WHITAKER'S ALMANACK
2008

The traditional design of the title page for Whitaker's Almanack which has appeared in each edition since 1868

WHITAKER'S ALMANACK

2008

A & C BLACK

LONDON

A & C Black Publishers Ltd
38 Soho Square, London W1D 3HB

Whitaker's Almanack published annually since 1868
140th edition © 2007 A & C Black Publishers Ltd

STANDARD EDITION
Cloth covers
978–0–7136–8554–1

CONCISE EDITION
Paperback
978–0–7136–8562–6

NORTH AMERICAN EDITION (THOMSON GALE)
Cloth covers
ISBN 10: 1–4144–3344–1
ISBN 13: 978–1–4144–3344–8

JACKET PHOTOGRAPHS
1. A helicopter drops water onto forest fires near the ancient city of Olympia in Greece during August 2007. © Louisa Gouliamaki/AFP/Getty Images
2. Residents in Johannesburg, South Africa, some originally from Zimbabwe, demonstrate against Robert Mugabe in March 2007. © Jerome Delay/AP/PA Photos
3. British Formula One driver Lewis Hamilton celebrates victory at the Canadian grand prix in June 2007. © Kerim Okten/epa/Corbis
4. A submerged road sign in Tewkesbury, Gloucestershire, during the July 2007 floods. © Rui Vieira/PA Wire/PA Photos
5. The new British prime minister, Gordon Brown, and his wife Sarah arrive at 10 Downing Street in June 2007. © Andrew Parsons/PA Wire/PA Photos
6. A cigarette stubbed out in an ashtray before the advent of the July 2007 smoking ban. © Matt Morton/PA Wire/PA Photos
7. Revd Ian Paisley and Gerry Adams share a press conference at the Stormont Assembly building in Belfast, in March 2007. © Paul Faith/POOL/PA Wire/PA Photos

Typeset in Great Britain by RefineCatch Ltd, Bungay, Suffolk

Printed and bound in Great Britain by William Clowes Ltd, Beccles, Suffolk

Whitaker's Almanack was compiled with the assistance of: Amnesty International; Christian Research; UK Hydrographic Office; Flag Institute; Met Office; Oxford Cartographers; Transparency International; WM/Reuters; Keesings Worldwide; World Health Organisation. Material was reproduced from: Thomas Brinkhoff *City Population* (www.citypopulation.de); *The Diplomatic List* © Crown Copyright; *International Financial Statistics Year Book* © International Monetary Fund; *Military Balance 2007* published by Taylor & Francis; *People in Power* © CIRCA; *2007 World Development Indicators* published by the World Bank; CIA *World Factbook 2007*. Crown copyright material is reproduced with the permission of the Controller of Her Majesty's Stationery Office.

A CIP catalogue record for this book is available from the British Library.

EDITORIAL STAFF
Editor-in-Chief: Inna Ward
UK Project Editors: Rob Hardy, Ruth Northey
International Project Editor: Mike Jakeman
Editorial Assistant: Clare Slaven

CONTRIBUTORS (where not listed)
Elizabeth Holmes (Education); Gordon Taylor (Astronomy); Hemant Kanitkar (Hindu calendar); John Noi (IT); Karen Harries-Rees (Environment); Clive Longhurst (Insurance); Duncan Murray, Chris Priestley (Legal Notes); Lisa Halborg (Mobile Communications); Jill Papworth (Taxation); Edward Gibbes, Stan Greenberg (Sport); Russell Ash (World in Figures) and Hilary Marsden (Countries of the World)

ILLUSTRATION DESIGN
Dermot O'Donnell

CONTENTS

PREFACE

Welcome to the 140th edition of *Whitaker's Almanack.* The past year has seen dramatic progress towards peaceful power sharing in Northern Ireland culminating in the reopening of Stormont and the unforgettable image we have chosen for this edition's cover, a photograph that will inspire hope in many nations torn apart by internal conflict.

Britain gained a new prime minister on 27 June. The new cabinet was put to the test almost as soon as it stepped into office, with a terrorist attack, a potentially disastrous foot-and-mouth outbreak and torrential downpours causing widespread flooding across the UK. After such a severe trial, the government's honeymoon period seemed to last and last with both the Tories and the Liberal Democrats lagging in the polls at the time of going to press. Following the reshuffles in all three parties, we have provided an up-to-date account of who is who in the new cabinet and new government departments. However, if the current media speculation about an early autumn election proves to be right, it will be too late to include in this edition.

Outside of the immediate political arena, the closely followed kidnapping of a British journalist (perhaps aided by his place of employment as much as his infallible reportage) ended happily with a smiling Alan Johnston providing a moving account of his imprisonment upon his release. British troops began pulling out of Basra marking the latest phase of Britain's disengagement in the conflict, while the media at large claimed London was experiencing a bigger wave of teenage gun violence than ever before. England, Wales and Northern Ireland followed Scotland by introducing nationwide public smoking bans and both interest rates and house prices continued to rise, fuelling tabloid speculation of an impending crash. The bubble nearly burst at the end of July when the world stock markets were rocked by severe volatility caused largely by the collapse of the sub-prime debt market in America. Whether it is the lenders or the borrowers behaving irresponsibly, one thing is clear: knowingly or otherwise, we are all part of the world's deeply entwined financial economy, be it through stocks, pensions, employment or home ownership.

As usual, all of the big and the not so big stories of the year are recorded in the *Almanack.* In the main edition, we have added a new section of colour maps showing a few key indicators in various countries of the world and a long overdue list of flags. We have also added a map of the current claims on the Antarctic territory, especially pertinent in view of the recently renewed race for the Arctic. We have expanded our clubs section, which now includes a map of London 'clubland' and, in most cases, a list of notable former members.

In the concise edition, we have added many new sections from the main book, including taxation and legal notes, UK press and broadcasting and an overview of the finance industry. Regional election results for Scotland, Wales and Northern Ireland are listed with details of the previous outcome for each constituency. We have revamped the education section with a new statistical summary, and added diagrams to our environment and architecture articles and countries of the world summaries. As ever, everything has been scrupulously updated using the most authoritative sources available. We are most grateful for the assistance of thousands of organisations and individuals who respond so readily to our requests for information. My personal thanks for their work also go to the Whitaker's team and our contributors, and to everyone involved in ensuring yet another great edition of the *Almanack.*

Inna Ward
Editor-in-Chief
Whitaker's Almanack
38 Soho Square
London
W1D 3HB

THE YEAR 2008

CHRONOLOGICAL CYCLES AND ERAS

Dominical Letter	FE
Epact	22
Golden Number (Lunar Cycle)	XIV
Julian Period	6721
Roman Indiction	1
Solar Cycle	1

	Beginning
Japanese year Heisei 20	1 Jan
Muslim year AH 1429*	10 Jan
Roman year 2761 AUC	14 Jan
Regnal year 57	6 Feb
Chinese year of the Rat	7 Feb
Sikh new year	14 Mar
Indian (Saka) year 1930	21 Mar
Hindu new year (Chaitra)	6 Apr
Jewish year AM 5769*	30 Sep

* Year begins at sunset

RELIGIOUS CALENDARS

CHRISTIAN

Epiphany	6 Jan
Presentation of Christ in the Temple	2 Feb
Ash Wednesday	6 Feb
Maundy Thursday	20 Mar
Good Friday	21 Mar
Easter Day (western churches)	23 Mar
The Annunciation	25 Mar
Easter Day (Eastern Orthodox)	27 Apr
Rogation Sunday	27 Apr
Ascension Day	1 May
Pentecost (Whit Sunday)	11 May
Trinity Sunday	18 May
Corpus Christi	25 May
All Saints' Day	1 Nov
Advent Sunday	30 Nov
Christmas Day	25 Dec

HINDU

Vasant Panchami (Sarasvati Puja)	11 Jan
Makara Sankranti	15 Jan
Mahashivaratri	6 Mar
Holi	21 Mar
Chaitra (Spring new year)	6 Apr
Ramanavami	13 Apr
Raksha Bandhan	16 Aug
Janmashtami	23 Aug
Ganesh Chaturthi	3 Sep
Navaratri festival (Durga Puja)	30 Sep
Dasara	9 Oct
Diwali (New Year festival of lights)	26 Oct

JEWISH

Purim	21 Mar
Pesach (Passover), first day	20 Apr
Shavuoth (Feast of Weeks), first day	9 Jun
Rosh Hashanah (Jewish new year)	30 Sep
Yom Kippur (Day of Atonement)	9 Oct
Succoth (Feast of Tabernacles), first day	14 Oct
Hanukkah, first day	22 Dec

MUSLIM

Muharram (Muslim new year)	10 Jan
Ashura	19 Jan
Ramadan, first day	2 Sep
Eid-ul-Fitr	1 Oct
Hajj	8 Dec
Eid-ul-Adha	11 Dec

SIKH

Birthday of Guru Gobind Singh Ji	5 Jan
Baisakhi Mela (Sikh new year)	14 Mar
Martyrdom of Guru Arjan Dev Ji	16 Jun
Birthday of Guru Nanak Dev Ji	13 Nov
Martyrdom of Guru Tegh Bahadur Ji	24 Nov

CIVIL CALENDAR

Countess of Wessex's birthday	20 Jan
Accession of the Queen	6 Feb
Duke of York's birthday	19 Feb
St David's Day	1 Mar
Earl of Wessex's birthday	10 Mar
Commonwealth Day	10 Mar
St Patrick's Day	17 Mar
Birthday of the Queen	21 Apr
St George's Day	23 Apr
Europe Day	9 May
Coronation Day	2 Jun
Duke of Edinburgh's birthday	10 Jun
The Queen's Official Birthday	14 Jun
Duchess of Cornwall's birthday	17 Jul
Princess Royal's birthday	15 Aug
Lord Mayor's Day	8 Nov
Remembrance Day	9 Nov
Prince of Wales' birthday	14 Nov
Wedding Day of the Queen	20 Nov
St Andrew's Day	30 Nov

LEGAL CALENDAR

LAW TERMS

Hilary Term	11 Jan to 19 Mar
Easter Term	1 Apr to 23 May
Trinity Term	3 Jun to 31 Jul
Michaelmas Term	1 Oct to 20 Dec

QUARTER DAYS *England, Wales and Northern Ireland*	TERM DAYS *Scotland*
Lady – 25 Mar	Candlemas – 28 Feb
Midsummer – 24 Jun	Whitsunday – 28 May
Michaelmas – 29 Sep	Lammas – 28 Aug
Christmas – 25 Dec	Martinmas – 28 Nov

2008

JANUARY

Sunday		6	13	20	27
Monday		7	14	21	28
Tuesday	1	8	15	22	29
Wednesday	2	9	16	23	30
Thursday	3	10	17	24	31
Friday	4	11	18	25	
Saturday	5	12	19	26	

FEBRUARY

Sunday		3	10	17	24
Monday		4	11	18	25
Tuesday		5	12	19	26
Wednesday		6	13	20	27
Thursday		7	14	21	28
Friday	1	8	15	22	29
Saturday	2	9	16	23	

MARCH

Sunday		2	9	16	23	30
Monday		3	10	17	24	31
Tuesday		4	11	18	25	
Wednesday		5	12	19	26	
Thursday		6	13	20	27	
Friday		7	14	21	28	
Saturday	1	8	15	22	29	

APRIL

Sunday		6	13	20	27
Monday		7	14	21	28
Tuesday	1	8	15	22	29
Wednesday	2	9	16	23	30
Thursday	3	10	17	24	
Friday	4	11	18	25	
Saturday	5	12	19	26	

MAY

Sunday		4	11	18	25
Monday		5	12	19	26
Tuesday		6	13	20	27
Wednesday		7	14	21	28
Thursday	1	8	15	22	29
Friday	2	9	16	23	30
Saturday	3	10	17	24	31

JUNE

Sunday	1	8	15	22	29
Monday	2	9	16	23	30
Tuesday	3	10	17	24	
Wednesday	4	11	18	25	
Thursday	5	12	19	26	
Friday	6	13	20	27	
Saturday	7	14	21	28	

JULY

Sunday		6	13	20	27
Monday		7	14	21	28
Tuesday	1	8	15	22	29
Wednesday	2	9	16	23	30
Thursday	3	10	17	24	31
Friday	4	11	18	25	
Saturday	5	12	19	26	

AUGUST

Sunday		3	10	17	24	31
Monday		4	11	18	25	
Tuesday		5	12	19	26	
Wednesday		6	13	20	27	
Thursday		7	14	21	28	
Friday	1	8	15	22	29	
Saturday	2	9	16	23	30	

SEPTEMBER

Sunday		7	14	21	28
Monday	1	8	15	22	29
Tuesday	2	9	16	23	30
Wednesday	3	10	17	24	
Thursday	4	11	18	25	
Friday	5	12	19	26	
Saturday	6	13	20	27	

OCTOBER

Sunday		5	12	19	26
Monday		6	13	20	27
Tuesday		7	14	21	28
Wednesday	1	8	15	22	29
Thursday	2	9	16	23	30
Friday	3	10	17	24	31
Saturday	4	11	18	25	

NOVEMBER

Sunday		2	9	16	23	30
Monday		3	10	17	24	
Tuesday		4	11	18	25	
Wednesday		5	12	19	26	
Thursday		6	13	20	27	
Friday		7	14	21	28	
Saturday	1	8	15	22	29	

DECEMBER

Sunday		7	14	21	28
Monday	1	8	15	22	29
Tuesday	2	9	16	23	30
Wednesday	3	10	17	24	31
Thursday	4	11	18	25	
Friday	5	12	19	26	
Saturday	6	13	20	27	

PUBLIC HOLIDAYS	*England and Wales*	*Scotland*	*Northern Ireland*
New Year	†1 January	1, †2 January	†1 January
St Patrick's Day	—	—	‡17 March
*Good Friday	21 March	21 March	21 March
Easter Monday	24 March	—	24 March
Early May	†5 May	5 May	†5 May
Spring	26 May	†26 May	26 May
Battle of the Boyne	—	—	‡12 July
Summer	25 August	4 August	25 August
*Christmas	25, 26 December	25, †26 December	25, 26 December

* In England, Wales and Northern Ireland, Christmas Day and Good Friday are common law holidays

† Subject to royal proclamation

‡ Subject to proclamation by the Secretary of State for Northern Ireland

Note: In the Channel Islands, Liberation Day is a bank and public holiday

2009

JANUARY

Sunday		4	11	18	25
Monday		5	12	19	26
Tuesday		6	13	20	27
Wednesday		7	14	21	28
Thursday	1	8	15	22	29
Friday	2	9	16	23	30
Saturday	3	10	17	24	31

FEBRUARY

Sunday	1	8	15	22
Monday	2	9	16	23
Tuesday	3	10	17	24
Wednesday	4	11	18	25
Thursday	5	12	19	26
Friday	6	13	20	27
Saturday	7	14	21	28

MARCH

Sunday	1	8	15	22	29
Monday	2	9	16	23	30
Tuesday	3	10	17	24	31
Wednesday	4	11	18	25	
Thursday	5	12	19	26	
Friday	6	13	20	27	
Saturday	7	14	21	28	

APRIL

Sunday		5	12	19	26
Monday		6	13	20	27
Tuesday		7	14	21	28
Wednesday	1	8	15	22	29
Thursday	2	9	16	23	30
Friday	3	10	17	24	
Saturday	4	11	18	25	

MAY

Sunday		3	10	17	24	31
Monday		4	11	18	25	
Tuesday		5	12	19	26	
Wednesday		6	13	20	27	
Thursday		7	14	21	28	
Friday	1	8	15	22	29	
Saturday	2	9	16	23	30	

JUNE

Sunday		7	14	21	28
Monday	1	8	15	22	29
Tuesday	2	9	16	23	30
Wednesday	3	10	17	24	
Thursday	4	11	18	25	
Friday	5	12	19	26	
Saturday	6	13	20	27	

JULY

Sunday		5	12	19	26
Monday		6	13	20	27
Tuesday		7	14	21	28
Wednesday	1	8	15	22	29
Thursday	2	9	16	23	30
Friday	3	10	17	24	31
Saturday	4	11	18	25	

AUGUST

Sunday		2	9	16	23	30
Monday		3	10	17	24	31
Tuesday		4	11	18	25	
Wednesday		5	12	19	26	
Thursday		6	13	20	27	
Friday		7	14	21	28	
Saturday	1	8	15	22	29	

SEPTEMBER

Sunday		6	13	20	27
Monday		7	14	21	28
Tuesday	1	8	15	22	29
Wednesday	2	9	16	23	30
Thursday	3	10	17	24	
Friday	4	11	18	25	
Saturday	5	12	19	26	

OCTOBER

Sunday		4	11	18	25
Monday		5	12	19	26
Tuesday		6	13	20	27
Wednesday		7	14	21	28
Thursday	1	8	15	22	29
Friday	2	9	16	23	30
Saturday	3	10	17	24	31

NOVEMBER

Sunday	1	8	15	22	29
Monday	2	9	16	23	30
Tuesday	3	10	17	24	
Wednesday	4	11	18	25	
Thursday	5	12	19	26	
Friday	6	13	20	27	
Saturday	7	14	21	28	

DECEMBER

Sunday		6	13	20	27
Monday		7	14	21	28
Tuesday	1	8	15	22	29
Wednesday	2	9	16	23	30
Thursday	3	10	17	24	31
Friday	4	11	18	25	
Saturday	5	12	19	26	

PUBLIC HOLIDAYS

PUBLIC HOLIDAYS	*England and Wales*	*Scotland*	*Northern Ireland*
New Year	†1 January	1, †2 January	†1 January
St Patrick's Day	—	—	‡17 March
*Good Friday	10 April	10 April	10 April
Easter Monday	13 April	—	13 April
Early May	†4 May	4 May	†4 May
Spring	25 May	†25 May	25 May
Battle of the Boyne	—	—	‡13 July
Summer	31 August	3 August	31 August
*Christmas	25, 28 December	25, †28 December	25, 28 December

* In England, Wales and Northern Ireland, Christmas Day and Good Friday are common law holidays

† Subject to royal proclamation

‡ Subject to proclamation by the Secretary of State for Northern Ireland

Note: In the Channel Islands, Liberation Day is a bank and public holiday

FORTHCOMING EVENTS

* Provisional dates
† Venue not confirmed

JANUARY

11–20	London Boat Show, ExCel, Docklands
11–27	London International Mime Festival
13	Russian Winter Festival, Trafalgar Square, London
16–20	London Art Fair, Business Design Centre
23–24	UK Dance Championships, Bournemouth International Centre
31–3 February	London Motorcycle Show, ExCel, Docklands

FEBRUARY

8–17	Leicester Comedy Festival
10	Orange British Academy Film Awards, Royal Opera House, London
23–2 March	Bath Literature Festival
29–1 March	Conservative Party Local Government Conference, Warwickshire
29–2 March	Ceramic Art London, Royal College of Art

MARCH

5–11	BADA Antiques and Fine Art Fair, Duke of York's Square, London
6	World Book Day
6–9	Crufts Dog Show, NEC, Birmingham
7–9	Liberal Democrat Party Spring Conference, Liverpool
7–16	National Science and Engineering Week
8	International Women's Day
14–6 April	Ideal Home Show, Earls Court

APRIL

April–September	Chichester Festival Theatre season
2–6	Oxford Literary Festival
14–16	London Book Fair, Earls Court

MAY

16–18	Battersea Contemporary Art Fair, London
18–31 August	Glyndebourne Festival Opera season
20–24	RHS Chelsea Flower Show, Royal Hospital, London
22–1 June	Hay Festival, Hay-on-Wye, Hereford

JUNE

*9–17 August	Royal Academy of Arts Summer Exhibition, Burlington House, London
14	Trooping the Colour, Horseguards Parade, London
16–29	Aldeburgh Festival of Music and the Arts, Snape, Suffolk
*27–29	Glastonbury Festival of Contemporary Performing Arts, Somerset

JULY

3–6	The Royal Show, Stoneleigh Park, Warwickshire
3–12	York Early Music Festival
3–13	New Designers Exhibition, Business Design Centre, London
4–20	Cheltenham Music Festival
8–13	RHS Hampton Court Palace Flower Show, Surrey
11–27	Buxton Festival, Derbyshire
17–26	The Welsh Proms, St David's Hall, Cardiff
*18–13 September	BBC Promenade Concerts, Royal Albert Hall, London
24–27	RHS Flower Show, Tatton Park, Cheshire
25–27	WOMAD Festival, Charlton Park, Wiltshire
*25–3 August	Edinburgh Jazz and Blues Festival
31–3 August	Cambridge Folk Festival

AUGUST

1–23	Edinburgh Military Tattoo, Edinburgh Castle
2–9	National Eisteddfod of Wales, Cardiff
2–9	Three Choirs Festival, Worcester
*8–31	Edinburgh International Festival
19–21	RHS Wisley Flower Show, RHS Garden, Wisley
*24–25	Notting Hill Carnival, Notting Hill, London
*29–2 November	Blackpool Illuminations, Blackpool Promenade

SEPTEMBER

1	Braemar Royal Highland Gathering, Aberdeenshire
*2	Mercury Music Prize
8	International Literacy Day
8–11	TUC Annual Congress, Brighton Centre, Brighton
12–21	Southampton Boat Show, Mayflower Park

13–18	Liberal Democrat Party Autumn Conference, Bournemouth
27–2 October	Labour Party Conference, Brighton
28–1 October	Conservative Party Conference, Birmingham

OCTOBER

7–4 January	Turner Prize Exhibition, Tate Britain, London
9	National Poetry Day
16–19	Frieze Art Fair, Regent's Park, London
Mid-October	Booker Prize
Mid-October	Classic Motor Show, NEC, Birmingham
Mid-October	London Film Festival

NOVEMBER

2	London to Brighton Veteran Car Run
8	Lord Mayor's Procession and Show, City of London
Mid-November	CBI Annual Conference, Business Design Centre, London
21–30	Huddersfield Contemporary Music Festival

SPORTS EVENTS

JANUARY

13–20	Snooker: Masters, Wembley Arena, London

FEBRUARY

2–15 March	Rugby Union: Six Nations Championship
24	Football: League Cup Final, Wembley Stadium, London

MARCH

5–26	Cricket: England Test series vs New Zealand
29	Rowing: Oxford and Cambridge Boat Race, Putney to Mortlake, London

APRIL

13	Athletics: London Marathon
19–5 May	Snooker: World Championship, Crucible Theatre, Sheffield

MAY

1–4	Badminton Horse Trials, Badminton
†4	Football: Welsh FA Cup Final
8–11	Royal Windsor Horse Show, Home Park, Windsor
14	Football: UEFA Cup Final, City of Manchester Stadium
15–9 June	Cricket: England Test series vs New Zealand
17	Football: FA Cup Final, Wembley Stadium, London
*17	Football: Scottish FA Cup Final, Hampden Park, Glasgow
21	Football: UEFA Champions League Final, Luzhniki Stadium, Moscow
*24	Rugby Union: Heineken Cup Final, Millennium Stadium, Cardiff
*24–6 June	Motorcycling: TT Races, Isle of Man

JUNE

7–29	Football: UEFA European Championship, Austria and Switzerland
16–21	British Amateur Golf Championship, Turnberry
23–6 July	Tennis: Wimbledon Championship, All England Lawn Tennis Club, London

JULY

2–6	Rowing: Henley Royal Regatta, Henley-on-Thames
6	Motorsport: British Formula 1 Grand Prix, Silverstone, Northants
10–11 August	Cricket: England Test series vs South Africa
12–26	Shooting: NRA Imperial Meeting, Bisley Camp, Surrey
17–20	Golf: Open Championship, Royal Birkdale
31–3 August	Golf: Women's British Open, Sunningdale

AUGUST

2–19	Sailing: Cowes Week, Isle of Wight
8–24	Olympic Games, Beijing
30	Rugby League: Challenge Cup Final, Wembley Stadium, London

SEPTEMBER

4–7	Burghley Horse Trials, Stamford, Lincolnshire
6–17	Paralympic Games, Beijing
16–21	Golf: Ryder Cup, Valhalla, Kentucky

OCTOBER

*8–12	Horse of the Year Show, NEC, Birmingham
Mid-October	Rugby League: Super League Final, Old Trafford, Manchester

HORSE RACING

30 March	Lincoln Handicap, Doncaster
3–5 April	Grand National, Aintree, Liverpool
3 May	Two Thousand Guineas, Newmarket
4 May	One Thousand Guineas, Newmarket
6 June	The Oaks, Epsom Downs
6 June	Coronation Cup, Epsom Downs
7 June	The Derby, Epsom Downs
17–21 June	Royal Ascot
26 July	King George VI and Queen Elizabeth Diamond Stakes, Ascot
10–13 September	St Leger, Doncaster
2–4 October	Cambridgeshire Meeting, Newmarket
17–18 October	Champions Meeting, Newmarket

CENTENARIES

2008

1608

9 Dec	John Milton, poet, born

1708

1 Oct	John Blow, organist and composer, died
15 Nov	William Pitt the Elder, prime minister 1766–8, born

1808

20 Apr	Napoleon III, emperor of France 1852–70, born
29 Dec	Andrew Johnson, president of the USA 1865–9, born

1908

9 Jan	Simone de Beauvoir, French writer and philosopher, born
26 Jan	Stephane Grappelli, French jazz violinist, born
11 Feb	Sir Vivian Fuchs, polar explorer and scientist, born
26 Feb	Frederick 'Tex' Avery, American cartoonist and director, born
5 Mar	Sir Reginald 'Rex' Harrison, actor, born
23 Mar	Joan Crawford, American actor, born
25 Mar	Sir David Lean, film director, born
5 Apr	Bette Davis, American actor, born
5 Apr	Herbert von Karajan, Austrian conductor, born
22 Apr	Sir Henry Campbell-Bannerman, prime minister 1906–8, died
28 Apr	Oskar Schindler, German industrialist who saved Jewish workers from the Holocaust, born
20 May	James Stewart, American actor, born
28 May	Ian Fleming, novelist, born
21 Jun	Nikolay Rimsky-Korsakov, Russian composer, died
24 Jun	Grover Cleveland, president of the USA 1885–9 and 1893–7, died
30 Jun	The Great Siberian Explosion occurred near the Tunguska river, felling an estimated 80 million trees
13 Jul	King Edward VII opened the first Olympic Games held in Britain
22 Jul	Sir William Randal Cremer, MP, pacifist and Nobel Peace Prize winner (1903), died
26 Jul	In the USA, the Federal Bureau of Investigation (FBI) was established
12 Aug	Ford's first Model T car came off the production line
22 Aug	Henri Cartier-Bresson, French photographer, born
27 Aug	Sir Donald Bradman, Australian cricketer, born
27 Aug	Lyndon B. Johnson, president of the USA 1963–9, born
20 Nov	Alistair Cooke, British-born American journalist and broadcaster, born
10 Dec	Olivier Messiaen, French composer, born
25 Dec	Quentin Crisp, author and actor, born

2009

1509

21 Apr	Henry VII, king of England 1485–1509, died
10 Jul	John Calvin, French reformationist, born

1709

18 Sep	Dr Samuel Johnson, lexicographer, critic and poet, born

1809

4 Jan	Louis Braille, French inventor of reading system for the blind, born
19 Jan	Edgar Allen Poe, American author, poet, critic and editor, born
3 Feb	Felix Mendelssohn-Bartholdy, German composer, born
12 Feb	Charles Darwin, naturalist and scientist, born
12 Feb	Abraham Lincoln, president of the USA 1860–5, born
27 Mar	Baron G.-E. Haussmann, French civic planner, financier and architect, born
31 Mar	Nikolai Gogol, Russian writer, born
31 Mar	Edward Fitzgerald, poet and scholar, born
24 May	Dartmoor prison opened to hold prisoners of the Napoleonic Wars
31 May	Franz Joseph Haydn, Austrian composer, died
8 Jun	Thomas Paine, writer, deist and radical, died
6 Aug	Lord Alfred Tennyson, poet, born
29 Dec	William Gladstone, four-time prime minister, born

1909

17 Feb	Geronimo, Apache Indian chief, died
10 Apr	Algernon Swinburne, poet and critic, died
15 May	James Mason, actor, born
18 May	Fred Perry, tennis player, born
26 May	Sir Matt Busby, football player and manager, born
6 Jun	Sir Isaiah Berlin, Latvian-born writer and historian, born
20 Jun	Errol Flynn, Australian actor, born
17 Jul	Sir Hardy Amies, costume designer and the Queen's official dressmaker, born
25 Jul	Louis Bleriot completed the first flight across the English Channel
14 Sep	Sir Peter Scott, conservationist, born
28 Oct	Francis Bacon, Anglo-Irish painter, born
26 Nov	Eugene Ionesco, French-Romanian playwright and dramatist, born
7 Dec	Leo Baekeland was awarded a patent for the first synthetic plastic (Bakelite)
9 Dec	Douglas Fairbanks Jr, American actor, born

THE UNITED KINGDOM

THE UK IN FIGURES

The United Kingdom comprises Great Britain (England, Wales and Scotland) and Northern Ireland. The Isle of Man and the Channel Islands are Crown dependencies with their own legislative systems, and not a part of the United Kingdom.

ABBREVIATIONS

AAS	*Annual Abstract of Statistics*
ST	*Social Trends*

All data is for the UK unless otherwise stated.

AREA OF THE UNITED KINGDOM

	sq. km	*sq. miles*
United Kingdom	242,495	93,627
England	130,279	50,301
Wales	20,733	8,005
Scotland	77,907	30,080
Northern Ireland	13,576	5,242

Source: ONS – *AAS 2006* (Crown copyright)

POPULATION

The first official census of population in England, Wales and Scotland was taken in 1801 and a census has been taken every ten years since, except in 1941 when there was no census because of war. The last official census in the United Kingdom was taken on 29 April 2001 and the next is due in April 2011.

The first official census of population in Ireland was taken in 1841. However, all figures given below refer only to the area which is now Northern Ireland. Figures for Northern Ireland in 1921 and 1931 are estimates based on the censuses taken in 1926 and 1937 respectively.

Estimates of the population of England before 1801, calculated from the number of baptisms, burials and marriages, are:

1570	4,160,221	1670	5,773,646
1600	4,811,718	1700	6,045,008
1630	5,600,517	1750	6,517,035

Further details are available on the Office for National Statistics (ONS) website (W www.statistics.gov.uk)

CENSUS RESULTS *Thousands*

	United Kingdom			England and Wales			Scotland			Northern Ireland		
Thousands	*Total*	*Male*	*Female*	*Total*	*Male*	*Female*	*Total*	*Male*	*Female*	*Total*	*Male*	*Female*
1801	—	—	—	8,893	4,255	4,638	1,608	739	869	—	—	—
1811	13,368	6,368	7,000	10,165	4,874	5,291	1,806	826	980	—	—	—
1821	15,472	7,498	7,974	12,000	5,850	6,150	2,092	983	1,109	—	—	—
1831	17,835	8,647	9,188	13,897	6,771	7,126	2,364	1,114	1,250	—	—	—
1841	20,183	9,819	10,364	15,914	7,778	8,137	2,620	1,242	1,378	1,649	800	849
1851	22,259	10,855	11,404	17,928	8,781	9,146	2,889	1,376	1,513	1,443	698	745
1861	24,525	11,894	12,631	20,066	9,776	10,290	3,062	1,450	1,612	1,396	668	728
1871	27,431	13,309	14,122	22,712	11,059	11,653	3,360	1,603	1,757	1,359	647	712
1881	31,015	15,060	15,955	25,974	12,640	13,335	3,736	1,799	1,936	1,305	621	684
1891	34,264	16,593	17,671	29,003	14,060	14,942	4,026	1,943	2,083	1,236	590	646
1901	38,237	18,492	19,745	32,528	15,729	16,799	4,472	2,174	2,298	1,237	590	647
1911	42,082	20,357	21,725	36,070	17,446	18,625	4,761	2,309	2,452	1,251	603	648
1921	44,027	21,033	22,994	37,887	18,075	19,811	4,882	2,348	2,535	1,258	610	648
1931	46,038	22,060	23,978	39,952	19,133	20,819	4,843	2,326	2,517	1,243	601	642
1951	50,225	24,118	26,107	43,758	21,016	22,742	5,096	2,434	2,662	1,371	668	703
1961	52,709	25,481	27,228	46,105	22,304	23,801	5,179	2,483	2,697	1,425	694	731
1971	55,515	26,952	28,562	48,750	23,683	25,067	5,229	2,515	2,714	1,536	755	781
1981	55,848	27,104	28,742	49,155	23,873	25,281	5,131	2,466	2,664	1,533*	750	783
1991	56,467	27,344	29,123	49,890	24,182	25,707	4,999	2,392	2,607	1,578	769	809
2001	58,789	28,581	30,208	52,042	25,327	26,715	5,062	2,432	2,630	1,685	821	864

* Figure includes 44,500 non-enumerated persons

Source: ONS – Census Reports (Crown copyright)

RESIDENT POPULATION *Thousands*

	United Kingdom			England and Wales			Scotland			Northern Ireland		
	Total	*Male*	*Female*	*Total*	*Male*	*Female*	*Total*	*Male*	*Female*	*Total*	*Male*	*Female*
2005	60,209	29,479	30,730	53,390	26,179	27,211	5,095	2,456	2,639	1,724	844	880
2006	60,533	29,668	30,864	53,691	26,357	27,334	5,108	2,463	2,646	1,733	848	884
2011	61,892	30,438	31,454	55,005	27,100	27,904	5,120	2,470	2,649	1,767	868	900
2021	64,727	31,943	32,784	57,770	28,572	28,198	5,127	2,471	2,656	1,830	900	930
2026	66,002	32,579	33,423	59,042	29,212	29,831	5,109	2,457	2,652	1,851	911	940

Source: ONS – *AAS 2007* (Crown copyright)

ISLANDS: CENSUS RESULTS

	Isle of Man			Jersey			*Guernsey		
	Total	*Male*	*Female*	*Total*	*Male*	*Female*	*Total*	*Male*	*Female*
1901	54,752	25,496	29,256	52,576	23,940	28,636	40,446	19,652	20,794
1911	52,016	23,937	28,079	51,898	24,014	27,884	41,858	20,661	21,197
1921	60,284	27,329	32,955	49,701	22,438	27,263	38,315	18,246	20,069
1931	49,308	22,443	26,865	50,462	23,424	27,038	40,643	19,659	20,984
1951	55,123	25,749	29,464	57,296	27,282	30,014	43,652	21,221	22,431
1961	48,151	22,060	26,091	57,200	27,200	30,000	45,068	21,671	23,397
1971	56,289	26,461	29,828	72,532	35,423	37,109	51,458	24,792	26,666
1981	64,679	30,901	33,778	77,000	37,000	40,000	53,313	25,701	27,612
1991	69,788	33,693	36,095	84,082	40,862	43,220	58,867	28,297	30,570
2001	76,315	37,372	38,943	87,186	42,485	44,701	59,807	29,138	30,669
2006†	80,058	39,523	40,535						

* Population of Guernsey, Herm, Jethou and Lithou

† The Isle of Man conducted a census in 2006

Figures for 1901–71 record all persons present on census night; census figures for 1981–2001 record all persons resident in the islands on census night. The 2001 population census also recorded the population of Alderney as 2,294 and an informal census of Sark gave its population as 591

Source: ONS – Census Reports (Crown copyright)

RESIDENT POPULATION

BY AGE AND SEX

Age Range	*Thousands* Men	Women
Under 1	367	349
1–4	1,389	1,323
5–9	1,823	1,737
10–14	1,962	1,859
15–19	2,038	1,927
20–29	3,847	3,794
30–44	6,645	6,763
45–59	5,746	5,878
60–64	1,519	1,595
65–74	2,389	2,659
75–84	1,403	2,022
85+	352	824

Source: ONS – *AAS 2007* (Crown copyright)

BY ETHNIC GROUP

Ethnic group	*Thousands*
White	
British	48,973
Other	2,570
Mixed	
White and Black Caribbean	211
White and Black African	76
White and Asian	151
Other Mixed	135
Asian	
Indian	1,081
Pakistani	829
Bangladeshi	334
Other Asian	380
Black	
Black Caribbean	583
Black African	653
Black Other	60
Chinese	228
Other	700
ALL*	58,692

* Includes those who did not state their ethnic origin

Source: ONS – *AAS 2007* (Crown copyright).

IMMIGRATION

ACCEPTANCES FOR SETTLEMENT IN THE UK

*Region**	*Number of persons* 2003	2005
Europe: total†	15,295	20,810
Bulgaria	750	1,225
Russia	2,160	1,795
Serbia and Montenegro	1,165	6,805
Turkey	4,365	5,330
Ukraine	805	1,195
Other former USSR	625	1,015
Americas: total	16,465	13,905
Canada	1,710	1,215
Colombia	1,000	1,555
Jamaica	4,500	2,780
USA	5,620	4,350
Africa: total	44,860	54,080
Angola	620	1,695
Dem. Rep. Congo	1,475	2,960
Ghana	4,015	2,880
Kenya	1,585	2,690
Nigeria	7,570	5,310
Sierra Leone	1,375	3,420
Somalia	6,305	8,255
South Africa	8,805	9,385
Uganda	830	1,065
Zimbabwe	3,675	4,520
Asia: total	54,945	83,740
Indian sub-continent: total	29,490	28,990
Bangladesh	5,590	3,085
India	10,955	16,720
Pakistan	12,945	9,185
Middle East: total	5,020	9,395
Iran	1,585	2,055
Iraq	1,440	4,675
Remainder of Asia: total	20,435	45,355
China	2,540	3,985
Japan	1,850	1,540
Malaysia	1,150	1,945
Philippines	3,810	14,710
Sri Lanka	2,555	5,475
Thailand	2,020	1,945
Oceania: total	7,125	6,335
Australia	4,120	3,740
New Zealand	2,920	2,505

British Overseas Citizens	265	95
Nationality unknown	330	160
ALL NATIONALITIES	139,280	179,120

* Country specified only when the figure for 2003 or 2005 is over 1,000

† Excluding European Economic Area and Swiss nationals

Source: ONS – *AAS 2007* (Crown copyright)

BIRTHS

	Live births	*Male*	*Female*	*Birth rate**
United Kingdom	723,000	370,000	353,000	12.0
England and Wales	646,000	331,000	315,000	12.1
Scotland	54,000	28,000	26,000	10.7
Northern Ireland	22,000	11,000	11,000	12.9

* Live births per 1,000 population

Source: ONS – *AAS 2007* (Crown copyright)

FERTILITY RATES

Live births per 1,000 women

Age of mother at childbirth	*1971*	*1991*	*2005*
Under 20	50.0	32.9	26.2
20–24	154.4	88.9	70.5
25–29	154.6	119.9	98.3
30–34	79.4	86.5	100.7
35–39	34.3	32.0	50.0
40+	9.2	5.3	10.6
Total fertility rate*	2.41	1.82	1.79
Total births (thousands)	901.6	792.3	722.5

* Number of children that would be born to a woman if current patterns of fertility persisted throughout her child-bearing life. For 1981 onwards, this is based on fertility rates for each single year of age, but for 1971 it is based on the rates for each five-year age group

Source: ONS – *ST 2007* (Crown copyright)

TOP TEN BABY NAMES

	1954		2006	
	Girls	*Boys*	*Girls*	*Boys*
1	Susan	David	Olivia	Jack
2	Linda	John	Grace	Thomas
3	Christine	Stephen	Jessica	Joshua
4	Margaret	Michael	Ruby	Oliver
5	Janet	Peter	Emily	Harry
6	Patricia	Robert	Sophie	James
7	Carol	Paul	Chloe	William
8	Elizabeth	Alan	Lucy	Samuel
9	Mary	Christopher	Lily	Daniel
10	Anne	Richard	Ellie	Charlie

Source: ONS (Crown copyright)

LEGAL ABORTIONS

	2000	*2005*
England and Wales	175,542	186,416
Scotland	11,997	12,603

Source: ONS – *AAS 2007* (Crown copyright)

DEATHS

Men	*Deaths*	*Death rate**
United Kingdom	276,803	9.4
England and Wales	243,324	
Scotland	26,522	
Northern Ireland	6,957	

Women	*Deaths*	*Death rate**
United Kingdom	305,860	10.0
England and Wales	269,368	
Scotland	29,225	
Northern Ireland	7,267	

* Per 1,000 population

Source: ONS – *AAS 2007* (Crown copyright)

INFANT MORTALITY RATE*

United Kingdom	5.1
England and Wales	5.0
Scotland	5.2
Northern Ireland	6.1

* Deaths of infants under one year of age per 1,000 live births

Source: ONS – *AAS 2007* (Crown copyright)

MARRIAGE AND DIVORCE

	Marriages	*Divorces*
United Kingdom*	283,731	155,052
England and Wales*	244,710	141,750
Scotland	30,881	10,940
Northern Ireland	8,140	2,362

* Provisional data

Source: ONS – *AAS 2007* (Crown copyright)

HOUSEHOLDS

BY TYPE (GREAT BRITAIN)

Percentages

	1971	*1991*	*2006*
One Person			
Under state pension age	6	11	14
Over state pension age	12	16	14
One family households			
Couple			
No children	27	28	28
1–2 dependent children	26	20	18
3 or more dependent children	9	5	4
Non-dependent children only	8	8	7
Lone parent			
Dependent children	3	6	7
Non-dependent children only	4	4	3
Two or more unrelated adults	4	3	3
Multi-family households	1	1	1
All households (=100%) *(millions)*	18.6	22.4	24.2

Source: ONS – *ST 2007* (Crown copyright)

BY SIZE (GREAT BRITAIN)

Percentages

	1971	*1991*	*2006*
One person	18	27	29
Two people	32	34	36
Three people	19	16	16
Four people	17	16	13
Five people	8	5	4
Six or more people	6	2	2
All households (=100%) *(millions)*	18.6	22.4	24.2
Average household size *(number of people)*	2.9	2.5	2.4

Source: ONS – *ST 2007* (Crown copyright)

DEPENDENT CHILDREN LIVING IN DIFFERENT FAMILY TYPES (GREAT BRITAIN)
Percentages

	1972	*1997*	*2006*
Couple families			
1 child	16	17	18
2 children	35	37	36
3 or more children	41	25	22
Lone mother families			
1 child	2	6	7
2 children	2	7	9
3 or more children	2	6	6
Lone father families			
1 child	–	1	1
2 or more children	1	1	1

Source: ONS – *ST 2007* (Crown copyright)

ADULTS LIVING WITH THEIR PARENTS (ENGLAND)
Percentages

Age/Gender	*1991*	*2002*	*2006*
Men			
20–24	50	56	58
25–29	19	19	22
30–34	9	8	9
Women			
20–24	32	37	39
25–29	9	10	11
30–34	5	2	3

Source: ONS – *ST 2007* (Crown copyright)

MORTGAGES

	1995	*2000*	*2005*
Mortgages* *(thousands)*	10,512	11,173	11,596
Arrears and repossessions* *(thousands)*			
Loans in arrears at end-period			
By 6–12 months	127	48	35
By 12+ months	85	21	14
Properties repossessed in period	49	23	10
Type of mortgage for house purchase† *(percentages)*			
Standard repayment	33.8	60.1	71.5
Endowment	52.0	17.5	3.8
Other‡	14.2	22.5	24.7

* Estimates cover only members of the Council of Mortgage Lenders, which account for 98 per cent of all outstanding mortgages

† Includes new mortgages advanced by building societies and other major lenders and includes sitting tenants

‡ Includes interest only, PEP/ISA and pension

Source: ONS – *AAS 2007* (Crown copyright)

TYPE OF ACCOMMODATION (GREAT BRITAIN)
Percentages by tenure 2005

	House or bungalow			*Flat or maisonette*	
	Detached	*Semi-detached*	*Terraced*	*Purpose-built*	*Other*
Owner-occupied	30	35	26	7	2
Owned outright	34	35	21	7	2
Owned with mortgage	26	34	30	7	2
Rented from social sector	1	24	30	42	3
Council	1	26	28	42	2
Housing association	1	19	34	41	5
Rented privately	11	19	32	22	16
Furnished	5	14	30	30	20
Unfurnished	14	20	33	18	15
All tenures	22	31	28	16	4

Source: ONS – *AAS 2007* (Crown copyright)

HEALTH

All data is for the UK unless otherwise stated.

LIFE EXPECTANCY

	2003	*2007 est*
Men	76.2	76.2
Women	80.5	81.3

Source: CIA World Factbook

DEATHS BY CAUSE

	England and Wales	*Scotland*	*N. Ireland*
Total Deaths	512,692	55,747	14,224
Deaths from natural causes	494,054	53,535	13,463
Certain infectious and parasitic diseases	6,141	719	162
Intestinal infectious diseases	2,221	99	16
Respiratory and other tuberculosis	406	49	4
Meningococcal infection	86	4	1
Viral hepatitis	205	16	2
AIDS (HIV – disease)	230	31	5

Neoplasms	138,454	15,408	3,826
Malignant neoplasms	135,252	15,135	3,735
Malignant neoplasm of oesophagus	6,490	798	162
Malignant neoplasm of stomach	4,927	590	161
Malignant neoplasm of colon	9,076	966	293
Malignant neoplasm of rectum and anus	3,995	367	99
Malignant neoplasm of pancreas	6,509	603	173
Malignant neoplasm of trachea, bronchus and lung	28,792	4,009	824
Malignant neoplasm of skin	1,622	158	43
Malignant neoplasm of breast	11,121	1,151	307
Malignant neoplasm of cervix uteri	911	127	20
Malignant neoplasm of prostate	9,042	765	222
Leukaemia	3,910	351	92
Diseases of the blood and blood-forming organs and certain disorders involving the immune mechanism	1,096	118	36
Endocrine, nutritional and metabolic diseases	7,433	988	302
Diabetes mellitus	5,677	745	224
Mental and behavioural disorders	14,563	2,454	408
Vascular and unspecified dementia	12,995	1,835	316
Alcohol abuse	523	343	86
Drug dependence and non-dependent abuse of drugs	762	217	2
Diseases of the nervous system and sense organs	15,253	1,306	484
Meningitis (excluding meningococcal)	187	18	2
Alzheimer's disease	4,914	415	207
Diseases of the circulatory system	183,997	20,060	5,002
Ischaemic heart diseases	88,271	10,331	2,708
Cerebrovascular diseases	50,772	5,789	1,307
Diseases of the respiratory system	72,517	7,093	1,921
Influenza	44	11	–
Pneumonia	31,443	2,483	895
Bronchitis, emphysema and other chronic obstructive pulmonary diseases	24,230	2,857	596
Asthma	1,186	100	32
Diseases of the digestive system	25,213	3,221	584
Gastric and duodenal ulcer	3,266	230	60
Chronic liver disease	5,873	1,152	150
Diseases of the skin and subcutaneous tissue	1,788	127	20
Diseases of the musculo-skeletal system and connective tissue	4,378	326	95
Rheumatoid arthritis and juvenile arthritis	835	109	28
Osteoporosis	1,416	47	12
Diseases of the genito-urinary system	10,231	1,063	351
Diseases of the kidney and ureter	3,967	617	210
Complications of pregnancy, childbirth and the puerperium	36	4	1
Certain conditions originating in the perinatal period	205*	164	81
Congenital malformations, deformations and chromosomal abnormalities	1,292*	159	82
Congenital malformations of the nervous system	123	15	10
Congenital malformations of the circulatory system	535	58	20
Symptoms, signs and abnormal findings not classified elsewhere	11,457	325	108
Senility without mention of psychosis (old age)	9,785	210	71
Sudden infant death syndrome	164	20	2
Deaths from external causes	16,411	2,212	761
All accidents	11,053	1,284	492
Land transport accidents	2,697	293	175
Accidental falls	3,006	676	99
Accidental poisonings	910	48	40
Suicide and intentional self-harm	3,172	547	186
Homicide and assault	326†	80	32
Event of undetermined intent	1,486	216	27

* Excludes neonatal deaths (those at age under 28 days): for England and Wales neonatal deaths are included in the total number of deaths but excluded from the cause figures

† This will not be a true figure as registration of homicide and assault deaths in England and Wales is often delayed by adjourned inquests

Source: ONS – *AAS 2007* (Crown copyright)

NOTIFICATIONS OF INFECTIOUS DISEASES

	2000	*2005*
Measles	2,865	2,326
Mumps	3,367	66,541
Rubella	2,064	1,327
Whooping cough	866	679
Scarlet fever	2,544	2,075
Dysentery	1,613	1,346
Food poisoning	98,076	78,959
Typhoid and paratyphoid fevers	205	300
Hepatitis	4,530	5,246
Tuberculosis	7,100	8,017
Malaria	1,166	700

Source: ONS – *AAS 2007* (Crown copyright)

IMMUNISATION OF CHILDREN BY THEIR SECOND BIRTHDAY*

Percentage

	1991–2	*2004–5*
Tetanus	94	94
Diphtheria	94	94
Poliomyelitis	94	94
Whooping cough	88	94
Measles, mumps, rubella (MMR)	90	82

* Excludes Scotland

Source: ONS – *ST 2006* (Crown copyright)

ALCOHOL CONSUMPTION* BY AGE (GREAT BRITAIN)

Percentages

	16–24	*25–44*	*45–64*	*65+*	*All 16+*
Men					
4–8 units	13	17	19	12	16
8+ units	30	25	16	4	19
4+ units	43	42	35	16	35
Women					
3–6 units	14	15	14	3	12
6+ units	22	11	4	1	8
3+ units	36	26	18	4	20

* On at least one day in the previous week. Current Department of Health advice is that consumption of between three and four units a day for men and between two and three units for women should not lead to significant health risks. A unit of alcohol is 8 grams by weight or 10ml by volume of pure alcohol, ie the amount contained in half a pint of ordinary strength beer or lager, a single pub measure of spirits or a small glass of ordinary strength wine.

Source: ONS – *ST 2007* (Crown copyright)

DRUG MISUSE BY YOUNG ADULTS* (ENGLAND AND WALES)

Percentages

	Males		*Females*	
	1996	*2004–5*	*1996*	*2004–5*
Cannabis	30	30	22	18
Ecstasy	9	7	4	3
Cocaine	2	7	–	3
Amphetamines	15	4	9	3
Magic mushrooms or LSD	9	5	2	2
All Class A drugs†	13	11	6	5
Any drug‡	34	33	25	21

* Aged 16–24 years

† Includes heroin, cocaine (powder and crack), ecstasy, magic mushrooms, LSD and unprescribed use of methadone

‡ Includes drugs not listed in the table

Source: ONS – *ST 2006* (Crown copyright)

THE NATIONAL FLAG

The national flag of the United Kingdom is the Union Flag, generally known as the Union Jack.

The Union Flag is a combination of the cross of St George, patron saint of England, the cross of St Andrew, patron saint of Scotland and the cross of St Patrick, patron saint of Ireland.

Cross of St George: cross Gules in a field Argent (red cross on a white ground)

Cross of St Andrew: saltire Argent in a field Azure (white diagonal cross on a blue ground)

Cross of St Patrick: saltire Gules in a field Argent (red diagonal cross on a white ground)

The Union Flag was first introduced in 1606 after the union of the kingdoms of England and Scotland under one sovereign. The cross of St Patrick was added in 1801 after the union of Great Britain and Ireland.

See also Flags of the World colour plates.

FLYING THE UNION FLAG

The correct orientation of the Union Flag when flying is with the broader diagonal band of white uppermost in the hoist (ie near the pole) and the narrower diagonal band of white uppermost in the fly (ie furthest from the pole).

It is the practice to fly the Union Flag daily on some customs houses. In all other cases, flags are flown on government buildings by command of the Queen. There is no formal definition of a government building but it is generally accepted to mean a building owned or used by the Crown and predominately occupied or used by civil servants or the Armed Forces. It is now customary for the Union Flag to be flown at Buckingham Palace, Windsor Castle and Sandringham when the Queen is not in residence. Individuals, local authorities and other organisations may fly the Union Flag whenever they wish, subject to compliance with local planning requirements.

The flying of the Union Flag is decided by the DCMS at the Queen's command.

FLAGS AT HALF-MAST

Flags are flown at half-mast (ie two-thirds up between the top and bottom of the flagstaff) on the following occasions:

- from the announcement of the death up to the funeral of the sovereign, except on Proclamation Day, when flags are hoisted right up from 11am to sunset
- the funerals of members of the royal family*
- the funerals of foreign rulers*
- the funerals of prime ministers and ex-prime ministers of the UK*
- other occasions by special command of the Queen

* Subject to special commands from the Queen in each case

On occasions when days for flying flags coincide with days for flying flags at half-mast, the following rules are observed. Flags are flown at full mast:

- although a member of the royal family, or a near relative of the royal family, may be lying dead, unless special commands are received from the Queen to the contrary
- although it may be the day of the funeral of a foreign ruler

If the body of a very distinguished subject is lying at a government office, the flag may fly at half-mast on that office until the body has left (provided it is a day on which the flag would fly) and then the flag is to be hoisted right up. On all other government buildings the flag will fly as usual.

DAYS FOR FLYING FLAGS

Flags are hoisted from 8am to sunset.

Countess of Wessex's birthday	20 January
Accession of the Queen	6 February
Duke of York's birthday	19 February
St David's Day (in Wales only)*	1 March
Earl of Wessex's birthday	10 March
Commonwealth Day (2008)	10 March
St Patrick's Day (in Northern Ireland only)†	17 March
Birthday of the Queen	21 April
St George's Day (in England only)*	23 April
Europe Day‡	9 May
Coronation Day	2 June
Duke of Edinburgh's birthday	10 June
The Queen's Official Birthday (2008)	14 June
Duchess of Cornwall's birthday	17 July
Princess Royal's birthday	15 August
Remembrance Day (2008)	9 November
Prince of Wales' birthday	14 November
Wedding Day of the Queen	20 November
St Andrew's Day (in Scotland only)*	30 November
Opening of Parliament by the Queen§	
Prorogation of Parliament by the Queen§	

* The appropriate national flag may be flown in addition to the Union Flag, but not in a superior position

† Only the Union Flag should be flown

‡ The Union Flag should fly alongside the European flag. On government buildings that have only one flagpole, the Union Flag should take precedence

§ Flags are flown whether or not the Queen performs the ceremony in person and only in the Greater London area

THE ROYAL STANDARD

The Royal Standard comprises four quarterings – two for England (three lions passant), one for Scotland* (a lion rampant) and one for Ireland (a harp).

The Royal Standard is flown when the Queen is in residence at a royal palace, on transport being used by the Queen for official journeys and from Victoria Tower when the Queen attends parliament. It may also be flown on any building (excluding ecclesiastical buildings) during a visit by the Queen. If the Queen is to be present in a building advice on flag flying can be obtained from the DCMS.

The Royal Standard is never flown at half-mast, even after the death of the Sovereign, as the new monarch immediately succeeds to the throne.

* In Scotland a version with two Scottish quarterings instead of two English quarterings is used

THE ROYAL FAMILY

THE SOVEREIGN

ELIZABETH II, by the Grace of God, of the United Kingdom of Great Britain and Northern Ireland and of her other Realms and Territories Queen, Head of the Commonwealth, Defender of the Faith
Her Majesty Elizabeth Alexandra Mary of Windsor, elder daughter of King George VI and of HM Queen Elizabeth the Queen Mother
Born 21 April 1926, at 17 Bruton Street, London W1
Ascended the throne 6 February 1952
Crowned 2 June 1953, at Westminster Abbey
Married 20 November 1947, in Westminster Abbey, HRH The Prince Philip, Duke of Edinburgh
Official residences: Buckingham Palace, London SW1A 1AA; Windsor Castle, Berks; Palace of Holyroodhouse, Edinburgh
Private residences: Sandringham, Norfolk; Balmoral Castle, Aberdeenshire

HUSBAND OF THE QUEEN

HRH THE PRINCE PHILIP, DUKE OF EDINBURGH, KG, KT, OM, GBE, AC, QSO, PC, Ranger of Windsor Park
Born 10 June 1921, son of Prince and Princess Andrew of Greece and Denmark, naturalised a British subject 1947, created Duke of Edinburgh, Earl of Merioneth and Baron Greenwich 1947

CHILDREN OF THE QUEEN

HRH THE PRINCE OF WALES (Prince Charles Philip Arthur George), KG, KT, GCB, OM and Great Master of the Order of the Bath, AK, QSO, PC, ADC(P)
Born 14 November 1948, created Prince of Wales and Earl of Chester 1958, succeeded as Duke of Cornwall, Duke of Rothesay, Earl of Carrick and Baron Renfrew, Lord of the Isles and Great Steward of Scotland 1952
Married (1) 29 July 1981 Lady Diana Frances Spencer (Diana, Princess of Wales (1961–97), youngest daughter of the 8th Earl Spencer and the Hon. Mrs Shand Kydd), marriage dissolved 1996; (2) 9 April 2005 Mrs Camilla Rosemary Parker Bowles, now HRH The Duchess of Cornwall (*born* 17 July 1947, daughter of Major Bruce Shand and the Hon. Mrs Rosalind Shand)
Residences: Clarence House, London SW1A 1BA; Highgrove, Doughton, Tetbury, Glos GL8 8TN; Birkhall, Ballater, Aberdeenshire
Issue:
1. HRH Prince William of Wales (Prince William Arthur Philip Louis), *born* 21 June 1982
2. HRH Prince Henry of Wales (Prince Henry Charles Albert David), *born* 15 September 1984

HRH THE PRINCESS ROYAL (Princess Anne Elizabeth Alice Louise), KG, KT, GCVO
Born 15 August 1950, declared The Princess Royal 1987
Married (1) 14 November 1973 Captain Mark Anthony Peter Phillips, CVO (*born* 22 September 1948); marriage dissolved 1992; (2) 12 December 1992 Captain Timothy James Hamilton Laurence, MVO, RN (*born* 1 March 1955)
Residence: Gatcombe Park, Minchinhampton, Glos GL6 9AT
Issue:
1. Peter Mark Andrew Phillips, *born* 15 November 1977
2. Zara Anne Elizabeth Phillips, *born* 15 May 1981

HRH THE DUKE OF YORK (Prince Andrew Albert Christian Edward), KG, KCVO, ADC(P)
Born 19 February 1960, created Duke of York, Earl of Inverness and Baron Killyleagh 1986
Married 23 July 1986 Sarah Margaret Ferguson, now Sarah, Duchess of York (*born* 15 October 1959, younger daughter of Major Ronald Ferguson and Mrs Hector Barrantes), marriage dissolved 1996
Residence: Royal Lodge, Windsor Great Park, Berks
Issue:
1. HRH Princess Beatrice of York (Princess Beatrice Elizabeth Mary), *born* 8 August 1988
2. HRH Princess Eugenie of York (Princess Eugenie Victoria Helena), *born* 23 March 1990

HRH THE EARL OF WESSEX (Prince Edward Antony Richard Louis), KG, KCVO
Born 10 March 1964, created Earl of Wessex, Viscount Severn 1999
Married 19 June 1999 Sophie Helen Rhys-Jones, now HRH The Countess of Wessex (*born* 20 January 1965, daughter of Mr and Mrs Christopher Rhys-Jones)
Residence: Bagshot Park, Bagshot, Surrey GU19 5HS
Issue:
1. Lady Louise Windsor (Louise Alice Elizabeth Mary Mountbatten-Windsor), *born* 8 November 2003

NEPHEW AND NIECE OF THE QUEEN

Children of HRH The Princess Margaret, Countess of Snowdon and the Earl of Snowdon (*see* House of Windsor):

DAVID ALBERT CHARLES ARMSTRONG-JONES, VISCOUNT LINLEY, *born* 3 November 1961, *married* 8 October 1993 the Hon. Serena Stanhope, and has issue, Hon. Charles Patrick Inigo Armstrong-Jones, *born* 1 July 1999; Hon. Margarita Elizabeth Alleyne Armstrong-Jones, *born* 14 May 2002

LADY SARAH CHATTO (Sarah Frances Elizabeth), *born* 1 May 1964, *married* 14 July 1994 Daniel Chatto, and has issue, Samuel David Benedict Chatto, *born* 28 July 1996; Arthur Robert Nathaniel Chatto, *born* 5 February 1999

COUSINS OF THE QUEEN

Child of HRH The Duke of Gloucester and HRH Princess Alice, Duchess of Gloucester (*see* House of Windsor):

HRH THE DUKE OF GLOUCESTER (Prince Richard Alexander Walter George), KG, GCVO, Grand Prior of the Order of St John of Jerusalem
Born 26 August 1944
Married 8 July 1972 Birgitte Eva van Deurs, now HRH The Duchess of Gloucester, GCVO (*born* 20 June 1946, daughter of Asger Henriksen and Vivian van Deurs)
Residence: Kensington Palace, London W8 4PU

Issue:
1. Earl of Ulster (Alexander Patrick Gregers Richard), *born* 24 October 1974, *married* 22 June 2002 Dr Claire Booth, and has issue, Lord Culloden (Xan Richard Anders), *born* 12 March 2007
2. Lady Davina Lewis (Davina Elizabeth Alice Benedikte), *born* 19 November 1977, *married* 31 July 2004 Gary Lewis
3. Lady Rose Windsor (Rose Victoria Birgitte Louise), *born* 1 March 1980

Children of HRH The Duke of Kent and Princess Marina, Duchess of Kent (*see* House of Windsor):

HRH THE DUKE OF KENT (Prince Edward George Nicholas Paul Patrick), KG, GCMG, GCVO, ADC(P)
Born 9 October 1935
Married 8 June 1961 Katharine Lucy Mary Worsley, now HRH The Duchess of Kent, GCVO (*born* 22 February 1933, daughter of Sir William Worsley, Bt.)
Residence: Wren House, Palace Green, London W8 4PY
Issue:
1. Earl of St Andrews (George Philip Nicholas), *born* 26 June 1962, *married* 9 January 1988 Sylvana Tomaselli, and has issue, Baron Downpatrick (Edward Edmund Maximilian George), *born* 2 December 1988; Lady Marina-Charlotte Windsor (Marina-Charlotte Alexandra Katharine Helen), *born* 30 September 1992; Lady Amelia Windsor (Amelia Sophia Theodora Mary Margaret), *born* 24 August 1995
2. Lady Helen Taylor (Helen Marina Lucy), *born* 28 April 1964, *married* 18 July 1992 Timothy Taylor, and has issue, Columbus George Donald Taylor, *born* 6 August 1994; Cassius Edward Taylor, *born* 26 December 1996; Eloise Olivia Katharine Taylor, *born* 3 March 2003; Estella Olga Elizabeth Taylor, *born* 21 December 2004
3. Lord Nicholas Windsor (Nicholas Charles Edward Jonathan), *born* 25 July 1970, *married* 4 November 2006 Paola Doimi de Frankopan

HRH PRINCESS ALEXANDRA, THE HON. LADY OGILVY (Princess Alexandra Helen Elizabeth Olga Christabel), KG, GCVO
Born 25 December 1936
Married 24 April 1963 The Rt. Hon. Sir Angus Ogilvy, KCVO (1928–2004), second son of 12th Earl of Airlie
Residence: Thatched House Lodge, Richmond Park, Surrey TW10 5HP
Issue:
1. James Robert Bruce Ogilvy, *born* 29 February 1964, *married* 30 July 1988 Julia Rawlinson, and has issue, Flora Alexandra Ogilvy, *born* 15 December 1994; Alexander Charles Ogilvy, *born* 12 November 1996
2. Marina Victoria Alexandra, Mrs Mowatt, *born* 31 July 1966, *married* 2 February 1990 Paul Mowatt (marriage dissolved 1997), and has issue, Zenouska May Mowatt, *born* 26 May 1990; Christian Alexander Mowatt, *born* 4 June 1993

HRH PRINCE MICHAEL OF KENT (Prince Michael George Charles Franklin), GCVO
Born 4 July 1942
Married 30 June 1978 Baroness Marie-Christine Agnes Hedwig Ida von Reibnitz, now HRH Princess Michael of Kent (*born* 15 January 1945, daughter of Baron Gunther von Reibnitz)
Residence: Kensington Palace, London W8 4PU
Issue:
1. Lord Frederick Windsor (Frederick Michael George David Louis), *born* 6 April 1979
2. Lady Gabriella Windsor (Gabriella Marina Alexandra Ophelia), *born* 23 April 1981

ORDER OF SUCCESSION

1	HRH The Prince of Wales
2	HRH Prince William of Wales
3	HRH Prince Henry of Wales
4	HRH The Duke of York
5	HRH Princess Beatrice of York
6	HRH Princess Eugenie of York
7	HRH The Earl of Wessex
8	Lady Louise Windsor
9	HRH The Princess Royal
10	Peter Phillips
11	Zara Phillips
12	Viscount Linley
13	Hon. Charles Armstrong-Jones
14	Hon. Margarita Armstrong-Jones
15	Lady Sarah Chatto
16	Samuel Chatto
17	Arthur Chatto
18	HRH The Duke of Gloucester
19	Earl of Ulster
20	Lord Culloden
21	Lady Davina Lewis
22	Lady Rose Windsor
23	HRH The Duke of Kent
24	Lady Marina-Charlotte Windsor
25	Lady Amelia Windsor
26	Lady Helen Taylor
27	Columbus Taylor
28	Cassius Taylor
29	Eloise Taylor
30	Estella Taylor
31	Lord Frederick Windsor
32	Lady Gabriella Windsor
33	HRH Princess Alexandra, the Hon. Lady Ogilvy
34	James Ogilvy
35	Alexander Ogilvy
36	Flora Ogilvy
37	Marina Ogilvy, Mrs Mowatt
38	Christian Mowatt
39	Zenouska Mowatt

HRH Prince Michael of Kent, and The Earl of St Andrews both lost the right of succession to the throne through marriage to a Roman Catholic. Lord Nicholas Windsor and Baron Downpatrick renounced their rights to the throne on converting to Roman Catholicism in 2001 and 2003 respectively. Their children remain in succession provided that they are in communion with the Church of England.

PRIVATE SECRETARIES TO THE ROYAL FAMILY

THE QUEEN
Office: Buckingham Palace, London SW1A 1AA
T 020-7930 4832 W www.royal.gov.uk
Private Secretary to the Queen, Christopher Geidt, OBE

PRINCE PHILIP, THE DUKE OF EDINBURGH
Office: Buckingham Palace, London SW1A 1AA
T 020-7930 4832
Private Secretary, Brig. Sir Miles Hunt-Davis, KCVO, CBE

THE PRINCE OF WALES AND THE DUCHESS OF CORNWALL
Office: Clarence House, London SW1A 1BA T 020-7930 4832
Principal Private Secretary, Sir Michael Peat, KCVO

PRINCES WILLIAM AND HENRY OF WALES
Office: Clarence House, London SW1A 1BA T 020-7930 4832
Private Secretary, James Lowther-Pinkerton, MVO, MBE

THE DUKE OF YORK
Office: Buckingham Palace, London SW1A 1AA
T 020-7930 4832
Private Secretary, Alastair Watson

THE EARL AND COUNTESS OF WESSEX
Office: Bagshot Park, Surrey GU19 5PL T 01276-707040
Private Secretary, Brig. J. Smedley

THE PRINCESS ROYAL
Office: Buckingham Palace, London SW1A 1AA
T 020-7930 4832
Private Secretary, Capt. N. P. Wright, LVO, RN

THE DUKE AND DUCHESS OF GLOUCESTER
Office: Kensington Palace, London W8 4PU T 020-7368 1000
Private Secretary, Alistair Wood, MBE

THE DUKE OF KENT
Office: St James's Palace, London SW1A 1BQ T 020-7930 4872
Private Secretary, N. Adamson, LVO, OBE

THE DUCHESS OF KENT
Office: Wren House, Palace Green, London W8 4PY
T 020-7937 2730
Personal Secretary, Virginia Utley

PRINCE AND PRINCESS MICHAEL OF KENT
Office: Kensington Palace, London W8 4PU T 020-7938 3519
W www.princemichael.org.uk
Private Secretary, N. Chance

PRINCESS ALEXANDRA, THE HON. LADY OGILVY
Office: Buckingham Palace, London SW1A 1AA
T 020-7024 4270
Private Secretary, Diane Duke

ROYAL SALUTES

ENGLAND

The basic royal salute is 21 rounds with an extra 20 rounds fired at Hyde Park because it is a royal park. At the Tower of London 62 rounds are fired on royal anniversaries (21 plus a further 20 because the Tower is a royal palace and a further 21 'for the City of London') and 41 on other occasions. Gun salutes occur on the following royal anniversaries:

- Accession Day
- The Queen's birthday
- Coronation Day
- Duke of Edinburgh's birthday
- The Queen's official birthday
- state opening of parliament

Gun salutes also occur when parliament is prorogued by the sovereign, on royal births and when a visiting head of state meets the sovereign in London, Windsor or Edinburgh.

In London, salutes are fired at Hyde Park and the Tower of London although on some occasions (state visits, state opening of parliament and the Queen's birthday parade) Green Park is used instead.

Constable of the Royal Palace and Fortress of London, Gen. Sir Roger Wheeler, GCB, CBE
Lieutenant of the Tower of London, Lt.-Gen. Sir Cedric Delves, KBE, DSO
Resident Governor and Keeper of the Jewel House, Maj.-Gen. Keith Cima, CB
Master Gunner of St James's Park, Gen. Sir Alex Harley, KBE, CB
Master Gunner within the Tower, Col. Simon Garrett

SCOTLAND

Royal salutes are authorised at Edinburgh Castle and Stirling Castle, although in practice Edinburgh Castle is the only operating saluting station in Scotland. A salute of 21 guns is fired on the following occasions:

- the anniversaries of the birth, accession and coronation of the sovereign
- the anniversary of the birth of the Duke of Edinburgh

A salute of 21 guns is fired in Edinburgh on the occasion of the opening of the general assembly of the Church of Scotland. A salute of 21 guns may also be fired in Edinburgh on the arrival of HM The Queen or a member of the royal family who is a Royal Highness on an official visit. Other military saluting stations are at Cardiff Castle in Wales and Hillsborough Castle, County Down in Northern Ireland.

ROYAL HOUSEHOLD

The PRIVATE SECRETARY is responsible for:

- informing and advising the Queen on constitutional, governmental and political matters in the UK, her other Realms and the wider Commonwealth, including communications with the prime minister and government departments
- organising the Queen's domestic and overseas official programme
- the Queen's speeches, messages, patronage, photographs, portraits and official presents
- communications in connection with the role of the royal family
- dealing with correspondence to the Queen from members of the public
- organising and coordinating royal travel
- coordinating and initiating research to support engagements by members of the royal family

The PRESS SECRETARY is in charge of Buckingham Palace's press office and reports to the private secretary. The press secretary is responsible for:

- developing communications strategies to enhance the public understanding of the role of the monarchy
- briefing the British and international media on the role and duties of the Queen and issues relating to the royal family
- responding to media enquiries
- arranging media facilities in the UK and overseas to support royal functions and engagements
- the management of the royal website

The private secretary is keeper of the Royal Archives and is responsible for the care of the records of the sovereign and the royal household from previous reigns, preserved in the Royal Archives at Windsor. As keeper, it is the private secretary's responsibility to ensure the proper management of the records of the present reign with a view to their transfer to the archives as and when appropriate. The private secretary is an *ex officio* trustee of the Royal Collection Trust.

The KEEPER OF THE PRIVY PURSE AND TREASURER to the Queen is responsible for:

- the Queen's Civil List, which is the money paid from the government's Consolidated Fund to meet official expenditure relating to the Queen's duties as head of state and head of the Commonwealth
- through the director of personnel, the planning and management of personnel policy across the royal household, the administration of all its pension schemes and private estates employees, and the allocation of employee and pensioner housing
- information technology systems
- internal audit services
- health and safety; insurance matters
- the privy purse, which is mainly financed by the net income of the Duchy of Lancaster, and meets both official and private expenditure incurred by the Queen
- liaison with other members of the royal family and their households on financial matters
- the Queen's private estates at Sandringham and Balmoral, the Queen's Racing Establishment and the Royal Studs and liaison with the Ascot Authority
- the Home Park at Windsor and liaison with the Crown Estate Commissioners concerning the Home Park and the Great Park at Windsor
- the Royal Philatelic Collection
- administrative aspects of the Military Knights of Windsor and the Royal Almonry
- administration of the Royal Victorian Order, of which the keeper of the privy purse is secretary, Long and Faithful Service Medals, and the Queen's cups, medals and prizes, and policy on commemorative medals

The keeper of the privy purse is one of three royal trustees (in respect of his responsibilities for the Civil List) and is receiver-general of the Duchy of Lancaster and a member of the Duchy's Council.

The keeper of the privy purse is also responsible for property services at occupied royal palaces in England, comprising Buckingham Palace, St James's Palace, Clarence House, Marlborough House Mews, the residential and office areas of Kensington Palace, Windsor Castle and buildings in the Home and Great Parks of Windsor and Hampton Court Mews and Paddocks. The costs of property services for occupied royal palaces are met from a grant-in-aid from the Department for Culture, Media and Sport.

The DIRECTOR OF PROPERTY SERVICES has day-to-day responsibility for the royal household's property section:

- fire safety issues
- repairs and refurbishment of buildings and new buildings work
- utilities and telecommunications
- putting up stages, tents and other work in connection with ceremonial occasions, garden parties and other official functions

The property section is also responsible, on a sub-contract basis from the DCMS, for the maintenance of Marlborough House (which is occupied by the Commonwealth Secretariat).

The keeper of the privy purse also oversees royal communications and information expenditure, which is met from the property services grant-in-aid, and the financial aspects of royal travel, met from a grant-in-aid provided by the Department for Transport.

The keeper of the privy purse is an *ex officio* trustee of the Historic Royal Palaces Trust and the Royal Collection Trust.

The Queen's Civil List and the grants-in-aid for property services and royal travel are provided by the government in return for the net surplus from the Crown Estate and other hereditary revenues.

The MASTER OF THE HOUSEHOLD is responsible for the staff and domestic arrangements at Buckingham Palace, Windsor Castle, the Palace of Holyroodhouse, Balmoral Castle and Sandringham House when the Queen is in residence. These arrangements include:

- the provision of meals for the Queen and other

members of the royal family, their guests and royal household employees
- service by liveried staff at meals, receptions and other events
- travel arrangements for employees and the movement of baggage between the royal residences
- cleaning and laundry
- furnishings and the internal decorative appearance of occupied royal palaces in collaboration with the director of the Royal Collection
- liaison with the royalty and diplomatic protection department of the Metropolitan Police concerning security procedures at occupied royal palaces
- the Queen's official entertaining, both at home and overseas, and overseeing aspects of the Queen's private entertaining

The COMPTROLLER, LORD CHAMBERLAIN'S OFFICE is responsible for:

- the organisation of all ceremonial engagements, including state visits to the Queen in the UK, royal weddings and funerals, the state opening of parliament, Guards of Honour at Buckingham Palace, investitures, and the Garter and Thistle ceremonies
- garden parties at Buckingham Palace and the Palace of Holyroodhouse (except for catering and tents)
- the Crown Jewels, which are part of the Royal Collection, when they are in use on state occasions
- coordination of the arrangements for the Queen to be represented at funerals and memorial services and at the arrival and departure of visiting heads of state
- advising on matters of precedence, style and titles, dress, flying of flags, gun salutes, mourning and other ceremonial issues
- supervising the applications from tradesmen for Royal Warrants of Appointment
- advising on the commercial use of royal emblems and contemporary royal photographs
- the ecclesiastical household, the medical household, the body guards and certain ceremonial appointments such as Gentlemen Ushers and Pages of Honour
- the lords in waiting, who represent the Queen on various occasions and escort visiting heads of state during incoming state visits
- the Queen's bargemaster and watermen and the Queen's swans

The comptroller is also responsible for the Royal Mews, assisted by the CROWN EQUERRY, who has day-to-day responsibility for:

- the provision of carriage processions for the state opening of parliament, state visits, Trooping of the Colour, Royal Ascot, the Garter Ceremony, the Thistle Service, the presentation of credentials to the Queen by incoming foreign ambassadors and high commissioners, and other state and ceremonial occasions
- the provision of chauffeur-driven cars
- coordinating travel arrangements by road in respect of the Queen's official engagements
- supervision and administration of the Royal Mews at Buckingham Palace, Windsor Castle, Hampton Court and the Palace of Holyroodhouse

The comptroller also has overall responsibility for the MARSHAL OF THE DIPLOMATIC CORPS, who is responsible for the relationship between the royal household and the Diplomatic Heads of Mission in London; and the SECRETARY OF THE CENTRAL CHANCERY OF THE ORDERS OF KNIGHTHOOD, who administers the Orders of Chivalry, makes arrangements for investitures and the distribution of insignia, and ensures the proper public notification of awards through the *London Gazette.*

The DIRECTOR OF THE ROYAL COLLECTION is responsible for:

- the administration and custodial control of the Royal Collection in all royal residences
- the care, display, conservation and restoration of items in the collection
- initiating and assisting research into the collection and publishing catalogues and books on the collection
- making the collection accessible to the public and educating and informing the public about the collection

The Royal Collection, which contains a large number of works of art, is held by the Queen as sovereign in trust for her successors and the nation and is not owned by her as an individual. The administration, conservation and presentation of the Royal Collection are funded by the Royal Collection Trust solely from income from visitors to Windsor Castle, Buckingham Palace and the Palace of Holyroodhouse. The Royal Collection Trust is chaired by the Prince of Wales. The Lord Chamberlain, the private secretary and the keeper of the privy purse are *ex officio* trustees and there are three external trustees appointed by the Queen.

The director of the Royal Collection is also at present the SURVEYOR OF THE QUEEN'S WORKS OF ART and is responsible for pictures and miniatures, the ROYAL LIBRARIAN is responsible for all books, manuscripts, coins and medals, insignia and works of art on paper including the watercolours, prints and drawings in the Print Room at Windsor Castle, and the SURVEYOR OF THE QUEEN'S WORKS OF ART is responsible for furniture, ceramics and the other decorative arts in the collection.

The director of the Royal Collection has overall responsibility for trading activities that fund the Royal Collection Department. These are administered by Royal Collection Enterprises Limited, the trading subsidiary of the Royal Collection Trust. The company, whose chair is the Keeper of the Privy Purse, is responsible for:

- Managing access by the public to Windsor Castle (including Frogmore House), Buckingham Palace (including the Royal Mews and the Queen's Gallery) and the Palace of Holyroodhouse
- Running shops at each location
- Managing the images and intellectual property rights of the Royal Collection

The director of the Royal Collection is also an *ex officio* trustee of the Historic Royal Palaces Trust.

SENIOR MANAGEMENT OF THE ROYAL HOUSEHOLD

Lord Chamberlain, Earl Peel, GCVO, PC
HEADS OF DEPARTMENT
Private Secretary to The Queen, Rt. Hon. Christopher Geidt, OBE
Keeper of the Privy Purse, Sir Alan Reid, KCVO
Master of the Household, Air Vice-Marshal David Walker, OBE, MVO
Comptroller, Lord Chamberlain's Office, Lt.-Col. Andrew Ford
Director of the Royal Collection, Sir Hugh Roberts, KCVO
NON-EXECUTIVE MEMBERS
Private Secretary to the Duke of Edinburgh, Brig. Sir Miles Hunt-Davis, KCVO, CBE
Private Secretary to the Prince of Wales, Sir Michael Peat, KCVO

THE POET LAUREATE

The post of Poet Laureate was officially established when John Dryden was appointed by royal warrant as Poet Laureate and Historiographer Royal in 1668. The post is attached to the royal household and was originally conferred on the holder for life; in 1999 the length of appointment was changed to a ten-year term. It is customary for the Poet Laureate to write verse to mark events of national importance. The postholder currently receives an honorarium of £5,000 a year.
The Poet Laureate, Prof. Andrew Motion, *apptd* 1999

ROYAL FINANCES

FUNDING

CIVIL LIST

The Civil List dates back to the late 17th century. It was originally used by the sovereign to supplement hereditary revenues for paying the salaries of judges, ambassadors and other government officers as well as the expenses of the royal household. In 1760, on the accession of George III, it was decided that the Civil List would be provided by parliament to cover all relevant expenditure in return for the king surrendering the hereditary revenues of the Crown (principally the net surplus of the Crown Estate). At that time parliament undertook to pay the salaries of judges, ambassadors, etc. In 1831 parliament agreed also to meet the costs of the royal palaces in return for a reduction in the Civil List. Each sovereign has agreed to continue this arrangement. The Civil List now meets the central staff costs and running expenses of the Queen's official household.

Until 1972, the amount of money allocated annually under the Civil List was set for the duration of a reign. The system was then altered to a fixed annual payment for ten years but from 1975 high inflation made an annual review necessary. The system of payments reverted to the practice of a fixed annual payment of £7.9m for a ten year period to 31 December 2000, during this period annual Civil List expenditure reached £6.5m, and a reserve of £35m was established. In order to draw down the reserve, the annual Civil List payment was left at £7.9m for a further ten years to 31 December 2010.

The legislative requirement is for Civil List accounts to be submitted to parliament, in the form of Royal Trustees Reports, at 10-yearly intervals, but from June 2002 accounts have been published annually. The sixth annual accounts for the year ending 31 December 2006 were published in June 2007:

	2005	*2006*
Civil List payment	£7,900,000	£7,900,000
Draw-down from the Civil List reserve	£3,400,000	£4,100,000
Net Receipts	£11,300,000	£12,000,000
Net Civil List Expenditure	(£11,300,000)	(£12,200,000)

PARLIAMENTARY ANNUITIES

The Civil List Acts provide for other members of the royal family to receive parliamentary annuities from government funds to meet the expenses of carrying out their official duties. Since 1993 the Queen has reimbursed all the annuities except those paid to the late Queen Elizabeth the Queen Mother and the Duke of Edinburgh.

The Prince of Wales does not receive a parliamentary annuity. He derives his income from the revenues of the Duchy of Cornwall and these monies meet the official and private expenses of the Prince of Wales and his family (*see* Prince of Wales' Funding).

In 2000 the annual amounts payable to members of the royal family, excluding the Earl of Wessex, were reset at their 1990 levels for the next ten years. The Earl of Wessex had his annuity increased by £45,000 to £141,000 on the occasion of his marriage in 1999.

The annual payments remain as follows until December 2010:

The Duke of Edinburgh	£359,000
The Duke of York	£249,000
The Earl of Wessex	£141,000
The Princess Royal	£228,000
The Duke and Duchess of Gloucester	£175,000
The Duke and Duchess of Kent	£236,000
Princess Alexandra	£225,000
Subtotal	£1,613,000
Refunded to the Treasury by the Queen	(£1,254,000)
TOTAL	£359,000

GRANTS-IN-AID

Grants-in-aid are provided to the royal household annually by the Department for Culture, Media and Sport for property services and communications and information, and by the Department for Transport for royal travel. Property services meets the cost of property maintenance, and of utilities, telephones and related services at the occupied royal palaces in England (*see* Royal Household section for a list of occupied palaces). Communications and Information meets the cost of communication and information services in connection with official royal functions and engagements in England and Scotland. Royal travel meets the cost of official royal travel by air and rail.

GRANTS-IN-AID 2006–7:

	Grant-in-aid voted by parliament	*Total net expenditure*
Property Services	£15,000,000	£14,500,000
Marlborough House Maintenance	£600,000	£400,000
Communications and Information	£500,000	£500,000
Royal Travel	£6,000,000	£5,600,000

THE PRIVY PURSE AND THE DUCHY OF LANCASTER
The funds received by the privy purse pay for official expenses incurred by the Queen as head of state and for some of the Queen's private expenditure. The revenues of the Duchy of Lancaster are the principal source of income for the privy purse. The revenues of the Duchy were retained by George III in 1760 when the hereditary revenues were surrendered in exchange for the Civil List. The Duchy's affairs are the responsibility of the Duchy Council which reports to the Chancellor of the Duchy of Lancaster, who in turn is accountable directly to the sovereign rather than to parliament. However the chancellor does answer parliamentary questions on matters relating to the Duchy of Lancaster's responsibilities.

THE DUCHY OF LANCASTER, Lancaster Place, London WC2E 7ED **E** info@duchyoflancaster.co.uk
W www.duchyoflancaster.co.uk
Chancellor of the Duchy of Lancaster, Rt Hon. Hilary Armstrong, MP, *apptd* 2006
Chair of the Council, Lord Shuttleworth
Clerk and Chief Executive, Paul Clarke, FRICS
Receiver-General, Sir Alan Reid, KCVO
Attorney-General, Robert Hildyard, QC

PERSONAL INCOME
The Queen's personal income derives mostly from investments, and is used to meet private expenditure.

EXPENDITURE MET BY GOVERNMENT DEPARTMENTS AND THE CROWN ESTATE 2006–7:

Administration of honours	£500,000
Equerries, orderlies and other personnel	£900,000
Maintenance of Holyroodhouse	£1,300,000
State visits to and by the Queen and liaison with the Diplomatic Corps	£600,000
Ceremonial occasions	£200,000
Maintenance of Home Park, Windsor Castle	£500,000
Other	£100,000
Total	£4,100,000

PRINCE OF WALES' FUNDING

The Duchy Estate was created in 1337 by Edward III for his son and heir Prince Edward (the Black Prince) who became the Duke of Cornwall. The Duchy's primary function is to provide an income from its assets for the Prince of Wales. Under a 1337 charter, confirmed by subsequent legislation, the Prince of Wales is not entitled to the proceeds or profit on the sale of Duchy assets but only to the annual income which is generated from these assets. The Duchy is responsible for the sustainable and commercial management of its properties, investment portfolio and approximately 54,764 hectares of land, based mostly in the southwest of England. The Prince of Wales has chosen to use a proportion of his income to meet the cost of his public and charitable work in addition to providing a private source of income. The Duchy also funds the public, charitable and private activities of the Duchess of Cornwall and princes William and Harry. Proceeds from the Duchy are voluntarily subject to income tax.

THE DUCHY OF CORNWALL, 10 Buckingham Gate, London SW1E 6L
T 0207-834 7346 **E** London@duchyofcornwall.gov.uk
W www.duchyofcornwall.org
Lord Warden of the Stannaries, Sir Nicholas Bacon, Bt.
Receiver-General, James Leigh-Pemberton
Attorney-General, Jonathan Crow, QC
Secretary and Keeper of the Records, Bertie Ross

TAXATION

The sovereign is not legally liable to pay income tax or capital gains tax. After income tax was reintroduced in 1842, some income tax was paid voluntarily by the sovereign but over a long period these payments were phased out. In 1992 the Queen offered to pay tax on a voluntary basis from 6 April 1993, and the Prince of Wales offered to pay tax on a voluntary basis on his income from the Duchy of Cornwall (he was already taxed in all other respects).

The main provisions for the Queen and the Prince of Wales to pay tax, set out in a Memorandum of Understanding on Royal Taxation presented to parliament on 11 February 1993, are that the Queen will pay income tax and capital gains tax in respect of her private income and assets, and on the proportion of the income and capital gains of the Privy Purse used for private purposes. Inheritance tax will be paid on the Queen's assets, except for those which pass to the next sovereign, whether automatically or by gift or bequest. The Prince of Wales will pay income tax on income from the Duchy of Cornwall used for private purposes.

The Prince of Wales has confirmed that he intends to pay tax on the same basis following his accession to the throne. Other members of the royal family are subject to tax as for any taxpayer.

MILITARY RANKS AND TITLES

THE QUEEN

ROYAL NAVY
Lord High Admiral of the United Kingdom

ARMY
Colonel-in-Chief
The Life Guards; The Blues and Royals (Royal Horse Guards and 1st Dragoons); The Royal Scots Dragoon Guards (Carabiniers and Greys); The Queen's Royal Lancers; Royal Tank Regiment; Corps of Royal Engineers; Grenadier Guards; Coldstream Guards; Scots Guards; Irish Guards; Welsh Guards; The Royal Regiment of Scotland; The Duke of Lancaster's Regiment; The Royal Welsh; Adjutant General's Corps; The Royal Mercian and Lancastrian Yeomanry; The Governor General's Horse Guards (of Canada); The King's Own Calgary Regiment (Royal Canadian Armoured Corps); Canadian Forces Military Engineers Branch; Royal 22e Regiment (of Canada); Governor General's Foot Guards (of Canada); The Canadian Grenadier Guards; Le Régiment de la Chaudière (of Canada); 2nd Battalion Royal New Brunswick Regiment (North Shore); The 48th Highlanders of Canada; The Argyll and Sutherland Highlanders of Canada (Princess Louise's); The Calgary Highlanders; Royal Australian Engineers; Royal Australian Infantry Corps; Royal Australian Army Ordnance Corps; Royal Australian Army Nursing Corps; The Corps of Royal New Zealand Engineers; Royal New Zealand Infantry Regiment; The Malawi Rifles; The Royal Malta Artillery

Affiliated Colonel-in-Chief
The Queen's Gurkha Engineers

Captain-General
Royal Regiment of Artillery; The Honourable Artillery Company; Combined Cadet Force; Royal Regiment of Canadian Artillery; Royal Regiment of Australian Artillery; Royal Regiment of New Zealand Artillery; Royal New Zealand Armoured Corps

Royal Colonel
The Argyll and Sutherland Highlanders, 5th Battalion The Royal Regiment of Scotland

Patron
Royal Army Chaplains' Department

ROYAL AIR FORCE
Air Commodore-in-Chief
Royal Auxiliary Air Force; Royal Air Force Regiment; Air Reserve of Canada; Royal Australian Air Force Reserve; Territorial Air Force (of New Zealand)

Commandant-in-Chief
Royal Air Force College, Cranwell

Royal Honorary Air Commodore
Royal Air Force Marham; 603 (City of Edinburgh) Squadron Royal Auxiliary Air Force

PRINCE PHILIP, DUKE OF EDINBURGH

ROYAL NAVY
Admiral of the Fleet
Admiral of the Fleet, Royal Australian Navy
Admiral of the Fleet, Royal New Zealand Navy
Admiral of the Royal Canadian Sea Cadets

ROYAL MARINES
Captain-General

ARMY
Field Marshal
Field Marshal, Australian Military Forces
Field Marshal, New Zealand Army

Colonel-in-Chief
The Queen's Royal Hussars (Queen's Own and Royal Irish); The Rifles; Corps of Royal Electrical and Mechanical Engineers; Intelligence Corps; Army Cadet Force Association; The Royal Canadian Regiment; The Royal Hamilton Light Infantry (Wentworth Regiment of Canada); The Cameron Highlanders of Ottawa; The Queen's Own Cameron Highlanders of Canada; The Seaforth Highlanders of Canada; The Royal Canadian Army Cadets; The Royal Australian Corps of Electrical and Mechanical Engineers; The Australian Army Cadet Corps

Colonel
Grenadier Guards

Royal Colonel
The Highlanders, 4th Battalion The Royal Regiment of Scotland

Hon. Colonel
City of Edinburgh University Officers' Training Corps; The Trinidad and Tobago Regiment

Member
Honourable Artillery Company

ROYAL AIR FORCE
Marshal of the Royal Air Force
Marshal of the Royal Australian Air Force
Marshal of the Royal New Zealand Air Force

Air Commodore-in-Chief
Air Training Corps; Royal Canadian Air Cadets

Hon. Air Commodore
Royal Air Force Kinloss

THE PRINCE OF WALES

ROYAL NAVY
Admiral
Commodore-in-Chief
Royal Naval Command Plymouth

ARMY
General

Colonel-in-Chief
The Royal Dragoon Guards; The 22nd Cheshire Regiment; The Parachute Regiment; The Royal Gurkha Rifles; Army Air Corps; The Royal Canadian Dragoons; Lord Strathcona's Horse (Royal Canadians); The Royal Regiment of Canada; Royal Winnipeg Rifles; Royal Australian Armoured Corps; The Royal Pacific Islands Regiment; 1st The Queen's Dragoon Guards; The Black Watch (Royal Highland Regiment) of Canada; The Toronto Scottish Regiment (Queen Elizabeth The Queen Mother's Own); The Welsh Guards

Royal Colonel
The Black Watch, 3rd Battalion The Royal Regiment of Scotland; 51st Highland, 7th Battalion The Royal Regiment of Scotland (Territorial Army)

Royal Honorary Colonel
The Queen's Own Yeomanry

ROYAL AIR FORCE
Air Chief Marshal

Hon. Air Commodore
Royal Air Force Valley

Air Commodore-in-Chief
Royal New Zealand Air Force

Colonel-in-Chief
Air Reserve Canada

THE DUCHESS OF CORNWALL

ROYAL NAVY
Commodore-in-Chief
Naval Medical Services

ARMY
Royal Colonel
4th Battalion The Rifles

PRINCE WILLIAM OF WALES

ROYAL NAVY
Commodore-in-Chief
Scotland Command; Submarines Command

ARMY
Second Lieutenant
The Blues and Royals (Royal Horse Guards and 1st Dragoons)

PRINCE HENRY OF WALES

ROYAL NAVY
Commodore-in-Chief
Small Ships and Diving Command

ARMY
Second Lieutenant
The Blues and Royals (Royal Horse Guards and 1st Dragoons)

THE DUKE OF YORK

ROYAL NAVY
Commander
Admiral of the Marine Society and Sea Cadets
Honorary Captain

ARMY
Colonel-in-Chief
The Royal Irish Regiment (27th (Inniskilling), 83rd, 87th and The Ulster Defence Regiment); 9th/12th Royal Lancers (The Prince of Wales's); The Royal Highland Fusiliers, 2nd Battalion The Royal Regiment of Scotland; The Yorkshire Regiment; Small Arms School Corps; The Queen's York Rangers (First Americans); Royal New Zealand Army Logistics Regiment; The Royal Highland Fusiliers of Canada; The Princess Louise Fusiliers (Canada)

ROYAL AIR FORCE
Hon. Air Commodore
Royal Air Force Lossiemouth

THE EARL OF WESSEX

ROYAL NAVY
Commodore-in-Chief
Royal Fleet Auxiliary

Patron
Royal Fleet Auxiliary Association

ARMY
Colonel-in-Chief
Hastings and Prince Edward Regiment; Saskatchewan Dragoons

Royal Hon. Colonel
Royal Wessex Yeomanry

THE COUNTESS OF WESSEX

ARMY
Colonel-in-Chief
Queen Alexandra's Royal Army Nursing Corps; The Lincoln and Welland Regiment

THE PRINCESS ROYAL

ROYAL NAVY
Rear-Admiral (Chief Commandant for Women in the Royal Navy)

ARMY
Colonel-in-Chief
The King's Royal Hussars; Royal Corps of Signals; Royal Logistic Corps; The Royal Army Veterinary Corps; 8th Canadian Hussars (Princess Louise's); Royal Newfoundland Regiment; Canadian Forces Communications and Electronics Branch; The Grey and Simcoe Foresters (Royal Canadian Armoured Corps); The Royal Regina Rifle Regiment; Canadian Forces Medical Branch; Royal Australian Corps of Signals; Royal New Zealand Corps of Signals; Royal New Zealand Nursing Corps

Affiliated Colonel-in-Chief
The Queen's Gurkha Signals; The Queen's Own Gurkha Transport Regiment

Royal Colonel
Royal Scots Borders, 1st Battalion The Royal Regiment of Scotland; 52nd Lowland, 6th Battalion The Royal Regiment of Scotland

Colonel
The Blues and Royals (Royal Horse Guards and 1st Dragoons)

Hon. Colonel
University of London Officers' Training Corps

Commandant-in-Chief
First Aid Nursing Yeomanry (Princess Royal's Volunteer Corps)

ROYAL AIR FORCE
Hon. Air Commodore
Royal Air Force Lyneham; University of London Air Squadron

THE DUKE OF GLOUCESTER

ARMY
Colonel-in-Chief
The Royal Anglian Regiment; Royal Army Medical Corps

Deputy Colonel-in-Chief
The Royal Gloucestershire, Berkshire and Wiltshire Regiment; The Royal Logistic Corps

Hon. Colonel
Royal Monmouthshire Royal Engineers (Militia)

ROYAL AIR FORCE
Hon. Air Marshal

Hon. Air Commodore
Royal Air Force Odiham; No. 501 (County of Gloucester) Squadron Royal Auxiliary Air Force

THE DUCHESS OF GLOUCESTER

ARMY
Colonel-in-Chief
Royal Army Dental Corps; Royal Australian Army Educational Corps; Royal New Zealand Army Educational Corps

Deputy Colonel-in-Chief
Adjutant-General's Corps

Vice-Patron
Adjutant-General's Corps Regimental Association

Patron
Royal Army Educational Corps Association; Army Families Federation

THE DUKE OF KENT

ARMY
Field Marshal

Colonel-in-Chief
The Royal Regiment of Fusiliers; Lorne Scots (Peel, Dufferin and Hamilton Regiment)

Deputy Colonel-in-Chief
The Royal Scots Dragoon Guards (Carabiniers and Greys)

Royal Colonel
1st Battalion The Rifles

Colonel
Scots Guards

ROYAL AIR FORCE
Hon. Air Chief Marshal

Hon. Air Commodore
Royal Air Force Leuchars

THE DUCHESS OF KENT

ARMY
Deputy Colonel-in-Chief
The Royal Dragoon Guards; Adjutant-General's Corps; The Royal Logistic Corps

PRINCE MICHAEL OF KENT

ROYAL NAVY
Honorary Rear Admiral Royal Naval Reserve

ARMY
Major (retd)
The Royal Hussars (Prince of Wales's Own)

Colonel-in-Chief
Essex and Kent Scottish Regiment (Ontario)

ROYAL AIR FORCE
Hon. Air Commodore
RAF Benson

PRINCESS ALEXANDRA, THE HON. LADY OGILVY

ROYAL NAVY
Patron
Queen Alexandra's Royal Naval Nursing Service

ARMY
Colonel-in-Chief
The Queen's Own Rifles of Canada; The Canadian Scottish Regiment (Princess Mary's)

Deputy Colonel-in-Chief
The Queen's Royal Lancers

Royal Colonel
3rd Battalion The Rifles

Honorary Royal Colonel
The Royal Yeomanry

ROYAL AIR FORCE
Patron and Air Chief Commandant
Princess Mary's Royal Air Force Nursing Service

Hon. Air Commodore
Royal Air Force Cottesmore

THE HOUSE OF WINDSOR

King George V assumed by royal proclamation (17 July 1917) for his House and family, as well as for all descendants in the male line of Queen Victoria who are subjects of these realms, the name of Windsor.

KING GEORGE V
(George Frederick Ernest Albert), second son of King Edward VII, *born* 3 June 1865; *married* 6 July 1893 HSH Princess Victoria Mary Augusta Louise Olga Pauline Claudine Agnes of Teck (Queen Mary, *born* 26 May 1867; *died* 24 March 1953); *succeeded* to the throne 6 May 1910; *died* 20 January 1936. *Issue:*

1. HRH PRINCE EDWARD Albert Christian George Andrew Patrick David, *born* 23 June 1894, *succeeded* to the throne as King Edward VIII, 20 January 1936; *abdicated* 11 December 1936; created *Duke of Windsor* 1937; *married* 3 June 1937, Mrs Wallis Simpson (Her Grace The Duchess of Windsor, *born* 19 June 1896; *died* 24 April 1986), *died* 28 May 1972

2. HRH PRINCE ALBERT Frederick Arthur George, *born* 14 December 1895, *created* Duke of York 1920; *married* 26 April 1923, Lady Elizabeth Bowes-Lyon, youngest daughter of the 14th Earl of Strathmore and Kinghorne (HM Queen Elizabeth the Queen Mother, *born* 4 August 1900; *died* 30 March 2002), *succeeded* to the throne as King George VI, 11 December 1936; *died* 6 February 1952. *Issue:*
(1) HRH Princess Elizabeth Alexandra Mary, *succeeded* to the throne as Queen Elizabeth II, 6 February 1952 (*see* Royal Family)
(2) HRH Princess Margaret Rose (later HRH The Princess Margaret, Countess of Snowdon), *born* 21 August 1930; *married* 6 May 1960, Anthony Charles Robert Armstrong-Jones, GCVO, *created* Earl of Snowdon 1961 (marriage dissolved 1978), *died* 9 February 2002, having had issue (*see* Royal Family)

3. HRH PRINCESS (Victoria Alexandra Alice) MARY, *born* 25 April 1897, *created* Princess Royal 1932; *married* 28 February 1922, Viscount Lascelles, later the 6th Earl of Harewood (1882–1947), *died* 28 March 1965. *Issue:*
(1) George Henry Hubert Lascelles, 7th Earl of Harewood, KBE, *born* 7 February 1923; *married* (1) 1949, Maria (Marion) Stein (marriage dissolved 1967); *issue, (a)* David Henry George, Viscount Lascelles, *born* 1950; *(b)* James Edward, *born* 1953; *(c)* (Robert) Jeremy Hugh, *born* 1955; (2) 1967, Mrs Patricia Tuckwell; *issue, (d)* Mark Hubert, *born* 1964
(2) Gerald David Lascelles (1924–98), *married* (1) 1952, Miss Angela Dowding (marriage dissolved 1978); *issue, (a)* Henry Ulick, *born* 1953; (2) 1978, Mrs Elizabeth Colvin; *issue, (b)* Martin David, *born* 1962

4. HRH PRINCE HENRY William Frederick Albert, *born* 31 March 1900, *created* Duke of Gloucester, Earl of Ulster and Baron Culloden 1928, *married* 6 November 1935, Lady Alice Christabel Montagu-Douglas-Scott, daughter of the 7th Duke of Buccleuch and Queensberry (HRH Princess Alice, Duchess of Gloucester, *born* 25 December 1901; *died* 29 October 2004); *died* 10 June 1974. *Issue:*
(1) HRH Prince William Henry Andrew Frederick, *born* 18 December 1941; *accidentally killed* 28 August 1972
(2) HRH Prince Richard Alexander Walter George (HRH The Duke of Gloucester)

5. HRH PRINCE GEORGE Edward Alexander Edmund, *born* 20 December 1902, *created* Duke of Kent, Earl of St Andrews and Baron Downpatrick 1934, *married* 29 November 1934, HRH Princess Marina of Greece and Denmark (*born* 30 November 1906; *died* 27 August 1968); *killed on active service,* 25 August 1942. *Issue:*
(1) HRH Prince Edward George Nicholas Paul Patrick (HRH The Duke of Kent)
(2) HRH Princess Alexandra Helen Elizabeth Olga Christabel (HRH Princess Alexandra, the Hon. Lady Ogilvy)
(3) HRH Prince Michael George Charles Franklin (HRH Prince Michael of Kent)

6. HRH PRINCE JOHN Charles Francis, *born* 12 July 1905; *died* 18 January 1919

DESCENDANTS OF QUEEN VICTORIA

QUEEN VICTORIA
(Alexandrina Victoria), *born* 24 May 1819; *succeeded* to the throne 20 June 1837; *married* 10 February 1840 (Francis) Albert Augustus Charles Emmanuel, Duke of Saxony, Prince of Saxe-Coburg and Gotha (HRH Albert, Prince Consort, *born* 26 August 1819, *died* 14 December 1861); *died* 22 January 1901. *Issue:*

I. HRH PRINCESS VICTORIA Adelaide Mary Louisa (Princess Royal) (1840–1901), *m.* 1858, Friedrich III (1831–88), German Emperor March–June 1888. *Issue:*
   1. HIM Wilhelm II (1859–1941), German Emperor 1888–1918, *m.* (1) 1881 Princess Augusta Victoria of Schleswig-Holstein-Sonderburg-Augustenburg (1858–1921); (2) 1922 Princess Hermine of Reuss (1887–1947). *Issue:*
      (a) Prince Wilhelm (1882–1951), *Crown Prince* 1888–1918, *m.* 1905 Duchess Cecilie of Mecklenburg-Schwerin; *issue:* Prince Wilhelm (1906–40); Prince Louis Ferdinand (1907–94), *m.* 1938 Grand Duchess Kira; Prince Hubertus (1909–50); Prince Friedrich Georg (1911–66); Princess Alexandrine Irene (1915–80); Princess Cecilie (1917–75)
      (b) Prince Eitel-Friedrich (1883–1942), *m.* 1906 Duchess Sophie of Oldenburg (marriage dissolved 1926)
      (c) Prince Adalbert (1884–1948), *m.* 1914 Princess Adelheid of Saxe-Meiningen; *issue:* Princess Victoria Marina (1917–81); Prince Wilhelm Victor (1919–89)
      (d) Prince August Wilhelm (1887–1949), *m.* 1908 Princess Alexandra of Schleswig-Holstein-Sonderburg-Glücksburg (marriage dissolved 1920); *issue:* Prince Alexander (1912–85)
      (e) Prince Oskar (1888–1958), *m.* 1914 Countess von Ruppin; *issue:* Prince Oskar (1915–39); Prince Burchard (1917–88); Princess Herzeleide (1918–89); Prince Wilhelm-Karl (1922–2007)
      (f) Prince Joachim (1890–1920), *m.* 1916 Princess Marie of Anhalt; *issue:* Prince (Karl) Franz Joseph (1916–75), and has issue
      (g) Princess Viktoria Luise (1892–1980), *m.* 1913 Ernst, Duke of Brunswick 1913–18 (1887–1953); *issue:* Prince Ernst (1914–87); Prince Georg (1915–2006), *m.* 1946 Princess Sophie of Greece and has issue (two sons, one daughter); Princess Frederika (1917–81), *m.* 1938 Paul I, King of the Hellenes; Prince Christian (1919–81); Prince Welf Heinrich (1923–97)
   2. Princess Charlotte (1860–1919), *m.* 1878 Bernhard, Duke of Saxe-Meiningen 1914 (1851–1928). *Issue:* Princess Feodora (1879–1945), *m.* 1898 Prince Heinrich XXX of Reuss
   3. Prince Heinrich (1862–1929), *m.* 1888 Princess Irene of Hesse. *Issue:*
      (a) Prince Waldemar (1889–1945), *m.* Princess Calixta Agnes of Lippe
      (b) Prince Sigismund (1896–1978), *m.* 1919 Princess Charlotte of Saxe-Altenburg; *issue:* Princess Barbara (1920–94); Prince Alfred (*b.* 1924)
      (c) Prince Heinrich (1900–4)
   4. Prince Sigismund (1864–6)
   5. Princess Victoria (1866–1929), *m.* (1) 1890, Prince Adolf of Schaumburg-Lippe (1859–1916); (2) 1927, Alexander Zubkov (1900–36)
   6. Prince Waldemar (1868–79)
   7. Princess Sophie (1870–1932), *m.* 1889 Constantine I (1868–1923), King of the Hellenes 1913–17, 1920–3. *Issue:*
      (a) George II (1890–1947), King of the Hellenes 1923–4 and 1935–47, *m.* 1921 Princess Elisabeth of Roumania (marriage dissolved 1935)
      (b) Alexander I (1893–1920), King of the Hellenes 1917–20, *m.* 1919 Aspasia Manos; *issue:* Princess Alexandra (1921–93), *m.* 1944 King Petar II of Yugoslavia
      (c) Princess Helena (1896–1982), *m.* 1921 King Carol of Roumania (marriage dissolved 1928) (*see* IV.2.(a))
      (d) Paul I (1901–64), King of the Hellenes 1947–64, *m.* 1938 Princess Frederika of Brunswick; *issue:* King Constantine II (*b.* 1940), *m.* 1964 Princess Anne-Marie of Denmark, and has issue (three sons, two daughters); Princess Sophie (*b.* 1938), *m.* 1962 Juan Carlos I of Spain; Princess Irene (*b.* 1942)
      (e) Princess Irene (1904–74), *m.* 1939 4th Duke of Aosta; *issue:* Prince Amedeo, 5th Duke of Aosta (*b.* 1943)
      (f) Princess Katherine (Lady Katherine Brandram) (*b.* 1913), *m.* 1947 Major R. C. A. Brandram, MC, TD; *issue:* R. Paul G. A. Brandram (*b.* 1948)
   8. Princess Margarethe (1872–1954), *m.* 1893 Prince Friedrich Karl of Hesse (1868–1940). *Issue:*
      (a) Prince Friedrich Wilhelm (1893–1916)
      (b) Prince Maximilian (1894–1914)
      (c) Prince Philipp (1896–1980), *m.* 1925 Princess Mafalda of Italy; *issue:* Prince Moritz (*b.* 1926); Prince Heinrich (1927–99); Prince Otto (1937–98); Princess Elisabeth (*b.* 1940)
      (d) Prince Wolfgang (1896–1989), *m.* (1) 1924 Princess Marie Alexandra of Baden; (2) 1948 Ottilie Möller
      (e) Prince Richard (1901–69)
      (f) Prince Christoph (1901–43), *m.* 1930 Princess Sophie of Greece (*see* III.1.(a)) and has issue (two sons, three daughters)

II. HRH PRINCE ALBERT EDWARD (HM KING EDWARD VII) (1841–1910), *m.* 1863 HRH Princess Alexandra of Denmark (1844–1925), *succeeded* to the throne 22 January 1901, *d.* 6 May 1910. *Issue:*
   1. Albert Victor, Duke of Clarence and Avondale (1864–92)
   2. George (HM KING GEORGE V) (1865–1936) (*see* House of Windsor)

3. Louise (1867–1931) Princess Royal 1905–31, *m.* 1889 1st Duke of Fife (1849–1912). *Issue:*
   (a) Princess Alexandra, Duchess of Fife (1891–1959), *m.* 1913 Prince Arthur of Connaught
   (b) Princess Maud (1893–1945), *m.* 1923 11th Earl of Southesk (1893–1992); *issue:* Duke of Fife (*b.* 1929)
4. Victoria (1868–1935)
5. Maud (1869–1938), *m.* 1896 Prince Carl of Denmark (1872–1957), later King Haakon VII of Norway 1905–57. *Issue:*
   (a) Olav V (1903–91), King of Norway 1957–91, *m.* 1929 Princess Märtha of Sweden (1901–54); *issue:* Princess Ragnhild (*b.* 1930); Princess Astrid (*b.* 1932); Harald V, King of Norway (*b.* 1937)
6. Alexander (6–7 April 1871)

III. HRH PRINCESS ALICE Maud Mary (1843–78), *m.* 1862 Prince Ludwig (1837–92), Grand Duke of Hesse 1877–92. *Issue:*

1. Victoria (1863–1950), *m.* 1884 *Admiral of the Fleet* Prince Louis of Battenberg (1854–1921), *cr.* 1st Marquess of Milford Haven 1917. *Issue:*
   (a) Alice (1885–1969), *m.* 1903 Prince Andrew of Greece (1882–1944); *issue:* Princess Margarita (1905–81), *m.* 1931 Prince Gottfried of Hohenlohe-Langenburg (*see* IV.4.(a)); Princess Theodora (1906–69), *m.* Prince Berthold of Baden (1906–63) and has issue (two sons, one daughter); Princess Cecilie (1911–37), *m.* George, Grand Duke of Hesse (*see* III.4.(b)); Princess Sophie (1914–2001), *m.* (1) 1930 Prince Christoph of Hesse (*see* I.8.(f)); (2) 1946 Prince Georg of Hanover; Prince Philip, Duke of Edinburgh (*b.* 1921)
   (b) Louise (1889–1965), *m.* 1923 Gustaf VI Adolf (1882–1973), King of Sweden 1950–73 (*see* VII.1.)
   (c) George, 2nd Marquess of Milford Haven (1892–1938), *m.* 1916 Countess Nadejda, daughter of Grand Duke Michael of Russia; *issue:* Lady Tatiana (1917–88); David Michael, 3rd Marquess (1919–70)
   (d) Louis, 1st Earl Mountbatten of Burma (1900–79), *m.* 1922 Edwina Ashley, daughter of Lord Mount Temple; *issue:* Patricia, Countess Mountbatten of Burma (*b.* 1924); Pamela (*b.* 1929)
2. Elizabeth (1864–1918), *m.* 1884 Grand Duke Sergius of Russia (1857–1905)
3. Irene (1866–1953), *m.* 1888 Prince Heinrich of Prussia
4. Ernst Ludwig (1868–1937), Grand Duke of Hesse 1892–1918, *m.* (1) 1894 Princess Victoria Melita of Saxe-Coburg (*see* IV.3) (marriage dissolved 1901); (2) 1905 Princess Eleonore of Solms-Hohensolmslich. *Issue:*
   (a) Princess Elizabeth (1895–1903)
   (b) George, Hereditary Grand Duke of Hesse (1906–37), *m.* Princess Cecilie of Greece (*see* III.1.(a)), and had issue, two sons, accidentally killed with parents, 1937
   (c) Ludwig, Prince of Hesse (1908–68), *m.* 1937 Margaret, daughter of 1st Lord Geddes
5. Frederick William (1870–3)
6. Alix (Tsaritsa of Russia) (1872–1918), *m.* 1894 Nicholas II (1868–1918) Tsar of All the Russias 1894–1917, assassinated 16 July 1918. *Issue:*
   (a) Grand Duchess Olga (1895–1918)
   (b) Grand Duchess Tatiana (1897–1918)
   (c) Grand Duchess Marie (1899–1918)
   (d) Grand Duchess Anastasia (1901–18)
   (e) Alexis, Tsarevich of Russia (1904–18)
7. Marie (1874–8)

IV. HRH PRINCE ALFRED Ernest Albert, Duke of Edinburgh, *Admiral of the Fleet* (1844–1900), *m.* 1874 Grand Duchess Marie Alexandrovna of Russia (1853–1920); succeeded as Duke of Saxe-Coburg and Gotha 22 August 1893. *Issue:*

1. Alfred, Prince of Saxe-Coburg (1874–99)
2. Marie (1875–1938), *m.* 1893 Ferdinand (1865–1927), King of Roumania 1914–27. *Issue:*
   (a) Carol II (1893–1953), King of Roumania 1930–40, *m.* (1) 1921 Princess Helena of Greece (*see* I.7.(c)) (marriage dissolved 1928), *issue:* Michael (*b.* 1921), King of Roumania 1927–30, 1940–7; (2) 1948 Princess Anne of Bourbon-Parma, and has issue (five daughters)
   (b) Elisabeth (1894–1956), *m.* 1921 George II, King of the Hellenes
   (c) Marie (1900–61), *m.* 1922 Alexander (1888–1934), King of Yugoslavia 1921–34; *issue:* Petar II (1923–70), King of Yugoslavia 1934–45, *m.* 1944 Princess Alexandra of Greece (*see* I.7.(b)) and has issue (Crown Prince Alexander, *b.* 1945); Prince Tomislav (1928–2000), *m.* (1) 1957 Princess Margarita of Baden (daughter of Princess Theodora of Greece and Prince Berthold of Baden (*see* III.1.(a))); (2) 1982 Linda Bonney; and has issue (three sons, one daughter); Prince Andrej (1929–90), *m.* (1) 1956 Princess Christina of Hesse (daughter of Prince Christoph of Hesse and Princess Sophie of Greece (*see* III.1.(a))); (2) 1963 Princess Kira-Melita of Leiningen (*see* IV.3.(a)); and has issue (three sons, two daughters)
   (d) Prince Nicolas (1903–78)
   (e) Princess Ileana (1909–91), *m.* (1) 1931 Archduke Anton of Austria; (2) 1954 Dr Stefan Issarescu; *issue:* Archduke Stefan (1932–98); Archduchess Maria Ileana (1933–59); Archduchess Alexandra (*b.* 1935); Archduke Dominic (*b.* 1937); Archduchess Maria Magdalena (*b.* 1939); Archduchess Elisabeth (*b.* 1942)
   (f) Prince Mircea (1913–16)
3. Victoria Melita (1876–1936), *m.* (1) 1894 Grand Duke Ernst Ludwig of Hesse (*see* III.4) (marriage dissolved 1901); (2) 1905 the Grand Duke Kirill of Russia (1876–1938). *Issue:*
   (a) Marie Kirillovna (1907–51), *m.* 1925 Prince Friedrich Karl of Leiningen; *issue:* Prince Emich (1926–91); Prince Karl (1928–90); Princess Kira-Melita (1930–2005), *m.* Prince Andrej of Yugoslavia (*see* IV.2.(c)); Princess Margarita (1932–96); Princess Mechtilde (*b.* 1936); Prince Friedrich (1938–98)
   (b) Kira Kirillovna (1909–67), *m.* 1938 Prince Louis Ferdinand of Prussia; *issue:* Prince Friedrich Wilhelm (*b.* 1939); Prince Michael

(*b.* 1940); Princess Marie (*b.* 1942); Princess Kira (1943–2004); Prince Louis Ferdinand (1944–77); Prince Christian (*b.* 1946); Princess Xenia (1949–92)

(c) Vladimir Kirillovich (1917–92), *m.* 1948 Princess Leonida Bagration-Mukhransky; *issue:* Grand Duchess Maria (*b.* 1953), and has issue

4. Alexandra (1878–1942), *m.* 1896 Ernst, Prince of Hohenlohe Langenburg. *Issue:*
   (a) Gottfried (1897–1960), *m.* 1931 Princess Margarita of Greece (*see* III.1.(a)); *issue:* Prince Kraft (1935–2004), Princess Beatrice (1936–97), Prince Georg Andreas (*b.* 1938), Prince Ruprecht (1944–76); Prince Albrecht (1944–92)
   (b) Maria (1899–1967), *m.* 1916 Prince Friedrich of Schleswig-Holstein-Sonderburg-Glücksburg; *issue:* Prince Peter (1922–80); Princess Marie (1927–2000)
   (c) Princess Alexandra (1901–63)
   (d) Princess Irma (1902–86)
5. Princess Beatrice (1884–1966), *m.* 1909 Alfonso of Orleans, Infante of Spain. *Issue:*
   (a) Prince Alvaro (1910–97), *m.* 1937 Carla Parodi-Delfino; *issue:* Doña Gerarda (*b.* 1939); Don Alonso (1941–75); Doña Beatriz (*b.* 1943); Don Alvaro (*b.* 1947)
   (b) Prince Alonso (1912–36)
   (c) Prince Ataulfo (1913–74)

V. HRH PRINCESS HELENA Augusta Victoria (1846–1923), *m.* 1866 Prince Christian of Schleswig-Holstein-Sonderburg-Augustenburg (1831–1917). *Issue:*
1. Prince Christian Victor (1867–1900)
2. Prince Albert (1869–1931), Duke of Schleswig-Holstein 1921–31
3. Princess Helena (1870–1948)
4. Princess Marie Louise (1872–1956), *m.* 1891 Prince Aribert of Anhalt (marriage dissolved 1900)
5. Prince Harold (12–20 May 1876)

VI. HRH PRINCESS LOUISE Caroline Alberta (1848–1939), *m.* 1871 Marquess of Lorne, afterwards 9th Duke of Argyll (1845–1914); without issue

VII. HRH PRINCE ARTHUR William Patrick Albert, Duke of Connaught, *Field Marshal* (1850–1942), *m.* 1879 Princess Louisa of Prussia (1860–1917). *Issue:*
1. Margaret (1882–1920), *m.* 1905 Crown Prince Gustaf Adolf (1882–1973), afterwards King of Sweden 1950–73 (*see* III.1.(b)). *Issue:*
   (a) Gustaf Adolf, Duke of Västerbotten (1906–47), *m.* 1932 Princess Sibylla of Saxe-Coburg-Gotha (*see* VIII.2.(b)); *issue:* Princess Margaretha (*b.* 1934); Princess Birgitta (*b.* 1937); Princess Désirée (*b.* 1938); Princess Christina (*b.* 1943); Carl XVI Gustaf, King of Sweden (*b.* 1946)
   (b) Count Sigvard Bernadotte (1907–2002), *m.* (1) 1934 Erika Patzeck; (2) 1943 Sonja Robbert; (3) 1961 Marianne Lindberg; *issue:* Count Michael (*b.* 1944)
   (c) Princess Ingrid (Queen Mother of Denmark) (1910–2000), *m.* 1935 Frederick IX (1899–1972), King of Denmark 1947–72; *issue:* Margrethe II, Queen of Denmark (*b.* 1940); Princess Benedikte (*b.* 1944); Princess Anne-Marfie (*b.* 1946), *m.* 1964 Constantine II of Greece
   (d) Prince Bertil, Duke of Halland (1912–97), *m.* 1976 Mrs Lilian Craig
   (e) Count Carl Bernadotte (*b.* 1916), *m.* (1) 1946 Mrs Kerstin Johnson; (2) 1988 Countess Gunnila Bussler
2. Arthur (1883–1938), *m.* 1913 HH Duchess of Fife. *Issue:* Alastair Arthur, 2nd Duke of Connaught (1914–43)
3. (Victoria) Patricia (1886–1974), *m.* 1919 Adm. Hon. Sir Alexander Ramsay. *Issue:* Alexander Ramsay of Mar (1919–2000), *m.* 1956 Hon. Flora Fraser (Lady Saltoun)

VIII. HRH PRINCE LEOPOLD George Duncan Albert, Duke of Albany (1853–84), *m.* 1882 Princess Helena of Waldeck (1861–1922). *Issue:*
1. Alice (1883–1981), *m.* 1904 Prince Alexander of Teck (1874–1957), *cr.* 1st Earl of Athlone 1917. *Issue:*
   (a) Lady May (1906–94), *m.* 1931 Sir Henry Abel-Smith, KCMG, KCVO, DSO; *issue:* Anne (*b.* 1932); Richard (1933–2004); Elizabeth (*b.* 1936)
   (b) Rupert, Viscount Trematon (1907–28)
   (c) Prince Maurice (March–September 1910)
2. Charles Edward (1884–1954), Duke of Albany 1884 until title suspended 1917, Duke of Saxe-Coburg-Gotha 1900–18, *m.* 1905 Princess Victoria Adelheid of Schleswig-Holstein-Sonderburg-Glücksburg. *Issue:*
   (a) Prince Johann Leopold (1906–72), and has issue
   (b) Princess Sibylla (1908–72), *m.* 1932 Prince Gustaf Adolf of Sweden (*see* VII.1.(a))
   (c) Prince Dietmar Hubertus (1909–43)
   (d) Princess Caroline (1912–83), and has issue
   (e) Prince Friedrich Josias (1918–98), and has issue

IX. HRH PRINCESS BEATRICE Mary Victoria Feodore (1857–1944), *m.* 1885 Prince Henry of Battenberg (1858–96). *Issue:*
1. Alexander, 1st Marquess of Carisbrooke (1886–1960), *m.* 1917 Lady Irene Denison. *Issue:*
   (a) Lady Iris Mountbatten (1920–82), *m.*; *issue:* Robin A. Bryan (*b.* 1957)
2. Victoria Eugénie (1887–1969), *m.* 1906 Alfonso XIII (1886–1941) King of Spain 1886–1931. *Issue:*
   (a) Prince Alfonso (1907–38)
   (b) Prince Jaime (1908–75), and has issue
   (c) Princess Beatriz (1909–2002), and has issue
   (d) Princess Maria (1911–96), and has issue
   (e) Prince Juan (1913–93), Count of Barcelona; *issue:* Princess Maria (*b.* 1936); Juan Carlos I, King of Spain (*b.* 1938), *m.* 1962 Princess Sophie of Greece and has issue (one son, two daughters); Princess Margarita (*b.* 1939)
   (f) Prince Gonzalo (1914–34)
3. Major Lord Leopold Mountbatten (1889–1922)
4. Maurice (1891–1914)

KINGS AND QUEENS

ENGLISH KINGS AND QUEENS 927 TO 1603

HOUSES OF CERDIC AND DENMARK

Reign

927–939 ÆTHELSTAN
Son of Edward the Elder, by Ecgwynn, and grandson of Alfred
Acceded to Wessex and Mercia *c.*924, established direct rule over Northumbria 927, effectively creating the Kingdom of England
Reigned 15 years

939–946 EDMUND I
Born 921, son of Edward the Elder, by Eadgifu
Married (1) Ælfgifu (2) Æthelflæd
Killed aged 25, *reigned* 6 years

946–955 EADRED
Son of Edward the Elder, by Eadgifu
Reigned 9 years

955–959 EADWIG
Born before 943, son of Edmund and Ælfgifu
Married Ælfgifu
Reigned 3 years

959–975 EDGAR I
Born 943, son of Edmund and Ælfgifu
Married (1) Æthelflæd (2) Wulfthryth (3) Ælfthryth
Died aged 32, *reigned* 15 years

975–978 EDWARD I (the Martyr)
*Born c.*962, son of Edgar and Æthelflæd
Assassinated aged *c.*16, *reigned* 2 years

978–1016 ÆTHELRED (the Unready)
*Born c.*968/969, son of Edgar and Ælfthryth
Married (1) Ælfgifu (2) Emma, daughter of Richard I, Count of Normandy
1013–14 dispossessed of kingdom by Swegn Forkbeard (King of Denmark 987–1014)
Died aged *c.*47, *reigned* 38 years

1016 EDMUND II (Ironside)
Born before 993, son of Æthelred and Ælfgifu
Married Ealdgyth
Died aged over 23, *reigned* 7 months (April–November)

1016–1035 CNUT (Canute)
*Born c.*995, son of Swegn Forkbeard, King of Denmark, and Gunhild
Married (1) Ælfgifu (2) Emma, widow of Æthelred the Unready
Gained submission of West Saxons 1015, Northumbrians 1016, Mercia 1016, King of all England after Edmund's death, King of Denmark 1019–35, King of Norway 1028–35
Died aged *c.*40, *reigned* 19 years

1035–1040 HAROLD I (Harefoot)
*Born c.*1016/17, son of Cnut and Ælfgifu
Married Ælfgifu
1035 recognised as regent for himself and his brother Harthacnut; 1037 recognised as king
Died aged *c.*23, *reigned* 4 years

1040–1042 HARTHACNUT (Harthacanute)
*Born c.*1018, son of Cnut and Emma
Titular king of Denmark from 1028
Acknowledged King of England 1035–7 with Harold I as regent; effective king after Harold's death
died aged *c.*24, *reigned* 2 years

1042–1066 EDWARD II (the Confessor)
Born between 1002 and 1005, son of Æthelred the Unready and Emma
Married Eadgyth, daughter of Godwine, Earl of Wessex
Died aged over 60, *reigned* 23 years

1066 HAROLD II (Godwinesson)
*Born c.*1020, son of Godwine, Earl of Wessex, and Gytha
Married (1) Eadgyth (2) Ealdgyth
Killed in battle aged *c.*46, *reigned* 10 months (January–October)

THE HOUSE OF NORMANDY

1066–1087 WILLIAM I (the Conqueror)
Born 1027/8, son of Robert I, Duke of Normandy; obtained the Crown by conquest
Married Matilda, daughter of Baldwin, Count of Flanders
Died aged *c.*60, *reigned* 20 years

1087–1100 WILLIAM II (Rufus)
Born between 1056 and 1060, third son of William I; succeeded his father in England only
Killed aged *c.*40, *reigned* 12 years

1100–1135 HENRY I (Beauclerk)
Born 1068, fourth son of William I
Married (1) Edith or Matilda, daughter of Malcolm III of Scotland (2) Adela, daughter of Godfrey, Count of Louvain
Died aged 67, *reigned* 35 years

1135–1154 STEPHEN
Born not later than 1100, third son of Adela, daughter of William I, and Stephen, Count of Blois
Married Matilda, daughter of Eustace, Count of Boulogne
1141 (February–November) held captive by adherents of Matilda, daughter of Henry I, who contested the crown until 1153
Died aged over 53, *reigned* 18 years

THE HOUSE OF ANJOU (PLANTAGENETS)

1154–1189 HENRY II (Curtmantle)
Born 1133, son of Matilda, daughter of Henry I, and Geoffrey, Count of Anjou
Married Eleanor, daughter of William, Duke of Aquitaine, and divorced queen of Louis VII of France
Died aged 56, *reigned* 34 years

1189–1199 RICHARD I (Coeur de Lion)
Born 1157, third son of Henry II
Married Berengaria, daughter of Sancho VI, King of Navarre
Died aged 42, *reigned* 9 years

1199–1216 JOHN (Lackland)
Born 1167, fifth son of Henry II

	Married (1) Isabella or Avisa, daughter of William, Earl of Gloucester (divorced) (2) Isabella, daughter of Aymer, Count of Angoulême *Died* aged 48, *reigned* 17 years
1216–1272	HENRY III *Born* 1207, son of John and Isabella of Angoulême *Married* Eleanor, daughter of Raymond, Count of Provence *Died* aged 65, *reigned* 56 years
1272–1307	EDWARD I (Longshanks) *Born* 1239, eldest son of Henry III *Married* (1) Eleanor, daughter of Ferdinand III, King of Castile (2) Margaret, daughter of Philip III of France *Died* aged 68, *reigned* 34 years
1307–1327	EDWARD II *Born* 1284, eldest surviving son of Edward I and Eleanor *Married* Isabella, daughter of Philip IV of France *Deposed* January 1327, *killed* September 1327 aged 43, *reigned* 19 years
1327–1377	EDWARD III *Born* 1312, eldest son of Edward II *Married* Philippa, daughter of William, Count of Hainault *Died* aged 64, *reigned* 50 years
1377–1399	RICHARD II *Born* 1367, son of Edward (the Black Prince), eldest son of Edward III *Married* (1) Anne, daughter of Emperor Charles IV (2) Isabelle, daughter of Charles VI of France *Deposed* September 1399, *killed* February 1400 aged 33, *reigned* 22 years

THE HOUSE OF LANCASTER

1399–1413	HENRY IV *Born* 1366, son of John of Gaunt, fourth son of Edward III, and Blanche, daughter of Henry, Duke of Lancaster *Married* (1) Mary, daughter of Humphrey, Earl of Hereford (2) Joan, daughter of Charles, King of Navarre, and widow of John, Duke of Brittany *Died* aged *c.*47, *reigned* 13 years
1413–1422	HENRY V *Born* 1387, eldest surviving son of Henry IV and Mary *Married* Catherine, daughter of Charles VI of France *Died* aged 34, *reigned* 9 years
1422–1471	HENRY VI *Born* 1421, son of Henry V *Married* Margaret, daughter of René, Duke of Anjou and Count of Provence *Deposed* March 1461, *restored* October 1470 *Deposed* April 1471, *killed* May 1471 aged 49, *reigned* 39 years

THE HOUSE OF YORK

1461–1483	EDWARD IV *Born* 1442, eldest son of Richard of York (grandson of Edmund, fifth son of Edward III, and son of Anne, great-granddaughter of Lionel, third son of Edward III) *Married* Elizabeth Woodville, daughter of Richard, Lord Rivers, and widow of Sir John Grey *Acceded* March 1461, *deposed* October 1470, *restored* April 1471 *Died* aged 40, *reigned* 21 years
1483	EDWARD V *Born* 1470, eldest son of Edward IV *Deposed* June 1483, *died* probably July–September 1483, aged 12, *reigned* 2 months (April–June)
1483–1485	RICHARD III *Born* 1452, fourth son of Richard of York *Married* Anne Neville, daughter of Richard, Earl of Warwick, and widow of Edward, Prince of Wales, son of Henry VI *Killed* in battle aged 32, *reigned* 2 years

THE HOUSE OF TUDOR

1485–1509	HENRY VII *Born* 1457, son of Margaret Beaufort (great-granddaughter of John of Gaunt, fourth son of Edward III) and Edmund Tudor, Earl of Richmond *Married* Elizabeth, daughter of Edward IV *Died* aged 52, *reigned* 23 years
1509–1547	HENRY VIII *Born* 1491, second son of Henry VII *Married* (1) Catherine, daughter of Ferdinand II, King of Aragon, and widow of his elder brother Arthur (divorced) (2) Anne, daughter of Sir Thomas Boleyn (executed) (3) Jane, daughter of Sir John Seymour (died in childbirth) (4) Anne, daughter of John, Duke of Cleves (divorced) (5) Catherine Howard, niece of the Duke of Norfolk (executed) (6) Catherine, daughter of Sir Thomas Parr and widow of Lord Latimer *Died* aged 55, *reigned* 37 years
1547–1553	EDWARD VI *Born* 1537, son of Henry VIII and Jane Seymour *Died* aged 15, *reigned* 6 years
1553	JANE *Born* 1537, daughter of Frances (daughter of Mary Tudor, the younger daughter of Henry VII) and Henry Grey, Duke of Suffolk *Married* Lord Guildford Dudley, son of the Duke of Northumberland *Deposed* July 1553, *executed* February 1554 aged 16, *reigned* 14 days
1553–1558	MARY I *Born* 1516, daughter of Henry VIII and Catherine of Aragon *Married* Philip II of Spain *Died* aged 42, *reigned* 5 years
1558–1603	ELIZABETH I *Born* 1533, daughter of Henry VIII and Anne Boleyn *Died* aged 69, *reigned* 44 years

BRITISH KINGS AND QUEENS SINCE 1603

THE HOUSE OF STUART

Reign	
1603–1625	JAMES I (VI OF SCOTLAND) *Born* 1566, son of Mary, Queen of Scots (granddaughter of Margaret Tudor, elder daughter of Henry VII), and Henry Stewart, Lord Darnley

Married Anne, daughter of Frederick II of Denmark
Died aged 58, *reigned* 22 years

1625–1649 CHARLES I
Born 1600, second son of James I
Married Henrietta Maria, daughter of Henry IV of France
Executed 1649 aged 48, *reigned* 23 years

INTERREGNUM 1649–60

1649–53 Government by a council of state
1653–8 Oliver Cromwell, Lord Protector
1658–9 Richard Cromwell, Lord Protector

Reign

1660–1685 CHARLES II
Born 1630, eldest son of Charles I
Married Catherine, daughter of John IV of Portugal
Died aged 54, *reigned* 24 years

1685–1688 JAMES II (VII OF SCOTLAND)
Born 1633, second son of Charles I
Married (1) Lady Anne Hyde, daughter of Edward, Earl of Clarendon (2) Mary, daughter of Alphonso, Duke of Modena
Reign ended with flight from kingdom December 1688
Died 1701 aged 67, *reigned* 3 years

INTERREGNUM
11 December 1688 to 12 February 1689

Reign

1689–1702 WILLIAM III
Born 1650, son of William II, Prince of Orange, and Mary Stuart, daughter of Charles I
Married Mary, elder daughter of James II
Died aged 51, *reigned* 13 years

and

1689–1694 MARY II
Born 1662, elder daughter of James II and Anne
Died aged 32, *reigned* 5 years

1702–1714 ANNE
Born 1665, younger daughter of James II and Anne
Married Prince George of Denmark, son of Frederick III of Denmark
Died aged 49, *reigned* 12 years

THE HOUSE OF HANOVER

1714–1727 GEORGE I (Elector of Hanover)
Born 1660, son of Sophia (daughter of Frederick, Elector Palatine, and Elizabeth Stuart, daughter of James I) and Ernest Augustus, Elector of Hanover
Married Sophia Dorothea, daughter of George William, Duke of Lüneburg-Celle
Died aged 67, *reigned* 12 years

1727–1760 GEORGE II
Born 1683, son of George I
Married Caroline, daughter of John Frederick, Margrave of Brandenburg-Anspach
Died aged 76, *reigned* 33 years

1760–1820 GEORGE III
Born 1738, son of Frederick, eldest son of George II
Married Charlotte, daughter of Charles Louis, Duke of Mecklenburg-Strelitz
Died aged 81, *reigned* 59 years

REGENCY 1811–20
Prince of Wales regent owing to the insanity of George III

Reign

1820–1830 GEORGE IV
Born 1762, eldest son of George III
Married Caroline, daughter of Charles, Duke of Brunswick-Wolfenbüttel
Died aged 67, *reigned* 10 years

1830–1837 WILLIAM IV
Born 1765, third son of George III
Married Adelaide, daughter of George, Duke of Saxe-Meiningen
Died aged 71, *reigned* 7 years

1837–1901 VICTORIA
Born 1819, daughter of Edward, fourth son of George III
Married Prince Albert of Saxe-Coburg and Gotha
Died aged 81, *reigned* 63 years

THE HOUSE OF SAXE-COBURG AND GOTHA

1901–1910 EDWARD VII
Born 1841, eldest son of Victoria and Albert
Married Alexandra, daughter of Christian IX of Denmark
Died aged 68, *reigned* 9 years

THE HOUSE OF WINDSOR

1910–1936 GEORGE V
Born 1865, second son of Edward VII
Married Victoria Mary, daughter of Francis, Duke of Teck
Died aged 70, *reigned* 25 years

1936 EDWARD VIII
Born 1894, eldest son of George V
Married (1937) Mrs Wallis Simpson
Abdicated 1936, *died* 1972 aged 77, *reigned* 10 months (20 January to 11 December)

1936–1952 GEORGE VI
Born 1895, second son of George V
Married Lady Elizabeth Bowes-Lyon, daughter of 14th Earl of Strathmore and Kinghorne
Died aged 56, *reigned* 15 years

1952– Elizabeth II
Born 1926, elder daughter of George VI
Married Philip, son of Prince Andrew of Greece

KINGS AND QUEENS OF SCOTS 1016 TO 1603

Reign

1016–1034 MALCOLM II
Born *c.*954, son of Kenneth II
Acceded to Alba 1005, secured Lothian *c.*1016, obtained Strathclyde for his grandson Duncan *c.*1016, thus reigning over an area approximately the same as that governed by later rulers of Scotland
Died aged *c.*80, *reigned* 18 years

THE HOUSE OF ATHOL

1034–1040 DUNCAN I
Son of Bethoc, daughter of Malcolm II, and Crinan, Mormaer of Atholl
Married a cousin of Siward, Earl of Northumbria
Reigned 5 years

1040–1057 MACBETH
*Born c.*1005, son of a daughter of Malcolm II and Finlaec, Mormaer of Moray
Married Gruoch, granddaughter of Kenneth III
Killed aged *c.*52, *reigned* 17 years

1057–1058 LULACH
*Born c.*1032, son of Gillacomgan, Mormaer of Moray, and Gruoch (and stepson of Macbeth)
Died aged *c.*26, *reigned* 7 months (August–March)

1058–1093 MALCOLM III (Canmore)
*Born c.*1031, elder son of Duncan I
Married (1) Ingibiorg (2) Margaret (St Margaret), granddaughter of Edmund II of England
Killed in battle aged *c.*62, *reigned* 35 years

1093–1097 DONALD III BÁN
*Born c.*1033, second son of Duncan I
Deposed May 1094, *restored* November 1094, *deposed* October 1097, *reigned* 3 years

1094 DUNCAN II
*Born c.*1060, elder son of Malcolm III and Ingibiorg
Married Octreda of Dunbar
Killed aged *c.*34, *reigned* 6 months (May–November)

1097–1107 EDGAR
*Born c.*1074, second son of Malcolm III and Margaret
Died aged *c.*32, *reigned* 9 years

1107–1124 ALEXANDER I (The Fierce)
*Born c.*1077, fifth son of Malcolm III and Margaret
Married Sybilla, illegitimate daughter of Henry I of England
Died aged *c.*47, *reigned* 17 years

1124–1153 DAVID I (The Saint)
*Born c.*1085, sixth son of Malcolm III and Margaret
Married Matilda, daughter of Waltheof, Earl of Huntingdon
Died aged *c.*68, *reigned* 29 years

1153–1165 MALCOLM IV (The Maiden)
*Born c.*1141, son of Henry, Earl of Huntingdon, second son of David I
Died aged *c.*24, *reigned* 12 years

1165–1214 WILLIAM I (The Lion)
*Born c.*1142, brother of Malcolm IV
Married Ermengarde, daughter of Richard, Viscount of Beaumont
Died aged *c.*72, *reigned* 49 years

1214–1249 ALEXANDER II
Born 1198, son of William I
Married (1) Joan, daughter of John, King of England (2) Marie, daughter of Ingelram de Coucy
Died aged 50, *reigned* 34 years

1249–1286 ALEXANDER III
Born 1241, son of Alexander II and Marie
Married (1) Margaret, daughter of Henry III of England (2) Yolande, daughter of the Count of Dreux
Killed accidentally aged 44, *reigned* 36 years

1286–1290 MARGARET (The Maid of Norway)
Born 1283, daughter of Margaret (daughter of Alexander III) and Eric II of Norway
Died aged 7, *reigned* 4 years

FIRST INTERREGNUM 1290–2

Throne disputed by 13 competitors. Crown awarded to John Balliol by adjudication of Edward I of England

THE HOUSE OF BALLIOL

Reign

1292–1296 JOHN (Balliol)
*Born c.*1250, son of Dervorguilla, great-great-granddaughter of David I, and John de Balliol
Married Isabella, daughter of John, Earl of Surrey
Abdicated 1296, *died* 1313 aged *c.*63, *reigned* 3 years

SECOND INTERREGNUM 1296–1306

Edward I of England declared John Balliol to have forfeited the throne for contumacy in 1296 and took the government of Scotland into his own hands

THE HOUSE OF BRUCE

Reign

1306–1329 ROBERT I (Bruce)
Born 1274, son of Robert Bruce and Marjorie, countess of Carrick, and great-grandson of the second daughter of David, Earl of Huntingdon, brother of William I
Married (1) Isabella, daughter of Donald, Earl of Mar (2) Elizabeth, daughter of Richard, Earl of Ulster
Died aged 54, *reigned* 23 years

1329–1371 DAVID II
Born 1324, son of Robert I and Elizabeth
Married (1) Joanna, daughter of Edward II of England (2) Margaret Drummond, widow of Sir John Logie (divorced)
Died aged 46, *reigned* 41 years
1332 Edward Balliol, son of John Balliol, crowned King of Scots September, expelled December
1333–6 Edward Balliol restored as King of Scots

THE HOUSE OF STEWART

1371–1390 ROBERT II (Stewart)
Born 1316, son of Marjorie (daughter of Robert I) and Walter, High Steward of Scotland
Married (1) Elizabeth, daughter of Sir Robert Mure of Rowallan (2) Euphemia, daughter of Hugh, Earl of Ross
Died aged 74, *reigned* 19 years

1390–1406 ROBERT III
*Born c.*1337, son of Robert II and Elizabeth
Married Annabella, daughter of Sir John Drummond of Stobhall
Died aged *c.*69, *reigned* 16 years

1406–1437 JAMES I
Born 1394, son of Robert III
Married Joan Beaufort, daughter of John, Earl of Somerset
Assassinated aged 42, *reigned* 30 years

1437–1460 JAMES II
Born 1430, son of James I
Married Mary, daughter of Arnold, Duke of Gueldres
Killed accidentally aged 29, *reigned* 23 years

1460–1488 JAMES III
Born 1452, son of James II

	Married Margaret, daughter of Christian I of Denmark
	Assassinated aged 36, *reigned* 27 years
1488–1513	JAMES IV
	Born 1473, son of James III
	Married Margaret Tudor, daughter of Henry VII of England
	Killed in battle aged 40, *reigned* 25 years
1513–1542	JAMES V
	Born 1512, son of James IV
	Married (1) Madeleine, daughter of Francis I of France (2) Mary of Lorraine, daughter of the Duc de Guise
	Died aged 30, *reigned* 29 years
1542–1567	MARY
	Born 1542, daughter of James V and Mary
	Married (1) the Dauphin, afterwards Francis II of France (2) Henry Stewart, Lord Darnley (3) James Hepburn, Earl of Bothwell
	Abdicated 1567, prisoner in England from 1568, *executed* 1587, *reigned* 24 years
1567–1625	JAMES VI (and I of England)
	Born 1566, son of Mary, Queen of Scots, and Henry, Lord Darnley
	Acceded 1567 to the Scottish throne, *reigned* 58 years
	Succeeded 1603 to the English throne, so joining the English and Scottish crowns in one person. The two kingdoms remained distinct until 1707 when the parliaments of the kingdoms became conjoined

WELSH SOVEREIGNS AND PRINCES

Wales was ruled by sovereign princes from the earliest times until the death of Llywelyn in 1282. The first English Prince of Wales was the son of Edward I, who was born in Caernarvon town on 25 April 1284. According to a discredited legend, he was presented to the Welsh chieftains as their prince, in fulfilment of a promise that they should have a prince who 'could not speak a word of English' and should be native born. This son, who afterwards became Edward II, was created 'Prince of Wales and Earl of Chester' at the Lincoln Parliament on 7 February 1301.

The title Prince of Wales is borne after individual conferment and is not inherited at birth, though some Princes have been declared and styled Prince of Wales but never formally so created (*s.*). The title was conferred on Prince Charles by the Queen on 26 July 1958. He was invested at Caernarvon on 1 July 1969.

INDEPENDENT PRINCES AD 844 TO 1282

844–878	Rhodri the Great
878–916	Anarawd, son of Rhodri
916–950	Hywel Dda, the Good
950–979	Iago ab Idwal (or Ieuaf)
979–985	Hywel ab Ieuaf, the Bad
985–986	Cadwallon, his brother
986–999	Maredudd ab Owain ap Hywel Dda
999–1008	Cynan ap Hywel ab Ieuaf
1018–1023	Llywelyn ap Seisyll
1023–1039	Iago ab Idwal ap Meurig
1039–1063	Gruffydd ap Llywelyn ap Seisyll
1063–1075	Bleddyn ap Cynfyn
1075–1081	Trahaern ap Caradog
1081–1137	Gruffydd ap Cynan ab Iago
1137–1170	Owain Gwynedd
1170–1194	Dafydd ab Owain Gwynedd
1194–1240	Llywelyn Fawr, the Great
1240–1246	Dafydd ap Llywelyn
1246–1282	Llywelyn ap Gruffydd ap Llywelyn

ENGLISH PRINCES SINCE 1301

1301	Edward (Edward II)
1343	Edward the Black Prince, son of Edward III
1376	Richard (Richard II), son of the Black Prince
1399	Henry of Monmouth (Henry V)
1454	Edward of Westminster, son of Henry VI
1471	Edward of Westminster (Edward V)
1483	Edward, son of Richard III (*d.* 1484)
1489	Arthur Tudor, son of Henry VII
1504	Henry Tudor (Henry VIII)
1610	Henry Stuart, son of James I (*d.* 1612)
1616	Charles Stuart (Charles I)
*c.*1638 (*s.*)	Charles Stuart (Charles II)
1688 (*s.*)	James Francis Edward Stuart (The Old Pretender), son of James II (*d.* 1766)
1714	George Augustus (George II)
1729	Frederick Lewis, son of George II (*d.* 1751)
1751	George William Frederick (George III)
1762	George Augustus Frederick (George IV)
1841	Albert Edward (Edward VII)
1901	George (George V)
1910	Edward (Edward VIII)
1958	Charles, son of Elizabeth II

PRINCESSES ROYAL

The style Princess Royal is conferred at the sovereign's discretion on his or her eldest daughter. It is an honorary title, held for life, and cannot be inherited or passed on. It was first conferred on Princess Mary, daughter of Charles I, in approximately 1642.

*c.*1642	Princess Mary (1631–60), daughter of Charles I
1727	Princess Anne (1709–59), daughter of George II
1766	Princess Charlotte (1766–1828), daughter of George III
1840	Princess Victoria (1840–1901), daughter of Victoria
1905	Princess Louise (1867–1931), daughter of Edward VII
1932	Princess Mary (1897–1965), daughter of George V
1987	Princess Anne (*b.* 1950), daughter of Elizabeth II

PRECEDENCE

ENGLAND AND WALES

The Sovereign
The Prince Philip, Duke of Edinburgh
The Prince of Wales
The Sovereign's younger sons
The Sovereign's grandsons
The Sovereign's cousins
Archbishop of Canterbury
Lord High Chancellor
Archbishop of York
The Prime Minister
Lord President of the Council
Speaker of the House of Commons
Lord Privy Seal
Ambassadors and High Commissioners
Lord Great Chamberlain
Earl Marshal
Lord Chamberlain of the Household
Lord Steward of the Household
Master of the Horse
Dukes, according to their patent of creation:
1. of England
2. of Scotland
3. of Great Britain
4. of Ireland
5. those created since the Union
Eldest sons of Dukes of the Blood Royal
Marquesses, according to their patent of creation:
1. of England
2. of Scotland
3. of Great Britain
4. of Ireland
5. those created since the Union
Dukes' eldest sons
Earls, according to their patent of creation:
1. of England
2. of Scotland
3. of Great Britain
4. of Ireland
5. those created since the Union
Younger sons of Dukes of Blood Royal
Marquesses' eldest sons
Dukes' younger sons
Viscounts, according to their patent of creation:
1. of England
2. of Scotland
3. of Great Britain
4. of Ireland
5. those created since the Union
Earls' eldest sons
Marquesses' younger sons
Bishop of London
Bishop of Durham
Bishop of Winchester
Other English Diocesan Bishops according to seniority of consecration
Suffragan Bishops, according to seniority of consecration
Secretaries of State, if of the degree of a Baron
Barons, according to their patent of creation:
1. of England
2. of Scotland
3. of Great Britain
4. of Ireland
5. those created since the Union, including Life Barons
Treasurer of the Household
Comptroller of the Household
Vice-Chamberlain of the Household
Secretaries of State under the degree of Baron
Viscounts' eldest sons
Earls' younger sons
Barons' eldest sons
Knights of the Garter
Privy Counsellors
Chancellor of the Exchequer
Chancellor of the Duchy of Lancaster
Lord Chief Justice of England and Wales
Master of the Rolls
President of the Queen's Bench Division
President of the Family Division
Chancellor of the High Court
Lords Justices of Appeal, according to seniority of appointment
Judges of the High Court, according to seniority of appointment
Viscounts' younger sons
Barons' younger sons
Sons of Life Peers and Lords of Appeal in Ordinary
Baronets, according to date of patent
Knights of the Thistle
Knights Grand Cross of the Bath
Knights Grand Commanders of the Star of India
Knights Grand Cross of St Michael and St George
Knights Grand Commanders of the Indian Empire
Knights Grand Cross of the Royal Victorian Order
Knights Grand Cross of the British Empire
Knights Commanders of the Bath
Knights Commanders of the Star of India
Knights Commanders of St Michael and St George
Knights Commanders of the Indian Empire
Knights Commanders of the Royal Victorian Order
Knights Commanders of the British Empire
Knights Bachelor
Circuit Judges, according to priority and order of their respective appointments
Companions of the Bath
Companions of the Star of India
Companions of St Michael and St George
Companions of the Indian Empire
Commanders of the Royal Victorian Order
Commanders of the British Empire
Companions of the Distinguished Service Order
Lieutenants of the Royal Victorian Order
Officers of the British Empire
Companions of the Imperial Service Order
Eldest sons of younger sons of Peers
Baronets' eldest sons
Eldest sons of Knights, in the same order as their fathers
Members of the Royal Victorian Order
Members of the British Empire
Younger sons of Baronets
Younger sons of Knights, in the same order as their fathers
Esquires
Gentlemen

SCOTLAND

The Sovereign
The Prince Philip, Duke of Edinburgh
The Lord High Commissioner to the General Assembly of the Church of Scotland (while that Assembly is sitting)
The Duke of Rothesay (eldest son of the Sovereign)
The Sovereign's younger sons
Grandsons of the Sovereign
The Sovereign's cousins
Lord-Lieutenants
Lord Provosts of cities being *ex-officio* Lord-Lieutenants of those cities during their term of office
Sheriffs Principal, successively, within their own localities and during holding of office
Lord Chancellor of Great Britain
Moderator of the General Assembly of the Church of Scotland
Keeper of the Great Seal of Scotland (The First Minister)
The Presiding Officer
The Secretary of State for Scotland
Hereditary High Constable of Scotland
Hereditary Master of the Household in Scotland
Dukes, in the same order as in England
Eldest sons of Dukes of the Blood Royal
Marquesses, as in England
Eldest sons of Dukes
Earls, as in England
Younger sons of Dukes of Blood Royal
Eldest sons of Marquesses
Dukes' younger sons
Lord Justice General
Lord Clerk Register
Lord Advocate
The Advocate-General
Lord Justice Clerk
Viscounts, as in England
Eldest sons of Earls
Marquesses' younger sons
Lord-Barons, as in England
Eldest sons of Viscounts
Earls' younger sons
Lord-Barons' eldest sons
Knights of the Garter
Knights of the Thistle
Privy Counsellors
Senators of College of Justice (Lords of Session)
Viscounts' younger sons
Lord-Barons' younger sons
Baronets
Knights Grand Cross and Knights Grand Commanders of Orders, as in England
Knights Commanders of Orders, as in England
Solicitor-General for Scotland
Lord Lyon King of Arms
Sheriffs Principal, when not within own county
Knights Bachelor
Sheriffs
Companions of Orders, as in England
Commanders of the Royal Victorian Order
Commanders of the British Empire
Companions of the Distinguished Service Order
Lieutenants of the Royal Victorian Order
Officers of the British Empire
Companions of the Imperial Service Order
Eldest sons of younger sons of Peers
Eldest sons of Baronets
Eldest sons of Knights, as in England
Members of the Royal Victorian Order
Members of the British Empire
Baronets' younger sons
Knights' younger sons
Esquires
Gentlemen

WOMEN

Women take the same rank as their husbands or as their brothers; but the daughter of a peer marrying a commoner retains her title as Lady or Honourable. Daughters of peers rank next immediately after the wives of their elder brothers, and before their younger brothers' wives. Daughters of peers marrying peers of a lower degree take the same order of precedence as that of their husbands; thus the daughter of a Duke marrying a Baron becomes of the rank of Baroness only, while her sisters married to commoners retain their rank and take precedence over the Baroness. Merely official rank on the husband's part does not give any similar precedence to the wife.

Peeresses in their own right take the same precedence as peers of the same rank, ie from their date of creation.

LOCAL PRECEDENCE

Scotland

The Lord Provosts of the city districts of Aberdeen, Dundee, Edinburgh and Glasgow are Lord-Lieutenants for those districts *ex officio* and take precedence as such.

THE PEERAGE

The rules which govern the creation and succession of peerages are extremely complicated. There are, technically, five separate peerages, the Peerage of England, of Scotland, of Ireland, of Great Britain, and of the United Kingdom. The Peerage of Great Britain dates from 1707 when an Act of Union combined the two kingdoms of England and Scotland and separate peerages were discontinued. The Peerage of the United Kingdom dates from 1801 when Great Britain and Ireland were combined under an Act of Union. Some Scottish peers have received additional peerages of Great Britain or of the United Kingdom since 1707, and some Irish peers additional peerages of the United Kingdom since 1801.

The Peerage of Ireland was not entirely discontinued from 1801 but holders of Irish peerages, whether predating or created subsequent to the Union of 1801, were not entitled to sit in the House of Lords if they had no additional English, Scottish, Great Britain or United Kingdom peerage. However, they are eligible for election to the House of Commons and to vote in parliamentary elections. An Irish peer holding a peerage of a lower grade which enabled him to sit in the House of Lords was introduced there by the title which enabled him to sit, though for all other purposes he was known by his higher title.

In the Peerage of Scotland there is no rank of Baron; the equivalent rank is Lord of Parliament, abbreviated to 'Lord' (the female equivalent is 'Lady').

All peers of England, Scotland, Great Britain or the United Kingdom who are 21 years or over, and of British, Irish or Commonwealth nationality were entitled to sit in the House of Lords until the House of Lords Act 1999, when hereditary peers lost the right to sit. However, section two of the act provided an exception for 90 hereditary peers plus the holders of the office of Earl Marshal and Lord Great Chamberlain to remain as members of the House of Lords for their lifetime or pending further reform. Of the 90 hereditary peers, 75 were elected by the hereditary peers in their political party, or Crossbench grouping, and the remaining 15 by the whole house. Until 7 November 2002 any vacancy arising due to the death of one of the 90 excepted hereditary peers was filled by the runner-up to the original election. From 7 November 2002 any vacancy due to a death has been filled by holding a by-election. By-elections are conducted in accordance with arrangements made by the Clerk of the Parliaments and have to take place within three months of a vacancy occurring. If the vacancy is among the 75, only the excepted hereditary peers in the relevant party or Crossbench grouping are entitled to vote. If the vacancy is among the other 15, the whole house is entitled to vote.

In the list below, peers currently holding one of the 92 hereditary places in the House of Lords are indicated by ** .

HEREDITARY WOMEN PEERS

Most hereditary peerages pass on death to the nearest male heir, but there are exceptions, and several are held by women.

A woman peer in her own right retains her title after marriage, and if her husband's rank is the superior she is designated by the two titles jointly, the inferior one second. Her hereditary claim still holds good in spite of any marriage whether higher or lower. No rank held by a woman can confer any title or even precedence upon her husband but the rank of a hereditary woman peer in her own right is inherited by her eldest son (or in some cases daughter).

After the Peerage Act 1963, hereditary women peers in their own right were entitled to sit in the House of Lords, subject to the same qualifications as men, until the House of Lords Act 1999.

LIFE PEERS

Since 1876 non-hereditary or life peerages have been conferred on certain eminent judges to enable the judicial functions of the House of Lords to be carried out. These lords are known as Lords of Appeal in Ordinary or law lords. In 2004 Baroness Hale of Richmond became the first female law lord.

Since 1958 life peerages have been conferred upon distinguished men and women from all walks of life, giving them seats in the House of Lords in the degree of Baron or Baroness. They are addressed in the same way as hereditary lords and barons, and their children have similar courtesy titles.

PEERAGES EXTINCT SINCE THE LAST EDITION

BARONY: Deramore (cr. 1885)
LIFE PEERAGES: Biffen (cr. 1997); Carter (cr. 1987); Cockfield (cr. 1978); Cooke of Thorndon (cr. 1996); Deedes (cr. 1986); Ewing of Kirkford (cr. 1992); Garden (cr. 2004); Forte (cr. 1982); Harris of High Cross (cr. 1979); Hussey of North Bradley (cr. 1996); Jauncey of Tullichettle (cr. 1988); Jeger (cr. 1979); Jellicoe of Southampton (cr. 1999); Kelvedon (cr. 1997); Nolan (cr. 1994); Peyton of Yeovil (cr. 1983); Renton (cr. 1979); Weatherill (cr. 1992)

DISCLAIMER OF PEERAGES

The Peerage Act 1963 enables peers to disclaim their peerages for life. Peers alive in 1963 could disclaim within twelve months after the passing of the act (31 July 1963); a person subsequently succeeding to a peerage may disclaim within 12 months (one month if an MP) after the date of succession, or of reaching 21, if later. The disclaimer is irrevocable but does not affect the descent of the peerage after the disclaimant's death, and children of a disclaimed peer may, if they wish, retain their precedence and any courtesy titles and styles borne as children of a peer. The disclaimer permitted the disclaimant to sit in the House of Commons if elected as an MP. As the House of Lords Act 1999 removed hereditary peers from the House of Lords, they are now entitled to sit in the House of Commons without having to disclaim their titles.

The following peerages are currently disclaimed:

EARLDOM: Selkirk (1994)
VISCOUNTCY: Stansgate (1963)
BARONIES: Merthyr (1977); Reith (1972); Sanderson of Ayot (1971)

PEERS WHO ARE MINORS (ie under 21 years of age)
EARL: Craven (*b.* 1989)
VISCOUNT: Selby (*b.* 1993)

FORMS OF ADDRESS

Forms of address are given under the style for each individual rank of the peerage. Both formal and social forms of address are given where usage differs; nowadays, the social form is generally preferred to the formal, which increasingly is used only for official documents and on very formal occasions.

ABBREVIATIONS AND SYMBOLS

S.	Scottish title
I.	Irish title
**	hereditary peer remaining in the House of Lords
°	there is no 'of' in the title
b.	born
s.	succeeded
m.	married
w.	widower or widow
M.	minor
†	heir not ascertained at time of going to press
F_	represents forename
S_	represents surname

ROLL OF THE PEERAGE

Crown Office, House of Lords, London SW1A 0PW

The Roll of the Peerage is kept at the Crown Office and maintained by the Registrar and Assistant Registrar of the Roll of the Perrage in accordance with the terms of a 2004 royal warrant. The roll records the names of all living life peers and hereditary peers who have proved their succession to the satisfaction of the Lord Chancellor. The Roll of the Peerage is maintained in addition to the Clerk of the Parliaments' register of hereditary peers eligable to stand for election in House of Lords' by-elections.

A person whose name is not entered on the Roll of Peerage can not be addressed or mentioned by the title of a peer in any official document.

Registrar, Ian Denyer, MVO
Assistant Registrar, Grant Bavister

HEREDITARY PEERS

as at 31 August 2007

PEERS OF THE BLOOD ROYAL

Style, His Royal Highness the Duke of _/His Royal Highness the Earl of_
Style of address (*formal*) May it please your Royal Highness; *(informal)* Sir

Created	*Title, order of succession, name, etc*	*Heir*
	Dukes	
1947	*Edinburgh (1st),* HRH the Prince Philip, Duke of Edinburgh	The Prince of Wales *
1337	*Cornwall,* HRH the Prince of Wales, *s.* 1952	‡
1398 S.	*Rothesay,* HRH the Prince of Wales, *s.* 1952	‡
1986	*York (1st),* Prince Andrew, HRH the Duke of York	None
1928	*Gloucester (2nd),* Prince Richard, HRH the Duke of Gloucester, *s.* 1974	Earl of Ulster
1934	*Kent (2nd),*Prince Edward, HRH the Duke of Kent, *s.* 1942	Earl of St Andrews
	Earl	
1999	*Wessex (1st),* Prince Edward, HRH the Earl of Wessex	None

* In June 1999 Buckingham Palace announced that the current Earl of Wessex will be granted the Dukedom of Edinburgh when the title reverts to the Crown. The title will only revert to the Crown on both the death of the current Duke of Edinburgh and the Prince of Wales' succession as king

‡ The title is held by the sovereign's eldest son from the moment of his birth or the sovereign's accession

DUKES

Coronet, Eight strawberry leaves

Style, His Grace the Duke of _
Envelope (formal), His Grace the Duke of _; *(social),* The Duke of _. *Letter (formal),* My Lord Duke; *(social),* Dear Duke. *Spoken (formal),* Your Grace; *(social),* Duke
Wife's style, Her Grace the Duchess of _
Envelope (formal), Her Grace the Duchess of _; *(social),* The Duchess of _. *Letter (formal),* Dear Madam; *(social),* Dear Duchess. *Spoken,* Duchess
Eldest son's style, Takes his father's second title as a courtesy title (*see* Courtesy Titles)
Younger sons' style, 'Lord' before forename (F_) and surname (S_)
Envelope, Lord F_ S_. *Letter (formal),* My Lord; *(social),* Dear Lord F_. *Spoken (formal),* My Lord; *(social),* Lord F_
Daughters' style, 'Lady' before forename (F_) and surname (S_)
Envelope, Lady F_ S_. *Letter (formal),* Dear Madam; *(social),* Dear Lady F_. *Spoken,* Lady F_

Created	*Title, order of succession, name, etc*	*Heir*
1868 I.	*Abercorn (5th),* James Hamilton, KG, *b.* 1934, *s.* 1979, *m., Lord Steward*	Marquess of Hamilton, *b.* 1969
1701 S.	*Argyll (13th),* Torquhil Ian Campbell, *b.* 1968, *s.* 2001	Marquess of Lorne, *b.* 2004
1703 S.	*Atholl (11th),* John Murray, *b.* 1929, *s.* 1996, *m.*	Marquis of Tullibardine, *b.* 1960
1682	*Beaufort (11th),* David Robert Somerset, *b.* 1928, *s.* 1984, *m.*	Marquess of Worcester, *b.* 1952
1694	*Bedford (15th),* Andrew Ian Henry Russell, *b.* 1962, *s.* 2003, *m.*	Lord Robin L. H. R., *b.* 1963
1663 S.	*Buccleuch (9th) and Queensberry (11th) (S. 1684),* Walter Francis John Montagu Douglas Scott, KT, VRD, *b.* 1923, *s.* 1973, *m.*	Earl of Dalkeith, KBE *b.* 1954
1694	*Devonshire (12th),* Peregrine Andrew Morny Cavendish, *b.* 1944, *s.* 2004, *m.*	Marquess of Hartington, *b.* 1969
1900	*Fife (3rd),* James George Alexander Bannerman Carnegie, *b.* 1929, *s.* 1959	Earl of Southesk, *b.* 1961
1675	*Grafton (11th),* Hugh Denis Charles FitzRoy, KG, *b.* 1919, *s.* 1970, *m.*	Earl of Euston, *b.* 1947
1643 S.	*Hamilton (15th) and Brandon (12th) (1711),* Angus Alan Douglas Douglas-Hamilton, *b.* 1938, *s.* 1973 *Premier Peer of Scotland*	Marquis of Douglas and Clydesdale, *b.* 1978
1766 I.	*Leinster (9th),* Maurice FitzGerald, *b.* 1948, *s.* 2004, *m. Premier Duke, Marquess and Earl of Ireland*	Lord John F., *b.* 1952

1719	*Manchester (13th),* Alexander Charles David Drogo Montagu, *b.* 1962, *s.* 2002, *m.*	Viscount Mandeville, *b.* 1993
1702	*Marlborough (11th),* John George Vanderbilt Henry Spencer-Churchill, *b.* 1926, *s.* 1972, *m.*	Marquess of Blandford, *b.* 1955
1707 S.	** *Montrose (8th),* James Graham, *b.* 1935, *s.* 1992, *m.*	Marquis of Graham, *b.* 1973
1483	** *Norfolk (18th),* Edward Wiliam Fitzalan-Howard, *b.* 1956, *s.* 2002, *m.* *Premier Duke and Earl Marshal*	Earl of Arundel and Surrey, *b.* 1987
1766	*Northumberland (12th),* Ralph George Algernon Percy, *b.* 1956, *s.* 1995, *m.*	Earl Percy, *b.* 1984
1675	*Richmond (10th) and Gordon (5th) (1876),* Charles Henry Gordon Lennox, *b.* 1929, *s.* 1989, *m.*	Earl of March and Kinrara, *b.* 1955
1707 S.	*Roxburghe (10th),* Guy David Innes-Ker, *b.* 1954, *s.* 1974, *m.* *Premier Baronet of Scotland*	Marquis of Bowmont and Cessford, *b.* 1981
1703	*Rutland (11th),* David Charles Robert Manners, *b.* 1959, *s.* 1999, *m.*	Marquess of Granby, *b.*1999
1684	*St Albans (14th),* Murray de Vere Beauclerk, *b.* 1939, *s.* 1988, *m.*	Earl of Burford, *b.* 1965
1547	*Somerset (19th),* John Michael Edward Seymour, *b.* 1952, *s.* 1984, *m.*	Lord Seymour, *b.* 1982
1833	*Sutherland (7th),* Francis Ronald Egerton, *b.* 1940, *s.* 2000, *m.*	Marquess of Stafford, *b.* 1975
1814	*Wellington (8th),* Arthur Valerian Wellesley, KG, LVO, OBE, MC, *b.* 1915, *s.* 1972, *m.*	Marquess of Douro, *b.* 1945
1874	*Westminster (6th),* Gerald Cavendish Grosvenor, KG, OBE, *b.* 1951, *s.* 1979, *m.*	Earl Grosvenor, *b.* 1991

MARQUESSES

Coronet, Four strawberry leaves alternating with four silver balls

Style, The Most Hon. the Marquess (of) _ . In Scotland the spelling 'Marquis' is preferred for pre-Union creations
Envelope (formal), The Most Hon. the Marquess of _; *(social),* The Marquess of _. *Letter (formal),* My Lord; *(social),* Dear Lord _. *Spoken (formal),* My Lord; *(social),* Lord _
Wife's style, The Most Hon. the Marchioness (of) _
Envelope (formal), The Most Hon. the Marchioness of _; *(social),* The Marchioness of _. *Letter (formal),* Madam; *(social),* Dear Lady _. *Spoken,* Lady _
Eldest son's style, Takes his father's second title as a courtesy title (*see* Courtesy Titles)
Younger sons' style, 'Lord' before forename and surname, as for Duke's younger sons
Daughters' style, 'Lady' before forename and surname, as for Duke's daughter

Created	*Title, order of succession, name, etc*	*Heir*
1916	*Aberdeen and Temair (7th),* Alexander George Gordon, *b.* 1955, *s.* 2002, *m.*	Earl of Haddo, *b.* 1983
1876	*Abergavenny (6th) and 10th Earl, Abergavenny, 1784,* Christopher George Charles Nevill, *b.* 1955, *s.* 2000, *m.*	To Earldom only, David M. R. N., *b.* 1941
1821	*Ailesbury (8th),* Michael Sidney Cedric Brudenell-Bruce, *b.* 1926, *s.* 1974	Earl of Cardigan, *b.* 1952
1831	*Ailsa (8th),* Archibald Angus Charles Kennedy, *b.* 1956, *s.* 1994	Lord David Kennedy, *b.* 1958
1815	*Anglesey (7th),* George Charles Henry Victor Paget, *b.* 1922, *s.* 1947, *m.*	Earl of Uxbridge, *b.* 1950
1789	*Bath (7th),* Alexander George Thynn, *b.* 1932, *s.* 1992, *m.*	Viscount Weymouth, *b.* 1974
1826	*Bristol (8th),* Frederick William Augustus Hervey, *b.* 1979, *s.* 1999	Timothy H. H., *b.* 1960
1796	*Bute (7th),* John Colum Crichton-Stuart, *b.* 1958, *s.* 1993, *m.*	Lord Mount Stuart, *b.* 1989
1812	° *Camden (6th),* David George Edward Henry Pratt, *b.* 1930, *s.* 1983	Earl of Brecknock, *b.* 1965
1815	** *Cholmondeley (7th),* David George Philip Cholmondeley, KCVO, *b.* 1960, *s.* 1990, *Lord Great Chamberlain*	Charles G. C., *b.* 1959
1816	° *Conyngham (7th),* Frederick William Henry Francis Conyngham, *b.* 1924, *s.* 1974, *m.*	Earl of Mount Charles, *b.* 1951
1791 I.	*Donegall (8th),* Arthur Patrick Chichester, *b.* 1952, *s.* 2007, *m.*	Earl of Belfast, *b.* 1990
1789 I.	*Downshire (9th),* (Arthur Francis) Nicholas Wills Hill, *b.* 1959, *s.* 2003, *m.*	Earl of Hillsborough, *b.* 1996
1801 I.	*Ely (9th),* Charles John Tottenham, *b.* 1943, *s.* 2006, *m.*	Lord Timothy C. T., *b.* 1948
1801	*Exeter (8th),* (William) Michael Anthony Cecil, *b.* 1935, *s.* 1988, *m.*	Lord Burghley, *b.* 1970

1800 I.	*Headfort (7th),* Thomas Michael Ronald Christopher Taylour, *b.* 1959, *s.* 2005, *m.*	Earl of Bective, *b.* 1989
1793	*Hertford (9th),* Henry Jocelyn Seymour, *b.* 1958, *s.* 1997, *m.*	Earl of Yarmouth, *b.* 1993
1599 S.	*Huntly (13th),* Granville Charles Gomer Gordon, *b.* 1944, *s.* 1987, *m.* *Premier Marquess of Scotland*	Earl of Aboyne, *b.* 1973
1784	*Lansdowne (9th),* Charles Maurice Mercer Nairne Petty-Fitzmaurice, LVO *b.* 1941, *s.* 1999, *m.*	Earl of Kerry, *b.* 1970
1902	*Linlithgow (4th),* Adrian John Charles Hope, *b.* 1946, *s.* 1987, *m.*	Earl of Hopetoun, *b.* 1969
1816 I.	*Londonderry (9th),* Alexander Charles Robert Vane-Tempest-Stewart, *b.* 1937, *s.* 1955, *m.*	Viscount Castlereagh, *b.* 1972
1701 S.	*Lothian (13th),* Michael Andrew Foster Jude Kerr (Michael Ancram), PC, *b.* 1945, *s.* 2004, *m.*	Lord Ralph W. F. J. K., *b.* 1957
1917	*Milford Haven (4th),* George Ivar Louis Mountbatten, *b.* 1961, *s.* 1970, *m.*	Earl of Medina, *b.* 1991
1838	*Normanby (5th),* Constantine Edmund Walter Phipps, *b.* 1954, *s.* 1994, *m.*	Earl of Mulgrave, *b.* 1994
1812	*Northampton (7th),* Spencer Douglas David Compton, *b.* 1946, *s.* 1978, *m.*	Earl Compton, *b.* 1973
1682 S.	*Queensberry (12th),* David Harrington Angus Douglas, *b.* 1929, *s.* 1954	Viscount Drumlanrig, *b.* 1967
1926	*Reading (4th),* Simon Charles Henry Rufus Isaacs, *b.* 1942, *s.* 1980, *m.*	Viscount Erleigh, *b.* 1986
1789	*Salisbury (7th) and Baron Gascoyne-Cecil (life peerage, 1999),* Robert Michael James Gascoyne-Cecil, PC, *b.* 1946, *s.* 2003, *m.*	Viscount Cranborne, *b.* 1970
1800 I.	*Sligo (11th),* Jeremy Ulick Browne, *b.* 1939, *s.* 1991, *m.*	Sebastian U. B., *b.* 1964
1787	° *Townshend (7th),* George John Patrick Dominic Townshend, *b.* 1916, *s.* 1921, *w.*	Viscount Raynham, *b.* 1945
1694 S.	*Tweeddale (14th),* Charles David Montagu Hay, *b.* 1947, *s.* 2005	Lord Andrew A. G. H., *b.* 1959
1789 I.	*Waterford (8th),* John Hubert de la Poer Beresford, *b.* 1933, *s.* 1934, *m.*	Earl of Tyrone, *b.* 1958
1551	*Winchester (18th),* Nigel George Paulet, *b.* 1941, *s.* 1968, *m. Premier Marquess of England*	Earl of Wiltshire, *b.* 1969
1892	*Zetland (4th),* Lawrence Mark Dundas, *b.* 1937, *s.* 1989, *m.*	Earl of Ronaldshay, *b.* 1965

EARLS

Coronet, Eight silver balls on stalks alternating with eight gold strawberry leaves

Style, The Right Hon. the Earl (of) _
Envelope (formal), The Right Hon. the Earl (of) _; *(social),* The Earl (of) _. *Letter (formal),* My Lord; *(social),* Dear Lord _. *Spoken (formal),* My Lord; *(social),* Lord _.
Wife's style, The Right Hon. the Countess (of) _
Envelope (formal), The Right Hon. the Countess (of) _; *(social),* The Countess (of) _. *Letter (formal),* Madam; *(social),* Lady _. *Spoken (formal),* Madam; *(social),* Lady _.
Eldest son's style, Takes his father's second title as a courtesy title (*see* Courtesy Titles)
Younger sons' style, 'The Hon.' before forename and surname, as for Baron's children
Daughters' style, 'Lady' before forename and surname, as for Duke's daughter

Created	*Title, order of succession, name, etc*	*Heir*
1639 S.	*Airlie (13th),* David George Coke Patrick Ogilvy, KT, GCVO, PC, Royal Victorian Chain, *b.* 1926, *s.* 1968, *m.*	Lord Ogilvy, *b.* 1958
1696	*Albemarle (10th),* Rufus Arnold Alexis Keppel, *b.* 1965, *s.* 1979, *m.*	Viscount Bury, *b.* 2003
1952	° *Alexander of Tunis (2nd),* Shane William Desmond Alexander, *b.* 1935, *s.* 1969, *m.*	Hon. Brian J. A., *b.* 1939
1662	*Annandale and Hartfell (11th),* Patrick Andrew Wentworth Hope Johnstone, *b.* 1941, *s.* 1983, *m.* claim established 1985	Lord Johnstone, *b.* 1971
1789 I.	° *Annesley (11th),* Philip Harrison Annesley, *b.* 1927, *s.* 2001, *m.*	Hon. Michael R. A., *b.* 1933
1785 I.	*Antrim (9th),* Alexander Randal Mark McDonnell, *b.* 1935, *s.* 1977, *m.*	Viscount Dunluce, *b.* 1967
1762 I.	** *Arran (9th),* Arthur Desmond Colquhoun Gore, *b.* 1938, *s.* 1983, *m.*	Paul A. G., CMG, CVO, *b.* 1921
1955	° ** *Attlee (3rd),* John Richard Attlee, *b.* 1956, *s.* 1991, *m.*	None
1714	*Aylesford (11th),* Charles Ian Finch-Knightley, *b.* 1918, *s.* 1958, *w.*	Lord Guernsey, *b.* 1947

1937	** *Baldwin of Bewdley (4th),* Edward Alfred Alexander Baldwin, *b.* 1938, *s.* 1976, *w.*	Viscount Corvedale, *b.* 1973
1922	*Balfour (5th),* Roderick Francis Arthur Balfour, *b.* 1948, *s.* 2003, *m.*	Charles G. Y. B., *b.* 1951
1772	° *Bathurst (8th),* Henry Allen John Bathurst, *b.* 1927, *s.* 1943, *m.*	Lord Apsley, *b.* 1961
1919	° *Beatty (3rd),* David Beatty, *b.* 1946, *s.* 1972, *m.*	Viscount Borodale, *b.* 1973
1797 I.	° *Belmore (8th),* John Armar Lowry-Corry, *b.* 1951, *s.* 1960, *m.*	Viscount Corry, *b.* 1985
1739 I.	*Bessborough (12th),* Myles Fitzhugh Longfield Ponsonby, *b.* 1941, *s.* 2002, *m.*	Viscount Duncannon, *b.* 1974
1815	*Bradford (7th),* Richard Thomas Orlando Bridgeman, *b.* 1947, *s.* 1981, *m.*	Viscount Newport, *b.* 1980
1469	*Buchan (17th),* Malcolm Harry Erskine, *b.* 1930, *s.* 1984, *m.*	Lord Cardross, *b.* 1960
1746	*Buckinghamshire (10th),* (George) Miles Hobart-Hampden, *b.* 1944, *s.* 1983, *m.*	Sir John Hobart, Bt., *b.* 1945
1800	° *Cadogan (8th),* Charles Gerald John Cadogan, *b.* 1937, *s.* 1997, *m.*	Viscount Chelsea, *b.* 1966
1878	° *Cairns (6th),* Simon Dallas Cairns, CVO, CBE, *b.* 1939, *s.* 1989, *m.*	Viscount Garmoyle, *b.* 1965
1455	** *Caithness (20th),* Malcolm Ian Sinclair, PC, *b.* 1948, *s.* 1965, *w.*	Lord Berriedale, *b.* 1981
1800 I.	*Caledon (7th),* Nicholas James Alexander, *b.* 1955, *s.* 1980, *m.*	Viscount Alexander, *b.* 1990
1661	*Carlisle (13th),* George William Beaumont Howard, *b.* 1949, *s.* 1994	Hon. Philip C. W. H., *b.* 1963
1793	*Carnarvon (8th),* George Reginald Oliver Molyneux Herbert, *b.* 1956, *s.* 2001, *m.*	Lord Porchester, *b.* 1992
1748 I.	*Carrick (10th),* David James Theobald Somerset Butler, *b.* 1953, *s.* 1992, *m.*	Viscount Ikerrin, *b.* 1975
1800 I.	° *Castle Stewart (8th),* Arthur Patrick Avondale Stuart, *b.* 1928, *s.* 1961, *w.*	Viscount Stuart, *b.* 1953
1814	°** *Cathcart (7th),* Charles Alan Andrew Cathcart, *b.* 1952, *s.* 1999, *m.*	Lord Greenock, *b.* 1986
1647 I.	*Cavan,* The 12th Earl died in 1988.	†Roger C. Lambart, *b.* 1944
1827	° *Cawdor (7th),* Colin Robert Vaughan Campbell, *b.* 1962, *s.* 1993, *m.*	Viscount Emlyn, *b.* 1998
1801	*Chichester (9th),* John Nicholas Pelham, *b.* 1944, *s.* 1944, *m.*	Richard A. H. P., *b.* 1952
1803 I.	*Clancarty (9th),* Nicholas Power Richard Le Poer Trench, *b.* 1952, *s.* 1995	None
1776 I.	*Clanwilliam (7th),* John Herbert Meade, *b.* 1919, *s.* 1989, *w.*	Lord Gillford, *b.* 1960
1776	*Clarendon (7th),* George Frederick Laurence Hyde Villiers, *b.* 1933, *s.* 1955, *m.*	Lord Hyde, *b.* 1976
1620 I.	*Cork and Orrery (15th),* John Richard Boyle, *b.* 1945, *s.* 2003, *m.*	Viscount Dungarvan, *b.* 1978
1850	*Cottenham (9th),* Mark John Henry Pepys, *b.* 1983, *s.* 2000	Hon. Sam R. P., *b.* 1986
1762 I.	** *Courtown (9th),* James Patrick Montagu Burgoyne Winthrop Stopford, *b.* 1954, *s.* 1975, *m.*	Viscount Stopford, *b.* 1988
1697	*Coventry (13th),* George William Coventry, *b.* 1939, *s.* 2004, *m.*	David D. S. C., *b.* 1973
1857	° *Cowley (7th),* Garret Graham Wellesley, *b.* 1934, *s.* 1975, *m.*	Viscount Dangan, *b.* 1965
1892	*Cranbrook (5th),* Gathorne Gathorne-Hardy, *b.* 1933, *s.* 1978, *m.*	Lord Medway, *b.* 1968
1801 M.	*Craven (9th),* Benjamin Robert Joseph Craven, *b.* 1989, *s.* 1990	Rupert J. E. C., *b.* 1926
1398 S.	*Crawford (29th) and Balcarres (12th) (S. 1651) and Baron Balniel (life peerage, 1974),* Robert Alexander Lindsay, KT, GCVO, PC, *b.* 1927, *s.* 1975, *m. Premier Earl on Union Roll*	Lord Balniel, *b.* 1958
1861	*Cromartie (5th),* John Ruaridh Blunt Grant Mackenzie, *b.* 1948, *s.* 1989, *m.*	Viscount Tarbat, *b.* 1987
1901	*Cromer (4th),* Evelyn Rowland Esmond Baring, *b.* 1946, *s.* 1991, *m.*	Viscount Errington, *b.* 1994
1633 S.	*Dalhousie (17th),* James Hubert Ramsay, *b.* 1948, *s.* 1999, *m.*	Lord Ramsay, *b.* 1981
1725 I.	*Darnley (11th),* Adam Ivo Stuart Bligh, *b.* 1941, *s.* 1980, *m.*	Lord Clifton, *b.* 1968
1711	*Dartmouth (10th),* William Legge, *b.* 1949, *s.* 1997	Hon. Rupert L., *b.* 1951
1761	° *De La Warr (11th),* William Herbrand Sackville, *b.* 1948, *s.* 1988, *m.*	Lord Buckhurst, *b.* 1979
1622	*Denbigh (12th) and Desmond (11th) (I. 1622),* Alexander Stephen Rudolph Feilding, *b.* 1970, *s.* 1995, *m.*	William D. F, *b.* 1939
1485	*Derby (19th),* Edward Richard William Stanley, *b.* 1962, *s.* 1994, *m.*	Lord Stanley, *b.* 1998
1553	*Devon (18th),* Hugh Rupert Courtenay, *b.* 1942, *s.* 1998, *m.*	Lord Courtenay, *b.* 1975
1800 I.	*Donoughmore (8th),* Richard Michael John Hely-Hutchinson, *b.* 1927, *s.* 1981, *w.*	Viscount Suirdale, *b.* 1952
1661 I.	*Drogheda (12th),* Henry Dermot Ponsonby Moore, *b.* 1937, *s.* 1989, *m.*	Viscount Moore, *b.* 1983
1837	*Ducie (7th),* David Leslie Moreton, *b.* 1951, *s.* 1991, *m.*	Lord Moreton, *b.* 1981
1860	*Dudley (4th),* William Humble David Ward, *b.* 1920, *s.* 1969, *m.*	Viscount Ednam, *b.* 1947
1660 S.	** *Dundee (12th),* Alexander Henry Scrymgeour, *b.* 1949, *s.* 1983, *m.*	Lord Scrymgeour, *b.* 1982
1669 S.	*Dundonald (15th),* Iain Alexander Douglas Blair Cochrane, *b.* 1961, *s.* 1986, *m.*	Lord Cochrane, *b.* 1991
1686 S.	*Dunmore (12th),* Malcolm Kenneth Murray, *b.* 1946, *s.* 1995, *m.*	Hon. Geoffrey C. M., *b.*1949
1822 I.	*Dunraven and Mount-Earl (7th),* Thady Windham Thomas Wyndham-Quin, *b.* 1939, *s.* 1965, *m.*	None

1833		*Durham (7th),* Edward Richard Lambton, *b.* 1961, *s.* 2006, *m.*	Viscount Lambton, *b.* 1985
1837		*Effingham (7th),* David Mowbray Algernon Howard, *b.* 1939, *s.* 1996, *m.*	Lord Howard of Effingham, *b.* 1971
1507 S.		*Eglinton (18th) and Winton (9th) (S. 1600),* Archibald George Montgomerie, *b.* 1939, *s.* 1966, *m.*	Lord Montgomerie, *b.* 1966
1733 I.		*Egmont (12th),* Thomas Frederick Gerald Perceval, *b.* 1934, *s.* 2001, *m.*	Hon. Donald W. P., *b.* 1954
1821		*Eldon (5th),* John Joseph Nicholas Scott, *b.* 1937, *s.* 1976, *m.*	Viscount Encombe, *b.* 1962
1633 S.		*Elgin (11th) and Kincardine (15th) (S. 1647),* Andrew Douglas Alexander Thomas Bruce, KT, *b.* 1924, *s.* 1968, *m.*	Lord Bruce, *b.* 1961
1789 I.		*Enniskillen (7th),* Andrew John Galbraith Cole, *b.* 1942, *s.* 1989, *m.*	Arthur G. C., *b.* 1920
1789 I.		*Erne (6th),* Henry George Victor John Crichton, *b.* 1937, *s.* 1940, *m.*	Viscount Crichton, *b.* 1971
1452 S.	**	*Erroll (24th),* Merlin Sereld Victor Gilbert Hay, *b.* 1948, *s.* 1978, *m.* *Hereditary Lord High Constable and Knight Marischal of Scotland*	Lord Hay, *b.* 1984
1661		*Essex (11th),* Frederick Paul de Vere Capell, *b.* 1944, *s.* 2005	William J. C., *b.* 1952
1711	° **	*Ferrers (13th),* Robert Washington Shirley, PC, *b.* 1929, *s.* 1954, *m.*	Viscount Tamworth, *b.* 1952
1789	°	*Fortescue (8th),* Charles Hugh Richard Fortescue, *b.* 1951, *s.* 1993, *m.*	John A. F. F., *b.* 1955
1841		*Gainsborough (5th),* Anthony Gerard Edward Noel, *b.* 1923, *s.* 1927, *m.*	Viscount Campden, *b.* 1950
1623 S.		*Galloway (13th),* Randolph Keith Reginald Stewart, *b.* 1928, *s.* 1978, *w.*	Andrew C. S., *b.* 1949
1703 S.	**	*Glasgow (10th),* Patrick Robin Archibald Boyle, *b.* 1939, *s.* 1984, *m.*	Viscount of Kelburn, *b.* 1978
1806 I.		*Gosford (7th),* Charles David Nicholas Alexander John Sparrow Acheson, *b.* 1942, *s.* 1966, *m.*	Hon. Patrick B. V. M. A., *b.* 1915
1945		*Gowrie (2nd),* Alexander Patrick Greysteil Hore-Ruthven, PC, *b.* 1939, *s.* 1955, *m.*	Viscount Ruthven of Canberra, *b.* 1964
1684 I.		*Granard (10th),* Peter Arthur Edward Hastings Forbes, *b.* 1957, *s.* 1992, *m.*	Viscount Forbes, *b.* 1981
1833	°	*Granville (6th),* Granville George Fergus Leveson-Gower, *b.* 1959, *s.* 1996, *m.*	Lord Leveson, *b.* 1999
1806	°	*Grey (6th),* Richard Fleming George Charles Grey, *b.* 1939, *s.* 1963, *m.*	Philip K. G., *b.* 1940
1752		*Guilford (10th),* Piers Edward Brownlow North, *b.* 1971, *s.* 1999, *m.*	Lord North, *b.* 2002
1619		*Haddington (13th),* John George Baillie-Hamilton, *b.* 1941, *s.* 1986, *m.*	Lord Binning, *b.* 1985
1919	°	*Haig (2nd),* George Alexander Eugene Douglas Haig, OBE, *b.* 1918, *s.* 1928, *m.*	Viscount Dawick, *b.* 1961
1944		*Halifax (3rd),* Charles Edward Peter Neil Wood, *b.* 1944, *s.* 1980, *m.*	Lord Irwin, *b.* 1977
1898		*Halsbury (4th),* Adam Edward Giffard, *b.* 1934, *s.* 2000, *m.*	None
1754		*Hardwicke (10th),* Joseph Philip Sebastian Yorke, *b.* 1971, *s.* 1974	Charles E. Y., *b.* 1951
1812		*Harewood (7th),* George Henry Hubert Lascelles, KBE, *b.* 1923, *s.* 1947, *m.*	Viscount Lascelles, *b.* 1950
1742		*Harrington (11th),* William Henry Leicester Stanhope, *b.* 1922, *s.* 1929, *m.*	Viscount Petersham, *b.* 1945
1809		*Harrowby (7th),* Dudley Danvers Granville Coutts Ryder, TD, *b.* 1922, *s.* 1987, *m.*	Viscount Sandon, *b.* 1951
1605	**	*Home (15th),* David Alexander Cospatrick Douglas-Home, CVO, CBE, *b.* 1943, *s.* 1995, *m.*	Lord Dunglass, *b.* 1987
1821	° **	*Howe (7th),* Frederick Richard Penn Curzon, *b.* 1951, *s.* 1984, *m.*	Viscount Curzon, *b.* 1994
1529		*Huntingdon (16th),* William Edward Robin Hood Hastings Bass, LVO, *b.* 1948, *s.* 1990, *m.*	Hon. Simon A. R. H. H. B., *b.* 1950
1885		*Iddesleigh (5th),* John Stafford Northcote, *b.* 1957, *s.* 2004, *m.*	Viscount St Cyres, *b.* 1985
1756		*Ilchester (10th),* Robin Maurice Fox-Strangways, *b.* 1942, *s.* 2006, *m.*	Lord Stavordale, *b.* 1972
1929		*Inchcape (4th),* (Kenneth) Peter (Lyle) Mackay, *b.* 1943, *s.* 1994, *m.*	Viscount Glenapp, *b.* 1979
1919		*Iveagh (4th),* Arthur Edward Rory Guinness, *b.* 1969, *s.* 1992	Viscount Elveden, *b.* 2003
1925	°	*Jellicoe (3rd),* Patrick John Bernard Jellicoe, *b.* 1950, *s.* 2007	Viscount Brocas, *b.* 1970
1697		*Jersey (10th),* George Francis William Child Villiers, *b.* 1976, *s.* 1998 *m.*	Hon. Jamie C. V., *b.* 1994
1822 I.		*Kilmorey (6th),* Sir Richard Francis Needham, PC, *b.* 1942, *s.* 1977, *m.*, (does not use title)	Viscount Newry and Mourne, *b.* 1966
1866		*Kimberley (5th),* John Armine Wodehouse, *b.* 1951, *s.* 2002, *m.*	Lord Wodehouse, *b.*1978
1768 I.		*Kingston (12th),* Robert Charles Henry King-Tenison, *b.* 1969, *s.* 2002, *m.*	Viscount Kingsborough, *b.* 2000
1633 S.		*Kinnoull (15th),* Arthur William George Patrick Hay, *b.* 1935, *s.* 1938, *m.*	Viscount Dupplin, *b.* 1962
1677 S.		*Kintore (14th),* James William Falconer Keith, *b.* 1976, *s.* 2004	Hon. Alexander D. B. K., *b.* 1946
1914	°	*Kitchener of Khartoum (3rd),* Henry Herbert Kitchener, TD, *b.* 1919, *s.* 1937	None
1624		*Lauderdale (17th),* Patrick Francis Maitland, *b.* 1911, *s.* 1968, *w.*	Viscount Maitland, *b.* 1937
1837		*Leicester (7th),* Edward Douglas Coke, *b.* 1936, *s.* 1994, *m.*	Viscount Coke, *b.* 1965

1641 S.	*Leven (14th) and Melville (13th) (S. 1690),* Alexander Robert Leslie Melville, *b.* 1924, *s.* 1947, *m.*	Lord Balgonie, *b.* 1984
1831	*Lichfield (6th),* Thomas William Robert Hugh Anson, *b.* 1978, *s.* 2005	George R. A., *b.* 1960
1803 I.	*Limerick (7th),* Edmund Christopher Pery, *b.* 1963, *s.* 2003, *m.*	Viscount Glentworth, *b.* 1991
1572	*Lincoln (19th),* Robert Edward Fiennes-Clinton, *b.* 1972, *s.* 2001	Hon. William R. F.-C., *b.* 1980
1633 S.	** *Lindsay (16th),* James Randolph Lindesay-Bethune, *b.* 1955, *s.* 1989, *m.*	Viscount Garnock, *b.* 1990
1626	*Lindsey (14th) and Abingdon (9th) (1682),* Richard Henry Rupert Bertie, *b.* 1931, *s.* 1963, *m.*	Lord Norreys, *b.* 1958
1776 I.	*Lisburne (8th),* John David Malet Vaughan, *b.* 1918, *s.* 1965, *m.*	Viscount Vaughan, *b.* 1945
1822 I.	** *Listowel (6th),* Francis Michael Hare, *b.* 1964, *s.* 1997, *m.*	Hon. Timothy P. H., *b.* 1966
1905	** *Liverpool (5th),* Edward Peter Bertram Savile Foljambe, *b.* 1944, *s.* 1969, *m.*	Viscount Hawkesbury, *b.* 1972
1945	° *Lloyd George of Dwyfor (3rd),* Owen Lloyd George, *b.* 1924, *s.* 1968, *m.*	Viscount Gwynedd, *b.* 1951
1785 I.	*Longford (8th),* Thomas Frank Dermot Pakenham, *b.* 1933, *s.* 2001, *m.*	Hon. Edward M. P., *b.* 1970
1807	*Lonsdale (8th),* Hugh Clayton Lowther, *b.* 1949, *s.* 2006, *m.*	Hon. William J. L., *b.* 1957
1633 S.	*Loudoun (14th),* Michael Edward Abney-Hastings, *b.* 1942, *s.* 2002, *m.*	Lord Mauchline, *b.* 1974
1838	*Lovelace (5th),* Peter Axel William Locke King, *b.* 1951, *s.* 1964, *m.*	None
1795 I.	*Lucan (7th),* Richard John Bingham, *b.* 1934, *s.* 1964, *m.* (missing since 8 November 1974)	Lord Bingham, *b.* 1967
1880	*Lytton (5th),* John Peter Michael Scawen Lytton, *b.* 1950, *s.* 1985, *m.*	Viscount Knebworth, *b.* 1989
1721	*Macclesfield (9th),* Richard Timothy George Mansfield Parker, *b.* 1943, *s.* 1992, *m.*	Hon. J. David G. P., *b.* 1945
1800	*Malmesbury (7th),* James Carleton Harris, *b.* 1946, *s.* 2000, *m.*	Viscount FitzHarris, *b.* 1970
1776	*Mansfield and Mansfield (8th) (1792),* William David Mungo James Murray, *b.* 1930, *s.* 1971, *m.*	Viscount Stormont, *b.* 1956
1565 S.	*Mar (14th) and Kellie (16th) (S. 1616) and Baron Erskine of Alloa Tower (life peerage, 2000),* James Thorne Erskine, *b.* 1949, *s.* 1994, *m.*	Hon. Alexander D. E., *b.* 1952
1785 I.	*Mayo (11th),* Charles Diarmuidh John Bourke, *b.* 1953, *s.* 2006, *m.*	Lord Naas, *b.* 1985
1627 I.	*Meath (15th),* John Anthony Brabazon, *b.* 1941, *s.* 1998, *m.*	Lord Ardee, *b.* 1977
1766 I.	*Mexborough (8th),* John Christopher George Savile, *b.* 1931, *s.* 1980, *m.*	Viscount Pollington, *b.* 1959
1813	*Minto (7th),* Gilbert Timothy George Lariston Elliot-Murray-Kynynmound, *b.* 1953, *s.* 2005, *m.*	Viscount Melgund, *b.* 1984
1562 S.	*Moray (20th),* Douglas John Moray Stuart, *b.* 1928, *s.* 1974, *m.*	Lord Doune, *b.* 1966
1815	*Morley (6th),* John St Aubyn Parker, KCVO, *b.* 1923, *s.* 1962, *m.*	Viscount Boringdon, *b.* 1956
1458	*Morton (22nd),* John Charles Sholto Douglas, *b.* 1927, *s.* 1976, *m.*	Lord Aberdour, *b.* 1952
1789	*Mount Edgcumbe (8th),* Robert Charles Edgcumbe, *b.* 1939, *s.* 1982	Piers V. E., *b.* 1946
1805	° *Nelson (9th),* Peter John Horatio Nelson, *b.* 1941, *s.* 1981, *m.*	Viscount Merton, *b.* 1971
1660 S.	*Newburgh (12th),* Don Filippo Giambattista Camillo Francesco Aldo Maria Rospigliosi, *b.* 1942, *s.* 1986, *m.*	Princess Donna Benedetta F. M. R., *b.* 1974
1827 I.	*Norbury (7th),* Richard James Graham-Toler, *b.* 1967, *s.* 2000	None
1806 I.	*Normanton (6th),* Shaun James Christian Welbore Ellis Agar, *b.* 1945, *s.* 1967, *m.*	Viscount Somerton, *b.* 1982
1647 S.	** *Northesk (14th),* David John MacRae Carnegie, *b.* 1954, *s.* 1994, *m.*	Patrick C. C., *b.* 1940
1801	** *Onslow (7th),* Michael William Coplestone Dillon Onslow, *b.* 1938, *s.* 1971, *m.*	Viscount Cranley, *b.* 1967
1696 S.	*Orkney (9th),* (Oliver) Peter St John, *b.* 1938, *s.* 1998, *m.*	Viscount Kirkwall, *b.* 1969
1328 I.	*Ormonde and Ossory (I. 1527),* The 25th/18th Earl (7th Marquess) died in 1988	†Viscount Mountgarret *b.* 1961 (*see* that title)
1925	*Oxford and Asquith (2nd),* Julian Edward George Asquith, KCMG, *b.* 1916, *s.* 1928, *w.*	Viscount Asquith, OBE, *b.* 1952
1929	° ** *Peel (3rd),* William James Robert Peel, GCVO, PC, *b.* 1947, *s.* 1969, *m.*	Viscount Clanfield, *b.* 1976
1551	*Pembroke (18th) and Montgomery (15th) (1605),* William Alexander Sidney Herbert, *b.* 1978, *s.* 2003	Earl of Carnarvon *b.* 1956 (*see* that title)
1605	*Perth (18th),* John Eric Drummond, *b.* 1935, *s.* 2002, *m.*	Viscount Strathallan, *b.* 1965
1905	*Plymouth (3rd),* Other Robert Ivor Windsor-Clive, *b.* 1923, *s.* 1943, *m.*	Viscount Windsor, *b.* 1951
1785	*Portarlington (7th),* George Lionel Yuill Seymour Dawson-Damer, *b.* 1938, *s.* 1959, *m.*	Viscount Carlow, *b.* 1965
1689	*Portland (12th),* Count Timothy Charles Robert Noel Bentinck, *b.* 1953, *s.* 1997, *m.*	Viscount Woodstock, *b.* 1984
1743	*Portsmouth (10th),* Quentin Gerard Carew Wallop, *b.* 1954, *s.* 1984, *m.*	Viscount Lymington, *b.* 1981
1804	*Powis (8th),* John George Herbert, *b.* 1952, *s.* 1993, *m.*	Viscount Clive, *b.* 1979
1765	*Radnor (8th),* Jacob Pleydell-Bouverie, *b.* 1927, *s.* 1968, *w.*	Viscount Folkestone, *b.* 1955
1831 I.	*Ranfurly (7th),* Gerald Françoys Needham Knox, *b.* 1929, *s.* 1988, *m.*	Viscount Northland, *b.* 1957
1771 I.	*Roden (10th),* Robert John Jocelyn, *b.* 1938, *s.* 1993, *m.*	Viscount Jocelyn, *b.* 1989
1801	*Romney (8th),* Julian Charles Marsham, *b.* 1948, *s.* 2004, *m.*	Viscount Marsham, *b.* 1977

1703 S.	*Rosebery (7th),* Neil Archibald Primrose, *b.* 1929, *s.* 1974, *m.*	Lord Dalmeny, *b.* 1967
1806 I.	*Rosse (7th),* William Brendan Parsons, *b.* 1936, *s.* 1979, *m.*	Lord Oxmantown, *b.* 1969.
1801	** *Rosslyn (7th),* Peter St Clair-Erskine, *b.* 1958, *s.* 1977, *m.*	Lord Loughborough, *b.* 1986
1457 S.	*Rothes (22nd),* James Malcolm David Leslie, *b.* 1958, *s.* 2005, *m.*	Alastair P. L., *b.* 1934
1861	° *Russell (6th),* Nicholas Lyulph Russell, *b.* 1968, *s.* 2004	Hon. John F. R., *b.* 1971
1915	° *St Aldwyn (3rd),* Michael Henry Hicks Beach, *b.* 1950, *s.* 1992, *m.*	Hon. David S. H. B., *b.* 1955
1815	*St Germans (10th),* Peregrine Nicholas Eliot, *b.* 1941, *s.* 1988	Lord Eliot, *b.* 2004
1660	** *Sandwich (11th),* John Edward Hollister Montagu, *b.* 1943, *s.* 1995, *m.*	Viscount Hinchingbrooke, *b.* 1969
1690	*Scarbrough (13th),* Richard Osbert Lumley, *b.* 1973, *s.* 2004	Hon. Thomas H. L., *b.* 1980
1701 S.	*Seafield (13th),* Ian Derek Francis Ogilvie-Grant, *b.* 1939, *s.* 1969, *m.*	Viscount Reidhaven, *b.* 1963
1882	** *Selborne (4th),* John Roundell Palmer, KBE, *b.* 1940, *s.* 1971, *m.*	Viscount Wolmer, *b.* 1971
1646 S.	*Selkirk,* Disclaimed for life 1994. (*see* Lord Selkirk of Douglas, Life Peers)	Master of Selkirk, *b.* 1978
1672	*Shaftesbury (12th),* Nicholas Edmund Anthony Ashley-Cooper, *b.* 1979, *s.* 2005	None
1756 I.	*Shannon (9th),* Richard Bentinck Boyle, *b.* 1924, *s.* 1963	Viscount Boyle, *b.* 1960
1442	** *Shrewsbury and Waterford (22nd) (I. 1446),* Charles Henry John Benedict Crofton Chetwynd Chetwynd-Talbot, *b.* 1952, *s.* 1980, *m. Premier Earl of England and Ireland*	Viscount Ingestre, *b.* 1978
1961	*Snowdon (1st) and Baron Armstrong-Jones (life peerage, 1999),* Antony Charles Robert Armstrong-Jones, GCVO, *b.* 1930, *m.*	Viscount Linley, *b.* 1961
1765	° *Spencer (9th),* Charles Edward Maurice Spencer, *b.* 1964, *s.* 1992, *m.*	Viscount Althorp, *b.* 1994
1703 S.	*Stair (14th),* John David James Dalrymple, *b.* 1961, *s.* 1996, *m.*	Hon. David H. D., *b.* 1963
1984	*Stockton (2nd),* Alexander Daniel Alan Macmillan, MEP, *b.* 1943, *s.* 1986, *m.*	Viscount Macmillan of Ovenden, *b.* 1974
1821	*Stradbroke (6th),* Robert Keith Rous, *b.* 1937, *s.* 1983, *m.*	Viscount Dunwich, *b.* 1961
1847	*Strafford (8th),* Thomas Edmund Byng, *b.* 1936, *s.* 1984, *m.*	Viscount Enfield, *b.* 1964
1606 S.	*Strathmore and Kinghorne (18th) (S. 1677),* Michael Fergus Bowes Lyon, *b.* 1957, *s.* 1987, *m.*	Lord Glamis, *b.* 1986
1603	*Suffolk (21st) and Berkshire (14th) (1626),* Michael John James George Robert Howard, *b.* 1935, *s.* 1941, *m.*	Viscount Andover, *b.* 1974
1955	*Swinton (3rd),* Nicholas John Cunliffe-Lister, *b.* 1939, *s.* 2006, *m.*	Lord Masham *b.* 1970
1714	*Tankerville (10th),* Peter Grey Bennet, *b.* 1956, *s.* 1980	Revd the Hon. George A. G. B., *b.* 1925
1822	° *Temple of Stowe (8th),* (Walter) Grenville Algernon Temple-Gore-Langton, *b.* 1924, *s.* 1988, *m.*	Lord Langton, *b.* 1955
1815	*Verulam (7th),* John Duncan Grimston, *b.* 1951, *s.* 1973, *m.*	Viscount Grimston, *b.* 1978
1729	° *Waldegrave (13th),* James Sherbrooke Waldegrave, *b.* 1940, *s.* 1995, *m.*	Viscount Chewton, *b.* 1986
1759	*Warwick (9th) and Brooke (9th) (1746),* Guy David Greville, *b.* 1957, *s.* 1996, *m.*	Lord Brooke, *b.* 1982
1633 S.	*Wemyss (12th) and March (8th),* Francis David Charteris, KT, *b.* 1912, *s.* 1937, *m.*	Lord Neidpath, *b.* 1948
1621 I.	*Westmeath (13th),* William Anthony Nugent, *b.* 1928, *s.* 1971, *m.*	Hon. Sean C. W. N., *b.* 1965
1624	*Westmorland (16th),* Anthony David Francis Henry Fane, *b.* 1951, *s.* 1993, *m.*	Hon. Harry St C. F., *b.* 1953
1876	*Wharncliffe (5th),* Richard Alan Montagu Stuart Wortley, *b.* 1953, *s.* 1987, *m.*	Viscount Carlton, *b.* 1980
1801	*Wilton (8th),* Francis Egerton Grosvenor, *b.* 1934, *s.* 1999, *m.*	Viscount Grey de Wilton, *b.*1959
1628	*Winchilsea (17th) and Nottingham (12th) (1681),* Daniel James Hatfield Finch Hatton, *b.* 1967, *s.* 1999, *m.*	Viscount Maidstone, *b.* 1998
1766	° *Winterton (8th),* (Donald) David Turnour, *b.* 1943, *s.* 1991, *m.*	Robert C. T., *b.* 1950
1956	*Woolton (3rd),* Simon Frederick Marquis, *b.* 1958, *s.* 1969, *m.*	None
1837	*Yarborough (8th),* Charles John Pelham, *b.* 1963, *s.* 1991, *m.*	Lord Worsley, *b.* 1990

COUNTESSES IN THEIR OWN RIGHT

Style, The Right Hon. the Countess (of) _
Envelope (formal), The Right Hon. the Countess (of) _; *(social),* The Countess (of) _. *Letter (formal),* Madam; *(social),* Lady _. *Spoken (formal),* Madam; *(social),* Lady _.
Husband, Untitled
Children's style, As for children of an Earl

Created	*Title, order of succession, name, etc*	*Heir*
1643 S.	*Dysart (12th in line),* Katherine Grant of Rothiemurchus, *b.* 1918, *s.* 2003 *w.*	Lord Huntingtower, *b.* 1946
c.1115 S.	** *Mar (31st in line),* Margaret of Mar, *b.* 1940, *s.* 1975, *m.* Premier Earldom of Scotland	Mistress of Mar, *b.* 1963
1947	° *Mountbatten of Burma (2nd in line),* Patricia Edwina Victoria Knatchbull, CBE, *b.* 1924, *s.* 1979, *w.*	Lord Romsey, (*also* Lord Brabourne (8th) *see* that title)
c.1235 S.	*Sutherland (24th in line),* Elizabeth Millicent Sutherland, *b.* 1921, *s.* 1963, *w.*	Lord Strathnaver, *b.* 1947

VISCOUNTS

Coronet, Sixteen silver balls

Style, The Right Hon. the Viscount _
Envelope (formal), The Right Hon. the Viscount _; *(social),* The Viscount _. *Letter (formal),* My Lord; *(social),* Dear Lord _. *Spoken,* Lord _.
Wife's style, The Right Hon. the Viscountess _
Envelope (formal), The Right Hon. the Viscountess _; *(social),* The Viscountess _. *Letter (formal),* Madam; *(social),* Dear Lady _. *Spoken,* Lady _.
Children's style, 'The Hon.' before forename and surname, as for Baron's children
In Scotland, the heir apparent to a Viscount may be styled 'The Master of _ (title of peer)'

Created	*Title, order of succession, name, etc*	*Heir*
1945	*Addison (4th),* William Matthew Wand Addison, *b.* 1945, *s.* 1992, *m.*	Hon. Paul W. A., *b.* 1973
1946	*Alanbrooke (3rd),* Alan Victor Harold Brooke, *b.* 1932, *s.* 1972	None
1919	** *Allenby (3rd),* Lt.-Col. Michael Jaffray Hynman Allenby, *b.* 1931, *s.* 1984, *m.*	Hon. Henry J. H. A., *b.* 1968
1911	*Allendale (4th),* Wentworth Peter Ismay Beaumont, *b.* 1948, *s.* 2002, *m.*	Hon. Wentworth A. I. B., *b.* 1979
1642 S.	*Arbuthnott (16th),* John Campbell Arbuthnott, KT, CBE, DSC, *b.* 1924, *s.* 1966, *m.*	Master of Arbuthnott, *b.* 1950
1751 I.	*Ashbrook (11th),* Michael Llowarch Warburton Flower, *b.* 1935, *s.* 1995, *m.*	Hon. Rowland F. W. F., *b.* 1975
1917	** *Astor (4th),* William Waldorf Astor, *b.* 1951, *s.* 1966, *m.*	Hon. William W. A., *b.* 1979
1781 I.	*Bangor (8th),* William Maxwell David Ward, *b.* 1948, *s.* 1993, *m.*	Hon. E. Nicholas W., *b.* 1953
1925	*Bearsted (5th),* Nicholas Alan Samuel, *b.* 1950, *s.* 1996, *m.*	Hon. Harry R. S., *b.* 1988
1963	*Blakenham (2nd),* Michael John Hare, *b.* 1938, *s.* 1982, *m.*	Hon. Caspar J. H., *b.* 1972
1935	** *Bledisloe (3rd),* Christopher Hiley Ludlow Bathurst, QC, *b.* 1934, *s.* 1979	Hon. Rupert E. L. B., *b.* 1964
1712	*Bolingbroke (7th) and St John (8th) (1716),* Kenneth Oliver Musgrave St John, *b.* 1927, *s.* 1974	Hon. Henry F. St J., *b.* 1957
1960	*Boyd of Merton (2nd),* Simon Donald Rupert Neville Lennox-Boyd, *b.* 1939, *s.* 1983, *m.*	Hon. Benjamin A. L.-B., *b.* 1964
1717 I.	*Boyne (11th),* Gustavus Michael Stucley Hamilton-Russell, *b.* 1965, *s.* 1995, *m.*	Hon. Gustavus A. E. H.-R., *b.* 1999
1929	*Brentford (4th),* Crispin William Joynson-Hicks, *b.* 1933, *s.* 1983, *m.*	Hon. Paul W. J.-H., *b.* 1971
1929	** *Bridgeman (3rd),* Robin John Orlando Bridgeman, *b.* 1930, *s.* 1982, *m.*	Hon. Luke R. O. B., *b.* 1971

1868		*Bridport (4th) and 7th Duke, Bronte in Sicily, 1799,* Alexander Nelson Hood, *b.* 1948, *s.* 1969, *m.*	Hon. Peregrine A. N. H., *b.* 1974
1952	**	*Brookeborough (3rd),* Alan Henry Brooke, *b.* 1952, *s.* 1987, *m.*	Hon. Christopher A. B., *b.* 1954
1933		*Buckmaster (4th),* Adrian Charles Buckmaster, *b.* 1949, *s.* 2007, *m.*	Hon. Andrew N. B., *b.* 1980
1939		*Caldecote (3rd),* Piers James Hampden Inskip, *b.* 1947, *s.* 1999, *m.*	Hon. Thomas J. H. I., *b.* 1985
1941		*Camrose (4th),* Adrian Michael Berry, *b.* 1937, *s.* 2001, *m.*	Hon. Jonathan W. B., *b.* 1970
1954		*Chandos (3rd) and Baron Lyttelton of Aldershot (life peerage, 2000),* Thomas Orlando Lyttelton, *b.* 1953, *s.* 1980, *m.*	Hon. Oliver A. L., *b.* 1986
1665 I.		*Charlemont (15th),* John Dodd Caulfeild, *b.* 1966, *s.* 2001, *m.*	Hon. Shane A. C., *b.* 1996
1921		*Chelmsford (4th)* Frederic Corin Piers Thesiger, *b.* 1962, *s.* 1999, *m.*	Hon. Frederic T. *b.* 2006
1717 I.		*Chetwynd (10th),* Adam Richard John Casson Chetwynd, *b.* 1935, *s.* 1965, *m.*	Hon. Adam D. C., *b.* 1969
1911		*Chilston (4th),* Alastair George Akers-Douglas, *b.* 1946, *s.* 1982, *m.*	Hon. Oliver I. A.-D., *b.* 1973
1902		*Churchill (3rd) and 5th UK Baron Churchill (1815),* Victor George Spencer, *b.* 1934, *s.* 1973	To Barony only, Richard H. R. S., *b.* 1926
1718		*Cobham (12th),* Christopher Charles Lyttelton, *b.* 1947, *s.* 2006, *m.*	Hon. Oliver C. L., *b.* 1976
1902	**	*Colville of Culross (4th),* John Mark Alexander Colville, QC, *b.* 1933, *s.* 1945, *m.*	Master of Colville, *b.* 1959
1826		*Combermere (6th),* Thomas Robert Wellington Stapleton-Cotton, *b.* 1969, *s.* 2000	Hon. David P. D. S.-C., *b.* 1932
1917		*Cowdray (4th),* Michael Orlando Weetman Pearson, *b.* 1944, *s.* 1995, *m.*	Hon. Peregrine J. D. P., *b.* 1994
1927	**	*Craigavon (3rd),* Janric Fraser Craig, *b.* 1944, *s.* 1974	None
1943		*Daventry (4th),* James Edward FitzRoy Newdegate, *b.* 1960, *s.* 2000, *m.*	Hon. Humphrey J. F. N., *b.* 1995
1937		*Davidson (2nd),* John Andrew Davidson, *b.* 1928, *s.* 1970, *m.*	Hon. Malcolm W. M. D., *b.* 1934
1956		*De L'Isle (2nd),* Philip John Algernon Sidney, MBE, *b.* 1945, *s.* 1991, *m.*	Hon. Philip W. E. S., *b.* 1985
1776 I.		*De Vesci (7th),* Thomas Eustace Vesey, *b.* 1955, *s.* 1983, *m.*	Hon. Oliver I. V., *b.* 1991
1917		*Devonport (3rd),* Terence Kearley, *b.* 1944, *s.* 1973	Chester D. H. K., *b.* 1932
1964		*Dilhorne (2nd),* John Mervyn Manningham-Buller, *b.* 1932, *s.* 1980, *m.*	Hon. James E. M.-B., *b.* 1956
1622 I.		*Dillon (22nd),* Henry Benedict Charles Dillon, *b.* 1973, *s.* 1982	Hon. Richard A. L. D., *b.* 1948
1785 I.		*Doneraile (10th),* Richard Allen St Leger, *b.* 1946, *s.* 1983, *m.*	Hon. Nathaniel W. R. St J. St L., *b.* 1971
1680 I.		*Downe (12th),* Richard Henry Dawnay, *b.* 1967, *s.* 2002	Thomas P. D., *b.* 1978
1959		*Dunrossil (3rd),* Andrew William Reginald Morrison, *b.* 1953, *s.* 2000, *m.*	Hon. Callum A. B. M., *b.* 1994
1964	**	*Eccles (2nd),* John Dawson Eccles, CBE, *b.* 1931, *s.* 1999, *m.*	Hon. William D. E., *b.* 1960
1897		*Esher (5th),* Christopher Lionel Baliol Brett, *b.* 1936, *s.* 2004, *m.*	Hon. Matthew C. A. B., *b.* 1963
1816		*Exmouth (10th),* Paul Edward Pellew, *b.* 1940, *s.* 1970, *m.*	Hon. Edward F. P., *b.* 1978
1620 S.	**	*Falkland (15th),* Lucius Edward William Plantagenet Cary, *b.* 1935, *s.* 1984, *m. Premier Scottish Viscount on the Roll*	Master of Falkland, *b.* 1963
1720		*Falmouth (9th),* George Hugh Boscawen, *b.* 1919, *s.* 1962, *w.*	Hon. Evelyn A. H. B., *b.* 1955
1720 I.		*Gage (8th),* (Henry) Nicolas Gage, *b.* 1934, *s.* 1993, *m.*	Hon. Henry W. G., *b.* 1975
1727 I.		*Galway (12th),* George Rupert Monckton-Arundell, *b.* 1922, *s.* 1980, *m.*	Hon. J. Philip M., *b.* 1952
1478 I.		*Gormanston (17th),* Jenico Nicholas Dudley Preston, *b.* 1939, *s.* 1940, *m. Premier Viscount of Ireland*	Hon. Jenico F. T. P., *b.* 1974
1816 I.		*Gort (9th),* Foley Robert Standish Prendergast Vereker, *b.* 1951, *s.* 1995, *m.*	Hon. Robert F. P. V., *b.* 1993
1900	**	*Goschen (4th),* Giles John Harry Goschen, *b.* 1965, *s.* 1977, *m.*	Hon. Alexander J. E. G., *b.* 2001
1849		*Gough (5th),* Shane Hugh Maryon Gough, *b.* 1941, *s.* 1951	None
1929		*Hailsham (3rd),* Douglas Martin Hogg, PC, QC, MP, *b.* 1945, *s.* 2001, *m.*	Hon. Quintin J. N. M. H., *b.* 1973
1891		*Hambleden (4th),* William Herbert Smith, *b.* 1930, *s.* 1948, *m.*	Hon. William H. B. S., *b.* 1955
1884		*Hampden (6th),* Anthony David Brand, *b.* 1937, *s.* 1975, *m.*	Hon. Francis A. B., *b.* 1970
1936		*Hanworth (3rd),* David Stephen Geoffrey Pollock, *b.* 1946, *s.* 1996, *m.*	Harold W. C. P., *b.* 1988
1791 I.		*Harberton (11th),* Henry Robert Pomeroy, *b.* 1958, *s.* 2004, *m.*	Hon. Patrick C. P., b. 1995
1846		*Hardinge (7th),* Andrew Hartland Hardinge, *b.* 1960, *s.* 2004, *m.*	Hon. Thomas H. de M. H., *b.* 1993
1791 I.		*Hawarden (9th),* (Robert) Connan Wyndham Leslie Maude, *b.* 1961, *s.* 1991, *m.*	Hon. Varian J. C. E. M., *b.* 1997
1960		*Head (2nd),* Richard Antony Head, *b.* 1937, *s.* 1983, *m.*	Hon. Henry J. H., *b.* 1980
1550		*Hereford (19th),* Charles Robin De Bohun Devereux, *b.* 1975, *s.* 2004, *Premier Viscount of England*	Hon. Edward M. de B. D., *b.* 1977
1842		*Hill (9th),* Peter David Raymond Charles Clegg-Hill, *b.* 1945, *s.* 2003	*Hon.* Paul A. R. C.-H., *b.* 1979

1796	*Hood (8th),* Henry Lyttleton Alexander Hood, *b.* 1958, *s.* 1999, *m.*	Hon. Archibald L. S. H., *b.* 1993
1956	*Ingleby (2nd),* Martin Raymond Peake, *b.* 1926, *s.* 1966, *w.*	None
1945	*Kemsley (3rd),* Richard Gomer Berry, *b.* 1951, *s.* 1999, *m.*	Hon. Luke G. B., *b.* 1998
1911	*Knollys (3rd),* David Francis Dudley Knollys, *b.* 1931, *s.* 1966, *m.*	Hon. Patrick N. M. K., *b.* 1962
1895	*Knutsford (6th),* Michael Holland-Hibbert, *b.* 1926, *s.* 1986, *m.*	Hon. Henry T. H.-H., *b.* 1959
1954	*Leathers (3rd),* Christopher Graeme Leathers, *b.* 1941, *s.* 1996, *m.*	Hon. James F. L., *b.* 1969
1781 I.	*Lifford (9th),* (Edward) James Wingfield Hewitt, *b.* 1949, *s.* 1987, *m.*	Hon. James T. W. H., *b.* 1979
1921	*Long (4th),* Richard Gerard Long, CBE, *b.* 1929, *s.* 1967, *m.*	Hon. James R. L., *b.* 1960
1957	*Mackintosh of Halifax (3rd),* (John) Clive Mackintosh, *b.* 1958, *s.* 1980, *m.*	Hon. Thomas H. G. M., *b.* 1985
1955	*Malvern (3rd),* Ashley Kevin Godfrey Huggins, *b.* 1949, *s.* 1978	Hon. M. James H., *b.* 1928
1945	*Marchwood (3rd),* David George Staveley Penny, *b.* 1936, *s.* 1979, *w.*	Hon. Peter G. W. P., *b.* 1965
1942	*Margesson (2nd),* Francis Vere Hampden Margesson, *b.* 1922, *s.* 1965, *m.*	Capt. Hon. Richard F. D. M., *b.* 1960
1660 I.	*Massereene (14th) and Ferrard (7th) (I. 1797),* John David Clotworthy Whyte-Melville Foster Skeffington, *b.* 1940, *s.* 1992, *m.*	Hon. Charles J. C. W.-M. F. S., *b.* 1973
1802	*Melville (9th),* Robert David Ross Dundas, *b.* 1937, *s.* 1971, *m.*	Hon. Robert H. K. D., *b.* 1984
1916	*Mersey (5th),* Edward John Hallam Bigham, *b.* 1966, *s.* 2006, *m.*	Hon. David E. H. B., *b.* 1938
1717 I.	*Midleton (12th),* Alan Henry Brodrick, *b.* 1949, *s.* 1988, *m.*	Hon. Ashley R. B., *b.* 1980
1962	*Mills (3rd),* Christopher Philip Roger Mills, *b.* 1956, *s.* 1988, *m.*	None
1716 I.	*Molesworth (12th),* Robert Bysse Kelham Molesworth, *b.* 1959, *s.* 1997	Hon. William J. C. M., *b.* 1960
1801 I.	*Monck (7th),* Charles Stanley Monck, *b.* 1953, *s.* 1982 (Does not use title)	Hon. George S. M., *b.* 1957
1957	*Monckton of Brenchley (3rd),* Christopher Walter Monckton, *b.* 1952, *s.* 2006, *m.*	Hon. Timothy D. R. M., *b.* 1955
1946	** *Montgomery of Alamein (2nd),* David Bernard Montgomery, CBE, *b.* 1928, *s.* 1976, *m.*	Hon. Henry D. M., *b.* 1954
1550 I.	*Mountgarret (18th),* Piers James Richard Butler, *b.* 1961, *s.* 2004	Hon. Edmund H. R. B., *b.* 1962
1952	*Norwich (2nd),* John Julius Cooper, CVO, *b.* 1929, *s.* 1954, *m.*	Hon. Jason C. D. B. C., *b.* 1959
1651 S.	*Oxfuird (14th),* Ian Arthur Alexander Makgill, *b.* 1969, *s.* 2003	Hon. Robert E. G. M., *b.* 1969
1873	*Portman (10th),* Christopher Edward Berkeley Portman, *b.* 1958, *s.* 1999, *m.*	Hon. Luke O. B. P., *b.* 1984
1743 I.	*Powerscourt (10th),* Mervyn Niall Wingfield, *b.* 1935, *s.* 1973, *m.*	Hon. Mervyn A. W., *b.* 1963
1900	*Ridley (4th),* Matthew White Ridley, KG, GCVO, TD, *b.* 1925, *s.* 1964, *w.*	Hon. Matthew W. R., *b.* 1958
1960	*Rochdale (2nd),* St John Durival Kemp, *b.* 1938, *s.* 1993, *m.*	Hon. Jonathan H. D. K., *b.* 1961
1919	*Rothermere (4th),* (Harold) Jonathan Esmond Vere Harmsworth, *b.* 1967, *s.* 1998, *m.*	Hon. Vere R. J. H. H., *b.* 1994
1937	*Runciman of Doxford (3rd),* Walter Garrison Runciman (Garry), CBE, *b.* 1934, *s.* 1989, *m.*	Hon. David W. R., *b.* 1967
1918	*St Davids (3rd),* Colwyn Jestyn John Philipps, *b.* 1939, *s.* 1991, *m.*	Hon. Rhodri C. P., *b.* 1966
1801	*St Vincent (8th),* Edward Robert James Jervis, *b.* 1951, *s.* 2006, *m.*	Hon. James R. A. J., *b.* 1982
1937	*Samuel (3rd),* David Herbert Samuel, OBE, PHD, *b.* 1922, *s.* 1978, *m.*	Hon. Dan J. S., *b.* 1925
1911	*Scarsdale (4th),* Peter Ghislain Nathaniel Curzon, *b.* 1949, *s.* 2000, *m.*	Hon. David J. N. C., *b.* 1958
1905 M.	*Selby (6th),* Christopher Rolf Thomas Gully, *b.* 1993, *s.* 2001	Hon. (James) Edward H. G. G., *b.* 1945
1805	*Sidmouth (8th),* Jeremy Francis Addington, *b.* 1947, *s.* 2005, *m.*	Hon. Steffan A., *b.* 1966
1940	** *Simon (3rd),* Jan David Simon, *b.* 1940, *s.* 1993, *m.*	None
1960	** *Slim (2nd),* John Douglas Slim, OBE, *b.* 1927, *s.* 1970, *m.*	Hon. Mark W. R. S., *b.* 1960
1954	*Soulbury (2nd),* James Herwald Ramsbotham, *b.* 1915, *s.* 1971, *w.*	Hon. Sir Peter E. R., GCMG, GCVO, *b.* 1919
1776 I.	*Southwell (7th),* Pyers Anthony Joseph Southwell, *b.* 1930, *s.* 1960, *m.*	Hon. Richard A. P. S., *b.* 1956
1942	*Stansgate,* Anthony Neil Wedgwood Benn, *b.* 1925, *s.* 1960, *w.* Disclaimed for life 1963.	Stephen M. W. B., *b.* 1951
1959	*Stuart of Findhorn (3rd),* James Dominic Stuart, *b.* 1948, *s.* 1999, *m.*	Hon. Andrew M. S., *b.* 1957
1957	** *Tenby (3rd),* William Lloyd George, *b.* 1927, *s.* 1983, *m.*	Hon. Timothy H. G. L. G., *b.* 1962
1952	*Thurso (3rd),* John Archibald Sinclair, *b.* 1953, *s.* 1995, *m.*	Hon. James A. R. S., *b.* 1984
1721	*Torrington (11th),* Timothy Howard St George Byng, *b.* 1943, *s.* 1961, *m.*	Colin H. C.-B., *b.* 1960
1936	** *Trenchard (3rd),* Hugh Trenchard, *b.* 1951, *s.* 1987, *m.*	Hon. Alexander T. T., *b.* 1978
1921	** *Ullswater (2nd),* Nicholas James Christopher Lowther, PC, LVO, *b.* 1942, *s.* 1949, *m.*	Hon. Benjamin J. L., *b.* 1975
1622 I.	*Valentia (15th),* Richard John Dighton Annesley, *b.* 1929, *s.* 1983, *m.*	Hon. Francis W. D. A., *b.* 1959
1952	** *Waverley (3rd),* John Desmond Forbes Anderson, *b.* 1949, *s.* 1990	Hon. Forbes A. R. A., *b.* 1996

1938	*Weir (3rd),* William Kenneth James Weir, *b.* 1933, *s.* 1975, *m.*	Hon. James W. H. W., *b.* 1965
1918	*Wimborne (4th),* Ivor Mervyn Vigors Guest, *b.* 1968, *s.* 1993	Hon. Julien J. G., *b.* 1945
1923	*Younger of Leckie (5th),* James Edward George Younger, *b.* 1955, *s.* 2003, *m.*	Hon. Alexander W. G. Y., *b.* 1993

BARONS/LORDS

Coronet, Six silver balls

Style, The Right Hon. the Lord _
Envelope (formal), The Right Hon. Lord _; *(social),* The Lord _. *Letter (formal),* My Lord; *(social),* Dear Lord _. *Spoken,* Lord _.
In the Peerage of Scotland there is no rank of Baron; the equivalent rank is Lord of Parliament and Scottish peers should always be styled 'Lord', never 'Baron'.
Wife's style, The Right Hon. the Lady _
Envelope (formal), The Right Hon. Lady _; *(social),* The Lady _. *Letter (formal),* My Lady; *(social),* Dear Lady _. *Spoken,* Lady _
Children's style, 'The Hon.' before forename (F_) and surname (S_)
Envelope, The Hon. F_ S_. *Letter,* Dear Mr/Miss/Mrs S_. *Spoken,* Mr/Miss/Mrs S_
In Scotland, the heir apparent to a Lord may be styled 'The Master of _ (title of peer)'

Created	*Title, order of succession, name, etc*	*Heir*
1911	*Aberconway (4th),* (Henry) Charles McLaren, *b.* 1948, *s.* 2003, *m.*	Hon. Charles S. M., *b.* 1984
1873	*Aberdare (5th),* Alastair John Lyndhurst Bruce, *b.* 1947, *s.* 2005, *m.*	Hon. Hector M. N. B., *b.* 1974
1835	*Abinger (9th),* James Harry Scarlett, *b.* 1959, *s.* 2002, *m.*	Hon. Peter R. S., *b.* 1961
1869	*Acton (4th) and Acton of Bridgnorth (life peerage, 2000),* Richard Gerald Lyon-Dalberg-Acton, *b.* 1941, *s.* 1989, *m.*	Hon. John C. F. H. L.-D.-A., *b.* 1966
1887	** *Addington (6th),* Dominic Bryce Hubbard, *b.* 1963, *s.* 1982	Hon. Michael W. L. H., *b.* 1965
1896	*Aldenham (6th) and Hunsdon of Hunsdon (4th) (1923),* Vicary Tyser Gibbs, *b.* 1948, *s.* 1986, *m.*	Hon. Humphrey W. F. G., *b.* 1989
1962	*Aldington (2nd),* Charles Harold Stuart Low, *b.* 1948, *s.* 2000, *m.*	Hon. Philip T. A. L., *b.* 1990
1945	*Altrincham (3rd),* Anthony Ulick David Dundas Grigg, *b.* 1934, *s.* 2001, *m.*	Hon. (Edward) Sebastian G., *b.* 1965
1929	*Alvingham (2nd),* Maj.-Gen. Robert Guy Eardley Yerburgh, CBE, *b.* 1926, *s.* 1955, *m.*	Capt. Hon. Robert R. G. Y., *b.* 1956
1892	*Amherst of Hackney (4th),* William Hugh Amherst Cecil, *b.* 1940, *s.* 1980, *m.*	Hon. H. William A. C., *b.* 1968
1881	** *Ampthill (4th),* Geoffrey Denis Erskine Russell, CBE, PC *b.* 1921, *s.* 1973	Hon. David W. E. R., *b.* 1947
1947	*Amwell (3rd),* Keith Norman Montague, *b.* 1943, *s.* 1990, *m.*	Hon. Ian K. M., *b.* 1973
1863	*Annaly (6th),* Luke Richard White, *b.* 1954, *s.* 1990, *m.*	Hon. Luke H. W., *b.* 1990
1885	*Ashbourne (4th),* Edward Barry Greynville Gibson, *b.* 1933, *s.* 1983, *m.*	Hon. Edward C. d'O. G., *b.* 1967
1835	*Ashburton (7th),* John Francis Harcourt Baring, KG, KCVO, *b.* 1928, *s.* 1991, *m.*	Hon. Mark F. R. B., *b.* 1958
1892	*Ashcombe (4th),* Henry Edward Cubitt, *b.* 1924, *s.* 1962, *m.*	Mark E. C., *b.* 1964
1911	*Ashton of Hyde (3rd),* Thomas John Ashton, TD, *b.* 1926, *s.* 1983, *m.*	Hon. Thomas H. A., *b.* 1958
1800 I.	*Ashtown (7th),* Nigel Clive Crosby Trench, KCMG, *b.* 1916, *s.* 1990, *m.*	Hon. Roderick N. G. T., *b.* 1944
1956	** *Astor of Hever (3rd),* John Jacob Astor, *b.* 1946, *s.* 1984, *m.*	Hon. Charles G. J. A., *b.* 1990
1789 I.	*Auckland (10th) and Auckland (10th) (1793),* Robert Ian Burnard Eden, *b.* 1962, *s.* 1997, *m.*	Hon. Ronald J. E., *b.* 1931
1313	*Audley,* Barony in abeyance between three co-heiresses since 1997	
1900	** *Avebury (4th),* Eric Reginald Lubbock, *b.* 1928, *s.* 1971, *m.*	Hon. Lyulph A. J. L., *b.* 1954
1718 I.	*Aylmer (14th),* (Anthony) Julian Aylmer, *b.* 1951, *s.* 2006, *m.*	Hon. Michael H. A., *b.* 1991
1929	*Baden-Powell (3rd),* Robert Crause Baden-Powell, *b.* 1936, *s.* 1962, *m.*	Hon. David M. B.-P., *b.* 1940
1780	*Bagot (10th),* (Charles Hugh) Shaun Bagot, *b.* 1944, *s.* 2001, *m.*	Richard C. V. B., *b.* 1941
1953	*Baillieu (3rd),* James William Latham Baillieu, *b.* 1950, *s.* 1973, *m.*	Hon. Robert L. B., *b.* 1979
1607 S.	*Balfour of Burleigh (8th),* Robert Bruce, *b.* 1927, *s.* 1967, *m.*	Hon. Victoria B., *b.* 1973
1945	*Balfour of Inchrye (2nd),* Ian Balfour, *b.* 1924, *s.* 1988, *w.*	None
1924	*Banbury of Southam (3rd),* Charles William Banbury, *b.* 1953, *s.* 1981, *m.*	None
1698	*Barnard (11th),* Harry John Neville Vane, TD, *b.* 1923, *s.* 1964	Hon. Henry F. C. V., *b.* 1959

1887		*Basing (5th),* Neil Lutley Sclater-Booth, *b.* 1939, *s.* 1983, *m.*	Hon. Stuart W. S.-B., *b.* 1969
1917		*Beaverbrook (3rd),* Maxwell William Humphrey Aitken, *b.* 1951, *s.* 1985, *m.*	Hon. Maxwell F. A., *b.* 1977
1647 S.		*Belhaven and Stenton (13th),* Robert Anthony Carmichael Hamilton, *b.* 1927, *s.* 1961, *m.*	Master of Belhaven, *b.* 1953
1848 I.		*Bellew (7th),* James Bryan Bellew, *b.* 1920, *s.* 1981, *w.*	Hon. Bryan E. B., *b.* 1943
1856		*Belper (5th),* Richard Henry Strutt, *b.* 1941, *s.* 1999, *m.*	Hon. Michael H. S., *b.* 1969
1421		*Berkeley (18th) and Gueterbock (life peerage, 2000),* Anthony Fitzhardinge Gueterbock, OBE, *b.* 1939, *s.* 1992, *m.*	Hon. Thomas F. G., *b.* 1969
1922		*Bethell (4th),* Nicholas William Bethell, *b.* 1938, *s.* 1967, *m.*	Hon. James N. B., *b.* 1967
1938		*Bicester (3rd),* Angus Edward Vivian Smith, *b.* 1932, *s.* 1968	Hugh C. V. S., *b.* 1934
1903		*Biddulph (5th),* (Anthony) Nicholas Colin Maitland Biddulph, *b.* 1959, *s.* 1988, *m.*	Hon. Robert J. M. B., *b.* 1994
1938		*Birdwood (3rd),* Mark William Ogilvie Birdwood, *b.* 1938, *s.* 1962, *m.*	None
1958		*Birkett (2nd),* Michael Birkett, *b.* 1929, *s.* 1962, *w.*	Hon. Thomas B., *b.* 1982
1907		*Blyth (4th),* Anthony Audley Rupert Blyth, *b.* 1931, *s.* 1977, *m.*	Hon. James A. I. B., *b.* 1970
1797		*Bolton (8th),* Harry Algar Nigel Orde-Powlett, *b.* 1954, *s.* 2001, *m.*	Hon. Thomas O.-P., *b.* 1979
1452 S.		*Borthwick (24th),* John Hugh Borthwick, *b.* 1940, *s.* 1996, *m.*	Hon. James H. A. B. of Glengelt, *b.* 1940
1922		*Borwick (5th),* (Geoffrey Robert) James Borwick, *b.* 1955, *s.* 2007, *m.*	Hon. Edwin D. W. B., *b.* 1984
1761		*Boston (11th),* George William Eustace Boteler Irby, *b.* 1971, *s.* 2007, *m.*	Hon. Thomas W. G. B. I., *b.* 1999
1942	**	*Brabazon of Tara (3rd),* Ivon Anthony Moore-Brabazon, *b.* 1946, *s.* 1974, *m.*	Hon. Benjamin R. M.-B., *b.* 1983
1880		*Brabourne (8th),* Norton Louis Philip Knatchbull, *b.* 1947, *s.* 2005, *m.* (*also* Lord Romsey heir to Countess Mountbatten of Burma, *see* that title)	Hon. Nicholas L. C. N. K., *b.* 1981
1925		*Bradbury (3rd),* John Bradbury, *b.* 1940, *s.* 1994, *m.*	Hon. John B., *b.* 1973
1962		*Brain (2nd),* Christopher Langdon Brain, *b.* 1926, *s.* 1966, *m.*	Hon. Michael C. B., *b.* 1928
1938		*Brassey of Apethorpe (3rd),* David Henry Brassey, OBE, *b.* 1932, *s.* 1967, *m.*	Hon. Edward B., *b.* 1964
1788		*Braybrooke (10th),* Robin Henry Charles Neville, *b.* 1932, *s.* 1990, *m.*	George N., *b.* 1943
1957	**	*Bridges (2nd),* Thomas Edward Bridges, GCMG, *b.* 1927, *s.* 1969, *m.*	Hon. Mark T. B., *b.* 1954
1945		*Broadbridge (4th),* Martin Hugh Broadbridge, *b.* 1929, *s.* 2000, *w.*	Hon. Richard J. M. B., *b.* 1959
1933		*Brocket (3rd),* Charles Ronald George Nall-Cain, *b.* 1952, *s.* 1967, *w.*	Hon. Alexander C. C. N.-C., *b.* 1984
1860	**	*Brougham and Vaux (5th),* Michael John Brougham, CBE, *b.* 1938, *s.* 1967	Hon. Charles W. B., *b.* 1971
1776		*Brownlow (7th),* Edward John Peregrine Cust, *b.* 1936, *s.* 1978, *m.*	Hon. Peregrine E. Q. C., *b.* 1974
1942		*Bruntisfield (3rd),* Michael John Victor Warrender, *b.* 1949, *s.* 2007, *m.*	Hon. John M. P. C. W., *b.* 1996
1950		*Burden (4th),* Fraser William Elsworth Burden, *b.* 1964, *s.* 2000, *m.*	Hon. Ian S. B., *b.* 1967
1529		*Burgh (8th),* (Alexander) Gregory Disney Leith, *b.* 1958, *s.* 2001, *m.*	Hon. Alexander J. S. L., *b.* 1986
1903		*Burnham (7th),* Harry Frederick Alan Lawson, *b.* 1968, *s.* 2005	None
1897		*Burton (3rd),* Michael Evan Victor Baillie, *b.* 1924, *s.* 1962, *m.*	Hon. Evan M. R. B., *b.* 1949
1643		*Byron (13th),* Robert James Byron, *b.* 1950, *s.* 1989, *m.*	Hon. Charles R. G. B., *b.* 1990
1937		*Cadman (3rd),* John Anthony Cadman, *b.* 1938, *s.* 1966, *m.*	Hon. Nicholas A. J. C., *b.* 1977
1945		*Calverley (3rd),* Charles Rodney Muff, *b.* 1946, *s.* 1971, *m.*	Hon. Jonathan E. M., *b.* 1975
1383		*Camoys (7th),* (Ralph) Thomas Campion George Sherman Stonor, GCVO, PC, *b.* 1940, *s.* 1976, *m.*	Hon. R. William R. T. S., *b.* 1974
1715 I.		*Carbery (11th),* Peter Ralfe Harrington Evans-Freke, *b.* 1920, *s.* 1970, *w.*	Hon. Michael P. E.-F., *b.* 1942
1834 I.		*Carew (7th) and Carew (7th) (1838),* Patrick Thomas Conolly-Carew, *b.* 1938, *s.* 1994, *m.*	Hon. William P. C.-C., *b.* 1973
1916		*Carnock (4th),* David Henry Arthur Nicolson, *b.* 1920, *s.* 1982	Adam N., *b.* 1957
1796 I.		*Carrington (6th) and Carrington (6th) (1797) and Carington of Upton (life peerage, 1999),* Peter Alexander Rupert Carington, KG, GCMG, CH, MC, PC, *b.* 1919, *s.* 1938, *m.*	Hon. Rupert F. J. C., *b.* 1948
1812 I.		*Castlemaine (8th),* Roland Thomas John Handcock, MBE, *b.* 1943, *s.* 1973, *m.*	Hon. Ronan M. E. H., *b.* 1989
1936		*Catto (3rd),* Innes Gordon Catto, *b.* 1950, *s.* 2001, *m.*	Hon. Alexander G. C., *b.* 1952
1918		*Cawley (4th),* John Francis Cawley, *b.* 1946, *s.* 2001, *m.*	Hon. William R. H. C., *b.* 1981
1937		*Chatfield (2nd),* Ernle David Lewis Chatfield, *b.* 1917, *s.* 1967, *m.*	None
1858		*Chesham (6th),* Nicholas Charles Cavendish, *b.* 1941, *s.* 1989, *m.*	Hon. Charles G. C. C., *b.* 1974
1945		*Chetwode (2nd),* Philip Chetwode, *b.* 1937, *s.* 1950, *m.*	Hon. Roger C., *b.* 1968
1945	**	*Chorley (2nd),* Roger Richard Edward Chorley, *b.* 1930, *s.* 1978, *m.*	Hon. Nicholas R. D. C., *b.* 1966
1858		*Churston (5th),* John Francis Yarde-Buller, *b.* 1934, *s.* 1991, *m.*	Hon. Benjamin F. A. Y.-B., *b.* 1974

1946	*Citrine (3rd),* Ronald Eric Citrine, *b.* 1919, *s.* 1997, *m.* (Does not use title)	None
1800 I.	*Clanmorris (8th),* Simon John Ward Bingham, *b.* 1937, *s.* 1988, *m.*	Robert D. de B. B., *b.* 1942
1672	*Clifford of Chudleigh (14th),* Thomas Hugh Clifford, *b.* 1948, *s.* 1988, *m.*	Hon. Alexander T. H. C., *b.* 1985
1299	*Clinton (22nd),* Gerard Nevile Mark Fane Trefusis, *b.* 1934, *s.* 1965, *m.*	Hon. Charles P. R. F. T., *b.* 1962
1955	*Clitheroe (2nd),* Ralph John Assheton, *b.* 1929, *s.* 1984, *m.*	Hon. Ralph C. A., *b.* 1962
1919	*Clwyd (4th),* (John) Murray Roberts, *b.* 1971, *s.* 2006	Hon. Jeremy T. R., *b.* 1973
1948	*Clydesmuir (3rd),* David Ronald Colville, *b.* 1949, *s.* 1996, *m.*	Hon. Richard C., *b.* 1980
1960	** *Cobbold (2nd),* David Antony Fromanteel Lytton Cobbold, *b.* 1937, *s.* 1987, *m.*	Hon. Henry F. L. C., *b.* 1962
1919	*Cochrane of Cults (4th),* (Ralph Henry) Vere Cochrane, *b.* 1926, *s.* 1990, *m.*	Hon. Thomas H. V. C., *b.* 1957
1954	*Coleraine (2nd),* (James) Martin (Bonar) Law, *b.* 1931, *s.* 1980, *m.*	Hon. James P. B. L., *b.* 1975
1873	*Coleridge (5th),* William Duke Coleridge, *b.* 1937, *s.* 1984, *m.*	Hon. James D. C., *b.* 1967
1946	*Colgrain (3rd),* David Colin Campbell, *b.* 1920, *s.* 1973, *m.*	Hon. Alastair C. L. C., *b.* 1951
1917	** *Colwyn (3rd),* (Ian) Anthony Hamilton-Smith, CBE, *b.* 1942, *s.* 1966, *m.*	Hon. Craig P. H.-S., *b.* 1968
1956	*Colyton (2nd),* Alisdair John Munro Hopkinson, *b.* 1958, *s.* 1996, *m.*	Hon. James P. M. H., *b.* 1983
1841	*Congleton (8th),* Christopher Patrick Parnell, *b.* 1930, *s.* 1967, *m.*	Hon. John P. C. P., *b.* 1959
1927	*Cornwallis (3rd),* Fiennes Neil Wykeham Cornwallis, OBE, *b.* 1921, *s.* 1982, *m.*	Hon. F. W. Jeremy C., *b.* 1946
1874	*Cottesloe (5th),*John Tapling Fremantle, *b.* 1927, *s.* 1994, *m.*	Hon. Thomas F. H. F., *b.* 1966
1929	*Craigmyle (4th),* Thomas Columba Shaw, *b.* 1960, *s.* 1998, *m.*	Hon. Alexander F. S., *b.* 1988
1899	*Cranworth (3rd),* Philip Bertram Gurdon, *b.* 1940, *s.* 1964, *m.*	Hon. Sacha W. R. G., *b.* 1970
1959	** *Crathorne (2nd),* Charles James Dugdale, *b.* 1939, *s.* 1977, *m.*	Hon. Thomas A. J. D., *b.* 1977
1892	*Crawshaw (5th),* David Gerald Brooks, *b.* 1934, *s.* 1997, *m.*	Hon. John P. B., *b.* 1938
1940	*Croft (3rd),* Bernard William Henry Page Croft, *b.* 1949, *s.* 1997, *m.*	None
1797 I.	*Crofton (7th),* Guy Patrick Gilbert Crofton, *b.* 1951, *s.* 1989, *m.*	Hon. E. Harry P. C., *b.* 1988
1375	*Cromwell (7th),* Godfrey John Bewicke-Copley, *b.* 1960, *s.* 1982, *m.*	Hon. David G. B.-C., *b.* 1997
1947	*Crook (3rd),* Robert Douglas Edwin Crook, *b.* 1955, *s.* 2001, *m.*	Hon. Matthew R. C., *b.* 1990
1920	*Cullen of Ashbourne (3rd),* Edmund Willoughby Marsham Cokayne, *b.* 1916, *s.* 2000, *w.*	(Hon.) John O'B. M. C., *b.*1920
1914	*Cunliffe (3rd),* Roger Cunliffe, *b.* 1932, *s.* 1963, *m.*	Hon. Henry C., *b.* 1962
1927	*Daresbury (4th),* Peter Gilbert Greenall, *b.* 1953, *s.* 1996, *m.*	Hon. Thomas E. G., *b.* 1984
1924	*Darling (3rd),* (Robert) Julian Henry Darling, *b.* 1944, *s.* 2003, *m.*	Hon. Robert J. C. D., *b.* 1972
1946	*Darwen (3rd),* Roger Michael Davies, *b.* 1938, *s.* 1988, *m.*	Hon. Paul D., *b.* 1962
1932	*Davies (3rd),* David Davies, *b.* 1940, *s.* 1944, *m.*	Hon. David D. D., *b.* 1975
1812 I.	*Decies (7th),* Marcus Hugh Tristram de la Poer Beresford, *b.* 1948, *s.* 1992, *m.*	Hon. Robert M. D. de la P. B., *b.* 1988
1299	*de Clifford (27th),* John Edward Southwell Russell, *b.* 1928, *s.* 1982, *m.*	Hon. William S. R., *b.* 1930
1851	*De Freyne (7th),* Francis Arthur John French, *b.* 1927, *s.* 1935, *m.*	Hon. Fulke C. A. J. F., *b.* 1957
1821	*Delamere (5th),* Hugh George Cholmondeley, *b.* 1934, *s.* 1979, *m.*	Hon. Thomas P. G. C., *b.* 1968
1838	** *de Mauley (7th),* Rupert Charles Ponsonby, *b.* 1957, *s.* 2002, *m.*	Ashley G. P., *b.* 1959
1937	** *Denham (2nd),* Bertram Stanley Mitford Bowyer, KBE, PC, *b.* 1927, *s.* 1948, *m.*	Hon. Richard G. G. B., *b.* 1959
1834	*Denman (5th),* Charles Spencer Denman, CBE, MC, TD, *b.* 1916, *s.* 1971, *w.*	Hon. Richard T. S. D., *b.* 1946
1887	*De Ramsey (4th),* John Ailwyn Fellowes, *b.* 1942, *s.* 1993, *m.*	Hon. Freddie J. F., *b.* 1978
1264	*de Ros (28th),* Peter Trevor Maxwell, *b.* 1958, *s.* 1983, *m. Premier Baron of England*	Hon. Finbar J. M., *b.* 1988
1881	*Derwent (5th),* Robin Evelyn Leo Vanden-Bempde-Johnstone, LVO, *b.* 1930, *s.* 1986, *m.*	Hon. Francis P. H. V.-B.-J., *b.* 1965
1831	*de Saumarez (7th),* Eric Douglas Saumarez, *b.* 1956, *s.* 1991, *m.*	Hon. Victor T. S., *b.* 1956
1910	*de Villiers (4th),* Alexander Charles de Villiers, *b.* 1940, *s.* 2001, *m.*	None
1930	*Dickinson (2nd),* Richard Clavering Hyett Dickinson, *b.* 1926, *s.* 1943, *m.*	Hon. Martin H. D., *b.* 1961
1620 I.	*Digby (12th) and Digby (5th) (1765),* Edward Henry Kenelm Digby, KCVO, *b.* 1924, *s.* 1964, *m.*	Hon. Henry N. K. D., *b.* 1954
1615	*Dormer (17th),* Geoffrey Henry Dormer, *b.* 1920, *s.* 1995, *m.*	Hon. William R. D., *b.* 1960
1943	*Dowding (3rd),* Piers Hugh Tremenheere Dowding, *b.* 1948, *s.* 1992	Hon. Mark D. J. D., *b.* 1949
1439	*Dudley (15th),* Jim Anthony Hill Wallace, *b.* 1930, *s.* 2002, *m.*	Hon. Jeremy W. G. W., *b.* 1964
1800 I.	*Dufferin and Clandeboye (11th),* John Francis Blackwood, *b.* 1944, *s.* 1991 (claim to the peerage not yet established), *m.*	*Hon.* Francis S. B., *b.* 1979
1929	*Dulverton (3rd),* (Gilbert) Michael Hamilton Wills, *b.* 1944, *s.* 1992, *m.*	Hon. Robert A. H. W., *b.* 1983
1800 I.	*Dunalley (7th),* Henry Francis Cornelius Prittie, *b.* 1948, *s.* 1992, *m.*	Hon. Joel H. P., *b.* 1981
1324 I.	*Dunboyne (29th),* John Fitzwalter Butler, *b.* 1951, *s.* 2004, *m.*	Hon. Richard P. T. B., *b.* 1983
1892	*Dunleath (6th),* Brian Henry Mulholland, *b.* 1950, *s.* 1997, *m.*	Hon. Andrew H. M., *b.* 1981

1439 I.		*Dunsany (20th),* Edward John Carlos Plunkett, *b.* 1939, *s.* 1999, *m.*	Hon. Randal P., *b.* 1983
1780		*Dynevor (9th),* Richard Charles Uryan Rhys, *b.* 1935, *s.* 1962	Hon. Hugo G. U. R., *b.* 1966
1963		*Egremont (2nd) and Leconfield (7th) (1859),* John Max Henry Scawen Wyndham, *b.* 1948, *s.* 1972, *m.*	Hon. George R. V. W., *b.* 1983
1643		*Elibank (14th),* Alan D'Ardis Erskine-Murray, *b.* 1923, *s.* 1973, *w.*	Master of Elibank, *b.* 1964
1802		*Ellenborough (8th),* Richard Edward Cecil Law, *b.* 1926, *s.* 1945, *m.*	Maj. Hon. Rupert E. H. L., *b.* 1955
1509 S.		*Elphinstone (19th) and Elphinstone (5th) (1885),* Alexander Mountstuart Elphinstone, *b.* 1980, *s.* 1994, *m.*	Hon. Angus J. E., *b.* 1982
1934	**	*Elton (2nd),* Rodney Elton, TD, *b.* 1930, *s.* 1973, *m.*	Hon. Edward P. E., *b.* 1966
1627 S.		*Fairfax of Cameron (14th),* Nicholas John Albert Fairfax, *b.* 1956, *s.* 1964, *m.*	Hon. Edward N. T. F., *b.* 1984
1961		*Fairhaven (3rd),* Ailwyn Henry George Broughton, *b.* 1936, *s.* 1973, *m.*	Maj. Hon. James H. A. B., *b.* 1963
1916		*Faringdon (3rd),* Charles Michael Henderson, *b.* 1937, *s.* 1977, *m.*	Hon. James H. H., *b.* 1961
1756 I.		*Farnham (13th),* Simon Kenlis Maxwell, *b.* 1933, *s.* 2001, *m.*	Hon. Robin S. M., *b.* 1965
1856 I.		*Fermoy (6th),* Patrick Maurice Burke Roche, *b.* 1967, *s.* 1984, *m.*	Hon. E. Hugh B. R., *b.* 1972
1826		*Feversham (6th),* Charles Antony Peter Duncombe, *b.* 1945, *s.* 1963, *m.*	Hon. Jasper O. S. D., *b.* 1968
1798 I.		*ffrench (8th),* Robuck John Peter Charles Mario ffrench, *b.* 1956, *s.* 1986, *m.*	Hon. John C. M. J. F. ff., *b.* 1928
1909		*Fisher (3rd),* John Vavasseur Fisher, DSC, *b.* 1921, *s.* 1955, *m.*	Hon. Patrick V. F., *b.* 1953
1295		*Fitzwalter (22nd),* Julian Brook Plumptre, *b.* 1952, *s. 2004, m.*	Hon. Edward B. P., *b.* 1989
1776		*Foley (8th),* Adrian Gerald Foley, *b.* 1923, *s.* 1927, *m.*	Hon. Thomas H. F., *b.* 1961
1445		*Forbes (22nd),* Nigel Ivan Forbes, KBE, *b.* 1918, *s.* 1953, *m. Premier Lord of Scotland*	Master of Forbes, *b.* 1946
1821		*Forester (9th),* Charles Richard George Weld-Forester, *b.* 1975, *s.* 2004,	Wolstan W. W.-F., *b.* 1941
1922		*Forres (4th),* Alastair Stephen Grant Williamson, *b.* 1946, *s.* 1978, *m.*	Hon. George A. M. W., *b.* 1972
1917		*Forteviot (4th),* John James Evelyn Dewar, *b.* 1938, *s.* 1993, *w.*	Hon. Alexander J. E. D., *b.* 1971
1951	**	*Freyberg (3rd),* Valerian Bernard Freyberg, *b.* 1970, *s.* 1993	None
1917		*Gainford (3rd),* Joseph Edward Pease, *b.* 1921, *s.* 1971, *m.*	Hon. George P., *b.* 1926
1818 I.		*Garvagh (5th),* (Alexander Leopold Ivor) George Canning, *b.* 1920, *s.* 1956, *m.*	Hon. Spencer G. S. de R. C., *b.* 1953
1942	**	*Geddes (3rd),* Euan Michael Ross Geddes, *b.* 1937, *s.* 1975, *m.*	Hon. James G. N. G., *b.* 1969
1876		*Gerard (5th),* Anthony Robert Hugo Gerard, *b.* 1949, *s.* 1992, *m.*	Hon. Rupert B. C. G., *b.* 1981
1824		*Gifford (6th),* Anthony Maurice Gifford, *b.* 1940, *s.* 1961, *m.*	Hon. Thomas A. G., *b.* 1967
1917		*Gisborough (3rd),* Thomas Richard John Long Chaloner, *b.* 1927, *s.* 1951, *m.*	Hon. T. Peregrine L. C., *b.* 1961
1960		*Gladwyn (2nd),* Miles Alvery Gladwyn Jebb, *b.* 1930, *s.* 1996	None
1899		*Glanusk (5th),* Christopher Russell Bailey, *b.* 1942, *s.* 1997, *m.*	Hon. Charles H. B., *b.* 1976
1918	**	*Glenarthur (4th),* Simon Mark Arthur, *b.* 1944, *s.* 1976, *m.*	Hon. Edward A. A., *b.* 1973
1911		*Glenconner (3rd),* Colin Christopher Paget Tennant, *b.* 1926, *s.* 1983, *m.*	Cody C. E. T., *b.* 1994
1964		*Glendevon (2nd),* Julian John Somerset Hope, *b.* 1950, *s.* 1996	Hon. Jonathan C. H., *b.* 1952
1922		*Glendyne (3rd),* Robert Nivison, *b.* 1926, *s.* 1967, *m.*	Hon. John N., *b.* 1960
1939	**	*Glentoran (3rd),* (Thomas) Robin (Valerian) Dixon, CBE, *b.* 1935, *s.* 1995, *m.*	Hon. Daniel G. D., *b.* 1959
1909		*Gorell (4th),* Timothy John Radcliffe Barnes, *b.* 1927, *s.* 1963, *m.*	Hon. Ronald A. H. B., *b.* 1931
1953	**	*Grantchester (3rd),* Christopher John Suenson-Taylor, *b.* 1951, *s.* 1995, *m.*	Hon. Jesse D. S.-T., *b.* 1977
1782		*Grantley (8th),* Richard William Brinsley Norton, *b.* 1956, *s.* 1995	Hon. Francis J. H. N., *b.* 1960
1794 I.		*Graves (10th),* Timothy Evelyn Graves, *b.* 1960, *s.* 2002	None
1445 S.		*Gray (23rd),* Andrew Godfrey Diarmid Stuart Campbell-Gray, *b.* 1964, *s.* 2003, *m.*	Master of Gray, *b.* 1996
1950		*Greenhill (3rd),* Malcolm Greenhill, *b.* 1924, *s.* 1989	None
1927	**	*Greenway (4th),* Ambrose Charles Drexel Greenway, *b.* 1941, *s.* 1975, *m.*	Hon. Nigel. P. G., *b.* 1944
1902		*Grenfell (3rd) and Grenfell of Kilvey (life peerage, 2000),* Julian Pascoe Francis St Leger Grenfell, *b.* 1935, *s.* 1976, *m.*	Francis P. J. G., *b.* 1938
1944		*Gretton (4th),* John Lysander Gretton, *b.* 1975, *s.* 1989	None
1397		*Grey of Codnor (6th),* Richard Henry Cornwall-Legh, *b.* 1936, *s.* 1996, *m.*	Hon. Richard S. C. C.-L., *b.* 1976
1955		*Gridley (3rd),* Richard David Arnold Gridley, *b.* 1956, *s.* 1996, *m.*	Peter A. C. G., *b.* 1940
1964		*Grimston of Westbury (3rd),* Robert John Sylvester Grimston, *b.* 1951, *s.* 2003, *m.*	Hon. Gerald C. W. G., *b.* 1953
1886		*Grimthorpe (5th),* Edward John Beckett, *b.* 1954, *s.* 2003, *m.*	Hon. Harry M. B., *b.* 1993
1945		*Hacking (3rd),* Douglas David Hacking, *b.* 1938, *s.* 1971, *m.*	Hon. Douglas F. H., *b.* 1968
1950		*Haden-Guest (5th),* Christopher Haden-Guest, *b.* 1948, *s.* 1996, *m.*	Hon. Nicholas H.-G., *b.* 1951

1886	*Hamilton of Dalzell (5th),* Gavin Goulburn Hamilton, *b.* 1968, *s.* 2006, *m.*	Hon. Robert P. H., *b.* 1971
1874	*Hampton (7th),* John Humphrey Arnott Pakington, *b.* 1964, *s.* 2003, *m.*	None
1939	*Hankey (3rd),* Donald Robin Alers Hankey, *b.* 1938, *s.* 1996, *m.*	Hon. Alexander M. A. H., *b.* 1947
1958	*Harding of Petherton (2nd),* John Charles Harding, *b.* 1928, *s.* 1989, *m.*	Hon. William A. J. H., *b.* 1969
1910	*Hardinge of Penshurst (4th),* Julian Alexander Hardinge, *b.* 1945, *s.* 1997	Hon. Hugh F. H., *b.* 1948
1876	*Harlech (6th),* Francis David Ormsby-Gore, *b.* 1954, *s.* 1985, *m.*	Hon. Jasset D. C. O.-G., *b.* 1986
1939	*Harmsworth (3rd),* Thomas Harold Raymond Harmsworth, *b.* 1939, *s.* 1990, *m.*	Hon. Dominic M. E. H., *b.* 1973
1815	*Harris (8th),* Anthony Harris, *b.* 1942, *s.* 1996, *m.*	Anthony J. T. H., *b.* 1915
1954	*Harvey of Tasburgh (2nd),* Peter Charles Oliver Harvey, *b.* 1921, *s.* 1968, *w.*	Charles J. G. H., *b.* 1951
1295	*Hastings (23rd),* Delaval Thomas Harold Astley, *b.* 1960, *s.* 2007, *m.*	Hon. Jacob A. A., *b.* 1991
1835	*Hatherton (8th),* Edward Charles Littleton, *b.* 1950, *s.* 1985, *m.*	Hon. Thomas E. L., *b.* 1977
1776	*Hawke (11th),* Edward George Hawke, TD, *b.* 1950, *s.* 1992, *m.*	Hon. William M. T. H., *b.* 1995
1927	*Hayter (4th),* George William Michael Chubb, *b.* 1943, *s.* 2003, *m.*	Hon. Thomas F. F. C., *b.*1986
1945	*Hazlerigg (3rd),* Arthur Grey Hazlerigg, *b.* 1951, *s.* 2002, *m.*	Hon. Arthur W. G. H. *b.* 1987
1943	*Hemingford (3rd),* (Dennis) Nicholas Herbert, *b.* 1934, *s.* 1982, *m.*	Hon. Christopher D. C. H., *b.* 1973
1906	*Hemphill (5th),* Peter Patrick Fitzroy Martyn Martyn-Hemphill, *b.* 1928, *s.* 1957, *m.*	Hon. Charles A. M. M.-H., *b.* 1954
1799 I.	** *Henley (8th) and Northington (6th) (1885),* Oliver Michael Robert Eden, *b.* 1953, *s.* 1977, *m.*	Hon. John W. O. E., *b.* 1988
1800 I.	*Henniker (9th) and Hartismere (6th) (1866),* Mark Ian Philip Chandos Henniker-Major, *b.* 1947, *s.* 2004, *m.*	Hon. Edward G. M. H.-M., *b.* 1985
1461	*Herbert (19th),* David John Seyfried Herbert, *b.* 1952, *s.* 2002, *m.*	Hon. Oliver R. S. H., *b.* 1976
1886	*Herschell (3rd),* Rognvald Richard Farrer Herschell, *b.* 1923, *s.* 1929, *m.*	None
1935	*Hesketh (3rd),* Thomas Alexander Fermor-Hesketh, KBE, PC, *b.* 1950, *s.* 1955, *m.*	Hon. Frederick H. F.-H., *b.* 1988
1828	*Heytesbury (7th),* James William Holmes à Court, *b.* 1967, *s.* 2004, *m.*	Peter M. H.. H. à. C., *b.* 1968
1886	*Hindlip (6th),* Charles Henry Allsopp, *b.* 1940, *s.* 1993, *m.*	Hon. Henry W. A., *b.* 1973
1950	*Hives (3rd),* Matthew Peter Hives, *b.* 1971, *s.* 1997	Hon. Michael B. H., *b.* 1926
1912	*Hollenden (4th),* Ian Hampden Hope-Morley, *b.* 1946, *s.* 1999, *m.*	Hon. Edward H.-M., *b.* 1981
1897	*Holm Patrick (4th),* Hans James David Hamilton, *b.* 1955, *s.* 1991, *m.*	Hon. Ion H. J. H., *b.* 1956
1797 I.	*Hotham (8th),* Henry Durand Hotham, *b.* 1940, *s.* 1967, *m.*	Hon. William B. H., *b.* 1972
1881	*Hothfield (6th),* Anthony Charles Sackville Tufton, *b.* 1939, *s.* 1991, *m.*	Hon. William S. T., *b.* 1977
1930	*Howard of Penrith (3rd),* Philip Esme Howard, *b.* 1945, *s.* 1999, *m.*	Hon. Thomas Philip H., *b.* 1974
1960	*Howick of Glendale (2nd),* Charles Evelyn Baring, *b.* 1937, *s.* 1973, *m.*	Hon. David E. C. B., *b.* 1975
1796 I.	*Huntingfield (7th),* Joshua Charles Vanneck, *b.* 1954, *s.* 1994, *m.*	Hon. Gerard C. A. V., *b.* 1985
1866	** *Hylton (5th),* Raymond Hervey Jolliffe, *b.* 1932, *s.* 1967, *m.*	Hon. William H. M. J., *b.* 1967
1933	*Iliffe (3rd),* Robert Peter Richard Iliffe, *b.* 1944, *s.* 1996, *m.*	Hon. Edward R. I., *b.* 1968
1543 I.	*Inchiquin (18th),* Conor Myles John O'Brien, *b.* 1943, *s.* 1982, *m.*	Conor J. A. O'B., *b.* 1952
1962	*Inchyra (2nd),* Robert Charles Reneke Hoyer Millar, *b.* 1935, *s.* 1989, *m.*	Hon. C. James C. H. M., *b.* 1962
1964	** *Inglewood (2nd),* (William) Richard Fletcher-Vane, *b.* 1951, *s.* 1989, *m.*	Hon. Henry W. F. F.-V., *b.* 1990
1919	*Inverforth (4th),* Andrew Peter Weir, *b.* 1966, *s.* 1982	Hon. John V. W., *b.* 1935
1941	*Ironside (2nd),* Edmund Oslac Ironside, *b.* 1924, *s.* 1959, *m.*	Hon. Charles E. G. I., *b.* 1956
1952	*Jeffreys (3rd),* Christopher Henry Mark Jeffreys, *b.* 1957, *s.* 1986, *m.*	Hon. Arthur M. H. J., *b.* 1989
1906	*Joicey (5th),* James Michael Joicey, *b.* 1953, *s.* 1993, *m.*	Hon. William J. J., *b.* 1990
1937	*Kenilworth (4th),* (John) Randle Siddeley, *b.* 1954, *s.* 1981, *m.*	Hon. William R. J. S., *b.* 1992
1935	*Kennet (2nd),* Wayland Hilton Young, *b.* 1923, *s.* 1960, *m.*	Hon. W. A. Thoby Y., *b.* 1957
1776 I.	*Kensington (8th) and Kensington (5th) (1886),* Hugh Ivor Edwardes, *b.* 1933, *s.* 1981, *m.*	Hon. W. Owen A. E., *b.* 1964
1951	*Kenswood (2nd),* John Michael Howard Whitfield, *b.* 1930, *s.* 1963, *m.*	Hon. Michael C. W., *b.* 1955
1788	*Kenyon (6th),* Lloyd Tyrell-Kenyon, *b.* 1947, *s.* 1993, *m.*	Hon. Lloyd N. T.-K., *b.* 1972
1947	*Kershaw (4th),* Edward John Kershaw, *b.* 1936, *s.* 1962, *m.*	Hon. John C. E. K., *b.* 1971
1943	*Keyes (3rd),* Charles William Packe Keyes, *b.* 1951, *s.* 2005, *m.*	Hon. Leopold R. J. K., *b.* 1956
1909	*Kilbracken (4th),* Christopher John Godley, *b.* 1945, *s.* 2006, *m.*	Hon. James J. G., *b.* 1972
1900	*Killanin (4th),* (George) Redmond Fitzpatrick Morris, *b.* 1947, *s.* 1999, *m.*	Hon. Luke M. G. M., *b.* 1975
1943	*Killearn (3rd),* Victor Miles George Aldous Lampson, *b.* 1941, *s.* 1996, *m.*	Hon. Miles H. M. L., *b.* 1977
1789 I.	*Kilmaine (7th),* John David Henry Browne, *b.* 1948, *s.* 1978, *m.*	Hon. John F. S. B., *b.* 1983

1831	*Kilmarnock (7th),* Alastair Ivor Gilbert Boyd, *b.* 1927, *s.* 1975, *m.*	Hon. Robin J. B., *b.* 1941
1941	*Kindersley (3rd),* Robert Hugh Molesworth Kindersley, *b.* 1929, *s.* 1976, *m.*	Hon. Rupert J. M. K., *b.* 1955
1223 I.	*Kingsale (36th),* Nevinson Mark de Courcy, *b.* 1958, *s.* 2005, *m., Premier Baron of Ireland*	Joseph K. C. de C., *b.* 1955
1902	*Kinross (5th),* Christopher Patrick Balfour, *b.* 1949, *s.* 1985, *m.*	Hon. Alan I. B., *b.* 1978
1951	*Kirkwood (3rd),* David Harvie Kirkwood, PHD, *b.* 1931, *s.* 1970, *m.*	Hon. James S. K., *b.* 1937
1800 I.	*Langford (9th),* Col. Geoffrey Alexander Rowley-Conwy, OBE, *b.* 1912, *s.* 1953, *m.*	Hon. Owain G. R.-C., *b.* 1958
1942	*Latham (2nd),* Dominic Charles Latham, *b.* 1954, *s.* 1970	Anthony M. L., *b.* 1954
1431	*Latymer (9th),* Crispin James Alan Nevill Money-Coutts, *b.* 1955, *s.* 2003, *m.*	Hon. Drummond W. T. M.-C., *b.* 1986
1869	*Lawrence (5th),* David John Downer Lawrence, *b.* 1937, *s.* 1968	None
1947	*Layton (3rd),* Geoffrey Michael Layton, *b.* 1947, *s.* 1989, *m.*	Hon. David L., *b.* 1914
1839	*Leigh (6th),* Christopher Dudley Piers Leigh, *b.* 1960, *s.* 2003, *m.*	Hon. Rupert D. L., *b.* 1994
1962	*Leighton of St Mellons (3rd),* Robert William Henry Leighton Seager, *b.* 1955, *s.* 1998	Hon. Simon J. L. S., *b.* 1957
1797	*Lilford (8th),* Mark Vernon Powys, *b.* 1975, *s.* 2005	Robert C. L. P., *b.* 1930
1945	*Lindsay of Birker (3rd),* James Francis Lindsay, *b.* 1945, *s.* 1994, *m.*	Alexander S. L., *b.* 1940
1758 I.	*Lisle (9th),* (John) Nicholas Geoffrey Lysaght, *b.* 1960, *s.* 2003	Hon. David J. L., *b.* 1963
1850	*Londesborough (9th),* Richard John Denison, *b.* 1959, *s.* 1968, *m.*	Hon. James F. D., *b.* 1990
1541 I.	*Louth (16th),* Otway Michael James Oliver Plunkett, *b.* 1929, *s.* 1950, *m.*	Hon. Jonathan O. P., *b.* 1952
1458 S.	*Lovat (16th) and Lovat (5th) (1837),* Simon Fraser, *b.* 1977, *s.* 1995	Hon. Jack F., *b.* 1984
1946	*Lucas of Chilworth (3rd),* Simon William Lucas, *b.* 1957, *s.* 2001, *m.*	Hon. John R. M. L., *b.* 1995
1663	** *Lucas (11th) and Dingwall (14th) (S. 1609),* Ralph Matthew Palmer, *b.* 1951, *s.* 1991	Hon. Lewis E. P., *b.* 1987
1929	** *Luke (3rd),* Arthur Charles St John Lawson-Johnston, *b.* 1933, *s.* 1996, *m.*	Hon. Ian J. St J. L.-J., *b.* 1963
1914	** *Lyell (3rd),* Charles Lyell, *b.* 1939, *s.* 1943	None
1859	*Lyveden (7th),* Jack Leslie Vernon, *b.* 1938, *s.* 1999, *m.*	Hon. Colin R. V., *b.* 1967
1959	*MacAndrew (3rd),* Christopher Anthony Colin MacAndrew, *b.* 1945, *s.* 1989, *m.*	Hon. Oliver C. J. M., *b.* 1983
1776 I.	*Macdonald (8th),* Godfrey James Macdonald of Macdonald, *b.* 1947, *s.* 1970, *m.*	Hon. Godfrey E. H. T. M., *b.* 1982
1937	*McGowan (4th),* Harry John Charles McGowan, *b.* 1971, *s.* 2003, *m.*	Hon. Dominic J. W. McG., *b.* 1951
1922	*Maclay (3rd),* Joseph Paton Maclay, *b.* 1942, *s.* 1969, *m.*	Hon. Joseph P. M., *b.* 1977
1955	*McNair (3rd),* Duncan James McNair, *b.* 1947, *s.* 1989, *m.*	Hon. William S. A. M., *b.* 1958
1951	*Macpherson of Drumochter (2nd),* (James) Gordon Macpherson, *b.* 1924, *s.* 1965, *m.*	Hon. James A. M., *b.* 1979
1937	** *Mancroft (3rd),* Benjamin Lloyd Stormont Mancroft, *b.* 1957, *s.* 1987, *m.*	Hon. Arthur L. S. M., *b.* 1995
1807	*Manners (5th),* John Robert Cecil Manners, *b.* 1923, *s.* 1972, *w.*	Hon. John H. R. M., *b.* 1956
1922	*Manton (4th),* Miles Ronald Marcus Watson, *b.* 1958, *s.* 2003, *m.*	Hon. Thomas N. C. D. W., *b.* 1985
1908	*Marchamley (4th),* William Francis Whiteley, *b.* 1968, *s.* 1994	None
1964	*Margadale (3rd),* Alastair John Morrison, *b.* 1958, *s.* 2003, *m.*	Hon. Declan J. M., *b.* 1993
1961	*Marks of Broughton (3rd),* Simon Richard Marks, *b.* 1950, *s.* 1998, *m.*	Hon. Michael M., *b.* 1989
1964	*Martonmere (2nd),* John Stephen Robinson, *b.* 1963, *s.* 1989	David A. R., *b.* 1965
1776 I.	*Massy (10th),* David Hamon Somerset Massy, *b.* 1947, *s.* 1995	Hon. John H. M., *b.* 1950
1935	*May (4th),* Jasper Bertram St John May, *b.* 1965, *s.* 2006	None
1928	*Melchett (4th),* Peter Robert Henry Mond, *b.* 1948, *s.* 1973	None
1925	*Merrivale (3rd),* Jack Henry Edmond Duke, *b.* 1917, *s.* 1951, *w.*	Hon. Derek J. P. D., *b.* 1948
1911	*Merthyr,* Trevor Oswin Lewis, CBE, *b.* 1935, *s.* 1977, *m.* Disclaimed for life 1977	David T. L., *b.* 1977
1919	*Meston (3rd),* James Meston, *b.* 1950, *s.* 1984, *m.*	Hon. Thomas J. D. M., *b.* 1977
1838	** *Methuen (7th),* Robert Alexander Holt Methuen, *b.* 1931, *s.* 1994, *m.*	James P. A. M.-C., *b.* 1952
1711	*Middleton (12th),* (Digby) Michael Godfrey John Willoughby, MC, *b.* 1921, *s.* 1970	Hon. Michael C. J. W., *b.* 1948
1939	*Milford (4th),* Guy Wogan Philipps, *b.* 1961, *s.* 1999, *m.*	Hon. Archie S. P., *b.* 1997
1933	*Milne (3rd),* George Alexander Milne, *b.* 1941, *s.* 2005	Hon. Iain C. L. M., *b.* 1949
1951	*Milner of Leeds (3rd),* Richard James Milner, *b.* 1959, *s.* 2003, *m.*	None
1947	*Milverton (2nd), Revd* Fraser Arthur Richard Richards, *b.* 1930, *s.* 1978, *m.*	Hon. Michael H. R., *b.* 1936
1873	*Moncreiff (6th),* Rhoderick Harry Wellwood Moncreiff, *b.* 1954, *s.* 2002, *m.*	Hon. Harry J. W. M., *b.* 1986

Created	Title, order of succession, name, etc.	Heir
1884	*Monk Bretton (3rd),* John Charles Dodson, *b.* 1924, *s.* 1933, *m.*	Hon. Christopher M. D., *b.* 1958
1885	*Monkswell (5th),* Gerard Collier, *b.* 1947, *s.* 1984, *m.*	Hon. James A. C., *b.* 1977
1728	** *Monson (11th),* John Monson, *b.* 1932, *s.* 1958, *m.*	Hon. Nicholas J. M., *b.* 1955
1885	** *Montagu of Beaulieu (3rd),* Edward John Barrington Douglas-Scott-Montagu, *b.* 1926, *s.* 1929, *m.*	Hon. Ralph D.-S.-M., *b.* 1961
1839	*Monteagle of Brandon (6th),* Gerald Spring Rice, *b.* 1926, *s.* 1946, *m.*	Hon. Charles J. S. R., *b.* 1953
1943	** *Moran (2nd),* (Richard) John (McMoran) Wilson, KCMG, *b.* 1924, *s.* 1977, *m.*	Hon. James M. W., *b.* 1952
1918	*Morris (3rd),* Michael David Morris, *b.* 1937, *s.* 1975, *m.*	Hon. Thomas A. S. M., *b.* 1982
1950	*Morris of Kenwood (3rd),* Jonathan David Morris, *b.* 1968, *s.* 2004, *m.*	None
1831	*Mostyn (6th),* Llewellyn Roger Lloyd-Mostyn, *b.* 1948, *s.* 2000, *m.*	Hon. Gregory P. R. L.-M., *b.* 1984
1933	*Mottistone (4th),* David Peter Seely, CBE, *b.* 1920, *s.* 1966, *m.*	Hon. Peter J. P. S., *b.* 1949
1945	*Mountevans (3rd),* Edward Patrick Broke Evans, *b.* 1943, *s.* 1974, *m.*	Hon. Jeffrey de C. R. E., *b.* 1948
1283	*Mowbray (27th), Segrave (28th) (1295) and Stourton (24th) (1448),* Edward William Stephen Stourton, *b.* 1953, *s.* 2006, *m.*	Hon. James C. P. S., *b.* 1991
1932	*Moyne (3rd),* Jonathan Bryan Guinness, *b.* 1930, *s.* 1992, *m.*	Hon. Jasper J. R. G., *b.* 1954
1929	** *Moynihan (4th),* Colin Berkeley Moynihan, *b.* 1955, *s.* 1997, *m.*	Hon. Nicholas E. B. M., *b.* 1994
1781 I.	*Muskerry (9th),* Robert Fitzmaurice Deane, *b.* 1948, *s.* 1988, *m.*	Hon. Jonathan F. D., *b.* 1986
1627 S.	*Napier (14th) and Ettrick (5th) (1872),* Francis Nigel Napier, KCVO, *b.* 1930, *s.* 1954, *m.*	Master of Napier, *b.* 1962
1868	*Napier of Magdala (6th),* Robert Alan Napier, *b.* 1940, *s.* 1987, *m.*	Hon. James R. N., *b.* 1966
1940	*Nathan (3rd),* Rupert Harry Bernard Nathan, *b.* 1957, *s.* 2007, *m.*	None
1960	*Nelson of Stafford (4th),* Alistair William Henry Nelson, *b.* 1973, *s.* 2006	Hon. James J. N., *b.* 1947
1959	*Netherthorpe (3rd),* James Frederick Turner, *b.* 1964, *s.* 1982, *m.*	Hon. Andrew J. E. T., *b.* 1993
1946	*Newall (2nd),* Francis Storer Eaton Newall, *b.* 1930, *s.* 1963, *m.*	Hon. Richard H. E. N., *b.* 1961
1776 I.	*Newborough (8th),* Robert Vaughan Wynn, *b.* 1949, *s.* 1998, *m.*	Hon. Charles H. R. W., *b.* 1923
1892	*Newton (5th),* Richard Thomas Legh, *b.* 1950, *s.* 1992, *m.*	Hon. Piers R. L., *b.* 1979
1930	*Noel-Buxton (3rd),* Martin Connal Noel-Buxton, *b.* 1940, *s.* 1980, *m.*	Hon. Charles C. N.-B., *b.* 1975
1957	*Norrie (2nd),* (George) Willoughby Moke Norrie, *b.* 1936, *s.* 1977, *m.*	Hon. Mark W. J. N., *b.* 1972
1884	** *Northbourne (5th),* Christopher George Walter James, *b.* 1926, *s.* 1982, *m.*	Hon. Charles W. H. J., *b.* 1960
1866	** *Northbrook (6th),* Francis Thomas Baring, *b.* 1954, *s.* 1990, *m.*	To the Baronetcy, Peter B. *b.* 1939
1878	*Norton (8th),* James Nigel Arden Adderley, *b.* 1947, *s.* 1993, *m.*	Hon. Edward J. A. A., *b.* 1982
1906	*Nunburnholme (6th),* Stephen Charles Wilson, *b.* 1973, *s.* 2000	Hon. David M. W., *b.* 1954
1950	*Ogmore (3rd),* Morgan Rees-Williams, *b.* 1937, *s.* 2004, *m.*	Hon. Tudor D. R.-W., *b.* 1991
1870	*O'Hagan (4th),* Charles Towneley Strachey, *b.* 1945, *s.* 1961	Hon. Richard T. S., *b.* 1950
1868	*O'Neill (4th),* Raymond Arthur Clanaboy O'Neill, TD, *b.* 1933, *s.* 1944, *m.*	Hon. Shane S. C. O'N., *b.* 1965
1836 I.	*Oranmore and Browne (5th) and Mereworth (3rd) (1926),* Dominick Geoffrey Thomas Browne, *b.* 1929, *s.* 2002	Hon. Martin M. D. B., *b.* 1931
1933	** *Palmer (4th),* Adrian Bailie Nottage Palmer, *b.* 1951, *s.* 1990, *m.*	Hon. Hugo B. R. P., *b.* 1980
1914	*Parmoor (4th),* (Frederick Alfred) Milo Cripps, *b.* 1929, *s.* 1977	Michael L. S. C., *b.* 1942
1937	*Pender (3rd),* John Willoughby Denison-Pender, *b.* 1933, *s.* 1965, *m.*	Hon. Henry J. R. D.-P., *b.* 1968
1866	*Penrhyn (7th),* Simon Douglas-Pennant, *b.* 1938, *s.* 2003, *m.*	Hon. Edward S. D.-P., *b.* 1966
1603	*Petre (18th),* John Patrick Lionel Petre, *b.* 1942, *s.* 1989, *m.*	Hon. Dominic W. P., *b.* 1966
1918	*Phillimore (5th),* Francis Stephen Phillimore, *b.* 1944, *s.* 1994, *m.*	Hon. Tristan A. S. P., *b.* 1977
1945	*Piercy (3rd),* James William Piercy, *b.* 1946, *s.* 1981	Hon. Mark E. P. P., *b.* 1953
1827	*Plunket (8th),* Robin Rathmore Plunket, *b.* 1925, *s.* 1975, *m.*	Hon. Shaun A. F. S. P., *b.* 1931
1831	*Poltimore (7th),* Mark Coplestone Bampfylde, *b.* 1957, *s.* 1978, *m.*	Hon. Henry A. W. B., *b.* 1985
1690 S.	*Polwarth (11th),* Andrew Walter Hepburne-Scott, *b.* 1947, *s.* 2005, *m.*	Master of Polwarth, *b.* 1973
1930	*Ponsonby of Shulbrede (4th) and Ponsonby of Roehampton (life peerage, 2000),* Frederick Matthew Thomas Ponsonby, *b.* 1958, *s.* 1990	None
1958	*Poole (2nd),* David Charles Poole, *b.* 1945, *s.* 1993, *m.*	Hon. Oliver J. P., *b.* 1972
1852	*Raglan (5th),* FitzRoy John Somerset, *b.* 1927, *s.* 1964	Hon. Geoffrey S., *b.* 1932
1932	*Rankeillour (5th),* Michael Richard Hope, *b.* 1940, *s.* 2005, *m.*	James F. H., *b.* 1968
1953	*Rathcavan (3rd),* Hugh Detmar Torrens O'Neill, *b.* 1939, *s.* 1994, *m.*	Hon. François H. N. O'N., *b.* 1984
1916	*Rathcreedan (3rd),* Christopher John Norton, *b.* 1949, *s.* 1990, *m.*	Hon. Adam G. N., *b.* 1952
1868 I.	*Rathdonnell (5th),* Thomas Benjamin McClintock-Bunbury, *b.* 1938, *s.* 1959, *m.*	Hon. William L. M.-B., *b.* 1966
1911	*Ravensdale (3rd),* Nicholas Mosley, MC, *b.* 1923, *s.* 1966, *m.*	Hon. Shaun N. M., *b.* 1949

1821	*Ravensworth (9th),* Thomas Arthur Hamish Liddell, *b.* 1954, *s.* 2004, *m.*	Hon. Henry A. T. L., *b.* 1987
1821	*Rayleigh (6th),* John Gerald Strutt, *b.* 1960, *s.* 1988, *m.*	Hon. John F. S., *b.* 1993
1937	** *Rea (3rd),* John Nicolas Rea, MD, *b.* 1928, *s.* 1981, *m.*	Hon. Matthew J. R., *b.* 1956
1628 S.	** *Reay (14th),* Hugh William Mackay, *b.* 1937, *s.* 1963, *m.*	Master of Reay, *b.* 1965
1902	*Redesdale (6th) and Mitford (life peerage 2000),* Rupert Bertram Mitford, *b.* 1967, *s.* 1991, *m.*	Hon. Bertram D. M., *b.* 2000
1940	*Reith,* Christopher John Reith, *b.* 1928, *s.* 1971, *m.* Disclaimed for life 1972.	Hon. James H. J. R., *b.* 1971
1928	*Remnant (3rd),* James Wogan Remnant, CVO, *b.* 1930, *s.* 1967, *m.*	Hon. Philip J. R., *b.* 1954
1806 I.	*Rendlesham (9th),* Charles William Brooke Thellusson, *b.* 1954, *s.* 1999, *m.*	Hon. Peter R. T., *b.* 1920
1933	*Rennell (4th),* James Roderick David Tremayne Rodd, *b.* 1978, *s.* 2006	None
1964	*Renwick (2nd),* Harry Andrew Renwick, *b.* 1935, *s.* 1973, *m.*	Hon. Robert J. R., *b.* 1966
1885	*Revelstoke (6th),* James Cecil Baring, *b.* 1938, *s.* 2003, *m.*	Hon. Alexander R. B., *b.* 1970
1905	*Ritchie of Dundee (5th),* (Harold) Malcolm Ritchie, *b.* 1919, *s.* 1978, *m.*	Hon. C. Rupert R. R., *b.* 1958
1935	*Riverdale (3rd),* Anthony Robert Balfour, *b.* 1960, *s.* 1998	Hon. David R. B., *b.* 1938
1961	*Robertson of Oakridge (2nd),* William Ronald Robertson, *b.* 1930, *s.* 1974, *m.*	Hon. William B. E. R., *b.* 1975
1938	*Roborough (3rd),* Henry Massey Lopes, *b.* 1940, *s.* 1992, *m.*	Hon. Massey J. H. L., *b.* 1969
1931	*Rochester (2nd),* Foster Charles Lowry Lamb, *b.* 1916, *s.* 1955, *w.*	Hon. David C. L., *b.* 1944
1934	*Rockley (3rd),* James Hugh Cecil, *b.* 1934, *s.* 1976, *m.*	Hon. Anthony R. C., *b.* 1961
1782	*Rodney (10th),* George Brydges Rodney, *b.* 1953, *s.* 1992, *m.*	Hon. John G. B. R., *b.* 1999
1651 S.	*Rollo (14th) and Dunning (5th) (1869),* David Eric Howard Rollo, *b.* 1943, *s.* 1997, *m.*	Master of Rollo, *b.* 1972
1959	*Rootes (3rd),* Nicholas Geoffrey Rootes, *b.* 1951, *s.* 1992, *m.*	William B. R., *b.* 1944
1796 I.	*Rossmore (7th) and Rossmore (6th) (1838),* William Warner Westenra, *b.* 1931, *s.* 1958, *m.*	Hon. Benedict W. W., *b.* 1983
1939	** *Rotherwick (3rd),* (Herbert) Robin Cayzer, *b.* 1954, *s.* 1996, *m.*	Hon. H. Robin C., *b.* 1989
1885	*Rothschild (4th),* (Nathaniel Charles) Jacob Rothschild, OM, GBE, *b.* 1936, *s.* 1990, *m.*	Hon. Nathaniel P. V. J. R., *b.* 1971
1911	*Rowallan (4th),* John Polson Cameron Corbett, *b.* 1947, *s.* 1993	Hon. Jason W. P. C. C., *b.* 1972
1947	*Rugby (3rd),* Robert Charles Maffey, *b.* 1951, *s.* 1990, *m.*	Hon. Timothy J. H. M., *b.* 1975
1919	*Russell of Liverpool (3rd),* Simon Gordon Jared Russell, *b.* 1952, *s.* 1981, *m.*	Hon. Edward C. S. R., *b.* 1985
1876	*Sackville (7th),* Robert Bertrand Sackville-West, *b.* 1958, *s.* 2004, *m.*	Hon. Arthur S-W., *b.* 2000
1964	*St Helens (2nd),* Richard Francis Hughes-Young, *b.* 1945, *s.* 1980, *m.*	Hon. Henry T. H.-Y., *b.* 1986
1559	** *St John of Bletso (21st),* Anthony Tudor St John, *b.* 1957, *s.* 1978, *m.*	Hon. Oliver B. St J., *b.* 1995
1887	*St Levan (4th),* John Francis Arthur St Aubyn, DSC, *b.* 1919, *s.* 1978, *w.*	James P. S. St. A., *b.* 1950
1885	*St Oswald (6th),* Charles Rowland Andrew Winn, *b.* 1959, *s.* 1999, *m.*	Hon. Rowland C. S. H. W., *b.* 1986
1960	*Sanderson of Ayot,* Alan Lindsay Sanderson, *b.* 1931, *s.* 1971, *m.* Disclaimed for life 1971.	Hon. Michael S., *b.* 1959
1945	*Sandford (2nd),* Revd John Cyril Edmondson, DSC, *b.* 1920, *s.* 1959, *m.*	Hon. James J. M. E., *b.* 1949
1871	*Sandhurst (6th),* Guy Rees John Mansfield, *b.* 1949, *s.* 2002, *m.*	Hon. Edward J. M., *b.* 1982
1802	*Sandys (7th),* Richard Michael Oliver Hill, *b.* 1931, *s.* 1961, *m.*	The Marquess of Downshire
1888	*Savile (3rd),* George Halifax Lumley-Savile, *b.* 1919, *s.* 1931	John A. T. L-S., *b.* 1947
1447	*Saye and Sele (21st),* Nathaniel Thomas Allen Fiennes, *b.* 1920, *s.* 1968, *m.*	Hon. Martin G. F., *b.* 1961
1826	*Seaford (6th),* Colin Humphrey Felton Ellis, *b.* 1946, *s.* 1999, *m.*	Hon. Benjamin F. T. E., *b.* 1976
1932	** *Selsdon (3rd),* Malcolm McEacharn Mitchell-Thomson, *b.* 1937, *s.* 1963, *m.*	Hon. Callum M. M. M.-T., *b.* 1969
1489 S.	*Sempill (21st),* James William Stuart Whitemore Sempill, *b.* 1949, *s.* 1995, *m.*	Master of Sempill, *b.* 1979
1916	*Shaughnessy (4th),* Michael James Shaughnessy, *b.* 1946, *s.* 2003	Charles, G. P. S., *b.* 1955
1946	*Shepherd (3rd),* Graham George Shepherd, *b.* 1949, *s.* 2001, *m.*	Hon. Patrick M. S., *b.* 19–
1964	*Sherfield (3rd),* Dwight William Makins, *b.* 1951, *s.* 2006, *m.*	None
1902	*Shuttleworth (5th),* Charles Geoffrey Nicholas Kay-Shuttleworth, *b.* 1948, *s.* 1975, *m.*	Hon. Thomas E. K.-S., *b.* 1976
1950	*Silkin (3rd),* Christopher Lewis Silkin, *b.* 1947, *s.* 2001	Rory L. S., *b.* 1954
1963	*Silsoe (3rd),* Simon Rupert Trustram Eve *b.* 1966, *s.* 2005	Hon. Peter N. T. E., *b.* 1930
1947	*Simon of Wythenshawe (3rd),* Matthew Simon, *b.* 1955, *s.* 2002	Martin S., *b.* 1944
1449 S.	*Sinclair (18th),* Matthew Murray Kennedy St Clair *b.* 1968, *s.* 2004, *m.*	Hugh A. C. St C., *b.* 1957
1957	*Sinclair of Cleeve (3rd),* John Lawrence Robert Sinclair, *b.* 1953, *s.* 1985	None
1919	*Sinha (6th),* Arup Kumar Sinha, *b.* 1966, *s.* 1999	Hon. Dilip K. S., *b.* 1967
1828	** *Skelmersdale (7th),* Roger Bootle-Wilbraham, *b.* 1945, *s.* 1973, *m.*	Hon. Andrew B.-W., *b.* 1977

Created	Title, order of succession, name, etc.	Heir
1916	*Somerleyton (3rd),* Savile William Francis Crossley, GCVO, *b.* 1928, *s.* 1959, *m.*	Hon. Hugh F. S. C., *b.* 1971
1784	*Somers (9th),* Philip Sebastian Somers Cocks, *b.* 1948, *s.* 1995	Alan B. C., *b.* 1930
1780	*Southampton (6th),* Charles James FitzRoy, *b.* 1928, *s.* 1989, *m.*	Hon. Edward C. F., *b.* 1955
1959	*Spens (4th),* Patrick Nathaniel George Spens, *b.* 1968, *s.* 2001, *m.*	Hon. Peter L. S., *b.* 2000
1640	*Stafford (15th),* Francis Melfort William Fitzherbert, *b.* 1954, *s.* 1986, *m.*	Hon. Benjamin J. B. F., *b.* 1983
1938	*Stamp (4th),* Trevor Charles Bosworth Stamp, MD, *b.* 1935, *s.* 1987, *m.*	Hon. Nicholas C. T. S., *b.* 1978
1839	*Stanley of Alderley (8th), Sheffield (8th) (I. 1738) and Eddisbury (7th) (1848),* Thomas Henry Oliver Stanley, *b.* 1927, *s.* 1971, *m.*	Hon. Richard O. S., *b.* 1956
1318	** *Strabolgi (11th),* David Montague de Burgh Kenworthy, *b.* 1914, *s.* 1953, *m.*	Andrew D. W. K., *b.* 1967
1954	*Strang (2nd),* Colin Strang, *b.* 1922, *s.* 1978, *m.*	None
1628	*Strange (17th),* Adam Humphrey Drummond of Megginch, *b.* 1953, *s.* 2005 *m.*	Hon. John A. H. D. of M. *b.* 1992
1955	*Strathalmond (3rd),* William Roberton Fraser, *b.* 1947, *s.* 1976, *m.*	Hon. William G. F., *b.* 1976
1936	*Strathcarron (3rd),* Ian David Patrick Macpherson, *b.* 1949, *s.* 2006, *m.*	Hon. Rory D. A. M., *b.* 1982
1955	** *Strathclyde (2nd),* Thomas Galloway Dunlop du Roy de Blicquy Galbraith, PC, *b.* 1960, *s.* 1985, *m.*	Hon. Charles W. du R. de B. G., *b.* 1962
1900	*Strathcona and Mount Royal (4th),* Donald Euan Palmer Howard, *b.* 1923, *s.* 1959, *m.*	Hon. D. Alexander S. H., *b.* 1961
1836	*Stratheden (6th) and Campbell (6th) (1841),* Donald Campbell, *b.* 1934, *s.* 1987, *m.*	Hon. David A. C., *b.* 1963
1884	*Strathspey (6th),* James Patrick Trevor Grant of Grant, *b.* 1943, *s.* 1992, *m.*	Hon. Michael P. F. G., *b.* 1953
1838	*Sudeley (7th),* Merlin Charles Sainthill Hanbury-Tracy, *b.* 1939, *s.* 1941	D. Andrew J. H.-T., *b.* 1928
1786	*Suffield (11th),* Anthony Philip Harbord-Hamond, MC, *b.* 1922, *s.* 1951, *w.*	Hon. Charles A. A. H.-H., *b.* 1953
1893	*Swansea (5th),* Richard Anthony Hussey Vivian, *b.* 1957, *s.* 2005, *m.*	Hon. James H. H. V., *b.* 1999
1907	*Swaythling (5th),* Charles Edgar Samuel Montagu, *b.* 1954, *s.* 1998, *m.*	Hon. Anthony T. S. M., *b.* 1931
1919	** *Swinfen (3rd),* Roger Mynors Swinfen Eady, *b.* 1938, *s.* 1977, *m.*	Hon. Charles R. P. S. E., *b.* 1971
1935	*Sysonby (3rd),* John Frederick Ponsonby, *b.* 1945, *s.* 1956	None
1831 I.	*Talbot of Malahide (10th),* Reginald John Richard Arundell, *b.* 1931, *s.* 1987, *m.*	Hon. Richard J. T. A., *b.* 1957
1946	*Tedder (3rd),* Robin John Tedder, *b.* 1955, *s.* 1994, *m.*	Hon. Benjamin J. T., *b.* 1985
1884	*Tennyson (6th),* David Harold Alexander Tennyson, *b.* 1960, *s.* 2006	Alan J. D. T., *b.* 1965
1918	*Terrington (6th),* Christopher Richard James Woodhouse, MB, *b.* 1946, *s.* 2001, *m.*	Hon. Jack H. L. W., *b.* 1978
1940	*Teviot (2nd),* Charles John Kerr, *b.* 1934, *s.* 1968, *m.*	Hon. Charles R. K., *b.* 1971
1616	*Teynham (20th),* John Christopher Ingham Roper-Curzon, *b.* 1928, *s.* 1972, *m.*	Hon. David J. H. I. R.-C., *b.* 1965
1964	*Thomson of Fleet (3rd),* David Kenneth Roy Thomson, *b.* 1957, *s.* 2006, *m.*	Hon. Benjamin T., *b.* 2006
1792	*Thurlow (8th),* Francis Edward Hovell-Thurlow-Cumming-Bruce, KCMG, *b.* 1912, *s.* 1971, *w.*	Hon. Roualeyn R. H.-T.-C.-B., *b.* 1952
1876	*Tollemache (5th),* Timothy John Edward Tollemache, *b.* 1939, *s.* 1975, *m.*	Hon. Edward J. H. T., *b.* 1976
1564 S.	*Torphichen (15th),* James Andrew Douglas Sandilands, *b.* 1946, *s.* 1975, *m.*	Robert P. S., *b.* 1950
1947	** *Trefgarne (2nd),* David Garro Trefgarne, PC, *b.* 1941, *s.* 1960, *m.*	Hon. George G. T., *b.* 1970
1921	*Trevethin (4th) and Oaksey (2nd) (1947),* John Geoffrey Tristram Lawrence, OBE, *b.* 1929, *s.* 1971, *m.*	Hon. Patrick J. T. L., *b.* 1960
1880	*Trevor (5th),* Marke Charles Hill-Trevor, *b.* 1970, *s.* 1997, *m.*	Hon. Iain R. H.-T., *b.* 1971
1461 I.	*Trimlestown (21st),* Raymond Charles Barnewall, *b.* 1930, *s.* 1997	None
1940	*Tryon (3rd),* Anthony George Merrik Tryon, *b.* 1940, *s.* 1976	Hon. Charles G. B. T., *b.* 1976
1935	*Tweedsmuir (3rd),* William de l'Aigle Buchan, *b.* 1916, *s.* 1996, *m.*	Hon. John W. H. de l'A. B., *b.* 1950
1523	*Vaux of Harrowden (11th),* Anthony William Gilbey, *b.* 1940, *s.* 2002, *m.*	Hon. Richard H. G. G., *b.*1965
1800 I.	*Ventry (8th),* Andrew Wesley Daubeny de Moleyns, *b.* 1943, *s.* 1987, *m.*	Hon. Francis W. D. de M., *b.* 1965
1762	*Vernon (11th),* Anthony William Vernon-Harcourt, *b.* 1939, *s.* 2000, *m.*	Hon. Simon A. V-H., *b.* 1969
1922	*Vestey (3rd),* Samuel George Armstrong Vestey, *b.* 1941, *s.* 1954, *m.*	Hon. William G. V., *b.* 1983
1841	*Vivian (7th),* Charles Crespigny Hussey Vivian, *b.* 1966, *s.* 2004	Hon. Victor A. R. B. V., *b.* 1940
1934	*Wakehurst (3rd),* (John) Christopher Loder, *b.* 1925, *s.* 1970, *m.*	Hon. Timothy W. L., *b.* 1958
1723	** *Walpole (10th) and Walpole of Wolterton (8th) (1756),* Robert Horatio Walpole, *b.* 1938, *s.* 1989, *m.*	Hon. Jonathan R. H. W., *b.* 1967

1780		*Walsingham (9th)*, John de Grey, MC, *b.* 1925, *s.* 1965, *m.*	Hon. Robert de. G., *b.* 1969
1936		*Wardington (3rd)*, William Simon Pease, *b.* 1925, *s.* 2005, *m.*	None
1792 I.		*Waterpark (7th)*, Frederick Caryll Philip Cavendish, *b.* 1926, *s.* 1948, *m.*	Hon. Roderick A. C., *b.* 1959
1942		*Wedgwood (4th)*, Piers Anthony Weymouth Wedgwood, *b.* 1954, *s.* 1970, *m.*	John W., *b.* 1919
1861		*Westbury (6th)*, Richard Nicholas Bethell, MBE, *b.* 1950, *s.* 2001, *m.*	Hon. Alexander B., *b.* 1986
1944		*Westwood (3rd)*, (William) Gavin Westwood, *b.* 1944, *s.* 1991, *m.*	Hon. W. Fergus W., *b.* 1972
1544/5		*Wharton (12th)*, Myles Christopher David Robertson, *b.* 1964, *s.* 2000, *m.*	Hon. Christopher J. R., *b.* 1969
1935		*Wigram (2nd)*, (George) Neville (Clive) Wigram, MC, *b.* 1915, *s.* 1960, *w.*	Maj. Hon. Andrew F. C. W., *b.* 1949
1491	**	*Willoughby de Broke (21st)*, Leopold David Verney, *b.* 1938, *s.* 1986, *m.*	Hon. Rupert G. V., *b.* 1966
1946		*Wilson (2nd)*, Patrick Maitland Wilson, *b.* 1915, *s.* 1964, *w.*	None
1937		*Windlesham (3rd) and Hennessy (life peerage, 1999)*, David James George Hennessy, CVO, PC, *b.* 1932, *s.* 1962, *w.*	Hon. James R. H., *b.* 1968
1951		*Wise (2nd)*, John Clayton Wise, *b.* 1923, *s.* 1968, *m.*	Hon. Christopher J. C. W., *b.* 1949
1869		*Wolverton (7th)*, Christopher Richard Glyn, *b.* 1938, *s.* 1988	Hon. Andrew J. G., *b.* 1943
1928		*Wraxall (3rd)*, Eustace Hubert Beilby Gibbs, KCVO, CMG, *b.* 1929, *s.* 2001, *m.*	Hon. Anthony H. G., *b.* 1958
1915		*Wrenbury (3rd)*, Revd John Burton Buckley, *b.* 1927, *s.* 1940, *m.*	Hon. William E. B., *b.* 1966
1838		*Wrottesley (6th)*, Clifton Hugh Lancelot de Verdon Wrottesley, *b.* 1968, *s.* 1977, *m.*	Hon. Stephen J. W., *b.* 1955
1829		*Wynford (9th)*, John Philip Robert Best, *b.* 1950, *s.* 2002, *m.*	Hon. Harry R. F. B., *b.* 1987
1308		*Zouche (18th)*, James Assheton Frankland, *b.* 1943, *s.* 1965, *m.*	Hon. William T. A. F., *b.* 1984

BARONESSES/LADIES IN THEIR OWN RIGHT

Style, The Right Hon. the Lady _ , *or* The Right Hon. the Baroness _ , according to her preference. Either style may be used, except in the case of Scottish titles (indicated by S.), which are not baronies (*see* page 44) and whose holders are always addressed as Lady.

Envelope, may be addressed in same way as a Baron's wife or, if she prefers *(formal)*, The Right Hon. the Baroness _; *(social)*, The Baroness _. Otherwise as for a Baron's wife

Husband, Untitled

Children's style, As for children of a Baron

Created		*Title, order of succession, name, etc*	*Heir*
1664		*Arlington*, Jennifer Jane Forwood, *b.* 1939, *s.* 1999, *w.* Title called out of abeyance 1999	Hon. Patrick J. D. F., *b.* 1967
1455		*Berners (16th)*, Pamela Vivien Kirkham, *b.* 1929, *s.* 1995, *m.*	Hon. Rupert W. T. K., *b.* 1953
1529		*Braye (8th)*, Mary Penelope Aubrey-Fletcher, *b.* 1941, *s.* 1985, *m.*	Two co-heiresses
1321		*Dacre (27th)*, Rachel Leila Douglas-Home, *b.* 1929, *s.* 1970, *w.*	Hon. James T. A. D.-H., *b.* 1952
1332	**	*Darcy de Knayth (18th)*, Davina Marcia Ingrams, DBE, *b.* 1938, *s.* 1943, *w.*	Hon. Caspar D. I., *b.* 1962
1490 S.		*Herries of Terregles (14th)*, Anne Elizabeth Fitzalan-Howard, *b.* 1938, *s.* 1975, *w.*	Lady Mary Mumford, *b.* 1940
1597		*Howard de Walden (10th)*, Mary Hazel Caridwen Czernin, *b.* 1935, *s.* 2004, *m.* Title called out of abeyance 2004	Hon. Peter J. J. C. *b.* 1966
1602 S.		*Kinloss (12th)*, Beatrice Mary Grenville Freeman-Grenville, *b.* 1922, *s.* 1944, *w.*	Master of Kinloss, *b.* 1953
1445 S.	**	*Saltoun (20th)*, Flora Marjory Fraser, *b.* 1930, *s.* 1979, *w.*	Hon. Katharine I. M. I. F., *b.* 1957
1313		*Willoughby de Eresby (27th)*, (Nancy) Jane Marie Heathcote-Drummond-Willoughby, *b.* 1934, *s.* 1983	Two co-heiresses

LIFE PEERS

Style, The Right Hon. the Lord _ /The Right Hon. the Lady _ , *or* The Right Hon. the Baroness _ , according to her preference
Envelope (formal), The Right Hon. Lord _/Lady_/ Baroness_; *(social),* The Lord _/Lady_/Baroness_
Letter (formal), My Lord/Lady; *(social),* Dear Lord/ Lady _. *Spoken,* Lord/Lady _
Wife's style, The Right Hon. the Lady _
Husband, Untitled
Children's style, 'The Hon.' before forename (F_) and surname (S_)
Envelope, The Hon. F_ S_. *Letter,* Dear Mr/Miss/Mrs S_. *Spoken,* Mr/Miss/Mrs S_

NEW LIFE PEERAGES

1 September 2006 to 31 August 2007:
Prof. Paul Anthony Elliott Bew; Dame Jane Susan Campbell; Jean Coussins; Sir Ara Warkes Darzi, KBE; Dr Khalid Hameed, CBE; Sir Robin Berry Janvrin, GCB, KCVO, PC; Sir Digby Marritt Jones; Prof, Sir John (Richard) Krebs, FRS; Sir George Mark Malloch Brown, KCMG, PC; Revd Andrew Mawson, OBE; Rt. Hon. Sir David Edmond Neuberger; Dame (Lilian) Pauline Neville-Jones, DCMG; Shriti Vadera; Gen. Sir Michael John Dawson Walker, GCB, CMG, CBE; Syeeda Warsi; Adm. Sir Alan William John West, GCB, DSC

SYMBOLS
* Hereditary peer who has been granted a life peerage. For further details, please refer to the Hereditary Peers section. For example, life peer *Balniel* can be found under his hereditary title *Earl of Crawford and Balcarres*
‡ Title not confirmed at time of going to press

CREATED UNDER THE APPELLATE JURISDICTION ACT 1876 (AS AMENDED)

BARONS
Created
1980 *Bridge of Harwich,* Nigel Cyprian Bridge, PC, *b.* 1917, *m.*
2004 *Brown of Eaton-under-Heywood,* Simon Denis Brown, PC, *b.* 1937, *m., Lord of Appeal in Ordinary*
1991 *Browne-Wilkinson,* Nicolas Christopher Henry Browne-Wilkinson, PC, *b.* 1930, *m.*
2004 *Carswell,* Robert Douglas Carswell, PC, *b.* 1934, *m., Lord of Appeal in Ordinary*
1996 *Clyde,* James John Clyde, PC, *b.* 1932, *m.*
1986 *Goff of Chieveley,* Robert Lionel Archibald Goff, PC, *b.* 1926, *m.*
1985 *Griffiths,* (William) Hugh Griffiths, MC, PC, *b.* 1923, *m.*
1995 *Hoffmann,* Leonard Hubert Hoffmann, PC, *b.* 1934, *m. Second Senior Lord of Appeal in Ordinary*
1997 *Hutton,* (James) Brian (Edward) Hutton, PC, *b.* 1931, *m.*
1993 *Lloyd of Berwick,* Anthony John Leslie Lloyd, PC, *b.* 1929, *m.*
2005 *Mance,* Jonathan Hugh Mance, PC, *b.* 1943, *m., Lord of Appeal in Ordinary*
1998 *Millett,* Peter Julian Millett, PC, *b.* 1932, *m.*
1992 *Mustill,* Michael John Mustill, PC, *b.* 1931, *m.*
2007 *Neuberger of Abbotsbury,* David Edmond Neuberger, PC, *b.* 1948, *m., Lord of Appeal in Ordinary*
1994 *Nicholls of Birkenhead,* Donald James Nicholls, PC, *b.* 1933, *m.*
1986 *Oliver of Aylmerton,* Peter Raymond Oliver, PC, *b.* 1921, *m.*
1999 *Phillips of Worth Matravers,* Nicholas Addison Phillips, b. 1938, *m. Lord Chief Justice of England and Wales*
1997 *Saville of Newdigate,* Mark Oliver Saville, PC, *b.* 1936, *m. Lord of Appeal in Ordinary*
2000 *Scott of Foscote,* Richard Rashleigh Folliott Scott, PC, *b.* 1934, *m. Lord of Appeal in Ordinary*
1992 *Slynn of Hadley,* Gordon Slynn, PC, *b.* 1930, *m.*
1995 *Steyn,* Johan van Zyl Steyn, PC, *b.* 1932, *m.*
1982 *Templeman,* Sydney William Templeman, MBE, PC, *b.* 1920, *m.*
2003 *Walker of Gestingthorpe,* Robert Walker, PC, *b.* 1938, *m. Lord of Appeal in Ordinary*
1992 *Woolf,* Harry Kenneth Woolf, PC, *b.* 1933, *m.*

BARONESSES
2004 *Hale of Richmond,* Brenda Marjorie Hale, DBE, PC, *b.* 1945, *m., Lord of Appeal in Ordinary*

CREATED UNDER THE LIFE PEERAGES ACT 1958

BARONS
Created
2000 **Acton of Bridgnorth,* Lord Acton, *b.* 1941, *m.* *(see* Hereditary Peers)
2001 *Adebowale,* Victor Olufemi Adebowale, CBE, *b.* 1962
2005 *Adonis,* Andrew Adonis, *b.* 1963, *m.*
1998 *Ahmed,* Nazir Ahmed, *b.* 1957, *m.*
1996 *Alderdice,* John Thomas Alderdice, *b.* 1955, *m.*
1976 *Allen of Abbeydale,* Philip Allen, GCB, *b.* 1912, *w.*
1998 *Alli,* Waheed Alli, *b.* 1964
2004 *Alliance,* David Alliance, CBE, *b.* 1932
1997 *Alton of Liverpool,* David Patrick Paul Alton, *b.* 1951, *m.*
2005 *Anderson of Swansea,* Donald Anderson, PC, *b.* 1939, *m.*
1992 *Archer of Sandwell,* Peter Kingsley Archer, PC, QC, *b.* 1926, *m.*
1992 *Archer of Weston-super-Mare,* Jeffrey Howard Archer, *b.* 1940, *m.*
1988 *Armstrong of Ilminster,* Robert Temple Armstrong, GCB, CVO, *b.* 1927, *m.*
1999 **Armstrong-Jones,* Earl of Snowdon, GCVO, *b.* 1930, *m.* *(see* Hereditary Peers)
2000 *Ashcroft,* Michael Anthony Ashcroft, KCMG,

2001 *Ashdown of Norton-sub-Hamdon,* Jeremy John Durham (Paddy) Ashdown, GCMG, KBE, PC, *b.* 1941, *m.*
1992 *Ashley of Stoke,* Jack Ashley, CH, PC, *b.* 1922, *w.*
1993 *Attenborough,* Richard Samuel Attenborough, CBE, *b.* 1923, *m.*
1998 *Bach,* William Stephen Goulden Bach, *b.* 1946, *m.*
1997 *Bagri,* Raj Kumar Bagri, CBE, *b.* 1930, *m.*
1997 *Baker of Dorking,* Kenneth Wilfred Baker, CH, PC, *b.* 1934, *m.*
2004 *Ballyedmond,* Dr Edward Haughey, OBE, *b.* 1944, *m.*
1974 **Balniel,* The Earl of Crawford and Balcarres, *b.* 1927, *m. (see* Hereditary Peers)
1992 *Barber of Tewkesbury,* Derek Coates Barber, *b.* 1918, *m.*
1983 *Barnett,* Joel Barnett, PC, *b.* 1923, *m.*
1997 *Bassam of Brighton,* (John) Steven Bassam, *b.* 1953
1967 *Beaumont of Whitley,* Revd Timothy Wentworth Beaumont, *b.* 1928, *m.*
1998 *Bell,* Timothy John Leigh Bell, *b.* 1941, *m.*
2000 *Bernstein of Craigweil,* Alexander Bernstein, *b.* 1936, *m.*
2001 *Best,* Richard Stuart Best, OBE, *b.* 1945, *m.*
2007 *Bew,* Prof. Paul Anthony Elliott Bew, PC, *b.* 1950, *m.*
2001 *Bhatia,* Amirali Alibhai Bhatia, OBE, *b.* 1932, *m.*
2004 *Bhattacharyya,* Prof. (Sushantha) Kumar Bhattacharyya, CBE *b.* 1932, *m.*
2006 *Bilimoria,* Karan Faridoon Bilimoria, CBE, *b.* 1961, *m.*
2005 *Bilston,* Dennis Turner, *b.* 1942, *m.*
1996 *Bingham of Cornhill,* Thomas Henry Bingham, KG, PC, *b.* 1933, *m. Senior Lord of Appeal in Ordinary*
2000 *Birt,* John Francis Hodgess Birt, *b.* 1944, *m.*
2001 *Black of Crossharbour,* Conrad Moffat Black, OC, PC, *b.* 1944, *m.*
1997 *Blackwell,* Norman Roy Blackwell, *b.* 1952, *m.*
1994 *Blaker,* Peter Allan Renshaw Blaker, KCMG, PC, *b.* 1922, *m.*
1978 *Blease,* William John Blease, *b.* 1914, *m.*
1995 *Blyth of Rowington,* James Blyth, *b.* 1940, *m.*
1996 *Borrie,* Gordon Johnson Borrie, QC, *b.* 1931, *m.*
1976 *Boston of Faversham,* Terence George Boston, QC, *b.* 1930, *m.*
1996 *Bowness,* Peter Spencer Bowness, CBE, *b.* 1943, *m.*
2003 *Boyce,* Michael Boyce, GCB, OBE, *b.* 1943
2006 *Boyd of Duncansby,* Colin David Boyd, PC, *b.* 1953, *m.*
2006 *Bradley,* Keith John Charles Bradley, PC, *b.* 1950, *m.*
1999 *Bradshaw,* William Peter Bradshaw, *b.* 1936, *m.*
1998 *Bragg,* Melvyn Bragg, *b.* 1939, *m.*
1987 *Bramall,* Edwin Noel Westby Bramall, KG, GCB, OBE, MC, *b.* 1923, *m.*
2000 *Brennan,* Daniel Joseph Brennan, QC, *b.* 1942, *m.*
1999 *Brett,* William Henry Brett, *b.* 1942, *m.*
1976 *Briggs,* Asa Briggs, FBA, *b.* 1921, *m.*
2000 *Brittan of Spennithorne,* Leon Brittan, PC, QC, *b.* 1939, *m.*
2004 *Broers,* Prof. Alec (Nigel) Broers, *b.* 1938, *m.*
1997 *Brooke of Alverthorpe,* Clive Brooke, *b.* 1942, *m.*
2001 *Brooke of Sutton Mandeville,* Peter Leonard Brooke, CH, PC, *b.* 1934, *m.*
1998 *Brookman,* David Keith Brookman, *b.* 1937, *m.*
1979 *Brooks of Tremorfa,* John Edward Brooks, *b.* 1927, *m.*
2006 *Browne of Belmont,* Wallace Hamilton Browne, *b.* 1947
2001 *Browne of Madingley,* Edmund John Phillip Browne, *b.* 1948
2006 *Bruce-Lockhart,* Alexander John (Sandy) Bruce-Lockhart, OBE, *b.* 1942, *m.*
1997 *Burlison,* Thomas Henry Burlison, *b.* 1936, *m.*
2006 *Burnett,* John Patrick Aubone Burnett, *b.* 1945, *m.*
1998 *Burns,* Terence Burns, GCB, *b.* 1944, *m.*
1998 *Butler of Brockwell,* (Frederick Edward) Robin Butler, KG, GCB, CVO, PC, *b.* 1938, *m.*
1978 *Buxton of Alsa,* Aubrey Leland Oakes Buxton, KCVO, MC, *b.* 1918, *m.*
2004 *Cameron of Dillington,* Ewen (James Hanning) Cameron, *b.* 1949, *m.*
1984 *Cameron of Lochbroom,* Kenneth John Cameron, PC, *b.* 1931, *m.*
1981 *Campbell of Alloway,* Alan Robertson Campbell, QC, *b.* 1917, *m.*
2001 *Campbell-Savours,* Dale Norman Campbell-Savours, *b.* 1943, *m.*
2002 *Carey of Clifton,* Rt. Revd George Leonard Carey, PC, *b.* 1935, *m.*
1999 **Carington of Upton,* Lord Carrington, GCMG, *b.* 1919, *m. (see* Hereditary Peers)
1999 *Carlile of Berriew,* Alexander Charles Carlile, QC, *b.* 1948, *m.*
1975 *Carr of Hadley,* (Leonard) Robert Carr, PC, *b.* 1916, *m.*
2004 *Carter of Coles,* Patrick Robert Carter, *b.* 1946, *m.*
1990 *Cavendish of Furness,* (Richard) Hugh Cavendish, *b.* 1941, *m.*
1996 *Chadlington,* Peter Selwyn Gummer, *b.* 1942, *m.*
1964 *Chalfont,* (Alun) Arthur Gwynne Jones, OBE, MC, PC, *b.* 1919, *m.*
2005 *Chidgey,* David William George Chidgey, *b.* 1942, *m.*
1987 *Chilver,* (Amos) Henry Chilver, FRS, FRENG, *b.* 1926, *m.*
1977 *Chitnis,* Pratap Chidamber Chitnis, *b.* 1936, *m.*
1998 *Christopher,* Anthony Martin Grosvenor Christopher, CBE, *b.* 1925, *m.*
2001 *Clark of Windermere,* David George Clark, PC, PHD, *b.* 1939, *m.*
1998 *Clarke of Hampstead,* Anthony James Clarke, CBE, *b.* 1932, *m.*
1998 *Clement-Jones,* Timothy Francis Clement-Jones, CBE, *b.* 1949, *m.*
1990 *Clinton-Davis,* Stanley Clinton Clinton-Davis, PC, *b.* 1928, *m.*
2000 *Coe,* Sebastian Newbold Coe, KBE, *b.* 1956, *m.*
2001 *Condon,* Paul Leslie Condon, QPM, *m.*
1992 *Cooke of Islandreagh,* Victor Alexander Cooke, OBE, *b.* 1920, *m.*
1997 *Cope of Berkeley,* John Ambrose Cope, PC, *b.* 1937, *m.*
2001 *Corbett of Castle Vale,* Robin Corbett, *b.* 1933, *m.*
2006 *Cotter,* Brian Joseph Michael Cotter, *b.* 1938, *m.*
1991 *Craig of Radley,* David Brownrigg Craig, GCB, OBE, *b.* 1929, *m.*
1987 *Crickhowell,* (Roger) Nicholas Edwards, PC, *b.* 1934, *m.*

2006 *Crisp,* (Edmund) Nigel (Ramsay) Crisp, KCB, *b.* 1952, *m.*
1978 *Croham,* Douglas Albert Vivian Allen, GCB, *b.* 1917, *w.*
1995 *Cuckney,* John Graham Cuckney, *b.* 1925, *m.*
2003 *Cullen of Whitekirk,* William Douglas Cullen, PC, *b.* 1935, *m.*
2005 *Cunningham of Felling,* John Anderson Cunningham, PC, *b.* 1939, *m.*
1996 *Currie of Marylebone,* David Anthony Currie, *b.* 1946, *m.*
1993 *Dahrendorf,* Ralf Dahrendorf, KBE, PHD, DPHIL, FBA, *b.* 1929, *m.*
2007 *Darzi of Denham,* Ara Warkes Darzi, KBE, *b.* 1960, *m.*
2006 *Davidson of Glen Clova,* Neil Forbes Davidson, QC, *b.* 1950, *m.*
1997 *Davies of Coity,* (David) Garfield Davies, CBE, *b.* 1935, *m.*
1997 *Davies of Oldham,* Bryan Davies, PC, *b.* 1939, *m.*
1993 *Dean of Harptree,* (Arthur) Paul Dean, PC, *b.* 1924, *m.*
2006 *Dear,* Geoffrey (James) Dear, QPM, *b.* 1937, *m.*
1998 *Dearing,* Ronald Ernest Dearing, *b.* 1930, *m.*
1991 *Desai,* Prof. Meghnad Jagdishchandra Desai, PHD, *b.* 1940, *m.*
1997 *Dholakia,* Navnit Dholakia, OBE, *b.* 1937, *m.*
1997 *Dixon,* Donald Dixon, PC, *b.* 1929, *m.*
1993 *Dixon-Smith,* Robert William Dixon-Smith, *b.* 1934, *m.*
1985 *Donoughue,* Bernard Donoughue, DPHIL, *b.* 1934
2004 *Drayson,* Paul Rudd Drayson, *b.* 1960, *m.*
1994 *Dubs,* Alfred Dubs, *b.* 1932, *m.*
2004 *Dykes,* Hugh John Maxwell Dykes, *b.* 1939, *m.*
1995 *Eames,* Robert Henry Alexander Eames, OM, PHD, *b.* 1937, *m.*
1992 *Eatwell,* John Leonard Eatwell, PHD, *b.* 1945
1983 *Eden of Winton,* John Benedict Eden, PC, *b.* 1925, *m*
1999 *Elder,* Thomas Murray Elder, *b.* 1950
1992 *Elis-Thomas,* Dafydd Elis Elis-Thomas, PC, *b.* 1946, *m.*
1985 *Elliott of Morpeth,* Robert William Elliott, *b.* 1920, *m.*
1981 *Elystan-Morgan,* Dafydd Elystan Elystan-Morgan, *b.* 1932, *w.*
2000 **Erskine of Alloa Tower,* Earl of Mar and Kellie, *b.* 1949, *m.* *(see* Hereditary Peers)
1997 *Evans of Parkside,* John Evans, *b.* 1930, *m.*
2000 *Evans of Temple Guiting,* Matthew Evans, CBE, *b.* 1941, *m.*
1998 *Evans of Watford,* David Charles Evans, *b.* 1942, *m.*
1983 *Ezra,* Derek Ezra, MBE, *b.* 1919, *m.*
1997 *Falconer of Thoroton,* Charles Leslie Falconer, QC, *b.* 1951, *m.*
1999 *Faulkner of Worcester,* Richard Oliver Faulkner, *b.* 1946, *m.*
2001 *Fearn, Ronald Cyril Fearn,* OBE, *b.* 1931, *m.*
1996 *Feldman,* Basil Feldman, *b.* 1926, *m.*
1999 *Fellowes,* Robert Fellowes, GCB, GCVO, PC, *b.* 1941, *m.*
1999 *Filkin,* David Geoffrey Nigel Filkin, CBE, *b.* 1944
1979 *Flowers,* Brian Hilton Flowers, FRS, *b.* 1924, *m.*
1999 *Forsyth of Drumlean,* Michael Bruce Forsyth, *b.* 1954, *m.*
2005 *Foster of Bishop Auckland,* Derek Foster, PC, *b.* 1937, *m.*
1999 *Foster of Thames Bank,* Norman Robert Foster, OM, *b.* 1935, *m.*
2005 *Foulkes of Cumnock,* George Foulkes, PC, *b.* 1942, *m.*
2001 *Fowler,* (Peter) Norman Fowler, PC, *b.* 1938, *m.*
1989 *Fraser of Carmyllie,* Peter Lovat Fraser, PC, QC, *b.* 1945, *m.*
1997 *Freeman,* Roger Norman Freeman, PC, *b.* 1942, *m.*
2000 *Fyfe of Fairfield,* George Lennox Fyfe, *b.* 1941, *m.*
1997 *Garel-Jones,* (William Armand) Thomas Tristan Garel-Jones, PC, *b.* 1941, *m.*
1999* *Gascoyne-Cecil,* The Marquess of Salisbury, PC , *b.* 1946, *m.* (*see* Hereditary Peers)
1999 *Gavron,* Robert Gavron, CBE, *b.* 1930, *m.*
2004 *George,* Edward (Alan John) George, GBE, PC, *b.* 1938, *m.*
2004 *Giddens,* Prof. Anthony Giddens, *b.* 1938, *m.*
1997 *Gilbert,* John William Gilbert, PC, PHD, *b.* 1927, *m.*
1992 *Gilmour of Craigmillar,* Ian Hedworth John Little Gilmour, PC, *b.* 1926, *w.*
1977 *Glenamara,* Edward Watson Short, CH, PC, *b.* 1912, *m.*
1999 *Goldsmith,* Peter Henry Goldsmith, QC, *b.* 1950, *m.*
1997 *Goodhart,* William Howard Goodhart, QC, *b.* 1933, *m.*
2005 *Goodlad,* Alastair Robertson Goodlad, KCMG, *b.* 1943, *m.*
1997 *Gordon of Strathblane,* James Stuart Gordon, CBE, *b.* 1936, *m.*
2004 *Gould of Brookwood,* Philip Gould *b.* 1950 *m.*
1999 *Grabiner,* Anthony Stephen Grabiner, QC, *b.* 1945, *m.*
1983 *Graham of Edmonton,* (Thomas) Edward Graham, *b.* 1925, *m.*
2000 *Greaves,* Anthony Robert Greaves, *b.* 1942, *m.*
1975 *Gregson,* John Gregson, *b.* 1924
2000 **Grenfell of Kilvey,* Lord Grenfell, *b.* 1935, *m.* *(see* Hereditary Peers)
2004 *Griffiths of Burry Port,* Revd Dr Leslie John Griffiths, *b.* 1942, *m.*
1991 *Griffiths of Fforestfach,* Brian Griffiths, *b.* 1941, *m.*
2001 *Grocott,* Bruce Joseph Grocott, PC, *b.* 1940, *m.*
2000 **Gueterbock,* Lord Berkley, OBE, *b.* 1939, *m.* *(see* Hereditary Peers)
2000 *Guthrie of Craigiebank,* Charles Ronald Llewelyn Guthrie, GCB, LVO, OBE *b.* 1938, *m.*
1995 *Habgood,* Rt. Revd John Stapylton Habgood, PC, PHD, *b.* 1927, *m.*
2007 *Hameed,* Dr Khalid Hameed, *b.* 1941, *m.*
2005 *Hamilton of Epsom,* Archibald Gavin Hamilton, PC, *b.* 1941, *m.*
2001 *Hannay of Chiswick,* David Hugh Alexander Hannay, GCMG, CH, *b.* 1935, *m.*
1998 *Hanningfield,* Paul Edward Winston White, *b.* 1940
1997 *Hardie,* Andrew Rutherford Hardie, QC, PC, *b.* 1946, *m.*
2006 *Harries of Pentregarth,* Rt. Revd Richard Douglas Harries, *b.* 1936, *m.*
1998 *Harris of Haringey,* (Jonathan) Toby Harris, *b.* 1953, *m.*

1996 *Harris of Peckham,* Philip Charles Harris, *b.* 1942, *m.*
1999 *Harrison,* Lyndon Henry Arthur Harrison, *b.* 1947, *m.*
2004 *Hart of Chilton,* Garry Richard Rushby Hart, *b.* 1940, *m.*
1993 *Haskel,* Simon Haskel, *b.* 1934, *m.*
1998 *Haskins,* Christopher Robin Haskins, *b.* 1937, *m.*
2005 *Hastings of Scarisbrick,* Michael John Hastings, CBE, *b.* 1958, *m.*
1997 *Hattersley,* Roy Sidney George Hattersley, PC, *b.* 1932, *m.*
2004 *Haworth,* Alan Robert Haworth, *b.* 1948, *m.*
1992 *Hayhoe,* Bernard John (Barney) Hayhoe, PC, *b.* 1925, *m.*
1992 *Healey,* Denis Winston Healey, CH, MBE, PC, *b.* 1917, *m.*
1999 **Hennessey,* Lord Windlesham, CVO, *b.* 1932, *m.* (*see* Hereditary Peers)
2001 *Heseltine,* Michael Ray Dibdin Heseltine, CH, PC, *b.* 1933, *m.*
1997 *Higgins,* Terence Langley Higgins, KBE, PC, *b.* 1928, *m.*
2000 *Hodgson of Astley Abbotts,* Robin Granville Hodgson, CBE, *b.* 1942, *m.*
1997 *Hogg of Cumbernauld,* Norman Hogg, *b.* 1938, *m.*
1991 *Hollick,* Clive Richard Hollick, *b.* 1945, *m.*
1990 *Holme of Cheltenham,* Richard Gordon Holme, CBE, *b.* 1936, *m.*
1979 *Hooson,* (Hugh) Emlyn Hooson, QC, *b.* 1925, *m.*
2005 *Hope of Thornes,* Rt. Revd David Michael Hope, KCVO, PC, *b.* 1940
1995 *Hope of Craighead,* (James Arthur) David Hope, PC, *b.* 1938, *m. Lord of Appeal in Ordinary*
2004 *Howard of Rising,* Greville Patrick Charles Howard, *b.* 1941, *m.*
2005 *Howarth of Newport,* Alan Thomas Howarth, CBE, PC, *b.* 1944
1992 *Howe of Aberavon,* (Richard Edward) Geoffrey Howe, CH, PC, QC, *b.* 1926, *m.*
1997 *Howell of Guildford,* David Arthur Russell Howell, PC, *b.* 1936, *m.*
1978 *Howie of Troon,* William Howie, *b.* 1924, *w.*
1997 *Hoyle,* (Eric) Douglas Harvey Hoyle, *b.* 1930, *w.*
1997 *Hughes of Woodside,* Robert Hughes, *b.* 1932, *m.*
2000 *Hunt of Chesterton,* Julian Charles Roland Hunt, CBE, *b.* 1941, *m.*
1997 *Hunt of Kings Heath,* Philip Alexander Hunt, OBE, *b.* 1949, *m.*
1980 *Hunt of Tanworth,* John Joseph Benedict Hunt, GCB, *b.* 1919, *w.*
1997 *Hunt of Wirral,* David James Fletcher Hunt, MBE, PC, *b.* 1942, *m.*
1997 *Hurd of Westwell,* Douglas Richard Hurd, CH, CBE, PC, *b.* 1930, *m.*
1978 *Hutchinson of Lullington,* Jeremy Nicolas Hutchinson, QC, *b.* 1915, *m.*
1999 *Imbert,* Peter Michael Imbert, QPM, *b.* 1933, *m.*
1997 *Inge,* Peter Anthony Inge, KG, GCB, PC, *b.* 1935, *m.*
1987 *Irvine of Lairg,* Alexander Andrew Mackay Irvine, PC, QC, *b.* 1940, *m.*
1997 *Jacobs,* (David) Anthony Jacobs, *b.* 1931, *m.*
2006 *James of Blackheath,* David Noel James, CBE, *b.* 1937, *m.*
1997 *Janner of Braunstone,* Greville Ewan Janner, QC, *b.* 1928, *w.*
2007 ‡*Janvrin,* Robin Berry Janvrin, GCB, KCVO, PC, *b.* 1946, *m.*
2006 *Jay of Ewelme,* Michael (Hastings) Jay, GCMG, *b.* 1946, *m.*
1987 *Jenkin of Roding,* (Charles) Patrick (Fleeming) Jenkin, PC, *b.* 1926, *m.*
2000 *Joffe,* Joel Goodman Joffe, CBE, *b.* 1932, *m.*
2001 *Jones,* (Stephen) Barry Jones, *b.* 1937, *m.*
2007 *Jones of Birmingham,* Digby Marritt Jones, *b.* 1955, *m.*
2005, *Jones of Cheltenham,* Nigel David Jones, *b.* 1948, *m.*
1997 *Jopling,* (Thomas) Michael Jopling, PC, *b.* 1930, *m.*
2000 *Jordan,* William Brian Jordan, CBE, *b.* 1936, *m.*
1991 *Judd,* Frank Ashcroft Judd, *b.* 1935, *m.*
2004 *Kalms,* Harold Stanley Kalms, *b.* 1931 *m.*
2004 *Kerr of Kinlochard,* John (Olav) Kerr, GCMG, *b.* 1942, *m.*
2001 *Kilclooney,* John David Taylor, PC (NI), *b.* 1937, *m.*
1996 *Kilpatrick of Kincraig,* Robert Kilpatrick, CBE, *b.* 1926, *m.*
1985 *Kimball,* Marcus Richard Kimball, *b.* 1928, *m.*
2001 *King of Bridgwater,* Thomas Jeremy King, CH, PC, *b.* 1933, *m.*
1999 *King of West Bromwich,* Tarsem King, *b.* 1937
1993 *Kingsdown,* Robert (Robin) Leigh-Pemberton, KG, PC, *b.* 1927, *m.*
1994 *Kingsland,* Christopher James Prout, TD, PC, QC, *b.* 1942
2005 *Kinnock,* Neil Gordon Kinnock, PC, *b.* 1942, *m.*
1999 *Kirkham,* Graham Kirkham, *b.* 1944, *m.*
1975 *Kirkhill,* John Farquharson Smith, *b.* 1930, *m.*
2005 *Kirkwood of Kirkhope,* Archibald Johnstone Kirkwood, *b.* 1946, *m.*
2007 *Krebs,* Prof. John (Richard) Krebs, FRS, *b.* 1945, *m.*
1987 *Knights,* Philip Douglas Knights, CBE, QPM, *b.* 1920, *m.*
2004 *Laidlaw,* Irvine Alan Stewart Laidlaw, *b.* 1942, *m.*
1991 *Laing of Dunphail,* Hector Laing, *b.* 1923, *m.*
1999 *Laird,* John Dunn Laird, *b.* 1944, *m.*
1998 *Laming,* (William) Herbert Laming, CBE, *b.* 1936, *m.*
1998 *Lamont of Lerwick,* Norman Stewart Hughson Lamont, PC, *b.* 1942, *m.*
1990 *Lane of Horsell,* Peter Stewart Lane, *b.* 1925, *w.*
1997 *Lang of Monkton,* Ian Bruce Lang, PC, *b.* 1940, *m.*
1992 *Lawson of Blaby,* Nigel Lawson, PC, *b.* 1932, *m.*
2000 *Layard,* Peter Richard Grenville Layard, *b.* 1934, *m.*
1999 *Lea of Crondall,* David Edward Lea, OBE, *b.* 1937
2006 *Leach of Fairford,* Charles Guy Rodney Leach, *b.* 1934, *m.*
2006 *Lee of Trafford,* John Robert Louis Lee, *b.* 1942, *m.*
2004 *Leitch,* Alexander Park Leitch, *b.* 1947, *m.*
1993 *Lester of Herne Hill,* Anthony Paul Lester, QC, *b.* 1936, *m.*
1997 *Levene of Portsoken,* Peter Keith Levene, KBE, *b.* 1941, *m.*
1997 *Levy,* Michael Abraham Levy, *b.* 1944, *m.*
1989 *Lewis of Newnham,* Jack Lewis, FRS, *b.* 1928, *m.*
1999 *Lipsey,* David Lawrence Lipsey, *b.* 1948, *m.*

2001 *Livsey of Talgarth,* Richard Arthur Lloyd Livsey, CBE, *b.* 1935, *m.*
1997 *Lloyd-Webber,* Andrew Lloyd Webber, *b.* 1948, *m.*
1997 *Lofthouse of Pontefract,* Geoffrey Lofthouse, *b.* 1925, *w.*
2006 *Low of Dalston,* Prof. Colin Mackenzie Low, CBE, *b.* 1942, *m.*
2000 *Luce,* Richard Napier Luce, GCVO, PC, *b.* 1936, *m.*
2005 *Lyell of Markyate,* Nicholas Walter Lyell, PC, QC, *b.* 1938, *m.*
2000 **Lyttleton of Aldershot,* The Viscount Chandos, *b.* 1953, *m.* *(see* Hereditary Peers)
1984 *McAlpine of West Green,* (Robert) Alistair McAlpine, *b.* 1942, *m.*
1988 *Macaulay of Bragar,* Donald Macaulay, QC, *b.* 1933, *m.*
1975 *McCarthy,* William Edward John McCarthy, DPHIL, *b.* 1925, *m.*
1976 *McCluskey,* John Herbert McCluskey, *b.* 1929, *m.*
1989 *McColl of Dulwich,* Ian McColl, CBE, FRCS, FRCSE, *b.* 1933, *m.*
1998 *Macdonald of Tradeston,* Angus John Macdonald, CBE, *b.* 1940, *m.*
1991 *Macfarlane of Bearsden,* Norman Somerville Macfarlane, KT, FRSE, *b.* 1926, *m.*
2001 *MacGregor of Pulham Market,* John Roddick Russell MacGregor, CBE, PC, *b.* 1937, *m.*
1982 *McIntosh of Haringey,* Andrew Robert McIntosh, *b.* 1933, *w.*
1979 *Mackay of Clashfern,* James Peter Hymers Mackay, KT, PC, FRSE, *b.* 1927, *m.*
1995 *Mackay of Drumadoon,* Donald Sage Mackay, PC, *b.* 1946, *m.*
2004 *McKenzie of Luton,* William David McKenzie, *b.* 1946, *m.*
1999 *Mackenzie of Culkein,* Hector Uisdean MacKenzie, *b.* 1940
1998 *Mackenzie of Framwellgate,* Brian Mackenzie, OBE, *b.* 1943, *m.*
1974 *Mackie of Benshie,* George Yull Mackie, CBE, DSO, DFC, *b.* 1919, *m.*
1996 *MacLaurin of Knebworth,* Ian Charter MacLaurin, *b.* 1937, *m.*
2001 *Maclennon of Rogart,* Robert Adam Ross Maclennan, PC, *b.* 1936, *m.*
1995 *McNally,* Tom McNally, PC, *b.* 1943, *m.*
2001 *Maginnis of Drumglass,* Kenneth Wiggins Maginnis, *b.* 1938, *m.*
2007 *Malloch-Brown,* George Mark Malloch Brown, KCMG, PC, *b.* 1953, *m.*
2006 *Marland,* Jonathan Peter Marland, *b.* 1956, *m.*
1991 *Marlesford,* Mark Shuldham Schreiber, *b.* 1931, *m.*
1981 *Marsh,* Richard William Marsh, PC, *b.* 1928, *m.*
1998 *Marshall of Knightsbridge,* Colin Marsh Marshall, *b.* 1933, *m.*
1987 *Mason of Barnsley,* Roy Mason, PC, *b.* 1924, *m.*
2005 *Mawhinney,* Brian Stanley Mawhinney, PC, *b.* 1940, *m.*
2007 *Mawson,* Revd Andrew Mawson, OBE, *b.* 1954, *m.*
2004 *Maxton,* John Alston Maxton, *b.* 1936, *m.*
2001 *May of Oxford,* Robert McCredie May, OM, *b.* 1936, *m.*
1997 *Mayhew of Twysden,* Patrick Barnabas Burke Mayhew, QC, PC, *b.* 1929, *m.*
2000 *Mitchell,* Parry Andrew Mitchell, *b.* 1943, *m.*
2000 **Mitford,* Lord Redesdale, *b.* 1967, *m.* *(see* Hereditary Peers)
1997 *Molyneaux of Killead,* James Henry Molyneaux, KBE, PC, *b.* 1920
2005 *Moonie,* Dr. Lewis George Moonie, *b.* 1947, *m.*
1992 *Moore of Lower Marsh,* John Edward Michael Moore, PC, *b.* 1937, *m.*
1986 *Moore of Wolvercote,* Philip Brian Cecil Moore, GCB, GCVO, CMG, PC, *b.* 1921, *m.*
2000 *Morgan,* Kenneth Owen Morgan, *b.* 1934, *m.*
2001 *Morris of Aberavon,* John Morris, KG, QC, *b.* 1931, *m.*
2006 *Morris of Handsworth,* William Manuel Morris, *b.* 1938, *m.*
1997 *Morris of Manchester,* Alfred Morris, PC, *b.* 1928, *m.*
2006 *Morrow,* Maurice George Morrow, *m.*
2001 *Moser,* Claus Adolf Moser, KCB, CBE, *b.* 1922, *m.*
1979 *Murton of Lindisfarne,* (Henry) Oscar Murton, OBE, TD, PC, *b.* 1914, *m.*
1997 *Naseby,* Michael Wolfgang Laurence Morris, PC, *b.* 1936, *m.*
1997 *Neill of Bladen,* (Francis) Patrick Neill, QC, *b.* 1926, *m.*
1997 *Newby,* Richard Mark Newby, OBE, *b.* 1953, *m.*
1997 *Newton of Braintree,* Antony Harold Newton, OBE, PC, *b.* 1937, *m.*
1994 *Nickson,* David Wigley Nickson, KBE, FRSE, *b.* 1929, *m.*
1975 *Northfield,* (William) Donald Chapman, *b.* 1923
1998 *Norton of Louth,* Philip Norton, *b.* 1951
2000 *Oakeshott of Seagrove Bay,* Matthew Alan Oakeshott, *b.* 1947, *m.*
2005 *O'Neill of Clackmannan,* Martin John O'Neill, *b.* 1945, *m.*
2001 *Ouseley,* Herman George Ouseley, *b.* 1945, *m.*
1992 *Owen,* David Anthony Llewellyn Owen, CH, PC, *b.* 1938, *m.*
1999 *Oxburgh,* Ernest Ronald Oxburgh, KBE, FRS, PHD, *b.* 1934, *m.*
1991 *Palumbo,* Peter Garth Palumbo, *b.* 1935, *m.*
2000 *Parekh,* Bhikhu Chhotalal Parekh, *b.* 1935, *m.*
1992 *Parkinson,* Cecil Edward Parkinson, PC, *b.* 1931, *m.*
1999 *Patel,* Narendra Babubhai Patel, *b.* 1938
2000 *Patel of Blackburn,* Adam Hafejee Patel, *b.* 1940
2006 *Patel of Bradford,* Prof. Kamlesh Kumar Patel, OBE, *b.* 1960 *m.*
2005 *Patten of Barnes,* Christopher Francis Patten, CH, PC, *b.* 1944, *m.*
1997 *Patten,* John Haggitt Charles Patten, PC, *b.* 1945, *m.*
1996 *Paul,* Swraj Paul, *b.* 1931, *m.*
1990 *Pearson of Rannoch,* Malcolm Everard MacLaren Pearson, *b.* 1942, *m.*
2001 *Pendry,* Thomas Pendry, *b.* 1934, *m.*
1987 *Peston,* Maurice Harry Peston, *b.* 1931, *m.*
1998 *Phillips of Sudbury,* Andrew Wyndham Phillips, OBE, *b.* 1939, *m.*
1996 *Pilkington of Oxenford,* Revd Canon Peter Pilkington, *b.* 1933, *w.*
1992 *Plant of Highfield,* Prof. Raymond Plant, PHD, *b.* 1945, *m.*
1987 *Plumb,* (Charles) Henry Plumb, *b.* 1925, *m.*

1981 *Plummer of St Marylebone,* (Arthur) Desmond (Herne) Plummer, TD, *b.* 1914, *m.*
2000 **Ponsonby of Roehampton,* Lord Ponsonby of Shulbrede, *b.* 1958 (*see* Hereditary Peers)
2000 *Powell of Bayswater,* Charles David Powell, KCMG, *b.* 1941
1987 *Prior,* James Michael Leathes Prior, PC, *b.* 1927, *m.*
1982 *Prys-Davies,* Gwilym Prys Prys-Davies, *b.* 1923, *m.*
1997 *Puttnam,* David Terence Puttnam, CBE, *b.* 1941, *m.*
1987 *Pym,* Francis Leslie Pym, MC, PC, *b.* 1922, *m.*
1982 *Quinton,* Anthony Meredith Quinton, FBA, *b.* 1925, *m.*
1994 *Quirk,* Prof. (Charles) Randolph Quirk, CBE, FBA, *b.* 1920, *m.*
2001 *Radice,* Giles Heneage Radice, PC, *b.* 1936
2005 *Ramsbotham,* Gen. David John Ramsbotham, GCB, CBE, *b.* 1934, *m.*
2004 *Rana,* Dr Diljit Singh Rana, MBE, *b.* 1938, *m.*
1997 *Randall of St Budeaux,* Stuart Jeffrey Randall, *b.* 1938, *m.*
1997 *Razzall,* (Edward) Timothy Razzall, CBE, *b.* 1943, *m.*
1987 *Rees,* Peter Wynford Innes Rees, PC, QC, *b.* 1926, *m.*
2005 *Rees of Ludlow,* Prof. Martin John Rees, OM, *b.* 1942, *m.*
1988 *Rees-Mogg,* William Rees-Mogg, *b.* 1928, *m.*
1991 *Renfrew of Kaimsthorn,* (Andrew) Colin Renfrew, FBA, *b.* 1937, *m.*
1999 *Rennard,* Christopher John Rennard, MBE, *b.* 1960
1997 *Renton of Mount Harry,* (Ronald) Timothy Renton, PC, *b.* 1932, *m.*
1997 *Renwick of Clifton,* Robin William Renwick, KCMG, *b.* 1937, *m.*
1990 *Richard,* Ivor Seward Richard, PC, QC, *b.* 1932, *m.*
1983 *Richardson of Duntisbourne,* Gordon William Humphreys Richardson, KG, MBE, TD, PC, *b.* 1915, *m.*
1992 *Rix,* Brian Norman Roger Rix, CBE, *b.* 1924, *m.*
2004 *Roberts of Llandudno,* Revd John Roger Roberts, *b.* 1935, *m.*
1997 *Roberts of Conwy,* (Ieuan) Wyn (Pritchard) Roberts, PC, *b.* 1930, *m.*
1999 *Robertson of Port Ellen,* George Islay MacNeill Robertson, KT, GCMG, PC, *b.* 1946, *m.*
1992 *Rodger of Earlsferry,* Alan Ferguson Rodger, PC, QC, FBA, *b.* 1944, *Lord of Appeal in Ordinary*
1992 *Rodgers of Quarry Bank,* William Thomas Rodgers, PC, *b.* 1928, *w.*
1999 *Rogan,* Dennis Robert David Rogan, *b.* 1942, *m.*
1996 *Rogers of Riverside,* Richard George Rogers, RA, RIBA, *b.* 1933, *m.*
2001 *Rooker,* Jeffrey William Rooker, PC, *b.* 1941, *m.*
2000 *Roper,* John Francis Hodgess Roper, PC, *b.* 1935, *m.*
2004 *Rosser,* Richard Andrew Rosser, *b.* 1944, *m.*
2006 *Rowe-Beddoe,* David (Sydney) Rowe-Beddoe, *b.* 1937, *m.*
2004 *Rowlands,* Edward Rowlands, CBE, *b.* 1940, *m.*
1997 *Russell-Johnston,* (David) Russell Russell-Johnston, *b.* 1932, *m.*
1997 *Ryder of Wensum,* Richard Andrew Ryder, OBE, PC, *b.* 1949, *m.*
1996 *Saatchi,* Maurice Saatchi, *b.* 1946, *m.*
1989 *Sainsbury of Preston Candover,* John Davan Sainsbury, KG, *b.* 1927, *m.*
1997 *Sainsbury of Turville,* David John Sainsbury, *b.* 1940, *m.*
1987 *St John of Fawsley,* Norman Antony Francis St John-Stevas, PC, *b.* 1929
1997 *Sandberg,* Michael Graham Ruddock Sandberg, CBE, *b.* 1927, *m.*
1985 *Sanderson of Bowden,* Charles Russell Sanderson, *b.* 1933, *m.*
1998 *Sawyer,* Lawrence (Tom) Sawyer, *b.* 1943
1997 *Selkirk of Douglas,* James Alexander Douglas-Hamilton, MSP, PC, QC, *b.* 1942, *m.*
1996 *Sewel,* John Buttifant Sewel, CBE, *b.* 1946
1999 *Sharman,* Colin Morven Sharman, OBE, *b.* 1943, *m.*
1994 *Shaw of Northstead,* Michael Norman Shaw, *b.* 1920, *m.*
2006 *Sheikh,* Mohamed Iltaf Sheikh, *b.* 1941, *m.*
2001 *Sheldon,* Robert Edward Sheldon, PC, *b.* 1923, *m.*
1994 *Sheppard of Didgemere,* Allan John George Sheppard, KCVO, *b.* 1932, *m.*
2000 *Shutt of Greetland,* David Trevor Shutt, OBE, *b.* 1942
1997 *Simon of Highbury,* David Alec Gwyn Simon, CBE, *b.* 1939, *m.*
1997 *Simpson of Dunkeld,* George Simpson, *b.* 1942, *m.*
1991 *Skidelsky,* Robert Jacob Alexander Skidelsky, DPHIL, *b.* 1939, *m.*
1997 *Smith of Clifton,* Trevor Arthur Smith, *b.* 1937, *m.*
2005 *Smith of Finsbury,* Christopher Robert Smith, PC, *b.* 1951
1999 *Smith of Leigh,* Peter Richard Charles Smith, *b.* 1945, *m.*
2004 *Snape,* Peter Charles Snape, *b.* 1942
2005 *Soley,* Clive Stafford Soley, *b.* 1939
1990 *Soulsby of Swaffham Prior,* Ernest Jackson Lawson Soulsby, PHD, *b.* 1926, *m.*
1983 *Stallard,* Albert William Stallard, *b.* 1921, *m.*
1997 *Steel of Aikwood,* David Martin Scott Steel, KT, KBE, PC, *b.* 1938, *m.*
2004 *Steinberg,* Leonard Steinberg, *b.* 1936
1991 *Sterling of Plaistow,* Jeffrey Maurice Sterling, GCVO, CBE, *b.* 1934, *m.*
2005 *Stevens of Kirkwhelpington,* John Arthur Stevens, *b.* 1942, *m.*
1987 *Stevens of Ludgate,* David Robert Stevens, *b.* 1936, *m.*
1999 *Stevenson of Coddenham,* Henry Dennistoun Stevenson, CBE, *b.* 1945, *m.*
1992 *Stewartby,* (Bernard Harold) Ian (Halley) Stewart, RD, PC, FBA, FRSE, *b.* 1935, *m.*
1983 *Stoddart of Swindon,* David Leonard Stoddart, *b.* 1926, *m.*
1969 *Stokes,* Donald Gresham Stokes, TD, FENG, *b.* 1914, *w.*
1997 *Stone of Blackheath,* Andrew Zelig Stone, *b.* 1942, *m.*
2001 *Sutherland of Houndwood,* Stewart Ross Sutherland, KT, *b.* 1941, *m.*
1971 *Tanlaw,* Simon Brooke Mackay, *b.* 1934, *m.*
1996 *Taverne,* Dick Taverne, QC, *b.* 1928, *m.*
1978 *Taylor of Blackburn,* Thomas Taylor, CBE, *b.* 1929, *m.*

2006 *Taylor of Holbeach,* John Derek Taylor, CBE, *b.* 1943, *m.*
1996 *Taylor of Warwick,* John David Beckett Taylor, *b.* 1952, *m.*
1992 *Tebbit,* Norman Beresford Tebbit, CH, PC, *b.* 1931, *m.*
2001 *Temple-Morris,* Peter Temple-Morris, *b.* 1938, *m.*
2006 *Teverson,* Robin Teverson, *b.* 1952, *m.*
1996 *Thomas of Gresford,* Donald Martin Thomas, OBE, QC, *b.* 1937, *m.*
1987 *Thomas of Gwydir,* Peter John Mitchell Thomas, PC, QC, *b.* 1920, *w.*
1997 *Thomas of Macclesfield,* Terence James Thomas, CBE, *b.* 1937, *m.*
1981 *Thomas of Swynnerton,* Hugh Swynnerton Thomas, *b.* 1931, *m.*
1977 *Thomson of Monifieth,* George Morgan Thomson, KT, PC, *b.* 1921, *m.*
1990 *Tombs,* Francis Leonard Tombs, FENG, *b.* 1924, *m.*
1998 *Tomlinson,* John Edward Tomlinson, *b.* 1939
1994 *Tope,* Graham Norman Tope, CBE, *b.* 1943, *m.*
1981 *Tordoff,* Geoffrey Johnson Tordoff, *b.* 1928, *m.*
2004 *Triesman,* David Maxim Triesman, *b.* 1943
2006 *Trimble,* William David Trimble, PC, *b.* 1944, *m.*
2004 *Truscott,* Dr Peter Derek Truscott, *b.* 1959 *m.*
1993 *Tugendhat,* Christopher Samuel Tugendhat, *b.* 1937, *m.*
2004 *Tunnicliffe,* Denis Tunnicliffe, CBE, *b.* 1943, *m.*
2000 *Turnberg,* Leslie Arnold Turnberg, MD, *b.* 1934, *m.*
2005 *Turnbull,* Andrew Turnbull, KCB, CVO, *b.* 1945, *m.*
2005 *Turner of Ecchinswell,* Jonathan Adair Turner, *b.* 1955, *m.*
2005 *Tyler,* Paul Archer Tyler, CBE, *b.* 1941, *m.*
2004 *Vallance of Tummel,* Iain (David Thomas) Vallance, *b.* 1943, *m.*
1990 *Varley,* Eric Graham Varley, PC, *b.* 1932, *m.*
1996 *Vincent of Coleshill,* Richard Frederick Vincent, GBE, KCB, DSO, *b.* 1931, *m.*
1985 *Vinson,* Nigel Vinson, LVO, *b.* 1931, *m.*
1990 *Waddington,* David Charles Waddington, GCVO, PC, QC, *b.* 1929, *m.*
1990 *Wade of Chorlton,* (William) Oulton Wade, *b.* 1932, *m.*
1992 *Wakeham,* John Wakeham, PC, *b.* 1932, *m.*
1999 *Waldegrave of North Hill,* William Arthur Waldegrave, PC, *b.* 1946, *m.*
2007 *Walker of Aldringham,* Michael John Dawson Walker, GCB, CMG, CBE, *b.* 1944, *m.*
1992 *Walker of Worcester,* Peter Edward Walker, MBE, PC, *b.* 1932, *m.*
1995 *Wallace of Saltaire,* William John Lawrence Wallace, PHD, *b.* 1941, *m.*
1989 *Walton of Detchant,* John Nicholas Walton, TD, FRCP, *b.* 1922, *w.*
1998 *Warner,* Norman Reginald Warner, PC, *b.* 1940, *m.*
1997 *Watson of Invergowrie,* Michael Goodall Watson, *b.* 1949, *m.*
1999 *Watson of Richmond,* Alan John Watson, CBE, *b.* 1941, *m.*
1977 *Wedderburn of Charlton,* (Kenneth) William Wedderburn, FBA, QC, *b.* 1927, *m.*
1976 *Weidenfeld,* (Arthur) George Weidenfeld, *b.* 1919, *m.*
2007 *West of Spithead,* Adm. Alan William John West, GCB, DSC, *b.* 1948, *m.*
1996 *Whitty,* John Lawrence (Larry) Whitty, *b.* 1943, *m.*
1985 *Williams of Elvel,* Charles Cuthbert Powell Williams, CBE, *b.* 1933, *m.*
1999 *Williamson of Horton,* David (Francis) Williamson, GCMG, CB, PC, *b.* 1934, *m.*
2002 *Wilson of Dinton,* Richard Thomas James Wilson, GCB, *b.* 1942, *m.*
1992 *Wilson of Tillyorn,* David Clive Wilson, KT, GCMG, PHD, *b.* 1935, *m.*
1995 *Winston,* Robert Maurice Lipson Winston, FRCOG, *b.* 1940, *m.*
1985 *Wolfson,* Leonard Gordon Wolfson, *b.* 1927, *m.*
1991 *Wolfson of Sunningdale,* David Wolfson, *b.* 1935, *m.*
1999 *Woolmer of Leeds,* Kenneth John Woolmer, *b.* 1940, *m.*
1994 *Wright of Richmond,* Patrick Richard Henry Wright, GCMG, *b.* 1931, *m.*
2004 *Young of Norwood Green,* Anthony (Ian) Young, *b.* 1942, *m.*
1984 *Young of Graffham,* David Ivor Young, PC, *b.* 1932, *m.*

BARONESSES

Created

2005 *Adams of Craigielea,* Katherine Patricia Irene Adams, *b.* 1947, *w.*
1997 *Amos,* Valerie Ann Amos, *b.* 1954
2000 *Andrews,* Elizabeth Kay Andrews, OBE, *b.* 1943, *m.*
1996 *Anelay of St Johns,* Joyce Anne Anelay, DBE, *b.* 1947, *m.*
1999 *Ashton of Upholland,* Catherine Margaret Ashton, PC, *b.* 1956, *m.*
1999 *Barker,* Elizabeth Jean Barker, *b.* 1961
2000 *Billingham,* Angela Theodora Billingham, DPHIL, *b.* 1939, *w.*
1987 *Blackstone,* Tessa Ann Vosper Blackstone, PHD, *b.* 1942
1999 *Blood,* May Blood, MBE, *b.* 1938
2000 *Boothroyd,* Betty Boothroyd, OM, PC, *b.* 1929
2004 *Bonham-Carter of Yarnbury,* Jane Bonham Carter, *b.* 1957, *w.*
2005 *Bottomley of Nettlestone,* Virginia Hilda Brunette Maxwell Bottomley, PC, *b.* 1948, *m.*
1998 *Buscombe,* Peta Jane Buscombe, *b.* 1954, *m.*
2006 *Butler-Sloss,* (Ann) Elizabeth (Oldfield) Butler-Sloss, GBE, PC *b.* 1933, *m.*
1996 *Byford,* Hazel Byford, DBE, *b.* 1941, *m.*
2007 *Campbell of Surbiton,* Jane Susan Campbell, DBE, PC, *b.* 1959, *m.*
1982 *Carnegy of Lour,* Elizabeth Patricia Carnegy of Lour, *b.* 1925
1992 *Chalker of Wallasey,* Lynda Chalker, PC, *b.* 1942, *m.*
2004 *Chapman,* Nicola Jane Chapman, *b.* 1961
2005 *Clark of Calton,* Dr Lynda Margaret Clark, QC, *b.* 1949
2000 *Cohen of Pimlico,* Janet Cohen, *b.* 1940, *m.*
2005 *Corston,* Jean Ann Corston, PC, *b.* 1942, *m.*
2007 *Coussins,* Jean Coussins, PC, *b.* 1950
1982 *Cox,* Caroline Anne Cox, *b.* 1937, *m.*
1998 *Crawley,* Christine Mary Crawley, *b.* 1950, *m.*

1990 *Cumberlege,* Julia Frances Cumberlege, CBE, *b.* 1943, *m.*
1978 *David,* Nora Ratcliff David, *b.* 1913, *w.*
1993 *Dean of Thornton-le-Fylde,* Brenda Dean, PC, *b.* 1943, *m.*
2005 *Deech,* Ruth Lynn Deech, DBE, *b.* 1943, *m.*
1974 *Delacourt-Smith of Alteryn,* Margaret Rosalind Delacourt-Smith, *b.* 1916, *m.*
2004 *D'Souza,* Dr Frances Gertrude Claire D'Souza, CMG, *b.* 1944 *m.*
1990 *Dunn,* Lydia Selina Dunn, DBE, *b.* 1940, *m.*
1990 *Eccles of Moulton,* Diana Catherine Eccles, *b.* 1933, *m.*
1972 *Elles,* Diana Louie Elles, *b.* 1921, *m.*
1997 *Emerton,* Audrey Caroline Emerton, DBE, *b.* 1935
1974 *Falkender,* Marcia Matilda Falkender, CBE, *b.* 1932
2004 *Falkner of Margravine,* Kishwer Falkner, *b.* 1955, *m.*
1994 *Farrington of Ribbleton,* Josephine Farrington, *b.* 1940, *m.*
2001 *Finlay of Llandaff,* Ilora Gillian Finlay, *b.* 1949, *m.*
1990 *Flather,* Shreela Flather, *m.*
1997 *Fookes,* Janet Evelyn Fookes, DBE, *b.* 1936
2006 *Ford,* Margaret Anne Ford, *b.* 1957, *m.*
2005 *Fritchie,* Irene Tordoff Fritchie, DBE, *b.* 1942, *m.*
1999 *Gale,* Anita Gale, *b.* 1940
1981 *Gardner of Parkes,* (Rachel) Trixie (Anne) Gardner, *b.* 1927, *w.*
2000 *Gibson of Market Rasen,* Anne Gibson, OBE, *b.* 1940, *m.*
2001 *Golding,* Llinos Golding, *b.* 1933, *m.*
1998 *Goudie,* Mary Teresa Goudie, *b.* 1946, *m.*
1993 *Gould of Potternewton,* Joyce Brenda Gould, *b.* 1932, *m.*
2001 *Greenfield,* Susan Adele Greenfield, CBE, *b.* 1950, *m.*
2000 *Greengross,* Sally Ralea Greengross, OBE, *b.* 1935, *m.*
1991 *Hamwee,* Sally Rachel Hamwee, *b.* 1947
1999 *Hanham,* Joan Brownlow Hanham, CBE, *b.* 1939, *m.*
1999 *Harris of Richmond,* Angela Felicity Harris, *b.* 1944
1996 *Hayman,* Helene Valerie Hayman, PC, *b.* 1949, *m.*
2004 *Henig,* Ruth Beatrice Henig, CBE, *b.* 1943, *m.*
1991 *Hilton of Eggardon,* Jennifer Hilton, QPM, *b.* 1936
1995 *Hogg,* Sarah Elizabeth Mary Hogg, *b.* 1946, *m.*
1990 *Hollis of Heigham,* Patricia Lesley Hollis, DPHIL, *b.* 1941, *m.*
1985 *Hooper,* Gloria Dorothy Hooper, CMG, *b.* 1939
2001 *Howarth of Breckland,* Valerie Georgina Howarth, OBE, *b.* 1940
2001 *Howe of Idlicote,* Elspeth Rosamond Morton Howe, CBE, *b.* 1932, *m.*
1999 *Howells of St Davids,* Rosalind Patricia-Anne Howells, *b.* 1931, *m.*
1991 *James of Holland Park,* Phyllis Dorothy White (P. D. James), OBE, *b.* 1920, *w.*
1992 *Jay of Paddington,* Margaret Ann Jay, PC, *b.* 1939, *m.*
2006 *Jones of Whitchurch,* Margaret Beryl Jones, *b.* 1955
1997 *Kennedy of the Shaws,* Helena Ann Kennedy, QC, *b.* 1950, *m.*
2006 *Kingsmill,* Denise Patricia Byrne Kingsmill, CBE, *b.* 1947, *m.*
1997 *Knight of Collingtree,* (Joan Christabel) Jill Knight, DBE, *b.* 1927, *w.*
1997 *Linklater of Butterstone,* Veronica Linklater, *b.* 1943, *m.*
1978 *Lockwood,* Betty Lockwood, *b.* 1924, *w.*
1997 *Ludford,* Sarah Ann Ludford, *b.* 1951
2004 *McDonagh,* Margaret Josephine McDonagh
1979 *McFarlane of Llandaff,* Jean Kennedy McFarlane, *b.* 1926
1999 *McIntosh of Hudnall,* Genista Mary McIntosh, *b.* 1946
1997 *Maddock,* Diana Margaret Maddock, *b.* 1945, *m.*
1991 *Mallalieu,* Ann Mallalieu, QC, *b.* 1945, *m.*
1970 *Masham of Ilton,* Susan Lilian Primrose Cunliffe-Lister, *b.* 1935, *w.*
1999 *Massey of Darwen,* Doreen Elizabeth Massey, *b.* 1938, *m.*
2006 *Meacher,* Molly Christine Meacher, *b.* 1940, *m.*
2001 *Michie of Gallanach,* Janet Ray Michie, *b.* 1934, *m.*
1998 *Miller of Chilthorne Domer,* Susan Elizabeth Miller, *b.* 1954
1993 *Miller of Hendon,* Doreen Miller, MBE, *b.* 1933, *m.*
2004 *Morgan of Drefelin,* Delyth Jane Morgan, *b.* 1961, *m.*
2001 *Morgan of Huyton,* Sally Morgan, *b.* 1959, *m.*
2004 *Morris of Bolton,* Patricia Morris, OBE, *b.* 1953
2005 *Morris of Yardley,* Estelle Morris, PC, *b.* 1952
2004 *Murphy,* Elaine Murphy, *b.* 1947, *m.*
2004 *Neuberger,* Rabbi Julia (Babette Sarah) Neuberger, DBE, *b.* 1950, *m.*
2007 ‡*Neville-Jones,* (Lilian) Pauline Neville-Jones, DCMG, *b.* 1939
1997 *Nicholson of Winterbourne,* Emma Harriet Nicholson, MEP, *b.* 1941, *m.*
1982 *Nicol,* Olive Mary Wendy Nicol, *b.* 1923, *m.*
2000 *Noakes,* Shiela Valerie Masters, DBE, *b.* 1949, *m.*
2000 *Northover,* Lindsay Patricia Granshaw, *b.* 1954
1991 *O'Cathain,* Detta O'Cathain, OBE, *b.* 1938, *m.*
1999 *O'Neill of Bengarve,* Onora Sylvia O'Neill, CBE, PHD, *b.* 1941
1989 *Oppenheim-Barnes,* Sally Oppenheim-Barnes, PC, *b.* 1930, *m.*
2006 *Paisley of St George's,* Eileen Emily Paisley, *m.*
1990 *Park of Monmouth,* Daphne Margaret Sybil Désirée Park, CMG, OBE, *b.* 1921
1991 *Perry of Southwark,* Pauline Perry, *b.* 1931, *m.*
1997 *Pitkeathley,* Jill Elizabeth Pitkeathley, OBE, *b.* 1940
1981 *Platt of Writtle,* Beryl Catherine Platt, CBE, FENG, *b.* 1923, *m.*
1999 *Prashar,* Usha Kumari Prashar, CBE, *b.* 1948, *m.*
2004 *Prosser,* Margaret Theresa Prosser, OBE, *b.* 1937
2006 *Quin,* Joyce Gwendoline Quin, PC *b.* 1944
1996 *Ramsay of Cartvale,* Margaret Mildred (Meta) Ramsay, *b.* 1936
1994 *Rawlings,* Patricia Elizabeth Rawlings, *b.* 1939
1997 *Rendell of Babergh,* Ruth Barbara Rendell, CBE, *b.* 1930, *m.*
1998 *Richardson of Calow,* Kathleen Margaret Richardson, OBE, *b.* 1938, *m.*
2004 *Royall of Blaisdon,* Janet Anne Royall, *b.* 1955, *m.*

1997 *Scotland of Asthal,* Patricia Janet Scotland, QC, *b.* 1955, *m.*
2000 *Scott of Needham Market,* Rosalind Carol Scott, *b.* 1957
1991 *Seccombe,* Joan Anna Dalziel Seccombe, DBE, *b.* 1930, *m.*
1998 *Sharp of Guildford,* Margaret Lucy Sharp, *b.* 1938, *m.*
1973 *Sharples,* Pamela Sharples, *b.* 1923, *m.*
2005 *Shephard of Northwold,* Gillian Patricia Shephard, PC, *b.* 1940, *m.*
1995 *Smith of Gilmorehill,* Elizabeth Margaret Smith, *b.* 1940, *w.*
1999 *Stern,* Vivien Helen Stern, CBE, *b.* 1941
1996 *Symons of Vernham Dean,* Elizabeth Conway Symons, *b.* 1951
2005 *Taylor of Bolton,* Winifred Ann Taylor, PC *b.* 1947, *m.*
1992 *Thatcher,* Margaret Hilda Thatcher, KG, OM, PC, FRS, *b.* 1925, *w.*
1994 *Thomas of Walliswood,* Susan Petronella Thomas, OBE, *b.* 1935, *m.*
2006 *Thomas of Winchester,* Celia Marjorie Thomas, MBE, *b.* 1945
1998 *Thornton,* (Dorothea) Glenys Thornton, *b.* 1952, *m.*
2005 *Tonge,* Dr. Jennifer Louise Tonge, *b.* 1941, *m.*
1980 *Trumpington,* Jean Alys Barker, DCVO, PC, *b.* 1922, *w.*
1985 *Turner of Camden,* Muriel Winifred Turner, *b.* 1927, *m.*
1998 *Uddin,* Manzila Pola Uddin, *b.* 1959, *m.*
2007 *Vadera,* Shriti Vadera
2005 *Valentine,* Josephine Clare Valentine
2006 *Verma,* Sandip Verma, *b.* 1959, *m.*
2004 *Wall of New Barnet,* Margaret Mary Wall, *b.* 1941, *m.*
2000 *Walmsley,* Joan Margaret Walmsley, *b.* 1943
1985 *Warnock,* Helen Mary Warnock, DBE, *b.* 1924, *w.*
2007 ‡*Warsi,* Syeeda Warsi, *b.* 1971, *m.*
1999 *Warwick of Undercliffe,* Diana Mary Warwick, *b.* 1945, *m.*
1999 *Whitaker,* Janet Alison Whitaker, *b.* 1936
1996 *Wilcox,* Judith Ann Wilcox, *b.* 1940, *w.*
1999 *Wilkins,* Rosalie Catherine Wilkins, *b.* 1946
1993 *Williams of Crosby,* Shirley Vivien Teresa Brittain Williams, PC, *b.* 1930, *w.*
2004 *Young of Hornsey,* Prof. Margaret Omolola Young, OBE, *b.* 1951, *m.*
1997 *Young of Old Scone,* Barbara Scott Young, *b.* 1948

LORDS SPIRITUAL

The Lords Spiritual are the Archbishops of Canterbury and York and 24 diocesan bishops of the Church of England. The Bishops of London, Durham and Winchester always have seats in the House of Lords; the other 21 seats are filled by the remaining diocesan bishops in order of seniority. The Bishop of Sodor and Man and the Bishop of Gibraltar are not eligible to sit in the House of Lords.

ARCHBISHOPS

Style, The Most Revd and Right Hon. the Lord Archbishop of_
Addressed as Archbishop *or* Your Grace

INTRODUCED TO HOUSE OF LORDS

2003 *Canterbury* (104th), Rowan Douglas Williams, PC, DPHIL, *b.* 1950, *m., cons.* 1992, *elected* 2002
2005 *York* (97th), John Mugabi Tucker Sentamu, PC, PHD, *b.* 1949, *m., cons.* 1996, *elected* 2005, *trans.* 2005

BISHOPS

Style, The Right Revd the Lord Bishop of _
Addressed as My Lord
elected date of confirmation as diocesan bishop

INTRODUCED TO HOUSE OF LORDS
(as at 31 August 2007)

1996 *London* (132nd), Richard John Carew Chartres, *b.* 1947, *m., cons.* 1992, *elected* 1995
2003 *Durham* (71st), Nicholas Thomas Wright, DPHIL, *b.* 1948, *m., cons.* 2003, *elected* 2003
1996 *Winchester* (96th), Michael Charles Scott-Joynt, *b.* 1943, *m., cons.* 1987, *elected* 1995
1997 *Southwark* (9th), Thomas Frederick Butler, *b.* 1940, *m., cons.* 1985, *elected* 1991, *trans.* 1998
1997 *Manchester* (11th), Nigel Simeon McCulloch, *b.* 1942, *m., cons.* 1986, *elected* 1992, *trans.* 2002
1998 *Salisbury* (77th), David Staffurth Stancliffe, *b.* 1942, *m., cons.* 1993, *elected* 1993
1999 *Rochester* (106th), Michael James Nazir-Ali, PHD, *b.* 1949, *m., cons.* 1984, *elected* 1994
1999 *Chelmsford* (9th), John Warren Gladwin, *b.* 1942, *m., cons.* 1994, *elected* 1994, *trans.* 2003
1999 *Portsmouth* (8th), Kenneth William Stevenson, *b.* 1949, *m., cons.* 1995, *elected* 1995
1999 *St Albans* (9th), Christopher William Herbert, *b.* 1944, *m., cons.* 1995, *elected* 1995
2001 *Peterborough* (37th), Ian Patrick Martyn Cundy, *b.* 1945, *m., cons.* 1992, *elected* 1996
2001 *Chester* (40th), Peter Robert Forster, PHD, *b.* 1950, *cons.* 1996, *elected* 1996
2002 *Truro* (14th), William Ind, *b.* 1942, *m., cons.* 1987, *elected* 1997
2003 *Newcastle* (11th), (John) Martin Wharton, *b.* 1944, *m., cons.* 1992, *elected* 1997
2003 *Sheffield* (6th), John Nicholls, *b.* 1943, *m., cons.* 1990, *elected* 1997
2003 *Coventry* (8th), Colin James Bennetts, *b.* 1940, *m., cons.* 1994, *elected* 1998
2003 *Liverpool* (7th), James Stuart Jones, *b.* 1948, *m., cons.* 1994, *elected* 1998
2003 *Leicester* (6th), Timothy John Stevens, *b.* 1946, *m., cons.* 1995, *elected* 1999
2004 *Southwell and Nottingham* (10th), George Henry Cassidy, *b.* 1942, *m., cons.* 1999, *elected* 1999
2004 *Norwich* (71st), Graham Richard James, *b.* 1951, *m., cons.* 1993, *elected* 1999
2005 *Exeter* (70th), Michael Lawrence Langrish, *b.* 1946, *m., cons.* 1993, *elected* 2000
2006 *Ripon and Leeds* (12th), John Richard Packer, *b.* 1946, *m., cons.* 1996, *elected* 2000
2007 *Ely* (68th), Dr Anthony John Russell, *b.* 1943, *m., cons.* 1988, *elected* 2000
2007 *Carlisle* (65th), (Geoffrey) Graham Dow, *b.* 1942, *m., cons.* 1985, *elected* 2000

BISHOPS AWAITING SEATS, in order of seniority
(as at 31 August 2007)

Chichester (102nd), John William Hind, *b.* 1945, *m., cons.* 1991, *elected* 2001
Lincoln (71st), Dr John Charles Saxbee, *b.* 1946, *m., cons.* 1994, *elected* 2001
Bath and Wells (77th), Peter Bryan Price, *b.* 1944, *m., cons.* 1997, *elected* 2002
Bradford (9th), David Charles James, *b.* 1945, *m., cons.* 1998, *elected* 2002
Wakefield (12th), Stephen George Platten, *b.* 1947, *m., cons.* 2003, *elected* 2003
Bristol (55th), Michael Arthur Hill, *b.* 1947, *m., cons.* 1998, *elected* 2003
Lichfield (98th), Jonathan Michael Gledhill, *b.* 1949, *m., cons.* 1996, *elected* 2003
Blackburn (8th), Nicholas Stewart Reade, *b.* 1946, *m., cons.* 2004, *elected* 2004
Hereford (104th), Anthony Martin Priddis, *b.* 1948, *m., cons.* 1996, *elected* 2004
Gloucester (40th), Michael Francis Perham, *b.* 1947, *m., cons.* 2004, *elected* 2004
Guildford (9th), Christopher John Hill, *b.* 1945, *m., cons.* 1996, *elected* 2004
Derby (7th), Alastair Llewellyn John Redfern, *b.* 1948, *m., cons.* 1997, *elected* 2005
Birmingham (9th), David Andrew Urquhart, *b.* 1952, *cons.* 2000, *elected* 2006
Oxford (42nd), John Lawrence Pritchard, *b.* 1948, *m., cons.* 2002 *elected* 2007
St Edmundsbury and Ipswich (10th), (William) Nigel Stock, *b.* 1950, *m., cons.* 2000, *elected* 2007
Worcester (113th), John Geoffrey Inge, PHD, *b.* 1955, *m., cons.* 2003, *elected* 2007

COURTESY TITLES AND PEERS' SURNAMES

COURTESY TITLES

The heir apparent to a Duke, Marquess or Earl uses the highest of his father's other titles as a courtesy title. For example, the Marquess of Blandford is heir to the Dukedom of Marlborough, and Viscount Amberley to the Earldom of Russell. Titles of second heirs (when in use) are also given, and the courtesy title of the father of a second heir is indicated by * eg Earl of Mornington, eldest son of *Marquess of Douro.

The holder of a courtesy title is not styled 'the Most Hon.' or 'the Right Hon.', and in correspondence 'the' is omitted before the title. The heir apparent to a Scottish title may use the title 'Master'.

MARQUESSES

*Blandford – *Marlborough, D.*
Bowmont and Cessford – *Roxburghe, D.*
Douglas and Clydesdale – *Hamilton, D.*
*Douro – *Wellington, D.*
Graham – *Montrose, D.*
Hamilton – *Abercorn, D.*
Hartington – *Devonshire, D.*
Lorne – *Argyll, D.*
Stafford – *Sutherland, D.*
Tullibardine – *Atholl, D.*
*Worcester – *Beaufort, D.*

EARLS

Aboyne – *Huntly, M.*
Arundel and Surrey – *Norfolk, D.*
Bective – *Headfort, M.*
Belfast – *Donegall, M.*
Brecknock – *Camden, M.*
Burford – *St Albans, D.*
*Cardigan – *Ailesbury, M.*
Compton – *Northampton, M.*
*Dalkeith – *Buccleuch, D.*
*Euston – *Grafton, D.*
Glamorgan – **Worcester, M.*
Grosvenor – *Westminster, D.*
Haddo – *Aberdeen and Temair, M.*
Hillsborough – *Downshire, M.*
Hopetoun – *Linlithgow, M.*
Kerry – *Lansdowne, M.*
March and Kinrara – *Richmond, D.*
Medina – *Milford Haven, M.*
*Mount Charles – *Conyngham, M.*
Mornington – **Douro, M.*
Mulgrave – *Normanby, M.*
Percy – *Northumberland, D.*
Ronaldshay – *Zetland, M.*
*St Andrews – *Kent, D.*
*Southesk – *Fife, D.*
Sunderland – **Blandford, M.*
*Tyrone – *Waterford, M.*
Ulster – *Gloucester, D.*
*Uxbridge – *Anglesey, M.*
Wiltshire – *Winchester, M.*
Yarmouth – *Hertford, M.*

VISCOUNTS

Alexander – *Caledon, E.*
Althorp – *Spencer, E.*
Andover – *Suffolk and Berkshire, E.*
Asquith – *Oxford and Asquith, E.*
Boringdon – *Morley, E.*
Borodale – *Beatty, E.*
Boyle – *Shannon, E.*
Brocas – *Jellicoe, E.*
Bury – *Albermarle, E.*
Campden – *Gainsborough, E.*
Carlow – *Portarlington, E.*
Carlton – *Wharncliffe, E.*
Castlereagh – *Londonderry, M.*
Chelsea – *Cadogan, E.*
Chewton – *Waldegrave, E.*
Clanfield – *Peel, E.*
Clive – *Powis, E.*
Coke – *Leicester, E.*
Corry – *Belmore, E.*
Corvedale – *Baldwin of Bewdley, E.*
Cranborne – *Salisbury, M.*
Cranley – *Onslow, E.*
Crichton – *Erne, E.*
Curzon – *Howe, E.*
Dangan – *Cowley, E.*
Dawick – *Haig, E.*
Drumlanrig – *Queensberry, M.*
Duncannon – *Bessborough, E.*
Dungarvan – *Cork and Orrery, E.*
Dunluce – *Antrim, E.*
Dunwich – *Stradbroke, E.*
Dupplin – *Kinnoull, E.*
Ednam – *Dudley, E.*
Elveden – *Iveagh, E.*
Emlyn – *Cawdor, E*
Encombe – *Eldon, E.*
Enfield – *Strafford, E.*
Erleigh – *Reading, M.*
Errington – *Cromer, E.*
FitzHarris – *Malmesbury, E.*
Folkestone – *Radnor, E.*
Forbes – *Granard, E.*
Garmoyle – *Cairns, E.*
Garnock – *Lindsay, E.*
Glenapp – *Inchcape, E.*
Glentworth – *Limerick, E.*
Grey de Wilton – *Wilton, E.*
Grimstone – *Verulam, E.*
Gwynedd – *Lloyd George of Dwyfor, E.*
Hawkesbury – *Liverpool, E.*
Hinchingbrooke – *Sandwich, E.*
Ikerrin – *Carrick, E.*
Ingestre – *Shrewsbury, E.*
Ipswich – **Euston, E.*
Jocelyn – *Roden, E.*
Kelburn – *Glasgow, E.*
Kingsborough – *Kingston, E.*
Kirkwall – *Orkney, E.*
Knebworth – *Lytton, E.*
Lambton – *Durham, E.*
Lascelles – *Harewood, E.*
Linley – *Snowdon, E.*
Lymington – *Portsmouth, E.*
Macmillan of Ovenden – *Stockton, E.*
Maidstone – *Winchilsea, E*
Maitland – *Lauderdale, E.*
Mandeville – *Manchester, D.*
Marsham – *Romney, E.*
Melgund – *Minto, E.*
Merton – *Nelson, E.*
Moore – *Drogheda, E.*
Newport – *Bradford, E.*
Northland – *Ranfurly, E*
Newry and Mourne – *Kilmorey, E.*
Petersham – *Harrington, E.*
Pollington – *Mexborough, E*
Raynham – *Townshend, M.*
Reidhaven – *Seafield, E.*
Ruthven of Canberra – *Gowrie, E.*
St Cyres – *Iddesleigh, E.*
Sandon – *Harrowby, E.*
Savernake – **Cardigan, E.*
Slane – **Mount Charles, E.*
Somerton – *Normanton, E.*
Stopford – *Courtown, E.*
Stormont – *Mansfield, E.*
Strathallan – *Perth, E.*
Stuart – *Castle Stewart, E.*
Suirdale – *Donoughmore, E.*
Tamworth – *Ferrers, E.*
Tarbat – *Cromartie, E.*
Vaughan – *Lisburne, E.*
Weymouth – *Bath, M.*
Windsor – *Plymouth, E.*
Wolmer – *Selborne, E.*
Woodstock – *Portland, E.*

BARONS (LORDS)

Aberdour – *Morton, E.*
Apsley – *Bathurst, E.*
Ardee – *Meath, E.*
Balgonie – *Leven and Melville, E.*
Balniel – *Crawford and Balcarres, E.*
Berriedale – *Caithness, E.*
Bingham – *Lucan, E.*
Binning – *Haddington, E.*
Brooke – *Warwick, E.*
Bruce – *Elgin, E.*
Burghley – *Exeter, M.*
Cardross – *Buchan, E.*
Carnegie – **Southesk, E.*
Clifton – *Darnley, E.*
Cochrane – *Dundonald, E.*
Courtenay – *Devon, E.*
Dalmeny – *Rosebery, E.*
Doune – *Moray, E.*
Downpatrick – **St Andrews, E.*
Dunglass – *Home, E.*
Eliot – *St Germans, E.*
Eskdail – **Dalkeith, E.*
Formartine – **Haddo, E.*
Gillford – *Clanwilliam, E.*
Glamis – *Strathmore, E.*
Greenock – *Cathcart, E.*
Guernsey – *Aylesford, E.*
Hay – *Erroll, E.*
Howard of Effingham – *Effingham, E.*
Huntingtower – *Dysart, C.*
Hyde – *Clarendon, E.*
Irwin – *Halifax, E.*

Johnstone – *Annandale and Hartfell, E.*
Langton – *Temple of Stowe, E.*
La Poer – **Tyrone, E.*
Leveson – *Granville, E*
Loughborough – *Rosslyn, E.*
Masham – *Swinton, E.*
Mauchline – *Loudoun, C.*
Medway – *Cranbrook, E.*
Montgomerie – *Eglinton and Winton, E.*
Moreton – *Ducie, E.*
Mount Stuart – *Bute, M*
Naas – *Mayo, E.*
Neidpath – *Wemyss and March, E.*
Norreys – *Lindsey and Abingdon, E.*
North – *Guilford, E.*
Ogilvy – *Airlie, E.*
Oxmantown – *Rosse, E.*
Paget de Beaudesert – **Uxbridge, E.*
Porchester – *Carnarvon, E.*
Ramsay – *Dalhousie, E.*
Romsey – *Mountbatten of Burma, C.*
Scrymgeour – *Dundee, E.*
Seymour – *Somerset, D.*
Stanley – *Derby, E.*
Stavordale – *Ilchester, E.*
Strathnaver – *Sutherland, C.*
Wodehouse – *Kimberley, E.*
Worsley – *Yarborough, E.*

PEERS' SURNAMES

The following symbols indicate the rank of the peer holding each title:

C. Countess
D. Duke
E. Earl
M. Marquess
V. Viscount
* Life Peer

Where no designation is given, the title is that of a hereditary Baron or Baroness.

Abney-Hastings – *Loudoun, C.*
Acheson – *Gosford, E.*
Adams – *A. of Craigielea**
Adderley – *Norton*
Addington – *Sidmouth, V.*
Adebowale – *A. of Thornes**
Agar – *Normanton, E.*
Aitken – *Beaverbrook*
Akers-Douglas – *Chilston, V.*
Alexander – *A. of Tunis, E.*
Alexander – *Caledon, E.*
Allen – *A. of Abbeydale**
Allen – *Croham**
Allsopp – *Hindlip*
Alton – *A. of Liverpool**
Anderson – *A. of Swansea**
Anderson – *Waverley, V.*
Anelay – *A. of St Johns**
Annesley – *Valentia, V.*
Anson – *Lichfield, E.*
Archer – *A. of Sandwell**
Archer – *A. of Weston-super-Mare**
Armstrong – *A. of Ilminster**
Armstrong-Jones – *Snowdon, E.*
Arthur – *Glenarthur*
Arundell – *Talbot of Malahide*
Ashdown – *A. of Norton-sub-Hamdon**
Ashley – *A. of Stoke**
Ashley-Cooper – *Shaftesbury, E.*
Ashton – *A. of Hyde*
Ashton – *A. of Upholland**
Asquith – *Oxford and Asquith, E.*
Assheton – *Clitheroe*
Astley – *Hastings*
Astor – *A. of Hever*
Aubrey-Fletcher – *Braye*
Bailey – *Glanusk*
Baillie – *Burton*
Baillie Hamilton – *Haddington, E.*
Baker – *B. of Dorking**
Baldwin – *B. of Bewdley, E.*
Balfour – *B. of Inchrye*
Balfour – *Kinross*
Balfour – *Riverdale*
Bampfylde – *Poltimore*
Banbury – *B. of Southam*
Barber – *B. of Tewkesbury**
Baring – *Ashburton*
Baring – *Cromer, E.*
Baring – *Howick of Glendale*
Baring – *Northbrook*
Baring – *Revelstoke*
Barker – *Trumpington**
Barnes – *Gorell*
Barnewall – *Trimlestown*
Bassam – *B. of Brighton**
Bathurst – *Bledisloe, V.*
Beauclerk – *St Albans, D.*
Beaumont – *Allendale, V.*
Beaumont – *B. of Whitley**
Beckett – *Grimthorpe*
Benn – *Stansgate, V.*
Bennet – *Tankerville, E.*
Bentinck – *Portland, E.*
Beresford – *Decies*
Beresford – *Waterford, M.*
Bernstein – *B. of Craigweil**
Berry – *Camrose, V.*
Berry – *Kemsley, V.*
Bertie – *Lindsey, E.*
Best – *Wynford*
Bethell – *Westbury*
Bewicke-Copley – *Cromwell*
Bigham – *Mersey, V.*
Bingham – *B. of Cornhill**
Bingham – *Clanmorris*
Bingham – *Lucan, E.*
Black – *B. of Crossharbour**
Bligh – *Darnley, E.*
Blyth – *B. of Rowington**
Bonham Carter – *B.-C. of Yarnbury**
Bootle-Wilbraham – *Skelmersdale*
Boscawen – *Falmouth, V.*
Boston – *B. of Faversham**
Bottomley – *B. of Nettlestone**
Bourke – *Mayo, E.*
Bowes Lyon – *Strathmore, E.*
Bowyer – *Denham*
Boyd – *Kilmarnock*
Boyd – *B. of Duncansby**
Boyle – *Cork and Orrery, E.*
Boyle – *Glasgow, E.*
Boyle – *Shannon, E.*
Brabazon – *Meath, E.*
Brand – *Hampden, V.*
Brassey – *B. of Apethorpe*
Brett – *Esher, V.*
Bridge – *B. of Harwich**
Bridgeman – *Bradford, E.*
Brittan – *B. of Spennithorne**
Brodrick – *Midleton, V.*
Brooke – *Alanbrooke, V.*
Brooke – *B. of Alverthorpe**
Brooke – *Brookeborough, V.*
Brooke – *B. of Sutton Mandeville**
Brooks – *B. of Tremorfa**
Brooks – *Crawshaw*
Brougham – *Brougham and Vaux*
Broughton – *Fairhaven*
Brown – *B. of Eaton-under-Heywood**
Browne – *B. of Belmont**
Browne – *B. of Madingley**
Browne – *Kilmaine*
Browne – *Oranmore and Browne*
Browne – *Sligo, M.*
Bruce – *Aberdare*
Bruce – *Balfour of Burleigh*
Bruce – *Elgin and Kincardine, E.*
Brudenell-Bruce – *Ailesbury, M.*
Buchan – *Tweedsmuir*
Buckley – *Wrenbury*
Butler – *B. of Brockwell**
Butler – *Carrick, E.*
Butler – *Dunboyne*
Butler – *Mountgarret, V.*
Buxton – *B. of Alsa**
Byng – *Strafford, E.*
Byng – *Torrington, V.*
Cambell-Savours – *C.-S. of Allerdale**
Cameron – *C. of Dillington**
Cameron – *C. of Lochbroom**
Campbell – *Argyll, D.*
Campbell – *C. of Alloway**
Campbell – *C. of Surbiton**
Campbell – *Cawdor, E.*
Campbell – *Colgrain*
Campbell – *Stratheden and Campbell*
Campbell-Gray – *Gray*
Canning – *Garvagh*
Capell – *Essex, E.*
Carey – *C. of Clifton**
Carington – *Carrington*
Carlisle – *C. of Berriew**
Carnegie – *Fife, D.*
Carnegie – *Northesk, E.*
Carr – *C. of Hadley**
Carter – *C. of Coles**
Cary – *Falkland, V.*
Caulfeild – *Charlemont, V.*
Cavendish – *C. of Furness**
Cavendish – *Chesham*
Cavendish – *Devonshire, D.*
Cavendish – *Waterpark*
Cayzer – *Rotherwick*
Cecil – *Amherst of Hackney*
Cecil – *Exeter, M.*
Cecil – *Rockley*
Chalker – *C. of Wallasey**
Chaloner – *Gisborough*
Chapman – *C. of Leeds**
Chapman – *Northfield**
Charteris – *Wemyss and March, E.*
Chetwynd-Talbot – *Shrewsbury, E.*
Chichester – *Donegall, M.*

Child Villiers – *Jersey, E.*
Cholmondeley – *Delamere*
Chubb – *Hayter*
Clark – *C. of Calton**
Clarke – *C. of Hampstead**
Clegg-Hill – *Hill, V.*
Clifford – *C. of Chudleigh*
Cochrane – *C. of Cults*
Cochrane – *Dundonald, E.*
Cocks – *Somers*
Cohen – *C. of Pimlico**
Cokayne – *Cullen of Ashbourne*
Coke – *Leicester, E.*
Cole – *Enniskillen, E.*
Collier – *Monkswell*
Colville – *Clydesmuir*
Colville – *C. of Culross, V.*
Compton – *Northampton, M.*
Conolly-Carew – *Carew*
Cooke – *C. of Islandreagh**
Cooper – *Norwich, V*
Cope – *C. of Berkeley**
Corbett – *C. of Castle Vale**.
Corbett – *Rowallan*
Cornwall-Leigh – *Grey of Condor*
Courtenay – *Devon, E.*
Craig – *C. of Radley**
Craig – *Craigavon, V.*
Crichton – *Erne, E.*
Crichton-Stuart – *Bute, M.*
Cripps – *Parmoor*
Crossley – *Somerleyton*
Cubitt – *Ashcombe*
Cunliffe-Lister – *Masham of Ilton**
Cunliffe-Lister – *Swinton, E.*
Cunningham – *C. of Felling**
Currie – *C. of Marylebone**
Curzon – *Howe, E.*
Curzon – *Scarsdale, V.*
Cust – *Brownlow*
Czernin – *Howard de Walden*
Dalrymple – *Stair, E.*
Darzi – *D. of Denham**
Daubeny de Moleyns – *Ventry*
Davidson – *D. of Glen Clova**
Davies – *D. of Coity**
Davies – *Darwen*
Davies – *D. of Oldham**
Dawnay – *Downe, V.*
Dawson-Damer – *Portarlington, E.*
Dean – *D. of Harptree**
Dean – *D. of Thornton-le-Fylde**
Deane – *Muskerry*
de Courcy – *Kingsale*
de Grey – *Walsingham*
Delacourt-Smith – *Delacourt Smith of Alteryn**
Denison – *Londesborough*
Denison-Pender – *Pender*
Devereux – *Hereford, V.*
Dewar – *Forteviot*
Dixon – *Glentoran*
Dodson – *Monk Bretton*
Douglas – *Morton, E.*
Douglas – *Queensberry, M.*
Douglas-Hamilton – *Hamilton, D.*
Douglas-Hamilton – *Selkirk, E.*
Douglas-Hamilton – *Selkirk of Douglas**
Douglas-Home – *Dacre*
Douglas-Home – *Home, E.*
Douglas-Pennant – *Penrhyn*
Douglas-Scott-Montagu – *Montagu of Beaulieu*
Drummond – *Perth, E.*
Drummond of Megginch – *Strange*
Dugdale – *Crathorne*
Duke – *Merrivale*
Duncombe – *Feversham*
Dundas – *Melville, V.*
Dundas – *Zetland, M.*
Eady – *Swinfen*
Eccles – *E. of Moulton**
Eden – *Auckland*
Eden – *E. of Winton**
Eden – *Henley*
Edgcumbe – *Mount Edgcumbe, E.*
Edmondson – *Sandford*
Edwardes – *Kensington*
Edwards – *Crickhowell**
Egerton – *Sutherland, D.*
Eliot – *St Germans, E.*
Elliott – *E. of Morpeth**
Elliot-Murray-Kynynmound – *Minto, E.*
Ellis – *Seaford*
Erskine – *Buchan, E.*
Erskine – *Mar and Kellie, E.*
Erskine-Murray – *Elibank*
Evans – *E. of Parkside**
Evans – *E. of Temple Guiting**
Evans – *E. of Watford**
Evans – *Mountevans*
Evans-Freke – *Carbery*
Eve – *Silsoe*
Fairfax – *F. of Cameron*
Falconer – *F. of Thoroton**
Falkner – *F. of Margravine**
Fane – *Westmorland, E.*
Farrington – *F. of Ribbleton**
Faulkner – *F. of Worcester**
Fearn – *F. of Southport**
Feilding – *Denbigh, E.*
Felton – *Seaford*
Fellowes – *De Ramsey*
Fermor-Hesketh – *Hesketh*
Fiennes – *Saye and Sele*
Fiennes-Clinton – *Lincoln, E.*
Finch Hatton – *Winchilsea, E.*
Finch-Knightley – *Aylesford, E.*
Finlay – *F. of Llandaff**
Fitzalan-Howard – *Herries of Terregles*
Fitzalan-Howard – *Norfolk, D.*
FitzGerald – *Leinster, D.*
Fitzherbert – *Stafford*
FitzRoy – *Grafton, D.*
FitzRoy – *Southampton*
FitzRoy Newdegate – *Daventry, V.*
Fletcher-Vane – *Inglewood*
Flower – *Ashbrook, V.*
Foljambe – *Liverpool, E.*
Forbes – *Granard, E*
Forsyth – *F. of Drumlean**
Forwood – *Arlington*
Foster – *F. of Thames Bank**
Foulkes – *F. of Cumnock**
Fowler – *F. of Sutton Caulfield**
Fox-Strangways – *Ilchester, E.*
Frankland – *Zouche*
Fraser – *F. of Carmyllie**
Fraser – *F. of Kilmorack**
Fraser – *Lovat*
Fraser – *Saltoun*
Fraser – *Strathalmond*
Freeman-Grenville – *Kinloss*
Fremantle – *Cottesloe*
French – *De Freyne*
Fyfe – *F. of Fairfield**
Galbraith – *Strathclyde*
Gardner – *G. of Parkes**
Gascoyne-Cecil – *M. of Salisbury**
Gathorne-Hardy – *Cranbrook, E.*
Gibbs – *Aldenham*
Gibbs – *Wraxall*
Gibson – *Ashbourne*
Gibson – *G. of Market Rasen**
Giffard – *Halsbury, E.*
Gilbey – *Vaux of Harrowden*
Gilmour – *G. of Craigmillar**
Glyn – *Wolverton*
Godley – *Kilbracken*
Goff – *G. of Chieveley**
Golding – *G. of Newcastle-under-Lyme**
Gordon – *Aberdeen, M.*
Gordon – *G. of Strathblane**
Gordon – *Huntly, M.*
Gordon Lennox – *Richmond, D.*
Gore – *Arran, E.*
Gould – *G. of Brookwood**
Gould – *G. of Potternewton**
Graham – *G. of Edmonton**
Graham – *Montrose, D.*
Graham-Toler – *Norbury, E.*
Granshaw – *Northover**
Grant of Grant – *Strathspey*
Grant of Rothiemurchus – *Dysart, C.*
Granville – *G. of Eye**
Greenall – *Daresbury*
Greville – *Warwick, E.*
Griffiths – *G. of Burry Port**
Griffiths – *G. of Fforestfach**
Grigg – *Altrincham*
Grimston – *G. of Westbury*
Grimston – *Verulam, E.*
Grosvenor – *Westminster, D.*
Grosvenor – *Wilton and Ebury, E*
Guest – *Wimborne, V*
Gueterbock – *Berkeley*
Guinness – *Iveagh, E.*
Guinness – *Moyne*
Gully – *Selby, V.*
Gummer – *Chadlington**
Gurdon – *Cranworth*
Guthrie – *G. of Craigiebank**
Gwynne Jones – *Chalfont**
Hale – *H. of Richmond**
Hamilton – *Abercorn, D.*
Hamilton – *Belhaven and Stenton*
Hamilton – *H. of Dalzell*
Hamilton – *H. of Epsom**
Hamilton – *Holm Patrick*
Hamilton-Russell – *Boyne, V.*
Hamilton-Smith – *Colwyn*
Hanbury-Tracy – *Sudeley*
Handcock – *Castlemaine*
Hannay – *H. of Chiswick**
Harbord-Hamond – *Suffield*
Harding – *H. of Petherton*
Hardinge – *H. of Penshurst*
Hare – *Blakenham, V.*
Hare – *Listowel, E.*
Harmsworth – *Rothermere, V.*
Harries – *H. of Pentregarth**
Harris – *H. of Haringey**
Harris – *H. of Peckham**
Harris – *H. of Richmond**

Harris – _Malmesbury, E._
Hart – _H. of Chilton_*
Harvey – _H. of Tasburgh_
Hastings – _H. of Scarisbrick_*
Hastings Bass – _Huntingdon, E._
Haughey – _Ballyedmond_*
Hay – _Erroll, E._
Hay – _Kinnoull, E._
Hay – _Tweeddale, M._
Heathcote-Drummond-Willoughby – _Willoughby de Eresby_
Hely-Hutchinson – _Donoughmore, E._
Henderson – _Faringdon_
Hennessy – _Windlesham_
Henniker-Major – _Henniker_
Hepburne-Scott – _Polwarth_
Herbert – _Carnarvon, E._
Herbert – _Hemingford_
Herbert – _Pembroke, E._
Herbert – _Powis, E._
Hervey – _Bristol, M._
Heseltine – _H. of Thenford_*
Hewitt – _Lifford, V._
Hicks Beach – _St Aldwyn, E._
Hill – _Downshire, M._
Hill – _Sandys_
Hill-Trevor – _Trevor_
Hilton – _H. of Eggardon_*
Hobart-Hampden – _Buckinghamshire, E._
Hodgson – _H. of Astley Abbotts_*
Hogg – _Hailsham, V._
Hogg – _H. of Cumbernauld_*
Holland-Hibbert – _Knutsford, V._
Hollis – _H. of Heigham_*
Holme – _H. of Cheltenham_*
Holmes à Court – _Heytesbury_
Hood – _Bridport, V._
Hope – _Glendevon_
Hope – _H. of Craighead_*
Hope – _H. of Thornes_*
Hope – _Linlithgow, M._
Hope – _Rankeillour_
Hope Johnstone – _Annandale and Hartfell, E._
Hope-Morley – _Hollenden_
Hopkinson – _Colyton_
Hore Ruthven – _Gowrie, E._
Hovell-Thurlow-Cumming-Bruce – _Thurlow_
Howard – _Carlisle, E._
Howard – _Effingham, E._
Howard – _H. of Penrith_
Howard – _H. of Rising_*
Howard – _Strathcona_
Howard – _Suffolk and Berkshire, E._
Howarth – _H. of Breckland_*
Howarth – _H. of Newport_*
Howe – _H. of Aberavon_*
Howe – _H. of Idlicote_*
Howell – _H. of Guildford_*
Howells – _H. of St. Davids_*
Howie – _H. of Troon_*
Hubbard – _Addington_
Huggins – _Malvern, V._
Hughes – _H. of Woodside_*
Hughes-Young – _St Helens_
Hunt – _H. of Chesterton_*
Hunt – _H. of Kings Heath_*
Hunt – _H. of Tanworth_*
Hunt – _H. of Wirral_*
Hurd – _H. of Westwell_*
Hutchinson – _H. of Lullington_*
Ingrams – _Darcy de Knayth_
Innes-Ker – _Roxburghe, D._
Inskip – _Caldecote, V._
Irby – _Boston_
Irvine – _I. of Lairg_*
Isaacs – _Reading, M._
James – _J. of Blackheath_*
James – _J. of Holland Park_*
James – _Northbourne_
Janner – _J. of Braunstone_*
Jay – _J. of Ewelme_*
Jay – _J. of Paddington_*
Jebb – _Gladwyn_
Jenkin – _J. of Roding_*
Jervis – _St Vincent, V._
Jocelyn – _Roden, E._
Jolliffe – _Hylton_
Jones – _J. of Birmingham_*
Jones – _J. of Cheltenham_*
Jones – _J. of Deeside_*
Jones – _J. of Whitchurch_*
Joynson-Hicks – _Brentford, V._
Kay-Shuttleworth – _Shuttleworth_
Kearley – _Devonport, V._
Keith – _Kintore, E._
Kemp – _Rochdale, V._
Kennedy – _Ailsa, M_
Kennedy – _K. of the Shaws_*
Kenworthy – _Strabolgi_
Keppel – _Albemarle, E._
Kerr – _K. of Kinlochard_*
Kerr – _Lothian, M._
Kerr – _Teviot_
Kilpatrick – _K. of Kincraig_*
King – _Lovelace, E._
King – _K. of West Bromwich_*
King-Tenison – _Kingston, E._
Kirkham – _Berners_
Kirkwood – _K. of Kirkhope_*
Kitchener – _K. of Khartoum, E._
Knatchbull – _Brabourne_
Knatchbull – _Mountbatten of Burma, C._
Knight – _K. of Collingtree_*
Knox – _Ranfurly, E._
Laing – _L. of Dunphail_*
Lamb – _Rochester_
Lambton – _Durham, E._
Lamont – _L. of Lerwick_*
Lampson – _Killearn_
Lane – _L. of Horsell_*
Lang – _L. of Monkton_*
Lascelles – _Harewood, E._
Law – _Coleraine_
Law – _Ellenborough_
Lawrence – _Trevethin and Oaksey_
Lawson – _Burnham_
Lawson – _L. of Blaby_*
Lawson-Johnston – _Luke_
Lea – _L. of Crondall_*
Leach – _L. of Fairford_*
Lee – _L. of Trafford_*
Legge – _Dartmouth, E._
Legh – _Grey of Codnor_
Legh – _Newton_
Leigh-Pemberton – _Kingsdown_*
Leith – _Burgh_
Lennox-Boyd – _Boyd of Merton, V._
Le Poer Trench – _Clancarty, E._
Leslie – _Rothes, E._
Leslie Melville – _Leven and Melville, E._
Lester – _L. of Herne Hill_*
Levene – _L. of Portsoken_*
Leveson-Gower – _Granville, E._
Lewis – _L. of Newnham_*
Lewis – _Merthyr_
Liddell – _Ravensworth_
Lindesay-Bethune – _Lindsay, E._
Lindsay – _Crawford, E._
Lindsay – _L. of Birker_
Linklater – _L. of Butterstone_*
Littleton – _Hatherton_
Lloyd – _L. of Berwick_*
Lloyd George – _Lloyd George of Dwyfor, E._
Lloyd George – _Tenby, V._
Lloyd-Mostyn – _Mostyn_
Loder – _Wakehurst_
Lofthouse – _L. of Pontefract_*
Lopes – _Roborough_
Lour – _Carnegy of Lour_*
Low – _Aldington_
Low – _L. of Dalston_*
Lowry-Corry – _Belmore, E._
Lowther – _Lonsdale, E._
Lowther – _Ullswater, V._
Lubbock – _Avebury_
Lucas – _L. of Chilworth_
Lumley – _Scarbrough, E._
Lumley-Savile – _Savile_
Lyell – _L. of Markyate_*
Lyon-Dalberg-Acton – _Acton_
Lysaght – _Lisle_
Lyttelton – _Chandos, V._
Lyttelton – _Cobham, V._
Lytton Cobbold – _Cobbold_
McAlpine – _M. of West Green_*
Macaulay – _M. of Bragar_*
McClintock-Bunbury – _Rathdonnell_
McColl – _M. of Dulwich_*
Macdonald – _M. of Tradeston_*
McDonnell – _Antrim, E._
Macfarlane – _M. of Bearsden_*
McFarlane – _M. of Llandaff_*
MacGregor – _M. of Pulham Market_*
McIntosh – _M. of Haringey_*
McIntosh – _M. of Hudnall_*
McKenzie – _M. of Luton_*
Mackay – _Inchcape, E._
Mackay – _M. of Clashfern_*
Mackay – _M. of Drumadoon_*
Mackay – _Reay_
Mackay – _Tanlaw_*
MacKenzie – _M. of Culkein_*
MacKenzie – _M. of Framwellgate_*
Mackenzie – _Cromartie, E._
Mackie – _M. of Benshie_*
Mackintosh – _M. of Halifax, V._
McLaren – _Aberconway_
_MacLaurin – M. of Knebworth_*
MacLennan – _M. of Rogart_*
Macmillan – _Stockton, E._
Macpherson – _M. of Drumochter_
Macpherson – _Strathcarron_
Maffey – _Rugby_
Maginnis – _M. of Drumglass_*
Maitland – _Lauderdale, E._
Makgill – _Oxfuird, V._
Makins – _Sherfield_
Manners – _Rutland, D._
Manningham-Buller – _Dilhorne, V._
Mansfield – _Sandhurst_
Marks – _M. of Broughton_
Marquis – _Woolton, E._

Marshall – *M. of Knightsbridge**
Marsham – *Romney, E.*
Martyn-Hemphill – *Hemphill*
Mason – *M. of Barnsley**
Massey – *M. of Darwen**
Masters – *Noakes**
Maude – *Hawarden, V.*
Maxwell – *de Ros*
Maxwell – *Farnham*
May – *M. of Oxford**
Mayhew – *M. of Twysden**
Meade – *Clanwilliam, E.*
Mercer Nairne Petty-Fitzmaurice – *Lansdowne, M.*
Millar – *Inchyra*
Miller – *M. of Chiltorne Domer**
Miller – *M. of Hendon**
Milner – *M. of Leeds*
Mitchell-Thomson – *Selsdon*
Mitford – *Redesdale*
Molyneaux – *M. of Killead**
Monckton – *M. of Brenchley, V.*
Monckton-Arundell – *Galway, V.*
Mond – *Melchett*
Money-Coutts – *Latymer*
Montagu – *Manchester, D.*
Montagu – *Sandwich, E.*
Montagu – *Swaythling*
Montagu Douglas Scott – *Buccleuch, D.*
Montagu Stuart Wortley – *Wharncliffe, E.*
Montague – *Amwell*
Montgomerie – *Eglinton, E.*
Montgomery – *M. of Alamein, V.*
Moore – *Drogheda, E.*
Moore – *M. of Lower Marsh**
Moore – *M. of Wolvercote**
Moore-Brabazon – *Brabazon of Tara*
Moreton – *Ducie, E*
Morgan – *M. of Drefelin**
Morgan – *M. of Huyton**
Morris – *Killanin*
Morris – *M. of Aberavon**
Morris – *M. of Bolton**
Morris – *M. of Handsworth**
Morris – *M. of Manchester**
Morris – *M. of Kenwood*
Morris – *M. of Yardley**
Morris – *Naseby**
Morrison – *Dunrossil, V.*
Morrison – *Margadale*
Moser – *M. of Regents Park**
Mosley – *Ravensdale*
Mountbatten – *Milford Haven, M.*
Muff – *Calverley*
Mulholland – *Dunleath*
Murray – *Atholl, D.*
Murray – *Dunmore, E.*
Murray – *Mansfield and Mansfield, E.*
Murton – *M. of Lindisfarne**
Nall-Cain – *Brocket*
Napier – *Napier and Ettrick*
Napier – *N. of Magdala*
Needham – *Kilmorey, E.*
Neill – *N. of Bladen**
Nelson – *N. of Stafford*
Neuberger – *N. of Abbotsbury**
Nevill – *Abergavenny, M.*
Neville – *Braybrooke*
Newton – *N. of Braintree**
Nicholls – *N. of Birkenhead**
Nicolson – *Carnock*
Nicholson – *N. of Winterboune**
Nivison – *Glendyne*
Noel – *Gainsborough, E.*
North – *Guilford, E.*
Northcote – *Iddesleigh, E.*
Norton – *Grantley*
Norton – *N. of Louth**
Norton – *Rathcreedan*
Nugent – *Westmeath, E.*
Oakeshott – *O. of Seagrove Bay**
O'Brien – *Inchiquin*
Ogilvie-Grant – *Seafield, E.*
Ogilvy – *Airlie, E.*
Oliver – *O. of Aylmerton**
O'Neill – *O'N. of Bengarve**
O'Neill – *O'N. of Clackmannan**
O'Neill – *Rathcavan*
Orde-Powlett – *Bolton*
Ormsby-Gore – *Harlech*
Ouseley – *O. of Peckham Rye**
Paget – *Anglesey, M.*
Paisley – *P. of St George's**
Pakenham – *Longford, E.*
Pakington – *Hampton*
Palmer – *Lucas and Dingwall*
Palmer – *Selborne, E.*
Park – *P. of Monmouth**
Parker – *Macclesfield, E.*
Parker – *Morley, E.*
Parnell – *Congleton*
Parsons – *Rosse, E.*
Patel – *P. of Blackburn**
Patel – *P. of Bradford**
Patten – *P. of Barnes**
Paulet – *Winchester, M.*
Peake – *Ingleby, V.*
Pearson – *Cowdray, V.*
Pearson – *P. of Rannoch**
Pease – *Gainford*
Pease – *Wardington*
Pelham – *Chichester, E.*
Pelham – *Yarborough, E.*
Pellew – *Exmouth, V*
Pendry – *P. of Stalybridge**.
Penny – *Marchwood, V.*
Pepys – *Cottenham, E.*
Perceval – *Egmont, E.*
Percy – *Northumberland, D.*
Perry – *P. of Southwark**
Pery – *Limerick, E.*
Philipps – *Milford*
Philipps – *St Davids, V.*
Phillips – *P. of Sudbury**
Phillips – *P. of Worth Matravers**
Phipps – *Normanby, M.*
Pilkington – *P. of Oxenford**
Plant – *P. of Highfield**
Platt – *P. of Writtle**
Pleydell-Bouverie – *Radnor, E.*
Plummer – *P. of St Marylebone**
Plumptre – *Fitzwalter*
Plunkett – *Dunsany*
Plunkett – *Louth*
Pollock – *Hanworth, V.*
Pomeroy – *Harberton, V.*
Ponsonby – *Bessborough, E.*
Ponsonby – *de Mauley*
Ponsonby – *P. of Shulbrede*
Ponsonby – *Sysonby*
Powell – *P. of Bayswater**
Powys – *Lilford*
Pratt – *Camden, M.*
Preston – *Gormanston, V.*
Primrose – *Rosebery, E.*
Prittie – *Dunalley*
Prout – *Kingsland**
Ramsay – *Dalhousie, E.*
Ramsay – *R. of Cartvale**
Ramsbotham – *Soulbury, V.*
Randall – *R. of St. Budeaux**
Rees – *R. of Ludlow**
Rees-Williams – *Ogmore*
Rendell – *R. of Babergh**
Renfrew – *R. of Kaimsthorn**
Renton – *R. of Mount Harry**
Renwick – *R. of Clifton**
Rhys – *Dynevor*
Richards – *Milverton*
Richardson – *R. of Calow**
Richardson – *R. of Duntisbourne**
Ritchie – *R. of Dundee*
Roberts – *Clwyd*
Roberts – *R. of Conway**
Roberts – *R. of Llandudno**
Robertson – *R. of Oakridge*
Robertson – *R. of Port Ellen**
Robertson – *Wharton*
Robinson – *Martonmere*
Roche – *Fermoy*
Rodd – *Rennell*
Rodger – *R. of Earlsferry**
Rodgers – *R. of Quarry Bank**
Rogers – *R. of Riverside**
Roper-Curzon – *Teynham*
Rospigliosi – *Newburgh, E.*
Rous – *Stradbroke, E.*
Rowley-Conwy – *Langford*
Royall – *R. of Blaisdon**
Runciman – *R. of Doxford, V.*
Russell – *Ampthill*
Russell – *Bedford, D.*
Russell – *de Clifford*
Russell – *R. of Liverpool*
Ryder – *Harrowby, E.*
Ryder – *R. of Wensum**
Sackville – *De La Warr, E.*
Sackville-West – *Sackville*
Sainsbury – *S. of Preston Candover**
Sainsbury – *S. of Turville**
St Aubyn – *St Levan*
St Clair – *Sinclair*
St Clair-Erskine – *Rosslyn, E.*
St John – *Bolingbroke and St John, V.*
St John – *St John of Blesto*
St John-Stevas – *St John of Fawsley**
St Leger – *Doneraile, V.*
Samuel – *Bearsted, V.*
Sanderson – *S. of Ayot*
Sanderson – *S. of Bowden**
Sandilands – *Torphichen*
Saumarez – *De Saumarez*
Savile – *Mexborough, E.*
Saville – *S. of Newdigate**
Scarlett – *Abinger*
Schreiber – *Marlesford**
Sclater-Booth – *Basing*
Scotland – *S. of Asthal**
Scott – *Eldon, E*
Scott – *S. of Foscotte**
Scott – *S. of Needham Market**.
Scrymgeour – *Dundee, E.*
Seager – *Leighton of St Mellons*
Seely – *Mottistone*
Seymour – *Hertford, M.*
Seymour – *Somerset, D.*
Sharp – *S. of Guildford**

Shaw – *Craigmyle*
Shaw – *S. of Northstead**
Shephard – *S. of Northwood**
Sheppard – *S. of Didgemere**
Shirley – *Ferrers, E.*
Short – *Glenamara**
Shutt – *S. of Greetland**
Siddeley – *Kenilworth*
Sidney – *De L'Isle, V.*
Simon – *S. of Highbury**
Simon – *S. of Wythenshawe*
Simpson – *S. of Dunkeld**
Sinclair – *Caithness, E.*
Sinclair – *S. of Cleeve*
Sinclair – *Thurso, V.*
Skeffington – *Massereene, V.*
Slynn – *S. of Hadley**
Smith – *Bicester*
Smith – *Hambleden, V.*
Smith – *Kirkhill**
Smith – *S. of Clifton**
Smith – *Smith of Finsbury**
Smith – *S. of Gilmorehill**
Smith – *S. of Leigh**
Somerset – *Beaufort, D.*
Somerset – *Raglan*
Soulsby – *S. of Swaffham Prior**
Spencer – *Churchill, V.*
Spencer-Churchill – *Marlborough, D.*
Spring Rice – *Monteagle of Brandon*
Stanhope – *Harrington, E.*
Stanley – *Derby, E.*
Stanley – *of Alderley and Sheffield*
Stapleton-Cotton – *Combermere, V.*
Steel – *S. of Aikwood**
Sterling – *S. of Plaistow**
Stevens – *S. of Kirkwhelpington**
Stevens – *S. of Ludgate**
Stevenson – *S. of Coddenham**
Stewart – *Galloway, E.*
Stewart – *Stewartby**
Stoddart – *S. of Swindon**
Stone – *S. of Blackheath**
Stonor – *Camoys*
Stopford – *Courtown, E.*
Stourton – *Mowbray*
Strachey – *O'Hagan*
Strutt – *Belper*
Strutt – *Rayleigh*
Stuart – *Castle Stewart, E.*
Stuart – *Moray, E.*
Stuart – *S. of Findhorn, V.*
Suenson-Taylor – *Grantchester*
Sutherland – *S. of Houndwood**
Symons – *S. of Vernham Dean**
Taylor – *Kilclooney**
Taylor – *T. of Blackburn**
Taylor – *T. of Bolton**
Taylor – *T. of Holbeach**
Taylor – *T. of Warwick**
Taylour – *Headfort, M.*
Temple-Gore-Langton – *Temple of Stowe, E*
Temple-Morris – *Temple-Morris of Llandaff**
Tennant – *Glenconner*
Thellusson – *Rendlesham*
Thesiger – *Chelmsford, V.*
Thomas – *T. of Gresford**
Thomas – *T. of Gwydir**
Thomas – *T. of Macclesfield**
Thomas – *T. of Swynnerton**
Thomas – *T. of Walliswood**
Thomas – *T. of Winchester**
Thomson – *T. of Fleet*
Thomson – *T. of Monifieth**
Thynn – *Bath, M.*
Tottenham – *Ely, M.*
Trefusis – *Clinton*
Trench – *Ashtown*
Tufton – *Hothfield*
Turner – *Bilston**
Turner – *Netherthorpe*
Turner – *T. of Camden**
Turner – *T. of Ecchinswell**
Turnour – *Winterton, E.*
Tyrell-Kenyon – *Kenyon*
Vanden-Bempde-Johnstone – *Derwent*
Vane – *Barnard*
Vane-Tempest-Stewart – *Londonderry, M.*
Vanneck – *Huntingfield*
Vaughan – *Lisburne, E.*
Vereker – *Gort, V.*
Verney – *Willoughby de Broke*
Vernon – *Lyveden*
Vesey – *De Vesci, V.*
Villiers – *Clarendon, E.*
Vincent – *V. of Coleshill**
Vivian – *Swansea*
Wade – *W. of Chorlton**
Waldegrave – *W. of North Hill**
Walker – *W. of Aldringham**
Walker – *W. of Gestingthorpe**
Walker – *W. of Worcester**
Wall – *W. of New Barnett**
Wallace – *Dudley*
Wallace – *W. of Saltaire**
Wallace – *W. of Tummel**
Wallop – *Portsmouth, E.*
Walton – *W. of Detchant**
Ward – *Bangor, V.*
Ward – *Dudley, E.*
Warrender – *Bruntisfield*
Warwick – *W. of Undercliffe**
Watson – *W. of Invergowrie**
Watson – *Manton*
Watson – *W. of Richmond**
Webber – *Lloyd-Webber**
Wedderburn – *W. of Charlton**
Weir – *Inverforth*
Weld-Forester – *Forester*
Wellesley – *Cowley, E.*
Wellesley – *Wellington, D.*
West – *W. of Spithead**
Westenra – *Rossmore*
White – *Annaly*
White – *Hanningfield**
Whiteley – *Marchamley*
Whitfield – *Kenswood*
Williams – *W. of Crosby**
Williams – *W. of Elvel**
Williamson – *Forres*
Williamson – *W. of Horton**
Willoughby – *Middleton*
Wills – *Dulverton*
Wilson – *Moran*
Wilson – *Nunburnholme*
Wilson – *W. of Dinton**
Wilson – *W. of Tillyorn**
Windsor – *Gloucester, D.*
Windsor – *Kent, D.*
Windsor-Clive – *Plymouth, E.*
Wingfield – *Powerscourt, V.*
Winn – *St Oswald*
Wodehouse – *Kimberley, E.*
Wolfson – *W. of Sunningdale**
Wood – *Halifax, E.*
Woodhouse – *Terrington*
Woolmer – *W. of Leeds**
Wright – *W. of Richmond**
Wyndham – *Egremont and Leconfield*
Wyndham-Quin – *Dunraven, E.*
Wynn – *Newborough*
Yarde-Buller – *Churston*
Yerburgh – *Alvingham*
Yorke – *Hardwicke, E.*
Young – *Kennet*
Young – *Y. of Graffham**
Young – *Y. of Hornsey**
Young – *Y. of Norwood Green**
Young – *Y. of Old Scone**
Younger – *Y. of Leckie, V.*

ORDERS OF CHIVALRY

THE MOST NOBLE ORDER OF THE GARTER (1348)

KG
Ribbon, Blue
Motto, Honi soit qui mal y pense
(Shame on him who thinks evil of it)

The number of Knights and Lady Companions is limited to 24

SOVEREIGN OF THE ORDER
The Queen

LADIES OF THE ORDER
HRH The Princess Royal, 1994
HRH Princess Alexandra, The Hon. Lady Ogilvy, 2003

ROYAL KNIGHTS
HRH The Prince Philip, Duke of Edinburgh, 1947
HRH The Prince of Wales, 1958
HRH The Duke of Kent, 1985
HRH The Duke of Gloucester, 1997
HRH The Duke of York, 2006
HRH The Earl of Wessex, 2006

EXTRA KNIGHT COMPANIONS AND LADIES
Grand Duke Jean of Luxembourg, 1972
HM The Queen of Denmark, 1979
HM The King of Sweden, 1983
HM The King of Spain, 1988
HM The Queen of the Netherlands, 1989
HIM The Emperor of Japan, 1998
HM The King of Norway, 2001

KNIGHTS AND LADY COMPANIONS
Duke of Grafton, 1976
Lord Richardson of Duntisbourne, 1983
Lord Carrington, 1985
Duke of Wellington, 1990
Lord Bramall, 1990
Viscount Ridley, 1992
Lord Sainsbury of Preston Candover, 1992
Lord Ashburton, 1994
Lord Kingsdown, 1994
Sir Ninian Stephen, 1994
Baroness Thatcher, 1995
Sir Edmund Hillary, 1995
Sir Timothy Colman, 1996
Duke of Abercorn, 1999
Sir William Gladstone, 1999
Lord Inge, 2001
Sir Anthony Acland, 2001
Duke of Westminster, 2003
Lord Butler of Brockwell, 2003
Lord Morris of Aberavon, 2003
Lady Soames, 2005
Lord Bingham of Cornhill, 2005
Sir John Major, 2005

Prelate, Bishop of Winchester
Chancellor, Lord Carrington, KG, GCMG, CH, MC
Register, Dean of Windsor
Garter King of Arms, Peter Gwynn-Jones, CVO
Gentleman Usher of the Black Rod, Lt.-Gen. Sir Michael Willcocks, KCB
Secretary, P. L. Dickinson, LVO

THE MOST ANCIENT AND MOST NOBLE ORDER OF THE THISTLE (REVIVED 1687)

KT
Ribbon, Green
Motto, Nemo me impune lacessit
(No one provokes me with impunity)

The number of Knights and Ladies of the Thistle is limited to 16

SOVEREIGN OF THE ORDER
The Queen

ROYAL LADY OF THE ORDER
HRH The Princess Royal, 2000

ROYAL KNIGHTS
HRH The Prince Philip, Duke of Edinburgh, 1952
HRH The Prince of Wales, Duke of Rothesay, 1977

KNIGHTS AND LADIES
Earl of Wemyss and March, 1966
Duke of Buccleuch and Queensberry, 1978
Earl of Elgin and Kincardine, 1981
Lord Thomson of Monifieth, 1981
Earl of Airlie, 1985
Viscount of Arbuthnott, 1996
Earl of Crawford and Balcarres, 1996
Lady Marion Fraser, 1996
Lord Macfarlane of Bearsden, 1996
Lord Mackay of Clashfern, 1997
Lord Wilson of Tillyorn, 2000
Lord Sutherland of Houndwood, 2002
Sir Eric Anderson, 2002
Lord Steel of Aikwood, 2004
Lord Robertson of Port Ellen, 2004

Chancellor, Duke of Buccleuch and Queensberry, KT, VRD
Dean, Very Revd Gilleasbuig Macmillan, CVO
Secretary and Lord Lyon King of Arms, Robin Blair, LVO, WS
Gentleman Usher of the Green Rod, Rear-Adm. Christopher Layman, CB, DSO, LVO

THE MOST HONOURABLE ORDER OF THE BATH (1725)

GCB *Military* GCB *Civil*

GCB	Knight (or Dame) Grand Cross
KCB	Knight Commander
DCB	Dame Commander
CB	Companion

Ribbon, Crimson
Motto, Tria juncta in uno
(Three joined in one)

Remodelled 1815, and enlarged many times since. The order is divided into civil and military divisions. Women became eligible for the order from 1 January 1971.

THE SOVEREIGN

GREAT MASTER AND FIRST OR PRINCIPAL KNIGHT GRAND CROSS
HRH The Prince of Wales, KG, KT, GCB, OM

Dean of the Order, Dean of Westminster
Bath King of Arms, Gen. Sir Brian Kenny, GCB, CBE
Registrar and Secretary, Rear-Adm. Iain Henderson, CB, CBE
Genealogist, Peter Gwynn-Jones, CVO
Gentleman Usher of the Scarlet Rod, Maj.-Gen. Charles Vyvyan, CB, CBE
Deputy Secretary, Secretary of the Central Chancery of the Orders of Knighthood

Chancery, Central Chancery of the Orders of Knighthood, St James's Palace, London SW1A 1BH

THE ORDER OF MERIT (1902)

OM *Military* OM *Civil*

OM
Ribbon, Blue and crimson

This order is designed as a special distinction for eminent men and women without conferring a knighthood upon them. The order is limited in numbers to 24, with the addition of foreign honorary members.

THE SOVEREIGN

HRH The Prince Philip, Duke of Edinburgh, 1968
Revd Prof. Owen Chadwick, KBE, 1983
Sir Andrew Huxley, 1983
Dr Frederick Sanger, 1986
Baroness Thatcher, 1990
Dame Joan Sutherland, 1991
Sir Michael Atiyah, 1992
Lucian Freud, 1993
Sir Aaron Klug, 1995
Lord Foster of Thames Bank, 1997
Sir Denis Rooke, 1997
Sir James Black, 2000
Sir Anthony Caro, 2000
Prof. Sir Roger Penrose, 2000
Sir Tom Stoppard, 2000
HRH The Prince of Wales, 2002
Lord May of Oxford, 2002
Lord Rothschild, 2002
Sir David Attenborough, 2005
Baroness Boothroyd, 2005
Sir Michael Howard, 2005
Sir Timothy Berners-Lee, KBE, 2007
Lord Eames, 2007
Lord Rees of Ludlow, 2007

Honorary Member, Nelson Mandela, 1995

Secretary and Registrar, Lord Fellowes, GCB, GCVO, PC, QSO
Chancery, Central Chancery of the Orders of Knighthood, St James's Palace, London SW1A 1BH

THE MOST DISTINGUISHED ORDER OF ST MICHAEL AND ST GEORGE (1818)

GCMG KCMG

GCMG Knight (or Dame) Grand Cross
KCMG Knight Commander
DCMG Dame Commander
CMG Companion

Ribbon, Saxon blue, with scarlet centre
Motto, Auspicium melioris aevi *(Token of a better age)*

THE SOVEREIGN

GRAND MASTER
HRH The Duke of Kent, KG, GCMG, GCVO, ADC

Prelate, Rt. Revd David Urquhart
Chancellor, Sir Christopher Mallaby, GCMG, GCVO
Secretary, Permanent Under-Secretary of State at the Foreign and Commonwealth Office and Head of the Diplomatic Service
Registrar, Lord Wilson of Tillyorn, KT, GCMG
King of Arms, Sir Ewen Fergusson, GCMG, GCVO
Gentleman Usher of the Blue Rod, Sir Anthony Figgis, KCVO, CMG
Dean, Dean of St Paul's
Deputy Secretary, Secretary of the Central Chancery of the Orders of Knighthood
Chancery, Central Chancery of the Orders of Knighthood, St James's Palace, London SW1A 1BH

THE MOST EMINENT ORDER OF THE INDIAN EMPIRE (1878)

GCIE Knight Grand Commander
KCIE Knight Commander
CIE Companion

Ribbon, Imperial purple
Motto, Imperatricis auspiciis *(Under the auspices of the Empress)*

THE SOVEREIGN

Registrar, Secretary of the Central Chancery of the Orders of Knighthood
No conferments have been made since 1947

HH Maharaja Shriraj Sahib of Halvad Dhrangadhara, 1947

THE IMPERIAL ORDER OF THE CROWN OF INDIA (1877) FOR LADIES

CI

Badge, the royal cipher of Queen Victoria in jewels within an oval, surmounted by an heraldic crown and attached to a bow of light blue watered ribbon, edged white

The honour does not confer any rank or title upon the recipient

No conferments have been made since 1947

HM The Queen, 1947

THE ROYAL VICTORIAN ORDER (1896)

GCVO KCVO

GCVO Knight or Dame Grand Cross
KCVO Knight Commander
DCVO Dame Commander
CVO Commander
LVO Lieutenant
MVO Member

Ribbon, Blue, with red and white edges
Motto, Victoria

THE SOVEREIGN
GRAND MASTER
HRH The Princess Royal

Chancellor, Lord Chamberlain
Secretary, Keeper of the Privy Purse
Registrar, Secretary of the Central Chancery of the Orders of Knighthood
Chaplain, Chaplain of the Queen's Chapel of the Savoy
Hon. Genealogist, D. H. B. Chesshyre, CVO

THE MOST EXCELLENT ORDER OF THE BRITISH EMPIRE (1917)

GBE KBE

The order was divided into military and civil divisions in December 1918

GBE	Knight or Dame Grand Cross
KBE	Knight Commander
DBE	Dame Commander
CBE	Commander
OBE	Officer
MBE	Member

Ribbon, Rose pink edged with pearl grey with vertical pearl stripe in centre (military division); without vertical pearl stripe (civil division)
Motto, For God and the Empire

THE SOVEREIGN

GRAND MASTER
HRH The Prince Philip, Duke of Edinburgh, KG, KT, OM, GBE, PC

Prelate, Bishop of London
King of Arms, Air Chief Marshal Sir Patrick Hine, GCB, GBE
Registrar, Secretary of the Central Chancery of the Orders of Knighthood
Secretary, Secretary of the Cabinet and Head of the Home Civil Service
Dean, Dean of St Paul's
Gentleman Usher of the Purple Rod, Sir Alexander Michael Graham, GBE, DCL
Chancery, Central Chancery of the Orders of Knighthood, St James's Palace, London SW1A 1BH

ORDER OF THE COMPANIONS OF HONOUR (1917)

CH

Ribbon, Carmine, with gold edges
This order consists of one class only and carries with it no title. The number of awards is limited to 65 (excluding honorary members).

Anthony, Rt. Hon. John, 1981
Ashley of Stoke, Lord, 1975
Attenborough, Sir David, 1995
Baker, Dame Janet, 1993
Baker of Dorking, Lord, 1992
Birtwistle, Sir Harrison, 2000
Brenner, Sydney, 1986
Brook, Peter, 1998
Brooke of Sutton Mandeville, Lord, 1992
Carrington, Lord, 1983
Christie, Sir George, 2001
Davis, Sir Colin, 2001
De Chastelain, Gen. John, 1999
Dench, Dame Judi, 2005
Fraser, Rt. Hon. Malcolm, 1977
Freud, Lucian, 1983
Glenamara, Lord, 1976
Hamilton, Richard, 1999
Hannay of Chiswick, Lord, 2003
Hawking, Prof. Stephen, 1989
Healey, Lord, 1979
Heseltine, Lord, 1997
Hobsbawm, Prof. Eric, 1998
Hockney, David, 1997
Hodgkin, Sir Howard, 2002
Howard, Sir Michael, 2002
Howe of Aberavon, Lord, 1996
Hurd of Westwell, Lord, 1995
Jones, James, 1977
King of Bridgewater, Lord, 1992
Lessing, Doris, 1999
Lovelock, Prof. James, 2002
McKenzie, Prof. Dan Peter, 2003
MacKerras, Sir Charles, 2003
Mahon, Sir Denis, 2002
Major, Rt. Hon. Sir John, 1998
Owen, Lord, 1994
Patten, Rt. Hon. Lord, 1997
Pawson, Prof. Anthony James, 2006
Pinter, Harold, 2002
Riley, Bridget, 1998
Sanger, Dr. Frederick, 1981
Scofield, Paul, 2000
Somare, Rt. Hon. Sir Michael, 1978
Talboys, Rt. Hon. Sir Brian, 1981
Tebbit, Lord, 1987
Varah, Revd Dr Chad, 1999

Honorary Members, Lee Kuan Yew, 1970; Prof. Amartya Sen, 2000; Bernard Haitink, 2002
Secretary and Registrar, Secretary of the Central Chancery of the Orders of Knighthood

THE DISTINGUISHED SERVICE ORDER (1886)

DSO

Ribbon, Red, with blue edges

Bestowed in recognition of especial services in action of commissioned officers in the Navy, Army and Royal Air Force and (since 1942) Mercantile Marine. The members are Companions only. A bar may be awarded for any additional act of service.

THE IMPERIAL SERVICE ORDER (1902)

ISO

Ribbon, Crimson, with blue centre

Appointment as companion of this order is open to members of the civil services whose eligibility is determined by the grade they hold. The order consists of the sovereign and companions to a number not exceeding 1,900, of whom 1,300 may belong to the home civil services and 600 to overseas civil services. The then prime minister announced in March 1993 that he would make no further recommendations for appointments to the order.

Secretary, Secretary of the Cabinet and Head of the Home Civil Service
Registrar, Secretary of the Central Chancery of the Orders of Knighthood

THE ROYAL VICTORIAN CHAIN (1902)

It confers no precedence on its holders

HM THE QUEEN

HM The King of Thailand, 1960
HM The Queen of Denmark, 1974
HM The King of Sweden, 1975
HM The Queen of the Netherlands, 1982
Gen. Antonio Eanes, 1985
HM The King of Spain, 1986
Dr Richard von Weizsäcker, 1992
HM The King of Norway, 1994
Earl of Airlie, 1997
Rt. Revd and Rt. Hon. Lord Carey of Clifton, 2002

BARONETAGE AND KNIGHTAGE

BARONETS

Style, 'Sir' before forename and surname, followed by 'Bt'.
Envelope, Sir F_ S_, Bt. *Letter (formal),* Dear Sir; *(social),* Dear Sir F_. *Spoken,* Sir F_
Wife's style, 'Lady' followed by surname
Envelope, Lady S_. *Letter (formal),* Dear Madam; *(social),* Dear Lady S_. *Spoken,* Lady S_
Style of Baronetess, 'Dame' before forename and surname, followed by 'Btss.' (*see also* Dames)

There are five different creations of baronetcies: Baronets of England (creations dating from 1611); Baronets of Ireland (creations dating from 1619); Baronets of Scotland or Nova Scotia (creations dating from 1625); Baronets of Great Britain (creations after the Act of Union 1707 which combined the kingdoms of England and Scotland); and Baronets of the United Kingdom (creations after the union of Great Britain and Ireland in 1801).

Badge of Baronets of the United Kingdom

Badge of Baronets of Nova Scotia

Badge of Ulster

The patent of creation limits the destination of a baronetcy, usually to male descendants of the first baronet, although special remainders allow the baronetcy to pass, if the male issue of sons fail, to the male issue of daughters of the first baronet. In the case of baronetcies of Scotland or Nova Scotia, a special remainder of 'heirs male and of tailzie' allows the baronetcy to descend to heirs general, including women. There are four existing Scottish baronets with such a remainder.

The Official Roll of the Baronetage is kept at the Crown Office and maintained by the Registrar and Assistant Registrar of the Baronetage. Anyone who considers that he or she is entitled to be entered on the roll may apply through the Crown Office to prove their succession. Every person succeeding to a baronetcy must exhibit proofs of succession to the Lord Chancellor. A person whose name is not entered on the official roll will not be addressed or mentioned by the title of baronet or baronetess in any official document, nor will he or she be accorded precedence as a baronet of baronetess.

BARONETCIES EXTINCT SINCE THE LAST EDITION

Echlin (cr. (I.) 1721); Prince-Smith (cr. 1911); Warren (cr.1784)

OFFICIAL ROLL OF THE BARONETAGE, Crown Office, House of Lords, London SW1A 0PW T 020-7219 2632
Registrar, Ian Denyer, MVO
Assistant Registrar, Grant Bavister

KNIGHTS

Style, 'Sir' before forename and surname, followed by appropriate post-nominal initials if a Knight Grand Cross, Knight Grand Commander or Knight Commander
Envelope, Sir F_ S_. *Letter (formal),* Dear Sir; *(social),* Dear Sir F_. *Spoken,* Sir F_
Wife's style, 'Lady' followed by surname
'*Envelope,* Lady S_. *Letter (formal),* Dear Madam; *(social),* Dear Lady S_. *Spoken,* Lady S_

The prefix 'Sir' is not used by knights who are clerics of the Church of England, who do not receive the accolade. Their wives are entitled to precedence as the wife of a knight but not to the style of 'Lady'.

ORDERS OF KNIGHTHOOD

Knight Grand Cross, Knight Grand Commander, and Knight Commander are the higher classes of the Orders of Chivalry (*see* Orders of Chivalry). Honorary knighthoods of these orders may be conferred on men who are citizens of countries of which the Queen is not head of state. As a rule, the prefix 'Sir' is not used by honorary knights.

KNIGHTS BACHELOR

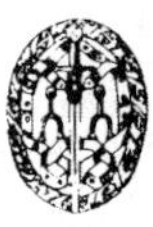

The Knights Bachelor do not constitute a royal order, but comprise the surviving representation of the ancient state orders of knighthood. The Register of Knights Bachelor, instituted by James I in the 17th century, lapsed, and in 1908 a voluntary association under the title of the Society of Knights (now the Imperial Society of Knights Bachelor) was formed with the primary objectives of continuing the various registers dating from 1257 and obtaining the uniform registration of every created Knight Bachelor. In 1926 a design for a badge to be worn by Knights Bachelor was approved and adopted; in 1974 a neck badge and miniature were added.

THE IMPERIAL SOCIETY OF KNIGHTS BACHELOR, 1 Throgmorton Avenue, London EC2N 2BY
Knight Principal, Sir Robert Balchin
Prelate, Rt. Revd and Rt. Hon. Bishop of London
Registrar, Sir Paul Judge
Hon. Treasurer, Sir Colin Berry
Clerk to the Council, Richard Jenkins, LVO, TD

LIST OF BARONETS AND KNIGHTS

as at 31 August 2007

† Not registered on the Official Roll of the Baronetage at the time of going to press
( ) The date of creation of the baronetcy is given in parentheses
I Baronet of Ireland
NS Baronet of Nova Scotia
S Baronet of Scotland

A full entry in italic type indicates that the recipient of a knighthood died during the year in which the honour was conferred. The name is included for purposes of record. Peers are not included in this list.

Aaronson, Sir Michael John, Kt., CBE
Abbott, *Adm.* Sir Peter Charles, GBE, KCB
Abdy, Sir Valentine Robert Duff, Bt. (1850)
Acheson, *Prof.* Sir (Ernest) Donald, KBE
Ackers, Sir James George, Kt.
Ackers-Jones, Sir David, KBE, CMG
Ackroyd, Sir Timothy Robert Whyte, Bt. (1956)
Acland, Sir Antony Arthur, KG, GCMG, GCVO
Acland, *Lt.-Col.* Sir (Christopher) Guy (Dyke), Bt. (1890), MVO
Acland, Sir John Dyke, Bt. (1644)
Adam, Sir Christopher Eric Forbes, Bt. (1917)
Adam, Sir Kenneth Hugo, Kt., OBE
Adams, Sir William James, KCMG
Adsetts, Sir William Norman, Kt., OBE
Adye, Sir John Anthony, KCMG
Aga Khan IV, HH Prince Karim, KBE
Agnew, Sir Crispin Hamlyn, Bt. (S. 1629)
Agnew, Sir John Keith, Bt. (1895)
Agnew, Sir Rudolph Ion Joseph, Kt.
Agnew-Somerville, Sir Quentin Charles Somerville, Bt. (1957)
Ah Koy, Sir James Michael, KBE
Aikens, *Hon.* Sir Richard John Pearson, Kt.
†Ainsworth, Sir Anthony Thomas Hugh, Bt. (1916)
Aird, *Capt.* Sir Alastair Sturgis, GCVO
Aird, Sir (George) John, Bt. (1901)
Airy, *Maj.-Gen.* Sir Christopher John, KCVO, CBE
Aitchison, Sir Charles Walter de Lancey, Bt. (1938)
Ajegbo, Sir Keith Onyema, Kt., OBE
Alberti, *Prof.* Sir Kurt George Matthew Mayer, Kt.
Albu, Sir George, Bt. (1912)
Alcock, *Air Chief Marshal* Sir (Robert James) Michael, GCB, KBE
Aldous, *Rt. Hon.* Sir William, Kt.
Alexander, Sir Charles Gundry, Bt. (1945)
Alexander, Sir Douglas, Bt. (1921)
Allen, *Prof.* Sir Geoffrey, Kt., PHD, FRS
Allen, Sir John Derek, Kt., CBE
Allen, Sir Mark John Spurgeon, Kt., CMG
Allen, *Hon.* Sir Peter Austin Philip Jermyn, Kt.
Allen, Sir Thomas Boaz, Kt., CBE
Allen, *Hon.* Sir William Clifford, KCMG
Allen, Sir William Guilford, Kt.
Alleyne, Sir George Allanmoore Ogarren, Kt.
Alleyne, *Revd* John Olpherts Campbell, Bt. (1769)
Allinson, Sir (Walter) Leonard, KCVO, CMG
Alliott, *Hon.* Sir John Downes, Kt.
Allison, *Air Chief Marshal* Sir John Shakespeare, KCB, CBE
Alun-Jones, Sir (John) Derek, Kt.
Ambo, *Rt. Revd* George, KBE
Amet, *Hon.* Sir Arnold Karibone, Kt.
Amory, Sir Ian Heathcoat, Bt. (1874)
Anderson, Sir John Anthony, KBE
Anderson, *Maj.-Gen.* Sir John Evelyn, KBE
Anderson, Sir Leith Reinsford Steven, Kt., CBE
Anderson, *Vice-Adm.* Sir Neil Dudley, KBE, CB
Anderson, *Prof.* Sir Roy Malcolm, Kt.
Anderson, Sir (William) Eric Kinloch, KT.
Anderson, *Prof.* Sir (William) Ferguson, Kt., OBE
Anderton, Sir (Cyril) James, Kt., CBE, QPM
Andrew, Sir Robert John, KCB
Andrews, Sir Derek Henry, KCB, CBE
Andrews, Sir Ian Charles Franklin, Kt., CBE, TD
Angus, Sir Michael Richardson, Kt.
Annesley, Sir Hugh Norman, Kt., QPM
Anson, *Vice-Adm.* Sir Edward Rosebery, KCB
Anson, Sir John, KCB
Anson, *Rear-Adm.* Sir Peter, Bt. CB (1831)
†Anstruther, Sir Sebastian Paten Campbell, Bt. (S. 1694)
†Anstruther, Sir Tobias Alexander Campbell, Bt. (1798)
Anstruther-Gough-Calthorpe, Sir Euan Hamilton, Bt. (1929)
Antrobus, Sir Edward Philip, Bt. (1815)
Appleyard, Sir Leonard Vincent, KCMG
Appleyard, Sir Raymond Kenelm, KBE
Arbib, Sir Martyn, Kt.
Arbuthnot, Sir Keith Robert Charles, Bt. (1823)
Arbuthnot, Sir William Reierson, Bt. (1964)
Arbuthnott, *Prof.* Sir John Peebles, Kt., PHD, FRSE
Archdale, *Capt.* Sir Edward Folmer, Bt. (1928), DSC, RN
Arculus, Sir Ronald, KCMG, KCVO
Arculus, Sir Thomas David Guy, Kt.
Armitage, *Air Chief Marshal* Sir Michael John, KCB, CBE
Armour, *Prof.* Sir James, Kt., CBE
Armstrong, Sir Christopher John Edmund Stuart, Bt. (1841), MBE
Armstrong, Sir Patrick John, Kt., CBE
Armstrong, Sir Richard, Kt., CBE
Armytage, Sir John Martin, Bt. (1738)
Arnold, Sir Thomas Richard, Kt.
Arnott, Sir Alexander John Maxwell, Bt. (1896)
Arrindell, Sir Clement Athelston, GCMG, GCVO, QC
Arthur, Sir Gavyn Farr, Kt.
Arthur, *Lt.-Gen.* Sir (John) Norman Stewart, KCB
Arthur, Sir Michael Anthony, KCMG
Arthur, Sir Stephen John, Bt. (1841)
Asbridge, Sir Jonathan Elliott, Kt.
Ash, *Prof.* Sir Eric Albert, Kt., CBE, FRS, FRENG
Ashburnham, Sir James Fleetwood, Bt. (1661)
Ashley, Sir Bernard Albert, Kt.
Ashmore, *Admiral of the Fleet* Sir Edward Beckwith, GCB, DSC
Aske, Sir Robert John Bingham, Bt. (1922)
Askew, Sir Bryan, Kt.
Asscher, Prof. Sir (Adolf) William, Kt., MD, FRCP
Astill, *Hon.* Sir Michael John, Kt.
Astley-Cooper, Sir Alexander Paston, Bt. (1821)
Aston, Sir Harold George, Kt., CBE
Astwood, *Hon.* Sir James Rufus, KBE
Atcherley, Sir Harold Winter, Kt.
Atiyah, Sir Michael Francis, Kt., OM, PHD, FRS
Atkins, *Rt. Hon.* Sir Robert James, Kt.
Atkinson, *Prof.* Sir Anthony Barnes, Kt.
Atkinson, *Air Marshal* Sir David William, KBE
Atkinson, Sir Frederick John, KCB
Atkinson, Sir John Alexander, KCB, DFC
Atkinson, Sir Robert, Kt., DSC, FRENG

Atopare, Sir Sailas, GCMG
Attenborough, Sir David Frederick, Kt., OM, CH, CVO, CBE, FRS
Aubrey-Fletcher, Sir Henry Egerton, Bt. (1782)
Audland, Sir Christopher John, KCMG
Audley, Sir George Bernard, Kt.
Augier, *Prof.* Sir Fitz-Roy Richard, Kt.
Auld, *Rt. Hon.* Sir Robin Ernest, Kt.
Austin, Sir Anthony Leonard, Bt. (1894)
Austin, *Air Marshal* Sir Roger Mark, KCB, AFC
Austen-Smith, *Air Marshal* Sir Roy David, KBE, CB, CVO, DFC
Avei, Sir Moi, KBE
Axford, Sir William Ian, Kt.
Ayckbourn, Sir Alan, Kt., CBE
Aykroyd, Sir James Alexander Frederic, Bt. (1929)
†Aykroyd, Sir Michael David, Bt. (1920)
Aylmer, Sir Richard John, Bt. (I. 1622)
Aynsley-Green, *Prof.* Sir Albert, Kt.
Bacha, Sir Bhinod, Kt., CMG
Backhouse, Sir Jonathan Roger, Bt. (1901)
Bacon, Sir Nicholas Hickman Ponsonby, Bt. (1611 and 1627), *Premier Baronet of England*
Bacon, Sir Sidney Charles, Kt., CB, FRENG.
Baddeley, Sir John Wolsey Beresford, Bt. (1922)
Baddiley, *Prof.* Sir James, Kt., PHD, FRS, FRSE
Badge, Sir Peter Gilmour Noto, Kt.
Baer, Sir Jack Mervyn Frank, Kt.
Bagge, Sir (John) Jeremy Picton, Bt. (1867)
Bagnall, *Air Chief Marshal* Sir Anthony, GBE, KCB
Bailey, Sir Alan Marshall, KCB
Bailey, Sir Brian Harry, Kt., OBE
Bailey, Sir Derrick Thomas Louis, Bt. (1919), DFC
Bailey, Sir John Bilsland, KCB
Bailey, *Rt. Revd* Jonathan Sansbury, KCVO
Bailey, Sir Richard John, Kt., CBE
Bailey, Sir Stanley Ernest, Kt., CBE, QPM
Bailhache, Sir Philip Martin, Kt.
Baillie, Sir Adrian Louis, Bt. (1823)
Bain, *Prof.* Sir George Sayers, Kt.
Baird, Sir Charles William Stuart, Bt. (1809)
†Baird, Sir James Andrew Gardiner, Bt. (S. 1695)
Baird, *Air Marshal* Sir John Alexander, KBE
Baird, *Vice-Adm.* Sir Thomas Henry Eustace, KCB
Bairsto, *Air Marshal* Sir Peter Edward, KBE, CB
Baker, Sir Bryan William, Kt.
Baker, *Prof.* Sir John Hamilton, Kt., QC
Baker, Sir John William, Kt., CBE
Baker, *Rt. Hon.* Sir (Thomas) Scott (Gillespie), Kt.
Balchin, Sir Robert George Alexander, Kt.
Balderstone, Sir James Schofield, Kt.
Baldwin, *Prof.* Sir Jack Edward, Kt., FRS
Baldwin, Sir Peter Robert, KCB
Ball, *Air Marshal* Sir Alfred Henry Wynne, KCB, DSO, DFC
Ball, Sir Christopher John Elinger, Kt.
Ball, *Prof.* Sir John Macleod, Kt.
Ball, Sir Richard Bentley, Bt. (1911)
Ball, *Prof.* Sir Robert James, Kt., PHD
Ballantyne, *Dr* Sir Frederick Nathaniel, GCMG
Bamford, Sir Anthony Paul, Kt.
Band, *Adm.* Sir Jonathon, KCB
Banham, Sir John Michael Middlecott, Kt.
Bannerman, Sir David Gordon, Bt., OBE (S. 1682)
Bannister, Sir Roger Gilbert, Kt., CBE, DM, FRCP
Barber, Sir Michael Bayldon, Kt.
Barber, Sir (Thomas) David, Bt. (1960)
Barbour, *Very Revd* Robert Alexander Stewart, KCVO, MC
Barclay, Sir Colville Herbert Sanford, Bt. (S. 1668)
Barclay, Sir David Rowat, Kt.
Barclay, Sir Frederick Hugh, Kt.
Barclay, Sir Peter Maurice, Kt., CBE
Barder, Sir Brian Leon, KCMG
Baring, Sir John Francis, Bt. (1911)
Barker, Sir Colin, Kt.
Barker, *Hon.* Sir (Richard) Ian, Kt.
Barlow, Sir Christopher Hilaro, Bt. (1803)
Barlow, Sir Frank, Kt., CBE
Barlow, Sir (George) William, Kt., FRENG
Barlow, Sir James Alan, Bt. (1902)
Barlow, Sir John Kemp, Bt. (1907)
Barnard, Sir Joseph Brian, Kt.
Barnes, *The Most Revd.* Brian James, KBE
Barnes, Sir (James) David (Francis), Kt., CBE
Barnes, Sir Kenneth, KCB
Barnewall, Sir Reginald Robert, Bt. (I. 1623)
Baron, Sir Thomas, Kt., CBE
Barraclough, *Air Chief Marshal* Sir John, KCB, CBE, DFC, AFC
Barran, Sir John Napoleon Ruthven, Bt. (1895)
Barratt, Sir Lawrence Arthur, Kt.
Barratt, Sir Richard Stanley, Kt., CBE, QPM
Barrett, Sir Stephen Jeremy, KCMG
†Barrett-Lennard,Sir Richard Fynes, Bt. (1801)
Barrington, Sir Benjamin, Bt. (1831)
Barrington, Sir Nicholas John, KCMG, CVO
Barrington-Ward, *Rt. Revd* Simon, KCMG
Barron, Sir Donald James, Kt.
Barrow, *Capt.* Sir Richard John Uniacke, Bt. (1835)
Barry, Sir (Lawrence) Edward (Anthony Tress), Bt. (1899)
Barter, Sir Peter Leslie Charles, Kt., OBE
†Bartlett, Sir Andrew Alan, Bt. (1913)
Barttelot, *Col.* Sir Brian Walter de Stopham, Bt. (1875), OBE
Bate, Sir David Lindsay, KBE
†Bates, Sir James Geoffrey, Bt. (1880)
Bates, Sir Malcolm Rowland, Kt.
Bates, Sir Richard Dawson Hoult, Bt. (1937)
Bateson, *Prof.* Sir Patrick, Kt.
Batho, Sir Peter Ghislain, Bt. (1928)
Bathurst, *Admiral of the Fleet* Sir (David) Benjamin, GCB
Batten, Sir John Charles, KCVO
Battersby, *Prof.* Sir Alan Rushton, Kt., FRS
Battishill, Sir Anthony Michael William, GCB
Baxendell, Sir Peter Brian, Kt., CBE, FRENG
Bayly, *Prof.* Sir Christopher Alan, Kt.
Bayne, Sir Nicholas Peter, KCMG
Baynes, Sir Christopher Rory, Bt. (1801)
Bazley, Sir Thomas John Sebastian, Bt. (1869)
Beach, *Gen.* Sir (William Gerald) Hugh, GBE, KCB, MC
Beache, *Hon.* Sir Vincent Ian, KCMG
Beale, *Lt.-Gen.* Sir Peter John, KBE, FRCP
Beamish, Sir Adrian John, KCMG
Bean, *Hon.* Sir David Michael, Kt
Beaumont, *Capt.* the Hon. Sir (Edward) Nicholas (Canning), KCVO
Beaumont, Sir George (Howland Francis), Bt. (1661)
Beaumont, Sir Richard Ashton, KCMG, OBE
Beatson, *Hon.* Sir Jack, Kt.
Beavis, *Air Chief Marshal* Sir Michael Gordon, KCB, CBE, AFC
Beck, Sir Edgar Philip, Kt.
Beckett, Sir Richard Gervase, Bt. (1921), QC
Beckett, Sir Terence Norman, KBE, FRENG
Beckwith, Sir John Lionel, Kt., CBE
Bedser, Sir Alec Victor, Kt., CBE
Beecham, Sir Jeremy Hugh, Kt.
Beecham, Sir John Stratford Roland, Bt. (1914)
Beetham, *Marshal of the Royal Air Force* Sir Michael James, GCB, CBE, DFC, AFC
Beevor, Sir Thomas Agnew, Bt. (1784)
Beldam, *Rt. Hon.* Sir (Alexander) Roy (Asplan), Kt.
Belich, Sir James, Kt.
Bell, Sir Brian Ernest, KBE
Bell, Sir David Charles Maurice, Kt.
Bell, Sir John Lowthian, Bt. (1885)

Bell, *Prof.* Sir Peter Robert Frank, Kt.
Bell, *Hon.* Sir Rodger, Kt.
Bell, Sir Stuart, Kt.
Bellamy, *Hon.* Sir Christopher William, Kt.
Bellingham, Sir Anthony Edward Norman, Bt. (1796)
Bender, Sir Brian Geoffrey, KCB
Benn, Sir (James) Jonathan, Bt. (1914)
Bennett, *Air Vice-Marshal* Sir Erik Peter, KBE, CB
Bennett, *Hon.* Sir Hugh Peter Derwyn, Kt.
Bennett, *Gen.* Sir Phillip Harvey, KBE, DSO
Bennett, Sir Richard Rodney, Kt., CBE
Bennett, Sir Ronald Wilfrid Murdoch, Bt. (1929)
Benson, Sir Christopher John, Kt.
Benyon, Sir William Richard, Kt.
Beresford, Sir (Alexander) Paul, Kt.
Beresford-Peirse, Sir Henry Grant de la Poer, Bt. (1814)
Berghuser, *Hon.* Sir Eric, Kt., MBE
Beringer, *Prof.* Sir John Evelyn, Kt., CBE
Berman, Sir Franklin Delow, KCMG
Berners-Lee, Sir Timothy John, KBE, OM, FRS
Bernard, Sir Dallas Edmund, Bt. (1954)
Bernstein, Sir Howard, Kt.
Berney, Sir Julian Reedham Stuart, Bt. (1620)
Berridge, *Prof.* Sir Michael John, Kt., FRS
Berrill, Sir Kenneth Ernest, GBE, KCB
Berriman, Sir David, Kt.
Berry, *Prof.* Sir Colin Leonard, Kt., FRCPATH
Berry, *Prof.* Sir Michael Victor, Kt., FRS
Berthoud, Sir Martin Seymour, KCVO, CMG
Best, Sir Richard Radford, KCVO, CBE
Best-Shaw, Sir John Michael Robert, Bt. (1665)
Bethel, Sir Baltron Benjamin, KCMG
Bett, Sir Michael, Kt., CBE
Bettison, Sir Norman George, Kt., QPM
Bevan, Sir Martyn Evan Evans, Bt. (1958)
Bevan, Sir Nicolas, Kt., CB
Bevan, Sir Timothy Hugh, Kt.
Beverley, *Lt.-Gen.* Sir Henry York La Roche, KCB, OBE, RM
Bibby, Sir Michael James, Bt. (1959)
Bichard, Sir Michael George, KCB
Bickersteth, *Rt. Revd* John Monier, KCVO
Biddulph, Sir Ian D'Olier, Bt. (1664)
Bide, Sir Austin Ernest, Kt.
Bidwell, Sir Hugh Charles Philip, GBE
Biggam, Sir Robin Adair, Kt.
Biggs, Sir Norman Paris, Kt.
Bilas, Sir Angmai Simon, Kt., OBE
Billière, *Gen.* Sir Peter Edgar de la Cour de la, KCB, KBE, DSO, MC
Bindman, Sir Geoffrey Lionel, Kt.
Bingham, *Hon.* Sir Eardley Max, Kt.
Birch, Sir John Allan, KCVO, CMG
Birch, Sir Roger, Kt., CBE, QPM
Bird, Sir Richard Geoffrey Chapman, Bt. (1922)
Birkin, Sir John Christian William, Bt. (1905)
Birkin, Sir (John) Derek, Kt., TD
Birkmyre, Sir James, Bt. (1921)
Birrell, Sir James Drake, Kt.
Birtwistle, Sir Harrison, Kt., CH
Bischoff, Sir Winfried Franz Wilhelm, Kt.
Bishop, Sir Michael David, Kt., CBE
Bisson, *Rt. Hon.* Sir Gordon Ellis, Kt.
Black, Sir James Whyte, Kt., OM, FRCP, FRS
Black, *Adm.* Sir (John) Jeremy, GBE, KCB, DSO
Black, Sir Robert David, Bt. (1922)
Blackburn, *Vice-Adm.* Sir David Anthony James, KCVO, CB, LVO
Blackburne, *Hon.* Sir William Anthony, Kt.
Blackett, Sir Hugh Francis, Bt. (1673)
Blackham, *Vice-Adm.* Sir Jeremy Joe, KCB
Blackman, Sir Frank Milton, KCVO, OBE
Blair, *Lt.-Gen.* Sir Chandos, KCVO, OBE, MC
†Blair, Sir Patrick David Hunter, Bt. (1786)
Blair, Sir Ian Warwick, Kt., QPM
Blake, Sir Alfred Lapthorn, KCVO, MC
Blake, Sir Francis Michael, Bt. (1907)
Blake, Sir Peter Thomas, Kt., CBE
Blake, Sir (Thomas) Richard (Valentine), Bt. (I. 1622)
Blaker, Sir John, Bt. (1919)
Blakiston, Sir Ferguson Arthur James, Bt. (1763)
Blanch, Sir Malcolm, KCVO
Bland, Sir (Francis) Christopher (Buchan), Kt.
Bland, *Lt.-Col.* Sir Simon Claud Michael, KCVO
Blank, Sir Maurice Victor, Kt.
Blatherwick, Sir David Elliott Spiby, KCMG, OBE
Blelloch, Sir John Nial Henderson, KCB
Blennerhassett, Sir (Marmaduke) Adrian Francis William, Bt. (1809)
Blewitt, *Maj.* Sir Shane Gabriel Basil, GCVO
Blofeld, *Hon.* Sir John Christopher Calthorpe, Kt.
Blois, Sir Charles Nicholas Gervase, Bt. (1686)
Blom-Cooper, Sir Louis Jacques, Kt., QC
Blomefield, Sir Thomas Charles Peregrine, Bt. (1807)
Bloomfield, Sir Kenneth Percy, KCB
Blundell, Sir Thomas Leon, Kt., FRS
Blunden, Sir George, Kt.
Blunden, Sir Philip Overington, Bt. (I. 1766)
Blunt, Sir David Richard Reginald Harvey, Bt. (1720)
Blyth, Sir Charles (Chay), Kt., CBE, BEM
Boardman, *Prof.* Sir John, Kt., FSA, FBA
Bodey, *Hon.* Sir David Roderick Lessiter, Kt.
Bodmer, Sir Walter Fred, Kt., PHD, FRS
Body, Sir Richard Bernard Frank Stewart, Kt.
Bogan, Sir Nagora, KBE
Boileau, Sir Guy (Francis), Bt. (1838)
Boles, Sir Jeremy John Fortescue, Bt. (1922)
Boles, Sir John Dennis, Kt., MBE
Bolland, Sir Edwin, KCMG
Bollers, *Hon.* Sir Harold Brodie Smith, Kt.
Bolt, *Air Marshal* Sir Richard Bruce, KBE, CB, DFC, AFC
Bona, Sir Kina, KBE
Bonallack, Sir Michael Francis, Kt., OBE
Bond, Sir John Reginald Hartnell, Kt.
Bond, *Prof.* Sir Michael Richard, Kt., FRCPSYCH, FRCPGLAS, FRCSE
Bone, Sir Roger Bridgland, KCMG
Bonfield, Sir Peter Leahy, Kt., CBE, FRENG
Bonham, *Maj.* Sir Antony Lionel Thomas, Bt. (1852)
Bonington, Sir Christian John Storey, Kt., CBE
Bonsall, Sir Arthur Wilfred, KCMG, CBE
Bonsor, Sir Nicholas Cosmo, Bt. (1925)
Boord, Sir Nicolas John Charles, Bt. (1896)
Boorman, *Lt.-Gen.* Sir Derek, KCB
Booth, Sir Christopher Charles, Kt., MD, FRCP
Booth, Sir Clive, Kt.
Booth, Sir Douglas Allen, Bt. (1916)
Booth, Sir Gordon, KCMG, CVO
Boothby, Sir Brooke Charles, Bt. (1660)
Bore, Sir Albert, Kt.
Boreel, Sir Stephan Gerard, Bt. (1645)
Borthwick, Sir Anthony Thomas, Bt. (1908)
Borysiewicz, *Prof.* Sir Leszek Krzysztof, Kt.
Bossom, *Hon.* Sir Clive, Bt. (1953)
Boswell, *Lt.-Gen.* Sir Alexander Crawford Simpson, KCB, CBE
Bosworth, Sir Neville Bruce Alfred, Kt., CBE
Botham, Sir Ian Terence, Kt., OBE
Bottoms, *Prof.* Sir Anthony Edward, Kt.
Bottomley, Sir James Reginald Alfred, KCMG

Boughey, Sir John George Fletcher, Bt. (1798)
Boulton, Sir Clifford John, GCB
Boulton, Sir William Whytehead, Bt. (1944), CBE, TD
Bourn, Sir John Bryant, KCB
Bouraga, Sir Phillip, KBE
Bourne, Sir Clive John, Kt.
Bowater, Sir Euan David Vansittart, Bt. (1939)
Bowater, Sir (John) Vansittart, Bt. (1914)
Bowden, Sir Andrew, Kt., MBE
Bowden, Sir Nicholas Richard, Bt. (1915)
Bowen, Sir Geoffrey Fraser, Kt.
Bowen, Sir Mark Edward Mortimer, Bt. (1921)
Bowes Lyon, Sir Simon Alexander, KCVO
Bowett, *Prof.* Sir Derek William, Kt., CBE, QC, FBA
†Bowlby, Sir Richard Peregrine Longstaff, Bt. (1923)
Bowman, Sir Edwin Geoffrey, KCB
Bowman, Sir Jeffery Haverstock, Kt.
Bowman-Shaw, Sir (George) Neville, Kt.
Bowness, Sir Alan, Kt., CBE
Bowyer-Smyth, Sir Thomas Weyland, Bt. (1661)
Boyce, Sir Graham Hugh, KCMG
Boyce, Sir Robert Charles Leslie, Bt. (1952)
Boyd, Sir Alexander Walter, Bt. (1916)
Boyd, Sir John Dixon Iklé, KCMG
Boyd, *Prof.* Sir Robert David Hugh, Kt.
Boyd-Carpenter, Sir (Marsom) Henry, KCVO
Boyd-Carpenter, *Lt.-Gen. Hon.* Sir Thomas Patrick John, KBE
Boyle, Sir Stephen Gurney, Bt. (1904)
Boyson, *Rt. Hon.* Sir Rhodes, Kt.
Brabham, Sir John Arthur, Kt., OBE
Bracewell-Smith, Sir Charles, Bt. (1947)
Bradbeer, Sir John Derek Richardson, Kt., OBE, TD
Bradfield, *Dr* Sir John Richard Grenfell, Kt., CBE
Bradford, Sir Edward Alexander Slade, Bt. (1902)
Bradshaw, Sir Kenneth Anthony, KCB
Brady, *Prof.* Sir John Michael, Kt., FRS
Braithwaite, *Rt. Hon.* Sir Nicholas Alexander, Kt., OBE
Braithwaite, Sir Rodric Quentin, GCMG
Bramley, *Prof.* Sir Paul Anthony, Kt.
Branson, Sir Richard Charles Nicholas, Kt.
Bratza, *Hon.* Sir Nicolas Dušan, Kt.
Breckenridge, *Prof.* Sir Alasdair Muir, Kt., CBE
Brennan, *Hon.* Sir (Francis) Gerard, KBE
Brenton, Sir Anthony Russell, KCMG
Brewer, Sir David William, Kt., CMG
Bridges, *Hon.* Sir Phillip Rodney, Kt., CMG
Brierley, Sir Ronald Alfred, Kt.
Briggs, *Hon.* Sir Michael Townley Featherstone, Kt.
Bright, Sir Graham Frank James, Kt.
Bright, Sir Keith, Kt.
Brigstocke, *Adm.* Sir John Richard, KCB
Brinckman, Sir Theodore George Roderick, Bt. (1831)
†Brisco, Sir Campbell Howard, Bt. (1782)
Briscoe, Sir Brian Anthony, Kt.
Briscoe, Sir John Geoffrey James, Bt. (1910)
Brittan, Sir Samuel, Kt.
†Broadbent, Sir Andrew George, Bt. (1893)
Broadbent, Sir Richard John, KCB
Brocklebank, Sir Aubrey Thomas, Bt. (1885)
Brodie, Sir Benjamin David Ross, Bt. (1834)
Brodie-Hall, Sir Laurence Charles, Kt., AO, CMG
Brooke, Sir Rodney George, Kt., CBE
Brooking, Sir Trevor, Kt., CBE
Bromhead, Sir John Desmond Gonville, Bt. (1806)
Bromley, Sir Michael Roger, KBE
Bromley, Sir Rupert Charles, Bt. (1757)
Brook, *Prof.* Sir Richard John, Kt. OBE
†Brooke, Sir Alistair Weston, Bt. (1919)
Brooke, Sir Francis George Windham, Bt. (1903)
Brooke, *Rt. Hon.* Sir Henry, Kt.
Brooke, Sir (Richard) David Christopher, Bt. (1662)
Brooking, Sir Trevor David, Kt., CBE
Brooks, Sir Timothy Gerald Martin, KCVO
Brooksbank, Sir (Edward) Nicholas, Bt. (1919)
Broomfield, Sir Nigel Hugh Robert Allen, KCMG
†Broughton, Sir David Delves, Bt. (1661)
Broun, Sir Wayne Hercules, Bt. (S. 1686)
Brown, Sir (Austen) Patrick, KCB
Brown, *Adm.* Sir Brian Thomas, KCB, CBE
Brown, Sir (Cyril) Maxwell Palmer, KCB, CMG
Brown, Sir David, Kt.
Brown, *Hon.* Sir Douglas Dunlop, Kt.
Brown, Sir George Francis Richmond, Bt. (1863)
Brown, Sir George Noel, Kt.
Brown, Sir Mervyn, KCMG, OBE
Brown, Sir Peter Randolph, Kt.
Brown, *Rt. Hon.* Sir Stephen, GBE
Brown, Sir Stephen David Reid, KCVO
Browne, Sir Nicholas Walker, KBE, CMG
Brownrigg, Sir Nicholas (Gawen), Bt. (1816)
Browse, *Prof.* Sir Norman Leslie, Kt., MD, FRCS
Bruce, Sir (Francis) Michael Ian, Bt. (S. 1628)
Bruce-Clifton, Sir Hervey James Hugh, Bt. (1804)
Bruce-Gardner, Sir Robert Henry, Bt. (1945)
Brunner, Sir John Henry Kilian, Bt. (1895)
Brunton, Sir (Edward Francis) Lauder, Bt. (1908)
Brunton, Sir Gordon Charles, Kt.
Bryan, Sir Arthur, Kt.
Buchan-Hepburn, Sir John Alastair Trant Kidd, Bt. (1815)
Buchanan, Sir Andrew George, Bt. (1878)
Buchanan, *Vice-Adm.* Sir Peter William, KBE
Buchanan, Sir Robert Wilson (Robin), Kt.
Buchanan-Jardine, *Maj.* Sir (Andrew) Rupert (John), Bt. (1885), MC
Buckland, Sir Ross, Kt.
Buckley, Sir Michael Sidney, Kt.
Buckley, *Lt.-Cdr.* Sir (Peter) Richard, KCVO
Buckley, *Hon.* Sir Roger John, Kt.
Buckworth-Herne-Soame, Sir Charles John, Bt. (1697)
Budd, Sir Alan Peter, Kt.
Budd, Sir Colin Richard, KCMG
Bull, Sir George Jeffrey, Kt.
Bull, Sir Simeon George, Bt. (1922)
Bullock, Sir Stephen Michael, Kt.
Bultin, Sir Bato, Kt., MBE
Bunbury, Sir Michael William, Bt. (1681), KCVO
Bunch, Sir Austin Wyeth, Kt., CBE
Bunyard, Sir Robert Sidney, Kt., CBE, QPM
Burbidge, Sir Peter Dudley, Bt. (1916)
Burden, Sir Anthony Thomas, Kt., QPM
Burdett, Sir Savile Aylmer, Bt. (1665)
Burgen, Sir Arnold Stanley Vincent, Kt., FRS
Burgess, *Gen.* Sir Edward Arthur, KCB, OBE
Burgess, Sir (Joseph) Stuart, Kt., CBE, PHD, FRSC
Burgh, Sir John Charles, KCMG, CB
Burke, Sir James Stanley Gilbert, Bt. (I. 1797)
Burke, Sir (Thomas) Kerry, Kt.
Burnell-Nugent, *Vice-Adm.* Sir James Michael, KCB, CBE, ADC
Burnet, Sir James William Alexander (Sir Alastair Burnet), Kt.
Burnett, *Air Chief Marshal* Sir Brian Kenyon, GCB, DFC, AFC
Burnett, Sir Charles David, Bt., (1913)
Burnett, Sir Walter John, Kt.
Burney, Sir Nigel Dennistoun, Bt. (1921)
Burns, Sir (Robert) Andrew, KCMG

Burnton, *Hon.* Sir Stanley Jeffrey, Kt.
Burrell, Sir John Raymond, Bt. (1774)
Burridge, *Air Chief Marshal* Sir Brian Kevin, KCB, CBE, ADC
Burston, Sir Samuel Gerald Wood, Kt., OBE
Burt, Sir Peter Alexander, Kt.
Burton, Sir Carlisle Archibald, Kt., OBE
Burton, Sir George Vernon Kennedy, Kt., CBE
Burton, *Lt.-Gen.* Sir Edmund Fortescue Gerard, KBE
Burton, Sir Graham Stuart, KCMG
Burton, *Hon.* Sir Michael John, Kt.
Burton, Sir Michael St Edmund, KCVO, CMG
Bush, *Adm.* Sir John Fitzroy Duyland, GCB, DSC
Butler, *Rt. Hon.* Sir Adam Courtauld, Kt.
Butler, *Hon.* Sir Arlington Griffith, KCMG
Butler, Sir Michael Dacres, GCMG
Butler, Sir (Reginald) Michael (Thomas), Bt. (1922)
Butler, Sir Percy James, Kt., CBE
Butler, *Hon.* Sir Richard Clive, Kt.
Butler, Sir Richard Pierce, Bt. (1628)
Butter, *Maj.* Sir David Henry, KCVO, MC
Butterfield, *Hon.* Sir Alexander Neil Logie, Kt.
Butterfill, Sir John Valentine, Kt.
Buxton, Sir Jocelyn Charles Roden, Bt. (1840)
Buxton, *Rt. Hon.* Sir Richard Joseph, Kt.
Buzzard, Sir Anthony Farquhar, Bt. (1929)
Byatt, Sir Hugh Campbell, KCVO, CMG
Byatt, Sir Ian Charles Rayner, Kt.
Byford, Sir Lawrence, Kt., CBE, QPM
Byron, *Rt. Hon.* Sir Charles Michael Dennis, Kt.
†Cable-Alexander, Sir Patrick Desmond William, Bt. (1809)
Cadbury, Sir (George) Adrian (Hayhurst), Kt.
Cadbury, Sir (Nicholas) Dominic, Kt.
Cadogan, *Prof.* Sir John Ivan George, Kt., CBE, FRS, FRSE
Cahn, Sir Albert Jonas, Bt. (1934)
Cain, Sir Henry Edney Conrad, Kt.
Caine, Sir Michael (Maurice Micklewhite), Kt., CBE
Caines, Sir John, KCB
Caldwell, Sir Edward George, KCB
Callaghan, Sir William Henry, Kt.
Callan, Sir Ivan Roy, KCVO, CMG
Calman, *Prof.* Sir Kenneth Charles, KCB, MD, FRCP, FRCS, FRSE
Calne, *Prof.* Sir Roy Yorke, Kt., FRS
Calvert-Smith, Sir David, Kt., QC
Cameron, Sir Hugh Roy Graham, Kt., QPM
Campbell, Sir Alan Hugh, GCMG
Campbell, *Prof.* Sir Colin Murray, Kt.
Campbell, Sir Ian Tofts, Kt., CBE, VRD
Campbell, Sir Ilay Mark, Bt. (1808)
Campbell, Sir James Alexander Moffat Bain, Bt. (S. 1668)
Campbell, Sir Lachlan Philip Kemeys, Bt. (1815)
Campbell, Sir Roderick Duncan Hamilton, Bt. (1831)
Campbell, Sir Robin Auchinbreck, Bt. (S. 1628)
Campbell, *Rt. Hon.* Sir Walter Menzies, Kt., CBE, QC
Campbell, *Rt. Hon.* Sir William Anthony, Kt.
Campbell-Orde, Sir John Alexander, Bt. (1790)
†Carden, Sir Christopher Robert, Bt. (1887)
Carden, Sir John Craven, Bt. (I. 1787)
Carew, Sir Rivers Verain, Bt. (1661)
Carey, Sir de Vic Graham, Kt.
Carey, Sir Peter Willoughby, GCB
Carleton-Smith, *Maj.-Gen.* Sir Michael Edward, Kt., CBE
Carlisle, Sir James Beethoven, GCMG
Carlisle, Sir John Michael, Kt.
Carlisle, Sir Kenneth Melville, Kt.
Carnegie, *Lt.-Gen.* Sir Robin Macdonald, KCB, OBE
Carnegie, Sir Roderick Howard, Kt.
Carnwath, *Rt. Hon.* Sir Robert John Anderson, Kt., CVO
Caro, Sir Anthony Alfred, Kt., OM, CBE
Carr, Sir (Albert) Raymond (Maillard), Kt.
Carr, Sir Peter Derek, Kt., CBE
Carr, *Very Revd Dr* Arthur Wesley, KCVO
Carr-Ellison, *Col.* Sir Ralph Harry, KCVO, TD
Carrick, *Hon.* Sir John Leslie, KCMG
Carrick, Sir Roger John, KCMG, LVO
Carruthers, Sir Ian James, Kt., OBE
Carsberg, *Prof.* Sir Bryan Victor, Kt.
Carter, *Prof.* Sir David Craig, Kt., FRCSE, FRCSGLAS, FRCPE
Carter, Sir John Alexander, Kt.
Carter, Sir John Gordon Thomas, Kt.
Carter, Sir Philip David, Kt., CBE
Carter, Sir Richard Henry Alwyn, Kt.
Cartland, Sir George Barrington, Kt., CMG
Cartledge, Sir Bryan George, KCMG
Cary, Sir Roger Hugh, Bt. (1955)
Casey, *Rt. Hon.* Sir Maurice Eugene, Kt.
Cass, Sir Geoffrey Arthur, Kt.
Cassel, Sir Timothy Felix Harold, Bt. (1920)
Cassels, Sir John Seton, Kt., CB
Cassels, *Adm.* Sir Simon Alastair Cassillis, KCB, CBE
Cassidi, *Adm.* Sir (Arthur) Desmond, GCB
Castell, Sir William Martin, Kt.
Castledine, *Prof.* Sir George, Kt.
Catford, Sir (John) Robin, KCVO, CBE
Catherwood, Sir (Henry) Frederick (Ross), Kt.
Catto, *Prof.* Sir Graeme Robertson Dawson, Kt.
Cave, Sir John Charles, Bt. (1896)
Cave-Browne-Cave, Sir Robert, Bt. (1641)
Cayley, Sir Digby William David, Bt. (1661)
Cayzer, Sir James Arthur, Bt. (1904)
Cazalet, *Hon.* Sir Edward Stephen, Kt.
Cazalet, Sir Peter Grenville, Kt.
Cecil, *Rear-Adm.* Sir (Oswald) Nigel Amherst, KBE, CB
Chadwick, *Revd Prof.* Henry, KBE
Chadwick, *Rt. Hon.* Sir John Murray, Kt.
Chadwick, Sir Joshua Kenneth Burton, Bt. (1935)
Chadwick, *Revd Prof.* (William) Owen, OM, KBE, FBA
Chadwyck-Healey, Sir Charles Edward, Bt. (1919)
Chakrabarti, Sir Sumantra, KCB
Chalmers, Sir Iain Geoffrey, Kt.
Chalmers, Sir Neil Robert, Kt.
Chalstrey, Sir (Leonard) John, Kt., MD, FRCS
Chan, *Rt. Hon.* Sir Julius, GCMG, KBE
Chan, Sir Thomas Kok, Kt., OBE
Chance, Sir (George) Jeremy ffolliott, Bt. (1900)
Chandler, Sir Colin Michael, Kt.
Chandler, Sir Geoffrey, Kt., CBE
Chantler, *Prof.* Sir Cyril, Kt., MD, FRCP
Chaplin, Sir Malcolm Hilbery, Kt., CBE
Chapman, Sir David Robert Macgowan, Bt. (1958)
Chapman, Sir George Alan, Kt.
Chapman, Sir Sidney Brookes, Kt., MP
Chapple, *Field Marshal* Sir John Lyon, GCB, CBE
Charles, *Hon.* Sir Arthur William Hessin, Kt.
Charles, Sir George Frederick Lawrence, KCMG, CBE
Charlton, Sir Robert (Bobby), Kt., CBE
Charnley, Sir (William) John, Kt., CB, FRENG
Chataway, *Rt. Hon.* Sir Christopher, Kt.
Chatfield, Sir John Freeman, Kt., CBE
†Chaytor, Sir Bruce Gordon, Bt. (1831)
Checketts, *Sqn. Ldr.* Sir David John, KCVO
Checkland, Sir Michael, Kt.
Cheshire, *Air Chief Marshal* Sir John Anthony, KBE, CB
Chessells, Sir Arthur David (Tim), Kt.
Chesterton, Sir Oliver Sidney, Kt., MC
Chetwood, Sir Clifford Jack, Kt.

†Chetwynd, Sir Robin John Talbot, Bt. (1795)
Cheyne, Sir Patrick John Lister, Bt. (1908)
†Chichester, Sir James Henry Edward, Bt. (1641)
Chichester-Clark, Sir Robin, Kt.
Chilcot, *Rt. Hon.* Sir John Anthony, GCB
Child, Sir (Coles John) Jeremy, Bt. (1919)
Chilton, *Brig.* Sir Frederick Oliver, Kt., CBE, DSO
Chilwell, *Hon.* Sir Muir Fitzherbert, Kt.
Chinn, Sir Trevor Edwin, Kt., CVO
Chipperfield, Sir Geoffrey Howes, KCB
Chisholm, Sir John Alexander Raymond, Kt., FRENG
Chitty, Sir Thomas Willes, Bt. (1924)
Cholmeley, Sir Hugh John Frederick Sebastian, Bt. (1806)
Chow, Sir Chung Kong, Kt.
Chow, Sir Henry Francis, Kt., OBE
Christie, Sir George William Langham, Kt., CH
Christie, Sir William, Kt., MBE
Christopher, Sir Duncan Robin Carmichael, KBE, CMG
Chung, Sir Sze-yuen, GBE, FRENG
Clark, Sir Francis Drake, Bt. (1886)
Clark, Sir John Arnold, Kt.
Clark, Sir Jonathan George, Bt. (1917)
Clark, Sir Robert Anthony, Kt., DSC
Clark, Sir Terence Joseph, KBE, CMG, CVO
Clarke, *Rt. Hon.* Sir Anthony Peter, Kt.
Clarke, Sir Arthur Charles, Kt., CBE
Clarke, Sir (Charles Mansfield) Tobias, Bt. (1831)
Clarke, *Hon.* Sir Christopher Simon Courtenay Stephenson, Kt.
Clarke, Sir Christopher James, Kt., OBE
Clarke, *Hon.* Sir David Clive, Kt.
Clarke, Sir Ellis Emmanuel Innocent, GCMG
Clarke, Sir Jonathan Dennis, Kt.
Clarke, Sir Robert Cyril, Kt.
†Clarke, Sir Rupert Grant Alexander, Bt. (1882)
Clay, Sir Edward, KCMG
Clay, Sir Richard Henry, Bt. (1841)
Clayton, Sir David Robert, Bt. (1732)
Cleaver, Sir Anthony Brian, Kt.
Clementi, Sir David Cecil, Kt.
Cleminson, Sir James Arnold Stacey, KBE, MC
Clerk, Sir Robert Maxwell, Bt. (1679), OBE
Clerke, Sir John Edward Longueville, Bt. (1660)
Clifford, Sir Roger Joseph, Bt. (1887)
Clifford, Sir Timothy Peter Plint, Kt.
Clothier, Sir Cecil Montacute, KCB, QC
Clucas, Sir Kenneth Henry, KCB
Clutterbuck, *Vice-Adm.* Sir David Granville, KBE, CB
Coates, Sir Anthony Robert Milnes, Bt. (1911)
Coates, Sir David Frederick Charlton, Bt. (1921)
Coats, Sir Alastair Francis Stuart, Bt. (1905)
Coats, Sir William David, Kt.
Cochrane, Sir (Henry) Marc (Sursock), Bt. (1903)
Cockburn, Sir John Elliot, Bt. (S. 1671)
Cockburn-Campbell, Sir Alexander Thomas, Bt. (1821)
Cockshaw, Sir Alan, Kt., FRENG
†Codrington, Sir Christopher George Wayne, Bt. (1876)
Codrington, Sir William Alexander, Bt. (1721)
Coghill, Sir Patrick Kendal Farley, Bt. (1778)
Coghlin, *Hon.* Sir Patrick, Kt.
Cohen, Sir Edward, Kt.
Cohen, Sir Ivor Harold, Kt., CBE, TD
Cohen, *Prof.* Sir Philip, Kt., PHD, FRS
Cohen, Sir Ronald, Kt.
Cole, Sir (Robert) William, Kt.
Coleman, Sir Robert John, KCMG
Coleridge, *Hon.* Sir Paul James Duke, Kt.
Coles, Sir (Arthur) John, GCMG
Colfox, Sir (William) John, Bt. (1939)
Collett, Sir Christopher, GBE
Collett, Sir Ian Seymour, Bt. (1934)
Collins, Sir Alan Stanley, KCVO, CMG
Collins, *Hon.* Sir Andrew David, Kt.
Collins, Sir Bryan Thomas Alfred, Kt., OBE, QFSM
Collins, Sir John Alexander, Kt
Collins, Sir Kenneth Darlingston, Kt.
Collins, *Hon.* Sir Lawrence Antony, Kt.
Collyear, Sir John Gowen, Kt.
Colman, *Hon.* Sir Anthony David, Kt.
Colman, Sir Michael Jeremiah, Bt. (1907)
Colman, Sir Timothy, KG
Colquhoun of Luss, Sir Ivar Iain, Bt. (1786)
Colt, Sir Edward William Dutton, Bt. (1694)
Colthurst, Sir Charles St John, Bt. (1744)
Colvin, Sir Howard Montagu, Kt., CVO, CBE, FBA
Compton, *Rt. Hon.* Sir John George Melvin, KCMG
Conant, Sir John Ernest Michael, Bt. (1954)
Connell, *Hon.* Sir Michael Bryan, Kt.
Connery, Sir Sean, Kt.
Connor, Sir William Joseph, Kt.
Conran, Sir Terence Orby, Kt.
Cons, *Hon.* Sir Derek, Kt.
Constantinou, Sir Georkios, Kt., OBE
Conway, *Prof.* Sir Gordon Richard, KCMG, FRS
Cook, Sir Christopher Wymondham Rayner Herbert, Bt. (1886)
Cook, *Prof.* Sir Peter Frederic Chester, Kt.
Cooke, *Col.* Sir David William Perceval, Bt. (1661)
Cooke, Sir Howard Felix Hanlan, GCMG, GCVO
Cooke, *Hon.* Sir Jeremy Lionel, Kt.
Cooke, *Prof.* Sir Ronald Urwick, Kt.
Cooksey, Sir David James Scott, GBE, Kt.
Cooper, *Gen.* Sir George Leslie Conroy, GCB, MC
Cooper, Sir Henry, Kt.
Cooper, Sir Richard Adrian, Bt. (1905)
Cooper, *Maj.-Gen.* Sir Simon Christie, GCVO
Cooper, Sir William Daniel Charles, Bt. (1863)
Coote, Sir Christopher John, Bt. (I. 1621), *Premier Baronet of Ireland*
Copas, *Most Revd* Virgil, KBE
Copisarow, Sir Alcon Charles, Kt.
Corbett, *Maj.-Gen.* Sir Robert John Swan, KCVO, CB
Corby, Sir (Frederick) Brian, Kt.
Cordy-Simpson, *Lt.-Gen.* Sir Roderick Alexander, KBE, CB
Corfield, Sir Kenneth George, Kt., FRENG
Cormack, Sir Patrick Thomas, Kt.
Cornelius-Wheeler, Sir Charles, Kt., CMG
Corness, Sir Colin Ross, Kt.
Cornforth, Sir John Warcup, Kt., CBE, DPHIL, FRS
Corry, Sir James Michael, Bt. (1885)
Cortazzi, Sir (Henry Arthur) Hugh, GCMG
Cory, Sir (Clinton Charles) Donald, Bt. (1919)
Cory-Wright, Sir Richard Michael, Bt. (1903)
Cossons, Sir Neil, Kt., OBE
Cotter, Sir Patrick Laurence Delaval, Bt. (I. 1763)
Cotterell, Sir John Henry Geers, Bt. (1805)
Cotton, *Hon.* Sir Robert Carrington, KCMG
Cotton, Sir William Frederick, Kt., CBE
Cottrell, Sir Alan Howard, Kt., PHD, FRS, FRENG
†Cotts, Sir Richard Crichton Mitchell, Bt. (1921)
Couper, Sir James George, Bt. (1841)
Court, *Hon.* Sir Charles Walter Michael, KCMG, OBE
Courtenay, Sir Thomas Daniel, Kt.
Cousins, *Air Chief Marshal* Sir David, KCB, AFC
Coville, *Air Marshal* Sir Christopher Charles Cotton, KCB
Cowan, *Gen.* Sir Samuel, KCB, CBE
Coward, *Vice-Adm.* Sir John Francis, KCB, DSO
Cowen, *Rt. Hon. Prof.* Sir Zelman, GCMG, GCVO
Cowie, Sir Thomas (Tom), Kt., OBE
Cowper-Coles, Sir Sherard Louis, KCMG, LVO

Cox, Sir Alan George, Kt., CBE
Cox, *Prof.* Sir David Roxbee, Kt.
Cox, Sir Geoffrey Sandford, Kt., CBE
Cox, Sir George Edwin, Kt.
Cradock, *Rt. Hon.* Sir Percy, GCMG
Craft, *Prof.* Sir Alan William, Kt.
Craig, Sir (Albert) James (Macqueen), GCMG
Craig-Cooper, Sir (Frederick Howard) Michael, Kt., CBE, TD
Crane, *Hon.* Sir Peter Francis, Kt.
Crane, *Prof.* Sir Peter Robert, Kt.
Craufurd, Sir Robert James, Bt. (1781)
Craven, Sir John Anthony, Kt.
Craven, Sir Philip Lee, Kt., MBE
Crawford, *Prof.* Sir Frederick William, Kt., FRENG
Crawford, Sir Robert William Kenneth, Kt. CBE
Crawley-Boevey, Sir Thomas Michael Blake, Bt. (1784)
Crew, Sir (Michael) Edward, Kt., QPM
Crewe, *Prof.* Sir Ivor Martin, Kt.
Cresswell, *Hon.* Sir Peter John, Kt.
Crichton-Brown, Sir Robert, KCMG, CBE, TD
Crick, *Prof.* Sir Bernard, Kt.
Crisp, Sir John Charles, Bt. (1913)
Critchett, Sir Charles George Montague, Bt. (1908)
Crockett, Sir Andrew Duncan, Kt.
Croft, Sir Owen Glendower, Bt. (1671)
Croft, Sir Thomas Stephen Hutton, Bt. (1818)
†Crofton, Sir Hugh Denis, Bt. (1801)
Crofton, *Prof.* Sir John Wenman, Kt.
†Crofton, Sir Julian Malby, Bt. (1838)
Crompton, Sir Dan, Kt., CBE, QPM
Crosby, Sir James Robert, Kt.
Crossland, *Prof.* Sir Bernard, Kt., CBE, FRENG
Crossley, Sir Sloan Nicholas, Bt. (1909)
Crowe, Sir Brian Lee, KCMG
Cruickshank, Sir Donald Gordon, Kt.
Cruthers, Sir James Winter, Kt.
Cubbon, Sir Brian Crossland, GCB
Cubitt, Sir Hugh Guy, Kt., CBE
Cullen, Sir (Edward) John, Kt., FRENG
Culme-Seymour, Sir Michael Patrick, Bt. (1809)
Culpin, Sir Robert Paul, Kt.
Cummins, Sir Michael John Austin, Kt.
Cunliffe, *Prof.* Sir Barrington, Kt., CBE
Cunliffe, Sir David Ellis, Bt. (1759)
Cunliffe-Owen, Sir Hugo Dudley, Bt. (1920)
Cunningham, *Lt.-Gen.* Sir Hugh Patrick, KBE
Cunningham, Sir Roger Keith, Kt., CBE
Cunynghame, Sir Andrew David Francis, Bt. (S. 1702)
†Currie, Sir Donald Scott, Bt. (1847)
Curry, Sir Donald Thomas Younger, Kt., CBE
Curtain, Sir Michael, KBE
Curtis, Sir Barry John, Kt.
Curtis, *Hon.* Sir Richard Herbert, Kt.
Curtis, Sir William Peter, Bt. (1802)
Curtiss, *Air Marshal* Sir John Bagot, KCB, KBE
Curwen, Sir Christopher Keith, KCMG
Cuschieri, *Prof.* Sir Alfred, Kt.
Cutler, Sir Charles Benjamin, KBE
Dain, Sir David John Michael, KCVO
Dales, Sir Richard Nigel, KCVO
Dalrymple-Hay, Sir John Hugh, Bt. (1798)
†Dalrymple-White, Sir Jan Hew, Bt. (1926)
Dalton, *Vice-Adm.* Sir Geoffrey Thomas James Oliver, KCB
Dalton, *Prof.* Sir Howard, Kt.
Dalton, Sir Richard John, KCMG
Dalyell, Sir Tam (Thomas), Bt. (NS 1685)
Daniel, Sir John Sagar, Kt., DSC
Dankworth, Sir John, Kt., CBE
Dannatt, *Lt.-Gen.* Sir Francis Richard, KCB, CBE
Darby, Sir Peter Howard, Kt., CBE, QFSM
Darell, Sir Jeffrey Lionel, Bt. (1795), MC
Darling, Sir Clifford, GCVO
Darrington, Sir Michael John, Kt.
Dasgupta, *Prof.* Sir Partha Sarathi, Kt.
†Dashwood, Sir Edward John Francis, Bt. (1707), *Premier Baronet of Great Britain*
Dashwood, Sir Richard James, Bt. (1684)
Daunt, Sir Timothy Lewis Achilles, KCMG
Davenport-Handley, Sir David John, Kt., OBE
David, Sir Jean Marc, Kt., CBE, QC
David, *His Hon.* Sir Robin (Robert) Daniel George, Kt.
Davies, Sir Alan Seymour, Kt.
Davies, Sir (Charles) Noel, Kt.
Davies, *Prof.* Sir David Evan Naughton, Kt., CBE, FRS, FRENG
Davies, *Hon.* Sir (David Herbert) Mervyn, Kt., MC, TD
Davies, Sir David John, Kt.
Davies, Sir Frank John, Kt., CBE
Davies, *Prof.* Sir Graeme John, Kt., FRENG
Davies, Sir John Howard, Kt.
Davies, Sir John Michael, KCB
Davies, *Vice-Adm.* Sir Lancelot Richard Bell, KBE
Davies, Sir Peter Maxwell, Kt., CBE
Davies, Sir Rhys Everson, Kt., QC
Davis, Sir Andrew Frank, Kt., CBE
Davis, Sir Colin Rex, Kt., CH, CBE
Davis, Sir Crispin Henry Lamert, Kt.
Davis, Sir John Gilbert, Bt. (1946)
Davis, *Hon.* Sir Nigel Anthony Lambert, Kt.
Davis, Sir Peter John, Kt.
Davis, *Hon.* Sir Thomas Robert Alexander Harries, KBE
Davis-Goff, Sir Robert (William), Bt. (1905)
Davison, *Rt. Hon.* Sir Ronald Keith, GBE, CMG
†Davson, Sir George Trenchard Simon, Bt. (1927)
Dawanincura, Sir John Norbert, Kt., OBE
Dawbarn, Sir Simon Yelverton, KCVO, CMG
Dawson, *Hon.* Sir Daryl Michael, KBE, CB
Dawson, Sir Hugh Michael Trevor, Bt. (1920)
Dawtry, Sir Alan (Graham), Kt., CBE, TD
Day, Sir Derek Malcolm, KCMG
Day, *Air Chief Marshal* Sir John Romney, KCB, OBE, ADC
Day, Sir (Judson) Graham, Kt.
Day, Sir Michael John, Kt., OBE
Day, Sir Simon James, Kt.
Deane, *Hon.* Sir William Patrick, KBE
Dearlove, Sir Richard Billing, KCMG, OBE
de Bellaigue, Sir Geoffrey, GCVO
†Debenham, Sir Thomas Adam, Bt. (1931)
de Deney, Sir Geoffrey Ivor, KCVO
Deeny, *Hon.* Sir Donnell Justin Patrick, Kt.
de Hoghton, Sir (Richard) Bernard (Cuthbert), Bt. (1611)
De la Bère, Sir Cameron, Bt. (1953)
de la Rue, Sir Andrew George Ilay, Bt. (1898)
De Silva, Sir George Desmond Lorenz, Kt., QC
Dellow, Sir John Albert, Kt., CBE
Delves, *Lt.-Gen.* Sir Cedric Norman George, KBE
Denholm, Sir John Ferguson (Ian), Kt., CBE
Denison-Smith, *Lt.-Gen.* Sir Anthony Arthur, KBE
Denny, Sir Anthony Coningham de Waltham, Bt. (I. 1782)
Denny, Sir Charles Alistair Maurice, Bt. (1913)
Derbyshire, Sir Andrew George, Kt.
Derham, Sir Peter John, Kt.
de Trafford, Sir Dermot Humphrey, Bt. (1841)
Deverell, *Gen.* Sir John Freegard, KCB, OBE
Devesi, Sir Baddeley, GCMG, GCVO
De Ville, Sir Harold Godfrey Oscar, Kt., CBE
Devitt, Sir James Hugh Thomas, Bt. (1916)
de Waal, Sir (Constant Henrik) Henry, KCB, QC
Dewey, Sir Anthony Hugh, Bt. (1917)
De Witt, Sir Ronald Wayne, Kt.
Dhenin, *Air Marshal* Sir Geoffrey Howard, KBE, AFC, GM, MD
Dhrangadhara, HH Maharaja Shriraj Sahib of Halvad, KCIE

Dick-Lauder, Sir Piers Robert, Bt. (S. 1690)
Dickinson, Sir Harold Herbert, Kt.
Dilke, Sir Charles John Wentworth, Bt. (1862)
Dillwyn-Venables-Llewelyn, Sir John Michael, Bt. (1890)
Dixon, Sir Jeremy, Kt.
Dixon, Sir Jonathan Mark, Bt. (1919)
Djanogly, Sir Harry Ari Simon, Kt., CBE
Dobson, *Vice-Adm.* Sir David Stuart, KBE
Dodds, Sir Ralph Jordan, Bt. (1964)
Dollery, Sir Colin Terence, Kt.
Don-Wauchope, Sir Roger (Hamilton), Bt. (S. 1667)
Donald, Sir Alan Ewen, KCMG
Donald, *Air Marshal* Sir John George, KBE
Donaldson, *Prof.* Sir Liam Joseph, Kt.
Donne, *Hon.* Sir Gaven John, KBE
Donne, Sir John Christopher, Kt.
Donnelly, Sir Joseph Brian, KBE, CMG
Dorey, Sir Graham Martyn, Kt.
Dorman, Sir Philip Henry Keppel, Bt. (1923)
Doughty, Sir Graham Martin, Kt.
Doughty, Sir William Roland, Kt.
Douglas, *Hon.* Sir Roger Owen, Kt.
Dover, *Prof.* Sir Kenneth James, Kt., DLITT, FBA, FRSE
Dowell, Sir Anthony James, Kt., CBE
Dowling, Sir Robert, Kt.
Downes, Sir Edward Thomas, Kt., CBE
Downey, Sir Gordon Stanley, KCB
Downs, Sir Diarmuid, Kt., CBE, FRENG
Downward, *Maj.-Gen.* Sir Peter Aldcroft, KCVO, CB, DSO, DFC
Dowson, Sir Philip Manning, Kt., CBE, PRA
Doyle, Sir Reginald Derek Henry, Kt., CBE
D'Oyly, Sir Hadley Gregory Bt. (1663)
Drake, *Hon.* Sir (Frederick) Maurice, Kt., DFC
Drewry, *Lt.-Gen.* Sir Christopher Francis, KCB, CBE
Drinkwater, Sir John Muir, Kt., QC
Driver, Sir Eric William, Kt.
Drury, Sir (Victor William) Michael, Kt., OBE
Dryden, Sir John Stephen Gyles, Bt. (1733 and 1795)
du Cann, *Rt. Hon.* Sir Edward Dillon Lott, KBE
†Duckworth, Sir James Edward Dyce, Bt. (1909)
du Cros, Sir Claude Philip Arthur Mallet, Bt. (1916)
Dudley-Williams, Sir Alastair Edgcumbe James, Bt. (1964)
Duff, *Prof.* Sir Gordon William, Kt.
Duff-Gordon, Sir Andrew Cosmo Lewis, Bt. (1813)
Duffell, *Lt.-Gen.* Sir Peter Royson, KCB, CBE, MC
Duffy, Sir (Albert) (Edward) Patrick, Kt., PHD
Dugdale, Sir William Stratford, Bt. (1936), MC
Duggin, Sir Thomas Joseph, Kt.
Dummett, *Prof.* Sir Michael Anthony Eardley, Kt., FBA
Dunbar, Sir Archibald Ranulph, Bt. (S. 1700)
Dunbar, Sir Robert Drummond Cospatrick, Bt. (S. 1698)
Dunbar, Sir James Michael, Bt. (S. 1694)
Dunbar of Hempriggs, Sir Richard Francis, Bt. (S. 1706)
Dunbar-Nasmith, *Prof.* Sir James Duncan, Kt., CBE
Duncan, Sir James Blair, Kt.
Dunlop, Sir Thomas, Bt. (1916)
Dunn, *Air Marshal* Sir Eric Clive, KBE, CB, BEM
Dunn, *Rt. Hon.* Sir Robin Horace Walford, Kt., MC
Dunne, Sir Thomas Raymond, KCVO
Dunning, Sir Simon William Patrick, Bt. (1930)
Dunnington-Jefferson, Sir Mervyn Stewart, Bt. (1958)
Dunstan, *Lt.-Gen.* Sir Donald Beaumont, KBE, CB
Dunt, *Vice-Adm.* Sir John Hugh, KCB
Duntze, Sir Daniel Evans Bt. (1774)
Dupre, Sir Tumun, Kt., MBE
Dupree, Sir (Thomas William James) David, Bt. (1921)
Durand, Sir Edward Alan Christopher David Percy, Bt. (1892)
Durant, Sir (Robert) Anthony (Bevis), Kt.
Durie, Sir David Robert Campbell, KCMG
Durrant, Sir William Alexander Estridge, Bt. (1784)
Duthie, *Prof.* Sir Herbert Livingston, Kt.
Duthie, Sir Robert Grieve (Robin), Kt., CBE
Dwyer, Sir Joseph Anthony, Kt.
Dyke, Sir David William Hart, Bt. (1677)
Dyson, Sir James, Kt., CBE
Dyson, *Rt. Hon.* Sir John Anthony, Kt.
Eady, *Hon.* Sir David, Kt.
Eardley-Wilmot, Sir Michael John Assheton, Bt. (1821)
Earle, Sir (Hardman) George (Algernon), Bt. (1869)
Easton, Sir Robert William Simpson, Kt., CBE
Eaton, *Adm.* Sir Kenneth John, GBE, KCB
Eberle, *Adm.* Sir James Henry Fuller, GCB
Ebrahim, Sir (Mahomed) Currimbhoy, Bt. (1910)
Eckersley, Sir Donald Payze, Kt., OBE
Eddington, Sir Roderick Ian, Kt.
Edge, *Capt.* Sir (Philip) Malcolm, KCVO
†Edge, Sir William, Bt. (1937)
Edmonstone, Sir Archibald Bruce Charles, Bt. (1774)
Edward, *Rt. Hon.* Sir David Alexander Ogilvy, KCMG
Edwardes, Sir Michael Owen, Kt.
Edwards, Sir Christopher John Churchill, Bt. (1866)
Edwards, Sir Llewellyn Roy, Kt.
Edwards, *Prof.* Sir Samuel Frederick, Kt., FRS
†Edwards-Moss, Sir David John, Bt. (1868)
Egan, Sir John Leopold, Kt.
Ehrman, Sir William Geoffrey, KCMG
Eichelbaum, *Rt. Hon.* Sir Thomas, GBE
Elias, *Hon.* Sir Patrick, Kt.
Eliott of Stobs, Sir Charles Joseph Alexander, Bt. (S. 1666)
Elliot, Sir Gerald Henry, Kt.
Elliott, Sir Clive Christopher Hugh, Bt. (1917)
Elliott, Sir David Murray, KCMG, CB
Elliott, *Prof.* Sir John Huxtable, Kt., FBA
Elliott, Sir Randal Forbes, KBE
Elliott, *Prof.* Sir Roger James, Kt., FRS
Elphinstone, Sir John, Bt. (S. 1701)
Elphinstone, Sir John Howard Main, Bt. (1816)
Elsmore, Sir Lloyd, Kt., OBE
Elton, Sir Arnold, Kt., CBE
Elton, Sir Charles Abraham Grierson, Bt. (1717)
Elton, Sir Leslie, Kt.
Elvidge, Sir John, KCB
Elwes, Sir Jeremy Vernon, Kt., CBE
Elwood, Sir Brian George Conway, Kt., CBE
Elworthy, *Air Cdre. Hon.* Sir Timothy Charles, KCVO, CBE
Empey, Sir Reginald Norman Morgan, Kt., OBE
Enderby, *Prof.* Sir John Edwin, Kt. CBE, FRS
Engle, Sir George Lawrence Jose, KCB, QC
English, Sir Terence Alexander Hawthorne, KBE, FRCS
Epstein, *Prof.* Sir (Michael) Anthony, Kt., CBE, FRS
Errington, *Col.* Sir Geoffrey Frederick, Bt. (1963), OBE
Errington, Sir Lancelot, KCB
Erskine, Sir (Thomas) Peter Neil, Bt. (1821)
Erskine-Hill, Sir Alexander Rodger, Bt. (1945)
Esmonde, Sir Thomas Francis Grattan, Bt. (I. 1629)
Esplen, Sir John Graham, Bt. (1921)
Essenhigh, *Adm.* Sir Nigel Richard, GCB
Etherton, *Hon.* Sir Terence Michael Elkan Barnet, Kt.
Evans, Sir Anthony Adney, Bt. (1920)
Evans, *Rt. Hon.* Sir Anthony Howell Meurig, Kt., RD

Evans, *Prof.* Sir Christopher Thomas, Kt., OBE
Evans, *Air Chief Marshal* Sir David George, GCB, CBE
Evans, *Hon.* Sir David Roderick, Kt.
Evans, Sir Harold Matthew, Kt.
Evans, *Hon.* Sir Haydn Tudor, Kt.
Evans, *Prof.* Sir John Grimley, Kt., FRCP
Evans, Sir John Stanley, Kt., QPM
Evans, *Prof.* Sir Martin John, Kt., FRS
Evans, Sir Richard Harry, Kt., CBE
Evans, Sir Richard Mark, KCMG, KCVO
Evans, Sir Robert, Kt., CBE, FRENG
Evans-Lombe, *Hon.* Sir Edward Christopher, Kt.
†Evans-Tipping, Sir David Gwynne, Bt. (1913)
Eveleigh, *Rt. Hon.* Sir Edward Walter, Kt., ERD
Everard, Sir Robin Charles, Bt. (1911)
Every, Sir Henry John Michael, Bt. (1641)
Ewans, Sir Martin Kenneth, KCMG
†Ewart, Sir William Michael, Bt. (1887)
Ewbank, *Hon.* Sir Anthony Bruce, Kt.
Eyre, Sir Reginald Edwin, Kt.
Eyre, Sir Richard Charles Hastings, Kt., CBE
Faber, Sir Richard Stanley, KCVO, CMG
Fagge, Sir John Christopher Frederick, Bt. (1660)
Fairbairn, Sir (James) Brooke, Bt. (1869)
Fairhall, *Hon.* Sir Allen, KBE
Fairlie-Cuninghame, Sir Robert Henry, Bt. (S. 1630)
Fairweather, Sir Patrick Stanislaus, KCMG
Falconer, *Hon.* Sir Douglas William, Kt., MBE
†Falkiner, Sir Benjamin Simon Patrick, Bt. (I. 1778)
Fall, Sir Brian James Proetel, GCVO, KCMG
Falle, Sir Samuel, KCMG, KCVO, DSC
Fang, *Prof.* Sir Harry, Kt., CBE
Fareed, Sir Djamil Sheik, Kt.
Farmer, Sir Thomas, Kt., CBE
Farquhar, Sir Michael Fitzroy Henry, Bt. (1796)
Farquharson, *Rt. Hon.* Sir Donald Henry, Kt.
Farrell, Sir Terence, Kt., CBE
Farrer, Sir (Charles) Matthew, GCVO
Farrington, Sir Henry William, Bt. (1818)
Fat, Sir (Maxime) Edouard (Lim Man) Lim, Kt.
Faulkner, Sir (James) Dennis (Compton), Kt., CBE, VRD
Fay, Sir (Humphrey) Michael Gerard, Kt.
Fayrer, Sir John Lang Macpherson, Bt. (1896)
Feachem, *Prof.* Sir Richard George Andrew, KBE
Fean, Sir Thomas Vincent, KCVO
Feilden, Sir Bernard Melchior, Kt., CBE
Feilden, Sir Henry Wemyss, Bt., (1846)
Fell, Sir David, KCB
Fender, Sir Brian Edward Frederick, Kt., CMG, PHD
Fenn, Sir Nicholas Maxted, GCMG
Fennell, *Hon.* Sir (John) Desmond Augustine, Kt., OBE
Fennessy, Sir Edward, Kt., CBE
Fergus, Sir Howard Archibald, KBE
Ferguson, Sir Alexander Chapman, Kt., CBE
Ferguson-Davie, Sir Michael, Bt. (1847)
Fergusson of Kilkerran, Sir Charles, Bt. (S. 1703)
Fergusson, Sir Ewan Alastair John, GCMG, GCVO
Fermor, Sir Patrick Michael Leigh, Kt., DSO, OBE
Feroze, Sir Rustam Moolan, Kt., FRCS
Fersht, *Prof.* Sir Alan Roy, Kt., FRS
Ferris, *Hon.* Sir Francis Mursell, Kt., TD
ffolkes, Sir Robert Francis Alexander, Bt. (1774), OBE
Field, Sir Malcolm David, Kt.
Field, *Hon.* Sir Richard Alan, Kt.
Fielding, Sir Colin Cunningham, Kt., CB
Fielding, Sir Leslie, KCMG
Fields, Sir Allan Clifford, KCMG
Fieldsend, *Hon.* Sir John Charles Rowell, KBE
Fiennes, Sir Ranulph Twisleton-Wykeham, Bt. (1916), OBE
Figg, Sir Leonard Clifford William, KCMG
Figgis, Sir Anthony St John Howard, KCVO, CMG
Finch, Sir Robert Gerard, Kt.
Finlay, Sir David Ronald James Bell, Bt. (1964)
Finlayson, Sir Garet Orlando, KCMG, OBE
Finney, Sir Thomas, Kt., OBE
Fison, Sir (Richard) Guy, Bt. (1905), DSC
Fitzalan-Howard, *Maj.-Gen.* Lord Michael, GCVO, CB, CBE, MC
†Fitzgerald, *Revd* Daniel Patrick, Bt. (1903)
FitzGerald, Sir Adrian James Andrew, Bt. (1880)
FitzHerbert, Sir Richard Ranulph, Bt. (1784)
Fitzpatrick, *Air Marshal* Sir John Bernard, KBE, CB
Flanagan, Sir Ronald, GBE
Fletcher, Sir James Muir Cameron, Kt.
Floissac, *Hon.* Sir Vincent Frederick, Kt., CMG, OBE
Floud, *Prof.* Sir Roderick Castle, Kt.
Floyd, Sir Giles Henry Charles, Bt. (1816)
Foley, *Lt.-Gen.* Sir John Paul, KCB, OBE, MC
Follett, *Prof.* Sir Brian Keith, Kt., FRS
Foot, Sir Geoffrey James, Kt.
Foots, Sir James William, Kt.
Forbes, *Maj.* Sir Hamish Stewart, Bt. (1823), MBE, MC
Forbes, *Adm.* Sir Ian Andrew, KCB, CBE
Forbes of Craigievar, Sir Andrew Iain Ochoncar, Bt. (S. 1630)
Forbes, *Vice-Adm.* Sir John Morrison, KCB
Forbes, *Hon.* Sir Thayne John, Kt.
Forbes-Leith, Sir George Ian David, Bt. (1923)
Ford, Sir Andrew Russell, Bt. (1929)
Ford, Sir David Robert, KBE, LVO
Ford, *Prof.* Sir Hugh, Kt., FRS, FRENG
Ford, Sir John Archibald, KCMG, MC
Ford, *Gen.* Sir Robert Cyril, GCB, CBE
Foreman, Sir Philip Frank, Kt., CBE, FRENG
Forestier-Walker, Sir Michael Leolin, Bt. (1835)
Forman, Sir John Denis, Kt., OBE
Forrest, *Prof.* Sir (Andrew) Patrick (McEwen), Kt.
Forte, Hon. Sir Rocco John Vincent, Kt.
Forwood, Sir Peter Noel, Bt. (1895)
Foster, Sir Andrew William, Kt.
Foster, *Prof.* Sir Christopher David, Kt.
Foster, Sir John Gregory, Bt. (1930)
Foulkes, Sir Arther Alexander, KCMG
Foulkes, Sir Nigel Gordon, Kt.
Fountain, *Hon.* Sir Cyril Stanley Smith, Kt.
Fowden, Sir Leslie, Kt., FRS
Fowke, Sir David Frederick Gustavus, Bt. (1814)
Fowler, Sir (Edward) Michael Coulson, Kt.
Fox, Sir Christopher, Kt., QPM
Fox, Sir Paul Leonard, Kt., CBE
France, Sir Christopher Walter, GCB
Francis, Sir Horace William Alexander, Kt., CBE, FRENG
Frank, Sir Robert Andrew, Bt. (1920)
Franklin, Sir Michael David Milroy, KCB, CMG
Franks, Sir Arthur Temple, KCMG
Fraser, Sir Alasdair MacLeod, Kt.
Fraser, Sir Charles Annand, KCVO
Fraser, *Gen.* Sir David William, GCB, OBE
Fraser, Sir Iain Michael Duncan, Bt. (1943)
Fraser, Sir James Murdo, KBE
Fraser, Sir William Kerr, GCB
Frayling, *Prof.* Sir Christopher John, Kt.
Frederick, Sir Christopher St John, Bt. (1723)
Freedman, *Prof.* Sir Lawrence David, KCMG, CBE
Freeland, Sir John Redvers, KCMG

Freeman, Sir James Robin, Bt. (1945)
Freer, *Air Chief Marshal* Sir Robert William George, GBE, KCB
French, *Air Marshal* Sir Joseph Charles, KCB, CBE
Frere, *Vice-Adm.* Sir Richard Tobias, KCB
Fretwell, Sir (Major) John (Emsley), GCMG
Freud, Sir Clement Raphael, Kt.
Friend *Prof.* Sir Richard Henry, Kt.
Froggatt, Sir Leslie Trevor, Kt.
Froggatt, Sir Peter, Kt.
Frossard, Sir Charles Keith, KBE
Frost, Sir David Paradine, Kt., OBE
Fry, Sir Graham Holbrook, KCMG
Fry, Sir Peter Derek, Kt.
Fry, *Lt.-Gen.* Sir Robert Allan, KCB, CBE
Fulford, *Hon.* Sir Adrian Bruce, Kt.
Fuller, Sir James Henry Fleetwood, Bt. (1910)
Fuller, *Hon.* Sir John Bryan Munro, Kt.
Fulton, *Lt.-Gen.* Sir Robert Henry Gervase, KBE
Furness, Sir Stephen Roberts, Bt. (1913)
Gage, *Rt. Hon.* Sir William Marcus, Kt.
Gains, Sir John Christopher, Kt.
Gainsford, Sir Ian Derek, Kt.
Gaius, *Rt. Revd* Saimon, KBE
Galsworthy, Sir Anthony Charles, KCMG
Galway, Sir James, Kt., OBE
Gamble, Sir David Hugh Norman, Bt. (1897)
Gambon, Sir Michael John, Kt., CBE
Gammell, Sir William Benjamin Bowring, Kt.
Gardiner, Sir John Eliot, Kt., CBE
Gardner, *Prof.* Sir Richard Lavenham, Kt.
Gardner, Sir Roy Alan, Kt.
Garland, *Hon.* Sir Patrick Neville, Kt.
Garland, *Hon.* Sir Ransley Victor, KBE
Garner, Sir Anthony Stuart, Kt.
Garnett, *Adm.* Sir Ian David Graham, KCB
Garnier, *Rear-Adm.* Sir John, KCVO, CBE
Garrard, Sir David Eardley, Kt.
Garrett, Sir Anthony Peter, Kt., CBE
Garrick, Sir Ronald, Kt., CBE, FRENG
Garrioch, Sir (William) Henry, Kt.
Garrod, *Lt.-Gen.* Sir (John) Martin Carruthers, KCB, OBE
Garthwaite, Sir (William) Mark (Charles), Bt. (1919)
Gaskell, Sir Richard Kennedy Harvey, Kt.
Geno, Sir Makena Viora, KBE
Gent, Sir Christopher Charles, Kt.
George, Sir Arthur Thomas, Kt.
George, *Prof.* Sir Charles Frederick, MD, FRCP
George, Sir Richard William, Kt., CVO
Gerken, *Vice-Adm.* Sir Robert William Frank, KCB, CBE
Gershon, Sir Peter Oliver, Kt., CBE
Gethin, Sir Richard Joseph St Lawrence, Bt. (I. 1665)
Ghurburrun, Sir Rabindrah, Kt.
Gibb, Sir Francis Ross (Frank), Kt., CBE, FRENG
Gibbings, Sir Peter Walter, Kt.
Gibbons, Sir (John) David, KBE
Gibbons, Sir William Edward Doran, Bt. (1752)
Gibbs, *Hon.* Sir Richard John Hedley, Kt.
Gibbs, Sir Roger Geoffrey, Kt.
†Gibson, *Revd* Christopher Herbert, Bt. (1931)
Gibson, Sir Ian, Kt., CBE
Gibson, *Rt. Hon.* Sir Peter Leslie, Kt.
Gibson-Craig-Carmichael, Sir David Peter William, Bt. (S. 1702 and 1831)
Giddings, *Air Marshal* Sir (Kenneth Charles) Michael, KCB, OBE, DFC, AFC
Gieve, Sir Edward John Watson, KCB
Giffard, Sir (Charles) Sydney (Rycroft), KCMG
Gilbart-Denham, *Lt.-Col.* Sir Seymour Vivian, KCVO
Gilbert, *Air Chief Marshal* Sir Joseph Alfred, KCB, CBE
Gilbert, Sir Martin John, Kt., CBE
†Gilbey, Sir Walter Gavin, Bt. (1893)
Gill, Sir Anthony Keith, Kt.
Gill, Sir Arthur Benjamin Norman, Kt., CBE
Gillam, Sir Patrick John, Kt.
Gillen, *Hon.* Sir John de Winter, Kt.
Gillett, Sir Robin Danvers Penrose, Bt. (1959), GBE, RD
Gillinson, Sir Clive Daniel, Kt., CBE
†Gilmour, Sir John, Bt. (1897)
Gina, Sir Lloyd Maepeza, KBE
Gingell, *Air Chief Marshal* Sir John, GBE, KCB, KCVO
Giordano, Sir Richard Vincent, KBE
Girolami, Sir Paul, Kt.
Girvan, *Rt. Hon.* Sir (Frederick) Paul, Kt.
Gladstone, Sir (Erskine) William, Bt. (1846), KG
Glenn, Sir (Joseph Robert) Archibald, Kt., OBE
Glidewell, *Rt. Hon.* Sir Iain Derek Laing, Kt.
Glover, Sir Victor Joseph Patrick, Kt.
Glyn, Sir Richard Lindsay, Bt. (1759 and 1800)
Gobbo, Sir James Augustine, Kt., AC
Godber, Sir George Edward, GCB, DM
Goldberg, *Prof.* Sir Abraham, Kt., MD, DSC, FRCP
Goldberg, *Prof.* Sir David Paul Brandes, Kt.
Goldring, *Hon.* Sir John Bernard, Kt.
Gomersall, Sir Stephen John, KCMG
Gonsalves-Sabola, *Hon.* Sir Joaquim Claudino, Kt
†Gooch, Sir Miles Peter, Bt. (1866)
Gooch, Sir Timothy Robert, Bt. (1746), MBE
Goodall, Sir (Arthur) David Saunders, GCMG
Goodall, *Air Marshal* Sir Roderick Harvey, KBE, CB, AFC
Goode, Prof. Sir Royston Miles, Kt., CBE, QC
Goodenough, Sir Anthony Michael, KCMG
Goodenough, Sir William McLernon, Bt. (1943)
Goodhart, Sir Philip Carter, Kt.
Goodhart, Sir Robert Anthony Gordon, Bt. (1911)
Goodison, Sir Nicholas Proctor, Kt.
Goodman, Sir Patrick Ledger, Kt., CBE
Goodson, Sir Mark Weston Lassam, Bt. (1922)
Goodwin, Sir Frederick, KBE
Goodwin, Sir Frederick Anderson, Kt.
Goodwin, Sir Matthew Dean, Kt., CBE
Goody, *Prof.* Sir John Rankine, Kt.
†Goold, Sir George William, Bt. (1801)
Gordon, Sir Charles Addison Somerville Snowden, KCB
Gordon, Sir Donald, Kt.
Gordon, Sir Gerald Henry, Kt., CBE, QC
Gordon, Sir Robert James, Bt. (S. 1706)
Gordon-Cumming, Sir Alexander Penrose, Bt. (1804)
†Gore, Sir Nigel Hugh St George, Bt. (I. 1622)
Gore-Booth, Sir Josslyn Henry Robert, Bt. (I. 1760)
Goring, Sir William Burton Nigel, Bt. (1627)
Gorman, Sir John Reginald, Kt., CVO, CBE, MC
Gorst, Sir John Michael, Kt.
Goschen, Sir (Edward) Alexander, Bt. (1916)
Gosling, Sir (Frederick) Donald, KCVO
Goswell, Sir Brian Lawrence, Kt.
Gough, Sir Charles Brandon, Kt.
Goulden, Sir (Peter) John, GCMG
Goulding, Sir Marrack Irvine, KCMG
Goulding, Sir (William) Lingard Walter, Bt. (1904)
Gourlay, *Gen.* Sir (Basil) Ian (Spencer), KCB, OBE, MC, RM
Gourlay, Sir Simon Alexander, Kt.
Govan, Sir Lawrence Herbert, Kt.
Gow, *Gen.* Sir (James) Michael, GCB
Gowans, Sir James Learmonth, Kt., CBE, FRCP, FRS
Gozney, Sir Richard Hugh Turton, KCMG
†Graaff, Sir David de Villiers, Bt. (1911)
Grabham, Sir Anthony Henry, Kt.
Graham, Sir Alexander Michael, GBE

Graham, Sir James Bellingham, Bt. (1662)
Graham, Sir James Fergus Surtees, Bt. (1783)
Graham, Sir James Thompson, Kt., CMG
Graham, Sir John Alexander Noble, Bt. (1906), GCMG
Graham, Sir John Alistair, Kt.
Graham, Sir John Moodie, Bt. (1964)
Graham, Sir Norman William, Kt., CB
Graham, Sir Peter, KCB, QC
Graham, Sir Peter Alfred, Kt., OBE
Graham, *Lt.-Gen.* Sir Peter Walter, KCB, CBE
†Graham, Sir Ralph Stuart, Bt. (1629)
Graham-Moon, Sir Peter Wilfred Giles, Bt. (1855)
Graham-Smith, *Prof.* Sir Francis, Kt.
Granger, *Prof.* Sir Clive William John, Kt.
Grant, Sir Archibald, Bt. (S. 1705)
Grant, Sir Clifford, Kt.
Grant, Sir (John) Anthony, Kt.
Grant, Sir John Douglas Kelso, KCMG
Grant, Sir Patrick Alexander Benedict, Bt. (S. 1688)
Grant, *Lt.-Gen.* Sir Scott Carnegie, KCB
Grant-Suttie, Sir James Edward, Bt. (S. 1702)
Granville-Chapman, *Lt.-Gen.* Sir Timothy John, GBE, KCB, ADC
Gratton-Bellew, Sir Henry Charles, Bt. (1838)
Gray, *Hon.* Sir Charles Anthony St John, Kt.
Gray, Sir Charles Ireland, Kt., CBE
Gray, *Prof.* Sir Denis John Pereira, Kt., OBE, FRCGP
Gray, Sir John Archibald Browne, Kt., SCD, FRS
Gray, *Dr.* Sir John Armstrong Muir, Kt., CBE
Gray, *Lt.-Gen.* Sir Michael Stuart, KCB, OBE
Gray, Sir Robert McDowall (Robin), Kt.
Gray, Sir William Hume, Bt. (1917)
Graydon, *Air Chief Marshal* Sir Michael James, GCB, CBE
Grayson, Sir Jeremy Brian Vincent Harrington, Bt. (1922)
Green, Sir Allan David, KCB, QC
Green, Sir Andrew Fleming, KCMG
Green, Sir Edward Patrick Lycett, Bt. (1886)
Green, Sir Gregory David, KCMG
Green, *Hon.* Sir Guy Stephen Montague, KBE
Green, Sir Kenneth, Kt.
Green, *Prof.* Sir Malcolm, Kt.
Green, Sir Owen Whitley, Kt.
Green, Sir Philip Green, Kt.
Green-Price, Sir Robert John, Bt. (1874)
Greenaway, Sir John Michael Burdick, Bt. (1933)
Greenbury, Sir Richard, Kt.
Greener, Sir Anthony Armitage, Kt.
Greengross, Sir Alan David, Kt.
Greening, *Rear-Adm.* Sir Paul Woollven, GCVO
Greenstock, Sir Jeremy Quentin, GCMG
Greenwell, Sir Edward Bernard, Bt. (1906)
Gregson, Sir Peter Lewis, GCB
Greig, Sir (Henry Louis) Carron, KCVO, CBE
Grey, Sir Anthony Dysart, Bt. (1814)
Grey-Egerton, Sir (Philip) John (Caledon), Bt. (1617)
Grierson, Sir Michael John Bewes, Bt. (S. 1685)
Grierson, Sir Ronald Hugh, Kt.
Griffin, *Maj.* Sir (Arthur) John (Stewart), KCVO
Griffiths, Sir Eldon Wylie, Kt.
Grigson, *Hon.* Sir Geoffrey Douglas, Kt.
Grimshaw, Sir Nicholas Thomas, Kt., CBE
Grimwade, Sir Andrew Sheppard, Kt., CBE
Grindrod, *Most Revd* John Basil Rowland, KBE
Grinstead, Sir Stanley Gordon, Kt.
Grose, *Vice-Adm.* Sir Alan, KBE
Gross, *Hon.* Sir Peter Henry, Kt.
Grossart, Sir Angus McFarlane McLeod, Kt., CBE
Grotrian, Sir Philip Christian Brent, Bt. (1934)
Grove, Sir Charles Gerald, Bt. (1874)
Grove, Sir Edmund Frank, KCVO
Grugeon, Sir John Drury, Kt.
Grundy, Sir Mark, Kt.
Guinness, Sir Howard Christian Sheldon, Kt., VRD
Guinness, Sir John Ralph Sidney, Kt., CB
Guinness, Sir Kenelm Ernest Lee, Bt. (1867)
†Guise, Sir Christopher James, Bt. (1783)
Gull, Sir Rupert William Cameron, Bt. (1872)
Gumbs, Sir Emile Rudolph, Kt.
Gunn, Sir Robert Norman, Kt.
†Gunning, Sir Charles Theodore, Bt. (1778)
Gunston, Sir John Wellesley, Bt. (1938)
Gurdon, *Prof.* Sir John Bertrand, Kt., DPHIL, FRS
Guthrie, Sir Malcolm Connop, Bt. (1936)
Haddacks, *Vice-Adm.* Sir Paul Kenneth, KCB
Hadfield, Sir Ronald, Kt., QPM
Hadlee, Sir Richard John, Kt., MBE
Hagart-Alexander, Sir Claud, Bt. (1886)
Hague, *Prof.* Sir Douglas Chalmers, Kt., CBE
Haines, *Prof.* Sir Andrew Paul, Kt.
Haji-Ioannou, Sir Stelios, Kt.
Halberg, Sir Murray Gordon, Kt., MBE
Hall, Sir Basil Brodribb, KCB, MC, TD
Hall, *Prof.* Sir David Michael Baldock, Kt.
Hall, Sir Ernest, Kt., OBE
Hall, Sir Graham Joseph, Kt.
Hall, Sir Iain Robert, Kt.
Hall, Sir (Frederick) John (Frank), Bt. (1923)
Hall, Sir John, Kt.
Hall, Sir John Bernard, Bt. (1919)
Hall, Sir John Douglas Hoste, Bt. (S. 1687)
Hall, Sir Peter Edward, KBE, CMG
Hall, *Prof.* Sir Peter Geoffrey, Kt., FBA
Hall, Sir Peter Reginald Frederick, Kt., CBE
Halliday, *Vice-Adm.* Sir Roy William, KBE, DSC
Halpern, Sir Ralph Mark, Kt.
Halsey, *Revd* John Walter Brooke, Bt. (1920)
Halstead, Sir Ronald, Kt., CBE
Hambling, Sir (Herbert) Hugh, Bt. (1924)
Hamilton, Sir Andrew Caradoc, Bt. (S. 1646)
Hamilton, Sir Edward Sydney, Bt. (1776 and 1819)
Hamilton, Sir James Arnot, KCB, MBE, FRENG
Hamilton-Dalrymple, *Maj.* Sir Hew Fleetwood, Bt. (S. 1697), GCVO
Hamilton-Spencer-Smith, Sir John, Bt. (1804)
Hammick, Sir Stephen George, Bt. (1834)
Hammond, Sir Anthony Hilgrove, KCB, QC
Hampel, Sir Ronald Claus, Kt.
Hampson, Sir Stuart, Kt.
Hampton, Sir (Leslie) Geoffrey, Kt.
Hampton, Sir Philip Roy, Kt.
Hanbury-Tenison, Sir Richard, KCVO
Hancock, Sir David John Stowell, KCB
Hanham, Sir Michael William, Bt. (1667), DFC
Hankes-Drielsma, Sir Claude Dunbar, KCVO
Hanley, *Rt. Hon.* Sir Jeremy James, KCMG
Hanmer, Sir John Wyndham Edward, Bt. (1774)
Hannam, Sir John Gordon, Kt.
Hanson, Sir (Charles) Rupert (Patrick), Bt. (1918)
Hanson, Sir John Gilbert, KCMG, CBE
Harcourt-Smith, *Air Chief Marshal* Sir David, GBE, KCB, DFC
Hardie Boys, *Rt. Hon.* Sir Michael, GCMG
Harding, Sir George William, KCMG, CVO
Harding, *Marshal of the Royal Air Force* Sir Peter Robin, GCB
Harding, Sir Roy Pollard, Kt., CBE
Hardy, Sir David William, Kt.
Hardy, Sir James Gilbert, Kt., OBE

Hardy, Sir Richard Charles Chandos, Bt. (1876)
Hare, Sir David, Kt., FRSL
Hare, Sir Nicholas Patrick, Bt. (1818)
Harford, Sir (John) Timothy, Bt. (1934)
Hargroves, *Brig.* Sir Robert Louis, Kt., CBE
Harington, Sir Nicholas John, Bt. (1611)
Harkness, *Very Revd* James, KCVO, CB, OBE
Harland, *Air Marshal* Sir Reginald Edward Wynyard, KBE, CB
Harley, *Gen.* Sir Alexander George Hamilton, KBE, CB
Harman, *Gen.* Sir Jack Wentworth, GCB, OBE, MC
Harman, *Hon.* Sir Jeremiah LeRoy, Kt.
Harman, Sir John Andrew, Kt.
Harmsworth, Sir Hildebrand Harold, Bt. (1922)
Harper, Sir Ewan William, Kt. CBE
Harper, *Prof.* Sir Peter Stanley, Kt., CBE
Harris, *Prof.* Sir Henry, Kt., FRCP, FRCPATH, FRS
Harris, Sir Jack Wolfred Ashford, Bt. (1932)
Harris, *Air Marshal* Sir John Hulme, KCB, CBE
Harris, *Prof.* Sir Martin Best, Kt., CBE
Harris, Sir Thomas George, KBE, CMG,
Harrison, *Prof.* Sir Brian Howard, Kt.
Harrison, Sir David, Kt., CBE, FRENG
Harrison, Sir Ernest Thomas, Kt., OBE
Harrison, *Surgeon Vice-Adm.* Sir John Albert Bews, KBE
Harrison, *Hon.* Sir Michael Guy Vicat, Kt.
Harrison, Sir Michael James Harwood, Bt. (1961)
Harrison, Sir (Robert) Colin, Bt. (1922)
Harrison, Sir Terence, Kt., FRENG
Harrop, Sir Peter John, KCB
Hart, *Hon.* Sir Anthony Ronald, Kt.
Hart, Sir David Michael, Kt., OBE
Hart, Sir Graham Allan, KCB
Hartwell, Sir (Francis) Anthony Charles Peter, Bt. (1805)
Harvey, Sir Charles Richard Musgrave, Bt. (1933)
Harvey-Jones, Sir John Henry, Kt., MBE
Harvie, Sir John Smith, Kt., CBE
Harvie-Watt, Sir James, Bt. (1945)
Haselhurst, *Rt. Hon.* Sir Alan Gordon Barraclough, Kt.
Haskard, Sir Cosmo Dugal Patrick Thomas, KCMG, MBE
Haslam, *Rear-Adm.* Sir David William, KBE, CB
Hassett, *Gen.* Sir Francis George, KBE, CB, DSO, LVO
Hastings, Sir Max Macdonald, Kt.
Hatter, Sir Maurice, Kt.
Havelock-Allan, Sir (Anthony) Mark David, Bt. (1858)
Hawkins, Sir Richard Caesar, Bt. (1778)
Hawley, Sir Donald Frederick, KCMG, MBE
†Hawley, Sir Henry Nicholas, Bt. (1795)
Haworth, Sir Philip, Bt. (1911)
Hawthorne, *Prof.* Sir William Rede, Kt., CBE, SCD, FRS, FRENG
Hay, Sir David Osborne, Kt., CBE, DSO
Hay, Sir David Russell, Kt., CBE, FRCP, MD
Hay, Sir Hamish Grenfell, Kt.
Hay, Sir John Erroll Audley, Bt. (S. 1663)
†Hay, Sir Ronald Frederick Hamilton, Bt. (S. 1703)
Hayes, Sir Brian, Kt., CBE, QPM
Hayes, Sir Brian David, GCB
Hayman-Joyce, *Lt.-Gen.* Sir Robert John, KCB, CBE
Hayter, Sir Paul David Grenville, KCB, LVO
Hayward, Sir Anthony William Byrd, Kt.
Hayward, Sir Jack Arnold, Kt., OBE
Haywood, Sir Harold, KCVO, OBE
Head, Sir Richard Douglas Somerville, Bt. (1838)
Heap, Sir Peter William, KCMG
Heap, *Prof.* Sir Robert Brian, Kt., CBE, FRS
Hearne, Sir Graham James, Kt., CBE
Heathcote, *Brig.* Sir Gilbert Simon, Bt. (1733), CBE
†Heathcote, Sir Timothy Gilbert, Bt. (1733)
Heatley, Sir Peter, Kt., CBE
Hedley, *Hon.* Sir Mark, Kt.
Hegarty, Sir John Kevin, Kt.
Heiser, Sir Terence Michael, GCB
Henao, Revd Ravu, Kt., OBE
Henderson, Sir Denys Hartley, Kt.
Henderson, Sir (John) Nicholas, GCMG, KCVO
Henderson, *Hon.* Sir Launcelot Dinadan James, Kt.
Henderson, *Maj.* Sir Richard Yates, KCVO
Hennessy, Sir James Patrick Ivan, KBE, CMG
†Henniker, Sir Adrian Chandos, Bt. (1813)
Henniker-Heaton, Sir Yvo Robert, Bt. (1912)
Henriques, *Hon.* Sir Richard Henry Quixano, Kt.
Henry, *Rt. Hon.* Sir Denis Robert Maurice, Kt.
Henry, *Hon.* Sir Geoffrey Arama, KBE
†Henry, Sir Patrick Denis, Bt. (1923)
Henry, *Hon.* Sir Trevor Ernest, Kt.
Henshaw, Sir David George, Kt.
Hepple, *Prof.* Sir Bob Alexander, Kt.
Herbecq, Sir John Edward, KCB
Herbert, *Adm.* Sir Peter Geoffrey Marshall, KCB, OBE
Hermon, Sir John Charles, Kt., OBE, QPM
Heron, Sir Conrad Frederick, KCB, OBE
Heron, Sir Michael Gilbert, Kt.
Heron-Maxwell, Sir Nigel Mellor, Bt. (S. 1683)
Hervey, Sir Roger Blaise Ramsay, KCVO, CMG
Hervey-Bathurst, Sir Frederick John Charles Gordon, Bt. (1818)
Heseltine, *Rt. Hon.* Sir William Frederick Payne, GCB, GCVO
Hewetson, Sir Christopher Raynor, Kt., TD
Hewett, Sir Richard Mark John, Bt. (1813)
Hewitt, Sir (Cyrus) Lenox (Simson), Kt., OBE
Hewitt, Sir Nicholas Charles Joseph, Bt. (1921)
Heygate, Sir Richard John Gage, Bt. (1831)
Heywood, Sir Peter, Bt. (1838)
Hezlet, *Vice-Adm.* Sir Arthur Richard, KBE, CB, DSO, DSC
Hibbert, Sir Jack, KCB
Hickey, Sir Justin, Kt.
Hickman, Sir (Richard) Glenn, Bt. (1903)
Hicks, Sir Robert, Kt.
Hidden, *Hon.* Sir Anthony Brian, Kt.
Hielscher, Sir Leo Arthur, Kt.
Higgins, *Rt. Hon.* Sir Malachy Joseph, Kt.
Higginson, Sir Gordon Robert, Kt., PHD, FRENG
Higgs, Sir Derek Alan, Kt.
Hill, Sir Arthur Alfred, Kt., CBE
Hill, Sir Brian John, Kt.
Hill, Sir James Frederick, Bt. (1917)
Hill, Sir John Alfred Rowley, Bt. (I 1779)
Hill, Sir John McGregor, Kt., PHD, FRENG
Hill, *Vice-Adm.* Sir Robert Charles Finch, KBE, FRENG
Hill-Norton, *Vice-Adm. Hon.* Sir Nicholas John, KCB
Hill-Wood, Sir Samuel Thomas, Bt. (1921)
Hillary, Sir Edmund, KG, KBE
Hillhouse, Sir (Robert) Russell, KCB
Hills, Sir Graham John, Kt.
Hine, *Air Chief Marshal* Sir Patrick Bardon, GCB, GBE
Hirsch, *Prof.* Sir Peter Bernhard, Kt., PHD., FRS
Hirst, *Rt. Hon.* Sir David Cozens-Hardy, Kt.
Hirst, Sir Michael William, Kt.
Hoare, *Prof.* Sir Charles Anthony Richard, Kt., FRS
Hoare, Sir David John, Bt. (1786)
Hoare, Sir Timothy Edward Charles, Bt. (I. 1784), OBE
Hobart, Sir John Vere, Bt. (1914)
Hobbs, *Maj.-Gen.* Sir Michael Frederick, KCVO, CBE
Hobday, Sir Gordon Ivan, Kt.
Hobhouse, Sir Charles John Spinney, Bt. (1812)

Hobson, Sir Ronald, KCVO
†Hodge, Sir Andrew Rowland, Bt. (1921)
Hodge, *Hon.* Sir Henry Egar Garfield, Kt.
Hodge, Sir James William, KCVO, CMG
Hodgkin, Sir (Gordon) Howard (Eliot), Kt., CH, CBE
Hodgkinson, Sir Michael Stewart, Kt.
Hodgkinson, *Air Chief Marshal* Sir (William) Derek, KCB, CBE, DFC, AFC
Hodgson, Sir Maurice Arthur Eric, Kt., FRENG
Hodson, Sir Michael Robin Adderley, Bt. (I. 1789)
Hogg, Sir Christopher Anthony, Kt.
†Hogg, Sir Piers Michael James, Bt. (1846)
Holcroft, Sir Peter George Culcheth, Bt. (1921)
Holderness, Sir Martin William, Bt. (1920)
Holden, Sir Paul, Bt. (1893)
Holden, Sir John David, Bt. (1919)
Holden-Brown, Sir Derrick, Kt.
Holder, Sir John Henry, Bt. (1898)
Holdgate, Sir Martin Wyatt, Kt., CB, PHD
Holdsworth, Sir (George) Trevor, Kt., CVO
Holland, *Hon.* Sir Alan Douglas, Kt.
Holland, *Hon.* Sir Christopher John, Kt.
Holland, Sir Clifton Vaughan, Kt.
Holland, Sir Geoffrey, KCB
Holland, Sir John Anthony, Kt.
Holland, Sir Philip Welsby, Kt.
Holliday, *Prof.* Sir Frederick George Thomas, Kt., CBE, FRSE
Hollings, *Hon.* Sir (Alfred) Kenneth, Kt., MC
Hollom, Sir Jasper Quintus, KBE
Holloway, *Hon.* Sir Barry Blyth, KBE
Holman, *Hon.* Sir (Edward) James, Kt.
Holmes, *Prof.* Sir Frank Wakefield, Kt.
Holmes, Sir John Eaton, GCVO, KBE, CMG
Holmes-Sellors, Sir Patrick John, KCVO
Holroyd, *Air Marshal* Sir Frank Martyn, KBE, CB
Holroyd, Sir Michael De Courcy Fraser, Kt., CBE
Holt, *Prof.* Sir James Clarke, Kt.
Holt, Sir Michael, Kt., CBE
Home, Sir William Dundas, Bt. (S. 1671)
Honeycombe, *Prof.* Sir Robert William Kerr, Kt., FRS, FRENG
Honywood, Sir Filmer Courtenay William, Bt. (1660)
†Hood, Sir John Joseph Harold, Bt. (1922)
Hookway, Sir Harry Thurston, Kt.
Hooper, *Rt. Hon.* Sir Anthony, Kt.
Hope, Sir Colin Frederick Newton, Kt.
Hope, Sir John Carl Alexander, Bt. (S. 1628)
Hope-Dunbar, Sir David, Bt. (S. 1664)
Hopkin, Sir Royston Oliver, KCMG
Hopkin, Sir (William Aylsham) Bryan, Kt., CBE
Hopkins, Sir Anthony Philip, Kt., CBE
Hopkins, Sir Michael John, Kt., CBE, RA, RIBA
Hopwood, *Prof.* Sir David Alan, Kt., FRS
Hordern, *Rt. Hon.* Sir Peter Maudslay, Kt.
Horlick, *Vice-Adm.* Sir Edwin John, KBE, FRENG
Horlick, Sir James Cunliffe William, Bt. (1914)
Horlock, *Prof.* Sir John Harold, Kt., FRS, FRENG
Horn, *Prof.* Sir Gabriel, Kt., FRS
Horn-Smith, Sir Julian Michael, Kt.
Hornby, Sir Derek Peter, Kt.
Hornby, Sir Simon Michael, Kt.
Horne, Sir Alan Gray Antony, Bt. (1929)
Horne, *Dr* Sir Alistair Allan, Kt. CBE
Horsbrugh-Porter, Sir John Simon, Bt. (1902)
Horsfall, Sir Edward John Wright, Bt. (1909)
†Hort, Sir Andrew Edwin Fenton, Bt. (1767)
Horton, Sir Robert Baynes, Kt.
Hosker, Sir Gerald Albery, KCB, QC
Hoskins, *Prof.* Sir Brian John, Kt. CBE, FRS
Hoskyns, Sir Benedict Leigh, Bt. (1676)
Hoskyns, Sir John Austin Hungerford Leigh, Kt.
Hotung, Sir Joseph Edward, Kt.
Houghton, Sir John Theodore, Kt., CBE, FRS
Houldsworth, Sir Richard Thomas Reginald, Bt. (1887)
Hourston, Sir Gordon Minto, Kt.
House, *Lt.-Gen.* Sir David George, GCB, KCVO, CBE, MC
Houssemayne du Boulay, Sir Roger William, KCVO, CMG
Houstoun-Boswall, Sir (Thomas) Alford, Bt. (1836)
Howard, Sir David Howarth Seymour, Bt. (1955)
Howard, *Prof.* Sir Michael Eliot, Kt., OM, CH, CBE, MC
Howard-Dobson, *Gen.* Sir Patrick John, GCB
Howard-Lawson, Sir John Philip, Bt. (1841)
Howell, Sir Ralph Frederic, Kt.
Howells, Sir Eric Waldo Benjamin, Kt., CBE
Howes, Sir Christopher Kingston, KCVO, CB
Howlett, *Gen.* Sir Geoffrey Hugh Whitby, KBE, MC
Huggins, *Hon.* Sir Alan Armstrong, Kt.
Hugh-Jones, Sir Wynn Normington, Kt., LVO
Hugh-Smith, Sir Andrew Colin, Kt.
Hughes, *Rt. Hon.* Sir Anthony Philip Gilson, Kt.
Hughes, Sir Thomas Collingwood, Bt. (1773)
Hughes, Sir Trevor Poulton, KCB
†Hughes-Morgan, Sir (Ian) Parry David, Bt. (1925)
Hull, *Prof.* Sir David, Kt.
Hulse, Sir Edward Jeremy Westrow, Bt. (1739)
Hum, Sir Christopher Owen, KCMG
Hunt, Sir John Leonard, Kt.
Hunt, *Adm.* Sir Nicholas John Streynsham, GCB, LVO
Hunt, Sir Rex Masterman, Kt., CMG
Hunt, *Dr* Sir Richard Timothy, Kt.
Hunt-Davis, *Brig.* Sir Miles Garth, KCVO, CBE
Hunter, Sir Alistair John, KCMG
Hunter, *Prof.* Sir Laurence Colvin, Kt., CBE, FRSE
Hunter, Sir Thomas Blane, Kt.
Huntington-Whiteley, Sir Hugo Baldwin, Bt. (1918)
Hurn, Sir (Francis) Roger, Kt.
Hurrell, Sir Anthony Gerald, KCVO, CMG
Hurst, Sir Geoffrey Charles, Kt., MBE
Husbands, Sir Clifford Straugh, GCMG
Hutchinson, *Hon.* Sir Ross, Kt., DFC
Hutchison, Sir James Colville, Bt. (1956)
Hutchison, *Rt. Hon.* Sir Michael, Kt.
Hutchison, Sir Robert, Bt. (1939)
Hutt, Sir Dexter Walter, Kt.
Huxley, *Prof.* Sir Andrew Fielding, Kt., OM, FRS
Huxtable, *Gen.* Sir Charles Richard, KCB, CBE
Ibbs, Sir (John) Robin, KBE
Imbert-Terry, Sir Michael Edward Stanley, Bt. (1917)
Imray, Sir Colin Henry, KBE, CMG
Ingham, Sir Bernard, Kt.
Ingilby, Sir Thomas Colvin William, Bt. (1866)
Inglis, Sir Brian Scott, Kt.
Inglis of Glencorse, Sir Roderick John, Bt. (S. 1703)
Ingram, Sir James Herbert Charles, Bt. (1893)
Ingram, Sir John Henderson, Kt., CBE
Inkin, Sir Geoffrey David, Kt., OBE
†Innes, Sir David Charles Kenneth Gordon, Bt. (NS 1686)
Innes of Edingight, Sir Malcolm Rognvald, KCVO
Innes, Sir Peter Alexander Berowald, Bt. (S. 1628)
Irvine, Sir Donald Hamilton, Kt., CBE, MD, FRCGP
Irving, *Prof.* Sir Miles Horsfall, Kt., MD, FRCS, FRCSE
Irwin, *Lt.-Gen.* Sir Alistair Stuart Hastings, KCB, CBE

Irwin, *Hon.* Sir Stephen John, Kt.
Isaacs, Sir Jeremy Israel, Kt.
Isham, Sir Ian Vere Gyles, Bt. (1627)
Ivory, Sir Brian Gammell, Kt., CBE
Jack, *Hon.* Sir Alieu Sulayman, Kt.
Jack, Sir David, Kt., CBE, FRS, FRSE
Jack, Sir David Emmanuel, GCMG, MBE
Jack, *Hon.* Sir Raymond Evan, Kt.
Jackling, Sir Roger Tustin, KCB, CBE
Jackson, Sir Barry Trevor, Kt.
Jackson, Sir Kenneth Joseph, Kt.
Jackson, *Gen.* Sir Michael David, GCB, CBE
Jackson, Sir Michael Roland, Bt. (1902)
Jackson, Sir Nicholas Fane St George, Bt. (1913)
Jackson, Sir Keith Arnold, Bt. (1815)
Jackson, *Hon.* Sir Rupert Matthew, Kt.
Jackson, Sir (William) Roland Cedric, Bt. (1869)
Jacob, *Rt. Hon.* Sir Robert Raphael Hayim (Robin), Kt.
Jacobi, Sir Derek George, Kt., CBE
Jacobi, *Dr* Sir James Edward, Kt., OBE
Jacobs, Sir Cecil Albert, Kt., CBE
Jacobs, *Rt. Hon.* Sir Francis Geoffrey, KCMG, QC
Jacobs, *Hon.* Sir Kenneth Sydney, KBE
Jacomb, Sir Martin Wakefield, Kt.
Jaffray, Sir William Otho, Bt. (1892)
Jagger, Sir Michael Philip, Kt.
James, Sir Cynlais Morgan, KCMG
James, Sir Jeffrey Russell, KBE
James, Sir John Nigel Courtenay, KCVO, CBE
James, Sir Stanislaus Anthony, GCMG, OBE
Jamieson, *Air Marshal* Sir David Ewan, KBE, CB
Jansen, Sir Ross Malcolm, KBE
Jardine of Applegirth, Sir Alexander Maule, Bt. (S. 1672)
Jardine, Sir Andrew Colin Douglas, Bt. (1916)
Jarman, *Prof.* Sir Brian, Kt., OBE
Jarratt, Sir Alexander Anthony, Kt., CB
Jarvis, Sir Gordon Ronald, Kt.
Jawara, *Hon.* Sir Dawda Kairaba, Kt.
Jay, Sir Antony Rupert, Kt., CVO
Jeewoolall, Sir Ramesh, Kt.
Jefferson, Sir George Rowland, Kt., CBE, FRENG
Jeffreys, *Prof.* Sir Alec John, Kt., FRS
Jeffries, *Hon.* Sir John Francis, Kt.
Jehangir, Sir Cowasji, Bt. (1908)
Jejeebhoy, Sir Jamsetjee, Bt. (1857)
Jenkins, Sir Brian Garton, GBE
Jenkins, Sir Elgar Spencer, Kt., OBE
Jenkins, Sir James Christopher, KCB, QC
Jenkins, Sir Michael Nicholas Howard, Kt., OBE
Jenkins, Sir Michael Romilly Heald, KCMG
Jenkins, Sir Simon, Kt.
Jenkinson, Sir John Banks, Bt. (1661)
Jenks, Sir (Richard) Peter, Bt. (1932)
Jenner, *Air Marshal* Sir Timothy Ivo, KCB
Jennings, Sir John Southwood, Kt., CBE, FRSE
Jennings, Sir Peter Neville Wake, Kt., CVO
Jephcott, Sir Neil Welbourn, Bt. (1962)
Jessel, Sir Charles John, Bt. (1883)
Jewkes, Sir Gordon Wesley, KCMG
Job, Sir Peter James Denton, Kt.
John, Sir David Glyndwr, KCMG
John, Sir Elton Hercules (Reginald Kenneth Dwight), Kt., CBE
Johns, *Air Chief Marshal* Sir Richard Edward, GCB, CBE, LVO
Johnson, Sir Colpoys Guy, Bt. (1755)
Johnson, *Gen.* Sir Garry Dene, KCB, OBE, MC
Johnson, Sir John Rodney, KCMG
†Johnson, Sir Patrick Eliot, Bt. (1818)
Johnson, *Hon.* Sir Robert Lionel, Kt.
Johnson, Sir Vassel Godfrey, Kt., CBE
Johnson-Ferguson, Sir Ian Edward, Bt. (1906)
Johnston, *Lt.-Gen.* Sir Maurice Robert, KCB, CVO, OBE
Johnston, Sir Thomas Alexander, Bt. (S. 1626)
Johnstone, Sir Geoffrey Adams Dinwiddie, KCMG
Johnstone, Sir (George) Richard Douglas, Bt. (S. 1700)
Johnstone, Sir (John) Raymond, Kt., CBE
Jolliffe, Sir Anthony Stuart, GBE
Jolly, Sir Arthur Richard, KCMG
Jonas, Sir John Peter Jens, Kt., CBE
Jones, Sir Alan Jeffrey, Kt.
Jones, Sir Harry George, Kt., CBE
Jones, Sir John Francis, Kt.
Jones, Sir Keith Stephen, Kt.
Jones, Sir Lyndon, Kt.
Jones, Sir (Owen) Trevor, Kt.
Jones, Sir Richard Anthony Lloyd, KCB
Jones, Sir Robert Edward, Kt.
Jones, Sir Roger Spencer, Kt., OBE
Jones, Sir Simon Warley Frederick Benton, Bt. (1919)
†Joseph, *Hon.* Sir James Samuel, Bt. (1943)
Jowitt, *Hon.* Sir Edwin Frank, Kt.
Judge, *Rt. Hon.* Sir Igor, Kt.
Judge, Sir Paul Rupert, Kt.
Jugnauth, *Rt. Hon.* Sir Anerood, KCMG
Jungius, *Vice-Adm.* Sir James George, KBE
Kaberry, *Hon.* Sir Christopher Donald, Bt. (1960)
Kadoorie, *Hon.* Sir Michael David, Kt.
Kakaraya, Sir Pato, KBE
Kan Yuet-Keung, Sir, GBE
Kapi, *Hon.* Sir Mari, Kt., CBE
Kaputin, Sir John Rumet, KBE, CMG
Kaufman, *Rt. Hon.* Sir Gerald Bernard, Kt.
Kausimae, Sir David Nanau, KBE
Kavali, Sir Thomas, Kt., OBE
Kawharu, *Prof.* Sir Ian Hugh, Kt.
Kay, *Prof.* Sir Andrew Watt, Kt.
Kay, *Rt. Hon.* Sir Maurice Ralph, Kt.
Kaye, Sir Paul Henry Gordon, Bt. (1923)
Keane, Sir Richard Michael, Bt. (1801)
Kearney, *Hon.* Sir William John Francis, Kt., CBE
Keeble, Sir (Herbert Ben) Curtis, GCMG
Keegan, Sir John Desmond Patrick, Kt., OBE
Keene, *Rt. Hon.* Sir David Wolfe, Kt.
Keith, *Hon.* Sir Brian Richard, Kt.
Keith, *Prof.* Sir James, KBE
†Kellett, Sir Stanley Charles, Bt. (1801)
Kelly, Sir Christopher William, KCB
Kelly, Sir David Robert Corbett, Kt., CBE
Kelly, *Rt. Hon.* Sir (John William) Basil, Kt.
Kemakeza, Sir Allan, Kt.
Kemball, *Air Marshal* Sir (Richard) John, KCB, CBE
Kemp, Sir (Edward) Peter, KCB
Kemp-Welch, Sir John, Kt.
Kenilorea, *Rt. Hon.* Sir Peter, KBE
Kennaway, Sir John Lawrence, Bt. (1791)
Kennedy, Sir Francis, KCMG, CBE
Kennedy, *Hon.* Sir Ian Alexander, Kt.
Kennedy, *Prof.* Sir Ian McColl, Kt.
Kennedy, Sir Ludovic Henry Coverley, Kt.
†Kennedy, Sir Michael Edward, Bt., (1836)
Kennedy, *Rt. Hon.* Sir Paul Joseph Morrow, Kt.
Kennedy, *Air Chief Marshal* Sir Thomas Lawrie, GCB, AFC
Kennedy-Good, Sir John, KBE
Kenny, Sir Anthony John Patrick, Kt., DPHIL, DLITT, FBA
Kenny, *Gen.* Sir Brian Leslie Graham, GCB, CBE
Kentridge, Sir Sydney Woolf, KCMG, QC
Kenyon, Sir George Henry, Kt.
Keogh, *Prof.* Sir Bruce Edward, KBE
Kermode, Sir (John) Frank, Kt., FBA
Kerr, *Rt. Hon.* Sir Brian Francis, Kt.
Kerr, *Adm.* Sir John Beverley, GCB
Kerry, Sir Michael James, KCB, QC
Kershaw, *Prof.* Sir Ian, Kt.
Kershaw, Sir (John) Anthony, Kt., MC
Kerslake, Sir Robert Walker, Kt.
Keswick, Sir John Chippendale Lindley, Kt.
Kevau, *Prof.* Sir Isi Henao, Kt., CBE
Kikau, *Ratu* Sir Jone Latianara, KBE
Kimber, Sir Charles Dixon, Bt. (1904)
King, *Prof.* Sir David Anthony, Kt., FRS
King, Sir John Christopher, Bt. (1888)

King, *Vice-Adm.* Sir Norman Ross Dutton, KBE
King, *Hon.* Sir Timothy Roger Alan, Kt.
King, Sir Wayne Alexander, Bt. (1815)
Kingman, *Prof.* Sir John Frank Charles, Kt., FRS
Kingsland, Sir Richard, Kt., CBE, DFC
Kingsley, Sir Ben, Kt.
Kinloch, Sir David, Bt. (S. 1686)
Kinloch, Sir David Oliphant, Bt. (1873)
Kipalan, Sir Albert, Kt.
Kirkpatrick, Sir Ivone Elliott, Bt. (S. 1685)
Kirkwood, *Hon.* Sir Andrew Tristram Hammett, Kt.
Kiszely, *Lt.-Gen.* Sir John Panton, KCB, MC
Kitchin, *Hon.* Sir David James Tyson, Kt.
Kitson, *Gen.* Sir Frank Edward, GBE, KCB, MC
Kitson, Sir Timothy Peter Geoffrey, Kt.
Kleinwort, Sir Richard Drake, Bt. (1909)
Klug, Sir Aaron, Kt., OM
Knight, Sir Harold Murray, KBE, DSC
Knight, Sir Kenneth John, Kt., CBE, QFSM
Knight, *Air Chief Marshal* Sir Michael William Patrick, KCB, AFC
Knight, *Prof.* Sir Peter, Kt.
†Knill, Sir Thomas John Pugin Bartholomew, Bt. (1893)
Knowles, Sir Charles Francis, Bt. (1765)
Knowles, Sir Durward Randolph, Kt., OBE
Knowles, Sir Richard Marchant, Kt.
Knox, Sir David Laidlaw, Kt.
Knox, *Hon.* Sir John Leonard, Kt.
Knox-Johnston, Sir William Robert Patrick (Sir Robin), Kt., CBE, RD
Koraea, Sir Thomas, Kt.
Kornberg, *Prof.* Sir Hans Leo, Kt., DSC, SCD, PHD, FRS
Korowi, Sir Wiwa, GCMG
Kroto, *Prof.* Sir Harold Walter, Kt., FRS
Kulukundis, Sir Elias George (Eddie), Kt., OBE
Kurongku, *Most Revd* Peter, KBE
Kwok-Po Li, *Dr* Sir David, Kt., OBE
Lachmann, *Prof.* Sir Peter Julius, Kt.
Lacon, Sir Edmund Vere, Bt. (1818)
Lacy, Sir Patrick Brian Finucane, Bt. (1921)
Lacy, Sir John Trend, Kt., CBE
Laddie, *Hon.* Sir Hugh Ian Lang, Kt.
Laidlaw, Sir Christopher Charles Fraser, Kt.
Laing, Sir (John) Martin (Kirby), Kt., CBE
Laing, Sir (John) Maurice, Kt.
Laing, Sir (William) Kirby, Kt., FRENG
Laird, Sir Gavin Harry, Kt., CBE
Lake, Sir (Atwell) Graham, Bt. (1711)
Lakin, Sir Michael, Bt. (1909)
Laking, Sir George Robert, KCMG
Lamb, Sir Albert Thomas, KBE, CMG, DFC
Lambert, Sir John Henry, KCVO, CMG
†Lambert, Sir Peter John Biddulph, Bt. (1711)
Lampl, Sir Frank William, Kt.
Lampl, Sir Peter, Kt., OBE
Lamport, Sir Stephen Mark Jeffrey, KCVO
Landale, Sir David William Neil, KCVO
Landau, Sir Dennis Marcus, Kt.
Lander, Sir Stephen James, KCB
Lane, Prof. Sir David Philip, Kt.
Langham, Sir John Stephen, Bt. (1660)
Langlands, Sir Robert Alan, Kt.
Langley, *Hon.* Sir Gordon Julian Hugh, Kt.
Langley, *Maj.-Gen.* Sir Henry Desmond Allen, KCVO, MBE
Langrishe, Sir James Hercules, Bt. (I. 1777)
Langstaff, *Hon.* Sir Brian Frederick James, Kt.
Lankester, Sir Timothy Patrick, KCB
Lapli, Sir John Ini, GCMG
Large, Sir Andrew McLeod Brooks, Kt.
Latasi, *Rt. Hon.* Sir Kamuta, KCMG, OBE
Latham, *Rt. Hon.* Sir David Nicholas Ramsey, Kt.
Latham, Sir Michael Anthony, Kt.
Latham, Sir Richard Thomas Paul, Bt. (1919)
Latimer, Sir (Courtenay) Robert, Kt., CBE
Latimer, Sir Graham Stanley, KBE
Latour-Adrien, *Hon.* Sir Maurice, Kt.
Laughton, Sir Anthony Seymour, Kt.
Laurence, Sir Peter Harold, KCMG, MC
Laurie, Sir Robert Bayley Emilius, Bt. (1834)
Lauterpacht, Sir Elihu, Kt., CBE, QC
Lauti, *Rt. Hon.* Sir Toaripi, GCMG
Lavan, *Hon.* Sir John Martin, Kt.
Lawes, Sir (John) Michael Bennet, Bt. (1882)
Lawler, Sir Peter James, Kt., OBE
Lawrence, Sir Clive Wyndham, Bt. (1906)
Lawrence, Sir Henry Peter, Bt. (1858)
Lawrence, Sir Ivan John, Kt., QC
Lawrence, Sir John Patrick Grosvenor, Kt., CBE
Lawrence, Sir William Fettiplace, Bt. (1867)
Lawrence-Jones, Sir Christopher, Bt. (1831)
Laws, *Rt. Hon.* Sir John Grant McKenzie, Kt.
Lawson, Sir Charles John Patrick, Bt. (1900)
Lawson, *Gen.* Sir Richard George, KCB, DSO, OBE
Lawson-Tancred, Sir Henry, Bt. (1662)
Lawton, *Prof.* Sir John Hartley, Kt., CBE, FRS
Layard, *Adm.* Sir Michael Henry Gordon, KCB, CBE
Lea, *Vice-Adm.* Sir John Stuart Crosbie, KBE
Lea, Sir Thomas William, Bt. (1892)
Leach, *Admiral of the Fleet* Sir Henry Conyers, GCB
Leahy, Sir Daniel Joseph, Kt.
Leahy, Sir John Henry Gladstone, KCMG
Leahy, Sir Terence Patrick, Kt.
Learmont, *Gen.* Sir John Hartley, KCB, CBE
Leaver, Sir Christopher, GBE
Le Bailly, *Vice-Adm.* Sir Louis Edward Stewart Holland, KBE, CB
Le Cheminant, *Air Chief Marshal* Sir Peter de Lacey, GBE, KCB, DFC
Lechmere, Sir Reginald Anthony Hungerford, Bt. (1818)
Ledger, Sir Philip Stevens, Kt., CBE, FRSE
Lee, *Brig.* Sir Leonard Henry, Kt., CBE
Lee, Sir Quo-wei, Kt., CBE
Leeds, Sir Christopher Anthony, Bt. (1812)
Lees, Sir David Bryan, Kt.
Lees, Sir Thomas Edward, Bt. (1897)
Lees, Sir Thomas Harcourt Ivor, Bt. (1804)
Lees, Sir (William) Antony Clare, Bt. (1937)
Leese, Sir Richard Charles, Kt., CBE
le Fleming, Sir David Kelland, Bt. (1705)
Legard, Sir Charles Thomas, Bt. (1660)
Legg, Sir Thomas Stuart, KCB, QC
Leggatt, *Rt. Hon.* Sir Andrew Peter, Kt.
Leggatt, Sir Hugh Frank John, Kt.
Leggett, *Prof.* Sir Anthony James, KBE
Leigh, Sir Geoffrey Norman, Kt.
Leigh, Sir Richard Henry, Bt. (1918)
Leighton, Sir Michael John Bryan, Bt. (1693)
Leitch, Sir George, KCB, OBE
Leith-Buchanan, Sir Gordon Kelly McNicol, Bt. (1775)
Le Marchant, Sir Francis Arthur, Bt. (1841)
Leng, *Gen.* Sir Peter John Hall, KCB, MBE, MC
Lennox-Boyd, The Hon. Sir Mark Alexander, Kt.
Leon, Sir John Ronald, Bt. (1911)
Leonard, *Rt. Revd Monsignor* and *Rt. Hon.* Graham Douglas, KCVO
Lepping, Sir George Geria Dennis, GCMG, MBE
Le Quesne, Sir (John) Godfray, Kt., QC
Lee-Steere, Sir Ernest Henry, KBE

Leslie, Sir Colin Alan Bettridge, Kt.
Leslie, Sir John Norman Ide, Bt. (1876)
Leslie, Sir Peter Evelyn, Kt.
Lester, Sir James Theodore, Kt.
Lethbridge, Sir Thomas Periam Hector Noel, Bt. (1804)
Lever, Sir Jeremy Frederick, KCMG, QC
Lever, Sir Paul, KCMG
Lever, Sir (Tresham) Christopher Arthur Lindsay, Bt. (1911)
Leveson, *Rt. Hon.* Sir Brian Henry, Kt.
Levey, Sir Michael Vincent, Kt., LVO
Levine, Sir Montague Bernard, Kt.
Levinge, Sir Richard George Robin, Bt. (I. 1704)
Lewinton, Sir Christopher, Kt.
Lewis, Sir David Courtenay Mansel, KCVO
Lewis, Sir John Anthony, Kt., OBE
Lewis, Sir Leigh Warren, KCB
Lewis, Sir Terence Murray, Kt., OBE, GM, QPM
Lewison, *Hon.* Sir Kim Martin Jordan, Kt.
Ley, Sir Ian Francis, Bt. (1905)
Li, Sir Ka-Shing, KBE
Lickiss, Sir Michael Gillam, Kt.
Liddington, Sir Bruce, Kt.
Liggins, *Prof.* Sir Graham Collingwood, Kt., CBE, FRS
Lightman, *Hon.* Sir Gavin Anthony, Kt.
Lighton, Sir Thomas Hamilton, Bt. (I. 1791)
Likierman, *Prof.* Sir John Andrew, Kt.
Lilleyman, *Prof.* Sir John Stuart, Kt.
Limon, Sir Donald William, KCB
Linacre, Sir (John) Gordon (Seymour), Kt., CBE, AFC, DFM
Lindop, Sir Norman, Kt.
Lindsay, Sir James Harvey Kincaid Stewart, Kt.
Lindsay, *Hon.* Sir John Edmund Frederic, Kt.
†Lindsay, Sir James Martin Evelyn, Bt. (1962)
†Lindsay-Hogg, Sir Michael Edward, Bt. (1905)
Lipton, Sir Stuart Anthony, Kt.
Lipworth, Sir (Maurice) Sydney, Kt.
Lister-Kaye, Sir John Phillip Lister, Bt. (1812)
Lithgow, Sir William James, Bt. (1925)
Little, *Most Revd* Thomas Francis, KBE
Littler, Sir (James) Geoffrey, KCB
Llewellyn, Sir David St Vincent, Bt. (1922)
Llewellyn-Smith, *Prof.* Sir Christopher Hubert, Kt.
Lloyd, *Prof.* Sir Geoffrey Ernest Richard, Kt., FBA
Lloyd, Sir Nicholas Markley, Kt.
Lloyd, *Rt. Hon.* Sir Peter Robert Cable, Kt.
Lloyd, Sir Richard Ernest Butler, Bt. (1960)
Lloyd, *Hon.* Sir Timothy Andrew Wigram, Kt.
Lloyd-Hughes, Sir Trevor Denby, Kt.
Lloyd Jones, Sir David, Kt.
Lloyd-Jones, Sir (Peter) Hugh (Jefferd), Kt.
Loader, Air Marshal Sir Clive Robert, KCB, OBE
Loane, *Most Revd* Marcus Lawrence, KBE
Lobo, Sir Rogerio Hyndman, Kt., CBE
†Loder, Sir Edmund Jeune, Bt. (1887)
Logan, Sir David Brian Carleton, KCMG
Logan, Sir Donald Arthur, KCMG
Lokoloko, Sir Tore, GCMG, GCVO, OBE
Longmore, *Rt. Hon.* Sir Andrew Centlivres, Kt.
Loram, *Vice-Adm.* Sir David Anning, KCB, CVO
Lord, Sir Michael Nicholson, Kt.
Lorimer, Sir (Thomas) Desmond, Kt.
Los, *Hon.* Sir Kubulan, Kt., CBE
Loughran, Sir Gerald Finbar, KCB
Louisy, *Rt. Hon.* Sir Allan Fitzgerald Laurent, KCMG
Lovell, Sir (Alfred Charles) Bernard, Kt., OBE, FRS
Lovelock, Sir Douglas Arthur, KCB
Loveridge, Sir John Warren, Kt.
Lovill, Sir John Roger, Kt., CBE
Lowe, *Air Chief Marshal* Sir Douglas Charles, GCB, DFC, AFC
Lowe, Sir Frank Budge, Kt.
Lowe, Sir Thomas William Gordon, Bt. (1918)
Lowson, Sir Ian Patrick, Bt. (1951)
Lowther, *Col.* Sir Charles Douglas, Bt. (1824)
Lowther, Sir John Luke, KCVO, CBE
Loyd, Sir Julian St John, KCVO
Lu, Sir Tseng Chi, Kt.
Lucas, *Prof.* Sir Colin Renshaw, Kt.
Lucas, Sir Thomas Edward, Bt. (1887)
Lucas-Tooth, Sir (Hugh) John, Bt. (1920)
Luddington, Sir Donald Collin Cumyn, KBE, CMG, CVO
Lumsden, Sir David James, Kt.
Lushington, Sir John Richard Castleman, Bt. (1791)
Lyall Grant, Sir Mark Justin, KCMG
Lygo, *Adm.* Sir Raymond Derek, KCB
Lyle, Sir Gavin Archibald, Bt. (1929)
Lynch-Blosse, *Capt.* Sir Richard Hely, Bt. (1622)
Lynch-Robinson, Sir Dominick Christopher, Bt. (1920)
Lyne, Sir Roderic Michael John, KBE, CMG
Lyons, Sir John, Kt.
Lyons, Sir Michael Thomas, Kt.
McAlpine, Sir William Hepburn, Bt. (1918)
Macara, Sir Alexander Wiseman, Kt., FRCP, FRCGP
†Macara, Sir Hugh Kenneth, Bt. (1911)
McCaffrey, Sir Thomas Daniel, Kt.
McCallum, Sir Donald Murdo, Kt., CBE, FRENG
McCamley, Sir Graham Edward, KBE
McCarthy, Sir Callum, Kt.
McCartney, Sir (James) Paul, Kt., MBE
Macartney, Sir John Ralph, Bt. (I. 1799)
McClay, *Dr* Sir Allen James, Kt., CBE
McClement, *Vice-Admiral* Sir Timothy Pentreath, KCB, OBE
McClintock, Sir Eric Paul, Kt.
McColl, Sir Colin Hugh Verel, KCMG
McCollum, *Rt. Hon.* Sir William, Kt.
McCombe, *Hon.* Sir Richard George Bramwell, Kt.
McConnell, Sir Robert Shean, Bt. (1900)
MacCormac, Sir Richard Cornelius, Kt., CBE
MacCormick, *Prof.* Sir Donald Neil, Kt., MEP, QC
†McCowan, Sir David William, Bt. (1934)
McCullough, *Hon.* Sir (Iain) Charles (Robert), Kt.
MacDermott, *Rt. Hon.* Sir John Clarke, Kt.
Macdonald, Sir Kenneth Carmichael, KCB
Macdonald, Sir Kenneth Donald John, Kt., QC
Mcdonald, Sir Trevor, Kt., OBE
Macdonald of Sleat, Sir Ian Godfrey Bosville, Bt. (S. 1625)
McDowell, Sir Eric Wallace, Kt., CBE
Mace, *Lt.-Gen.* Sir John Airth, KBE, CB
McEwen, Sir John Roderick Hugh, Bt. (1953)
McFarland, Sir John Talbot, Bt. (1914)
MacFarlane, *Prof.* Sir Alistair George James, Kt., CBE, FRS
McFarlane, Sir Andrew Ewart, Kt.
Macfarlane, Sir (David) Neil, Kt.
McFarlane, Sir Ian, Kt.
McGrath, Sir Brian Henry, GCVO
Macgregor, Sir Ian Grant, Bt. (1828)
McGregor, Sir James David, Kt., OBE
MacGregor of MacGregor, Sir Malcolm Gregor Charles, Bt. (1795)
McGrigor, *Capt.* Sir Charles Edward, Bt. (1831)
McIntosh, Sir Neil William David, Kt., CBE
McIntosh, Sir Ronald Robert Duncan, KCB
McIntyre, Sir Donald Conroy, Kt., CBE
McIntyre, Sir Meredith Alister, Kt.
Mackay, *Hon.* Sir Colin Crichton, Kt.
MacKay, *Prof.* Sir Donald Iain, Kt.
MacKay, Sir Francis Henry, Kt.
McKay, Sir William Robert, KCB

Mackay-Dick, *Maj.-Gen.* Sir Iain Charles, KCVO, MBE
Mackechnie, Sir Alistair John, Kt.
McKellen, Sir Ian Murray, Kt., CBE
Mackenzie, Sir (James William) Guy, Bt. (1890)
Mackenzie, *Gen.* Sir Jeremy John George, GCB, OBE
†Mackenzie, Sir Peter Douglas, Bt. (S. 1673)
†Mackenzie, Sir Roderick McQuhae, Bt. (S. 1703)
McKenzie, Sir Roy Allan, KBE
Mackerras, Sir (Alan) Charles (MacLaurin), Kt., CH, CBE
Mackeson, Sir Rupert Henry, Bt. (1954)
McKillop, Sir Thomas Fulton Wilson, Kt.
McKinnon, Sir James, Kt.
McKinnon, *Hon.* Sir Stuart Neil, Kt.
Mackintosh, Sir Cameron Anthony, Kt.
Mackworth, Sir Digby (John), Bt. (1776)
McLaren, Sir Robin John Taylor, KCMG
McLaughlin, Sir Richard, Kt.
Maclean of Dunconnell, Sir Charles Edward, Bt. (1957)
Maclean, Sir Donald Og Grant, Kt.
Maclean, Sir Lachlan Hector Charles, Bt. (NS 1631)
Maclean, Sir Murdo, Kt.
McLeod, Sir Charles Henry, Bt. (1925)
MacLeod, Sir (John) Maxwell Norman, Bt. (1924)
Macleod, Sir (Nathaniel William) Hamish, KBE
McLintock, Sir Michael William, Bt. (1934)
Maclure, Sir John Robert Spencer, Bt. (1898)
McMahon, Sir Brian Patrick, Bt. (1817)
McMahon, Sir Christopher William, Kt.
McMaster, Sir Brian John, Kt., CBE
Macmillan, Sir (Alexander McGregor) Graham, Kt.
MacMillan, *Lt.-Gen.* Sir John Richard Alexander, KCB, CBE
McMullin, *Rt. Hon.* Sir Duncan Wallace, Kt.
McMurtry, Sir David, Kt., CBE
†Macnaghten, Sir Malcolm Francis, Bt. (1836)
McNair-Wilson, Sir Patrick Michael Ernest David, Kt.
McNamara, *Air Chief Marshal* Sir Neville Patrick, KBE
Macnaughton, *Prof.* Sir Malcolm Campbell, Kt.
McNee, Sir David Blackstock, Kt., QPM
McNulty, Sir (Robert William) Roy, Kt., CBE
MacPhail, Sir Bruce Dugald, Kt.
Macpherson, Sir Ronald Thomas Steward (Tommy), CBE, MC, TD
Macpherson of Cluny, *Hon.* Sir William Alan, Kt., TD
McQuarrie, Sir Albert, Kt.
MacRae, Sir (Alastair) Christopher (Donald Summerhayes), KCMG
Macready, Sir Nevil John Wilfrid, Bt. (1923)
MacSween, *Prof.* Sir Roderick Norman McIver, Kt.
Mactaggart, Sir John Auld, Bt. (1938)
McWilliam, Sir Michael Douglas, KCMG
McWilliams, Sir Francis, GBE
Madden, Sir David Christopher Andrew, KCMG
†Madden, Sir Charles Jonathan, Bt. (1919)
Maddox, Sir John Royden, Kt.
Madel, Sir (William) David, Kt.
Magee, Sir Ian Bernard Vaughan, Kt., CB
Magnus, Sir Laurence Henry Philip, Bt. (1917)
Mahon, Sir (John) Denis, Kt., CH, CBE
Mahon, Sir William Walter, Bt. (1819)
Maiden, Sir Colin James, Kt., DPHIL
Main, Sir Peter Tester, Kt., ERD
Maingard de la Ville ès Offrans, Sir Louis Pierre René, Kt., CBE
Maini, *Prof.* Sir Ravinder Nath, Kt.
Maino, Sir Charles, KBE
†Maitland, Sir Charles Alexander, Bt. (1818)
Maitland, Sir Donald James Dundas, GCMG, OBE
Major, *Rt. Hon.* Sir John, KG, CH
Malbon, *Vice-Adm.* Sir Fabian Michael, KBE
Malcolm, Sir James William Thomas Alexander, Bt. (S. 1665)
Malet, Sir Harry Douglas St Lo, Bt. (1791)
Mallaby, Sir Christopher Leslie George, GCMG, GCVO
Mallet, Sir William George, GCMG, CBE
Mallick, *Prof.* Sir Netar Prakash, Kt.
Mallinson, Sir William James, Bt. (1935)
Malpas, Sir Robert, Kt., CBE
Mamo, Sir Anthony Joseph, Kt., OBE
Mancham, Sir James Richard Marie, KBE
†Mander, Sir (Charles) Nicholas, Bt. (1911)
Manduell, Sir John, Kt., CBE
Mann, *Hon.* Sir George Anthony, Kt.
Mann, *Rt. Revd* Michael Ashley, KCVO
Mann, Sir Rupert Edward, Bt. (1905)
Manning, Sir David Geoffrey, KCMG, CVO
Mansel, Sir Philip, Bt. (1622)
Mansfield, *Prof.* Sir Peter, Kt.
Mantell, *Rt. Hon.* Sir Charles Barrie Knight, Kt.
Manuella, Sir Tulaga, GCMG, MBE
Manzie, Sir (Andrew) Gordon, KCB
Margetson, Sir John William Denys, KCMG
Margetts, Sir Robert John, Kt., CBE
Mark, Sir Robert, GBE
Markesinis, *Prof.* Sir Basil Spyridonos, Kt. QC
Markham, Sir (Arthur) David, Bt. (1911)
Marling, Sir Charles William Somerset, Bt. (1882)
Marmot, Prof. Sir Michael Gideon, Kt.
Marr, Sir Leslie Lynn, Bt. (1919)
Marriner, Sir Neville, Kt., CBE
†Marsden, Sir Simon Neville Llewelyn, Bt. (1924)
Marsh, *Prof.* Sir John Stanley, Kt., CBE
Marshall, Sir Denis Alfred, Kt.
Marshall, *Prof.* Sir (Oshley) Roy, Kt., CBE
Marshall, Sir Peter Harold Reginald, KCMG
Martin, Sir Clive Haydon, Kt., OBE
Martin, Sir George Henry, Kt., CBE
Martin, *Vice-Adm.* Sir John Edward Ludgate, KCB, DSC
Martin, *Prof.* Sir Laurence Woodward, Kt.
Martin, Sir (Robert) Bruce, Kt., QC
Marychurch, Sir Peter Harvey, KCMG
Masefield, Sir Charles Beech Gordon, Kt.
Mason, *Hon.* Sir Anthony Frank, KBE
Mason, Sir (Basil) John, Kt., CB, DSC, FRS
Mason, *Prof.* Sir David Kean, Kt., CBE
Mason, Sir Frederick Cecil, KCVO, CMG
Mason, Sir Gordon Charles, Kt., OBE
Mason, Sir John Charles Moir, KCMG
Mason, Sir John Peter, Kt., CBE
Mason, Sir Peter James, KBE
Mason, *Prof.* Sir Ronald, KCB, FRS
Massie, Sir Herbert William, Kt., CBE
Matane, HE Sir Paulias Nguna, GCMG, OBE
Mathers, Sir Robert William, Kt.
Matheson of Matheson, Sir Fergus John, Bt. (1882)
Mathewson, Sir George Ross, Kt., CBE, PHD, FRSE
Matthews, Sir Terence Hedley, Kt., OBE
Maud, *Hon.* Sir Humphrey John Hamilton, KCMG
Maughan, Sir Deryck, Kt.
Mawer, Sir Philip John Courtney, Kt.
Maxwell, Sir Michael Eustace George, Bt. (S. 1681)
Maxwell-Hyslop, Sir Robert John (Robin), Kt.
Maxwell-Scott, Sir Dominic James, Bt. (1642)
May, *Rt. Hon.* Sir Anthony Tristram Kenneth, Kt.
Mayhew-Sanders, Sir John Reynolds, Kt.

Maynard, *Hon.* Sir Clement Travelyan, Kt.
Meadow, *Prof.* Sir (Samuel) Roy, Kt., FRCP, FRCPE
Medlycott, Sir Mervyn Tregonwell, Bt. (1808)
Meldrum, Sir Graham, Kt., CBE, QFSM
Melhuish, Sir Michael Ramsay, KBE, CMG
Mellon, Sir James, KCMG
Melmoth, Sir Graham John, Kt.
Melville, *Prof.* Sir David, Kt., CBE
Merifield, Sir Anthony James, KCVO, CB
†Meyer, Sir (Anthony) Ashley Frank, Bt. (1910)
Meyer, Sir Christopher John Rome, KCMG
Meyjes, Sir Richard Anthony, Kt.
†Meyrick, Sir Timothy Thomas Charlton, Bt. (1880)
Miakwe, *Hon.* Sir Akepa, KBE
Michael, Sir Duncan, Kt.
Michael, *Dr* Sir Jonathan, Kt.
Michael, Sir Peter Colin, Kt., CBE
Michels, Sir David Michael Charles, Kt.
Middleton, Sir John Maxwell, Kt.
Middleton, Sir Peter Edward, GCB
Miers, Sir (Henry) David Alastair Capel, KBE, CMG
Milbank, Sir Anthony Frederick, Bt. (1882)
Milborne-Swinnerton-Pilkington, Sir Thomas Henry, Bt. (S. 1635)
Milburn, Sir Anthony Rupert, Bt. (1905)
Miles, Sir Peter Tremayne, KCVO
Miles, Sir William Napier Maurice, Bt. (1859)
Millais, Sir Geoffrey Richard Everett, Bt. (1885)
Millard, Sir Guy Elwin, KCMG, CVO
Miller, Sir Albert Joel, KCMG, MVO, MBE, QPM, CPM
Miller, Sir Donald John, Kt., FRSE, FRENG
Miller, *Air Marshal* Sir Graham Anthony, KBE
Miller, Sir Harry Holmes, Bt. (1705)
Miller, Sir Hilary Duppa (Hal), Kt.
Miller, Sir Jonathan Wolfe, Kt., CBE
Miller, Sir Peter North, Kt.
Miller, Sir Robin Robert William, Kt.
Miller, Sir Ronald Andrew Baird, Kt., CBE
Miller of Glenlee, Sir Stephen William Macdonald, Bt. (1788)
Mills, Sir Ian, Kt.
Mills, Sir Keith, Kt.
Mills, Sir Peter Frederick Leighton, Bt. (1921)
Milman, Sir David Patrick, Bt. (1800)
Milne, Sir John Drummond, Kt.
Milne-Watson, Sir Andrew Michael, Bt. (1937)
Milner, Sir Timothy William Lycett, Bt. (1717)
Milton, Sir Simon, Kt.
Milton-Thompson, *Surgeon Vice-Adm.* Sir Godfrey James, KBE
Mirrlees, *Prof.* Sir James Alexander, Kt., FBA
Mitchell, Sir David Bower, Kt.
Mitchell, Sir Derek Jack, KCB, CVO
Mitchell, *Rt. Hon.* Sir James FitzAllen, KCMG
Mitchell, *Very Revd* Patrick Reynolds, KCVO
Mitchell, *Hon.* Sir Stephen George, Kt.
Mitting, *Hon.* Sir John Edward, Kt.
Moate, Sir Roger Denis, Kt.
Moberly, Sir Patrick Hamilton, KCMG
Moffat, Sir Brian Scott, Kt., OBE
Moffat, *Lt.-Gen.* Sir (William) Cameron, KBE
Mogg, Sir John Frederick, KCMG
Moir, Sir Christopher Ernest, Bt. (1916)
†Molesworth-St Aubyn, Sir William, Bt. (1689)
†Molony, Sir Thomas Desmond, Bt. (1925)
Monck, Sir Nicholas Jeremy, KCB
Money-Coutts, Sir David Burdett, KCVO
Montagu, Sir Nicholas Lionel John, KCB
Montagu-Pollock, Sir Giles Hampden, Bt. (1872)
Montague, Sir Adrian Alastair, Kt., CBE
Montague-Browne, Sir Anthony Arthur Duncan, KCMG, CBE, DFC
Montgomery, Sir (Basil Henry) David, Bt. (1801), CVO
Montgomery, Sir (William) Fergus, Kt.
Montgomery-Cuninghame, Sir John Christopher Foggo, Bt. (NS 1672)
Moody-Stuart, Sir Mark, KCMG
Moollan, Sir Abdool Hamid Adam, Kt.
Moollan, *Hon.* Sir Cassam (Ismael), Kt.
†Moon, Sir Roger, Bt. (1887)
Moore, *Most Revd* Desmond Charles, KBE
Moore, Sir Francis Thomas, Kt.
Moore, *Maj.-Gen.* Sir (John) Jeremy, KCB, OBE, MC
Moore, Sir John Michael, KCVO, CB, DSC
Moore, *Vice Adm.* Sir Michael Antony Claës, KBE, LVO
Moore, *Prof.* Sir Norman Winfrid, Bt. (1919)
Moore, Sir Patrick Alfred Caldwell, Kt., CBE
Moore, Sir Patrick William Eisdell, Kt., OBE
Moore, Sir Roger George, KBE
Moore, Sir William Roger Clotworthy, Bt. (1932), TD
Moore-Bick, *Rt. Hon.* Sir Martin James, Kt.
Moores, Sir Peter, Kt., CBE
Morauta, Sir Mekere, Kt.
Mordaunt, Sir Richard Nigel Charles, Bt. (1611)
Moreton, Sir John Oscar, KCMG, KCVO, MC
Morgan, *Vice-Adm.* Sir Charles Christopher, KBE
Morgan, *Hon.* Sir Charles Declan, Kt.
Morgan, Sir Graham, Kt.
Morgan, Sir John Albert Leigh, KCMG
Morgan-Giles, *Rear-Adm.* Sir Morgan Charles, Kt., DSO, OBE, GM
Morison, *Hon.* Sir Thomas Richard Atkin, Kt.
Morland, *Hon.* Sir Michael, Kt.
Morland, Sir Robert Kenelm, Kt.
Morpeth, Sir Douglas Spottiswoode, Kt., TD
†Morris, Sir Allan Lindsay, Bt. (1806)
Morris, *Air Marshal* Sir Arnold Alec, KBE, CB
Morris, Sir Derek James, Kt.
Morris, Sir (James) Richard (Samuel), Kt., CBE
Morris, Sir Keith Elliot Hedley, KBE, CMG
Morris, *Prof.* Sir Peter John, Kt.
Morris, Sir Trefor Alfred, Kt., CBE, QPM
Morris, *Very Revd* William James, KCVO
Morrison, Sir (Alexander) Fraser, Kt., CBE
Morrison, Sir Howard Leslie, Kt., OBE
Morrison, Sir Kenneth Duncan, Kt., CBE
Morrison-Bell, Sir William Hollin Dayrell, Bt. (1905)
Morrison-Low, Sir James Richard, Bt. (1908)
Morritt, *Rt. Hon.* Sir (Robert) Andrew, Kt., CVO
Morse, Sir Christopher Jeremy, KCMG
Mortimer, Sir John Clifford, Kt., CBE, QC
Moseley, Sir George Walker, KCB
Moses, *Rt. Hon.* Sir Alan George, Kt.
Moses, Very Revd Dr John Henry, KCVO
Moss, Sir David Joseph, KCVO, CMG
Moss, Sir Stephen Alan, Kt.
Moss, Sir Stirling Craufurd, Kt., OBE
Mostyn, Sir William Basil John, Bt. (1670)
Mott, Sir John Harmer, Bt. (1930)
Mottram, Sir Richard Clive, GCB
†Mount, Sir (William Robert) Ferdinand, Bt. (1921)
†Mountain, Sir Edward Brian Stanford, Bt. (1922)
Mountfield, Sir Robin, KCB
Mowbray, Sir John Robert, Bt. (1880)
Moylan, *Hon.* Sir Andrew John Gregory, Kt.
Muir, Sir Laurence Macdonald, Kt.
†Muir, Sir Richard James Kay, Bt. (1892)

Muir-Mackenzie, Sir Alexander Alwyne Henry Charles Brinton, Bt. (1805)
Mulcahy, Sir Geoffrey John, Kt.
Mullens, *Lt.-Gen.* Sir Anthony Richard Guy, KCB, OBE
Mummery, *Rt. Hon.* Sir John Frank, Kt.
Munby, *Hon.* Sir James Lawrence, Kt.
Munn, Sir James, Kt., OBE
Munro, Sir Alan Gordon, KCMG
†Munro, Sir Kenneth Arnold William, Bt. (S. 1634)
Munro, Sir Alasdair Thomas Ian, Bt. (1825)
Muria, *Hon.* Sir Gilbert John Baptist, Kt.
Murphy, Sir Leslie Frederick, Kt.
Murray, Sir David Edward, Kt.
Murray, *Rt. Hon.* Sir Donald Bruce, Kt.
Murray, Sir James, KCMG
Murray, *Prof.* Sir Kenneth, Kt.
Murray, Sir Nigel Andrew Digby, Bt. (S. 1628)
Murray, Sir Patrick Ian Keith, Bt. (S. 1673)
†Murray, Sir Rowland William, Bt. (S. 1630)
Mursell, Sir Peter, Kt., MBE
Musgrave, Sir Christopher John Shane, Bt. (1782)
Musgrave, Sir Christopher Patrick Charles, Bt. (1611)
Musson, *Gen.* Sir Geoffrey Randolph Dixon, GCB, CBE, DSO
Myers, Sir Philip Alan, Kt., OBE, QPM
Myers, *Prof.* Sir Rupert Horace, KBE
Mynors, Sir Richard Baskerville, Bt. (1964)
Naipaul, Sir Vidiadhar Surajprasad, Kt.
Nairn, Sir Michael, Bt. (1904)
Nairne, *Rt. Hon.* Sir Patrick Dalmahoy, GCB, MC
Naish, Sir (Charles) David, Kt.
Nall, Sir Edward William Joseph Bt. (1954)
Namaliu, *Rt. Hon.* Sir Rabbie Langanai, KCMG
†Napier, Sir Charles Joseph, Bt. (1867)
Napier, Sir John Archibald Lennox, Bt. (S. 1627)
Napier, Sir Oliver John, Kt.
Naylor-Leyland, Sir Philip Vyvyan, Bt. (1895)
Neal, Sir Eric James, Kt., CVO
Neal, Sir Leonard Francis, Kt., CBE
Neale, Sir Gerrard Anthony, Kt.
Neave, Sir Paul Arundell, Bt. (1795)
Neill, *Rt. Hon.* Sir Brian Thomas, Kt.
Neill, Sir (James) Hugh, KCVO, CBE, TD
†Nelson, Sir Jamie Charles Vernon Hope, Bt. (1912)
Nelson, *Hon.* Sir Robert Franklyn, Kt.
Neubert, Sir Michael John, Kt.
New, *Maj.-Gen.* Sir Laurence Anthony Wallis, Kt., CB, CBE
Newall, Sir Paul Henry, Kt., TD
Newby, *Prof.* Sir Howard Joseph, Kt., CBE
Newington, Sir Michael John, KCMG
Newman, Sir Francis Hugh Cecil, Bt. (1912)
Newman, Sir Geoffrey Robert, Bt. (1836)
Newman, *Hon.* Sir George Michael, Kt.
Newman, Sir Kenneth Leslie, GBE, QPM
Newman, *Vice-Adm.* Sir Roy Thomas, KCB
Newsam, Sir Peter Anthony, Kt.
†Newson-Smith, Sir Peter Frank Graham, Bt. (1944)
Newton, Sir (Charles) Wilfred, Kt., CBE
Newton, Sir (Harry) Michael (Rex), Bt. (1900)
Newton, Sir Kenneth Garnar, Bt. (1924), OBE, TD
Ngata, Sir Henare Kohere, KBE
Nice, Sir Geoffrey, Kt., QC
Nichol, Sir Duncan Kirkbride, Kt., CBE
Nicholas, Sir David, Kt., CBE
Nicholas, Sir John William, KCVO, CMG
Nicholls, Sir Nigel Hamilton, KCVO, CBE
Nichols, Sir Richard Everard, Kt.
Nicholson, Sir Bryan Hubert, GBE, Kt.
†Nicholson, Sir Charles Christian, Bt. (1912)
Nicholson, *Rt. Hon.* Sir Michael, Kt.
Nicholson, Sir Paul Douglas, Kt.
Nicholson, Sir Robin Buchanan, Kt., PHD, FRS, FRENG
Nicoll, Sir William, KCMG
Nightingale, Sir Charles Manners Gamaliel, Bt. (1628)
Nixon, Sir Simon Michael Christopher, Bt. (1906)
Nixon, Sir Edwin Ronald, Kt., CBE
Noble, Sir David Brunel, Bt. (1902)
Noble, Sir Iain Andrew, Bt., OBE (1923)
Nombri, Sir Joseph Karl, Kt., ISO, BEM
Noon, Sir Gulam Kaderbhoy, Kt., MBE
Norman, Sir Arthur Gordon, KBE, DFC
Norman, Sir Mark Annesley, Bt. (1915)
Norman, Sir Robert Henry, Kt., OBE
Norman, Sir Ronald, Kt., OBE
Norman, Sir Torquil Patrick Alexander, Kt., CBE
Normington, Sir David John, KCB
Norrington, Sir Roger Arthur Carver, Kt., CBE
Norriss, Air Marshal Sir Peter Coulson, KBE, CB, AFC
North, Sir Peter Machin, Kt., CBE, QC, DCL, FBA
North, Sir Thomas Lindsay, Kt.
North, Sir (William) Jonathan (Frederick), Bt. (1920)
Norton-Griffiths, Sir John, Bt. (1922)
Nossal, Sir Gustav Joseph Victor, Kt., CBE
Nott, *Rt. Hon.* Sir John William Frederic, KCB
Nourse, *Rt. Hon.* Sir Martin Charles, Kt.
Nugent, Sir John Edwin Lavallin, Bt. (I. 1795)
†Nugent, Sir Christopher George Ridley, Bt. (1806)
†Nugent, Sir (Walter) Richard Middleton, Bt. (1831)
Nunn, Sir Trevor Robert, Kt., CBE
Nunneley, Sir Charles Kenneth Roylance, Kt.
Nursaw, Sir James, KCB, QC
Nurse, Sir Paul Maxime, Kt.
†Nuttall, Sir Harry, Bt. (1922)
Nutting, Sir John Grenfell, Bt. (1903), QC
Oakeley, Sir John Digby Atholl, Bt. (1790)
Oakes, Sir Christopher, Bt. (1939)
†Oakshott, Hon. Sir Michael Arthur John, Bt. (1959)
Oates, Sir Thomas, Kt., CMG, OBE
O'Brien, Sir Frederick William Fitzgerald, Kt.
O'Brien, Sir Richard, Kt., DSO, MC
O'Brien, Sir Timothy John, Bt. (1849)
O'Brien, *Adm.* Sir William Donough, KCB, DSC
O'Connell, Sir Bernard, Kt.
O'Connell, Sir Maurice James Donagh MacCarthy, Bt. (1869)
O'Dea, Sir Patrick Jerad, KCVO
Odell, Sir Stanley John, Kt.
Odgers, Sir Graeme David William, Kt.
O'Donnell, Sir Augustine Thomas, KCB
O'Donnell, Sir Christopher John, Kt.
O'Donoghue, *Lt.-Gen.* Sir Kevin, KCB, CBE
O'Dowd, Sir David Joseph, Kt., CBE, QPM
Ogden, *Dr* Sir Peter James, Kt.
Ogden, Sir Robert, Kt., CBE
Ogilvy, Sir Francis Gilbert Arthur, Bt. (S. 1626)
Ogilvy-Wedderburn, Sir Andrew John Alexander, Bt. (1803)
Ognall, *Hon.* Sir Harry Henry, Kt.
Ohlson, Sir Brian Eric Christopher, Bt. (1920)
Oldham, *Dr* Sir John, Kt., OBE
Oliver, Sir James Michael Yorrick, Kt.
Oliver, Sir Stephen John Lindsay, Kt., QC
O'Loghlen, Sir Colman Michael, Bt. (1838)
Olver, Sir Stephen John Linley, KBE, CMG
Omand, Sir David Bruce, GCB
O'Nions, Prof. Sir Robert Keith, Kt., FRS, PHD
Ondaatje, Sir Christopher, Kt., CBE
Onslow, Sir John Roger Wilmot, Bt. (1797)

Oppenheimer, Sir Michael Bernard Grenville, Bt. (1921)
Oppenshaw, Sir Charles Peter Lawford, Kt., QC
Orde, Sir Hugh Stephen Roden, Kt., OBE
O'Regan, *Dr* Sir Stephen Gerard (Tipene), Kt.
O'Reilly, Sir Anthony John Francis, Kt.
O'Reilly, *Prof.* Sir John James, Kt.
Orr, Sir David Alexander, Kt., MC
Orr, Sir John, Kt., OBE
Orr-Ewing, Sir (Alistair) Simon, Bt. (1963)
Orr-Ewing, Sir Archibald Donald, Bt. (1886)
Osborn, Sir John Holbrook, Kt.
Osborn, Sir Richard Henry Danvers, Bt. (1662)
Osborne, Sir Peter George, Bt. (I. 1629)
Osmotherly, Sir Edward Benjamin Crofton, Kt., CB
O'Sullevan, Sir Peter John, Kt., CBE
Oswald, *Admiral of the Fleet* Sir (John) Julian Robertson, GCB
Oswald, Sir (William Richard) Michael, KCVO
Otton, Sir Geoffrey John, KCB
Otton, *Rt. Hon.* Sir Philip Howard, Kt.
Oulton, Sir Antony Derek Maxwell, GCB, QC
Ouseley, *Hon.* Sir Brian Walter, Kt.
Outram, Sir Alan James, Bt. (1858)
Owen, Sir Geoffrey, Kt.
Owen, *Hon.* Sir John Arthur Dalziel, Kt.
Owen, *Hon.* Sir Robert Michael, Kt.
Owen-Jones, Sir Lindsay Harwood, KBE
Packer, Sir Richard John, KCB
Page, Sir (Arthur) John, Kt.
Paget, Sir Julian Tolver, Bt. (1871), CVO
Paget, Sir Richard Herbert, Bt. (1886)
Paine, Sir Christopher Hammon, Kt., FRCP, FRCR
Pakenham, *Hon.* Sir Michael Aiden, KBE, CMG
Palin, *Air Chief Marshal* Sir Roger Hewlett, KCB, OBE
Palliser, *Rt. Hon.* Sir (Arthur) Michael, GCMG
Palmer, Sir Albert Rocky, Kt.
Palmer, Sir (Charles) Mark, Bt. (1886)
Palmer, Sir Geoffrey Christopher John, Bt. (1660)
Palmer, *Rt. Hon.* Sir Geoffrey Winston Russell, KCMG
Palmer, Sir John Edward Somerset, Bt. (1791)
Palmer, *Maj.-Gen.* Sir (Joseph) Michael, KCVO
Palmer, Sir Reginald Oswald, GCMG, MBE
Pantlin, Sir Dick Hurst, Kt., CBE
Parbo, Sir Arvi Hillar, Kt.
Park, *Hon.* Sir Andrew Edward Wilson, Kt.
Parker, Sir Alan William, Kt., CBE
Parker, Sir Eric Wilson, Kt.
Parker, *Rt. Hon.* Sir Jonathan Frederic, Kt.
Parker, *Maj.* Sir Michael John, KCVO, CBE
Parker, Sir Richard (William) Hyde, Bt. (1681)
Parker, *Rt. Hon.* Sir Roger Jocelyn, Kt.
Parker, Sir (Thomas) John, Kt.
Parker, Sir William Peter Brian, Bt. (1844)
Parkes, Sir Edward Walter, Kt., FRENG
Parry, Sir Emyr Jones, GCMG
Parry-Evans, *Air Chief Marshal* Sir David, GCB, CBE
Parsons, Sir John Christopher, KCVO
Parsons, Sir (John) Michael, Kt.
Parsons, Sir Richard Edmund (Clement Fownes), KCMG
Partridge, Sir Michael John Anthony, KCB
Pascoe, *Gen.* Sir Robert Alan, KCB, MBE
Pasley, Sir Robert Killigrew Sabine, Bt. (1794)
Paston-Bedingfeld, *Capt.* Sir Edmund George Felix, Bt. (1661)
Paterson, Sir Dennis Craig, Kt.
Patnick, Sir (Cyril) Irvine, Kt., OBE
Patten, *Hon.* Mr Justice, Sir Nicholas John, Kt.
Pattie, *Rt. Hon.* Sir Geoffrey Edwin, Kt.
Pattison, *Prof.* Sir John Ridley, Kt., DM, FRCPATH
Pattullo, Sir (David) Bruce, Kt., CBE
Pauncefort-Duncombe, Sir Philip Digby, Bt. (1859)
Payne, Sir Norman John, Kt., CBE, FRENG
Payne-Gallwey, Sir Philip Frankland, Bt. (1812)
Peach, Sir Leonard Harry, Kt.
Peacock, *Prof.* Sir Alan Turner, Kt., DSC
Pearce, Sir (Daniel Norton) Idris, Kt., CBE, TD
Pearse, Sir Brian Gerald, Kt.
Pearson, Sir Francis Nicholas Fraser, Bt. (1964)
Pearson, *Gen.* Sir Thomas Cecil Hook, KCB, CBE, DSO
Peart, *Prof.* Sir William Stanley, Kt., MD, FRS
Pease, Sir (Alfred) Vincent, Bt. (1882)
Pease, Sir Richard Thorn, Bt. (1920)
Peat, Sir Gerrard Charles, KCVO
Peat, Sir Michael Charles Gerrard, KCVO
Peck, Sir Edward Heywood, GCMG
Peckham, *Prof.* Sir Michael John, Kt.
Pedelty, Sir Mervyn Kay, Kt.
Peek, *Vice-Adm.* Sir Richard Innes, KBE, CB, DSC
Peek, Sir Richard Grenville, Bt. (1874)
Peirse, *Air Vice-Marshal* Sir Richard Charles Fairfax, KCVO, CB
Pelgen, Sir Harry Friedrich, Kt., MBE
Peliza, Sir Robert John, KBE, ED
Pelly, Sir Richard John, Bt. (1840)
Pemberton, Sir Francis Wingate William, Kt., CBE
Pendry, *Prof.* Sir John Brian, Kt., FRS
Penrose, *Prof.* Sir Roger, Kt., OM, FRS
Penry-Davey, *Hon.* Sir David Herbert, Kt.
Pepper, *Dr.* Sir David Edwin, KCMG
Pepper, *Prof.* Sir Michael, Kt.
Perowne, *Vice-Adm.* Sir James Francis, KBE
Perring, Sir John Raymond, Bt. (1963)
Perris, Sir David (Arthur), Kt., MBE
Perry, Sir David Howard, KCB
Perry, Sir (David) Norman, Kt., MBE
Perry, Sir Michael Sydney, GBE
Pervez, Sir Mohammed Anwar, Kt., OBE
Peters, *Prof.* Sir David Keith, Kt., FRCP
Peterson, Sir Christopher Matthew, Kt., CBE, TD
†Petit, Sir Jehangir, Bt. (1890)
Peto, Sir Henry George Morton, Bt. (1855)
Peto, Sir Michael Henry Basil, Bt. (1927)
Peto, *Prof.* Sir Richard, Kt., FRS
Petrie, Sir Peter Charles, Bt. (1918), CMG
Pettigrew, Sir Russell Hilton, Kt.
Pettit, Sir Daniel Eric Arthur, Kt.
Pettitt, Sir Dennis, Kt.
†Philipson-Stow, Sir (Robert) Matthew, Bt. (1907)
Phillips, Sir Fred Albert, Kt., CVO
Phillips, Sir (Gerald) Hayden, GCB
Phillips, Sir John David, Kt., QPM
Phillips, Sir Peter John, Kt., OBE
Phillips, Sir Robin Francis, Bt. (1912)
Phillis, Sir Robert Weston, Kt.
Pickard, Sir (John) Michael, Kt.
Pickthorn, Sir James Francis Mann, Bt. (1959)
Pidgeon, Sir John Allan Stewart, Kt.
†Piers, Sir James Desmond, Bt. (I. 1661)
Piggott-Brown, Sir William Brian, Bt. (1903)
Pigot, Sir George Hugh, Bt. (1764)
Pigott, *Lt.-Gen.* Sir Anthony David, KCB, CBE
Pigott, Sir Berkeley Henry Sebastian, Bt. (1808)
Pike, *Lt.-Gen.* Sir Hew William Royston, KCB, DSO, MBE
Pike, Sir Michael Edmund, KCVO, CMG
Pike, Sir Philip Ernest Housden, Kt., QC
Pilditch, Sir Richard Edward, Bt. (1929)
Pile, Sir Frederick Devereux, Bt. (1900), MC
Pill, *Rt. Hon.* Sir Malcolm Thomas, Kt.

Pilling, Sir Joseph Grant, KCB
Pinsent, Sir Christopher Roy, Bt. (1938)
Pinsent, Sir Matthew Clive, Kt., CBE
Pippard, *Prof.* Sir (Alfred) Brian, Kt., FRS
Pitakaka, Sir Moses Puibangara, GCMG
Pitcher, Sir Desmond Henry, Kt.
Pitchers, *Hon.* Sir Christopher (John), Kt.
Pitchford, *Hon.* Sir Christopher John, Kt.
Pitman, Sir Brian Ivor, Kt.
Pitoi, Sir Sere, Kt., CBE
Pitt, Sir Michael Edward, Kt.
Pitts, Sir Cyril Alfred, Kt.
Plastow, Sir David Arnold Stuart, Kt.
Platt, Sir Harold Grant, Kt.
Platt, Sir Martin Philip, Bt. (1959)
Pledger, *Air Chief Marshal* Sir Malcolm David, KCB, OBE, AFC
Plumbly, Sir Derek John, KCMG
Pogo, *Most Revd.* Ellison Leslie, KBE
Pohai, Sir Timothy, Kt., MBE
Pole, Sir (John) Richard (Walter Reginald) Carew, Bt. (1628)
Pole, Sir Peter Van Notten, Bt. (1791)
Polkinghorne, *Revd Canon* John Charlton, KBE, FRS
Pollard, Sir Charles, Kt.
†Pollen, Sir Richard John Hungerford, Bt. (1795)
Pollock, Sir George Frederick, Bt. (1866)
Ponsonby, Sir Ashley Charles Gibbs, Bt., KCVO, MC (1956)
Poore, Sir Roger Ricardo, Bt. (1795)
Pope, Sir Joseph Albert, Kt., DSC, PHD
Popplewell, *Hon.* Sir Oliver Bury, Kt.
†Porritt, Sir Jonathon Espie, Bt. (1963)
Portal, Sir Jonathan Francis, Bt. (1901)
Porter, *Rt. Hon.* Sir Robert Wilson, Kt., PC (NI)
Posnett, Sir Richard Neil, KBE, CMG
Potter, *Rt. Hon.* Sir Mark Howard, Kt.
Potts, *Hon.* Sir Francis Humphrey, Kt.
Pound, Sir John David, Bt. (1905)
Povey, Sir Keith, Kt., QPM
Powell, Sir Nicholas Folliott Douglas, Bt. (1897)
Power, Sir Alastair John Cecil, Bt. (1924)
Power, *Hon.* Sir Noel Plunkett, Kt.
Prance, *Prof.* Sir Ghillean Tolmie, Kt., FRS
Prendergast, Sir (Walter) Kieran, KCVO, CMG
Prescott, Sir Mark, Bt. (1938)
†Preston, Sir Philip Charles Henry Hulton, Bt. (1815)
Prevost, Sir Christopher Gerald, Bt. (1805)
Price, Sir David Ernest Campbell, Kt.
Price, Sir Francis Caradoc Rose, Bt. (1815)
Price, Sir Frank Leslie, Kt.
Prickett, *Air Chief Marshal* Sir Thomas Other, KCB, DSO, DFC
Prideaux, Sir Humphrey Povah Treverbian, Kt., OBE
Priestly, Sir Julian Gordon, KCMG
†Primrose, Sir John Ure, Bt. (1903)
Pringle, *Air Marshal* Sir Charles Norman Seton, KBE, FRENG
Pringle, *Hon.* Sir John Kenneth, Kt.
Pringle, *Lt.-Gen.* Sir Steuart (Robert), Bt. (S. 1683), KCB
Pritchard, Sir Neil, KCMG
Prichard-Jones, Sir John, Bt. (1910)
Proby, Sir William Henry, Bt. (1952)
Proctor-Beauchamp, Sir Christopher Radstock, Bt. (1745)
Prosser, Sir David John, Kt.
Prosser, Sir Ian Maurice Gray, Kt.
Pryke, Sir Christopher Dudley, Bt. (1926)
Puapua, *Rt. Hon.* Sir Tomasi, GCMG, KBE
Pugh, Sir Idwal Vaughan, KCB
Pumfrey, *Hon.* Sir Nicholas Richard, Kt.
Pumphrey, Sir (John) Laurence, KCMG
Purves, Sir William, Kt., CBE, DSO
Purvis, *Vice-Adm.* Sir Neville, KCB
Quan, Sir Henry (Francis), KBE
Quicke, Sir John Godolphin, Kt., CBE
Quigley, Sir (William) George (Henry), Kt., CB, PHD
Quilter, Sir Anthony Raymond Leopold Cuthbert, Bt. (1897)
Quinlan, Sir Michael Edward, GCB
Quinton, Sir James Grand, Kt.
Radcliffe, Sir Sebastian Everard, Bt. (1813)
Radda, *Prof.* Sir George Karoly, Kt., CBE, FRS
Rae, Sir William, Kt., QPM
Raeburn, Sir Michael Edward Norman, Bt. (1923)
Raikes, *Vice-Adm.* Sir Iwan Geoffrey, KCB, CBE, DSC
Raison, *Rt. Hon.* Sir Timothy Hugh Francis, Kt.
Rake, Sir Michael Derek Vaughan, Kt.
Ralli, Sir Godfrey Victor, Bt., TD (1912)
Ramdanee, Sir Mookteswar Baboolall Kailash, Kt.
Ramphal, Sir Shridath Surendranath, GCMG
Ramphul, Sir Baalkhristna, Kt.
Ramphul, Sir Indurduth, Kt.
Ramsay, Sir Alexander William Burnett, Bt. (1806)
Ramsay, Sir Allan John (Hepple), KBE, CMG
Ramsay-Fairfax-Lucy, Sir Edmund John William Hugh, Bt. (1836)
Ramsbotham, *Hon.* Sir Peter Edward, GCMG, GCVO
Ramsden, Sir John Charles Josslyn, Bt. (1689)
Ramsey, *Dr* Sir Frank Cuthbert, KCMG
Ramsey, *Hon.* Sir Vivian Arthur, Kt.
Rankin, Sir Ian Niall, Bt. (1898)
Rasch, Sir Simon Anthony Carne, Bt. (1903)
Rashleigh, Sir Richard Harry, Bt. (1831)
Ratford, Sir David John Edward, KCMG, CVO
Rattee, *Hon.* Sir Donald Keith, Kt.
Rattle, Sir Simon Dennis, Kt., CBE
Rawlins, *Surgeon Vice-Adm.* Sir John Stuart Pepys, KBE
Rawlins, *Prof.* Sir Michael David, Kt., FRCP, FRCPED
Rawlinson, Sir Anthony Henry John, Bt. (1891)
Rea, *Prof.* Sir Desmond, Kt., OBE
Read, *Air Marshal* Sir Charles Frederick, KBE, CB, DFC, AFC
Read, *Prof.* Sir David John, Kt.
Read, Sir John Emms, Kt.
†Reade, Sir Kenneth Ray, Bt. (1661)
Reardon-Smith, Sir (William) Antony (John), Bt. (1920)
Reay, *Lt.-Gen.* Sir (Hubert) Alan John, KBE
Redgrave, *Maj.-Gen.* Sir Roy Michael Frederick, KBE, MC
Redgrave, Sir Steven Geoffrey, Kt., CBE
Redmayne, Sir Nicholas, Bt. (1964)
Redwood, Sir Peter Boverton, Bt. (1911)
Reece, Sir Charles Hugh, Kt.
Reedie, Sir Craig Collins, Kt., CBE
Rees, Sir Richard Ellis Meuric, Kt., CBE
Reeve, Sir Anthony, KCMG, KCVO
Reeves, *Most Revd* Paul Alfred, GCMG, GCVO
Reffell, *Adm.* Sir Derek Roy, KCB
Refshauge, *Maj.-Gen.* Sir William Dudley, Kt., CBE
Reid, Sir Alexander James, Bt. (1897)
Reid, Sir Hugh, Bt. (1922)
Reid, Sir Norman Robert, Kt.
Reid, Sir (Philip) Alan, KCVO
Reid, Sir Robert Paul, Kt.
Reid, Sir William Kennedy, KCB
Reiher, Sir Frederick Bernard Carl, KBE, CMG
Reilly, *Lt.-Gen.* Sir Jeremy Calcott, KCB, DSO
Renals, Sir Stanley, Bt. (1895)
Renouf, Sir Clement William Bailey, Kt.
Renshaw, Sir John David Bine, Bt. (1903)
Renwick, Sir Richard Eustace, Bt. (1921)
Reporter, Sir Shapoor Ardeshirji, KBE
Reynolds, Sir David James, Bt. (1923)
Reynolds, Sir Peter William John, Kt., CBE
Rhodes, Sir John Christopher Douglas, Bt. (1919)
Rice, *Maj.-Gen.* Sir Desmond Hind Garrett, KCVO, CBE
Rice, Sir Timothy Miles Bindon, Kt.
Richard, Sir Cliff, Kt., OBE

Richards, Sir Brian Mansel, Kt., CBE, PHD
Richards, *Hon.* Sir David Anthony Stewart, Kt.
Richards, Sir David Gerald, Kt.
Richards, *Lt.-Gen.* Sir David, Julian, KCB, CBE, DSO
Richards, Sir Francis Neville, KCMG, CVO
Richards, *Rt. Hon.* Sir Stephen Price, Kt.
Richardson, Sir Anthony Lewis, Bt. (1924)
Richardson, *Rt. Hon.* Sir Ivor Lloyd Morgan, Kt.
Richardson, *Lt.-Gen.* Sir Robert Francis, KCB, CVO, CBE
Richardson, Sir Thomas Legh, KCMG
Richardson-Bunbury, Sir (Richard David) Michael, Bt. (I. 1787)
Richmond, *Prof.* Sir Mark Henry, Kt., FRS
Ricketts, Sir (Robert) Tristram, Bt. (1828)
Riddell, Sir John Charles Buchanan, Bt. (S. 1628), CVO
Ridley, Sir Adam (Nicholas), Kt.
Ridley, Sir Michael Kershaw, KCVO
Rifkind, *Rt. Hon.* Sir Malcolm Leslie, KCMG
Rigby, Sir Anthony John, Bt. (1929)
Rigby, Sir Peter, Kt.
Rimer, *Hon.* Sir Colin Percy Farquharson, Kt.
Ripley, Sir William Hugh, Bt. (1880)
Risk, Sir Thomas Neilson, Kt.
Ritako, Sir Thomas Baha, Kt., MBE
Ritblat, Sir John Henry, Kt.
Rivett-Carnac, Sir Miles James, Bt. (1836)
Rix, *Rt. Hon.* Sir Bernard Anthony, Kt.
Rix, Sir John, Kt., MBE, FRENG
Robati, Sir Pupuke, KBE
Robb, Sir John Weddell, Kt.
Roberts, *Hon.* Sir Denys Tudor Emil, KBE,
Roberts, Sir Derek Harry, Kt., CBE, FRS, FRENG
Roberts, *Prof.* Sir Edward Adam, KCMG
Roberts, Sir Gilbert Howland Rookehurst, Bt. (1809)
Roberts, Sir Hugh Ashley, KCVO
Roberts, Sir Ivor Anthony, KCMG
Roberts, *Maj.-Gen.* Sir Sebastian John Lechmere, KCVO, OBE
Roberts, Sir Samuel, Bt. (1919)
Roberts, Sir William James Denby, Bt. (1909)
Robertson, Sir Lewis, Kt., CBE, FRSE
Robins, Sir Ralph Harry, Kt., FRENG
Robinson, Sir Albert Edward Phineas, Kt.
†Robinson, Sir Christopher Philipse, Bt. (1854)
Robinson, Sir Gerrard Jude, Kt.
Robinson, Sir Ian, Kt.
Robinson, Sir John James Michael Laud, Bt. (1660)
Robinson, *Dr* Sir Kenneth, Kt.
Robinson, Sir Wilfred Henry Frederick, Bt. (1908)
Robson, Sir John Adam, KCMG
Robson, Sir Stephen Arthur, Kt., CB
Robson, Sir Robert William, Kt., CBE
Roch, *Rt. Hon.* Sir John Ormond, Kt.
Roche, Sir David O'Grady, Bt. (1838)
Roche, Sir Henry John, Kt.
Rodgers, Sir (Andrew) Piers (Wingate Aikin-Sneath), Bt. (1964)
Rodley, *Prof.* Sir Nigel, KBE
Rodrigues, Sir Alberto Maria, Kt., CBE, ED
Rogers, *Air Chief Marshal* Sir John Robson, KCB, CBE
Rooke, Sir Denis Eric, Kt., OM, CBE, FRS, FRENG
Ropner, Sir John Bruce Woollacott, Bt. (1952)
Ropner, Sir Robert Clinton, Bt. (1904)
Rose, Sir Arthur James, Kt., CBE
Rose, *Rt. Hon.* Sir Christopher Dudley Roger, Kt.
Rose, Sir Clive Martin, GCMG
Rose, Sir David Lancaster, Bt. (1874)
Rose, *Gen.* Sir (Hugh) Michael, KCB, CBE, DSO, QGM
Rose, Sir John Edward Victor, Kt.
Rose, Sir Julian Day, Bt. (1872 and 1909)
Rosenthal, Sir Norman Leon, Kt.
Ross, *Maj.* Sir Andrew Charles Paterson, Bt. (1960)
Ross, *Lt.-Gen.* Sir Robert Jeremy, KCB, OBE
Ross, *Lt.-Col.* Sir Walter Hugh Malcolm, GCVO, OBE
Rossi, Sir Hugh Alexis Louis, Kt.
Rothschild, Sir Evelyn Robert Adrian de, Kt.
Rougier, *Hon.* Sir Richard George, Kt.
Rove, *Revd* Ikan, KBE
Rowe, *Rear-Adm.* Sir Patrick Barton, KCVO, CBE
Rowe-Ham, Sir David Kenneth, GBE
Rowland, Sir (John) David, Kt.
Rowlands, Sir David, KCB
Rowley, Sir Charles Robert, Bt. (1836)
Rowling, Sir John Reginald, Kt.
Rowlinson, *Prof.* Sir John Shipley, Kt., FRS
Royce, *Hon.* Sir Roger John, Kt.
Royden, Sir Christopher John, Bt. (1905)
Rudd, Sir (Anthony) Nigel (Russell), Kt.
Rudge, Sir Alan Walter, Kt., CBE, FRS
Rugge-Price, Sir James Keith Peter, Bt. (1804)
Ruggles-Brise, Sir Timothy Edward, Bt. (1935)
Rumbold, Sir Henry John Sebastian, Bt. (1779)
Runchorelal, Sir (Udayan) Chinubhai Madhowlal, Bt. (1913)
Rusby, *Vice-Adm.* Sir Cameron, KCB, LVO
Rushdie, Sir (Ahmed) Salman, Kt.
†Russell, Sir (Arthur) Mervyn, Bt. (1812)
Russell, Sir Charles Dominic, Bt. (1916)
Russell, Sir George, Kt., CBE
Russell, Sir Muir, KCB
Rutter, *Prof.* Sir Michael Llewellyn, Kt., CBE, MD, FRS
Ryan, Sir Derek Gerald, Bt. (1919)
Rycroft, Sir Richard John, Bt. (1784)
Ryder, *Hon.* Sir Ernest Nigel Ryder, Kt., TD
Ryrie, Sir William Sinclair, KCB
Sacks, *Chief Rabbi Dr* Jonathan, Kt.
Sacranie, Sir Iqbal Abdul Karim Mussa, Kt., OBE
Sainsbury, *Rt. Hon.* Sir Timothy Alan Davan, Kt.
St Clair-Ford, Sir James Anson, Bt. (1793)
St George, Sir John Avenel Bligh, Bt. (I. 1766)
St John-Mildmay, Sir Walter John Hugh, Bt. (1772)
Sainty, Sir John Christopher, KCB
Salisbury, Sir Robert William, Kt.
Salt, Sir Patrick MacDonnell, Bt. (1869)
Salt, Sir (Thomas) Michael John, Bt. (1899)
Salusbury-Trelawny, Sir John Barry, Bt. (1628)
Sampson, Sir Colin, Kt., CBE, QPM
Samuel, Sir John Michael Glen, Bt. (1898)
Samuelson, Sir (Bernard) Michael (Francis), Bt. (1884)
Samuelson, Sir Sydney Wylie, Kt., CBE
Sanders, Sir Robert Tait, KBE, CMG
Sanders, Sir Ronald Michael, KCMG
Sanderson, Sir Frank Linton, Bt. (1920)
Sands, Sir Roger Blakemore, KCB
Sarei, Sir Alexis Holyweek, Kt., CBE
Satchwell, Sir Kevin Joseph, Kt.
Saunders, *Hon.* Sir John Henry Boulton, Kt.
Savile, Sir James Wilson Vincent, Kt., OBE
Savory, Sir Michael Berry, Kt.
Sawers, Sir Robert John, KCMG
Saxby, *Prof.* Sir Robin Keith, Kt.
Scarlett, Sir John McLeod, KCMG, OBE
Scheele, Sir Nicholas Vernon, KCMG
Schiemann, *Rt. Hon.* Sir Konrad Hermann Theodor, Kt.
Scholar, Sir Michael Charles, KCB
Scholey, Sir David Gerald, Kt., CBE
Scholey, Sir Robert, Kt., CBE, FRENG
Scholtens, Sir James Henry, KCVO
Schreier, Sir Bernard, Kt.
Schubert, Sir Sydney, Kt.
Scipio, Sir Hudson Rupert, Kt.

Scoon, Sir Paul, GCMG, GCVO, OBE
Scott, Sir Anthony Percy, Bt. (1913)
Scott, Sir David Aubrey, GCMG
Scott, *Prof.* Sir George Peter, Kt.
Scott, Sir James Jervoise, Bt. (1962)
Scott, Sir Kenneth Bertram Adam, KCVO, CMG
Scott, Sir Oliver Christopher Anderson, Bt. (1909)
Scott, *Prof.* Sir Philip John, KBE
Scott, Sir Ridley, Kt.
Scott, Sir Robert David Hillyer, Kt.
Scott, Sir Walter John, Bt. (1907)
Scott-Lee, Sir Paul Joseph, Kt., QPM
Seale, Sir Clarence David, Kt.
Seale, Sir John Henry, Bt. (1838)
Seaman, Sir Keith Douglas, KCVO, OBE
Sebastian, Sir Cuthbert Montraville, GCMG, OBE
†Sebright, Sir Rufus Hugo Giles, Bt. (1626)
Seccombe, Sir (William) Vernon Stephen, Kt.
Seconde, Sir Reginald Louis, KCMG, CVO
Sedley, *Rt. Hon.* Sir Stephen John, Kt.
Seely, Sir Nigel Edward, Bt. (1896)
Seeto, Sir Ling James, Kt., MBE
Seeyave, Sir Rene Sow Choung, Kt., CBE
Seligman, Sir Peter Wendel, Kt., CBE
Semple, Sir John Laughlin, KCB
Sergeant, Sir Patrick, Kt.
Series, Sir (Joseph Michel) Emile, Kt., CBE
Serota, Sir Nicholas Andrew, Kt.
Serpell, Sir David Radford, KCB, CMG, OBE
†Seton, Sir Charles Wallace, Bt. (S. 1683)
Seton, Sir Iain Bruce, Bt. (S. 1663)
Severne, *Air Vice-Marshal* Sir John de Milt, KCVO, OBE, AFC
Shaffer, Sir Peter Levin, Kt., CBE
Shakerley, Sir Geoffrey Adam, Bt. (1838)
Shakespeare, Sir Thomas William, Bt. (1942)
Sharp, Sir Adrian, Bt. (1922)
Sharp, Sir Kenneth Johnston, Kt., TD
Sharp, Sir Leslie, Kt., QPM
Sharp, Sir Sheridan Christopher Robin, Bt. (1920)
Sharples, Sir James, Kt., QPM
Shattock, Sir Gordon, Kt.
Shaw, Sir Brian Piers, Kt.
Shaw, Sir (Charles) Barry, Kt., CB, QC
Shaw, Sir Charles De Vere, Bt. (1821)
Shaw, *Prof.* Sir John Calman, Kt., CBE
Shaw, Sir Neil McGowan, Kt.
Shaw, Sir Roy, Kt.
Shaw, Sir Run Run, Kt., CBE
Shaw-Stewart, Sir Ludovic Houston, Bt. (S. 1667)
Shearing, Sir George Albert, Kt. OBE
Shebbeare, Sir Thomas Andrew, KCVO
Sheehy, Sir Patrick, Kt.
Sheffield, Sir Reginald Adrian Berkeley, Bt. (1755)
Shehadie, Sir Nicholas Michael, Kt., OBE
Sheil, *Rt. Hon.* Sir John, Kt.
Sheinwald, Sir Nigel Elton, KCMG
Shelley, Sir John Richard, Bt. (1611)
Shepherd, Sir Colin Ryley, Kt.
Shepherd, Sir John Alan, KCVO, CMG
Shepperd, Sir Alfred Joseph, Kt.
Sher, Sir Antony, KBE
Sherbourne, Sir Stephen Ashley, Kt., CBE
Sherston-Baker, Sir Robert George Humphrey, Bt. (1796)
Shields, *Prof.* Sir Robert, Kt., MD
Shiffner, Sir Henry David, Bt. (1818)
Silber, *Hon.* Sir Stephen Robert, Kt.
Shinwell, Sir (Maurice) Adrian, Kt.
Shock, Sir Maurice, Kt.
Short, Sir Apenera Pera, KBE
Shortridge, Sir Jon Deacon, KCB
Shuckburgh, Sir Rupert Charles Gerald, Bt. (1660)
Sieff, *Hon.* Sir David, Kt.
Silber, *Rt. Hon.* Sir Stephen Robert, Kt.
Simeon, Sir Richard Edmund Barrington, Bt. (1815)
Simmonds, *Rt. Hon. Dr* Sir Kennedy Alphonse, KCMG
Simmons, *Air Marshal* Sir Michael George, KCB, AFC
Simmons, Sir Stanley Clifford, Kt.
Simms, Sir Neville Ian, Kt., FRENG
Simon, *Hon.* Sir Peregrine Charles Hugh, Kt.
Simonet, Sir Louis Marcel Pierre, Kt., CBE
Simpson, *Dr* Sir Peter Jeffery, Kt.
Sims, Sir Roger Edward, Kt
Sinclair, Sir Clive Marles, Kt.
Sinclair, Sir Ian McTaggart, KCMG, QC
Sinclair, Sir Patrick Robert Richard, Bt. (S. 1704)
Sinclair, Sir Robert John, Kt.
Sinclair-Lockhart, Sir Simon John Edward Francis, Bt. (S. 1636)
Sinden, Sir Donald Alfred, Kt., CBE
Singer, *Hon.* Sir Jan Peter, Kt.
Singh, Sir Pritpal, Kt.
Singleton, Sir Roger, Kt., CBE
Sione, Sir Tomu Malaefone, GCMG, OBE
Sitwell, Sir (Sacheverell) Reresby, Bt. (1808)
Skeggs, Sir Clifford George, Kt.
Skehel, Sir John James, Kt., FRS
Skingsley, *Air Chief Marshal* Sir Anthony Gerald, GBE, KCB
Skinner, Sir (Thomas) Keith (Hewitt), Bt. (1912)
Skipwith, Sir Patrick Alexander d'Estoteville, Bt. (1622)
Slack, Sir William Willatt, KCVO, FRCS
Slade, Sir Benjamin Julian Alfred, Bt. (1831)
Slade, *Rt. Hon.* Sir Christopher John, Kt.
Slaney, *Prof.* Sir Geoffrey, KBE
Slater, *Adm.* Sir John (Jock) Cunningham Kirkwood, GCB, LVO
Sleight, Sir Richard, Bt. (1920)
Sloan, Sir Andrew Kirkpatrick, Kt., QPM
Sloman, Sir Albert Edward, Kt., CBE
Smart, Sir Jack, Kt., CBE
Smiley, *Lt.-Col.* Sir John Philip, Bt. (1903)
Smith, Sir Alan, Kt., CBE, DFC
Smith, *Hon.* Sir Andrew Charles, Kt.
Smith, Sir Andrew Thomas, Bt. (1897)
†Smith, Sir Robert Christopher Sydney Winwood, Bt. (1809)
Smith, *Prof.* Sir Colin Stansfield, Kt., CBE
Smith, Sir Cyril, Kt., MBE
Smith, *Prof.* Sir David Cecil, Kt., FRS
Smith, Sir David Iser, KCVO
Smith, Sir Dudley (Gordon), Kt.
Smith, *Prof.* Sir Eric Brian, Kt., PHD
Smith, Sir Geoffrey Johnson, Kt.
Smith, Sir John Alfred, Kt., QPM
Smith, Sir Joseph William Grenville, Kt.
Smith, Sir Kevin, Kt., CBE
Smith, Sir Michael John Llewellyn, KCVO, CMG
Smith, Sir (Norman) Brian, Kt., CBE, PHD
Smith, Sir Paul Brierley, Kt., CBE
Smith, *Hon.* Sir Peter (Winston), Kt.
Smith, Sir Robert Courtney, Kt., CBE
Smith, Sir Robert Haldane, Kt
Smith, Sir Robert Hill, Bt. (1945)
Smith, *Gen.* Sir Rupert Anthony, KCB, DSO, OBE, QGM
Smith-Dodsworth, Sir John Christopher, Bt. (1784)
Smith-Gordon, Sir (Lionel) Eldred (Peter), Bt. (1838)
Smith-Marriott, Sir Hugh Cavendish, Bt. (1774)
Smurfit, *Dr.* Sir Michael William Joseph, KBE
Smyth, Sir Timothy John, Bt. (1955)
Sobers, Sir Garfield St Auburn, Kt.
Solomon, Sir Harry, Kt.
Somare, *Rt. Hon.* Sir Michael Thomas, GCMG, CH
Somerville, *Brig.* Sir John Nicholas, Kt., CBE
Sorrell, Sir Martin Stuart, Kt.
Soulsby, Sir Peter Alfred, Kt.
Soutar, *Air Marshal* Sir Charles John Williamson, KBE
Southby, Sir John Richard Bilbe, Bt. (1937)
Southern, *Prof.* Sir Edwin Mellor, Kt.
Southgate, Sir Colin Grieve, Kt.
Southgate, Sir William David, Kt.
Southward, *Dr* Sir Nigel Ralph, KCVO
Souyave, *Hon.* Sir (Louis) Georges, Kt.

Sowrey, *Air Marshal* Sir Frederick Beresford, KCB, CBE, AFC
Sparrow, Sir John, Kt.
Spearman, Sir Alexander Young Richard Mainwaring, Bt. (1840)
Spedding, *Prof.* Sir Colin Raymond William, Kt., CBE
Speed, Sir (Herbert) Keith, Kt., RD
Speelman, Sir Cornelis Jacob, Bt. (1686)
Speight, *Hon.* Sir Graham Davies, Kt.
Spencer, Sir Derek Harold, Kt., QC
Spencer, *Vice-Adm.* Sir Peter, KCB
Spencer-Nairn, Sir Robert Arnold, Bt. (1933)
Spicer, Sir James Wilton, Kt.
Spicer, Sir Nicholas Adrian Albert, Bt. (1906)
Spicer, Sir (William) Michael Hardy, Kt.
Spiers, Sir Donald Maurice, Kt., CB, TD
Spooner, Sir James Douglas, Kt.
Spratt, *Col.* Sir Greville Douglas, GBE, TD
Spring, Sir Dryden Thomas, Kt.
Squire, *Air Chief Marshal* Sir Peter Ted, GCB, DFC, AFC, ADC
Stainton, Sir (John) Ross, Kt., CBE
Staite, Sir Richard John, Kt., OBE
Stamer, Sir (Lovelace) Anthony, Bt. (1809)
Stanhope, *Adm.* Sir Mark, KCB, OBE
Stanier, Sir Beville Douglas, Bt. (1917)
Stanier, *Field Marshal* Sir John Wilfred, GCB, MBE
Stanley, *Rt. Hon.* Sir John Paul, Kt., MP
Staples, Sir Richard Molesworth, Bt. (I. 1628)
Starkey, Sir John Philip, Bt. (1935)
Staughton, *Rt. Hon.* Sir Christopher Stephen Thomas Jonathan Thayer, Kt.
Staveley, Sir John Malfroy, KBE, MC
Stear, *Air Chief Marshal* Sir Michael James Douglas, KCB, CBE
Steel, *Hon.* Sir David William, Kt.
Steer, Sir Alan William, Kt.
Stephen, *Rt. Hon.* Sir Ninian Martin, KG, GCMG, GCVO, KBE
Stephens, Sir (Edwin) Barrie, Kt.
Stephens, Sir William Benjamin Synge, Kt.
Stephenson, Sir Henry Upton, Bt. (1936)
Stern, *Prof.* Sir Nicholas Herbert, Kt.
Sternberg, Sir Sigmund, Kt.
Stevens, Sir Jocelyn Edward Greville, Kt., CVO
Stevens, Sir Laurence Houghton, Kt., CBE
Stevenson, Sir Simpson, Kt.
Stewart, Sir Alan d'Arcy, Bt. (I. 1623)
Stewart, Sir Brian John, Kt., CBE
Stewart, Sir David James Henderson, Bt. (1957)
Stewart, Sir David John Christopher, Bt. (1803)
Stewart, Sir James Douglas, Kt.
Stewart, Sir James Moray, KCB
Stewart, Sir (John) Simon (Watson), Bt. (1920)
Stewart, Sir John Young, Kt., OBE
Stewart, *Lt.-Col.* Sir Robert Christie, KCVO, CBE, TD
Stewart, Sir Robertson Huntly, Kt., CBE
Stewart, Sir Robin Alastair, Bt. (1960)
Stewart, *Prof.* Sir William Duncan Paterson, Kt., FRS, FRSE
Stewart-Clark, Sir John, Bt. (1918)
Stewart-Richardson, Sir Simon Alaisdair, Bt. (S. 1630)
Stewart-Wilson, *Lt.-Col.* Sir Blair Aubyn, KCVO
Stibbon, *Gen.* Sir John James, KCB, OBE
Stirling, Sir Alexander John Dickson, KBE, CMG
Stirling, Sir Angus Duncan Aeneas, Kt.
Stirling-Hamilton, Sir Malcolm William Bruce, Bt. (S. 1673)
Stirling of Fairburn, Sir Roderick William Kenneth, KCVO
Stirling of Garden, *Col.* Sir James, KCVO, CBE, TD
Stirrup, *Air Chief Marshal* Sir Graham Eric (Jock), GCB, AFC, ADC
Stockdale, Sir Thomas Minshull, Bt. (1960)
Stoddart, *Prof.* Sir James Fraser, Kt.
Stoddart, *Wg Cdr.* Sir Kenneth Maxwell, KCVO, AE
Stoker, *Prof.* Sir Michael George Parke, Kt., CBE, FRCP, FRS, FRSE
Stones, Sir William Frederick, Kt., OBE
Stonhouse, *Revd* Michael Philip, Bt. (1628 and 1670)
Stonor, *Air Marshal* Sir Thomas Henry, KCB
Stoppard, Sir Thomas, Kt., OM, CBE
Storey, *Hon.* Sir Richard, Bt., CBE (1960)
Stothard, Sir Peter Michael, Kt.
Stott, Sir Adrian George Ellingham, Bt. (1920)
Stoute, Sir Michael Ronald, Kt.
Stowe, Sir Kenneth Ronald, GCB, CVO
Stracey, Sir John Simon, Bt. (1818)
Strachan, Sir Curtis Victor, Kt., CVO
Strachey, Sir Charles, Bt. (1801)
Straker, Sir Louis Hilton, KCMG
Strang Steel, Sir (Fiennes) Michael, Bt. (1938)
Street, *Hon.* Sir Laurence Whistler, KCMG
Streeton, Sir Terence George, KBE, CMG
Strickland-Constable, Sir Frederic, Bt. (1641)
Stringer, Sir Donald Edgar, Kt., CBE
Stringer, Sir Howard, Kt.
Strong, Sir Roy Colin, Kt., PHD, FSA
Stronge, Sir James Anselan Maxwell, Bt. (1803)
Stuart, Sir James Keith, Kt.
Stuart, Sir Kenneth Lamonte, Kt.
†Stuart, Sir Phillip Luttrell, Bt. (1660)
†Stuart-Forbes, Sir William Daniel, Bt. (S. 1626)
Stuart-Menteth, Sir James Wallace, Bt. (1838)
Stuart-Paul, *Air Marshal* Sir Ronald Ian, KBE
Stuart-Smith, *Rt. Hon.* Sir Murray, Kt.
Stubbs, Sir William Hamilton, Kt., PHD
Stucley, *Lt.* Sir Hugh George Coplestone Bampfylde, Bt. (1859)
Studd, Sir Edward Fairfax, Bt. (1929)
Studholme, Sir Henry William, Bt. (1956)
Sturridge, Sir Nicholas Anthony, KCVO
†Style, Sir William Frederick, Bt. (1627)
Sugar, Sir Alan Michael, Kt.
Sullivan, *Hon.* Sir Jeremy Mirth, Kt.
Sullivan, Sir Richard Arthur, Bt. (1804)
Sulston, Sir John Edward, Kt.
Sumner, *Hon.* Sir Christopher John, Kt.
Sunderland, Sir John Michael, Kt.
Sutherland, Sir John Brewer, Bt. (1921)
Sutherland, Sir William George MacKenzie, Kt.
Sutton, Sir Frederick Walter, Kt., OBE
Sutton, *Air Marshal* Sir John Matthias Dobson, KCB
Sutton, Sir Richard Lexington, Bt. (1772)
Swaffield, Sir James Chesebrough, Kt., CBE, RD
Swaine, Sir John Joseph, Kt., CBE
Swan, Sir Conrad Marshall John Fisher, KCVO, PHD
Swan, Sir John William David, KBE
Swann, Sir Michael Christopher, Bt. (1906), TD
Swartz, *Hon.* Sir Reginald William Colin, KBE, ED
Sweeney, Sir George, Kt.
Sweeting, *Prof.* Sir Martin Nicholas, Kt., OBE, FRS
Sweetnam, Sir (David) Rodney, KCVO, CBE, FRCS
Swinburn, *Lt.-Gen.* Sir Richard Hull, KCB
Swinnerton-Dyer, *Prof.* Sir (Henry) Peter (Francis), Bt. (1678), KBE, FRS
Swinton, *Maj.-Gen.* Sir John, KCVO, OBE
Swire, Sir Adrian Christopher, Kt.
Swire, Sir John Anthony, Kt., CBE
Sykes, Sir David Michael, Bt. (1921)
Sykes, Sir Francis John Badcock, Bt. (1781)
Sykes, Sir Hugh Ridley, Kt.
Sykes, *Prof.* Sir (Malcolm) Keith, Kt.
Sykes, Sir Richard, Kt.
Sykes, Sir Tatton Christopher Mark, Bt. (1783)

Symington, *Prof.* Sir Thomas, Kt., MD, FRSE
Symons, *Vice-Adm.* Sir Patrick Jeremy, KBE
Synge, Sir Robert Carson, Bt. (1801)
Synnott, Sir Hilary Nicholas Hugh, KCMG
Talboys, *Rt. Hon.* Sir Brian Edward, CH, KCB
Tangaroa, *Hon.* Sir Tangoroa, Kt., MBE
Tapps-Gervis-Meyrick, Sir George Christopher Cadafael, Bt. (1791)
Tapsell, Sir Peter Hannay Bailey, Kt., MP
Tate, Sir (Henry) Saxon, Bt. (1898)
Taureka, *Dr* Sir Reubeh, KBE
Tauvasa, Sir Joseph James, KBE
Tavare, Sir John, Kt., CBE
Tavener, *Prof.* Sir John Kenneth, Kt.
Taylor, Sir (Arthur) Godfrey, Kt.
Taylor, Sir Cyril Julian Hebden, GBE
Taylor, Sir Edward Macmillan (Teddy), Kt.
Taylor, *Rt. Revd* John Bernard, KCVO
Taylor, *Dr.* Sir John Michael, Kt., OBE
Taylor, Sir Nicholas Richard Stuart, Bt. (1917)
Taylor, Sir Robert Richard, KCVO, OBE
Taylor, *Prof.* Sir William, Kt., CBE
Taylor, Sir William George, Kt.
Teagle, *Vice-Adm.* Sir Somerford Francis, KBE
Teare, *Hon.* Sir Nigel John Martin, Kt.
Teasdale, *Prof.* Sir Graham Michael, Kt.
Tebbit, Sir Donald Claude, GCMG
Tebbit, Sir Kevin Reginald, KCB, CMG
Telford, Sir Robert, Kt., CBE, FRENG
Telito, *HE Revd* Filoimea, GCMG, MBE
Temple, *Prof.* Sir John Graham, Kt.
Temple, *Maj.* Sir Richard Anthony Purbeck, Bt. (1876), MC
Templeton, Sir John Marks, Kt.
Tennant, Sir Anthony John, Kt.
Tennyson-D'Eyncourt, Sir Mark Gervais, Bt. (1930)
Terry, *Air Marshal* Sir Colin George, KBE, CB
Terry, *Air Chief Marshal* Sir Peter David George, GCB, AFC
Thatcher, Sir Mark, Bt. (1990)
Thomas, Sir David John Godfrey, Bt. (1694)
Thomas, Sir Derek Morison David, KCMG
Thomas, Sir Gilbert Stanley, Kt., OBE
Thomas, Sir Jeremy Cashel, KCMG
Thomas, Sir (John) Alan, Kt.
Thomas, *Prof.* Sir John Meurig, Kt., FRS
Thomas, Sir Keith Vivian, Kt.
Thomas, Sir Philip Lloyd, KCVO, CMG
Thomas, Sir Quentin Jeremy, Kt., CB
Thomas, *Rt. Hon.* Sir Roger John Laugharne, Kt.
Thomas, *Hon.* Sir Swinton Barclay, Kt.
Thomas, Sir William Michael, Bt. (1919)
Thomas, Sir (William) Michael (Marsh), Bt. (1918)
Thompson, Sir Christopher Peile, Bt. (1890)
Thompson, Sir Clive Malcolm, Kt.
Thompson, Sir David Albert, KCMG
Thompson, Sir Gilbert Williamson, Kt., OBE
Thompson, *Prof.* Sir Michael Warwick, Kt., DSC
Thompson, Sir Nicholas Annesley, Bt. (1963)
Thompson, Sir Nigel Cooper, KCMG, CBE
Thompson, Sir Paul Anthony, Bt. (1963)
Thompson, Sir Peter Anthony, Kt.
Thompson, *Dr* Sir Richard Paul Hepworth, KCVO
Thompson, Sir Thomas d'Eyncourt John, Bt. (1806)
Thomson, Sir (Frederick Douglas) David, Bt. (1929)
Thomson, Sir John Adam, GCMG
Thomson, Sir John (Ian) Sutherland, KBE, CMG
Thomson, Sir Mark Wilfrid Home, Bt. (1925)
Thomson, Sir Thomas James, Kt., CBE, FRCP
Thorn, Sir John Samuel, Kt., OBE
Thorne, Sir Neil Gordon, Kt., OBE, TD
Thornton, *Air Marshal* Sir Barry Michael, KCB
Thornton, Sir (George) Malcolm, Kt.
Thornton, Sir Peter Eustace, KCB
Thornton, Sir Richard Eustace, KCVO, OBE
†Thorold, Sir (Anthony) Oliver, Bt. (1642)
Thorpe, *Rt. Hon.* Sir Mathew Alexander, Kt.
Thurecht, Sir Ramon Richard, Kt., OBE
Thwaites, Sir Bryan, Kt., PHD
Tickell, Sir Crispin Charles Cervantes, GCMG, KCVO
Tikaram, Sir Moti, KBE
Tilt, Sir Robin Richard, Kt.
Tiltman, Sir John Hessell, KCVO
Timmins, *Col.* Sir John Bradford, KCVO, OBE, TD
Tims, Sir Michael David, KCVO
Tindle, Sir Ray Stanley, Kt., CBE
Tirvengadum, Sir Harry Krishnan, Kt.
Tjoeng, Sir James Neng, KBE
Tod, *Vice-Adm.* Sir Jonathan James Richard, KCB, CBE
Todd, *Prof.* Sir David, Kt., CBE
Todd, Sir Ian Pelham, KBE, FRCS
Tollemache, Sir Lyonel Humphry John, Bt. (1793)
Tomkins, Sir Edward Emile, GCMG, CVO
Tomkys, Sir (William) Roger, KCMG
Tomlinson, *Prof.* Sir Bernard Evans, Kt., CBE
Tomlinson, Sir John Rowland, Kt., CBE
Tomlinson, Sir Michael John, Kt., CBE
Tomlinson, *Hon.* Sir Stephen Miles, Kt.
Tooke, *Prof.* Sir John Edward, Kt.
Tooley, Sir John, Kt.
ToRobert, Sir Henry Thomas, KBE
Torpy, *Air Marshal* Sir Glenn Lester, KCB, CBE, DSO
Torry, Sir Peter James, GCVO, KCMG
Tory, Sir Geofroy William, KCMG
Touche, Sir Anthony George, Bt. (1920)
Touche, Sir Rodney Gordon, Bt. (1962)
Toulson, *Rt. Hon.* Sir Roger Grenfell, Kt.
Tovadek, Sir Martin, Kt. CMG
Tovey, Sir Brian John Maynard, KCMG
ToVue, Sir Ronald, Kt., OBE
Towneley, Sir Simon Peter Edmund Cosmo William, KCVO
Townsend, Sir Cyril David, Kt.
Traill, Sir Alan Towers, GBE
Trant, *Gen.* Sir Richard Brooking, KCB
Treacher, *Adm.* Sir John Devereux, KCB
Treacy, *Hon.* Sir Colman Maurice, Kt.
Treacy, *Hon.* Sir (James Mary) Seamus, Kt.
Treitel, *Prof.* Sir Guenter Heinz, Kt., FBA, QC
Trescowthick, Sir Donald Henry, KBE
Trevelyan, Sir Geoffrey Washington, Bt. (1662 and 1874)
Trezise, Sir Kenneth Bruce, Kt., OBE
Trippier, Sir David Austin, Kt., RD
Tritton, Sir Anthony John Ernest, Bt. (1905)
Trollope, Sir Anthony Simon, Bt. (1642)
Trotman-Dickenson, Sir Aubrey Fiennes, Kt.
Trotter, Sir Neville Guthrie, Kt.
Trotter, Sir Ronald Ramsay, Kt.
Troubridge, Sir Thomas Richard, Bt. (1799)
Troup, *Vice-Adm.* Sir (John) Anthony (Rose), KCB, DSC
Trousdell, *Lt.-Gen.* Sir Philip Charles Cornwallis, KBE, CB
Truscott, Sir Ralph Eric Nicholson, Bt. (1909)
Tsang, Sir Donald Yam-keun, KBE
Tuamure-Maoate, *Dr* Sir Terepai, KBE
Tuck, Sir Bruce Adolph Reginald, Bt. (1910)
Tucker, *Hon.* Sir Richard Howard, Kt.
Tuckey, *Rt. Hon.* Sir Simon Lane, Kt.
Tugendhat, *Hon.* Sir Michael George, Kt.
Tuita, Sir Mariano Kelesimalefo, KBE

Tuite, Sir Christopher Hugh, Bt. (1622), PHD
Tuivaga, Sir Timoci Uluiburotu, Kt.
Tully, Sir William Mark, KBE
Tupper, Sir Charles Hibbert, Bt. (1888)
Turbott, Sir Ian Graham, Kt., CMG, CVO
Turing, Sir John Dermot, Bt. (S. 1638)
Turner, Sir Colin William Carstairs, Kt., CBE, DFC
Turner, *Hon.* Sir Michael John, Kt.
Turnquest, Sir Orville Alton, GCMG, QC
Tusa, Sir John, Kt.
Tuti, *Revd* Dudley, KBE
Tweedie, *Prof.* Sir David Philip, Kt.
Tyree, Sir (Alfred) William, Kt., OBE
Tyrwhitt, Sir Reginald Thomas Newman, Bt. (1919)
Underhill, *Hon.* Sir Nicholas Edward, Kt.
Underwood, *Prof.* Sir James Cressee Elphinstone, Kt.
Unwin, Sir (James) Brian, KCB
Ure, Sir John Burns, KCMG, LVO
Urquhart, Sir Brian Edward, KCMG, MBE
Urwick, Sir Alan Bedford, KCVO, CMG
Usher, Sir Andrew John, Bt. (1899)
Utting, Sir William Benjamin, Kt., CB
Vallat, Sir Francis Aimé, GBE, KCMG, QC
Vallings, *Vice-Adm.* Sir George Montague Francis, KCB
Vanderfelt, Sir Robin Victor, KBE
Vardy, Sir Peter, Kt.
Varney, Sir David Robert, Kt.
Vasquez, Sir Alfred Joseph, Kt., CBE, QC
Vassar-Smith, Sir John Rathbone, Bt. (1917)
Vavasour, Sir Eric Michael Joseph Marmaduke, Bt. (1828)
Veness, Sir David, Kt., CBE, QPM
Venner, Sir Kenneth Dwight Vincent, KBE
Vereker, Sir John Michael Medlicott, KCB
†Verney, Sir John Sebastian, Bt. (1946)
Verney, *Hon.* Sir Lawrence John, Kt., TD
†Verney, Sir Edmund Ralph, Bt. (1818)
Vernon, Sir Nigel John Douglas, Bt. (1914)
Vernon, Sir (William) Michael, Kt.
Vestey, Sir Paul Edmund, Bt. (1921)
Vickers, Sir John Stuart, Kt.
Vickers, *Lt.-Gen.* Sir Richard Maurice Hilton, KCB, CVO, OBE
Viggers, *Lt-Gen.* Sir Frederick Richard, KCB, CMG, MBE
Vincent, Sir William Percy Maxwell, Bt. (1936)
Vineall, Sir Anthony John Patrick, Kt.
Vines, Sir William Joshua, Kt., CMG
von Schramek, Sir Eric Emil, Kt.
†Vyvyan, Sir Ralph Ferrers Alexander, Bt. (1645)
Wade-Gery, Sir Robert Lucian, KCMG, KCVO
Waena, Sir Nathaniel Rahumaea, GCMG
Waine, *Rt. Revd* John, KCVO
Waite, *Rt. Hon.* Sir John Douglas, Kt.
Waka, Sir Lucas Joseph, Kt., OBE
Wake, Sir Hereward, Bt. (1621), MC
Wakefield, Sir (Edward) Humphry (Tyrell), Bt. (1962)
Wakefield, Sir Norman Edward, Kt.
Wakefield, Sir Peter George Arthur, KBE, CMG
Wakeford, Sir Geoffrey Michael Montgomery, Kt., OBE
Wakeley, Sir John Cecil Nicholson, Bt. (1952), FRCS
†Wakeman, Sir Edward Offley Bertram, Bt. (1828)
Wales, Sir Robert Andrew, Kt.
Waley-Cohen, Sir Stephen Harry, Bt. (1961)
Walford, Sir Christopher Rupert, Kt.
Walker, *Gen.* Sir Antony Kenneth Frederick, KCB
†Walker, Sir Christopher Robert Baldwin, Bt. (1856)
Walker, Sir David Alan, Kt.
Walker, Sir Harold Berners, KCMG
†Walker, Sir Roy Edward, Bt. (1906)
Walker, Sir James Graham, Kt., MBE
Walker, Sir John Ernest, Kt., DPHIL, FRS
Walker, *Air Marshal* Sir John Robert, KCB, CBE, AFC
Walker, Sir Miles Rawstron, Kt., CBE
Walker, Sir Patrick Jeremy, KCB
Walker, *Hon.* Sir Paul James, Kt.
Walker, Sir Rodney Myerscough, Kt.
Walker, *Hon.* Sir Timothy Edward, Kt.
Walker, Sir Victor Stewart Heron, Bt. (1868)
Walker-Okeover, Sir Andrew Peter Monro, Bt. (1886)
Walker-Smith, Sir John Jonah, Bt. (1960)
Wall, Sir John Anthony, Kt., CBE
Wall, Sir (John) Stephen, GCMG, LVO
Wall, *Rt. Hon.* Sir Nicholas Peter Rathbone, Kt.
Wall, Sir Robert William, Kt., OBE
Wallace, *Lt.-Gen.* Sir Christopher Brooke Quentin, KBE
Wallace, *Prof.* David James, Kt., CBE, FRS
Wallace, Sir Ian James, Kt., CBE
Waller, *Rt. Hon.* Sir (George) Mark, Kt.
Waller, Sir John Michael, Bt. (I. 1780)
Wallis, Sir Peter Gordon, KCVO
Wallis, Sir Timothy William, Kt.
Walmsley, *Vice-Adm.* Sir Robert, KCB
†Walsham, Sir Timothy John, Bt. (1831)
Walters, *Prof.* Sir Alan Arthur, Kt.
Walters, Sir Dennis Murray, Kt., MBE
Walters, Sir Frederick Donald, Kt.
Walters, Sir Peter Ingram, Kt.
Walters, Sir Roger Talbot, KBE, FRIBA
Wamiri, Sir Akapite, KBE
Wan, Sir Wamp, Kt., MBE
Wanless, Sir Derek, Kt.
Ward, *Rt. Hon.* Sir Alan Hylton, Kt.
Ward, Sir Austin, Kt., QC
Ward, Sir John Devereux, Kt., CBE
Ward, *Prof.* Sir John MacQueen, Kt., CBE
Ward, Sir Joseph James Laffey, Bt. (1911)
Ward, Sir Timothy James, Kt.
Wardale, Sir Geoffrey Charles, KCB
Wardlaw, Sir Henry (John), Bt. (NS. 1631)
Waring, Sir (Alfred) Holburt, Bt. (1935)
Warmington, Sir Rupert Marshall, Bt. (1908)
Warner, Sir (Edward Courtenay) Henry, Bt. (1910)
Warner, *Prof.* Sir Frederick Edward, Kt., FRS, FRENG
Warner, Sir Gerald Chierici, KCMG
Warren, Sir (Frederick) Miles, KBE
Warren, Sir Kenneth Robin, Kt.
Warren, Sir Nicholas Roger, Kt.
Wass, Sir Douglas William Gretton, GCB
Waterhouse, *Hon.* Sir Ronald Gough, GBE
Waterlow, Sir Christopher Rupert, Bt. (1873)
Waterlow, Sir (James) Gerard, Bt. (1930)
Waters, *Gen.* Sir (Charles) John, GCB, CBE
Waters, Sir (Thomas) Neil (Morris), Kt.
Waterworth, Sir Alan William, KCVO
Wates, Sir Christopher Stephen, Kt.
Watkins, *Rt. Hon.* Sir Tasker, VC, GBE
Watson, Sir Bruce Dunstan, Kt.
Watson, *Prof.* Sir David John, Kt., PHD
Watson, Sir (James) Andrew, Bt. (1866)
Watson, *Vice-Adm.* Sir Philip Alexander, KBE, LVO
Watson, Sir Ronald Matthew, Kt., CBE
Watson, Sir Simon Conran Hamilton, Bt. (1895)
Watt, *Gen.* Sir Charles Redmond, KCVO, CBE
Watt, *Surgeon Vice-Adm.* Sir James, KBE, FRCS
Watts, Sir Arthur Desmond, KCMG
Watts, Sir John Augustus Fitzroy, KCMG, CBE
Watts, Sir Philip Beverley, KCMG
Weatherall, *Prof.* Sir David John, Kt., FRS
Weatherall, *Vice-Adm.* Sir James Lamb, KCVO, KBE
Weatherstone, Sir Dennis, KBE
Weatherup, *Hon.* Sir Ronald Eccles, Kt.

Webb, *Prof.* Sir Adrian Leonard, Kt.
Webb-Carter, *Gen.* Sir Evelyn John, KCVO, OBE
Webster, *Very Revd* Alan Brunskill, KCVO
Webster, *Vice-Adm.* Sir John Morrison, KCB
Webster, *Hon.* Sir Peter Edlin, Kt.
Wedgwood, Sir (Hugo) Martin, Bt. (1942)
Weekes, Sir Everton DeCourcey, KCMG, OBE
Weinberg, Sir Mark Aubrey, Kt.
Weir, *Hon.* Sir Reginald George, Kt.
Weir, Sir Roderick Bignell, Kt.
Welby, Sir (Richard) Bruno Gregory, Bt. (1801)
Welch, Sir John Reader, Bt. (1957)
Weldon, Sir Anthony William, Bt. (I. 1723)
Weller, Sir Arthur Burton, Kt., CBE
Wellings, Sir Jack Alfred, Kt., CBE
†Wells, Sir Christopher Charles, Bt. (1944)
Wells, Sir John Julius, Kt.
Wells, Sir William Henry Weston, Kt., FRICS
Wesker, Sir Arnold, Kt.
Westbrook, Sir Neil Gowanloch, Kt., CBE
Westmacott, Sir Peter John, KCMG
Weston, Sir Michael Charles Swift, KCMG, CVO
Weston, Sir (Philip) John, KCMG
Whalen, Sir Geoffrey Henry, Kt., CBE
Wheeler, Sir Harry Anthony, Kt., OBE
Wheeler, *Air Chief Marshal* Sir (Henry) Neil (George), GCB, CBE, DSO, DFC, AFC
Wheeler, *Rt. Hon.* Sir John Daniel, Kt.
Wheeler, Sir John Frederick, Bt. (1920)
Wheeler, *Gen.* Sir Roger Neil, GCB, CBE
Wheeler-Booth, Sir Michael Addison John, KCB
Wheler, Sir Edward Woodford, Bt. (1660)
Whishaw, Sir Charles Percival Law, Kt.
Whitaker, Sir John James Ingham (Jack), Bt. (1936)
Whitchurch, Sir Graeme Ian, Kt., OBE
White, *Prof.* Sir Christopher John, Kt., CVO
White, Sir Christopher Robert Meadows, Bt. (1937)
White, Sir David (David Jason), Kt., OBE
White, Sir David Harry, Kt.
White, *Hon.* Sir Frank John, Kt.
White, Sir George Stanley James, Bt. (1904)
White, *Adm.* Sir Hugo Moresby, GCB, CBE
White, *Hon.* Sir John Charles, Kt., MBE
White, Sir John Woolmer, Bt. (1922)
White, Sir Nicholas Peter Archibald, Bt. (1802)
White, *Adm.* Sir Peter, GBE
White, Sir Willard Wentworth, Kt., CBE
Whitehead, Sir John Stainton, GCMG, CVO
†Whitehead, Sir Philip Henry Rathbone, Bt. (1889)
Whiteley, *Gen.* Sir Peter John Frederick, GCB, OBE, RM
Whitfield, Sir William, Kt., CBE
Whitmore, Sir Clive Anthony, GCB, CVO
Whitmore, Sir John Henry Douglas, Bt. (1954)
Whitney, Sir Raymond William, Kt., OBE
Whitson, Sir Keith Roderick, Kt.
Wickerson, Sir John Michael, Kt.
Wicks, Sir Nigel Leonard, GCB, CVO, CBE
†Wigan, Sir Michael Iain, Bt. (1898)
Wiggin, Sir Alfred William (Jerry), Kt., TD
†Wiggin, Sir Charles Rupert John, Bt. (1892)
†Wigram, Sir John Woolmore, Bt. (1805)
Wilbraham, Sir Richard Baker, Bt. (1776)
Wiles, *Prof.* Sir Andrew John, KBE
Wilkes, *Prof.* Sir Maurice Vincent, Kt.
Wilkes, *Gen.* Sir Michael John, KCB, CBE
Wilkie, *Hon.* Sir Alan Fraser, Kt.
Wilkinson, Sir (David) Graham (Brook) Bt. (1941)
Wilkinson, *Prof.* Sir Denys Haigh, Kt., FRS
Willcocks, Sir David Valentine, Kt., CBE, MC
Willcocks, *Lt.-Gen.* Sir Michael Alan, KCB
Williams, Sir Arthur Dennis Pitt, Kt.
Williams, Sir (Arthur) Gareth Ludovic Emrys Rhys, Bt. (1918)
Williams, *Prof.* Sir Bruce Rodda, KBE
Williams, Sir Charles Othniel, Kt.
Williams, Sir Daniel Charles, GCMG, QC
Williams, *Adm.* Sir David, GCB
Williams, *Prof.* Sir David Glyndwr Tudor, Kt.
Williams, Sir David Innes, Kt.
Williams, Sir David Reeve, Kt., CBE
Williams, *Hon.* Sir Denys Ambrose, KCMG
Williams, Sir Donald Mark, Bt. (1866)
Williams, *Prof.* Sir (Edward) Dillwyn, Kt., FRCP
Williams, Sir Francis Owen Garbett, Kt., CBE
Williams, *Hon.* Sir (John) Griffith, Kt.
Williams, Sir (Lawrence) Hugh, Bt. (1798)
Williams, Sir Osmond, Bt. (1909), MC
Williams, Sir Peter Michael, Kt.
Williams, Sir (Robert) Philip Nathaniel, Bt. (1915)
Williams, Sir Robin Philip, Bt. (1953)
Williams, *Prof.* Sir Roger, Kt.
Williams, Sir (William) Maxwell (Harries), Kt.
Williams, *Hon.* Sir Wyn Lewis
Williams-Bulkeley, Sir Richard Thomas, Bt. (1661)
Williams-Wynn, Sir David Watkin, Bt. (1688)
Williamson, Sir George Malcolm, Kt.
Williamson, *Marshal of the Royal Air Force* Sir Keith Alec, GCB, AFC
Williamson, Sir Robert Brian, Kt., CBE
Willink, Sir Charles William, Bt. (1957)
Willis, *Air Chief Marshal* Sir John Frederick, GBE, KCB
Willison, *Lt.-Gen.* Sir David John, KCB, OBE, MC
Wills, Sir David James Vernon, Bt. (1923)
Wills, Sir David Seton, Bt. (1904)
Wilmot, Sir David, Kt., QPM
Wilmot, Sir Henry Robert, Bt. (1759)
Wilsey, *Gen.* Sir John Finlay Willasey, GCB, CBE
Wilshaw, Sir Michael, Kt.
Wilson, *Prof.* Sir Alan Geoffrey, Kt.
Wilson, Sir Anthony, Kt.
Wilson, *Vice-Adm.* Sir Barry Nigel, KCB
Wilson, Sir David, Bt. (1920)
Wilson, Sir David Mackenzie, Kt.
Wilson, Sir James William Douglas, Bt. (1906)
Wilson, *Brig.* Sir Mathew John Anthony, Bt. (1874), OBE, MC
Wilson, *Rt. Hon.* Sir Nicholas Allan Roy, Kt.
Wilson, Sir Robert Peter, KCMG
Wilson, *Air Chief Marshal* Sir (Ronald) Andrew (Fellowes), KCB, AFC
Wilton, Sir (Arthur) John, KCMG, KCVO, MC
Wingate, *Capt.* Sir Miles Buckley, KCVO
Winkley, Sir David Ross, Kt.
Winnington, Sir Anthony Edward, Bt. (1755)
Winship, Sir Peter James Joseph, Kt., CBE
Winter, *Dr* Sir Gregory Winter, Kt., CBE
Winterton, Sir Nicholas Raymond, Kt.
Winton, Sir Nicholas George, Kt., MBE
Wisdom, Sir Norman, Kt., OBE
Wiseman, Sir John William, Bt. (1628)
Wolfendale, *Prof.* Sir Arnold Whittaker, Kt., FRS
Wolseley, Sir Charles Garnet Richard Mark, Bt. (1628)
†Wolseley, Sir James Douglas, Bt. (I. 1745)
†Wombell, Sir George Philip Frederick, Bt. (1778)

Womersley, Sir Peter John Walter, Bt. (1945)
Woo, Sir Leo Joseph, Kt.
Woo, Sir Po-Shing, Kt.
Wood, Sir Alan Marshall Muir, Kt., FRS, FRENG
Wood, Sir Andrew Marley, GCMG
Wood, Sir Anthony John Page, Bt. (1837)
Wood, Sir Ian Clark, Kt., CBE
Wood, *Hon.* Sir John Kember, Kt., MC
Wood, Sir Martin Francis, Kt., OBE
Wood, Sir Michael Charles, KCMG
Wood, *Hon.* Sir Roderic Lionel James, Kt.
Wood, Sir Russell Dillon, KCVO, VRD
Wood, Sir William Alan, KCVO, CB
Woodard, *Rear Adm.* Sir Robert Nathaniel, KCVO
Woodcock, Sir John, Kt., CBE, QPM
Woodhead, *Vice-Adm.* Sir (Anthony) Peter, KCB
Woodhouse, *Rt. Hon.* Sir (Arthur) Owen, KBE, DSC
Woodroffe, *Most Revd* George Cuthbert Manning, KBE
Woods, Sir Robert Kynnersley, Kt., CBE
Woodward, *Hon.* Sir (Albert) Edward, Kt., OBE
Woodward, Sir Clive Ronald, Kt., OBE
Woodward, *Adm.* Sir John Forster, GBE, KCB
Woodward, Sir Thomas Jones (Tom Jones), Kt., OBE
Worsley, *Gen.* Sir Richard Edward, GCB, OBE
Worsley, Sir (William) Marcus (John), Bt. (1838)
Worsthorne, Sir Peregrine Gerard, Kt.
Wratten, *Air Chief Marshal* Sir William John, GBE, CB, AFC
Wraxall, Sir Charles Frederick Lascelles, Bt. (1813)
Wrey, Sir George Richard Bourchier, Bt. (1628)
Wrigglesworth, Sir Ian William, Kt.
Wright, Sir Allan Frederick, KBE
Wright, Sir David John, GCMG, LVO
Wright, *Hon.* Sir (John) Michael, Kt.
Wright, Sir (John) Oliver, GCMG, GCVO, DSC
Wright, *Prof.* Sir Nicholas Alcwyn, Kt.
Wright, Sir Peter Robert, Kt., CBE
Wright, *Air Marshal* Sir Robert Alfred, KBE, AFC
Wright, Sir Stephen John Leadbetter, KCMG
Wrightson, Sir Charles Mark Garmondsway, Bt. (1900)
Wrigley, *Prof.* Sir Edward Anthony (Sir Tony), Kt., PHD, PBA
Wrixon-Becher, Sir John William Michael, Bt. (1831)
Wu, Sir Gordon Ying Sheung, KCMG
Yacoub, *Prof.* Sir Magdi Habib, Kt., FRCS
Yaki, Sir Roy, KBE
Yang, *Hon.* Sir Ti Liang, Kt.
Yapp, Sir Stanley Graham, Kt.
Yardley, Sir David Charles Miller, Kt., LLD
Yarrow, Sir Eric Grant, Bt. (1916), MBE
Yocklunn, Sir John (Soong Chung), KCVO
Yoo Foo, Sir (François) Henri, Kt.
Young, Sir Brian Walter Mark, Kt.
Young, Sir Colville Norbert, GCMG, MBE
Young, Sir Dennis Charles, KCMG
Young, *Rt. Hon.* Sir George Samuel Knatchbull, Bt. (1813)
Young, *Hon.* Sir Harold William, KCMG
Young, Sir Jimmy Leslie Ronald, Kt. CBE
Young, Sir John Kenyon Roe, Bt. (1821)
Young, *Hon.* Sir John McIntosh, KCMG
Young, Sir John Robertson, GCMG
Young, Sir Leslie Clarence, Kt., CBE
Young, Sir Nicholas Charles, Kt.
Young, Sir Richard Dilworth, Kt.
Young, Sir Robin Urquhart, KCB
Young, Sir Roger William, Kt.
Young, Sir Stephen Stewart Templeton, Bt. (1945)
Young, Sir William Neil, Bt. (1769)
Younger, Sir Julian William Richard, Bt. (1911)
Yuwi, Sir Matiabe, KBE
Zeeman, *Prof.* Sir (Erik) Christopher, Kt., FRS
Zissman, Sir Bernard Philip, Kt.
Zochonis, Sir John Basil, Kt.
Zunz, Sir Gerhard Jacob (Jack), Kt., FRENG
Zurenuoc, Sir Zibang, KBE

BARONETESS

Stirling-Maxwell, Dame Ann Maxwell Macdonald, Btss. (NS 1682)

DAMES

DAMES GRAND CROSS AND DAMES COMMANDERS

Style, 'Dame' before forename and surname, followed by appropriate post-nominal initials. Where such an award is made to a lady already in possession of a higher title, the appropriate initials follow her name

Envelope, Dame F_ S_, followed by appropriate post-nominal letters. *Letter (formal),* Dear Madam; *(social),* Dear Dame F_. *Spoken,* Dame F_

Husband, Untitled

Dame Grand Cross and Dame Commander are the higher classes for women of the Order of the Bath, the Order of St Michael and St George, the Royal Victorian Order, and the Order of the British Empire. Dames Grand Cross rank after the wives of Baronets and before the wives of Knights Grand Cross. Dames Commanders rank after the wives of Knights Grand Cross and before the wives of Knights Commanders.

Honorary Dames Commanders may be conferred on women who are citizens of countries of which the Queen is not head of state.

LIST OF DAMES

As at 31 August 2007

Women peers in their own right and life peers are not included in this list. Female members of the royal family are not included in this list; details of the orders they hold can be found within the Royal Family section.

If a dame has a double barrelled or hyphenated surname, she is listed under the first element of the name.

A full entry in italic type indicates that the recipient of an honour died during the year in which the honour was conferred. The name is included for the purposes of record.

Abaijah, Dame Josephine, DBE
Airlie, The Countess of, DCVO
Albemarle, The Countess of, DBE
Allen, *Prof.* Dame Ingrid Victoria, DBE
Andrews, Dame Julie, DBE
Anglesey, The Marchioness of, DBE
Anson, Lady (Elizabeth Audrey), DBE
Anstee, Dame Margaret Joan, DCMG
Arden, *Rt. Hon.* Dame Mary Howarth (Mrs Mance), DBE
Atkins, Dame Eileen, DBE
Bainbridge, Dame Beryl, DBE
Baker, Dame Janet Abbott (Mrs Shelley), CH, DBE
Barbour, Dame Margaret (Mrs Ash), DBE
Baron, *Hon.* Dame Florence Jacqueline, DBE
Barrow, Dame Jocelyn Anita (Mrs Downer), DBE
Barstow, Dame Josephine Clare (Mrs Anderson), DBE
Bassey, Dame Shirley, DBE
Beaurepaire, Dame Beryl Edith, DBE
Beer, *Prof.* Dame Gillian Patricia Kempster, DBE, FBA
Bergquist, *Prof.* Dame Patricia Rose, DBE
Bevan, Dame Yasmin, DBE
Bewley, Dame Beulah Rosemary, DBE
Bibby, Dame Enid, DBE
Black, *Prof.* Dame Carol Mary, DBE
Black, *Hon.* Dame Jill Margaret, DBE
Blackadder, Dame Elizabeth Violet, DBE
Blaize, Dame Venetia Ursula, DBE
Blaxland, Dame Helen Frances, DBE
Booth, *Hon.* Dame Margaret Myfanwy Wood, DBE
Bowtell, Dame Ann Elizabeth, DCB
Boyd, Dame Vivienne Myra, DBE
Brain, Dame Margaret Anne (Mrs Wheeler), DBE
Brennan, Dame Maureen, DBE
Bridges, Dame Mary Patricia, DBE
Brittan, Dame Diana (Lady Brittan of Spennithorne), DBE
Browne, Lady Moyra Blanche Madeleine, DBE
Buckland, Dame Yvonne Helen Elaine, DBE
Burnell, *Prof.* Dame Susan Jocelyn Bell, DBE
Burslem, Dame Alexandra Vivien, DBE
Byatt, Dame Antonia Susan, DBE, FRSL
Bynoe, Dame Hilda Louisa, DBE
Caldicott, Dame Fiona, DBE, FRCP, FRCPSYCH
Cameron, *Prof.* Dame Averil Millicent, DBE
Campbell-Preston, Dame Frances Olivia, DCVO
Cartwright, Dame Silvia Rose, DBE
Clark, *Prof.* Dame Jill MacLeod, DBE
Clark, *Prof.* Dame (Margaret) June, DBE, PHD
Clayton, Dame Barbara Evelyn (Mrs Klyne), DBE
Collarbone, Dame Patricia, DBE
Contreras, *Prof.* Dame Marcela, DBE
Corsar, *Hon.* Dame Mary Drummond, DBE
Coward, Dame Pamela Sarah, DBE
Cox, *Hon.* Dame Laura Mary, DBE
Davies, Dame Wendy Patricia, DBE
Davis, Dame Karlene Cecile, DBE
Daws, Dame Joyce Margaretta, DBE
Dawson, *Prof.* Dame Sandra Jane Noble, DBE
Dell, Dame Miriam Patricia, DBE
Dench, Dame Judith Olivia (Mrs Williams), CH, DBE
Descartes, Dame Marie Selipha Sesenne, DBE, BEM
Devonshire, The Duchess of, DCVO
Digby, Lady, DBE
Dobbs, *Hon.* Dame Linda Penelope, DBE
Docherty, Dame Jacqueline, DBE
Douglas, Prof. Dame Margaret Mary, DBE
Dowling, *Prof.* Dame Ann Patricia, DBE
Duffield, Dame Vivien Louise, DBE
Dumont, Dame Ivy Leona, DCMG
Dyche, Dame Rachael Mary, DBE
Elcoat, Dame Catherine Elizabeth, DBE
Ellison, Dame Jill, DBE
Else, Dame Jean, DBE
Engel, Dame Pauline Frances (Sister Pauline Engel), DBE
Esteve-Coll, Dame Elizabeth Anne Loosemore, DBE
Evans, Dame Anne Elizabeth Jane, DBE
Evans, Dame Madeline Glynne Dervel, DBE, CMG
Evison, Dame Helen June Patricia, DBE
Fenner, Dame Peggy Edith, DBE
Fielding, Dame Pauline, DBE
Forgan, Dame Elizabeth Anne Lucy, DBE
Fort, Dame Maeve Geraldine, DCMG, DCVO
Fraser, Dame Dorothy Rita, DBE
Friend, Dame Phyllis Muriel, DBE

Fry, Dame Margaret Louise, DBE
Gallagher, Dame Monica Josephine, DBE
Gardiner, Dame Helen Louisa, DBE, MVO
Glen-Haig, Dame Mary Alison, DBE
Glenn, *Prof.* Dame Hazel Gillian, DBE
Glennie, *Dr* Dame Evelyn Elizabeth Ann, DBE
Gloster, *Hon.* Dame Elisabeth (Lady Popplewell), DBE
Glover, Dame Audrey Frances, DBE, CMG
Goodall, *Dr* Dame (Valerie) Jane, DBE
Goodman, Dame Barbara, DBE
Gordon, Dame Minita Elmira, GCMG, GCVO
Gordon, *Hon.* Dame Pamela Felicity, DBE
Gow, Dame Jane Elizabeth (Mrs Whiteley), DBE
Grafton, The Duchess of, GCVO
Grant, Dame Mavis, DBE
Green, Dame Pauline, DBE
Grey, Dame Beryl Elizabeth (Mrs Svenson), DBE
Grey-Thompson, Dame Tanni Carys Davina, DBE
Griffiths, Dame Anne, DCVO
Grimthorpe, The Lady, DCVO
Guilfoyle, Dame Margaret Georgina Constance, DBE
Guthardt, *Revd Dr* Dame Phyllis Myra, DBE
Hallett, *Rt. Hon.* Dame Heather Carol, DBE
Harbison, Dame Joan Irene, DBE
Harper, Dame Elizabeth Margaret Way, DBE
Harris, Lady Pauline, DBE
Hassan, Dame Anna Patricia Lucy, DBE
Hedley-Miller, Dame Mary Elizabeth, DCVO, CB
Henderson, Dame Fiona Douglas, DCVO
Herbison, Dame Jean Marjory, DBE, CMG
Hercus, *Hon.* Dame (Margaret) Ann, DCMG
Higgins, *Prof.* Dame Joan Margaret, DBE
Higgins, *Prof.* Dame Julia Stretton, DBE, FRS
Higgins, *Prof.* Dame Rosalyn, DBE, QC
Hill, *Air Cdre* Dame Felicity Barbara, DBE
Hine, Dame Deirdre Joan, DBE, FRCP
Hodgson, Dame Patricia Anne, DBE
Hogg, *Hon.* Dame Mary Claire (Mrs Koops), DBE
Hollows, Dame Sharon, DBE
Holmes, Dame Kelly, DBE
Hoodless, Dame Elisabeth Anne, DBE
Hufton, *Prof.* Dame Olwen, DBE
Husband, *Prof.* Dame Janet Elizabeth Siarey, DBE
Hussey, Dame Susan Katharine (Lady Hussey of North Bradley), DCVO
Hutton, Dame Deirdre Mary, DBE
Imison, Dame Tamsyn, DBE
Isaacs, Dame Albertha Madeline, DBE
James, Dame Naomi Christine (Mrs Haythorne), DBE
Jenkins, Dame (Mary) Jennifer (Lady Jenkins of Hillhead), DBE
Johnson, *Prof.* Dame Louise Napier, DBE, FRS
Jonas, Dame Judith Mayhew
Jones, Dame Gwyneth (Mrs Haberfeld-Jones), DBE
Jordan, *Prof.* Dame Carole, DBE
Keegan, Dame Elizabeth Mary, DBE
Keegan, Dame Geraldine Mary Marcella, DBE
Kekedo, Dame Rosalina Violet, DBE
Kelleher, Dame Joan, DBE
Kellett-Bowman, Dame (Mary) Elaine, DBE
Kelly, Dame Barbara Mary, DBE
Kelly, Dame Lorna May Boreland, DBE
Kershaw, Dame Janet Elizabeth Murray (Dame Betty), DBE
Kettlewell, *Comdt.* Dame Marion Mildred, DBE
Kidu, Lady, DBE
Kirby, Dame Carolyn Emma, DBE
Kirby, Dame Georgina Kamiria, DBE
Kramer, *Prof.* Dame Leonie Judith, DBE
Laine, Dame Cleo (Clementine) Dinah (Lady Dankworth), DBE
Lamb, Dame Dawn Ruth, DBE
Leather, Dame Susan Catherine, DBE
Leslie, Dame Ann Elizabeth Mary, DBE
Lewis, Dame Edna Leofrida (Lady Lewis), DBE
Lott, Dame Felicity Ann Emwhyla (Mrs Woolf), DBE
Louisy, Dame (Calliopa) Pearlette, GCMG
Lynn, Dame Vera (Mrs Lewis), DBE
MacArthur, Dame Ellen Patricia, DBE
Macdonald, Dame Mary Beaton, DBE
McDonald, Dame Mavis, DCB
Mackinnon, Dame (Una) Patricia, DBE
Macmillan of Ovenden, Katharine, Viscountess, DBE
Macur, *Hon.* Dame Julia Wendy, DBE
Mayhew, Dame Judith, DBE
Major, Dame Malvina Lorraine (Mrs Fleming), DBE
Major, Dame Norma Christina Elizabeth, DBE
Manningham-Buller, *Hon.* Dame Elizabeth, DCB
Marsh, Dame Mary Elizabeth, DBE
Mellor, Dame Julie Thérèse Mellor, DBE
Metge, *Dr* Dame (Alice) Joan, DBE
Middleton, Dame Elaine Madoline, DCMG, MBE
Mills, Dame Barbara Jean Lyon, DBE, QC
Mirren, Dame Helen, DBE
Moores, Dame Yvonne, DBE
Morgan, *Dr* Dame Gillian Margaret, DBE
Morrison, *Hon.* Dame Mary Anne, DCVO
Muirhead, Dame Lorna Elizabeth Fox, DBE
Muldoon, Lady Thea Dale, DBE, QSO
Mullally, *Revd* Dame Sarah Elisabeth, DBE
Mumford, Lady Mary Katharine, DCVO
Munro, Dame Alison, DBE
Murdoch, Dame Elisabeth Joy, DBE
Nelson, *Prof.* Dame Janet Laughland, DBE
Neville, Dame Elizabeth, DBE, QPM
Ogilvie, Dame Bridget Margaret, DBE, PHD, DSC
Oliver, Dame Gillian Frances, DBE
Ollerenshaw, Dame Kathleen Mary, DBE, DPHIL
Oxenbury, Dame Shirley Anne, DBE
Park, Dame Merle Florence (Mrs Bloch), DBE
Pauffley, *Hon.* Dame Anna Evelyn Hamilton, DBE
Penhaligon, Dame Annette (Mrs Egerton), DBE
Perkins, Dame Mary Lesley, DBE
Peters, Dame Mary Elizabeth, DBE
Pindling, Lady (Marguerite M.), DCMG
Platt, Dame Denise, DBE
Plowright, Dame Joan Ann, DBE
Polak, *Prof.* Dame Julia Margaret, DBE
Poole, Dame Avril Anne Barker, DBE
Porter, Dame Shirley (Lady Porter), DBE
Powell, Dame Sally Ann Vickers, DBE
Prendergast, Dame Simone Ruth, DBE
Price, Dame Margaret Berenice, DBE
Pugh, *Dr* Dame Gillian Mary, DBE
Purves, Dame Daphne Helen, DBE
Quinn, Dame Sheila Margaret Imelda, DBE
Rafferty, *Hon.* Dame Anne Judith, DBE
Rawson, *Prof.* Dame Jessica Mary, DBE
Rees, *Prof.* Dame Lesley Howard, DBE
Reeves, Dame Helen May, DBE
Richardson, Dame Mary, DBE
Ridsdale, Dame Victoire Evelyn Patricia (Lady Ridsdale), DBE
Rigg, Dame Diana, DBE
Rimington, Dame Stella, DCB
Ritterman, Dame Janet, DBE

Roberts, Dame Jane Elisabeth, DBE
Robins, Dame Ruth Laura, DBE
Robottom, Dame Marlene, DBE
Roe, Dame Marion Audrey, DBE
Roe, Dame Raigh Edith, DBE
Ronson, Dame Gail, DBE
Rothwell, *Prof.* Dame Nancy Jane, DBE
Rumbold, *Rt. Hon.* Dame Angela Claire Rosemary, DBE
Runciman of Doxford, The Viscountess, DBE
Salas, Dame Margaret Laurence, DBE
Salmond, *Prof.* Dame Mary Anne, DBE
Sawyer, *Hon.* Dame Joan Augusta, DBE
Scardino, Dame Marjorie, DBE
Scott, Dame Catherine Margaret (Mrs Denton), DBE
Seward, Dame Margaret Helen Elizabeth, DBE
Shedrick, *Dr* Dame Daphne Marjorie, DBE
Shirley, Dame Stephanie, DBE
Shovelton, Dame Helena, DBE
Sibley, Dame Antoinette (Mrs Corbett), DBE
Silver, *Dr* Dame Ruth Muldoon, DBE
Smith, Dame Dela, DBE
Smith, *Rt. Hon.* Dame Janet Hilary (Mrs Mathieson), DBE
Smith, *Hon.* Dame Jennifer Meredith, DBE
Smith, Dame Margaret Natalie (Maggie) (Mrs Cross), DBE
Soames, Lady Mary, KG, DBE
Southgate, *Prof.* Dame Lesley Jill, DBE
Spencer, Dame Rosemary Jane, DCMG
Steel, *Hon.* Dame (Anne) Heather (Mrs Beattie), DBE
Strachan, Dame Valerie Patricia Marie, DCB
Strathern, *Prof.* Dame Anne Marilyn, DBE
Street, Dame Susan Ruth, DCB
Sutherland, Dame Joan (Mrs Bonynge), OM, DBE
Sutherland, Dame Veronica Evelyn, DBE, CMG
Swift, *Hon.* Dame Caroline Jane (Mrs Openshaw), DBE, QC
Symmonds, Dame Olga Patricia, DBE
Taylor, Dame Elizabeth, DBE
Taylor, Dame Meg, DBE
Te Kanawa, Dame Kiri Janette, DBE
Thomas, *Prof.* Dame Jean Olwen, DBE
Thomas, Dame Maureen Elizabeth (Lady Thomas), DBE
Tinson, Dame Sue, DBE
Tizard, Dame Catherine Anne, GCMG, GCVO, DBE
Tokiel, Dame Rosa, DBE
Trotter, Dame Janet Olive, DBE
Turner-Warwick, Dame Margaret Elizabeth Harvey, DBE, FRCP, FRCPED
Uprichard, Dame Mary Elizabeth, DBE
Varley, Dame Joan Fleetwood, DBE
Wagner, Dame Gillian Mary Millicent (Lady Wagner), DBE
Wall, Dame (Alice) Anne, (Mrs Michael Wall), DCVO
Wallis, Dame Sheila Ann, DBE
Warburton, Dame Anne Marion, DCVO, CMG
Waterhouse, Dame Rachel Elizabeth, DBE, PHD
Waterman, *Dr* Dame Fanny, DBE
Webb, *Prof.* Dame Patricia, DBE
Weir, Dame Gillian Constance (Mrs Phelps), DBE
Weller, Dame Rita, DBE
Weston, Dame Margaret Kate, DBE
Westwood, Dame Vivienne Isabel, DBE
Wheldon, Dame Juliet Louise, DCB, QC
Williams, Dame Josephine, DBE
Wilson-Barnett, *Prof.* Dame Jenifer, DBE
Winstone, Dame Dorothy Gertrude, DBE, CMG
Wong Yick-ming, Dame Rosanna, DBE

DECORATIONS AND MEDALS

PRINCIPAL DECORATIONS AND MEDALS
IN ORDER OF WEAR

VICTORIA CROSS (VC), 1856 (*see* below)
GEORGE CROSS (GC), 1940 (*see* below)

BRITISH ORDERS OF KNIGHTHOOD (*see also* Orders of Chivalry)
Order of the Garter
Order of the Thistle
Order of St Patrick
Order of the Bath
Order of Merit
Order of the Star of India
Order of St Michael and George
Order of the Indian Empire
Order of the Crown of India
Royal Victorian Order (Classes I, II and III)
Order of the British Empire (Classes I, II and III)
Order of the Companions of Honour
Distinguished Service Order
Royal Victorian Order (Class IV)
Order of the British Empire (Class IV)
Imperial Service Order
Royal Victorian Order (Class V)
Order of the British Empire (Class V)

BARONET'S BADGE

KNIGHT BACHELOR'S BADGE

INDIAN ORDER OF MERIT (MILITARY)

DECORATIONS
Conspicuous Gallantry Cross (CGC), 1995
Royal Red Cross Class I (RRC), 1883
Distinguished Service Cross (DSC), 1914
Military Cross (MC), December 1914
Distinguished Flying Cross (DFC), 1918
Air Force Cross (AFC), 1918
Royal Red Cross Class II (ARRC)
Order of British India
Kaisar-i-Hind Medal
Order of St John

MEDALS FOR GALLANTRY AND DISTINGUISHED CONDUCT
Union of South Africa Queen's Medal for Bravery, in Gold
Distinguished Conduct Medal (DCM), 1854
Conspicuous Gallantry Medal (CGM), 1874
Conspicuous Gallantry Medal (Flying)
George Medal (GM), 1940
Queen's Police Medal for Gallantry
Queen's Fire Service Medal for Gallantry
Royal West African Frontier Force Distinguished Conduct Medal
King's African Rifles Distinguished Conduct Medal
Indian Distinguished Service Medal
Union of South Africa Queen's Medal for Bravery, in Silver
Distinguished Service Medal (DSM), 1914
Military Medal (MM), 1916
Distinguished Flying Medal (DFM), 1918
Air Force Medal (AFM)
Constabulary Medal (Ireland)
Medal for Saving Life at Sea (Sea Gallantry Medal)
Indian Order of Merit (Civil)
Indian Police Medal for Gallantry
Ceylon Police Medal for Gallantry
Sierra Leone Police Medal for Gallantry
Sierra Leone Fire Brigades Medal for Gallantry
Colonial Police Medal for Gallantry (CPM)
Queen's Gallantry Medal (QGM), 1974
Royal Victorian Medal (RVM), Gold, Silver and Bronze
British Empire Medal (BEM)
Canada Medal
Queen's Police Medal for Distinguished Service (QPM)
Queen's Fire Service Medal for Distinguished Service (QFSM)
Queen's Volunteer Reserves Medal
Queen's Medal for Chiefs

CAMPAIGN MEDALS AND STARS
Including authorised United Nations, European Community/Union and North Atlantic Treaty Organisation medals (in order of date of campaign for which awarded)

POLAR MEDALS (in order of date)

IMPERIAL SERVICE MEDAL

POLICE MEDALS FOR VALUABLE SERVICE
Indian Police Medal for Meritorious Service
Ceylon Police Medal for Merit
Sierra Leone Police Medal for Meritorious Service
Sierra Leone Fire Brigades Medal for Meritorious Service
Colonial Police Medal for Meritorious Service

BADGE OF HONOUR

JUBILEE, CORONATION AND DURBAR MEDALS
Queen Victoria, King Edward VII, King George V, King George VI, Queen Elizabeth II, Visit Commemoration and Long and Faithful Service Medals

EFFICIENCY AND LONG SERVICE DECORATIONS AND MEDALS
Medal for Meritorious Service
Accumulated Campaign Service Medal
Medal for Long Service and Good Conduct (Military)
Naval Long Service and Good Conduct Medal
Medal for Meritorious Service (Royal Navy 1918–28)
Indian Long Service and Good Conduct Medal
Indian Meritorious Service Medal
Royal Marines Meritorious Service Medal (1849–1947)
Royal Air Force Meritorious Service Medal (1918–1928)
Royal Air Force Long Service and Good Conduct Medal
Medal for Long Service and Good Conduct (Ulster Defence Regiment)
Indian Long Service and Good Conduct Medal
Royal West African Frontier Force Long Service and Good Conduct Medal

yal Sierra Leone Military Forces Long Service and Good Conduct Medal
ing's African Rifles and Long Service and Good Conduct Medal
dian Meritorious Service Medal
lice Long Service and Good Conduct Medal
re Brigade Long Service and Good Conduct Medal
frican Police Medal for Meritorious Service
oyal Canadian Mounted Police Long Service Medal
eylon Police Long Service Medal
eylon Fire Services Long Service Medal
erra Leone Police Long Service Medal
olonial Police Long Service Medal
erra Leone Fire Brigades Long Service Medal
lauritius Police Long Service and Good Conduct Medal
lauritius Fire Services Long Service and Good Conduct Medal
lauritius Prisons Service Long Service and Good Conduct Medal
olonial Fire Brigades Long Service Medal
olonial Prison Service Medal
long Kong Disciplined Services Medal
rmy Emergency Reserve Decoration (ERD)
olunteer Officers' Decoration (VD)
olunteer Long Service Medal
olunteer Officers' Decoration (for India and the Colonies)
olunteer Long Service Medal (for India and the Colonies)
olonial Auxiliary Forces Officers' Decoration
olonial Auxiliary Forces Long Service Medal
ledal for Good Shooting (Naval)
lilitia Long Service Medal
mperial Yeomanry Long Service Medal
erritorial Decoration (TD), 1908
eylon Armed Services Long Service Medal
fficiency Decoration (ED)
erritorial Efficiency Medal
fficiency Medal
pecial Reserve Long Service and Good Conduct Medal
ecoration for Officers of the Royal Navy Reserve (RD), 1910
ecoration for Officers of the Royal Naval Volunteer Reserve (VRD)
oyal Naval Reserve Long Service and Good Conduct Medal
oyal Naval Volunteer Reserve Long Service and Good Conduct Medal
oyal Naval Auxiliary Sick Berth Reserve Long Service and Good Conduct Medal
oyal Fleet Reserve Long Service and Good Conduct Medal
oyal Naval Wireless Auxiliary Reserve Long Service and Good Conduct Medal
oyal Naval Auxiliary Service Medal
ir Efficiency Award (AE), 1942
olunteer Reserves Service Medal
lster Defence Regiment Medal
orthern Ireland Home Service Medal
Queen's Medal (for Champion Shots of the RN and RM)
Queen's Medal (for Champion Shots of the New Zealand Naval Forces)
Queen's Medal (for Champion Shots in the Military Forces)
Queen's Medal (for Champion Shots of the Air Forces)
Cadet Forces Medal, 1950
Coastguard Auxiliary Service Long Service Medal
Special Constabulary Long Service Medal
Canadian Forces Decoration
Royal Observer Corps Medal
Civil Defence Long Service Medal
Ambulance Service (Emergency Duties) Long Service and Good Conduct Medal
Royal Fleet Auxiliary Service Medal Rhodesia Medal
Royal Ulster Constabulary Service Medal
Northern Ireland Prison Service Medal
Union of South Africa Commemoration Medal
Indian Independence Medal
Pakistan Medal
Ceylon Armed Services Inauguration Medal
Ceylon Police Independence Medal (1948)
Sierra Leone Independence Medal
Jamaica Independence Medal
Uganda Independence Medal
Malawi Independence Medal
Fiji Independence Medal
Papua New Guinea Independence Medal
Solomon Islands Independence Medal
Service Medal of the Order of St John
Badge of the Order of the League of Mercy
Voluntary Medical Service Medal (1932)
Women's Royal Voluntary Service Medal
South African Medal for War Services
Colonial Special Constabulary Medal

HONORARY MEMBERSHIP OF COMMONWEALTH ORDERS

OTHER COMMONWEALTH MEMBERS' ORDERS, DECORATIONS AND MEDALS

FOREIGN ORDERS

FOREIGN DECORATIONS

FOREIGN MEDALS

THE VICTORIA CROSS (1856)

FOR CONSPICUOUS BRAVERY

VC

Ribbon, Crimson, for all Services (until 1918 it was blue for the Royal Navy)

Instituted on 29 January 1856, the Victoria Cross was awarded retrospectively to 1854, the first being held by Lt. C. D. Lucas, RN, for bravery in the Baltic Sea on 21 June 1854 (gazetted 24 February 1857). The first 62 crosses were presented by Queen Victoria in Hyde Park, London, on 26 June 1857.

The Victoria Cross is worn before all other decorations, on the left breast, and consists of a cross-pattée of bronze, 3.8cm in diameter, with the royal crown surmounted by a lion in the centre, and beneath there is the inscription *For Valour.* Holders of the VC currently receive a tax-free annuity of £1,500, irrespective of need or other conditions. In 1911, the right to receive the cross was extended to Indian soldiers, and in 1920 to matrons, sisters and nurses, the staff of the nursing services and other services pertaining to hospitals and nursing, and to civilians of either sex regularly or temporarily under the orders, direction or supervision of the naval, military, or air forces of the crown.

SURVIVING RECIPIENTS OF THE VICTORIA CROSS
as at 31 August 2007

Beharry, *Pte.* J. G. (Princess of Wales's Royal Regiment)
2005 *Iraq*
Bhan Bhagta Gurung, *Havildar* (2nd Gurkha Rifles)
1945 *World War*
Cruickshank, *Flt. Lt.* J. A. (RAFVR)
1944 *World War*
Fraser, *Lt.-Cdr.* I. E., DSC, RD and bar (RNR)
1945 *World War*
Kenna, *Pte.* E. (Australian Military Forces, 2/4th (NSW))
1945 *World War*
Lachhiman Gurung, *Havildar* (8th Gurkha Rifles)
1945 *World War*
Payne, *WO* K., DSC (USA) (Australian Army Training Team)
1969 *Vietnam*
Rambahadur Limbu, *Capt.*, MVO (10th Princess Mary's Gurkha Rifles)
1965 *Sarawak*
Speakman-Pitts, *Sgt.* W. (Black Watch, attached KOSB)
1951 *Korea*
Tulbahadur Pun, *Lt.* (6th Gurkha Rifles)
1944 *World War*
Watkins, *Maj. Rt. Hon.* Sir Tasker, GBE (Welch Regiment)
1944 *World War*
Wilson, *Lt.-Col.* E. C. T. (East Surrey Regiment)
1940 *World War*

AWARDED POSTHUMOUSLY IN 2006–7
Budd, *Cpl.* B. J. (Parachute Regiment), killed in action
2006 *Afghanistan*

THE GEORGE CROSS (1940)
FOR GALLANTRY

GC

Ribbon, Dark blue, threaded through a bar adorned with laurel leaves
Instituted 24 September 1940 (with amendments, 3 November 1942)

The George Cross is worn before all other decorations (except the VC) on the left breast (when worn by a woman it may be worn on the left shoulder from a ribbon of the same width and colour fashioned into a bow). It consists of a plain silver cross with four equal limbs, the cross having in the centre a circular medallion bearing a design showing St George and the Dragon. The inscription *F[or] Gallantry* appears round the medallion and in the ang[le] of each limb of the cross is the royal cypher 'G V' forming a circle concentric with the medallion. Th[e] reverse is plain and bears the name of the recipient an[d] the date of the award. The cross is suspended by a rin[g] from a bar adorned with laurel leaves on dark blu[e] ribbon 3.8cm wide.

The cross is intended primarily for civilians; awards t[o] the fighting services are confined to actions for whic[h] purely military honours are not normally granted. It [is] awarded only for acts of the greatest heroism or of th[e] most conspicuous courage in circumstances of extrem[e] danger. From 1 April 1965, holders of the cross hav[e] received a tax-free annuity, which is currently £1,50[0]. The cross has twice been awarded collectively rather tha[n] to an individual: to Malta (1942) and the Royal Ulst[er] Constabulary (1999).

In October 1971 all surviving holders of the Albe[rt] Medal and the Edward Medal exchanged thos[e] decorations for the George Cross.

SURVIVING RECIPIENTS OF THE GEORGE CROSS
as at 31 August 2007

If the recipient originally received the Albert Medal (AM) or the Edward Medal (EM), this is indicated by the initial in parentheses.

Archer, *Col.* B. S. T., GC, OBE, ERD, 1941
Bamford, J., GC, 1952
Beaton, J., GC, CVO, 1974
Butson, *Lt.-Col.* A. R. C., GC, CD, MD (AM), 1948
Finney, *Trooper* C., GC, 2003
Flintoff, H. H., GC (EM), 1944
Gledhill, A. J., GC, 1967
Gregson, J. S., GC (AM), 1943
Johnson, *WO1 (SSM)* B., GC, 1990
Kinne, D. G., GC, 1954
Lowe, A. R., GC (AM), 1949
Norton, *Capt.* P. A., GC, 2006
Pratt, M. K., GC, 1978
Purves, Mrs M., GC (AM), 1949
Raweng, Awang anak, GC, 1951
Stevens, H. W., GC, 1958
Walker, C., GC, 1972
Walker, C. H., GC (AM), 1942
Walton, E. W. K., GC (AM), DSO, 1948
Wooding, E. A., GC (AM), 1945

AWARDED POSTHUMOUSLY IN 2006–7
Wright, *Cpl.* M. W., GC, 2006

CHIEFS OF CLANS IN SCOTLAND

Only chiefs of whole Names or Clans are included, except certain special instances (marked *) who, though not chiefs of a whole Name, were or are for some reason (eg the Macdonald forfeiture) independent. Under decision (*Campbell-Gray*, 1950) that a bearer of a 'double or triple-barrelled' surname cannot be held chief of a part of such, several others cannot be included in the list at present.

THE ROYAL HOUSE: HM The Queen
AGNEW: Sir Crispin Agnew of Lochnaw, Bt.
ANSTRUTHER: Tobias Anstruther of Anstruther and Balcaskie
ARBUTHNOTT: Viscount of Arbuthnott, KT, CBE, DSC
BANNERMAN: Sir David Bannerman of Elsick, Bt.
BARCLAY: Peter C. Barclay of Towie Barclay and of that Ilk
BORTHWICK: Lord Borthwick
BOYD: Lord Kilmarnock, MBE
BOYLE: Earl of Glasgow
BRODIE: Alexander Brodie of Brodie
BROUN OF COLSTOUN: Sir Wayne Broun of Colstoun, Bt.
BRUCE: Earl of Elgin and Kincardine, KT
BUCHAN: David Buchan of Auchmacoy
BURNETT: J. C. A. Burnett of Leys
CAMERON: Donald Cameron of Lochiel
CAMPBELL: Duke of Argyll
CARMICHAEL: Richard Carmichael of Carmichael
CARNEGIE: Duke of Fife
CATHCART: Earl Cathcart
CHARTERIS: Earl of Wemyss and March, KT
CLAN CHATTAN: K. Mackintosh of Clan Chattan
CHISHOLM: Hamish Chisholm of Chisholm *(The Chisholm)*
COCHRANE: Earl of Dundonald
COLQUHOUN: Sir Ivar Colquhoun of Luss, Bt.
CRANSTOUN: David Cranstoun of that Ilk
CUMMING: Sir Alastair Cumming of Altyre, Bt.
DARROCH: Capt. Duncan Darroch of Gourock
DAVIDSON: Alister Davidson of Davidston
DEWAR: Michael Dewar of that Ilk and Vogrie
DRUMMOND: Earl of Perth
DUNBAR: Sir James Dunbar of Mochrum, Bt.
DUNDAS: David Dundas of Dundas
DURIE: Andrew Durie of Durie, CBE
ELIOTT: Mrs Margaret Eliott of Redheugh
ERSKINE: Earl of Mar and Kellie
FARQUHARSON: Capt. A. Farquharson of Invercauld, MC
FERGUSSON: Sir Charles Fergusson of Kilkerran, Bt.
FORBES: Lord Forbes, KBE
FORSYTH: Alistair Forsyth of that Ilk
FRASER: Lady Saltoun
*FRASER (OF LOVAT): Lord Lovat
GAYRE: R. Gayre of Gayre and Nigg
GORDON: Marquess of Huntly
GRAHAM: Duke of Montrose
GRANT: Lord Strathspey
GRIERSON: Sir Michael Grierson of Lag, Bt.
GUTHRIE: Alexander Guthrie of Guthrie
HAIG: Earl Haig, OBE
HALDANE: Martin Haldane of Gleneagles
HANNAY: David Hannay of Kirkdale and of that Ilk
HAY: Earl of Erroll
HENDERSON: Alistair Henderson of Fordell
HUNTER: Pauline Hunter of Hunterston
IRVINE OF DRUM: David Irvine of Drum
JARDINE: Sir Alexander Jardine of Applegirth, Bt.
JOHNSTONE: Earl of Annandale and Hartfell
KEITH: Earl of Kintore
KENNEDY: Marquess of Ailsa
KERR: Marquess of Lothian, PC
KINCAID: Madam Arabella Kincaid of Kincaid
LAMONT: Revd Peter Lamont of that Ilk
LEASK: Madam Leask of Leask
LENNOX: Edward Lennox of that Ilk
LESLIE: Earl of Rothes
LINDSAY: Earl of Crawford and Balcarres, KT, GCVO, PC
LIVINGSTONE (or MACLEA): Alastair Livingstone of Bachuil
LOCKHART: Angus Lockhart of the Lee
LUMSDEN: Gillem Lumsden of that Ilk and Blanerne
MACALESTER: William St J. McAlester of Loup and Kennox
MACARTHUR; John MacArthur of that Ilk
MCBAIN: J. H. McBain of McBain
MACDONALD: Lord Macdonald *(The Macdonald of Macdonald)*
*MACDONALD OF CLANRANALD: Ranald Macdonald of Clanranald
MACDONALD OF KEPPOCH: Ranald MacDonald of Keppoch
*MACDONALD OF SLEAT (CLAN HUSTEAIN): Sir Ian Macdonald of Sleat, Bt.
*MACDONELL OF GLENGARRY: Ranald MacDonell of Glengarry
MACDOUGALL: Morag MacDougall of MacDougall
MACDOWALL: Fergus Macdowall of Garthland
MACGREGOR: Sir Malcolm MacGregor of MacGregor, Bt.
MACINTYRE: Donald MacIntyre of Glenoe
MACKAY: Lord Reay
MACKENZIE: Earl of Cromartie
MACKINNON: Anne Mackinnon of Mackinnon
MACKINTOSH: John Mackintosh of Mackintosh *(The Mackintosh of Mackintosh)*
MACLACHLAN: Euan MacLachlan of MacLachlan
MACLAREN: Donald MacLaren of MacLaren and Achleskine
MACLEAN: Hon. Sir Lachlan Maclean of Duart, Bt., CVO
MACLENNAN: Ruaraidh MacLennan of MacLennan
MACLEOD: Hugh MacLeod of MacLeod
MACMILLAN: George MacMillan of MacMillan
MACNAB: J. C. Macnab of Macnab *(The Macnab)*
MACNAGHTEN: Sir Patrick Macnaghten of Macnaghten and Dundarave, Bt.
MACNEACAIL: John Macneacail of Macneacail and Scorrybreac

MACNEIL OF BARRA: Ian Macneil of Barra *(The Macneil of Barra)*
MACPHERSON: Hon. Sir William Macpherson of Cluny, TD
MACTHOMAS: Andrew MacThomas of Finegand
MAITLAND: Earl of Lauderdale
MAKGILL: Viscount of Oxfuird
MALCOLM (MACCALLUM): Robin N. L. Malcolm of Poltalloch
MAR: Countess of Mar
MARJORIBANKS: Andrew Marjoribanks of that Ilk
MATHESON: Maj. Sir Fergus Matheson of Matheson, Bt.
MENZIES: David Menzies of Menzies
MOFFAT: Madam Moffat of that Ilk
MONCREIFFE: Hon. Peregrine Moncreiffe of that Ilk
MONTGOMERIE: Earl of Eglinton and Winton
MORRISON: Dr Iain Morrison of Ruchdi
MUNRO: Hector Munro of Foulis
MURRAY: Duke of Atholl
NESBITT (or NISBET): Mark Nesbitt of that Ilk
NICOLSON: Lord Carnock
OGILVY: Earl of Airlie, KT, GCVO, PC
OLIPHANT: Richard Oliphant of that Ilk
RAMSAY: Earl of Dalhousie
RIDDELL: Sir John Riddell of Riddell, Bt., CVO
ROBERTSON: Alexander Robertson of Struan *(Struan-Robertson)*
ROLLO: Lord Rollo
ROSE: Miss Elizabeth Rose of Kilravock
ROSS: David Ross of that Ilk and Balnagowan
RUTHVEN: Earl of Gowrie, PC
SCOTT: Duke of Buccleuch and Queensberry, KT, VRD
SCRYMGEOUR: Earl of Dundee
SEMPILL: Lord Sempill
SHAW: John Shaw of Tordarroch
SINCLAIR: Earl of Caithness
SKENE: Danus Skene of Skene
STIRLING: Fraser Stirling of Cader
STRANGE: Maj. Timothy Strange of Balcaskie
SUTHERLAND: Countess of Sutherland
SWINTON: John Swinton of that Ilk
TROTTER: Alexander Trotter of Mortonhall
URQUHART: Kenneth Urquhart of Urquhart
WALLACE: Ian Wallace of that Ilk
WEDDERBURN: Master of Dundee
WEMYSS: Michael Wemyss of that Ilk

THE PRIVY COUNCIL

The sovereign in council, or Privy Council, was the chief source of executive power until the system of cabinet government developed in the 18th century. Now the Privy Council's main functions are to advise the sovereign and to exercise its own statutory responsibilities independent of the sovereign in council.

Membership of the Privy Council is automatic upon appointment to certain government and judicial positions in the United Kingdom, eg cabinet ministers must be Privy Counsellors and are sworn in on first assuming office. Membership is also accorded by the Queen to eminent people in the UK and independent countries of the Commonwealth of which she is Queen, on the recommendation of the British prime minister. Membership of the council is retained for life, except for very occasional removals.

The administrative functions of the Privy Council are carried out by the Privy Council Office under the direction of the president of the council, who is always a member of the cabinet.

President of the Council, Rt. Hon. Baroness Ashton of Upholland
Clerk of the Council, Judith Simpson

MEMBERS *as at August 2007*

Style The Right (or Rt.) Hon._
Envelope, The Right (or Rt.) Hon. F_ S_. *Letter,* Dear Mr/Miss/Mrs S_. *Spoken,* Mr/Miss/Mrs S_
It is incorrect to use the letters PC after the name in conjunction with the prefix The Right Hon., unless the Privy Counsellor is a peer below the rank of Marquess and so is styled The Right Hon. because of his/her rank. In this case only, the post-nominal letters may be used in conjunction with the prefix The Right Hon.

HRH The Duke of Edinburgh, 1951
HRH The Prince of Wales, 1977

Abernethy, *Hon.* Lord (Alastair Cameron), 2005
Ainsworth, Robert, 2005
Airlie, Earl of, 1984
Aldous, Sir William, 1995
Alebua, Ezekiel, 1988
Alexander, Douglas, 2005
Amos, Baroness, 2003
Ampthill, Lord, 1995
Ancram, Michael, 1996
Anderson of Swansea, Lord, 2000
Angiolini, Elish, 2006
Anthony, Douglas, 1971
Arbuthnot, James, 1998
Archer of Sandwell, Lord, 1977
Arden, Dame Mary, 2000
Armstrong, Hilary, 1999
Arthur, *Hon.* Owen, 1995
Ashdown of Norton-sub-Hamdon, Lord, 1989
Ashley of Stoke, Lord, 1979
Ashton of Upholland, Baroness, 2006
Atkins, Sir Robert, 1995
Auld, Sir Robin, 1995
Baker, Sir Thomas, 2002
Baker of Dorking, Lord, 1984
Balls, Ed, 2007
Barnett, Lord, 1975
Barron, Kevin, 2001
Battle, John, 2002
Beckett, Margaret, 1993
Beith, Alan, 1992
Beldam, Sir Roy, 1989
Benn, Anthony, 1964
Benn, Hilary, 2003
Bew, Lord, 2007
Bingham of Cornhill, Lord, 1986
Birch, William, 1992
Bisson, Sir Gordon, 1987
Blackstone, Baroness, 2001
Blair, Anthony, 1994
Blaker, Lord, 1983
Blanchard, Peter, 1998
Blears, Hazel, 2005
Blunkett, David, 1997
Boateng, Paul, 1999
Bolger, James, 1991
Booth, Albert, 1976
Boothroyd, Baroness, 1992
Boscawen, *Hon.* Robert, 1992
Bottomley of Nettlestone, Baroness, 1992
Boyd of Duncansby, Lord, 2000
Boyson, Sir Rhodes, 1987
Bradley, Lord, 2001
Brathwaite, Sir Nicholas, 1991
Bridge of Harwich, Lord, 1975
Brittan of Spennithorne, Lord, 1981
Brooke, Sir Henry, 1996
Brooke of Sutton Mandeville, Lord, 1988
Brown, Gordon, 1996
Brown, Nicholas, 1997
Brown, Sir Stephen, 1983
Brown of Eaton-under-Heywood, Lord, 1992
Browne, Desmond, 2005
Browne-Wilkinson, Lord, 1983
Bruce, Malcolm, 2006
Burnham, Andy, 2007
Butler, Sir Adam, 1984
Butler of Brockwell, Lord, 2004
Butler-Sloss, Baroness, 1988
Buxton, Sir Richard, 1997
Byers, Stephen, 1998
Bryon, Sir Dennis, 2004
Caborn, Richard, 1999
Caithness, Earl of, 1990
Cameron, David, 2005
Cameron of Lochbroom, Lord, 1984
Camoys, Lord, 1997
Campbell, Sir Walter Menzies, 1999
Campbell, Sir William, 1999
Campbell of Surbiton, Baroness, 2007
Canterbury, Archbishop of, 2002
Carey of Clifton, Lord, 1991
Carnwath, Sir Robert, 2002
Carr of Hadley, Lord, 1963
Carrington, Lord, 1959
Carswell, Lord, 1993
Casey, Sir Maurice, 1986
Chadwick, Sir John, 1997
Chalfont, Lord, 1964
Chalker of Wallasey, Baroness, 1987
Chan, Sir Julius, 1981
Chataway, Sir Christopher, 1970
Chilcot, Sir John, 2004
Christie, Perry, 2004
Clark of Windermere, Lord, 1997
Clark, Helen, 1990
Clarke, Sir Anthony, 1998
Clarke, Charles, 2001
Clarke, Kenneth, 1984
Clarke, Thomas, 1997
Clinton-Davis, Lord, 1998
Clwyd, Ann, 2004
Clyde, Lord, 1996
Colman, Fraser, 1986
Compton, Sir John, 1983
Cope of Berkeley, Lord, 1988
Corston, Baroness, 2003
Cosgrove, *Hon.* Lady (Hazel Cosgrove), 2003
Coulsfield, *Hon.* Lord (John Coulsfield), 2000
Coussins, Baroness, 2007
Cowen, Sir Zelman, 1981
Cradock, Sir Percy, 1993
Crawford and Balcarres, Earl of, 1972
Creech, *Hon.* Wyatt, 1999
Crickhowell, Lord, 1979
Cullen of Whitekirk, *Hon.* Lord, 1997
Cunningham of Felling, Lord, 1993
Curry, David, 1996
Darling, Alistair, 1997
Davies, Denzil, 1978
Davies, Ronald, 1997
Davies of Oldham, Lord, 2006
Davis, David, 1997
Davis, Terence, 1999
Davison, Sir Ronald, 1978
de la Bastide, Michael, 2004
Dean of Harptree, Lord, 1991
Dean of Thornton-le-Fylde, Baroness, 1998
Denham, John, 2000
Denham, Lord, 1981
Dixon, Lord, 1996
Dobson, Frank, 1997
Donaldson, Jeffrey, 2007
Dorrell, Stephen, 1994
du Cann, Sir Edward, 1964
Duncan Smith, Iain, 2001

Dunn, Sir Robin, 1980
Dyson, Sir John, 2001
Eassie, *Hon.* Lord (Ronald Mackay), 2006
East, Paul, 1998
Eden of Winton, Lord, 1972
Edward, Sir David, 2005
Eggar, Timothy, 1995
Eichelbaum, Sir Thomas, 1989
Elias, *Hon.* Dame, Sian, 1999
Elis-Thomas, Lord, 2004
Esquivel, Manuel, 1986
Evans, Sir Anthony, 1992
Eveleigh, Sir Edward, 1977
Falconer of Thoroton, Lord, 2003
Farquharson, Sir Donald, 1989
Fellowes, Lord, 1990
Ferrers, Earl, 1982
Field, Frank, 1997
Floissac, Sir Vincent, 1992
Foot, Michael, 1974
Forsyth of Drumlean, Lord, 1995
Foster of Bishop Auckland, Lord, 1993
Foulkes of Cumnock, Lord, 2002
Fowler, Lord, 1979
Fraser, Malcolm, 1976
Fraser of Carmyllie, Lord, 1989
Freeman, John, 1966
Freeman, Lord, 1993
Gage, Sir William, 2004
Garel-Jones, Lord, 1992
Gault, Thomas, 1992
Geidt, Christopher, 2007
George, Bruce, 2000
George, Lord, 1999
Gibson, Sir Peter, 1993
Gilbert, Lord, 1978
Gill, *Hon.* Lord (Brian Gill), 2002
Gilmour of Craigmillar, Lord, 1973
Girvan, Sir (Frederick) Paul, 2007
Glenamara, Lord, 1964
Glidewell, Sir Iain, 1985
Goff of Chieveley, Lord, 1982
Goldsmith, Lord, 2002
Goodlad, Lord, 1992
Gowrie, Earl of, 1984
Graham, Sir Douglas, 1998
Graham of Edmonton, Lord, 1998
Griffiths, Lord, 1980
Grocott, Lord, 2002
Gummer, John, 1985
Habgood, Rt. Revd Lord, 1983
Hague, William, 1995
Hain, Peter, 2001
Hale of Richmond, Baroness, 1999
Hallett, Dame Heather, 2005
Hameed, Lord, 2007
Hamilton, *Hon.* Lord (Arthur Hamilton), 2002
Hamilton of Epsom, Lord, 1991
Hanley, Sir Jeremy, 1994
Hanson, David, 2007
Hardie, Lord, 1997
Hardie Boys, Sir Michael, 1989
Harman, Harriet, 1997
Harrison, Walter, 1977
Haselhurst, Sir Alan, 1999
Hattersley, Lord, 1975
Hayhoe, Lord, 1985
Hayman, Baroness, 2000
Healey, Lord, 1964
Heathcoat-Amory, David, 1996
Henry, Sir Denis, 1993
Henry, John, 1996
Heseltine, Lord, 1979
Heseltine, Sir William, 1986
Hesketh, Lord, 1991
Hewitt, Patricia, 2001
Higgins, Lord, 1979
Higgins, Sir Malachy, 2007
Hill, Keith, 2003
Hirst, Sir David, 1992
Hodge, Margaret, 2003
Hoffmann, Lord, 1992
Hogg, *Hon.* Douglas, 1992
Hollis of Heigham, Baroness, 1999
Holme of Cheltenham, Lord, 2000
Hoon, Geoffrey, 1999
Hooper, Sir Anthony, 2004
Hope of Craighead, Lord, 1989
Hope of Thornes, Lord, 1991
Hordern, Sir Peter, 1993
Howard, Michael, 1990
Howarth, George, 2005
Howarth of Newport, Lord, 2000
Howe of Aberavon, Lord, 1972
Howell of Guildford, Lord, 1979
Hughes, Sir Anthony, 2006
Hughes, Beverley, 2004
Hunt, Jonathan, 1989
Hunt of Wirral, Lord, 1990
Hurd of Westwell, Lord, 1982
Hutchison, Sir Michael, 1995
Hutton, Lord, 1988
Hutton, John, 2001
Inge, Lord, 2004
Ingraham, Hubert, 1993
Ingram, Adam, 1999
Irvine of Lairg, Lord, 1997
Jack, Michael, 1997
Jacob, Sir Robert, 2004
Jacobs, Francis, 2005
Janvrin, Lord, 1998
Jay of Paddington, Baroness, 1998
Jenkin of Roding, Lord, 1973
Johnson, Alan, 2003
Johnson Smith, Sir Geoffrey, 1996
Johnston, *Hon.* Lord (Alan Johnston), 2005
Jones, Lord, 1999
Jopling, Lord, 1979
Jowell, Tessa, 1998
Judge, Sir Igor, 1996
Jugnauth, Sir Anerood, 1987
Kaufman, Sir Gerald, 1978
Kay, Sir Maurice, 2004
Keene, Sir David, 2000
Keith, Sir Kenneth, 1998
Kelly, Sir Basil, 1984
Kelly, Ruth, 2004
Kenilorea, Sir Peter, 1979
Kennedy, Charles, 1999
Kennedy, Jane, 2003
Kennedy, Sir Paul, 1992
Kerr, Sir Brian, 2004
King of Bridgwater, Lord, 1979
Kingarth, *Hon.* Lord (Derek Emslie)
Kingsdown, Lord, 1987
Kingsland, Lord, 1994
Kinnock, Lord, 1983
Kirkwood, *Hon.* Lord (Ian Kirkwood), 2000
Knight, Gregory, 1995
Lamont of Lerwick, Lord, 1986
Lang of Monkton, Lord, 1990
Latasi, Sir Kamuta, 1996
Latham, Sir David, 2000
Lauti, Sir Toaripi, 1979
Lawrence, John, 2005
Laws, Sir John, 1999
Lawson of Blaby, Lord, 1981
Leggatt, Sir Andrew, 1990
Leonard, Rt. Revd Graham, 1981
Letwin, Oliver, 2002
Leveson, Sir Brian, 2006
Liddell, Mrs Helen, 1998
Lilley, Peter, 1990
Lloyd of Berwick, Lord, 1984
Lloyd, Sir Peter, 1994
Lloyd, Sir Timothy, 2005
London, Bishop of, 1995
Longmore, Sir Andrew, 2001
Louisy, Sir Allan, 1981
Luce, Lord, 1986
Lyell of Markyate, Lord, 1990
Mabon, Dickson, 1977
McAvoy, Thomas, 2003
McCartney, Ian, 1999
McCollum, Sir Liam, 1997
McConnell, Jack, 2001
McCowan, Sir Anthony, 1989
MacDermott, Sir John, 1987
Macdonald of Tradeston, Lord, 199
Macfadyen, *Hon.* Lord (Donald MacFadyen), 2002
McFall, John, 2004
MacGregor of Pulham Market, Lord, 1985
McIntosh of Haringey, Lord, 2002
Mackay, Andrew, 1998
McKay, Ian, 1992
Mackay of Clashfern, Lord, 1979
Mackay of Drumadoon, Lord, 1996
McKinnon, Donald, 1992
Maclean, David, 1995
Maclean, *Hon.* Lord (Ranald MacLean), 2001
McLeish, Henry, 2000
Maclennan of Rogart, Lord, 1997
McLoughlin, Patrick, 2005
McMullin, Sir Duncan, 1980
McNally, Lord, 2005
McNulty, Anthony, 2007
McShane, Denis, 2005
Major, Sir John, 1987
Malloch-Brown, Lord, 2007
Mance, Lord, 1999
Mandelson, Peter, 1998
Mantell, Sir Charles, 1997
Marnoch, *Hon.* Lord (Michael Marnoch), 2001
Marsh, Lord, 1966
Martin, Michael, 2000
Mason of Barnsley, Lord, 1968
Mates, Michael, 2004
Maude, *Hon.* Francis, 1992
Mawhinney, Lord, 1994
May, Sir Anthony, 1998
May, Theresa, 2003
Mayhew of Twysden, Lord, 1986
Meacher, Michael, 1997
Mellor, David, 1990
Michael, Alun, 1998
Milburn, Alan, 1998
Miliband, David, 2005
Miliband, Ed, 2007
Millan, Bruce, 1975
Millett, Lord, 1994
Mitchell, Sir James, 1985
Mitchell, Dr Keith, 2004
Molyneaux of Killead, Lord, 1983
Moore, Michael, 1990
Moore of Lower Marsh, Lord, 1986
Moore of Wolvercote, Lord, 1977
Moore-Bick, Sir Martin, 2005
Morgan, Rhodri, 2000
Morley, Elliot, 2007
Morris, Charles, 1978
Morris of Aberavon, Lord, 1970
Morris of Manchester, Lord, 1979

Morris of Yardley, Baroness, 1999
Morritt, Sir Robert, 1994
Moses, Sir Alan, 2005
Moyle, Roland, 1978
Mummery, Sir John, 1996
Murphy, Paul, 1999
Murray, *Hon.* Lord (Ronald Murray), 1974
Murray, Sir Donald, 1989
Murton of Lindisfarne, Lord, 1976
Musa, Wilbert, 2005
Mustill, Lord, 1985
Nairne, Sir Patrick, 1982
Namaliu, Sir Rabbie, 1989
Naseby, Lord, 1994
Needham, Sir Richard, 1994
Neill, Sir Brian, 1985
Neuberger of Abbotsbury, Lord, 2004
Newton of Braintree, Lord, 1988
Nicholls of Birkenhead, Lord, 1995
Nicholson, Sir Michael, 1995
Nimmo Smith, *Hon.* Lord (William Nimmo Smith), 2005
Nott, Sir John, 1979
Nourse, Sir Martin, 1985
O'Donnell, Turlough, 1979
Oliver of Aylmerton, Lord, 1980
Oppenheim-Barnes, Baroness, 1979
Osborne, *Hon.* Lord (Kenneth Osborne), 2001
Otton, Sir Philip, 1995
Owen, Lord, 1976
Paeniu, Bikenibeu, 1991
Paisley, Dr Ian, 2005
Palliser, Sir Michael, 1983
Palmer, Sir Geoffrey, 1986
Parker, Sir Jonathan, 2000
Parker, Sir Roger, 1983
Parkinson, Lord, 1981
Paton, *Hon.* Lady (Ann Paton), 2007
Patten, Lord, 1990
Patten of Barnes, Lord, 1989
Patterson, Percival, 1993
Pattie, Sir Geoffrey, 1987
Peel, Earl, 2006
Pendry, Lord, 2000
Penrose, *Hon.* Lord (George Penrose), 2000
Peters, Winston, 1998
Philip, *Hon.* Lord (Alexander Philip), 2005
Phillips of Worth Matravers, Lord, 1995
Pill, Sir Malcolm, 1995
Portillo, Michael, 1992
Potter, Sir Mark, 1996
Prescott, John, 1994
Price, George, 1982
Primarolo, Dawn, 2002
Prior, Lord, 1970
Prosser, *Hon.* Lord (William Prosser), 2000
Puapua, Sir Tomasi, 1982
Purnell, James, 2007
Pym, Lord, 1970
Quin, Baroness, 1998
Radice, Lord, 1999
Raison, Sir Timothy, 1982
Ramsden, James, 1963
Raynsford, Nick, 2001
Redwood, John, 1993
Rees, Lord, 1983
Reid, George, 2004
Reid, John, 1998
Renton of Mount Harry, Lord, 1989
Richard, Lord, 1993
Richards, Sir Stephen, 2005
Richardson, Sir Ivor, 1978
Richardson of Duntisbourne, Lord, 1976
Rifkind, Sir Malcolm, 1986
Rix, Sir Bernard, 2000
Roberts of Conwy, Lord, 1991
Robertson of Port Ellen, Lord, 1997
Robinson, Peter, 2007
Roch, Sir John, 1993
Rodger of Earlsferry, Lord, 1992
Rodgers of Quarry Bank, Lord, 1975
Rooker, Lord, 1999
Roper, Lord, 2005
Rose, Sir Christopher, 1992
Ross, *Hon.* Lord (Donald MacArthur), 1985
Rumbold, Dame Angela, 1991
Ryan, Joan, 2007
Ryder of Wensum, Lord, 1990
Sainsbury, Sir Timothy, 1992
St John of Fawsley, Lord, 1979
Salisbury, Marquess of, 1994
Salmond, Alex, 2007
Sandiford, Erskine, 1989
Saville of Newdigate, Lord, 1994
Sawyer, Dame Joan, 2004
Schiemann, Sir Konrad, 1995
Scotland of Asthal, Baroness, 2001
Scott of Foscote, Lord, 1991
Seaga, Edward, 1981
Sedley, Sir Stephen, 1999
Selkirk of Douglas, Lord, 1996
Sheldon, Lord, 1977
Shephard of Northwold, Baroness, 1992
Sheil, Sir John, 2005
Shipley, Jennifer, 1998
Short, Clare, 1997
Simmonds, Kennedy Sir, 1984
Sinclair, Ian, 1977
Slade, Sir Christopher, 1982
Slynn of Hadley, Lord, 1992
Smith, Andrew, 1997
Smith, Dame Janet, 2002
Smith, Jacqueline, 2003
Smith of Finsbury, Lord, 1997
Somare, Sir Michael, 1977
Spellar, John, 2001
Stanley, Sir John, 1984
Staughton, Sir Christopher, 1988
Steel of Aikwood, Lord, 1977
Stephen, Sir Ninian, 1979
Stewartby, Lord, 1989
Steyn, Lord, 1992
Strang, Gavin, 1997
Strathclyde, Lord, 1995
Straw, Jack, 1997
Stuart-Smith, Sir Murray, 1988
Sutherland, *Hon.* Lord (Ranald Sutherland), 2000
Symons of Vernham Dean, Baroness, 2001
Talboys, Sir Brian, 1977
Taylor of Bolton, Baroness, 1997
Tebbit, Lord, 1981
Templeman, Lord, 1978
Thatcher, Baroness, 1970
Thomas, Edmund, 1996
Thomas of Gwydir, Lord, 1964
Thomas, Sir Roger, 2003
Thomas, Sir Swinton, 1994
Thomson of Monifieth, Lord, 1966
Thorpe, Jeremy, 1967
Thorpe, Sir Matthew, 1995
Timms, Stephen, 2006
Tipping, Andrew, 1998
Tizard, Robert, 1986
Touhig, Don, 2006
Toulson, Sir Roger, 2007
Trefgarne, Lord, 1989
Trimble, Lord, 1997
Trumpington, Baroness, 1992
Tuckey, Sir Simon, 1998
Ullswater, Viscount, 1994
Upton, Simon, 1999
Varley, Lord, 1974
Vaz, Keith, 2006
Waddington, Lord, 1987
Waite, Sir John, 1993
Wakeham, Lord, 1983
Waldegrave of North Hill, Lord, 1990
Walker of Gestingthorpe, Lord, 1997
Walker of Worcester, Lord, 1970
Wall, Sir Nicholas, 2004
Wallace, James, 2000
Waller, Sir Mark, 1996
Ward, Sir Alan, 1995
Warner, Lord, 2006
Watkins, Sir Tasker, 1980
Wheatley, *Hon.* Lord (John Wheatley), 2007
Wheeler, Sir John, 1993
Whitty, Lord, 2005
Widdecombe, Ann, 1997
Wigley, Dafydd, 1997
Williams, Alan, 1977
Williams of Crosby, Baroness, 1974
Williamson of Horton, Lord, 2007
Wilson, Brian, 2003
Wilson, Sir Nicholas, 2005
Windlesham, Lord, 1973
Winterton, Rosie, 2006
Winti, Paias, 1987
Withers, Reginald, 1977
Woodhouse, Sir Owen, 1974
Woodward, Shaun, 2007
Woolf, Lord, 1986
York, Archbishop of, 2005
Young, Sir George, 1993
Young of Graffham, Lord, 1984
Zacca, Edward, 1992

PRIVY COUNCIL OF NORTHERN IRELAND

The Privy Council of Northern Ireland had responsibilities in Northern Ireland similar to those of the Privy Council in Great Britain until the Northern Ireland Act 1974.

Membership of the Privy Council of Northern Ireland is retained for life. Since the Northern Ireland Constitution Act 1973 no further appointments have been made. The postnominal initials PC (NI) are used to differentiate its members from those of the Privy Council.

MEMBERS *as at August 2007*

Bailie, Robin, 1971
Bleakley, David, 1971
Craig, William, 1963
Dobson, John, 1969
Kelly, Sir Basil, 1969
Kilclooney, Lord, 1970
Kirk, Herbert, 1962
Long, William, 1966
Porter, Sir Robert, 1969

PARLIAMENT

The United Kingdom constitution is not contained in any single document but has evolved over time, formed partly by statute, partly by common law and partly by convention. A constitutional monarchy, the United Kingdom is governed by ministers of the crown in the name of the sovereign, who is head both of the state and of the government.

The organs of government are the legislature (parliament), the executive and the judiciary. The executive consists of HM government (the cabinet and other ministers), government departments and local authorities (*see* Local Government, Government Departments and Public Bodies sections). The judiciary (*see* Law Courts and Offices section) pronounces on the law, both written and unwritten, interprets statutes and is responsible for the enforcement of the law; the judiciary is independent of both the legislature and the executive.

THE MONARCHY

The sovereign personifies the state and is, in law, an integral part of the legislature, head of the executive, head of the judiciary, commander-in-chief of all armed forces of the crown and supreme governor of the Church of England. The seat of the monarchy is in the United Kingdom. In the Channel Islands and the Isle of Man, which are crown dependencies, the sovereign is represented by a lieutenant-governor. In the member states of the Commonwealth of which the sovereign is head of state, her representative is a governor-general; in UK dependencies the sovereign is usually represented by a governor, who is responsible to the British government.

Although in practice the powers of the monarchy are now very limited, and restricted mainly to the advisory and ceremonial, there are important acts of government which require the participation of the sovereign. These include summoning, proroguing and dissolving parliament, giving royal assent to bills passed by parliament, appointing important office-holders, eg government ministers, judges, bishops and governors, conferring peerages, knighthoods and other honours, and granting pardon to a person wrongly convicted of a crime. The sovereign appoints the prime minister; by convention this office is held by the leader of the political party which enjoys, or can secure, a majority of votes in the House of Commons. In international affairs the sovereign as head of state has the power to declare war and make peace, to recognise foreign states and governments, to conclude treaties and to annex or cede territory. However, as the sovereign entrusts executive power to ministers of the crown and acts on the advice of her ministers, which she cannot ignore, royal prerogative powers are in practice exercised by ministers, who are responsible to parliament.

Ministerial responsibility does not diminish the sovereign's importance to the smooth working of government. She holds meetings of the Privy Council (*see* below), gives audiences to her ministers and other officials at home and overseas, receives accounts of cabinet decisions, reads dispatches and signs state papers; she must be informed and consulted on every aspect of national life; and she must show complete impartiality.

COUNSELLORS OF STATE

In the event of the sovereign's absence abroad, it is necessary to appoint counsellors of state under letters patent to carry out the chief functions of the monarch, including the holding of Privy Councils and giving royal assent to acts passed by parliament. The normal procedure is to appoint as counsellors three or four members of the royal family among those remaining in the UK.

In the event of the sovereign on accession being under the age of 18 years, or at any time unavailable or incapacitated by infirmity of mind or body for the performance of the royal functions, provision is made for a regency.

THE PRIVY COUNCIL

The sovereign in council, or Privy Council, was the chief source of executive power until the system of cabinet government developed. Its main function today is to advise the sovereign on the approval of various statutory functions and acts of the royal prerogative. These powers are exercised through orders in council and royal proclamations, approved by the Queen at meetings of the Privy Council. The council is also able to exercise a number of statutory duties without approval from the sovereign, including powers of supervision over the registering bodies for the medical and allied professions. These duties are exercised through orders in council.

Although appointment as a privy counsellor is for life, only those who are currently government ministers are involved in the day-to-day business of the council. A full council is summoned only on the death of the sovereign or when the sovereign announces his or her intention to marry. (For a full list of privy counsellors, *see* the Privy Council section.)

There are a number of advisory Privy Council committees whose meetings the sovereign does not attend. Some are prerogative committees, such as those dealing with legislative matters submitted by the legislatures of the Channel Islands and the Isle of Man or with applications for charters of incorporation; and some are provided for by statute, eg those for the universities of Oxford and Cambridge and the Scottish universities.

The Judicial Committee of the Privy Council is the court of final appeal from courts of the UK dependencies, courts of independent Commonwealth countries which have retained the right of appeal and courts of the Channel Islands and the Isle of Man.

It also has certain jurisdiction within the United Kingdom, the most important of which is that it is the court of final appeal for 'devolution issues', ie issues as to the legal competences and functions of the legislative and executive authorities established in Scotland, Wales and Northern Ireland by the devolution legislation of 1998.

The committee is composed of privy counsellors who hold, or have held, high judicial office, although usually only three or five hear each case.

Administrative work is carried out by the Privy Council Office under the direction of the Lord President of the Council, a cabinet minister.

PARLIAMENT

Parliament is the supreme law-making authority and can legislate for the UK as a whole or for any parts of it separately (the Channel Islands and the Isle of Man are crown dependencies and not part of the UK). The main functions of parliament are to pass laws, to provide (by voting taxation) the means of carrying on the work of government and to scrutinise government policy and administration, particularly proposals for expenditure. International treaties and agreements are by custom presented to parliament before ratification.

Parliament emerged during the late 13th and early 14th centuries. The officers of the king's household and the king's judges were the nucleus of early parliaments, joined by such ecclesiastical and lay magnates as the king might summon to form a prototype 'House of Lords', and occasionally by the knights of the shires, burgesses and proctors of the lower clergy. By the end of Edward III's reign a 'House of Commons' was beginning to appear; the first known Speaker was elected in 1377.

Parliamentary procedure is based on custom and precedent, partly formulated in the standing orders of both houses of parliament, and each house has the right to control its own internal proceedings and to commit for contempt. The system of debate in the two houses is similar; when a motion has been moved, the Speaker proposes the question as the subject of a debate. Members speak from wherever they have been sitting. Questions are decided by a vote on a simple majority. Draft legislation is introduced, in either house, as a bill. Bills can be introduced by a government minister or a private member, but in practice the majority of bills which become law are introduced by the government. To become law, a bill must be passed by each house (for parliamentary stages, *see* Parliamentary Information) and then sent to the sovereign for the royal assent, after which it becomes an act of parliament.

Proceedings of both houses are public, except on extremely rare occasions. The minutes (called *Votes and Proceedings in the Commons,* and *Minutes of Proceedings in the Lords*) and the speeches (*The Official Report of Parliamentary Debates,* Hansard) are published daily. Proceedings are also recorded for transmission on radio and television and stored in the Parliamentary Recording Unit before transfer to the National Sound Archive. Television cameras have been allowed into the House of Lords since 1985 and into the House of Commons since 1989; committee meetings may also be televised.

By the Parliament Act of 1911, the maximum duration of a parliament is five years (if not previously dissolved), the term being reckoned from the date given on the writs for the new parliament. The maximum life has been prolonged by legislation in such rare circumstances as the two World Wars (31 January 1911 to 25 November 1918; 26 November 1935 to 15 June 1945). Dissolution and writs for a general election are ordered by the sovereign on the advice of the prime minister. The life of a parliament is divided into sessions, usually of one year in length, beginning and ending most often in October or November.

DEVOLUTION

The Scottish parliament has legislative power over all devolved matters, ie matters not reserved to Westminster or otherwise outside its powers. The National Assembly for Wales has power to make secondary legislation in the areas where executive functions have been transferred to it. The Northern Ireland Assembly has legislative authority in the fields previously administered by the Northern Ireland departments. The assembly was suspended in October 2002 and dissolved in April 2003, before being reinstated on 8 May 2007. For further information, *see* the Regional Government section.

THE HOUSE OF LORDS

London SW1A 0PW
T 020-7219 3000 Information Office 020-7219 3107
E hlinfo@parliament.uk **W** www.parliament.uk

The House of Lords is the second chamber, or 'Upper House', of the UK's bicameral parliament. Until the beginning of the twentieth century, the House of Lords had considerable power, being able to veto any bill submitted to it by the House of Commons. Today the main functions of the House of Lords are to revise legislation, to act as a check on the government, to provide a forum of independent expertise and to act as a final court of appeal.

The House of Lords has a number of select committees. Some relate to the internal affairs of the house – such as its management and administration – while others carry out important investigative work on matters of public interest. There are four main areas of work – Europe, science, the economy and the constitution. House of Lords investigative committees look at broader issues and do not mirror government departments as the select committees in the House of Commons do.

The House of Lords has judicial powers as the ultimate court of appeal for courts in Great Britain and Northern Ireland, except for criminal cases in Scotland. These powers are exercised by the Lords of Appeal in Ordinary (the law lords) – (*see* Law Courts and Offices section). On 12 June 2003 the government announced reforms affecting the role of the Lord Chancellor as a judge and Speaker of the House of Lords, and establishing a separate supreme court (*see* Government Departments section). The supreme court is expected to be established in late 2009, when the judicial function of the House of Lords will cease. In 2006 the position of Lord Chancellor was significantly altered by the Constitutional Reform Act 2005. The office holder is no longer speaker of the House of Lords nor head of the judiciary in England and Wales, and is instead a cabinet minister (the Secretary of State for Justice). The function of speaker of the House of Lords was devolved to the newly created post of Lord Speaker. The Rt. Hon. Baroness Hayman was elected as the first Lord Speaker by the house on 4 July 2006.

Members of the House of Lords comprise life peers created under the Life Peerages Act 1958, 92 hereditary peers under the House of Lords Act 1999 and Lords of Appeal in Ordinary, ie law lords, under the Appellate Jurisdiction Act 1876. The Archbishops of Canterbury and York, the Bishops of London, Durham and Winchester, and the 21 senior diocesan bishops of the Church of England are also members.

The House of Lords Act provides for 90 elected hereditary peers to remain in the House of Lords until longer-term reform of the House has been carried out; 42 Conservative, 28 crossbench, three Liberal Democrat and two Labour. Elections for each of the party groups and the crossbenches were held in October and November 1999. Fifteen office holders were elected by the whole house. Two hereditary peers, the Earl Marshal and the Lord Great Chamberlain, are also members.

Peers are disqualified from sitting in the house if they are:

- aliens, ie any peer who is not a British citizen, a Commonwealth citizen (under the British Nationality Act 1981) or a citizen of the Republic of Ireland
- under the age of 21
- undischarged bankrupts or, in Scotland, those whose estate is sequestered
- convicted of treason

Bishops retire at the age of 70 and cease to be members of the house at that time.

Members who do not wish to attend sittings of the House of Lords may apply for leave of absence for the duration of a parliament.

Members of the House of Lords are unpaid but are entitled to allowances for attendance at sittings of the house. The daily maxima, between 1 August 2006 and 31 July 2007, were £159.50 for overnight subsistence, £79.50 for day subsistence and incidental travel, and £69.00 for office costs.

COMPOSITION *as at 2 July 2007*

Archbishops and bishops	26
Life peers under the Appellate Jurisdiction Act 1876	26
Life peers under the Life Peerages Act 1958	603
Peers under the House of Lords Act 1999	92
Total	747

STATE OF THE PARTIES *as at 2 July 2007**

Conservative	204
Labour	211
Liberal Democrat	77
Crossbench	205
Archbishops and bishops	26
Other	12
Total	735

* Excluding 12 peers on leave of absence from the house

HOUSE OF LORDS PAY BANDS

Staff are placed in the following pay bands according to their level of responsibility and taking account of other factors such as experience and marketability.

Judicial group 4	£165,900
Senior band 3	£97,852–£139,974
Senior band 2	£79,433–£129,729
Senior band 1A	£66,771–£108,806
Senior band 1	£57,561–£96,477
Band A1	£53,221–£70,019
Band A2	£44,253–£57,931

OFFICERS AND OFFICIALS

The house is presided over by the Lord Speaker, whose powers differ from those of the Speaker of the House of Commons. The Lord Speaker has no power to maintain order because the House of Lords is self-regulating.

A panel of deputy speakers is appointed by Royal Commission. The first deputy speaker is the chair of committees, appointed at the beginning of each session, who is a salaried officer of the house. He or she takes the chair when the whole house is in committee and in some select committees. He or she is assisted by a panel of deputy chairs, headed by the salaried principal deputy chair of committees, who is also chair of the European Communities Committee of the house.

The Clerk of the Parliaments is the accounting officer and the chief permanent official responsible for the administration of the house. The Gentleman Usher of the Black Rod is responsible for security and other services and also has royal duties as secretary to the Lord Great Chamberlain.

Lord Speaker (£104,386), Rt. Hon. Baroness Hayman
Chair of Committees (£81,504), Lord Brabazon of Tara
Principal Deputy Chair of Committees (£76,250), Lord Grenfell
Clerk of the Parliaments (Judicial Group 4), Sir Paul Hayter, KCB, LVO
Clerk Assistant (Senior Band 3), M. G. Pownall
Reading Clerk and Clerk of the Overseas Office (Senior Band 2), D. R. Beamish, LLM
Clerk of the Committees (Senior Band 2), Dr R. H. Walters, DPHIL
Finance Director (Senior Band 1A), E. C. Ollard
Head of Human Resources (Senior Band 1A), Dr F. P. Tudor
Clerk of the Judicial Office and Registrar of Lords Interests (Senior Band 1A), B. P. Keith
Director of Information Services and Librarian (Senior Band 2), Dr E. Hallam Smith
Clerk of Public and Private Bill Office and Examiner of Petitions for Private Bills in the House of Lords (Senior Band 1A), T. V. Mohan
Editor of the Official Report (Senior Band 1), A. S. Nicholls
Clerk of the Records (Senior Band 1), S. K. Ellison
Deputy Finance Director and Head of Finance (Senior Band 1), A. D. Underwood
Director of Public Information (Band A1), Miss M. L. Morgan
Counsel to the Chairman of Committees (Senior Band 2), A. Roberts
Second Counsel to the Chairman of Committees (Senior Band 2), Dr C. S. Kerse, CB, PHD
Legal Adviser to the Human Rights Committee (Senior Band 2), M. Hunt
Change Manager (Senior Band 1), Mrs M. E. Ollard
Clerk of the Journals (Senior Band 1), A. Makower
Clerk of the European Union Committee (Senior Band 1A), S. P. Burton
Clerk of Pre-Legislative Scrutiny (Senior Band 1), Mrs K. S. Lawrence
Gentleman Usher of the Black Rod and Serjeant-at-Arms (Senior Band 2), Lt.-Gen. Sir Michael Willcocks, KCB
Yeoman Usher of the Black Rod and Deputy Serjeant-at-Arms (Band A2), Brig. H. D. C. Duncan, MBE

LORD GREAT CHAMBERLAIN'S OFFICE

Lord Great Chamberlain, Marquess of Cholmondeley
Secretary to the Lord Great Chamberlain, Lt.-Gen. Sir Michael Willcocks, KCB

SELECT COMMITTEES

The main House of Lords select committees, *as at June 2007*, are as follows:

European Union – Chair, Lord Grenfell; *Clerk,* S. Burton
European Union – Sub-committees:
A (Economic and Financial Affairs and International Trade) – Chair, Baroness Cohen of Pimlico; *Clerk,* Simon Blackburn

B (Internal Market) – *Chair,* Lord Freeman; *Clerk,* Judith Brooke
C (Foreign Affairs, Defence and Development Policy) – *Chair,* Lord Roper; *Clerk,* Kathryn Colvin
D (Agriculture and the Environment) – *Chair,* Lord Sewel; *Clerk,* Robert Preston
E (Law and Institutions) – *Chair,* Lord Brown of Eaton-under-Heywood; *Clerk,* Susanna Street
F (Home Affairs) – *Chair,* Lord Wright of Richmond; *Clerk,* Michael Collon
G (Social and Consumer Affairs) – *Chair,* Baroness Thomas of Walliswood; *Clerk,* Barry Werner
Constitution Committee – *Chair,* Lord Holme of Cheltenham; *Clerk,* Tom Wilson
Delegated Powers and Regulatory Reform – *Chair,* Lord Goodhart; *Clerk,* A. Mackersie
Economic Affairs – *Chair,* Lord Wakeham; *Clerk,* Robert Graham-Harrison
Science and Technology – *Chair,* Lord Broers; *Clerk,* Dr Christopher Johnson
I – *Chair,* Baroness Finlay of Llandaff; *Clerk,* Sarah Jones
II – *Chair,* Lord Broers; *Clerk,* Dr Christopher Johnson
Human Rights Joint Committee – *Chair,* Andrew Dismore, MP; *Lords Clerk,* Bill Sinton
Merits of Statutory Instruments Committee – *Chair,* Lord Filkin; *Clerk,* A. Mackersie

THE HOUSE OF COMMONS

London SW1A 0AA
T 020-7219 3000
Information Office 020-7219 4272
Forthcoming business 020-7219 5532
E hcinfo@parliament.uk W www.parliament.uk

The members of the House of Commons are elected by universal adult suffrage. For electoral purposes, the United Kingdom is divided into constituencies, each of which returns one member to the House of Commons, the member being the candidate who obtains the largest number of votes cast in the constituency. To ensure equitable representation, the four Boundary Commissions keep constituency boundaries under review and recommend any redistribution of seats which may seem necessary because of population movements, etc. The number of seats was raised to 640 in 1945, reduced to 625 in 1948, and subsequently rose to 630 in 1955, 635 in 1970, 650 in 1983, 651 in 1992 and 659 in 1997, before falling to 646 in 2005. Of the present 646 seats, there are 529 for England, 40 for Wales, 59 for Scotland and 18 for Northern Ireland.

ELECTIONS

Elections are by secret ballot, each elector casting one vote; voting is not compulsory. For entitlement to vote in parliamentary elections, *see* Legal Notes section. When a seat becomes vacant between general elections, a by-election is held.

British subjects and citizens of the Irish Republic can stand for election as MPs provided they are 21 or over and not subject to disqualification. Those disqualified from sitting in the house include:

- undischarged bankrupts
- people sentenced to more than one year's imprisonment
- members of the House of Lords (but hereditary peers not sitting in the Lords are eligible)
- holders of certain offices listed in the House of Commons Disqualification Act 1975, eg members of the judiciary, civil service, regular armed forces, police forces, some local government officers and some members of public corporations and government commissions

A candidate does not require any party backing but his or her nomination for election must be supported by the signatures of ten people registered in the constituency. A candidate must also deposit £500 with the returning officer, which is forfeit if the candidate does not receive more than 5 per cent of the votes cast. All election expenses at a general election, except the candidate's personal expenses, are subject to a statutory limit of £7,150, plus five pence for each elector in a borough constituency or seven pence for each elector in a county constituency.

See pages 139–146 for an alphabetical list of MPs, results of the last general election in 2005 and results of by-elections since the general election.

STATE OF THE PARTIES *as at 1 August 2007**

Labour, 352
Conservative, 196
Liberal Democrats, 63
Democratic Unionist Party, 9
Scottish National Party, 6
Sinn Fein (have not taken their seats), 5
Plaid Cymru, 3
Social Democratic Labour Party, 3
Independent, 2
Independent Labour, 1
Respect, 1
Ulster Unionist, 1
The Speaker and three Deputy Speakers, 4
Total, 646

* Working majority of 67; 352 Labour MPs less 285 of all other parties (excluding the speaker, deputy speakers and Sinn Fein)

BUSINESS

The week's business of the house is outlined each Thursday by the leader of the house, after consultation between the chief government whip and the chief opposition whip. A quarter to a third of the time will be taken up by the government's legislative programme and the rest by other business. As a rule, bills likely to raise political controversy are introduced in the Commons before going on to the Lords, and the Commons claims exclusive control in respect of national taxation and expenditure. Bills such as the finance bill, which imposes taxation, and the consolidated fund bills, which authorise expenditure, must begin in the Commons. A bill of which the financial provisions are subsidiary may begin in the Lords; and the Commons may waive its rights in regard to Lords' amendments affecting finance.

The Commons has a public register of MPs' financial and certain other interests; this is published annually as a House of Commons paper. Members must also disclose any relevant financial interest or benefit in a matter before the house when taking part in a debate, in certain other proceedings of the house, or in consultations with other MPs, with ministers or with civil servants.

MEMBERS' PAY AND ALLOWANCES

Since 1911 members of the House of Commons have received salary payments; facilities for free travel were introduced in 1924. Salary rates since 1911 are as follows:

1911	£400	1987 Jan	£18,500
1931	360	1988 Jan	22,548
1934	380	1989 Jan	24,107
1935	400	1990 Jan	26,701
1937	600	1991 Jan	28,970
1946	1,000	1992 Jan	30,854
1954	1,250	1994 Jan	31,687
1957	1,750	1995 Jan	33,189
1964	3,250	1996 Jan	34,085
1972 Jan	4,500	1996 Jul	43,000
1975 Jun	5,750	1997 Apr	43,860
1976 Jun	6,062	1998 Apr	45,066
1977 Jul	6,270	1999 Apr	47,008
1978 Jun	6,897	2000 Apr	48,371
1979 Jun	9,450	2001 Apr	49,822
1980 Jun	11,750	2002 Apr	55,118
1981 Jun	13,950	2003 Apr	56,358
1982 Jun	14,510	2004 Apr	57,485
1983 Jun	15,308	2005 Apr	59,095
1984 Jan	16,106	2006 Apr	59,686
1985 Jan	16,904	2007 Apr	60,675

In 1969 MPs were granted an annual allowance for secretarial and research expenses, revised in July 2001. Members receive an incidental expenses provision (£21,339), a staffing allowance (up to £90,505) and a communications allowance (£10,000).

Since 1972 MPs have been able to claim reimbursement for the additional cost of staying overnight away from their main residence while on parliamentary business; this is known as the additional costs allowance and from April 2007 is £23,083 per year.

Members of staff who are paid out of the allowances can benefit from a sum not exceeding 10 per cent of their gross salary which is paid into the Portcullis Pension Plan. This sum comes from a central budget.

MEMBERS' PENSIONS

Pension arrangements for MPs were first introduced in 1964. Under the Parliamentary Contributory Pension Fund (PCPF), MPs receive a pension on retirement based upon their salary in their final year, and upon their number of years' service as an MP. Members may pay a contribution rate of 10 per cent or 6 per cent and build up a pension of 2.5 per cent or 2 per cent of salary for each year of service. Pensions are normally payable at age 65; upon retirement at 65, the pension payable is subject to a maximum of 66.6 per cent of salary, inclusive of pensions from employment or self-employment prior to becoming an MP. There are provisions in place for: early retirement for those MPs who cease to serve between the ages of 50 and 65; MPs of any age who retire due to ill health; and pensions for widows/widowers of MPs. All pensions are index-linked. There is an Exchequer contribution to ensure that shortfalls are made up; currently 8.7 per cent of an MP's salary for 15 years from 2006/7.

The House of Commons Members' Fund provides for annual or lump sum grants to ex-MPs, their widows or widowers, and children of those who either ceased to serve as an MP prior to the PCPF being established or who are experiencing hardship. Members contribute £24 a year and the Exchequer £215,000 a year to the fund.

HOUSE OF COMMONS PAY BANDS

Staff are placed in the following Senior Civil Service pay bands. These pay bands apply to the most senior staff in departments and agencies.

Pay Band 1	£56,100–£92,000
Pay Band 1A	£65,280–£104,000
Pay Band 2	£81,600–£123,000
Pay Band 3	£99,960–£137,763

OFFICERS AND OFFICIALS

The House of Commons is presided over by the Speaker, who has considerable powers to maintain order. A deputy speaker, called the chairman of ways and means, and two deputy chairs may preside over sittings of the House of Commons; they are elected by the house, and, like the Speaker, neither speak nor vote other than in their official capacity.

The staff of the house are employed by a commission chaired by the Speaker. The heads of the six House of Commons departments are permanent officers of the house, not MPs. The Clerk of the House is the principal adviser to the Speaker on the privileges and procedures of the house, the conduct of the business of the house, and committees. The Serjeant-at-Arms is responsible for security, ceremonial, and for accommodation in the Commons part of the Palace of Westminster.

Speaker (£137,579), Rt. Hon. Michael J. Martin, MP (Glasgow Springburn)
Chairman of Ways and Means (£100,567), Sir Alan Haselhurst, MP (Saffron Walden)
First Deputy Chairman of Ways and Means (£95,736), Sylvia Heal, MP (Halesowen and Rowley Regis)
Second Deputy Chairman of Ways and Means (£95,736), Sir Michael Lord, MP (Suffolk Central and Ipswich North)

OFFICES OF THE SPEAKER AND CHAIRMAN OF WAYS AND MEANS

Speaker's Secretary (£65,280–£104,000), A. Sinclair
Chaplain to the Speaker, Revd Canon R. Wright
Secretary to the Chairman of Ways and Means (£40,723–£55,539), J. Whatley

DEPARTMENT OF THE CLERK OF THE HOUSE

Clerk of the House of Commons (£165,900), Dr M. R. Jack
Clerk Assistant (£99,960–£137,763), D. G. Millar
Clerk of Committees (£99,960–£137,763), Ms H. E. Irwin
Clerk of Legislation (£99,960–£137,763), R. J. Rogers
Principal Clerks (£81,600–£123,000)
Table Office, D. L. Natzler
Journals, Ms J. Sharpe
Principal Clerk and Deputy Head of Committee Office, R. W. G. Wilson
Principal Clerks (£65,280–£104,000)
Overseas Office, L. C. Laurence Smyth
Bills, D. W. N. Doig
Clerk of Domestic Committees/Secretary to the Commission, A. R. Kennon
Select Committees, P. A. Evans; D. J. Gerhild
Delegated Legislation, S. J. Patrick
Deputy Principal Clerks (£56,100–£92,000), J. S. Benger, DPHIL; Mrs S. A. R. Davies; A. H. Doherty; Mrs E. J. Flood; K. C. Fox; Miss L. M. Gardner; M. D. Hamlyn; D. F. Harrison; T. W. P. Healey; Ms P. A. Helme; M. Hennessy; B. M. Hutton; Dr R. G. James; C. G. Lee; D. R. Lloyd; S. Mark; Mrs J. N. St J. Mulley; Mrs C. Oxborough; R. I. S. Phillips; S. J. Priestly; F. J. Reid; D. W. Rhys; Ms E. C. Samson; A. Sandall; C. A. Shaw; C. D. Stanton; N. P. Walker; Dr C. R. M. Ward; H. A. Yardley
Senior Clerks (£40,723–£55,539), M. P. Atkins; T. Byrne;

M. Clark; G. K. Clarke; Ms E. Commander; Ms O. Davidson; J. H. Davies; Dr R. Davies; M. Egan; Ms K. Emms; M. Etherton; G. F. J. Farrar; Miss T. S. Garratty; J. Gearson; T. Goldsmith; D. H. Griffiths; Ms S. Griffiths; P. Harborne; M. Hedges; M. Hillyard; Miss S. F. Ioannou; Ms S. Jones; Ms C. A. Littleboy; Ms J. E. McCullogh; G. McKee; Miss F. McLean; Sir Edward Osmotherly; Ms A. Toft; Ms E. Webbon; Ms N. Welfoot; J. D. Whatley; N. P. Wright

Examiners of Petitions for Private Bills, D. W. N. Doig; T. Mohan

Registrar of Members' Interests (£56,100–£92,000), Ms A. Barry

Taxing Officer, D. W. N. Doig

VOTE OFFICE

Deliverer of the Vote (£56,100–£92,000), J. F. Collins

Deputy Deliverers of the Vote (£40,723–£55,539), O. B. T. Sweeney *(Parliamentary)*; R. Brook *(Development)*; Ms J. Pitt *(Production)*; A. Powell *(Systems)*

LEGAL SERVICES OFFICE

Speaker's Counsel and Head of Legal Services Office (£81,600–£123,000), J. E. G. Vaux

Counsel for European Legislation (£65,280–£104,000), M. Carpenter

Counsel for Legislation, (£65,280–£104,000), Peter Davis

Deputy Counsel (£56,100–£92,000), A. Akbar; P. Brooksbank; Ms V. Rose

Assistant Counsel (£40,723–£55,539), Ms H. Emes

DEPARTMENT OF THE SERJEANT-AT-ARMS

Serjeant-at-Arms (£81,600–£123,000), vacant

Deputy Serjeant-at-Arms (£65,280–£104,000), R. M. Morton

Assistant Serjeants-at-Arms, (£40,723–£67,340), Ms R. Beech; Mrs J. Pay; J. M. Robertson

DEPARTMENT OF THE LIBRARY

Librarian (£81,600–£123,000), J. Pullinger

Directors (£56,100–£92,000), R. Clements *(Research Services)*; Ms B. McInnes *(Departmental Services)*; S. Wise *(Service Delivery and Development)*; E. Wood *(Information Services)*

Heads of Sections (£40,723–£67,340), C. Barclay; R. Cracknell; T. Edmonds; O. Gay; Mrs C. Gillie; V. Miller; B. Morgan; Dr C. Pond; Ms P. J. Strickland; A Walker *(acting)*

Senior Library Clerks (£40,723–£55,539), G. Allen; J. Anseau; E. Ares; E. Beale; G. Berman; P. Bolton; P. Bowers; Ms B. Brevitt; A. Brown; L. Butcher; Ms D. Clark; G. Danby; C. Fairbairn; M. Gheera; V. Gialias; Ms D. Gore; V. Griffin; Ms H. Holden; A. Horne; J. Hough; S. Hubble; R. Kelly; S. Kennedy; V. Keter; Dr J. Lunn; L. Maer; S. McGinness; K. Parry; M. Peck; E. Potton; Ms J. Roll; A. Seely; C. Taylor; Ms A. Thorp; D. Thurley; P. Ward; D. Webb; C. Weeds; Ms I. White; M. Whittaker; Ms F. Whittle; Ms W. Wilson; R. Winstone; R. Young; T. Youngs

DEPARTMENT OF FINANCE AND ADMINISTRATION

Director of Finance and Administration (£81,600–£123,000), A. J. Walker

Deputy Director of Finance and Administration (£56,100–£92,000), Ms E. Honer

Director of Operations (£65,280–£104,000), T. M. Bird

Director of Human Resource Management (£56,100–£92,000), Mrs H. Bryson

Director of Finance Policy (£56,100–£92,000), C. Ridley

Director of Internal Review Services (£56,100–£92,000), R. Russell

DEPARTMENT OF THE OFFICIAL REPORT

Editor (£65,280–£104,000), Miss L. Sutherland

Deputy Editors (£56,100–£92,000), Ms C. Fogarty; V. A. Widgery

REFRESHMENT DEPARTMENT

Director of Catering Services (£65,280–£104,000), Mrs S. Harrison

Business Development Manager (£49,392–£67,340), Mrs J. Rissen

Catering Operations Manager (Outbuildings) (£40,723–£55,539), Ms D. Herd

Food and Beverage Operations Manager, Palace of Westminster (£40,723–£55,539), R. Gibbs

Executive Chef (£40,723–£55,539), M. Hill

Retail Manager (£40,723–£55,539), Mrs M. DeSouza

Human Resources and Development Manager (£40,723–£55,539), J. van den Broek

PARLIAMENTARY INFORMATION AND COMMUNICATION TECHNOLOGY (ICT)

Director of Parliamentary ICT (£65,280–£104,000), Ms J. Miller

Director of Business Information Systems Directorate (£56,100–£92,000), I. Montgomery *(acting)*

Director of Operations (£56,100–£92,000), M. Taylor

Director of Resources (£56,100–£92,000), R. Ware

Director of Programmes and Project Development (£56,100–£92,000), Ms N. Woods *(acting)*

NATIONAL AUDIT OFFICE

157–197 Buckingham Palace Road, London SW1W 9SP
T 020-7798 7000 **F** 020-7798 7070
E enquiries@nao.gsi.gov.uk **W** www.nao.org.uk

The National Audit Office came into existence under the National Audit Act 1983 to replace and continue the work of the former Exchequer and Audit Department. The act reinforced the office's total financial and operational independence from the government and brought its head, the Comptroller and Auditor-General, into a closer relationship with parliament as an officer of the House of Commons.

The National Audit Office provides independent information, advice and assurance to parliament and the public about all aspects of the financial operations of government departments and many other bodies receiving public funds. It does this by examining and certifying the accounts of these organisations. It also regularly publishes reports to parliament on the results of its value for money investigations of the economy, namely the efficiency and effectiveness with which public resources have been used. The National Audit Office is also the auditor by agreement of the accounts of certain international and other organisations. In addition, the office authorises the issue of public funds to government departments.

Comptroller and Auditor-General, Sir John Bourn, KCB

Private Secretary, Dean Parker

Deputy Comptroller and Auditor-General, Tim Burr

Assistant Auditors-General, Gabrielle Cohen; Wendy Kenway-Smith; Caroline Mawhood; Jim Rickleton; Anna Simons; Martin Sinclair; Michael Whitehouse

SELECT COMMITTEES

The more significant committees, as at June 2007, are:

DEPARTMENTAL COMMITTEES

Communities and Local Government – Chair, Dr Phyllis Starkey, MP; *Clerk,* Jessica Mulley
Constitutional Affairs – Chair,* Rt. Hon. Alan Beith, MP; *Clerk,* Roger Phillips
Culture, Media and Sport – Chair, John Whittingdale, MP; *Clerk,* Kenneth Fox
Defence – Chair, Rt. Hon. James Arbuthnot, MP; *Clerk,* Philippa Helme
Education and Skills – Chair,* Barry Sheerman, MP; *Clerk,* David Lloyd
Environment, Food and Rural Affairs – Chair, Rt. Hon. Michael Jack, MP; *Clerk,* Chris Stanton
Foreign Affairs – Chair, Mike Gapes, MP; *Clerk,* Steve Priestley
Health – Chair, Rt. Hon. Kevin Barron, MP; *Clerk,* Dr David Harrison
Home Affairs – Chair, Rt. Hon. John Denham, MP; *Clerk,* Dr Robin James
International Development – Chair, Malcolm Bruce, MP; *Clerk,* Carol Oxborough
Northern Ireland Affairs – Chair, Sir Patrick Cormack, MP; *Clerk,* James Rhys
Scottish Affairs – Chair, Mohammad Sarwar, MP; *Clerk,* Mike Clark
Standards and Privileges – Chair, Rt. Hon. Sir George Young, Bt., MP; *Clerk,* Dr Christopher Ward
Trade and Industry – Chair,* Peter Luff, MP; *Clerk,* Elizabeth Flood
Transport – Chair, Gwyneth Dunwoody, MP; *Clerks,* Tom Healey; Annette Toft
Treasury – Chair, Rt. Hon. John McFall, MP; *Clerk,* Colin Lee
Welsh Affairs – Chair, Dr Hywel Francis, MP; *Clerk,* Nick Wright
Work and Pensions – Chair, Terry Rooney, MP; *Clerk,* Sarah Davies

* From the beginning of the parliamentary session on 6 November 2007, these committees were due to be disbanded with four new committees being formed in their place (Business, Enterprise and Regulatory Reform; Children, Schools and Families; Innovation, Universities and Skills; and Justice)

NON-DEPARTMENTAL COMMITTEES

Environmental Audit – Chair, Tim Yeo, MP; *Clerk,* Mike Hennessy
European Scrutiny – Chair, Michael Connarty, MP; *Clerk,* Alistair Doherty
Finance and Services – Chair, Sir Stuart Bell, MP; *Clerk,* Andrew Kennon
Human Rights (Joint Committee) – Chair, Andrew Dismore, MP; *Clerks,* Dr Mark Egan; Bill Sinton
Intelligence and Security (Cabinet Office) – Chair, Rt. Hon. Paul Murphy, MP; *Clerk,* Emma-Louise Avery
Modernisation of the House of Commons – Chair, Rt. Hon. Jack Straw, MP; *Clerk,* Helen Irwin
Procedure – Chair, Rt. Hon. Greg Knight, MP; *Clerk,* Mark Hutton
Public Accounts – Chair, Edward Leigh, MP; *Clerk,* Mark Etherton
Public Administration – Chair, Dr Tony Wright, MP; *Clerk,* Eve Samson
Regulatory Reform – Chair, Andrew Miller, MP; *Clerk,* Mick Hillyard
Science and Technology – Chair,* Phil Willis, MP; *Clerk,* Dr Lynn Gardner
Statutory Instruments (Joint Committee) – Chair, Rt. Hon. David Maclean, MP; *Clerk,* Mick Hillyard

DOMESTIC COMMITTEE

Administration – Chair, Frank Doran, MP; *Clerk,* Steven Mark

PARLIAMENTARY INFORMATION

The following is a short glossary of aspects of the work of parliament. Unless otherwise stated, references are to House of Commons procedures.

BILL – Proposed legislation is termed a bill. The stages of a public bill (for private bills, *see* below) in the House of Commons are as follows:
First Reading: This stage merely constitutes an order to have the bill printed.
Second Reading: The debate on the principles of the bill.
Committee Stage: The detailed examination of a bill, clause by clause. In most cases this takes place in a public bill committee, or the whole house may act as a committee. Public bill committees may take evidence before embarking on detailed scrutiny of the bill. Very rarely, a bill may be examined by a select committee.
Report Stage: Detailed review of a bill as amended in committee, on the floor of the house.
Third Reading: Final debate on a bill. Public bills go through the same stages in the House of Lords, but with important differences: the committee stage is taken in committee of the whole house or in a grand committee, in which any peer may participate. There are no time limits, and no selection of amendments can be made at third reading.

A bill may start in either house, and has to pass through both houses to become law. Both houses have to agree the final text of a bill, so that amendments made by the second house are then considered in the originating house, and if not agreed, sent back or themselves amended, until agreement is reached.

CHILTERN HUNDREDS – A nominal office of profit under the crown, the acceptance of which requires an MP to vacate his/her seat. The Manor of Northstead is similar. These are the only means by which an MP may resign.

CONSOLIDATED FUND BILL – A bill to authorise issue of money to maintain government services. The bill is dealt with without debate.

EARLY DAY MOTION – A motion put on the notice paper by an MP without, in general, the real prospect of its being debated. Such motions are expressions of back-bench opinion.

FATHER OF THE HOUSE – The MP whose continuous service in the House of Commons is the longest. The present Father of the House is the Rt. Hon. Alan Williams, MP.

HOURS OF MEETING – The House of Commons normally meets on Mondays and Tuesdays at 2.30pm, Wednesdays at 11.30am, Thursdays at 10.30am and some Fridays at 9.30am. (*See also* Westminster Hall Sittings, below.) The House of Lords normally meets at 2.30pm Mondays and Tuesdays, 3pm on Wednesdays and at 11am on Thursdays. The House of Lords often sits on Fridays at 11am.

LEADER OF THE OPPOSITION – In 1937 the office of leader of the opposition was recognised and a salary was assigned to the post. Since April 2007 this has been £131,172 (including a parliamentary salary of £60,675).

The present leader of the opposition is the Rt. Hon. David Cameron, MP.

THE LORD CHANCELLOR – The office of Lord High Chancellor of Great Britain was significantly altered by the Constitutional Reform Act 2005. Previously, the Lord Chancellor was (*ex officio*) the Speaker of the House of Lords, and took part in debates and voted in divisions in the House of Lords. The Department for Constitutional Affairs was created in 2003, which became the Ministry of Justice in 2007, incorporating most of the responsibilities of the Lord Chancellor's department. The role of Speaker has been transferred to the newly created post of Lord Speaker. The Constitutional Reform Act 2005 also brought to an end the Lord Chancellor's role as head of the judiciary. A new Judicial Appointments Commission was created in April 2006, and a new supreme court (separate from the House of Lords) is being established (scheduled to open in 2009).

THE LORD SPEAKER – The first Lord Speaker of the House of Lords, the Rt. Hon. Baroness Hayman, took up office on 4 July 2006. Unlike in the case of the Lord Chancellor, the Lord Speaker is independent of the government and elected by members of the House of Lords rather than appointed by the prime minister. Although the Lord Speaker's primary role is to preside over proceedings in the House of Lords, she does not have the same powers as the speaker of the House of Commons. For example, the Lord Speaker is not responsible for maintaining order during debates, as this is the responsibility of the house as a whole. The Lord Speaker sits in the Lords on one of the woolsacks, which are couches covered in red cloth and stuffed with wool.

THE LORD GREAT CHAMBERLAIN – The Lord Great Chamberlain is a Great Officer of State, the office being hereditary since the grant of Henry I to the family of De Vere, Earls of Oxford. It is now a joint hereditary office rotating on the death of the sovereign between the Cholmondeley, Carington and Ancaster families.

The Lord Great Chamberlain, currently the Marquess of Cholmondeley, is responsible for the royal apartments in the Palace of Westminster, the Royal Gallery, the administration of the Chapel of St Mary Undercroft and, in conjunction with the Lord Speaker and the Speaker of the House of Commons, Westminster Hall. The Lord Great Chamberlain has the right to perform specific services at a coronation, he carries out ceremonial duties in the Palace of Westminster when the sovereign visits the palace and has particular responsibility for the internal administrative arrangements within the House of Lords for state openings of parliament.

NORTHERN IRELAND GRAND COMMITTEE – The Northern Ireland Grand Committee consists of all MPs representing constituencies in Northern Ireland, together with not more than 25 other MPs nominated by the committee of selection. The business of the committee includes questions, short debates, ministerial statements, bills, legislative proposals and other matters relating exclusively to Northern Ireland, and delegated legislation.

The Northern Ireland Affairs Committee is one of the departmental select committees, empowered to examine the expenditure, administration and policy of the Northern Ireland Office and the administration and expenditure of the Crown Solicitor's Office.

OPPOSITION DAY – A day on which the topic for debate is chosen by the opposition. There are 20 such days in a normal session. On 17 days, subjects are chosen by the leader of the opposition; on the remaining three days by the leader of the next largest opposition party.

PARLIAMENT ACTS 1911 AND 1949 – Under these acts, bills may become law without the consent of the Lords, though the House of Lords has the power to delay a public bill for a parliamentary session.

PRIME MINISTER'S QUESTIONS – The prime minister answers questions from 12.00 to 12.30pm on Wednesdays.

PRIVATE BILL – A bill promoted by a body or an individual to give powers additional to, or in conflict with, the general law, and to which a special procedure applies to enable people affected to object.

PRIVATE MEMBER'S BILL – A public bill promoted by an MP or peer who is not a member of the government.

PRIVATE NOTICE QUESTION – A question adjudged of urgent importance on submission to the Speaker (in the Lords, the Lord Speaker), answered at the end of oral questions.

PRIVILEGE – The House of Commons has rights and immunities to protect it from obstruction in carrying out its duties. These are known as parliamentary privilege and enable Members of Parliament to debate freely. The most important privilege is that of freedom of speech. MPs cannot be prosecuted for sedition or sued for libel or slander over anything said during proceedings in the house. This enables them to raise in the house questions affecting the public good which might be difficult to raise outside owing to the possibility of being sued. The House of Lords has similar privileges.

QUESTION TIME – Oral questions are answered by ministers in the Commons from 2.30 to 3.30pm on Mondays and Tuesdays, 11.30am to 12.30pm on Wednesdays, and 10.30 to 11.30am on Thursdays. Questions are also taken at the start of the Lords sittings, with a daily limit of four oral questions.

ROYAL ASSENT – The royal assent is signified by letters patent to such bills and measures as have passed both Houses of Parliament (or bills which have been passed under the Parliament Acts 1911 and 1949). The sovereign has not given royal assent in person since 1854. On occasion, for instance in the prorogation of parliament, royal assent may be pronounced to the two houses by Lords Commissioners. More usually royal assent is notified to each house sitting separately in accordance with the Royal Assent Act 1967. The old French formulae for royal assent are then endorsed on the acts by the Clerk of the Parliaments.

The power to withhold assent resides with the sovereign but has not been exercised in the UK since 1707.

SELECT COMMITTEES – Consisting usually of 10 to 15 members of all parties, select committees are a means used by both houses in order to investigate certain matters.

Most select committees in the House of Commons are tied to departments: each committee investigates subjects within a government department's remit. There are other select committees dealing with matters such as public accounts (ie the spending by the government of money voted by parliament) and European legislation, and also committees advising on procedures and domestic administration of the house. Major select committees usually take evidence in public; their evidence and reports are published on the parliament website and in hard copy by TSO (The Stationery Office). House of Commons select committees are reconstituted after a general election.

In the House of Lords, select committees do not mirror

government departments but cover broader issues. There is a select committee on the European Union (EU), which has seven sub-committees dealing with specific areas of EU policy, a select committee on science and technology, which appoints sub-committees to deal with specific subjects, a select committee on economic affairs and also one on the constitution. There is also a select committee on delegated powers and regulatory reform and one on the merits of statutory instruments. In addition, *ad hoc* select committees have been set up from time to time to investigate specific subjects. There are also joint committees of the two houses, eg the committees on statutory instruments and on human rights.

THE SPEAKER – The Speaker of the House of Commons is the spokesperson and chair of the Chamber. He or she is elected by the house at the beginning of each parliament or when the previous Speaker retires or dies. The Speaker neither speaks in debates nor votes in divisions except when the voting is equal.

VACANT SEATS – When a vacancy occurs in the House of Commons during a session of parliament, the writ for the by-election is moved by a whip of the party to which the member whose seat has been vacated belonged. If the house is in recess, the Speaker can issue a warrant for a writ, should two members certify to him that a seat is vacant.

WELSH AFFAIRS COMMITTEE — The Welsh Affairs Committee is one of the Commons departmental select committees, empowered to examine matters within the responsibility of the Secretary of State for Wales (including relations with the National Assembly for Wales).

WESTMINSTER HALL SITTINGS – Following a report by the Modernisation of the House of Commons Select Committee, the Commons decided in May 1999 to set up a second debating forum. It is known as 'Westminster Hall' and sittings are in the Grand Committee Room on Tuesdays from 9.30am to 2pm, Wednesdays from 9.30 to 11.30am and from 2.30 to 5pm, and Thursdays from 2.30 to 5.30pm. Sittings will be open to the public at the times indicated.

WHIPS – In order to secure the attendance of members of a particular party in parliament, particularly on the occasion of an important vote, whips (originally known as 'whippers-in') are appointed. The written appeal or circular letter issued by them is also known as a 'whip', its urgency being denoted by the number of times it is underlined. Failure to respond to a three-line whip is tantamount in the Commons to secession (at any rate temporarily) from the party. Whips are provided with office accommodation in both houses, and government and some opposition whips receive salaries from public funds.

HOUSE OF COMMONS INFORMATION OFFICE
Norman Shaw Building (North), London SW1A 2TT
T 020-7219 4272 E hcinfo@parliament.uk
W www.parliament.uk

PARLIAMENTARY ARCHIVES
Houses of Parliament, London SW1A 0PW
T 020-7219 3074 F 020-7219 2570
E archives@parliament.uk W www.parliament.uk/archives

Since 1497, the records of parliament have been kept within the Palace of Westminster. They are in the custody of the Clerk of the Parliaments. In 1946 the House of Lords Record Office, which became the Parliamentary Archives in 2006, was established to supervise their preservation and their availability to the public. Some three million documents are preserved, including acts of parliament from 1497, journals of the House of Lords from 1510, minutes and committee proceedings from 1610, and papers laid before parliament from 1531. Amongst the records are the Petition of Right, the death warrant of Charles I, the Declaration of Breda, and the Bill of Rights. Records are available through a public search room.
Clerk of the Records, S. K. Ellison

GOVERNMENT OFFICE

The government is the body of ministers responsible for the administration of national affairs, determining policy and introducing into parliament any legislation necessary to give effect to government policy. The majority of ministers are members of the House of Commons but members of the House of Lords, or of neither house, may also hold ministerial responsibility. The Lord Chancellor is always a member of the House of Lords. The prime minister is, by current convention, always a member of the House of Commons.

THE PRIME MINISTER

The office of prime minister, which had been in existence for nearly 200 years, was officially recognised in 1905 and its holder was granted a place in the table of precedence. The prime minister, by tradition also First Lord of the Treasury and Minister for the Civil Service, is appointed by the sovereign and is usually the leader of the party which enjoys, or can secure, a majority in the House of Commons. Other ministers are appointed by the sovereign on the recommendation of the prime minister, who also allocates functions amongst ministers and has the power to obtain their resignation or dismissal individually.

The prime minister informs the sovereign of state on political matters, advises on the dissolution of parliament, and makes recommendations for important crown appointments, ie the award of honours, etc.

As the chair of cabinet meetings and leader of a political party, the prime minister is responsible for translating party policy into government activity. As leader of the government, the prime minister is responsible to parliament and to the electorate for the policies and their implementation.

The prime minister also represents the nation in international affairs, eg summit conferences.

THE CABINET

The cabinet developed during the 18th century as an inner committee of the Privy Council, which was the chief source of executive power until that time. The cabinet is composed of about 20 ministers chosen by the prime minister, usually the heads of government departments (generally known as secretaries of state unless they have a special title, eg Chancellor of the Exchequer), the leaders of the two houses of parliament, and the holders of various traditional offices.

The cabinet's functions are the final determination of policy, control of government and coordination of government departments. The exercise of its functions is dependent upon enjoying majority support in the House of Commons. Cabinet meetings are held in private, taking place once or twice a week during parliamentary sittings and less often during a recess. Proceedings are confidential, the members being bound by their oath as privy counsellors not to disclose information about the proceedings.

The convention of collective responsibility means that the cabinet acts unanimously even when cabinet ministers do not all agree on a subject. The policies of departmental ministers must be consistent with the policies of the government as a whole, and once the government's policy has been decided, each minister is expected to support it or resign.

The convention of ministerial responsibility holds a minister, as the political head of his or her department, accountable to parliament for the department's work. Departmental ministers usually decide all matters within their responsibility, although on matters of political importance they normally consult their colleagues collectively. A decision by a departmental minister is binding on the government as a whole.

POLITICAL PARTIES

Before the reign of William and Mary the principal officers of state were chosen by and were responsible to the sovereign alone, and not to parliament or the nation at large. Such officers acted sometimes in concert with one another but more often independently, and the fall of one did not, of necessity, involve that of others, although all were liable to be dismissed at any moment.

In 1693 the Earl of Sunderland recommended to William III the advisability of selecting a ministry from the political party which enjoyed a majority in the House of Commons, and the first united ministry was drawn in 1696 from the Whigs, to which party the king owed his throne. This group became known as the 'Junto' and was regarded with suspicion as a novelty in the political life of the nation, being a small section meeting in secret apart from the main body of ministers. It may be regarded as the forerunner of the cabinet and in the course of time it led to the establishment of the principle of joint responsibility of ministers, so that internal disagreement caused a change of personnel or resignation of the whole body of ministers.

The accession of George I, who was unfamiliar with the English language, led to a disinclination on the part of the sovereign to preside at meetings of his ministers and caused the emergence of a prime minister, a position first acquired by Robert Walpole in 1721 and retained by him without interruption for 20 years and 326 days.

DEVELOPMENT OF PARTIES

In 1828 the Whigs became known as Liberals, a name originally given by opponents to imply laxity of principles, but gradually accepted by the party to indicate its claim to be pioneers and champions of political reform and progressive legislation. In 1861 a Liberal Registration Association was founded and Liberal Associations became widespread. In 1877 a National Liberal Federation was formed, with its headquarters in London. The Liberal Party was in power for long periods during the second half of the 19th century and for several years during the first quarter of the 20th century, but after a split in the party in 1931, the numbers elected remained small. In 1988, a majority of the Liberals agreed on a merger with the Social Democratic Party under the title Social and Liberal Democrats; since 1989 they have been known as the Liberal Democrats. A minority continue separately as the Liberal Party.

Soon after the change from Whig to Liberal, the Tory Party became known as Conservative, a name believed to have been invented by John Wilson Croker in 1830 and to have been generally adopted around the time of the passing of the Reform Act of 1832 – to indicate that the preservation of national institutions was the leading principle of the party. After the Home Rule crisis of 1886 the dissentient Liberals entered into a compact with the Conservatives, under which the latter undertook not to contest their seats, but a separate Liberal Unionist organisation was maintained until 1912, when it was united with the Conservatives.

Labour candidates for parliament made their first appearance at the general election of 1892, when there were 27 standing as Labour or Liberal-Labour. In 1900 the Labour Representation Committee (LRC) was set up in order to establish a distinct Labour group in parliament, with its own whips, its own policy, and a readiness to cooperate with any party which might be engaged in promoting legislation in the direct interests of labour. In 1906 the LRC became known as the Labour Party.

The Council for Social Democracy was announced by four former Labour cabinet ministers in January 1981 and in March 1981 the Social Democratic Party (SDP) was launched. Later that year the SDP and the Liberal Party formed an electoral alliance. In 1988 a majority of the SDP agreed on a merger with the Liberal Party but a minority continued as a separate party under the SDP title. In 1990 it was decided to wind up the party organisation and its three sitting MPs were known as independent social democrats. None were returned at the 1992 general election.

Plaid Cymru was founded in 1926 to provide an independent political voice for Wales and to campaign for self-government in Wales.

The Scottish National Party was founded in 1934 to campaign for independence for Scotland.

The Social Democratic and Labour Party was founded in 1970, emerging from the civil rights movement of the 1960s, with the aim of promoting reform, reconciliation and partnership across the sectarian divide in Northern Ireland, and of opposing violence from any quarter.

The Democratic Unionist Party was founded in 1971 to resist moves by the Ulster Unionist Party which were considered a threat to the Union. Its aim is to maintain Northern Ireland as an integral part of the UK.

The Ulster Unionist Council first met formally in 1905. Its objectives are to maintain Northern Ireland as an integral part of the UK and to promote the aims of the Ulster Unionist Party.

Sinn Fein first emerged in the 1900s as a federation of nationalist clubs. It is a left-wing republican and labour party that seeks to end British governance in Ireland and achieve a 32-county republic.

GOVERNMENT AND OPPOSITION

The government of the day is formed by the party which wins the largest number of seats in the House of Commons at a general election, or which has the support of a majority of members in the House of Commons. By tradition, the leader of the majority party is asked by the sovereign to form a government, while the largest minority party becomes the official opposition with its own leader and a shadow cabinet. Leaders of the government and opposition sit on the front benches of the Commons with their supporters (the back-benchers) sitting behind them.

'INANCIAL SUPPORT

'inancial support for opposition parties in the House of Commons was introduced in 1975 and is commonly known as Short Money, after Edward Short, the leader of he house at that time, who introduced the scheme. Short Aoney allocation for 2007–8 is:

Conservative	£3,816,074
Liberal Democrats	£1,626,225
Plaid Cymru	£63,378
SNP	£135,103
SDLP	£56,817
Democratic Unionists	£152,448

specific allocation for the leader of the opposition's ffice was introduced in April 1999 and has been set at 622,223 for the years 2007–8.

Financial support for opposition parties in the House of ords was introduced in 1996 and is commonly known as ranborne Money.

'he parties included here are those with MPs sitting in he House of Commons in the present parliament.

ONSERVATIVE PARTY

onservative Campaign Headquarters, 30 Millbank, London W1P 4DP
020-7222 9000 **F** 020-7222 1135
ccoffice@conservatives.com
V www.conservatives.com

HADOW CABINET *as at July 2007*

eader of the Opposition, Rt. Hon. David Cameron, MP
enior Member and Secretary of State for Foreign Affairs, Rt. Hon. William Hague, MP
hancellor of the Exchequer and General Election Campaign Coordinator, George Osborne, MP
ecretary of State for Home Affairs, Rt. Hon. David Davis, MP
arty Chair, Caroline Spelman, MP
hair of Policy Review and of Conservative Research Department, Rt. Hon. Oliver Letwin, MP
Ainister for the Cabinet Office, Chancellor of the Duchy of Lancaster, Rt. Hon. Francis Maude, MP
ecretary of State for Business, Enterprise and Regulatory Reform, Alan Duncan, MP
ecretary of State for Children, School and Families, Michael Gove, MP
ecretary of State for Communities and Local Government, Eric Pickles, MP
Ainister for Community Cohesion, Sayeeda Warsi, MP
ecretary of State for Culture, Media and Sport, Jeremy Hunt, MP
ecretary of State for Defence, Dr Liam Fox, MP
ecretary of State for Environment, Food and Rural Affairs, Peter Ainsworth, MP
ecretary of State for Health, Andrew Lansley, CBE, MP
ecretary of State for Innovation, Universities and Skills, David Willetts, MP
ecretary of State for International Development, Andrew Mitchell, MP
ecretary of State for Justice, Nick Herbert, MP
eader in the House of Commons, Rt. Hon. Theresa May, MP
eader in the House of Lords, Rt. Hon. Lord Strathclyde
ecretary of State for Northern Ireland, Owen Paterson, MP
ecretary of State for Scotland, David Mundell, MP
Ainister for Security and National Security Adviser to the Leader of the Opposition, Dame Pauline Neville-Jones, DCMG
Secretary of State for Transport, Theresa Villiers, MP
Chief Secretary to the Treasury, Philip Hammond, MP
Secretary of State for Wales, Cheryl Gillan, MP
Secretary of State for Work and Pensions, Chris Grayling, MP

CONSERVATIVE WHIPS

House of Lords, Baroness Anelay of St Johns, DBE
House of Commons, Rt. Hon. Patrick McLoughlin, MP

LABOUR PARTY

Eldon House, Regent Centre, Newcastle upon Tyne NE3 3PW
T 0870-590 0200 **W** www.labour.org.uk
Parliamentary Party Leader, Rt. Hon. Gordon Brown, MP
Deputy Party Leader, Leader in the Commons and Party Chair, Rt. Hon. Harriet Harman, QC, MP
Leader in the Lords, Rt. Hon. Baroness Ashton of Upholland
General Secretary, Peter Watt
General Secretary, Scottish Labour Party, Lesley Quinn

LIBERAL DEMOCRATS

4 Cowley Street, London SW1P 3NB
T 020-7222 7999 **F** 020-7799 2170
E info@libdems.org.uk **W** www.libdems.org.uk
President and Leader in the Commons, Simon Hughes, MP
Hon. Treasurer, Lord Razzall
Chief Executive, Lord Rennard
Parliamentary Party Leader, Rt. Hon. Sir Menzies Campbell, QC, MP
Leader in the Lords, Rt. Hon. Lord McNally

LIBERAL DEMOCRAT SPOKESMEN *as at July 2007*

Deputy Leader and Shadow Chancellor of the Exchequer, Dr Vincent Cable, MP
Attorney-General, Lord Thomas of Gresford
Business, Enterprise and Regulatory Reform, Lembit Opik, MP
Cabinet Office, Norman Baker, MP
Children, Schools and Families, David Laws, MP
Communities and Local Government, Andrew Stunell, MP
Culture, Media and Sport, Don Foster, MP
Defence, Nick Harvey, MP
Environment, Food and Rural Affairs, Chris Huhne, MP
Foreign and Commonwealth Affairs, Michael Moore, MP
Health, Norman Lamb, MP
Home Affairs, Nick Clegg, MP
Housing, Paul Holmes, MP
Innovation, Universities and Skills, Sarah Teather, MP
International Development, Lynne Featherstone, MP
Justice, David Heath, MP
Scotland and Northern Ireland, Alistair Carmichael, MP
Solicitor-General, David Howarth, MP
Transport, Susan Kramer, MP
Treasury, Julia Goldsworthy, MP
Wales, Roger Williams, MP
Work and Pensions, Danny Alexander, MP
Chair of the Manifesto Group, Prof. Steve Webb, MP
Chair of the Parliamentary Party, Paul Holmes, MP
Chief of Staff and Chair of Campaigns and Communications, Ed Davey, MP
Parliamentary Private Secretary to the Leader, Tim Farron, MP

LIBERAL DEMOCRAT WHIPS
House of Lords, Lord Shutt of Greetland
House of Commons, Paul Burstow, MP

NORTHERN IRELAND DEMOCRATIC UNIONIST PARTY
91 Dundela Avenue, Belfast BT4 3BU
T 028-9065 4479 F 028-9065 4480
E info@dup.org.uk W www.dup2win.com
Parliamentary Party Leader, Dr Ian Paisley, MP, MLA
Deputy Leader, Peter Robinson, MP, MLA
Chair, Lord Morrow, MLA
Hon. Treasurer, Gregory Campbell, MP, MLA
Party Secretary, Nigel Dodds, MP, MLA

PLAID CYMRU – THE PARTY OF WALES
Ty Gwynfor, 18 Park Grove, Cardiff CF10 3BN
T 029-2064 6000
E post@plaidcymru.org W www.plaidcymru.org
Party Leader, Ieuan Wyn Jones, AM
Party President, Dafydd Iwan
Party Vice-President, Jill Evans, MEP
Parliamentary Group Leader, Elfyn Llwyd
Chief Executive, Dafydd Trystan

RESPECT – THE UNITY COALITION
9 Club Row, London E1 6JX
T 0870-850 1978
E office@respectcoalition.org W www.respectcoalition.org
Chair, Linda Smith
Vice-Chair, Salma Yaqoob
National Secretary, John Rees
Treasurer, Elaine Graham-Leigh

SCOTTISH NATIONAL PARTY
107 McDonald Road, Edinburgh EH7 4NW
T 0131-525 8900 F 0131-525 8901
E snp.hq@snp.org W www.snp.org
Westminster Parliamentary Party Leader, Alex Salmond, MP
Westminster Parliamentary Party Chief Whip, Pete Wishart, MP
Scottish Parliamentary Party Leader, Alex Salmond, MSP
Scottish Parliamentary Party Chief Whip, Bruce Crawford, MSP
National Treasurer, Colin Beattie
National Secretary, Dr Duncan Ross
Chief Executive, Peter Murrell

SINN FEIN
53 Falls Road, Belfast BT12 4PD
T 028-9022 3000 F 028-9022 3001
E sfadmin@eircom.net W www.sinnfein.ie
Party President, Gerry Adams, MP, MLA
Vice-President, Pat Doherty, MP, MLA
Chair, Mary Lou McDonald, MEP
Chief Negotiator, Martin McGuinness, MP, MLA
General Secretary, Rita O'Hare

SOCIAL DEMOCRATIC AND LABOUR PARTY
121 Ormeau Road, Belfast BT7 1SH
T 028-9024 7700 F 028-9023 6699
E sdlp@indigo.ie W www.sdlp.ie
Parliamentary Party Leader, Mark Durkan, MP, MLA
Deputy Leader, Dr Alasdair McDonnell, MP, MLA
Chief Whip, John Dallat
Chair, Sean Farren, MLA
Treasurer, Peter McEvoy
General Secretary, Gerry Cosgrove

ULSTER UNIONIST PARTY
429 Holywood Road, Belfast BT4 2LN
T 028-9076 5500 F 028-9076 9419
E uup@uup.org W www.uup.org
Party Leader, Sir Reg Empey, OBE, MLA
Chief Whip, David McNarry, MLA

ULSTER UNIONIST COUNCIL
President, John White, OBE
Leader, Sir Reg Empey, OBE, MLA
Chair of the Executive Committee, David Campbell, CBE
Hon. Treasurer, Lord Maginnis of Drumglass
Vice-Chair, Tom Fleming
Party Officers, Johnny Andrews; Joan Carson; Cllr. Mark Cosgrove; Kenny Donaldson; Richard Holmes; Terry Wright
Officers from Elected Representatives, David McNarry, MLA Jim Nicholson, MEP; Cllr. Trevor Wilson

The following parties have sitting MEPs, *see* European Parliament section.

GREEN PARTY
1A Waterlow Road, London N19 5NJ
T 020-7272 4474 F 020-7272 6653
E office@greenparty.org.uk W www.greenparty.org.uk
Chair, Richard Mallender
Principal Speakers, Siân Berry; Dr Derek Wall
Registered Treasurer, Khalid Hussenbux

UK INDEPENDENCE PARTY
Lexdrum House, Unit 1, King Charles Industrial Estate, Bovey Tracey, Devon TQ12 6UT
T 01626-831290 F 01626-831348
E mail@ukip.org W www.ukip.org
Party Leader, Nigel Farage, MEP
Chair, Dr John Whittaker, MEP
Party Secretary, Michael Zuckerman

MEMBERS OF PARLIAMENT as at 1 September 2007

New MP
Previously MP in another seat
Previously MP for another party

bbott, Diane (*b.* 1953) *Lab., Hackney North & Stoke Newington,* Maj. 7,427
dams, Gerry (*b.* 1948) *SF, Belfast West,* Maj. 19,315
Afriyie, Adam (*b.* 1965) *C., Windsor,* Maj. 10,292
inger, Nick (*b.* 1949) *Lab., Carmarthen West & Pembrokeshire South,* Maj. 1,910
insworth, Peter (*b.* 1956) *C., Surrey East,* Maj. 15,921
insworth, Rt. Hon. Robert (*b.* 1952) *Lab., Coventry North East,* Maj. 14,222
Alexander, Danny (*b.* 1972) *LD, Inverness, Nairn, Badenoch & Strathspey,* Maj. 4,148
lexander, Rt. Hon. Douglas (*b.* 1967) *Lab., Paisley & Renfrewshire South,* Maj. 13,232
llen, Graham (*b.* 1953) *Lab., Nottingham North,* Maj. 12,171
mess, David (*b.* 1952) *C., Southend West,* Maj. 8,959
ncram, Rt. Hon. Michael (*b.* 1945) *C., Devizes,* Maj. 13,194
Anderson, David (*b.* 1953) *Lab., Blaydon,* Maj. 5,335
nderson, Janet (*b.* 1949) *Lab., Rossendale & Darwen,* Maj. 3,676
rbuthnot, Rt. Hon. James (*b.* 1952) *C., Hampshire North East,* Maj. 12,549
rmstrong, Rt. Hon. Hilary (*b.* 1945) *Lab., Durham North West,* Maj. 13,443
tkins, Charlotte (*b.* 1950) *Lab., Staffordshire Moorlands,* Maj. 2,438
tkinson, Peter (*b.* 1943) *C., Hexham,* Maj. 5,020
Austin, Ian (*b.* 1965) *Lab., Dudley North,* Maj. 5,432
ustin, John (*b.* 1944) *Lab., Erith & Thamesmead,* Maj. 11,500
acon, Richard (*b.* 1962) *C., Norfolk South,* Maj. 8,782
ailey, Adrian (*b.* 1945) *Lab. (Co-op), West Bromwich West,* Maj. 10,894
aird, Vera (*b.* 1950) *Lab., Redcar,* Maj. 12,116
aker, Norman (*b.* 1957) *LD, Lewes,* Maj. 8,474
aldry, Tony (*b.* 1950) *C., Banbury,* Maj. 10,797
Balls, Ed (*b.* 1967) *Lab. (Co-op), Normanton,* Maj. 10,002
Banks, Gordon (*b.* 1955) *Lab., Ochil & Perthshire South,* Maj. 688
arker, Gregory (*b.* 1966) *C., Bexhill & Battle,* Maj. 13,449
Barlow, Celia (*b.* 1955) *Lab., Hove,* Maj. 420
aron, John (*b.* 1959) *C., Billericay,* Maj. 11,206
arrett, John (*b.* 1954) *LD, Edinburgh West,* Maj. 13,600
arron, Rt. Hon. Kevin (*b.* 1946) *Lab., Rother Valley,* Maj. 14,224
attle, Rt. Hon. John (*b.* 1951) *Lab., Leeds West,* Maj. 12,810
ayley, Hugh (*b.* 1952) *Lab., York, City of,* Maj. 10,472
eckett, Rt. Hon. Margaret (*b.* 1943) *Lab., Derby South,* Maj. 5,657
egg, Anne (*b.* 1955) *Lab., Aberdeen South,* Maj. 1,348
eith, Rt. Hon. Alan (*b.* 1943) *LD, Berwick-upon-Tweed,* Maj. 8,632
ell, Sir Stuart (*b.* 1938) *Lab., Middlesbrough,* Maj. 12,567
ellingham, Henry (*b.* 1955) *C., Norfolk North West,* Maj. 9,180
enn, Rt. Hon. Hilary (*b.* 1953) *Lab., Leeds Central,* Maj. 11,866
enton, Joe (*b.* 1933) *Lab., Bootle,* Maj. 16,357
***Benyon**, Richard (*b.* 1960) *C., Newbury,* Maj. 3,460
Bercow, John (*b.* 1963) *C., Buckingham,* Maj. 18,129
Beresford, Sir Paul (*b.* 1946) *C., Mole Valley,* Maj. 11,997
Berry, Dr Roger (*b.* 1948) *Lab., Kingswood,* Maj. 7,873
Betts, Clive (*b.* 1950) *Lab., Sheffield Attercliffe,* Maj. 15,967
***Binley**, Brian (*b.* 1942) *C., Northampton South,* Maj. 4,419
Blackman, Liz (*b.* 1949) *Lab., Erewash,* Maj. 7,084
***Blackman-Woods**, Dr Roberta (*b.* 1957) *Lab., Durham, City of,* Maj. 3,274
Blears, Rt. Hon. Hazel (*b.* 1956) *Lab., Salford,* Maj. 7,945
Blizzard, Bob (*b.* 1950) *Lab., Waveney,* Maj. 5,915
Blunkett, Rt. Hon. David (*b.* 1947) *Lab., Sheffield Brightside,* Maj. 13,644
Blunt, Crispin (*b.* 1960) *C., Reigate,* Maj. 10,988
***Bone**, Peter (*b.* 1952) *C., Wellingborough,* Maj. 687
Borrow, David (*b.* 1952) *Lab., Ribble South,* Maj. 2,184
Boswell, Tim (*b.* 1942) *C., Daventry,* Maj. 14,686
Bottomley, Peter (*b.* 1944) *C., Worthing West,* Maj. 9,379
Bradshaw, Ben (*b.* 1960) *Lab., Exeter,* Maj. 7,665
Brady, Graham (*b.* 1967) *C., Altrincham & Sale West,* Maj. 7,159
Brake, Tom (*b.* 1962) *LD, Carshalton & Wallington,* Maj. 1,068
Brazier, Julian (*b.* 1953) *C., Canterbury,* Maj. 7,471
Breed, Colin (*b.* 1947) *LD, Cornwall South East,* Maj. 6,507
Brennan, Kevin (*b.* 1959) *Lab., Cardiff West,* Maj. 8,167
***Brokenshire**, James (*b.* 1968) *C., Hornchurch,* Maj. 480
Brooke, Annette (*b.* 1947) *LD, Dorset Mid & Poole North,* Maj. 5,482
Brown, Rt. Hon. Gordon (*b.* 1951) *Lab., Kirkcaldy & Cowdenbeath,* Maj. 18,216
***Brown**, Lyn (*b.* 1960) *Lab., West Ham,* Maj. 9,801
Brown, Rt. Hon. Nick (*b.* 1950) *Lab., Newcastle upon Tyne East & Wallsend,* Maj. 7,565
Brown, Russell (*b.* 1951) *Lab., Dumfries & Galloway,* Maj. 2,922
Browne, Rt. Hon. Desmond (*b.* 1952) *Lab., Kilmarnock & Loudoun,* Maj. 8,703
***Browne**, Jeremy (*b.* 1970) *LD, Taunton,* Maj. 573
Browning, Angela (*b.* 1946) *C., Tiverton & Honiton,* Maj. 11,051
Bruce, Malcolm (*b.* 1944) *LD, Gordon,* Maj. 11,026
Bryant, Chris (*b.* 1962) *Lab., Rhondda,* Maj. 16,242
Buck, Karen (*b.* 1958) *Lab., Regent's Park & Kensington North,* Maj. 6,131
Burden, Richard (*b.* 1954) *Lab., Birmingham Northfield,* Maj. 6,454
Burgon, Colin (*b.* 1948) *Lab., Elmet,* Maj. 4,528
Burnham, Andy (*b.* 1970) *Lab., Leigh,* Maj. 17,272
Burns, Simon (*b.* 1952) *C., Chelmsford West,* Maj. 9,620
***Burrowes**, David (*b.* 1969) *C., Enfield Southgate,* Maj. 1,747
Burstow, Paul (*b.* 1962) *LD, Sutton & Cheam,* Maj. 2,846
Burt, Alistair (*b.* 1955) *C., Bedfordshire North East,* Maj. 12,251
***Burt**, Lorely (*b.* 1957) *LD, Solihull,* Maj. 279
***Butler**, Dawn (*b.* 1969) *Lab., Brent South,* Maj. 11,326
Butterfill, Sir John (*b.* 1941) *C., Bournemouth West,* Maj. 4,031

Byers, Rt. Hon. Stephen (*b.* 1953) *Lab., Tyneside North,* Maj. 15,037
Byrne, Liam (*b.* 1970) *Lab., Birmingham Hodge Hill,* Maj. 5,449
Cable, Dr Vincent (*b.* 1943) *LD, Twickenham,* Maj. 9,965
Caborn, Rt. Hon. Richard (*b.* 1943) *Lab., Sheffield Central,* Maj. 7,055
Cairns, David (*b.* 1966) *Lab., Inverclyde,* Maj. 11,259
Cameron, Rt. Hon. David (*b.* 1966) *C., Witney,* Maj. 14,156
Campbell, Alan (*b.* 1957) *Lab., Tynemouth,* Maj. 4,143
Campbell, Gregory (*b.* 1953) *DUP, Londonderry East,* Maj. 7,727
Campbell, Rt. Hon. Sir Menzies (*b.* 1941) *LD, Fife North East,* Maj. 12,571
Campbell, Ronnie (*b.* 1943) *Lab., Blyth Valley,* Maj. 8,527
Carmichael, Alistair (*b.* 1965) *LD, Orkney & Shetland,* Maj. 6,627
***Carswell**, Douglas (*b.* 1971) *C., Harwich,* Maj. 920
Cash, Bill (*b.* 1940) *C., Stone,* Maj. 9,089
Caton, Martin (*b.* 1951) *Lab., Gower,* Maj. 6,703
Cawsey, Ian (*b.* 1960) *Lab., Brigg & Goole,* Maj. 2,894
Challen, Colin (*b.* 1953) *Lab., Morley & Rothwell,* Maj. 12,343
Chapman, Ben (*b.* 1940) *Lab., Wirral South,* Maj. 3,724
Chaytor, David (*b.* 1949) *Lab., Bury North,* Maj. 2,926
Chope, Christopher (*b.* 1947) *C., Christchurch,* Maj. 15,559
Clapham, Michael (*b.* 1943) *Lab., Barnsley West & Penistone,* Maj. 11,314
Clappison, James (*b.* 1956) *C., Hertsmere,* Maj. 11,093
***Clark**, Greg (*b.* 1967) *C., Tunbridge Wells,* Maj. 9,988
***Clark**, Katy (*b.* 1967) *Lab., Ayrshire North & Arran,* Maj. 11,296
Clark, Paul (*b.* 1957) *Lab., Gillingham,* Maj. 254
Clarke, Rt. Hon. Charles (*b.* 1950) *Lab., Norwich South,* Maj. 3,653
Clarke, Rt. Hon. Kenneth (*b.* 1940) *C., Rushcliffe,* Maj. 12,974
Clarke, Rt. Hon. Thomas (*b.* 1941) *Lab., Coatbridge, Chryston & Bellshill,* Maj. 19,519
***Clegg**, Nick (*b.* 1967) *LD, Sheffield Hallam,* Maj. 8,682
Clelland, David (*b.* 1943) *Lab., Tyne Bridge,* Maj. 10,400
Clifton-Brown, Geoffrey (*b.* 1953) *C., Cotswold,* Maj. 9,688
Clwyd, Rt. Hon. Ann (*b.* 1937) *Lab., Cynon Valley,* Maj. 13,259
Coaker, Vernon (*b.* 1953) *Lab., Gedling,* Maj. 3,811
Coffey, Ann (*b.* 1946) *Lab., Stockport,* Maj. 9,163
Cohen, Harry (*b.* 1949) *Lab., Leyton & Wanstead,* Maj. 6,857
Connarty, Michael (*b.* 1947) *Lab., Linlithgow & Falkirk East,* Maj. 11,202
Conway, Derek (*b.* 1953) *C., Old Bexley & Sidcup,* Maj. 9,920
Cook, Frank (*b.* 1935) *Lab., Stockton North,* Maj. 12,437
***Cooper**, Rosie (*b.* 1950) *Lab., Lancashire West,* Maj. 6,084
Cooper, Yvette (*b.* 1969) *Lab., Pontefract & Castleford,* Maj. 15,246
Corbyn, Jeremy (*b.* 1949) *Lab., Islington North,* Maj. 6,716
Cormack, Sir Patrick (*b.* 1939) *C., Staffordshire South,* Maj. 8,847
Cousins, Jim (*b.* 1944) *Lab., Newcastle upon Tyne Central,* Maj. 3,982
***Cox**, Geoffrey (*b.* 1960) *C., Devon West & Torridge,* Maj. 3,236
***Crabb**, Stephen (*b.* 1973) *C., Preseli Pembrokeshire,* Maj. 607
Crausby, David (*b.* 1946) *Lab., Bolton North East,* Maj. 4,103
***Creagh**, Mary (*b.* 1967) *Lab., Wakefield,* Maj. 5,154
Cruddas, Jonathan (*b.* 1965) *Lab., Dagenham,* Maj. 7,605
Cryer, Ann (*b.* 1939) *Lab., Keighley,* Maj. 4,852
Cummings, John (*b.* 1943) *Lab., Easington,* Maj. 18,636
Cunningham, Jim (*b.* 1941) *Lab., Coventry South,* Maj. 6,255
Cunningham, Tony (*b.* 1952) *Lab., Workington,* Maj. 6,895
Curry, Rt. Hon. David (*b.* 1944) *C., Skipton & Ripon,* Maj. 11,620
Curtis-Thomas, Claire (*b.* 1958) *Lab., Crosby,* Maj. 5,840
Darling, Rt. Hon. Alistair (*b.* 1953) *Lab., Edinburgh South West,* Maj. 7,242
Davey, Edward (*b.* 1965) *LD, Kingston & Surbiton,* Maj. 8,966
David, Wayne (*b.* 1957) *Lab., Caerphilly,* Maj. 15,359
Davidson, Ian (*b.* 1950) *Lab. (Co-op), Glasgow South West,* Maj. 13,896
***Davies**, Dai (*b.* 1959) *Ind., Blaenau Gwent,* Maj. 2,484
***Davies**, David (*b.* 1970) *C., Monmouth,* Maj. 4,527
***Davies**, Philip (*b.* 1972) *C., Shipley,* Maj. 422
‡**Davies**, Quentin (*b.* 1944) *Lab., Grantham & Stamford,* Maj. 7,445
Davis, Rt. Hon. David (*b.* 1948) *C., Haltemprice & Howden,* Maj. 5,116
Dean, Janet (*b.* 1949) *Lab., Burton,* Maj. 1,421
Denham, Rt. Hon. John (*b.* 1953) *Lab., Southampton Itchen,* Maj. 9,302
***Devine**, Jim (*b.* 1953) *Lab., Livingston,* Maj. 2,680
Dhanda, Parmjit (*b.* 1971) *Lab., Gloucester,* Maj. 4,271
Dismore, Andrew (*b.* 1954) *Lab., Hendon,* Maj. 2,699
Djanogly, Jonathan (*b.* 1965) *C., Huntingdon,* Maj. 12,847
Dobbin, Jim (*b.* 1941) *Lab. (Co-op), Heywood & Middleton,* Maj. 11,083
Dobson, Rt. Hon. Frank (*b.* 1940) *Lab., Holborn & St Pancras,* Maj. 4,787
Dodds, Nigel (*b.* 1958) *DUP, Belfast North,* Maj. 5,188
Doherty, Pat (*b.* 1945) *SF, Tyrone West,* Maj. 5,005
‡**Donaldson**, Jeffrey (*b.* 1962) *DUP, Lagan Valley,* Maj. 14,117
Donohoe, Brian (*b.* 1948) *Lab., Ayrshire Central,* Maj. 10,423
Doran, Frank (*b.* 1949) *Lab., Aberdeen North,* Maj. 6,795
Dorrell, Rt. Hon. Stephen (*b.* 1952) *C., Charnwood,* Maj. 8,809
***Dorries**, Nadine (*b.* 1958) *C., Bedfordshire Mid,* Maj. 11,355
Dowd, Jim (*b.* 1951) *Lab., Lewisham West,* Maj. 9,932
Drew, David (*b.* 1952) *Lab. (Co-op), Stroud,* Maj. 350
***Duddridge**, James (*b.* 1971) *C., Rochford & Southend East,* Maj. 5,494
Duncan Smith, Rt. Hon. Iain (*b.* 1954) *C., Chingford & Woodford Green,* Maj. 10,641
Duncan, Alan (*b.* 1957) *C., Rutland & Melton,* Maj. 12,930
***Dunne**, Philip (*b.* 1958) *C., Ludlow,* Maj. 2,027
Dunwoody, Gwyneth (*b.* 1930) *Lab., Crewe & Nantwich,* Maj. 7,078
***Durkan**, Mark (*b.* 1960) *SDLP, Foyle,* Maj. 5,957
Eagle, Angela (*b.* 1961) *Lab., Wallasey,* Maj. 9,109
Eagle, Maria (*b.* 1961) *Lab., Liverpool Garston,* Maj. 7,193

fford, Clive (*b.* 1958) *Lab., Eltham,* Maj. 3,276
llman, Louise (*b.* 1945) *Lab. (Co-op), Liverpool Riverside,* Maj. 10,214
Ellwood, Tobias (*b.* 1966) *C., Bournemouth East,* Maj. 5,244
Engel, Natascha (*b.* 1967) *Lab., Derbyshire North East,* Maj. 10,065
nnis, Jeff (*b.* 1952) *Lab., Barnsley East & Mexborough,* Maj. 14,125
therington, Bill (*b.* 1941) *Lab., Sunderland North,* Maj. 9,995
vans, Nigel (*b.* 1957) *C., Ribble Valley,* Maj. 14,171
Evennett, David (*b.* 1949) *C., Bexleyheath & Crayford,* Maj. 4,551
abricant, Michael (*b.* 1950) *C., Lichfield,* Maj. 7,080
allon, Michael (*b.* 1952) *C., Sevenoaks,* Maj. 12,970
arrelly, Paul (*b.* 1962) *Lab., Newcastle-under-Lyme,* Maj. 8,108
Farron, Tim (*b.* 1970) *LD, Westmorland & Lonsdale,* Maj. 267
Featherstone, Lynne (*b.* 1951) *LD, Hornsey & Wood Green,* Maj. 2,395
ield, Rt. Hon. Frank (*b.* 1942) *Lab., Birkenhead,* Maj. 12,934
ield, Mark (*b.* 1934) *C., Cities of London & Westminster,* Maj. 8,095
isher, Mark (*b.* 1944) *Lab., Stoke-on-Trent Central,* Maj. 9,774
itzpatrick, Jim (*b.* 1952) *Lab., Poplar & Canning Town,* Maj. 7,129
Flello, Robert (*b.* 1966) *Lab., Stoke-on-Trent South,* Maj. 8,681
lint, Caroline (*b.* 1961) *Lab., Don Valley,* Maj. 8,598
lynn, Paul (*b.* 1935) *Lab., Newport West,* Maj. 5,458
ollett, Barbara (*b.* 1942) *Lab., Stevenage,* Maj. 3,139
oster, Don (*b.* 1947) *LD, Bath,* Maj. 4,638
oster, Michael (*b.* 1946) *Lab., Hastings & Rye,* Maj. 2,026
oster, Michael (*b.* 1963) *Lab., Worcester,* Maj. 3,144
ox, Dr Liam (*b.* 1961) *C., Woodspring,* Maj. 6,016
rancis, Dr Hywel (*b.* 1946) *Lab., Aberavon,* Maj. 13,937
rancois, Mark (*b.* 1965) *C., Rayleigh,* Maj. 14,726
Fraser, Christopher (*b.* 1962) *C., Norfolk South West,* Maj. 10,086
ale, Roger (*b.* 1943) *C., Thanet North,* Maj. 7,634
‡**Galloway**, George (*b.* 1954) *Respect, Bethnal Green & Bow,* Maj. 823
apes, Mike (*b.* 1952) *Lab. (Co-op), Ilford South,* Maj. 9,228
ardiner, Barry (*b.* 1957) *Lab., Brent North,* Maj. 5,641
arnier, Edward (*b.* 1952) *C., Harborough,* Maj. 3,892
Gauke, David (*b.* 1971) *C., Hertfordshire South West,* Maj. 8,473
eorge, Andrew (*b.* 1958) *LD, St Ives,* Maj. 11,609
eorge, Rt. Hon. Bruce (*b.* 1942) *Lab., Walsall South,* Maj. 7,946
errard, Neil (*b.* 1942) *Lab., Walthamstow,* Maj. 7,993
ibb, Nick (*b.* 1960) *C., Bognor Regis & Littlehampton,* Maj. 7,822
ibson, Dr Ian (*b.* 1938) *Lab., Norwich North,* Maj. 5,459
idley, Sandra (*b.* 1957) *LD, Romsey,* Maj. 125
ildernew, Michelle (*b.* 1970) *SF, Fermanagh & South Tyrone,* Maj. 4,582
illan, Cheryl (*b.* 1952) *C., Chesham & Amersham,* Maj. 13,798
ilroy, Linda (*b.* 1949) *Lab. (Co-op), Plymouth Sutton,* Maj. 4,109
Godsiff, Roger (*b.* 1946) *Lab., Birmingham Sparkbrook & Small Heath,* Maj. 3,289
Goggins, Paul (*b.* 1953) *Lab., Wythenshawe & Sale East,* Maj. 10,827
***Goldsworthy**, Julia (*b.* 1978) *LD, Falmouth & Camborne,* Maj. 1,886
***Goodman**, Helen (*b.* 1958) *Lab., Bishop Auckland,* Maj. 10,047
Goodman, Paul (*b.* 1960) *C., Wycombe,* Maj. 7,051
***Goodwill**, Robert (*b.* 1956) *C., Scarborough & Whitby,* Maj. 1,245
***Gove**, Michael (*b.* 1967) *C., Surrey Heath,* Maj. 10,845
Gray, James (*b.* 1954) *C., Wiltshire North,* Maj. 5,303
Grayling, Chris (*b.* 1962) *C., Epsom & Ewell,* Maj. 16,447
Green, Damian (*b.* 1956) *C., Ashford,* Maj. 13,298
***Greening**, Justine (*b.* 1969) *C., Putney,* Maj. 1,766
Greenway, John (*b.* 1946) *C., Ryedale,* Maj. 10,469
Grieve, Dominic (*b.* 1956) *C., Beaconsfield,* Maj. 15,253
***Griffith**, Nia (*b.* 1956) *Lab., Llanelli,* Maj. 7,234
Griffiths, Nigel (*b.* 1955) *Lab., Edinburgh South,* Maj. 405
Grogan, John (*b.* 1961) *Lab., Selby,* Maj. 467
Gummer, Rt. Hon. John (*b.* 1939) *C., Suffolk Coastal,* Maj. 9,685
***Gwynne**, Andrew (*b.* 1974) *Lab., Denton & Reddish,* Maj. 13,498
Hague, Rt. Hon. William (*b.* 1961) *C., Richmond (Yorks),* Maj. 17,807
Hain, Rt. Hon. Peter (*b.* 1950) *Lab., Neath,* Maj. 12,710
Hall, Mike (*b.* 1952) *Lab., Weaver Vale,* Maj. 6,855
Hall, Patrick (*b.* 1951) *Lab., Bedford,* Maj. 3,383
Hamilton, David (*b.* 1950) *Lab., Midlothian,* Maj. 7,265
Hamilton, Fabian (*b.* 1955) *Lab., Leeds North East,* Maj. 5,262
Hammond, Philip (*b.* 1955) *C., Runnymede & Weybridge,* Maj. 12,349
***Hammond**, Stephen (*b.* 1962) *C., Wimbledon,* Maj. 2,301
Hancock, Mike (*b.* 1946) *LD, Portsmouth South,* Maj. 3,362
***Hands**, Greg (*b.* 1965) *C., Hammersmith & Fulham,* Maj. 5,029
Hanson, David (*b.* 1957) *Lab., Delyn,* Maj. 6,644
Harman, Rt. Hon. Harriet (*b.* 1950) *Lab., Camberwell & Peckham,* Maj. 13,483
***Harper**, Mark (*b.* 1970) *C., Forest of Dean,* Maj. 2,049
Harris, Dr Evan (*b.* 1965) *LD, Oxford West & Abingdon,* Maj. 7,683
Harris, Tom (*b.* 1964) *Lab., Glasgow South,* Maj. 10,832
Harvey, Nick (*b.* 1961) *LD, Devon North,* Maj. 4,972
Haselhurst, Rt. Hon. Sir Alan (*b.* 1937) *C., Saffron Walden,* Maj. 13,008
Havard, Dai (*b.* 1949) *Lab., Merthyr Tydfil & Rhymney,* Maj. 13,934
Hayes, John (*b.* 1958) *C., South Holland & The Deepings,* Maj. 15,780
Heal, Sylvia (*b.* 1942) *Lab., Halesowen & Rowley Regis,* Maj. 4,337
Heald, Oliver (*b.* 1954) *C., Hertfordshire North East,* Maj. 9,138
Healey, John (*b.* 1960) *Lab., Wentworth,* Maj. 15,056
Heath, David (*b.* 1954) *LD, Somerton & Frome,* Maj. 812
Heathcoat-Amory, Rt. Hon. David (*b.* 1949) *C., Wells,* Maj. 3,040
***Hemming**, John (*b.* 1960) *LD, Birmingham Yardley,* Maj. 2,672
Henderson, Doug (*b.* 1949) *Lab., Newcastle upon Tyne North,* Maj. 7,023

Hendrick, Mark (*b.* 1958) *Lab. (Co-op), Preston,* Maj. 9,407
Hendry, Charles (*b.* 1959) *C., Wealden,* Maj. 15,921
Hepburn, Stephen (*b.* 1959) *Lab., Jarrow,* Maj. 13,904
Heppell, John (*b.* 1948) *Lab., Nottingham East,* Maj. 6,939
***Herbert**, Nick (*b.* 1963) *C., Arundel & South Downs,* Maj. 11,309
Hermon, Lady Sylvia (*b.* 1956) *UUP, Down North,* Maj. 4,944
Hesford, Stephen (*b.* 1957) *Lab., Wirral West,* Maj. 1,097
Hewitt, Rt. Hon. Patricia (*b.* 1948) *Lab., Leicester West,* Maj. 9,070
Heyes, David (*b.* 1946) *Lab., Ashton-under-Lyne,* Maj. 13,952
Hill, Rt. Hon. Keith (*b.* 1943) *Lab., Streatham,* Maj. 7,466
***Hillier**, Meg (*b.* 1969) *Lab. (Co-op), Hackney South & Shoreditch,* Maj. 10,204
Hoban, Mark (*b.* 1964) *C., Fareham,* Maj. 11,702
Hodge, Rt. Hon. Margaret (*b.* 1944) *Lab., Barking,* Maj. 8,883
***Hodgson**, Sharon (*b.* 1966) *Lab., Gateshead East & Washington West,* Maj. 13,407
Hoey, Kate (*b.* 1946) *Lab., Vauxhall,* Maj. 9,977
Hogg, Rt. Hon. Douglas (*b.* 1945) *C., Sleaford & North Hykeham,* Maj. 12,705
***Hollobone**, Philip (*b.* 1964) *C., Kettering,* Maj. 3,301
***Holloway**, Adam (*b.* 1965) *C., Gravesham,* Maj. 654
Holmes, Paul (*b.* 1957) *LD, Chesterfield,* Maj. 3,045
Hood, Jimmy (*b.* 1948) *Lab., Lanark & Hamilton East,* Maj. 11,947
Hoon, Rt. Hon. Geoff (*b.* 1953) *Lab., Ashfield,* Maj. 10,213
Hope, Phil (*b.* 1955) *Lab. (Co-op), Corby,* Maj. 1,517
Hopkins, Kelvin (*b.* 1941) *Lab., Luton North,* Maj. 6,487
Horam, John (*b.* 1939) *C., Orpington,* Maj. 4,947
***Horwood**, Martin (*b.* 1962) *LD, Cheltenham,* Maj. 2,303
***Hosie**, Stewart (*b.* 1963) *SNP, Dundee East,* Maj. 383
Howard, Rt. Hon. Michael (*b.* 1941) *C., Folkestone & Hythe,* Maj. 11,680
***Howarth**, David (*b.* 1958) *LD, Cambridge,* Maj. 4,339
Howarth, Rt. Hon. George (*b.* 1949) *Lab., Knowsley North & Sefton East,* Maj. 16,269
Howarth, Gerald (*b.* 1947) *C., Aldershot,* Maj. 5,334
Howells, Dr Kim (*b.* 1946) *Lab., Pontypridd,* Maj. 13,191
Hoyle, Lindsay (*b.* 1957) *Lab., Chorley,* Maj. 7,625
Hughes, Rt. Hon. Beverley (*b.* 1950) *Lab., Stretford & Urmston,* Maj. 7,851
Hughes, Simon (*b.* 1951) *LD, Southwark North & Bermondsey,* Maj. 5,406
***Huhne**, Chris (*b.* 1954) *LD, Eastleigh,* Maj. 568
Humble, Joan (*b.* 1951) *Lab., Blackpool North & Fleetwood,* Maj. 5,062
***Hunt**, Jeremy (*b.* 1966) *C., Surrey South West,* Maj. 5,711
***Hunter**, Mark (*b.* 1957) *LD, Cheadle,* Maj. 3,657
***Hurd**, Nick (*b.* 1962) *C., Ruislip-Northwood,* Maj. 8,910
Hutton, Rt. Hon. John (*b.* 1955) *Lab., Barrow & Furness,* Maj. 6,037
Iddon, Dr Brian (*b.* 1940) *Lab., Bolton South East,* Maj. 11,638
Illsley, Eric (*b.* 1955) *Lab., Barnsley Central,* Maj. 12,732
Ingram, Rt. Hon. Adam (*b.* 1947) *Lab., East Kilbride, Strathaven & Lesmahagow,* Maj. 14,723
Irranca-Davies, Huw (*b.* 1963) *Lab., Ogmore,* Maj. 13,703
Jack, Rt. Hon. Michael (*b.* 1946) *C., Fylde,* Maj. 12,459
Jackson, Glenda (*b.* 1936) *Lab., Hampstead & Highgate,* Maj. 3,729
***Jackson**, Stewart (*b.* 1965) *C., Peterborough,* Maj. 2,740
***James**, Sian (*b.* 1959) *Lab., Swansea East,* Maj. 11,249
Jenkin, Bernard (*b.* 1959) *C., Essex North,* Maj. 10,903
Jenkins, Brian (*b.* 1942) *Lab., Tamworth,* Maj. 2,569
Johnson, Boris (*b.* 1964) *C., Henley,* Maj. 12,793
Johnson, Rt. Hon. Alan (*b.* 1950) *Lab., Hull West & Hessle,* Maj. 9,450
***Johnson**, Diana (*b.* 1966) *Lab., Hull North,* Maj. 7,351
***Jones**, David (*b.* 1952) *C., Clwyd West,* Maj. 133
Jones, Helen (*b.* 1954) *Lab., Warrington North,* Maj. 12,204
Jones, Kevan (*b.* 1964) *Lab., Durham North,* Maj. 16,781
Jones, Dr Lynne (*b.* 1951) *Lab., Birmingham Selly Oak,* Maj. 8,851
Jones, Martyn (*b.* 1947) *Lab., Clwyd South,* Maj. 6,348
Jowell, Rt. Hon. Tessa (*b.* 1947) *Lab., Dulwich & West Norwood,* Maj. 8,807
Joyce, Eric (*b.* 1960) *Lab., Falkirk,* Maj. 13,475
Kaufman, Rt. Hon. Sir Gerald (*b.* 1930) *Lab., Manchester Gorton,* Maj. 5,808
***Kawczynski**, Daniel (*b.* 1972) *C., Shrewsbury & Atcham,* Maj. 1,808
Keeble, Sally (*b.* 1951) *Lab., Northampton North,* Maj. 3,960
***Keeley**, Barbara (*b.* 1952) *Lab., Worsley,* Maj. 9,368
Keen, Alan (*b.* 1937) *Lab. (Co-op), Feltham & Heston,* Maj. 6,820
Keen, Ann (*b.* 1948) *Lab., Brentford & Isleworth,* Maj. 4,411
Keetch, Paul (*b.* 1961) *LD, Hereford,* Maj. 962
Kelly, Rt. Hon. Ruth (*b.* 1968) *Lab., Bolton West,* Maj. 2,064
Kemp, Fraser (*b.* 1958) *Lab., Houghton & Washington East,* Maj. 16,065
Kennedy, Rt. Hon. Charles (*b.* 1959) *LD, Ross, Skye & Lochaber,* Maj. 14,249
Kennedy, Rt. Hon. Jane (*b.* 1958) *Lab., Liverpool Wavertree,* Maj. 5,173
Key, Robert (*b.* 1945) *C., Salisbury,* Maj. 11,142
***Khan**, Sadiq (*b.* 1970) *Lab., Tooting,* Maj. 5,381
Kidney, David (*b.* 1955) *Lab., Stafford,* Maj. 2,121
Kilfoyle, Peter (*b.* 1946) *Lab., Liverpool Walton,* Maj. 15,957
Kirkbride, Julie (*b.* 1960) *C., Bromsgrove,* Maj. 10,080
Knight, Rt. Hon. Greg (*b.* 1949) *C., Yorkshire East,* Maj. 6,283
Knight, Jim (*b.* 1965) *Lab., Dorset South,* Maj. 1,812
***Kramer**, Susan (*b.* 1950) *LD, Richmond Park,* Maj. 3,731
Kumar, Dr Ashok (*b.* 1956) *Lab., Middlesbrough South & Cleveland East,* Maj. 8,000
Ladyman, Dr Stephen (*b.* 1952) *Lab., Thanet South,* Maj. 664
Laing, Eleanor (*b.* 1958) *C., Epping Forest,* Maj. 14,358
Lait, Jacqui (*b.* 1947) *C., Beckenham,* Maj. 8,401
Lamb, Norman (*b.* 1957) *LD, Norfolk North,* Maj. 10,606
Lammy, David (*b.* 1972) *Lab., Tottenham,* Maj. 13,034
***Lancaster**, Mark (*b.* 1970) *C., Milton Keynes North East,* Maj. 1,665
Lansley, Andrew (*b.* 1956) *C., Cambridgeshire South,* Maj. 8,001
Laws, David (*b.* 1965) *LD, Yeovil,* Maj. 8,562
Laxton, Bob (*b.* 1944) *Lab., Derby North,* Maj. 3,757
Lazarowicz, Mark (*b.* 1953) *Lab. (Co-op), Edinburgh North & Leith,* Maj. 2,153
***Leech**, John (*b.* 1971) *LD, Manchester Withington,* Maj. 667

Leigh, Edward (*b.* 1950) *C., Gainsborough,* Maj. 8,003
Lepper, David (*b.* 1945) *Lab. (Co-op), Brighton Pavilion,* Maj. 5,030
Letwin, Rt. Hon. Oliver (*b.* 1956) *C., Dorset West,* Maj. 2,461
Levitt, Tom (*b.* 1954) *Lab., High Peak,* Maj. 735
Lewis, Ivan (*b.* 1967) *Lab., Bury South,* Maj. 8,912
Lewis, Dr Julian (*b.* 1951) *C., New Forest East,* Maj. 6,551
Liddell-Grainger, Ian (*b.* 1959) *C., Bridgwater,* Maj. 8,469
Lidington, David (*b.* 1956) *C., Aylesbury,* Maj. 11,065
Lilley, Rt. Hon. Peter (*b.* 1943) *C., Hitchin & Harpenden,* Maj. 11,393
Linton, Martin (*b.* 1944) *Lab., Battersea,* Maj. 163
Lloyd, Tony (*b.* 1950) *Lab., Manchester Central,* Maj. 9,776
Llwyd, Elfyn (*b.* 1951) *PC, Meirionnydd Nant Conwy,* Maj. 6,614
Lord, Sir Michael (*b.* 1938) *C., Suffolk Central & Ipswich North,* Maj. 7,856
Loughton, Tim (*b.* 1962) *C., Worthing East & Shoreham,* Maj. 8,183
Love, Andy (*b.* 1949) *Lab. (Co-op), Edmonton,* Maj. 8,075
Lucas, Ian (*b.* 1960) *Lab., Wrexham,* Maj. 6,819
Luff, Peter (*b.* 1955) *C., Worcestershire Mid,* Maj. 13,327
McAvoy, Rt. Hon. Thomas (*b.* 1943) *Lab. (Co-op), Rutherglen & Hamilton West,* Maj. 16,112
McCabe, Stephen (*b.* 1955) *Lab., Birmingham Hall Green,* Maj. 5,714
McCafferty, Christine (*b.* 1945) *Lab., Calder Valley,* Maj. 1,367
***McCarthy**, Kerry (*b.* 1965) *Lab., Bristol East,* Maj. 8,621
***McCarthy-Fry**, Sarah (*b.* 1955) *Lab. (Co-op), Portsmouth North,* Maj. 1,139
McCartney, Rt. Hon. Ian (*b.* 1951) *Lab., Makerfield,* Maj. 18,149
***McCrea**, Dr William (*b.* 1948) *DUP, Antrim South,* Maj. 3,448
McDonagh, Siobhain (*b.* 1960) *Lab., Mitcham & Morden,* Maj. 12,560
***McDonnell**, Dr Alasdair (*b.* 1949) *SDLP, Belfast South,* Maj. 1,235
McDonnell, John (*b.* 1951) *Lab., Hayes & Harlington,* Maj. 10,847
MacDougall, John (*b.* 1947) *Lab., Glenrothes,* Maj. 10,664
***McFadden**, Pat (*b.* 1965) *Lab., Wolverhampton South East,* Maj. 10,495
McFall, Rt. Hon. John (*b.* 1944) *Lab. (Co-op), Dunbartonshire West,* Maj. 12,553
***McGovern**, James (*b.* 1956) *Lab., Dundee West,* Maj. 5,379
McGrady, Edward (*b.* 1935) *SDLP, Down South,* Maj. 9,140
McGuinness, Martin (*b.* 1950) *SF, Ulster Mid,* Maj. 10,976
McGuire, Anne (*b.* 1949) *Lab., Stirling,* Maj. 4,767
McIntosh, Anne (*b.* 1954) *C., Vale of York,* Maj. 13,712
McIsaac, Shona (*b.* 1960) *Lab., Cleethorpes,* Maj. 2,642
Mackay, Rt. Hon. Andrew (*b.* 1949) *C., Bracknell,* Maj. 12,036
McKechin, Ann (*b.* 1961) *Lab., Glasgow North,* Maj. 3,338
McKenna, Rosemary (*b.* 1941) *Lab., Cumbernauld, Kilsyth & Kirkintilloch East,* Maj. 11,562
Mackinlay, Andrew (*b.* 1949) *Lab., Thurrock,* Maj. 6,375
Maclean, Rt. Hon. David (*b.* 1953) *C., Penrith & The Border,* Maj. 11,904
McLoughlin, Rt. Hon. Patrick (*b.* 1957) *C., Derbyshire West,* Maj. 10,753
***MacNeil**, Angus (*b.* 1970) *SNP, Na h-Eileanan an Iar,* Maj. 1,441
McNulty, Tony (*b.* 1958) *Lab., Harrow East,* Maj. 4,730
MacShane, Rt. Hon. Denis (*b.* 1948) *Lab., Rotherham,* Maj. 10,681
Mactaggart, Fiona (*b.* 1953) *Lab., Slough,* Maj. 7,851
Mahmood, Khalid (*b.* 1961) *Lab., Birmingham Perry Barr,* Maj. 7,948
***Main**, Anne (*b.* 1957) *C., St Albans,* Maj. 1,361
***Malik**, Shahid (*b.* 1967) *Lab., Dewsbury,* Maj. 4,615
Malins, Humfrey (*b.* 1945) *C., Woking,* Maj. 6,612
Mallaber, Judith (*b.* 1951) *Lab., Amber Valley,* Maj. 5,275
Mann, John (*b.* 1960) *Lab., Bassetlaw,* Maj. 10,837
Maples, John (*b.* 1943) *C., Stratford-upon-Avon,* Maj. 12,184
Marris, Rob (*b.* 1955) *Lab., Wolverhampton South West,* Maj. 2,879
Marsden, Gordon (*b.* 1953) *Lab., Blackpool South,* Maj. 7,922
Marshall, David (*b.* 1941) *Lab., Glasgow East,* Maj. 13,507
Marshall-Andrews, Bob (*b.* 1944) *Lab., Medway,* Maj. 213
Martin, Rt. Hon. Michael (*b.* 1945) *The Speaker, Glasgow North East,* Maj. 10,134
Martlew, Eric (*b.* 1949) *Lab., Carlisle,* Maj. 5,695
Mates, Rt. Hon. Michael (*b.* 1934) *C., Hampshire East,* Maj. 5,509
Maude, Rt. Hon. Francis (*b.* 1953) *C., Horsham,* Maj. 12,627
May, Rt. Hon. Theresa (*b.* 1956) *C., Maidenhead,* Maj. 6,231
Meacher, Rt. Hon. Michael (*b.* 1939) *Lab., Oldham West & Royton,* Maj. 10,454
Meale, Alan (*b.* 1949) *Lab., Mansfield,* Maj. 11,365
Mercer, Patrick (*b.* 1956) *C., Newark,* Maj. 6,464
Merron, Gillian (*b.* 1959) *Lab., Lincoln,* Maj. 4,614
Michael, Rt. Hon. Alun (*b.* 1943) *Lab. (Co-op), Cardiff South & Penarth,* Maj. 9,237
Milburn, Rt. Hon. Alan (*b.* 1958) *Lab., Darlington,* Maj. 10,404
Miliband, Rt. Hon. David (*b.* 1966) *Lab., South Shields,* Maj. 12,312
***Miliband**, Edward (*b.* 1969) *Lab., Doncaster North,* Maj. 12,656
Miller, Andrew (*b.* 1949) *Lab., Ellesmere Port & Neston,* Maj. 6,486
***Miller**, Maria (*b.* 1964) *C., Basingstoke,* Maj. 4,680
***Milton**, Anne (*b.* 1955) *C., Guildford,* Maj. 347
Mitchell, Andrew (*b.* 1956) *C., Sutton Coldfield,* Maj. 12,283
Mitchell, Austin (*b.* 1934) *Lab., Great Grimsby,* Maj. 7,654
Moffat, Anne (*b.* 1958) *Lab., East Lothian,* Maj. 7,620
Moffatt, Laura (*b.* 1954) *Lab., Crawley,* Maj. 37
Mole, Chris (*b.* 1958) *Lab., Ipswich,* Maj. 5,332
***Moon**, Madeleine (*b.* 1950) *Lab., Bridgend,* Maj. 6,523
Moore, Michael (*b.* 1965) *LD, Berwickshire, Roxburgh & Selkirk,* Maj. 5,901
Moran, Margaret (*b.* 1955) *Lab., Luton South,* Maj. 5,650
***Morden**, Jessica (*b.* 1968) *Lab., Newport East,* Maj. 6,838
Morgan, Julie (*b.* 1944) *Lab., Cardiff North,* Maj. 1,146
Morley, Elliot (*b.* 1952) *Lab., Scunthorpe,* Maj. 8,963
Moss, Malcolm (*b.* 1943) *C., Cambridgeshire North East,* Maj. 8,901

Mountford, Kali (*b.* 1954) *Lab., Colne Valley,* Maj. 1,501
Mudie, George (*b.* 1945) *Lab., Leeds East,* Maj. 11,578
***Mulholland**, Greg (*b.* 1970) *LD, Leeds North West,* Maj. 1,877
Mullin, Chris (*b.* 1947) *Lab., Sunderland South,* Maj. 11,059
***Mundell**, David (*b.* 1962) *C., Dumfriesshire, Clydesdale & Tweeddale,* Maj. 1,738
Munn, Meg (*b.* 1959) *Lab. (Co-op), Sheffield Heeley,* Maj. 11,370
***Murphy**, Conor (*b.* 1963) *SF, Newry & Armagh,* Maj. 8,195
Murphy, Denis (*b.* 1948) *Lab., Wansbeck,* Maj. 10,581
Murphy, Jim (*b.* 1967) *Lab., Renfrewshire East,* Maj. 6,657
Murphy, Rt. Hon. Paul (*b.* 1948) *Lab., Torfaen,* Maj. 14,791
Murrison, Dr Andrew (*b.* 1961) *C., Westbury,* Maj. 5,349
Naysmith, Dr Doug (*b.* 1941) *Lab. (Co-op), Bristol North West,* Maj. 8,962
***Neill**, Bob (*b.* 1952) *C., Bromley & Chislehurst,* Maj. 633
***Newmark**, Brooks (*b.* 1958) *C., Braintree,* Maj. 3,893
Norris, Dan (*b.* 1960) *Lab., Wansdyke,* Maj. 1,839
Oaten, Mark (*b.* 1964) *LD, Winchester,* Maj. 7,476
O'Brien, Mike (*b.* 1954) *Lab., Warwickshire North,* Maj. 7,553
O'Brien, Stephen (*b.* 1957) *C., Eddisbury,* Maj. 6,195
O'Hara, Eddie (*b.* 1937) *Lab., Knowsley South,* Maj. 17,688
Olner, Bill (*b.* 1942) *Lab., Nuneaton,* Maj. 2,280
Opik, Lembit (*b.* 1965) *LD, Montgomeryshire,* Maj. 7,173
Osborne, George (*b.* 1971) *C., Tatton,* Maj. 11,731
Osborne, Sandra (*b.* 1956) *Lab., Ayr, Carrick & Cumnock,* Maj. 9,997
Ottaway, Richard (*b.* 1945) *C., Croydon South,* Maj. 13,528
Owen, Albert (*b.* 1960) *Lab., Ynys Mon,* Maj. 1,242
Paice, James (*b.* 1949) *C., Cambridgeshire South East,* Maj. 8,624
Paisley, Revd Rt. Hon. Ian (*b.* 1926) *DUP, Antrim North,* Maj. 17,965
Palmer, Dr Nick (*b.* 1950) *Lab., Broxtowe,* Maj. 2,296
Paterson, Owen (*b.* 1956) *C., Shropshire North,* Maj. 11,020
Pearson, Ian (*b.* 1959) *Lab., Dudley South,* Maj. 4,244
***Pelling**, Andrew (*b.* 1959) *C., Croydon Central,* Maj. 75
***Penning**, Michael (*b.* 1957) *C., Hemel Hempstead,* Maj. 499
***Penrose**, John (*b.* 1964) *C., Weston-Super-Mare,* Maj. 2,079
Pickles, Eric (*b.* 1952) *C., Brentwood & Ongar,* Maj. 11,612
Plaskitt, James (*b.* 1954) *Lab., Warwick & Leamington,* Maj. 266
Pope, Greg (*b.* 1960) *Lab., Hyndburn,* Maj. 5,587
Pound, Stephen (*b.* 1948) *Lab., Ealing North,* Maj. 7,059
Prentice, Bridget (*b.* 1952) *Lab., Lewisham East,* Maj. 6,751
Prentice, Gordon (*b.* 1951) *Lab., Pendle,* Maj. 2,180
Prescott, Rt. Hon. John (*b.* 1938) *Lab., Hull East,* Maj. 11,747
Price, Adam (*b.* 1968) *PC, Carmarthen East & Dinefwr,* Maj. 6,718
Primarolo, Rt. Hon. Dawn (*b.* 1954) *Lab., Bristol South,* Maj. 11,142
Prisk, Mark (*b.* 1962) *C., Hertford & Stortford,* Maj. 13,097
***Pritchard**, Mark (*b.* 1966) *C., The Wrekin,* Maj. 942
Prosser, Gwyn (*b.* 1943) *Lab., Dover,* Maj. 4,941
Pugh, Dr John (*b.* 1948) *LD, Southport,* Maj. 3,838
Purchase, Ken (*b.* 1939) *Lab. (Co-op), Wolverhampton North East,* Maj. 8,156
Purnell, James (*b.* 1970) *Lab., Stalybridge & Hyde,* Maj. 8,348
Rammell, Bill (*b.* 1959) *Lab., Harlow,* Maj. 97
Randall, John (*b.* 1955) *C., Uxbridge,* Maj. 6,171
Raynsford, Rt. Hon. Nick (*b.* 1945) *Lab., Greenwich & Woolwich,* Maj. 10,146
Redwood, Rt. Hon. John (*b.* 1951) *C., Wokingham,* Maj. 7,240
Reed, Andy (*b.* 1964) *Lab. (Co-op), Loughborough,* Maj. 1,996
***Reed**, Jamie (*b.* 1973) *Lab., Copeland,* Maj. 6,320
Reid, Alan (*b.* 1954) *LD, Argyll & Bute,* Maj. 5,636
Reid, Rt. Hon. Dr John (*b.* 1947) *Lab., Airdrie & Shotts,* Maj. 14,084
***Rennie**, Willie (*b.* 1967) *LD, Dunfermline & Fife West,* Maj. 1,800
†**Rifkind**, Rt. Hon. Sir Malcolm (*b.* 1946) *C., Kensington & Chelsea,* Maj. 12,418
***Riordan**, Linda (*b.* 1953) *Lab. (Co-op), Halifax,* Maj. 3,417
Robathan, Andrew (*b.* 1951) *C., Blaby,* Maj. 7,873
Robertson, Angus (*b.* 1969) *SNP, Moray,* Maj. 5,676
Robertson, Hugh (*b.* 1962) *C., Faversham & Kent Mid,* Maj. 8,720
Robertson, John (*b.* 1952) *Lab., Glasgow North West,* Maj. 10,093
Robertson, Laurence (*b.* 1958) *C., Tewkesbury,* Maj. 9,892
Robinson, Geoffrey (*b.* 1938) *Lab., Coventry North West,* Maj. 9,315
Robinson, Iris (*b.* 1949) *DUP, Strangford,* Maj. 13,049
Robinson, Peter (*b.* 1948) *DUP, Belfast East,* Maj. 5,877
***Rogerson**, Dan (*b.* 1975) *LD, Cornwall North,* Maj. 3,076
Rooney, Terry (*b.* 1950) *Lab., Bradford North,* Maj. 3,511
Rosindell, Andrew (*b.* 1966) *C., Romford,* Maj. 11,589
***Rowen**, Paul (*b.* 1955) *LD, Rochdale,* Maj. 442
Roy, Frank (*b.* 1958) *Lab., Motherwell & Wishaw,* Maj. 15,222
Ruane, Christopher (*b.* 1958) *Lab., Vale of Clwyd,* Maj. 4,669
Ruddock, Joan (*b.* 1943) *Lab., Lewisham Deptford,* Maj. 11,811
Ruffley, David (*b.* 1962) *C., Bury St Edmunds,* Maj. 9,930
Russell, Bob (*b.* 1946) *LD, Colchester,* Maj. 6,277
Russell, Christine (*b.* 1945) *Lab., Chester, City of,* Maj. 915
Ryan, Joan (*b.* 1955) *Lab., Enfield North,* Maj. 1,920
Salmond, Alex (*b.* 1954) *SNP, Banff & Buchan,* Maj. 11,837
Salter, Martin (*b.* 1954) *Lab., Reading West,* Maj. 4,682
Sanders, Adrian (*b.* 1959) *LD, Torbay,* Maj. 2,029
Sarwar, Mohammad (*b.* 1952) *Lab., Glasgow Central,* Maj. 8,531
***Scott**, Lee (*b.* 1956) *C., Ilford North,* Maj. 1,653
***Seabeck**, Alison (*b.* 1954) *Lab., Plymouth Devonport,* Maj. 8,103
Selous, Andrew (*b.* 1962) *C., Bedfordshire South West,* Maj. 8,277
***Shapps**, Grant (*b.* 1968) *C., Welwyn Hatfield,* Maj. 5,946
Sharma, Virendra (*b.* 1947) *Lab., Ealing Southall,* Maj. 5,070
Shaw, Jonathan (*b.* 1966) *Lab., Chatham & Aylesford,* Maj. 2,332
Sheerman, Barry (*b.* 1940) *Lab. (Co-op), Huddersfield,* Maj. 8,351

Shepherd, Richard (*b.* 1942) *C., Aldridge-Brownhills,* Maj. 5,507
Sheridan, James (*b.* 1952) *Lab., Paisley & Renfrewshire North,* Maj. 11,001
‡**Short**, Rt. Hon. Clare (*b.* 1946) *Ind., Birmingham Ladywood,* Maj. 6,801
Simmonds, Mark (*b.* 1964) *C., Boston & Skegness,* Maj. 5,907
Simon, Sion (*b.* 1969) *Lab., Birmingham Erdington,* Maj. 9,575
Simpson, Alan (*b.* 1948) *Lab., Nottingham South,* Maj. 7,486
*__Simpson__, David (*b.* 1959) *DUP, Upper Bann,* Maj. 5,298
Simpson, Keith (*b.* 1949) *C., Norfolk Mid,* Maj. 7,560
Singh, Marsha (*b.* 1954) *Lab., Bradford West,* Maj. 3,026
Skinner, Dennis (*b.* 1932) *Lab., Bolsover,* Maj. 18,437
*__Slaughter__, Andrew (*b.* 1960) *Lab., Ealing, Acton & Shepherd's Bush,* Maj. 5,520
Smith, Rt. Hon. Andrew (*b.* 1951) *Lab., Oxford East,* Maj. 963
*__Smith__, Angela C. (*b.* 1961) *Lab., Sheffield Hillsborough,* Maj. 11,243
Smith, Angela E. (*b.* 1959) *Lab. (Co-op), Basildon,* Maj. 3,142
Smith, Geraldine (*b.* 1961) *Lab., Morecambe & Lunesdale,* Maj. 4,768
Smith, Rt. Hon. Jacqui (*b.* 1962) *Lab., Redditch,* Maj. 2,716
Smith, John (*b.* 1951) *Lab., Vale of Glamorgan,* Maj. 1,808
Smith, Sir Robert (*b.* 1958) *LD, Aberdeenshire West & Kincardine,* Maj. 7,471
*__Snelgrove__, Anne (*b.* 1957) *Lab., Swindon South ,* Maj. 1,353
Soames, Hon. Nicholas (*b.* 1948) *C., Sussex Mid,* Maj. 5,890
*__Soulsby__, Sir Peter (*b.* 1948) *Lab., Leicester South,* Maj. 3,717
Southworth, Helen (*b.* 1956) *Lab., Warrington South,* Maj. 3,515
Spellar, Rt. Hon. John (*b.* 1947) *Lab., Warley,* Maj. 10,147
Spelman, Caroline (*b.* 1958) *C., Meriden,* Maj. 7,009
Spicer, Sir Michael (*b.* 1943) *C., Worcestershire West,* Maj. 2,475
Spink, Dr Robert (*b.* 1948) *C., Castle Point,* Maj. 8,201
Spring, Richard (*b.* 1946) *C., Suffolk West,* Maj. 8,909
Stanley, Rt. Hon. Sir John (*b.* 1942) *C., Tonbridge & Malling,* Maj. 13,352
Starkey, Dr Phyllis (*b.* 1947) *Lab., Milton Keynes South West,* Maj. 4,010
Steen, Anthony (*b.* 1939) *C., Totnes,* Maj. 1,947
Stewart, Ian (*b.* 1950) *Lab., Eccles,* Maj. 12,886
Stoate, Dr Howard (*b.* 1954) *Lab., Dartford,* Maj. 706
Strang, Rt. Hon. Gavin (*b.* 1943) *Lab., Edinburgh East,* Maj. 6,202
Straw, Rt. Hon. Jack (*b.* 1946) *Lab., Blackburn,* Maj. 8,009
Streeter, Gary (*b.* 1955) *C., Devon South West,* Maj. 10,141
Stringer, Graham (*b.* 1950) *Lab., Manchester Blackley,* Maj. 12,027
Stuart, Gisela (*b.* 1955) *Lab., Birmingham Edgbaston,* Maj. 2,349
*__Stuart__, Graham (*b.* 1962) *C., Beverley & Holderness,* Maj. 2,580
Stunell, Andrew (*b.* 1942) *LD, Hazel Grove,* Maj. 7,748
Sutcliffe, Gerry (*b.* 1953) *Lab., Bradford South,* Maj. 9,167
Swayne, Desmond (*b.* 1956) *C., New Forest West,* Maj. 17,285
*__Swinson__, Jo (*b.* 1980) *LD, Dunbartonshire East,* Maj. 4,061
Swire, Hugo (*b.* 1959) *C., Devon East,* Maj. 7,936
Syms, Robert (*b.* 1956) *C., Poole,* Maj. 5,988
Tami, Mark (*b.* 1963) *Lab., Alyn & Deeside,* Maj. 8,378
Tapsell, Sir Peter (*b.* 1930) *C., Louth & Horncastle,* Maj. 9,896
Taylor, Dari (*b.* 1944) *Lab., Stockton South,* Maj. 6,139
Taylor, David (*b.* 1946) *Lab. (Co-op), Leicestershire North West,* Maj. 4,477
Taylor, Ian (*b.* 1945) *C., Esher & Walton,* Maj. 7,727
Taylor, Matthew (*b.* 1963) *LD, Truro & St Austell,* Maj. 7,403
Taylor, Dr Richard (*b.* 1935) *KHHC, Wyre Forest,* Maj. 5,250
Teather, Sarah (*b.* 1974) *LD, Brent East,* Maj. 2,712
Thomas, Gareth (*b.* 1967) *Lab. (Co-op), Harrow West,* Maj. 2,028
*__Thornberry__, Emily (*b.* 1960) *Lab., Islington South & Finsbury,* Maj. 484
Thurso, John (*b.* 1953) *LD, Caithness, Sutherland & Easter Ross,* Maj. 8,168
Timms, Stephen (*b.* 1955) *Lab., East Ham,* Maj. 13,155
Tipping, Paddy (*b.* 1949) *Lab., Sherwood,* Maj. 6,652
Todd, Mark (*b.* 1954) *Lab., Derbyshire South,* Maj. 4,495
Touhig, Don (*b.* 1947) *Lab. (Co-op), Islwyn,* Maj. 15,740
Tredinnick, David (*b.* 1950) *C., Bosworth,* Maj. 5,319
Trickett, Jon (*b.* 1950) *Lab., Hemsworth,* Maj. 13,481
Truswell, Paul (*b.* 1955) *Lab., Pudsey,* Maj. 5,870
Turner, Andrew (*b.* 1953) *C., Isle of Wight,* Maj. 12,978
Turner, Dr Desmond (*b.* 1939) *Lab., Brighton Kemptown,* Maj. 2,737
Turner, Neil (*b.* 1945) *Lab., Wigan,* Maj. 11,767
Twigg, Derek (*b.* 1959) *Lab., Halton,* Maj. 14,606
Tyrie, Andrew (*b.* 1957) *C., Chichester,* Maj. 10,860
*__Ussher__, Kitty (*b.* 1971) *Lab., Burnley,* Maj. 5,778
*__Vaizey__, Ed (*b.* 1969) *C., Wantage,* Maj. 8,017
*__Vara__, Shailesh (*b.* 1960) *C., Cambridgeshire North West,* Maj. 9,833
Vaz, Keith (*b.* 1956) *Lab., Leicester East,* Maj. 15,876
Viggers, Peter (*b.* 1938) *C., Gosport,* Maj. 5,730
*__Villiers__, Theresa (*b.* 1968) *C., Chipping Barnet,* Maj. 5,960
Vis, Dr Rudi (*b.* 1941) *Lab., Finchley & Golders Green,* Maj. 741
*__Walker__, Charles (*b.* 1967) *C., Broxbourne,* Maj. 11,509
*__Wallace__, Ben (*b.* 1970) *C., Lancaster & Wyre,* Maj. 4,171
Walley, Joan (*b.* 1949) *Lab., Stoke-on-Trent North,* Maj. 10,036
Walter, Robert (*b.* 1948) *C., Dorset North,* Maj. 2,244
*__Waltho__, Lynda (*b.* 1960) *Lab., Stourbridge,* Maj. 407
Ward, Claire (*b.* 1972) *Lab., Watford,* Maj. 1,148
Wareing, Robert (*b.* 1930) *Lab., Liverpool West Derby,* Maj. 15,225
Waterson, Nigel (*b.* 1950) *C., Eastbourne,* Maj. 1,124
Watkinson, Angela (*b.* 1941) *C., Upminster,* Maj. 6,042
Watson, Tom (*b.* 1967) *Lab., West Bromwich East,* Maj. 11,652
Watts, Dave (*b.* 1951) *Lab., St Helens North,* Maj. 13,962
Webb, Prof. Steve (*b.* 1965) *LD, Northavon,* Maj. 11,033
Weir, Michael (*b.* 1957) *SNP, Angus,* Maj. 1,601
Whitehead, Dr Alan (*b.* 1950) *Lab., Southampton Test,* Maj. 7,018

Whittingdale, John (*b.* 1959) *C., Maldon & Chelmsford East,* Maj. 12,573
Wicks, Malcolm (*b.* 1947) *Lab., Croydon North,* Maj. 13,888
Widdecombe, Rt. Hon. Ann (*b.* 1947) *C., Maidstone & The Weald,* Maj. 14,856
Wiggin, Bill (*b.* 1966) *C., Leominster,* Maj. 13,187
Willetts, David (*b.* 1956) *C., Havant,* Maj. 6,508
Williams, Rt. Hon. Alan (*b.* 1930) *Lab., Swansea West,* Maj. 4,269
Williams, Betty (*b.* 1944) *Lab., Conwy,* Maj. 3,081
Williams, Hywel (*b.* 1953) *PC, Caernarfon,* Maj. 5,209
***Williams**, Mark (*b.* 1966) *LD, Ceredigion,* Maj. 219
Williams, Roger (*b.* 1948) *LD, Brecon & Radnorshire,* Maj. 3,905
***Williams**, Stephen (*b.* 1966) *LD, Bristol West,* Maj. 5,128
Willis, Phil (*b.* 1941) *LD, Harrogate & Knaresborough,* Maj. 10,429
***Willott**, Jenny (*b.* 1974) *LD, Cardiff Central,* Maj. 5,593
Wills, Michael (*b.* 1952) *Lab., Swindon North,* Maj. 2,571
Wilshire, David (*b.* 1943) *C., Spelthorne,* Maj. 9,936
***Wilson**, Phil (*b.* 1959) *Lab., Sedgefield,* Maj. 6,956
***Wilson**, Rob (*b.* 1965) *C., Reading East,* Maj. 475
***Wilson**, Sammy (*b.* 1953) *DUP, Antrim East,* Maj. 7,304
Winnick, David (*b.* 1933) *Lab., Walsall North,* Maj. 6,640
Winterton, Lady Ann (*b.* 1941) *C., Congleton,* Maj. 8,246
Winterton, Sir Nicholas (*b.* 1938) *C., Macclesfield,* Maj. 9,401
Winterton, Rosie (*b.* 1958) *Lab., Doncaster Central,* Maj. 9,802
Wishart, Peter (*b.* 1962) *SNP, Perth & Perthshire North,* Maj. 1,521
Wood, Mike (*b.* 1946) *Lab., Batley & Spen,* Maj. 5,788
Woodward, Shaun (*b.* 1958) *Lab., St Helens South,* Maj. 9,309
Woolas, Phil (*b.* 1959) *Lab., Oldham East & Saddleworth,* Maj. 3,590
Wright, Anthony (*b.* 1954) *Lab., Great Yarmouth,* Maj. 3,055
Wright, David (*b.* 1967) *Lab., Telford,* Maj. 5,406
Wright, Iain (*b.* 1972) *Lab., Hartlepool,* Maj. 7,478
***Wright**, Jeremy (*b.* 1972) *C., Rugby & Kenilworth,* Maj. 1,556
Wright, Dr Tony (*b.* 1948) *Lab., Cannock Chase,* Maj. 9,227
Wyatt, Derek (*b.* 1949) *Lab., Sittingbourne & Sheppey,* Maj. 79
Yeo, Tim (*b.* 1945) *C., Suffolk South,* Maj. 6,606
Young, Rt. Hon. Sir George (*b.* 1941) *C., Hampshire North West,* Maj. 13,264
Younger-Ross, Richard (*b.* 1953) *LD, Teignbridge,* Maj. 6,215

GENERAL ELECTION RESULTS

The results of voting in each parliamentary division at the general election of 5 May 2005 are given below.

SCOTTISH BOUNDARY CHANGES

The number of Scottish constituencies was reduced from 72 to 59 for the 2005 general election, bringing the average electorate of each constituency in line with that of England.

For the majority of constituencies where a boundary change has taken place, it is not appropriate to make a straight comparison between the results of 2001 and 2005. The seat of Dundee East, for example, comprises 80 per cent of the old Dundee East constituency and 30 per cent of the old Angus constituency; it cannot therefore be described as a simple gain for the Scottish National Party from Labour. The term 'notional' used here refers to a theoretical set of results, published by Professors Rallings and Thrasher of Plymouth University, that estimates the way each new constituency might have voted in the 2001 general election.

KEY

* New MP

† Previously MP in another seat

‡ Previously MP for another party

§ Notional result; *see* explanation of Scottish boundary changes

E. Electorate T. Turnout

Abbreviations of parties standing in the General Election in 2005:

AFC	Alliance for Change
Alliance	Alliance
AP	Alternative Party
Baths	Save the Bristol North Baths Party
Bean	New Millennium Bean
BMG	Blair Must Go Party
BNP	British National Party
BPP	British Public Party
Bridges	Build Duddon and Morecambe Bridges
Burnley	Burnley First Independent
C.	Conservative
CAP	Community Action Party
CG	Community Group
CL	Communist League
Clause 28	Clause 28 Children's Protection Christian Democrats
Comm.	Communist Party
Comm. Brit.	Communist Party of Britain
Community	Community
CP	Civilisation Party
CPA	Christian Peoples Alliance
Croydon	Croydon Pensions Alliance
Currency	Virtue Currency Cognitive Appraisal Party
DDTP	Death, Dungeons & Taxes Party
Dem. Lab.	Democratic Labour Party
Dem. Soc. All.	Democratic Socialist Alliance – People Before Profit
DUP	Democratic Unionist Party
EDP	English Democratic Party
EPP	English Parliamentary Party
Elvis	Church of the Militant Elvis Party
Eng. Dem.	English Democrats Party
Eng. Ind.	English Independence Party
FF	familiesfirst.uk.net
Fit	Fit Party For Integrity And Trust
Forum	Open-Forum
FP	Freedom Party
Free Scot.	Free Scotland Party
FWP	Forward Wales Party
GBB	Get Britain Back Party
Good	Common Good
Green	Green
Green Soc.	Alliance for Green Socialism
Honesty	Demanding Honesty in Politics and Whitehall
Ind. Green	Independent Green Voice
Ind.	Independent
Ind. Pr. Lab.	Independent Progressive Labour
IP	Imperial Party
Iraq	Iraq War, Not in My Name
IWCA	Independent Working Class Association
IZB	Islam Zinda Baad Platform
JP	Justice Party
KHHC	Kidderminster Hospital and Health Concern
Lab.	Labour
Lab. (Co-op)	Labour (Cooperative)
LCA	Legalise Cannabis Alliance
LD	Liberal Democrat
Lib.	Liberal
Local	Local Community Party
Loony	Monster Raving Loony Party
Masts	Removal of Tetra Masts in Cornwall
MC	The Millenium Council
Meb. Ker.	Mebyon Kernow
MNP	Motorcycle News Party
NACVP	Newcastle Academy with Christian Values Party
NEP	New England Party
NF	National Front
Northern	Northern Progress for You
OCV	Operation Christian Vote
OFD	Organisation of Free Democrats
Online	Seeks a Worldwide Online Participatory Directory
Paisley	Pride in Paisley Party
PC	Plaid Cymru
PDP	Progressive Democratic Party
PHF	People of Horsham First
Power	Max Power Party
PPN-V	Peace Party, Non-Violence, Justice, Environment
PPS	Pensioners Party Scotland
Progress	Peace and Progress Party
Protest	Protest Vote Party
PRTYP	Personality and Rational Thinking? Yes! Party
Publican	Publican Party – Free to Smoke (Pubs)
RA	Residents Association
R & R Loony	Rock & Roll Loony Party
Respect	Respect – the Unity Coalition
RP	The Resolutionist Party
St Albans	St Albans Party
Scot. Green	Scottish Green Party
Scot. Ind.	Scottish Independence Party
Scot. Senior	Scottish Senior Citizens Party
Scot. U.	Scottish Unionist
SDLP	Social Democratic and Labour Party
Senior	Senior Citizens Party
SF	Sinn Fein
Silent	Silent Majority Party
SNH	Safeguard the National Health Service
SNP	Scottish National Party
Soc. All.	Socialist Alliance
Soc. Alt.	Socialist Alternative Party
Socialist	Socialist
Soc. Lab.	Socialist Labour Party
Soc. Unity	Socialist Unity Network
SOS	SOS! Voters Against Overdevelopment of Northampton
Speaker	The Speaker
SSCUP	Scottish Senior Citizens Unity Party
SSP	Scottish Socialist Party
Tele.	telepathicpartnership.com
TEPK	Tigers Eye the Party for Kids
Third	Third Way
TP	Their Party
UKC	UK Community Issues Party
UKIP	UK Independence Party
UK Path	UK Pathfinders
UKPP	UK Pensioners Party
UUP	Ulster Unionist Party
Veritas	Veritas
Vote Dream	Vote for Yourself Rainbow Dream Ticket
Wessex Reg.	Wessex Regionalist
Work	The People's Choice Making Politicians Work
WP	Workers' Party
WRP	Workers' Revolutionary Party
XPP	Xtraordinary People Party
YPB	Your Party (Banbury)

PARLIAMENTARY CONSTITUENCIES AS AT MAY 2005 GENERAL ELECTION

ENGLAND

ALDERSHOT
E. 78,553 T. 48,141 (61.28%) C. hold
Gerald Howarth, C. 20,572
Adrian Collett, LD 15,238
Howard Linsley, Lab. 9,895
Derek Rumsey, UKIP 1,182
Gary Cowd, Eng. Dem. 701
Howling Lord Hope, Loony 553
C. maj. 5,334 (11.08%)
1.74% swing C. to LD
(2001: C. maj. 6,564 (14.49%))

ALDRIDGE-BROWNHILLS
E. 61,761 T. 39,556 (64.05%) C. hold
Richard Shepherd, C. 18,744
Jon Phillips, Lab. 13,237
Roy Sheward, LD 4,862
William Vaughan, BNP 1,620
Graham Eardley, UKIP 1,093
C. maj. 5,507 (13.92%)
1.98% swing Lab. to C.
(2001: C. maj. 3,768 (9.97%))

ALTRINCHAM & SALE WEST
E. 67,247 T. 44,310 (65.89%) C. hold
Graham Brady, C. 20,569
John Stockton, Lab. 13,410
Ian Chappell, LD 9,595
Gary Peart, UKIP 736
C. maj. 7,159 (16.16%)
4.70% swing Lab. to C.
(2001: C. maj. 2,941 (6.75%))

AMBER VALLEY
E. 75,376 T. 47,391 (62.87%) Lab. hold
Judy Mallaber, Lab. 21,593
Gillian Shaw, C. 16,318
Kate Smith, LD 6,225
Paul Snell, BNP 1,243
Alexander Stevenson, Veritas 1,224
Hugh Price, UKIP 788
Lab. maj. 5,275 (11.13%)
2.55% swing Lab. to C.
(2001: Lab. maj. 7,227 (16.24%))

ARUNDEL & SOUTH DOWNS
E. 72,535 T. 49,690 (68.50%) C. hold
*Nick Herbert, C. 24,752
Derek Deedman, LD 13,443
Sharon Whitlam, Lab. 8,482
Andrew Moffat, UKIP 2,700
Mark Stack, Protest 313
C. maj. 11,309 (22.76%)
3.55% swing C. to LD
(2001: C. maj. 13,704 (29.86%))

ASHFIELD
E. 73,403 T. 42,051 (57.29%) Lab. hold
Rt. Hon. Geoff Hoon, Lab. 20,433
Giles Inglis-Jones, C. 10,220
Wendy Johnson, LD 5,829
Roy Adkins, Ind. 2,292
Kathryn Allsop, Ind. 1,900
Sarah Hemstock, Veritas 1,108
Eddie Grenfell, Ind. 269
Lab. maj. 10,213 (24.29%)
4.72% swing Lab. to C.
(2001: Lab. maj. 13,268 (33.72%))

ASHFORD
E. 79,493 T. 51,685 (65.02%) C. hold
Damian Green, C. 26,651
Valerie Whitaker, Lab. 13,353
Chris Took, LD 8,308
Richard Boden, Green 1,753
Bernard Stroud, UKIP 1,620
C. maj. 13,298 (25.73%)
5.19% swing Lab. to C.
(2001: C. maj. 7,359 (15.35%))

ASHTON UNDER LYNE
E. 72,000 T. 36,967 (51.34%) Lab. hold
David Heyes, Lab. 21,211
Graeme Brown, C. 7,259
Les Jones, LD 5,108
Anthony Jones, BNP 2,051
Dr John Whittaker, UKIP 768
Jack Crossfield, Local 570
Lab. maj. 13,952 (37.74%)
2.82% swing Lab. to C.
(2001: Lab. maj. 15,518 (43.39%))

AYLESBURY
E. 82,428 T. 51,458 (62.43%) C. hold
David Lidington, C. 25,252
Peter Jones, LD 14,187
Mohammed Khaliel, Lab. 9,540
Christopher Adams, UKIP 2,479
C. maj. 11,065 (21.50%)
0.56% swing LD to C.
(2001: C. maj. 10,009 (20.39%))

BANBURY
E. 87,168 T. 56,209 (64.48%) C. hold
Tony Baldry, C. 26,382
Les Sibley, Lab. 15,585
Zoe Patrick, LD 10,076
Alyson Duckmanton, Green 1,590
Dianna Heimann, UKIP 1,241
James Starkey, NF 918
Christopher Rowe, YPB 417
C. maj. 10,797 (19.21%)
4.54% swing Lab. to C.
(2001: C. maj. 5,219 (10.13%))

BARKING
E. 57,658 T. 28,906 (50.13%) Lab. hold
Rt. Hon. Margaret Hodge, Lab. 13,826
Keith Prince, C. 4,943
Richard Barnbrook, BNP 4,916
Toby Wickenden, LD 3,211
Terry Jones, UKIP 803
Laurie Cleeland, Green 618
Demetrious Panton, Ind. 530
Michael Saxby, WRP 59
Lab. maj. 8,883 (30.73%)
3.61% swing Lab. to C.
(2001: Lab. maj. 9,534 (37.94%))

BARNSLEY CENTRAL
E. 60,592 T. 28,615 (47.23%) Lab. hold
Eric Illsley, Lab. 17,478
Miles Crompton, LD 4,746
Peter Morel, C. 3,813
Geoff Broadley, BNP 1,403
Donald Wood, Ind. 1,175
Lab. maj. 12,732 (44.49%)
5.22% swing Lab. to LD
(2001: Lab. maj. 15,130 (54.93%))

BARNSLEY EAST & MEXBOROUGH
E. 66,941 T. 33,026 (49.34%) Lab. hold
Jeff Ennis, Lab. 20,779
Sharron Brook, LD 6,654
Carolyn Abbott, C. 4,853
Terence Robinson, Soc. Lab. 740
Lab. maj. 14,125 (42.77%)
4.44% swing Lab. to LD
(2001: Lab. maj. 16,789 (51.64%))

BARNSLEY WEST & PENISTONE
E. 66,985 T. 36,852 (55.02%) Lab. hold
Michael Clapham, Lab. 20,372
Clive Watkinson, C. 9,058
Alison Brelsford, LD 7,422
Lab. maj. 11,314 (30.70%)
2.52% swing Lab. to C.
(2001: Lab. maj. 12,352 (35.74%))

BARROW & FURNESS
E. 61,883 T. 36,493 (58.97%) Lab. hold
Rt. Hon. John Hutton, Lab. 17,360
Bill Dorman, C. 11,323
Barry Rabone, LD 6,130
Alan Beach, UKIP 758
Timothy Bell, Bridges 409
Brian Greaves, Veritas 306
Helene Young, Ind. 207
Lab. maj. 6,037 (16.54%)
4.40% swing Lab. to C.
(2001: Lab. maj. 9,889 (25.34%))

BASILDON
E. 73,912 T. 43,141 (58.37%)
Lab. (Co-op) hold
Angela Smith, Lab. (Co-op) 18,720
Aaron Powell, C. 15,578
Martin Thompson, LD 4,473
Emma Colgate, BNP 2,055
Alix Blythe, UKIP 1,143
Vikki Copping, Green 662
Kim Gandy, Eng. Dem. 510
Lab. (Co-op) maj. 3,142 (7.28%)
5.82% swing Lab. (Co-op) to C.
(2001: Lab. (Co-op) maj. 7,738 (18.93%))

BASINGSTOKE
E. 76,404 T. 48,123 (62.98%) C. gain
*Maria Miller, C. 19,955
Paul Harvey, Lab. 15,275
Jen Smith, LD 9,952
Peter Effer, UKIP 1,044
Darren Shirley, Green 928
Roger Robertson, BNP 821
Roger Macnair, MC 148
C. maj. 4,680 (9.73%)
3.95% swing Lab. to C.
(C. gain because previous MP defected to DUP in 2004)
(2001: C. maj. 880 (1.83%))

BASSETLAW
E. 69,389 T. 40,342 (58.14%) Lab. hold
John Mann, Lab. 22,847
Jonathan Sheppard, C. 12,010
David Dobbie, LD 5,485
Lab. maj. 10,837 (26.86%)
0.90% swing C. to Lab.
(2001: Lab. maj. 9,748 (25.06%))

BATH
E. 66,824 T. 45,836 (68.59%) LD hold
Don Foster, LD 20,101
Sian Dawson, C. 15,463
Harriet Ajderian, Lab. 6,773
Eric Lucas, Green 2,494
Richard Crowder, UKIP 770
Patrick Cobbe, Ind. 177
Graham Walker, Ind. 58
LD maj. 4,638 (10.12%)
5.63% swing LD to C.
(2001: LD maj. 9,894 (21.37%))

BATLEY & SPEN
E. 62,948 T. 39,208 (62.29%) Lab. hold
Mike Wood, Lab. 17,974
Robert Light, C. 12,186
Neil Bentley, LD 5,731
Colin Auty, BNP 2,668
Clive Lord, Green 649
Lab. maj. 5,788 (14.76%)
0.81% swing C. to Lab.
(2001: Lab. maj. 5,064 (13.14%))

BATTERSEA
E. 69,548 T. 41,049 (59.02%) Lab. hold
Martin Linton, Lab. 16,569
Dominic Schofield, C. 16,406
Norsheen Bhatti, LD 6,006
Hugo Charlton, Green 1,735
Terence Jones, UKIP 333
Lab. maj. 163 (0.40%)
6.67% swing Lab. to C.
(2001: Lab. maj. 5,053 (13.73%))

BEACONSFIELD
E. 68,083 T. 43,523 (63.93%) C. hold
Dominic Grieve, C. 24,126
Peter Chapman, LD 8,873
Alex Sobel, Lab. 8,422
John Fagan, UKIP 2,102
C. maj. 15,253 (35.05%)
1.96% swing LD to C.
(2001: C. maj. 13,065 (31.07%))

BECKENHAM
E. 74,738 T. 48,964 (65.51%) C. hold
Jacqui Lait, C. 22,183
Liam Curran, Lab. 13,782
Jef Foulger, LD 10,862
James Cartwright, UKIP 1,301
Roderick Reed, Ind. 836
C. maj. 8,401 (17.16%)
3.14% swing Lab. to C.
(2001: C. maj. 4,959 (10.88%))

BEDFORD
E. 70,629 T. 42,072 (59.57%) Lab. hold
Patrick Hall, Lab. 17,557
Richard Fuller, C. 14,174
Michael Headley, LD 9,063
Peter Conquest, UKIP 995
John McCready, Ind. 283
Lab. maj. 3,383 (8.04%)
3.57% swing Lab. to C.
(2001: Lab. maj. 6,157 (15.17%))

BEDFORDSHIRE MID
E. 73,768 T. 50,420 (68.35%) C. hold
*Nadine Dorries, C. 23,345
Mark Chapman, LD 11,990
Martin Lindsay, Lab. 11,351
Richard Joselyn, UKIP 1,372
Ben Foley, Green 1,292
Howard Martin, Veritas 769
Saqhib Ali, Ind. 301
C. maj. 11,355 (22.52%)
2.55% swing C. to LD
(2001: C. maj. 8,066 (17.29%))

BEDFORDSHIRE NORTH EAST
E. 72,757 T. 49,505 (68.04%) C. hold
Alistair Burt, C. 24,725
Keith White, Lab. 12,474
Stephen Rutherford, LD 10,320
James May, UKIP 1,986
C. maj. 12,251 (24.75%)
2.9% swing Lab. to C.
(2001: C. maj. 8,577 (18.96%))

BEDFORDSHIRE SOUTH WEST
E. 74,096 T. 45,814 (61.83%) C. hold
Andrew Selous, C. 22,114
Joyce Still, Lab. 13,837
Andy Strange, LD 7,723
Tom Wise, UKIP 1,923
Kenson Gurney, Forum 217
C. maj. 8,277 (18.07%)
8.15% swing Lab. to C.
(2001: C. maj. 776 (1.77%))

BERWICK-UPON-TWEED
E. 56,944 T. 36,090 (63.38%) LD hold
Rt. Hon. Alan Beith, LD 19,052
Mike Elliott, C. 10,420
Glen Reynolds, Lab. 6,618
LD maj. 8,632 (23.92%)
0.31% swing C. to LD
(2001: LD maj. 8,458 (23.30%))

BETHNAL GREEN & BOW
E. 85,950 T. 44,007 (51.20%) Respect gain
†‡George Galloway, Respect 15,801
Oona King, Lab. 14,978
Shahagir Bakth Faruk, C. 6,244
Syed Nurul Islam Dulu, LD 4,928
John Foster, Green 1,950
Ejiro Etefia, AFC 68
Celia Pugh, CL 38
Respect maj. 823 (1.87%)
26.20% swing Lab. to Respect
(2001: Lab. maj. 10,057 (26.14%))

BEVERLEY & HOLDERNESS
E. 77,460 T. 50,202 (64.81%) C. hold
*Graham Stuart, C. 20,434
George McManus, Lab. 17,854
Brian Willie, LD 9,578
Oliver Marriott, UKIP 2,336
C. maj. 2,580 (5.14%)
1.73% swing Lab. to C.
(2001: C. maj. 781 (1.68%))

BEXHILL & BATTLE
E. 69,676 T. 46,834 (67.22%) C. hold
Greg Barker, C. 24,629
Mary Varrall, LD 11,180
Michael Jones, Lab. 8,457
Anthony Smith, UKIP 2,568
C. maj. 13,449 (28.72%)
2.63% swing LD to C.
(2001: C. maj. 10,503 (23.45%))

BEXLEYHEATH & CRAYFORD
E. 65,025 T. 42,580 (65.48%) C. gain
†David Evennett, C. 19,722
Nigel Beard, Lab. 15,171
David Raval, LD 5,144
John Dunford, UKIP 1,302
Jay Lee, BNP 1,241
C. maj. 4,551 (10.69%)
7.17% swing Lab. to C.
(2001: Lab. maj. 1,472 (3.65%))

BILLERICAY
E. 79,537 T. 48,858 (61.43%) C. hold
John Baron, C. 25,487
Anneliese Dodds, Lab. 14,281
Mike Hibbs, LD 6,471
Bryn Robinson, BNP 1,435
Seantino Callaghan, UKIP 1,184
C. maj. 11,206 (22.94%)
5.97% swing Lab. to C.
(2001: C. maj. 5,013 (10.99%))

BIRKENHEAD
E. 57,097 T. 27,786 (48.66%) Lab. hold
Rt. Hon. Frank Field, Lab. 18,059
Stuart Kelly, LD 5,125
Howard Morton, C. 4,602
Lab. maj. 12,934 (46.55%)
5.54% swing Lab. to LD
(2001: Lab. maj. 15,591 (53.82%))

BIRMINGHAM EDGBASTON
E. 64,893 T. 37,631 (57.99%) Lab. hold
Gisela Stuart, Lab. 16,465
Deirdre Alden, C. 14,116
Mike Dixon, LD 5,185
Peter Beck, Green 1,116
Stephen White, UKIP 749
Lab. maj. 2,349 (6.24%)
3.10% swing Lab. to C.
(2001: Lab. maj. 4,698 (12.45%))

BIRMINGHAM ERDINGTON
E. 64,951 T. 31,746 (48.88%) Lab. hold
Sion Simon, Lab. 16,810
Victoria Elvidge, C. 7,235
Jerry Evans, LD 5,027
Sharon Ebanks, BNP 1,512
Rannal Hepburn, UKIP 746
Terry Williams, NF 416
Lab. maj. 9,575 (30.16%)
1.20% swing Lab. to C.
(2001: Lab. maj. 9,962 (32.55%))

BIRMINGHAM HALL GREEN
E. 57,222 T. 34,536 (60.35%) Lab. hold
Stephen McCabe, Lab. 16,304
Eddie Hughes, C. 10,590
Roger Harmer, LD 6,682
David Melhuish, UKIP 960
Lab. maj. 5,714 (16.55%)
1.77% swing Lab. to C.
(2001: Lab. maj. 6,648 (20.09%))

BIRMINGHAM HODGE HILL
E. 53,903 T. 28,417 (52.72%) Lab. hold
Liam Byrne, Lab. 13,822
Nicola Davies, LD 8,373
Deborah Thomas, C. 3,768
Denis Adams, BNP 1,445
Adrian Duffen, UKIP 680
Azmat Begg, Progress 329
Lab. maj. 5,449 (19.18%)
18.29% swing Lab. to LD
(2004 July by-election: Lab. maj. 460 (2.25%))
(2001: Lab. maj. 11,618 (43.90%))

BIRMINGHAM LADYWOOD
E. 70,977 T. 33,246 (46.84%) Lab. hold
Rt. Hon. Clare Short, Lab. 17,262
Ayoub Khan, LD 10,461
Philippa Stroud, C. 3,515
Lynette Nazemi-Afshar, UKIP 2,008
Lab. maj. 6,801 (20.46%)
20.11% swing Lab. to LD
(2001: Lab. maj. 18,143 (57.61%))

BIRMINGHAM NORTHFIELD
E. 54,868 T. 31,056 (56.60%) Lab. hold
Richard Burden, Lab. 15,419
Vicky Ford, C. 8,965
Trevor Sword, LD 4,171
Mark Cattell, BNP 1,278
Gillian Chant, UKIP 641
Richard Rodgers, Good 428
Louise Houldey, Soc. Alt. 120
Francis Sweeney, WRP 34
Lab. maj. 6,454 (20.78%)
2.81% swing Lab. to C.
(2001: Lab. maj. 7,798 (26.40%))

BIRMINGHAM PERRY BARR
E. 70,126 T. 38,911 (55.49%) Lab. hold
Khalid Mahmood, Lab. 18,269
Jon Hunt, LD 10,321
Naweed Khan, C. 6,513
Dr Mohammad Naseem, Respect 2,173
Rajinder Clair, Soc. Lab. 890
Bimla Balu, UKIP 745
Lab. maj. 7,948 (20.43%)
1.61% swing Lab. to LD
(2001: Lab. maj. 8,753 (23.39%))

BIRMINGHAM SELLY OAK
E. 70,162 T. 41,740 (59.49%) Lab. hold
Dr Lynne Jones, Lab. 19,226
Joe Tildesley, C. 10,375
Richard Brighton, LD 9,591
Barney Smith, Green 1,581
Ronan Burnett, UKIP 967
Lab. maj. 8,851 (21.21%)
2.29% swing Lab. to C.
(2001: Lab. maj. 10,339 (25.78%))

BIRMINGHAM SPARKBROOK & SMALL HEATH
E. 73,721 T. 38,192 (51.81%) Lab. hold
Roger Godsiff, Lab. 13,787
Salma Yaqoob, Respect 10,498
Talib Hussain, LD 7,727
Sameer Mirza, C. 3,480
Jennifer Brookes, UKIP 1,342
Ian Jamieson, Green 855
Abdul Chaudhary, Ind. 503
Lab. maj. 3,289 (8.61%)
24.4% swing Lab. to Respect
(2001: Lab. maj. 16,246 (44.33%))

BIRMINGHAM YARDLEY
E. 50,975 T. 29,431 (57.74%) LD gain
*John Hemming, LD 13,648
Jayne Innes, Lab. 10,976
Paul Uppal, C. 2,970
Robert Purcell, BNP 1,523
Mohammed Yaqub, UKIP 314
LD maj. 2,672 (9.08%)
8.83% swing Lab. to LD
(2001: Lab. maj. 2,578 (8.59%))

BISHOP AUCKLAND
E. 67,534 T. 38,128 (56.46%) Lab. hold
*Helen Goodman, Lab. 19,065
Chris Foote-Wood, LD 9,018
Richard Bell, C. 8,736
Margaret Hopson, UKIP 1,309
Lab. maj. 10,047 (26.35%)
8.36% swing Lab. to LD
(2001: Lab. maj. 13,926 (36.12%))

BLABY
E. 75,444 T. 49,388 (65.46%) C. hold
Andrew Robathan, C. 22,487
David Morgan, Lab. 14,614
Jeff Stephenson, LD 9,382
Michael Robinson, BNP 1,704
Delroy Young, UKIP 1,201
C. maj. 7,873 (15.94%)
1.45% swing Lab. to C.
(2001: C. maj. 6,209 (13.03%))

BLACKBURN
E. 73,494 T. 41,805 (56.88%) Lab. hold
Rt. Hon. Jack Straw, Lab. 17,562
Imtiaz Ameen, C. 9,553
Tony Melia, LD 8,608
Nicholas Holt, BNP 2,263
Craig Murray, Ind. 2,082
Dorothy Baxter, UKIP 954
Graham Carter, Green 783
Lab. maj. 8,009 (19.16%)
1.90% swing Lab. to C.
(2001: Lab. maj. 9,249 (22.85%))

BLACKPOOL NORTH & FLEETWOOD
E. 74,975 T. 43,290 (57.74%) Lab. hold
Joan Humble, Lab. 20,620
Gavin Williamson, C. 15,558
Steven Bate, LD 5,533
Roy Hopwood, UKIP 1,579
Lab. maj. 5,062 (11.69%)
0.87% swing Lab. to C.
(2001: Lab. maj. 5,721 (13.44%))

BLACKPOOL SOUTH
E. 73,529 T. 38,342 (52.15%) Lab. hold
Gordon Marsden, Lab. 19,375
Michael Winstanley, C. 11,453
Doreen Holt, LD 5,552
Roy Goodwin, BNP 1,113
John Porter, UKIP 849
Lab. maj. 7,922 (20.66%)
0.32% swing Lab. to C.
(2001: Lab. maj. 8,262 (21.30%))

BLAYDON
E. 62,413 T. 39,053 (62.57%) Lab. hold
*David Anderson, Lab. 20,120
Peter Maughan, LD 14,785
Dorothy Luckhurst, C. 3,129
Norman Endacott, UKIP 1,019
Lab. maj. 5,335 (13.66%)
3.70% swing Lab. to LD
(2001: Lab. maj. 7,809 (21.06%))

BLYTH VALLEY
E. 63,640 T. 35,773 (56.21%) Lab. hold
Ronnie Campbell, Lab. 19,659
Jeffrey Reid, LD 11,132
Michael Windridge, C. 4,982
Lab. maj. 8,527 (23.84%)
5.72% swing Lab. to LD
(2001: Lab. maj. 12,188 (35.28%))

BOGNOR REGIS & LITTLEHAMPTON
E. 65,591 T. 40,747 (62.12%) C. hold
Nick Gibb, C. 18,183
George O'Neill, Lab. 10,361
Simon McDougall, LD 8,927
Adrian Lithgow, UKIP 3,276
C. maj. 7,822 (19.20%)
2.36% swing Lab. to C.
(2001: C. maj. 5,643 (14.48%))

BOLSOVER
E. 67,568 T. 38,699 (57.27%) Lab. hold
Dennis Skinner, Lab. 25,217
Denise Hawksworth, LD 6,780
Hasan Imam, C. 6,702
Lab. maj. 18,437 (47.64%)
4.53% swing Lab. to LD
(2001: Lab. maj. 18,777 (49.06%))

BOLTON NORTH EAST
E. 67,394 T. 36,911 (54.77%) Lab. hold
David Crausby, Lab. 16,874
Paul Brierley, C. 12,771
Adam Killeya, LD 6,044
Kevin Epsom, UKIP 640
Alan Ainscow, Veritas 375
Lynne Lowe, Soc. Lab. 207
Lab. maj. 4,103 (11.12%)
5.25% swing Lab. to C.
(2001: Lab. maj. 8,422 (21.62%))

BOLTON SOUTH EAST
E. 63,697 T. 31,850 (50.00%) Lab. hold
Dr Brian Iddon, Lab. 18,129
Deborah Dunleavy, C. 6,491
Frank Harasiwka, LD 6,047
Florence Bates, UKIP 840
David Jones, Veritas 343
Lab. maj. 11,638 (36.54%)
0.57% swing Lab. to C.
(2001: Lab. maj. 12,871 (37.69%))

BOLTON WEST
E. 63,836 T. 40,543 (63.51%) Lab. hold
Rt. Hon. Ruth Kelly, Lab. 17,239
Philip Allott, C. 15,175
Tim Perkins, LD 7,241
Marjorie Ford, UKIP 524
Michael Ford, Veritas 290
Kate Griggs, XPP 74
Lab. maj. 2,064 (5.09%)
4.15% swing Lab. to C.
(2001: Lab. maj. 5,518 (13.39%))

BOOTLE
E. 53,700 T. 25,622 (47.71%) Lab. hold
Joe Benton, Lab. 19,345
Chris Newby, LD 2,988
Wafik Moustafa, C. 1,580
Paul Nuttall, UKIP 1,054
Peter Glover, Soc. Alt. 655
Lab. maj. 16,357 (63.84%)
2.59% swing Lab. to LD
(2001: Lab. maj. 19,043 (69.01%))

BOSTON & SKEGNESS
E. 71,212 T. 41,869 (58.79%) C. hold
Mark Simmonds, C. 19,329
Paul Kenny, Lab. 13,422
Dr Richard Horsnell, UKIP 4,024
Alan Riley, LD 3,649
Wendy Russell, BNP 1,025
Marcus Petz, Green 420
C. maj. 5,907 (14.11%)
6.42% swing Lab. to C.
(2001: C. maj. 515 (1.28%))

BOSWORTH
E. 71,596 T. 47,499 (66.34%) C. hold
David Tredinnick, C. 20,212
Rupert Herd, Lab. 14,893
James Moore, LD 10,528
Denis Walker, UKIP 1,866
C. maj. 5,319 (11.20%)
3.07% swing Lab. to C.
(2001: C. maj. 2,280 (5.05%))

BOURNEMOUTH EAST
E. 63,426 T. 37,599 (59.28%) C. hold
*Tobias Ellwood, C. 16,925
Andrew Garratt, LD 11,681
David Stokes, Lab. 7,191
Thomas Collier, UKIP 1,802
C. maj. 5,244 (13.95%)
2.18% swing LD to C.
(2001: C. maj. 3,434 (9.59%))

BOURNEMOUTH WEST
E. 63,658 T. 33,924 (53.29%) C. hold
Sir John Butterfill, C. 14,057
Richard Renaut, LD 10,026
Dafydd Williams, Lab. 7,824
Michael Maclaire-Hillier, UKIP 2,017
C. maj. 4,031 (11.88%)
2.90% swing C. to LD
(2001: C. maj. 4,718 (14.02%))

BRACKNELL
E. 80,657 T. 51,141 (63.41%) C. hold
Rt. Hon. Andrew Mackay, C. 25,412
Janet Keene, Lab. 13,376
Lee Glendon, LD 10,128
Vincent Pearson, UKIP 1,818
Dominica Roberts, Ind. 407
C. maj. 12,036 (23.53%)
4.95% swing Lab. to C.
(2001: C. maj. 6,713 (13.64%))

BRADFORD NORTH
E. 64,515 T. 34,397 (53.32%) Lab. hold
Terry Rooney, Lab. 14,622
David Ward, LD 11,111
Teck Khong, C. 5,569
Lynda Cromie, BNP 2,061
Steve Schofield, Green 560
Umit Yildiz, Respect 474
Lab. maj. 3,511 (10.21%)
9.88% swing Lab. to LD
(2001: Lab. maj. 8,969 (25.61%))

BRADFORD SOUTH
E. 67,576 T. 36,605 (54.17%) Lab. hold
Gerry Sutcliffe, Lab. 17,954
Geraldine Carter, C. 8,787
Mike Doyle, LD 5,334
Dr James Lewthwaite, BNP 2,862
Derek Curtis, Green 695
Jason Smith, UKIP 552
Therese Muchewicz, Veritas 421
Lab. maj. 9,167 (25.04%)
1.23% swing Lab. to C.
(2001: Lab. maj. 9,662 (27.50%))

BRADFORD WEST
E. 67,356 T. 36,369 (54.00%) Lab. hold
Marsha Singh, Lab. 14,570
Haroon Rashid, C. 11,544
Mukhtar Ali, LD 6,620
Paul Cromie, BNP 2,525
Parvez Darr, Green 1,110
Lab. maj. 3,026 (8.32%)
1.27% swing Lab. to C.
(2001: Lab. maj. 4,165 (10.85%))

BRAINTREE
E. 80,458 T. 53,055 (65.94%) C. gain
*Brooks Newmark, C. 23,597
Alan Hurst, Lab. 19,704
Peter Turner, LD 7,037
James Abbott, Green 1,308
Roger Lord, UKIP 1,181
Buster Michael Nolan, Ind. 228
C. maj. 3,893 (7.34%)
4.02% swing Lab. to C.
(2001: Lab. maj. 358 (0.71%))

BRENT EAST
E. 56,227 T. 31,068 (55.25%) LD hold
Sarah Teather, LD 14,764
Yasmin Qureshi, Lab. 12,052
Kwasi Kwarteng, C. 3,193
Shahrar Ali, Green 905
Michelle Weininger, Ind. 115
Rainbow George Weiss, Vote Dream 39
LD maj. 2,712 (8.73%)
30.68% swing Lab. to LD
(2003 Sept. by-election: LD maj. 1,118 (5.36%))
(2001: Lab. maj. 13,047 (45.00%))

BRENT NORTH
E. 60,148 T. 35,682 (59.32%) Lab. hold
Barry Gardiner, Lab. 17,420
Bob Blackman, C. 11,779
Havard Hughes, LD 5,672
Babar Ahmad, Progress 685
Rainbow George Weiss, Vote Dream 126
Lab. maj. 5,641 (15.81%)
7.13% swing Lab. to C.
(2001: Lab. maj. 10,205 (30.07%))

BRENT SOUTH
E. 56,508 T. 29,764 (52.67%) Lab. hold
*Dawn Butler, Lab. 17,501
James Allie, LD 6,175
Rishi Saha, C. 4,485
Rowan Langley, Green 957
Shaun Wallace, Ind. 297
Rocky Fernandez, Ind. 288
Rainbow George Weiss, Vote Dream 61
Lab. maj. 11,326 (38.05%)
12.20% swing Lab. to LD
(2001: Lab. maj. 17,380 (60.69%))

BRENTFORD & ISLEWORTH
E. 84,366 T. 46,017 (54.54%) Lab. hold
Ann Keen, Lab. 18,329
Alexander Northcote, C. 13,918
Andrew Dakers, LD 10,477
John Hunt, Green 1,652
Phillip Andrews, Community 1,118
Michael Stoneman, NF 523
Lab. maj. 4,411 (9.59%)
6.80% swing Lab. to C.
(2001: Lab. maj. 10,318 (23.18%))

BRENTWOOD & ONGAR
E. 64,496 T. 44,145 (68.45%) C. hold
Eric Pickles, C. 23,609
Gavin Stollar, LD 11,997
John Adams, Lab. 6,579
Stuart Gulleford, UKIP 1,805
Anthony Appleton, Ind. 155
C. maj. 11,612 (26.30%)
1.91% swing LD to C.
(2001: C. maj. 2,821 (6.48%))

BRIDGWATER
E. 75,790 T. 48,109 (63.48%) C. hold
Ian Liddell-Grainger, C. 21,240
Matthew Burchell, Lab. 12,771
James Main, LD 10,940
Ray Weinstein, UKIP 1,767
Charlie Graham, Green 1,391
C. maj. 8,469 (17.60%)
1.96% swing Lab. to C.
(2001: C. maj. 4,987 (10.42%))

BRIGG & GOOLE
E. 67,364 T. 42,578 (63.21%) Lab. hold
Ian Cawsey, Lab. 19,257
Matthew Bean, C. 16,363
Gary Johnson, LD 5,690
Stephen Martin, UKIP 1,268
Lab. maj. 2,894 (6.80%)
1.43% swing Lab. to C.
(2001: Lab. maj. 3,961 (9.65%))

BRIGHTON KEMPTOWN
E. 65,985 T. 39,719 (60.19%) Lab. hold
Dr Desmond Turner, Lab. 15,858
Judith Symes, C. 13,121
Marina Pepper, LD 6,560
Simon Williams, Green 2,800
Dr James Chamberlain-Webber, UKIP 758
Caroline O'Reilly, PPN-V 172
John McLeod, Soc. Lab. 163
Elaine Cook, Ind. 127
Phil Clarke, Soc. Alt. 113
Gene Dobbs, Ind. 47
Lab. maj. 2,737 (6.89%)
2.83% swing Lab. to C.
(2001: Lab. maj. 4,922 (12.56%))

BRIGHTON PAVILION
E. 68,087 T. 43,578 (64.00%) Lab. (Co-op) hold
David Lepper, Lab. (Co-op) 15,427
Mike Weatherley, C. 10,397
Keith Taylor, Green 9,571
Hazel Thorpe, LD 7,171
Kimberley Crisp-Comotto, UKIP 508
Tony Greenstein, Green Soc. 188
Ian Fyvie, Soc. Lab. 152
Christopher Rooke, Ind. 122
Keith Jago, Ind. 42
Lab. (Co-op) maj. 5,030 (11.55%)
6.06% swing Lab. (Co-op) to C.
(2001: Lab. (Co-op) maj. 9,643 (23.68%))

BRISTOL EAST
E. 68,096 T. 41,720 (61.27%) Lab. hold
*Kerry McCarthy, Lab. 19,152
Philip James, LD 10,531
Julia Manning, C. 8,787
Arjuna Krishna-Das, Green 1,586
Jean Smith, UKIP 1,132
Paulette North, Respect 532
Lab. maj. 8,621 (20.66%)
8.59% swing Lab. to LD
(2001: Lab. maj. 13,392 (33.20%))

BRISTOL NORTH WEST
E. 77,703 T. 47,492 (61.12%) Lab. (Co-op) hold
Dr Doug Naysmith, Lab. (Co-op) 22,192
Alastair Watson, C. 13,230
Bob Hoyle, LD 9,545
Christopher Lees, UKIP 1,132
Michael Blundell, EDP 828
Graeme Jones, Soc. Alt. 565
Lab. (Co-op) maj. 8,962 (18.87%)
2.28% swing Lab. (Co-op) to C.
(2001: Lab. (Co-op) maj. 11,087 (23.74%))

BRISTOL SOUTH
E. 70,835 T. 42,328 (59.76%) Lab. hold
Rt. Hon. Dawn Primarolo, Lab. 20,778
Kay Barnard, LD 9,636
Graham Hill, C. 8,466
Charlie Bolton, Green 2,127
Mark Dent, UKIP 1,321
Lab. maj. 11,142 (26.32%)
7.86% swing Lab. to LD
(2001: Lab. maj. 14,181 (34.61%))

BRISTOL WEST
E. 81,382 T. 57,396 (70.53%) LD gain
*Stephen Williams, LD 21,987
Valerie Davey, Lab. 16,859
David Martin, C. 15,429
Justin Quinnell, Green 2,163
Simon Muir, UKIP 439
Bernard Kennedy, Soc. Lab. 329
Doug Reid, Baths 190
LD maj. 5,128 (8.93%)
8.44% swing Lab. to LD
(2001: Lab. maj. 4,426 (7.95%))

BROMLEY & CHISLEHURST
E. 71,173 T. 46,137 (64.82%) C. hold
Rt. Hon. Eric Forth, C. 23,583
Rachel Reeves, Lab. 10,241
Peter Brooks, LD 9,368
David Hooper, UKIP 1,475
Ann Garrett, Green 1,470
C. maj. 13,342 (28.92%)
4.01% swing Lab. to C.
(2001: C. maj. 9,037 (20.90%))

BROMSGROVE
E. 70,762 T. 47,810 (67.56%) C. hold
Julie Kirkbride, C. 24,387
David Jones, Lab. 14,307
Sue Haswell, LD 7,197
Paul Buckingham, UKIP 1,919
C. maj. 10,080 (21.08%)
1.63% swing Lab. to C.
(2001: C. maj. 8,138 (17.81%))

BROXBOURNE
E. 68,106 T. 40,628 (59.65%) C. hold
*Charles Walker, C. 21,878
Jamie Bolden, Lab. 10,369
Andrew Porrer, LD 4,973
Dr Andrew Emerson, BNP 1,929
Martin Harvey, UKIP 1,479
C. maj. 11,509 (28.33%)
2.28% swing Lab. to C.
(2001: C. maj. 8,993 (23.76%))

BROXTOWE
E. 71,121 T. 48,806 (68.62%) Lab. hold
Dr Nick Palmer, Lab. 20,457
Bob Seely, C. 18,161
David Watts, LD 7,837
Paul Anderson, Green 896
Patricia Wolfe, UKIP 695
Damian Hockney, Veritas 590
Mark Gregory, Ind. 170
Lab. maj. 2,296 (4.70%)
3.64% swing Lab. to C.
(2001: Lab. maj. 5,873 (11.98%))

BUCKINGHAM
E. 70,265 T. 48,307 (68.75%) C. hold
John Bercow, C. 27,748
David Greene, Lab. 9,619
Luke Croydon, LD 9,508
David Williams, UKIP 1,432
C. maj. 18,129 (37.53%)
4.05% swing Lab. to C.
(2001: C. maj. 13,325 (29.43%))

BURNLEY
E. 65,869 T. 38,983 (59.18%) Lab. hold
*Kitty Ussher, Lab. 14,999
Gordon Birtwistle, LD 9,221
Harry Brooks, Burnley 5,786
Yousuf Miah, C. 4,206
Len Starr, BNP 4,003
Dr Jeff Slater, Ind. 392
Robert McDowell, UKIP 376
Lab. maj. 5,778 (14.82%)
9.15% swing Lab. to LD
(2001: Lab. maj. 10,498 (28.46%))

BURTON
E. 78,556 T. 47,882 (60.95%) Lab. hold
Janet Dean, Lab. 19,701
Adrian Pepper, C. 18,280
Sandra Johnson, LD 6,236
Julie Russell, BNP 1,840
Philip Lancaster, UKIP 913
Brian Buxton, Veritas 912
Lab. maj. 1,421 (2.97%)
3.73% swing Lab. to C.
(2001: Lab. maj. 4,849 (10.44%))

BURY NORTH
E. 72,268 T. 44,439 (61.49%) Lab. hold
David Chaytor, Lab. 19,130
David Nuttall, C. 16,204
Wilf Davison, LD 6,514
Stewart Clough, BNP 1,790
Philip Silver, UKIP 476
Ryan O'Neill, Soc. Lab. 172
Ian Upton, Veritas 153
Lab. maj. 2,926 (6.58%)
4.00% swing Lab. to C.
(2001: Lab. maj. 6,532 (14.58%))

BURY SOUTH
E. 66,898 T. 39,154 (58.53%) Lab. hold
Ivan Lewis, Lab. 19,741
Alex Williams, C. 10,829
Victor D'Albert, LD 6,968
Jim Greenhalgh, UKIP 1,059
Yvonne Hossack, Ind. 557
Lab. maj. 8,912 (22.76%)
4.77% swing Lab. to C.
(2001: Lab. maj. 12,772 (32.30%))

BURY ST EDMUNDS
E. 79,658 T. 52,619 (66.06%) C. hold
David Ruffley, C. 24,332
David Monaghan, Lab. 14,402
David Chappell, LD 10,423
Dr John Howlett, UKIP 1,859
Graham Manning, Green 1,603
C. maj. 9,930 (18.87%)
6.95% swing Lab. to C.
(2001: C. maj. 2,503 (4.98%))

CALDER VALLEY
E. 71,325 T. 47,770 (66.98%) Lab. hold
Christine McCafferty, Lab. 18,426
Liz Truss, C. 17,059
Liz Ingleton, LD 9,027
John Gregory, BNP 1,887
Paul Palmer, Green 1,371
Lab. maj. 1,367 (2.86%)
1.83% swing Lab. to C.
(2001: Lab. maj. 3,094 (6.52%))

CAMBERWELL & PECKHAM
E. 55,739 T. 28,991 (52.01%) Lab. hold
Rt. Hon. Harriet Harman, Lab. 18,933
Richard Porter, LD 5,450
Jessica Lee, C. 2,841
Paul Ingram, Green 1,172
Derek Penhallow, UKIP 350
Margaret Sharkey, Soc. Lab. 132
Sanjay Kulkarni, WRP 113
Lab. maj. 13,483 (46.51%)
4.88% swing Lab. to LD
(2001: Lab. maj. 14,123 (56.26%))

CAMBRIDGE
E. 70,154 T. 43,569 (62.10%) LD gain
*David Howarth, LD 19,152
Anne Campbell, Lab. 14,813
Ian Lyon, C. 7,193
Martin Lucas-Smith, Green 1,245
Helene Davies, UKIP 569
Tom Woodcock, Respect 477
Suzon Forscey-Moore, Ind. 60
Graham Wilkinson, Ind. 60
LD maj. 4,339 (9.96%)
14.99% swing Lab. to LD
(2001: Lab. maj. 8,579 (20.03%))

CAMBRIDGESHIRE NORTH EAST
E. 85,079 T. 50,877 (59.80%) C. hold
Malcolm Moss, C. 24,181
Ffinlo Costain, Lab. 15,280
Alan Dean, LD 8,693
Leonard Baynes, UKIP 2,723
C. maj. 8,901 (17.50%)
2.12% swing Lab. to C.
(2001: C. maj. 6,373 (13.26%))

CAMBRIDGESHIRE NORTH WEST
E. 79,694 T. 49,092 (61.60%) C. hold
*Shailesh Vara, C. 22,504
Ayfer Orhan, Lab. 12,671
John Souter, LD 11,232
Robert Brown, UKIP 2,685
C. maj. 9,833 (20.03%)
0.80% swing Lab. to C.
(2001: C. maj. 8,101 (18.43%))

AMBRIDGESHIRE SOUTH
77,022 T. 52,648 (68.35%) C. hold
ndrew Lansley, C. 23,676
ndrew Dickson, LD 15,675
ndra Wilson, Lab. 10,189
obin Page, UKIP 1,556
mon Saggers, Green 1,552
. maj. 8,001 (15.20%)
09% swing C. to LD
001: C. maj. 8,403 (17.38%))

AMBRIDGESHIRE SOUTH EAST
85,901 T. 56,060 (65.26%) C. hold
mes Paice, C. 26,374
nathan Chatfield, LD 17,750
ona Ross, Lab. 11,936
. maj. 8,624 (15.38%)
97% swing C. to LD
001: C. maj. 8,990 (17.33%))

ANNOCK CHASE
75,194 T. 43,155 (57.39%) Lab. hold
r Tony Wright, Lab. 22,139
n Collard, C. 12,912
nny Pinkett, LD 5,934
oy Jenkins, UKIP 2,170
ab. maj. 9,227 (21.38%)
34% swing Lab. to C.
001: Lab. maj. 10,704 (26.07%))

ANTERBURY
. 72,046 T. 47,587 (66.05%) C. hold
lian Brazier, C. 21,113
lex Hilton, Lab. 13,642
nny Barnard-Langston, LD 10,059
eoff Meaden, Green 1,521
hn Moore, UKIP 926
ocky van de Benderskum, LCA 326
. maj. 7,471 (15.70%)
.56% swing Lab. to C.
001: C. maj. 2,069 (4.58%))

ARLISLE
. 59,508 T. 35,394 (59.48%) Lab. hold
ric Martlew, Lab. 17,019
like Mitchelson, C. 11,324
teven Tweedie, LD 5,916
teven Cochrane, UKIP 792
ezley Gibson, LCA 343
ab. maj. 5,695 (16.09%)
.12% swing Lab. to C.
001: Lab. maj. 5,702 (16.33%))

ARSHALTON & WALLINGTON
. 67,844 T. 43,061 (63.47%) LD hold
om Brake, LD 17,357
en Andrew, C. 16,289
ndrew Theobald, Lab. 7,396
rancis Day, UKIP 1,111
ob Steel, Green 908
D maj. 1,068 (2.48%)
.36% swing LD to C.
001: LD maj. 4,547 (11.20%))

ASTLE POINT
. 69,480 T. 45,802 (65.92%) C. hold
r Robert Spink, C. 22,118
uke Akehurst, Lab. 13,917
mes Sandbach, LD 4,719
eil Hamper, UKIP 3,431
ene Willis, Green 1,617
. maj. 8,201 (17.91%)
.71% swing Lab. to C.
001: C. maj. 985 (2.48%))

CHARNWOOD
E. 76,274 T. 50,616 (66.36%) C. hold
Rt. Hon. Stephen Dorrell, C. 23,571
Richard Robinson, Lab. 14,762
Sue King, LD 9,057
Andrew Holders, BNP 1,737
Jamie Bye, UKIP 1,489
C. maj. 8,809 (17.40%)
0.68% swing Lab. to C.
(2001: C. maj. 7,739 (16.03%))

CHATHAM & AYLESFORD
E. 70,515 T. 42,080 (59.68%) Lab. hold
Jonathan Shaw, Lab. 18,387
Anne Jobson, C. 16,055
Debra Enever, LD 5,744
Jeffrey King, UKIP 1,226
Michael Russell, Eng. Dem. 668
Lab. maj. 2,332 (5.54%)
2.69% swing Lab. to C.
(2001: Lab. maj. 4,340 (10.92%))

CHEADLE
E. 68,123 T. 47,437 (69.63%) LD hold
Patsy Calton, LD 23,189
Stephen Day, C. 19,169
Martin Miller, Lab. 4,169
Vincent Cavanagh, UKIP 489
Richard Chadfield, BNP 421
LD maj. 4,020 (8.47%)
4.20% swing C. to LD
(2001: LD maj. 33 (0.08%))

CHELMSFORD WEST
E. 82,489 T. 51,052 (61.89%) C. hold
Simon Burns, C. 22,946
Stephen Robinson, LD 13,326
Russell Kennedy, Lab. 13,236
Kenneth Wedon, UKIP 1,544
C. maj. 9,620 (18.84%)
0.18% swing C. to LD
(2001: C. maj. 6,261 (13.01%))

CHELTENHAM
E. 71,541 T. 43,621 (60.97%) LD hold
*Martin Horwood, LD 18,122
Dr Vanessa Gearson, C. 15,819
Christopher Evans, Lab. 4,988
Dr Robert Hodges, Ind. 2,651
Keith Bessant, Green 908
Niall Warry, UKIP 608
Dancing Ken Hanks, Loony 525
LD maj. 2,303 (5.28%)
3.64% swing LD to C.
(2001: LD maj. 5,255 (12.56%))

CHESHAM & AMERSHAM
E. 69,217 T. 47,097 (68.04%) C. hold
Cheryl Gillan, C. 25,619
John Ford, LD 11,821
Rupa Huq, Lab. 6,610
Nick Wilkins, Green 1,656
David Samuel-Camps, UKIP 1,391
C. maj. 13,798 (29.30%)
1.53% swing LD to C.
(2001: C. maj. 11,882 (26.24%))

CHESTER, CITY OF
E. 69,785 T. 44,903 (64.34%) Lab. hold
Christine Russell, Lab. 17,458
Paul Offer, C. 16,543
Mia Jones, LD 9,818
Allan Weddell, UKIP 776
Ed Abrams, Eng. Dem. 308
Lab. maj. 915 (2.04%)
6.66% swing Lab. to C.
(2001: Lab. maj. 6,894 (15.36%))

CHESTERFIELD
E. 74,007 T. 44,121 (59.62%) LD hold
Paul Holmes, LD 20,875
Simon Rich, Lab. 17,830
Mark Kreling, C. 3,605
Christopher Brady, UKIP 997
Ian Jerram, Eng. Dem. 814
LD maj. 3,045 (6.90%)
0.54% swing Lab. to LD
(2001: LD maj. 2,586 (5.82%))

CHICHESTER
E. 78,645 T. 52,401 (66.63%) C. hold
Andrew Tyrie, C. 25,302
Alan Hilliar, LD 14,442
Jonathan Austin, Lab. 9,632
Douglas Denny, UKIP 3,025
C. maj. 10,860 (20.72%)
1.09% swing C. to LD
(2001: C. maj. 11,355 (22.93%))

CHINGFORD & WOODFORD GREEN
E. 61,386 T. 38,648 (62.96%) C. hold
Rt. Hon. Iain Duncan Smith, C. 20,555
Simon Wright, Lab. 9,914
John Beanse, LD 6,832
Michael McGough, UKIP 1,078
Barry White, Ind. 269
C. maj. 10,641 (27.53%)
6.35% swing Lab. to C.
(2001: C. maj. 5,487 (14.84%))

CHIPPING BARNET
E. 66,143 T. 42,381 (64.07%) C. hold
*Theresa Villiers, C. 19,744
Pauline Coakley-Webb, Lab. 13,784
Sean Hooker, LD 6,671
Audrey Poppy, Green 1,199
Victor Kaye, UKIP 924
Rainbow George Weiss, Vote Dream 59
C. maj. 5,960 (14.06%)
3.85% swing Lab. to C.
(2001: C. maj. 2,701 (6.36%))

CHORLEY
E. 78,838 T. 49,569 (62.87%) Lab. hold
Lindsay Hoyle, Lab. 25,131
Simon Mallett, C. 17,506
Alexander Wilson-Fletcher, LD 6,932
Lab. maj. 7,625 (15.38%)
1.11% swing Lab. to C.
(2001: Lab. maj. 8,444 (17.61%))

CHRISTCHURCH
E. 74,109 T. 51,565 (69.58%) C. hold
Christopher Chope, C. 28,208
Leslie Coman, LD 12,649
Jim King, Lab. 8,051
David Hughes, UKIP 2,657
C. maj. 15,559 (30.17%)
1.42% swing LD to C.
(2001: C. maj. 13,544 (27.32%))

CITIES OF LONDON & WESTMINSTER
E. 72,577 T. 36,487 (50.27%) C. hold
Mark Field, C. 17,260
Hywel Lloyd, Lab. 9,165
Marie-Louise Rossi, LD 7,306
Tristan Smith, Green 1,544
Colin Merton, UKIP 399
Brian Haw, Ind. 298
Jill McLachlan, CPA 246
David Harris, Veritas 218
Cass Jean-Claude Cass-Horne, Ind. 51
C. maj. 8,095 (22.19%)
4.47% swing Lab. to C.
(2001: C. maj. 4,499 (13.24%))

CLEETHORPES
E. 70,746 T. 43,589 (61.61%) Lab. hold
Shona McIsaac, Lab. 18,889
Martin Vickers, C. 16,247
Geoff Lowis, LD 6,437
Bill Hardie, UKIP 2,016
Lab. maj. 2,642 (6.06%)
3.59% swing Lab. to C.
(2001: Lab. maj. 5,620 (13.25%))

COLCHESTER
E. 79,010 T. 44,899 (56.83%) LD hold
Bob Russell, LD 21,145
Kevin Bentley, C. 14,868
Laura Bruni, Lab. 8,886
LD maj. 6,277 (13.98%)
0.64% swing C. to LD
(2001: LD maj. 5,553 (12.70%))

COLNE VALLEY
E. 74,121 T. 48,920 (66.00%) Lab. hold
Kali Mountford, Lab. 17,536
Maggie Throup, C. 16,035
Elisabeth Wilson, LD 11,822
Barry Fowler, BNP 1,430
Lesley Hedges, Green 1,295
Helen Martinek, Veritas 543
Ian Mumford, Loony 259
Lab. maj. 1,501 (3.07%)
3.40% swing Lab. to C.
(2001: Lab. maj. 4,639 (9.87%))

CONGLETON
E. 72,770 T. 46,682 (64.15%) C. hold
Lady Ann Winterton, C. 21,189
Nicholas Milton, Lab. 12,943
Eleanor Key, LD 12,550
C. maj. 8,246 (17.66%)
0.92% swing Lab. to C.
(2001: C. maj. 7,134 (15.82%))

COPELAND
E. 54,206 T. 33,757 (62.28%) Lab. hold
*Jamie Reed, Lab. 17,033
Chris Whiteside, C. 10,713
Frank Hollowell, LD 3,880
Edward Caley-Knowles, UKIP 735
Brian Earley, Ind. 734
Alan Mossop, Eng. Dem. 662
Lab. maj. 6,320 (18.72%)
2.22% swing C. to Lab.
(2001: Lab. maj. 4,964 (14.28%))

CORBY
E. 73,000 T. 48,527 (66.48%) Lab. (Co-op) hold
Phil Hope, Lab. (Co-op) 20,913
Andrew Griffith, C. 19,396
David Radcliffe, LD 6,184
Ian Gillman, UKIP 1,278
Steve Carey, Soc. Lab. 499
John Morris, Ind. 257
Lab. (Co-op) maj. 1,517 (3.13%)
4.47% swing Lab. (Co-op) to C.
(2001: Lab. (Co-op) maj. 5,700 (12.07%))

CORNWALL NORTH
E. 86,841 T. 55,982 (64.46%) LD hold
*Dan Rogerson, LD 23,842
Mark Formosa, C. 20,766
David Acton, Lab. 6,636
David Campbell-Bannerman, UKIP 3,063
Dick Cole, Meb. Ker. 1,351
Alan Eastwood, Veritas 324
LD maj. 3,076 (5.49%)
6.36% swing LD to C.
(2001: LD maj. 9,832 (18.21%))

CORNWALL SOUTH EAST
E. 80,704 T. 53,455 (66.24%) LD hold
Colin Breed, LD 24,986
Ashley Gray, C. 18,479
Colin Binley, Lab. 6,069
David Lucas, UKIP 2,693
Graham Sandercock, Meb. Ker. 769
Anne Assheton-Salton, Veritas 459
LD maj. 6,507 (12.17%)
0.89% swing C. to LD
(2001: LD maj. 5,375 (10.39%))

COTSWOLD
E. 71,039 T. 47,351 (66.65%) C. hold
Geoffrey Clifton-Brown, C. 23,326
Philip Beckerlegge, LD 13,638
Mark Dempsey, Lab. 8,457
Richard Buckley, UKIP 1,538
James Derieg, Ind. 392
C. maj. 9,688 (20.46%)
2.80% swing C. to LD
(2001: C. maj. 11,983 (26.06%))

COVENTRY NORTH EAST
E. 70,225 T. 37,195 (52.97%) Lab. hold
Rt. Hon. Robert Ainsworth, Lab. 21,178
Jaswant Singh Birdi, C. 6,956
Russell Field, LD 6,123
Dave Nellist, Soc. Alt. 1,874
Paul Sootheran, UKIP 1,064
Lab. maj. 14,222 (38.24%)
2.02% swing Lab. to C.
(2001: Lab. maj. 15,751 (42.27%))

COVENTRY NORTH WEST
E. 73,180 T. 43,438 (59.36%) Lab. hold
Geoffrey Robinson, Lab. 20,942
Brian Connell, C. 11,627
Iona Anderson, LD 7,932
David Clarke, BNP 1,556
Sandra List, UKIP 766
Nicola Downes, Soc. Alt. 615
Lab. maj. 9,315 (21.44%)
2.06% swing Lab. to C.
(2001: Lab. maj. 10,874 (25.56%))

COVENTRY SOUTH
E. 68,884 T. 40,685 (59.06%) Lab. ho
Jim Cunningham, Lab. 18,64
Heather Wheeler, C. 12,39
Vincent McKee, LD 7,22
Rob Windsor, Soc. Alt. 1,09
William Brown, UKIP 82
Irene Rogers, Ind. 34
James Rooney, FF 14
Lab. maj. 6,255 (15.37%)
2.64% swing Lab. to C.
(2001: Lab. maj. 8,279 (20.65%))

CRAWLEY
E. 71,911 T. 41,973 (58.37%) Lab. hol
Laura Moffatt, Lab. 16,41
Henry Smith, C. 16,37
Rupert Sheard, LD 6,50
Richard Trower, BNP 1,27
Ronald Walters, UKIP 93
Robin Burnham, Dem. Soc. All. 26
Arshad Khan, JP 21
Lab. maj. 37 (0.09%)
8.52% swing Lab. to C.
(2001: Lab. maj. 6,770 (17.13%))

CREWE & NANTWICH
E. 72,472 T. 43,485 (60.00%) Lab. hol
Gwyneth Dunwoody, Lab. 21,24
Eveleigh Moore-Dutton, C. 14,16
Paul Roberts, LD 8,08
Lab. maj. 7,078 (16.28%)
3.78% swing Lab. to C.
(2001: Lab. maj. 9,906 (23.84%))

CROSBY
E. 54,255 T. 36,194 (66.71%) Lab. hol
Claire Curtis-Thomas, Lab. 17,46
Debi Jones, C. 11,62
Jim Murray, LD 6,29
Dr John Whittaker, UKIP 45
Geoffrey Bottoms, Comm. Brit. 19
David Braid, Clause 28 15
Lab. maj. 5,840 (16.14%)
3.26% swing Lab. to C.
(2001: Lab. maj. 8,353 (22.66%))

CROYDON CENTRAL
E. 80,825 T. 48,957 (60.57%) C. gai
*Andrew Pelling, C. 19,97
Geraint Davies, Lab. 19,89
Jeremy Hargreaves, LD 6,38
Ian Edwards, UKIP 1,06
Bernice Golberg, Green 1,03
Marianne Bowness, Veritas 30
John Cartwright, Loony 19
Janet Stears, Work 10
C. maj. 75 (0.15%)
4.42% swing Lab. to C.
(2001: Lab. maj. 3,984 (8.69%))

CROYDON NORTH
E. 83,796 T. 43,847 (52.33%) Lab. hol
Malcolm Wicks, Lab. 23,55
Tariq Ahmad, C. 9,66
Adrian Gee-Turner, LD 7,56
Shasha Khan, Green 1,24
Henry Pearce, UKIP 77
Peter Gibson, Croydon 39
Winston McKenzie, Veritas 32
Farhan Rasheed, Ind. 19
Michelle Chambers, Work 13
Lab. maj. 13,888 (31.67%)
4.29% swing Lab. to C.
(2001: Lab. maj. 16,858 (40.25%))

ROYDON SOUTH
76,872 T. 48,897 (63.61%) C. hold
chard Ottaway, C. 25,320
ul Smith, Lab. 11,792
ndra Lawman, LD 10,049
nes Feisenberger, UKIP 1,054
aham Dare, Veritas 497
ark Samuel, Work 185
maj. 13,528 (27.67%)
18% swing Lab. to C.
001: C. maj. 8,697 (19.30%))

AGENHAM
60,141 T. 30,841 (51.28%) Lab. hold
nathan Cruddas, Lab. 15,446
ichael White, C. 7,841
nes Kempton, LD 3,106
wrence Rustem, BNP 2,870
erard Batten, UKIP 1,578
b. maj. 7,605 (24.66%)
43% swing Lab. to C.
001: Lab. maj. 8,693 (31.52%))

ARLINGTON
65,281 T. 39,388 (60.34%) Lab. hold
. Hon. Alan Milburn, Lab. 20,643
nthony Frieze, C. 10,239
obert Adamson, LD 7,269
hn Hoodless, UKIP 730
ai Davies, Veritas 507
b. maj. 10,404 (26.41%)
19% swing C. to Lab.
001: Lab. maj. 9,529 (23.38%))

ARTFORD
74,028 T. 46,779 (63.19%) Lab. hold
r Howard Stoate, Lab. 19,909
areth Johnson, C. 19,203
eter Bucklitsch, LD 5,036
ark Croucher, UKIP 1,407
ichael Tibby, NEP 1,224
b. maj. 706 (1.51%)
94% swing Lab. to C.
001: Lab. maj. 3,306 (7.39%))

AVENTRY
88,758 T. 60,439 (68.09%) C. hold
m Boswell, C. 31,206
ndrew Hammond, Lab. 16,520
annah Saul, LD 9,964
arry Mahoney, UKIP 1,927
arrie Wilkins, Veritas 822
. maj. 14,686 (24.30%)
64% swing Lab. to C.
001: C. maj. 9,649 (17.02%))

ENTON & REDDISH
68,267 T. 35,442 (51.92%) Lab. hold
Andrew Gwynne, Lab. 20,340
lex Story, C. 6,842
llison Seabourne, LD 5,814
hn Edgar, BNP 1,326
erald Price, UKIP 1,120
b. maj. 13,498 (38.08%)
77% swing Lab. to C.
001: Lab. maj. 15,330 (45.63%))

ERBY NORTH
68,173 T. 43,818 (64.27%) Lab. hold
ob Laxton, Lab. 19,272
ichard Aitken-Davies, C. 15,515
remy Beckett, LD 7,209
artin Bardoe, Veritas 958
ichelle Medgyesy, UKIP 864
b. maj. 3,757 (8.57%)
64% swing Lab. to C.
001: Lab. maj. 6,982 (15.85%))

DERBY SOUTH
E. 70,397 T. 43,373 (61.61%) Lab. hold
Rt. Hon. Margaret Beckett, Lab. 19,683
Lucy Care, LD 14,026
David Brackenbury, C. 8,211
David Black, UKIP 845
Frank Leeming, Veritas 608
Lab. maj. 5,657 (13.04%)
12.05% swing Lab. to LD
(2001: Lab. maj. 13,855 (32.16%))

DERBYSHIRE NORTH EAST
E. 70,981 T. 43,434 (61.19%) Lab. hold
*Natascha Engel, Lab. 21,416
Dominic Johnson, C. 11,351
Tom Snowdon, LD 8,812
Kenneth Perkins, UKIP 1,855
Lab. maj. 10,065 (23.17%)
2.96% swing Lab. to C.
(2001: Lab. maj. 12,258 (29.10%))

DERBYSHIRE SOUTH
E. 85,049 T. 55,820 (65.63%) Lab. hold
Mark Todd, Lab. 24,823
Simon Spencer, C. 20,328
Deborah Newton-Cook, LD 7,600
David Joines, BNP 1,797
Edward Spalton, Veritas 1,272
Lab. maj. 4,495 (8.05%)
3.53% swing Lab. to C.
(2001: Lab. maj. 7,851 (15.11%))

DERBYSHIRE WEST
E. 73,865 T. 51,143 (69.24%) C. hold
Patrick McLoughlin, C. 24,378
David Menon, Lab. 13,625
Ray Dring, LD 11,408
Michael Cruddas, UKIP 1,322
Nick Delves, Loony 405
Martin Kyslun, Ind. 5
C. maj. 10,753 (21.03%)
3.23% swing Lab. to C.
(2001: C. maj. 7,370 (14.57%))

DEVIZES
E. 86,168 T. 56,146 (65.16%) C. hold
Rt. Hon. Michael Ancram, C. 27,253
Fiona Hornby, LD 14,059
Sharon Charity, Lab. 12,519
Alan Wood, UKIP 2,315
C. maj. 13,194 (23.50%)
0.84% swing C. to LD
(2001: C. maj. 11,896 (22.34%))

DEVON EAST
E. 71,000 T. 49,247 (69.36%) C. hold
Hugo Swire, C. 23,075
Tim Dumper, LD 15,139
James Court, Lab. 7,598
Colin McNamee, UKIP 3,035
Christopher Way, Ind. 400
C. maj. 7,936 (16.11%)
0.51% swing C. to LD
(2001: C. maj. 8,195 (17.13%))

DEVON NORTH
E. 76,203 T. 51,930 (68.15%) LD hold
Nick Harvey, LD 23,840
Orlando Fraser, C. 18,868
Mark Cann, Lab. 4,656
John Browne, UKIP 2,740
Richard Knight, Green 1,826
LD maj. 4,972 (9.57%)
1.76% swing C. to LD
(2001: LD maj. 2,984 (6.06%))

DEVON SOUTH WEST
E. 71,307 T. 48,885 (68.56%) C. hold
Gary Streeter, C. 21,906
Judy Evans, LD 11,765
Christopher Mavin, Lab. 11,545
Hugh Williams, UKIP 3,669
C. maj. 10,141 (20.74%)
3.86% swing C. to LD
(2001: C. maj. 7,144 (15.23%))

DEVON WEST & TORRIDGE
E. 83,489 T. 58,584 (70.17%) C. gain
*Geoffrey Cox, C. 25,013
David Walter, LD 21,777
Rebecca Richards, Lab. 6,001
Matthew Jackson, UKIP 3,790
Peter Christie, Green 2,003
C. maj. 3,236 (5.52%)
3.83% swing LD to C.
(2001: LD maj. 1,194 (2.14%))

DEWSBURY
E. 62,243 T. 38,595 (62.01%) Lab. hold
*Shahid Malik, Lab. 15,807
Sayeeda Warsi, C. 11,192
Kingsley Hill, LD 5,624
David Exley, BNP 5,066
Brenda Smithson, Green 593
Alan Girvan, Ind. 313
Lab. maj. 4,615 (11.96%)
4.18% swing Lab. to C.
(2001: Lab. maj. 7,449 (20.32%))

DON VALLEY
E. 66,993 T. 36,864 (55.03%) Lab. hold
Caroline Flint, Lab. 19,418
Adam Duguid, C. 10,820
Stewart Arnold, LD 6,626
Lab. maj. 8,598 (23.32%)
1.33% swing Lab. to C.
(2001: Lab. maj. 9,520 (25.99%))

DONCASTER CENTRAL
E. 65,731 T. 34,351 (52.26%) Lab. hold
Rosie Winterton, Lab. 17,617
Patrick Wilson, LD 7,815
Stefan Kerner, C. 6,489
John Wilkinson, BNP 1,239
Alan Simmons, UKIP 1,191
Lab. maj. 9,802 (28.53%)
8.80% swing Lab. to LD
(2001: Lab. maj. 11,999 (35.39%))

DONCASTER NORTH
E. 61,741 T. 31,578 (51.15%) Lab. hold
*Ed Miliband, Lab. 17,531
Martin Drake, C. 4,875
Doug Pickett, LD 3,800
Martin Williams, CG 2,365
Lee Hagan, BNP 1,506
Robert Nixon, UKIP 940
Michael Cassidy, Eng. Dem. 561
Lab. maj. 12,656 (40.08%)
4.17% swing Lab. to C.
(2001: Lab. maj. 15,187 (48.42%))

DORSET MID & POOLE NORTH
E. 65,924 T. 45,159 (68.50%) LD hold
Annette Brooke, LD 22,000
Simon Hayes, C. 16,518
Philip Murray, Lab. 5,221
Avril King, UKIP 1,420
LD maj. 5,482 (12.14%)
5.63% swing C. to LD
(2001: LD maj. 384 (0.88%))

DORSET NORTH
E. 74,286 T. 52,815 (71.10%) C. hold
Robert Walter, C. 23,714
Emily Gasson, LD 21,470
John Yarwood, Lab. 4,596
Richard Frampton Hobbs, UKIP 1,918
Ralph Arliss, Green 1,117
C. maj. 2,244 (4.25%)
1.85% swing C. to LD
(2001: C. maj. 3,797 (7.94%))

DORSET SOUTH
E. 70,668 T. 48,584 (68.75%) Lab. hold
Jim Knight, Lab. 20,231
Ed Matts, C. 18,419
Graham Oakes, LD 7,647
Hugh Chalker, UKIP 1,571
Vic Hamilton, LCA 282
Bernard Parkes, Respect 219
Andrew Kirkwood, PRTYP 107
Colin Bex, Wessex Reg. 83
David Marchesi, Soc. Lab. 25
Lab. maj. 1,812 (3.73%)
1.70% swing C. to Lab.
(2001: Lab. maj. 153 (0.34%))

DORSET WEST
E. 69,764 T. 53,225 (76.29%) C. hold
Rt. Hon. Oliver Letwin, C. 24,763
Justine McGuinness, LD 22,302
Dave Roberts, Lab. 4,124
Linda Guest, UKIP 1,084
Susan Greene, Green 952
C. maj. 2,461 (4.62%)
0.89% swing LD to C.
(2001: C. maj. 1,414 (2.85%))

DOVER
E. 70,884 T. 47,884 (67.55%) Lab. hold
Gwyn Prosser, Lab. 21,680
Paul Watkins, C. 16,739
Antony Hook, LD 7,607
Mike Wiltshire, UKIP 1,252
Vic Matcham, Ind. 606
Lab. maj. 4,941 (10.32%)
0.62% swing Lab. to C.
(2001: Lab. maj. 5,199 (11.56%))

DUDLEY NORTH
E. 68,766 T. 41,408 (60.22%) Lab. hold
*Ian Austin, Lab. 18,306
Ian Hillas, C. 12,874
Gerry Lewis, LD 4,257
Simon Darby, BNP 4,022
Malcolm Davis, UKIP 1,949
Lab. maj. 5,432 (13.12%)
2.26% swing Lab. to C.
(2001: Lab. maj. 6,800 (17.63%))

DUDLEY SOUTH
E. 65,228 T. 39,276 (60.21%) Lab. hold
Ian Pearson, Lab. 17,800
Marco Longhi, C. 13,556
Jonathan Bramall, LD 4,808
John Salvage, BNP 1,841
Andrew Benion, UKIP 1,271
Lab. maj. 4,244 (10.81%)
3.98% swing Lab. to C.
(2001: Lab. maj. 6,817 (18.76%))

DULWICH & WEST NORWOOD
E. 72,232 T. 41,989 (58.13%) Lab. hold
Rt. Hon. Tessa Jowell, Lab. 19,059
Jonathan Mitchell, LD 10,252
Kim Humphreys, C. 9,200
Jenny Jones, Green 2,741
Ralph Atkinson, UKIP 290
David Heather, Veritas 241
Amanda Rose, Soc. Lab. 149
Judy Weleminsky, Fit 57
Lab. maj. 8,807 (20.97%)
9.37% swing Lab. to LD
(2001: Lab. maj. 12,310 (32.19%))

DURHAM NORTH
E. 67,506 T. 37,341 (55.32%) Lab. hold
Kevan Jones, Lab. 23,932
Philip Latham, LD 7,151
Mark Watson, C. 6,258
Lab. maj. 16,781 (44.94%)
4.12% swing Lab. to LD
(2001: Lab. maj. 18,683 (48.44%))

DURHAM NORTH WEST
E. 68,130 T. 39,509 (57.99%) Lab. hold
Rt. Hon. Hilary Armstrong, Lab. 21,312
Alan Ord, LD 7,869
Jamie Devlin, C. 6,463
Watts Stelling, Ind. 3,865
Lab. maj. 13,443 (34.03%)
6.80% swing Lab. to LD
(2001: Lab. maj. 16,333 (41.64%))

DURHAM, CITY OF
E. 71,441 T. 44,364 (62.10%) Lab. hold
*Dr Roberta Blackman-Woods, Lab. 20,928
Carol Woods, LD 17,654
Ben Rogers, C. 4,179
Anthony Martin, Veritas 1,603
Lab. maj. 3,274 (7.38%)
12.51% swing Lab. to LD
(2001: Lab. maj. 13,441 (32.40%))

EALING ACTON & SHEPHERD'S BUSH
E. 70,454 T. 39,623 (56.24%) Lab. hold
*Andrew Slaughter, Lab. 16,579
Jonathan Gough, C. 11,059
Gary Malcolm, LD 9,986
Geoff Burgess, Green 1,999
Lab. maj. 5,520 (13.93%)
7.54% swing Lab. to C.
(2001: Lab. maj. 10,789 (29.00%))

EALING NORTH
E. 78,298 T. 46,507 (59.40%) Lab. hold
Stephen Pound, Lab. 20,956
Roger Curtis, C. 13,897
Francesco Fruzza, LD 9,148
Alan Outten, Green 1,319
Robin Lambert, UKIP 692
David Malindine, Veritas 495
Lab. maj. 7,059 (15.18%)
5.58% swing Lab. to C.
(2001: Lab. maj. 11,837 (26.33%))

EALING SOUTHALL
E. 83,738 T. 47,045 (56.18%) Lab. hold
Piara Khabra, Lab. 22,937
Nigel Bakhai, LD 11,497
Mark Nicholson, C. 10,147
Sarah Edwards, Green 2,175
Malkiat Bilku, WRP 289
Lab. maj. 11,440 (24.32%)
6.59% swing Lab. to LD
(2001: Lab. maj. 13,683 (29.22%))

EASINGTON
E. 61,084 T. 31,855 (52.15%) Lab. ho
John Cummings, Lab. 22,73
Christopher Ord, LD 4,09
Lucille Nicholson, C. 3,40
Ian McDonald, BNP 1,04
Dave Robinson, Soc. Lab. 58
Lab. maj. 18,636 (58.50%)
4.00% swing Lab. to LD
(2001: Lab. maj. 21,949 (66.49%))

EAST HAM
E. 78,104 T. 39,569 (50.66%) Lab. ho
Stephen Timms, Lab. 21,32
Abdul Khaliq Mian, Respect 8,17
Sarah Macken, C. 5,19
Ann Haigh, LD 4,29
David Bamber, CPA 58
Lab. maj. 13,155 (33.25%)
19.95% swing Lab. to Respect
(2001: Lab. maj. 21,032 (56.42%))

EASTBOURNE
E. 74,628 T. 48,392 (64.84%) C. hol
Nigel Waterson, C. 21,03
Stephen Lloyd, LD 19,90
Andrew Jones, Lab. 5,26
Andrew Meggs, UKIP 1,23
Clive Gross, Green 94
C. maj. 1,124 (2.32%)
1.24% swing C. to LD
(2001: C. maj. 2,154 (4.81%))

EASTLEIGH
E. 76,844 T. 49,771 (64.77%) LD hol
*Christopher Huhne, LD 19,21
Conor Burns, C. 18,64
Chris Watt, Lab. 10,23
Christopher Murphy, UKIP 1,66
LD maj. 568 (1.14%)
2.64% swing LD to C.
(2001: LD maj. 3,058 (6.43%))

ECCLES
E. 69,006 T. 34,632 (50.19%) Lab. hol
Ian Stewart, Lab. 19,70
Thelma Matuk, C. 6,81
Jane Brophy, LD 6,42
Peter Reeve, UKIP 1,68
Lab. maj. 12,886 (37.21%)
3.29% swing Lab. to C.
(2001: Lab. maj. 14,528 (43.78%))

EDDISBURY
E. 72,249 T. 45,674 (63.22%) C. hol
Stephen O'Brien, C. 21,18
Mark Green, Lab. 14,98
Joanne Crotty, LD 8,18
Steve Roxborough, UKIP 1,32
C. maj. 6,195 (13.56%)
1.64% swing Lab. to C.
(2001: C. maj. 4,568 (10.29%))

EDMONTON
E. 58,764 T. 34,703 (59.05%) Lab. (Co-op) hol
Andy Love, Lab. (Co-op) 18,45
Lionel Zetter, C. 10,38
Dr Iarla Kilbane-Dawe, LD 4,16
Nina Armstrong, Green 88
Gwyneth Rolph, UKIP 81
Lab. (Co-op) maj. 8,075 (23.27%)
2.42% swing Lab. (Co-op) to C.
(2001: Lab. (Co-op) maj. 9,772 (28.10%))

.LLESMERE PORT & NESTON
68,249 T. 42,069 (61.64%) Lab. hold
ndrew Miller, Lab. 20,371
yles Hogg, C. 13,885
eve Cooke, LD 6,607
enry Crocker, UKIP 1,206
ab. maj. 6,486 (15.42%)
37% swing Lab. to C.
001: Lab. maj. 10,861 (26.15%))

.MET
68,514 T. 47,146 (68.81%) Lab. hold
olin Burgon, Lab. 22,260
ndrew Millard, C. 17,732
adeleine Kirk, LD 5,923
acy Andrews, BNP 1,231
ab. maj. 4,528 (9.60%)
26% swing C. to Lab.
001: Lab. maj. 4,171 (9.08%))

.THAM
57,236 T. 35,305 (61.68%) Lab. hold
live Efford, Lab. 15,381
pencer Drury, C. 12,105
n Gerrard, LD 5,669
remy Elms, UKIP 1,024
arry Roberts, BNP 979
ndrew Graham, Ind. 147
ab. maj. 3,276 (9.28%)
71% swing Lab. to C.
001: Lab. maj. 6,996 (20.70%))

NFIELD NORTH
66,460 T. 40,749 (61.31%) Lab. hold
oan Ryan, Lab. 18,055
ick de Bois, C. 16,135
mon Radford, LD 4,642
erence Farr, BNP 1,004
ary Robbens, UKIP 750
atrick Burns, Ind. 163
ab. maj. 1,920 (4.71%)
63% swing Lab. to C.
001: Lab. maj. 2,291 (6.01%))

NFIELD SOUTHGATE
63,613 T. 42,210 (66.35%) C. gain
David Burrowes, C. 18,830
ephen Twigg, Lab. 17,083
iz Kakoulakis, LD 4,724
revor Doughty, Green 1,083
rian Hall, UKIP 490
. maj. 1,747 (4.14%)
.69% swing Lab. to C.
001: Lab. maj. 5,546 (13.23%))

PPING FOREST
72,776 T. 44,860 (61.64%) C. hold
leanor Laing, C. 23,783
ambos Charalambous, Lab. 9,425
ichael Heavens, LD 8,279
ulian Leppert, BNP 1,728
ndrew Smith, UKIP 1,014
obin Tilbrook, Eng. Dem. 631
. maj. 14,358 (32.01%)
.07% swing Lab. to C.
001: C. maj. 8,426 (19.87%))

PSOM & EWELL
75,515 T. 49,879 (66.05%) C. hold
hris Grayling, C. 27,146
onathan Lees, LD 10,699
harles Mansell, Lab. 10,265
eter Kefford, UKIP 1,769
. maj. 16,447 (32.97%)
.50% swing LD to C.
001: C. maj. 10,080 (21.61%))

EREWASH
E. 78,376 T. 50,553 (64.50%) Lab. hold
Liz Blackman, Lab. 22,472
David Simmonds, C. 15,388
Martin Garnett, LD 7,073
Robert Kilroy-Silk, Veritas 2,957
Sadie Graham, BNP 1,319
Geoffrey Kingscott, UKIP 941
R. U. Seerius, Loony 287
David Bishop, Elvis 116
Lab. maj. 7,084 (14.01%)
0.13% swing Lab. to C.
(2001: Lab. maj. 6,932 (14.26%))

ERITH & THAMESMEAD
E. 72,058 T. 37,651 (52.25%) Lab. hold
John Austin, Lab. 20,483
Chris Bromby, C. 8,983
Steven Toole, LD 5,088
Brian Ravenscroft, BNP 1,620
Barrie Thomas, UKIP 1,477
Lab. maj. 11,500 (30.54%)
1.47% swing Lab. to C.
(2001: Lab. maj. 11,167 (33.48%))

ESHER & WALTON
E. 76,926 T. 47,878 (62.24%) C. hold
Ian Taylor, C. 21,882
Mark Marsh, LD 14,155
Richard Taylor, Lab. 9,309
Bernard Collignon, UKIP 1,582
Chinners Chinnery, Loony 608
Richard Cutler, Soc. Lab. 342
C. maj. 7,727 (16.14%)
5.17% swing C. to LD
(2001: C. maj. 11,538 (25.34%))

ESSEX NORTH
E. 73,037 T. 47,959 (65.66%) C. hold
Bernard Jenkin, C. 22,811
Elizabeth Hughes, Lab. 11,908
James Raven, LD 9,831
Christopher Fox, Green 1,718
George Curtis, UKIP 1,691
C. maj. 10,903 (22.73%)
3.37% swing Lab. to C.
(2001: C. maj. 7,186 (15.99%))

EXETER
E. 84,964 T. 55,068 (64.81%) Lab. hold
Ben Bradshaw, Lab. 22,619
Peter Cox, C. 14,954
Jon Underwood, LD 11,340
Margaret Danks, Lib. 2,214
Tim Brenan, Green 1,896
Mark Fitzgeorge-Parker, UKIP 1,854
John Stuart, Ind. 191
Lab. maj. 7,665 (13.92%)
4.21% swing Lab. to C.
(2001: Lab. maj. 11,759 (22.35%))

FALMOUTH & CAMBORNE
E. 71,509 T. 48,015 (67.15%) LD gain
*Julia Goldsworthy, LD 16,747
Candy Atherton, Lab. 14,861
Ashley Crossley, C. 12,644
Michael Mahon, UKIP 1,820
David Mudd, Ind. 961
Paul Holmes, Lib. 423
Hilda Wasley, Meb. Ker. 370
Peter Gifford, Veritas 128
Richard Smith, Masts 61
LD maj. 1,886 (3.93%)
9.52% swing Lab. to LD
(2001: Lab. maj. 4,527 (9.67%))

FAREHAM
E. 72,599 T. 48,576 (66.91%) C. hold
Mark Hoban, C. 24,151
James Carr, Lab. 12,449
Richard De Ste-Croix, LD 10,551
Peter Mason-Apps, UKIP 1,425
C. maj. 11,702 (24.09%)
4.33% swing Lab. to C.
(2001: C. maj. 7,009 (15.42%))

FAVERSHAM & KENT MID
E. 66,411 T. 43,626 (65.69%) C. hold
Hugh Robertson, C. 21,690
Andrew Bradstock, Lab. 12,970
David Naghi, LD 7,204
Robert Thompson, UKIP 1,152
Norman Davidson, Loony 610
C. maj. 8,720 (19.99%)
4.90% swing Lab. to C.
(2001: C. maj. 4,183 (10.19%))

FELTHAM & HESTON
E. 75,391 T. 37,282 (49.45%)
Lab. (Co-op) hold
Alan Keen, Lab. (Co-op) 17,741
Mark Bowen, C. 10,921
Satnam Kaur Khalsa, LD 6,177
Graham Kemp, NF 975
Elizabeth Anstis, Green 815
Leon Mullett, UKIP 612
Warwick Prachar, Ind. 41
Lab. (Co-op) maj. 6,820 (18.29%)
8.35% swing Lab. (Co-op) to C.
(2001: Lab. (Co-op) maj. 12,657 (34.99%))

FINCHLEY & GOLDERS GREEN
E. 69,808 T. 43,214 (61.90%) Lab. hold
Dr Rudi Vis, Lab. 17,487
Andrew Mennear, C. 16,746
Sue Garden, LD 7,282
Noel Lynch, Green 1,136
Jeremy Jacobs, UKIP 453
Rainbow George Weiss, Vote Dream 110
Lab. maj. 741 (1.71%)
3.40% swing Lab. to C.
(2001: Lab. maj. 3,716 (8.51%))

FOLKESTONE & HYTHE
E. 70,914 T. 48,503 (68.40%) C. hold
Rt. Hon. Michael Howard, C. 26,161
Peter Carroll, LD 14,481
Maureen Tomison, Lab. 6,053
Dr Hazel Dawe, Green 688
Petrina Holdsworth, UKIP 619
Lord Toby Jug, Loony 175
Rodney Hylton-Potts, GBB 153
Grahame Leon-Smith, Senior 151
Sylvia Dunn, Progress 22
C. maj. 11,680 (24.08%)
5.60% swing LD to C.
(2001: C. maj. 5,907 (12.88%))

FOREST OF DEAN
E. 67,225 T. 47,640 (70.87%) C. gain
*Mark Harper, C. 19,474
Isabel Owen, Lab. 17,425
Christopher Coleman, LD 8,185
Patricia Hill, UKIP 1,140
Stephen Tweedie, Green 991
Anthony Reeve, Ind. 300
Gerald Morgan, EPP 125
C. maj. 2,049 (4.30%)
4.45% swing Lab. to C.
(2001: Lab. maj. 2,049 (4.59%))

FYLDE
E. 75,703 T. 45,510 (60.12%) C. hold
Rt. Hon. Michael Jack, C. 24,287
William Parbury, Lab. 11,828
Bill Winlow, LD 7,748
Tim Akeroyd, Lib. 1,647
C. maj. 12,459 (27.38%)
2.95% swing Lab. to C.
(2001: C. maj. 9,610 (21.48%))

GAINSBOROUGH
E. 70,733 T. 45,681 (64.58%) C. hold
Edward Leigh, C. 20,040
Adrian Heath, LD 12,037
John Knight, Lab. 11,744
Steven Pearson, UKIP 1,860
C. maj. 8,003 (17.52%)
1.02% swing C. to LD
(2001: C. maj. 8,071 (19.07%))

GATESHEAD EAST & WASHINGTON WEST
E. 61,421 T. 34,668 (56.44%) Lab. hold
*Sharon Hodgson, Lab. 20,997
Frank Hindle, LD 7,590
Lee Martin, C. 4,812
Jim Batty, UKIP 1,269
Lab. maj. 13,407 (38.67%)
7.29% swing Lab. to LD
(2001: Lab. maj. 17,904 (53.26%))

GEDLING
E. 68,917 T. 44,069 (63.95%) Lab. hold
Vernon Coaker, Lab. 20,329
Anna Soubry, C. 16,518
Raymond Poynter, LD 6,070
Alan Margerison, UKIP 741
Deborah Johnson, Veritas 411
Lab. maj. 3,811 (8.65%)
2.06% swing Lab. to C.
(2001: Lab. maj. 5,598 (12.78%))

GILLINGHAM
E. 72,223 T. 45,167 (62.54%) Lab. hold
Paul Clark, Lab. 18,621
Tim Butcher, C. 18,367
Andrew Stamp, LD 6,734
Craig MacKinlay, UKIP 1,191
Gordon Bryan, Ind. 254
Lab. maj. 254 (0.56%)
2.41% swing Lab. to C.
(2001: Lab. maj. 2,272 (5.38%))

GLOUCESTER
E. 82,500 T. 51,803 (62.79%) Lab. hold
Parmjit Dhanda, Lab. 23,138
Paul James, C. 18,867
Jeremy Hilton, LD 7,825
Gary Phipps, UKIP 1,116
Bryan Meloy, Green 857
Lab. maj. 4,271 (8.24%)
0.10% swing C. to Lab.
(2001: Lab. maj. 3,880 (8.05%))

GOSPORT
E. 71,119 T. 43,034 (60.51%) C. hold
Peter Viggers, C. 19,268
Richard Williams, Lab. 13,538
Roger Roberts, LD 7,145
John Bowles, UKIP 1,825
Andrea Smith, Green 1,258
C. maj. 5,730 (13.32%)
3.36% swing Lab. to C.
(2001: C. maj. 2,621 (6.59%))

GRANTHAM & STAMFORD
E. 74,074 T. 47,147 (63.65%) C. hold
Quentin Davies, C. 22,109
Ian Selby, Lab. 14,664
Patrick O'Connor, LD 7,838
Stuart Rising, UKIP 1,498
Benedict Brown, Eng. Dem. 774
John Andrews, OFD 264
C. maj. 7,445 (15.79%)
3.02% swing Lab. to C.
(2001: C. maj. 4,518 (9.76%))

GRAVESHAM
E. 68,705 T. 45,179 (65.76%) C. gain
*Adam Holloway, C. 19,739
Chris Pond, Lab. 19,085
Bruce Parmenter, LD 4,851
Geoff Coates, UKIP 850
Christopher Nickerson, Eng. Ind. 654
C. maj. 654 (1.45%)
6.29% swing Lab. to C.
(2001: Lab. maj. 4,862 (11.14%))

GREAT GRIMSBY
E. 63,711 T. 32,964 (51.74%) Lab. hold
Austin Mitchell, Lab. 15,512
Giles Taylor, C. 7,858
Andrew de Freitas, LD 6,356
Stephen Fyfe, BNP 1,338
Martin Grant, UKIP 1,239
David Brooks, Green 661
Lab. maj. 7,654 (23.22%)
5.78% swing Lab. to C.
(2001: Lab. maj. 11,484 (34.78%))

GREAT YARMOUTH
E. 68,887 T. 41,378 (60.07%) Lab. hold
Anthony Wright, Lab. 18,850
Mark Fox, C. 15,795
Stephen Newton, LD 4,585
Bertie Poole, UKIP 1,759
Michael Skipper, LCA 389
Lab. maj. 3,055 (7.38%)
1.96% swing Lab. to C.
(2001: Lab. maj. 4,564 (11.31%))

GREENWICH & WOOLWICH
E. 64,033 T. 35,615 (55.62%) Lab. hold
Rt. Hon. Nick Raynsford, Lab. 17,527
Christopher Le Breton, LD 7,381
Alistair Craig, C. 7,142
David Sharman, Green 1,579
Garry Bushell, Eng. Dem. 1,216
Stanley Gain, UKIP 709
Puvarani Nagalingam, Ind. 61
Lab. maj. 10,146 (28.49%)
8.21% swing Lab. to LD
(2001: Lab. maj. 13,433 (41.29%))

GUILDFORD
E. 75,566 T. 51,631 (68.33%) C. gain
*Anne Milton, C. 22,595
Sue Doughty, LD 22,248
Karen Landles, Lab. 5,054
John Pletts, Green 811
Martin Haslam, UKIP 645
John Morris, PPN-V 166
Victoria Lavin, Ind. 112
C. maj. 347 (0.67%)
0.90% swing LD to C.
(2001: LD maj. 538 (1.12%))

HACKNEY NORTH & STOKE NEWINGTON
E. 59,260 T. 29,380 (49.58%) Lab. ho
Diane Abbott, Lab. 14,26
James Blanchard, LD 6,84
Ertan Hurer, C. 4,21
Mischa Borris, Green 2,90
David Vail, Ind. 60
Nusrat Sen, Soc. Lab. 29
Nigel Barrow, Loony 24
Lab. maj. 7,427 (25.28%)
10.84% swing Lab. to LD
(2001: Lab. maj. 13,651 (46.09%))

HACKNEY SOUTH & SHOREDITCH
E. 64,818 T. 32,237 (49.73%)
Lab. (Co-op) ho
*Meg Hillier, Lab. (Co-op) 17,04
Gavin Baylis, LD 6,84
John Moss, C. 4,52
Ipemndoh dan Iyan, Green 1,77
Dean Ryan, Respect 1,43
Benjamin Rae, Lib. 31
Monty Goldman, Comm. 20
Jonty Leff, WRP 9
Lab. (Co-op) maj. 10,204 (31.65%)
8.97% swing Lab. (Co-op) to LD
(2001: Lab. (Co-op) maj. 15,049 (49.59%))

HALESOWEN & ROWLEY REGIS
E. 65,748 T. 41,327 (62.86%) Lab. hol
Sylvia Heal, Lab. 19,24
Les Jones, C. 14,90
Martin Turner, LD 5,20
Nikki Sinclaire, UKIP 1,97
Lab. maj. 4,337 (10.49%)
4.12% swing Lab. to C.
(2001: Lab. maj. 7,359 (18.74%))

HALIFAX
E. 64,861 T. 39,659 (61.14%)
Lab. (Co-op) hol
*Linda Riordan, Lab. (Co-op) 16,57
Kris Hopkins, C. 13,16
Michael Taylor, LD 7,10
Geoff Wallace, BNP 2,62
Thomas Holmes, NF 19
Lab. (Co-op) maj. 3,417 (8.62%)
3.28% swing Lab. (Co-op) to C.
(2001: Lab. (Co-op) maj. 6,129 (15.17%))

HALTEMPRICE & HOWDEN
E. 68,471 T. 48,029 (70.15%) C. hol
Rt. Hon. David Davis, C. 22,79
Jon Neal, LD 17,67
Edward Hart, Lab. 6,10
Jonathan Mainprize, BNP 79
Philip Lane, UKIP 65
C. maj. 5,116 (10.65%)
3.16% swing LD to C.
(2001: C. maj. 1,903 (4.33%))

HALTON
E. 64,379 T. 34,183 (53.10%) Lab. hol
Derek Twigg, Lab. 21,46
Colin Bloom, C. 6,85
Roger Barlow, LD 5,86
Lab. maj. 14,606 (42.73%)
3.92% swing Lab. to C.
(2001: Lab. maj. 17,428 (50.56%))

AMMERSMITH & FULHAM
. 79,082 T. 49,327 (62.37%) C. gain
Greg Hands, C. 22,407
Melanie Smallman, Lab. 17,378
lan Bullion, LD 7,116
ona Harrold, Green 1,933
iles Fisher, UKIP 493
. maj. 5,029 (10.20%)
.35% swing Lab. to C.
2001: Lab. maj. 2,015 (4.51%))

AMPSHIRE EAST
. 79,801 T. 53,139 (66.59%) C. hold
t. Hon. Michael Mates, C. 24,273
uth Bright, LD 18,764
larjory Broughton, Lab. 8,519
avid Samuel, UKIP 1,583
. maj. 5,509 (10.37%)
.66% swing C. to LD
2001: C. maj. 8,890 (17.68%))

AMPSHIRE NORTH EAST
. 72,939 T. 47,287 (64.83%) C. hold
t. Hon. James Arbuthnot, C. 25,407
dam Carew, LD 12,858
evin McGrath, Lab. 7,630
aul Birch, UKIP 1,392
. maj. 12,549 (26.54%)
.81% swing C. to LD
2001: C. maj. 13,257 (30.17%))

AMPSHIRE NORTH WEST
. 79,763 T. 51,265 (64.27%) C. hold
t. Hon. Sir George Young, C. 26,005
lartin Tod, LD 12,741
lichael Mumford, Lab. 10,594
eter Sumner, UKIP 1,925
. maj. 13,264 (25.87%)
.50% swing C. to LD
2001: C. maj. 12,009 (24.69%))

AMPSTEAD & HIGHGATE
. 68,737 T. 38,173 (55.53%) Lab. hold
lenda Jackson, Lab. 14,615
iers Wauchope, C. 10,886
d Fordham, LD 10,293
ian Berry, Green 2,013
lagnus Nielsen, UKIP 275
Rainbow George Weiss, Vote Dream 91
ab. maj. 3,729 (9.77%)
.24% swing Lab. to C.
2001: Lab. maj. 7,876 (22.24%))

ARBOROUGH
. 74,583 T. 47,922 (64.25%) C. hold
dward Garnier, C. 20,536
ill Hope, LD 16,644
eter Evans, Lab. 9,222
larietta King, UKIP 1,520
. maj. 3,892 (8.12%)
.60% swing C. to LD
2001: C. maj. 5,252 (11.31%))

ARLOW
. 63,500 T. 39,733 (62.57%) Lab. hold
Bill Rammell, Lab. 16,453
Robert Halfon, C. 16,356
orna Spenceley, LD 5,002
ohn Felgate, UKIP 981
Anthony Bennett, Veritas 941
ab. maj. 97 (0.24%)
.39% swing Lab. to C.
2001: Lab. maj. 5,228 (13.03%))

HARROGATE & KNARESBOROUGH
E. 65,622 T. 42,858 (65.31%) LD hold
Phil Willis, LD 24,113
Maggie Punyer, C. 13,684
Lorraine Ferris, Lab. 3,627
Chris Royston, UKIP 845
Colin Banner, BNP 466
John Allman, AFC 123
LD maj. 10,429 (24.33%)
1.68% swing C. to LD
(2001: LD maj. 8,845 (20.97%))

HARROW EAST
E. 84,033 T. 50,823 (60.48%) Lab. hold
Tony McNulty, Lab. 23,445
David Ashton, C. 18,715
Pash Nandhra, LD 7,747
Paul Cronin, UKIP 916
Lab. maj. 4,730 (9.31%)
6.92% swing Lab. to C.
(2001: Lab. maj. 11,124 (23.14%))

HARROW WEST
E. 74,228 T. 47,759 (64.34%)
Lab. (Co-op) hold
Gareth Thomas, Lab. (Co-op) 20,298
Mike Freer, C. 18,270
Christopher Noyce, LD 8,188
Janice Cronin, UKIP 576
Berjis Daver, Ind. 427
Lab. (Co-op) maj. 2,028 (4.25%)
4.48% swing Lab. (Co-op) to C.
(2001: Lab. (Co-op) maj. 6,156 (13.20%))

HARTLEPOOL
E. 68,776 T. 35,436 (51.52%) Lab. hold
Iain Wright, Lab. 18,251
Jody Dunn, LD 10,773
Amanda Vigar, C. 4,058
George Springer, UKIP 1,256
Frank Harrison, Soc. Lab. 373
Iris Ryder, Green 288
John Hobbs, Ind. 275
Sausage Supremo Headbanger, Loony 162
Lab. maj. 7,478 (21.10%)
11.51% swing Lab. to LD
(2004 Sept. by-election: Lab. maj. 2,033 (6.48%))
(2001: Lab. maj. 14,571 (38.29%))

HARWICH
E. 80,474 T. 50,408 (62.64%) C. gain
*Douglas Carswell, C. 21,235
Ivan Henderson, Lab. 20,315
Keith Tully, LD 5,913
Jeffrey Titford, UKIP 2,314
John Tipple, Respect 477
Christopher Humphrey, Ind. 154
C. maj. 920 (1.83%)
3.61% swing Lab. to C.
(2001: Lab. maj. 2,596 (5.40%))

HASTINGS & RYE
E. 72,765 T. 43,004 (59.10%) Lab. hold
Michael Foster, Lab. 18,107
Mark Coote, C. 16,081
Richard Stevens, LD 6,479
Terry Grant, UKIP 1,098
Sally Phillips, Green 1,032
John Ord-Clarke, Loony 207
Lab. maj. 2,026 (4.71%)
2.87% swing Lab. to C.
(2001: Lab. maj. 4,308 (10.45%))

HAVANT
E. 68,545 T. 41,351 (60.33%) C. hold
David Willetts, C. 18,370
Sarah Bogle, Lab. 11,862
Alex Bentley, LD 8,358
Timothy Dawes, Green 1,006
Steve Harris, UKIP 998
Ian Johnson, BNP 562
Russell Thomas, Veritas 195
C. maj. 6,508 (15.74%)
2.67% swing Lab. to C.
(2001: C. maj. 4,207 (10.40%))

HAYES & HARLINGTON
E. 57,493 T. 32,389 (56.34%) Lab. hold
John McDonnell, Lab. 19,009
Richard Worrall, C. 8,162
Jon Ball, LD 3,174
Tony Hazel, BNP 830
Martin Haley, UKIP 552
Brian Outten, Green 442
Paul Goddard, Ind. 220
Lab. maj. 10,847 (33.49%)
4.03% swing Lab. to C.
(2001: Lab. maj. 13,466 (41.56%))

HAZEL GROVE
E. 64,376 T. 39,117 (60.76%) LD hold
Andrew Stunell, LD 19,355
Alan White, C. 11,607
Andrew Graystone, Lab. 6,834
Keith Ryan, UKIP 1,321
LD maj. 7,748 (19.81%)
1.06% swing LD to C.
(2001: LD maj. 8,435 (21.92%))

HEMEL HEMPSTEAD
E. 73,095 T. 47,108 (64.45%) C. gain
*Michael Penning, C. 19,000
Tony McWalter, Lab. (Co-op) 18,501
Dr Richard Grayson, LD 8,089
Barry Newton, UKIP 1,518
C. maj. 499 (1.06%)
4.61% swing Lab. (Co-op) to C.
(2001: Lab. (Co-op) maj. 3,742 (8.16%))

HEMSWORTH
E. 67,339 T. 36,792 (54.64%) Lab. hold
Jon Trickett, Lab. 21,630
Jonathan Mortimer, C. 8,149
David Hall-Matthews, LD 5,766
John Burdon, Veritas 1,247
Lab. maj. 13,481 (36.64%)
3.87% swing Lab. to C.
(2001: Lab. maj. 15,636 (44.39%))

HENDON
E. 71,764 T. 41,839 (58.30%) Lab. hold
Andrew Dismore, Lab. 18,596
Dr Richard Evans, C. 15,897
Nahid Boethe, LD 5,831
David Williams, Green 754
Melvyn Smallman, UKIP 637
Rainbow George Weiss, Vote Dream 68
Michael Stewart, PDP 56
Lab. maj. 2,699 (6.45%)
5.85% swing Lab. to C.
(2001: Lab. maj. 7,417 (18.16%))

HENLEY
E. 68,538 T. 46,537 (67.90%) C. hold
Boris Johnson, C. 24,894
David Turner, LD 12,101
Kaleem Saeed, Lab. 6,862
Mark Stevenson, Green 1,518
Delphine Gray-Fisk, UKIP 1,162
C. maj. 12,793 (27.49%)
4.22% swing LD to C.
(2001: C. maj. 8,458 (19.05%))

HEREFORD
E. 71,813 T. 46,894 (65.30%) LD hold
Paul Keetch, LD 20,285
Virginia Taylor, C. 19,323
Tom Calver, Lab. 4,800
Brian Lunt, Green 1,052
Christopher Kingsley, UKIP 1,030
Peter Morton, Ind. 404
LD maj. 962 (2.05%)
0.06% swing LD to C.
(2001: LD maj. 968 (2.17%))

HERTFORD & STORTFORD
E. 73,394 T. 49,692 (67.71%) C. hold
Mark Prisk, C. 25,074
Richard Henry, Lab. 11,977
James Lucas, LD 9,129
Peter Hart, Green 1,914
David Sodey, UKIP 1,026
Debbie Le May, Veritas 572
C. maj. 13,097 (26.36%)
7.24% swing Lab. to C.
(2001: C. maj. 5,603 (11.88%))

HERTFORDSHIRE NORTH EAST
E. 72,190 T. 47,374 (65.62%) C. hold
Oliver Heald, C. 22,402
Andrew Harrop, Lab. 13,264
Iain Coleman, LD 10,147
David Hitchman, UKIP 1,561
C. maj. 9,138 (19.29%)
5.79% swing Lab. to C.
(2001: C. maj. 3,444 (7.71%))

HERTFORDSHIRE SOUTH WEST
E. 73,170 T. 50,088 (68.45%) C. hold
*David Gauke, C. 23,494
Ed Featherstone, LD 15,021
Kerron Cross, Lab. 10,466
Colin Rodden, UKIP 1,107
C. maj. 8,473 (16.92%)
0.54% swing C. to LD
(2001: C. maj. 8,181 (17.31%))

HERTSMERE
E. 67,572 T. 42,572 (63.00%) C. hold
James Clappison, C. 22,665
Kelly Tebb, Lab. 11,572
Jonathan Davies, LD 7,817
James Dry, Soc. Lab. 518
C. maj. 11,093 (26.06%)
7.12% swing Lab. to C.
(2001: C. maj. 4,902 (11.81%))

HEXHAM
E. 60,374 T. 41,513 (68.76%) C. hold
Peter Atkinson, C. 17,605
Kevin Graham, Lab. 12,585
Andrew Duffield, LD 10,673
Ian Riddell, Eng. Dem. 521
Thomas Davison, IP 129
C. maj. 5,020 (12.09%)
3.06% swing Lab. to C.
(2001: C. maj. 2,529 (5.96%))

HEYWOOD & MIDDLETON
E. 71,510 T. 39,053 (54.61%)
Lab. (Co-op) hold
Jim Dobbin, Lab. (Co-op) 19,438
Stephen Pathmarajah, C. 8,355
Crea Lavin, LD 7,261
Gary Aronsson, BNP 1,855
Phil Burke, Lib. 1,377
Dr John Whittaker, UKIP 767
Lab. (Co-op) maj. 11,083 (28.38%)
0.86% swing Lab. (Co-op) to C.
(2001: Lab. (Co-op) maj. 11,670 (30.09%))

HIGH PEAK
E. 75,275 T. 49,989 (66.41%) Lab. hold
Tom Levitt, Lab. 19,809
Andrew Bingham, C. 19,074
Marc Godwin, LD 10,000
Michael Schwartz, UKIP 1,106
Lab. maj. 735 (1.47%)
3.93% swing Lab. to C.
(2001: Lab. maj. 4,489 (9.33%))

HITCHIN & HARPENDEN
E. 67,207 T. 47,387 (70.51%) C. hold
Rt. Hon. Peter Lilley, C. 23,627
Hannah Hedges, LD 12,234
Paul Orrett, Lab. 10,499
John Saunders, UKIP 828
Peter Rigby, Ind. 199
C. maj. 11,393 (24.04%)
2.66% swing C. to LD
(2001: C. maj. 6,663 (14.83%))

HOLBORN & ST PANCRAS
E. 68,237 T. 34,359 (50.35%) Lab. hold
Rt. Hon. Frank Dobson, Lab. 14,857
Jill Fraser, LD 10,070
Margot James, C. 6,482
Adrian Oliver, Green 2,798
Rainbow George Weiss, Vote Dream 152
Lab. maj. 4,787 (13.93%)
10.98% swing Lab. to LD
(2001: Lab. maj. 11,175 (35.90%))

HORNCHURCH
E. 59,773 T. 38,169 (63.86%) C. gain
*James Brokenshire, C. 16,355
John Cryer, Lab. 15,875
Nat Green, LD 2,894
Ian Moore, BNP 1,313
Lawrence Webb, UKIP 1,033
Malvin Brown, RA 395
Graham Williamson, Third 304
C. maj. 480 (1.26%)
2.71% swing Lab. to C.
(2001: Lab. maj. 1,482 (4.17%))

HORNSEY & WOOD GREEN
E. 76,621 T. 47,330 (61.77%) LD gain
*Lynne Featherstone, LD 20,512
Barbara Roche, Lab. 18,117
Peter Forrest, C. 6,014
Jayne Forbes, Green 2,377
Roy Freshwater, UKIP 310
LD maj. 2,395 (5.06%)
14.57% swing Lab. to LD
(2001: Lab. maj. 10,614 (24.09%))

HORSHAM
E. 80,974 T. 54,495 (67.30%) C. hol
Rt. Hon. Francis Maude, C. 27,24
Rosie Sharpley, LD 14,61
Rehman Chishti, Lab. 9,32
Hugo Miller, UKIP 2,55
Jim Duggan, Ind. 41
Martin Jeremiah, PHF 35
C. maj. 12,627 (23.17%)
1.87% swing C. to LD
(2001: C. maj. 13,666 (26.92%))

HOUGHTON & WASHINGTON EAST
E. 67,089 T. 34,694 (51.71%) Lab. hol
Fraser Kemp, Lab. 22,31
Mark Greenfield, LD 6,24
Anthony Devenish, C. 4,77
John Richardson, BNP 1,36
Lab. maj. 16,065 (46.30%)
7.20% swing Lab. to LD
(2001: Lab. maj. 19,818 (58.91%))

HOVE
E. 69,939 T. 44,796 (64.05%) Lab. hol
*Celia Barlow, Lab. 16,78
Nicholas Boles, C. 16,36
Paul Elgood, LD 8,00
Anthea Ballam, Green 2,57
Stuart Bower, UKIP 57
Paddy O'Keeffe, Respect 26
Bob Dobbs, Ind. 9
Richard Franklin, Silent 7
Brian Ralfe, Ind. 5
Lab. maj. 420 (0.94%)
3.31% swing Lab. to C.
(2001: Lab. maj. 3,171 (7.55%))

HUDDERSFIELD
E. 61,723 T. 34,940 (56.61%)
Lab. (Co-op) hol
Barry Sheerman, Lab. (Co-op) 16,34
Emma Bone, LD 7,99
David Meacock, C. 7,59
Julie Stewart-Turner, Green 1,65
Karl Hanson, BNP 1,03
Theresa Quarmby, Ind. 32
Lab. (Co-op) maj. 8,351 (23.90%)
7.18% swing Lab. (Co-op) to LD
(2001: Lab. (Co-op) maj. 10,046 (28.39%))

HULL EAST
E. 65,407 T. 31,022 (47.43%) Lab. hol
Rt. Hon. John Prescott, Lab. 17,60
Andy Sloan, LD 5,86
Katy Lindsay, C. 4,03
Alan Siddle, BNP 1,02
Janet Toker, Lib. 1,01
Graham Morris, Veritas 75
Ronald Noon, Ind. 33
Linda Muir, Soc. Lab. 20
Carl Wagner, LCA 18
Lab. maj. 11,747 (37.87%)
5.88% swing Lab. to LD
(2001: Lab. maj. 15,325 (49.64%))

ULL NORTH
. 62,590 T. 29,584 (47.27%) Lab. hold
Diana Johnson, Lab. 15,364
enis Healy, LD 8,013
ydia Rivlin, C. 3,822
lartin Deane, Green 858
rian Wainwright, BNP 766
ineke Robinson, Veritas 389
hristopher Veasey, Northern 193
arl Wagner, LCA 179
ab. maj. 7,351 (24.85%)
.30% swing Lab. to LD
2001: Lab. maj. 10,721 (37.44%))

ULL WEST & HESSLE
. 61,494 T. 27,818 (45.24%) Lab. hold
.t. Hon. Alan Johnson, Lab. 15,305
avid Nolan, LD 5,855
aren Woods, C. 5,769
tephen Wallis, Veritas 889
ab. maj. 9,450 (33.97%)
.66% swing Lab. to LD
2001: Lab. maj. 10,951 (37.87%))

UNTINGDON
. 83,843 T. 52,418 (62.52%) C. hold
onathan Djanogly, C. 26,646
ulian Huppert, LD 13,799
tephen Sartain, Lab. 9,821
erek Norman, UKIP 2,152
. maj. 12,847 (24.51%)
.78% swing C. to LD
2001: C. maj. 12,792 (26.06%))

IYNDBURN
. 67,086 T. 39,449 (58.80%) Lab. hold
reg Pope, Lab. 18,136
ames Mawdsley, C. 12,549
ill Greene, LD 5,577
hristian Jackson, BNP 2,444
r John Whittaker, UKIP 743
ab. maj. 5,587 (14.16%)
.66% swing Lab. to C.
2001: Lab. maj. 8,219 (21.49%))

LFORD NORTH
. 70,718 T. 43,000 (60.80%) C. gain
Lee Scott, C. 18,781
inda Perham, Lab. 17,128
lark Gayler, LD 5,896
ndrew Cross, UKIP 902
lartin Levin, Ind. 293
. maj. 1,653 (3.84%)
.55% swing Lab. to C.
2001: Lab. maj. 2,115 (5.26%))

LFORD SOUTH
. 79,639 T. 42,693 (53.61%)
Lab. (Co-op) hold
like Gapes, Lab. (Co-op) 20,856
tephen Metcalfe, C. 11,628
latthew Lake, LD 8,761
ashif Rana, BPP 763
olin Taylor, UKIP 685
ab. (Co-op) maj. 9,228 (21.61%)
.14% swing Lab. (Co-op) to C.
2001: Lab. (Co-op) maj. 13,997
33.90%))

IPSWICH
E. 68,825 T. 41,878 (60.85%) Lab. hold
Chris Mole, Lab. 18,336
Paul West, C. 13,004
Richard Atkins, LD 8,464
Alison West, UKIP 1,134
Jervis Kay, Eng. Dem. 641
Sally Wainman, Ind. 299
Lab. maj. 5,332 (12.73%)
4.03% swing Lab. to C.
(2001 Nov. by-election: Lab. maj. 4,087 (14.91%))
(2001: Lab. maj. 8,081 (20.79%))

ISLE OF WIGHT
E. 109,046 T. 66,843 (61.30%) C. hold
Andrew Turner, C. 32,717
Anthony Rowlands, LD 19,739
Mark Chiverton, Lab. 11,484
Michael Tarrant, UKIP 2,352
Edward Corby, Ind. 551
C. maj. 12,978 (19.42%)
7.48% swing LD to C.
(2001: C. maj. 2,826 (4.45%))

ISLINGTON NORTH
E. 58,427 T. 31,494 (53.90%) Lab. hold
Jeremy Corbyn, Lab. 16,118
Laura Willoughby, LD 9,402
Nicola Talbot, C. 3,740
Jon Nott, Green 2,234
Lab. maj. 6,716 (21.32%)
10.78% swing Lab. to LD
(2001: Lab. maj. 12,958 (42.88%))

ISLINGTON SOUTH & FINSBURY
E. 57,748 T. 30,961 (53.61%) Lab. hold
*Emily Thornberry, Lab. 12,345
Bridget Fox, LD 11,861
Melanie McLean, C. 4,594
James Humphries, Green 1,471
Patricia Theophanides, UKIP 470
Andy the Hat Gardner, Loony 189
Chris Gidden, Ind. 31
Lab. maj. 484 (1.56%)
12.12% swing Lab. to LD
(2001: Lab. maj. 7,280 (25.81%))

JARROW
E. 61,814 T. 33,978 (54.97%) Lab. hold
Stephen Hepburn, Lab. 20,554
Bill Schardt, LD 6,650
Linkson Jack, C. 4,807
Alan Badger, UKIP 1,567
Roger Nettleship, SNH 400
Lab. maj. 13,904 (40.92%)
5.06% swing Lab. to LD
(2001: Lab. maj. 17,595 (51.03%))

KEIGHLEY
E. 68,229 T. 46,312 (67.88%) Lab. hold
Ann Cryer, Lab. 20,720
Karl Poulsen, C. 15,868
Nader Fekri, LD 5,484
Nick Griffin, BNP 4,240
Lab. maj. 4,852 (10.48%)
0.62% swing C. to Lab.
(2001: Lab. maj. 4,005 (9.24%))

KENSINGTON & CHELSEA
E. 62,662 T. 31,336 (50.01%) C. hold
†Rt. Hon. Sir Malcolm Rifkind, C. 18,144
Jennifer Kingsley, LD 5,726
Catherine Atkinson, Lab. 5,521
Julia Stephenson, Green 1,342
Mildred Eilorat, UKIP 395
Alfred Bovill, Ind. 107
Eddie Adams, Green Soc. 101
C. maj. 12,418 (39.63%)
0.46% swing LD to C.
(2001: C. maj. 8,771 (31.28%))

KETTERING
E. 81,887 T. 55,646 (67.95%) C. gain
*Philip Hollobone, C. 25,401
Phil Sawford, Lab. 22,100
Roger Aron, LD 6,882
Rosemarie Clark, UKIP 1,263
C. maj. 3,301 (5.93%)
3.58% swing Lab. to C.
(2001: Lab. maj. 665 (1.24%))

KINGSTON & SURBITON
E. 72,671 T. 49,750 (68.46%) LD hold
Edward Davey, LD 25,397
Kevin Davis, C. 16,431
Nick Parrott, Lab. 6,553
Barry Thornton, UKIP 657
John Hayball, Soc. Lab. 366
David Henson, Veritas 200
Rainbow George Weiss, Vote Dream 146
LD maj. 8,966 (18.02%)
6.95% swing LD to C.
(2001: LD maj. 15,676 (31.93%))

KINGSWOOD
E. 84,400 T. 56,311 (66.72%) Lab. hold
Dr Roger Berry, Lab. 26,491
Owen Inskip, C. 18,618
Geoff Brewer, LD 9,089
John Knight, UKIP 1,444
David Burnside, Ind. 669
Lab. maj. 7,873 (13.98%)
6.26% swing Lab. to C.
(2001: Lab. maj. 13,962 (26.51%))

KNOWSLEY NORTH & SEFTON EAST
E. 70,403 T. 37,053 (52.63%) Lab. hold
George Howarth, Lab. 23,461
Flo Clucas, LD 7,192
Naman Purewal, C. 5,064
Michael McDermott, BNP 872
Stephen Whatham, Soc. Lab. 464
Lab. maj. 16,269 (43.91%)
4.52% swing Lab. to LD
(2001: Lab. maj. 18,927 (50.45%))

KNOWSLEY SOUTH
E. 70,726 T. 36,444 (51.53%) Lab. hold
Eddie O'Hara, Lab. 24,820
David Smithson, LD 7,132
Andrea Leadsom, C. 4,492
Lab. maj. 17,688 (48.53%)
4.86% swing Lab. to LD
(2001: Lab. maj. 21,316 (58.26%))

LANCASHIRE WEST
E. 74,777 T. 43,155 (57.71%) Lab. hold
*Rosie Cooper, Lab. 20,746
Alf Doran, C. 14,662
Richard Kemp, LD 6,059
Alan Freeman, UKIP 871
Stephen Garrett, Eng. Dem. 525
David Braid, Clause 28 292
Lab. maj. 6,084 (14.10%)
4.17% swing Lab. to C.
(2001: Lab. maj. 9,643 (22.44%))

LANCASTER & WYRE
E. 80,739 T. 52,061 (64.48%) C. gain
*Ben Wallace, C. 22,266
Anne Sacks, Lab. 18,095
Stuart Langhorn, LD 8,453
Jon Barry, Green 2,278
John Mander, UKIP 969
C. maj. 4,171 (8.01%)
4.47% swing Lab. to C.
(2001: Lab. maj. 481 (0.92%))

LEEDS CENTRAL
E. 62,939 T. 29,186 (46.37%) Lab. hold
Rt. Hon. Hilary Benn, Lab. 17,526
Ruth Coleman, LD 5,660
Brian Cattell, C. 3,865
Mark Collett, BNP 1,201
Peter Sewards, UKIP 494
Mick Dear, Ind. 189
Oluwole Taiwo, Ind. 126
Julian Fitzgerald, AFC 125
Lab. maj. 11,866 (40.66%)
6.53% swing Lab. to LD
(2001: Lab. maj. 14,381 (52.67%))

LEEDS EAST
E. 54,691 T. 30,077 (54.99%) Lab. hold
George Mudie, Lab. 17,799
Andrew Tear, LD 6,221
Dominic Ponniah, C. 5,557
Peter Socrates, Ind. 500
Lab. maj. 11,578 (38.49%)
5.48% swing Lab. to LD
(2001: Lab. maj. 12,643 (43.51%))

LEEDS NORTH EAST
E. 63,304 T. 41,467 (65.50%) Lab. hold
Fabian Hamilton, Lab. 18,632
Matthew Lobley, C. 13,370
Jonathan Brown, LD 8,427
Celia Foote, Green Soc. 1,038
Lab. maj. 5,262 (12.69%)
2.57% swing Lab. to C.
(2001: Lab. maj. 7,089 (17.82%))

LEEDS NORTH WEST
E. 71,644 T. 44,711 (62.41%) LD gain
*Greg Mulholland, LD 16,612
Judith Blake, Lab. 14,735
George Lee, C. 11,510
Martin Hemingway, Green 1,128
Adrian Knowles, Eng. Dem. 545
Jeannie Sutton, Green Soc. 181
LD maj. 1,877 (4.20%)
9.59% swing Lab. to LD
(2001: Lab. maj. 5,236 (12.33%))

LEEDS WEST
E. 62,882 T. 33,718 (53.62%) Lab. hold
Rt. Hon. John Battle, Lab. 18,704
Darren Finlay, LD 5,894
Tim Metcalfe, C. 4,807
David Blackburn, Green 2,519
Julie Day, BNP 1,166
David Sewards, UKIP 628
Lab. maj. 12,810 (37.99%)
6.85% swing Lab. to LD
(2001: Lab. maj. 14,935 (46.54%))

LEICESTER EAST
E. 66,383 T. 41,306 (62.22%) Lab. hold
Keith Vaz, Lab. 24,015
Suella Fernandes, C. 8,139
Susan Cooper, LD 7,052
Colin Brown, Veritas 1,666
Valerie Smalley, Soc. Lab. 434
Lab. maj. 15,876 (38.44%)
2.69% swing C. to Lab.
(2001: Lab. maj. 13,442 (33.06%))

LEICESTER SOUTH
E. 72,310 T. 42,411 (58.65%) Lab. gain
*Sir Peter Soulsby, Lab. 16,688
Parmjit Singh Gill, LD 12,971
Martin McElwee, C. 7,549
Yvonne Ridley, Respect 2,720
Matthew Follett, Green 1,379
Ken Roseblade, Veritas 573
Dave Roberts, Soc. Lab. 315
Paul Lord, Ind. 216
Lab. maj. 3,717 (8.76%)
14.26% swing Lab. to LD
(2004 July by-election: LD maj.1,654 (5.62%))
(2001: Lab. maj. 13,243 (31.43%))

LEICESTER WEST
E. 62,389 T. 33,224 (53.25%) Lab. hold
Rt. Hon. Patricia Hewitt, Lab. 17,184
Sarah Richardson, C. 8,114
Zuffar Haq, LD 5,803
Geoff Forse, Green 1,571
Steve Score, Soc. Alt. 552
Lab. maj. 9,070 (27.30%)
0.86% swing Lab. to C.
(2001: Lab. maj. 9,639 (29.02%))

LEICESTERSHIRE NORTH WEST
E. 70,519 T. 47,140 (66.85%) Lab. (Co-op) hold
David Taylor, Lab. (Co-op) 21,449
Nicola Le Page, C. 16,972
Rod Keyes, LD 5,682
John Blunt, UKIP 1,563
Clive Potter, BNP 1,474
Lab. (Co-op) maj. 4,477 (9.50%)
4.31% swing Lab. (Co-op) to C.
(2001: Lab. (Co-op) maj. 8,157 (18.12%))

LEIGH
E. 72,473 T. 36,488 (50.35%) Lab. hold
Andy Burnham, Lab. 23,097
Laurance Wedderburn, C. 5,825
Dave Crowther, LD 4,962
Ian Franzen, CAP 2,189
Thomas Hampson, LCA 415
Lab. maj. 17,272 (47.34%)
0.49% swing C. to Lab.
(2001: Lab. maj. 16,362 (46.35%))

LEOMINSTER
E. 70,587 T. 48,793 (69.12%) C. hol
Bill Wiggin, C. 25,40
Caroline Williams, LD 12,22
Paul Bell, Lab. 7,42
Felicity Norman, Green 2,19
Peter Venables, UKIP 1,55
C. maj. 13,187 (27.03%)
2.42% swing LD to C.
(2001: C. maj. 10,367 (22.19%))

LEWES
E. 67,073 T. 46,552 (69.40%) LD hol
Norman Baker, LD 24,37
Rory Love, C. 15,90
Richard Black, Lab. 4,16
Susan Murray, Green 1,07
John Petley, UKIP 1,03
LD maj. 8,474 (18.20%)
1.58% swing LD to C.
(2001: LD maj. 9,710 (21.37%))

LEWISHAM DEPTFORD
E. 59,018 T. 30,393 (51.50%) Lab. hol
Joan Ruddock, Lab. 16,90
Columba Blango, LD 5,09
James Cartlidge, C. 3,77
Darren Johnson, Green 3,36
Ian Page, Soc. Alt. 74
Dr David Holland, UKIP 51
Lab. maj. 11,811 (38.86%)
7.21% swing Lab. to LD
(2001: Lab. maj. 15,293 (52.54%))

LEWISHAM EAST
E. 59,135 T. 31,127 (52.64%) Lab. hol
Bridget Prentice, Lab. 14,26
James Cleverly, C. 7,51
Richard Thomas, LD 6,78
Anna Baker, Green 1,24
Arnold Tarling, UKIP 69
Bernard Franklin, NF 62
Lab. maj. 6,751 (21.69%)
4.12% swing Lab. to C.
(2001: Lab. maj. 8,959 (29.82%))

LEWISHAM WEST
E. 58,349 T. 31,923 (54.71%) Lab. hol
Jim Dowd, Lab. 16,61
Alex Feakes, LD 6,67
Evett McAnuff, C. 6,39
Nick Long, Green 1,46
Jens Winton, UKIP 77
Lab. maj. 9,932 (31.11%)
8.25% swing Lab. to LD
(2001: Lab. maj. 11,920 (38.68%))

LEYTON & WANSTEAD
E. 60,444 T. 33,272 (55.05%) Lab. hol
Harry Cohen, Lab. 15,23
Meher Khan, LD 8,37
Julien Foster, C. 7,39
Ashley Gunstock, Green 1,52
Nick Jones, UKIP 59
Marc Robertson, Ind. 15
Lab. maj. 6,857 (20.61%)
10.71% swing Lab. to LD
(2001: Lab. maj. 12,904 (38.27%))

LICHFIELD
E. 65,565 T. 43,744 (66.72%) C. hol
Michael Fabricant, C. 21,27
Nigel Gardner, Lab. 14,19
Ian Jackson, LD 6,80
Malcolm McKenzie, UKIP 1,47
C. maj. 7,080 (16.19%)
2.78% swing Lab. to C.
(2001: C. maj. 4,426 (10.62%))

LINCOLN
E. 65,203 T. 36,857 (56.53%) Lab. hold
Gillian Merron, Lab. 16,724
Karl McCartney, C. 12,110
Lisa Gabriel, LD 6,715
Nicholas Smith, UKIP 1,308
Lab. maj. 4,614 (12.52%)
5.08% swing Lab. to C.
(2001: Lab. maj. 8,420 (22.68%))

LIVERPOOL GARSTON
E. 63,669 T. 34,974 (54.93%) Lab. hold
Maria Eagle, Lab. 18,900
Paula Keaveney, LD 11,707
Amber Rudd, C. 3,424
Kevin Kearney, UKIP 780
David Oatley, WRP 163
Lab. maj. 7,193 (20.57%)
8.85% swing Lab. to LD
(2001: Lab. maj. 12,494 (38.27%))

LIVERPOOL RIVERSIDE
E. 75,171 T. 31,191 (41.49%) Lab. (Co-op) hold
Louise Ellman, Lab. (Co-op) 17,951
Richard Marbrow, LD 7,737
Gabrielle Howatson, C. 2,843
Peter Cranie, Green 1,707
Beth Marshall, Soc. Lab. 498
Ann Irving, UKIP 455
Lab. (Co-op) maj. 10,214 (32.75%)
10.98% swing Lab. (Co-op) to LD
(2001: Lab. (Co-op) maj. 13,950 (54.70%))

LIVERPOOL WALTON
E. 62,044 T. 27,930 (45.02%) Lab. hold
Peter Kilfoyle, Lab. 20,322
Kiron Reid, LD 4,365
Sharon Buckle, C. 1,655
Joseph Moran, UKIP 1,108
Daniel Wood, Lib. 480
Lab. maj. 15,957 (57.13%)
3.05% swing Lab. to LD
(2001: Lab. maj. 17,996 (63.24%))

LIVERPOOL WAVERTREE
E. 69,189 T. 35,171 (50.83%) Lab. hold
Rt. Hon. Jane Kennedy, Lab. 18,441
Colin Eldridge, LD 13,268
Jason Steen, C. 2,331
Mark Bill, UKIP 660
Gary Theys, Soc. Lab. 244
Paul Filby, Dem. Soc. All. 227
Lab. maj. 5,173 (14.71%)
11.81% swing Lab. to LD
(2001: Lab. maj. 12,319 (38.33%))

LIVERPOOL WEST DERBY
E. 64,591 T. 30,464 (47.16%) Lab. hold
Robert Wareing, Lab. 19,140
Patrick Maloney, LD 3,915
Steve Radford, Lib. 3,606
Peter Garrett, C. 2,567
Kai Andersen, Soc. Lab. 698
Peter Baden, UKIP 538
Lab. maj. 15,225 (49.98%)
2.66% swing Lab. to LD
(2001: Lab. maj. 15,853 (51.29%))

LOUGHBOROUGH
E. 72,351 T. 46,140 (63.77%) Lab. (Co-op) hold
Andy Reed, Lab. (Co-op) 19,098
Nicky Morgan, C. 17,102
Graeme Smith, LD 8,258
Bernard Sherratt, UKIP 1,094
John McVay, Veritas 588
Lab. (Co-op) maj. 1,996 (4.33%)
5.04% swing Lab. (Co-op) to C.
(2001: Lab. (Co-op) maj. 6,378 (14.41%))

LOUTH & HORNCASTLE
E. 75,313 T. 46,683 (61.99%) C. hold
Sir Peter Tapsell, C. 21,744
Frank Hodgkiss, Lab. 11,848
Fiona Martin, LD 9,480
Christopher Pain, UKIP 3,611
C. maj. 9,896 (21.20%)
2.10% swing Lab. to C.
(2001: C. maj. 7,554 (16.99%))

LUDLOW
E. 64,572 T. 46,540 (72.07%) C. gain
*Philip Dunne, C. 20,979
Matthew Green, LD 18,952
Nigel Knowles, Lab. 4,974
Jim Gaffney, Green 852
Michael Zuckerman, UKIP 783
C. maj. 2,027 (4.36%)
4.07% swing LD to C.
(2001: LD maj. 1,630 (3.78%))

LUTON NORTH
E. 68,175 T. 39,122 (57.38%) Lab. hold
Kelvin Hopkins, Lab. 19,062
Hannah Hall, C. 12,575
Linda Jack, LD 6,081
Colin Brown, UKIP 1,255
Kayson Gurney, Forum 149
Lab. maj. 6,487 (16.58%)
4.46% swing Lab. to C.
(2001: Lab. maj. 9,977 (25.50%))

LUTON SOUTH
E. 71,949 T. 38,918 (54.09%) Lab. hold
Margaret Moran, Lab. 16,610
Richard Stay, C. 10,960
Qurban Hussain, LD 8,778
Charles Lawman, UKIP 957
Marc Scheimann, Green 790
Mohammed Ilyas, Respect 725
Arthur Lynn, WRP 98
Lab. maj. 5,650 (14.52%)
5.62% swing Lab. to C.
(2001: Lab. maj. 10,133 (25.75%))

MACCLESFIELD
E. 72,267 T. 45,621 (63.13%) C. hold
Sir Nicholas Winterton, C. 22,628
Stephen Carter, Lab. 13,227
Catherine O'Brien, LD 8,918
John Scott, Veritas 848
C. maj. 9,401 (20.61%)
2.41% swing Lab. to C.
(2001: C. maj. 7,200 (15.79%))

MAIDENHEAD
E. 63,978 T. 45,850 (71.67%) C. hold
Rt. Hon. Theresa May, C. 23,312
Kathryn Newbound, LD 17,081
Janet Pritchard, Lab. 4,144
Tim Rait, BNP 704
Douglas Lewis, UKIP 609
C. maj. 6,231 (13.59%)
3.00% swing LD to C.
(2001: C. maj. 3,284 (7.58%))

MAIDSTONE & THE WEALD
E. 74,054 T. 48,755 (65.84%) C. hold
Rt. Hon. Ann Widdecombe, C. 25,670
Beth Breeze, Lab. 10,814
Mark Corney, LD 10,808
Anthony Robertson, UKIP 1,463
C. maj. 14,856 (30.47%)
3.92% swing Lab. to C.
(2001: C. maj. 10,318 (22.64%))

MAKERFIELD
E. 69,039 T. 35,580 (51.54%) Lab. hold
Rt. Hon. Ian McCartney, Lab. 22,494
Kulveer Ranger, C. 4,345
Trevor Beswick, LD 3,789
Peter Franzen, CAP 2,769
Dennis Shambley, BNP 1,221
Gregory Atherton, UKIP 962
Lab. maj. 18,149 (51.01%)
0.04% swing C. to Lab.
(2001: Lab. maj. 17,750 (50.92%))

MALDON & CHELMSFORD EAST
E. 69,502 T. 46,091 (66.32%) C. hold
John Whittingdale, C. 23,732
Sue Tibballs, Lab. 11,159
Matthew Lambert, LD 9,270
Jesse Pryke, UKIP 1,930
C. maj. 12,573 (27.28%)
4.05% swing Lab. to C.
(2001: C. maj. 8,462 (19.19%))

MANCHESTER BLACKLEY
E. 60,229 T. 27,591 (45.81%) Lab. hold
Graham Stringer, Lab. 17,187
Iain Donaldson, LD 5,160
Amar Ahmed, C. 3,690
Roger Bullock, UKIP 1,554
Lab. maj. 12,027 (43.59%)
6.99% swing Lab. to LD
(2001: Lab. maj. 14,464 (54.53%))

MANCHESTER CENTRAL
E. 69,656 T. 29,264 (42.01%) Lab. hold
Tony Lloyd, Lab. 16,993
Marc Ramsbottom, LD 7,217
Tom Jackson, C. 2,504
Steven Durrant, Green 1,292
Richard Kemp, NF 421
Damien O'Connor, Ind. Pr. Lab. 382
Dr John Whittaker, UKIP 272
Ronald Sinclair, Soc. Lab. 183
Lab. maj. 9,776 (33.41%)
9.80% swing Lab. to LD
(2001: Lab. maj. 13,742 (53.00%))

MANCHESTER GORTON
E. 64,696 T. 29,123 (45.02%) Lab. hold
Rt. Hon. Sir Gerald Kaufman, Lab. 15,480
Qassim Afzal, LD 9,672
Amanda Byrne, C. 2,848
Gregory Beaman, UKIP 783
Dan Waller, WRP 181
Matthew Kay, RP 159
Lab. maj. 5,808 (19.94%)
10.79% swing Lab. to LD
(2001: Lab. maj. 11,304 (41.51%))

MANCHESTER WITHINGTON
E. 67,781 T. 37,458 (55.26%) LD gain
*John Leech, LD 15,872
Rt. Hon. Keith Bradley, Lab. 15,205
Karen Bradley, C. 3,919
Brian Candeland, Green 1,595
Dr Robert Gutfreund-Walmsley, UKIP 424
Ivan Benett, Ind. 243
Yasmin Zalzala, Ind. 153
Richard Reed, TP 47
LD maj. 667 (1.78%)
17.33% swing Lab. to LD
(2001: Lab. maj. 11,524 (32.88%))

MANSFIELD
E. 69,131 T. 38,276 (55.37%) Lab. hold
Alan Meale, Lab. 18,400
Anne Wright, C. 7,035
Stewart Rickersey, Ind. 6,491
Roger Shelley, LD 5,316
Michael Harvey, Veritas 1,034
Lab. maj. 11,365 (29.69%)
0.13% swing Lab. to C.
(2001: Lab. maj. 11,038 (29.95%))

MEDWAY
E. 67,251 T. 41,093 (61.10%) Lab. hold
Bob Marshall-Andrews, Lab. 17,333
Mark Reckless, C. 17,120
Geoffrey Juby, LD 5,152
Robert Oakley, UKIP 1,488
Lab. maj. 213 (0.52%)
4.64% swing Lab. to C.
(2001: Lab. maj. 3,780 (9.79%))

MERIDEN
E. 77,342 T. 46,503 (60.13%) C. hold
Caroline Spelman, C. 22,416
Jim Brown, Lab. 15,407
William Laitinen, LD 7,113
Denis Brookes, UKIP 1,567
C. maj. 7,009 (15.07%)
3.29% swing Lab. to C.
(2001: C. maj. 3,784 (8.49%))

MIDDLESBROUGH
E. 65,924 T. 32,140 (48.75%) Lab. hold
Sir Stuart Bell, Lab. 18,562
Joe Michna, LD 5,995
Caroline Flynn-Macleod, C. 5,263
Ron Armes, BNP 819
Michael Landers, UKIP 768
Jackie Elder, Ind. 503
Derrick Arnott, Ind. 230
Lab. maj. 12,567 (39.10%)
9.03% swing Lab. to LD
(2001: Lab. maj. 16,330 (48.43%))

MIDDLESBROUGH SOUTH & CLEVELAND EAST
E. 71,883 T. 43,696 (60.79%) Lab. hold
Dr Ashok Kumar, Lab. 21,945
Mark Brooks, C. 13,945
Carl Minns, LD 6,049
Geoffrey Groves, BNP 1,099
Charlotte Bull, UKIP 658
Lab. maj. 8,000 (18.31%)
1.47% swing Lab. to C.
(2001: Lab. maj. 9,351 (21.26%))

MILTON KEYNES NORTH EAST
E. 78,758 T. 50,104 (63.62%) C. gain
*Mark Lancaster, C. 19,674
Brian White, Lab. 18,009
Jane Carr, LD 9,789
Michael Phillips, UKIP 1,400
Peter Richardson, Green 1,090
Anant Vyas, Ind. 142
C. maj. 1,665 (3.32%)
3.60% swing Lab. to C.
(2001: Lab. maj. 1,829 (3.88%))

MILTON KEYNES SOUTH WEST
E. 82,228 T. 48,709 (59.24%) Lab. hold
Dr Phyllis Starkey, Lab. 20,862
Iain Stewart, C. 16,852
Neil Stuart, LD 7,909
George Harlock, UKIP 1,750
Alan Francis, Green 1,336
Lab. maj. 4,010 (8.23%)
3.57% swing Lab. to C.
(2001: Lab. maj. 6,978 (15.38%))

MITCHAM & MORDEN
E. 65,172 T. 39,868 (61.17%) Lab. hold
Siobhain McDonagh, Lab. 22,489
Andrew Shellhorn, C. 9,929
Jo Christie-Smith, LD 5,583
Tom Walsh, Green 1,395
Adrian Roberts, Veritas 286
Rathy Alagaratnam, Ind. 186
Lab. maj. 12,560 (31.50%)
2.40% swing Lab. to C.
(2001: Lab. maj. 13,785 (36.31%))

MOLE VALLEY
E. 68,181 T. 49,415 (72.48%) C. hold
Sir Paul Beresford, C. 27,060
Nasser Butt, LD 15,063
Farmida Bi, Lab. 5,310
David Payne, UKIP 1,475
Roger Meekins, Veritas 507
C. maj. 11,997 (24.28%)
1.35% swing LD to C.
(2001: C. maj. 10,153 (21.57%))

MORECAMBE & LUNESDALE
E. 67,775 T. 41,635 (61.43%) Lab. hold
Geraldine Smith, Lab. 20,331
James Airey, C. 15,563
Alex Stone, LD 5,741
Lab. maj. 4,768 (11.45%)
0.39% swing Lab. to C.
(2001: Lab. maj. 5,092 (12.22%))

MORLEY & ROTHWELL
E. 72,248 T. 42,495 (58.82%) Lab. hold
Colin Challen, Lab. 20,570
Nick Vineall, C. 8,227
Stewart Golton, LD 6,819
Robert Finnigan, Ind. 4,608
Chris Beverley, BNP 2,271
Lab. maj. 12,343 (29.05%)
1.20% swing Lab. to C.
(2001: Lab. maj. 12,090 (31.45%))

NEW FOREST EAST
E. 68,633 T. 45,235 (65.91%) C. hold
Dr Julian Lewis, C. 21,975
Brian Dash, LD 15,424
Stephen Roberts, Lab. 5,492
Katy Davies, UKIP 2,344
C. maj. 6,551 (14.48%)
2.70% swing LD to C.
(2001: C. maj. 3,829 (9.08%))

NEW FOREST WEST
E. 69,232 T. 46,067 (66.54%) C. hold
Desmond Swayne, C. 26,004
Murari Kaushik, LD 8,719
Janice Hurne, Lab. 7,590
Brian Lawrence, UKIP 1,917
Janet Richards, Green 1,837
C. maj. 17,285 (37.52%)
3.80% swing LD to C.
(2001: C. maj. 13,191 (29.92%))

NEWARK
E. 72,249 T. 45,696 (63.25%) C. hold
Patrick Mercer, C. 21,946
Jason Reece, Lab. 15,482
Stuart Thompstone, LD 7,276
Charlotte Creasy, UKIP 992
C. maj. 6,464 (14.15%)
2.56% swing Lab. to C.
(2001: C. maj. 4,073 (9.02%))

NEWBURY
E. 75,903 T. 54,673 (72.03%) C. gain
*Richard Benyon, C. 26,771
David Rendel, LD 23,311
Oscar Van Nooijen, Lab. 3,239
David McMahon, UKIP 857
Nicholas Cornish, Ind. 409
Barrie Singleton, Ind. 86
C. maj. 3,460 (6.33%)
5.54% swing LD to C.
(2001: LD maj. 2,415 (4.75%))

NEWCASTLE-UNDER-LYME
E. 68,414 T. 39,788 (58.16%) Lab. hold
Paul Farrelly, Lab. 18,053
Jeremy Lefroy, C. 9,945
Trevor Johnson, LD 7,528
David Nixon, UKIP 1,436
John Dawson, BNP 1,390
Prof. Andrew Dobson, Green 918
Marian Harvey-Lover, Veritas 518
Lab. maj. 8,108 (20.38%)
2.72% swing Lab. to C.
(2001: Lab. maj. 9,986 (25.82%))

NEWCASTLE UPON TYNE CENTRAL
E. 62,734 T. 35,920 (57.26%) Lab. hold
Jim Cousins, Lab. 16,211
Greg Stone, LD 12,229
Wendy Morton, C. 5,749
Joe Hulm, Green 1,254
Clive Harding, NACVP 477
Lab. maj. 3,982 (11.09%)
11.10% swing Lab. to LD
(2001: Lab. maj. 11,605 (33.28%))

NEWCASTLE UPON TYNE EAST & WALLSEND
E. 56,900 T. 31,678 (55.67%) Lab. hold
Rt. Hon. Nick Brown, Lab. 17,462
David Ord, LD 9,897
Norma Dias, C. 3,532
William Hopwood, Soc. Alt. 582
Martin Levy, Comm. Brit. 205
Lab. maj. 7,565 (23.88%)
9.81% swing Lab. to LD
(2001: Lab. maj. 14,223 (43.50%))

NEWCASTLE UPON TYNE NORTH
E. 64,599 T. 38,444 (59.51%) Lab. hold
Doug Henderson, Lab. 19,224
Ron Beadle, LD 12,201
Neil Hudson, C. 6,022
Roland Wood, NF 997
Lab. maj. 7,023 (18.27%)
11.22% swing Lab. to LD
(2001: Lab. maj. 14,450 (39.73%))

NORFOLK MID
E. 81,738 T. 54,734 (66.96%) C. hold
Keith Simpson, C. 23,564
Daniel Zeichner, Lab. 16,004
Vivienne Clifford-Jackson, LD 12,988
Simon Fletcher, UKIP 2,178
C. maj. 7,560 (13.81%)
2.57% swing Lab. to C.
(2001: C. maj. 4,562 (8.68%))

NORFOLK NORTH
E. 80,784 T. 58,965 (72.99%) LD hold
Norman Lamb, LD 31,515
Iain Dale, C. 20,909
Philip Harris, Lab. 5,447
Stuart Agnew, UKIP 978
Justin Appleyard, Ind. 116
LD maj. 10,606 (17.99%)
8.56% swing C. to LD
(2001: LD maj. 483 (0.86%))

NORFOLK NORTH WEST
E. 82,171 T. 50,649 (61.64%) C. hold
Henry Bellingham, C. 25,471
Damien Welfare, Lab. 16,291
Simon Higginson, LD 7,026
Michael Stone, UKIP 1,861
C. maj. 9,180 (18.12%)
5.66% swing Lab. to C.
(2001: C. maj. 3,485 (6.81%))

NORFOLK SOUTH
E. 85,896 T. 58,974 (68.66%) C. hold
Richard Bacon, C. 26,399
Dr Ian Mack, LD 17,617
John Morgan, Lab. 13,262
Philip Tye, UKIP 1,696
C. maj. 8,782 (14.89%)
1.28% swing LD to C.
(2001: C. maj. 6,893 (12.32%))

NORFOLK SOUTH WEST
E. 88,260 T. 55,127 (62.46%) C. hold
†Christopher Fraser, C. 25,881
Charmaine Morgan, Lab. 15,795
April Pond, LD 10,207
Delia Hall, UKIP 2,738
Kim Hayes, Ind. 506
C. maj. 10,086 (18.30%)
0.30% swing Lab. to C.
(2001: C. maj. 9,366 (17.69%))

NORMANTON
E. 65,129 T. 37,424 (57.46%)
Lab. (Co-op) hold
*Ed Balls, Lab. (Co-op) 19,161
Andrew Percy, C. 9,159
Simone Butterworth, LD 6,357
John Aveyard, BNP 1,967
Mark Harrop, Ind. 780
Lab. (Co-op) maj. 10,002 (26.73%)
1.18% swing Lab. (Co-op) to C.
(2001: Lab. (Co-op) maj. 9,937 (29.09%))

NORTHAMPTON NORTH
E. 73,926 T. 42,048 (56.88%) Lab. hold
Sally Keeble, Lab. 16,905
Damian Collins, C. 12,945
Andrew Simpson, LD 10,317
John Howsam, UKIP 1,050
Paul Withrington, SOS 495
Andrew Otchie, CPA 336
Lab. maj. 3,960 (9.42%)
4.80% swing Lab. to C.
(2001: Lab. maj. 7,893 (19.02%))

NORTHAMPTON SOUTH
E. 89,722 T. 54,481 (60.72%) C. gain
*Brian Binley, C. 23,818
Tony Clarke, Lab. 19,399
Kevin Barron, LD 8,327
Derek Clark, UKIP 1,032
Anthony Green, Veritas 508
John Harrisson, SOS 437
John Percival, Loony 354
Fitzy Fitzpatrick, Ind. 346
Tim Webb, CPA 260
C. maj. 4,419 (8.11%)
4.92% swing Lab. to C.
(2001: Lab. maj. 885 (1.73%))

NORTHAVON
E. 81,800 T. 59,056 (72.20%) LD hold
Prof. Steve Webb, LD 30,872
Chris Butt, C. 19,839
Patricia Gardener, Lab. 6,277
Adrian Blake, UKIP 1,032
Alan Pinder, Green 922
Thomas Beacham, Ind. 114
LD maj. 11,033 (18.68%)
0.48% swing C. to LD
(2001: LD maj. 9,877 (17.71%))

NORWICH NORTH
E. 76,992 T. 47,033 (61.09%) Lab. hold
Dr Ian Gibson, Lab. 21,097
James Tumbridge, C. 15,638
Robin Whitmore, LD 7,616
Adrian Holmes, Green 1,252
John Youles, UKIP 1,122
Bill Holden, Ind. 308
Lab. maj. 5,459 (11.61%)
0.62% swing Lab. to C.
(2001: Lab. maj. 5,863 (12.85%))

NORWICH SOUTH
E. 70,409 T. 42,190 (59.92%) Lab. hold
Rt. Hon. Charles Clarke, Lab. 15,904
Andrew Aalders-Dunthorne, LD 12,251
Antony Little, C. 9,567
Adrian Ramsay, Green 3,101
Vandra Ahlstrom, UKIP 597
Christine Constable, Eng. Dem. 466
Don Barnard, LCA 219
Roger Blackwell, WRP 85
Lab. maj. 3,653 (8.66%)
7.09% swing Lab. to LD
(2001: Lab. maj. 8,816 (20.70%))

NOTTINGHAM EAST
E. 60,634 T. 30,091 (49.63%) Lab. hold
John Heppell, Lab. 13,787
Issan Ghazni, LD 6,848
Jim Thornton, C. 6,826
Ashley Baxter, Green 1,517
Anthony Ellwood, UKIP 740
Pete Ratcliff, Soc. Unity 373
Lab. maj. 6,939 (23.06%)
11.44% swing Lab. to LD
(2001: Lab. maj. 10,320 (34.71%))

NOTTINGHAM NORTH
E. 61,894 T. 30,383 (49.09%) Lab. hold
Graham Allen, Lab. 17,842
Priti Patel, C. 5,671
Tim Ball, LD 5,190
Irena Marriott, UKIP 1,680
Lab. maj. 12,171 (40.06%)
0.34% swing Lab. to C.
(2001: Lab. maj. 12,240 (40.74%))

NOTTINGHAM SOUTH
E. 68,921 T. 34,840 (50.55%) Lab. hold
Alan Simpson, Lab. 16,506
Sudesh Mattu, C. 9,020
Tony Sutton, LD 7,961
Ken Browne, UKIP 1,353
Lab. maj. 7,486 (21.49%)
2.90% swing Lab. to C.
(2001: Lab. maj. 9,989 (27.29%))

NUNEATON
E. 73,440 T. 45,280 (61.66%) Lab. hold
Bill Olner, Lab. 19,945
Mark Pawsey, C. 17,665
Ali Asghar, LD 5,884
Keith Tyson, UKIP 1,786
Lab. maj. 2,280 (5.04%)
6.18% swing Lab. to C.
(2001: Lab. maj. 7,535 (17.40%))

OLD BEXLEY & SIDCUP
E. 68,227 T. 44,572 (65.33%) C. hold
Derek Conway, C. 22,191
Gavin Moore, Lab. 12,271
Nickolas O'Hare, LD 6,564
Michael Barnbrook, UKIP 2,015
Claire Sayers, BNP 1,227
Gregory Peters, Ind. 304
C. maj. 9,920 (22.26%)
7.16% swing Lab. to C.
(2001: C. maj. 3,345 (7.94%))

OLDHAM EAST & SADDLEWORTH
E. 75,680 T. 43,367 (57.30%) Lab. hold
Phil Woolas, Lab. 17,968
Tony Dawson, LD 14,378
Keith Chapman, C. 7,901
Michael Treacy, BNP 2,109
Valerie Nield, UKIP 873
Philip O'Grady, Ind. 138
Lab. maj. 3,590 (8.28%)
1.14% swing LD to Lab.
(2001: Lab. maj. 2,726 (6.00%))

OLDHAM WEST & ROYTON
E. 70,496 T. 37,562 (53.28%) Lab. hold
Rt. Hon. Michael Meacher, Lab. 18,452
Sean Moore, C. 7,998
Stuart Bodsworth, LD 7,519
Anita Corbett, BNP 2,606
David Short, UKIP 987
Lab. maj. 10,454 (27.83%)
2.81% swing Lab. to C.
(2001: Lab. maj. 13,365 (33.44%))

ORPINGTON
E. 78,276 T. 54,734 (69.92%) C. hold
John Horam, C. 26,718
Chris Maines, LD 21,771
Emily Bird, Lab. 4,914
Mick Greenhough, UKIP 1,331
C. maj. 4,947 (9.04%)
4.25% swing LD to C.
(2001: C. maj. 269 (0.53%))

OXFORD EAST
E. 72,234 T. 41,790 (57.85%) Lab. hold
Rt. Hon. Andrew Smith, Lab. 15,405
Steve Goddard, LD 14,442
Virginia Morris, C. 6,992
Jacob Sanders, Green 1,813
Honest Blair, Ind. 1,485
Maurice Leen, IWCA 892
Peter Gardner, UKIP 715
Pat Mylvaganam, Ind. 46
Lab. maj. 963 (2.30%)
11.83% swing Lab. to LD
(2001: Lab. maj. 10,344 (25.96%))

OXFORD WEST & ABINGDON
E. 80,195 T. 52,600 (65.59%) LD hold
Dr Evan Harris, LD 24,336
Amanda McLean, C. 16,653
Antonia Bance, Lab. 8,725
Tom Lines, Green 2,091
Marcus Watney, UKIP 795
LD maj. 7,683 (14.61%)
1.60% swing LD to C.
(2001: LD maj. 9,185 (17.81%))

PENDLE
E. 64,917 T. 41,132 (63.36%) Lab. hold
Gordon Prentice, Lab. 15,250
Jane Ellison, C. 13,070
Shazad Anwar, LD 9,528
Thomas Boocock, BNP 2,547
Graham Cannon, UKIP 737
Lab. maj. 2,180 (5.30%)
2.73% swing Lab. to C.
(2001: Lab. maj. 4,275 (10.76%))

PENRITH & THE BORDER
E. 70,922 T. 46,882 (66.10%) C. hold
Rt. Hon. David Maclean, C. 24,046
Geyve Walker, LD 12,142
Michael Boaden, Lab. 8,958
William Robinson, UKIP 1,187
Mark Gibson, LCA 549
C. maj. 11,904 (25.39%)
3.89% swing C. to LD
(2001: C. maj. 14,677 (33.17%))

PETERBOROUGH
E. 67,499 T. 41,204 (61.04%) C. gain
*Stewart Jackson, C. 17,364
Rt. Hon. Helen Clark, Lab. 14,624
Nick Sandford, LD 6,876
Mary Herdman, UKIP 1,242
Terry Blackham, NF 931
Marc Potter, MNP 167
C. maj. 2,740 (6.65%)
6.91% swing Lab. to C.
(2001: Lab. maj. 2,854 (7.17%))

PLYMOUTH DEVONPORT
E. 72,848 T. 42,013 (57.67%) Lab. hold
*Alison Seabeck, Lab. 18,612
Richard Cuming, C. 10,509
Judith Jolly, LD 8,000
Bill Wakeham, UKIP 3,324
Keith Greene, Ind. 747
Robert Hawkins, Soc. Lab. 445
Tony Staunton, Respect 376
Lab. maj. 8,103 (19.29%)
5.98% swing Lab. to C.
(2001: Lab. maj. 13,033 (31.24%))

PLYMOUTH SUTTON
E. 67,202 T. 38,192 (56.83%)
Lab. (Co-op) hold
Linda Gilroy, Lab. (Co-op) 15,497
Oliver Colvile, C. 11,388
Karen Gillard, LD 8,685
Robert Cumming, UKIP 2,392
Rob Hawkins, Soc. Lab. 230
Lab. (Co-op) maj. 4,109 (10.76%)
4.24% swing Lab. (Co-op) to C.
(2001: Lab. (Co-op) maj. 7,517 (19.24%))

PONTEFRACT & CASTLEFORD
E. 61,871 T. 32,947 (53.25%) Lab. hold
Yvette Cooper, Lab. 20,973
Simon Jones, C. 5,727
Wesley Paxton, LD 3,942
Suzy Cass, BNP 1,835
Bob Hague, Green Soc. 470
Lab. maj. 15,246 (46.27%)
2.95% swing Lab. to C.
(2001: Lab. maj. 16,378 (52.17%))

POOLE
E. 64,178 T. 40,513 (63.13%) C. hold
Robert Syms, C. 17,571
Mike Plummer, LD 11,583
Darren Brown, Lab. 9,376
John Barnes, UKIP 1,436
Peter Pirnie, BNP 547
C. maj. 5,988 (14.78%)
2.42% swing C. to LD
(2001: C. maj. 7,166 (18.27%))

POPLAR & CANNING TOWN
E. 81,544 T. 39,010 (47.84%) Lab. hold
Jim Fitzpatrick, Lab. 15,628
Tim Archer, C. 8,499
Oliur Rahman, Respect 6,573
Janet Ludlow, LD 5,420
Terry McGrenera, Green 955
Aminul Hoque, Ind. 815
Tony Smith, Veritas 650
Simeon Ademolake, CPA 470
Lab. maj. 7,129 (18.27%)
11.55% swing Lab. to C.
(2001: Lab. maj. 14,104 (41.35%))

PORTSMOUTH NORTH
E. 62,884 T. 37,717 (59.98%)
Lab. (Co-op) hold
*Sarah McCarthy-Fry, Lab. (Co-op) 15,412
Penny Mordaunt, C. 14,273
Gary Lawson, LD 6,684
Mike Smith, UKIP 1,348
Lab. (Co-op) maj. 1,139 (3.02%)
5.45% swing Lab. (Co-op) to C.
(2001: Lab. (Co-op) maj. 5,134 (13.93%))

PORTSMOUTH SOUTH
E. 70,969 T. 40,374 (56.89%) LD hold
Mike Hancock, LD 17,047
Caroline Dinenage, C. 13,685
Mark Button, Lab. 8,714
Dennis Pierson, UKIP 928
LD maj. 3,362 (8.33%)
3.60% swing LD to C.
(2001: LD maj. 6,094 (15.54%))

PRESTON
E. 63,351 T. 34,081 (53.80%)
Lab. (Co-op) hold
Mark Hendrick, Lab. (Co-op) 17,210
Fiona Bryce, C. 7,803
William Parkinson, LD 5,701
Michael Lavalette, Respect 2,318
Ellen Boardman, UKIP 1,049
Lab. (Co-op) maj. 9,407 (27.60%)
3.22% swing Lab. (Co-op) to C.
(2001: Lab. (Co-op) maj. 12,268 (34.04%))

PUDSEY
E. 70,411 T. 46,444 (65.96%) Lab. hold
Paul Truswell, Lab. 21,261
Pamela Singleton, C. 15,391
James Keeley, LD 8,551
David Daniel, UKIP 1,241
Lab. maj. 5,870 (12.64%)
0.09% swing C. to Lab.
(2001: Lab. maj. 5,626 (12.45%))

PUTNEY
E. 61,498 T. 36,574 (59.47%) C. gain
*Justine Greening, C. 15,497
Tony Colman, Lab. 13,731
Jeremy Ambache, LD 5,965
Keith Magnum, Green 993
Anthony Gahan, UKIP 388
C. maj. 1,766 (4.83%)
6.46% swing Lab. to C.
(2001: Lab. maj. 2,771 (8.09%))

RAYLEIGH
E. 71,996 T. 46,193 (64.16%) C. hold
Mark Francois, C. 25,609
Julian Ware-Lane, Lab. 10,883
Sid Cumberland, LD 7,406
Janet Davies, UKIP 2,295
C. maj. 14,726 (31.88%)
6.25% swing Lab. to C.
(2001: C. maj. 8,290 (19.38%))

READING EAST
E. 72,806 T. 43,912 (60.31%) C. gain
*Rob Wilson, C. 15,557
Tony Page, Lab. 15,082
Prof. John Howson, LD 10,619
Rob White, Green 1,548
David Lamb, UKIP 849
Jan Lloyd, Ind. 135
Rex Hora, Ind. 122
C. maj. 475 (1.08%)
6.95% swing Lab. to C.
(2001: Lab. maj. 5,588 (12.81%))

READING WEST
E. 69,011 T. 42,103 (61.01%) Lab. hold
Martin Salter, Lab. 18,940
Ewan Cameron, C. 14,258
Denise Gaines, LD 6,663
Peter Williams, UKIP 1,180
Adrian Windisch, Green 921
Dave Boyle, Veritas 141
Lab. maj. 4,682 (11.12%)
4.98% swing Lab. to C.
(2001: Lab. maj. 8,849 (21.08%))

REDCAR
E. 66,947 T. 38,861 (58.05%) Lab. hold
Vera Baird, Lab. 19,968
Ian Swales, LD 7,852
Jonathan Lehrle, C. 6,954
Christopher McGlade, Ind. 2,379
Andrew Harris, BNP 985
Edward Walker, UKIP 564
John Taylor, Soc. Lab. 159
Lab. maj. 12,116 (31.18%)
8.25% swing Lab. to LD
(2001: Lab. maj. 13,443 (35.19%))

REDDITCH
E. 64,121 T. 40,291 (62.84%) Lab. hold
Rt. Hon. Jacqui Smith, Lab. 18,012
Karen Lumley, C. 15,296
Nigel Hicks, LD 5,602
John Ison, UKIP 1,381
Lab. maj. 2,716 (6.74%)
0.02% swing C. to Lab.
(2001: Lab. maj. 2,484 (6.71%))

REGENT'S PARK & KENSINGTON NORTH
E. 78,975 T. 40,680 (51.51%) Lab. hold
Karen Buck, Lab. 18,196
Jeremy Bradshaw, C. 12,065
Rabi Martins, LD 7,569
Dr Paul Miller, Green 1,985
Pamela Perrin, UKIP 456
Rezouk Boufas, CP 227
Abby Dharamsey, Ind. 182
Lab. maj. 6,131 (15.07%)
6.32% swing Lab. to C.
(2001: Lab. maj. 10,266 (27.71%))

REIGATE
E. 65,719 T. 42,605 (64.83%) C. hold
Crispin Blunt, C. 20,884
Jane Kulka, LD 9,896
Sam Townend, Lab. 8,896
Jeremy Wraith, UKIP 1,921
Harold Green, EDP 600
Michael Selby, Ind. 408
C. maj. 10,988 (25.79%)
0.46% swing C. to LD
(2001: C. maj. 8,025 (20.33%))

RIBBLE SOUTH
E. 75,357 T. 47,511 (63.05%) Lab. hold
David Borrow, Lab. 20,428
Lorraine Fullbrook, C. 18,244
Mark Alcock, LD 7,634
Kenneth Jones, UKIP 1,205
Lab. maj. 2,184 (4.60%)
1.82% swing Lab. to C.
(2001: Lab. maj. 3,792 (8.22%))

RIBBLE VALLEY
E. 75,692 T. 49,766 (65.75%) C. hold
Nigel Evans, C. 25,834
Julie Young, LD 11,663
Jack Davenport, Lab. 10,924
Kevin Henry, UKIP 1,345
C. maj. 14,171 (28.48%)
2.81% swing LD to C.
(2001: C. maj. 11,238 (22.85%))

RICHMOND (YORKS)
E. 69,521 T. 45,200 (65.02%) C. hold
Rt. Hon. William Hague, C. 26,722
Neil Foster, Lab. 8,915
Jacquie Bell, LD 7,982
Leslie Rowe, Green 1,581
C. maj. 17,807 (39.40%)
1.17% swing Lab. to C.
(2001: C. maj. 16,319 (37.06%))

RICHMOND PARK
E. 70,555 T. 51,374 (72.81%) LD hold
*Susan Kramer, LD 24,011
Marco Forgione, C. 20,280
James Butler, Lab. 4,768
James Page, Green 1,379
Peter Dul, UKIP 458
Peter Flower, CPA 288
Margaret Harrison, Ind. 83
Rainbow George Weiss, Vote Dream 63
Richard Meacock, Ind. 44
LD maj. 3,731 (7.26%)
1.42% swing LD to C.
(2001: LD maj. 4,964 (10.10%))

ROCHDALE
E. 69,894 T. 40,836 (58.43%) LD gain
*Paul Rowen, LD 16,787
Lorna Fitzsimons, Lab. 16,345
Khalid Hussain, C. 4,270
Derek Adams, BNP 1,773
Dr John Whittaker, UKIP 499
Samir Chatterjee, Green 448
Mohammed Salim, IZB 361
Carl Faulkner, Veritas 353
LD maj. 442 (1.08%)
7.72% swing Lab. to LD
(2001: Lab. maj. 5,655 (14.35%))

ROCHFORD & SOUTHEND EAST
E. 71,186 T. 39,462 (55.44%) C. hold
*James Duddridge, C. 17,874
Fred Grindrod, Lab. 12,380
Graham Longley, LD 5,967
John Croft, UKIP 1,913
Andrew Vaughan, Green 1,328
C. maj. 5,494 (13.92%)
2.43% swing C. to Lab.
(2001: C. maj. 7,034 (18.78%))

ROMFORD
E. 58,571 T. 36,482 (62.29%) C. hold
Andrew Rosindell, C. 21,560
Margaret Mullane, Lab. 9,971
Geoffrey Seeff, LD 3,066
John McCaffrey, BNP 1,088
Terry Murray, UKIP 797
C. maj. 11,589 (31.77%)
7.51% swing Lab. to C.
(2001: C. maj. 5,977 (16.74%))

ROMSEY
E. 72,177 T. 50,311 (69.71%) LD hold
Sandra Gidley, LD 22,465
Caroline Nokes, C. 22,340
Matthew Stevens, Lab. 4,430
Michael Wigley, UKIP 1,076
LD maj. 125 (0.25%)
2.32% swing LD to C.
(2001: LD maj. 2,370 (4.89%))

ROSSENDALE & DARWEN
E. 72,207 T. 44,437 (61.54%) Lab. hold
Janet Anderson, Lab. 19,073
Nigel Adams, C. 15,397
Mike Carr, LD 6,670
Anthony Wentworth, BNP 1,736
Graeme McIver, Green 821
David Duthie, UKIP 740
Lab. maj. 3,676 (8.27%)
1.85% swing Lab. to C.
(2001: Lab. maj. 5,223 (12.63%))

ROTHER VALLEY
E. 67,973 T. 39,495 (58.10%) Lab. hold
Rt. Hon. Kevin Barron, Lab. 21,871
Colin Phillips, C. 7,647
Phillip Bristow, LD 6,272
Nicholas Cass, BNP 2,020
Gordon Brown, UKIP 1,685
Lab. maj. 14,224 (36.01%)
2.21% swing Lab. to C.
(2001: Lab. maj. 14,882 (40.44%))

ROTHERHAM
E. 54,410 T. 29,978 (55.10%) Lab. hold
Rt. Hon. Denis MacShane, Lab. 15,840
Timothy Gordon, LD 5,159
Lee Rotherham, C. 4,966
Marlene Guest, BNP 1,986
David Cutts, UKIP 1,122
Richard Penycate, Green 905
Lab. maj. 10,681 (35.63%)
8.83% swing Lab. to LD
(2001: Lab. maj. 13,077 (44.55%))

RUGBY & KENILWORTH
E. 83,303 T. 56,949 (68.36%) C. gain
*Jeremy Wright, C. 23,447
Andy King, Lab. 21,891
Richard Allanach, LD 10,143
John Thurley, UKIP 911
Brian Hadland, Ind. 299
Lillian Pallikaropoulos, Ind. 258
C. maj. 1,556 (2.73%)
4.04% swing Lab. to C.
(2001: Lab. maj. 2,877 (5.35%))

RUISLIP-NORTHWOOD
E. 60,774 T. 39,670 (65.27%) C. hold
*Nick Hurd, C. 18,939
Mike Cox, LD 10,029
Ashley Riley, Lab. 8,323
Graham Lee, Green 892
Ian Edward, NF 841
Roland Courtenay, UKIP 646
C. maj. 8,910 (22.46%)
3.49% swing C. to LD
(2001: C. maj. 7,537 (20.29%))

RUNNYMEDE & WEYBRIDGE
E. 74,172 T. 43,524 (58.68%) C. hold
Philip Hammond, C. 22,366
Paul Greenwood, Lab. 10,017
Henry Bolton, LD 7,771
Anthony Micklethwait, UKIP 1,719
Charles Gilman, Green 1,180
Mad Crab Collett, Loony 358
Katrina Osman, UKC 113
C. maj. 12,349 (28.37%)
4.33% swing Lab. to C.
(2001: C. maj. 8,360 (19.70%))

RUSHCLIFFE
E. 79,913 T. 56,311 (70.47%) C. hold
Rt. Hon. Kenneth Clarke, C. 27,899
Edward Gamble, Lab. 14,925
Karrar Khan, LD 9,813
Simon Anthony, Green 1,692
Matthew Faithfull, UKIP 1,358
Daniel Moss, Veritas 624
C. maj. 12,974 (23.04%)
4.76% swing Lab. to C.
(2001: C. maj. 7,357 (13.51%))

RUTLAND & MELTON
E. 75,823 T. 49,284 (65.00%) C. hold
Alan Duncan, C. 25,237
Linda Arnold, Lab. 12,307
Grahame Hudson, LD 9,153
Peter Baker, UKIP 1,554
Duncan Shelley, Veritas 696
Helen Pender, Ind. 337
C. maj. 12,930 (26.24%)
3.97% swing Lab. to C.
(2001: C. maj. 8,612 (18.30%))

RYEDALE
E. 67,770 T. 44,120 (65.10%) C. hold
John Greenway, C. 21,251
Gordon Beever, LD 10,782
Paul Blanchard, Lab. 9,148
Stephen Feaster, UKIP 1,522
John Clarke, Lib. 1,417
C. maj. 10,469 (23.73%)
6.31% swing LD to C.
(2001: C. maj. 4,875 (11.11%))

SAFFRON WALDEN
E. 77,600 T. 53,020 (68.32%) C. hold
Rt. Hon. Sir Alan Haselhurst, C. 27,263
Elfreda Tealby-Watson, LD 14,255
Swatantra Nandanwar, Lab. 8,755
Raymond Tyler, UKIP 1,412
Raymond Brown, Eng. Dem. 860
Trevor Hackett, Veritas 475
C. maj. 13,008 (24.53%)
0.27% swing LD to C.
(2001: C. maj. 12,004 (23.99%))

ST ALBANS
E. 64,595 T. 45,462 (70.38%) C. gain
*Anne Main, C. 16,953
Kerry Pollard, Lab. 15,592
Michael Green, LD 11,561
Richard Evans, UKIP 707
Janet Girsman, St Albans 430
Mark Reynolds, Ind. 219
C. maj. 1,361 (2.99%)
6.60% swing Lab. to C.
(2001: Lab. maj. 4,466 (10.21%))

ST HELENS NORTH
E. 69,834 T. 39,271 (56.23%) Lab. hold
Dave Watts, Lab. 22,329
John Beirne, LD 8,367
Paul Oakley, C. 7,410
Sylvia Hall, UKIP 1,165
Lab. maj. 13,962 (35.55%)
3.99% swing Lab. to LD
(2001: Lab. maj. 15,901 (42.29%))

ST HELENS SOUTH
E. 65,441 T. 35,473 (54.21%) Lab. hold
Shaun Woodward, Lab. 19,345
Brian Spencer, LD 10,036
Una Riley, C. 4,602
Malcolm Nightingale, UKIP 847
Michael Perry, Soc. Lab. 643
Lab. maj. 9,309 (26.24%)
0.17% swing Lab. to LD
(2001: Lab. maj. 8,985 (26.58%))

ST IVES
E. 74,716 T. 50,417 (67.48%) LD hold
Andrew George, LD 25,577
Christian Mitchell, C. 13,968
Michael Dooley, Lab. 6,583
Michael Faulkner, UKIP 2,551
Katrina Slack, Green 1,738
LD maj. 11,609 (23.03%)
1.31% swing C. to LD
(2001: LD maj. 10,053 (20.41%))

SALFORD
E. 53,294 T. 22,600 (42.41%) Lab. hold
Rt. Hon. Hazel Blears, Lab. 13,007
Norman Owen, LD 5,062
Laetitia Cash, C. 3,440
Lisa Duffy, UKIP 1,091
Lab. maj. 7,945 (35.15%)
6.88% swing Lab. to LD
(2001: Lab. maj. 11,012 (48.91%))

SALISBURY
E. 80,385 T. 54,322 (67.58%) C. hold
Robert Key, C. 25,961
Richard Denton-White, LD 14,819
Clare Moody, Lab. 9,457
Frances Howard, UKIP 2,290
Hamish Soutar, Green 1,555
John Holme, Ind. 240
C. maj. 11,142 (20.51%)
1.98% swing LD to C.
(2001: C. maj. 8,703 (16.54%))

SCARBOROUGH & WHITBY
E. 73,806 T. 46,912 (63.56%) C. gain
*Robert Goodwill, C. 19,248
Lawrence Quinn, Lab. 18,003
Tania Exley-Moore, LD 7,495
Jonathan Dixon, Green 1,214
Paul Abbott, UKIP 952
C. maj. 1,245 (2.65%)
5.10% swing Lab. to C.
(2001: Lab. maj. 3,585 (7.54%))

SCUNTHORPE
E. 62,669 T. 32,664 (52.12%) Lab. hold
Elliot Morley, Lab. 17,355
Julian Sturdy, C. 8,392
Neil Poole, LD 5,556
David Baxendale, UKIP 1,361
Lab. maj. 8,963 (27.44%)
1.70% swing Lab. to C.
(2001: Lab. maj. 10,372 (30.85%))

SEDGEFIELD
E. 66,666 T. 41,483 (62.23%) Lab. hold
Rt. Hon. Tony Blair, Lab. 24,429
Grp Capt Al Lockwood, C. 5,972
Robert Browne, LD 4,935
Reg Keys, Ind. 4,252
William Brown, UKIP 646
Mark Farrell, NF 253
Fiona Luckhurst-Matthews, Veritas 218
Berony Abraham, Ind. 209
Boney Maroney, Loony 157
Jonathan Cockburn, BMG 103
Terry Pattinson, Senior 97
Cherri Gilham, UKPP 82
Helen John, Ind. 68
John Barker, Ind. 45
Julian Brennan, Ind. 17
Lab. maj. 18,457 (44.49%)
0.25% swing C. to Lab.
(2001: Lab. maj. 17,713 (44.00%))

SELBY
E. 78,111 T. 52,549 (67.27%) Lab. hold
John Grogan, Lab. 22,623
Mark Menzies, C. 22,156
Ian Cuthbertson, LD 7,770
Lab. maj. 467 (0.89%)
1.68% swing Lab. to C.
(2001: Lab. maj. 2,138 (4.25%))

SEVENOAKS
E. 65,109 T. 43,298 (66.50%) C. hold
Michael Fallon, C. 22,437
Ben Abbotts, LD 9,467
Tim Stanley, Lab. 9,101
Robert Dobson, UKIP 1,309
John Marshall, Eng. Dem. 751
Mark Ellis, UK Path 233
C. maj. 12,970 (29.96%)
1.09% swing LD to C.
(2001: C. maj. 10,154 (23.83%))

SHEFFIELD ATTERCLIFFE
E. 67,815 T. 37,019 (54.59%) Lab. hold
Clive Betts, Lab. 22,250
Kevin Moore, LD 6,283
Tracy Critchlow, C. 5,329
Jonathan Arnott, UKIP 1,680
Beverley Jones, BNP 1,477
Lab. maj. 15,967 (43.13%)
5.22% swing Lab. to LD
(2001: Lab. maj. 18,844 (52.60%))

SHEFFIELD BRIGHTSIDE
E. 51,379 T. 24,629 (47.94%) Lab. hold
Rt. Hon. David Blunkett, Lab. 16,876
Jonathan Harston, LD 3,232
Tim Clark, C. 2,205
Christopher Hartigan, BNP 1,537
Judith Clarke, UKIP 779
Lab. maj. 13,644 (55.40%)
6.37% swing Lab. to LD
(2001: Lab. maj. 17,049 (66.72%))

SHEFFIELD CENTRAL
E. 59,862 T. 29,985 (50.09%) Lab. hold
Rt. Hon. Richard Caborn, Lab. 14,950
Ali Qadar, LD 7,895
Samantha George, C. 3,094
Bernard Little, Green 1,808
Maxine Bowler, Respect 1,284
Mark Payne, BNP 539
Charlotte Arnott, UKIP 415
Lab. maj. 7,055 (23.53%)
9.09% swing Lab. to LD
(2001: Lab. maj. 12,544 (41.72%))

SHEFFIELD HALLAM
E. 59,606 T. 40,427 (67.82%) LD hold
*Nick Clegg, LD 20,710
Spencer Pitfield, C. 12,028
Mahroof Hussain, Lab. 5,110
Rob Cole, Green 1,331
Sid Cordle, CPA 441
Nigel James, UKIP 438
Ian Senior, BNP 369
LD maj. 8,682 (21.48%)
1.48% swing LD to C.
(2001: LD maj. 9,347 (24.44%))

SHEFFIELD HEELEY
E. 59,748 T. 34,093 (57.06%)
Lab. (Co-op) hold
Meg Munn, Lab. (Co-op) 18,405
Colin Ross, LD 7,035
Aster Crawshaw, C. 4,987
John Beatson, BNP 1,314
Rob Unwin, Green 1,312
Mark Suter, UKIP 775
Mark Dunnell, Soc. Alt. 265
Lab. (Co-op) maj. 11,370 (33.35%)
0.47% swing Lab. (Co-op) to LD
(2001: Lab. (Co-op) maj. 11,704 (34.28%))

SHEFFIELD HILLSBOROUGH
E. 75,706 T. 45,884 (60.61%) Lab. hold
*Angela Smith, Lab. 23,477
John Commons, LD 12,234
Jackie Doyle-Price, C. 6,890
David Wright, BNP 2,010
Maurice Patterson, UKIP 1,273
Lab. maj. 11,243 (24.50%)
4.87% swing Lab. to LD
(2001: Lab. maj. 14,569 (34.25%))

SHERWOOD
E. 75,913 T. 47,117 (62.07%) Lab. hold
Paddy Tipping, Lab. 22,824
Bruce Laughton, C. 16,172
Peter Harris, LD 6,384
Moritz Dawkins, UKIP 1,737
Lab. maj. 6,652 (14.12%)
3.15% swing Lab. to C.
(2001: Lab. maj. 9,373 (20.42%))

SHIPLEY
E. 69,575 T. 47,666 (68.51%) C. gain
*Philip Davies, C. 18,608
Christopher Leslie, Lab. 18,186
John Briggs, LD 7,018
Tom Linden, BNP 2,000
Quentin Deakin, Green 1,665
David Crabtree, Iraq 189
C. maj. 422 (0.89%)
1.99% swing Lab. to C.
(2001: Lab. maj. 1,428 (3.10%))

SHREWSBURY & ATCHAM
E. 73,193 T. 50,296 (68.72%) C. gain
*Daniel Kawczynski, C. 18,960
Michael Ion, Lab. 17,152
Richard Burt, LD 11,487
Peter Lewis, UKIP 1,349
Emma Bullard, Green 1,138
James Gollins, Ind. 126
Nigel Harris, Online 84
C. maj. 1,808 (3.59%)
5.38% swing Lab. to C.
(2001: Lab. maj. 3,579 (7.17%))

SHROPSHIRE NORTH
E. 73,477 T. 46,510 (63.30%) C. hold
Owen Paterson, C. 23,061
Sandra Samuels, Lab. 12,041
Steven Bourne, LD 9,175
Ian Smith, UKIP 2,233
C. maj. 11,020 (23.69%)
5.14% swing Lab. to C.
(2001: C. maj. 6,241 (13.42%))

SITTINGBOURNE & SHEPPEY
E. 62,950 T. 40,803 (64.82%) Lab. hold
Derek Wyatt, Lab. 17,051
Gordon Henderson, C. 16,972
Jane Nelson, LD 5,183
Stephen Dean, UKIP 926
Mad MikeYoung, R & R Loony 479
David Cassidy, Veritas 192
Lab. maj. 79 (0.19%)
4.54% swing Lab. to C.
(2001: Lab. maj. 3,509 (9.27%))

SKIPTON & RIPON
E. 76,485 T. 50,521 (66.05%) C. hold
Rt. Hon. David Curry, C. 25,100
Paul English, LD 13,480
Paul Baptie, Lab. 9,393
Ian Bannister, UKIP 2,274
Robert Leakey, Currency 274
C. maj. 11,620 (23.00%)
1.66% swing C. to LD
(2001: C. maj. 12,930 (26.32%))

SLEAFORD & NORTH HYKEHAM
E. 79,612 T. 53,397 (67.07%) C. hold
Rt. Hon. Douglas Hogg, C. 26,855
Katrina Bull, Lab. 14,150
David Harding-Price, LD 9,710
Guy Croft, UKIP 2,682
C. maj. 12,705 (23.79%)
3.05% swing Lab. to C.
(2001: C. maj. 8,622 (17.70%))

SLOUGH
E. 71,595 T. 37,095 (51.81%) Lab. hold
Fiona Mactaggart, Lab. 17,517
Sheila Gunn, C. 9,666
Thomas McCann, LD 5,739
Ajaz Khan, Respect 1,632
Geoff Howard, UKIP 1,415
David Wood, Green 759
Paul Janik, Ind. 367
Lab. maj. 7,851 (21.16%)
5.45% swing Lab. to C.
(2001: Lab. maj. 12,508 (32.07%))

SOLIHULL
E. 77,910 T. 52,313 (67.15%) LD gain
*Lorely Burt, LD 20,896
John Taylor, C. 20,617
Rory Vaughan, Lab. 8,058
Diane Carr, BNP 1,752
Andrew Moore, UKIP 990
LD maj. 279 (0.53%)
10.01% swing C. to LD
(2001: C. maj. 9,407 (19.49%))

SOMERTON & FROME
E. 77,806 T. 54,102 (69.53%) LD hold
David Heath, LD 23,759
Clive Allen, C. 22,947
Joseph Pestell, Lab. 5,865
William Lukins, UKIP 1,047
Carleton Beaman, Veritas 484
LD maj. 812 (1.50%)
0.12% swing C. to LD
(2001: LD maj. 668 (1.27%))

SOUTH HOLLAND & THE DEEPINGS
E. 77,453 T. 48,249 (62.29%) C. hold
John Hayes, C. 27,544
Linda Woodings, Lab. 11,764
Steve Jarvis, LD 6,244
Jamie Corney, UKIP 1,950
Paul Poll, Ind. 747
C. maj. 15,780 (32.71%)
4.34% swing Lab. to C.
(2001: C. maj. 11,099 (24.02%))

SOUTH SHIELDS
E. 59,403 T. 30,206 (50.85%) Lab. hold
Rt. Hon. David Miliband, Lab. 18,269
Stephen Psallidas, LD 5,957
Richard Lewis, C. 5,207
Nader Afshari-Naderi, Ind. 773
Lab. maj. 12,312 (40.76%)
2.78% swing Lab. to LD
(2001: Lab. maj. 14,090 (46.28%))

SOUTHAMPTON ITCHEN
E. 78,818 T. 43,225 (54.84%) Lab. hold
Rt. Hon. John Denham, Lab. 20,871
Flick Drummond, C. 11,569
David Goodall, LD 9,162
Kim Rose, UKIP 1,623
Lab. maj. 9,302 (21.52%)
2.80% swing Lab. to C.
(2001: Lab. maj. 11,223 (27.13%))

SOUTHAMPTON TEST
E. 72,833 T. 41,783 (57.37%) Lab. hold
Dr Alan Whitehead, Lab. 17,845
Stephen MacLoughlin, C. 10,827
Steve Sollitt, LD 10,368
John Spottiswoode, Green 1,482
Peter Day, UKIP 1,261
Lab. maj. 7,018 (16.80%)
5.08% swing Lab. to C.
(2001: Lab. maj. 11,207 (26.96%))

SOUTHEND WEST
E. 64,915 T. 39,830 (61.36%) C. hold
David Amess, C. 18,408
Peter Wexham, LD 9,449
Jan Etienne, Lab. 9,072
Carole Sampson, UKIP 1,349
Dr Marimuthu Velmurugan, Ind. 745
Jeremy Moss, Eng. Dem. 701
Dan Anslow, Power 106
C. maj. 8,959 (22.49%)
0.55% swing LD to C.
(2001: C. maj. 7,941 (21.25%))

SOUTHPORT
E. 67,977 T. 41,201 (60.61%) LD hold
Dr John Pugh, LD 19,093
Mark Bigley, C. 15,255
Paul Brant, Lab. 5,277
Terry Durrance, UKIP 749
Bill Givens, YPB 589
Harry Forster, Veritas 238
LD maj. 3,838 (9.32%)
1.00% swing C. to LD
(2001: LD maj. 3,007 (7.31%))

SOUTHWARK NORTH & BERMONDSEY
E. 77,084 T. 37,959 (49.24%) LD hold
Simon Hughes, LD 17,874
Kirsty McNeill, Lab. 12,468
David Branch, C. 4,752
Storm Poorun, Green 1,137
Linda Robson, UKIP 791
Paul Winnett, NF 704
Simi Lawanson, CPA 233
LD maj. 5,406 (14.24%)
5.94% swing LD to Lab.
(2001: LD maj. 9,632 (26.13%))

SPELTHORNE
E. 69,650 T. 42,829 (61.49%) C. hold
David Wilshire, C. 21,620
Keith Dibble, Lab. 11,684
Simon James, LD 7,318
Christopher Browne, UKIP 1,968
Caroline Schwark, UKC 239
C. maj. 9,936 (23.20%)
7.70% swing Lab. to C.
(2001: C. maj. 3,262 (7.80%))

STAFFORD
E. 70,359 T. 45,554 (64.75%) Lab. hold
David Kidney, Lab. 19,889
David Chambers, C. 17,768
Barry Stamp, LD 6,390
Frederick Goode, UKIP 1,507
Lab. maj. 2,121 (4.66%)
3.34% swing Lab. to C.
(2001: Lab. maj. 5,032 (11.34%))

STAFFORDSHIRE MOORLANDS
E. 69,136 T. 44,253 (64.01%) Lab. hold
Charlotte Atkins, Lab. 18,126
Marcus Hayes, C. 15,688
John Fisher, LD 6,927
Steve Povey, UKIP 3,512
Lab. maj. 2,438 (5.51%)
4.09% swing Lab. to C.
(2001: Lab. maj. 5,838 (13.69%))

STAFFORDSHIRE SOUTH
Deferred until 23 June 2005 due to the death of the Liberal Democrat candidate during the general election campaign (*see* by-elections)

STALYBRIDGE & HYDE
E. 66,013 T. 35,314 (53.50%) Lab. hold
James Purnell, Lab. 17,535
Lisa Boardman, C. 9,187
Viv Bingham, LD 5,532
Nigel Byrne, BNP 1,399
Mike Smee, Green 1,088
Dr John Whittaker, UKIP 573
Lab. maj. 8,348 (23.64%)
2.00% swing Lab. to C.
(2001: Lab. maj. 8,859 (27.64%))

STEVENAGE
E. 66,889 T. 41,934 (62.69%) Lab. hold
Barbara Follett, Lab. 18,003
George Freeman, C. 14,864
Julia Davies, LD 7,610
Victoria Peebles, UKIP 1,305
Antal Losonczi, Ind. 152
Lab. maj. 3,139 (7.49%)
6.35% swing Lab. to C.
(2001: Lab. maj. 8,566 (20.18%))

STOCKPORT
E. 65,593 T. 35,771 (54.53%) Lab. hold
Ann Coffey, Lab. 18,069
Elizabeth Berridge, C. 8,906
Lyn-Su Floodgate, LD 7,832
Richard Simpson, UKIP 964
Lab. maj. 9,163 (25.62%)
3.54% swing Lab. to C.
(2001: Lab. maj. 11,569 (32.70%))

STOCKTON NORTH
E. 63,271 T. 36,428 (57.57%) Lab. hold
Frank Cook, Lab. 20,012
Harriett Baldwin, C. 7,575
Neil Hughes, LD 6,869
Kevin Hughes, BNP 986
Gordon Parkin, UKIP 986
Lab. maj. 12,437 (34.14%)
3.60% swing Lab. to C.
(2001: Lab. maj. 14,647 (41.34%))

STOCKTON SOUTH
E. 71,286 T. 44,923 (63.02%) Lab. hold
Dari Taylor, Lab. 21,480
James Gaddas, C. 15,341
Mike Barker, LD 7,171
Sandra Allison, UKIP 931
Lab. maj. 6,139 (13.67%)
3.44% swing Lab. to C.
(2001: Lab. maj. 9,086 (20.55%))

STOKE-ON-TRENT CENTRAL
E. 57,643 T. 27,907 (48.41%) Lab. hold
Mark Fisher, Lab. 14,760
John Redfern, LD 4,986
Esther Baroudy, C. 4,823
Michael Coleman, BNP 2,178
Joseph Bonfiglio, UKIP 914
Jim Cessford, Soc. Alt. 246
Lab. maj. 9,774 (35.02%)
5.50% swing Lab. to LD
(2001: Lab. maj. 11,845 (41.86%))

STOKE-ON-TRENT NORTH
E. 58,422 T. 30,760 (52.65%) Lab. hold
Joan Walley, Lab. 16,191
Benjamin Browning, C. 6,155
Henry Jebb, LD 4,561
Spencer Cartlidge, BNP 2,132
Eileen Braithwaite, UKIP 696
Ian Taylor, Veritas 689
Harry Chesters, Ind. 336
Lab. maj. 10,036 (32.63%)
3.25% swing Lab. to C.
(2001: Lab. maj. 11,784 (39.13%))

STOKE-ON-TRENT SOUTH
E. 70,612 T. 37,820 (53.56%) Lab. hold
*Robert Flello, Lab. 17,727
Mark Deaville, C. 9,046
Andrew Martin, LD 5,894
Mark Leat, BNP 3,305
Neville Benson, UKIP 1,043
Grant Allen, Veritas 805
Lab. maj. 8,681 (22.95%)
3.08% swing Lab. to C.
(2001: Lab. maj. 10,489 (29.11%))

STONE
E. 70,359 T. 47,036 (66.85%) C. hold
Bill Cash, C. 22,733
Mark Davis, Lab. 13,644
Peter Stevens, LD 9,111
Michael Nattrass, UKIP 1,548
C. maj. 9,089 (19.32%)
3.05% swing Lab. to C.
(2001: C. maj. 6,036 (13.22%))

STOURBRIDGE
E. 64,479 T. 41,708 (64.68%) Lab. hold
*Lynda Waltho, Lab. 17,089
Diana Coad, C. 16,682
Chris Bramall, LD 6,850
Daniel Pui Chai Mau, UKIP 1,087
Lab. maj. 407 (0.98%)
4.29% swing Lab. to C.
(2001: Lab. maj. 3,812 (9.55%))

STRATFORD-UPON-AVON
E. 84,591 T. 58,240 (68.85%) C. hold
John Maples, C. 28,652
Dr Susan Juned, LD 16,468
Rachel Blackmore, Lab. (Co-op) 10,145
Harry Cottam, UKIP 1,621
Mick Davies, Green 1,354
C. maj. 12,184 (20.92%)
0.29% swing C. to LD
(2001: C. maj. 11,802 (21.49%))

STREATHAM
E. 79,193 T. 40,615 (51.29%) Lab. hold
Rt. Hon. Keith Hill, Lab. 18,950
Darren Sanders, LD 11,484
James Sproule, C. 7,238
Shane Collins, Green 2,245
Trevor Gittings, UKIP 396
William Colvill, WRP 127
Philippa Stone, Ind. 100
Robert West, Ind. 40
Sarah Acheng, Ind. 35
Lab. maj. 7,466 (18.38%)
10.09% swing Lab. to LD
(2001: Lab. maj. 14,270 (38.57%))

STRETFORD & URMSTON
E. 61,979 T. 38,101 (61.47%) Lab. hold
Rt. Hon. Beverley Hughes, Lab. 19,417
Damian Hinds, C. 11,566
Faraz Bhatti, LD 5,323
Mark Krantz, Respect 950
Michael McManus, UKIP 845
Lab. maj. 7,851 (20.61%)
6.71% swing Lab. to C.
(2001: Lab. maj. 13,239 (33.97%))

STROUD
E. 79,748 T. 56,875 (71.32%) Lab. (Co-op) hold
David Drew, Lab. (Co-op) 22,527
Neil Carmichael, C. 22,177
Peter Hirst, LD 8,026
Martin Whiteside, Green 3,056
Edward Noble, UKIP 1,089
Lab. (Co-op) maj. 350 (0.62%)
4.26% swing Lab. (Co-op) to C.
(2001: Lab. (Co-op) maj. 5,039 (9.13%))

SUFFOLK CENTRAL & IPSWICH NORTH
E. 76,271 T. 50,866 (66.69%) C. hold
Sir Michael Lord, C. 22,333
Neil MacDonald, Lab. 14,477
Andrew Houseley, LD 10,709
John West, UKIP 1,754
Martin Wolfe, Green 1,593
C. maj. 7,856 (15.44%)
4.04% swing Lab. to C.
(2001: C. maj. 3,469 (7.36%))

SUFFOLK COASTAL
E. 77,423 T. 52,557 (67.88%) C. hold
Rt. Hon. John Gummer, C. 23,415
David Rowe, Lab. 13,730
David Young, LD 11,637
Richard Curtis, UKIP 2,020
Paul Whitlow, Green 1,755
C. maj. 9,685 (18.43%)
4.92% swing Lab. to C.
(2001: C. maj. 4,326 (8.58%))

SUFFOLK SOUTH
E. 70,237 T. 48,707 (69.35%) C. hold
Tim Yeo, C. 20,471
Kathy Pollard, LD 13,865
Kevin Craig, Lab. 11,917
James Carver, UKIP 2,454
C. maj. 6,606 (13.56%)
1.45% swing C. to LD
(2001: C. maj. 5,081 (11.22%))

SUFFOLK WEST
E. 72,856 T. 44,205 (60.67%) C. hold
Richard Spring, C. 21,682
Michael Jefferys, Lab. 12,773
Adrian Graves, LD 7,573
Ian Smith, UKIP 2,177
C. maj. 8,909 (20.15%)
5.02% swing Lab. to C.
(2001: C. maj. 4,295 (10.12%))

SUNDERLAND NORTH
E. 58,146 T. 28,913 (49.72%) Lab. hold
Bill Etherington, Lab. 15,719
Stephen Daughton, C. 5,724
James Hollern, LD 4,277
Neil Herron, Ind. 2,057
Debra Hiles, BNP 1,136
Lab. maj. 9,995 (34.57%)
5.11% swing Lab. to C.
(2001: Lab. maj. 13,354 (44.78%))

SUNDERLAND SOUTH
E. 62,256 T. 30,712 (49.33%) Lab. hold
Chris Mullin, Lab. 17,982
Robert Oliver, C. 6,923
Gareth Kane, LD 4,492
David Guynan, BNP 1,166
Rosalyn Warner, Loony 149
Lab. maj. 11,059 (36.01%)
3.91% swing Lab. to C.
(2001: Lab. maj. 13,667 (43.82%))

SURREY EAST
E. 73,948 T. 49,253 (66.60%) C. hold
Peter Ainsworth, C. 27,659
Jeremy Pursehouse, LD 11,738
James Bridge, Lab. 7,288
Tony Stone, UKIP 2,158
Winston Matthews, LCA 410
C. maj. 15,921 (32.32%)
2.13% swing LD to C.
(2001: C. maj. 13,203 (28.06%))

SURREY HEATH
E. 76,090 T. 47,858 (62.90%) C. hold
*Michael Gove, C. 24,642
Rosalyn Harper, LD 13,797
Chris Lowe, Lab. 7,989
Steve Smith, UKIP 1,430
C. maj. 10,845 (22.66%)
0.66% swing C. to LD
(2001: C. maj. 10,819 (23.99%))

SURREY SOUTH WEST
E. 72,977 T. 52,409 (71.82%) C. hold
*Jeremy Hunt, C. 26,420
Simon Cordon, LD 20,709
Thomas Sleigh, Lab. 4,150
Timothy Clark, UKIP 958
Glenn Platt, Veritas 172
C. maj. 5,711 (10.90%)
4.58% swing LD to C.
(2001: C. maj. 861 (1.74%))

SUSSEX MID
E. 72,114 T. 49,494 (68.63%) C. hold
Hon. Nicholas Soames, C. 23,765
Serena Tierney, LD 17,875
Robert Fromant, Lab. 6,280
Harold Piggott, UKIP 1,574
C. maj. 5,890 (11.90%)
1.58% swing C. to LD
(2001: C. maj. 6,898 (15.05%))

SUTTON & CHEAM
E. 63,319 T. 41,932 (66.22%) LD hold
Paul Burstow, LD 19,768
Richard Willis, C. 16,922
Anand Shukla, Lab. 4,954
Rainbow George Weiss, Vote Dream 288
LD maj. 2,846 (6.79%)
2.02% swing LD to C.
(2001: LD maj. 4,304 (10.84%))

SUTTON COLDFIELD
E. 72,995 T. 46,318 (63.45%) C. hold
Andrew Mitchell, C. 24,308
Robert Pocock, Lab. 12,025
Craig Drury, LD 7,710
Stephen Shorrock, UKIP 2,275
C. maj. 12,283 (26.52%)
1.63% swing Lab. to C.
(2001: C. maj. 10,104 (23.25%))

SWINDON NORTH
E. 73,636 T. 44,885 (60.96%) Lab. hold
Michael Wills, Lab. 19,612
Justin Tomlinson, C. 17,041
Mike Evemy, LD 6,831
Robert Tingey, UKIP 998
Andy Newman, Soc. Unity 208
Ernest Reynolds, Ind. 195
Lab. maj. 2,571 (5.73%)
6.71% swing Lab. to C.
(2001: Lab. maj. 8,105 (19.15%))

SWINDON SOUTH
E. 72,267 T. 43,472 (60.15%) Lab. hold
*Anne Snelgrove, Lab. 17,534
Robert Buckland, C. 16,181
Sue Stebbing, LD 7,322
Bill Hughes, Green 1,234
Stephen Halden, UKIP 955
Alan Hayward, Ind. 193
John Williams, Ind. 53
Lab. maj. 1,353 (3.11%)
6.90% swing Lab. to C.
(2001: Lab. maj. 7,341 (16.92%))

TAMWORTH
E. 71,675 T. 43,740 (61.03%) Lab. hold
Brian Jenkins, Lab. 18,801
Christopher Pincher, C. 16,232
Phillip Bennion, LD 6,175
Patrick Eston, Veritas 1,320
Tom Simpson, UKIP 1,212
Lab. maj. 2,569 (5.87%)
2.78% swing Lab. to C.
(2001: Lab. maj. 4,598 (11.42%))

TATTON
E. 64,140 T. 41,414 (64.57%) C. hold
George Osborne, C. 21,447
Justin Madders, Lab. 9,716
Ainsley Arnold, LD 9,016
Diane Bowler, UKIP 996
Michael Gibson, Ind. 239
C. maj. 11,731 (28.33%)
3.73% swing Lab. to C.
(2001: C. maj. 8,611 (20.86%))

TAUNTON
E. 85,466 T. 59,528 (69.65%) LD gain
*Jeremy Browne, LD 25,764
Adrian Flook, C. 25,191
Andrew Govier, Lab. 7,132
Helen Miles, UKIP 1,441
LD maj. 573 (0.96%)
0.69% swing C. to LD
(2001: C. maj. 235 (0.43%))

TEIGNBRIDGE
E. 88,674 T. 60,898 (68.68%) LD hold
Richard Younger-Ross, LD 27,808
Stanley Johnson, C. 21,593
Chris Sherwood, Lab. 6,931
Trevor Colman, UKIP 3,881
Reginald Wills, Lib. 685
LD maj. 6,215 (10.21%)
2.56% swing C. to LD
(2001: LD maj. 3,011 (5.08%))

TELFORD
E. 59,277 T. 34,206 (57.71%) Lab. hold
David Wright, Lab. 16,506
Stella Kyriazis, C. 11,100
Ian Jenkins, LD 4,941
Tom McCartney, UKIP 1,659
Lab. maj. 5,406 (15.80%)
5.67% swing Lab. to C.
(2001: Lab. maj. 8,383 (27.15%))

TEWKESBURY
E. 72,145 T. 45,453 (63.00%) C. hold
Laurence Robertson, C. 22,339
Alistair Cameron, LD 12,447
Charles Mannan, Lab. 9,179
Robert Rendell, Green 1,488
C. maj. 9,892 (21.76%)
0.96% swing LD to C.
(2001: C. maj. 8,663 (19.17%))

THANET NORTH
E. 72,734 T. 43,732 (60.13%) C. hold
Roger Gale, C. 21,699
Iris Johnston, Lab. 14,065
Mark Barnard, LD 6,279
Timothy Stocks, UKIP 1,689
C. maj. 7,634 (17.46%)
0.79% swing Lab. to C.
(2001: C. maj. 6,650 (15.88%))

THANET SOUTH
E. 63,436 T. 41,242 (65.01%) Lab. hold
Dr Stephen Ladyman, Lab. 16,660
Mark MacGregor, C. 15,996
Guy Voizey, LD 5,431
Nigel Farage, UKIP 2,079
Howard Green, Green 888
Maude Kinsella, Ind. 188
Lab. maj. 664 (1.61%)
1.47% swing Lab. to C.
(2001: Lab. maj. 1,792 (4.54%))

THURROCK
E. 79,545 T. 43,692 (54.93%) Lab. hold
Andrew Mackinlay, Lab. 20,636
Garry Hague, C. 14,261
Earnshaw Palmer, LD 4,770
Nick Geri, BNP 2,526
Carol Jackson, UKIP 1,499
Lab. maj. 6,375 (14.59%)
6.08% swing Lab. to C.
(2001: Lab. maj. 9,997 (26.76%))

TIVERTON & HONITON
E. 83,375 T. 58,168 (69.77%) C. hold
Angela Browning, C. 27,838
David Nation, LD 16,787
Fiona Bentley, Lab. 7,944
Robert Edwards, UKIP 2,499
Roy Collins, Lib. 1,701
Colin Matthews, Green 1,399
C. maj. 11,051 (19.00%)
3.87% swing LD to C.
(2001: C. maj. 6,284 (11.26%))

TONBRIDGE & MALLING
E. 68,444 T. 46,063 (67.30%) C. hold
Rt. Hon. Sir John Stanley, C. 24,357
Victoria Hayman, Lab. 11,005
John Barstow, LD 8,980
David Waller, UKIP 1,721
C. maj. 13,352 (28.99%)
4.77% swing Lab. to C.
(2001: C. maj. 8,250 (19.44%))

TOOTING
E. 70,504 T. 41,568 (58.96%) Lab. hold
*Sadiq Khan, Lab. 17,914
James Bethell, C. 12,533
Stephanie Dearden, LD 8,110
Siobhan Vitelli, Green 1,695
Ali Zaidi, Respect 700
Strachan McDonald, UKIP 424
Ian Perkin, Ind. 192
Lab. maj. 5,381 (12.95%)
7.36% swing Lab. to C.
(2001: Lab. maj. 10,400 (27.67%))

TORBAY
E. 76,474 T. 47,303 (61.86%) LD hold
Adrian Sanders, LD 19,317
Marcus Wood, C. 17,288
David Pedrick-Friend, Lab. 6,972
Graham Booth, UKIP 3,726
LD maj. 2,029 (4.29%)
4.91% swing LD to C.
(2001: LD maj. 6,708 (14.10%))

TOTNES
E. 74,744 T. 50,575 (67.66%) C. hold
Anthony Steen, C. 21,112
Michael Treleaven, LD 19,165
Valerie Burns, Lab. 6,185
Roger Knapman, UKIP 3,914
Michael Thompson, Ind. 199
C. maj. 1,947 (3.85%)
1.73% swing C. to LD
(2001: C. maj. 3,597 (7.30%))

TOTTENHAM
E. 66,231 T. 31,664 (47.81%) Lab. hold
David Lammy, Lab. 18,343
Wayne Hoban, LD 5,309
William MacDougall, C. 4,278
Janet Alder, Respect 2,014
Pete McAskie, Green 1,457
Jaamit Durrani, Soc. Lab. 263
Lab. maj. 13,034 (41.16%)
8.39% swing Lab. to LD
(2001: Lab. maj. 16,916 (53.53%))

TRURO & ST AUSTELL
E. 80,256 T. 51,564 (64.25%) LD hold
Matthew Taylor, LD 24,089
Dr Fiona Kemp, C. 16,686
Dr Charlotte Mackenzie, Lab. 6,991
David Noakes, UKIP 2,736
Conan Jenkin, Meb. Ker. 1,062
LD maj. 7,403 (14.36%)
0.84% swing LD to C.
(2001: LD maj. 8,065 (16.04%))

TUNBRIDGE WELLS
E. 64,630 T. 42,482 (65.73%) C. hold
*Greg Clark, C. 21,083
Laura Murphy, LD 11,095
Jacqui Jedrzejewski, Lab. 8,736
Victor Webb, UKIP 1,568
C. maj. 9,988 (23.51%)
0.35% swing C. to LD
(2001: C. maj. 9,730 (24.20%))

TWICKENHAM
E. 72,015 T. 51,687 (71.77%) LD hold
Dr Vincent Cable, LD 26,696
Paul Maynard, C. 16,731
Brian Whitington, Lab. 5,868
Henry Gower, Green 1,445
Douglas Orchard, UKIP 766
Brian Gilbert, Ind. 117
Rainbow George Weiss, Vote Dream 64
LD maj. 9,965 (19.28%)
1.98% swing C. to LD
(2001: LD maj. 7,655 (15.33%))

TYNE BRIDGE
E. 53,565 T. 26,383 (49.25%) Lab. hold
David Clelland, Lab. 16,151
Chris Boyle, LD 5,751
Tom Fairhead, C. 2,962
Kevin Scott, BNP 1,072
Jill Russell, Respect 447
Lab. maj. 10,400 (39.42%)
9.35% swing Lab. to LD
(2001: Lab. maj. 14,889 (57.19%))

TYNEMOUTH
E. 64,023 T. 42,859 (66.94%) Lab. hold
Alan Campbell, Lab. 20,143
Michael McIntyre, C. 16,000
Colin Finlay, LD 6,716
Lab. maj. 4,143 (9.67%)
5.05% swing Lab. to C.
(2001: Lab. maj. 8,678 (19.77%))

TYNESIDE NORTH
E. 64,634 T. 36,939 (57.15%) Lab. hold
Rt. Hon. Stephen Byers, Lab. 22,882
Duncan McLellan, C. 7,845
Gillian Ferguson, LD 6,212
Lab. maj. 15,037 (40.71%)
7.09% swing Lab. to C.
(2001: Lab. maj. 20,668 (55.01%))

UPMINSTER
E. 55,075 T. 34,676 (62.96%) C. hold
Angela Watkinson, C. 16,820
Keith Darvill, Lab. 10,778
Peter Truesdale, LD 3,128
Ronald Ower, RA 1,455
Chris Roberts, BNP 1,173
Alan Hindle, UKIP 701
Melanie Collins, Green 543
David Durant, Third 78
C. maj. 6,042 (17.42%)
6.88% swing Lab. to C.
(2001: C. maj. 1,241 (3.67%))

UXBRIDGE
E. 57,878 T. 34,378 (59.40%) C. hold
John Randall, C. 16,840
Rod Marshall, Lab. 10,669
Dr Tariq Mahmood, LD 4,544
Cliff Le May, BNP 763
Stephen Young, Green 725
Robert Kerby, UKIP 553
Peter Shaw, NF 284
C. maj. 6,171 (17.95%)
5.84% swing Lab. to C.
(2001: C. maj. 2,098 (6.28%))

VALE OF YORK
E. 76,000 T. 50,378 (66.29%) C. hold
Anne McIntosh, C. 26,025
David Scott, Lab. 12,313
Jeremy Wilcock, LD 12,040
C. maj. 13,712 (27.22%)
0.70% swing Lab. to C.
(2001: C. maj. 12,517 (25.81%))

VAUXHALL
E. 79,637 T. 37,353 (46.90%) Lab. hold
Kate Hoey, Lab. 19,744
Charles Anglin, LD 9,767
Edward Heckels, C. 5,405
Tim Summers, Green 1,705
Robert McWhirter, UKIP 271
Daniel Lambert, Socialist 240
Janus Polenceus, Eng. Dem. 221
Lab. maj. 9,977 (26.71%)
6.14% swing Lab. to LD
(2001: Lab. maj. 13,018 (38.99%))

WAKEFIELD
E. 73,118 T. 43,381 (59.33%) Lab. hold
*Mary Creagh, Lab. 18,802
Alec Shelbrooke, C. 13,648
David Ridgway, LD 7,063
Grant Rowe, BNP 1,328
Derek Hardcastle, Green 1,297
John Upex, UKIP 467
Paul McEnhill, Eng. Dem. 356
Mick Griffiths, Soc. Alt. 319
Linda Sheridan, Soc. Lab. 101
Lab. maj. 5,154 (11.88%)
3.70% swing Lab. to C.
(2001: Lab. maj. 7,954 (19.28%))

WALLASEY
E. 63,764 T. 36,671 (57.51%) Lab. hold
Angela Eagle, Lab. 20,085
Leah Fraser, C. 10,976
Joanna Pemberton, LD 4,770
Philip Griffiths, UKIP 840
Lab. maj. 9,109 (24.84%)
4.02% swing Lab. to C.
(2001: Lab. maj. 12,276 (32.87%))

WALSALL NORTH
E. 63,268 T. 33,428 (52.84%) Lab. hold
David Winnick, Lab. 15,990
Ian Lucas, C. 9,350
Douglas Taylor, LD 4,144
William Locke, BNP 1,992
Anthony Lenton, UKIP 1,182
Peter Smith, Dem. Lab. 770
Lab. maj. 6,640 (19.86%)
4.60% swing Lab. to C.
(2001: Lab. maj. 9,391 (29.06%))

WALSALL SOUTH
E. 60,370 T. 35,315 (58.50%) Lab. hold
Rt. Hon. Bruce George, Lab. 17,633
Kabir Sabar, C. 9,687
Mohamed Hanif Asmal, LD 3,240
Derek Bennett, UKIP 1,833
Kevin Smith, BNP 1,776
Nadia Fazal, Respect 1,146
Lab. maj. 7,946 (22.50%)
2.98% swing Lab. to C.
(2001: Lab. maj. 9,931 (28.46%))

WALTHAMSTOW
E. 63,079 T. 34,444 (54.60%) Lab. hold
Neil Gerrard, Lab. 17,323
Farid Ahmed, LD 9,330
Jane Wright, C. 6,254
Robert Brock, UKIP 810
Nancy Taaffe, Soc. Alt. 727
Lab. maj. 7,993 (23.21%)
12.18% swing Lab. to LD
(2001: Lab. maj. 15,181 (44.09%))

WANSBECK
E. 63,096 T. 36,809 (58.34%) Lab. hold
Denis Murphy, Lab. 20,315
Simon Reed, LD 9,734
Ginny Scrope, C. 5,515
Dr Nic Best, Green 1,245
Lab. maj. 10,581 (28.75%)
3.13% swing Lab. to LD
(2001: Lab. maj. 13,101 (35.01%))

WANSDYKE
E. 70,359 T. 50,933 (72.39%) Lab. hold
Dan Norris, Lab. 20,686
Chris Watt, C. 18,847
Gail Coleshill, LD 10,050
Peter Sandell, UKIP 1,129
Geoffrey Parkes, Ind. 221
Lab. maj. 1,839 (3.61%)
3.86% swing Lab. to C.
(2001: Lab. maj. 5,113 (10.42%))

WANTAGE
E. 76,156 T. 51,931 (68.19%) C. hold
*Ed Vaizey, C. 22,354
Andrew Crawford, LD 14,337
Mark McDonald, Lab. 12,464
Adam Twine, Green 1,332
Nikolai Tolstoy-Miloslavsky, UKIP 798
Gerald Lambourne, Eng. Dem. 646
C. maj. 8,017 (15.44%)
1.92% swing LD to C.
(2001: C. maj. 5,600 (11.40%))

WARLEY
E. 56,171 T. 32,087 (57.12%) Lab. hold
Rt. Hon. John Spellar, Lab. 17,462
Karen Bissell, C. 7,315
Tony Ferguson, LD 4,277
Simon Smith, BNP 1,761
Malcolm Connigale, Soc. Lab. 637
David Matthews, UKIP 635
Lab. maj. 10,147 (31.62%)
3.05% swing Lab. to C.
(2001: Lab. maj. 11,850 (37.72%))

WARRINGTON NORTH
E. 73,352 T. 40,418 (55.10%) Lab. hold
Helen Jones, Lab. 21,632
Andrew Ferryman, C. 9,428
Peter Walker, LD 7,699
John Kirkham, UKIP 1,086
Mike Hughes, CAP 573
Lab. maj. 12,204 (30.19%)
4.38% swing Lab. to C.
(2001: Lab. maj. 15,156 (38.95%))

WARRINGTON SOUTH
E. 75,724 T. 46,797 (61.80%) Lab. hold
Helen Southworth, Lab. 18,972
Fiona Bruce, C. 15,457
Ian Marks, LD 11,111
Gerald Kelley, UKIP 804
Paul Kennedy, Ind. 453
Lab. maj. 3,515 (7.51%)
4.37% swing Lab. to C.
(2001: Lab. maj. 7,387 (16.24%))

WARWICK & LEAMINGTON
E. 81,205 T. 54,784 (67.46%) Lab. hold
James Plaskitt, Lab. 22,238
Chris White, C. 21,972
Linda Forbes, LD 8,119
Ian Davison, Green 1,534
Greville Warwick, UKIP 921
Lab. maj. 266 (0.49%)
5.32% swing Lab. to C.
(2001: Lab. maj. 5,953 (11.12%))

WARWICKSHIRE NORTH
E. 75,435 T. 46,939 (62.22%) Lab. hold
Mike O'Brien, Lab. 22,561
Ian Gibb, C. 15,008
Jerry Roodhouse, LD 6,212
Michaela Mackenzie, BNP 1,910
Iain Campbell, UKIP 1,248
Lab. maj. 7,553 (16.09%)
2.81% swing Lab. to C.
(2001: Lab. maj. 9,639 (21.71%))

WATFORD
E. 76,280 T. 49,394 (64.75%) Lab. hold
Claire Ward, Lab. 16,575
Sal Brinton, LD 15,427
Ali Miraj, C. 14,634
Steve Rackett, Green 1,466
Kenneth Wight, UKIP 1,292
Lab. maj. 1,148 (2.32%)
12.75% swing Lab. to LD
(2001: Lab. maj. 5,555 (11.98%))

WAVENEY
E. 77,138 T. 49,653 (64.37%) Lab. hold
Bob Blizzard, Lab. 22,505
Peter Aldous, C. 16,590
Nick Bromley, LD 7,497
Brian Aylett, UKIP 1,861
Graham Elliott, Green 1,200
Lab. maj. 5,915 (11.91%)
3.11% swing Lab. to C.
(2001: Lab. maj. 8,553 (18.13%))

WEALDEN
E. 82,261 T. 55,653 (67.65%) C. hold
Charles Hendry, C. 28,975
Christopher Wigley, LD 13,054
Dudley Rose, Lab. 9,360
Julian Salmon, Green 2,150
Keith Riddle, UKIP 2,114
C. maj. 15,921 (28.61%)
1.25% swing LD to C.
(2001: C. maj. 13,772 (26.11%))

WEAVER VALE
E. 69,072 T. 39,420 (57.07%) Lab. hold
Mike Hall, Lab. 18,759
Jonathan Mackie, C. 11,904
Nigel Griffiths, LD 7,723
Brenda Swinscoe, UKIP 1,034
Lab. maj. 6,855 (17.39%)
3.58% swing Lab. to C.
(2001: Lab. maj. 9,637 (24.54%))

WELLINGBOROUGH
E. 79,679 T. 53,005 (66.52%) C. gain
*Peter Bone, C. 22,674
Paul Stinchcombe, Lab. 21,987
Richard Church, LD 6,147
James Wrench, UKIP 1,214
Nicholas Alex, Veritas 749
Andy Dickson, Soc. Lab. 234
C. maj. 687 (1.30%)
2.96% swing Lab. to C.
(2001: Lab. maj. 2,355 (4.62%))

WELLS
E. 77,842 T. 52,965 (68.04%) C. hold
Rt. Hon. David Heathcoat-Amory, C. 23,071
Tessa Munt, LD 20,031
Dan Whittle, Lab. 8,288
Steven Reed, UKIP 1,575
C. maj. 3,040 (5.74%)
0.15% swing LD to C.
(2001: C. maj. 2,796 (5.45%))

WELWYN HATFIELD
E. 65,617 T. 44,716 (68.15%) C. gain
*Grant Shapps, C. 22,172
Melanie Johnson, Lab. 16,226
Sara Bedford, LD 6,318
C. maj. 5,946 (13.30%)
8.05% swing Lab. to C.
(2001: Lab. maj. 1,196 (2.79%))

WENTWORTH
E. 63,561 T. 35,596 (56.00%) Lab. hold
John Healey, Lab. 21,225
Mark Hughes, C. 6,169
Keith Orrell, LD 4,800
Jonathan Pygott, BNP 1,798
John Wilkinson, UKIP 1,604
Lab. maj. 15,056 (42.30%)
3.20% swing Lab. to C.
(2001: Lab. maj. 16,449 (48.70%))

WEST BROMWICH EAST
E. 60,565 T. 35,512 (58.63%) Lab. hold
Tom Watson, Lab. 19,741
Rosemary Bromwich, C. 8,089
Ian Garrett, LD 4,386
Carl Butler, BNP 2,329
Steven Grey, UKIP 607
Judith Sambrook, Soc. Lab. 200
Margaret Macklin, Ind. 160
Lab. maj. 11,652 (32.81%)
1.46% swing C. to Lab.
(2001: Lab. maj. 9,763 (29.89%))

WEST BROMWICH WEST
E. 66,752 T. 34,917 (52.31%) Lab. (Co-op) hold
Adrian Bailey, Lab. (Co-op) 18,951
Mimi Harker, C. 8,057
Martyn Smith, LD 3,583
James Lloyd, BNP 3,456
Kevin Walker, UKIP 870
Lab. (Co-op) maj. 10,894 (31.20%)
2.23% swing Lab. (Co-op) to C.
(2001: Lab. (Co-op) maj. 11,355 (35.66%))

WEST HAM
E. 62,184 T. 30,966 (49.80%) Lab. hold
*Lyn Brown, Lab. 15,840
Lindsey German, Respect 6,039
Chris Whitbread, C. 3,618
Alexandra Sugden, LD 3,364
Jane Lithgow, Green 894
Stephen Hammond, CPA 437
Henry Mayhew, UKIP 409
Generoso Alcantara, Veritas 365
Lab. maj. 9,801 (31.65%)
19.12% swing Lab. to Respect
(2001: Lab. maj. 15,645 (53.45%))

WESTBURY
E. 83,039 T. 55,604 (66.96%) C. hold
Dr Andrew Murrison, C. 24,749
Duncan Hames, LD 19,400
Phil Gibby, Lab. 9,640
Lincoln Williams, UKIP 1,815
C. maj. 5,349 (9.62%)
0.42% swing C. to LD
(2001: C. maj. 5,294 (10.46%))

WESTMORLAND & LONSDALE
E. 69,363 T. 49,636 (71.56%) LD gain
*Tim Farron, LD 22,569
Tim Collins, C. 22,302
John Reardon, Lab. 3,796
Robert Gibson, UKIP 660
Anthony Kemp, Ind. 309
LD maj. 267 (0.54%)
3.55% swing C. to LD
(2001: C. maj. 3,147 (6.57%))

WESTON-SUPER-MARE
E. 74,900 T. 49,095 (65.55%) C. gain
*John Penrose, C. 19,804
Brian Cotter, LD 17,725
Damien Egan, Lab. 9,169
Paul Spencer, UKIP 1,207
Clive Courtney, BNP 778
William Human, Ind. 225
Paul Hemingway-Arnold, Honesty 187
C. maj. 2,079 (4.23%)
2.48% swing LD to C.
(2001: LD maj. 338 (0.72%))

WIGAN
E. 64,267 T. 34,278 (53.34%) Lab. hold
Neil Turner, Lab. 18,901
John Coombes, C. 7,134
Denise Capstick, LD 6,051
Dr John Whittaker, UKIP 1,166
Kevin Williams, CAP 1,026
Lab. maj. 11,767 (34.33%)
3.29% swing Lab. to C.
(2001: Lab. maj. 13,743 (40.91%))

WILTSHIRE NORTH
E. 80,896 T. 56,061 (69.30%) C. hold
James Gray, C. 26,282
Paul Fox, LD 20,979
David Nash, Lab. 6,794
Neil Dowdney, UKIP 1,428
Philip Allnatt, Ind. 578
C. maj. 5,303 (9.46%)
1.07% swing LD to C.
(2001: C. maj. 3,878 (7.32%))

WIMBLEDON
E. 63,714 T. 43,404 (68.12%) C. gain
*Stephen Hammond, C. 17,886
Roger Casale, Lab. 15,585
Stephen Gee, LD 7,868
Giles Barrow, Green 1,374
Andrew Mills, UKIP 408
Christopher Coverdale, Ind. 211
Alastair Wilson, TEPK 50
Rainbow George Weiss, Vote Dream 22
C. maj. 2,301 (5.30%)
7.20% swing Lab. to C.
(2001: Lab. maj. 3,744 (9.11%))

WINCHESTER
E. 85,810 T. 61,658 (71.85%) LD hold
Mark Oaten, LD 31,225
George Hollingbery, C. 23,749
Patrick Davies, Lab. 4,782
Dr David Abbott, UKIP 1,321
Arthur Uther Pendragon, Ind. 581
LD maj. 7,476 (12.12%)
2.08% swing LD to C.
(2001: LD maj. 9,634 (16.29%))

WINDSOR
E. 68,290 T. 43,693 (63.98%) C. hold
*Adam Afriyie, C. 21,646
Antony Wood, LD 11,354
Mark Muller, Lab. 8,339
David Black, UKIP 1,098
Derek Wall, Green 1,074
Peter Hooper, Ind. 182
C. maj. 10,292 (23.56%)
1.22% swing LD to C.
(2001: C. maj. 8,889 (21.11%))

WIRRAL SOUTH
E. 58,834 T. 39,704 (67.48%) Lab. hold
Ben Chapman, Lab. 16,892
Carl Cross, C. 13,168
Simon Holbrook, LD 8,568
David Scott, UKIP 616
Laurence Jones, Ind. 460
Lab. maj. 3,724 (9.38%)
1.65% swing Lab. to C.
(2001: Lab. maj. 5,049 (12.68%))

WIRRAL WEST
E. 61,050 T. 41,233 (67.54%) Lab. hold
Stephen Hesford, Lab. 17,543
Esther McVey, C. 16,446
Jeff Clarke, LD 6,652
John Moore, UKIP 429
Roger Taylor, AP 163
Lab. maj. 1,097 (2.66%)
3.65% swing Lab. to C.
(2001: Lab. maj. 4,035 (9.97%))

WITNEY
E. 78,053 T. 53,869 (69.02%) C. hold
David Cameron, C. 26,571
Liz Leffman, LD 12,415
Tony Gray, Lab. 11,845
Richard Dossett-Davies, Green 1,682
Paul Wesson, UKIP 1,356
C. maj. 14,156 (26.28%)
0.79% swing LD to C.
(2001: C. maj. 7,973 (16.20%))

WOKING
E. 72,676 T. 46,045 (63.36%) C. hold
Humfrey Malins, C. 21,838
Anne Lee, LD 15,226
Ellie Blagbrough, Lab. 7,507
Matthew Davies, UKIP 1,324
Michael Osman, UKC 150
C. maj. 6,612 (14.36%)
0.70% swing C. to LD
(2001: C. maj. 6,759 (15.75%))

WOKINGHAM
E. 68,614 T. 46,072 (67.15%) C. hold
Rt. Hon. John Redwood, C. 22,174
Prue Bray, LD 14,934
David Black, Lab. 6,991
Frank Carstairs, UKIP 994
Top Cat Owen, Loony 569
Richard Colborne, BNP 376
Michael Hall, Tele. 34
C. maj. 7,240 (15.71%)
1.02% swing LD to C.
(2001: C. maj. 5,994 (13.67%))

WOLVERHAMPTON NORTH EAST
E. 60,595 T. 32,956 (54.39%)
Lab. (Co-op) hold
Ken Purchase, Lab. (Co-op) 17,948
Alexandra Robson, C. 9,792
David Jack, LD 3,845
Lydia Simpson, UKIP 1,371
Lab. (Co-op) maj. 8,156 (24.75%)
3.45% swing Lab. (Co-op) to C.
(2001: Lab. (Co-op) maj. 9,965 (31.64%))

WOLVERHAMPTON SOUTH EAST
E. 54,047 T. 28,251 (52.27%) Lab. hold
*Pat McFadden, Lab. 16,790
James Fairbairn, C. 6,295
David Murray, LD 3,682
Kevin Simmons, UKIP 1,484
Lab. maj. 10,495 (37.15%)
4.26% swing Lab. to C.
(2001: Lab. (Co-op) maj. 12,464 (45.66%))

WOLVERHAMPTON SOUTH WEST
E. 67,096 T. 41,679 (62.12%) Lab. hold
Rob Marris, Lab. 18,489
Sandy Verma, C. 15,610
Colin Ross, LD 5,568
Douglas Hope, UKIP 1,029
Edward Mullins, BNP 983
Lab. maj. 2,879 (6.91%)
0.81% swing Lab. to C.
(2001: Lab. maj. 3,487 (8.53%))

WOODSPRING
E. 71,662 T. 51,618 (72.03%) C. hold
Dr Liam Fox, C. 21,587
Mike Bell, LD 15,571
Chanel Stevens, Lab. 11,249
Rebecca Lewis, Green 1,309
Anthony Butcher, UKIP 1,269
Michael Howson, BNP 633
C. maj. 6,016 (11.65%)
3.90% swing C. to LD
(2001: C. maj. 8,798 (18.04%))

WORCESTER
E. 72,384 T. 46,388 (64.09%) Lab. hold
Michael Foster, Lab. 19,421
Margaret Harper, C. 16,277
Mary Dhonau, LD 7,557
Richard Chamings, UKIP 1,113
Martin Roberts, BNP 980
Chris Lennard, Green 921
Prudence Dowson, Ind. 119
Lab. maj. 3,144 (6.78%)
3.13% swing Lab. to C.
(2001: Lab. maj. 5,766 (13.04%))

WORCESTERSHIRE MID
E. 71,546 T. 48,127 (67.27%) C. hold
Peter Luff, C. 24,783
Matt Gregson, Lab. 11,456
Margaret Rowley, LD 9,796
Tony Eaves, UKIP 2,092
C. maj. 13,327 (27.69%)
2.01% swing Lab. to C.
(2001: C. maj. 10,627 (23.67%))

WORCESTERSHIRE WEST
E. 66,999 T. 47,077 (70.27%) C. hold
Sir Michael Spicer, C. 20,959
Tom Wells, LD 18,484
Qamar Bhatti, Lab. 4,945
Caroline Bovey, UKIP 1,590
Malcolm Victory, Green 1,099
C. maj. 2,475 (5.26%)
3.37% swing C. to LD
(2001: C. maj. 5,374 (11.99%))

WORKINGTON
E. 61,441 T. 39,737 (64.68%) Lab. hold
Tony Cunningham, Lab. 19,554
Judith Pattinson, C. 12,659
Kate Clarkson, LD 5,815
Mark Richardson, UKIP 1,328
John Peacock, LCA 381
Lab. maj. 6,895 (17.35%)
4.30% swing Lab. to C.
(2001: Lab. maj. 10,850 (25.94%))

WORSLEY
E. 69,534 T. 36,946 (53.13%) Lab. hold
*Barbara Keeley, Lab. 18,859
Graham Evans, C. 9,491
Richard Clayton, LD 6,902
Bernard Gill, UKIP 1,694
Lab. maj. 9,368 (25.36%)
3.99% swing Lab. to C.
(2001: Lab. maj. 11,787 (33.33%))

WORTHING EAST & SHOREHAM
E. 72,302 T. 44,543 (61.61%) C. hold
Tim Loughton, C. 19,548
Daniel Yates, Lab. 11,365
James Doyle, LD 10,844
Richard Jelf, UKIP 2,109
Chris Baldwin, LCA 677
C. maj. 8,183 (18.37%)
2.06% swing Lab. to C.
(2001: C. maj. 6,139 (14.25%))

WORTHING WEST
E. 71,780 T. 44,941 (62.61%) C. hold
Peter Bottomley, C. 21,383
Claire Potter, LD 12,004
Antony Bignell, Lab. 8,630
Timothy Cross, UKIP 2,374
Chris Baldwin, LCA 550
C. maj. 9,379 (20.87%)
0.02% swing C. to LD
(2001: C. maj. 9,037 (20.91%))

WREKIN, THE
E. 67,291 T. 45,054 (66.95%) C. gain
*Mark Pritchard, C. 18,899
Peter Bradley, Lab. 17,957
Bill Tomlinson, LD 6,608
Bruce Lawson, UKIP 1,590
C. maj. 942 (2.09%)
5.37% swing Lab. to C.
(2001: Lab. maj. 3,587 (8.65%))

WYCOMBE
E. 71,464 T. 44,427 (62.17%) C. hold
Paul Goodman, C. 20,331
Julia Wassell, Lab. 13,280
James Oates, LD 8,780
Robert Davis, UKIP 1,735
David Fitton, Ind. 301
C. maj. 7,051 (15.87%)
4.41% swing Lab. to C.
(2001: C. maj. 3,168 (7.04%))

WYRE FOREST
E. 73,192 T. 46,987 (64.20%)
KHHC hold
Dr Richard Taylor, KHHC 18,739
Mark Garnier, C. 13,489
Marc Bayliss, Lab. 10,716
Fran Oborski, Lib. 2,666
Rustie Lee, UKIP 1,074
Bert Priest, Loony 303
KHHC maj. 5,250 (11.17%)
13.92% swing KHHC to C.
(2001: KHHC maj. 17,630 (35.93%))

WYTHENSHAWE & SALE EAST
E. 71,766 T. 36,184 (50.42%) Lab. hold
Paul Goggins, Lab. 18,878
Jane Meehan, C. 8,051
Alison Firth, LD 7,766
William Ford, UKIP 1,120
Lynn Worthington, Soc. Alt. 369
Lab. maj. 10,827 (29.92%)
3.02% swing Lab. to C.
(2001: Lab. maj. 12,608 (35.97%))

YEOVIL
E. 77,668 T. 49,913 (64.26%) LD hold
David Laws, LD 25,658
Ian Jenkins, C. 17,096
Colin Rolfe, Lab. 5,256
Graham Livings, UKIP 1,903
LD maj. 8,562 (17.15%)
4.50% swing C. to LD
(2001: LD maj. 3,928 (8.16%))

YORK, CITY OF
E. 75,555 T. 46,597 (61.67%) Lab. hold
Hugh Bayley, Lab. 21,836
Clive Booth, C. 11,364
Andrew Waller, LD 10,166
Andy D'Agorne, Green 2,113
Richard Jackson, UKIP 832
Ken Curran, Ind. 121
Damien Fleck, DDTP 93
Andrew Hinkles, Ind. 72
Lab. maj. 10,472 (22.47%)
3.12% swing Lab. to C.
(2001: Lab. maj. 13,779 (28.72%))

YORKSHIRE EAST
E. 76,648 T. 46,925 (61.22%) C. hold
Rt. Hon. Greg Knight, C. 21,215
Emma Hoddinott, Lab. 14,932
Jim Wastling, LD 9,075
Christopher Tresidder, UKIP 1,703
C. maj. 6,283 (13.39%)
1.29% swing Lab. to C.
(2001: C. maj. 4,682 (10.81%))

WALES

ABERAVON
E. 51,080 T. 30,104 (58.94%) Lab. hold
Dr Hywel Francis, Lab. 18,077
Claire Waller, LD 4,140
Philip Evans, PC 3,545
Annunziata Rees-Mogg, C. 3,064
Walter Wright, Veritas 768
Miranda La Vey, Green 510
Lab. maj. 13,937 (46.30%)
3.57% swing Lab. to LD
(2001: Lab. maj. 16,108 (53.36%))

ALYN & DEESIDE
E. 58,939 T. 35,496 (60.22%) Lab. hold
Mark Tami, Lab. 17,331
Lynne Hale, C. 8,953
Paul Brighton, LD 6,174
Richard Coombs, PC 1,320
William Crawford, UKIP 918
Klaus Armstrong-Braun, FWP 378
Judith Kilshaw, Ind. 215
Glyn Davies, Comm Brit 207
Lab. maj. 8,378 (23.60%)
1.22% swing Lab. to C.
(2001: Lab. maj. 9,222 (26.04%))

BLAENAU GWENT
E. 53,301 T. 35,251 (66.14%) Ind. gain
*Peter Law, Ind. 20,505
Maggie Jones, Lab. 11,384
Brian Thomas, LD 1,511
John Price, PC 843
Dr Phillip Lee, C. 816
Peter Osborne, UKIP 192
Ind. maj. 9,121 (25.87%)
43.38% swing Lab. to Ind.
(2001: Lab. maj. 19,313 (60.88%))

BRECON & RADNORSHIRE
E. 55,171 T. 38,341 (69.49%) LD hold
Roger Williams, LD 17,182
Andrew Davies, C. 13,277
Leighton Veale, Lab. 5,755
Mabon ap Gwynfor, PC 1,404
Elizabeth Phillips, UKIP 723
LD maj. 3,905 (10.18%)
4.09% swing C. to LD
(2001: LD maj. 751 (2.00%))

BRIDGEND
E. 63,936 T. 37,859 (59.21%) Lab. hold
*Madeleine Moon, Lab. 16,410
Helen Baker, C. 9,887
Paul Warren, LD 7,949
Gareth Clubb, PC 2,527
Jonathan Spink, Green 595
Kunnathur Rajan, UKIP 491
Lab. maj. 6,523 (17.23%)
4.96% swing Lab. to C.
(2001: Lab. maj. 10,045 (27.15%))

CAERNARFON
E. 46,393 T. 27,999 (60.35%) PC hold
Hywel Williams, PC 12,747
Martin Eaglestone, Lab. 7,538
Melfyn ab Owain, LD 3,508
Guy Opperman, C. 3,483
Elwyn Williams, UKIP 723
PC maj. 5,209 (18.60%)
3.26% swing Lab. to PC
(2001: PC maj. 3,511 (12.08%))

CAERPHILLY
E. 66,939 T. 39,229 (58.60%) Lab. hold
Wayne David, Lab. 22,190
Lindsay Whittle, PC 6,831
Stephen Watson, C. 5,711
Ashgar Ali, LD 3,861
Graeme Beard, FWP 636
Lab. maj. 15,359 (39.15%)
1.00% swing PC to Lab.
(2001: Lab. maj. 14,425 (37.15%))

CARDIFF CENTRAL
E. 61,001 T. 36,132 (59.23%) LD gain
*Jenny Willott, LD 17,991
Jon Owen Jones, Lab. (Co-op) 12,398
Gotz Mohindra, C. 3,339
Richard Grigg, PC 1,271
Raja Gul Raiz, Respect 386
Frank Hughes, UKIP 383
Anne Savoury, Ind. 168
Captain Beany, Bean 159
Catherine Taylor-Dawson, Vote Dream 37
LD maj. 5,593 (15.48%)
8.69% swing Lab. (Co-op) to LD
(2001: Lab. (Co-op) maj. 659 (1.89%))

CARDIFF NORTH
E. 64,341 T. 45,360 (70.50%) Lab. hold
Julie Morgan, Lab. 17,707
Jonathan Morgan, C. 16,561
John Dixon, LD 8,483
John Rowlands, PC 1,936
Don Hulston, UKIP 534
Alison Hobbs, FWP 138
Catherine Taylor-Dawson, Vote Dream 1
Lab. maj. 1,146 (2.53%)
5.87% swing Lab. to C.
(2001: Lab. maj. 6,165 (14.26%))

CARDIFF SOUTH & PENARTH
E. 65,710 T. 36,912 (56.17%) Lab. (Co-op) hold
Rt. Hon. Alun Michael, Lab. (Co-op) 17,447
Victoria Green, C. 8,210
Gavin Cox, LD 7,529
Jason Toby, PC 2,023
John Matthews, Green 729
Jennifer Tuttle, UKIP 522
Dave Bartlett, Soc. Alt. 269
Andrew Taylor, Ind. 104
Catherine Taylor-Dawson, Vote Dream 79
Lab. (Co-op) maj. 9,237 (25.02%)
4.67% swing Lab. (Co-op) to C.
(2001: Lab. (Co-op) maj. 12,287 (34.37%))

CARDIFF WEST
E. 59,847 T. 34,561 (57.75%) Lab. hold
Kevin Brennan, Lab. 15,729
Simon Baker, C. 7,562
Alison Goldsworthy, LD 6,060
Neil McEvoy, PC 4,316
Joe Callan, UKIP 727
Catherine Taylor-Dawson, Vote Dream 167
Lab. maj. 8,167 (23.63%)
4.79% swing Lab. to C.
(2001: Lab. maj. 11,321 (33.22%))

CARMARTHEN EAST & DINEFWR
E. 53,484 T. 38,291 (71.59%) PC hold
Adam Price, PC 17,561
Ross Hendry, Lab. 10,843
Suzy Davies, C. 5,235
Juliana Hughes, LD 3,719
Mike Squires, UKIP 661
Sid Whitworth, LCA 272
PC maj. 6,718 (17.54%)
5.37% swing Lab. to PC
(2001: PC maj. 2,590 (6.81%))

CARMARTHEN WEST & PEMBROKESHIRE SOUTH
E. 56,245 T. 37,863 (67.32%) Lab. hold
Nick Ainger, Lab. 13,953
David Morris, C. 12,043
John Dixon, PC 5,582
John Allen, LD 5,399
Josie MacDonald, UKIP 545
Alex Daszak, LCA 237
Nick Turner, Ind. 104
Lab. maj. 1,910 (5.04%)
3.62% swing Lab. to C.
(2001: Lab. maj. 4,538 (12.29%))

CEREDIGION
E. 53,493 T. 35,947 (67.20%) LD gain
*Mark Williams, LD 13,130
Simon Thomas, PC 12,911
John Harrison, C. 4,455
Alun Davies, Lab. 4,337
Dave Bradney, Green 846
Iain Sheldon, Veritas 268
LD maj. 219 (0.61%)
6.00% swing PC to LD
(2001: PC maj. 3,944 (11.40%))

CLWYD SOUTH
E. 52,353 T. 32,931 (62.90%) Lab. hold
Martyn Jones, Lab. 14,808
Tom Biggins, C. 8,460
Deric Burnham, LD 5,105
Mark Strong, PC 3,111
Alwyn Humphreys, FWP 803
Nick Powell, UKIP 644
Lab. maj. 6,348 (19.28%)
3.64% swing Lab. to C.
(2001: Lab. maj. 8,898 (26.56%))

CLWYD WEST
E. 55,642 T. 35,614 (64.01%) C. gain
*David Jones, C. 12,909
Gareth Thomas, Lab. 12,776
Frank Taylor, LD 4,723
Eilian Williams, PC 3,874
Warwick Nicholson, UKIP 512
Jimmy James, Ind. 507
Patrick Keenan, Soc. Lab. 313
C. maj. 133 (0.37%)
1.80% swing Lab. to C.
(2001: Lab. maj. 1,115 (3.22%))

CONWY
E. 53,987 T. 33,657 (62.34%) Lab. hold
Betty Williams, Lab. 12,479
Guto Bebb, C. 9,398
Gareth Roberts, LD 6,723
Paul Rowlinson, PC 3,730
Jim Killock, Green 512
David Lloyd Jones, Soc. Lab. 324
Kenneth Khambatta, UKIP 298
Tim Evans, LCA 193
Lab. maj. 3,081 (9.15%)
4.47% swing Lab. to C.
(2001: Lab. maj. 6,219 (18.10%))

CYNON VALLEY
E. 45,369 T. 26,647 (58.73%) Lab. hold
Rt. Hon. Ann Clwyd, Lab. 17,074
Geraint Benney, PC 3,815
Margaret Phelps, LD 2,991
Antonia Dunn, C. 2,062
Susan Davies, UKIP 705
Lab. maj. 13,259 (49.76%)
0.77% swing PC to Lab.
(2001: Lab. maj. 12,998 (48.22%))

DELYN
E. 52,766 T. 34,004 (64.44%) Lab. hold
David Hanson, Lab. 15,540
John Bell, C. 8,896
Tudor Jones, LD 6,089
Phil Thomas, PC 2,524
May Crawford, UKIP 533
Nigel Williams, Ind. 422
Lab. maj. 6,644 (19.54%)
2.65% swing Lab. to C.
(2001: Lab. maj. 8,605 (24.84%))

GOWER
E. 60,925 T. 39,542 (64.90%) Lab. hold
Martin Caton, Lab. 16,786
Mike Murray, C. 10,083
Nick Tregoning, LD 7,291
Sian Caiach, PC 3,089
Richard Lewis, UKIP 1,264
Rhodri Griffiths, Green 1,029
Lab. maj. 6,703 (16.95%)
1.42% swing Lab. to C.
(2001: Lab. maj. 7,395 (19.80%))

ISLWYN
E. 50,595 T. 30,865 (61.00%) Lab. (Co-op) hold
Don Touhig, Lab. (Co-op) 19,687
Jim Criddle, PC 3,947
Lee Dillon, LD 3,873
Phillip Howells, C. 3,358
Lab. (Co-op) maj. 15,740 (51.00%)
0.67% swing PC to Lab. (Co-op)
(2001: Lab. (Co-op) maj. 15,309 (48.31%))

LLANELLI
E. 55,678 T. 35,344 (63.48%) Lab. hold
*Nia Griffith, Lab. 16,592
Neil Baker, PC 9,358
Adrian Phillips, C. 4,844
Ken Rees, LD 4,550
Lab. maj. 7,234 (20.47%)
1.39% swing PC to Lab.
(2001: Lab. maj. 6,403 (17.69%))

MEIRIONNYDD NANT CONWY
E. 33,443 T. 20,640 (61.72%) PC hold
Elfyn Llwyd, PC 10,597
Rhodri Jones, Lab. 3,983
Dan Munford, C. 3,402
Adrian Fawcett, LD 2,192
Francis Wykes, UKIP 466
PC maj. 6,614 (32.04%)
2.53% swing Lab. to PC
(2001: PC maj. 5,684 (26.98%))

MERTHYR TYDFIL & RHYMNEY

E. 54,579 T. 29,976 (54.92%) Lab. hold

Dai Havard, Lab.	18,129
Ceirion Rees, LD	4,195
Noel Turner, PC	2,972
Roger Berry, C.	2,680
Neil Greer, FWP	1,030
Gwyn Parry, UKIP	699
na Marsden, Soc. Lab.	271

Lab. maj. 13,934 (46.48%)

3.88% swing Lab. to LD

(2001: Lab. maj. 14,923 (47.10%))

MONMOUTH

E. 63,093 T. 45,653 (72.36%) C. gain

*David Davies, C.	21,396
Huw Edwards, Lab.	16,869
Phil Hobson, LD	5,852
Jonathan Clark, PC	993
John Bufton, UKIP	543

C. maj. 4,527 (9.92%)

5.39% swing Lab. to C.

(2001: Lab. maj. 384 (0.86%))

MONTGOMERYSHIRE

E. 46,766 T. 30,097 (64.36%) LD hold

Lembit Opik, LD	15,419
Simon Baynes, C.	8,246
David Tinline, Lab.	3,454
Ellen ap Gwynn, PC	2,078
Clive Easton, UKIP	900

LD maj. 7,173 (23.83%)

1.16% swing C. to LD

(2001: LD maj. 6,234 (21.51%))

NEATH

E. 57,607 T. 35,817 (62.17%) Lab. hold

Rt. Hon. Peter Hain, Lab.	18,835
Geraint Owen, PC	6,125
Sheila Waye, LD	5,112
Harri Lloyd Davies, C.	4,136
Susan Jay, Green	658
Gerry Brienza, Ind.	360
Pat Tabram, LCA	334
Heather Falconer, Respect	257

Lab. maj. 12,710 (35.49%)

3.41% swing Lab. to PC

(2001: Lab. maj. 14,816 (42.31%))

NEWPORT EAST

E. 54,956 T. 31,825 (57.91%) Lab. hold

*Jessica Morden, Lab.	14,389
Ed Townsend, LD	7,551
Matthew Collings, C.	7,459
Mohammad Asghar, PC	1,221
Roger Thomas, UKIP	945
Liz Screen, Soc. Lab.	260

Lab. maj. 6,838 (21.49%)

9.60% swing Lab. to LD

(2001: Lab. maj. 9,874 (31.56%))

NEWPORT WEST

E. 60,287 T. 35,732 (59.27%) Lab. hold

Paul Flynn, Lab.	16,021
Dr William Morgan, C.	10,563
Nigel Flanagan, LD	6,398
Tony Salkeld, PC	1,278
Hugh Moelwyn Hughes, UKIP	848
Peter Varley, Green	540
Saeid Arjomand, Ind.	84

Lab. maj. 5,458 (15.27%)

5.63% swing Lab. to C.

(2001: Lab. maj. 9,304 (26.54%))

OGMORE

E. 52,349 T. 30,278 (57.84%) Lab. hold

Huw Irranca-Davies, Lab.	18,295
Jackie Radford, LD	4,592
Dr Norma Lloyd-Nesling, C.	4,243
John Williams, PC	3,148

Lab. maj. 13,703 (45.26%)

2.01% swing Lab. to LD

(2002 Feb. by-election: Lab maj. 5,721 (31.13%))

(2001: Lab. maj. 14,574 (48.02%))

PONTYPRIDD

E. 65,074 T. 39,634 (60.91%) Lab. hold

Dr Kim Howells, Lab.	20,919
Mike Powell, LD	7,728
Quentin Gwynne Edwards, C.	5,321
Julie Richards, PC	4,420
David Bevan, UKIP	1,013
Robert Griffiths, Comm.	233

Lab. maj. 13,191 (33.28%)

7.91% swing Lab. to LD

(2001: Lab. maj. 17,684 (46.16%))

PRESELI PEMBROKESHIRE

E. 55,502 T. 38,587 (69.52%) C. gain

*Stephen Crabb, C.	14,106
Sue Hayman, Lab.	13,499
Dewi Smith, LD	4,963
Matt Mathias, PC	4,752
James Carver, UKIP	498
Molly Scott-Cato, Green	494
Trish Bowen, Soc. Lab.	275

C. maj. 607 (1.57%)

4.79% swing Lab. to C.

(2001: Lab. maj. 2,946 (8.01%))

RHONDDA

E. 51,041 T. 31,148 (61.03%) Lab. hold

Chris Bryant, Lab.	21,198
Layton Percy Jones, PC	4,956
Karen Roberts, LD	3,264
Paul Stuart-Smith, C.	1,730

Lab. maj. 16,242 (52.14%)

2.48% swing PC to Lab.

(2001: Lab. maj. 16,047 (47.19%))

SWANSEA EAST

E. 58,813 T. 30,834 (52.43%) Lab. hold

*Sian James, Lab.	17,457
Robert Speht, LD	6,208
Ellenor Bland, C.	3,103
Carolyn Shan Couch, PC	2,129
Kevin Holloway, BNP	770
Timothy Jenkins, UKIP	674
Tony Young, Green	493

Lab. maj. 11,249 (36.48%)

9.27% swing Lab. to LD

(2001: Lab. maj. 16,148 (53.70%))

SWANSEA WEST

E. 57,946 T. 33,086 (57.10%) Lab. hold

Rt. Hon. Alan Williams, Lab.	13,833
Rene Kinzett, LD	9,564
Mohammed Abdel-Haq, C.	5,285
Harri Roberts, PC	2,150
Martyn Shrewsbury, Green	738
Martyn Ford, UKIP	609
Yvonne Holley, Veritas	401
Robert Williams, Soc. Alt.	288
Steve Pank, LCA	218

Lab. maj. 4,269 (12.90%)

9.64% swing Lab. to LD

(2001: Lab. maj. 9,550 (29.75%))

TORFAEN

E. 60,669 T. 35,979 (59.30%) Lab. hold

Rt. Hon. Paul Murphy, Lab.	20,472
Nick Ramsay, C.	5,681
Veronica Watkins, LD	5,678
Aneurin Preece, PC	2,242
David Rowlands, UKIP	1,145
Richard Turner-Thomas, Ind.	761

Lab. maj. 14,791 (41.11%)

2.54% swing Lab. to C.

(2001: Lab. maj. 16,280 (46.19%))

VALE OF CLWYD

E. 51,982 T. 32,313 (62.16%) Lab. hold

Christopher Ruane, Lab.	14,875
Felicity Elphick, C.	10,206
Elizabeth Jewkes, LD	3,820
Mark Jones, PC	2,309
Mark Young, Ind.	442
Edna Khambatta, UKIP	375
Jeff Ditchfield, LCA	286

Lab. maj. 4,669 (14.45%)

1.68% swing Lab. to C.

(2001: Lab. maj. 5,761 (17.81%))

VALE OF GLAMORGAN

E. 68,657 T. 47,324 (68.93%) Lab. hold

John Smith, Lab.	19,481
Alun Cairns, C.	17,673
Mark Hooper, LD	6,140
Barry Shaw, PC	2,423
Richard Suchorzewski, UKIP	840
Karl-James Langford, Lib.	605
Paul Mules, Soc. Lab.	162

Lab. maj. 1,808 (3.82%)

3.29% swing Lab. to C.

(2001: Lab. maj. 4,700 (10.40%))

WREXHAM

E. 48,016 T. 30,385 (63.28%) Lab. hold

Ian Lucas, Lab.	13,993
Tom Rippeth, LD	7,174
Dr Therese Coffey, C.	6,079
Sion Owen, PC	1,744
John Walker, BNP	919
Janet Williams, FWP	476

Lab. maj. 6,819 (22.44%)

6.72% swing Lab. to LD

(2001: Lab. maj. 9,188 (30.58%))

YNYS MON

E. 52,512 T. 35,462 (67.53%) Lab. hold

Albert Owen, Lab.	12,278
Eurig Wyn, PC	11,036
Peter Rogers, Ind.	5,216
James Roach, C.	3,915
Sarah Green, LD	2,418
Elaine Gill, UKIP	367
Tim Evans, LCA	232

Lab. maj. 1,242 (3.50%)

0.58% swing PC to Lab.

(2001: Lab. maj. 800 (2.35%))

SCOTLAND

ABERDEEN NORTH
E. 65,714 T. 36,634 (55.75%) Lab. win
Frank Doran, Lab. 15,557
Steve Delaney, LD 8,762
Kevin Stewart, SNP 8,168
David Anderson, C. 3,456
John Connon, SSP 691
Lab. maj. 6,795 (18.55%)
§ 9.25% swing Lab. to LD
(§ 2001 Lab. maj. 9,294 (23.66%))

ABERDEEN SOUTH
E. 67,012 T. 41,621 (62.11%) Lab. win
Anne Begg, Lab. 15,272
Vicki Harris, LD 13,924
Stewart Whyte, C. 7,134
Maureen Watt, SNP 4,120
Rhonda Reekie, Scot. Green 768
Donald Munro, SSP 403
Lab. maj. 1,348 (3.24%)
§ 3.13% swing Lab. to LD
(§ 2001 Lab. maj. 3,931 (9.49%))

ABERDEENSHIRE WEST & KINCARDINE
E. 65,548 T. 41,648 (63.54%) LD win
Sir Robert Smith, LD 19,285
Alex Johnstone, C. 11,814
James Barrowman, Lab. 5,470
Caroline Little, SNP 4,700
Lorna Grant, SSP 379
LD maj. 7,471 (17.94%)
§ 2.25% swing C. to LD
(§ 2001 LD maj. 5,146 (13.44%))

AIRDRIE & SHOTTS
E. 61,955 T. 33,158 (53.52%) Lab. win
Rt. Hon. Dr John Reid, Lab. 19,568
Malcolm Balfour, SNP 5,484
Helen Watt, LD 3,792
Stuart Cottis, C. 3,271
Fraser Coats, SSP 706
Joseph Rowan, Scot. Ind. 337
Lab. maj. 14,084 (42.48%)
§ 1.51% swing SNP to Lab.
(§ 2001 Lab. maj. 13,545 (39.46%))

ANGUS
E. 63,093 T. 38,186 (60.52%) SNP win
Mike Weir, SNP 12,840
Sandy Bushby, C. 11,280
Douglas Bradley, Lab. 6,850
Scott Rennie, LD 6,660
Alan Manley, SSP 556
SNP maj. 1,601 (4.20%)
§ 1.34% swing C. to SNP
(§ 2001 SNP maj. 532 (1.52%))

ARGYLL & BUTE
E. 67,325 T. 43,229 (64.21%) LD win
Alan Reid, LD 15,786
James McGrigor, C. 10,150
Carolyn Manson, Lab. 9,696
Isobel Strong, SNP 6,716
Deirdre Henderson, SSP 881
LD maj. 5,636 (13.04%)
§ 1.94% swing C. to LD
(§ 2001 LD maj. 3,832 (9.16%))

AYR, CARRICK & CUMNOCK
E. 73,448 T. 45,048 (61.33%) Lab. win
Sandra Osborne, Lab. 20,433
Mark Jones, C. 10,436
Colin Waugh, LD 6,341
Charles Brodie, SNP 5,932
Donald Sharp, SSCUP 592
Murray Steele, SSP 554
James McDaid, Soc. Lab. 395
Bryan McCormack, UKIP 365
Lab. maj. 9,997 (22.19%)
§ 2.18% swing Lab. to C.
(§ 2001 Lab. maj. 12,387 (26.56%))

AYRSHIRE CENTRAL
E. 68,643 T. 42,871 (62.46%) Lab. win
Brian Donohoe, Lab. 19,905
Garry Clark, C. 9,482
Iain Kennedy, LD 6,881
Jahangir Hanif, SNP 4,969
Denise Morton, SSP 820
Robert Cochrane, Soc. Lab. 468
Jim Groves, UKIP 346
Lab. maj. 10,423 (24.31%)
§ 0.68% swing C. to Lab.
(§ 2001 Lab. maj. 9,772 (22.96%))

AYRSHIRE NORTH & ARRAN
E. 72,986 T. 44,205 (60.57%) Lab. win
*Katy Clark, Lab. 19,417
Stewart Connell, C. 8,121
Tony Gurney, SNP 7,938
George White, LD 7,264
Colin Turbett, SSP 780
John Pursley, UKIP 382
Louise McDaid, Soc. Lab. 303
Lab. maj. 11,296 (25.55%)
§ 2.68% swing Lab. to C.
(§ 2001 Lab. maj. 12,140 (27.33%))

BANFF & BUCHAN
E. 65,570 T. 37,216 (56.76%) SNP win
Alex Salmond, SNP 19,044
Sandy Wallace, C. 7,207
Eleanor Anderson, LD 4,952
Rami Okasha, Lab. 4,476
Victor Ross, OCV 683
Kathleen Kemp, UKIP 442
Steve Will, SSP 412
SNP maj. 11,837 (31.81%)
§ 2.22% swing C. to SNP
(§ 2001 SNP maj. 9,744 (27.37%))

BERWICKSHIRE, ROXBURGH & SELKIRK
E. 71,702 T. 45,388 (63.30%) LD win
Michael Moore, LD 18,993
John Lamont, C. 13,092
Sam Held, Lab. 7,206
Aileen Orr, SNP 3,885
John Hein, Lib. 916
Graeme McIver, SSP 695
Peter Neilson, UKIP 601
LD maj. 5,901 (13.00%)
§ 5.90% swing LD to C.
(§ 2001 LD maj. 10,770 (24.80%))

CAITHNESS, SUTHERLAND & EASTER ROSS
E. 46,837 T. 27,663 (59.06%) LD win
John Thurso, LD 13,957
Alan Jamieson, Lab. 5,789
Karen Shirron, SNP 3,686
Angus Ross, C. 2,835
Gordon Campbell, Ind. 848
Luke Ivory, SSP 548
LD maj. 8,168 (29.53%)
§ 7.60% swing Lab. to LD
(§ 2001 LD maj. 4,078 (14.33%))

COATBRIDGE, CHRYSTON & BELLSHILL
E. 67,385 T. 38,344 (56.90%) Lab. win
Rt. Hon. Thomas Clarke, Lab. 24,725
Duncan Ross, SNP 5,206
Rodney Ackland, LD 4,605
Lindsay Paterson, C. 2,775
Joan Kinloch, SSP 1,033
Lab. maj. 19,519 (50.90%)
§ 1.82% swing Lab. to SNP
(§ 2001 Lab. maj. 22,092 (54.55%))

CUMBERNAULD, KILSYTH & KIRKINTILLOCH EAST
E. 64,748 T. 39,088 (60.37%) Lab. win
Rosemary McKenna, Lab. 20,251
James Hepburn, SNP 8,689
Hugh O'Donnell, LD 5,817
James Boswell, C. 2,718
Willie O'Neill, SSP 1,141
Patrick Elliott, OCV 472
Lab. maj. 11,562 (29.58%)
§ 1.11% swing Lab. to SNP
(§ 2001 Lab. maj. 12,667 (31.79%))

DUMFRIES & GALLOWAY
E. 74,273 T. 50,891 (68.52%) Lab. win
Russell Brown, Lab. 20,924
Peter Duncan, C. 18,002
Douglas Henderson, SNP 6,182
Keith Legg, LD 4,259
John Schofield, Scot. Green 745
John Dennis, SSP 497
Mark Smith, OCV 282
Lab. maj. 2,922 (5.74%)
§ 2.73% swing C. to Lab.
(§ 2001 Lab. maj. 141 (0.28%))

DUMFRIESSHIRE, CLYDESDALE & TWEEDDALE
E. 66,045 T. 44,616 (67.55%) C. win
*David Mundell, C. 16,141
Sean Marshall, Lab. 14,403
Patsy Kenton, LD 9,046
Andrew Wood, SNP 4,075
Sarah MacTavish, SSP 521
Tony Lee, UKIP 430
C. maj. 1,738 (3.90%)
§ 7.98% swing Lab. to C.
(§ 2001 Lab. maj. 5,254 (12.06%))

DUNBARTONSHIRE EAST
E. 64,763 T. 46,724 (72.15%) LD win
*Jo Swinson, LD 19,533
John Lyons, Lab. 15,472
David Jack, C. 7,708
Chris Sagan, SNP 2,716
Stuart Callison, Scot. Green 876
Pamela Page, SSP 419
LD maj. 4,061 (8.69%)
§ 7.49% swing Lab. to LD
(§ 2001 Lab. maj. 2,601 (6.29%))

DUNBARTONSHIRE WEST
E. 67,805 T. 41,589 (61.34%) Lab. (Co-op) win
Rt. Hon. John McFall, Lab. (Co-op) 21,600
Tom Chalmers, SNP 9,047
Niall Walker, LD 5,999
Campbell Murdoch, C. 2,679
Les Robertson, SSP 1,708
Bryan Maher, UKIP 354
Marlon Dawson, OCV 202
Lab. (Co-op) maj. 12,553 (30.18%)
§ 4.65% swing Lab. (Co-op) to SNP
(§ 2001 Lab. (Co-op) maj. 18,169 (39.49%))

DUNDEE EAST
E. 63,335 T. 39,540 (62.43%) SNP win
*Stewart Hosie, SNP 14,708
Iain Luke, Lab. 14,325
Christopher Bustin, C. 5,061
Clive Sneddon, LD 4,498
Harvey Duke, SSP 537
Donald Low, UKIP 292
David Allison, Ind. 119
SNP maj. 383 (0.97%)
§ 1.13% swing Lab. to SNP
(§ 2001 Lab. maj. 496 (1.29%))

DUNDEE WEST
E. 65,857 T. 36,936 (56.09%) Lab. win
*James McGovern, Lab. 16,468
Joe Fitzpatrick, SNP 11,089
Nykoma Garry, LD 5,323
Christopher McKinlay, C. 3,062
Jim McFarlane, SSP 994
Lab. maj. 5,379 (14.56%)
§ 3.99% swing Lab. to SNP
(§ 2001 Lab. maj. 8,410 (22.54%))

DUNFERMLINE & FIFE WEST
E. 70,775 T. 42,394 (59.90%) Lab. win
Rachel Squire, Lab. 20,111
David Herbert, LD 8,549
Douglas Chapman, SNP 8,026
Roger Smillie, C. 4,376
Susan Archibald, SSP 689
Ian Borland, UKIP 643
Lab. maj. 11,562 (27.27%)
§ 6.47% swing Lab. to LD
(§ 2001 Lab. maj. 14,845 (36.64%))

EAST KILBRIDE, STRATHAVEN & LESMAHAGOW
E. 75,132 T. 47,733 (63.53%) Lab. win
Rt. Hon. Adam Ingram, Lab. 23,264
Douglas Edwards, SNP 8,541
John Oswald, LD 7,904
Tony Lewis, C. 4,776
Kirsten Robb, Scot. Green 1,575
Rose Gentle, Ind. 1,513
John Houston, Ind. 160
Lab. maj. 14,723 (30.84%)
§ 0.78% swing SNP to Lab.
(§ 2001 Lab. maj. 13,999 (29.29%))

EAST LOTHIAN
E. 70,989 T. 45,776 (64.48%) Lab. win
Anne Picking, Lab. 18,983
Chris Butler, LD 11,363
William Stevenson, C. 7,315
Paul McLennan, SNP 5,995
Michael Collie, Scot. Green 1,132
Gary Galbraith, SSP 504
Eric Robb, UKIP 306
William Thompson, OCV 178
Lab. maj. 7,620 (16.65%)
§ 7.54% swing Lab. to LD
(§ 2001 Lab. maj. 14,011 (31.73%))

EDINBURGH EAST
E. 64,826 T. 39,709 (61.25%) Lab. win
Rt. Hon. Gavin Strang, Lab. 15,899
Gordon Mackenzie, LD 9,697
Stefan Tymkewycz, SNP 6,760
Mev Brown, C. 4,093
Cara Gillespie, Scot. Green 2,266
Catriona Grant, SSP 868
Brett Harris, DDTP 89
Peter Clifford, Ind. 37
Lab. maj. 6,202 (15.62%)
§ 8.47% swing Lab. to LD
(§ 2001 Lab. maj. 12,808 (32.56%))

EDINBURGH NORTH & LEITH
E. 68,038 T. 42,640 (62.67%) Lab. (Co-op) win
Mark Lazarowicz, Lab. (Co-op) 14,597
Mike Crockart, LD 12,444
Iain Whyte, C. 7,969
Davie Hutchison, SNP 4,344
Mark Sydenham, Scot. Green 2,482
Bill Scott, SSP 804
Lab. (Co-op) maj. 2,153 (5.05%)
§ 8.26% swing Lab. (Co-op) to LD
(§ 2001 Lab. (Co-op) maj. 8,688 (21.56%))

EDINBURGH SOUTH
E. 60,993 T. 42,698 (70.00%) Lab. win
Nigel Griffiths, Lab. 14,188
Marilyne MacLaren, LD 13,783
Gavin Brown, C. 10,291
Graham Sutherland, SNP 2,635
Dr Steve Burgess, Scot. Green 1,387
Morag Robertson, SSP 414
Lab. maj. 405 (0.95%)
§ 6.50% swing Lab. to LD
(§ 2001 Lab. maj. 5,785 (13.95%))

EDINBURGH SOUTH WEST
E. 67,135 T. 43,926 (65.43%) Lab. win
Rt. Hon. Alistair Darling, Lab. 17,476
Gordon Buchan, C. 10,234
Simon Clark, LD 9,252
Nick Elliott-Cannon, SNP 4,654
John Blair-Fish, Scot. Green 1,520
Pat Smith, SSP 585
William Boys, UKIP 205
Lab. maj. 7,242 (16.49%)
§ 0.71% swing Lab. to C.
(§ 2001 Lab. maj. 7,951 (17.91%))

EDINBURGH WEST
E. 65,741 T. 45,265 (68.85%) LD win
John Barrett, LD 22,417
David Brogan, C. 8,817
Navraj Singh Ghaleigh, Lab. 8,433
Sheena Cleland, SNP 4,124
Ailsa Spindler, Scot. Green 964
Gary Clark, SSP 510
LD maj. 13,600 (30.05%)
§ 6.71% swing C. to LD
(§ 2001 LD maj. 5,320 (11.86%))

FALKIRK
E. 76,784 T. 45,750 (59.58%) Lab. win
Eric Joyce, Lab. 23,264
Laura Love, SNP 9,789
Callum Chomczuk, LD 7,321
David Potts, C. 4,538
Danny Quinlan, SSP 838
Lab. maj. 13,475 (29.45%)
§ 0.36% swing Lab. to SNP
(§ 2001 Lab. maj. 13,555 (30.17%))

FIFE NORTH EAST
E. 62,057 T. 38,556 (62.13%) LD win
Rt. Hon. Sir Menzies Campbell, LD 20,088
Mike Scott-Hayward, C. 7,517
Anthony King, Lab. 4,920
Rod Campbell, SNP 4,011
Jim Park, Scot. Green 1,071
Dr Duncan Pickard, UKIP 533
Jack Ferguson, SSP 416
LD maj. 12,571 (32.60%)
§ 3.20% swing C. to LD
(§ 2001 LD maj. 9,686 (26.20%))

GLASGOW CENTRAL
E. 64,053 T. 28,037 (43.77%) Lab. win
Mohammad Sarwar, Lab. 13,518
Isabel Nelson, LD 4,987
Bill Kidd, SNP 4,148
Richard Sullivan, C. 1,757
Gordon Masterton, Scot. Green 1,372
Marie Gordon, SSP 1,110
Walter Hamilton, BNP 671
Ian Johnson, Soc. Lab. 255
Thomas Greig, OCV 139
Elinor McKenzie, Comm. Brit. 80
Lab. maj. 8,531 (30.43%)
§ 7.36% swing Lab. to LD
(§ 2001 Lab. maj. 9,382 (33.82%))

GLASGOW EAST
E. 64,130 T. 30,939 (48.24%) Lab. win
David Marshall, Lab. 18,775
Lachlan McNeill, SNP 5,268
David Jackson, LD 3,665
Carl Thomson, C. 2,135
George Savage, SSP 1,096
Lab. maj. 13,507 (43.66%)
§ 1.48% swing Lab. to SNP
(§ 2001 Lab. maj. 15,238 (46.62%))

GLASGOW NORTH
E. 55,419 T. 27,921 (50.38%) Lab. win
Ann McKechin, Lab. 11,001
Amy Rodger, LD 7,663
Kenneth McLean, SNP 3,614
Brian Pope, C. 2,441
Martin Bartos, Scot. Green 2,135
Nick Tarlton, SSP 1,067
Lab. maj. 3,338 (11.96%)
§ 8.70% swing Lab. to LD
(§ 2001 Lab. maj. 8,023 (29.36%))

GLASGOW NORTH EAST
E. 62,042 T. 28,418 (45.80%) Speaker win
Rt. Hon. Michael Martin, Speaker 15,153
John McLaughlin, SNP 5,019
Doris Kelly, Soc. Lab. 4,036
Graham Campbell, SSP 1,402
Daniel Houston, Scot. U. 1,266
Scott McLean, BNP 920
Joe Chambers, Ind. 622
Speaker maj. 10,134 (35.66%)
§ 6.62% swing Speaker to SNP
(§ 2001 Speaker maj. 15,203 (48.90%))

GLASGOW NORTH WEST
E. 61,880 T. 34,061 (55.04%) Lab. win
John Robertson, Lab. 16,748
Paul Graham, LD 6,655
Graeme Hendry, SNP 4,676
Murray Roxburgh, C. 3,262
Martha Wardrop, Scot. Green 1,333
Anthea Irwin, SSP 1,108
Colin Muir, Soc. Lab. 279
Lab. maj. 10,093 (29.63%)
§ 6.80% swing Lab. to LD
(§ 2001 Lab. maj. 13,231 (38.83%))

GLASGOW SOUTH
E. 68,837 T. 38,431 (55.83%) Lab. win
Tom Harris, Lab. 18,153
Arthur Sanderson, LD 7,321
Finlay MacLean, SNP 4,860
Dr Janette McAlpine, C. 4,836
Kay Allan, Scot. Green 1,692
Ronnie Stevenson, SSP 1,303
Dorothy Entwistle, Soc. Lab. 266
Lab. maj. 10,832 (28.19%)
§ 4.93% swing Lab. to LD
(§ 2001 Lab. maj. 13,042 (33.15%))

GLASGOW SOUTH WEST
E. 62,005 T. 30,977 (49.96%)
Lab. (Co-op) win
Ian Davidson, Lab. (Co-op) 18,653
James Dornan, SNP 4,757
Katy Gordon, LD 3,593
Scott Brady, C. 1,786
Keith Baldassara, SSP 1,666
Alistair McConnachie, Ind. Green 379
Violet Shaw, Soc. Lab. 143
Lab. (Co-op) maj. 13,896 (44.86%)
§ 0.22% swing SNP to Lab. (Co-op)
(§ 2001 Lab. (Co-op) maj. 14,687
(44.42%))

GLENROTHES
E. 66,563 T. 37,366 (56.14%) Lab. win
John MacDougall, Lab. 19,395
John Beare, SNP 8,731
Elizabeth Riches, LD 4,728
Belinda Don, C. 2,651
George Rodger, PPS 716
Morag Balfour, SSP 705
Paul Smith, UKIP 440
Lab. maj. 10,664 (28.54%)
§ 2.71% swing Lab. to SNP
(§ 2001 Lab. maj. 12,988 (33.95%))

GORDON
E. 71,925 T. 44,438 (61.78%) LD win
Malcolm Bruce, LD 20,008
Iain Brotchie, Lab. 8,982
Philip Atkinson, C. 7,842
Joanna Strathdee, SNP 7,098
Tommy Paterson, SSP 508
LD maj. 11,026 (24.81%)
§ 3.73% swing Lab. to LD
(§ 2001 LD maj. 6,845 (17.36%))

INVERCLYDE
E. 59,291 T. 36,098 (60.88%) Lab. win
David Cairns, Lab. 18,318
Stuart McMillan, SNP 7,059
Douglas Herbison, LD 6,123
Gordon Fraser, C. 3,692
David Landels, SSP 906
Lab. maj. 11,259 (31.19%)
§ 2.51% swing Lab. to SNP
(§ 2001 Lab. maj. 11,314 (29.06%))

INVERNESS, NAIRN, BADENOCH & STRATHSPEY
E. 69,636 T. 44,255 (63.55%) LD win
*Danny Alexander, LD 17,830
David Stewart, Lab. 13,682
David Thompson, SNP 5,992
Robert Rowantree, C. 4,579
Donnie MacLeod, Scot. Green 1,065
Donald Lawson, Publican 678
George MacDonald, SSP 429
LD maj. 4,148 (9.37%)
§ 6.01% swing Lab. to LD
(§ 2001 Lab. maj. 1,134 (2.65%))

KILMARNOCK & LOUDOUN
E. 72,851 T. 44,383 (60.92%) Lab. win
Rt. Hon. Desmond Browne, Lab. 20,976
Daniel Coffey, SNP 12,273
Gary Smith, C. 5,026
Kevin Lang, LD 4,945
Hugh Kerr, SSP 833
Ronnie Robertson, UKIP 330
Lab. maj. 8,703 (19.61%)
§ 5.45% swing Lab. to SNP
(§ 2001 Lab. maj. 13,621 (30.51%))

KIRKCALDY & COWDENBEATH
E. 71,606 T. 41,796 (58.37%) Lab. win
Rt. Hon. Gordon Brown, Lab. 24,278
Alan Bath, SNP 6,062
Alex Cole-Hamilton, LD 5,450
Stuart Randall, C. 4,308
Steve West, SSP 666
Peter Adams, UKIP 516
James Parker, Scot. Senior 425
Elizabeth Kwantes, Ind. 47
Pat Sargent, Ind. 44
Lab. maj. 18,216 (43.58%)
§ 1.84% swing SNP to Lab.
(§ 2001 Lab. maj. 16,238 (39.91%))

LANARK & HAMILTON EAST
E. 73,736 T. 43,589 (59.11%) Lab. win
Jimmy Hood, Lab. 20,072
Fraser Grieve, LD 8,125
John Wilson, SNP 7,746
Robert Pettigrew, C. 5,576
Dennis Reilly, SSP 802
Donald Mackay, UKIP 437
Duncan McFarlane, Ind. 416
Robin Mawhinney, OCV 415
Lab. maj. 11,947 (27.41%)
§ 5.89% swing Lab. to LD
(§ 2001 Lab. maj. 12,861 (28.59%))

LINLITHGOW & FALKIRK EAST
E. 76,739 T. 46,389 (60.45%) Lab. win
Michael Connarty, Lab. 22,121
Gordon Guthrie, SNP 10,919
Stephen Glenn, LD 7,100
Michael Veitch, C. 5,486
Ally Hendry, SSP 763
Lab. maj. 11,202 (24.15%)
§ 1.16% swing Lab. to SNP
(§ 2001 Lab. maj. 11,796 (26.46%))

LIVINGSTON
E. 76,353 T. 44,337 (58.07%) Lab. win
Rt. Hon. Robin Cook, Lab. 22,657
Angela Constance, SNP 9,560
Charles Dundas, LD 6,832
Alison Ross, C. 4,499
Steven Nimmo, SSP 789
Lab. maj. 13,097 (29.54%)
§ 1.17% swing Lab. to SNP
(§ 2001 Lab. maj. 13,638 (31.88%))

MIDLOTHIAN
E. 60,644 T. 37,704 (62.17%) Lab. win
David Hamilton, Lab. 17,153
Fred Mackintosh, LD 9,888
Colin Beattie, SNP 6,400
Iain McGill, C. 3,537
Norman Gilfillan, SSP 726
Lab. maj. 7,265 (19.27%)
§ 6.98% swing Lab. to LD
(§ 2001 Lab. maj. 12,017 (31.29%))

MORAY
E. 66,463 T. 38,793 (58.37%) SNP win
Angus Robertson, SNP 14,196
Jamie Halcro-Johnston, C. 8,520
Kevin Hutchens, Lab. 7,919
Linda Gorn, LD 7,460
Norma Anderson, SSP 698
SNP maj. 5,676 (14.63%)
§ 4.07% swing C. to SNP
(§ 2001 SNP maj. 1,852 (5.06%))

MOTHERWELL & WISHAW
E. 66,987 T. 37,109 (55.40%) Lab. win
Frank Roy, Lab. 21,327
Ian MacQuarrie, SNP 6,105
Conor Snowden, LD 4,464
Peter Finnie, C. 3,440
Gregor MacEwan, SSP 1,019
Dallas Carter, Free Scot. 384
Coral Thompson, OCV 370
Lab. maj. 15,222 (41.02%)
§ 2.35% swing SNP to Lab.
(§ 2001 Lab. maj. 13,778 (36.33%))

NA H-EILEANAN AN IAR
E. 21,576 T. 13,836 (64.13%) SNP gain
*Angus MacNeil, SNP 6,213
Calum MacDonald, Lab. 4,772
Dr Jean Davis, LD 1,096
James Hargreaves, OCV 1,048
Andy Maciver, C. 610
Joanne Telfer, SSP 97
SNP maj. 1,441 (10.41%)
9.29% swing Lab. to SNP
(2001: Lab. maj. 1,074 (8.16%))

OCHIL & PERTHSHIRE SOUTH
E. 70,731 T. 46,697 (66.02%) Lab. win
*Gordon Banks, Lab. 14,645
Annabelle Ewing, SNP 13,957
Elizabeth Smith, C. 10,021
Catherine Whittingham, LD 6,218
George Baxter, Scot. Green 978
Iain Campbell, SSP 420
David Bushby, UKIP 275
Maitland Kelly, Free Scot. 183
Lab. maj. 688 (1.47%)
§ 0.18% swing Lab. to SNP
(§ 2001 Lab. maj. 821 (1.83%))

ORKNEY & SHETLAND
E. 33,048 T. 17,742 (53.69%) LD hold
Alistair Carmichael, LD 9,138
Richard Meade, Lab. 2,511
Frank Nairn, C. 2,357
John Mowat, SNP 1,833
John Aberdein, SSP 992
Scott Dyble, UKIP 424
Paul Cruickshank, LCA 311
Brian Nugent, Free Scot. 176
LD maj. 6,627 (37.35%)
8.29% swing Lab. to LD
(2001: LD maj. 3,475 (20.77%))

PAISLEY & RENFREWSHIRE NORTH
E. 63,076 T. 40,885 (64.82%) Lab. win
ames Sheridan, Lab. 18,697
Bill Wilson, SNP 7,696
Lewis Hutton, LD 7,464
Philip Lardner, C. 5,566
Angela McGregor, SSP 646
Katharine McGavigan, Soc. Lab. 444
ohn Pearson, UKIP 372
Lab. maj. 11,001 (26.91%)
§ 1.34% swing Lab. to SNP
(§ 2001 Lab. maj. 12,417 (29.58%))

PAISLEY & RENFREWSHIRE SOUTH
E. 60,181 T. 37,860 (62.91%) Lab. win
Douglas Alexander, Lab. 19,904
Eileen McCartin, LD 6,672
Andrew Doig, SNP 6,653
Thomas Begg, C. 3,188
Iain Hogg, SSP 789
Gordon Matthew, Paisley 381
Robert Rodgers, Ind. 166
Howard Broadbent, Soc. Lab. 107
Lab. maj. 13,232 (34.95%)
§ 6.24% swing Lab. to LD
(§ 2001 Lab. maj. 13,968 (36.10%))

PERTH & PERTHSHIRE NORTH
E. 70,895 T. 45,930 (64.79%) SNP win
Peter Wishart, SNP 15,469
Douglas Taylor, C. 13,948
Doug Maughan, Lab. 8,601
Gordon Campbell, LD 7,403
Philip Stott, SSP 509
SNP maj. 1,521 (3.31%)
§ 3.85% swing SNP to C.
(§ 2001 SNP maj. 5,020 (11.01%))

RENFREWSHIRE EAST
E. 65,714 T. 47,405 (72.14%) Lab. hold
Jim Murphy, Lab. 20,815
Richard Cook, C. 14,158
Dr Gordon Macdonald, LD 8,659
Osama Bhutta, SNP 3,245
Ian Henderson, SSP 528
Lab. maj. 6,657 (14.04%)
2.43% swing Lab. to C.
(2001: Lab. maj. 9,141 (18.90%))

ROSS, SKYE & LOCHABER
E. 50,507 T. 32,538 (64.42%) LD win
Rt. Hon. Charles Kennedy, LD 19,100
Christine Conniff, Lab. 4,851
John Hodgson, C. 3,275
Mhairi Will, SNP 3,119
David Jardine, Scot. Green 1,097
Phillip Anderson, UKIP 500
Anne Macleod, SSP 412
Morris Grant, Ind. 184
LD maj. 14,249 (43.79%)
§ 11.27% swing Lab. to LD
(§ 2001 LD maj. 6,567 (21.26%))

RUTHERGLEN & HAMILTON WEST
E. 73,998 T. 43,261 (58.46%)
Lab. (Co-op) win
Rt. Hon. Thomas McAvoy, Lab. (Co-op) 24,054
Ian Robertson, LD 7,942
Margaret Park, SNP 6,023
Peter Crerar, C. 3,621
Bill Bonnar, SSP 1,164
Janice Murdoch, UKIP 457
Lab. (Co-op) maj. 16,112 (37.24%)
§ 5.37% swing Lab. (Co-op) to LD
(§ 2001 Lab. (Co-op) maj. 18,504 (44.42%))

STIRLING
E. 64,554 T. 43,691 (67.68%) Lab. win
Anne McGuire, Lab. 15,729
Stephen Kerr, C. 10,962
Kelvin Holdsworth, LD 9,052
Frances McGlinchey, SNP 5,503
Duncan Illingworth, Scot. Green 1,302
Rowland Sheret, SSP 458
James McDonald, Ind. 261
Michael Willis, OCV 215
Matthew Desmond, UKIP 209
Lab. maj. 4,767 (10.91%)
§ 4.18% swing Lab. to C.
(§ 2001 Lab. maj. 8,303 (19.28%))

NORTHERN IRELAND

ANTRIM EAST
E. 58,335 T. 31,767 (54.46%)
DUP gain
*Sammy Wilson, DUP 15,766
Roy Beggs, UUP 8,462
Sean Neeson, Alliance 4,869
Danny O'Connor, SDLP 1,695
James McKeown, SF 828
David Kerr, Vote Dream 147
DUP maj. 7,304 (22.99%)
11.67% swing UUP to DUP
(2001: UUP maj. 128 (0.36%))

ANTRIM NORTH
E. 74,450 T. 45,926 (61.69%)
DUP hold
Revd Ian Paisley, DUP 25,156
Philip McGuigan, SF 7,191
Rodney McCune, UUP 6,637
Sean Farren, SDLP 5,585
Jayne Dunlop, Alliance 1,357
DUP maj. 17,965 (39.12%)
0.47% swing DUP to SF
(2001: DUP maj. 14,224 (28.90%))

ANTRIM SOUTH
E. 66,931 T. 37,957 (56.71%)
DUP gain
†Revd William McCrea, DUP 14,507
David Burnside, UUP 11,059
Noreen McClelland, SDLP 4,706
Henry Cushinan, SF 4,407
David Ford, Alliance 3,278
DUP maj. 3,448 (9.08%)
5.69% swing UUP to DUP
(2001: UUP maj. 1,011 (2.29%))

BELFAST EAST
E. 53,176 T. 30,831 (57.98%)
DUP hold
Peter Robinson, DUP 15,152
Sir Reg Empey, UUP 9,275
Naomi Long, Alliance 3,746
Deborah Devenny, SF 1,029
Mary Muldoon, SDLP 844
Alan Greer, C. 434
Joe Bell, WP 179
Lynda Gilby, Vote Dream 172
DUP maj. 5,877 (19.06%)
0.13% swing DUP to UUP
(2001: DUP maj. 7,117 (19.32%))

BELFAST NORTH
E. 52,853 T. 30,540 (57.78%)
DUP hold
Nigel Dodds, DUP 13,935
Gerry Kelly, SF 8,747
Alban Maginness, SDLP 4,950
Fred Cobain, UUP 2,154
Marjorie Hawkins, Alliance 438
Marcella Delaney, WP 165
Lynda Gilby, Vote Dream 151
DUP maj. 5,188 (16.99%)
0.69% swing SF to DUP
(2001: DUP maj. 6,387 (15.60%))

BELFAST SOUTH
E. 52,668 T. 32,028 (60.81%)
SDLP gain
*Dr Alasdair McDonnell, SDLP 10,339
James Spratt, DUP 9,104
Michael McGimpsey, UUP 7,263
Alex Maskey, SF 2,882
Geraldine Rice, Alliance 2,012
Lynda Gilby, Vote Dream 235
Paddy Lynn, WP 193
SDLP maj. 1,235 (3.86%)
11.91% swing UUP to SDLP
(2001: UUP maj. 5,399 (14.23%))

BELFAST WEST
E. 53,831 T. 34,545 (64.17%) SF hold
Gerry Adams, SF 24,348
Alex Attwood, SDLP 5,033
Diane Dodds, DUP 3,652
Chris McGimpsey, UUP 779
John Lowry, WP 432
Lynda Gilby, Vote Dream 154
Liam Kennedy, Ind. 147
SF maj. 19,315 (55.91%)
4.36% swing SDLP to SF
(2001: SF maj. 19,342 (47.20%))

DOWN NORTH
E. 59,748 T. 32,290 (54.04%)
UUP hold

Lady Sylvia Hermon, UUP	16,268
Peter Weir, DUP	11,324
David Alderdice, Alliance	2,451
Liam Logan, SDLP	1,009
Julian Robertson, C.	822
Christopher Carter, Ind.	211
Janet McCrory, SF	205

UUP maj. 4,944 (15.31%)
20.35% swing UUP to DUP
(2001: UUP maj. 7,324 (19.69%))

DOWN SOUTH
E. 73,668 T. 48,177 (65.40%)
SDLP hold

Edward McGrady, SDLP	21,557
Caitriona Ruane, SF	12,417
Jim Wells, DUP	8,815
Dermot Nesbitt, UUP	4,775
Julian Crozier, Alliance	613

SDLP maj. 9,140 (18.97%)
3.82% swing SDLP to SF
(2001: SDLP maj. 13,858 (26.61%))

FERMANAGH & SOUTH TYRONE
E. 67,174 T. 48,793 (72.64%) SF hold

Michelle Gildernew, SF	18,638
Arlene Foster, DUP	14,056
Tom Elliott, UUP	8,869
Tommy Gallagher, SDLP	7,230

SF maj. 4,582 (9.39%)
12.35% swing SF to DUP
(2001: SF maj. 53 (0.10%))

FOYLE
E. 69,207 T. 45,609 (65.90%)
SDLP hold

*Mark Durkan, SDLP	21,119
Mitchel McLaughlin, SF	15,162
William Hay, DUP	6,557
Eammon McCann, Soc EA	1,649
Earl Storey, UUP	1,091
Ben Reel, Vote Dream	31

SDLP maj. 5,957 (13.06%)
5.28% swing SDLP to SF
(2001: SDLP maj. 11,550 (23.63%))

LAGAN VALLEY
E. 70,742 T. 42,572 (60.18%)
DUP gain

‡Jeffrey Donaldson, DUP	23,289
Basil McCrea, UUP	9,172
Seamus Close, Alliance	4,316
Paul Butler, SF	3,197
Patricia Lewsley, SDLP	2,598

DUP maj. 14,117 (33.16%)
38.13% swing UUP to DUP
(2001: UUP maj. 18,342 (39.93%))

LONDONDERRY EAST
E. 58,861 T. 35,504 (60.32%)
DUP hold

Gregory Campbell, DUP	15,225
David McClarty, UUP	7,498
John Dallat, SDLP	6,077
Billy Leonard, SF	5,709
Yvonne Boyle, Alliance	924
Malcolm Samuel, Ind.	71

DUP maj. 7,727 (21.76%)
8.50% swing UUP to DUP
(2001: DUP maj. 1,901 (4.77%))

NEWRY & ARMAGH
E. 72,448 T. 50,696 (69.98%) SF gain

*Conor Murphy, SF	20,965
Dominic Bradley, SDLP	12,770
Paul Berry, DUP	9,311
Danny Kennedy, UUP	7,025
Gerry Markey, Ind.	625

SF maj. 8,195 (16.16%)
11.30% swing SDLP to SF
(2001: SDLP maj. 3,575 (6.43%))

STRANGFORD
E. 69,040 T. 37,032 (53.64%)
DUP hold

Iris Robinson, DUP	20,921
Gareth McGimpsey, UUP	7,872
Kieran McCarthy, Alliance	3,332
Joe Boyle, SDLP	2,496
Terry Dick, C.	1,462
Dermot Kennedy, SF	949

DUP maj. 13,049 (35.24%)
16.34% swing UUP to DUP
(2001: DUP maj. 1,110 (2.57%))

TYRONE WEST
E. 60,286 T. 43,487 (72.13%) SF hold

Pat Doherty, SF	16,910
Dr Kieran Deeny, Ind.	11,905
Thomas Buchanan, DUP	7,742
Eugene McMenamin, SDLP	3,949
Derek Hussey, UUP	2,981

SF maj. 5,005 (11.51%)
14.65% swing SF to Ind.
(2001: SF maj. 5,040 (10.39%))

ULSTER MID
E. 62,666 T. 45,426 (72.49%) SF hold

Martin McGuinness, SF	21,641
Ian McCrea, DUP	10,665
Patsy McGlone, SDLP	7,922
Billy Armstrong, UUP	4,853
Francis Donnelly, WP	345

SF maj. 10,976 (24.16%)
2.12% swing DUP to SF
(2001: SF maj. 9,953 (19.93%))

UPPER BANN
E. 72,402 T. 44,422 (61.35%)
DUP gain

*David Simpson, DUP	16,679
David Trimble, UUP	11,381
John O'Dowd, SF	9,305
Dolores Kelly, SDLP	5,747
Alan Castle, Alliance	955
Tom French, WP	355

DUP maj. 5,298 (11.93%)
7.98% swing UUP to DUP
(2001: UUP maj. 2,058 (4.03%))

BY-ELECTIONS 2005–7

Abbreviations of parties standing in the 2005–7 by-elections (see also General Election Results):

Money	Money Reform Party
SCP	Scottish Christian Party (formerly Operation Christian Vote)
SPGB	Socialist Party of Great Britain
Tolls	Abolish Forth Bridge Tolls Party

BLAENAU GWENT

E. 52,508 T. 27,165 (51.73%) Ind hold

Dai Davis, Ind.	12,543
Owen Smith, Lab.	10,059
Steffan Lewis, PC	1,755
Amy Kitcher, LD	1,477
Margrit Williams, C.	1,013
Alan Hope, Loony	318

Ind maj. 2,484 (9.14%)
8.37% swing Ind. to Lab.
(2005: Ind. maj. 9,121 (25.81%))

BROMLEY & CHISLEHURST

E. 71,818 T. 29,052 (40.45%) C. hold

Bob Neill, C.	11,621
Ben Abbotts, LD	10,988
Nigel Farage, UKIP	2,347
Rachel Reeves, Lab	1,925
Anne Garrett, Green	811
Paul Winnett, NF	476
John Hemming-Clarke, Ind.	442
Stevens Uncles, Eng. Dem.	212
John Cartwright, Loony	132
Nick Hadziannis, Ind.	65
Anne Belsey, Money	33

C. maj. 633 (2.18%)
14.32% swing C. to LD
(2005: C. maj. 13,342 (28.92%))

CHEADLE

E. 68,051 T. 37,567 (55.20%) LD hold

*Mark Hunter, LD	19,593
Stephen Day, C.	15,936
Martin Miller, Lab.	1,739
Leslie Leggett, Veritas	218
John Allman, AFC	81

LD maj. 3,657 (9.73%)
0.63% swing C. to LD
(2005: LD maj. 4,020 (8.47%))

DUNFERMLINE & FIFE WEST

E. 71,017 T. 34,578 (48.69%) LD gain

*Willie Rennie, LD	12,391
Catherine Stihler, Lab.	10,591
Douglas Chapman, SNP	7,261
Carrie Ruxton, C.	2,702
John McAllion, SSP	537
James Hargreaves, SCP	411
Thomas Minogue, Tolls	374
Ian Borland, UKIP	208
Dick Rodgers, Good	103

LD maj. 1,800 (5.21%)
16.24% swing Lab. to LD
(2005: Lab maj. 11,562 (27.27%))

EALING SOUTHALL

E. 85,423 T. 36,618 (42.87%) Lab. hold

*Virendra Sharma, Lab.	15,188
Nigel Bakhai, LD	10,118
Tony Lit, C.	8,230
Sarah Edwards, Green	1,135
Salvinder Dhillon, Respect	588
Dr Kunnathur Rajan, UKIP	285
Yaqub Masih, Christian Party	280
Jasdev Rai, Ind.	275
John Cartwright, Loony	188
Sati Chaggar, Eng. Dem.	152
Gulbash Singh, Ind.	92
Kuldeep Grewal, Ind.	87

Lab. maj. 5,070 (13.85%)
5.24% swing Lab. to LD
(2005: Lab. maj. 11,440 (24.32%))

LIVINGSTON

E. 76,376 T. 29,477 (38.59%) Lab. hold

*Jim Devine, Lab.	12,319
Angela Constance, SNP	9,639
Charles Dundas, LD	4,362
Gordon Lindhurst, C.	1,993
David Robertson, Green	529
Steven Nimmo, SSP	407
Peter Adams, UKIP	108
Melville Brown, Ind.	55
John Allman, AFC	33
Brian Gardner, SPGB	32

Lab. maj. 2,680 (9.09%)
10.22% swing Lab. to SNP
(2005: Lab. maj. 13,097 (29.54%))

SEDGEFIELD

E. 67,339 T. 27,980 (41.55%) Lab. hold

*Phil Wilson, Lab.	12,528
Greg Stone, LD	5,572
Graham Robb, C.	4,082
Andrew Spence, BNP	2,494
Paul Gittins, Ind.	1,885
Toby Horton, UKIP	536
Chris Haine, Green	348
Stephen Gash, Eng. Dem.	177
Tim Grainger, Christian Party	177
Alan Hope, Loony	147
Norman Scarth, Anti-Crime Party	34

Lab. maj. 6,956 (24.86%)
11.06% swing Lab. to LD
(2005: Lab. maj. 18,457 (44.49%))

STAFFORDSHIRE SOUTH

(23 June 2005; not strictly a by-election, the Staffordshire South poll was deferred until this date as a result of the death of the Liberal Democrat candidate during the general election campaign)

E. 68,763 T. 25,635 (37.28%) C. hold

Sir Patrick Cormack, C.	13,343
Paul Kalinauckas, Lab.	4,496
Jo Crotty, LD	3,540
Malcolm Hurst, UKIP	2,675
Garry Bushell, Eng. Dem.	643
Kate Spohrer, Green	437
Adrian Davies, FP	434
The Rev David Braid, Clause 28	67

C. maj. 8,847 (34.51%)
9.10% swing Lab. to C.
(2001: C. maj. 6,881 (16.31%))

THE GOVERNMENT

as at 1 September 2007

THE CABINET

Prime Minister, First Lord of the Treasury and Minister for the Civil Service
Rt. Hon. Gordon Brown, MP (since June 2007)
Chancellor of the Exchequer
Rt. Hon. Alistair Darling, MP (since June 2007)
Chancellor of the Duchy of Lancaster and Minister for the Cabinet Office
Rt. Hon. Ed Miliband, MP (since June 2007)
Chief Secretary to the Treasury
Rt. Hon. Andy Burnham, MP (since June 2007)
Leader of the House of Commons and Lord Privy Seal, Deputy Leader and Chair of Labour Party, and Minister for Women
Rt. Hon. Harriet Harman, QC, MP (since June 2007)
Leader of the House of Lords and Lord President of the Council
Rt. Hon. Baroness Ashton of Upholland (since June 2007)
Parliamentary Secretary to the Treasury and Chief Whip
Rt. Hon. Geoff Hoon, MP (since June 2007)
Secretary of State for Business, Enterprise and Regulatory Reform
Rt. Hon. John Hutton, MP (since June 2007)
Secretary of State for Children, Schools and Families
Rt. Hon. Ed Balls, MP (since June 2007)
Secretary of State for Communities and Local Government
Rt. Hon. Hazel Blears, MP (since June 2007)
Secretary of State for Culture, Media and Sport
Rt. Hon. James Purnell, MP (since June 2007)
Secretary of State for Defence (since May 2006) *and Secretary of State for Scotland* (since June 2007)
Rt. Hon. Des Browne, MP
Secretary of State for Environment, Food and Rural Affairs
Rt. Hon. Hilary Benn, MP (since June 2007)
Secretary of State for Foreign and Commonwealth Affairs
Rt. Hon. David Miliband, MP (since June 2007)
Secretary of State for Health
Rt. Hon. Alan Johnson, MP (since June 2007)
Secretary of State for the Home Department
Rt. Hon. Jacqui Smith, MP (since June 2007)
Secretary of State for Innovation, Universities and Skills
Rt. Hon. John Denham, MP (since June 2007)
Secretary of State for International Development
Rt. Hon. Douglas Alexander, MP (since June 2007)
Secretary of State for Justice and Lord Chancellor
Rt. Hon. Jack Straw, MP (since June 2007)
Secretary of State for Northern Ireland
Rt. Hon. Shaun Woodward, MP (since June 2007)
Secretary of State for Transport
Rt. Hon. Ruth Kelly, MP (since June 2007)
Secretary of State for Work and Pensions (since June 2007) *and Secretary of State for Wales* (since October 2002)
Rt. Hon. Peter Hain, MP

The Attorney-General (Rt. Hon. Baroness Scotland of Asthal, QC), the Minister of State for the Olympics and London (Rt. Hon. Tessa Jowell, MP), the Minister of State for Housing (Yvette Cooper, MP), the Minister of State for Africa, Asia and the UN (Lord Malloch Brown, KCMG), the Minister for the North-West (Rt. Hon Beverley Hughes, MP), the Parliamentary Private Secretaries to the Prime Minister (Ian Austin, MP; Angela E. Smith, MP) and the Chief Whip in the House of Lords and Captain of the Gentlemen-at-Arms (Rt. Hon. Lord Grocott) attend cabinet meetings although they are not members of the cabinet.

LAW OFFICERS

Attorney-General
Rt. Hon. Baroness Scotland, QC (since June 2007)
Solicitor-General
Vera Baird, QC, MP (since June 2007)
Advocate-General for Scotland
Lord Davidson of Glen Clova, QC (since May 2006)

MINISTERS OF STATE

Business, Enterprise and Regulatory Reform
Lord Drayson*
Sir Digby Jones†
Pat McFadden, MP
Rt. Hon. Stephen Timms, MP
Malcolm Wicks, MP
Cabinet Office
Rt. Hon. Ed Miliband, MP *(Chancellor of the Duchy of Lancaster)*
Rt. Hon. Tessa Jowell, MP
Children, Schools and Families
Rt. Hon. Beverley Hughes, MP
Jim Knight, MP
Communities and Local Government
Yvette Cooper, MP
John Healey, MP
Culture, Media and Sport
Rt. Hon. Margaret Hodge, MBE, MP
Defence
Rt. Hon. Bob Ainsworth, MP
Environment, Food and Rural Affairs
Rt. Hon. Lord Rooker
Phil Woolas, MP
Foreign and Commonwealth Office
Dr Kim Howells, MP
Lord Malloch Brown, KCMG
Rt. Hon. Jim Murphy, MP
Health
Ben Bradshaw, MP
Rt. Hon. Dawn Primarolo, MP
Home Office
Liam Byrne, MP
Tony McNulty, MP
Innovation, Universities and Skills
Ian Pearson, MP
Bill Rammell, MP
Justice
Rt. Hon. David Hanson, MP
Michael Wills, MP

Northern Ireland Office
Paul Goggins, MP
Scotland Office
David Cairns, MP
Transport
Rt. Hon. Rosie Winterton, MP
Work and Pensions
Mike O'Brien, MP
Caroline Flint, MP

* Also works in the Ministry of Defence
† Also works in the Foreign and Commonwealth Office

UNDER-SECRETARIES OF STATE

Business, Enterprise and Regulatory Reform
Gareth Thomas, MP*
Children, Schools and Families
Lord Adonis
Kevin Brennan, MP
Communities and Local Government
Parmjit Dhanda, MP
Iain Wright, MP
Culture, Media and Sport
Gerry Sutcliffe, MP
Defence
Derek Twigg, MP
Environment, Food and Rural Affairs
Joan Ruddock, MP
Jonathan Shaw, MP
Foreign and Commonwealth Office
Meg Munn, MP
Health
Prof. Sir Ara Darzi
Ann Keen, MP
Ivan Lewis, MP
Home Office
Vernon Coaker, MP
Meg Hillier, MP
Adm. Sir Alan West
Innovation, Universities and Skills
David Lammy, MP
Lord Triesman
International Development
Shahid Malik, MP
Baroness Vadera
Justice
Maria Eagle, MP
Lord Hunt of King's Heath, OBE
Transport
Jim Fitzpatrick, MP
Tom Harris, MP
Wales Office
Huw Irranca-Davies, MP
Work and Pensions
Barbara Follett, MP
Anne McGuire, MP
Lord McKenzie of Luton
James Plaskitt, MP

* Also in the Department for International Development

OTHER MINISTERS

Parliamentary Private Secretary to the Prime Minister
Ian Austin, MP
Cabinet Office
Rt. Hon. Tessa Jowell, MP *(Paymaster-General)*
Phil Hope, MP *(Parliamentary Secretary)*
Gillian Merron, MP *(Parliamentary Secretary)*
Leader of the Commons
Harriet Harman, QC, MP *(Lord Privy Seal, Labour Party Chair and Minister for Women)*
Helen Goodman, MP *(Parliamentary Secretary)*
Treasury
Rt. Hon. Jane Kennedy, MP *(Financial Secretary)*
Kitty Ussher, MP *(Economic Secretary)*
Angela Eagle, MP *(Exchequer Secretary)*

GOVERNMENT WHIPS

HOUSE OF LORDS

Captain of the Honourable Corps of the Gentlemen-at-Arms (Chief Whip)
Rt. Hon. Lord Grocott
Captain of the Queen's Bodyguard of the Yeomen of the Guard (Deputy Chief Whip)
Rt. Hon. Lord Davies of Oldham
Lords-in-Waiting
Lord Bassam of Brighton
Lord Evans of Temple Guiting, CBE
Lord Truscott
Baronesses-in-Waiting
Baroness Crawley
Baroness Farrington of Ribbleton
Baroness Morgan of Drefelin
Baroness Royall of Blaisdon

HOUSE OF COMMONS

Parliamentary Secretary to the Treasury (Chief Whip)
Rt. Hon. Geoff Hoon, MP
Treasurer of HM Household (Deputy Chief Whip)
Rt. Hon. Nicholas Brown, MP
Comptroller of HM Household
Rt. Hon. Thomas McAvoy, MP
Vice-Chamberlain of HM Household
Liz Blackman, MP
Lords Commissioners of HM Treasury
Alan Campbell, MP; Stephen McCabe, MP; Frank Roy, MP; Claire Ward, MP; Dave Watts, MP
Assistant Whips
Bob Blizzard, MP; Tony Cunningham, MP; Wayne David, MP; Michael Foster, MP; Diana R. Johnson, MP; Sadiq Khan, MP; Siobhain McDonagh, MP; Alison Seabeck, MP; Mark Tami, MP

GOVERNMENT DEPARTMENTS

THE CIVIL SERVICE

Under the Next Steps programme, launched in 1988, many semi-autonomous executive agencies were established to carry out much of the work of the civil service. Executive agencies operate within a framework set by the responsible minister which specifies policies, objectives and available resources. All executive agencies are set annual performance targets by their minister. Each agency has a chief executive, who is responsible for the day-to-day operations of the agency and who is accountable to the minister for the use of resources and for meeting the agency's targets. The minister accounts to parliament for the work of the agency. Nearly 75 per cent of civil servants now work in executive agencies. In June 2006 there were about 524,000 permanent civil servants, down from about 537,000 in June 2005.

The Senior Civil Service was created in 1996 and on 1 April 2007 comprised about 4,000 staff from permanent secretary to the former grade 5 level, including all agency chief executives. All government departments and executive agencies are now responsible for their own pay and grading systems for civil servants outside the Senior Civil Service.

SALARIES 2006–7

MINISTERIAL SALARIES *from 1 April 2007*

Ministers who are members of the House of Commons receive a parliamentary salary (£60,675) in addition to their ministerial salary.

Prime minister	£128,174
Cabinet minister (Commons)	£76,704
Cabinet minister (Lords)	£104,386
Minister of state (Commons)	£39,893
Minister of state (Lords)	£81,504
Parliamentary under-secretary (Commons)	£30,280
Parliamentary under-secretary (Lords)	£70,986

SPECIAL ADVISERS' SALARIES *from 1 April 2007*

Special advisers to government ministers are paid out of public funds; their salaries are negotiated individually, but are usually in the range of £38,862 to £102,918.

CIVIL SERVICE SALARIES *from 1 April 2007*

Senior Civil Servants	
Permanent secretary	£139,740–£273,250
Band 3	£99,960–£205,000
Band 2	£81,580–£160,000
Band 1A	£65,280–£127,000
Band 1	£56,100–£116,000

Staff are placed in pay bands according to their level of responsibility and taking account of other factors such as experience and marketability. Movement within and between bands is based on performance. Following the delegation of responsibility for pay and grading to government departments and agencies from 1 April 1996, it is no longer possible to show service-wide pay rates for staff outside the Senior Civil Service.

GOVERNMENT DEPARTMENTS

CABINET OFFICE

70 Whitehall, London SW1A 2AS
Switchboard 020-7276 3000 T 020-7276 1234
W www.cabinet-office.gov.uk

The Cabinet Office, alongside the Treasury, sits at the centre of the government. It has three core functions: to support the prime minister in defining and delivering the government's objectives; to support the cabinet in ensuring the coherence, quality and delivery of policy and operations across departments; and strengthening the Civil Service's capabilities in terms of organisation, leadership and skills. The department is headed by the Chancellor of the Duchy of Lancaster.

Prime Minister and Minister for the Civil Service, Rt. Hon. Gordon Brown, MP
Principal Private Secretary to the Prime Minister, Tom Scholar
Chancellor of the Duchy of Lancaster and Minister for the Cabinet Office, Rt. Hon. Ed Miliband, MP
Parliamentary Private Secretary, Jeffrey Ennis, MP
Principal Private Secretary, Lee O'Rourke
Private Secretary, Louise Coward
Parliamentary Secretary, Phil Hope, MP
Assistant Private Secretaries, Gemma Lobb; Kate Wilson
Parliamentary Secretary, Gillian Merron, MP
Private Secretary, Sarah Goulbourne
Secretary of the Cabinet and Head of the Home Civil Service, Sir Gus O'Donnell, KCB
Principal Private Secretary, Ciaran Martin
Private Secretary, Paul Rennie
Assistant Private Secretary, Jackie Fraser *(Diary)*
Permanent Secretary, Sir Richard Mottram, GCB *(Intelligence, Security and Resilience)*
Principal Private Secretary, Dominic Fagan
Private Secretary, Stephen Knight
Minister for the Olympics and London, Rt. Hon. Tessa Jowell, MP
Private Secretary, Alec Taylor
Parliamentary Private Secretary, John Mann, MP

The TRANSFORMATIONAL GOVERNMENT TEAM comprises Transformational Government, Cabinet Office Management, Business Support Group and Change Team. It was established to provide overall technology leadership in three key areas of government: the transformation of public services for the benefit of citizens, businesses, taxpayers and front-line staff; the efficiency of the corporate services and infrastructure of government organisations; and the steps necessary to achieve the effective delivery of technology for government.

TRANSFORMATIONAL GOVERNMENT

1 Horse Guards Road, London SW1A 2HQ
T 020-7276 3248
HM Government Chief Information Officer, John Suffolk

CABINET OFFICE MANAGEMENT

Admiralty Arch, The Mall, London SW1A 2WH
T 020-7276 3090

Director-General, Transformational Government and Cabinet Office Management, Alexis Cleveland

BUSINESS SUPPORT GROUP
Kirkland House, 22–26 Whitehall, London SW1A 2WH
T 020-7276 0530
Director-General, Strategic Finance and Operations, Roger Marsh

CHANGE TEAM
Kirkland House, 22–26 Whitehall, London SW1A 2WH
T 020-7276 2160
Director, Sarah Cox

The CIVIL SERVICE CAPABILITY GROUP comprises Cabinet Office Human Resources, the Leadership and Development Strategy Directorate and Capability Review. The group is responsible for recruiting and developing staff and raising the capability of HR management throughout the civil service.
Director-General, Leadership, People and Change, Gill Rider

CABINET OFFICE HUMAN RESOURCES
Admiralty Arch South, The Mall, London SW1A 2WH
T 020-7276 6200
Director, Helen Dudley

LEADERSHIP AND DEVELOPMENT STRATEGY DIRECTORATE
Admiralty Arch, The Mall, London SW1A 2WH
T 020-7276 2006
Director, Anne-Marie Lawlor

CAPABILITY REVIEW
1 Horse Guards Road, London SW1A 2HQ
T 020-7270 5884
Director, Peter Thomas

The DOMESTIC POLICY GROUP comprises the Ceremonial Secretariat, the Economic and Domestic Affairs Secretariat, the Office of the Third Sector, the Social Exclusion Task Force and the Strategy Unit.

CEREMONIAL SECRETARIAT
35 Great Smith Street, London SW1P 3BQ
T 020-7276 2777
Ceremonial Officer, Denis Brennan

ECONOMIC AND DOMESTIC AFFAIRS SECRETARIAT
Cabinet Office, 70 Whitehall, London SW1A 2WH
T 020-7276 0055
Director, Paul Britton, CB

OFFICE OF THE THIRD SECTOR
35 Great Smith Street, London SW1P 3BQ
T 020-7276 6400
Director-General, Campbell Robb

SOCIAL EXCLUSION TASK FORCE
Admiralty Arch, The Mall, London SW1A 2WH
T 020-7276 2323
Director, Naomi Eisenstadt

STRATEGY UNIT
Admiralty Arch, The Mall, London SW1A 2WH
T 020-7276 1881 W www.strategy.gov.uk
Director, Stephen Aldridge

EUROPEAN SECRETARIAT
70 Whitehall, London SW1A 2WH
T 020-7276 1234
Prime Minister's Adviser on International Economic Affairs and Europe, Jon Cunliffe

The COMMUNICATION AND INFORMATION GROUP comprises Cabinet Office Communication, Government Communication and the Histories, Openness and Records Unit.

CABINET OFFICE COMMUNICATIONS
22 Whitehall, London SW1A 2WH
T 020-7276 0432/0400
Director, vacant

GOVERNMENT COMMUNICATION
26 Whitehall, London SW1A 2WH
T 020-7276 2712 W www.comms.gov.uk
Permanent Secretary, Howell James, CBE
Director, John Worne

HISTORIES OPENNESS AND RECORDS UNIT
Admiralty Arch, The Mall, London SW1A 2WH
T 020-7276 6326
Departmental Records Officer and Adviser, Tessa Stirling

The INTELLIGENCE, SECURITY AND RESILIENCE GROUP comprises the Civil Contingencies Secretariat, the Emergency Planning College and the Intelligence and Security Secretariat (including the Central Sponsor for Information Assurance).

CIVIL CONTINGENCIES SECRETARIAT
10 Great George Street, London SW1P 3AE
T 020-7276 5117
Director, Bruce Mann

EMERGENCY PLANNING COLLEGE
The Hawkhills, Easingwold, York YO61 3EG
T 01347-822877 W www.epcollege.gov.uk
Chief Executive, Michael Charlton-Weedy

INTELLIGENCE AND SECURITY SECRETARIAT
70 Whitehall, London SW1A 2WH
T 020-7276 0333
Director, Chris Wright

CENTRAL SPONSOR FOR INFORMATION ASSURANCE
2nd Floor, Cabinet Office, 26 Whitehall, London SW1A 2WH
T 020-7276 3108
W www.cabinetoffice.gov.uk/csia
Director, Roger Styles

DEFENCE AND OVERSEAS SECRETARIAT
70 Whitehall, London SW1A 2WH
T 020-7276 1234
Prime Minister's Foreign Policy Adviser and Head of Secretariat, Sir Nigel Sheinwald, KCMG

PRIME MINISTER'S OFFICE
10 Downing Street, London SW1A 2AA
T 020-7270 3000 F 020-7925 0918
W www.number-10.gov.uk
Prime Minister, Rt. Hon Gordon Brown, MP
Parliamentary Private Secretaries, Ian Austin, MP; Angela E. Smith, MP
Chief of Staff and Principal Private Secretary, Tom Scholar

Prime Minister's Spokesman and Director of Communications, Michael Ellam
Deputy Chief of Staff, Gavin Kelly
Directors, Sue Nye *(Government Relations)*; Spencer Livermore *(Political Strategy)*
Heads of Units, Jeremy Heywood *(Domestic Policy and Strategy)*; Simon McDonald *(Foreign and Defence Policy)*; Jon Cunliffe *(International Economic Affairs, Europe and G8 Sherpa)*; Dan Corry *(Policy)*
Special Advisers, Dan Corry; Gavin Kelly; Spencer Livermore; Damian McBride; Sue Nye

CROSS GOVERNMENT UNITS in the Cabinet Office comprises the Committee on Standards in Public Life (*see* Public Bodies section), Independent Offices and the Office of the Parliamentary Counsel.

INDEPENDENT OFFICES

OFFICE OF THE COMMISSIONER FOR PUBLIC APPOINTMENTS (OCPA)
3rd Floor, 35 Great Smith Street, London SW1P 3BQ
T 020-7276 2625 F 020-7276 2633
E ocpa@gtnet.gov.uk W www.ocpa.gov.uk

The Commissioner for Public Appointments is responsible for monitoring, regulating and reporting on ministerial appointments to public bodies. The commissioner can investigate complaints about the way in which appointments were made or applicants treated.
Commissioner for Public Appointments, Janet Gaymer, CBE
Secretary to the Commissioner and Head of the Independent Offices, Jim Barron, CBE

OFFICE OF THE CIVIL SERVICE COMMISSIONERS (OCSC)
35 Great Smith Street, London SW1P 3BQ
T 020-7276 2617 W www.civilservicecommissioners.gov.uk

The Civil Service Commissioners are the custodians of the principle of selection on merit by fair and open competition; they publish a recruitment code and audit departments' and agencies' performance against it. When the most senior posts are opened to people from outside the service, the commissioners normally chair the recruitment process.
First Commissioner, Janet Paraskeva
Commissioners (part-time), Sir Michael Aaronson, CBE; Mark Addison; James Boyle; Dame A. Burslem, DBE; Janet Gaymer, CBE; Ms M. J. Jacobi; Bernard Knight; J. MacAuslan; A. MacDonald, CB; Ms E. McMeikan; Anthea Millett, CBE; Ms S. Pantelides; Ranjit Sondhi; C. Stephens; Libby Watkins
Secretary to the Commissioners and Head of the Independent Offices, Jim Barron, CBE

OFFICE OF THE PARLIAMENTARY COUNSEL
35 Whitehall, London SW1A 2AY
T 020-7210 2588 W www.parliamentary-counsel.gov.uk
First Parliamentary Counsel, Stephen Laws, CB
Chief Executive, John Gilhooly, CB

INTELLIGENCE AND SECURITY COMMITTEE SECRETARIAT
70 Whitehall, London SW1A 2AS
T 020-7276 1215 W www.cabinetoffice.gov.uk/intelligence
Head of Management Unit, Emma-Louise Avery

INTERNAL AUDIT SERVICE
9th Floor, Ashdown House, 123 Victoria Street, London SW1E 6DE
T 020-7944 6882
Head, Steve Simmonds

ATTORNEY-GENERAL'S OFFICE

Attorney-General's Office, 20 Victoria Street, London SW1H 0NF
T 020-7271 2492 F 020-7271 2434
Attorney-General's Chambers, Royal Courts of Justice, Belfast BT1 3JY
T 028-9054 6082 F 028-9054 6049
E correspondenceunit@attorneygeneral.gsi.gov.uk
W www.attorneygeneral.gov.uk

The law officers of the crown for England and Wales are the Attorney-General and the Solicitor-General. The Attorney-General, assisted by the Solicitor-General, is the chief legal adviser to the government and is also ultimately responsible for all crown litigation. He has overall responsibility for the work of the Law Officers' Departments (the Treasury Solicitor's Department, the Crown Prosecution Service, the Serious Fraud Office, the Revenue and Customs Prosecution Office, the Army Prosecuting Authority, HM Crown Prosecution Service Inspectorate and the Attorney-General's Office). He has a specific statutory duty to superintend the discharge of their duties by the Director of Public Prosecutions (who heads the Crown Prosecution Service) and the Director of the Serious Fraud Office. The Director of Public Prosecutions for Northern Ireland and the Crown Solicitor for Northern Ireland are also responsible to the Attorney-General for the performance of their functions. The Attorney-General has specific responsibilities for the enforcement of the criminal law and also performs certain public interest functions, eg protecting charities and appealing unduly lenient sentences. He also deals with questions of law arising in bills and with issues of legal policy.
Attorney-General, Rt. Hon. Lord Goldsmith, QC
Private Secretary, W. Hart
Solicitor-General, Hon. Mike O'Brien, QC, MP
Legal Secretary, J. Jones
Deputy Legal Secretary, H. Heycock

DEPARTMENT FOR BUSINESS, ENTERPRISE AND REGULATORY REFORM

1 Victoria Street, London SW1H 0ET
T 020-7215 5000 F 020-7215 0105
W www.berr.gov.uk

The Department for Business, Enterprise and Regulatory Reform (BERR) was established in June 2007 after the Department of Trade and Industry was disbanded. BERR promotes best practice in design and manufacture, and investment opportunities, and champions different industries' legitimate interests through policy and regulation. The department aims to create the conditions required for business success through competitive and flexible markets that provide value for businesses, consumers and employers. It is responsible for regulatory reform and works across government and the UK's regions to raise levels of UK productivity, and has joint responsibility – with the Department for International Development and the Foreign and Commonwealth Office respectively – for trade policy, and trade promotion and inward investment. BERR also works closely with the newly established Department for Innovation, Universities and Skills.

Secretary of State for Business, Enterprise and Regulatory Reform, Rt. Hon. John Hutton, MP
Principal Private Secretary, Dr Philippa Lloyd
Senior Private Secretary, Catherine Capon
Private Secretaries, Emily Bourne; Dr Matthew Clarke
Parliamentary Private Secretary, Eric Joyce, MP
Special Advisers, John Williams; John Woodcock
Minister of State, Rt. Hon. Stephen Timms, MP *(Competitiveness)*
Private Secretary, vacant
Parliamentary Private Secretary, Stephen Pound, MP
Minister of State, Malcolm Wicks, MP *(Energy)*
Private Secretary, David Curran
Parliamentary Private Secretary, Dr Nick Palmer, MP
Minister of State, Lord Jones of Birmingham *(Trade and Investment)*
Private Secretary, vacant
Parliamentary Private Secretary, Andy Slaughter, MP
Minister of State, Pat McFadden, MP *(Employment Relation and Postal Affairs)*
Private Secretary, Dominic Scullard
Parliamentary Private Secretary, Jim McGovern, MP
Minister of State, Lord Drayson *(Business and Regulatory Reform; also a minister with MoD)*
Private Secretary, vacant
Parliamentary Private Secretary, Russell Brown, MP
Parliamentary Under-Secretary of State, Gareth Thomas, MP *(Trade and Consumer Affairs; also a minister with DfID)*
Private Secretary, vacant
Permanent Secretary, Sir Brian Bender, KCB
Private Secretary, John Sartin
Head of Parliamentary Unit, Ian Webster

MANAGEMENT BOARD
Chair, Sir Brian Bender
Members, Hilary Douglas *(Chief Operating Officer)*; Vicky Pryce *(Economics, Director-General; Chief Economic Adviser)*; Willy Rickett *(Energy Group, Director-General)*; Mark Gibson *(Enterprise and Business Group, Director-General)*; John Alty *(Fair Markets Group, Director-General)*; Mark Clarke *(Finance and Strategy, Director-General)*; Anthony Inglese *(Legal Services, Director-General; Solicitor and Deputy Chair)*; Sir Keith O'Nions *(Science and Innovation, Director-General)*; Andrew Cahn *(UK Trade and Industry, Chief Executive)*
Independent Members, Arnoud De Meyer; Roger Urwin; Fields Wicker-Miurin; Dr Brian Woods-Scawen

BETTER REGULATION EXECUTIVE
22 Whitehall, London SW1A 2WH
T 020-7276 2828 W www.betterregulation.gov.uk

The Better Regulation Executive works across government to minimise bureaucracy by reducing and removing unnecessary regulation from the public, private and voluntary sectors.
Chair, William Sargent
Chief Executive, Jitinder Kohli

SHAREHOLDER EXECUTIVE
1 Victoria Street, London SW1H 0ET
T 020-7215 6830 F 020-7215 5494
W www.shareholderexecutive.gov.uk

The Shareholder Executive was established in September 2003 to improve the government's performance as a shareholder in government-owned businesses and to provide a source of corporate finance expertise within government; currently the executive's remit covers 27 businesses.
Chair, Philip Remnant
Chief Executive (acting), Stephen Lovegrove

DEPARTMENT FOR CHILDREN, SCHOOLS AND FAMILIES

Sanctuary Buildings, Great Smith Street, London SW1P 3BT
Caxton House, Tothill Street, London SW1H 9NA
Castle View House, East Lane, Runcorn WA7 2GJ
Mowden Hall, Staindrop Road, Darlington DL3 9BG
Moorfoot, Sheffield S1 4PQ
T 0870-001 2345 Public Enquiries 0870-000 2288
F 01928-794248
E info@dcsf.gsi.gov.uk W www.dcsf.gov.uk

The Department for Children, Schools and Families (DCSF) was established in June 2007 in place of the Department for Education and Skills (DfES), in order to achieve better integrated children's services and improved educational standards; higher education and lifelong learning directorates moved to the new Department for Innovation, Universities and Skills.

The DCSF is responsible for everything affecting children and young people under the age of 19, including schools and relevant services. The department's objectives are to raise standards in order to increase the number of children reaching expected standards; help children out of poverty; and re-engage disaffected young people. It also aims to respond to factors affecting children and families, such as demographic and socio-economic change, developing technology and increasing global competition.

Secretary of State for Children, Schools and Families, Rt. Hon. Ed Balls, MP
Principal Private Secretary, Mela Watts
Private Secretary, Hannah Sheehan
Special Advisers, Francine Bates; Alex Belardinelli
Parliamentary Private Secretary, Paul Clark, MP
Minister of State, Jim Knight, MP *(Schools and Learners)*
Private Secretary, Charles Deighton-Fox
Parliamentary Private Secretary, Madeline Moon, MP
Minister of State, Rt. Hon. Beverley Hughes, MP *(Children, Young People and Families)*
Private Secretary, Jo Hawley
Parliamentary Private Secretary, Christine Russell, MP
Parliamentary Under-Secretary of State, Lord Adonis *(Schools and Learners)*
Private Secretary, Dunstan Hadley
Parliamentary Under-Secretary of State, Kevin Brennan, MP *(Children, Young People and Families)*
Private Secretary, Nicola Sams
Parliamentary Clerk, Mike Watts
Spokesperson in the House of Lords, Lord Adonis
Permanent Secretary, David Bell
Private Secretary, Lucy Andrew

BOARD MEMBERS
Chair, David Bell
Directors-General, Tom Jeffrey *(Children and Families)*; Jon Thompson *(Corporate Services)*; Ralph Tabberer *(Schools)*; Lesley Longstone *(Young People)*
Director of Communications, Caroline Wright
Non-Executive Members, Philip Augar; Katherine Kerswell

CORPORATE SERVICES DIRECTORATE
Chief Information Officer, Tim Wright

INTERNAL AUDIT
Head of Internal Audit, Suzanne Orr

LEGAL ADVISER'S OFFICE
Legal Adviser, David Noble

DEPARTMENT FOR COMMUNITIES AND LOCAL GOVERNMENT

Eland House, London SW1E 5DU
T 020-7944 4400 F 020-7944 9645
W www.communities.gov.uk

The Department for Communities and Local Government (DCLG) was formed in May 2006 with a remit to promote community cohesion and equality, as well as responsibility for housing, urban regeneration and planning. It unites the communities and civil renewal functions previously undertaken by the Home Office, with responsibility for regeneration, neighbourhood renewal and local government (previously held by the Office of the Deputy Prime Minister, which was abolished following a cabinet reshuffle in May 2006).

The DCLG also brings together responsibility for equality policy, including policy on race, faith, gender and sexual orientation (functions that were previously split between several government departments). The department will also sponsor the Commission for Equality and Human Rights.

Secretary of State for the Department for Communities and Local Government, Minister for Women, Rt. Hon. Hazel Blears, MP
Private Secretary, Daniel Thornton
Parliamentary Private Secretary, Robert Flello, MP
Minister of State, Rt. Hon. John Healey, MP *(Local Government)*
Private Secretary, Mark Doran
Parliamentary Private Secretary, Chris Mole, MP
Minister of State, Yvette Cooper, MP *(Housing)*
Private Secretary, Mark Livesey
Parliamentary Private Secretary, Angela C. Smith, MP
Parliamentary Under-Secretary of State, Parmjit Dhanda, MP
Private Secretary, Ian Hardy
Parliamentary Under-Secretary of State, Baroness Andrews, OBE
Private Secretary, Alistair MacDonald
Parliamentary Under-Secretary of State, Iain Wright, MP
Private Secretary, Stella Michael
Permanent Secretary, Peter Housden
Private Secretary, Tanya Ferguson
Chief Scientist, Prof. Michael Kelly

DEPARTMENT FOR COMMUNITIES AND LOCAL GOVERNMENT BOARD
Chair, Peter Housden *(Permanent Secretary)*
Members, Susan Scholefield *(Director-General, Equalities)*; Joe Montgomery *(Director-General, Places and Communities)*; Richard McCarthy *(Director-General, Programmes, Policy and Innovation)*

SENIOR STAFF
Directors-General, Susan Scholefield *(Equalities)*; Hunada Nouss *(Finance and Corporate Service Delivery)*; Chris Wormald *(Governance and Communications)*; Joe Montgomery *(Places and Communities)*; Richard McCarthy *(Programmes, Policy and Innovation)*; Alun Evans *(Transformation)*
Directors, Michael Kell *(Analytical Services)*; John Shield *(Communications)*; Peter Betts *(Fire and Resilience)*; Colin Byrne *(Home Information Packs)*; Terrie Alafat *(Housing Strategy and Support)*; Clive Norris *(Human Resources)*; Roy Marshall *(Knowledge, IT and Working Environment)*; Sandra Unerman *(Legal)*; David Rossington *(Local Democracy)*; Ros Dunn *(Local Development and Renewal)*; Lindsay Bell *(Local Government Finance)*; Andrew Campbell *(Local Strategic Partnerships and Performance)*; Andrew Wells *(New Homes and Sustainable Development)*; Neil McDonald *(Planning Policy)*; Mark Carroll *(Race, Faith and Cohesion)*; Teresa Vokes *(Regional and Cross Government Delivery)*; Mark Kleinman *(Regional, Urban and Economic Policy)*
Chief Executive of Thames Gateway and Olympics, Judith Armitt

DEPARTMENT FOR CULTURE, MEDIA AND SPORT

2–4 Cockspur Street, London SW1Y 5DH
T 020-7211 6200 F 020-7211 6032
E enquiries@culture.gov.uk W www.culture.gov.uk

The Department for Culture, Media and Sport (DCMS) was established in July 1997 and aims to improve the quality of life for all those in the UK through cultural and sporting activities while championing the tourism, creative and leisure industries. It is responsible for government policy relating to the arts, sport, the National Lottery, tourism, libraries, museums and galleries, broadcasting, creative industries – including film and the music industry – press freedom and regulation, licensing, gambling and the historic environment.

The department is also responsible for 63 public bodies that help deliver the department's strategic aims and objectives, the 2012 Olympic Games and Paralympic Games, the listing of historic buildings and scheduling of ancient monuments, the export licensing of cultural goods, and the management of the Government Art Collection and the Royal Parks (its sole executive agency). In May 2005 the DCMS assumed responsibility for fashion design, advertising and the arts market from the then Department for Trade and Industry – now the Department for Business, Enterprise and Regulatory Reform – which it also works jointly with on design issues (including sponsorship of the Design Council) and on relations with the computer games and publishing industries.

Secretary of State for Culture, Media and Sport, Rt. Hon. James Purnell, MP
Principal Private Secretary, Rita Patel
Special Advisers, vacant
Parliamentary Private Secretary, Gordon Banks, MP
Minister of State, Rt. Hon. Margaret Hodge, MBE, MP *(Culture, Creative Industries and Tourism)*
Private Secretary, James Bird
Parliamentary Private Secretary, Derek Wyatt, MP
Parliamentary Under-Secretary of State, Gerry Sutcliffe, MP *(Sport)*
Private Secretary, vacant
Permanent Secretary, Jonathan Stephens
Private Secretary, Sarah Taylor

MANAGEMENT BOARD
Chair, Jonathan Stephens
Directors-General, Andrew Ramsay, CB *(Culture, Creativity and Economy)*; Jeremy Beeton *(Government Olympic Executive)*
Chief Operating Officer, Nicholas Holgate
Directors, Anita Charlesworth *(Active Generation)*; Jon Zeff

(Broadcasting); Paddy Feeny *(Communications)*; Alan Davey *(Culture)*; David Goldstone *(Finance)*; Brian Leonard *(Industry)*; Patrick Kilgarriff *(Legal)*; Andrew Lean *(Olympics)*; Nicky Roche *(Olympics)*; David Roe *(Strategy)*
Non-Executive Directors, Clive Elphick; Parminder Vir
Royal Parks Chief Executive, Mark Camley

MINISTRY OF DEFENCE

see Defence section

DEPARTMENT FOR ENVIRONMENT, FOOD AND RURAL AFFAIRS

Nobel House, 17 Smith Square, London SW1P 3JR
T 020-7238 3000 F 020-7238 6591
Helpline 0845-933 5577
E helpline@defra.gsi.gov.uk W www.defra.gov.uk

The Department for Environment, Food and Rural Affairs (DEFRA) is responsible for government policy on the environment, rural matters, farming and food production; its central aim is sustainable development. In association with the agriculture departments of the Scottish Executive, the National Assembly for Wales and the Northern Ireland Office, and with the Intervention Board, the department is responsible for negotiations in the EU on the common agricultural and fisheries policies, and for single European market questions relating to its responsibilities. Its remit includes international agricultural and food trade policy.

The department's five strategic priorities, published in *DEFRA's Five-Year Strategy: Delivering the Essentials of Life,* are climate change and energy; sustainable consumption and production; the protection of natural resources and the countryside; sustainable rural communities; and sustainable farming and food, including animal health and welfare. DEFRA is also the lead government department for emergencies in animal and plant diseases, flooding, food and water supply, dealing with the consequences of a chemical, biological, radiological or nuclear incident, and certain other threats to the environment.

Secretary of State for Environment, Food and Rural Affairs, Rt. Hon. Hilary Benn, MP
Principal Private Secretary, Rory O'Donnell
Private Secretaries, Beth Crook; Rebecca Evernden; Sharee Samuel
Parliamentary Private Secretary, Dr Ashok Kumar, MP
Minister of State, Phil Woolas, MP *(Environment)*
Senior Private Secretary, Neil Hornby
Private Secretary, Kathryn Wood
Parliamentary Private Secretary, Nia Griffith, MP
Minister of State, Rt. Hon. Lord Rooker *(Sustainable Food and Farming, and Animal Health)*
Senior Private Secretary, Rhian Mewis
Private Secretaries, Amelia Munn; Vincent Venturotti
Parliamentary Under-Secretary of State, Joan Ruddock, MP *(Climate Change, Biodiversity and Waste)*
Senior Private Secretary, Naomi Matthiessen
Private Secretaries, Liz Kitchen; David Miller
Parliamentary Under-Secretary of State, Jonathan Shaw, MP *(Marine, Landscape and Rural Affairs)*
Senior Private Secretary, Deborah Wells
Private Secretaries, Anna Sanders; Joe Speck
Permanent Secretary, Helen Ghosh
Private Secretary, Jenny McClelland

MANAGEMENT BOARD
Chair, Helen Ghosh *(Permanent Secretary)*
Directors-General, Prof. Howard Dalton *(Chief Scientific Adviser)*; Mike Anderson *(Climate Change)*; Ian Grattidge *(Finance)*; Andy Lebrecht *(Food and Farming)*; Debby Reynolds *(Food and Farming, and Chief Veterinary Officer)*; Gill Aitken *(Legal Services, and Solicitor)*; Peter Unwin *(Natural Environment Group)*; Liz Sands *(Renew Programme)*; Andrew Burchell *(Service Transformation)*; Bill Stow *(Strategy and Evidence)*
Non-Executive Members, Bill Griffiths; Janet Grossman

FOREIGN AND COMMONWEALTH OFFICE

King Charles Street, London SW1A 2AH
T 020-7008 1500 W www.fco.gov.uk

The Foreign and Commonwealth Office (FCO) provides, through its staff in the UK and through its diplomatic missions abroad, the means of communication between the British government and other governments – and international governmental organisations – on all matters falling within the field of international relations.

It is responsible for alerting the British government to the implications of developments overseas; promoting British interests overseas; protecting British citizens abroad; explaining British policies to, and cultivating relationships with, governments overseas; the discharge of British responsibilities to the overseas territories; entry clearance UK visas (with the Home Office); and promoting British business overseas (jointly with the Department for Business, Enterprise and Regulatory Reform through UK Trade and Investment).

Secretary of State for Foreign and Commonwealth Affairs, Rt. Hon. David Miliband, MP
Principal Private Secretary, Matthew Gould
Special Advisers, Ravi Gurumurthy; Madlin Sadler; Sarah Schaefer
Parliamentary Private Secretary, Dan Norris, MP
Minister of State, Jim Murphy, MP *(Europe)*
Private Secretary, Nicholas Catsaras
Parliamentary Private Secretary, Neil Turner, MP
Minister of State, Dr Kim Howells, MP *(Middle East)*
Private Secretary, Scott Furssedonn
Parliamentary Private Secretary, John Robertson, MP
Minister of State, Lord Jones of Birmingham *(Trade and Investment)*
Minister of State, Lord Malloch-Brown, KCMG *(Africa, Asia and the UN)*
Private Secretary, Craig Fulton
Parliamentary Private Secretary, Andy Slaughter, MP
Parliamentary Under-Secretary of State, Meg Munn, MP
Private Secretary, Darren James
Permanent Under-Secretary of State and Head of HM Diplomatic Service, Sir Peter Ricketts, CMG
Private Secretary, Jill Parkinson
Group Chief Executive, UK Trade and Investment, Andrew Cahn
Directors-General, Dickie Stagg, CMG *(Change and Delivery)*; David Richmond, CMG *(Defence/Intelligence)*; Nicola Brewer, CMG *(EU Policy)*; Martin Donnelly, CMG *(Europe and Globalisation)*; Keith Luck *(Finance)*; Mark Lyall Grant *(Political)*; Daniel Bethlehem *(Legal Adviser)*
Non-Executive Board Members, Alistair Johnson; Alison Platt

SENIOR PERSONNEL
Directors, Andrew Lloyd *(Africa)*; Chris Wood *(Americas)*; John Dennis *(Asia)*; Sebastian Wood *(Asia Pacific)*;

Lucian Hudson *(Communications, and Press Secretary)*; Rob Macaire *(Consular Services)*; Mariot Leslie *(Defence and Strategic Threats)*; Geoff Gillham *(Estates)*; Anthony Smith *(European Political Affairs)*; Shan Morgan *(European Union)*; Ric Todd *(Finance)*; Scott Wightman *(Global and Economic Issues)*; Darren Warren *(Human Resources)*; Tony Mather *(Information and Technology)*; Stephen Pattison *(International Security)*; Simon McDonald *(Iraq)*; Peter Gooderham *(Middle East and North Africa)*; Judith Gregor *(Migration)*; Sarah Gillot *(Protocol)*; Simon Smith *(Russia, South Caucasus and Central Asia)*; Andrew Noble *(Security)*; Adam Thomson *(South Asia and Afghanistan)*; Anne Pringle, CMG *(Strategy and Information)*; Mark Sedwell *(UK Visas)*
Chief Executive, FCO Services, Chris Moxey
Legal Adviser, Sir Michael Wood, KCMG

UK SPECIAL REPRESENTATIVES
Afghanistan, Tom Phillips, CMG
Climate Change, John Ashton
South Caucasus, Sir Brian Fall, KCMG
Sudan, Rod Pullen

UK VISAS (JOINT FCO/HOME OFFICE DIRECTORATE)
Directors-General, Dickie Stagg, CMG *(Corporate Affairs)*; Lin Homer *(Immigration and Nationality Directorate)*
Director, UK Visas, Mark Sedwill
Head of Directorate, Mandie Campbell

DEPARTMENT OF HEALTH

Richmond House, 79 Whitehall, London SW1A 2NS
T 020-7210 3000
W www.dh.gov.uk

The Department of Health is responsible for the provision of the National Health Service (NHS) in England and for social care. The department's aims are to support, protect, promote and improve the nation's health; to secure the provision of comprehensive, high-quality care for all those who need it, regardless of their ability to pay, where they live or their age; and to provide responsive social care and child protection for those who lack the support they need.

The Department of Health is responsible for setting health and social care policy in England. The department's work sets standards and drives modernisation across all areas of the NHS, social care and public health.

Secretary of State for Health, Rt. Hon. Alan Johnson, MP
Principal Private Secretary, Clara Swinson
Parliamentary Private Secretary, Laura Moffat, MP
Minister of State, Ben Bradshaw, MP *(Health Services)*
Private Secretary, Kirsten Hubble
Parliamentary Private Secretary, Rosie Cooper, MP
Minister of State, Rt. Hon. Dawn Primarolo, MP *(Public Health)*
Private Secretary, Sarah Hall
Parliamentary Private Secretary, Helen Jones, MP
Parliamentary Under-Secretary of State, Prof. Lord Darzi, KBE
Private Secretary, Julia Scott
Parliamentary Under-Secretary of State, Ivan Lewis, MP *(Care Services)*
Private Secretary, Edward Scully
Parliamentary Under-Secretary of State, Ann Keen, MP *(Health)*
Private Secretary, Thomas Strickland
Parliamentary Clerk, Tim Elms

DEPARTMENTAL BOARD MEMBERS
Chief Executive of the NHS, David Nicholson, CBE
Permanent Secretary of State, Hugh Taylor, CB
Chief Medical Officer, Prof. Sir Liam Donaldson, KB
Directors-General, Chan Wheeler *(Commercial)*; Mark Britnell *(Commissioning and System Management)*; Sian Jarvis *(Communications)*; Alan Doran *(Departmental Management)*; Richard Douglas *(Finance and Investment)*; Richard Granger *(IT)*; David Flory *(NHS Finance, Performance and Operations)*; Una O'Brien *(Policy and Strategy, acting)*; David Behan *(Social Care, Local Government and Care Partnerships)*; Prof. Christine Beasley, CBE *(Chief Nursing Officer, and Director-General of User Experience and Involvement, and Professional Leadership)*; Clare Chapman *(Workforce)*
Non-Executive Directors, Julie Baddeley; Derek Myers; Mike Wheeler

NON-BOARD DIRECTORS
Deputy Chief Medical Officer, Dr Fiona Adshead
Director for Equality and Human Rights, Surinder Sharma
National Director for Social Care, Kathryn Hudson

NATIONAL CLINICAL DIRECTORS
Cancer, Prof. Mike Richards
Children, Dr Sheila Shribman
Diabetes, Dr Sue Roberts
Emergency Access, Prof. Sir George Alberti
Heart Disease and Stroke, Dr Roger Boyle
Kidney Services, Donal J. O'Donoghue
Learning Disabilities, Nicola Smith
Mental Health, Prof. Louis Appleby
Older People's Services, Ian Philp
Pandemic Influenza Preparedness, Prof. Lindsey Davies
Patients and the Public, Harry Cayton
Primary Care, David Colin-Thome
Valuing People, Rob Greig
Widening Participation in Learning, Prof. Bob Fryer, CBE

SOLICITOR'S OFFICE, DEPARTMENT FOR WORK AND PENSIONS
Solicitor, Richard Heaton
Director of Legal Services, John Catlin; Greer Kerrigan, CB

SPECIAL HEALTH AUTHORITIES

HEALTH PROTECTION AGENCY
W www.hpa.org.uk
MENTAL HEALTH ACT COMMISSION
W www.mhac.org.uk
NATIONAL BLOOD SERVICE
W www.blood.co.uk
NATIONAL CLINICAL ASSESSMENT SERVICE
W www.ncas.nhs.uk
NATIONAL INSTITUTE FOR CLINICAL EXCELLENCE
W www.nice.org.uk
NATIONAL TREATMENT AGENCY FOR SUBSTANCE MISUSE
W www.nta.nhs.uk
NATIONAL PATIENT SAFETY AGENCY
W www.npsa.nhs.uk

NHS APPOINTMENTS COMMISSION
W www.appointments.org.uk
NHS BUSINESS SERVICES AUTHORITY
W www.nhsbsa.nhs.uk
NHS LITIGATION AUTHORITY
W www.nhsla.com
UK TRANSPLANT
W www.uktransplant.org.uk

HOME OFFICE

2 Marsham Street, London SW1P 4DF
T 020-7035 4848 F 020-7035 4745
E public.enquiries@homeoffice.gsi.gov.uk
W www.homeoffice.gov.uk

The Home Office deals with those internal affairs in England and Wales which have not been assigned to other government departments. The Secretary of State for the Home Department is the link between the Queen and the public, and exercises certain powers on her behalf, including that of the royal pardon.

The Home Office aims to build a safe, just and tolerant society and to maintain and enhance public security and protection; to support and mobilise communities so that they are able to shape policy and improvement for their locality, overcome nuisance and anti-social behaviour, maintain and enhance social cohesion and enjoy their homes and public spaces peacefully; to deliver departmental policies and responsibilities fairly, effectively and efficiently; and to make the best use of resources. These objectives reflect the priorities of the government and the home secretary in areas of crime, citizenship and communities, namely to reduce crime and the fear of crime through visible, responsive and accountable policing; to reduce organised and international crime; to combat terrorism and other threats to national security; to ensure the effective delivery of justice; to reduce re-offending and protect the public; to reduce the availability and abuse of dangerous drugs; to regulate entry to, and settlement in, the UK in the interests of sustainable growth and social inclusion; and to support strong, active communities in which people of all races and backgrounds are valued and participate on equal terms.

The Home Office delivers these aims through the immigration services, its agencies and non-departmental public bodies, and by working with partners in private, public and voluntary sectors, individuals and communities. The home secretary is also the link between the UK government and the governments of the Channel Islands and the Isle of Man.

Secretary of State for the Home Department, Rt. Hon. Jacqui Smith, MP
Principal Private Secretary, Richard Westlake
Private Secretaries, Chris Felton; Mark Williams; Paul Wylie
Special Adviser, Susan Jackson
Minister of State, Tony McNulty, MP *(Security, Counter-Terrorism, Crime and Policing)*
Private Secretary, Neil Roberts
Minister of State, Liam Byrne, MP *(Borders and Immigration)*
Private Secretary, Thomas Grieg
Parliamentary Under-Secretary of State, Lord West of Spithead *(Security and Counter-Terrorism)*
Private Secretary, Caroline Smith
Parliamentary Under-Secretary of State, Vernon Coaker, MP *(Crime Reduction)*
Private Secretary, Suzanne Jacob
Parliamentary Under-Secretary of State, Meg Hiller, MP *(Identity)*
Private Secretary, Jacob Hawkins
Permanent Secretary of State, Sir David Normington, KCB
Private Secretary, Isobel Arthur
Parliamentary Clerk, Phil Rawlinson

HOME OFFICE BOARD MEMBERS
Permanent Secretary of State, Sir David Normington, KCB *(Chair)*
Chief Executive of Border and Immigration Agency, Lin Homer
Chief Executive of Office for Criminal Justice Reform, Ursula Brennan
Director-General of Crime, Policing and Counter-Terrorism, Moira Wallace
Director-General of Financial and Commercial, Helen Kilpatrick
Director-General of Performance and Reform, Peter Makeham
Group Director of Human Resources, Kevin White
Non-Executive Members, Derrick Anderson; Patrick Carter

COMMUNICATION DIRECTORATE
Director, Julia Simpson
Head of News (Press Office), Michael Winders

SHARED SERVICES DIRECTORATE
Director, David Myers

STRATEGY AND REFORM DIRECTORATE
Director, Peter Makeham

CRIME REDUCTION AND COMMUNITY SAFETY GROUP
Director-General, Moira Wallace
Directors, Vanessa Nicholls *(Crime Drug Strategy)*; Paul Evans *(Police and Crime Standards)*; Vic Hogg *(Policing Policy and Operations)*; Stephen Kershaw *(Police Reform and Resources)*; Alastair Bridges *(Strategic Support)*

OFFICE FOR SECURITY AND COUNTER-TERRORISM
Director-General, Charles Farr
Directors, William Nye; Jaee Samant; Stephen Smith

OFFICE FOR CRIMINAL JUSTICE REFORM
Chief Executive, Ursula Brennan
Directors, Stephen Jenner *(Criminal Justice IT, acting)*; Catherine Lee *(Delivery and Communications, acting)*; David Wood *(Policy and Process)*; Jonathan Sedgwick *(Strategy and Planning)*

Note: The OCJR is a cross-departmental organisation, also reporting to the Ministry of Justice and the Office of the Attorney-General

HUMAN RESOURCES DIRECTORATE
Director, Kevin White
Directors, Dusty Amroliwala *(Services)*; Mandie Campbell *(Leadership and Learning)*

BORDER AND IMMIGRATION AGENCY
Chief Executive, Lin Homer
Deputy Chief Executive, Ken Sutton
Strategic Directors, Matthew Coats *(Asylum)*; Brodie Clark *(Borders)*; Jonathan Lindley *(Enforcement)*; Joe Dugdale *(HR and Organisational Development)*; Paula Higson

(Managed Migration); Justin Holiday *(Resource Management)*

LEGAL ADVISERS' BRANCH
Senior Legal Adviser, David Seymour
Deputy Legal Advisers, Steven Bramley; Iain Macleod

PERFORMANCE AND FINANCE DIRECTORATE
Director, Peter Kane

INTERNATIONAL DIRECTORATE
Director, Peter Storr

COMMERCIAL DIRECTORATE
Director, John Collington

SCIENCE AND RESEARCH GROUP
Director and Chief Scientific Adviser, Prof. Paul Wiles

DEPARTMENT FOR INNOVATION, UNIVERSITIES AND SKILLS

1 Victoria Street, London SW1H 0ET
T 020-7215 5555 W www.dfid.gov.uk

The Department for Innovation, Universities and Skills (DIUS) was established in June 2007, and brings together functions from the former Department for Trade and Industry – including responsibilities for science and innovation – with functions from the former Department for Education and Skills (further and higher education and skills). The DIUS works particularly closely with the Department for Business, Enterprise and Regulatory Reform and with the Department for Children, Schools and Families.

The DIUS aims to sustain and develop a world-class research base; maximise the exploitation of said base to support innovation across all sectors of the economy; increase and widen participation in higher education; raise participation and attainment by young people and adults in post-16 education and learning; reduce the skills gap amongst adults, particularly in terms of numeracy and literacy; and increase the supply of people in the fields of science, technology, engineering and mathematics.

Secretary of State for Innovation, Universities and Skills, Rt. Hon. John Denham, MP
Principal Private Secretary, Claire Burton
Private Secretary, Kate McAleenan
Parliamentary Private Secretary, Lyn Brown, MP
Minister of State, Ian Pearson, MP *(Science and Innovation)*
Private Secretary, Georgiana Glaysher
Parliamentary Private Secretary, Celia Barlow, MP
Minister of State, Bill Rammell, MP *(Lifelong Learning, Further and Higher Education)*
Private Secretary, Lisa Glover
Parliamentary Private Secretary, David Anderson, MP
Parliamentary Under-Secretary of State, David Lammy, MP *(Skills)*
Private Secretary, Luke Owen
Parliamentary Under-Secretary of State, Lord Triesman *(Intellectual Property and Quality)*
Private Secretary, Francesca Orpen

MANAGEMENT BOARD
Permanent Secretary, Ian Watmore *(Chair)*
Government Chief Scientific Adviser and Head of Government Office for Science, Prof. Sir David King
Directors-General, Simon Morys *(Business Operations)*; Nick Edmonds *(Finance and Performance)*; Stephen Marston *(Further Education and Skills)*; Ruth Thompson *(Higher Education)*; Shirley Pointer *(Human Resources)*; Sir Keith O'Nions *(Science and Innovation)*; Zina Etheridge *(Strategy and Communications)*

SENIOR STAFF
Directors, David Williams *(British National Space Centre)*; Susan Pember *(Further Education and Skills Performance Group)*; Jeremy Clayton *(Government Office for Science)*; Martin Williams *(Higher Education Strategy)*; John Landeryou *(Improvement Group)*; Win Harris *(Joint International Unit)*; Jeff Llewellyn *(National Weights and Measures Laboratory)*; John Neilson *(Research Base)*; Stephen Hillier *(Skills Group)*; Michael Hipkins *(Student Finance Strategy)*; David Evans *(Technology and Innovation)*; Ian Fletcher *(UK Intellectual Property Office)*

DEPARTMENT FOR INTERNATIONAL DEVELOPMENT

1 Palace Street, London SW1 5HE
T 020-7023 0000 F 020-7023 0016
Abercrombie House, Eaglesham Road, East Kilbride, Glasgow G75 8EA T 01355-844000 F 01355-844099
Public Enquiries 0845-300 4100
E enquiry@dfid.gov.uk W www.dfid.gov.uk

The Department for International Development (DFID) is responsible for promoting sustainable development and reducing poverty. The central focus of the government's policy, based on the 1997, 2000 and 2006 white papers on international development, is a commitment to the internationally agreed Millennium Development Goals, to be achieved by 2015. These seek to eradicate extreme poverty and hunger; achieve universal primary education; promote gender equality and empower women; reduce child mortality; improve maternal health; combat HIV/AIDS, malaria and other diseases; ensure environmental sustainability; and encourage a global partnership for development.

DFID's assistance is concentrated in the poorest countries of sub-Saharan Africa and Asia, but also contributes to poverty reduction and sustainable development in middle-income countries, including those in Latin America and Eastern Europe. The department works in partnership with governments committed to the Millennium Development Goals, and with the private sector and the research community. It also works with multilateral institutions, including the World Bank, United Nations agencies and the European Commission. The department has headquarters in London and East Kilbride, offices in many developing countries, and staff based in British embassies and high commissions around the world.

Secretary of State for International Development, Rt. Hon. Douglas Alexander, MP
Principal Private Secretary, Howard Taylor
Private Secretary, Helen Winterton
Special Advisers, Paul Sinclair; Anthony Vigor
Parliamentary Private Secretary, Kerry McCarthy, MP
Parliamentary Clerk, Richard Haviland
Parliamentary Under-Secretary of State, Gareth R. Thomas, MP *(also a minister with BERR)*
Private Secretary, Eleanor Briers
Parliamentary Under-Secretary of State, Shahid Malik, MP
Private Secretary, Charlotte Pierre
Parliamentary Under-Secretary of State, Baroness Vadera
Private Secretary, Hugh Walker
House of Lords Spokesperson, Baroness Amos
Liaison Peer, Baroness Whitaker

Whips, Bob Blizzard, MP *(Commons)*; Baroness Royall *(Lords)*
Permanent Secretary, Suma Chakrabarti

MANAGEMENT BOARD
Directors-General, Sue Owen *(Corporate Performance and Knowledge Sharing)*; Mark Lowcock *(Policy and International)*; Minouche Shafik *(Regional Programmes)*
Non-Executive Directors, Helen Ghosh; Bill Griffiths

DIVISIONS
Directors, Paul Mylrea *(Communications)*; Dave Fish *(East and Central Africa)*; Sue Wardell *(Europe, Middle East, Americas, Central and East Asia Division)*; Sam Sharpe *(Finance and Corporate Performance)*; Owen Barder *(Global Development Effectiveness)*; Liz Davies *(Human Resources)*; Marcus Manuel *(Pan-Africa Strategy and Programmes)*; Andrew Steer *(Policy and Research)*; Jim Drummond *(South Asia)*; Martin Dinham *(UN, Conflict and Humanitarian)*; Beverley Warmington *(West and Southern Africa)*

CDC GROUP
5 Duke Street, London SW1Y 6BN
T 020-7484 7700 **W** www.cdcgroup.com

Founded in 1948, CDC is a government-owned fund of funds that provides capital to invest through third-party fund managers in private equity funds focused on emerging economies; it covers countries in Africa, Asia and Latin America. CDC is a public limited company with the Department for International Development as its 100 per cent shareholder.
Chair, Sir Malcolm Williamson
Chief Executive, Richard Laing

MINISTRY OF JUSTICE

Selbourne House, 54 Victoria Street, London SW1E 6QW
T 020-7210 8500 **E** general.enquiries@justice.gsi.gov.uk
W www.justice.gov.uk

The Ministry of Justice (MoJ) was established in May 2007 and the responsibilities of the Department for Constitutional Affairs (DCA) were transferred to it. The MoJ's priorities are to protect the public; reduce reoffending; promote and provide access to justice; engender confidence in the justice system; uphold people's human rights, alongside their information and democratic rights; and to safeguard and modernise the constitution.

The MoJ incorporates the National Offender Management Service, which includes HM Prison Service and the National Probation Service, and the Office for Criminal Justice Reform (a cross-departmental organisation also reporting to the Home Office and the Office of the Attorney-General). In April 2006 the largest central government tribunals were incorporated into the MoJ (then, the DCA) as the Tribunals Service (*see* Tribunals section). The remit of the Lord Chancellor was also altered: he continues to be the government minister responsible to parliament for the judiciary and the courts system, but is no longer the head of the judiciary. The Lord Chief Justice has taken on the role of head of the judiciary and now performs many of the judicial functions formerly undertaken by the Lord Chancellor.

The MoJ established an independent Judicial Appointments Commission and related bodies, and retains its association with several associated departments, non-departmental public bodies and executive agencies, including the Northern Ireland Court Service, Her Majesty's Land Registry, the National Archives, the Legal Service Commission, and the Public Guardianship Office. The administrative functions of the Scotland Office and the Wales Office transferred to the MoJ in June 2003. Responsibilities for the maintenance of the relationship between Westminster and the devolved administrations in Edinburgh and Cardiff remain with the Secretary of State for Scotland and the Secretary of State for Wales respectively.

Secretary of State for Justice and Lord Chancellor, Rt. Hon. Jack Straw, MP
Principal Private Secretary, Antonia Romeo
Special Advisers, Mark Davies; Declan McHugh
Parliamentary Private Secretary, Mark Hendrick, MP
Minister of State, Rt. Hon. David Hanson, MP
Private Secretary, Philip Lawley
Parliamentary Private Secretary, Lynda Waltho, MP
Minister of State, Michael Wills, MP
Private Secretary, Martyn Taylor
Parliamentary Private Secretary, Gordon Marsden, MP
Parliamentary Under-Secretary of State, Lord Hunt of Kings Heath, OBE
Private Secretary, Alexandra Knapton
Parliamentary Under-Secretary of State, Bridget Prentice, MP
Private Secretary, Adam Rothapel
Parliamentary Under-Secretary of State, Maria Eagle, MP
Private Secretary, Dileeni Daniel-Selvaratnam
Permanent Secretary, Alex Allan
Private Secretary, Jennifer Hepker
Parliamentary Clerk, Ann Nixon

MINISTRY OF JUSTICE BOARD
Chair, Rt. Hon. Jack Straw, MP *(Lord Chancellor and Secretary of State for Justice)*
Members, MoJ Ministers of State; MoJ Parliamentary Under-Secretaries of State; Peter Brook *(Director-General, Financial and Commercial, acting)*; Sir Ron de Witt *(Chief Executive, HM Courts Service)*; Phil Wheatley *(Director-General, HM Prison Service for England and Wales)*; John Lyon, CB *(Director-General, Legal and Judicial)*; Carolyn Regan *(Chief Executive, Legal Services Commission)*; Helen Edwards *(Chief Executive, National Offender Management Service)*; Ursula Brennan *(Chief Executive, Office for Criminal Justice Reform)*; Alex Allan *(Permanent Secretary)*; Rod Clark *(Director-General, Strategy)*
Non-Executive Directors, Sir Peter Bonfield; Prof. George M. Selim

DEPARTMENTAL MANAGEMENT BOARD
Chair, Alex Allan *(Permanent Secretary)*
Members, Yvonne Gallagher *(Chief Information Officer)*; Peter Brook *(Director-General, Financial and Commercial, acting)*; Sir Ron de Witt *(Chief Executive, HM Courts Service)*; Phil Wheatley *(Director-General, HM Prison Service for England and Wales)*; Beverley Shears *(Human Resources, Director)*; John Lyon, CB *(Director-General, Legal and Judicial)*; Carolyn Regan *(Chief Executive, Legal Services Commission)*; Helen Edwards *(Chief Executive, National Offender Management Service)*; Ursula Brennan *(Chief Executive, Office for Criminal Justice Reform)*; Rod Clark *(Director-General, Strategy)*; Peter Handcock, CBE *(Chief Executive, The Tribunals Service)*

LORD CHANCELLOR'S DEPARTMENT

See Ministry of Justice

NORTHERN IRELAND OFFICE

11 Millbank, London SW1P 4PN
T 020-7210 3000
Castle Buildings, Stormont, Belfast BT4 3SG
T 028-9052 0700 E mail@nio.gov.uk
W www.nio.gov.uk

The Northern Ireland Office was established in 1972, when the Northern Ireland (Temporary Provisions) Act transferred the legislative and executive powers of the Northern Ireland parliament and government to the UK parliament and a secretary of state.

The Northern Ireland Office is responsible primarily for security issues, law and order and prisons, and for matters relating to the political and constitutional future of the province. It also deals with international issues as they affect Northern Ireland.

Under the terms of the 1998 Good Friday Agreement, power was devolved to the Northern Ireland Assembly in 1999. The assembly took on responsibility for the relevant areas of work previously undertaken by the departments of the Northern Ireland Office, covering agriculture and rural development, the environment, regional development, social development, education, higher education, training and employment, enterprise, trade and investment, culture, arts and leisure, health, social services, public safety and finance and personnel. In October 2002 the Northern Ireland Assembly was suspended and Northern Ireland returned to direct rule, but despite repeated setbacks, devolution was restored on 8 May 2007. For further details, *see* Regional Government section.

Secretary of State for Northern Ireland, Rt. Hon. Shaun Woodward, MP
Parliamentary Private Secretary, Rob Marris, MP
Minister of State, Paul Goggins, MP
Parliamentary Private Secretary, vacant
Permanent Secretary, Jonathan Phillips
Head of the Northern Ireland Civil Service, Nigel Hamilton

NORTHERN IRELAND INFORMATION SERVICE
Castle Buildings, Stormont Estate, Belfast BT4 3SG
T 028-9052 0700

OFFICE OF THE ADVOCATE-GENERAL FOR SCOTLAND

Dover House, Whitehall, London SW1A 2AU
T 020-7270 6720 F 020-7270 6813
1 Melville Crescent, Edinburgh EH3 7HW
T 0131-244 9033 F 0131-244 9034
E ps/advocategeneral@scotland.gsi.gov.uk
W www.oag.gov.uk

The Advocate-General for Scotland is one of the three law officers of the crown, alongside the Attorney-General and the Solicitor-General for England and Wales. He is the legal adviser to the UK government on Scottish law and is supported by staff in the Office of the Advocate-General for Scotland.

The post was created as a consequence of the constitutional changes set out in the Scotland Act 1998, which created a devolved Scottish parliament. The Lord Advocate and the Solicitor-General for Scotland were then transferred to the Scottish Executive and the Advocate-General took over their previous role as legal adviser to the government on Scottish law. *See also* Regional Government section and Ministry of Justice.

Advocate-General for Scotland, Lord Davidson of Glen Clova, QC
Private Secretary, Chris Fawcett

OFFICE OF THE LEADER OF THE HOUSE OF COMMONS

26 Whitehall, London SW1A 2WH
T 020-7276 1005 F 020-7276 1006
E leader@commonsleader.x.gsi.gov.uk
W www.commonsleader.gov.uk

The Office of the Leader of the House of Commons is responsible for the arrangement of government business in the House of Commons and for planning and supervising the government's legislative programme. The Leader of the House of Commons upholds the rights and privileges of the house and acts as a spokesperson for the government as a whole.

The leader reports regularly to the cabinet on parliamentary business and the legislative programme. In her capacity as leader of the house, she is a member of the Public Accounts Commission and of the House of Commons Commission. She also chairs the cabinet committee on the legislative programme. As Lord Privy Seal, she is chair of the board of trustees of the Chevening Estate.

The Deputy Leader of the House of Commons supports the leader in handling the government's business in the house. She is responsible for monitoring MPs' and peers' correspondence and is a member of several committees, including the Ministerial Committee on the Law Commission.

Leader of the House of Commons and Lord Privy Seal, Rt. Hon. Harriet Harman, QC, MP
Principal Private Secretary, Stephen Hillcoat
Private Secretary, Mike Winter
Deputy Leader of the House of Commons, Helen Goodman, MP
Private Secretary, Frances Slee

PRIVY COUNCIL OFFICE

2 Carlton Gardens, London SW1Y 5AA
T 020-7210 1033 F 020-7210 1071
W www.privy-council.gov.uk

The office is responsible for the arrangements leading to the making of all royal proclamations and orders in council; for certain formalities connected with ministerial changes; for considering applications for the granting (or amendment) of royal charters; for the scrutiny and approval of by-laws and statutes of chartered bodies; and for the appointment of high sheriffs and many crown and Privy Council appointments to governing bodies.

The Lord President of the Council presides at meetings of the Privy Council, is a member of the cabinet and Leader of the House of Lords. She has no departmental portfolio but is a member of several cabinet committees, and supports the Lord Chancellor in his responsibility for the House of Lords reform. She is the Lords' spokesperson on equality and human rights issues, and is responsible to the prime minister for the organisation of government business in the house as well as repeating in the House of Lords statements made by the prime minister in the House of Commons. She also gives guidance to the house on matters of order and procedure.

Lord President of the Council (and Leader of the House of Lords), Baroness Ashton of Upholland, PC
Principal Private Secretary, Tanya Ferguson
Clerk of the Council, Judith Simpson
Head of Secretariat, Ceri King
Senior Clerks, Christopher Berry; Meriel McCullagh
Registrar of the Judicial Committee, Mary MacDonald

SCOTLAND OFFICE

Dover House, Whitehall, London SW1A 2AU
T 020-7270 6754 F 020-7270 6812
1 Melville Crescent, Edinburgh EH3 7HW
T 0131-244 9010 F 0131-244 9028
E scottish.secretary@scotland.gsi.gov.uk
W www.scotlandoffice.gov.uk

The Scotland Office is the department of the Secretary of State for Scotland which represents Scottish interests within the UK government in matters reserved to the UK parliament. The Secretary of State for Scotland also exercises certain specific functions in relation to devolution, including those provided for in the Scotland Act 1998; maintains the stability of the devolution settlement for Scotland; and pays grants to the Scottish Consolidated Fund and manages other financial transactions.

Reserved matters include the constitution, foreign affairs, defence, international development, the civil service, financial and economic matters, national security, immigration and nationality, misuse of drugs, trade and industry, various aspects of energy regulation (eg coal, electricity, oil, gas and nuclear energy), various aspects of transport, social security, employment, abortion, genetics, surrogacy, medicines, broadcasting and equal opportunities. Devolved matters include health and social work, education and training, local government and housing, justice and police, agriculture, forestry, fisheries, the environment, tourism, sports, heritage, economic development and internal transport. *See also* Regional Government section and Ministry of Justice.

Secretary of State for Scotland, Rt. Hon. Des Browne, MP
Private Secretary, Amy Bishop
Parliamentary Private Secretary, Russell Brown, MP
Minister of State, David Cairns, MP
Private Secretary, Amy Bishop
Parliamentary Private Secretary, Mike Lazarowicz, MP
Spokesperson in the House of Lords, Lord Evans of Temple Guiting, CBE

DEPARTMENT FOR TRANSPORT

Great Minster House, 76 Marsham Street, London SW1P 4DR
T 020-7944 8300 W www.dft.gov.uk

The Department for Transport (DfT) was established in May 2002 following the de-merger of the Department of Transport, Local Government and the Regions. The department's role is to oversee the delivery of a reliable, safe and secure transport system and to determine overall transport strategy; its main responsibilities are aviation, freight, health and safety, integrated and local transport, London Underground, maritime, mobility and inclusion, railways, roads and road safety, shipping and vehicles.

The DfT's work is focused around the following tasks: improving the current operation and capacity of transport networks and services, and providing better information for travellers; shaping the future pattern of demand for transport, including through land-use planning and appropriate pricing; tackling the environmental impact of transport through pricing, regulation, technology, consumer information and promoting efficient use of resources; planning and managing long-term investment programmes; regulating and licensing certain transport services and operators; and managing information and delivering services to support wider government objectives.

Secretary of State for Transport, Rt. Hon Ruth Kelly, MP
Principal Private Secretary, Lara Sherwin
Minister of State, Rt. Hon. Rosie Winterton, MP
Private Secretary, Peter Lee
Parliamentary Under-Secretary of State, Tom Harris, MP
Private Secretary, Roy Cahill
Parliamentary Under-Secretary of State, Jim Fitzpatrick, MP
Private Secretary, Eamonn Beirne
Permanent Secretary, Robert Devereux
Private Secretary, Suzanne Roddie

MANAGEMENT BOARD
Chair, Robert Devereux
Members, Ann Hemingway *(Non-Executive)*; Barbara Moorhouse; Archie Robertson; Deborah Williams *(Non-Executive)*

SENIOR STAFF
Directors-General, Bronwyn Hill *(City and Regional Networks Group)*; Barbara Moorhouse *(Corporate Resources)*; Simon Webb *(International Networks and Environment)*; Mike Mitchell *(Rail and National Networks)*; Stephen Hickey *(Safety, Service Delivery and Logistics)*
Director, Legal Services, Christopher Muttukumaru
Chief Scientific Adviser, Brian Collins

HM TREASURY

1 Horse Guards Road, London SW1A 2HQ
T 020-7270 4558 F 020-7270 4861
E public.enquiries@hm-treasury.gov.uk
W www.hm-treasury.gov.uk

HM Treasury is the country's economics and finance ministry, and is responsible for formulating and implementing the government's financial and economic policy. It aims to raise the rate of sustainable growth, boost prosperity, and provide the conditions necessary for universal economic and employment opportunities. The Office of the Lord High Treasurer has been continuously in commission for over 200 years. The Lord High Commissioners of HM Treasury are the First Lord of the Treasury (who is also the prime minister), the Chancellor of the Exchequer and five junior lords. This board of commissioners is assisted at present by the chief secretary, the parliamentary secretary (who is also the government chief whip in the House of Commons), the financial secretary, the economic secretary and the exchequer secretary. The prime minister as first lord is not primarily concerned with the day-to-day aspects of Treasury business; neither are the parliamentary secretary and the junior lords as government whips. Treasury business is managed by the Chancellor of the Exchequer and the other Treasury ministers, assisted by the permanent secretary.

The chief secretary is responsible for public expenditure, including spending reviews and strategic planning; in-year control; public sector pay and pensions; efficiency in public services; capital investment; and public service delivery and performance. He also has responsibility for the Treasury's interest in devolution, assists the Chancellor of the Exchequer where necessary on international and European issues, and oversees the integration of the tax and benefit system.

The financial secretary is the departmental minister for HM Revenue and Customs and the Valuation Office Agency and has strategic oversight of the UK tax system as a whole. She is the lead minister on European and international tax issues, and her responsibilities include the Finance Bill, the voluntary sector and charities, childcare issues and tax credits.

The exchequer secretary is a title only used

occasionally, normally when the post of paymaster-general is allocated to a minister outside of the Treasury (as it is at present; Rt. Hon. Tessa Jowell, MP was appointed paymaster-general as Olympic minister within the Cabinet Office in June 2007). Her responsibilities include enterprise and productivity; competition and better regulation; science, innovation and skills policy; regional economic policy and environmental issues.

The economic secretary's responsibilities include financial services policy, including tax issues; personal savings policy; foreign exchange reserves and debt management policy; stamp duty land tax and real estate investment trusts; and EMU preparations.

Prime Minister and First Lord of the Treasury, Rt. Hon. Gordon Brown, MP
Chancellor of the Exchequer, Rt. Hon. Alistair Darling, MP
Principal Private Secretary, James Bowler
Private Secretaries, Jonathan Black; Lewis Neal
Parliamentary Private Secretary, Ann Coffey, MP
Special Advisers, Emily Thomas; Sam White
Chief Secretary to the Treasury, Rt. Hon. Andy Burnham, MP
Private Secretary, Matthew Style
Parliamentary Private Secretary, Mary Creagh, MP
Financial Secretary to the Treasury, Rt. Hon. Jane Kennedy, MP
Private Secretary, Cerys Morgan
Parliamentary Private Secretary, David Wright, MP
Exchequer Secretary to the Treasury, Angela Eagle, MP
Private Secretary, Su Viner
Economic Secretary to the Treasury, Kitty Ussher, MP
Private Secretary, Hermione Gough
Permanent Secretary to the Treasury, Nick Macpherson
Private Secretary, Dan Mobley
Parliamentary Secretary to the Treasury and Government Chief Whip, Rt. Hon. Geoff Hoon, MP
Parliamentary Private Secretary, Sarah McCarthy-Fry, MP
Economic Adviser, Andrew Maugham
Lords Commissioners of HM Treasury (Whips), Alan Campbell, MP; Stephen McCabe, MP; Frank Roy, MP; Clarie Ward, MP; Dave Watts, MP
Assistant Whips, Bob Blizzard, MP; Tony Cunningham, MP; Wayne David, MP; Michael Foster, MP; Diana R. Johnson, MP; Sadiq Khan, MP; Siobhain McDonagh, MP; Alison Seabeck, MP; Mark Tami, MP; Tom Watson, MP

TREASURY BOARD

Permanent Secretary, Nick Macpherson *(Chair)*
Managing Directors, Mark Neale *(Budget, Tax and Revenue)*; Mary Keegan *(Government Financial Management)*; Stephen Pickford *(International and Finance)*; Dave Ramsden *(Macroeconomic and Fiscal Policy)*; John Kingman *(Public Services and Growth)*
Chief Executive of Office of Government Commerce, Nigel Smith
Directors, Louise Tulett *(Group Finance, Procurement and Operations)*; Sam Beckett *(Policy and Planning)*
Non-Executive Directors, Sir Peter Gershon; Stella Manzie; William Sargent; Sir David Varney

OTHER BODIES

OFFICE OF GOVERNMENT COMMERCE (OGC)
1 Horse Guards Road, London SW1A 2HQ
T 0845-000 4999 E servicedesk@ogc.gsi.gov.uk
W www.ogc.gov.uk

The Office of Government Commerce was set up in April 2000. It is responsible for increasing the government's value for money by improving standards and capability in procurement, for example by commodities buying, delivering major capital projects, and maximising the effective use of 60 per cent of government spending and a £30bn property estate.
Chief Executive, Nigel Smith

WALES OFFICE

Gwydyr House, Whitehall, London SW1A 2ER
T 020-7270 0534
E walesoffice@walesoffice.gsi.gov.uk
W www.walesoffice.gov.uk

The Wales Office was established in 1999 when most of the powers of the Welsh Office were handed over to the National Assembly for Wales. It is the department of the Secretary of State for Wales, who is the key government figure liaising with the devolved government in Wales and who represents Welsh interests in the cabinet and parliament. The secretary of state has the right to attend and speak at sessions of the National Assembly (and must consult the assembly on the government's legislative programme). *See also* Regional Government section and Ministry of Justice.
Secretary of State for Wales, Rt. Hon. Peter Hain, MP
Principal Private Secretary, Glynne Jones
Parliamentary Under-Secretary, Huw Irranca-Davies, MP
Director of Office, Alan Cogbill

DEPARTMENT FOR WORK AND PENSIONS

Caxton House, Tothill Street, London SW1H 9NA
T 020-7962 8000 E enquiries@dwp.gsi.gov.uk
W www.dwp.gov.uk

The Department for Work and Pensions was formed in June 2001 from parts of the former Department of Social Security, the Department for Education and Employment and the Employment Service. The department helps unemployed people of working age into work, helps employers to fill their vacancies and provides financial support to people unable to help themselves, through back-to-work programmes. The department also administers the child support system, social security benefits and the social fund. In addition, the department has reciprocal social security arrangements with other countries.

In April 2002 the Benefits Agency and the Employment Service were replaced by the Jobcentre Plus network (responsible for helping to find jobs and paying benefits to people of working age), and the Pension Service which administers the Benefits Agency's pension-related services.

Secretary of State for Work and Pensions, Rt. Hon. Peter Hain, MP
Principal Private Secretary, John Oliver
Private Secretaries, Helen Bache; Tom Fox; Zoe Rigden; Antonia Williams
Special Advisers, Matthew Burchell; Claire McCarthy
Parliamentary Private Secretary, Natascha Engel, MP
Minister of State, Caroline Flint, MP *(Employment and Welfare Reform)*
Private Secretary, Laura Timms
Parliamentary Private Secretary, vacant
Assistant Private Secretaries, Jessica Hodgson; Linda Reynolds
Minister of State, Mike O'Brien, MP *(Pensions Reform)*
Private Secretary, Jean-Paul Marks

Parliamentary Private Secretary, Jim Cunningham, MP
Assistant Private Secretaries, Michael Cordy; Helen Hutchings
Parliamentary Under-Secretary of State (Commons), James Plaskitt, MP
Private Secretary, Robin Gordon-Farleigh
Assistant Private Secretaries, Anahita Easton; Christopher Raitt
Parliamentary Under-Secretary of State (Lords), Lord McKenzie of Luton
Private Secretary, Sarah Kelly
Assistant Private Secretaries, Janet Smith; Maxine Thompson
Parliamentary Under-Secretary of State (Commons), Anne McGuire, MP *(Disabled People)*
Private Secretary, Lisa Pinnell
Assistant Private Secretaries, Kevin Green; Paul Warren
Parliamentary Under-Secretary of State, Barbara Follett, MP *(Equality)*
Permanent Secretary, Leigh Lewis
Private Secretaries, Phil Hall; Judith Tunstall; Lucy Wyatt

PENSIONS CLIENT DIRECTORATE
Director-General, Phil Wynn Owen
Directors, Caroline Rookes *(Private Pensions, Planning for Retirement and Older People)*; Alan Woods *(State Pensions and Pensions Reform)*; Robert Laslett *(Strategic Analysis and Stewardship, Chief Economist)*

GROUP FINANCE DIRECTORATE
Director-General, John Codling
Deputy Director-General, Howard Orme
Directors, David Smith *(Commercial)*; Jeremy Moore *(Planning and Performance Management)*; Richard Paul *(Risk Assurance)*

PROGRAMME AND SYSTEM DELIVERY
Director-General, Chief Information Officer, Joe Harley
Chief Operating Officer, Dean James

HUMAN RESOURCES GROUP
Director-General (acting), Jane Saint
Directors, Debbie Haigh *(Diversity and Equality)*; Alison Stanley *(HR Policy)*; Jerry Arnott *(Organisational Capability)*

HEALTH, WORK AND WELLBEING DIRECTORATE
Director, Chief Medical Adviser, Chief Scientist, Dr Bill Gunnyeon
Deputy Director, Principal Scientific Adviser, Dr Peter Wright
Principal Occupational Physician, Dr Nerys Williams
Chief Psychologist, David Carew

LAW, GOVERNANCE AND SPECIAL POLICY GROUP
Director-General, Richard Heaton
Directors, Ronald Powell *(Commercial and Employment)*; Frances Logan *(Legal Services)*; Mark Gidden *(Litigation)*; Amanda de Blaquiere *(Prosecutions)*; Greer Kerrigan, CB *(Social Security)*

COMMUNICATIONS NETWORK
Director, Sue Garrard

WORK, WELFARE AND EQUALITY GROUP
Director-General, Adam Sharples
Directors, Shirley Trundle *(Benefit Strategy)*; Hilary Reynolds *(Child Maintenance Redesign)*; Alan Cave *(Delivery)*; Bruce Calderwood *(Disability and Carers)*; Ian Scott *(Finance)*; Dr Bill Gunnyeon *(Health, Work and Wellbeing)*; Win Harris *(Joint International Unit)*; Cay Stratton *(National Employment Panel)*; Jonathan Portes *(Poverty and Analysis)*; Sharon White *(Welfare to Work)*

EXECUTIVE AGENCIES

Executive agencies are well-defined business units that carry out services with a clear focus on delivering specific outputs within a framework of accountability to ministers. They can be set up or disbanded without legislation, and they are organisationally independent from the department they are answerable to. In the following list the agencies are shown in the accounts of their sponsor departments. Legally they act on behalf of the relevant secretary of state. Their chief executives also perform the role of accounting officers, which means they are responsible for the money spent by their organisations. Staff employed by agencies are civil servants.

CABINET OFFICE

COI (CENTRAL OFFICE OF INFORMATION)
Hercules Road, London SE1 7DU
T 020-7928 2345 F 020-7928 5037
W www.coi.gov.uk
The COI is the principal agency within government for the provision and procurement of marketing and communications services. Administrative responsibility for the COI rests with the minister for the Cabinet Office.
Chief Executive, A. Bishop
Deputy Chief Executive, P. Buchanan

MANAGEMENT BOARD
Members, G. Beasant; Ms A. Butler; R. Haslam; I. Hamilton; G. Hooper; Ms E. Lochhead; A. Wade; Mrs S. Whetton

ATTORNEY-GENERAL'S OFFICE

TREASURY SOLICITOR'S DEPARTMENT
1 Kemble Street, London WC2B 4TS
T 020-7210 3000 F 020-7210 3004
E thetreasurysolicitor@tsol.gsi.gov.uk
W www.tsol.gov.uk
The Treasury Solicitor's Department, which became an executive agency in 1996, provides legal services for many government departments and is answerable to the Attorney-General. Those departments without their own lawyers are provided with legal advice, and both they and other departments are provided with litigation services. The Treasury Solicitor is also the Queen's Proctor, and is responsible for collecting ownerless goods *(bona vacantia)* on behalf of the crown.
HM Procurator-General and Treasury Solicitor, Permanent Secretary, Paul Jenkins

BONA VACANTIA DIVISION
Head of Division, Valerie Cain

CABINET OFFICE AND CENTRAL ADVISORY DIVISION
Head of Division, Peter Fish

DEPARTMENT OF CULTURE, MEDIA AND SPORT DIVISION
Legal Adviser, Patrick Kilgarriff

DEPARTMENT FOR CHILDREN, SCHOOLS AND FAMILIES DIVISION
Legal Adviser, David Noble

DIRECTORATE OF CORPORATE STRATEGY
Director, Julie Anderson

EUROPEAN DIVISION
Head of Division, Frances Nash

HM TREASURY ADVISORY DIVISION
Legal Adviser, Stephen Parker

LITIGATION GROUP
Head of Division, David Pearson

DEPARTMENT FOR BUSINESS, ENTERPRISE AND REGULATORY REFORM

COMPANIES HOUSE
Crown Way, Cardiff CF14 3UZ
T 0870-333 3636 F 029-2038 0517
E enquiries@companieshouse.gov.uk
W www.companieshouse.gov.uk
Companies House incorporates companies, registers company documents and provides company information.
Registrar of Companies for England and Wales, Gareth Jones
Registrar of Companies for Scotland, Dorothy Blair

THE INSOLVENCY SERVICE
21 Bloomsbury Street, London WC1B 3QW
Insolvency Enquiry Line 0845-602 9848
Redundancy Enquiry Line 0845-145 0004
W www.insolvency.gov.uk
The role of the service includes administration and investigation of the affairs of bankrupts, partners and companies in compulsory liquidation; dealing with the disqualification of directors in all corporate failures; authorising and regulating the insolvency profession; providing banking and investment services for bankruptcy and liquidation estate funds; assessing and paying statutory entitlement to redundancy payments when an employer cannot, or will not, pay its employees; and advising ministers on insolvency, redundancy and related issues.
Inspector-General and Chief Executive, Stephen Speed
Deputy Inspectors-General, L. T. Cramp; G. Horne
Inspector of Companies, Robert Burns

DEPARTMENT FOR COMMUNITIES AND LOCAL GOVERNMENT

FIRE SERVICE COLLEGE
Moreton-in-Marsh, Gloucestershire GL56 0RH
T 01608-650831 F 01608-651788
W www.fireservicecollege.ac.uk
The Fire Service College provides unique facilities for both practical and theoretical fire fighting, fire safety and accident and emergency training, including urban search and rescue and community safety.
Chief Executive, Gill Newton

ORDNANCE SURVEY
Romsey Road, Southampton SO16 4GU
T 0845-605 0505 F 023-8079 2615
E customerservices@ordnancesurvey.co.uk
W www.ordnancesurvey.co.uk
Ordnance Survey is the national mapping agency for Great Britain. It is a government department and executive agency operating as a trading fund since 1999.
Director-General and Chief Executive, Vanessa Lawrence

PLANNING INSPECTORATE
Temple Quay House, 2 The Square, Temple Quay, Bristol BS1 6PN
T 0117-372 6372 E enquiries@planning-inspectorate.gsi.gov.uk
Crown Buildings, Cathays Park, Cardiff CF10 3NQ
T 029-2082 3866 E wales@planning-inspectorate.gsi.gov.uk
W www.planning-inspectorate.gov.uk
The main work of the inspectorate consists of the processing of planning and enforcement appeals, and holding inquiries into local development plans and frameworks. It also deals with appeals against the decisions of local authorities on planning applications; appeals against local authority enforcement notices; listed building consent appeals; advertisement appeals; rights of way cases; and cases arising from the Environmental Protection and Water acts, the Transport and Works Act 1992 and other highways legislation.
Chief Executive, Katrine Sporle

THE QUEEN ELIZABETH II CONFERENCE CENTRE
Broad Sanctuary, London SW1P 3EE
T 020-7222 5000 F 020-7798 4200
E info@qeiicc.co.uk W www.qeiicc.co.uk
The centre provides secure conference facilities for national and international government and private sector use.
Chief Executive, Ernest Vincent

DEPARTMENT FOR CULTURE, MEDIA AND SPORT

THE ROYAL PARKS
The Old Police House, Hyde Park, London W2 2UH
T 020-7298 2000 F 020-7298 2005
E hq@royalparks.gsi.gov.uk W www.royalparks.org.uk
Royal Parks is responsible for maintaining and developing over 2,000 hectares (5,000 acres) of urban parkland contained within the eight royal parks in London: Bushy Park (with the Longford River); Green Park; Greenwich Park; Hyde Park; Kensington Gardens; Regent's Park (with Primrose Hill); Richmond Park and St James's Park.
Chief Executive, Mark Camley

DEPARTMENT FOR ENVIRONMENT, FOOD AND RURAL AFFAIRS

ANIMAL HEALTH
Corporate Centre, Block C, Government Buildings, Whittington Road, Worcester WR5 2LQ
T 01905-767111 F 01905-768854
E corporate-office@animalhealth.gsi.gov.uk
W www.svs.gov.uk
Animal Health, formerly the State Veterinary Service, is the government's delivery agent for animal health and welfare in England, Scotland and Wales. It is responsible for the prevention, detection and management of diseases in animals; protecting the welfare of farmed animals; the

ıdication of endemic disease; import and export ɪrtification; animal by-product regulation; preparedness : managing exotic animal diseases; and licensing the de in endangered species for conservation purposes.
ɪief Executive, Glenys Stacey

ːNTRAL SCIENCE LABORATORY (CSL)
ɪd Hutton, York YO41 1LZ
01904-462000 F 01904-462111
cience@csl.gov.uk W www.csl.gov.uk
ıe Central Science Laboratory specialises in the sciences derpinning sustainable land use, environmental otection and food safety. It provides a wide range of alytical, diagnostic and consultancy services to ganisations in both the public and private sectors, signed to support the international land-based and od industries.
ɪief Executive, Prof. Michael Roberts

ːNTRE FOR ENVIRONMENT, FISHERIES AND QUACULTURE SCIENCE (CEFAS)
ːefield Road, Lowestoft, Suffolk NR33 0HT
01502-562244 F 01502-513865
www.cefas.co.uk
tablished in April 1997, the agency provides research d consultancy services in fisheries science and ınagement, aquaculture, fish health and hygiene, vironmental impact assessment, and environmental ality assessment.
ɪief Executive, Richard Judge

ƆVERNMENT DECONTAMINATION SERVICE
ɔD Stafford, Beaconside, Stafford ST18 0AQ
)845-850 1323 F 01785-216363
ıds@gds.gsi.gov.uk W www.gds.gov.uk
ıe Government Decontamination Service boosts the <'s capacity to resist and recover from deliberate and cidental releases of chemical, biological, radiological d nuclear materials, and from major accidental releases hazardous materials.
ɪief Executive, Robert Bettley-Smith, FRICS

ARINE AND FISHERIES AGENCY
8 Whitehall Place, London SW1A 2HH
)20-7270 8328 F 020-7270 8345
nfo@mfa.gsi.gov.uk W www.mfa.gov.uk
ıe Marine and Fisheries Agency was established in ːtober 2005 to coordinate for the first time the service livery, inspection and enforcement of activities ɔvided by the government to the fishing industry and ıer marine stakeholders in England and Wales.
ɪief Executive, Nigel Gooding

ːSTICIDES SAFETY DIRECTORATE
ıllard House, Kings Pool, 3 Peasholme Green, York YO1 7PX
01904-455775 F 01904-455733
nformation@psd.defra.gsi.gov.uk W www.pesticides.gov.uk
ıe Pesticides Safety Directorate aims to ensure the safe : of pesticides and detergents for the public and the vironment; to harmonise pesticide regulation within the ıropean Community; and to reduce negative impacts of sticides on the environment.
ɪief Executive, Dr H. K. Wilson

JRAL PAYMENTS AGENCY
ıgs House, 33 Kings Road, Reading RG1 3BU
)845-603 7777 F 0118-959 7736
ɪnquiries@rpa.gsi.gov.uk W www.rpa.gov.uk
The RPA was established in 2001. It is the single paying agency responsible for Common Agricultural Policy (CAP) schemes in England and for certain schemes throughout the UK; it intends to deliver over £2bn of payments to farmers and traders per year.
Chief Executive, Tony Cooper
Chief Operating Officer, Hugh Taylor

VETERINARY LABORATORIES AGENCY
Woodham Lane, New Haw, Addlestone, Surrey KT15 3NB
T 01932-341111 F 01932-347046
E enquiries@vla.defra.gov.uk W www.vla.gov.uk
The Veterinary Laboratories Agency is a regional network of 16 veterinary laboratories and two surveillance centres, which provides all sectors of the animal health industry with animal disease surveillance, diagnostic services and veterinary scientific research.
Chief Executive, Prof. S. Edwards

VETERINARY MEDICINES DIRECTORATE
Woodham Lane, New Haw, Addlestone, Surrey KT15 3LS
T 01932-336911 F 01932-336618
W www.vmd.gov.uk
The Veterinary Medicines Directorate is responsible for all aspects of the authorisation and control of veterinary medicines, including post-authorisation surveillance of residues in animals and animal products, and also for the provision of policy advice to ministers.
Chief Executive, Steve Dean

FOREIGN AND COMMONWEALTH OFFICE

FCO SERVICES
Hanslope Park, Milton Keynes MK19 7BH
T 01908-515789 E fco.serv@fco.gov.uk
W www.fcoservices.gov.uk
FCO Services was established in April 2006. It delivers a combination of secure business-to-business services to the FCO in the UK and at its missions overseas, other UK government departments and public bodies, friendly foreign governments and private sector organisations.

The Corps of Queen's Messengers, couriers of confidential and important documents, was transferred to FCO Services in 2006.
Chief Executive, Chris Moxey
Superintendent of the Corps of Queen's Messengers, Sqn. Ldr. J. S. Frizzell
Queen's Messengers, S. J. Addy; P. Allen; R. Allen; Maj. A. N. D. Bols; Maj. S. Cambridge; Maj. P. C. H. Dening-Smitherman; J. A. Hatfield; Sqn. Ldr. P. J. Hearn; Sqn. Ldr. A. Hill; W. Lisle; Maj. K. J. Rowbottom; Maj. J. H. Steele; R. T. Wilson

WILTON PARK CONFERENCE CENTRE
Wiston House, Steyning, W. Sussex BN44 3DZ
T 01903-815020 F 01903-816373
E admin@wiltonpark.org.uk W www.wiltonpark.org.uk
Wilton Park organises international affairs conferences and is hired out to government departments and commercial users.
Chief Executive, Donald Lamont

DEPARTMENT OF HEALTH

MEDICINES AND HEALTHCARE PRODUCTS REGULATORY AGENCY (MHRA)
Market Towers, 1 Nine Elms Lane, London SW8 5NQ
T 020-7084 2000 F 020-7084 2353
E info@mhra.gsi.gov.uk W www.mhra.gov.uk

The MHRA is responsible for protecting and promoting public and patient safety by ensuring that medicines, healthcare products and medical equipment meet appropriate standards of safety, quality, performance and effectiveness, and are used safely.
Chair, Prof. Sir Alasdair Breckenridge, CBE
Chief Executive, Prof. Kent Woods

NHS PURCHASING AND SUPPLY AGENCY
Premier House, 60 Caversham Road, Reading RG1 7EB
T 0118-980 8600 F 0118-980 8650
E pasa@pasa.nhs.uk W www.pasa.nhs.uk
The agency was established in April 2000 and is responsible for ensuring that the NHS makes the most effective use of its resources by getting the best value for money possible when purchasing goods and services. It works with around 400 NHS trusts and health authorities, and manages in the region of 3,000 national purchasing contracts.
Chief Operating Officer, John Cooper

HOME OFFICE

CRIMINAL RECORDS BUREAU
PO Box 110, Liverpool L69 3EF
T 0870-909 0811 W www.crb.gov.uk
The Criminal Records Bureau was launched in March 2002 and provides access to criminal record information to enable organisations in the public, private and voluntary sectors to make safer recruitment decisions by identifying candidates who may be unsuitable for certain work – especially that which involves children or vulnerable adults.
Chief Executive, Vincent Gaskell

FORENSIC SCIENCE SERVICE (FSS)
see Police Service section

HM PRISON SERVICE
see Prison Service section

IDENTITY AND PASSPORT SERVICE
Globe House, 89 Ecclestone Square, London SW1V 1PN
T Advice Line 0870-521 0410
E info@passport.gov.uk W www.passport.gov.uk
The Identity and Passport Service was established on in April 2006 and incorporates the UK Passport Service. Its role is to provide passport services and, in the future (as part of the National Identity Scheme), identity cards for British and foreign nationals resident in the UK.
Chief Executive, James Hall

DEPARTMENT FOR INNOVATION, UNIVERSITIES AND SKILLS

NATIONAL WEIGHTS AND MEASURES LABORATORY
Stanton Avenue, Teddington, Middx TW11 0JZ
T 020-8943 7272 F 020-8943 7270
E info@nwml.gov.uk W www.nwml.gov.uk
The laboratory is responsible for ensuring all trade measurements are accurate, legal and fair to both buyer and seller. It provides the following services: type approval; mass, length and volume calibration; ISO 9001 certification; metrology training; and consultancy. It is also responsible for the implementation of European directives on measuring instruments.
Chief Executive, Dr Jeff Llewellyn

UK INTELLECTUAL PROPERTY OFFICE
Concept House, Cardiff Road, Newport NP10 8QQ
T 0845-950 0505 F 01633-814444
E enquiries@ipo.gov.uk W www.ipo.gov.uk
The UK Intellectual Property Office, formerly known the Patent Office, was established in 1990 and became trading fund in 1991. The office is responsible f intellectual property (IP) policy and operation in the U and aims to educate business, researchers and the publ about the IP system; facilitate the appropriate protecti and use of rights; design and provide commercial servic to assist business use of the IP system; and create domestic and international legal and political framewor which balances the interests of rights holders with t need for open competition and free markets.
Comptroller-General and Chief Executive, Ian Fletcher

MINISTRY OF JUSTICE

HER MAJESTY'S COURTS SERVICE
see Law Courts and Offices section

LAND REGISTRY
Lincoln's Inn Fields, London WC2A 3PH
T 020-7917 8888 F 020-7955 0110
E propertyinformationteam@landregistry.gsi.gov.uk
W www.landregistry.gov.uk
The registration of title to land was first introduced England and Wales by the Land Registry Act 1862. La Registry keeps and maintains the Land Register f England and Wales, and is an executive agency a trading fund responsible to the Secretary of State f Justice. The Land Register has been open to publ inspection since 1990.
Chief Land Registrar and Chief Executive, Peter Collis, C
Deputy Chief Executive and Business Development Directo, Ted Beardsall, CBE

NATIONAL ARCHIVES
Kew, Richmond, Surrey TW9 4DU
T 020-8876 3444 F 020-8878 8905
E enquiries@nationalarchives.gov.uk
W www.nationalarchives.gov.uk
The National Archives, a government department and executive agency reporting to the Secretary of State f Justice, was formed in April 2003 by bringing togeth the Public Record Office (founded in 1838) and t Historical Manuscripts Commission (founded in 1869).

The National Archives leads on record manageme policy with government, and provides access government records at its sites in Kew and Islington a through digital resources available online. The Nation Archives also oversees information and archi management across the UK, setting standards a providing advice and support to raise the standards information management. OPSI – with its copyrigh legislation and official publishing roles – operates fro within the National Archives.

The organisation administers the UK's public recor system under the Public Records Acts of 1958 and 196 The records it holds span 1,000 years – from t Domesday Book to the latest government papers to released – and fill more than 160km (100 miles) shelving.
Chief Executive, Ms N. Ceeney
Directors, Dr D. Thomas *(Collections and Technology)*; Ms E. Stoddart *(Finance and Corporate Services)*; M. Lamb *(Human Resources and Organisational*

Development); Ms C. Tullo *(Public Sector Information)*; J. Strachan *(Public Services and Marketing)*

)FFICE OF PUBLIC SECTOR INFORMATION
: Clements House, 2–16 Colegate, Norwich NR3 1BQ
01603-723011 W www.opsi.gov.uk
'he Office of Public Sector Information (OPSI) operates 'om within the National Archives as of October 2006, fter previously being attached to the Cabinet Office. It is :sponsible for policy in relation to access and re-use of K public sector information. The legal and statutory :sponsibilities of Her Majesty's Stationery Office HMSO), in relation to statutory publishing and the ıanagement of crown copyright, operate from within the)PSI's wider remit.
)irector/Controller, Carol Tullo

)FFICE OF THE PUBLIC GUARDIAN
rchway Tower, 2 Junction Road, London N19 5SZ
0845-330 2900 F 020-7664 7705
customerservices@publicguardian.gsi.gov.uk
/ www.publicguardian.gov.uk
'he Office of the Public Guardian was established on 1)ctober 2007, in place of the Public Guardianship)ffice. It is responsible for providing services that support ıe financial, property, health and welfare matters of eople lacking in the mental capacity to make decisions ı a particular area. Capacity is assessed in accordance ith the requirements set out in the Mental Capacity Act 005.
'hief Executive and Public Guardian Designate, Richard Brook

RIBUNALS SERVICE
:e Tribunals section

NORTHERN IRELAND OFFICE

:OMPENSATION AGENCY
ɔyston House, 34 Upper Queen Street, Belfast BT1 6FD
028-9024 9944 E comp-agency@nics.gov.uk
/ www.compensationni.gov.uk
he Compensation Agency supports the victims of violent :ime by providing compensation to those who sustain ›ss as a result of actions taken under emergency rovisions legislation.
'hief Executive, Gareth Johnston

ORENSIC SCIENCE NORTHERN IRELAND
51 Belfast Road, Carrickfergus, Co. Antrim BT38 8PL
028-9036 1888 F 028-9036 1900
forensic.science@fsni.gov.uk W www.fsni.gov.uk
orensic Science Northern Ireland aims to enhance the elivery of justice by providing scientific support and dvice for the police and the legal profession, and training ıd analytical support for pathologists.
'hief Executive, Stanley Brown

ORTHERN IRELAND PRISON SERVICE
'e Prison Service section

OUTH JUSTICE AGENCY
orporate Headquarters, 41–43 Waring Street, Belfast BT1 2DY
028-9031 6400 F 028-9031 6402/3
info@yjani.gov.uk W www.youthjusticeagencyni.gov.uk
he Youth Justice Agency aims to prevent children ɔmmitting criminal offences through provision of community-based services, youth conferencing services, attendance centres and secure custody.
Chief Executive, Bill Lockhart, OBE

DEPARTMENT FOR TRANSPORT

DRIVER AND VEHICLE LICENSING AGENCY (DVLA)
Longview Road, Swansea SA6 7JL
T 01792-782341 W www.dvla.gov.uk
The agency was established as an executive agency in 1990 and became a trading fund in 2004. It is responsible for registering and licensing drivers and vehicles, and the collection and enforcement of vehicle excise duty (some £4.9bn annually). The DVLA also maintains records of all those who are entitled to drive various types of vehicle (currently 39 million people), all vehicles entitled to travel on public roads (currently 32 million), and drivers' endorsements, disqualifications and medical conditions.
Chief Executive, Clive Bennett

DRIVING STANDARDS AGENCY
Stanley House, 56 Talbot Street, Nottingham NG1 5GU
T 0115-901 2500 F 0115-901 2510
E customer.services@dsa.gsi.gov.uk
W www.dsa.gov.uk
The agency is responsible for carrying out theory and practical driving tests for car drivers, motorcyclists, bus and lorry drivers, and for maintaining the registers of approved driving instructors and large goods vehicle instructors. It also supervises Compulsory Basic Training (CBT) for learner motorcyclists. There are two area offices, which manage over 400 practical driving test centres across Britain.
Chief Executive, Rosemary Thew

GOVERNMENT CAR AND DESPATCH AGENCY
46 Ponton Road, London SW8 5AX
T 020-7217 3839 F 020-7217 3859
W www.gcda.gov.uk
The agency provides secure transport and mail distribution to government and the public sector.
Chief Executive, Roy Burke

HIGHWAYS AGENCY
123 Buckingham Palace Road, London SW1W 9HA
T 0845-955 6575 Information Line 0845-750 4030
E ha_info@highways.gsi.gov.uk W www.highways.gov.uk
The agency is responsible for delivering the Department for Transport's road programme and for maintaining the 7,754km (4,818 miles) of strategic road network in England (made up of motorways and trunk roads and valued at over £65bn).
Chief Executive, Archie Robertson

MARITIME AND COASTGUARD AGENCY
Spring Place, 105 Commercial Road, Southampton SO15 1EG
T 023-8032 9100 F 023-8032 9374
W www.mcga.gov.uk
The agency's aims are to prevent loss of life, continuously improve maritime safety and protect the marine environment.
Chief Executive, Peter Cardy
Chief Coastguard, Peter Dymond

VEHICLE CERTIFICATION AGENCY
1 Eastgate Office Centre, Eastgate Road, Bristol BS5 6XX
T 0117-952 4235 F 0117-952 4104
E enquiries@vca.gov.uk W www.vca.gov.uk

The agency is the UK authority responsible for ensuring that vehicles and vehicle parts have been designed and constructed to meet internationally agreed standards of safety and environmental protection.
Chief Executive, P. Markwick

VEHICLE AND OPERATOR SERVICES AGENCY
Berkeley House, Croydon Street, Bristol BS5 0DA
T 0117-954 3200 F 0117-954 3212
Enquiry Line 0870-606 0440
E enquiries@vosa.gov.uk W www.vosa.gov.uk
The Vehicle and Operator Services Agency was formed in April 2003 from the merger of the Vehicle Inspectorate and the Traffic Area Network. The agency works with the independent traffic commissioners to improve road safety and the environment; safeguard fair competition by promoting and enforcing compliance with commercial operator licensing requirements; process applications for licences to operate lorries and buses; register bus services; operate and administer testing schemes for all vehicles, including the supervision of the MOT testing scheme; enforce the law on vehicles to ensure that they comply with legal standards and regulations; enforce drivers' hours and licensing requirements; provide training and advice for commercial operators; and investigate vehicle accidents, defects and recalls.
Chief Executive, Stephen J. Tetlow, MBE

HM TREASURY

NATIONAL SAVINGS AND INVESTMENTS
375 Kensington High Street, London W14 8SD
T 020-7348 9200 F 020-7048 9698
E customerenquiries@nsandi.com
W www.nsandi.com
National Savings and Investments came into being in 1861 when the Palmerston government set up the Post Office Savings Bank, a savings scheme which aimed to encourage ordinary wage earners 'to provide for themselves against adversity and ill health'. National Savings and Investments was established as a government department in 1969. It became an executive agency of the Treasury in 1996 and is responsible for the design, marketing and administration of savings and investment products for personal savers and investors. It has approximately 26 million customers with over £70bn invested. *See also* Finance section.
Chief Executive, Jane Platt

OFFICE FOR NATIONAL STATISTICS
1 Drummond Gate, London SW1V 2QQ
T 0845-601 3034 E info@statistics.gov.uk
W www.statistics.gov.uk
ONS was created in 1996 by the merger of the Central Statistical Office and the Office of Population Censuses and Surveys. It is both a government department and an executive agency of the Treasury and is responsible for preparing, interpreting and publishing key statistics on the government, economy and society of the UK. Its key responsibilities include the provision of population estimates and projections and statistics on health and other demographic matters in England and Wales; the production of the UK National Accounts and other key economic indicators; the organisation of population censuses in England and Wales and surveys for government departments and public bodies.

Following a consultation period that ended in June 2006, plans are underway to establish ONS as a non-ministerial department fully independent of government, with governing board that will report directly to parliament.

The General Register Office is part of the ONS and responsible for ensuring the registration of all birth marriages and deaths in England and Wales, and fc maintaining a central archive dating back to 1837.
National Statistician, Director of ONS, Registrar-General for England and Wales, Karen Dunnell

OGC BUYING SOLUTIONS
5th Floor, Royal Liver Building, Pier Head, Liverpool L3 1PE
T 0845-410 2222 F 0151-227 3315
W www.ogcbuyingsolutions.gov.uk
The agency provides a professional procurement service t government departments and other public bodies. Fro April 2000 it became part of the Office of Governme Commerce in the Treasury.
Chief Executive, Alison Littley

ROYAL MINT
Llantrisant, Pontyclun CF72 8YT
T 01443-222111 F 01443-623148
E information.office@royalmint.gov.uk
W www.royalmint.gov.uk
The Royal Mint has operated as a trading fund since 197 and was established as an executive agency in 1990.

The prime responsibility of the Royal Mint is th provision of United Kingdom coinage, but it activel competes in world markets for a share of the availab circulating coin business and about half of the coins an blanks it produces annually are exported. It als manufactures special proof and uncirculated quality coir in gold, silver and other metals; military and civ decorations and medals; commemorative and priz medals; and royal and official seals. In 1999 the Roy Mint was given greater commercial freedom to expand i business into new areas and develop partnerships with th private sector.
Master of the Mint, Chancellor of the Exchequer *(ex officio)*
Chief Executive, D. Barrass

UK DEBT MANAGEMENT OFFICE
Eastcheap Court, 11 Philpot Lane, London EC3M 8UD
T 0845-357 6500 F 0845-357 6509
W www.dmo.gov.uk
The UK Debt Management Office (DMO) was launche as an executive agency of HM Treasury in April 199 The Chancellor of the Exchequer determines the polic and financial framework within which the DMO operate but delegates operational decisions on debt and cas management and the day-to-day running of the office t the chief executive. The DMO's remit is to carry out th government's debt management policy of minimisin financing costs over the long term, and to minimise th cost of offsetting the government's net cash flows ov time, while operating at a level of risk approved b ministers in both cases.
Chief Executive, Robert Stheeman

DEPARTMENT FOR WORK AND PENSIONS

CHILD SUPPORT AGENCY (CSA)
PO Box 55, Brierly Hill, West Midlands DY5 1YL
T 0845-713 3133 F 0845-713 8924
W www.csa.gov.uk

'he CSA was set up in April 1993. It is responsible for the dministration of the Child Support Act and for the ssessment, collection and enforcement of maintenance ayments. Government plans to establish a new rganisation, the Child Maintenance and Enforcement Commission, were outlined in the Child Maintenance Vhite Paper; the commission was due to be in place, with tatutory authority, by the end of 2009.
'hief Executive, Stephen Geraghty

)ISABILITY AND CARERS SERVICE
lock 1, Room 112, Government Buildings, Norcross Lane, lackpool, Lancs FY5 3TA T 0800-882 200
dbu-customer-service@dwp.gsi.gov.uk
V www.dwp.gov.uk/dcs
'he Disability and Carers Service (DCS) aims to enable ie independence of disabled people and carers through ie financial support available from the disability living llowance, attendance allowance and carer's allowance. 'he DCS also delivers payments to those who have ecome disabled as a result of vaccine damage. Currently ie service provides in excess of £13bn per year to over 4 iillion disabled people and carers.
'hief Executive, Terry Moran
'hief Operating Officer, Vivien Hopkins

OBCENTRE PLUS
rst Floor, Steel City House, West Street, Sheffield S1 2GQ
0845-606 0234 E contact-us@jobcentreplus.gsi.gov.uk
V www.jobcentreplus.gov.uk
obcentre Plus was formed in April 2002 following the ierger of the Employment Service and some parts of the enefits Agency. The agency administers claims for, and ayment of, social security benefits to help people gain mployment or improve their prospects for work, as well s helping employers to fill their vacancies.
'hief Executive, Lesley Strathie

'HE PENSION SERVICE
oom 204, Richmond House, 79 Whitehall, London SW1A 2NS
0207-271 2601 Public Enquiries 0845-606 0265
V www.thepensionservice.gov.uk
he Pension Service was launched in April 2002 as an rganisation dedicated to understanding the wishes and eeds of today's and future pensioners, and to providing ate financial support for pensioners.
'hief Executive, Alexis Cleveland

'HE RENT SERVICE
Welbeck Street, London W1G 9YQ
020-7023 6000 F 020-7023 6222
customer.services@therentservice.gov.uk
V www.therentservice.gov.uk
he Rent Service provides a rental valuation service to cal authorities in England, supplying them with a range f valuations to assist them in settling claims for housing enefit. It also provides fair rent determinations for ndlords and tenants under the provisions laid down in ie Rent Act 1977.
'hief Executive, Patrick Boyle

JON-MINISTERIAL GOVERNMENT)EPARTMENTS

SSETS RECOVERY AGENCY
) Box 39992, London EC4M 7XQ
020-7029 5700 E enquiries@ara.gsi.gov.uk
V www.assetsrecovery.gov.uk

The Assets Recovery Agency became operational in February 2003. It reports to the home secretary and was established to disrupt organised criminal enterprises through the recovery of criminal assets. It also works to promote the use of financial investigation as an integral part of criminal investigations.

Subject to the passing of the necessary legislation, a proposed merger of the Assets Recovery Agency and the Serious Organised Crime Agency will take place in April 2008.
Director (acting), Alan McQuillan

CHARITY COMMISSION
PO Box 1227, Liverpool L69 3UG
T 0845-300 0218 E enquiries@charitycommission.gsi.gov.uk
W www.charitycommission.gov.uk

The Charity Commission for England and Wales is the government department whose aim is to give the public confidence in the integrity of charities. It also carries out the functions of the registration, monitoring and support of charities and the investigation of alleged wrongdoing. The commission maintains a computerised register of some 187,000 charities. It is accountable to the courts and, for its efficiency, to the home secretary. There are five commissioners appointed by the Home Office for a fixed term and the commission has offices in London, Liverpool, Taunton and Newport.
Chair, Dame Suzi Leather
Chief Executive, Andrew Hind

CROWN ESTATE
16 New Burlington Place, London W1S 2HX
T 020-7851 5000 F 020-7851 5128
W www.thecrownestate.co.uk

The Crown Estate is valued at more than £5bn, and includes substantial blocks of urban property, primarily in London, almost 108,000 hectares (266,800 acres) of rural land, almost half of the foreshore, and the sea bed out to the twelve nautical mile territorial limit throughout the UK. The Crown Estate is part of the hereditary possessions of the sovereign 'in right of the crown', managed under the provisions of the Crown Estate Act 1961. The Crown Estate has a duty to maintain and enhance the capital value of estate and the income obtained from it. Under the terms of the act, the Crown Estate pays its revenue surplus to the Treasury every year.
Chair, Ian Grant, CBE
Chief Executive, Roger Bright
Board Members, Chris Bartram, FRICS; Sir Donald Curry, KB, CBE; Hugh Duberly, CBE; Jenefer Greenwood, FRICS; Martin Moore; Dinah Nichols, CB
Directors, John Lelliot *(Finance and Information Services)*; Giles Clarke *(Investment and Asset Management)*; Rob Hastings *(Marine Estate)*; Chris Bourchier *(Rural Estate)*

CROWN PROSECUTION SERVICE
50 Ludgate Hill, London EC4M 7EX
T 020-7796 8000 F 020-7796 8680
E enquiries@cps.gsi.gov.uk W www.cps.gov.uk

The Crown Prosecution Service (CPS) is the independent body responsible for prosecuting people in England and Wales. The CPS was established as a result of the Prosecution of Offences Act 1985. It works closely with the police to advise on lines of inquiry and to decide on appropriate charges and other disposals in all but minor cases. *See also* Law Courts and Offices section.

Director of Public Prosecutions, Sir Ken Macdonald, QC
Chief Executive, Peter Lewis

EXPORT CREDITS GUARANTEE DEPARTMENT (ECGD)

PO Box 2200, 2 Exchange Tower, Harbour Exchange Square, London E14 9GS
T 020-7512 7000 F 020-7512 7649
E help@ecgd.gsi.gov.uk W www.ecgd.gov.uk

ECGD is the UK's official export credit agency and was established in 1919. A separate government department reporting to the Secretary of State for Business, Enterprise and Regulatory Reform, it has more than 80 years' experience of working closely with exporters, project sponsors, banks and buyers to help UK exporters of capital equipment and project-related goods and services. ECGD does this by providing help in arranging finance packages for buyers of UK goods by guaranteeing bank loans; insurance against non-payment to UK exporters; and overseas investment insurance – a facility that gives UK investors up to 15 years' insurance against political risks such as war, expropriation and restrictions on remittances.

Chief Executive and Accounting Officer, P. Crawford
Non-Executive Chair, G. Pimlott
Group Directors, S. R. Dodgson *(Business Group)*; David Havelock *(Credit Risk Group)*; Nigel Addison-Smith *(Finance)*; D. N. Ridley *(General Counsel)*; S. Johnson *(Human Resources)*
Non-Executive Directors, D. Godfrey; D. Harrison; P. Haslehurst; K. Letsinger; G. Pimlott

FOOD STANDARDS AGENCY

Aviation House, 125 Kingsway, London WC2B 6NH
T 020-7276 8000 F 020-7276 8004
E helpline@foodstandards.gsi.gov.uk
W www.food.gov.uk

The FSA was established in April 2000 to protect public health from risks arising in connection with the consumption of food, and otherwise to protect the interests of consumers in relation to food. The agency has the general function of developing policy in these areas and provides information and advice to the government, other public bodies and consumers. It also sets standards for and monitors food law enforcement by local authorities. The agency is a UK-wide non-ministerial government body, led by a board which has been appointed to act in the public interest. It has executive offices in Scotland, Wales and Northern Ireland. It is advised by advisory committees on food safety matters of special interest to each of these areas.

Chair, Dame Deirdre Hutton, CBE
Deputy Chair, Dr Ian Reynolds
Chief Executive, John Harwood

FOOD STANDARDS AGENCY NORTHERN IRELAND, 10C Clarendon Road, Belfast BT1 3BG T 028-9041 7700 E infofsani@foodstandards.gsi.gov.uk
FOOD STANDARDS AGENCY SCOTLAND, St Magnus House, 6th Floor, 25 Guild Street, Aberdeen AB11 6NJ T 01224-285100 E scotland@foodstandards.gsi.gov.uk
FOOD STANDARDS AGENCY WALES, 11th Floor, Southgate House, Wood Street, Cardiff CF10 1EW T 029-2067 8999 E wales@foodstandards.gsi.gov.uk

MEAT HYGIENE SERVICE
Kings Pool, Peasholme Green, York YO1 7PR
T 01904-455501 F 01904-455502
E mhs.enquiries@mhs.gov.uk

The Meat Hygiene Service was launched in April 1995 a[s] an agency of the former Ministry of Agriculture, Fisherie[s] and Food, and became an executive agency of the Foo[d] Standards Agency in April 2000. It protects public healt[h] and animal welfare at slaughter through veterinar[y] supervision and meat inspection in approved fresh mea[t] establishments in Great Britain.

Chief Executive, Steve McGrath

FORESTRY COMMISSION

Silvan House, 231 Corstorphine Road, Edinburgh EH12 7AT
T 0131-334 0303 F 0131-334 3047
E enquiries@forestry.gsi.gov.uk W www.forestry.gov.uk

The Forestry Commission is the government departmen[t] responsible for forestry policy in Great Britain. It report[s] directly to forestry ministers (ie the Secretary of State fo[r] Environment, Food and Rural Affairs, the Scottis[h] ministers and the National Assembly for Wales), to whon[n] it is responsible for advice on forestry policy and for th[e] implementation of that policy.

The commission's principal objectives are to protec[t] Britain's forests and woodlands; expand Britain's fores[t] area; enhance the economic value of forest resources[;] conserve and improve the biodiversity, landscape an[d] cultural heritage of forests and woodlands; develo[p] opportunities for woodland recreation; and increas[e] public understanding of, and community participation in forestry.

Chair (part-time), Rt. Hon. Lord Clark of Windermere
Director-General and Deputy Chair, T. Rollinson

FORESTRY COMMISSION ENGLAND, Great Easter[n] House, Tenison Road, Cambridge CB1 2DU T 01223-31454[6]
FORESTRY COMMISSION SCOTLAND, Silvan House[,] 231 Corstorphine Road, Edinburgh EH12 7AT T 0131-334 0303
FORESTRY COMMISSION WALES, Victoria Terrace[,] Aberystwyth, Ceredigion SY23 2DQ T 0845-604 0845
NORTHERN RESEARCH STATION, Roslin, Midlothia[n] EH25 9SY T 0131-445 2176

FOREST ENTERPRISE
Forest Enterprise England, 340 Bristol Business Park, Coldharbour Lane, Bristol BS16 1EJ
T 0117-906 6000 F 0117-931 2859
Forest Enterprise Scotland, 1 Highlander Way, Inverness Busines[s] and Retail Park, Inverness IV2 6GB
T 01463-232811 F 01463-243846

Forest Enterprise was established as an executiv[e] agency of the Forestry Commission in 1996 to manag[e] the UK's forest estate; it ceased to exist as a singl[e] executive agency in March 2003, when three nev[w] agencies were created – one each for England, Wales an[d] Scotland. Forest Enterprise Wales has since been woun[d] up, with its responsibilities reabsorbed by the Forestr[y] Commission.

The agencies in England and Scotland take thei[r] direction from their respective country governments bu[t] their basic remit is to provide environmental, social an[d] economic benefits from the forests they manage.

Chief Executives, Simon Hodgson *(England)*; Dr Hugh Insley *(Scotland)*

OREST RESEARCH

ice Holt Lodge, Farnham, Surrey GU10 4LH
01420-22255 F 01420-23653
' www.forestresearch.gov.uk

orest Research is also an executive agency of the Forestry ommissions. Its objectives are to inform and support restry's contribution to the development and delivery of e policies of the government and devolved ministrations; to provide research, development and onitoring services relevant to UK forestry interests; and transfer knowledge actively and appropriately.
hief Executive, Prof. Jim Lynch
esearch Director, Dr Peter Freer-Smith

M REVENUE AND CUSTOMS

oard of HM Revenue and Customs, 100 Parliament Street, ndon SW1A 2BQ
' www.hmrc.gov.uk

MRC was formed following the integration of the land Revenue and HM Customs and Excise, which was ade formal by parliament in April 2005. It administers, d advises the Chancellor of the Exchequer on, any atters connected with the following areas: income, rporation, capital gains, inheritance, insurance emium, stamp, land and petroleum revenue taxes; vironmental taxes (climate change and aggregates levy, ndfill tax); value added tax (VAT); customs duties and ontier protection; excise duties; National Insurance; tax edits, child benefit and the Child Trust Fund; forcement of the minimum wage; and recovery of udent loan repayments.
hair, Paul Gray, CB
irectors, Stuart Cruickshank; Mike Eland; Mike Hanson, MBE; Dave Hartnett, CB; Steve Heminsley; David Hogg; Chris Hopson; Bernadette Kenny; Steve Lamey

ALUATION OFFICE AGENCY

ew Court, 48 Carey Street, London WC2A 2JE
020-7506 1700 F 020-7506 1998
customerservices@voa.gsi.gov.uk W www.voa.gov.uk

tablished in 1991, the Valuation Office is an executive ency of HM Revenue and Customs. It is responsible for mpiling and maintaining the business rating and uncil tax valuation lists for England and Wales; valuing operty throughout Great Britain for the purposes of xes administered by the Inland Revenue; providing atutory and non-statutory property valuation services in gland, Wales and Scotland; and giving policy advice to inisters on property valuation matters.
hief Executive, Andrew Hudson

ATIONAL SCHOOL OF GOVERNMENT

nningdale Park, Larch Avenue, Ascot, Berks SL5 0QE
01344-634000 F 01344-634233
customer.services@nationalschool.gsi.gov.uk
www.nationalschool.gov.uk

he National School of Government became a separate n-ministerial department on 1 January 2007. It works th nationally and internationally to help government partments and public sector organisations build pacity in good governance and offer more effective, tter value services.
hair, Sir Brian Bender
incipal and Chief Executive, David Spencer

OFFICE OF FAIR TRADING (OFT)

Fleetbank House, 2–6 Salisbury Square, London EC4Y 8JX
T 020-7211 8000
E enquiries@oft.gsi.gov.uk W www.oft.gov.uk

The OFT is a non-ministerial government department established by statute in 1973, and it is the UK's consumer and competition authority. It encourages businesses to comply with competition and consumer law and to improve their trading practices through self-regulation. It acts decisively to stop hardcore or flagrant offenders, studies markets and recommends action where required, and empowers consumers with the knowledge and skills to make informed choices.
Chair, Philip Collins
Chief Executive Officer, John Fingleton

OFFICE OF GAS AND ELECTRICITY MARKETS (OFGEM)

9 Millbank, London SW1P 3GE
T 020-7901 7295 F 020-7901 7196
E consumeraffairs@ofgem.gov.uk W www.ofgem.gov.uk

OFGEM is the regulator for Britain's gas and electricity industries. Its role is to protect and advance the interests of consumers by promoting competition where possible, and through regulation only where necessary. OFGEM operates under the direction and governance of the Gas and Electricity Markets Authority, which makes all major decisions and sets policy priorities for OFGEM. OFGEM's powers are provided for under the Gas Act 1986 and the Electricity Act 1989, as amended by the Utilities Act 2000. It also has enforcement powers under the Competition Act 1998.
Chair, Sir John Mogg
Chief Executive, Alistair Buchanan

OFFICE OF RAIL REGULATION

1 Kemble Street, London WC2B 4AN
T 020-7282 2000 F 020-7282 2045
E rail.library@orr.gsi.gov.uk W www.rail-reg.gov.uk

The Office of the Rail Regulator was set up under the Railways Act 1993. It became the ORR in July 2004, under the provisions of the Railways and Transport Safety Act 2003. On 1 April 2006, in addition to its role as economic regulator, the ORR became the health and safety regulator for the rail industry. This transfer of responsibility from the Health and Safety Executive was given effect under the Railways Act 2005. The board and chair are appointed by the Secretary of State for Transport. The ORR's key roles are to ensure that Network Rail, the owner and operator of the national railway infrastructure (the track and signalling), manages the network efficiently and in a way that meets the needs of its users; to encourage continuous improvement in health and safety performance while securing compliance with relevant health and safety law, including taking enforcement action as necessary; and to develop policy and enhance relevant railway health and safety legislation. It is also responsible for licensing operators of railway assets, setting the terms for access by operators to the network and other railway facilities, and enforcing competition law in the rail sector.
Chair, Chris Bolt
Chief Executive, Bill Emery

OFFICE FOR STANDARDS IN EDUCATION, CHILDREN'S SERVICES AND SKILLS (OFSTED)

Royal Exchange Buildings, St Ann's Square, Manchester M2 7LA
T 0845-404040 W www.ofsted.gov.uk

OFSTED was established under the Education (Schools Act) 1992 and was relaunched on 1 April 2007 with a wider remit, bringing together four formerly separate inspectorates. It inspects and regulates care for children and young people, and inspects education and training for learners of all ages. *See also* The Education System.
HM Chief Inspector, Christine Gilbert, CBE
Chair, Zenna Atkins

POSTAL SERVICES COMMISSION (POSTCOMM)

Hercules House, 6 Hercules Road, London SE1 7DB
T 020-7593 2100 W www.psc.gov.uk

Postcomm is an independent regulator set up by the Postal Services Act 2000 to secure the universal postal service, improve postal services by introducing competition to the UK postal market, and ensure that postal operators, including Royal Mail, meet the needs of their customers throughout the UK. Postcomm also monitors – and reports to the Department for Business, Enterprise and Regulatory Reform on – the network of post offices in the UK.
Chair, Nigel Stapleton
Chief Executive, Sarah Chambers

REVENUE AND CUSTOMS PROSECUTIONS OFFICE (RCPO)

New Kings Beam House, 22 Upper Ground, London SE1 9BT
E enquiries@rcpo.gsi.gov.uk W www.rcpo.gov.uk

The RCPO prosecutes major drug trafficking and tax fraud cases in the UK, currently at a rate of around 2,500 each year. Prior to the establishment of the RCPO in April 2005, criminal prosecutions were handled separately by Customs and Excise and Inland Revenue Lawyers. The RCPO's director is appointed by the attorney-general.
Director, David Green, QC

SECURITY AND INTELLIGENCE SERVICES

GOVERNMENT COMMUNICATIONS HEADQUARTERS (GCHQ)

Hubble Road, Cheltenham GL51 0EX
T 01242-221491 F 01242-574349
E pressoffice@gchq.gsi.gov.uk W www.gchq.gov.uk

GCHQ produces signals intelligence in support of national security and the UK's economic wellbeing, and in the prevention or detection of serious crime. Additionally, GCHQ Communications-Electronics Security Group (CESG) is the national authority for information assurance, and provides advice and assistance to government departments, the armed forces and other national infrastructure bodies on the security of their communications and information systems. GCHQ was placed on a statutory footing by the Intelligence Services Act 1994 and is headed by a director who is directly accountable to the foreign secretary.
Director, Sir David Pepper

SECRET INTELLIGENCE SERVICE (MI6)

PO Box 1300, London SE1 1BD
W www.mi6.gov.uk

The Secret Intelligence Service produces secr intelligence in support of the government's securi defence, foreign and economic policies. It was placed on statutory footing by the Intelligence Services Act 199 and is headed by a chief, known as 'C', who is direct accountable to the foreign secretary.
Chief, Sir J. M. Scarlett, KCMG, OBE

SECURITY SERVICE (MI5)

PO Box 3255, London SW1P 1AE
T 020-7930 9000
W www.mi5.gov.uk

The Security Service is responsible for securi intelligence work against covertly organised threats to tl UK. These include terrorism, espionage and tl proliferation of weapons of mass destruction. Tl Security Service also provides security advice to a wi range of organisations to help reduce vulnerability threats from individuals, groups or countries hostile to U interests. The home secretary has parliamenta accountability for the Security Service.
Director-General, Jonathan Evans

SERIOUS FRAUD OFFICE

Elm House, 10–16 Elm Street, London WC1X 0BJ
T 020-7239 7272 F 020-7837 1689
E public.enquiries@sfo.gsi.gov.uk
W www.sfo.gov.uk

The Serious Fraud Office is an independent governme department that investigates and prosecutes serious complex fraud. It is part of the UK Criminal Justi System. The office is headed by a director who appointed by and accountable to the Attorney-Gener and has jurisdiction over England, Wales and Northe Ireland but not Scotland, the Isle of Man or the Chann Islands.
Director, Robert Wardle

UK TRADE AND INVESTMENT

Kingsgate House, 66–74 Victoria Street, London SW1E 6SW
T 020-7215 8000 W www.uktradeinvest.gov.uk

UK Trade and Investment is a government organisati that aims to enhance the competitiveness of companies the UK through overseas trade and investments, and attract high-quality foreign direct investment.
Chief Executive, Andrew Cahn

WATER SERVICES REGULATION AUTHORITY (OFWAT)

Centre City Tower, 7 Hill Street, Birmingham B5 4UA
T 0121-625 1300 F 0121-625 1400
E enquiries@ofwat.gsi.gov.uk W www.ofwat.gov.uk

OFWAT succeeded the director-general of Water Servic on 1 April 2006. It is the independent economic regulat of the water and sewerage companies in England ar Wales. OFWAT's main duties are to ensure that tl companies can finance and carry out the functio specified in the Water Industry Act 1991 and to prote the interests of water customers, by promoting effecti competition wherever appropriate.
Chair, Philip Fletcher
Chief Executive, Regina Finn

PUBLIC BODIES

The following section is a listing of public bodies, ombudsman services and selected other civil service organisations.

Whereas executive agencies are either part of a government department or are one in their own right (*see* Government Departments section), public bodies carry out their functions to a greater or lesser extent at arm's length from central government. Ministers are ultimately responsible to parliament for the activities of the public bodies sponsored by their department and in almost all cases (except where there is separate statutory provision) ministers make the appointments to their boards. Departments are responsible for funding and ensuring good governance of their public bodies.

The term 'public body' is a general one which includes public corporations, such as the BBC; NHS bodies; and non-departmental public bodies (NDPBs). There were 883 public bodies sponsored by UK government departments as at 31 March 2006. This figure is made up of 21 public corporations, the Bank of England, two public broadcasting authorities, 23 NHS bodies and 836 NDPBs. The NDPB group is made up of 199 executive NDPBs, 448 advisory NDPBs, 40 tribunal NDPBs (counted on the basis of tribunal systems rather than individual boards; *see* Tribunals section) and 149 independent monitoring boards. The following is not a complete listing of these organisations.

ADJUDICATOR'S OFFICE

6th Floor, Haymarket House, 28 Haymarket, London SW1Y 4SP
T 020-7930 2292 F 020-7930 2298
E adjudicators@gtnet.gov.uk W www.adjudicatorsoffice.gov.uk

The Adjudicator's Office opened in 1993 and investigates complaints about the way HM Revenue and Customs, the Valuation Office Agency, the Public Guardianship Office and the Insolvency Service have handled a person's affairs.
The Adjudicator, Dame Barbara Mills, DBE, QC

ADVISORY, CONCILIATION AND ARBITRATION SERVICE (ACAS)

Brandon House, 180 Borough High Street, London SE1 1LW
T 020-7210 3613 Helpline 0845-747 4747 F 020-7210 3708
W www.acas.org.uk

ACAS was set up under the Employment Protection Act 1975 (the provisions now being found in the Trade Union and Labour Relations (Consolidation) Act 1992).

ACAS is funded by the Department for Business, Enterprise and Regulatory Reform and overall guidance is provided by a council consisting of a full-time chair and part-time members from businesses, trade unions and independent sectors. The chair and members are appointed by the Secretary of State for Business, Enterprise and Regulatory Reform. ACAS aims to promote the improvement of industrial relations in general, to provide facilities for conciliation, mediation and arbitration as means of avoiding and resolving industrial disputes, and to provide advisory and information services on industrial relations matters to employers, employees and their representatives.

ACAS has 13 regional offices in Birmingham, Bury St Edmunds, Bristol, Cardiff, Fleet, Glasgow, Leeds, Liverpool, London, Manchester, Newcastle upon Tyne, Nottingham and Paddock Wood.
Chair, Rita Donaghy, CBE
Chief Executive, John Taylor

ADVISORY COUNCIL ON NATIONAL RECORDS AND ARCHIVES

Secretariat : The National Archives, Kew, Surrey TW9 4DU
T 020-8392 5381 F 020-8392 9198
W www.nationalarchives.gov.uk/advisorycouncil

Following the bringing together of the Public Record Office and the Historical Manuscripts Commission to form the National Archives, the advisory council advises on all matters relating to the preservation, use of, and access to historical manuscripts, records and archives of all kinds. The Advisory Council on National Records and Archives encompasses the statutory Advisory Council on Public Records, and advises on public records issues as before.
Chair, Rt. Hon. Sir Anthony Clarke *(Master of the Rolls)*

ANCIENT MONUMENTS BOARD FOR WALES (CADW)

Plas Carew, Unit 5–7 Cefn Coed, Parc Nantgarw,
Cardiff CF15 7QQ
T 01443-336000 F 01443-336001
E cadw@wales.gsi.gov.uk W www.cadw.wales.gov.uk

The Ancient Monuments Advisory Board for Wales advises the Welsh Assembly Government on its statutory functions in respect of ancient monuments.
Chair, Richard Brewer
Members, Prof. Miranda Aldhouse-Green, FSA; Dr Nancy Edwards; Prof. Ralph Griffiths, DLITT; John Hilling; Christopher Musson, MBE, FSA; Dr Emma Plunkett Dillon; Dr Anthony Ward; Prof. Alasdair Whittle, FBA, DPHIL

ARCHITECTURE AND DESIGN SCOTLAND (A+DS)

Bakehouse Close, 146 Canongate, Edinburgh EH8 8DD
T 0131-556 6699 F 0131-556 6633
E info@ads.org.uk W www.ads.org.uk

Architecture and Design Scotland (A+DS) was established in 2005 by the Scottish Executive as the national champion for good architecture, design and planning in the built environment; it works with a wide range of organisations at national, regional and local levels. A+DS also assumed the independent design review and advisory role of the Royal Fine Art Commission for Scotland.
Chair, Raymond Young
Chief Executive, Sebastian Tombs

ARMED FORCES' PAY REVIEW BODY

6th Floor, Kingsgate House, 66–74 Victoria Street,
London SW1E 6SW
T 020-7215 8534 W www.ome.uk.com

The Armed Forces' Pay Review Body was appointed in 1971. It advises the prime minister and the Secretary of State for Defence on the pay and allowances of members of naval, military and air forces of the crown.

Chair, Prof. David Greenaway

Members, Robert Burgin; Alison Gallico; Dr Peter Knight; Prof. Derek Leslie; Keith McNeish; Neil Sherlock; Air Vice-Marshall (retd) Ian Stewart, CB; Dr Anne Wright; Lord Young of Norwood Green

ARTS COUNCIL ENGLAND

14 Great Peter Street, London SW1P 3NQ
T 0845-300 6200 **F** 020-7973 6590
E enquiries@artscouncil.org.uk
W www.artscouncil.org.uk

Arts Council England is the national development agency for the arts in England, distributing public money from government and the National Lottery. Between 2006 and 2008 Arts Council England plans to invest £1.1bn of public funds in the arts in England. Arts Council grants are for individuals, arts organisations, national touring and other people who use the arts in their work.

In 2002, the Arts Council of England and nine regional arts boards joined together to form a single development organisation for the arts. The governing council's members and chair are appointed by the Secretary of State for Culture, Media and Sport usually for a term of four years, and meet approximately five times a year.

Chair, Prof. Sir Christopher Frayling

Members, Diran Adebayo; Janet Barnes; Tom Bloxham, MBE; Kentake Chinyelu-Hope; Lady Hollick; Keith Khan; Prof. Alan Livingston; Sir Brian McMaster, CBE; Francois Matarasso; Elsie Owusu, OBE; Alice Rawsthorn; Dr Tom Shakespeare; Prof. Stuart Timperley; Dorothy Wilson

Chief Executive, Peter Hewitt

ARTS COUNCIL OF NORTHERN IRELAND

77 Malone Road, Belfast BT9 6AQ
T 028-9038 5200 **F** 028-9066 1715
E info@artscouncil-ni.org **W** www.artscouncil-ni.org

The Arts Council of Northern Ireland is the prime distributor of government funds in support of the arts in Northern Ireland. It is funded by the Department of Culture, Arts and Leisure and from National Lottery funds. In January 2007, the council launched a five-year plan which aims to increase arts funding from £6 to £10 per capita (an increase of approximately £20m for the period up to 2012).

Chair, Rosemary Kelly

Members, Eithne Benson; Kate Bond; Martin Bradley *(Vice-Chair)*; Lucy Finnegan; Raymond Fullerton; Anthony Kennedy; Tim Kerr; Jill McEneaney; Bill Montgomery; Sharon O'Connor; Gearoid O'Heara; Peter Spratt

Chief Executive, Roisin McDonough

ARTS COUNCIL OF WALES

9 Museum Place, Cardiff CF10 3NX
T 029-2037 6500 **F** 029-2022 1447
E feedback@artswales.org.uk
W www.artswales.org.uk

The Arts Council of Wales was established in 1994 by royal charter and is the development body for the arts in Wales. It funds arts organisations with funding from the National Assembly for Wales and is the distributor of National Lottery funds to the arts in Wales. The grant for 2006–7 was £26.6m from the National Assembly and £11.3m from the National Lottery.

Chair, Prof. Dai Smith

Members, Simon Dancey; Maggie Hampton; John Metcalf; Robin Morrison; Christopher O'Neil; Dr Ian J. Rees; Clive Sefia; Ruth Till; David Vokes; Debbie Wilcox; Rhiannon Wyn Hughes

Chief Executive, Peter Tyndall

AUDIT COMMISSION

1st Floor, Millbank Tower, London SW1P 4HQ
T 020-7828 1212 **F** 020-7976 6187
E enquiries@audit-commission.gov.uk
W www.audit-commission.gov.uk

The Audit Commission was set up in 1983 and is an independent body responsible for ensuring that public money is spent economically, efficiently and effectively, to achieve high-quality local services for the public. Its remit covers around 11,000 bodies in England, which between them spend more than £180bn of public money each year. Its work covers local government, health, criminal justice organisations and public services.

The commission has a chair, a deputy chair and a board of up to 20 commissioners who are appointed by the Department of Communities and Local Government following consultation with key stakeholders.

Chair, Michael Higgins

Members, S. Bundred *(ex officio)*; Jim Coulter; Dr Jennifer Dixon; Sheila Drew Smith; Cllr Stephen Houghton; Cllr Peter Jones; Sir Thomas Legg; David Moss; Brian Pomeroy, CBE; Prof. Peter Smith; Cllr Chris White

Chief Executive, Steve Bundred

BANK OF ENGLAND

Threadneedle Street, London EC2R 8AH
T 020-7601 4444 **F** 020-7601 4771
E enquiries@bankofengland.co.uk
W www.bankofengland.co.uk

The Bank of England was incorporated in 1694 under royal charter. It is the banker of the government and it manages the issue of banknotes. Since 1997 it has been operationally independent and its Monetary Policy Committee has had responsibility for setting short-term interest rates to meet the government's inflation target. As the central reserve bank of the country, the Bank of England keeps the accounts of British banks, who maintain with it a proportion of their cash resources, and of most overseas central banks. The bank's core purposes are monetary stability and financial stability. Its responsibility for banking supervision was transferred to the Financial Services Authority in 1998.

Governor, M. A. King

Deputy Governors, Sir John Gieve, CB; Ms R. Lomax

Non-Executive Directors, B. Barber; Ms A. C. Fawcett, CBE; Mrs M. Francis, LVO; Sir Graham Hall; Hon. Peter Jay; Prof. Sir John Likierman; C. McCarthy; P. Myners; Sir Thomas Parker; Dr D. Potter, CBE; Ms H. Rabbats, CBE; David Rhind; A. Sarin; James Strachan; G. Wilkinson; Bob Wigley

Monetary Policy Committee, The Governor; the Deputy Governors; Mrs K. Barker; C. Bean; Prof. Tim Besley; D. Blanchflower; Dr Andrew Sentance; P. Tucker

Advisers to the Governor, M. Blejer; Juliet Wheldon
Chief Cashier and Executive Director, Banking Services, A. Bailey
The Auditor, S. Brown

BIG LOTTERY FUND

1 Plough Place, London EC4A 1DE
T 020-7211 1800 F 020-7211 1750
Advice Line 0845-410 2030
E general.enquiries@biglotteryfund.org.uk
W www.biglotteryfund.org.uk

The Big Lottery Fund was launched in 2004, merging the New Opportunities Fund and the Community Fund. The fund receives 50 per cent of the proceeds raised for good causes through the sale of lottery tickets, which is currently between £600m and £700m per year (this level of funding is guaranteed until the current Camelot licence expires in 2009). The money is distributed to charitable, benevolent and philanthropic organisations in the voluntary and community sectors, as well as health, education and environmental projects. The Big Lottery Fund also assumed the Millennium Commission's role of supporting large-scale regenerative projects.

Chair, Prof. Sir Clive Booth
Vice-Chair, Anna Southall
Regional Chairs, Sanjay Dighe *(England)*; Breidge Gadd, CBE *(Northern Ireland)*; Alison Magee *(Scotland)*; Huw Vaughan *(Wales)*
General Members, Judith Donovan, CBE; Roland Doven, MBE; John Gartside, OBE; Esther O'Callaghan; Albert Tucker; Diana Whitworth
Chief Executive, Stephen Dunmore
Directors, Walter Rader *(Northern Ireland)*; Dharmendra Kanani *(Scotland)*; Ceri Doyle *(Wales)*

BOUNDARY COMMISSIONS

The commissions, established in 1944, are constituted under the Parliamentary Constituencies Act 1986 (as amended). The Speaker of the House of Commons is *ex officio* chair of all four commissions in the UK. Each of the four commissions is required by law to keep the parliamentary constituencies in their part of the UK under review. The latest Boundary Commission report for England was laid before parliament in February 2007, and the proposals outlined will take effect at the next general election. The latest report from Northern Ireland was published in May 2006, from Wales in January 2005 and the most recent Scottish report was completed in December 2004.

ENGLAND

1 Drummond Gate, London SW1V 2QQ
T 020-7533 5177 F 020-7533 5176
E bcomm.england@ons.gov.uk W www.statistics.gov.uk/pbc/
Deputy Chair, Hon. Mr Justice Sullivan

WALES

1st Floor, Caradog House, 1–6 St Andrews Place, Cardiff CF10 3BE
T 029-2039 5031 F 029-2039 5250
E bcomm.wales@wales.gsi.gov.uk
W www.bcomm-wales.gov.uk
Deputy Chair, Hon. Justice Lloyd Jones

SCOTLAND

3 Drumsheugh Gardens, Edinburgh EH3 7QJ
T 0131-538 7200 F 0131-538 7240
E secretariat@bcomm-scotland.gov.uk
W www.bcomm-scotland.gov.uk
Deputy Chair, Hon. Lord McEwan

NORTHERN IRELAND

Forestview, Purdy's Lane, Newtownbreda, Belfast BT8 7AR
T 028-9069 4800 F 028-9069 4801
E bcni@belfast.org.uk W www.boundarycommission.org.uk
Deputy Chair, Hon. Mr Justice Coghlin

BRITISH BROADCASTING CORPORATION (BBC)

Television Centre, Wood Lane, London W12 7RJ
T 020-8743 8000 BBC Information Line 0870-010 0222
W www.bbc.co.uk

The BBC was incorporated under royal charter in 1926 as successor to the British Broadcasting Company Ltd. The BBC's current charter, which came into force on 1 January 2007 and extends to 31 December 2016, recognises the BBC's editorial independence and sets out its public purposes. The BBC Trust was formed under the new charter and replaces the Board of Governors; it sets the strategic direction of the BBC and has a duty to represent the interests of licence fee payers. The chair, vice-chair and other trustees are appointed by the Queen-in-Council. The BBC is financed by revenue from receiving licences for the home services and by grant-in-aid from parliament for the World Service (radio). *See also* Broadcasting section.

BBC TRUST MEMBERS

Chair, Sir Michael Lyons
Vice-Chair, Chitra Bharucha
National Trustees, Alison Hastings *(England)*; Rotha Johnston *(N. Ireland)*; Janet Lewis-Jones *(Wales)*; Jeremy Peat *(Scotland)*
Trustees, Diane Coyle; Dermot Gleeson; Patricia Hodgson; David Liddiment; Mehmuda Mian Pritchard; Richard Tait

EXECUTIVE BOARD

Director-General and Chair, Mark Thompson
Deputy Director-General, Mark Byford
Directors, Jenny Abramsky *(Audio and Music)*; Jana Bennett *(Vision)*; Tim Davie *(Marketing, Communications and Audiences)*; Ashley Highfield *(Future Media and Technology)*; Stephen Kelly *(People)*; Zarin Patel *(Group Finance)*
Chief Executive, BBC Worldwide, John Smith
Chief Operating Officer, Caroline Thomas
Senior Independent Director, Marcus Agius
Non-Executive Directors, Dr Mike Lynch, OBE; David Robbie; Dr Samir Shah, OBE; Robert Webb, QC

STATION CONTROLLERS

BBC1, Peter Fincham
BBC2, Roly Keating
BBC3, Danny Cohen
BBC4, Janice Hadlow
BBC News 24, Kevin Bakhurst
BBC Parliament, Peter Knowles
BBC Northern Ireland, Peter Johnston
BBC Scotland, Ken MacQuarrie
BBC Wales, Menna Richards
Radio 1, Andy Parfitt
Radio 2, Lesley Douglas
Radio 3, Roger Wright

Radio 4, Mark Damazer
Radio 5 Live, Bob Shennan

BRITISH COUNCIL

Bridgewater House, 58 Whitworth Street, Manchester M1 6BB
T 0161-957 7755 F 0161-957 7762
E general.enquiries@britishcouncil.org
W www.britishcouncil.org

The British Council was established in 1934, incorporated by royal charter in 1940 and granted a supplemental charter in 1993. It is an independent, non-political organisation which promotes Britain abroad and is the UK's international organisation for educational and cultural relations. The British Council is represented in 216 towns and cities in 109 countries. Turnover in 2005–6, including Foreign and Commonwealth Office grants and contracted money, was £512m.
Chair, Lord Kinnock, PC
Chief Executive, Martin Davidson, CMG

BRITISH FILM INSTITUTE (BFI)

21 Stephen Street, London W1T 1LN
T 020-7255 1444 F 020-7436 0165
W www.bfi.org.uk

The BFI, established in 1933, offers opportunities for people throughout the UK to experience, learn and discover more about the world of film and moving image culture. It incorporates the BFI National Archive, the BFI National Library, a range of video and DVD releases, publications and educational materials (including the monthly *Sight and Sound* magazine), BFI Southbank, BFI Distribution, the annual BFI London Film Festival as well as the BFI London Lesbian and Gay Film Festival, and the BFI IMAX cinema, and provides advice and support for regional cinemas and film festivals across the UK.
Chair, Anthony Minghella, CBE
Director, Amanda Nevill

BRITISH LIBRARY

96 Euston Road, London NW1 2DB
T 020-7412 7332 F 020-7412 7340
E visitor-services@bl.uk W www.bl.uk

The British Library was established in 1973. It is the UK's national library and occupies a key position in the library and information network. It aims to serve scholarship, research, industry, commerce and all other major users of information. Its services are based on a collection of 150 million separate items, including books, journals, manuscripts, maps, stamps, music, patents, newspapers and sound recordings in all written and spoken languages. The library is now based at three sites: London (St Pancras and Colindale) and Boston Spa, W. Yorks. The library's sponsoring department is the Department for Culture, Media and Sport.

Access to the reading rooms at St Pancras is limited to holders of a British Library reader's pass; information about eligibility is available from the reader admissions office. The exhibition galleries and public areas are open to all, free of charge.

BRITISH LIBRARY BOARD
Chair, Sir Colin Lucas
Chief Executive and Deputy Chair, Mrs L. Brindley
Members, Ms D. Airey; H. Boyd-Carpenter, KCVO; R. S. Broadhurst, CBE; Prof. R. Burgess; Sir K. Calman; Ms S. Forbes, CBE; Prof. W. Hall, CBE; Ms E. Mackay, CB; Prof. K. McLuskie; S. Olswang; Dr G. W. Roberts; M. Semple, OBE

SCHOLARSHIP AND COLLECTIONS
Americas Collections, T 020-7412 7743
Asia, Pacific and Africa Collections, T 020-7412 7873
British and Irish Collections, T 020-7412 7538
British Library Newspapers, Colindale Avenue, London NW9 5HE T 020-7412 7353
British Library Sound Archive, T 020-7412 7676
Early Printed Collections, T 020-7412 7676
Map Library, T 020-7412 7702
Music Library, T 020-7412 7772
Philatelic Collections, T 020-7412 7635
Reader Information, T 020-7412 7676
West European Collections, T 020-7412 7572

OPERATIONS AND SERVICES
Permission Clearance, T 020-7412 7755
Research Services, T 020-7412 7797

SCIENCE, TECHNOLOGY AND INNOVATION
Business, T 020-7412 7454
National Preservation Office, T 020-7412 7612
Patents, T 020-7412 7919
Science and Technology, T 020-7412 7494/7288
Social Science, Law and Official Publications, T 020-7412 7536

BRITISH LIBRARY, BOSTON SPA
Boston Spa, Wetherby, W. Yorks LS23 7BQ
T 01937-546000

BRITISH MUSEUM

Great Russell Street, London WC1B 3DG
T 020-7323 8000 F 020-7323 8616
E information@thebritishmuseum.ac.uk
W www.thebritishmuseum.ac.uk

The British Museum houses the national collection of antiquities, ethnography, coins and paper money, medals, prints and drawings. The British Museum may be said to date from 1753, when parliament approved the holding of a public lottery to raise funds for the purchase of the collections of Sir Hans Sloane and the Harleian manuscripts, and for their proper housing and maintenance. The building (Montagu House) was opened in 1759. The existing buildings were erected between 1823 and the present day, and the original collection has increased to its current dimensions by gifts and purchases. Total government grant-in-aid for 2006–7 was in the region of £40m.

BOARD OF TRUSTEES
Appointed by the Sovereign, HRH The Duke of Gloucester, KG, GCVO
Appointed by the Prime Minister, Chief Emeka Anyaoku; Lord Broers; Sir Ronald Cohen; Prof. Sir Barry Cunliffe, CBE; Francis Finlay; Niall FitzGerald, KBE *(Chair)*; Val Gooding, OBE; Bonnie Greer; Baroness Kennedy; Richard Lambert; David Lindsell; Dr David Norgrove; Eric Salama; Vikram Seth, CBE
Appointed by the Trustees of the British Museum, Stephen Green; Lord Powell of Bayswater, KCMG; Sir John Tusa
Appointed by the Royal Society, Dr Olga Kennard; Ms Edmee P. Leventis

Appointed by the Royal Academy, Antony Gormley, OBE
Appointed by the British Academy, Sir Keith Thomas, FBA

OFFICERS
Director, Neil MacGregor
Deputy Director, Andrew Burnett
Director of Communications, Joanna Mackle
Director of Marketing and Public Affairs, Gillian Marsh
Director of Operations, Chris Rofe
Heads of Departments, Simon Neale *(Capital Projects)*; Joanna Mackle *(Communications)*; Xerxes Mazda *(Education)*; Stephen Gill *(Facilities)*; Zoe Hancock *(Finance, acting)*; Carolyn Young *(Membership Development)*

KEEPERS
Keeper of Ancient Near East Antiquities, Dr John Curtis
Keeper of Coins and Medals, Joe Cribb
Keeper of Department of Asia, Jan Stuart
Keeper of Ancient Egypt and Sudan, Vivian Davies
Keeper of Africa, Oceania and the Americas, Jonathan King
Keeper of Greek and Roman Antiquities, Dr Dyfri Williams
Keeper of Prehistory and Europe, Jonathan Williams
Keeper of Prints and Drawings, Antony Griffiths
Conservation, Documentation and Science, David Saunders

BRITISH PHARMACOPOEIA COMMISSION

Market Towers, 1 Nine Elms Lane, London SW8 5NQ
T 020-7084 2561 E bpcom@mhra.gsi.gov.uk
W www.pharmacopoeia.org.uk

The British Pharmacopoeia Commission sets standards for medicinal products used in human and veterinary medicines and is responsible for publication of the *British Pharmacopoeia* (a publicly available statement of the standard that a product must meet throughout its shelf-life), the *British Pharmacopoeia (Veterinary)* and the *British Approved Names.* It has 17 members, including two lay members, who are appointed by the NHS Appointments Commission (the body responsible for appointments to all of the Medicines Act advisory bodies).
Chair, Prof. A. D. Woolfson
Vice-Chair, V'lain Fenton-May
Secretary and Scientific Director, Dr M. G. Lee

BRITISH WATERWAYS

Willow Grange, Church Road, Watford WD17 4QA
T 01923-201120 F 01923-201400
E enquiries.hq@britishwaterways.co.uk
W www.britishwaterways.co.uk

British Waterways conserves and manages the network of over 3,540km (2,200 miles) of canals and rivers in England, Scotland and Wales. Its sponsoring departments are the Department for Environment, Food and Rural Affairs in England and Wales, and the Enterprise, Transport and Lifelong Learning Department in Scotland.

Its responsibilities include maintaining the waterways and structures on and around them; looking after wildlife and the waterway environment; and ensuring that canals and rivers are safe and enjoyable places to visit.
Chair, Tony Hales
Vice-Chair, Dr Campbell Christie, CBE
Chief Executive, Robin Evans, FRICS

CENTRAL ARBITRATION COMMITTEE (CAC)

PO Box 51547, London SE1 1ZG
T 020-7904 2300 F 020-7904 2301
E enquiries@cac.gov.uk W www.cac.gov.uk

The CAC is a permanent independent body with statutory powers whose main function is to adjudicate on applications relating to the statutory recognition and de-recognition of trade unions for collective bargaining purposes, where such recognition or de-recognition cannot be agreed voluntarily. In addition, the CAC has a statutory role in determining disputes between trade unions and employers over the disclosure of information for collective bargaining purposes, and in resolving applications and complaints under the information and consultation regulations, and performs a similar role in relation to the legislation on the European Works Council, European companies and the European cooperative societies. The CAC also provides voluntary arbitration in industrial disputes.

The committee consists of a chair and 11 deputy chairs, 29 members experienced as representatives of employers and 26 members experienced as representatives of workers. All members of the committee are appointed by the Secretary of State for Business, Enterprise and Regulatory Reform after consulting ACAS.
Chair, Sir Michael Burton
Chief Executive, Graeme Charles

CERTIFICATION OFFICE FOR TRADE UNIONS AND EMPLOYERS' ASSOCIATIONS

Brandon House, 180 Borough High Street, London SE1 1LW
T 020-7210 3734 F 020-7210 3612
E info@certoffice.org W www.certoffice.org

The Certification Office is an independent statutory authority. The certification officer is appointed by the Secretary of State for Business, Enterprise and Regulatory Reform and is responsible for receiving and scrutinising annual returns from trade unions and employers' associations; for determining complaints concerning trade union elections, certain ballots and certain breaches of trade union rules; for ensuring observance of statutory requirements governing mergers between trade unions and employers' associations; for overseeing the political funds and finances of trade unions and employers' associations; and for certifying the independence of trade unions.
Certification Officer, David Cockburn

SCOTLAND
69A George Street, Edinburgh EH2 2JG
T 0131-220 7660
Certification Officer for Scotland, Christine Stuart

CHURCH COMMISSIONERS

Church House, Great Smith Street, London SW1P 3AZ
T 020-7898 1000 F 020-7898 1131
E commissioners.enquiry@c-of-e.org
W www.cofe.anglican.org/about/churchcommissioners

The Church Commissioners were established in 1948 by the amalgamation of Queen Anne's Bounty (established 1704) and the Ecclesiastical Commissioners (established 1836). They are responsible for the management of some of the Church of England's assets, the income from which is predominantly used to help pay for the stipend and pension of the clergy. The commissioners own over 48,500ha (120,000 acres) of agricultural land, a residential estate in central London, and commercial property across Great Britain. They also carry out administrative duties in connection with pastoral reorganisation and redundant churches.

The commissioners are: the Archbishops of Canterbury and of York; four bishops, three clergy and four lay persons elected by the respective houses of the General Synod; two deans elected by all the deans; three persons nominated by the Queen; three persons nominated by the Archbishops of Canterbury and York; three persons nominated by the archbishops after consultation with others including the Lord Mayors of London and York and the vice-chancellors of the universities of Oxford and Cambridge; the First Lord of the Treasury; the Lord President of the Council; the home secretary; the Lord Chancellor; the Secretary of State for Culture, Media and Sport; and the Speaker of the House of Commons.

CHURCH ESTATES COMMISSIONERS
First, A. Whittam Smith
Second, Sir Stuart Bell, MP
Third, T. E. H. Walker

OFFICERS
Secretary, A. C. Brown

ASSISTANT SECRETARIES
Chief Surveyor, P. Clark
Chief Investments Manager, M. Chaloner
Pastoral and Redundant Churches, P. Lewis
Official Solicitor, S. Jones

CIVIL AVIATION AUTHORITY (CAA)

CAA House, 45–59 Kingsway, London WC2B 6TE
T 020-7379 7311 E infoservices@caa.co.uk
W www.caa.co.uk

The CAA is the UK's specialist aviation regulator. Its responsibilities include ensuring that the aviation industry meets the highest technical and operational safety standards; preventing holidaymakers from being stranded abroad or losing money because of tour operator insolvency; planning and regulating all UK airspace; regulating airports, air traffic services and airlines; and providing advice on aviation policy from an economic standpoint. The government provides no direct funding; the CAA must meet its costs entirely from charges on those whom it regulates.
Chair, Sir Roy McNulty, CBE

THE COAL AUTHORITY

200 Lichfield Lane, Mansfield, Notts NG18 4RG
T 01623-637000 F 01623-622072
E thecoalauthority@coal.gov.uk W www.coal.gov.uk

The Coal Authority was established under the Coal Industry Act 1994 to manage certain functions previously undertaken by British Coal, including ownership of unworked coal. It is responsible for licensing coal mining operations and for providing information on coal reserves and past and future coal mining. It settles subsidence damage claims which are not the reponsibility of licensed coal mining operators. It deals with the management and disposal of property, and with surface hazards such as abandoned coal mine shafts.
Chair, Dr Helen Mounsey
Chief Executive, Philip Lawrence

COLLEGE OF ARMS (HERALDS' COLLEGE)

Queen Victoria Street, London EC4V 4BT
T 020-7248 2762 F 020-7248 6448
E enquiries@college-of-arms.gov.uk
W www.college-of-arms.gov.uk

The Sovereign's Officers of Arms (Kings, Heralds and Pursuivants of Arms) were first incorporated by Richard III in 1484. The powers vested by the crown in the Earl Marshal (the Duke of Norfolk) with regard to state ceremonial are largely exercised through the college. The college is also the official repository of the arms and pedigrees of English, Welsh, Northern Irish and Commonwealth (except Canadian) families and their descendants, and its records include official copies of the records of the Ulster King of Arms, the originals of which remain in Dublin. The 13 officers of the college specialise in genealogical and heraldic work for their respective clients.

Arms have long been, and still are, granted by letters patent from the Kings of Arms. A right to arms can only be established by the registration in the official records of the College of Arms of a pedigree showing direct male line descent from an ancestor already appearing therein as being entitled to arms, or by making application through the College of Arms for a grant of arms. Grants are made to corporations as well as to individuals.
Earl Marshal, Duke of Norfolk

KINGS OF ARMS
Garter, P. L. Gwynn-Jones, CVO, FSA
Clarenceux, D. H. B. Chesshyre, CVO, FSA
Norroy and Ulster, T. Woodcock, LVO, FSA

HERALDS
Richmond (and Earl Marshal's Secretary), P. L. Dickinson, LVO
York, H. E. Paston-Bedingfeld
Chester, T. H. S. Duke
Lancaster, R. J. B. Noel
Windsor (and Registrar), W. G. Hunt, TD
Somerset, D. V. White

PURSUIVANTS
Rouge Dragon, C. E. A. Cheesman
Bluemantle, M. P. D. O'Donoghue

COMMISSION FOR ARCHITECTURE AND THE BUILT ENVIRONMENT (CABE)

1 Kemble Street, London WC2B 4AN
T 020-7070 6700 F 020-7070 6777
E enquiries@cabe.org.uk W www.cabe.org.uk

CABE was established in 1999 and is responsible for promoting the importance of high-quality architecture and urban design, and for encouraging the understanding of architecture through educational and regional initiatives. The commission offers free advice to local authorities, public sector clients and others embarking on building projects of any size or purpose. CABE has a board of 16 commissioners, appointed by the Secretary of State for Culture, Media and Sport for a maximum of two four-year terms.
Chair, John Sorrell
Chief Executive, Richard Simmons

COMMISSION FOR INTEGRATED TRANSPORT (CFIT)

1/F16, Ashdown House, 123 Victoria Street, London SW1E 6DE
T 020-7944 8131 F 020-7944 8643
E cfit@dft.gsi.gov.uk W www.cfit.gov.uk

The CfIT was established in June 1999. Its role is to provide independent expert advice to the government in order to achieve a transport system that supports sustainable development. The CfIT also encourages best practice amongst local authorities and delivery agencies, and assesses both the impact of new technology on future policy options and transport policy initiatives from outside the UK. Members of the commission are appointed by the transport secretary.

Chair, Peter Hendy
Vice-Chair, David Leeder

COMMISSION FOR EQUALITY AND HUMAN RIGHTS (CEHR)

Kingsgate House, 66–74 Victoria Street, London SW1E 6SW
T 020-7215 8415 F 020-7215 8225
W www.cehr.org.uk

The CEHR is a statutory body, established under the Equality Act 2006 and launched in October 2007. It inherited the responsibilities of the Commission for Racial Equality, the Disability Rights Commission and the Equal Opportunities Commission. The CEHR's purpose is to reduce inequality, eliminate discrimination, strengthen relations between people, and promote and protect human rights. It enforces equality legislation on age, disability and health, gender, race, religion and belief, sexual orientation or transgender status, and encourages compliance with the Human Rights Act 1998 throughout England, Wales and Scotland.

The Secretary of State for Communities and Local Government appoints the chair and commissioners of the board, which has a maximum of 15 members including a commissioner each for Wales and Scotland, and one who is or has been a disabled person.

Chair, Trevor Phillips
Deputy Chair, Baroness Prosser, OBE
Commissioners, Morag Alexander; Kay Allen; Dame Jane Campbell, DBE; Kay Carberry; Jeannie Drake, CBE; Baroness Greengross, OBE; Prof. Kay Hampton; Francesca Klug; Sir Bert Massie, CBE; Ziauddin Sardar; Ben Summerskill; Dr Neil Wooding
Chief Executive, Dr Nicola Brewer

COMMISSION FOR RURAL COMMUNITIES

John Dower House, Crescent Place, Cheltenham GL50 3RA
T 01242-521381 E info@ruralcommunities.gov.uk
W www.ruralcommunities.gov.uk

The Commission for Rural Communities was established in October 2006; it was formerly an operating division of the now-defunct Countryside Agency. It is a statutory body under the Natural Environment and Rural Communities Act 2006 and it aims to provide well-informed, independent advice to government and to ensure that policies reflect the needs of people living and working in rural England, with a particular focus on tackling disadvantage. Its three key roles are to be a rural advocate, an expert adviser and an independent watchdog. The commission is funded by an annual grant from the Department for Environment, Food and Rural Affairs and board members are appointed by the secretary of state.

Chair and Rural Advocate, Dr Stuart Burgess
Members, Prof. Sheena Asthana; Richard Burge; Dr Jim Cox, OBE; Elinor Goodman; Alison McLean; Howard Petch, CBE; Prof. Mark Shucksmith; John Varley; Prof. Michael Winter, OBE
Chief Executive, Graham Garbutt

COMMITTEE ON STANDARDS IN PUBLIC LIFE

35 Great Smith Street, London SW1P 3BQ
T 020-7276 2595 F 020-7276 2585
E standards@evidence.x.gsi.gov.uk
W www.public-standards.gov.uk

The Committee on Standards in Public Life was set up in October 1994. It is a standing body whose chair and members are appointed by the prime minister; three members are nominated by the leaders of the three main political parties. The committee's remit is to examine concerns about standards of conduct of all holders of public office, including arrangements relating to financial and commercial activities, and to make recommendations as to any changes in present arrangements which might be required to ensure the highest standards of propriety in public life. It is also charged with reviewing issues in relation to the funding of political parties. The committee does not investigate individual allegations of misconduct.

Chair (acting), Rita Donaghy, CBE
Members, Lloyd Clark, QPM; Prof. Hazel Genn, CBE; Dame Patricia Hodgson, DBE; Baroness Maddock; Rt. Hon. Baroness Shephard of Northwold; Dr Elizabeth Vallance; Dr Brian Woods-Scawen

COMMONWEALTH WAR GRAVES COMMISSION

2 Marlow Road, Maidenhead, Berks SL6 7DX
T 01628-634221 F 01628-771208
E casualty.enq@cwgc.org W www.cwgc.org

The Commonwealth War Graves Commission (formerly Imperial War Graves Commission) was founded by royal charter in 1917. It is responsible for the commemoration of around 1.7 million members of the forces of the Commonwealth who lost their lives in the two world wars. More than one million graves are maintained in 23,274 burial grounds throughout the world. Over three-quarters of a million men and women who have no known grave or who were cremated are commemorated by name on memorials built by the commission.

The funds of the commission are derived from the six participating governments, ie the UK, Canada, Australia, New Zealand, South Africa and India.

President, HRH The Duke of Kent, KG, GCMG, GCVO, ADC
Chair, Secretary of State for Defence (UK)
Vice-Chair, Air Chief Marshal Sir Peter Squire, GCB, DFC, AFC, DSC
Members, High Commissioners in London for Australia, Canada, South Africa, New Zealand and India; Adm. Sir Ian Garnett, KCB; Lt.-Gen. Sir Alistair Irwin, KCB, CBE; Ian Henderson, CBE, FRICS; Sara Jones, CBE; Alan Meale, MP; Hon. Nicholas Soames, MP; Prof. Huw Strachan, FRSE; Sir Rob Young, GCMG

Director-General and Secretary to the Commission, R. E. Kellaway, CBE
Deputy Director-General, T. V. Reeves
Legal Adviser and Solicitor, G. C. Reddie

COMPETITION COMMISSION

Victoria House, Southampton Row, London WC1B 4AD
T 020-7271 0100
E info@cc.gsi.gov.uk W www.competition-commission.org.uk

The commission was established in 1948 as the Monopolies and Restrictive Practices Commission (later the Monopolies and Mergers Commission); it became the Competition Commission in April 1999 under the Competition Act 1998. The commission conducts in-depth inquiries into mergers, markets, and the regulation of major industries. Every inquiry the commission undertakes is in response to a reference made to it by another authority, usually the Office of Fair Trading. The commission has no power to conduct inquiries on its own initiative. The Enterprise Act 2002 introduced a new regime for the assessment of mergers and markets in the UK – in most related investigations the commission is responsible for making decisions on the competition questions and for making and implementing decisions on appropriate remedies.

The commission has a full-time chair and three deputy chairs. There are usually around 50 part-time commission members, who usually carry out investigations in groups of four or five after appointment by the chair. All are appointed by the Secretary of State for Business, Enterprise and Regulatory Reform for eight-year terms.

Chair, Peter Freeman
Deputy Chairs, Christopher Clarke; Dr Peter Davis; Diana Guy
Members, Jayne Almond; Prof. John Baillie; Christopher Bright; Laura Carstensen; Dr John Collings; Dr Diane Coyle; Prof. John Cubbin; Roger Davis; Carolan Dobson; Barbara Donoghue; Laurence Elks; Richard Farrant; Christopher Goodall; Prof. Alan Gregory, FCMA; Ivar Grey; Prof. Alan Hamlin; Prof. Jonathan Haskel; Peter Hazell; Jill Hill; Richard Holroyd; Alexander Johnston; Ian Jones; Peter Jones; Prof. Bruce Lyons; Dame Barbara Mills, DBE, QC; Prof. Peter Moizer, FCA; Jeremy Peat; Prof. Mahendra Raj; Christopher Smallwood; John Smith; Anthony Stern; Peter Stoddart, FCA; Prof. Sudi Sudarsanam; Richard Taylor; Robert Turgoose; Prof. Catherine Waddams; Steven Walzer; Prof. Michael Waterson; Jonathan Whiticar; Prof. Stephen Wilks, FCA; Fiona Woolf, CBE
Non-Executive Directors, Tony Foster; Dame Patricia Hodgson, DBE
Chief Executive and Secretary, Martin Stanley

COMPETITION SERVICE

Victoria House, Bloomsbury Place, London WC1A 2EB
T 020-7979 7979 F 020-7979 7978
E info@catribunal.org.uk W www.catribunal.org.uk

The Enterprise Act 2002 created the Competition Service, a non-departmental public body whose purpose is to fund and provide support services to the Competition Appeal Tribunal. Support services include everything necessary to facilitate the carrying out by the Competition Appeal Tribunal of its statutory functions such as administration, accommodation and office equipment.

Director, Operations, Jeremy Straker

CONSUMER COUNCIL FOR WATER (CCW)

Victoria Square House, Victoria Square, Birmingham B2 4AJ
T 0121-345 1000 F 0121-345 1001
E enquiries@ccwater.org.uk W www.ccwater.org.uk

The CCW was established in 2005 under the Water Act 2003 to represent customers' interests in respect of price, service and value for money from their water and sewerage services, and to investigate complaints from customers about their water company. There are nine regional committees in England and one in Wales.

Chair, Dame Yve Buckland, DBE

CORPORATION OF TRINITY HOUSE

Trinity House, Tower Hill, London EC3N 4DH
T 020-7481 6900 F 020-7480 7662
E enquiries@thls.org W www.trinityhouse.co.uk

The Corporation of Trinity House is the general lighthouse authority for England, Wales and the Channel Islands, and was granted its first charter by Henry VIII in 1514. Its remit is to assist the safe passage of a variety of vessels through some of the busiest sea-lanes in the world; it does this by deploying and maintaining approximately 600 aids to navigation, ranging from lighthouses to a satellite navigation service. The corporation also has certain statutory jurisdiction over aids to navigation maintained by local harbour authorities and is responsible for marking or dispersing wrecks dangerous to navigation, except those occurring within port limits or wrecks of HM ships.

The statutory duties of Trinity House are funded by the General Lighthouse Fund, which is provided from light duties levied on ships calling at ports of the UK and the Republic of Ireland. The corporation is a deep-sea pilotage authority, authorised by the Secretary of State for Transport to license deep-sea pilots. In addition Trinity House is a charitable organisation that maintains a number of retirement homes for mariners and their dependants, funds a four-year training scheme for those seeking a career in the merchant navy, and also dispenses grants to a wide range of maritime charities. The charity work is wholly funded by its own activities.

The corporation is controlled by a board of Elder Brethren; a separate board controls the Lighthouse Service. The Elder Brethren also act as nautical assessors in marine cases in the Admiralty Division of the High Court.

ELDER BRETHREN

Master, HRH The Prince Philip, Duke of Edinburgh, KG, KT, PC
Deputy Master, Rear-Adm. Jeremy de Halpert, CB
Wardens, Cdre. Peter Melson, CBE, RN *(Rental)*; Douglas Potter *(Nether)*
Elder Brethren, HRH The Prince of Wales, KG, KT, GCB; HRH The Duke of York, KG, KCVO, ADC; HRH The Princess Royal, KG, KT, GCVO; Adm. Lord Boyce, GCB, OBE; Lord Browne of Madingley; Capt. John Burton-Hall, RD; Rt. Hon. Lord Carrington, KG, GCMG, CH; Capt. David Cloke; Rt. Hon. Lord Cuckney of Millbank; Capt. Sir Malcolm Edge, KCVO; Capt. Ian Gibb; Cdr. Sir Robin Gillett, Bt., GBE, RD; Capt. Duncan Glass; Lord Greenway; Hon. Christopher Lyttelton; Rt. Hon. Lord Mackay of Clashfern, KT; Capt. Peter Mason, CBE; Capt. David Orr; Capt. Nigel Pryke, MCIT, FNI; Capt. Derek Richards, RD, RNR;

Cdr. Miles Rivett-Carnac, RN; Rt. Hon. Lord Robertson of Port Ellen, KT, GCMG; Rear-Adm. Sir Patrick Rowe, KCVO, CBE; Cdre. Jim Scorer; Sir Brian Shaw; Simon Sherard; Adm. Sir Jock Slater, GCB, LVO; Capt. David Smith, OBE, RN; Capt. David Squire, CBE, RFA; Cdre. Rt. Hon. Lord Sterling of Plaistow, CBE, GCVO, RNR; Capt. Colin Stewart, LVO; Sir Adrian Swire, AE; Capt. Sir Miles Wingate, KCVO; Capt. Thomas Woodfield, OBE

FFICERS
cretary, Peter Galloway
rector of Finance, Jerry Wedge
rector of Operations and Asset Management, Cdre. Jim Scorer
rector of Navigation, Capt. Duncan Glass

OUNCIL ON TRIBUNALS

Chancery Lane, London WC2A 1BQ
020-7855 5200 F 020-7855 5201
nquiries@cot.gsi.gov.uk
www.council-on-tribunals.gov.uk

e Council on Tribunals is a permanent standing visory body that operates under the Tribunals and quiries Act 1992. It consists of 17 members appointed the Secretary of State for Justice and the Scottish nisters; one member is appointed to represent the terests of people in Wales. The Scottish Committee of e Council generally considers Scottish tribunals and atters relating only to Scotland. The Parliamentary mmissioner for Administration is an *ex officio* member the council and the Scottish Committee.

The council advises on, and keeps under review, the nstitution and working of the tribunals listed in the ibunals and Inquiries Act 1992, and considers and ports on administrative procedures relating to statutory quiries. Some 80 tribunals are currently under the uncil's supervision. It is consulted by and advises vernment departments on a wide range of subjects ating to adjudicative procedures.

air, Rt. Hon. Lord Newton of Braintree, OBE
embers, The Parliamentary Commissioner *(ex officio),* Ann Abraham; Carolyn Berkeley; Prof. Alice Brown *(ex officio)*; Elizabeth Cameron; Sue Davis; Judith Edwards; Susan Howdle; Penny Letts; Prof. Alistair MacLeary; Stephen Mannion, QPM; Bernard Quoroll; Prof. Genevra Richardson, CBE; Dr Jonathan Spencer, CB; Dr Adrian Stokes, OBE; Pat Thomas, CBE; Heather Wilcox

COTTISH COMMITTEE OF THE COUNCIL ON RIBUNALS
orge House, 126 George Street, Edinburgh EH2 4HH
0131-271 4300 F 0131-271 4309
sccot@gtnet.gov.uk
hair, Prof. A. MacLeary
embers, The Parliamentary Commissioner for Administration *(ex officio)*; The Scottish Public Services Ombudsman *(ex officio)*; Elizabeth C. Cameron; Douglas Graham; Stephen Mannion; Lyndy Roberts; Audrey Watson; Mary Wood

COUNTRYSIDE COUNCIL FOR WALES/CYNGOR CEFN GWLAD CYMRU

Maes-y-Ffynnon, Penrhosgarnedd, Bangor, Gwynedd LL57 2DW
T 0845-130 6229 F 01248-355782
E enquiries@ccw.gov.uk W www.ccw.gov.uk

The Countryside Council for Wales is the government's statutory adviser on sustaining natural beauty, wildlife and the opportunity for outdoor enjoyment in Wales and its inshore waters. It is funded by the National Assembly for Wales and accountable to the First Secretary, who appoints its members.

Chair, John Lloyd Jones, OBE
Chief Executive, Roger Thomas
Directors, Dr David Parker *(Science)*; Dr John Taylor *(Policy)*

COVENT GARDEN MARKET AUTHORITY

Covent House, New Covent Garden Market, London SW8 5NX
T 020-7720 2211 F 020-7622 5307
E info@cgma.gov.uk W www.cgma.gov.uk

The Covent Garden Market Authority is constituted under the Covent Garden Market Acts 1961 to 1977, the board being appointed by the Department of Environment, Food and Rural Affairs. The authority owns and operates the 22 hectare (56 acre) New Covent Garden Markets (fruit, vegetables, flowers), which have been trading at the site since 1974.

Chair (part-time), Rt. Hon. Baroness Dean of Thornton-le-Fylde
Chief Executive, Jan Lloyd

CRIMINAL CASES REVIEW COMMISSION

Alpha Tower, Suffolk Street, Queensway, Birmingham B1 1TT
T 0121-633 1800 F 0121-633 1823/1804
E info@ccrc.x.gsi.gov.uk W www.ccrc.gov.uk

The Criminal Cases Review Commission is an independent body set up under the Criminal Appeal Act 1995. It is a non-departmental public body reporting to parliament via the Lord Chancellor and Secretary of State for Justice. It is responsible for investigating possible miscarriages of justice in England, Wales and Northern Ireland, and deciding whether or not to refer cases back to an appeal court. Membership of the commission is by royal appointment; the senior executive staff are appointed by the commission.

Chair, Prof. Graham Zellick
Members, M. Allen; Ms P. Barrett; M. Emerton; J. England; Ms J. Goulding; D. Jessel; A. MacGregor, QC; I. Nicholl, E. Smith; J. Weeden
Principal Director, C. Albert

CRIMINAL INJURIES COMPENSATION AUTHORITY (CICA)

Tay House, 300 Bath Street, Glasgow G2 4LN
T 0141-331 2726 Freephone 0800-358 3601
F 0141-331 2287
E enquiries@cica.gsi.gov.uk W www.cica.gov.uk

All applications for compensation for personal injury arising from crimes of violence in England, Scotland and Wales are dealt with at the above location (separate arrangements apply in Northern Ireland). Applications received up to 31 March 1996 are assessed on the basis of common law damages under the 1990 compensation

scheme. Applications received on or after 1 April 1996 are assessed under a tariff-based scheme, made under the Criminal Injuries Compensation Act 1995, by the CICA. There is a separate avenue of appeal to the Criminal Injuries Compensation Appeals Panel (CICAP – *see* Tribunals section).
Chief Executive, Joanne Drean

CROFTERS COMMISSION

Castle Wynd, Inverness IV2 3EQ
T 01463-663450 F 01463-711820
E info@crofterscommission.org.uk
W www.crofterscommission.org.uk

The Crofters Commission, established in 1955 under the Crofters (Scotland) Act, is a government-funded organisation tasked with overseeing crofting legislation and developing crofting. It works with communities to regulate crofting and assist local development initiatives. It also advises Scottish ministers on crofting matters. The commission administers the Crofting Counties Agricultural Grants Scheme, the Highlands and Islands Croft Entrant Scheme, the Crofters' Cattle Improvement Scheme and the Crofting Community Development Scheme. It also provides a free enquiry service.
Chair, Drew Ratter
Chief Executive, Nick Reiter

DEER COMMISSION FOR SCOTLAND

Great Glen House, Leachkin Road, Inverness IV3 8NW
T 01463-725000 F 01463-725048
E enquiries@deercom.com W www.dcs.gov.uk

The Deer Commission for Scotland has the general functions of furthering the conservation and control of deer in Scotland. It has the statutory duty, with powers, to prevent damage to agriculture, forestry and the habitat by deer. It is funded by the Scottish Executive.
Chair (part-time), Prof. J. Milne, MBE
Director, N. Halfhide

DESIGN COUNCIL

34 Bow Street, London WC2E 7DL
T 020-7420 5200 F 020-7420 5300
E info@designcouncil.org.uk W www.design-council.org.uk

The Design Council is a campaigning organisation which works with partners in business, education and government to promote the effective use of good design; its aim is to make businesses more competitive and public services more effective. It is a registered charity with a royal charter and is funded jointly by grant-in-aid from the Department for Business, Enterprise and Regulatory Reform and the Department for Culture, Media and Sport; the secretaries of state of these two departments appoint the chair and members of the council.
Chair, Sir George Cox
Chief Executive, David Kester

ENGLISH HERITAGE (HISTORIC BUILDINGS AND MONUMENTS COMMISSION FOR ENGLAND)

1 Waterhouse Square, 138–142 Holborn, London EC1N 2ST
T 020-7973 3000 F 020-7973 3001
W www.english-heritage.org.uk

English Heritage was established under the National Heritage Act 1983. On 1 April 1999 it merged with the Royal Commission on the Historical Monuments of England to become the new lead body for Englan historic environment. It is sponsored by the Department Culture, Media and Sport and its duties are to carry out a sponsor archaeological, architectural and scientific surve and research designed to increase the understanding England's past and its changing condition; to ident buildings, monuments and landscapes for protection whi also offering expert advice, skills and grants to conser these sites; to encourage town planners to make imaginati re-use of historic buildings to aid regeneration of t centres of cities, towns and villages; to manage and cur selected sites; and to curate and make publicly accessib the National Monuments Record, whose records of ov one million historic sites and buildings, and extensi collections of photographs, maps, drawings and repo constitute the central database and archive of Englan historic environment.
Chair, Sir Neil Cossons, OBE, FSA, FMA
Commissioners, Maria Adebowale; Joyce Bridges, CBE; B Bryson; Michael Cairns; Prof. David Cannadine, DPHIL, LITT D, FBA; Manish Chande; Barry Cunlif CBE; Gilly Drummond; Marquess of Douro, OBE; Ja Grenville, FSA; Michael Jolly, CBE; Jane Kennedy; E of Leicester, CBE; Les Sparks, OBE, FRSA; Elizabeth Williamson, FSA
Chief Executive, Dr Simon Thurley

CUSTOMER SERVICES DEPARTMENT, PO Box 569, Swindon SN2 2YP T 0870-333 1181
E customers@english-heritage.org.uk
NATIONAL MONUMENTS RECORD CENTRE, Kemble Drive, Swindon SN2 2GZ T 01793-414600
F 01793-414606

ENVIRONMENT AGENCY

Rio House, Waterside Drive, Aztec West, Almondsbury, Bristol BS32 4UD
T 0870-850 6506 F 01709-312820
E enquiries@environment-agency.gov.uk
W www.environment-agency.gov.uk

The Environment Agency was established in 1996 und the Environment Act 1995 and is a non-department public body sponsored by the Department f Environment, Food and Rural Affairs and the Nation Assembly for Wales – around 60 per cent of the agency funding is from the government, with the rest raised fro various charging schemes. The agency is responsible f pollution prevention and control in England and Wal helping businesses use resources more effectively, and f the management and use of water resources, includir flood defences, fisheries and navigation. It has he offices in London and Bristol, and eight regional offices.

THE BOARD
Chair, Sir John Harman
Members, James Braithwaite, CBE; Peter Bye; Ted Cantl CBE; John Edmonds; Prof. Ruth Hall; Richard Percy; Dr Lyndon Stanton; Cllr Kay Twitchen, OBE; Dr Malcolm Smith; Lady Warner, OBE; Prof. Lynda Warren; Lord Whitty
Chief Executive, Barbara Young

EQUALITY COMMISSION FOR NORTHERN IRELAND

Equality House, 7–9 Shaftesbury Square, Belfast BT2 7DP
T 028-9050 0600 F 028-9024 8687
E information@equalityni.org W www.equalityni.org

he Equality Commission was set up in 1999 under the orthern Ireland Act 1998 and is responsible for romoting equality, keeping the relevant legislation under view, eliminating discrimination on the grounds of race, isability, sexual orientation, gender, religion and political pinion and for overseeing the statutory duty on public ithorities to promote equality of opportunity.
hief Commissioner, Bob Collins
eputy Chief Commissioner, Anne O'Reilly
hief Executive, Evelyn Collins

OREIGN COMPENSATION OMMISSION (FCC)

ld Admiralty Building, London SW1A 2PA
020-7008 1321 **F** 020-7008 0160
/ www.fcc.gov.uk

he FCC was set up by the Foreign Compensation Act 950 primarily to distribute, under orders in council, inds received from other governments in accordance ith agreements to pay compensation for expropriated ritish property and other losses sustained by British ationals. The FCC carries out both judicial and dministrative functions, including the adjudication of aims by applicants and the investment and management f compensation funds. There are no active compensation rogrammes at present.
hair, Dr John Barker

AMBLING COMMISSION

ctoria Square House, Victoria Square, Birmingham B2 4BP
0121-230 6666 **F** 0121-233 6720
info@gamblingcommission.gov.uk
/ www.gamblingcommission.gov.uk

he Gambling Commission was established under the ambling Act 2005, and took over the role previously ccupied by the Gaming Board for Great Britain in egulating and licensing all commercial gambling – apart om spread betting and the National Lottery – ie casinos, ingo, remote gambling, gaming machines and lotteries. It so advises local and central government on related sues, and is responsible for the protection of children nd the vulnerable. The commission is sponsored by the epartment for Culture, Media and Sport, with its work inded mainly by licence fees paid by the gambling idustry.
hair, Peter Dean, CBE
hief Executive, Jenny Williams

OVERNMENT OFFICES FOR THE EGIONS

he nine Government Offices for the Regions (GOs) are e primary means by which a wide range of government olicies are delivered in the English regions. The overnment Offices bring together the activities and terests of eleven 'sponsor' government departments: the epartment for Business, Enterprise and Regulatory eform; the Cabinet Office; the Department for hildren, Schools and Families; the Department for ommunities and Local Government; the Department or Culture, Media and Sport; the Department for nvironment, Food and Rural Affairs; the Department of lealth; the Home Office; the Ministry of Justice; the epartment for Transport; and the Department for Work nd Pensions.

GOs contribute to the delivery of over 40 public service agreements (PSAs) on behalf of their sponsor departments. These PSAs cover a diverse range of tasks including regenerating communities, fighting crime, tackling housing needs, improving public health, raising standards in education and skills, tackling countryside issues, and reducing unemployment. GOs also manage European funds.

GOs directly manage the spending programmes of the government departments listed above. They oversee budgets and contracts delegated to regional organisations, as well as carrying out regulatory functions and sponsoring Regional Development Agencies. As part of central government, their role also includes providing a regional perspective to inform the development and evaluation of policy.

The Government Office Network comprises the nine regional Government Offices, and the Regional Coordination Unit.

REGIONAL COORDINATION UNIT

2nd Floor, Riverwalk House, 157–161 Millbank, London SW1P 4RR
T 020–7217 3111 **F** 020–7217 3590
E rcuenquiries@rcu.gsi.gov.uk **W** www.gos.gov.uk
Director-General, Joe Montgomery

EAST MIDLANDS

The Belgrave Centre, Stanley Place, Talbot Street, Nottingham NG1 5GG
T 0115–971 9971 **F** 0115–971 2404
E enquiries@goem.gsi.gov.uk
W www.goem.gov.uk
Regional Director, Jane Todd

EAST OF ENGLAND

Eastbrook, Shaftesbury Road, Cambridge CB2 2DF
T 01223–372500 **F** 01223–372501
W www.go-east.gov.uk
Regional Director, Brian Hackland

LONDON

Riverwalk House, 157–161 Millbank, London SW1P 4RR
T 020–7217 3151 **F** 020–7217 3450
W www.gol.gov.uk
Regional Director, Liz Meek

NORTH EAST

Citygate, Gallowgate, Newcastle upon Tyne NE1 4WH
T 0191–201 3300 **F** 0191–202 3998
W www.go-ne.gov.uk
Regional Director, Jonathan Blackie

NORTH WEST

City Tower, Piccadilly Plaza, Manchester M1 4BE
T 0161–952 4000 **F** 0161–952 4099
W www.go-nw.gov.uk
Regional Director, Keith Barnes

SOUTH EAST

Bridge House, 1 Walnut Tree Close, Guildford GU1 4GA
T 01483–882255 **F** 01483–882259
W www.go-se.gov.uk
Regional Director, Rolande Anderson

SOUTH WEST
2 Rivergate, Temple Quay, Bristol BS1 6ED
T 0117–900 1700 F 0117–900 1900
W www.gosw.gov.uk
Regional Director (acting), Richard Sheard

WEST MIDLANDS
5 St Phillips Place, Colmore Row, Birmingham B3 2PW
T 0121–352 5050 F 0121–352 1010
W www.go-wm.gov.uk
Regional Director, Trudi Elliot

YORKSHIRE AND THE HUMBER
8 City Walk, Leeds LS11 9AT
T 0113–341 3000 W www.goyh.gov.uk
Regional Director, Felicity Everiss

HEALTH PROTECTION AGENCY (HPA)

7th Floor, Holborn Gate, 330 High Holborn, London WC1V 7PP
T 020-7759 2700 F 020-7759 2733
E webteam@hpa.org.uk W www.hpa.org.uk

The HPA was set up in 2003 and is responsible for providing an integrated approach to protecting public health through the provision of support and advice to the NHS, local authorities, emergency services, other NDPBs, the Department of Health and the devolved administrations.

The HPA works at local, regional, national and international levels to reduce the impact of infectious diseases and reduce exposure to chemicals, radiation and poisons, as well as ensuring a rapid response when hazards occur. The HPA provides services in Northern Ireland and works closely with the devolved administrations, so that there is a coordinated response to incidents, trends and outbreaks on a national level. Research and development projects conducted by HPA scientists are primarily concerned with new methods of treating illness and assessing exposure to chemicals or radiation, ie developing new vaccines and biomarkers of chemical exposure.

Chair, Sir William Stewart
Board Members, Dr Parvaiz Ali; Dr Barbara Bannister, FRCP; Michael Beaumont, CBE, FCA; James T. Brown; Ian Cranston, FCA; Dr Paul Darragh, TD; Prof. Charles Easmon, CBE; Prof. William Gelletly; Prof. Rod Griffiths, CBE; Prof. Andrew Hall; Prof. David Latchman, FRSA; Dr Vanessa Mayatt; Prof. Karl Nicholson; John Wyn Owen, CB; Prof. Sandy Primrose; Dr Geoffrey Schild, CBE; Prof. Richard Wise
Chief Executive, Prof. Pat Troop

HEALTH AND SAFETY COMMISSION

Rose Court, 2 Southwark Bridge, London SE1 9HS
T 0845-345 0055 E hse.infoline@natbrit.com
W www.hse.gov.uk

The Health and Safety Commission was created under the Health and Safety at Work etc Act 1974, and is responsible for health and safety regulation in Great Britain. The Health and Safety Executive and local government are the enforcing authorities who work in support of the commission. Its aim is to ensure risks in the workplace are properly controlled and generally to promote the protection of people at work and the public from hazards arising from industrial and commercial activity, including major industrial accidents and the transportation of hazardous materials.

Its members are appointed by the Secretary of State for Work and Pensions following consultation with representative groups (employers, employees, local authorities and others).

Chair, Sir Bill Callaghan
Members, S. Blair; D. Carrigan; R. Dahlberg; Ms J. Donovan; S. Khan; J. Longworth; H. Robertson; Ms E Snape; J. Spanswick

HEALTH AND SAFETY EXECUTIVE

Rose Court, 2 Southwark Bridge, London SE1 9HS
T 0845-345 0055 F 0845-408 9566
E hse.infoline@natbrit.com W www.hse.gov.uk

The Health and Safety Executive is the Health and Safety Commission's major instrument. Through its inspectorates it enforces health and safety law in the majority of industrial premises. The executive advises the commission in its major task of laying down safety standards through regulations and practical guidance for many industrial processes. The executive is also the licensing authority for nuclear installations, the reporting officer on the severity of nuclear incidents in Britain and it is responsible for the Channel Tunnel Safety Authority.

Chief Executive, Geoffrey Podger
Deputy Chief Executive, Operations, Justin McCracken
Deputy Chief Executive, Policy, Jonathan Rees
Director and HM Chief Inspector of the Nuclear Installations Inspectorate, Dr Mike Weightman
Chief Scientist and Director of Corporate Science and Analytical Service Directorate, Dr Patrick McDonald

HIGHLANDS AND ISLANDS ENTERPRISE (HIE)

Cowan House, Inverness Retail and Business Park, Inverness IV2 7GF
T 01463-234171 F 01463-244469
E hie.general@hient.co.uk W www.hie.co.uk

HIE was set up under the Enterprise and New Towns (Scotland) Act 1991. Its role is to design, direct and deliver enterprise development, training and environmental and social projects and services. HIE is made up of a strategic core body and nine local enterprise companies (LECs), to which many of its individual functions are delegated.

Chair, W. Roe
Chief Executive, I. J. R. S. Cumming

HISTORIC ENVIRONMENT ADVISORY COUNCIL FOR SCOTLAND

Longmore House, Salisbury Place, Edinburgh EH9 1SH
T 0131-668 8810 F 0131-668 8987
E heacs@scotland.gsi.gov.uk W www.heacs.org.uk

The Historic Environment Advisory Council for Scotland, established in 2003, is the advisory body set up to provide Scottish ministers with advice on issues affecting the historic environment and how the functions of the Scottish ministers may be exercised effectively for the benefit of said historic environment. In this context the historic environment means any or all structures and places in Scotland of historical, archaeological or architectural interest or importance.

Chair, Elizabeth Burns, CMG, OBE

IISTORIC ROYAL PALACES

partment 39A, Hampton Court Palace, Surrey KT8 9AU
0870-751 5172 **F** 020-8781 9754
operators@hrp.org.uk **W** www.hrp.org.uk

istoric Royal Palaces was established in 1998 as a royal iarter body with charitable status and is contracted by ie Secretary of State for Culture, Media and Sport to ianage the palaces on her behalf. The palaces – the ower of London, Hampton Court Palace, the anqueting House, Kensington Palace and Kew Palace – e owned by the Queen on behalf of the nation.

The organisation is governed by a board comprising a iair and ten non-executive trustees. The chief executive accountable to the board of trustees and ultimately to arliament. Historic Royal Palaces receives no funding om the government or the crown.

RUSTEES
hair, Charles Mackay
ppointed by the Queen, Sir Trevor McDonald, OBE; Sir Alan Reid, KCVO; Sir Hugh Roberts, KCVO, FSA
ppointed by the Secretary of State, Dawn Austwick, OBE; Dr Bridget Cherry, OBE, FSA; Sue Farr; John Hamer; Malcolm Reading
x officio, Gen. Sir Roger Wheeler, GCB, CBE *(Constable of the Tower of London)*

)FFICERS
hief Executive, Michael Day
esident Governor, HM Tower of London, Maj.-Gen. Keith Cima

IOME-GROWN CEREALS AUTHORITY

aledonia House, 223 Pentonville Road, London N1 9HY
020-7520 3926 **F** 020-7520 3954
communications@hgca.com **W** www.hgca.com

et up under the Cereals Marketing Act 1965, the Home-irown Cereals Authority (HGCA) board consists of: even members representing UK cereal growers; seven epresenting dealers in, or processors of, grain; and two idependent members. HGCA's functions are to improve ie production and marketing of UK-grown cereals and ilseeds through a research and development programme, provide a market information service and to promote JK cereals in export markets.
hair, J. Page
hief Executive, J. Cowens

IORSERACE TOTALISATOR BOARD

ouglas House, Chapel Lane, Wigan WN3 4HS
01942-617500 **F** 01942-617701
V www.totesport.com

he Horserace Totalisator Board (the Tote) was stablished by the Betting, Gaming and Lotteries Act 963. Its function is to operate totalisators on approved acecourses in Great Britain, and it also provides on and ff-course cash and credit offices. Under the Horserace otalisator and Betting Levy Board Act 1972, it is further mpowered to offer bets at starting price (or other bets at ixed odds) on any sporting event, and under the Iorserace Totalisator Board Act 1997 to take bets on any vent, except the National Lottery. The chair and iembers of the board are appointed by the Secretary of tate for Culture, Media and Sport.

The government announced in March 2001 that the Tote would eventually be sold to a racing trust. The necessary legislation was passed in 2004 and the privatisation of the Tote is expected to be completed during the 2007 financial year.
Chair, P. I. Jones
Chief Executive, T. Beaumont

HOUSING CORPORATION

Maple House, 149 Tottenham Court Road, London W1T 7BN
T 0845-230 7000 **F** 0113-233 7101
E enquiries@housingcorp.gsx.gov.uk
W www.housingcorp.gov.uk

Established by parliament in 1964, the Housing Corporation funds new affordable housing and is the statutory regulator for housing associations. Under the Housing Act 1996, the corporation's regulatory role was widened to embrace new types of landlords, in particular local housing companies. The corporation is funded by the Department for Communities and Local Government; the £3.9bn programme of investment for 2006–8 is set to create 84,000 new affordable homes.
Chair, Peter Dixon
Chief Executive, Jon Rouse

HUMAN FERTILISATION AND EMBRYOLOGY AUTHORITY (HFEA)

21 Bloomsbury Street, London WC1B 3HF
T 020-7291 8200 **F** 020-7291 8201
E admin@hfea.gov.uk **W** www.hfea.gov.uk

The HFEA was established in 1991 under the Human Fertilisation and Embryology Act 1990. It is the UK's independent regulator tasked with overseeing safe and appropriate practice in fertility treatment and embryo research, including licensing and monitoring centres carrying out IVF, donor insemination and human embryo research. HFEA also provides a range of detailed information for patients, professionals and government, and maintains a formal register of information about donors, fertility treatments and children born as a result of those treatments.
Chair, Shirley Harrison
Chief Executive, Angela McNab

HUMAN GENETICS COMMISSION

Area 605, Wellington House, 133–155 Waterloo Road, London SE1 8UG
T 020-7972 4351 **F** 020-7972 4300
E hgc@dh.gsi.gov.uk **W** www.hgc.gov.uk

The Human Genetics Commission was established in 1999, subsuming three previous advisory committees. Its remit is to give ministers strategic advice on how developments in human genetics will impact on people and healthcare, focusing in particular on the social and ethical implications.
Chair, Baroness H. Kennedy of the Shaws, QC
Vice Chair, Sir John Sulston
Members, Prof. Emerita Brenda Almond; Prof. Stephen Bain; Dr Celia Brazell; Prof. Angus Clarke; Prof. Sarah Cunningham-Burley; Dr Paul Darragh; Dr Paul Debenham; Dr Frances Flinter; Ros Gardner; Prof. John Harris; Michael Harrison; Shirley Harrison; Prof. Christopher Higgins; Alastair Kent; Dr Rosemary Leonard; Alice Maynard; Lola Oni; Dr Christine Patch; Peter Sayers; Dr Rosalind Skinner; Dr Anita Thomas

HUMAN TISSUE AUTHORITY (HTA)

Ground Floor, Finlaison House, 15–17 Furnival Street, London EC4A 1AB
T 020-7211 3400 F 020-7211 3430
E enquiries@hta.gov.uk W www.hta.gov.uk

The HTA was established on 1 April 2005 under the Human Tissue Act 2004, and is sponsored and part-funded by the Department of Health. Its role is to inform the public and Secretary of State for Health about issues within its remit, which include the import, export, storage and use of human bodies and tissue for scheduled purposes, and disposal of human tissue following its use in medical treatment or for scheduled purposes. The HTA is the competent authority under the EU Tissues and Cells Directive for regulating human tissue banking for transplant services.

The HTA also supersedes and extends the role that was previously performed by the now-defunct Unrelated Live Transplant Regulatory Authority (ULTRA) in setting out the circumstances in which live 'transplantable material' (from both related and unrelated donors) will be allowed.

Chair, Shirley Harrison
Chief Executive, Adrian McNeil

IMPERIAL WAR MUSEUM

Lambeth Road, London SE1 6HZ
T 020-7416 5320 F 020-7416 5374
E mail@iwm.org.uk W www.iwm.org.uk

The museum, founded in 1917, illustrates and records all aspects of the two world wars and other military operations involving Britain and the Commonwealth since 1914. It was opened in its present home, formerly Bethlem Royal Hospital, in 1936. The museum is a multi-branch organisation that also includes the Churchill Museum and Cabinet War Rooms in Whitehall; HMS *Belfast* in the Pool of London; Imperial War Museum Duxford in Cambridgeshire; and Imperial War Museum North in Trafford, Manchester.

The total grant-in-aid (including grants for special projects) for 2007–8 is £22.18m.

OFFICERS

Chair of Trustees, Air Chief Marshal Sir Peter Squire, GCB, DFC, AFC
Director-General, Sir Robert Crawford, CBE
Directors, Richard Ashton *(Imperial War Museum Duxford)*; Jon Card *(Secretary, Finance)*; Jim Forrester *(Imperial War Museum North)*; Angela Godwin *(Public Services)*; Brad King *(HMS Belfast)*; Phil Reed *(Churchill Museum and Cabinet War Rooms)*; Alan Stoneman *(Corporate Services)*; Mark Whitmore *(Collections)*

INDEPENDENT HOUSING OMBUDSMAN

81 Aldwych, London WC2B 4HN
T 020-7421 3800 F 020-7831 1942
E info@housing-ombudsman.org.uk
W www.housing-ombudsman.org.uk

The Housing Ombudsman Service, established in 1997, deals with complaints from residents concerning shortcomings in the way homes are managed by landlords and housing agents. The ombudsman has a statutory jurisdiction over all registered social landlords in England. Private and other landlords can join the service on voluntary basis.

Ombudsman, Dr Mike Biles
Deputy Ombudsman, Rafael Runco

INDEPENDENT POLICE COMPLAINTS COMMISSION (IPCC)

90 High Holborn, London WC1V 6BH
T 0845-300 2002 F 020-7404 0430
E enquiries@ipcc.gsi.gov.uk W www.ipcc.gov.uk

The IPCC succeeded the Police Complaints Authority i 2004. It was established under the Police Reform Ac 2002. The IPCC has teams of investigators headed b directors in each of its regions to assist with th supervision and management of some polic investigations. They also carry out independer investigations into serious incidents or allegations c misconduct by persons serving with the police. Fror April 2006 the IPCC took on responsibility fc investigating complaints of serious incidents, includin death or injury, made against staff of HM Revenue an Customs and the Serious Organised Crime Agency. Th 17 commissioners of the IPCC must not previously hav worked for the police.

Chair, N. Hardwick
Deputy Chair, J. Wadham
Commissioners, I. Bynoe; J. Crawley; T. Davies; M. Franklin; G. Garland; Ms D. Glass; L. Jackson; N. Long L. Lustgarten; Ms N. Malik; Ms R. Marsh; D. Petch; M M. Mian Pritchard; Ms A. Somal; Ms N. Williams
Chief Executive, Jane Furniss

INDEPENDENT REVIEW SERVICE FOR THE SOCIAL FUND

4th Floor, Centre City Podium, 5 Hill Street, Birmingham B5 4U
T 0800-096 1926 F 0121-606 2172
E sfc@irs-review.org.uk W www.irs-review.org.uk

The Social Fund Commissioner is appointed by th Secretary of State for Work and Pensions. Th commissioner appoints Social Fund Inspectors, wh provide an independent review for customers dissatisfie with decisions made in Jobcentre Plus offices throughou England, Scotland and Wales regarding the grants an loans available from the Discretionary Social Fund.

Social Fund Commissioner, Sir Richard Tilt

INDUSTRIAL INJURIES ADVISORY COUNCIL

6th Floor, The Adelphi, 1–11 John Adam Street, London WC2N 6HT
T 020-7962 8066 F 020-7712 2255
E iiac@dwp.gsi.gov.uk W www.iiac.org.uk

The Industrial Injuries Advisory Council was establishe under the Social Security Administration Act 1992, wit statutory provisions governing its work set out i section 171 of the act. The council consists of 1 members appointed by the Secretary of State for Wor and Pensions, and has three roles: to advise on th prescription of diseases; to advise on matters referred t the council by the secretary of state or proposal concerning the Industrial Injuries Disablement Benef Scheme; and to advise on any other matter relating t industrial injuries benefit or its administration.

Chair, Prof. A. J. Newman Taylor, CB, FRCP

{FORMATION COMMISSIONER'S FFICE

cliffe House, Water Lane, Wilmslow, Cheshire SK9 5AF
845-630 6060 **F** 01625-524510
ıail@ico.gsi.gov.uk **W** www.ico.gov.uk

e Information Commissioner's Office is sponsored by : Ministry of Justice and oversees and enforces the edom of Information Act 2000 and the Data otection Act 1998, with the objective of promoting blic access to official information and protecting rsonal information.

The Data Protection Act 1998 sets out rules for the ocessing of personal information and applies to records ld on computers and some paper files. It works in two ys: it dictates that those who record and use personal ormation (data controllers) must be open about how : information is used and must follow the eight nciples of 'good information handling', and it gives lividuals certain rights to access their personal ormation.

The Freedom of Information Act 2000 is designed to lp end the culture of unnecessary secrecy and open up : inner workings of the public sector to citizens and sinesses. Under the Freedom of Information Act, public thorities must produce a publication scheme that sets t what information the public authority is obliged to blish by law.

The Information Commissioner reports annually to rliament on the performance of his functions under the ts and has obligations to assess breaches of the acts.

formation Commissioner, Richard Thomas

VESTIGATORY POWERS TRIBUNAL

Box 33220, London SW1H 9ZQ
)20-7035 3711 **W** www.ipt-uk.com

e Investigatory Powers Tribunal replaced the terception of Communications Tribunal, the telligence Services Tribunal, the Security Services ibunal and the complaints function of the commissioner pointed under the Police Act 1997.

The Regulation of Investigatory Powers Act 2000 IPA) provides for a tribunal made up of senior embers of the legal profession, independent of the vernment and appointed by the Queen, to consider all mplaints against the intelligence services and those ainst public authorities in respect of powers covered by IPA; and to consider proceedings brought under ction 7 of the Human Rights Act 1998 against the telligence services and law enforcement agencies in spect of these powers.

esident, Rt. Hon. Lord Justice John Mummery
ce-President, Mr Justice Michael Burton
embers, W. Carmichael; Sir Richard Gaskell; Sheriff Principal J. McInnes, QC; P. Scott, QC; R. Seabrook, QC

)INT NATURE CONSERVATION OMMITTEE

onkstone House, City Road, Peterborough PE1 1JY
)1733-562626 **F** 01733-555948
comment@jncc.gov.uk **W** www.jncc.gov.uk

ıe committee was established under the Environmental otection Act 1990 and was reconstituted by the atural Environment and Rural Communities Act 2006. advises the government and others on UK and international nature conservation issues and disseminates knowledge on these subjects. It establishes common standards for the monitoring of nature conservation and research, and provides guidance to Natural England, Scottish Natural Heritage, the Council for Nature Conservation and the Countryside, and the Countryside Council for Wales.

Chair, Adrian Darby, OBE
Deputy Chair, Prof. David Ingram, OBE

LAW COMMISSION

Conquest House, 37–38 John Street, London WC1N 2BQ
T 020-7453 1220 **F** 020-7453 1297
E chief.executive@lawcommission.gsi.gov.uk
W www.lawcom.gov.uk

The Law Commission was set up under the Law Commissions Act 1965, to make proposals to the government for the examination of the law in England and Wales and for its revision where it is unsuited for modern requirements, obscure, or otherwise unsatisfactory. It recommends to the Lord Chancellor programmes for the examination of different branches of the law and suggests whether the examination should be carried out by the commission itself or by some other body. The commission is also responsible for the preparation of Consolidation and Statute Law (Repeals) Bills.

Chair, Hon. Mr Justice Etherton
Commissioners, S. Bridge; David Hertzell; Dr Jeremy Horder; Kenneth Parker, QC; Prof. M. Partington, CBE
Chief Executive, S. Humphreys

LEARNING AND SKILLS COUNCIL (LSC)

Cheylesmore House, Quinton Road, Coventry CV1 2WT
T 0870-900 6800 **F** 02476-823675
E info@lsc.gov.uk **W** www.lsc.gov.uk

The LSC was established in 2001 to replace the Further Education Funding and the Training and Enterprise Councils. It is a non-departmental public body responsible for the planning and funding of post-16 education and training outside of universities. Its remit is to ensure that high-quality post-16 provision is available to meet the needs of employers, individuals and communities. The LSC operates through a national office based in Coventry and also through local departments, which work to promote the equality of opportunity in the workplace; its budget for 2006–7 was £10.4bn.

Chair, Chris Banks, CBE
Chief Executive, Mark Haysom

LEGAL SERVICES COMMISSION

85 Gray's Inn Road, London WC1X 8TX
T 020-7759 0000
W www.legalservices.gov.uk

The Legal Services Commission was created under the Access to Justice Act 1999 and replaced the Legal Aid Board in April 2000. It is a non-departmental public body which is sponsored by the Ministry of Justice.

The commission is responsible for two schemes. The Community Legal Service funds the delivery of civil legal and advice services, identifies priorities and unmet needs, and develops suppliers and services to meet those needs. The Criminal Defence Service provides free legal advice and representation for people involved in criminal investigations or proceedings.

The commission produces free information leaflets which are available from solicitors' and advisory offices, and from the commission's website.

Chief Executive, Carolyn Regan
Chair, Sir Michael Bichard

MENTAL HEALTH ACT COMMISSION (MHAC)

Maid Marian House, 56 Hounds Gate, Nottingham NG1 6BG
T 0115-943 7100 F 0115-943 7101
E chiefexec@mhac.org.uk W www.mhac.org.uk

The MHAC was established in 1983. Its functions are to keep under review the operation of the Mental Health Act 1983; to visit and meet patients detained under the act; to investigate complaints falling within the commission's remit; to operate the 'consent to treatment' safeguards in the Mental Health Act; to publish a biennial report on its activities; to monitor the implementation of the code of practice; and to advise ministers.

The MHAC is comprised of approximately 100 part-time commission members, who are appointed by the Secretary of State for Health.

Chair, Prof. Lord Patel of Bradford
Vice-Chair, Deborah Jenkins, MBE
Chief Executive, Chris Heginbotham

MUSEUM OF LONDON

150 London Wall, London EC2Y 5HN
T 0870-444 3852 F 0870-444 3853
E info@museumoflondon.org.uk
W www.museumoflondon.org.uk

The Museum of London illustrates the history of London from prehistoric times to the present day. It opened in 1976 and is based on the amalgamation of the former Guildhall Museum and London Museum. The museum is controlled by a board of governors, appointed (nine each) by the government and the Corporation of London. The museum is currently funded by grants from the Department for Culture, Media and Sport and the Corporation of London. The total grant-in-aid for 2007–8 is £13.6m.

Chair of Board of Governors, Michael Cassidy, CBE
Director, Prof. Jack Lohman

MUSEUMS, LIBRARIES AND ARCHIVES COUNCIL (MLA)

Victoria House, Southampton Row, London WC1B 4EA
T 020-7273 1444 F 020-7273 1404
E info@mla.gov.uk W www.mla.gov.uk

The MLA was launched in April 2000 and is the lead strategic agency for museums, libraries and archives. It works with nine regional agencies and is a non-departmental public body sponsored by the Department for Culture, Media and Sport. The MLA replaced the Museums and Galleries Commission (MGC) and the Library and Information Commission (LIC).

Chair, Mark Wood
Chief Executive, Chris Batt, OBE
Board Members, Geoffrey Bond; Sarah Carthew; Roy Clare; Alex Cunningham; Nick Dodd; Yinnon Ezra; Helen Forde; John Hicks; Sir Geoffrey Holland; Glen Lawes; Prof. Sara Selwood; John Tarrant; Michael Walsh; Robert Wand

NATIONAL ARMY MUSEUM

Royal Hospital Road, London SW3 4HT
T 020-7730 0717
E info@national-army-museum.ac.uk
W www.national-army-museum.ac.uk

The National Army Museum was established by ro charter in 1960, and covers the history of five centuries the British Army. It chronicles the campaigns and batt fought over this time as well as the social history a development of the Army, and its impact on Britain a the world. The museum houses a wide array of artefac paintings, photographs, uniforms and equipment.

Chair, General Sir Jack Deverell, KCB, OBE
Director, Dr Alan J. Guy

NATIONAL CONSUMER COUNCIL (NCC

20 Grosvenor Gardens, London SW1W 0DH
T 020-7730 3469 F 020-7730 0191
E info@ncc.org.uk W www.ncc.org.uk

The NCC was set up by the government in 1975 to gi an independent voice to consumers in the UK. Its role to advocate the consumer interest to decision-makers national and local government, industry and regulato bodies, business and the professions. It does this throu a combination of research and campaigning. The NCC a non-profit-making company limited by guarantee a is largely funded by grant-in-aid from the Departme for Business, Enterprise and Regulatory Reform, and t secretary of state appoints the chair and board membe The council is not a consumer advice or complair body.

Chair, Lord Whitty
Chief Executive, Ed Mayo

NATIONAL ENDOWMENT FOR SCIENC TECHNOLOGY AND THE ARTS (NESTA)

1 Plough Place, London EC4A 1DE
T 020-7438 2500 F 020-7438 2501
E nesta@nesta.org.uk W www.nesta.org.uk

NESTA was established under the National Lottery A 1998 with a £200m endowment from the proceeds of t National Lottery. Its endowment is presently over £250 making it the largest single source of early-stage busine funding in the UK. NESTA's aim is to improve the UK capacity for innovation by investing in ventures th stimulate entrepreneurship and by instigatir programmes of business mentoring and support.

Chair, Chris Powell
Chief Executive, Jonathan Kestenbaum

NATIONAL GALLERIES OF SCOTLAND

The Dean Gallery, 73 Belford Road, Edinburgh EH4 3DS
T 0131-624 6200 F 0131-623 7133
E enquiries@nationalgalleries.org W www.nationalgalleries.or

The National Galleries of Scotland comprise the Nation Gallery of Scotland, the Scottish National Portra Gallery, the Scottish National Gallery of Modern Art, th Dean Gallery and the Royal Scottish Academy Buildin There are also outstations at Paxton House, Berwickshir and Duff House, Banffshire. Total government grant-i aid for 2006–7 was £12.43m.

TRUSTEES
Chair, Sir Brian Ivory, CBE
Trustees, Ian Barr; Anne Bonnar; Richard Burns; James Dawney; Marc Ellington; James Knox; Ray Macfarlane; Gordon Mackie; Alasdair Morton; Prof. Richard Thomson; Dr Ruth Wishart

OFFICERS
Director-General, John Leighton
Directors, M. Clarke *(National Gallery of Scotland)*; Keith Hartley *(Scottish National Gallery of Modern Art and Dean Gallery – acting)*; J. Holloway *(Scottish National Portrait Gallery)*

NATIONAL GALLERY

Trafalgar Square, London WC2N 5DN
T 020-7747 2885 F 020-7747 2423
W www.nationalgallery.org.uk

The National Gallery, which houses a permanent collection of western European painting from the 13th to the 20th century, was founded in 1824, following a parliamentary grant of £60,000 for the purchase and exhibition of the Angerstein collection of pictures. The present site was first occupied in 1838; an extension to the north of the building with a public entrance in Orange Street was opened in 1975; the Sainsbury wing was opened in 1991; and the Getty Entrance opened off Trafalgar Square at the east end of the main building in 2004. Total government grant-in-aid for 2007–8 is £25.57m.

BOARD OF TRUSTEES
Chair, P. Scott, QC
Trustees, V. Barnsley; S. Burke; Prof. D. Ekserdjian; J. Fenton; M. Getty; Prof. J. Higgins; Lord Kerr of Kinlochard; Prof. M. King; J. Lessore; D. A. Moore; Lady Normanby; J. Snow; R. Sondhi

OFFICERS
Director, Dr C. Saumarez Smith
Director of Collections, Dr S. Foister
Director of Communications, Clare Gough
Director of Conservation, M. H. Wyld, CBE
Director of Education, K. Adler
Director of Scientific Research, Dr A. Roy
Senior Curator, D. Jaffé

NATIONAL HERITAGE MEMORIAL FUND

7 Holbein Place, London SW1W 8NR
T 020-7591 6042 E enquire@hlf.org.uk
W www.nhmf.org.uk

The National Heritage Memorial Fund was set up under the National Heritage Act 1980 in memory of people who have given their lives for the United Kingdom. The fund is one of 'last resort', focusing on saving heritage which is under threat – whether from sale overseas, the break-up of collections or, in the case of land, from unsympathetic development. The fund is administered by a chair and 14 trustees who are appointed by the prime minister.

The National Lottery etc Act 1993 designated the fund as distributor of the heritage share of proceeds from the National Lottery. As a result, the fund now operates a National Heritage Memorial Fund and a Heritage Lottery Fund. The National Heritage Memorial Fund receives an annual grant from the Department for Culture, Media and Sport.
Chair, Dame Liz Forgan, OBE
Director, Robert Bewley

NATIONAL LIBRARY OF SCOTLAND

George IV Bridge, Edinburgh EH1 1EW
T 0131-623 3700 F 0131-623 3701
E enquiries@nls.uk W www.nls.uk

The library, which was founded as the Advocates' Library in 1682, became the National Library of Scotland (NLS) in 1925. It is funded by the Scottish Executive. It contains about 13 million books and pamphlets, two million maps, 20,000 current periodicals, 350 newspaper titles and 120,000 manuscripts, including the recently acquired John Murray Archive. It has an unrivalled Scottish collection as well as online catalogues and digital resources which can be accessed through the NLS website.

Material can be consulted in the reading rooms, which are open to anyone with a valid reader's ticket.
Chair of the Trustees, Prof. Michael Anderson, OBE, FBA, FRSE
National Librarian and Secretary to the Trustees, M. Wade
Directors, C. Newton *(Collection Development)*; D. Campbell *(Corporate Services)*; G. Hunt *(Customer Services)*; G. Dove *(Development)*; A. Miller *(Strategy and Communications)*

NATIONAL LIBRARY OF WALES/LLYFRGELL GENEDLAETHOL CYMRU

Aberystwyth SY23 3BU
T 01970-632800 F 01970-615709
E holi@llgc.org.uk W www.llgc.org.uk

The National Library of Wales was founded by royal charter in 1907, and is funded by the National Assembly for Wales. It contains about four million printed books, 40,000 manuscripts, four million deeds and documents, numerous maps, prints and drawings, and a sound and moving image collection. It specialises in manuscripts and books relating to Wales and the Celtic peoples. It is the repository for pre-1858 Welsh probate records, manorial records and tithe documents, and certain legal records. Admission is by reader's ticket to the reading rooms but entry to the exhibition programme is free.
President, Dr R. Brinley Jones
Heads of Departments, G. Jenkins *(Collection Services)*; M. W. Mainwaring *(Corporate Services)*; Dr W. R. M. Griffiths *(Public Services)*
Librarian, A. M. W. Green

NATIONAL LOTTERY COMMISSION

101 Wigmore Street, London W1U 1QU
T 0845-712 5596 F 020-7016 3401
W www.natlotcomm.gov.uk

The National Lottery Commission replaced the Office of the National Lottery (OFLOT) in 1999 under the National Lottery Act 1998. The commission is responsible for the granting, varying and enforcing of licences to run the National Lottery. It also runs the competition to award the next licence. Its duties are to ensure that the National Lottery is run with all due propriety, that the interests of players are protected, and, subject to these two objectives, that returns to the good causes are maximised. The commission does not have a role in the distribution of funds to good causes, this is undertaken by 14 distributors, visit www.lotteryfunding.org.uk for further information. Gaming and lotteries in the UK are officially regulated and may only be run by licensed operators or in licensed premises.

The Department of Culture, Media and Sport (DCMS) is responsible for gaming and lottery policy and laws. Empowered by the National Lottery Act 1993 (as amended), the DCMS directs the National Lottery Commission, who in turn regulates Camelot, the lottery operator. Camelot, a private company wholly owned by five shareholders, was granted a second seven-year licence to run the Lottery, which began on 27 January 2002 and ends on 31 January 2009.

Chair, Anne Wright, CBE
Chief Executive, Mark Harris

NATIONAL MARITIME MUSEUM

Park Row, Greenwich, London SE10 9NF
T 020-8858 4422 F 020-8312 6632
W www.nmm.ac.uk

Established in 1934, the National Maritime Museum provides information on the maritime history of Great Britain and is the largest institution of its kind in the world, with over two million items in its collections related to searfaring, navigation and astronomy. The museum is in three groups of buildings in Greenwich Park: the main building, the Queen's House (built by Inigo Jones, 1616–35) and the Royal Observatory (including Christopher Wren's Flamsteed House). In 1999 a £20m Heritage Lottery-supported project opened 16 new galleries in a glazed courtyard in the museum's west wing.

Director, Kevin Fewster
Chair, Lord Sterling of Plaistow, GCVO, CBE

NATIONAL MUSEUMS AND GALLERIES NORTHERN IRELAND

Botanic Gardens, Belfast BT9 5AB
T 028-9038 3000 F 028-9038 3006
W www.magni.org.uk

The organisation of National Museums and Galleries of Northern Ireland was established under the Museums and Galleries (Northern Ireland) Order in 1998 and includes the Ulster Museum with Armagh Museum, the Ulster Folk and Transport Museum, the Ulster American Folk Park and W5 at Odyssey (a wholly owned subsidiary).

Legislation requires National Museums and Galleries of Northern Ireland's board of trustees to care for, preserve and add to the collections; ensure that the collections are exhibited to the public; ensure that the significance of the collections is interpreted; and promote the awareness, appreciation and understanding of the public in relation to art, history and science.

Chair, Margaret Elliott, CBE
Vice-Chair, Sir Kenneth Bloomfield
Trustees, Linda Beers; Lt.-Col. Reginald Harvey Bickers; Patricia Flanagan; Dan Harvey; Dame Geraldine Keegan; Prof. Eithne McLaughlin; William Montgomery; Sean Neeson, MLA; Wendy Osborne; Thomas Shaw; Dr Alastair Walker
Chief Executive, Tim Cooke

NATIONAL MUSEUM WALES – AMGUEDDFA CYMRU

Cathays Park, Cardiff CF10 3NP
T 029-2039 7951 F 029-2057 3321
E post@museumwales.ac.uk W www.museumwales.ac.uk

National Museum Wales – Amgueddfa Cymru aims to provide a complete illustration of the geology, mineralogy, zoology, botany, ethnography, archaeology, art, history and special industries of Wales. It is comprised of the National Museum Cardiff; St Fagans National History Museum; Big Pit – National Coal Museum, Blaenafon; the National Roman Legion Museum, Caerleon; the National Slate Museum, Llanberis; the National Wool Museum, Dre-fach Felindre; and the National Waterfront Museum, Swansea. Total funding from the Welsh Assembly government for 2006–7 was £22.45m.

President, Paul E. Loveluck, CBE
Vice-President, Dr Susan J. Davies
Director-General, Michael Houlihan
Trustees, D. Bowen Lewis; Elisabeth Elias; Dr Iolo ap Gwynn; Prof. Colin L. Jones, OBE; Prof. J. W. Last, CBE; Peter W. Morgan; J. E. Peirson Jones; M. C. T. Prichard, CBE; Gareth Williams; H. R. C. Williams; Dr Brian Willott, CB; Rhiannon Wyn Hughes, MBE; J. Wynford Evans, CBE

NATIONAL MUSEUMS LIVERPOOL

127 Dale Street, Liverpool L2 2JH
T 0151-207 0001 F 0151-478 4790
W www.liverpoolmuseums.org.uk

The board of trustees of the National Museums Liverpool (formerly National Museums and Galleries on Merseyside) is responsible for the World Museum Liverpool, the Merseyside Maritime Museum (incorporating HM Customs and Excise National Museum), the Museum of Liverpool, the Lady Lever Art Gallery, the Walker Art Gallery, Sudley House, the National Conservation Centre and the International Slavery Museum. Total government grant-in-aid for 2005–6 was £17.6m.

Chair of the Board of Trustees, Loyd Grossman, OBE
Director, Dr David Fleming
Keeper of Art Galleries, R. King
Keeper, World Museum Liverpool, J. Millard
Keeper, Merseyside Maritime Museum, T. Tibbles
Keeper, Museum of Liverpool, J. Dugdale
Head of Collections Management, National Conservation Centre, Sally Ann Yates
Head of International Slavery Museum, Dr Richard Benjamin

NATIONAL MUSEUMS OF SCOTLAND

Chambers Street, Edinburgh EH1 1JF
T 0131-247 4422 E info@nms.ac.uk W www.nms.ac.uk

National Museums Scotland provides advice and expertise to the museums community across Scotland, and comprise the National Museum of Scotland, the National War Museum, the National Museum of Rural Life, the National Museum of Flight, the National Museum of Costume and the National Museums Collection Centre. Total grant-in-aid funding from the Scottish Executive for 2007–8 is £20.3m.

Trustees are appointed by the Minister for Tourism, Culture and Sport for a term of four years, and may serve a second term.

Chair, Sir Angus Grossart, CBE, LLD, DLITT

Trustees, James Fiddes, OBE, FRICS; Lesley Hart, MBE; Michael Kirwan, FCA; Prof. Michael Lynch, FRSE, FSA (SCOT); Neena Mahal; Sir Neil McIntosh, CBE; Prof. Malcolm McLeod, CBE, FRSE; Dr Stuart Munro, OBE; Ian Ritchie, CBE, FRENG, FRSE; Sir John Ward, CBE, FRSE, FRSA; Iain Watt
Director, Dr Gordon Rintoul

NATIONAL PORTRAIT GALLERY

St Martin's Place, London WC2H 0HE
T 020-7306 0055 **F** 020-7306 0056
W www.npg.org.uk

The National Portrait Gallery was formed after a grant was made in 1856 to form a gallery of the portraits of the most eminent persons in British history. The present building was opened in 1896 and the Ondaatje Wing (including a new Balcony Gallery, Tudor Gallery, IT Gallery, lecture theatre and roof-top restaurant) opened in May 2000. There are three regional partnerships displaying portraits at Montacute House, Beningbrough Hall and Bodelwyddan Castle. Total government grant-in-aid for 2007–8 is £7.03m.

BOARD OF TRUSTEES
Chair, Prof. David Cannadine, FBA, FRSL
Trustees, Rt. Hon. Baroness Amos; Zeinab Badawi; Nicholas Blake, QC; Prof. R. Boucher, CBE, FRENG; Marchioness of Douro; Amelia Fawcett, CBE; Flora Fraser; Sir Nicholas Grimshaw, CBE, PRA; Prof. Ludmilla Jordanova; David Mach, RA; Sir Christopher Ondaatje, CBE, OC; David Ross; Prof. Sara Selwood; Alexandra Shulman, OBE; Sir John Weston, KCMG
Director, Sandy Nairne

NATURAL ENGLAND

1 East Parade, Sheffield S1 2ET
T 0845-600 3078
E enquiries@naturalengland.org.uk
W www.naturalengland.org.uk

Natural England was established on 1 October 2006 after the Natural Environment and Rural Communities Act received royal assent in March 2006. The organisation encompasses three previous bodies: English Nature, the environmental land management elements of the Rural Development Service and the Countryside Agency's landscape, access and recreation division. It is responsible for enhancing biodiversity, landscapes and wildlife in rural, urban, coastal and marine areas; promoting access, recreation and public wellbeing; designating sites of special scientific interest, national parks and areas of outstanding natural beauty; managing national nature reserves; enforcing associated regulations; and contributing to the way natural resources are managed.
Chief Executive, Dr Helen Phillips

NATURAL HISTORY MUSEUM

Cromwell Road, London SW7 5BD
T 020-7942 5000 **W** www.nhm.ac.uk

The Natural History Museum originates from the natural history departments of the British Museum, which grew extensively during the 19th century; in 1860 the natural history collection was moved from Bloomsbury to a new location. Part of the site of the 1862 International Exhibition in South Kensington was acquired for the new museum, and the museum opened to the public in 1881. In 1963 the Natural History Museum became completely independent with its own board of trustees. The Natural History Museum at Tring, bequeathed by the second Lord Rothschild, has formed part of the museum since 1938. The Geological Museum merged with the Natural History Museum in 1985. Total government grant-in-aid for 2006–7 was £42.8m.
Chair, Oliver Stacken
Trustees, Sir William Castell; Prof. Dianne Edwards, CBE, FRS; Prof. M. Hassell, CBE, FRS; Prof. C. Leaver, CBE, FRS; Prof. Georgina Mace, OBE; Dame Judith Mayhew, DBE; Prof. J. McGlade; Lord Palumbo; Prof. Linda Partridge, FRS, FRSE; Sir Richard Sykes, FRS

SENIOR STAFF
Director, Dr Michael Dixon
Director of Estates and Services, David Sanders
Director of Finance, N. Greenwood
Director of Human Resources, P. Brereton
Director, Natural History Museum at Tring, Mrs T. Wild
Director of Public Engagement Group, Sharon Ament
Director of Science, R. Lane
Head of Audit and Review, D. Thorpe
Head of Library and Information Services, G. Higley
Keeper of Botany, Dr J. Vogel
Keeper of Entomology, Dr M. Scoble
Keeper of Mineralogy, Prof. A. Fleet
Keeper of Palaeontology, Dr N. MacLeod
Keeper of Zoology, Prof. P. Rainbow
Museum Manager, I. Jenkinson

NORTHERN IRELAND HUMAN RIGHTS COMMISSION

Temple Court, 39 North Street, Belfast BT1 1NA
T 028-9024 3987 Textphone 028-9024 9066
F 028-9024 7844
E information@nihrc.org **W** www.nihrc.org

The Northern Ireland Human Rights Commission was set up in March 1999. Its main functions are to keep under review the law and practice relating to human rights in Northern Ireland, to advise the government and to promote an awareness of human rights in Northern Ireland. It can also take cases to court. The members of the commission are appointed by the Secretary of State for Northern Ireland.
Chief Commissioner, Prof. Monica McWilliams
Commissioners, Jonathan Bell; Thomas Duncan; Lady Christine Eames; Prof. Colin Harvey; Alan Henry; Ann Hope; Kevin McLaughlin; Eamonn O'Neill; Geraldine Rice

NORTHERN LIGHTHOUSE BOARD

84 George Street, Edinburgh EH2 3DA
T 0131-473 3100 **F** 0131-220 2093
E enquiries@nlb.org.uk **W** www.nlb.org.uk

The Northern Lighthouse Board is the general lighthouse authority for Scotland and the Isle of Man and owes its origin to an act of parliament passed in 1786. At present there are 19 commissioners who operate under the Merchant Shipping Act 1995.

The commissioners control 212 lighthouses, many lighted and unlighted buoys, a DGPS (differential global positioning system) station and a LORAN (long-range navigation) system (class C) on a trial basis. *See also* Transport section.

Chair, Capt. George Sutherland
Commissioners, Lord Advocate; Solicitor-General for Scotland; Lord Provosts of Edinburgh, Glasgow and Aberdeen; Convener of Highland Council; Convener of Argyll and Bute Council; Sheriffs-Principal of North Strathclyde, Tayside, Central and Fife, Grampian, Highlands and Islands, South Strathclyde, Dumfries and Galloway, Lothians and Borders and Glasgow and Strathkelvin; Peter MacKay, CB; Dr Andrew Cubie, CBE, FRSE; Capt. Kenneth MacLeod; Robert Quayle; Alistair Whyte
Chief Executive, Roger Lockwood, CB

OFFICE OF COMMUNICATIONS (OFCOM)

Riverside House, 2A Southwark Bridge Road, London SE1 9HA
T 020-7981 3000 **F** 020-7981 3033
E contact@ofcom.org.uk **W** www.ofcom.org.uk

OFCOM was established in 2003 under the Office of Communications Act 2002 as the independent regulator and competition authority for the UK communications industries with responsibility for television, radio, telecommunications and wireless communications services. It merged the functions of five regulatory bodies: the Independent Television Commission (ITC), the Broadcasting Standards Commission (BSC), the Office of Telecommunications (OFTEL), the Radio Authority (RAu) and the Radiocommunications Agency (RA).
Chief Executive, Ed Richards
Chair, David Currie
Deputy Chair, Philip Graf, CBE
Board Members, Millie Banerjee; Ian Hargreaves; Stephanie Liston; Sara Nathan; Philip Rutnam

OFFICE OF THE LEGAL SERVICES OMBUDSMAN

3rd Floor, Sunlight House, Quay Street, Manchester M3 3JZ
T 0161-839 7262; 0845-601 0794 **F** 0161-832 5446
E lso@olso.gsi.gov.uk **W** www.olso.org

The Legal Services Ombudsman oversees the handling of complaints against solicitors, barristers, licensed conveyancers, legal executives and patent agents by their professional bodies. A complainant must first complain to the relevant professional body before raising the matter with the ombudsman, who will then investigate the way the complaint was dealt with. The ombudsman is independent of the legal profession and her services are free of charge, although she is unable to give legal advice.
Legal Services Ombudsman, Zahida Manzoor, CBE
Operations Director, Gavin Brown

OFFICE OF MANPOWER ECONOMICS (OME)

6th Floor, Kingsgate House, 66–74 Victoria Street, London SW1E 6SW
T 020-7215 8252 **F** 020-7215 4445
W www.ome.uk.com

OME was set up in 1971. It is an independent non-statutory organisation which is responsible for servicing independent review bodies which advise on the pay of various public service groups, the Police Negotiating Board and the Police Advisory Board for England and Wales. The OME is also responsible for servicing *ad hoc* bodies of inquiry and for undertaking research into pay and associated matters as requested by the government.
OME Director, Ian Jones
Director, Health Secretariats, Research and Analysis Group and OME Deputy Director, David Miner
Director, Armed Forces' and Prison Service Secretariats, Christine Haworth
Director, Senior Salaries Secretariat, Keith Masson
Director, School Teachers', Police Negotiating Board and Police Advisory Board for England and Wales Secretariats, David Wilson

OFFICE OF THE PENSIONS OMBUDSMAN

6th Floor, 11 Belgrave Road, London SW1V 1RB
T 020-7834 9144 **F** 020-7821 0065
E enquiries@pensions-ombudsman.org.uk
W www.pensions-ombudsman.org.uk

The Pensions Ombudsman is appointed by the Secretary of State for Work and Pensions, under the Pension Schemes Act 1993 as amended by the Pensions Act 1995. He independently investigates and decides complaints and disputes concerning pension schemes. The Pension Ombudsman's decision is final and binding to all parties concerned in the complaint or dispute, and it can be legally enforced.
Pensions Ombudsman, David Laverick

OFFICE OF THE SCOTTISH LEGAL SERVICES OMBUDSMAN

17 Waterloo Place, Edinburgh EH1 3DL
T 0131-556 9123 **F** 0131-556 9292
E ombudsman@slso.org.uk **W** www.slso.org.uk

The ombudsman investigates complaints about the way in which Scottish professional bodies have handled a complaint against a practitioner.

The ombudsman also examines complaints about the unwillingness of a professional body to investigate a complaint against a practitioner.
Scottish Legal Services Ombudsman, Jane Irvine

PARADES COMMISSION

Windsor House, 9–15 Bedford Street, Belfast BT2 7EL
T 028-9089 5900 **F** 028-9032 2988
E info@paradescommission.com
W www.paradescommission.org

The Parades Commission was set up under the Public Processions (Northern Ireland) Act 1998. Its function is to encourage and facilitate local accommodation on contentious parades; where this is not possible, the commission is empowered to make legal determinations about such parades, which may include imposing conditions on aspects of the notified parade (such as restrictions on routes/areas and exclusion of certain groups with a record of bad behaviour).

The chair and members are appointed by the Secretary of State for Northern Ireland; the membership must, as far as is practicable, be representative of the community in Northern Ireland.
Chair, Roger Poole
Vice-Chair, Vilma Patterson, MBE
Members, Kelly Andrews; David Burrows; Dr Joe Hendron; Anne Monaghan; Alison Scott-McKinley

PARLIAMENTARY AND HEALTH SERVICE OMBUDSMAN

Millbank Tower, Millbank, London SW1P 4QP
T 0845-015 4033 F 020-7217 4000
E phso.enquiries@ombudsman.org.uk
W www.ombudsman.org.uk

The Parliamentary Ombudsman is independent of government and is an officer of parliament. She is responsible for investigating complaints referred to her by MPs from members of the public who claim to have sustained injustice in consequence of maladministration by or on behalf of government departments and certain non-departmental public bodies. In 1999 an additional 158 public bodies were brought within the jurisdiction of the Parliamentary Ombudsman. Certain types of action by government departments or bodies are excluded from investigation. The Parliamentary Ombudsman is also responsible for investigating complaints, referred by MPs, alleging that access to official information has been wrongly refused under the Code of Practice on Access to Government Information 1994.

The Health Service Ombudsman for England is responsible for investigating complaints against National Health Service authorities and trusts that are not dealt with by those authorities to the satisfaction of the complainant. Complaints can be referred directly by the member of the public who claims to have sustained injustice or hardship in consequence of the failure in a service provided by a relevant body. The ombudsman's jurisdiction now covers complaints about family doctors, dentists, pharmacists and opticians, and complaints about actions resulting from clinical judgement.

The Health Service Ombudsman is also responsible for investigating complaints that information has been wrongly refused under the Code of Practice on Openness in the National Health Service 1995. The parliamentary and the health offices are presently held by the same person.

Parliamentary Ombudsman and Health Service Ombudsman, Ms A. Abraham
Deputy Parliamentary Commissioner, Ms T. Longdon

PAROLE BOARD FOR ENGLAND AND WALES

Grenadier House, 99–105 Horseferry Road, London SW1P 2DD
T 0870-420 3505 F 020-7217 0118
E info@paroleboard.gov.uk W www.paroleboard.gov.uk

The Parole Board was established under the Criminal Justice Act 1967 and became an independent executive non-departmental public body under the Criminal Justice and Public Order Act 1994. It is the body that protects the public by making risk assessments about prisoners to decide who may safely be released into the community and who must remain in, or be returned to, custody. Board decisions are taken at two main types of three-member panels: 'paper panels' for the vast majority of cases, or oral hearings for finely balanced decisions concerning prisoners serving life or on extended sentences.

Chair, Prof. Sir Duncan Nichol, CBE
Chief Executive, Christine Glenn

PAROLE BOARD FOR SCOTLAND

Saughton House, Broomhouse Drive, Edinburgh EH11 3XD
T 0131-244 8373 F 0131-244 6974
W www.scottishparoleboard.gov.uk

The board directs and advises the Scottish ministers on the release of prisoners on licence, and related matters.

Chair, Prof. Sandy Cameron
Vice-Chair, Sheriff Rita Rae, QC

PENSION PROTECTION FUND (PPF)

Knollys House, 17 Addiscombe Road, Croydon CR0 6SR
T 0845-600 2541 F 020-8633 4903
E information@ppf.gsi.gov.uk
W www.pensionprotectionfund.org.uk

The PPF became operational in 2005. It was established to pay compensation to members of eligible defined-benefit pension schemes where a qualifying insolvency event in relation to the employer occurs, or where there is a lack of sufficient assets in the pension scheme. The PPF is also responsible for the Fraud Compensation Fund (which provides compensation to occupational pension schemes that suffer a loss that can be attributed to dishonesty). The chair and board of the PPF are appointed by, and accountable to, the Secretary of State for Work and Pensions, and are responsible for paying compensation, calculating annual levies (which help fund the PPF), and setting and overseeing investment strategy.

Chair, Lawrence Churchill
Chief Executive, Partha Dasgupta

THE PENSIONS REGULATOR

Napier House, Trafalgar Place, Brighton BN1 4DW
T 0870-606 3636 F 0870-241 1144
E customersupport@thepensionsregulator.gov.uk
W www.thepensionsregulator.gov.uk

The Pensions Regulator was established in 2005 as the regulator of work-based pensions in the UK, replacing the Occupational Pensions Regulatory Authority (OPRA). It aims to protect the benefits of occupational and personal pension scheme members, while reducing the risk of situations leading to claims on the Pension Protection Fund. The regulator is able to collect detailed scheme information, issue improvement notices and third-party notices, disqualify trustees deemed unfit to carry out their duties, issue a contribution notice or financial support direction, and freeze a scheme at risk while it investigates.

Chair, David Norgrove
Chief Executive, Tony Hobman

POLICE ADVISORY BOARD FOR ENGLAND AND WALES

6th Floor, Kingsgate House, 66–74 Victoria Street, London SW1E 6SW
T 020-7215 8101 F 020-7215 4445
W www.ome.uk.com

The Police Advisory Board for England and Wales was established in 1965 and provides advice to the home secretary on general questions affecting the police in England and Wales. It also considers draft regulations which the secretary of state proposes to make with respect to matters other than hours of duty, leave, pay and allowances or the issue, use and return of police clothing, personal equipment and other effects.

Independent Chair, John Randall
Independent Deputy Chair, Prof. Gillian Morris

POLICE NEGOTIATING BOARD (PNB)

6h Floor, Kingsgate House, 66–74 Victoria Street, London SW1E 6SW
T 020-7215 8101 F 020-7215 4445
W www.ome.uk.com

The PNB was established in 1980 to negotiate pay, allowances, hours of duty, leave and pensions of United Kingdom police officers and to make recommendations on these matters to the Secretary of State for Home Affairs, Northern Ireland secretary, and Scottish ministers.
Independent Chair, John Randall
Independent Deputy Chair, Prof. Gillian Morris

POLICE OMBUDSMAN FOR NORTHERN IRELAND

New Cathedral Buildings, St Anne's Square, Belfast BT1 1PG
T 028-9082 8600 F 028-9082 8659
E info@policeombudsman.org W www.policeombudsman.org

Founded in November 2000 under the Police (Northern Ireland) Act 1998, the function of the Office of the Police Ombudsman for Northern Ireland is to investigate complaints against the police in an impartial, efficient, effective and (as far as is possible) transparent way, to win the confidence of the public and the police. It must report on trends in complaints and react to incidents involving the police, where it is in the public interest, even if no individual complaint has been made.
Police Ombudsman, N. O'Loan

PRISONS AND PROBATION OMBUDSMAN FOR ENGLAND AND WALES

Ashley House, 2 Monck Street, London SW1P 2BQ
T 020-7035 2876 F 020-7035 2860
E mail@ppo.gsi.gov.uk W www.ppo.gov.uk

The ombudsman provides a free and independent complaints investigation service for prisoners, those held in immigration detention and those under probation supervision who have been unable to resolve their grievances with the Prison, Immigration and Probation Services. He also conducts independent investigations into the deaths of prisoners, residents of probation hostels and people detained by the immigration authorities.
Ombudsman, Stephen Shaw, CBE

PRISON SERVICE PAY REVIEW BODY (PSPRB)

6th Floor, Kingsgate House, 66–74 Victoria Street, London SW1E 6SW
T 020-7215 8503 F 020-7215 4445
W www.ome.uk.com

The PSPRB was set up in 2001. It makes independent recommendations on the pay of prison governors, operational managers, prison officers and related grades for the Prison Service in England and Wales and for the Northern Ireland Prison Service.
Chair, Jerry Cope
Members, Beryl Brewer; Dr Henrietta Campbell; Richard Childs, QPM; Ray Coughlin; Bronwen Curtis; John Davies; Joseph Magee; Sarah Murray; Dr Peter Riach; Ann Robinson; Peter Tett

REGIONAL DEVELOPMENT AGENCIES (RDAS)

Broadway House, Tothill Street, London SW1H 9NQ
T 020-7222 8180 F 020-7222 8182
E natsec@rda-secretariat.com
W www.englandsrdas.com

RDAs were established to help the English regions improve their relative economic performance and reduce social and economic disparities within and between regions. Their five statutory objectives are to further economic development and regeneration; to promote business efficiency and competitiveness; to promote employment; to enhance the development and application of skills relevant to employment; and to contribute to sustainable development. There are nine RDAs in England, and they are financed through a single fund provided by contributing government departments (BERR, DCSF, DIUS, DEFRA and DCMS). In 2005–6 the RDA's budget was £2.2bn.

RDA REGIONS
NORTH WEST – PO Box 37, Renaissance House, Centre Park, Warrington WA1 1XB T 01925-400100
Chair, Bryan Gray, MBE
YORKSHIRE – Victoria House, 2 Victoria Place, Leeds LS11 5AE T 0113-394 9600 *Chair,* Terry Hodgkinson
NORTH EAST – Stella House, Goldcrest Way, Newburn Riverside, Newcastle upon Tyne NE15 8NY T 0191-229 6200
Chair, Margaret Fay
WEST MIDLANDS – 3 Priestley Wharf, Holt Street, Aston Science Park, Birmingham B7 4BN T 0121-380 3500
Chair, Nick Paul
EAST MIDLANDS – Apex Court, City Link, Nottingham NG2 4LA T 0115-988 8300 *Chair,* Dr Bryan Jackson
EAST OF ENGLAND – The Business Centre, Station Road, Histon, Cambridge CB4 9LQ T 01223-713900
Chair, Richard Ellis
SOUTH WEST – Sterling House, Dix's Field, Exeter EX1 1QA T 01392-214747 *Chair,* Juliet Williams
LONDON – Palestra, 197 Blackfriars Road, London SE1 8AA T 020-7593 8700 *Chair,* Mary Reilly
SOUTH EAST – Cross Lanes, Guildford GU1 1YA T 01483-484200 *Chair,* Jim Braithwaite

REGISTRAR OF PUBLIC LENDING RIGHT

Richard House, Sorbonne Close, Stockton on Tees TS17 6DA
T 01642-604699 F 01642-615641
E authorservices@plr.uk.com W www.plr.uk.com

Under the Public Lending Right system, in operation since 1983, payment is made from public funds to authors whose books are lent out from public libraries. Payment is made once a year and the amount each author receives is proportionate to the number of times (established from a sample) that each registered book has been lent out during the previous year. The registrar of PLR, who is appointed by the Secretary of State for Culture, Media and Sport, compiles the register of authors and books. Authors resident in all EU countries are eligible to apply. (The term 'author' covers writers, illustrators, translators, and some editors/compilers.)

A payment of 5.98 pence was made in 2006–7 for each estimated loan of a registered book, up to a top limit of £6,600 for the books of any one registered author; the money for loans above this level is used to augment the remaining PLR paymensts. In 2007 the sum of £6.81m was paid out to 23,869 registered authors and assignees as the annual payment of PLR.

Registrar, Dr J. G. Parker
Chair of Advisory Committee, S. Brett

REVIEW BODY FOR NURSING AND OTHER HEALTH PROFESSIONS

6th Floor, Kingsgate House, 66–74 Victoria Street, London SW1E 6SW
T 020-7215 4453 **F** 020-7215 4445
W www.ome.uk.com

The Review Body for Nurses and Allied Health Professions was set up in 1983, and following the Agenda for Change in 2004 the body changed its name to recognise its broader staff remit. It advises the prime minister and the Secretary of State for Health, and ministers of the Scottish Executive and Welsh Assembly on the remuneration of nursing staff and other health professions employed in the National Health Service, which is currently around 700,000 people.

Chair, Prof. Gillian Morris
Members, Philip Ashmore; Lucinda Bolton; Prof. Richard Disney; Wilma MacPherson, CBE; Prof. Alan Manning; Ian McKay; Sharon Whitlam

REVIEW BODY ON DOCTORS' AND DENTISTS' REMUNERATION

6th Floor, Kingsgate House, 66–74 Victoria Street, London SW1E 6SW
T 020-7215 8407 **F** 020-7215 4445
W www.ome.uk.com

The Review Body on Doctors' and Dentists' Remuneration was set up in 1971. It advises the prime minister and the Secretaries of State for Health, Scotland and Wales on the remuneration of doctors and dentists taking any part in the National Health Service.

Chair, Ronald Amy, OBE
Members, Prof. John Beath; Dr Margaret Collingwood, TD; Hugh Donaldson; Katrina Easterling; David Grafton

ROYAL AIR FORCE MUSEUM

Grahame Park Way, London NW9 5LL
T 020-8205 2266 **F** 020-8200 1751
E london@rafmuseum.org **W** www.rafmuseum.org

The museum has two sites, one at the former airfield at Hendon and the second at Cosford, in the West Midlands, both of which illustrate the development of aviation from before the Wright brothers to the present-day RAF with over 100 aircraft, as well as artefacts, aviation memorabilia, fine art and photographs. Total government grant-in-aid for 2005–6, provided by the Ministry of Defence, was £7.03m.

Director-General, Dr M. A. Fopp

ROYAL BOTANIC GARDEN EDINBURGH (RBGE)

20A Inverleith Row, Edinburgh EH3 5LR
T 0131-552 7171 **F** 0131-248 2901
E info@rbge.org.uk **W** www.rbge.org.uk

The RBGE originated as the Physic Garden, established in 1670 beside the Palace of Holyroodhouse. The garden moved to its present 28-hectare site at Inverleith, Edinburgh, in 1821. There are also three regional gardens: Benmore Botanic Garden, near Dunoon, Argyll; Logan Botanic Garden, near Stranraer, Wigtownshire; and Dawyck Botanic Garden, near Stobo, Peeblesshire. Since 1986 RBGE has been administered by a board of trustees established under the National Heritage (Scotland) Act 1985. It receives an annual grant from the Environment and Rural Affairs Department of the Scottish Executive.

The RBGE is an international centre for scientific research on plant diversity and for horticulture education and conservation. It has an extensive library, a herbarium with over two million preserved plant specimens, and over 16,500 species in the living collections.

Chair of the Board of Trustees, Dr Paul Nicholson
Regius Keeper, Prof. Stephen Blackmore, FRSE

ROYAL BOTANIC GARDENS (RBG) KEW

Richmond, Surrey TW9 3AB
T 020-8332 5000 **F** 020-8332 5197
Wakehurst Place, Ardingly, W. Sussex RH17 6TN
T 01444-89000 **F** 01444-894069
E info@kew.org **W** www.kew.org

The Royal Botanic Gardens (RBG) Kew were originally laid out as a private garden for Kew House for George III's mother, Princess Augusta, in 1759. The gardens were much enlarged in the 19th century, notably by the inclusion of the grounds of the former Richmond Lodge. In 1965 the garden at Wakehurst Place was acquired; it is owned by the National Trust and managed by RBG Kew. Under the National Heritage Act 1983 a board of trustees was set up to administer the gardens, which in 1984 became an independent body supported by grant-in-aid from the Department of Environment, Food and Rural Affairs.

The functions of RBG Kew are to carry out research into plant sciences, to disseminate knowledge about plants and to provide the public with the opportunity to gain knowledge and enjoyment from the gardens' collections. There are extensive national reference collections of living and preserved plants and a comprehensive library and archive. The main emphasis is on plant conservation and biodiversity; Wakehurst Place houses the Millennium Seed Bank, which is the largest *ex situ* conservation project ever conceived – its aim is to acquire seed from ten per cent of Earth's wild plant species by 2010.

BOARD OF TRUSTEES
Chair, Lord Selborne
Members, Marcus Agius; Tanya Burman; Andrew Cahn; Richard Deverell; Prof. Jonathan Drori, CBE; Prof. Charles Godfray; Dr Sandy Harrison; Richard Lapthorne, CBE; David Norman; Marion Regan; Prof. Sir William Stewart; Sir Richard Sykes
Director, Prof. Stephen Hopper

ROYAL COMMISSION ON ENVIRONMENTAL POLLUTION

3rd Floor, 5–8 The Sanctuary, Westminster, London SW1P 3JS
T 020-7799 8970 **F** 020-7799 8971
E enquiries@rcep.org.uk **W** www.rcep.org.uk

The commission was set up in 1970 to advise on national and international matters concerning the pollution of the environment. The commission's advice is mainly in the form of reports which are the outcome of studies, the most recent of which relates to the urban environment.

Members are appointed by the Queen on the advice of the prime minister.

Chair, Prof. Sir John Lawton, CBE, FRS

Members, Prof. Nicholas Cumpsty, FRENG; Prof. Michael H. Depledge; Dr Paul Ekins; Dr I. Graham-Bryce, CBE, FRSE; Prof. Stephen Holgate, FRCP; Prof. J. Jowell, QC; Prof. Peter Liss; Prof. Susan Owens, OBE; Prof. Judith Petts; Prof. S. Rayner; John Speirs, CBE, LVO; Prof. Janet Sprent, OBE, FRSE; Prof. Lynda Warren

ROYAL COMMISSION ON THE ANCIENT AND HISTORICAL MONUMENTS OF SCOTLAND

John Sinclair House, 16 Bernard Terrace, Edinburgh EH8 9NX
T 0131-662 1456 F 0131-662 1477
E info@rcahms.gov.uk W www.rcahms.gov.uk

The Royal Commission was established by a royal warrant in 1908, which was revised in 1992, and is appointed to provide for the survey and recording of ancient and historical monuments connected with the culture, civilisation and conditions of life of the people in Scotland from the earliest times. It is funded by the Scottish Executive. The commission compiles, maintains and makes available the National Monuments Record of Scotland as the national record of the archaeological and historical environment.

Chair, Prof. John Hume, OBE, FSA (SCOT)

Commissioners, Kate Byrne; Mark Hopton, FSA (SCOT); Prof. John Hunter, FSA, FSA (SCOT); Prof. Angus Macdonald, FSA (SCOT); Dr Margaret Mackay, FSA (SCOT); Gordon Masterton; Prof. Christopher Morris, FSA, FRSE, FSA (SCOT); Dr Jane Murray, FSA (SCOT); Dr Stana Nenadic, FSA (SCOT)

Chief Executive, Diana Murray, FSA, FSA (SCOT)

ROYAL COMMISSION ON THE ANCIENT AND HISTORICAL MONUMENTS OF WALES

Crown Building, Plas Crug, Aberystwyth SY23 1NJ
T 01970-621200 F 01970-627701
E nmr.wales@rcahmw.gov.uk W www.rcahmw.gov.uk

The Royal Commission was established in 1908 and is currently empowered by a royal warrant of 2001 to survey, record, publish and maintain a database of ancient and historical and maritime sites and structures, and landscapes, in Wales. The commission is funded by the National Assembly for Wales and is also responsible for the National Monuments Record of Wales, which is open daily for public reference and has a public enquiry service. The commission is responsible for supplying archaeological information to Ordnance Survey, for the coordination of archaeological aerial photography in Wales, and for sponsorship of the regional Sites and Monuments Records.

Chair, Prof. Ralph A. Griffiths, DLITT, FRHISTS

Vice-Chair, Dr Llinos Smith, FRHISTS

Commissioners, Prof. Anthony D. Carr, FSA, FRHISTS; David W. Crossley, FSA; Mrs A. Eastham; Neil Harries; John W. Lloyd, CB; Jonathan Matthews Hudson; John Newman, FSA; Henry Owen-John; Prof. Patrick Sims-Williams, FBA

ROYAL MAIL GROUP

148 Old Street, London EC1V 9HQ
T 020-7250 2888
W www.royalmailgroup.com

Crown services for the carriage of government dispatches were set up in about 1516. The conveyance of public correspondence began in 1635 and the mail service was made a parliamentary responsibility with the setting up of a Post Office in 1657. Telegraphs came under Post Office control in 1870 and the Post Office Telephone Service began in 1880. The National Girobank service of the Post Office began in 1968. The Post Office ceased to be a government department in 1969 when responsibility for the running of the postal, telecommunications, giro and remittance services was transferred to a public authority of the same name.

The British Telecommunications Act 1981 separated the functions of the Post Office, making it solely responsible for postal services and Girobank. Girobank was privatised in 1990. The Postal Services Act 2000 turned the Post Office into a wholly owned public limited company establishing a regulatory regime under the Postal Service Commission. The Post Office Group changed its name to Consignia plc in March 2001 when its new corporate structure took effect; in November 2001 the name was changed to Royal Mail Group plc. As of 1 January 2006 the UK postal service market was fully liberalised, and any licensed operator is now able to deliver mail to businesses and residential customers.

The chair, chief executive and members of the board are appointed by the Secretary of State for Business, Enterprise and Regulatory Reform but responsibility for the running of Royal Mail Group as a whole rests with the board in its corporate capacity.

BOARD

Chair, Allan Leighton

Chief Executive (Royal Mail Group), Adam Crozier

Managing Director, Alan Cook, CBE *(Post Office Ltd)*

Members, David Burden *(Group Technology Director)*; Ian Duncan *(Group Finance Director)*; Tony McCarthy *(Group Director, People and Organisational Development)*

Non-Executive Directors, David Fish; Richard Handover; Sir Mike Hodgkinson; John Neill, CBE; Baroness Prosser, OBE; Helen Weir

ROYAL NAVAL MUSEUM

HM Naval Base (PP66), Portsmouth PO1 3NH
T 023-9272 7562 F 023-9272 7575
W www.royalnavalmuseum.org

The Royal Naval Museum is a non-departmental public body sponsored by the Ministry of Defence, and is a registered charity governed by a board of trustees. Lord Nelson's flagship, HMS *Victory*, is in dry dock and is part of the museum. The museum aims to provide an effective and accessible repository for the heritage of the Navy, and to raise public awareness, and encourage scholarship and research into, the history and achievements of the Royal Navy.

Chair, Adm. Sir Peter Abbott, GBE, KCB

SCHOOL TEACHERS' REVIEW BODY (STRB)

6th Floor, Kingsgate House, 66–74 Victoria Street, London SW1E 6SW
T 020-7215 8297 F 020-7215 4445
W www.ome.uk.com

The STRB was set up under the School Teachers' Pay and Conditions Act 1991. It is required to examine and report on such matters relating to the statutory conditions of employment of school teachers in England and Wales as may be referred to it by the education secretary.

Chair, Bill Cockburn, CBE, TD

Members, Jennifer Board; Monojit Chatterji; Mark Goodridge; Dewi Jones; Elizabeth Kidd; Esmond Lindop; Bruce Warman; Anne Watts

SCIENCE MUSEUM

Exhibition Road, London SW7 2DD

T 0870-870 4868 **E** sciencemuseum@nmsi.ac.uk

W www.sciencemuseum.org.uk

The Science Museum, part of the National Museum of Science and Industry (NMSI), houses the national collections of science, technology, industry and medicine. The museum began as the science collection of the South Kensington Museum and first opened in 1857. In 1883 it acquired the collections of the Patent Museum and in 1909 the science collections were transferred to the new Science Museum, leaving the art collections with the Victoria and Albert Museum. The Wellcome Wing was opened in July 2000.

Some of the museum's larger objects, ranging across aircraft, agricultural machinery, computing, mechanical engineering, and road and rail transport collections, are at Science Museum Swindon, Wilts. The NMSI also incorporates the National Railway Museum, York, the National Museum of Photography, Film and Television, Bradford, and Locomotion: the National Railway Museum at Shildon.

Total government grant-in-aid for 2007–8 is £38.61m.

Chair, Rt. Hon. Lord Waldegrave of North Hill

Trustees, Lady Chisholm; Prof. Sir Ron U. Cooke, DSC; Prof. Dame Ann Dowling, CBE, FRENG; Lord Faulkner of Worcester; Dr Douglas Gurr; Richard Haythornthwaite; Lord Rees of Ludlow, FRS; Prof. Sir Howard Newby, KB, CBE; Prof. Simon J. Schaffer; Dr Maggie Semple, OBE; Dr Tony Sewell; Martin G. Smith; Prof. Roderick A. Smith, FRENG; Prof. Kathy Sykes; Sir William Wells; Michael G. Wilson

Director of NMSI, Martin Earwicker

Director of Science Museum, Prof. Chris Rapley, CBE

Director of National Media Museum, Colin Philpott

Director of National Railway Museum, Andrew Scott

SCOTTISH ARTS COUNCIL

12 Manor Place, Edinburgh EH3 7DD

T 0131-226 6051 **F** 0131-225 9833

E help.desk@scottisharts.org.uk **W** www.scottisharts.org.uk

The Scottish Arts Council is the main arts development agency in Scotland. It is a non-departmental public body, accountable to the Scottish Executive. The Scottish Arts Council invests funds from the Scottish Executive and National Lottery and works with partners to support and develop artistic excellence and creativity throughout Scotland.

Chair, Richard Holloway

Members, Dinah Caine; Donald Emslie; Steven Grimmond; Charles Lovatt; Ray Macfarlane *(Vice-Chair)*; Barbara McKissack; Jim McSharry; John Mulgrew; Rab Noakes; Ian Smith; Ben Twist

Chief Executive (acting), Jim Tough

SCOTTISH CRIMINAL CASES REVIEW COMMISSION

5th Floor, Portland House, 17 Renfield Street, Glasgow G2 5AH

T 0141-270 7030 **F** 0141-270 7040/23

E info@sccrc.org.uk **W** www.sccrc.org.uk

The commission is a non-departmental public body, funded by the Scottish Executive Justice Department, and established in April 1999. It assumed the role previously performed by the Secretary of State for Scotland to consider alleged miscarriages of justice in Scotland and refer cases meeting the relevant criteria to the High Court for determination. Members are appointed by the Queen on the recommendation of the First Minister; senior executive staff are appointed by the commission.

Chair, Very Revd Graham Forbes, CBE

Members, David Belfall; Graham Bell, QC; Prof. Brian Caddy; Stewart Campbell; Sir Gerald Gordon, CBE, QC; Robert Gordon, QC; James Mackay, QPM; Gerard McClay

Chief Executive, Gerard Sinclair

SCOTTISH ENTERPRISE

5 Atlantic Quay, 150 Broomielaw, Glasgow G2 8LU

T 0141-248 2700 Helpline 0845-607 8787 **F** 0141-221 3217

E network.helpline@scotent.co.uk

W www.scottish-enterprise.com

Scottish Enterprise was established in 1991 and its purpose is to create jobs and prosperity for the people of Scotland. It is funded by the Scottish Executive and is responsible to the Scottish ministers. Working in partnership with the private and public sectors, Scottish Enterprise aims to further the development of Scotland's economy, to enhance the skills of the Scottish workforce and to promote Scotland's international competitiveness. Scottish Enterprise is concerned with attracting firms to Scotland and, through Scottish Trade International, it helps Scottish companies to compete in world export markets. Scottish Enterprise has a network of 12 local enterprise companies that deliver economic development services at local level.

Chair, Sir John Ward, CBE

Chief Executive, Jack Perry

SCOTTISH ENVIRONMENT PROTECTION AGENCY (SEPA)

Erskine Court, Castle Business Park, Stirling FK9 4TR

T 01786-457700 Hotline 0800-807060

F 01786-446885 **E** info@sepa.org.uk

W www.sepa.org.uk

SEPA was established in 1996 and is the public body responsible for environmental protection in Scotland. It regulates potential pollution to land, air and water; the storage, transport and disposal of controlled waste; and the safekeeping and disposal of radioactive materials. It does this within a complex legislative framework of acts of parliament, EC directives and regulations, granting licences to operations of industrial processes and waste disposal. SEPA also operates Floodline, 0845-988 1188, a public service providing information on the possible risk of flooding 24 hours a day, 365 days a year.

Chair, Sir Ken Collins

Chief Executive, Campbell Gemmell

Directors, Colin Bayes *(Environmental Regulation and Improvement)*; Calum MacDonald *(Environmental and Organisational Development)*; Chris Spray *(Environmental Science)*

SCOTTISH LAW COMMISSION

140 Causewayside, Edinburgh EH9 1PR
T 0131-668 2131 F 0131-662 4900
E info@scotlawcom.gov.uk W www.scotlawcom.gov.uk

The Scottish Law Commission, established in 1965, keeps the law in Scotland under review and makes proposals for its development and reform. It is responsible to the Scottish ministers through the Scottish Executive Justice Department.
Chair (part-time), Hon. Lord Drummond Young
Chief Executive, C. M. A. Lugton
Commissioners, Prof. G. L. Gretton; Prof. G. Maher, QC; Prof. J. M. Thomson; C. J. Tyre, QC

SCOTTISH LEGAL AID BOARD

44 Drumsheugh Gardens, Edinburgh EH3 7SW
T 0131-226 7061 Helpline 0845-122 8686
F 0131-220 4878
E general@slab.org.uk W www.slab.org.uk

The Scottish Legal Aid Board was set up under the Legal Aid (Scotland) Act 1986 to manage legal aid in Scotland. It reports to the Scottish Executive. Board members are appointed by Scottish ministers.
Chair, Iain A. Robertson, CBE
Members, Graham Bell, QC; Les Campbell; William Gallagher; Joseph Hughes; Denise Loney; Paul McBride, QC; Susan McPhee; Ellen Morton; David Nicol; Elaine Rosie; Prof. Mahendra Raj; Sheriff Kenneth Ross; Graham Watson
Chief Executive, Lindsay Montgomery

SCOTTISH NATURAL HERITAGE (SNH)

Great Glen House, Leachkin Road, Inverness IV3 8NW
T 01463-725000 F 01463-725067
E enquiries@snh.gov.uk W www.snh.org.uk

SNH was established in 1992 under the Natural Heritage (Scotland) Act 1991. It provides advice on nature conservation to all those whose activities affect wildlife, landforms and features of geological interest in Scotland, and seeks to develop and improve facilities for the enjoyment and understanding of the Scottish countryside. It is funded by the Scottish Executive.
Chair, Andrew Thin
Chief Executive, I. Jardine
Chief Scientific Adviser, C. Galbraith
Directors of Operations, A. Bachell *(East)*; J. Watson *(North)*; J. Thomson *(West)*
Director of Corporate Services, J. Moore

SCOTTISH PRISONS COMPLAINTS COMMISSION

Government Buildings, Broomhouse Drive, Edinburgh EH11 3XD
T 0131-244 8423 F 0131-244 8430
E spcc@scotland.gsi.gov.uk W www.scotland.gov.uk/spcc

The commission was established in 1994. It is an independent body to which prisoners in Scottish prisons can make applications in relation to any matter where they have failed to obtain satisfaction from the Scottish Prison Service's internal grievance procedures. Clinical judgements made by medical officers, matters which are the subject of legal proceedings and matters relating to sentence, conviction and parole decision-making are excluded from the commission's jurisdiction. The commissioner is appointed by the Scottish ministers.
Commissioner, Vaughan Barrett

SCOTTISH PUBLIC SERVICES OMBUDSMAN

Freepost EH641, Edinburgh EH3 0BR
T 0800-377 7330 F 0800-377 7331
E ask@spso.org.uk W www.spso.org.uk

The Scottish Public Services Ombudsman was established in 2002. The ombudsman investigates complaints about Scottish Executive departments and agencies, councils, housing associations, the National Health Service (NHS) and other public bodies. The public bodies which the Scottish Public Services Ombudsman may consider investigating are contained in a list outlined in the Scottish Public Services Ombudsman Act 2002. The ombudsman's remit was extended in 2005 to cover Scotland's further education colleges and higher education institutions. Complaints considered by the ombudsman can range from complaints about poor service, failure to provide a service, administrative failure and complaints about the NHS including hospital staff, GPs, dentists and other health professionals.
Scottish Public Services Ombudsman, Prof. Alice Brown

SCOTTISH RECORDS ADVISORY COUNCIL

HM General Register House, Edinburgh EH1 3YY
T 0131-535 1403 F 0131-535 1430
W www.scottishrecordsadvisorycouncil.info

The council was established under the Public Records (Scotland) Act 1937. Its members are appointed by the First Minister and it may submit proposals or make representations to the First Minister, the Lord Justice General or the Lord President of the Court of Session on questions relating to the public records of Scotland.
Chair, Prof. H. MacQueen

SEAFISH INDUSTRY AUTHORITY

18 Logie Mill, Logie Green Road, Edinburgh EH7 4HS
T 0131-558 3331 F 0131-558 1442
E seafish@seafish.co.uk W www.seafish.org

Established under the Fisheries Act 1981, the authority works with all sectors of the UK seafood industry to satisfy consumers, raise standards, improve efficiency and secure a sustainable and profitable future. It is sponsored by the four UK fisheries departments, which appoint the board, and is funded by a levy on seafood.
Chair, Andrew Dewar-Durie
Chief Executive, John Rutherford

SENIOR SALARIES REVIEW BODY

6th Floor, Kingsgate House, 66–74 Victoria Street, London SW1E 6SW
T 020-7215 8276 F 020-7215 4445
W www.ome.uk.com

The Senior Salaries Review Body (formerly the Top Salaries Review Body) was set up in 1971 to advise the prime minister on the remuneration of the judiciary, senior civil servants and senior officers of the armed forces. In 1993 its remit was extended to cover the pay, pensions and allowances of MPs, ministers and others whose pay is determined by the Ministerial and Other Salaries Act 1975, and also the allowances of peers. It

asked, it advises on the pay of officers and members of the devolved parliament and assemblies.
Chair, John Baker, CBE
Members, Mark Baker, CBE; Mary Galbraith; Prof. David Greenaway; Michael Langley; Jim McKenna; Mei Sim Lai, OBE; Sir Peter North, CBE, QC; Richard Pearson; Paul Williams

SERIOUS ORGANISED CRIME AGENCY (SOCA)

PO Box 8000, London SE11 5EN
T 020-7238 8000 W www.soca.gov.uk

SOCA was established in April 2006. It took over the functions of the National Criminal Intelligence Service and the National Crime Squad, as well as the role of HM Revenue and Customs in investigating drug trafficking and related criminal finance, and some of the functions of the UK Immigration Service in dealing with organised immigration crime. Its remit is to prevent and detect serious organised crime and to gather, store, analyse and disseminate information on crime. SOCA is also tasked with providing support to law enforcement partners.

The Secretary of State for Home Affairs appoints the chair and director-general, may set SOCA strategies and judges the success of its efforts. Grant-in-aid is provided by the Home Office and for 2006–7 was set provisionally at £416m in resource funding and £41m in capital provision.
Chair, Sir Stephen Lander
Director-General, Bill Hughes
Directors, David Bolt *(Intelligence)*; Malcolm Cornberg *(Corporate Services)*; Paul Evans *(Intervention)*; Trevor Pearce *(Enforcement)*
Non-Executive Directors, Stephen Barrett; Elizabeth France; Ken Jarrold; Janet Paraskeva; Gen. Sir Roger Wheeler

STATISTICS COMMISSION

Artillery House, 11–19 Artillery Row, London SW1P 1RT
T 020-7273 8008 F 020-7273 8019
E statscom@statscom.org.uk W www.statscom.org.uk

The Statistics Commission was set up in 2000 to advise on the quality, quality assurance and priority-setting for official statistics, and on the procedures designed to deliver statistical integrity, to help ensure official statistics are trustworthy and responsive to public needs. It is independent of both ministers and the producers of National Statistics. It operates in a transparent way with the minutes of its meetings, correspondence and evidence it receives, and advice it gives, all normally publicly available for scrutiny.
Chair, Prof. D. Rhind, CBE, FRS, FBA
Vice-Chair, Sir Derek Wanless
Members, Ian Beesley; Miss C. Bowe; H. J. Dixon; Dr Isabelle Low; Mrs J. Trewsdale; M. Weale

STUDENT LOANS COMPANY LTD

100 Bothwell Street, Glasgow G2 7JD
T 0141-306 2000 F 0141-306 2005
W www.slc.co.uk

The Student Loans Company Ltd is wholly owned by the government. It administers the Student Loan Scheme (established in 1990) and the Income Contingent Loans Scheme (established in 1998), and provides loans to eligible students in higher education in the United Kingdom. In the region of £2.95bn of loans were distributed during 2006–7. As at 31 March 2007 there were 2.5 million borrowers, and a total of £18.13bn of outstanding loans to be repaid.
Chair, Keith Bedell-Pearce
Chief Executive, Ralph Seymour-Jackson

TATE BRITAIN

Millbank, London SW1P 4RG
T 020-7887 8888
E visiting.britain@tate.org.uk W www.tate.org.uk
Tate Britain displays the national collection of British art from 1500 to the present day – with special attention and dedicated space given to Blake, Turner and Constable. The gallery opened in 1897, the cost of building (£80,000) being defrayed by Sir Henry Tate, who also contributed the nucleus of the present collection. The Turner wing was opened in 1910, and further galleries and a new sculpture hall followed in 1937. In 1979 a further extension was built, and the Clore Gallery was opened in 1987. The Centenary Development was opened in 2001.

There are four Tate galleries: Tate Britain and Tate Modern in London, Tate Liverpool and Tate St Ives; the entire Tate collection is available to view online.

BOARD OF TRUSTEES
Chair, Paul Myners, CBE
Trustees, Helen Alexander; Victoria Barnsley; Melanie Clore; Sir Howard Davies; Jeremy Deller; Anish Kapoor; Patricia Lankester; Prof. Jennifer Latto; Fiona Rae; Jon Snow; John Studzinski

OFFICERS
Director, Sir Nicholas Serota
Director, Tate Britain, Dr Stephen Deuchar
Director, Tate Liverpool, Dr Christoph Grunenberg
Director, Tate Modern, Vicente Todoli
Director, Tate St Ives, Susan Daniel-McElroy

TATE MODERN

Bankside, London SE1 9TG
T 020-7887 8888 E visiting.modern@tate.org.uk
W www.tate.org.uk

Opened in May 2000, Tate Modern displays the Tate collection of international modern art dating from 1900 to the present day. It includes works by Dalí, Picasso, Matisse and Warhol as well as many contemporary works. It is housed in the former Bankside Power Station in London, which was redesigned by the Swiss architects Herzog and de Meuron.
Director, Vicente Todoli

TOURISM BODIES

Visit Britain, Visit Scotland, the Wales Tourist Board and the Northern Ireland Tourist Board are responsible for developing and marketing the tourist industry in their respective countries.

VISIT BRITAIN
Thames Tower, Blacks Road, London W6 9EL T 020-8846 9000
F 020-8563-0302 W www.visitbritain.com
Chair, Christopher Rodrigues, CBE
Chief Executive, Tom Wright

VISIT SCOTLAND
94 Ocean Drive, Leith, Edinburgh EH6 6JH T 0131-472 2222
E generalenquiries@visitscotland.com
W www.visitscotland.com
Chair, Peter Lederer, CBE
Chief Executive, Philip Riddle

WALES TOURIST BOARD
Brunel House, 2 Fitzalan Road, Cardiff CF24 0UY
T 0870-830 0306 F 0870-121 1259
E info@visitwales.co.uk W www.visitwales.com
Directors, Gareth Hall; Jonathan Jones

NORTHERN IRELAND TOURIST BOARD
59 North Street, Belfast BT1 1NB T 028-9023 1221
F 028-9024 0960 E info@nitb.com
W www.discovernorthernireland.com
Chair, Tom McGrath, OBE
Chief Executive, Alan Clarke

TRAINING AND DEVELOPMENT AGENCY (TDA)
151 Buckingham Palace Road, London SW1W 9SZ
T 020-7023 8001 W www.tda.gov.uk

The TDA was launched in September 2005 and took on the role, and expanded the remit of, the Teacher Training Agency. The TDA aims to attract able and committed people to teaching, concentrating specifically on subjects where teachers are in short supply; provide schools and their staff with good information on training and development opportunities; and ensure that new teachers enter schools with appropriate skills and knowledge, through working closely with providers of initial teacher training.
Chief Executive, Graham Holley

TRANSPORT FOR LONDON (TFL)
Windsor House, 42–50 Victoria Street, London SW1H 0TL
T 020-7222 5600
E enquire@tfl.gov.uk W www.tfl.gov.uk

TfL was formed in July 2000 as a functional body of the Greater London Authority and is responsible for the capital's transport system. Its role is to implement the Mayor of London's transport strategy and manage the transport services across London for which the mayor has responsibility.

As a result, TfL is responsible for London's buses, the Underground, the Docklands Light Railway (DLR) and the management of Croydon Tramlink and London River Services. It also runs Victoria Coach Station and London's Transport Museum, manages the Congestion Charging scheme and regulates the city's taxis and private hire trade.
Chair, Ken Livingstone
Vice-Chair, Dave Wetzel
Commissioner, Peter Hendy

UK ATOMIC ENERGY AUTHORITY (UKAEA)
Harwell Science and Innovation Campus, Oxon OX11 0RA
T 01235-820220 F 01235-436899
W www.ukaea.org.uk

The UKAEA was established by the Atomic Energy Authority Act 1954 and took over responsibility for the research and development of the civil nuclear power programme. The UKAEA is now responsible for the safe management and decommissioning of its radioactive plants and for leading the development of the Harwell Science and Innovation Campus. The UKAEA also undertakes the UK's contribution to the international fusion programme.
Chair, Hon. Barbara Thomas Judge
Chief Executive, Norman Harrison

UK FILM COUNCIL
10 Little Portland Street, London W1W 7JG
T 020-7861 7861 F 020-7861 7862
E info@ukfilmcouncil.org.uk W www.ukfilmcouncil.org.uk

The council was created in April 2000 by the Department for Culture, Media and Sport. The council's board is comprised of 15 directors and has been established as a private company limited by guarantee, with an intention to move it to a statutory basis at a later stage. It invests grant-in-aid and National Lottery funds in film development and production, training, international development and export promotion, distribution and exhibition, and education.

UK Film Council International (formerly the British Film Commission) is part of the same organisation, and was originally established in 1991. Its remit is to attract inward investment by promoting the UK as an international production centre to the film and television industries and encouraging the use of British locations, services, facilities and personnel.
Chair, Stewart Till, CBE
Chief Executive, John Woodward
British Film Commissioner, Colin Brown

UNITED KINGDOM SPORTS COUNCIL (UK SPORT)
40 Bernard Street, London WC1N 1ST
T 020-7211 5100 F 020-7211 5246
E info@uksport.gov.uk W www.uksport.gov.uk

UK Sport was established by royal charter in 1996 and is accountable to parliament through the Department for Culture, Media and Sport. Its role is to lead the UK to sporting excellence by supporting winning athletes, world-class events, world-class standards and ethically fair and drug-free sport. UK Sport is responsible for managing and distributing public investment (£60m annually) and is a statutory distributor of funds raised by the National Lottery.
Chair, Sue Campbell, CBE
Chief Executive, John Steele

VICTORIA AND ALBERT MUSEUM
Cromwell Road, London SW7 2RL
T 020-7942 2000 W www.vam.ac.uk

The Victoria and Albert Museum (V&A) is the national museum of fine and applied art and design. It descends directly from the Museum of Manufactures, which opened in Marlborough House in 1852 after the Great Exhibition of 1851. The museum was moved in 1857 to become part of the South Kensington Museum. It was renamed the Victoria and Albert Museum in 1899. It also houses the National Art Library and Print Room.

The museum administers the V&A Museum of Childhood at Bethnal Green, which was opened in 1872; the building is the most important surviving example of the type of glass and iron construction used by Paxton for the Great Exhibition. Total government grant-in-aid for 2007–8 is £41.7m.

BOARD OF TRUSTEES

Chair, Paula Ridley, OBE

Members, E. Davies, OBE; T. Dixon, OBE; Mrs J. Gordon Clark; Prof. Sir Christopher Frayling, PHD; Ms B. Jackson, MBE; Prof. Lisa Jardine, CBE; R. Mather; P. Rogers, CBE; P. Ruddock; Rt. Hon. Sir Timothy Sainsbury; Dame Marjorie Scardino, DBE; S. Shah, OBE

OFFICERS

Managing Director of V&A Enterprises Ltd, Ms. J. Prosser

Director of the V&A, M. Jones

Deputy Director, I. Blatchford

Directors, Ms B. McKillop *(Collections; Keeper of the Asian Department)*; N. Umney *(Collections Services)*; Ms J. Lawson *(Development)*; A. Ganguli *(Finance)*; A. Hill *(Human Resources)*; D. Anderson, OBE *(Learning and Interpretation)*; Ms M. Gemmill *(Projects and Design)*; P. Catlow *(Property Services)*; D. Whitmore *(Public Affairs)*; Ms S. Ridley *(Security and Visitor Services)*; G. Marsh *(Theatre Collections)*; Ms D. Lees *(V&A Museum of Childhood)*

Keepers of Departments, C. Wilk *(Furniture, Fashion and Textiles)*; Dr P. E. D. Williamson *(Sculpture, Metalwork, Ceramics and Glass)*; J. Bryant *(Word and Image)*

WALLACE COLLECTION

Hertford House, Manchester Square, London W1U 3BN
T 020-7563 9500 **F** 020-7224 2155
E enquiries@wallacecollection.org
W www.wallacecollection.org

The Wallace Collection was bequeathed to the nation by the widow of Sir Richard Wallace, in 1897, and Hertford House was subsequently acquired by the government. The collection contains works by Titian and Rembrandt, and includes porcelain, furniture and an array of arms and armour. Total government grant-in-aid for 2006–7 was £3.53m.

Director, Rosalind Savill

WOMEN'S NATIONAL COMMISSION

1/F6 Ashdown House, 123 Victoria Street, London SW1E 5DE
T 020-7944 0585 **F** 020-7944 0583
E wnc@communities.gsi.gov.uk **W** www.thewnc.org.uk

The Women's National Commission was established in 1969 as an independent advisory committee to the government. It is an umbrella organisation representing women and women's organisations in the UK. Its remit is to ensure that the informed opinions of women are given their due weight in the deliberations of the government and in public debate on matters of public interest, including those of special interest to women. The commission is an advisory NDPB based within the Department for Communities and Local Government alongside the Women and Equality Unit.

Chair (acting), Baroness Gould of Potternewton

Director (acting), Susan Green

REGIONAL GOVERNMENT

LONDON

GREATER LONDON AUTHORITY (GLA)

City Hall, The Queen's Walk, London SE1 2AA
T 020-7983 4000 E mayor@london.gov.uk
W www.london.gov.uk

On 7 May 1998 London voted in favour of the formation of the Greater London Authority (GLA). The first elections to the GLA took place on 4 May 2000 and the new authority took over its responsibilities on 3 July 2000. In July 2002 the GLA moved to one of London's most spectacular buildings, newly built on a brownfield site on the south bank of the Thames, adjacent to Tower Bridge. The second election to the GLA took place on 10 June 2004.

The structure and objectives of the GLA stem from its eight main areas of responsibility. These are transport, planning, economic development and regeneration, the environment, police, fire and emergency planning, culture and health. The bodies that coordinate these functions and report to the GLA are Transport for London (TfL), the London Development Agency (LDA), the Metropolitan Police Authority (MPA), and the London Fire and Emergency Planning Authority (LFEPA). The GLA also absorbed a number of other London bodies, such as the London Planning Advisory Committee, the London Ecology Unit and the London Research Centre.

The GLA consists of a directly elected mayor, the Mayor of London, and a separately elected assembly, the London Assembly. The mayor has the key role of decision making, with the assembly performing the tasks of regulating and scrutinising these decisions. In addition, the GLA has around 600 permanent staff to support the activities of the mayor and the assembly, which are overseen by a head of paid service. The mayor may appoint two political advisers, though does not necessarily exercise this power, but he may not appoint the chief executive, the monitoring officer or the chief finance officer. These must be appointed by the assembly.

Every aspect of the assembly and its activities must be open to public scrutiny and therefore accountable. The assembly holds the mayor to account through scrutiny of his strategies, decisions and actions. This is carried out by direct questioning at assembly meetings and by conducting detailed investigations in committee.

People's Question Time gives Londoners the chance to question the mayor and the London Assembly about plans, priorities and policies for London. It is held twice a year in different areas of London.

The role of the mayor can be broken down into a number of key areas: to represent and promote London at home and abroad and speak up for Londoners; to devise strategies and plans to tackle London-wide issues, such as transport, economic development and regeneration, air quality, environment, noise, waste, bio-diversity, planning and culture; and to set budgets for TFL, the LDA, the MPA and the LFEPA. The mayor is chair of TFL and has the power to appoint the members of their board and those of the LDA; he also makes appointments to the police and fire authorities. With London's successful bid to host the 2012 Olympic and Paralympic Games, the mayor is the signatory to the contract with the International Olympic Committee undertaking that the games will be delivered.

The role of the assembly can be broken down into a number of key areas:

- to check on and balance the mayor
- to scrutinise the mayor
- to have the power to amend the mayor's budget by a majority of two-thirds
- to investigate issues of London-wide significance and make proposals to the mayor
- to provide the deputy mayor and the members serving on the police, fire and emergency planning authorities with advice

Mayor, Ken Livingstone
Deputy Mayor, Nicky Gavron
Chair of the London Assembly, Sally Hamwee
Deputy Chair of the Assembly, Brian Coleman

ELECTIONS AND THE VOTING SYSTEMS

The assembly is elected every four years at the same time as the mayor, and consists of 25 members. There is one member from each of the 14 GLA constituencies topped up with 11 London members who are representatives of political parties or individuals standing as independent candidates. The next election will be on 1 May 2008.

The GLA constituencies are Barnet and Camden; Bexley and Bromley; Brent and Harrow; City and East, covering Barking and Dagenham, the City of London, Newham and Tower Hamlets; Croydon and Sutton; Ealing and Hillingdon; Enfield and Haringey; Greenwich and Lewisham; Havering and Redbridge; North East, covering Hackney, Islington and Waltham Forest; Lambeth and Southwark; West Central, covering Hammersmith and Fulham, Kensington and Chelsea and Westminster; South West, covering Hounslow, Kingston upon Thames and Richmond upon Thames; Merton and Wandsworth.

Two distinct voting systems are used to appoint the existing mayor and the assembly. The mayor is elected using the supplementary vote system (SVS). With SVS, electors have two votes: one to give a first choice for mayor and one to give a second choice. Electors cannot vote twice for the same candidate. If one candidate gets more than half of all the first-choice votes, he or she becomes mayor. If no candidate gets more than half of the first-choice votes, the two candidates with the most first-choice votes remain in the election and all the other candidates drop out. The second-choice votes on the ballot papers of the candidates who drop out are then counted. Where these second-choice votes are for the two remaining candidates they are added to the first-choice votes these candidates already have. The candidate with the most first- and second-choice votes combined becomes the Mayor of London.

The assembly is appointed using the additional member system (AMS). Under AMS, electors have two votes. The first vote is for a constituency candidate. The second vote is for a party list or individual candidate contesting the London-wide assembly seats. The 14 constituency members are elected under the first-past-the-post system, the same system used in general and local elections. Electors vote for one candidate and the candidate with the most votes wins. The additional (London) members are drawn from party lists or are independent candidates who stand as London members.

The Greater London Returning Officer (GLRO) is the independent official responsible for running the election in London. The GLRO has overall responsibility for running a free, fair and efficient election. He is supported in this by returning officers in each of the 14 London constituencies.

GLRO, Anthony Mayer

TRANSPORT FOR LONDON (TfL)

TfL is the integrated body responsible for London's transport system. Its role is to implement the mayor's transport strategy for London and manage transport services across the capital for which the mayor has responsibility. TfL is directed by a management board whose members are chosen for their understanding of transport matters and are appointed by the mayor, who chairs the board. TfL's role is:

- to manage the London Underground, buses, Croydon Tramlink and the Docklands Light Railway (DLR)
- to manage a 580km (360 miles) network of main roads and all of London's 4,600 traffic lights
- to regulate taxis and minicabs
- to run the London River Services, Victoria Coach Station and London's Transport Museum
- to help to coordinate the Dial-a-Ride and Taxicard schemes for door-to-door services for transport users with mobility problems

The London Borough Councils maintain the role of highway and traffic authorities for 95 per cent of London's roads. A £5 congestion charge for motorists driving into central London between the hours of 7am and 6.30pm, Monday to Friday (excluding public holidays) was introduced on 17 February 2003, and was subsequently raised to £8 on 4 July 2005. On 19 February 2007, the charge zone roughly doubled in size after a westward expansion, and the time zone changed to finish earlier at 6pm.

From 11 November 2007, responsibility for running the Silverlink overland train service was due to be transferred to TfL.

Transport Commissioner for London, Peter Hendy

LONDON DEVELOPMENT AGENCY (LDA)

The LDA promotes economic development and regeneration. It is one of the nine regional development agencies set up around the country to perform this task. It is run by a board of 14 members appointed by the mayor. The key aspects of the LDA's role are:

- to promote business efficiency, investment and competitiveness
- to promote employment
- to enhance the skills of local people
- to create sustainable development

The London boroughs retain powers to promote economic development in their local areas.

Chair, Mary Reilly

THE ENVIRONMENT

The mayor is required to formulate strategies to tackle London's environmental issues including the quality of water, air and land; the use of energy and London's contribution to climate change targets; groundwater levels and traffic emissions; and municipal waste management.

METROPOLITAN POLICE AUTHORITY (MPA)

This body, which oversees the policing of London, consists of 23 members; 12 from the assembly, including the deputy mayor, four magistrates and seven independents. One of the independents is appointed directly by the home secretary. The role of the MPA is:

- to maintain an efficient and effective police force
- to publish an annual policing plan
- to set police targets and monitor performance
- to be part of the appointment, discipline and removal of senior officers
- to be responsible for the performance budget
- to oversee formal inquiries and the implementation of their recommendations

The boundaries of the metropolitan police districts have been changed to be consistent with the 32 London boroughs. Areas beyond the GLA remit have been incorporated into the Surrey, Hertfordshire and Essex police areas. The City of London has its own police force.

Chair, Len Duvall

LONDON FIRE AND EMERGENCY PLANNING AUTHORITY (LFEPA)

In July 2000 the London Fire and Civil Defence Authority became the London Fire and Emergency Planning Authority. It consists of 17 members, 9 drawn from the assembly and 8 from the London boroughs. The role of the LFEPA is:

- to set the strategy for the provision of fire services
- to ensure that the fire brigade can meet all the normal requirements efficiently
- to ensure that effective arrangements are made for the fire brigade to receive emergency calls and deal with them promptly
- to ensure that information useful to the development of the fire brigades is gathered
- to assist the boroughs with their emergency planning training and exercises

Chair, Valerie Shawcross

SALARIES *as at June 2007*	
Mayor	£137,579
Deputy Mayor	£90,954
Chair of the Assembly	£60,675
Assembly Member	£50,582

LONDON ASSEMBLY COMMITTEES

Chair, Audit Panel, Peter Hulme Cross
Chair, Budget Committee, Andrew Pelling
Chair, Business Management and Appointments Committee, Elections Review Committee, Brian Coleman
Chair, Economic Development, Culture, Sport and Tourism Committee, Dee Doocey
Chair, Environment Committee, Darren Johnson
Chair, Health and Public Services Committee, Joanne McCartney
Chair, Planning and Spatial Development Committee, Tony Arbour
Chair, Standards Committee, Prof. Malcolm Grant
Chair, Transport Committee, Roger Evans

GLA ORGANISATIONAL STRUCTURE

MAYOR'S OFFICE
Public Affairs (International and European Relations, London Stakeholders, Government and Parliamentary Liaison, Public Consultation, Public Affairs Publications)
Best Value Partnership (Borough Liaison)
Economic and Business Policy (Private Sector, Strategic Evaluation Unit)
Equalities and Policing
Environment
Tourism and Creative Industries
London House (Brussels)
Administration Manager

SECRETARIAT
Assembly Support
Scrutiny and Investigations
Committee Services
Assembly's Media Relations

CHIEF EXECUTIVE'S OFFICE
Governance
Marketing
Mayor's Media Relations

POLICY AND PARTNERSHIPS
Spatial Development Strategy
Planning Decisions
Architecture and Urbanism Unit
Environment
Culture
Policy Support (Health, Housing and Homelessness, Social Inclusion, Sustainable Development)
Business Support

CORPORATE SERVICES
GLA Economics
Information and Communication Technology
Legal
HR and Administration (Facilities Management and Internal Communications)
Research Library
Data Management
Public Liaison
Business Support

FINANCE AND PERFORMANCE
Core Performance and Project Management
Strategic Performance
Core Finance
Strategic Finance

LONDON ASSEMBLY MEMBERS

as at 1 July 2007

Arbour, Anthony, *C., South West,* Maj. 4,067
Arnold, Jennette Sarah Alfreda, *Lab., North East,* Maj. 13,338
Barnes, Richard Michael, *C., Ealing and Hillingdon,* Maj. 11,016
Biggs, John Robert, *Lab., City and East,* Maj. 14,336
Blackman, Robert, *C., Brent and Harrow,* Maj. 4,686
Bray, Angela Lavinia, *C., West Central,* Maj. 29,944
Coleman, Brian, *C., Barnet and Camden,* Maj. 11,519
Doocey, Dee, *LD, London List*
Duvall, Leonard Lloyd, *Lab., Greenwich and Lewisham,* Maj. 14,083
Evans, Jeremy Roger, *C., Havering and Redbridge,* Maj. 16,706
Gavron, Felicia Nicolette, *Lab., London List*
Hamwee, Sally Rachel, *LD, London List*
Hockney, Nicholas Damian, *One London, London List*
Howlett, Elizabeth, *C., Merton and Wandsworth,* Maj. 16,878
Hulme-Cross, Peter Kenneth, *One London, London List*
Johnson, Darren, *Green, London List*
Jones, Jenny, *Green, London List*
McCartney, Joanne, *Lab., Enfield and Haringey,* Maj. 1,574
Neill, Robert James Macgillivray, *C., Bexley and Bromley,* Maj. 34,254
Pelling, Andrew John, *C., Croydon and Sutton,* Maj. 23,694
***Pope**, Geoff, *LD, London List*
Qureshi, Murad, *Lab., London List*
Shawcross, Valerie, *Lab., Lambeth and Southwark,* Maj. 5,475
Tope, Graham Norman, *LD, London List*
Tuffrey, Michael William, *LD, London List*

* Lynne Featherstone stepped down after her election to parliament and was replaced by Geoff Pope on 6 June 2005

STATE OF THE PARTIES *as at 1 July 2007*

Party	*Seats*	*Gain/Loss*
Conservative (C.)	9	0
Labour (Lab.)	7	–2
Liberal Democrats (LD)	5	+1
Green	2	–1
One London	2	+2

MAYORAL ELECTION RESULTS
10 June 2004
E. 5,197,647 T. 1,920,533 (36.95%)
Change in turnout from 2000: +2.52%
Good votes 1st choice 1,863,671 (97.04%); 2nd choice 1,591,443 (82.86%)
Rejected votes 1st choice 56,862 (2.96%); 2nd choice 329,090 (17.14%)

First	*Party*	*Votes*	*%*
Ken Livingstone	Lab.	685,541	35.70
Steven Norris	C.	542,423	28.24
Simon Hughes	LD	284,645	14.82
Frank Maloney	UKIP	115,665	6.02
Lindsey German	Respect	61,731	3.21
Julian Leppert	BNP	58,405	3.04
Darren Johnson	Green	57,331	2.99
Ram Gidoomal	CPA	41,696	2.17
Lorna Reid	Ind. Working Class	9,542	0.50
Tammy Nagalingam	Ind.	6,692	0.35

Second	*Party*	*Votes*	*%*
Simon Hughes	LD	465,704	24.25
Ken Livingstone	Lab.	250,517	13.04
Steven Norris	C.	222,559	11.59
Darren Johnson	Green	208,686	10.87
Frank Maloney	UKIP	193,157	10.06
Julian Leppert	BNP	70,736	3.68
Lindsey German	Respect	63,294	3.30
Ram Gidoomal	CPA	56,721	2.95
Lorna Reid	Ind. Working Class	39,678	2.07
Tammy Nagalingam	Ind.	20,391	1.06

LONDON ASSEMBLY ELECTION RESULTS

as at June 2004

E. Electorate T. Turnout
See General Election Results for a list of party abbreviations

CONSTITUENCIES

BARNET AND CAMDEN
E. 371,186 T. 38.41%

Brian Coleman, C.	47,640
Lucy Anderson, Lab.	36,121
Jonathan Simpson, LD	23,603
Miranda Dunn, Green	11,921
Magnus Nielsen, UKIP	8,685
Elisabeth Wheatley, Respect	5,150
Humberto Heliotrope, CPA	1,914

C. majority 11,519

BEXLEY AND BROMLEY
E. 397,075 T. 41.48%

Robert Neill, C.	64,246
Duncan Borrowman, LD	29,992
Heather Bennett, UKIP	26,703
Charles Mansell, Lab.	24,848
Ann Garrett, Green	8,069
Miranda Suit, CPA	3,397
Alun Morinan, Respect	1,673

C. majority 34,254

BRENT AND HARROW
E. 332,723 T. 38.03%

Robert Blackman, C.	39,900
Toby Harris, Lab.	35,214
Havard Hughes, LD	20,782
Daniel Moss, UKIP	7,199
Mohammad Ali, Green	6,975
Albert Harriott, Respect	4,586
Gladstone Macaulay, CPA	2,734

C. majority 4,686

CITY AND EAST
E. 437,298 T. 33.43%

John Biggs, Lab.	38,085
Shafi Choudhury, C.	23,749
Oliur Rahman, Respect	19,675
Guy Burton, LD	18,255
Christopher Pratt, UKIP	17,997
Terry McGrenera, Green	8,687
Christopher Gill, CPA	4,461

Lab. majority 14,336

CROYDON AND SUTTON
E. 376,175 T. 37.82%

Andrew Pelling, C.	52,330
Steven Gauge, LD	28,636
Sean Fitzsimons, Lab.	25,861
James Feisenberger, UKIP	15,203
Shasha Khan, Green	6,175
David Campanale, CPA	4,234
Waqas Hussain, Respect	3,108

C. majority 23,694

EALING AND HILLINGDON
E. 397,564 T. 37.28%

Richard Barnes, C.	45,230
Gurcharan Singh, Lab.	34,214
Michael Cox, LD	23,440
David Malindine, UKIP	14,698
Sarah Edwards, Green	9,395
Dalawar Chaudhry, Ind.	5,285
Salvinder Dhillon, Respect	4,229
Genevieve Hibbs, CPA	3,024

C. majority 11,016

ENFIELD AND HARINGEY
E. 343,617 T. 36.14%

Joanne McCartney, Lab.	33,955
Peter Forrest, C.	32,381
Wayne Hoban, LD	19,720
Brian Hall, UKIP	10,652
Jayne Forbes, Green	10,310
Sait Akgul, Respect	6,855
Peter Wolstenholme, CPA	2,365

Lab. majority 1,574

GREENWICH AND LEWISHAM
E. 329,450 T. 35.10%

Leonard Duvall, Lab.	36,251
Gareth Bacon, C.	22,168
Alexander Feakes, LD	19,183
Timothy Reynolds, UKIP	13,454
Susan Luxton, Green	11,271
Stephen Hammond, CPA	3,619
Ian Page, Respect/Soc. Alt.	2,825

Lab. majority 14,083

HAVERING AND REDBRIDGE
E. 350,652 T. 38.96%

Jeremy Evans, C.	44,723
Keith Darvill, Lab.	28,017
Lawrence Webb, UKIP	18,297
Matthew Lake, LD	13,646
Malvin Brown, Residents Assn. of London	6,925
Ashley Gunstock, Green	6,009
Abdurahman Jafar, Respect	5,185
Juliet Hawkins, CPA	2,917
David Stephens, Third Way	2,031
Peter Thorogood, Ind.	1,597

C. majority 16,706

LAMBETH AND SOUTHWARK
E. 373,293 T. 33.38%

Valerie Shawcross, Lab.	36,280
Caroline Pidgeon, LD	30,805
Bernard Gentry, C.	17,379
Shane Collins, Green	11,900
Frank Maloney, UKIP	8,776
Janet Noble, Respect	4,930
Simisola Lawanson, CPA	3,655
Navindh Baburam, Ind.	608

Lab. majority 5,475

MERTON AND WANDSWORTH
E. 340,792 T. 38.55%

Elizabeth Howlett, C.	48,295
Kathryn Smith, Lab.	31,417
Andrew Martin, LD	17,864
Roy Vickery, Green	10,163
Adrian Roberts, UKIP	8,327
Ruairidh Maclean, Respect	4,291
Ellen Greco, CPA	2,782
Rathy Alagaratnam, Ind.	1,240

C. majority 16,878

NORTH EAST
E. 410,719 T. 33.93%

Jennette Arnold, Lab.	37,380
Terry Stacy, LD	24,042
Andrew Boff, C.	23,264
Jon Nott, Green	16,739
Robert Selby, UKIP	11,459
Dean Ryan, Respect	11,184
Andrew Otchie, CPA	3,219
James Beavis, Comm.	1,378

Lab. majority 13,338

SOUTH WEST
E. 384,450 T. 40.31%

Tony Arbour, C.	48,858
Dee Doocey, LD	44,791
Seema Malhotra, Lab.	25,225
Alan Hindle, UKIP	12,477
Judy Maciejowska, Green	9,866
Omar Waraich, Respect	3,785
Peter Flower, CPA	3,008

C. majority 4,067

WEST CENTRAL
E. 352,653 T. 35.28%

Angela Bray, C.	51,884
Ansuya Sodha, Lab.	21,940
Francesco Fruzza, LD	17,478
Julia Stephenson, Green	10,762
Damian Hockney, UKIP	7,219
Kevin Cobham, Respect	4,825
Jillian McLachlan, CPA	1,993

C. majority 29,944

TOP-UP MEMBERS

LABOUR
Felicia Nicolette Gavron
Murad Qureshi

LIBERAL DEMOCRAT
Dee Doocey
Lynne Featherstone*
Sally Hamwee
Graham Tope
Michael Tuffey

ONE LONDON GROUP†
Damian Hockney
Peter Hulme-Cross

GREEN PARTY
Darren Johnson
Jenny Jones

* Lynne Featherstone stepped down after her election to parliament and was replaced by Geoff Pope on 6 June 2005

† On 1 September 2005, Damian Hockney and Peter Hulme-Cross formed the One London Group; both members were originally elected to the assembly as UK Independence Party (UKIP) representatives

VALES

NATIONAL ASSEMBLY FOR WALES

ardiff Bay, Cardiff CF99 1NA
0845-010 5500 **E** webmaster@assemblywales.org
V www.assemblywales.org

n July 1997 the government announced plans to stablish a National Assembly for Wales. In a referendum n September 1997 about 50 per cent of the electorate oted, of whom 50.3 per cent voted in favour of the ssembly. Elections are held every four years and the first lections took place on 6 May 1999, the second on 1 Aay 2003 and the third on 3 May 2007.

Until 2007 the National Assembly for Wales had esponsibility in Wales for ministerial functions relating to ealth and personal social services; education; the Welsh anguage, arts and culture; local government; housing; vater and sewerage; environmental protection; sport; griculture and fisheries; forestry; land use, including own and country planning and conservation; roads; ourism; and European Union matters.

The Government of Wales Act 2006 introduced a adical change to the functions and status of the National Assembly for Wales. With effect from 25 May 2007 the ct formally separated the National Assembly for Wales the legislature – made up of 60 elected assembly nembers) and the Welsh Assembly Government (the executive – comprising the first minister, Welsh ministers, leputy Welsh ministers and the counsel general). It also nade changes to the electoral process: candidates are no onger permitted to stand for both a constituency and on a egional list. The act enabled the National Assembly for Wales to formulate its own legislation (assembly measures) on devolved matters such as health, education, social services and local government; the assembly is given egislative competence (the legal authority to pass neasures) on a case-by-case basis by the UK parliament.

The role of the National Assembly for Wales is to scrutinise and monitor the Welsh Assembly Government. t meets in the Senedd debating chamber. The 60 assembly nembers examine and approve assembly measures and approve certain items of subordinate legislation; approve budgets for the Welsh Assembly Government's programmes; hold Welsh ministers to account; and analyse and debate their decisions and policies.

Presiding Officer, Lord Dafydd Elis-Thomas, AM

SALARIES *as at 1 April 2007*

First Minister*	£76,996
Minister/Presiding Officer*	£39,939
Deputy Presiding Officer*	£25,121
Assembly Members (AM)†	£46,496

* Also receives the assembly member salary
† Reduced by two-thirds if the member is already an MP or an MEP

WELSH ASSEMBLY GOVERNMENT

Cathays Park, Cardiff CF10 3NQ
T 0845-010 3300 **W** http://new.wales.gov.uk

The Welsh Assembly Government is comprised of the first minister, the Welsh ministers, the counsel general – a newly created position, the counsel general is the chief legal adviser – and the deputy Welsh ministers. The 60 assembly members delegate their executive powers, including the implementation of policies and legislation, to the first minister – who is elected by the whole assembly and is therefore usually the leader of the largest political party. In turn, the first minister delegates responsibility for delivering the executive functions to Welsh ministers, who together form the cabinet.

The Welsh Assembly Government has responsibility over the following devolved areas: agriculture, fisheries, forestry and rural development; ancient monuments and historic buildings; culture; economic development; education and training; environment; fire and rescue services; food; health and health services; highways and transport; housing; local government; public administration; social welfare; sport and recreation; tourism; town and county planning; water and flood defence; and the Welsh language.

First Minister for Wales, Rt. Hon. Rhodri Morgan, AM
Minister for Budget and Business Management, Jane Hutt, AM
Minister for the Economy and Transport, Dr Brian Gibbons, AM
Minister for Education, Culture and the Welsh Language, Carwyn Jones, AM
Minister for Health and Social Services, Edwina Hart, MBE, AM
Minister for Social Justice and Public Service Delivery, Andrew Davies, AM
Minister for Sustainability and Rural Development, Jane Davidson, AM
Chief Whip and Deputy Business Minister, Carl Sargeant, AM
Deputy Minister for the Economy and Transport, Huw Lewis, AM
Deputy Minister for Education, Culture and Welsh Language, John Griffiths, AM
Deputy Minister for Health and Social Services, Gwenda Thomas, AM
Deputy Minister for Social Justice and Public Service Delivery, Leighton Andrews, AM
Counsel General, Carwyn Jones, AM
Clerk to the Assembly and Chief Executive of Assembly Commission, Claire Clancy

MANAGEMENT BOARD
Permanent Secretary, Sir Jon Shortridge
Senior Director, Derek Jones
Director, Business Development, June Milligan
Director, Corporate Information and Services, Dr Michael Harrington
Director, Economy and Transport, Gareth Hall
Director, Education, Culture and the Welsh Language, Steven Marshall
Director, Finance, Christine Daws
Director, Health and Social Services, Ann Lloyd
Director, Human Resources, Bernard Galton
Director, Legal Services, Jeff Godfrey
Director, Public Health and Health Professions, and Chief Medical Officer, Dr Tony Jewell
Director, Public Services and Performance, Richard Davies
Director, Social Justice and Local Government, Dr Emyr Roberts
Director, Strategic Policy, Legislation and Communications, Hugh Rawlings
Director, Sustainability and Rural Development, Huw Brodie
Non-Executive Directors, Kathryn Bishop; Adrian Webb

DEPARTMENTS
Economy and Transport
Education, Culture and Welsh Language

Health and Social Services
Public Services and Performance
Social Justice and Local Government
Strategic Policy, Legislation and Communications
Sustainability and Rural Development

EXECUTIVE AGENCIES
Planning Inspectorate
Welsh European Funding Office

COMMITTEES
Audit
Business
Communities and Culture
Enterprise and Learning
Equality of Opportunity
European and External Affairs
Finance
Health, Wellbeing and Local Government
Petitions
Standards of Conduct
Subordinate Legislation
Sustainability

PUBLIC SERVICES OMBUDSMAN FOR WALES
1 Ffordd yr Hen Gae, Pencoed CF35 5LJ
T 01656-641150 F 01656-641199
E ask@ombudsman-wales.org.uk
W www.ombudsman-wales.org.uk
Ombudsman, Adam Peat

MEMBERS OF THE NATIONAL ASSEMBLY FOR WALES

as at 4 May 2007

Andrews, Leighton, *Lab., Rhondda,* Maj. 6,215
Ashgar, Mohammad, *PC, South Wales East region*
Barrett, Lorraine Jayne, *Lab., Cardiff South and Penarth,* Maj. 2,754
Bates, Michael, *LD, Montgomeryshire,* Maj. 1,979
Black, Peter, *LD, South Wales West region*
Bourne, Prof. Nicholas, *C., Mid and West Wales region*
Burnham, Eleanor, *LD, North Wales region*
Burns, Angela, *C., Carmarthen West and South Pembrokeshire,* Maj. 98
Butler, Rosemary Janet Mair, *Lab., Newport West,* Maj. 1,401
Cairns, Alun, *C., South Wales West region*
Chapman, Christine, *Lab., Cynon Valley,* Maj. 5,623
Cuthbert, Jeffrey, *Lab., Caerphilly,* Maj. 2,287
Davidson, Jane Elizabeth, *Lab., Pontypridd,* Maj. 3,347
Davies, Alun, *Lab., Mid and West Wales region*
Davies, Andrew David, *Lab., Swansea West,* Maj. 1,511
Davies, Andrew Robert, *C., South Wales Central region*
Davies, Jocelyn, *PC, South Wales East region*
Davies, Paul, *C., Preseli Pembrokeshire,* Maj. 3,205
Elis-Thomas, Lord Dafydd, *PC, Dwyfor Meirionnydd,* Maj. 8,868
Evans, Nerys, *PC, Mid and West Wales region*
Franks, Christopher, *PC, South Wales Central region*
German, Michael, *LD, South Wales East region*
Gibbons, Brian, *Lab., Aberavon,* Maj. 6,571
Graham, William, *C., South Wales East region*
Gregory, Janice, *Lab., Ogmore,* Maj. 7,900
Griffiths, Albert John, *Lab., Newport East,* Maj. 875
Griffiths, Lesley, *Lab., Wrexham,* Maj. 1,250
Hart, Edwina, *Lab., Gower,* Maj. 1,192
Hutt, Jane, *Lab., Vale of Glamorgan,* Maj. 83
Isherwood, Mark, *C., North Wales region*
James, Irene, *Lab., Islwyn,* Maj. 2,218
Jenkins, Bethan, *PC, South Wales West region*
Jones, Alun, *PC, Arfon,* Maj. 5,018
Jones, Carwyn Howell, *Lab., Bridgend,* Maj. 2,556
Jones, Elin, *PC, Ceredigion,* Maj. 3,955
Jones, Gareth, *PC, Aberconwy,* Maj. 1,693
Jones, Helen Mary, *PC, Llanelli,* Maj. 3,884
Jones, Margaret Ann (Ann), *Lab., Vale of Clwyd,* Maj. 92
Law, Trish, *Ind., Blaenau Gwent,* Maj. 5,357
Lewis, Huw, *Lab., Merthyr Tydfil and Rhymney,* Maj. 4,581
Lloyd, Dr David, *PC, South Wales West region*
Lloyd, Val, *Lab., Swansea East,* Maj. 4,961
Melding, David, *C., South Wales Central region*
Mewies, Sandra Elaine, *Lab., Delyn,* Maj. 511
Millar, Darren, *C., Clwyd West,* Maj. 1,596
Morgan, Hywel Rhodri, *Lab., Cardiff West,* Maj. 3,698
Morgan, Jonathan, *C., Cardiff North,* Maj. 4,844
Neagle, Lynne, *Lab., Torfaen,* Maj. 5,396
Ramsay, Nicholas, *C., Monmouth,* Maj. 8,469
Randerson, Jennifer Elizabeth, *LD, Cardiff Central,* Maj 6,565
Ryder, Janet, *PC, North Wales region*
Sargeant, Carl, *Lab., Alyn and Deeside,* Maj. 3,362
Sinclair, Karen, *Lab., Clwyd South,* Maj. 1,119
Thomas, Gwenda, *Lab., Neath,* Maj. 1,944
Thomas, Rhodri, *PC, Carmarthen East and Dinefwr,* Maj 8,469
Watson, Joyce, *Lab., Mid and West Wales region*
Williams, Brynle, *C., North Wales region*
Williams, Kirsty, *LD, Brecon and Radnorshire,* Maj. 5,354
Wood, Leanne, *PC, South Wales Central region*
Wyn Jones, Ieuan, *PC, Ynys Mon,* Maj. 4,392

STATE OF THE PARTIES *as at 4 May 2007*

	Constituency AMs	*Regional AMs*	*AM total*
Labour (Lab.)	23*	2	25*
Plaid Cymru (PC)	6*	8	14*
Conservative (C.)	5	7	12
Liberal Democrats (LD)	3	3	6
Others	1	0	1
The Presiding Officer	1	0	1
The Deputy Presiding Officer	1	0	1
Total	40	20	60

* Excludes the presiding officer (PC) and deputy presiding officer (Lab.), who have no party allegiance while in post

NATIONAL ASSEMBLY ELECTION RESULT

As at May 2007

E. Electorate T. Turnout

See General Election Results for a list of party abbreviations

CONSTITUENCIES

ABERAVON (S. WALES WEST)
E. 51,536 T. 20,528 (39.83%)

Brian Gibbons, Lab.	10,129
Linet Purcell, PC	3,558
Andrew Tutton, Neath Port Talbot Ratepayers Association	2,561
Daisy Meyland-Smith, C.	1,990
Claire Waller, LD	1,450
Captain Beany, Bean	840

Lab. majority 6,571 (32.01%)
4.82% swing Lab. to PC

ALYN AND DEESIDE (WALES N.)
E. 59,355 T. 21,095 (35.54%)

Carl Sargeant, Lab.	8,196
Will Gallagher, C.	4,834
Dennis Hutchinson, Ind.	3,241
Paul Brighton, LD	2,091
Dafydd Passe, PC	1,398
William Crawford, UKIP	1,335

Lab. majority 3,362 (15.94%)
3.66% swing Lab. to C.

BLAENAU GWENT (S. WALES EAST)
E. 52,816 T. 23,518 (44.53%)

Trish Law, Ind.	12,722
Keren Bender, Lab.	7,365
Gareth Lewis, LD	1,351
Natasha Asghar, PC	1,129
Bob Hayward, C.	951

Ind. majority 5,357 (22.78%)
46.5% swing Lab. to Ind.

BRECON AND RADNORSHIRE (WALES MID AND W.)
E. 55,428 T. 28,748 (51.87%)

Kirsty Williams, LD	15,006
Suzy Davies, C.	9,652
Neil Stone, Lab.	2,514
Arwel Lloyd, PC	1,576

LD majority 5,354 (18.62%)
0.58% swing LD to C.

BRIDGEND (S. WALES WEST)
E. 59,550 T. 24,552 (41.23%)

Carwyn Jones, Lab.	9,889
Emma Greenow, C.	7,333
Paul Warren, LD	3,730
Nicholas Thomas, PC	3,600

Lab. majority 2,556 (10.41%)
0.71% swing Lab. to C.

CAERNARFON (WALES N.)
E. 39,891 T. 19,573 (49.07%)

Alun Ffred Jones, PC	10,260
Martin Eaglestone, Lab.	5,242
Gerry Frobisher, C.	1,858
Mel ab Owain, LD	1,424
Elwyn Williams, UKIP	789

PC majority 5,018 (25.64%)
3.43% swing Lab. to PC

CAERPHILLY (S. WALES EAST)
E. 62,046 T. 26,922 (43.39%)

Jeff Cuthbert, Lab.	8,937
Lindsay Whittle, PC	7,000
Ron Davies, Ind.	6,071
Richard Foley, C.	3,227
Huw Price, LD	1,687

Lab. majority 1,937 (7.19%)
5.07% swing Lab. to PC

CARDIFF CENTRAL (S. WALES CENTRAL)
E. 62,202 T. 22,397 (36.01%)

Jenny Randerson, LD	11,462
Sue Lent, Lab.	4,897
Andrew Murphy, C.	3,137
Thomas Whitfield, PC	1,855
Frank Hughes, UKIP	1,046

LD majority 6,565 (29.31%)
2.71% swing LD to Lab.

CARDIFF NORTH (S. WALES CENTRAL)
E. 65,687 T. 33,702 (51.31%)

Jonathan Morgan, C.	15,253
Sophie Howe, Lab.	10,409
Ed Bridges, LD	4,287
Wyn Jones, PC	2,491
Dai Llewellyn, UKIP	1,262

C. majority 4,844 (14.37%)
8.16% swing Lab. to C.

CARDIFF SOUTH AND PENARTH (S. WALES CENTRAL)
E. 71,312 T. 26,728 (37.48%)

Lorraine Barrett, Lab.	10,106
Karen Robson, C.	7,352
Dominic Hannigan, LD	5,445
Jason Toby, PC	3,825

Lab. majority 2,754 (10.30%)
4.22% swing Lab. to C.

CARDIFF WEST (S. WALES CENTRAL)
E. 64,588 T. 26,889 (41.63%)

Rhodri Morgan, Lab.	10,390
Craig Williams, C.	6,692
Neil McEvoy, PC	5,719
Alison Goldsworthy, LD	4,088

Lab. majority 3,698 (13.75%)
8.77% swing Lab. to C.

CARMARTHEN EAST AND DINEFWR (WALES MID AND W.)
E. 52,528 T. 29,269 (55.72%)

Rhodri Glyn Thomas, PC	15,655
Kevin Madge, Lab.	7,186
Henrietta Hensher, C.	4,676
Ian Walton, LD	1,752

PC majority 8,469 (28.94%)
5.85% swing Lab. to PC

CARMARTHEN WEST AND SOUTH PEMBROKESHIRE (WALES MID AND W.)
E. 57,477 T. 28,568 (49.70%)

Angela Burns, C.	8,590
Christine Gwyther, Lab.	8,492
John Dixon, PC	8,340
John Gossage, LD	1,806
Malcolm Calver, Ind.	1,340

C. majority 98 (0.34%)
7.45% swing Lab. to C.

CEREDIGION (WALES MID AND W.)
E. 54,071 T. 30,108 (55.68%)

Elin Jones, PC	14,818
John Davies, LD	10,863
Trefor Jones, C.	2,369
Linda Grace, Lab.	1,530
Emyr Morgan, Ind.	528

PC majority 3,955 (13.14%)
2.20% swing PC to LD

CLWYD SOUTH (WALES N.)
E. 51,865 T. 19,498 (37.59%)

Karen Sinclair, Lab.	6,838
John Bell, C.	5,719
Nia Davies, PC	3,894
Frank Biggs, LD	1,838
David Rowlands, UKIP	1,209

Lab. majority 1,119 (5.74%)
6.04% swing Lab. to C.

CLWYD WEST (WALES N.)
E. 57,312 T. 26,205 (45.72%)

Darren Millar, C.	8,905
Alun Pugh, Lab.	7,309
Philip Edwards, PC	7,162
Simon Croft, LD	1,705
Warwick Nicholson, UKIP	1,124

C. majority 1,596 (6.09%)
4.13% swing Lab. to C.

CONWY (WALES N.)
E. 44,143 T. 20,699 (46.89%)

Gareth Jones, PC	7,983
Dylan Jones-Evans, C.	6,290
Denise Idris Jones, Lab.	4,508
Euron Hughes, LD	1,918

PC majority 1,693 (8.18%)
2.86% swing C. to PC

CYNON VALLEY (S. WALES CENTRAL)
E. 50,846 T. 19,517 (38.38%)

Christine Chapman, Lab.	11,058
Liz Walters, PC	5,435
Neill John, C.	2,024
Margaret Phelps, LD	1,000

Lab. majority 5,623 (28.81%)
7.16% swing Lab. to PC

DELYN (WALES N.)
E. 52,733 T. 21,668 (41.09%)

Sandy Mewies, Lab.	7,506
Antoinette Sandbach, C.	6,996
Meg Ellis, PC	3,179
Ian Matthews, LD	2,669
Derek Bigg, UKIP	1,318

Lab. majority 510 (2.35%)
3.63% swing Lab. to C.

GOWER (S. WALES WEST)
E. 61,520 T. 27,545 (44.77%)

Edwina Hart, Lab.	9,406
Byron Davis, C.	8,214
Darren Price, PC	5,106
Nick Tregoning, LD	2,924
Alex Lewis, UKIP	1,895

Lab. majority 1,192 (4.33%)
9.84% swing Lab. to C.

ISLWYN (S. WALES EAST)
E. 54,795 T. 23,564 (43.00%)

Irene James, Lab.	8,883
Kevin Etheridge, Ind.	6,665
Allan Pritchard, PC	5,084
Paul Williams, C.	1,797
Mark Maguire, LD	1,135

Lab. majority 2,218 (9.41%)
23.3% swing Lab. to Ind.

LLANELLI (WALES MID AND W.)
E. 56,154 T. 27,602 (49.15%)

Helen Mary Jones, PC	13,839
Catherine Thomas, Lab.	9,955
Andrew Morgan, C.	2,757
Jeremy Townsend, LD	1,051

PC majority 3,884 (14.07%)
7.08% swing Lab. to PC

MEIRIONNYDD NANT CONWY (WALES MID AND W.)
E. 46,718 T. 22,122 (47.35%)

Dafydd Elis-Thomas, PC	13,201
Mike Wood, C.	4,333
David Phillips, Lab.	2,749
Steve Churchman, LD	1,839

PC majority 8,868 (40.09%)
1.57% swing PC to C.

MERTHYR TYDFIL AND RHYMNEY (S. WALES EAST)
E. 54,025 T. 21,028 (38.92%)

Huw Lewis, Lab.	7,776
Amy Kitcher, LD	3,195
Clive Tovey, Ind.	2,622
Glyndwr Jones, PC	2,519
Jeff Edwards, Ind.	1,950
Giles Howard, C.	1,151
Jock Greer, Ind.	844
Vivienne Hadley, Ind.	809
Richard Williams, Ind.	162

Lab. majority 4,581 (21.79%)
15.77% swing Lab. to LD

MONMOUTH (S. WALES EAST)
E. 63,000 T. 29,565 (46.93%)

Nick Ramsay, C.	15,389
Richard Clark, Lab.	6,920
Jacqui Sullivan, LD	4,359
Jonathan Clark, PC	2,093
Ed Abrams, Eng. Dem.	804

C. majority 8,469 (28.65%)
0.99% swing C. to Lab.

MONTGOMERYSHIRE (WALES MID AND W.)
E. 48,377 T. 22,300 (46.10%)

Mick Bates, LD	8,704
Don Munford, C.	6,725
David Thomas, PC	3,076
Charles Lawson, UKIP	2,251
Rachel Maycock, Lab.	1,544

LD majority 1,979 (8.87%)
1.18% swing LD to C.

NEATH (S. WALES WEST)
E. 57,952 T. 25,200 (43.48%)

Gwenda Thomas, Lab.	10,934
Alun Llewelyn, PC	8,990
Andrew Sivertsen, C.	2,956
Sheila Waye, LD	2,320

Lab. majority 1,944 (7.71%)
7.29% swing Lab. to PC

NEWPORT EAST (S. WALES EAST)
E. 53,060 T. 19,906 (37.52%)

John Griffiths, Lab.	6,395
Ed Townsend, LD	5,520
Peter Fox, C.	4,512
Trefor Puw, PC	1,696
James Harris, Ind.	1,354
Mike Blundell, Eng. Dem.	429

Lab. majority 875 (4.40%)
12.00% swing Lab. to LD

NEWPORT WEST (S. WALES EAST)
E. 58,981 T. 23,659 (40.11%)

Rosemary Butler, Lab.	9,582
Matthew Evans, C.	8,181
Nigel Flanagan, LD	2,813
Brian Hancock, PC	2,449
Andrew Constantine, Eng. Dem.	634

Lab. majority 1,401 (5.92%)
5.79% swing Lab. to C.

OGMORE (S. WALES WEST)
E. 56,973 T. 22,766 (39.96%)

Janice Gregory, Lab.	11,761
Sian Caiach, PC	3,861
Norma Lloyd-Nesling, C.	2,663
Steve Smith, Ind.	2,337
Martin Plant, LD	2,144

Lab. majority 7,900 (34.70%)
2.65% swing Lab. to PC

PONTYPRIDD (S. WALES CENTRAL)
E. 57,512 T. 23,501 (40.86%)

Jane Davidson, Lab.	9,836
Michael Powell, LD	6,449
Richard Grigg, PC	4,181
Janice Charles, C.	3,035

Lab. majority 3,387 (14.41%)
11.08% swing Lab. to LD

PRESELI PEMBROKESHIRE (WALES MID AND W.)
E. 56,435 T. 28,720 (50.89%)

Paul Davies, C.	11,086
Tamsin Dunwoody, Lab.	7,881
John Osmond, PC	7,101
Hywel Davies, LD	2,652

C. majority 3,205 (11.16%)
3.52% swing Lab. to C.

RHONDDA (S. WALES CENTRAL)
E. 52,478 T. 22,107 (42.13%)

Leighton Andrews, Lab.	12,875
Jill Evans, PC	6,660
Karen Roberts, LD	1,441
Howard Parsons, C.	1,131

Lab. majority 6,215 (28.11%)
3.23% swing Lab. to PC

SWANSEA EAST (S. WALES WEST)
E. 59,186 T. 20,717 (35.00%)

Val Lloyd, Lab.	8,590
Helen Clarke, LD	3,629
Danny Bowles, PC	3,218
Bob Dowdle, C.	2,025
David Robinson, Ind.	1,618
Ray Welsby, Ind.	1,177
Gary Evans, Ind.	460

Lab. majority 4,961 (23.95%)
0.49% swing LD to Lab.

SWANSEA WEST (S. WALES WEST)
E. 61,469 T. 22,879 (37.22%)

Andrew Davies, Lab.	7,393
Peter May, LD	5,882
Harri Davies, C.	4,379
Ian Titherington, PC	3,583
Richard Lewis, UKIP	1,642

Lab. majority 1,511 (6.60%)
5.75% swing Lab. to LD

TORFAEN (S. WALES EAST)
E. 62,592 T. 23,215 (37.09%)

Lynne Neagle, Lab.	9,921
Graham Smith, C.	4,525
Ian Williams, Ind.	3,348
Rhys ab Elis, PC	2,762
Patrick Legge, LD	2,659

Lab. majority 5,396 (23.24%)
6.18% swing Lab. to C.

VALE OF CLWYD (WALES N.)
E. 55,234 T. 22,275 (40.33%)

Ann Jones, Lab.	8,104
Matt Wright, C.	8,012
Mark Jones, PC	3,884
Mark Young, LD	2,275

Lab. majority 92 (0.41%)
7.40% swing Lab. to C.

VALE OF GLAMORGAN (S. WALES CENTRAL)
E. 68,856 T. 33,686 (48.92%)

Jane Hutt, Lab.	11,515
Gordon Kemp, C.	11,432
Barry Shaw, PC	4,671
Mark Hooper, LD	3,758
Kevin Mahoney, UKIP	2,310

Lab. majority 83 (0.25%)
4.02% swing Lab. to C.

WREXHAM (WALES N.)
E. 50,759 T. 19,567 (38.55%)

Lesley Griffiths, Lab.	5,633
John Marek, Ind.	4,383
Felicity Elphick, C.	3,372
Bruce Roberts, LD	3,268
Sion Aled Owen, PC	1,878
Peter Lewis, UKIP	1,033

Lab. majority 1,250 (6.39%)
6.0% swing Ind. to Lab.

YNYS MON (WALES N.)
E. 51,814 T. 26,820 (51.76%)

Ieuan Wyn Jones, PC	10,653
Peter Rogers, Ind.	6,261
Jonathan Austin, Lab.	4,681
James Roach, C.	3,480
Mandi Abrahams, LD	912
Francis Wykes, UKIP	833

PC majority 4,392 (16.38%)
10.5% swing PC to Ind.

REGIONS

MID AND WEST WALES
E. 427,188 T. 216,957 (50.79%)

PC	67,258 (31.00%)
C.	49,606 (22.86%)
Lab.	39,979 (18.43%)
LD	28,790 (13.27%)
Green	8,768 (4.04%)
UKIP	8,191 (3.78%)
BNP	6,389 (2.94%)
Soc. Lab.	2,196 (1.01%)
Ind.	1,598 (0.74%)
Welsh Christian Party	1,493 (0.69%)
Ind. Evans	1,108 (0.51%)
Comm. Brit.	666 (0.31%)
Veritas	502 (0.23%)
CPA	413 (0.19%)

PC majority 17,652 (8.14%)
1.16% swing PC to C. (2003 PC majority 5,423)

ADDITIONAL MEMBERS
Nick Bourne, *C.*
Alun Davies, *Lab.*
Joyce Watson, *Lab.*
Nerys Evans, *PC*

NORTH WALES
E. 463,106 T. 196,442 (42.42%)

Lab.	51,831 (26.38%)
PC	50,558 (25.74%)
C.	50,266 (25.59%)
LD	15,275 (7.78%)
BNP	9,986 (5.08%)
UKIP	8,015 (4.08%)
Green	5,660 (2.88%)
Soc. Lab.	2,209 (1.12%)
Welsh Christian Party	1,300 (0.66%)
Comm. Brit.	700 (0.36%)
CPA	642 (0.33%)

Lab. majority 1,273 (0.65%)
4.72% swing Lab. to PC (2003 Lab. majority 13,610)

ADDITIONAL MEMBERS
Brynle Williams, *C.*
Mark Isherwood, *C.*
Eleanor Burnham, *LD*
Janet Ryder, *PC*

SOUTH WALES CENTRAL
E. 493,481 T. 208,294 (42.21%)

Lab.	70,799 (33.99%)
C.	45,147 (21.67%)
PC	32,207 (15.46%)
LD	29,262 (14.05%)
BNP	7,889 (3.79%)
Green	7,831 (3.76%)
UKIP	7,645 (3.67%)
Welsh Christian Party	1,987 (0.95%)
Soc. Lab.	1,744 (0.84%)
Respect	1,079 (0.52%)
Soc. Alt.	838 (0.40%)
Comm. Brit.	817 (0.39%)
CPA	757 (0.36%)
Socialist Equality Party	292 (0.14%)

Lab. majority 25,652 (12.32%)
5.16% swing Lab. to C. (2003 Lab. majority 40,965)

ADDITIONAL MEMBERS
David Melding, *C.*
Andrew Davies, *C.*
Leanne Wood, *PC*
Chris Franks, *PC*

SOUTH WALES EAST
E. 461,315 T. 190,064 (41.20%)

Lab.	67,998 (35.78%)
C.	37,935 (19.96%)
PC	25,915 (13.63%)
LD	20,947 (11.02%)
BNP	8,940 (4.70%)
UKIP	8,725 (4.59%)
Green	5,414 (2.85%)
Ind.	4,876 (2.57%)
Soc. Lab.	3,693 (1.94%)
Welsh Christian Party	2,498 (1.31%)
Eng. Dem.	1,655 (0.87%)
Comm. Brit.	979 (0.52%)
CPA	489 (0.26%)

Lab. majority 30,063 (15.82%)
4.55% swing Lab. to C. (2003 Lab. majority 42,291)

ADDITIONAL MEMBERS
William Graham, *C.*
Michael German, *LD*
Jocelyn Davies, *PC*
Mohammed Asghar, *PC*

SOUTH WALES WEST
E. 408,186 T. 163,127 (39.96%)

Lab.	58,347 (35.77%)
PC	28,819 (17.67%)
C.	26,199 (16.06%)
LD	20,226 (12.40%)
BNP	8,993 (5.51%)
Green	6,130 (3.76%)
UKIP	5,914 (3.63%)
Soc. Lab.	2,367 (1.45%)
Welsh Christian Party	1,685 (1.03%)
Ind. James	1,186 (0.73%)
Soc. Alt.	1,027 (0.63%)
Respect	713 (0.44%)
Ind.	582 (0.36%)
Comm. Brit.	546 (0.33%)
CPA	393 (0.24%)

Lab. majority 29,528 (18.10%)
2.87% swing Lab. to PC (2003 Lab. majority 33,267)

ADDITIONAL MEMBERS
Alun Cairns, *C.*
Peter Black, *LD*
Bethan Jenkins, *PC*
Dai Lloyd, *PC*

COTLAND

COTTISH PARLIAMENT

inburgh EH99 1SP
)131-348 5000/0845-278 1999 Textphone 0845-270 0152
131-348 5601
p.info@scottish.parliament.uk
www.scottish.parliament.uk

July 1997 the government announced plans to ablish a Scottish parliament. In a referendum on 11 ptember 1997 about 60 per cent of the electorate ted. Of those who voted, 74.3 per cent voted in favour the parliament and 63.5 per cent in favour of it having -raising powers. Elections are held every four years. e first elections were held on 6 May 1999, when about per cent of the electorate voted. The first meeting was ld on 12 May 1999 and the Scottish parliament was ficially opened on 1 July 1999 at the Assembly Hall, inburgh. A new building to house parliament was ened, in the presence of the Queen, at Holyrood on 9 ctober 2004. On 3 May 2007 the third elections to the ottish parliament took place.

The Scottish parliament has 129 members (including e presiding officer), comprising 73 constituency embers and 56 additional regional members, mainly m party lists. It can introduce primary legislation and s the power to raise or lower the basic rate of income by up to three pence in the pound.

The areas for which the Scottish parliament is sponsible include: education, health, law, environment, onomic development, local government, housing, lice, fire services, planning, financial assistance to dustry, tourism, some transport, heritage and the arts, riculture, forestry and food standards.

LARIES *as at 1 April 2007*

rst Minister*	£76,907
inisters*	£39,897
rd Advocate*	£52,123
licitor-General for Scotland*	£37,690
nior Ministers*	£24,989
SPs†	£53,091
esiding Officer*	£39,897
eputy Presiding Officer*	£24,989

n addition to the MSP salary
Reduced by two-thirds if the member is already an MP or an MEP

COTTISH EXECUTIVE

Andrew's House, Regent Road, Edinburgh EH1 3DG
0845-774 1741 Enquiry Line 0131-556 8400
eu@scotland.gov.uk W www.scotland.gov.uk

e Scottish Executive is the devolved government for otland. It is responsible for most of the issues of day-to-y concern to the people of Scotland, including health, ucation, justice, rural affairs and transport, and manages annual budget of around £30bn.

The executive was established in 1999, following the st elections to the Scottish parliament, and the current ministration was formed after elections in May 2007.

The executive is led by a first minister who is minated by the parliament and in turn appoints the her Scottish ministers.

Scottish Executive civil servants are accountable to ottish ministers, who are themselves accountable to the ottish parliament.

CABINET
First Minister, Rt. Hon. Alex Salmond, MSP
Minister for EU, International and Culture, Linda Fabiani, MSP
Minister for Parliamentary Business, Bruce Crawford, MSP
Deputy First Minister and Cabinet Secretary for Health and Wellbeing, Nicola Sturgeon, MSP
Minister for Communities and Sport, Stewart Maxwell, MSP
Minister for Public Health, Shona Robison, MSP
Cabinet Secretary for Education and Lifelong Learning, Fiona Hyslop, MSP
Minister for Children and Early Years, Adam Ingram, MSP
Minister for Schools and Skills, Maureen Watt, MSP
Cabinet Secretary for Finance and Sustainable Growth, John Swinney, MSP
Minister for Enterprise, Energy and Tourism, Jim Mather, MSP
Minister for Transport, Infrastructure and Climate Change, Stewart Stevenson, MSP
Cabinet Secretary for Justice, Kenny MacAskill, MSP
Minister for Community Safety, Fergus Ewing, MSP
Cabinet Secretary for Rural Affairs and the Environment, Richard Lochhead, MSP
Minister for Environment, Michael Russel, MSP

LAW OFFICERS
Lord Advocate, Elish Angiolini, QC
Solicitor-General for Scotland, John Beckett, QC

STRATEGIC BOARD
Permanent Secretary, Sir John Elvidge, KCB
Director-General, Economy, and Chief Economic Adviser, Dr Andrew Goudie
Director-General, Education, Philip Rycroft
Director-General, Environment, Richard Wakeford
Director-General, Health, and Chief Executive of NHS Scotland, Dr Kevin Woods
Director-General, Justice and Communities, Robert Gordon, CB
Non-Executive Directors, Prof. William Bound, David Fisher; Shonaig Macpherson

CHANGE AND CORPORATE SERVICES
Saughton House, Broomhouse Drive, Edinburgh EH11 3XD
T 0845-774 1741
Director of Change and Corporate Services, Paul Pagliari

ECONOMY DEPARTMENT
Victoria Quay, Edinburgh EH6 6QQ
T 0845-774 1741
Directorates: Europe; External Affairs and Culture; Finance; Inquiry Reporters; Planning; Public Service Reform; Scottish Development International; Transport
Director-General and Chief Economic Adviser, Dr Andrew Goudie

EXECUTIVE AGENCIES
General Register Office of Scotland
Historic Scotland
National Archives for Scotland
Registers of Scotland
Scottish Building Standards Agency
Scottish Public Pensions Agency
Scottish Water
Transport Scotland
Water Industry Commission

EDUCATION DEPARTMENT
Pentland House, 47 Robb's Loan, Edinburgh EH14 1TY
T 0845-774 1741 F 01397-795001
Directorates: Analytical Services; Chief Scientific Adviser; Children; Enterprise and Industrial Affairs and Tourism; Lifelong Learning; School; Young People and Social Care
Director-General, Philip Ryecroft

EXECUTIVE AGENCIES
HM Inspectorate of Education
Social Work Inspection Agency
Student Awards Agency for Scotland

ENVIRONMENT DEPARTMENT
Pentland House, 47 Robb's Loan, Edinburgh EH14 1TY
T 0845-774 1741
Directorates: Environment; Marine; Operations; Rural; Science and Analysis
Director-General, Richard Wakeford

EXECUTIVE AGENCIES
Animal Health Agency
Cairngorms National Park Authority
Crofters Commission
Deer Commission Scotland
Fisheries Research Service
Forest Enterprise
Forestry Commission Scotland
Loch Lomond and Trossach National Park Authority
Royal Botanic Gardens
Scottish Agricultural Science Agency
Scottish Agricultural Wages Board
Scottish Environmental Protection Agency
Scottish Fisheries Protection Service

HEALTH DEPARTMENT
St Andrew's House, Regent Road, Edinburgh EH1 3DG
T 0131-244 2440
Directorates: Chief Medical Officer; Chief Nursing Officer; Delivery; eHealth; Finance; Health Improvement; Primary and Community Care; Service Policy and Planning; Workforce
Director-General and Chief Executive of NHS Scotland, Dr Kevin Woods

EXECUTIVE AGENCIES
Mental Health Tribunal (Scotland)
Scottish Commission for the Regulation of Care

JUSTICE AND COMMUNITIES DEPARTMENT
St Andrew's House, Regent Road, Edinburgh EH1 3DG
T 0131-244 2120 F 0131-244 2121
Directorates: Courts; Civil and International Justice; Constitutional and Legal Services; Criminal Justice; Housing and Regeneration; Office of the First Scottish Parliamentary Counsel; Police and Community Safety; Solicitor
Director-General, Robert Gordon, CB

EXECUTIVE AGENCIES
Accountant in Bankruptcy
Communities Scotland
HM Inspector Constabulary
HMC Inspector Fire Rescue Service
HMC Inspector Prisons
Office of Scottish Charities Regulator
Scottish Courts Service
Scottish Prison Service

CROWN OFFICE AND PROCURATOR FISCAL SERVICE
29 Chambers Street, Edinburgh EH1 1LD
T 0131-226 4962
Chief Executive and Crown Agent, Norman McFadyen

OFFICE OF THE PERMANENT SECRETARY
St Andrew's House, Regent Road, Edinburgh EH1 3DG
T 0131-244 4028 F 0131-244 2756
Permanent Secretary, Sir John Elvidge, KCB

AUDIT SCOTLAND
110 George Street, Edinburgh EH2 4LH
T 0845-146 1010 F 0845-146 1009
W www.audit-scotland.gov.uk
Auditor-General, Robert W. Black
Accounts Commission Chair, Alastair MacNish

COURT OF THE LORD LYON
HM New Register House, Edinburgh EH1 3YT
T 0131-556 7255 F 0131-557 2148
W www.lyon-court.com
Lord Lyon King of Arms, Robin O. Blair, LVO, WS

MEMBERS OF THE SCOTTISH PARLIAMENT

as at 3 May 2007

Adam, Brian, *SNP, Aberdeen North,* Maj. 3,749
Ahmad, Bashir, *SNP, Glasgow region*
Aitken, Bill, *C., Glasgow region*
Alexander, Wendy, *Lab., Paisley North,* Maj. 5,113
Allan, Alasdair, *SNP, Western Isles,* Maj. 987
Baillie, Jackie, *Lab., Dumbarton,* Maj. 1,611
Baker, Claire, *Lab., Mid Scotland and Fife region*
Baker, Richard, *Lab., North East Scotland region*
Boyack, Sarah, *Lab., Edinburgh Central,* Maj. 1,193
Brankin, Rhona, *Lab., Midlothian,* Maj. 1,702
Brocklebank, Ted, *C., Mid Scotland and Fife region*
Brown, Gavin, *C., Lothians region*
Brown, Keith, *SNP, Ochil,* Maj. 490
Brown, Robert E., *LD, Glasgow region*
Brownlee, Derek, *C., South of Scotland region*
Butler, Bill, *Lab., Glasgow Anniesland,* Maj. 4,306
Campbell, Aileen, *SNP, South of Scotland region*
Carlaw, Jackson, *C., West of Scotland region*
Chisholm, Malcolm, *Lab., Edinburgh North and Lei* Maj. 2,444
Coffey, Willie, *SNP, Kilmarnock and Loudon,* Maj. 1,342
Constance, Angela, *SNP, Livingston,* Maj. 870
Craigie, Cathie, *Lab., Cumbernauld and Kilsyth,* Ma 2,079
Crawford, Bruce, *SNP, Stirling,* Maj. 620
Cunningham, Roseanna, *SNP, Perth,* Maj. 2,495
Curran, Margaret, *Lab., Glasgow Baillieston,* Maj. 3,934
Don, Nigel, *SNP, North East Scotland region*
Doris, Bob, *SNP, Glasgow region*
Eadie, Helen, *Lab., Dunfermline East,* Maj. 3,993
Ewing, Fergus, *SNP, Inverness East, Nairn and Lochab* Maj. 5,471
Fabiani, Linda, *SNP, Central Scotland region*
Ferguson, Patricia, *Lab., Glasgow Maryhill,* Maj. 2,310
Fergusson, Alex, *C., Galloway and Upper Nithsdale,* Ma 3,333
Finnie, Ross, *LD, West of Scotland region*
Fitzpatrick, Joe, *SNP, Dundee West,* Maj. 1,946
Foulkes, George, *Lab., Lothians region*
Fraser, Murdo, *C., Mid Scotland and Fife region*
Gibson, Kenneth, *SNP, Cunninghame North,* Maj. 48

ibson, Rob, *SNP, Highlands and Islands region*
illon, Karen, *Lab., Clydesdale,* Maj. 2,893
len, Marlyn, *Lab., North East Scotland region*
odman, Trish, *Lab., Renfrewshire West,* Maj. 2,178
oldie, Annabel, *C., West of Scotland region*
ordon, Charlie, *Lab., Glasgow Cathcart,* Maj. 2,189
rahame, Christine, *SNP, South of Scotland region*
rant, Rhoda, *Lab., Highlands and Islands region*
ray, Ian, *Lab., East Lothian,* Maj. 2,448
arper, Robin, *Scot. Green, Lothians region*
arvie, Christopher, *SNP, Mid Scotland and Fife region*
arvie, Patrick, *Scot. Green, Glasgow region*
enry, Hugh, *Lab., Paisley South,* Maj. 4,230
epburn, Jamie, *SNP, Central Scotland region*
ume, Jim, *LD, South of Scotland region*
yslop, Fiona, *SNP, Lothians region*
gram, Adam, *SNP, South of Scotland region*
mieson, Cathy, *Lab., Carrick, Cumnock and Doon Valley,* Maj. 3,986
hnstone, Alex, *C., North East Scotland region*
elly, James, *Lab., Glasgow Rutherglen,* Maj. 4,378
err, Andy, *Lab., East Kilbride,* Maj. 1,972
idd, Bill, *SNP, Glasgow region*
mont, Johann, *Lab., Glasgow Pollok,* Maj. 4,393
mont, John, *C., Roxburgh and Berwickshire,* Maj. 1,985
vingstone, Marilyn, *Lab., Kirkcaldy,* Maj. 2,622
ochhead, Richard, *SNP, Moray,* Maj. 7,924
acAskill, Kenny, *SNP, Edinburgh East and Musselburgh,* Maj. 1,382
acdonald, Lewis, *Lab., Aberdeen Central,* Maj. 382
acDonald, Margo, *Ind., Lothians region*
acintosh, Kenneth, *Lab., Eastwood,* Maj. 891
cArthur, Liam, *LD, Orkney,* Maj. 2,476
cAveety, Frank, *Lab., Glasgow Shettleston,* Maj. 2,881
cCabe, Tom, *Lab., Hamilton South,* Maj. 3,652
cConnell, Jack, *Lab., Motherwell and Wishaw,* Maj. 5,938
cGrigor, Jamie, *C., Highlands and Islands region*
cInnes, Alison, *LD, North East Scotland region*
cKee, Ian, *SNP, Lothians region*
cKelvie, Christina, *SNP, Central Scotland region*
cLetchie, David, *C., Edinburgh Pentlands,* Maj. 4,525
cMahon, Michael, *Lab., Hamilton North and Bellshill,* Maj. 4,865
cMillan, Stuart, *SNP, West of Scotland region*
cNeil, Duncan, *Lab., Greenock and Inverclyde,* Maj. 3,024
cNeill, Pauline, *Lab., Glasgow Kelvin,* Maj. 1,207
cNulty, Des, *Lab., Clydebank and Milngavie,* Maj. 3,179
artin, Paul, *Lab., Glasgow Springburn,* Maj. 5,095
arwick, Tricia, *SNP, Central Fife,* Maj. 1,166
ather, Jim, *SNP, Argyll and Bute,* Maj. 815
atheson, Michael, *SNP, Falkirk West,* Maj. 776
axwell, Stewart, *SNP, West of Scotland region*
ilne, Nanette, *C., North East Scotland region*
itchell, Margaret, *C., Central Scotland region*
organ, Alasdair, *SNP, South of Scotland region*
ulligan, Mary, *Lab., Linlithgow,* Maj. 1,160
unro, John F., *LD, Ross, Skye and Inverness West,* Maj. 3,486
urray, Dr Elaine, *Lab., Dumfries,* Maj. 2,839
eil, Alex, *SNP, Central Scotland region*
'Donnell, Hugh, *LD, Central Scotland region*
ldfather, Irene, *Lab., Cunninghame South,* Maj. 2,168
ark, John, *Lab., Mid Scotland and Fife region*
Paterson, Gil, *SNP, West of Scotland region*
Peacock, Peter, *Lab., Highlands and Islands region*
Peattie, Cathy, *Lab., Falkirk East,* Maj. 1,872
Pringle, Mike, *LD, Edinburgh South,* Maj. 1,929
Purvis, Jeremy, *LD, Tweeddale, Ettrick and Lauderdale,* Maj. 598
Robison, Shona, *SNP, Dundee East,* Maj. 4,524
Rumbles, Mike, *LD, Aberdeenshire West and Kincardine,* Maj. 5,170
Russell, Michael, *SNP, South of Scotland region*
Salmond, Alex, *SNP, Gordon,* Maj. 2062
Scanlon, Mary, *C., Highlands and Islands region*
Scott, John, *C., Ayr,* Maj. 3,906
Scott, Tavish, *LD, Shetland,* Maj. 4,909
Simpson, Richard, *Lab., Mid Scotland and Fife region*
Smith, Elaine, *Lab., Coatbridge and Chryston,* Maj. 4,510
Smith, Elizabeth, *C., Mid Scotland and Fife region*
Smith, Iain, *LD, Fife North East,* Maj. 5,016
Smith, Margaret, *LD, Edinburgh West,* Maj. 5,886
Stephen, Nicol, *LD, Aberdeen South,* Maj. 2,732
Stevenson, Stewart, *SNP, Banff and Buchan,* Maj. 10,530
Stewart, David, *Lab., Highlands and Islands region*
Stone, Jamie, *LD, Caithness, Sutherland and Easter Ross,* Maj. 2,323
Sturgeon, Nicola, *SNP, Glasgow Govan,* Maj. 744
Swinney, John, *SNP, North Tayside,* Maj. 7,584
Thompson, Dave, *SNP, Highlands and Islands region*
Tolson, Jim, *LD, Dunfermline West,* Maj. 476
Tymkewycz, Stefan, *SNP, Lothians region*
Watt, Maureen, *SNP, North East Scotland region*
Welsh, Andrew, *SNP, Angus,* Maj. 8,243
White, Sandra, *SNP, Glasgow region*
Whitefield, Karen, *Lab., Airdrie and Shotts,* Maj. 1,446
Whitton, David, *Lab., Strathkelvin and Bearsden,* Maj. 3,388
Wilson, Bill, *SNP, West of Scotland region*
Wilson, John, *SNP, Central Scotland region*

STATE OF THE PARTIES *as at 3 May 2007*

	Constituency MSPs	*Regional MSPs*	*Total*
Scottish Labour Party (Lab.)	37	9	46
Scottish National Party (SNP)	21	26	47
Scottish Conservative and Unionist Party (C.)	3	13	16
Scottish Liberal Democrats (LD)	11	5	16
Scottish Green Party (Scot. Green)	0	2	2
Independent (Ind.)*	9	1	1
Presiding Officer†	1	0	1
Total	73	56	129

* Independent MSP is Margo MacDonald
† The presiding officer was elected as a constituency member for the Conservatives but has no party allegiance while in post

The Presiding Officer, Alex Fergusson, MSP
Deputy Presiding Officers, Trish Godman, MSP *(Lab.)*; Alasdair Morgan, MSP *(SNP)*

SCOTTISH PARLIAMENT CONSTITUENCIES

as at May 2007
E. Electorate T. Turnout
See General Election Results for a list of party abbreviations

ABERDEEN CENTRAL
(Scotland North East Region)
E. 46,588 T. 21,120 (45.33%)
Lewis Macdonald, Lab. 7,232
Karen Shirron, SNP 6,850
John Stewart, LD 4,693
Andrew Jones, C. 2,345
Lab. majority 382 (1.81%)
2.06% swing Lab. to SNP

ABERDEEN NORTH
(Scotland North East Region)
E. 51,507 T. 24,891 (48.33%)
Brian Adam, SNP 11,406
Elaine Thomson, Lab. 7,657
Steve Delaney, LD 3,836
Carol Garvie, C. 1,992
SNP majority 3,749 (15.06%)
6.62% swing Lab. to SNP

ABERDEEN SOUTH
(Scotland North East Region)
E. 56,700 T. 29,885 (52.71%)
Nicol Stephen, LD 10,843
Maureen Watt, SNP 8,111
Rami Okasha, Lab. 5,499
David Davidson, C. 5,432
LD majority 2,732 (9.14%)
11.21% swing LD to SNP

ABERDEENSHIRE WEST AND KINCARDINE
(Scotland North East Region)
E. 65,233 T. 34,823 (53.38%)
Mike Rumbles, LD 14,314
Dennis Robertson, SNP 9,144
Stewart Whyte, C. 8,604
James Noble, Lab. 2,761
LD majority 5,170 (14.85%)
8.48% swing LD to SNP

AIRDRIE AND SHOTTS
(Scotland Central Region)
E. 57,660 T. 27,160 (47.10%)
Karen Whitefield, Lab. 11,907
Sophia Coyle, SNP 10,461
Iain McGill, C. 2,370
Robert Gorrie, LD 1,452
Mev Brown, Scottish Voice 970
Lab. majority 1,446 (5.32%)
15.23% swing Lab. to SNP

ANGUS
(Scotland North East Region)
E. 61,362 T. 31,960 (52.08%)
Andrew Welsh, SNP 15,686
Alex Johnstone, C. 7,443
Doug Bradley, Lab. 5,032
Scott Rennie, LD 3,799
SNP majority 8,243 (25.79%)
1.67% swing C. to SNP

ARGYLL AND BUTE
(Highlands and Islands Region)
E. 48,846 T. 28,792 (58.94%)
Jim Mather, SNP 9,9
George Lyon, LD 9,1
Jamie McGrigor, C. 5,5
Mary Galbraith, Lab. 4,1
SNP majority 815 (2.83%)
9.17% swing LD to SNP

AYR
(Scotland South Region)
E. 55,034 T. 31,025 (56.37%)
John Scott, C. 12,6
John Duncan, Lab. 8,7
Iain White, SNP 7,9
Stuart Ritchie, LD 1,7
C. majority 3,906 (12.59%)
3.30% swing Lab. to C.

BANFF AND BUCHAN
(Scotland North East Region)
E. 56,324 T. 27,285 (48.44%)
Stewart Stevenson, SNP 16,0
Geordie Burnett-Stuart, C. 5,5
Kay Barnett, Lab. 3,1
Alison McInnes, LD 2,6
SNP majority 10,530 (38.59%)
3.30% swing C. to SNP

CAITHNESS, SUTHERLAND AND EASTER ROSS
(Highlands and Islands Region)
E. 41,789 T. 22,334 (53.44%)
Jamie Stone, LD 8,9
Rob Gibson, SNP 6,6
John McKendrick, Lab. 3,1
Donald MacDonald, C. 2,5
Gordon Campbell, Ind. 9
LD majority 2,323 (10.40%)
4.38% swing LD to SNP

CARRICK, CUMNOCK AND DOON VALLEY
(Scotland South Region)
E. 65,166 T. 33,785 (51.84%)
Cathy Jamieson, Lab. 14,3
Adam Ingram, SNP 10,3
Tony Lewis, C. 6,7
Paul McGreal, LD 1,4
Hugh Hill, Ind. 8
Ray Barry, Equal Parenting Alliance 1
Lab. majority 3,986 (11.80%)
9.61% swing Lab. to SNP

CLYDEBANK AND MILNGAVIE
(Scotland West Region)
E. 48,700 T. 26,765 (54.96%)
Des McNulty, Lab. 11,61
Gil Paterson, SNP 8,43
Murray Roxburgh, C. 3,54
Ashay Ghai, LD 3,16
Lab. majority 3,179 (11.88%)
2.61% swing Lab. to SNP

:YDESDALE
cotland South Region)
66,011 T. 33,332 (50.49%)

aren Gillon, Lab.	13,835
leen Campbell, SNP	10,942
olin McGavigan, C.	5,604
aser Grieve, LD	2,951

ab. majority 2,893 (8.68%)
94% swing Lab. to SNP

OATBRIDGE AND CHRYSTON
cotland Central Region)
54,423 T. 25,725 (47.27%)

aine Smith, Lab.	11,860
ances McGlinchey, SNP	7,350
oss Thomson, C.	2,305
lie McAnulty, Ind.	1,843
oreen Nisbet, LD	1,519
aille McCann, Scottish Voice	848

ab. majority 4,510 (17.53%)
19% swing Lab. to SNP

UMBERNAULD AND KILSYTH
cotland Central Region)
49,197 T. 26,382 (53.63%)

athie Craigie, Lab.	12,672
mie Hepburn, SNP	10,593
ugh O'Donnell, LD	1,670
nne Harding, C.	1,447

ab. majority 2,079 (7.88%)
87% swing SNP to Lab.

UNNINGHAME NORTH
cotland West Region)
55,925 T. 30,241 (54.07%)

enneth Gibson, SNP	9,295
llan Wilson, Lab.	9,247
hilip Lardner, C.	5,466
ampbell Martin, Ind.	4,423
ewis Hutton, LD	1,810

NP majority 48 (0.16%)
99% swing Lab. to SNP

UNNINGHAME SOUTH
cotland South Region)
49,969 T. 23,422 (46.87%)

ene Oldfather, Lab.	10,270
uncan Ross, SNP	8,102
at McPhee, C.	3,073
in Dale, LD	1,977

ab. majority 2,168 (9.26%)
.71% swing Lab. to SNP

UMBARTON
cotland West Region)
54,023 T. 30,054 (55.63%)

ckie Baillie, Lab.	11,635
raeme McCormick, SNP	10,024
rian Pope, C.	4,701
lex Mackie, LD	3,385
ohn Black, Scottish Jacobite Party	309

ab. majority 1,611 (5.36%)
.79% swing Lab. to SNP

DUMFRIES
(Scotland South Region)
E. 53,518 T. 33,419 (62.44%)

Elaine Murray, Lab.	13,707
Murray Tosh, C.	10,868
Michael Russell, SNP	6,306
Lynne Hume, LD	2,538

Lab. majority 2,839 (8.50%)
2.54% swing C. to Lab.

DUNDEE EAST
(Scotland North East Region)
E. 53,804 T. 26,869 (49.94%)

Shona Robison, SNP	13,314
Iain Luke, Lab.	8,790
Chris Bustin, C.	2,976
Clive Sneddon, LD	1,789

SNP majority 4,524 (16.84%)
8.25% swing Lab. to SNP

DUNDEE WEST
(Scotland North East Region)
E. 49,711 T. 24,268 (48.82%)

Joe Fitzpatrick, SNP	10,955
Jill Shimi, Lab.	9,009
Michael Charlton, LD	2,517
Belinda Don, C.	1,787

SNP majority 1,946 (8.02%)
6.14% swing Lab. to SNP

DUNFERMLINE EAST
(Scotland Mid and Fife Region)
E. 51,115 T. 24,568 (48.06%)

Helen Eadie, Lab.	10,995
Ewan Dow, SNP	7,002
Graeme Brown, C.	3,718
Karen Utting, LD	2,853

Lab. majority 3,993 (16.25%)
7.62% swing Lab. to SNP

DUNFERMLINE WEST
(Scotland Mid and Fife Region)
E. 56,953 T. 29,525 (51.84%)

Jim Tolson, LD	9,952
Scott Barrie, Lab.	9,476
Len Woods, SNP	7,296
Peter Lyburn, C.	2,363
Susan Archibald, Scottish Voice	438

LD majority 476 (1.61%)
10.77% swing Lab. to LD

EAST KILBRIDE
(Scotland Central Region)
E. 66,935 T. 35,902 (53.64%)

Andy Kerr, Lab.	15,334
Linda Fabiani, SNP	13,362
Graham Simpson, C.	4,114
David Clark, LD	3,092

Lab. majority 1,972 (5.49%)
5.00% swing Lab. to SNP

EAST LOTHIAN
(Scotland South Region)
E. 61,378 T. 34,471 (56.16%)
Iain Gray, Lab. 12,219
Andrew Sharp, SNP 9,771
Judy Hayman, LD 6,249
Bill Stevenson, C. 6,232
Lab. majority 2,448 (7.10%)
10.08% swing Lab. to SNP

EASTWOOD
(Scotland West Region)
E. 67,347 T. 42,187 (62.64%)
Ken Macintosh, Lab. 15,099
Jackson Carlaw, C. 14,186
Stewart Maxwell, SNP 7,972
Gordon MacDonald, LD 3,603
Frank McGhee, Ind. 1,327
Lab. majority 913 (2.16%)
3.68% swing Lab. to C.

EDINBURGH CENTRAL
(Lothians Region)
E. 55,953 T. 29,396 (52.54%)
Sarah Boyack, Lab. 9,155
Siobhan Mathers, LD 7,962
Shirley-Anne Somerville, SNP 7,496
Fiona Houston, C. 4,783
Lab. majority 1,193 (4.06%)
2.73% swing Lab. to LD

EDINBURGH EAST AND MUSSELBURGH
(Lothians Region)
E. 56,578 T. 29,967 (52.97%)
Kenny MacAskill, SNP 11,209
Norman Murray, Lab. 9,827
Gillian Cole-Hamilton, LD 5,473
Christine Wright, C. 3,458
SNP majority 1,382 (4.61%)
12.91% swing Lab. to SNP

EDINBURGH NORTH AND LEITH
(Lothians Region)
E. 60,340 T. 31,685 (52.51%)
Malcolm Chisholm, Lab. 11,020
Mike Crockart, LD 8,576
Davie Hutchison, SNP 8,044
Iain Whyte, C. 4,045
Lab. majority 2,444 (7.71%)
6.92% swing Lab. to LD

EDINBURGH PENTLANDS
(Lothians Region)
E. 57,891 T. 34,377 (59.38%)
David McLetchie, C. 12,927
Sheila Gilmore, Lab. 8,402
Ian McKee, SNP 8,234
Simon Clark, LD 4,814
C. majority 4,525 (13.16%)
3.42% swing Lab. to C.

EDINBURGH SOUTH
(Lothians Region)
E. 57,621 T. 32,573 (56.53%)
Mike Pringle, LD 11,39
Donald Anderson, Lab. 9,46
Robert Holland, SNP 6,11
Gavin Brown, C. 5,58
LD majority 1,929 (5.92%)
2.71% swing Lab. to LD

EDINBURGH WEST
(Lothians Region)
E. 59,814 T. 34,752 (58.10%)
Margaret Smith, LD 13,67
Sheena Cleland, SNP 7,79
Gordon Lindhurst, C. 7,36
Richard Meade, Lab. 5,34
John Wilson, Ind. 58
LD majority 5,886 (16.94%)
7.00% swing LD to SNP

FALKIRK EAST
(Scotland Central Region)
E. 57,663 T. 30,333 (52.60%)
Cathy Peattie, Lab. 13,18
Annabelle Ewing, SNP 11,31
Scott Campbell, C. 3,70
Natalie Maver, LD 2,13
Lab. majority 1,872 (6.17%)
9.00% swing Lab. to SNP

FALKIRK WEST
(Scotland Central Region)
E. 56,254 T. 28,785 (51.17%)
Michael Matheson, SNP 12,06
Dennis Goldie, Lab. 11,29
Stephen O'Rourke, C. 2,88
Callum Chomczuk, LD 2,53
SNP majority 776 (2.70%)
1.13% swing Lab. to SNP

FIFE CENTRAL
(Scotland Mid and Fife Region)
E. 58,215 T. 26,965 (46.32%)
Tricia Marwick, SNP 11,92
Christine May, Lab. 10,75
Elizabeth Riches, LD 2,28
Maurice Golden, C. 2,00
SNP majority 1,166 (4.32%)
7.56% swing Lab. to SNP

FIFE NORTH EAST
(Scotland Mid and Fife Region)
E. 61,078 T. 31,552 (51.66%)
Iain Smith, LD 13,30
Ted Brocklebank, C. 8,29
Roderick Campbell, SNP 6,73
Kenny Young, Lab. 2,55
Tony Campbell, Ind. 66
LD majority 5,016 (15.90%)
0.68% swing LD to C.

LLOWAY AND UPPER NITHSDALE
otland South Region)
52,583 T. 30,318 (57.66%)

ex Fergusson, C.	13,387
asdair Morgan, SNP	10,054
ephen Hodgson, Lab.	4,935
astair Cooper, LD	1,631
ndy Richardson, Ind.	311

majority 3,333 (10.99%)
33% swing SNP to C.

ASGOW ANNIESLAND
lasgow Region)
48,344 T. 22,139 (45.79%)

ll Butler, Lab.	10,483
ll Kidd, SNP	6,177
ll Aitken, C.	3,154
anica Gilland, LD	2,325

b. majority 4,306 (19.45%)
38% swing Lab. to SNP

ASGOW BAILLIESTON
lasgow Region)
44,367 T. 17,272 (38.93%)

argaret Curran, Lab.	9,141
chie McNeill, SNP	5,207
chard Sullivan, C.	1,276
avid Jackson, LD	1,060
eorge Hargreaves, Scottish Christian Party	588

b. majority 3,934 (22.78%)
52% swing Lab. to SNP

ASGOW CATHCART
lasgow Region)
47,822 T. 21,657 (45.29%)

arlie Gordon, Lab.	8,476
mes Dornan, SNP	6,287
avid Smith, Ind.	2,911
avena Rankin, C.	2,324
abnum Mustapha, LD	1,659

b. majority 2,189 (10.11%)
40% swing Lab. to SNP

ASGOW GOVAN
lasgow Region)
47,405 T. 21,521 (45.40%)

icola Sturgeon, SNP	9,010
ordon Jackson, Lab.	8,266
hris Young, LD	1,891
artyn McIntyre, C.	1,680
sif Nasir, Ind.	423
inor McKenzie, Comm. Brit.	251

VP majority 744 (3.46%)
65% swing Lab. to SNP

LASGOW KELVIN
lasgow Region)
55,096 T. 23,500 (42.65%)

auline McNeill, Lab.	7,875
andra White, SNP	6,668
artin Bartos, Green	2,971
aty Gordon, LD	2,843
rian Cooklin, C.	1,943
iall Walker, Ind.	744
obel Macleod, Scottish Christian Party	456

ab. majority 1,207 (5.14%)
88% swing Lab. to SNP

GLASGOW MARYHILL
(Glasgow Region)
E. 46,060 T. 16,564 (35.96%)

Patricia Ferguson, Lab.	7,955
Bob Doris, SNP	5,645
Kenn Elder, LD	1,936
Heather MacLeod, C.	1,028

Lab. majority 2,310 (13.95%)
7.74% swing Lab. to SNP

GLASGOW POLLOK
(Glasgow Region)
E. 47,189 T. 19,416 (41.15%)

Johann Lamont, Lab.	10,456
Chris Stephens, SNP	6,063
Gerald Michaluk, C.	1,460
Christine Gilmore, LD	1,437

Lab. majority 4,393 (22.63%)
0.85% swing Lab. to SNP

GLASGOW RUTHERGLEN
(Glasgow Region)
E. 50,005 T. 24,252 (48.50%)

James Kelly, Lab.	10,237
Margaret Park, SNP	5,857
Robert Brown, LD	5,516
Christina Harcus, C.	2,094
Tom Greig, Scottish Christian Party	548

Lab. majority 4,380 (18.06%)
6.43% swing Lab. to SNP

GLASGOW SHETTLESTON
(Glasgow Region)
E. 44,278 T. 14,801 (33.43%)

Frank McAveety, Lab.	7,574
John McLaughlin, SNP	4,693
Ross Renton, LD	1,182
William MacNair, C.	946
Bob Graham, Scottish Christian Party	406

Lab. majority 2,881 (19.46%)
9.45% swing Lab. to SNP

GLASGOW SPRINGBURN
(Glasgow Region)
E. 47,021 T. 17,612 (37.46%)

Paul Martin, Lab.	10,024
Anne McLaughlin, SNP	4,929
Katy McCloskey, LD	1,108
Gordon Wilson, C.	1,067
David Johnston, Scottish Christian Party	484

Lab. majority 5,095 (28.93%)
7.09% swing Lab. to SNP

GORDON
(Scotland North East Region)
E. 65,431 T. 35,363 (54.05%)

Alex Salmond, SNP	14,650
Nora Radcliffe, LD	12,588
Nanette Milne, C.	5,348
Neil Cardwell, Lab.	2,276
Donald Marr, Ind.	199
Dave Mathers, Ind.	185
Bob Ingram, Scottish Enterprise Party	117

SNP majority 2,062 (5.83%)
10.66% swing LD to SNP

GREENOCK AND INVERCLYDE
(Scotland West Region)
E. 44,646 T. 23,105 (51.75%)

Duncan McNeil, Lab.	10,035
Stuart McMillan, SNP	7,011
Ross Finnie, LD	3,893
Charles Ferguson, C.	2,166

Lab. majority 3,024 (13.09%)
6.37% swing Lab. to SNP

HAMILTON NORTH AND BELLSHILL
(Scotland Central Region)
E. 53,854 T. 25,366 (47.10%)

Michael McMahon, Lab.	12,334
Alex Neil, SNP	7,469
James Callander, C.	2,835
Douglas Herbison, LD	1,726
Joe Gorman, Scottish Voice	571
Gordon Weir, Ind.	431

Lab. majority 4,865 (19.18%)
6.75% swing Lab. to SNP

HAMILTON SOUTH
(Scotland Central Region)
E. 48,838 T. 23,211 (47.53%)

Tom McCabe, Lab.	10,280
Christina McKelvie, SNP	6,628
Margaret Mitchell, C.	2,929
Michael McGlynn, Ind.	1,764
John Oswald, LD	1,610

Lab. majority 3,652 (15.73%)
3.89% swing Lab. to SNP

INVERNESS EAST, NAIRN AND LOCHABER
(Highlands and Islands Region)
E. 71,609 T. 39,609 (55.31%)

Fergus Ewing, SNP	16,443
Craig Harrow, LD	10,972
Linda Stewart, Lab.	7,559
Jamie Halcro-Johnston, C.	4,635

SNP majority 5,471 (13.81%)
0.48% swing SNP to LD

KILMARNOCK AND LOUDOUN
(Scotland Central Region)
E. 60,753 T. 33,435 (55.03%)

Willie Coffey, SNP	14,297
Margaret Jamieson, Lab.	12,955
Janette McAlpine, C.	4,127
Ron Aitken, LD	2,056

SNP majority 1,342 (4.01%)
3.93% swing Lab. to SNP

KIRKCALDY
(Scotland Mid and Fife Region)
E. 50,761 T. 24,195 (47.66%)

Marilyn Livingstone, Lab.	10,627
Chris Harvie, SNP	8,005
Alice Soper, LD	3,361
David Potts, C.	2,202

Lab. majority 2,622 (10.84%)
5.58% swing Lab. to SNP

LINLITHGOW
(Lothians Region)
E. 56,175 T. 29,637 (52.76%)

Mary Mulligan, Lab.	12,7
Fiona Hyslop, SNP	11,5
Donald Cameron, C.	3,1
Martin Oliver, LD	2,2

Lab. majority 1,150 (3.88%)
1.62% swing Lab. to SNP

LIVINGSTON
(Lothians Region)
E. 66,348 T. 33,224 (50.08%)

Angela Constance, SNP	13,1
Bristow Muldoon, Lab.	12,2
Ernie Walker, Action to Save St John's Hospital	2,8
David Brown, C.	2,8
Evan Bell, LD	2,1

SNP majority 870 (2.62%)
7.31% swing Lab. to SNP

MIDLOTHIAN
(Lothians Region)
E. 48,395 T. 25,111 (51.89%)

Rhona Brankin, Lab.	10,6
Colin Beattie, SNP	8,9
Ross Laird, LD	2,7
P.J. Lewis, C.	2,2
George McCleery, Had Enough Party	4

Lab. majority 1,702 (6.78%)
8.37% swing Lab. to SNP

MORAY
(Highlands and Islands Region)
E. 60,959 T. 30,274 (49.66%)

Richard Lochhead, SNP	15,04
Mary Scanlon, C.	7,12
Lee Butcher, Lab.	4,5
Dominique Rommel, LD	3,5

SNP majority 7,924 (26.17%)
3.24% swing C. to SNP

MOTHERWELL AND WISHAW
(Scotland Central Region)
E. 53,875 T. 26,150 (48.54%)

Jack McConnell, Lab.	12,57
Marion Fellows, SNP	6,63
Diane Huddleston, C.	1,9
John Swinburne, SSCUP	1,7
Stuart Douglas, LD	1,57
Tom Selfridge, Scottish Christian Party	1,49
Richard Leat, Anti-Trident Party	18

Lab. majority 5,938 (22.71%)
6.88% swing Lab. to SNP

OCHIL
(Scotland Mid and Fife Region)
E. 58,104 T. 31,553 (54.30%)

Keith Brown, SNP	12,14
Brian Fearon, Lab.	11,65
George Murray, C.	4,28
Lorraine Caddell, LD	3,46

SNP majority 490 (1.55%)
0.29% swing Lab. to SNP

ORKNEY
(Highlands and Islands Region)
E. 16,195 T. 8,653 (53.43%)

Liam McArthur, LD	4,113
John Mowat, SNP	1,637
Helen Gardiner, C.	1,632
Iain MacDonald, Lab.	1,134
Barrie Johnson, Ind.	137

LD majority 2,476 (28.61%)
1.95% swing LD to SNP

PAISLEY NORTH
(Scotland West Region)
E. 44,081 T. 23,206 (52.64%)

Wendy Alexander, Lab.	12,111
Andy Doig, SNP	6,998
Malcolm MacAskill, C.	1,721
Angela McGarrigle, LD	1,570
Iain Hogg, SSP	525
John Plott, Ind.	281

Lab. majority 5,113 (22.03%)
1.31% swing SNP to Lab.

PAISLEY SOUTH
(Scotland West Region)
E. 49,175 T. 25,527 (51.91%)

Hugh Henry, Lab.	12,123
Fiona McLeod, SNP	7,893
Eileen McCartin, LD	3,434
Tom Begg, C.	2,077

Lab. majority 4,230 (16.57%)
3.38% swing SNP to Lab.

PERTH
(Scotland and Mid Fife Region)
E. 62,220 T. 34,862 (56.03%)

Roseanna Cunningham, SNP	13,751
Liz Smith, C.	11,256
Peter Barrett, LD	4,767
Doug Maughan, Lab.	4,513
Jim Fairlie, Free Scot.	575

SNP majority 2,495 (7.16%)
2.43% swing C. to SNP

RENFREWSHIRE WEST
(Scotland West Region)
E. 50,787 T. 29,129 (57.36%)

Trish Godman, Lab.	10,467
Annabel Goldie, C.	8,289
Bill Wilson, SNP	8,167
Simon Hutton, LD	2,206

Lab. majority 2,178 (7.48%)
1.22% swing Lab. to C.

ROSS, SKYE AND INVERNESS WEST
(Highlands and Islands Region)
E. 59,237 T. 31,719 (53.55%)

John Farquhar Munro, LD	13,501
Dave Thompson, SNP	10,015
Maureen Macmillan, Lab.	4,789
John Hodgson, C.	3,122
Iain Brodie, Scottish Enterprise Party	292

LD majority 3,486 (10.99%)
6.32% swing LD to SNP

ROXBURGH AND BERWICKSHIRE
(Scotland South Region)
E. 47,862 T. 25,680 (53.65%)

John Lamont, C.	10,556
Euan Robson, LD	8,571
Aileen Orr, SNP	4,127
Mary Lockhart, Lab.	2,108
Jesse Rae, No Description	318

C. majority 1,985 (7.73%)
9.40% swing LD to C.

SHETLAND
(Highlands and Islands Region)
E. 17,108 T. 9,795 (57.25%)

Tavish Scott, LD	6,531
Val Simpson, SNP	1,622
Mark Jones, C.	972
Scott Burnett, Lab.	670

LD majority 4,909 (50.12%)
11.99% swing SNP to LD

STIRLING
(Scotland and Mid Fife Region)
E. 52,864 T. 32,625 (61.71%)

Bruce Crawford, SNP	10,447
Sylvia Jackson, Lab.	9,827
Bob Dalrymple, C.	8,081
Alex Cole-Hamilton, LD	3,693
Liz Law, Peace Party	577

SNP majority 620 (1.90%)
9.41% swing Lab. to SNP

STRATHKELVIN AND BEARSDEN
(Scotland West Region)
E. 60,389 T. 36,595 (60.60%)

David Whitton, Lab.	11,396
Robin Easton, SNP	8,008
Jean Turner, Ind.	6,742
Stephanie Fraser, C.	5,178
Cathy McInnes, LD	4,658
Bob Handyside, Scottish Christian Party	613

Lab. majority 3,388 (9.26%)
3.91% swing Lab. to SNP

TAYSIDE NORTH
(Scotland Mid and Fife Region)
E. 62,133 T. 35,396 (56.97%)

John Swinney, SNP	18,281
Murdo Fraser, C.	10,697
Michael Marna, Lab.	3,243
James Taylor, LD	3,175

SNP majority 7,584 (21.43%)
3.96% swing C. to SNP

TWEEDDALE, ETTRICK AND LAUDERDALE
(Scotland South Region)
E. 53,588 T. 30,327 (56.59%)

Jeremy Purvis, LD	10,656
Christine Grahame, SNP	10,058
Derek Brownlee, C.	5,594
Catherine Maxwell-Stuart, Lab.	4,019

LD majority 598 (1.97%)
0.02% swing LD to SNP

WESTERN ISLES
(Highlands and Islands Region)
E. 22,051 T. 13,625 (61.79%)

Alasdair Allan, SNP	6,354
Alasdair Morrison, Lab.	5,667
Ruaraidh Ferguson, LD	852
Dave Petrie, C.	752

SNP majority 687 (5.04%)
5.43% swing Lab. to SNP

ADDITIONAL MEMBERS
Mary Scanlon, *C.*
Jamie McGrigor, *C.*
Peter Peacock, *Lab.*
Rhoda Grant, *Lab.*
David Stewart, *Lab.*
Rob Gibson, *SNP*
Dave Thompson, *SNP*

REGIONS

GLASGOW
E. 477,587 T. 206,618 (43.26%)

Lab.	78,838 (38.16%)
SNP	55,832 (27.02%)
LD	14,767 (7.15%)
C.	13,781 (6.67%)
Green	10,759 (5.21%)
Solidarity	8,525 (4.13%)
BNP	3,865 (1.87%)
SSCUP	3,703 (1.79%)
Scottish Christian Party	2,991 (1.45%)
Soc. Lab.	2,680 (1.30%)
CPA	2,626 (1.27%)
SSP	2,579 (1.25%)
Scottish Unionist Party	1,612 (0.78%)
Publican Party Smoking-Room in Pubs	952 (0.46%)
Ind. Shoaib	582 (0.28%)
Ind. Green	496 (0.24%)
UKIP	405 (0.20%)
Scottish Voice	389 (0.19%)
Ind. Nasir	317 (0.15%)
Scotland Against Crooked Lawyers	293 (0.14%)
Ind.	286 (0.14%)
Comm. Brit.	260 (0.13%)
Nine Per Cent Growth Party	80 (0.04%)

Lab. majority 23,006 (11.13%)
4.75% swing Lab. to SNP (2003 Lab. majority 42,146)

ADDITIONAL MEMBERS
Bill Aitken, *C.*
Robert Brown, *LD*
Bashir Ahmad, *SNP*
Sandra White, *SNP*
Bob Doris, *SNP*
Bill Kidd, *SNP*
Patrick Harvie, *Green*

HIGHLANDS AND ISLANDS
E. 337,794 T. 185,773 (55.00%)

SNP	63,979 (34.44%)
LD	37,001 (19.92%)
Lab.	32,952 (17.74%)
C.	23,334 (12.56%)
Green	8,602 (4.63%)
Scottish Christian Party	6,332 (3.41%)
SSCUP	3,841 (2.07%)
BNP	2,152 (1.16%)
Solidarity	1,833 (0.99%)
UKIP	1,287 (0.69%)
Soc. Lab.	1,027 (0.55%)
SSP	973 (0.52%)
Publican Party Smoking-Room in Pubs	914 (0.49%)
CPA	885 (0.48%)
Scottish Voice	450 (0.24%)
Scottish Enterprise Party	211 (0.11%)

SNP majority 26,978 (14.52%)
4.94% swing LD to SNP (2003 SNP majority 1,892)

LOTHIANS
E. 519,115 T. 287,039 (55.29%)

SNP	76,019 (26.48%)
Lab.	75,495 (26.30%)
C.	37,548 (13.08%)
LD	36,571 (12.74%)
Green	20,147 (7.02%)
Ind.	19,256 (6.71%)
SSCUP	4,176 (1.45%)
Solidarity	2,998 (1.04%)
BNP	2,637 (0.92%)
Soc. Lab.	2,190 (0.76%)
Scottish Christian Party	2,002 (0.70%)
SSP	1,994 (0.69%)
Publican Party Smoking-Room in Pubs	1,230 (0.43%)
Witchery Tour Party	867 (0.30%)
CPA	848 (0.30%)
UKIP	834 (0.29%)
Had Enough Party	670 (0.23%)
Scottish Voice	661 (0.23%)
Scotland Against Crooked Lawyers	322 (0.11%)
Ind. Scott	189 (0.07%)
Scottish Enterprise Party	183 (0.06%)
Ind. Wilson	129 (0.04%)
Ind. Thorp	73 (0.03%)

SNP majority 524 (0.18%)
4.22% swing Lab. to SNP (2003 Lab. majority 21,960)

ADDITIONAL MEMBERS
Gavin Brown, *C.*
George Foulkes, *Lab.*
Fiona Hyslop, *SNP*
Ian McKee, *SNP*
Stefan Tymkewycz, *SNP*
Robin Harper, *Green*
Margo MacDonald, *Ind.*

SCOTLAND CENTRAL
E. 559,452 T. 284,512 (50.86%)

Lab.	112,596 (39.58%)
SNP	89,210 (31.36%)
C.	24,253 (8.52%)
LD	14,648 (5.15%)
Green	7,204 (2.53%)
SSCUP	7,060 (2.48%)
Scottish Christian Party	5,575 (1.96%)
Solidarity	5,012 (1.76%)
CPA	4,617 (1.62%)
BNP	4,125 (1.45%)
Soc. Lab.	2,303 (0.81%)
SSP	2,188 (0.77%)
Scottish Voice	1,955 (0.69%)
Scottish Unionist Party	1,544 (0.54%)
Publican Party Smoking-Room in Pubs	1,500 (0.53%)
UKIP	722 (0.25%)

Lab. majority 23,386 (8.22%)
4.83% swing Lab. to SNP (2003 Lab. majority 47,044)

ADDITIONAL MEMBERS
Margaret Mitchell, *C.*
Hugh O'Donnell, *LD*
Alex Neil, *SNP*
Linda Fabiani, *SNP*
Jamie Hepburn, *SNP*
Christina McKelvie, *SNP*
John Wilson, *SNP*

SCOTLAND MID AND FIFE
E. 513,443 T. 273,083 (53.19%)

SNP	90,090 (32.99%)
Lab.	71,922 (26.34%)
C.	44,341 (16.24%)
LD	36,195 (13.25%)
Green	10,318 (3.78%)
SSCUP	5,523 (2.02%)
BNP	2,620 (0.96%)
Solidarity	2,468 (0.90%)
Scottish Christian Party	1,698 (0.62%)
UKIP	1,587 (0.58%)
Soc. Lab.	1,523 (0.56%)
Publican Party Smoking-Room in Pubs	1,309 (0.48%)
SSP	1,116 (0.41%)
Scottish Voice	919 (0.34%)
CPA	790 (0.29%)
Free Scotland Party	664 (0.24%)

SNP majority 18,168 (6.65%)
4.45% swing Lab. to SNP (2003 Lab. majority 5,608)

ADDITIONAL MEMBERS
Murdo Fraser, *C.*
Liz Smith, *C.*
Ted Brocklebank, *C.*
John Park, *Lab.*
Claire Baker, *Lab.*
Richard Simpson, *Lab.*
Chris Harvie, *SNP*

SCOTLAND NORTH EAST
E. 506,660 T. 256,282 (50.58%)

SNP	105,265 (41.07%)
Lab.	52,125 (20.34%)
LD	40,934 (15.97%)
C.	37,666 (14.70%)
Green	8,148 (3.18%)
BNP	2,764 (1.08%)
Solidarity	2,004 (0.78%)
Scottish Christian Party	1,895 (0.74%)
CPA	1,173 (0.46%)
SSP	1,051 (0.41%)
UKIP	1,045 (0.41%)
SSCUP	930 (0.36%)
Scottish Voice	569 (0.22%)
Soc. Lab.	491 (0.19%)
Scottish Enterprise Party	222 (0.09%)

SNP majority 53,140 (20.73%)
5.82% swing Lab. to SNP (2003 SNP majority 17,274)

ADDITIONAL MEMBERS
Alex Johnstone, *C.*
Nanette Milne, *C.*
Richard Baker, *Lab.*
Marlyn Glen, *Lab.*
Alison McInnes, *LD*
Maureen Watt, *SNP*
Nigel Don, *SNP*

SCOTLAND SOUTH
E. 514,105 T. 276,910 (53.86%)

Lab.	79,762 (28.80%)
SNP	77,053 (27.83%)
C.	62,475 (22.56%)
LD	28,040 (10.13%)
Green	9,254 (3.34%)
SSCUP	5,335 (1.93%)
Solidarity	3,433 (1.24%)
BNP	3,212 (1.16%)
Scottish Christian Party	2,353 (0.85%)
Soc. Lab.	1,633 (0.59%)
UKIP	1,429 (0.52%)
SSP	1,114 (0.40%)
CPA	839 (0.30%)
Scottish Voice	490 (0.18%)
Ind.	488 (0.18%)

Lab. majority 2,709 (0.98%)
5.32% swing Lab. to SNP (2003 Lab. majority 15,128)

ADDITIONAL MEMBERS
Derek Brownlee, *C.*
Jim Hume, *LD*
Christine Grahame, *SNP*
Michael Russell, *SNP*
Adam Ingram, *SNP*
Alasdair Morgan, *SNP*
Aileen Campbell, *SNP*

SCOTLAND WEST
E. 475,073 T. 268,179 (56.45%)

Lab.	91,725 (34.20%)
SNP	75,953 (28.32%)
C.	40,637 (15.15%)
LD	22,515 (8.40%)
Green	8,152 (3.04%)
SSCUP	5,231 (1.95%)
Solidarity	4,774 (1.78%)
Scottish Christian Party	3,729 (1.39%)
BNP	3,241 (1.21%)
CPA	3,027 (1.13%)
Save Our NHS Group	2,682 (1.00%)
SSP	1,716 (0.64%)
Soc. Lab.	1,557 (0.58%)
Scottish Unionist Party	1,245 (0.46%)
UKIP	888 (0.33%)
Scottish Voice	522 (0.19%)
Scottish Jacobite Party	446 (0.17%)
Socialist Equality Party	139 (0.05%)

Lab. majority 15,772 (5.88%)
2.70% swing Lab. to SNP (2003 Lab. majority 12,351)

ADDITIONAL MEMBERS
Annabel Goldie, *C.*
Jackson Carlaw, *C.*
Ross Finnie, *LD*
Stewart Maxwell, *SNP*
Gil Paterson, *SNP*
Bill Wilson, *SNP*
Stuart McMillan, *SNP*

NORTHERN IRELAND

NORTHERN IRELAND ASSEMBLY

Parliament Buildings, Stormont, Belfast BT4 3XX
T 028-9052 1333 **F** 028-9052 1961
W www.niassembly.gov.uk

The Northern Ireland Assembly was established as a result of the Belfast Agreement (also known as the Good Friday Agreement) in April 1998. The agreement was endorsed through a referendum held in May 1998 and subsequently given legal force through the Northern Ireland Act 1998.

The Northern Ireland Assembly has full legislative and executive authority for all matters that are the responsibility of the government's Northern Ireland departments – known as transferred matters. Excepted and reserved matters are defined in schedules 2 and 3 of the Northern Ireland Act 1998 and remain the responsibility of UK parliament.

The first assembly election occurred on 25 June 1998 and the 108 members elected met for the first time on 1 July 1998. The 108 members are elected by the single transferable vote system from 18 constituencies – six per constituency. The first minister and deputy first minister head the executive committee of ministers and, acting jointly, determine the total number of ministers in the executive. First and deputy first ministers are elected by members through a formula of parallel consent that requires a majority of designated unionists, a majority of designated nationalists and a majority of the whole assembly. The parties elected to the assembly select ministerial portfolios in proportion to party strengths using the d'Hondt nominating procedure.

On 29 November 1999 the assembly appointed ten ministers as well as the chairs and deputy chairs for the ten statutory departmental committees. Devolution of powers to the Northern Ireland Assembly occurred on 2 December 1999, following several delays concerned with Sinn Fein's inclusion in the executive while Irish Republican Army (IRA) weapons were yet to be decommissioned.

Since the devolution of powers, the assembly has been suspended by the Secretary of State for Northern Ireland on four occasions. The first was between 11 February and 30 May 2000, with two 24-hour suspensions on 10 August and 22 September 2001– all owing to a lack of progress in decommissioning. The final suspension took place on 14 October 2002 after unionists walked out of the executive following a police raid on Sinn Fein's office investigating alleged intelligence gathering.

The assembly was formally dissolved in April 2003 in anticipation of an election, which eventually took place on 26 November 2003. The results of the election changed the balance of power between the political parties, with an increase in the number of seats held by the Democratic Unionist Party (DUP) and Sinn Fein (SF), so that they became the largest parties. The assembly was restored to a state of suspension following the November election while political parties engaged in a review of the Belfast Agreement aimed at fully restoring the devolved institutions.

In July 2005 the leadership of the IRA formally ordered an end to its armed campaign; it authorised a representative to engage with the Independent International Commission on Decommissioning in order to verifiably put the arms beyond use. On 26 September 2005 General John de Chastelain, the chair of the commission, along with two independent church witnesses confirmed that the IRA's entire arsenal of weapons had been decommissioned.

Following the passing of the Northern Ireland Act 2006 the secretary of state created a non-legislative fixed term assembly, whose membership consisted of the 108 members elected in the 2003 election. It first met on 15 May 2006 with the remit of making preparations for the restoration of devolved government; its discussions informed the next round of talks called by the British and Irish governments held at St Andrews. The St Andrews agreement of 13 October 2006 led to the establishment of the transitional assembly.

The Northern Ireland (St Andrews Agreement) Act 2006 set out a timetable to restore devolution, and also set the date for the third election to the assembly as 7 March 2007. The DUP and SF again had the largest number of Members of the Legislative Assembly (MLAs) elected, and although the initial restoration deadline of 26 March was missed, the leaders of the DUP and SF (Revd Dr Ian Paisley, MP, MLA and Gerry Adams, MLA, respectively) took part in a historic meeting and made a joint commitment to establish an executive committee in the assembly to which devolved powers were restored on 8 May 2007.

SALARIES *as at May 2007*

Assembly Member	£31,817

NORTHERN IRELAND EXECUTIVE

Stormont Castle, Stormont, Belfast BT4 3TT
T 028-9052 0700 **F** 028-9052 8195
W www.northernireland.gov.uk

The executive committee includes five DUP ministers, four SF ministers, two Ulster Unionist members, one Social Democratic and Labour Party minister alongside the first minister, Ian Paisley MP, MLA, of the DUP, and the deputy first minister, Martin McGuinness, MLA, of SF.

EXECUTIVE COMMITTEE

First Minister, Rt. Hon. Revd Ian Paisley, MP, MLA
Deputy First Minister, Martin McGuinness, MP, MLA
Junior Ministers, Gerry Kelly, MLA; Ian Paisley Jr, MLA
Minister for Agriculture and Rural Development, Michelle Gildernew, MP, MLA
Minister for Culture, Arts and Leisure, Edwin Poots, MLA
Minister for Education, Caitriona Ruane, MLA
Minister for Employment and Learning, Sir Reg Empey, MLA
Minister for Enterprise, Trade and Investment, Nigel Dodds OBE, MP, MLA
Minister for Environment, Arlene Foster, MLA
Minister for Finance and Personnel, Rt. Hon. Peter Robinson, MP, MLA
Minister for Health, Social Services and Public Safety, Michael McGimpsey, MLA
Minister for Regional Development, Conor Murphy, MP, MLA
Minister for Social Development, Margaret Ritchie, MLA

OFFICE OF THE FIRST MINISTER AND DEPUTY FIRST MINISTER

Stormont Castle, Stormont, Belfast BT4 3TT
T 028-9052 8400 **W** www.ofmdfmni.gov.uk

DEPARTMENT OF AGRICULTURE AND RURAL DEVELOPMENT

Dundonald House, Upper Newtownards Road, Belfast BT4 3SB
T 028-9052 0100 **W** www.dardni.gov.uk

EXECUTIVE AGENCIES
Forest Service
Rivers Agency

DEPARTMENT OF CULTURE, ARTS AND LEISURE
Interpoint, 20–24 York Street, Belfast BT15 1AQ
T 028-9025 8825 **W** www.dcalni.gov.uk

EXECUTIVE AGENCIES
Ordnance Survey of Northern Ireland
Public Record Office of Northern Ireland

DEPARTMENT OF EDUCATION
Rathgael House, Balloo Road, Bangor, Co. Down BT19 7PR
T 028-9127 9279 **W** www.deni.gov.uk

DEPARTMENT FOR EMPLOYMENT AND LEARNING
Adelaide House, 39–49 Adelaide Street, Belfast BT2 8FD
T 028-9025 7777 **W** www.delni.gov.uk

DEPARTMENT OF ENTERPRISE, TRADE AND INVESTMENT
Netherleigh, Massey Avenue, Belfast BT4 2JP
T 028-9052 9900 **F** 028-9052 9550
W www.detini.gov.uk

EXECUTIVE AGENCY
Health and Safety Executive

DEPARTMENT OF THE ENVIRONMENT
Clarence Court, 10–18 Adelaide Street, Belfast BT2 8GB
T 028-9054 0540 **W** www.doeni.gov.uk

EXECUTIVE AGENCIES
Driver and Vehicle Agency (Northern Ireland)
Environment and Heritage Service
Planning Service

DEPARTMENT OF FINANCE AND PERSONNEL
Rathgael House, Balloo Road, Bangor BT19 7PR
T 028-9185 8111 **W** www.dfpni.gov.uk

EXECUTIVE AGENCIES
Land Registers of Northern Ireland
Northern Ireland Statistics and Research Agency*
Land and Property Services
* Incorporates the General Register Office (Northern Ireland)

DEPARTMENT OF HEALTH, SOCIAL SERVICES AND PUBLIC SAFETY
Castle Buildings, Stormont, Belfast BT4 3SJ **T** 028-9052 0500
W www.dhsspsni.gov.uk

EXECUTIVE AGENCY
Northern Ireland Health and Social Services Agency

DEPARTMENT FOR REGIONAL DEVELOPMENT
Clarence Court, 10–18 Adelaide Street, Belfast BT2 8GB
T 028-9054 0540 **W** www.drdni.gov.uk

EXECUTIVE AGENCY
Roads Agency

DEPARTMENT FOR SOCIAL DEVELOPMENT
Lighthouse Building, 1 Cromac Place, Gasworks Business Park, Ormeau Road, Belfast BT7 2JB **T** 028-9082 9028
W www.dsdni.gov.uk

NORTHERN IRELAND AUDIT OFFICE
106 University Street, Belfast BT7 1EU
T 028-9025 1000 **F** 028-9025 1106
E info@niauditoffice.gov.uk **W** www.niauditoffice.gov.uk
Comptroller and Auditor-General for Northern Ireland, J. M. Dowdall, CB

NORTHERN IRELAND AUTHORITY FOR ENERGY REGULATION
Queens House, 10–14 Queen Street, Belfast BT1 6ER
T 028-9031 1575 **F** 028-9031 1740
E ofreg@nics.gov.uk **W** http://ofreg.nics.gov.uk
Chair, Prof. Peter Matthews

NORTHERN IRELAND ASSEMBLY MEMBERS

as at 8 May 2007

Adams, Gerry, *SF, West Belfast*
Anderson, Martina, *SF, Foyle*
Armstrong, Billy, *UUP, Mid Ulster*
Attwood, Alex, *SDLP, West Belfast*
Beggs, Roy, *UUP, East Antrim*
Boylan, Cathal, *SF, Newry and Armagh*
Bradley, Dominic, *SDLP, Newry and Armagh*
Bradley, Mary, *SDLP, Foyle*
Bradley, P. J., *SDLP, South Down*
Brady, Mickey, *SF, Newry and Armagh*
Bresland, Allan, *DUP, West Tyrone*
Brolly, Francie, *SF, East Londonderry*
Browne of Belmont, Lord, *DUP, East Belfast*
Buchanan, Thomas, *DUP, West Tyrone*
Burns, Thomas, *SDLP, South Antrim*
Burnside, David, *UUP, South Antrim*
Butler, Paul, *SF, Lagan Valley*
Campbell, Gregory, *DUP, East Londonderry*
Clarke, Trevor, *DUP, South Antrim*
Clarke, Willie, *SF, South Down*
Cobain, Fred, *UUP, North Belfast*
Coulter, Revd Dr Robert, *UUP, North Antrim*
Craig, Jonathan, *DUP, Lagan Valley*
Cree, Leslie, *UUP, North Down*
Dallat, John, *SDLP, East Londonderry*
Deeny, Dr Kieran, *Ind., West Tyrone*
Dodds, Nigel, *DUP, North Belfast*
Doherty, Pat, *SF, West Tyrone*
Donaldson, Jeffrey, *DUP, Lagan Valley*
Durkan, Mark, *SDLP, Foyle*
Easton, Alex, *DUP, North Down*
Elliot, Tom, *UUP, Fermanagh and South Tyrone*
Empey, Sir Reg, *UUP, East Belfast*
Farry, Stephen, *All., North Down*
Ford, David, *All., South Antrim*
Foster, Arlene, *DUP, Fermanagh and South Tyrone*
Gallagher, Tommy, *SDLP, Fermanagh and South Tyrone*
Gardiner, Samuel, *UUP, Upper Bann*
Gildernew, Michelle, *SF, Fermanagh and South Tyrone*
Hamilton, Simon, *DUP, Strangford*
Hanna, Carmel, *SDLP, South Belfast*
Hay, William, *DUP, Foyle*
Hilditch, David, *DUP, East Antrim*
Irwin, William, *DUP, Newry and Armagh*
Kelly, Dolores, *SDLP, Upper Bann*
Kelly, Gerry, *SF, North Belfast*
Kennedy, Danny, *UUP, Newry and Armagh*
Lo, Anna, *All., South Belfast*
Long, Naomi, *All., East Belfast*
Lunn, Trevor, *All., Lagan Valley*
Maginness, Alban, *SDLP, North Belfast*
Maskey, Alex, *SF, South Belfast*
Maskey, Paul, *SF, West Belfast*
McCallister, John, *UUP, South Down*
McCann, Fra, *SF, West Belfast*

McCann, Jennifer, *SF, West Belfast*
McCarthy, Kieran, *All., Strangford*
McCartney, Raymond, *SF, Foyle*
McCausland, Nelson, *DUP, North Belfast*
McClarty, David, *UUP, East Londonderry*
McCrea, Basil, *UUP, Lagan Valley*
McCrea, Ian, *DUP, Mid Ulster*
McCrea, Dr William, *DUP, South Antrim*
McDonnell, Dr Alasdair, *SDLP, South Belfast*
McElduff, Barry, *SF, West Tyrone*
McFarland, Alan, *UUP, North Down*
McGill, Claire, *SF, West Tyrone*
McGimpsey, Michael, *UUP, South Belfast*
McGlone, Patsy, *SDLP, Mid Ulster*
McGuinness, Martin, *SF, Mid Ulster*
McHugh, Gerry, *SF, Fermanagh and South Tyrone*
McIlveen, Michelle, *DUP, Strangford*
McKay, Daithí, *SF, North Antrim*
McLaughlin, Mitchel, *SF, South Antrim*
McNarry, David, *UUP, Strangford*
McQuillan, Adrian, *DUP, East Londonderry*
Molloy, Francie, *SF, Mid Ulster*
Morrow, Lord, *DUP, Fermanagh and South Tyrone*
Moutray, Stephen, *DUP, Upper Bann*
Murphy, Conor, *SF, Newry and Armagh*
Neeson, Sean, *All., East Antrim*
Newton, Robin, *DUP, East Belfast*
Ní Chuilín, Carál, *SF, North Belfast*
O'Dowd, John, *SF, Upper Bann*
O'Loan, Declan, *SDLP, North Antrim*
O'Neill, Michelle, *SF, Mid Ulster*
Paisley, Revd Dr Ian, PC, *DUP, North Antrim*
Paisley, Ian Jr, *DUP, North Antrim*
Poots, Edwin, *DUP, Lagan Valley*
Purvis, Dawn, *PUP, East Belfast*
Ramsey, Pat, *SDLP, Foyle*
Ramsey, Sue, *SF, West Belfast*
Ritchie, Margaret, *SDLP, South Down*
Robinson, George, *DUP, East Londonderry*
Robinson, Iris, *DUP, Strangford*
Robinson, Ken, *UUP, East Antrim*
Robinson, Peter, *DUP, East Belfast*
***Ross**, Alastair, *DUP, East Antrim*
Ruane, Caitriona, *SF, South Down*
Savage, George, *UUP, Upper Bann*
Shannon, Jim, *DUP, Strangford*
Simpson, David, *DUP, Upper Bann*
Spratt, Jimmy, *DUP, South Belfast*
Storey, Mervyn, *DUP, North Antrim*
Weir, Peter, *DUP, North Down*
Wells, Jim, *DUP, South Down*
Wilson, Brian, *Green, North Down*
Wilson, Sammy, *DUP, East Antrim*

* George Dawson died on 7 May 2007 and was replaced by Alastair Ross, whose appointment was notified by the Chief Electoral Officer with effect from 14 May 2007

POLITICAL COMPOSITION

Party	Seats
Democratic Unionist Party (DUP)	36
Sinn Fein (SF)	28
Ulster Unionist Party (UUP)	18
Social Democratic and Labour Party (SDLP)	16
Alliance Party (Alliance)	7
Independent (Ind.)	1
Progressive Unionist Party (PUP)	1
Green Party	1

NORTHERN IRELAND ASSEMBLY ELECTION RESULTS

as at March 2007

E. Electorate T. Turnout
First = first-preference votes
Final = final total for that candidate, after all necessary transfers of lower-preference votes
See General Election Results for a list of party abbreviations

ANTRIM EAST

E. 56,666 T. 30,293 (53.46%)	*First*	*Final*	*Elected (Round)*
Sammy Wilson, DUP	6,755	6,755	First (1)
George Dawson, DUP	4,167	4,777	Second (2)
Sean Neeson, Alliance	3,114	5,191	Fourth (10)
Roy Beggs, UUP	3,076	5,115	Fifth (12)
David Hilditch, DUP	2,732	4,587	Third (3)
Ken Robinson, UUP	1,881	4,195	Sixth (13)
Danny O'Connor, SDLP *(Eliminated last)*	1,769	3,298	
Stewart Dickson, Alliance	1,624		
Mark Dunn, UUP	1,617		
Oliver McMullan, SF	1,168		
Tom Robinson, UK Unionist Party	731		
Mark Bailey, Green	612		
John Anderson, Ind.	398		
Tim Lewis, C.	395		

ANTRIM NORTH

E. 72,814 T. 44,655 (61.33%)	*First*	*Final*	*Elected (Round)*
Revd Ian Paisley , DUP	7,716	7,716	First (1)
Daithi McKay, SF	7,065	7,065	Second (1)
Ian Paisley Jr, DUP	6,106	7,264	Third (2)
Mervyn Storey, DUP	5,171	6,924	Fifth (8)
Revd Robert Coulter, UUP	5,047	6,579	Fourth (7)
Declan O'Loan, SDLP	3,281	6,498	Sixth (10)
Deirdre Nelson, DUP *(Eliminated last)*	2,740	4,092	
Orla Black, SDLP	2,129		
Lyle Cubitt, UK Unionist Party	1,848		
Robert Swann, UUP	1,281		
Jayne Dunlop, Alliance	1,254		
Paul McGlinchey, Ind.	383		
James Gregg, Ind.	310		

ANTRIM SOUTH

E. 65,654 T. 38,481 (58.61%)	*First*	*Final*	*Elected (Round)*
Mitchel McLaughlin, SF	6,313	6,313	First (1)
Revd William McCrea, DUP	6,023	6,023	Second (1)
David Ford, Alliance	5,007	5,495	Third (5)
David Burnside, UUP	4,507	6,926	Fourth (7)
Trevor Clarke, DUP	4,302	5,544	Fifth (8)
Mel Lucas, DUP *(Eliminated last)*	2,840	4,429	
Thomas Burns, SDLP	2,721	5,396	Sixth (8)
Danny Kinahan, UUP	2,391		
Noreen McClelland, SDLP	1,526		
Stephen Nicholl, UUP	927		

Candidate	First	Final	Elected (Round)
Robert McCartney, UK Unionist Party	893		
Pete Whitcroft, Green	507		
Stephen O'Brien, C.	129		
Marcella Delaney, WP	89		

BELFAST EAST

E. 49,757 T. 29,873 (60.04%)

Candidate	*First*	*Final*	*Elected (Round)*
Peter Robinson, DUP	5,635	5,635	First (1)
Naomi Long, Alliance	5,585	5,585	Second (1)
Sir Reg Empey, UUP	4,139	4,620	Third (3)
Lord Wallace Browne, DUP	3,185	3,734	Fifth (10)
Dawn Purvis, Progressive Unionist Party	3,045	4,208	Fourth (10)
Robin Newton, DUP	2,335	3,517	Sixth (10)
Michael Copeland, UUP *(Eliminated last)*	1,557	2,999	
Niall O'Donnghaile, SF	1,055		
Jim Rodgers, UUP	820		
Mary Muldoon, SDLP	816		
Steve Agnew, Green	653		
Glyn Chambers, C.	427		
Thomas Black, Socialist Party	225		
Joe Bell, WP	107		
Rainbow George, Make Politicians History	47		

BELFAST NORTH

E. 49,372 T. 30,067 (60.90%)

Candidate	*First*	*Final*	*Elected (Round)*
Nigel Dodds, DUP	6,973	6,973	First (1)
Gerry Kelly, SF	5,414	5,414	Second (1)
Caral Ni Chuilin, SF	3,680	4,587	Third (3)
Fred Cobain, UUP	2,498	3,967	Fifth (10)
Nelson McCausland, DUP	2,462	3,818	Sixth (10)
Alban Maginness, SDLP	2,212	4,830	Fourth (9)
Pat Convery, SDLP	1,868		
William Humphrey, DUP *(Eliminated last)*	1,673	3,327	
Raymond McCord, Ind.	1,320		
Peter Emerson, Green	590		
Tommy McCullough, Alliance	486		
Robert McCartney, UK Unionist Party	360		
John Lavery, WP	139		
Rainbow George, Make Politicians History	40		

BELFAST SOUTH

E. 48,923 T. 30,533 (62.41%)

Candidate	*First*	*Final*	*Elected (Round)*
Jimmy Spratt, DUP	4,762	4,762	First (1)
Dr Alasdair McDonnell, SDLP	4,379	4,379	Second (1)
Alex Maskey, SF	3,996	4,167	Sixth (10)
Anna Lo, Alliance	3,829	4,415	Third (8)
Carmel Hanna, SDLP	3,748	4,262	Fifth (10)
Michael McGimpsey, UUP	2,647	4,927	Fourth (10)
Christopher Stalford, DUP *(Eliminated last)*	2,035	3,275	
Dr Esmond Birnie, UUP	1,804		
Bob Stoker, UUP	1,122		
Brenda Cooke, Green	737		
Andrew Park, Progressive Unionist Party	410		
David Hoey, UK Unionist Party	298		
Jim Barbour, Socialist Party	248		
Paddy Lynn, WP	123		
Roger Lomas, C.	108		
Rainbow George, Make Politicians History	66		
Charles Smyth, Pro-Capitalism	22		
Geoffrey Wilson, Ind.	10		

BELFAST WEST

E. 50,792 T. 34,238 (67.41%)

Candidate	*First*	*Final*	*Elected (Round)*
Gerry Adams, SF	6,029	6,029	First (1)
Sue Ramsey, SF	4,715	5,267	Second (2)
Paul Maskey, SF	4,368	5,075	Third (6)
Jennifer McCann, SF	4,265	4,849	Fourth (6)
Fra McCann, SF	4,254	4,647	Sixth (6)
Diane Dodds, DUP *(Eliminated last)*	3,661	4,166	
Alex Attwood, SDLP	3,036	4,779	Fifth (6)
Margaret Walsh, SDLP	1,074		
Sean Mitchell, People Before Profit	774		
Louis West, UUP	558		
John Lowry, WP	434		
Geraldine Taylor, Republican Sinn Fein	427		
Dan McGuinness, Alliance	127		
Rainbow George, Make Politicians History	68		

DOWN NORTH

E. 57,525 T. 30,930 (53.77%)

Candidate	*First*	*Final*	*Elected (Round)*
Alex Easton, DUP	4,946	4,946	First (1)
Peter Weir, DUP	3,376	4,380	Fifth (10)
Stephen Farry, Alliance	3,131	4,466	Second (8)
Leslie Cree, UUP	2,937	4,687	Third (10)
Brian Wilson, Green	2,839	4,572	Fourth (10)
Alan McFarland, UUP	2,245	3,986	Sixth (10)
Alan Graham, DUP *(Eliminated last)*	2,147	3,255	
Marion Smith, UUP	2,098		
Robert McCartney, UK Unionist Party	1,806		
Brian Rowan, Ind.	1,194		
Alan Chambers, Ind.	1,129		
Liam Logan, SDLP	1,115		
James Leslie, C.	864		
Deaglan Page, SF	390		
Elaine Martin, Progressive Unionist Party	367		
Chris Carter, Ind.	123		

DOWN SOUTH

E. 71,704 T. 46,623 (65.02%)

	First	Final	Elected (Round)
Catriona Ruane, SF	6,334	6,676	First (7)
Margaret Ritchie, SDLP	5,838	6,945	Third (8)
P. J. Bradley, SDLP	5,652	6,650	Fourth (9)
Jim Wells, DUP	5,542	8,463	Fifth (10)
Willie Clarke, SF	5,138	7,382	Second (8)
John McCallister, UUP	4,447	7,721	Sixth (11)
Michael Carr, SDLP *(Eliminated last)*	2,972	3,883	
Eamonn McConvey, SF	2,662		
William Burns, DUP	2,611		
Ciaran Mussen, Green	1,622		
Henry Reilly, UKIP	1,229		
David Griffin, Alliance	691		
Martin Cunningham, Ind.	434		
Nelson Wharton, UK Unionist Party	424		
Peter Bowles, C.	391		
Malachi Curran, Lab.	123		

FERMANAGH AND SOUTH TYRONE

E. 65,826 T. 46,845 (71.16%)

	First	Final	Elected (Round)
Arlene Foster, DUP	7,138	7,138	First (1)
Michelle Gildernew, SF	7,026	7,026	Second (1)
Tom Elliott, UUP	6,603	6,680	Third (2)
Gerry McHugh, SF	5,103	5,777	Sixth (8)
Sean Lynch, SF *(Eliminated last)*	4,704	5,188	
Lord Morrow, DUP	4,700	7,014	Fifth (8)
Tommy Gallagher, SDLP	4,440	6,640	Fourth (7)
Kenny Donaldson, UUP	2,531		
Vincent Currie, SDLP	2,043		
Gerry McGeough, Ind.	814		
Allan Leonard, Alliance	521		
Michael McManus, Republican Sinn Fein	431		
Robert McCartney, UK Unionist Party	388		

FOYLE

E. 64,889 T. 41,455 (63.89%)

	First	Final	Elected (Round)
William Hay, DUP	6,960	6,960	First (1)
Mark Durkan, SDLP	6,401	6,401	Second (1)
Martina Anderson, SF	5,414	5,972	Third (6)
Raymond McCartney, SF	4,321	7,275	Fourth (8)
Pat Ramsey, SDLP	3,242	5,396	Fifth (10)
Lynn Fleming, SF	2,914		
Mary Bradley, SDLP	2,891	4,419	Sixth (10)
Helen Quigley, SDLP *(Eliminated last)*	2,648		
Eamonn McCann, Socialist Environmental Alliance	2,045		
Peggy O'Hara, Ind.	1,789		
Peter Munce, UUP	1,755		
Adele Corry, Green	359		
Yvonne Boyle, Alliance	224		
Willie Frazer, Ind.	73		

LAGAN VALLEY

E. 70,101 T. 42,058 (60.00%)

	First	Final	Elected (Round)
Jeffrey Donaldson, DUP	9,793	9,793	First (1)
Paul Butler, SF	5,098	6,387	Second (6)
Basil McCrea, UUP	4,031	6,712	Third (7)
Trevor Lunn, Alliance	3,765	6,264	Fourth (7)
Jonathan Craig, DUP	3,471	6,147	Fifth (8)
Edwin Poots, DUP	3,457	5,386	Sixth (9)
Paul Givan, DUP *(Eliminated last)*	3,377	4,728	
Marietta Farrell, SDLP	2,839		
Billy Bell, UUP	2,599		
Ronnie Crawford, UUP	1,147		
Michael Rogan, Green	922		
Robert McCartney, UK Unionist Party	853		
Neil Johnston, C.	387		
John Magee, WP	83		

LONDONDERRY EAST

E. 56,104 T. 34,180 (60.92%)

	First	Final	Elected (Round)
Gregory Campbell, DUP	6,845	6,845	First (1)
Francie Brolly, SF	4,476	5,003	Third (7)
George Robinson, DUP	3,991	4,869	Second (5)
David McClarty, UUP	2,875	4,409	Fifth (9)
Adrian McQuillan, DUP	2,650	4,074	Sixth (9)
John Dallat, SDLP	2,638	6,380	Fourth (8)
Billy Leonard, SF	2,321		
Norman Hillis, UUP *(Eliminated last)*	2,054	3,195	
Orla Beattie, SDLP	1,797		
Barney Fitzpatrick, Alliance	1,401		
Edwin Stevenson, UUP	1,338		
Leslie Cubitt, UK Unionist Party	549		
Phillippe Moison, Green	521		
Michael McGonigle, Republican Sinn Fein	393		
Victor Christie, Ind.	73		

NEWRY AND ARMAGH

E. 70,823 T. 50,165 (70.83%)

	First	Final	Elected (Round)
Conor Murphy, SF	7,437	7,437	First (1)
Cathal Boylan, SF	7,105	7,105	Second (1)
Danny Kennedy, UUP	6,517	7,653	Fifth (5)
William Irwin, DUP	6,418	8,008	Fourth (5)
Mickey Brady, SF	6,337	7,514	Third (4)
Dominic Bradley, SDLP	5,318	6,311	Sixth (7)
Sharon Haughey, SDLP *(Eliminated last)*	4,500	5,368	
Paul Berry, Ind.	2,317		
Davy Hyland, Ind.	2,188		
Willie Frazer, Ind.	605		
Arthur Morgan, Green	599		
Maire Hendron, Alliance	278		

STRANGFORD

E. 66,648 T. 36,340 (54.53%)

	First	Final	Elected (Round)
Iris Robinson, DUP	5,917	5,917	First (1)
Jim Shannon, DUP	4,788	5,178	Second (6)
Kieran McCarthy, Alliance	4,085	5,207	Third (9)

	First	Final	Elected (Round)
mon Hamilton, DUP	3,889	4,998	Fifth (13)
avid McNarry, UUP	3,709	6,036	Fourth (10)
ichelle McIlveen, DUP	3,468	4,579	Sixth (13)
e Boyle, SDLP *(Eliminated last)*	3,068	4,548	
ngus Carson, UUP	2,128		
ermot Kennedy, SF	1,089		
eorge Ennis, UK Unionist Party	872		
ephanie Sim, Green	868		
ichael Henderson, UUP	675		
avid Gregg, Ind.	650		
ob Little, C.	508		
edric Wilson, Ind.	305		

YRONE WEST

58,367 T. 41,839 (71.68%)

	First	*Final*	*Elected (Round)*
arry McElduff, SF	6,971	6,971	First (1)
at Doherty, SF	6,709	6,709	Second (1)
lare McGill, SF	4,757	6,217	Third (3)
om Buchanan, DUP	4,625	6,208	Fourth (6)
llan Bresland, DUP	4,244	5,543	Sixth (7)
r Kieran Deeny, Ind.	3,776	5,616	Fifth (7)
erek Hussey, UUP	3,686		
sephine Deehan, SDLP *(Eliminated last)*	2,689	5,186	
ugene McMenamin, SDLP	2,272		
eamus Shiels, SDLP	1,057		
e O'Neill, Republican Sinn Fein	448		
obert McCartney, UK Unionist Party	220		

ULSTER MID

E. 61,223 T. 44,728 (73.06%)

	First	*Final*	*Elected (Round)*
Martin McGuinness, SF	8,065	8,065	First (1)
Ian McCrea, DUP	7,608	7,608	Second (1)
Francie Molloy, SF	6,597	6,597	Third (1)
Michelle O'Neill, SF	6,432	6,432	Fourth (1)
Patsy McGlone, SDLP	4,976	6,430	Fifth (5)
Billy Armstrong, UUP	4,781	6,355	Sixth (7)
Kate Lagan, SDLP *(Eliminated last)*	2,759	3,531	
Walter Millar, UK Unionist Party	1,210		
Ann Forde, DUP	1,021		
Brendan McLaughlin, Republican Sinn Fein	437		
Margaret Marshall, Alliance	221		
Harry Hutchinson, Ind.	170		

UPPER BANN

E. 70,716 T. 43,235 (61.14%)

	First	*Final*	*Elected (Round)*
John O'Dowd, SF	7,733	7,733	First (1)
David Simpson, DUP	6,828	6,828	Second (1)
Samuel Gardiner, UUP	5,135	7,265	Fourth (9)
Dolores Kelly, SDLP	4,689	6,191	Third (8)
Stephen Moutray, DUP	3,663	7,550	Fifth (11)
Dessie Ward, SF *(Eliminated last)*	3,118	4,732	
Junior McCrum, DUP	2,975		
George Savage, UUP	2,167	5,998	Sixth (12)
Arnold Hatch, UUP	1,815		
David Calvert, No Description	1,332		
Helen Corry, Green	1,156		
Sheila McQuaid, Alliance	798		
Pat McAleenan, SDLP	761		
Barry Toman, Republican Sinn Fein	386		
David Fry, C.	248		
Suzanne Peeples, Ind.	78		

LOCAL GOVERNMENT

Major changes in local government were introduced in England and Wales in 1974 and in Scotland in 1975 by the Local Government Act 1972 and the Local Government (Scotland) Act 1973. Further significant alterations were made in England by the Local Government Acts of 1985, 1992 and 2000.

The structure in England was based on two tiers of local authorities (county councils and district councils) in the non-metropolitan areas; and a single tier of metropolitan councils in the six metropolitan areas of England and London borough councils in London.

Following reviews of the structure of local government in England by the Local Government Commission, 46 unitary (all-purpose) authorities were created between April 1995 and April 1998 to cover certain areas in the non-metropolitan counties. The remaining county areas continue to have two tiers of local authorities. The county and district councils in the Isle of Wight were replaced by a single unitary authority on 1 April 1995; the former counties of Avon, Cleveland, Humberside and Berkshire were replaced by unitary authorities; and Hereford and Worcester was replaced by a new county council for Worcestershire (with district councils) and a unitary authority for Herefordshire.

The Local Government (Wales) Act 1994 and the Local Government etc (Scotland) Act 1994 abolished the two-tier structure in Wales and Scotland with effect from 1 April 1996, replacing it with a single tier of unitary authorities.

ELECTIONS

Local elections are normally held on the first Thursday in May. Generally, all British subjects, citizens of the Republic of Ireland, Commonwealth and other European Union citizens who are 18 years or over and resident on the qualifying date in the area for which the election is being held, are entitled to vote at local government elections. A register of electors is prepared and published annually by local electoral registration officers.

A returning officer has the overall responsibility for an election. Voting takes place at polling stations, arranged by the local authority and under the supervision of a presiding officer specially appointed for the purpose. Candidates, who are subject to various statutory qualifications and disqualifications designed to ensure that they are suitable to hold office, must be nominated by electors for the electoral area concerned.

In England, the Boundary Committee for England is responsible for carrying out periodic reviews of electoral arrangements and making recommendations to the Electoral Commission.

In Wales and Scotland these matters are the responsibility of the Local Government Boundary Commission for Wales and the Boundary Commission for Scotland respectively. The Local Government Act 2000 provided for the secretary of state to change the frequency and phasing of elections.

THE BOUNDARY COMMITTEE FOR ENGLAND, Trevelyan House, Great Peter Street, London SW1P 2HW T 020-7271 0500 W www.boundarycommittee.org.uk

LOCAL GOVERNMENT BOUNDARY COMMISSION FOR WALES, Caradog House, 1–6 St Andrew's Place, Cardiff CF10 3BE T 029-2039 5031 W www.lgbc-wales.gov.uk

THE BOUNDARY COMMISSION FOR SCOTLAND, 3 Drumsheugh Gardens, Edinburgh EH3 7QJ T 0131-538 7200 W www.bcomm-scotland.gov.uk

INTERNAL ORGANISATION

The council as a whole is the final decision-making bod within any authority. Councils are free to a great extent t make their own internal organisational arrangements. Th Local Government Act, given royal assent on 28 Jul 2000, allows councils to adopt one of three broa categories of a new constitution which include a separa executive.

These three categories are:

- A directly elected mayor with a cabinet selected by th mayor
- A cabinet, either elected by the council or appointed b its leader
- A directly elected mayor and council manager

Normally, questions of policy are settled by the fu council, while the administration of the various services the responsibility of committees of councillors. Day-to day decisions are delegated to the council's officers, wh act within the policies laid down by the councillors.

FINANCE

Local government in England, Wales and Scotland financed from four sources: the council tax, non-domest rates, government grants and income from fees an charges for services.

COUNCIL TAX

Under the Local Government Finance Act 1992, from April 1993 the council tax replaced the communi charge (which had been introduced in April 1989 i Scotland and April 1990 in England and Wales in place o domestic rates).

The council tax is a local tax levied by each loc council. Liability for the council tax bill usually falls o the owner-occupier or tenant of a dwelling which is the sole or main residence. Council tax bills may be reduce because of the personal circumstances of people reside in a property, and there are discounts in the case o dwellings occupied by fewer than two adults.

In England, each county council, each district counc and each police authority sets its own council tax rat The district councils collect the combined council tax, an the county councils and police authorities claim the share from the district councils' collection funds. In Wale each unitary authority and each police authority sets i own council tax rate. The unitary authorities collect th combined council tax and the police authorities clai their share from the funds. In Scotland, each loc authority sets its own rate of council tax.

The tax relates to the value of the dwelling. In Englan and Scotland each dwelling is placed in one of eig aluation bands, ranging from A to H, based on the roperty's estimated market value as at 1 April 1991. In Vales there are nine bands, ranging from A to I, based on he estimated market value of property as at 1 April 2003.

The valuation bands and ranges of values in England, Vales and Scotland are:

ngland

A	Up to £40,000	E	£88,001–£120,000
B	£40,001–£52,000	F	£120,001–£160,000
C	£52,001–£68,000	G	£160,001–£320,000
D	£68,001–£88,000	H	Over £320,001

Vales

A	Up to £44,000	F	£223,001–£324,000
B	£44,001–£65,000	G	£223,001–£324,000
C	£65,001–£91,000	H	£324,001–£424,000
D	£91,001–£123,000	I	Over £424,001
E	£123,001–£162,000		

cotland

A	Up to £27,000	E	£58,001–£80,000
B	£27,001–£35,000	F	£80,001–£106,000
C	£35,001–£45,000	G	£106,001–£212,000
D	£45,001–£58,000	H	Over £212,001

he council tax within a local area varies between the ifferent bands according to proportions laid down by w. The charge attributable to each band as a proportion f the Band D charge set by the council is approximately:

A	67%	F	144%
B	78%	G	167%
C	89%	H	200%
D	100%	I	233%*
E	122%		

Wales only

he average Band D council tax bill for each authority rea is given in the tables on the following pages. There ay be variations from the given figure within each istrict council area because of different parish or ommunity precepts being levied.

ON-DOMESTIC RATES

on-domestic (business) rates are collected by billing uthorities; these are the district councils in those areas of ngland with two tiers of local government and unitary uthorities in other parts of England, in Wales and in cotland. In respect of England and Wales, the Local overnment Finance Act 1988 provides for liability for tes to be assessed on the basis of a poundage (multiplier) x on the rateable value of property (hereditaments). eparate multipliers are set by the Department for ommunities and Local Government in England, the Velsh Assembly Government and the Scottish Executive. ates are collected by the billing authority for the area here a property is located. Rate income collected by illing authorities is paid into a national non-domestic ting (NNDR) pool and redistributed to individual uthorities on the basis of the adult population figure as rescribed by the Department for Communities and Local overnment, the Welsh Assembly Government or the cottish Executive. The rates pools are maintained eparately in England, Wales and Scotland. Actual ayment of rates in certain cases is subject to transitional rrangements, to phase in the larger increases and reductions in rates resulting from the effects of the latest revaluation.

Rateable values for the 2005 rating lists came into effect on 1 April 2005. They are derived from the rental value of property as at 1 April 2003 and determined on certain statutory assumptions by the Valuation Office Agency in England and Wales, and by local area assessors in Scotland. New property which is added to the list, and significant changes to existing property, necessitate amendments to the rateable value on the same basis. Rating lists (valuation rolls in Scotland) remain in force until the next general revaluation. Such revaluations take place every five years, the next being in 2010.

Certain types of property are exempt from rates, eg agricultural land and buildings, certain businesses and places of public religious worship. Charities and other non-profit-making organisations may receive full or partial relief. The owner or leaseholder of an empty property is liable to pay rates but at a reduced level, except for some types of premises, such as factories, which are entirely exempt.

GOVERNMENT GRANTS

In addition to specific grants in support of revenue expenditure on particular services, central government pays a revenue support grant to local authorities. This grant is paid to each local authority so that if each authority spends at the level of its standard spending assessment, all authorities in the same class can set broadly the same council tax.

COMPLAINTS

ENGLAND

In England the Local Government Ombudsmen investigate complaints of injustice arising from maladministration by local authorities and certain other bodies. The Local Government Ombudsman will not usually consider a complaint unless the local authority concerned has had an opportunity to investigate and reply to a complainant. Details about how to make a complaint are given in *Complaint about the Council?* and *How to complain to the Local Government Ombudsman* from the Commission for Local Administration in England (W www.lgo.org.uk).

The Local Government Act 2000 established a Standards Board and an independent tribunal known as the Adjudication Panel for England. The Standards Board's main task is to ensure that standards of ethical conduct are maintained and to investigate any allegations that councillors have breached the council's Code of Conduct. At the end of the investigation, the case may be referred to either the relevant local authority's standards committee or the Adjudication Panel, which has a number of sanctions at its disposal, up to and including the disqualification of a member from holding office for five years. Unlike the ombudsmen, the Standards Board does not deal with issues of corporate maladministration nor seek to secure financial recompense for complainants.

Local Government Ombudsmen, Tony Redmond, Anne Seex, Jerry White

COMMISSION FOR LOCAL ADMINISTRATION IN ENGLAND, 10th Floor, Millbank Tower, Millbank, London SW1P 4QP T 020-7217 4620

THE STANDARDS BOARD FOR ENGLAND, 4th Floor, Griffin House, 40 Lever Street, Manchester M1 1BB T 0161-817 5300 W www.standardsboard.gov.uk

THE ADJUDICATION PANEL FOR ENGLAND,
23 Victoria Avenue, Harrogate, North Yorkshire HG1 5RD
T 01423-538783 W www.adjudicationpanel.co.uk

WALES

The office of Public Services Ombudsman for Wales came into force on 1 April 2006 incorporating the functions of the Local Government Ombudsman for Wales.

Public Service Ombudsman for Wales, Adam Peat

PUBLIC SERVICES OMBUDSMAN FOR WALES,
1 Ffordd yr Hen Gae, Pencoed CF35 5LJ T 01656-641150
W www.ombudsman-wales.org.uk

SCOTLAND

The Scottish Public Services Ombudsman is responsible for complaints regarding the maladaministration of local government in Scotland.

Scottish Public Services Ombudsman, Prof. Alice Brown

SCOTTISH PUBLIC SERVICES OMBUDSMAN,
Freepost EH641, Edinburgh EH3 0BR T 0800-377 7330
W www.spso.org.uk

NORTHERN IRELAND

The Northern Ireland Commissioner for Complaints fulfils a similar function in Northern Ireland, investigating complaints about local authorities and certain public bodies. Complaints are made to the relevant local authority in the first instance but may also be made directly to the Commissioner.

Northern Ireland Commissioner for Complaints, Tom Frawley

NORTHERN IRELAND COMMISSIONER FOR COMPLAINTS, Freepost BEL 1478, Belfast BT1 6LR
T 0800-343424 W www.ni-ombudsman.org.uk

THE QUEEN'S REPRESENTATIVES

The lord-lieutenant of a county is the permanent local representative of the Crown in that county. The appointment of lord-lieutenants is now regulated by the Lieutenancies Act 1997. They are appointed by the sovereign on the recommendation of the prime minister. The retirement age is 75. The office of lord-lieutenant dates from 1551, and its holder was originally responsible for maintaining order and for local defence in the county. The duties of the post include attending on royalty during official visits to the county, performing certain duties in connection with armed forces of the Crown (and in particular the reserve forces), and making presentations of honours and awards on behalf of the Crown. In England, Wales and Northern Ireland, the lord-lieutenant usually also holds the office of *Custos Rotulorum.* As such, he or she acts as head of the county's commission of the peace (which recommends the appointment of magistrates).

The office of sheriff (from the Old English shire-reeve) of a county was created in the tenth century. The sheriff was the special nominee of the sovereign, and the office reached the peak of its influence under the Norman kings. The Provisions of Oxford (1258) laid down a yearly tenure of office. Since the mid-16th century the office has been purely civil, with military duties taken over by the lord-lieutenant of the county. The sheriff (commonly known as 'high sheriff') attends on royalty during official visits to the county, acts as the returning officer during parliamentary elections in county constituencies, attends the opening ceremony when a high court judge goes on circuit, executes high court writs, and appoints under-sheriffs to act as deputies. The appointments and duties o the sheriffs in England and Wales are laid down by th Sheriffs Act 1887.

The serving high sheriff submits a list of names c possible future sheriffs to a tribunal which chooses thre names to put to the sovereign. The tribunal nominates th high sheriff annually on 12 November and the sovereig picks the name of the sheriff to succeed in the followin year. The term of office runs from 25 March to th following 24 March (the civil and legal year befor 1752). No person may be chosen twice in three years there is any other suitable person in the county.

CIVIC DIGNITIES

District councils in England may petition for a roya charter granting borough or 'city' status to the distric Local councils in Wales may petition for a roya charter granting county borough or 'city' status to th council.

In England and Wales the chairman of a borough o county borough council may be called a mayor, and th chairman of a city council may be called a lord mayor lord mayoralty has been conferred on that city. Paris councils in England and community councils in Wale may call themselves 'town councils', in which case the chairman is the town mayor.

In Scotland the chairman of a local council may b known as a convenor; a provost is the mayoral equivalen The chairmen of the councils for the cities of Aberdeer Dundee, Edinburgh and Glasgow are lord provosts.

ENGLAND

There are currently 34 counties; all are divided int districts. In addition, there are 46 unitary authorities plu the Isles of Scilly and 238 district councils. Th populations of most of the unitary authorities are in th range of 100,000 to 300,000. The district councils hav populations broadly in the range of 60,000 to 100,00 some, however, have larger populations, because of th need to avoid dividing large towns, and some in mainl rural areas have smaller populations.

The main conurbations outside Greater London – Tyn and Wear, West Midlands, Merseyside, Greate Manchester, West Yorkshire and South Yorkshire – a divided into 36 metropolitan boroughs, most of whic have a population of over 200,000.

There are also about 10,000 parishes, in 219 of th district councils and 18 of the metropolitan boroughs.

ELECTIONS

For districts, counties and for about 8,000 parishes, ther are elected councils, consisting of directly electe councillors. The councillors elect annually one of the number as chair.

Generally, councillors serve four years and there are n elections of district and parish councillors in count election years. In metropolitan boroughs, one-third of th councillors for each ward are elected each year except i the year when county elections take place elsewher District councils can choose whether to have elections b thirds or whole council elections. In the former case, one third of the council (or as near as possible) is elected i each year of metropolitan borough elections. If whol council elections are chosen, these are held in the yea midway between county elections.

FUNCTIONS
In non-metropolitan areas, functions are divided between the districts and counties (those requiring the larger area or population are generally the responsibility of the county). The metropolitan councils, with the larger population in their areas, already had wider functions than non-metropolitan councils, and following the abolition of the metropolitan county councils were also given most of their functions. A few functions continue to be exercised over the larger area by joint bodies, made up of councillors from each district.

The allocation of functions is as follows:

County councils: education; strategic planning; traffic, transport and highways; fire service; consumer protection; refuse disposal; smallholdings; social services; libraries

District councils: local planning; housing; highways (maintenance of certain urban roads and off-street car parks); building regulations; environmental health; refuse collection; cemeteries and crematoria

Unitary and metropolitan councils: their functions are all those listed above, except that the fire service is exercised by a joint body

Concurrently by county and district councils: recreation (parks, playing fields, swimming pools); museums; encouragement of the arts, tourism and industry

The Police and Magistrates Court Act 1994 set up police authorities in England and Wales separate from the local authorities.

PARISH COUNCILS
Parishes with 200 or more electors must generally have parish councils, which means that over three-quarters of the parishes have councils. A parish council comprises at least five members, the number being fixed by the district council. Elections are held every four years, at the time of the election of the district councillor for the ward including the parish. All parishes have parish meetings comprising the electors of the parish. Where there is no council, the meeting must be held at least twice a year.

Parish council functions include: allotments; encouragement of arts and crafts; community halls, recreational facilities (eg open spaces, swimming pools); cemeteries and crematoria; and many minor functions. They must also be given an opportunity to comment on planning applications. They may, like county and district councils, spend limited sums for the general benefit of the parish. They levy a precept on the district councils for their funds. Parish precepts for 2007–8 totalled £299m, an increase of 6.7 per cent on 2006–7.

REGIONAL ASSEMBLIES
Voluntary regional chambers were established in each of the eight english regions outside London under the Regional Development Agencies Act 1998. The chambers operate within the same boundaries as the Government Offices in the Regions and the Regional Development Agencies.

The Regional Assemblies (Preparations) Act received royal assent on 8 May 2003, giving the chambers responsibility to act as regional planning bodies and to receive direct funding from central government for fulfilling this role. Regional assemblies are mainly funded by central government although some assemblies also receive money from other sources such as local authority subscriptions.

The profile and number of assembly members varies from region to region but under guidance issued by the secretary of state, generally comprises 70 per cent elected local authority councillors and 30 per cent drawn from other sectors, including education, business, arts and culture, faith groups, community, voluntary and environmental organisations.

ROLE OF THE CHAMBERS
All assemblies perform four core functions: acting as regional planning bodies and housing boards, advising the government and European institutions on matters of regional strategic and policy development and scrutinising the work of the Regional Development Agencies. They may also engage in other work according to regional circumstances and priorities. Principal areas of policy development include regional planning and transport, the environment, sustainable development, rural issues and equalities.

EAST MIDLANDS REGIONAL ASSEMBLY, First Floor Suite, Council Offices, Nottingham Road, Melton Mowbray, Leicestershire LE13 0UL **T** 01664-502555 **W** www.emra.gov.uk

EAST OF ENGLAND REGIONAL ASSEMBLY, Flempton House, Flempton, Bury St Edmunds, Suffolk IP28 6EG **T** 01284-728151 **W** www.eera.gov.uk

NORTH EAST ASSEMBLY, The Axis Building, Kingsway North, Team Valley, Gateshead NE11 0NQ **T** 0845-673 3343 **W** www.northeastassembly.gov.uk

NORTH WEST REGIONAL ASSEMBLY, Wigan Investment Centre, Waterside Drive, Wigan WN3 5BA **T** 01942-737916 **W** www.nwra.gov.uk

SOUTH EAST ENGLAND REGIONAL ASSEMBLY, Berkeley House, Cross Lanes, Guildford, Surrey GU1 1UN **T** 01483-555200 **W** www.southeast-ra.gov.uk

SOUTH WEST REGIONAL ASSEMBLY, Dennett House, 11 Middle Street, Taunton, Somerset TA1 1SH **T** 01823-270101 **W** www.southwest-ra.gov.uk

WEST MIDLANDS REGIONAL ASSEMBLY, Regional Partnership Centre, Albert House, Quay Place, 92–93 Edward Street, Birmingham B1 2RA **T** 0121-245 0200 **W** www.wmra.gov.uk

YORKSHIRE AND HUMBER ASSEMBLY, 18 King Street, Wakefield, West Yorkshire WF1 2SQ **T** 01924-331555 **W** www.yhassembly.gov.uk

The English Regions Network is the umbrella organisation for England's eight regional assemblies (c/o West Midlands Regional Assembly)

FINANCE
Budgeted revenue expenditure in 2007–8 is £97.3bn; 24 per cent of this is to be raised through council tax (£23.6bn), 26 per cent from formula grant (comprises revenue support grant £3.1bn, redistributed business rates £18.5bn and £4.0bn police grant) and 44 per cent from specific grants (estimated at £43bn).

In England, the average council tax per dwelling for 2007–8 is £1,101, up from £1,056 in 2006–7, an increase of 4.3 per cent. The average council tax for 2007–8 is £1,148 in shire areas, £1,167 in London and £919 in metropolitan areas. In England, the average council tax bill for a Band D dwelling (occupied by two adults, including parish precepts) for 2007–8 is £1,321, an average increase of 4.2 per cent from 2006–7. The average Band D council tax is £1,348 in shire areas, £1,284 in metropolitan areas and £1,258 in London. Since 2006–7 the London figure includes a levy to fund the 2012 Olympic Games which equates to a £20 a year increase on Band D council tax.

The provisional amount estimated to be raised from national non-domestic rates from central and local lists is £18.5bn. The non-domestic rating multiplier for England for 2007–8 is 44.4p (44.1p for small businesses). The City of London is able to set a different multiplier from the rest of England; for 2007–8 this is 44.8p (44.5p for small businesses).

Under the Local Government and Housing Act 1989, local authorities have four main ways of paying for capital expenditure: borrowing and other forms of extended credit; capital grants from central government towards some types of capital expenditure; 'usable' capital receipts from the sale of land, houses and other assets; and revenue.

The amount of capital expenditure which a local authority can finance by borrowing (or other forms of credit) is effectively limited by the credit approvals issued to it by central government. Most credit approvals can be used for any kind of local authority capital expenditure; these are known as basic credit approvals. Others (supplementary credit approvals) can be used only for the kind of expenditure specified in the approval, and so are often given to fund particular projects or services.

Local authorities can use all capital receipts from the sale of property or assets for capital spending, except in the case of sales of council houses. Generally, the 'usable' part of a local authority's capital receipts consists of 25 per cent of receipts from the sale of council houses and 50 per cent of other housing assets such as shops or vacant land. The balance has to be set aside as provision for repaying debt and meeting other credit liabilities.

EXPENDITURE

Local authority budgeted net expenditure for 2007–8 is:

Service	*£ million*
Education	39,620
Highways and transport	5,600
Social services	18,469
Housing (excluding HRA)	2,452
Cultural, environment and planning	9,902
Police	11,609
Fire and rescue	2,227
Courts	62
Central services	3,350
Other	248
Mandatory rent allowances	8,365
Mandatory rent rebates	626
Rent rebates granted to HRA tenants	3,803
Net current expenditure	106,333
Capital financing	3,352
Capital expenditure charged to revenue account	1,245
Council tax benefit	3,338
Discretionary non-domestic rate relief	25
Bad debt provision	29
Flood defence payments to Environment Agency	26
Pensions interest cost and expected return on pensions assets	3,531
Less interest receipts	(1,123)
Less specific grants outside AEF	(19,444)
Gross revenue expenditure	97,312
Less specific grants inside AEF	(43,035)
Net revenue expenditure	54,277
Less appropriations from pensions reserves	(3,990)
Less appropriations from other revenue reserves	(890)
Less adjustments	(0)
BUDGET REQUIREMENT	49,398

HRA = Housing Revenue Account
AEF = aggregate external finance

LONDON

The Greater London Council was abolished in 1986 and London was divided into 32 borough councils, which have a status similar to the metropolitan borough councils in the rest of England, and the Corporation of the City of London.

In March 1998 the government announced proposals for a Greater London Authority (GLA) covering the area of the 32 London boroughs and the City of London, which would comprise a directly elected mayor and a 25-member assembly. A referendum was held in London on 7 May 1998; the turnout was approximately 34 per cent and 72 per cent of electors voted in favour of the GLA. The independent candidate for London mayor, Ken Livingstone, was elected on 4 May 2000 and the Authority assumed its responsibilities on 3 July 2000. He was re-elected on 10 June 2004 as a Labour candidate. The next mayoral election is due on 1 May 2008.

The GLA is responsible for transport, economic development, strategic planning, culture, health, the environment, the police and fire and emergency planning. The separately elected assembly scrutinises the mayor's activities and approves plans and budgets. There are 14 constituency assembly members, each representing a separate area of London (each constituency is made up of two or three complete London boroughs). Eleven additional members, making up the total assembly complement of 25 members, are elected on a London-wide basis, either as independents or from party political lists on the basis of proportional representation.

LONDON BOROUGH COUNCILS

The London boroughs have whole council elections every four years, in the year immediately following the county council election year. The most recent elections took place on 4 May 2006.

The borough councils have responsibility for the following functions: building regulations; cemeteries and crematoria; consumer protection; education; youth employment; environmental health; electoral registration; food; drugs; housing; leisure services; libraries; local planning; local roads; museums; parking; recreation (parks, playing fields, swimming pools); refuse collection and street cleansing; social services; town planning; and traffic management.

CORPORATION OF LONDON

The Corporation of London is the local authority for the City of London. Its legal definition is the 'Mayor and Commonalty and Citizens of the City of London'. It is governed by the court of common council, which consists of the lord mayor, 25 other aldermen, and about 100 common councilmen. The lord mayor and two sheriffs are nominated annually by the City guilds (the livery companies) and elected by the court of aldermen. Aldermen and councilmen are elected from the 25 wards into which the City is divided; councilmen must stand for re-election annually. The council is a legislative assembly and there are no political parties.

The corporation has the same functions as the London borough councils. In addition, it runs the City of London Police; is the health authority for the Port of London; has health control of animal imports throughout Greater London, including at Heathrow airport; owns and manages public open spaces throughout Greater London; runs the central criminal court; and runs Billingsgate, Smithfield and Spitalfields markets.

'HE CITY GUILDS (LIVERY COMPANIES)

he livery companies of the City of London grew out of arly medieval religious fraternities and began to emerge s trade and craft guilds, retaining their religious aspect, in ie 12th century. From the early 14th century, only ıembers of the trade and craft guilds could call ıemselves citizens of the City of London. The guilds egan to be called livery companies, because of the istinctive livery worn by the most prosperous guild ıembers on ceremonial occasions, in the late 15th entury.

By the early 19th century the power of the companies ithin their trades had begun to wane, but those wearing ie livery of a company continued to play an important ɔle in the government of the City of London. Liverymen ill have the right to nominate the lord mayor and ıeriffs, and most members of the court of common ɔuncil are liverymen.

VALES

he Local Government (Wales) Act 1994 abolished the vo-tier structure of eight county and 37 district councils hich had existed since 1974, and replaced it, from 1 pril 1996, with 22 unitary authorities. The new ıthorities were elected in May 1995. Each unitary ıthority inherited all the functions of the previous ɔunty and district councils, except fire services (which e provided by three combined fire authorities, composed f representatives of the unitary authorities) and national arks (which are the responsibility of three independent ational Park Authorities).

OMMUNITY COUNCILS

ı Wales community councils are the equivalent of arishes in England. Unlike England, where many areas e not in any parish, communities have been established r the whole of Wales, approximately 865 communities ı all. Community meetings may be convened as and hen desired.

Community or town councils exist in 736 of the ɔmmunities and further councils may be established at e request of a community meeting. Community councils ave broadly the same range of powers as English parish ɔuncils. Community councillors are elected for a term of ur years.

INANCE

otal budgeted revenue expenditure for 2007–8 is 6.7bn, an increase of 5.5 per cent on 2006–7. Total udget requirement, which excludes expenditure financed y specific and special government grants and any use of serves, is £5.2bn. This comprises revenue support grant f £3bn, support from the national non-domestic rate ɔol of £791m, police grant of £225m and £1.1bn to be ised through council tax. The non-domestic rating ultiplier for Wales for 2007–8 is 44.8p. The average and D council tax levied in Wales for 2007–8 is £1,005, ɔmprising unitary authorities £829, police authorities 153 and community councils £23.

XPENDITURE

ocal authority budgeted net revenue expenditure for 007–8 is:

rvice	*£ million*
ducation	2,312.7
ɔcial services	1,307.8
Council fund housing, including housing benefit	730.7
Local environmental services	358.9
Roads and transport	300.3
Libraries, culture, heritage, sport and recreation	263.0
Planning, economic and community development	111.2
Council tax collection	30.0
Debt financing costs: counties	312.9
Central administrative and other revenue expenditure	239.1
Police	616.4
Fire	137.2
National parks	17.1
Gross revenue expenditure	6,737.3
Less specific and special government grants	(1,489.4)
Net revenue expenditure	5,247.9
Less appropriations from reserves	(42.1)
BUDGET REQUIREMENT	5,205.8

SCOTLAND

The Local Government etc (Scotland) Act 1994 abolished the two-tier structure of nine regional and 53 district councils which had existed since 1975 and replaced it, from 1 April 1996, with 29 unitary authorities on the mainland; the three islands councils remained. The new authorities were elected in April 1995.

In July 1999 the Scottish parliament assumed responsibility for legislation on local government. The government had established a commission on local government and the Scottish parliament (the McIntosh Commission) to make recommendations on the relationship between local authorities and the Scottish parliament and on increasing local authorities' accountability.

The local government in Scotland bill was introduced to the Scottish parliament in May 2002. The bill focused on three integrated core elements:

- A power for local authorities to promote and improve the well-being of their area and/or persons in it
- Statutory underpinning for community planning through the introduction of a duty on local authorities and key partners, including police, health boards and enterprise agencies
- A duty to secure best value

ELECTIONS

The unitary authorities consist of directly elected councillors. The Scottish Local Government (Elections) Act 2002 moved elections from a three-year to a four-year cycle; the last elections took place in May 2007.

FUNCTIONS

The functions of the councils and islands councils are: education; social work; strategic planning; the provision of infrastructure such as roads; consumer protection; flood prevention; coast protection; valuation and rating; the police and fire services; civil defence; electoral registration; public transport; registration of births, deaths and marriages; housing; leisure and recreation; development and building control; environmental health; licensing; allotments; public conveniences; and the administration of district courts.

COMMUNITY COUNCILS

Scottish community councils differ from those in England and Wales. Their purpose as defined in statute is to ascertain and express the views of the communities they represent, and to take in the interests of their communities such action as appears to be expedient or practicable. Around 1,200 community councils have been established under schemes drawn up by local authorities in Scotland.

FINANCE

Budgeted aggregate external finance for 2007–8 is £8.7bn, comprising £6bn revenue support grant, non-domestic rate income of £1.9bn and specific grants of £861m. The non-domestic rate multiplier or poundage for 2007–8 is 44.1p. All non-domestic properties in with a rateable value of £11,500 or less are eligible for a discount of between 5 and 50 per cent in the rate poundage. The average band D council tax for 2007–8 is £1,149.

EXPENDITURE

The 2007–8 net expenditure budget estimates for local authorities in Scotland were:

Service	*£ million*
Education	4,372.5
Cultural and related services	576.2
Social work services	2,275.6
Police	1,099.2
Roads and transport	473.8
Environmental services	511.8
Fire	291.3
Planning and development services	183.1
Other	1,248.7
TOTAL	11,032.2

NORTHERN IRELAND

For the purpose of local government Northern Ireland has a system of 26 single-tier district councils.

ELECTIONS

Council members are elected for periods of four years at a time on the principle of proportional representation.

FUNCTIONS

The district councils have three main roles. These are:

Executive: responsibility for a wide range of local services including building regulations; community services; consumer protection; cultural facilities; environmental health; miscellaneous licensing and registration provisions, including dog control; litter prevention; recreational and social facilities; refuse collection and disposal; street cleaning; and tourist development

Representative: nominating representatives to sit as members of the various statutory bodies responsible fc the administration of regional services such as drainag education, fire, health and personal social services, housing, and libraries

Consultative: acting as the medium through which the views of local people are expressed on the operation i their area of other regional services – notably conservation (including water supply and sewerage services), planning and roads – provided by those departments of central government which have an obligation, statutory or otherwise, to consult the district councils about proposals affecting their areas

FINANCE

Local government in Northern Ireland is funded by system of rates. The ratepayer receives a combined tax bi consisting of the regional rate and the district rate, whic is set by each district council. The regional and distric rates are both collected by the Land and Property Service Agency (formerly the Rate Collection Agency). Th product of the district rates is paid over to each counc whilst the product of the regional rate suppor expenditure by the departments of the executive an assembly.

Since April 2007 domestic rates bills have bee based on the capital value of a property, rather than th rental value. The capital value is defined as the price th property might reasonably be expected to realise had been sold on the open market on 1 January 200 Non-domestic rates bills are based on 2001 rent values.

Rate bills are calculated by multiplying the property net annual rental value (NAV) (in the case of non-domesti property), or capital value (in the case of domesti property), by the regional and district rate poundage respectively.

For 2007–8 the overall average domestic poundage 0.6285p (direct comparisons can not be made betwee 2007–8 and 2006–7 poundages due to the change fro rental to capital values). For 2007–8 the overall averag non-domestic rate poundage is 49.37p compared t 47.71p in 2006–7.

POLITICAL COMPOSITION OF LOCAL COUNCILS

as at May 2007

Abbreviations

All.	Alliance
BNP	British National Party
C.	Conservative
DUP	Democratic Unionist Party
Green	Green
Ind.	Independent
Ind. Un.	Independent Unionist
Lab.	Labour
LD	Liberal Democrat
Lib.	Liberal
O.	Other
PC	Plaid Cymru
R	Residents Associations/Ratepayers
SD	Social Democrat
SDLP	Social Democratic and Labour Party
SF	Sinn Fein
SNP	Scottish National Party
Soc.	Socialist
UUP	Ulster Unionist Party
v.	Vacant

Total number of seats is given in parentheses after council name.

ENGLAND

COUNTY COUNCILS

Bedfordshire (52)	C. 35; LD 9; Lab. 7; Ind. 1
Buckinghamshire (57)	C. 44; LD 11; Lab. 2
Cambridgeshire (69)	C. 43; LD 22; Lab. 4
Cheshire (51)	C. 26; Lab. 16; LD 8; Ind. 1
Cornwall (82)	LD 48; Ind. 19; C. 9; Lab. 5; Lib. 1
Cumbria (84)	Lab. 39; C. 32; LD 11; Ind. 2
Derbyshire (64)	Lab. 38; C. 15; LD 10; Ind. 1
Devon (62)	LD 33; C. 23; Lab. 4; Ind. 2
Dorset (45)	C. 24; LD 16; Lab. 4; Ind. 1
Durham (63)	Lab. 53; LD 5; Ind. 3; C. 2
East Sussex (49)	C. 29; LD 13; Lab. 5; Ind. 1; O. 1
Essex (75)	C. 50; Lab. 13; LD 8; Green 2; Ind. 2
Gloucestershire (63)	C. 34; LD 13; Lab. 12; Ind. 3; O. 1
Hampshire (78)	C. 46; LD 28; Lab. 4
Hertfordshire (77)	C. 46; Lab. 16; LD 14; Green 1
Kent (84)	C. 57; Lab. 21; LD 5; v. 1
Lancashire (84)	Lab. 43; C. 31; LD 6; Ind. 2; Green 1; O. 1
Leicestershire (55)	C. 31; Lab. 13; LD 11
Lincolnshire (77)	C. 45; Lab. 20; LD 8; Ind. 3; v. 1
Norfolk (84)	C. 47; Lab. 22; LD 13; Green 2
North Yorkshire (72)	C. 42; LD 19; Lab. 8; Ind. 3
Northamptonshire (73)	C. 45; Lab. 19; LD 8; v. 1
Northumberland (67)	Lab. 35; C. 17; LD 14; Ind. 1
Nottinghamshire (67)	Lab. 36; C. 26; LD 5
Oxfordshire (74)	C. 44; LD 16; Lab. 8; Green 5; Ind. 1
Shropshire (48)	C. 25; LD 12; Lab. 9; Ind. 2
Somerset (58)	LD 30; C. 24; Lab. 4
Staffordshire (62)	Lab. 32; C. 26; LD 2; Ind. 1; v. 1
Suffolk (75)	C. 45; Lab. 21; LD 7; Ind. 1; v. 1
Surrey (80)	C. 58; LD 12; R 8; Lab. 2
Warwickshire (62)	C. 28; Lab. 23; LD 10; Ind. 1
West Sussex (70)	C. 46; LD 16; Lab. 7; v. 1
Wiltshire (49)	C. 29, LD 16; Lab. 3; Ind. 1
Worcestershire (57)	C. 29; Lab. 17; LD 8; Lib. 2; Ind. 1

DISTRICT COUNCILS

Adur (29)	C. 26; Ind. 2; LD 1
Allerdale (56)	O. 33; Lab. 21; Ind. 2
Alnwick (30)	LD 11; C. 9; Ind. 6; Lab. 2; O. 2
Amber Valley (45)	C. 28; Lab. 17
Arun (56)	C. 42; LD 9; Lab. 3; Ind. 2
Ashfield (33)	LD 10; Ind. 9; Lab. 9; C. 3; O. 2
Ashford (43)	C. 28; LD 8; O. 3; Ind. 2; Lab. 2
Aylesbury Vale (59)	C. 37; LD 21; Ind. 1
Babergh (43)	C. 19; LD 16; Ind. 7; O. 1
Barrow-in-Furness (38)	C. 19; Lab. 16; Ind. 2; O. 1
Basildon (42)	C. 28; Lab. 11; LD 3
Basingstoke and Deane (60)	C. 31; LD 15; Lab. 11; Ind. 3
Bassetlaw (48)	C. 28; Lab. 16; Ind. 4
Bedford (54)	C. 19; LD 16; Lab. 12; Ind. 4; O. 3
Berwick-upon-Tweed (29)	LD 13; C. 10; Ind. 6
Blaby (39)	C. 27; LD 7; Lab. 4; Ind. 1
Blyth Valley (50)	Lab. 30; LD 13; Ind. 5; C. 2
Bolsover (37)	Lab. 27; Ind. 7; R 2; O. 1
Boston (32)	O. 25; C. 5; Ind. 2
Braintree (60)	C. 42; Lab. 9; R 5; Green 2; Ind. 1; LD 1
Breckland (54)	C. 48; Ind. 3; Lab. 3
Brentwood (37)	C. 28; LD 6; Lab. 3
Bridgnorth (34)	Ind. 23; C. 6; O. 4; Lab. 1
Broadland (47)	C. 35; LD 9; Ind. 3
Bromsgrove (39)	C. 26; Lab. 6; Ind. 4; R 2; LD 1
Broxbourne (38)	C. 36; Lab. 2
Broxtowe (44)	C. 16; LD 15; Lab. 10; Ind. 2; BNP 1
Burnley (45)	LD 18; Lab. 17; C. 6; BNP 4
Cambridge (42)	LD 28; Lab. 13; Ind. 1
Cannock Chase (41)	Lab. 16; LD 14; C. 10; v. 1
Canterbury (50)	C. 29; LD 19; Lab. 2
Caradon (42)	LD 23; C. 9; Ind. 9; O. 1
Carlisle (52)	Lab. 25; C. 19; LD 7; Ind. 1
Carrick (47)	C. 19; LD 18; Ind. 8; Lab. 1; O. 1
Castle Morpeth (33)	C. 12; LD 12; Lab. 6; Ind. 2; Green 1
Castle Point (41)	C. 26; Ind. 15
Charnwood (52)	C. 32; Lab. 13; LD 5; BNP 1; Ind. 1
Chelmsford (57)	C. 33; LD 24
Cheltenham (40)	C. 17; LD 17; O. 5; Lab. 1
Cherwell (50)	C. 42; Lab. 4; LD 4
Chester (60)	C. 33; Lab. 13; LD 13; Ind. 1
Chester-le-Street (34)	Lab. 26; Ind. 5; C. 2; LD 1
Chesterfield (48)	LD 35; Lab. 12; Ind. 1
Chichester (48)	C. 34; LD 11; Ind. 3
Chiltern (40)	C. 30; LD 9; Ind. 1
Chorley (47)	C. 25; Lab. 15; Ind. 4; LD 3
Christchurch (24)	C. 17; LD 4; Ind. 3
Colchester (60)	C. 30; LD 21; Lab. 6; Ind. 3
Congleton (48)	C. 26; LD 14; O. 6; Ind. 2

Copeland (51)	Lab. 31; C. 19; Ind. 1
Corby (29)	Lab. 16; C. 8; LD 5
Cotswolds (44)	C. 38; LD 4; Ind. 2
Craven (30)	C. 13; Ind. 10; LD 6; v. 1
Crawley (37)	C. 22; Lab. 12; LD 3
Crewe and Nantwich (56)	C. 28; Lab. 17; LD 6; O. 3; Ind. 2
Dacorum (51)	C. 44; LD 5; Lab. 2
Dartford (44)	C. 26; Lab. 12; R 6
Daventry (38)	C. 35; LD 2; Lab. 1
Derbyshire Dales (39)	C. 26; LD 8; Lab. 4; Ind. 1
Derwentside (55)	Lab. 29; Ind. 24; LD 2
Dover (45)	C. 28; Lab. 14; LD 2; v. 1
Durham (50)	LD 30; Lab. 17; Ind. 3
Easington (51)	Lab. 47; Ind. 2; LD 2
East Cambridgeshire (39)	C. 24; LD 13; Ind. 2
East Devon (59)	C. 43; LD 10; Ind. 6
East Dorset (36)	C. 25; LD 11
East Hampshire (44)	C. 30; LD 14
East Hertfordshire (50)	C. 42; LD 4; Ind. 2; O. 2
East Lindsey (60)	C. 28; Ind. 19; Lab. 8; LD 3; O. 2
East Northamptonshire (40)	C. 38; Ind. 1; v. 1
East Staffordshire (39)	C. 25; Lab. 12; LD 2
Eastbourne (27)	LD 20; C. 7
Eastleigh (44)	LD 37; C. 5; Lab. 2
Eden (38)	Ind. 18; C. 14; LD 5; O. 1
Ellesmere Port and Neston (43)	Lab. 24; C. 17; LD 2
Elmbridge (60)	C. 28; R 23; LD 8; O. 1
Epping Forest (58)	C. 32; LD 11; BNP 6; R 5; Ind. 2; Lab. 1; O. 1
Epsom and Ewell (38)	R 25; LD 11; C. 2
Erewash (51)	C. 30; Lab. 18; LD 2; Ind. 1
Exeter (40)	Lab. 14; LD 12; C. 10; Lib. 4
Fareham (31)	C. 22; LD 9
Fenland (40)	C. 39; Ind. 1
Forest Heath (27)	C. 22; LD 2; O. 2; Ind. 1
Forest of Dean (48)	C. 30; Ind. 8; Lab. 8; LD 2
Fylde (51)	C. 29; Ind. 14; R 4; LD 2; O. 2
Gedling (50)	C. 28; Lab. 9; LD 9; Ind. 4
Gloucester (36)	C. 15; LD 12; Lab. 9
Gosport (34)	C. 17; LD 9; Lab. 7; Ind. 1
Gravesham (44)	C. 26; Lab. 16; v. 2
Great Yarmouth (39)	C. 22; Lab. 17
Guildford (48)	C. 26; LD 22
Hambleton (44)	C. 39; Ind. 3; LD 2
Harborough (37)	C. 26; LD 11
Harlow (33)	C. 12; Lab. 12; LD 8; Ind. 1
Harrogate (54)	C. 25; LD 23; Ind. 6
Hart (35)	C. 15; LD 12; O. 6; Ind. 2
Hastings (32)	C. 15; Lab 12; LD 5
Havant (38)	C. 31; Lab 4; LD 3
Hertsmere (39)	C. 28; LD 7; Lab. 4
High Peak (43)	C. 24; Lab. 9; LD 6; Ind. 4
Hinckley and Bosworth (34)	LD 19; C. 13; Lab. 2
Horsham (44)	C. 31; LD 11; Ind. 2
Huntingdonshire (52)	C. 39; LD 11; Ind. 2
Hyndburn (35)	C. 18; Lab. 15; Ind. 2
Ipswich (48)	C. 20; Lab. 18; LD 9; v. 1
Kennet (43)	C. 34; Ind. 5; O. 3; LD 1
Kerrier (44)	Ind. 21; LD 11; C. 5; O. 4; Lab. 2; Lib. 1
Kettering (36)	C. 28; Lab. 6; Ind. 2
King's Lynn and West Norfolk (62)	C. 52; Lab. 4; LD 4; Ind. 2
Lancaster (60)	O. 16; Lab. 14; C. 12; Green 12; LD 5; Ind. 1
Lewes (41)	LD 23; C. 17; Ind. 1
Lichfield (56)	C. 44; Lab. 7; LD 4; Ind. 1
Lincoln City (33)	C. 17; Lab. 15; LD 1
Macclesfield (60)	C. 38; LD 12; Lab. 6; Ind. 2; R 2
Maidstone (55)	C. 26; LD 21; Ind. 4; Lab. 4
Maldon (31)	C. 25; Ind. 4; v. 2
Malvern Hills (38)	C. 29; LD 5; Ind. 3; Green 1
Mansfield (46)	O. 28; Lab. 12; LD 4; C. 1; Ind. 1
Melton (28)	C. 20; Ind. 5; Lab. 3
Mendip (47)	C. 24; LD 23
Mid Bedfordshire (53)	C. 38; LD 11; Ind. 4
Mid Devon (42)	C. 17; Ind. 14; LD 10; v. 1
Mid Suffolk (40)	C. 25; LD 10; Green 2; O. 2; Ind. 1
Mid Sussex (54)	C. 30; LD 23; Lab. 1
Mole Valley (41)	C. 22; LD 16; Ind. 3
New Forest (60)	C. 45; LD 14; Ind. 1
Newark and Sherwood (46)	C. 26; Ind. 10; Lab. 6; LD 4
Newcastle-under-Lyme (60)	C. 20; Lab. 20; LD 18; O. 2
North Cornwall (36)	Ind. 15; LD 14; C. 6; O. 1
North Devon (43)	C. 22; LD 17; Ind. 4
North Dorset (33)	C. 17; LD 13; Lab. 3
North East Derbyshire (53)	Lab. 29; C. 10; Ind. 7; LD 7
North Hertfordshire (49)	C. 30; LD 9; O. 8; Lab. 2
North Kesteven (43)	C. 25; Ind. 14; LD 4
North Norfolk (48)	LD 29; C. 17; Ind. 2
North Shropshire (40)	C. 26; Ind. 12; Lab. 2
North Warwickshire (35)	C. 21; Lab. 14
North West Leicestershire (38)	C. 27; Lab. 5; LD 3; BNP 2; Ind. 1
North Wiltshire (54)	C. 39; LD 14; Lab. 1
Northampton (47)	LD 26; C. 15; Lab. 5; Ind. 1
Norwich (39)	Lab. 15; LD 11; Green 10; C. 3
Nuneaton and Bedworth (34)	Lab. 18; C. 14; LD 1; v. 1
Oadby and Wigston (26)	LD 21; C. 5
Oswestry (29)	C. 17; O. 6; LD 4; Ind. 2
Oxford (48)	Lab. 18; LD 16; Green 8; O. 4; C. 2
Pendle (49)	LD 27; C. 14; Lab. 6; BNP 1; v. 1
Penwith (35)	C. 17; LD 12; Ind. 6
Preston (57)	Lab. 24; C. 20; LD 10; O. 2; Ind. 1
Purbeck (24)	C. 13; LD 9; Ind. 2
Redditch (29)	Lab. 14; C. 11; LD 3; BNP 1
Reigate and Banstead (51)	C. 41; R 6; LD 2; Ind. 1; Lab. 1
Restormel (45)	LD 20; Ind. 13; C. 10; O. 2
Ribble Valley (40)	C. 29; LD 10; Ind. 1
Richmondshire (34)	C. 17; O. 11; LD 6
Rochford (39)	C. 31; LD 5; Ind. 1; R 1; v. 1
Rossendale (36)	C. 22; Lab. 12; Ind. 1; LD 1
Rother (38)	C. 28; LD 8; Ind. 2
Rugby (48)	C. 27; Lab. 11; LD 10
Runnymede (42)	C. 36; R 6
Rushcliffe (50)	C. 34; LD 11; Green 2; Lab. 2; Ind. 1
Rushmoor (42)	C. 28; LD 8; Lab. 5; Ind. 1
Ryedale (30)	C. 14; LD 8; Ind. 5; Lib. 1; R 1; v. 1

St Albans (58)	LD 29; C. 19; Lab. 8; Ind. 2
St Edmundsbury (45)	C. 36; Lab. 3; LD 3; Ind. 2; O. 1
Salisbury (55)	C. 22; LD 19; Lab. 10; Ind. 4
Scarborough (50)	C. 23; Ind. 15; LD 6; Lab. 4; Green 2
Sedgefield (50)	Lab. 28; Ind. 14; LD 6; C. 1; O. 1
Sedgemoor (50)	C. 35; Lab. 11; LD 4
Selby (41)	C. 29; Lab. 9; Ind. 3
Sevenoaks (54)	C. 41; LD 7; Lab. 5; Ind. 1
Shepway (46)	C. 34; LD 10; O. 2
Shrewsbury and Atcham (40)	C. 22; Lab. 10; LD 5; Ind. 3
South Bedfordshire (50)	C. 34; LD 12; Lab. 4
South Bucks (40)	C. 36; Ind. 2; LD 2
South Cambridgeshire (57)	C. 31; LD 16; Ind. 8; O. 2
South Derbyshire (36)	C. 21; Lab. 14; Ind. 1
South Hams (40)	C. 28; LD 9; Ind. 3
South Holland (37)	C. 26; Ind. 11
South Kesteven (58)	C. 35; Ind. 15; LD 6; Lab. 2
South Lakeland (52)	LD 34; C. 15; Lab. 2; Ind. 1
South Norfolk (46)	C. 39; LD 7
South Northamptonshire (42)	C. 35; Ind. 7
South Oxfordshire (48)	C. 38; LD 6; Ind. 2; Lab. 1; R 1
South Ribble (55)	C. 44; Lab. 8; O. 2; LD 1
South Shropshire (34)	C. 18; LD 11; Ind. 3; O. 2
South Somerset (60)	LD 38; C. 17; Ind. 5
South Staffordshire (49)	C. 42; Ind. 3; Lab. 1; LD 1; v. 2
Spelthorne (39)	C. 31; LD 8
Stafford (59)	C. 40; Lab. 13; O. 6
Staffordshire Moorlands (56)	C. 28; Ind. 11; LD 6; Lab. 5; R 3; O. 2; BNP 1
Stevenage (39)	Lab. 32; LD 4; C. 3
Stratford-on-Avon (53)	C. 37; LD 14; Ind. 2
Stroud (51)	C. 31; Lab. 9; Green 5; LD 4; Ind. 1; O. 1
Suffolk Coastal (55)	C. 45; LD 9; Lab. 1
Surrey Heath (40)	C. 30; LD 7; Lab. 2; Ind. 1
Swale (47)	C. 26; Lab. 10; LD 6; Ind. 5
Tamworth (30)	C. 24; Lab. 5; Ind. 1
Tandridge (42)	C. 30; LD 10; Lab. 2; Ind. 1
Taunton Deane (56)	LD 26; C. 25; Ind. 4; Lab. 1
Teesdale (32)	Ind. 16; Lab. 6; O. 6; C. 4
Teignbridge (46)	LD 21; C. 19; Ind. 6
Tendring (60)	C. 28; O. 15; Lab. 6; LD 6; Ind. 5
Test Valley (48)	C. 33; LD 15
Tewkesbury (38)	C. 19; LD 17; Ind. 2
Thanet (56)	C. 33; Lab. 19; Ind. 3; O. 1
Three Rivers (48)	LD 30; C. 11; Lab. 7
Tonbridge and Malling (53)	C. 46; LD 7
Torridge (36)	C. 13; Ind. 12; LD 8; O. 3
Tunbridge Wells (48)	C. 41; LD 7
Tynedale (52)	C. 30; LD 9; Lab. 8; Ind. 5
Uttlesford (44)	C. 26; LD 15; Ind. 3
Vale of White Horse (51)	LD 34; C. 17
Vale Royal (57)	C. 29; Lab. 17; LD 11
Wansbeck (45)	Lab. 26; C. 16; O. 3
Warwick (46)	C. 24; Lab. 9; LD 9; Ind. 4
Watford (37)	LD 29; C. 3; Green 3; Ind. 1; Lab. 1
Waveney (48)	C. 30; Lab. 12; LD 3; Ind. 2; Green 1
Waverley (57)	C. 51; Ind. 3; LD 3
Wealden (55)	C. 34; LD 12; O. 6; Green 2; Ind. 1
Wear Valley (40)	Lab. 18; LD 16; Ind. 6
Wellingborough (36)	C. 30; O. 6
Welwyn and Hatfield (48)	C. 35; Lab. 10; LD 3
West Devon (31)	C. 14; Ind. 10; LD 7
West Dorset (48)	C. 26; LD 16; Ind. 6
West Lancashire (54)	C. 33; Lab. 21
West Lindsey (37)	LD 20; C. 16; Ind. 1
West Oxfordshire (49)	C. 36; LD 8; Ind. 4; Lab. 1
West Somerset (31)	Ind. 16; C. 13; Lab. 1; LD 1
West Wiltshire (44)	C. 26; LD 14; Ind. 2; O. 2
Weymouth and Portland (36)	C. 14; LD 11; Lab. 6; Ind. 5
Winchester (57)	C. 29; LD 23; Ind. 4; Lab. 1
Woking (36)	C. 19; LD 17
Worcester (35)	C. 18; Lab. 12; LD 3; Ind. 1; O. 1
Worthing (37)	C. 24; LD 12; Ind. 1
Wychavon (45)	C. 35; LD 10
Wycombe (60)	C. 49; Lab. 5; LD 4; Ind. 2
Wyre (55)	C. 45; Lab. 9; LD 1
Wyre Forest (42)	C. 18; O. 10; Lib. 7; Lab. 3; Ind. 2; LD 2

LONDON BOROUGH COUNCILS

Barking and Dagenham (51)	Lab. 38; BNP 12; C. 1
Barnet (63)	C. 37; Lab. 20; LD 6
Bexley (63)	C. 54; Lab. 9
Brent (63)	LD 27; Lab. 21; C. 15
Bromley (60)	C. 49; LD 7; Lab. 4
Camden (54)	LD 21; Lab. 17; C. 14; Green 2
Croydon (70)	C. 43; Lab. 27
Ealing (69)	C. 37; Lab. 29; LD 3
Enfield (63)	C. 34; Lab. 27; O. 2
Greenwich (51)	Lab. 36; C. 13; LD 2
Hackney (58)	Lab. 45; C. 9; LD 3; Green 1
Hammersmith and Fulham (46)	C. 33; LD 13
Haringey (57)	Lab. 30; LD 27
Harrow (63)	C. 37; Lab. 24; LD 2
Havering (54)	C. 34; R 16; Lab. 2; BNP 1; O. 1
Hillingdon (65)	C. 45; Lab. 18; LD 2
Hounslow (60)	Lab. 24; C. 23; O. 6; LD 4; Ind. 3
Islington (48)	LD 24; Lab. 23; Green 1
Kensington and Chelsea (54)	C. 45; Lab. 9
Kingston upon Thames (48)	LD 25; C. 21; Lab. 1; Ind. 1
Lambeth (63)	Lab. 39; LD 17; C. 6; Green 1
Lewisham (55)	Lab. 27; LD 16; Green 6; C. 3; Soc. 2; Ind. 1
Merton (60)	C. 30; Lab. 27; R 3
Newham (60)	Lab. 54; O. 6
Redbridge (63)	C. 34; Lab. 18; LD 10; BNP 1
Richmond upon Thames (54)	LD 36; C. 18
Southwark (63)	Lab. 29; LD 27; C. 6; Green 1
Sutton (54)	LD 32; C. 22
Tower Hamlets (51)	Lab. 27; O. 11; C. 7; LD 6
Waltham Forest (60)	Lab. 26; LD 19; C. 15
Wandsworth (60)	C. 51; Lab. 9
Westminster (60)	C. 48; Lab. 12

METROPOLITAN BOROUGHS

Barnsley (63)	Lab. 33; Ind. 21; C. 5; LD 2; O. 2
Birmingham (120)	C. 44; Lab. 41; LD 32; O. 2; Ind. 1
Bolton (60)	Lab. 26; C. 22; LD 12
Bradford (90)	Lab. 39; C. 32; LD 14; Green 3; BNP 2
Bury (51)	C. 23; Lab. 20; LD 8
Calderdale (51)	C. 18; LD 16; Lab. 11; Ind. 4; BNP 1; O. 1
Coventry (54)	C. 28; Lab. 23; Soc. 2; LD 1
Doncaster (63)	Lab. 29; LD 12; Ind. 10; C. 9; O. 3
Dudley (72)	C. 39; Lab. 28; LD 5
Gateshead (66)	Lab. 41; LD 23; Lib. 1; v. 1
Kirklees (69)	Lab. 22; C. 20; LD 18; Green 4; BNP 3; Ind. 2
Knowsley (63)	Lab. 50; LD 13
Leeds (99)	Lab. 43; LD 24; C. 22; O. 5; Green 3; BNP 1; Ind. 1
Liverpool (90)	LD 51; Lab 34; Lib. 3; Green 1; Ind. 1
Manchester (96)	Lab. 61; LD 34; Green 1
Newcastle-upon-Tyne (78)	LD 45; Lab. 31; v. 2
North Tyneside (60)	C. 28; Lab. 23; LD 9
Oldham (60)	Lab. 30; LD 26; C. 3; Ind. 1
Rochdale (60)	LD 32; Lab. 20; C. 8
Rotherham (63)	Lab. 53; C. 7; Ind. 2; v. 1
St Helens (48)	Lab. 21; LD 21; C. 6
Salford (60)	Lab. 42; C. 10; LD 8
Sandwell (72)	Lab. 51; C. 10; LD 6; BNP 4; v. 1
Sefton (66)	LD 26; Lab. 22; C. 18
Sheffield (84)	Lab. 41; LD 39; Green 2; C. 1; Ind. 1
Solihull (51)	C. 24; LD 18; Lab. 7; BNP 1; Ind. 1
South Tyneside (54)	Lab. 35; O. 7; Ind. 6; C. 3; LD 3
Stockport (63)	LD 36; Lab. 15; C. 9; R 3
Sunderland (75)	Lab. 54; C. 16; Ind. 4; LD 1
Tameside (57)	Lab. 45; C. 8; Ind. 3; LD 1
Trafford (63)	C. 39; Lab. 20; LD 4
Wakefield (63)	Lab. 40; C. 16; Ind. 4; LD 3
Walsall (60)	C. 33; Lab. 18; LD 6; Ind. 2; O. 1
Wigan (75)	Lab. 46; C. 10; O. 10; Ind. 5; LD 3; v. 1
Wirral (66)	Lab. 25; C. 21; LD 19; O. 1
Wolverhampton (60)	Lab. 36; C. 19; LD 3; Ind. 1; O. 1

UNITARY COUNCILS

Bath and North East Somerset (65)	LD 29; C. 26; Lab. 6; Ind. 4
Blackburn with Darwen (64)	Lab. 31; C. 17; LD 13; O. 3
Blackpool (42)	C. 26; Lab. 13; LD 3
Bournemouth (54)	C. 41; LD 7; Lab. 3; Ind. 3
Bracknell Forest (42)	C. 39; Lab. 3
Brighton and Hove (54)	C. 26; Lab. 13; Green 12; LD 2; Ind. 1
Bristol (70)	LD 31; Lab. 25; C. 13; Green 1
Darlington (53)	Lab. 29; C. 18; LD 5; Ind. 1
Derby (51)	Lab. 24; LD 13; C. 12; Ind. 2
East Riding of Yorkshire (67)	C. 47; LD 12; Ind. 4; Lab. 3; SD 1
Halton (56)	Lab. 33; LD 15; C. 8
Hartlepool (47)	Lab. 24; O. 12; LD 7; C. 4
Herefordshire (58)	C. 31; Ind. 14; LD 10; Lab. 2; O. 1
Isles of Scilly (21)*	O. 21
Isle of Wight (48)	C. 35; Ind. 4; LD. 4; O. 3; Lab 2
Kingston-upon-Hull (59)	LD 30; Lab. 20; O. 6; C. 2; Ind. 1
Leicester (54)	Lab. 38; C. 8; LD 6; Green 2
Luton (48)	Lab. 26; LD 17; C. 5
Medway (55)	C. 33; Lab. 13; LD 8; Ind. 1
Middlesbrough (48)	Lab. 26; Ind. 10; C. 6; LD 5; O. 1
Milton Keynes (51)	LD 22; C. 15; Lab. 13; O. 1
North East Lincolnshire (42)	LD 19; C. 15; Lab. 6; Ind. 2
North Lincolnshire (43)	Lab. 22; C. 18; Ind. 2; LD 1
North Somerset (61)	C. 46; Ind. 7; LD 5; Lab. 3
Nottingham (55)	Lab. 42; C. 7; LD 6
Peterborough (57)	C. 40; Ind. 6; O. 5; LD 4; Lab. 2
Plymouth (57)	C. 31; Lab. 26
Poole (42)	C. 25; LD 17
Portsmouth (42)	LD 19; C. 17; Lab. 5; Ind. 1
Reading (46)	Lab. 25; C. 14; LD 7
Redcar and Cleveland (59)	Lab. 28; LD 13; C. 11; Ind. 7
Rutland (26)	C. 19; Ind. 5; LD 2
Slough (41)	Lab. 19; C. 7; LD 4; Ind. 3; Lib. 3; R 3; O. 2
South Gloucestershire (70)	C. 34; LD 27; Lab. 9
Southampton (48)	C. 18; Lab. 18; LD 12
Southend-on-Sea (51)	C. 30; LD 10; Lab. 7; Ind. 4
Stockton-on-Tees (56)	Lab. 22; C. 13; Ind. 13; LD 8
Stoke-on-Trent (60)	Lab. 24; O. 13; Ind. 12; BNP 6; LD 5
Swindon (59)	C. 43; Lab. 12; LD 3; Ind. 1
Telford and Wrekin (54)	C. 25; Lab. 19; Ind. 4; LD 3; O. 3
Thurrock (49)	C. 24; Lab. 22; Ind. 2; O. 1
Torbay (36)	C. 24; LD 9; Ind. 3
Warrington (57)	LD 27; Lab. 24; C. 5; Ind. 1
West Berkshire (52)	C. 36; LD 16
Windsor and Maidenhead (57)	C. 36; LD 16; Ind. 5
Wokingham (54)	C. 43; LD 11
York (47)	LD 19; Lab. 18; C. 8; Green 2

* Thirteen councillors are elected by the residents of the isle of St Mary's and two councillors each are elected by the residents of the four other islands (Bryher, St Martins, St Agnes and Tresco)

WALES

Blaenau Gwent (42)	Lab. 29; Ind. 11; LD 1; v. 1
Bridgend (54)	Lab. 22; LD 13; C. 8; O. 6; Ind. 4; PC 1
Caerphilly (73)	Lab. 41; PC 26; Ind. 6
Cardiff (75)	LD 32; Lab. 27; C. 10; PC 4; Ind. 2
Carmarthenshire (74)	Ind. 31; Lab. 25; PC 16; O. 2
Ceredigion (42)	Ind. 16; PC 16; LD 9; Lab. 1
Conwy (59)	Ind. 17; C. 15; Lab. 11; PC 11; LD 4; v. 1
Denbighshire (47)	Ind. 18; C. 9; Lab. 7; PC 7; O. 6
Flintshire (70)	Lab. 36; Ind. 18; LD 10; C. 4; O. 1; PC 1
Gwynedd (75)	PC 44; Ind. 14; Lab. 9; LD 6; O. 2
Merthyr Tydfil (33)	Lab. 16; O. 9; Ind. 8
Monmouthshire (43)	C. 24; Lab. 9; Ind. 3; LD 3; O. 2; PC 2

Neath Port Talbot (64)	Lab. 36; PC 10; R 9; Ind. 4; SD 3; LD 2
Newport (50)	Lab. 31; C. 11; LD 6; Ind. 1; PC 1
Pembrokeshire (60)	Ind. 39; Lab. 11; PC 5; LD 4; O. 1
Powys (73)	Ind. 53; LD 15; Lab. 4; v. 1
Rhondda Cynon Taff (75)	Lab. 57; PC 13; Ind. 2; O. 2; LD 1
Swansea (72)	Lab. 31; O. 31; C. 4; PC 4; Ind. 1; v. 1
Torfaen (44)	Lab. 34; Ind. 7; LD 2; C. 1
Vale of Glamorgan (47)	C. 20; Lab. 16; PC 8; Ind. 3
Wrexham (52)	Lab. 19; LD 15; O. 9; Ind. 5; C. 4
Ynys Mon (Isle of Anglesey) (40)	Ind. 28; PC 6; C. 2; O. 2; Lab. 1; LD 1

SCOTLAND

Aberdeen (43)	LD 15; SNP 12; Lab. 10; C. 5; Ind. 1
Aberdeenshire (68)	LD 24; SNP 22; C. 14; Ind. 8
Angus (29)	SNP 13; Ind. 6; C. 5; LD 3; Lab. 2
Argyll and Bute (36)	Ind. 16; SNP 10; LD 7; C. 3
Clackmannanshire (18)	Lab. 8; SNP 7; C. 1; Ind. 1; LD 1
Dumfries and Galloway (47)	C. 18; Lab. 14; SNP 10; LD 3; Ind. 2
Dundee (29)	SNP 13; Lab. 10; C. 3; LD 2; Ind. 1
East Ayrshire (32)	Lab. 14; SNP 14; C. 3; Ind. 1
East Dunbartonshire (24)	SNP 8; Lab. 6; C. 5; LD 3; Ind. 2
East Lothian (23)	Lab. 7; SNP 7; LD 6; C. 2; Ind. 1
East Renfrewshire (20)	C. 7; Lab. 7; SNP 3; Ind. 2; LD 1
Edinburgh (58)	LD 17; Lab. 15; SNP 12; C. 11; Green 3
Eilean Siar (Western Isles) (31)	Ind. 25; SNP 4; Lab. 2
Falkirk (32)	Lab. 14; SNP 13; Ind. 3; C. 2
Fife (78)	Lab. 24; SNP 23; LD 21; C. 5; Ind. 3; O. 2
Glasgow (79)	Lab 45; SNP 22; LD 5; Green 5; C. 1; O. 1
Highland (80)	Ind. 34; LD 22; SNP 17; Lab. 7
Inverclyde (20)	Lab. 9; SNP 5; LD 4; C. 1; Ind. 1
Midlothian (18)	Lab. 9; SNP 6; LD 3
Moray (26)	Ind. 12; SNP 9; C. 3; Lab. 2
North Ayrshire (30)	Lab. 12; SNP 8; Ind. 5; C. 3; LD 2
North Lanarkshire (70)	Lab. 40; SNP 23; Ind. 5; C. 1; O. 1
Orkney Islands (21)	Ind. 21
Perth and Kinross (41)	SNP 18; C. 12; LD 8; Lab. 3
Renfrewshire (40)	Lab. 17; SNP 17; LD 4; C. 2
Scottish Borders (34)	C. 11; LD 10; SNP 6; Ind. 5; O. 2
Shetland Islands (22)	O. 12; Ind. 10
South Ayrshire (30)	C. 12; Lab. 9; SNP 8; Ind. 1
South Lanarkshire (67)	Lab. 30; SNP 24; C. 8; Ind. 3; LD 2
Stirling (22)	Lab. 8; SNP 7; C. 4; LD 3
West Dunbartonshire (22)	Lab. 10; SNP 9; Ind. 2; Soc. 1
West Lothian (32)	Lab. 14; SNP 13; O. 3; C. 1; Ind. 1

NORTHERN IRELAND

Antrim (19)	DUP 6; UUP 5; SF 3; All. 2; SDLP 2; Ind. 1
Ards (23)	DUP 11; UUP 6; All. 3; Ind. 1; O. 1; SDLP 1
Armagh City (22)	SDLP 6; DUP 5; SF 5; UUP 5; Ind. Un. 1
Ballymena (24)	DUP 9; O. 6; UUP 4; Ind. 2; SDLP 2; SF 1
Ballymoney (16)	DUP 7; SF 3; Ind. Un. 2; SDLP 2; UUP 2
Banbridge (17)	DUP 6; UUP 5; SDLP 3; All. 1; Ind. Un. 1; SF 1
Belfast (51)	DUP 14; SF 14; SDLP 8; UUP 8; All. 4; O. 2; Ind. 1
Carrickfergus (17)	DUP 8; UUP 4; All. 3; Ind. 1; O. 1
Castlereagh (24)	DUP 13; All. 4; UUP 4; SDLP 3
Coleraine (22)	DUP 8; UUP 8; SDLP 3; All. 1; Ind. Un. 1; SF 1
Cookstown (16)	SDLP 5; SF 5; DUP 3; UUP 3
Craigavon (26)	DUP 8; SF 6; UUP 6; Ind. 3; SDLP 3
Derry City (30)	SDLP 14; SF 10; DUP 5; UUP 1
Down (23)	SDLP 10; SF 5; DUP 3; UUP 3; C. 1; Green 1
Dungannon and South Tyrone (22)	SF 9; DUP 5; SDLP 4; UUP 4
Fermanagh (23)	SF 9; SDLP 5; UUP 5; DUP 4
Larne (15)	DUP 4; UUP 4; Ind. 3; All. 2; SDLP 2
Limavady (15)	SF 6; SDLP 3; DUP 2; O. 2; UUP 2
Lisburn (30)	DUP 12; UUP 7; SF 4; All. 3; SDLP 3; Ind. Un. 1
Magherafelt (16)	SF 6; DUP 4; O. 2; SDLP 2; UUP 2
Moyle (15)	SF 4; DUP 3; Ind. Un. 3; SDLP 3; UUP 2
Newry and Mourne (30)	SF 12; SDLP 9; DUP 2; Ind. 2; UUP 2; Green 1; Ind. Un. 1; O. 1
Newtownabbey (25)	DUP 12; UUP 6; Ind. Un. 3; All. 2; SDLP 1; SF 1
North Down (25)	DUP 8; UUP 8; All. 6; Ind. 2; Green 1
Omagh (21)	SF 10; DUP 3; SDLP 3; UUP 3; Ind. Un. 2
Strabane (16)	SF 8; DUP 3; SDLP 2; UUP 2; Ind. Un. 1

ENGLAND

The Kingdom of England lies between 55° 46′ and 49° 57′ 30″ N. latitude (from a few miles north of the mouth of the Tweed to the Lizard), and between 1° 46′ E. and 5° 43′ W. longitude (from Lowestoft to Land's End). England is bounded on the north by the Cheviot Hills; on the south by the English Channel; on the east by the Straits of Dover (Pas de Calais) and the North Sea; and on the west by the Atlantic Ocean, Wales and the Irish Sea. It has a total area of 130,432 sq. km (50,360 sq. miles): land 130,279 sq. km (50,301 sq. miles); inland water 153 sq. km (59 sq. miles).

POPULATION

The population at the 2001 census was 49,138,831. The average density of the population in 2001 was 377 persons per sq. km (976 per sq. mile).

FLAG

The flag of England is the cross of St George, a red cross on a white field (cross gules in a field argent). The cross of St George, the patron saint of England, has been used since the 13th century.

RELIEF

There is a marked division between the upland and lowland areas of England. In the extreme north the Cheviot Hills (highest point, the Cheviot, 815m/2,674ft) form a natural boundary with Scotland. Running south from the Cheviots, though divided from them by the Tyne Gap, is the Pennine range (highest point, Cross Fell, 893m/2,930ft), the main orological feature of the country. The Pennines culminate in the Peak District of Derbyshire (Kinder Scout, 636m/2,088ft). West of the Pennines are the Cumbrian mountains, which include Scafell Pike (978m/3,210ft), the highest peak in England, and to the east are the Yorkshire Moors, their highest point being Urra Moor (454m/1,490ft).

In the west, the foothills of the Welsh mountains extend into the bordering English counties of Shropshire (the Wrekin, 407m/1,334ft; Long Mynd, 516m/1,694ft) and Hereford and Worcester (the Malvern Hills – Worcestershire Beacon, 425m/1,394ft). Extensive areas of highland and moorland are also to be found in the south-western peninsula formed by Somerset, Devon and Cornwall, principally Exmoor (Dunkery Beacon, 519m/1,704ft), Dartmoor (High Willhays, 621m/2,038ft) and Bodmin Moor (Brown Willy, 420m/1,377ft). Ranges of low, undulating hills run across the south of the country, including the Cotswolds in the Midlands and south-west, the Chilterns to the north of London, and the North (Kent) and South (Sussex) Downs of the south-east coastal areas.

The lowlands of England lie in the Vale of York, East Anglia and the area around the Wash. The lowest-lying are the Cambridgeshire Fens in the valleys of the Great Ouse and the River Nene, which are below sea-level in places. Since the 17th century extensive drainage has brought much of the Fens under cultivation. The North Sea coast between the Thames and the Humber, low-lying and formed of sand and shingle for the most part, is subject to erosion and defences against further incursion have been built along many stretches.

HYDROGRAPHY

The Severn is the longest river in Great Britain, rising in the north-eastern slopes of Plynlimon (Wales) and entering England in Shropshire, with a total length of 354km (220 miles) from its source to its outflow into the Bristol Channel, where it receives the Bristol Avon on the east and the Wye on the west; its other tributaries are the Vyrnwy, Tern, Stour, Teme and Upper (or Warwickshire) Avon. The Severn is tidal below Gloucester, and a high bore or tidal wave sometimes reverses the flow as high as Tewkesbury (21.75km/13.5 miles above Gloucester). The scenery of the greater part of the river is very picturesque, and the Severn is a noted salmon river, with some of its tributaries being famous for trout. Navigation is assisted by the Gloucester and Berkeley Ship Canal (26km/16.25 miles), which admits vessels of 350 tons to Gloucester. The Severn Tunnel was begun in 1873 and completed in 1886 at a cost of £2m and after many difficulties caused by flooding. It is 7km (4 miles 628 yards) in length (of which 3.67km/2.25 miles are under the river). The Severn road bridge between Haysgate, Gwent, and Almondsbury, Glos, with a centre span of 988m (3,240ft), was opened in 1966.

The longest river wholly in England is the Thames, with a total length of 346km (215 miles) from its source in the Cotswold hills to the Nore, and is navigable by ocean-going ships to London Bridge. The Thames is tidal to Teddington (111km/69 miles from its mouth) and forms county boundaries almost throughout its course; on its banks are situated London, Windsor Castle, Eton College and Oxford University. Of the remaining English rivers, those flowing into the North Sea are the Tyne, Wear, Tees, Ouse and Trent from the Pennine Range, the Great Ouse (257km/160 miles), which rises in Northamptonshire, and the Orwell and Stour from the hills of East Anglia. Flowing into the English Channel are the Sussex Ouse from the Weald, the Itchen from the Hampshire Hills, and the Axe, Teign, Dart, Tamar and Exe from the Devonian hills. Flowing into the Irish Sea are the Mersey, Ribble and Eden from the western slopes of the Pennines and the Derwent from the Cumbrian mountains.

The English Lakes, notable for their picturesque scenery and poetic associations, lie in Cumbria's Lake District; the largest are Windermere (14.7 sq. km/5.7 sq. miles), Ullswater (8.8 sq. km/3.4 sq. miles) and Derwent Water (5.3 sq. km/2.0 sq. miles).

ISLANDS

The Isle of Wight is separated from Hampshire by the Solent. The capital, Newport, stands at the head of the estuary of the Medina, and Cowes (at the mouth) is the chief port. Other centres are Ryde, Sandown, Shanklin, Ventnor, Freshwater, Yarmouth, Totland Bay, Seaview and Bembridge.

Lundy (the name means Puffin Island), 18km (11 miles) north-west of Hartland Point, Devon, is around 5km (3 miles) long and almost 1km (half a mile) wide on average, with a total area of around 452 hectares (1,116 acres), and a population of around 18. It became the property of the National Trust in 1969 and is now principally a bird sanctuary.

The Isles of Scilly comprise around 140 islands and

skerries (total area, 10 sq. km/6 sq. miles) situated 45 km (28 miles) south-west of Land's End in Cornwall. Only five are inhabited: St Mary's, St Agnes, Bryher, Tresco and St Martin's. The population at the 2001 census was 2,153. The entire group has been designated an Area of Outstanding Natural Beauty because of its unique flora and fauna. Tourism and the winter/spring flower trade for the home market form the basis of the economy of the islands. The island group is a recognised rural development area.

EARLY HISTORY

Archaeological evidence suggests that England has been inhabited since at least the Palaeolithic period, though the extent of the various Palaeolithic cultures was dependent upon the degree of glaciation. The succeeding Neolithic and Bronze Age cultures have left abundant remains throughout the country; the best-known of these are the henges and stone circles of Stonehenge (ten miles north of Salisbury, Wilts) and Avebury (Wilts), both of which are believed to have been of religious significance. In the latter part of the Bronze Age the Goidels, a people of the Celtic race, invaded the country and brought with them Celtic civilisation and dialects; as a result place names in England bear witness to the spread of the invasion across the whole kingdom.

THE ROMAN CONQUEST

The Roman conquest of Gaul (57–50 BC) brought Britain into close contact with Roman civilisation, but although Julius Caesar raided the south of Britain in 55 and 54 BC, conquest was not undertaken until nearly 100 years later. In AD 43 the Emperor Claudius dispatched Aulus Plautius, with a well-equipped force of 40,000, and himself followed with reinforcements in the same year. Success was delayed by the resistance of Caratacus (Caractacus), the British leader from AD 48–51, who was finally captured and sent to Rome, and by a great revolt in AD 61 led by Boudicca (Boadicea), Queen of the Iceni, but the south of Britain was secured by AD 70, and Wales and the area north to the Tyne by about AD 80.

In AD 122, the Emperor Hadrian visited Britain and built a continuous rampart, since known as Hadrian's Wall, from Wallsend to Bowness (Tyne to Solway). The work was entrusted by the Emperor Hadrian to Aulus Platorius Nepos, legate of Britain from AD 122 to 126, and it was intended to form the northern frontier of the Roman Empire.

The Romans administered Britain as a province under a governor, with a well-defined system of local government, each Roman municipality ruling itself and its surrounding territory, while London was the centre of the road system and the seat of the financial officials of the Province of Britain. Colchester, Lincoln, York, Gloucester and St Albans stand on the sites of five Roman municipalities, and Wroxeter, Caerleon, Chester, Lincoln and York were at various times the sites of legionary fortresses. Well-preserved Roman towns have been uncovered at or near Silchester *(Calleva Atrebatum)*, ten miles south of Reading, Wroxeter *(Viroconium Cornoviorum)*, near Shrewsbury, and St Albans *(Verulamium)* in Hertfordshire.

Four main groups of roads radiated from London, and a fifth (the Fosse) ran obliquely from Lincoln through Leicester, Cirencester and Bath to Exeter. Of the four groups radiating from London, one ran south-east to Canterbury and the coast of Kent, a second to Silchester and thence to parts of western Britain and south Wales, a third (later known as Watling Street) ran through St Albans to Chester, with various branches, and the fourth reached Colchester, Lincoln, York and the eastern counties.

In the fourth century Britain was subjected to raids along the east coast by Saxon pirates, which led to the establishment of a system of coastal defences from the Wash to Southampton Water, with forts at Brancaster, Burgh Castle (Yarmouth), Walton (Felixstowe), Bradwell, Reculver, Richborough, Dover, Lympne, Pevensey and Porchester (Portsmouth). The Irish (Scoti) and Picts in the north were also becoming more aggressive and from around AD 350 incursions became more frequent and more formidable. As the Roman Empire came increasingly under attack towards the end of the fourth century, many troops were removed from Britain for service in other parts of the empire. The island was eventually cut off from Rome by the Teutonic conquest of Gaul, and with the withdrawal of the last Roman garrison early in the fifth century, the Romano-British were left to themselves.

SAXON SETTLEMENT

According to legend, the British King Vortigern called in the Saxons to defend his lands against the Picts. The Saxon chieftains Hengist and Horsa landed at Ebbsfleet, Kent, and established themselves in the Isle of Thanet, but the events during the one-and-a-half centuries between the final break with Rome and the re-establishment of Christianity are unclear. However, it would appear that over the course of this period the raids turned into large-scale settlement by invaders traditionally known as Angles (England north of the Wash and East Anglia), Saxons (Essex and southern England) and Jutes (Kent and the Weald), which pushed the Romano-British into the mountainous areas of the north and west. Celtic culture outside Wales and Cornwall survives only in topographical names. Various kingdoms established at this time attempted to claim overlordship of the whole country, hegemony finally being achieved by Wessex (with the capital at Winchester) in the ninth century. This century also saw the beginning of raids by the Vikings (Danes), which were resisted by Alfred the Great (871–899), who fixed a limit on the advance of Danish settlement by the Treaty of Wedmore (878), giving them the area north and east of Watling Street on the condition that they adopt Christianity.

In the tenth century the kings of Wessex recovered the whole of England from the Danes, but subsequent rulers were unable to resist a second wave of invaders. England paid tribute *(Danegeld)* for many years, and was invaded in 1013 by the Danes and ruled by Danish kings (including Cnut) from 1016 until 1042, when Edward the Confessor was recalled from exile in Normandy. On Edward's death in 1066 Harold Godwinson (brother-in-law of Edward and son of Earl Godwin of Wessex) was chosen to be King of England. After defeating (at Stamford Bridge, Yorkshire, 25 September) an invading army under Harald Hadraada, King of Norway (aided by the outlawed Earl Tostig of Northumbria, Harold's brother), Harold was himself defeated at the Battle of Hastings on 14 October 1066, and the Norman conquest secured the throne of England for Duke William of Normandy, a cousin of Edward the Confessor.

CHRISTIANITY

Christianity reached the Roman province of Britain from Gaul in the third century (or possibly earlier). Alban, traditionally Britain's first martyr, was put to death as a

Christian during the persecution of Diocletian (22 June 303) at his native town *Verulamium,* and the Bishops of *Londinium, Eboracum* (York), and *Lindum* (Lincoln) attended the Council of Arles in 314. However, the Anglo-Saxon invasions submerged the Christian religion in England until the sixth century: conversion was undertaken in the north from 563 by Celtic missionaries from Ireland led by St Columba, and in the south by a mission sent from Rome in 597 which was led by St Augustine, who became the first archbishop of Canterbury. England appears to have been converted again by the end of the seventh century and followed, after the Council of Whitby in 663, the practices of the Roman Church, which brought the kingdom into the mainstream of European thought and culture.

PRINCIPAL CITIES

There are 50 cities in England and space constraints prevent us from including profiles of them all. Below is a selection of England's principal cities with the date on which city status was conferred in parenthesis. Other cities are: Chichester (pre-1900), Derby (1977), Ely (pre-1900), Exeter (pre-1900), Gloucester (pre-1900), Hereford (pre-1900), Lancaster (1937), Lichfield (pre-1900), London (pre-1900), Peterborough (pre-1900), Plymouth (1928), Portsmouth (1926), Preston (2002), Ripon (pre-1900), Salford (1926), Sunderland (1992), Truro (pre-1900), Wakefield (pre-1900), Wells (pre-1900), Westminster (pre-1900), Wolverhampton (2000) and Worcester (pre-1900).

Certain cities have also been granted a lord mayoralty – this grant confers no additional powers or functions and is purely honorific. Cities with lord mayors are: Birmingham, Bradford, Bristol, Canterbury, Chester, Coventry, Exeter, Kingston-upon-Hull, Leeds, Leicester, Liverpool, London, Manchester, Newcastle-upon-Tyne, Norwich, Nottingham, Oxford, Plymouth, Portsmouth, Sheffield, Stoke-on-Trent, Westminster and York.

BATH (PRE-1900)

Bath stands on the River Avon between the Cotswold Hills to the north and the Mendips to the south. In the early 18th century, Bath became England's premier spa town where the rich and celebrated members of fashionable society gathered to 'take the waters' and enjoy the town's theatres and concert rooms. During this period the architect John Wood laid the foundations for a new Georgian city to be built using the honey-coloured stone for which Bath is famous today.

Contemporary Bath is a thriving tourist destination and remains a leading cultural, religious and historical centre with many art galleries and historic sites including the Pump Room (1790); the Royal Crescent (1767); the Circus (1754); the 18th-century Assembly Rooms (housing the Museum of Costume); Pulteney Bridge (1771); the Guildhall and the Abbey, now over 500 years old, which is built on the site of a Saxon monastery. In 2006 the Bath Thermae Spa was completed and the hot springs re-opened to the public for the first time since 1978; combining five historic spa buildings with contemporary architecture, it is the only spa in the UK to utilise naturally occurring thermal waters.

BIRMINGHAM (PRE-1900)

Birmingham is Britain's second largest city, with a population of nearly one million. The generally accepted derivation of 'Birmingham' is the *ham* (dwelling-place) of the *ing* (family) of *Beorma,* presumed to have been Saxon. During the Industrial Revolution the town grew into a major manufacturing centre and in 1889 was granted city status.

Recent developments include Millennium Point, which houses Thinktank, the Birmingham science museum, and Brindleyplace, a development of shops, offices and leisure facilities on a former industrial site clustered around canals. In 2003 the Bullring shopping centre was officially opened as part of the city's urban regeneration programme.

The principal buildings are the Town Hall (1834–50), the Council House (1879), Victoria Law Courts (1891), the University of Birmingham (1906–9), the 13th-century Church of St Martin-in-the-Bull-Ring (rebuilt 1873), the cathedral (formerly St Philip's Church) (1711), the Roman Catholic cathedral of St Chad (1839–41), the Assay Office (1773), the Rotunda (1964) and the National Exhibition Centre (1976). There is also the Birmingham Museum and Art Gallery which was founded in 1885 and is home to a collection of Pre-Raphaelite paintings.

BRADFORD (PRE-1900)

During the Industrial Revolution of the 18th and 19th centuries Bradford expanded rapidly, largely as a result of the thriving wool industry.

Bradford city centre has a host of buildings with historical and cultural interest, including City Hall, with its 19th-century Lord Mayor's rooms and Victorian law court; Bradford Cathedral; the Priestley, a theatre and arts centre originally established as the Bradford Civic Playhouse by J. B. Priestley and friends; the Colour Museum; the National Museum of Photography, Film and Television which houses five floors of interactive displays and three cinemas; Piece Hall Yard which incorporates the Bradford Club, a Victorian Gothic style building dating from 1837, and the Peace Museum.

BRIGHTON AND HOVE (2000)

Brighton and Hove is situated on the south coast of England, around 96 km (60 miles) south of London. Originally a fishing village called Brighthelmstone, it was transformed into a fashionable seaside resort in the 18th century when Dr Richard Russell popularised the benefits of his 'sea-water cure'; as one of the closest beaches to London, Brighton began to attract wealthy visitors. One of these was the Prince Regent (the future King George IV), who first visited in 1783 and became so fond of the city that in 1807 he bought the former farmhouse he had been renting, and gradually turned it into Brighton's most recognisable building, the Royal Pavilion. The Pavilion is renowned for its Indo-Saracenic exterior, featuring minarets and an enormous central dome designed by John Nash, combined with the lavish chinoiserie of Frederick Crace's and Robert Jones' interiors.

Brighton and Hove's Regency heritage can also be seen in the numerous elegant squares and crescents designed by Amon Wilds and Augustin Busby that dominate the seafront.

Brighton and Hove is once again a fashionable resort, known for its cafe culture, lively nightlife and thriving gay scene.

BRISTOL (PRE-1900)

Bristol was a royal borough before the Norman conquest. The earliest form of the name is *Bricgstow.*

The principal buildings include the 12th-century

athedral with Norman chapter house and gateway; the 4th-century Church of St Mary Redcliffe; Wesley's hapel, Broadmead; the Merchant Venturers' Almshouses; e Council House (1956); the Guildhall; the Exchange ected from the designs of John Wood in 1743); Cabot wer; the University and Clifton College. The Roman atholic cathedral at Clifton was opened in 1973.

The Clifton Suspension Bridge, with a span of 214m 02ft) over the Avon, was projected by Isambard ngdom Brunel in 1836 but was not completed until 64. Brunel's SS *Great Britain,* the first ocean-going opeller-driven ship, now forms a museum at the Western ockyard, from where she was originally launched in 43. The docks themselves have been extensively stored and redeveloped; the 19th-century two-storey rmer tea warehouse is now the Arnolfini centre for ntemporary arts, and an 18th-century sail loft houses e Architecture Centre. Behind the baroque-domed cade of the former 'E' Shed are shops, cafes, restaurants d the Watershed Media Centre, and on Princes Wharf sused transit sheds house the Industrial Museum.

AMBRIDGE (1951)

ambridge, a settlement far older than its ancient iversity, lies on the River Cam (or Granta). The city is a unty town and regional headquarters. Its industries clude technology research and development, and otechnology. Among its open spaces are Jesus Green, eep's Green, Coe Fen, Parker's Piece, Christ's Pieces, e University Botanic Garden, and the 'Backs' – lawns d gardens through which the Cam winds behind the incipal line of college buildings. Historical sites east of e Cam include King's Parade, Great St Mary's Church, bbs' Senate House and King's College Chapel.

University and college buildings provide the itstanding features of Cambridge's architecture but veral churches (especially St Benet's, the oldest building the city, and Holy Sepulchre or the Round Church) are so notable. The Guildhall (1937) stands on a site, of hich at least part has held municipal buildings since 224.

ANTERBURY (PRE-1900)

anterbury, seat of the Archbishop of Canterbury, the imate of the Church of England, dates back to ehistoric times. It was the Roman *Durovernum antiacorum* and the Saxon *Cant-wara-byrig* (stronghold the men of Kent). It was here in 597 that St Augustine gan the conversion of the English to Christianity, when helbert, King of Kent, was baptised.

Of the Benedictine St Augustine's Abbey, burial place the Jutish Kings of Kent, only ruins remain. St Martin's hurch, on the eastern outskirts of the city, is stated by de to have been the place of worship of Queen Bertha, e Christian wife of King Ethelbert, before the advent of Augustine.

In 1170 the rivalry of Church and State culminated in e murder in Canterbury Cathedral, by Henry II's ights, of Archbishop Thomas Becket. His shrine came a great centre of pilgrimage, as described in haucer's *Canterbury Tales.* After the Reformation lgrimages ceased, but the prosperity of the city was engthened by an influx of Huguenot refugees, who troduced weaving. The poet and playwright hristopher Marlowe was born and raised in Canterbury, d there are also literary associations with Defoe, ickens, Joseph Conrad and Somerset Maugham.

The cathedral, its architecture ranging from the 11th to the 15th centuries, is famous worldwide. Visitors are attracted particularly to the Martyrdom, the Black Prince's Tomb, the Warriors' Chapel and the many examples of medieval stained glass.

The medieval city walls are built on Roman foundations and the 14th-century West Gate is one of the finest buildings of its kind in the country.

The 1,000-seat Marlowe Theatre is a centre for the Canterbury Arts Festival each autumn.

CARLISLE (PRE-1900)

Carlisle is situated at the confluence of the River Eden and River Caldew, 497km (309 miles) north-west of London and around 16km (10 miles) from the Scottish border. It was granted a charter in 1158.

The city stands at the western end of Hadrian's Wall and dates from the original Roman settlement of *Luguvalium.* Granted to Scotland in the tenth century, Carlisle is not included in the Domesday Book. William Rufus reclaimed the area in 1092 and the castle and city walls were built to guard Carlisle and the western border; the citadel is a Tudor addition to protect the south of the city. Border disputes were common until the problem of the Debateable Lands was settled in 1552. During the Civil War the city remained Royalist; in 1745 Carlisle was besieged for the last time by the Young Pretender (Bonnie Prince Charlie).

The cathedral, originally a 12th-century Augustinian priory, was enlarged in the 13th and 14th centuries after the diocese was created in 1133. To the south is a restored tithe barn and nearby the 18th-century church of St Cuthbert, the third to stand on a site dating from the seventh century.

Carlisle is the major shopping, commercial and agricultural centre for the area, and industries include the manufacture of metal goods, biscuits and textiles. However, the largest employer is the services sector, most notably in central and local government, retailing and transport. The city occupies an important position at the centre of a network of major roads, as a stage on the main west coast rail services, and with its own airport at Crosby-on-Eden.

CHESTER (PRE-1900)

Chester is situated on the River Dee. Its recorded history dates from the first century when the Romans founded the fortress of *Deva.* The city's name is derived from the Latin *castra* (a camp or encampment). During the Middle Ages, Chester was the principal port of north-west England but declined with the silting of the Dee estuary and competition from Liverpool. The city was also an important military centre, notably during Edward I's Welsh campaigns and the Elizabethan Irish campaigns. During the Civil War, Chester supported the King and was besieged from 1643 to 1646. Chester's first charter was granted *c.*1175 and the city was incorporated in 1506. The office of sheriff is the earliest created in the country (1120s), and in 1992 the mayor was granted the title of Lord Mayor, who also enjoys the title 'Admiral of the Dee'.

The city's architectural features include the city walls (an almost complete two-mile circuit), the unique 13th-century Rows (covered galleries above the street-level shops), the Victorian Gothic Town Hall (1869), the castle (rebuilt 1788 and 1822) and numerous half-timbered buildings. The cathedral was a Benedictine abbey until the Dissolution of the Monasteries. Remaining monastic buildings include the chapter house, refectory and cloisters and there is a modern free-standing bell tower. The Norman church of St John the Baptist was a cathedral church in the early Middle Ages.

COVENTRY (PRE-1900)

Coventry is an important industrial centre, producing vehicles, machine tools, agricultural machinery, man-made fibres, aerospace components and telecommunications equipment. New investment has come from financial services, power transmission, professional services, leisure and education.

The city owes its beginning to Leofric, Earl of Mercia, and his wife Godiva who, in 1043, founded a Benedictine monastery. The guildhall of St Mary and three of the city's churches date from the 14th and 15th centuries, and 16th-century almshouses can still be seen. Coventry's first cathedral was destroyed during the Reformation, its second in the 1940 blitz (the walls and spire remain) and the new cathedral designed by Sir Basil Spence, consecrated in 1962, now draws numerous visitors.

Coventry is the home of the University of Warwick, Coventry University, the Westwood Business Park, the Museum of British Road Transport and the Skydome Arena.

DURHAM (PRE-1900)

The city of Durham is a major tourist attraction and its prominent Norman cathedral and castle are set high on a wooded peninsula overlooking the River Wear. The cathedral was founded as a shrine for the body of St Cuthbert in 995. The present building dates from 1093 and among its many treasures is the tomb of the Venerable Bede (673–735). Durham's prince bishops had unique powers up to 1836, being lay rulers as well as religious leaders. As a palatinate, Durham could have its own army, nobility, coinage and courts. The castle was the main seat of the prince bishops for nearly 800 years; it is now used as a college by the University of Durham. The university, founded in the early 19th century on the initiative of Bishop William Van Mildert, is England's third oldest.

Among other buildings of interest is the Guildhall in the Market Place which dates from the 14th century. Work has been carried out to conserve this area as part of the city's contribution to the Council of Europe's Urban Renaissance Campaign. Annual events include Durham's regatta in June (claimed to be the oldest rowing event in Britain) and the annual Gala (formerly Durham Miners' Gala) in July.

The economy has undergone a significant change with the replacement of mining as the dominant industry by 'white collar' employment. Although still a predominantly rural area, the industrial and commercial sectors are growing and a wide range of manufacturing and service industries are based on industrial estates in and around the city. A research and development centre, linked to the university, also plays an important role in the local economy.

KINGSTON-UPON-HULL (PRE-1900)

Hull (officially Kingston-upon-Hull, so named by Edward I) lies at the junction of the River Hull with the Humber, 35km (22 miles) from the North Sea. It is one of the major seaports of the United Kingdom. The port provides a wide range of cargo services, including ro-ro and container traffic, and handles an estimated million passengers annually on daily sailings to Rotterdam and Zeebrugge. There is a variety of manufacturing and service industries. City status was accorded in 1897 and the office of mayor raised to the dignity of Lord Mayor 1914.

The city, restored after heavy air raid damage duri the Second World War, has good educational faciliti with both the University of Hull and the Universi of Lincoln being within its boundaries. Hull is home the world's only submarium, The Deep, a £45.5 project which opened in 2002, and the Kingst Communications Stadium, with a seating capacity f 25,000, which was also completed in 2002.

Tourism is a growing industry; the old town area h been renovated and includes museums, a marina and shopping complex. Just west of the city is the Humb Bridge, the fourth-largest suspension bridge in the worl

LEEDS (PRE-1900)

Leeds, situated in the lower Aire Valley, is a junction f road, rail, canal and air services and an importa commercial centre. It was first incorporated by Charles in 1626. The earliest forms of the name are *Loidis* *Ledes,* the origins of which are obscure.

The principal buildings are the Civic Hall (1933), t Town Hall (1858), the Municipal Buildings and A Gallery (1884) with the Henry Moore Gallery (1982), t Corn Exchange (1863) and the University. The pari church (St Peter's) was rebuilt in 1841; the 17th-centu St John's Church has a fine interior with a famous Engli Renaissance screen; the last remaining 18th-centu church in the city is Holy Trinity in Boar Lane (172 Kirkstall Abbey (about three miles from the centre of t city), founded by Henry de Lacy in 1152, is one of t most complete examples of a Cistercian house no remaining. Temple Newsam, birthplace of Lord Darnl and largely rebuilt by Sir Arthur Ingram *c.*1620, w acquired by the council in 1922. Adel Church, about fi miles from the centre of the city, is a fine Norm structure. The Royal Armouries Museum forms part of group of museums, including the Tower of Londo which house the national collection of antique arms ar armour.

LEICESTER (1919)

Leicester is situated in central England. The city was important Roman settlement and also one of the fi Danish boroughs of Danelaw. In 1485 Richard III w buried in Leicester following his death at the nearb Battle of Bosworth. In 1589 Queen Elizabeth I granted charter to the city and the ancient title was confirmed letters patent in 1919.

The textile industry, responsible for Leicester's ear expansion, has declined in recent years, although the ci still maintains a strong manufacturing base. Cotton mi and factories are now undergoing extensive regeneratic and are being converted into offices, apartments, bars ar restaurants. The principal buildings include the tw universities (the University of Leicester and De Montfo University), as well as the Town Hall, the 13th-centu Guildhall, De Montfort Hall, Leicester Cathedral, th Jewry Wall (the UK's highest standing Roman wall), Nicholas Church and St Mary de Castro church. Th motte and Great Hall of Leicester can be seen from th castle gardens, situated next to the River Soar.

Leicester is now one of the UK's most ethnical diverse cities – home to the only Jain temple in th western world and hosting the country's second-large Caribbean carnival.

INCOLN (PRE-1900)

tuated 64km (40 miles) inland on the River Witham, ncoln derives its name from a contraction of *Lindum olonia*, the settlement founded in AD 48 by the Romans command the crossing of Ermine Street and Fosse Way. ctions of the third-century Roman city wall can be seen, cluding an extant gateway (Newport Arch), and cavations have discovered traces of a sewerage system ique in Britain. The Romans also drained the rrounding fenland and created a canal system, laying e foundations of Lincoln's agricultural prosperity and so the city's importance in the medieval wool trade as a rt and staple town.

As one of the five boroughs of Danelaw, Lincoln was an portant trading centre in the ninth and tenth centuries d prosperity from the wool trade lasted until the 14th ntury. This wealth enabled local merchants to build rish churches, of which three survive, and there are also mains of a 12th-century Jewish community (Jew's ouse and Court, Aaron's House). However, the removal the staple to Boston in 1369 heralded a decline, from hich the city only recovered fully in the 19th century, hen improved fen drainage made Lincoln agriculturally portant. Improved canal and rail links led to industrial velopment, mainly in the manufacture of machinery, mponents and engineering products.

The castle was built shortly after the Norman Conquest d is unusual in having two mounds; on one motte ands a keep (Lucy's Tower) added in the 12th century. It rrently houses one of the four surviving copies of the agna Carta. The cathedral was begun *c.*1073 when the st Norman bishop moved the see of Lindsey to Lincoln, t was mostly destroyed by fire and earthquake in the 2th century. Rebuilding was begun by St Hugh and mpleted over a century later. Other notable architectural atures are the 12th-century High Bridge, the oldest in itain still to carry buildings, and the Guildhall, situated ove the 15th–16th-century Stonebow gateway.

IVERPOOL (PRE-1900)

verpool, on the north bank of the River Mersey, 5km (3 iles) from the Irish Sea, is the United Kingdom's remost port for Atlantic trade. Tunnels link Liverpool ith Birkenhead and Wallasey.

There are 2,100 acres of dockland on both sides of the ver and the Gladstone and Royal Seaforth Docks can commodate tanker-sized vessels. Liverpool Free Port as opened in 1984.

Liverpool was created a free borough in 1207 and a ty in 1880. From the early 18th century it expanded pidly with the growth of industrialisation and Atlantic ade. Surviving buildings from this period include the uecoat Chambers (1717, formerly the Bluecoat School), e Town Hall (1754, rebuilt to the original design 795), and buildings in Rodney Street, Canning Street d the suburbs. Notable from the 19th and 20th nturies are the Anglican cathedral, built from the signs of Sir Giles Gilbert Scott (the foundation stone as laid in 1904, but the building was only completed in 980); the Catholic Metropolitan Cathedral (designed by r Frederick Gibberd, consecrated 1967) and St George's all (1842), regarded as one of the finest modern camples of classical architecture. The refurbished Albert ock (designed by Jesse Hartley) contains the Merseyside aritime Museum and Tate Gallery, Liverpool.

In 1852 an act was passed establishing a public library, useum and art gallery; as a result Liverpool had one of e first public libraries in the country. The Brown, Picton and Hornby libraries form one of the country's major collections. The Victoria Building of Liverpool University; the Royal Liver, Cunard and Mersey Docks & Harbour Company buildings at the Pier Head; the Municipal Buildings and the Philharmonic Hall are other examples of the city's fine architecture.

Six areas of Liverpool's maritime mercantile city were designated as UNESCO World Heritage Sites in 2004, and Liverpool has been elected as European Capital of Culture for 2008.

MANCHESTER (PRE-1900)

Manchester (the *Mamucium* of the Romans, who occupied it in AD 79) is a commercial and industrial centre engaged in the engineering, chemical, clothing, food processing and textile industries and in education. Banking, insurance and a growing leisure industry are among the prime commercial activities. The city is connected with the sea by the Manchester Ship Canal, opened in 1894, 57km (35.5 miles) long, and accommodating ships up to 15,000 tons.

The principal buildings are the Town Hall, erected in 1877 from the designs of Alfred Waterhouse, with a large extension of 1938; the Royal Exchange (1869, enlarged 1921); the Central Library (1934); Heaton Hall; the 17th-century Chetham Library; the Rylands Library (1900), which includes the Althorp collection; the university precinct; the 15th-century cathedral (formerly the parish church); the Manchester Central conference and exhibition centre and the Bridgewater Hall (1996) concert venue. Manchester is the home of the Hallé Orchestra, the Royal Northern College of Music, the Royal Exchange Theatre and numerous public art galleries.

To accommodate the Commonwealth Games held in the city in 2002, new sports facilities were built including a stadium, swimming pool complex and the National Cycling Centre.

The town received its first charter of incorporation in 1838 and was created a city in 1853.

NEWCASTLE UPON TYNE (PRE-1900)

Newcastle upon Tyne, on the north bank of the River Tyne, is 13km (8 miles) from the North Sea. A cathedral and university city, it is the administrative, commercial and cultural centre for north-east England and the principal port. It is an important manufacturing centre with a wide variety of industries.

The principal buildings include the Castle Keep (12th century), Black Gate (13th century), Blackfriars (13th century), West Walls (13th century), St Nicholas's Cathedral (15th century, fine lantern tower), St Andrew's Church (12th–14th century), St John's (14th–15th century), All Saints (1786 by Stephenson), St Mary's Roman Catholic Cathedral (1844), Trinity House (17th century), Sandhill (16th-century houses), Guildhall (Georgian), Grey Street (1834–9), Central Station (1846–50), Laing Art Gallery (1904), University of Newcastle Physics Building (1962) and Medical Building (1985), Civic Centre (1963), Central Library (1969) and Eldon Square shopping development (1976). Open spaces include the Town Moor (927 acres) and Jesmond Dene. Ten bridges span the Tyne at Newcastle, including the tilting Millennium Bridge (2001), which links the city with Gateshead to the south.

The city's name is derived from the 'new castle' (1080) erected as a defence against the Scots. In 1400 it was made a county, and in 1882 a city.

NORWICH (PRE-1900)

Norwich grew from an early Anglo-Saxon settlement near the confluence of the rivers Yare and Wensum, and now serves as provincial capital for the predominantly agricultural region of East Anglia. The name is thought to relate to the most northerly of a group of Anglo-Saxon villages or *wics*. The city's first known charter was granted in 1158 by Henry II.

Norwich serves its surrounding area as a market town and commercial centre, with banking and insurance prominent among the city's businesses. From the 14th century until the Industrial Revolution, Norwich was the regional centre of the woollen industry, but now the biggest single industry is financial services and principal trades are engineering, printing, shoemaking, the production of chemicals and clothing, food processing and technology. Norwich is accessible to seagoing vessels by means of the River Yare, entered at Great Yarmouth, 32km (20 miles) to the east.

Among many historic buildings are the cathedral (completed in the 12th century and surmounted by a 15th-century spire 96m (315ft) in height); the keep of the Norman castle (now a museum and art gallery); the 15th-century flint-walled Guildhall; some thirty medieval parish churches; St Andrew's and Blackfriars' Halls; the Tudor houses preserved in Elm Hill and the Georgian Assembly House. The University of East Anglia is on the city's western boundary.

NOTTINGHAM (PRE-1900)

Nottingham stands on the River Trent. *Snotingaham* or *Notingeham,* literally the homestead of the people of Snot, is the Anglo-Saxon name for the Celtic settlement of *Tigguocobauc,* or the house of caves. In 878, Nottingham became one of the five boroughs of Danelaw. William the Conqueror ordered the construction of Nottingham Castle, while the town itself developed rapidly under Norman rule. Its laws and rights were later formally recognised by Henry II's charter in 1155. The castle became a favoured residence of King John. In 1642 King Charles I raised his personal standard at Nottingham Castle at the start of the Civil War.

Nottingham is home to Notts County FC (the world's oldest football league side), Nottingham Forest FC, Nottingham Racecourse, Trent Bridge cricket ground and the National Watersports Centre. The principal industries include textiles, pharmaceuticals, food manufacturing, engineering and telecommunications. There are two universities within the city boundaries.

Architecturally, Nottingham has a wealth of notable buildings, particularly those designed in the Victorian era by T. C. Hine and Watson Fothergill. The city council owns the castle, of Norman origin but restored in 1878, Wollaton Hall (1580–8), Newstead Abbey (home of Lord Byron), the Guildhall (1888) and Council House (1929). St Mary's, St Peter's and St Nicholas' churches are of interest, as is the Roman Catholic cathedral (Pugin, 1842–4). Nottingham was granted city status in 1897.

OXFORD (PRE-1900)

Oxford is a university city, an important industrial centre and a market town. Industry played a minor part in Oxford until the motor industry was established in 1912.

Oxford is known for its architecture, its oldest specimens being the reputedly Saxon tower of St Michael's Church, the remains of the Norman castle and city walls, and the Norman church at Iffley. It also has many Gothic buildings, such as the Divinity Schools, the Old Library at Merton College, William of Wykeham New College, Magdalen and Christ Church colleges ar many other college buildings. Later centuries a represented by the Laudian quadrangle at St John College, the Renaissance Sheldonian Theatre by Wre Trinity College Chapel, All Saints Church, Hawksmoo mock-Gothic at All Souls College, and the 18th-centu Queen's College. In addition to individual building High Street and Radcliffe Square both form interestir architectural compositions. Most of the colleges ha gardens, those of Magdalen, New College, St John's ar Worcester being the largest.

ST ALBANS (PRE-1900)

The origins of St Albans, situated on the River Ver, ste from the Roman town of *Verulamium.* Named after th first Christian martyr in Britain, who was executed ther St Albans has developed around the Norman abbey ar cathedral church (consecrated 1115), built partly materials from the old Roman city. The museums hou Iron Age and Roman artefacts and the Roman theat unique in Britain, has a stage as opposed to amphitheatre. Archaeological excavations in the ci centre have revealed evidence of pre-Roman, Saxon ar medieval occupation.

The town's significance grew to the extent that it was signatory and venue for the drafting of the Magna Cart It was also the scene of riots during the Peasants' Revo the French King John was imprisoned there after th Battle of Poitiers, and heavy fighting took place the during the Wars of the Roses.

Previously controlled by the Abbot, the town achieve a charter in 1553 and city status in 1877. The stre market, first established in 1553, is still an importa feature of the city, as are many hotels and inns, survivin from the days when St Albans was an important coac stop. Tourist attractions include historic churches ar houses and a 15th-century clock tower.

The city is now home to a wide range of businesse with special emphasis on information and legal service In addition, it is home to the Royal National Rose Socie and Rothamsted Park, the agricultural research centre.

SALISBURY (PRE-1900)

The history of Salisbury centres around the cathedral an cathedral close. The city evolved from an Iron Age camp mile to the north of its current position which w strengthened by the Romans and called *Serviodunum.* Th Normans built a castle and cathedral on the site an renamed it Sarum. In 1220 Bishop Richard Poore and th architect Elias de Derham decided to build a new Goth style cathedral. The cathedral was completed 38 yea later and a community known as New Sarum, now calle Salisbury, grew around it. Originally the cathedral had squat tower; the 404ft spire that makes the cathedral th tallest medieval structure in the world was added *c.*131 A walled close with houses for the clergy was built arour the cathedral; the Medieval Hall still stands toda alongside buildings dating from the 13th to the 20 century, some designed by Sir Christopher Wren.

A prosperous wool and cloth trade allowed Salisbury flourish until the 17th century. When the wool trac declined new crafts were established including cutler leather and basket work, saddlery, lacemaking, joine and malting. By 1750 it had become an important ro junction and coaching centre and in the Victorian era th railways enabled a new age of expansion and prosperi Today Salisbury is a thriving tourist centre.

HEFFIELD (PRE-1900)

ıeffield is situated at the junction of the Sheaf, Porter, ıvelin and Loxley valleys with the River Don and was eated a city in 1893. Though its cutlery, silverware and ate have long been famous, Sheffield has other and now ore important industries: special and alloy steels, ıgineering, tool-making, medical equipment and media-lated industries (in its new cultural industries quarter). ıeffield has two universities and is an important research ntre.

The parish church of St Peter and St Paul, founded in e 12th century, became the cathedral church of the iocese of Sheffield in 1914. The Roman Catholic athedral Church of St Marie (founded 1847) was eated a cathedral for the new diocese of Hallam in)80. Parts of the present building date from *c.*1435. ıe principal buildings are the Town Hall (1897), the utlers' Hall (1832), City Hall (1932), Graves Art allery (1934), Mappin Art Gallery, the Crucible Theatre ıd the restored Lyceum theatre, which dates from 1897 ıd was reopened in 1990. Three major sports venues ere opened between 1990 and 1991: Sheffield Arena, on Valley Stadium and Pond's Forge. The Millennium allcries opened in 2001.

OUTHAMPTON (1964)

)uthampton is a major seaport on the south coast of ıgland, situated between the mouths of the Test and chen rivers. Southampton's natural deep-water harbour ıs made the area an important settlement since the omans built the first port (known as *Clausentum*) in the ·st century, and Southampton's port has witnessed veral important departures, including those of King enry V in 1415 for the Battle of Agincourt, RMS *itanic* in 1912, and the *Mayflower* in 1620.

The city's strategic importance, not only as a seaport ıt also as a centre for aircraft production, meant that it as heavily bombed during the Second World War; ɔwever, many historically significant structures remain, cluding the Wool House, dating from 1417 and now ;ed as the Maritime Museum; parts of the Norman city alls which are among the most complete in the UK; the argate, which was originally the main gateway into the ty; God's House Tower, now the Museum of rchaeology; St Michael's, the city's oldest church; and ıe Tudor Merchants Hall.

Home to the National Oceanography Centre, the ıternational Boat Show and some of the country's :incipal watersports venues, Southampton's coastal :tting and maritime history remain its main focus, but it so features extensive parks and a thriving entertainment :ene.

TOKE-ON-TRENT (1925)

:oke-on-Trent, standing on the River Trent and miliarly known as 'the potteries', is the main centre of nployment for the population of north Staffordshire. he city is the largest clayware producer in the world hina, earthenware, sanitary goods, refractories, bricks ıd tiles) and also has a wide range of other ıanufacturing industries, including steel, chemicals, ıgineering and tyres. Extensive reconstruction has been ırried out in recent years.

The city was formed by the federation of the separate ıunicipal authorities of Tunstall, Burslem, Hanley, Stoke, enton, and Longton in 1910 and received its city status ı 1925.

WINCHESTER (PRE-1900)

Winchester, the ancient capital of England, is situated on the River Itchen. The city is rich in architecture of all types, especially notable is the cathedral. Built in 1079–93 the cathedral exhibits examples of Norman, early English and Perpendicular styles and is the burial place of author Jane Austen. Winchester College, founded in 1382, is one of the country's most famous public schools, and the original building (1393) remains largely unaltered. St Cross Hospital, another great medieval foundation, lies one mile south of the city. The almshouses were founded in 1136 by Bishop Henry de Blois, and Cardinal Henry Beaufort added a new almshouse of 'Noble Poverty' in 1446. The chapel and dwellings are of great architectural interest, and visitors may still receive the 'Wayfarer's Dole' of bread and ale.

Excavations have done much to clarify the origins and development of Winchester. Part of the forum and several of the streets from the Roman town have been discovered. Excavations in the Cathedral Close have uncovered the entire site of the Anglo-Saxon cathedral (known as the Old Minster) and parts of the New Minster which was built by Alfred's son, Edward the Elder, and is the burial place of the Alfredian dynasty. The original burial place of St Swithun, before his remains were translated to a site in the present cathedral, was also uncovered.

Excavations in other parts of the city have thrown much light on Norman Winchester, notably on the site of the Royal Castle (adjacent to which the new Law Courts have been built) and in the grounds of Wolvesey Castle, where the great house built by Bishops Giffard and Henry de Blois in the 12th century has been uncovered. The Great Hall, built by Henry III between 1222 and 1236, survives and houses the Arthurian Round Table.

YORK (PRE-1900)

The city of York is an archiepiscopal seat. Its recorded history dates from AD 71, when the Roman Ninth Legion established a base under Petilius Cerealis that would later become the fortress of *Eburacum,* or *Eboracum.* In Anglo-Saxon times the city was the royal and ecclesiastical centre of Northumbria, and after capture by a Viking army in AD 866 it became the capital of the Viking kingdom of Jorvik. By the 14th century the city had become a great mercantile centre, mainly because of its control of the wool trade, and was used as the chief base against the Scots. Under the Tudors its fortunes declined, although Henry VIII made it the headquarters of the Council of the North. Excavations on many sites, including Coppergate, have greatly expanded knowledge of Roman, Viking and medieval urban life.

With its development as a railway centre in the 19th century the commercial life of York expanded, and today the city is home to the award-winning National Railway Museum. The principal industries are the manufacture of chocolate, scientific instruments and sugar.

The city is rich in examples of architecture of all periods. The earliest church was built in AD 627 and, from the 12th to 15th centuries, the present Minster was built in a succession of styles. Other examples within the city are the medieval city walls and gateways, churches and guildhalls. Domestic architecture includes the Georgian mansions of The Mount, Micklegate and Bootham.

LORD-LIEUTENANTS AND HIGH SHERIFFS

Area	*Lord-Lieutenant*	*High Sheriff (2007–8)*
Bedfordshire	S. Whitbread	Dr Vaughan Southgate
Berkshire	P. Wroughton	Harry Henderson
Bristol	Mary Prior, MBE	William Durie
Buckinghamshire	Sir Henry Aubrey-Fletcher	Amanda Nicholson
Cambridgeshire	Hugh Duberly, CBE	Col. Peter Horrell, TD
Cheshire	W. Bromley-Davenport	Nicholas Bromley-Davenport
Cornwall	Lady Mary Holborow	Hon. Evelyn Boscawen
Cumbria	J. Cropper	Claire Hensman
Derbyshire	J. Bather	Roger Wardle
Devon	E. Dancer, CBE	Anthony Mildmay-White
Dorset	Valerie Pitt-Rivers	Adrian Scott
Durham	Sir Paul Nicholson	Ian Dewhirst
East Riding of Yorkshire	Hon. Susan Cunliffe-Lister	Nicholas Hildyard
East Sussex	Mrs P. Stewart-Roberts, OBE	Caroline Mayhew
Essex	Lord Petre	Lady Kemp-Welch
Gloucestershire	Henry Elwes	Jonathan Carr
Greater London	Lord Imbert, QPM	Jan Pethick
Greater Manchester	Warren Smith	Michael Oglesby
Hampshire	Mrs M. Fagan	Sarah Thorne
Herefordshire	Sir Thomas Dunne, KCVO	John Yorke
Hertfordshire	Countess of Verulam	Howard Guard
Isle of Wight	Maj.-Gen. Martin White, CB, CBE	Lt.-Col. David Langford
Kent	Allan Willett, CMG	Nigel Wheeler
Lancashire	Lord Shuttleworth	Ruth Winterbottom
Leicestershire	Lady Gretton	Barry Jackson
Lincolnshire	Mrs B. Cracroft-Eley	Patricia Ware
Merseyside	Dame Lorna Fox Muirhead, DBE	Prof. Philip Love, CBE
Norfolk	Richard Jewson	Earl of Romney
North Yorkshire	Lord Crathorne	Philip Ingham
Northamptonshire	Lady Juliet Townsend	Lady Harper
Northumberland	Sir John Riddell, CVO	Sir Hugh Blackett, Bt.
Nottinghamshire	Sir Andrew Buchanan, Bt.	Cdr. Peter Moore, RD
Oxfordshire	H. Brunner	Thomas Loyd
Rutland	Dr Laurence Howard, OBE	Barbara Gilman
Shropshire	A. Heber-Percy	Meriel Afia, LVO
Somerset	Lady Gass	David Medlock
South Yorkshire	David Moody	Col. Jonathan Hunt, OBE, TD
Staffordshire	J. Hawley, TD	Graham Stow, CBE
Suffolk	Lord Tollemache	Air Marshal Sir Richard Kemball, KCB, CB
Surrey	Mrs S. Goad	Nicholas Sealy
Tyne and Wear	N. Sherlock, OBE	Hon. Nigel Westwood
Warwickshire	M. Dunne	Andrew Arkwright
West Midlands	Paul Sabapathy, CBE	Robert Tomlinson
West Sussex	H. Wyatt	Colin Field
West Yorkshire	Dr Ingrid Roscoe	Rhona Hartley, MBE
Wiltshire	John Bush, OBE	Hon. Peter Pleydell-Bouverie
Worcestershire	M. Brinton	John Yorke

COUNTY COUNCILS

uncil & Administrative Headquarters	*Telephone*	*Population**	*Council Tax†*	*Chief Executive*
dfordshire, Bedford	01234-363222	397,700	£1,082	Andrea Hill
ckinghamshire, Aylesbury	01296-395000	481,500	£975	Chris Williams
mbridgeshire, Cambridge	01223-717111	588,900	£932	Mike Parsons *(acting)*
eshire, Chester	0845-113 3311	679,900	£1,002	Jeremy Taylor
rnwall, Truro	01872-322000	519,400	£970	Sheila Healy
mbria, Carlisle	01228-606060	498,900	£1,070	Peter Stybelski
rbyshire, Matlock	01629-580000	747,500	£996	Nick Hodgson
von, Exeter	01392-382000	731,000	£1,024	Phil Norrey
rset, Dorchester	01305-251000	401,100	£1,049	David Jenkins
rham, Durham	0191-383 3000	499,800	£995	Mark Lloyd
st Sussex, Lewes	01273-481000	497,900	£1,048	Cheryl Miller, CBE
sex, Chelmsford	01245-492211	1,340,000	£1,004	Joanna Killian
oucestershire, Gloucester	01452-425000	575,200	£988	Peter Bungard
mpshire, Winchester	01962-841841	1,259,500	£956	Peter Robertson
rtfordshire, Hertford	01992-555555	1,048,200	£1,034	Caroline Tapster
nt, Maidstone	01622-671411	1,369,900	£964	Peter Gilroy
ncashire, Preston	0545-053 0000	1,156,100	£1,046	Chris Trinick
icestershire, Leicester	0116-232 3232	627,800	£970	John Sinnott
ncolnshire, Lincoln	01522-552222	678,700	£987	Tony McArdle
orfolk, Norwich	0844-800 8020	824,200	£1,052	David White
orth Yorkshire, Northallerton	01609-780780	582,000	£944	John Marsden
orthamptonshire, Northampton	01604-236236	651,800	£918	Rory Borealis *(acting)*
orthumberland, Morpeth	01670-533000	311,300	£1,111	Mark Henderson
ottinghamshire, Nottingham	0115-982 3823	762,700	£1,125	Roger Latham
xfordshire, Oxford	01865-792422	626,900	£1,049	Joanna Simons
ropshire, Shrewsbury	0845-678 9000	289,000	£976	Carolyn Downs
merset, Taunton	0845-345 9166	515,600	£963	Alan Jones
affordshire, Stafford	01785-223121	816,700	£948	Nigel Pursey
ffolk, Ipswich	0845-606 6067	692,100	£1,035	Mike More
rrey, Kingston upon Thames	020-8541 8800	1,075,500	£1,010	Richard Shaw
arwickshire, Warwick	01926-410410	533,900	£1,045	Jim Graham
est Sussex, Chichester	01243-777100	764,400	£1,051	Mark Hammond
iltshire, Trowbridge	01225-713000	446,600	£974	Dr Keith Robinson
orcestershire, Worcester	01905-763763	555,800	£944	Rob Sykes

ource: The Office of National Statistics – *Mid-2005 Population Estimates* (Crown copyright)
Average 2007–8 Band D council tax in the county area exclusive of precepts for fire and police authorities. County councils claim heir share of the combined council tax from the collection funds of the district authorities into whose area they fall. Average Band D council tax bills for the billing authority are given on the following pages

DISTRICT COUNCILS

District Council	*Telephone*	*Population**	*Council Tax*†	*Chief Executive*
Adur	01273-263000	59,100	£1,432	Ian Lowrie
Allerdale	01900-326333	96,300	£1,401	Gillian Bishop
Alnwick	01665-510505	32,200	£1,369	William Batey
Amber Valley	01773-570222	118,600	£1,370	Peter Carney
Arun	01903-737500	144,500	£1,373	Ian Sumnall
Ashfield	01623-450000	114,000	£1,489	Alan Mellor
Ashford	01233-637311	110,000	£1,285	David Hill
Aylesbury Vale	01296-585858	168,100	£1,346	Andrew Grant
Babergh	01473-822801	85,100	£1,354	Patricia Rockall
Barrow-in-Furness	01229-894900	70,100	£1,435	Tom Campbell
Basildon	01268-533333	167,000	£1,417	Bala Mahendran
Basingstoke and Deane	01256-844844	156,900	£1,247	Gordon Holdcroft
Bassetlaw	01909-533533	110,700	£1,490	David Hunter
Bedford	01234-267422	153,000	£1,443	Shaun Field
Berwick-upon-Tweed	01289-330044	26,200	£1,370	Jane Pannell
Blaby	0116-275 0555	91,400	£1,340	Sandra Whiles
Blyth Valley	01670-542000	81,600	£1,337	Geoff Paul
Bolsover	01246-240000	73,200	£1,431	Wes Lumley
Boston	01205-314200	58,000	£1,293	Michael Gallagher
Braintree	01376-552525	137,800	£1,358	Allan Reid
Breckland	01362-695333	127,100	£1,327	Trevor Holden
Brentwood	01277-312500	70,900	£1,345	Bob McLintock
Bridgnorth	01746-713100	52,200	£1,375	John Harmeston
Broadland	01603-431133	121,100	£1,372	Colin Bland
Bromsgrove	01527-873232	91,500	£1,355	Kevin Dicks
Broxbourne	01992-785555	86,400	£1,269	Mike Walker
Broxtowe	0115-917 7777	109,100	£1,491	Ruth Hyde
Burnley	01282-425011	87,700	£1,463	Steve Rumbelow
CAMBRIDGE CITY	01223-457000	124,000	£1,283	Rob Hammond
Cannock Chase	01543-462621	93,200	£1,362	Stephen Brown
CANTERBURY CITY	01227-862000	143,700	£1,317	Colin Carmichael
Caradon	01579-341000	82,100	£1,315	Byron Davies
CARLISLE CITY	01228-817000	105,200	£1,430	Maggie Mooney
Carrick	01872-224400	90,600	£1,314	John Winskill
Castle Morpeth	01670-535000	49,900	£1,406	Ken Dunbar
Castle Point	01268-882200	87,000	£1,393	David Marchant
Charnwood	01509-263151	160,100	£1,313	Brian Hayes
Chelmsford	01245-606606	161,100	£1,352	Steve Packham
Cheltenham	01242-262626	111,700	£1,342	Andrew North
Cherwell	01295-252535	134,200	£1,379	Clive Baynes *(acting)*
CHESTER CITY	01244-324324	118,600	£1,361	Paul Durham
Chesterfield	01246-345345	100,000	£1,333	David Shaw
Chester-le-Street	0191-387 1919	53,200	£1,399	Roy Templeman
Chichester	01243-785166	109,300	£1,332	John Marsland
Chiltern	01494-729000	89,800	£1,359	Alan Goodrum
Chorley	01257-515151	103,700	£1,417	Donna Hall
Christchurch	01202-495000	45,100	£1,416	Michael Turvey
Colchester	01206-282222	163,400	£1,355	Adrian Pritchard
Congleton	01270-763231	91,800	£1,371	Glyn Chambers
Copeland	0845-054 8600	71,500	£1,419	Liam Murphy
Corby	01536-464000	53,500	£1,250	Chris Mallender
Cotswold	01285-623000	83,100	£1,345	Bob Austin
Craven	01756-700600	54,400	£1,368	Gill Dixon
Crawley	01293-438000	98,500	£1,352	Michael Coughlin
Crewe and Nantwich	01270-537777	113,600	£1,331	Paul Ancell
Dacorum	01442-228000	138,500	£1,325	Daniel Zammit
Dartford	01322-343434	87,400	£1,313	Graham Harris

* *Source:* ONS – *Mid-2005 Population Estimates* (Crown copyright)
† Average Band D council tax bill for 2007–8

District Council	*Telephone*	*Population**	*Council Tax†*	*Chief Executive*
Daventry	01327-871100	75,900	£1,259	Ian Vincent
Derbyshire Dales	01629-761100	69,800	£1,403	David Wheatcroft
Derwentside	01207-218000	86,300	£1,462	Mike Clark
Dover	01304-821199	106,100	£1,326	Nadeem Aziz
DURHAM CITY	0191-386 6111	92,200	£1,409	Brian Spears
Easington	0191-527 0501	93,300	£1,539	Janet Johnson
East Cambridgeshire	01353-665555	78,500	£1,300	John Hill
East Devon	01395-516551	129,800	£1,357	Mark Williams
East Dorset	01202-886201	85,200	£1,459	Alan Breakwell
East Hampshire	01730-266551	111,300	£1,314	Will Godfrey
East Hertfordshire	01279-655261	131,800	£1,365	Anne Freimanis
East Lindsey	01507-601111	137,400	£1,245	Nigel Howells
East Northamptonshire	01832-742000	81,500	£1,253	David Oliver
East Staffordshire	01283-508000	106,900	£1,367	Simon Baker *(acting)*
Eastbourne	01323-410000	92,900	£1,448	Martin Ray
Eastleigh	023-8068 8000	116,600	£1,311	Bernie Topham
Eden	01768-817817	52,800	£1,413	Kevin Douglas
Ellesmere Port and Neston	0151-356 6789	80,600	£1,353	Stephen Ewbank
Elmbridge	01372-474474	130,300	£1,372	Rob Moran *(acting)*
Epping Forest	01992-564000	122,000	£1,372	Peter Hayward
Epsom and Ewell	01372-732000	68,500	£1,327	David Smith
Erewash	0115-907 2244	109,800	£1,359	Jeremy Jaroszek
EXETER CITY	01392-277888	117,600	£1,329	Philip Bostock
Fareham	01329-236100	108,500	£1,270	Alan Davies
Fenland	01354-654321	87,200	£1,370	Tim Pilsbury
Forest Heath	01638-719000	63,100	£1,359	David Burnip
Forest of Dean	01594-810000	80,900	£1,360	Tim Perrin
Fylde	01253-658658	76,400	£1,395	Phillip Woodward
Gedling	0115-901 3901	111,200	£1,470	Peter Murdock
GLOUCESTER CITY	01452-522232	111,300	£1,335	Julian Wain
Gosport	023-9258 4242	77,300	£1,328	Ian Lycett
Gravesham	01474-337000	95,200	£1,300	Jim Wintour
Great Yarmouth	01493-856100	92,500	£1,359	Richard Packham
Guildford	01483-505050	132,200	£1,336	David Hill
Hambleton	0845-121 1555	85,000	£1,291	Peter Simpson
Harborough	01858-828282	80,400	£1,342	Sue Smith
Harlow	01279-446611	77,700	£1,416	Malcolm Morley
Harrogate	01423-500600	155,300	£1,396	Michael Walsh
Hart	01252-622122	87,800	£1,325	Geoff Bonner
Hastings	0845-274 1066	84,600	£1,460	Roy Mawford
Havant	023 9247 4174	115,300	£1,314	Gwen Andrews
Hertsmere	020-8207 2277	93,900	£1,333	Eden Lee
High Peak	0845-129 7777	91,100	£1,377	Peter Sloman
Hinckley and Bosworth	01455-238141	102,800	£1,295	Steve Atkinson
Horsham	01403-215100	125,800	£1,337	Tom Crowley
Huntingdonshire	01480-388388	162,000	£1,306	David Monks
Hyndburn	01254-388111	81,600	£1,439	David Welsby
Ipswich	01473-432000	118,200	£1,462	James Hehir
Kennet	01380-724911	77,400	£1,345	Mark Boden
Kerrier	01209-614000	96,200	£1,316	Barry Manning
Kettering	01536-410333	86,000	£1,269	David Cook
King's Lynn and West Norfolk	01553 616200	140,400	£1,358	Ray Harding
LANCASTER CITY	01524-582000	138,000	£1,406	Mark Cullinan
Lewes	01273-471600	93,400	£1,479	John Crawford
Lichfield	01543-308000	95,500	£1,331	Nina Dawes
LINCOLN CITY	01522-881188	87,000	£1,331	Andrew Taylor
Macclesfield	01625-500500	150,500	£1,345	Vivienne Horton
Maidstone	01622-602000	143,400	£1,363	David Petford
Maldon	01621-854477	60,700	£1,375	Steve Watson
Malvern Hills	01684-862151	75,100	£1,337	Chris Bocock
Mansfield	01623-463463	99,000	£1,497	Ruth Marlow
Melton	01664-502502	48,300	£1,338	Lynn Aisbett
Mendip	01749-343399	107,300	£1,357	David Thomson
Mid Bedfordshire	08452-304040	129,400	£1,456	Jaki Salisbury
Mid Devon	01884-255255	73,000	£1,413	David Ablett *(acting)*
Mid Suffolk	01449-720711	89,900	£1,355	Andrew Good
Mid Sussex	01444-458166	129,000	£1,357	John Jory

District Council	*Telephone*	*Population**	*Council Tax†*	*Chief Executive*
Mole Valley	01306-885001	81,100	£1,325	Darren Mepham
New Forest	023-8028 5000	171,700	£1,338	David Yates
Newark and Sherwood	01636-650000	110,800	£1,540	Andrew Muter
Newcastle-under-Lyme	01782-717717	123,400	£1,340	Mark Barrow
North Cornwall	01208-893333	84,100	£1,322	Mark Hall
North Devon	01271-327711	90,200	£1,405	John Sunderland
North Dorset	01258-454111	65,400	£1,411	Elizabeth Goodall
North East Derbyshire	01246-231111	97,300	£1,426	Mrs Lee Adams
North Hertfordshire	01462-474000	120,700	£1,361	John Campbell
North Kesteven	01529-414155	101,700	£1,297	Ian Fytche
North Norfolk	01263-513811	100,200	£1,371	Philip Burton
North Shropshire	01939-232771	59,100	£1,406	Nicola Yates
North Warwickshire	01827-715341	62,300	£1,420	Jeremy Hutchinson
North West Leicestershire	01530-454545	88,800	£1,364	Christine Fisher
North Wiltshire	01249-706111	129,400	£1,381	Delwyn Burbidge
Northampton	01604-837837	195,000	£1,289	John Edwards *(acting)*
NORWICH CITY	01603-212212	127,600	£1,422	Laura McGillivray
Nuneaton and Bedworth	02476-376376	120,700	£1,383	Christine Kerr
Oadby and Wigston	0116-288 8961	56,000	£1,345	Wendy Back
Oswestry	01691-671111	39,200	£1,440	Paul Shevlin
OXFORD CITY	01865-249811	149,800	£1,429	Peter Sloman
Pendle	01282-661661	89,300	£1,466	Stephen Barnes
Penwith	01736-362341	64,000	£1,263	Jim McKenna
PRESTON CITY	01772-906900	131,300	£1,463	Jim Carr
Purbeck	01929-556561	45,100	£1,443	Steve Mackenzie
Redditch	01527-64252	79,600	£1,354	Christopher Smith
Reigate and Banstead	01737-276000	127,200	£1,366	Nigel Clifford
Restormel	01726-223300	100,300	£1,276	Gareth Pinwell
Ribble Valley	01200-425111	56,900	£1,373	David Morris
Richmondshire	01748-829100	50,700	£1,383	Jack Neal
Rochford	01702-546366	79,500	£1,389	Paul Warren
Rossendale	01706-217777	66,000	£1,471	Carolyn Wilkins
Rother	01424-787878	86,000	£1,431	Derek Stevens
Rugby	01788-533533	91,600	£1,369	Simon Warren
Runnymede	01932-838383	79,600	£1,302	Tim Williams
Rushcliffe	0115-981 9911	107,800	£1,488	Allen Graham
Rushmoor	01252-398398	89,200	£1,307	Andrew Lloyd
Ryedale	01653-600666	52,000	£1,379	Janet Waggott
ST ALBANS CITY	01727-866100	133,500	£1,361	Daniel Goodwin
St Edmundsbury	01284-763233	101,500	£1,370	Deborah Cadman
SALISBURY CITY	01722-336272	115,800	£1,323	David Crook *(acting)*
Scarborough	01723-232323	107,000	£1,391	Jim Dillon
Sedgefield	01388-816166	87,800	£1,566	Brian Allen
Sedgemoor	0845-408 2540	109,900	£1,322	Mr Kerry Rickards
Selby	01757-705101	77,600	£1,370	Martin Connor
Sevenoaks	01732-227000	111,100	£1,363	Robin Hales
Shepway	01303-853000	99,500	£1,396	Alistair Stewart
Shrewsbury and Atcham	01743-281000	96,300	£1,366	Robin Hooper
South Bedfordshire	01582-472222	115,300	£1,527	Jon Ruddick
South Bucks	01895-837200	63,500	£1,341	Chris Furness
South Cambridgeshire	08450-450500	137,200	£1,293	Greg Harlock
South Derbyshire	01283-221000	87,700	£1,353	Frank McArdle
South Hams	01803-861234	82,800	£1,379	Ruth Bagley
South Holland	01775-761161	81,200	£1,288	Terry Huggins
South Kesteven	01476-406080	128,500	£1,265	Duncan Kerr
South Lakeland	01539-733333	102,900	£1,421	Peter Ridgway
South Norfolk	01508-533633	115,300	£1,393	Geoff Rivers
South Northamptonshire	0845-230 0226	86,000	£1,287	Jean Morgan
South Oxfordshire	01491-823000	128,200	£1,364	David Buckle
South Ribble	01772-421491	105,800	£1,426	Jean Hunter
South Shropshire	01584-813000	42,300	£1,443	Graham Biggs
South Somerset	01935-462462	156,100	£1,361	Philip Dolan
South Staffordshire	01902-696000	105,300	£1,301	Rolf Levesley
Spelthorne	01784-451499	88,500	£1,335	Roberto Tambini
Stafford	01785-619000	123,600	£1,320	David Rawlings
Staffordshire Moorlands	01538-483483	94,600	£1,340	Simon Baker
Stevenage	01438-242242	79,000	£1,339	Peter Ollis

District Council	*Telephone*	*Population**	*Council Tax†*	*Chief Executive*
Stratford-on-Avon	01789-267575	119,000	£1,355	Paul Lankester
Stroud	01453-766321	110,000	£1,388	David Hagg
Suffolk Coastal	01394-383789	119,600	£1,342	Stephen Baker
Surrey Heath	01276-707100	81,500	£1,362	Barry Catchpole
Swale	01795-424341	126,800	£1,303	Mark Bilsborough
Tamworth	01827-709709	74,200	£1,301	David Weatherley
Tandridge	01883-722000	79,400	£1,366	Stephen Weigel
Taunton Deane	01823-356356	106,800	£1,312	Penny James
Teesdale	01833-690000	24,900	£1,433	Neil Stokell
Teignbridge	01626-361101	124,500	£1,383	Nicola Bulbeck
Tendring	01255-686868	141,800	£1,344	John Hawkins
Test Valley	01264-368000	112,300	£1,270	Roger Tetstall
Tewkesbury	01684-295010	78,400	£1,288	Bob Austin
Thanet	01843-577000	128,100	£1,348	Richard Samuel
Three Rivers	01923-776611	84,600	£1,353	Steven Halls
Tonbridge and Malling	01732-844522	112,400	£1,332	David Hughes
Torridge	01237-428700	62,500	£1,385	John van de Laarschot
Tunbridge Wells	01892-526121	106,200	£1,306	Sheila Wheeler
Tynedale	01434-652121	59,800	£1,381	Richard Robson
Uttlesford	01799-510400	71,100	£1,363	Alasdair Bovaird
Vale of White Horse	01235-520202	117,000	£1,336	Terry Stock
Vale Royal	01606-862862	124,600	£1,357	Anne Bingham-Holmes
Wansbeck	01670-532200	61,700	£1,356	Bob Stephenson
Warwick	01926-450000	140,300	£1,342	Chris Elliott
Watford	01923-226400	79,300	£1,409	Alastair Robertson
Waveney	01502-562111	114,700	£1,317	Glen Garrod
Waverley	01483-523333	116,800	£1,365	Mary Orton
Wealden	01892-653311	141,000	£1,470	Charles Lant
Wear Valley	01388-765555	62,100	£1,423	Michael Lainge
Wellingborough	01933-229777	73,900	£1,227	Lyn Martin-Bennison
Welwyn & Hatfield	01707-357000	100,500	£1,383	Michel Saminaden
West Devon	01822-813600	50,600	£1,434	David Incoll
West Dorset	01305-251010	95,800	£1,432	David Clarke
West Lancashire	01695-577177	109,500	£1,416	William Taylor
West Lindsey	01427-676676	84,900	£1,329	Duncan Sharkey
West Oxfordshire	01993-861000	97,700	£1,309	David Neudegg
West Somerset	01643-703704	35,500	£1,334	Tim Howes
West Wiltshire	01225-776655	124,100	£1,369	Andrew Pate
Weymouth and Portland	01305-838000	64,600	£1,501	Tom Grainger
WINCHESTER CITY	01962-840222	112,500	£1,308	Simon Eden
Woking	01483-755855	90,500	£1,372	Ray Morgan
WORCESTER CITY	01905-723471	94,300	£1,314	David Wareing
Worthing	01903-239999	98,100	£1,367	Ian Lowrie
Wychavon	01386-565000	116,900	£1,305	Jack Hegarty
Wycombe	01494-461000	160,200	£1,320	Ms K. Satterford
Wyre	01253-891000	109,900	£1,397	Jim Corry
Wyre Forest	01562-732928	98,500	£1,361	Walter Delin

Councils in CAPITAL LETTERS have city status

METROPOLITAN BOROUGH COUNCILS

Metropolitan Borough Councils	*Telephone*	*Population**	*Council Tax†*	*Chief Executive*
Barnsley	01226-770770	222,100	£1,278	Philip Coppard
BIRMINGHAM CITY	0121-303 9944	1,001,200	£1,189	Stephen Hughes
Bolton	01204-333333	265,400	£1,321	Bernard Knight
BRADFORD CITY	01274-432001	485,000	£1,206	Tony Reeves
Bury	0161-253 5000	183,500	£1,289	Mark Sanders
Calderdale	01422-357257	195,300	£1,360	Paul Sheehan
COVENTRY CITY	024-7683 3333	304,200	£1,349	Stella Manzie
Doncaster	01302-734444	289,600	£1,179	Paul Hart *(acting)*
Dudley	01384-812345	305,600	£1,145	Andrew Sparke
Gateshead	0191-433 3000	191,500	£1,468	Roger Kelly
Kirklees	01484-221000	394,600	£1,290	Rob Vincent
Knowsley	0151-489 6000	149,400	£1,297	Sheena Ramsey
LEEDS CITY	0113-234 8080	723,100	£1,188	Paul Rogerson
LIVERPOOL CITY	0151-233 3000	447,500	£1,379	Colin Hilton
MANCHESTER CITY	0161-234 5000	441,200	£1,235	Sir Howard Bernstein
NEWCASTLE UPON TYNE CITY	0191-232 8520	276,400	£1,396	Ian Stratford
North Tyneside	0191-200 6565	192,300	£1,367	Andrew Kerr
Oldham	0161-911 3000	219,200	£1,481	Andrew Kilburn
Rochdale	01706-647474	206,400	£1,317	Roger Ellis
Rotherham	01709-382121	253,200	£1,320	Mike Cuff
St Helens	01744-456000	176,300	£1,279	Carole Hudson
SALFORD CITY	0161-794 4711	216,400	£1,414	Barbara Spicer
Sandwell	0121-569 2200	286,300	£1,248	Allison Fraser
Sefton	0151-922 4040	280,900	£1,351	Graham Haywood
SHEFFIELD CITY	0114-272 6444	520,700	£1,386	Sir Robert Kerslake
Solihull	0121-704 6000	200,900	£1,200	Katherine Kerswell
South Tyneside	0191-427 1717	151,300	£1,331	Irene Lucas
Stockport	0161-480 4949	281,600	£1,376	John Schultz
SUNDERLAND CITY	0191-553 1000	283,700	£1,247	Jed Fitzgerald
Tameside	0161-342 8355	214,100	£1,251	Janet Callender
Trafford	0161-912 1212	213,200	£1,152	David McNulty
WAKEFIELD CITY	01924-306090	320,600	£1,172	John Foster
Walsall	01922-650000	253,500	£1,383	Dave Martin *(acting)*
Wigan	01942-244991	306,700	£1,277	Joyce Redfern
Wirral	0151-638 7070	313,100	£1,330	Stephen Maddox
WOLVERHAMPTON CITY	01902-556556	239,600	£1,348	Richard Carr

* *Source:* ONS – *Mid-2005 Population Estimates* (Crown copyright)
† Average Band D council tax bill for 2007–8
Councils in CAPITAL LETTERS have city status

UNITARY COUNCILS

Unitary Councils	*Telephone*	*Population**	*Council Tax†*	*Chief Executive*
Bath and North East Somerset	01225-477000	173,700	£1,318	John Everitt
Blackburn with Darwen	01254-585585	140,200	£1,381	Graham Burgess
Blackpool	01253-477477	142,900	£1,359	Steve Weaver
Bournemouth	01202-451451	163,600	£1,330	Pam Donnellan
Bracknell Forest	01344-424642	111,200	£1,210	Timothy Wheadon
BRIGHTON AND HOVE CITY	01273-290000	255,000	£1,342	Alan McCarthy
BRISTOL CITY	0117-922 2000	398,300	£1,424	Nick Gurney
Darlington	01325-380651	99,200	£1,278	Ada Burns
DERBY CITY	01332-293111	233,700	£1,217	Ray Cowlishaw
East Riding of Yorkshire	01482-887700	327,400	£1,356	Nigel Pearson
Halton	0151-424 2061	118,800	£1,221	Tony McDermot
Hartlepool	01429-266522	90,000	£1,497	Paul Walker
Herefordshire	01432-260000	178,800	£1,336	Neil Pringle
Isle of Wight	01983-821000	140,000	£1,319	Joe Duckworth
Isles of Scilly‡	01720-422537	2,100	£1,028	Philip Hygate
KINGSTON UPON HULL CITY	01482-609100	249,100	£1,244	Mr Kim Ryley
LEICESTER CITY	0116-254 9922	288,000	£1,248	Rodney Green
Luton	01582-546000	184,900	£1,234	Kevin Crompton
Medway	01634-306000	251,100	£1,178	Neil Davies
Middlesbrough	01642-245432	137,600	£1,337	Jan Richmond
Milton Keynes	01908-691691	218,500	£1,261	John Best
North East Lincolnshire	01472-313131	157,500	£1,407	George Krawiec
North Lincolnshire	01724-296296	157,100	£1,400	Simon Driver
North Somerset	01934-888888	195,100	£1,319	Graham Turner
NOTTINGHAM CITY	0115-915 5555	278,700	£1,418	Michael Frater
PETERBOROUGH CITY	01733-563141	159,700	£1,235	Gillian Beasley
PLYMOUTH CITY	01752-668000	246,100	£1,295	Barry Keel
Poole	01202-633633	137,100	£1,279	John McBride
PORTSMOUTH CITY	023-9282 2251	189,600	£1,226	David Williams
Reading	0118-939 0900	145,100	£1,379	Trish Haines
Redcar and Cleveland	0845-612 6126	138,600	£1,383	Colin Moore
Rutland	01572-722577	37,300	£1,534	Helen Briggs
Slough	01753-475111	117,500	£1,219	Ruth Bagley
South Gloucestershire	01454-868686	248,100	£1,371	Amanda Deeks
SOUTHAMPTON CITY	023-8022 3855	222,000	£1,316	Brad Roynon
Southend-on-Sea	01702-215000	159,300	£1,174	Robert Tinlin
Stockton-on-Tees	01642-393939	186,700	£1,321	George Garlick
STOKE-ON-TRENT CITY	01782-234567	238,300	£1,262	Steve Robinson
Swindon	01793-463000	184,000	£1,271	Gavin Jones
Telford and Wrekin	01952-202100	161,600	£1,296	Steve Wellings
Thurrock	01375-652652	146,600	£1,188	Angie Ridgwell
Torbay	01803-201201	132,800	£1,332	Colin Gamble
Warrington	01925-444400	194,700	£1,217	Diana Terris
West Berkshire	01635-42400	146,300	£1,362	Nick Carter
Windsor and Maidenhead	01628-683800	138,500	£1,215	David Lunn, OBE
Wokingham	0118-974 6000	153,600	£1,308	Doug Patterson
YORK CITY	01904-613161	186,800	£1,232	David Atkinson

* *Source:* ONS – *Mid-2005 Population Estimates* (Crown copyright)
† Average Band D council tax bill for 2007–8
‡ Under the Isles of Scilly Clause the council has additional functions to other unitary authorities and certain other functions are performed by Cornwall County Council for the benefit of the Isles of Scilly
Councils in CAPITAL LETTERS have city status

MAP OF COUNCILS IN ENGLAND

LONDON

THE CITY OF LONDON CORPORATION

The City of London is the historic centre at the heart of London known as 'the square mile' around which the vast metropolis has grown over the centuries. The City's residential population is roughly 9,000 and in addition, over 320,000 people work in the City. The civic government is carried on by the City of London Corporation through the court of Common Council.

The City is an international financial and business centre, generating about £30bn a year for the British economy. It includes the head offices of the principal banks, insurance companies and mercantile houses, in addition to buildings ranging from the historic Roman Wall and the 15th-century Guildhall, to the massive splendour of St Paul's Cathedral and the architectural beauty of Wren's spires.

The City of London was described by Tacitus in AD 62 as 'a busy emporium for trade and traders'. Under the Romans it became an important administration centre and hub of the road system. Little is known of London in Saxon times, when it formed part of the kingdom of the East Saxons. In 886 Alfred recovered London from the Danes and reconstituted it a burgh under his son-in-law. In 1066 the citizens submitted to William the Conqueror who in 1067 granted them a charter, which is still preserved, establishing them in the rights and privileges they had hitherto enjoyed.

THE MAYORALTY

The mayoralty was probably established about 1189, the first mayor being Henry Fitz Ailwyn who filled the office for 23 years and was succeeded by Fitz Alan (1212–14). A new charter was granted by King John in 1215, directing the mayor to be chosen annually, which has been done ever since, though in early times the same individual often held the office more than once. A familiar instance is that of 'Whittington, thrice Lord Mayor of London' (in reality four times, 1397, 1398, 1406, 1419); and many modern cases have occurred. The earliest instance of the phrase 'lord mayor' in English is in 1414. It was used more generally in the latter part of the 15th century and became invariable from 1535 onwards. At Michaelmas the liverymen in Common Hall choose two aldermen who have served the office of sheriff for presentation to the Court of Aldermen, and one is chosen to be lord mayor for the following mayoral year.

LORD MAYOR'S DAY

The lord mayor of London was previously elected on the feast of St Simon and St Jude (28 October), and from the time of Edward I, at least, was presented to the King or to the Barons of the Exchequer on the following day, unless that day was a Sunday. The day of election was altered to 16 October in 1346, and after some further changes was fixed for Michaelmas Day in 1546, but the ceremonies of admittance and swearing-in of the lord mayor continued to take place on 28 and 29 October respectively until 1751. In 1752, at the reform of the calendar, the lord mayor was continued in office until 8 November, the 'new style' equivalent of 28 October. The lord mayor is now presented to the lord chief justice at the royal courts of justice on the second Saturday in November to make the final declaration of office, having been sworn in at Guildhall on the preceding day. The procession to the royal courts of justice is popularly known as the Lord Mayor's Show.

REPRESENTATIVES

Aldermen are mentioned in the 11th century and their office is of Saxon origin. They were elected annually between 1377 and 1394, when an act of parliament of Richard II directed them to be chosen for life.

The Common Council was, at an early date, substituted for a popular assembly called the *Folkmote*. At first only two representatives were sent from each ward, but now each of the City's 25 wards is represented by an alderman and at least two Common Councilmen (the number depending on the size of the ward).

OFFICERS

Sheriffs were Saxon officers; their predecessors were the *wic-reeves* and *portreeves* of London and Middlesex. At first they were officers of the Crown, and were named by the Barons of the Exchequer; but Henry I (in 1132) gave the citizens permission to choose their own Sheriffs, and the annual election of Sheriffs became fully operative under King John's charter of 1199. The citizens lost this privilege, as far as the election of the Sheriff of Middlesex was concerned, by the Local Government Act 1888; but the liverymen continue to choose two Sheriffs of the City of London, who are appointed on Midsummer Day and take office at Michaelmas.

The office of Chamberlain is an ancient one, the first contemporary record of which is 1237. The town clerk (or Common Clerk) is first mentioned in 1274.

ACTIVITIES

The work of the City of London Corporation is assigned to a number of committees which present reports to the Court of Common Council. These committees are: Barbican Centre; Barbican Residential; Board of Governors of the City of London Freeman's School, the City of London School, the City of London School for Girls, the Guildhall School of Music and Drama and the Museum of London; City Bridge Trust; City Lands and Bridge House Estates; Community and Children's Services; Court of Alderman; Court of Common Council; Education; Epping Forest and Commons; Establishment; Finance; Freedom Applications; Gresham (city side); Guildhall Improvement; Guildhall Yard East Building; Hampstead Heath Consultative; Hampstead Heath Management; Joint Working Party of the Three Schools; Keats House Management; Libraries, Archives and Guildhall Art Gallery; Licensing; Livery; London Drug Policy Forum; Managers of West Ham Park; Markets; Open Spaces; Planning and Transportation; Police; Policy and Resources; Port Health and Environmental Services; Queen's Park and Highgate Wood Management and Standards Committees.

The City's estate, in the possession of which the City of London Corporation differs from other municipalities, is managed by the City Lands and Bridge House Estates Committee, the chairmanship of which carries with it the title of Chief Commoner.

The Honourable the Irish Society, which manages the City Corporation's estates in Ulster, consists of a governor and five other aldermen, the recorder, and 19 Common Councilmen, of whom one is elected deputy governor.

THE LORD MAYOR 2007–8

The Rt. Hon. the Lord Mayor, David Lewis*
Private Secretary, Kay Brock
* Provisional at time of going to press

THE SHERIFFS 2007–8

Michael Bear (Portsoken); Ian Luder (Castle Baynard)

OFFICERS, ETC

Town Clerk, Chris Duffield
Chamberlain, Chris Bilsland
Chief Commoner (2007), Pauline Halliday
Clerk, The Honourable the Irish Society, C. Fisher

THE ALDERMEN

with office held and date of appointment to that office

Name and Ward	*CC*	*Ald.*	*Shff*	*Lord Mayor*
Sir Richard Nichols, *Candlewick*	1983	1984	1994	1997
Lord Levene of Portsoken, KBE, *Aldgate*	1983	1984	1995	1998
Sir David Howard, Bt., *Cornhill*	1972	1986	1997	2000
Sir Michael Oliver, *Bishopsgate*	1980	1987	1997	2001
Sir Gavyn Arthur, *Cripplegate*	1988	1991	1998	2002
Sir Robert Finch, *Coleman Street*	–	1992	1999	2003
Sir Michael Savory, *Bread Street*	1980	1996	2001	2004
Sir David Brewer, *Bassishaw*	1992	1996	2002	2005
John Stuttard, *Lime Street*	–	2001	2005	2006

All the above have passed the Civic Chair

Nicholas Anstee, *Aldersgate*	1987	1996	2003
John Hughesdon, *Billingsgate*	1991	1997	2004
David Lewis, *Broad Street*	–	2001	2007
Dr Andrew Parmley, *Vintry*	1992	2001	
Simon Walsh, *Farringdon Wt.*	1989	2000	
Robert Hall, *Farringdon Wn.*	1995	2002	
Alison Gowman, *Dowgate*	1991	2002	
Richard Walduck, OBE, *Tower*	–	2003	
Gordon Haines, *Queenhithe*	–	2004	
Colin Hart, *Cheap*	–	2004	
Roger Gifford, *Cordwainer*	–	2004	
David Mauleverer, *Walbrook*	–	2005	2001
Ian Luder, *Castle Baynard*	1998	2005	
Michael Bear, *Portsoken*	2003	2005	
David Wootton, *Langbourn*	2002	2005	
Alan Yarrow, *Bridge*	–	2007	

THE COMMON COUNCIL

Deputy: each Common Councilman so described serves as deputy to the alderman of her/his ward.

Abrahams, G. C. (2000)	*Farringdon Wt.*
Absalom, J. D. (1994)	*Farringdon Wt.*
Altman, L. P., CBE (1996)	*Cripplegate Wn.*
Ayers, K. E. (1996)	*Bassishaw*
Bain-Stewart, A. (2005)	*Farringdon Wn.*
Barker, *Deputy* J. A., OBE (1981)	*Cripplegate*
Bennett, J. A. (2005)	*Broad Street*
Bird, J. L., OBE (1977)	*Tower*
Boleat, M. J. (2002)	*Cordwainer*
Bradshaw, D. J. (1991)	*Cripplegate Wn.*
Brewster, J. W., OBE (1994)	*Bassishaw*
Burleigh, I. B. (2005)	*Portsoken*
Campbell-Taylor, Revd W. G. (2005)	*Portsoken*
Carrington, M. L. (2004)	*Lime Street*
Cassidy, *Deputy* M. J., CBE (1989)	*Coleman Street*
Catt, R. M. (2004)	*Castle Baynard*
Cenci Di Bello, Mrs P. J. (2004)	*Farringdon Wn.*
Chadwick, R. A. H. (1994)	*Tower*
Challis, N. K. (2005)	*Castle Baynard*
Chapman, N. K. (2006)	*Langbourn*
Cohen, Mrs C. M., OBE (1986)	*Lime Street*
Cotgrove, D. (1991)	*Lime Street*
Currie, *Deputy* Miss S. E. M. (1985)	*Cripplegate Wt.*
Day, M. J. (2005)	*Bishopsgate*
Dove, W. H., MBE (1993)	*Bishopsgate*
Duckworth, S. (2000)	*Bishopsgate*
Dudley, Revd Dr M. R. (2002)	*Aldersgate*
Duffield, R. W. (2004)	*Farringdon Wn.*
Eskenzi, *Deputy* A. N., CBE (1970)	*Farringdon Wn.*
Eve, *Deputy* R. A. (1980)	*Cheap*
Everett, K. M. (1984)	*Candlewick*
Farr, M. C. (1998)	*Walbrook*
Farrow, *Deputy* M. W. W. (1996)	*Farringdon Wt.*
FitzGerald, *Deputy* R. C. A. (1981)	*Bread Street*
Fraser, S. J. (1993)	*Coleman Street*
Fraser, *Deputy* W. B., OBE (1981)	*Vintry*
Galloway, *Deputy* A. D., OBE (1981)	*Broad Street*
Gillon, G. M. F. (1995)	*Cordwainer*
Ginsburg, *Deputy* S. (1990)	*Bishopsgate*
Graves, A. C. (1985)	*Bishopsgate*
Haines, Revd S. D. (2005)	*Cornhill*
Halliday, *Deputy* Mrs P. A. (1992)	*Walbrook*
Hardwick, Dr P. B. (1987)	*Aldgate*
Harris, B. N. (2004)	*Bridge*
Henderson-Begg, M. (1977)	*Coleman Street*
Hilliard, N. R. M. (2005)	*Farringdon Wt.*
Hoffman, T. D. D. (2002)	*Vintry*
Holland, *Deputy* J., CBE (1972)	*Aldgate*
Hudson, M. (2007)	*Castle Baynard*
Hughes-Penney, R. C. (2004)	*Farringdon Wn.*
Hunt, W. G. (2004)	*Castle Baynard*
Jackson, L. St J. T. (1978)	*Bread Street*
Jones, H. L. M. (2004)	*Portsoken*
Kellett, Mrs M. W. F. (1986)	*Tower*
Kemp, D. L. (1984)	*Coleman Street*
King, *Deputy* A. J. N. (1999)	*Queenhithe*
Knowles, *Deputy* S. K. (1984)	*Candlewick*
Lawrence, *Deputy* G. A. (2002)	*Farringdon Wt.*
Leck, P. (1998)	*Aldersgate*
Lee, *Deputy* Revd Dr B. J. (2001)	*Portsoken*
Lord, C. E. (2001)	*Coleman Street*
Luder, I. D. (1998)	*Castle Baynard*
McGuinness, *Deputy* C. S. (1997)	*Castle Baynard*
Malins, J. H., QC (1981)	*Farringdon Wt.*
Martinelli, *Deputy* P. J. (1994)	*Bassishaw*
Mayhew, J. P. (1996)	*Aldersgate*
Mead, Mrs W. (1997)	*Farringdon Wt.*
Mobsby, *Deputy* D. J. L. (1985)	*Billingsgate*

Mooney, B. D. F. (1998) *Queenhithe*
Moss, A. D. (1989) *Tower*
Moys, Mrs S. D. (2001) *Aldgate*
Nash, *Deputy* Mrs J. C., OBE (1983) *Aldersgate*
Newman, Mrs P. B., CBE (1989) *Aldersgate*
Nove, P. R., CBE (2004) *Castle Baynard*
Owen, *Deputy* Mrs J., MBE (1975) *Langbourn*
Owen-Ward, J. R. (1983) *Bridge*
Page, M. (2002) *Farringdon Wn.*
Pembroke, *Deputy* Mrs A. M. F. (1978) *Cheap*
Pollard, J. H. G. (2002) *Dowgate*
Price, E. E. (1996) *Farringdon Wt.*
Pulman, *Deputy* G. A. G. (1983) *Tower*
Punter, C. (1993) *Cripplegate Wn.*
Quilter, S. D. (1998) *Cripplegate Wt.*
Regan, R. D. (1998) *Farringdon Wn.*
Robinson, Mrs D. C. (1989) *Bishopsgate*
Roney, *Deputy* E. P. T., CBE (1974) *Bishopsgate*
Scott, J. G. S. (1999) *Broad Street*
Shalit, *Deputy* D. M. (1972) *Farringdon Wn.*
Sherlock, *Deputy* M. R. C. (1992) *Dowgate*
Simons, J. L. (2004) *Castle Baynard*
Snyder, *Deputy* M. J. (1986) *Cordwainer*
Spanner, J. H. (2001) *Farringdon Wt.*
Starling, Mrs A. J. (2006) *Cripplegate Wt.*
Stevenson, F. P. (1994) *Cripplegate Wn.*
Thompson, D. J. (2004) *Aldgate*
Tomlinson, J. (2004) *Cripplegate Wt.*
Twogood, M. (2004) *Farringdon Wt.*
Wang, *Deputy* Mrs C. A. M. (2004) *Cornhill*
Welbank, J. M. (2005) *Billingsgate*
Willoughby, *Deputy* P. J. (1985) *Bishopsgate*

THE CITY GUILDS (LIVERY COMPANIES)

he constitution of the livery companies has been nchanged for centuries. There are three ranks of nembership: freemen, liverymen and assistants. A person an become a freeman by patrimony (through a parent aving been a freeman); by servitude (through having erved an apprenticeship to a freeman); or by redemption by purchase).

Election to the livery is the prerogative of the company, who can elect any of its freemen as liverymen. Assistants re usually elected from the livery and form a Court of ssistants which is the governing body of the company. he master (in some companies called the prime warden) s elected annually from the assistants.

The register for 2007–8 lists 24,344 liverymen of the uilds entitled to vote at elections at Common Hall.

The order of precedence, omitting extinct companies, is iven in parentheses after the name of each company in he list below. In certain companies the election of Master r Prime Warden for the year does not take place until the utumn. In such cases the master or prime warden for 006–7, rather than 2007–8, is given.

HE TWELVE GREAT COMPANIES

n order of civic precedence

MERCERS *(1). Hall,* Mercers' Hall, Ironmonger Lane, London EC2V 8HE *Livery,* 244. *Clerk,* Charles Parker *Master,* Frederick Hohler

GROCERS *(2). Hall,* Grocers' Hall, Princes Street, London EC2R 8AD *Livery,* 349. *Clerk,* Brig. Robert Pridham, OBE *Master,* J. Scott

DRAPERS *(3). Hall,* Drapers' Hall, Throgmorton Avenue, London EC2N 2DQ *Livery,* 293. *Clerk,* Rear-Adm. Alastair Ross, CB, CBE *Master,* Stephen Foakes, TD

FISHMONGERS *(4). Hall,* Fishmongers' Hall, London Bridge, London EC4R 9EL *Livery,* 342. *Clerk,* Keith Waters *Prime Warden,* Sir Matthew Farrer, GCVO

GOLDSMITHS *(5). Hall,* Goldsmiths' Hall, Foster Lane, London EC2V 6BN *Livery,* 260. *Clerk,* R. Melly *Prime Warden,* Prof. R. Himsworth, FRCP

SKINNERS *(6/7). Hall,* Skinners' Hall, 8 Dowgate Hill, London EC4R 2SP *Livery,* 400. *Clerk,* Maj.-Gen. Brian Plummer, CBE *Master,* Patrick Tudor Crosthwaite

MERCHANT TAYLORS *(6/7). Hall,* Merchant Taylors' Hall, 30 Threadneedle Street, London EC2R 8JB *Livery,* 285. *Clerk,* Rear-Adm. Nick Harris, CB, MBE *Master,* H. Stubbs

HABERDASHERS *(8). Hall,* 18 West Smithfield, London EC1A 9HQ *Livery,* 285. *Clerk,* Rear-Adm. Richard Phillips, CB *Master,* M. Jeans (from November 2007, subject to election), MBE

SALTERS *(9). Hall,* Salters' Hall, 4 Fore Street, London EC2Y 5DE *Livery,* 159. *Clerk,* Capt. D. Morris, RN *Master,* D. Blackwell

IRONMONGERS *(10). Hall,* Ironmongers' Hall, 1 Shaftesbury Place, London EC2Y 8AA *Livery,* 133. *Clerk,* Col. Hamon Massey *Master,* Jonathan Hudson

VINTNERS *(11). Hall,* Vintners' Hall, Upper Thames Street, London EC4V 3BG *Livery,* 312. *Clerk,* Brig. Michael Smythe, OBE *Master,* A. Edwards

CLOTHWORKERS *(12). Hall,* Clothworkers' Hall, Dunster Court, Mincing Lane, London EC3R 7AH *Livery,* 228. *Clerk,* Andrew Blessley *Master,* Christopher Jonas

OTHER CITY GUILDS

In alphabetical order

ACTUARIES *(91).* 3rd Floor Cheapside House, 138 Cheapside, London EC2V 6BW *Livery,* 221. *Clerk,* David Johnson *Master,* Chris Ide

AIR PILOTS AND AIR NAVIGATORS *(81). Hall,* Cobham House, 9 Warwick Court, Gray's Inn, London WC1R 5DJ *Livery,* 600. *Clerk,* Paul Tacon *Grand Master,* HRH The Duke of York, KG, KCVO, ADC(P) *Master,* Gp Capt. R. Gault

APOTHECARIES *(58). Hall,* Apothecaries' Hall, 14 Black Friars Lane, London EC4V 6EJ *Livery,* 1,274. *Clerk,* A. Wallington-Smith *Master,* Ami Paris, FRCS

ARBITRATORS *(93).* 13 Hall Gardens, Colney Heath, St Albans, Herts AL4 0QF *Livery,* 175. *Clerk,* Gaye Duffy *Master,* Michael Stevens

ARMOURERS AND BRASIERS *(22). Hall,* Armourers' Hall, 81 Coleman Street, London EC2R 5BJ *Livery,* 122. *Clerk,* Cdre Christopher Waite *Master,* Prof. William Bonfield, CBE, FRS, FRENG

BAKERS *(19). Hall,* Bakers' Hall, Harp Lane, London EC3R 6DP *Livery,* 300. *Clerk,* John Tompkins *Master,* J. Renshaw (from 26 November subject to election)

BARBERS *(17). Hall,* Barber-Surgeons' Hall, Monkwell Square, Wood Street, London EC2Y 5BL *Livery,* 210. *Clerk,* Col. Peter Durrant, MBE *Master,* Prof. John Christopher Buckland-Wright, DSC

BASKETMAKERS *(52).* 29 Ingram House, Park Road, Hampton Wick, Surrey KT1 4BA *Livery,* 300. *Clerk,* Roger de Pilkyngton *Prime Warden,* Richard Walduck, OBE

BLACKSMITHS *(40).* 48 Upwood Road, London SE12 8AN *Livery,* 235. *Clerk,* Christopher Jeal *Prime Warden,* John McCuin

BOWYERS *(38).* 5 Archer House, Vicarage Crescent, London SW11 3LF *Livery,* 97. *Clerk,* Richard Wilkinson *Master,* Richard Model

BREWERS *(14). Hall,* Brewers' Hall, Aldermanbury Square, London EC2V 7HR *Livery,* 180. *Clerk,* Brig. D. Ross, CBE *Master,* M. Thomas

BRODERERS *(48)*. Ember House, 35–37 Creek Road, East Molesey, Surrey KT8 9BE *Livery*, 154. *Clerk*, Peter Crouch *Master*, Brig. D. Chaundler, OBE

BUILDERS MERCHANTS *(88)*. 4 College Hill, London EC4R 2RB *Livery*, 202. *Clerk*, T. Statham *Master*, John O'Carroll-Bailey

BUTCHERS *(24)*. *Hall*, Butchers' Hall, 87 Bartholomew Close, London EC1A 7EB *Livery*, 635. *Clerk*, Cdre Anthony Morrow, CVO *Master*, John Tuckwell

CARMEN *(77)*. 5 Kings House, 1 Queen Street Place, London EC4R 1QS *Livery*, 500. *Clerk*, Walter Gill *Master*, Montague Meyer

CARPENTERS *(26)*. *Hall*, Carpenters' Hall, 1 Throgmorton Avenue, London EC2N 2JJ *Livery*, 184. *Clerk*, Brig. T. Gregson *Master*, Michael Mathews

CHARTERED ACCOUNTANTS *(86)*. The Rustlings, Valley Close, Studham, Dunstable LU6 2QN *Livery*, 340. *Clerk*, Clifford Bygrave *Master*, H. P. Gold

CHARTERED ARCHITECTS *(98)*. 82A Muswell Hill Road, London N10 3JR *Livery*, 142. *Clerk*, David Cole-Adams *Master*, Jonathan Ball, MBE

CHARTERED SECRETARIES AND ADMINISTRATORS *(87)*. 3rd Floor, Saddlers' House, 40 Gutter Lane, London EC2V 6BR *Livery*, 261. *Clerk*, Col. Michael Dudding, OBE, TD *Master*, Adèle Thorpe

CHARTERED SURVEYORS *(85)*. 75 Meadway Drive, Horsell, Woking, Surrey GU21 4TF *Livery*, 345. *Clerk*, Amanda Jackson *Master*, David Larkin

CLOCKMAKERS *(61)*. Salters' Hall, 4 Fore Street, London EC2Y 5DE *Livery*, 270. *Clerk*, Joseph Buxton *Master*, David Poole

COACHMAKERS AND COACH-HARNESS MAKERS *(72)*. Elm Tree Cottage, Bottom House Farm Lane, Chalfont St Giles, Buckinghamshire HP8 4EE *Livery*, 400. *Clerk*, Gp Capt. Gerry Bunn, CBE *Master*, Andrew Love

CONSTRUCTORS *(99)*. Forge Farmhouse, Glassenbury, Cranbrook, Kent TN17 2QE *Livery*, 135. *Clerk*, Tim Nicholson *Master*, Martin Wade, FRICS

COOKS *(35)*. Coombe Ridge, Thursley Road, Churt, Farnham, Surrey GU10 2LQ *Livery*, 76. *Clerk*, Michael Thatcher, LLB *Master* (subject to election), Alan Granger Fairbrass

COOPERS *(36)*. *Hall*, Coopers' Hall, 13 Devonshire Square, London EC2M 4TH *Livery*, 260. *Clerk*, Lt.-Col. Adrian Carroll *Master*, Richard Sibley

CORDWAINERS *(27)*. Clothworkers' Hall, Dunster Court, Mincing Lane, London EC3R 7AH *Livery*, 168. *Clerk*, John Miller *Master*, James Calder

CURRIERS *(29)*. Hedgerley, 10 The Leaze, Ashton Keynes, Wiltshire SN6 6PE *Livery*, 93. *Clerk*, Gp Capt. David Moss *Master*, His Hon. Judge Lawson, QC

CUTLERS *(18)*. *Hall*, Cutlers' Hall, Warwick Lane, London EC4M 7BR *Livery*, 100. *Clerk*, J. Allen *Master*, R. Randolph

DISTILLERS *(69)*. 71 Lincoln's Inn Fields, London WC2A 3JF *Livery*, 260. *Clerk*, C. Hughes *Master*, Derek Plant

DYERS *(13)*. *Hall*, Dyers' Hall, 10 Dowgate Hill, London EC4R 2ST *Livery*, 129. *Clerk*, J. Vaizey *Prime Warden*, J. Chambers

ENGINEERS *(94)*. Wax Chandlers' Hall, 6 Gresham Street, London EC2V 7AD *Livery*, 300. *Clerk*, Air Vice-Marshal Graham Skinner, CBE *Master*, Rear-Adm. David Bawtree, CB

ENVIRONMENTAL CLEANERS *(97)*. 6 Grange Meadows, Elmswell, Bury St Edmunds, Suffolk IP30 9GE *Livery*, 268. *Clerk*, Michael Bizley *Master*, Michael Bayless

FAN MAKERS *(76)*. Skinners' Hall, 8 Dowgate Hill, London EC4R 2SP *Livery*, 202. *Clerk*, Keith Patterson *Master*, His Hon. Judge Connor

FARMERS *(80)*. *Hall*, The Farmers' and Fletchers' Hall, 3 Cloth Street, London EC1A 7LD *Livery*, 300. *Clerk*, Col. David King, OBE *Master*, T. Copas

FARRIERS *(55)*. 19 Queen Street, Chipperfield, Kings Langley, Herts WD4 9BT *Livery*, 321. *Clerk*, Charlotte Clifford *Master*, Col. Richard Kinsella-Bevan

FELTMAKERS *(63)*. Post Cottage,Greywell, Hook, Hampshire RG29 1DA *Livery*, 171. *Clerk*, Maj. J. Coombs *Master*, Derek Bonham

FIREFIGHTERS *(103)*. The Insurance Hall, 20 Aldermanbury, London EC2V 7HY *Livery*, 76. *Clerk*, Martin Bonham *Master*, Vivian Jones

FLETCHERS *(39)*. *Hall*, The Farmers' and Fletchers' Hall, 3 Cloth Street, London EC1A 7LD *Livery*, 143. *Clerk*, Capt. Michael Johnson, RN *Master*, Peter Scott

FOUNDERS *(33)*. *Hall*, Founders' Hall, 1 Cloth Fair, London EC1A 7JQ *Livery*, 155. *Clerk*, A. Gillett *Master*, J. Kelly, RD

FRAMEWORK KNITTERS *(64)*. 86 Park Drive, Upminster, Essex RM14 3AS *Livery*, 215. *Clerk*, Alan Clark *Master*, Hugh Stevenson

FRUITERERS *(45)*. Chapelstones, 84 High Street, Codford St Mary, Warminster BA12 0ND *Livery*, 283. *Clerk*, Lt.-Col. L. French *Master*, I. Robins

FUELLERS *(95)*. 26 Merrick Square, London SE1 4JB *Livery*, 125. *Clerk*, Sir Anthony Reardon Smith, Bt. *Master*, David Bell

FURNITURE MAKERS *(83)*. *Hall*, Furniture Makers' Hall, 12 Austin Friars, London EC2N 2HE *Livery*, 295. *Clerk*, Mrs J. Wright *Master*, George Mitchell

GARDENERS *(66)*. 25 Luke Street, London EC2A 4AR *Livery*, 285. *Clerk*, Trevor Hines *Master*, Alderman Sir Gavyn Arthur

GIRDLERS *(23)*. *Hall*, Girdlers' Hall, Basinghall Avenue, London EC2V 5DD *Livery*, 80. *Clerk*, Brig. I. Rees *Master*, R. Roberts

GLASS SELLERS *(71)*. 57 Witley Court, Coram Street, London WC1N 1HD *Livery*, 230. *Clerk*, Col. Audrey Smith *Master*, Sir Anthony Hammond, KCB, QC

GLAZIERS AND PAINTERS OF GLASS *(53)*. *Hall*, Glaziers' Hall, 9 Montague Close, London SE1 9DD *Livery*, 240. *Clerk*, Alex Galloway, CVO *Master*, David Ball, FRENG

GLOVERS *(62)*. Oscar Court, 17A Tite Street, London SW3 4JR *Livery*, 250. *Clerk*, Carole Blackshaw *Master*, John Brown, CBE

GOLD AND SILVER WYRE DRAWERS *(74)*. Middleton House, Winterslow, Salisbury, Wiltshire SP5 1QR *Livery*, 305. *Clerk*, Cdr. R. House, RN *Master*, J. Simmons

GUNMAKERS *(73)*. The Proof House, 48–50 Commercial Road, London E1 1LP *Livery*, 310. *Clerk*, Col. W. Chesshyre *Master*, S. Urry

HACKNEY CARRIAGE DRIVERS *(104)*. 25 The Grove, Parkfield, Latimer, Buckinghamshire HP5 1UE *Livery*, 98. *Clerk*, Mary Whitworth *Master*, Alan Parker

HORNERS *(54)*. c/o Clergy House, Hide Place, London SW1P 4NJ *Livery*, 224. *Clerk*, Raymond Layard *Master*, David Oxley

INFORMATION TECHNOLOGISTS *(100)*. *Hall*, Information Technologists' Hall, 39A Bartholomew Close, London EC1A 7JN *Livery*, 287. *Clerk*, Michael Grant *Master*, David Morriss

INNHOLDERS *(32)*. *Hall*, Innholders' Hall, 30 College Street, London EC4R 2RH *Livery*, 154. *Clerk*, Dougal Bulger *Master*, Cdr. Hugh Evans

INSURERS *(92)*. The Hall, 20 Aldermanbury, London

EC2V 7HY *Livery,* 380. *Clerk,* L. Walters *Master,* Graham Doswell

INTERNATIONAL BANKERS *(106).* 12 Austin Friars, London EC2N 2HE *Livery,* 109. *Clerk,* Wg Cdr Tim Woods, BEM *Master,* Angus MacLennan

JOINERS AND CEILERS *(41).* 75 Meadway Drive, Horsell, Woking, Surrey GU21 4TF *Livery,* 128. *Clerk,* Amanda Jackson *Master,* David Latham

LAUNDERERS *(89). Hall,* Launderers' Hall, 9 Montague Close, London Bridge, London SE1 9DD *Livery,* 240. *Clerk,* Mrs J. Polek *Master,* Selwin Burchhardt

LEATHERSELLERS *(15). Hall,* Leathersellers' Hall, 15 St Helen's Place, London EC3A 6DQ *Livery,* 150. *Clerk,* Jonathan Cooke *Master,* Anthony Collinson

LIGHTMONGERS *(96).* Crown Wharf, 11A Coldharbour, Blackwall Reach, London E14 9NS *Livery,* 194. *Clerk,* Derek Wheatley *Master,* Martin Tratte

LORINERS *(57).* Hampton House, High Street, East Grinstead, West Sussex RH19 3AW *Livery,* 344. *Clerk,* Peter Lusty *Master,* Dr Nigel Berman

MAKERS OF PLAYING CARDS *(75).* 2 Cannon Way, West Molesey, Surrey KT8 2NB *Livery,* 146. *Clerk,* Paul Bowen *Master,* Adrian Maurice

MANAGEMENT CONSULTANTS *(105).* Copperfield, The Ridgeway, Cranleigh GU6 7HR *Livery,* 170. *Clerk,* Lt.-Col. Dennis Hall *Master,* H. Morris

MARKETORS *(90).* 13 Hall Gardens, Colney Heath, St Albans, Herts AL4 0QF *Livery,* 298. *Clerk,* Mrs G. Duffy *Master,* Keith Arundale

MASONS *(30).* 22 Cannon Hill, Southgate, London N14 6LG *Livery,* 132. *Clerk,* P. Clark *Master,* G. Everett

MASTER MARINERS *(78). Hall,* HQS Wellington, Temple Stairs, Victoria Embankment, London WC2R 2PN *Livery,* 197. *Clerk,* Cdr. Rod Craig, RN *Master,* Capt. E. Scott

MUSICIANS *(50).* 6th Floor, 2 London Wall Building, London EC2M 5PP *Livery,* 381. *Clerk,* Mrs M. Alford *Master,* Leslie East

NEEDLEMAKERS *(65).* PO Box 3682, Windsor, Berkshire SL4 3WR *Livery,* 200. *Clerk,* Philip Grant *Master,* Dr Simon Fradd

PAINTER-STAINERS *(28). Hall,* Painters' Hall, 9 Little Trinity Lane, London EC4V 2AD *Livery,* 320. *Clerk,* Chris Twyman *Master,* P. Gandy

PATTENMAKERS *(70).* 3 The High Street, Sutton Valence, Kent ME17 3AG *Livery,* 200. *Clerk,* Col. R. W. Murfin, TD *Master,* Prof. B. A. K. Rider

PAVIORS *(56).* 3 Ridgemount Gardens, Enfield, Middx EN2 8QL *Livery,* 269. *Clerk,* John White *Master,* Oliver Whitehead

PEWTERERS *(16). Hall,* Pewterers' Hall, Oat Lane, London EC2V 7DE *Livery,* 80. *Clerk,* Capt. Paddy Watson, RN *Master,* Peter Errington Gibbs

PLAISTERERS *(46). Hall,* Plaisterers' Hall, 1 London Wall, London EC2Y 5JU *Livery,* 210. *Clerk,* Hilary Machtus *Master,* Nicholas Carr

PLUMBERS *(31).* Wax Chandlers' Hall, 6 Gresham Street, London EC2V 7AD *Livery,* 340. *Clerk,* Lt.-Col. Anthony Paterson-Fox *Master,* D. W. Alexander

POULTERS *(34).* The Old Butchers, Station Road, Groombridge, Kent TN3 9QX *Livery,* 204. *Clerk,* Gwen Butcher *Master,* John Nokes

SADDLERS *(25). Hall,* Saddlers' Hall, 40 Gutter Lane, London EC2V 6BR *Livery,* 75. *Clerk,* Col. N. Lithgow, CBE *Master,* I. Pulley

SCIENTIFIC INSTRUMENT MAKERS *(84).* 9 Montague Close, London SE1 9DD *Livery,* 230. *Clerk,* Neville Watson *Master,* D. Smith

SCRIVENERS *(44).* HQS Wellington, Temple Stairs, Victoria Embankment, London WC2R 2PN *Livery,* 200. *Clerk,* P. Elliott *Master,* Syliva Tutt

SHIPWRIGHTS *(59).* Ironmongers Hall, Barbican, London EC2Y 8AA *Livery,* 463. *Clerk,* Rear-Adm. Derek Anthony, MBE *Permanent Master,* HRH the Duke of Edinburgh, KG, KT, OM *Prime Warden,* A. Marsh

SOLICITORS *(79).* 4 College Hill, London EC4R 2RB *Livery,* 350. *Clerk,* Neil Cameron *Master,* William Knight

SPECTACLE MAKERS *(60).* Apothecaries' Hall, Black Friars Lane, London EC4V 6EL *Livery,* 380. *Clerk,* Lt.-Col. John Salmon, OBE *Master,* Rubin Weathersbee

STATIONERS AND NEWSPAPER MAKERS *(47). Hall,* Stationers' Hall, Ave Maria Lane, London EC4M 7DD *Livery,* 441. *Clerk,* Brig. D. Sharp, AFC *Master,* J. Waterlow

TALLOW CHANDLERS *(21). Hall,* Tallow Chandlers' Hall, 4 Dowgate Hill, London EC4R 2SH *Livery,* 175. *Clerk,* Brig. R. Wilde, CBE *Master,* Philip Edwards

TAX ADVISERS *(107).* 191 West End Road, Ruislip, Middlesex HA4 6LD *Freemen,* 121. *Clerk,* Paul Herbage *Master,* W. Norris

TIN PLATE WORKERS (ALIAS WIRE WORKERS) *(67).* Highbanks, Ferry Road, Surlingham, Norwich, Norfolk NR14 7AR *Livery,* 210. *Clerk,* Michael Henderson-Begg *Master,* D. Saunders, RD

TOBACCO PIPE MAKERS AND TOBACCO BLENDERS *(82).* Green Meadow Island, Steep, Hampshire GU32 1AE *Livery,* 150. *Clerk,* Barbara Hines *Master,* George Lankester

TURNERS *(51).* 182 Temple Chambers, Temple Avenue, London EC4Y 0HP *Livery,* 175. *Clerk,* Edward Windsor Clive *Master,* G. Kieffer

TYLERS AND BRICKLAYERS *(37).* 30 Shelley Avenue, Tiptree CO5 0SF *Livery,* 151. *Clerk,* Barry Blumson *Master,* Dr George Bird

UPHOLDERS *(49).* Hall in the Wood, 46 Quail Gardens, Selsdon Vale, Croydon CR2 8TF *Livery,* 213. *Clerk,* Jean Cody *Master,* Peter Lawton

WATER CONSERVATORS *(102).* The Lark, 2 Bell Lane, Worlington, Bury St Edmunds, Suffolk IP28 8SE *Livery,* 210. *Clerk,* Ralph Riley *Master,* Colin Drummond

WAX CHANDLERS *(20). Hall,* Wax Chandlers' Hall, 6 Gresham Street, London EC2V 7AD *Livery,* 130. *Clerk,* Richard Percival *Master,* T. Willcox

WEAVERS *(42).* Saddlers' House, Gutter Lane, London EC2V 6BR *Livery,* 125. *Clerk,* John Snowdon *Upper Bailiff,* Julian Birchall

WHEELWRIGHTS *(68).* 7 Glengall Road, Bexleyheath, Kent DA7 4AL *Livery,* 218. *Clerk,* Brian François *Master,* K. Davidson

WOOLMEN *(43).* The Old Post Office, 56 Lower Way, Great Brickhill, Bucks MK17 9AG *Livery,* 141. *Clerk,* Gillian Wilson *Master,* Gavin Hamilton-Deeley

WORLD TRADERS *(101).* 36 Ladbroke Grove, London W11 2PA *Livery,* 208. *Clerk,* Nigel Pullman *Master,* Robert Alston, CMG

SECURITY PROFESSIONALS *(No Livery).* 1 Wallis Mews, Guildford Road, Leatherhead, Surrey KT22 9DQ *Freemen,* 282. *Clerk,* John Maddock *Master,* Peter French

PARISH CLERKS *(No Livery*).* Acreholt, 33 Medstead Road, Beech, Alton, Hampshire GU34 4AD *Members,* 95. *Clerk,* Lt.-Col. Brian Coombes *Master,* R.F. S. Townend

WATERMEN AND LIGHTERMEN *(No Livery*). Hall,* Watermen's Hall, 16 St Mary-at-Hill, London EC3R 8EF *Craft Owning Freemen,* 340. *Clerk,* Colin Middlemiss *Master,* K. Dwan

* Parish Clerks and Watermen and Lightermen have requested to remain with no livery

LONDON BOROUGH COUNCILS

Council	*Telephone*	*Population**	*Council Tax†*	*Chief Executive*
Barking and Dagenham	020-8592 4500	164,500	£1,278	Robert Whiteman
Barnet	020-8359 2000	329,700	£1,350	Leo Boland
Bexley	020-8303 7777	220,300	£1,362	Nick Johnson
Brent	020-8937 1234	270,100	£1,299	Gareth Daniel
Bromley	020-8464 3333	301,900	£1,218	Doug Patterson
Camden	020-7278 4444	226,100	£1,301	Moira Gibb, CBE
CITY OF LONDON CORPORATION	020-7606 3030	9,200	£900	Chris Duffield
Croydon	020-8686 4433	342,700	£1,358	Jon Rouse
Ealing	020-8825 5000	301,800	£1,344	Darra Singh
Enfield	020-8379 1000	280,500	£1,337	Rob Leak
Greenwich	020-8854 8888	228,100	£1,266	Mary Ney
Hackney	020-8356 5000	207,700	£1,302	Tim Shields *(acting)*
Hammersmith and Fulham	020-8748 3020	179,900	£1,193	Geoff Alltimes
Haringey	020-8489 0000	224,500	£1,432	Ita O'Donovan
Harrow	020-8863 5611	214,000	£1,423	Michael Lockwood
Havering	01708-434343	226,200	£1,433	Cheryl Coppell
Hillingdon	01895-250111	252,400	£1,384	Hugh Dunnachie *(acting)*
Hounslow	020-8583 2000	212,500	£1,395	Mark Gilks
Islington	020-7527 2000	182,600	£1,219	Helen Bailey
Kensington and Chelsea	020-7937 5464	196,200	£1,043	Derek Myers
Kingston upon Thames	020-8547 5757	153,000	£1,523	Bruce McDonald
Lambeth	020-7926 1000	269,100	£1,187	Derrick Anderson
Lewisham	020-8314 6000	247,500	£1,296	Barry Quirk, CBE
Merton	020-8543 2222	194,700	£1,358	Ged Curran
Newham	020-8430 2000	246,200	£1,220	Chris Wood *(acting)*
Redbridge	020-8554 5000	251,500	£1,331	Roger Hampson
Richmond upon Thames	020-8891 1411	186,300	£1,491	Gillian Norton
Southwark	020-7525 5000	257,700	£1,181	Annie Shepperd
Sutton	020-8770 5000	177,700	£1,376	Paul Martin
Tower Hamlets	020-7364 5000	213,200	£1,140	Martin Smith
Waltham Forest	020-8496 3000	224,100	£1,407	Roger Taylor *(acting)*
Wandsworth	020-8871 6000	281,400	£681	Gerald Jones
WESTMINSTER	020-7641 6000	244,400	£682	Peter Rogers

* *Source:* ONS – *Mid-2005 Population Estimates* (Crown copyright)

† Average Band D council tax bill for 2007–8

Councils in CAPITAL LETTERS have city status

WALES

Cymru

The Principality of Wales (Cymru) occupies the extreme west of the central southern portion of the island of Great Britain, with a total area of 20,778 sq. km (8,022 sq. miles): land 20,733 sq. km (8,005 sq. miles); inland water 45 sq. km (17 sq. miles). It is bordered in the north by the Irish Sea, in the south by the Bristol Channel, in the east by the English counties of Cheshire, Shropshire, Herefordshire and Gloucestershire, and in the west by St George's Channel.

Across the Menai Straits is Ynys Mon (Isle of Anglesey) (715 sq. km/276 sq. miles), communication with which is facilitated by the Menai Suspension Bridge (305m/1,000ft long) built by Telford in 1826, and by the tubular railway bridge (335m/1,100ft long) built by Stephenson in 1850. Holyhead harbour, on Holy Isle (north-west of Anglesey), provides ferry services to Dublin (113km/70 miles).

POPULATION

The population at the 2001 census was 2,903,085 (men 1,403,782; women 1,499,303). The average density of population in 2001 was 140 persons per sq. km (362 per sq. mile).

RELIEF

Wales is a country of extensive tracts of high plateau and shorter stretches of mountain ranges deeply dissected by river valleys. Lower-lying ground is largely confined to the coastal belt and the lower parts of the valleys. The highest mountains are those of Snowdonia in the north west (Snowdon, 1,085m/3,559ft), Berwyn (Aran Fawddwy, 906m/2,971ft), Cader Idris (Pen y Gadair, 892m/2,928ft), Dyfed (Plynlimon, 752m/2,467ft), and the Black Mountains, Brecon Beacons and Black Forest ranges in the south-east (Pen y Fan, 886m/2,906ft; Waun Fâch, 811m/2,660ft; Carmarthen Van, 802m/2,630ft).

HYDROGRAPHY

The principal river in Wales is the Severn, which flows from the slopes of Plynlimon to the English border. The Wye (209km/130 miles) also rises in the slopes of Plynlimon. The Usk (90km/56 miles) flows into the Bristol Channel through Gwent. The Dee (113km/70 miles) rises in Bala Lake and flows through the Vale of Llangollen, where an aqueduct (built by Telford in 1805) carries the Pontcysyllte branch of the Shropshire Union Canal across the valley. The estuary of the Dee is the navigable portion, it is 23km (14 miles) in length and about 8km (5 miles) in breadth. The Towy (109km/68 miles), Teifi (80km/50 miles), Taff (64km/40 miles), Dovey (48km/30 miles), Taf (40km/25 miles) and Conway (39km/24 miles) are wholly Welsh rivers.

The largest natural lake is Bala (Llyn Tegid) in Gwynedd, nearly 7km (4 miles) long and 1.6km (1 mile) wide. Lake Vyrnwy is an artificial reservoir, about the size of Bala, it forms the water supply of Liverpool; Birmingham's water is supplied from reservoirs in the Elan and Claerwen valleys.

WELSH LANGUAGE

According to the 2001 census results, the percentage of people aged three years and over who are able to speak Welsh is:

Blaenau Gwent	9.1	Neath Port Talbot	17.8
Bridgend	10.6	Newport	9.6
Caerphilly	10.9	Pembrokeshire	21.5
Cardiff	10.9	Powys	20.8
Carmarthenshire	50.1	Rhondda Cynon Taf	12.3
Ceredigion	51.8	Swansea	13.2
Conwy	29.2	Torfaen	10.7
Denbighshire	26.1	Vale of Glamorgan	11.1
Flintshire	14.1	Wrexham	14.4
Gwynedd	68.7	Ynys Mon (Isle of Anglesey)	59.8
Merthyr Tydfil	10.0		
Monmouthshire	9.0	*Total in Wales*	20.5

FLAG

The flag of Wales, the Red Dragon (Y Ddraig Goch), is a red dragon on a field divided white over green (per fess argent and vert a dragon passant gules). The flag was augmented in 1953 by a royal badge on a shield encircled with a riband bearing the words *Ddraig Goch Ddyry Cychwyn* and imperially crowned, but this augmented flag is rarely used.

EARLY HISTORY

The earliest inhabitants of whom there is any record appear to have been subdued or exterminated by the Goidels (a people of Celtic race) in the Bronze Age. A further invasion of Celtic Brythons and Belgae followed in the ensuing Iron Age. The Roman conquest of southern Britain and Wales was for some time successfully opposed by Caratacus (Caractacus or Caradog), chieftain of the Catuvellauni and son of Cunobelinus (Cymbeline). South-east Wales was subjugated and the legionary fortress at Caerleon-on-Usk established by around AD 75–7; the conquest of Wales was completed by Agricola around AD 78. Communications were opened up by the construction of military roads from Chester to Caerleon-on-Usk and Caerwent, and from Chester to Conwy (and thence to Carmarthen and Neath). Christianity was introduced in the fourth century, during the Roman occupation.

ANGLO-SAXON ATTACKS

The Anglo-Saxon invaders of southern Britain drove the Celts into the mountain stronghold of Wales, and into Strathclyde (Cumberland and south-west Scotland) and Cornwall, giving them the name of *Waelisc* (Welsh), meaning 'foreign'. The West Saxons' victory of Deorham (AD 577) isolated Wales from Cornwall and the battle of Chester (AD 613) cut off communication with Strathclyde and northern Britain. In the eighth century the boundaries of the Welsh were further restricted by the annexations of Offa, King of Mercia, and counter-attacks were largely prevented by the construction of an artificial boundary from the Dee to the Wye (Offa's Dyke).

In the ninth century Rhodri Mawr (844–878) united

the country and successfully resisted further incursions of the Saxons by land and raids of Norse and Danish pirates by sea, but at his death his three provinces of Gwynedd (north), Powys (central) and Deheubarth (south) were divided among his three sons, Anarawd, Mervyn and Cadell. Cadell's son Hywel Dda ruled a large part of Wales and codified its laws but the provinces were not united again until the rule of Llewelyn ap Seisyllt (husband of the heiress of Gwynedd) from 1018 to 1023.

THE NORMAN CONQUEST

After the Norman conquest of England, William I created palatine counties along the Welsh frontier, and the Norman barons began to make encroachments into Welsh territory. The Welsh princes recovered many of their losses during the civil wars of Stephen's reign (1135–54), and in the early 13th century Owen Gruffydd, prince of Gwynedd, was the dominant figure in Wales. Under Llywelyn ap Iorwerth (1194–1240) the Welsh united in powerful resistance to English incursions and Llywelyn's privileges and *de facto* independence were recognised in the Magna Carta. His grandson, Llywelyn ap Gruffydd, was the last native prince; he was killed in 1282 during hostilities between the Welsh and English, allowing Edward I of England to establish his authority over the country. On 7 February 1301, Edward of Caernarvon, son of Edward I, was created Prince of Wales, a title subsequently borne by the eldest son of the sovereign.

Strong Welsh national feeling continued, expressed in the early 15th century in the rising led by Owain Glyndwr, but the situation was altered by the accession to the English throne in 1485 of Henry VII of the Welsh House of Tudor. Wales was politically annexed by England under the Act of Union of 1535, which extended English laws to the principality and gave it parliamentary representation for the first time.

EISTEDDFOD

The Welsh are a distinct nation, with a language and literature of their own; the national bardic festival (Eisteddfod), instituted by Prince Rhys ap Griffith in 1176, is still held annually. These *Eisteddfodau* (sessions) form part of the *Gorsedd* (assembly) and are believed to date from the time of Prydian, a ruling prince in an age many centuries before the Christian era.

PRINCIPAL CITIES

There are five cities in Wales (with date city status conferred): Bangor (pre-1900), Cardiff (1905), St David's (1994), Newport (2002) and Swansea (1969).

Cardiff and Swansea have also been granted Lord Mayoralities.

CARDIFF

Cardiff, at the mouth of the rivers Taff, Rhymney and Ely, is the capital city of Wales and at the 2001 census had a population of 305,353. The city has changed dramatically in recent years following the regeneration of Cardiff Bay and construction of a barrage, which has created a permanent freshwater lake and waterfront for the city. As the capital city, Cardiff is home to the National Assembly for Wales and is a major administrative, retail, business and cultural centre.

The city is home to many fine buildings including the City Hall, Cardiff Castle, Llandaff Cathedral, the National Museum of Wales, university buildings, law courts and the Temple of Peace and Health. The Millennium Stadium opened in 1999 and has hosted FA Cup finals and other high-profile English football matches since 2001.

SWANSEA

Swansea *(Abertawe)* is a seaport with a population of 223,293 at the 2001 census. The Gower peninsula was brought within the city boundary under local government reform in 1974.

The principal buildings are the Norman Castle (rebuilt *c.*1330), the Royal Institution of South Wales, founded in 1835 (including library), the University of Wales Swansea at Singleton and the Guildhall, containing Frank Brangwyn's British Empire panels. The Dylan Thomas Centre, formerly the old Guildhall, was restored in 1995. More recent buildings include the County Hall, the Maritime Quarter Marina, the Wales National Pool and the National Waterfront Museum.

Swansea was chartered by the Earl of Warwick (1158–84), and further charters were granted by King John, Henry III, Edward II, Edward III and James II, Oliver Cromwell and the Marcher Lord William de Breos. It was formally invested with city status in 1969 by HRH The Prince of Wales.

LORD-LIEUTENANTS AND HIGH SHERIFFS

Area	*Lord-Lieutenant*	*High Sheriff (2007–8)*
Clwyd	T. Jones, CBE	Jonathan Major
Dyfed	Hon. Robin Lewis, OBE	Col. David Davies, TD
Gwent	S. Boyle	Lt.-Col. Michael Harry
Gwynedd	Gruffydd Daniel	Dr Dewi Roberts
Mid Glamorgan	Kate Thomas	Charles Knight
Powys	Hon. Mrs E. Legge-Bourke, LVO	John Turner
S. Glamorgan	Capt. N. Lloyd-Edwards	Paul Williams, OBE
W. Glamorgan	R. Hastie, CBE	Martin Trainer

LOCAL COUNCILS

Council	*Administrative Headquarters*	*Telephone*	*Population**	*Council Tax†*	*Chief Executive*
Blaenau Gwent	Ebbw Vale	01495-350555	68,400	£1,215	Robin Morrison
Bridgend	Bridgend	01656-643643	130,800	£1,085	Dr Jo Farrar
Caerphilly	Hengoed	01443-815588	170,200	£993	Stewart Rosser
CARDIFF CITY	Cardiff	029-2087 2000	319,700	£949	Byron Davies
Carmarthenshire	Carmarthen	01267-234567	178,100	£1,033	Mark James
Ceredigion	Aberaeron	01545-570881	78,300	£969	Bronwen Morgan
Conwy	Conwy	01492-574000	111,500	£915	Derek Barker
Denbighshire	Ruthin	01824-706000	96,000	£1,123	Ian Miller
Flintshire	Mold	01352-752121	150,200	£1,006	Colin Everett
Gwynedd	Caernarfon	01286-672255	118,000	£1,060	Harry Thomas
Merthyr Tydfil	Merthyr Tydfil	01685-725000	54,900	£1,169	Alistair Neill
Monmouthshire	Cwmbran	01633-644644	87,700	£1,041	Colin Berg
Neath Port Talbot	Port Talbot	01639-763333	135,600	£1,204	Ken Sawyers
NEWPORT CITY	Newport	01633-656656	139,600	£854	Chris Freegard
Pembrokeshire	Haverfordwest	01437-764551	117,500	£796	Bryn Parry-Jones
Powys	Llandrindod Wells	01597-826000	131,500	£985	Mark Kerr
Rhondda Cynon Taff	Tonypandy	01443-424000	231,600	£1,103	Keith Griffiths
SWANSEA CITY	Swansea	01792-636000	226,400	£990	Paul Smith
Torfaen	Pontypool	01495-762200	90,300	£1,030	Alison Ward
Vale of Glamorgan	Barry	01446-700111	122,900	£959	John Maitland-Evans
Wrexham	Wrexham	01978-292000	130,500	£1,002	Isobel Garner
Ynys Mon (Isle of Anglesey)	Ynys Mon	01248-750057	68,900	£959	Derrick Jones

* *Source:* ONS – *Mid-2005 Population Estimates* (Crown copyright)
† Average Band D council tax bill 2007–8
Councils in CAPITAL LETTERS have city status

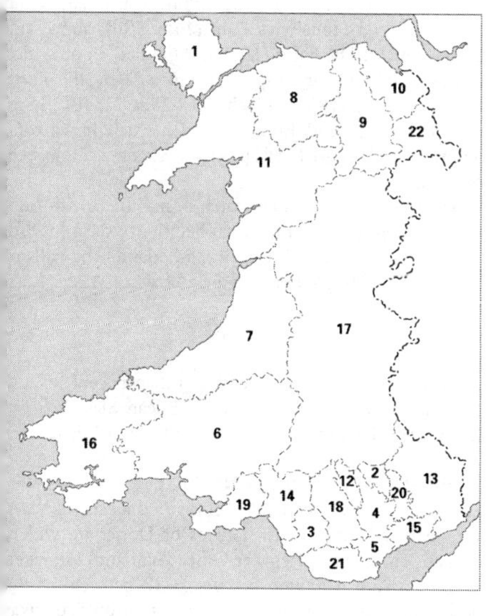

Key	*Council*
1	Anglesey (Ynys Mon)
2	Blaenau Gwent
3	Bridgend
4	Caerphilly
5	Cardiff
6	Carmarthenshire
7	Ceredigion
8	Conwy
9	Denbighshire
10	Flintshire
11	Gwynedd
12	Merthyr Tydfil
13	Monmouthshire
14	Neath Port Talbot
15	Newport
16	Pembrokeshire
17	Powys
18	Rhondda, Cynon, Taff
19	Swansea
20	Torfaen
21	Vale of Glamorgan
22	Wrexham

SCOTLAND

The Kingdom of Scotland occupies the northern portion of the main island of Great Britain and includes the Inner and Outer Hebrides, Orkney, Shetland and many other islands. It lies between 60° 51′ 30″ and 54° 38′ N. latitude and between 1° 45′ 32″ and 6° 14′ W. longitude, with England to the south, the Atlantic Ocean on the north and west, and the North Sea on the east.

The greatest length of the mainland (Cape Wrath to the Mull of Galloway) is 441km (274 miles), and the greatest breadth (Buchan Ness to Applecross) is 248km (154 miles). The customary measurement of the island of Great Britain is from the site of John o' Groats house, near Duncansby Head, Caithness, to Land's End, Cornwall, a total distance of 970km (603 miles) in a straight line and approximately 1,448km (900 miles) by road.

The total area of Scotland is 78,807 sq. km (30,427 sq. miles): land 77,907 sq. km (30,080 sq. miles), inland water 900 sq. km (347 sq. miles).

POPULATION

The population at the 2001 census was 5,062,011 (men 2,432,494; women 2,629,517). The average density of the population in 2001 was 64 persons per sq. km (166 per sq. mile).

RELIEF

There are three natural orographic divisions of Scotland. The southern uplands have their highest points in Merrick (843m/2,766ft), Rhinns of Kells (814m/2,669ft) and Cairnsmuir of Carsphairn (797m/2,614ft), in the west; and the Tweedsmuir Hills in the east (Broad Law 840m/2,756ft; Dollar Law 817m/2,682ft; Hartfell 808m/2,651ft).

The central lowlands, formed by the valleys of the Clyde, Forth and Tay, divide the southern uplands from the northern Highlands, which extend almost from the extreme north of the mainland to the central lowlands, and are divided into a northern and a southern system by the Great Glen.

The Grampian Mountains, which entirely cover the southern Highland area, include in the west Ben Nevis (1,343m/4,406ft), the highest point in the British Isles, and in the east the Cairngorm Mountains (Ben Macdui 1,309m/4,296ft; Braeriach 1,295m/4,248ft; Cairn Gorm 1,245m/4,084ft). The north-western Highland area contains the mountains of Wester and Easter Ross (Carn Eige 1,183m/3,880ft; Sgurr na Lapaich 1,151m/3,775ft).

Created, like the central lowlands, by a major geological fault, the Great Glen (97km/60 miles long) runs between Inverness and Fort William, and contains Loch Ness, Loch Oich and Loch Lochy. These are linked to each other and to the north-east and south-west coasts of Scotland by the Caledonian Canal, providing a navigable passage between the Moray Firth and the Inner Hebrides.

HYDROGRAPHY

The western coast is fragmented by peninsulas and islands, and indented by fjords (sea-lochs), the longest of which is Loch Fyne (68km/42 miles long) in Argyll. Although the east coast tends to be less fractured and lower, there are several great drowned inlets (firths), eg Firth of Forth, Firth of Tay and Moray Firth, as well as the Firth of Clyde in the west.

The lochs are the principal hydrographic feature. The largest in Scotland and in Britain is Loch Lomond (70 sq km/27 sq. miles), in the Grampian valleys and the longest and deepest is Loch Ness (39km/24 miles long and 244m/800ft deep), in the Great Glen.

The longest river is the Tay (188km/117 miles), noted for its salmon. It flows into the North Sea, with Dundee on the estuary, which is spanned by the Tay Bridge (3,136m/10,289ft) opened in 1887 and the Tay Road Bridge (2,245m/7,365ft) opened in 1966. Other noted salmon rivers are the Dee (145km/90 miles) which flows into the North Sea at Aberdeen, and the Spey (177km/110 miles), the swiftest flowing river in the British Isles, which flows into Moray Firth. The Tweed which gave its name to the woollen cloth produced along its banks, marks in the lower stretches of its 154km (96 mile) course the border between Scotland and England.

The most important river commercially is the Clyde (171km/106 miles), formed by the junction of the Daer and Portrail water, which flows through the city of Glasgow to the Firth of Clyde. During its course it passes over the picturesque Falls of Clyde, Bonnington Linn (9m/30ft), Corra Linn (26m/84ft), Dundaff Linn (3m/10ft) and Stonebyres Linn (24m/80ft), above and below Lanark. The Forth (106km/66 miles), upon which stands Edinburgh, the capital, is spanned by the Forth Railway Bridge (1890), which is 1,625m (5,330ft) long and the Forth Road Bridge (1964), which has a total length of 1,876m (6,156ft) (over water) and a single span of 914m (3,000ft).

The highest waterfall in Scotland, and the British Isles is Eas a'Chal Aluinn with a total height of 201m (658ft) which falls from Glas Bheinn in Sutherland. The Falls of Glomach, on a head-stream of the Elchaig in Wester Ross have a drop of 113m (370ft).

GAELIC LANGUAGE

According to the 2001 census, 1.2 per cent of the population of Scotland, mainly in Eilean Siar (Western Isles), were able to speak the Scottish form of Gaelic.

LOWLAND SCOTTISH LANGUAGE

Several regional lowland Scottish dialects, known variously as Scots, Scotch, Lallans or Doric, are widely spoken. The General Register Office (Scotland) estimated in 1996 that 1.5 million people, or 30 per cent of the population, are Scots speakers. A question on Scots was not included in the 2001 census.

FLAG

The flag of Scotland is known as the Saltire. It is a white diagonal cross on a blue field (saltire argent in a field azure) and represents St Andrew, the patron saint of Scotland.

THE SCOTTISH ISLANDS

ORKNEY

The Orkney Islands (total area 972 sq. km/376 sq. miles) lie about ten km (six miles) north of the mainland, separated from it by the Pentland Firth. Of the 90 islands and islets (holms and skerries) in the group, about one-third are inhabited.

The total population at the 2001 census was 19,245; the 2001 populations of the islands shown here include those of smaller islands forming part of the same council district.

Mainland, 15,339
Burray, 357
Eday, 121
Flotta, 81
Hoy, 392
North Ronaldsay, 70
Papa Westray, 65
Rousay, 267
Sanday, 478
Shapinsay, 300
South Ronaldsay, 854
Stronsay, 358
Westray, 563

The islands are rich in prehistoric and Scandinavian remains, the most notable being the Stone Age village of Skara Brae, the burial chamber of Maes Howe, the many brochs (towers) and the 12th-century St Magnus Cathedral. Scapa Flow, between the Mainland and Hoy, was the war station of the British Grand Fleet from 1914 to 1919 and the scene of the scuttling of the surrendered German High Seas Fleet (21 June 1919).

Most of the islands are low-lying and fertile, and farming (principally beef cattle) is the main industry. Flotta, to the south of Scapa Flow, is the site of the oil terminal for the Piper, Claymore and Tartan fields in the North Sea.

The capital is Kirkwall (population 6,206) situated on Mainland.

SHETLAND

The Shetland Islands have a total area of 1,427 sq. km (551 sq. miles) and a population at the 2001 census of 21,988. They lie about 80km (50 miles) north of the Orkneys, with Fair Isle about half way between the two groups. Out Stack, off Muckle Flugga, 1.6km (one mile) north of Unst, is the most northerly part of the British Isles (60° 51′ 30″ N. lat.).

There are over 100 islands, of which 16 are inhabited. Populations at the 2001 census were:

Mainland, 17,575
Bressay, 384
East Burra, 66
Fair Isle, 69
Fetlar, 86
Housay, 76
Muckle Roe, 104
Trondra, 133
Unst, 720
West Burra, 784
Whalsay, 1,034
Yell, 957

Shetland's many archaeological sites include Jarlshof, Mousa and Clickhimin, and its long connection with Scandinavia has resulted in a strong Norse influence on its placenames and dialect.

Industries include fishing, knitwear and farming. In addition to the fishing fleet there are fish processing factories, and the traditional handknitting of Fair Isle and Unst is now supplemented with machine-knitted garments. Farming is mainly crofting, with sheep being raised on the moorland and hills of the islands. Latterly the islands have become a centre of the North Sea oil industry, with pipelines from the Brent and Ninian fields running to the terminal at Sullom Voe, the largest of its kind in Europe.

The capital is Lerwick (population 6,830) situated on Mainland. Lerwick is the main centre for supply services for offshore oil exploration and development.

THE HEBRIDES

Until the late 13th century the Hebrides included other Scottish islands in the Firth of Clyde, the peninsula of Kintyre (Argyll), the Isle of Man, and the (Irish) Isle of Rathlin. The origin of the name is probably the Greek *Eboudai,* latinised as *Hebudes* by Pliny, and corrupted to its present form. The Norwegian name *Sudreyjar* (Southern Islands) was latinised as *Sodorenses,* a name that survives in the Anglican bishopric of Sodor and Man.

There are over 500 islands and islets, of which about 100 are inhabited, though mountainous terrain and extensive peat bogs mean that only a fraction of the total area is under cultivation. Stone, Bronze and Iron Age settlement has left many remains, including those at Callanish on Lewis, and Norse colonisation influenced language, customs and placenames. Occupations include farming (mostly crofting and stock-raising), fishing and the manufacture of tweeds and other woollens. Tourism is also an important part of the economy.

The Inner Hebrides lie off the west coast of Scotland and are relatively close to the mainland. The largest and best-known is Skye (area 1,665 sq. km/643 sq. miles; pop. 9,251; chief town, Portree), which contains the Cuillin Hills (Sgurr Alasdair 993m/3,257ft); Bla Bheinn (928m/3,046ft); the Storr (719m/2,358ft) and the Red Hills (Beinn na Caillich 732m/2,403ft). Other islands in the Highland council area include Raasay (pop. 194), Rum, Eigg (pop. 131) and Muck.

Further south the Inner Hebridean islands include Arran (pop. 5,058) containing Goat Fell (874m/2,868ft); Coll and Tiree (pop. 934); Colonsay and Oronsay (pop. 113); Easdale (pop. 58); Gigha (pop. 110); Islay (area 608 sq. km/235 sq. miles; pop. 3,457); Jura (area 414 sq. km/160 sq. miles; pop. 188) with a range of hills culminating in the Paps of Jura (Beinn-an-Oir, 785m/2,576ft, and Beinn Chaolais, 755m/2,477ft); Lismore (pop. 146); Luing (pop. 220); and Mull (area 950 sq. km/367 sq. miles; pop. 2,696; chief town Tobermory) containing Ben More (967m/3,171ft).

The Outer Hebrides, separated from the mainland by the Minch, now form the Eilean Siar (Western Isles) council area (area 2,897 sq. km/1,119 sq. miles; pop. 26,502). The main islands are Lewis with Harris (area 1,994 sq. km/770 sq. miles, pop. 19,918), whose chief town, Stornoway, is the administrative headquarters; North Uist (pop. 1,320); South Uist (pop. 1,818); Benbecula (pop. 1,249) and Barra (pop. 1,078). Other inhabited islands include Bernera (233), Berneray (136), Eriskay (133), Grimsay (201), Scalpay (322) and Vatersay (94).

EARLY HISTORY

There is evidence of human settlement in Scotland dating from the third millennium BC, the earliest settlers being Middle Stone Age hunters and fishermen. Early in the second millennium BC, New Stone Age farmers began to cultivate crops and rear livestock; their settlements were on the west coast and in the north, and included Skara Brae and Maeshowe (Orkney). Settlement by the early Bronze Age 'Beaker Folk', so-called from the shape of their drinking vessels, in eastern Scotland dates from about 1800 BC. Further settlement is believed to have occurred from 700 BC onwards, as tribes were displaced from further south by new incursions from the Continent and the Roman invasions from AD 43.

Julius Agricola, the Roman governor of Britain AD 77–84, extended the Roman conquests in Britain by advancing into Caledonia, culminating with a victory at Mons Graupius, probably in AD 84; he was recalled to Rome shortly afterwards and his forward policy was not pursued. Hadrian's Wall, mostly completed by AD 30, marked the northern frontier of the Roman empire except for the period between about AD 144 and 190 when the frontier moved north to the Forth-Clyde isthmus and a turf wall, the Antonine Wall, was manned.

After the Roman withdrawal from Britain, there were centuries of warfare between the Picts, Scots, Britons, Angles and Vikings. The Picts, believed to be a non-Indo-European race, occupied the area north of the Forth. The Scots, a Gaelic-speaking people of northern Ireland, colonised the area of Argyll and Bute (the kingdom of Dalriada) in the fifth century AD and then expanded eastwards and northwards. The Britons, speaking a Brythonic Celtic language, colonised Scotland from the south from the first century BC; they lost control of south-eastern Scotland (incorporated into the kingdom of Northumbria) to the Angles in the early seventh century but retained Strathclyde (south-western Scotland and Cumbria). Viking raids from the late eighth century were followed by Norse settlement in the western and northern isles, Argyll, Caithness and Sutherland from the mid-ninth century onwards.

UNIFICATION

The union of the areas which now comprise Scotland began in AD 843 when Kenneth mac Alpin, king of the Scots from *c.*834, also became king of the Picts, joining the two lands to form the kingdom of Alba (comprising Scotland north of a line between the Forth and Clyde rivers). Lothian, the eastern part of the area between the Forth and the Tweed, seems to have been leased to Kenneth II of Alba (reigned 971–995) by Edgar of England *c.*973, and Scottish possession was confirmed by Malcolm II's victory over a Northumbrian army at Carham *c.*1016. At about this time Malcolm II (reigned 1005–34) placed his grandson Duncan on the throne of the British kingdom of Strathclyde, bringing under Scots rule virtually all of what is now Scotland.

The Norse possessions were incorporated into the kingdom of Scotland from the 12th century onwards. An uprising in the mid-12th century drove the Norse from most of mainland Argyll. The Hebrides were ceded to Scotland by the treaty of Perth in 1266 after a Norwegian expedition in 1263 failed to maintain Norse authority over the islands. Orkney and Shetland fell to Scotland in 1468–9 as a pledge for the unpaid dowry of Margaret of Denmark, wife of James III, although Danish claims of suzerainty were relinquished only with the marriage of Anne of Denmark to James VI in 1590.

From the 11th century, there were frequent wars between Scotland and England over territory and the extent of England's political influence. The failure of the Scottish royal line with the death of Margaret of Norway in 1290 led to disputes over the throne which were resolved by the adjudication of Edward I of England. He awarded the throne to John Balliol in 1292 but Balliol's refusal to be a puppet king led to war. Balliol surrendered to Edward I in 1296 and Edward attempted to rule Scotland himself. Resistance to Scotland's loss of independence was led by William Wallace, who defeated the English at Stirling Bridge (1297), and Robert Bruce crowned in 1306, who held most of Scotland by 131[?] and routed Edward II's army at Bannockburn (1314). England recognised the independence of Scotland in the treaty of Northampton in 1328. Subsequent clashes include the disastrous battle of Flodden (1513) in which James IV and many of his nobles fell.

THE UNION

In 1603 James VI of Scotland succeeded Elizabeth I on the throne of England (his mother, Mary Queen of Scots was the great-granddaughter of Henry VII), his successors reigning as sovereigns of Great Britain. Political union of the two countries did not occur until 1707.

THE JACOBITE REVOLTS

After the abdication (by flight) in 1688 of James VII and II, the crown devolved upon William III (grandson of Charles I) and Mary II (elder daughter of James VII and II). In 1689 Graham of Claverhouse roused the Highlands on behalf of James VII and II, but died after a military success at Killiecrankie.

After the death of Anne (younger daughter of James VII and II), the throne devolved upon George I (great-grandson of James VI and I). In 1715, armed risings on behalf of James Stuart (the Old Pretender, son of James VII and II) led to the indecisive battle of Sheriffmuir, and the Jacobite movement died down until 1745, when Charles Stuart (the Young Pretender) defeated the Royalist troops at Prestonpans and advanced to Derby (1746). From Derby, the adherents of 'James VIII and III' (the title claimed for his father by Charles Stuart) fell back on the defensive and were finally crushed at Culloden (16 April 1746) by an army led by by the Duke of Cumberland, son of George II.

PRINCIPAL CITIES

ABERDEEN

Aberdeen, 209km (130 miles) north-east of Edinburgh received its charter as a Royal Burgh in 1124. Scotland's third largest city, Aberdeen lies between two rivers, the Dee and the Don, facing the North Sea; the city has a strong maritime history and is today a major centre for offshore oil exploration and production. It is also an ancient university town and distinguished research centre. Other industries include engineering, food processing, textiles, paper manufacturing and chemicals.

Places of interest include King's College, St Machar's Cathedral, Brig o' Balgownie, Duthie Park and Winter Gardens, Hazlehead Park, the Kirk of St Nicholas, Mercat Cross, Marischal College and Marischal Museum, Provost Skene's House, Art Gallery, Gordon Highlanders Museum, Satrosphere Hands-On Discovery Centre, and Aberdeen Maritime Museum.

DUNDEE

The Royal Burgh of Dundee is situated on the north bank of the Tay estuary. The city's port and dock installations are important to the offshore oil industry and the airport also provides servicing facilities. Principal industries include textiles, biotechnology and digital media, lasers, printing, tyre manufacture, food processing, engineering and tourism.

The unique City Churches – three churches under one roof, together with the 15th-century St Mary's Tower – are the most prominent architectural feature. Dundee is ome to two historic ships: the Dundee-built RRS *)iscovery* which took Capt. Scott to the Antarctic lies longside Discovery Quay, and the frigate *Unicorn,* the nly British-built wooden warship still afloat, is moored ı Victoria Dock. Places of interest include Mills Public)bservatory, the Tay road and rail bridges, Dundee :ontemporary Arts Centre, McManus Galleries, Claypotts :astle, Broughty Castle, Verdant Works (Textile Heritage :entre) and the Sensation Science Centre.

:DINBURGH

dinburgh is the capital city and seat of government in cotland. The city is built on a group of hills and contains ı Princes Street one of the most beautiful thoroughfares ı the world. Edinburgh has many strong literary ssociations and was named UNESCO city of literature in 005.

The principal buildings are the castle, which houses the tone of Scone and also includes St Margaret's Chapel, ne oldest building in Edinburgh, and near it, the Scottish lational War Memorial; the Palace of Holyroodhouse; 'arliament House, the present seat of the judicature; three niversities (Edinburgh, Heriot-Watt, Napier); St Giles' :athedral; St Mary's (Scottish Episcopal) Cathedral (Sir ;eorge Gilbert Scott); the General Register House Robert Adam); the National and Signet libraries; the lational Gallery of Scotland; the Royal Scottish cademy; the Scottish National Portrait Gallery and the dinburgh International Conference Centre.

;LASGOW

;lasgow, a Royal Burgh, is Scotland's largest city and its rincipal commercial and industrial centre. The city ccupies the north and south banks of the Clyde, formerly ne of the chief commercial estuaries in the world. The ıain industries include engineering, electronics, finance, chemicals and printing. The city is also a key tourist and conference destination.

The chief buildings are the 13th-century Gothic cathedral, the university (Sir George Gilbert Scott), the City Chambers, the Royal Concert Hall, St Mungo Museum of Religious Life and Art, Pollok House, the School of Art (Charles Rennie Mackintosh), Kelvingrove Art Galleries, the Gallery of Modern Art, the Burrell Collection museum and the Mitchell Library. The city is home to the Scottish National Orchestra, Scottish Opera, Scottish Ballet and BBC Scotland and Scottish Television.

INVERNESS

Inverness was granted city status in 2000. The city's name is derived from the Gaelic for 'the mouth of the Ness', referring to the river on which it lies. Inverness is recorded as being at the junction of the old trade routes since AD 565. Today the city is the main administrative centre for the north of Scotland and is the capital of the Highlands. Tourism is one of the city's main industries.

Among the city's most notable buildings is Abertarff House, built in 1593 and the oldest secular building remaining in Inverness. Balnain House, built as a town house in 1726, is a fine example of early Georgian architecture. Once a hospital for Hanoverian soldiers after the battle of Culloden and as billets for the Royal Engineers when completing the first Ordnance Survey, today Balnain House is the National Trust for Scotland's regional HQ. The Old High Church, on St Michael's Mount, is the original parish church of Inverness and is built on the site of the earliest Christian church in the city. Parts of the church date back to the 14th century.

Stirling was granted city status in 2002. Aberdeen, Dundee, Edinburgh and Glasgow have also been granted Lord Mayoralty/Lord Provostship.

.ORD-LIEUTENANTS

Title	*Name*
berdeen City*	Lord Provost Peter Stephen
berdeenshire	A. Farquharson, OBE
ngus	Mrs G. Osborne
rgyll and Bute	K. Mackinnon
yrshire and Arran	John Duncan, QPM
3anffshire	Clare Russell
3erwickshire	Maj. A. Trotter
:aithness	Miss M. Dunnett
:lackmannan	Mrs S. Cruickshank
)umfries	Jean Tulloch
)unbartonshire	Col. Donald Ross, OBE
)undee City*	Lord Provost John Letford
:ast Lothian	W. Garth Morrison, CBE
:dinburgh City*	Rt. Hon. Lord Provost George Grubb
:ilean Siar (Western Isles)	A. Matheson, OBE
'ife	Mrs C. Dean
;lasgow City*	Rt. Hon. Lord Provost Robert Winter
nverness	Donald Angus Cameron of Lochiel
Kincardineshire	Carol Kinghorn
Lanarkshire	G. Cox, MBE
Midlothian	Patrick Prenter, CBE
Moray	Grenville Shaw Johnston, OBE, TD
Nairn	Ewen Brodie of Lethan
Orkney	Dr Anthony Trickett, MBE
Perth and Kinross	Brig. Melville Jameson, CBE
Renfrewshire	Guy Clark
Ross and Cromarty	Janet Bowen
Roxburgh, Ettrick and Lauderdale	Hon. Capt. Gerald Maitland-Carew
Shetland	J. Scott
Stirling and Falkirk	Mrs M. McLachlan
Sutherland	Dr Monica Maitland Main
The Stewartry of Kirkcudbright	Lt.-Col. Sir Malcolm Walter Hugh Ross, GCVO, OBE
Tweeddale	Capt. D. Younger
West Lothian	Mrs I. Brydie, MBE
Wigtown	Marion Brewis

* The Lord Provosts of the four cities of Aberdeen, Dundee, Edinburgh and Glasgow are Lord-Lieutenants *ex officio* for those districts

LOCAL COUNCILS

Council	*Administrative Headquarters*	*Telephone*	*Population**	*Council Tax*†	*Chief Executive*
ABERDEEN	Aberdeen	01224-522000	202,400	£1,230	Douglas Paterson
Aberdeenshire	Aberdeen	01467-620981	235,400	£1,141	Alan Campbell
Angus	Forfar	01307-461460	109,200	£1,072	David Sawers
Argyll and Bute	Lochgilphead	01546-602127	90,900	£1,178	James McLellan
Clackmannanshire	Alloa	01259-452000	48,600	£1,148	Dave Jones
Dumfries and Galloway	Dumfries	01387-260000	148,300	£1,049	Philip Jones
DUNDEE	Dundee	01382-434000	142,200	£1,211	Alex Stephen
East Ayrshire	Kilmarnock	01563-576000	119,400	£1,189	Fiona Lees
East Dunbartonshire	Kirkintilloch	0141-578 8000	106,000	£1,142	Sue Bruce
East Lothian	Haddington	01620-827827	91,800	£1,118	Alex McCrorie
East Renfrewshire	Giffnock	0141-577 3000	89,600	£1,126	David Dippie
EDINBURGH	Edinburgh	0131-200 2000	457,800	£1,169	Tom Aitchison
Eilean Siar (Western Isles)	Stornoway	01851-703773	26,400	£1,024	Malcolm Burr
Falkirk	Falkirk	01324-506070	149,200	£1,070	Mary Pitcaithly
Fife	Glenrothes	01592-414141	356,700	£1,118	Ronnie Hinds
GLASGOW	Glasgow	0141-287 2000	578,800	£1,213	George Black
Highland	Inverness	01463-702000	213,600	£1,163	Arthur McCourt
Inverclyde	Greenock	01475-717171	82,100	£1,198	John Mundell
Midlothian	Dalkeith	0131-270 7500	79,200	£1,210	Trevor Muir
Moray	Elgin	01343-543451	88,100	£1,135	Alastair Keddie
North Ayrshire	Irvine	0845-324100	135,800	£1,152	Ian Snodgrass
North Lanarkshire	Motherwell	01698-302222	323,400	£1,098	Gavin Whitefield
Orkney	Kirkwall	01856-873535	19,600	£1,037	Alistair Buchan
Perth and Kinross	Perth	01738-475000	138,400	£1,158	Bernadette Malone
Renfrewshire	Paisley	0141-842 5000	170,000	£1,165	David Martin
Scottish Borders	Melrose	01835-824000	109,700	£1,084	David Hume
Shetland	Lerwick	01595-693535	22,000	£1,053	Morgan Goodlad
South Ayrshire	Ayr	01292-612000	111,800	£1,154	Tom Cairns
South Lanarkshire	Hamilton	01698-454444	306,300	£1,101	Archie Streng
STIRLING	Stirling	0845-277 7000	86,900	£1,223	Keith Yates
West Dunbartonshire	Dumbarton	01389-737000	91,400	£1,163	David McMillian
West Lothian	Livingston	01506-777000	163,800	£1,128	Alex Linkston

* *Source:* ONS – *Mid-2005 Population Estimates* (Crown copyright)
† Average Band D council tax bill 2007–8
Councils in CAPITAL LETTERS have city status

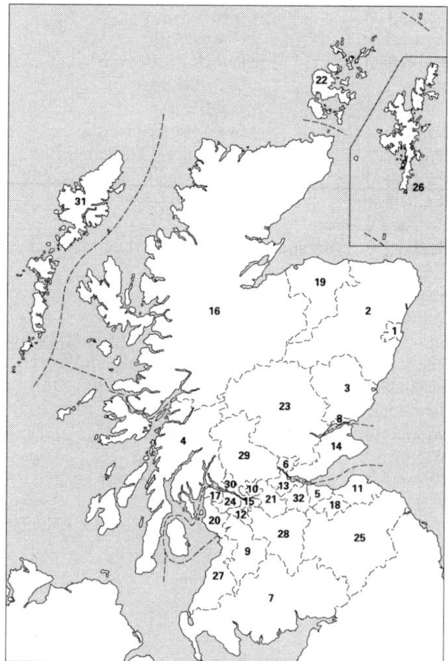

Key	*Council*	*Key*	*Council*
1	Aberdeen City	18	Midlothian
2	Aberdeenshire	19	Moray
3	Angus	20	North Ayrshire
4	Argyll and Bute	21	North Lanarkshire
5	City of Edinburgh	22	Orkney
6	Clackmannanshire	23	Perth and Kinross
7	Dumfries and Galloway	24	Renfrewshire
8	Dundee City	25	Scottish Borders
9	East Ayrshire	26	Shetland
10	East Dunbartonshire	27	South Ayrshire
11	East Lothian	28	South Lanarkshire
12	East Renfrewshire	29	Stirling
13	Falkirk	30	West Dunbartonshire
14	Fife	31	Western Isles (Eilean Siar)
15	Glasgow City	32	West Lothian
16	Highland		
17	Inverclyde		

NORTHERN IRELAND

Northern Ireland has a total area of 14,149 sq. km (5,463 q. miles): land, 13,576 sq. km (5,242 sq. miles); inland vater, 573 sq. km (221 sq. miles).

The population of Northern Ireland at the 2001 census vas 1,685,267 (men 821,449; women 863,818). The verage density of population in 2001 was 119 persons er sq. km (308 per sq. mile).

In 2001 the number of persons in the various religious enominations (expressed as percentages of the total opulation) were: Catholic, 40.26; Presbyterian, 20.69; Church of Ireland, 15.30; Methodist Church in Ireland, .51; other Christian (including Christian related) 6.07; ther religions and philosophies, 0.3; no religion or eligion not stated, 13.88.

FLAG

The official national flag of Northern Ireland is now the Jnion Flag. The flag formerly in use (a white, six-pointed tar in the centre of a red cross on a white field, enclosing red hand and surmounted by a crown) has not been used ince the imposition of direct rule.

PRINCIPAL CITIES

BELFAST

Belfast, the administrative centre of Northern Ireland, is ituated at the mouth of the River Lagan at its entrance to Belfast Lough. The city grew to be a great industrial entre, owing to its easy access by sea to Scottish coal and ron.

The principal buildings are of a relatively young age nd include the parliament buildings at Stormont, the City Hall, Waterfront Hall, the Law Courts, the Public Library and the Museum and Art Gallery.

Belfast received its first charter of incorporation in 613 and was created a city in 1888; the title of lord nayor was conferred in 1892.

LONDONDERRY

Londonderry (originally Derry) is situated on the River Foyle, and has important associations with the City of London. The Irish Society was created by the City of London in 1610, and under its royal charter of 1613 it ortified the city and was for a long time closely associated vith its administration. Because of this connection the city was incorporated in 1613 under the new name of Londonderry.

The city is famous for the great siege of 1688–9, when or 105 days the town held out against the forces of James I. The city walls are still intact and form a circuit of 1.6 km (one mile) around the old city.

Interesting buildings are the Protestant cathedral of St Columb's (1633) and the Guildhall, reconstructed in 1912 and containing a number of beautiful stained glass windows, many of which were presented by the livery companies of London.

Three other places in Northern Ireland have been granted city status: Armagh (1994), Lisburn (2002) and Newry (2002).

CONSTITUTIONAL DEVELOPMENTS

Northern Ireland is subject to the same fundamental constitutional provisions which apply to the rest of the United Kingdom. It had its own parliament and government from 1921 to 1972, but after increasing civil unrest the Northern Ireland (Temporary Provisions) Act 1972 transferred the legislative and executive powers of the Northern Ireland parliament and government to the UK parliament and a secretary of state. The Northern Ireland Constitution Act 1973 provided for devolution in Northern Ireland through an assembly and executive, but a power-sharing executive formed by the Northern Ireland political parties in January 1974 collapsed in May 1974. Following the collapse of the power-sharing executive Northern Ireland returned to direct rule governance under the provisions of the Northern Ireland Act 1974, placing the Northern Ireland department under the direction and control of the Northern Ireland secretary.

In December 1993 the British and Irish governments published the Joint Declaration complementing their political talks, and making clear that any settlement would need to be founded on principles of democracy and consent. The declaration also stated that all democratically mandated parties could be involved in political talks as long as they permanently renounced paramilitary violence.

On 12 January 1998 the British and Irish governments issued a joint document, *Propositions on Heads of Agreement,* proposing the establishment of various new cross-border bodies; further proposals were presented on 27 January. A draft peace settlement was issued by the talks' chairman, US Senator George Mitchell, on 6 April 1998 but was rejected by the Unionists the following day. On 10 April agreement was reached between the British and Irish governments and the eight Northern Ireland political parties still involved in the talks (the Good Friday Agreement). The agreement provided for an elected Northern Ireland Assembly, a North/South Ministerial Council, and a British-Irish Council comprising representatives of the British, Irish, Channel Islands and Isle of Man governments and members of the new assemblies for Scotland, Wales and Northern Ireland. Further points included the abandonment of the Republic of Ireland's constitutional claim to Northern Ireland; the decommissioning of weapons; the release of paramilitary prisoners and changes in policing.

Referendums on the agreement were held in Northern Ireland and the Republic of Ireland on 22 May 1998. In Northern Ireland the turnout was 81 per cent, of which 71.12 per cent voted in favour of the agreement. In the Republic of Ireland, the turnout was about 55 per cent, of which 94.4 per cent voted in favour of both the agreement and the necessary constitutional change. In the UK, the Northern Ireland Act 1998, enshrining the provisions of the agreement, received royal assent in November 1998.

On 28 April 2003 the secretary of state again assumed responsibility for the direction of the Northern Ireland departments on the dissolution of the Northern Ireland Assembly, following its initial suspension from midnight on 14 October 2002. In 2006, following the passing of the Northern Ireland Act, the secretary of state created a non-legislative fixed-term assembly which would cease to operate either when the political parties agreed to restore devolution, or on 24 November 2006 (whichever occurred first). In October 2006 a timetable to restore devolution was drawn up (St Andrews Agreement) and a transitional Northern Ireland Assembly was formed on 24 November. The transitional assembly was dissolved in January 2007 in preparation for elections to be held on 7 March; following the elections a power-sharing executive was formed and the new 108-member Northern Ireland Assembly became operational on 8 May 2007.

See also Regional Government and Events of the Year.

FINANCE

Northern Ireland's expenditure is funded through th Northern Ireland Consolidated Fund (NICF). Up unt devolution on 2 December 1999, the NICF was large financed by Northern Ireland's attributed share of U taxation and supplemented by a grant-in-aid. Fro devolution, these separate elements have been subsume into a single block grant. The Northern Irelan Departmental Expenditure Limit for 2007–8 was set £8,612m.

LORD-LIEUTENANTS AND HIGH SHERIFFS

County	*Lord-Lieutenant*	*High Sheriff (2007)*
Antrim	The Lord O'Neill, TD	Dr Joseph Wilson
Armagh	The Earl of Caledon	Dr Colin Mathews
Belfast City	Lady Carswell, OBE	Thomas Kirkpatrick
Down	William Hall	John Fisher
Fermanagh	The Earl of Erne	Rosemary Forde
Londonderry	Denis Desmond, CBE	Sharyn Griffith
Londonderry City	Dr Donal Keegan, OBE	Richard Sterling, OBE
Tyrone	The Duke of Abercorn	John Little

LOCAL COUNCILS

Council	*Telephone*	*Population**	*Chief Executive*
Antrim, Co. Down	028-9446 3113	50,500	David McCammick
Ards, Co. Down	028-9182 4000	75,300	Ashley Boreland
ARMAGH CITY, Co. Armagh	028-3752 9600	55,800	John Briggs *(acting)*
Ballymena, Co. Antrim	028-2566 0300	60,700	*vacant*
Ballymoney, Co. Antrim	028-2766 0200	28,700	John Dempsey
Banbridge, Co. Down	028-4066 0600	44,800	Liam Hannaway
BELFAST CITY, Co. Antrim and Co. Down	028-9032 0202	268,000	Peter McNaney
Carrickfergus, Co. Antrim	028-9335 8000	39,200	Alan Cardwell
Castlereagh, Co. Down	028-9046 4500	65,700	Adrian Donaldson
Coleraine, Co. Londonderry	028-7034 7034	56,600	Davy Wreath *(acting*
Cookstown, Co. Tyrone	028-8676 2205	34,100	Michael McGuckin
Craigavon, Co. Armagh	028-3831 2400	84,700	Francis Rock
DERRY CITY, Co. Londonderry	028-7136 5151	107,300	Anthony McGurk
Down, Co. Down	028-4461 0800	67,400	John McGrillen
Dungannon and South Tyrone, Co. Tyrone	028-8772 0300	50,700	Alan Burke *(acting)*
Fermanagh, Co. Fermanagh	028-6632 5050	59,700	Rodney Connor
Larne, Co. Antrim	028-2827 2313	31,100	Geraldine McGahey
Limavady, Co. Londonderry	028-7772 2226	34,100	Liam Flanigan
LISBURN CITY, Co. Antrim	028-9250 9250	111,500	Norman Davidson
Magherafelt, Co. Londonderry	028-7939 7979	41,800	John McLaughlin
Moyle, Co. Antrim	028-2076 2225	16,500	Richard Lewis
NEWRY and Mourne, Co. Down and Co. Armagh	028-3031 3031	91,600	Thomas McCall
Newtownabbey, Co. Antrim	028-9034 0000	80,800	Norman Dunn
North Down, Co. Down	028-9127 0371	78,300	Trevor Polley
Omagh, Co. Tyrone	028 8224 5321	50,700	Daniel McSorley
Strabane, Co. Tyrone	028-7138 2204	38,700	Philip Faithfull

* *Source:* ONS – *Mid-2005 Population Estimates* (Crown copyright)
Councils in CAPITAL LETTERS have city status

THE ISLE OF MAN

Ellan Vannin

The Isle of Man is an island situated in the Irish Sea, at latitude 54° 3′–54° 25′ N. and longitude 4° 18′–4° 47′ W., nearly equidistant from England, Scotland and Ireland. Although the early inhabitants were of Celtic origin, the Isle of Man was part of the Norwegian Kingdom of the Hebrides until 1266, when this was ceded to Scotland. Subsequently granted to the Stanleys (Earls of Derby) in the 15th century and later to the Dukes of Atholl, it was brought under the administration of the crown in 1765. The island forms the bishopric of Sodor and Man.

The total land area is 572 sq. km (221 sq. miles). The 2006 census showed a resident population of 80,058 (men, 39,523; women, 40,535). The main language in use is English. There are no remaining native speakers of Manx Gaelic but around 1,550 people are able to speak the language.

CAPITAL – ΨDouglas; population, 26,218 (2006). ΨCastletown (3,109) is the ancient capital; the other towns are ΨPeel (4,280) and ΨRamsey (7,309)

FLAG – A red flag charged with three conjoined armoured legs in white and gold

NATIONAL DAY – 5 July (Tynwald Day)

GOVERNMENT

The Isle of Man is a self-governing crown dependency, with its own parliamentary, legal and administrative system. The British government is responsible for international relations and defence. Under the UK Act of Accession, Protocol 3, the island's relationship with the European Union is limited to trade alone and does not extend to financial aid. The Lieutenant-Governor is the Queen's personal representative on the island.

The legislature, Tynwald, is the oldest parliament in the world in continuous existence. It has two branches: the Legislative Council and the House of Keys. The council consists of the President of Tynwald, the Bishop of Sodor and Man, the Attorney-General (who does not have a vote) and eight members elected by the House of Keys. The House of Keys has 24 members, elected by universal adult suffrage. The branches sit separately to consider legislation and sit together, as Tynwald Court, for most other parliamentary purposes.

The presiding officer of Tynwald Court is the President of Tynwald, elected by the members, who also presides over sittings of the Legislative Council. The presiding officer of the House of Keys is the Speaker, who is elected by members of the house.

The principal members of the Manx government are the chief minister and nine departmental ministers, who comprise the Council of Ministers.

Lieutenant-Governor, HE Vice-Adm. Sir Paul Kenneth Haddacks, KCB
ADC to the Lieutenant-Governor, C. J. Tummon
President of Tynwald, Hon. Noel Cringle
Speaker, House of Keys, Hon. Steve Rodan, SHK
The First Deemster and Clerk of the Rolls, John Michael Kerruish
Clerk of Tynwald, Secretary to the House of Keys and Counsel to the Speaker, Malachy Cornwell-Kelly
Clerk of the Legislative Council and Deputy Clerk of Tynwald, Mrs M. Cullen
Attorney-General, W. J. H. Corlett, QC
Chief Minister, Hon. Tony Brown, MHK
Chief Secretary, Mrs M. Williams

ECONOMY

Most of the income generated in the island is earned in the services sector with financial and professional services accounting for just over half of the national income. Tourism and manufacturing are also major generators of income whilst the island's other traditional industries of agriculture and fishing now play a smaller role in the economy. Under the terms of Protocol 3, the island has tariff-free access to EU markets for its goods.

In May 2007 the island's unemployment rate was 1.4 per cent and inflation (RPI) was 4.2 per cent.

FINANCE

The budget for 2007–8 provides for net revenue expenditure of £538.2m. The principal sources of government revenue are taxes on income and expenditure. Income tax is payable at a rate of 10 per cent on the first £10,500 of taxable income for single resident individuals and 18 per cent on the balance, after personal allowances of £8,850. These bands are doubled for married couples. The rate of income tax for trading companies is zero per cent except for income from banking and land and property, which is taxed at 10 per cent. By agreement with the British government, the island keeps most of its rates of indirect taxation (VAT and duties) the same as those in the UK. However, VAT on tourist accommodation, property, repairs and renovations is charged at 5 per cent. A reciprocal agreement on national insurance benefits and pensions exists between the governments of the Isle of Man and the UK. Taxes are also charged on property (rates), but these are comparatively low.

The major government expenditure items are health, social security, social services and education, which account for 59 per cent of the government budget. The island makes an annual contribution to the UK for defence and other external services.

The island has a special relationship with the European Union and neither contributes money to nor receives funds from the EU budget.

Ψ = sea port

THE CHANNEL ISLANDS

The Channel Islands, situated off the north-west coast of France (at a distance of 16km (10 miles) at their closest point), are the only portions of the Dukedom of Normandy still belonging to the crown, to which they have been attached since the Norman Conquest of 1066. They were the only British territory to come under German occupation during the Second World War, following invasion on 30 June and 1 July 1940. The islands were relieved by British forces on 9 May 1945, and 9 May (Liberation Day) is now observed as a bank and public holiday.

The islands consist of Jersey (11,630ha/28,717 acres), Guernsey (6,340ha/15,654 acres), and the dependencies of Guernsey: Alderney (795ha/1,962 acres), Brecqhou (30ha/74 acres), Great Sark (419ha/1,035 acres), Little Sark (97ha/239 acres), Herm (130ha/320 acres), Jethou (18ha/44 acres) and Lihou (15ha/38 acres) – a total of 19,474ha/48,083 acres, or 194 sq. km/75 sq. miles. The 2001 census showed the population of Jersey as 87,186; Guernsey, 59,807 and Alderney, 2,294. Sark did not complete the same census but a recent informal census gave its population figure as 591. The official languages are English and French. In country districts of Jersey and Guernsey and throughout Sark a Norman-French *patois* is also in use, though to a lesser extent.

GOVERNMENT

The islands are crown dependencies with their own legislative assemblies (the States in Jersey, Guernsey and Alderney and the Chief Pleas in Sark), systems of local administration and law, and their own courts. Acts passed by the States require the sanction of the Queen-in-council. The British government is responsible for defence and international relations. The Channel Islands have trading rights only (not including financial aid) within the European Union.

In both Jersey and Guernsey bailiwicks the Lieutenant-Governor and Commander-in-Chief, who is appointed by the crown, is the personal representative of the Queen and the channel of communication between the crown (via the Privy Council) and the island's government.

In 2001 a ministerial system of government was introduced in Jersey to replace the previous committee system. The executive consists of a chief minister and nine ministers who form the Council of Ministers. Ministers are assisted by up to 13 assistant ministers. Members of the States who are not in the executive are able to sit on a number of scrutiny panels and the Public Accounts Committee to examine the policy of the executive and hold ministers to account. On 1 May 2004 Guernsey also introduced a ministerial governance system – a Policy Council comprising a chief minister and ten departmental ministers. There are also five specialist committees, each led by a chairman, responsible for public sector pay negotiations, parliamentary procedural matters and for scrutinising policy, finance and legislation. Justice is administered by the royal courts of Jersey and Guernsey, each consisting of the bailiff and 12 elected jurats. The bailiffs of Jersey and Guernsey, appointed by the crown, are presidents of the states and of the royal courts of their respective islands.

Each bailiwick constitutes a deanery under th jurisdiction of the Bishop of Winchester.

ECONOMY

A mild climate and good soil have led to the developmen of intensive systems of agriculture and horticulture, whic form a significant part of the economy. Equally importan are earnings from tourism and banking and finance: th low rates of income and corporation tax and the absenc of death duties and VAT make the islands an importan offshore financial centre.

Principal exports are agricultural produce and flowers imports are chiefly machinery, manufactured goods, food fuel and chemicals. Trade with the UK is regarded a internal.

British currency is legal tender in the Channel Island but each bailiwick issues its own coins and notes (*se* Currency section). They also issue their own postag stamps; UK stamps are not valid.

JERSEY

Lieutenant-Governor and Commander-in-Chief of Jersey, HE Lt.-Gen. Andrew Peter Ridgway, CB, CBE, *apptd* 200
Secretary and ADC, Lt.-Col. A. J. C. Woodrow, OBE, MC
Bailiff of Jersey, Sir Philip Bailhache, Kt.
Deputy Bailiff, M. C. St J. Birt
Attorney-General, W. J. Bailhache, QC
Receiver-General, P. Lewin
Solicitor-General, Miss S. C. Nicolle, QC
Greffier of the States, M. N. de la Haye
States Treasurer, Mr I. Black

FINANCE

	2005	*200*
Revenue income	£699,100,000	£732,557,00
Revenue expenditure	£652,479,000	£670,749,00
Capital expenditure	£56,686,000	£58,090,00

CHIEF TOWN – ΨSt Helier, on the south coast
FLAG – A white field charged with a red saltire cross, and the arms of Jersey in the upper centre

GUERNSEY AND DEPENDENCIES

Lieutenant-Governor and Commander-in-Chief of the Bailiwick of Guernsey and its Dependencies, HE Vice-Adm. Sir Fabian Malbon, KBE, *apptd* 2005
Secretary and ADC, Col. R Graham, MBE
Bailiff of Guernsey, Geoffrey Rowland
Deputy Bailiff, Richard Collas
HM Procureur and Receiver-General, John van Leuven, QC
HM Comptroller, Howard Roberts, QC
Chief Minister, Deputy Mike Torode
Chief Executive, Mike Brown

FINANCE

	2005	*2006*
Revenue	£310,481,250	£325,098,105
Expenditure	£291,604,688	£294,612,476

HIEF TOWNS – Ψ St Peter Port, on the east coast of Guernsey; St Anne on Alderney
AG – White, bearing a red cross of St George, with a gold cross of Normandy overall in the centre

.DERNEY
esident of the States, Sir Norman Browse, OBE
ief Executive, David Jeremiah, OBE, QC
effier, Sarah Kelly

RK*
gneur of Sark, John Beaumont, OBE
neschal, Lt.-Col. R Guille, MBE
effier, Trevor Hamon

OTHER DEPENDENCIES
Herm and Lihou are owned by the States of Guernsey; Herm is leased. Jethou is leased by the Crown to the States of Guernsey and is sub-let by the States. Brecqhou is within the legislative and judicial territory of Sark.

* On 4 October 2006 the islanders of Sark voted in favour of establishing a 28-member elected assembly from December 2008; *see also* UK Events of the Year

Ψ = sea port

EUROPEAN PARLIAMENT

European parliament elections take place at five-yearly intervals; the first direct elections to the parliament were held in 1979. In mainland Britain, members of the European parliament (MEPs) were elected in all constituencies on a first-past-the-post basis until 1999 when a regional system of proportional representation was introduced; in Northern Ireland three MEPs have been elected by the single transferable vote system of proportional representation since 1979. From 1979 to 1994 the number of seats held by the UK in the European parliament was 81, which increased to 87 in the 1994 election and decreased to 78 (England 64, Wales 4, Scotland 7, Northern Ireland 3) following EU enlargement in 2004.

At the 2004 European parliament elections all UK MEPs were elected under a 'closed-list' regional system of proportional representation, with England being divided into nine regions and Scotland, Wales and Northern Ireland each constituting a region. Since June 2004 residents of Gibraltar vote in the South West region. Parties submitted a list of candidates for each region in their own order of preference. Voters voted for a party or an independent candidate, and the first seat in each region was allocated to the party or candidate with the highest number of votes. The rest of the seats in each region were then allocated broadly in proportion to each party's share of the vote. Each region returned the following number of members: East Midlands, 6; Eastern, 7; London, 9; North East, 3; North West, 9; South East, 10; South West, 7; West Midlands, 7; Yorkshire and the Humber, 6; Wales, 4; Northern Ireland, 3; Scotland, 7.

If a vacancy occurs due to the resignation or death of an MEP, it is filled by the next available person on that party's list. If an independent MEP resigns or dies, a by-election is held. Where an MEP leaves the party on whose list he/she was elected, there is no requirement to resign and he/she can remain in office until the next election.

British subjects and nationals of member states of the European Union are eligible for election to the European parliament provided they are 21 or over and not subject to disqualification. Since 1994, eligible citizens have had the right to vote in elections to the European parliament in the UK as long as they are entered on the electoral register.

MEPs currently receive a salary from the parliaments or governments of their respective member states, set at the level of the national parliamentary salary and subject to national taxation. British MEPs receive a salary of £60,277.

From 2009 a new MEP statute will take effect introducing the same salary for all MEPs at a rate of 38.5 per cent of the basic salary of a European court of justice judge.

The next elections to the European parliament will take place in June 2009. For further information visit the European parliament's website (W www.europarl.org.uk).

UK MEMBERS *as at June 2007*

* Denotes membership of the last European parliament
† Replacements since the last election
‡ Previously a member of UKIP
** Previously a member of DUP

**Allister, James (b. 1953), *NI, Northern Ireland*
Ashworth, Richard (b. 1947), *C., South East*
***Atkins**, Rt. Hon. Sir Robert (b. 1946), *C., North West*
***Attwooll**, Elspeth M. A. (b. 1943), *LD, Scotland*
Batten, Gerard (b. 1972), *UKIP, London*
***Beazley**, Christopher J. P. (b. 1952), *C., Eastern*
Bloom, Godfrey (b. 1949), *UKIP, Yorkshire and the Humber*
***Booth**, Graham (b. 1940), *UKIP, South West*
***Bowis**, John C., OBE (b. 1945), *C., London*
†**Bowles**, Sharon M. (b. 1953), *LD, South East*
***Bradbourn**, Philip, OBE (b. 1951), *C., West Midlands*
***Bushill-Matthews**, Philip (b. 1943), *C., West Midlands*
***Callanan**, Martin (b. 1961), *C., North East*
***Cashman**, Michael (b. 1950), *Lab., West Midlands*
***Chichester**, Giles B. (b. 1946), *C., South West*
Clark, Derek (b. 1933), *UKIP, East Midlands*
***Corbett**, Richard (b. 1955), *Lab., Yorkshire and the Humber*
***Davies**, Christopher G. (b. 1954), *LD, North West*
de Brún, Bairbre (b. 1954), *SF, Northern Ireland*
***Deva**, Niranjan J. A. (Nirj), FRSA (b. 1948), *C., South East*
***Dover**, Densmore (b. 1938), *C., North West*
***Duff**, Andrew N. (b. 1950), *LD, Eastern*
***Elles**, James E. M. (b. 1949), *C., South East*
***Evans**, Jillian R. (b. 1959), *PC, Wales*
***Evans**, Jonathan P., FRSA (b. 1950), *C., Wales*
***Evans**, Robert J. E. (b. 1956), *Lab., London*
***Farage**, Nigel P. (b. 1964), *UKIP, South East*
***Ford**, Glyn J. (b. 1950), *Lab., South West*
***Gill**, Neena (b. 1956), *Lab., West Midlands*
Hall, Fiona (b. 1955), *LD, North East*
***Hannan**, Daniel J. (b. 1971), *C., South East*
***Harbour**, Malcolm (b. 1947), *C., West Midlands*
***Heaton-Harris**, Christopher (b. 1967), *C., East Midlands*
***Helmer**, Roger (b. 1944), *C., East Midlands*
***Honeyball**, Mary (b. 1952), *Lab., London*
***Howitt**, Richard (b. 1961), *Lab., Eastern*
***Hudghton**, Ian (b. 1951), *SNP, Scotland*
***Hughes**, Stephen (b. 1952), *Lab., North East*
***Jackson**, Caroline F., DPHIL (b. 1946), *C., South West*
†**Kamall**, Syed S. (b. 1967), *C., London*
Karim, Sajjad (b. 1970), *LD, North West*
‡**Kilroy-Silk**, Robert (b. 1942), *NI, East Midlands*
***Kinnock**, Glenys (b. 1944), *Lab., Wales*
***Kirkhope**, Timothy J. R. (b. 1945), *C., Yorkshire and the Humber*
Knapman, Roger (b. 1944), *UKIP, South West*
***Lambert**, Jean D. (b. 1950), *Green, London*
***Lucas**, Dr Caroline (b. 1960), *Green, South East*
***Ludford**, Baroness (b. 1951), *LD, London*
***Lynne**, Elizabeth (b. 1948), *LD, West Midlands*
***McAvan**, Linda (b. 1962), *Lab., Yorkshire and the Humber*

McCarthy, Arlene (b. 1960), *Lab., North West*
McMillan-Scott, Edward H. C. (b. 1949), *C., Yorkshire and the Humber*
Martin, David W. (b. 1954), *Lab., Scotland*
Moraes, Claude (b. 1965), *Lab., London*
Morgan, Eluned (b. 1967), *Lab., Wales*
Mote, Ashley (b. 1936), *NI, South East*
attrass, Mike (b. 1945), *UKIP, West Midlands*
Newton Dunn, William F. (Bill) (b. 1941), *LD, East Midlands*
Nicholson, James (b. 1945), *UUP, Northern Ireland*
Nicholson of Winterbourne, Baroness (b. 1941), *LD, South East*
Parish, Neil (b. 1956), *C., South West*
Purvis, John R., CBE (b. 1938), *C., Scotland*
Simpson, Brian (b. 1953), *Lab., North West*
***Skinner**, Peter W. (b. 1959), *Lab., South East*
Smith, Alyn (b. 1973), *SNP, Scotland*
***Stevenson**, Struan (b. 1948), *C., Scotland*
***Stihler**, Catherine D. (b. 1973), *Lab., Scotland*
***Sturdy**, Robert W. (b. 1944), *C., Eastern*
***Sumberg**, David (b. 1941), *C., North West*
***Tannock**, Dr Charles (b. 1957), *C., London*
***Titford**, Jeffrey (b. 1933), *UKIP, Eastern*
***Titley**, Gary (b. 1950), *Lab., North West,*
***Van Orden**, Geoffrey (b. 1945), *C., Eastern*
***Wallis**, Diana (b. 1954), *LD, Yorkshire and the Humber*
***Watson**, Graham R. (b. 1956), *LD, South West*
Whittaker, John (b. 1945), *UKIP, North West*
†Willmott, Glenis (b. 1951), *Lab., East Midlands*
Wise, Tom (b. 1948), *UKIP, Eastern*

K REGIONS *as at 10 June 2004 election*

bbreviations

GS	Alliance for Green Socialism
ommon	The Common Good
D	English Democrats
FP	English Freedom Party
W	Forward Wales
I	Non-attached Members
CV	Operation Christian Vote
ace	Peace Party
PBG	People's Party for Better Government
espect	Respect – Unity Coalition
EA	Socialist Environmental Alliance
nior	Senior Citizens
c. All.	Socialist Alliance
SP	Scottish Socialist Party
WW	Scottish Wind Watch

or other abbreviations, *see* UK eneral Election Results
or detailed information on which eas of the country are covered by a rticular region, please contact the ome Office.

ASTERN

edfordshire, Cambridgeshire, ssex, Hertfordshire, Luton, Norfolk, eterborough, Southend-on-Sea, uffolk, Thurrock)

4,137,210	T. 36.73%
.	465,526 (30.8%)
KIP	296,160 (19.6%)
ab.	244,929 (16.2%)
D	211,378 (14.0%)
d.	93,028 (6.2%)
reen	84,068 (5.6%)
NP	65,557 (4.3%)
D	26,807 (1.8%)
espect	13,904 (0.9%)
d.	5,137 (0.3%)
roLife	3,730 (0.3%)
majority	169,366

une 1999, C. maj. 174,959)

MEMBERS ELECTED
G. van Orden, *C.*
*J. Titford, *UKIP*
*R. Howitt, *Lab.*
*R. Sturdy, *C.*
A. Duff, *LD*
*C. Beazley, *C.*
T. Wise, *UKIP*

EAST MIDLANDS

(Derby, Derbyshire, Leicester, Leicestershire, Northamptonshire, Nottingham, Nottinghamshire, Rutland)

E. 3,220,019	T. 43.88%
C.	371,362 (26.4%)
UKIP	366,498 (26.1%)
Lab.	294,918 (21.0%)
LD	181,964 (12.9%)
BNP	91,860 (6.5%)
Green	76,633 (5.5%)
Respect	20,009 (1.4%)
Ind.	2,615 (0.2%)
Ind.	847 (0.1%)
C. majority	4,864

(June 1999, C. maj. 78,906)

MEMBERS ELECTED
*R. Helmer, *C.*
‡R. Kilroy-Silk, *NI*
*P. Whitehead, *Lab.*
*C. Heaton-Harris, *C.*
D. Clark, *UKIP*
*W. Newton Dunn, *LD*

LONDON

E. 5,054,957	T. 37.65%
C.	504,941 (26.5%)
Lab.	466,584 (24.5%)
LD	288,790 (15.2%)
UKIP	232,633 (12.2%)
Green	158,986 (8.4%)
Respect	91,175 (4.8%)
BNP	76,152 (4.0%)
CPA	45,038 (2.4%)
ED	15,945 (0.8%)
PPBG	5,205 (0.3%)
C. majority	38,357

(June 1999, Lab. maj. 26,477)

MEMBERS ELECTED
†S. Kamall, *C.*
*C. Moraes, *Lab.*
*Baroness Ludford, *LD*
*J. Bowis, *C.*
*M. Honeyball, *Lab.*
G. Batten, *UKIP*
*C. Tannock, *C.*
*J. Lambert, *Green*
*R. Evans, *Lab.*

NORTH EAST

(Co. Durham, Darlington, Hartlepool, Middlesbrough, Northumberland, Redcar and Cleveland, Stockton-on-Tees, Tyne and Wear)

E. 1,905,132	T. 41.54%
Lab.	266,057 (34.1%)
C.	144,969 (18.6%)
LD	138,791 (17.8%)
UKIP	94,887 (12.2%)
BNP	50,249 (6.4%)
Ind.	39,658 (5.1%)
Green	37,247 (4.8%)
Respect	8,633 (1.1%)
Lab. majority	121,088

(June 1999, Lab. maj. 57,000)

MEMBERS ELECTED
*S. Hughes, *Lab.*
*M. Callanan, *C.*
Ms F. Hall, *LD*

NORTHERN IRELAND

(Northern Ireland forms a three-member seat with a single transferable vote system)

E. 1,072,669	T. 51.72%
Jim Allister, *NI*	175,761 (31.9%)
Bairbre de Brún, *SF*	144,541 (26.3%)
Jim Nicholson, *UUP*	91,164 (16.6%)
Martin Morgan, *SDLP*	87,559 (15.9%)
John Gilliland, *Ind.*	36,270 (6.6%)

Eamonn McCann, *SEA*	9,172 (1.6%)
Lindsay Whitcroft, *Green*	4,810 (0.9%)

MEMBERS ELECTED
**J. Allister, *NI*
B. de Brún, *SF*
*J. Nicholson, *UUP*

NORTH WEST

(Blackburn-with-Darwen, Blackpool, Cheshire, Cumbria, Greater Manchester, Halton, Lancashire, Merseyside, Warrington)

E. 5,151,488	T. 41.46%
Lab.	576,388 (27.3%)
C.	509,446 (24.1%)
LD	335,063 (15.8%)
UKIP	257,158 (12.2%)
BNP	134,959 (6.4%)
Green	117,393 (5.6%)
Lib.	96,325 (4.6%)
ED	34,110 (1.6%)
Respect	24,636 (1.2%)
Country	11,283 (0.5%)
ProLife	10,084 (0.5%)
Ind.	8,318 (0.4%)
Lab. majority	66,942

(June 1999, C. maj. 9,516)

MEMBERS ELECTED
*G. Titley, *Lab.*
*D. Dover, *C.*
*C. Davies, *LD*
*A. McCarthy, *Lab.*
J. Whittaker, *UKIP*
*D. Sumberg, *C.*
*T. Wynn, *Lab.*
*Sir Robert Atkins, *C.*
S. Karim, *LD*

SCOTLAND

E. 3,839,952	T. 30.75%
Lab.	310,865 (26.4%)
SNP	231,505 (19.7%)
C.	209,028 (17.8%)
LD	154,178 (13.1%)
Green	79,695 (6.8%)
UKIP	78,828 (6.7%)
SSP	61,356 (5.2%)
OCV	21,056 (1.8%)
BNP	19,427 (1.6%)
SWW	7,255 (0.6%)
Ind.	3,624 (0.3%)
Lab. majority	79,360

(June 1999, Lab. maj. 14,962)

MEMBERS ELECTED
*D. Martin, *Lab.*
*I. Hudghton, *SNP*
*S. Stevenson, *C.*
*C. Stihler, *Lab.*
*E. Attwooll, *LD*
A. Smith, *SNP*
*J. Purvis, *C.*

SOUTH EAST

(Bracknell Forest, Brighton and Hove, Buckinghamshire, East Sussex, Hampshire, Isle of Wight, Kent, Medway, Milton Keynes, Oxfordshire, Portsmouth, Reading, Slough, Southampton, Surrey, West Berkshire, West Sussex, Windsor and Maidenhead, Wokingham)

E. 6,034,549	T. 36.78%
C.	776,370 (35.2%)
UKIP	431,111 (19.5%)
LD	338,342 (15.3%)
Lab.	301,398 (13.7%)
Green	173,351 (7.9%)
BNP	64,877 (2.9%)
Senior	42,681 (1.9%)
ED	29,126 (1.3%)
Respect	13,426 (0.9%)
Peace	12,572 (0.6%)
CPA	11,733 (0.5%)
ProLife	6,579 (0.3%)
Ind.	5,671 (0.3%)
C. majority	345,259

(June 1999, C. maj. 369,785)

MEMBERS ELECTED
*D. Hannan, *C.*
*N. Farage, *UKIP*
*N. Deva, *C.*
†S. Bowles, *LD*
*P. Skinner, *Lab.*
*J. Elles, *C.*
‡A. Mote, *NI*
R. Ashworth, *C.*
*Dr Caroline Lucas, *Green*
*Baroness Nicholson of Winterbourne, *LD*

SOUTH WEST

(Bath and North East Somerset, Bournemouth, Bristol, Cornwall, Devon, Dorset, Gloucestershire, North Somerset, South Gloucestershire, Swindon, Torbay, Wiltshire)

E. 3,845,210	T. 37.80%
C.	457,371 (31.6%)
UKIP	326,784 (22.5%)
LD	265,619 (18.3%)
Lab.	209,908 (14.5%)
Green	103,821 (7.2%)
BNP	43,653 (3.0%)
Country	30,824 (2.1%)
Respect	10,437 (0.7%)
C. majority	130,587

(June 1999, C. maj. 246,283)

MEMBERS ELECTED
*N. Parish, *C.*
G. Booth, *UKIP*
*G. Watson, *LD*
*Dr Caroline Jackson, *C.*
*G. Ford, *Lab.*
R. Knapman, *UKIP*
*G. Chichester, *C.*

WALES

E. 2,218,649	T. 41.86
Lab.	297,810 (32.1
C.	177,771 (19.1
PC	159,888 (17.2
UKIP	96,677 (10.4
LD	96,116 (10.4
Green	32,761 (3.5
BNP	27,135 (2.9
FW	17,280 (1.9
Ch. D	6,821 (0.7
Respect	5,427 (0.6
Lab. majority	120,03

(June 1999, Lab. maj. 14,455)

MEMBERS ELECTED
*G. Kinnock, *Lab.*
*J. Evans, *C.*
*J. Evans, *PC*
*E. Morgan, *Lab.*

WEST MIDLANDS

(Herefordshire, Shropshire, Staffordshire, Stoke-on-Trent, Telford and Wrekin, Warwickshire, West Midlands Metropolitan area, Worcestershire)

E. 3,957,848	T. 36.63
C.	392,937 (27.3
Lab.	336,613 (23.4
UKIP	251,366 (17.5
LD	197,479 (13.7
BNP	107,794 (7.5
Green	73,991 (5.2
Respect	34,704 (2.4
Pensioner	33,501 (2.3
Common	8,650 (0.6
C. majority	56,32

(June 1999, C. maj. 84,048)

MEMBERS ELECTED
*P. Bushill-Matthews, *C.*
*M. Cashman, *Lab.*
M. Nattrass, *UKIP*
*E. Lynne, *LD*
*P. Bradbourn, *C.*
*N. Gill, *Lab.*
*M. Harbour, *C.*

ORKSHIRE AND THE UMBER

:ast Riding of Yorkshire, Kingston-
on-Hull, North East Lincolnshire,
orth Lincolnshire, North Yorkshire,
outh Yorkshire, West Yorkshire,
ork)

. 3,719,717	T. 42.93%
ab.	413,213 (26.3%)
	387,369 (24.6%)
D	244,607 (15.6%)
KIP	228,666 (14.0%)
NP	126,538 (8.0%)
reen	90,337 (5.7%)
espect	29,865 (1.9%)
D	24,068 (1.5%)
ıd.	14,762 (0.9%)
GS	13,776 (0.9%)
ab. majority	25,844

une 1999, C. maj. 39,629)

IEMBERS ELECTED
Linda McAvan, *Lab.*
T. Kirkhope, *C.*
D. Wallis, *LD*
. Bloom, *UKIP*
R. Corbett, *Lab.*
E. McMillan-Scott, *C.*

LAW COURTS AND OFFICES

HIERARCHY OF ENGLISH COURTS

Court	*Courts it binds*	*Courts it follows*
European Court of Justice	The court making the preliminary reference	None
House of Lords	All English courts	None
Court of Appeal	Divisional Courts High Court Crown Court County courts Magistrates' courts	House of Lords
Divisional Courts	High Court Crown Court County courts Magistrates' courts	House of Lords Court of Appeal
High Court	County courts Magistrates' courts	House of Lords Court of Appeal Divisional Courts
Crown Court	None	House of Lords
County courts	None	Court of Appeal
Magistrates' courts	None	Divisional Courts High Court

JUDICATURE OF ENGLAND AND WALES

The legal system in England and Wales is divided into criminal law and civil law. Criminal law is concerned with acts harmful to the community and the rules laid down by the state for the benefit of citizens, whereas civil law governs the relationships and transactions between individuals. Administrative law is a kind of civil law usually concerning the interaction of individuals and the state, and most cases are heard in tribunals specific to the subject (*see* Tribunals section). Scotland and Northern Ireland possess legal systems that differ from the system in England and Wales in law, judicial procedure and court structure, but retain the distinction between criminal and civil law.

The appellate committee of the House of Lords is the supreme judicial authority. It is the ultimate court of appeal for all courts in Great Britain and Northern Ireland (except criminal courts in Scotland) for all cases except those concerning the interpretation and application of European Community law, including preliminary rulings requested by British courts and tribunals, which are decided by the European court of justice (*see* European Union section). As a court of appeal the House of Lords consists of 12 Lords of Appeal in Ordinary (law lords); virtually all appeals concern the meaning of the law, rather than the evidence in a particular case.

Under the provisions of the Criminal Appeal Act 1995, a commission was set up to direct and supervise investigations into possible miscarriages of justice and to refer cases to the courts on the grounds of conviction and sentence; these functions were formerly the responsibility of the home secretary.

SUPREME COURT OF JUDICATURE

The supreme court of judicature comprises the high cou of justice, the crown court and the court of appeal. Th President of the Courts of England and Wales, a new tit given to the Lord Chief Justice under the Constitution Reform Act 2005, is the head of the judiciary.

The high court was created in 1875 and combine many previously separate courts. Sittings are held at th royal courts of justice in London or at about 120 distri registries outside the capital. It is the superior civil cou and is split into three divisions – the chancery divisio the Queen's bench division and the family division – eac of which is further divided. The chancery division headed by the Chancellor of the High Court and concerned mainly with equity, trusts, tax and bankruptc while also including two specialist courts, the paten court and the companies court. The Queen's benc division (QBD) is the largest of the three divisions, and headed by its own president, who is also Head c Criminal Justice. It deals with common law (ie tor contract, debt and personal injuries), some tax law, e VAT tribunal appeals, and encompasses the admiralt court and the commercial court. The QBD als administers the technology and construction court. Th family division was created in 1970 and is headed by i own president, who is also Head of Family Justice, an hears cases concerning divorce, access to and custody c children, and other family matters. The divisional court c the high court sits in the family and chancery division and hears appeals from the magistrates' courts and count courts.

The crown court was set up in 1972 and sits at abou 90 centres throughout England and Wales. It deals wit more serious (indictable) criminal offences, which ar able before a judge and jury, including treason, murder, pe, kidnapping, armed robbery and Official Secrets Act fences. It also handles cases transferred from the agistrates' courts where the magistrate decides his or her wn power of sentence is inadequate, or where someone peals against a magistrate's decision, or in a case that is able 'either way' where the accused has chosen a jury al. The crown court centres are divided into three tiers: gh court judges, and sometimes circuit judges and corders (part-time circuit judges), sit in first-tier centres d deal with the most serious (Class 1) criminal offences g murder, treason) and with some civil high court cases; e second-tier centres are presided over by high court dges, circuit judges or recorders and deal with Class 2 iminal offences (eg rape, manslaughter); third-tier courts al with Class 3 criminal offences, with circuit judges or corders presiding.

The court of appeal hears appeals against both fact and w, and was last restructured in 1966 when it replaced e court of criminal appeal. It is split into the civil vision (which hears appeals from the high court, bunals and in certain cases, the county courts) and the iminal division (which hears appeals from the crown urt). Cases are heard by Lord Justices of Appeal if emed suitable for reconsideration.

The Constitutional Reform Act 2005 instigated several y changes to the judiciary in England and Wales. These clude the provision for the establishment of an dependent supreme court, scheduled to open in ctober 2009; the reform of the post of Lord Chancellor, ansferring its judicial functions to the President of the ourts of England and Wales; a duty on government inisters to uphold the independence of the judiciary by rring them from trying to influence judicial decisions rough any special access to judges; the formation of a lly transparent and independent Judicial Appointments ommission that is responsible for selecting candidates to commend for judicial appointment to the Secretary of ate for Justice; and the creation of the post of Judicial ppointments and Conduct Ombudsman.

RIMINAL CASES

criminal matters the decision to prosecute (in the ajority of cases) rests with the Crown Prosecution rvice (CPS), which is the independent prosecuting body England and Wales. The CPS is headed by the director public prosecutions, who works under the perintendence of the Attorney-General. Certain tegories of offence continue to require the Attorney-eneral's consent for prosecution.

Most minor criminal cases (summary offences) are dealt ith in magistrates' courts, usually by a bench of three paid lay magistrates (justices of the peace) sitting ithout a jury and assisted on points of law and ocedure by a legally trained clerk. There were around),828 justices of the peace in April 2007. In busier urts a full-time, salaried and legally qualified 'district dge (magistrates' court)' – formerly known as a ipendiary judge – presides alone. There were 139 strict judges (magistrates' courts) as at 1 April 2007. agistrates' courts oversee the completion of 95 per cent all criminal cases. Magistrates' courts also house some mily proceedings courts (which deal with relationship eakdown and childcare cases) and youth courts. Cases medium seriousness (known as 'offences triable either ay') where the defendant pleads not guilty can be heard the crown court for a trial by jury, if the defendant so ooses. Preliminary proceedings in a serious case to decide whether there is evidence to justify committal for trial in the crown court are dealt with in the magistrates' courts.

The 91 centres that the crown court sits in are divided into seven regions; a case is presided over by high court judges, circuit judges or recorders. There were 1,201 recorders as at 1 April 2007; they must sit a minimum of 15 days per year and are usually subject to a maximum of 30. A jury is present in all trials that are contested.

Appeals from magistrates' courts against sentence or conviction are made to the crown court, and appeals upon a point of law are made to the high court, which may ultimately be appealed to the House of Lords. Appeals from the crown court, either against sentence or conviction, are made to the court of appeal (criminal division), presided over by the Lord Chief Justice. Again, these appeals may be brought to the House of Lords if a point of law is contested, and if the house considers it is of sufficient importance.

CIVIL CASES

Most minor civil cases – including contract, tort (especially personal injuries), property, divorce and other family matters, bankruptcy etc – are dealt with by the county courts, of which there are 225 (*see* the Court Service website, www.hmcourts-service.gov.uk, for further details). Cases are heard by circuit judges, recorders or district judges. For cases involving small claims (with certain exceptions, where the amount claimed is £5,000 or less) there are informal and simplified procedures designed to enable parties to present their cases themselves without recourse to lawyers. Where there are financial limits on county court jurisdiction, claims that exceed those limits may be tried in the county courts with the consent of the parties, subject to the court's agreement, or in certain circumstances on transfer from the high court. Outside London, bankruptcy proceedings can be heard in designated county courts. Magistrates' courts also deal with certain classes of civil case and committees of magistrates license public houses, clubs and betting shops. For the implementation of the Children Act 1989, a new structure of hearing centres was set up in 1991 for family proceedings cases, involving magistrates' courts (family proceedings courts), divorce county courts, family hearing centres and care centres.

Appeals in certain family matters heard in the family proceedings courts go to the family division of the high court. Appeals against decisions made in magistrates' courts are heard in the crown court. Appeals from county courts may be heard in the court of appeal (civil division), presided over by the Master of the Rolls, and may go on to the House of Lords.

CORONERS' COURTS

The coroners' courts investigate violent and unnatural deaths or sudden deaths where the cause is unknown. Doctors, the police, various public authorities or members of the public may bring cases before a local coroner (a senior lawyer or doctor), in order to determine whether further criminal investigation is necessary. Where a death is sudden and the cause is unknown, the coroner may order a post-mortem examination to determine the cause of death rather than hold an inquest in court. An inquest must be held however if a person died in a violent or unnatural way, or died in prison or other unusual circumstances. If the coroner suspects murder, manslaughter or infanticide, he or she must summon a jury.

HOUSE OF LORDS

AS FINAL COURT OF APPEAL

Senior Lord of Appeal in Ordinary (£205,700), Rt. Hon. Lord Bingham of Cornhill, KG, *born* 1933, *apptd* 2000

LORDS OF APPEAL IN ORDINARY *as at 1 July 2007* (each £198,700)
Style, The Rt. Hon. Lord/Lady–

Rt. Hon. Lord Hoffmann, *born* 1934, *apptd* 1995
Rt. Hon. Lord Hope of Craighead, *born* 1938, *apptd* 1996
Rt. Hon. Lord Saville of Newdigate, *born* 1936, *apptd* 1997
Rt. Hon. Lord Scott of Foscote, *born* 1934, *apptd* 2000
Rt. Hon. Lord Rodger of Earlsferry, *born* 1944, *apptd* 2001
Rt. Hon. Lord Walker of Gestingthorpe, *born* 1938, *apptd* 2002
Rt. Hon. Lady Hale of Richmond, *born* 1945, *apptd* 2004
Rt. Hon. Lord Carswell, *born* 1934, *apptd* 2004
Rt. Hon. Lord Brown of Eaton-under-Heywood, *born* 1937, *apptd* 2004
Rt. Hon. Lord Mance, *born* 1943, *apptd* 2005
Rt. Hon. Lord Neuberger, *born* 1948, *apptd* 2007

JUDICIAL OFFICE OF THE HOUSE OF LORDS
House of Lords, London SW1A 0PW **T** 020-7219 3111
Registrar, Clerk of the Parliaments

SENIOR JUDICIARY OF ENGLAND AND WALES

Lord Chief Justice of England and Wales (£230,400), Rt. Hon. Lord Phillips of Worth Matravers, *born* 1938, *apptd* 2005
Master of the Rolls and Head of Civil Justice (£205,700), Rt. Hon. Sir Anthony Clarke, *born* 1943, *apptd* 2005
President of the Queen's Bench Division and Head of Criminal Justice (£198,700), Rt. Hon. Sir Igor Judge, *born* 1941, *apptd* 2005
President of the Family Division and Head of Family Justice (£198,700), Rt. Hon. Sir Mark Potter, *born* 1937, *apptd* 2005
Chancellor of the High Court (£198,700), Rt. Hon. Sir Robert Morritt, CVO, *born* 1938, *apptd* 2000

SUPREME COURT OF JUDICATURE

COURT OF APPEAL
Master of the Rolls (£205,700), Rt. Hon. Sir Anthony Clarke, *born* 1943, *apptd* 2005
Secretary, Ms J. Sears
Clerk, Dawn Rollason

LORD JUSTICES OF APPEAL *as at 1 July 2007* (each £188,900)
Style, The Rt. Hon. Lord/Lady Justice [surname]

Rt. Hon. Sir Robin Auld, *born* 1937, *apptd* 1995
Rt. Hon. Sir Malcolm Pill, *born* 1938, *apptd* 1995
Rt. Hon. Sir Alan Ward, *born* 1938, *apptd* 1995
Rt. Hon. Sir Mathew Thorpe, *born* 1938, *apptd* 1995
Rt. Hon. Sir George Waller, *born* 1940, *apptd* 1996
Rt. Hon. Sir John Mummery, *born* 1938, *apptd* 1996
Rt. Hon. Sir John Chadwick, ED, *born* 1941, *apptd* 1997
Rt. Hon. Sir Richard Buxton, *born* 1938, *apptd* 1997
Rt. Hon. Sir Anthony May, *born* 1940, *apptd* 1997
Rt. Hon. Sir Simon Tuckey, *born* 1941, *apptd* 1998
Rt. Hon. Sir John Laws, *born* 1945, *apptd* 1999
Rt. Hon. Sir Stephen Sedley, *born* 1939, *apptd* 1999
Rt. Hon. Sir David Latham, *born* 1942, *apptd* 2000
Rt. Hon. Sir Bernard Rix, *born* 1944, *apptd* 2000
Rt. Hon. Dame Mary Arden, DBE, *born* 1947, *apptd* 2000
Rt. Hon. Sir David Keene, *born* 1941, *apptd* 2000
Rt. Hon. Sir John Dyson, *born* 1943, *apptd* 2001
Rt. Hon. Sir Andrew Longmore, *born* 1944, *apptd* 200
Rt. Hon. Sir Robert Carnwath, CVO, *born* 1945, *apptd* 2002
Rt. Hon. Sir Scott Baker, *born* 1937, *apptd* 2002
Rt. Hon. Dame Janet Smith, DBE, *born* 1940, *apptd* 20
Rt. Hon. Sir Roger Thomas, *born* 1947, *apptd* 2003
Rt. Hon. Sir Robin Jacob, *born* 1941, *apptd* 2003
Rt. Hon. Sir Nicholas Wall, *born* 1945, *apptd* 2004
Rt. Hon. Sir Maurice Kay, *born* 1942, *apptd* 2004
Rt. Hon. Sir Anthony Hooper, *born* 1937, *apptd* 2004
Rt. Hon. Sir William Gage, *born* 1938, *apptd* 2004
Rt. Hon. Sir Timothy Lloyd, *born* 1946, *apptd* 2005
Rt. Hon. Sir Martin Moore-Bick, *born* 1948, *apptd* 200
Rt. Hon. Sir Nicholas Wilson, *born* 1945, *apptd* 2005
Rt. Hon. Sir Alan Moses, *born* 1945, *apptd* 2005
Rt. Hon. Sir Stephen Richards, *born* 1950, *apptd* 2005
Rt. Hon. Dame Heather Hallett, DBE, *born* 1949, *apptc* 2005
Rt. Hon. Sir Anthony Hughes, *born* 1948, *apptd* 2006
Rt. Hon. Sir Brian Leveson, *born* 1949, *apptd* 2006
Rt. Hon. Sir Lawrence Collins, *born* 1941, *apptd* 2007
Rt. Hon. Sir Roger Toulson, *born* 1946, *apptd* 2007

Ex Officio Judges, Lord Chief Justice of England and Wales; Master of the Rolls; President of the Queen's Bench Division; President of the Family Division; an Chancellor of the High Court

COURT OF APPEAL (CIVIL DIVISION)
Vice-President, Rt. Hon. Sir Mark Waller

COURT OF APPEAL (CRIMINAL DIVISION)
Vice-President, Rt. Hon. Sir David Latham
Judges, Lord Chief Justice of England and Wales; Master the Rolls; Lord Justices of Appeal; and Judges of the High Court of Justice

COURTS-MARTIAL APPEAL COURT
Judges, Lord Chief Justice of England and Wales; Master the Rolls; Lord Justices of Appeal; and Judges of the High Court of Justice

HIGH COURT OF JUSTICE

CHANCERY DIVISION
Chancellor of the High Court (£198,700), Rt. Hon. Sir Andrew Morritt, CVO, *born* 1938, *apptd* 2000
Secretary, Ms E. Harbert
Clerk, Sheila Glasgow

JUDGES *as at 1 July 2007* (each £165,900)
Style, The Hon. Mr/Mrs Justice [surname]

Hon. Sir John Lindsay, *born* 1935, *apptd* 1992
Hon. Sir Edward Evans-Lombe, *born* 1937, *apptd* 1993
Hon. Sir William Blackburne, *born* 1944, *apptd* 1993
Hon. Sir Gavin Lightman, *born* 1939, *apptd* 1994
Hon. Sir Colin Rimer, *born* 1944, *apptd* 1994

on. Sir Nicholas Pumfrey, *born* 1951, *apptd* 1997
on. Sir Nicholas Patten, *born* 1950, *apptd* 2000
on. Sir Terrence Etherton, *born* 1951, *apptd* 2001
on. Sir Peter Smith, *born* 1952, *apptd* 2002
on. Sir Kim Lewison, *born* 1952, *apptd* 2003
on. Sir David Richards, *born* 1951, *apptd* 2003
on. Sir George Mann, *born* 1951, *apptd* 2004
on. Sir Nicholas Warren, *born* 1949, *apptd* 2005
on. Sir David Kitchin, *born* 1955, *apptd* 2005
on. Sir Michael Briggs, *born* 1954, *apptd* 2006
on. Sir Launcelot Henderson, *born* 1951, *apptd* 2006

e Chancery Division also includes three specialist urts: the Companies Court, the Patents Court and the nkruptcy Court.

JEEN'S BENCH DIVISION
rd Chief Justice of England and Wales (£230,400), Rt. Hon. Lord Phillips of Worth Matravers, *born* 1938, *apptd* 2005
cretary, Michèle Souris
erk, Helen Tyler
esident (£198,700), Rt. Hon. Sir Igor Judge, *born* 1941, *apptd* 2005
ce-President (£188,900), Rt. Hon. Sir Anthony May, *born* 1940, *apptd* 2002

DGES *as at 1 July 2007* (each £165,900)
yle, The Hon. Mr/Mrs Justice [surname]

on. Sir Stuart McKinnon, *born* 1938, *apptd* 1988
on. Sir Peter Cresswell, *born* 1944, *apptd* 1991
on. Sir Christopher Holland, *born* 1937, *apptd* 1992
on. Sir John Forbes, *born* 1938, *apptd* 1993
on. Sir Andrew Collins, *born* 1942, *apptd* 1994
on. Sir Alexander Butterfield, *born* 1942, *apptd* 1995
on. Sir George Newman, *born* 1941, *apptd* 1995
on. Sir Gordon Langley, *born* 1943, *apptd* 1995
on. Sir Robert Nelson, *born* 1942, *apptd* 1996
on. Sir David Eady, *born* 1943, *apptd* 1997
on. Sir Jeremy Sullivan, *born* 1945, *apptd* 1997
on. Sir David Penry-Davey, *born* 1942, *apptd* 1997
on. Sir David Steel, *born* 1943, *apptd* 1998
on. Sir Charles Gray, *born* 1942, *apptd* 1998
on. Sir Nicolas Bratza, *born* 1945, *apptd* 1998
on. Sir Michael Burton, *born* 1946, *apptd* 1998
on. Sir Rupert Jackson, *born* 1948, *apptd* 1999
on. Sir Patrick Elias, *born* 1947, *apptd* 1999
on. Sir Richard Aikens, *born* 1948, *apptd* 1999
on. Sir Stephen Silber, *born* 1944, *apptd* 1999
on. Sir John Goldring, *born* 1944, *apptd* 1999
on. Dame Anne Rafferty, DBE, *born* 1950, *apptd* 2000
on. Sir Geoffrey Grigson, *born* 1944, *apptd* 2000
on. Sir Richard Gibbs, *born* 1941, *apptd* 2000
on. Sir Richard Henriques, *born* 1943, *apptd* 2000
on. Sir Stephen Tomlinson, *born* 1952, *apptd* 2000
on. Sir Andrew Smith, *born* 1947, *apptd* 2000
on. Sir Stanley Burnton, *born* 1942, *apptd* 2000
on. Sir Christopher Pitchford, *born* 1947, *apptd* 2000
on. Sir Duncan Ouseley, *born* 1950, *apptd* 2000
on. Sir Richard McCombe, *born* 1952, *apptd* 2001
on. Sir Raymond Jack, *born* 1942, *apptd* 2001
on. Sir Robert Owen, *born* 1944, *apptd* 2001
on. Sir Colin Mackay, *born* 1943, *apptd* 2001
on. Sir John Mitting, *born* 1947, *apptd* 2001
on. Sir Roderick Evans, *born* 1946, *apptd* 2001
on. Sir Nigel Davis, *born* 1951, *apptd* 2001
on. Sir Peter Gross, *born* 1952, *apptd* 2001
Hon. Sir Brian Keith, *born* 1944, *apptd* 2001
Hon. Sir Jeremy Cooke, *born* 1949, *apptd* 2001
Hon. Sir Richard Field, *born* 1947, *apptd* 2002
Hon. Sir Christopher Pitchers, *born* 1942, *apptd* 2002
Hon. Sir Colman Treacy, *born* 1949, *apptd* 2002
Hon. Sir Peregrine Simon, *born* 1950, *apptd* 2002
Hon. Sir Roger Royce, *born* 1944, *apptd* 2002
Hon. Dame Laura Cox, DBE, *born* 1951, *apptd* 2002
Hon. Sir Adrian Fulford, *born* 1953, *apptd* 2002
Hon. Sir Jack Beatson, *born* 1948, *apptd* 2003
Hon. Sir Michael Tugendhat, *born* 1944, *apptd* 2003
Hon. Sir David Clarke, *born* 1942, *apptd* 2003
Hon. Dame Elizabeth Gloster, DBE, *born* 1949, *apptd* 2004
Hon. Sir David Bean, *born* 1954, *apptd* 2004
Hon. Sir Alan Wilkie, *born* 1947, *apptd* 2004
Hon. Dame Linda Dobbs, DBE, *born* 1951, *apptd* 2004
Hon. Sir Henry Hodge, OBE, *born* 1944, *apptd* 2004
Hon. Sir Paul Walker, *born* 1954, *apptd* 2004
Hon. Sir David Calvert-Smith, *born* 1945, *apptd* 2005
Hon. Sir Christopher Clarke, *born* 1947, *apptd* 2005
Hon. Sir Charles Openshaw, *born* 1947, *apptd* 2005
Hon. Dame Caroline Swift, DBE, *born* 1955, *apptd* 2005
Hon. Sir Brian Langstaff, *born* 1948, *apptd* 2005
Hon. Sir David Jones, *born* 1952, *apptd* 2005
Hon. Sir Vivian Ramsey, *born* 1950, *apptd* 2005
Hon. Sir Nicholas Underhill, *born* 1952, *apptd* 2006
Hon. Sir Stephen Irwin, *born* 1953, *apptd* 2006
Hon. Sir Nigel Teare, *born* 1952, *apptd* 2006
Hon. Sir John Griffith Williams, *born* 1944, *apptd* 2007
Hon. Sir Wyn Williams, *born* 1951, *apptd* 2007
Hon. Sir Timothy King, *born* 1946, *apptd* 2007

The Queen's Bench Division also includes three specialist courts – the Commercial Court, the Admiralty Court and the Administration Court – and administers the Technology and Construction Court.

FAMILY DIVISION
President (£198,700), Rt. Hon. Sir Mark Potter, *born* 1937, *apptd* 2005
Secretary, Mrs S. Leung
Clerk, Miss Ayo Onatade

JUDGES *as at 3 July 2006* (each £165,900)
Style, The Hon. Mr/Mrs Justice [surname]

Hon. Sir Jan Singer, *born* 1944, *apptd* 1993
Hon. Sir Andrew Kirkwood, *born* 1944, *apptd* 1993
Hon. Sir Hugh Bennett, *born* 1943, *apptd* 1995
Hon. Sir Edward Holman, *born* 1947, *apptd* 1995
Hon. Dame Mary Hogg, DBE, *born* 1947, *apptd* 1995
Hon. Sir Christopher Sumner, *born* 1939, *apptd* 1996
Hon. Sir Arthur Charles, *born* 1948, *apptd* 1998
Hon. Sir David Bodey, *born* 1947, *apptd* 1999
Hon. Dame Jill Black, DBE, *born* 1954, *apptd* 1999
Hon. Sir James Munby, *born* 1948, *apptd* 2000
Hon. Sir Paul Coleridge, *born* 1949, *apptd* 2000
Hon. Sir Mark Hedley, *born* 1946, *apptd* 2002
Hon. Dame Anna Pauffley, DBE, *born* 1956, *apptd* 2003
Hon. Sir Roderic Wood, *born* 1951, *apptd* 2004
Hon. Dame Florence Baron, DBE, *born* 1952, *apptd* 2004
Hon. Sir Ernest Ryder, *born* 1957, *apptd* 2004
Hon. Sir Andrew McFarlane, *born* 1954, *apptd* 2005
Hon. Dame Julia Macur, DBE, *born* 1957, *apptd* 2005
Hon. Sir Andrew Moylan, *born* 1953, *apptd* 2007

SUPREME COURT DEPARTMENTS AND OFFICES
Royal Courts of Justice, London WC2A 2LL
T 020-7947 6000

DIRECTOR'S OFFICE
T 020-7947 6159
Director, Alastair Clegg
Area Directors, Loraine Ladlow *(Court of Appeal)*; Stephen Fash *(High Court Group)*; Helen Smith *(Probate Service)*
Managers, Keith Richardson *(Finance)*; Amanda Monsarrat *(Regional Change and Performance)*

ADMIRALTY AND COMMERCIAL REGISTRY AND MARSHAL'S OFFICE
T 020-7947 6112
Registrar (£98,900), P. Miller
Admiralty Marshal and Court Manager, K. Houghton

BANKRUPTCY AND COMPANIES COURT
T 020-7947 6441
Chief Registrar (£123,200), S. Baister
Bankruptcy Registrars (£98,900), C. Derrett; G. W. Jaques; W. Nicholls; P. J. S. Rawson; J. A. Simmonds
Court Manager, Pauline O'Brien

CENTRAL OFFICE OF THE SUPREME COURT
Senior Master of the Supreme Court (QBD), and Queen's Remembrancer (£123,200), R. L. Turner
Masters of the Supreme Court (QBD) (£98,900), P. G. A. Eyre; B. J. F. Fontaine; I. H. Foster; H. J. Leslie; P. Miller; G. H. Rose; J. G. G. Ungley; S. Whitaker; B. Yoxall
Court Manager, M. A. Brown

CHANCERY CHAMBERS
T 020-7947 7785
Chief Master of the Supreme Court (£123,200), J. I. Winegarten
Masters of the Supreme Court (£98,900), T. J. Bowles; N. W. Bragge; J. A. Moncaster; N. S. Price; P. R. Teverson
Court Manager, Jane O'Connor

COURT OF APPEAL CIVIL DIVISION
T 020-7947 6533
Registrar (£98,900), David Gladwell
Court Manager, Michael O'Neill

COURT OF APPEAL CRIMINAL DIVISION
T 020-7947 6011
Registrar (£98,900), R. A. Venne
Deputy Registrar, Ms P. Donnelly
Group Manager, Ann Lee

ADMINISTRATIVE OFFICE OF THE SUPREME COURT
T 020-7947 6655
Master of the Crown Office, and Queen's Coroner and Attorney (£98,900), R. A. Venne
Head of Crown Office, Mrs L. G. Knapman
Group Manager, Ann Lee

EXAMINERS OF THE COURT
Empowered to take examination of witnesses in all divisions of the High Court.
Examiners, M. W. M. Chism; A. G. Dyer; A. W. Hughes; Mrs G. M. Keene; R. M. Planterose

SUPREME COURT COSTS OFFICE
T 020-7947 6423
Senior Cost Judge (£123,200), P. T. Hurst
Masters of the Supreme Court (£98,900), C. D. N. Campbell; A. Gordon-Saker; P. Haworth; J. E. O'Har
P. R. Rogers; J. Simons; C. C. Wright
Court Manager, vacant

COURT OF PROTECTION
11th Floor, Archway Towers, 2 Junction Road, London N19 5
T 0845-330 2900
Senior Judge (£123,200), Denzil Lush

ELECTION PETITIONS OFFICE
Room E19, Royal Courts of Justice, London WC2A 2LL
T 020-7947 7529

The office accepts petitions and deals with all matt relating to the questioning of parliamentary, Europe parliament and local government elections, and w applications for relief under the 'representation of t people' legislation.
Prescribed Officer (£123,200), R. L. Turner
Chief Clerk, Ms H. L. Newman

OFFICE OF THE LORD CHANCELLOR'S VISITORS
Archway Towers, 11th Floor, 2 Junction Road, London N19 5
T 020-7664 7317

The Mental Capacity Act 2005 came into force on October 2007, and it makes provision for there to be t panels of court of protection visitors (special visitors general visitors). At the time of going to press, appointments had been made to either panel.

OFFICIAL RECEIVERS' DEPARTMENT
21 Bloomsbury Street, London WC1B 3QW
T 020-7637 1110
Inspector-General, Des Flynn
Deputies, L. Gramp; G. Horn

OFFICIAL SOLICITOR'S DEPARTMENT
81 Chancery Lane, London WC2A 1DD
T 020-7911 7127
Official Solicitor to the Supreme Court, Alastair Pitblado
Deputy Official Solicitor, May Maughan
Public Trustee, David Thompson

PRINCIPAL REGISTRY (FAMILY DIVISION)
First Avenue House, 42–49 High Holborn, London WC1V 6N
T 020-7947 6000
Senior District Judge (£123,200), P. Waller
District Judges (£98,900), A. R. S. Bassett-Cross; M. C. Berry; Ms H. Black; Ms S. M. Bowman; Ms H. C. Bradley; G. C. Brasse; Ms P. Cushing; Ms K. E. Gree
P. Greene; R. Harper; Ms H. MacGregor; K. Malik; C Million; Ms D. Redgrave; Ms C. Reid; Ms L. D. Rober
R. Robinson; Ms S. Walker; K. J. White
Director for the Probate Service, Helen Smith
Family Business Director, John Miller

DISTRICT PROBATE REGISTRARS
Probate Manager of London, Kevin Donnelly
Birmingham District, Pam Walbeoff
Brighton District, Phil Ellwood
Bristol District, Russell Joyce
Ipswich District, Helen Whitby
Leeds District, Angela Parry
Liverpool District, Karen Clark-Rimmer
Manchester District, Paul Burch
Newcastle District, Christine Riley

xford District, Roland D'Costa
Vales District, Paul Curran
Vinchester District, Alan Butler

UDGE ADVOCATES

he Judge Advocates are the officers in supreme control of e courts martial in the armed forces; historically, the dge Advocate of the Fleet for the Royal Navy and the dge Advocate-General for the Army and Royal Air orce. However, since 2004 the functions of the Judge dvocate of the Fleet have been largely delegated to the dge Advocate-General; it is planned that the two offices ill be amalgamated by the end of 2008, when the rmed Forces Act 2006 is fully in force.

HE JUDGE ADVOCATE OF THE FLEET
o Chichester Combined Court, Southgate, Chichester
019 1SX T 01243-520741
dge Advocate of the Fleet, His Hon. Judge Sessions

FFICE OF THE JUDGE ADVOCATE-GENERAL OF THE ORCES
1 Chancery Lane, London WC2A IBQ
020-7218 8089
dge Advocate-General (£133,100), His Hon. Judge Blackett
ice-Judge Advocate-General (£116,700), Michael Hunter
dge Advocates (£102,900)*, J. F. T. Bayliss; C. R. Burn; J. P. Camp; M. R. Elsom; R. D. Hill; A. J. B. McGrigor; R. C. C. Seymour
yle for Judge Advocates, Judge Advocate [surname]

Salary includes £2,000 London salary lead and a London allowance of £2,000

IGH COURT AND CROWN COURT ENTRES

rst-tier centres deal with both civil and criminal cases d are served by high court and circuit judges. Second-er centres deal with criminal cases only and are served high court and circuit judges. Third-tier centres deal ith criminal cases only and are served only by circuit dges.

ONDON REGION
rst-tier – None
cond-tier – Central Criminal Court
hird-tier – Blackfriars, Harrow, Inner London Sessions House, Isleworth, Kingston, Snaresbrook, Southwark, Wood Green, Woolwich & Croydon
egional Director, Kevin Pogson, 2nd Floor, Rose Court, 2 Southwark Bridge, London SE1 9HS T 020-7921 2010
rea Directors (London Crown), Sarah McAdam *(Central and South)*; Sandra Aston *(North and West)*
rea Director (London Civil and Family), Linda Lennon

he High Court in Greater London sits at the Royal ourts of Justice.

IDLAND REGION
rst-tier – Birmingham, Lincoln, Nottingham, Stafford, Warwick
cond-tier – Leicester, Northampton, Shrewsbury, Worcester, Wolverhampton
hird-tier – Coventry, Derby, Hereford, Stoke-on-Trent
egional Director, Alan Eccles, PO Box 11772, 6th Floor, Temple Court, Bull Street, Birmingham B4 6WF T 0121-250 6162
Area Directors, Kelvin Launchbury *(Birmingham, Coventry, Solihull and Warwickshire)*; Peter Hammersley *(Black Country, Staffordshire and West Mercia)*; Mark Swales *(Derbyshire and Nottinghamshire)*; Richard Redgrave *(Leicestershire, Lincolnshire and Northamptonshire)*

NORTH-EAST REGION
First-tier – Leeds, Newcastle upon Tyne, Sheffield, Teesside
Second-tier – Bradford, York
Third-tier – Doncaster, Durham, Kingston-upon-Hull, Great Grimsby
Regional Director, S. Caven, 18th Floor, West Riding House, Albion Street, Leeds LS1 5AA T 0113-251 1200
Area Directors, Sheila Proudlock *(Cleveland, Durham and Northumbria)*; Paul Bradley *(South Yorkshire and Humber)*; Dyfed Foulkes *(North and West Yorkshire)*

NORTH-WEST REGION
First-tier – Carlisle, Chester, Liverpool, Manchester (Crown Square), Preston
Third-tier – Barrow-in-Furness, Bolton, Burnley, Knutsford, Lancaster, Manchester (Minshull Street), Warrington
Regional Director, Christine Mayer, 15 Quay Street, Manchester M60 9FD T 0161-833 1005
Area Directors, Shaun McNally *(Cheshire and Merseyside)*; Gill Hague *(Cumbria and Lancashire)*; Richard Knott *(Greater Manchester)*

SOUTH-EAST REGION
First-tier – Cambridge, Chelmsford, Lewes, Norwich, Oxford
Second-tier – Ipswich, Luton, Maidstone, Reading, St Albans
Third-tier – Aylesbury, Basildon, Canterbury, Chichester, Croydon, Guildford, King's Lynn, Peterborough, Southend
Regional Director, Keith Budgen, 3rd Floor, Rose Court, 2 Southwark Bridge, London SE1 9HS T 020-7921 2061
Area Directors, Mark Littlewood *(Bedfordshire, Essex and Hertfordshire)*; Dave Weston *(Kent)*; Pauline Cornford *(Norfolk, Suffolk and Cambridgeshire)*; Julia Eeles *(Sussex and Surrey)*; Jonathan Lane *(Thames Valley)*

SOUTH-WEST REGION
First-tier – Bristol, Exeter, Truro, Winchester
Second-tier – Dorchester & Weymouth, Gloucester, Plymouth
Third-tier – Barnstaple, Bournemouth, Newport (IoW), Portsmouth, Salisbury, Southampton, Swindon, Taunton
Regional Director, Peter Risk, 5th Floor, Greyfriars, Lewins Mead, Bristol BS1 2NR T 0117-910 3600
Area Directors, Rod White *(Avon and Somerset)*; David Gentry *(Devon and Cornwall)*; Rod Brummitt *(Dorset, Gloucestershire and Wiltshire)*; Simon Townley *(Hampshire and Isle of Wight)*

WALES REGION
First-tier – Caernarfon, Cardiff, Mold, Swansea
Second-tier – Carmarthen, Merthyr Tydfil, Newport, Welshpool
Third-tier – Dolgellau, Haverfordwest
Regional Director, N. Chibnall, Churchill House, Churchill Way, Cardiff CF10 2HH T 029-2041 5505
Area Directors, Luigi Strinati *(Mid and West Wales)*; Clare Pillman *(North Wales)*; Alan Davies *(South-East Wales)*

CIRCUIT JUDGES

Circuit judges are barristers of at least seven years' standing or recorders of at least five years' standing. Circuit judges serve in the county courts and the crown court.

Style, His/Her Hon. Judge [surname]
Senior Presiding Judge, Rt. Hon. Lord Justice Leveson
Senior Circuit Judges, each £133,100
Circuit Judges at the Central Criminal Court, London (Old Bailey Judges), each £133,100
Circuit Judges, each £123,200

LONDON REGION
Presiding Judges, Hon. Mr Justice Bean; Hon. Mr Justice Calvert-Smith; Hon. Mr Justice Cooke; Hon. Mr Justice Gross

MIDLAND REGION
Presiding Judges, Hon. Mr Justice Gibbs; Hon. Mr Justice Treacy

NORTH-EAST REGION
Presiding Judges, Hon. Mr Justice Simon; Hon. Mr Justice Wilkie

NORTH-WEST REGION
Presiding Judges, Hon. Mr Justice David Clarke; Hon. Mr Justice McCombe

SOUTH-EAST REGION
Presiding Judges, Hon. Mr Justice Bean; Hon. Mr Justice Calvert-Smith; Hon. Mr Justice Cooke; Hon. Mr Justice Gross

SOUTH-WEST REGION
Presiding Judges, Hon. Mr Justice Owen; Hon. Mr Justice Royce

WALES REGION
Presiding Judges, Hon. Mr Justice Roderick Evans; Hon. Mr Justice Davis

DISTRICT JUDGES

District judges, formerly known as registrars of the court, are solicitors of at least seven years' standing and serve in county courts.
District Judges (each £98,900)

DISTRICT JUDGES (MAGISTRATES' COURTS)

District judges (magistrates' courts), formerly known as stipendiary magistrates, must be barristers or solicitors of at least seven years' standing (including at least two years' experience as a deputy district judge), and serve in magistrates' courts. All former provincial and metropolitan stipendiary magistrates can serve nationally within any district.
District Judges, each £102,900 (salary includes £4,000 inner London weighting)

CROWN PROSECUTION SERVICE

50 Ludgate Hill, London EC4M 7EX
T 020-7796 8000 **E** enquiries@cps.gsi.gov.uk
W www.cps.gov.uk

The Crown Prosecution Service (CPS) is responsible for prosecuting cases investigated by the police in England and Wales, with the exception of cases conducted by the Serious Fraud Office and certain minor offences.

The CPS is headed by the director of publ prosecutions (DPP), who works under th superintendence of the attorney-general. The servi comprises a headquarters and 43 areas (including tw head offices in London and York), with each ar corresponding to a police area in England and Wal Each area is headed by a chief crown prosecut supported by an area business manager.

Director of Public Prosecutions, Sir Ken Macdonald, QC
Chief Executive, Peter Lewis
Directors, vacant *(Business Development)*; Ms C. Hamon *(Business Information Systems)*; Sue Hemming *(Counter Terrorism)*; Seamus Taylor *(Equality and Diversity)*; J. Graham *(Finance)*; Ros McCool *(Human Resources)*; Alison Saunders *(Organised Crime)*; P. Geering *(Polic* C. Newell *(Principal Legal Adviser)*; Carmen David *(Special Crime)*
Head of Strategic Communications, P. Teare

CPS AREAS ENGLAND

CPS DIRECT, 6th Floor, United House, Piccadilly, York YO1 9PQ **T** 01904-545594
Chief Crown Prosecutor, Barry Hughes

AVON AND SOMERSET, 2nd Floor, Froomsgate House, Rupert Street, Bristol BS1 2QJ **T** 0117-930 2800
Chief Crown Prosecutor, David Archer

BEDFORDSHIRE, Sceptre House, 7–9 Castle Street, Lutor LU1 3AJ **T** 01582-816600
Chief Crown Prosecutor, Richard Newcombe

CAMBRIDGESHIRE, Justinian House, Spitfire Close, Ermir Business Park, Huntingdon, Cambs PE29 6XY **T** 01480-825200
Chief Crown Prosecutor, Richard Crowley

CHESHIRE, 2nd Floor, Windsor House, Pepper Street, Chester CH1 1TD **T** 01244-408600
Chief Crown Prosecutor, Ian Rushton

CLEVELAND, 5 Linthorpe Road, Middlesbrough, Cleveland TS1 1TX **T** 01642-204500
Chief Crown Prosecutor, Martin Goldman

CUMBRIA, 1st Floor, Stocklund House, Castle Street, Carlis CA3 8SY **T** 01228-882900
Chief Crown Prosecutor, Claire Lindley

DERBYSHIRE, 7th Floor, St Peter's House, Gower Street, Derby DE1 1SB **T** 01332-614000
Chief Crown Prosecutor, Brian Gunn

DEVON AND CORNWALL, Hawkins House, Pynes Hill, Rydon Lane, Exeter EX2 5SS **T** 01392-288000
Chief Crown Prosecutor, Roger Coe-Salazar, OBE

DORSET, Ground Floor, Oxford House, Oxford Road, Bournemouth BH8 8HA **T** 01202-498700
Chief Crown Prosecutor (acting), Kate Brown

DURHAM, Elvet House, Hallgarth Street, Durham DH1 3AT **T** 0191-383 5800
Chief Crown Prosecutor, Ms Portia Ragnauth

ESSEX, County House, 100 New London Road, Chelmsford CM2 0RG **T** 01245-455800
Chief Crown Prosecutor, Paula Abrahams

GLOUCESTERSHIRE, 2 Kimbrose Way, Gloucester GL1 2DB **T** 01452-872400
Chief Crown Prosecutor, Adrian Foster

GREATER MANCHESTER, PO Box 237, 8th Floor, Sunlight House, Quay Street, Manchester M60 3PS **T** 0161-827 4700
Chief Crown Prosecutor, John Holt

HAMPSHIRE AND ISLE OF WIGHT, 3rd Floor, Black Horse House, 8–10 Leigh Road, Eastleigh, Hants SO50 9FH **T** 023-8067 3800
Chief Crown Prosecutor, Nick Hawkins

ERTFORDSHIRE, Queen's House, 58 Victoria Street, St Albans, Herts AL1 3HZ **T** 01727-798700
Chief Crown Prosecutor, Charles Ingham
UMBERSIDE, Citadel House, 58 High Street, Kingston-upon-Hull HU1 1QD **T** 01482-621000
Chief Crown Prosecutor, Nigel Cowgill
ENT, Priory Gate, 29 Union Street, Maidstone ME14 1PT **T** 01622-356300
Chief Crown Prosecutor, Elizabeth Howe
ANCASHIRE, 2nd Floor Podium, Unicentre, Lord's Walk, Preston PR1 1OH **T** 01772-208100
Chief Crown Prosecutor, Robert Marshall
EICESTERSHIRE, Beaumont Leys Police Station, 2 Beaumont Way, Beaumont Leys, Leicester LE4 1OS **T** 0116-222 2222
Chief Crown Prosecutor, Janet Meek, OBE
INCOLNSHIRE, Crosstrend House, 10A Newport, Lincoln LN1 3DF **T** 01522-585900
Chief Crown Prosecutor, Colin Chapman
ONDON, 7th Floor, CPS HQ, 50 Ludgate Hill, London EC4M 7EX **T** 020-7796 8000
Chief Crown Prosecutor, Dru Sharpling
ERSEYSIDE, 7th Floor (South), Royal Liver Building, Pier Head, Liverpool L3 1HN **T** 0151-239 6400
Chief Crown Prosecutor, Paul Whittaker
ORFOLK, Carmelite House, St James Court, Whitefriars, Norwich NR3 1SL **T** 01603-693000
Chief Crown Prosecutor, Peter Tidey
ORTH YORKSHIRE, Athena House, Kettlestring Lane, Clifton Moor, York YO30 4XF **T** 01904-731700
Chief Crown Prosecutor, Robert Turnbull
ORTHAMPTONSHIRE, Beaumont House, Cliftonville, Northampton NN1 5BE **T** 01604-823600
Chief Crown Prosecutor, Grace Ononiwu
ORTHUMBRIA, St Ann's Quay, 122 Quayside, Newcastle upon Tyne NE1 3BD **T** 0191-260 4200
Chief Crown Prosecutor, Nicola Reasbeck
OTTINGHAMSHIRE, 2 King Edward Court, King Edward Street, Nottingham NG1 1EL **T** 0115-852 3300
Chief Crown Prosecutor, Kate Carty
OUTH YORKSHIRE, Greenfield House, 32 Scotland Street, Sheffield S3 7DQ **T** 0114-229 8600
Chief Crown Prosecutor, Judith Walker
TAFFORDSHIRE, Building 3, Etruria Valley Office Village, Etruria, Stoke-on-Trent ST1 5RU **T** 01782-664560
Chief Crown Prosecutor, Harry Ireland
UFFOLK, 9th Floor, St Vincent's House, 1 Cutler Street, Ipswich IP1 1UL **T** 01473-282100
Chief Crown Prosecutor, Ken Caley
URREY, Saxon House, 3 Onslow Street, Guildford, Surrey GU1 4YA **T** 01483-468200
Chief Crown Prosecutor, Tracey Easton
USSEX, City Gates, 185 Dyke Road, Brighton BN3 1TL **T** 01273-765600
Chief Crown Prosecutor, Mrs Sarah Jane Gallagher
HAMES VALLEY, Eaton Court, 112 Oxford Road, Reading RG1 7LL **T** 01189-513265
Chief Crown Prosecutor, Baljit Ubhey
ARWICKSHIRE, Rossmore House, 10 Newbold Terrace, Leamington Spa CV32 4EA **T** 01926-455000
Chief Crown Prosecutor, Mark Lynn
EST MERCIA, Artillery House, Heritage Way, Droitwich, Worcester WR9 8YB **T** 01905-825000
Chief Crown Prosecutor, Chris Enzor
EST MIDLANDS, Colmore Gate, 2 Colmore Row, Birmingham B3 2QA **T** 0121-262 1300
Chief Crown Prosecutor, David Blundell
WEST YORKSHIRE, Oxford House, Oxford Row, Leeds LS1 3BE **T** 0113-290 2700
Chief Crown Prosecutor, Neil Franklin
WILTSHIRE, 2nd Floor, Fox Talbot House, Bellinger Close, Malmesbury Road, Chippenham SN15 1BN **T** 01249-766100
Chief Crown Prosecutor, Karen Harrold

CPS AREAS WALES
DYFED POWYS, Heol Penlanffos, Tanerdy, Carmarthen, Dyfed SA31 2EZ **T** 01267-242100
Chief Crown Prosecutor, Iwan Jenkins
GWENT, 6th Floor, Chartist Tower, Upper Dock Street, Newport, Gwent NP20 1DW **T** 01633-261100
Chief Crown Prosecutor, Christopher Woolley
NORTH WALES, Bromfield House, Ellice Way, Wrexham LL13 7YW **T** 01978-346000
Chief Crown Prosecutor, Ed Beltrami
SOUTH WALES, 20th Floor, Capital House, Greyfriars Road, Cardiff CF10 3PL **T** 029-2080 3900
Chief Crown Prosecutor, Christopher Woolley

HER MAJESTY'S COURTS SERVICE

5th Floor, Clive House, Petty France, London SW1H 9HD
T 0845-456 8770 **F** 020-7189 2732
E customerservicecshq@hmcourts-service.gsi.gov.uk
W www.hmcourts-service.gov.uk

Her Majesty's Courts Service (HMCS) was launched on 1 April 2005, bringing together the Magistrates' Courts Service and the Court Service into a single organisation, and is responsible for the administration of the court of appeal, the high court, the crown court, the magistrates' courts, the county courts and the Probate Service. HMCS is an executive agency of the Ministry of Justice, and provides information on procedures and processes for the public, hearing lists, and address details for all relevant courts.
Chief Executive, Sir Ron De Witt, KB

JUDICIAL APPOINTMENTS COMMISSION

Steel House, 11 Tothill Street, London SW1H 9LJ
T 020-7210 1453 **E** enquiries@jac.gsi.gov.uk
W www.judicialappointments.gov.uk

The Judicial Appointments Commission was established as an independent non-departmental public body in April 2006 by the Constitutional Reform Act 2005. Its role is to select judicial office holders independently of government (a responsibility previously held by the Lord Chancellor). It has a statutory duty to encourage diversity in the range of persons available for selection and is sponsored by the Ministry of Justice and accountable to parliament through the Lord Chancellor. It is made up of 15 commissioners, including a chair.
Chair, Baroness Prashar, CBE
Commissioners, Rt. Hon. Lord Justice Auld; Dame Boreland-Kelly, DBE, FRSA; Dame Prof. Hazel Genn, DBE; Hon. Mr Justice Goldring; Rt. Hon. Lady Justice Hallett, DBE; Sir Geoffrey Inkin, OBE; Her Hon. Judge Kirkham; Edward Nally; Sara Nathan; Charles Newman; His Hon. Judge Pearl; Francis Plowden; Harriet Spicer; Jonathan Sumption, OBE, QC
Chief Executive, Clare Pelham

DIRECTORATE OF JUDICIAL OFFICES

The Directorate of Judicial Offices for England and Wales was established in April 2006 following the implementation of the Constitutional Reform Act 2005, and incorporates the Judicial Office, the Judicial Communications Office and the Judicial Studies Board. It provides the Lord Chief Justice and the judiciary with the support they need to fulfil the new responsibilities which transferred to the judiciary in April 2006. Although part of the directorate is based at the royal courts of justice (which is managed by HM Courts Service), the directorate works independently from government departments and agencies.

DIRECTOR'S OFFICE
T 020-7947 7598
Director, Debora Matthews
Secretary, Sarah Welfoot

JUDICIAL OFFICE
T 020-7073 4858
Heads, Jonathan Creer *(Judicial HR Services)*; Amanda Jeffrey *(Planning and Governance)*
Secretary to the Judges' Council, Barbara Flaxman

JUDICIAL COMMUNICATIONS OFFICE
T 020-7073 4852
Heads, Phillip Golding *(Corporate Communications)*; Mike Wicksteed *(Judicial Communications)*
Chief Public Information Officer, Peter Farr

JUDICIAL STUDIES BOARD
Millbank Tower, London SW1P 4QU
T 020-7217 4708 W www.jsboard.co.uk
Executive Directors, Judith Kilick; Maggy Piggot
Heads, Mark Shore *(Corporate Services)*; Helen Baker *(Judicial Training)*; Lynne McGechie *(Magistrates' Training Unit and Senior Adviser)*; Mary Holmes *(Tribunals and Training Unit and Senior Adviser)*

JUDICIAL COMMITTEE OF THE PRIVY COUNCIL

The Judicial Committee of the Privy Council is the final court of appeal for the United Kingdom overseas territories (*see* UK Overseas Territories section), crown dependencies and those independent Commonwealth countries which have retained this avenue of appeal (Antigua and Barbuda, Bahamas, Barbados, Belize, Brunei, Cook Islands and Niue, Dominica, Grenada, Jamaica, Kiribati, Mauritius, St Christopher and Nevis, St Lucia, St Vincent and the Grenadines, Trinidad and Tobago, and Tuvalu) and the sovereign base areas of Akrotiri and Dhekelia in Cyprus. The committee also hears appeals against pastoral schemes under the Pastoral Measure 1983, and deals with appeals from veterinary disciplinary bodies.

Under the devolution legislation enacted in 1998, the Judicial Committee of the Privy Council is the final arbiter in disputes as to the legal competence of matters done or proposed by the devolved legislative and executive authorities in Scotland, Wales and Northern Ireland.

In 2006 the Judicial Committee dealt with a total of 70 appeals and 60 petitions for special leave to appeal.

The members of the Judicial Committee are the Lords of Appeal in Ordinary, and other Privy Counsellors who hold or have held high judicial office in the United Kingdom or in certain designated courts o Commonwealth countries from which appeals are taken t committee.

JUDICIAL COMMITTEE OF THE PRIVY COUNCIL
Downing Street, London SW1A 2AJ T 020-7276 0483/5
Registrar of the Privy Council, Mary Macdonald
Group Manager, Jackie Lindsay

SCOTTISH JUDICATURE

Scotland has a legal system separate from, and differing greatly from, the English legal system in enacted law judicial procedure and the structure of courts.

In Scotland the system of public prosecution is heade by the Lord Advocate and is independent of the police who have no say in the decision to prosecute. The Lor Advocate, discharging his functions through the Crown Office in Edinburgh, is responsible for prosecutions in th high court, sheriff courts and district courts. Prosecution in the high court are prepared by the Crown Office an conducted in court by one of the law officers, by a advocate-depute, or by a solicitor advocate. In the inferio courts the decision to prosecute is made and prosecutio is preferred by procurators fiscal, who are lawyers an full-time civil servants subject to the directions of th Crown Office. A permanent legally qualified civil servant known as the crown agent, is responsible for the running of the Crown Office and the organisation of th Procurator Fiscal Service, of which he or she is the head.

Scotland is divided into six sheriffdoms, each with full-time sheriff principal. The sheriffdoms are furthe divided into sheriff court districts, each of which has legally qualified resident sheriff or sheriffs, who are th judges of the court.

In criminal cases sheriffs principal and sheriffs have th same powers; sitting with a jury of 15 members, they ma try more serious cases on indictment, or, sitting alone may try lesser cases under summary procedure. Mino summary offences are dealt with in district courts which are administered by the district and the islands loca government authorities and presided over by lay justice of the peace (of whom some 500 regularly sit in court and, in Glasgow only, by stipendiary magistrates. Juvenil offenders (children under 16) may be brought before a informal children's hearing comprising three local la people. The superior criminal court is the high court o justiciary which is both a trial and an appeal court. Case on indictment are tried by a high court judge, sitting with a jury of 15, in Edinburgh and on circuit in othe towns. Appeals from the lower courts against convictio or sentence are also heard by the high court, which sits a an appeal court only in Edinburgh. There is no furthe appeal to the House of Lords in criminal cases.

In civil cases the jurisdiction of the sheriff cour extends to most kinds of action. Appeals against decision of the sheriff may be made to the sheriff principal an thence to the court of session, or direct to the court o session, which sits only in Edinburgh. The court o session is divided into the inner and the outer house. Th outer house is a court of first instance in which cases ar heard by judges sitting singly, sometimes with a jury o 12. The inner house, itself subdivided into two division of equal status, is mainly an appeal court. Appeals may b made to the inner house from the outer house as well a from the sheriff court. An appeal may be made from th inner house to the House of Lords.

The judges of the court of session are the same as thos

the high court of justiciary, with the Lord President of e court of session also holding the office of Lord Justice eneral in the high court. Senators of the College of stice are Lords Commissioners of Justiciary as well as dges of the court of session. On appointment, a senator kes a judicial title, which is retained for life. Although yled The Hon./Rt. Hon. Lord, the senator is not a peer, though some judges are peers in their own right.

The office of coroner does not exist in Scotland. The cal procurator fiscal inquires privately into sudden or spicious deaths and may report findings to the crown ent. In some cases a fatal accident inquiry may be held fore the sheriff.

OURT OF SESSION AND HIGH COURT F JUSTICIARY

he Lord President and Lord Justice General (£205,700), Rt. Hon. Lord Hamilton, *born* 1942, *apptd* 2005
ivate Secretary, A. Maxwell

NER HOUSE
rds of Session (each £188,900)

RST DIVISION
1e Lord President
. Hon. Lord Nimmo Smith (William Nimmo Smith), *born* 1942, *apptd* 1996
. Hon. Lord Philip (Alexander Philip), *born* 1942, *apptd* 1996
. Hon. Lord Kingarth (Derek Emslie), *born* 1945, *apptd* 1997

COND DIVISION
rd Justice Clerk (£198,700), Rt. Hon. Lord Gill (Brian Gill), *born* 1942, *apptd* 2001
. Hon. Lord Osborne (Kenneth Osborne), *born* 1937, *apptd* 1990
. Hon. Lord Abernethy (Alistair Cameron), *born* 1938, *apptd* 1992
. Hon. Lord Johnston (Alan Johnston), *born* 1942, *apptd* 1994
. Hon. Lord MacFadyen (Donald MacFadyen), *born* 1945, *apptd* 1995
. Hon. Lord Eassie (Ronald Mackay), *born* 1945, *apptd* 1997
. Hon. Lord Wheatley (John Wheatley), *born* 1941, *apptd* 2000
. Hon. Lady Paton (Ann Paton), *born* 1952, *apptd* 2000

UTER HOUSE
rds of Session (each £165,900)
on. Lord Reed (Robert Reed), *born* 1956, *apptd* 1998
on. Lord Carloway (Colin Sutherland), *born* 1954, *apptd* 2000
on. Lord Clarke (Matthew Clarke), *born* 1947, *apptd* 2000
. Hon. Lord Hardie (Andrew Hardie), *born* 1946, *apptd* 2000
. Hon. Lord Mackay of Drumadoon (Donald Mackay), *born* 1946, *apptd* 2000
on. Lord McEwan (Robin McEwan), *born* 1943, *apptd* 2000
on. Lord Menzies (Duncan Menzies), *born* 1953, *apptd* 2001
on. Lord Drummond Young (James Drummond Young), *born* 1950, *apptd* 2001
on. Lord Emslie (Nigel Emslie), *born* 1947, *apptd* 2001
on. Lady Smith (Anne Smith), *born* 1955, *apptd* 2001
Hon. Lord Brodie (Philip Brodie), *born* 1950, *apptd* 2002
Hon. Lord Bracadale (Alastair Campbell), *born* 1949, *apptd* 2003
Hon. Lady Dorrian (Leeona Dorrian), *born* 1959, *apptd* 2005
Hon. Lord Hodge (Patrick Hodge), *born* 1953, *apptd* 2005
Hon. Lord Macphail (Iain Macphail), *born* 1938, *apptd* 2005
Hon. Lord Glennie (Angus Glennie), *born* 1950, *apptd* 2005
Hon. Lord Kinclaven (Alexander F. Wylie), *born* 1951, *apptd* 2005
Hon. Lady Clark of Calton (Lynda Clark), *born* 1946, *apptd* 2006
Hon. Lord Turnbull (Alan Turnbull), *born* 1958, *apptd* 2006
Hon. Lord Brailsford (Sidney Brailsford), *born* 1954, *apptd* 2006
Hon. Lord Uist (Roderick Macdonald), *born* 1951, *apptd* 2006
Hon. Lord Malcolm (Colin M. Campbell), *born* 1953, *apptd* 2007
Hon. Lord Matthews (Hugh Matthews), *born* 1953, *apptd* 2007

COURT OF SESSION AND HIGH COURT OF JUSTICIARY
Parliament House, Parliament Square, Edinburgh EH1 1HQ
T 0131-225 2595
Principal Clerk of Session and Justiciary, Graham Marwick
Deputy Principal Clerk of Justiciary, F. Shannly
Deputy Principal Clerk of Session and Principal Extractor, R. Cockburn
Depute in Charge of Offices of Court, Y. Anderson
Keeper of the Rolls, A. Moffat
Depute Clerks of Session and Justiciary, J. Atkinson; D. Bruton; A. Corr; D. Cullen; L. Curran; E. Dickson; W. Dunn; P. Fiddes; A. Finlayson; C. Fyffe; A. Hutchinson; T. Kell; A. Lynch; J. Lynn; L. MacLachlan; D. MacLeod; R. MacPherson; L. MacNamara; I. Martin; A. McArdle; N. McGinley; A. McKay; D. Morrison; J. Moyes; R. Newlands; Q. Oliver; R. Phillips; C. Reid; C. Richardson; N. Robertson; C. Scott; B. Sinclair; R. Sinclair; A. Thompson; K. Todd; C. Truby; P. Weir

SCOTTISH EXECUTIVE COURTS DIRECTORATE
Hayweight House, 23 Lauriston Street, Edinburgh EH3 9DQ
T 0131-229 9200

The Scottish Executive Courts Directorate is responsible for the provision of sufficient judges and sheriffs to meet the needs of the business of the supreme and sheriffs court in Scotland. It is also responsible for the efficient administration of a number of specialist courts and tribunals.
Deputy Director, J. L. Anderson

JUDICIAL APPOINTMENTS BOARD FOR SCOTLAND
9–10 St Andrew Square, Edinburgh EH2 2AF
T 0131-718 6045

The board's remit is to provide the first minister with a list of candidates recommended for appointment to the posts of senator of the court of session, sheriff principal, sheriff and part-time sheriff.
Chair, Sir Neil McIntosh, CBE

SCOTTISH COURT SERVICE
Hayweight House, 23 Lauriston Street, Edinburgh EH3 9DQ
T 0131-229 9200 W www.scotcourts.gov.uk

The Scottish Court Service is an executive agency within the Scottish Executive Justice Department. It is responsible to the Scottish ministers for the provision of staff, courthouses and associated services for the supreme and sheriff courts.
Chief Executive, Eleanor Emberson

SHERIFF COURT OF CHANCERY
27 Chambers Street, Edinburgh EH1 1LB
T 0131-225 2525

The court deals with service of heirs and completion of title in relation to heritable property.
Sheriff Principal, Edward F. Bowen, QC

HM COMMISSARY OFFICE
27 Chambers Street, Edinburgh EH1 1LB
T 0131-225 2525

The office is responsible for issuing confirmation, a legal document entitling a person to execute a deceased person's will, and other related matters.
Commissary Clerk, David Fyfe

SCOTTISH LAND COURT
126 George Street, Edinburgh EH2 4HH
T 0131-271 4360

The court deals with disputes relating to agricultural and crofting land in Scotland.
Chair (£133,100), Hon. Lord McGhie (James McGhie), QC
Members, D. J. Houston; A. Macdonald *(part-time)*; J. A. Smith *(part-time)*
Principal Clerk, K. H. R. Graham, WS

SHERIFFDOMS

SALARIES

Sheriff Principal	£133,100
Sheriff	£123,200

Floating Sheriffs are denoted with an *.

GLASGOW AND STRATHKELVIN
Sheriff Principal, James A. Taylor
Sheriffdom Business Manager, Stephen Bain

SHERIFFS AND SHERIFF CLERK
Glasgow, J. A. Baird; Mrs P. M. M. Bowman; S. Cathcart; D. Convery; A. F. Deutsch; A. C. Henry; *M. Jones, QC; B. Kearney; *Mrs M. H. Liddell; *A. R. Mackenzie; Miss D. M. MacNeill, QC; C. W. McFarlane, QC; I. H. L. Miller; J. K. Mitchell; S. Murphy; A. W. Noble; A. C. Normand; I. A. S. Peebles, QC; J. Platt; Miss R. E. A. Rae, QC; Miss S. A. O. Raeburn, QC; *N. C. Ritchie, QC; *N. A. Ross; Miss L. M. Ruxton; C. A. L. Scott; W. J. Totten; L. Wood
Sheriff Clerk, Stephen Bain

GRAMPIAN, HIGHLAND AND ISLANDS
Sheriff Principal, Sir Stephen S. T. Young, Bt., QC
Sheriffdom Business Manager, David Fraser

SHERIFFS AND SHERIFF CLERKS
Aberdeen and Stonehaven, G. K. Buchanan; Ms A. M. Cowan; D. J. Cusine; *P. P. Davies; C. J. Harris, QC; A S. Jessop; K. A. McLernan; *K. M. Stewart; J. K. Tierney; *Sheriff Clerks,* Mrs F. Hendry *(Aberdeen)*; Mrs L. McKnight *(Stonehaven)*
Banff, P. P. Davies; *Sheriff Clerk Depute,* Melissa McLean
Dingwall, A. L. MacFadyen; *Sheriff Clerk Depute,* M. McBey
Dornoch, D. O. Sutherland; *Sheriff Clerk Depute,* Ken Ker
Elgin, I. A. Cameron; *Sheriff Clerk,* Mrs F. MacPherson
Fort William, W. D. Small *(also Oban)*; *Sheriff Clerk Depute,* S. McKenna
Inverness, Portree, Stornoway, Tain and Wick, D. Booker-Milburn; A. Pollock; *Sheriff Clerk,* A. Bayliss *(Inverness)*; *Sheriff Clerks Depute,* Miss M. Campbell *(Lochmaddy and Portree)*; K. Finnie *(Stornoway)*; R. M Hughes *(Tain)*; Mrs J. McEwan *(Wick)*
Kirkwall and Lerwick, G. Napier; *Sheriff Clerks Depute,* A Moore *(Kirkwall)*; Christina Bardsley *(Lerwick)*
Peterhead, *M. Garden; *Sheriff Clerk,* R. Cantwell *(Peterhead*
Lochmaddy, A. L. MacFadyen; *Sheriff Clerk Depute,* Miss M. Campbell

LOTHIAN AND BORDERS
Sheriff Principal, E. F. Bowen, QC
Sheriffdom Business Manager, David Shand

SHERIFFS AND SHERIFF CLERKS
Edinburgh, J. D. Allan; *F. R. Crowe; J. A. Farrell; J. M. S. Horsburgh, QC; Mrs M. L. E. Jarvie, QC; G. W. M. Liddle; A. Lothian; *Mrs K. E. C. Mackie; K. M. MacIver; I. McColl; *D. W. M. McIntyre; N. McPartli QC; N. M. P. Morrison, QC; F. Reith, QC; *J. P. Scott Miss M. M. Stephen; C. N. Stoddart; *Sheriff Clerk,* David Shand
Linlithgow, *M. G. R. Edington; G. R. Fleming; D. A. Kinloch; W. D. Muirhead; *Sheriff Clerk,* D. Fyffe
Haddington, P. Gillam; *Sheriff Clerk,* I. Munro
Jedburgh and Duns, T. A. K. Drummond, QC; *Sheriff Cler* J. O'Donnell
Peebles, Rota system is used; *Sheriff Clerk Depute,* H. Johnston
Selkirk, T. A. K. Drummond, QC; *Interim Sheriff Clerk,* M McCabe

NORTH STRATHCLYDE
Sheriff Principal, B. A. Kerr, QC
Sheriffdom Business Manager (acting), Christine Cockburn

SHERIFFS AND SHERIFF CLERKS
Campbeltown, *Ms R. Anderson *(also Paisley)*; *Sheriff Clerk Depute,* Ms. E. Harvey
Dumbarton, W. Dunlop; S. W. H. Fraser; S. Pender; *Sherif Clerk,* K. Carter
Dunoon, Ms C. Kelly; *Sheriff Clerk Depute,* Ms K. Wilson
Greenock, J. Herald *(also Rothesay)*; V. J. Canavan; *Mrs R Swanney; *Sheriff Clerk,* Ms J. G. Blackstock
Kilmarnock, W. S. Ireland; Mrs I. S. McDonald; Ms E. MacFarlane; A. G. Watson; *Sheriff Clerk,* C. Cockburn
Oban, W. D. Small *(also Fort William)*; *Sheriff Clerk Depute,* G. Whitelaw
Paisley, *Ms R. Anderson *(also Campbeltown)*; N. Dougla G. C. Kavanagh; D. J. Pender; *C. W. Pettigrew; Ms S. M. Sinclair; J. Spy; *Sheriff Clerk,* C. McGrane
Rothesay, J. Herald *(also Greenock)*; *Sheriff Clerk Depute,* Mrs C. K. McCormick

SOUTH STRATHCLYDE, DUMFRIES AND GALLOWAY
Sheriff Principal, B. A. Lockhart
Sheriffdom Business Manager, Sheila Hindes

SHERIFFS AND SHERIFF CLERKS
Airdrie, P. M. Collins *(also Lanark)*; R. H. Dickson; Mrs M. M. Galbraith; J. C. Morris, QC; A. D. Vannet; *Sheriff Clerk,* J. Hamilton
Ayr, *D. A. Brown; J. McGowan; C. B. Miller; J. Montgomery; *Sheriff Clerk,* Mrs O. McShane
Dumfries, K. G. Barr; K. A. Ross; *Sheriff Clerk,* Ms E. Young
Hamilton, D. M. Bicket; J. Miller; F. L. Pieri; Miss J. Powrie; D. Scullion; H. K. Small; Mrs M. Smart; V. J. Smith; J. H. Stewart; S. A. Waldron; T. Welsh, QC; *Sheriff Clerk,* F. Petrie
Lanark, P. M. Collins *(also Airdrie)*; Ms N. C. Stewart; *Sheriff Clerk,* J. Foy
Stranraer and Kirkcudbright, J. R. Smith; *Sheriff Clerks,* D. Hood *(Kirkcudbright)*; B. Lindsay *(Stranraer)*

TAYSIDE, CENTRAL AND FIFE
Sheriff Principal, R. A. Dunlop, QC
Sheriffdom Business Manager, Gillian Prentice

SHERIFFS AND SHERIFF CLERKS
Alloa, D. M. Mackie; *Sheriff Clerk,* L. Reid
Arbroath, C. N. R. Stein; *Sheriff Clerk,* S. Munro
Cupar, G. J. Evans; *Sheriff Clerk,* C. Donald
Dundee, R. A. Davidson; A. J. M. Duff; T. G. Hughes; A. G. McCulloch; E. Munro; *Sheriff Clerk,* R. McMillan
Dunfermline, I. D. Dunbar; J. C. C. McSherry; *Sheriff Clerk,* J. Murphy
Falkirk, C. Caldwell; N. J. Mackinnon; *Sheriff Clerk,* P. McFarlane
Forfar, K. A. Veal; *Sheriff Clerk,* M. Herbertson
Kirkcaldy, *P. Braid; B. G. Donald; W. H. Holligan; *Sheriff Clerk,* S. Walker
Perth, M. J. Fletcher; L. D. R. Foulis; R. A. McCreadie, QC; *Sheriff Clerk,* A. Nicol
Stirling, A. Cubie; A. W. Robertson; *Sheriff Clerk,* M. McLean

STIPENDIARY MAGISTRATES

GLASGOW
R. B. Christie, *apptd* 1985; Mrs J. A. M. MacLean, *apptd* 1990

CROWN OFFICE AND PROCURATOR FISCAL SERVICE

CROWN OFFICE
25 Chambers Street, Edinburgh EH1 1LA
T 0131-226 2626 W www.crownoffice.gov.uk
Crown Agent, Norman McFadyen
Deputy Crown Agent, James Brisbane

PROCURATORS FISCAL

SALARIES

Area Fiscals	£55,000–£160,000
District Procurator Fiscal	£39,270–£59,464

GRAMPIAN AREA
Area Procurator Fiscal, Ms M. McLaughlin *(Aberdeen)*
Procurators Fiscal, Ms C. Frame; A. B. Hutchinson; Ms S. Ralph

HIGHLAND AND ISLANDS AREA
Area Procurator Fiscal, A. Laing *(Inverness)*
Procurators Fiscal, G. Aitken; Ms S. Foard; A. MacDonald; D. S. Teale; S. T. Swan; Ms A. Wyllie

LANARKSHIRE AREA
Area Procurator Fiscal, Ms J. Cameron *(Hamilton)*
Procurators Fiscal, Mrs A. C. Donaldson; S. Houston; D. Spiers

CENTRAL AREA
Area Procurator Fiscal, Mrs G. W. Watt *(Stirling)*
Procurators Fiscal, K. Donnelly; Ms R. McQuaid

DUNDEE AREA
Area Procurator Fiscal, D. Howdle *(Dundee)*
Procurators Fiscal, A. Grant; Dr David Griffiths; Ms E. Miller

FIFE AREA
Area Procurator Fiscal, C. Ritchie *(Kirkcaldy)*
Procurators Fiscal, J. Robertson; E. B. Russell

LOTHIAN AND BORDERS AREA
Area Procurator Fiscal, F. Mulholland *(Edinburgh)*
Procurators Fiscal, A. R. G. Fraser; M. R. MacLeod; Ms L. Thomson

AYRSHIRE AREA
Area Procurator Fiscal, John Dunn *(Kilmarnock)*
Procurators Fiscal, L. Brown; I. L. Murray

ARGYLL AND CLYDE AREA
Area Procurator Fiscal, J. Watt *(Paisley)*
Procurators Fiscal, J. E. Farrell; A. Miller; S. Pattison; M. Ramage; D. Webster

DUMFRIES AND GALLOWAY AREA
Area Procurator Fiscal, T. Dysart *(Dumfries)*
Procurators Fiscal, K. Grieve; J. Service

GLASGOW AREA
Area Procurator Fiscal, Ms C. Dyer *(Glasgow)*
Procurators Fiscal, A. Currie; D. Green; Ms J. Harrower; M. Watson

NORTHERN IRELAND JUDICATURE

In Northern Ireland the legal system and the structure of courts closely resemble those of England and Wales; there are, however, often differences in enacted law.

The supreme court of judicature of Northern Ireland comprises the court of appeal, the high court of justice and the crown court. The practice and procedure of these courts is similar to that in England. The superior civil court is the high court of justice, from which an appeal lies to the Northern Ireland court of appeal; the House of Lords is the final civil appeal court.

The crown court, served by high court and county court judges, deals with criminal trials on indictment. Cases are heard before a judge and, except those involving offences specified under emergency legislation, a jury. Appeals from the crown court against conviction or sentence are heard by the Northern Ireland court of appeal; the House of Lords is the final court of appeal.

The decision to prosecute in cases tried on indictment and in summary cases of a serious nature rests in Northern Ireland with the director of public prosecutions, who is responsible to the attorney-general. Minor summary offences are prosecuted by the police.

Minor criminal offences are dealt with in magistrates' courts by a legally qualified resident magistrate and, where an offender is under the age of 17, by juvenile courts each consisting of a resident magistrate and two lay members specially qualified to deal with juveniles (at least one of whom must be a woman). On 1 July 2006 there were 800 justices of the peace in Northern Ireland. Appeals from magistrates' courts are heard by the county court, or by the court of appeal on a point of law or an issue as to jurisdiction.

Magistrates' courts in Northern Ireland can deal with certain classes of civil case but most minor civil cases are dealt with in county courts. Judgments of all civil courts are enforceable through a centralised procedure administered by the Enforcement of Judgments Office.

SUPREME COURT OF JUDICATURE

The Royal Courts of Justice, Belfast BT1 3JF
T 028-9023 5111

Lord Chief Justice of Northern Ireland (£205,700), Rt. Hon. Sir Brian Kerr, *born* 1948, *apptd* 2004
Principal Secretary, S. T. A. Rogers

LORD JUSTICES OF APPEAL (£188,900)
Style, The Rt. Hon. Lord Justice [surname]
Rt. Hon. Sir Anthony Campbell, *born* 1936, *apptd* 1998
Rt. Hon. Sir Malachy Higgins, *born* 1944, *apptd* 2007
Rt. Hon. Sir Paul Girvan, *born* 1948, *apptd* 2007

PUISNE JUDGES (£165,900)
Style, The Hon. Mr Justice [surname]
Hon. Sir Patrick Coghlin, *born* 1945, *apptd* 1997
Hon. Sir John Gillen, *born* 1947, *apptd* 1998
Hon. Sir Richard McLaughlin, *born* 1947, *apptd* 1999
Hon. Sir Ronald Weatherup, *born* 1947, *apptd* 2001
Hon. Sir Reginald Weir, *born* 1947, *apptd* 2003
Hon. Sir Declan Morgan, *born* 1952, *apptd* 2004
Hon. Sir Donnell Deeny, *born* 1950, *apptd* 2004
Hon. Sir Anthony Hart, *born* 1946, *apptd* 2005
Hon. Sir Seamus Treacy, *born* 1956, *apptd* 2007
Hon. Sir William Benjamin Synge Stephens, *born* 1954, *apptd* 2007

MASTERS OF THE SUPREME COURT (£98,900)
Master, Queen's Bench and Appeals, C. J. McCorry
Master, Office of Care and Protection, H. Wells
Master, Chancery and Probate, R. A. Ellison
Master, Matrimonial, C. W. G. Redpath
Master, Queen's Bench and Matrimonial, E. Bell
Master, Taxing Office, J. Boullie
Master, Bankruptcy, F. Kelly

OFFICIAL SOLICITOR
Official Solicitor to the Supreme Court of Northern Ireland, Miss B. M. Donnelly

COUNTY COURTS

JUDGES (£123,200)
Style, His/Her Hon. Judge [surname]

Judge Babington; Judge Finnegan; Judge Gibson, QC; Her Hon. Judge Kennedy; Judge Lockie; Judge Loughran; Judge Lynch; Judge McFarland; Judge McKay, QC; Judge McReynolds; Judge Markey, QC; Judge Marrinan, QC; Judge Martin *(Chief Social Security and Child Support Commissioner)*; Judge Rodgers; Judge Smyth, QC

RECORDERS
Belfast (£143,748), Judge Burgess
Londonderry (£123,200), Her Hon. Judge Philpott, QC

MAGISTRATES' COURTS

RESIDENT MAGISTRATES (£98,900)
There are 20 resident magistrates in Northern Ireland.

CROWN SOLICITOR'S OFFICE
PO Box 410, Royal Courts of Justice, Belfast BT1 3JY
T 028-9054 2555
Crown Solicitor, J. Conn

DEPARTMENT OF THE DIRECTOR OF PUBLIC PROSECUTIONS
93 Chichester Street, Belfast BT1 3TR
T 028-9054 2444
Director of Public Prosecutions, Sir Alasdair Fraser, CB, QC

NORTHERN IRELAND COURT SERVICE
Windsor House, Bedford Street, Belfast BT2 7LT
T 028-9032 8594 W www.courtsni.gov.uk
Director, D. A. Lavery

TRIBUNALS

THE TRIBUNALS SERVICE

'ictory House, 30–34 Kingsway, London WC2B 6EX
' 0845-600 0877 E customer.services@tribunals.gsi.gov.uk
V www.tribunals.gov.uk

The Tribunals Service, launched in April 2006, is an xecutive agency within the Ministry of Justice that rovides common administrative support to 21 central overnment tribunals (plus the Adjudicator to HM Land Registry and the Gender Recognition Panel, which are ot technically tribunals). The service also aims to deliver reater consistency in practice and procedure, to ensure ribunals are manifestly independent from those whose ecisions are being reviewed, and to provide increased ccess to information for the public.

A number of government tribunals are expected to join he Tribunals Service in the future and all new, on-devolved, central government tribunals will be stablished as part of the service.

hief Executive, Peter Handcock

AGRICULTURAL LAND TRIBUNALS

/o DEFRA, Ergon House, Horseferry Road, London SW1P 2AL
0845-933 5577 E helpline@defra.gsi.gov.uk
V www.defra.gov.uk

Agricultural Land Tribunals settle disputes and other ssues between agricultural landlords and tenants under he Agricultural Holdings Act 1986, and drainage lisputes between neighbours under the Land Drainage Act 1991.

There are seven tribunals covering England and one overing Wales. For each tribunal the Lord Chancellor ppoints a chair and one or more deputies (barristers or olicitors of at least seven years' standing). The Lord Chancellor also appoints lay members to three statutory anels: the 'landowners' panel, the 'farmers' panel and the lrainage' panel.

Each tribunal is an independent statutory body with urisdiction only within its own geographical area. A eparate tribunal is constituted for each case, and consists f a chair and two lay members nominated by the chair.

hairs (England), Shirley Evans; His Hon. Judge Machin; George Newsom; Paul de la Piquerie; His Hon. Judge Taylor; Nigel Thomas; Martin Wood

hair (Wales), James Buxton

ASYLUM AND IMMIGRATION TRIBUNAL

O Box 6987, Leicester LE1 6ZX
0845-600 0877 E customer.service@tribunals.gsi.gov.uk
V www.ait.gov.uk

The Asylum and Immigration Tribunal (AIT) is part of the ribunals Service and hears appeals against decisions nade by the Home Office; its powers are derived from the mmigration and Asylum Act 1999. This tribunal replaced ne two-tiered Immigration Appellate Authority in 2005 y merging the Immigration Adjudicators and the mmigration Appeal Tribunal under Section 26 of the sylum and Immigration (Treatment of Claimants, etc) ct 2004. Immigration judges are appointed by the Lord Chancellor and hear appeals against decisions to: refuse sylum under the Refugee Convention; refuse entry into the UK; refuse to issue or extend a visa; deport a person from the UK; or deprive a person of UK citizenship. An appeal against a decision will go before a hearing, where the appellant, his/her representative and a representative from the Home Office will attend before an immigration judge (or panel, sometimes including non-legal members) who will make a determination on whether the appeal should be allowed or dismissed. In certain circumstances, either side may apply for a reconsideration of the determination. Depending on how the appeal was heard (by a single immigration judge or by a panel) will dictate where any applications for reconsideration will be lodged.

President, Hon. Mr Justice Hodge, OBE

Deputy Presidents, Libby Arfon-Jones; Mark Ockelton

CARE STANDARDS TRIBUNAL

18 Pocock Street, London SE1 0BW
T 020-7960 0660 E cst@tribunals.gsi.gov.uk
W www.carestandardstribunal.gov.uk

The tribunal was established under the Protection of Children Act 1999 and considers appeals in relation to decisions made about the inclusion of individuals' names on the list of those considered unsuitable to work with children, restrictions from teaching and employment in schools/further education institutions, and the registration of independent schools. It also deals with general registration decisions made about care homes, children's homes, nurses' agencies, residential family centres and fostering agencies. The tribunal's president appoints the panels for each case and each appeal is heard by a legally qualified chair and two lay members with expertise in the field.

President, His Hon. Judge Pearl

CIVIL AVIATION AUTHORITY

CAA House, 45–59 Kingsway, London WC2B 6TE
T 020-7453 6162 E legal@caa.co.uk
W www.caa.co.uk

The Civil Aviation Authority (CAA) does not have a separate tribunal department as such, however for certain purposes the CAA must conform to tribunal requirements. For example, to deal with appeals against the refusal or revocation of aviation licences and certificates issued by the CAA, and the allocation of routes outside of the EU to airlines.

The chair and four non-executive members who may sit on panels for tribunal purposes are appointed by the Secretary of State for Transport.

Chair, Sir Roy McNulty, CBE

COMMONS COMMISSIONERS

Room 1/14, Temple Quay House, 2 The Square, Temple Quay, Bristol BS1 6EB
T 0117-372 8973 E commons.commissioners@defra.gsi.gov.uk

The Commons Commissioners are responsible for deciding disputes arising under the Commons Registration Act 1965. They also enquire into the ownership of unclaimed common land and village greens. Commissioners must be barristers or solicitors of at least seven years' standing and are appointed by the Lord Chancellor.

Chief Commons Commissioner, Edward Cousins

COMPETITION APPEAL TRIBUNAL

Victoria House, Bloomsbury Place, London WC1A 2EB
T 020-7979 7979 **E** info@catribunal.org.uk
W www.catribunal.org.uk

The Competition Appeal Tribunal (CAT) is a specialist tribunal established to hear certain cases in the sphere of UK competition and economic regulatory law. It hears appeals against decisions of the Office of Fair Trading (OFT) and their sectoral regulators under the Competition Act 1998, and also decisions against the OFT, Secretary of State for Trade and Industry and Competition Commission under the merger control and market investigation provisions of the Enterprise Act 2002. The CAT also has jurisdiction under the Competition Act 1998 to award damages in respect of infringements of EC or UK competition law and to hear appeals against decisions of OFCOM under the Communications Act 2003.

Cases are heard before a panel consisting of three members: either the president or a member of the panel of chairs and two ordinary members. The members of the panel are judges of the Chancery Division of the high court and other senior lawyers. The ordinary members have expertise in law and/or related fields. The president and chairs are appointed by the Lord Chancellor; the ordinary members are appointed by the secretary of state.
President, vacant

COPYRIGHT TRIBUNAL

Room 2G31, Concept House, Cardiff Road, Newport NP10 9FU
T 01633-811035 **E** copyright.tribunal@ipo.gov.uk
W www.ipo.gov.uk/copy/tribunal

The Copyright Tribunal resolves disputes over the terms and conditions of licences offered by, or licensing schemes operated by, collective licensing bodies in the copyright and related rights area. Its decisions are appealable to the high court on points of law only.

The chair and two deputy chairs are appointed by the Lord Chancellor. Up to eight ordinary members are appointed by the Secretary of State for Trade and Industry. The tribunal operates on a panel basis and its members have wide expertise in business, public administration, and the professions.
Chair, Judge Fysh, QC

CRIMINAL INJURIES COMPENSATION APPEALS PANEL

11th Floor, Cardinal Tower, Farringdon Road, London EC1M 3HS
T 020-7549 4600 **E** enquiries-cicap@tribunals.gsi.gov.uk
W www.cicap.gov.uk

The Criminal Injuries Compensation Appeals Panel determines appeals against review decisions made by the Criminal Injuries Compensation Authority on applications for compensation received from victims of crimes of violence. The chair and members of the panel are appointed by the Secretary of State for the Home Department. Each hearing panel consists of two or three members, one of whom will be a qualified lawyer.
Chair, Roger Goodier

EMPLOYMENT APPEAL TRIBUNAL

London Office: Audit House, 58 Victoria Embankment, London EC4Y 0DS **T** 020-7273 1041
Edinburgh Office: 52 Melville Street, Edinburgh EH3 7HF
T 0131-225 3963 **W** www.employmentappeals.gov.uk

The Employment Appeal Tribunal hears appeals (on points of law only) arising from any decision of an employment tribunal. Hearings are conducted by a judge either alone or accompanied by two lay members who have practical experience in employment relations. Administrative support is provided by the Tribunals Service.
President, Hon. Mr Justice Elias
Scottish Chair, Hon. Lady Smith

EMPLOYMENT TRIBUNALS (ENGLAND AND WALES)

Ground Floor, Victory House, 30–34 Kingsway, London WC2B 6EX
T 0845-795 9775 **W** www.employmenttribunals.gov.uk

Employment Tribunals for England and Wales sit in 12 regions. The tribunals deal with matters of employment law, redundancy, dismissal, contract disputes, sexual, racial and disability discrimination and related areas of dispute which may arise in the workplace. A public register of judgments is held at 100 Southgate Street, Bury St Edmunds, Suffolk IP33 2AQ.

Chairs, who may be full-time or part-time, are legally qualified. They, along with the tribunal members, are appointed by the Ministry of Justice.
President, His Hon. Judge Meeran

EMPLOYMENT TRIBUNALS (SCOTLAND)

Central Office, Eagle Building, 215 Bothwell Street, Glasgow G2 7TS
T 0141-204 0730

Tribunals in Scotland have the same remit as those in England and Wales. Chairs are appointed by the Lord President of the Court of Session and lay members by the Secretary of State for Trade and Industry.
President, C. M. Milne

FAMILY HEALTH SERVICES APPEAL AUTHORITY

30 Victoria Avenue, Harrogate HG1 5PR
T 01423-530280 **E** mail@fhsaa.nhs.uk **W** www.fhsaa.org.uk

The Family Health Services Appeal Authority (FHSAA) is completely independent of the Department of Health and considers appeals against the decisions of primary care trusts (PCTs), for example appeals by GPs, dentists, pharmacists and opticians against action taken against them. The president allocates appeals and applications to panels normally consisting of a legal chair, a professional member and a lay member. The FHSAA's president and members are appointed by the Lord Chancellor.
President, Paul Kelly

FINANCIAL SERVICES AND MARKETS TRIBUNAL

15–19 Bedford Avenue, London WC1B 3AS
T 020-7612 9700 **E** fs&mt@tribunals.gsi.gov.uk
W www.financeandtaxtribunals.gov.uk

The Financial Services and Markets Tribunal hears cases arising from decisions issued by the Financial Services Authority against financial service providers, including banks, clearing houses, stockbrokers and mortgage advisers. The president, a panel of legally qualified chairs and a panel of lay members are all appointed by the Lord Chancellor.
President, Sir Stephen Oliver, QC

GENERAL COMMISSIONERS OF INCOME TAX

Selborne House, 54–60 Victoria Street, London SW1E 6QW
T 020-7210 0670

General commissioners of income tax operate under the Taxes Management Act 1970. They are unpaid judicial officers who sit in some 350 divisions throughout the UK to hear appeals against decisions by HM Revenue and Customs on a variety of taxation matters. The commissioners' jurisdiction was extended in 1999 to hear National Insurance appeals. The Lord Chancellor appoints general commissioners (except in Scotland, where they are appointed by the Scottish Executive). There are approximately 1,700 general commissioners appointed throughout the United Kingdom. In each division, commissioners appoint a clerk, who is normally legally qualified, who makes the administrative arrangements for appeal hearings and advises the commissioners on points of law and procedure. The Ministry of Justice pays the clerks' remuneration.

Appeals from the general commissioners are by way of case stated, on a point of law, to the high court (the court of session in Scotland or the court of appeal in Northern Ireland).

IMMIGRATION SERVICES TRIBUNAL

Procession House, 55 Ludgate Hill, London EC4M 7JW
T 020-7029 9790 E imset@tribunals.gsi.gov.uk
W www.immigrationservicestribunal.gov.uk

The Immigration Services Tribunal is an independent judicial body established in 2000 to provide a forum in which appeals against decisions of the Immigration Services Commissioner and complaints made by the Immigration Services Commissioner can be heard and determined. The cases exclusively concern people providing advice and representation services in connection with immigration matters.

The tribunal forms part of the Ministry of Justice. There is a president, who is the judicial head; other judicial members, who must be legally qualified; lay members, who must have substantial experience in immigration services or in the law and procedure relating to immigration; and a secretary, who is responsible for administration. The tribunal can sit anywhere in the UK.
President, His Hon. Judge Cripps

INDUSTRIAL TRIBUNALS AND THE FAIR EMPLOYMENT TRIBUNAL (NORTHERN IRELAND)

Long Bridge House, 20–24 Waring Street, Belfast BT1 2EB
T 028-9032 7666 E mail@employmenttribunalsni.org
W www.employmenttribunalsni.co.uk

The industrial tribunal system in Northern Ireland was set up in 1965 and has a similar remit to the employment tribunals in the rest of the UK. There is also a Fair Employment Tribunal, which hears and determines individual cases of alleged religious or political discrimination in employment. Employers can appeal to the Fair Employment Tribunal if they consider the directions of the Equality Commission to be unreasonable, inappropriate or unnecessary, and the Equality Commission can make application to the tribunal for the enforcement of undertakings or directions with which an employer has not complied.

The president, vice-president and part-time chairs of the Fair Employment Tribunal are appointed by the Lord Chancellor. The full-time chair and the part-time chairs of the industrial tribunals and the panel members to both the industrial tribunals and the Fair Employment Tribunal are appointed by the Department for Employment and Learning.
President of the Industrial Tribunals and the Fair Employment Tribunal, Eileen McBride

INFORMATION TRIBUNAL

Arnhem House Support Centre, PO Box 6987, Leicester LE1 6ZX
T 0845-6000 877 E informationtribunal@tribunals.gsi.gov.uk
W www.informationtribunal.gov.uk

The Information Tribunal determines appeals against notices issued by the Information Commissioner. The chair and deputy chair are appointed by the Lord Chancellor and must be legally qualified. Lay members are appointed by the Lord Chancellor to represent the interests of data users or data subjects. A tribunal consists of a chair sitting with equal numbers of the lay members. There is a separate panel of the tribunal which hears national security appeals; the president of this panel is Sir Stephen Mitchell.
Chair, John Angel

LANDS TRIBUNAL

Procession House, 55 Ludgate Hill, London EC4M 7JW
T 020-7029 9780 E lands@tribunals.gsi.gov.uk
W www.landstribunal.gov.uk

The Lands Tribunal is an independent judicial body which determines questions relating to the valuation of land, rating appeals from valuation tribunals, appeals from leasehold valuation tribunals, the discharge or modification of restrictive covenants, and compulsory purchase compensation. The tribunal may also arbitrate under references by consent. The president and members are appointed by the Lord Chancellor. Cases are usually heard by a single member but they may sometimes be heard by two or three members.
President, G. R. Bartlett, QC

LANDS TRIBUNAL FOR SCOTLAND

George House, 126 George Street, Edinburgh EH2 4HH
T 0131-271 4350 E mailbox@lands-tribunal-scotland.org.uk
W www.lands-tribunal-scotland.org.uk

The Lands Tribunal for Scotland has much the same remit as the tribunal for England and Wales but also covers questions relating to tenants' rights to buy their homes under the Housing (Scotland) Act 1987. The president is appointed by the Lord President of the Court of Session.
President, Hon. Lord McGhie, QC

MENTAL HEALTH REVIEW TRIBUNALS

Secretariat: 5th Floor, 11 Belgrave Road, London SW1V 1RS
T 020-7592 1007 W www.mhrt.org.uk

The Mental Health Review Tribunals are independent judicial bodies which review the cases of patients compulsorily detained under the provisions of the Mental Health Act 1983. They have the power to discharge the patient, to recommend leave of absence, to delay discharge, transfer to another hospital or that a guardianship order be made, to reclassify both restricted and unrestricted patients, and to recommend consideration of a supervision application. There are three tribunals in England and Wales, each headed by a regional chair who is appointed by the Lord Chancellor on a

part-time basis. Each tribunal is made up of at least three members, and must include a lawyer, who acts as president, a medical member and a lay member.
Liaison Judge, His Hon. Judge Sycamore

NATIONAL HEALTH SERVICE TRIBUNAL (SCOTLAND)

40 Craiglockhart Road North, Edinburgh EH14 1BT
T 0131-443 2575

The Scottish National Health Service Tribunal considers representations that the continued inclusion of a doctor, dentist, optometrist or pharmacist on a health board's list would be prejudicial to the efficiency of the service concerned, by virtue either of fraudulent practices or unsatisfactory personal or professional conduct. The tribunal sits when required and is composed of a chair, one lay member, and one practitioner member drawn from a representative professional panel. The chair is appointed by the Lord President of the Court of Session, and the lay member and the members of the professional panel are appointed by the Scottish ministers.
Chair, J. Michael D. Graham

NATIONAL PARKING ADJUDICATION SERVICE

Barlow House, Minshull Street, Manchester M1 3DZ
T 0161-242 5252 E npas@parking-adjudication.gov.uk
W www.parking-appeals.gov.uk

The National Parking Adjudication Service considers appeals from motorists against penalty charge notices issued by councils in England and Wales under the Road Traffic Act 1991, including appeals against bus lane contraventions. Parking adjudicators are appointed with the express consent of the Lord Chancellor and must be lawyers of five years' standing. Cases are decided by a single adjudicator, either in a postal, telephone or a personal hearing.
Head of Service, Louise Hutchinson

OFFICE OF THE SOCIAL SECURITY AND CHILD SUPPORT COMMISSIONERS

3rd Floor, Procession House, 55 Ludgate Hill, London EC4M 7JW
T 020-7029 9850 E osscsc@tribunals.gsi.gov.uk
George House, 126 George Street, Edinburgh EH2 4HH
T 0131-271 4310 E ossc@ossc-scotland.org.uk
W www.osscsc.gov.uk

Commissioners are the final statutory authority to decide appeals on points of law in social security, tax credit, child support, housing benefit, council tax benefit and compensation recovery cases. They also decide appeals from Pensions Appeal Tribunals relating to war pensions and cases which have been referred to them under the Forfeiture Act 1982. The commissioners' jurisdiction covers England, Wales and Scotland. There are 18 commissioners, all of whom are qualified lawyers.
Chief Commissioner for Great Britain, His Hon. Judge Hickinbottom
Senior Commissioner for Scotland, D. J. May, QC

OFFICE OF THE SOCIAL SECURITY COMMISSIONERS AND CHILD SUPPORT COMMISSIONERS FOR NORTHERN IRELAND

Headline Building, 10–14 Victoria Street, Belfast BT1 3GG
T 028-9033 2344
E socialsecuritycommissioners@courtsni.gov.uk
W www.courtsni.gov.uk

The role of Northern Ireland Social Security Commissioners and Child Support Commissioners is similar to that of the commissioners in Great Britain; they also have jurisdiction to deal with questions arising under the Forfeiture (Northern Ireland) Order 1982. There are two commissioners for Northern Ireland.
Chief Commissioner, His Hon. Judge Martin, QC
Commissioner, Mrs M. F. Brown, LLB

PENSIONS APPEAL TRIBUNAL

Procession House, 55 Ludgate Hill, London EC4M 7JW
T 020-7029 9800 E pensions.appeal@tribunals.gsi.gov.uk
W www.pensionsappealtribunals.gov.uk

The Pensions Appeal Tribunals are independent from the Service Personnel and Veterans Agency and the Ministry of Defence, and deal with appeals concerning the two schemes that provide compensation for injuries sustained in the armed forces. Established in 1919, the war pensions scheme is applicable in respect of injuries that occurred before 5 April 2005. The tribunals adjudicate on entitlement to a war pension, the percentage at which the War Pensions Agency has assessed a disablement and whether an allowance is justified (ie for mobility needs). For injuries after that date, the armed forces compensation scheme applies, and tribunals decide on entitlement to and amount of the award. The tribunal members are appointed by the Secretary of State for Justice.
President, Dr H. M. G. Concannon, LLM

PENSIONS APPEAL TRIBUNALS FOR SCOTLAND
126 George Street, Edinburgh EH2 4HH
T 0131-271 4340 E info@patscotland.org.uk
W www.patscotland.org.uk
President, C. N. McEachran, QC

RESIDENTIAL PROPERTY TRIBUNAL SERVICE

10 Alfred Place, London WC1E 7LR
T 0845-600 3178 E rptscorporateunit@communities.gsi.gov.uk
W www.rpts.gov.uk

The Residential Property Tribunal Service provides members to sit on panels for the Rent Assessment Committees, Residential Property Tribunals and Leasehold Valuation Tribunals, and serves the private-rented and leasehold property market in England by resolving disputes between leaseholders, tenants and landlords. The president and chair are appointed by the Lord Chancellor and other members are appointed by the Department for Communities and Local Government and the Ministry of Justice.
Senior President, Siobhan McGrath

SOCIAL SECURITY AND CHILD SUPPORT APPEALS

4th Floor, 14 Grays Inn Road, Fox Court, London WC1X 8HN
T 020-7712 2640 W www.appeals-service.gov.uk

The Social Security and Child Support Appeals Tribunal arranges and hears appeals on a range of decisions including those concerned with social security, child support, child tax credit, pensions credit, housing benefit, council tax benefit, vaccine damage, tax credits and compensation recovery.

Judicial authority rests with the president, while administrative responsibility is exercised by the Tribunals Service, which is an executive agency of the Ministry of Justice.
President, vacant

SOLICITORS' DISCIPLINARY TRIBUNAL

3rd Floor, Gate House, 1 Farringdon Street, London EC4M 7NS
T 020-7329 4808 **E** enquiries@solicitorsdt.com
W www.solicitorstribunal.org.uk

The Solicitors' Disciplinary Tribunal is an independent statutory body whose members are appointed by the Master of the Rolls. The tribunal considers applications made to it alleging either professional misconduct and/or a breach of the statutory rules by which solicitors are bound against an individually named solicitor, former solicitor, registered foreign lawyer, or solicitor's clerk. The tribunal has around 50 members, two thirds are solicitor members and one third are lay members. The president and solicitor members do not receive remuneration and lay members are remunerated by the Ministry of Justice.
President, A. Isaacs

SOLICITORS' DISCIPLINE TRIBUNAL (SCOTTISH)

Unit 3.5, The Granary Business Centre, Coal Road, Cuper, Fife KY15 5YQ
T 01334-659088 **W** www.ssdt.org.uk

The Scottish Solicitors' Discipline Tribunal is an independent statutory body with a panel of 22 members, 14 of whom are solicitors; members are appointed by the Lord President of the Court of Session. Its principal function is to consider complaints of misconduct against solicitors in Scotland.
Chair, A. Cockburn

SPECIAL COMMISSIONERS

15–19 Bedford Avenue, London WC1B 3AS
T 020-7612 9700 **E** sc@tribunals.gsi.gov.uk
W www.financeandtaxtribunals.gov.uk

The Special Commissioners are an independent body appointed by the Lord Chancellor to hear complex appeals against decisions of HM Revenue and Customs relating to direct tax matters.
Presiding Special Commissioner, Sir Stephen Oliver, QC

SPECIAL EDUCATIONAL NEEDS AND DISABILITY TRIBUNAL

Central Office, Procession House, 55 Ludgate Hill, London EC4M 7JW **T** 0870-241 2555
Darlington Office, Ground Floor, Mowden Hall, Staindrop Road DL3 9BG
E sendistqueries@tribunals.gsi.gov.uk **W** www.sendist.gov.uk

The Special Educational Needs and Disability Tribunal considers parents' appeals against the decisions of local education authorities (LEAs) about children's special educational needs and claims of disability discrimination in schools. Its president, chairs and specialist members are appointed by the Lord Chancellor.
President, Lady Rosemary Hughes

SPECIAL IMMIGRATION APPEALS COMMISSION

15 Breams Buildings, London EC4A 1DZ
T 0845-600 0877 **W** www.siac.tribunals.gov.uk

The commission was set up under the Special Immigration Appeals Commission Act 1997. Its main function is to consider appeals against orders for deportations in cases which involve, in the main, considerations of national security or the public interest. The commission also hears appeals against decisions to deprive persons of citizenship status. Members are appointed by the Lord Chancellor.
Chair, Hon. Mr Justice Mitting

TRANSPORT TRIBUNAL

Procession House, 55 Ludgate Hill, London EC4M 7JW
T 020-7029 9780 **E** transport@tribunals.gsi.gov.uk
W www.transporttribunal.gov.uk

The Transport Tribunal has three jurisdictions: it hears appeals against decisions made by Traffic Commissioners at public inquiries, appeals against decisions of the Registrar of the Driving Standards Agency and is able to resolve disputes under the Postal Services Act 2000. The tribunal consists of a legally qualified president, other judicial members, and lay members. The president and legal members are appointed by the Lord Chancellor and the lay members by the transport secretary. Members of the Transport Tribunal also act as the London Service Permit Appeals Panel.
President, H. B. H. Carlisle, QC

VALUATION TRIBUNAL SERVICE

Chief Executive's Office, Block 1, Angel Square, 1 Torrens Street, London EC1V 1NY
T 020-7841 8700 **W** www.valuation-tribunals.gov.uk

The Valuation Tribunal Service (VTS) was created as a corporate body by the Local Government Finance Act 2003, and is responsible for providing or arranging the services required for the operation of valuation tribunals in England. The VTS board is comprised of a chair and members appointed by the secretary of state. There are 56 tribunals in England that hear appeals concerning council tax and non-domestic rating and land drainage rates. The VTS is funded by the Department for Communities and Local Government. A separate tribunal is constituted for each hearing, and consists of a chair and two or three other members. A clerk, who is a paid employee of the VTS, is present to advise on points of procedure and law. Members are appointed by a representative of the local authorities and the valuation tribunal president, and serve on a voluntary basis.
Chair, VTS Board, Anne Galbraith, OBE

VALUATION TRIBUNAL SERVICE FOR WALES

Governing Council of VTSW, Dinerth Road, Rhos on Sea, Colwyn Bay LL28 4UL
T 01492-546610 **E** northwales.vt@vto.gsx.gov.uk

The Valuation Tribunal Service for Wales (VTSW) was created under the Valuation Tribunals (Wales) Regulations 2005, and is responsible for providing or arranging the services required for the operation of the four tribunals in Wales. The governing council of the VTSW is comprised of four regional presidents, one of whom is elected director together with one member who is appointed by the National Assembly for Wales. The VTSW hear appeals concerning council tax and non-domestic rating, and land drainage rates in Wales. An individual tribunal, supported

by a clerk, is constituted for each hearing and is normally serviced by three members, one of whom also chairs.
Director, J. H. Owens

VAT AND DUTIES TRIBUNALS

15–19 Bedford Avenue, London WC1B 3AS
T 020-7612 9700 E vatlon@tribunals.gsi.gov.uk
W www.financeandtaxtribunals.gov.uk

VAT and Duties Tribunals are independent and decide disputes between taxpayers and HM Revenue and Customs. In England and Wales, the president and chairs are appointed by the Lord Chancellor and members by the Treasury. Chairs in Scotland are appointed by the Lord President of the Court of Session.
President, Sir Stephen Oliver, QC
Vice-President, England and Wales, J. D. Demack
Vice-President, Scotland, T. G. Coutts, QC

TRIBUNAL CENTRES
EDINBURGH, 126 George Street, Edinburgh EH2 4HH T 0131-271 4330
LONDON, 15–19 Bedford Avenue, London WC1B 3AS T 020-7612 9700
MANCHESTER, 9th Floor, Westpoint, 501 Chester Road, Manchester M16 5HU T 0161-868 6600

ˈHE POLICE SERVICE

ıere are 52 police forces in the United Kingdom: 43 in ıgland and Wales, including the Metropolitan Police ıd the City of London Police, eight in Scotland and the ılice Service of Northern Ireland. Most forces' areas are terminous with one or more local authority areas. The ıe of Man, States of Jersey and Guernsey have their own ɾces responsible for policing in their respective islands d bailiwicks. The Serious Organised Crime Agency OCA), which became operational in April 2006, is ponsible for the investigation of national and ernational serious organised crime.

Police authorities are independent bodies, responsible r the supervision of local policing. There are 43 police thorities in England and Wales, plus an additional one r British Transport Police. Most police authorities have members, comprising nine local councillors, five dependent members and three magistrates. Authorities ıich are responsible for larger areas may have more embers, such as the Metropolitan Police Authority ıich has 23 members: 12 drawn from the London ssembly, seven independent members and four agistrates. The Corporation of London acts as the police thority for the City of London Police. In Scotland, six the forces are maintained by joint police boards, made of local councillors from each council in the force area; e other two constabularies (Dumfries & Galloway and fe) are directly administered by their respective councils. ıe Northern Ireland Policing Board is an independent ıblic body consisting of 19 political and independent embers.

Police forces in England, Scotland and Wales are ıanced by central and local government grants and a ecept on the council tax. The Police Service of orthern Ireland is wholly funded by central government. ıe police authorities, subject to the approval of the home cretary (in England and Wales), the Northern Ireland cretary and to regulations, are responsible for pointing the Chief Constable. In England and Wales e latter are responsible for the force's budget, levying e precept on the council tax, publishing annual policing ans and reports, setting local objectives, monitoring rformance targets and appointing or dismissing senior ficers. In Scotland the police authorities are responsible r setting the force's budget, providing the resources cessary to police the area adequately and appointing ficers of the rank of Assistant Chief Constable and ove. In Northern Ireland, the Northern Ireland Policing oard exercises similar functions.

The home secretary, the Northern Ireland secretary and ıe Scottish Executive are responsible for the ganisation, administration and operation of the police rvice. They regulate police ranks, discipline, hours of ıty and pay and allowances. All police forces are subject inspection by HM Inspectors of Constabulary, who port to the home secretary, Scottish Executive or the orthern Ireland secretary.

COMPLAINTS

The Independent Police Complaints Commission (IPCC) has overall responsibility for the system of complaints against the police in England and Wales. Complaints can be made directly to the local police force or to the IPCC which will contact the police force concerned on the complainant's behalf. All complaints are reviewed by the police force. If the complaint is relatively minor, the police force will attempt to resolve it internally and an official investigation may not be required. Serious complaints are reported to the IPCC immediately and are formerly investigated by a senior officer. The Crown Prosecution Service then decides whether or not to bring criminal charges against the officer(s) involved. The IPCC has the power to initiate, carry out and oversee investigations and is also responsible for the way complaints are handled by local police forces. An officer who is dismissed, required to resign or reduced in rank, whether as a result of a complaint or not, may appeal to a police appeals tribunal established by the relevant police authority.

Under the Police, Public Order and Criminal Justice (Scotland) Act 2006, which came into force on 1 April 2007, the Police Complaints Commissioner for Scotland is responsible for providing independent scrutiny of the way Scottish police forces, authorities and policing agencies handle complaints from the public. The commissioner also has the power to direct police forces to re-examine any complaints which are not considered to have been dealt with satisfactorily. If there is a suggestion of criminal activity, the complaint is investigated by a procurator fiscal.

The Police Ombudsman for Northern Ireland provides an independent police complaints system for Northern Ireland, dealing with all stages of the complaints procedure. Complaints which cannot be resolved informally are investigated and the ombudsman recommends a suitable course of action to the Chief Constable of the Police Service of Northern Ireland or the Northern Ireland Policing Board based on the investigation's findings. The ombudsman may recommend that a police officer be prosecuted although the decision to prosecute a police officer rests with the Director of Public Prosecutions.

RATES OF PAY

London weighting of £2,055 per annum (from 1 July 2006) is awarded to all police officers working in London irrespective of their ranks and in addition to the salaries listed below:

BASIC RATES OF PAY *at 1 September 2006*

Chief Constables of Greater Manchester, Strathclyde and West Midlands*	£161,178–£163,908
Chief Constable*	£114,735–£152,982
Deputy Chief Constable*	£98,346–£125,667
Assistant Chief Constable and Commanders*	£81,954–£95,613
Chief Superintendent	£67,200–£71,031
Superintendent Range 2†	£64,434–£68,571

Superintendent	£56,274–£65,565
Chief Inspector‡§	£46,779 (£48,645)–£48,705 (£50,568)
Inspector‡§	£42,264 (£44,118)–£45,843 (£47,709)
Sergeant‡	£32,985–£37,071
Constable‡	£21,009–£32,985
Metropolitan Police	
Commissioner	£234,939
Deputy Commissioner	£193,959
City of London Police	
Commissioner	£145,344
Assistant Commissioner	£119,883
Police Service of Northern Ireland	
Chief Constable	£174,834
Deputy Chief Constable	£142,053

* Chief Officers may receive a bonus of at least five per cent of pensionable pay if their performance is deemed exceptional

† For Superintendents who were not promoted to the rank of Chief Superintendent on its re-introduction on 1 January 2002

‡ Officers who have been on the highest available salary for one year have access to a competence-related threshold payment of £1,095 per annum

§ London salary in parentheses (applicable only to officers in the Metropolitan and City of London police forces)

POLICE SERVICES

FORENSIC SCIENCE SERVICE

Headquarters: Trident Court, 2920 Solihull Parkway, Birmingham Business Park, Birmingham B37 7YN
T 0121-329 5200 **W** www.forensic.gov.uk

The Forensic Science Service (FSS) is a government-owned company which provides forensic science and technology services for UK police forces and other law enforcement agencies. Services are also available to defence lawyers and commercial companies. The FSS employs more than 2,500 staff and operates from 12 facilities across the UK.
Chief Executive, David Werrett, PHD

NATIONAL EXTREMISM TACTICAL COORDINATION UNIT

PO Box 525, Huntingdon PE29 9AL
T 01480-425091 **E** mailbox@netcu.pnn.police.uk
W www.netcu.org.uk

The National Extremism Tactical Coordination Unit (NETCU) provides the police service of England and Wales and other law enforcement agencies with tactical advice and guidance on policing domestic extremism and associated criminality. The unit also supports organisations and companies that are the targets of domestic extremism campaigns. NETCU is funded by the Home Office and accountable to the Association of Chief Police Officers' Terrorism and Allied Matters Committee.

NATIONAL POLICING IMPROVEMENT AGENCY

4th Floor, 10 Victoria Street, London SW1H 0NN
T 020-7084 8841 **W** www.npia.police.uk

The National Policing Improvement Agency (NPIA) was established under the Police and Justice Act 2006 and became operational on 1 April 2007. NPIA has taken on the functions of the Police Information Technology Organisation (PITO) and the Central Police Training and Development Authority (CENTREX), which have bee abolished. In addition NPIA has assumed responsibili for some Home Office and Association of Chief Poli Officers (ACPO) functions which relate directly policing.

The NPIA is a police-owned body whose remit is ensure that agreed programmes of reforms a implemented and good practice is applied throughout tl police service. It is also responsible for the procureme and deployment of information and communicatio technology systems to support and improve policing ar is active in helping to recruit and train police personne The NPIA is charged with improving policing in Englar and Wales but it is also connected to policing bodies Scotland and Northern Ireland and collaborates wi them on some initiatives.
Chairman, Peter Holland, CBE
Director of Policing Policy and Practice, Deputy Chi Constable Chris Sims

SERIOUS ORGANISED CRIME AGENCY

PO Box 8000, London SE11 5EN **W** www.soca.gov.uk

The Serious Organised Crime Agency (SOCA) is a executive non-departmental public body sponsored b but operationally independent from, the Home Offic The agency was formed in April 2006 from th amalgamation of the National Crime Squad, Nation Criminal Intelligence Service, the part of HM Revenu and Customs responsible for dealing with drug traffickin and associated criminal finance and the part of the U Immigration Service responsible for dealing wit organised immigration crime.

SOCA broadly aims to apportion around 40 per cent c its operational effort in tackling primarily Class A drug trafficking, around 25 per cent of its capabilities towarc organised immigration crime, 10 per cent on individu and private sector fraud and 15 per cent to deal with othe organised crime. SOCA works closely with other la enforcement agencies and organisations and th remaining 10 per cent of its capabilities is specifically se aside for assisting its law enforcement partners i achieving their objectives.
Chair (non-executive), Sir Stephen Lander
Director-General, Bill Hughes

UK POLICE NATIONAL MISSING PERSONS BUREAU

Room 209, New Scotland Yard, 10 Broadway, London SW1H 0BG
T 0207-230 4029 **E** pnmpb.enquiries@met.pnn.police.uk
W www.missingpersons.police.uk

The Police National Missing Persons Bureau (PNMPB acts as a central clearing house for all missing person information. The bureau receives information on missin person cases that are still outstanding after 14 days (o earlier if it is felt that some harm may have befallen them) unidentified persons who are unable or unwilling t identify themselves and unidentified bodies or remain within 48 hours of being found with a view t cross-matching the missing against the found Information is forwarded to the PNMPB from all forces i the UK and from foreign police forces via Interpol. Th bureau also manages the Missing Kids website.
W http://uk.missingkids.com

OLICE FORCES

rength: size of force as known at February 2007
urce: Police and Constabulary Almanac 2007, R. Hazell
Co.

NGLAND

or the City of London Police and the Metropolitan olice Service *see* London Forces.

VON AND SOMERSET CONSTABULARY PO Box 37, Portishead, Bristol BS20 8QJ T 0845-456 7000 *Strength,* 3,380
Chief Constable, C. Port

EDFORDSHIRE POLICE Woburn Road, Kempston, Bedford MK43 9AX T 01234-841212 *Strength,* 1,250
Chief Constable, Gillian Parker, QPM

AMBRIDGESHIRE CONSTABULARY Hinchingbrooke Park, Huntingdon PE29 6NP T 0845-456 4564 *Strength,* 1,414
Chief Constable, Julie Spence

HESHIRE CONSTABULARY Clemonds Hey, Oakmere Road, Winsford CW7 2UA T 01244-350000 *Strength,* 2,292
Chief Constable, P. Fahy, QPM

LEVELAND POLICE PO Box 70, Ladgate Lane, Middlesbrough TS8 9EH T 01642-326326 *Strength,* 1,728
Chief Constable, Sean Price, QPM

UMBRIA CONSTABULARY Carleton Hall, Penrith CA10 2AU T 0845-330 0247 *Strength,* 1,275
Chief Constable, Michael Baxter, QPM

ERBYSHIRE CONSTABULARY Butterley Hall, Ripley DE5 3RS T 0845-123 3333 *Strength,* 2,081
Chief Constable, D. Coleman, QPM

EVON AND CORNWALL CONSTABULARY Middlemoor, Exeter EX2 7HQ T 08452-777444 *Strength,* 3,485
Chief Constable, Stephen Otter

ORSET POLICE Winfrith, Dorchester DT2 8DZ T 01929-462727 W www.dorset.police.uk *Strength,* 1,502
Chief Constable, M. Baker, QPM

URHAM CONSTABULARY Aykley Heads, Durham DH1 5TT T 0845-606 0365 *Strength,* 1,733
Chief Constable, Thomas Stoddart QPM

SSEX POLICE PO Box 2, Springfield, Chelmsford CM2 6DA T 01245-491491 W www.essex.police.uk *Strength,* 3,159
Chief Constable, R. Baker

LOUCESTERSHIRE CONSTABULARY 1 Waterwells, Waterwells Drive, Quedgeley, Gloucester GL2 2AN T 0845-090 1234 *Strength,* 1,354
Chief Constable, Timothy Brain, QPM, PHD

REATER MANCHESTER POLICE PO Box 22 Chester House, Boyer Street, Manchester M16 0RE T 0161-872 5050 *Strength,* 7,930
Chief Constable, Michael Todd, QPM

IAMPSHIRE CONSTABULARY West Hill, Winchester SO22 5DB T 0845-045 4545 *Strength,* 3,812
Chief Constable, Paul Kernaghan, CBE, QPM

IERTFORDSHIRE CONSTABULARY Stanborough Road, Welwyn Garden City AL8 6XF T 01707-354000 *Strength,* 2,167
Chief Constable, Frank Whiteley

IUMBERSIDE POLICE Priory Road Police Station, Priory Road, Hull HU1 5SF T 0845-606 0222 *Strength,* 2,245
Chief Constable, Tim Hollis, QPM

ENT POLICE Sutton Road, Maidstone ME15 9BZ T 01622-690690 W www.kent.police.uk *Strength,* 3,732
Chief Constable, Michael Fuller, QPM

LANCASHIRE CONSTABULARY PO Box 77, Hutton, Nr. Preston PR4 5SB T 01772-614444 *Strength,* 3,616
Acting Chief Constable, Stephen Finnigan, QPM

LEICESTERSHIRE CONSTABULARY St John's, Enderby, Leicester LE19 2BX T 0116-222 2222 W www.leics.police.uk *Strength,* 2,183
Chief Constable, Matthew Baggott, QPM

LINCOLNSHIRE POLICE PO Box 999, Lincoln LN5 7PH T 01522-532222 *Strength,* 1,236
Chief Constable, Tony Lake, QPM

MERSEYSIDE POLICE PO Box 59, Liverpool L69 1JD T 0151-709 6010 *Strength,* 4,500
Chief Constable, B. Hogan-Howe, QPM

NORFOLK CONSTABULARY Falconers Chase, Wymondham, NR18 0WW T 0845-456 4567 *Strength,* 1,568
Chief Constable, Ian McPherson

NORTHAMPTONSHIRE POLICE Wootton Hall, Northampton NN4 0JQ T 01604-700700 *Strength,* 1,347
Chief Constable, Peter Maddison

NORTHUMBRIA POLICE Ponteland, Newcastle upon Tyne NE20 0BL T 01661-872555 *Strength,* 4,031
Chief Constable, M. Craik, QPM

NORTH YORKSHIRE POLICE Newby Wiske Hall, Northallerton DL7 9HA T 0845-606 0247 *Strength,* 1,633
Chief Constable, Ms. D. Cannings, QPM

NOTTINGHAMSHIRE POLICE Sherwood Lodge, Arnold, Nottingham NG5 8PP T 0115-967 0999 *Strength,* 2,484
Chief Constable, S. Green, QPM

SOUTH YORKSHIRE POLICE Snig Hill, Sheffield S3 8LY T 0114-220 2020 *Strength,* 3,278
Chief Constable, M. Hughes, QPM

STAFFORDSHIRE POLICE Cannock Road, Stafford ST17 0QG T 0845-330 2010 *Strength,* 2,332
Acting Chief Constable, David Swift, QPM

SUFFOLK CONSTABULARY Martlesham Heath, Ipswich IP5 3QS T 01473-613500 *Strength,* 1,337
Chief Constable, Alastair McWhirter, QPM

SURREY POLICE Mount Browne, Sandy Lane, Guildford GU3 1HG T 0845-125 2222 W www.surrey.police.uk *Strength,* 1,778
Chief Constable, Robert Quick, QPM

SUSSEX POLICE Police Headquarters, Lewes BN7 2DZ T 0845-607 0999 *Strength,* 3,123
Chief Constable, Joe Edwards, QPM

THAMES VALLEY POLICE Oxford Road, Kidlington OX5 2NZ T 0845-8505 505 *Strength,* 4,275
Chief Constable, Sara Thornton

WARWICKSHIRE POLICE PO Box 4, Leek Wootton, Warwick CV35 7QB T 01926-415000 *Strength,* 1,042
Chief Constable, Keith Bristow

WEST MERCIA CONSTABULARY Hindlip Hall, Hindlip, Worcester WR3 8SP T 08457-444888 W www.westmercia.police.uk *Strength,* 2,524
Chief Constable, Paul West, QPM

WEST MIDLANDS POLICE PO Box 52, Lloyd House, Colmore Circus, Queensway, Birmingham B4 6NQ T 0845-113 5000 *Strength,* 8,311
Chief Constable, Paul Scott-Lee, QPM

WEST YORKSHIRE POLICE PO Box 9, Wakefield WF1 3QP T 01924-375222 *Strength,* 5,732
Chief Constable, Sir Norman Bettison

WILTSHIRE CONSTABULARY London Road, Devizes SN10 2DN T 0845-408 7000 *Strength,* 1,259
Chief Constable, Martin Richards

WALES

DYFED-POWYS POLICE PO Box 99, Llangunnor, Carmarthen SA31 2PF T 0845-330 2000 *Strength,* 1,201
Chief Constable, T. Grange, QPM

GWENT POLICE Croesyceiliog, Cwmbran NP44 2XJ T 01633-838111 W www.gwent.police.uk *Strength,* 1,483
Chief Constable, Michael Tonge

NORTH WALES POLICE Glan-y-Don, Colwyn Bay LL29 8AW T 0845-607 1001 *Strength,* 1,649
Chief Constable, R. Brunstrom

SOUTH WALES POLICE Cowbridge Road, Bridgend CF31 3SU T 01656-655555 *Strength,* 3,401
Chief Constable, Barbara Wilding, CBE, QPM

SCOTLAND

CENTRAL SCOTLAND POLICE Randolphfield, Stirling FK8 2HD T 01786-456000 W www.centralscotland.police.uk *Strength,* 827
Chief Constable, Andrew Cameron, QPM

DUMFRIES AND GALLOWAY CONSTABULARY Cornwall Mount, Dumfries DG1 1PZ T 0845-600 5701 W www.dumfriesandgalloway.police.uk *Strength,* 509
Chief Constable, David Strang, QPM

FIFE CONSTABULARY Detroit Road, Glenrothes KY6 2RJ T 01592-418888 W www.fife.police.uk *Strength,* 1,046
Chief Constable, Peter Wilson, QPM

GRAMPIAN POLICE Queen Street, Aberdeen AB10 1ZA T 0845-600 5700 W www.grampian.police.uk *Strength,* 1,399
Chief Constable, Colin McKerracher, QPM

LOTHIAN AND BORDERS POLICE Fettes Avenue, Edinburgh EH4 1RB T 0131-311 3131 W www.lbp.police.uk *Strength,* 2,848
Chief Constable, Paddy Tomkins

NORTHERN CONSTABULARY Old Perth Road, Inverness IV2 3SY T 01463-715555 *Strength,* 705
Chief Constable, Ian Latimer

STRATHCLYDE POLICE 173 Pitt Street, Glasgow G2 4JS T 0141-532 2000 W www.strathclyde.police.uk *Strength,* 7,945
Chief Constable, Sir William Rae, QPM

TAYSIDE POLICE PO Box 59, West Bell Street, Dundee DD1 9JU T 01382-223200 W www.tayside.police.uk *Strength,* 1,173
Chief Constable, John Vine, QPM

NORTHERN IRELAND

POLICE SERVICE OF NORTHERN IRELAND Brooklyn, 65 Knock Road, Belfast BT5 6LE T 028-9065 0222 W www.psni.police.uk *Strength,* 8,888
Chief Constable, Sir Hugh Orde, OBE

ISLANDS

GUERNSEY POLICE Hospital Lane, St Peter Port, Guernsey GY1 2QN T 01481-725111 *Strength,* 177
Chief Officer, G. Le Page

ISLE OF MAN CONSTABULARY Glencrutchery Road, Douglas IM2 4RG T 01624-631212 *Strength,* 236
Chief Constable, Mike Culverhouse

STATES OF JERSEY POLICE PO Box 789, St Helier, Jersey JE4 8ZD T 01534-612612 W www.police.gov.je *Strength,* 245
Chief Officer, Graham Power, QPM

LONDON FORCES

CITY OF LONDON POLICE

37 Wood Street, London EC2P 2NQ T 020-7601 2222
W www.cityoflondon.police.uk

Strength (February 2007), 856
Though small, the City of London has one of the mos important financial centres in the world and the force ha particular expertise in areas such as fraud investigation a well as the areas required of any police force. The forc has a wholly elected police authority, the polic committee of the Corporation of London, which appoint the commissioner.
Commissioner (acting), Mike Bowron
Assistant Commissioner (acting), Frank Armstrong
Commander (acting), Patrick Rice

METROPOLITAN POLICE SERVICE

New Scotland Yard, 8–10 Broadway, London SW1H 0BG
T 020-7230 1212 W www.met.police.uk

Strength (February 2007), 31,141
The Metropolitan Police Service is divided into thre main areas for operational purposes:

TERRITORIAL POLICING
Most of the day-to-day policing of London is carried ou by 33 borough operational command units; 32 comman units operate within the same boundaries as the Londo borough councils, plus there is an additional unit which i responsible for policing Heathrow airport.

SPECIALIST OPERATIONS
Specialist Operations is divided into three sections know as commands:

- *Protection Command* is responsible for the protection an security of high-profile persons, key public figures an official delegations in the UK and overseas. Thes include the current and former prime ministers, foreig dignitaries visiting the UK under the Vienn Convention, members of the British royal family an visiting European royal families, ambassadors diplomats, MPs, peers and others
- *Security Command* is responsible for aviation security a Heathrow and London City airports, including policin the terminal buildings and local areas, maintaining a effective response to terrorist activity and working wit the airports, airlines, government departments an agencies to prevent crime and dismantle organise criminal networks
- *Counter Terrorism Command* is responsible for th prevention and disruption of terrorist activity, domesti extremism and related offences both within London an nationally, providing a bomb disposal capability withi London, assisting the security services in fulfilling thei roles and providing a single point of contact fo international partners in counter-terrorism matters

SPECIALIST CRIME DIRECTORATE
The Specialist Crime Directorate's main areas of focus ar dismantling organised criminal networks and seizing thei assets; safeguarding children and young people fro physical, sexual and emotional abuse; and the investigation and prevention of homicide.

Commissioner, Sir Ian Blair, QPM
Deputy Commissioner, Paul Stephenson, QPM

ssistant Commissioners, Tarique Ghaffur, CBE, QPM *Central Operations)*; Tim Godwin, OBE *(Territorial olicing)*; Andy Hayman, CBE, QPM *(Specialist perations)*; Stephen House, QPM *(Specialist Crime irectorate)*; John Yates, QPM *(Operational Services)*
irectors, Ailsa Beaton *(Information)*; Sharon Burd *Resources (acting))*; Dick Fedorico *(Public Affairs and nternal Communication)*; Stephen Rimmer *(Strategy, Modernisation and Performance)*; Martin Tiplady *(Human esources)*

PECIALIST FORCES

RITISH TRANSPORT POLICE

5–27 Camden Road, London NW1 9LN **T** 020-7388 7541
/ www.btp.police.uk

trength (February 2007), 2,177
ritish Transport Police is the national police force for the ailways in England, Wales and Scotland, including the ondon Underground system, Docklands Light Railway, Midland Metro Tram system and Croydon Tramlink. The hief constable reports to the British Transport Police uthority. The members of the authority are appointed by he transport secretary and include representatives from he rail industry as well as independent members. Officers re paid the same as other police forces.
hief Constable, Ian Johnston, CBE, QPM
eputy Chief Constable, Andy Trotter, QPM

IVIL NUCLEAR CONSTABULARY

uilding F6, Culham Science Centre, Abingdon,
xfordshire OX14 3DB **T** 01235-466606 **W** www.cnc.police.uk

trength (March 2007), 670
he Civil Nuclear Constabulary (CNC) operates under he strategic direction of the Department of Trade and ndustry. The CNC is a specialised armed force whose role s the protection of civil nuclear sites and nuclear naterials. The constabulary is responsible for policing UK ivil nuclear industry facilities and for escorting nuclear naterial between establishments within the UK and vorldwide.
hief Constable (acting), James Smith
eputy Chief Constable, James Coupland

MINISTRY OF DEFENCE POLICE

Ministry of Defence Police and Guarding Agency, Wethersfield, raintree, Essex CM7 4AZ **T** 01371-854000

trength (January 2007), 3,917
art of the Ministry of Defence Police and Guarding Agency, the Ministry of Defence Police is a statutory civil olice force with particular responsibility for the security nd policing of the MoD environment. It contributes to he physical protection of property and personnel within ts jurisdiction and provides a comprehensive police ervice to the MoD as a whole.
hief Constable/Chief Executive, Steve Love
eputy Chief Constable, David Ray, QPM
irector of Resources and Planning, Daniel Applegate
ssistant Chief Constables: Director of Professional Development, R. Chidley; *Director of Operational Support,* J. Bligh; *Director of Divisional Operations,* G McAuley; *Director of Regional Operations (MoD Guard Service),* A. MacCormick

THE SPECIAL CONSTABULARY

The Special Constabulary is a force of trained volunteers who support and work with their local police force for a minimum of four hours a week. Special Constables are thoroughly grounded in the basic aspects of police work, such as self-defence, powers of arrest, common crimes and preparing evidence for court, before they can begin to carry out any police duties. Once they have completed their training, they have the same powers as a regular officer and wear a similar uniform.
W http://specials.homeoffice.gov.uk

STAFF ASSOCIATIONS

Police officers are not permitted to join a trade union or to take strike action. All ranks have their own staff associations.

ASSOCIATION OF CHIEF POLICE OFFICERS OF ENGLAND, WALES AND NORTHERN IRELAND, 10 Victoria Street, London SW1H 0NN **T** 020-7084 8950
Secretary, T. Flaherty

ENGLAND AND WALES

POLICE FEDERATION OF ENGLAND AND WALES, 15–17 Langley Road, Surbiton, Surrey KT6 6LP
T 020-8335 1000 **W** www.polfed.org
General Secretary, John Francis

POLICE SUPERINTENDENTS' ASSOCIATION OF ENGLAND AND WALES, 67A Reading Road, Pangbourne, Reading RG8 7JD **T** 0118-984 4005
National Secretary, Chief Supt. Philip Aspey

SCOTLAND

ASSOCIATION OF CHIEF POLICE OFFICERS IN SCOTLAND, Police Headquarters, 173 Pitt Street, Glasgow G2 4JS **T** 0141-532 2052
E secretariat@acpos.pnn.police.uk
Hon. Secretary, Sir William Rae, QPM

ASSOCIATION OF SCOTTISH POLICE SUPERINTENDENTS, Secretariat, 173 Pitt Street, Glasgow G2 4JS **T** 0141-221 5796
E secretariat@scottishpolicesupers.org.uk
W www.asps.org.uk
General Secretary, Carol Forfar

SCOTTISH POLICE FEDERATION, 5 Woodside Place, Glasgow G3 7QF **T** 0141-332 5234 **W** www.spf.org.uk
General Secretary and Treasurer, Joe Grant

NORTHERN IRELAND

POLICE FEDERATION FOR NORTHERN IRELAND, 77–79 Garnerville Road, Belfast BT4 2NX **T** 028-9076 4200
E office.pfni@btconnect.com **W** www.policefed-ni.org.uk
Secretary (acting), Larry Williams

SUPERINTENDENTS' ASSOCIATION OF NORTHERN IRELAND, PSNI College, Garnerville Road, Belfast BT4 2NX **T** 028-9092 2201 **E** mail@psani.org
W www.psani.org
Hon. Secretary, Supt. G. Thomson

THE PRISON SERVICE

The prison services in the United Kingdom are the responsibility of the Secretary of State for Justice, the Scottish Executive Justice Department and the Secretary of State for Northern Ireland. The chief directors-general (chief executive in Scotland, director in Northern Ireland), officers of the Prison Service, the Scottish Prison Service and the Northern Ireland Prison Service are responsible for the day-to-day running of the system.

There are 140 prison establishments in England and Wales, 15 in Scotland and three in Northern Ireland. Convicted prisoners are classified according to their assessed security risk and are housed in establishments appropriate to that level of security. There are no open prisons in Northern Ireland. Female prisoners are housed in women's establishments or in separate wings of mixed prisons. Remand prisoners are, where possible, housed separately from convicted prisoners. Offenders under the age of 21 are usually detained in a Young Offender Institution, which may be a separate establishment or part of a prison. Appellant and failed asylum seekers are held in Immigration Removal Centres, or in separate units of other prisons.

Eleven prisons are now run by the private sector, and in England, Wales and Scotland all escort services have been contracted out to private companies. In Scotland, one prison (Kilmarnock) was built and financed by the private sector and is being operated by private contractors.

There are independent prison inspectorates in England, Wales and Scotland which report annually on conditions and the treatment of prisoners. The Chief Inspector of Criminal Justice in Northern Ireland and HM Chief Inspector of Prisons for England and Wales perform an inspectorate role for prisons in Northern Ireland. Every prison establishment also has an independent monitoring board made up of local volunteers.

Any prisoner whose complaint is not satisfied by the internal complaints procedures may complain to the prisons ombudsman for England and Wales, the Scottish Prisons Complaints Commission or the prisoner ombudsman for Northern Ireland.

The 11 private sector prisons in England and Wales are the direct responsibility of the chief executive of the National Offender Management Service (NOMS). The NOMS was created in January 2004, in order to integrate prisons and probation into a system whereby end-to-end management of offenders is provided; this is expected to reduce re-offending and cut the growth rate of the prison population. The chief executive, Helen Edwards, also has responsibility for public prisons, the National Probation Service, the Youth Justice Board and NOMS policy. In May 2007 NOMS was amalgamated into the Ministry of Justice. The prisons and probation inspectors, the prisons ombudsman and the independent monitoring boards report to the home secretary.

PRISON STATISTICS

PRISON POPULATION (UK)
as at April 2007
The projected 'high scenario' prison population for 201 in England and Wales is 106,550; the 'low scenario' i 90,250.

	Remand	*Sentenced*	*Othe*
ENGLAND AND WALES			
Male	11,859	62,591	1,44
Female	918	3,403	4
Total	12,777	65,994	1,49
SCOTLAND*			
Male	1,159	5,364	[illegible]
Female	83	251	–
Total	1,242	5,614	[illegible]
N. IRELAND			
Male	510	920	–
Female	17	27	–
Total	527	947	–
UK TOTAL	14,546	72,555	1,49

* Figures for Scotland are an average for 2005–6
Sources: Home Office – *Research Development Statistics*; Scottis Prison Service – *Annual Report and Accounts 2005–6*; Norther Ireland Prison Service – www.niprisonservice.gov.uk

SENTENCED PRISON POPULATION BY SEX AND OFFENCE (ENGLAND AND WALES)
as at April 2007

	Male	*Femal*
Violence against the person	17,014	684
Sexual offences	7,240	46
Burglary	7,810	206
Robbery	8,297	304
Theft, handling	3,433	441
Fraud and forgery	1,515	242
Drugs offences	9,639	1,038
Motoring offences	1,608	26
Other offences	5,646	383
Offence not recorded	319	25
*Total**	62,521	3,395

* Figures do not include civil (non-criminal) prisoners or fine defaulters
Source: Home Office – *Research Development Statistics*

SENTENCED POPULATION BY LENGTH OF SENTENCE (ENGLAND AND WALES)
as at April 2007

	Adults	*Young offenders*
Less than 12 months	6,091	2,022
12 months to less than 4 years	18,042	4,775
4 years to less than life	24,077	1,787
Life	8,494	630
*Total**	56,704	9,214

* Figures do not include civil (non-criminal) prisoners or fine defaulters
Source: Home Office – *Research Development Statistics*

'ERAGE DAILY SENTENCED POPULATION BY LENGTH
' SENTENCE 2005–6 (SCOTLAND)

	Adults	*Young offenders*
ss than 4 years	2,266	460
years or over (including life)	2,723	165
tal	4,989	625

urce: Scottish Prison Service – *Annual Report and Accounts 2005–6*

LF-INFLICTED DEATHS IN PRISON APRIL 2006 – ARCH 2007 (ENGLAND AND WALES)

en	68
omen	5
tal	73
te per 100,000 prisoners in custody	95.5

urce: Home Office – *Research Development Statistics*

PERATING COSTS OF PRISON SERVICE IN ENGLAND ND WALES 2006–7

aff costs	£1,586,126,000
her operating costs	£649,184,000
perating income	(£299,026,000)
t operating costs for the year	£1,936,284,000
erage cost per prisoner place	£28,734

urce: HM Prison Service – *Annual Report and Accounts 2006–7*

PERATING COSTS OF SCOTTISH PRISON SERVICE 06–7

tal income	(£2,140,000)
tal expenditure	£264,753,000
Staff costs	£131,984,000
Running costs	£90,947,000
Other current expenditure	£41,822,000
perating cost	£262,613,000
Cost of capital charges	£18,840,000
Interest payable and similar charges	£16,000
Interest receivable	(£8,000)
et operating cost	£281,461,000

urce: Scottish Prison Service – *Annual Report and Accounts 2006–7*

PERATING COSTS OF NORTHERN IRELAND PRISON RVICE 2006–7

aff costs	£89,443,000
et running costs	£29,319,000
epreciation	£8,921,000
nance charges	£6,231,000
npairment of fixed assets	£1,804,000
perating expenditure	£135,718,000
ther current expenditure	£930,000
et operating costs for the year	£136,648,000

urce: Northern Ireland Prison Service – *Annual Report and Accounts 2006–7*

THE PRISON SERVICES

HM PRISON SERVICE

Cleland House, Page Street, London SW1P 4LN
T 0870-000 1397 E public.enquiries@hmps.gsi.gov.uk
W www.hmprisonservice.gov.uk

SALARIES
from 1 April 2007

Senior Manager A	£60,442–£78,732
Senior Manager B	£55,528–£76,796
Senior Manager C	£53,357–£69,157
Senior Manager D	£44,589–£63,535
Manager E	£29,184–£43,927
Manager F	£26,280–£37,262
Manager G	£23,434–£30,676

THE PRISON SERVICE MANAGEMENT

Director-General (SCS), Phil Wheatley, CB
Deputy Director-General (SCS), Michael Spurr
Director of High Security Prisons (SCS), Steve Wagstaffe
Director of Operational Policy (SCS), Ian Poree
Director of Finance (SCS), Ann Beasley
Director of Personnel (SCS), Robin Wilkinson
Director of Prison Health (SCS), Richard Bradshaw
Board Secretary and Head of Secretariat (SMB), Ken Everett
Legal Adviser, Andrew Dodsworth
Media Relations, Simon Watts
Race Equality Adviser, Beverley Thompson

AREA MANAGERS

Phil Copple *(North-East)*; Ian Lockwood *(North-West)*; Tony Hassall *(Yorkshire and Humberside)*; Bob Perry *(East Midlands)*; Geoff Hughes *(Wales)*; Sue McAllister *(West Midlands)*; Danny McAllister *(Eastern)*; Alan Scott *South-West)*; Nick Pascoe *(London)*; Colin McConnell *(South Central)*; Adrian Smith *(Kent and Sussex)*; Michelle Jaran-Howe *(Contracted Prisons)*

PRISON ESTABLISHMENTS – ENGLAND AND WALES

POPULATION STATISTICS
as at 15 June 2007

Male prisoners	76,140
Female prisoners	4,398
Number of prisoners held in police cells under Operation Safeguard	413
Total	80,951
Useable operational capacity	81,058
Spaces available under Operation Safeguard*	400
Total	81,458
Number under home detention curfew supervision	2,296

* These vary from night to night and up to a 400 place ceiling

PRISON ESTABLISHMENTS KEY
* Women's establishment or establishment with units for women
† Remand Centre (other establishments may contain units for remand prisoners)
‡ Young Offender Institution or establishment with units for young offenders
§ Immigration Removal Centre or establishment with units for immigration detainees

as at April 2007

ACKLINGTON, nr. Morpeth, Northumberland NE65 9XF *Prisoners,* 849 *Governor,* Mick Lees

ALBANY, 55 Parkhurst Road, Newport, Isle of Wight PO30 5RS *Prisoners,* 525 *Governor,* Mel Jones

†‡ALTCOURSE (private prison), Higher Lane, Fazakerley, Liverpool L9 7LH *Prisoners,* 1,105 *Director,* John McLaughlin

†‡ASHFIELD (private prison), Shortwood Road, Pucklechurch, Bristol BS16 9QJ *Prisoners,* 386 *Director,* Vicky O'Dea

ASHWELL, Oakham, Rutland, Leics LE15 7LF *Prisoners,* 544 *Governor (acting),* Deborah McGivern

*ASKHAM GRANGE, Askham Richard, York YO23 3FT *Prisoners,* 99 *Governor,* Alec McCrystal

‡AYLESBURY, Bierton Road, Aylesbury, Bucks HP20 1FH *Prisoners,* 443 *Governor,* David Kennedy

‡BEDFORD, St Loyes Street, Bedford MK40 1HG *Prisoners,* 478 *Governor,* Paul Kempster

‡BELMARSH, Western Way, Thamesmead, London SE28 0EB *Prisoners,* 919 *Governor,* Claudia Sturt

‡BIRMINGHAM, Winson Green Road, Birmingham B18 4AS *Prisoners,* 1,452 *Governor,* Mike Shann

‡BLAKENHURST, Hewell Lane, Redditch, Worcs B97 6QS *Prisoners,* 1,070 *Governor,* Terry Witton

BLANTYRE HOUSE, Horden, Goudhurst, Kent TN17 2NH *Prisoners,* 120 *Governor,* Dave Atkinson

BLUNDESTON, Lowestoft, Suffolk NR32 5BG *Prisoners,* 464 *Governor,* Paul Cawkwell

†‡BRINSFORD, New Road, Featherstone, Wolverhampton WV10 7PY *Prisoners,* 476 *Governor,* Pete Knapton

‡BRISTOL, 19 Cambridge Road, Horfield, Bristol BS7 8PS *Prisoners,* 607 *Governor,* Suzy Dymond-White

‡BRIXTON, Jebb Avenue, London SW2 5XF *Prisoners,* 806 *Governor,* Paul McDowell

*†‡BROCKHILL, Hewell Lane, Redditch, Worcs B97 6RD *Prisoners,* 169 *Governor,* Alison Gomme

*‡BRONZEFIELD (private prison), Woodthorpe Road, Ashford, Middlesex TW15 3JZ *Prisoners,* 447 *Director,* Janine McDowell

*†‡BUCKLEY HALL, Buckley Hall Road, Rochdale, Lancs OL12 9DP *Prisoners,* 384 *Governor,* Mick Regan

‡BULLINGDON, PO Box 50, Bicester, Oxon OX25 1WD *Prisoners,* 961 *Governor,* Phil Taylor

*‡BULLWOOD HALL, High Road, Hockley, Essex SS5 4TE *Prisoners,* 182 *Governor,* Roger Plant

CAMP HILL, Newport, Isle of Wight PO30 5PB *Prisoners,* 594 *Governor,* Ian Young

CANTERBURY, 46 Longport, Canterbury, Kent CT1 1PJ *Prisoners,* 276 *Governor,* Chris Bartlett

‡CARDIFF, Knox Road, Cardiff CF24 0UG *Prisoners,* 760 *Governor,* Sian West

‡CASTINGTON, Morpeth, Northumberland NE65 9XG *Prisoners,* 385 *Governor,* Bill Shaw

CHANNINGS WOOD, Denbury, Newton Abbott, Devon TQ12 6DW *Prisoners,* 658 *Governor,* Jeannine Hendrick

†‡CHELMSFORD, 200 Springfield Road, Chelmsford, Essex CM2 6LQ *Prisoners,* 723 *Governor,* Nigel Smith

COLDINGLEY, Shaftesbury Road, Bisley, Woking, Surrey GU24 9EX *Prisoners,* 390 *Governor,* John Robinson

*COOKHAM WOOD, Rochester, Kent ME1 3LU *Prisoner* 186 *Governor,* Ed Tullet

DARTMOOR, Princetown, Yelverton, Devon PL20 6RR *Prisoners,* 629 *Governor,* Serena Watts

‡DEERBOLT, Bowes Road, Barnard Castle, Co. Durham DL12 9BG *Prisoners,* 403 *Governor,* Debra Baldwin

†‡DONCASTER (private prison), off North Bridge Road, Marshgate, Doncaster DN5 8UX *Prisoners,* 1,142 *Directo* Brian Anderson

‡DORCHESTER, North Square, Dorchester, Dorset DT1 1 *Prisoners,* 245 *Governor,* Tony Corcoran

DOVEGATE (private prison), Uttoxeter, Staffs ST14 8XR *Prisoners,* 833 *Director,* Wyn Jones

DOVER, The Citadel, Western Heights, Dover, Kent CT17 9D *Prisoners,* 309 *Governor,* Jim Carmichael

*DOWNVIEW, Sutton Lane, Sutton, Surrey SM2 5PD *Prisoners,* 353 *Governor,* Ian Murray

*DRAKE HALL, Eccleshall, Staffs ST21 6LQ *Prisoners,* 246 *Governor,* John Huntington

*‡DURHAM, Old Elvet, Durham DH1 3HU *Prisoners,* 975 *Governor,* Alan Tallentire

*EAST SUTTON PARK, Sutton Valence, Maidstone, Kent ME17 3DF *Prisoners,* 100 *Governor,* Ed Tullett

*†‡EASTWOOD PARK, Falfield, Wotton-under-Edge, Glc GL12 8DB *Prisoners,* 348 *Governor,* Tim Beeston

†EDMUNDS HILL, Stradishall, Newmarket, Suffolk CB8 9YN *Prisoners,* 366 *Governor,* Norma Harrington

†‡ELMLEY, Church Road, Eastchurch, Sheerness, Kent ME12 4DZ *Prisoners,* 986 *Governor,* Helen Rinaldi

ERLESTOKE, Devizes, Wilts SN10 5TU *Prisoners,* 418 *Governor,* Doug Moon

EVERTHORPE, Beck Road, Brough, E. Yorks HU15 1RB *Prisoners,* 678 *Governor,* Gary Monaghan

‡EXETER, 30 New North Road, Exeter, Devon EX4 4EX *Prisoners,* 495 *Governor,* Mark Flinton

FEATHERSTONE, New Road, Featherstone, Wolverhampton WV10 7PU *Prisoners,* 609 *Governor,* Simon Cartwright

†‡FELTHAM, Bedfont Road, Feltham, Middx TW13 4ND *Prisoners,* 629 *Governor,* vacant

FORD, Arundel, W. Sussex BN18 0BX *Prisoners,* 457 *Governor,* Fiona Radford

‡FOREST BANK (private prison), Agecroft Road, Pendlebury, Manchester M27 8FB *Prisoners,* 1,060 *Director,* Ivor Woods

*‡FOSTON HALL, Foston, Derby DE65 5DN *Prisoners,* 24 *Governor,* Paddy Scriven

FRANKLAND, Brasside, Durham DH1 5YD *Prisoners,* 714 *Governor,* Bob Mullen

FULL SUTTON, York YO41 1PS *Prisoners,* 582 *Governor,* Steve Tilley

GARTH, Ulnes Walton Lane, Leyland, Preston PR26 8NE *Prisoners,* 611 *Governor,* Terry Williams

GARTREE, Gallow Field Road, Market Harborough, Leics LE16 7RP *Prisoners,* 575 *Governor,* Julia Morgan

†‡GLEN PARVA, 10 Tigers Road, Wigston, Leicester LE18 4TN *Prisoners,* 810 *Governor,* Alison Perry

‡GLOUCESTER, Barrack Square, Gloucester GL1 2JN *Prisoners,* 306 *Governor,* David Chalmers

GRENDON, Grendon Underwood, Bucks HP18 0TL *Prisoners,* 547 *Governor,* Dr Peter Bennett

‡GUYS MARSH, Shaftesbury, Dorset SP7 0AH *Prisoners,* 562 *Governor,* Barry Greenberry

§HASLAR, 2 Dolphin Way, Gosport, Hampshire PO12 2AW *Prisoners,* 119 *Manager,* Julia Killick

IAVERIGG, Millom, Cumbria LA18 4NA *Prisoners,* 568 *Governor,* Clive Chatterton

IEWELL GRANGE, Redditch, Worcs B97 6QQ *Prisoners,* 181 *Governor,* Alison Gomme

‡HIGH DOWN, High Down Lane, Sutton, Surrey SM2 5PJ *Prisoners,* 762 *Governor,* Peter Dawson

‡HIGHPOINT, Stradishall, Newmarket, Suffolk CB8 9YG *Prisoners,* 812 *Governor,* Sue Doolan

‡HINDLEY, Gibson Street, Bickershaw, Wigan, Lancs WN2 5TH *Prisoners,* 493 *Governor,* Ray Hill

:HOLLESLEY BAY, Woodbridge, Suffolk IP12 3JW *Prisoners,* 305 *Governor,* Declan Moore

†‡HOLLOWAY, Parkhurst Road, London N7 0NU *Prisoners,* 441 *Governor,* Sue Saunders

IOLME HOUSE, Holme House Road, Stockton-on-Tees TS18 2QU *Prisoners,* 1,002 *Governor,* Matt Spencer

:HULL, Hedon Road, Hull HU9 5LS *Prisoners,* 1,055 *Governor,* Paul Foweather

:HUNTERCOMBE, Nuffield, Henley-on-Thames, Oxon RG9 5SB *Prisoners,* 362 *Governor,* Kevin Leggett

KENNET, Parkbourn, Maghull, Liverpool, Merseyside L31 1HX *Prisoners,* 350 *Governor,* Steve Lawrence

KINGSTON, 122 Milton Road, Portsmouth PO3 6AS *Prisoners,* 198 *Governor,* Ian Telfer

KIRKHAM, Freckleton Road, Kirkham, Preston, Lancs PR4 2RN *Prisoners,* 508 *Governor,* John Hewitson

KIRKLEVINGTON GRANGE, Yarm, Cleveland TS15 9PA *Prisoners,* 222 *Governor,* Alan Richer

.ANCASTER, The Castle, Lancaster LA1 1YL *Prisoners,* 237 *Governor,* Peter Francis

‡LANCASTER FARMS, Far Moor Lane, Stone Row Head, Off Quernmore Road, Lancaster LA1 3QZ *Prisoners,* 512 *Governor,* Paul Holland

.ATCHMERE HOUSE, Church Road, Ham Common, Richmond, Surrey TW10 5HH *Prisoners,* 207 *Governor,* Steve Metcalf

.EEDS, 2 Gloucester Terrace, Stanningley Road, Leeds LS12 2TJ *Prisoners,* 1,019 *Governor,* Rob Kellet

.EICESTER, Welford Road, Leicester LE2 7AJ *Prisoners,* 362 *Governor,* Danny Mulligan

‡LEWES, Brighton Road, Lewes, E. Sussex BN7 1EA *Prisoners,* 532 *Governor,* Eoin McLennan-Murray

.EYHILL, Wotton-under-Edge, Glos GL12 8BT *Prisoners,* 432 *Governor,* Mick Bell

‡LINCOLN, Greetwell Road, Lincoln LN2 4BD *Prisoners,* 534 *Governor,* Lynne Saunders

.INDHOLME, Bawtry Road, Hatfield Woodhouse, Doncaster DN7 6EE *Prisoners,* 1,015 *Governor,* Martin Ward

.ITTLEHEY, Perry, Huntingdon, Cambs PE28 0SR *Prisoners,* 697 *Governor,* David Taylor

‡LIVERPOOL, 68 Hornby Road, Liverpool L9 3DF *Prisoners,* 1,347 *Governor,* Alan Brown

.ONG LARTIN, South Littleton, Evesham, Worcs WR11 8TZ *Prisoners,* 442 *Governor,* Ferdie Parker

†‡LOW NEWTON, Brasside, Durham DH1 5YA *Prisoners,* 262 *Governor,* Paddy Fox

.OWDHAM GRANGE (private prison), Lowdham, Notts NG14 7DA *Prisoners,* 609 *Director,* Guy Baulf

MAIDSTONE, 36 County Road, Maidstone, Kent ME14 1UZ *Prisoners,* 575 *Governor,* Jane Galbally

MANCHESTER, 1 Southall Street, Manchester M60 9AH *Prisoners,* 1,247 *Governor,* Chris Sheffield

‡MOORLAND CLOSED, Bawtry Road, Hatfield Woodhouse, Doncaster DN7 6BW *Prisoners,* 784 *Governor,* Jacqui Tilley

‡MOORLAND OPEN, Thorne Road, Hatfield, Doncaster DN7 6EL *Prisoners,* 222 *Governor,* Jacqui Tilley

*MORTON HALL, Swinderby, Lincoln LN6 9PT *Prisoners,* 297 *Governor,* Susan Howard

THE MOUNT, Molyneaux Avenue, Bovingdon, Hemel Hempstead, Herts HP3 0NZ *Prisoners,* 719 *Governor,* Damian Evans

*†‡NEW HALL, Dial Wood, Flockton, Wakefield, W. Yorks WF4 4XX *Prisoners,* 371 *Governor,* Sara Snell

NORTH SEA CAMP, Freiston, Boston, Lincs PE22 0QX *Prisoners,* 303 *Governor,* Norman Warwick

‡NORTHALLERTON, East Road, Northallerton, N. Yorks DL6 1NW *Prisoners,* 244 *Governor,* Norman Griffin

†‡NORWICH, Knox Road, Norwich, Norfolk NR1 4LU *Prisoners,* 611 *Governor,* James Shanley

NOTTINGHAM, Perry Road, Sherwood, Nottingham NG5 3AG *Prisoners,* 550 *Governor,* Tom Wheatley

‡ONLEY, Willoughby, Rugby, Warks CV23 8AP *Prisoners,* 619 *Governor,* Robin Eldridge

†‡PARC (private prison), Heol Hopcyn John, Bridgend, S. Wales CF35 6AR *Prisoners,* 1,128 *Director,* Janet Wallsgrove

‡PARKHURST, Newport, Isle of Wight PO30 5NX *Prisoners,* 525 *Governor,* Carole Draper

‡PENTONVILLE, Caledonian Road, London N7 8TT *Prisoners,* 1,155 *Governor,* Nick Leader

*‡PETERBOROUGH (private prison), Saville Road, Westfield, Peterborough PE3 7PD *Prisoners,* 576 *Director,* Mike Conway

‡PORTLAND, Easton, Portland, Dorset DT5 1DL *Prisoners,* 447 *Governor,* Steve Holland

‡PRESCOED, Coed-y-Paen, Pontypool, Monmouthshire NP4 0TB *Prisoners,* 170 *Governor,* David Ward

‡PRESTON, 2 Ribbleton Lane, Preston, Lancs PR1 5AB *Prisoners,* 737 *Governor,* Richard Vince

RANBY, Retford, Notts DN22 8EU *Prisoners,* 1,024 *Governor,* Louise Taylor

†‡READING, Forbury Road, Reading, Berks RG1 3HY *Prisoners,* 262 *Governor,* Pauline Bryant

RISLEY, Warrington Road, Risley, Warrington, Cheshire WA3 6BP *Prisoners,* 1,081 *Governor,* Bob McColm

‡ROCHESTER, 1 Fort Road, Rochester, Kent ME1 3QS *Prisoners,* 388 *Governor (acting),* John Wilson

RYE HILL (private prison), Willoughby, nr. Rugby, Warks CV23 8SZ *Prisoners,* 646 *Director,* Dave McDonnell

*SEND, Ripley Road, Woking, Surrey GU23 7LJ *Prisoners,* 208 *Governor,* Brian Ritchie

SHEPTON MALLET, Cornhill, Shepton Mallet, Somerset BA4 5LU *Prisoners,* 188 *Governor,* Nick Evans

‡SHREWSBURY, The Dana, Shrewsbury, Shropshire SY1 2HR *Prisoners,* 338 *Governor,* Gerry Hendry

SPRING HILL, Grendon Underwood, nr. Aylesbury, Bucks HP18 0TL *Prisoners,* 314 *Governor,* Dr Peter Bennett

STAFFORD, 54 Gaol Road, Stafford ST16 3AW *Prisoners,* 672 *Governor,* Peter Small

STANDFORD HILL, Church Road, Eastchurch, Sheerness, Kent ME12 4AA *Prisoners,* 419 *Governor,* Kieron Taylor

STOCKEN, Stocken Hall Road, Stretton, nr. Oakham, Leics LE15 7RD *Prisoners,* 621 *Governor,* Steve Turner

‡STOKE HEATH, Market Drayton, Shropshire TF9 2JL *Prisoners,* 661 *Governor,* Teresa Clarke

*†‡STYAL, Wilmslow, Cheshire SK9 4HR *Prisoners,* 432 *Governor,* Steve Hall

SUDBURY, Ashbourne, Derbyshire DE6 5HW *Prisoners,* 500 *Governor,* Chris Davidson

SWALESIDE, Brabazon Road, Eastchurch, Isle of Sheppey, Kent ME12 4AX *Prisoners,* 776 *Governor,* Stephen O'Connell

‡SWANSEA, 200 Oystermouth Road, Swansea SA1 3SR *Prisoners,* 419 *Governor,* Andrea Whitfield

‡SWINFEN HALL, Lichfield, Staffs WS14 9QS *Prisoners,* 618 *Governor,* Tom Watson

‡THORN CROSS, Arley Road, Appleton Thorn, Warrington, Cheshire WA4 4RL *Prisoners,* 223 *Governor,* Derek Harrison

USK, 47 Maryport Street, Usk, Monmouthshire NP15 1XP *Prisoners,* 394 *Governor,* David Ward

THE VERNE, Portland, Dorset DT5 1EQ *Prisoners,* 590 *Governor,* Denise Hodder

WAKEFIELD, 5 Love Lane, Wakefield, West Yorks WF2 9AG *Prisoners,* 745 *Governor,* David Thompson

‡WANDSWORTH, PO Box 757, Heathfield Road, London SW18 3HS *Prisoners,* 1,482 *Governor,* Ian Mulholland

‡WARREN HILL, Hollesley, Woodbridge, Suffolk IP12 3JW *Prisoners,* 217 *Governor,* Ken Kan

WAYLAND, Griston, Thetford, Norfolk IP25 6RL *Prisoners,* 697 *Governor,* Michael Wood

WEALSTUN, Wetherby, W. Yorks LS23 7AZ *Prisoners,* 796 *Governor,* Amy Rice

WELLINGBOROUGH, Millers Park, Doddington Road, Wellingborough, Northants NN8 2NH *Prisoners,* 643 *Governor,* Peter Siddons

‡WERRINGTON, Stoke-on-Trent ST9 0DX *Prisoners,* 156 *Governor,* Frank Flynn

‡WETHERBY, York Road, Wetherby, W. Yorks LS22 5ED *Prisoners,* 323 *Governor,* Will Styles

WHATTON, 14 Cromwell Road, Whatton, Nottingham NG13 9FQ *Prisoners,* 755 *Governor,* Peter Wright

WHITEMOOR, Longhill Road, March, Cambs PE15 0PR *Prisoners,* 448 *Governor,* Steve Rodford

WINCHESTER, Romsey Road, Winchester SO22 5DF *Prisoners,* 544 *Governor,* Andy Lattimore

WOLDS (private prison), Everthorpe, Brough, E. Yorks HU15 2JZ *Prisoners,* 373 *Director,* Dave McDonnell

†‡§WOODHILL, Tattenhoe Street, Milton Keynes, Bucks MK4 4DA *Prisoners,* 826 *Governor,* Luke Serjeant

†WORMWOOD SCRUBS, PO Box 757, Du Cane Road, London W12 0AE *Prisoners,* 1,289 *Governor,* Steve Metcalf

WYMOTT, Ulnes Walton Lane, Leyland, Preston PR26 8LW *Prisoners,* 1,064 *Governor,* Jayne Blake

SCOTTISH PRISON SERVICE (SPS)

Calton House, 5 Redheughs Rigg, Edinburgh EH12 9HW
T 0131-244 8747 E gaolinfo@sps.gov.uk
W www.sps.gov.uk

SALARIES 2007–8

Senior managers in the Scottish Prison Service, including governors and deputy governors of prisons, are paid across three pay bands:

Band I	£50,823–£63,317
Band H	£40,341–£52,465
Band G	£31,765–£43,624

SPS BOARD

Chief Executive, Mike Ewart

Directors, Rachel Gwyon *(Corporate Services)*; Willie Pretswell *(Finance and Business Services)*; Dr Andrew Fraser *(Health and Care)*; Barbara Allison *(Human Resources)*; Eric Murch *(Partnerships and Commissioning)*; Mike Duffy *(Prisons)*

Non-Executive Directors, Bill Carr; Eric Jackson; Elinor Smith

PRISON ESTABLISHMENTS

Average prisoner numbers 2005–6

*ABERDEEN, Craiginches, 4 Grampian Place, Aberdeen AB11 8FN *Prisoners,* 225 *Governor,* Mike Inglis

†BARLINNIE, Glasgow G33 2QX *Prisoners,* 1,195 *Governor,* Bill McKinlay

CASTLE HUNTLY, Longforgan, Dundee DD2 5HL *Prisoners* 155 *Governor,* Ian Whitehead

*‡CORNTON VALE, Cornton Road, Stirling FK9 5NU *Prisoners,* 246 *Governor,* Ian Gunn

†DUMFRIES, Terregles Street, Dumfries DG2 9AX *Prisoners,* 182 *Governor,* Nigel Ironside

‡EDINBURGH, 33 Stenhouse Road, Edinburgh EH11 3LN *Prisoners,* 701 *Governor,* Dan Gunn

GLENOCHIL, King O'Muir Road, Tullibody FK10 3AD *Prisoners,* 485 *Governor,* Audrey Park

‡GREENOCK, Gateside, Greenock PA16 9AH *Prisoners,* 323 *Governor,* Tony Simpson

*INVERNESS, Porterfield, Inverness IV2 3HH *Prisoners,* 150 *Governor,* Eric Fairbairn

‡KILMARNOCK (private prison), Bowhouse, Kilmarnock KA1 5AA *Prisoners,* 583 *Director,* Wendy Sinclair

NORANSIDE, Fern By Forfar, Angus DD8 3QY *Prisoners,* 135 *Governor,* Ian Whitehead

PERTH, 3 Edinburgh Road, Perth PH2 8AT *Prisoners,* 655 *Governor,* Kate Donegan

PETERHEAD, Aberdeenshire AB42 2YY *Prisoners,* 298 *Governor,* vacant

‡POLMONT, Falkirk FK2 0AB *Prisoners,* 632 *Governor,* Derek McGill

SHOTTS, Canthill Road, Lanarkshire ML7 4LE *Prisoners,* 515 *Governor,* Rona Sweeney

NORTHERN IRELAND PRISON SERVICE

Dundonald House, Upper Newtownards Road, Belfast BT4 3SU
T 028-9052 2922
E info@niprisonservice.gov.uk
W www.niprisonservice.gov.uk

SALARIES 2006–7

Governor 1	£66,638–£71,823
Governor 2	£60,612–£64,351
Governor 3	£52,448–£55,962
Governor 4	£45,612–£49,401
Governor 5	£40,066–£44,934

SENIOR STAFF

Director, Robin Masefield, CBE

Deputy Directors, Mark McGuckin *(Finance and Personnel)*; Max Murray *(Operations)*; Anne McCleary *(Services)*

Associate Director of Health and Healthcare, Philip McClements

PRISON ESTABLISHMENTS

*‡§HYDEBANK WOOD, Hospital Road, Belfast BT8 8NA *Governor,* Stephen Davis

§MAGHABERRY, Old Road, Ballinderry Upper, Lisburn, Co. Antrim BT28 2NF *Governor,* Alan Longwell

MAGILLIGAN, Point Road, Limavady, Co. Londonderry BT49 0LR *Governor,* Tom Woods

)EFENCE

he armed forces of the United Kingdom comprise the oyal Navy, the Army and the Royal Air Force (RAF). The ueen is Commander-in-Chief of all the armed forces. he Secretary of State for Defence is responsible for the rmulation and content of defence policy and for oviding the means by which it is conducted. The formal gal basis for the conduct of defence in the UK rests on a nge of powers vested by statute and Letters Patent in the efence Council, chaired by the Secretary of State for efence. Beneath the ministers lies the top management the Ministry of Defence (MoD), headed jointly by the ermanent Secretary and the Chief of Defence Staff. The ermanent Secretary is the government's principal civilian lviser on defence and has the primary responsibility for olicy, finance, management and administration. He is so personally accountable to parliament for the xpenditure of all public money allocated to defence urposes. The Chief of the Defence Staff is the rofessional head of the armed forces in the UK and e principal military adviser to the secretary of state and e government.

The Defence Management Board (DMB) is the xecutive board of the Defence Council. Chaired by the ermanent Secretary, it acts as the main executive board of e Ministry of Defence, providing senior level leadership nd strategic management of defence.

The Central Staff, headed by the Vice-Chief of the efence Staff and the Second Permanent Under-Secretary f State, is the policy core of the department. Defence quipment and Support, headed by the Chief of Defence laterial, is responsible for purchasing defence equipment nd providing logistical support to the armed forces.

A permanent Joint Headquarters for the conduct of int operations was set up at Northwood in 1996. The int Headquarters connects the policy and strategic nctions of the MoD head office with the conduct of perations and is intended to strengthen the olicy/executive division.

The UK pursues its defence and security policies rough its membership of NATO (to which most of its med forces are committed), the European Union, the rganisation for Security and Cooperation in Europe and e UN (*see* International Organisations section).

TRENGTH OF THE ARMED FORCES

	Royal Navy	*Army*	*RAF*	*All Services*
1975 strength	76,200	167,100	95,000	338,300
1990 strength	63,210	152,810	89,680	305,700
2001 strength	42,420	109,530	53,700	205,650
2002 strength	41,630	110,050	53,000	204,680
2003 strength	41,550	112,130	53,240	206,920
2004 strength	40,880	112,750	53,390	207,020
2005 strength	39,940	109,290	51,870	201,100
2006 strength	39,390	107,730	48,730	195,850
2007 strength	38,860*	106,200	45,360*	190,420*

provisional figures
ource: MoD Defence Analytical Services Agency *National atistics* (Crown copyright)

SERVICE PERSONNEL BY RANK AND GENDER

	Officers		*Other ranks*	
	Males	*Females*	*Males*	*Females*
All services	28,410*	3,720*	144,330*	13,960*
Royal Navy	6,900*	680*	28,310*	2,970*
Army	13,040	1,640	84,940	6,590
RAF	8,480*	1,410*	31,080*	4,400*

* provisional figures
Source: MoD Defence Analytical Services Agency *National Statistics* (Crown copyright)

UK regular forces include trained and untrained personnel and nursing services, but exclude Gurkhas, full-time reserve service personnel, the home service battalions of the Royal Irish Regiment, mobilised reservists and naval activated reservists. As at 1 June 2007 these groups number:

All Gurkhas	3,710
Full-time reserve service	1,570*
Royal Irish Regiment (Home Service)	1,230
Mobilised reservists	
Army	1,140
RAF	230*
Naval activated reservists	150*

* provisional figures
Source: MoD Defence Analytical Services Agency *National Statistics* (Crown copyright)

CIVILIAN PERSONNEL

1993 level	159,600
2000 level	121,300
2001 level	118,200
2002 level	110,100
2003 level	107,600
2004 level	108,990
2005 level	107,680
2006 level	102,970
2007 level	95,790

Source: MoD Defence Analytical Services Agency *National Statistics* (Crown copyright)

UK REGULAR FORCES: DEATHS

In 2005 there were a total of 158 deaths among the UK regular armed forces, of which 27 were serving in the Royal Navy and Royal Marines, 91 in the Army and 40 in the RAF. Accidents accounted for 79 deaths (50 per cent) and the largest single cause of death was road traffic accidents, which accounted for 52 deaths (33 per cent) in 2005. Eighteen regular service personnel were killed in action and three died of wounds while in Iraq; accounting for 13 per cent of the total deaths.

NUMBER OF DEATHS AND MORTALITY RATES

	1997	*2000*	*2004*	*2005*	*2006*
Total number	164	147	169	158	190
Royal Navy	39	25	37	27	33
Army	92	88	95	91	109
RAF	33	34	37	40	48
Mortality rates per thousand					
Tri-service rate	0.81	0.71	0.81	0.78	0.96
Navy	0.87	0.63	0.92	0.69	0.84
Army*	0.93	0.78	0.78	0.81	0.93
RAF	0.47	0.61	0.63	0.71	0.83

* includes personnel deaths in the Brigade of Gurkhas

Source: MoD Defence Analytical Services Agency *National Statistics* (Crown copyright)

NUCLEAR FORCES

The Vanguard Class SSBN (ship submersible ballistic nuclear) provides the UK's strategic nuclear deterrent. Each Vanguard Class submarine is capable of carrying 16 Trident D5 missiles equipped with nuclear warheads.

There is a ballistic missile early warning system station at RAF Fylingdales in North Yorkshire.

ARMS CONTROL

The 1990 Conventional Armed Forces in Europe (CFE) treaty, which commits all NATO and former Warsaw Pact members to limiting their holdings of five major classes of conventional weapons, has been adapted to reflect the changed geo-strategic environment and negotiations continue for its implementation. The Open Skies Treaty, which the UK signed in 1992 and entered into force in 2002, allows for the overflight of States Parties by other States Parties using unarmed observation aircraft.

In 1968 the UK signed and ratified the Nuclear Non-Proliferation Treaty, which came into force in 1970 and was indefinitely and unconditionally extended in 1995. In 1996 the UK signed the Comprehensive Nuclear Test Ban Treaty and ratified it in 1998. The UK is a party to the 1972 Biological and Toxin Weapons Convention, which provides for a worldwide ban on biological weapons, and the 1993 Chemical Weapons Convention, which came into force in 1997 and provides for a verifiable worldwide ban on chemical weapons.

DEFENCE BUDGET DEPARTMENTAL EXPENDITURE LIMITS (DEL) *(£ billion)*

	Resource budget	*Capital budget*	*Total DEL*
2005–6 (outturn)	33.4	6.4	39.8
2006–7 (estimate)	33.7	7.1	40.8
2007–8 (projection)	32.8	7.6	40.4

Source: HM Treasury – *Budget 2007* (Crown copyright)

MINISTRY OF DEFENCE

Main Building, Whitehall, London SW1A 2HB
T 020-7218 9000 W www.mod.uk

Secretary of State for Defence, Rt. Hon. Des Browne, MP
Private Secretary, Ian Forber
Special Advisers, Matthew Cavangh; Alena McDonald
Parliamentary Private Secretary, Dr Roberta Blackman-Woods, MP
Minister of State for the Armed Forces, Rt. Hon. Bob Ainsworth, MP
Private Secretary, Richard Johnson
Parliamentary Private Secretary, Adrian Bailey, MP
Minister of State for Defence Equipment and Support, Lord Drayson
Private Secretary, Conrad Bailey
Parliamentary Private Secretary, Russell Brown, MP
Under-Secretary of State for Defence and Minister for Veterans, Derek Twigg, MP
Private Secretary, Jeremy Williams

CHIEFS OF STAFF

Chief of the Defence Staff, Air Chief Marshal Sir Jock Stirrup, GCB, AFC, ADC
Vice Chief of the Defence Staff, Gen. Sir Timothy Granville-Chapman, GBE, KCB, CBE
First Sea Lord and Chief of the Naval Staff, Adm. Sir Jonathon Band, KCB, ADC
Assistant Chief of the Naval Staff, Rear-Adm. Alan Massey, CBE
Chief of the General Staff, Gen. Sir Richard Dannatt, KCB CBE, MC
Assistant Chief of the General Staff, Maj.-Gen. S. Mayall
Chief of the Air Staff, Air Chief Marshal Sir Glenn Torpy, KCB, CBE, DSO
Assistant Chief of the Air Staff, Air Vice-Marshal T. Anderson, DSO

SENIOR OFFICIALS

Permanent Under-Secretary of State, Bill Jeffrey, CB
Second Permanent Under-Secretary of State, Sir Ian Andrews, CBE, TD
Chief of Defence Material, Gen. Sir Kevin O'Donoghue, KCB, CBE
Chief Scientific Adviser, Prof. Roy Anderson, FRS
Finance Director, Trevor Woolley, CB

THE DEFENCE COUNCIL

The Defence Council is the senior committee of the Ministry of Defence, and was established by royal prerogative under the Letters Patent in April 1964. The Letters Patent confer on the Defence Council the command over all of the armed forces and charge the council with such matters relating to the administration of the armed forces as the Secretary of State for Defence should direct them to execute. It is chaired by the Secretary of State for Defence and consists of the Minister of State for the Armed Forces, the Minister of State for Defence Equipment and Support, the Under-Secretary of State for Defence and the Minister for Veterans, the Chief of Defence Staff, the Permanent Under-Secretary of State, the First Sea Lord and Chief of the Naval Staff, the Chief of the General Staff, the Chief of the Air Staff, the Vice Chief of Defence Staff, the Second Permanent Under-Secretary of State, the Chief Scientific Adviser and the Finance Director.

CENTRAL STAFF

Vice-Chief of the Defence Staff, Gen. Sir Timothy Granville-Chapman, GBE, KCB, CBE
Second Permanent Under-Secretary of State, Sir Ian Andrews, CBE, TD

PERMANENT JOINT HQ

Chief of Joint Operations, Lt.-Gen. J. Houghton, CBE
Deputy Chief of Joint Operations, Maj.-Gen. J. Dutton, CBE

LEET COMMAND
'ommander-in-Chief Fleet, Adm. Sir James Burnell-Nugent, KCB, CBE
eputy Commander-in-Chief Fleet, Vice-Adm. Paul Boissier, CB

AVAL HOME COMMAND
econd Sea Lord and Commander-in-Chief Naval Home Command, Vice-Adm. Adrian Johns, CBE, ADC
'hief of Staff to Second Sea Lord and Commander-in-Chief Naval Home Command, Rear-Adm. Michael Kimmons

AND COMMAND
'ommander-in-Chief Land Command, Gen. Sir Redmond Watt, KCVO, CBE, ADC
'hief of Staff Land Command, Maj.-Gen. J. Shaw, CBE

DJUTANT-GENERAL'S COMMAND
djutant-General, Lt.-Gen. Sir Frederick Viggers, KCB, CMG, MBE
)eputy Adjutant-General and Director-General Service Conditions (Army), Maj.-Gen. M. Mans, CBE

IR COMMAND
'ommander-in-Chief Air Command, Air Chief Marshal Sir Clive Loader, KCB, OBE, DC
)eputy Commander-in-Chief Operations, Air Marshal Iain McNicoll, CB, CBE
)eputy Commander-in-Chief Personnel, Air Marshal Stephen Dalton, CB

)EFENCE EQUIPMENT AND SUPPORT
'hief of Defence Material, Gen. Sir Kevin O'Donoghue, KCB, CBE
'hief Operating Officer, D. Gould
'hief of Corporate Services, T. Flesher
'hief of Material (Fleet), Vice-Adm. Trevor Soar, OBE
'hief of Material (Land), Lt.-Gen. R. Applegate, OBE
'hief of Material (Air), Air Marshal B. Thornton, CB

:XECUTIVE AGENCIES

RMY BASE REPAIR ORGANISATION (ABRO)
Portway, Monxton Road, Andover, Hampshire SP11 8HT T 01264-383295

RITISH FORCES POST OFFICE
Corporate Headquarters, Inglis Barracks, Mill Hill, London NW7 1PX T 0845-7769 7978

)EFENCE ANALYTICAL SERVICES AGENCY (DASA)
Level 32, 1K, Main Building, Whitehall, London SW1A 2HB T 020-7218 1474

)EFENCE AVIATION REPAIR AGENCY
St Athan, Barry, Vale of Glamorgan CF62 4WA T 01446-755000

)EFENCE BILLS AGENCY
Mersey House, Drury Lane, Liverpool L2 7PX T 0151-237 6500

)EFENCE COMMUNICATION SERVICES AGENCY
Building 111, Basil Hill Site, Park Lane, Corsham, Wiltshire SN13 9NR T 01225-814750

)EFENCE ESTATES
St George's House, Kingston Road, Sutton Coldfield, West Midlands B75 7RL T 0121-311 2140

)EFENCE MEDICAL EDUCATION AND TRAINING AGENCY
MacKenzie Block, Fort Blockhouse, Gosport, Hampshire PO12 2AB T 023-9276 5438

)EFENCE SCIENCE AND TECHNOLOGY LABORATORY
Porton Down, Salisbury, Wiltshire SP4 0JQ T 01980-613121

DEFENCE STORAGE AND DISTRIBUTION AGENCY
Ploughley Road, Lower Arncott, Bicester, Oxon OX25 2LD T 01869-256804

DEFENCE TRANSPORT AND MOVEMENTS AGENCY
Building 400, Monxton Road, Andover, Hampshire SP11 8HT T 01264-381125

DEFENCE VETTING AGENCY
Building 107, Imphal Barracks, Fulford Road, York YO10 4AS T 01904–662644

DISPOSAL SERVICES AGENCY
2nd Floor, St George's Court, 2–12 Bloomsbury Way, London WC1A 2SH T 020-7305 3156

THE DUKE OF YORK'S ROYAL MILITARY SCHOOL
Dover, Kent CT15 5EQ T 01304-245024

MET OFFICE
Fitzroy Road, Exeter EX1 3PB T 0870-900 0100

MINISTRY OF DEFENCE POLICE AND GUARDING AGENCY
Weathersfield, Braintree, Essex CM7 4AZ T 01371-854000

PEOPLE, PAY AND PENSIONS AGENCY
J Block Foxhill, Combe Down, Bath BA1 5AB T 0800-345 7772

SERVICE CHILDREN'S EDUCATION
HQ SCE, Building 5, Military Complex, Wegberg BFPO 40 T (+49) (2161) 908 2371

SERVICE PERSONNEL AND VETERANS AGENCY (SPVA)
Norcross, Blackpool FY5 3WP T 0800-169 2277

UK HYDROGRAPHIC OFFICE
Admiralty Way, Taunton, Somerset TA1 2DN T 01823-337900

ARMED FORCES TRAINING AND RECRUITMENT

In April 2006 the MoD removed agency status from three armed forces training agencies which now function as an integral part of their respective service.

The Naval Training Command provides training at six establishments: Britannia Royal Naval College; Commando Training Centre, RM Lympstone; the Maritime Warfare School (comprising HMS Collingwood; HMS Dryad and HMS Excellent); and HMS Sultan.

The Army Recruiting and Training Division (ARTD) consists of a number of operating groups : Armour Centre; Army Staff Leadership School; Defence College of Electro-Mechanical Engineering; Defence College of Intelligence, Defence College of Logistics; Defence College of Police and Guarding; Defence Medical Education and Training Agency; Initial Training Group; Recruiting Group; Royal Military Academy Sandhurst; Royal School of Artillery; Royal School of Military Engineering; School of Army Aviation and the School of Infantry.

The Royal Air Force No. 22 (Training) Group exists to recruit RAF personnel and provide trained specialist personnel to the armed forces as a whole, such as providing the army air corps with trained helicopter pilots. The group is split into seven areas: RAF College Cranwell and Director of Recruiting; the Directorate of Flying Training (DFT); the Directorate of Joint Technical Training (DJTT); the Air Cadet Organisation; Core Headquarters; the Defence College of Aeronautical Engineering (DCAE) and the Defence College of Communications and Information Systems (DCCIS).

USEFUL WEBSITES
W www.rncom.mod.uk
W www.army.mod.uk
W www.tgda.gov.uk

THE ROYAL NAVY

LORD HIGH ADMIRAL OF THE UNITED KINGDOM
HM The Queen

ADMIRALS OF THE FLEET
HRH The Prince Philip, Duke of Edinburgh, KG, KT, OM, GBE, AC, QSO, PC, *apptd* 1953
Sir Edward Ashmore, GCB, DSC, *apptd* 1977
Sir Henry Leach, GCB, *apptd* 1982
Sir Julian Oswald, GCB, *apptd* 1993
Sir Benjamin Bathurst, GCB, *apptd* 1995

ADMIRALS
(Former Chiefs or Vice Chiefs of Defence Staff and First Sea Lords who remain on the active list)

Slater, Sir Jock, GCB, LVO, *apptd* 1991
Boyce, Lord, GCB, OBE, *apptd* 1995
Abbott, Sir Peter, GBE, KCB, *apptd* 1995
Essenhigh, Sir Nigel, GCB, *apptd* 1998
West of Spithead, Lord, GCB, DSC, *apptd* 2000

ADMIRALS
Band, Sir Jonathon, KCB, ADC *(First Sea Lord and Chief of Naval Staff)*
Stanhope, Sir Mark, KCB, OBE *(Deputy Supreme Allied Commander Transformation)*
Burnell-Nugent, Sir James, KCB, CBE *(Commander-in-Chief Fleet)*
HRH The Prince of Wales, KG, KT, GCB, OM, AK, QSO, PC, ADC

VICE-ADMIRALS
Johns, Adrian, CBE, ADC *(Second Sea Lord and Commander-in-Chief Naval Home Command, Rear-Adm. Fleet Air Arm (Head of Fighting Arm))*
Style, Charles, CBE *(Deputy Chief of Defence Staff (Commitments))*
Dymock, Anthony, CB *(UK Military Representative to NATO and the European Union)*
Boissier, (Robin) Paul, CB *(Deputy Commander-in-Chief Fleet and Chief Naval Warfare Officer)*
Soar, Trevor, OBE *(Chief of Material (Fleet) and Chief of Fleet Support to the Naval Board)*
Laurence, Timothy, CB, MVO *(Chief Executive Defence Estates)*
Wilkinson, Peter *(Deputy Chief of Defence Staff (Personnel))*

REAR-ADMIRALS
HRH The Princess Royal, KG, KT, GCVO *(Chief Commandant for Women in the Royal Navy)*
Ward, Rees, CB *(Director-General Information Systems Services))*
Guild, Nigel, CB *(Director-General Capability (Carrier Strike) and Chief Naval Engineering Officer)*
Spires, Trevor *(Chief Executive Service Personnel and Veterans Agency)*
Wilcocks, Philip, CB, DSC *(Chief of Staff (Capability) to Commander-in-Chief Fleet, Rear-Adm. Surface Ships (Head of Fighting Arm))*
Lambert, Paul *(Capability Manager (Precision Attack), Controller of the Navy)*
Cooke, David, MBE *(Cdr. (Operations) to Commander-in-Chief Fleet, Rear-Adm. Submarines (Head of Fighting Arm))*
Parry, Christopher, CBE *(Director-General Development, Concepts and Doctrine)*
Latham, Neil *(Commandant, College of Management and Technology, Shrivenham)*
Kimmons, Michael *(Chief of Staff (Support and Transformation) to Commander-in-Chief Fleet and Chief Naval Logistics Officer)*
Mathews, Andrew *(Director-General Submarines)*
Ibbotson, Richard, DSC *(Flag Officer Sea Training)*
Massey, Alan, CBE *(Assistant Chief of the Naval Staff)*
Leaman, Richard, OBE *(Deputy Chief of Staff to the Supreme Allied Cdr. Transformation)*
Morisetti, Neil *(Commandant, Joint Services Command and Staff College)*
Rix, Anthony *(Chief of Staff to the Cdr. Allied Naval Force Southern Europe)*
Zambellas, George, DSC *(Cdr. UK Maritime Forces)*
Cooling, Robert *(Deputy Cdr. Striking Force NATO)*
Hussain, Amjad *(Director-General Weapons)*
Moncrieff, Ian *(National Hydrographer and Deputy Chief Executive UK Hydrographic Office)*
Johnstone-Burt, (Charles) Anthony, OBE (Flag Officer Scotland, Northern England and Northern Ireland and Flag Officer Reserves)
Snow, Christopher *(Senior Naval Member, Royal College of Defence Studies)*
Love, Robert, OBE *(CV(F) Team Leader)*
Montgomery, Charles, CBE *(Naval Secretary and Chief of Staff (Personnel))*
Tibbitt, Ian *(Director-General Safety and Engineering)*
Richards, Alan *(Assistant Chief of Defence Staff (Policy))*

ROYAL MARINES

MAJOR-GENERALS
Dutton, James, CBE *(Deputy Chief of Joint Operations (Operations))*
Rose, John, MBE *(Director-General Intelligence Collection)*
Robison, Garry *(Commandant General Royal Marines and Cdr. UK Amphibious Forces)*
Thomas, Jeremy *(Senior British Military Adviser to US Central Command)*

The Royal Marines were formed in 1664 and are part of the Naval Service. Their primary purpose is to conduct amphibious and land warfare. The principal operational units are

- Three Commando Brigade, an amphibious all-arms brigade trained to operate in arduous environments (a core element of the UK's Joint Rapid Reaction Force). The commando units each have a strength of around 700 and are based in Taunton (40 Commando), Plymouth (42 Commando) and Arbroath (45 Commando)
- Fleet Protection Group, responsible for a wide range of tasks worldwide in support of the Royal Navy. The group is over 500 strong and is based at HM Naval Base Clyde on the west coast of Scotland
- Assault Group, responsible for landing craft training. Based at Poole, Dorset

The Royal Marines also provide detachments for warships and land-based naval parties as required.

ROYAL MARINES RESERVES (RMR)
The Royal Marines Reserve is a commando-trained volunteer force with the principal role, when mobilised, of supporting the Royal Marines. The RMR consists of approximately 600 trained ranks who are distributed between the five RMR centres in the UK. Approximately 10 per cent of the RMR are working with the regular corps on long-term attachments within all of the Royal Marines regular units.

OTHER PARTS OF THE NAVAL SERVICE

FLEET AIR ARM
The Fleet Air Arm (FAA) provides the Royal Navy with a multi-role aviation combat capability able to operate autonomously at short notice worldwide in all environments, over the sea and land. The FAA numbers some 6,200 people, which comprises 11.5 per cent of the total Royal Naval strength. It operates some 200 combat aircraft and more than 50 support/training aircraft.

ROYAL FLEET AUXILIARY SERVICE (RFA)
The Royal Fleet Auxiliary Service is a civilian-manned flotilla of 18 ships. Its primary role is to supply the Royal Navy at sea with fuel, ammunition, food and spares, enabling it to maintain operations away from its home ports. It also provides amphibious support and secure sea transport for Army units and their equipment and aviation support for the Royal Navy.

ROYAL NAVAL RESERVE (RNR)
The Royal Naval Reserve is an integral part of the Naval Service. It comprises up to 3,250 men and women who volunteer to train in their spare time to enable the Royal Navy to meet its operational commitments, at sea and ashore, in crisis or war.

The standard annual training commitment in peacetime is 12 days operational training per annum together with a number of training nights and some weekends. Most new entrants are expected to attend training nights once a week at their nearest RNR unit.

QUEEN ALEXANDRA'S ROYAL NAVAL NURSING SERVICE
The first nursing sisters were appointed to naval hospitals in 1884 and the Queen Alexandra's Royal Naval Nursing Service (QARNNS) gained its current title in 1902. Nursing ratings were introduced in 1960 and men were integrated into the service in 1982; QARNNS recruits qualified nurses as both officers and ratings, and student nurse training can be undertaken in the service.

Patron, HRH Princess Alexandra, the Hon. Lady Ogilvy, KG, GCVO
Director of Naval Nursing Services and Matron-in-Chief, Capt. L. Gibbon, ARRC, QHN, QARNNS

HM FLEET

as at 1 June 2007

Submarines	
Vanguard Class	Vanguard, Vengeance, Victorious, Vigilant
Swiftsure Class	Sceptre, Superb
Trafalgar Class	Talent, Tireless, Torbay, Trafalgar, Trenchant, Triumph, Turbulent
Aircraft Carriers	Ark Royal, Illustrious, Invincible*
Amphibious Assault Ships	Ocean, Albion, Bulwark
Destroyers	
Type 42 Batch 2	Exeter, Liverpool, Nottingham, Southampton
Type 42 Batch 3	Edinburgh, Gloucester, Manchester, York
Frigates	
Type 22	Campbeltown, Chatham, Cornwall, Cumberland
Type 23	Argyll, Iron Duke, Kent, Lancaster, Monmouth, Montrose, Northumberland, Portland, Richmond, St Albans, Somerset, Sutherland, Westminster
Minehunters	
Hunt Class	Atherstone, Brocklesby, Cattistock, Chiddingfold, Hurworth, Ledbury, Middleton, Quorn
Sandown Class	Bangor, Blyth, Grimsby, Pembroke, Penzance, Ramsey, Shoreham, Walney
Patrol Class	
Archer Class P2000 Training Boats	Archer, Biter, Blazer, Charger, Dasher†, Example, Exploit, Explorer, Express, Puncher, Pursuer†, Raider, Ranger, Smiter, Tracker, Trumpeter
Gibraltar Squadron 16m Fast Patrol Class	Sabre, Scimitar
Castle Class Patrol Vessel	Dumbarton Castle‡
River Class Patrol Vessels	Mersey, Severn, Tyne
Survey Vessels	
Antarctic Patrol Ship	Endurance
Ocean Survey Vessels	Scott
Coastal Survey Vessels	Gleaner, Roebuck
Multi-Role Survey Vessels	Echo, Enterprise

* HMS Invincible is currently being held at very low readiness
† HMS Dasher and HMS Pursuer form the Royal Navy Cyprus Squadron
‡ HMS Dumbarton Castle is due to leave service around the end of 2007

ROYAL FLEET AUXILIARY

Landing Ship Logistic	RFA Sir Bedivere
Landing Ship Dock (Auxiliary)	RFA Cardigan Bay, RFA Mounts Bay, RFA Largs Bay
Wave Class	RFA Wave Knight, RFA Wave Ruler
Rover Class	RFA Black Rover, RFA Gold Rover
Leaf Class	RFA Orangeleaf, RFA Bayleaf, RFA Brambleleaf, RFA Oakleaf
Fort Class	RFA Fort Austin, RFA Fort George, RFA Fort Rosalie, RFA Fort Victoria
Forward Repair Ship	RFA Diligence
Joint Casualty Treatment Ship/Maritime Afloat Training Capability	RFA Angus

THE ARMY

THE QUEEN

FIELD MARSHALS

HRH The Prince Philip, Duke of Edinburgh, KG, KT, OM, GBE, AC, QSO, PC, *apptd* 1953
Lord Bramall, KG, GCB, OBE, MC, *apptd* 1982
Sir John Stanier, GCB, MBE, *apptd* 1985
Lord Vincent of Coleshill, GBE, KCB, DSO, *apptd* 1991
Sir John Chapple, GCB, CBE, *apptd* 1992
HRH The Duke of Kent, KG, GCMG, GCVO, ADC, *apptd* 1993
Lord Inge, KG, GCB *apptd* 1994

FORMER CHIEFS OF STAFF

Gen. Lord Guthrie of Craigiebank, GCB, LVO, OBE, *apptd* 1992
Gen. Sir Roger Wheeler, GCB, CBE, *apptd* 1995
Gen. Sir Michael Walker, GCB, CMG, CBE, *apptd* 1997
Gen. Sir Mike Jackson, GCB, CBE, DSO, *apptd* 2000

GENERALS

Granville-Chapman, Sir Timothy, GBE, KCB, CBE *(Vice-Chief of the Defence Staff)*
Reith, Sir John, KCB, CBE *(held strength pending retirement)*
O'Donoghue, Sir Kevin, KCB, CBE *(Chief of Defence Material)*
Dannatt, Sir Richard, KCB, CBE, MC *(Chief of the General Staff)*
Watt, Sir Redmond, KCVO, CBE, ADC *(Commander-in-Chief Land Command)*
HRH The Prince of Wales, KG, KT, GCB, OM, AK, QSO, PC, ADC
McColl, J., CBE, DSO *(Deputy Supreme Allied Cdr. Europe)*

LIEUTENANT-GENERALS

Kiszely, Sir John, KCB, MC *(Director Defence Academy)*
Richards, Sir David, KCB, CBE, DSO *(Cdr. Allied Rapid Reaction Corps)*
Brims, R., CB, CBE, DSO *(held strength pending retirement)*
Viggers, Sir Frederick, KCB, CMG, MBE *(Adjutant-General)*
Houghton, J., CBE *(Chief of Joint Operations)*
Figgures, A., CBE *(Deputy Chief of the Defence Staff (Equipment Capability))*
Parker, N., CBE *(Cdr. Regional Forces, Land Command)*
Lamb, G., CMG, DSO, OBE *(Cdr. Field Army, Land Command)*
Lillywhite, L., MBE, QHS *(Surgeon General)*
Applegate, R., OBE *(Chief of Material (Land) and Quartermaster General)*
Leakey, A., CMG, CBE *(Director-General European Union Military Staff)*
Baxter, R., CBE *(Deputy Chief of the Defence Staff (Health))*
Rollo, W., CBE *(Deputy Commanding Gen. Multi-National Force, Iraq and Senior British Military Representative, Iraq)*
Pearson, P., CBE *(Deputy Cdr. Allied Joint Force Command, Naples)*
Wall, P., CBE *(Deputy Chief of the Defence Staff (Commitments))*

MAJOR-GENERALS

Gilchrist, P., CB *(Head of British Defence Staff US)*
Howell, D., CB, OBE *(Director Army Legal Services)*
Cottam, N., CB, OBE *(Military Secretary)*
Wood, M., CBE *(Director-General Joint Supply Chain)*
Shirreff, A., CBE *(held strength pending next appointment)*
Roberts, Sir Sebastian, KCVO, OBE *(Senior Army Member Royal College of Defence Studies)*
Bill, D., CB *(Deputy Cdr. NATO Rapid Deployable Corps, Italy)*
Stewart, A., CB, CBE *(held strength pending retirement)*
Whitley, A., CBE, CMG *(Senior British Loan Service Officer, Oman)*
Brown, C., CBE *(GOC Northern Ireland)*
Graham, A., CBE *(Director-General Army Training and Recruiting)*
Tyler, T. *(Director-General Land Equipment)*
Cooper, J., DSO, MBE *(Director-General Training Support)*
Wilkes, Revd D., OBE, QHC *(Chaplain General)*
Farquhar, A., CBE *(GOC 5th Division)*
Riley, J., DSO *(next appointment not yet announced)*
Wilson, C., CBE *(Capability Manager (Battlespace Manoeuvre) and Master General of the Ordnance)*
Mans, M., CBE *(Deputy Adjutant-General and Director-General Service Conditions (Army))*
White-Spunner, B., CBE *(GOC 3rd (UK) Division)*
Hawley, A., OBE, QHP *(Director-General Army Medical Services)*
Coward, G., OBE *(Cdr. Joint Helicopter Command)*
Steirn, C., CBE *(held strength pending retirement)*
Everson, P., OBE *(GOC 4th Division)*
Newton, P., OBE *(Director-General Engagements Multi-National Force, Iraq)*
Gregory, A. *(HQ Land Command and HQ Adjutant-General Collocation Implementation Team Leader)*
Melvin, R., OBE *(GOC UK Support Command, Germany)*
Mayall, S. *(Assistant Chief of the General Staff)*
Bucknall, J., CBE *(Chief of Staff Allied Rapid Reaction Corps)*
Binns, G., CBE, DSO, MC *(GOC 1st (UK) Armoured Division)*
Von Bertele, M., OBE *(Chief Executive Defence Medical Education and Training Agency)*
Rollo, N., CBE *(GOC Theatre Troops)*
Macklin, A. *(Armoured Fighting Vehicles Group Leader)*
Berragan, G. *(Deputy Commanding Gen. Multi-National Corps, Iraq)*
Shaw, J., CBE *(Chief of Staff Land Command)*
McDowall, D., MBE *(GOC 2nd Division)*
Lalor, S., TD *(Assistant Chief of the Defence Staff (Reserves and Cadets))*
Sykes, R. *(Defence Services Secretary)*
Page, J., OBE *(Cdr. Regional Command (South), Afghanistan)*
Shouesmith, D. *(Assistant Chief of the Defence Staff (Logistic Operations))*
Moore, W., CBE *(Director-General Logistics, Supply and Equipment (Land Command))*
Cubitt, W., CBE *(GOC London District and Maj.-Gen. Commanding The Household Division)*
Rutherford-Jones, D. *(Commandant Royal Military Academy Sandhurst)*
Rutledge, M., OBE *(Kosovo Protection Corps Coordinator)*

:ONSTITUTION OF THE ARMY

he army consists of the Regular Army, the Regular eserve and the Territorial Army (TA). It is commanded y the Chief of the General Staff, who is the professional lead of Service and Chair of the Executive Committee of ie Army Board, which provides overall strategic policy ıd direction to the commands. These are: Land ommand, which comprises the Field Army, Regional orces, the Joint Helicopter Command, the Theatre roops and Land Support; and the Adjutant General's ommand, responsible for army personnel matters and ducation and training. The army is divided into ınctional arms and services, sub-divided into regiments ıd corps (listed below in order of precedence). The army currently nearing completion of the first phase of a ıajor reform programme known as the Future Army tructure (FAS). The FAS incorporates changes in tactical octrine, organisational structure, personnel terms and onditions of service and the introduction of new quipment. Under the programme, the infantry has been -structured into large multi-battalion regiments, which ıvolved amalgamations and changes in title for some giments. The first phase of FAS is expected to be ompleted during 2008.

Further information in the public domain on the omposition of the Army Board, Headquarters, Arms and ervices, including addresses, can be obtained from the rmy List, which is published annually by the Stationery ffice and held in most public libraries. Members of the ublic can write for general information to Headquarters djutant General Secretariat, Trenchard Lines, Upavon, Viltshire SN9 6BE. Information on how to make requests or information under the Freedom of Information Act 000 can be found at www.foi.mod.uk, which includes an ectronic request form. All enquiries with regard to cords of serving personnel (Regular and Territorial rmy) should be directed to The Army Personnel Centre elp Desk, Kentigern House, 65 Brown Street, Glasgow 2 8EX T 0141-224 2023/3303. Enquirers should note that ıe Army is governed in the release of personal ıformation by various Acts of Parliament.

ORDER OF PRECEDENCE OF CORPS AND REGIMENTS OF THE BRITISH RMY

RMS

OUSEHOLD CAVALRY
he Life Guards
he Blues and Royals (Royal Horse Guards and 1st Dragoons)

OYAL HORSE ARTILLERY
when on parade with their guns, the Royal Horse Artillery take precedence over the Household Cavalry)

OYAL ARMOURED CORPS
st the Queen's Dragoon Guards
he Royal Scots Dragoon Guards (Carabiniers and Greys)
he Royal Dragoon Guards
he Queen's Royal Hussars (The Queen's Own and Royal Irish)
th/12th Royal Lancers (Prince of Wales')
he King's Royal Hussars
he Light Dragoons
he Queen's Royal Lancers
oyal Tank Regiment

ROYAL REGIMENT OF ARTILLERY
(with the exception of the Royal Horse Artillery *(see above)*)

CORPS OF ROYAL ENGINEERS

ROYAL CORPS OF SIGNALS

REGIMENTS OF FOOT GUARDS
Grenadier Guards
Coldstream Guards
Scots Guards
Irish Guards
Welsh Guards

REGIMENTS OF INFANTRY
The Royal Regiment of Scotland
The Princess of Wales' Royal Regiment (Queen and Royal Hampshire's)
The Duke of Lancaster's Regiment (King's, Lancashire and Border)
The Royal Regiment of Fusiliers
The Royal Anglian Regiment
The Rifles
The Yorkshire Regiment
The Mercian Regiment
The Royal Welsh
The Royal Irish Regiment
The Parachute Regiment
The Royal Gurkha Rifles

SPECIAL AIR SERVICE

ARMY AIR CORPS

SERVICES

ROYAL ARMY CHAPLAINS' DEPARTMENT

THE ROYAL LOGISTIC CORPS

ROYAL ARMY MEDICAL CORPS

CORPS OF ROYAL ELECTRICAL AND MECHANICAL ENGINEERS

ADJUTANT-GENERAL'S CORPS

ROYAL ARMY VETERINARY CORPS

SMALL ARMS SCHOOL CORPS

ROYAL ARMY DENTAL CORPS

INTELLIGENCE CORPS

ARMY PHYSICAL TRAINING CORPS

QUEEN ALEXANDRA'S ROYAL ARMY NURSING CORPS

CORPS OF ARMY MUSIC

THE ROYAL MONMOUTHSHIRE ROYAL ENGINEERS (MILITIA) (TA)

THE HONOURABLE ARTILLERY COMPANY (TA)

REST OF THE TERRITORIAL ARMY (TA)

ARMY EQUIPMENT

Tanks	386
Challenger 2	386
Reconnaissance vehicles	475
Fuchs	11
Scimitar	327
Sabre	137
Reconnaissance aircraft	3
Armoured Infantry Fighting Vehicle	575
Armoured Personnel Carrier	2,611
Artillery pieces	877
Anti-tank missile	800+
Helicopters	324
Attack	176
Apache	67
Lynx	109
Support	148
Gazelle	133
Scout	15
Unmanned aerial vehicle	8
Surface-to-air missile	339+
Land radar	4+
Miscellaneous boats/craft	4
Amphibious craft	4
Logistics and support vehicles	6

Source: Military Balance 2007

THE TERRITORIAL ARMY (TA)

The Territorial Army is part of the UK's reserve lar forces and provides support to the regular army at hon and overseas. The TA is divided into three types of un national, regional, and sponsored. TA soldiers serving regional units complete a minimum of 27 days training year, comprising some evenings, weekends and an annu two-week camp. National units normally specialise in specific role or trade, such as logistics, IT, communicatio or medical services. Members of national units have lower level of training commitment because of the trav involved and complete 19 days training a yea comprising two to three weekends and an annual tw week camp. At the end of 2006 the TA's total streng was 36,260 (the established liability is 42,000).

QUEEN ALEXANDRA'S ROYAL ARMY NURSING CORPS

The Queen Alexandra's Royal Army Nursing Cor (QARANC) was founded in 1902 as Queen Alexandra Imperial Military Nursing Service and gained its prese title in 1949. The QARANC has trained nurses for th register since 1950 and also trains and employs heal care assistants to Level 2 NVQ, with the option to train Level 3. The corps recruits qualified nurses as officers an other ranks and in 1992 male nurses already serving the army were transferred to the QARANC.

Colonel-in-Chief, HRH The Countess of Wessex
Colonel Commandant, Brig. Jane Arigho, CBE

THE ROYAL AIR FORCE

THE QUEEN

MARSHAL OF THE ROYAL AIR FORCE
HRH The Prince Philip, Duke of Edinburgh, KG, KT, OM, GBE, AC, QSO, PC, *apptd* 1953

FORMER CHIEFS OF THE AIR STAFF

MARSHALS OF THE ROYAL AIR FORCE
Sir Michael Beetham, GCB, CBE, DFC, AFC, *apptd* 1982
Sir Keith Williamson, GCB, AFC, *apptd* 1985
Lord Craig of Radley, GCB, OBE, *apptd* 1988

AIR CHIEF MARSHALS
Sir Michael Graydon, GCB, CBE, *apptd* 1991
Sir Richard Johns, GCB, OBE, LVO *apptd* 1994
Sir Peter Squire, GCB, DFC, AFC *apptd* 1999

AIR RANK LIST

AIR CHIEF MARSHALS
Stirrup, Sir Jock, GCB, AFC, ADC *(Chief of the Defence Staff)*
Torpy, Sir Glenn, KCB, CBE, DSO, ADC *(Chief of the Air Staff)*
HRH The Prince of Wales, KG, KT, GCB, OM, AK, QSO, PC, ADC
Loader, Sir Clive, KCB, OBE, DC *(Commander-in-Chief Air Command)*

AIR MARSHALS
Thornton, Sir Barry, KCB *(Chief of Material (Air) and Air Member for Material)*
Peach, S., CBE *(Chief of Defence Intelligence)*
McNicoll, I., CB, CBE *(Deputy Commander-in-Chief Operations, Air Command)*
Dalton, S., CB *(Deputy Commander-in-Chief Personnel and Air Member for Personnel, Air Command)*
Moran, C., OBE, MVO *(Deputy Cdr. Allied Joint Force Command, Brunssum)*
Walker, D., CBE, AFC *(Deputy Cdr. Allied Air Component Command, Ramstein)*

AIR VICE-MARSHALS
Charles, R., CB *(Director RAF Legal Services)*
Ness, C. *(Director-General Combat (Air))*
Walker, D. A., OBE, MVO *(Master of the Royal Household)*
Cliffe, J., OBE *(Director-General Training and Education, MoD)*
Thornton, E., QHP *(Director-General Healthcare)*
Ruddock, P., CBE *(Director-General Saudi Arabia Armed Forces Project)*
Chisnall, S. *(Senior Directing Staff (Air), Royal College of Defence Studies)*
Leeson, K., CBE *(Assistant Chief of the Defence Staff (Resources and Plans)*
Dougherty, S., QHP *(Chief of Staff (Health) and Director-General RAF Medical Services)*
Ponsonby, J., OBE *(Chief of Staff (Operations) Air Command)*
Dye, P., OBE *(Head of RAF Transformation)*
Nickols, C., CBE *(Assistant Chief of the Defence Staff (Operations), MoD)*
Harper, C., CBE *(Air Officer Commanding No. 1 Group)*
Walton, A., CBE *(Deputy Chief of Joint Operations (Operations Support), Permanent Joint HQ)*
Mills, Revd P., QHC *(Director-General Chaplaincy Services)*
Butler, S. *(Capability Manager (Information Superiority) and Air Member Equipment Capability)*
Lacey, R., CBE *(Cdr. British Forces Cyprus)*
Bryant, S., CBE *(Chief of Staff Personnel and Air Secretary)*
Pulford, A., CBE *(Air Officer Commanding No. 2 Group)*
Allan, R., OBE *(Director-General Information Systems and Services)*
Anderson, T., DSO *(Assistant Chief of the Air Staff)*
Routledge, M. *(Chief of Staff Strategy, Policy and Plans, Air Command)*
Garwood, R., CBE, DFC *(Air Officer Commanding No. 22 Training Group)*
Kurth, N., CBE *(Chief of Staff (Support) Air Command)*
Wiles, M. *(Director-General Joint Supply Chain)*

CONSTITUTION OF THE RAF

The RAF consists of a single command, Air Command, based at RAF High Wycombe. RAF Air Command was formed on 1 April 2007 from the amalgamation of Strike Command and Personnel and Training Command.

Air Command consists of three groups, each organised around specific operational duties, and the Expeditionary Air Wings. No. 1 Group is the coordinating organisation for the tactical fast-jet forces responsible for attack, offensive support and air defence operations. No. 2 Group provides air combat support including air transport and air to air refuelling; intelligence surveillance; targeting and reconnaissance; and force protection. No. 22 (Training) Group recruits personnel and provides trained specialist personnel to the RAF, as well as to the Royal Navy and the Army (*see also* Armed Forces Training and Recruitment).

RAF EQUIPMENT

Aircraft	
BAe 125	5
BAe 146	2
Dominie	9
Firefly	38
Globemaster	4
Harrier	42
Hawk	99
Hercules	44
Islander	2
Jaguar	14
Jetstream	11
King Air (leased)	7
Nimrod	22
Sentinel	1
Sentry	6
Tornado	234
Tristar	8
Tucano	67
Tutor	99
Typhoon	25
VC10	17

Helicopters	
Chinook	34
Ecureuil	31
Griffin	14
Merlin	22
Puma	33
Sea King	20

Source: Military Balance 2007

ROYAL AUXILIARY AIR FORCE

The Auxiliary Air Force was formed in 1924 to train an elite corps of civilians to serve their country in flying squadrons in their spare time. In 1947 the force was awarded the prefix 'royal' in recognition of its distinguished war service and the Sovereign's Colour for the Royal Auxiliary Air Force (RAuxAF) was presented in 1989. The RAuxAF continues to recruit civilians who undertake military training in their spare time to support the Royal Air Force in times of emergency or war.

Air Commodore-in-Chief, HM The Queen
Honorary Inspector-General Royal Auxiliary Air Force, Air Vice-Marshal Barry Newton, CB, CVO, OBE
Inspector Royal Auxiliary Air Force, Gp Capt. Gary Bunkell, QVRM, AE, ADC

PRINCESS MARY'S ROYAL AIR FORCE NURSING SERVICE

The Princess Mary's Royal Air Force Nursing Service (PMRAFNS) was formed on 1 June 1918 as the Royal Ai Force Nursing Service. In June 1923, His Majesty King George V gave his royal assent for the Royal Air Force Nursing Service to be known as the Princess Mary's Roya Air Force Nursing Service. Men were integrated into the PMRAFNS in 1980 and now serve as officers and othe ranks.

Patron and Air Chief Commandant, HRH Princess Alexandra, The Hon. Lady Ogilvy, KG, GCVO
Director of Nursing Services and Matron-in-Chief, Gp Capt W. B. Williams, RRC, QHN

SERVICE SALARIES

The following rates of pay apply from 1 April 2007.

The pay rates shown are for army personnel. The rates also apply to personnel of equivalent rank and pay band in the other services (*see* below for table of relative ranks).

Rank	*Annual salary*
SECOND LIEUTENANT	£22,679.76
LIEUTENANT	
On appointment	£27,260.04
After 1 year in rank	£27,980.88
After 2 years in rank	£28,697.76
After 3 years in rank	£29,410.80
After 4 years in rank	£30,131.40
CAPTAIN	
On appointment	£34,934.52
After 1 year in rank	£35,870.28
After 2 years in rank	£36,817.32
After 3 years in rank	£37,768.08
After 4 years in rank	£38,707.56
After 5 years in rank	£39,654.60
After 6 years in rank	£40,594.08
After 7 years in rank	£41,073.24
After 8 years in rank	£41,544.84
MAJOR	
On appointment	£44,004.96
After 1 year in rank	£45,091.56
After 2 years in rank	£46,170.48
After 3 years in rank	£47,264.76
After 4 years in rank	£48,347.76
After 5 years in rank	£49,441.80
After 6 years in rank	£50,528.52
After 7 years in rank	£51,611.28
After 8 years in rank	£52,701.72
LIEUTENANT-COLONEL	
On appointment	£61,760.76
After 1 year in rank	£62,579.52
After 2 years in rank	£63,390.72
After 3 years in rank	£64,202.04
After 4 years in rank	£65,013.12
After 5 years in rank	£65,824.32
After 6 years in rank	£66,635.52
After 7 years in rank	£67,454.28
After 8 years in rank	£68,272.92
COLONEL	
On appointment	£71,521.56
After 1 year in rank	£72,461.04
After 2 years in rank	£73,404.36
After 3 years in rank	£74,343.84
After 4 years in rank	£75,283.32
After 5 years in rank	£76,222.80
After 6 years in rank	£77,162.28
After 7 years in rank	£78,105.48
After 8 years in rank	£79,048.68
BRIGADIER	
On appointment	£85,787.52
After 1 year in rank	£86,700.60
After 2 years in rank	£87,613.68
After 3 years in rank	£88,522.92
After 4 years in rank	£89,443.56

PAY SYSTEM FOR SENIOR MILITARY OFFICERS

Revised pay rates effective from 1 April 2007 for all military officers of 2* rank and above (excluding medical and dental officers).

MAJOR-GENERAL (2*)	*Annual salary*
Scale 1	£94,749.96
Scale 2	£96,174.96
Scale 3	£98,060.04
Scale 4	£100,310.04
Scale 5	£102,561.00
Scale 6	£104,811.00
Scale 7	£107,060.04
LIEUTENANT-GENERAL (3*)	*Annual salary*
Scale 1	£111,753.96
Scale 2	£118,821.96
Scale 3	£125,889.00
Scale 4	£130,356.96
Scale 5	£134,826.96
Scale 6	£139,295.04
Scale 7	n/a
GENERAL (4*)	*Annual salary*
Scale 1	£151,370.04
Scale 2	£154,386.96
Scale 3	£157,475.04
Scale 4	£160,625.04
Scale 5	£163,836.00
Scale 6	£167,114.04
Scale 7	n/a

Field Marshal – appointments to this rank will not usually be made in peacetime. The salary for holders of the rank is equivalent to the salary of a 5-star General, a salary created only in times of war. In peacetime, the equivalent rank to Field Marshal is the Chief of the Defence Staff. From 1 April 2007, the annual salary range for the Chief of the Defence Staff is: £217,572.00–£230,889.00.

OFFICERS COMMISSIONED FROM THE SENIOR RANKS

Rank	*Annual salary*
Level 15	£46,695.12
Level 14	£46,389.60
Level 13	£46,068.72
Level 12	£45,446.16
Level 11	£44,827.44
Level 10	£44,201.04
Level 9	£43,578.48
Level 8	£42,956.04
Level 7*	£42,178.80
Level 6	£41,699.52
Level 5	£41,212.80
Level 4†	£40,250.64
Level 3	£39,771.48
Level 2	£39,281.04
Level 1‡	£38,322.72

* Officers commissioned from the ranks with more than 15 years' service enter on level 7

† Officers commissioned from the ranks with between 12 and 15 years' service enter on level 4

‡ Officers commissioned from the ranks with less than 12 years' service enter on level 1

SOLDIERS' SALARIES

Under the Pay 2000 scheme, personnel are paid in either a high or low band in accordance with how their trade has been allocated to those bands at each rank. Pay is based on trade and rank, not on individual appointment, or in response to temporary changes in role.

Rates of pay effective from 1 April 2007 are:

PRIVATE	*Lower Band*	*Higher Band*
Level 1	£15,677.04	£15,677.04
Level 2	£16,110.72	£16,899.48
Level 3	£16,544.64	£18,657.72
Level 4	£17,993.52	£20,061.36
LANCE CORPORAL (levels 5–7 also applicable to Privates)		
Level 5	£18,963.24	£22,181.64
Level 6	£19,755.72	£23,260.80
Level 7	£20,600.76	£24,328.44
Level 8	£21,543.96	£25,422.84
Level 9	£22,325.04	£26,664.00

CORPORAL	*Lower Band*	*Higher Band*
Level 1	£24,328.44	£25,422.84
Level 2	£25,422.84	£26,664.00
Level 3	£26,664.00	£27,969.48
Level 4	£26,867.76	£28,622.16
Level 5	£27,079.08	£29,312.64
Level 6	£27,294.24	£29,920.20
Level 7	£27,494.16	£30,572.88

SERGEANT	*Lower Band*	*Higher Band*
Level 1	£27,652.68	£30,180.48
Level 2	£28,377.00	£30,961.56
Level 3	£29,090.04	£31,746.24
Level 4	£29,384.40	£32,146.32
Level 5	£30,150.36	£32,772.60
Level 6	£31,191.72	£33,398.88
Level 7	£31,429.32	£34,025.16

STAFF SERGEANT	*Lower Band*	*Higher Band*
Level 1	£30,610.80	£34,047.84
Level 2	£31,010.52	£34,870.32
Level 3	£32,018.04	£35,704.20
Level 4	£32,768.88	£36,530.52
WARRANT OFFICER II (levels 5–7 also applicable to Staff Sergeants)		
Level 5	£33,213.96	£37,360.68
Level 6	£34,715.76	£38,186.88
Level 7	£35,247.60	£38,737.80
Level 8	£35,704.20	£39,288.60
Level 9	£36,511.68	£39,850.80

WARRANT OFFICER I	*Lower Band*	*Higher Band*
Level 1	£35,564.52	£38,771.52
Level 2	£36,255.00	£39,533.88
Level 3	£36,986.88	£40,212.96
Level 4	£37,718.88	£40,952.52
Level 5	£38,454.72	£41,684.52
Level 6	£39,533.88	£42,427.80
Level 7	£40,650.60	£43,076.76

RELATIVE RANK – ARMED FORCES

Royal Navy
1 Admiral of the Fleet
2 Admiral (Adm.)
3 Vice-Admiral (Vice-Adm.)
4 Rear-Admiral (Rear-Adm.)
5 Commodore (Cdre)
6 Captain (Capt.)
7 Commander (Cdr)
8 Lieutenant-Commander (Lt.-Cdr)
9 Lieutenant (Lt.)
10 Sub-Lieutenant (Sub-Lt.)
11 Acting Sub-Lieutenant (Acting Sub-Lt.)

Army
1 Field Marshal
2 General (Gen.)
3 Lieutenant-General (Lt.-Gen.)
4 Major-General (Maj.-Gen.)
5 Brigadier (Brig.)
6 Colonel (Col.)
7 Lieutenant-Colonel (Lt.-Col.)
8 Major (Maj.)
9 Captain (Capt.)
10 Lieutenant (Lt.)
11 Second Lieutenant (2nd Lt.)

Royal Air Force
1 Marshal of the RAF
2 Air Chief Marshal
3 Air Marshal
4 Air Vice-Marshal
5 Air Commodore (Air Cdre)
6 Group Captain (Gp Capt.)
7 Wing Commander (Wg Cdr)
8 Squadron Leader (Sqn Ldr)
9 Flight Lieutenant (Flt Lt)
10 Flying Officer (FO)
11 Pilot Officer (PO)

ERVICE RETIRED PAY

n compulsory retirement

hose who leave the services having served at least five ears, but not long enough to qualify for the appropriate mmediate pension, now qualify for a preserved pension nd terminal grant, both of which are payable at age 60. he tax-free resettlement grants shown below are ayable on release to those who qualify for a preserved ension and who have completed nine years' service rom age 21 (officers) or 12 years from age 18 (other anks).

The annual rates for army personnel are given. The ates also apply to personnel of equivalent rank in the ther services, including the nursing services.

OFFICERS

Applicable to officers who give full pay service on the active list on or after 31 March 2007. Pensionable earnings for senior officers (*) is defined as the total amount of basic pay received during the year ending on the day prior to retirement, or the amount of basic pay received during any 12-month period within 3 years prior to retirement, whichever is the higher. Figures for senior officers are percentage rates of pensionable earnings on final salary arrangements on or after 31 March 2007.

o. of years eckonable ervice	*Capt. and below*	*Major*	*Lt.-Col.*	*Colonel*	*Brigadier*	*Major-General**	*Lieutenant-General**	*General**
6	£11,569	£13,779	£18,066	£20,920	£24,970	—	—	—
7	£12,103	£14,434	£18,902	£21,888	£25,943	—	—	—
8	£12,636	£15,088	£19,738	£22,856	£26,917	—	—	—
9	£13,169	£15,743	£20,574	£23,823	£27,890	—	—	—
0	£13,702	£16,397	£21,410	£24,791	£28,864	—	—	—
1	£14,236	£17,052	£22,246	£25,759	£29,837	—	—	—
2	£14,769	£17,706	£23,082	£26,726	£30,811	—	—	—
3	£15,302	£18,361	£23,918	£27,694	£31,784	—	—	—
4	£15,835	£19,015	£24,753	£28,662	£32,758	38.5%	—	—
5	£16,369	£19,670	£25,589	£29,629	£33,731	39.7%	—	—
6	£16,902	£20,324	£26,425	£30,597	£34,705	40.8%	—	—
7	£17,435	£20,979	£27,261	£31,565	£35,678	42.0%	42.0%	—
8	£17,968	£21,633	£28,097	£32,532	£36,652	43.1%	43.1%	—
9	£18,502	£22,288	£28,933	£33,500	£37,625	44.3%	44.3%	—
0	£19,035	£22,942	£29,769	£34,468	£38,599	45.4%	45.4%	45.4%
1	£19,568	£23,597	£30,605	£35,436	£39,572	46.6%	46.6%	46.6%
2	£20,102	£24,251	£31,441	£36,403	£40,546	47.7%	47.7%	47.7%
3	£20,635	£24,906	£32,276	£37,371	£41,519	48.9%	48.9%	48.9%
4	£21,168	£25,560	£33,112	£38,339	£42,493	50.0%	50.0%	50.0%

VARRANT OFFICERS, NCOS AND PRIVATES

Applicable to soldiers who give full pay service on or after 31 March 2007)

o. of years eckonable ervice	*Below Corporal*	*Corporal*	*Sergeant*	*Staff Sergeant*	*Warrant Officer Level II*	*Warrant Officer Level I*
2	£6,847	£8,833	£9,683	£11,030	£11,776	£12,521
3	£7,086	£9,141	£10,021	£11,415	£12,187	£12,958
4	£7,325	£9,449	£10,359	£11,800	£12,598	£13,395
5	£7,564	£9,757	£10,697	£12,185	£13,009	£13,832
6	£7,803	£10,066	£11,035	£12,570	£13,420	£14,269
7	£8,042	£10,374	£11,373	£12,955	£13,831	£14,706
8	£8,281	£10,682	£11,711	£13,340	£14,242	£15,144
9	£8,520	£10,991	£12,049	£13,725	£14,653	£15,581
0	£8,759	£11,299	£12,387	£14,110	£15,064	£16,018
1	£8,998	£11,607	£12,725	£14,495	£15,475	£16,455
2	£9,237	£11,916	£13,063	£14,880	£15,886	£16,892
3	£9,476	£12,224	£13,401	£15,265	£16,297	£17,329
4	£9,715	£12,532	£13,739	£15,650	£16,708	£17,766
5	£9,954	£12,840	£14,077	£16,035	£17,119	£18,203
6	£10,193	£13,149	£14,415	£16,420	£17,530	£18,640
7	£10,432	£13,457	£14,753	£16,805	£17,941	£19,077

GRANTS AND GRATUITIES

erminal grants are in each case three times the rate of etired pay or pension. There are special rates of retired ay for certain other ranks not shown above. Lower rates re payable in cases of voluntary retirement.

A gratuity of £3,935 is payable for officers with short service commissions for each year completed. Resettlement grants are £13,531 for officers and £9,249 for other ranks.

THE EDUCATION SYSTEM

Responsibility for education in England lies with the Secretaries of State for Children, Schools and Families (DCSF) and Innovation, Universities and Skills (DIUS); in Wales, with Welsh ministers; in Scotland, with Scottish ministers; and in Northern Ireland with the education minister and the Minister for Employment and Learning.

EXPENDITURE

Most education expenditure is incurred by local authorities, which make their own expenditure decisions according to their local situations and needs. Expenditure for higher and further education in England and Scotland is met by the respective funding agencies; in Wales it is provided directly to post-16 providers; and in Northern Ireland it is met by the Department for Employment and Learning for the Further Education (FE) sector.

The bulk of direct expenditure by the DIUS, the Welsh Assembly Government and the Scottish Executive is directed towards supporting post-16 education. Funding for higher education in universities and colleges is channelled through the Higher Education Funding Councils (HEFCs) and through the Department for Employment and Learning in Northern Ireland. Funding for further education, sixth form provision, work based learning and adult and community education is channelled through the funding councils for that sector, but in Wales is provided directly to post-16 providers through the Welsh Assembly Government's Department for Children, Education, Lifelong Learning and Skills (DCELLS). In addition, the DIUS currently funds student support for students from England and the Welsh Assembly Government is responsible for student support in Wales for students who live in Wales. The DCSF is responsible for the City Technology Colleges, the City College for the Technology of the Arts, and pays grants under the specialist schools programme in England.

LOCAL EDUCATION ADMINISTRATION

In England and Wales the school education service is administered by local authorities, which have day-to-day responsibility for providing state primary and secondary education and special schools for pupils in their areas. They share with the appropriate funding bodies (in Wales with the Assembly Government) the duty to provide adult education to meet local needs.

There are four categories of state-funded mainstream schools: community, foundation, voluntary controlled and voluntary aided. In these schools the role of the governing bodies and ownership of assets varies but they all have a lot in common – they are self-managing and do not charge fees. The majority of pupils go to state schools. Unlike other services, where local authorities are financed largely from the council tax and aggregate external finance from Communities and Local Government in England and the National Assembly for Wales, since 2006–7 funding for schools and other pupil provision in England is provided through the new Dedicated Schools Grant from the DCSF to each local authority. Authority-maintained schools usually manage their own budgets: the local authority allocates funds to the school, largely on the basis of pupil numbers, and the school governing body is responsible for overseeing spending and for most aspects of staffing, including appointments and dismissals. Local authorities also have intervention powers to add additional governors, take back control of a school's budget or replace the governing body of a school with an interim executive when a school is placed under special measures, is judged to have serious weaknesses or is causing concern and has not complied with a formal warning from the authority. The duty of providing education locally in Scotland rests with the education authorities. They are responsible for the construction of buildings, the employment of teachers and other staff, and the provision of equipment and materials.

Devolved school management is in place for all primary, secondary and special schools. Since August 2007, arrangements for parental involvement in schools have changed, to enable parents to get more involved in their child's education. School Boards were replaced by parent councils. The structure of these councils is decided by parents. Headteachers are involved, and the council can invite members of the school or wider community to attend meetings.

Scotland has primary, secondary and special schools. A select group of secondary schools which have found new ways to inspire pupils to get the most from education are on the Schools of Ambition programme. There are currently 52 schools on the scheme, which allocates them extra funding and support. Scotland has 395 state-funded faith schools: 391 Catholic, one Jewish and three Episcopalian.

Education, with the exception of further and higher education, is administered locally in Northern Ireland by five education and library boards (ELBs), which fund controlled and maintained schools and whose costs are met in full by the Northern Ireland Executive. All grant-aided schools include elected parents and teachers on their boards of governors. All schools and colleges of further education have full responsibility for their own budgets, including staffing costs.

EDUCATION IN FIGURES

EXPENDITURE

UK MANAGED EXPENDITURE ON EDUCATION AND TRAINING *(Percentage of GDP)*

	2004–5 outturn	*2005–6 outturn*	*2006–7 outturn (est)*
Education and training	5.4	5.6	5.7
Education	5.3	5.4	5.5

Source: PESA 2007

UK EXPENDITURE ON EDUCATION AND TRAINING *(£m)*

	2005–6 outturn accruals	*2006–7 est. outturn accruals*
Under-fives	4,299	4,142
Primary schools	18,616	19,426
Secondary schools	21,119	22,136
Post-secondary non-tertiary education	8,033	8,365

Tertiary education	9,069	10,738
Training	2,163	2,408
Other education and training	5,969	6,461
Total	69,268	73,946

Source: PESA 2007

UK MANAGED EXPENDITURE ON EDUCATION AND TRAINING *(£bn)*

1997–8	46.5	2002–3	58.6
1998–9	47.1	2003–4	63.3
1999–2000	48.6	2004–5	65.8
2000–1	52.2	2005–6	69.3
2001–2	56.9	2006–7	72.2
of which on education (£bn)			
1997–8	45.1	2002–3	56.6
1998–9	45.5	2003–4	61.2
1999–2000	47.0	2004–5	63.7
2000–1	50.5	2005–6	67.1
2001–2	55.2	2006–7	69.8

UK EXPENDITURE ON EDUCATION BY THE GOVERNMENT AND LOCAL AUTHORITIES (2005–6) *(£m)*

Local authorities	
Current	42,292
Capital	3,737
Total	46,029
Central government	
Current	26,326
Capital	3,737
Total	30,039
All public authorities	
Current	68,618
Capital	7,450
TOTAL	76,068

PUPILS AND SCHOOLS

UK PRE-SCHOOL EDUCATION (2006) *(percentage)*

	Public sector	*Private and voluntary*	*Total*
UK	64	35	99
England	64	38	102
Wales	83	—	83
Scotland	64	25	89
Northern Ireland	59	13	72

UK SCHOOLS BY CATEGORY (2005–6)

	England	*Wales*
Maintained nursery schools	455	33
Maintained primary and secondary schools	20,871	1,779
Community	13,009	1,500
Voluntary aided	4,302	163
Voluntary controlled	2,667	104
Foundation	893	12
Pupil referral units	449	32
Maintained special schools	1,033	43
Non-maintained special schools	72	—
City Technology Colleges and City Colleges for the Technology of the Arts	11	—
Academies	27	—
Independent schools	2,261	56
Total	25,179	1,943

Scotland	
Publicly funded schools	2,755
Independent schools	150
Total	2,905
Northern Ireland	
Grant-aided mainstream	
Nursery*	99
Primary	879
Secondary	228
grammar	69
other	159
Non-maintained mainstream	18
Special (maintained)	48†
Total	1,272

* Excludes voluntary and private pre-school education centres
† Figure includes three hospital schools

UK PUPILS IN THE MAINTAINED SECTOR (2005–6)

Nursery pupils	150,800
Primary pupils	4,974,900
Secondary pupils	3,987,500
Pupils in special schools	101,300
Pupils in pupil referral units	15,600
Total	9,229,100

SPECIAL NEEDS PUPILS (2005–6)

	Number of pupils	*Percentage of all pupils*
England	236,700	2.9
Wales	15,800	3.2
Scotland	13,800	1.6
Northern Ireland	12,000	3.5
Total	278,300	2.8

TEACHERS

FULL-TIME QUALIFIED TEACHERS (2005–6 EST) *(THOUSANDS)*

	E&W	*Scotland*	*NI*	*UK*
Maintained nursery and primary schools	179.0	21.6	7.9	208.5
Maintained secondary schools	199.3	23.2	10.0	232.5
Non-maintained mainstream schools	53.7	2.5	0.1	56.3
All special schools	17.2	2.1	0.7	19.9
Total	449.1	49.4	18.7	517.2

UK PRIMARY SCHOOL PUPIL–TEACHER RATIOS

	England	*Wales*	*Scotland*	*NI*
2003–4	22.7	20.7	18.2	19.9
2004–5	22.5	20.7	17.6	20.0
2005–6	22.0	19.8	17.1	20.5

* The average size of classes 'as taught' was 25.9 in 2005–6 (Figures refer to 'all classes' rather than 'one-teacher classes' only).

UK SECONDARY SCHOOLS (2005–6)

	England	*Wales*	*Scotland*	*NI*
No. of pupils	3,306,800	213,000	315,800	151,800
Average class size	21.5	20.6	—	—
Pupil–teacher ratio	16.6	16.6	12.3	14.4

POST-16 AND HIGHER EDUCATION

POST-16 STUDENTS IN THE UK (2005–6)

	Full-time	*Part-time*
UK	1,083,500	3,963,700
England	967,300	3,367,200
Wales	41,400	193,400
Scotland*	47,300	294,400
Northern Ireland	27,500	108,700

* Enrolments, not head count

HIGHER EDUCATION STUDENTS IN THE UK* (2005–6)

	Part-time	*Full-time*	*Total*
HE students	–	–	2,336,110
Postgraduate students	311,150	234,220	545,370
Undergraduate students	591,925	1,198,820	1,790,740

*Includes UK, EU and non-EU students

UK HIGHER EDUCATION QUALIFICATIONS AWARDED (2005–6)

	Full-time	*Part-time*
First degrees	278,385	37,600
Higher degrees	90,895	34,180
Other postgraduate	40,705	32,505
Other graduate	48,565	78,020
Total	458,550	182,300

UK HIGHER EDUCATION INCOME BY SOURCE (2005–6)

	£ thousand	*Percentage of total*
Funding council grants	7,544,078	38.7
Tuition fees, education grants and contracts	4,640,799	23.8
Research grants and contracts	3,120,606	16.0
Endowment and investment	343,083	1.8
Other	3,854,546	19.7
Total	19,503,112	100

UK HIGHER EDUCATION EXPENDITURE (2005–6)

	£ thousand	*Percentage of total*
Staff costs	11,188,241	57.9
Other operating expenses	6,908,704	35.8
Depreciation	961,211	5.0
Interest payable	254,012	1.3
Total	17,779,680	100

Statistics are published by each of the home education departments through press notices, bulletins and statistical volumes. These can be found on the following websites:
ENGLAND **W** www.dcsf.gov.uk
WALES **W** www.wales.gov.uk
SCOTLAND **W** www.scotland.gov.uk
NORTHERN IRELAND **W** www.deni.gov.uk

THE INSPECTORATE

ENGLAND

The Office for Standards in Education, Children's Services and Skills (OFSTED) was created on 1 April 2007. It has responsibility for the regulatory and inspection activities of the former Office for Standards in Education; inspection of adult learning and training formerly undertaken by the Adult Learning Inspectorate; the regulation and inspection of children's social care formerly undertaken by the Commission for Social Care Inspection; and the inspection of the Children and Family Court Advisory and Support Service formerly undertaken by Her Majesty's Inspectorate of Court Administration.

OFSTED is a non-ministerial government department whose executive head is Her Majesty's Chief Inspector of Education, Children's Services and Skills (HMCI). OFSTED is responsible for the registration and inspection of childcare, arrangements for social care and support of children and young people, and the inspection of all maintained and some independent schools. It is also responsible for the inspection of further education, all publicly funded adult education and training and some privately funded training provision, and the inspection of teacher training.

The inspection of the Children and Family Court Advisory and Support Service (CAFCASS) is also undertaken by OFSTED. Joint Area Reviews and Annual Performance Assessments of local children's services provision continue to be led by OFSTED. The post of the Children's Rights Director (CRD) transferred to OFSTED from the Commission for Social Care Inspection on 1 April 2007.

The Education and Inspections Act that established the new OFSTED requires the inspectorate to promote improvement in the public services it inspects and regulates; ensure that these services focus on the interests of children, parents, learners and employers; and ensure that these services are efficient and effective. The act also established a board to provide strategic oversight of OFSTED. The non-executive board has a duty to have regard to the views of service users as well as a statutory purpose to encourage improvement.

WALES

Estyn: Arolygiaeth Ei Mawrhydi dros Addysg a Hyfforddiant yng Nghymru (Her Majesty's Inspectorate for Education and Training in Wales) is responsible for inspecting early years provision in the non-maintained sector, primary schools, secondary schools, special schools (including independent special schools), pupil referral units, independent schools, further education, youth support services, local education authorities, teacher education and training, work-based learning, Careers Wales companies, the education, guidance and training elements of the New Deal and adult community based learning. Its remit from the Welsh Assembly Government also includes providing advice on a wide range of education and training matters.

SCOTLAND

HM Inspectorate of Education (HMIE) is an executive agency of the Scottish Executive. HM Inspectors (HMIs) inspect or review and report on education provision in primary, secondary and special schools, further education institutions (under contract to the Scottish Further Education Funding Council), initial teacher education, community learning and development, care and welfare of pupils, the education functions of local authorities, prison education, children's services and in other contexts as necessary. They work in collaboration with the Care Commission in integrated inspection of pre-school education centres and residential schools. They work with Audit Scotland on the inspection of education authorities and on behalf of the Scottish Further Education Funding Council in the review of Scotland's 43 further education colleges. The HMIs work in teams alongside lay members (who are volunteer members of the public) and associate assessors (who are practising teachers or senior educationalists seconded for the inspection). HMIE is led y the senior chief inspector, supported by six chief nspectors (five of whom head inspectorates) and twelve ssistant chief inspectors. The Scottish Higher Education 'unding Council has a duty to assess quality in higher ducation institutions and universities, a responsibility vhich it sub-contracts to the Quality Assurance Agency or Higher Education (QAA) Scotland office. The Further nd Higher Education (Scotland) Act 2005 extends this luty on the council to ensure that provision is made for ssessing and enhancing the quality of education rovided.

NORTHERN IRELAND

nspection is carried out in Northern Ireland by the :ducation and Training Inspectorate, which provides nspection services for the Department of Education lorthern Ireland (DENI), the Department for mployment and Learning and the Department of Culture, Arts and Leisure. Schools are currently inspected nce every five to seven years. In further education and raining, extended inspections are carried out once every ight years and focused inspections at least every four ears. In addition, the inspectorate provides evidence-based advice to ministers and departments to assist in the ormulation and evaluation of policies in education, raining and youth.

SCHOOLS

ull-time education is compulsory in Great Britain for all hildren between five and 16 years and between four and 6 years in Northern Ireland. About 93 per cent of hildren in the United Kingdom receive free education om public funds and the rest attend fee-charging schools r are educated at home. Provision is being increased for re-school children and many pupils remain at school fter the minimum leaving age. No fees are charged in any ublicly maintained school in England, Wales and cotland. In Northern Ireland, fees may be charged in oluntary schools and are paid by pupils in preparatory epartments of grammar schools, but pupils admitted to ne secondary departments of grammar schools, unless ney come from outside Northern Ireland, do not pay fees. tudents under 19 years of age attending courses at urther education colleges are not charged course fees.

ENGLAND AND WALES

here are two main types of school in England and Wales: chools maintained by the state, which charge no fees; and ndependent schools, which charge fees. Schools naintained by the state, with the exception of the cademies and city technology colleges, which exist in ngland alone, are maintained by local authorities. chools maintained by the state are classified as ommunity, voluntary or foundation schools. Community chools are owned by local authorities and wholly funded y them (although sixth forms have separate funding rrangements). They are non-denominational and provide rimary and secondary education. Schools in the oluntary category provide primary and secondary ducation and many have a particular religious ethos. lthough the school buildings are in many cases provided y the voluntary body (known as the foundation), the uthority financially maintains them.

There are two subdivisions in the voluntary category: *oluntary controlled,* and *voluntary aided.* In the case of oluntary controlled schools, the authority bears all the osts. In voluntary aided schools, the governing body is responsible for capital expenditure on the buildings, perimeter walls and fences, playgrounds, furniture fixtures and fittings (including ICT), and the Secretary of State for Children, Schools and Families may pay a capital grant of up to 90 per cent of approved capital expenditure. The local authority is responsible for capital work to playing fields and buildings on those fields related to their use as playing fields, and for all revenue funding. Sixth forms have separate funding arrangements. The arrangements in Wales are similar but the rate of grant support is 85 per cent.

Foundation schools provide primary and secondary education. They can have a religious character, although most do not. They are funded by the local authority, and, via the local authority, by the relevant funding bodies in respect of sixth form provision, although the land and buildings will be owned by a foundation or by the governors. The government's policy is to encourage community and voluntary controlled schools to become self-governing as foundation schools. The government is also encouraging schools to acquire foundations (known as Trusts) as a means of forming permanent relationships with external partners. Foundation schools with foundations are known as Trust schools.

Local authorities are required to provide the schools that they maintain with a delegated budget to cover their running costs, including staffing costs. Authorities can retain funding of various centrally provided services, including transport and some special educational needs. The authority acts as admission authority for most community and some voluntary schools.

Academies (England only) – are all-ability independent state schools with a mission to transform education where the status quo is simply not good enough. They are established and managed by independent sponsors, and funded by the government at a level comparable to other local schools. No fees are paid by parents. There are currently 47 academies open as at April 2007 and a further 37 are scheduled to open by the end of September 2007.

City Technology Colleges (CTCs) and *City Colleges for the Technology of the Arts (CCTAs)* are found in England only, and are state-aided but independent of local authorities. Their aim is to widen the choice of secondary education in disadvantaged urban areas and to teach a broad curriculum with an emphasis on science, technology, business understanding and arts technologies. Capital costs are shared by government and business sponsors, and running costs are covered by a per capita grant from the DCSF in line with an average of the comparable costs in authority-maintained schools in the areas where CTCs are located. CTCs are now being encouraged to convert to academies. To date five have converted and a further seven are considering converting over the next few years.

Education Action Zones (EAZs) were established in England from 1998 to develop local partnerships between schools, parents, the community, businesses and local authorities to find solutions to educational underachievement. They were set up as statutory bodies with a maximum five-year lifespan. After five years EAZs in rural areas changed into *Excellence Clusters* and those in urban areas into *Excellence in Cities (EiC)* action zones.

Education Improvement Partnerships are a way of enabling schools and other education providers to work together to raise standards; extend opportunities; and provide high quality services. They have the potential to become the delivery structure for a child-centred, local community agenda, capable of efficiently and effectively coordinating multi-agency working to ensure the broadest range and richest quality of service provision for every child.

Federations – the term describes groups of two or more governing bodies with a formal agreement for their schools to share governance arrangements and to work together for the benefit of all pupils and their school communities; this could entail sharing the curriculum, teaching resources, staff, ICT facilities, sports facilities or budgets. Federations can involve a mix of primary and secondary schools.

Governing bodies – all publicly maintained schools have a governing body, usually made up of a number of parent and local community representatives, governors appointed by the authority if the school is local authority-maintained, the headteacher (unless he or she chooses otherwise) and serving teachers and other staff. Voluntary schools and some foundation schools (including Trust schools) have foundation governors who are generally appointed to protect the ethos of the school. All schools can also appoint up to two sponsor governors and, since August 2005 in England, maintained secondary schools can appoint up to four sponsor governors. Sponsor governors are persons who give substantial assistance to the school, financially or in kind, or who provide services to the school. Governing bodies are responsible for the overall conduct and policies of schools including their academic aims and objectives.

Independent/State School Partnerships were launched in 1998 to forge links between independent and state schools and enhance the opportunities on offer to pupils. In 2006–7 a £2m government package funded 18 new partnership projects.

The *Leading Edge Partnership Programme* involves secondary schools working together to address some of the most critical learning challenges facing the education system. Partnerships focus on raising the performance of schools which are struggling to improve standards or close the achievement gap by addressing issues of under-performance among groups of pupils from poorer socio-economic backgrounds and from particular ethnic minority groups. There are currently 210 Leading Edge Partnerships already established across nearly 100 local authorities. Participation in the Leading Edge Partnership Programme is open to specialist schools which meet high performance criteria at re-designation.

Specialist Schools Programme – is open to all maintained secondary schools in England, including special schools with secondary aged pupils, that wish to develop a curriculum specialism in one of ten specialist areas: arts, business and enterprise, engineering, humanities, languages, mathematics and computing, music, science, sport, and technology. A new specialism for Special Educational Needs (SEN) for SEN schools was also introduced in 2005. Specialist schools receive additional recurrent funding to support the targets within their plan. This is currently calculated at a rate of £129 per pupil per annum. In addition, they receive a one-off capital grant of £100,000 supplemented by sponsorship, to improve their specialist facilities. Specialist schools are expected to include sponsors, local businesses and/or employers on their governing bodies. In January 2007 there were around 2,700 designated specialist schools, representing over 85 per cent of England's total number of secondary schools. Re-designation to the programme is reviewed at the time the school has an OFSTED section 5 inspection, usually every three years. At this point, schools which meet certain prescribed criteria are also invited to take o extra roles under the High Performing Specialist Schoo element of the programme. These include the opportunit to take up additional roles to support system-wide refor including taking a second curricular or vocational o SEN/inclusion specialism, raising standards through focus on underperformance, or a teacher training rol Around 400 have already established their options.

Trust schools are foundation schools supported by charitable foundation or 'Trust' that shares the school' aspirations for their pupils and can support them i continuing improvement. They are funded on exactly th same basis as other local authority maintained schools Through the Trust, they employ their own staff, set thei own admission arrangements in accordance with th admissions code, and manage their own land an buildings. Trust schools are supported by the Trus through the appointment of governors to the school' governing body. The Trust allows schools to build long term relationships with partners such as businesses charities, universities and other schools to help rais standards and widen opportunities for pupils. By Ma 2007 there were over 200 schools working towards Trus status.

SCOTLAND

Education authority schools (known as publicly-funde schools) are financed by local government, partly throug revenue support grants from central government, an partly from local taxation. Devolved management fro the local authority to the school is in place for more tha 88 per cent of all school-level expenditure. A sma number of grant-aided schools, mainly in the specia sector, are conducted by boards of managers and receiv grants direct from the Scottish Executive Educatio Department. Independent schools charge fees and receiv no direct grant, but are subject to inspection an registration.

NORTHERN IRELAND

Controlled schools are managed by the education an library boards (ELBs) through boards of governor consisting of representatives of transferors (mainly th Protestant churches), parents, teachers and the ELE Within the controlled sector there is a small number c controlled integrated schools. There are also gra maintained integrated schools which are funded directl by the Department of Education.

Voluntary maintained schools are managed by board of governors consisting of members nominated b trustees (mainly Roman Catholic) with representatives o teachers, parents and the ELB. Voluntary schools receiv grants towards capital costs and running costs in whole c in part. A majority are entitled to capital grants at 100 pe cent. Voluntary non-maintained schools are mainl voluntary grammar schools managed by boards c governors consisting of representatives of parent teachers and, in most cases, the Department of Educatio and the ELB, as well as those appointed as provided i each school's scheme of management. Integrated schoo exist to educate Protestant and Roman Catholic childre as well as those of other faiths and no faith, togethe Latest figures show that there are currently 56 integrate schools, comprising 19 integrated second level college and 37 integrated primary schools.

There are a number of Irish-language schools and unit and in June 2007 there were 21 freestanding Irish medium schools (19 of which received recurrent fundin rom the Department) and 12 Irish-medium units attached o schools in the English language sector. Of the 19 chools, 18 are Irish-medium primary schools. There are lso 3 Irish-medium nursery units.

HE STATE SYSTEM

URE START

ure Start is a programme in England designed to deliver he best start in life for every child. It increases the vailability of childcare; improves health, education and motional development for young people; and supports arents in their role including increasing their chances to vork, train and study. Children's Centres providing ntegrated services for under-fives are now being rolled ut to all communities, with the goal of opening 3,500 cross England by 2010. Sure Start's remit is confined to he under-fives, but other Sure Start group programmes re targeted at older children, including as part of the xtended schools initiative ensuring that accessible and ffordable care is available for all children up to the age of 4, or 16 for children with a special need.

RE-SCHOOL EDUCATION

re-school education is for children from 3 to 5 years of ge. It is not compulsory, parents can take as little or as nuch of their entitlement as they choose, although a free lace is available for every 3- and 4-year-old whose arents want one. In England since April 2006 all 3- and -year-olds are entitled to 12½ hours per week of free arly education over 38 weeks of the year. Children are ligible from 1 January, 1 April or 1 September, following heir third birthday. By 2010 the free early education ntitlement will increase from 12½ hours per week to 15 ours and parents will be able to use their entitlement for onger periods over a minimum of three days. Free places re funded via local authorities and are delivered by a ange of providers in the maintained and non-maintained ectors – nursery schools; nursery classes in primary chools; private schools; private day nurseries; voluntary laygroups; pre-schools and registered childminders (who re part of a network approved to deliver early education). n order to receive funding, providers should be working owards the early learning goals and other features of the oundation Stage curriculum; they should be inspected on regular basis by education inspectors appointed by the Office for Standards in Education, Children's Services and kills (OFSTED) and meet any conditions set by the local uthority.

From September 2008 the Foundation Stage urriculum, Birth to Three Matters and relevant elements f the National Daycare Standards will be consolidated nto the Early Years Foundation Stage (EYFS). This will be single quality framework for the development, learning nd care of all children in all early years settings. The atest available data (January 2006) shows that around 96 er cent of 3-year-olds and virtually all 4-year-olds in ngland were receiving at least some free early education. n Wales, a free part-time place in a maintained or funded on-maintained setting is available for each child from the erm following their third birthday. In Scotland, councils ave a duty to provide pre-school education for all 3- and -year-olds whose parents request one. In August 2007, he legal duty for provision increased to 475 hours of free re-school education per year, although local authorities ave the power to provide more if they choose. Most rovision is delivered in daily 2.5 hour sessions, but lternative arrangements are possible. In Northern Ireland children who have reached the age of 4 on or before 1 July will commence primary school at the beginning of the September following. In Northern Ireland approximately 30 per cent of pre-school education takes place in voluntary/private sector playgroups funded by the Department of Education.

PRIMARY EDUCATION

Primary education begins at 5 years in Great Britain and 4 years in Northern Ireland. In England, Wales and Northern Ireland the transfer to secondary school is generally made at 11 years.

Primary schools consist mainly of infant schools for children aged 5 to 7, junior schools for those aged 7 to 11, and combined junior and infant schools for both age groups. First schools in some parts of England cater for ages 5 to 10 as the first stage of a three-tier system of first, middle and secondary schools. Unlike England, Scotland has only primary schools.

MIDDLE SCHOOLS

Middle schools take children from first schools, mostly in England, cover varying age ranges between 8 and 14 and usually lead on to comprehensive upper schools.

SECONDARY EDUCATION

Secondary schools are for children aged 11 to 16 and for those who choose to stay on to 18. At 16, many students prefer to move on to tertiary or sixth form colleges or into further education colleges or work-based training. Most secondary schools in England, Wales and Scotland are co-educational. The largest secondary schools have over 1,500 pupils, but only 5.5 per cent of schools in the United Kingdom take over 1,000 pupils.

In England and Wales the main types of maintained secondary schools are: comprehensive schools, whose admission arrangements are without reference to ability or aptitude; deemed middle schools (in England), for children aged between eight and 14 years who then move on to senior comprehensive schools at 12, 13 or 14; and (in England) secondary grammar schools, with selective intake, providing an academic course from 11 to 16–18 years.

In Scotland all pupils in education authority secondary schools attend schools with a comprehensive intake. Most of these schools provide a full range of courses appropriate to all levels of ability from first to sixth year.

In Northern Ireland the process of selection (currently the 11-plus examination) is a key factor of the education system. Children are admitted to either grammar (42 per cent of pupils in 2006) or secondary schools (58 per cent of pupils in 2006) based on the grade they achieve in two tests taken during their seventh year at school when they are 10 or 11 years of age. Following a major review of post-primary education, which included research into the selective education system, extensive consultation and recommendations from the Post-Primary Review Working Group (Costello), Northern Ireland's education system was to embark on a process of major reform. However, following the restoration of the Northern Ireland Assembly a vote by the assembly will be required to end academic selection.

New arrangements for post-primary education, in particular the means by which pupils transfer from primary to post-primary schools, are being introduced. The key aspects of the new arrangements are:

- The last transfer tests will be held in autumn 2008
- Transfer from primary to post-primary will be based on informed parental choice

- A pupil profile will be developed for each child, detailing his or her progress

The new post-primary arrangements will guarantee all pupils access to a much wider range of courses, with a minimum of 24 courses at key stage 4, and 27 at post-16. At least one third of the courses on offer will be general (academic) in nature, and at least one third will be (applied vocational/professional/technical). Legislation has been made to give effect to these changes and to enable schools to enter into collaborative arrangements with other schools, FE colleges or other providers.

SPECIAL EDUCATION

Wherever appropriate, taking parents' wishes into account, children with special educational needs are educated in ordinary schools, which are required to publish their policy for pupils with such needs. Schools and local authorities in England and Wales and education and library boards in Northern Ireland are required to identify and secure provision for children with special educational needs and to involve the parents in decisions.

In Scotland, school placing is a matter of agreement between education authorities and parents. Parents have the right to say which school they want their child to attend, and a right of appeal where their wishes are not being met.

In Northern Ireland grant-aided special schools are funded by local education and library boards (ELBs) and have partially delegated budgets. ELBs can also fund places in a small number of local independent schools, recognised by the Department of Education as providers of special education.

Maintained special schools are run by education authorities which pay all the costs of maintenance, but under the terms of local management, all maintained schools must have a delegated budget including maintained special schools. Non-maintained special schools are run by voluntary bodies; they may receive grants from central government for capital expenditure and for equipment but their current expenditure is met primarily from the fees charged to education authorities for pupils placed in the schools. Some independent schools provide education wholly or mainly for children with special educational needs.

Of all the pupils with statements of special educational needs in 2005–6, 63 per cent were educated in mainstream schools.

ELECTIVE HOME EDUCATION

There is no legal obligation on parents in the UK to educate their children at school provided that the local authority is satisfied that the child is receiving full-time education suited to its age, abilities and aptitudes and any special needs. The education authority need not be informed that a child is being educated at home unless the child is currently attending school. In that case the parents must arrange for the child's name to be removed from the school's register (by writing to the headteacher) before education at home can begin. Failure to do so leaves the parents liable to prosecution for condoning non-attendance. There are no official figures on the numbers of pupils educated outside school.

THE CURRICULUM

ENGLAND

The national curriculum was introduced in England from 1988 for the period of compulsory schooling from 5 to 16. It is mandatory in all maintained schools. Following a review in 1999, a revised curriculum was introduced in schools from September 2000.

The Foundation Stage was introduced in September 2000 for children aged 3–5. It sets out six areas of learning:

- Personal, social and emotional development
- Communication
- Mathematical development
- Knowledge and understanding of the world
- Physical development
- Creative development

The Education Act 2002 extended the national curriculum to include the Foundation Stage. This act also established a single national assessment system for the Foundation Stage called the Foundation Stage Profile.

At key stages 1 and 2, the statutory subjects in the national curriculum are:

Core subjects	*Foundation subjects*
English	Design and Technology
Mathematics	Information and Communication Technology
Science	History
	Geography
	Art and Design
	Music
	Physical Education

At key stage 3 (11- to 14-year-olds) a modern foreign language and citizenship are introduced. At key stage 4 (14- to 16-year-olds) pupils are required to continue to study the core subjects, plus physical education, information and communication technology and citizenship. Careers and sex education are also statutory subjects for all secondary pupils and work-related learning is statutory for all pupils at key stage 4. In addition, schools must provide access for each key stage 4 pupil to a minimum of one course in the arts (art and design, music, dance, drama and media arts), one course in the humanities (history and geography), at least one modern foreign language and design and technology. Other subjects, such as drama, dance and classical languages, are taught when the resources of individual schools permit. Religious education must be taught across all key stages. Parents have the right to withdraw their children from religious education and sex education classes.

Statutory assessment takes place at the end of the Foundation Stage and national tests and tasks take place in English and mathematics at the end of key stage 1 (seven-year-olds), with the addition of science at the end of key stage 2 (11-year-olds). At key stage 1 the results of tasks and tests are not reported but are used to underpin teachers' overall assessment of pupils. At key stages 2 and 3 separate teacher assessments of pupils' progress are made to set alongside the test results. At key stage 4, the GCSE and vocational equivalents are the main form of assessment.

Each year, the Department for Children, Schools and Families (DCSF) in England publishes four sets of achievement and attainment tables showing performance measures for every school and local authority based on results at key stages 2 and 3, GCSE, A-level and equivalent qualifications.

The Qualifications and Curriculum Authority (QCA) is an independent government agency funded by the DCSF. It is responsible for setting the national curriculum and for ensuring that the curriculum and qualifications available to young people and adults are of high quality, coherent and flexible; its remit ranges from the under-fives to higher level vocational qualifications.

The National Assessment Agency (NAA) was launched in April 2004 by the DfES to develop and deliver high quality national curriculum tests and supervise the delivery and modernisation of GCSE and A-level examinations. The NAA is a subsidiary of the QCA.

WALES

A national curriculum was introduced simultaneously in Wales and, although it is broadly similar to that of England, it has separate and distinctive characteristics which are reflected in the programmes of study where appropriate. Welsh is compulsory for pupils at all key stages, either as a first or as a second language. Between 8 January and 30 March 2007, a series of consultation exercises was undertaken as part of the review of the school curriculum in Wales. Following this consultation, recommendations will be made to the Minister for Education, Lifelong Learning and Skills and it is anticipated that the revised curriculum will be implemented from September 2008.

In July 2003 the minister announced that statutory testing would be removed for pupils in Wales at the end of key stage 2 from 2004–5 and from 2005–6 for key stage 3. Statutory teacher assessment remains and will be strengthened by moderation and accreditation arrangements. It is the only form of statutory assessment from key stages 1–3.

On 1 April 2006, Awdurdod Cymwysterau, Cwricwlwm ac Asesu Cymru (ACCAC – the Qualifications, Curriculum and Assessment Authority for Wales) merged with the Department of Training and Education, ELWa, Dysg and the Welsh Youth Agency to create the Department for Education, Lifelong Learning and Skills.

SCOTLAND

The content and management of the curriculum in Scotland are not prescribed by statute but are the responsibility of education authorities and individual headteachers. Advice and guidance are provided by the Scottish Executive Education Department and Learning and Teaching Scotland, which also has a developmental role. Those bodies have produced guidelines on the structure and balance of the curriculum as well as for each of five broad curriculum areas for the five to 14 age group. There are also guidelines on assessment across the whole curriculum, on reporting to parents, and on the use of national tests for reading, writing and mathematics at six levels. Testing is carried out by the school when the teacher judges that a pupil has completed a level; most pupils are expected to move from one level to the next at roughly 18-month to two-year intervals. Guidance on the curriculum for 14- to 16-year-olds recommends study within each of eight modes: language and communication; mathematical studies; science; technology; social studies; creative activities; physical education; and religious and moral education. There is also a recommended percentage of time to be devoted to each area over the two years. Provision is also made for teaching in Gaelic in many parts of Scotland and the number of pupils, from nursery to secondary, in Gaelic-medium education is growing. Local authorities must ensure that local education provision meets demand and consider whether they need a Gaelic-medium class, school or unit. For 16- to 18-year-olds, National Qualifications, a unified framework of courses and awards which brings together both academic and vocational courses, was introduced in 1999. The Scottish Qualifications Authority awards the certificates.

NORTHERN IRELAND

The statutory Northern Ireland curriculum is made up of religious education and five broad areas of study at primary level and six at secondary level. Provided the requirements of the statutory curriculum are met, it is for each school to decide what additional subjects should be made available for pupils. Pupils at key stages 1 and 2 study religious education, English, mathematics, science, history and geography (known as the environment and society area of study), art and design, music and PE (the creative and expressive area of study), Irish (in Irish-language schools only) and four educational cross-curricular themes (education for mutual understanding, cultural heritage, health education and information technology). At key stage 3, pupils also study technology and design, plus a foreign language (pupils in Irish-language schools can study a foreign language or continue studying Irish) and two extra cross-curricular themes (economic awareness and careers education). At key stage 4, pupils can drop technology and design, art and design, and music and can choose one subject from history, geography, business studies, home economics, economics, political studies or social and environmental studies.

The government accepted proposals from the Northern Ireland Council for the Curriculum Examinations and Assessment (CCEA) for a revised Northern Ireland curriculum in June 2004. The new curriculum will be phased in over a number of years from September 2007 to allow schools to plan for and implement the changes. A number of elements of the revised curriculum are being piloted in advance of implementation. The revised curriculum will be less prescriptive in terms of content, and more holistic and flexible. There will be greater emphasis on developing skills (such as communication, using mathematics and using ICT, along with thinking skills such as creativity, teamwork and problem-solving) and a new area of Learning for Life and Work at key stages 3 and 4 that will include education for employability, citizenship and personal development. In addition to religious education, the other learning areas (which will replace areas of study) are:

Foundation Stage, Key Stages 1 and 2	*Key Stages 3 and 4*
The Arts	Learning for Life and Work
Language and Literacy	The Arts
Mathematics and Numeracy	Language and Literacy
Personal Development and Mutual Understanding	Mathematics and numeracy
Physical Education	Modern Languages
The World Around Us	Physical Education
	Science and Technology
	Environment and Society

A new key stage known as the Foundation Stage, which covers years 1 and 2 of primary school, will be introduced. This is to allow a more appropriate learning style for the youngest pupils and to ease the transition from pre-school.

The assessment of pupils is broadly in line with practice in England and Wales and currently takes place at the ages of eight, 11 and 14, ie end of key stage assessment. With the introduction of the revised curriculum, this will be replaced by annual assessment reported to parents in the form of a pupil profile. Teachers will assess pupils in the cross-curricular skills of communication, using mathematics and using ICT. Teachers will also comment on a pupil's progress and areas for future development in the other thinking skills and in the learning areas. Teacher assessment can be suported by objective computer-based diagnostic assessments. The GCSE is used to assess 16-year-olds.

The CCEA is a unique education body in the UK in that it combines the three functions of a curriculum advisory body, an awarding body and a qualifications regulatory body. It monitors and advises the Department of Education and teachers on all matters relating to the curriculum, assessment arrangements and examinations in grant-aided schools. It conducts GCSE, A- and AS-level examinations, pupil assessment at key stages 1, 2 and 3 and administers the transfer procedure tests. It also ensures that qualifications offered by awarding bodies in Northern Ireland are of an appropriate quality and standard.

PUBLIC EXAMINATIONS AND QUALIFICATIONS

ENGLAND, WALES AND NORTHERN IRELAND

In 1988 a single system of examinations, the General Certificate of Secondary Education (GCSE), which is usually taken after five years of secondary education, was introduced. The GCSE is the main method of assessing the performance of pupils on a subject-specific basis. The structure of the examination reflects national curriculum requirements where these apply. GCSE short-course qualifications are available in some subjects. As a rule the syllabus comprises half the content of a full GCSE course. In September 2002 eight GCSEs in vocational subjects were introduced (known as Applied GCSEs) and they are: applied art and design, applied business, engineering, health and social care, applied ICT, leisure and tourism, manufacturing, and applied science.

The GCSE differs from its predecessors in that there are syllabuses based on national criteria covering course objectives, content and assessment methods; differentiated assessment (ie different papers or questions for different ranges of ability) and grade-related criteria (ie grades awarded on absolute rather than relative performance). The GCSE certificates are awarded on an eight-point scale, A* to G. All GCSE syllabuses, assessments and grading procedures are monitored by qualification regulators for England, Wales and Northern Ireland (QCA, DELLS and CCEA) to ensure that they conform to the national criteria. In England in 2005, 56.3 per cent of 15-year-olds (at the beginning of the academic year) gained at least five results at grade C or better at GCSE or General National Vocational Qualification (GNVQ) equivalent (61 per cent in Northern Ireland), while 89.0 per cent achieved five or more at grade G or above. Students are increasingly encouraged to continue their education post-16. For those who do so, in addition to the vocational qualifications outlined below, there are GCE (General Certificate of Education), AS (Advanced Subsidiary) and A (Advanced) Levels and the Advanced Applied A-levels. Since September 2005 Applied A-levels have AS/A2 units, bringing them into line with GCE A-levels. At the same time the formal distinction between GCEs and VCEs was dropped and both vocational and academic qualifications are now known as GCEs. However, a small number of subjects – art and design, business, ICT and science – were available as GCEs and VCEs. In order to distinguish between the different patterns of study and assessment in these qualifications, the term 'applied' was introduced into the current vocational qualification in these subjects: for example, the current VCE in art and design is known as the GCE A-level in applied art and design. A-level courses usually last two years and have traditionally provided the foundation for entry to higher education. AS-level qualifications were introduced in September 2000 and represent the first half of a full A-level and are assessed accordingly. Following extensive consultations in 1996 and 1997 which indicated the need to broaden the post-16 curriculum, new A-level qualifications were introduced in September 2000. The new A-level qualification consists of six units (three AS units and three A2 units). Students who go on to complete the full A-level will be assessed on their attainment in all six units, which may be taken either in stages or at the end of the course. A-levels and AS-levels are marked on a six-point scale from A to E. There is also the opportunity for A-level candidates to take additional papers known as Advanced Extension Awards (which replaced Special papers) and these are designed to challenge the most able A-level students.

VOCATIONAL QUALIFICATIONS

There are two broad categories of vocational qualifications: National Vocational Qualifications (NVQs), which demonstrate competence in a specific occupation (or aspect of an occupation), and vocationally related qualifications, which usually give a broader, more general preparation for an industry or wider occupational area. All vocational qualifications are based upon national occupational standards, which are designed by employers. Vocational qualifications are accredited into the national qualifications framework by the QCA at nine levels:

- Entry level
- Level 1 – Foundation Skills
- Level 2 – Operative/Semiskilled
- Level 3 – Technician/Craft/Skilled/Supervisory
- Level 4 – Technical/Middle Management
- Level 5 – Chartered/Professional/Senior Management
- Level 6 – Knowledge Based Professionals
- Level 7 – High Level Specialist Professional/Senior Professionals
- Level 8 – Leading Experts/Practitioners

General National Vocational Qualifications (GNVQs) are now being replaced by vocational GCSEs (*see* above). The Advanced Vocational Certificate of Education (VCE), replaced Advanced GNVQs. It is available in different forms: the three-unit Advanced Subsidiary (equivalent to one GCE AS-level), the six-unit Advanced Level (equivalent to one GCE A-level), and the 12-unit Double Award (equivalent to two GCE A-levels).

WELSH BACCALAUREATE

The Welsh Baccalaureate is a new qualification for 16–19 year olds that incorporates current approved qualifications like A-levels, GCSEs and NVQs and adds breadth and balance through a core programme of activities. It is currently being piloted in 31 schools and colleges roughout Wales at both intermediate and advanced level nd, subject to ministerial decisions following external valuation which was reported in the summer of 2006, it as planned to be rolled out nationally from September 007. In addition, the pilot has now been extended to clude the development of a foundation level Welsh accalaureate since September 2006. This is being iloted in pre-16 settings along with limited intermediate rovision. The Welsh Baccalaureate allows students exibility of study in the range of traditional ualifications and the opportunity to develop key skills nd wider learning experiences.

COTLAND

cotland has its own system of public examinations, and 1999 a new system of National Qualifications was troduced. Five levels of study are offered: Access, ntermediate 1, Intermediate 2, Higher and Advanced igher. The new Higher National course and Advanced igher National course are direct replacements for the old CE Higher grade and the Certificate of Sixth Year tudies respectively. National Qualifications are included n the Scottish Credit and Qualifications Framework SCQF) (*see* below), with Access equating to levels 1 to 3, ntermediate 1 to level 4, Intermediate 2 to level 5, igher to level 6 and Advanced Higher to level 7.

National courses consist of blocks of study called ational units. A unit usually consists of around 40 hours f study and there are three units in a course. Unit awards emonstrate that a learner has achieved competence in a articular area of study. National course awards are graded y external assessment, which consists of an examination, oursework or performance, or a combination of two or ore of these. National course awards also require andidates to pass all unit assessments of the course. A ypical national course external assessment requires andidates to demonstrate long-term retention of nowledge, high levels of problem solving, integration f knowledge across a whole course and an ability to pply knowledge and skills in novel situations. The range f subjects has been expanded to include vocational ualifications.

A number of schools use the new National Qualifications system for pupils in their fourth year of econdary education, but the majority of this lower age roup still take the traditional Standard Grade xaminations at the end of a two-year course. Awards at tandard Grade are set at three levels: Credit (leading to wards at grade 1 or 2); General (leading to awards at rade 3 or 4); and Foundation (leading to awards at grade or 6). Grade 7 is awarded to those who, although they ave completed the course, have not attained any of these evels. Normally pupils will take examinations covering wo pairs of grades, either grades 1–4 or grades 3–6. Most candidates take seven or eight Standard Grade xaminations. The three levels of Standard Grade equate o levels 3 to 5 of the SCQF.

NTERNATIONAL BACCALAUREATE

The International Baccalaureate (IB) Organisation is a on-profit foundation that offers three challenging ducational programmes – the Primary Years Programme or students aged 3 to 12, the Middle Years Programme or students aged 11 to 16 and the Diploma Programme for tudents aged 16 to 19. Each programme can be taught in ts own right, but, when linked together, they form a ontinuum of education for students aged 3 to 19. The rogrammes consist of a curriculum or curriculum framework and a pedagogy promoting good teaching practice; methods of student assessment appropriate to the age range; professional development and support opportunities for educators; and an ongoing process of school evaluation. The programmes are offered through IB World Schools (of which there are 87 in the UK and over 1,800 worldwide) and are well recognized by governments and universities around the world. More than half of the students currently participating in IB programmes are in state funded schools.

POST-16 EDUCATION

In the UK in 2004–5, 77 per cent of 16-year-olds and 64 per cent of 17-year-olds were in post-compulsory education, either at school or in further education. There were over 5 million further education students in the UK during the academic year 2004–5, of which 79 per cent were part-time. In 2005–6, there were 476 further education colleges in the UK of which 102 were sixth form colleges. In 2004–5, there were 60,000 full-time academic staff in further education institutions.

ENGLAND

The further education (FE) system provides a wide range of education and training opportunities for individuals from age 14 upwards and employers. Learning opportunities are provided at all levels from basic skills to higher education. The central policy aim is to build a further education system that provides the skills the economy needs to sustain quality of life and to contribute to the UK's international standing. The goal is to lead the world in skills development – with virtually all young people staying on in education and training to age 19 and half progressing to higher education; all adults having the support they need to improve their skills throughout life; and all employers seeing skills as key to their success.

In March 2006 a reform strategy *Further Education: Raising Skills, Improving Life Chances* was launched which set out a programme of changes to deliver this aim. Key aspects include:

- a new economic mission for FE
- providers of learning and skills to specialise to supply world class services
- an enhanced role for employers and learners in shaping development
- new entitlements to learning and support for those who most need it – free tuition for first level 3 for 19–25 year olds and learner accounts for adults on level 3 programmes
- a new strategy for raising quality, with intervention to eliminate poor quality provision
- public funding focused on delivery priorities
- less bureaucracy along with more autonomy for effective providers

The English FE system includes independent providers (voluntary and private sector) who offer a range of work-based and personal and community learning. Personal and community development learning takes place in a wide range of settings usually community based and delivered via local authorities. Post-16 education and training (excluding Higher Education) in England is funded through the Learning and Skills Council (LSC).

WORK-BASED LEARNING

Apprenticeships are a way for learners to get practical experience while gaining nationally recognised qualifications. The LSC in England and the Welsh

Assembly Government in Wales contribute towards the cost of the training and assessment. Apprenticeships normally last between one and three years (four in Wales) and there are two levels: apprenticeships and advanced apprenticeships at levels 2 and 3 respectively. Both of these lead to:

- National Vocational Qualifications (NVQs)
- Key Skills qualifications – transferable work-related skills such as IT and communication and problem solving
- Technical certificates – vocationally related qualifications that provide the basic knowledge of the NVQ

There are currently over 250,000 young people aged between 16 to 24 on apprenticeships in England alone, with similar programmes in place in Scotland, Northern Ireland and Wales.

In May 2004 a new set of apprenticeships was announced, incorporating Young Apprenticeships for 14- to 16-year-olds, which was launched in September 2004 with 1,000 young people. A further 2,000 young people joined the programme from September 2005. The reforms also led to the opening up of adult apprenticeships by scrapping the arbitrary 25-year-old age limit. Following a successful series of trials additional funding has been put in place for around 8,000 adults to take up apprenticeships in 2007–8.

Diplomas are new qualifications which will give young people a real alternative to traditional learning. Combining theoretical and applied learning they provide a package that ensures that young people are both educated and employable. Employers will know that a young person has mastered functional skills in English, Maths and ICT, and can apply these in work situations. Diploma Development Partnerships (DDPs) have been established to explore content development. These DDPs, led by Sector Skills Councils and including employers, higher education, school and college and awarding body representatives, specify the content of the diplomas. Awarding bodies will then develop the qualifications. The diplomas will be available in 14 lines of learning. The content for the first five lines (ICT; health and social care, engineering, creative and media and construction and the built environment) can be accessed via the QCA website. These qualifications will be available for teaching from September 2008. A further five diplomas, in business administration and finance; hair and beauty; hospitality and catering; land-based and environmental; and manufacturing will be available for teaching in 2009. The final four diplomas, in public services; sport and leisure; retail; and travel and tourism will be available in 2010. A new statutory entitlement will be in place for all 14-19 year olds from September 2013.

WALES

In Wales, the aims and makeup of the FE system are very similar to those outlined for England, although, as the education portfolio is devolved to the Welsh Assembly, the policy documents vary. Current thinking is outlined in *The Learning Country: Vision into Action* which was published in October 2006. This document focuses on improving basic skills and aims for 70 per cent of working age adults to be educated to at least level 2, 50 per cent to level 3 and 40 per cent to level 4 and above by 2010.

SCOTLAND

Since Autumn 2005, the Scottish Funding Council h been the statutory body responsible for fundir Scotland's 46 further education colleges. The Scottis Qualifications Authority (SQA) is the statutory awardir body for qualifications in the national education ar training system. It is both the main awarding body f qualifications for work including Scottish Vocation Qualifications (SVQs) and is also their accrediting bod The SQA is by statute required clearly to separate awarding and accrediting functions. There are three mai qualification 'families' in Scottish further educatio National Qualifications; Higher National Qualificatio (HNC and HND); and SVQs. In addition to Standa Grade qualifications, National Qualifications are availab at five levels. Another feature of the qualifications syste is the Scottish Group Award (SGA). SGAs are built up un by unit and allow opportunity for credit transfer fro other qualifications (such as Standard Grade or SVQ providing a further option, especially for adult learne SVQs are competence-based qualifications suitable f workplace delivery but they can also be taken in furth education colleges and other centres where workpla conditions can be simulated. The Scottish Credit ar Qualifications Framework includes qualifications acro academic and vocational sectors in a single credit-base framework. It comprises 12 levels, covering a mainstream qualifications from Access level in Nation Qualifications to postgraduate qualifications, an including SVQs. In the academic year 2004–5 there we 450,435 student enrolments on vocational and nor vocational courses in further education colleges. Of th total, higher education courses accounted for 29 per ce of college activity.

NORTHERN IRELAND

All further education colleges are independent corpora bodies like their counterparts in the rest of the UK Responsibility for the sector lies with the Department fc Employment and Learning (DELNI), which funds th colleges directly. The colleges own their own property, a responsible for their own services and employ their ow staff.

The governing bodies of the colleges must include a least 50 per cent membership from those who ar engaged or employed in business, industry, or an profession. The composition of governing bodies is bein reviewed as part of the planned restructuring of the F sector from August 2007.

Northern Ireland has 16 institutions of furthe education. This was reduced to six area-based colleges i August 2007. In 2005–6 there were 33,353 full-time an 133,003 part-time enrolments on vocational furthe education courses.

STUDENT SUPPORT

Education maintenance allowance (EMA) is an incom tested allowance that supports young people in post-1 learning across the UK. EMA consists of a weekl allowance of up to £30, plus periodic bonus payment and is available to learners from low-income household who stay on at school, college, LSC-funded Entry t Employment (E2E) or programme led apprenticeship EMA is available for up to three years. Also available t students in England aged 16-19 are learner support fund These funds, which are targeted at those students i greatest need, have four separate strands: transpor childcare (Care2Learn), residential and general funding

Vhilst the funding for both transport and childcare are niversal, the discretionary nature of the other funds llows local learning institutions to provide targeted help nd support where it is needed. Hardship funds are vailable to learners in E2E or programme led pprenticeships and replicate the general learner support und available to learners in further education. For adults 19 and over) in England similar discretionary learner upport funds are available for the most disadvantaged tudents with the greatest need. These provide financial elp with the costs of childcare, books, equipment and ransport and residential funding. Funds are administered y colleges and other providers. In England, the adult earning grant (ALG) is an income assessed grant of up to 30 per week for adults who are on low incomes. It is aid to learners who are studying full time for their first ull level 2 (five GCSEs or equivalent) or level 3 ualification (two A-levels or equivalent). ALG is dministered by the LSC and is currently piloted in urther education providers across 25 LSC areas. It has een available throughout England since September 2007.

For students over 18 in the UK who choose to fund heir course themselves, career development loans are vailable from three high street banks. Loans of between 300 and £8,000 can be used to pay for the costs of ocational training courses. Interest on the loan is paid by he LSC while the student is completing the course. ligible Welsh-domiciled students aged 19 years or over n further education courses, whether full-time or part-ime (subject to a minimum contact requirement), receive a neans-tested non-repayable assembly learning grant. Discretionary financial contingency funds are also vailable to all students suffering hardship and are dministered by the institutions themselves. In addition, ndividual learning accounts are available in Wales, vhich provide adults with means-tested support of up to 200 to undertake a wide range of learning. Eligible cottish-domiciled further education students can apply o their college for discretionary support in the form of ursaries. These can include allowances for maintenance, ravel, study, dependants and additional support needs. College students receiving EMAs may also be eligible for he non-maintenance elements. Colleges administer liscretionary funds in the form of hardship funds. They lso have a childcare fund which is used to pay for egistered childcare. Some colleges may offer different nethods of childcare support and provision, for example n-site nurseries or childcare vouchers.

Full-time students over 19 years of age, resident in Northern Ireland and on certain vocational courses, may benefit from discretionary non-repayable further ducation bursaries. The bursaries are administered by the ducation and library boards. Support includes free tuition o all full-time students up to age 18 and to all full-time tudents over 18 undertaking a vocational course at level 3 or below. In addition, financial help is provided by colleges through a discretionary support fund for both full-time and part-time students whose access to and participation in further education is inhibited by financial considerations.

TEACHERS

ENGLAND AND WALES

All teachers working in maintained primary, special and secondary schools, non-maintained special schools and pupil referral units are required to register with the General Teaching Council for England (GTCE) in England and the General Teaching Council for Wales (GTCW) in Wales.

New entrants to the teaching profession in state primary and secondary schools are required to be graduates and to have qualified teacher status (QTS). QTS is achieved by successfully completing a course of initial teacher training, traditionally either a Bachelor of Education (BEd) degree, BA with QTS, BSc with QTS or the Postgraduate Certificate of Education (PGCE) at an accredited institution. New entrants are statutorily required to serve a three term (full-time, pro rata part-time) induction period during which they will have a structured programme of support. All initial teacher training has a strong element of practical school-based work, with student teachers spending significant periods of their training in the classroom.

In addition to the traditional routes, in recent years various employment-based routes to QTS have been developed. The Graduate Teacher Programme (GTP) is designed for mature, well-qualified people who can quickly take on teaching responsibilities and who need to earn a living while they train. Trainees are paid a salary and undergo up to a year of school-based training. The Registered Teacher Programme (RTP) is designed for people without a degree or formal teaching qualification but with at least two years of higher education; entrants are paid a salary and complete a degree while undergoing training for up to two years. Employment-based training routes account for about 15 per cent of all teacher training places.

Teachers in further education (FE) are not required to have QTS, though roughly half have a teaching qualification and most have industrial, commercial or professional experience. Since July 2002, all new entrants to FE teaching in Wales are required to have, or to be working towards, a specified FE teaching qualification. A qualification for aspiring headteachers, the National Professional Qualification for Headship (NPQH), has been introduced. The National College for School Leadership administers this qualification and others and acts as a focus for development and support. In Wales, the NPQH and other headship programmes are administered by the Welsh Assembly Government and consideration is being given to establishing a similar scheme in respect of FE principals, in association with powers under the Education Act 2002 allowing the making of regulations requiring FE principals to have a specified qualification.

New financial incentives for trainee teachers were introduced from September 2006. Maths and science postgraduate trainees may be eligible for a £9,000 tax free bursary while they train, and a £5,000 taxable 'golden hello' after successfully completing the induction period. Modern languages, English or drama, design and technology, ICT, music and religious education postgraduate trainees may be eligible for a £9,000 training bursary and a £2,500 'golden hello'. A £6,000 training bursary is available for other postgraduate secondary and primary trainees. In Wales a similar scheme operates, on a pilot basis, for those undertaking the full-time PGCE (FE) or PGCE (PcET) (Post-compulsory Education and Training). Eligible students receive a bursary of £6,000 (£7,000 for mathematics and science courses since September 2005), paid in instalments whilst studying. In England, other training awards may be available through the secondary shortage subject scheme (SSSS). This is an additional, means-tested hardship fund from the Training and Development Agency for Schools. The subjects currently included are: design and technology, geography, information technology, mathematics, modern languages, music, religious education and science.

In Wales, placement grants supported by the Higher Education Funding Council for Wales (HEFCW) provide £1,000 per funded student on undergraduate priority courses – the same subjects that attract the £4,000 training grant – and £600 to students on other undergraduate courses.

The Teacher Training Agency became the Training and Development Agency for Schools (TDA) in September 2005 and in early 2006 it incorporated the work of the National Remodelling Team. In addition to attracting quality people to initial teacher training (ITT), funding universities, colleges and schools to deliver ITT and working to improve the quality of training, the agency's new role is to work with schools to help them develop and train their whole school team. The TDA administers a returners' programme for qualified teachers who wish to refresh their skills before returning to the profession. Participants are entitled to a bursary of up to £150 a week to a total of £1,500 and additional childcare support. The TDA supports the sharing of good practice in teacher training, encourages schools to offer placements for trainee teachers, and funds training and assessment for higher level teaching assistant (HLTA) status.

In Wales funding of ITT is undertaken by the HEFCW. On an integrated England and Wales basis the TDA also acts as a central source of information and advice on entry to teaching.

The General Teaching Council for England (GTCE), an independent professional council, acts as a disciplinary body dealing with cases of misconduct and incompetence in England. The GTCE also hears appeal hearings for registered teachers who have failed their induction year. In addition, it is responsible for promoting the profession and professional standards and for advising the secretary of state. The separate General Teaching Council for Wales (GTCW) fulfils a similar role in Wales and provides advice to the Welsh Assembly Government.

The Specialist Teacher Assistant scheme provides trained support to qualified teachers in the teaching of reading, writing and arithmetic to young pupils.

In January 2003 the DfES, Welsh Assembly Government, employers and teaching unions signed a national agreement, *Raising Standards and Tackling Workload,* setting out a three-year programme of reforms to provide more classroom support for teachers.

SCOTLAND

The General Teaching Council for Scotland (GTCS) advises central government on matters relating to teacher supply and the professional suitability of all teacher training courses. It is also the body responsible for disciplinary procedures in cases of professional misconduct. All teachers in maintained schools must be registered with the GTCS. Only graduates are accepted as entrants to the profession; primary school teachers undertake either a four-year vocational degree course or a one-year postgraduate course, while teachers of academic subjects in secondary schools undertake the latter. There is also a combined degree sometimes known as a concurrent degree.

The Scottish Qualification for Headship has been introduced for aspiring headteachers. Universities with specialist education departments provide both in-service and pre-service training for teachers. The universities are funded by the Scottish Higher Education Funding Council, which also sets intake levels for teach education courses in line with guidance provided by th Scottish Executive.

NORTHERN IRELAND

All new entrants to teaching in grant-aided schools ar graduates and hold an approved teaching qualification. fully integrated programme of Initial Teacher Educatio (ITE), induction and early professional development a well as the Professional Qualification for Headshi programme, is in place in Northern Ireland. ITE provided by Queen's University, Belfast, University c Ulster, Stranmillis University College, St Mary University College and the Open University (NI). Th university colleges are concerned with teacher educatio mainly for the primary school sector and the universitie mainly for the post-primary sector. The General Teachin Council for Northern Ireland (GTCNI) advise government on professional issues, maintains a register c professional teachers and acts as a disciplinary body.

SALARIES

Qualified teachers in England and Wales, other than th leadership group (which includes headteachers, deput headteachers and advanced skills teachers) are paid on six-point main pay scale. Teachers who demonstrat exceptional ability have the opportunity to be assesse against national standards and moving to the three poin upper scale. An 'Excellent Teacher' scheme has bee available to schools since September 2006. This allow eligible teachers to access a 'spot' salary. There ar teaching and learning responsibility payments fo specific posts, special needs work and recruitment an retention factors which may be awarded at the discretio of the relevant body, ie the governing body or the loca authority. The advanced skills teacher grade wa introduced to enhance prospects in the classroom for th most able teachers. Experienced teachers are assesse against national standards to move onto the upper pa scale, after which they receive performance-related pa increases. There is a statutory superannuation scheme Teachers working in the London area are paid on separat pay scales. As at September 2007, salary scales fo teachers in England and Wales are:

Headteacher	£39,525–£98,02
Advanced skills teacher	£34,938–£53,11
Classroom teacher (upper pay scale)	£31,878–£34,28
Classroom teacher (main pay scale)	£20,133–£29,42
Unqualified teachers	£14,751–£23,33
Inner London	
Headteacher	£46,134–£104,62
Advanced skills teacher	£41,541–£59,72
Classroom teacher (upper pay scale)	£37,809–£41,00
Classroom teacher (main pay scale)	£24,168–£33,93
Unqualified teachers	£18,552–£27,12

Teachers in Scotland are paid on a seven-point scale. The entry point depends on type of qualification and additional allowances are payable under a range of circumstances. As at 1 April 2006, salary scales for teachers in Scotland were:

Headteacher/deputy headteacher	£39,207–£76,527
Principal teacher	£34,566–£44,616
Chartered teacher	£32,688–£38,868
Main grade	£19,878–£31,707

Teachers in Northern Ireland have broadly similar pay and working conditions as teachers in England and Wales, although negotiated through separate local negotiating machinery. There are a few exceptions to this, for example there is no advanced skills teacher grade. As at September 2007, salary scales for teachers in Northern Ireland are:

Principal	£39,525–£98,022
Vice-Principal	From £34,938
Classroom teacher	£20,133–£34,281

HIGHER EDUCATION

The term higher education is used to describe education above A-level, Higher and Advanced Higher Grade and their equivalent, which is provided in universities, colleges of higher education and in some FE colleges.

The main purposes of higher education are:

- to enable people to develop their capabilities and fulfil their potential, both personally and at work
- to advance knowledge and understanding through scholarship and research
- to contribute to an economically successful and culturally diverse nation

Advice to government on matters relating to higher education is provided by the separate Higher Education Funding Councils for England, Wales and Scotland, and by the Northern Ireland Higher Education Council. The former receive a block grant from central government which they allocate to the universities and colleges. In Northern Ireland the grant is allocated directly to institutions by the Department for Employment and Learning.

The Scottish Funding Council (SFC) funds 20 institutions of higher education, including 14 universities. The universities are broadly managed as described above and the remaining colleges are managed by independent governing bodies which include representatives of industrial, commercial, professional and educational interests.

In Northern Ireland higher education is provided in six regional further education colleges, the two universities and the two university colleges. These institutions offer a range of courses, including first and postgraduate degrees, PGCEs, undergraduate diplomas and certificates, foundation degrees, Higher National Diplomas and professional qualifications.

TYPES OF HIGHER EDUCATION INSTITUTION

The Further and Higher Education Act 1992 and parallel legislation in Scotland removed the distinction between higher education provided by the universities and that provided in England, Scotland and Wales by the former polytechnics and colleges of higher education. It allowed all polytechnics, and other higher education institutions which satisfy the necessary criteria, to award their own taught course and research degrees and to adopt the title of university. All the polytechnics and some colleges of higher education have since done so. The change of name does not affect the legal constitution of the institutions. Funding is by the Higher Education Funding Councils for England, Wales and Scotland and directly by the Department for Employment and Learning in Northern Ireland. There are now 106 universities in the UK, up from the 48 which existed prior to the Further and Higher Education Acts 1992. Of the 106, 88 are in England (including the University of London, which has a federal structure), 13 in Wales, 14 in Scotland (including the Open University) and four (including two university colleges) in Northern Ireland. There are also 46 colleges of higher education in the UK, some of which are multidisciplinary while others specialise, for example, in initial teacher training. Some award their own degrees and qualifications, while others are validated by a university or a national body.

GOVERNANCE OF UNIVERSITIES AND COLLEGES

The pre-1992 universities each have their own system of internal governance but broad similarities exist. They are run by a council which is the executive governing body and is responsible for all the affairs of the university including appointments, promotions and bidding for and allocation of financial resources. At least half the members of the council are drawn from outside the university. Many of the council's functions are carried out through committees. The senate reports to the council and deals primarily with academic issues. It consists of the council and members elected from within the university. The 1992 Act, and the Education Reform Act 1988, set out the system of governance for universities which were formerly polytechnics or other higher education institutions and for the colleges of higher education. Each institution has an instrument and articles of government that are approved by the Privy Council. These post-1992 institutions are run by boards of governors, which are responsible for the mission, finances and all appointments. Much of the board's business is delegated to committees. In particular, there is usually an academic board that deals with all matters relating to teaching and research. Most of the newest universities to be created were originally established by Trust Deed and have become incorporated as companies limited by guarantee. Their memorandum and articles of association incorporate the instrument and articles of government and are subject to Privy Council approval.

OPEN UNIVERSITY AND THE UNIVERSITY FOR INDUSTRY

The non-residential Open University provides a modular programme of courses throughout the UK and most of Europe leading to first and higher degrees, diplomas and certificates. Students are taught through distance learning, using written and audio-visual materials and the internet, supported by tutorials and short residential courses. No qualifications are needed for entry at undergraduate level. In 2005–6 the Open University received £201.1m in public funding and there was a total of 156,000 undergraduate students, 19,000 postgraduate students and a further 32,000 students on programmes at other institutions validated by the university. More than 625,000 degrees, certificates and diplomas have been awarded since the university's first students started to study in 1971. Research across a wide range of disciplines feeds directly into the university's teaching. The university has five Centres of Research Excellence – in citizenship, identities and governance; comparative criminological research; computing; education and educational technology; and earth, planetary, space and astronomical research. In addition, it carries out internationally recognised research in geography, design, art history, music, history, literature, pure mathematics, statistics, materials engineering and biological sciences. The university's new open content initative is making educational resources freely available on the internet, with learning support and collaboration tools to connect students and educators.

- the Open University is the UK's largest university, teaching 33 per cent of all part-time undergraduate students in the UK each year
- thirty-four per cent of new OU undergraduate students in the UK have fewer than two A-levels
- the most popular courses (for 2005–6) were an introduction to the social sciences (7,800 students); an introduction to the humanities (5,200); understanding health and social care (4,900); data, computing and information (4,100); and discovering science (3,900)
- the median age of new undergraduate level students is 32
- in 2005–6, more than 30,000 students received financial help in paying their fees.

The University for Industry (Ufi) Ltd operates Learndirect and UK Online network and is the largest government-backed e-learning organisation in the world. Ufi aims to boost people's employability, by helping them gain skills and qualifications, as well as improve organisations' productivity and competitiveness. Through the national network of over 800 Learndirect centres in England and Wales and 6,000 UK Online centres in England, Ufi provides access and support to a range of services from taster and skills-check activities to e-learning courses which are linked to qualifications. In addition, Learndirect careers advice provides free impartial information and advice to people online and over the telephone on more than 900,000 courses nationally from thousands of providers as well as free careers guidance.

ACADEMIC STAFF

Each university and college appoints its own academic staff. The Universities and Colleges Employers Association (UCEA) is the employers' association for subscribing universities and other higher education institutions in the UK. It provides a framework within which representatives of institutions can discuss salaries, conditions of service, employee relations and all matters connected with the employment of staff and employees. The services of the UCEA include collective bargaining and an annual salary survey. Teaching staff in higher education require no formal teaching qualification. However, the Higher Education Academy leads, supports and informs the professional development and recognition of staff in higher education as well as promoting good practice and providing information, advice and resources. Teacher trainers are required to spend a certain amount of time in schools to ensure that they have sufficient recent practical experience.

In the academic year 2005–6 there were 164,665 academic staff in all higher education institutions in the UK, of which 111,410 were full-time. Of these, 70,665 were male and 40,745 were female.

As a result of the National Framework Agreement, staff working in higher education should be, since August 2006, paid on a single national pay scale, which is used as the basis for locally negotiated pay and grading structures. The framework sought to unify pay arrangements as well as address concerns about equal pay. Since August 2006 the 51-point National Pay Spine has ranged from £11,575 to £49,116 and from February 2008, it will start from £12,461 to £52,628.

COURSES

In the UK all universities and some colleges award their own degrees and other qualifications and may act as awarding and validating bodies for colleges. The power to award degrees is regulated by law and it is an offence to purport to award a UK degree unless authorised to do so. The Quality Assurance Agency for Higher Education advises government on applications for degree-awarding powers.

The Quality Assurance Agency for Higher Education (QAA) was established in 1997 and is an independent public body funded by subscriptions from universities and colleges of higher education, and through contracts with the main higher education funding bodies. Its principal role is to safeguard and help to improve the academic standards and quality of higher education. It does this by working with universities and colleges to define standards for higher education, through a framework known as the academic infrastructure, which includes the qualifications frameworks for the United Kingdom. QAA also carries out reviews of higher education institutions against these standards and publishes their outcomes. It advises governments on applications for the grant of degree awarding powers, university title or designation as a higher education institution. QAA is governed by a board, which has overall responsibility for the conduct and strategic direction of its business. The board has 14 members. Four are appointed by the representative bodies of the heads of higher education institutions; four are appointed by the funding bodies in higher education; and six are independent directors who have wide practical experience of industry, commerce, finance or the practice of a profession, and are appointed by the board as a whole. The chair is appointed by the board from among the independent members.

Facilities exist for full-time and part-time study, day release, sandwich or block release. Credit accumulation and transfer systems allow a student to achieve a final qualification by accumulating credits for courses of study successfully achieved, or even professional experience, over a period of time.

Higher education courses comprise: first degree and postgraduate (including research); Diploma in Higher Education (DipHE); BTEC Higher National Diplomas (HND) and Higher National Certificates (HNC); and preparation for professional examinations.

The DipHE is commonly a two-year diploma usually intended to serve as a stepping stone to a degree course or other further study. The DipHE is awarded by the institution itself if it is accredited or by an accredited institution of its choice if it is not. The HNCs are awarded after two years' part-time study. The HNDs are awarded after two years' full-time, or three years' sandwich-course or part-time study.

The foundation degree, launched in 2001, is a two-ar vocational higher education qualification which rms either a self-contained qualification or a basis for rther study leading to an honours degree or further ofessional qualifications.

Undergraduate courses lead to the title of Bachelor, achelor of Arts (BA) and Bachelor of Science (BSc) being e most common, except in certain Scottish universities here Master is sometimes used for a first degree in arts bjects. For a higher degree the titles are Master of Arts 1A), Master of Science (MSc) and the research degrees of aster of Philosophy (MPhil) and Doctor of Philosophy hD or, at a few universities, DPhil).

Most undergraduate courses at universities and colleges higher education run for three years, but some take four ars or longer. Postgraduate studies vary in length.

Post-experience short courses form a significant part of gher education provision, reflecting the demand for ofessional and technical training. Most of these courses nd themselves.

DMISSIONS

he government's target is to increase participation in gher education to 50 per cent of 18- to 30-year-olds by)10. Institutions suffer financial penalties if the number students laid down for them by the funding councils is ceeded, but the individual university or college decides hich students to accept. The formal entry requirements most degree courses are two or more A-levels at grade or above (or equivalent), and to HND courses one A-vel (or equivalent). In practice, most offers of places quire qualifications in excess of this, higher quirements usually reflecting the popularity of a course institution. These requirements do not, however, clude applications from students with a variety of non-CSE qualifications or unquantified experience and skills.

For admission to a degree, DipHE or HND, potential udents apply through UCAS, the organisation sponsible for managing applications to higher education ourses in the UK. UCAS operates an online application stem and provides services to applicants, advisory rvices, schools, colleges and universities and facilitates d promotes access to higher education. Application rvices exist across a range of subject areas and for UK iversities and colleges. More than 500,000 people anting to study at a university or college of higher lucation use the service each year and 100,000 of them e the specialist services: the Graduate Teacher Training egistry (GTTR) and the Conservatoires UK Admissions ervice (CUKAS). The Open University conducts its own lmissions. Details of initial teacher training courses in otland can be obtained from those universities offering ich courses, from Universities Scotland, and from the ebsite created by the Scottish Executive to promote aching: W www.teachinginscotland.com.

For admission as a postgraduate student, universities id colleges normally require a good first degree in a sub-ct related to the proposed course of study or research. pplications can be made to individual institutions, xcept for teaching and social work. There is also now an ternative to applying to postgraduate courses; UKPASS an online application service created by UCAS. It was t up in 2007 following demand from the higher lucation sector to have a centralised admissions service at would not only help institutions to monitor their pplicants but would also enable them to get to know ore about this particular group, which is the fastest rowing sector of the UK higher education marketplace.

FEES AND GRANTS

FEES FOR FULL TIME STUDENTS IN 2007–8

The Higher Education Act 2004 introduced variable tuition fees for full time higher education courses at English and Welsh institutions, and these came into effect for courses starting in September 2006 or later. In Northern Ireland variable tuition fees were introduced under the Higher Education (Northern Ireland) Order 2005. Fees are capped at £3,000 subject only to inflationary increases until 2010. In the academic year 2006–7 the maximum an institution could charge new students was £3,000 a year, and in 2007–8 this rose to £3,070.

However, students who started their course before September 2006 would still be treated under the old student finance regime and make an annual contribution to their tuition fees depending on their own level of income and that of their household. In 2006 this was up to a maximum of £1,200 and in 2007 this could be up to £1,225 (There are a few exceptions to these rules; for example gap year students who started their course in September 2006 instead of September 2005).

From September 2006 no student – no matter when they started – has to pay tuition fees before they start their course or whilst they are studying as student loans for tuition fees are available (*see* below). These cover the full amount of any fees charged.

Welsh Higher Education institutions also charge fees (up to £3,070 in 2007–8). Students who normally live in Wales (and EU students) are entitled to a fee grant up to a maximum of £1,845.

ENGLAND

The following table gives a brief breakdown of what help is available to full time higher education students in England in 2007–8:

Type of support	*Old system students**	*New system students†*
Student loan for tuition fees	Yes	Yes
Student loan for maintenance	Yes	Yes
Extra help for disabled students	Yes	Yes
Extra help for students with dependents	Yes	Yes
Help towards tuition fees	Yes	No
Higher education grant	Yes	No
Maintenance (or special support) grant	No	Yes
Access to learning fund (from institutions)	Yes	Yes

* Old system students are on higher education courses living in England who started (or are treated as starting) their course before September 2006

† New system students are on higher education courses which began in September 2006 or after

A maintenance grant of up to £2,765 to help with living costs is available to new system students only. Any amount due is assessed on income and does not have to be repaid. The full grant is available to students living with a household income lower than £17,910. Partial grants are available for household incomes up to £38,300. For students entitled to benefits, maintenance grants could be replaced by a non-repayable special support grant which will not affect Department for Work and Pensions benefit entitlement.

REPAYMENT OF STUDENT LOANS

Repayment of both student loans for maintenance and student loans for tuition fees does not start until the April after the student has left their course and is earning more than £15,000 a year. Repayments are calculated at 9 per cent of income over the threshold of £15,000, so someone earning £18,000 would pay back around £5.19 a week. If income falls below the threshold, repayments cease until income rises above it again. Those who pay tax through PAYE have repayments deducted from their salaries, whilst the self-employed make repayments through their tax returns.

PART TIME HIGHER EDUCATION STUDENTS

Part-time higher education students on courses in England that are at least 50 per cent of an equivalent full-time course may be entitled to a grant towards their fees, and a grant towards their course costs. This help does not have to be repaid, and entitlement to the fee grant and the course grant depends on the student's income and that of their husband, wife or partner. Students who already have a degree cannot usually apply for this support.

For 2007–8, there are three different rates of fee grant depending on how intensive the course undertaken is:

Course intensity	*Maximum fee grant*
50–59 per cent of a full time course	£750
60–74 per cent of a full time course	£900
75 per cent or more of a full time course	£1,125

For 2007–8 the maximum course grant is £250 and does not depend on the intensity of the course. Students who receive the part-time grant for fees, but whose tuition fees are more than the amount of support available may be eligible for extra help from their institution. Part-time students with disabilities may be eligible for disabled students allowances.

WALES

Since 2007, students who started in 2006 and 2007 have been charged a deferred flexible fee of up to £3,070. However, students who normally live in Wales and study at a university or college in Wales can apply for a fee grant of up to £1,845 a year which does not have to be repaid. This tuition fee grant is available regardless of family income and is paid directly to the place of study. Since September 2006 eligible full-time undergraduate students who live in Wales have not had to pay fees before starting their course or whilst they are studying. Instead, a student loan for fees can be taken out, which does not have to be repaid until the course is finished and earnings are over £15,000 a year.

Other aspects of Student Finance Wales student support arrangements for 2007 starters include:

- an assembly learning grant worth up to £2,765 for eligible students from low income households
- all eligible students can also apply for a student loan for maintenance of up to £6,320 to help with living costs

Students who normally live in Wales but choose to study elsewhere in the UK will be charged fees according to the fee regime of the country in which they study and that set by the institution. Student Finance Wales will provide a loan to defer this fee but students who live in Wales and are studying elsewhere in the UK will not be entitled to the fee grant.

Fee levels in Wales are the same for students wh normally live elsewhere in the UK and began studying Wales in the academic year 2006–7. However, the students are not eligible to receive Student Finance Wal services. A national bursary scheme is planned for Wale to commence in the academic year 2007–8. Eligib students will receive a bursary of around £305, which wi be additional to other support received and will not b offset by any reductions in other forms of support.

SCOTLAND

The arrangements for Scottish students in Scotland fro 2008 are as follows:

Tuition fees – tuition fee contributions have bee abolished for all eligible full-time Scottish domiciled an EU students studying in Scotland.

Student Loans – living cost support is mainly provide through a means-tested student loan. An additional loa of £560 is available to young students from low incom backgrounds.

Bursaries – the young students' bursary (YSB) available to young students from low-incom backgrounds. It is non-repayable and reduces the level debt which eligible students accrue during a course study. In 2007–8 the maximum annual support provide through YSB is £2,510.

SUPPLEMENTARY GRANTS

Depending on eligibility, students in Scotland may als receive: the adult dependants grant; the lone paren grant; childcare fund support; travel costs; the disable students allowance; the basic allowance; the speci equipment allowance; and non-medical personal help.

HARDSHIP FUNDS

Students who are experiencing particular financi difficulty can apply for assistance from their institution hardship funds.

NORTHERN IRELAND

The arrangements for Northern Ireland are very similar t those for England with these differences:

- the maintenance grant is worth up to £3,265
- the higher education bursary is up to £2,000
- the access to learning fund is known as the suppo fund in Northern Ireland and is allocated by centr government directly to the institution

POSTGRADUATE AWARDS

In general, postgraduate students do not qualify fo mandatory support (including student loans and tuitio fee assistance). An exception to this is the PGCE.

Awards for postgraduate courses are the responsibilit of the Research Councils, depending on the field of stud Research Councils are independent bodies and make thei own decisions about expenditure on postgraduate suppo according to the resources available to them. The fact tha a course lies within its remit does not oblige the Researc Councils to support every or indeed any student applyin for awards.

It is for institutions to decide the level of their fees. Th government is raising the levels of award available t postgraduates under the competitive merit-based syster provided by the Research Councils: the minimum PhI stipend will be £12,600 in 2007–8.

Targeted support is also available to meet particula needs: postgraduate students can apply through thei colleges for discretionary help from the access to learnin nd. Disabled students allowances are also available to igible students undertaking postgraduate study.

There is support available to students in Scotland for ›stgraduate study through the Postgraduate Students' llowances Scheme (PSAS), which is administered by the udent Awards Agency for Scotland (SAAS). Eligible udents can apply for an award consisting of a means sted maintenance grant and payment of tuition fees. ourses supported under PSAS are generally nine-month-ng, taught postgraduate diploma courses on largely cational subjects. Awards from PSAS are discretionary, ɔt mandatory, so there is no guarantee of an award at ›stgraduate level.

There is support available to students who wish to ɪrsue postgraduate study in Northern Ireland (at either ueen's University of Belfast or University of Ulster). All udents should apply to the university for an application rm. Students should apply for a place on the course and r an award. As there are always more applicants than vards, not all applicants who secure a place on the urses will be successful in obtaining an award. *See also* esearch Councils section

IFELONG LEARNING

the UK, the duty of securing adult and continuing lucation leading to academic or vocational qualifications statutory. The Learning and Skills Council (LSC) in ngland, the Welsh Assembly Government and the cottish Funding Council are responsible for and fund ose courses which take place in their sector and lead to :ademic and vocational qualifications, prepare students undertake further or higher education courses, or ›nfer basic skills; the Higher Education Funding ouncils fund advanced courses of continuing education. ɔcal authorities have the power, although not the duty, provide those courses which do not fall within the mit of the funding bodies. In Northern Ireland the epartment for Employment and Learning is responsible r the funding of the statutory further education sector.

In January 2007 Lord Leitch delivered his interim port into skills. This showed that England lags behind :her major economies in terms of skills development. he LSC is working together with the government to ise the nation's skills levels and increase the numbers of lults gaining Level 2 and higher qualifications. The LSC responsible for funding and planning provision for ›prenticeships, adult learning, offender learning and :ills, Train to Gain, Basic Skills and leisure learning. It orks closely with employers providing vocational lucation and work based learning. Twelve new national :ills academies are to be opened this year in sectors cluding manufacturing, retail and financial services. rain to Gain provides employers with free and bsidised training for their employees and also provides em with independent advice and guidance via an npartial skills brokerage service. There are currently over 50,000 apprentices working in over 80 subject areas and e LSC has been challenged by government to double is figure to 500,000. In the summer of 2006, the LSC ok over responsibility for offender learning across ngland. The LSC also provides several learner support nds to support those learners who cannot afford to ›ntinue in education or training. These include lucation maintenance allowances (EMA) for young eople, the Care2Learn scheme for young parents and lult learning grants.

Of the many voluntary bodies providing adult lucation, the biggest is the Workers' Educational Association (WEA), which operates throughout England and Scotland to provide over 14,000 courses each year, reaching more than 95,000 adults. The WEA is a charity supported by funding from the LSC in England, and by the Scottish Executive and local authorities in Scotland. Similar but separate organisations operate in Wales and Northern Ireland: Coleg Harlech WEA (covering North Wales), WEA South Wales and WEA Northern Ireland. The National Institute of Adult Continuing Education, has a broad remit to promote lifelong learning opportunities for adults.

NIACE Dysgu Cymru, the Welsh committee, receives financial support from the National Assembly for Wales and support in kind from local authorities, and advises government, voluntary bodies and education providers on adult continuing education and training matters in Wales. In Scotland, policy responsibility for community learning and development lies with Learning Connections and the Directorate General for Education of the Scottish Executive. In Northern Ireland, those functions are undertaken by the Department for Employment and Learning.

CONTACTS

APPRENTICESHIPS **T** 0800-015 0600
W www.apprenticeships.co.uk

COUNCIL FOR THE CURRICULUM EXAMINATIONS AND ASSESSMENT (NORTHERN IRELAND) **T** 028-9026 1200 **W** www.ccea.org.uk

DEPARTMENT FOR CHILDREN, SCHOOLS AND FAMILIES (ENGLAND) **T** 0870-000 2288
W www.dcsf.gov.uk

DEPARTMENT FOR EDUCATION NORTHERN IRELAND **T** 028-9127 9279 **W** www.deni.gov.uk

DEPARTMENT FOR EMPLOYMENT AND LEARNING NORTHERN IRELAND **T** 028 9025 7777
W www.delni.gov.uk

DEPARTMENT FOR INNOVATION, UNIVERSITIES AND SKILLS (ENGLAND) **T** 0870-001 0336
W www.dius.gov.uk

DIPLOMAS **T** 0870 000 2288 **W** www.dfes.gov.uk/14-19

EDUCATION DEPARTMENT, SCOTTISH EXECUTIVE **T** 0845-345 4745
W www.teachinginscotland.com

EDUCATION OTHERWISE **T** 0870-730 0074
W www.education-otherwise.org

EDUCATION AND TRAINING INSPECTORATE (NORTHERN IRELAND) **T** 028-9127 9726
W www.etini.gov.uk

EUROPEAN SOCIAL FUND **W** www.esf.gov.uk

GENERAL TEACHING COUNCIL FOR ENGLAND **T** 08700-010 308
W www.gtce.org.uk

GENERAL TEACHING COUNCIL FOR NORTHERN IRELAND **T** 028-9033 3390 **W** www.gtcni.org.uk

GENERAL TEACHING COUNCIL FOR SCOTLAND
T 0131-314 6000 **W** www.gtcs.org.uk

GENERAL TEACHING COUNCIL FOR WALES
T 029-2055 0350 **W** www.gtcw.org.uk

HER MAJESTY'S CHIEF INSPECTOR OF EDUCATION AND TRAINING IN WALES
T 029-2044 6446 **W** www.estyn.gov.uk

HER MAJESTY'S INSPECTORATE OF EDUCATION IN SCOTLAND **T** 01506-600200 **W** www.hmie.gov.uk

HIGHER EDUCATION ACADEMY **T** 01904-717500
W www.heacademy.ac.uk

HIGHER EDUCATION FUNDING COUNCIL FOR ENGLAND **T** 0117-931 7317 **W** www.hefce.ac.uk

HIGHER EDUCATION FUNDING COUNCIL FOR WALES T 029-2076 1861 W www.hefcw.ac.uk
HOME EDUCATION ADVISORY SERVICE T 01707-371854 W www.heas.org.uk
INTERNATIONAL BACCALAUREATE ORGANISATION T (+41) (22) 791 7740 W www.ibo.org
LEARNING AND SKILLS COUNCIL (ENGLAND) T 0845-019 4170 W www.lsc.gov.uk
LEARNING AND TEACHING SCOTLAND T 08700-100 297 W www.ltscotland.org.uk
NATIONAL ASSESSMENT AGENCY T 0870-0600 622 W www.naa.org.uk
NATIONAL INSTITUTE OF ADULT CONTINUING EDUCATION T 0116-204 4200 W www.niace.org.uk
OFFICE FOR STANDARDS IN EDUCATION, CHILDREN'S SERVICES AND SKILLS (ENGLAND) T 08456-404045 W www.ofsted.gov.uk
OPEN UNIVERSITY T 0870-333 4340 W www.open.ac.uk
PROFESSIONAL QUALIFICATION FOR HEADSHIP (NORTHERN IRELAND) T 028-9061 8121 W www.rtuni.org/pqhni.cfm
QUALITY ASSURANCE AGENCY T 0141-572 3420 W www.qaa.ac.uk
QUALIFICATIONS AND CURRICULUM AUTHORITY T 020-7509 5556 W www.qca.org.uk
SCOTTISH EXECUTIVE T 08457-741 741 W www.scotland.gov.uk
SCOTTISH FUNDING COUNCIL T 0131-313 6500 W www.sfc.ac.uk
SCOTTISH QUALIFICATION FOR HEADSHIP T 0131-651 6179 W www.sqh.ed.ac.uk
SCOTTISH QUALIFICATIONS AUTHORITY T 0845-279 1000 W www.sqa.org.uk
STUDENT AWARDS AGENCY FOR SCOTLAND T 0845-111 1711 W www.student-support-saas.gov.uk
STUDENT FINANCE DIRECT T 0845-607 7577 W www.studentsupportdirect.co.uk
STUDENT FINANCE WALES T 0845-602 8845 W www.studentfinancewales.co.uk
SURE START T 0870-000 2288 W www.surestart.gov.uk
TRAINING AND DEVELOPMENT AGENCY FOR SCHOOLS T 020-7023 8001 W www.tda.gov.uk
UCAS T 0871-468 0468 W www.ucas.com
UNIVERSITIES AND COLLEGES EMPLOYERS ASSOCIATION T 020-7383 2444 W www.ucea.ac.uk
UNIVERSITY FOR INDUSTRY T 0114-291 5000 W www.ufi.com
WELSH ASSEMBLY T 0845-010 5500 W www.wales.gov.uk
WORKERS' EDUCATION ASSOCIATION T 020-7426 3450 W www.wea.org.uk

.OCAL EDUCATION AUTHORITIES

·NGLAND

·OUNTY COUNCILS

·DFORDSHIRE Children's Services, County Hall, Cauldwell Street, Bedford MK42 9AP **T** 01234-363222 **E** education@bedscc.gov.uk **W** www.bedfordshire.gov.uk
Director, Malcolm Newsam

·JCKINGHAMSHIRE Children's Services, County Hall, Walton Street, Aylesbury HP20 1UA **T** 01296-395000 **E** simbriano@buckscc.gov.uk **W** www.buckscc.gov.uk
Director, Sue Imbriano

·MBRIDGESHIRE Children and Young People's Services, ELH 1000, Castle Court, Shire Hall, Cambridge CB3 0AP **T** 01223-717970 **E** elh.webmaster@cambridgeshire.gov.uk **W** www.cambridgeshire.gov.uk
Deputy Chief Executive, Gordon Jeyes

·IESHIRE Children's Services, County Hall, Chester CH1 1SQ **T** 01244-602201 **W** www.cheshire.gov.uk
Director, Joan Feenan

·)RNWALL Children, Young People and Families, New County Hall, Treyew Road, Truro TR1 3AY **T** 01872-322003 **E** childrenservices@cornwall.gov.uk **W** www.cornwall.gov.uk
Director, Dean Ashton

·JMBRIA Children's Services Department, 5 Portland Square, Carlisle CA1 1PU **T** 01228-606877 **E** education@cumbriacc.gov.uk **W** www.cumbria.gov.uk/education
Corporate Director, Moira Swann

·:RBYSHIRE Children and Younger Adults Department, County Hall, Matlock DE4 3AG **T** 01629-585814 **W** www.derbyshire.gov.uk
Strategic Director, Bruce Buckley

·:VON Children and Young People's Services, County Hall, Topsham Road, Exeter EX2 4QG **T** 01392-382000 **E** edmail@devon.gov.uk **W** www.devon.gov.uk
Director, Anne Whiteley

·)RSET Children's Services, County Hall, Dorchester DT1 1XJ **T** 01305-251000 **W** www.dorsetforyou.com
Director, Stephen Prewett

·JRHAM Children and Young People's Services, County Hall, Durham DH1 5UL **T** 0191-383 3000 **W** www.durham.gov.uk
Corporate Director, David Williams

·ST SUSSEX Children's Services, County Hall, St Anne's Crescent, Lewes BN7 1SG **T** 01273-481000 **E** childrenservices@eastsussex.gov.uk **W** www.eastsussex.gov.uk
Director, Matt Dunkley

SEX Children and Young People, County Hall, Market Road, Chelmsford CM1 1QH **T** 0845-603 7627 **W** www.essexcc.gov.uk
Director, Carey Bennet

·.OUCESTERSHIRE Children and Young People's Services, Shire Hall, Westgate Street, Gloucester GL1 2TG **T** 01452-425000 **W** www.gloucestershire.gov.uk
Group Director, Jo Davidson

·MPSHIRE Children's Services, County Office, The Castle, Winchester SO23 8UG **T** 01962-846452 **E** children.services.enquiries@hants.gov.uk **W** www.hants.gov.uk/education
Director, John Coughlan

HERTFORDSHIRE Children, Schools and Families, County Hall, Pegs Lane, Hertford SG13 8DQ **T** 01438-737500 **W** www.hertsdirect.org
Director, John Harris

KENT Children, Families and Education, Sessions House, County Hall, Maidstone ME14 1XQ **T** 01622-671411 **W** www.kent.gov.uk
Managing Director, Graham Badman

LANCASHIRE Children's Services, PO Box 61, County Hall, Preston PR1 8RJ **T** 01772-531854 **W** www.lancashire.gov.uk
Executive Director, Pat Jefferson

LEICESTERSHIRE Children and Young People's Service, County Hall, Glenfield, LE3 8RA **T** 0116-265 6631 **E** childrensservices@leics.gov.uk **W** www.leics.gov.uk
Director, Gareth Williams

LINCOLNSHIRE Children's Services, County Offices, Newland, Lincoln LN1 1YQ **T** 01522-552222 **W** www.lincolnshire.gov.uk **E** customer_services@lincolnshire.gov.uk
Director, Mr P. Duxbury

NORFOLK Children's Services, County Hall, Martineau Lane, Norwich NR1 2DH **T** 0844-800 8001 **E** information@norfolk.gov.uk **W** www.norfolk.gov.uk
Director, Lisa Christensen

NORTHAMPTONSHIRE Children and Young People's Service, PO Box 93, County Hall, Northampton NN1 1AN **T** 01604-237619 **E** citizensfirst@northamptonshire.gov.uk **W** www.northamptonshire.gov.uk
Director, Andrew Sortwell

NORTHUMBERLAND Children's Services, County Hall, Morpeth NE61 2EF **T** 01670-533000 **E** childrensservices@northumberland.gov.uk **W** www.northumberland.gov.uk
Executive Director, Trevor Doughty

NORTH YORKSHIRE Children and Young People's Service, County Hall, Northallerton DL7 8AE **T** 01609-780780 **E** cyp@northyorks.gov.uk **W** www.northyorks.gov.uk
Director, Cynthia Welbourn, FRSA

NOTTINGHAMSHIRE Children and Young People's Services, County Hall, West Bridgford, Nottingham NG2 7QP **T** 0115-982 3823 **E** communications.cyp@nottsc.gov.uk **W** www.nottinghamshire.gov.uk
Director, Dr Robert Garnett

OXFORDSHIRE Children, Young People and Families, Macclesfield House, New Road, Oxford OX1 1NA **T** 01865-815449 **E** learning@oxfordshire.gov.uk **W** www.oxfordshire.gov.uk
Director, Janet Tomlinson

SHROPSHIRE Children and Young People, The Shirehall, Abbey Foregate, Shrewsbury SY2 6ND **T** 01743-254307 **E** children&youngpeople@shropshire-cc.gov.uk **W** www.shropshire.gov.uk
Director, Liz Nicholson

SOMERSET Education Service, County Hall, Taunton TA1 4DY **T** 0845-345 9122 **W** www.somerset.gov.uk
Corporate Director, David Taylor

STAFFORDSHIRE Children and Lifelong Learning, Tipping Street, Stafford ST16 2DH **T** 01785-223121 **E** education@staffordshire.gov.uk **W** www.staffordshire.gov.uk
Corporate Director, Peter Traves

SUFFOLK Children and Young People, Endeavour House, Russell Road, Ipswich IP1 2BX T 01473-583000 W www.suffolk.gov.uk
Director, Rosalind Turner

SURREY Services for Families, County Hall, Penrhyn Road, Kingston upon Thames KT1 2DJ T 0845-600 9009 W www.surreycc.gov.uk
Strategic Director, Andrew Webster

WARWICKSHIRE Children, Young People and Families, 22 Northgate Street, Warwick CV34 4SP T 01926-410410 E edcomms@warwickshire.gov.uk W www.warwickshire.gov.uk
Strategic Director, Marion Davis

WEST SUSSEX Children and Young People's Services, County Hall, Chichester PO19 1RQ T 0845-075 1007 E cyps@westsussex.gov.uk W www.westsussex.gov.uk
Director, Robert Back

WILTSHIRE Children, Education and Libraries, County Hall, Bythesea Road, Trowbridge BA14 8JB T 01225-713000 E directorcel@wiltshire.gov.uk W www.wiltshire.gov.uk
Director, Carolyn Godfrey

WORCESTERSHIRE Children's Services Directorate, PO Box 73, Worcester WR5 2YA T 01905-763763 W www.worcestershire.gov.uk
Director, Richard Hubbard

UNITARY AND METROPOLITAN BOROUGH COUNCILS

BARNSLEY Directorate for Children, Young People and Families, Berneslai Close, Barnsley S70 2HS T 01226-773500 E education@barnsley.gov.uk W www.barnsley.gov.uk
Executive Director, E. Sutton

BATH AND NORTH EAST SOMERSET Children's Services, PO Box 25, Riverside, Temple Street, Keynsham BS31 1DN T 01225-477000 E children's_services@bathnes.gov.uk W www.bathnes.gov.uk
Director, Ashley Ayre

BIRMINGHAM Children, Young People and Families, Room 183, Council House Extension, Margaret Street, Birmingham B3 3BU T 0121-303 3541 W www.bgfl.org
Strategic Director, Tony Howell

BLACKBURN WITH DARWEN Children's Services, Town Hall, Blackburn BB1 7DY T 01254-585585 W www.blackburn.gov.uk
Director, Peter Morgan

BLACKPOOL Children and Young People's Department, Progress House, Clifton Road, Blackpool FY4 4US T 01253-477668 E social.services@blackpool.gov.uk W www.blackpool.gov.uk
Director, David Lund

BOLTON Children's Services, Paderborn House, Civic Centre, Bolton BL1 1JW T 01204-333333 E ea.strategy@bolton.gov.uk W www.boltonlea.org.uk
Director, Margaret Asquith

BOURNEMOUTH Children's Services, Dorset House, 20–22 Christchurch Road, Bournemouth BH1 3NL T 01202-456219 E cs@bournemouth.gov.uk W www.bournemouth.gov.uk
Corporate Director, J. Portman

BRACKNELL FOREST Education, Children's Services and Libraries, Seymour House, 38 Broadway, Bracknell RG12 1AU T 01344-354000 E ecsl@bracknell-forest.gov.uk W www.bracknell-forest.gov.uk
Director, T. Eccleston

BRADFORD Education Bradford, Future House, Bolling Road, Bradford BD4 7EB T 01274-385500 E feedback@educationbradford.com W www.educationbradford.com
Managing Director, John Gaskin

BRIGHTON AND HOVE Children and Young People's Trust, Kings House, Grand Avenue, Hove BN3 2LS T 01273-290000 E cis@brighton-hove.gov.uk W www.brighton-hove.gov.uk
Director of Children's Services, David Hawker

BRISTOL Children and Young People's Services, The Council House, College Green, Bristol BS99 7EB T 0117-903 7900 W www.bristol-cyps.org.uk
Director, Heather Tomlinson

BURY Children's Services, Athenaeum House, Market Street, Bury BL9 0BN T 0161-253 5652 E children.services@bury.gov.uk W www.bury.gov.uk
Executive Director, Eleni Ioannides

CALDERDALE Children and Young People's Services, Town Hall, Halifax HX1 1UJ T 01422-392500 E customer.first@calderdale.gov.uk W www.calderdale.gov.uk
Group Director, Carol White

COVENTRY Children, Learning and Young People's Directorate, Civic Centre 1, Earl Street, Coventry CV1 5RS T 024-7683 1500 W www.coventry.gov.uk
Director, Colin Green

DARLINGTON Children's Services, Town Hall, Darlington DL1 5QT T 01325-380651 E education.feedback@darlington.gov.uk W www.darlington.gov.uk
Director, Murry Rose

DERBY Children and Young People, Middleton House, 27 St Mary's Gate, Derby DE1 3NN T 01332-716924 E education@derby.gov.uk W www.derby.gov.uk
Corporate Director, A. Flack

DONCASTER Children's Services, PO Box 251, Council House, College Road, Doncaster DN1 3AD T 01302-737777 E general.enquiries@doncaster.gov.uk W www.doncaster.gov.uk
Director, Tom Common

DUDLEY Children's Services, Westox House, 1 Trinity Road, Dudley DY1 1JQ T 01384-818181 E director.children@dudley.gov.uk W www.dudley.gov.uk
Director, John Freeman

EAST RIDING OF YORKSHIRE Children, Family and Adult Services, County Hall, Beverley HU17 9BA T 01482-392020 E june.leech@eastriding.gov.uk W www.eastriding.gov.uk
Director, Andrew Williams

GATESHEAD Learning and Children, Civic Centre, Regent Street, Gateshead NE8 1HH T 0191-433 3000 E enquiries@gateshead.gov.uk W www.gateshead.gov.uk
Director, Maggie Atkinson

HALTON Children and Young People, Grosvenor House, Halton Lea, Runcorn WA7 2ED T 0151-907 8300 W www.halton.gov.uk
Strategic Director, Gerald Meehan

HARTLEPOOL Children's Services, Civic Centre, Victoria Road, Hartlepool TS24 8AY T 01429-266522 E children@hartlepool.gov.uk W www.hartlepool.gov.uk
Director, Adrienne Simcock

HEREFORDSHIRE Children and Young People's Directorate, PO Box 185, Blackfriars Street, Hereford HR4 9ZR T 01432-260900 E education@herefordshire.gov.uk W www.education.herefordshire.gov.uk
Director, S. Menghini

KINGSTON UPON HULL Children and Young People's Services, Essex House, Manor Street, Kingston upon Hull HU1 1YD T 01482-613007 E childrenandyoungpeople@hullcc.gov.uk W www.hullcc.gov.uk
Director, Nigel Richardson

RKLEES Children and Young People Service, Oldgate House, 2 Oldgate, Huddersfield HD1 6QW T 01484-225242 E chyps@kirklees.gov.uk W www.kirklees.gov.uk
Director, Alison O'Sullivan

NOWSLEY Children's Services, Education Offices, Huyton Hey Road, Huyton L36 5YH T 0151-443 3232 W www.knowsley.gov.uk
Executive Director, Damian Allen

EDS Education Leeds, 10th Floor East, 110 Merrion Centre, Leeds LS2 8DT T 0113-247 5590 E educ.info@educationleeds.co.uk W www.educationleeds.co.uk
Chief Executive, Chris Edwards

ICESTER Children and Young People's Services, Marlborough House, 38 Welford Road, Leicester LE2 7AA T 0116-252 7807 W www.leicester.gov.uk
Corporate Director, Sheila Lock

VERPOOL Education and Lifelong Learning, Municipal Buildings, Dale Street, Liverpool L2 2DH T 0151-233 3000 W www.liverpool.gov.uk
Executive Director, Colin Hilton

JTON Children and Learning, Unity House, 111 Stuart Street, Luton LU1 5NP T 01582-548005 E feedback@luton.gov.uk W www.luton.gov.uk
Corporate Director, T. Dessent

ANCHESTER Children's Services, Overseas House, Quay Street, Manchester M3 3BB T 0161-234 5000 E education.enquiries@manchester.gov.uk W www.manchester.gov.uk/education
Director, Pauline Newman

EDWAY Children's Services, Civic Centre, Strood, Rochester ME2 4AU T 01634-306000 E childrens.services@medway.gov.uk W www.medway.gov.uk
Director, Rose Collinson

IDDLESBROUGH Children, Families and Learning, PO Box 69, Vancouver House, Gurney Street TS1 1EL T 01642-728301 E jan_douglas@middlesbrough.gov.uk W www.middlesbrough.gov.uk
Interim Executive Director, Jan Douglas

ILTON KEYNES Learning and Development Directorate, Saxon Court, Avebury Boulevard, Milton Keynes MK9 3HS T 01908-691691 W www.mkweb.co.uk
Group Director, School Improvement and Planning, David Gamble

EWCASTLE UPON TYNE Children's Services, Civic Centre, Newcastle upon Tyne NE99 2BN T 0191-232 8520 E education.directorate@newcastle.gov.uk W www.newcastle.gov.uk
Executive Director, Catherine Fitt

ORTH EAST LINCOLNSHIRE Children's Services, Municipal Offices, Town Hall Square, Grimsby DN31 1HU T 01472-323021 W www.nelincs.gov.uk
Executive Director, Andrew Samson

ORTH LINCOLNSHIRE Education, Learning and Achievement Service, PO Box 35, Hewson House, Station Road, Brigg DN20 8XJ T 01724-297240 E suzanne.watson@northlincs.gov.uk W www.northlincs.gov.uk
Head, D. Lea

ORTH SOMERSET Children and Young People's Services, Town Hall, Weston-super-Mare BS23 1UJ T 01934-888888 E colin.diamond@n-somerset.gov.uk W www.n-somerset.gov.uk
Director, Colin Diamond

ORTH TYNESIDE Education Services, Stephenson House, Stephenson Street, North Shields NE30 1QA T 0191-200 5006 E gill.alexander@northtyneside.gov.uk W www.northtyneside.gov.uk
Director, Gill Alexander

NOTTINGHAM Children's Services, Sandfield Centre, Sandfield Road, Nottingham NG7 1HQ T 0115-915 0800 E education@lea.nottinghamcity.gov.uk W www.nottinghamcity.gov.uk
Director, Edwina Grant

OLDHAM Children, Young People and Families, Civic Centre, West Street, Oldham OL1 1XJ T 0161-770 4260 E general.enquiry@oldham.gov.uk W www.oldham.gov.uk
Executive Director, Ruth M. Baldwin

PETERBOROUGH Children's Services, Bayard Place, Broadway, Peterborough PE1 1FB T 01733-748444 E leonie.owens@peterborough.gov.uk W www.thelearningcity.co.uk
Director, Mohammed Mehmet

PLYMOUTH Children's Services, Windsor House, Plymouth PL1 2AA T 01752-307400 E childrens.services@plymouth.gov.uk W www.plymouth.gov.uk
Director, Bronwen Lacey

POOLE Children's Services, Civic Centre, Sandbanks Road, Poole BH15 2RU T 01202-633633 E enquiries@boroughofpoole.com W www.boroughofpoole.com
Strategic Director, John Nash

PORTSMOUTH Children, Families and Learning, Civic Offices, Guildhall Square, Portsmouth PO1 2AL T 023-9284 1202 W www.portsmouth.gov.uk
Strategic Director, Lynda Fisher

READING Education and Children's Services, Civic Centre, Reading RG1 7WA T 0118-939 0900 W www.reading.gov.uk
Director, Anna Wright

REDCAR AND CLEVELAND Children's Services, Redcar and Cleveland House, Kirkleatham Street, Redcar TS10 1YA T 01642-441121 E contactus@redcar-cleveland.gov.uk W www.redcar-cleveland.gov.uk
Director, Jenny Lewis

ROCHDALE Children's Services, Municipal Offices, Smith Street, Rochdale OL16 1YD T 01706-924 7474 E education@rochdale.gov.uk W www.rochdale.gov.uk
Executive Director, Terry Piggott

ROTHERHAM Children and Young People's Services, Norfolk House, Walker Place, Rotherham S65 1AS T 01709-382121 E education@rotherham.gov.uk W www.rotherham.gov.uk
Strategic Director, Sonia Sharp

ROYAL BOROUGH OF WINDSOR AND MAIDENHEAD Education Department, Town Hall, St Ives Road, Maidenhead SL6 1RF T 01628-798888 E jim.gould@rbwm.gov.uk W www.rbwm.gov.uk
Director of Learning and Care, Jim Gould

RUTLAND Children and Young People's Services, Catmose, Oakham LE15 6HP T 01572-722577 E enquiries@rutland.gov.uk W www.rutland.gov.uk
Director, Carol Chambers

SALFORD Children's Services, Minerva House, Pendlebury Road, Swinton M27 4EQ T 0161-778 0123 E sue.atkinson@salford.gov.uk W www.salford.gov.uk
Director, Jill Baker

SANDWELL Education and Children's Services, Shaftesbury House, 402 High Street, West Bromwich B70 9LT T 0121-569 2200 E education@sandwell.gov.uk W www.sandwell.gov.uk
Executive Director, Roger Crouch

SEFTON Children's Services, 9th Floor, Merton House, Stanley Road, Bootle L20 3JA T 0845-140 0845

W www.sefton.gov.uk
Director, Bryn Marsh

SHEFFIELD Children and Young People's Service, Town Hall, Pinstone Street, Sheffield S1 2HH T 0114-273 5722 E cypdinformation@sheffield.gov.uk W www.sheffield.gov.uk
Executive Director, Jonathan Crossley-Holland

SLOUGH Education and Children's Services, Town Hall, Bath Road, Slough SL1 3UQ T 01753-875700 E edhelp@slough.gov.uk W www.slough.gov.uk
Strategic Director, Janet Tomlinson

SOLIHULL Education and Children's Services, PO Box 20, Council House, Homer Road B91 9QU T 0121-704 6000 E childrensservices@solihull.gov.uk W www.solihull.gov.uk
Corporate Director, Mark Rogers

SOUTHAMPTON Children's Services and Learning, Frobisher House, Nelson Gate, Commercial Road, Southampton SO15 1BZ T 023-8083 3466 E education.enquiries@southampton.gov.uk W www.southampton.gov.uk
Executive Director, Clive Webster

SOUTHEND-ON-SEA Department of Children and Learning, Civic Centre, Victoria Avenue, Southend-on-Sea SS2 6ER T 01702-215000 W www.southend.gov.uk
Corporate Director, Paul Greenhalgh

SOUTH GLOUCESTERSHIRE Children and Young People, Bowling Hill, Chipping Sodbury BS37 6JX T 01454-868008 E educ_service@southglos.gov.uk W www.southglos.gov.uk
Director, Therese Gillespie

SOUTH TYNESIDE Lifelong Learning and Leisure, Town Hall and Civic Offices, Westoe Road, South Shields NE33 2RL T 0191-427 1717 W www.southtyneside.info
Executive Director, Kim Bromley-Derry

ST HELENS Children and Young People's Service, Rivington Centre, Rivington Road, St Helens WA10 4ND T 01744-455328 W www.sthelens.gov.uk
Director, Susan Richardson

STOCKPORT Children and Young People's Directorate, Town Hall, Stockport SK1 3XE T 0161-474 3813 E cypd@stockport.gov.uk W www.stockport.gov.uk
Corporate Director, Andrew Webb

STOCKTON-ON-TEES Children, Education and Social Care, Municipal Buildings, Church Road, Stockton-on-Tees TS18 1LD T 01642-393939 W www.stockton.gov.uk
Director, Ann Baxter

STOKE-ON-TRENT Children and Young People's Services, Civic Centre, Glebe Street, Stoke-on-Trent ST4 1HH T 01782-234567 E children@stoke.gov.uk W www.stoke.gov.uk/children
Director, D. Jones

SUNDERLAND Children's Services, Civic Centre, Sunderland SR2 7DN T 0191-520 5555 E enquiries@sunderland.gov.uk W www.sunderland.gov.uk
Director Dr Helen Paterson

SWINDON Children Services, Sanford House, Sanford Street, Swindon SN1 1QH T 01793-463000 E hpitts@swindon.gov.uk W www.swindon.gov.uk
Group Director, Hilary Pitts

TAMESIDE Education Department, Council Offices, Wellington Road, Ashton under Lyne OL6 6DL T 0161-342 8355 E lifelong.learning@tameside.gov.uk W www.tameside.gov.uk
Director, Jim Taylor

TELFORD AND WREKIN Children and Young People, Civic Offices, Telford TF3 4WF T 01952-385385 E children&youngpeople@telford.gov.uk W www.telford.gov.uk
Corporate Director, vacant

THURROCK Children, Education and Families, Civic Offices, New Road, Grays RM17 6SL T 01375-652652 E education@thurrock.gov.uk W www.thurrock.gov.uk/education
Interim Corporate Director, Julien Kramer

TORBAY Children's Services, Oldway Mansion, Paignton TQ3 2TE T 01803-208227 E csenquiries@torbay.gov.uk W www.torbay.gov.uk
Strategic Director, Margaret Dennison

TRAFFORD Children and Young People's Service, Sale Waterside, Waterside House, Sale M33 7ZF T 0161-912 2000 E trafford.direct@trafford.gov.uk W www.trafford.gov.uk
Corporate Director, Chris Pratt

WAKEFIELD Family Services, County Hall, Bond Street, Wakefield WF1 2QL T 01924-306090 W www.wakefield.gov.uk
Corporate Director, Elaine McHale

WALSALL Children's Services, The Civic Centre, Walsall WS1 1TP T 01922-650000 E info@walsall.gov.uk W www.walsall.gov.uk
Director, David Brown

WARRINGTON Children's Services Directorate, New Town House, Buttermarket Street, Warrington WA1 2NJ T 01925-444400 E education@warrington.gov.uk W www.warrington.gov.uk
Strategic Director, Norma Cadwallader

WEST BERKSHIRE Children and Young People, Avonbank House, West Street, Newbury RG14 1BZ T 01635-519027 E mgoldie@westberks.gov.uk W www.westberks.gov.uk
Head of Education Service, Margaret Goldie

WIGAN Children's and Young People's Services, Progress House, Westwood Park Drive, Wigan WN3 4HH T 01942-486123 E education@wigan.gov.uk W www.wigan.gov.uk
Director, Ged Rowney

WIRRAL Children and Young People's Department, Hamilto[n] Building, Conway Street, Birkenhead CH41 4FD T 0151-60[...] 2000 E childrens@wirral.gov.uk W www.wirral.gov.uk/ed
Director, Howard Cooper

WOKINGHAM Children's Services, PO Box 156, Shute End, Wokingham RG40 1WN T 0118-974 6134 E childrensservicesreception@wokingham.gov.uk W www.wokingham.gov.uk
Corporate Head, Wendy Woodcock

WOLVERHAMPTON Children and Young People, Civic Centre, St Peter's Square, Wolverhampton WV1 1RR T 01902-556556 E educ.mail@wolverhampton.gov.uk W www.wolverhampton.gov.uk
Director, Roy Lockwood

YORK Learning, Culture and Children's Services, Mill House, North Street, York YO1 6JD T 01904-613161 E education.queries@york.gov.uk W www.york.gov.uk
Director, Pete Dwyer

LONDON

*Inner London borough

BARKING AND DAGENHAM Children's Services, Town Ha[ll], Barking IG11 7LU T 020-8227 3181 E enquiries@lbbd.gov.uk W www.lbbd.gov.uk
Corporate Director, Roger Luxton, OBE

BARNET Barnet Children's Service, Building 4, North Londo[n] Business Park, Oakleigh Road South, London N11 1NP T 020-8359 7618 E education.info@barnet.gov.uk W www.barnet.gov.uk
Director, Gillian Palmer

BEXLEY Children and Young People's Services, Hill View, Hil[l] View Drive, Welling DA16 3RY T 020-8303 7777

E knowledgemanagement@bexley.gov.uk
W www.bexley.gov.uk
Director, Dr Deborah Absalom

RENT Children and Families Department, Brent House Annexe, 356–358 High Road, Wembley HA9 6BX T 020-8937 4715 E childrenandfamilies@brent.gov.uk W www.brent.gov.uk
Director, Janet Palmer

ROMLEY Children and Young People Services, Civic Centre, Stockwell Close, Bromley BR1 3UH T 020-8464 3333 W www.bromley.gov.uk
Director, Gillian Pearson

AMDEN Education Department, Crowndale Centre, 218 Eversholt Street, London NW1 1BD T 020-7974 1525 W www.camden.gov.uk
Director, Heather Schroeder

ITY OF LONDON Education Service, Corporation of London, PO Box 270, Guildhall, London EC2P 2EJ T 020-7332 1750 E fyi@cityoflondon.gov.uk
Family and Young People's Director, Gillian Humble

ROYDON Education Department, Taberner House, Park Lane, Croydon CR9 3JS T 020-8726 6400 E contact.thecouncil@croydon.gov.uk W www.croydon.gov.uk
Director, Peter Wylie

ALING Schools Service, Perceval House, 14–16 Uxbridge Road, London W5 2HL T 020-8825 5599 E education@ealing.gov.uk W www.ealing.gov.uk
Director, Rachael Black

NFIELD Education, Children's Services and Leisure, 7th Floor, Civic Centre, Silver Street, Enfield EN1 3XQ T 020-8379 1000 W www.enfield.gov.uk
Director, Peter Lewis

GREENWICH Children's Services, Riverside House, Woolwich High Street, London SE18 6DF T 020-8854 8888 W www.greenwich.gov.uk
Director, Paul Burnett

HACKNEY Hackney Technology and Learning Centre, 1 Reading Lane, London E8 1GQ T 020-8820 7000 E info@learningtrust.co.uk W www.learningtrust.co.uk
Chief Executive, Alan Wood

HAMMERSMITH AND FULHAM Children's Services, Town Hall, King Street, London W6 9JU T 020-8753 3621 E educationenquiries@lbhf.gov.uk W www.lbhf.gov.uk
Director, Andrew Christie

ARINGEY Children's Service, 48 Station Road, London N22 7TY T 020-8489 3767 E customer.services@haringey.gov.uk W www.haringey.gov.uk
Director, Sharon Shoesmith

ARROW Children's Services, PO Box 22, Civic Centre, Station Road, Harrow HA1 2UW T 020-8863 5611 E info@harrow.gov.uk W www.harrow.gov.uk
Director, Paul Clark

AVERING Children's Services, Town Hall, Main Road, Romford RM1 3BB T 01708-434343 E info@havering.gov.uk W www.havering.gov.uk
Group Director, Andrew Ireland

ILLINGDON Education Department, Civic Centre, High Street, Uxbridge UB8 1UW T 01895-250529 E cspencer@hillingdon.gov.uk W www.hillingdon.gov.uk
Corporate Director, Christopher Spencer

OUNSLOW Children's Services and Lifelong Learning, Civic Centre, Lampton Road, Hounslow TW3 4DN T 020-8583 2600 W www.hounslow.gov.uk
Director, Dr Robert Garnett

*ISLINGTON Education Services, Laycock Street, Islington, London N1 1TH T 020-7527 5800 E admissions.cea@islington.gov.uk W www.islington.gov.uk
Director, Eleanor Schooling

*ROYAL BOROUGH OF KENSINGTON AND CHELSEA Family and Children's Services, The Town Hall, Hornton Street, London W8 7NX T 020-7361 3009 E education@rbkc.gov.uk W www.rbkc.gov.uk
Executive Director, Anne Marie Carrie

KINGSTON UPON THAMES Children's Services, Guildhall 2, Kingston upon Thames KT1 1EU T 020-8546 2121 W www.kingston.gov.uk
Director, P. Leeson

*LAMBETH Children and Young People's Service, International House, Canterbury Crescent, London SW9 7QE T 020-7926 1000 E infoservice@lambeth.gov.uk W www.lambeth.gov.uk
Executive Director, Phyllis Dunipace

*LEWISHAM Children and Young People, 3rd Floor, Laurence House, 1 Catford Road, London SE6 4RU T 020-8314 6000 E frankie.sulke@lewisham.gov.uk W www.lewisham.gov.uk
Executive Director, Frankie Sulke

MERTON Children, Schools and Families, 10th Floor Civic Centre, London Road, Morden SM4 5DX T 020-8274 4901 E education@merton.gov.uk W www.merton.gov.uk
Director, Dave Hill

NEWHAM Children and Young People's Services, Broadway House, High Street, Stratford E15 1AJ T 020-8430 2000 W www.newham.gov.uk
Executive Director, Pauline Maddison

REDBRIDGE Children's Services, Lynton House, 255–259 High Road, Ilford IG1 1NN T 020-8478 3020 W www.redbridge.gov.uk
Director, Pat Reynolds

RICHMOND UPON THAMES Education and Leisure Services, 1st Floor, Regal House, London Road, Twickenham TW1 3QB T 020-8891 7500 E a.phillips@richmond.gov.uk W www.richmond.gov.uk
Director, Anji Phillips

*SOUTHWARK Education Department, John Smith House, 144–152 Walworth Road, London SE17 1JL T 020-7525 5050 E childrens.info@southwark.gov.uk W www.southwark.gov.uk
Strategic Director, Romi Bowen

SUTTON Learning for Life, The Grove, Carshalton SM5 3AL T 020-8770 5000 W www.sutton.gov.uk
Strategic Director, Dr I. Birnbaum

*TOWER HAMLETS Children's Services, Mulberry Place, 5 Clove Crescent, London E14 2BG T 020-7364 5006 E childrensservices@towerhamlets.gov.uk W www.towerhamlets.org.uk
Corporate Director, Kevan Collins

WALTHAM FOREST Children's Services, Silver Birch House, Uplands Business Park, Blackhorse Lane, London E17 5SD T 020-8496 3000 W www.walthamforest.gov.uk E chris.kiernan@walthamforest.gov.uk
Executive Director, Christopher Kiernan

*WANDSWORTH Education Department, Town Hall, Wandsworth High Street, London SW18 2PU T 020-8871 8013 E edadmin@wandsworth.gov.uk W www.wandsworth.gov.uk
Director, Paul Robinson

*CITY OF WESTMINSTER Education Department, City Hall, 13th Floor, 64 Victoria Street, London SW1E 6QP T 020-7641 6000 W www.westminster.gov.uk
Director of Schools and Learning, Steve Farnsworth

WALES

ANGLESEY County Offices, Llangefni LL77 7TW T 01248-752900 W www.anglesey.gov.uk
Director, Richard Parry Jones

BLAENAU GWENT Central Depot, Barleyfields, Brynmaur NP23 4YF T 01495-355294
E education.department@blaenau-gwent.gov.uk
W www.blaenau-gwent.gov.uk
Director, Dr Brett Pugh

BRIDGEND Education Department, Sunnyside, Bridgend CF31 4AR T 01656-642600 E education@bridgend.gov.uk
W www.bridgend.gov.uk
Executive Director, Hilary Anthony

CAERPHILLY Education Offices, Caerphilly Road, Ystrad Mynach, Hengoed CF82 7EP T 01443-815588
E info@caerphilly.gov.uk W www.caerphilly.gov.uk
Director, David Hopkins

CARDIFF Schools and Lifelong Learning, County Hall, Atlantic Wharf, Cardiff CF10 4UW T 029-2087 2000
E cardiff.webmaster@cardiff.gov.uk W www.cardiff.gov.uk
Chief Officer, Chris Jones

CARMARTHENSHIRE Education and Children's Services, Pibwrlwyd, Carmarthen SA31 2NH T 01267-224532
E lll@carmarthenshire.gov.uk
W www.carmarthenshire.gov.uk
Director, Vernon Morgan

CEREDIGION Education and Community Services, Swyddfa'r Sir, Glan y Mor, Aberystwyth SY23 2DE T 01970-633600
E education@ceredigion.gov.uk W www.ceredigion.gov.uk
Director, Gareth Jones

CONWY Education Services, Government Buildings, Dinerth Road, Colwyn Bay LL28 4UL T 01492-575031
E education@conwy.gov.uk W www.conwy.gov.uk
Chief Education Officer, R. Geraint James

DENBIGHSHIRE Lifelong Learning Department, County Hall, Wynnstay Road, Ruthin LL15 1YN T 01824-706000
E education@denbighshire.gov.uk
W www.denbighshire.gov.uk
Corporate Director, Huw Griffiths

FLINTSHIRE Education and Children's Services, County Hall, Mold CH7 6ND T 01352-752121 W www.flintshire.gov.uk
Director, Alan Davies

GWYNEDD Schools Services, Council Offices, Caernarfon LL55 1SH T 01286-672255 E education@gwynedd.gov.uk
W www.gwynedd.gov.uk
Director, Dr Gwynne Jones

MERTHYR TYDFIL Integrated Children's Services, Ty Keir Hardie, Riverside Court, Avenue De Clichy, Merthyr Tydfil CF47 8XD T 01685-724600 E officeservices@merthyr.gov.uk
W www.merthyr.gov.uk
Director, C. A. Abbott

MONMOUTHSHIRE Lifelong Learning and Leisure, County Hall, Cwmbran NP44 2XH T 01633-644644
E andrewkeep@monmouthshire.gov.uk
W www.monmouthshire.gov.uk
Corporate Director, Andrew Keep

NEATH PORT TALBOT Education, Leisure and Lifelong Learning Directorate, Civic Centre, Port Talbot SA13 1PJ
T 01639-763298 E education@npt.gov.uk
W www.neath-porttalbot.gov.uk
Director, Karl Napieralla

NEWPORT Education Department, Civic Centre, Newport NP20 4UR T 01633-656656 E education@newport.gov.uk
W www.newport.gov.uk
Chief Education Officer, Dr B. Pugh

PEMBROKESHIRE Education Department, County Hall, Haverfordwest SA61 1TP T 01437-764551
E enquiries@pembrokeshire.gov.uk
W www.pembrokeshire.gov.uk
Director, Gerson Davies

POWYS Education Department, County Hall, Llandrindod Wells LD1 5LG T 01597-826422
W www.education.powys.gov.uk
Head of Schools and Inclusion, Douglas Wilson

RHONDDA CYNON TAF Education Department, Ty Trevithick, Abercynon, Mountain Ash CF45 4UQ
T 01443-744000 W www.rhondda-cynon-taf.gov.uk
Director, Mike Keating

SWANSEA Education Department, County Hall, Oystermouth Road, Swansea SA1 3SN T 01792-63600
E education.department@swansea.gov.uk
W www.swansea.gov.uk/education
Director, Richard Parry

TORFAEN County Hall, Croesyceiliog, Cwmbran NP44 2WN T 01495-762200 E your.call@torfaen.gov.uk
W www.torfaen.gov.uk
Chief Education Officer, Catherine Simpson

VALE OF GLAMORGAN Learning and Development, Civic Offices, Holton Road, Barry CF63 4RU T 01446-700111
W www.valeofglamorgan.gov.uk
Director of Learning and Development, Bryan Jeffreys

WREXHAM Children and Young People Service, Ty Henblas, Queen's Square, Wrexham LL13 8AZ T 01978-297505
E education@wrexham.gov.uk W www.wrexham.gov.uk
Strategic Director, Terry Garner

SCOTLAND

ABERDEEN Strategic Leadership, Summerhill Centre, Stronsa Drive, Aberdeen AB15 6JA T 01224-522000
W www.aberdeencity.gov.uk
Director, Abigail Tierney

ABERDEENSHIRE Education and Recreation, Woodhill House, Westburn Road, Aberdeen AB16 5GB
T 01224-664630 W www.aberdeenshire.gov.uk
Director, Bruce Robertson, OBE

ANGUS Educational Services, County Buildings, Market Street Forfar DD8 3WE T 01307-461460
E education@angus.gov.uk W www.angus.gov.uk
Director of Education, Jim Anderson

ARGYLL AND BUTE Community Services, Argyll House, Alexandra Parade, Dunoon PA23 8AJ T 01369-704000
W www.argyll-bute.gov.uk
Director, Douglas Hendry

CLACKMANNANSHIRE Services to People, Lime Tree House Alloa FK10 1EX T 01259-450000
E servicestopeople@clacks.gov.uk
W www.clacksweb.org.uk
Head of Schools, Jim Goodall

DUMFRIES AND GALLOWAY Education and Community Services, Woodbank, 30 Edinburgh Road, Dumfries DG1 1NW T 01387-260400 E frasers@dumgal.gov.uk
W www.dumgal.gov.uk
Corporate Director, Fraser Sanderson

DUNDEE Education Department, Tayside House, Crichton Street, Dundee DD1 3RJ T 01382-434000
E education@dundeecity.gov.uk W www.dundeecity.gov.uk
Director, A. Wilson

EAST AYRSHIRE Education Department, Council Headquarters, London Road, Kilmarnock KA3 7BU
T 01563-576000 E education@east-ayrshire.gov.uk
W www.east-ayrshire.gov.uk
Executive Director, Graham Short

EAST DUNBARTONSHIRE Community Department, Boclair House, 100 Milngavie Road, Bearsden, Glasgow G61 2TQ

T 0141-578 8000 E education@eastdunbarton.gov.uk
W www.eastdunbarton.gov.uk
Corporate Director, David Anderson

EAST LOTHIAN Education and Children's Services, John Muir House, Haddington EH41 3HA T 01620-827631
W www.eastlothian.gov.uk
Director, Alan J. Blackie

EAST RENFREWSHIRE Education Department, Council Offices, 211 Main Street, Barrhead G78 1SY
T 0141-577 3404 W www.eastrenfrewshire.gov.uk
Director, John Wilson

CITY OF EDINBURGH Children and Families, Waverley Court, 4 East Market Street, Edinburgh EH8 8BG
T 0131-469 3000 E gillian.tee@edinburgh.gov.uk
W www.edinburgh.gov.uk
Director, Gillian Tee

EILEAN SIAR (WESTERN ISLES) Education Department, Council Offices, Sandwick Road, Stornoway HS1 2BW
T 01851-709431 E dsmith@cne-siar.gov.uk
W www.cne-siar.gov.uk
Director, Murdo Macleod

FALKIRK Education Services, McLaren House, Marchmont Avenue, Polmont, Falkirk FK2 0NZ
T 01324-506600 E director.educ@falkirk.gov.uk
W www.falkirk.gov.uk
Director, Julia Swan

FIFE Education Service, Rothesay House, Rothesay Place, Glenrothes KY7 5PQ T 01592-583372
E education.services@fife.gov.uk W www.fifedirect.co.uk
Executive Director, Kenneth Greer

GLASGOW Education, Training and Young People, Wheatley House, 25 Cochrane Street, Merchant City, Glasgow G1 1HL
T 0141-287 2000 E education@glasgow.gov.uk
W www.glasgow.gov.uk
Executive Director, Ronnie O'Connor

HIGHLAND Education, Culture and Sport Service, Council Offices, Glenurquhart Road, Inverness IV3 5NX
T 01463-702074 E ecs@highland.gov.uk
W www.highland.gov.uk
Director, Hugh Fraser

INVERCLYDE Education Services, 105 Dalrymple Street, Greenock PA15 1HT T 01475-712850
W www.inverclyde.gov.uk
Director, Ian Fraser

MIDLOTHIAN Communications, Midlothian House, Buccleuch Street, Dalkeith EH22 1DJ T 0131-270 7500
E education.services@midlothian.gov.uk
W www.midlothian.gov.uk
Director, D. MacKay

MORAY Educational Services, Council Offices, High Street, Elgin IV30 1BX T 01343-563397
E elaine.bain@moray.gov.uk W www.moray.gov.uk
Director, Donald M. Duncan

NORTH AYRSHIRE Educational Services, Cunninghame House, Friars Croft, Irvine KA12 8EE T 01294-324400
E education@north-ayrshire.gov.uk
W www.north-ayrshire.gov.uk
Corporate Director, John Travers

NORTH LANARKSHIRE Learning and Leisure Services, Municipal Buildings, Kildonan Street, Coatbridge ML5 3BT
T 01236-812222 E lls.enquiries@northlan.gov.uk
W www.northlan.gov.uk
Executive Director, Christine Pollock

ORKNEY ISLANDS Education and Recreation Services, Council Offices, School Place, Kirkwall, Orkney KW15 1NY
T 01856-873535 E education@orkney.gov.uk
W www.orkney.gov.uk
Director, Leslie Manson

PERTH AND KINROSS Education and Children's Services, Pullar House, 35 Kinnoull Street, Perth PH1 5GD
T 01738-476200 E ecsgeneralenquiries@pkc.gov.uk
W www.pkc.gov.uk
Executive Director (interim), David Montgomery

RENFREWSHIRE South Building, Council Headquarters, Cotton Street, Paisley PA1 1LE T 0141-842 5663
E schools.els@renfrewshire.gov.uk
W www.renfrewshire.gov.uk
Director, John Rooney

SCOTTISH BORDERS Education and Lifelong Learning, Council Headquarters, Newtown St Boswells, Melrose TD6 0SA T 01835-824000
E ellinfo@scotborders.gov.uk
W www.scotborders.gov.uk
Director, Glenn Rodger

SHETLAND ISLANDS Education Service, Hayfield House, Hayfield Lane, Lerwick ZE1 0QD
T 01595-744000
E education.and.social.service@shetland.gov.uk
W www.shetland.gov.uk
Head of Education Service, Helen Budge

SOUTH AYRSHIRE Education, Culture and Lifelong Learning, County Buildings, Wellington Square, Ayr KA7 1DR T 01292-612285
E cst@south-ayrshire.gov.uk
W www.south-ayrshire.gov.uk
Director, Mike McCabe

SOUTH LANARKSHIRE Education Resources, Council Offices, Almada Street, Hamilton ML3 0AE T 01698-454444
E education@southlanarkshire.gov.uk
W www.southlanarkshire.gov.uk
Executive Director, Larry Forde

STIRLING Children's Services, Viewforth, Stirling FK8 2ET
T 01786-442666 E camerond@stirling.gov.uk
W www.stirling.gov.uk
Director, David Cameron

WEST DUNBARTONSHIRE Education and Cultural Services, Council Offices, Garshake Road, Dumbarton G82 3PU
T 01389-737309
E education.centralregistry@west-dunbarton.gov.uk
Director, Liz McGinlay

WEST LOTHIAN Education and Cultural Services, West Lothian House, Almondvale Boulevard, Livingston EH54 6QG T 01506-776000
E education@westlothian.gov.uk
Director, Gordon Ford

NORTHERN IRELAND

BELFAST Education and Library Board, 40 Academy Street, Belfast BT1 2NQ T 028-9056 4000 E info@belb.co.uk
W www.belb.org.uk
Chief Executive, David Cargo

NORTH EAST North Eastern Education and Library Board, Library HQ, 25–31 Demesne Avenue, Ballymena BT43 7BG
T 028-2566 4119 W www.neelb.org.uk
Chief Executive, G. Topping

SOUTH Southern Education and Library Board, 3 Charlemont Place, The Mall, Armagh BT61 9AX T 028-3751 2200
E selb.hq@selb.org W www.selb.org
Chief Executive, Helen McClenaghan

SOUTH EAST South Eastern Education and Library Board, Headquarters Offices, Grahamsbridge Road, Dundonald, Belfast BT16 2HS T 028-9056 6200 E info@seelb.org.uk
W www.seelb.org.uk
Chief Executive, I. Knox

WEST Western Education and Library Board, 1 Hospital Road, Omagh BT79 0AW **T** 028-8241 1411 **E** info@welbni.org **W** www.welbni.org
Chief Executive, B. Mulholland

ISLANDS

GUERNSEY Education Department, PO Box 32, The Grange, St Peter Port, Guernsey GY1 3AU **T** 01481-710821 **E** enquiries@education.gov.gg **W** www.education.gg
Director, D. T. Neale

ISLE OF MAN Department of Education, St. George's Court, Upper Church Street, Douglas, Isle of Man IM1 2SG **T** 01624-685808 **E** admin@doe.gov.im **W** www.gov.im
Director, John Cain

ISLE OF WIGHT County Hall, High Street, Newport PO30 1UD **T** 01983-821000 **W** www.iwight.com
Director of Children's Services, Steve Beynon

ISLES OF SCILLY Education Department, Town Hall, Hugh Town, St Mary's TR21 0LW **T** 01720-422537 **E** enquiries@scilly.gov.uk **W** www.scilly.gov.uk
Chief Executive, Philip Hygate

JERSEY Education, Sport and Culture, PO Box 142, Jersey JE4 8QJ **T** 01534-445504 **E** esc@gov.je **W** www.gov.je
Director, T. W. McKeon

ᴵNIVERSITIES

he following is a list of universities, which are those stitutions that have been granted degree awarding owers by either a royal charter or an act of parliament nd have been granted permission to use the word niversity' (or 'university college') by the Privy Council. here are other recognised bodies in the UK with degree warding powers, as well as institutions offering courses ading to a degree from a recognised body. Further formation is available at W www.dfes.gov.uk.

Where available, student numbers represent the number f full-time undergraduates for the academic year 2006– , with the exception of the Open University, where all udents study part time.

Fees listed are per annum for students beginning ıll-time undergraduate courses in the academic year 007–8 (variations apply on certain courses). Whether e fees apply varies depending on where the student is om. English and Northern Irish students pay top-up fees herever they study in the UK; Welsh students pay p-up fees in England, Scotland and Northern Ireland, ut are entitled to a partial tuition fee grant if they remain Wales or attend a course that is not available at any /elsh university; Scottish students only pay top-up fees in ngland, Wales and Northern Ireland. EU students pay es as if they came from the country they are studying in the lowest amount) and international students pay their niversity's international fees, which are typically much igher than top-up fees.

NIVERSITY OF ABERDEEN (1495)
ng's College, Aberdeen AB24 3FX T 01224-272000
 www.abdn.ac.uk
udents: 8,716 *Fees:* £1,735
hancellor, Lord Wilson of Tillyorn, KT, GCMG, FRSE
rincipal and Vice-Chancellor, Prof. C. Duncan Rice, FRSE
cademic Registrar, Dr Gillian Macintosh

NIVERSITY OF ABERTAY DUNDEE (1994)
ell Street, Dundee DD1 1HG T 01382-308000
 www.abertay.ac.uk
udents: 3,165 *Fees:* £1,735
hancellor, The Rt. Hon. the Earl of Airlie, KT, GCVO
ice-Chancellor, Prof. Bernard King, CBE
cademic Registrar, Dr Colin Fraser

NGLIA RUSKIN UNIVERSITY (1992)
vermead Campus, Bishop Hall Lane, Chelmsford, Essex M1 1SQ T 01245-493131 W www.anglia.ac.uk
udents: 9,100 *Fees:* £3,070
hancellor, Lord Ashcroft, KCMG
ice-Chancellor, Prof. Michael Thorne, FRSA
he Secretary and Clerk, Stephen Bennett

NIVERSITY OF THE ARTS LONDON (Formerly he London Institute (1986), University of the Arts ondon was formed in 2004)
5 Davies Street, London W1K 5DA T 020-7514 6000
 www.arts.ac.uk
udents: 18,797 *Fees:* £3,070
hancellor, Lord Stevenson of Coddenham, CBE
ector, Sir Michael Bichard, KCB
niversity Secretary, Martin Prince

COLLEGES

CAMBERWELL COLLEGE OF ARTS (1898)
Peckham Road, London SE5 8UF T 020-7514 6302
W www.camberwell.arts.ac.uk
Head of College, Chris Wainwright

CENTRAL SAINT MARTINS COLLEGE OF ART & DESIGN (1854)
Southampton Row, London WC1B 4AP T 020-7514 7022
W www.csm.arts.ac.uk
Head of College, Jane Rapley, OBE

CHELSEA COLLEGE OF ART & DESIGN (1895)
Millbank, London SW1P 4RJ T 020-7514 7751
W www.chelsea.arts.ac.uk
Head of College, Chris Wainwright

LONDON COLLEGE OF COMMUNICATION (1894)
Elephant & Castle, London SE1 6SB T 020-7514 6500
W www.lcc.arts.ac.uk
Head of College, Dr William Bridge

LONDON COLLEGE OF FASHION (1963)
20 John Princes Street, London W1G 0BJ T 020-7514 7500
W www.fashion.arts.ac.uk
Head of College, Dr Frances Corner

WIMBLEDON COLLEGE OF ART (1930)
Merton Hall Road, London SW19 3QA T 020-7514 9641
W www.wimbledon.arts.ac.uk
Head of College, Chris Wainwright

ASTON UNIVERSITY (1966)
Aston Triangle, Birmingham B4 7ET T 0121-204 3000
W www.aston.ac.uk
Students: 7,087 *Fees:* £3,070
Chancellor, Prof. Michael Bett, CBE
Vice-Chancellor, Prof. Julia King, CBE, FRENG, FRSA
Registrar, David Packham, FRSA

UNIVERSITY OF BATH (1966)
Bath BA2 7AY T 01225-388388 W www.bath.ac.uk
Students: 8,621 *Fees:* £3,070
Chancellor, Lord Tugendhat
Vice-Chancellor, Prof. Glynis Breakwell, PHD, FRSA
University Secretary, Mark Humphriss

BATH SPA UNIVERSITY (2005)
Newton Park, Newton St Loe, Bath BA2 9BN T 01225-875875
W www.bathspa.ac.uk
Students: 5,500 *Fees:* £3,070
Vice-Chancellor, Prof. Frank Morgan
Academic Registrar, Christopher Ellicott

UNIVERSITY OF BEDFORDSHIRE (1993)
Park Square, Luton LU1 3JU T 01582-734111
W www.beds.ac.uk
Students: 8,298 *Fees:* £3,000
Chancellor, Sir Robin Biggam
Vice-Chancellor, Prof. Les Ebdon
Registrar, Dr Jim Franklin

UNIVERSITY OF BIRMINGHAM (1900)
Edgbaston, Birmingham B15 2TT T 0121-414 3344
W www.bham.ac.uk
Students: 16,639 *Fees:* £3,070
Chancellor, Sir Dominic Cadbury
Vice-Chancellor, Prof. M. Sterling
Registrar and Secretary, Mrs G. Ball

UNIVERSITY OF BOLTON (2005)
Deane Road, Bolton BL3 5AB T 01204-903903
W www.bolton.ac.uk
Students: 2,760 *Fees:* £3,070
Vice-Chancellor, Dr George Holmes

BOURNEMOUTH UNIVERSITY (1992)
Fern Barrow, Poole, Dorset BH12 5BB T 01202-524111
W www.bournemouth.ac.uk
Students: 10,106 *Fees:* £3,070
Chancellor, Lady Digby, DBE, DL
Vice-Chancellor, Prof. Paul Curran
Registrar, Noel Richardson

UNIVERSITY OF BRADFORD (1966)
Richmond Building, Richmond Road, Bradford, W. Yorks
BD7 1DP T 01274-232323 W www.brad.ac.uk
Students: 7,502 *Fees:* £3,070
Chancellor, Imran Khan
Vice-Chancellor, Prof. Mark Cleary
University Secretary, Mary Rose Millin

UNIVERSITY OF BRIGHTON (1992)
Mithras House, Lewes Road, Brighton BN2 4AT
T 01273-600900 W www.bton.ac.uk
Students: 12,649 *Fees:* £3,070
Chancellor, Sir John Mogg
Vice-Chancellor, Prof. Julian Crampton
Registrar and Secretary, Christine Moon

UNIVERSITY OF BRISTOL (1909)
Senate House, Tyndall Avenue, Bristol BS8 1TH T 0117-928 9000 W www.bristol.ac.uk
Students: 12,000 *Fees:* £3,070
Chancellor, Baroness Hale of Richmond, DBE, PC
Vice Chancellor, Prof. Eric Thomas
Registrar, Derek Pretty

BRUNEL UNIVERSITY (1966)
Uxbridge, Middx UB8 3PH T 01895-274000
W www.brunel.ac.uk
Students: 11,000 *Fees:* £3,000
Chancellor, The Rt. Hon. Lord Wakeham
Vice-Chancellor and Principal, Prof. C. Jenks
Secretary and Registrar, J. Weale

UNIVERSITY OF BUCKINGHAM (1983)
Buckingham MK18 1EG T 01280-814080
W www.buckingham.ac.uk
Students: 600 *Fees:* £7,500
Chancellor, Sir Martin Jacomb
Vice-Chancellor, Terence Kealey, DPHIL
Registrar, Prof. Len Evans

UNIVERSITY OF CAMBRIDGE (1209)
The Old Schools, Trinity Lane, Cambridge CB2 1TN
T 01223-337733 W www.cam.ac.uk
Students: 11,825 *Fees:* £3,000
Chancellor, HRH The Prince Philip, Duke of Edinburgh, KG, KT, OM, GBE, PC, FRS
Vice-Chancellor, Prof. Alison Richard (Newnham)
High Steward, Dame Bridget Ogilvie, DBE, FRS (Girton
Deputy High Steward, Lord Richardson of Duntisbourne, KG, MBE, TD, PC (Gonville and Caius)
Commissary, Lord Mackay of Clashfern, KT, PC, FRSE (Trinity)
Pro-Vice-Chancellors, Prof. A. D. Cliff (Christ's); Prof. I. M. Leslie (Christ's); Prof. M. C. McKendrick (Girton); Prof. A. C. Minson (Wolfson); Dr K. B. Pretty (Homerton)
Proctors, Revd R. Greeves (Clare), Dr P. Sarris (Trinity)
Orator, A. J. Bowen (Jesus)
Registrary, Dr J. W. Nichols (Emmanuel)
Librarian, P. K. Fox (Selwyn)
Director of the Fitzwilliam Museum, D. D. Robinson (Magdalene)
Academic Secretary, G. P. Allen (Wolfson)
Director of Finance, A. M. Reid (Wolfson)

COLLEGES AND HALLS *with dates of foundation*
CHRIST'S (1505)
Master, Prof. Frank Kelly, FRS
CHURCHILL (1960)
Master, Prof. Sir David Wallace, CBE, FRS
CLARE (1326)
Master, Prof. A. J. Badger
CLARE HALL (1966)
President, Prof. E. K. H. Salje, FRS
CORPUS CHRISTI (1352)
Master, Prof. Sir Alan Wilson
DARWIN (1964)
Master, Prof. W. A. Brown, CBE
DOWNING (1800)
Master, Prof. B. J. Everitt, FRS
EMMANUEL (1584)
Master, Lord Wilson of Dinton, GCB
FITZWILLIAM (1966)
Master, Prof. R. D. Lethbridge
GIRTON (1869)
Mistress, Prof. Dame Marilyn Strathern, DBE, FBA
GONVILLE AND CAIUS (1348)
Master, Sir Christopher Hum, KCMG
HOMERTON (1824)
Principal, Dr K. B. Pretty
HUGHES HALL (1985)
President, Mrs S. Squire
JESUS (1496)
Master, Prof. R. Mair, FRS, FRENG
KING'S (1441)
Provost, Prof. T. R. Harrison
LUCY CAVENDISH (1965)
President, Dame Veronica Sutherland, DBE, CMG
MAGDALENE (1542)
Master, D. D. Robinson
NEW HALL (1954)
President, Mrs A. M. Lonsdale, CBE
NEWNHAM (1871)
Principal, Dame Patricia Hodgson, DBE
PEMBROKE (1347)
Master, Sir Richard Dearlove, KCMG, OBE
PETERHOUSE (1284)
Master, Lord Wilson of Tillyorn, KT, GCMG, FRSE
QUEENS' (1448)
President, Prof. Lord Eatwell
ROBINSON (1977)
Warden, A. D. Yates
ST CATHARINE'S (1473)
Master, Prof. Dame Jean Thomas, DBE, FRS

T EDMUND'S (1896)
Master, Prof. J. P. Luzio
T JOHN'S (1511)
Master, Prof. C. Dobson, FRS
ELWYN (1882)
Master, Prof. R. J. Bowring
IDNEY SUSSEX (1596)
Master, Prof. Dame Sandra Dawson, DBE
RINITY (1546)
Master, Prof. Lord Rees of Ludlow, PRS
RINITY HALL (1350)
Master, Prof. M. J. Daunton, FBA
/OLFSON (1965)
President, G. Johnson

ANTERBURY CHRIST CHURCH UNIVERSITY
2005)
orth Holmes Road, Canterbury CT1 1QU **T** 01227-767700
/ www.canterbury.ac.uk
tudents: 5,421 *Fees:* £3,070
'hancellor, Most Revd Rowan Williams, PC, DPHIL
'ice-Chancellor and Principal, Prof. Michael Wright
cademic Registrar, Kevin Tomlinson

ARDIFF UNIVERSITY (1883)
ardiff CF10 3XQ **T** 029-2087 4000 **W** www.cardiff.ac.uk
tudents: 22,000 *Fees:* £3,000
'resident, Lord Kinnock, PC
'ice-Chancellor, Dr David Grant, CBE, FRENG
)irector of Registry, Prof. Tony Cryer

NIVERSITY OF CENTRAL LANCASHIRE (1992)
'eston PR1 2HE **T** 01772-201201 **W** www.uclan.ac.uk
tudents: 18,648 *Fees:* £3,070
'hancellor, Sir Richard Evans, CBE
'ice-Chancellor, Dr Malcolm McVicar
)irector of Student Affairs, Ian McMillan

NIVERSITY OF CHESTER (2005)
arkgate Road, Chester CH1 4BJ **T** 01244-511000
/ www.chester.ac.uk
tudents: 5,768 *Fees:* £3,070
'hancellor, His Grace, The Duke of Westminster
'ice-Chancellor and Principal, Prof. Tim Wheeler, DL
'niversity Secretary/Bursar, David Stevens

JNIVERSITY OF CHICHESTER (2005)
'shop Otter Campus, College Lane, Chichester PO19 6PE
01243-816000 **W** www.chi.ac.uk
tudents: 4,243 *Fees:* £3,100
'ice-Chancellor, Dr Robin Baker

ITY UNIVERSITY (1966)
orthampton Square, London EC1V 0HB **T** 020-7040 5060
/ www.city.ac.uk
tudents: 8,550 *Fees:* £3,070
'ro-Chancellor, John Stuttard, BT., DSC
'ice-Chancellor, Prof. Malcolm Gillies
'egistrar, Eamon Martin

OVENTRY UNIVERSITY (1992)
riory Street, Coventry CV1 5FB **T** 024-7688 7688
/ www.coventry.ac.uk
tudents: 10,910 *Fees:* £3,070
'hancellor, Sir John Egan
'ice-Chancellor, Prof. Madeleine Atkins, CBE
cademic Registrar and Secretary, Kate Quantrell

DE MONTFORT UNIVERSITY (1992)
The Gateway, Leicester LE1 9BH **T** 08459-454647
W www.dmu.ac.uk
Students: 14,024 *Fees:* £3,070
Chancellor, Lord Alli
Vice-Chancellor, Prof. Philip Tasker
Registrar, Eugene Critchlow

UNIVERSITY OF DERBY (1992)
Kedleston Road, Derby DE22 1GB **T** 01332-590500
W www.derby.ac.uk
Students: 9,000 *Fees:* £3,070
Chancellor, Prof. Leslie Wagner, CBE
Vice-Chancellor, Prof. John Coyne
Deputy Vice-Chancellor, Jennifer Fry

UNIVERSITY OF DUNDEE (1967)
Nethergate, Dundee DD1 4HN **T** 01382-384000
W www.dundee.ac.uk
Students: 9,500 *Fees:* £1,735
Chancellor, Lord Patel, FRSE
Vice-Chancellor, Sir Alan Langlands, FRSE

DURHAM UNIVERSITY (1832)
The University Office, Durham DH1 3HP **T** 0191-334 2000
W www.dur.ac.uk
Students: 15,057 *Fees:* £3,070
Chancellor, Bill Bryson
Vice-Chancellor and Warden, Prof. C. F. Higgins, FRSE, FRSA, FMEDSCI
Registrar and Secretary, L. Sanders

COLLEGES
COLLINGWOOD
Principal, Prof. J. Taylor until January 2008, Prof. E. Corrigan, FRS, thereafter
GEORGE STEPHENSON
Principal, Prof. A. C. Darnell
GREY
Master, Prof. J. M. Chamberlain, DPHIL
HATFIELD
Master, Prof. T. P. Burt, DSC
JOHN SNOW
Principal, Prof. H. M. Evans
JOSEPHINE BUTLER
Principal, A. Simpson
ST AIDAN'S
Principal, Prof. J. S. Ashworth
ST CHAD'S
Principal, Revd J. P. M. Cassidy, PHD
ST CUTHBERT'S SOCIETY
Principal, Prof. R. D. Boyne
ST HILD AND ST BEDE
Principal, J. A. Pearson
ST JOHN'S
Principal, Revd D. Wilkinson, PHD
ST MARY'S
Principal (acting), Dr Gillian Boughton
TREVELYAN
Principal, N. Martin
UNIVERSITY
Master, Prof. M. E. Tucker
USHAW
Rector, Revd T. Drainey
USTINOV
Principal, Penelope B. Wilson, DPHIL
VAN MILDERT
Master, Prof. P. O'Meara, DPHIL

UNIVERSITY OF EAST ANGLIA (1963)
Norwich NR4 7TJ T 01603-456161 W www.uea.ac.uk
Students: 8,524 *Fees:* £3,070
Chancellor, Sir Brandon Gough
Vice-Chancellor, Dr Bill Macmillan
Academic Registrar, Brian Summers

UNIVERSITY OF EAST LONDON (1898)
University Way, London E16 2RD T 020-8223 3000
W www.uel.ac.uk
Students: 10,000 *Fees:* £3,000
Chancellor, Lord Rix, CBE
Vice-Chancellor, Prof. Martin Everett
Registrar and Secretary, Alan Ingle

EDGE HILL UNIVERSITY (2006)
St Helens Road, Ormskirk, Lancs L39 4QP T 01695-575171
W www.edgehill.ac.uk
Students: 12,229 *Fees:* £3,070
Vice-Chancellor, John Cater
University Secretary, Lesley Munro

UNIVERSITY OF EDINBURGH (1583)
Old College, South Bridge, Edinburgh EH8 9YL T 0131-650 1000 W www.ed.ac.uk
Students: 18,378 *Fees:* £1,735
Chancellor, HRH The Prince Philip, Duke of Edinburgh, KG, KT, OM
Principal and Vice-Chancellor, Prof. Timothy O'Shea, FRSE

UNIVERSITY OF ESSEX (1965)
Wivenhoe Park, Colchester CO4 3SQ T 01206-873333
W www.essex.ac.uk
Students: 6,000 *Fees:* £3,070
Chancellor, Lord Phillips of Sudbury, OBE
Vice-Chancellor, Prof. Colin Riordan
Academic Registrar, Dr Tony Rich

UNIVERSITY OF EXETER (1955)
The Queen's Drive, Exeter EX4 4QJ T 01392-661000
W www.exeter.ac.uk
Students: 9,123 *Fees:* £3,070
Chancellor, Floella Benjamin, OBE
Vice Chancellor, Prof. Steve Smith
Registrar and Secretary, David Allen

UNIVERSITY OF GLAMORGAN (1992)
Pontypridd CF37 1DL T 0800-716925 W www.glam.ac.uk
Students: 9,833 *Fees:* £3,070
Chancellor, Lord Morris of Aberavon, KG, PC, QC
Vice-Chancellor, Prof. David Halton
Academic Registrar, John O'Shea

UNIVERSITY OF GLASGOW (1451)
Gilbert Scott Building, University Avenue, Glasgow G12 8QQ
T 0141-330 2000 W www.gla.ac.uk
Students: 14,980 *Fees:* £1,735–£2,760
Chancellor, Prof. Sir Kenneth Calman, KCB, MD, FRCS
Vice-Chancellor, Sir Muir Russell, KCB, FRSE
Secretary of Court, David Newall

GLASGOW CALEDONIAN UNIVERSITY (1993)
City Campus, 70 Cowcaddens Road, Glasgow G4 0BA
T 0141-331 3000 W www.caledonian.ac.uk
Students: 10,072 *Fees:* £1,735
Vice-Chancellor and Principal, Prof. Pamela Gillies, FRSA, FFPH
Registrar, Alison Rooney

UNIVERSITY OF GLOUCESTERSHIRE (2001)
The Park, Cheltenham GL50 2RH T 08707-210210
W www.glos.ac.uk
Students: 5,375 *Fees:* £3,070
Chancellor, Lord Carey of Clifton, PC
Vice-Chancellor, Prof. Patricia Broadfoot, CBE
Academic Registrar, Paul Van Rossum

UNIVERSITY OF GREENWICH (1992)
Old Royal Naval College, Park Row, Greenwich, London SE10 9LS T 020-8331 8000 W www.gre.ac.uk
Students: 12,255 *Fees:* £2,560
Chancellor, Lord Holme of Cheltenham, CBE, PC
Vice-Chancellor, Baroness Blackstone, PHD
Secretary and Registrar, Linda Cording

HERIOT-WATT UNIVERSITY (1966)
Edinburgh EH14 4AS T 0131-449 5111 W www.hw.ac.uk
Students: 5,298 *Fees:* £1,700
Chancellor, Susan Greenfield, BT., CBE, FRCP
Principal and Vice-Chancellor, Prof. Anton Muscatelli
Secretary, Peter Wilson

UNIVERSITY OF HERTFORDSHIRE (1992)
College Lane, Hatfield, Herts AL10 9AB T 01707-284000
W www.herts.ac.uk
Students: 18,188 *Fees:* £3,075
Chancellor, The Marquess of Salisbury, PC
Vice-Chancellor, Prof. Tim Wilson
Registrar and Secretary, Philip Waters

UNIVERSITY OF HUDDERSFIELD (1992)
Queensgate, Huddersfield HD1 3DH T 01484-422288
W www.hud.ac.uk
Students: 6,495 *Fees:* £3,070
Chancellor, Patrick Stewart, OBE
Vice-Chancellor, Prof. Bob Cryan
Academic Registrar, Kathy Sherlock

UNIVERSITY OF HULL (1927)
Cottingham Road, Hull HU6 7RX T 01482-346311
W www.hull.ac.uk
Students: 10,568 *Fees:* £3,070
Chancellor, Baroness Bottomley of Nettlestone, PC, LLD
Vice-Chancellor, Prof. David J. Drewry, FRSA
Quality Director, Registrar and Secretary, Frances Owen

IMPERIAL COLLEGE LONDON (1907)
South Kensington, London SW7 2AZ T 020-7589 5111
W www.imperial.ac.uk
Students: 8,050 *Fees:* £3,070
Rector, Sir Richard Sykes
Deputy Rector, Prof. Sir Leszek Borysiewicz
Academic Registrar, Vernon McClure

KEELE UNIVERSITY (1962)
Keele, Staffs ST5 5BG T 01782-621111 W www.keele.ac.uk
Students: 4,800 *Fees:* £3,000
Chancellor, Prof. Sir David Weatherall, FRS
Vice-Chancellor, Prof. Janet Finch, CBE
Registrar and Secretary, Mr S. J. Morris

UNIVERSITY OF KENT (1965)
Canterbury, Kent CT2 7NZ **T** 01227-764000
W www.kent.ac.uk
Students: 11,122 *Fees:* £3,070
Chancellor, Prof. Sir Robert Worcester, KBE
Vice-Chancellor, Prof. Julia Goodfellow, CBE
Secretary of the Council, Karen Griffin

KINGSTON UNIVERSITY (1992)
River House, 53–57 High Street, Kingston upon Thames, Surrey KT1 1LQ **T** 020-8547 2000 **W** www.kingston.ac.uk
Students: 21,059 *Fees:* £3,000
Chancellor, Sir Peter Hall
Vice-Chancellor, Prof. Peter Scott
Academic Registrar, Alison Stokes

UNIVERSITY OF LANCASTER (1964)
Bailrigg, Lancaster LA1 4YW **T** 01524-65201
W www.lancs.ac.uk
Students: 8,323 *Fees:* £3,070
Chancellor, Sir Christian Bonington, CBE
Vice-Chancellor, Prof. Paul Wellings
University Secretary, Fiona Aiken

UNIVERSITY OF LEEDS (1904)
Leeds LS2 9JT **T** 0113-243 1751 **W** www.leeds.ac.uk
Students: 22,391 *Fees:* £3,070
Chancellor, Lord Bragg
Vice-Chancellor, Prof. Michael Arthur
Secretary, Roger Gair

LEEDS METROPOLITAN UNIVERSITY (1992)
Civic Quarter, Leeds LS1 3HE **T** 0113-283 2600
W www.leedsmet.ac.uk
Students: 14,202 *Fees:* £2,000
Chancellor, Brendan Foster, MBE
Vice-Chancellor, Prof. Simon Lee
Registrar and Secretary, Stephen Denton

UNIVERSITY OF LEICESTER (1957)
University Road, Leicester LE1 7RH **T** 0116-252 2522
W www.le.ac.uk
Students: 7,426 *Fees:* £3,070
Chancellor, Sir Peter Williams, CBE, FRS, FRENG
Vice-Chancellor, Prof. Robert Burgess
Registrar and Secretary, Dave Hall

UNIVERSITY OF LINCOLN (1992)
Brayford Pool, Lincoln LN6 7TS **T** 01522-882000
W www.lincoln.ac.uk
Students: 8,236 *Fees:* £3,000
Chancellor, Dame Elizabeth Esteve-Coll
Vice-Chancellor, Prof. David Chiddick
Registrar, Edmund Fitzpatrick

UNIVERSITY OF LIVERPOOL (1903)
Liverpool, Merseyside L69 72X **T** 0151-794 2000
W www.liv.ac.uk
Students: 13,880 *Fees:* £3,000
Chancellor, Lord Owen, CH, PC, FRCP
Vice-Chancellor, Prof. James Drummond Bone, FRSA
Chief Operating Officer, Ron Calvert

LIVERPOOL HOPE UNIVERSITY (2005)
Hope Park, Liverpool L16 9JD **T** 0151-291 3000
W www.hope.ac.uk
Students: 6,000 *Fees:* £3,000
Chancellor, Baroness Cox
Vice-Chancellor, Prof. Gerald Pillay, FRSA
University Secretary, Graham Donelan

LIVERPOOL JOHN MOORES UNIVERSITY (1992)
Egerton Court, 2 Rodney Street, Liverpool L3 5UX **T** 0151-231 2121 **W** www.ljmu.ac.uk
Students: 14,433 *Fees:* £3,070
Chancellor, vacant
Vice-Chancellor, Prof. Michael Brown
Secretary, Alison Wild

UNIVERSITY OF LONDON (1836)
Senate House, Malet Street, London WC1E 7HU **T** 020-7862 8000 **W** www.london.ac.uk
Students: 56,040 *Fees:* variable; contact individual colleges for details
Chancellor, HRH the Princess Royal, KG, GCVO, FRS
Vice-Chancellor, Prof. Sir Graeme Davies, FRENG, FRSE
Chair of the Council, Lord Sutherland of Houndwood, KT, FBA
Director of Administration, Catherine Swarbrick

COLLEGES

BIRKBECK COLLEGE
Malet Street, London WC1E 7HX
Master, Prof. D. Latchman

CENTRAL SCHOOL OF SPEECH AND DRAMA
Embassy Theatre, Eton Avenue, London NW3 3HY
Principal, Prof. Gavin Henderson, CBE

COURTAULD INSTITUTE OF ART
North Block, Somerset House, Strand, London WC2R 0RN
Director, Dr Deborah Swallow

GOLDSMITHS COLLEGE
Lewisham Way, New Cross, London SE14 6NW
Warden, Prof. Geoffrey Crossick

HEYTHROP COLLEGE
Kensington Square, London W8 5HQ
Principal, Revd Dr J. McDade, SJ, BD

INSTITUTE OF CANCER RESEARCH
Royal Cancer Hospital, Chester Beatty Laboratories, 237 Fulham Road, London SW3 6JB
Chief Executive, Prof. P. Rigby

INSTITUTE OF EDUCATION
20 Bedford Way, London WC1H 0AL
Director, Prof. G. Whitty

KING'S COLLEGE LONDON
(includes Guy's, King's and St Thomas's Schools of Medicine, Dentistry and Biomedical Sciences) Strand, London WC2R 2LS
Principal, Prof. R. Trainor

LONDON BUSINESS SCHOOL
Sussex Place, Regent's Park, London NW1 4SU
Dean, Robin Buchanan

LONDON SCHOOL OF ECONOMICS AND POLITICAL SCIENCE
Houghton Street, London WC2A 2AE
Director, Sir Howard Davies

LONDON SCHOOL OF HYGIENE AND TROPICAL MEDICINE
Keppel Street, London WC1E 7HT
Dean, Prof. Sir Andrew Haines

QUEEN MARY
(incorporating St Bartholomew's and the Royal London School of Medicine and Dentistry) Mile End Road, London E1 4NS
Principal, Prof. A. Smith, FRS

ROYAL ACADEMY OF MUSIC
Marylebone Road, London NW1 5HT
Principal, Prof. Curtis Price, KBE

ROYAL HOLLOWAY
Egham Hill, Egham, Surrey TW20 0EX
Principal, Prof. S. Hill, MPHIL

ROYAL VETERINARY COLLEGE
Royal College Street, London NW1 0TU
Principal and Dean, Prof. Q. McKellar

ST GEORGE'S
Cranmer Terrace, London SW17 0RE
Acting Principal, Prof. Sean Hilton, FRCGP

SCHOOL OF ORIENTAL AND AFRICAN STUDIES
Thornhaugh Street, Russell Square, London WC1H 1AX
Director, Prof. Paul Webley

SCHOOL OF PHARMACY
29–39 Brunswick Square, London WC1N 1AX
Dean, Prof. Anthony Smith

UNIVERSITY COLLEGE LONDON
(including UCL Medical School) Gower Street, London WC1E 6BT
Provost and President, Prof. Malcolm Grant, CBE

INSTITUTES
UNIVERSITY OF LONDON INSTITUTE IN PARIS
9–11 rue de Constantine, 75340 Paris, Cedex 07
Director, Dr David Shepheard

UNIVERSITY MARINE BIOLOGICAL STATION
Millport, Isle of Cumbrae KA28 0EG
Acting Director, Prof. P. G. Moore

SCHOOL OF ADVANCED STUDY
Senate House, Malet Street, London WC1E 7HU
Dean, vacant

INSTITUTE OF ADVANCED LEGAL STUDIES
Charles Clore House, 17 Russell Square, London WC1B 5DR
Director, Prof. Avrom Sherr

INSTITUTE OF CLASSICAL STUDIES
Senate House, Malet Street, London WC1E 7HU
Director, Prof. M. Edwards

INSTITUTE OF COMMONWEALTH STUDIES
28 Russell Square, London WC1B 5DS
Director, Prof. R. Crook

INSTITUTE OF ENGLISH STUDIES
Senate House, Malet Street, London WC1E 7HU
Director, Prof. W. Gould

INSTITUTE OF GERMANIC AND ROMANCE STUDIES
Senate House, Malet Street, London WC1E 7HU
Director, Prof. Naomi Segal

INSTITUTE OF HISTORICAL RESEARCH
Senate House, Malet Street, London WC1E 7HU
Director, Prof. David Bates

INSTITUTE OF MUSICAL RESEARCH
Senate House, Malet Street, London WC1E 7HU
Director, Prof. Katharine Ellis

INSTITUTE OF PHILOSOPHY
Senate House, Malet Street, London WC1E 7HU
Director, Prof. Tim Crane

INSTITUTE FOR THE STUDY OF THE AMERICAS
31 Tavistock Square, London WC1H 9HA
Director, Prof. J. Dunkerley

WARBURG INSTITUTE
Woburn Square, London WC1H 0AB
Director, Prof. C. Hope

DISTANCE LEARNING
EXTERNAL PROGRAMME
Senate House, Malet Street, London WC1E 7HU
Director, J. M. McConnell
Dean, Prof. J. Kydd

LONDON METROPOLITAN UNIVERSITY (2002)
31 Jewry Street, London EC3N 2EY **T** 020-7423 0000
W www.londonmet.ac.uk
Students: 21,000 *Fees:* £3,000
Vice-Chancellor and Chief Executive, Brian Roper
Academic Registrar, Dr Ray Smith

LONDON SOUTH BANK UNIVERSITY (1992)
103 Borough Road, London SE1 0AA **T** 020-7815 7815
W www.lsbu.ac.uk
Students: 9,000 *Fees:* £3,000
Chancellor, Jane Newell, OBE
Vice-Chancellor, Prof. Deian Hopkin, FRSA

LOUGHBOROUGH UNIVERSITY (1966)
Ashby Road, Loughborough, Leics LE11 3TU **T** 01509-263171
W www.lboro.ac.uk
Students: 10,505 *Fees:* £3,070
Chancellor, Sir John Jennings, CBE, FRSE
Vice-Chancellor, Prof. Shirley Pearce, CBE
Academic Registrar, John Town

UNIVERSITY OF MANCHESTER (2004)
Oxford Road, Manchester M13 9PL **T** 0161-306 6000
W www.manchester.ac.uk
Students: 26,440 *Fees:* £3,000
Co-Chancellors, Anna Ford and Sir Terry Leahy
President and Vice-Chancellor, Prof. Alan Gilbert
Registrar and Secretary, Albert McMenemy

MANCHESTER METROPOLITAN UNIVERSITY (1992)
All Saints, Manchester M15 6BH **T** 0161-247 2000
W www.mmu.ac.uk
Students: 24,127 *Fees:* £3,070
Chancellor, Dame Janet Smith, DBE, PC
Vice-Chancellor, Prof. John Brooks, DSC, FINSTP
Registrar, Gwyn Arnold

IDDLESEX UNIVERSITY (1992)
orth London Business Park, Oakleigh Road South, London
1 1QS **T** 020-8411 5555 **W** www.mdx.ac.uk
udents: 14,230 *Fees:* £3,070
hancellor, Lord Sheppard of Didgemere, KT, KCVO
ice-Chancellor, Prof. Michael Driscoll
gistrar, Colin Davis

APIER UNIVERSITY (1992)
aighouse Road, Edinburgh EH10 5LG **T** 0845-260 6040
www.napier.ac.uk
udents: 11,690 *Fees:* £1,735
incipal and Vice-Chancellor, Prof. Joan Stringer, CBE
gistrar and Secretary, Dr Gerry Webber

NIVERSITY OF NEWCASTLE UPON TYNE (1963)
Kensington Terrace, Newcastle upon Tyne NE1 7RU
0191-222 6000 **W** www.ncl.ac.uk
udents: 14,058 *Fees:* £3,070
hancellor, Rt. Hon. Lord Patten of Barnes, CH
ice-Chancellor, Prof. Chris Brink, FRS, DPHIL, PHD
gistrar, Dr John Hogan

NIVERSITY OF NORTHAMPTON (2005)
rk Campus, Boughton Green Road, Northampton NN2 7AL
01604-735500 **W** www.northampton.ac.uk
udents: 6,761 *Fees:* £3,070
ice-Chancellor, Ann Tate
gistrar, Jane Bunce

ORTHUMBRIA UNIVERSITY AT NEWCASTLE
992)
ison Building, Ellison Place, Newcastle upon Tyne NE1 8ST
0191-232 6002 **W** www.northumbria.ac.uk
udents: 19,507 *Fees:* £3,070
hancellor, Lord Stevens of Kirkwhelpington, QPM, FRSA
ice-Chancellor, Prof. Kel Fidler, FRENG
gistrar, Paul Kelly

NIVERSITY OF NOTTINGHAM (1948)
ng's Meadow Campus, Lenton Lane, Nottingham NG7 2NR
0115-951 5151 **W** www.nottingham.ac.uk
udents: 20,282 *Fees:* £3,070
hancellor, Prof. Yang Fujia, LITTD
ce Chancellor, Prof. Sir Colin Campbell
gistrar, Dr Paul Greatrix

OTTINGHAM TRENT UNIVERSITY (1992)
rton Street, Nottingham NG1 4BU **T** 0115-941 8418
www.ntu.ac.uk
udents: 18,459 *Fees:* £3,070
nior Pro-Vice-Chancellor, Peter Jones
ce-Chancellor, Prof. Neil Gorman

PEN UNIVERSITY (1969)
alton Hall, Milton Keynes MK7 6AA **T** 01908-274066
www.open.ac.uk
udents: 150,000 (all part-time) *Fees:* £3,500–£4,000
hancellor, Lord Puttnam of Queensgate
ce-Chancellor, Prof. Brenda Gourley
niversity Secretary, Fraser Woodburn

NIVERSITY OF OXFORD (c.12th century)
iversity Offices, Wellington Square, Oxford OX1 2JD
01865-270000 **W** www.ox.ac.uk
udents: 11,185 *Fees:* £3,070
Chancellor, Lord Patten of Barnes, CH, PC (Balliol, St Antony's)
High Steward, Lord Bingham of Cornhill, PC (Balliol, Nuffield)
Vice-Chancellor, Dr John Hood (All Souls, Templeton, Worcester)
Pro-Vice-Chancellors, Dame Fiona Caldicott (Somerville); Dr J. S. Dellandrea (Magdalen); Prof. E. A. Fallaize (St John's); Prof. E. G. McKendrick (Lady Margaret Hall); Prof. A. P. Monaco (Merton)
Registrar, Dr J. K. Maxton (University)
Secretary of the Faculties and Academic Registrar, M. D. Sibly (St Anne's)
Proctors, Dr J. Forder (Balliol); Prof. M. J. Banks (Wolfson)
Assessor, Dr P. Coones (Hertford)
Public Orator, R. H. A. Jenkyns
Director of University Library Services and Bodley's Librarian, Dr S. E. Thomas (Balliol)
Director of the Ashmolean Museum, Dr C. Brown (Worcester)
Keeper of Archives, S. Bailey
Director of Estates, Ms J. Wood
Director of Finance, G. F. B. Kerr

COLLEGES AND HALLS *with dates of foundation*
ALL SOULS (1438)
Warden, Prof. J. Davis, FBA
BALLIOL (1263)
Master, A. Graham
BLACKFRIARS (1221)
Regent, Revd Richard Finn
BRASENOSE (1509)
Principal, Prof. R. Cashmore, FRS
CAMPION HALL (1896)
Master, Revd Dr P. l'Estrange
CHRIST CHURCH (1546)
Dean, Very Revd C. A. Lewis
CORPUS CHRISTI (1517)
President, Timothy Lankester, KCB
EXETER (1314)
Rector, Ms Frances Cairncross, CBE
GREEN (1979)
Warden, Dr Colin Bundy
GREYFRIARS (1910)
Warden, Dr Nicholas Richardson
HARRIS MANCHESTER (1786)
Principal, Revd R. Waller
HERTFORD (1974)
Principal, Dr John Landers
JESUS (1571)
Principal, Lord Krebs, FRS
KEBLE (1868)
Warden, Prof. A. Cameron, CBE, FBA
KELLOGG (1990)
President, Dr G. P. Thomas
LADY MARGARET HALL (1878)
Principal, Dr Frances Lannon
LINACRE (1962)
Principal, Prof. P. A. Slack, FBA
LINCOLN (1427)
Rector, Prof. P. Langford
MAGDALEN (1458)
President, Prof. David Clary, FRS
MANSFIELD (1886)
Principal, Dr D. Walford, FRCP
MERTON (1264)
Warden, Prof. Dame J. Rawson, CBE, FBA

NEW COLLEGE (1379)
Warden, Prof. A. J. Ryan, FBA
NUFFIELD (1958)
Warden, Prof. Stephen Nickell, FBA
ORIEL (1326)
Provost, Sir Derek Morris
PEMBROKE (1624)
Master, Giles Henderson, CBE
QUEEN'S (1340)
Provost, Sir Alan Budd
REGENT'S PARK (1820)
Principal, Revd Dr P. S. Fiddes
ST ANNE'S (1952)
Principal, Tim Gardam
ST ANTONY'S (1953)
Warden, Prof. Margaret MacMillan
ST BENET'S HALL (1897)
Master, Father Leo Chamberlain
ST CATHERINE'S (1963)
Master, Prof. Roger Ainsworth
ST CROSS (1965)
Master, Prof. Andrew Goudie
ST EDMUND HALL (c.1278)
Principal, Prof. D. M. P. Mingos, FRS
ST HILDA'S (1893)
Principal, Sheila Forbes, CBE
ST HUGH'S (1886)
Principal, A. Dilnot, CBE
ST JOHN'S (1555)
President, Sir Michael Scholar, KCB
ST PETER'S (1929)
Master, Prof. Bernard Silverman, FRS
ST STEPHEN'S HOUSE (1876)
Principal, Revd Dr Robin Ward
SOMERVILLE (1879)
Principal, Dame Fiona Caldicott, DBE, FRCP, FRCPSYCH
TEMPLETON (1965)
Dean, Prof. Michael Earl
TRINITY (1554)
President, Sir Ivor Roberts, KCMG
UNIVERSITY (1249)
Master, Lord Butler of Brockwell, GCB, CVO
WADHAM (1610)
Warden, Sir Neil Chalmers, CBE
WOLFSON (1966)
President (acting), Prof. John Stallworthy, FBA, FRSL
WORCESTER (1714)
Provost, R. G. Smethurst
WYCLIFFE HALL (1877)
Principal, Revd Dr Richard Turnbull

OXFORD BROOKES UNIVERSITY (1992)
Gipsy Lane, Oxford OX3 0BP T 01865-741111
W www.brookes.ac.uk
Students: 13,670 *Fees:* £3,070
Chancellor, Jon Snow
Vice-Chancellor, Prof. Graham Upton
Academic Registrar, Stephen Marshall

UNIVERSITY OF PAISLEY (1992)
Paisley PA1 2BE T 0141-848 3000 W www.paisley.ac.uk
Students: 5,873 *Fees:* £1,700
Chancellor, Sir Robert Smith, FSA
Principal and Vice-Chancellor, Prof. Seamus McDaid
Secretary, David Rigg
Academic Registrar, Donna McMillan

UNIVERSITY OF PLYMOUTH (1992)
Drake Circus, Plymouth PL4 8AA T 01752-600600
W www.plymouth.ac.uk
Students: 24,250 *Fees:* £3,070
Vice-Chancellor (acting), Prof. Steve Newstead
Academic Registrar and Secretary, Jane Hopkinson

UNIVERSITY OF PORTSMOUTH (1992)
University House, Winston Churchill Avenue, Portsmouth PO1 2UP T 023-9284 8484 W www.port.ac.uk
Students: 15,287 *Fees:* £3,000
Chancellor, Lord Palumbo
Vice-Chancellor, Prof. John Craven
Academic Registrar, Andy Rees

QUEEN'S UNIVERSITY BELFAST (1908)
University Road, Belfast BT7 1NN T 028-9024 5133
W www.qub.ac.uk
Students: 15,200 *Fees:* £3,070
Chancellor, Senator George Mitchell
Vice-Chancellor, Prof. Peter Gregson, FRENG
Registrar, James O'Kane

UNIVERSITY OF READING (1926)
Whiteknights, PO Box 217, Reading RG6 6AH T 0118-987 51[illegible]
W www.reading.ac.uk
Students: 8,840 *Fees:* £3,070
Chancellor, Rt. Hon. Lord Carrington of Upton, KG, GCMG, CH
Vice-Chancellor, Prof. Gordon Marshall, CBE, FBA
Director of Student Services, W. D. Watts

ROBERT GORDON UNIVERSITY (1992)
Schoolhill, Aberdeen AB10 1FR T 01224-262000
W www.rgu.ac.uk
Students: 6,850 *Fees:* £1,735
Chancellor, Sir Ian Wood, CBE
Vice-Chancellor, Prof. R. Michael Pittilo
Academic Registrar, Hilary Douglas

ROEHAMPTON UNIVERSITY (2004)
Erasmus House, Roehampton Lane, London SW15 5PU
T 020-8392 3000 W www.roehampton.ac.uk
Students: 6,351 *Fees:* £3,070
Chancellor, John Simpson, CBE
Vice-Chancellor, Prof. Paul O'Prey
Academic Secretary, Andrew Skinner

ROYAL COLLEGE OF ART (1967)
Kensington Gore, London SW7 2EU T 020-7590 4444
W www.rca.ac.uk
Students: 850 (postgraduate only) *Fees:* £4,250
Provost, Sir Terence Conran
Rector and Vice-Provost, Prof. Sir Christopher Frayling, PHD
Registrar, Alan Selby

ROYAL COLLEGE OF MUSIC (1882)
Prince Consort Road, London SW7 2BS T 020-7589 3643
W www.rcm.ac.uk
Students: 350 *Fees:* £3,000
President, HRH Prince of Wales, KG, KT, GCB
Vice-Chancellor, Dr Colin Lawson, DMUS, FRCM
Registrar and Secretary, Kevin Porter

UNIVERSITY OF ST ANDREWS (1413)
College Gate, St Andrews, Fife KY16 9AJ T 01334-476161
W www.st-andrews.ac.uk

Students: 5,746 *Fees:* £1,735
Chancellor, Rt. Hon. Sir Menzies Campbell, CBE, QC, MP
Principal and Vice-Chancellor, Dr Brian Lang
Secretary and Registrar, Mark Butler

UNIVERSITY OF SALFORD (1967)
Salford, Greater Manchester M5 4WT **T** 0161-295 5000
W www.salford.ac.uk
Students: 12,753 *Fees:* £3,070
Chancellor, Prof. Sir Martin Harris
Vice-Chancellor, Prof. Michael Harloe
Registrar, Dr Adrian Graves

UNIVERSITY OF SHEFFIELD (1905)
Western Bank, Sheffield S10 2TN **T** 0114-222 2000
W www.shef.ac.uk
Students: 16,877 *Fees:* £3,070
Chancellor, Sir Peter Middleton, GCB
Vice-Chancellor, Prof. R. F. Boucher, CBE, FRENG
Registrar and Secretary, Dr D. E. Fletcher

SHEFFIELD HALLAM UNIVERSITY (1992)
City Campus, Howard Street, Sheffield S1 1WB **T** 0114-225 5555 **W** www.shu.ac.uk
Students: 17,500 *Fees:* £3,070
Chancellor, Prof. Lord Winston, FRCOG, FRCP
Vice-Chancellor, Prof. Philip Jones, LLB, LLM
Secretary and Registrar, Liz Winders

UNIVERSITY OF SOUTHAMPTON (1952)
Building 37, Highfield, Southampton SO17 1BJ **T** 023-8059 5000 **W** www.soton.ac.uk
Students: 13,850 *Fees:* £3,070
Chancellor, Sir John Parker
Vice-Chancellor, Prof. William A. Wakeham
Registrar and Chief Operating Officer, Simon Higman

SOUTHAMPTON SOLENT UNIVERSITY (2005)
East Park Terrace, Southampton SO14 0YN **T** 023-8031 9000
W www.solent.ac.uk
Students: 8,900 *Fees:* £3,070
Chancellor, Sir Alan West, GCB, DSC
Vice-Chancellor, Prof. Van Gore

STAFFORDSHIRE UNIVERSITY (1992)
Federation House, Stoke-on-Trent, Staffs ST4 2DE
T 01782-294000 **W** www.staffs.ac.uk
Students: 8,895 *Fees:* £3,000
Chancellor, Lord Morris of Handsworth
Vice-Chancellor, Prof. Christine E. King, CBE
University Secretary, Ken Sproston

UNIVERSITY OF STIRLING (1967)
Stirling FK9 4LA **T** 01786-473171 **W** www.stir.ac.uk
Students: 6,050 *Fees:* £1,735
Chancellor, Dame Diana Rigg, CBE
Vice-Chancellor, Prof. Christine Hallett, FRSE
Registrar, Joanna Morrow

UNIVERSITY OF STRATHCLYDE (1964)
16 Richmond Street, Glasgow G1 1XQ **T** 0141-552 4400
W www.strath.ac.uk
Students: 11,400 *Fees:* £1,700
Chancellor, Rt. Hon. Lord Hope of Craighead, FRSE
Vice-Chancellor and Principal, Prof. Andrew Hamnett, DPHIL, FRSC, FRSE
Secretary, Dr Peter West, OBE

UNIVERSITY OF SUNDERLAND (1992)
Edinburgh Building, Chester Road, Sunderland SR1 3SD
T 0191-515 2000 **W** www.sunderland.ac.uk
Students: 8,500 *Fees:* £3,070
Chancellor, vacant
Vice-Chancellor, Prof. Peter Fidler
Academic Registrar, Beatrice Ollerenshaw

UNIVERSITY OF SURREY (1966)
Guildford, Surrey GU2 7XH **T** 01483-300800
W www.surrey.ac.uk
Students: 7,000 *Fees:* £3,070
Chancellor, HRH the Duke of Kent, KG, KT, OM
Vice-Chancellor, Prof. Christopher Snowden, FRS, FRENG
Registrar, P. Henry, TD

UNIVERSITY OF SUSSEX (1961)
Sussex House, Falmer, Brighton BN1 9RH **T** 01273-606755
W www.sussex.ac.uk
Students: 7,427 *Fees:* £3,070
Chancellor, Lord Attenborough, CBE
Vice-Chancellor, Prof. Alasdair Smith
Academic Registrar, Dr Philip Harvey

UNIVERSITY OF TEESSIDE (1992)
Middlesbrough, Tees Valley TS1 3BA **T** 01642-218121
W www.tees.ac.uk
Students: 8,308 *Fees:* £3,070
Chancellor, Lord Sawyer
Vice-Chancellor, Prof. Graham Henderson
Registrar, Morgan McClintock

THAMES VALLEY UNIVERSITY (1992)
St Mary's Road, Ealing, London W5 5RF **T** 020-8579 5000
W www.tvu.ac.uk
Students: 6,115 *Fees:* £2,770
Chancellor, Lord Bilimoria, CBE
Vice-Chancellor, Prof. Geoff Crispin
Registrar, Chris Broomfield

UCE BIRMINGHAM (1992)
Perry Barr, Birmingham B42 2SU **T** 0121-331 5595 **W** www.uce.ac.uk
Students: 19,628 *Fees:* £3,000
Chancellor, Lord Mayor of Birmingham, Councillor Mike Sharpe
Vice-Chancellor, Prof. David H. Tidmarsh, FIMECHE, FCMI
Registrar, Maxine Penlington

UNIVERSITY OF ULSTER (1984)
Cromore Road, Coleraine, Co. Londonderry BT52 1SA
T 0870-040 0700 **W** www.ulster.ac.uk
Students: 17,100 *Fees:* £3,070
Chancellor, Sir Richard Nichols
Vice-Chancellor, Prof. Richard Barnett
Director of Corporate and Governance, Irene Aston

UNIVERSITY OF WALES (1893)
King Edward VII Avenue, Cathays Park, Cardiff CF10 3NS
T 029-2038 2656 **W** www.wales.ac.uk
Students: variable; contact individual institutions for details *Fees:* variable; contact individual institutions for details
Chancellor, HRH The Prince of Wales, KG, KT, GCB
Senior Vice-Chancellor, Prof. A. J. Chapman, FRSA
Secretary-General, Dr L. E. Williams

MEMBER INSTITUTIONS

UNIVERSITY OF WALES, ABERYSTWYTH
Old College, King Street, Aberystwyth SY23 2AX
T 01970-623111
Vice-Chancellor, Prof. N. G. Lloyd

UNIVERSITY OF WALES, BANGOR
Gwynedd LL57 2DG T 01248-351151
Vice-Chancellor, Prof. R. M. Jones

UNIVERSITY OF WALES, LAMPETER
Lampeter SA48 7ED T 01570-422351
Vice-Chancellor, Prof. R. A. Pearce

UNIVERSITY OF WALES, NEWPORT
Caerleon Campus, PO Box 179, Newport NP6 1YG
T 01633-430088
Vice-Chancellor, Dr P. Noyes

UNIVERSITY OF WALES, SWANSEA
Singleton Park SA2 8PP T 01792-205678
Vice-Chancellor, Prof. R. B. Davies

UNIVERSITY OF WALES INSTITUTE, CARDIFF
Llandaff Centre, Western Avenue, Cardiff CF5 2SG
T 029-2041 6070
Vice-Chancellor, Prof. A. J. Chapman

NORTH EAST WALES INSTITUTE OF HIGHER EDUCATION
Plas Coch, Mold Road, Wrexham LL11 2AW T 01978-290666
Principal, Prof. M. Scott

SWANSEA INSTITUTE OF HIGHER EDUCATION
Mount Pleasant, Swansea SA1 6ED T 01792-481000
Principal, Prof. D. Warner

TRINITY COLLEGE, CARMARTHEN
Carmarthen SA31 3EP T 01267-676767
Principal, Dr M. Hughes

UNIVERSITY OF WARWICK (1965)
Coventry CV4 7AL T 024-7652 3523 W www.warwick.ac.uk
Students: 11,315 *Fees:* £3,070
Chancellor, Sir Nicholas Scheele
Vice-Chancellor, Prof. Nigel Thrift
Registrar, Jon Baldwin

UNIVERSITY OF WESTMINSTER (1992)
309 Regent Street, London W1B 2UW T 020-7911 5000
W www.wmin.ac.uk
Students: 10,839 *Fees:* £3,070
Chancellor, Lord Paul
Vice-Chancellor, Dr Geoffrey Copland
Academic Registrar, Evelyne Rugg

UNIVERSITY OF THE WEST OF ENGLAND (1992)
Frenchay Campus, Coldharbour Lane, Bristol BS16 1QY
T 0117-965 6261 W www.uwe.ac.uk
Students: 16,891 *Fees:* £3,070
Chancellor, Rt. Hon. Dame Elizabeth Butler-Sloss, CBE
Vice-Chancellor, Sir Howard Newby, KB, CBE
Registrar, Tessa Harrison

UNIVERSITY OF WINCHESTER (2005)
West Hill, Winchester SO22 4NR T 01962-841515
W www.winchester.ac.uk
Students: 3,300 *Fees:* £3,070
Chancellor, Mary Fagan
Vice-Chancellor, Prof. Joy Carter
Registrar, Lyn Black

UNIVERSITY OF WOLVERHAMPTON (1992)
Wulfruna Street, Wolverhampton WV1 1SB T 01902-321000
W www.wlv.ac.uk
Students: 12,534 *Fees:* £3,070
Chancellor, Lord Paul
Vice-Chancellor, Prof. Caroline Gipps
Registrar, Paul Travill

UNIVERSITY OF WORCESTER (2005)
Henwick Grove, Worcester WR2 6AJ T 01905-855000
W www.worcester.ac.uk
Students: 8,000 *Fees:* £3,070
Vice-Chancellor and Chief Executive, Prof. David Green
Registrar and Secretary, John Ryan

UNIVERSITY OF YORK (1963)
Heslington, York YO10 5DD T 01904-430000
W www.york.ac.uk
Students: 7,923 *Fees:* £3,070
Chancellor, Greg Dyke
Vice-Chancellor, Prof. Brian Cantor, FRENG, FIM, FRMS
Registrar, Sally Neocosmos

PROFESSIONAL EDUCATION

The organisations selected below provide specialist training, conduct examinations or are responsible for maintaining a register of those with professional qualifications in their sector, thereby controlling entry into a profession.

EU RECOGNITION

It is possible for those with professional qualifications obtained in the UK to have these recognised in other European countries. Further information can be obtained online (**W** www.dfes.gov.uk/europeopen) or from:

DEPARTMENT FOR CHILDREN, SCHOOLS AND FAMILIES Sanctuary Buildings, Great Smith Street, London SW1P 3BT **T** 0870-000 2288 **E** info@dfes.gsi.gov.uk

ACCOUNTANCY

The vast majority of chartered accountancy trainees are graduates, and entry to the profession is open to graduates of all disciplines. The undergraduate degree is followed by a three-year training contract with an approved employer culminating in professional exams provided by the Institute of Chartered Accountants in England and Wales (ICAEW), the Institute of Chartered Accountants of Scotland (ICAS) or the Institute of Chartered Accountants in Ireland (ICAI). Success in the examination and membership of one of the institutes allows the use of the designation 'chartered accountant' and the letters ACA or CA.

The training route for chartered certified accountants is similar to that of chartered accountants and is taken by students in a range of business sectors and countries. The Association of Chartered Certified Accountants (ACCA) qualification involves up to 14 examinations and a minimum of three years of relevant supervised experience. Chartered certified accountants can use the designatory letters ACCA.

Chartered management accountants focus on accounting for businesses, and most do not work in accountancy practices but in industry, commerce, not-for-profit and public sector organisations. Graduates who have not studied a business or accounting undergraduate degree must gain the Chartered Institute of Management Accountants (CIMA) Certificate in Business Accounting (formerly known as the foundation level) before studying for the CIMA Professional Qualification. The qualification requires three years of practical experience combined with nine examinations and a pass in the Institute's Test of Professional Competence in Management Accounting (TOPCIMA).

Chartered public finance accountants usually work for public bodies, but they can also work in the private sector. To gain chartered public finance accountant status (CPFA), trainees must complete the three parts of the Chartered Institute of Public Finance and Accountancy (CIPFA) Professional Accountancy Qualification (PAQ), which takes approximately three years. The first stage is the certificate level, which leads to affiliate membership of CIPFA, the second is the diploma level which leads to associate membership, and finally completion of the Final Test of Professional Competence leads to full membership of CIPFA.

ASSOCIATION OF CHARTERED CERTIFIED ACCOUNTANTS (ACCA) 29 Lincoln's Inn Fields, London WC2A 3EE **T** 020-7059 5000 **E** info@accaglobal.com **W** www.accaglobal.com
Chief Executive, Allen Blewitt

CHARTERED INSTITUTE OF MANAGEMENT ACCOUNTANTS (CIMA) 26 Chapter Street, London SW1P 4NP **T** 020-7663 5441 **W** www.cimaglobal.com
Chief Executive, Charles Tilley

CHARTERED INSTITUTE OF PUBLIC FINANCE AND ACCOUNTANCY (CIPFA) 3 Robert Street, London WC2N 6RL **T** 030-7543 5600 **E** corporate@cipfa.org **W** www.cipfa.org.uk
Chief Executive, Steve Freer

INSTITUTE OF CHARTERED ACCOUNTANTS IN ENGLAND AND WALES (ICAEW) Chartered Accountants' Hall, PO Box 433, London EC2P 2BJ **T** 020-7920 8100 **W** www.icaew.com
Chief Executive, Michael Izza

INSTITUTE OF CHARTERED ACCOUNTANTS IN IRELAND (ICAI) The Linenhall, 32–38 Linenhall Street, Belfast BT2 8BG **T** 028-9032 1600 **E** ca@icai.ie **W** www.icai.ie
Chief Executive, Pat Costello

INSTITUTE OF CHARTERED ACCOUNTANTS OF SCOTLAND (ICAS) CA House, 21 Haymarket Yards, Edinburgh EH12 5BH **T** 0131-347 0100 **E** enquiries@icas.org.uk **W** www.icas.org.uk
Chief Executive, Anton Colella

ACTUARIAL SCIENCE

The UK actuarial profession is controlled by the Institute of Actuaries in London and the Faculty of Actuaries in Edinburgh (operating together as 'the actuarial profession'). The faculty and institute together issue technical guidance, develop actuarial techniques and set examinations, professional codes and disciplinary standards, and they develop actuarial techniques and guidance. UK qualified actuaries may be fellows of either organisation. On average, it takes five years to qualify as an actuary; examinations are held twice a year, and applicants to the profession must also have completed three years of actuarial work experience before gaining fellowship.

In March 2005, HM Treasury asked the Financial Reporting Council (FRC) to oversee the actuarial profession. The FRC established a new body, the Board for Actuarial Standards, to set and maintain actuarial standards independently of the profession while the Professional Oversight Board of the FRC oversees the actuarial profession and is responsible for accountancy, audit and corporate reporting and governance.

FACULTY OF ACTUARIES Maclaurin House, 18 Dublin Street, Edinburgh EH1 3PP **T** 0131-240 1300 **E** faculty@actuaries.org.uk **W** www.actuaries.org.uk
Secretary, Richard Maconachie

FINANCIAL REPORTING COUNCIL (FRC) 5th Floor, Aldwych House, 71–91 Aldwych, London WC2B 4HN **T** 020-7492 2300 **W** www.frc.org.uk
Chief Executive, Paul Boyle

INSTITUTE OF ACTUARIES Staple Inn Hall, High Holborn, London WC1V 7QJ T 020-7632 2100 E institute@actuaries.org.uk W www.actuaries.org.uk
Chief Executive, Caroline Instance

ARCHITECTURE

It takes a minimum of seven years to become an architect, involving three stages: a three-year first degree, a two-year second degree or diploma and two years of professional experience followed by the successful completion of a professional practice examination. Architectural qualifications are validated by the Royal Institute of British Architects (RIBA).

The Architects Registration Board (ARB) is the independent regulator for the profession. It was set up by an act of parliament in 1997 and is responsible for maintaining the register of UK architects, prescribing qualifications that lead to registration as an architect, the conduct and competence of architects, and ensuring only those who are registered with ARB use the title of 'architect'. It is only following registration with ARB that an architect can apply for chartered membership of RIBA. RIBA received its royal charter in 1837 and recognises courses at 40 schools of architecture in the UK for exemption from their own examinations as well as courses at 57 overseas schools.

The Chartered Institute of Architectural Technologists is the qualifying body for chartered architectural technologists (MCIAT) and architectural technicians (TCIAT).

ARCHITECTS REGISTRATION BOARD (ARB) 8 Weymouth Street, London W1W 5BU T 020-7580 5861 E info@arb.org.uk W www.arb.org.uk
Registrar and Chief Executive, Alison Carr

CHARTERED INSTITUTE OF ARCHITECTURAL TECHNOLOGISTS 397 City Road, London EC1V 1NH T 020-7278 2206 E info@ciat.org.uk W www.ciat.org.uk
Chief Executive, Francesca Berriman

ROYAL INSTITUTE OF BRITISH ARCHITECTS (RIBA) 66 Portland Place, London W1B 1AD T 020-7580 5533 E info@inst.riba.org W www.riba.org
Chief Executive, Richard Hastilow, CBE

ENGINEERING

The Engineering Council UK (ECUK) sets standards of professional competence and ethics for engineers, technologists and technicians, and regulates the profession through the 35 institutions (Licensed Members) listed below who are licensed to put suitably qualified members on the ECUK's Register of Engineers. All candidates for registration as Chartered Engineer, Incorporated Engineer or Engineering Technician must satisfy the competence standards set by ECUK and be members of the appropriate institution. Applicants must show that they have a satisfactory educational base, have undergone approved professional development, and, at interview, must demonstrate their professional competence against specific criteria.

ENGINEERING COUNCIL 10 Maltravers Street, London WC2R 3ER T 020-3206 0500 E info@engc.org.uk W www.engc.org.uk
Chief Executive Officer, Andrew Ramsay

LICENSED MEMBERS

BRITISH COMPUTER SOCIETY W www.bcs.org.uk

BRITISH INSTITUTE OF NON-DESTRUCTIVE TESTING W www.bindt.org

CHARTERED INSTITUTION OF BUILDING SERVICES ENGINEERS W www.cibse.org

CHARTERED INSTITUTION OF WATER AND ENVIRONMENTAL MANAGEMENT W www.ciwem.org.uk

ENERGY INSTITUTE W www.energyinst.org.uk

INSTITUTE OF ACOUSTICS W www.ioa.org.uk

INSTITUTE OF CAST METALS ENGINEERS W www.icme.org.uk

INSTITUTE OF HEALTHCARE ENGINEERING AND ESTATE MANAGEMENT W www.iheem.org.uk

INSTITUTE OF HIGHWAY INCORPORATED ENGINEERS W www.ihie.org.uk

INSTITUTE OF MARINE ENGINEERING, SCIENCE AND TECHNOLOGY W www.imarest.org

INSTITUTE OF MATERIALS, MINERALS AND MINING W www.iom3.org

INSTITUTE OF MEASUREMENT AND CONTROL W www.instmc.org.uk

INSTITUTE OF THE MOTOR INDUSTRY W www.motor.org.uk

INSTITUTE OF PHYSICS W www.iop.org

INSTITUTE OF PHYSICS AND ENGINEERING IN MEDICINE W www.ipem.org.uk

INSTITUTE OF PLUMBING AND HEATING ENGINEERING W www.iphe.org.uk

INSTITUTION OF AGRICULTURAL ENGINEERS W www.iagre.org

INSTITUTION OF CHEMICAL ENGINEERS W www.icheme.org

INSTITUTION OF CIVIL ENGINEERS W www.ice.org.uk

INSTITUTION OF ENGINEERING DESIGNERS W www.ied.org.uk

INSTITUTION OF ENGINEERING AND TECHNOLOGY W www.theiet.org

INSTITUTION OF FIRE ENGINEERS W www.ife.org.uk

INSTITUTION OF GAS ENGINEERS AND MANAGERS W www.igem.org.uk

INSTITUTION OF HIGHWAYS AND TRANSPORTATION W www.iht.org

INSTITUTION OF LIGHTING ENGINEERS W www.ile.org.uk

INSTITUTION OF MECHANICAL ENGINEERS W www.imeche.org.uk

INSTITUTION OF NUCLEAR ENGINEERS W www.inuce.org.uk

INSTITUTION OF RAILWAY SIGNAL ENGINEERS W www.irse.org

INSTITUTION OF STRUCTURAL ENGINEERS W www.istructe.org.uk

INSTITUTION OF WATER OFFICERS W www.iwo.org.uk

ROYAL AERONAUTICAL SOCIETY W www.raes.org.uk

ROYAL INSTITUTION OF NAVAL ARCHITECTS W www.rina.org.uk

SOCIETY OF ENVIRONMENTAL ENGINEERS W www.environmental.org.uk

SOCIETY OF OPERATIONS ENGINEERS W www.soe.org.uk

WELDING INSTITUTE W www.twi.co.uk

IEALTHCARE

:HIROPRACTIC

he General Chiropractic Council (GCC) is the statutory :gulatory body for chiropractors and its role and remit is efined in the Chiropractors Act 1994. The GCC sets the riteria for the recognition of chiropractic degrees and for :andards of proficiency and conduct. Details of the ıstitutions offering degree programmes are available on ıe GCC website (*see* below). It is illegal for anyone in the K to use the title 'chiropractor' unless registered with ıe GCC.

The British Chiropractic Association, McTimoney :hiropractic Association, Scottish Chiropractic ssociation and the United Chiropractic Association are presentative bodies for the profession and are sources of ırther information about chiropractic.

RITISH CHIROPRACTIC ASSOCIATION 59 Castle Street, Reading RG1 7SN T 0118-950 5950 E enquiries@chiropractic-uk.co.uk
Executive Director, Sue Wakefield

ENERAL CHIROPRACTIC COUNCIL 44 Wicklow Street, London WC1X 9HL T 020-7713 5155 E enquiries@gcc-uk.org W www.gcc-uk.org
Chief Executive, Margaret Coats

ICTIMONEY CHIROPRACTIC ASSOCIATION Crowmarsh Gifford, Wallingford OX10 8DJ T 01491-829211 E admin@mctimoney-chiropractic.org W www.mctimoney-chiropractic.org
Chair, Christina Cunliffe

COTTISH CHIROPRACTIC ASSOCIATION Laigh Hatton Farm, Old Greenock Road, Bishopton, Renfrewshire PA7 5BP T 01505-863151 E admin@sca-chiropractic.org W www.sca-chiropractic.org
Chief Executive, Morag Cairns

NITED CHIROPRACTIC ASSOCIATION 17 Fore Street, Ivybridge PL21 9AB T 01752-896223 E admin@united-chiropractic.org W www.united-chiropractic.org
Secretary, Melissa Sandford

ENTISTRY

he General Dental Council (GDC) is the organisation ıat regulates dental professionals in the United ingdom. All dentists, dental hygienists, dental therapists, inical dental technicians and orthodontic therapists must : registered with the GDC to work in the UK, whether ıey work in the NHS, in private practice or any other ırm of practice. From July 2008 by law all dental nurses ıd technicians will need to be registered with the GDC.

There are various different routes to qualify for :gistration, including holding a degree or licentiate in :ntal surgery from a UK university or Royal Surgical ollege; completing the GDC's qualifying examination; : holding a relevant European Economic Area or verseas diploma. The GDC works to set standards of :ntal practice, behaviour and education, and helps to :otect patients by hearing complaints and taking action :ainst professionals where necessary.

The British Dental Association is a membership :ganisation that provides dentists with professional and lucational services. It has over 18,000 qualified embers and over 3,500 student members.

RITISH DENTAL ASSOCIATION 64 Wimpole Street, London W1G 8YS T 020-7935 0875 E enquiries@bda.org W www.bda.org
Chief Executive, Peter Ward

ENERAL DENTAL COUNCIL 37 Wimpole Street, London W1G 8DQ T 020-7887 3800 E information@gdc-uk.org W www.gdc-uk.org
Chief Executive, Duncan Rudkin

MEDICINE

The General Medical Council (GMC) sets the standard for basic medical education; this covers undergraduate study (usually five years) and the first year of training after graduation. Subsequent training is regulated by the Postgraduate Medical Education and Training Board (PMETB). The first two years of training after graduation are collectively called the 'foundation programme'.

All doctors must be registered with the GMC, which is responsible for protecting the public. It does this by setting standards for professional practice, overseeing medical education, keeping a register of qualified doctors and taking action where a doctor's fitness to practise is in doubt. Doctors are eligible for full registration upon successful completion of the first year of training after graduation.

Following the foundation programme, many doctors then undertake specialist training (provided by the colleges and faculties listed below) to become either a consultant or a GP. Once specialist training has been completed, doctors are awarded the Certificate of Completion of Training (CCT) and are eligible to be placed on either the GMC's specialist register or its GP register. The responsibility for awarding CCTs lies with the PMETB.

GENERAL MEDICAL COUNCIL (GMC) 350 Euston Road, London NW1 3JN T 0845-357 3456 E gmc@gmc-uk.org W www.gmc-uk.org
Chief Executive, Finlay Scott

POSTGRADUATE MEDICAL EDUCATION AND TRAINING BOARD (PMETB) Hercules House, Hercules Road, London SE1 7DU T 020-7160 6100 E info@pmetb.org.uk W www.pmetb.org.uk
Chief Executive, Paul Streets

SOCIETY OF APOTHECARIES OF LONDON Black Friars Lane, London EC4V 6EJ T 020-7236 1189 E clerk@apothecaries.org W www.apothecaries.org
Clerk, A. M. Wallington-Smith

SPECIALIST TRAINING COLLEGES AND FACULTIES

COLLEGE OF EMERGENCY MEDICINE W www.emergencymed.org.uk

FACULTY OF PHARMACEUTICAL MEDICINE W www.fpm.org.uk

FACULTY OF PUBLIC HEALTH W www.fphm.org.uk

ROYAL COLLEGE OF ANAESTHETISTS W www.rcoa.ac.uk

ROYAL COLLEGE OF GENERAL PRACTITIONERS W www.rcgp.org.uk

ROYAL COLLEGE OF OBSTETRICIANS AND GYNAECOLOGISTS W www.rcog.org.uk

ROYAL COLLEGE OF OPHTHALMOLOGISTS W www.rcophth.ac.uk

ROYAL COLLEGE OF PAEDIATRICS AND CHILD HEALTH W www.rcpch.ac.uk

ROYAL COLLEGE OF PATHOLOGISTS W www.rcpath.org

ROYAL COLLEGE OF PHYSICIANS W www.rcplondon.ac.uk

ROYAL COLLEGE OF PHYSICIANS AND SURGEONS OF GLASGOW W www.rcpsg.ac.uk

ROYAL COLLEGE OF PHYSICIANS OF EDINBURGH W www.rcpe.ac.uk

ROYAL COLLEGE OF PSYCHIATRISTS
W www.rcpsych.ac.uk
ROYAL COLLEGE OF RADIOLOGISTS
W www.rcr.ac.uk
ROYAL COLLEGE OF SURGEONS OF EDINBURGH
W www.rcsed.ac.uk
ROYAL COLLEGE OF SURGEONS OF ENGLAND
W www.rcseng.ac.uk

MEDICINE, SUPPLEMENTARY PROFESSIONS

The standard of professional education for arts therapists, biomedical scientists, chiropodists and podiatrists, clinical scientists, dietitians, occupational therapists, operating department practitioners, orthoptists, paramedics, physiotherapists, prosthetists and orthotists, radiographers, and speech and language therapists is regulated by the Health Professions Council (HPC), who only register those practitioners who meet certain standards of training, performance and conduct. Other than biomedical science and clinical science, all the professions listed below are described by the NHS as 'allied health professions'. The HPC currently registers over 170,000 professionals.

HEALTH PROFESSIONS COUNCIL Park House, 184 Kennington Park Road, London SE11 4BU T 020-7582 0866 E info@hpc-uk.org W www.hpc-uk.org
Chief Executive and Registrar, Marc Seale

ART, DRAMA AND MUSIC THERAPIES

An art, drama or music therapist encourages people to express their feelings and emotions through art, such as painting and drawing, drama or music. A postgraduate qualification in the relevant therapy is required. Details of accredited training programmes in the UK can be obtained from the following organisations:

ASSOCIATION OF PROFESSIONAL MUSIC THERAPISTS 61 Church Hill Road, East Barnet, Herts EN4 8SY T 020-8440 4153 E apmtoffice@aol.com W www.apmt.org
Administrator, Louise Karena

BRITISH ASSOCIATION OF ART THERAPISTS 24–27 White Lion Street, London N1 9PD T 020-7686 4216 E info@baat.org W www.baat.org
Chief Executive, Val Huet

BRITISH ASSOCIATION OF DRAMA THERAPISTS Waverley, Battledown Approach, Cheltenham, Gloucestershire GL52 6RE T 01242-235515 E enquiries@badth.org.uk W www.badth.org.uk
Chair, Madeleine Andersen-Warren

BIOMEDICAL SCIENCES

Biomedical scientists analyse specimens from patients in order to assist doctors in their diagnoses. Qualifications from higher education establishments and training in medical laboratories are required for membership of the Institute of Biomedical Science, which sets the professional standards of competence for biomedical scientists.

INSTITUTE OF BIOMEDICAL SCIENCE 12 Coldbath Square, London EC1R 5HL T 020-7713 0214 E mail@ibms.org W www.ibms.org
Chief Executive, Alan Potter

CHIROPODY AND PODIATRY

Chiropodists and podiatrists assess, diagnose and treat problems of the lower leg and foot. The Society of Chiropodists and Podiatrists is the professional body and trade union for the profession. Qualifications granted an degrees recognised by the society are approved by th Health Professions Council (HPC). HPC registration required in order to use the titles chiropodist an podiatrist.

SOCIETY OF CHIROPODISTS AND PODIATRISTS 1 Fellmonger's Path, Tower Bridge Road, London SE1 3LY T 0845-450 3720 E enq@scpod.org W www.feetforlife.org
Chief Executive, Joanna Brown

CLINICAL SCIENCE

Clinical scientists conduct tests in laboratories in order t diagnose and manage disease. The Association of Clinic Scientists is responsible for setting the criteria fc competence of applicants to the HPC's register and t present a Certificate of Attainment to candidat following a successful assessment. This certificate wi allow direct registration with the HPC.

ASSOCIATION OF CLINICAL SCIENTISTS c/o Association for Clinical Biochemistry, 130–132 Tooley Stree London SE1 2TU T 020-7940 8960 E info@assclinsci.org W www.assclinsci.org
Chair, Derek Pearson

DIETETICS

Dietitians advise patients on how to improve their healt and counter specific health problems by eating a health diet. The British Dietetic Association, established i 1936, is the professional association for dietitians. Fu membership is open to UK registered dietitians, who mu also be registered with the Health Professions Council.

BRITISH DIETETIC ASSOCIATION 5th Floor, Charles House, 148–149 Great Charles Street Queensway, Birmingham B3 3HT T 0121-200 8080 E info@bda.uk.com W www.bda.uk.com
Chief Executive, Andy Burman

OCCUPATIONAL THERAPY

Occupational therapists work with people who ha physical, mental and/or social problems, either from bir or as a result of accident, illness or ageing, and aim make them as independent as possible. The professiona qualification and eligibility for registration may b obtained upon successful completion of a validated cours in any of the educational institutions approved by th College of Occupational Therapists, which is th professional body for occupational therapy in the U The courses are normally degree-level courses based higher education institutions.

COLLEGE OF OCCUPATIONAL THERAPISTS 106–114 Borough High Street, London SE1 1LB T 020-7357 6480 W www.cot.org.uk
Chief Executive, Julia Scott

ORTHOPTICS

Orthoptists undertake the diagnosis and treatment of a types of squint and other anomalies of binocular visio working in close collaboration with ophthalmologist The professional body is the British and Irish Orthopt Society and training is at degree level.

BRITISH AND IRISH ORTHOPTIC SOCIETY Tavistock House North, Tavistock Square, London WC1H 9HX T 020-7387 7992 W www.orthoptics.org.uk
Chair, Rosemary Auld

PARAMEDICAL SERVICES

Paramedics deal with accidents and emergencies, assessing patients and carrying out any specialist treatment and care needed in the first instance. The body that represents ambulance professionals is the British Paramedic Association.

BRITISH PARAMEDIC ASSOCIATION 28 Wilfred Street, Derby DE23 8GF **T** 01332-746356
E exec.bpa@britishparamedic.org
W www.britishparamedic.org
Chief Executive, Roland Furber

Physiotherapists are concerned with movement and function and deal with problems arising from injury, illness and ageing. Full-time three- or four-year degree courses are available at over 30 higher education institutions in the UK. Information about courses leading to state registration is available from the Chartered Society of Physiotherapy.

CHARTERED SOCIETY OF PHYSIOTHERAPY
14 Bedford Row, London WC1R 4ED **T** 020-7306 6666
W www.csp.org.uk
Chief Executive, Phil Gray

PROSTHETICS AND ORTHOTICS

Prosthetists provide artificial limbs, while orthotists provide devices to support or control a part of the body. It is necessary to obtain an honours degree to become a prosthetist or orthotist. Training is centred at the universities of Salford and Strathclyde.

BRITISH ASSOCIATION OF PROSTHETISTS AND ORTHOTISTS Sir James Clark Building, Abbey Mill Business Centre, Paisley PA1 1TJ **T** 0141-561 7217
E admin@bapo.com **W** www.bapo.org
Chair, Sophie Hill

RADIOGRAPHY

In order to practise both diagnostic and therapeutic radiography in the UK, it is necessary to have successfully completed a course of education and training recognised by the Privy Council. Such courses are offered by universities throughout the UK and lead to the award of a degree in radiography. Further information is available from the Society and College of Radiographers.

SOCIETY AND COLLEGE OF RADIOGRAPHERS
207 Providence Square, Mill Street, London SE1 2EW
T 020-7740 7200 **E** info@sor.org **W** www.sor.org
Chief Executive, Richard Evans

SPEECH AND LANGUAGE THERAPY

Speech and language therapists (SLTs) work with people with speech, voice and swallowing problems. The Royal College of Speech and Language Therapists is the professional body for speech and language therapists and support workers. Alongside the Health Professions Council, it accredits education and training courses leading to qualification.

ROYAL COLLEGE OF SPEECH AND LANGUAGE THERAPISTS 2 White Hart Yard, London SE1 1NX
T 020-7378 1200 **E** info@rcslt.org **W** www.rcslt.org
Chief Executive, Kamini Gadhok

NURSING

In order to practice in the UK all nurses and midwives must be registered with the Nursing and Midwifery Council (NMC). Courses leading to registration are at a minimum of diploma in higher education, although some are offered at degree level and all are a minimum of three years if undertaken full-time. The NMC approves programmes run jointly by higher education institutions with their healthcare service partners who offer clinical placements. The nursing part of the register has four fields of practice: adult, children's, learning disability and mental health nursing. During the first year of a nursing course, the common foundation programme, students have experience of the first four fields of practice. In addition those studying to become adult nurses have experience of nursing in relation to medicine, surgery, maternity care and nursing in the home. The NMC also sets standards for programmes leading to registration as a midwife and a range of post–registration courses including specialist practice programmes, nurse prescribing and those for teachers of nursing and midwifery. The NMC has a part of the register for specialist community public health nurses and approves programmes for health visitors, occupational health nurses and school nurses.

The Royal College of Nursing is the largest professional union representing nurses, and provides higher education through its institute.

NURSING AND MIDWIFERY COUNCIL 23 Portland Place, London W18 1PZ **T** 020-7637 7181
E communications@nmc-uk.org **W** www.nmc-uk.org
Chief Executive and Registrar, Sarah Thewlis

ROYAL COLLEGE OF NURSING 20 Cavendish Square, London W1G 0RN **T** 020-740 3333 **W** www.rcn.org.uk
General Secretary, Dr Peter Carter

OPTOMETRY AND DISPENSING OPTICS

There are various routes to qualification as a dispensing optician. Qualification takes three years in total, and can be completed by combining a distance learning course or day release while working as a trainee under the supervision of a qualified and registered optician. Alternatively, students can do a two-year full-time course followed by one year of supervised practice with a qualified and registered optician. Training must be done at a training establishment approved by the regulatory body – the General Optical Council (GOC). There are six training establishments which are approved by the GOC: the Association of British Dispensing Opticians (ABDO), Anglia Ruskin University, Bradford College, the City and Islington College, City University and Glasgow Caledonian University. All routes are concluded by ABDO examinations, successful completion of which leads to registration with the GOC, which is compulsory for all practising dispensing opticians. After qualifying as a dispensing optician and completing training to fit contact lenses, students have the option to take a career progression course at the University of Bradford that allows them to graduate with a degree in optometry in one calendar year.

Optometrists must obtain an undergraduate optometry degree from one of the eight institutions approved by the GOC (Anglia Ruskin University, Aston University, the University of Bradford, Cardiff University, City University, Glasgow Caledonian University, the University of Manchester and the University of Ulster). Following graduation, trainees must complete a year of supervised salaried training with a registered optometrist during which they must successfully complete the assessments within the scheme for registration set by the College of Optometrists. As with dispensing opticians, optometrists must then register with the GOC in order to practise.

ASSOCIATION OF BRITISH DISPENSING OPTICIANS 199 Gloucester Terrace W2 6LD
T 020-7298 5100 **E** general@abdo.org.uk
W www.abdo.org.uk
General Secretary, Sir Anthony Garrett, CBE

COLLEGE OF OPTOMETRISTS 42 Craven Street, London WC2N 5NG T 020-7839 6000
E optometry@college-optometrists.org
W www.college-optometrists.org
Chief Executive, Bryony Pawinska

GENERAL OPTICAL COUNCIL (GOC) 1 Harley Street, London W1G 8DJ T 020-7580 3898 E goc@optical.org
W www.optical.org
Chief Executive and Registrar, Peter Coe

OSTEOPATHY

Osteopathy is a statutorily self-regulated healthcare profession. The General Osteopathic Council (GOsC) maintains a register of those entitled to practise osteopathy in the UK. It is a criminal offence for anyone to describe themselves as an osteopath unless they are registered with the GOsC.

To gain entry to the register, applicants must hold a recognised qualification from an osteopathic education institute accredited by the GOsC; this involves a four to five year honours degree programme combined with clinical training.

GENERAL OSTEOPATHIC COUNCIL Osteopathy House, 176 Tower Bridge Road, London SE1 3LU
T 020-7357 6655 E info@osteopathy.org.uk
W www.osteopathy.org.uk
Chief Executive and Registrar, Madeleine Craggs

PHARMACY

The Royal Pharmaceutical Society of Great Britain (RPSGB) is the regulatory and professional body for pharmacists in all aspects of practice. It has a statutory duty to maintain the registers of pharmacists and pharmacy premises. The Pharmaceutical Society of Northern Ireland performs the same role in Northern Ireland. In order to register, students must complete a four-year degree in pharmacy that is accredited by either the RPSGB or the Pharmaceutical Society of Northern Ireland followed by one year of pre-registration training at an approved pharmacy, and must then pass an entrance examination.

PHARMACEUTICAL SOCIETY OF NORTHERN IRELAND 73 University Street, Belfast BT7 1HL
T 02890-326927 E mail@psni.org.uk W www.psni.org.uk
Director, Raymond Blaney

ROYAL PHARMACEUTICAL SOCIETY OF GREAT BRITAIN (RPSGB) 1 Lambeth High Street, London SE1 7JN T 020-7735 9141 E enquiries@rpsgb.org
W www.rpsgb.org
Secretary and Registrar, Jeremy Holmes

LAW

There are two types of practising lawyers: barristers and solicitors. Solicitors tend to work as a group in firms, and can be approached directly by individuals. They advise on a variety of legal issues and must decide the most appropriate course of action, if any. Barristers, on the other hand, are usually self-employed. If a solicitor believes that a barrister is required, he or she will instruct one on behalf of the client; the client will not have contact with the barrister without the solicitor being present.

When specialist expertise is needed, barristers give opinions on complex matters of law, and when clients require representation in the higher courts (crown courts, high courts, the court of appeal and the House of Lords), barristers provide a specialist advocacy service. However, solicitors – who represent their clients in the lower courts such as tribunals, magistrates' courts and county courts – can also apply for advocacy rights in the higher courts instead of briefing a barrister.

THE BAR

The governing body of the Bar of England and Wales is the General Council of the Bar, also known as the Bar Council. Since January 2006, the regulatory functions of the Bar Council (including regulating the education and training requirements for those wishing to enter the profession) have been undertaken by the Bar Standards Board.

In the first (or 'academic') stage of training, aspiring barristers must obtain a law degree of a good standard (at least second class). Alternatively, a non-law degree (at least second class) followed by a one-year full-time or two-year part-time Common Professional Examination (CPE) or an approved Postgraduate Diploma in Law (PgDL).

The second (vocational) stage is the completion of the Bar Vocational Course (BVC), which is available at eight validated institutions in the UK and must be applied for around one year in advance (W www.bvconline.co.uk). All barristers must join one of the four Inns of Court prior to commencing the BVC.

Students are 'called to the Bar' by their Inn after completion of the vocational stage, but cannot practise as a barrister until completion of the third stage, which is called 'pupillage'. Call to the Bar does not entitle a person to practise as a barrister – successful completion of pupillage is now a pre-requisite. Pupillage lasts for two six-month periods: the 'non-practising six' and the 'practising six'. The former consists of shadowing an experienced barrister, while the latter involves appearing in court as a barrister.

Admission to the Bar of Northern Ireland is controlled by the Honorable Society of the Inn of Court of Northern Ireland; admission as an Advocate to the Scottish Bar is through the Faculty of Advocates.

BAR STANDARDS BOARD The Bar Council, 289–293 High Holborn, London WC1V 7HZ T 020-7611 1444
W www.barstandardsboard.org.uk
Director of Regulation, Mark Stobbs

FACULTY OF ADVOCATES Parliament House, Edinburgh EH1 1RF T 0131-226 5071 W www.advocates.org.uk
Chief Executive Officer, Tony Parker

GENERAL COUNCIL OF THE BAR 289–293 High Holborn, London WC1V 7HZ T 020-7242 0082
E chiefexec@barcouncil.org.uk W www.barcouncil.org.uk
Chief Executive, David Hobart

GENERAL COUNCIL OF THE BAR OF NORTHERN IRELAND The Bar Library, 91 Chichester Street, Belfast BT1 3JQ T 028-9056 2349
E chief.executive@barcouncil-ni.org.uk
W www.barlibrary.com
Chief Executive, Brendan Garland

HONOURABLE SOCIETY OF THE INN OF COURT OF NORTHERN IRELAND The Under-Treasurer's Office, Room 1–3, Royal Courts of Justice, Belfast BT1 3JF
T 028-9072 4699
Under-Treasurer, J. W. Wilson QC

THE INNS OF COURT

HONOURABLE SOCIETY OF GRAY'S INN 8 South Square, London WC1R 5ET T 020-7458 7800
W www.graysinn.org.uk
Under-Treasurer, Maj.-Gen. David Jenkins, CB, CBE

HONOURABLE SOCIETY OF LINCOLN'S INN Treasury Office, Lincoln's Inn, London WC2A 3TL
T 020-7405 1393 E mail@lincolnsinn.org.uk

W www.lincolnsinn.org.uk
Under-Treasurer, Col. D. Hills, MBE
ONOURABLE SOCIETY OF THE INNER TEMPLE
Inner Temple, London EC4Y 7HL T 020-7797 8250
E enquiries@innertemple.org.uk
W www.innertemple.org.uk
Sub-Treasurer, Patrick Maddams
ONOURABLE SOCIETY OF THE MIDDLE TEMPLE
Middle Temple Lane, London EC4Y 9AT T 020-7427 4800
E studentenquiries@middletemple.org.uk
W www.middletemple.org.uk
Under-Treasurer, Air Cdre Peter Hilling

OLICITORS

raduates from any discipline can train to be a solicitor; owever, if the undergraduate degree is not in law, a one-ear conversion course (either the Common Professional xamination (CPE) or the Graduate Diploma in Law GDL)) must be completed. The next stage, and the eginning of the vocational phase, is the Legal Practice ourse (LPC), which takes one year and is obligatory for oth law and non-law graduates. The LPC provides ofessional instruction for prospective solicitors and can e completed on a full-time or part-time basis. Trainee olicitors then enter the final stage, which is a paid period f supervised work that lasts two years for full-time ontracts. The employer that provides the training ontract must be authorised by the Solicitors Regulation uthority (SRA) (the regulatory body of the Law Society f England and Wales), the Law Society of Scotland, or e Law Society of Northern Ireland. The SRA also onitors the training contract to ensure that it provides e trainee with the necessary expertise to qualify as a olicitor.

HE LAW SOCIETY OF ENGLAND AND WALES The Law Society's Hall, 113 Chancery Lane, London WC2A 1PL
T 020-7242 1222 E enquiries@lawsociety.org.uk
W www.lawsociety.org.uk
Chief Executive, Des Hudson
AW SOCIETY OF NORTHERN IRELAND 40 Linenhall Street, Belfast BT2 8BA T 028-9023 1614
E info@lawsoc-ni.org W www.lawsoc-ni.org
Chief Executive and Secretary, John Bailie
AW SOCIETY OF SCOTLAND 26 Drumsheugh Gardens, Edinburgh EH3 7YR T 0131-226 7411
E lawscot@lawscot.org.uk W www.lawscot.org.uk
Chief Executive, Douglas Mill
OLICITORS REGULATION AUTHORITY Ipsley Court, Berrington Close, Redditch, Worcs B98 0TD
T 0870-606 2555 E info.services@sra.org.uk
W www.sra.org.uk
Chair, Peter Williamson

URVEYING

he Royal Institution of Chartered Surveyors (RICS) is e professional body that represents and regulates roperty professionals including land surveyors, valuers, uctioneers, quantity surveyors and project managers. ntry to the institution, following completion of a RICS-ccredited degree, is through completion of the ssessment of Professional Competence (APC), which volves a period of practical training concluded by a final ssessment of competence. Entry as a technical surveyor equires completion of the Assessment of Technical Competence (ATC), which mirrors the format of the APC. he different levels of RICS membership are MRICS member) or FRICS (fellow) for chartered surveyors, and echRICS for technical surveyors.

Relevant courses can also be accredited by the Chartered Institute of Building (CIOB), which represents managers working in a range of construction disciplines; CIOB offers four levels of membership to those who satisfy its requirements: FCIOB (fellow), MCIOB (member), ICIOB (incorporated) and ACIOB (associate).

CHARTERED INSTITUTE OF BUILDING Englemere, King's Ride, Ascot SL5 7TB T 01344-630700
E reception@ciob.org.uk W www.ciob.org.uk
Chief Executive, Chris Blythe
ROYAL INSTITUTION OF CHARTERED SURVEYORS (RICS) 12 Great George Street, Parliament Square, London SW1P 3AD T 0870-333 1600
E contactrics@rics.org W www.rics.org
Chief Executive, J. H. Armstrong

TEACHING

(*See also* Education section)

The General Teaching Councils for England, Northern Ireland, Scotland and Wales maintain registers of qualified teachers in their respective countries, and registration is a legal requirement in order to teach in local authority schools.

Further information on how to become a teacher in England and Wales is available on the Training and Development Agency for Schools website (*see* below). Personal advice is available from the Teaching Information Line (T 0845-600 0991; T 0845-600 0992 for Welsh speakers). Details on courses in Scotland can be obtained from universities and the Graduate Teacher Training Registry. Details of the courses in Northern Ireland can be obtained from individual universities and the Department of Education for Northern Ireland.

The College of Teachers, under the terms of its royal charter, provides professional qualifications in the field of Teaching English to Speakers of Other Languages (TESOL) for teachers based in the UK and overseas.

COLLEGE OF TEACHERS Institute of Education, 20 Bedford Way, London WC1H 0AL T 020-7911 5536
E enquiries@cot.ac.uk W www.cot.ac.uk
President, Prof. Geoff Whitty, FRSA
DEPARTMENT OF EDUCATION NORTHERN IRELAND Rathgael House, Balloo Road, Bangor BT19 7PR
T 028-9127 9279 E mail@deni.gov.uk W www.deni.gov.uk
Permanent Secretary, Will Haire
GENERAL TEACHING COUNCIL FOR ENGLAND Whittington House, 19–30 Alfred Place, London WC1E 7EA
T 0870-001 0308 E info@gtce.org.uk W www.gtce.org.uk
Chief Executive, Keith Bartley
GENERAL TEACHING COUNCIL FOR NORTHERN IRELAND 4th Floor, Albany House, 73–75 Great Victoria Street, Belfast BT2 7AF T 028-9033 3390
E info@gtcni.org.uk W www.gtcni.org.uk
Registrar, Eddie McArdle
GENERAL TEACHING COUNCIL FOR SCOTLAND Clerwood House, 96 Clermiston Road, Edinburgh EH12 6UT
T 0131-314 6000 E gtcs@gtcs.org.uk W www.gtcs.org.uk
Chief Executive, Matthew MacIver
GENERAL TEACHING COUNCIL FOR WALES 4th Floor, Southgate House, Wood Street, Cardiff CF10 1EW
T 029-2055 0350 E information@gtcw.org.uk
W www.gtcw.org.uk
Chief Executive, Gary Brace
GRADUATE TEACHER TRAINING REGISTRY Rosehill, New Barn Lane, Cheltenham GL52 3LZ
T 0871-468 0469 E enquiries@gttr.ac.uk W www.gttr.ac.uk
Chief Executive, Anthony McClaran

TRAINING AND DEVELOPMENT AGENCY FOR SCHOOLS 151 Buckingham Palace Road, London SW1W 9SZ T 020-7023 8001 W www.tda.gov.uk
Chief Executive, Graham Holley

VETERINARY MEDICINE

The regulatory body for veterinary surgeons in the UK is the Royal College of Veterinary Surgeons (RCVS), which keeps the register of those entitled to practise veterinary medicine as well as the list of qualified veterinary nurses. Holders of recognised degrees from any of the six UK university veterinary schools or from certain EU or overseas universities are entitled to be registered, and holders of certain other degrees may take a statutory membership examination. The UK's veterinary schools are located at the University of Bristol, the University of Cambridge, the University of Edinburgh, the University of Glasgow, the University of Liverpool and the Royal Veterinary College in London; all veterinary degrees last for five years except that offered at Cambridge, which lasts for six. A seventh school at the University of Nottingham has not received RCVS accreditation because no student has yet completed the degree course.

The British Veterinary Association is the profession[al] body representing veterinary surgeons. The Britis[h] Veterinary Nursing Association is the professional bod[y] representing veterinary nurses.

BRITISH VETERINARY ASSOCIATION 7 Mansfield Street, London W1G 9NQ T 020-7636 6541 E bvahq@bva.co.uk W www.bva.co.uk
Company Secretary, Henrietta Alderman

BRITISH VETERINARY NURSING ASSOCIATION 8[illegible] Greenway Business Centre, Harlow Business Park, Harlow CM19 5QE T 01279-408644 E bvna@bvna.co.uk W www.bvna.org.uk

ROYAL COLLEGE OF VETERINARY SURGEONS Belgravia House, 62–64 Horseferry Road, London SW1P 2A[illegible] T 020-7222 2001 E admin@rcvs.org.uk W www.rcvs.org.uk
Registrar, Jane Hern

NDEPENDENT SCHOOLS

ndependent schools (non-maintained mainstream hools) charge fees and are owned and managed under ecial trusts, with profits being used for the benefit of the hools concerned. In 2005–6 there were 2,493 non-aintained mainstream schools (of which 27 were cademies) in the United Kingdom, educating over 50,000 pupils, or approximately 7 per cent of the total hool-age population. The number of pupils at non-aintained mainstream schools in 2005–6 was:

JK	658,500
England	618,300
Wales	9,600
Scotland	29,700
Northern Ireland	800

he Independent Schools Council (ISC), formed in 1974, cts on behalf of the seven independent schools' ssociations which constitute it. These associations are: eadmasters' and Headmistresses' Conference, the Girls' chools Association, the Independent Schools ssociation, the Society of Headmasters and eadmistresses of Independent Schools, the Incorporated ssociation of Preparatory Schools, the Association of overning Bodies of Independent Schools and the ndependent Schools Bursars Association. There were 510,000 pupils being educated in 1,275 Independent Schools Council (ISC) accredited schools in 2007. Most of the schools outside ISC membership are likely to be privately owned. The ISC has overall responsibility for the Independent Schools Inspectorate (ISI), which works under a framework agreed with the DfES and OFSTED. A school must pass an ISI accreditation inspection to qualify for membership of an association within ISC. Schools are evaluated on their educational standards (including attainment, learning and behaviour), quality of teaching, assessment and recording, curriculum, staffing, premises and resources, links with parents and the community, pupils' personal development and pastoral care, management, efficiency, aims and ethos. ISC schools are subject to inspection every six years.

In 2006 at GCSE 57.2 per cent of all exams taken by independent school candidates achieve either an A* or A grade (compared to the national average of 19.1 per cent), and at A-level 74.3 per cent of entries were awarded an A or B grade (national average, 48.1 per cent). In 2007 over 125,000 pupils at ISC schools received help with their fees in the form of bursaries and scholarships from the schools. These cost the schools over £300m.

INDEPENDENT SCHOOLS COUNCIL
St Vincent House, 30 Orange Street, London WC2H 7HH
T 020-7766 7070 W www.isc.co.uk

he fees shown below represent the upper limits payable during 2007–8 (fees noted with an * are for 2006–7) for UK upils who do not qualify for any reduction; please note that scholarships and bursaries are available at many of the sted establishments.

The list was compiled with the assistance of Judy Mott, editor of *Independent Schools Yearbook 2007–8*, published by &C Black. Further details are available online (W www.isyb.co.uk).

chool	*Web Address*	*Termly fees* *Day*	*Board*	*Head*
NGLAND				
bbey Gate College, Cheshire	www.abbeygatecollege.co.uk	£2,915	–	Mrs L. M. Horner
he Abbey School, Berks	www.theabbey.co.uk	£3,420	–	Mrs B. Stanley
bbots Bromley School for Girls, Staffs	www.abbotsbromley.staffs.sch.uk	£3,985	£6,670	Mrs P. J. Woodhouse
bbot's Hill School, Herts	www.abbotshill.herts.sch.uk	£4,145	–	Mrs K. Lewis
bbotsholme School, Derbyshire	www.abbotsholme.com	£5,200	£7,700	S. Fairclough
bingdon School, Oxon	www.abingdon.org.uk	£3,980	£7,590	M. Turner
ckworth School, W. Yorks	www.ackworthschool.com	£3,422	£5,582	P. J. Simpson
ldenham School, Herts	www.aldenham.com	£5,319	£7,731	J. C. Fowler
lderley Edge School for Girls, Cheshire	www.aesg.info	£2,627	–	Mrs K. Mills
lleyn's School, London SE2	www.alleyns.org.uk	£4,095	–	C. Diggory
mberfield School, Suffolk	www.amberfield.suffolk.sch.uk	£2,905	–	Mrs H. Kay
mpleforth College, N. Yorks	www.ampleforthcollege.york.sch.uk	£4,682	£8,090	Revd C. G. Everitt
rdingly College, W. Sussex	www.ardingly.com	£5,900	£7,800	P. Green
rnold School, Lancs	www.arnoldschool.com	£2,645	–	B. M. Hughes
shford School, Kent	www.ashfordschool.co.uk	£4,084	£7,577	M. Buchanan
shville College, N. Yorks	www.ashville.co.uk	£3,280	£6,435	A. A. P. Fleck
ustin Friars St Monica's School, Cumbria	www.austinfriars.cumbria.sch.uk	£3,240	–	C. J. Lumb
ablake School, W. Midlands	www.bablake.com	£2,660	–	J. W. Watson
adminton School, Bristol	www.badminton.bristol.sch.uk	£4,580	£8,130	Mrs J. A. Scarrow
ancroft's School, Essex	www.bancrofts.essex.sch.uk	£3,665	–	P. R. Scott
arnard Castle School, Durham	www.barnardcastleschool.org.uk	£3,220	£5,542	D. H. Ewart
atley Grammar School, W. Yorks	www.batleygrammar.co.uk	£2,622	–	B. Battye
attle Abbey School, E. Sussex	www.battleabbeyschool.com	£3,995	£6,585	R. C. Clark

Bearwood College, Berks	www.bearwoodcollege.co.uk	£4,695	£7,905	S. G. G. Aiano
Bedales School, Hants	www.bedales.org.uk	£6,675	£8,547	K. J. Budge
Bedford High School, Beds	www.bedfordhigh.co.uk	£3,386	£6,288	Mrs J. A. Eldridge
Bedford Modern School, Beds	www.bedmod.co.uk	£3,166	–	S. Smith
Bedford School, Beds	www.bedfordschool.org.uk	£4,595	£7,225	I. P. Evans
Bedstone College, Shropshire	www.bedstone.org	£3,390*	£6,200*	M. S. Symonds
Beechwood Sacred Heart, Kent	www.beechwood.org.uk	£4,150	£6,960	N. Beesley
Benenden School, Kent	www.benenden.kent.sch.uk	–	£8,225*	Mrs C. M. Oulton
Berkhamsted Collegiate School, Herts	www.berkhamstedcollegiateschool.org.uk	£4,690	£7,409	Dr P. Chadwick
Bethany School, Kent	www.bethanyschool.org.uk	£4,382	£6,817	N. D. B. Dorey
Birkdale School, S. Yorks	www.birkdaleschool.org.uk	£3,112	–	R. J. Court
Birkenhead High School, Merseyside	www.gdst.net/birkenheadhigh	£2,798	–	Mrs C. H. Evans
Birkenhead School, Merseyside	www.birkenheadschool.co.uk	£2,797	–	D. J. Clark
Bishop's Stortford College, Herts	www.bishops-stortford-college.herts.sch.uk	£4,347	£6,045	J. G. Trotman
Blackheath High School, London SE3	www.blackheathhighschool.gdst.net	£3,490	–	Mrs E. A. Laws
Bloxham School, Oxon	www.bloxhamschool.com	£6,213	£8,040	M. E. Allbrook
Blundell's School, Devon	www.blundells.org	£4,920	£7,625	I. R. Davenport
Bolton School Boys' Division, Lancs	www.boltonschool.org/seniorboys	£2,797	–	M. E. W. Brooker
Bolton School Girls' Division, Lancs	www.boltonschool.org/seniorgirls	£2,797	–	Mrs G. Richards
Bootham School, N. Yorks	www.bootham.york.sch.uk	£4,285	£6,880	J. F. J. Taylor
Box Hill School, Surrey	www.boxhillschool.org.uk	£4,200	£6,940	M. Eagers
Bradfield College, Berks	www.bradfieldcollege.org.uk	£6,500	£8,125	P. J. M. Roberts
Bradford Girls' Grammar School, W. Yorks	www.bggs.com	£3,297	–	Mrs L. J. Warrington
Bradford Grammar School, W. Yorks	www.bradfordgrammar.com	£3,050	–	S. R. Davidson
Brentwood School, Essex	www.brentwoodschool.co.uk	£4,048	£7,142	D. I. Davies
Brighton and Hove High School, E. Sussex	www.gdst.net/bhhs	£2,798	–	Mrs A. Greatorex
Brighton College, E. Sussex	www.brightoncollege.net	£5,178	£8,026	R. J. Cairns
Brigidine School Windsor, Berks	www.brigidine.org.uk	£3,955	–	Mrs J. Dunn
Bristol Cathedral School, Bristol	www.bristolcathedral.bristol.sch.uk	£3,080	–	A. H. Monro
Bristol Grammar School, Bristol	www.bristolgrammarschool.co.uk	£3,099	–	Dr D. J. Mascord
Bromley High School, Kent	www.bromleyhigh.gdst.net	£3,490	–	Mrs L. Duggleby
Bromsgrove School, Worcs	www.bromsgrove-school.co.uk	£3,760	£7,200	C. J. Edwards
Bruton School for Girls, Somerset	www.brutonschool.co.uk	£3,658	£6,141	J. Burrough
Bryanston School, Dorset	www.bryanston.co.uk	–	£8,495	Ms S. J. Thomas
Burgess Hill School for Girls, W. Sussex	www.burgesshill-school.com	£3,800	£6,595	Mrs A. Aughwane
Bury Grammar School Boys, Lancs	www.bgsboys.co.uk	£2,442	–	Revd S. C. Harvey
Bury Grammar School Girls, Lancs	www.bgsg.bury.sch.uk	£2,442	–	Mrs R. Georghiou
Canford School, Dorset	www.canford.com	£6,306	£8,190	J. D. Lever
Casterton School, Lancs	www.castertonschool.co.uk	£3,977	£6,646	P. McLaughlin
Caterham School, Surrey	www.caterhamschool.co.uk	£4,093	£7,636	J. P. Thomas
Central Newcastle High School, Tyne and Wear	www.newcastlehigh.gdst.net	£2,798	–	Mrs H. J. French
Channing School, London N6	www.channing.co.uk	£3,910	–	Mrs B. Elliott
Charterhouse, Surrey	www.charterhouse.org.uk	£7,192	£8,700	Revd J. S. Witheridge
Cheadle Hulme School, Cheshire	www.cheadlehulmeschool.co.uk	£2,759	–	P. V. Dixon
Cheltenham College, Glos	www.cheltcoll.gloucs.sch.uk/cc	£6,455	£8,615	J. S. Richardson
The Cheltenham Ladies' College, Glos	www.cheltladiescollege.org	£5,490	£8,176	Mrs V. Tuck
Chetham's School of Music, Manchester	www.chethams.com	sliding scale		Mrs C. Hickman
Chetwynde School, Cumbria	www.chetwynde.co.uk	£2,215	–	Mrs I. Nixon
Chigwell School, Essex	www.chigwell-school.org	£4,156	£6,316	M. E. Punt
Christ's Hospital, W. Sussex	www.christs-hospital.org.uk	–	£6,392	J. Franklin
Churcher's College, Hants	www.churcherscollege.com	£3,270	–	S. H. L. Williams
City of London Freemen's School, Surrey	www.clfs.surrey.sch.uk	£4,290	£6,822	P. MacDonald

City of London School, London EC4	www.clsb.org.uk	£4,008	–	D. R. Levin
City of London School for Girls, London EC2	www.clsg.org.uk	£3,855	–	Miss D. Vernon
Claremont Fan Court School, Surrey	www.claremont-school.co.uk	£3,852	–	Mrs P. B. Farrar
Clayesmore School, Dorset	www.clayesmore.com	£5,788	£7,910	M. G. Cooke
Clifton College, Bristol	www.cliftoncollegeuk.com	£5,415	£8,025	M. J. Moore
Clifton High School, Bristol	www.cliftonhigh.bristol.sch.uk	£2,935	£4,955	Mrs C. Culligan
Cobham Hall, Kent	www.cobhamhall.com	£5,500	£7,950	Mrs H. Davy
Cokethorpe School, Oxon	www.cokethorpe.org.uk	£4,295	–	D. J. Ettinger
Colfe's School, London SE12	www.colfes.com	£3,561*	–	R. F. Russell
Colston's Girls' School, Bristol	www.colstonsgirls.bristol.sch.uk	£2,536*	–	Mrs L. Jones
Colston's School, Bristol	www.colstons.bristol.sch.uk	£2,895	£6,200	P. T. Fraser
Combe Bank School, Kent	www.combebank.kent.sch.uk	£4,075*	–	Mrs R. Martin
Concord College, Shropshire	www.concordcollegeuk.com	£3,323	£6,993	N. G. Hawkins
Cranford House School, Oxon	www.cranfordhouse.oxon.sch.uk	£3,695	–	Mrs C. Hamilton
Cranleigh School, Surrey	www.cranleigh.org	£6,790	£8,330	G. Waller
Croham Hurst School, Surrey	www.crohamhurst.com	£3,475	–	Mrs E. J. Abbotts
Croydon High School, Surrey	www.gdst.net/croydonhigh	£3,490	–	Mrs Z. M. Braganza
Culford School, Suffolk	www.culford.co.uk	£4,610	£7,240	J. F. Johnson-Munday
Dame Alice Harpur School, Beds	www.dahs.co.uk	£3,170	–	Mrs J. Berry
Dame Allan's Boys' School, Tyne and Wear	www.dameallans.co.uk	£2,735	–	Dr J. R. Hind
Dame Allan's Girls' School, Tyne and Wear	www.dameallans.co.uk	£2,735	–	Dr J. R. Hind
Dauntsey's School, Wilts	www.dauntseys.wilts.sch.uk	£4,465	£7,535	S. Roberts
Dean Close School, Glos	www.deanclose.co.uk	£5,870	£8,315	Revd T. M. Hastie-Smith
Denstone College, Staffs	www.denstonecollege.org	£3,290	£5,729	D. M. Derbyshire
Derby High School, Derbyshire	www.derbyhigh.derby.sch.uk	£2,760	–	C. T. Callaghan
Dodderhill School, Worcs	www.dodderhill.co.uk	£2,790	–	Mrs J. M. Mumby
Dover College, Kent	www.dovercollege.org.uk	£3,590	£7,190	S. Jones
Downe House, Berks	www.downehouse.net	£6,267	£8,656	Mrs E. McKendrick
Downside School, Somerset	www.downside.co.uk	£3,630*	£6,954*	Dom Leo Maidlow Davis
Duke of York's Royal Military School, Kent	www.doyrms.mod.uk	–	£2,275	C. H. Johnson
Dulwich College, London SE21	www.dulwich.org.uk	£4,193	£8,443	G. G. Able
Dunottar School, Surrey	www.dunottar.surrey.sch.uk	£3,525	–	Mrs J. Hellier
Durham High School for Girls, Durham	www.dhsfg.org.uk	£2,840	–	Mrs A. J. Templeman
Durham School, Durham	www.durhamschool.co.uk	£4,413	£6,663	N. G. Kern
Eastbourne College, E. Sussex	www.eastbourne-college.co.uk	£4,770*	£7,205*	S. P. Davies
Edgbaston High School, W. Midlands	www.edgbastonhigh.bham.sch.uk	£2,715	–	Dr Ruth A. Weeks
Ellesmere College, Shropshire	www.ellesmere.com	£4,254*	£6,666*	B. J. Wignall
Eltham College, London SE9	www.eltham-college.org.uk	£3,696	–	P. J. Henderson
Emanuel School, London SW11	www.emanuel.org.uk	£4,165	–	M. D. Hanley-Browne
Epsom College, Surrey	www.epsomcollege.org.uk	£5,828	£8,456	S. R. Borthwick
Eton College, Berks	www.etoncollege.com	–	£8,830	A. R. M. Little
Ewell Castle School, Surrey	www.ewellcastle.co.uk	£3,340	–	A. J. Tibble
Exeter School, Devon	www.exeterschool.org.uk	£2,960	–	R. Griffin
Farlington School, W. Sussex	www.farlingtonschool.net	£3,735*	£5,940*	Mrs J. Goyer
Farnborough Hill, Hants	www.farnborough-hill.org.uk	£3,130	–	Mrs S. Buckle
Farringtons School, Kent	www.farringtons.org.uk	£3,390	£6,230	Mrs C. James
Felsted School, Essex	www.felsted.org	£5,596	£7,477	S. C. Roberts
Forest School, London E17	www.forest.org.uk	£3,938	–	A. G. Boggis
Framlingham College, Suffolk	www.framlingham.suffolk.sch.uk	£4,433	£6,897	Mrs G. M. Randall
Francis Holland School, London NW1	www.francisholland.org	£4,065	–	Mrs V. M. Durham
Francis Holland School, London SW1	www.fhs-sw1.org.uk	£3,950*	–	Miss S. J. Pattenden
Frensham Heights, Surrey	www.frensham-heights.org.uk	£4,670	£7,065	A. Fisher

Friends' School, Essex	www.friends.org.uk	£4,060	£6,325	G. Wigley
Fulneck School, W. Yorks	www.fulneckschool.co.uk	£3,025	£5,540	T. Kernohan
Gateways School, W. Yorks	www.gatewayschool.co.uk	£2,958	–	Mrs D. Davidson
Giggleswick School, N. Yorks	www.giggleswick.org.uk	£5,272	£7,775	G. P. Boult
The Godolphin and Latymer School, London W6	www.godolphinandlatymer.com	£4,197	–	Miss M. Rudland
The Godolphin School, Wilts	www.godolphin.org	£4,793	£7,097	Miss M. J. Horsburgh
The Grange School, Cheshire	www.grange.org.uk	£2,515	–	C. P. Jeffery
Greenacre School for Girls, Surrey	www.greenacre.surrey.sch.uk	£3,600	–	Mrs P. M. Wood
Grenville College, Devon	www.grenvillecollege.co.uk	£3,250	£6,495	A. Waters
Gresham's School, Norfolk	www.greshams.com	£5,830	£7,595	A. R. Clark
Guildford High School, Surrey	www.guildfordhigh.surrey.sch.uk	£3,705	–	Mrs F. J. Boulton
The Haberdashers' Aske's Boys' School, Herts	www.habsboys.org.uk	£4,025	–	P. B. Hamilton
The Haberdashers' Aske's School for Girls, Herts	www.habsgirls.org.uk	£3,344	–	Mrs E. Radice
Haileybury, Herts	www.haileybury.com	£6,040	£8,040	S. A. Westley
Halliford School, Middx	www.hallifordschool.co.uk	£3,200	–	P. V. Cottam
Hampshire Collegiate School, Hants	www.hampshirecs.org.uk	£3,794	£6,278	D. F. Chapman
Hampton School, Middx	www.hamptonschool.org.uk	£4,040	–	B. R. Martin
Harrogate Ladies' College, N. Yorks	www.hlc.org.uk	£3,910	£6,690	G. F. Hazell
Harrow School, Middx	www.harrowschool.org.uk	–	£8,815	B. J. Lenon
Headington School, Oxon	www.headington.org	£3,750	£7,200	Mrs A. Coutts
Heathfield St Mary's, Berks	www.heathfieldstmarys.net	–	£7,630	Mrs F. King
Heathfield School, Middx	www.heathfield.gdst.net	£3,490	–	Miss C. M. Juett
Hereford Cathedral School, Herefordshire	www.hcsch.org	£3,153	–	P. A. Smith
Hethersett Old Hall School, Norfolk	www.hohs.co.uk	£3,300	£6,195	Mrs J. M. Mark
Highclare School, W. Midlands	www.highclareschool.co.uk	£2,890	–	Mrs M. Viles
Highgate School, London N6	www.highgateschool.org.uk	£4,545	–	A. S. Pettitt
Hipperholme Grammar School, W. Yorks	www.hipperholmegrammar.org.uk	£2,665	–	Dr J. Scarth
Hollygirt School, Notts	www.hollygirt.co.uk	£2,600	–	Mrs P. S. Hutley
Holy Trinity School, Worcs	www.holytrinity.co.uk	£2,795	–	Mrs Y. Wilkinson
Hull Collegiate School, E. Yorks	www.hullcollegiateschool.co.uk	£2,616*	–	R. Haworth
Hurstpierpoint College, W. Sussex	www.hppc.co.uk	£5,495	£7,395	T. J. Manly
Hymers College, E. Yorks	www.hymerscollege.co.uk	£2,469	–	D. C. Elstone
Immanuel College, Herts	www.immanuelcollege.co.uk	£3,832	–	P. Skelker
Ipswich High School, Suffolk	www.ipswichhigh.gdst.net	£2,798	–	Ms E. Purves
Ipswich School, Suffolk	www.ipswich.suffolk.sch.uk	£3,295	£5,752	I. G. Galbraith
James Allen's Girls' School, London SE22	www.jags.org.uk	£3,900	–	Mrs M. Gibbs
The John Lyon School, Middx	www.johnlyon.org	£3,975	–	K. J. Riley
Kelly College, Devon	www.kellycollege.com	£4,250	£7,450	M. S. Steed
Kent College, Kent	www.kentcollege.com	£4,400	£7,570	D. J. Lamper
Kent College Pembury, Kent	www.kent-college.co.uk	£4,630	£7,465	Mrs A. Upton
Kimbolton School, Cambs	www.kimbolton.cambs.sch.uk	£3,610	£5,980	J. Belbin
King Edward VI High School for Girls, W. Midlands	www.kehs.org.uk	£2,810	–	Miss S. H. Evans
King Edward VI School, Hants	www.kes.hants.sch.uk	£3,315	–	A. J. Thould
King Edward VII and Queen Mary School, Lancs	www.keqms.co.uk	£2,492	–	R. J. Karling
King Edward's School, Somerset	www.kesbath.com	£3,119*	–	C. Rowe
King Edward's School, Surrey	www.kesw.surrey.sch.uk	£5,100	£7,100	P. Kerr Fulton-Peebles
King Edward's School, W. Midlands	www.kes.bham.sch.uk	£2,850	–	J. A. Claughton
King Henry VIII School, W. Midlands	www.khviii.com	£2,660	–	G. Fisher
King William's College, Isle of Man	www.kwc.sch.im	£5,289	£7,703	P. D. John
Kingham Hill School, Oxon	www.kingham-hill.oxon.sch.uk	£4,820	£7,110	M. J. Morris

ıg's College School, London SW19	www.kcs.org.uk	£4,775	–	A. C. V. Evans
ıg's College, Somerset	www.kings-taunton.co.uk	£5,070	£7,490	R. R. Biggs
ıg's High School, Warks	www.kingshighwarwick.co.uk	£2,900	–	Mrs E. Surber
e King's School, Cambs	www.kingsschoolely.co.uk	£4,955	£7,170	Mrs S. E. Freestone
e King's School, Canterbury, Kent	www.kings-school.co.uk	£6,510	£8,770	N. Clements
e King's School, Chester, Cheshire	www.kingschester.co.uk	£2,975	–	C. D. Ramsey
e King's School, Gloucester	www.thekingsschool.co.uk	£4,322*	–	A. K. Macnaughton
e King's School, Macclesfield, Cheshire	www.kingsmac.co.uk	£2,665	–	S. Coyne
ıg's School, Rochester, Kent	www.kings-school-rochester.co.uk	£4,920	£8,270	Dr I. R. Walker
ıg's School, Somerset	www.kingsbruton.com	£5,470	£7,535	N. M. Lashbrook
e King's School, Tyne and Wear	www.kings-tynemouth.org.uk	£2,810	–	P. J. S. Cantwell
e King's School, Worcs	www.ksw.org.uk	£3,261	–	T. H. Keyes
e Kingsley School, Warks	www.thekingsleyschool.com	£3,010	–	Mrs C. A. Mannion Watson
ıgston Grammar School, Surrey	www.kingston-grammar.surrey.sch.uk	£4,078	–	C. D. Baxter
ıgswood School, Somerset	www.kingswood.bath.sch.uk	£3,263	£7,276	G. M. Best
ːkham Grammar School, Lancs	www.kirkhamgrammar.co.uk	£2,568	£4,783	D. R. Walker
e Lady Eleanor Holles School, Middx	www.lehs.org.uk	£3,900	–	Mrs G. Low
ncing College, W. Sussex	www.lancingcollege.co.uk	£5,695	£8,200	J. W. J. Gillespie
ngley School, Norfolk	www.langleyschool.co.uk	£3,060	£6,225	D. K. Findlay
Sagesse School, Tyne and Wear	www.lasagesse.org.uk	£2,985	–	Miss L. Clark
ːymer Upper School, London W6	www.latymer-upper.org	£4,280	–	P. J. Winter
vant House, W. Sussex	www.lavanthouse.org.uk	£3,750	£5,930	Mrs M. Scott
eds Girls' High School, W. Yorks	www.lghs.org	£2,875*	–	Ms S. Fishburn
e Grammar School at Leeds, W. Yorks	www.gsal.org.uk	£3,075	–	M. Bailey
icester Grammar School, Leics	www.leicestergrammar.org.uk	£2,900	–	C. P. M. King
icester High School for Girls, Leics	www.leicesterhigh.co.uk	£2,800	–	Mrs J. Burns
ighton Park School, Berks	www.leightonpark.com	£5,045	£7,700	J. H. Dunston
weston School, Dorset	www.leweston.co.uk	£4,565	£6,590	A. J. F. Aylward
e Leys School, Cambs	www.theleys.net	£4,935	£7,634	M. Slater
e Licensed Victuallers' School, Berks	www.lvs.ascot.sch.uk	£3,930	£6,905	G. Best
ıcoln Minster School, Lincs	www.lincolnminsterschool.co.uk	£3,000*	£5,677*	C. Rickart
'erpool College, Merseyside	www.liverpoolcollege.org.uk	£2,760	–	S. Buglass
dge School, Surrey	www.lodgeschool.co.uk	£3,500	–	Miss P. A. Maynard
ngridge Towers School, Northumberland	www.lts.org.uk	£2,995	£6,280	A. E. Clemit
rd Wandsworth College, Hants	www.lordwandsworth.org	£5,325	£7,505	I. G. Power
ughborough Grammar School, Leics	www.loughgs.leics.sch.uk	£3,006	£5,338	P. B. Fisher
ughborough High School, Leics	www.loughhs.leics.sch.uk	£2,787	–	Miss B. A. O'Connor
ckley-Oakfield School, Berks	www.luckley.wokingham.sch.uk	£3,869	£6,624	Miss V. A. Davis
ıgdalen College School, Oxon	www.mcsoxford.org	£3,728	–	A. D. Halls
ılvern College, Worcs	www.malcol.org	£5,591	£8,731	Dr S. J. Welch
ılvern St James, Worcs	www.malvernstjames.co.uk	£3,995*	£7,750*	Mrs R. Hayes
ıe Manchester Grammar School, Manchester	www.mgs.org	£2,784	–	C. Ray
ınchester High School for Girls, Manchester	www.manchesterhigh.co.uk	£2,720	–	Mrs C. Lee-Jones
ınor House School, Surrey	www.manorhouse.surrey.sch.uk	£3,795	–	Mrs A. Morris
ıe Marist Senior School, Berks	www.themaristschools.com	£3,095	–	K. McCloskey
ırlborough College, Wilts	www.marlboroughcollege.org	£6,550	£8,730	N. A. Sampson

Marymount International School, Surrey	www.marymountlondon.com	£5,350	£8,983	Sr Kathleen Fag
The Maynard School, Devon	www.maynard.co.uk	£3,010	–	Dr D. West
Merchant Taylors' Boys' School, Merseyside	www.merchanttaylors.com	£2,586	–	D. H. I. Cook
Merchant Taylors' Girls' School, Merseyside	www.mtgs.co.uk	£2,586	–	Mrs L. A. Robinson
Merchant Taylors' School, Middx	www.mtsn.org.uk	£4,470	–	S. N. Wright
Mill Hill School, London NW7	www.millhill.org.uk	£4,849	£7,661	Dr D. Luckett
Millfield, Somerset	www.millfieldschool.com	£5,710	£8,365	P. M. Johnson
Milton Abbey School, Dorset	www.miltonabbey.co.uk	£6,370	£8,490	W. J. Hughes-D'Aeth
Moira House Girls School, E. Sussex	www.moirahouse.co.uk	£4,200	£7,240	Mrs L. Watson
Monkton Senior, Somerset	www.monktoncombeschool.com	£5,261	£7,789	R. P. Backhouse
More House School, London SW1	www.morehouse.org.uk	£3,995	–	R. Carlysle
Moreton Hall, Shropshire	www.moretonhall.org	£6,400	£7,950	J. Forster
The Mount School, London NW7	www.mountschool.com	£3,175	–	Mrs J. K. Jackson
The Mount School, N. Yorks	www.mountschoolyork.co.uk	£4,195	£6,515	Mrs D. J. Gant
Mount St Mary's College, Derbyshire	www.msmcollege.com	£3,135	£5,820	L. E. McKell
New Hall School, Essex	www.newhallschool.co.uk	£4,520	£6,790	Mrs K. Jeffrey
Newcastle-under-Lyme School, Staffs	www.nuls.org.uk	£2,616	–	N. Rugg
The Newcastle upon Tyne Church High School, Tyne and Wear	www.churchhigh.com	£2,885	–	Mrs L. G. Smith
North Cestrian Grammar School, Cheshire	www.ncgs.co.uk	£2,370	–	D. G. Vanstone
North London Collegiate School, Middx	www.nlcs.org.uk	£3,715	–	Mrs B. McCabe
Northampton High School, Northants	www.northamptonhigh.co.uk	£2,990	–	Mrs S. A. Dixon
Northamptonshire Grammar School, Northants	www.ngs-school.com	£3,372	–	N. R. Toone
Northwood College, Middx	www.northwoodcollege.co.uk	£3,610	–	Mrs R. Mercer
Norwich High School, Norfolk	www.gdst.net/norwich	£2,798	–	Mrs V. C. Bidwe
Norwich School, Norfolk	www.norwich-school.org.uk	£3,284	–	J. B. Hawkins
Notre Dame Senior School, Surrey	www.notredame.co.uk	£3,500	–	Mrs B. Williams
Notting Hill and Ealing High School, London W13	www.nhehs.gdst.net	£3,490	–	Mrs S. M. Whitfield
Nottingham High School, Notts	www.nottinghamhigh.co.uk	£3,171	–	K. D. Fear
Nottingham High School for Girls, Notts	www.gdst.net/nottinghamgirlshigh	£2,798	–	Mrs S. Gorham
Oakham School, Rutland	www.oakham.rutland.sch.uk	£4,760	£7,950	Dr J. A. F. Spenc
Ockbrook School, Derbyshire	www.ockbrook.derby.sch.uk	£2,780	£5,145	Mrs A. M. Steele
The Old Palace School of John Whitgift, Surrey	www.oldpalace.croydon.sch.uk	£3,190	–	Ms J. Harris
Oldham Hulme Grammar Schools, Lancs	www.hulme-grammar.oldham.sch.uk	£2,475	–	Dr P. G. Neeson
The Oratory School, Berks	www.oratory.co.uk	£5,705	£7,900	C. I. Dytor
Oswestry School, Shropshire	www.oswestryschool.org.uk	£3,775	£6,425	P. D. Stockdale
Oundle School, Northants	www.oundleschool.org.uk	£5,200	£7,980	C. M. P. Bush
Our Lady of Sion School, W. Sussex	www.sionschool.org.uk	£2,935	–	M. Scullion
Our Lady's Convent Senior School, Oxon	www.olcss.org.uk	£3,003	–	Mrs L. Renwick
Oxford High School, Oxon	www.gdst.net/oxfordhigh	£2,798	–	Miss O. F. S. Lus
Palmers Green High School, London N21	www.pghs.co.uk	£3,265	–	Mrs C. Edmundson
Pangbourne College, Berks	www.pangbournecollege.com	£5,457	£7,780	T. J. C. Garnier
The Perse School, Cambs	www.perse.co.uk	£3,908	–	N. P. V. Richardson
The Perse School for Girls, Cambs	www.perse.cambs.sch.uk	£3,915	–	Miss P. M. Kelleh
Peterborough High School, Cambs	www.peterboroughhigh.co.uk	£3,323	£6,120	A. Meadows
Pipers Corner School, Bucks	www.piperscorner.co.uk	£3,765	£6,225	Mrs H. J. Ness-Gifford

lymouth College, Devon	www.plymouthcollege.com	£3,482	£6,613	Dr S. J. Wormleighton
ocklington School, E. Yorks	www.pocklingtonschool.com	£3,365	£6,025	N. Clements
olam Hall School, Durham	www.polamhall.com	£3,290	£6,440	Miss M. Green
he Portsmouth Grammar School, Hants	www.pgs.org.uk	£3,392	–	T. R. Hands
ortsmouth High School, Hants	www.gdst.net/portsmouthhigh	£2,798	–	Mrs J. Clough
he Princess Helena College, Herts	www.phc.herts.sch.uk	£4,845	£6,995	Mrs A-M. Hodgkiss
rincethorpe College, Warks	www.wcisf.co.uk	£2,685	–	J. M. Shinkwin
rior Park College, Somerset	www.priorparkschools.co.uk	£3,942	£7,108	R. G. G. Mercer
rior's Field, Surrey	www.priorsfieldschool.com	£4,160	£6,735	Mrs J. A. Roseblade
he Purcell School, Herts	www.purcell-school.org	£7,128*	£9,116*	P. Crook
utney High School, London SW15	www.gdst.net/putneyhigh	£3,490	–	Dr D. V. Lodge
ueen Anne's School, Berks	www.qas.org.uk	£5,425	£8,005	Mrs J. Harrington
ueen Elizabeth's Grammar School, Lancs	www.qegs.blackburn.sch.uk	£2,816	–	S. A. Corns
ueen Elizabeth Grammar School, W. Yorks	www.wgsf.org.uk	£2,895	–	M. R. Gibbons
ueen Elizabeth's Hospital, Bristol	www.qehbristol.co.uk	£3,035	–	S. W. Holliday
ueen Margaret's School, N. Yorks	www.queenmargaretsschool.co.uk	£4,432	£6,995	G. A. H. Chapman
ueen Mary's School, N. Yorks	www.queenmarys.org	£4,185	£5,450	R. A. McKenzie Johnston
ueen's College, London W1	www.qcl.org.uk	£4,200	–	Miss M. M. Connell
ueen's College, Somerset	www.queenscollege.org.uk	£4,225	£6,494	C. J. Alcock
ueen's Gate School, London SW7	www.queensgate.org	£4,100	–	Mrs R. M. Kamaryc
he Queen's School, Cheshire	www.queens.cheshire.sch.uk	£2,965	–	Mrs C. M. Buckley
ueenswood, Herts	www.queenswood.org	£6,245	£8,090	Mrs P. C. Edgar
adley College, Oxon	www.radley.org.uk	–	£8,330	A. W. McPhail
atcliffe College, Leics	www.ratcliffecollege.com	£3,968	£5,975	P. Farrar
he Read School, N. Yorks	www.readschool.co.uk	£2,543	£5,504	R. A. Hadfield
eading Blue Coat School, Berks	www.blue-coat.reading.sch.uk	£3,640	–	S. J. W. McArthur
he Red Maids' School, Bristol	www.redmaids.bristol.sch.uk	£2,840	–	Mrs I. Tobias
edland High School for Girls, Bristol	www.redland.bristol.sch.uk	£2,880	–	Mrs C. P. Bateson
eed's School, Surrey	www.reeds.surrey.sch.uk	£5,555	£7,350	D. W. Jarrett
eigate Grammar School, Surrey	www.reigategrammar.org	£4,024	–	D. S. Thomas
endcomb College, Glos	www.rendcombcollege.co.uk	£5,235	£7,020	G. Holden
epton School, Derbyshire	www.repton.org.uk	£5,875	£7,920	R. A. Holroyd
ishworth School, W. Yorks	www.rishworth-school.co.uk	£3,070	£5,865	R. A. Baker
oedean School, E. Sussex	www.roedean.co.uk	£5,000	£8,650	Mrs C. Shaw
ossall School, Lancs	www.rossallschool.org.uk	£3,315	£8,315	T. J. Wilbur
he Royal Grammar School, Surrey	www.rgs-guildford.co.uk	£3,752	–	J. M. Cox
oyal Grammar School, Tyne and Wear	www.rgs.newcastle.sch.uk	£2,610*	–	J. F. X. Miller
GS Worcester and The Alice Ottley School, Worcs	www.rgsao.org.uk	£2,898	–	A. R. Rattue
he Royal High School, Bath, Somerset	www.gdst.net/royalhighbath	£2,798	£5,486	J. Graham-Brown
he Royal Hospital School, Suffolk	www.royalhospitalschool.org	£3,308	£6,214	H. W. Blackett
he Royal Masonic School for Girls, Herts	www.royalmasonic.herts.sch.uk	£4,040	£6,450	Mrs D. Rose
oyal Russell School, Surrey	www.royalrussell.co.uk	£3,985	£7,880	J. R. Jennings
he Royal School, Surrey	www.royal-school.org	£4,250	£2,624	Mrs L. Taylor-Gooby
oyal School Hampstead, London NW3	www.royalschoolhampstead.net	£2,965	£5,890	Mrs J. Ebner-Landy
he Royal Wolverhampton School, W. Midlands	www.theroyalschool.co.uk	£3,550	£7,420	T. L. Waters
ugby School, Warks	www.rugbyschool.net	£5,250	£8,305	P. S. J. Derham

Ryde School with Upper Chine, Isle of Wight	www.rydeschool.org.uk	£2,865	£5,855	Dr N. J. England
Rye St Antony School, Oxon	www.ryestantony.co.uk	£3,400	£5,700	Miss A. M. Jones
St Albans High School, Herts	www.sahs.org.uk	£3,445	–	Ms Jacqualyn Pai
St Albans School, Herts	www.st-albans.herts.sch.uk	£3,942	–	A. R. Grant
St Andrew's School, Beds	www.standrewsschoolbedford.com	£3,020	–	Mrs J. E. Marslan
St Bede's College, Manchester	www.stbedescollege.co.uk	£2,532	–	J. Byrne
St Bede's School, E. Sussex	www.stbedesschool.org	£4,555	£7,410	S. Cole
St Bees School, Cumbria	www.st-bees-school.org	£4,425	£7,383	P. J. Capes
St Benedict's School, London W5	www.stbenedictsealing.org.uk	£3,670	–	C. J. Cleugh
St Catherine's School, Middx	www.stcatherineschool.co.uk	£3,190	–	Sr Paula Thomas
St Catherine's School, Surrey	www.stcatherines.info	£3,920	£6,450	Mrs A. M. Phillip
St Christopher School, Herts	www.stchris.co.uk	£4,275	£7,500	R. Palmer
St Columba's College, Herts	www.stcolumbascollege.net	£3,180	–	J. Stuart
St David's School, Middx	www.stdavidsschool.com	£3,703	£6,858	Mrs T. Smith
St Dominic's Priory School, Staffs	www.st-dominics.co.uk	£2,586	–	A. Egan
St Dominic's School, Staffs	www.stdominicsschool.co.uk	£2,990*	–	Mrs S. White
St Dunstan's College, London SE6	www.stdunstans.org.uk	£3,854	–	Mrs J. D. Davies
St Edmund's College, Herts	www.stedmundscollege.org	£4,280	£6,940	C. P. Long
St Edmund's School, Kent	www.stedmunds.org.uk	£4,908	£7,601	J. M. Gladwin
St Edward's, Oxford, Oxon	www.stedwards.oxon.sch.uk	£6,795	£8,495	A. F. Trotman
St Edward's School, Glos	www.stedwards.co.uk	£3,598	–	A. J. Nash
Saint Felix School, Suffolk	www.stfelix.co.uk	£3,950	£6,550	D. A. T. Ward
St Francis' College, Herts	www.st-francis.herts.sch.uk	£3,195*	£6,285*	Miss M. Hegarty
St Gabriel's School, Berks	www.st-gabriels.w-berks.sch.uk	£3,620	–	A. Jones
St George's College, Surrey	www.st-georges-college.co.uk	£4,255	–	J. A. Peake
St George's School, Berks	www.stgeorges-ascot.org.uk	£5,170	£7,950	Mrs C. L. Jordan
St George's School, W. Midlands	www.sgse.co.uk	£2,675*	–	Miss H. Phillips
The School of St Helen and St Katharine, Oxon	www.shsk.org.uk	£3,203	–	Mrs C. L. Hall
St Helen's School for Girls, Middx	www.sthelensnorthwood.co.uk	£3,795	£7,038	Mrs M. Morris
St James Independent School for Senior Girls, London W14	www.stjamesschools.co.uk	£3,460	–	Mrs L. Hyde
St John's College, Hants	www.stjohnscollege.co.uk	£2,625	£5,750	N. W. Thorne
St John's School, Surrey	www.stjohnsleatherhead.co.uk	£5,515	£7,580	N. J. R. Haddock
St Joseph's College, Suffolk	www.stjos.co.uk	£3,350	£5,500	Mrs S. Grant
St Joseph's Convent School, Berks	www.st-josephs.reading.sch.uk	£3,300	–	Mrs M. Sheridan
St Lawrence College, Kent	www.slcuk.com	£4,300	£7,342	Revd M. Aitken
St Leonards-Mayfield School, E. Sussex	www.stlm.e-sussex.sch.uk	£4,710	£7,090	Mrs J. Dalton
St Margaret's School, Devon	www.stmargarets-school.co.uk	£2,860	–	Miss R. Edbrooke
St Margaret's School, Herts	www.stmargaretsbushey.org.uk	£3,885	£6,995	Mrs L. Crighton
Saint Martin's, W. Midlands	www.saintmartins-school.com	£2,935	–	Mrs J. Carwithen
St Mary's College, Merseyside	www.stmaryscrosby.co.uk	£2,392*	–	Mrs J. M. Marsh
St Mary's Hall, E. Sussex	www.stmaryshall.co.uk	£3,965	£6,546	Mrs S. M. Meek
St Mary's School, Berks	www.st-marys-ascot.co.uk	£5,925	£8,325	Mrs M. Breen
St Mary's School, Bucks	www.stmarysschool.co.uk	£3,610	–	Mrs F. A. Balcombe
St Mary's School, Cambs	www.stmaryscambridge.co.uk	£3,690	£7,400	Miss C. F. Avery
St Mary's School, Dorset	www.st-marys-shaftesbury.co.uk	£4,750	£6,980	R. James
St Mary's School, Essex	www.stmarysschool.org.uk	£2,705	–	Mrs H. Vipond
St Mary's School, Wilts	www.stmaryscalne.org	£5,850	£8,350	Mrs H. Wright
St Mary's School, Worcs	www.stmarys.org.uk	£2,885	–	Mrs S. K. Cookso
St Nicholas' School, Hants	www.st-nicholas.hants.sch.uk	£3,166	–	Mrs A. V. Whatmough
St Paul's Girls' School, London W6	www.spgs.org	£4,541	–	Ms C. M. Farr
St Paul's School, London SW13	www.stpaulsschool.org.uk	£5,123	£7,624	G. M. Stephen
St Peter's School, N. Yorks	www.st-peters.york.sch.uk	£3,998	£6,760	R. I. Smyth
St Swithun's School, Hants	www.stswithuns.com	£4,425	£7,290	Dr H. L. Harvey
St Teresa's School, Surrey	www.stteresasschool.com	£4,100	£6,970	Mrs L. Falconer
Scarborough College, N. Yorks	www.scarboroughcollege.co.uk	£3,300	£5,633	T. L. Kirkup
Seaford College, W. Sussex	www.seaford.org	£4,650	£7,100	T. J. Mullins
Sedbergh School, Cumbria	www.sedberghschool.org	£5,640	£7,555	C. H. Hirst
Sevenoaks School, Kent	www.sevenoaksschool.org	£5,047	£8,093	Mrs C. L. Ricks
Shebbear College, Devon	www.shebbearcollege.co.uk	£3,025	£5,650	R. S. Barnes
Sheffield High School, S. Yorks	www.sheffieldhighschool.org.uk	£2,798	–	Mrs V. A. Dunsford

herborne School, Dorset	www.sherborne.org	£6,735	£8,415	S. F. Eliot
herborne School for Girls, Dorset	www.sherborne.com	£6,200	£8,500	Mrs J. Dwyer
hiplake College, Oxon	www.shiplake.org.uk	£4,901	£7,266	A. G. S. Davies
hrewsbury High School, Shropshire	www.gdst.net/shrewsburyhigh	£2,798	–	Mrs M. Cass
hrewsbury School, Shropshire	www.shrewsbury.org.uk	£5,800	£8,370	J. W. R. Goulding
ibford School, Oxon	www.sibford.oxon.sch.uk	£3,195*	£6,208*	M. Goodwin
idcot School, Somerset	www.sidcot.org.uk	£3,660	£6,150	J. Walmsley
ilcoates School, W. Yorks	www.silcoates.com	£3,448	–	A. P. Spillane
ir William Perkins's School, Surrey	www.swps.org.uk	£3,454	–	Mrs S. D. Cooke
olihull School, W. Midlands	www.solsch.org.uk	£2,943	–	P. J. Griffiths
outh Hampstead High School, London NW3	www.gdst.net/shhs	£3,490	–	Mrs J. E. Stephen
tafford Grammar School, Staffs	www.stafford-grammar.co.uk	£2,676	–	M. R. Darley
tamford High School, Lincs	www.ses.lincs.sch.uk	£3,380	£6,328	Dr P. R. Mason
tamford School, Lincs	www.ses.lincs.sch.uk	£3,380	£6,328	Dr P. R. Mason
tanbridge Earls School, Hants	www.stanbridgeearls.co.uk	£5,600	£7,534	G. P. Link
tockport Grammar School, Cheshire	www.stockportgrammar.co.uk	£2,571	–	A. H. Chicken
tonar School, Wilts	www.stonarschool.com	£3,600	£6,350	Mrs S. Shayler
tonyhurst College, Lancs	www.stonyhurst.ac.uk	£4,553	£7,754	A. R. Johnson
tover School, Devon	www.stover.co.uk	£2,995	£6,195	Mrs S. Bradley
towe School, Bucks	www.stowe.co.uk	£6,305	£8,525	A. K. Wallersteiner
treatham and Clapham High School, London SW16	www.gdst.net/streathamhigh	£3,490	–	Mrs S. Mitchell
underland High School, Tyne and Wear	www.sunderlandhigh.co.uk	£2,306*	–	Dr A. Slater
urbiton High School, Surrey	www.surbitonhigh.com	£3,619	–	Dr J. Longhurst
utton High School, Surrey	www.gdst.net/suttonhigh	£3,490	–	S. J. Callaghan
utton Valence School, Kent	www.svs.org.uk	£5,010	£7,920	J. S. Davies
ydenham High School, London SE26	www.gdst.net/sydenhamhigh	£3,490	–	Mrs K. E. Pullen
albot Heath, Dorset	www.talbotheath.org.uk	£3,122	£5,199	Mrs C. Dipple
aunton School, Somerset	www.tauntonschool.co.uk	£4,290*	£6,720*	Dr J. H. Newton
eesside High School, Cleveland	www.teessidehigh.co.uk	£2,975	–	T. A. Packer
ettenhall College, W. Midlands	www.tettenhallcollege.co.uk	£3,367*	£5,908*	P. C. Bodkin
hetford Grammar School, Norfolk	www.thetgram.norfolk.sch.uk	£2,993	–	G. J. Price
hornton College, Bucks	www.thorntoncollege.com	£2,885*	£4,775*	Miss A. T. Williams
horpe House School, Norfolk	www.thorpehouseschool.com	£2,240*	–	A. Todd
onbridge School, Kent	www.tonbridge-school.co.uk	£6,575	£8,942	T. H. P. Haynes
ormead School, Surrey	www.tormeadschool.org.uk	£3,535	–	Mrs S. E. Marks
rent College, Notts	www.trentcollege.net	£3,999	£4,994	Mrs G. Dixon
rinity School, Surrey	www.trinity-school.org	£3,622	–	M. J. Bishop
ruro High School for Girls, Cornwall	www.trurohigh.co.uk	£3,065	£5,780	M. A. McDowell
ruro School, Cornwall	www.truroschool.com	£3,200	£6,150	P. K. Smith
udor Hall, Oxon	www.tudorhallschool.com	£4,741	£7,354	Miss W. Griffiths
niversity College School, London NW3	www.ucs.org.uk	£4,620	–	K. J. Durham
ppingham School, Rutland	www.uppingham.co.uk	£5,810	£8,300	R. Harman
Vakefield Girls' High School, W. Yorks	www.wgsf.org.uk	£2,895	–	Mrs P. A. Langham
Valthamstow Hall, Kent	www.walthamstow-hall.co.uk	£4,280	–	Mrs J. Milner
Varminster School, Wilts	www.warminsterschool.org.uk	£3,730	£6,480	M. J. Priestley
Varwick School, Warks	www.warwickschool.org	£3,106	£6,627	E. B. Halse
Vellingborough School, Northants	www.wellingboroughschool.org	£3,500	–	G. R. Bowe
Vellington College, Berks	www.wellingtoncollege.org.uk	£6,405	£8,540	A. F. Seldon
Vellington School, Somerset	www.wellington-school.org.uk	£3,160	£5,618	M. S. Reader
Vells Cathedral School, Somerset	www.wells-cathedral-school.com	£4,249	£7,102	Mrs E. C. Cairncross
Ventworth College, Dorset	www.wentworthcollege.com	£3,475	£5,725	Miss S. Coe
Vest Buckland School, Devon	www.westbuckland.devon.sch.uk	£3,390	£5,780	J. F. Vick
Vestfield School, Tyne and Wear	www.westfield.newcastle.sch.uk	£2,880	–	Mrs M. Farndale

Westholme School, Lancs	www.westholmeschool.com	£2,388	–	Mrs L. Croston
Westminster School, London SW1	www.westminster.org.uk	£5,992	£8,652	M. S. Spurr
Westonbirt, Glos	www.westonbirt.gloucs.sch.uk	£5,460	£7,867	Mrs M. Henderso
Whitgift School, Surrey	www.whitgift.co.uk	£3,940*	–	C. A. Barnett
Wimbledon High School, London SW19	www.gdst.net/wimbledon	£3,490	–	Mrs P. H. Wilkes
Winchester College, Hants	www.winchestercollege.co.uk	£8,385	£8,827	R. D. Townsend
Windermere St Anne's School, Cumbria	www.wsaschool.com	£3,860	£6,970	A. Graham
Wisbech Grammar School, Cambs	www.wgs.cambs.sch.uk	£3,050	–	R. S. Repper
Wispers School for Girls, Surrey	www.wispers.org.uk	£4,405	£6,988	L. H. Beltran
Withington Girls' School, Manchester	www.withington.manchester.sch.uk	£2,680	–	Mrs J. D. Pickerin
Woldingham School, Surrey	www.woldinghamschool.co.uk	£4,730	£7,915	Mrs J. Triffitt
Wolverhampton Grammar School, W. Midlands	www.wgs.org.uk	£3,231	–	B. St J. Trafford
Woodbridge School, Suffolk	www.woodbridge.suffolk.sch.uk	£3,828	£6,728	S. H. Cole
Woodhouse Grove School, W. Yorks	www.woodhousegrove.co.uk	£3,110	£5,900	D. C. Humphreys
Worksop College, Notts	www.worksopcollege.notts.sch.uk	£4,640	£6,845	R. A. Collard
Worth School, W. Sussex	www.worthschool.co.uk	£5,707	£7,704	G. G. Carminati
Wrekin College, Shropshire	www.wrekincollege.com	£4,410	£7,282	S. G. Drew
Wychwood School, Oxon	www.wychwood-school.org.uk	£3,325	£5,395	Mrs S. Wingfield Digby
Wycliffe College, Glos	www.wycliffe.co.uk	£4,960	£7,405	Mrs M. E. Burnet Ward
Wycombe Abbey School, Bucks	www.wycombeabbey.com	£6,450	£8,600	Mrs P. E. Davies
Wykeham House School, Hants	www.wykehamhouse.hants.sch.uk	£2,810	–	Mrs L. R. Clarke
Yarm School, Cleveland	www.yarmschool.org	£3,019	–	D. M. Dunn
The Yehudi Menuhin School, Surrey	www.yehudimenuhinschool.co.uk	sliding scale		N. Chisholm

WALES

Christ College, Brecon	www.christcollegebrecon.com	£4,155	£6,425	Mrs E. Taylor
Haberdashers' Monmouth School for Girls, Monmouth	www.habs-monmouth.org	£3,303*	£5,893*	Dr B. Despontin
Howell's School, Denbigh	www.howells.org	£3,500	£5,650	Miss R. Hodgson
Howell's School Llandaff, Cardiff	www.gdst.net/howells-llandaff	£2,816	–	Mrs S. Davis
Llandovery College, Llandovery	www.llandoverycollege.com	£4,077	£6,027	P. A. Hogan
Monmouth School, Monmouth	www.habs-monmouth.org	£3,559	£5,991	S. G. Connors
Rougemont School, Newport	www.rougemontschool.co.uk	£2,896	–	Dr J. Tribbick
Ruthin School, Ruthin	www.ruthinschool.co.uk	£3,520	£5,795	J. S. Rowlands
Rydal Penrhos School, Colwyn Bay	www.rydal-penrhos.com	£4,140	£7,100	M. S. James
St David's College, Llandudno	www.stdavidscollege.co.uk	£3,748*	£5,766*	C. Condrup

NORTHERN IRELAND

Bangor Grammar School, Bangor	www.bangorgrammarschool.org.uk	–	–	S. D. Connolly
Belfast Royal Academy, Belfast	www.belfastroyalacademy.com	£40	–	W. S. F. Young
Campbell College, Belfast	www.campbellcollege.co.uk	£633	£3,099	J. A. Piggot
Coleraine Academical Institution, Coleraine	www.coleraineai.com	£120	–	Dr D. R. J. Carruthers
Foyle and Londonderry College, Londonderry	www.foylenet.org/foyleandlondonderry	£40	–	W. J. Magill
Methodist College, Belfast	www.methody.org	£40*	£2,433*	J. S. W. Naismith
Portora Royal School, Enniskillen	www.portoraroyal.co.uk	£14	–	J. N. Morton
The Royal Belfast Academical Institution, Belfast	www.rbai.org.uk	£245	–	Miss J. Williamsor
The Royal School Dungannon, Dungannon	www.royaldungannon.com	£45	£1,917	P. D. Hewitt

SCOTLAND

Dollar Academy, Dollar	www.dollaracademy.org.uk	£2,862	£6,531	J. S. Robertson
The High School of Dundee, Dundee	www.highschoolofdundee.co.uk	£2,904	–	A. M. Duncan
The Edinburgh Academy, Edinburgh	www.edinburghacademy.org.uk	£2,580	£5,790	J. V. Light
Fettes College, Edinburgh	www.fettes.com	£5,632	£7,833	M. C. B. Spens

orge Heriot's School, Edinburgh	www.george-heriots.com	£2,774	–	A. G. Hector
orge Watson's College, Edinburgh	www.gwc.org.uk	£2,827	–	G. Edwards
e Glasgow Academy, Glasgow	www.theglasgowacademy.org.uk	£2,825	–	P. J. Brodie
enalmond College, Perth	www.glenalmondcollege.co.uk	£5,380	£7,885	G. C. Woods
e High School of Glasgow, Glasgow	www.glasgowhigh.com	£2,829	–	C. D. R. Mair
tchesons' Grammar School, Glasgow	www.hutchesons.org	£2,748	–	Dr K. M. Greig
lvinside Academy, Glasgow	www.kelvinsideacademy.org.uk	£2,965	–	J. L. Broadfoot
graston, Bridge of Earn	www.kilgraston.com	£4,100	£6,995	M. Farmer
mond School, Helensburgh	www.lomond-school.org	£2,590*	£5,540*	A. D. Macdonald
retto School, Edinburgh	www.loretto.com	£5,310	£7,825	M. B. Mavor
e Mary Erskine School, Edinburgh	www.esms.edin.sch.uk	£2,728	£5,443	J. N. D. Gray
erchiston Castle School, Edinburgh	www.merchiston.co.uk	£5,465	£7,615	A. R. Hunter
orrison's Academy, Crieff	www.morrisonsacademy.org	£2,851	–	G. S. H. Pengelley
bert Gordon's College, Aberdeen	www.rgc.aberdeen.sch.uk	£2,830	–	H. Ouston
Aloysius' College, Glasgow	www.staloysius.org	£2,518	–	J. Stoer
Columba's School, Kilmacolm	www.st-columbas.org	£2,823	–	D. G. Girdwood
George's School for Girls, Edinburgh	www.st-georges.edin.sch.uk	£3,210	£6,360	Dr J. McClure
Margaret's School for Girls, Aberdeen	www.st-margaret.aberdeen.sch.uk	£2,860	–	Mrs A. Everest
Margaret's School, Edinburgh	www.st-margarets.edin.sch.uk	£3,008	£6,512	Mrs E. M. Davis
ewart's Melville College, Edinburgh	www.esms.edin.sch.uk	£2,728	£5,443	J. N. D. Gray
athallan School, Perth	www.strathallan.co.uk	£5,112	£7,535	B. K. Thompson

HANNEL ISLANDS

izabeth College, Guernsey	www.elizcoll.org	£2,178	–	N. D. Argent
e Ladies' College, Guernsey	www.ladiescollege.sch.gg	£1,700	–	Miss M. E. Macdonald
ctoria College, Jersey	www.vcj.sch.je	£1,260	–	R. G. Cook

NATIONAL ACADEMIES OF SCHOLARSHIP

The national academies are self-governing bodies whose members are elected as a result of achievement and distinction in the academy's field. Within their discipline, the academies provide advice, support education and exceptional scholars, stimulate debate, promote UK research worldwide and collaborate with international counterparts.

In addition to income from donations, membership contributions, trading and investments, the English academies receive grant-in-aid funding from the science budget, administered by the Department for Innovation, Universities and Skills*; the allocations for the year 2007–8 are as follows:

	£ thousand
Royal Society	41,072
British Academy	21,385
Royal Academy of Engineering	9,752

* The Academy of Medical Sciences receives grant-in-aid funding from the Department of Health. It was allocated £1.75m spread over five years from 2004.

ACADEMY OF MEDICAL SCIENCES (1998)

10 Carlton House Terrace, London SW1Y 5AH
T 020-7969 5288
W www.acmedsci.ac.uk

The Academy of Medical Sciences was established in 1998 to promote advances in medical science and to ensure these are converted as quickly as possible into healthcare benefits for society.

The academy campaigns for the development, protection and promotion of careers for academics in the biomedical sciences and encourages good practice in training and development.

The academy is independent and self-governing and receives funding from a variety of sources including the fellowship, charitable donations, government and industry.

Fellows are elected from a broad range of medical sciences: biomedical, clinical and population based. The academy includes in its remit vetinary medicine, dentistry, nursing, medical law, economics, sociology and ethics. Elections are from nominations put forward by existing fellows.

At June 2007 there were 881 fellows and 23 honorary fellows.

President, Prof. John Bell, PMedSci
Vice-Presidents, Sir John Skehel, FRS, FMedSci; Sir Michael Rutter, CBE, FRS, FMedSci
Treasurer, Prof. Ian Lauder, FMedSci
Registrar, Prof. Patrick Maxwell, FMedSci
Executive Director, Mary Manning

BRITISH ACADEMY (1902)

10 Carlton House Terrace, London SW1Y 5AH
T 020-7969 5200
W www.britac.ac.uk

The British Academy is an independent, self-governing learned society for the promotion of the humanities and social sciences. It supports advanced academic resea and is a channel for the government's support of resear in those disciplines.

The fellows are scholars who have attained distincti in one of the branches of study that the academy exists promote. Candidates must be nominated by existi fellows. There are 770 ordinary fellows, 15 honora fellows and 306 corresponding fellows overseas.

President, Baroness O'Neill, FBA
Chief Executive, Dr R. Jackson
Treasurer, Prof. R. J. P. Kain, FBA
Foreign Secretary, Prof. D. I. D. Gallie, FBA
Publications Secretary, Dr D. J. McKitterick, FBA

ROYAL ACADEMY OF ENGINEERING (1

29 Great Peter Street, London SW1P 3LW
T 020-7227 0500
W www.raeng.org.uk

The Royal Academy of Engineering was established as t Fellowship of Engineering in 1976. It was granted a ro charter in 1983 and its present title in 1992. It is independent, self-governing body whose object is t pursuit, encouragement and maintenance of excellence the whole field of engineering, in order to promote t advancement of science, art and practice of engineeri for the benefit of the public.

Election to the fellowship is by invitation only, fro nominations supported by the body of fellows. At Ju 2007 there were 1,339 fellows. The Duke of Edinbur is the senior fellow and the Duke of Kent is a royal fello

President, Lord Browne of Madingley, FRENG
Senior Vice-President, Prof. W. Hall, CBE, FRENG
Vice-Presidents, Prof. W. R. Eatock Taylor, FRENG; Dr E. Ion, OBE, FRENG; P. Saraga, OBE, FRENG; Dr F S. Steedman, FRENG; Prof. R. A. Williams, FRENG
Hon. Treasurer, F. C. Price, FRENG
Hon. Secretaries, P. Saraga, OBE, FRENG (International Activities); Dr D. Grant, CBE, FRENG (Education an Training)
Chief Executive, P. D. Greenish, CBE

ROYAL SOCIETY (1660)

6–9 Carlton House Terrace, London SW1Y 5AG
T 020-7451 2500
W www.royalsoc.ac.uk

The Royal Society is an independent academy promoti the natural and applied sciences. Founded in 1660, t society has three roles, as the UK academy of science, as learned society and as a funding agency. It is independent, self-governing body under a royal chart promoting and advancing all fields of physical ar biological sciences, of mathematics and engineerin medical and agricultural sciences and their application.

Fellows are elected for their contributions to scienc both in fundamental research resulting in great understanding, and also in leading and directing scienti and technological progress in industry and resear establishments. A maximum of 44 new fellows, who mu be citizens or residents of the British Commonweal countries or Ireland, may be elected annually.

Up to eight foreign members, who are selected from ose not eligible to become fellows because of :izenship or residency, are elected annually for their ntributions to science.

One honorary fellow may be elected each year from ose not eligible for election as fellows or foreign embers. There are approximately 1,400 fellows and reign members covering all scientific disciplines.

esident, Prof. Lord Rees of Ludlow, PRS
easurer, Prof. Sir D. Wallace, CBE, FRS, FRENG
ological Secretary, Prof. D. Read, FRS
ysical Secretary, Prof. M. Taylor, FRS
reign Secretary, Prof. L. Casselton, FRS
ecutive Secretary, S. Cox, CVO

OYAL SOCIETY OF EDINBURGH (1783)

–26 George Street, Edinburgh EH2 2PQ
0131-240 5000
www.royalsoced.org.uk

e Royal Society of Edinburgh (RSE) is an educational arity and Scotland's National Academy of Science and tters. An independent body with charitable status, its ultidisciplinary membership of around 1,400 fellows presents a knowledge resource for the people of otland. Granted its royal charter in 1783 for the dvancement of learning and useful knowledge', the ciety organises conferences, debates and lectures; nducts independent inquiries; facilitates international llaboration and showcases the country's research and velopment capabilities; provides educational activities r primary and secondary school students and awards izes and medals. The society also awards over £1.7m nually to Scotland's top researchers and entrepreneurs orking in Scotland.

At May 2007 there were 1,462 fellows.

esident, Sir Michael Atiyah, OM, PPRS, FRSE
ce-Presidents, Prof. Janet McDonald, FRSE; Prof. John Mavor, FRSE; Lord Patel, FRSE
easurer, Edward Cunningham, CBE, FRSE
eneral Secretary (acting), Prof. Andrew Miller, CBE, FRSE

PRIVATELY FUNDED ARTS ACADEMIES

The Royal Academy and the Royal Scottish Academy support the visual arts community in the UK, hold educational events and promote interest in the arts. They are entirely privately funded through contributions by 'friends' (regular donors who receive benefits such as free entry, previews and magazines), bequests, corporate donations and exhibitions.

ROYAL ACADEMY OF ARTS (1768)

Burlington House, Piccadilly, London W1J 0BD
T 020-7300 8000
W www.royalacademy.org.uk

The Royal Academy of Arts is an independent, self-governing society devoted to the encouragement and promotion of the fine arts.

Membership of the academy is limited to 80 academicians, all being painters, engravers, sculptors or architects. Candidates are nominated and elected by the existing academicians. There is also a limited class of honorary academicians, of whom as of October 2007 there were 20.

President, Sir Nicholas Grimshaw, PRA
Treasurer, Prof. Paul Huxley, RA
Keeper, Prof. Maurice Cockrill, RA
Secretary and Chief Executive, Charles Saumarez Smith

ROYAL SCOTTISH ACADEMY (1838)

The Mound, Edinburgh EH2 2EL
T 0131-225 6671
W www.royalscottishacademy.org

Founded in 1826 and granted a Royal Charter in 1838, The Royal Scottish Academy is an independent institution led by prominent Scottish artists and architects. It promotes and supports the visual arts through an ongoing exhibitions programme, related educational events and through a series of awards, bursaries and scholarships for artists at all stages of their careers.

Members are elected from the disciplines of art and architecture and elections are from nominations put forward by the existing membership. At mid-2007 there were 20 honorary members and 91 members.

President, I. McKenzie Smith, OBE, PRSA
Secretary, W. Scott, RSA
Treasurer, I. Metzstein, OBE, RSA
Administrative Secretary, B. Laidlaw, ACIS

RESEARCH COUNCILS

The government funds basic and applied civil science research, mostly through seven research councils, which are established under royal charter and supported by the Department for Innovation, Universities and Skills (DIUS). The councils support research and training in universities and other higher education establishments. The science budget, administered by the DIUS, contributes around 30 per cent of public sector investment in research, with funding from other government departments (including higher education funding) and regional development making up the remaining investment. The councils also receive income for research commissioned by government departments and the private sector, in addition to income from charitable sources. The annual science budget has risen from £2.73bn in 2004–5 to almost £3.45bn in 2007–8.

The government science budget for 2007–8 includes the following allocations:

	£ thousand
Arts and Humanities Research Council	97,092
Biotechnology and Biological Sciences Research Council	381,829
Economic and Social Research Council	150,336
Engineering and Physical Sciences Research Council	721,172
Medical Research Council	546,514
Natural Environment Research Council	367,248
Science and Technology Facilities Council	530,000
Higher Education Innovation Fund	85,000
Science Research Investment Fund	300,000

Source: DTI (DIUS) – Science Budget Allocations 2004–5 to 2007–8

ALCOHOL EDUCATION AND RESEARCH COUNCIL

Room 178, Queen Anne Business Centre, 28 Broadway, London SW1H 9JX **T** 020-7340 9502 **F** 020-7340 9505
W www.aerc.org.uk

The AERC was established by act of parliament in 1982 to administer the Alcohol Education and Research Fund. The government fund is used in UK education and research projects to develop new ways to help those with drinking problems. The AERC aims to increase awareness of alcohol issues, to reduce alcohol-related harm and to encourage best practice.
Chair, Dr Noel Olsen
Director, Prof. Ray Hodgson

ARTS AND HUMANITIES RESEARCH COUNCIL

Whitefriars, Lewins Mead, Bristol BS1 2AE
T 0117-987 6500 **W** www.ahrc.ac.uk

Launched in April 2005 as the successor organisation to the Arts and Humanities Research Board, the AHRC funds postgraduate training and research in the arts and humanities, encompassing disciplines such as English literature, history, modern languages, archaeology, mus and drama.

With a budget of around £90m, the AHRC provic support for research and postgraduate study within t UK's higher education institutions. In any one year, t AHRC makes approximately 700 research awards ar around 1,500 postgraduate awards. Awards are made af a rigorous peer review process, to ensure the quality applications.
Chair, Prof. Sir Brian Follett
Chief Executive, Prof. Philip Esler

BIOTECHNOLOGY AND BIOLOGICAL SCIENCES RESEARCH COUNCIL

Polaris House, North Star Avenue, Swindon SN2 1UH
T 01793-413200

Established by royal charter in 1994, the BBSRC fun basic and strategic biological research in order to advan UK expertise on the understanding and exploitation biological systems. It funds research into how all livi organisms function and behave. To deliver its mission, t BBRC supports research and training in universities a research centres throughout the UK, including t institutes listed below.
Chair, Dr P. Ringose
Chief Executive, Steve Visscher *(acting)*

INSTITUTES

BABRAHAM INSTITUTE, Babraham Hall, Babraham, Cambridge CB2 4AT **T** 01223-496000
Director, Prof. Michael Wakelam

INSTITUTE FOR ANIMAL HEALTH, Compton Laboratory, Compton, Newbury, Berks RG20 7NN **T** 01635-578411
Director, Prof. M. Shirley

NEUROPATHOGENESIS UNIT, Ogston Building, West Mains Road, Edinburgh EH9 3JF **T** 0131-667 5204

IAH PIRBRIGHT LABORATORY, Ash Road, Pirbright, Woking, Surrey GU24 0NF **T** 01483-232441
Head, Dr David Mackay

ROTHAMSTED RESEARCH, Rothamsted, Harpenden, Herts AL5 2JQ **T** 01582-763133
Director, Prof. I. R. Crute

ROTHAMSTED RESEARCH, BROOM'S BARN RESEARCH STATION, Higham, Bury St. Edmunds, Suffolk IP28 6NP **T** 01284-812200
Director, Bill Clark

INSTITUTE OF FOOD RESEARCH, Norwich Research Park, Colney Lane, Norwich NR4 7UA **T** 01603-255000
Director, Prof. D. White

INSTITUTE OF GRASSLAND AND ENVIRONMENTAL RESEARCH (IGER), Aberystwy Research Centre, Plas Gogerddan, Aberystwyth SY23 3EB **T** 01970-823000
Director (interim), Prof. Mervyn Humphrys

IGER NORTH WYKE RESEARCH STATION, Okehampton, Devon EX20 2SB **T** 01837-883500
Head, vacant

JOHN INNES CENTRE, Norwich Research Park, Colney, Norwich NR4 7UH **T** 01603-450000
Director, Prof. C. Lamb

)SLIN INSTITUTE, Roslin, Midlothian EH25 9PS
T 0131-527 4200
Director, Dr Harry Griffin

:ONOMIC AND SOCIAL RESEARCH)UNCIL

aris House, North Star Avenue, Swindon SN2 1UJ
1793-413000
omms@esrc.ac.uk W www.esrcsocietytoday.ac.uk

e purpose of the ESRC is to promote and support earch and postgraduate training in the social sciences. also provides advice, disseminates knowledge and)motes public understanding in these areas.
air, Lord A. Turner
ief Executive, I. Diamond

:SEARCH CENTRES
.NTRE FOR MARKET AND PUBLIC ORGANISATION, University of Bristol, Bristol BS8 1TN T 0117-928 8436
Director, Prof. S. Burgess
:NTRE ON MIGRATION, POLICY AND SOCIETY, University of Oxford, Oxford OX2 6QS T 01865-274711
Director, Prof. S. Vertovec
:NTRE FOR MICROECONOMIC ANALYSIS OF PUBLIC POLICY, Institute for Fiscal Studies, 7 Ridgmount Street, London WC1E 7AE T 020-7291 4800
Director, Prof. R. Blundell
:NTRE FOR ORGANISATION AND INNOVATION, University of Sheffield, Sheffield S10 2TN T 0114-222 3254
Directors, Prof. C. Clegg; Prof. T. Wall; Prof. S. Wood
:NTRE FOR RESEARCH ON INNOVATION AND COMPETITION, University of Manchester M13 9QH T 0161-275 7374
Director, Prof. J. Howells
:NTRE FOR RESEARCH ON SOCIO-CULTURAL CHANGE, University of Manchester, Manchester M13 9PL T 0161-275 8985
Directors, Prof. M. Savage; Prof. K. Williams
:NTRE ON SKILLS, KNOWLEDGE AND ORGANISATIONAL PERFORMANCE, University of Oxford, Oxford OX1 3UQ T 01865-276434
Director, K. Mayhew
:NTRE FOR SOCIAL AND ECONOMIC RESEARCH ON THE GLOBAL ENVIRONMENT, University of East Anglia, Norwich NR4 7TJ T 01603-592551
Director, Prof. K. Turner
:NTRE FOR SOCIAL AND ECONOMIC RESEARCH ON INNOVATION IN GENOMICS, University of Edinburgh, Edinburgh EH1 1LZ T 0131-650 9174
Director, Prof. J. Tait
.NTRE FOR THE STUDY OF GLOBALISATION AND REGIONALISATION, University of Warwick, Coventry CV4 7AL T 024-7652 4633
Directors, Prof. R. Higgott; Prof. J. Scholte
)MPLEX PRODUCT SYSTEMS INNOVATION CENTRE, University of Sussex, Brighton BN1 9RH T 01273-642188
Directors, Prof. M. Hobday; Prof. H. Rush
RC CENTRE FOR GENOMICS IN SOCIETY, University of Exeter, Exeter, Devon EX4 4RJ T 01392-262049
Director, J. Dupré
:SEARCH CENTRE ON MICRO-SOCIAL CHANGE, University of Essex, Colchester, Essex CO4 3SQ T 01206-872957
Director, Prof. S. Pudney

TYNDALL CENTRE FOR CLIMATE CHANGE RESEARCH, University of East Anglia, Norwich NR4 7TJ T 01603-593162
Directors, Prof. M. Hulme; Prof. J. Schellnhuber

RESOURCE CENTRES
CENTRE FOR LONGITUDINAL STUDIES, Institute of Education, London WC1H 0AL T 020-7612 6901
Director, Prof. H. Joshi
NATIONAL CENTRE FOR RESEARCH METHODS, University of Southampton, Southampton SO17 1BJ T 023-8059 4539
Director, Prof. C. Skinner
UK LONGITUDINAL STUDIES CENTRE, University of Essex, Colchester CO4 3SQ T 01206-873066
Director, Prof. N. Buck

ENGINEERING AND PHYSICAL SCIENCES RESEARCH COUNCIL

Polaris House, North Star Avenue, Swindon SN2 1ET
T 01793-444000, Helpline: 01793-444100 W www.epsrc.ac.uk

The EPSRC is the UK government's main funding agency for research and training in engineering and the physical sciences in universities and other organisations throughout the UK. It also provides advice, disseminates knowledge and promotes public understanding in these areas.
Chair, John Armitt, CBE, FRENG
Interim Chief Executive, Prof. Randal Richards

HEALTH PROTECTION AGENCY

7th Floor, Holborn Gate, 330 High Holborn, London WC1V 7PP
T 020-7759 2700 F 020-7759 2733 W www.hpa.org.uk

The Health Protection Agency is a Special Health Authority, established in 2003 (merged with the National Radiological Protection Board in 2005), it gives advice to the public, health authorities and the government. It works to reduce the impact of infectious diseases and exposure to chemicals, poisons and radiation at local, national and regional levels and in emergency situations. The agency researches new ways to combat illness and to assess exposure to chemicals and radiation to determine whether treatment is needed.
Chairman, Sir William Stewart
Chief Executive, Prof. Pat Troop

RESEARCH CENTRES
CENTRE FOR INFECTIONS, 61 Colindale Avenue, London NW9 5EQ T 020-8200 4400
Director, Prof. Peter Borriello
CENTRE FOR EMERGENCY PREPAREDNESS AND RESPONSE Porton Down, Salisbury SP4 0JG T 01980-612100
Director, Dr Stephen Chatfield
CENTRE FOR RADIATION, CHEMICAL AND ENVIRONMENTAL HAZARDS, Chilton, Didcot OX11 0RQ T 01235-831600
Director, Dr Roger Cox

MEDICAL RESEARCH COUNCIL

20 Park Crescent, London W1B 1AL T 020-7636 5422
W www.mrc.ac.uk

The purpose of the MRC is to promote medical and related biological research. The council employs its own research staff and funds research by other institutions and individuals, complementing the research resources of the universities and hospitals.

Chair, Sir John Chisholm
Chief Executive, Prof. Colin Blakemore
Chair, Neurosciences and Mental Health Board, Prof. C. Kennard
Chair, Molecular and Cellular Medicine Board, Prof. P. Luzio
Chair, Infections and Immunity Board, Prof. D. Smith
Chair, Health Services and Public Health Research Board, Dr D. Armstrong
Chair, Physiological and Clinical Sciences Board, Prof. S. Holgate

MRC RESEARCH CENTRES
MRC/Asthma UK Centre in Allergic Mechanisms of Asthma T 020-7188 1943
Anatomical Neuropharmacology Unit W mrcanu.pharm.ox.ac.uk
Biostatistics Unit W www.mrc-bsu.cam.ac.uk
Cambridge Behavioural and Clinical Neuroscience Institute W www.psychol.cam.ac.uk/bcni
Cancer Cell Unit W www.hutchison-mrc.cam.ac.uk
Cell Biology Unit W www.ucl.ac.uk/lmcb
Centre for Developmental Neurobiology at King's College London W www.kcl.ac.uk/depsta/biomedical/mrc
Clinical Sciences Centre W www.csc.mrc.ac.uk
MRC/Cancer Research UK/BHF Clinical Trial Service Unit & Epidemiological Studies Unit W www.ctsu.ox.ac.uk
Clinical Trials Unit W www.ctu.mrc.ac.uk
Cognition and Brain Sciences Unit W www.mrc-cbu.cam.ac.uk
Centre for Developmental and Biomedical Genetics W cdbg.shef.ac.uk
Dunn Human Nutrition Unit W www.mrc-dunn.cam.ac.uk
Epidemiology Resource Centre W www.mrc.soton.ac.uk
Epidemiology Unit W www.mrc-epid.cam.ac.uk
Functional Genetics Unit W www.mrcfgu.ox.ac.uk
Laboratories, the Gambia W www.mrc.gm
MRC/University of Sussex Centre in Genome Damage and Stability W www.sussex.ac.uk/gdsc
Health Services Research Collaboration W www.hsrc.ac.uk
Human Genetics Unit W www.hgu.mrc.ac.uk
Human Immunology Unit T 01865-222336
Collaborative Centre for Human Nutrition Research W www.mrc-hnr.cam.ac.uk
Human Reproductive Sciences Unit W www.hrsu.mrc.ac.uk
MRC/University of Birmingham Centre for Immune Regulation W www.bham.ac.uk/mrcbcir
Immunochemistry Unit W www2.bioch.ox.ac.uk/immunoch
MRC/University of Edinburgh Centre for Inflammation Research W www.cir.med.ed.ac.uk
Institute of Hearing Research W www.ihr.mrc.ac.uk
Mammalian Genetics Unit W www.mgu.har.mrc.ac.uk
MRC/UCL Centre for Medical Molecular Virology T 020-7504 9343
Laboratory of Molecular Biology W www2.mrc-lmb.cam.ac.uk
Molecular Haemotology Unit W www.imm.ox.ac.uk/groups/mrc_molhaem
National Institute for Medical Research W www.nimr.mrc.ac.uk
Centre for Neurodegenerative Research W cnr.iop.kcl.ac.uk
Centre for Nutritional Epidemiology in Cancer Prevention and Survival W www.srl.cam.ac.uk
Centre for Protein Engineering W www.mrc-cpe.cam.ac.uk
Prion Unit W www.prion.ucl.ac.uk
Protein Phosphorylation Unit W www.dundee.ac.uk/lifesciences/mrcppu
Radiation and Genome Damage Stability Unit W www.ragsu.har.mrc.ac.uk
Social and Public Health Sciences Unit W www.msoc-mrc.gla.ac.uk
Social, Genetic and Developmental Psychiatry Research Centre T 020-7848 0871
Centre for Stem Cell Biology and Medicine W www.stemcells.cam.ac.uk
Centre for Stem Cell Research W www.iscr.ed.ac.uk
MRC/University of Bristol Centre for Synaptic Plasticity W www.bris.ac.uk/depts/synaptic
Toxicology Unit W www.le.ac.uk/mrctox
Uganda Research Unit on AIDS T (+256) (41) 320272
Virology Unit W www.mrcvu.gla.ac.uk

MILK DEVELOPMENT COUNCIL

Stroud Road, Cirencester GL7 6JN T 01285-646500 F 01285-646501 W www.mdc.org.uk

The MDC was founded in 1994 and is funded by government as an independent public body. It aims help dairy farmers throughout Britain increase th profits, by offering advice on production efficiency a expertise and opportunities that can increase the dema or value of milk, or stop its value declining. It aims create better supply chain relationships to ensure t farmers profit as well as retailers.
Chair, Brian Peacock
Chief Executive, Kevin Bellamy

NATIONAL PHYSICAL LABORATORY

Hampton Road, Teddington, Middlesex TW11 0LW T 020-89 3222 F 020-8943 6458 W www.npl.co.uk

The NPL is the UK's national standards laboratory a has been operating since 1900. It is an independ laboratory for research, development and knowled transfer in measurement and materials science. The N develops the national measurement standards for physi quantities
Managing Director, Steve McQuillan

ATURAL ENVIRONMENT RESEARCH OUNCIL

aris House, North Star Avenue, Swindon SN2 1EU
1793-411500 W www.nerc.ac.uk

e NERC funds and carries out impartial scientific earch in the sciences relating to natural environment. work covers the full range of atmospheric, earth, ological, terrestrial and aquatic sciences, from the pths of the oceans to the upper atmosphere. Its mission to gather and apply knowledge, create understanding d predict the behaviour of the natural environment and resources.

air, Rob Margetts, CBE, FRENG
ief Executive, Prof. Alan Thorpe

ESEARCH CENTRES

ITISH ANTARCTIC SURVEY, High Cross, Madingley Road, Cambridge CB3 OET T 01223-221400
Director, Prof. Chris Rapley, CBE

ITISH GEOLOGICAL SURVEY, Kingsley Dunham Centre, Keyworth, Nottingham NG12 5GG
T 0115-936 3100
Executive Director, Dr John Ludden

NTRE FOR ECOLOGY AND HYDROLOGY, Polaris House, North Star Avenue, Swindon SN2 1EU
T 01793-442516
Director, Prof. Patricia Nuttall, OBE

OUDMAN OCEANOGRAPHIC LABORATORY, Joseph Proudman Building, 6 Brownlow Street, Liverpool L3 5DA T 0151-795 4800
Director, Prof. Andrew Willmott

OLLABORATIVE CENTRES

NTRE FOR OBSERVATION OF AIR-SEA INTERACTIONS AND FLUXES, Plymouth Marine Laboratory, Prospect Place, Plymouth PL1 3DH
T 01752-633429
Director, Prof. Jim Aiken

NTRE FOR OBSERVATION AND MODELLING OF EARTHQUAKES AND TECTONICS, Department of Earth Sciences, University of Oxford, Parks Road, Oxford OX1 3PR T 01865-272030
Director, Prof. Barry Parsons

NTRE FOR POLAR OBSERVATION AND MODELLING, Department of Space and Climate Physics, Pearson Building, University College London, Gower Street, London WC1E 6BT T 020-7679 3031
Director, Prof. Duncan Wingham

NTRE FOR POPULATION BIOLOGY, Imperial College London, Silwood Park Campus, Ascot SL5 7PY
T 020-7594 2475
Director, Prof. Georgina Mace, FRS

IMATE AND LAND SURFACE SYSTEMS INTERACTION CENTRE, School of Engineering, Computer Science and Mathematics, Harrison building, North Park Road, University of Exeter EX4 4QF
T 01792-295144
Director, Prof. Peter Cox

ATA ASSIMILATION RESEARCH CENTRE, Department of Meteorology, University of Reading, PO Box 243, Earley Gate, Reading RG6 6BB T 0118-378 6728
Director, Prof. Alan O'Neill

VIRONMENTAL SYSTEMS SCIENCE CENTRE, University of Reading, PO Box 238, Harry Pitt Building, 3 Earley Gate, Reading RG6 6AL T 0118-378 8741
Director, Prof. Robert Gurney, OBE

NATIONAL INSTITUTE FOR ENVIRONMENTAL E-SCIENCE, Department of Earth Sciences, University of Cambridge, Downing Street, Cambridge CB2 3EQ
T 01223-764917
Director, Dr Martin Dove

NATIONAL OCEANOGRAPHY CENTRE, SOUTHAMPTON, University of Southampton, Waterfront Campus, European Way, Southampton SO14 3ZH T 023-8059 6666
Director, Prof. Ed Hill

NATIONAL CENTRES FOR ATMOSPHERIC SCIENCE, School of Earth and Environment, University of Leeds LS2 9JT T 0113-343 5158
Director, Prof. Stephen Mobbs

NCAS GLOBAL COMPOSITION AND CLIMATE RESEARCH, Department of Chemistry, University of Cambridge, Lensfield Road, Cambridge CB2 1EW
T 01223-336473
Director, Prof. John Pyle, FRS

NCAS BRITISH ATMOSPHERIC DATA CENTRE, Rutherford Appleton Laboratory, Chilton, Didcot OX11 0QX
T 01235-446432
Director, Dr Bryan Lawrence

NCAS-CLIMATE, Department of Meteorology, University of Reading, PO Box 243, Earley Gate, Reading RG6 6BB
T 0118-378 8424
Director, Prof. Julia Slingo

NCAS DISTRIBUTED INSTITUTE FOR ATMOSPHERIC COMPOSITION, School of Chemistry, University of Leeds, Leeds LS2 9JT
T 0113-343 6450
Director, Prof. Mike Pilling

NCAS FACILITY FOR AIRBORNE ATMOSPHERIC MEASUREMENTS, Building 125, Cranfield University, Cranfield, Bedford MK43 0AL T 01234-754411
Head of Facility, Steve Ball

NCAS UNIVERSITIES FACILITY FOR ATMOSPHERIC MEASUREMENTS, School of Earth and Environment, University of Leeds, Leeds LS2 9JT
T 0113-343 6408
Director, Dr Alan Blyth

NCAS UNIVERSITIES WEATHER RESEARCH NETWORK, Department of Meteorology, University of Reading, PO Box 243, Earley Gate, Reading, RG6 6BB
T 0118-378 8957
Director, Prof. P. Mason

NERC CENTRE FOR TERRESTRIAL CARBON DYNAMICS, University of Sheffield, Hicks Building, Hounsfield Road, Sheffield S3 7RH T 0114-222 3803
Director, Prof. Shaun Quegan

PLYMOUTH MARINE LABORATORY, Prospect Place, Plymouth PL1 3DH T 01752-633100
Director, Prof. Nicholas Owens

SCOTTISH ASSOCIATION FOR MARINE SCIENCE, Dunstaffnage Marine Laboratory, Oban PA37 1QA
T 01631-559000
Director, Prof. Graham Shimmield

SEA MAMMAL RESEARCH UNIT, Gatty Marine Laboratory, University of St Andrews, St Andrews KY16 8LB
T 01334-462630
Director, Prof. Ian Boyd

TYNDALL CENTRE FOR CLIMATE CHANGE RESEARCH, School of Environmental Sciences, University of East Anglia, Norwich, Norfolk NR4 7TJ T 01603-593900
Executive Director, Prof. Mike Hulme

SCIENCE AND TECHNOLOGY FACILITIES COUNCIL

Polaris House, North Star Avenue, Swindon SN2 1SZ
T 01793-442000 F 01793-442002 W www.scitech.ac.uk

Formed by royal charter on 1 April 2007, through the merger of the Council for the Central Laboratory of the Research Councils and the Particle Physics and Astronomy Research Council, the STFC is a non-departmental public body reporting to the Department for Innovation, Universities and Skills.

The STFC invests in large national and international research facilities, whilst delivering science, technology and expertise for the UK. The council is involved in research projects including the Diamond Light Source Synchrotron and the Large Hadron Collider, and develops new areas of science and technology. The EPSRC has transferred its responsibility for nuclear physics to the STFC.

Chair, Peter Warry
Chief Executive, Prof. Keith Mason
CHILBOLTON OBSERVATORY, Stockbridge, Hampshire SO20 6BJ T 01264-860391
DARESBURY LABORATORY, Daresbury Science and Innovation Campus, Daresbury WA4 4AD T 01925-603000
RUTHERFORD APPLETON LABORATORY, Harwell Science and Innovation Campus, Didcot OX11 0QX T 01235-445000
UK ASTRONOMY TECHNOLOGY CENTRE, Royal Observatory, Edinburgh, Blackford Hill, Edinburgh EH9 3H T 0131-668 8100

RESEARCH AND TECHNOLOGY ORGANISATIONS

Over 30 industrial and technological research bodies a members of the Association of Independent Research a Technology Organisations Limited (AIRTO). Membe activities span a wide range of disciplines from sciences to engineering. Their work includes ba research, development and design of innovative produ or processes, instrumentation testing and certification, a technology and management consultancy. AIRT publishes a directory to help clients identify t organisations that might be able to assist them. For a f list of members, see AIRTO's website.

AIRTO LTD, c/o CCFRA, Station Road, Chipping Campden, Glos GL55 6LD T 01386-842247
E airto@campden.co.uk W www.airto.co.uk
President, Prof. R. Brook

HEALTH

NATIONAL HEALTH SERVICE

he National Health Service (NHS) came into being on 5 ıly 1948 under the National Health Service Act 1946, overing England and Wales and, under separate gislation, Scotland and Northern Ireland. The NHS is ow administered by the Secretary of State for Health (in ngland), the Welsh Assembly Government, the Scottish xecutive and the Secretary of State for Northern Ireland.

The function of the NHS is to provide a comprehensive ealth service designed to secure improvement in the hysical and mental health of the people and to prevent, iagnose and treat illness. It was founded on the principle hat treatment should be provided according to clinical eed rather than ability to pay, and should be free at the oint of delivery.

Hospital, mental, dental, nursing, ophthalmic and mbulance services and facilities for the care of expectant nd nursing mothers and young children are provided by he NHS to meet all reasonable requirements. Rehabilitation services such as occupational therapy, hysiotherapy, speech therapy and surgical and medical ppliances are supplied where appropriate. Specialists and onsultants who work in NHS hospitals can also engage n private practice, including the treatment of their private atients in NHS hospitals.

STRUCTURE

The structure of the NHS remained relatively stable for he first 30 years of its existence. In 1974, a three-tier nanagement structure comprising regional health uthorities, area health authorities and district nanagement teams was introduced in England, and the NHS became responsible for community health services. n 1979 area health authorities were abolished and istrict management teams were replaced by district ealth authorities.

The National Health Service and Community Care Act 990 provided for more streamlined regional health uthorities and district health authorities, and for the stablishment of family health services authorities (FHSA) nd NHS trusts. The concept of the 'internal market' was ntroduced into health care, whereby care was provided hrough NHS contracts where health authorities or oards and GP fundholders (the purchasers) were esponsible for buying health care from hospitals, non-undholding GPs, community services and ambulance ervices (the providers). The Act also paved the way for he community care reforms, which were introduced in April 1993, and changed the way care is administered for lder people, the mentally ill, the physically disabled and eople with learning disabilities.

ENGLAND

Regional health authorities in England were abolished in April 1996 and replaced by eight regional offices which, ogether with the headquarters in Leeds, formed the NHS xecutive (which has since been merged with the Department of Health). In April 2002, as an interim rrangement, the eight regional offices were replaced by four directorates of health and social care (DHSC). In April 2003, the DHSCs were abolished.

HEALTH AUTHORITIES

In April 1996 the district health authorities and family health service authorities were merged to form 100 unified health authorities (HAs) in England. In April 2002, 28 new health authorities were formed from the existing HAs. In October 2002, as part of the new arrangements set out in the NHS Reform and Health Care Professions Act 2002, these new health authorities were renamed strategic health authorities. The whole of England is now split into 10 strategic health authorities (SHAs) each of which is divided into various types of trusts that take responsibilty for running different NHS services locally. The different types of trusts comprise acute trusts (also known as NHS or foundation trusts), ambulance trusts, care trusts, mental health trusts and primary care trusts. SHAs are charged with improving and monitoring the performance of the trusts in their area.

PRIMARY CARE TRUSTS

The first 17 primary care trusts (PCTs) became operational in England on 1 April 2000. There are currently 152 PCTs in England. PCTs were created to give primary care professionals greater control over how resources are best used to benefit patients. PCTs are free-standing statutory bodies responsible for securing the provision of services and integrating health and social care locally. PCTs receive most of their funding directly from the Department of Health and can use this to purchase hospital and other services from NHS trusts and other healthcare providers. They are also responsible for making payments to independent primary care contractors such as GPs and dentists.

Each PCT is overseen by a board, typically comprising a chair; at least five non-executive directors who are appointed by the Appointments Commission; at least five executive members, including the chief executive, finance director and director of public health; and at least two members of the PCT's professional executive committee (PEC), which is made up of health professionals. Clinical expertise is provided by the PEC with representation from local GPs, nurses, other health professionals and social services. The board concentrates on the overall strategies for the trust and ensures the trust meets its statutory, financial and legal obligations.

ACUTE TRUSTS AND FOUNDATION TRUSTS

Hospitals are managed by acute trusts (also known as NHS trusts) that are responsible for the quality of hospital health care and for spending funds efficiently.

First introduced in April 2004, there are now 73 foundation trusts in England. NHS foundation trusts are NHS hospitals, but have their own accountability and governance systems, which function outside of the Department of Health's framework, giving them greater freedom to run their own affairs. NHS foundation trusts treat patients according to NHS principles and standards and are inspected by the Healthcare Commission. The government's aim is that by 2008, all NHS trusts will have reached a standard which will enable them to apply for NHS foundation trust status.

STRATEGIC HEALTH AUTHORITIES

EAST OF ENGLAND, Victoria House, Capital Park, Fulbourn, Cambridge CB21 5XB T 01223-597500 W www.eoe.nhs.uk

EAST MIDLANDS, Octavia House, Bostocks Lane, Sandiacre, Nottingham NG10 5QG T 0115-968 4444 W www.eastmidlands.nhs.uk

LONDON, Southside, 105 Victoria Street, London SW1E 6QT T 020-7932 3700 W www.london.nhs.uk

NORTH EAST, Riverside House, Goldcrest Way, Newcastle upon Tyne NE15 8NY T 0191-210 6400 W www.northeast.nhs.uk

NORTH WEST, 7th Floor Gateway House, Piccadilly South, Manchester M60 7LP T 0161-236 9456 W www.northwest.nhs.uk

SOUTH CENTRAL, 1st Floor Rivergate House, Newbury Business Park, London Road, Newbury, Berks RG14 2PZ T 01635-275500 W www.southcentral.nhs.uk

SOUTH EAST, York House, 18–20 Masetts Road, Horley, Surrey RH6 7DE, T 01293-778899 W www.southeastcoast.nhs.uk

SOUTH WEST, Wellsprings Road, Taunton, Somerset TA2 7PQ T 01823-333491 W www.southwest.nhs.uk

WEST MIDLANDS, St Chad's Court, 213 Hagley Road, Edgbaston, Birmingham B16 9RG T 0845-155 1022 W www.westmidlands.nhs.uk

YORKSHIRE AND THE HUMBER, Blenheim House, West One, Duncombe Street, Leeds LS1 4PL T 0113-295 2000 W www.yorkshireandhumber.nhs.uk

Contact details for PCTs and other NHS trusts in England can be found on the NHS Choices website (W www.nhs.uk).

WALES

LOCAL HEALTH BOARDS AND COMMUNITY HEALTH COUNCILS

In Wales there were five HAs which replaced the former 17 HAs and FHSAs in April 1996. The HAs set up 22 local health groups (LHGs), coterminous with local authority areas (*see* Local Government section), which began work in April 1999. Originally they advised HAs, but in March 2003 the five HAs were abolished and the LHGs, were renamed local health boards (LHB) and took up a role similar to PCTs, assuming responsibility for commissioning services and devising strategies for improving health. They also integrate the delivery of primary and community care. Each local health board has a governing body made up of local doctors, a nurse, other health professionals, members of the local authority and voluntary organisations and others to represent the interests of patients. There is also a small executive team to take action on decisions and provide services for the public. There are also 19 community health councils (CHCs).

SPECIALISED SERVICES AND PUBLIC HEALTH

Although LHBs plan and fund most hospital and family health services there are a few specialised services which are overseen at national level. These services are the responsibility of the Health Commission Wales (specialised services), which was setup in April 2003. The National Public Health Service for Wales also gives advice and guidance to LHBs on a range of issues such as communicable disease protection and control as well as childhood immunisation.

NHS TRUSTS AND HOSPITALS

There are 14 NHS trusts in Wales, including one all-Wales ambulance trust. Between them, the trusts are responsible for managing 119 hospitals.

REGIONAL OFFICES

There are three regional offices of the Welsh Assembly Government for mid and west Wales, north Wales and south east Wales. The regional offices support coordination at local level between LHBs, local authorities and NHS trusts. They have a specific role in ensuring that Welsh Assembly Government initiatives are carried out.

Contact details for the LHBs, community health councils, NHS trusts and all other NHS national and local services in Wales are available in the *NHS Wales Directory* on the NHS Wales website (W www.wales.nhs.uk).

SCOTLAND

In Scotland, the Scottish Executive Health Department leads the central management of the NHS, heading the Management Executive, which oversees the work of 14 area health boards responsible for all health services in their area. On 31 March 2006 Argyll and Clyde health board was dissolved and the administrative boundaries for the Greater Glasgow and Highland health boards were changed to allow them to take responsibility for managing the delivery of health services in relevant parts of the Argyll and Clyde area. Greater Glasgow health board took responsibility for healthcare services in Inverclyde, Renfrewshire, West Dunbartonshire and East Renfrewshire and was re-named the Greater Glasgow and Clyde health board. Highland health board took responsibility for healthcare services in Argyll and Bute.

HEALTH BOARDS

AYRSHIRE AND ARRAN, 3 Lister Street, Crosshouse Hospital, Kilmarnock KA2 0BE T 01563-577037 W www.nhsayrshireandarran.com

BORDERS, Newstead, Melrose TD6 9BD T 01896-828282 W www.nhsborders.org.uk

DUMFRIES AND GALLOWAY, Mid North, Crichton Hall, Dumfries DG1 4TG T 01387-246246 W www.nhsdg.scot.nhs.uk

FIFE, Hayfield House, Hayfield Road, Kirkcaldy, Fife KY2 5AH T 01592-643355 W www.nhsfife.scot.nhs.uk

FORTH VALLEY, Carseview House, Castle Business Park, Stirling FK9 4SW T 01786-463031 W www.nhsforthvalley.com

GRAMPIAN, Summerfield House, 2 Eday Road, Aberdeen AB15 6RE T 0845-456 6000 W www.nhsgrampian.org

GREATER GLASGOW AND CLYDE, Dalian House, 350 St Vincent Street, Glasgow G3 8YZ T 0141-201 4444 W www.nhsggc.org.uk

HIGHLAND, Assynt House, Beechwood Park, Inverness IV2 3HG T 01463-717123 W www.nhshighland.scot.nhs.uk

LANARKSHIRE, 14 Beckford Street, Hamilton, Lanarkshire ML3 0TA T 01698-281313 W www.nhslanarkshire.org.uk

LOTHIAN, Deaconess House, 148 Pleasance, Edinburgh EH8 9RS T 0131-536 9000 W www.nhslothian.scot.nhs.uk

ORKNEY, Garden House, New Scapa Road, Kirkwall, Orkney KW15 1BQ T 01856-888000 W www.ohb.scot.nhs.uk

SHETLAND, Brevik House, South Road, Lerwick ZE1 0TG T 01595-743060 W www.shb.scot.nhs.uk

TAYSIDE, Kings Cross, Clepington Road, Dundee DD3 8EA T 01382-818479 W www.nhstayside.scot.nhs.uk

WESTERN ISLES, 37 South Beach Street, Stornoway, Isle of Lewis HS1 2BB T 01851-702997 W www.wihb.scot.nhs.uk

NORTHERN IRELAND

In Northern Ireland there are four health and social services boards responsible for commissioning services to meet the needs of their respective populations. They are also responsible for assessing the needs of that population, establishing objectives and developing policies and priorities to meet these objectives.

EASTERN, Champion House, 12–22 Linenhall Street, Belfast BT2 8BS T 028-9032 1313 W www.ehssb.n-i.nhs.uk

NORTHERN, County Hall, 182 Galgorm Road, Ballymena BT42 1QB T 028-2531 1000 W www.nhssb.n-i.nhs.uk

SOUTHERN, Tower Hill, Armagh BT61 9DR T 028-3741 0041 W www.shssb.org

WESTERN, 15 Gransha Park, Clooney Road, Londonderry BT47 6FN T 028-7186 0086 W www.whssb.n-i.nhs.uk

THE NHS PLAN

In July 2000 the government launched the NHS Plan, a ten-year strategy to modernise the health service. In June 2004 it also launched the NHS Improvement Plan, which set out the next stage of NHS reform, moving the focus from access to services towards the broader issues of public health and chronic disease management. The core aims are to sustain increased levels of investment in the NHS and to continue to focus on the improvements outlined in the NHS Plan, while delivering greater levels of choice and information to patients. In July 2004, the Department of Health published *National Standards, Local Action: Health and Social Care Standards and Planning Framework 2005/6–2007/8,* which cut the number of national targets that NHS providers must comply with from 62 to 20. These national targets, which cover areas such as waiting times for accident and emergency treatment, have become national core standards which all providers of care must maintain from April 2005. Alongside this, NHS providers have been given power to set more locally relevant targets.

FINANCE

The NHS is still funded mainly through general taxation, although in recent years more reliance has been placed on the NHS element of national insurance contributions, patient charges and other sources of income.

In the April 2002 budget, the chancellor announced a five-year spending plan for the NHS. Over the years 2003–4 to 2007–8, these plans mean that expenditure on the NHS in the UK will increase on average by 7.2 per cent a year over and above inflation, 7.4 per cent a year for England. The spending plans are set out in the table below:

	UK £ million	*% real terms increase**	*England £ million*	*% real terms increase**
2003–4	74,800	7.0	61,300	7.1
2004–5	82,200	7.1	67,400	7.2
2005–6	90,500	7.4	74,400	7.6
2006–7	99,400	7.2	81,800	7.3
2007–8	109,400	7.4	90,200	7.5

* Calculated using GDP deflator at 27 June 2003
Source: Department of Health

PRIVATE FINANCE INITIATIVE

The Private Finance Initiative (PFI) was launched in 1992, and involves the private sector in designing, building, financing and operating new hospitals and primary care premises, which are then leased to the NHS. The NHS Plan committed the NHS to entering into a new public private partnership, Partnerships for Health, a joint venture between the Department of Health and Partnerships UK plc established in September 2001. Its role is to support the development of NHS Local Improvement Finance Trusts (LIFT) by implementing a standard approach to procurement as well as providing some equity. LIFTs are set up as limited companies with the local NHS, Partnerships for Health and the private sector as shareholders. LIFT schemes build and refurbish primary care premises, which the schemes own and then rent to GPs on a lease basis (as well as other parties such as chemists, opticians, dentists etc).

As at April 2007, there were 49 approved LIFT projects in England; of these, 42 had reached financial close. Forty of these schemes now have buildings open to patients. The total capital cost of all schemes at April 2007 was £1045.35m.

EMPLOYEES AND SALARIES

NHS HEALTH SERVICE STAFF (GREAT BRITAIN)
Full-time equivalent

All hospital and community medical staff	93,532
All hospital and community dental staff	3,680
Nursing and midwifery staff	492,391
General medical practitioners	42,531
General dental practitioners	24,123
Ophthalmic medical practitioners	498
Ophthalmic opticians	9,599

Source: ONS – *Annual Abstract of Statistics 2007* (Crown copyright)

SALARIES

General practitioners (GPs), dentists, optometrists and pharmacists are self-employed, and are employed by the NHS under contract. On 20 June 2003 GPs accepted a new practice-based contract which rewards practices for delivering quality and a wider range of services. Dentists receive payment for items of treatment for individual adult patients and, in addition, a continuing care payment for those registered with them. Optometrists receive approved fees for each sight test they carry out. Pharmacists receive professional fees from the NHS and are refunded the cost of prescriptions supplied. Doctors in training receive additional supplements reflecting the intensity and out-of-hours elements of their duties.

SALARIES FOR HOSPITAL MEDICAL AND DENTAL STAFF* *as at 1 April 2007*

Consultant (2003 contract)	£71,822–£96,831
Consultant (pre-2003 contract)	£59,512–£77,300
Senior Registrar	£33,825–£44,581
Specialist Registrar	£29,364–£44,581
Registrar	£29,364–£35,619
Senior House Officer	£26,270–£36,837
House Officer	£21,052–£23,762

* These figures do not include merit awards, discretionary points or banding supplements

NURSES

From 1 December 2004 a new pay system *Agenda for Change* was introduced throughout the UK for all NHS staff with the exception of medical and dental staff, doctors in public health medicine and the community health service. Nurses' salaries are incorporated in the *Agenda for Change* nine pay band structure, which provides additional payments for flexible working such as providing out-of-hours services, working weekends and nights and being 'on-call'. All employers were expected to have moved their staff to the new pay structure by the end of 2006 and all pay and terms and conditions were backdated to 1 October 2004. Under the nine pay band system the minimum starting salary for a registered nurse is £19,166 per annum.

HEALTH SERVICES

PRIMARY CARE

Primary care comprises the services provided by general practitioners, community health centres, pharmacies, dental surgeries and opticians. Primary nursing care includes the work carried out by practice nurses, community nurses, community midwives and health visitors.

PRIMARY MEDICAL SERVICES

In England, primary medical services are the responsibility of primary care trusts (PCT) who contract with healthcare providers – GPs, dentists, pharmacists etc – to provide the service to the NHS. There are four different contracts available to PCTs: the General Medical Services (GMS) contract, which provides flexibility for GPs; the Personal Medical Services (PMS) contract, which is largely locally determined; the Primary Care Trust Medical Services contract (PCTMS), under which PCTs are able to provide services themselves by directly employing staff and the Alternative Provider Medical Services (APMS) contract, which is particularly useful in areas of under-provision as it allows for substantial restructuring of services.

In Wales, responsibility for primary medical services rests with local health boards (LHB), in Scotland with the 14 health boards and in Northern Ireland with the four health and social services boards.

Any vocationally trained doctor may provide general or personal medical services. GPs may also have private fee-paying patients, but not if that patient is already an NHS patient on that doctor's patient list.

A person who is ordinarily resident in the UK is eligible to register with a GP (or PMS provider) for free primary care treatment. Should a patient have difficulty in registering with a doctor, he or she should contact the local PCT for help. When a person is away from home he/she can still access primary care treatment from a GP if they ask to be treated as a temporary resident. In an emergency any doctor in the service will give treatment and advice.

GPs are responsible for the care of their patients 24 hours a day, seven days a week, but can fulfil the terms of their contract by delegating or transferring responsibility for out-of-hours (OOH) care to an accredited provider. Under the GMS contract, practices can opt out of responsibility for patient care during the OOH period. When they do so it becomes the responsibility of the PCT, who can either provide the OOH cover themselves or commission the service from an OOH provider.

Increasingly, some secondary care services, such as minor operations and consultations, can be provided in a primary care setting. The number of such practitioners is growing and the GMS contract provides a platform for further expansion.

In addition a total of 72 NHS walk-in centres are currently operational across the country, with a further 16 centres under development. Usually open seven days a week, from early in the morning until late in the evening, they are nurse-led and provide treatment for minor ailments and injuries, health information and self-help advice.

HEALTH COSTS

Some people are exempt from, or entitled to help with, health costs such as prescription charges, ophthalmic and dental costs, and in some cases help towards travel costs to and from hospital.

The following list is intended as a general guide to those who may be entitled to help, or who are exempt from some of the charges relating to the above:

- children under 16 and young people in full time education who are under 19
- people aged 60 or over
- pregnant women and women who have had a baby in the last 12 months
- people, or their partners, who are in receipt of income support and/or income-based jobseeker's allowance
- people in receipt of the pension credit guarantee credit
- people with a specified medical condition or disability who have a valid exemption certificate
- diagnosed glaucoma patients, people who have been advised by an ophthalmologist that they are at risk of glaucoma and people aged 40 or over who have an immediate family member who is a diagnosed glaucoma patient
- diagnosed diabetic patients
- NHS in-patients
- NHS out-patients for all prescribed contraceptives, medication given at a hospital, NHS walk-in centre personally administered by a GP or supplied at a hospital or primary care trust clinic for the treatment of a sexually transmissable infection
- patients of the Community Dental Service or an out-patient of the NHS Hospital Dental Service
- people registered blind or partially sighted
- people who need complex lenses
- war pensioners whose treatment/prescription is for their accepted disablement and who have a valid exemption certificate
- people who are entitled to, or named on, a valid NHS tax credit exemption or HC2 certificate

People in other circumstances may also be eligible for help; Booklet HC11 outlines further details and is available from main post offices, local social security offices or online (**W** www.direct.gov.uk).

WALES

On 1 April 2007 all prescription charges (including those for medical supports and appliances and wigs) for people living in Wales were abolished. The above guide still applies for NHS dental and optical charges although all people aged under 25 living in Wales are also entitled to free dental examinations.

PHARMACEUTICAL SERVICES

Patients may obtain medicines and appliances under the NHS from any pharmacy whose owner has entered into arrangements with the PCT to provide this service. There are also some suppliers who only provide special appliances. In rural areas, where access to a pharmacy may be difficult, patients may be able to obtain medicines, etc, from a dispensing doctor.

In England, a charge of £6.85 is payable for each item

supplied (except for contraceptives for which there is no charge), unless the patient is exempt and the declaration on the back of the prescription form is completed. Prepayment certificates (£26.85* valid for three months, £98.70 valid for a year) may be purchased by those patients not entitled to exemption who require frequent prescriptions. Prescription charges in Scotland and Northern Ireland are currently the same. In Wales NHS prescription charges were abolished on 1 April 2007.

* In Scotland there is only a four month prepayment certificate available at £35.85

DENTAL SERVICES

Dentists, like doctors, may take part in the NHS and also have private patients. Dentists are responsible to the local health provider in whose areas they provide services. Patients may go to any dentist who is taking part in the NHS and is willing to accept them. On 1 April 2006 the charging system for NHS dentistry in England and Wales was changed. There is now a three-tier payment system based on the individual course of treatment required.

COURSE OF TREATMENT COSTS 2007–8

Examination, diagnosis, preventive care* (eg x-rays, scale and polish)	£15.90/£12.00
Examination, diagnosis, preventive care and basic additional treatment (eg fillings, root canal treatment and extractions)	£43.60/£39.00
Examination, diagnosis, preventive care and all other treatment (eg more complex procedures such as crowns, dentures or bridges)	£194.00/£177.00

* Urgent and out-of-hours treatment will also be charged at this payment tier

The cost of individual treatment plan should be known prior to treatment and some dental practices may require payment in advance. There is no charge for writing a prescription or removing stitches and only one charge is payable for each course of treatment even if more than one visit to the dentist is required. If additional treatment is required within two months of visiting the dentist and this is covered by the course of treatment most recently paid for (eg payment was made for the second tier of treatment but an additional filling is required) then this will be provided free of charge.

SCOTLAND

In Scotland, NHS dental patients pay 80 per cent of the total cost of the treatment up to a maximum of £384 during 2007–8. Basic and extensive examinations are free.

GENERAL OPHTHALMIC SERVICES

General ophthalmic services are administered by local health providers. Testing of sight may be carried out by any ophthalmic medical practitioner or ophthalmic optician (optometrist). The optician must give the prescription to the patient, who can take this to any supplier of glasses to have them dispensed. Only registered opticians can supply glasses to children and to people registered as blind or partially sighted.

As at 1 July 2007 the NHS sight test cost was £18.85 in England and Wales. Free eyesight tests and help towards the cost are available to people in certain circumstances. Help is also available for the purchase of glasses or contact lenses (*see* Health Costs section or booklet HC11). In Scotland eye examinations, which include a sight test, are free to all. Help is also available for the purchase of glasses or contact lenses to those entitled to help with health costs in the same way it is available to those in England and Wales.

CHILD HEALTH SERVICES

Pre-school services at GP surgeries or child health clinics provide regular monitoring of children's physical, mental and emotional health and development and advise parents on their children's health and welfare.

NHS DIRECT AND NHS 24

NHS Direct is a 24-hour nurse-led advice telephone service for England and Wales. It provides medical advice as well as directing people to the appropriate part of the NHS for treatment if necessary (T 0845-4647).

NHS 24 provides an equivalent service for Scotland (T 0845-424 2424).

SECONDARY CARE AND OTHER SERVICES

HOSPITALS

NHS hospitals provide acute and specialist care services, treating conditions which normally cannot be dealt with by primary care specialists, and provide for medical emergencies.

NUMBER OF BEDS 2005

In-patients	*Average daily*	
	available beds	*occupation of beds*
England	176,000	149,000
Wales	14,000	11,000
Scotland	28,100	22,500
Northern Ireland	8,238	6,887

PATIENT ACTIVITY 2005

Out-patient attendances	*New patients*	*Total*
England*	13,370,000	44,768,000
Wales	776,000	2,882,000
Scotland	2,720,000	5,990,000
Northern Ireland	1,043,000	2,221,000

* 2004 figures

Source: ONS – *Annual Abstract of Statistics 2007* (Crown copyright)

HOSPITAL CHARGES

Acute or foundation trusts can provide hospital accommodation in single rooms or small wards, if not required for patients who need privacy for medical reasons. The patient is still an NHS patient, but there may be a charge for these additional facilities. Acute or foundation trusts can charge for certain patient services that are considered to be additional treatments over and above the normal hospital service provision. There is no blanket policy to cover this and each case is considered in the light of the patient's clinical need. However, if an item or service is considered to be an integral part of a patient's treatment by their clinician, then a charge should not be made.

In some NHS hospitals, accommodation and services are available for the treatment of private patients where it does not interfere with care for NHS patients. Income generated by treating private patients is then put back into local NHS services. Private patients undertake to pay the full costs of medical treatment, accommodation, medication and other related services. Charges for private patients are set locally.

WAITING LISTS

England

Under the charter *Your Guide to the NHS,* patients were guaranteed admission within 18 months of being placed on a waiting list. In July 2004 a new target, of an 18 week maximum wait from start time (ie seeing a GP) to treatment, was set to be achieved by 2008. Known as the referral to treatment (RTT) pathway, monthly data is published on the NHS 18-weeks website (W www.18weeks.nhs.uk). In May 2007 the number of patients who completed their RTT pathway totalled 277,540; of which 53 per cent were seen within 18 weeks.

Wales

In Wales the number of patients waiting for in-patient or day case treatment totalled 61,267 on 30 June 2007, a decrease from 67,163 in June 2006; of these, 8,085 had been waiting between 22 and 36 weeks, 15,091 between 13 and 22 weeks and 38,090 under 13 weeks. The number of patients waiting for a first out-patient appointment totalled 171,097 in June 2007, compared with 200,550 in June 2006; of these, 65 had been waiting over 36 weeks, 16,426 had been waiting between 22 and 36 weeks, 36,278 between 13 and 22 weeks and 118,328 under 13 weeks.

Scotland

In 2005 the Scottish Executive Health Department published *Delivering for Health* in which is pledged that by the end of 2007 no patient will wait more than 18 weeks from GP or dentist referral to their first out-patient appointment or between a decision being made to undertake treatment and the start of that treatment. At the end of March 2007 84 per cent of patients had been seen within 18 weeks from point of referral, compared with 78.5 per cent of patients in March 2006, and no patients had been waiting more than 18 weeks for in-patient or day-case treatment at the end of March 2007, compared with 6,117 patients at the end of March 2006.

Northern Ireland

Overall the total number of patients waiting to be admitted to hospitals in Northern Ireland at the end of March 2007 was 37,978, compared with 41,448 in March 2006. The number of patients waiting six months and over for an initial out-patient appointment at the end of March 2007 was 32, a reduction of almost 100 per cent from March 2006, when the figure stood at 73,915. Following the achievement of the waiting time targets for 2006–7 the health minister set new targets to ensure that by March 2008 no patient will wait more than 13 weeks for a first out-patient appointment and no more than 21 weeks for in-patient or day-case treatment.

AMBULANCE SERVICE

The NHS provides emergency ambulance services free of charge via the 999 emergency telephone service. Air ambulances, provided through local charities and partially funded by the NHS, are used throughout the UK. They assist with cases where access may be difficult or heavy traffic could hinder road progress. Non-emergency ambulance services are provided free of charge to patients who are deemed to require them on medical grounds.

In 2006–7 in England approximately 6.3 million emergency calls were made to the ambulance service, an increase of 6.3 per cent on the previous year. There were about 3.6 million emergency patient journeys. Since 1 April 2001 all services have had a system of call prioritisation. The prioritisation procedures require all emergency calls to be classified as either immediately life threatening (category A) or other emergency (category B). Services are expected to reach 75 per cent of Category A (life threatening) calls within eight minutes and 95 per cent of category B calls within 19 minutes (since April 2006 there has been no difference in response time for urban or rural areas). In 2006–7, 74.6 per cent of life threatening calls resulted in emergency response arriving at the scene of the incident within eight minutes. For category B calls, 90.5 per cent of incidents were responded to within 19 minutes.

BLOOD SERVICES

There are four national bodies which coordinate the blood donor programme in the UK. Donors give blood at local centres on a voluntary basis.

NATIONAL BLOOD SERVICE, Oak House, Reeds Crescent, Watford, Herts WD24 4QN **T** 0845-771 1711 **W** www.blood.co.uk

WELSH BLOOD SERVICE, Ely Valley Road, Talbot Green, Pontyclun CF72 9WB **T** 01443-622000 **W** www.welsh-blood.org.uk

SCOTTISH NATIONAL BLOOD TRANSFUSION SERVICE, 21 Ellen's Glen Road, Edinburgh EH17 7QT **T** 0845-909 0999 **W** www.scotblood.co.uk

NORTHERN IRELAND BLOOD TRANSFUSION SERVICE, Belfast City Hospital Complex, Lisburn Road, Belfast BT9 7TS **T** 028-9032 1414 **W** www.nibts.org

HOSPICES

Hospice or palliative care may be available for patients with life-threatening illnesses. It may be provided at the patient's home or in a voluntary or NHS hospice or in hospital, and is intended to ensure the best possible quality of life for the patient during their illness, and to provide help and support to both the patient and the patient's family. The National Council for Palliative Care coordinates NHS and voluntary services in England, Wales and Northern Ireland; the Scottish Partnership for Palliative Care performs the same function in Scotland.

NATIONAL COUNCIL FOR PALLIATIVE CARE, The Fitzpatrick Building, 188–194 York Way, London N7 9AS **T** 020-7697 1520 **W** www.ncpc.org.uk

SCOTTISH PARTNERSHIP FOR PALLIATIVE CARE, 1A Cambridge Street, Edinburgh EH1 2DY **T** 0131-229 0538 **W** www.palliativecarescotland.org.uk

NHS CHARTERS

The original Patient's Charter was published in 1991 and came into force in 1992; an expanded version was published in 1995. The charter set out the rights of patients in relation to the standards of service they should expect to receive at all times and standards of service that the NHS aimed to provide.

The Patient's Charter was replaced nationally in 2001 with *Your Guide to the NHS,* which provided information on how to get treatment and gave specific details on minimum standards for patients, targets for the NHS and improvements in the NHS Plan. It also detailed what patients had a right to expect from the NHS and what is expected from patients.

Information for patients about all aspects of the NHS has now been reorganised and is available on the NHS Choices website (W www.nhs.uk).

COMPLAINTS

Firstly, an attempt must be made to resolve the complaint at a local level directly with the healthcare provider concerned. Patient advice and liaison services (PALS) have been established for every NHS and primary care trust in England. PALS are not part of the complaints procedure itself, but can give advice on local complaints procedure, or resolve concerns informally. Secondly, if the case is not resolved locally, an independent review can be requested by the Healthcare Commission in England or by the relevant health and social services board in Northern Ireland. As a final resort, complainants may approach the Health Service Ombudsman in England, the Scottish Public Services Ombudsman, Public Services Ombudsman for Wales or the Commissioner for Complaints in Northern Ireland.

RECIPROCAL ARRANGEMENTS

UK residents are entitled to medical treatment that becomes necessary, at a reduced cost or free of charge, when temporarily visiting a European Union country, Iceland, Liechtenstein, Norway or Switzerland. Only treatment provided under the country's state scheme is covered. A European Health Insurance Card (EHIC) should be obtained before travelling either from the post office, by telephone (T 0845-606 2030) or online (W www.ehic.org.uk).

The UK also has bilateral agreements with several other countries, including Australia and New Zealand, for the free provision of urgent medical treatment.

European Economic Area nationals visiting the UK and visitors from other countries with which the UK has bilateral health care agreements, are entitled to receive emergency health care on the NHS on the same terms as it is available to UK residents.

SOCIAL WELFARE

SOCIAL SERVICES

The Secretary of State for Health (in England), the National Assembly of Wales, the Scottish Executive and the Secretary of State for Northern Ireland are responsible, under the Local Authority Social Services Act 1970, for the provision of social services for older people, disabled people, families and children, and those with mental disorders. Personal social services are administered by local authorities according to policies, with standards set by central and devolved government. Each authority has a director and a committee responsible for the social services functions placed upon them. Local authorities provide, enable and commission care after assessing the needs of their population. The private and voluntary sectors also play an important role in the delivery of social services, and an estimated six million people in the UK provide substantial regular care for a member of their family.

Under the Health and Social Care (Community Health and Standards) Act 2003 the Commission for Social Care Inspection (CSCI) was established in April 2004. The CSCI was established as a single, regulatory authority, to ensure that local authority, private and voluntary care services throughout England are run in accordance with the national minimum standards and regulations that have been set by the government through a system of inspections and self-assessment. In April 2007 the Office for Standards in Education, Children's Services and Skills (OFSTED) was made responsible for inspecting and regulating all care services for children and young people in England; the CSCI is now only responsible for all adult social care services. Both OFSTED and the CSCI collate information on local care services and make this information available to the public.

The Care and Social Services Inspectorate Wales (CSSIW), an operationally independent part of the Welsh Assembly Government, is reponsible for the regulation and inspection of all social care services in Wales and the Scottish Commission for the Regulation of Care (the Care Commission), established in April 2002 under the Regulation of Care (Scotland) Act 2001, is the independent care services regulator for Scotland. The Department of Health, Social Services and Public Safety is responsible for social care services in Northern Ireland.

COMMISSION FOR SOCIAL CARE INSPECTION (CSCI), 33 Greycoat Street, London SW1P 2QF **T** 020-7979 2000 **E** enquiries@csci.gsi.gov.uk **W** www.csci.org.uk

OFFICE FOR STANDARDS IN EDUCATION, CHILDREN'S SERVICES AND SKILLS (OFSTED), Royal Exchange Buildings, St Ann's Square, Manchester M2 7LA **T** 0845-640 4040 **E** enquiries@ofsted.gov.uk **W** www.ofsted.gov.uk

CARE AND SOCIAL SERVICES INSPECTORATE WALES (CSSIW), Cathays Park, Cardiff CF10 3NQ **T** 01443-848450 **E** cssiw@wales.gsi.gov.uk **W** www.cssiw.org.uk

SCOTTISH COMMISSION FOR THE REGULATION OF CARE, Compass House, 11 Riverside Drive, Dundee DD1 4NY **T** 01382-207100 **W** www.carecommission.com

DEPARTMENT OF HEALTH, SOCIAL SERVICES AND PUBLIC SAFETY, Castle Buildings, Stormont, Belfast BT4 3SJ **T** 028-9052 0500 **W** www.dhsspsni.gov.uk

STAFF

Total social service staff England and Wales	216,500
Home help service	38,200
Field social workers	40,800
Day care establishments staff	30,600
Residential care staff	52,200

Source: ONS – *Annual Abstract of Statistics 2007* (Crown copyright)

OLDER PEOPLE

Services for older people are designed to enable them to remain living in their own homes for as long as possible. Local authority services include advice, domestic help, meals in the home, alterations to the home to aid mobility, emergency alarm systems, day and/or night attendants, laundry services and the provision of day centres and recreational facilities. Charges may be made for these services. Respite care may also be provided in order to allow carers temporary relief from their responsibilities.

Local authorities and the private sector also provide 'sheltered housing' for older people, sometimes with resident wardens.

If an older person is admitted to a residential home, charges are made according to a means test; if the person cannot afford to pay, the costs are met by the local authority.

In March 2001 a National Service Framework for Older People was published. The framework set national standards and service models of care across health and social services for older people whether they live at home, in residential care or are being cared for in hospital.

DISABLED PEOPLE

Services for disabled people are designed to enable them to remain living in their own homes wherever possible. Local authority services include advice, adaptations to the home, meals in the home, help with personal care, occupational therapy, educational facilities and recreational facilities. Respite care may also be provided in order to allow carers temporary relief from their responsibilities.

Special housing may be available for disabled people who can live independently, and residential accommodation for those who cannot.

FAMILIES AND CHILDREN

Local authorities are required to provide services aimed at safeguarding the welfare of children in need and, wherever possible, allowing them to be brought up by their families. Services include advice, counselling, help in the home and the provision of family centres. Many authorities also provide short-term refuge accommodation for women and children.

DAY CARE

In allocating day care places to children, local authorities give priority to children with special needs, whether in terms of their health, learning abilities or social needs. Since September 2001 OFSTED has been responsible for the regulation and registration of all early years childcare and education provision in England (previously the responsibility of the local authorities). All day care and childminding services which care for children under eight years of age for more than two hours a day must register with OFSTED and are inspected at least every two years. As at 30 June 2007 there were 1,551,200 registered childcare places and 104,616 registered childcare providers in England.

CHILD PROTECTION

Children considered to be at risk of physical injury, neglect or sexual abuse are placed on the local authority's child protection register. Local authority social services staff, schools, health visitors and other agencies work together to prevent and detect cases of abuse. In England as at 31 March 2006 there were 26,400 children on child protection registers. Of the children registered during 2005–6, 13,700 were at risk of neglect, 5,100 of physical abuse, 2,600 of sexual abuse and 6,700 of emotional abuse. At 31 March 2006 there were 2,163 children on child protection registers in Wales, 2,288 in Scotland and 1,639 in Northern Ireland.

LOCAL AUTHORITY CARE

Local authorities are required to provide accommodation for children who have no parents or guardians or whose parents or guardians are unable or unwilling to care for them. A family proceedings court may also issue a care order where a child is being neglected or abused, or is not attending school; the court must be satisfied that this would positively contribute to the well-being of the child.

The welfare of children in local authority care must be properly safeguarded. Children may be placed with foster families, who receive payments to cover the expenses of caring for the child or children, or in residential care.

Children's homes may be run by the local authority or by the private or voluntary sectors; all homes are subject to inspection procedures. In England as at 31 March 2006, 60,300 children were in the care of local authorities, of these, 42,000 were in foster placements. In Wales 4,529 children were being looked after by local authorities on 31 March 2006, 12,966 in Scotland and 2,436 children in Northern Ireland.

ADOPTION

Local authorities are required to provide an adoption service, either directly or via approved voluntary societies. In the UK, in 2005, 6,161 children (under 18 years of age) were entered onto the Adopted Children Register: 5,582 in England and Wales, 439 in Scotland and 140 in Northern Ireland.

PEOPLE WITH LEARNING DISABILITIES

Services for people with learning disabilities are designed to enable them to remain living in the community wherever possible. Local authority services include short-term care, support in the home, the provision of day care centres, and help with other activities outside the home. Residential care is provided for the severely or profoundly disabled.

MENTALLY ILL PEOPLE

Under the care programme approach, mentally ill people should be assessed by specialist services, receive a care plan and a key worker should be appointed for each patient. Regular reviews of the person's progress should be conducted. Local authorities provide help and advice to mentally ill people and their families, and places in day centres and social centres. Social workers can apply for a mentally disturbed person to be compulsorily detained in hospital. Where appropriate, mentally ill people are provided with accommodation in special hospitals, local authority accommodation, or at homes run by private or voluntary organisations. Patients who have been discharged from hospitals may be placed on a supervision register. *Mental Health National Service Framework* was published in September 1999 setting national standards on how to prevent and treat mental illness.

NATIONAL INSURANCE

The National Insurance (NI) scheme operates under the Social Security Contributions and Benefits Act 1992 and the Social Security Administration Act 1992, and orders and regulations made thereunder. The scheme is financed by contributions payable by earners, employers and others (*see* below). Money collected under the scheme is used to finance the National Insurance Fund (from which contributory benefits are paid) and to contribute to the cost of the National Health Service.

NATIONAL INSURANCE FUND

Estimated receipts, payments and statement of balances of the National Insurance Fund for 2007–8:

Receipts	*£ million*
Net national insurance contributions	71,747
Compensation from the Consolidated Fund for statutory sick, maternity, paternity and adoption pay recoveries	1,397
Income from investments	1,799
State scheme premiums	118
Other receipts	69
TOTAL RECEIPTS	75,130

Payments	*£ million*
Benefits	
At present rates	63,574
Increase due to proposed rate changes	2,170
Personal and stakeholder pensions contracted-out rebates	2,156
Age-related rebates for contracted-out money purchase schemes	205
Administration costs	1,470
Redundancy fund payments	251
Transfer to Northern Ireland	452
Other payments	33
TOTAL PAYMENTS	70,313

Balances	*£ million*
Opening balance	38,475
Excess of receipts over payments	4,817
BALANCE AT END OF YEAR	43,292

CONTRIBUTIONS

There are six classes of National Insurance contributions (NICs):

Class 1	paid by employees and their employers
Class 1A	paid by employers who provide employees with certain benefits in kind for private use, such as company cars
Class 1B	paid by employers who enter into a pay as you earn (PAYE) settlement agreement with HM Revenue and Customs
Class 2	paid by self-employed people
Class 3	voluntary contributions paid to protect entitlement to the state pension for those who do not pay enough NI contributions in another class
Class 4	paid by the self-employed on their taxable profits over a set limit. These are normally paid by self-employed people in addition to class 2 contributions. Class 4 contributions do not count towards benefits.

The lower and upper earnings limits and the percentage rates referred to below apply from April 2007 to April 2008.

CLASS 1

Class 1 contributions are paid where a person:

- is an employed earner (employee), office holder (eg company director) or employed under a contract of service in Great Britain or Northern Ireland
- is 16 or over and under state pension age
- earns at or above the earnings threshold of £100.00 per week (including overtime pay, bonus, commission, etc, without deduction of superannuation contributions)

Class 1 contributions are made up of primary and secondary contributions. Primary contributions are those paid by the employee and these are deducted from earnings by the employer. Since 6 April 2001 the employee's and employer's earnings thresholds have been the same and are referred to as the earnings threshold. Primary contributions are not paid on earnings below the earnings threshold of £100.00 per week. However, between the lower earnings limit of £87.00 per week and the earnings threshold of £100.00 per week, NI contributions are treated as having been paid to protect the benefit entitlement position of lower earners. Contributions are payable at the rate of 11 per cent on earnings between the earnings threshold and the upper earnings limit of £670.00 per week (9.4 per cent for contracted-out employment). Above the upper earnings limit 1 per cent is payable.

Some married women or widows pay a reduced rate of 4.85 per cent on earnings between the earnings threshold and upper earnings limits and 1 per cent above this. It is no longer possible to elect to pay the reduced rate but those who had reduced liability before 12 May 1977 may retain it for as long as certain conditions are met. *See* leaflet *Married Women Paying Reduced Rate National Insurance Contributions (NICs).*

Secondary contributions are paid by employers of employed earners at the rate of 12.8 per cent on all earnings above the earnings threshold of £97.00 per week. There is no upper earnings limit for employers' contributions. Employers operating contracted-out salary related schemes pay reduced contributions of 9.3 per cent; those with contracted-out money-purchase schemes pay 11.8 per cent. The contracted-out rate applies only to that portion of earnings between the earnings threshold and the upper earnings limits. Employers' contributions below and above those respective limits are assessed at the appropriate not contracted-out rate.

CLASS 2

Class 2 contributions are paid where a person is self-employed and is 16 or over and under state pension age. Contributions are paid at a flat rate of £2.20 per week regardless of the amount earned. However, those with earnings of less than £4,635 a year can apply for small earnings exception, eg exemption from liability to pay class 2 contributions. Those granted exemption from class 2 contributions may pay class 2 or class 3 contributions voluntarily. Self-employed earners (whether or not they pay class 2 contributions) may also be liable to pay class 4 contributions based on profits. There are special rules for those who are concurrently employed and self-employed.

Married women and widows can no longer choose not to pay class 2 contributions but those who elected not to pay class 2 contributions before 12 May 1977 may tain the right for as long as certain conditions are met.

Class 2 contributions are collected by the national surance contributions department of HM Revenue and ustoms (HMRC), by direct debit or quarterly bills. *See* aflet CA04.

LASS 3

lass 3 contributions are voluntary flat-rate contributions f £7.80 per week payable by persons over the age of 16 ho would otherwise be unable to qualify for retirement ension and certain other benefits because they have an sufficient record of class 1 or class 2 contributions. This ay include those who are not working, those not liable r class 1 or class 2 contributions or those excepted from ass 2 contributions. Married women and widows who n or before 11 May 1977 elected not to pay class 1 (full te) or class 2 contributions cannot pay class 3 ontributions while they retain this right. Class 3 ontributions are collected by HMRC by quarterly bills or rect debit. *See* leaflet CA04.

LASS 4

elf employed people whose profits and gains are over 5,225 a year pay class 4 contributions in addition to ass 2 contributions. This applies to self-employed arners over 16 and under the state pension age. Class 4 ontributions are calculated at 8 per cent of annual profits r gains between £5,225 and £34,840 and 1 per cent bove. Class 4 contributions are assessed and collected by MRC. It is possible, in some circumstances, to apply for xceptions from liability to pay class 4 contributions or to ave the amount of contribution reduced.

ENSIONS

lany people will qualify for a state pension; however, ere are further pension choices available, such as ersonal and stakeholder pensions. There are also other on-pension savings and investment options. The llowing section provides background information on xisting pension schemes.

TATE PENSION SCHEME

he state pension scheme consists of:

- basic state pension
- additional state pension

eople may be able to get both or either when they reach ate pension age and meet the qualifying conditions.

The state pension does not have to be claimed at state ension age, people can delay claiming it to earn extra eekly state pension or a lump sum payment.

asic State Pension

he amount of basic state pension paid is dependent on ne number of 'qualifying years' a person has established uring their working life. In 2007–8, the full basic state ension is £87.30 a week and the minimum basic state ension is £21.83 a week (*see also* Benefits, State Pension: ategories A and B).

ualifying Years

'qualifying year' is a tax year in which a person has nough earnings on which they have paid, are treated as aving paid, or have been credited with national nsurance (NI) contributions (*see* National Insurance redits section). By state pension age, a person needs to ave one qualifying year from NI contributions paid or from NI contributions treated as being paid to be eligible for any basic state pension. The number of qualifying years can be reduced if a person qualifies for home responsibilities protection (*see* below).

National Insurance Credits

Those in receipt of carer's allowance, working tax credit (with a disability element), jobseeker's allowance, incapacity benefit, statutory sick pay or statutory maternity pay may have class 1 NI contributions credited to them. Persons undertaking certain training courses or jury service or who have been wrongly imprisoned for a conviction which is quashed on appeal may also get class 1 NI credits for each week they receive benefit or fulfil certain conditions. Class 1 credits are also available to men for the tax years in which they reach age 60 up to age 64, if they are not liable to pay contributions. Class 1 NI credits count toward all future contributory benefits. A class 3 NI credit for basic state pension and bereavement benefit purposes is awarded, where required, for each week the working tax credit (without a disability element) has been received. Class 3 credits are also awarded automatically to young people aged 16 to 18 if they have not paid enough contributions to gain a qualifying year. However, a state pension will not be paid based on a record of NI credits alone.

Working Life

Working life is counted from the start of the tax year in which a person reaches 16 to the end of the tax year before the one in which they reach state pension age: for men this is normally 49 years and for women this varies between 44 and 49 years depending on their birth date (*see* State Pension Age). To get the full rate (100 per cent) basic state pension a person must normally have qualifying years for about 90 per cent of their working life. To get the minimum basic state pension (25 per cent) a person will normally need ten or eleven qualifying years.

State Pension Age

State pension age is:

- 65 for men
- 60 for women born on or before 5 April 1950
- 65 for women born on or after 6 April 1955

Women born between 6 April 1950 and 5 April 1955 will have a state pension age between 60 and 65 depending on their date of birth. Further information can be obtained from the online state pension calculator (W www.thepensionservice.gov.uk/resourcecentre/statepensioncalc.asp).

Using the NI Contribution Record of Another Person to Claim a State Pension

Married women who are not entitled to a state pension on their own NI contributions may get a basic state pension calculated using their husband's NI contribution record. A basic state pension may be paid of up to 60 per cent of the husband's entitlement (up to £52.30 a week in 2007–8). From 6 April 2010, married men and civil partners will be able to claim a basic state pension based on their wife or civil partner's NI contributions if better than one based on their own record and if their wife or civil partner was born after 6 April 1950. A state pension is also payable to widows, widowers, surviving civil partners, and people who are divorced or whose civil partnership has been dissolved, based on their late or ex-spouse's/civil partner's NI contributions.

Non-contributory State Pensions

A non-contributory state pension may be payable to those aged 80 or over who live in England, Scotland or Wales, and have done so for a total of ten years or more for any continuous period in the 20 years after their 60th birthday, if they are not entitled to another category of state pension, or are entitled to one below the rate of £52.30 a week in 2007–8 (*see also* Benefits, State Pension: Category D).

Graduated Retirement Benefit

Graduated Retirement Benefit (GRB) is based on the amount of graduated NI contributions paid into the GRB scheme between April 1961 and April 1975.

Home Responsibilities Protection

It is possible for people who have a low income or are unable to work because they care for children or a sick or disabled person at home to reduce the number of qualifying years required. This is called home responsibilities protection (HRP) and can be given for any tax year since April 1978; the number of years for which HRP is given is deducted from the number of qualifying years needed. HRP may, in some cases, also qualify the recipient for additional state pension. Since April 2003, HRP has also been available to approved foster carers.

Additional State Pension

The amount of additional state pension paid depends on the amount of earnings a person has, or is treated as having, between the lower and upper earnings limits for each complete tax year between 6 April 1978 (when the scheme started) and the tax year before they reach state pension age. The right to additional state pension does not depend on the person's right to basic state pension.

From 1978 to 2002, additional state pension was called the State Earnings-Related Pension Scheme (SERPS). SERPS covered all earnings by employees from 6 April 1978 to 5 April 1997 on which standard rate class 1 NI contributions had been paid, and earnings between 6 April 1997 and 5 April 2002 if the standard rate class 1 NI contributions had been contracted-in.

In 2002, SERPS was reformed through the state second pension, by improving the pension available to low and moderate earners and extending access to certain carers and people with long-term illness or disability. If earnings on which class 1 NI contributions have been paid or can be treated as paid are above the annual NI lower earnings limit (£4,524 for 2007–8) but below the statutory low earnings threshold (£13,000 for 2007–8), the state second pension regards this as earnings of £13,000 and it is treated as equivalent. Certain carers and people with long-term illness and disability will be considered as having earned at the low earnings threshold for each complete tax year since 2002–3 even if they do not work at all, or earn less than the annual NI lower earnings limit.

The amount of additional state pension paid also depends on when a person reaches state pension age; changes phased in from 6 April 1999 mean that pensions are calculated differently from that date.

Inheritance

Men or women widowed before 6 October 2002 can inherit all of their late spouse's SERPS pension. From 6 October 2002, the maximum percentage of SERPS pension that a person can inherit from a late spouse or civil partner depends on their late spouse or civil partne[r's] date of birth:

Maximum SERPS entitlement	*d.o.b (men)*	*d.o.b (wome[n])*
100%	5/10/37 or earlier	5/10/42 or earli[er]
90%	6/10/37 to 5/10/39	6/10/42 to 5/10/[illegible]
80%	6/10/39 to 5/10/41	6/10/44 to 5/10/[illegible]
70%	6/10/41 to 5/10/43	6/10/46 to 5/10/[illegible]
60%	6/10/43 to 5/10/45	6/10/48 to 5/7/[illegible]
50%	6/10/45 or later	6/7/50 or lat[er]

The maximum state second pension a person can inhe[rit] from a late spouse or civil partner is 50 per cent.

Pension Forecasts

The Pension Service provides a state pension forecasti[ng] service by phone (T 0845-300 0168) or online (W ww[w.] thepensionservice.gov.uk).

PRIVATE PENSION SCHEMES

Contracted-Out Appropriate Personal Pension Schemes

Since July 1988 an employee has been able to start [a] personal pension which, if it meets certain conditions, ca[n] be used in place of the additional state pension. The[se] pensions are known as appropriate personal pensio[ns] (APPs). The part of an APP derived from the protecte[d] rights (rights comprising mainly the NI contributio[n] rebate and its investment return) is intended to provi[de] benefits broadly equivalent to those given up in th[e] additional state pension. At retirement, a contracted-ou[t] deduction will be made from additional state pensio[n] built up from 6 April 1987 to 5 April 1997. Th[e] reduction may be more or less than that part of th[e] pension derived from the protected rights. From 6 Apr[il] 1997 to 5 April 2002, members of an APP scheme wi[ll] not have built up any entitlement to additional sta[te] pension during the period of their membership. From [6] April 2002, employees contracted-out into a person[al] pension and earning between the lower earnings limit an[d] the low earnings threshold (£4,524 and £13,000 i[n] 2007–8) will be entitled to a reduced amount [of] additional state pension.

Contracted-Out Salary-Related (COSR) Scheme

- these schemes (also known as contracted-out define[d] benefit (DB) schemes) provide a pension related t[o] earnings and the length of pensionable service
- any notional additional state pension built up from [6] April 1978 to 5 April 1997 will be reduced by th[e] amount of guaranteed minimum pension (GMP) bui[lt] up during that period (the contracted-out deduction)
- from 6 April 1997 these schemes no longer provide GMP. Instead, as a condition of contracting out the[y] have to satisfy a reference scheme test to ensure that th[e] benefits provided are at least as good as a prescribe[d] standard
- when someone contracts out of the additional sta[te] pension through a COSR scheme, both the schem[e] member and the employer, pay a reduced rate of N[I] contributions (known as the contracted-out rebate) t[o] compensate for the additional state pension given up

Contracted-Out Money Purchase (COMP) Scheme

- these schemes (also known as contracted-out define[d] contribution (DC) schemes) provide a pension based o[n] the value of the fund at retirement, ie the money pai[d] in, along with the investment return the part of the COMP fund derived from protected rights (rights made up mainly from the contracted-out rebate and its investment return) is intended to provide benefits broadly equivalent to those given up in the additional state pension

a contracted-out deduction, which may be more or less than that part of the pension derived from the protected rights, will be made from any notional additional pension built up from 6 April 1988 to 5 April 1997

as with a COSR scheme, when someone contracts out of the additional state pension through a COMP scheme, both the scheme member and the employer pay a reduced rate of NI contributions (the contracted-out rebate) to compensate for the state pension given up. In addition, at the end of each tax year, HM Revenue and Customs pays an additional age-related rebate direct to the scheme for investment on behalf of the employee

ntracted-Out Mixed Benefit (COMB) Scheme
mixed benefit scheme is a single scheme with both a ary related section and a money purchase section. ıeme rules set out which section individual employees y join and the circumstances (if any), in which mbers may move between sections. Each section must isfy the respective contracting-out conditions for OSR and COMP schemes.

r more information on contracted-out pension schemes the Department for Work and Pensions' leaflet PM7 *ntracting out of State Second Pension – Your Guide.*

AKEHOLDER PENSION SCHEMES
troduced in 2001, stakeholder pensions are available to eryone but are principally for moderate earners who do t have access to a good value company pension scheme. akeholder pensions must meet a number of minimum ndards to make sure they are flexible, portable and nual management charges are capped. The minimum ntribution is £20 per month.

As with personal pensions it is possible to invest up to ,600 (including tax relief) into stakeholder pensions ch year without evidence of earnings. Contributions can made on someone else's behalf, for example, a non-orking partner. If it meets certain conditions, it can be ed to contract out of the additional state pension rmerly SERPS). When someone contracts out of the te scheme with either an APP or a stakeholder pension, th the employee and their employers pay NI ntributions at the full not contracted-out rate. At the d of the tax year to which those NI contributions relate, M Revenue and Customs pays an age-related rebate hich increases with age) and tax relief on the ployee's share of the rebate directly into the scheme for estment on behalf of the employee.

OMPLAINTS
ıe Pensions Advisory Service gives free help and advice people who have problems with occupational or rsonal pensions. There are two bodies for pension mplaints. The Financial Ombudsman Service deals with mplaints which predominantly concern the sale and/or arketing of occupational, stakeholder and personal nsions. The Pensions Ombudsman deals with mplaints which predominantly concern the anagement (after sale or marketing) of occupational, akeholder and personal pensions. The Pensions gulator is the UK regulator for work-based pension schemes; it concentrates its resources on schemes where there is the greatest risk to the security of members' benefits, promotes good administration practice for all work-based schemes and works with trustees, employers and professional advisers to put things right when necessary.

WAR PENSIONS AND THE ARMED FORCES COMPENSATION SCHEME

The Service Personnel and Veterans Agency (SPVA), formerly the Veterans Agency, is an executive agency of the Ministry of Defence. SPVA was formed on 1 April 2007 from the former Armed Services Personnel Administration Agency and the Veterans Agency to provide services to both serving personnel and veterans.

SPVA is responsible for the administration of the war pensions scheme and the armed forces compensation scheme (AFCS) to members of the armed forces in respect of disablement or death due to service. There is also a scheme for civilians and civil defence workers in respect of the Second World War, and other schemes for groups such as merchant seamen and Polish armed forces who served under British command during the Second World War. The agency is also responsible for the administration of the armed forces pension scheme, which provides occupational pensions for ex-service personnel (*see* Defence).

THE WAR PENSIONS SCHEME

War disablement pension is awarded for the disabling effects of any injury, wound or disease which was the result of, or was aggravated by, conditions of service in the armed forces prior to 6 April 2005. Claims are only considered once the person has left the armed forces. The amount of pension paid depends on the severity of disablement, which is assessed by comparing the health of the claimant with that of a healthy person of the same age and sex. The person's earning capacity or occupation are not taken into account in this assessment. A pension is awarded if the person has a disablement of 20 per cent or more and a lump sum is usually payable to those with a disablement of less than 20 per cent. No award is made for noise-induced sensorineural hearing loss where the assessment of disablement is less than 20 per cent.

A pension is payable to war widows, widowers and surviving civil partners where the spouse's or civil partner's death was due to, or hastened by, service in the armed forces, prior to 6 April 2005, or where the spouse or civil partner was in receipt of a war disablement pension constant attendance allowance (or would have been if not in hospital) at the time of death. A pension is also payable to widows, widowers or surviving civil partners if the spouse or civil partner was receiving the war disablement pension at the 80 per cent rate or higher in conjunction with unemployability supplement at the time of death. War widows, widowers and surviving civil partners receive a standard rank-related rate, but a lower weekly rate is payable to war widows, widowers and surviving civil partners of personnel below the rank of Major who are under the age of 40, without children and capable of maintaining themselves. This is increased to the standard rate at age 40. Allowances are paid for children (in addition to child benefit) and adult dependants. An age allowance is automatically given when the widow, widower or surviving civil partner reaches 65 and increased at ages 70 and 80.

All war pensions and pensions for war widows,

widowers and surviving civil partners are tax-free and pensioners living overseas receive the same amount as those resident in the UK.

SUPPLEMENTARY ALLOWANCES

A number of supplementary allowances may be awarded to a war pensioner which are intended to meet various needs which may result from disablement or death and take account of its particular effect on the pensioner, pensioner's spouse or civil partner. The principal supplementary allowances are unemployability supplement, allowance for lowered standard of occupation and constant attendance allowance. Others include exceptionally severe disablement allowance, severe disablement occupational allowance, treatment allowance, mobility supplement, comforts allowance, clothing allowance, age allowance and widow/widower/surviving civil partner's age allowance. Rent and children's allowances are also available on pensions for war widows, widowers and surviving civil partners.

ARMED FORCES COMPENSATION SCHEME

The armed forces compensation scheme (AFCS) became effective on 6 April 2005 and covers all regular (including Gurkhas) and reserve personnel whose injury, ill health or death is caused by service on or after 6 April 2005. Ex-members of the armed forces who served prior to this date or who are in receipt of any pension under the war pensions scheme will continue to receive their pension and any associated benefits in the normal way. The new scheme affects only those who served after 6 April 2005.

The AFCS provides compensation where service in the armed forces is the only or main cause of injury, illness or death. Compensation can also be paid in certain exceptional circumstances to off-duty personnel, for example, to victims of a terrorist attack targeted due their position in the armed forces. Under the terms of scheme a lump sum is payable to service or ex-serv personnel based on a 15-level tariff, graduated accordi to the seriousness of the condition. A guaranteed inco payment (GIP), payable for life, is received by those w could be expected to experience a serious loss of earni capability. A GIP will also be paid to surviving partn (including spouses, civil and unmarried partners). GIP calculated by multiplying the pensionable pay of service person by a factor which depends on the age the person's last birthday. The younger the person, higher the factor, because there are more years to norm retirement age.

DEPARTMENT FOR WORK AND PENSIONS BENEFITS

Most benefits are paid in addition to those in receipt payments under the AFCS and the war pensions scher but may be affected by any supplementary allowances payment. Any state pension for which a war wid widower or surviving civil partner qualifies for on th own NI contribution record can be paid in addition monies received under the war pensions scheme.

CLAIMS AND QUESTIONS

Further information on the war pensions scheme, t armed forces compensation scheme and the nearest W Pensioners' Welfare Office can be obtained from t Service Personnel and Veterans Agency by telepho (T 0800-169 2277, if calling from the UK or, if livi overseas, T (+44) (125) 386-6043).

SERVICE PERSONNEL AND VETERANS AGENCY, Norcross, Blackpool FY5 3WP E veterans.help@spva.gsi.gov.u W www.veterans-uk.info

AX CREDITS

x credits are administered by HM Revenue and stoms and are awarded for up to 12 months, although y can be adjusted during the year to reflect changes in ome or circumstances.

ORKING TAX CREDIT

orking tax credit is made up of a basic payment with ditional payments for couples, lone parents, people rking over 30 hours a week, disabled workers and ople aged 50 or over returning to work after a period of nefits. The tax credit is paid with wages to people who employed and directly to the self-employed. It is ilable to:

people with dependent children and/or a disability, working at least 16 hours a week
people aged 25 or over and working at least 30 hours a week

The aim of the tax credit system is to provide a aranteed minimum income from full-time work for ose aged 25 or over, of £212 a week for couples, and 80 a week for single people. This is increased for those th a disability or for those with children. The system kes assumptions based on the national minimum wage d the number of hours worked per week. An annual come of £8,479 represents the 2007–8 income of an ult working 30 hours a week at the national minimum ge: six months at the 2006-7 rate of £5.35 per hour d six months at the rate of £5.52 per hour (national nimum wage from October 2007).

ORKING TAX CREDIT 2007–8

nual Income/Status	*Tax credit per annum*
*,000**	
Single	–
Couple	–
Single adult with a disability	£4,040
,479†	
Single	£1,230
Couple	£2,930
Single adult with a disability	£3,540
0,000	
Single	£665
Couple	£2,370
Single adult with a disability	£2,980
5,000	
Single	–
Couple	£520
Single adult with a disability	£1,130

Those with incomes of £5,000 a year are assumed to work rt-time (working between 16 and 30 hours a week).
ncome of £8,479 represents the income of an adult working hours per week at the national minimum wage rate (*see* above explanation). In families with an income of £8,479 a year or ore, at least one adult is assumed to be working 30 or more urs a week.

CHILDCARE

In families with children where a lone parent or both partners in a couple work for at least 16 hours a week, or where one partner works and the other is disabled, the family is entitled to the childcare element of working tax credit. This payment can contribute up to 70 per cent of childcare costs up to a maximum of £175 a week for one child and up to £300 a week for two or more children. Families can only claim if they use an approved or registered childcare provider.

CHILD TAX CREDIT

Child tax credit combines all income-related support for children and is paid direct to the main carer. The credit is made up of a main 'family' payment with additional payments for each extra child in the household, for children with a disability and an extra payment for children who are severely disabled. Child tax credit is available to households where:

- there is at least one dependant under 16-years-old
- there is at least one dependant under 19-years-old and in full-time non-advanced education or registered with the Careers or Connexions Service (does not include Scotland or Northern Ireland)

CHILD TAX CREDIT AND WORKING TAX CREDIT 2007–8 *(£ PER YEAR)*

	One Child		*Two Children*	
Annual Income	*No Childcare*	*Maximum Childcare*	*No Childcare*	*Maximum Childcare*
0	2,390	2,390	4,240	4,240
5,000*	5,825	13,145	7,675	20,220
8,479*	5,325	12,645	7,175	19,720
10,000†	4,760	12,080	6,610	19,160
15,000	2,910	10,230	4,760	17,310
20,000	1,060	8,380	2,910	15,460
25,000	545	6,530	1,060	13,610
30,000	545	4,680	545	11,760
35,000	545	2,830	545	9,910
40,000	545	980	545	8,060
45,000	545	545	545	6,210
50,000	545	545	545	4,360
60,000	–	–	–	660
65,000	–	–	–	230
70,000	–	–	–	–

* At income levels of £5,000 and £8,479 awards are shown for lone parents. At an income level of £5,000 the award is shown for a lone parent working part-time (between 16 and 30 hours a week). At an income level of £8,479 the award is shown for a lone parent working 30 hours a week.

† At an income level of £10,000 awards are shown for two parents working part-time (between 16 and 30 hours per week)

BENEFITS

The following is intended as a general guide to the benefits system. Conditions of entitlement and benefit rates change annually and all prospective claimants should check exact entitlements and rates of benefit directly with their local Jobcentre Plus office, pension centre or online (W www.direct.gov.uk). Leaflets relating to the various benefits and contribution conditions for different benefits are available from local Jobcentre Plus offices; leaflet BRA5DWP *Social Security Benefit Rates* is a general guide to benefit rates and contributions.

CONTRIBUTORY BENEFITS

Entitlement to contributory benefits depends on national insurance contribution conditions being satisfied either by the claimant or by someone on the claimant's behalf (depending on the kind of benefit). The class or classes of national insurance contribution relevant to each benefit are:

Jobseeker's allowance (contribution-based)	Class 1
Incapacity benefit	Class 1 or 2
Widow's benefit and bereavement benefit	Class 1, 2 or 3
State pensions, categories A and B	Class 1, 2 or 3

The system of contribution conditions relates to yearly levels of earnings on which national insurance (NI) contributions have been paid.

JOBSEEKER'S ALLOWANCE

Jobseeker's allowance (JSA) replaced unemployment benefit and income support for unemployed people under state pension age from 7 October 1996. There are two routes of entitlement. Contribution-based JSA is paid at a personal rate (ie additional benefit for dependants is not paid) to those who have made sufficient NI contributions in two particular tax years. Savings and partner's earnings are not taken into account and payment can be made for up to six months. Rates of JSA correspond to income support rates.

Claims are made through Jobcentre Plus. A person wishing to claim JSA must generally be unemployed or working on average less than 16 hours a week, capable of work and available for any work which he or she can reasonably be expected to do, usually for at least 40 hours per week. The claimant must agree and sign a 'jobseeker's agreement', which will set out his or her plans to find work, and must actively seek work. If the claimant refuses work or training the benefit may be sanctioned for between one and 26 weeks.

A person will be sanctioned from JSA for up to 26 weeks if he or she has left a job voluntarily without just cause or through misconduct. In these circumstances, it may be possible to receive hardship payments, particularly where the claimant or the claimant's family is vulnerable, eg if sick or pregnant, or with children or caring responsibilities. *See* leaflet JSAL5 *(JSA – Helping You Back to Work).*

INCAPACITY BENEFIT

Incapacity benefit is available to those who are incapable of work but cannot get statutory sick pay from their employer. It is not payable to those over state pension age. However, people who are already in receipt of short-term incapacity benefit when they reach state pension age may continue to receive this benefit for up to 52 weeks. Apart from those who qualify under the special provisions for people incapacitated in youth, entitlement is based o person's NI contribution record. In order to qualify incapacity benefit, two contribution conditions, based the last three tax years before the year in which benefi claimed, must be satisfied. The amount of incapac benefit payable may be reduced where a claimant recei more than a specified amount of occupational or perso pension. People who became incapable of work before t age of 20 (or 25 for those who were in education training before the age of 20) may receive incapac benefit without meeting the NI contribution conditio There are three rates of incapacity benefit:

- short-term lower rate for the first 28 weeks of sickn
- short-term higher rate from weeks 29 to 52
- long-term rate from week 53 onwards

The terminally ill and those entitled to the highest r care component of disability living allowance are paid long-term rate after 28 weeks. Incapacity benefit is taxa after 28 weeks.

Two rates of age addition are paid, with long-te benefit based on the claimant's age when incapac started. The higher rate is payable where incapacity work commenced before the age of 35, and the lower r where incapacity commenced before the age of 45.

Increases are made for claimants over the age of 60 a for adult dependants. Dependent children are provid for through the child tax credit system.

There are two medical tests of incapacity: the 'o occupation' test and the 'personal capability' assessme Those who worked before becoming incapable working will be assessed, for the first 28 weeks incapacity, on their ability to do their own job. After weeks (or from the start of incapacity for those who w not working) claimants are assessed on their ability carry out a range of work-related activities. *See* leaflets I and IB214. New incapacity benefit claimants will invited back for work-focused interviews at intervals not longer than three years. The interviews do not inclu medical tests, but if the claimant is due for a medical t around the same time, their local office will aim schedule both together. People who are severely disab and those who are terminally ill will not be asked attend these interviews.

BEREAVEMENT BENEFITS

Bereavement benefits replaced widow's benefit on 9 Ap 2001. Those claiming widow's benefit before this d will continue to receive them under the old scheme for long as they qualify. The new system provid bereavement benefits for widows, widowers and, from December 2005, surviving civil partners (providing t their deceased spouse or civil partner paid contributions). The new system offers benefits in th forms:

- *Bereavement payment* – may be received by a man woman who is under the state pension age at the ti of their spouse or civil partner's death, or whose hu band, wife or civil partner was not entitled to a c egory A retirement pension when he or she died. It i single tax-free lump sum of £2,000 payable immec ately on widowhood or loss of a civil partner
- *Widowed parent's allowance* – a taxable benefit payal to the surviving partner if he or she is entitled treated as entitled to child benefit, or to a widow if s is expecting her husband's baby at the time of his dea
- *Bereavement allowance* – a taxable weekly benefit pa for 52 weeks after the spouse or civil partner's death. aged over 55 and under state pension age the f

allowance is payable, if aged between 45 and 54 a percentage of the full rate is paid. A widow, widower or surviving civil partner may receive this allowance if his or her widowed parent's allowance ends before 52 weeks.

is not possible to receive widowed parent's allowance ıd bereavement allowance at the same time. Bereavement nefits and widow's benefit, in any form, cease upon marriage or a new civil partnership or are suspended ıring a period of cohabitation as partners without being gally married or in a civil partnership. *See* leaflets GL14 ıd D49 (D49S for deaths that occur in Scotland).

ATE PENSION: CATEGORIES A AND B

ategory A pension is payable for life to men and women ho reach state pension age, who satisfy the contributions nditions and who claim for it. Category B pension is ıyable for life to married women, widows, widowers and rviving civil partners and is based on their wife, ısband or civil partner's contributions. It is payable to a arried woman only when both the wife and husband ıve claimed their state pension and they have both ached state pension age. From April 2010 a married an and civil partner will be able to qualify for a category pension from their wife's or civil partner's contributions oviding the wife or civil partner were born on or after 6 pril 1950. Category B pension is also payable on idowhood or death of a civil partner after state pension ge. Category B pension is payable to widows regardless the age of their husband when he died, although at esent, it is only paid to widowers and civil partners if ıeir wife or civil partner had reached state pension age hen they died. Widowers or surviving civil partners ho reach state pension age on or after 6 April 2010 ill be able to get a category B pension on the same rms as widows. There are special rules for those whose ouse or civil partner dies before reaching state pension ge.

Where a person is entitled to both a category A and tegory B pension then they can be combined to give a mposite pension, but this cannot be more than the full te pension. Where a person is entitled to more than ıe category A or category B pension then only one can paid. In such cases the person can choose which to et; if no choice is made, the most favourable one is ıid.

A person may defer claiming their pension beyond ate pension age. In doing so they may earn increments hich will increase the weekly amount paid by one per nt per five weeks of deferral (equivalent to 10.4 per nt/year) when they claim their state pension. If a person elays claiming for at least 12 months they are given the ption of a one-off taxable lump sum, instead of a pension crease, based on the weekly pension deferred, plus terest. If a married man defers his category A pension, is wife cannot claim a category B pension on his ontributions but she may earn increments on her state ension during this time. A woman can defer her category pension, and earn increments, even if her husband is aiming his category A pension.

The basic state pension is £87.30 per week plus any dditional (earnings-related) state pension the person may e entitled to. An increase of £52.30 is paid for an adult ependant, providing the dependant's earnings do not xceed the rate of Jobseeker's Allowance for a single erson (*see* below) and the couple are living together. If ıe couple are not living together an increase is payable if ıe dependant's earnings are not above £52.30. Before April 2003 it was also possible to get an increase of category A and B pensions for a child or children, since this date provision for children has been made through child tax credits. An age addition of 25p per week is payable with a state pension if a pensioner is aged 80 or over.

The category B pension provides up to £52.30 a week for a married woman and up to £87.30 a week for a widow, widower or surviving civil partner.

Since 1989 pensioners have been allowed to have unlimited earnings without affecting their state pension.

GRADUATED RETIREMENT BENEFIT

Graduated NI contributions were first payable from April 1961 and were calculated as a percentage of earnings between certain bands. The graduated retirement benefit scheme existed until April 1975, however, it is still paid in addition to any state pension, to those who made the relevant contributions. A person will receive graduated retirement benefit based on their own contributions, even if not entitled to a basic state pension. Widows, widowers and surviving civil partners may inherit half of their deceased spouse's or civil partner's entitlement, but none that the deceased spouse or civil partner may have been eligible for from a former spouse or civil partner.

Graduated retirement benefit is calculated using a weekly rate for each 'unit' of graduated contributions paid by the employee (half a unit or more counts as a whole unit); the rate varies from person to person. A unit of graduated retirement benefit can be calculated by adding together all graduated contributions and dividing by 7.5 (men) or 9 (women). If a person defers making a claim beyond state pension age, they may earn an increase or a one-off lump sum payment in respect of their deferred graduated retirement benefit; calculated in the same way as for the category A or B state pension.

WEEKLY RATES OF CONTRIBUTORY BENEFITS
from April 2007

Jobseeker's allowance (JSA) (contribution-based)	
Person under 18	£35.65
Person aged 18–24	£46.85
Person aged 25 to state pension age*	£59.15

* Since October 2003 people aged between 60 and state pension age can choose to claim pension credits instead of JSA.

Short-term incapacity benefit	
Person under state pension age	
Lower rate	£61.35
Higher rate	£72.55
Increase for adult dependant	£37.90
Person over state pension age	
Lower rate	£78.05
Higher rate	£81.35
Increase for adult dependant	£46.80

Long-term incapacity benefit	
Person under state pension age	£81.35
Increase for adult dependant	£48.65
Age addition – lower rate	£8.55
Age addition – higher rate	£17.10

Widow's benefits	
Widowed mother's allowance	£87.30
Widow's pension, full entitlement (aged 55 or over at time of spouse's death)	£87.30

Amount of widow's pension by age of widow at spouse's death (for deaths occurring before 11 April 1988 refer to the age-points in brackets):

aged 54 (49)	£81.19
aged 53 (48)	£75.08
aged 52 (47)	£68.97
aged 51 (46)	£62.86
aged 50 (45)	£56.75
aged 49 (44)	£50.63
aged 48 (43)	£44.52
aged 47 (42)	£38.41
aged 46 (41)	£32.30
aged 45 (40)	£26.19

Bereavement benefit

Bereavement payment (lump sum)	£2,000
Widowed parent's allowance	£87.30
Bereavement allowance, full entitlement (aged 55 and over at time of spouse's or civil partner's death)	£87.30

Amount of bereavement allowance by age of widow/widower or surviving civil partner at spouse's or civil partner's death:

aged 54	£81.19
aged 53	£75.08
aged 52	£68.97
aged 51	£62.86
aged 50	£56.75
aged 49	£50.63
aged 48	£44.52
aged 47	£38.41
aged 46	£32.30
aged 45	£26.19

State Pension: Categories A and B

Category A or B pension for a single person	£87.30
Category B pension (married women)	£52.30
Increase for adult dependant	£52.30
Age addition at age 80	£0.25

NON-CONTRIBUTORY BENEFITS

These benefits are paid from general taxation and are not dependent on NI contributions.

JOBSEEKER'S ALLOWANCE (INCOME-BASED)

Those who do not qualify for contribution-based jobseeker's allowance (JSA(c)), those who have exhausted their entitlement to contribution-based JSA or those for whom contribution-based JSA provides insufficient income may qualify for income-based JSA. The amount paid depends on age, whether they are single or a couple, number of dependants and amount of income and savings. Income-based JSA is comprised of three parts:

- a personal allowance for the jobseeker and his/her partner*
- premiums for people with special needs
- amounts for housing costs

* Since April 2003, child dependants have been provided for through the child tax credit system, although an increase in JSA for dependent children is still available for existing claimants.

The rules of entitlement are the same as for contribution-based JSA.

If one person in a couple was born after 28 Octob 1957 and neither person in the couple has responsibili for a child or children, then the couple will have to make joint claim for JSA if they wish to receive income-bas JSA.

MATERNITY ALLOWANCE

Maternity allowance (MA) is a benefit available f pregnant women who are self-employed or otherwise c not qualify for statutory maternity pay (SMP) from the employers. In order to qualify for payment, a woman mu have been employed and/or self-employed for at least 2 weeks in the 66 week period up to and including t week before the baby is due (test period). She must al have average weekly earning of at least £30 (materni allowance threshold) over any 13 weeks of the woman choice within the test period. Women who are se employed are deemed to have enough earnings (£125.2 a week) to result in the standard rate of MA being payab Self-employed women holding a small earnings exceptic certificate are treated as having earnings equal to t maternity allowance threshold. A woman can choose start receiving MA from the 11th week before the week which the baby is due up to the day following the day birth. The exact date MA starts will depend on when t woman stops work to have her baby or if the baby is bo before she stops work. However, where the woman absent from work wholly or partly due to pregnancy c or after the Sunday of the 4th week before the baby is du to be born, MA will start the day following the first day absence from work. MA is paid for a maximum of 3 weeks regardless of when the baby is actually born.

For more information *see* leaflet NI17A *A Guide Maternity Benefits* available on the Department for Wo and Pensions website (W www.dwp.gov.uk/advisers/ni17a/)

CHILD BENEFIT

Child benefit is payable for virtually all children age under 16, for those aged 16 to 18 in full-time educatio or in a programme of approved training, for those aged 1 or 17 who have registered with Connexions or th Careers Service (or the equivalent in Northern Irelan and those aged 19 who are in full-time education approved training which started before their 19 birthday.

GUARDIAN'S ALLOWANCE

Guardian's allowance is payable to a person who bringing up a child or young person because the child parents have died, or in some circumstances, where on one parent has died. To receive the allowance the persc must be in receipt of child benefit for the child or youn person, although they do not have to be the child's leg guardian.

CARER'S ALLOWANCE

Carer's allowance (CA) is a benefit payable to people wh spend at least 35 hours per week caring for a severel disabled person. To qualify for CA a person must b caring for someone in receipt of one of the followin benefits:

- the middle or highest rate of disability living allowanc care component
- either rate of attendance allowance
- constant attendance allowance, paid at not less than th normal maximum rate or basic (full-day) rate, under th industrial injuries or war pension schemes

See leaflet CAA5DCS.

EVERE DISABLEMENT ALLOWANCE

ince April 2001 severe disablement allowance (SDA) as not been available to new claimants. Those claiming DA before that date will continue to receive it for as long s they qualify.

TTENDANCE ALLOWANCE

'his may be payable to disabled people who claim after he age of 65 and who need a lot of care or supervision ecause of physical or mental disability, and who have eeded help for a period of at least six months. ttendance allowance has two rates: the lower rate is for ay or night care, and the higher rate is for day and night are. People not expected to live for more than six months ecause of a progressive disease can receive the highest ate of attendance allowance straight away. *See* leaflet *ttendance Allowance.*

ISABILITY LIVING ALLOWANCE

'his may be payable to disabled people who claim before he age of 65 who have personal care and/or mobility eeds because of an illness or disability for a period of at east three months and are likely to have those needs for a urther six months or more. The allowance has two omponents: the care component, which has three rates, nd the mobility component, which has two rates. The ates depend on the care and mobility needs of the laimant. People not expected to live for more than six nonths because of a progressive disease will automatically eceive the highest rate of the care component. *See* leaflets *isability Living Allowance* and *Disability Living llowance for Children.*

TATE PENSION: CATEGORY D

Category D pension is provided for people aged 80 and ver if they are not entitled to another category of ension or are entitled to a state pension that is less than ne category D rate. The person must also normally live in reat Britain and have done so for a continuous period of n years within any 20-year period since their 60th irthday.

VEEKLY RATES OF NON-CONTRIBUTORY BENEFITS
om April 2007

obseeker's allowance (income-based)	
erson under 18	£35.65
erson aged 18–24	£46.85
erson aged 25 to state pension age	£59.15
ouple with one or both under 18*	£35.65–£59.15
Couple aged 18 to state pension age	£92.80
one parents*	£35.65–£59.15
ependent children (from birth to the day before 20th birthday)	£47.45
amily premium	£16.43

depending on circumstances

Iaternity allowance	
tandard rate	£112.75 or 90 per cent of the women's average weekly earnings if less than £112.75
ncrease for adult dependant	£37.90

Child benefit	
Eldest/only child	£18.10
Each subsequent child	£12.10

Guardian's allowance	
Each child	£12.95

Carer's allowance	£48.65
Increase for dependent adult	£29.05

Severe disablement allowance	
Basic rate	£49.15
Age related addition*:	
Under 40	£17.10
40–49	£11.00
50–59	£5.50

* The age addition applies to the age when incapacity began

Attendance allowance	
Higher rate	£64.50
Lower rate	£43.15

Disability living allowance	
Care component	
Higher rate	£64.50
Middle rate	£43.15
Lowest rate	£17.10
Mobility component	
Higher rate	£45.00
Lower rate	£17.10

State pension: category D	
Single person	£52.30
Age addition to State Pension at age 80	£0.25

INCOME SUPPORT

Income support is a benefit for those aged 16 and over whose income is below a certain level. It can be paid to people who are not expected to sign on as unemployed (income support for unemployed people was replaced by jobseeker's allowance in October 1996) and who are:

- incapable of work due to sickness or disability
- bringing up children alone
- looking after a person who has a disability
- registered blind

Pension credit replaced income support for people aged 60 or over on 6 October 2003. Some people who are not in the above categories may also be able to claim income support.

Income support is also payable to people who work fewer than 16 hours a week on average (or 24 hours for a partner). Some people can claim income support if they work longer hours.

Income support is not payable if the claimant, or claimant and partner, have capital or savings in excess of £16,000. For capital and savings in excess of £6,000, a deduction of £1 a week is made for every £250 or part of £250 held. Different limits apply to people permanently in residential care and nursing homes: the upper limit is £16,000 and deductions apply for capital in excess of £10,000.

Sums payable depend on fixed allowances laid down by law for people in different circumstances. If both partners are eligible for income support, either may claim it for the couple. People receiving income support may be able to receive housing benefit, help with mortgage or home loan interest and help with healthcare. They may also be eligible for help with exceptional expenses from the Social Fund. Special rates may apply to some people living in residential care or nursing homes. Leaflet IS20 (only available online) gives a detailed explanation of income support.

In October 1998 the government's voluntary *New Deal for Lone Parents* programme became available throughout the UK. All lone parents receiving income support are assigned a personal adviser at a Jobcentre who will provide guidance and support with a view to enabling the claimant to find work.

INCOME SUPPORT PREMIUMS

Income support premiums are additional weekly payments for those with special needs. People qualifying for more than one premium will normally only receive the highest single premium for which they qualify. However, family premium, disabled child premium, severe disability premium and carer premium are payable in addition to other premiums.

People with children may qualify for:

- the family premium if they have at least one child (a higher rate is paid to lone parents whose claim was made prior to 6 April 1998)
- the disabled child premium if they have a child who receives disability living allowance or is registered blind

Carers may qualify for:

- the carer premium if they or their partner are in receipt of carer's allowance

Long-term sick or disabled people may qualify for:

- the disability premium if they or their partner are receiving certain benefits because they are disabled or cannot work; are registered blind; or if the claimant has been incapable of work or receiving statutory sick pay for at least 364 days (196 days if the person is terminally ill), including periods of incapacity separated by eight weeks or less
- the severe disability premium if the person lives alone and receives attendance allowance or the middle or higher rate of disability living allowance care component and no one receives carer's allowance for caring for that person. This premium is also available to couples where both partners meet the above conditions

WEEKLY RATES OF INCOME SUPPORT

From April 2007

Single person	
under 18	£35.65
under 18 (higher)	£46.85
aged 18–24	£46.85
aged 25 and over	£59.15
aged under 18 and a single parent (lower)	£35.65
aged under 18 and a single parent (higher)	£46.85
aged 18 and over and a single parent	£59.15
Couples	
Both under 18	£35.65
Both under 18, one disabled	£46.85
Both under 18 with responsibility for a child	£70.70
One under 18, one aged 18–24	£46.85
One under 18, one aged 25+	£59.15
Both aged 18+	£92.80
For each child in a family from birth to day before 19th birthday	£47.45
Dependent children	
From birth to September following 16th birthday	£47.75
From September following 16th birthday to day before 20th birthday	£47.75

Premiums	
Family premium	£16.4
Family (lone parent) premium	£16.4
Disabled child premium	£46.6
Carer premium	£27.1
Disability premium	
Single person	£25.2
Couples	£17.7
Enhanced disability premium	
Single person	£12.3
Couples	£17.7
Enhanced disabled child premium	£18.7
Severe disability premium	
Lower rate (single person and some couples)	£48.4
Higher rate (couples)	£96.9

PENSION CREDIT

Pension credit was introduced on 6 October 2003 an replaced income support for those aged 60 and over. There are two elements to pension credit:

THE GUARANTEE CREDIT

The guarantee credit provides a guaranteed minimur income, with additional elements for people who have:

- eligible housing costs
- severe disabilities
- caring responsibilities

Income from state pension, private pensions, earnings an certain benefits are taken into account when calculatin the guarantee credit. For savings and capital in excess c £6,000 a deduction of £1 per week is made for ever £500 or part of £500 held.

People receiving the guarantee credit element c pension credit will be able to receive housing benefi council tax benefit and help with healthcare costs.

THE SAVINGS CREDIT

Single people aged 65 or over (and couples where on member is 65 or over) may be entitled to a savings credi which will reward pensioners who have modest income c savings. The savings credit is calculated by taking int account any qualifying income above the savings credi threshold. For 2007–8 the threshold is £87.30 for singl people and £139.60 for couples. The savings credit give pensioners a cash addition calculated at 60p for ever pound of qualifying income they have between th savings credit threshold and the guarantee credit. Afte this, the maximum reward will be reduced by 40p fc every pound of income above the guarantee level. Th maximum savings credit is £19.05 per week (£25.26 week for couples).

Income that qualifies towards the savings credi includes state pensions, earnings, second pensions an capital above £6,000.

Some people will be entitled to the guarantee credi some to the savings credit and some to both.

Where only the savings credit is in payment, peopl need to claim standard housing benefit or council ta benefit. Although local authorities take any savings cred into account in the housing benefit or council tax benef assessment, for people aged 65 and over housing benef or council tax benefit is enhanced to ensure that gains i pension credit are not depleted.

WEEKLY RATES OF PENSION CREDIT
from April 2007

Standard minimum guarantee	
Single	£119.05
Couple	£181.70
Additional amount for	
Severe disability	£48.45
Carers	£27.15

HOUSING BENEFIT
Housing benefit is designed to help people with rent (including rent for accommodation in guesthouses, lodgings or hostels). It does not cover mortgage payments. The amount of benefit paid depends on:

- the income of the claimant, and partner if there is one, including earned income, unearned income (any other income including some other benefits) and savings
- number of dependants
- certain extra needs of the claimant, partner or any dependants
- number and gross income of people sharing the home who are not dependent on the claimant
- how much rent is paid

Housing benefit is not payable if the claimant, or claimant and partner, have savings in excess of £16,000. The amount of benefit is affected if savings held exceed £6,000 (£10,000 for pensioners and people living in care homes). Housing benefit is not paid for meals, fuel or certain service charges that may be included in the rent. Deductions are also made for most non-dependants who live in the same accommodation as the claimant (and their partner).

The maximum amount of benefit (which is not necessarily the same as the amount of rent paid) may be paid where the claimant is in receipt of income support, income-based jobseeker's allowance, the guarantee element of pension credit or where the claimant's income is less than the amount allowed for their needs. Any income over that allowed for their needs will mean that their benefit is reduced. *See* leaflets HBA5DWP and RR2 (only available online).

COUNCIL TAX BENEFIT
Nearly all the rules which apply to housing benefit apply to council tax benefit, which helps people on low incomes to pay council tax bills. The amount payable depends on how much council tax is paid and who lives with the claimant. The benefit may be available to those receiving income support, income-based jobseeker's allowance, the guarantee element of pension credit or to those whose income is less than that allowed for their needs. Any income over that allowed for their needs will mean that their council tax benefit is reduced. Deductions are made for non-dependants.

The maximum amount that is payable for those living in properties in council tax bands A to E is 100 per cent of the claimant's council tax liability. This also applies to those living in properties in bands F to H who were in receipt of the benefit at 31 March 1998 if they have remained in the same property.

If a person shares a home with one or more adults (not their partner) who are on a low income, it may be possible to claim a second adult rebate. Those who are entitled to both council tax benefit and second adult rebate will be awarded whichever is the greater. Second adult rebate may be claimed by those not in receipt of or eligible for council tax benefit.

THE SOCIAL FUND

REGULATED PAYMENTS
Sure Start Maternity Grant
The Sure Start maternity grant (SSMG) is a one-off payment of £500 to help people on low incomes pay for essential items for new babies that are expected, born, adopted, the subject of a parental order (following a surrogate birth) or, in certain circumstances, the subject of a residency order. SSMG can be claimed any time from the 29th week of pregnancy up to three months after the birth, adoption or date of parental or residency order. Those eligible are people in receipt of income support, income-based jobseeker's allowance, pension credit, child tax credit at a rate higher than the family element or working tax credit where a disability or severe disability element is in payment.

Funeral Payments
Payable to help cover the necessary cost of burial or cremation, plus certain other funeral expenses incurred up to £700. Those eligible are people receiving income support, income-based jobseeker's allowance, pension credit, child tax credit at a higher rate than the family element, working tax credit where a disability or severe disability element is in payment, council tax benefit or housing benefit who have good reason for taking responsibility for the funeral expenses. These payments are recoverable from any estate of the deceased.

Cold Weather Payments
A payment of £8.50 when the average temperature is recorded at or forecast to be 0°C or below over seven consecutive days in the qualifying person's area. Payments are made to people on pension credit, income support and those on income-based jobseeker's allowance who have a child who is disabled or under the age of five, or whose benefit includes a pensioner or disability premium. Payments are made automatically and do not have to be repaid.

Winter Fuel Payments
An annual payment of at least £200 per household paid to most people aged 60 or over. Where the household includes someone aged 80 or over, the amount is £300. The majority of eligible people are paid automatically before Christmas, although a few need to claim. Payments do not have to be repaid.

DISCRETIONARY PAYMENTS
Community Care Grants
These are intended to help people on income support, income-based jobseeker's allowance, in receipt of pension credit, or receiving payments on account of such benefits (or those likely to receive these benefits on leaving residential or institutional accommodation) to live as independently as possible in the community; ease exceptional pressures on families; care for a prisoner or young offender released on temporary licence; help people set up home as part of a resettlement programme and/or assist with certain travelling expenses. They do not have to be repaid.

Budgeting Loans
These are interest-free loans to people who have been receiving income support, income-based jobseeker's allowance, pension credit or payments on account of such

benefits for at least 26 weeks, for intermittent expenses that may be difficult to budget for.

Crisis Loans
These are interest-free loans to anyone, whether receiving benefits or not, who is without resources in an emergency or due to a disaster, where there is no other means of preventing serious damage or serious risk to their, or their family members' health or safety.

SAVINGS
Savings over £500 (£1,000 for people aged 60 or over) are taken into account for community care grants and savings of £1,000 (£2,000 for people aged 60 or over) are taken into account for budgeting loans. All savings are taken into account for crisis loans. Savings are not taken into account for Sure Start maternity grant, funeral payments, cold weather or winter fuel payments.

INDUSTRIAL INJURIES AND DISABLEMENT BENEFITS

The Industrial Injuries Scheme, administered under the Social Security Contributions and Benefits Act 1992, provides a range of benefits designed to compensate for disablement resulting from an industrial accident (ie an accident arising out of and in the course of an earner's employment) or from a prescribed disease due to the nature of a person's employment. Those who are self-employed are not covered by this scheme.

INDUSTRIAL INJURIES DISABLEMENT BENEFIT
A person must be at least 14 per cent disabled (except for certain respiratory diseases) in order to qualify for this benefit. The amount paid depends on the degree of disablement:

- those assessed as 14–19 per cent disabled are paid at the 20 per cent rate
- those with disablement of over 20 per cent will have the percentage rounded up or down to the nearest 10 per cent, eg a disablement of 44 per cent will be paid at the 40 per cent rate while a disablement of 45 per cent will be paid at the 50 per cent rate

Except for certain respiratory diseases for which industrial injuries disablement benefit is paid immediately, most benefit is payable 15 weeks (90 days) after the date of the accident or onset of the disease (subject to backdating limits) and may be payable for a limited period or for life. The benefit is payable whether the person works or not and those who are incapable of work are entitled to draw statutory sick pay or incapacity benefit in addition to industrial injuries disablement benefit. It may also be possible to claim the following allowances:

- reduced earnings allowance for those who are unable to return to their regular work or work of the same standard and who had their accident (or whose disease started) before 1 October 1990. At state pension age this is converted to retirement allowance
- constant attendance allowance for those with a disablement of 100 per cent who need constant care. There are four rates of allowance depending on how much care the person needs
- exceptionally severe disablement allowance for those who are entitled to constant care attendance allowance at one of the higher rates and who need constant care permanently

See leaflets IIDBAA5JP, IIDBASA5JP and IIDBDA5JP.

OTHER BENEFITS
People who are disabled because of an accident or disease that was the result of work that they did before 5 July 1948 are not entitled to industrial injuries disablement benefit. They may, however, be entitled to payment under the Workmen's Compensation Scheme or the Pneumoconiosis, Byssinosis and Miscellaneous Diseases Benefit Scheme. *See* leaflet GL23. People who suffer from certain industrial diseases caused by dust, or their dependants, can make a claim for an additional payment under the Pneumoconiosis etc (Workers' Compensation) Act 1979 if they are unable to get damages from the employer who caused or contributed to the disease.

WEEKLY RATES OF BENEFIT *FROM APRIL 2007*
*Disablement benefit/pension**

Degree of disablement:	
100 per cent	£137.70
90	£118.53
80	£105.36
70	£92.19
60	£79.02
50	£65.85
40	£52.68
30	£39.51
20	£26.34
Unemployability supplement	£81.35
Addition for adult dependant (subject to earnings rule)	£48.65
Reduced earnings allowance (maximum)	£52.68
Retirement allowance (maximum)	£13.17
Constant attendance allowance (normal maximum rate)	£52.70
Exceptionally severe disablement allowance	£52.70

* There is a weekly benefit for those under 18 with no dependants which is set at a lower rate

CLAIMS AND QUESTIONS

Entitlement to benefit and regulated Social Fund payments is determined by a decision maker on behalf of the Secretary of State for the Department for Work and Pensions. A claimant who is dissatisfied with that decision can ask for an explanation. He or she can dispute the decision by applying to have it revised or, in particular circumstances, superseded. The claimant can go to the Appeals Service where the case will be heard by an independent tribunal. There is a further right of appeal to a social security commissioner against the tribunal's decision but this is on a point of law only and leave to appeal must first be obtained.

Decisions on claims and applications for housing benefit and council tax benefit are made by local authorities. The explanation, dispute and appeals process is the same as for other benefits. *See* leaflets GL24DWP and NI260DMA.

All decisions on applications to the discretionary Social Fund are made by Jobcentre Plus Social Fund decision makers. Applicants can ask for a review of the decision within 28 days of the date on the decision letter. The Social Fund review officer will review the case and there is a further right of review by an independent Social Fund inspector.

EMPLOYER PAYMENTS

STATUTORY MATERNITY PAY

Employers pay statutory maternity pay (SMP) to pregnant women who have been employed by them full or part-time continuously for at least 26 weeks into the 15th week before the week the baby is due, and whose earnings on average at least equal the lower earnings limit applied to NI contributions (£87 per week from April 2007). All women who meet these conditions receive payment of 90 per cent of their average earnings for the first six weeks; the remaining weeks are paid at £112.75 or 90 per cent of the woman's average weekly earnings if this is less than £112.75. SMP can be paid, at the earliest, 11 weeks before the week in which the baby is due, up to the day following the birth. Women can decide when they wish their maternity leave to start and can work until the baby is born. However, where the woman is absent from work wholly or partly due to pregnancy on or after the Sunday of the 4th week before the baby is due to be born, SMP will start the day following the first day of absence from work. SMP is paid for a maximum of 39 weeks regardless of when the baby is actually born.

Employers are reimbursed for 92 per cent of the SMP they pay. Small employers with annual gross NI payments of £45,000 or less recover 100 per cent of the SMP paid plus 4.5 per cent in compensation for the secondary NI contributions paid on SMP.

For more information *see* leaflet NI7A *A Guide to Maternity Benefits* available on the Department for Work and Pensions website (W www.dwp.gov.uk/advisers/ni17a/).

STATUTORY PATERNITY PAY

Employers pay statutory paternity pay (SPP) to employees who are taking leave when a child is born or placed for adoption. To qualify the employee must:

- have responsibility for the child's upbringing
- be the biological father of the child (or the child's adopter), or the spouse/civil partner/partner of the mother or adopter
- be taking time off work to care for the child and/or support the mother or adopter
- have been employed by the same employer for at least 26 weeks ending with the 15th week before the baby is due (or the week in which the adopter is notified of having been matched with a child)
- continue working for the employer up to the child's birth (or placement for adoption)
- have earnings on average at least equal to the lower earnings limit applied to NI contributions (£87 per week from April 2007)

Employees who meet these conditions receive payment of £112.75 or 90 per cent of the employee's average weekly earnings if this is less than £112.75. The employee can choose to be paid for one or two consecutive weeks. The earliest the SPP period can begin is the date of the child's birth or placement for adoption. The SPP period must be completed within eight weeks of that date. SPP is not payable for any week in which the employee works. Employers are reimbursed in the same way as for statutory maternity pay. *See* Department for Business, Enterprise and Regulatory Reform leaflet *Working fathers: rights to leave and pay available* online (W www.berr.gov.uk).

STATUTORY ADOPTION PAY

Employers pay statutory adoption pay (SAP) to employees taking adoption leave from their employers. To qualify for SAP the employee must:

- be newly matched with a child by an adoption agency
- have been employed by the same employer for at least 26 weeks ending the week in which they have been notified of being matched with a child
- have earnings at least equal to the lower earnings limit applied to NI contributions (£87 per week from April 2007)

Employees who meet these conditions receive payment of £112.75 or 90 per cent of their average weekly earnings if this is less than £112.75 for up to 39 weeks. The SAP period can start from the date of the child's placement. SAP is not payable for any week in which the employee works. Where a couple adopt a child, only one of them may receive SAP, the other may be able to receive statutory paternity pay (SPP) if they meet the eligibility criteria. Employers are reimbursed in the same way as for statutory maternity pay. *See* Department for Business, Enterprise and Regulatory Reform leaflet *Adoptive parents: rights to leave and pay available* online (W www.berr.gov.uk).

STATUTORY SICK PAY

Employers pay statutory sick pay (SSP) for up to a maximum of 28 weeks to any employee incapable of work for four or more consecutive days, who has average earnings, in a specified period, at or above the point at which earnings become relevant for NI purposes (£87 from April 2007). SSP is paid at £72.55 per week and is subject to PAYE and NI contributions. Employees who cannot obtain SSP may be able to claim incapacity benefit. Employers may be able to recover some SSP costs. *See* HM Revenue and Customs Leaflets CA86 *Employees Guide to Statutory Sick Pay,* available online (W www.hmrc.gov.uk).

THE WATER INDUSTRY

Water services in England and Wales are provided by private companies. In Scotland there is a single authority, Scottish Water, that is answerable to the Scottish Executive, and in Northern Ireland all services are provided by the Water Service, which remains in the public sector as an executive agency within Northern Ireland's Department for Regional Development. In the UK the water industry provides services to over 20 million properties and has an annual turnover of £7bn. It also manages assets that include over 2,500 water and 9,000 sewerage treatment plants, 1,000 reservoirs and over 700,000km of water mains and sewers.

ENGLAND AND WALES

The water industry supplies around 18,000 million litres of water every day. In 2002 water companies in England and Wales carried out around 2.9 million tests on drinking water samples, of which 99.87 per cent met all British and European standards. In England and Wales the Secretary of State for Environment, Food and Rural Affairs and the National Assembly for Wales have overall responsibility for water policy and oversee environmental standards for the water industry.

Water UK is the industry association that represents all UK water and wastewater service suppliers at national and European level and is funded directly by its members who are the service suppliers for England, Scotland, Wales and Northern Ireland; every member has a seat on the Water UK Council.

WATER UK, 1 Queen Anne's Gate, London SW1H 9BT
T 020-7344 1844 W www.water.org.uk
Chief Executive, Pamela Taylor

WATER SERVICE COMPANIES
(members of Water UK)

ANGLIAN WATER SERVICES LTD, Customer Services, PO Box 770, Lincoln LN5 7WX T 08457-145145 W www.anglianwater.co.uk

BOURNEMOUTH & WEST HAMPSHIRE WATER PLC, George Jessel House, Francis Avenue, Bournemouth, Dorset BH11 8NX T 01202-590059 W www.bwhwater.co.uk

BRISTOL WATER PLC, PO Box 218, Bridgwater Road, Bristol BS99 7AU T 0117-966 5881 W www.bristolwater.co.uk

CAMBRIDGE WATER PLC, 90 Fulbourn Road, Cambridge CB1 9JN T 01223-706050 W www.cambridge-water.co.uk

CHOLDERTON & DISTRICT WATER COMPANY, Estate Office, Cholderton, Salisbury, Wiltshire SP4 0DR T 01980-629203

DEE VALLEY WATER PLC, Packsaddle, Wrexham Road, Rhostyllen, Wrexham LL14 4EH T 01978-846946 W www.deevalleygroup.com

DWR CYMRU CYFYNGEDIG (WELSH WATER), Pentwyn Road, Nelson, Treharris, Mid Glamorgan CF46 6LY T 0800-052 0145 W www.dwrcymru.co.uk

ESSEX & SUFFOLK WATER PLC (subsidiary of Northumbrian Water Ltd), Hall Street, Chelmsford, Essex CM2 0HH T 0845-782 0999 W www.eswater.co.uk

FOLKESTONE & DOVER WATER SERVICES LTD, Cherry Garden Lane, Folkestone, Kent CT19 4QB T 0845-888 5888 W www.fdws.co.uk

MID KENT WATER PLC, Snodland, Kent ME6 5AH T 0845-850 6060 W www.midkentwater.co.uk

NORTHUMBRIAN WATER LTD, Abbey Road, Pity Me, Durham DH1 5FJ T 0845 717 1100 W www.nwl.co.uk

PORTSMOUTH WATER PLC, PO Box 8, West Street, Havant, Hampshire PO9 1LG T 023-9249 9888 W www.portsmouthwater.co.uk

SEVERN TRENT PLC, 2297 Coventry Road, Birmingham B26 3PU T 0121-722 4000 W www.severntrent.com

SOUTH EAST WATER PLC, 3 Church Road, Haywards Heath, West Sussex RH16 3NY T 0845-301 0845 W www.southeastwater.co.uk

SOUTH STAFFORDSHIRE WATER PLC, PO Box 63, Walsall WS2 7PJ T 0845-607 0456 W www.south-staffs-water.co.uk

SOUTH WEST WATER LTD, Peninsula House, Rydon Lane, Exeter EX2 7HS T 0800-169 1144 W www.swwater.co.uk

SOUTHERN WATER, Southern House, Yeoman Road, Worthing, W. Sussex BN13 3NX T 0845-278 0845 W www.southernwater.co.uk

SUTTON AND EAST SURREY WATER PLC, London Road, Redhill, Surrey RH1 1LJ T 01737-772000 W www.waterplc.com

TENDRING HUNDRED WATER SERVICES LTD, Mill Hill, Manningtree, Essex CO11 2AZ T 01206-399200 W www.thws.co.uk

THAMES WATER UTILITIES LTD, PO Box 436, Swindon SN38 ITU T 0845-920 0888 W www.thameswater.com

THREE VALLEYS WATER PLC, PO Box 48, Bishops Rise, Hatfield, Hertfordshire AL10 9HL T 01707-268111 W www.3valleys.co.uk

UNITED UTILITIES WATER PLC, Haweswater House, Lingley Mere Business Park, Lingley Green Avenue, Great Sankey, Warrington, WA5 3LP T 0845-7462222 W www.unitedutilities.com

WESSEX WATER SERVICES LTD, Claverton Down Road, Bath BA2 7WW T 01225-526000 W wessexwater.co.uk

YORKSHIRE WATER SERVICES LTD, PO Box 52, Bradford BD3 7YD T 0845-124 2424 W www.yorkshirewater.com

ISLAND WATER AUTHORITIES
(not members of Water UK)

COUNCIL OF THE ISLES OF SCILLY, Town Hall, St Mary's, Isles of Scilly TR21 0LW T 01720-422537

ISLE OF MAN WATER AUTHORITY, Tromode Road, Douglas, Isle of Man IM2 5PA T 01624-695949 W www.gov.im/water

JERSEY WATER, PO Box 69, Mulcaster House, Westmount Road, St. Helier, Jersey JE4 9PN T 01534-707301 W www.jerseywater.je

STATES OF GUERNSEY WATER BOARD, PO Box 30, South Esplanade, St Peter Port, Guernsey GY1 3AS T 01481-724552 W www.gov.gg

VATER SUPPLY AND CONSUMPTION 2005–6

	Supply		*Consumption*			
	Supply from Treatment Works (megalitres/day)	*Total Leakage (megalitres/day)*	*Household (litres/head/day)*		*Non-household (litres/property/day)*	
			Unmetered	*Metered*	*Unmetered*	*Metered*
WATER AND SEWERAGE COMPANIES						
Anglian	1,164	214	160	128	229	2,889
Dwr Cymru	866	224	154	129	426	2,247
Northumbrian	722	157	148	143	786	3,432
Severn Trent	1,946	542	137	118	535	2,239
South West	450	84	165	139	1,003	1,602
Southern	582	93	157	139	705	2,524
Thames	2,801	862	167	154	807	3,297
United Utilities	1,940	477	144	132	739	2,692
Wessex	371	73	157	136	3,251	2,232
Yorkshire	1,295	297	148	134	127	2,757
Total	12,135	3,024	—	—	—	—
Average	—	—	154	135	861	2,591
WATER ONLY COMPANIES						
Total	3,221	553	—	—	—	—
Average	—	—	162	141	747	2,558

ource: OFWAT

₹EGULATORY BODIES

'he Water Services Regulation Authority (OFWAT) was et up under the Water Act 1989 and is the independent conomic regulator of the water and sewerage companies 1 England and Wales. Overall responsibility for water olicy and overseeing environmental standards for the vater industry lies with DEFRA and the Welsh Assembly.)FWAT's main duties are to ensure that the companies an finance and carry out their statutory functions and to rotect the interests of water customers. OFWAT is a non-iinisterial government department headed by a board ollowing a change in legislation set out in the Water Act :003.

Under the Competition Act 1998, from 1 March 2000 he Competition Appeal Tribunal has heard appeals gainst the regulator's decisions regarding anti-ompetitive agreements and abuse of a dominant position n the marketplace. The Water Act 2003 placed a new duty n OFWAT to have regard to sustainable development.

The Environment Agency was set up by the :nvironment Act 1995 as a non-departmental public ody and is sponsored largely by DEFRA and the Welsh ssembly. The Environment Agency has statutory duties nd powers in relation to water resources, pollution ontrol, flood defence, fisheries, recreation, conservation nd navigation in England and Wales. They are also esponsible for issuing permits, licences, consents and egistrations such as industrial licences to extract water nd fishing licences.

The Drinking Water Inspectorate (DWI) is the drinking vater quality regulator for England and Wales, esponsible for assessing the quality of the drinking water upplied by the water companies and investigating any ıcidents affecting drinking water quality, initiating rosecution where necessary. The DWI also provides scientific advice on drinking water policy issues to DEFRA and the Welsh Assembly.

OFWAT, Centre City Tower, 7 Hill Street, Birmingham B5 4UA
T 0121-625 1300 E enquiries@ofwat.gsi.gov.uk
W www.ofwat.gov.uk
Chairman, Philip Fletcher

METHODS OF CHARGING

In England and Wales, most domestic customers still pay for domestic water supply and sewerage services through charges based on the rateable value of their property. Overall, companies expect about 33 per cent of household customers in England and Wales to have metered supplies in 2007–8. Industrial and most commercial customers are charged according to consumption.

Under the Water Industry Act 1999, water companies can continue basing their charges on the old rateable value of property. Domestic customers can continue paying on an unmeasured basis unless they choose to pay according to consumption. After having a meter installed (which is free of charge), a customer can revert to unmeasured charging within 12 months. Domestic, school and hospital customers cannot be disconnected for non-payment.

Price limits for the period 2005–10 were set by OFWAT in December 2004.

AVERAGE HOUSEHOLD WATER BILLS (2007–8)

	Unmetered (£)	*Metered (£)*
Water	157	134
Sewerage	167	151
Combined	325	285

SCOTLAND

Overall responsibility for national water policy in Scotland rests with the Scottish ministers. Until the Local Government (Scotland) Act 1994, water supply and sewerage services were local authority responsibilities. The Central Scotland Water Development Board had the function of developing new sources of water supply for the purpose of providing water in bulk to water authorities whose limits of supply were within the board's area. Under the act, three new public water authorities, covering the north, east and west of Scotland respectively, took over the provision of water and sewerage services from April 1996. The Central Scotland Water Development Board was then abolished. The act also established the Scottish Water and Sewerage Customers Council representing consumer interests. It monitored the performance of the authorities; approved charges schemes; investigated complaints; and advised the secretary of state. The Water Industry Act 1999, whose Scottish provisions were accepted by the Scottish Executive, abolished the Scottish Water and Sewerage Customers Council and replaced it in November 1999 with a Water Industry Commissioner.

The Water Industry (Scotland) Act 2002 resulted from the Scottish Executive's proposal that a single authority was better placed than three separate authorities to harmonise changes across the Scottish water industry. In 2002 the three existing water authorities (East of Scotland Water, North of Scotland Water and West of Scotland Water) merged to form Scottish Water. Scottish Water is a public sector company, structured and managed like a private company, but remains answerable to the Scottish Parliament. Scottish Water is regulated by the Water Industry Commissioner for Scotland, the Scottish Environment Protection Agency (SEPA), and the Drinking Water Quality Regulator for Scotland. The Water Industry Commissioner is responsible for regulating all aspects of economic and customer service performance, including water and sewerage charges. SEPA is responsible for environmental issues, including controlling pollution and promoting the cleanliness of Scotland's rivers, lochs and coastal waters.

METHODS OF CHARGING

Scottish Water sets charges for domestic and non-domestic water and sewerage provision through charges schemes which are regulated by the Water Industries Commissioner for Scotland. In February 2004 the harmonisation of all household charges across the country was completed following the merger of the separate authorities under Scottish Water.

SCOTTISH WATER, PO Box 8855, Edinburgh EH10 6YQ T 0845-601 8855 W www.scottishwater.co.uk

SCOTTISH ENVIRONMENT PROTECTION AGENCY, Erskine Court, Castle Business Park, Stirling FK9 4TR T 01786-457700 W www.sepa.org.uk

WATER INDUSTRY COMMISSIONER FOR SCOTLAND, Ochil House, Springkerse Business Park, Stirling FK7 7XE T 01786-430200 W www.watercommissioner.co.uk

NORTHERN IRELAND

In Northern Ireland ministerial responsibility for wate services lies with the minister of the Department fo Regional Development. The Water Service, which is a executive agency of the Department for Region Development, is responsible for policy and coordinatio with regard to supply, distribution and cleanliness o water, and the provision and maintenance of sewerag services.

The Water Service comprises four divisions: Easterr Northern, Western and Southern. The main division offices are based in Belfast, Ballymena, Londonderry an Craigavon.

METHODS OF CHARGING

The Water Service is currently funded from public fund and direct charges. The department's policy is to meter a properties that are not exclusively domestic. They ar however, granted an allowance of 200 cubic metres pe annum to reflect domestic usage, known as the domesti usage allowance. Customers are charged only for wate used in excess of this allowance together with a standin charge, which is intended to cover the costs of mete provision, maintenance, reading and billing. Th allowance is not granted if rates are not paid on th property. Traders operating from de-rated, rate exempt o rate rebated premises are required to pay for the treatmer and disposal of trade effluent which they discharge int the public sewer.

Water and sewerage services in Northern Irelan became self-financed in 2006. Under new legislatio domestic customers are charged directly for water an sewerage services, currently a proportion of the rates pai on domestic properties. Following a public consultatio document *The Reform of the Water and Sewerage Services I Northern Ireland* the initial conclusion from th Department for Regional Development was that the nev domestic charge would include a fixed element and variable element, the latter determined by property valu or consumption.

NORTHERN IRELAND WATER SERVICE, PO Box 126 Belfast BT1 9DJ T 08457-440088 W www.waterni.gov.uk

ENERGY

he main primary sources of energy in Britain are oil, atural gas, coal, nuclear power and water power. The ain secondary sources (ie sources derived from the rimary sources) are electricity, coke and smokeless fuels nd petroleum products. The Department for the nvironment, Food and Rural Affairs (DEFRA) is sponsible for promoting energy efficiency.

IDIGENOUS PRODUCTION OF PRIMARY FUELS
Iillion tonnes of oil equivalent

	2006
Coal	11.4
Primary oils	84.0
Natural gas	80.0
Primary electricity	17.7
Renewable and waste	3.6
Total	196.7

urce: Department for Business, Enterprise and Regulatory Reform

ILAND ENERGY CONSUMPTION BY PRIMARY FUEL
Iillion tonnes of oil equivalent, seasonally adjusted

	2006
Coal	43.4
Petroleum	77.1
Natural gas	89.2
Nuclear electricity	17.0
Hydro electricity	0.8
Net Imports	0.6
Renewables and waste	4.1
Total	232.1

urce: Department for Business, Enterprise and Regulatory Reform

RADE IN FUELS AND RELATED MATERIALS (2006)

	Quantity million tonnes of oil equivalent	*Value £m*
nports		
oal and other solid fuel	34.6	2,203
rude petroleum	60.8	14,580
etroleum products	35.3	10,019
atural gas	21.0	2,512
lectricity	0.8	445
otal	152.5	29,759
xports		
oal and other solid fuel	0.4	49
rude petroleum	51.8	12,849
etroleum products	37.3	9,571
atural gas	10.4	1,315
lectricity	0.2	92
otal	100.1	23,876

urce: HM Customs & Excise

OIL

Until the 1960s Britain imported almost all its oil supplies. In 1969 oil was discovered in the Arbroath field of the UK Continental Shelf (UKCS). The first oilfield to be brought into production was the Argyll field in 1975, and since the mid-1970s Britain has been a major producer of crude oil.

Licences for exploration and production are granted to companies by the Department for Business, Enterprise and Regulatory Reform; the leading British oil companies are BP and Shell. At the end of 2004, 565 seaward production licences and 101 onshore petroleum exploration and development licences had been awarded, and there were a total of 264 offshore oil and gas fields in production. In 2003 there were 9 oil refineries and three smaller refining units processing crude and process oils. Oil remaining in the UKCS is estimated at 1,267 million tonnes. Royalties are payable on fields approved before April 1982 and petroleum revenue tax is levied on fields approved between 1975 and March 1993.

DRILLING ACTIVITY (2006)
by number of wells started

	Offshore	*Onshore*
Exploration	29	8
Appraisal	40	7
Development	211	12

Source: Department for Business, Enterprise and Regulatory Reform

INDIGENOUS PRODUCTION AND REFINERY RECEIPTS
Thousand tonnes

	2005	*2006*
Indigenous production	84,721	76,579
Crude oil	77,179	69,666
NGLs*	7,543	6,913
Refinery receipts	80,221	75,844

* Natural Gas Liquids: condensates and petroleum gases derived at onshore treatment plants

Source: Department for Business, Enterprise and Regulatory Reform

DELIVERIES OF PETROLEUM PRODUCTS FOR INLAND CONSUMPTION BY ENERGY USE
Thousand tonnes

	2005	*2006*
Industry	6,424	6,553
Transport	52,908	53,457
Domestic	2,782	2,926
Other	1,603	1,399
Total	63,717	64,335

Source: Department for Business, Enterprise and Regulatory Reform

COAL

Coal has been mined in Britain for centuries and the availability of coal was crucial to the industrial revolution of the 18th and 19th centuries. Mines were in private ownership until 1947 when they were nationalised and came under the management of the National Coal Board, later the British Coal Corporation. The corporation held a monopoly on coal production until 1994 when the industry was restructured. Under the Coal Industry Act 1994, the Coal Authority was established to take over ownership of coal reserves and to issue licences to private mining companies. The Coal Authority was also given the responsibility of dealing with the physical legacy of mining, eg subsidence damage claims, and is responsible for holding and making available all existing records.

UK mines were sold as five separate businesses in 1994 and coal production is now undertaken entirely in the private sector. Coal output was around 50 million tonnes a year in 1994. Since then coal output has declined and today there are 7 major deep mines, 11 smaller mines and 30 opencast sites. In 2003 the government launched Coal Investment Aid with a budget of up to £60m to be allocated to coal producers for projects that maintain access to coal reserves.

The main consumer of coal in the UK is the electricity supply industry. Coal still supplies a third of the UK's electricity needs but as indigenous production has declined, imports have risen to make up the shortfall. An energy white paper, published in 2003, had four policy goals, one of which was to cut carbon dioxide emissions by 60 per cent by 2050. This recognised that for a low-carbon economy the development of cleaner coal technologies is required. In November 2005 the government announced an energy policy review and published a report in July 2006. This was the foundation for a further energy white paper published on 23 May 2007 which set out the government's international and domestic energy strategy to meet the long-term challenges posed by climate change to ensure secure, clean and affordable energy. Coal continues to play an important role in the future generating mix, but there is a need to tackle carbon emissions through the introduction of abatement technologies and, in the long term, the introduction of carbon capture and storage.

INLAND COAL USE
Thousand tonnes

	2005	*2006*
Fuel producers		
Electricity generators	52,084	57,323
Heat generation	450	450
Coke manufacture	5,564	5,929
Blast furnaces	1,039	1,121
Other conversion industries†	266	276
Final consumption		
Industry	1,791	1,714
Domestic	614	547
Public administration	22	9
Commerce	6	6
Agriculture	9	5

† Mainly recycled products
Source: Department for Business, Enterprise and Regulatory Reform

COAL PRODUCTION AND FOREIGN TRADE
Thousand tonnes

	2005	*200(*
Deep-mined	9,563	9,44
Opencast	10,445	8,63
Imports	43,968	50,45
Exports	536	–44
Total supply	61,802*	67,267*
TOTAL	61,853	67,38

* Includes an estimate for slurry and stock change
Source: Department for Business, Enterprise and Regulato Reform

GAS

From the late 18th century gas in Britain was produce from coal. In the 1960s town gas began to be produce from oil-based feedstocks using imported oil. In 1965 g was discovered in the North Sea in the West Sole fiel which became the first gasfield in production in 196 and from the late 1960s natural gas began to replace tow gas. Britain is the world's sixth largest producer of gas ar in 1998 only 1.5 per cent of gas available fo consumption in the UK was imported. From Octob 1998 Britain was connected to the continental Europea gas system via a pipeline from Bacton, Norfolk Zeebrugge, Belgium. Gas is transported throug 275,000km of mains pipeline including 6,400km high-pressure gas pipelines owned and operated in th UK by National Grid Gas plc.

The gas industry in Britain was nationalised in 194 and operated as the Gas Council. The Gas Council w replaced by the British Gas Corporation in 1972 and th industry became more centralised. The British G Corporation was privatised in 1986 as British Gas plc. 1993 the Monopolies and Mergers Commission foun that British Gas' integrated business in Great Britain as gas trader and the owner of the gas transportation syste could operate against the public interest. In Februa 1997, British Gas demerged its trading arm to becom two separate companies, BG plc and Centrica plc. B Group, as the company is now known, is an internation natural gas company whose principal business is findir and developing gas reserves and building gas markets. core operations are located in the UK, South Americ Egypt, Trinidad and Tobago, Kazakhstan and Indi Centrica runs the trading and services operations und the British Gas brand name in Great Britain. In Octob 2000 BG demerged its pipeline business, Transco, whic became part of Lattice Group, finally merging with th National Grid Group in 2002 to become National Gr Transco plc.

In July 2005 National Grid Transco plc changed i name to National Grid plc and Transco plc becam National Grid Gas plc. In the same year National Grid G also completed the sale of four of its eight gas distributio networks. The distribution networks transport gas lower pressures, which eventually supply the consume such as domestic customers. The Scotland and south-ea of England networks were sold to Scotia Gas Network The Wales and south-west network was sold to Wales

West Utilities and the network in the north-east to Northern Gas Networks. This was the biggest change in the corporate structure of gas infrastructure since privatisation in 1986.

Competition was gradually introduced into the industrial gas market from 1986. Supply of gas to the domestic market was opened to companies other than British Gas, starting in April 1996 with a pilot project in the West Country and Wales, with the rest of the UK following soon after. Since competition was introduced in domestic retail of gas, around half of Britain's 20 million gas customers have changed their supplier.

BG GROUP PLC, Thames Valley Park, Reading RG6 1PT T 0118-935 3222 W www.bg-group.com
Chairman, Sir Robert Wilson
Chief Executive, Frank Chapman

CENTRICA PLC, Millstream, Maidenhead Road, Windsor, Berkshire SL4 5GD T 01753-494000 W www.centrica.co.uk
Chairman, Roger Carr
Chief Executive, Sam Laidlaw

NATIONAL GRID TRANSCO PLC, 1–3 Strand, London WC2N 5EH T 020-7004 3000 W www.ngtgroup.com
Chairman, Sir John Parker
Deputy Group Chief Executive, Steve Holliday

UK NATURAL GAS PRODUCTION
GWh

	2004	*2005*
Power stations	341,111	333,834
Petroleum refineries	1,797	1,987
Nuclear fuel production	201	202
Production and distribution of other energy	721	715
Total final producers	343,830	336,738

Source: Annual Abstract of Statistics 2007 (Crown copyright)

UK GAS CONSUMPTION BY INDUSTRY
GWh

	2004	*2005*
Iron and steel industry	9,715	8,410
Other industries	143,959	140,271
Domestic	396,411	381,879
Public administration	50,934	49,385
Agriculture	2,355	2,201
Miscellaneous	68,797	64,788
Total final users	672,171	646,990

Source: Annual Abstract of Statistics 2007 (Crown copyright)

ELECTRICITY

The first power station in Britain generating electricity for public supply began operating in 1882. In the 1930s a national transmission grid was developed and it was reconstructed and extended in the 1950s and 1960s. Power stations were operated by the Central Electricity Generating Board.

Under the Electricity Act 1989, 12 regional electricity companies, responsible for the distribution of electricity from the national grid to consumers, were formed from the former area electricity boards in England and Wales. Four companies were formed from the Central Electricity Generating Board: three generating companies (National Power plc, Nuclear Electric plc and Powergen plc) and the National Grid Company plc, which owned and operated the transmission system in England and Wales. National Power and Powergen were floated on the stock market in 1991.

National Power was demerged in October 2000 to form two separate companies: International Power plc and Innogy plc, which manages the bulk of National Power's UK assets. Nuclear Electric was split into two parts in 1996: British Energy (*see* Nuclear Energy) and Magnox Electric, which owns the magnox nuclear reactors, remained in the public sector. Magnox was integrated into British Nuclear Fuels (BNFL) in 1998.

The National Grid Company was floated on the stock market in 1995 and formed a new holding company, National Grid Group. National Grid Group completed a merger with Lattice in 2002 to form National Grid Transco, a public limited company. National Grid Transco has since undergone a series of name changes (*see* Gas).

Following privatisation, generators and suppliers in England and Wales traded via the Electricity Pool. A competitive wholesale trading market known as NETA (New Electricity Trading Arrangements) replaced the Electicity Pool in March 2001, which was extended to include Scotland via the British Electricity Transmissions and Trading Arrangements (BETTA) in 2005. As part of BETTA, National Grid became the system operator for all transmission. The introduction of competition into the domestic electricity market was completed in May 1999. With the gas market also open, most suppliers now offer their customers both gas and electricity. Since competition was introduced, around half of Britain's 26 million electricity customers have switched their supplier.

In Scotland, three new companies were formed under the Electricity Act 1989: Scottish Power plc and Scottish Hydro-Electric plc, which were responsible for generation, transmission, distribution and supply; and Scottish Nuclear Ltd. Scottish Power and Scottish Hydro-Electric were floated on the stock market in 1991. Scottish Hydro-Electric merged with Southern Electric in 1998 to become Scottish and Southern Energy plc. Scottish Nuclear was incorporated into British Energy in 1996. BETTA opened the Scottish market to the same competition that had applied in England and Wales.

In Northern Ireland, Northern Ireland Electricity plc was set up in 1993 under a 1991 Order in Council. In 1993 it was floated on the stock market and in 1998 it became part of the Viridian Group and is responsible for distribution and supply.

On 30 September 2003 the Electricity Association, the industry's main trade association, was replaced with three separate trade bodies:

ASSOCIATION OF ELECTRICITY PRODUCERS, 1st Floor, 17 Waterloo Place, London SW1Y 4AR T 020-7930 9390 W www.aepuk.com
ENERGY NETWORKS ASSOCIATION, 18 Stanhope Place, London W2 2HH T 020-7706 5100 W www.energynetworks.org
ENERGY RETAIL ASSOCIATION, 4th Floor, 17 Waterloo Place, London SW1Y 4AR T 020-7930 9175 W www.energy-retail.org.uk

ELECTRICITY GENERATION, SUPPLY AND CONSUMPTION
GWh

	2004	2005
Electricity generated		
Conventional thermal and other*	130,882	136,348
Combined cycle gas turbine stations	139,405	136,084
Nuclear stations	79,999	81,618
Hydroelectric stations		
Natural flow	4,000	3,993
Pumped storage	2,649	2,930
Renewables other than hydro	1,471	1,406
Major power producers: total	358,406	362,379
Other generators	36,900	38,145
Electricity used on works: total	17,081	17,832
Electricity supplied (gross)		
Conventional thermal and other*	124,052	129,156
Combined cycle gas turbine stations	137,170	133,713
Nuclear stations	73,682	75,172
Hydroelectric stations		
Natural flow	3,993	3,987
Pumped storage	2,559	2,776
Renewables other than hydro	1,367	1,309
Major power producers: total	342,824	346,113
Other generators total	35,401	36,579
Electricity used in pumping	3,497	3,707
Electricity consumed		
Fuel industries	8,491	9,162
Final users total	339,641	345,926
Industrial sector	116,531	119,515
Domestic sector	115,526	116,811
Other sectors	107,584	109,600
Total	348,134	355,088

* Includes electricity supplied by gas turbines, oil engines and plants producing electricity from renewable resources other than hydro

Source: Annual Abstract of Statistics 2007 (Crown copyright)

GAS AND ELECTRICITY SUPPLIERS

With the gas and electricity markets open, most suppliers offer their customers both services. The majority of gas/electricity companies have become part of larger multi-utility companies, often operating internationally. The following list comprises a selection of suppliers offering gas and electricity. Organisations in italics are subsidiaries of the companies listed in capital letters directly above.

ENGLAND, SCOTLAND AND WALES

CE ELECTRIC UK, W www.ce-electricuk.com
Northern Electric Distribution Ltd, Manor House, Station Road, New Penshaw, Houghton-le-Spring DH4 7LA T 0800-668877
Yorkshire Electricity Distribution, 161 Gelderd Road, Leeds LS1 1QZ T 0800-375675

CENTRICA PLC, Millstream, Maidenhead Road, Windsor, Berkshire SL4 5GD T 01753-494000 W www.centrica.com
British Gas/Scottish Gas, T 0845-955 5200 W www.house.co.uk

EDF ENERGY, 40 Grosvenor Place, Victoria, London SW1X 7EN T 020-7242 9050 W www.edfenergy.com

E.ON, Westwood Way, Westwood Business Park, Coventry, CV4 8LG T 024-7642 4000 W www.eon-uk.com
Powergen, PO Box 7750, Nottingham NG1 6WR T 0800-052 0346

NPOWER, PO Box 93, Peterlee SR8 2XX T 08457-7145 146 W www.npower.com

SCOTTISH AND SOUTHERN ENERGY PLC, Inveralmond House, 200 Dunkeld Road, Perth PH1 3AQ T 01738 456000 W www.scottish-southern.co.uk
Scottish Hydro Electric, PO Box 7506, Perth PH1 3QR T 0845-300 2141 W www.hydro.co.uk
Southern Electric, PO Box 7506, Perth PH1 3QR T 0845-744 4555 W www.southern-electric.co.uk
SWALEC, PO Box 7506, Perth PH1 3QR T 0800-052 5252 W www.swalec.co.uk

SCOTTISHPOWER, Cathcart House, Cathcart Business Park, Spean Street, Glasgow G44 4BE T 0845-273 4444 W www.scottishpower.co.uk

NORTHERN IRELAND

VIRIDIAN GROUP PLC, 120 Malone Road, Belfast BT9 5HT T 028-9066 8416 W www.viridiangroup.co.uk
Energia, Energia House, 62 Newforge Lane, Belfast BT9 5NF T 028-9068 5900 W www.viridianenergia.co.uk
Northern Ireland Electricity, 120 Malone Road, Belfast BT9 5HT T 028-9066 1100 W www.nie.co.uk

REGULATION OF THE GAS AND ELECTRICITY INDUSTRIES

The Office of the Gas and Electricity Markets (OFGEM) regulates the gas and electricity industries in Great Britain. It was formed in 1999 by the merger of the Office of Gas Supply and the Office of Electricity Regulation. OFGEM's overriding aim is to protect and promote the interests of all gas and electricity customers by promoting competition and regulating monopolies. It is governed by an authority and its powers are provided for under the Gas Act 1986, the Electricity Act 1989 and the Utilities Act 2000.

THE OFFICE OF THE GAS AND ELECTRICTY MARKETS (OFGEM), 9 Millbank, London SW1 3GE T 020-7901 7000 W www.ofgem.gov.uk

NUCLEAR POWER

Nuclear reactors began to supply electricity to the national grid in 1956; in 2006 nuclear power generated 26 per cent of the UK electricity at six magnox reactors, seven advanced gas-cooled reactors (AGR) and one pressurised water reactor (PWR), Sizewell 'B' in Suffolk. In 1989 nuclear stations were withdrawn from privatisation. In 1996 Nuclear Electric Ltd and Scottish Nuclear Ltd became operating subsidiaries of British Energy and the magnox stations were transferred to Nuclear Electric which became Magnox Electric, later part of British Nuclear Fuels Ltd. British Energy manages eight nuclear power stations (seven AGRs and one PWR) and generates around one-fifth of the UK's electricity.

In April 2005 the responsibility for the decommissioning of civil nuclear reactors and other nuclear facilities used in research and development was handed from the UK Atomic Energy Authority (UKAEA) to a new body, the Nuclear Decommissioning Authority (NDA). The NDA is a non-departmental public body funded mainly by the Department for Business, Enterprise and Regulatory Reform. UK Nirex, which was set up by the nuclear generating companies with the agreement of the government, is responsible for the disposal of intermediate and some low-level nuclear waste. The UKAEA now operates on a private contractor basis and is currently decommissioning the nuclear power stations at Dounreay, Harwell, Windscale, Withrin and the JET facilities at Culham.

SAFETY AND REGULATION

The Nuclear Safety Directorate of the Health and Safety Executive is the nuclear industry's regulator. Operations at all UK nuclear power stations are governed by a site licence which is issued under the Nuclear Installations Act. The Nuclear Installations Inspectorate (NII) monitors compliance with each licence through an NII inspector that is assigned to each station and has the jurisdiction to close down a reactor if the terms of the licence are breached. The Department for Business, Enterprise and Regulatory Reform is responsible for security at all the UK's nuclear power stations which are policed by the Civil Nuclear Constabulary, a specialised armed force created in April 2005.

THE NUCLEAR DILEMMA

In February 2007 the high court ruled that the consultation conducted during the government's 2006 review on nuclear energy, which advocated the building of new power plants to provide up to 40 per cent of the country's energy, was 'misleading' and 'seriously flawed'. This ruling has brought energy back into public consideration. Both the former prime minister Tony Blair and the former trade and industry secretary, Alistair Darling, have endorsed nuclear power as the best immediate option.

There are a number of factors which have affected the government's backing of nuclear power: domestic gas supplies are running low, oil and gas prices are rising, carbon emissions must be cut to comply with EU legislation and a number of coal-fired power stations that fail to meet clean air requirements are due to be closed. The government has long foreseen an energy gap in the country's future generating capacity due to the decommissioning of current nuclear stations and the necessity of cutting back on fossil fuels.

- Nuclear power provides over 16 per cent of the world's electricity, almost 24 per cent of electricity in OECD countries, and 34 per cent in the EU.
- All but one of the UK nuclear power stations are set to close by 2023. They produce 20 per cent of the UK electricity.

Nuclear power has a number of advantages: reactors emit virtually no carbon dioxide, uranium prices have remained steady for decades and supply does not depend on agreements with unstable foreign regimes. The advantages of low emissions are countered by the high costs of construction. There are difficulties in disposing of nuclear waste; currently the only method is to store it securely until it has slowly decayed to safe levels. Countries that have sought to develop nuclear weapons in the last 50 years – including North Korea and Iran – have done so through manipulating their nuclear power programmes to create an undeniable and difficult link between nuclear energy and warfare. Finally, public distrust persists with the images of disasters such as Chernobyl difficult to forget, despite the advances in safety technology.

RENEWABLE SOURCES

Renewable sources of energy principally include biofuels, hydro, wind and solar. Renewable sources produced over 4.4 million tonnes of oil equivalent for primary energy usage in 2006; of this, about 3.9 million tonnes was used to generate electricity and 0.5 million tonnes to generate heat. In 2006, the UK generated 4.5 per cent of its total energy production from renewable sources.

The government's principal mechanism for developing renewable energy sources are Non-Fossil Fuel Obligation Renewables Orders. Under the terms of the orders, regional electricity companies are required to buy specified amounts of electricity from specified non-fossil fuel sources. The Renewables Obligation (RO) aims to increase the contribution of electricity from renewables in the UK, so that 10 per cent of licensed UK electricity sales should be from renewable sources eligible for the RO by 2010, and 15 per cent should be eligible by 2015.

A renewables obligation has been in place in England and Wales since April 2002 to give incentives to generators to supply progressively higher levels of renewable energy over time. These measures included exempting renewable energy sources from the climate change levy, capital grants, enhanced research funding and regional planning to meet renewables targets. These developments prompted the British government to approve an EU-wide agreement in March 2007 to generate 20 per cent of energy production from renewable sources by 2020. Former prime minister Tony Blair described the deal as 'groundbreaking, bold and ambitious'. A document produced by the Department for Business, Enterprise and Regulatory Reform in the summer of 2007 cast doubt on the government's ability to achieve its ambitions, suggesting that the UK is capable only of generating 9 per cent by the end of the target period.

RENEWABLE ENERGY SOURCES (2006)

	Percentage
Biofuels and wastes	82.0
Landfill gas	33.1
Sewage gas	4.5
Wood combustion	6.4
Waste combustion	11.6
Other biofuels	7.7
Hydro	9.0
Large-scale	8.0
Small-scale	1.0
Wind and wave	8.2
Geothermal and active solar heating	0.7
Total	100

Source: Department for Business, Enterprise and Regulatory Reform

TRANSPORT

CIVIL AVIATION

Since the privatisation of British Airways in 1987, UK airlines have been operated entirely by the private sector. In 2006, total capacity of British airlines amounted to 50 billion tonne km, of which 39 billion tonne km was on scheduled services. British airlines carried 127 million passengers, 98 million on scheduled services and 30 million on charter flights. Overall, passenger traffic grew by 3 per cent. Traffic at the five main London airports grew by 2 per cent over 2006 and regional airlines saw a growth of 4 per cent, largely due to the expansion of 'no-frills' airlines. Leading British airlines include BMI, British Airways, EasyJet, First Choice Airways, Monarch, My Travel Airways, Thomas Cook Airlines, Thomsonfly and Virgin Atlantic. Irish airline Ryanair also operates frequent flights from Britain.

There are around 140 licensed civil aerodromes in Britain, with Heathrow and Gatwick handling the highest volume of passengers. BAA plc owns and operates the seven major airports: Heathrow, Gatwick, Stansted, Southampton, Glasgow, Edinburgh and Aberdeen, which between them handle about 63 per cent of air passengers and a high percentage of air cargo traffic in Britain. Other airports are controlled by local authorities or private companies.

The Civil Aviation Authority (CAA), an independent statutory body, is responsible for the regulation of UK airlines. This includes economic and airspace regulation, air safety, consumer protection and environmental research and consultancy. All commercial airline companies must be granted an air operator's certificate, which is issued by the CAA to operators meeting the required safety standards. The CAA issues airport safety licences, which must be obtained by any airport used for public transport and training flights. All British-registered aircraft must be granted an airworthiness certificate, and the CAA issues professional licences to pilots, flight crew, ground engineers and air traffic controllers. The CAA also manages the Air Travel Organiser's Licence (ATOL), the UK's principal travel protection scheme. The CAA's costs are met entirely from charges on those whom it regulates; there is no direct government funding of the CAA's work.

The Transport Act, passed by parliament on 29 November 2000, separated the CAA from its subsidiary, National Air Traffic Services (NATS), which provides air traffic control services to aircraft flying in UK airspace and over the eastern part of the North Atlantic. In March 2001 the Airline Group, a consortium of seven UK airlines (British Airways, BMI, Virgin Atlantic, Britannia, Monarch, EasyJet and Airtours), was selected by the government as its strategic partner for NATS. Financial restructuring of NATS was completed in March 2003 with additional equity investment of £65m each from BAA and the government. The new structure enabled NATS to begin a ten-year £1bn investment programme, to increase its flight handling capability to three million flights per annum by 2010. NATS is a public private partnership between the Airline Group, which holds 42 per cent of the shares; NATS staff, who hold 5 per cent; BAA, which holds 4 per cent, and the government, which holds 49 per cent and a golden share. In 2006 NATS handled a total of 2,386,105 flights, an increase of 3.5 per cent on 2005.

AIR PASSENGERS 2006

ALL UK AIRPORTS: TOTAL	235,139,346
Aberdeen (BAA)	3,162,624
Barra (HIAL)†	9,808
Belfast City	2,105,597
Belfast International	5,015,264
Benbecula (HIAL)†	33,433
Biggin Hill	220
Birmingham	9,056,004
Blackpool	552,641
Bournemouth	960,773
Bristol	5,710,222
Cambridge	1,391
Campbeltown (HIAL)†	8,928
Cardiff	1,993,097
City of Derry (Eglinton)	341,719
Coventry	609,859
Doncaster Sheffield	899,307
Dundee	51,496
Durham Tees Valley	900,107
Edinburgh (BAA)	8,606,651
Exeter	970,614
Gatwick (BAA)	34,080,345
Glasgow (BAA)	8,820,462
Gloucestershire	166
Hawarden*	–
Heathrow (BAA)	67,339,227
Humberside	515,889
Inverness (HIAL)†	670,894
Islay (HIAL)†	26,218
Isle of Man	782,734
Isles of Scilly (St Mary's)	128,093
Isles of Scilly (Tresco)	41,906
Kent International	9,845
Kirkwall (HIAL)†	116,837
Lands End (St Just)	23,380
Leeds Bradford	2,787,217
Lerwick (Tingwall)	4,438
Liverpool	4,962,460
London City	2,358,159
Luton	9,414,829
Lydd	2,754
Manchester	22,123,762
Newcastle	5,407,362
Newquay	343,143
Norwich	745,192
Nottingham East Midlands International	4,720,819
Penzance Heliport	93,958
Plymouth	76,568
Prestwick	2,394,928
Scatsta	255,147
Shoreham	4,508
Southampton (BAA)	1,912,702
Southend	30,222
Stansted (BAA)	23,680,352
Stornoway (HIAL)†	120,288

Sumburgh (HIAL)†	128,233
Tiree (HIAL)†	7,016
Wick (HIAL)†	19,538
:HANNEL ISLANDS AIRPORTS: TOTAL	2,420,723
Alderney	76,806
Guernsey	864,764
Jersey	1,479,153

Figure not supplied by airport
· Highlands and Islands Airports Ltd (HIAL)
ource: Civil Aviation Authority

:AA, CAA House, 45–59 Kingsway, London WC2B 6TE
T 020-7379 7311 W www.caa.co.uk

3AA, Belgrave House, London SW1W 9TQ T 020-7834 9449
W www.baa.com

Gatwick Airport	T 0870-000 2468
Heathrow Airport	T 0870-000 0123
Southampton Airport	T 0870-040 0009
Stansted Airport	T 0870-000 0303
Aberdeen Airport	T 0870-040 0006
Edinburgh Airport	T 0870-040 0007
Glasgow Airport	T 0870-040 0008

3MI, Donington Hall, Castle Donington, Derby DE74 2SB
T 01332-854000 W www.flybmi.com

3RITISH AIRWAYS, Waterside, PO Box 365, Harmondsworth UB7 0GB T 0870-850 9850
W www.britishairways.com

:ASYJET, Hangar 89, London Luton Airport LU2 9PF
T 0871-244 2366 W www.easyjet.com

'IRST CHOICE AIRWAYS, Diamond House, Peel Cross Road, Salford, Manchester M5 4DT T 0871-664 0144
W www.firstchoice.co.uk

ИONARCH, Prospect House, Prospect Way, London Luton Airport LU2 9NU T 0870-040 5040
W www.flymonarch.com

ИY TRAVEL AIRWAYS, Holiday House, Sandbrook Park, Sandbrook Way, Rochdale OL11 1SA T 0161-498 4498
W www.mytravel.com

'HOMAS COOK AIRLINES, Thomas Cook Business Park, Coningsby Road, Peterborough PE3 8SB T 0870-243 0416
W www.thomascookairlines.com

'HOMSONFLY, Wigmore House, Wigmore Lane, Luton LU2 9TN T 0870-1900 737 W www.thomsonfly.com

'IRGIN ATLANTIC, The Office, Crawley, Sussex RH10 9NU
T 01293-562345 W www.virgin-atlantic.com

RAILWAYS

'he railway network in Britain was developed by private ompanies in the 19th century. In 1948 the main railway ompanies were nationalised and were run by a public uthority, the British Transport Commission. The ommission was replaced by the British Railways Board n 1963, operating as British Rail. On 1 April 1994, esponsibility for managing the track and railway nfrastructure passed to a newly formed company, Railtrack plc. In October 2001 Railtrack was put into dministration under the Railways Act 1993 and Ernst nd Young was appointed as administrator. In October 002 Railtrack was taken out of administration and eplaced by the not-for-profit company Network Rail. 'he British Railways Board continued as operator of all rain services until 1996–7, when they were sold or ranchised to the private sector.

The Strategic Rail Authority (SRA) was created to provide strategic leadership to the rail industry and formally came into being on 1 February 2001 following the passing of the Transport Act 2000. In January 2002 it published its first strategic plan, setting out the strategic priorities for Britain's railways over the next ten years. In addition to its coordinating role, the SRA was responsible for allocating government funding to the railways and awarding and monitoring the franchises for operating rail services.

On 15 July 2004 the transport secretary announced a new structure for the rail industry in the white paper *The Future of Rail.* These proposals were implemented under the Railways Act 2005, which abolished the Strategic Rail Authority, passing most of its functions to the Department for Transport; established the Rail Passengers Council (RPC) as a single national body, dissolving the regional committees; and gave devolved governments in Scotland and Wales more say in decisions at a local level. In addition, responsibility for railway safety regulation was transferred to the Office of Rail Regulation from the Health and Safety Executive.

OFFICE OF RAIL REGULATION

The Office of Rail Regulation (ORR) was established on 5 July 2004 by the Railways and Transport Safety Act 2003, replacing the Office of the Rail Regulator. As the railway industry's economic and safety regulator, the ORR's principal function is to regulate Network Rail's stewardship of the national network. The ORR also licenses operators of railway assets, approves agreements for access by operators to track, stations and light maintenance depots, and enforces domestic competition law. The ORR is led by a board appointed by the Secretary of State for Transport, under the chairmanship of Chris Bolt. Mr Bolt also fulfils the role of International Rail Regulator (IRR), a statutory office separate from the ORR, which licenses both the operation of certain international rail services in the European Economic Area and access to railway infrastructure in Great Britain for the purpose of operating international services.

SERVICES

For privatisation, under the Railways Act 1993, domestic passenger services were divided into 25 train operating units, which were franchised to private sector operators via a competitive tendering process. The train operators formed the Association of Train Operating Companies (ATOC) to act as the official voice of the passenger rail industry and provide its members with a range of services enabling them to comply with conditions imposed on them through their franchise agreements and operating licences.

As at June 2007 there were 24 passenger train operating companies (TOCs): Arriva Trains Wales; c2c; Central Trains; Chiltern Railways; Eurostar; First Capital Connect; First Great Western; First ScotRail; Gatwick Express; GNER; Heathrow Connect; Heathrow Express; Hull Trains; Island Line (Isle of Wight); Merseyrail; Midland Mainline; Northern Rail; One; Silverlink; South West Trains; Southeastern; Southern; TransPennine Express and Virgin Trains.

Network Rail publishes a national timetable which contains details of rail services operated over the UK network and sea ferry services which provide connections with Ireland, the Isle of Man, the Isle of Wight, the Channel Islands and some European destinations.

The national rail enquiries service offers information about train times and fares for any part of the country,

Transport for London (TfL) provides London-specific travel information for all modes of travel and Eurostar provides information for international channel tunnel rail services:

NATIONAL RAIL ENQUIRIES
T 08457-484950
W www.nationalrail.co.uk
TRANSPORT FOR LONDON
T 020-7222 1234
W www.tfl.gov.uk
EUROSTAR
T 08705-186 186
W www.eurostar.com

PASSENGER FOCUS AND LONDON TRAVELWATCH

Passenger Focus is the operating name of the Rail Passengers' Council, a single national consumer body for rail, which is funded by the Department for Transport but whose independence is guaranteed by an act of parliament. Rail Users' Consultative Committees were set up under the Railways Act 1993 to protect the interests of users of the services and facilities provided on Britain's rail network. The Transport Act 2000 changed their name to Rail Passenger Committees (RPCs) and brought the committees under the overall sponsorship of the Strategic Rail Authority. There were eight RPCs nationwide, one for each of the six English regions and one each for Scotland and Wales. Under the Railways Act 2005, the eight regional committees were disbanded in June 2005 and their functions and duties transferred to the Rail Passengers' Council , the Strategic Rail Authority was abolished and sponsorship for the Rail Passengers' Council transferred to the Department for Transport.

Established in July 2000, London TravelWatch is the operating name of the official watchdog organisation representing the interests of transport users in and around the capital. Officially known as the London Transport Users' Committee, it is sponsored and funded by the London Assembly and is independent of the transport operators. London TravelWatch represents users of buses, the Underground, river and rail services in and around London, including Eurostar and Heathrow Express, Croydon Tramlink and the Docklands Light Railway. The interests of pedestrians, cyclists and motorists are also represented, as are those of taxi users.

FREIGHT

Rail freight services are provided by a small number of companies. On privatisation, British Rail's bulk freight operations were sold to English, Welsh and Scottish Railways (EWS). The other major companies in the rail freight sector are Freightliner Ltd (formerly the British Rail container business), Direct Rail Service (DRS) and GB Railfreight. In 2005 22.1 billion tonne kilometres of freight was moved by rail.

NETWORK RAIL

Network Rail is responsible for the tracks, bridges, tunnels, level crossings, viaducts and 17 main stations that form Britain's rail network. In addition to providing the timetables for the passenger and freight operators, Network Rail is also responsible for all the signalling and electrical control equipment needed to operate the rail network and for monitoring and reporting performance across the industry.

Network Rail is a private company run as a commercial business; it is directly accountable to its members and regulated by the ORR. The members have similar rights to those of shareholders in a public company except they do not receive dividends or share capital and thereby have no financial or economic interest in Network Rail. All of Network Rail's profits are reinvested into maintaining and upgrading the rail infrastructure.

ASSOCIATION OF TRAIN OPERATING COMPANIES, 3rd Floor, 40 Bernard Street, London WC1N 1BY T 020-7841 8000 W www.atoc.org
LONDON TRAVELWATCH, 6 Middle Street, London EC1A 7JA T 020-7505 9000
W www.londontravelwatch.org.uk
NETWORK RAIL, 40 Melton Street, London NW1 2EE
T 020-7557 8000 W www.networkrail.co.uk
OFFICE OF RAIL REGULATION, 1 Kemble Street, London WC2B 4AN T 020-7282 2000
W www.rail-reg.gov.uk
Chair/International Rail Regulator, Chris Bolt
PASSENGER FOCUS, Freepost WA1521, Warrington WA4 6GP T 0845-3022 022
W www.railpassengers.org.uk

RAIL SAFETY

On 1 April 2006 responsibility for health and safety policy and enforcement on the railways transferred from the Health and Safety Executive to the Office of Rail Regulation.

In 2006 a total of 20 passengers, railway staff and other members of the public were fatally injured in rail incidents, compared with 33 in 2005. There were no passenger fatalities resulting from train incidents in 2006.

ACCIDENTS ON RAILWAYS

	2005	*2006*
Total train incidents	1,057	1,061
Total train incident fatalities	7	[illegible]
Passengers	0	[illegible]
Railway employees	1	[illegible]
Others	6	[illegible]
Total train incident injuries	51	4[illegible]
Passengers	22	2[illegible]
Railway staff	20	1[illegible]
Others	9	[illegible]

TRESPASSERS, SUICIDES AND ATTEMPTED SUICIDES 2006*

Total fatalities	321
Total injuries	140

*Includes all incidents on rail (network rail, London Underground and other rail systems, such as trams). Fatality data is subject to change pending the outcome of Coroners' inquests
Source: Office of Rail Regulation – *Railway Safety Statistical Report 2006*

OTHER RAIL SYSTEMS

Responsibility for the London Underground passed from the government to the Mayor and Transport for London on 15 July 2003, with a public-private partnership (PPP) already in place. Plans for a public-private partnership for London Underground were pushed through by the government in February 2002 despite opposition from the Mayor of London and a range of transport organisations. Under the PPP, long-term contracts with private companies were estimated to enable around £16bn to be invested in renewing and upgrading the Underground's infrastructure over 15 years. Responsibility for stations, trains, operations, signalling nd safety remains in the public sector. In 2005–6 there vere 970 million passenger journeys on the London Jnderground, a decrease of 0.6 per cent on the previous 'ear.

Britain has nine other light rail, tram or underground ystems: Blackpool Tramway, Croydon Tramlink, Dockands Light Railway (DLR), Glasgow Subway, Manchester Metrolink, Midland Metro, Nottingham Express Transit NET), Sheffield Supertram and Tyne and Wear Metro.

Light rail and metro systems in Great Britain ontributed to the growth in public transport, with 175 nillion passenger journeys in 2005–6, an increase of 1.7 er cent on the previous year. In England there were 162 nillion passenger journeys in 2005–6, compared with 24 million in 2000–1. The government's ten-year 'ransport Plan target is to double light rail use in England measured by number of passenger journeys) by 2010 ompared to 2000 levels.

'HE CHANNEL TUNNEL

he earliest recorded scheme for a submarine transport onnection between Britain and France was in 1802. 'unnelling began simultaneously on both sides of the Channel three times: in 1881, in the early 1970s, and on December 1987, when construction workers bored the rst of the three tunnels which form the Channel Tunnel. ngineers 'holed through' the first tunnel (the service unnel) on 1 December 1990 and tunnelling was ompleted in June 1991. The tunnel was officially naugurated by the Queen and President Mitterrand of rance on 6 May 1994.

The submarine link comprises two rail tunnels, each arrying trains in one direction, which measure 7.6m 24.93ft) in diameter. Between them lies a smaller service unnel, measuring 4.8m (15.75ft) in diameter. The service unnel is linked to the rail tunnels by 130 cross-passages or maintenance and safety purposes. The tunnels are 0km (31 miles) long, 38km (24 miles) of which is under he seabed at an average depth of 40m (132ft). The rail erminals are situated at Folkestone and Calais, and the unnels go underground at Shakespeare Cliff, Dover, and angatte, west of Calais.

Eurostar is the high-speed passenger train service onnecting London with Paris in 2 hours 15 minutes and russels in 1 hours 51 minutes, via the Channel Tunnel rom 14 November 2007). Some trains stop en route t Ashford (Kent) and Calais, Disneyland Paris and Lille in rance.

RAIL LINKS

he route for the British Channel Tunnel Rail Link will un from Folkestone to a new terminal at St Pancras tation, London, with new intermediate stations at bbsfleet, Kent, and Stratford, east London. International ervices presently running into a terminal at Waterloo tation, London, will discontinue.

Construction of the rail link is being financed by the rivate sector with a substantial government contribution. private sector consortium, London and Continental Railways Ltd (LCR), is responsible for the design, onstruction and ownership of the rail link, and omprises Union Railways and the UK operator of urostar. Construction was expected to be completed in 003, but on 28 January 1998 LCR informed the overnment that it was unable to fulfil its obligations. On June 1998 the government announced a new funding greement with LCR. The rail link will be constructed in wo phases: phase one, from the Channel Tunnel to Fawkham Junction, North Kent, began in October 1998 and opened to fare-paying passengers on 28 September 2003; phase two, from Southfleet Junction to St Pancras, was due to be completed in November 2007. Infrastructure developments in France have been completed and high-speed trains run from Calais to Paris and from Lille to the south of France.

ROADS

HIGHWAY AUTHORITIES

The powers and responsibilities of highway authorities in England and Wales are set out in the Highways Act 1980; for Scotland there is separate legislation.

Responsibility for trunk road motorways and other trunk roads in Great Britain rests in England with the Secretary of State for Transport, in Scotland with the Scottish Executive, and in Wales with the Welsh Assembly. The costs of construction, improvement and maintenance are paid for by central government in England and by the Welsh Assembly Government in Wales. The highway authority for non-trunk roads in England, Wales and Scotland is, in general, the local authority in whose area the roads lie. With the establishment of the Greater London Authority in July 2000, Transport for London became the highway authority for roads in London.

In Northern Ireland the Department of Regional Development is the statutory road authority responsible for public roads and their maintenance and construction; the Roads Service executive agency carries out these functions on behalf of the department.

FINANCE

In England all aspects of trunk road and motorway funding are provided directly by the government to the Highways Agency, which operates, maintains and improves a network of motorways and trunk roads over 7,200km (4,500 miles) long, on behalf of the secretary of state. Since 2001 the length of the network that the Highways Agency is responsible for has been decreasing due to a policy of de-trunking, which transfers responsibility for non-core roads to local authorities. For the financial year 2007–8 the Highways Agency's total planned expenditure is £6,470m: £839m for maintenance, £789m for major improvements, £197m revenue support for major private investment, £312m for existing network improvements and technology and the remainder for other programmes and administration costs.

Government support for local authority capital expenditure on roads and other transport infrastructure is provided through grant and credit approvals as part of the Local Transport Plan (LTP). Local authorities bid for resources on the basis of a five-year programme built around delivering integrated transport strategies. As well as covering the structural maintenance of local roads and the construction of major new road schemes, LTP funding also includes smaller-scale safety and traffic management measures with associated improvements for public transport, cyclists and pedestrians.

For the financial year 2007–8, planned expenditure in the form of LTP funding for local authorities is £1.7bn. £683m for road maintenance, £571m for small-scale integrated transport measures and £481m for new and existing major projects.

Total expenditure by the Welsh Assembly Government on trunk roads, motorways, rail, bus and other transport services (including grants to local authorities) in 2006–7 was £537m. Planned expenditure for 2007–8 is £542m.

Until 1999 the Scottish Office received a block vote from parliament and the Secretary of State for Scotland determined how much was spent on roads. Since 1 July 1999 all decisions on transport expenditure have been devolved to the Scottish Executive. Total expenditure on motorways and trunk roads in Scotland during 2006–7 was £907.2m, including depreciation and cost of capital charge. Planned expenditure for 2007–8 is £895m.

In Northern Ireland total expenditure by the Roads Service on all roads in 2006–7 was £121.1m, with £118.8m spent on trunk roads and motorways. Planned expenditure for 2007–8 is £101.8m, with £85.5m allocated for trunk roads and motorways.

The Transport Act 2000 gave English and Welsh local authorities (outside London) powers to introduce road-user charging or workplace parking levy schemes. The act requires that the net revenue raised is used to improve local transport services and facilities for at least ten years. The aim is to reduce congestion and encourage greater use of alternative modes of transport. Schemes developed by local authorities require government approval. The government's 2000 Ten Year Plan for Transport assumes that eight large road user charging schemes and 12 large workplace parking levy schemes will be developed by 2010. The UK's first toll road, the M6 Toll, opened in December 2003 and runs for 43.5km (27 miles) around Birmingham from junction 3a to junction 11a on the M6.

Charging schemes in London are allowed under the 1999 Greater London Authority Act. The Central London Congestion Charge Scheme began on 17 February 2003 (*see also* Regional Government).

TARGETED PROGRAMME OF IMPROVEMENTS

The Targeted Programme of Improvements constitutes the Highway Agency's investment programme in the trunk road and motorway networks. The programme comprises 80 major road schemes, each costing more than £5m, funded either conventionally or by public-private partnerships.

ROAD LENGTHS 2005
Kilometres

	England	*Wales*	*Scotland*	*Great Britain*
Motorways	2,992	141	386	3,519
Dual carriageway	6,569	553	783	7,905
Single carriageway	25,646	3,619	9,487	38,752
B roads	19,863	2,981	7,345	30,189
C roads	64,294	9,841	10,324	84,459
Unclassified roads	178,548	16,098	28,538	223,184
TOTAL	297,912	33,233	56,864	388,008

Source: Department for Transport

ROAD USE

ROAD TRAFFIC BY TYPE OF VEHICLE (GREAT BRITAIN) 2005
Million vehicle kilometres

All motor vehicles	499,400
Cars and taxis	397,200
Motorcycles	5,400
Buses and coaches	5,200
Light vans	62,600
Other goods vehicles	29,000
Pedal cycles	4,400

Source: Department for Transport

FREIGHT TRANSPORT BY ROAD (GREAT BRITAIN) 2005

GOODS MOVED	
By mode of working (billion tonne kilometres)	
All modes	153
Own account	43
Public haulage	110
By gross weight of vehicle (billion tonne kilometres)	
All vehicles	153
3.5–25 tonnes	17
Over 25 tonnes	136
GOODS LIFTED	
By mode of working (million tonnes)	
All modes	1,746
Own account	667
Public haulage	1,079
By gross weight of vehicle (million tonnes)	
All vehicles	1,746
3.5–25 tonnes	257
Over 25 tonnes	1,489

Source: Department for Transport

BUSES

Nearly all bus and coach services in Great Britain ar provided by private sector companies. The Transport Ac 2000 outlines a ten-year transport plan intended t promote bus use, through agreements between loca authorities and bus operators, and to improve the standar and efficiency of services. The ten-year plan sets targets fo bus patronage and reliability of services. There are number of ways in which the government supports bu services:

- Bus Service Operators Grant (BSOG) is paid directly t bus operators and reimburses the major part of th excise duty paid on the fuel used in operating locall registered bus services
- Rural Bus Subsidy Grant (RBSG) is paid to loca authorities with rural areas to fund socially necessar bus services that are not provided commercially
- Payments to local authorities to fund existing Rural an Urban Bus Challenge (RUBC) schemes aimed a providing innovative and flexible transport solutions such as taxi bus services, in public transport deprive rural and urban areas.

In 2007–8 planned expenditure by central governmen on BSOG is £405m and £67m on RBSG and RUB schemes.

Since April 2006 it has been a statutory minimum requirement for all local authorities to provide free loca bus travel between 9.30am and 11pm, and all day a weekends and bank holidays, to people aged 60 and ove and disabled people who qualify under the categorie listed in the Transport Act 2000. Local authoritie recompense operators for the reduced fare revenue.

In London, Transport for London (TfL) has overal responsibility for setting routes, service standards an fares for the bus network. Almost all routes ar competitively tendered to commercial operators.

In Northern Ireland, passenger transport services ar provided by Ulsterbus and Metro (formerly Citybus), tw wholly owned subsidiaries of the Northern Irelan Transport Holding Company. Along with Norther Ireland Railways, Ulsterbus and Metro operate under th brand name of Translink and are publicly owne Ulsterbus is responsible for virtually all bus services i Northern Ireland except Belfast city services, which ar operated by Metro.

JS PASSENGER JOURNEYS 2005–6 (GREAT BRITAIN)
o. of journeys (millions)

ngland	4,125
London	1,810
Vales	117
cotland	477
'OTAL	4,719

ource: Department for Transport

AXIS AND PRIVATE HIRE VEHICLES
taxi is a public transport vehicle with fewer than nine ssenger seats, which is licensed to 'ply for hire'. This stinguishes taxis from private hire vehicles which must booked in advance through an operator. In London, xis and private hire vehicles are licensed by the Public rriage Office (PCO), part of TfL. Outside of London, cal authorities are responsible for the licensing of taxis d private hire vehicles operational in their respective ministrative areas. At the end of March 2005 there were ,957 taxis and 79,305 licensed private hire vehicles in gland, of these, 20,750 taxis and 40,000 private hire hicles were licensed by the PCO in London.

OAD SAFETY
March 2000, the government published a new road fety strategy, *Tomorrow's Roads – Safer for Everyone,* ich set new casualty reduction targets for 2010. The w targets include a 40 per cent reduction in the overall mber of people killed or seriously injured in road cidents, a 50 per cent reduction in the number of children led or seriously injured and a 10 per cent reduction in slight casualty rate (per 100 million vehicle ometres), all compared with the average for 1994–8.

There were 258,404 reported casualties on roads in eat Britain in 2006, 5 per cent less than in 2005. Child sualties fell by 9 per cent with 169 child fatalities, an rease of 20 per cent compared to 2005 figures. Car er casualties decreased by 4 per cent on the 2005 level 171,000 and fatalities decreased by 4 per cent to 1,612 m 1,675. Pedestrian casualties were 30,982 in 2006, 7 r cent less than 2005, although pedestrian deaths were er cent higher compared to 2005 at 675. Compared to 05, pedal cyclist casualties fell by 2 per cent to 16,196 d the number of pedal cyclists killed on British roads creased by 1 per cent from 148 to 146.

OAD ACCIDENT CASUALTIES 2006

	Fatal	*Serious*	*Slight*	*All Severities*
erage for 1994–8	3,578	44,078	272,272	319,928
gland	2,695	24,856	201,026	228,577
les	163	1,210	11,319	12,692
otland	314	2,607	14,214	17,135
eat Britain	3,172	28,673	226,559	258,404

	Killed	*Injured*
65	7,952	389,985
70	7,499	355,869
75	6,366	318,584
80	6,010	323,000
85	5,165	312,359
90	5,217	335,924
95	3,621	306,885
00	3,409	316,872
05	3,201	267,816
06	3,172	255,232

rce: Department for Transport

DRIVING LICENCES
It is necessary to hold a valid full licence in order to drive unaccompanied on public roads in the UK. Learner drivers must obtain a provisional driving licence before starting to learn to drive and must then pass theory and practical tests to obtain a full driving licence.

There are separate tests for driving motorcycles, cars, passenger-carrying vehicles (PCVs) and large goods vehicles (LGVs). Drivers must hold full car entitlement before they can apply for PCV or LGV entitlements.

The Driver and Vehicle Licensing Agency (DVLA) ceased the issue of paper licences in March 2000, however, those currently in circulation will remain valid until they expire or the details on them change. The photocard driving licence was introduced to comply with the second EC directive on driving licences. This requires a photograph of the driver to be included on all UK licences issued from July 2001.

To apply for a first photocard driving licence, individuals are required to complete the form *Application for a Driving Licence* (D1).

The minimum age for driving motor cars, light goods vehicles up to 3.5 tonnes and motorcycles is 17 (moped, 16). Since June 1997, drivers who collect six or more penalty points within two years of qualifying lose their licence and are required to take another test. All forms and leaflets including *What You Need to Know About Driving Licences* (D100), are available from post offices, DVLA local offices and online (W www.dvla.gov.uk or W www.direct.gov.uk).

The DVLA is responsible for issuing driving licences, registering and licensing vehicles, and collecting excise duty in Great Britain. Driver and Vehicle Licensing Northern Ireland (DVLNI), part of the Driver and Vehicle Agency (DVA), has similar responsibilities in Northern Ireland.

DRIVING LICENCE FEES*
valid from February 2007 to March 2008

Provisional licence	
Car, motorcycle or moped	£45.00
Bus or lorry	Free
After disqualification until passing re-test	Free
Changing a provisional licence to a full licence	Free
Renewal	
At age 70 and over	Free
For medical reasons	Free
Bus or lorry licence	Free
After disqualification	£60.00
After disqualification for some drink driving offences†	£85.00
After revocation	£45.00
Replacing a lost or stolen licence	£22.00
Adding an entitlement to a full licence	Free
Removing expired endorsements	
from a photocard licence	£22.00
from a paper licence (while exchanging it for a photocard licence)	£10.00
Exchanging	
a paper licence for a photocard licence	£10.00
a photocard for a photocard licence	£22.00
a full GB licence for a full Northern Ireland licence	Free
a full GB licence for a full EC/EEA or other foreign licence (including Channel Islands and Isle of Man)	Free
a full EC/EEA or other foreign licence (including Channel Islands and Isle of Man) for a full GB licence	£45.00

Change of name or address (existing licence must be surrendered)	Free

* If the application involves two separate fees only the higher fee is payable
† For an alcohol-related offence where the DVLA needed to arrange medical enquiries

DRIVING TESTS

The Driving Standards Agency (DSA) is responsible for carrying out driving tests and approving driving instructors in Great Britain. Driver and Vehicle Testing, part of the Driver and Vehicle Agency, is responsible for testing drivers and vehicles in Northern Ireland.

DRIVING TESTS TAKEN AND PASSED

April 2006–March 2007

Type of Test	*Number Taken*	*Percentage Passed*
Practical Test		
Car	1,789,882	43
Motorcycle	77,007	65
Large goods vehicle	78,140	46
Passenger-carrying vehicle	9,922	46
Theory Test		
Car	1,306,335	68
Motorcycle	71,831	84
Large goods vehicle	41,725	75
Passenger-carrying vehicle	8,919	70

Source: DSA

The theory and practical driving tests can be booked with a postal application, online (W www.dsa.gov.uk or W www.direct.gov.uk) or by phone (T 0870-010 1372).

DRIVING TEST FEES (Weekday rate/evening* and weekend rate)

from September 2007

Theory tests	
Car and motorcycle	£28.50
Lorry and bus	£32.00
Practical tests:	
Car	£48.50/£58.00
Tractors and other specialist vehicles	£48.50/£58.00
Motorcycle	£60.00/£70.00
Lorry and bus	£89.00/£107.00
Car and trailer	£89.00/£107.00
Extended tests for disqualified drivers:	
Car	£97.00/£116.00
Motorcycle	£120.00/£140.00

* after 4.30pm

VEHICLE LICENCES

Registration and first licensing of vehicles is through local offices of the DVLA in Swansea. Local facilities for relicensing are available at any post office which deals with vehicle licensing. Applicants will need to take their vehicle registration document (V5C) or, if this is not available, the applicant must complete form V62. Postal applications can be made to the post offices shown in the V100 booklet, which also provides guidance on registering and licensing vehicles. All forms and booklets are available at post offices, DVLA local offices and online (W www.dvla.gov.uk or W www.direct.gov.uk)

MOTOR VEHICLES LICENSED 2006 (GREAT BRITAIN)

	Thousand
All cars	27,83
Taxis (black cabs only)	4
Motorcycles, mopeds and scooters	1,22
Buses and coaches	18
Light goods vehicles	3,05
Heavy goods vehicles	41
Other vehicles	61
TOTAL	33,36

Source: Department for Transport

VEHICLE EXCISE DUTY

Details of the present duties chargeable on motor vehicl are available at DVLA local offices, post offices and onli (W www.dvla.gov.uk or W www.direct.gov.uk). The Vehic Excise and Registration Act 1994 provides *inter alia* th any vehicle kept on a public road but not used on roads chargeable to excise duty as if it were in use. All no commercial vehicles constructed before 1 January 19 are exempt from vehicle excise duty. Any vehicle licens on or after 31 January 1998, not in use and not kept public roads must be registered as SORN (Statutory C Road Notification) to be exempted from vehicle exc duty. From 1 January 2004 the registered keeper of vehicle remains responsible for taxing a vehicle or maki a SORN declaration until that liability is forma transferred to a new keeper.

	12 months rate £	*6 montl rate*
Private/light goods vehicles registered before 1 March 200 (not over 3,500kg)		
Under 1,549cc	115.00	63.2
Over 1,549cc	180.00	99.0
Motorcycles (with or without sidecar)		
Not over 150cc	15.00	
151–400cc	32.00	
401–600cc	47.00	
600cc+	64.00	35.2
Tricycles		
Not over 150cc	15.00	
All others	64.00	35.2
Light goods vehicles (not over 3,500kg) registered on or after 1 March 2001	175.00	96.2
Euro 4 light goods vehicles registered between 1 March 2003 and 31 December 2006	115.00	63.2
*Buses**		
Seating 10–17 persons	165.00 (165.00)	90.75 (90.7
Seating 18–36 persons	220.00 (165.00)	121.00 (90.7
Seating 37–61 persons	330.00 (165.00)	181.50 (90.7
Seating 61+ persons	500.00 (165.00)	275.00 (90.7

* Figures in parentheses refer to reduced pollution vehicl
Seating capacity includes driver

ATES OF EXCISE DUTY *from March 2007*

3and	CO_2 Emissions (g/km)	Diesel Car 12 months	Diesel Car 6 months	Petrol Car 12 months	Petrol Car 6 months	Alternative Fuel Car 12 months	Alternative Fuel Car 6 months
'rivate vehicles registered on or after 1 March 2001							
A	Up to 100	£0.00	–	£0.00	–	£0.00	–
B	101–120	£35.00	–	£35.00	–	£15.00	–
C	121–150	£115.00	£63.25	£115.00	£63.25	£95.00	£52.25
D	151–165	£140.00	£77.00	£140.00	£77.00	£120.00	£66.00
E	166–185	£165.00	£90.75	£165.00	£90.75	£145.00	£79.75
F	186–225	£205.00	£112.75	£205.00	£112.75	£190.00	£104.50
'rivate vehicles registered on or after 23 March 2006							
G	225+	£300.00	£165.00	£300.00	£165.00	£285.00	£156.75

OT TESTING

ars, motorcycles, motor caravans, light goods and dual-urpose vehicles more than three years old must be overed by a current MOT test certificate. However, some hicles (ie minibuses, ambulances and taxis) may require certificate at one year old. All certificates must be newed annually. The MOT testing scheme is lministered by the Vehicle and Operator Services gency (VOSA) on behalf of the Secretary of State for ansport.

A fee is payable to MOT testing stations, which must be thorised to carry out tests. The maximum fees, which e prescribed by regulations as at 7 November 2006, are:

or cars and public service vehicles (up to eight seats), motor caravans, dual purpose, ambulances and taxis	£50.35	
or motorcycles	£27.15	
or motorcycles with sidecar	£34.65	
or three-wheeled vehicles	£34.65	
ivate passenger vehicles and ambulances with:		
9–12 passenger seats	£52.60	£58.75†
13–16 passenger seats	£54.65	£74.10†
16+ passenger seats	£73.95	£114.45†
oods vehicles (3,000–3,500kg)	£53.80	

Including seatbelt installation check

HIPPING AND PORTS

a trade has always played a central role in Britain's onomy. By the 17th century Britain had built up a bstantial merchant fleet and by the early 20th century it ominated the world shipping industry. Until the late 90s the size and tonnage of the UK-registered trading et had been steadily declining. In December 1998 the vernment published *British Shipping: Charting a New ourse,* which outlined strategies to promote the long-rm interests of British shipping. By the end of 2006 the mber of ships in the UK fleet had increased by 66 per nt whilst tonnage had more than tripled. The UK-gged merchant fleet now constitutes 1.3 per cent of the orld fleet in terms of vessels and 1.7 per cent in terms of nnage.

Freight is carried by liner and bulk services, almost all heduled liner services being containerised. About 95 r cent by weight of Britain's overseas trade is carried by a; this amounts to 75 per cent of its total value. ssengers and vehicles are carried by roll-on, roll-off rries, hovercraft, hydrofoils and high-speed catamarans. There were about 45 million ferry passengers in 2006, of whom 23 million travelled internationally.

Lloyd's of London provides the most comprehensive shipping intelligence service in the world. *Lloyd's Shipping Index,* published daily, lists some 25,000 ocean-going vessels and gives the latest known report of each.

PORTS

There are more than 650 ports in Great Britain for which statutory harbour powers have been granted. Of these about 120 are commercially significant ports. In 2006* the largest ports in terms of freight tonnage were Grimsby and Immingham (64.0 million tonnes), Tees and Hartlepool (53.3 million tonnes), London (51.9 million tonnes), Southampton (40.5 million tonnes), Milford Haven (34.3 million tonnes), Liverpool (33.6 million tonnes), Forth (31.1 million tonnes), Felixstowe (24.4 million tonnes), Dover (23.8 million tonnes) and Sullom Voe (19.4 million tonnes). Belfast is the principal freight port in Northern Ireland.

Broadly speaking, ports are owned and operated by private companies, local authorities or trusts. The largest operator is Associated British Ports which owns 21 ports. Provisional port traffic results show that 580 million tonnes were handled by UK ports in 2006, an decrease of 1.0 per cent on the previous year's figure of 585 million tonnes.

* Provisional data

MARINE SAFETY

The Maritime and Coastguard Agency is an executive agency of the Department for Transport. Working closely with the shipping industry and the public its aims are to:

- reduce accidents and accident related deaths within UK search and rescue waters and coastline
- reduce accidents and accident related deaths from UK registered merchant ships and fishing vessels
- reduce the number of incidents of pollution from shipping activities in the UK pollution control zone

HM Coastguard maintains a 24-hour search and rescue response and coordination capability for the whole of the UK coast and the internationally agreed search and rescue region. HM Coastguard is responsible for mobilising and organising resources in response to people in distress at sea, or at risk of injury or death on the UK's cliffs or shoreline. There are around 500 coastguards and a further 3,000 voluntary auxiliary coastguards that form over 400 local coastguard rescue teams. In 2006 HM Coastguard rescued 4,809 people whose life was at risk and gave assistance to a further 23,113 people whose life was not at risk. Of the total number of 371 deaths recorded by the coastguard, 124 resulted from maritime accidents.

Locations hazardous to shipping in coastal waters are marked by lighthouses and other lights and buoys. The lighthouse authorities are the Corporation of Trinity House (for England, Wales and the Channel Islands), the Northern Lighthouse Board (for Scotland and the Isle of Man), and the Commissioners of Irish Lights (for Northern Ireland and the Republic of Ireland). Trinity House maintains 72 lighthouses, 10 light vessels/floats, 412 buoys, 19 beacons, 48 radar beacons and seven DGPS (Differential Global Positioning System) stations*. The Northern Lighthouse Board maintains 215 lighthouses, 157 buoys, 40 beacons, 26 radar beacons, four DGPS stations and one LORAN (long-range navigation) station; and Irish Lights looks after 80 lighthouses, 149 buoys, 47 beacons, 22 radar beacons, three DGPS stations, two LANBYs (large automatic navigational buoys) and one light float.

Harbour authorities are responsible for pilotage within their harbour areas; and the Ports Act 1991 provides for the transfer of lights and buoys to harbour authorities where these are used for mainly local navigation.

* DGPS is a satellite-based navigation system

UK-OWNED TRADING VESSELS
100 gross tons and over, as at end 2005

Type of vessel	*No.*	*Gross tonnage*
Liquid	169	4,147,000
Dry bulk	60	2,753,000
Specialised carrier	19	263,000
Container	75	3,297
Ro-Ro	137	1,413
Other general cargo	179	920,000
Passenger	49	926,000
All trading vessels	688	13,719
of which registered in the UK	382	5,739

Source: Department for Transport

UK SEA PASSENGER MOVEMENTS 2006

Type of journey	*No. of passenger movements**
International†	23,465,000
Domestic	3,476,000

* Passengers are included at both departure and arrival if their journeys begin and end at a UK seaport

† Routes to Belgium, Denmark, Faroe Islands, Finland, France, Germany, Ireland, the Netherlands, Norway, Spain and Sweden

Source: Department for Transport

MARINECALL WEATHER FORECAST SERVICE

Marinecall offers a wide range of inshore, offshore ar European forecasts from the Met Office which incluc gale and strong wind warnings, the general situatio wind speed and direction, probability and strength gusts, developing weather conditions, visibility and se state. Information is provided by various means includin telephone, fax, SMS etc. Marinecall 10-day forecas contain a 48-hour inshore/offshore sea area summar followed by a 1–5 day forecast for the local sea area, 6–1 day national forecast and an outlook for the month ahea In addition fax forecasts provide a synopic chart. Oth services such as area specific, current weather reports an 6-hour forecasts are also available.

MARINECALL 10-DAY FORECAST

	By Phone	By Fa
INSHORE AREA	09068-500+	09065-30C
Cape Wrath – Rattray Head	451	25
Rattray Head – Berwick	452	25
Berwick – Whitby	453	25
Whitby – Gibraltar Point	454	25
Gibraltar Point – North Foreland	455	25
North Foreland – Selsey Bill	456	25
Selsey Bill – Lyme Regis	457	25
Lyme Regis – Hartland Point	458	25
Hartland Point – St David's Head	459	25
St David's Head – Great Ormes Head	460	26
Great Ormes Head – Mull of Galloway	461	26
Mull of Galloway – Mull of Kintyre	462	26
Mull of Kintyre – Ardnamurchan	463	26
Ardnamurchan – Cape Wrath	464	26
Lough Foyle – Carlingford Lough	465	26
Channel Islands	432	
OFFSHORE AREA		
English Channel	992	27
Southern North Sea	991	27
Irish Sea	954	27
Biscay	953	27
North-west Scotland	955	27
Northern North Sea	985	27

Marinecall by UK landline is charged at 60p per minu and Marinecall by fax at £1.50 per minute. Calls fro mobiles may be subject to network operator surcharges.

UK SHIPPING FORECAST AREAS

Weather bulletins for shipping are broadcast daily on BBC Radio 4 at the following times: 0048 and 0520, 1201 and 1754 on long wave at 1515m (198kHz). The bulletins consist of a gale warning summary, general synopsis, sea-area forecasts and coastal station reports. In addition, gale warnings are broadcast at the first available programme break after receipt. If this does not coincide with a news bulletin, the warning is repeated after the next news bulletin. Shipping forecasts and gale warnings are also available online (W www.bbc.co.uk/weather/coast/shipping).

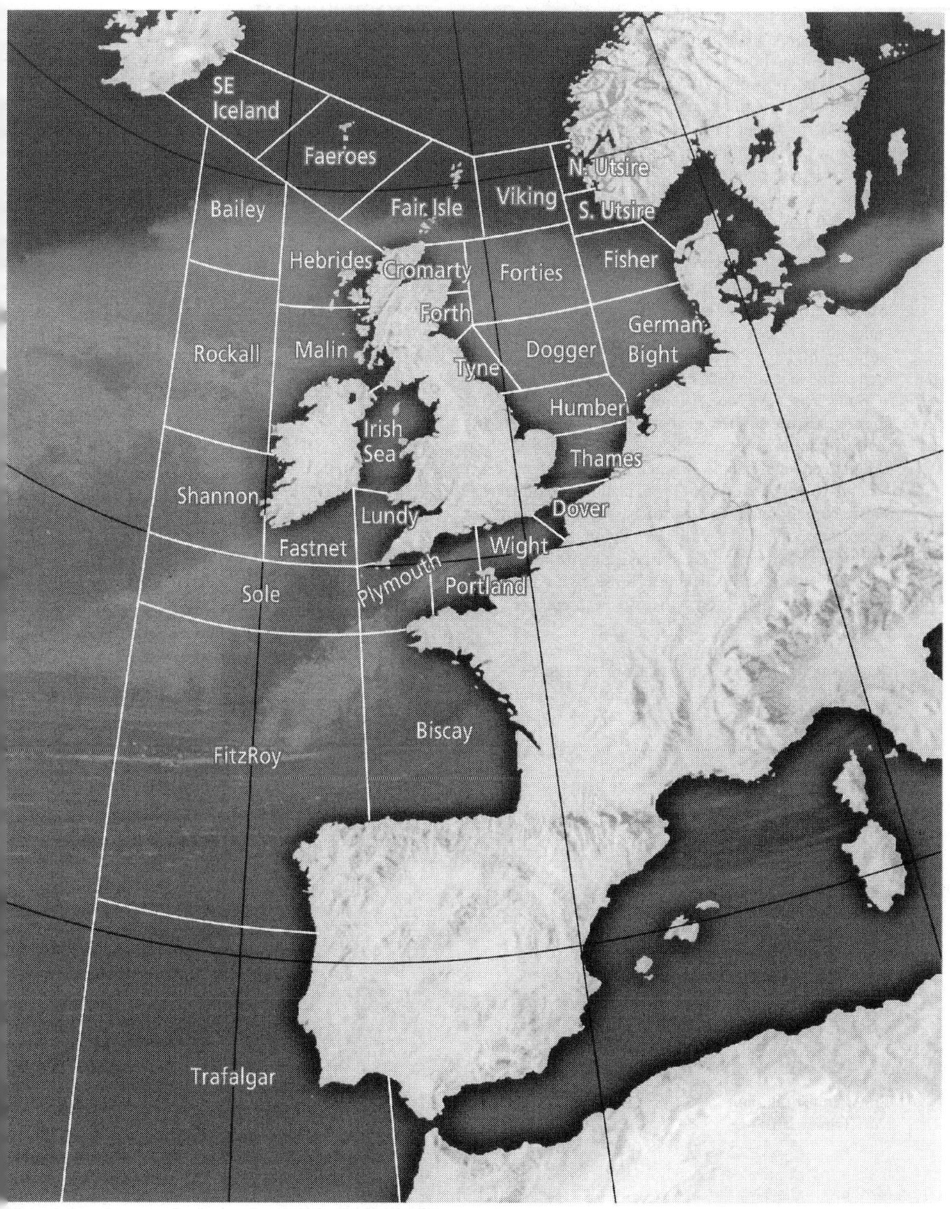

RELIGION IN THE UK

The 2001 census included a voluntary question on religion for the first time (although the question had been included in previous censuses in Northern Ireland); 92 per cent of people chose to answer the question. In the UK, 71.6 per cent of people in Britain identified themselves as Christian (42.1 million people). After Christianity, the next most prevalent faith was Islam with 2.7 per cent describing their religion as Muslim (1.6 million people). The next largest religious groups were Hindus (559,000), followed by Sikhs (336,000), Jews (267,000), Buddhists (152,000) and people from other religions (179,000). Together, these groups accounted for less than 3 per cent of the total UK population. People in Northern Ireland were most likely to say that they identified with a religion (86 per cent) compared with 77 per cent in England and Wales and 67 per cent in Scotland. The English counties with the highest proportion of Christians are Durham, Merseyside and Cumbria, each with 82 per cent or more; in Wales it is Ynys Mon (Isle of Anglesey) (79 per cent). London has the highest proportion of Muslims (8.5 per cent), Hindus (4.1 per cent), Jews (2.1 per cent), Buddhists (0.8 per cent) and people of other religions (0.5 per cent). Around 16 per cent of the UK population stated that they had no religion. The districts with the highest proportions of people with no religion were Norwich, Brighton and Hove and Cambridge, all with over 25 per cent. This category included those who identified themselves as agnostics, atheists, heathens and Jedi Knights.

CENSUS 2001 RESULTS – RELIGIONS IN THE UK

	thousand	*per cent*
Christian	42,079	71.6
Buddhist	152	0.3
Hindu	559	1.0
Jewish	267	0.5
Muslim	1,591	2.7
Sikh	336	0.6
Other religion	179	0.3
All religions	45,163	76.8
No religion	9,104	15.5
Not stated	4,289	7.3
All no religion/not stated	13,626	23.2
TOTAL	58,789	100

Source: Census 2001

ADHERENTS TO RELIGIONS IN THE UK
(million people)

	1975	*1985*	*1995*	*2000*
Christian (Trinitarian)	40.2	39.1	38.1	37.5
Non-Trinitarian	0.7	1.0	1.3	1.3
Hindu	0.3	0.4	0.4	0.5
Jew	0.4	0.3	0.3	0.3
Muslim	0.4	0.9	1.2	1.4
Sikh	0.2	0.3	0.6	0.6
Other	0.1	0.3	0.3	0.4
Total	42.3	42.3	42.2	42.0

Source: Christian Research – *UK Christian Handbook Religious Trends 3*

INTER-CHURCH AND INTER-FAITH COOPERATION

The main umbrella body for the Christian churches in the UK is Churches Together in Britain and Ireland. There are also ecumenical bodies in each of the constituen countries of the UK: Churches Together in England, Action of Churches Together in Scotland, CYTUN (Churches Together in Wales), and the Irish Counci of Churches. The Free Churches Group (formerly the Free Churches Council), which is closely associated wit Churches Together in England, represents most of the free churches in England and Wales, and the Evangelica Alliance represents evangelical Christians.

The Inter Faith Network for the United Kingdom promotes cooperation between faiths, and the Council o Christians and Jews works to improve relations between the two religions. Churches Together in Britain and Ireland also has a commission on inter faith relations.

ACTION OF CHURCHES TOGETHER IN SCOTLAND, 7 Forrester Lodge, Inglewood, Alloa FK10 2HU **T** 01259-216980 **E** ecumenical@acts-scotland.org **W** www.acts-scotland.org
General Secretary, Brother Stephen Smyth

CHURCHES TOGETHER IN BRITAIN AND IRELAND, Bastille Court, 2 Paris Garden, London SE1 8ND **T** 020-7654 7254 **E** info@ctbi.org.uk **W** www.ctbi.org.uk
General Secretary, Revd Bob Fyffe

CHURCHES TOGETHER IN ENGLAND, 27 Tavistock Square, London WC1H 9HH **T** 020-7529 8131 **E** office@cte.org.uk **W** www.churches-together.org.uk
General Secretary, Revd Bill Snelson

COUNCIL OF CHRISTIANS AND JEWS, 1st Floor, Camelford House, 87–89 Albert Embankment, London SE1 7TP **T** 020-7820 0090 **E** cjrelations@ccj.org.uk **W** www.ccj.org.uk
Chief Executive, David Gifford

CYTUN (CHURCHES TOGETHER IN WALES), 58 Richmond Road, Cardiff CF24 3UR **T** 029-2046 4204 **E** post@cytun.org.uk **W** www.cytun.org.uk
Chief Executive, Revd Aled Edwards

EVANGELICAL ALLIANCE, 186 Kennington Park Road, London SE11 4BT **T** 020-7207 2100 **E** info@eauk.org **W** www.eauk.org
General Director, Revd Joel Edwards

FREE CHURCHES GROUP, 27 Tavistock Square, London WC1H 9HH **T** 020-7529 8131 **E** freechurch@cte.org.uk
Executive Secretary, Revd Mark Fisher

INTER-FAITH NETWORK FOR THE UNITED KINGDOM, 8A Lower Grosvenor Place, London SW1W 0EN **T** 020-7931 7766 **E** ifnet@interfaith.org.uk **W** www.interfaith.org.uk
Director, Dr Harriet Crabtree

IRISH COUNCIL OF CHURCHES, Inter-Church Centre, 48 Elmwood Avenue, Belfast BT9 6AZ **T** 028-9066 3145 **E** irish.churches@btconnect.com **W** www.irishchurches.org
General Secretary, Michael Earle

:HRISTIANITY

:hristianity is a monotheistic faith based on the person nd teachings of Jesus Christ, and all Christian enominations claim his authority. Central to its teaching the concept of God and his son Jesus Christ, who was rucified and resurrected in order to enable mankind to ttain salvation.

The Jewish scriptures predicted the coming of a *Aessiah,* an 'anointed one', who would bring salvation. To :hristians, Jesus of Nazareth, a Jewish rabbi (teacher) who vas born in Palestine, was the promised Messiah. Jesus' irth, teachings, crucifixion and subsequent resurrection re recorded in the *Gospels,* which, together with other criptures that summarise Christian belief, form the *New 'estament.* This, together with the Hebrew scriptures – ntitled the *Old Testament* by Christians – makes up the ible, the sacred texts of Christianity.

BELIEFS

:hristians believe that sin distanced mankind from God, nd that Jesus was the son of God, sent to redeem nankind from sin by his death. In addition, many believe hat Jesus will return again at some future date, triumph ver evil and establish a kingdom on earth, thus naugurating a new age. The Gospel assures Christians hat those who believe in Jesus and obey his teachings vill be forgiven their sins and will be resurrected from the ead.

PRACTICES

:hristian practices vary widely between different :hristian churches, but prayer, charity and giving (for the naintenance of the church buildings, for the work of the hurch, and to the poor and needy) are common to all. In ddition, certain days of observance, ie the *Sabbath, Easter* nd *Christmas,* are celebrated by most Christians. The)rthodox, Roman Catholic and Anglican churches elebrate many more days of observance, based on saints nd significant events in the life of Jesus. The belief in acraments, physical signs believed to have been rdained by Jesus Christ to symbolise and convey piritual gifts, varies greatly between Christian lenominations; *baptism* and the *Eucharist* are practised y most Christians. Baptism, symbolising repentance nd faith in Jesus, is an act marking entry into the :hristian community; the Eucharist, the ritual re-enactment of the Last Supper, Jesus' final meal with his lisciples, is also practised by most denominations. Other acraments, such as anointing the sick; the laying on of nands to symbolise the passing on of the office of riesthood or to heal the sick and speaking in tongues, vhere it is believed that the person is possessed by the Holy Spirit, are less common. In denominations where nfant baptism is practised, confirmation (where the erson repeats the commitments made for him or her at nfancy) is common. Matrimony and the ordination of riests are also widely believed to be sacraments. Many Protestants regard only baptism and the Eucharist to be acraments; the Quakers and the Salvation Army reject he use of sacraments.

Most Christians believe that God actively guides the :hurch.

THE EARLY CHURCH

The Apostles were Jesus' first converts and are recognised by Christians as the founders of the Christian community. The new faith spread rapidly throughout the eastern provinces of the Roman Empire. Early Christianity was subjected to great persecution until AD 313, when Emperor Constantine's Edict of Toleration confirmed its right to exist and it was established as the religion of the Roman Empire in AD 381.

The Christian faith was slowly formulated in the first millennium of the Christian era. Between AD 325 and 787 there were seven Oecumenical Councils at which bishops from the entire Christian world assembled to resolve various doctrinal disputes. The estrangement between East and West began after Constantine moved the centre of the Roman Empire from Rome to Constantinople, and it grew after the division of the Roman Empire into eastern and western halves. Linguistic and cultural differences between Greek East and Latin West served to encourage separate ecclesiastical developments which became pronounced in the tenth and early 11th centuries.

Administration of the church was divided between five ancient patriarchates: Rome and all the West, Constantinople (the imperial city – the 'New Rome'), Jerusalem and all of Palestine, Antioch and all the East and Alexandria and all of Africa. Of these, only Rome was in the Latin West and after the schism in 1054, Rome developed a structure of authority centralised on the Papacy, while the Orthodox East maintained the style of localised administration.

Papal authority over the doctrine and jurisdiction of the church in Western Europe was unrivalled after the split with the Eastern Orthodox Church until the Protestant Reformation in the 16th century.

CHRISTIANITY IN BRITAIN

An English church already existed when Pope Gregory sent Augustine to evangelise the English in AD 596. Conflicts between Church and State during the Middle Ages culminated in the Act of Supremacy in 1534, which repudiated papal supremacy and declared King Henry VIII to be the supreme head of the church in England. Since 1559 the English monarch has been termed the Supreme Governor of the Church of England.

In 1560 the jurisdiction of the Roman Catholic Church in Scotland was abolished and the first assembly of the Church of Scotland ratified the Confession of Faith, drawn up by a committee led by John Knox. In 1592 parliament passed an act guaranteeing the liberties of the church and its Presbyterian government. King James VI (James I of England) and later Stuart monarchs attempted to reintroduce episcopacy, but a Presbyterian church was finally restored in 1690 and secured by the Act of Settlement (1690) and the Act of Union (1707).

PORVOO DECLARATION

The Porvoo Declaration was drawn up by representatives of the British and Irish Anglican churches and the Nordic and Baltic Lutheran churches and was approved by the General Synod of the Church of England in July 1995. Churches that approve the declaration regard baptised members of each other's churches as members of their own, and allow free interchange of episcopally ordained ministers within the rules of each church.

NON-CHRISTIAN RELIGIONS AND BELIEFS

BAHA'I FAITH

Mirza Husayn-'Ali, known as *Baha'u'llah* (Glory of God) was born in Iran in 1817 and became a follower of the *Bab,* a religious reformer and prophet who was imprisoned for his beliefs and executed on the grounds of heresy in 1850. Baha'u'llah was himself imprisoned in 1852, and in 1853 he had a vision that he was the 'promised one' foretold by the Bab. He was exiled after his release from prison and eventually arrived in Acre, now in Israel, where he continued to compose the Baha'i sacred scriptures. He died in 1892 and was succeeded by his son, Abdu'l-Baha, as spiritual leader, under whose guidance the faith spread to Europe and North America. He was followed by Shoghi Effendi, his grandson, who translated many of Baha'u'llah's works into English. Upon his death in 1957, a democratic system of leadership was brought into operation.

The Baha'i faith espouses the unity and relativity of religious truth and teaches that there is only one God, whose will has been revealed to mankind by a series of messengers, such as Zoroaster, Abraham, Moses, Buddha, Krishna, Christ, Muhammad, the Bab and Baha'u'llah, who were seen as the founders of separate religions, but whose common purpose was to bring God's message to mankind. It teaches that all races and both sexes are equal and deserving of equal opportunities and treatment, that education is a fundamental right and encourages a fair distribution of wealth. In addition, the faith exhorts mankind to establish a world federal system to promote peace and tolerance.

A feast is held every 19 days, which consists of prayer and readings of Baha'i scriptures, consultation on community business, and social activities. Music, food and beverages usually accompany the proceedings. There is no clergy; each local community elects a local assembly, which coordinates community activities, enrols new members, counsels and assists members in need, and conducts Baha'i marriages and funerals. A national assembly is elected annually by locally elected delegates, and every five years the national spiritual assemblies meet together to elect the Universal House of Justice, the supreme international governing body of the Baha'i Faith. Worldwide there are over 13,000 local spiritual assemblies; there are around five million members residing in about 235 countries, of which 179 have national organisations.

THE BAHA'I OFFICE OF PUBLIC INFORMATION, 27 Rutland Gate, London SW7 1PD **T** 020-7584 2566 **E** nsa@bahai.org.uk **W** www.bahai.org.uk
Secretary of the National Spiritual Assembly, Dr Kishan Manocha
Secretary for External Affairs, Robert Weinberg

BUDDHISM

Buddhism originated in what is now the Bihar area of northern India in the teachings of Siddhartha Gautama, who became the *Buddha* (Enlightened One). The Buddhist era is dated from his passing away 45 years after his enlightenment; the year 2008 is 2551 by the Buddhist reckoning.

Fundamental to Buddhism is the concept of rebirth, whereby each life carries with it the consequences of the conduct of earlier lives (known as the law of *karma*) and this cycle of death and rebirth is broken only when the state of *nirvana* has been reached. Buddhism steers middle path between belief in personal continuity and the belief that death results in total extinction.

While doctrine does not have a pivotal position in Buddhism, a statement of four 'Noble Truths' is common to all its schools and varieties. These are: suffering is inescapable in even the most fortunate of existences; craving is the root cause of suffering; abandonment of the selfish mindset is the way to end suffering; and bodily and mental discipline, accompanied by the cultivation of wisdom and compassion, provides the spiritual path ('Noble Eightfold Path') to accomplish this. Buddhists deny the idea of a creator and prefer to emphasise the practical aspects of moral and spiritual development.

The schools of Buddhism can be broadly divided into three: *Theravada,* the generally monastic-led tradition practised in Sri Lanka and south-east Asia; *Mahayana,* the philosophical and popular traditions of the Far East; and *Esoteric,* the Tantric-derived traditions found in Tibet and Mongolia and, to a lesser extent, China and Japan. The extensive Theravada scriptures are contained in the *Pali Canon,* which dates in its written form from the first century BC. Mahayana and Esoteric schools have Sanskrit-derived translations of these plus many more additional scriptures as well as exegetical material.

In the East the new and full moons and the lunar quarter days were (and to a certain extent, still are) significant in determining the religious calendar. Most private homes contain a shrine where offerings, worship and other spiritual practices (such as meditation, chanting or mantra recitation) take place on a daily basis. Buddhist festivals vary according to local traditions within the different schools and there is very little uniformity – even in commemorating the birth, enlightenment and death of the Buddha.

There is no governing authority for Buddhism in the UK. Communities representing all schools of Buddhism operate independently. The Buddhist Society was established in 1924; it runs courses, lectures and meditation groups, and publishes books about Buddhism. The Network of Buddhist Organisations was founded in 1993 to promote fellowship and dialogue between Buddhist organisations and to facilitate cooperation in matters of common interest.

There are estimated to be at least 300 million Buddhists worldwide. Of the 152,000 Buddhists in the UK (according to the 2001 census), 60,000 are white British (the majority are converts), 36,000 Chinese, 15,000 Asian and 36,000 'other ethnic'.

THE BUDDHIST SOCIETY, 58 Eccleston Square, London SW1V 1PH **T** 020-7834 5858 **E** info@thebuddhistsociety.org **W** www.thebuddhistsociety.org

FRIENDS OF THE WESTERN BUDDHIST ORDER, The London Buddhist Centre, 51 Roman Road, London E2 0HU **T** 0845-458 4716 **E** info@lbc.org.uk **W** www.lbc.org.uk

THE NETWORK OF BUDDHIST ORGANISATIONS, 6 Tyne Road, Bishopston, Bristol BS7 8EE **T** 0845-345 8978 **E** secretary@nbo.org.uk **W** www.nbo.org.uk

TIBET HOUSE TRUST, Tibet House, 1 Culworth Street, London NW8 7AF **T** 020-7722 5378 **E** secretary@tibet-house-trust.co.uk **W** www.tibet-house-trust.co.uk

SOKA GAKKAI UK, Taplow Court Grand Cultural Centre, Taplow, Maidenhead, Berkshire SL6 0ER **T** 01628-773163 **W** www.sgi-uk.org

HINDUISM

Hinduism has no historical founder but had become highly developed in India by *c.*2500 BC. Its adherents originally called themselves Aryans; Muslim invaders first called the Aryans 'Hindus' (derived from 'Sindhu', the name of the river Indus) in the eighth century.

Most Hindus hold that *satya* (truthfulness), honesty, sincerity and devotion to God are essential for good living. They believe in one supreme spirit *(Brahman),* and in the transmigration of *atman* (the soul). Most Hindus accept the doctrine of *karma* (consequences of actions), the concept of *samsara* (successive lives) and the possibility of all atmans achieving *moksha* (liberation from samsara) through *jnana* (knowledge), *yoga* (meditation), *karma* (work or action) and *bhakti* (devotion).

Most Hindus offer worship to *murtis* (images of deities) representing different incarnations or aspects of Brahman, and follow their *dharma* (religious and social duty) according to the traditions of their *varna* (social class), *ashrama* (stage in life), *jaiti* (caste) and *kula* (family).

Hinduism's sacred texts are divided into *shruti* ('that which is heard'), including the *Vedas,* and *smriti* ('that which is remembered'), including the *Ramayana,* the *Mahabharata,* the *Puranas* (ancient myths), and the sacred law books. Most Hindus recognise the authority of the *Vedas,* the oldest holy books, and accept the philosophical teachings of the *Upanishads,* the *Vedanta Sutras* and the *Bhagavad-Gita.*

Hindus believe Brahman to be omniscient, omnipotent, limitless and all-pervading. Brahman is usually worshipped in its deity form. Brahma, Vishnu and Shiva are the most important deities or aspects of Brahman worshipped by Hindus; their respective consorts are Saraswati, Lakshmi and Durga or Parvati, also known as Shakti. There are believed to have been ten *avatars* (incarnations) of Vishnu, of whom the most important are Rama and Krishna. Other popular gods are Ganesha, Hanuman and Subrahmanyam. All Hindu gods are seen as aspects of the supreme spirit (Brahman), not as competing deities.

Orthodox Hindus revere all gods and goddesses equally, but there are many denominations, including the Hare-Krishna movement (ISKCon), the Arya Samaj and the Swaminarayan Hindu mission, in which worship is concentrated on one deity. The *guru* (spiritual teacher) is seen as the source of spiritual guidance.

Hinduism does not have a centrally trained and ordained priesthood. The pronouncements of the *shankaracharyas* (heads of monasteries) of Shringeri, Puri, Dwarka and Badrinath are heeded by the orthodox but may be ignored by the various sects.

The commonest form of worship is *puja,* in which water, flowers, food, fruit, incense and light are offered to the deity. Puja may be done either in a home shrine or a *mandir* (temple). Many British Hindus celebrate *samskars* (purification rites), for example to name a baby, the sacred thread (an initiation ceremony), marriage and cremation.

The largest communities of Hindus in Britain are in Leicester, London, Birmingham and Bradford, and developed as a result of immigration from India, eastern Africa and Sri Lanka.

There are an estimated 800 million Hindus worldwide; there are around 559,000 adherents, according to the 2001 UK census, and over 140 temples in the UK.

ARYA SAMAJ LONDON, 69A Argyle Road, London W13 0LY T 020-8991 1732
E aryasamajlondon@yahoo.co.uk
General Secretary, Amrit Lal Bhardwaj

BHARATIYA VIDYA BHAVAN, Institute of Indian Art and Culture, 4A Castletown Road, London W14 9HE
T 020-7381 3086 E info@bhavan.net W www.bhavan.net
Executive Director, Dr M. N. Nandakumara

INTERNATIONAL SOCIETY FOR KRISHNA CONSCIOUSNESS (ISKCON), Bhaktivedanta Manor, Dharam Marg, Hilfield Lane, Aldenham, Watford, Herts WD25 8EZ T 01923-857244
E bhaktivendanta.manor@pamho.net
W www.krishnatemple.com
Temple President, Gauri das

NATIONAL COUNCIL OF HINDU TEMPLES (UK), Shree Sanatan Mandir, 84 Weymoth Street, Leicester LE4 6FQ T 0116-266 1402 E info@nchtuk.org
W www.nchtuk.org
General Secretary, Sanjay Jagatia

SWAMINARAYAN HINDU MISSION (SHRI SWAMINARAYAN MANDIR), 105–119 Brentfield Road, London NW10 8LD T 020-8965 2651
E info@mandir.org W www.mandir.org

HUMANISM

Humanism traces its roots back to ancient times, with Indian, Chinese, Greek and Roman philosophers expressing Humanist ideas some 2,500 years ago. Confucius, the Chinese philosopher who lived *c.*500 BC, believed that religious observances should be replaced with moral values as the basis of social and political order and that 'the true way' is based on reason and humanity. He also stressed the importance of benevolence and respect for others, and believed that the individual situation should be considered rather than the global application of traditional rules.

Humanists believe that there is no God or other supernatural being, that humans have only one life (Humanists do not believe in an after-life or reincarnation) and that humans can live ethical and fulfilling lives without religious beliefs through a moral code derived from a shared history, personal experience and thought. There are no sacred Humanist texts. Particular emphasis is placed on science as the only reliable source of knowledge of the universe. Many Humanists recognise a need for ceremonies to mark important occasions in life and the British Humanist Association has a network of officiants and celebrants who are trained and accredited to conduct baby namings, weddings and funerals. The British Humanist Association's campaigns for a secular society (a society based on freedom of religious or non-religious belief with no privileges for any particular set of beliefs) are based on equality and human rights, and the association also campaigns for inclusive schools that meet the needs of all parents and pupils, regardless of their religious or non-religious beliefs.

BRITISH HUMANIST ASSOCIATION, 1 Gower Street, London WC1E 6HD T 020-7079 3580 F 020-7079 3588
E info@humanism.org.uk W www.humanism.org.uk
Chief Executive, Hanne Stinson

ISLAM

Islam (which means 'peace arising from submission to the will of Allah' in Arabic) is a monotheistic religion which was taught in Arabia by the Prophet Muhammad, who was born in Mecca (Al-Makkah) in 570 AD. Islam spread to Egypt, north Africa, Spain and the borders of China in the century following the Prophet's death, and is now the predominant religion in Indonesia, the near and Middle East, northern and parts of western Africa, Pakistan, Bangladesh, Malaysia and some of the former Soviet republics. There are also large Muslim communities in other countries.

For Muslims (adherents of Islam), there is one God *(Allah)*, who holds absolute power. Muslims believe that Allah's commands were revealed to mankind through the prophets, who include Abraham, Moses and Jesus, but that Allah's message was gradually corrupted until revealed finally and in perfect form to Muhammad through the angel *Jibril* (Gabriel) over a period of 23 years. This last, incorruptible message is said to have been recorded in the *Qur'an* (Koran), which contains 114 divisions called *surahs*, each made up of *ayahs* of various lengths, and is held to be the essence of all previous scriptures. The *Ahadith* are the records of the Prophet Muhammad's deeds and sayings (the *Sunnah*) as practised and recounted by his immediate followers. A culture and a system of law and theology gradually developed to form a distinctive Islamic civilisation. Islam makes no distinction between sacred and worldly affairs and provides rules for every aspect of human life. The *Shariah* is the sacred law of Islam based primarily upon prescriptions derived from the *Qur'an* and the *Sunnah* of the Prophet.

The 'five pillars of Islam' are *shahadah* (a declaration of faith in the oneness and supremacy of Allah and the messengership of Muhammad); *salat* (formal prayer, to be performed five times a day facing the *Ka'bah* (the most sacred shrine in the holy city of Mecca)); *zakat* (welfare due, paid annually on all savings at the rate of 2.5 per cent); *sawm* (fasting during the month of Ramadan from dawn until sunset); and *hajj* (pilgrimage to Mecca made once in a lifetime if the believer is financially and physically able). Some Muslims would add *jihad* as the sixth pillar (striving for the cause of good and resistance to evil).

Two main groups developed among Muslims. *Sunni* Muslims accept the legitimacy of Muhammad's first four *caliphs* (successors as head of the Muslim community) and of the authority of the Muslim community as a whole. About 90 per cent of Muslims are Sunni Muslims.

Shi'ites recognise only Muhammad's son-in-law Ali as his rightful successor and the *Imams* (descendants of Ali, not to be confused with *imams*, who are prayer leaders or religious teachers) as the principal legitimate religious authority. The largest group within Shi'ism is *Twelver Shi'ism*, which has been the official school of law and theology in Iran since the 16th century; other subsects include the *Ismailis*, the *Druze* and the *Alawis*, the latter two differing considerably from the main body of Muslims. The *Ibadis* of Oman are neither Sunni nor Shia, deriving from the strictly observant *Khariji* (Seceeders). There is no organised priesthood, but learned men such as imams, *ulama*, and *ayatollahs* are accorded great respect. The *Sufis* are the mystics of Islam. Mosques are centres for worship and teaching and also for social and welfare activities.

Islam was first recorded in western Europe in the eighth century AD when 800 years of Muslim rule began in Spain. Later, Islam spread to eastern Europe. More recently, Muslims came to Europe from Africa, the Middle East and Asia in the late 19th century. Both the Sunni and Shi'a traditions are represented in Britain, but the majority of Muslims in Britain adhere to Sunni Islam. Efforts to establish a representative national body for Muslims in Britain resulted in the founding, in 1997, of the Muslim Council of Britain. In addition, there are many other Muslim organisations in the UK. There are around 1,200 million Muslims worldwide, with nearly two million adherents and about 1,632 mosques in the UK.

IMAMS AND MOSQUES COUNCIL, 20–22 Creffield Road, London W5 3RP **T** 020-8992 6636
E msraza@muslimcollege.ac.uk
Executive Secretary, Moulana M. S. Raza

ISLAMIC CULTURAL CENTRE – THE LONDON CENTRAL MOSQUE, 146 Park Road, London NW8 7RG
T 020-7724 3363 **E** info@iccuk.org **W** www.iccuk.org
Director, Dr Ahmad Al-Dubayan

MUSLIM COUNCIL OF BRITAIN, PO Box 57330, London E1 2WJ **T** 0845-262 6786 **E** admin@mcb.org.uk
W www.mcb.org.uk
Secretary-General, Dr Muhammad Abdul Bari

MUSLIM WORLD LEAGUE LONDON, 46 Goodge Street, London W1T 4LU **T** 020-7636 7568
Director, Abdul Aziz al-Harbi

UNION OF MUSLIM ORGANISATIONS OF THE UK AND EIRE, 109 Campden Hill Road, London W8 7TL
T 020-7221 6608
Secretary-General, Dr Syed A. Pasha

JAINISM

Jainism traces its history to Vardhamana Jnatriputra, known as *Tirthankara Mahavira* (The Great Hero) whose traditional dates were 599–527 BC. He was the last of a series of 24 *Jinas* (those who overcome all passions and desires) or *Tirthankaras* (those who show a way across the ocean of life) stretching back to remote antiquity. Born to a noble family in north-eastern India, he renounced the world for the life of a wandering ascetic and after 12 years of austerity and meditation he attained enlightenment. He then preached his message until, at the age of 72, he passed away and reached *moksha*, total liberation from the cycle of death and rebirth.

Jains declare that the Hindu rituals of transferring merit are not acceptable as each living being is responsible for its own actions. They recognise some of the minor deities of the Hindu pantheon, but the supreme objects of worship are the Tirthankaras. The pious Jain does not ask favours from the Tirthankaras, but seeks to emulate their example in his or her own life.

Jains believe that the universe is eternal and self-subsisting, that there is no omnipotent creator God ruling it and the destiny of the individual is in his or her own hands. *Karma*, the fruit of past actions, is believed to determine the place of every living being and rebirth may be in the heavens, on earth as a human, an animal or other lower being, or in the hells. The ultimate goal of existence for Jains is *moksha* or *nirvana*, a state of perfect knowledge and tranquility for each individual soul, which can be achieved only by gaining enlightenment.

The Jainist path to liberation is defined by the Three Jewels, *samyak darshana* (right perception), *samyak jnana* (right knowledge) and *samyak charitra* (right conduct). Of the five fundamental precepts of the Jains, *Ahimsa* (non-injury to any form of being, in any mode) is the first and foremost, and was popularised by Gandhi as *Ahimsa paramo dharma*.

There are around 25,000 Jains in Britain, sizeable communities in North America and east Africa and smaller groups in many other countries.

INSTITUTE OF JAINOLOGY, Unit 18, Silicon Business Centre, 28 Wadsworth Road, Perivale, Greenford, Middx UB6 7JZ **T** 020-8997 2300 **E** enquiries@jainology.org
W www.jainology.org
Secretary, Harshad Sanghrajka

JUDAISM

Judaism is the oldest monotheistic faith. The primary text of Judaism is the Hebrew bible or *Tanakh,* which records how the descendants of Abraham were led by Moses out of their slavery in Egypt to Mount Sinai where God's law *(Torah)* was revealed to them as the chosen people. The *Talmud,* which consists of commentaries on the *Mishnah* (the first text of rabbinical Judaism), is also held to be authoritative, and may be divided into two main categories: the *halakah* (dealing with legal and ritual matters) and the *aggadah* (dealing with theological and ethical matters not directly concerned with the regulation of conduct). The *midrash* comprises rabbinic writings containing biblical interpretations in the spirit of the aggadah. The halakah has become a source of division: orthodox Jews regard Jewish law as derived from God and therefore unalterable; progressive Jews seek to interpret it in the light of contemporary considerations; and conservative Jews aim to maintain most of the traditional rituals but to allow changes in accordance with tradition. Reconstructionist Judaism, a 20th-century movement, regards Judaism as a culture rather than a theological system and accepts all forms of Jewish practice.

The family is the basic unit of Jewish ritual, with the synagogue playing an important role as the centre for public worship and religious study. A synagogue is led by a group of laymen who are elected to office. The Rabbi is primarily a teacher and spiritual guide. The Sabbath is the central religious observance. Most British Jews are descendants of either the *Ashkenazim* of central and eastern Europe or the *Sephardim* of Spain, Portugal and the Middle East.

The Chief Rabbi of the United Hebrew Congregations of the Commonwealth is appointed by a Chief Rabbinate Conference, and is the rabbinical authority of the mainstream Orthodox sector of the Ashkenazi Jewish community, the largest body of which is the United Synagogue. His formal ecclesiastical authority is not recognised by the Reform Synagogues of Great Britain (the largest progressive group), the Union of Liberal and Progressive Synagogues, the Sephardi community or the Assembly of Masorti Synagogues. He is, however, generally recognised both outside the Jewish community and within it as the public religious representative of the totality of British Jewry. The Chief Rabbi is President of the London *Beth Din* (Court of Judgement), a rabbinic court. The *Dayanim* (Assessors) adjudicate in disputes or on matters of Jewish law and tradition; they also oversee dietary law administration, marriage, divorce and issues of personal status.

The Board of Deputies of British Jews, established in 1760, is the representative body of British Jewry. The basis of representation is through the election of deputies by synagogues and communal organisations. It protects and promotes the interests of British Jewry, acts as the central voice of the community and seeks to counter anti-Jewish discrimination and anti-Semitic activities.

There are over 12.5 million Jews worldwide; in Great Britain and Ireland there are an estimated 285,000 adherents and about 365 synagogues. Of these, 191 congregations and about 175 rabbis and ministers are under the jurisdiction of the Chief Rabbi; 99 orthodox congregations have a more independent status; and 79 congregations are outside the jurisdiction of the Chief Rabbi.

OFFICE OF THE CHIEF RABBI, Adler House, 735 High Road, London N12 0US T 020-8343 6301 F 020-8343 6310 E info@chiefrabbi.org W www.chiefrabbi.org
Chief Rabbi, Sir Jonathan Sacks

BETH DIN (COURT OF THE CHIEF RABBI), 735 High Road, London N12 0US T 020-8343 6270 E info@bethdin.org.uk W www.theus.org.uk
Registrar, David Frei
Dayanim, Rabbi Chanoch Ehrentreu *(Consultant Dayan);* Menachem Gelley *(Senior Dayan);* Ivan Binstock; Yonason Abraham; Shmuel Simons

ASSEMBLY OF MASORTI SYNAGOGUES, Alexander House, 3 Shakespeare Road, London N3 1XE T 020-8349 6650 E enquiries@masorti.org.uk W www.masorti.org.uk
Executive Director, Michael Gluckman

BOARD OF DEPUTIES OF BRITISH JEWS, 6 Bloomsbury Square, London WC1A 2LP T 020-7543 5400 F 020-7543 0010 E info@bod.org.uk W www.bod.org.uk
President, Henry Grunwald, QC

FEDERATION OF SYNAGOGUES, 65 Watford Way, London NW4 3AQ T 020-8202 2263 E info@federationofsynagogues.com W www.federationofsynagogues.com
President, Alan Finlay

LIBERAL JUDAISM, The Montagu Centre, 21 Maple Street, London W1T 4BE T 020-7580 1663 E montagu@liberaljudaism.org W www.liberaljudaism.org
Chief Executive, Rabbi Danny Rich

THE MOVEMENT FOR REFORM JUDAISM, The Sternberg Centre for Judaism, 80 East End Road, London N3 2SY T 020-8349 5640 E admin@reformjudaism.org.uk W www.reformjudaism.org.uk
Head of Movement, Rabbi Tony Bayfield

SPANISH AND PORTUGUESE JEWS' CONGREGATION, 2 Ashworth Road, London W9 1JY T 020-7289 2573 E howardmiller@spsyn.org.uk W www.sandp.org
Chief Executive, Howard Miller

UNION OF ORTHODOX HEBREW CONGREGATIONS, 140 Stamford Hill, London N16 6QT T 020-8802 6226 F 020-8809 6590
Principal Rabbinical Authority, Rabbi Ephraim Padwa

UNITED SYNAGOGUE HEAD OFFICE, Adler House, 735 High Road, London N12 0US T 020-8343 8989 F 020-8343 6262 E info@unitedsynagogue.org.uk W www.theus.org.uk
Chief Executive, Rabbi Saul Zneimer

PAGANISM

Paganism draws on the ideas of the Celtic people of pre-Roman Europe and is closely linked to Druidism. The first historical record of Druidry comes from classical Greek and Roman writers of the third century BC, who noted the existence of Druids among a people called the Keltoi who inhabited central and southern Europe. The word druid may derive from the Indo-European 'dreo-vid', meaning 'one who knows the truth'. In practice it was probably understood to mean something like 'wise-one' or 'philosopher-priest'.

Paganism is a pantheistic nature-worshipping religion which incorporates beliefs and ritual practices from ancient times. Pagans place much emphasis on the natural world and the ongoing cycle of life and death is central to their beliefs. Most Pagans believe that they are part of nature and not separate from, or superior to it, and seek to live in a way that minimises harm to the natural environment (the word Pagan derives from the Latin

Paganus, meaning 'rural'). Paganism strongly emphasises the equality of the sexes, with women playing a prominent role in the modern Pagan movement and goddess worship featuring in most ceremonies. Paganism cannot be defined by any principal beliefs because it is shaped by each individual's experiences.

The Pagan Federation was founded in 1971 to provide information on Paganism, campaigns on issues which affect Paganism and provides support to members of the Pagan community. Within the UK the Pagan Federation is divided into 13 districts each with a district manager, regional and local coordinators. Local meetings are called 'moots' and take place in private homes, pubs or coffee bars. The Pagan Federation publishes a quarterly journal, *Pagan Dawn*, formerly *The Wiccan* (founded in 1968). The federation also publishes other material, arranges members-only and public events and maintains personal contact by letter with individual members and the wider Pagan community. An annual conference is held at the end of each November and there are regional gatherings throughout the year.

THE PAGAN FEDERATION, BM Box 7097, London WC1N 3XX **T** 0798-603 4378 **E** secretary@paganfed.org
W www.paganfed.org
President, Lindsey Heffern

SIKHISM

The Sikh religion dates from the birth of Guru Nanak in the Punjab in 1469. 'Guru' means teacher but in Sikh tradition has come to represent the divine presence of God giving inner spiritual guidance. Nanak's role as the human vessel of the divine guru was passed on to nine successors, the last of whom (Guru Gobind Singh) died in 1708. The immortal guru is now held to reside in the sacred scripture, *Guru Granth Sahib*, and so to be present in all Sikh gatherings.

Guru Nanak taught that there is one God and that different religions are like different roads leading to the same destination. He condemned religious conflict, ritualism and caste prejudices. The fifth Guru, Guru Arjan Dev, largely compiled the Sikh Holy scripture, a collection of hymns *(gurbani)* known as the *Adi Granth*. It includes the writings of the first five gurus and the ninth guru, and selected writings of Hindu and Muslim saints whose views are in accord with the gurus' teachings. Guru Arjan Dev also built the Golden Temple at Amritsar, the centre of Sikhism. The tenth guru, Guru Gobind Singh, passed on the guruship to the sacred scripture, Guru Granth Sahib and founded the *Khalsa*, an order intended to fight against tyranny and injustice. Male initiates to the order added 'Singh' to their given names and women added 'Kaur'. Guru Gobind Singh also made the wearing of five symbols obligatory: *kaccha* (a special undergarment), *kara* (a steel bangle), *kirpan* (a small sword), *kesh* (long unshorn hair, and consequently the wearing of a turban) and *kangha* (a comb). These practices are still compulsory for those Sikhs who are initiated into the Khalsa (the *Amritdharis*). Those who do not seek initiation are known as *Sehajdharis*.

There are no professional priests in Sikhism; anyone with a reasonable proficiency in the Punjabi language can conduct a service. Worship can be offered individually or communally, and in a private house or a *gurdwara* (temple). Sikhs are forbidden to eat meat prepared by ritual slaughter; they are also asked to abstain from smoking, alcohol and other intoxicants. Such abstention is compulsory for the Amritdharis.

There are about 20 million Sikhs worldwide and, according to the 2001 census, there are 336,000 adherents in the UK. Every gurdwara manages its own affairs; there is no central body in the UK. The Sikh Missionary Society provides an information service.

SIKH MISSIONARY SOCIETY UK, 10 Featherstone Road, Southall, Middx UB2 5AA **T** 020-8574 1902
E info@sikhmissionarysociety.org
W www.sikhmissionarysociety.org
Hon. General Secretary, Surinder Singh Purewal

ZOROASTRIANISM

Zoroastrians are followers of the Iranian prophet Spitaman Zarathushtra (or Zoroaster in its hellenised form) who lived *c*.1200 BC. Zoroastrians were persecuted in Iran following the Arab invasion of Persia in the seventh century AD and a group (who are known as Parsis) migrated to India in the eighth century AD to avoid harassment and persecution. Zarathushtra's words are recorded in five poems called the *Gathas*, which, together with other scriptures, forms the *Avesta*.

Zoroastrianism teaches that there is one God, *Ahura Mazda* (the Wise Lord), and that all creation stems ultimately from God; the Gathas teach that human beings have free will, are responsible for their own actions and can choose between good and evil. It is believed that choosing *Asha* (truth or righteousness), with the aid of *Vohu Manah* (good mind), leads to happiness for the individual and society, whereas choosing evil leads to unhappiness and conflict. The *Gathas* also encourage hard work, good deeds and charitable acts. Zoroastrians believe that after death the immortal soul is judged by God, and is then sent to paradise or hell, where it will stay until the end of time to be resurrected for the final judgement.

In Zoroastrian places of worship, an urn containing fire is the central feature; the fire symbolises purity, light and truth and is a visible symbol of the *Fravashi* or *Farohar*, the presence of Ahura Mazda in every human being. Zoroastrians respect nature and much importance is attached to cultivating land and protecting air, earth and water.

The Zoroastrian Trust Funds of Europe is the main body for Zorastrians in the UK. Founded in 1861 as the Relgious Funds of the Zorastrians of Europe, it disseminates information on the Zoroastrian faith, provides a place of worship and maintains separate burial grounds for Zoroastrians. It also holds religious and social functions and provides assistance to Zoroastrians as considered necessary, including the provision of loans and grants to students of Zoroastrianism.

There are approximately 140,000 Zoroastrians worldwide, of which around 7,000 reside in Britain, mainly in London and the South East.

ZOROASTRIAN TRUST FUNDS OF EUROPE, Zoroastrian Centre, 440 Alexandra Avenue, Harrow, Middx HA2 9TL **T** 020-8866 0765 **E** secretary@ztfe.com
W www.ztfe.com
President, Paurushasp B. Jila

;HURCHES

here are two established (ie state) churches in the United ingdom: the Church of England and the Church of cotland. There are no established churches in Wales or orthern Ireland, though the Church in Wales, the cottish Episcopal Church and the Church of Ireland are embers of the Anglican Communion.

;HURCH OF ENGLAND

he Church of England is the established (ie national) urch in England and is organised locally into dioceses nd parishes. It traces its life back to the first coming of hristianity to England. Its position is defined by the ncient creeds of the church and by the 39 Articles of eligion (1571), the Book of Common Prayer (1662) nd the Ordinal. The Church of England is thus both atholic and reformed. It is the mother church of the nglican Communion.

HE ANGLICAN COMMUNION

he Anglican Communion consists of 38 independent rovincial or national Christian churches throughout the orld, many of which are in Commonwealth countries nd originate from missionary activity by the Church of ngland. Every ten years all the bishops in the ommunion meet at the Lambeth Conference, convened y the Archbishop of Canterbury. The conference has no olicy-making authority but is an important forum for iscussing and forming consensus around issues of ommon concern. The Anglican Consultative Council was rmed following a resolution of the 1968 Lambeth onference which discerned the need for more frequent nd representative contact than was possible through a nce-a-decade conference of bishops. The council came nto being in 1969 and meets every two to three years to aise between the member churches and provinces of the nglican Communion.

There are about 70 million Anglicans organised into 500 ioceses and 64,000 individual congregations worldwide.

TRUCTURE

he Church of England is divided into the two provinces f Canterbury and York, each under an archbishop. The wo provinces are subdivided into 44 dioceses.

Legislative provision for the Church of England is ade by the General Synod, established in 1970. It also iscusses and expresses opinion on any other matter of eligious or public interest. The General Synod has 467 embers in total, divided between three houses: the louse of Bishops, the House of Clergy and the House of aity. It is presided over jointly by the Archbishops of anterbury and York and normally meets twice a year. he synod has the power, delegated by parliament, to ame statute law (known as a 'measure') on any matter oncerning the Church of England. A measure must be id before both houses of parliament, who may accept or eject it but cannot amend it. Once accepted the measure s submitted for royal assent and then has the full force of law. In addition to the General Synod, there are synods at diocesan level.

The Archbishops' Council was established in January 1999. Its creation was the result of changes to the Church of England's national structure proposed in 1995 and subsequently approved by the synod and parliament. The council's purpose, set out in the National Institutions Measure 1998, is 'to coordinate, promote and further the work and mission of the Church of England'. It reports to the General Synod. The Archbishops' Council comprises the Archbishops of Canterbury and York, *ex officio,* the prolocutors elected by the convocations of Canterbury and York, the chair and vice-chair of the House of Laity, elected by that house, two bishops, two clergy and two lay persons elected by their respective houses of the General Synod, and up to six persons appointed jointly by the two archbishops with the approval of the General Synod.

There are also a number of national boards, councils and other bodies working on matters such as social responsibility, mission, Christian unity and education which report to the General Synod through the Archbishops' Council.

GENERAL SYNOD OF THE CHURCH OF ENGLAND, Church House, Great Smith Street, London SW1P 3NZ T 020-7898 1000
Joint Presidents, Archbishops of Canterbury and York
HOUSE OF BISHOPS: *Chair,* Archbishop of Canterbury; *Vice-Chair,* Archbishop of York
HOUSE OF CLERGY: *Chairs (alternating),* Ven. Norman Russell; Canon Glyn Webster
HOUSE OF LAITY: *Chair,* Dr Christina Baxter; *Vice-Chair,* Dr Philip Giddings
ARCHBISHOPS' COUNCIL, Church House, Great Smith Street, London SW1P 3NZ T 020-7898 1000
Joint Presidents, Archbishops of Canterbury and York; *Secretary-General,* William Fittall

THE ORDINATION OF WOMEN

The canon making it possible for women to be ordained to the priesthood was promulgated in the General Synod in February 1994 and the first 32 women priests were ordained on 12 March 1994.

MEMBERSHIP

In 2005, 140,700 people were baptised, the Church of England had an electoral roll membership of 1.3 million, and each week about 1.2 million people attended services. As at December 2006 there were over 16,000 churches and places of worship. At December 2006 there were 354 dignitaries (including bishops, archdeacons and cathedral clergy); 7,890 full-time parochial stipendiary clergy; 337 full-time non parochial stipendiary clergy; 1,230 chaplains etc; 410 lay workers and Church Army evangelists; 8,010 licensed readers and 2,210 readers with permission to officiate and active emeriti; and approximately 4,446 active retired ordained clergy.

	Full-time Diocesan Clergy 2006		Electoral Roll Membership 2005
	Male	Female	
Bath and Wells	175	42	39,000
Birmingham	141	33	18,900
Blackburn	196	21	35,800
Bradford	87	15	12,200
Bristol	113	22	17,000
Canterbury	131	19	22,300
Carlisle	115	24	22,000
Chelmsford	333	68	50,100
Chester	207	40	48,700
Chichester	295	18	55,700
Coventry	109	21	16,900
Derby	134	26	20,100
Durham	157	38	24,900
Ely	109	31	19,500
Europe	80	5	10,400
Exeter	198	28	32,200
Gloucester	111	29	24,100
Guildford	138	29	30,800
Hereford	76	26	18,600
Leicester	109	34	17,700
Lichfield	252	52	47,800
Lincoln	153	39	28,600
Liverpool	168	46	29,800
London	447	69	69,400
Manchester	218	49	35,800
Newcastle	114	28	16,900
Norwich	152	33	23,400
Oxford	298	88	57,400
Peterborough	124	30	18,800
Portsmouth	99	16	18,300
Ripon and Leeds	99	31	18,200
Rochester	186	34	31,700
St Albans	202	64	41,800
St Edmundsbury and Ipswich	115	24	24,700
Salisbury	175	39	45,100
Sheffield	133	35	20,000
Sodor and Man	17	2	2,700
Southwark	275	68	47,300
Southwell and Nottingham	115	36	19,200
Truro	92	18	17,000
Wakefield	120	34	21,700
Winchester	200	22	39,800
Worcester	116	29	20,400
York	197	45	35,900
Total	7,081	1,500	1,268,600

STIPENDS 2007–8*

Archbishop of Canterbury	£66,750
Archbishop of York	£57,210
Bishop of London	£52,440
Other diocesan bishops	£36,230
Suffragan bishops	£29,560
Assistant bishops (full-time)	£28,610
Deans	£30,200
Archdeacons (recommended)	£28,610
Residentiary canons	£22,880†
Incumbents and clergy of similar status	£20,980†

* Rates are for those appointed on or after 1 April 2004, transitional arrangements are in place for those appointed prior to this date.

† National Stipend Benchmark (adjusted regionally to reflect variations in the cost of living)

CANTERBURY

104TH ARCHBISHOP AND PRIMATE OF ALL ENGLAND

Most Revd and Rt. Hon. Rowan Williams, *cons.* 1992, *apptd* 2002; Lambeth Palace, London SE1 7JU
Signs Rowan Cantuar:

BISHOPS SUFFRAGAN

Dover, Rt. Revd Stephen Venner, *cons.* 1994, *apptd* 1999; Upway, St Martin's Hill, Canterbury, Kent CT1 1PR

Maidstone, Rt. Revd Graham Cray, *cons.* 2001, *apptd* 2001; Bishop's House, Pett Lane, Charing, Ashford, Kent TN27 0DL

Ebbsfleet, Rt. Revd Andrew Burnham, *cons.* 2000, *apptd* 2000 (provincial episcopal visitor); Bishop's House, Dry Sandford, Abingdon, Oxon OX13 6JP

Richborough, Rt. Revd Keith Newton, *cons.* 2002, *apptd* 2002 (provincial episcopal visitor); 6 Mellis Gardens, Woodford Green, Essex IG8 0BH

DEAN

Very Revd Robert Willis, *apptd* 2001

Organist, D. Flood, FRCO, *apptd* 1988

ARCHDEACONS

Canterbury, Ven. Sheila Watson, *apptd* 2007
Maidstone, Ven. Philip Down, *apptd* 2002

Vicar-General of Province and Diocese, Chancellor Sheila Cameron, QC
Commissary-General, His Hon. Richard Walker
Joint Registrars of the Province, Canon John Rees; Stephen Slack
Diocesan Registrar and Legal Adviser, Richard Sturt
Diocesan Secretary, Julian Hills, Diocesan House, Lady Wootton's Green, Canterbury CT1 1NQ **T** 01227-459401

YORK

97TH ARCHBISHOP AND PRIMATE OF ENGLAND

Most Revd and Rt. Hon. Dr John Sentamu, *cons.* 1996, *trans.* 2005; Bishopthorpe, York YO23 2GE
Signs Sentamu Ebor:

BISHOPS SUFFRAGAN

Beverley, Rt. Revd Martyn Jarrett (provincial episcopal visitor), *cons.* 1994, *apptd* 2000; 3 North Lane, Roundhay, Leeds LS8 2QJ

Hull, Rt. Revd Richard Frith, *cons.* 1998, *apptd* 1998; Hullen House, Woodfield Lane, Hessle, Hull HU13 0ES

Selby, Rt. Revd Martin Wallace, *cons.* 2003, *apptd* 2003; Bishop's House, Barton le Street, Malton, York YO17 6PL

Whitby, Rt. Revd Robert Ladds, *cons.* 1999, *apptd* 1999; 60 West Green, Stokesley, Middlesbrough TS9 5BD

DEAN

Very Revd Keith Jones, *apptd* 2004

Master of the Music, Philip Moore, FRCO, *apptd* 1983

ARCHDEACONS

Cleveland, Ven. Paul Ferguson, *apptd* 2001
East Riding, Ven. David Butterfield, *apptd* 2006
York, Ven. Richard Seed, *apptd* 1999

Chancellor of the Diocese, Revd Peter Collier, QC, *apptd* 2006
Registrar and Legal Secretary, Lionel Lennox
Diocesan Secretary, Peter Warry, Diocesan House, Aviator Court, Clifton Moor, York YO30 4WJ **T** 01904-699500

ONDON (Canterbury)

32ND BISHOP

:. Revd and Rt. Hon Richard Chartres, *cons.* 1992, *apptd* 1995; The Old Deanery, Dean's Court, London EC4V 5AA
Signs Richard Londin:

REA BISHOPS

lmonton, Rt. Revd Peter Wheatley, *cons.* 1999, *apptd* 1999; 27 Thurlow Road, London NW3 5PP
ensington, Rt. Revd Michael Colclough, *cons.* 1996, *apptd* 1996; Dial House, Riverside, Twickenham, Middx TW1 3DT
epney, Rt. Revd Canon Stephen Oliver, *cons.* 2003, *apptd* 2003; 63 Coborn Road, London E3 2DB
'illesden, Rt. Revd Peter Broadbent, *cons.* 2001, *apptd* 2001; 173 Willesden Lane, London NW6 7YN

ISHOP SUFFRAGAN

ilham, Rt. Revd John Broadhurst, *cons.* 1996, *apptd* 1996; 26 Canonbury Park South, London N1 2FN

EAN OF ST PAUL'S

t. Revd Graeme Knowles, *apptd* 2007

rganist, Malcolm Archer, *apptd* 2004

RCHDEACONS

haring Cross, Ven. Dr William Jacob, *apptd* 1996
ackney, Ven. Lyle Dennen, *apptd* 1999
ampstead, Ven. Michael Lawson, *apptd* 1999
ondon, Ven. Peter Delaney, *apptd* 1999
iddlesex, Ven. Stephen Welch, *apptd* 2006
ortholt, Ven. Rachel Treweek, *apptd* 2006

hancellor, Nigel Seed, QC, *apptd* 2002
egistrar and Legal Secretary, Paul Morris
iocesan Secretary, Keith Robinson, London Diocesan House, 36 Causton Street, London SW1P 4AU
T 020-7932 1226

URHAM (York)

1ST BISHOP

t. Revd Dr N. Thomas Wright, *cons.* 2003, *apptd* 2003; Auckland Castle, Bishop Auckland DL14 7NR
Signs Thomas Dunelm:

ISHOP SUFFRAGAN

rrow, Rt. Revd Mark Bryant, *cons.* 2007, *apptd* 2007; Bishop's House, Ivy Lane, Low Fell, Gateshead NE9 6QD

EAN

ery Revd Michael Sadgrove, *apptd* 2003

rganist, James Lancelot, FRCO, *apptd* 1985

RCHDEACONS

uckland, Ven. Nicholas Barker, *apptd* 2007
urham, Ven. Ian Jagger, *apptd* 2006
inderland, Ven. Stuart Bain, *apptd* 2002

hancellor, The Worshipful Revd Dr Rupert Bursell, QC, *apptd* 1989
egistrar and Legal Secretary, Hilary Monckton-Milnes
iocesan Secretary, Ian Boothroyd, Diocesan Office, Auckland Castle, Bishop Auckland, Co. Durham DL14 7QJ
T 01388-604515

WINCHESTER (Canterbury)

96TH BISHOP

Rt. Revd Michael C. Scott-Joynt, *cons.*1987, *trans.* 1995; Wolvesey, Winchester SO23 9ND
Signs Michael Winton:

BISHOPS SUFFRAGAN

Basingstoke, Rt. Revd Trevor Willmott, *cons.* 2002, *apptd* 2002; Bishopswood End, Kingswood Rise, Four Marks, Alton, Hants GU34 5BD
Southampton, Rt. Revd Paul Butler, *cons.* 2004, *apptd* 2004; Ham House, The Crescent, Romsey SO51 7NG

DEAN

Very Revd James Atwell, *apptd* 2005
Dean of Jersey (A Peculiar), Very Revd Robert Key, *apptd* 2005
Dean of Guernsey (A Peculiar), Very Revd Paul Mellor, *apptd* 2003
Director of Music, Andrew Lumsden, *apptd* 2002

ARCHDEACONS

Bournemouth, Ven. Adrian Harbidge, *apptd* 1998
Winchester, vacant

Chancellor, Christopher Clark, *apptd* 1993
Registrar and Legal Secretary, Peter White
Diocesan Secretary, Andrew Howard, Church House, 9 The Close, Winchester, Hants SO23 9LS T 01962-624742

BATH AND WELLS (Canterbury)

78TH BISHOP

Rt. Revd Peter Price, *cons.* 1997, *apptd* 2002; The Palace, Wells BA5 2PD
Signs Peter Bath & Wells

BISHOP SUFFRAGAN

Taunton, Rt. Revd Peter Maurice, *cons.* 2006, *apptd* 2006; The Palace, Wells BA5 2PD

DEAN

Very Revd John Clarke, *apptd* 2004

Organist, Matthew Owens, *apptd* 2005

ARCHDEACONS

Bath, Ven. Andrew Piggott, *apptd* 2005
Taunton, Ven. John Reed, *apptd* 1999
Wells, Ven. Nicola Sullivan, *apptd* 2006

Chancellor, Timothy Briden, *apptd* 1993
Registrar and Legal Secretary, Tim Berry
Diocesan Secretary, Nicholas Denison, The Old Deanery, Wells, Somerset BA5 2UG T 01749-670777

BIRMINGHAM (Canterbury)

8TH BISHOP

Rt. Revd David Urquhart, *cons.* 2000, *apptd* 2006; Bishop's Croft, Old Church Road, Harborne, Birmingham B17 0BG
Signs David Birmingham

BISHOP SUFFRAGAN

Aston, vacant

DEAN

Very Revd Bob Wilkes, *apptd* 2006

Organist, Marcus Huxley, FRCO, *apptd* 1986

ARCHDEACONS
Aston, Ven. Dr Brian Russell, *apptd* 2005
Birmingham, Ven. Hayward Osborne, *apptd* 2001
Chancellor, Martin Cardinal, *apptd* 2005
Registrar and Legal Secretary, Hugh Carslake
Diocesan Secretary, Jim Drennan, 175 Harborne Park Road, Harborne, Birmingham B17 0BH **T** 0121-426 0400

BLACKBURN *(York)*
8TH BISHOP
Rt. Revd Nicholas Reade, *apptd* 2003, *cons.* March 2004; Bishop's House, Ribchester Road, Blackburn BB1 9EF
Signs Nicholas Blackburn

BISHOPS SUFFRAGAN
Burnley, Rt. Revd John Goddard, *cons.* 2000, *apptd* 2000; Dean House, 449 Padiham Road, Burnley BB12 6TE
Lancaster, Rt. Revd Geoffrey Pearson, *cons.* 2006, *apptd* 2006; The Vicarage, Whinney Brow Lane, Shireshead, Forton, Preston PR3 0AE

DEAN
Very Revd Christopher Armstrong, *apptd* 2001

Organist, Richard Tanner, *apptd* 1998

ARCHDEACONS
Blackburn, Ven. John Hawley, *apptd* 2002
Lancaster, Ven. Peter Ballard, *apptd* 2006

Chancellor, John Bullimore, *apptd* 1990
Registrar and Legal Secretary, Thomas Hoyle
Diocesan Secretary, Graeme Pollard, Diocesan Office, Cathedral Close, Blackburn BB1 5AA **T** 01254-54421

BRADFORD *(York)*
9TH BISHOP
Rt. Revd David James, *apptd* 2002; Bishopscroft, Ashwell Road, Heaton, Bradford BD9 4AU
Signs David Bradford

DEAN
Very Revd Dr David Ison, *apptd* 2005

Organist, Andrew Teague, FRCO, *apptd* 2003

ARCHDEACONS
Bradford, Ven. David Lee, *apptd* 2004
Craven, Ven. Paul Slater, *apptd* 2005

Chancellor, John de G. Walford, *apptd* 1999
Registrar and Legal Secretary, Peter Foskett
Diocesan Secretary, Malcolm Halliday, Kadugli House, Elmsley Street, Steeton, Keighley BD20 6SE **T** 01535-650555

BRISTOL *(Canterbury)*
55TH BISHOP
Rt. Revd Michael Hill, *cons.* 1998, *apptd* 2003; Wethered House, 11 The Avenue, Clifton, Bristol BS8 3HG
Signs Michael Bristol

BISHOP SUFFRAGAN
Swindon, Rt. Revd Dr Lee Rayfield, *cons.* 2005, *apptd* 2005; Mark House, Field Rise, Swindon, Wiltshire, SN1 4HP

DEAN
Very Revd Robert W. Grimley, *apptd* 1997

Organist and Director of Music, Mark Lee, *apptd* 1998

ARCHDEACONS
Bristol, Ven. Tim McClure, *apptd* 1999
Malmesbury, Ven. Alan Hawker, *apptd* 1998

Chancellor, Dr James Behrens, *apptd* 2005
Registrar and Legal Secretary, Tim Berry
Diocesan Secretary, Lesley Farrall, Diocesan Church House, 23 Great George Street, Bristol BS1 5QZ **T** 0117-906 0100

CARLISLE *(York)*
66TH BISHOP
Rt. Revd Graham Dow, *cons.* 1985, *apptd* 2000; Rose Castle, Dalston, Carlisle CA5 7BZ
Signs Graham Carlisle:

BISHOP SUFFRAGAN
Penrith, Rt. Revd James Newcome, *cons.* 2002, *apptd* 2002; Holm Croft, Castle Road, Kendal, Cumbria LA9 7A

DEAN
Very Revd Mark Boyling, *apptd* 2004

Organist, Jeremy Suter, FRCO, *apptd* 1991

ARCHDEACONS
Carlisle, Ven. David Thomson, *apptd* 2002
West Cumberland, Ven. Colin Hill, *apptd* 2004
Westmorland and Furness, Ven. George Howe, *apptd* 200

Chancellor, Geoffrey Tattersall, QC, *apptd* 2003
Registrar and Legal Secretary, Jane Lowdon
Diocesan Secretary, Derek Hurton, Church House, West Walls, Carlisle CA3 8UE **T** 01228-522573

CHELMSFORD *(Canterbury)*
9TH BISHOP
Rt. Revd John Warren Gladwin, *cons.* 1994, *apptd* 2003 *trans.* 2004; Bishopscourt, Margaretting, Ingatestone CM4 0HD
Signs John Chelmsford

BISHOPS SUFFRAGAN
Barking, Rt. Revd David Hawkins, *apptd* 2003; Barking Lodge, Verulam Avenue, London E17 8ES
Bradwell, Rt. Revd Laurence Green, *cons.* 1993, *apptd* 1993; Bishop's House, Orsett Road, Horndon-on-the-Hill, Stanford-le-Hope, Essex SS17 8NS
Colchester, Rt. Revd Christopher Morgan, *cons.* 2001, *apptd* 2001; 1 Fitzwalter Road, Colchester, Essex CO3 3S

DEAN
Very Revd Peter S. M. Judd, *apptd* 1997

Master of Music, Peter Nardone, *apptd* 2000

ARCHDEACONS
Colchester, Ven. Annette Cooper, *apptd* 2004
Harlow, Ven. Peter Taylor, *apptd* 1996
Southend, Ven. David Lowman, *apptd* 2001
West Ham, Ven. Elwin Cockett, *apptd* 2007

Chancellor, George Pulman, QC, *apptd* 2001
Registrar and Legal Secretary, Brian Hood
Chief Executive, Steven Webb, 53 New Street, Chelmsford, Essex CM1 1AT **T** 01245-294400

CHESTER *(York)*
40TH BISHOP
Rt. Revd Peter R. Forster, PHD, *cons.* 1996, *apptd* 1996 Bishop's House, Chester CH1 2JD
Signs Peter Cestr:

;HOPS SUFFRAGAN
kenhead, Rt. Revd Keith Sinclair, *cons.* 2007, *apptd* 2007; Bishop's Lodge, 67 Bidston Road, Prenton CH43 6TR
:kport, vacant

AN
'y Revd Dr Gordon McPhate, *apptd* 2002

ganist and Director of Music, David Poulter, FRCO, *apptd* 1997

CHDEACONS
ester, Ven. Donald Allister, *apptd* 2002
cclesfield, Ven. Richard Gillings, *apptd* 1994

ancellor, His Hon. Judge Turner, QC, *apptd* 1998
istrar and Legal Secretary, Alan McAllester
ocesan Secretary, Dr John Mason, Church House, Lower Lane, Aldford, Chester CH3 6HP T 01244-620444

IICHESTER *(Canterbury)*
2ND BISHOP
Revd John Hind, *cons.* 1991, *apptd* 2001; The Palace, Chichester PO19 1PY
Signs John Cicestr:

;HOPS SUFFRAGAN
rsham, Rt. Revd Lindsay G. Urwin, *cons.* 1993, *apptd* 1993; Bishop's House, 21 Guildford Road, Horsham, W. Sussex RH12 1LU
ves, Rt. Revd Wallace P. Benn, *cons.* 1997, *apptd* 1997; Bishop's Lodge, 16A Prideaux Road, Eastbourne, E. Sussex BN21 2NB

AN
'y Revd Nicholas Frayling, *apptd* 2002

ganist, Alan Thurlow, FRCO, *apptd* 1980

CHDEACONS
ichester, Ven. Douglas McKittrick, *apptd* 2002
rsham, Ven. Roger Combes, *apptd* 2003
ves and Hastings, Ven. Philip Jones, *apptd* 2005

ancellor, Mark Hill
istrar and Legal Secretary, John Stapleton
ocesan Secretary, Jonathan Prichard, Diocesan Church House, 211 New Church Road, Hove, E. Sussex BN3 4ED T 01273-421021

OVENTRY *(Canterbury)*
H BISHOP
Revd Colin J. Bennetts, *cons.* 1994, *apptd* 1997; The Bishop's House, 23 Davenport Road, Coventry CV5 6PW
Signs Colin Coventry

;HOP SUFFRAGAN
rwick, Rt. Revd John Stroyan, *cons.* 2005, *apptd* 2005; rwick House, 139 Kenilworth Road, Coventry CV4 7AP

AN
'y Revd John Irvine, *apptd* 2001

ector of Music, Mr Kerry Beaumont, *apptd* 2006

CHDEACONS
ventry, Ven. Mark Bryant, *apptd* 2001
rwick, Ven. Michael Paget-Wilkes, *apptd* 1990

ancellor, Sir William Gage, *apptd* 1980
istrar and Legal Secretary, David Dumbleton
ocesan Secretary, Simon Lloyd, Cathedral & Diocesan Offices, 1 Hilltop, Coventry CV1 5AB T 024-7652 1200

DERBY *(Canterbury)*
7TH BISHOP
Rt. Revd Alastair Redfern, *cons.*1997, *apptd* 2005; Bishop's House, 6 King Street, Duffield, Belper, Derbyshire DE56 4EU
Signs Alastair Derby

BISHOP SUFFRAGAN
Repton, Rt. Revd Humphrey Southern, *cons.* 2007, *apptd* 2007; Repton House, Lea, Matlock, Derbyshire DE4 5JP

DEAN
Very Revd Martin Kitchen, PHD, *apptd* 2005

Organist, Peter Gould, *apptd* 1982

ARCHDEACONS
Chesterfield, Ven. David Garnett, *apptd* 1996
Derby, Ven. Christopher Cunliffe, *apptd* 2006

Chancellor, His Hon. Judge John Bullimore, *apptd* 1981
Registrar and Legal Secretary, Mrs Nadine Waldron
Diocesan Secretary, Bob Carey, Derby Church House, Full Street, Derby DE1 3DR T 01332-388650

ELY *(Canterbury)*
68TH BISHOP
Rt. Revd Dr Anthony Russell, *cons.* 1988, *apptd* 2000; The Bishop's House, Ely, Cambs CB7 4DW
Signs Anthony Ely

BISHOP SUFFRAGAN
Huntingdon, vacant

DEAN
Very Revd Dr Michael Chandler, *apptd* 2003

Director of Music, Paul Trepte, FRCO, *apptd* 1991

ARCHDEACONS
Cambridge, Ven. John Beer, *apptd* 2004
Huntingdon and Wisbech, Ven. Hugh McCurdy, *apptd* 2005

Chancellor, The Hon. Mr Justice Gage, QC
Registrar, Peter Beesley
Diocesan Secretary, Dr Matthew Lavis, Bishop Woodford House, Barton Road, Ely, Cambs CB7 4DX T 01353-652701

EXETER *(Canterbury)*
70TH BISHOP
Rt. Revd Michael Langrish, *cons.* 1993, *apptd* 2000; The Palace, Exeter EX1 1HY
Signs Michael Exon:

BISHOPS SUFFRAGAN
Crediton, Rt. Revd Robert Evens, *cons.* 2004, *apptd* 2004; 32 The Avenue, Tiverton EX16 4HW
Plymouth, Rt. Revd John Ford, *cons.* 2006, *apptd* 2005; 31 Riverside Walk, Tamerton Foliot, Plymouth PL5 4AQ

DEAN
Very Revd Cyril Meyrick, *apptd* 2005

Director of Music, Andrew Millington, *apptd* 1999

ARCHDEACONS
Barnstaple, Ven. David Gunn-Johnson, *apptd* 2003
Exeter, Ven. Penny Driver, *apptd* 2006
Plymouth, Ven. Tony Wilds, *apptd* 2001
Totnes, Ven. John Rawlings, *apptd* 2006

Chancellor, Hon. Sir Andrew McFarlane

Registrar and Legal Secretary, C. Butcher
Diocesan Secretary, Mark Beedell, The Old Deanery, The Cloisters, Exeter EX1 1HS T 01392-272686

GIBRALTAR IN EUROPE *(Canterbury)*
BISHOP
Rt. Revd Dr Geoffrey Rowell, *cons.* 1994, *apptd* 2001; Bishop's Lodge, Church Road, Worth, Crawley, West Sussex RH10 7RT

BISHOP SUFFRAGAN
In Europe, Rt. Revd David Hamid, *cons.* 2002, *apptd* 2002; 14 Tufton Street, London SW1P 3QZ
Dean, Cathedral Church of the Holy Trinity, Gibraltar, Very Revd Alan Woods
Chancellor, Pro-Cathedral of St Paul, Valletta, Malta, Canon Thomas Mendel
Chancellor, Pro-Cathedral of the Holy Trinity, Brussels, Belgium, Canon Dr Robert Innes

ARCHDEACONS
Eastern, Ven. Patrick Curran
North-West Europe, Ven. Dirk Van Leeuwen
France, Ven. Kenneth Letts
Gibraltar, Very Revd Alan Woods
Italy, Ven. Arthur Siddall
Scandinavia and Germany, Ven. Mark Oakley
Switzerland, Ven. Arthur Siddall

Chancellor, Mark Hill
Registrar and Legal Secretary, John Underwood
Diocesan Secretary, Adrian Mumford, 14 Tufton Street, London SW1P 3QZ T 020-7898 1155

GLOUCESTER *(Canterbury)*
40TH BISHOP
Rt. Revd Michael Perham, *cons.* 2004, *apptd* 2004; Bishopscourt, Pitt Street, Gloucester GL1 2BQ
Signs Michael Gloucestr

BISHOP SUFFRAGAN
Tewkesbury, Rt. Revd John S. Went, *cons.* 1995, *apptd* 1995; Bishop's House, Staverton, Cheltenham GL51 0TW

DEAN
Very Revd Nicholas Bury, *apptd* 1997

Director of Music, Adrian Partington, *apptd* 2007

ARCHDEACONS
Cheltenham, Ven. Hedley Ringrose, *apptd* 1998
Gloucester, Ven. Geoffrey Sidaway, *apptd* 2000

Chancellor and Vicar-General, June Rodgers, *apptd* 1990
Registrar and Legal Secretary, Chris Peak
Diocesan Secretary, Dr Kevin Brown, Church House, College Green, Gloucester GL1 2LY T 01452-410022

GUILDFORD *(Canterbury)*
9TH BISHOP
Rt. Revd Christopher Hill, *cons.* 1996, *apptd* 2004; Willow Grange, Woking Road, Guildford GU4 7QS
Signs Christopher Guildford

BISHOP SUFFRAGAN
Dorking, Rt. Revd Ian Brackley, *cons.* 1996, *apptd* 1995; Dayspring, 13 Pilgrims Way, Guildford GU4 8AD

DEAN
Very Revd Victor Stock, *apptd* 2002

Organist, Stephen Farr, FRCO, *apptd* 1999

ARCHDEACONS
Dorking, Ven. Julian Henderson, *apptd* 2005
Surrey, Ven. Stuart Beake, *apptd* 2005

Chancellor, Andrew Jordan
Registrar and Legal Secretary, Peter Beesley
Diocesan Secretary, Stephen Marriott, Diocesan House, Quarry Street, Guildford GU1 3AG T 01483-571826

HEREFORD *(Canterbury)*
104TH BISHOP
Rt. Revd Anthony Priddis, *cons.* 1996, *apptd* 2004; Th Bishop's House, Hereford HR4 9BN
Signs Anthony Hereford

BISHOP SUFFRAGAN
Ludlow, Rt. Revd Michael Wrenford Hooper, *cons.* 200 *apptd* 2002; Bishop's House, Corvedale Road, Craven Arms, Shropshire SY7 9BT

DEAN
Very Revd Michael Tavinor, *apptd* 2002

Organist, Geraint Bowen, FRCO, *apptd* 2001

ARCHDEACONS
Hereford, Ven. Malcom Colmer, *apptd* 2005
Ludlow, Rt. Revd Michael Hooper, *apptd* 2002

Chancellor, Roger Kaye
Registrar and Legal Secretary, Tom Jordan; Peter Beesley
Diocesan Secretary, John Clark, The Palace, Hereford HR4 T 01432-373300

LEICESTER *(Canterbury)*
6TH BISHOP
Rt. Revd Timothy J. Stevens, *cons.* 1995, *apptd* 1999; Bishop's Lodge, 10 Springfield Road, Leicester LE2 3BD
Signs Timothy Leicester

DEAN
Very Revd Vivienne F. Faull, *apptd* 2000

Master of Music, Jonathan Gregory, *apptd* 1994

ARCHDEACONS
Leicester, Ven. Richard Atkinson, *apptd* 2002
Loughborough, Ven. Paul Hackwood, *apptd* 2005

Chancellor, Dr James Behrens
Registrar and Legal Secretary, Trevor Kirkman
Diocesan Secretary, Jane Easton, Church House, 3–5 St Martin's East, Leicester LE1 5FX T 0116-248 7400

LICHFIELD *(Canterbury)*
98TH BISHOP
Rt. Revd Jonathan Gledhill *cons.* 1996, *apptd* 2003; Bishop's House, The Close, Lichfield WS13 7LG
Signs Jonathan Lichfield

BISHOPS SUFFRAGAN
Shrewsbury, Rt. Revd Dr Alan Smith, *cons.* 2001, *apptd* 2002; 68 London Road, Shrewsbury SY2 6PG
Stafford, Rt. Revd A. Gordon Mursell, *cons.* 2005, *appt* 2005; Ash Garth, 6 Broughton Crescent, Barlaston, Stok on Trent, ST12 9DD

olverhampton, Rt. Revd Clive Gregory, *cons.* 2007, *apptd* 2007

EAN
ry Revd Adrian Dorber, *apptd* 2005

ganist, Philip Scriven, *apptd* 2002

RCHDEACONS
chfield, Ven. Christopher Liley, *apptd* 2001
op, Ven. John Hall, *apptd* 1998
ke-on-Trent, Ven. Godfrey Owen Stone, *apptd* 2002
alsall, Revd Robert Jackson, *apptd* 2004

ancellor, His Hon. Judge Marten Coates
nt Registrars and Legal Secretaries, J. P. Thorneycroft; N. Blackie
ocesan Secretary, D. R. Taylor, St Mary's House, The Close, Lichfield, Staffs WS13 7LD T 01543-306030

NCOLN *(Canterbury)*
ST BISHOP
Revd Dr John Saxbee, *cons.* 1994, *apptd* 2002; Bishop's House, Eastgate, Lincoln LN2 1QQ
Signs John Lincoln

SHOPS SUFFRAGAN
antham, Rt. Revd Dr Timothy Ellis, *cons.* 2006, *apptd* 2006; Saxonwell Vicarage, Church Street, Long Bennington, Newark NG23 5ES
imsby, Rt. Revd David D. J. Rossdale, *cons.* 2000, *apptd* 2000; Bishop's House, Church Lane, Irby-upon-Humber, Grimsby DN37 7JR

EAN
ry Revd Philip Buckler, *apptd* 2007

rector of Music, A. Prentice, *apptd* 2003

RCHDEACONS
ncoln, Ven. Arthur Hawes, *apptd* 1995
ndsey and Stow, Ven. Jane Sinclair, *apptd* 2007

ancellor, Mark Bishop, QC, *apptd* 2007
gistrar and Legal Secretary, Derek Wellman
ocesan Secretary, Max Manin, The Old Palace, Lincoln LN2 1PU T 01522-504050

VERPOOL *(York)*
H BISHOP
Revd James Jones, *cons.* 1994, *apptd* 1998; Bishop's Lodge, Woolton Park, Liverpool L25 6DT *Signs* James Liverpool

SHOP SUFFRAGAN
arrington, Rt. Revd David Jennings, *cons.* 2000, *apptd* 2000; 34 Central Avenue, Eccleston Park, Prescot, Merseyside L34 2QP

EAN
vd Justin Welby, *apptd* 2007

ganist, Prof. Ian Tracey, *apptd* 1980

RCHDEACONS
verpool, Ven. Richard Panter, *apptd* 2002
arrington, Ven. Peter Bradley, *apptd* 2001

hancellor, Hon. Sir Mark Hedley
gistrar and Legal Secretary, Roger Arden
ocesan Secretary, Mike Eastwood, Church House, 1 Hanover Street, Liverpool L1 3DW T 0151-709 9722

MANCHESTER *(York)*
11TH BISHOP
Rt. Revd Nigel McCulloch, *cons.* 1986, *apptd* 2002, *trans.* 2002; Bishopscourt, Bury New Road, Manchester M7 4LE
Signs Nigel Manchester

BISHOPS SUFFRAGAN
Bolton, Rt. Revd David Gillett, *cons.* 1999, *apptd* 1999; 4 Bishop's Lodge, Bolton Road, Hawkshaw, Bury BL8 4JN
Hulme, Rt. Revd Stephen Lowe, *cons.* 1999, *apptd* 1999; 14 Moorgate Avenue, Withington, Manchester M20 1HE
Middleton, Rt. Revd Michael Lewis, *cons.* 1999, *apptd* 1999; The Hollies, Manchester Road, Rochdale OL11 3QY

DEAN
Revd Rogers Govender, *apptd* 2006

Organist, Christopher Stokes, *apptd* 1992

ARCHDEACONS
Bolton, Ven. John Applegate, *apptd* 2002
Manchester, Ven. Andrew Ballard, *apptd* 2005
Rochdale, Ven. Mark Davies, *apptd* 2005

Chancellor, G. Tattersall
Registrar and Legal Secretary, Michael Darlington
Diocesan Secretary, Nigel Spraggins, Diocesan Church House, 90 Deansgate, Manchester M3 2GH T 0161-828 1400

NEWCASTLE *(York)*
11TH BISHOP
Rt. Revd J. Martin Wharton, *cons.* 1992, *apptd* 1997; Bishop's House, 29 Moor Road South, Gosforth, Newcastle upon Tyne NE3 1PA
Signs Martin Newcastle

ASSISTANT BISHOP
Rt. Revd Paul Richardson, *cons.* 1987, *apptd* 1999

DEAN
Very Revd Christopher C. Dalliston, *apptd* 2003

Director of Music, Scott Farrell, *apptd* 2002

ARCHDEACONS
Lindisfarne, Ven. Robert Langley, *apptd* 2001
Northumberland, Ven. Geoffrey Miller, *apptd* 2004

Chancellor, Prof. David McClean, *apptd* 1998
Registrar and Legal Secretary, Jane Lowdon
Diocesan Secretary, Philip Davies, Church House, St John's Terrace, North Shields NE29 6HS T 0191-270 4100

NORWICH *(Canterbury)*
71ST BISHOP
Rt. Revd Graham R. James, *cons.* 1993, *apptd* 2000; Bishop's House, Norwich NR3 1SB *Signs* Graham Norvic:

BISHOPS SUFFRAGAN
Lynn, Rt. Revd James Langstaff, *cons.* 2004, *apptd* 2004; The Old Vicarage, Castle Acre, King's Lynn PE32 2AA
Thetford, Rt. Revd David J. Atkinson, *cons.* 2001, *apptd* 2001; The Red House, 53 Norwich Road, Stoke Holy Cross, Norwich NR14 8AB

DEAN
Very Revd Graham Smith, *apptd* 2004

Organist, David Dunnett, *apptd* 1996

ARCHDEACONS
Lynn, Ven. Martin Gray, *apptd* 1999
Norfolk, Ven. David Hayden, *apptd* 2002
Norwich, Ven. Clifford Offer, *apptd* 1994

Chancellor, His Hon. Judge Paul Downes, *apptd* 2007
Registrar and Legal Secretary, Ian Mayers
Diocesan Secretary, Revd Canon Richard Bowett, Diocesan House, 109 Dereham Road, Easton, Norwich, Norfolk NR9 5ES T 01603-880853

OXFORD *(Canterbury)*

42ND BISHOP
Rt. Revd John Pritchard *cons.* 2002, *apptd* 2007; Diocesan Church House, North Hinksey Lane, Oxford OX2 0NB
Signs John Oxon:

AREA BISHOPS
Buckingham, Rt. Revd Dr Alan Wilson *cons.* 2003, *apptd* 2003; Sheridan, Grimms Hill, Great Missenden, Bucks HP16 9BD
Dorchester, Rt. Revd Colin Fletcher, *cons.* 2000, *apptd* 2000; Arran House, Sandy Lane, Yarnton, Oxon OX5 1PB
Reading, Rt. Revd Stephen Cottrell, *cons.* 2004, *apptd* 2004; Bishop's House, Tidmarsh Lane, Tidmarsh, Reading RG8 8HA

DEAN OF CHRIST CHURCH
Very Revd Dr Christopher Lewis, *apptd* 2003

Organist, Dr Stephen Darlington, FRCO, *apptd* 1985

ARCHDEACONS
Berkshire, Ven. Norman Russell, *apptd* 1998
Buckingham, vacant
Oxford, Ven. Julian Hubbard, *apptd* 2005

Chancellor, Revd Dr Rupert Bursell, *apptd* 2001
Registrars and Legal Secretaries, Dr F. E. Robson and Revd. Canon John Rees
Diocesan Secretary, Rosemary Pearce, Diocesan Church House, North Hinksey, Oxford OX2 0NB T 01865-208202

PETERBOROUGH *(Canterbury)*

37TH BISHOP
Rt. Revd Ian P. M. Cundy, *cons.* 1992, *apptd* 1996; Bishop's Lodging, The Palace, Peterborough PE1 1YA
Signs Ian Petriburg:

BISHOP SUFFRAGAN
Brixworth, Rt. Revd Frank White, *cons.* 2002, *apptd* 2002; 4 The Avenue, Dallington, Northampton NN1 4RZ

DEAN
Very Revd Charles Taylor, *apptd* 2007

Organist, Andrew Reid, *apptd* 2004

ARCHDEACONS
Northampton, Ven. Christine Allsopp, *apptd* 2005
Oakham, Ven. David Painter, *apptd* 2000

Chancellor, David Pittaway, QC, *apptd* 2005
Registrar and Legal Secretary, Revd Canon Raymond Hemingray
Diocesan Secretary, Canon Richard Pestell, Diocesan Office, The Palace, Peterborough PE1 1YB T 01733-887000

PORTSMOUTH *(Canterbury)*

8TH BISHOP
Rt. Revd Dr Kenneth Stevenson, *cons.* 1995, *apptd* 19[illegible]
Bishopsgrove, 26 Osborn Road, Fareham, Hants PO16 7D[illegible]
Signs Kenneth Portsmouth

DEAN
Very Revd David Brindley, *apptd* 2002

Organist, David Price, *apptd* 1996

ARCHDEACONS
Isle of Wight, Ven. Caroline Baston, *apptd* 2006
Portsdown, Ven. Trevor Reader, *apptd* 2006
The Meon, Ven. Peter Hancock, *apptd* 1999

Chancellor, C. Clark, QC
Registrar and Legal Secretary, Hilary Tyler
Diocesan Secretary, Wendy Kennedy, Diocesan Offices, 1st Floor, Peninsular House, Wharf Road, Portsmouth PO2 8H[illegible] T 023-9289 9664

RIPON AND LEEDS *(York)*

12TH BISHOP
Rt. Revd John Packer, *cons.* 1996, *apptd* 2000; Bishop Mount, Ripon HG4 5DP
Signs John Ripon and Leeds

BISHOP SUFFRAGAN
Knaresborough, Rt. Revd James Bell, *cons.* 2004, *apptd* 2004; Thistledown, Main Street, Exelby, Bedale DL8 2HD

DEAN
Revd Keith Jukes, *apptd* 2007

Director of Music, Andrew Bryden, *apptd* 2003

ARCHDEACONS
Leeds, Ven. Peter Burrows, *apptd* 2005
Richmond, Ven. Janet Henderson, *apptd* 2007

Chancellor, His Hon. Judge Grenfell, *apptd* 1992
Registrars and Legal Secretaries, Christopher Tunnard; Nichola Harding
Diocesan Secretary, Philip Arundel, Diocesan Office, St Mary's Street, Leeds LS9 7DP T 0113-200 0540

ROCHESTER *(Canterbury)*

106TH BISHOP
Rt. Revd Dr Michael Nazir-Ali, *cons.* 1984, *apptd* 1994
Bishopscourt, Rochester ME1 1TS
Signs Michael Roffen:

BISHOP SUFFRAGAN
Tonbridge, Rt. Revd Dr Brian C. Castle, *cons.* 2002, *apptd* 2002; Bishop's Lodge, 48 St Botolph's Road, Sevenoaks TN13 3AG

DEAN
Very Revd Adrian Newman, *apptd* 2004

Director of Music, Roger Sayer, FRCO, *apptd* 1995

ARCHDEACONS
Bromley, Ven. Paul Wright, *apptd* 2003
Rochester, Ven. Peter Lock, *apptd* 2000
Tonbridge, Ven. Clive Mansell, *apptd* 2002

Chancellor, John Gallagher, *apptd* 2006
Registrar and Legal Secretary, Owen Carew-Jones
Diocesan Secretary, Canon Louise Gilbert, St Nicholas Church, Boley Hill, Rochester ME1 1SL T 01634-560000

T ALBANS *(Canterbury)*
TH BISHOP
t. Revd Christopher W. Herbert, *cons.* 1995, *apptd* 1995; Abbey Gate House, St Albans AL3 4HD
Signs Christopher St Albans

ISHOPS SUFFRAGAN
edford, Rt. Revd Richard N. Inwood, *cons.* 2003, *apptd* 2003; Bishop's Lodge, Bedford Road, Cardington, Bedford MK44 3SS
ertford, Rt. Revd Christopher R. J. Foster, *cons.* 2001, *apptd* 2001; Hertford House, Abbey Mill Lane, St Albans AL3 4HE

EAN
ery Revd Dr Jeffrey John, *apptd* 2004

rganist, Andrew Lucas, *apptd* 1998

RCHDEACONS
edford, Ven. Paul Hughes, *apptd* 2004
ertford, Ven. Trevor Jones, *apptd* 1997
Albans, Ven. Helen Cunliffe, *apptd* 2003

hancellor, Roger Kaye, *apptd* 2002
egistrar and Legal Secretary, David Cheetham
iocesan Secretary, Susan Pope, Holywell Lodge, 41 Holywell Hill, St Albans AL1 1HE T 01727-854532

T EDMUNDSBURY AND IPSWICH *Canterbury)*
0TH BISHOP
t. Revd Nigel Stock, *cons.* 2000, *apptd* 2007; Bishop's House, 4 Park Road, Ipswich IP1 3ST
Signs Nigel St Edmundsbury and Ipswich

ISHOP SUFFRAGAN
unwich, Rt. Revd Clive Young, *cons.* 1999, *apptd* 1999; 28 Westerfield Road, Ipswich IP4 2UJ

EAN
ery Revd Neil Collings, *apptd* 2006

rganist, James Thomas, *apptd* 1997

RCHDEACONS
pswich, vacant
udbury, Ven. David Brierley, *apptd* 2006
uffolk, Ven. Geoffrey Arrand, *apptd* 1994

hancellor, The Hon. Mr Justice Blofeld, *apptd* 1974
egistrar and Legal Secretary, James Hall
iocesan Secretary, Nicholas Edgell, Diocesan Office, St Nicholas Centre, 4 Cutler Street, Ipswich IP1 1UQ T 01473-298500

ALISBURY *(Canterbury)*
7TH BISHOP
t. Revd Dr David S. Stancliffe, *cons.* 1993, *apptd* 1993; South Canonry, The Close, Salisbury SP1 2ER
Signs David Sarum

ISHOPS SUFFRAGAN
amsbury, Rt. Revd Stephen Conway, *cons.* 2006, *apptd* 2006; Southbroom House, London Road, Devizes, Wiltshire SN10 1LT
herborne, Rt. Revd Timothy M. Thornton, *cons.* 2001, *apptd* 2001; Sherborne Office, Little Bailie, Dullar Lane, Sturminster Marshall, Wimborne, Dorset BH21 4AD

DEAN
Very Revd June Osborne, *apptd* 2004

Organist, David Halls, *apptd* 2005

ARCHDEACONS
Dorset, Ven. Alistair Magowan, *apptd* 2000
Sherborne, Ven. Paul Taylor, *apptd* 2004
Wilts, Ven. John Wraw, *apptd* 2004
Sarum, Ven. Alan Jeans, *apptd* 2003

Chancellor, His Hon. Judge Samuel Wiggs, *apptd* 1997
Registrar and Legal Secretary, Andrew Johnson
Diocesan Secretary, Lucinda Herklots, Church House, Crane Street, Salisbury SP1 2QB T 01722-411922

SHEFFIELD *(York)*
6TH BISHOP
Rt. Revd John (Jack) Nicholls, *cons.* 1990, *apptd* 1997; Bishopscroft, Snaithing Lane, Sheffield S10 3LG
Signs Jack Sheffield

BISHOP SUFFRAGAN
Doncaster, Rt. Revd Cyril Guy Ashton, *cons.* 2000, *apptd* 2000; Bishop's House, 3 Farrington Court, Wickersley, Rotherham S66 1JQ

DEAN
Very Revd Peter Bradley, *apptd* 2003

Master of Music, Neil Taylor, *apptd* 1997

ARCHDEACONS
Doncaster, Ven. Robert Fitzharris, *apptd* 2001
Sheffield and Rotherham, Ven. Richard Blackburn, *apptd* 1999

Chancellor, Prof. David McClean, *apptd* 1992
Registrar and Legal Secretary, Miranda Myers
Diocesan Secretary, Malcolm Fair, Diocesan Church House, 95–99 Effingham Street, Rotherham S65 1BL T 01709-309100

SODOR AND MAN *(York)*
81st BISHOP
vacant

ARCHDEACON OF MAN
Ven. Brian Smith, *apptd* 2005

Vicar-General and Chancellor, Clare Faulds
Registrar and Legal Secretary, Jonathan Kewley
Diocesan Secretary, Barbara Brereton, Silverdene, Station Road, Ballasalla, Isle of Man IM9 2DQ T 01624-827644

SOUTHWARK *(Canterbury)*
9TH BISHOP
Rt. Revd Dr Tom F. Butler, *cons.* 1985, *apptd* 1998; Bishop's House, 38 Tooting Bec Gardens, London SW16 1QZ
Signs Thomas Southwark

AREA BISHOPS
Croydon, Rt. Revd Nicholas Baines, *cons.* 2003, *apptd* 2003; St Matthew's House, 100 George Street, Croydon, Surrey CR0 1PE
Kingston upon Thames, Rt. Revd Richard Cheetham, *cons.* 2002, *apptd* 2002; Kingston Episcopal Area Office, St Cecilia's, Sutherland Grove, London SW18 5JR
Woolwich, Rt. Revd Christopher Chessun, *cons.* 2005, *apptd* 2005; Diocesan Office (*see* below)

DEAN
Very Revd Colin B. Slee, OBE, *apptd* 1994

Organist, Peter Wright, FRCO, *apptd* 1989

ARCHDEACONS
Croydon, Ven. Tony Davies, *apptd* 1994
Lambeth, Ven. Christopher Skilton, *apptd* 2003
Lewisham, Ven. Christine Hardman, *apptd* 2001
Reigate, Ven. Daniel Kajumba, *apptd* 2001
Southwark, Revd Dr Michael Ipgrave, *apptd* 2004
Wandsworth, Ven. Stephen Roberts, *apptd* 2005

Chancellor, Charles George, QC
Registrar and Legal Secretary, Paul Morris
Diocesan Secretary, Simon Parton, Trinity House, 4 Chapel Court, Borough High Street, London SE1 1HW T 020-7939 9400

SOUTHWELL AND NOTTINGHAM *(York)*

10TH BISHOP
Rt. Revd George H. Cassidy, *cons.* 1999, *apptd* 1999; Bishop's Manor, Southwell NG25 0JR
Signs George Southwell

BISHOP SUFFRAGAN
Sherwood, Rt. Revd Anthony Porter, *cons.* 2006, *apptd* 2006; Dunham House, 8 Westgate, Southwell NG25 0JL

DEAN
Very Revd John Guille, *apptd* 2007

Organist, Paul Hale, *apptd* 1989

ARCHDEACONS
Newark, Ven. Nigel Peyton, *apptd* 1999
Nottingham, Ven. Peter Hill, *apptd* 2007

Chancellor, Linda Box, *apptd* 2005
Registrar and Legal Secretary, Christopher Hodson
Diocesan Secretary, Dunham House, Westgate, Southwell, Notts NG25 0JL T 01636-817204

TRURO *(Canterbury)*

14TH BISHOP
Rt. Revd William Ind, *cons.* 1987, *apptd* 1997; Lis Escop, Truro TR3 6QQ
Signs William Truro

BISHOP SUFFRAGAN
St Germans, Rt. Revd Royden Screech, *cons.* 2000, *apptd* 2000; Royden Screech, 32 Falmouth Road, Truro, Cornwall TR1 2HX

DEAN
Very Revd Dr Christopher Hardwick, *apptd* 2005

Organist, Robert Sharpe, *apptd* 2002

ARCHDEACONS
Cornwall, Ven. Roger Bush, *apptd* 2006
Bodmin, Ven. Clive Cohen, *apptd* 2000

Chancellor, Timothy Briden, *apptd* 1998
Registrar and Legal Secretary, Martin Follett
Diocesan Secretary, Sheri Sturgess, Diocesan House, Kenwyn, Truro TR1 1JQ T 01872-274351

WAKEFIELD *(York)*

12TH BISHOP
Rt. Revd Stephen Platten, *cons.* 2003, *apptd* 2003; Bishop's Lodge, Woodthorpe Lane, Wakefield WF2 6JL
Signs Stephen Wakefield

BISHOP SUFFRAGAN
Pontefract, Rt. Revd Anthony William Robinson, *cons.* 2003, *apptd* 2002; Pontefract House, 181A Manygates Lane, Wakefield WF2 7DR

DEAN
vacant

Organist, Jonathan Bielby, FRCO, *apptd* 1972

ARCHDEACONS
Halifax, Ven. Robert Freeman, *apptd* 2003
Pontefract, Ven. Jonathan Greener, *apptd* 2003

Chancellor, Paul Downes, *apptd* 2006
Registrar and Legal Secretaries, Julian Gill; Julia Wilding
Diocesan Secretary, Ashley Ellis, Church House, 1 South Parade, Wakefield WF1 1LP T 01924-371802

WORCESTER *(Canterbury)*

113TH BISHOP
Rt. Revd Dr John Inge, *cons.* 2003, *apptd* 2007; The Bishop's House, Hartlebury Castle, Kidderminster DY11 7X
Signs John Wigorn

SUFFRAGAN BISHOP
Dudley, Rt. Revd Dr David S. Walker, *cons.* 2000, *apptd* 2000; The Bishop's House, Bishop's Walk, Cradley Heath B64 7JF

DEAN
Revd Peter Atkinson, *apptd* 2006

Organist, Adrian Lucas, *apptd* 1996

ARCHDEACONS
Dudley, Ven. Fred Trethewey, *apptd* 2001
Worcester, Ven. Dr Joy Tetley, *apptd* 1999

Chancellor, Charles Mynors, *apptd* 1999
Registrar and Legal Secretary, Michael Huskinson
Diocesan Secretary, Robert Higham, The Old Palace, Deansway, Worcester WR1 2JE T 01905-20537

ROYAL PECULIARS *(Canterbury)*

WESTMINSTER
The Collegiate Church of St Peter
Dean, Canon John Hall
Sub Dean and Archdeacon, Canon Robert Wright, *apptd* 2005
Chapter Clerk and Receiver-General, Maj.-Gen. David Burden, CB, CBE, Chapter Office, 20 Dean's Yard, London SW1P 3PA
Organist, James O'Donnell, *apptd* 1999
Registrar, Stuart Holmes, MVO
Legal Secretary, Christopher Vyse, *apptd* 2000

WINDSOR
The Queen's Free Chapel of St George within Her Castle of Windsor
Dean, Rt. Revd David Conner, *apptd* 1998
Chapter Clerk, Charlotte Manley, LVO, OBE, *apptd* 2003 Chapter Office, The Cloisters, Windsor Castle, Windsor, Berks SL4 1NJ
Director of Music, Timothy Byram-Wigfield, *apptd* 2004

)THER ANGLICAN CHURCHES

'HE CHURCH IN WALES

'he Anglican Church was the established church in Wales ·om the 16th century until 1920, when the estrangement f the majority of Welsh people from Anglicanism :sulted in disestablishment. Since then the Church in Vales has been an autonomous province consisting of six :es. The bishops are elected by an electoral college omprising elected lay and clerical members, who also lect one of the diocesan bishops as Archbishop of Wales.

The legislative body of the Church in Wales is the ;overning Body, which has 207 members divided etween the three orders of bishops, clergy and laity. Its resident is the Archbishop of Wales and it meets twice nnually. Its decisions are binding upon all members of ie church. The church's property and finances are the :sponsibility of the Representative Body. There are about 8,700 members of the Church in Wales, with 584 :ipendiary clergy and 977 parishes.

HE GOVERNING BODY OF THE CHURCH IN WALES, 39 Cathedral Road, Cardiff CF11 9XF T 029-2034 8200 *Lay Secretary,* John Shirley

2th ARCHBISHOP OF WALES, Most Revd Dr Barry Morgan (Bishop of Llandaff), *elected* 2003 *Signs* Barry Cambrensis

·ISHOPS

'angor (80th), Rt. Revd Anthony Crockett, *b.* 1945, *cons.* 2004, *elected* 2004; Ty'r Esgob, Bangor, Gwynedd LL57 2SS *Signs* Anthony Bangor. *Stipendiary clergy,* 51

landaff (102nd), Most Revd Dr Barry Morgan (*also* Archbishop of Wales), *b.* 1947, *cons.* 1993, *trans.* 1999; Llys Esgob, The Cathedral Green, Llandaff, Cardiff CF5 2YE *Signs* Barry Cambrensis. *Stipendiary clergy,* 143

1onmouth (9th), Rt. Revd Dominic Walker, *b.* 1948, *cons.* 1997, *elected* 2003; Bishopstow, Stow Hill, Newport NP20 4EA *Signs* Dominic Monmouth. *Stipendiary clergy,* 90

t Asaph (74th), Rt. Revd John Davies, *b.* 1943, *cons.* 1999, *elected* 1999; Esgobty, Upper Denbigh Road, St Asaph, Denbighshire LL17 0TW *Signs* John St Asaph. *Stipendiary clergy,* 102

t David's (127th), Rt. Revd Carl Cooper, *b.* 1960, *cons.* 2002, *elected* 2002; Llys Esgob, Abergwili, Carmarthen SA31 2JG *Signs* Carl St Davids. *Stipendiary clergy,* 126

wansea and Brecon (8th), Rt. Revd Anthony Pierce, *b.* 1941, *cons.* 1999, *elected* 1999; Ely Tower, Brecon, Powys LD3 9DE *Signs* Anthony Swansea & Brecon. *Stipendiary clergy,* 76

he stipend for a diocesan bishop of the Church in Wales £35,073 a year for 2007–8.

COTTISH EPISCOPAL CHURCH

he Scottish Episcopal Church was founded after the Act f Settlement (1690) established the presbyterian nature f the Church of Scotland. The Scottish Episcopal Church a member of the worldwide Anglican Communion. The overning authority is the General Synod, an elected ody of approximately 140 members which meets once a ear. The bishop who convenes and presides at meetings f the General Synod is called the 'primus' and is elected y his fellow bishops.

There are 42,290 members of the Scottish Episcopal :hurch, of whom 28,589 are communicants. There are :ven bishops, approximately 482 serving clergy, and 313 hurches and places of worship.

THE GENERAL SYNOD OF THE SCOTTISH EPISCOPAL CHURCH, 21 Grosvenor Crescent, Edinburgh EH12 5EE T 0131-225 6357 W www.scotland-anglican.org *Secretary-General,* J. F. Stuart

PRIMUS OF THE SCOTTISH EPISCOPAL CHURCH, Most Revd Dr Idris Jones (Bishop of Glasgow and Galloway), *elected* 2006

BISHOPS

Aberdeen and Orkney, Very Revd Bob Gillies, *b.* 1951, *cons.* 2007, *elected* 2007. *Clergy,* 54

Argyll and the Isles, Rt. Revd Martin Shaw, *b.* 1944, *cons.* 2004, *elected* 2004. *Clergy* 22

Brechin, Rt. Revd John Mantle, *b.* 1946, *cons.* 2005, *elected* 2005. *Clergy,* 35

Edinburgh, Rt. Revd Brian Smith, *b.* 1943, *cons.* 1993, *elected* 2001. *Clergy,* 162

Glasgow and Galloway, Most Revd Idris Jones, *b.* 1943, *cons.* 1998, *elected* 1998. *Clergy,* 99

Moray, Ross and Caithness, Rt. Revd John Crook, *b.* 1940, *cons.* 1999, *elected* 1999. *Clergy,* 31

St Andrews, Dunkeld and Dunblane, Rt. Revd Mark Strange, *b.* 1961, *cons.* 2007, *elected* 2007. *Clergy,* 86

The minimum stipend of a diocesan bishop of the Scottish Episcopal Church for 2007 is £31,470 (ie 1.5 times the standard clergy stipend of £20,980).

CHURCH OF IRELAND

The Anglican Church was the established church in Ireland from the 16th century but never secured the allegiance of the majority and was disestablished in 1871. The Church of Ireland is divided into the provinces of Armagh and Dublin, each under an archbishop. The provinces are subdivided into 12 dioceses.

The legislative body is the General Synod, which has 660 members in total, divided between the House of Bishops and the House of Representatives. The Archbishop of Armagh is elected by the House of Bishops; other episcopal elections are made by an electoral college.

There are about 400,000 members of the Church of Ireland, with two archbishops, ten bishops, about 600 clergy and about 1,100 churches and places of worship.

CENTRAL OFFICE, Church of Ireland House, Church Avenue, Rathmines, Dublin 6 T (+353) (1) 497 8422 *Chief Officer and Secretary of the Representative Church Body,* D. C. Reardon

PROVINCE OF ARMAGH

ARCHBISHOP OF ARMAGH, PRIMATE OF ALL IRELAND AND METROPOLITAN, Most Revd Alan Harper, OBE, *b.* 1944, *cons.* 2002, *trans.* 2007. *Clergy,* 55

BISHOPS

Clogher, Rt. Revd Michael Jackson, PHD, DPHIL, *b.* 1956, *cons.* 2002, *apptd* 2002. *Clergy,* 32

Connor, Rt. Revd Alan Abernethy, *b.* 1957, *cons.* 2007, *apptd* 2007. *Clergy,* 106

Derry and Raphoe, Rt. Revd Kenneth Good, *b.* 1952, *cons.* 2002, *apptd* 2002. *Clergy,* 51

Down and Dromore, Rt. Revd Harold Miller, *b.* 1950, *cons.* 1997, *apptd* 1997. *Clergy,* 116

Kilmore, Elphin and Ardagh, Rt. Revd Kenneth Clarke, *b.* 1949, *cons.* 2001, *apptd* 2001. *Clergy,* 21
Tuam, Killala and Achonry, Rt. Revd Richard Henderson, DPHIL, *b.* 1957, *cons.* 1998, *apptd* 1998. *Clergy,* 13

PROVINCE OF DUBLIN
ARCHBISHOP OF DUBLIN, BISHOP OF GLENDALOUGH, PRIMATE OF IRELAND AND METROPOLITAN, Most Revd John R. W. Neill, *b.* 1945, *apptd* 2002. *Clergy,* 86

BISHOPS
Cashel and Ossory, Rt. Revd Michael Burrows, *b.* 1961, *cons.* 2006, *apptd* 2006. *Clergy,* 42
Cork, Cloyne and Ross, Rt. Revd W. Paul Colton, *b.* 1960, *cons.* 1999, *apptd* 1999. *Clergy,* 30
Limerick and Killaloe, Rt. Revd Michael Mayes, *b.* 1941, *cons.* 1993, *trans.* 2000. *Clergy,* 19
Meath and Kildare, Most Revd Richard Clarke, PHD, *b.* 1949, *cons.* 1996, *apptd* 1996. *Clergy,* 26

OVERSEAS

PRIMATES
PRIMATE AND PRESIDING BISHOP OF AOTEAROA, NEW ZEALAND AND POLYNESIA, Most Revd William Brown Turei
PRIMATE OF AUSTRALIA, Most Revd Phillip Aspinall
PRIMATE OF BRAZIL, Most Revd Maurício Araújo de Andrade
ARCHBISHOP OF THE PROVINCE OF BURUNDI, Most Revd Bernard Ntahoturi
ARCHBISHOP AND PRIMATE OF CANADA, Most Revd Andrew Sandford Hutchison
ARCHBISHOP OF THE PROVINCE OF CENTRAL AFRICA, Most Revd Bernard Amos Malango
PRIMATE OF THE CENTRAL REGION OF AMERICA, Most Revd Martin de Jesus Barahona
ARCHBISHOP OF THE PROVINCE OF CONGO, Most Revd Dr Dirokpa Balufuga Fidèle
PRIMATE OF THE PROVINCE OF HONG KONG SHENG KUNG HUI, Most Revd Paul Kwong
ARCHBISHOP OF THE PROVINCE OF THE INDIAN OCEAN, Most Revd Gerald James Ernest
PRIMATE OF JAPAN (NIPPON SEI KO KAI), Most Revd Nathaniel Makoto Uematsu
PRESIDENT-BISHOP OF JERUSALEM AND THE MIDDLE EAST, Most Revd Dr Mouneer Hanna Anis
ARCHBISHOP OF THE PROVINCE OF KENYA, Most Revd Benjamin M. P. Nzimbi
ARCHBISHOP OF THE PROVINCE OF KOREA, Most Revd Francis Kyung Jo Park
ARCHBISHOP OF THE PROVINCE OF MELANESIA, Most Revd Sir Ellison Leslie Pogo, KBE
ARCHBISHOP OF MEXICO, Most Revd Carlos Touche-Porter
ARCHBISHOP OF THE PROVINCE OF MYANMAR, Most Revd Samuel San Si Htay
ARCHBISHOP OF THE PROVINCE OF NIGERIA, Most Revd Peter Akinola
ARCHBISHOP OF PAPUA NEW GUINEA, Most Revd James Ayong
PRIME BISHOP OF THE PHILIPPINES, Most Revd Ignacio Capuyan Soliba
ARCHBISHOP OF THE PROVINCE OF RWANDA, Most Revd Emmanuel Musaba Kolini
PRIMATE OF THE PROVINCE OF SOUTH EAST ASIA, Most Revd Dr John Chew
METROPOLITAN OF THE PROVINCE OF SOUTHERN AFRICA, Most Revd Njongonkulu W. H Ndungane
PRESIDING BISHOP OF THE SOUTHERN CONE O AMERICA, Most Revd Gregory James Venables
ARCHBISHOP OF THE PROVINCE OF THE SUDAN Most Revd Joseph Biringi Hassan Marona
ARCHBISHOP OF THE PROVINCE OF TANZANIA, Most Revd Donald Leo Mtetemela
ARCHBISHOP OF THE PROVINCE OF UGANDA, Most Revd Henry Luke Orombi
PRESIDING BISHOP AND PRIMATE OF THE USA, Most Revd Katharine Jefferts Schori
ARCHBISHOP OF THE PROVINCE OF WEST AFRICA, Most Revd Justice Ofei Akrofi
ARCHBISHOP OF THE PROVINCE OF THE WEST INDIES, Most Revd Drexel Wellington Gomez

OTHER CHURCHES AND EXTRA-PROVINCIAL DIOCESES
ANGLICAN CHURCH OF BERMUDA, *extra-provincia to Canterbury*
Bishop, Rt. Revd Ewen Ratteray
CHURCH OF CEYLON, *extra-provincial to Canterbury*
Bishop of Colombo, Rt. Revd Duleep de Chickera
Bishop of Kurunagala, Rt. Revd Kumara Illangasinghe
EPISCOPAL CHURCH OF CUBA, Rt. Revd Miguel Tamayo *(interim)*
FALKLAND ISLANDS, *extra-provincial to Canterbury*
Episcopal Commissary, Rt. Revd Stephen Venner (Bishop of Dover)
LUSITANIAN CHURCH *(Portuguese Episcopal Church), extra-provincial to Canterbury*
Bishop, Rt. Revd Fernando Soares
REFORMED EPISCOPAL CHURCH OF SPAIN, *extra-provincial to Canterbury*
Bishop, Rt. Revd Carlos López-Lozano

MODERATION OF CHURCHES IN FULL COMMUNION WITH THE ANGLICAN COMMUNION
CHURCH OF BANGLADESH, Rt. Revd Michael Baroi
CHURCH OF NORTH INDIA, Most Revd Joel Vidyasagar Mal
CHURCH OF SOUTH INDIA, Most Revd Badda Peter Sugandhar
CHURCH OF PAKISTAN, Rt. Revd Dr Alexander John Malik

CHURCH OF SCOTLAND

The Church of Scotland is the established (ie nationa church of Scotland. The church is reformed in doctrin and presbyterian in constitution, ie based on a hierarch of councils of ministers and elders and, since 1990, c members of a diaconate. At local level the Kirk Sessio consists of the parish minister and ruling elders. At distric level the presbyteries, of which there are 44 in Britai consist of all the ministers in the district, one ruling eld from each congregation, and those members of th diaconate who qualify for membership. The Gener Assembly is the supreme authority, and is presided over b a Moderator chosen annually by the Assembly. Th sovereign, if not present in person, is represented by Lord High Commissioner who is appointed each year b the crown.

The Church of Scotland has about 504,363 member 1,004 ministers and 1,191 churches. There are about 2

ministers and other personnel working overseas.
Lord High Commissioner (2007–8), HRH The Duke of York, KG, KCVO
Moderator of the General Assembly (2007–8), Rt. Revd Sheilagh Kesting
Principal Clerk, Very Revd Dr F. Macdonald
Depute Clerk, Revd. Dr M. MacLean
Procurator, L. Dunlop
Law Agent and Solicitor of the Church, Mrs J. Wilson
Parliamentary Agent, I. McCulloch *(London)*
General Treasurer, I. Grimmond
Secretary, Church and Society Council, Revd Dr David Sinclair
CHURCH OFFICE, 121 George Street, Edinburgh EH2 4YN T 0131-225 5722

PRESBYTERIES AND CLERKS
Edinburgh, Revd W. Graham
West Lothian, Revd D. Shaw
Lothian, J. McCulloch
Melrose and Peebles, Jack Stewart
Duns, Peter Johnson
Jedburgh, Revd W. Frank Campbell
Annandale and Eskdale, Revd C. Haston
Dumfries and Kirkcudbright, Revd G. Savage
Wigtown and Stranraer, Revd D. Dutton
Ayr, Revd J. Crichton
Irvine and Kilmarnock, Revd C. Brockie
Ardrossan, Revd J. Mackay
Lanark, Revd J. Cutler
Greenock and Paisley, Revd A. Ward
Glasgow, Revd D. Lunan
Hamilton, Revd S. Paterson
Dumbarton, Revd C. Caskie
Argyll, I. Maclagan
Falkirk, Revd I. Black
Stirling, Revd M. MacCormick
Dunfermline, Revd E. Kenny
Kirkcaldy, Rosemary Frew
St Andrews, Dr R. Mackie
Dunkeld and Meigle, Revd J. Russell
Perth, Revd D. Main
Dundee, Revd J. Wilson
Angus, Revd M. Bicket
Aberdeen, Revd I. MacLean
Kincardine and Deeside, Revd J. Holt
Gordon, Revd Euan Glen
Buchan, George Berstan
Moray, Revd Hugh Smith
Abernethy, Revd J. MacEwan
Inverness, Revd A. Younger
Lochaber, Revd D. Anderson
Ross, Revd T. McWilliam
Sutherland, Revd J. Goskirk
Caithness, J. Houston
Lochcarron-Skye, Revd A. MacArthur
Uist, Revd M. Smith
Lewis, Revd T. Sinclair
Orkney, Revd T. Hunt
Shetland, Revd C. Greig
England, Revd Scott Brown
Europe, Revd J. Cowie

The stipends for ministers in the Church of Scotland in 2007 range from £21,466–£28,500, depending on length of service. In addition, congregations can make extra payments.

ROMAN CATHOLIC CHURCH

The Roman Catholic Church is one worldwide Christian church acknowledging as its head the Bishop of Rome, known as the Pope (Father). He leads a communion of followers of Christ, who believe they continue his presence in the world as servants of faith, hope and love to all society. The Pope is held to be the successor of St Peter and thus invested with the power which was entrusted to St Peter by Jesus Christ. A direct line of succession is therefore claimed from the earliest Christian communities. With the fall of the Roman Empire the Pope also became an important political leader. His territory is now limited to the 0.44 sq. km. (0.17 sq. miles) of the Vatican City State, created to provide some independence to the Pope from Italy and other nations.

The Pope exercises spiritual authority over the church with the advice and assistance of the Sacred College of Cardinals, the supreme council of the church. He is also advised by bishops in communion with him, by a group of officers which form the Roman Curia and by his ambassadors, called Apostolic Nuncios, who liaise with the Bishops' Conference in each country.

Those members of the College of Cardinals who are under the age of 80 elect a successor of the Pope following his death. The assembly of the cardinals called to the Vatican for the election of a new Pope is known as the conclave. In complete seclusion the cardinals vote by a secret ballot; a two-thirds majority is necessary before the vote can be accepted as final. When a cardinal receives the necessary number of votes, the Dean of the Sacred College formally asks him if he will accept election and the name by which he wishes to be known. On his acceptance of the office of Supreme Pontiff, the conclave is dissolved and the first Cardinal Deacon announces the election to the assembled crowd in St Peter's Square.

The number of cardinals was fixed at 70 by Pope Sixtus V in 1586 but has been steadily increased since the pontificate of John XXIII and at the end of March 2005 stood at 183, plus one cardinal 'in pectore' (their name kept secret by the Pope for fear of persecution). At the end of March 2005, 117 of the 183 cardinals were cardinal electors, who took part in the election of Pope Benedict XVI, following the death of Pope John Paul II in April 2005.

The Pope has full legislative, judicial and administrative power over the whole church. He is aided in his administration by the curia, which is made up of a number of departments. The Secretariat of State is the central office for carrying out the Pope's instructions and is presided over by the Cardinal Secretary of State. It maintains relations with the departments of the curia, with the episcopate, with the representatives of the Holy See in various countries, governments and private persons. The congregations and pontifical councils are the Pope's ministries and include departments such as the Congregation for the Doctrine of Faith, whose field of competence concerns faith and morals; the Congregation for the Clergy and the Congregation for the Evangelisation of Peoples, the Pontifical Council for the Family and the Pontifical Council for the Promotion of Christian Unity.

The Vatican State does not have diplomatic representatives. The Holy See, composed of the Pope and those who help him in his mission for the church, is recognised by the Conventions of Vienna as an international moral body. The representatives of the Holy See are known as Apostolic Nuncios. Where representation is only to the local churches and not to the government of a country, the papal representative is known as an apostolic delegate. The Roman Catholic Church has an estimated 840 million adherents under the care of some 2,500 diocesan bishops worldwide.

SOVEREIGN PONTIFF

His Holiness Pope Benedict XVI (Joseph Ratzinger), *born* Bavaria, Germany, 16 April 1927; *ordained priest* 1951; *appointed Archbishop* (of Munich), March 1977; *created Cardinal* June 1977; *assumed pontificate* 19 April 2005

SECRETARIAT OF STATE

Secretary of State, HE Cardinal Tarcisio Bertone
First Section (General Affairs), Most Revd Leonardo Sandri (Titular Archbishop of Cittanova)
Second Section (Relations with Other States), Most Revd Dominique Mamberti (Titular Archbishop of Sagona)

BISHOPS' CONFERENCE

The Catholic Church in England and Wales consists of a total of 22 dioceses. The Bishops' Conference, which coordinates the church, includes the diocesan bishops, the Apostolic Exarch of the Ukrainians, the Bishop of the Forces and the auxiliary bishops. The conference is headed by the president (HE Cardinal Cormac Murphy-O'Connor, Archbishop of Westminster) and vice-president (The Most Revd Patrick Kelly, Archbishop of Liverpool). There are six departments, each with an episcopal chair: the Department for Christian Life and Worship (the Bishop of Leeds), the Department for Dialogue and Unity (the Archbishop of Southwark), the Department for Catholic Education and Formation (the Archbishop of Birmingham), the Department for Christian Responsibility and Citizenship (the Archbishop of Cardiff), the Department for International Affairs (the Bishop of Portsmouth) and the Department for Evangelisation and Catechesis (the Bishop of Nottingham).

The Bishops' Conference Standing Committee is made up of two directly elected bishops in addition to the Metropolitan Archbishops and chairs from each of the above departments. The committee has general responsibility for continuity of policy between the plenary sessions of the conference, preparing the conference agenda and implementing its decisions.

The administration of the Bishops' Conference is funded by a levy on each diocese, according to income. A general secretariat in London coordinates and supervises the Bishops' Conference administration activities. There are also other agencies and consultative bodies affiliated to the conference.

The Bishops' Conference of Scotland is the permanently constituted assembly of the bishops of Scotland. The conference is headed by the president (HE Cardinal Keith Patrick O'Brien, Archbishop of St. Andrews and Edinburgh). The conference establishes various agencies which have an advisory function in relation to the conference. The more important of these agencies are called commissions and each one has a bishop president who, with the other members of the commissions, are appointed by the conference.

The Irish Episcopal Conference has as its president Archbishop Brady of Armagh. Its membership comprises all the archbishops and bishops of Ireland and it appoints various commissions to assist it in its work. There are three types of commissions: (a) those made up of lay and clerical members chosen for their skills and experience, and staffed by full-time expert secretariats; (b) commissions whose members are selected from existing institutions and whose services are supplied on a part-time basis; and (c) commissions of bishops only.

The Catholic Church in the UK has an estimated 5,631,449 members, 6,583 priests and 4,475 churches.

Bishops' Conferences secretariats:

ENGLAND AND WALES, 39 Eccleston Square, London SW1V 1BX T 020-7630 8220 F 020-7901 4821
E secretariat@cbcew.org.uk W www.catholicchurch.org.uk
General Secretary, Mgr Andrew Summersgill

SCOTLAND, 64 Aitken Street, Airdrie, Lanarkshire ML6 6LT T 01236-764061 E gensec@bpsconfscot.com
General Secretary, Revd Paul Conroy

IRELAND, Columba Centre, Maynooth, County Kildare T (+353) (1) 505 3000 W www.catholiccommunications.ie
Secretary, Most Revd William Lee (Bishop of Waterford and Lismore)
Executive Secretary, Revd Aidan O'Boyle

GREAT BRITAIN

APOSTOLIC NUNCIO TO GREAT BRITAIN

Most Revd Faustino Sainz Muñoz, 54 Parkside, London SW19 5NE T 020-8944 7189

ENGLAND AND WALES

THE MOST REVD ARCHBISHOPS

Westminster, HE Cardinal Cormac Murphy-O'Connor, *cons.* 1977, *apptd* 2000 *Auxiliaries,* George Stack, *cons.* 2001; Bernard Longley *cons.* 2003; Alan Hopes *cons.* 2003; John Arnold *cons.* 2006. *Clergy,* 690. *Archbishop's Residence,* Archbishop's House, Ambrosden Avenue, London SW1P 1QJ T 020-7798 9033

Birmingham, Vincent Nichols, *cons.* 1992, *apptd* 2000 *Auxiliaries,* Philip Pargeter, *cons.* 1990; David McGough, *cons.* 2005; William Kenney, *cons.* 1987. *Clergy,* 443. *Archbishop's Residence,* Archbishop's House, 8 Shadwell Street, Birmingham B4 6EY T 0121-236 9090

Cardiff, Peter Smith, *cons.* 1995, *apptd* 2001. *Clergy,* 96. *Archbishop's Residence,* Archbishop's House, 43 Cathedral Road, Cardiff CF11 9HD T 029-2022 0411

Liverpool, Patrick Kelly, *cons.* 1984, *apptd* 1996 *Auxiliary,* Thomas Williams, *cons.* 2003. *Clergy,* 474. *Diocesan Curia,* Archdiocese of Liverpool, Centre for Evangelisation, Croxteth Drive, Sefton Park, Liverpool L17 1AA T 0151-522 1000

Southwark, Kevin McDonald, *cons.* 2001, *apptd* 2003 *Auxiliaries,* John Hine, *cons.* 2001; Patrick Lynch, *cons.* 2006; Paul Hendricks, *cons.* 2006. *Clergy,* 518. *Diocesan Curia,* Archbishop's House, 150 St George's Road, London SE1 6HX T 020-7928 5592

THE RT. REVD BISHOPS

Arundel and Brighton, Kieran Conry, *cons.* 2001, *apptd* 2001. *Clergy,* 105. *Diocesan Curia,* Bishop's House, The Upper Drive, Hove, E. Sussex BN3 6NE T 01273-506387

Brentwood, Thomas McMahon, *cons.* 1980, *apptd* 1980. *Clergy,* 121. *Bishop's Office,* Cathedral House, Ingrave Road, Brentwood, Essex CM15 8AT T 01277-232266

Clifton, Declan Lang, *cons.* 2001, *apptd* 2001. *Clergy,* 251. *Bishop's House,* St Ambrose, North Road, Leigh Woods, Bristol BS8 3PW T 0117-973 3072

East Anglia, Michael Evans, *cons* 2003, *apptd* 2003. *Clergy,* 129. *Diocesan Curia,* The White House, 21 Upgate, Poringland, Norwich NR14 7SH T 01508-492202

Hallam, John Rawsthorne, *cons.* 1981, *apptd* 1997. *Clergy,* 75. *Bishop's House,* 75 Norfolk Road, Sheffield S2 2SZ T 0114-278 7988

Hexham and Newcastle, Kevin Dunn, *cons.* 2004, *apptd* 2004. *Clergy,* 211. *Diocesan Curia,* Bishop's House, East Denton Hall, 800 West Road, Newcastle upon Tyne NE5 2BJ T 0191-228 0003

Lancaster, Patrick O'Donoghue, *cons.* 1993, *apptd* 2001. *Clergy,* 248. *Bishop's Residence,* Bishop's Apartment, Cathedral House, Balmoral Road, Lancaster LA1 3BT T 01524-596050

Leeds, Arthur Roche, *cons.* 2001, *apptd* 2004. *Clergy,* 226. *Diocesan Curia,* Hinsley Hall, 62 Headingley Lane, Leeds LS6 2BX T 0113-261 8022

Menevia (Wales), Mark Jabalé, *cons.* 2001, *apptd* 2001. *Clergy,* 60. *Diocesan Curia,* 27 Convent Street, Swansea SA1 2BX T 01792-644017

Middlesbrough, vacant. *Clergy,* 113. *Diocesan Curia,* 50A The Avenue, Linthorpe, Middlesbrough TS5 6QT T 01642-850505

Northampton, Peter Doyle, *Clergy,* 163. *Diocesan Curia,* Bishop's House, Marriott Street, Northampton NN2 6AW T 01604-715635

Nottingham, Malcolm McMahon, *cons.* 2000, *apptd* 2000. *Clergy,* 162. *Bishop's House,* 27 Cavendish Road East, The Park, Nottingham NG7 1BB T 0115-947 4786

Plymouth, Christopher Budd, *cons.* 1986, *apptd* 1985. *Clergy,* 132. *Bishop's Residence,* Bishop's House, 31 Wyndham Street West, Plymouth PL1 5RZ T 01752-224414

Portsmouth, Crispian Hollis, *cons.* 1987, *apptd* 1989. *Clergy,* 282. *Bishop's Residence,* Bishop's House, Edinburgh Road, Portsmouth, Hants PO1 3HG T 023-9282 0894

Salford, Terence Brain, *cons.* 1991, *apptd* 1997. *Clergy,* 387. *Diocesan Curia,* 5 Gerald Road, Pendleton, Salford M6 6DL T 0161-736 1421

Shrewsbury, Brian Noble, *cons.* 1995, *apptd* 1995. *Clergy* 203. *Diocesan Curia,* 2 Park Road South, Prenton, Wirral CH43 4UX T 0151-652 9855

Wrexham (Wales), Edwin Regan, *cons.*1994, *apptd* 1994. *Clergy,* 45. *Diocesan Curia,* Bishop's House, Sontley Road, Wrexham LL13 7EW T 01978-262726

SCOTLAND

THE MOST REVD ARCHBISHOPS

St Andrews and Edinburgh, HE Cardinal Keith Patrick O'Brien, *cons.* 1985, *apptd* 1985, *elevated* 2003. *Clergy,* 150. *Diocesan Office,* 100 Strathearn Road, Edinburgh EH9 1BB T 0131-623 8900

Glasgow, Mario Joseph Conti, *cons.* 1977, *apptd* 2002. *Clergy,* 233. *Diocesan Curia,* 196 Clyde Street, Glasgow G1 4JY T 0141-226 5898

THE RT. REVD BISHOPS

Aberdeen, Peter Moran, *cons.* 2003, *apptd* 2003. *Clergy,* 43. *Diocesan Curia,* Bishop's House, 3 Queen's Cross, Aberdeen AB15 4XU T 01224-319154

Argyll and the Isles, Ian Murray, *cons.* 1999, *apptd* 1999. *Clergy,* 32. *Bishop's House,* Esplanade, Oban, Argyll PA34 5AB T 01631-571395

Dunkeld, Vincent Logan, *cons.* 1981. *Clergy,* 42. *Diocesan Curia,* 24–28 Lawside Road, Dundee DD3 6XY T 01382-225453

Galloway, John Cunningham, *cons.* 2004, *apptd* 2004. *Clergy* 56. *Diocesan Curia,* Candida Casa, 8 Corsehill Road, Ayr KA7 2ST T 01292-266750

Motherwell, Joseph Devine, *cons.* 1977, *apptd* 1983. *Clergy,* 123. *Diocesan Curia,* Coursington Road, Motherwell ML1 1PP T 01698-269114

Paisley, Philip Tartaglia, *cons.* 2005, *apptd* 2005. *Clergy,* 85. *Diocesan Curia,* Diocesan Centre, Cathedral Precincts, Incle Street, Paisley PA1 1HR T 0141-847 6130

BISHOPRIC OF THE FORCES

Rt. Revd Thomas Matthew Burns, *cons.* 2002, *apptd* 2002. *Administration,* Bishopric of the Forces, Middle Hill, Aldershot, Hants GU11 1PP T 01252-349004

IRELAND

There is one hierarchy for the whole of Ireland. Several of the dioceses have territory partly in the Republic of Ireland and partly in Northern Ireland.

APOSTOLIC NUNCIO TO IRELAND

HE Most Revd Dr Giuseppe Lazzarotto (Titular Archbishop of Numana), 183 Navan Road, Dublin 7 T (+353) (1) 838 0577 F (+353) (1) 838 0276

THE MOST REVD ARCHBISHOPS

Armagh, Seán Brady (*also* Primate of all Ireland), *cons.* 1995, *apptd* 1996. *Archbishop Emeritus,* HE Cardinal Cahal Daly *cons.* 1967, *elevated* 1991. *Auxiliary Bishop,* Most Revd Gerard Clifford, *cons.* 1991. *Clergy,* 165. *Bishop's Residence,* Ara Coeli, Armagh BT61 7QY T 028-3752 2045

Cashel and Emly, Dermot Clifford, *cons.* 1986, *apptd* 1988. *Clergy,* 103. *Archbishop's Residence,* Archbishop's House, Thurles, Co. Tipperary T (+353) (504) 21512

Dublin, Diarmuid Martin, *cons.* 1999, *apptd Coadjutor Archbishop* 2003, *succeeded as Archbishop* 2004. *Emeritus Archbishop,* HE Cardinal Desmond Connell, *cons.* 1988, *elevated* 2001. *Auxiliaries,* Eamonn Walsh, *cons.* 1990; Fiachra O'Ceallaigh, *cons* 1994; Raymond Field, *cons.* 1997. *Clergy,* 994. *Communications Office,* Archbishop's House, Drumcondra, Dublin 9 T (+353) (1) 836 0723

Tuam, Michael Neary, *cons.* 1992, *apptd* 1995. *Clergy,* 141. *Archbishop's Residence,* Archbishop's House, Tuam, Co. Galway T (+353) (93) 24166

THE RT. REVD BISHOPS

Achonry, Thomas Flynn, *cons.* 1977, *apptd* 1976. *Clergy,* 53. *Diocesan Office,* The Presbytery, Ballaghaderreen, Co. Roscommon T (+353) (94) 986 0011

Ardagh and Clonmacnois, Colm O'Reilly, *cons.* 1983, *apptd* 1983. *Clergy,* 65. *Diocesan Office,* Ballinalee Road, Longford, Co. Longford T (+353) (43) 46432

Clogher, Joseph Duffy, *cons.* 1979, *apptd* 1979. *Clergy,* 74. *Bishop's Residence,* Bishop's House, Monaghan T (+353) (47) 81019

Clonfert, John Kirby, *cons.* 1988 *apptd* 1988. *Clergy,* 46. *Bishop's Residence,* St Brendan's, Coorheen, Loughrea, Co. Galway T (+353) (91) 841560

Cloyne, John Magee, *cons.* 1987, *apptd* 1987. *Clergy,* 145. *Diocesan Centre,* Cobh, Co. Cork T (+353) (21) 481 1430

Cork and Ross, John Buckley, *cons.* 1984, *apptd* 1998. *Clergy,* 136. *Diocesan Office,* Cork and Ross Offices, Redemption Road, Cork T (+353) (21) 430 1717

Derry, Seamus Hegarty, *cons.* 1982, *apptd* 1994. *Auxiliary,* Francis Lagan, *cons.* 1988. *Clergy,* 138. *Bishop's Residence,* PO Box 227, Bishop's House, St Eugene's Cathedral, Derry BT48 9YG T 028-7126 2894

Down and Connor, Patrick Walsh, *cons.* 1983, *apptd* 1991. *Auxiliaries,* Anthony Farquhar, *cons.* 1983; Donal McKeown, *cons.* 2001. *Clergy,* 240. *Bishop's Residence,* Lisbreen, 73 Somerton Road, Belfast, Co. Antrim BT15 4DE T 028-9077 6185

Dromore, John McAreavey, *cons.* 1999, *apptd* 1999. *Clergy,* 43. *Bishop's Residence,* Bishop's House, 44 Armagh Road, Newry, Co. Down BT35 6PN T 028-3026 2444

Elphin, Christopher Jones, *cons.* 1994, *apptd* 1994. *Clergy,* 70. *Bishop's Residence,* St Mary's, Sligo T (+353) (71) 916 2670
Ferns, Denis Brennan, *cons.* 2006, *apptd* 2006. *Clergy,* 130. *Bishop's Residence,* Bishop's House, Summerhill, Wexford T (+353) (53) 912 2177
Galway, Kilmacduagh and Kilfenora, Martin Drennan, *cons.* 1997, *apptd* 2005. *Clergy,* 81. *Bishop's Residence,* Mount Saint Mary's, Taylor's Hill, Galway T (+353) (91) 563566
Kerry, William Murphy, *cons.* 1995, *apptd* 1995. *Clergy,* 126. *Bishop's Residence,* Bishop's House, Killarney, Co. Kerry T (+353) (64) 31168
Kildare and Leighlin, James Moriarty, *cons.* 1991, *apptd* 2002. *Clergy,* 110. *Bishop's Residence,* Bishop's House, Dublin Road, Carlow T (+353) (59) 917 6725
Killala, John Fleming, *cons.* 2002, *apptd* 2002. *Clergy,* 54. *Bishop's Residence,* Bishop's House, Ballina, Co. Mayo T (+353) (96) 21518
Killaloe, William Walsh, *cons.* 1994 *apptd* 1994. *Clergy,* 149. *Bishop's Residence,* Westbourne, Ennis, Co. Clare T (+353) (65) 682 8638
Kilmore, Leo O'Reilly, *cons.* 1997, *apptd* 1998. *Clergy,* 98. *Bishop's Residence,* Bishop's House, Cullies, Co. Cavan T (+353) (49) 433 1496
Limerick, Donal Murray, *cons.* 1982, *apptd* 1996. *Clergy,* 110. *Diocesan Office,* Social Service Centre, Henry Street, Limerick T (+353) (61) 315856
Meath, Michael Smith, *cons.* 1984, *apptd* 1990. *Clergy,* 141. *Bishop's Residence,* Bishop's House, Dublin Road, Mullingar, Co. Westmeath T (+353) (44) 934 8841
Ossory, Laurence Forristal, *cons.* 1980, *apptd* 1981. *Clergy,* 91. *Bishop's Residence,* Sion House, Kilkenny T (+353) (56) 62448
Raphoe, Philip Boyce, *cons.* 1995, *apptd* 1995. *Clergy,* 82. *Bishop's Residence,* Ard Adhamhnáin, Letterkenny, Co. Donegal T (+353) (74) 912 1208
Waterford and Lismore, William Lee, *cons.* 1993, *apptd* 1993. *Clergy,* 114. *Bishop's Residence,* John's Hill, Waterford T (+353) (51) 874463

OTHER CHURCHES IN THE UK

AFRICAN AND AFRO-CARIBBEAN CHURCHES

There are more than 160 Christian churches or groups of African or Afro-Caribbean origin in the UK. These include the Apostolic Faith Church, the Cherubim and Seraphim Church, the New Testament Church Assembly, the New Testament Church of God, the Wesleyan Holiness Church and the Aladura Churches. The Afro-West Indian United Council of Churches and the Council of African and Afro-Caribbean Churches UK (which was initiated as the Council of African and Allied Churches in 1979) are the media through which the member churches can work jointly to provide services they cannot easily provide individually.

There are about 70,000 adherents of African and Afro-Caribbean churches in the UK, and over 1,000 congregations. The Council of African and Afro-Caribbean Churches UK has about 17,000 members, 250 ministers and 125 congregations.

There are also numerous African and Caribbean Pentecostal churches and ministries which are members of the African Caribbean Evangelical Alliance.

COUNCIL OF AFRICAN AND AFRO-CARIBBEAN CHURCHES UK, 31 Norton House, Sidney Road, London SW9 0UJ T 020-7274 5589 E olu_abiola@lineone.net
Chair, HG Most Revd Father Olu A. Abiola, OBE

ASSOCIATED PRESBYTERIAN CHURCHES OF SCOTLAND

The Associated Presbyterian Churches came into being in 1989 as a result of a division within the Free Presbyterian Church of Scotland. Following two controversial disciplinary cases, the culmination of deepening differences within the church, a presbytery was formed calling itself the Associated Presbyterian Churches (APC). The Associated Presbyterian Churches has about 900 members, 9 ministers and 16 churches.

ASSOCIATED PRESBYTERIAN CHURCHES OF SCOTLAND, APC Manse, Polvinster Road, Oban PA34 5TN T 01631-567076 E archibald.mcphail@ntlworld.com W www.apchurches.org
Clerk of Presbytery, Revd A. N. McPhail

BAPTIST CHURCH

Baptists trace their origins to John Smyth, who in 1609 in Amsterdam reinstituted the baptism of conscious believers as the basis of the fellowship of a gathered church. Members of Smyth's church established the first Baptist church in England in 1612. They came to be known as 'General' Baptists and their theology was Arminian, whereas a later group of Calvinists who adopted the baptism of believers came to be known as 'Particular' Baptists. The two sections of the Baptists were united into one body, the Baptist Union of Great Britain and Ireland, in 1891. In 1988 the title was changed to the Baptist Union of Great Britain.

Baptists emphasise the complete autonomy of the local church, although individual churches are linked in various kinds of associations. There are international bodies (such as the Baptist World Alliance) and national bodies, but some Baptist churches belong to neither. However, in Great Britain the majority of churches and associations belong to the Baptist Union of Great Britain. There are also Baptist Unions in Wales, Scotland and Ireland which are much smaller than the Baptist Union of Great Britain, and there is some overlap of membership.

There are currently some 150,000 members and 2,150 churches associated with the Baptist Union of Great Britain. The Baptist Union of Great Britain is one of the founder members of the European Baptist Federation (1948) and the Baptist World Alliance (1905) which represents nearly 150,000 churches and over 40 million members worldwide.

In the Baptist Union of Scotland there are 13,625 members, 140 pastors and 173 churches.

In the Baptist Union of Wales (Undeb Bedyddwyr Cymru) there are about 15,500 members, 100 pastors and 450 churches, including those in England.

BAPTIST UNION OF GREAT BRITAIN, Baptist House, PO Box 44, 129 Broadway, Didcot, Oxon OX11 8RT T 01235-517700 E info@baptist.org.uk W www.baptist.org.uk
General Secretary, Revd Jonathan Edwards

BAPTIST UNION OF SCOTLAND, 14 Aytoun Road, Glasgow G41 5RT T 0141-423 6169 F 0141-424 1422 E director@scottishbaptist.org.uk
General Director, Revd William Slack

BAPTIST UNION OF WALES, 94 Mansel Street, Swansea SA1 5TZ T 01792-655468
President of the English Assembly (2007–8), Revd Richard Harrison

President of the Welsh Assembly (2007–8), Revd Alwyn Daniels
General Secretary of the Baptist Union of Wales, Revd Peter Thomas

CONGREGATIONAL FEDERATION

The Congregational Federation was founded by members of Congregational churches in England and Wales who did not join the United Reformed Church in 1972. There are also churches in Scotland and France affiliated to the federation. The federation exists to encourage congregations of believers to worship in free assembly, but it has no authority over them and emphasises their right to independence and self-governance.

The federation has 9,286 members, 80 accredited ministers and 293 churches in England, Wales and Scotland.

CONGREGATIONAL FEDERATION, 8 Castle Gate, Nottingham NG1 7AS T 0115-911 1460
E admin@congregational.org.uk
W www.congregational.org.uk
President of the Federation (2007–8), Revd Dr Alan Argent
General Secretary, Revd M. Heaney

FELLOWSHIP OF INDEPENDENT EVANGELICAL CHURCHES

The Fellowship of Independent Evangelical Churches was founded by Revd E. J. Poole-Connor (1872–1962) in 1922. In 1923 the fellowship published its first register of non-denominational pastors, evangelists and congregations who had accepted the doctrinal basis for the fellowship.

Members of the fellowship have two primary convictions, firstly to defend the evangelical faith, and secondly that evangelicism is the bond that unites the fellowship, rather than forms of worship or church government.

The Fellowship of Independent Evangelical Churches exists to promote the welfare of non-denominational bible churches and to give expression to the fundamental doctrines of evangelical Christianity. It supports individual churches by gathering and disseminating information and resources, advising churches on current theological, moral, social and practical issues and seeking to uphold the quality and integrity of church leaders through the Pastors' Association.

More than 480 churches are linked through the fellowship, which has 11 regions covering the whole of the UK. There are more than 330 pastors and approximately 35,000 people worship in fellowship churches every Sunday.

FELLOWSHIP OF INDEPENDENT EVANGELICAL CHURCHES, 39 The Point, Market Harborough, Leics LE16 7QU T 01858-434540 E admin@fiec.org.uk
W www.fiec.org.uk
President, Revd Rupert Bentley-Taylor
General Secretary, Richard Underwood

FREE CHURCH OF ENGLAND

The Free Church of England, otherwise called the Reformed Episcopal Church, is an independent church, constituted according to the historic faith, tradition and practice of the Church of England. Its roots lie in the 18th century, but most of its growth took place from the 1840s onwards, as clergy and congregations joined it from the established church in protest against the Oxford Movement. The historic episcopate was conferred on the English church in 1876 through bishops of the Reformed Episcopal Church (which had broken away from the Protestant Episcopal Church in the USA in 1873). A branch of the Reformed Episcopal Church was founded in the UK and this merged with the Free Church of England in 1927 to create the present church.

Worship is according to the *Book of Common Prayer* and some modern liturgy is permissable. Only men are ordained to the orders of deacon, presbyter and bishop.

The Free Church of England has 25 congregations, now mainly confined to England. It also has a few members in New Zealand and one congregation in St Petersburg, Russia.

THE FREE CHURCH OF ENGLAND, 329 Wolverhampton Road West, Willenhall WV13 2RL
T 01902-607335 W www.fcofe.org.uk
General Secretary, Rt. Revd Paul Hunt

FREE CHURCH OF SCOTLAND

The Free Church of Scotland was formed in 1843 when over 400 ministers withdrew from the Church of Scotland as a result of interference in the internal affairs of the church by the civil authorities. In 1900, all but 26 ministers joined with others to form the United Free Church (most of which rejoined the Church of Scotland in 1929). In 1904 the remaining 26 ministers were recognised by the House of Lords as continuing the Free Church of Scotland.

The church maintains strict adherence to the Westminster Confession of Faith (1648) and accepts the Bible as the sole rule of faith and conduct. Its general assembly meets annually. It also has links with reformed churches overseas. The Free Church of Scotland has about 12,000 members, 90 ministers and 100 congregations.

FREE CHURCH OF SCOTLAND, 15 North Bank Street, The Mound, Edinburgh EH1 2LS T 0131-226 5286
E offices@freechurchofscotland.org.uk
Chief Administrative Officer, R. M. Morrison

FREE PRESBYTERIAN CHURCH OF SCOTLAND

The Free Presbyterian Church of Scotland was formed in 1893 by two ministers of the Free Church of Scotland who refused to accept a Declaratory Act passed by the Free Church General Assembly in 1892. The Free Presbyterian Church of Scotland is Calvinistic in doctrine and emphasises observance of the Sabbath. It adheres strictly to the Westminster Confession of Faith of 1648.

The church has about 3,000 members in Scotland and about 4,000 in overseas congregations. It has 20 ministers and 50 churches in the UK.

FREE PRESBYTERIAN CHURCH OF SCOTLAND, Free Presbyterian Manse, Laide, Ross-shire IV22 2NB
T 0141-332 9283
Moderator, Revd D. A. Ross
Clerk of the Synod, Revd John MacLeod

HOLY APOSTOLIC CATHOLIC ASSYRIAN CHURCH OF THE EAST

The Holy Apostolic Catholic Assyrian Church of the East traces its beginnings to the middle of the first century. It spread from Upper Mesopotamia throughout the territories of the Persian Empire. The Assyrian Church of the East became theologically separated from the rest of the Christian community following the Council of Ephesus in 431. The church is headed by the Catholicos Patriarch and is episcopal in government. The liturgical language is Syriac (Aramaic). The Assyrian Church of the

East and the Roman Catholic Church agreed a common Christological declaration in 1994 and a process of dialogue between the Assyrian Church of the East and the Chaldean Catholic Church, which is in communion with Rome but shares the Syriac liturgy, was instituted in 1996.

The church has about 400,000 members in the Middle East, India, Europe, North America and Australasia.

The church in Great Britain forms part of the diocese of Europe under Mar Odisho Oraham.

HOLY APOSTOLIC CATHOLIC ASSYRIAN CHURCH OF THE EAST, 66 Montague Road, London W7 3PQ T 020-8579 7259
Representative in Great Britain, Very Revd Younan Y. Younan

INDEPENDENT METHODIST CHURCHES

The Independent Methodist Churches were formed in 1805 and remained independent when the Methodist Church in Great Britain was formed in 1932. They are mainly concentrated in the industrial areas of the north of England.

The churches are Methodist in doctrine but their organisation is congregational. All the churches are members of the Independent Methodist Connexion of Churches. The controlling body of the Connexion is the Annual Meeting, to which churches send delegates. The Connexional President is elected annually. Between annual meetings the affairs of the Connexion are handled by departmental committees. Ministers are appointed by the churches and trained through the Connexion. The ministry is open to both men and women and is unpaid.

There are 2,000 members, 90 ministers and 86 churches in Great Britain.

INDEPENDENT METHODIST RESOURCE CENTRE, Fleet Street, Pemberton, Wigan, WN5 0DS T 01942-223526
E resourcecentre@imcgb.org.uk
General Secretary, W. C. Gabb

LUTHERAN CHURCH

Lutheranism is based on the teachings of Martin Luther, the German leader of the Protestant Reformation. The authority of the scriptures is held to be supreme over church tradition. The teachings of Lutheranism are explained in detail in 16th-century confessional writings, particularly the Augsburg Confession. Lutheranism is one of the largest Protestant denominations and it is particularly strong in northern Europe and the USA. Some Lutheran churches are episcopal, while others have a synodal form of organisation; unity is based on doctrine rather than structure. Most Lutheran churches are members of the Lutheran World Federation, based in Geneva.

Lutheran services in Great Britain are held in 18 languages to serve members of different nationalities. Services usually follow ancient liturgies. English-language congregations are members either of the Lutheran Church in Great Britain or of the Evangelical Lutheran Church of England. The Lutheran Church in Great Britain and other Lutheran churches in Britain are members of the Lutheran Council of Great Britain, which represents them and coordinates their common work.

There are over 70 million Lutherans worldwide; in Great Britain there are about 100,000 members, 50 clergy and 100 congregations.

THE LUTHERAN COUNCIL OF GREAT BRITAIN, 30 Thanet Street, London WC1H 9QH T 020-7554 2900
F 020-7383 3081 E enquiries@lutheran.org.uk
W www.lutheran.org.uk
General Secretary, Revd Thomas Bruch

METHODIST CHURCH

The Methodist movement started in England in 1729 when the Revd John Wesley, an Anglican priest, and his brother Charles met with others in Oxford and resolved to conduct their lives and study by 'rule and method'. In 1739 the Wesleys began evangelistic preaching and the first Methodist chapel was founded in Bristol in the same year. In 1744 the first annual conference was held, at which the Articles of Religion were drawn up. Doctrinal emphases included repentance, faith, the assurance of salvation, social concern and the priesthood of all believers. After John Wesley's death in 1791 the Methodists withdrew from the established church to form the Methodist Church. Methodists gradually drifted into many groups, but in 1932 the Wesleyan Methodist Church, the United Methodist Church and the Primitive Methodist Church united to form the Methodist Church of Great Britain.

The governing body of the Methodist Church is the conference. The conference is held in June each year and consists of three parts: the diaconal, ministerial and representative sessions. In addition, there are 32 district synods whose purpose is to decide policy for the district and be the link between the conference and the circuits. The circuit is the basic structure of the Methodist Church and is usually formed from the local churches in a defined area; a number of circuits make up each district. There are over 60 million Methodists worldwide; in Great Britain in 2007 there were 272,500 members, 3,603 ministers and 239 deacons.

THE METHODIST CHURCH OF GREAT BRITAIN, Methodist Church House, 25 Marylebone Road, London NW1 5JR T 020-7486 5502
E generalsecretary@methodistchurch.org.uk
W www.methodist.org.uk
President of the Conference (2007–8), Revd Dr Martyn Atkins
Vice-President of the Conference (2007–8), Ruby Beech
Secretary of the Conference, Revd David Deeks

IRELAND

The Methodist Church in Ireland is autonomous but has close links with British Methodism. It has a community roll of 54,079, 15,600 members, 230 ministers, 218 lay preachers and 220 churches.

METHODIST CHURCH IN IRELAND, 1 Fountainville Avenue, Belfast BT9 6AN T 028-9032 4554
E secretary@irishmethodist.org W www.irishmethodist.org
President (2007–8), Revd Roy Cooper
Secretary, Revd Donald Ker

ORTHODOX CHURCHES

EASTERN ORTHODOX CHURCH

The Eastern (or Byzantine) Orthodox Church is a communion of self-governing Christian churches that recognises the honorary primacy of the Oecumenical Patriarch of Constantinople.

The position of Orthodox Christians is that the faith was fully defined during the period of the Oecumenical Councils. In doctrine it is strongly trinitarian, and stresses the mystery and importance of the sacraments. It is episcopal in government. The structure of the Orthodox Christian year differs from that of western churches.

Orthodox Christians throughout the world are estimated to number about 300 million; there are an estimated 271,158 in the UK.

GREEK ORTHODOX CHURCH (PATRIARCHATE OF ANTIOCH)

There are sixteen parishes in the UK. The Diocese of Western and Central Europe is led by HE Metropolitan Gabriel.

DIOCESE OF WESTERN AND CENTRAL EUROPE, 22 Avenue Kleber, 75116 Paris T (+33) (145) 01 8356
Bishop, HE Metropolitan Gabriel

PATRIARCHATE OF ANTIOCH IN THE UK, St George's Cathedral, 1A Redhill Street, London NW1 4BG T 020-7383 0403 E info@antiochgreekorth.co.uk W www.antiochgreekorth.co.uk
Priest, Fr. Samir Gholam

GREEK ORTHODOX CHURCH (PATRIARCHATE OF CONSTANTINOPLE)

The presence of Greek Orthodox Christians in Britain dates back at least to 1677 when Archbishop Joseph Geogirenes of Samos fled from Turkish persecution and came to London. The present Greek cathedral in Moscow Road, Bayswater, was opened for public worship in 1879 and the Diocese of Thyateira and Great Britain was established in 1922. There are now 120 parishes and other communities (including monasteries) in the UK, served by five bishops, 105 clergy, nine cathedrals and about 93 churches.

THE PATRIARCHATE OF CONSTANTINOPLE IN GREAT BRITAIN, Thyateira House, 5 Craven Hill, London W2 3EN T 020-7723 4787 F 020-7224 9301 E mail@thyateira.org.uk W www.thyateira.org.uk
Archbishop, Gregorios of Thyateira and Great Britain

RUSSIAN ORTHODOX CHURCH

The records of Russian Orthodox Church activities in Britain date from the visit to England of Tsar Peter I in the early 18th century. Clergy were sent from Russia to serve the chapel established to minister to the staff of the Imperial Russian Embassy in London.

In 2007, after an 80-year division, the Russian Orthodox Church Outside Russia agreed to become an autonomous part of the Russian Orthodox Church, Patriarchate of Moscow. The reunification agreement was signed by Patriarch Alexy II, Patriarch of the Russian Orthodox Church and Metropolitan Lavy, leader of the Russian Orthodox Church Outside Russia on 17 May at a ceremony at Christ the Saviour Cathedral in Moscow.

The diocese of Sourozh is the diocese of the Russian Orthodox Church in Great Britain and Ireland and is currently led by Archbishop Innokenty of Korsun. The local administration of the diocese is the responsibility of Bishop Elisey of Bogorodsk and 19 diocesan clergy.

DIOCESE OF SOUROZH, Diocesan Office, Cathedral of the Dormition and All Saints, 67 Ennismore Gardens, London SW7 1NH T 020-7584 0096 W www.sourozh.org
Bishop of Bogorodsk, Rt. Revd Elisey

SERBIAN ORTHODOX CHURCH (PATRIARCHATE OF SERBIA)

There are around 40,000 members in the UK served by 11 clergy. The Patriarchate of Serbia is represented by Bishop Dositej of Great Britain and Scandinavia.

SERBIAN ORTHODOX CHURCH IN GREAT BRITAIN, Saint Sava, 89 Lancaster Road, London W11 1QQ T 020-7727 8367 E crkva@spclondon.org W www.spclondon.org
Representative, Very Revd Milun Kostic

OTHER NATIONALITIES

The Patriarchates of Romania and Bulgaria have memberships of around 3,000 and 86 respectively, while the Ukrainian Autocephalous Patriarchate has around 1,000 members. The Belarusian (membership estimated at 2,300) and Latvian (membership of around 110) Orthodox churches are part of the Patriarchate of Constantinople.

ORIENTAL ORTHODOX CHURCHES

The term 'Oriental Orthodox Churches' is now generally used to describe a group of six ancient eastern churches which reject the Christological definition of the Council of Chalcedon (AD 451) and use Christological terms in different ways from the Eastern Orthodox Church. There are estimated to be around 50 million members worldwide of the Oriental Orthodox Churches and about 22,020 in the UK.

ARMENIAN ORTHODOX CHURCH (PATRIARCHATE OF ETCHMIADZIN)

The Armenian Orthodox Church is led by HH Karekin II, Catholicos of All Armenians. Bishop Nathan Hovhannisian is the Primate of the Armenian Church of Great Britain and President of the Armenian Community and Church Council.

ARMENIAN CHURCH OF GREAT BRITAIN, The Armenian Vicarage, Iverna Gardens, London W8 6TP T 020-7937 0152 E arajnortaran@aol.com W www.accc.org.uk
Primate, Bishop Nathan Hovhannisian

COPTIC ORTHODOX CHURCH

The Coptic Orthodox Church is led by HH Pope Shenouda III and is represented in Great Britain by Bishop Angaelos at the Coptic Orthodox Cathedral of St George at the Coptic Orthodox Church Centre. The Coptic Orthodox Church is the largest Oriental Orthodox community in Great Britain.

COPTIC ORTHODOX CHURCH CENTRE, Shephalbury Manor, Broadhall Way, Stevenage, Herts SG2 8RH T 01438-745232 E info@copticcentre.com W www.copticcentre.com
Bishop, Bishop Angaelos

BRITISH ORTHODOX CHURCH

The British Orthodox Church is canonically part of the Coptic Orthodox Patriarchate of Alexandria. As it ministers to British people all its services are in English.

THE BRITISH ORTHODOX CHURCH, 10 Heathwood Gardens, Charlton, London SE7 8EP T 020-8854 3090 E boc@nildram.co.uk W www.britishorthodox.org
Metropolitan, Abba Seraphim

INDIAN ORTHODOX CHURCH

The Indian Orthodox Church, also known as the Malankara Orthodox Church, is part of the Diocese of Europe, UK and Canada under Metropolitan Thomas Mar Makarios. The church in Great Britain can be contacted via Fr. Abraham Thomas.

INDIAN ORTHODOX CHURCH, St Gregorios Indian Orthodox Church, Cranfield Road, Brockley, London SE4 1UF T 020-8691 9456 E vicar@indian-orthodox.co.uk W www.indian-orthodox.co.uk
Vicar, Fr. Abraham Thomas

SYRIAN ORTHODOX CHURCH

The Patriarchate Vicariate of the Syrian Orthodox Church

in the United Kingdom is represented by HE Archbishop Athanasius Toma Dawod.

SYRIAN ORTHODOX CHURCH IN THE UK, 5 Canning Road, Croydon CR0 6QA T 020-8654 7531 E info-uk@syrianorthodoxchurch.net W www.syrianorthodoxchurch.net
Archbishop, HE Athanasius Toma Dawod

PENTECOSTAL CHURCHES

Pentecostalism is inspired by the descent of the Holy Spirit upon the apostles at Pentecost. The movement began in Los Angeles, USA, in 1906 and is characterised by baptism with the Holy Spirit, divine healing, speaking in tongues (glossolalia), and a literal interpretation of the scriptures.

The Pentecostal movement in Britain dates from 1907. Initially, groups of Pentecostalists were led by laymen and did not organise formally. However, in 1915 the Elim Foursquare Gospel Alliance (more usually called the Elim Pentecostal Church) was founded in Ireland by George Jeffreys and currently has about 550 churches, 68,500 adherents and 650 accredited ministers. In 1924 about 70 independent assemblies formed a fellowship, the Assemblies of God in Great Britain and Ireland, which now incorporates around 600 churches and is known as the Assemblies of God.

The Apostolic Church grew out of the 1904–5 revivals in South Wales and was established in 1916. The Apostolic Church of Great Britain and Northern Ireland has around 116 churches, 5,500 adherents and 76 ministers. The New Testament Church of God was established in England in 1953 and has about 120 congregations, around 40,000 followers and more than 300 ministers across England and Wales. In recent years many aspects of Pentecostalism have been adopted by the growing charismatic movement within the Roman Catholic, Protestant and Eastern Orthodox churches. There are about 105 million Pentecostalists worldwide, with about 280,260 adherents in Great Britain and Ireland.

THE APOSTOLIC CHURCH OF GREAT BRITAIN AND NORTHERN IRELAND, International Administration Offices, PO Box 389, Swansea SA7 9LA T 01792-790300 E admin@apostolic-church.org
National Leader, Warren Jones

THE ASSEMBLIES OF GOD INCORPORATED, PO Box 7634, Nottingham NG11 6ZY T 0115-921 7272 E info@aog.org.uk W www.aog.org.uk
General Superintendent, Paul C. Weaver

THE ELIM PENTECOSTAL CHURCH, PO Box 38, Cheltenham, Glos GL50 3HN T 01242-519904 E info@elimhq.net W www.elim.org.uk
General Superintendent, Revd John Glass

THE NEW TESTAMENT CHURCH OF GOD, Main House, Overstone Park, Overstone, Northampton NN6 0AD T 01604-643311 E bigmove@ntcg.org.uk W www.ntcg.org.uk
Administrative Bishop, Bishop Eric Arthur Brown

PLYMOUTH BRETHREN

The Brethren was founded in Dublin in 1827–8. It rejected denominationalism and clericalism and based itself on the structures and practices of the early church. Many groups sprang up and that at Plymouth became the best known, which resulted in the designation by others as Plymouth Brethren.

Early worship had a prescribed form but quickly assumed an unstructured, non-liturgical format. There were services devoted to worship, usually involving the breaking of bread, and separate preaching meetings. There is no salaried ministry.

A theological dispute led in 1848 to schism between the Open Brethren and the Closed or Exclusive Brethren, each branch later suffering further divisions.

Open Brethren churches are completely independent, but freely cooperate with each other. Open Brethren churches are run by appointed elders. Exclusive Brethren churches believe in a universal fellowship between congregations. They do not have elders, but appoint respected members of their congregation to perform certain administrative functions.

The Brethren are established throughout the UK, Ireland, Europe, India, Africa and Australasia. They do not maintain lists of their members. There are a few publishing houses which publish Brethren related literature. Chapter Two is the main supplier of such literature in the UK and also has a Brethren history archive which is available for use by appointment.

CHAPTER TWO, Conduit Mews, London SE18 7AP T 020-8316 5389 E chapter2uk@aol.com W www.chaptertwobooks.org.uk

PRESBYTERIAN CHURCH IN IRELAND

The Presbyterian Church in Ireland is reformed in doctrine and presbyterian in constitution. Presbyterianism was established in Ireland as a result of the Ulster plantation in the early 17th century when English and Scottish Protestants settled in the north of Ireland.

There are 21 presbyteries under the chief court known as the general assembly. The general assembly meets annually and is presided over by a moderator who is elected for one year. The ongoing work of the church is undertaken by 15 boards under which there are specialist committees.

There are around 300,000 Presbyterians in Ireland and Northern Ireland, forming over 560 congregations.

THE PRESBYTERIAN CHURCH IN IRELAND, Church House, Belfast BT1 6DW T 028-9032 2284 E info@presbyterianireland.org W www.presbyterianireland.org
Moderator (2007–8), Rt. Revd Dr John Finlay
Clerk of Assembly and General Secretary, Revd Dr Donald Watts

PRESBYTERIAN CHURCH OF WALES

The Presbyterian Church of Wales or Calvinistic Methodist Church of Wales is Calvinistic in doctrine and presbyterian in constitution. It was formed in 1811 when Welsh Calvinists severed the relationship with the established church by ordaining their own ministers. It secured its own confession of faith in 1823 and a Constitutional Deed in 1826, and since 1864 the General Assembly has met annually, presided over by a moderator elected for a year. The doctrine and constitutional structure of the Presbyterian Church of Wales was confirmed by act of parliament in 1931–2.

The Church has around 33,363 members, 89 ministers and 745 churches.

THE PRESBYTERIAN CHURCH OF WALES, Tabernacle Chapel, 81 Merthyr Road, Whitchurch, Cardiff CF14 1DD T 029-2062 7465 E swyddfa.office@ebcpcw.org.uk W www.ebcpcw.org.uk
Moderator (2007–8), Revd John Owen
General Secretary, Revd Ifan Roberts

RELIGIOUS SOCIETY OF FRIENDS (QUAKERS)

Quakerism is a religious denomination which was ounded in the 17th century by George Fox and others in n attempt to revive what they saw as the original primitive Christianity'. The movement, at first called riends of the Truth, started in the Midlands, Yorkshire nd north-west England, but there are now Quakers all ver Britain and in 36 countries around the world. The olony of Pennsylvania, founded by William Penn, was riginally Quaker.

Emphasis is placed on the experience of God in daily ife rather than on sacraments or religious occasions. here is no church calendar. Worship is largely silent and here are no appointed ministers; the responsibility for onducting a meeting is shared equally among those resent. Religious tolerance and social reform have always een important to Quakers, together with a commitment o peace and non-violence in resolving disputes.

There are more than 27,000 'friends' or Quakers in ireat Britain. There are about 500 places where Quaker neetings are held, many of them Quaker owned Friends leeting Houses. The Britain Yearly Meeting is the name iven to the central organisation of Quakers in Britain.

HE RELIGIOUS SOCIETY OF FRIENDS (QUAKERS) IN BRITAIN, Friends House, 173–177 Euston Road, London NW1 2BJ T 020-7663 1000
E enquiries@quaker.org.uk W www.quaker.org.uk
Recording Clerk, Elsa Dicks

SALVATION ARMY

he Salvation Army is an international Christian rganisation working in 111 countries worldwide. As a hurch and registered charity, the Salvation Army is unded through donations from its members, the general ublic and, where appropriate, government grants.

The Salvation Army was founded by a Methodist ninister, William Booth, in the East End of London in 865, and now has 755 local church centres, 50 esidential centres for the homeless, 18 elderly care entres and six substance misuse centres. It also runs a lothing recycling programme, charity shops, a prison isiting service and a family tracing service. In 1878 it dopted a quasi-military command structure intended to ispire and regulate its endeavours and to reflect its view hat the church was engaged in spiritual warfare. alvationists emphasise evangelism and the provision of ocial welfare.

K TERRITORIAL HEADQUARTERS, 101 Newington Causeway, London SE1 6BN T 0845-634 0101
E press.office@salvationarmy.org.uk
W www.salvationarmy.org.uk
International Leader, Gen. Shaw Clifton
UK Territorial Commander, Commissioner John Matear

SEVENTH-DAY ADVENTIST CHURCH

he Seventh-day Adventist Church was founded in 1863 n the USA and the first church in the UK was established n 1886. It is a worldwide Christian church with 14.75 nillion members worshipping in 121,564 congregrations n 202 countries. Slightly more than 70 per cent of all eventh-day Adventists live in Africa, the Caribbean and entral and South America. In the UK there are 27,079 nembers worshipping in 279 churches and companies.

The beliefs and practices of the church are rooted in the ible and are summarised under 28 core beliefs. The nission of the church is to proclaim to all people the verlasting gospel of the three angels' messages of Revelation 14:6–12, leading them to accept Jesus as their personal saviour and to prepare for his imminent return.

The world church is divided administratively into 13 divisions, each made up of 'unions' of churches. The British Isles headquarters is known as the British Union Conference of Seventh-day Adventists.

BRITISH UNION CONFERENCE OF SEVENTH-DAY ADVENTISTS, Stanborough Park, Watford WD25 9JZ
T 01923-672251 W www.adventist.org.uk
President, Don McFarlane

THE (SWEDENBORGIAN) NEW CHURCH

The New Church is based on the teachings of the 18th century Swedish scientist and theologian Emanuel Swedenborg (1688–1772), who believed that Jesus Christ appeared to him and instructed him to reveal the spiritual meaning of the Bible. He claimed to have visions of the spiritual world, including heaven and hell, and conversations with angels and spirits. He published several theological works, including descriptions of the spiritual world and a Bible commentary.

The second coming of Jesus Christ is believed to have already taken place and is still taking place, being not an actual physical reappearance of Christ, but rather his return in spirit. It is also believed that concurrent with our life on earth is life in a parallel spiritual world, of which we are usually unconscious until death. There are around 30,000 Swedenborgians worldwide, with 850 members, 24 Churches and 10 ministers in the UK.

THE GENERAL CONFERENCE OF THE NEW CHURCH, Swedenborg House, 20 Bloomsbury Way, London WC1A 2TH T 020-7229 9340
E enquiries@generalconference.org.uk
W www.thenewchurch.org.uk
Chief Executive, Michael Hindley

UNDEB YR ANNIBYNWYR CYMRAEG

Undeb Yr Annibynwyr Cymraeg, the Union of Welsh Independents, was formed in 1872 and is a voluntary association of Welsh Congregational churches and personal members. It is mainly Welsh speaking. Congregationalism in Wales dates back to 1639 when the first Welsh Congregational church was opened in Gwent. Member churches are traditionally Calvinistic in doctrine, although a wide range of interpretations are permitted, and congregationalist in organisation. Each church has complete independence in the government and administration of its affairs.

The Union has 28,892 members, 98 ministers and 449 member churches.

UNDEB YR ANNIBYNWYR CYMRAEG, 5 Axis Court, Riverside Business Park, Swansea Vale, Swansea SA7 0AJ
T 01792-795888 E undeb@annibynwyr.org
W www.annibynwyr.org
President of the Union (2007–8), Revd Dewi Myrddin Hughes
General Secretary, Revd Dr Geraint Tudur

UNITED REFORMED CHURCH

The United Reformed Church (URC) was first formed by the union of most of the Congregational churches in England and Wales with the Presbyterian Church of England in 1972. Congregationalism dates from the mid-16th century. It is Calvinistic in doctrine, and its followers form independent self-governing congregations bound under God by covenant, a principle laid down in the writings of Robert Browne (1550–1633). From the late 16th century the movement was driven underground by persecution, but the cause was defended at the Westminster Assembly in 1643 and the Savoy Declaration of 1658 laid down its principles. Congregational churches formed county associations for mutual support and in 1832 these associations merged to form the Congregational Union of England and Wales.

Presbyterianism in England also dates from the mid 16th century, and was Calvinistic and evangelical in its doctrine. It was governed by a hierarchy of courts.

In the 1960s there was close cooperation locally and nationally between congregational and presbyterian churches. This led to union negotiations and a Scheme of Union, supported by act of parliament in 1972. In 1981 a further unification took place, with the Reformed Association of Churches of Christ becoming part of the URC. In 2000 a third union took place, with the Congregational Union of Scotland. In its basis the United Reformed Church reflects local church initiative and responsibility with a conciliar pattern of oversight. The general assembly is the central body, and is made up of equal numbers of ministers and lay members.

The United Reformed Church is divided into 81 district councils which form 13 Synods, each with a Synod Moderator. There are around 1,800 congregations which serve around 150,000 adults and 100,000 children and young people. There are around 1,000 serving ministers.

The General Assembly is the central body, and comprises around 700 representatives, mainly appointed by the district councils, of which half are lay persons and half are ministers. Each year the General Assembly elects a Moderator, either lay or ordained, who then becomes the national representative of the URC.

UNITED REFORMED CHURCH, 86 Tavistock Place, London WC1H 9RT **T** 020-7916 2020 **E** urc@urc.org.uk
W www.urc.org.uk
Moderator of the General Assembly (2007–8), Revd Stephen Orchard
General Secretary, Revd Dr David Cornick

WESLEYAN REFORM UNION

The Wesleyan Reform Union was founded by Methodists who left or were expelled from Wesleyan Methodism in 1849 following a period of internal conflict. Its doctrine is conservative evangelical and its organisation is congregational, each church having complete independence in the government and administration of its affairs. The union has 1,843 members, 15 ministers, 115 lay preachers and 108 churches.

THE WESLEYAN REFORM UNION, Wesleyan Reform Church House, 123 Queen Street, Sheffield S1 2DU
T 0114-272 1938 **E** admin@thewru.co.uk
W www.thewru.com
President (2007–8), Revd David Mills
General Secretary, Revd Colin Braithwaite

NON-TRINITARIAN CHURCHES

CHRISTADELPHIAN

Christadelphians believe that the Bible is the word of God and that it reveals both God's dealings with mankind in the past and his plans for the future. These plans centre on the work of Jesus Christ, who it is believed will return to Earth to establish God's kingdom. Christadelphians have existed since the 1850s, beginning in the USA through the work of an Englishman, Dr John Thomas.

THE CHRISTADELPHIAN MAGAZINE AND PUBLISHING ASSOCIATION, 404 Shaftmoor Lane, Birmingham B28 8SZ **T** 0121-777 6324 **F** 0121-778 5024
E enquiries@thechristadelphian.com
W www.thechristadelphian.com

CHURCH OF CHRIST, SCIENTIST

The Church of Christ, Scientist was founded by Mary Baker Eddy in the USA in 1879 to 'reinstate primitive Christianity and its lost element of healing'. Christian Science teaches the need for spiritual regeneration and salvation from sin, but is best known for its reliance on prayer alone in the healing of sickness. Adherents believe that such healing is a law, or divine science, and is in direct line with that practised by Jesus Christ (revered, not as God, but as the son of God) and by the early Christian church.

The denomination consists of The First Church of Christ, Scientist, in Boston, Massachusetts, USA (the 'mother church') and its branch churches in almost 8[illegible] countries worldwide. The Bible and Mary Baker Eddy's book, *Science and Health with Key to the Scriptures,* are used for daily spiritual guidance and healing by all members and are read at services; there are no clergy. Those engaged in full-time healing are called practitioners, of whom there are 1,500 worldwide. The church also publishes *The Christian Science Monitor.*

No membership figures are available, since Mary Baker Eddy felt that numbers are no measure of spiritual vitality and ruled that such statistics should not be published. There are almost 2,000 branch churches worldwide, including over 100 in the UK.

CHRISTIAN SCIENCE COMMITTEE ON PUBLICATION, Claridge House, 29 Barnes High Street, London SW13 9LW **T** 020-8282 1645 **E** londoncs@csps.com
W www.christianscience.com
District Manager for the UK and the Republic of Ireland, Tony Lobl

CHURCH OF JESUS CHRIST OF LATTER-DAY SAINTS

The Church of Jesus Christ of Latter-Day Saints (often referred to as 'Mormons') was founded in New York State, USA, in 1830, and came to Britain in 1837. The oldest continuous congregation of the church is in Preston, Lancashire.

Mormons are Christians who claim to belong to the 'restored church' of Jesus Christ. They believe that true Christianity died when the last original apostle died, but that it was given back to the world by God and Christ through Joseph Smith, the church's founder and first president. They accept and use the Bible as scripture, but believe in continuing revelation from God and use additional scriptures, including *The Book of Mormon: Another Testament of Jesus Christ.* The importance of the family is central to the church's beliefs and practice. Church members set aside Monday evenings as family home evenings when Christian family values are taught. Polygamy was formally discontinued in 1890.

The church has no paid ministry: local congregations are headed by a leader chosen from amongst their number. The world governing body, based in Utah, USA, is led by a president, believed to be the chosen prophet, and his two counsellors. There are more than 12.5 million members worldwide, with over 190,000 adherents and 411 congregations in the UK.

CHURCH OF JESUS CHRIST OF LATTER-DAY SAINTS, British Headquarters, 751 Warwick Road, Solihull, W. Midlands B91 3DQ **T** 0121-712 1200 **W** www.lds.org.uk

JEHOVAH'S WITNESSES

The movement now known as Jehovah's Witnesses grew from a Bible study group formed by Charles Taze Russell in 1872 in Pennsylvania, USA. In 1896 it adopted the name of the Watch Tower Bible and Tract Society, and in 1931 its members became known as Jehovah's Witnesses.

Jehovah's (God's) Witnesses believe in the Bible as the word of God, and consider it to be inspired and historically accurate. They take the scriptures literally, except where there are obvious indications that they are figurative or symbolic, and reject the doctrine of the Trinity. Witnesses also believe that the earth will remain for ever and that all those approved of by Jehovah will have eternal life on a cleansed and beautified earth; only 144,000 will go to heaven to rule with Christ. They believe that the second coming of Christ began in 1914 and his thousand-year reign on earth is imminent, and that armageddon (a final battle in which evil will be defeated) will precede Christ's rule of peace. They refuse to take part in military service and do not accept blood transfusions.

The nine-member world governing body is based in New York, USA. There is no paid ministry, but each congregation has elders assigned to look after various duties and every Witness is assigned homes to visit in their congregation. There are over 6.7 million Jehovah's Witnesses worldwide, with 130,000 Witnesses in the UK organised into more than 1,500 congregations.

BRITISH ISLES HEADQUARTERS, Watch Tower House, The Ridgeway, London NW7 1RN **T** 020-8906 2211
E opi@wtbts.org.uk **W** www.watchtower.org

UNITARIAN AND FREE CHRISTIAN CHURCHES

Unitarianism has its historical roots in the Judaeo-Christian tradition but rejects the deity of Christ and the doctrine of the Trinity. It allows the individual to embrace insights from all the world's faiths and philosophies, as there is no fixed creed. It is accepted that beliefs may evolve in the light of personal experience.

Unitarian communities first became established in Poland and Transylvania in the 16th century. The first avowedly Unitarian place of worship in the British Isles opened in London in 1774. The General Assembly of Unitarian and Free Christian Churches came into existence in 1928 as the result of the amalgamation of two earlier organisations.

There are about 4,400 Unitarians in Great Britain and Ireland and about 72 Unitarian ministers. Nearly 200 self-governing congregations and fellowship groups, including a small number overseas, are members of the General Assembly.

GENERAL ASSEMBLY OF UNITARIAN AND FREE CHRISTIAN CHURCHES, Essex Hall, 1–6 Essex Street, London WC2R 3HY **T** 020-7240 2384
E ga@unitarian.org.uk **W** www.unitarian.org.uk
President 2007–8, Revd Celia Midgley

COMMUNICATIONS

POSTAL SERVICES

The Royal Mail Group plc operates Parcelforce Worldwide, Post Office and Royal Mail, which handles around 84 million items of mail each day. The Postal Services Commission (Postcomm), an independent regulator accountable to parliament, oversees postal operations in the UK. It is responsible for the smooth introduction of competition into postal services, and the market was opened to full competition in January 2006. All postal operators, including Royal Mail, are licensed by Postcomm; the licence requires the operators to ensure that the mail they handle is always secure and to maintain certain standards. Postwatch is the consumer organisation responsible for postal services and takes up complaints on behalf of consumers against any licensed provider of postal services.

POSTCOMM, Hercules House, 6 Hercules Road, London SE1 7DB **T** 020-7593 2100 **W** www.psc.gov.uk

POSTWATCH, Freepost, Postwatch **T** 08456-013265 **W** www.postwatch.co.uk

PRICING IN PROPORTION

In August 2006 Royal Mail introduced a new pricing system, whereby the pricing of mail depends upon its size as well as its weight. The system is designed to rebalance postage prices to reflect the fact that larger, bulkier items cost more to handle than smaller, lighter ones. There are three basic categories of correspondence:

LETTER
Length up to 240mm, *width* up to 165mm, *thickness* up to 5mm, *weight* up to 100g, eg most cards, postcards and bills

LARGE LETTER
Length up to 353mm, *width* up to 250mm, *thickness* up to 25mm, *weight* up to 750g, eg most A4 documents, CDs and magazines

PACKET
Length over 353mm, *width* over 250mm, *thickness* over 25mm, *weight* over 750g, eg VHS cassettes, books, prints and posters in cylindrical packaging

INLAND POSTAL SERVICES

Below are details of a number of popular postal services along with prices correct as at August 2007.

INLAND POST RATES

Format	*Maximum weight*	*First class*	*Second class†*
Letter*	100g	£0.34	£0.24
Large letter	100g	£0.48	£0.40
	250g	£0.70	£0.60
	500g	£0.98	£0.83
	750g	£1.42	£1.20
Packet	100g	£1.09	£0.92
	250g	£1.38	£1.20
	500g	£1.84	£1.52
	750g	£2.38	£1.92
	1,000g‡	£2.92	£2.30

* Includes postcards
† First class post is normally delivered on the following working day and second class within three working days
‡ Packets weighing over 1kg cost £4.25 plus £0.75 for every additional 250g or part thereof and can only be sent by first class post

UK PARCEL RATES

Maximum weight	*Standard tariff**
1kg	£3.85
1.5kg	£4.95
2kg	£5.68
4kg	£8.24
6kg	£9.35
8kg	£10.67
10kg	£11.45
20kg	£13.33

* Standard parcels are normally delivered within three to five working days

OVERSEAS POSTAL SERVICES

Royal Mail divides the world into three zones: **Europe** (Albania, Andorra, Armenia, Austria, Azerbaijan, Azores, Balearic Islands, Belarus, Belgium, Bosnia and Hercegovina, Bulgaria, Canary Islands, Corsica, Croatia, Cyprus, Czech Republic, Denmark, Estonia, Faroe Islands, Finland, France, Georgia, Germany, Gibraltar, Greece, Greenland, Hungary, Iceland, Ireland, Italy, Kazakhstan, Kyrgyzstan, Latvia, Liechtenstein, Lithuania, Luxembourg, Macedonia, Madeira, Malta, Moldova, Monaco, Montenegro, the Netherlands, Norway, Poland, Portugal, Romania, Russian Federation, San Marino, Serbia, Slovakia, Slovenia, Spain, Spitzbergen, Sweden, Switzerland, Tajikistan, Turkey, Turkmenistan, Ukraine, Uzbekistan, Vatican City State); **World Zone 1** (All countries that are not listed under Europe or World Zone 2); **World Zone 2** (American Samoa, Australia, China, East Timor, Fiji, French Polynesia, French Southern and Antarctic Territories*, Guam, Japan, Kiribati, Democratic People's Republic of Korea, Republic of Korea, Marshall Islands, Micronesia, Mongolia, Nauru, New Caledonia, New Zealand and Territories, Norfolk Island, Northern Mariana Islands, Palau, Papua New Guinea, Philippines, Pitcairn Island, Solomon Islands, Taiwan, Tonga, Tuvalu, Vanuatu, Wake Island, Wallis and Futuna Island, Western Samoa).

* There are no Airmail services to the French Southern and Antarctic Territories

OVERSEAS SURFACE MAIL RATES (WORLD ZONES 1 & 2*)

Letters

Maximum weight		*Maximum weight*	
20g†	£0.46	150g	£1.55
60g	£0.78	200g	£1.99
100g	£1.10	250g	£2.43

300g	£2.86	1,000g	£8.88
350g	£3.29	1,250g	£11.03
400g	£3.72	1,500g	£13.18
450g	£4.15	1,750g	£15.33
500g	£4.58	2,000g	£17.48
750g	£6.73		

* Letters and postcards to Europe are sent by Airmail
† Includes postcards

Small packets and printed papers

Maximum weight		*Maximum weight*	
100g	£0.77	450g	£2.60
150g	£1.04	500g	£2.86
200g	£1.30	750g	£4.16
250g	£1.56	1,000g	£5.46
300g	£1.82	1,500g	£8.06
350g	£2.08	2,000g*	£10.66
400g	£2.34		

* Maximum weight. For printed papers only: add £0.26 for each additional 50g up to maximum weight of 5kg

AIRMAIL LETTERS

Europe

Maximum weight		*Maximum weight*	
20g*	£0.48	300g	£3.34
40g	£0.69	320g	£3.52
60g	£0.90	340g	£3.70
80g	£1.10	360g	£3.88
100g	£1.31	380g	£4.06
120g	£1.52	400g	£4.24
140g	£1.73	420g	£4.42
160g	£1.94	440g	£4.60
180g	£2.15	460g	£4.78
200g	£2.35	480g	£4.96
220g	£2.54	500g	£5.14
240g	£2.74	1,000g	£9.64
260g	£2.94	2,000g	£18.64
280g	£3.13		

* Includes postcards

World Zones 1 and 2

Maximum weight	*World zone 1*	*World zone 2*
Postcards	£0.54	£0.54
20g	£0.78	£0.78
40g	£1.17	£1.24
60g	£1.58	£1.74
80g	£2.00	£2.24
100g	£2.42	£2.74
500g	£10.14	£11.91
1,000g	£19.39	£22.91
2,000g	£37.89	£44.91

Note that there are different rates for small packets and printed matter. *See* W www.royalmail.com for further details.

SPECIAL DELIVERY SERVICES

SPECIAL DELIVERY NEXT DAY
A guaranteed next working day delivery service by 1pm to 99 per cent of the UK for first class letters and packets (maximum item weight is 10kg). Prices start at £4.30. There is also a service which guarantees delivery by 9am (maximum item weight is 2kg). Prices start at £9.35.

INTERNATIONAL SIGNED FOR AND AIRSURE
Express airmail services (maximum weight 2kg) that include £34 compensation in case of loss or damage. The fee for International Signed For is £3.50 plus airmail postage. The fee for Airsure is £4.20 plus airmail postage.

RECORDED SIGNED FOR
Provides a record of posting and delivery of letters and ensures a signature on delivery. This service is recommended for items of little or no monetary value. All packets must be handed to the post office and a receipt issued as proof of posting. *Charge:* 70p plus the standard first or second class postage.

OTHER SERVICES

BUSINESS SERVICES
A range of postal services are available to businesses including business collection, freepost, business reply services, business packaging for special deliveries and international bulk mailing options.

COMPENSATION
Compensation for loss or damage to an item sent varies according to the service used to send the item.

PASSPORT APPLICATIONS
Around 2,000 post offices process passport applications. To find out your nearest office, and for further information, see W www.postoffice.co.uk.

TRACK AND TRACE
This online service, accessible from www.royalmail.com and www.postoffice.co.uk, enables customers to track the progress of items sent using the special delivery services listed above.

REDIRECTION
A printed form obtainable from the Post Office or from www.royalmail.com must be signed by the person to whom the letters are to be addressed. A fee is payable for each different surname on the application form. *Charges:* one month, £7.10 (abroad via airmail, £14.30); three months, £15.55 (£31.10); six months, £23.95 (£47.90); 12 months, £35.95 (£71.90).

KEEPSAFE
Mail is held for up to two months while the addressee is away and is delivered when the addressee returns. Prices start at £5.70. Perishable items are returned to the sender. Recorded items are held for a week before being returned to the sender, and Special Delivery items for three weeks beyond the keepsafe expiry date.

POST OFFICE BOX
A PO Box provides a short and memorable alternative address. Mail is held at a local delivery office until the addressee is ready to collect it. A PO Box costs £46.95 for six months or £57.85 for a year.

CONTACTS

Royal Mail general enquiries: T 08457-740740
W www.royalmail.com
Royal Mail business enquiries: T 08457-950950
Postcode enquiry line: T 0906-302 1222 / 08457-111222
Parcelforce Worldwide: T 08708-501150
W www.parcelforce.com
Post Office enquiries: T 08457-223344
W www.postoffice.co.uk

INTERNATIONAL DIRECT DIALLING

International dialling (IDD) codes are composed of four elements which are dialled in sequence:

(i) the international code
(ii) the country code
(iii) the area code
(iv) the telephone number

Calls to Midway Island, Tristan da Cunha and Wake Island must be made by calling the international operator on 155.

* Varies depending on area and/or carrier

	IDD from UK	*IDD to UK*
Afghanistan	00 93	00 44
Albania	00 355	00 44
Algeria	00 213	00 44
American Samoa	00 1 684	011 44
Andorra	00 376	00 44
Angola	00 244	00 44
Anguilla	00 1 264	011 44
Antigua and Barbuda	00 1 268	011 44
Argentina	00 54	00 44
Armenia	00 374	00 44
Aruba	00 297	00 44
Ascension Island	00 247	00 44
Australia	00 61	00 11 44
Austria	00 43	00 44
Azerbaijan	00 994	810 44
Azores	00 351	00 44
Bahamas	00 1 242	011 44
Bahrain	00 973	00 44
Balearic Islands	00 34	00 44
Bangladesh	00 880	00 44
Barbados	00 1 246	011 44
Belarus	00 375	810 44
Belgium	00 32	00 44
Belize	00 501	00 44
Benin	00 229	00 44
Bermuda	00 1 441	011 44
Bhutan	00 975	00 44
Bolivia	00 591	0010 44*
		0011 44*
		0012 44*
		0013 44*
Bosnia and Hercegovina	00 387	00 44
Botswana	00 267	00 44
Brazil	00 55	0014 44*
		0015 44*
		0021 44*
		0023 44*
		0031 44*
British Virgin Islands	00 1 284	011 44
Brunei	00 673	00 44
Bulgaria	00 359	00 44
Burkina Faso	00 226	00 44
Burundi	00 257	00 44
Cambodia	00 855	001 44
Cameroon	00 237	00 44
Canada	00 1	011 44
Canary Islands	00 34	00 44
Cape Verde	00 238	0 44
Cayman Islands	00 1 345	011 44
Central African Republic	00 236	19 44
Chad	00 235	15 44
Chile	00 56	00 44
China	00 86	00 44
Colombia	00 57	009 44
The Comoros	00 269	00 44
Congo, Dem. Rep. of	00 243	00 44
Congo, Rep. of	00 242	00 44
Cook Islands	00 682	00 44
Costa Rica	00 506	00 44
Côte d'Ivoire	00 225	00 44
Croatia	00 385	00 44
Cuba	00 53	119 44
Cyprus	00 357	00 44
Czech Rep.	00 420	00 44
Denmark	00 45	00 44
Djibouti	00 253	00 44
Dominica	00 1 767	011 44
Dominican Rep.	00 1 809	011 44
	00 1 829	
East Timor	00 670	00 44
Ecuador	00 593	00 44
Egypt	00 20	00 44
El Salvador	00 503	00 44
Equatorial Guinea	00 240	00 44
Eritrea	00 291	00 44
Estonia	00 372	00 44
Ethiopia	00 251	00 44
Falkland Islands	00 500	00 44
Faeroe Islands	00 298	00 44
Fiji	00 679	00 44
Finland	00 358	00 44*
France	00 33	00 44
French Guiana	00 594	00 44
French Polynesia	00 689	00 44
Gabon	00 241	00 44
The Gambia	00 220	00 44
Georgia	00 995	810 44
Germany	00 49	00 44
Ghana	00 233	00 44
Gibraltar	00 350	00 44
Greece	00 30	00 44
Greenland	00 299	00 44
Grenada	00 1 473	011 44
Guadeloupe	00 590	00 44
Guam	00 1 671	011 44
Guatemala	00 502	00 44
Guinea	00 224	00 44
Guinea-Bissau	00 245	00 44
Guyana	00 592	001 44
Haiti	00 509	00 44
Honduras	00 504	00 44
Hong Kong	00 852	001 44
Hungary	00 36	00 44
Iceland	00 354	00 44
India	00 91	00 44
Indonesia	00 62	001 44*
		007 44*
Iran	00 98	00 44
Iraq	00 964	00 44
Ireland	00 353	00 44
Israel	00 972	00 44*
Italy	00 39	00 44
Jamaica	00 1 876	011 44
Japan	00 81	001 010 44*
		0033 010 44*
		0041 010 44*
		0061 010 44*
		010 44*

rdan	00 962	00 44*
azakhstan	00 7	810 44
enya	00 254	000 44
ribati	00 686	00 44
orea, Dem. People's Rep. of	00 850	00 44
orea, Republic of	00 82	001 44* 002 44*
uwait	00 965	00 44
yrgyzstan	00 996	00 44
os	00 856	00 44
tvia	00 371	00 44
banon	00 961	00 44
sotho	00 266	00 44
beria	00 231	00 44
bya	00 218	00 44
echtenstein	00 423	00 44
thuania	00 370	00 44
uxembourg	00 352	00 44
acao	00 853	00 44
acedonia	00 389	00 44
adagascar	00 261	00 44
adeira	00 351	00 44
alawi	00 265	00 44
alaysia	00 60	00 44
aldives	00 960	00 44
ali	00 223	00 44
alta	00 356	00 44
arshall Islands	00 692	011 44
artinique	00 596	00 44
auritania	00 222	00 44
auritius	00 230	00 44
ayotte	00 269	10 44
exico	00 52	98 44
icronesia, Federated States of	00 691	011 44
oldova	00 373	00 44
onaco	00 377	00 44
ongolia	00 976	001 44
ontenegro	00 382	00 44
ontserrat	00 1 664	011 44
orocco	00 212	00 44
ozambique	00 258	00 44
yanmar	00 95	00 44
amibia	00 264	00 44
auru	00 674	00 44
epal	00 977	00 44
he Netherlands	00 31	00 44
etherlands Antilles	00 599	00 44
ew Caledonia	00 687	00 44
ew Zealand	00 64	00 44
icaragua	00 505	00 44
iger	00 227	00 44
igeria	00 234	009 44
iue	00 683	00 44
orfolk Island	00 672	00 44
orthern Mariana Islands	00 1 670	011 44
orway	00 47	00 44
man	00 968	00 44
akistan	00 92	00 44
alau	00 680	011 44
anama	00 507	00 44
apua New Guinea	00 675	05 44
araguay	00 595	002 44
eru	00 51	00 44
he Philippines	00 63	00 44
oland	00 48	00 44
ortugal	00 351	00 44
Puerto Rico	00 1 787 00 1 939	011 44
Qatar	00 974	00 44
Réunion	00 262	00 44
Romania	00 40	00 44
Russian Federation	00 7	810 44
Rwanda	00 250	00 44
St Christopher and Nevis	00 1 869	011 44
St Helena	00 290	00 44
St Lucia	00 1 758	011 44
St Pierre and Miquelon	00 508	00 44
St Vincent and the Grenadines	00 1 784	011 44
Samoa	00 685	0 44
San Marino	00 378	00 44
Sao Tome and Principe	00 239	00 44
Saudi Arabia	00 966	00 44
Senegal	00 221	00 44
Serbia	00 381	00 44
Seychelles	00 248	00 44
Sierra Leone	00 232	00 44
Singapore	00 65	001 44
Slovakia	00 421	00 44
Slovenia	00 386	00 44
Solomon Islands	00 677	00 44
Somalia	00 252	00 44
South Africa	00 27	00 44
Spain	00 34	00 44
Sri Lanka	00 94	00 44
Sudan	00 249	00 44
Suriname	00 597	00 44
Swaziland	00 268	00 44
Sweden	00 46	00 44
Switzerland	00 41	00 44
Syria	00 963	00 44
Taiwan	00 886	002 44
Tajikistan	00 992	810 44
Tanzania	00 255	000 44
Thailand	00 66	001 44
Tibet	00 86	00 44
Togo	00 228	00 44
Tokelau	00 690	00 44
Tonga	00 676	00 44
Trinidad and Tobago	00 1 868	011 44
Tunisia	00 216	00 44
Turkey	00 90	00 44
Turkmenistan	00 993	810 44
Turks and Caicos Islands	00 1 649	011 44
Tuvalu	00 688	00 44
Uganda	00 256	000 44
Ukraine	00 380	810 44
United Arab Emirates	00 971	00 44
United States of America	00 1	011 44
Uruguay	00 598	00 44
Uzbekistan	00 998	810 44
Vanuatu	00 678	00 44
Vatican City State	00 39	00 44
Venezuela	00 58	00 44
Vietnam	00 84	00 44
Virgin Islands	00 1 340	011 44
Yemen	00 967	00 44
Zambia	00 260	00 44
Zimbabwe	00 263	00 44

MOBILE COMMUNICATIONS

In *The Telecommunications Market 2006* report, UK regulator OFCOM revealed that year-on-year growth in mobile revenues continued during 2005, with income from users totalling £13.1bn and representing 34 per cent of all retail telecoms revenue. Moreover, for the first time, revenue from mobile calls surpassed that from fixed lines. This is largely due to a rise in the number of mobile subscriptions in the UK, which, at its current level of 66.2 million, exceeds the size of the UK population. This is due to a number of people having more than one mobile subscription, either for a second mobile phone or a substitute wireless device such as a Blackberry.

UK MOBILE SUBSCRIBER STATISTICS (MILLIONS)

Date	*1999*	*2001*	*2003*	*2004*	*2005*	*2006*
Subscriber base	13.0	40.1	46.9	50.2	61.2	65.7

Source: OFCOM Telecommunications Reviews 2005 and 2006

INDUSTRY STRUCTURE

With various technologies converging, the structure of the mobile communications industry is becoming increasingly complex. This has resulted in new services being delivered to consumers over multiple platforms, thereby blurring the industry structure somewhat. In spite of this, two main types of players can be identified in the mobile sector, namely network operators, such as Vodafone and Orange, who own the infrastructure, set tariffs and bill customers; and service providers, who lease network capacity from the operators, with Mobile Virtual Network Operators (MVNOs), such as Virgin Mobile, being the most common service provider in the UK. OFCOM is responsible for setting the controls in this market and for ensuring that industry players do not behave in an anti-competitive manner. Unlike in other European countries, where the regulator forced operators to sell capacity, UK operators originally opened their networks voluntarily, with no regulatory intervention required.

NETWORK OPERATORS

There were five licensed network operators in the UK at the end of 2006:

Operator	*Owned by*	*Subscriber numbers (millions)*
Hutchison 3G	Hutchison Whampoa Ltd	3.8
O2	Telefónica O2 Europe	19.0*
Orange	France Telecom SA	15.3
T-Mobile	100Deutsche Telekom AG	16.8
Vodafone	Vodafone Group Plc	14.7

Source: Ofcom operators

* O2 subscriber figures include Tesco Mobile subscribers

ALTERNATIVE SERVICE PROVIDERS

Service providers were introduced into the UK market as a means of stimulating competition, with Singlepoint (acquired by Vodafone in 2003) being an early example. These players buy wholesale airtime from netwo operators and sell it on to users at a discount. They do n own any infrastructure or SIM cards. Service provide still exist in the UK market, though the business moc has changed somewhat, with MVNOs now representi the most significant service provider model in the UK. with their predecessors, they also resell wholesale minut purchased from network operators, but are distinct inso as they may – under the conditions of their agreeme with the operator – set prices, manage accounts, own t customer database, perform customer service activities a manage distribution, marketing and branding. Moreov MVNOs typically own, issue and activate SIM cards.

The world's first MVNO was Virgin Mobile, whi launched in 1999. By the end of 2005 it had an estimat active subscriber base of four million. MVNOs have al been launched by existing telecoms companies such BT, and by companies in non-related sectors such supermarkets. There are now an estimated 230 MVN worldwide.

MVNO (launched)	*Network operator*	*Active subscribers (est)*	*Further information*
Virgin (1999)	T-Mobile	4,000,000	Virgin Mobile mergec with NTL Telewest in July 2006
Tesco (2003)	O2	1,000,000	Joint venture with O2
BT Mobile (2003)	Vodafone	250,000	Deal for a five-year period
Sainsbury's (2004)	O2	30,000	Controlled by Carphone Warehouse
Easy (2005)	T-Mobile	23,000	Joint venture with TDC

Source: OFCOM, Interim Review of the Telecommunicatio Market 2006

TYPES OF MOBILE SUBSCRIPTIONS

There are two basic types of mobile subscriptior contracts and pre-paid, also known as pay-as-you-go PAYG. A contract, generally paid on a monthly basis ar fixed to a minimum contract term, requires the user to pa a fixed subscription fee each month entitling him or h to a certain number of services. More recently, there ha been a trend towards 18-month contracts by operato through the offer of reduced line rental or complimenta services for the contract duration. Such moves a designed to reduce customer switching between operator thereby reducing the cost of new customer acquisitio Operators have also introduced more generous servic bundles to those customers signing up directly, in an effo to reduce payments to third-party retailers.

By contrast, pre-paid subscribers have access to th same services but pay in advance and simply top up the account when credit is running low. New payme channels, such as bank ATMs, have emerged for PAY customers to encourage additional spending. Th introduction of pre-paid services has allowed the industr o target new areas of the market that would otherwise be neligible for a contract, either for age or credit rating easons. PAYG contracts have moved towards more omprehensive packages of multimedia services such as lownloadable games, access to news and information ipdates, and typically offer a certain amount of omplimentary airtime.

There has been little change over the past years in terms of the proportion of contract to PAYG customers in the JK; OFCOM's 2006 *Telecommunications Review* reports hat at the end of 2005 there were 22.2 million total ctive contract subscribers and 43.2 million pre-pay ustomers.

NETWORK TECHNOLOGY

Network technology has improved dramatically since the aunch in 1985 of the first-generation 900 MHz analogue GSM service (known as TACS), which offered little or no lata capability. In 1992 Vodafone launched a new digital GSM network, usually referred to as 2G or second generation. This technology used digital encoding and llowed voice and low-speed data communications. 2G echnology was later extended to 2.5G, allowing dditional features such as an enhanced data transfer ate.

More recently, the development of 3G technology has provided increased data transmission speeds, supporting nultimedia applications such as video-conferencing and nternet access. Since 3G uses an entirely new network, operators are required to hold a licence to offer it. The UK was the third European country to license 3G operators, fter Finland and Spain, with five licences being granted o Hutchinson 3G, O2, Orange, T-Mobile and Vodafone. Under the terms of the licence, operators are required to offer a service with coverage for at least 80 per cent of the population by the end of 2007.

MOBILE SERVICES

The upgrade from analogue to 2G brought clearer voice quality, while later moves to 2.5G and 3G opened the loor for new data services. In a mature market mobile evenues are expected to come from enhanced mobile ervices, so pressure is on operators to provide innovative olutions and to encourage upgrades to new handsets with added functionality. This section outlines the array of mobile services available to today's consumer and gives examples by operator, where appropriate.

Aside from voice services, which represent 80 per cent of all mobile retail revenues, SMS, or more colloquially, ext messaging, is the secondary source of mobile retail evenue, accounting for 16 per cent of mobile retail evenues, according to OFCOM's *Telecommunications Review 2006*. The number of SMS messages has been ncreasing dramatically year-on-year, with 3.5 billion text nessages sent in 2005.

The technological move to 2G and 2.5G enabled nobile phones to access the internet, thereby allowing for emails and photos to be sent, and for downloading ingtones and games. Such services are referred to as nultimedia messaging (MMS). The use of MMS remains elatively low compared to SMS, despite the increasing number of camera phones in circulation.

3G technology provides higher quality audio and video content, so that consumers can access information, entertainment and communication on the move, eg live mobile internet, music downloads and TV streaming. The table below shows the monthly consumption of services by UK mobile subscribers and highlights the continuing dominance of SMS.

UK CONSUMPTION OF MOBILE CONTENT AND APPLICATIONS (AS AT DECEMBER 2006)

Activity	*Subscribers (per cent)*
Sent text message	86.3
Used photo messaging	30.3
Browsed news and information	14.5
Used email	11.1
Downloaded mobile game	4.9
Purchased ringtone	4.8
Used instant messenger	4.2
Purchased wallpaper or screensaver	2.1

Source: M:Metrics Inc Benchmark Survey, Dec. 2006

Technological developments have merged the previously distinct areas of television, internet and telephony. During the second half of 2005, operators introduced live streaming television over 3G networks, with deals struck between broadcasters (including BSkyB, Granada and Disney) and mobile operators. In May 2005 Orange was the first operator in the UK to launch a mobile television service, through which subscribers could access a variety of entertainment channels, including ITV and Cartoon Network. Rival operators have since introduced similar services. The pricing structure of mobile TV varies by operator, but subscribers typically pay to view a bundle of programmes.

The convergence of technologies has also encouraged online businesses to offer services to mobile customers. Examples of recent deals include Vodafone's agreement with the social networking site MySpace.com, to distribute software that allows consumers to update their MySpace page from their mobile. Similarly, 3 launched a music download service and SeeMeTV, enabling users to upload videos shot on their phones. 3G handsets also allow users to search the internet, although this process is still slow compared to equivalent searches on personal computers. Advertisers, too, have begun to explore the possibilities of improved mobile technology. Where phone advertising used to be limited to the sending of text messages, in the last year Orange announced a full-scale mobile advertising trial across its Orange World portal, with advertising banners appearing on Orange World web pages as users browsed the internet via their phone. Likewise, Yahoo! announced a deal to create mobile advertising for Vodafone. Meanwhile, Unilever, Coca-Cola and Land Rover were among the brands to launch the first ad-supported mobile content trial across multiple network operators.

REGULATION

Competition in the UK telecommunications market is regulated by OFCOM, a statutory corporation established by Act of Parliament and independent of government. OFCOM replaced the former communications and broadcasting regulators, OFTEL and the Radio-communications Agency. The Communications Act of 2003 governs regulation of the telecoms market and OFCOM's responsibilities cover television, radio, telecoms and wireless communications services. The regulator's principal duty under the Communications Act is to further the interests of (i) citizens in relation to communications matters and (ii) consumers in relevant markets, where appropriate by promoting competition.

Competition in the communications market is also regulated by the Office of Fair Trading (OFT), the main UK regulator. The OFT and OFCOM consult one another, however OFCOM takes the lead in competition investigations in the UK market. The Competition Appeals Tribunal (CAT) hears appeals against OFCOM's decisions, while price-related appeals are referred to the Competition Commission.

HEALTH

The possible health implications of mobile phone use have received a great deal of media coverage. The widespread use of mobile phones is still relatively recent and technologies are continuing to develop at a pace that is outstripping analyses of any potential impact on health. A report produced by the National Radiological Protection Board (NRPB) in 2004 identified a possible danger concerning mobiles with a high specific energy absorption rate (SAR) – a measure of the energy absorbed by the user's head while he or she is using the phone. Different phones have different SAR values, but the SAR also depends on the proximity of a user to a mobile phone mast and the length of time the handset is in use. Presently, the long-term effects are unknown. The NRPB's report concluded that while 'there is as yet no hard evidence of adverse health effects on the general public', the discussion about SAR and mobile phone safety is ongoing.

SAFETY WHILE DRIVING

Numerous studies have shown that motorists risk a higher chance of collision and losing control of their vehicle if talking on a mobile phone while driving, even whe using a hands-free kit. In 2003, a new regulation cam into force making it an offence to use a hand-held phon or similar hand-held device, when driving a moto vehicle on the road. The term hand-held refers to mobile telephone or similar device held at some poin during the course of making or receiving a call o performing any other interactive function. The penalt was a £30 fixed fine or up to £1,000 on conviction i court (£2,500 for drivers of goods vehicles, buses c coaches). Tougher penalties were introduced to clam down on this offence in 2007; the maximum penalty i now a £60 fine and offenders risk three points bein added to their licence.

CONTACTS

COMPETITION APPEAL TRIBUNAL (CAT)
Victoria House, Bloomsbury Place, London WC1A 2E
T 020-7979 7979 W www.catribunal.org.uk

DEPARTMENT FOR BUSINESS, ENTERPRISE AND REGULATORY REFORM
1 Victoria Street, London SW1V 0ET
T 020-7215 5000 W www.berr.gov.uk

OFCOM
Riverside House, 2A Southwark Bridge Road, London SE1 9HA
T 020-7981 3000 W www.ofcom.org.uk

OFFICE OF FAIR TRADING (OFT)
Fleetbank House, 2-6 Salisbury Square, London EC4Y 8J
T 020-7211 8000 W www.oft.gov.uk

NFORMATION TECHNOLOGY

OPULAR WEBSITES OF 2007

AILYMOTION.COM: A video-sharing website that allows users to share personal videos, privately or publicly, with a video-blogging component

EL.ICIO.US: A social bookmarking website allowing users to store bookmarks online, allowing them access to the same bookmarks from any computer and the ability to add them from anywhere

IGG.COM: A user-driven social content website where 100 per cent of the news stories are submitted by their community of users. Popular submissions are promoted to the front page through a system of votes – 'diggs'

ACEBOOK.COM: A social networking website that connects people with friends, allowing them to upload photos, and share links and videos

LICKR.COM: An online photo-management and sharing website which allows users to make their personal photos available through the web, RSS feeds, email and blogs

AST.FM: A social music website that through a user's music collection creates personal recommendations, music lists, and allows connection with other users who share similar music tastes

IVEJOURNAL.COM: An online blogging community where people from around the world share stories, discuss topics and keep in touch with friends

YSPACE.COM: A social networking website that allows users to create private communities and blogs where photos, music and video can be shared with friends

ENDSPACE.COM: A file-sharing website used to send large files too big for email attachments to friends, family and businesses

VIKIPEDIA.ORG: A multilingual, web-based, free content encyclopaedia project written collaboratively by volunteers from all around the world. Articles can be edited by anyone with access to the internet

OUTUBE.COM: A video-sharing website used to watch and share videos worldwide. YouTube allows people to upload and share videos through websites, mobile devices, blogs and email

A SHORT HISTORY OF THE INTERNET

rior to the advent of the internet, computers tended to e connected together by hardware and protocols that vere specific to each particular connection. Typically, inks were point-to-point (physically established between he two computers). In 1969 ARPANET was formed by he US department of defence to establish a way for the omputer capability of the military to be dispersed so that o single centre was critical to the operation of the etwork as a whole. This was achieved by interconnecting omputers both directly and by way of other intermediary omputers; thus if one computer was destroyed, other athways of communication could be established. These nterconnections, when drawn, appeared as a net or web. ARPANET was extended to non-military users such as universities early in the 1970s, with initial international links appearing in 1972.

The introduction of domain names (eg www.whitakersalmanack.com) in 1984 offered an easier means of using the web. Prior to domain names, IP addresses (eg 192.168.1.100) were used for accessing destination computers. However, before 1989 the internet was still primarily limited to government agencies, the military, academic and research organisations and some big businesses.

In 1989, what most people perceive as 'the internet' was born. It was effectively invented at CERN (the European Particle Physics Laboratory) by Tim Berners-Lee as a way for scientists to share information by placing it in a prescribed format on a server. Initially text only, development of computer capability allowed the inclusion of images.

The internet is effectively a very large network of computers, connected through various telecommunications links. Millions of routers (*see* Glossary) around the world link together massive networks of computers to form a backbone to the internet. Most home and business users will connect up to an ISP (internet service provider) via a telephone or a digital line. ISPs have their own routers, which all the lines connect to. The internet 'traffic' is then routed to another (often larger) telecommunications company, which is also connected by fibre-optic lines to other such companies across the globe. Websites are stored on servers that are designed for hosting, running a special program that 'serves' up the content.

As use of technology has increased, the downloading of music, pictures and video from the internet has become faster and more practical. Analogue media, such as music stored on a tape, or a painting, loses quality in reproduction. Digital media on the other hand can be copied flawlessly between computers, as it is the simple process of replicating a string of zeros and ones.

The Data Protection Act 1984 (revised 1998) was introduced to ensure the correct and proper handling of personal and sensitive data held on computer databases. During the 1980s computer hacking was still not illegal, but the number of serious computer attacks was rapidly increasing. Failed attempts to prosecute these hackers brought about the Computer Misuse Act, passed in 1990 to protect computer systems from unauthorised access. Copyright law has also been amended to encompass the concept of 'digital property' and include criminal sanctions for breaching the copyright of protected music, video, books, software and website material.

INTERNET TRENDS

While the internet has always been used as a key method of dispersing information, increased internet speeds and accessibility of cheaper broadband have prompted the advent of Web 2.0, a second generation of web-based services enabling more people to reach higher quality content online. Music, high-resolution images and video files can be downloaded in seconds, compared to hours when accessed via telephone modems.

This new era has led to a wave of new photo-sharing websites such as Flickr.com and YouTube.com that allow users to upload photographs and share multimedia files online, and also of file-sharing services such as Sendpsace.com and Bittorrent.com. Websites that promote social networking and user-generated content are also on the rise. Myspace.com and Facebook.com have created international communities of millions of people where users interact and converse via photo and music sharing, blogs and even popularity contests.

The number of web office applications has grown with the merging of traditional desktop applications and web-based technology. Often utilising AJAX, many web-based applications such as Google's Docs and Spreadsheets, Zoho, and Thinkfree, offer free alternatives to Microsoft's Office.

RSS feeds are expected to continue to play an important role in the growth of the internet, and directly related to Web 2.0 is the increase in the use of mobile web. Cheaper internet access plans, mobile banking, mobile-linked user-generated content and even the appearance of the iPhone, Apple's much-touted webphone, are helping make mobile phones a popular browsing device.

INTERNET STATISTICS

- Between 2002 and 2006 the proportion of adults in Great Britain who had used the internet in the last three months increased by almost one-quarter, from 48 per cent to 60 per cent.
- 59 per cent of internet users over the age of 16 went online every day or almost every day in 2006, while 4 per cent went online less than once a month.
- Internet use declines with age. In 2006, 84 per cent of people aged 16 to 24 had used the internet within the last three months, compared with 52 per cent of people aged 55 to 64 and 15 per cent of those aged 65 and over.
- For users aged 16 and over the most common location to access the internet was at home. In 2006, 85 per cent of internet users aged 16 and over who had accessed the internet in the last three months had done so at home.
- For those who did not have household access to the internet, the most common places to go online were at work (46 per cent) and at another person's home (also 46 per cent).
- Information research and using email were the two most common online activities of internet users in 2006.
- Two in five adults said they had purchased items online for private or personal reasons. The most common items bought online were travel and holidays (51 per cent), followed by films, videos and DVDs (42 per cent). 18 per cent of internet users had sold goods or services online in 2006, more than double that in 2004.
- The majority (70 per cent) of those who had shopped online had not encountered any problems doing so. For those who had, the most common problem was that delivery took longer than expected.

Source: National Statistics Omnibus Survey

TOP 10 BROADBAND SUBSCRIBERS BY COUNTRY

Country	*2005*	*2006*
1. USA	46,110,191	57,330,216
2. China	37,504,000	51,899,000
3. Japan	22,647,830	26,095,919
4. Germany	10,706,648	14,660,084
5. South Korea	12,199,666	14,042,698
6. France	9,958,086	13,983,900
7. UK	9,828,900	13,116,600
8. Italy	6,977,404	8,826,803
9. Canada	6,854,994	7,876,487
10. Spain	4,852,388	6,726,756

Source: www.dslforum.org

GLOSSARY OF INTERNET TERMS

The following is a selected list of modern computing terms. It is by no means exhaustive but is intended to cover those that the average computer user might encounter.

3G: Third Generation wireless – a term commonly used to describe high-bandwidth (2 Mbps) wireless technologies for mobile phones. 3G is still in its infancy, but when fully deployed 3G technology will offer high speed and capacity transmission of sound, vision and data to and from wireless devices and networks. *See also* Mobile Communications section.

ADSL: Asymmetric Digital Subscriber Line – high-speed internet connection, four or more times faster than a modem, but using the same standard cables as a regular telephone. Faster at downloading than uploading.

AJAX: Asynchronous JavaScript and XML – a way of including content in a web page in which JavaScript code in the web page fetches some data from a server and displays it without re-fetching the entire surrounding page at the same time (hence 'asynchronous'). The intention is to make web pages feel more responsive by exchanging small amounts of data with the server behind the scenes, so that an entire web page does not have to be reloaded each time the user makes a change, thereby increasing its interactivity, speed and usability.

APACHE: The most common web server (or HTTP server) software on the internet. Apache is an open-source application originally created from a series of changes ('patches') made to a web server written at the National Centre for Supercomputing Applications in the USA. It is designed as a set of modules, enabling administrators to choose which features they wish to use to meet specific needs, including handling protocols other than the web-standard HTTP.

ASCII: American Standard Code for Information Interchange – a widely used character-encoding system, expressing letters, numbers and other symbols as binary numbers. It employs a string of eight binary digits or bits to represent 128 characters, enough for all the letters of the Roman alphabet and various permutations of every number between zero and nine.

BANDWIDTH: Determines how much data can be sent through a connection. Usually measured in bits-per-second (bps). A full page of English text is about 16,000 bits. A fast modem can move about 57,000bps. Full-motion, full-screen video would require roughly 10,000,000bps, depending on compression.

BLOG: A blog (short for web log) is an online personal journal that is frequently updated and intended to be read by the public. Blogs generally represent the personality of the author and may include philosophy, commentary on the internet and other social issues and links to favourite websites. Blogs are kept by 'bloggers' and are commonly available as RSS feeds.

.UETOOTH: Standard for short-range (10m) wireless connectivity between devices such as laptops, cell phones and printers to interact without cables. Bluetooth can presently operate at speeds of up to 2Mbps.

OADBAND: Generic term to describe high-speed internet-using technologies such as ISDN, ADSL etc as opposed to narrowband connections via modem.

OWSER: Typically referring to a 'web browser' program that allows a computer user to view web page content on their computer, eg Microsoft Explorer, Netscape Navigator, AOL or Safari.

OOKIE: A piece of information sent by a web server to a web browser which is then saved and sent back to the server whenever the browser makes requests from the server. Cookies contain information such as login, registration or online 'shopping cart' data, user preferences, etc and are usually set to expire after a predetermined length of time.

SS: Cascading Style Sheet – a standard for specifying the appearance of text and other elements. CSS was developed for use with HTML in web pages, but can be used in other contexts. CSS provides a single 'library' of styles that are used over and over throughout a large number of related documents. A CSS file might specify for example that all numbered lists are to appear in italics.

GERATI: The elite of the computer industry and online communities. Famous computer scientists, magazine writers and well-known bloggers are included among the digerati.

NS: Domain Name Server – a server that translates domain names into the IP addresses used by programs to directly access computers on the internet. Each server has an IP address and a name. DNS is analogous to the telephone directory enquiry service, providing a means of looking up and locating a computer connected to the internet.

OMAIN: A set of words, numbers and letters separated by dots used to identify an internet server or group of servers, eg www.whitakersalmanack.co.uk, where 'www' denotes a web (http) server, 'whitakersalmanack' denotes the organisation name, 'co' denotes that the organisation is a company and 'uk' indicates United Kingdom. (For a complete list of country suffixes *see* Internet Domain Names section.)

MAIL: Electronic mail – an email message is a document that is addressed to one or more persons from an individual address. Usually containing a message, it can also include other documents. It has superseded the telex, telegram, postcard and letter for rapidly exchanging information. The advent of the internet has seen an explosion in the use of email in modern life. Without encryption or digital signature, an email is not secure.

XTRANET: An extranet is a secure and private subset of the internet, protected by security protocols and typically used for exchanging information and services within a specific group.

LE SERVER: A computer on a network that stores computer files which users can access from other computers on the network. Popular modern systems include Microsoft Windows, UNIX, Novell NetWare, and MacOS Server.

REWALL: Computer or device to protect a network from security risks posed by the internet. Just as a firewall protects parts of a building from a fire raging on the other side, a network firewall stops risks posed by the internet from egressing into a private network.

FLAME: Flaming (or trolling) has come to refer to any kind of derogatory comment, no matter how witless or crude, which takes place in an online discussion. A situation where an online discussion degenerates into a series of personal attacks against the debaters, rather than a discussion of their positions, is known as a 'flame war'.

FTP: File Transfer Protocol – an internet protocol whereby an FTP client program can exchange files with a remote server.

GBPS: Gigabits per second – denoting 1,000 million bits transmitted per second.

GPRS: General Packet Radio Services – a service for continuous wireless communication over the internet from mobile phones and computers. Presently available in data rates of between 56 and 114Kbps, GPRS tends to be charged by volume of information transferred rather than by time, which allows a more economic continuous connection compared with direct dial over a modem.

GZIP: Compression – a common mechanism on UNIX and Linux operating systems to compress information in order to save resources.

HIT: In reference to the internet, a 'hit' means a single request from a web browser for a single item from a web server; thus in order for a web browser to display a page that contains three graphics, four 'hits' would occur at the server: one for the HTML page, and one for each of the three graphics. The number of hits on a website is not synonymous with the number of distinct visitors.

HTML: HyperText Mark-up Language – a small programming language used to denote or mark-up how an internet page should be presented to a user from an HTTP server via a web browser. HTML is an evolving standard that has grown greatly from its first version to accommodate new types of web content and features provided by the different web browsers (eg Netscape and Internet Explorer).

HTTP: HyperText Transfer Protocol – an internet protocol whereby a web server sends web pages, images and files to a web browser.

IMAP: Internet Mail Access Protocol – allows a user to review, manipulate and store email on a central server from one or more workstations without necessitating message removal from the server.

INTRANET: Subset of the internet, using internet protocols over a local area network, common today for publishing information and services within an organisation.

IRC: Internet Relay Chat – a protocol that allows users to 'chat' online using their keyboards. Under IRC a user can log into various chat rooms under their own name or an alias and have a text 'conversation' in real time.

JAVA: a high-level, object-orientated computer language developed by Sun Microsystems, especially designed for use via the web.

KBPS: Kilobits per second – measure of transmission speed, denoting 1,000 bits transmitted per second.

LINUX: A UNIX-like operating system first developed as a free or low-cost system for personal computers. *See also* Operating Systems in main article.

MASHUP: A web page or site made by automatically combining content from other sources, usually by using material available via RSS feeds.

MBPS: Megabits per second – denoting 1 million bits transmitted per second.

META TAG: A specific kind of HTML tag that contains information not normally displayed to the user. Meta tags contain information about the page itself, hence the name (meta means 'about this subject'). Meta tags are typically used to include information for search engines to help them better categorise a page and can be viewed in the source code.

MODEM: Modulator-Demodulator – a device that modulates digital signals from a computer into analogue signals for transmission over a standard telephone line, and demodulates an incoming analogue signal and converts it to a digital signal for the computer.

MP3: A popular format for compressing audio information for transmission over the internet for later playback on personal computers, music players and other devices.

MPEG: Motion Picture Encoding Group – popular format standard for compressing video and audio information for transmission over the internet for later playback on personal computers and on hand-held devices.

MS-DOS: Microsoft Corporation's Disk Operating System – an early OS commercially developed, but not invented, by Microsoft for use on early Intel-based personal computers. *See also* Operating System.

NETIQUETTE: Conventions of politeness on electronic forums such as internet message boards.

NETIZEN: A person actively involved in online communications. The term implies civic responsibility and participation in improving and developing the internet, while encouraging free speech and open access.

OPEN CONTENT: Copyrighted information that is made available by the owner to the general public under licence terms that allow reuse of the material, often with the requirement that the reuser grant the public the same rights to the modified version. Information that is in the 'public domain' might also be considered a form of open content.

OPEN-SOURCE: A computer program that has its source-code (the instructions that make up a program) freely available for viewing and modification is said to be open-source.

OPERATING SYSTEM (OS): Computer software developed to provide computer programs with standard facilities to interact with users and with computer hardware (via drivers). *See also* MS-DOS, UNIX, MacOS.

PDF: Portable Document Format – a file format designed to enable printing and viewing of documents with all their formatting (typefaces, images, layout, etc.) appearing the same regardless of what operating system is used. The PDF format is based on the widely used Postscript document-description language. Both PDF and Postscript were developed by the Adobe Corporation.

PODCASTING: A form of audio broadcasting using the internet, podcasting takes its name from a combination of 'iPod' and broadcasting, though it does not require the use of an iPod. Podcasting involves making one or more audio files available as 'enclosures' in an RSS feed. A podcaster creates a list of music and/or other sound files and makes that list available in the RSS 2.0 format. The list can then be obtained using various podcast 'retriever' software which makes the audio files available to digital audio devices (including, but not limited to, iPods) where users may then listen to th at their convenience.

POP3: Post Office Protocol 3 – an internet proto whereby a workstation can collect email from personal mailbox on an email server and move it to user's own machine.

RAM: Random Access Memory – the main memory t is used by a computer to store temporary data (wh accessing or altering individual storage locations) t is lost when the computer is turned off.

ROUTER: Where multiple networks are joined togethe router acts like a fast sorting office, examining t destination address of each information packet a passing or routing it to the appropriate netwo Routers can select the most efficient route for packet

RSS: Rich Site Summary or RDF Site Summary or R Simple Syndication – a commonly used protocol f syndication and sharing of content, origina developed to facilitate the syndication of news articl now widely used to share the contents of blo Mashups are often made using RSS feeds.

SERVER: A node on a network that provides service the terminals on the network. These computers ha higher hardware specifications, ie more resources a greater speed, in order to handle large amounts of da

SOCIAL BOOKMARKING: Web-based service to sha internet bookmarks.

SPAM: A term used for unsolicited, generally junk, ema To spam someone is to send them (multiple) ju emails. Junk email is becoming a major issue with so estimates suggesting that spam is becoming m prevalent than legitimate email. Most spam conta offers of pornography, get-rich schemes, prescripti drugs, low-cost finance or discount goods or servic Many legislatures around the globe are taking steps ban or regulate spam.

TAG: As a noun, a tag is a basic element of the languag used to create web pages (HTML) and simil languages such as XML.

TCP/IP: Transmission Control Protocol/Intern Protocol – the lifeblood of the internet, TCP/ defines how information and requests generated by other protocols are transmitted over the intern Information on the internet is chopped up into sm chunks or packets which are addressed with destination and origination address. It sometim happens that a packet gets lost and TCP/IP dicta how such a loss is handled.

UNIX: *See* Operating Systems in main article. Mode versions include Linux, MacOS X, Solaris, FreeBSD.

USB: Universal Serial Bus – standard for connecting ser devices such as scanners, digital cameras, keyboar modems and printers to computers. With USB, spee of 10Mbps and higher are possible.

URL: Uniform Resource Locator – address of an intern file accessible on the internet, eg http://www.whitakersalmanack.com

USER-GENERATED CONTENT (UGC): Refers various media content produced or primar influenced by end-users, as opposed to tradition media producers such as licensed broadcasters a production companies. These forms of media inclu digital video, blogging, podcasting, mobile pho photography and wikis.

VIRUS: A computer program or script written for t express purpose of replicating itself onto as ma machines as possible (much like its biologi namesake), often with negative side effects to the ho computer and computer network. Such effects vary from harmless screen messages to corruption of document integrity, network overload or the compromising of data security or privacy. Historically transmitted slowly by floppy disk and over networks within offices, the prevalence of email means viruses can spread globally within minutes.

OIP: Voice Over IP – various technologies used to make telephone calls over IP networks, especially the internet. Just as modems allow computers to connect to the internet over regular telephone lines, VOIP technology allows humans to talk over internet connections. Costs for VOIP calls can be much lower than for traditional telephone calls. Because the IP networks are packet-switched, this allows for vastly different ways of handling connections and more efficient use of network resources.

PN: Virtual Private Network – usually refers to a network parts of which are connected using the public internet, but the data sent across the internet is encrypted, so the entire network is 'virtually' private.

AP: Wireless Application Protocol – a set of standards to define how portable devices connected via radio waves (such as mobile phones) can access internet services.

EBDAV: Web-based Distributed Authoring and Versioning – a set of extensions to the HTTP protocol that allows multiple users not only to read but also to add, delete and change documents residing on a web server.

EB 2.0: Generally refers to a second generation of services available on the web that lets people collaborate and share information online. In contrast to the first generation, Web 2.0 gives users an experience closer to desktop applications than traditional static web pages. The term was popularised as the name for a series of web development conferences that started in October 2004. Web 2.0 applications often use a combination of techniques including AJAX and web syndication. They also allow for mass publishing (web-based social software).

I-FI: Industry brand name for the increasingly popular high frequency wireless local area Ethernet networking technology. Wi-Fi is also a popular term for a form of wireless data communication.

IKI: Software that allows users to freely create and edit web pages' content using any web browser. Theoretically this encourages democratic use of the internet and promotes content composition by non-technical users.

LAN: Wireless Local Area Network – a network where information is transferred by radio frequency rather than wires between computers and base stations. As radio waves can pass through objects such as walls, it is becoming increasingly important for WLANs to be secured by encryption against unauthorised access.

HTML: eXtensible HyperText Mark-up Language – essentially HTML expressed as valid XML. XHTML is intended to be used for the same purpose as HTML (creating web pages) but is much more strictly defined, which makes it easier to create software that can read, edit and check it for errors. XHTML is expected to eventually replace HTML.

ML: eXtensible Mark-up Language – similar to HTML but more powerful, XML allows information to be encoded or tagged in a manner that is both human and computer readable. The advent of XML has greatly simplified the exchange of information between many formerly incompatible systems.

DEVELOPMENT OF COMPUTERS

The abacus was the first true calculating machine and was probably invented in China around 500 BC. The invention of the first mechanical calculating machine in 1623 is credited to Wilhelm Schickard, a friend of the astronomer Johannes Kepler. Unfortunately there are no surviving examples of this machine, so the machine built by French scientist and philosopher Blaise Pascal between 1642 and 1645 tends to be credited as the first true mechanical calculator. This was a device that used cogs and wheels to perform addition and subtraction over eight columns of digits. In 1673 Gottfried Leibniz invented an improved calculator that could be used to multiply, divide and find square roots.

The next significant step towards the modern computer occurred in 1804 when Joseph-Marie Jacquard invented an automated loom. Patterns in cloth woven on the loom were dictated by a series of punchcards. This was the first time that data had been stored on cards and then processed in a machine.

The closest ancestors of the modern computer are the Difference Engine and the Analytical Engine devised by mathematician Charles Babbage 30 years after the Jacquard Loom. The Difference Engine, a clockwork-like mechanism, designed to compute mathematical tables, was abandoned by Babbage in the 1840s due to the limitations of the technology of the period and a lack of funds. Unlike the Difference Engine, the Analytical Engine was designed as a general-purpose tool capable of storing information. Babbage's work relied heavily on mechanics and physical machinery and it was not until the 20th-century invention of the electrical vacuum tube, and then the transistor, that computers became a feasible means of solving problems.

FIRST GENERATION

War has played a significant role in the development of the computer. In 1943, during the Second World War, British and American scientists started work on electro-mechanical computers. Colossus, a British effort, was specifically developed to crack German coding ciphers, whilst the US machine, Harvard Mark I, was developed as a more general-purpose electro-mechanical programmable computer (partly intended for atom bomb research). Regarded as early 'first generation' computers, these machines primarily comprised wired circuits and vacuum tubes. Punched cards and paper tape were largely employed as the input, output and main storage systems. In 1946 ENIAC (Electronic Numerical Integrator and Computer) was completed at the University of Pennsylvania, USA. Capable of carrying out 100,000 calculations a second, it was remarkable for its day despite weighing 30 tons.

SECOND GENERATION

Similar to light bulbs, vacuum tubes (more commonly known as 'valves') were prone to failure, requiring tedious checks to resolve problems (ENIAC alone contained 18,000 vacuum valves). In 1947 the transistor was invented, initially to replace vacuum tubes used in amplifiers. Performing the same role as a vacuum tube but less prone to failure, smaller and more efficient, the transistor allowed smaller 'second generation' computers to be developed throughout the 1950s and early 1960s.

THIRD GENERATION
In 1958 Jack St Claire Kilby, of Texas Instruments, invented the first integrated circuit (or 'microchip'). Six months later Robert Noyce of Fairchild Semiconductors independently produced a similar integrated circuit. A microchip is comprised of a large number of transistors and other components fabricated from a wafer ('chip') of silicon, interconnected by a surface film of conductive material rather than by wires. By reducing distance between components, savings are made in both size and electricity. In 1963 the first 'third generation' computers based on microchip technology appeared.

FOURTH GENERATION
In 1971 Intel produced the first 'microprocessor', heralding a 'fourth generation' of computers. The Intel 4004 (capable of 60,000 instructions per second) grouped much of the processing functions onto a single microchip. Around the same time, Intel invented the RAM (random access memory) chip, which grouped significant amounts of memory onto a single chip. Supercomputers and mainframes, utilising scores of microprocessors, had terrific power, capable of 150 million instructions per second. Developments such as multi-layer circuits, and the use of copper instead of gold in microchips, yielded improvements in size and performance through miniaturisation. The size of the transistor was scaled down from thumb size to far smaller than the thickness of a human hair, allowing for greater density and thus exponentially increasing the total power of the computer.

NEXT GENERATION
Most modern computers are still regarded as 'fourth generation' as they use essentially the same technology, albeit highly miniaturised. Gordon Moore, co-founder of Intel, observed in 1965 that the number of transistors per square inch had doubled every 12 months since the inception of the integrated circuit. The widely recognised current definition of the so-called 'Moore's Law' is that the number of transistors on a microprocessor doubles every 18 months and is likely to do so for the next fe decades. Moore underestimated the improvement microprocessing power that has occurred since then microprocessing 'clock' speeds are now measured mega- and even gigahertz.

Processor	*Clock speed*	*Year of launc*
Intel 80286	8MHz	1982
Intel 80386	16MHz	1985
Intel 80486	25Mhz	1989
Intel Pentium	60MHz	1993
Intel Pentium II	350MHz	1997
Intel Pentium 4	1,500MHz	2000

There are many technological paradigms currently research that could shape the next generation computers. The future of computer technology could f example be dependent on the physics of light. Alrea used extensively in the computer industry for high-spe communications, light offers future possibilities for bo calculation and storage. Another strong candidate is t use of quantum computing, where data is not held in b (zeros and ones) but 'qubits' that, when combined, c hold a greater magnitude of information. Next generati computers may also utilise technology such as neu interfaces, joining the human central nervous system to computer input and output system. Nanotechnology, new manufacturing technology that works on a molecul level, is fast becoming a major subject of researc Continuing miniaturisation in computer architecture has great deal of scope to advance many areas of science, su as medicine, robotics and materials. Theoris applications in medicine include the ability to produ cell-like structures that combat certain diseases or ev destroy cancerous cells. Nanorobotics also presents t ability to construct devices that can regenerate wh damaged, particularly useful in space exploration. Wi the current high investment in research, nanotechnolo seems likely to become one of the next technologic revolutions.

INTERNET DOMAIN NAMES

Internet top-level domains names are two-letter codes that appear at the end of a website address to identify its origi Websites that use a country code top-level domain must be registered with the individual country or dependent territor The list below is of active domain names for countries only.*

ad	Andorra
ae	United Arab Emirates
af	Afghanistan
aq	The Antarctic
ag	Antigua and Barbuda
al	Albania
am	Armenia
ao	Angola
ar	Argentina
at	Austria
au	Australia
az	Azerbaijan
ba	Bosnia and Hercegovina
bb	Barbados
bd	Bangladesh
be	Belgium
bf	Burkina Faso
bg	Bulgaria
bh	Bahrain
bi	Burundi
bj	Benin
bn	Brunei
bo	Bolivia
br	Brazil
bt	Bhutan
bw	Botswana
by	Belarus
bz	Belize
ca	Canada
cd	Congo, Dem. Republic of
cf	Central African Republic
cg	Congo, Republic of
ch	Switzerland
ci	Côte d'Ivoire
cl	Chile
cm	Cameroon
cn	China
co	Colombia
cr	Costa Rica
cs	Serbia; Montenegro
cu	Cuba
cv	Cape Verde
cy	Cyprus
cz	Czech Republic
de	Germany
dj	Djibouti
dk	Denmark
dm	Dominica
do	Dominican Republic
dz	Algeria
ec	Ecuador

* North Korea has no internet country code top-level domain, but .kp is reserved for the country

Estonia	li	Liechtenstein	sa	Saudi Arabia
Egypt	lk	Sri Lanka	sb	Solomon Islands
Eritrea	lr	Liberia	sc	Seychelles
Spain	ls	Lesotho	sd	Sudan
Ethiopia	lt	Lithuania	se	Sweden
European Union	lu	Luxembourg	sg	Singapore
Finland	lv	Latvia	si	Slovenia
Fiji	ly	Libya	sk	Slovakia
Micronesia, Federated States of	ma	Morocco	sl	Sierra Leone
France	mc	Monaco	sn	Senegal
Gabon	md	Moldova	so	Somalia
Grenada	mg	Madagascar	sr	Suriname
Georgia	mh	Marshall Islands	st	São Tomé and Príncipe
Ghana	mk	Macedonia	sv	El Salvador
The Gambia	ml	Mali	sy	Syria
Guinea	mm	Myanmar	sz	Swaziland
Equatorial Guinea	mn	Mongolia	td	Chad
Greece	mr	Mauritania	tg	Togo
Guatemala	mt	Malta	th	Thailand
Guinea-Bissau	mu	Mauritius	tj	Tajikistan
Guyana	mv	Maldives	tl	East Timor
Honduras	mw	Malawi	tm	Turkmenistan
Croatia	mx	Mexico	tn	Tunisia
Haiti	my	Malaysia	to	Tonga
Hungary	mz	Mozambique	tp	East Timor
Indonesia	na	Namibia	tr	Turkey
Ireland	ne	Niger	tt	Trinidad and Tobago
Israel	ng	Nigeria	tv	Tuvalu
India	ni	Nicaragua	tw	Taiwan
Iraq	nl	The Netherlands	tz	Tanzania
Iran	no	Norway	ua	Ukraine
Iceland	np	Nepal	ug	Uganda
Italy	nz	New Zealand	uk	United Kingdom
Jamaica	om	Oman	us	United States of America
Jordan	pa	Panama	uy	Uruguay
Japan	pe	Peru	uz	Uzbekistan
Kenya	pg	Papua New Guinea	va	Vatican City State (Holy See)
Kyrgyzstan	ph	The Philippines	vc	St Vincent and the Grenadines
Cambodia	pk	Pakistan	ve	Venezuela
Kiribati	pl	Poland	vn	Vietnam
The Comoros	pt	Portugal	vu	Vanuatu
St Christopher and Nevis	pw	Palau	ws	Samoa
Korea, Republic of	py	Paraguay	ye	Yemen
Kuwait	qa	Qatar	yu	Montenegro; Serbia†
Kazakhstan	ro	Romania	za	South Africa
Laos	ru	Russian Federation	zm	Zambia
Lebanon	rw	Rwanda	zw	Zimbabwe

Montenegro and Serbia have been assigned new codes, me and rs. They are not yet active as of April 2007

THE ENVIRONMENT

The 11 warmest years on record have all occurred in the last 12 years. The second half of the 20th century was the warmest period in the northern hemisphere for 1,300 years and Europe has warmed by about 1°C over the past 100 years according to the United Nations latest climate change report. The report also concludes that the frequency of extreme weather events has increased and regional climate patterns are changing. Heat waves and changes in storm tracks and precipitation can now be traced back to climate change caused by human activity. The European Environment Agency (EEA) has described climate change as Europe's most pressing challenge. Other areas of concern include biodiversity, marine ecosystems and land and water resources air pollution.

This year marks 35 years of environmental legislation. There is strong evidence that past regulation has worked. Water and air have been cleaned up, ozone-depleting substances have been phased out, and waste recycling has risen.

GLOBAL PRODUCTION OF CFCs: 1986–2004

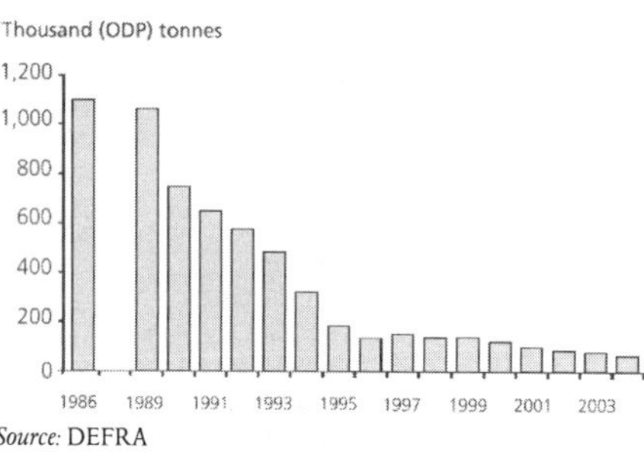

Source: DEFRA

However, these successes have been overshadowed by changes in personal consumption patterns. Europeans are living longer and more live alone, putting greater demands on living space. They travel further and more frequently and are consuming the planet's natural resources at twice the average global rate. Transport is the fastest growing contributor to greenhouse gas emissions and will continue to be for the foreseeable future. It is currently responsible for 21 per cent of total greenhouse gas emissions. Between 1990 and 2003, passenger transport volumes in Europe grew by 20 per cent and emissions from aviation increased by 86 per cent between 1990 and 2004.

With this in mind, attention is turning to individuals and to what they can do to reduce their carbon footprint. This is a measure of the amount of carbon dioxide emitted through the burning of fossil fuels as part of a person's daily life or, in the case of an organisation, as part of its everyday operations. The UK's carbon footprint is currently 648 million tonnes of CO_2 per year, according to the Carbon Trust. This means the average Briton's annual carbon footprint is 10.92 tonnes. By contrast, the average American generates 20 tonnes of carbon dioxide each year. Initiatives aimed at individuals are being launched, such as the UK's *We're in this together* campaign which aims to provide people with practical solutions to reduce their household emissions by a target of one to each over the next three years.

SELECTED UK TARGETS

AIR QUALITY AND ATMOSPHERE

- Reduce carbon dioxide emissions to 26–32 per c below 1990 levels by 2020, and by 60 per cent 2050
- Reduce emissions of volatile organic compounds by per cent below 1990 levels by 2010
- UK to reduce greenhouse gas emission by 12.5 per c below 1990 levels by 2008–12

FRESH WATER AND SEA

- All inland and coastal water to reach good st (ecological, chemical and quantitative) by 2015

WASTE

- Recycle or compost 40 per cent of household waste 2010, 45 per cent by 2015 and 50 per cent by 202
- Reduce residual household waste by 29 per cent 2010, 35 per cent by 2015 and 45 per cent by 2 from 2000 levels
- Reduce commercial and industrial waste landfilled 20 per cent by 2010, based on 2004 levels

ENERGY

- Provide 10 per cent of UK electricity from renew sources by 2010 and 20 per cent by 2020
- Scotland to generate 18 per cent of electricity by 2 from renewable sources, rising to 40 per cent by 202
- 10 per cent use of bio-fuels by 2020

EUROPEAN UNION MEASURES

The EU is developing an interlinked set of policies – sixth environment action programme, the Cardiff Pro and the EU sustainable development strategy – that f the framework for more detailed strategies. The Europ Commission (EC) is also diversifying the methods it u in particular to include market-based instruments such environmental taxes and voluntary measures. These increasingly being used across Europe. At EU le several are in use, such as the emissions trading scheme greenhouse gas emissions.

The environment action programme began in 1970s. The sixth of these, *Environment 2010: our fut our choice,* was adopted in 2001 and represents cornerstone of EU policy. It focuses on four topics: clim change, nature and biodiversity, environment and hea and natural resources and waste.

EU environmental legislation is based on the princi that the polluter pays. The environmental liabi directive, adopted in 2004, will be used to hold pollut financially liable for damage they cause. The EU is a attempting to look beyond current legislation. T prospective environmental analysis of land development in Europe (PRELUDE) project looks at w Europe's society and environment might be like 30 ye from now with the aim of illustrating key trends support strategic decision making.

JSTAINABLE DEVELOPMENT

e environmental agenda has become part of a wider ve to address sustainability that incorporates social, ironmental and economic development. During the rld summit on sustainable development, held in annesburg in 2002, governments agreed on a series of nmitments in five priority areas: water and sanitation, rgy, health, agriculture and biodiversity. Targets and etables approved included halving the number of ople who lack access to clean water or proper sanitation 2015, and reducing the rate of biodiversity loss by 10. Following the summit, the UN commission on tainable development agreed its programme for the t 15 years. In addition, 2005–15 has been named as ter for life' decade.

The EU's latest sustainable development strategy, nched in 2005, focuses on climate change and clean rgy; public health threats; social exclusion, nography and migration; management of natural ources; sustainable transport and global poverty and relopment. There are multiple links between these llenges; for example between the use of renewable rgy and climate change or climate change and poverty.

In 2005, the UK government published *Securing the ure*, its revised sustainable development strategy, ngside *Framework for sustainable development across the , our future – different paths,* shared between the vernment, the devolved administrations and the rthern Ireland office. The key aspects of the UK ategy include: a task force on sustainable public ocurement that published a national action plan – *ocuring our future*; a scheme to enable government partments to offset the carbon impacts of their air vel; and *Together we can,* which enables groups to help luence authorities' sustainability strategies and velopment plans at a local level.

The Scottish Executive's vision, priorities and licators for sustainable development are set out in *oosing our future*, published in 2005. In October 2006, ew set of indicators was published to reflect the key comes in the strategy, including new measures on bon emissions. The indicators are also more closely gned to the joint UK framework for sustainable velopment.

The Welsh National Assembly published sustainability emes in 2000 and 2004. Its programme for putting new scheme into effect is set out in its *Sustainable elopment action plan 2004–2007*. Recommendations a full set of sustainable development indicators re accepted in 2006.

'ASTE

ste policy in the UK follows a number of principles: waste hierarchy of reduce, reuse, recycle, dispose; the oximity principle of disposing of waste close to its neration; and national self-sufficiency. EU directives y an important role in driving UK policy, particularly garding commercial and industrial waste. For example, response to the landfill directive, adopted in July 1999, government established a landfill allowance trading eme, under which the amount of biodegradable nicipal waste local authorities can dispose of in landfill es is limited. These landfill allowances are tradable and thorities can buy, sell or save surplus allowances.

The proposed European integrated products policy ns to internalise the environmental costs of products throughout their life cycle using market forces, by focusing on eco-design and incentives to ensure increased demand for greener products. The policy will culminate in 2007 with the identification of a first set of products with the greatest potential for environmental improvement.

The EU is already addressing greater responsibility for end-of-life products. Producer responsibility directives, which had to be enacted in member states by August 2004, include: the directive for packaging waste; the end-of-life vehicle directive; and directives on waste from electrical and electronic equipment (and on the restriction of the use of certain hazardous substances in such equipment). The directive on batteries has also been adopted, requiring all batteries on the EU market to be collected and recycled.

The proportion of household waste recycled (including composting) in the UK has been steadily increasing, from 22.5 per cent in 2004–5 to 26.7 per cent in 2005–6. Scotland recycled 24.4 per cent of municipal waste in 2005–6, up from 17.3 per cent in the previous year. However, the total amount of waste produced per person per year has grown from 450kg in 1995–6 to 517 in 2004–5.

UK HOUSEHOLD WASTE AND RECYCLING

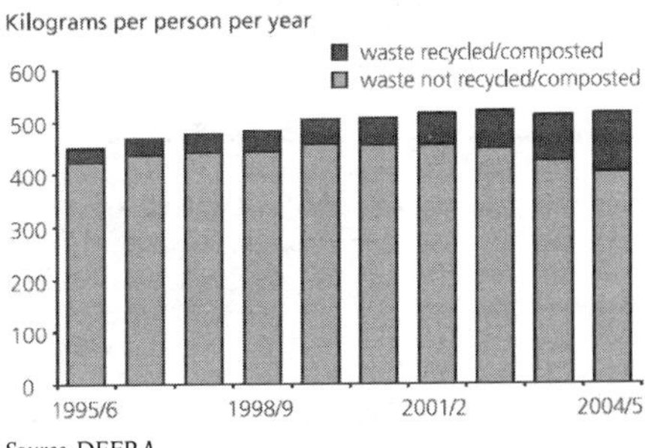

Source: DEFRA

In May 2007, the UK government published a new waste strategy. Targets for household recycling have been increased significantly and there is a strong emphasis on waste prevention with a new target to help measure waste reduction. Businesses will also have a greater responsibility to minimise and recycle packaging. In addition, the government aims to increase the amount of energy produced from waste schemes. Meanwhile, in March 2006, Northern Ireland launched a new waste management strategy – *Towards resource management* – that outlines plans to modernise waste management policies.

CLIMATE CHANGE AND AIR POLLUTION

The UK's response to climate change has been driven by the UN framework convention on climate change. This is a binding agreement that came into force in March 1994. It aims to reduce the risks of global warming by limiting greenhouse gas emissions.

Progress towards the convention's targets is assessed at regular conferences. In 1997, the Kyoto protocol was adopted. It covers the six main greenhouse gases – carbon dioxide, methane, nitrous oxide, hydrofluorocarbons (HFCs), perfluorocarbons (PFCs) and sulphur hexafluoride. Under the protocol, industrialised countries agreed to legally binding targets for cutting emissions of greenhouse gases by 5.2 per cent below 1990 levels by 2008–12. EU members agreed to an 8 per cent reduction and the UK to 12.5 per cent. The new EU member states have all ratified the protocol and have their own targets of between 6 and 8 per cent. The protocol entered into force in 2005 after it was ratified by Russia; the USA and Australia have stated that they will not ratify the treaty. The EC expects the EU to meet its Kyoto targets, provided all the measures in the pipeline are implemented. The UK is currently on course to meet its Kyoto target. In 2005, emissions of the six greenhouse gases were 15.3 per cent below 1990 levels, and 18.8 per cent below when the effect of the EU emissions trading scheme is taken into account, against the Kyoto target of 12.5 per cent.

In the new member states, emissions have declined substantially. In 2004, emissions were 23 per cent below 1990 levels. This is mainly due to the restructuring or closure of heavily polluting and energy-intensive industries. Greenhouse gas emissions from transport decreased by 5 per cent between 1990 and 1995 but increased after 1995. In 2004, they exceeded 1990 levels by 28 per cent.

EU EMISSIONS OF GREENHOUSE GASES AGAINST KYOTO PROTOCOL TARGET

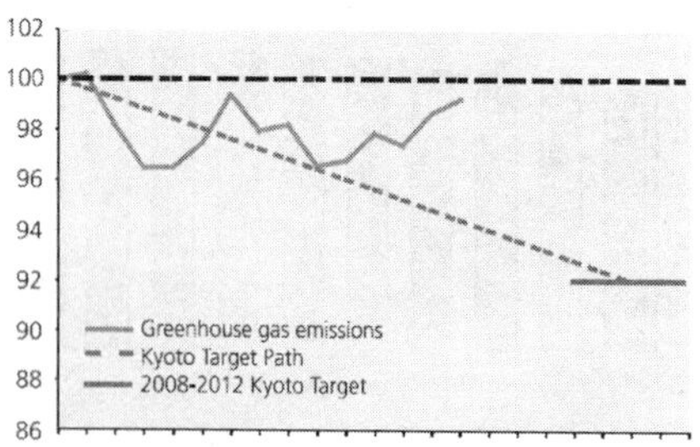

Source: DEFRA

The EC launched a second European climate change programme in 2005 that places a greater emphasis on adaptation to climate change. There are five working groups in this programme: review of the first climate change programme; carbon dioxide capture and geological storage; impacts and adaptation; aviation; and carbon dioxide and cars.

In January, the EC set out proposals and options for keeping climate change to manageable levels in *Limiting global climate change to 2° Celsius: the way ahead for 2020 and beyond*. This is part of a package of measures to establish a new energy policy for Europe. It also contributes to the international discussions on a future global agreement to combat climate change after 2012, when the Kyoto emissions targets expire. An EC impact assessment says investment in a low-carbon economy will require about 0.5 per cent of global GDP over the period 2013–20, compared with the government commissioned Stern Review's estimate that uncontrolled climate change will cost 5–20 per cent of GDP in the longer term.

The EU's national emission ceilings directive sets upper limits for each member state for the total emissions in 2010 of the four pollutants responsible for acidification, eutrophication and ground-level ozone pollution (sulphur dioxide, nitrogen oxides, volatile organic compounds and ammonia), but leaves it largely to the member states decide which measures to take in order to comply.

In March 2007, the EU heads of state and governm agreed a firm target of cutting 20 per cent of the E greenhouse gas emissions by 2020, rising to 30 per c if the USA, Canada and India make similar commitme

Current measures to tackle climate change in the are covered by a programme launched in March 20 The measures to reduce emissions target every sector the economy and include: a stricter cap for indus measures to encourage the uptake of biofuels in pet tighter building regulations; measures to impr household energy efficiency; a renewed emphasis encouraging and enabling the general public, busines and public authorities to help achieve the governme targets; and increased levels of micro-generation. T programme is expected to reduce the UK's emissions greenhouse gases to 23–25 per cent below base y levels and reduce the UK's carbon dioxide emissions 15–18 per cent below 1990 levels by 2010. Howe higher than anticipated levels of economic growth the recent rises in global energy prices, which in turn h altered the relative price of coal and gas, have led increased emissions and have made the target m challenging. The government recently admitted that 2010 target is looking increasingly difficult to achieve.

In March, the UK government issued a draft clim change bill. The bill, and the accompanying strategy, out a framework to move the UK to a low-carb economy. The bill proposes a legally binding target c 60 per cent reduction in carbon dioxide emissions bel 1990 levels by 2050 with an interim target of a reduct of 26–32 per cent over the period 2008–12. It a proposes five-year carbon budgets. These will require government to set binding limits on CO_2 emissi during five-year budget periods.

Scotland launched its new climate change program – *Changing our ways* – in March 2006. It quantifies carbon terms the contribution Scotland must ma towards UK commitments to reduce greenhouse gas The Scottish share has been calculated at 1.7 mill tonnes of carbon savings by 2010. The Scottish Execut will report annually on progress with the climate char programme. The first report was published in Ma 2007 and showed that in the first year, Scotland h increased investment in renewable technology and met renewable energy target for 2010 ahead of schedule.

WATER

Water quality targets are set at both EU and UK level drinking water sources, wastewater discharges, rive coastal water and bathing water. The EU's wa framework directive, which entered into force in 200 aims to achieve 'good' water status throughout the EU 2015. Member states are obliged to monitor and ass groundwater quality on the basis of common criteria a to identify and reverse trends in groundwater polluti Information on local water quality can be obtained fr the water information system for Europe (WISE), a n interactive internet tool, run by the EC.

Under the UK Water Act of 2003, a new water servi regulatory authority replaced OFWAT in April 200 although it carries the same name. The Wa Environment and Water Services Bill for Scotland a completed its passage through the Scottish parliament 2003. It established a source-to-sea planning framewo for river basin management.

The EC has adopted a new bathing water directive in :bruary, which sets a tighter bathing water quality andard than the previous directive. Results for 2006 ıow that only two out of the 413 bathing areas onitored in the UK failed to meet the directive's inimum requirements, while 75 per cent met the tighter andard. These figures show a great improvement since ıe early 1990s, when less than a third of England's :aches reached the toughest standards. Scotland has a :w better bathing waters strategy to raise standards to eet the European directive.

K COMPLIANCE WITH BATHING WATER
TANDARDS

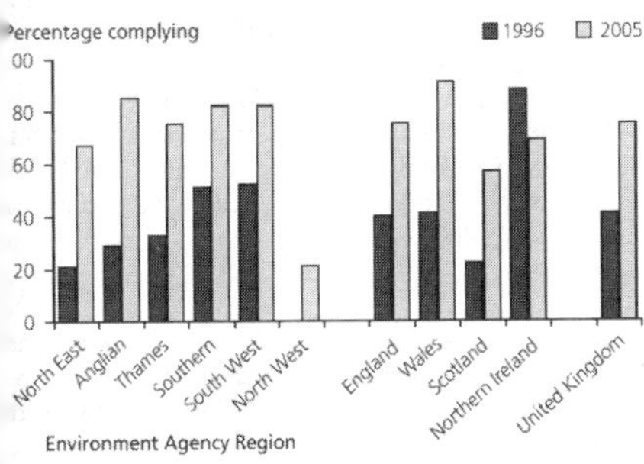

urce: DEFRA

The Environment Agency sets river quality objectives ır each stretch of river. In 2005, 72 per cent of rivers ere of good quality, compared with 69 per cent in 2000. etween 1990 and 2005, the biological quality of 31 per :nt of rivers improved. Most of this improvement :curred in the first five years and has since levelled off. In ıme places, such as parts of Wales, biological quality has eteriorated since 1995.

The European urban waste water treatment directive ts minimum standards for sewage treatment before ischarge into coastal waters, with the levels of treatment :eded depending on the sensitivity of the receiving ater.

NERGY

ıergy used in the home is responsible for 25 per cent of ıe UK's carbon dioxide emissions. In 2003, the UK ıvernment published a white paper, *Our energy future – eating a low carbon economy,* setting out a long-term rategy for UK energy policy to 2050, combining ıvironmental, competitiveness, social and security of ıpply goals. It built on the Performance and Innovation nit's *Energy review,* published a year earlier. An energy ıll was also introduced in 2003.

In 2004 the government launched its *UK international riorities – the energy strategy,* which set out how it plans to ıeet the international energy challenge over the next five ı ten years. The UK has a target to increase the ıntribution of renewables to 10 per cent of electricity by 010, with an aspiration to reach 20 per cent by 2020. enewables capacity is increasing. By the beginning of 006, the UK installed over 1,300MW of wind capacity.

In July 2006, the UK government published its third ınual report on the implementation of the white paper. his detailed the progress made and summarised the way ıead to achieving the four energy policy goals – cutting carbon dioxide emissions, maintaining reliable energy supplies, promoting competitive energy markets, and ensuring homes are affordably heated.

Also in July, the government published its report on the *Energy review – The energy challenge.* Proposals to tackle climate change by reducing carbon dioxide emissions and to deliver secure, clean energy and affordable prices will feed into the energy white paper. The paper was due in 2007, but was delayed by a court ruling, following legal action by Greenpeace, which found that consultation on nuclear power prior to the review being published was inadequate.

A new framework directive for eco-design for energy-using products will set efficiency standards for household items such as boilers, computers and washing machines, as well as commercial equipment and component parts. The EU's renewables directive has been in place since 2001. It aims to increase the EU's share of electricity produced from renewable energy sources to 21 per cent by 2010 (up from 15.2 per cent in 2001). However, current figures show it will fall short, reaching 19 per cent by 2010.

ENVIRONMENT AND HEALTH

Concerns about the impact of pollution on health are covered in the *Environment and health action plan 2004–10,* launched in 2004. The plan proposes an integrated approach involving closer cooperation between the health, environment and research areas.

A new chemicals policy, under which industry will have to provide information on the effects of chemicals on human health and the environment, as well as on safe ways of handling them, has also been set up. It replaces 40 existing pieces of legislation and will be managed by a new European Chemicals Agency, in Helsinki. It will enter into force in 2007.

CONTACTS

DEPARTMENT OF ENVIRONMENT, FOOD AND RURAL AFFAIRS
Eastbury House, 30–34 Albert Embankment, London SE1 7TL
T 08459-335577 **W** www.defra.gov.uk

DEPARTMENT OF THE ENVIRONMENT, NORTHERN IRELAND
Clarence Court, 10–18 Adelaide Street, Belfast BT2 8GB
T 028-9054 0540 **W** www.doeni.gov.uk

ENVIRONMENT AGENCY
Rio House, Almonsbury, Bristol BS32 4UD **T** 08708-506506
W www.environment-agency.gov.uk

EUROPEAN ENVIRONMENT AGENCY
Kongens Nytorv 6, DK-1050 Copenhagen K, Denmark
W www.eea.europa.eu

ROYAL COMMISSION ON ENVIRONMENTAL POLLUTION
Third Floor, The Sanctuary, London SW1P 3JS **T** 020-7799 8970
W www.rcep.org.uk

SCOTTISH EXECUTIVE, ENVIRONMENT AND RURAL AFFAIRS DEPARTMENT
Pentland House, 47 Robb's Loan, Edinburgh EH14 1TY
T 0131-556 8400 **W** www.scotland.gov.uk

CONSERVATION AND HERITAGE

NATIONAL PARKS

ENGLAND AND WALES

With the designation of the New Forest as a national park on 1 March 2005, there are now eight national parks in England and three in Wales. In addition, the Norfolk and Suffolk Broads are considered to have equivalent status to a national park. Under the provisions of the National Parks and Access to the Countryside Act 1949, as clarified by the Natural Environment and Rural Communities Act 2006, areas designated as national parks have a statutory requirement to conserve and protect scenic landscapes from inappropriate development and to provide access to the land for public enjoyment.

Natural England (formerly the Countryside Agency) is the statutory body which has the power to designate national parks in England, and the Countryside Council for Wales is responsible for national parks in Wales. Designations in England are confirmed by the Secretary of State for Environment, Food and Rural Affairs and those in Wales by the National Assembly for Wales. The designation of a national park does not affect the ownership of the land or remove the rights of the local community. The majority of the land in the national parks is owned by private landowners (74 per cent) or by bodies such as the National Trust (7 per cent) and the Forestry Commission (7 per cent). The national park authorities own only around 2 per cent of the land.

The Environment Act 1995 replaced the existing national park boards and committees with free-standing national park authorities (NPAs). NPAs are the sole local planning authorities for their areas and as such influence land use and development, and deal with planning applications. Their duties include conserving and enhancing the natural beauty, wildlife and cultural heritage of the parks; promoting opportunities for public understanding and enjoyment; and fostering the economic and social well-being of the communities within national parks. The NPAs publish management plans as statements of their policies and appoint their own officers and staff.

The Broads Authority was established under the Norfolk and Suffolk Broads Act 1998 and meets the requirement for the authority to have a navigation function in addition to a regard for the needs of agriculture, forestry and the economic and social interests of those who live or work in the Broads.

The New Forest NPA was established on 1 April 2005. Following an interim year, in which the authority had a limited range of statutory powers and functions, it became fully operational on 1 April 2006.

MEMBERSHIP

Membership of English NPAs comprises local authority appointees, members directly appointed by the environment secretary of state and members appointed by him after a consultation with local parishes. Under the Natural Environment and Rural Communities Act 2006 every district, county or unitary authority with land in a national park is entitled to appoint at least one member unless it chooses to opt out. The total number of local authority and parish members must exceed the number national members. Since 1 April 2007 all NPAs have : members, except for the Peak District which has 30.

The Broads Authority has 21 members: nine appoint by the constituent local authorities, two appointed by t Navigation Committee and ten appointed by t Secretary of State. The Secretary of State's appointe include at least three which are appointed aft consultation with representatives of boating interests a at least two which are appointed after consultation wi representatives of landowning and farming interests.

In Wales two-thirds of NPA members are appointed the constituent local authorities and one-third by t Welsh Assembly Government, advised by the Countrysi Council for Wales.

FUNDING

The English NPAs and the Broads Authority are fund by central government. In the financial year 2007–8 core grant totalling £44.24m was allocated between t authorities.

In Wales, national parks are funded via a grant from t National Assembly. In addition, the three Welsh NPAs c levy a further third of their monies from their constitue local authorities.

All NPAs and the Broads Authority can take advanta of grants from other bodies including lottery a European grants.

The national parks (with date designation confirmed) a

BRECON BEACONS (1957), Powys (66 per cent)/Carmarthenshire/Rhondda, Cynon and Taff/Merthyr Tydfil/Blaenau Gwent/Monmouthshir 1,344 sq. km/519 sq. miles – The park is centred on the Beacons, Pen y Fan, Corn Du and Cribyn, but als includes the valley of the Usk, the Black Mountains t the east and the Black Mountain to the west. There are information centres at the national park visitor centre near Libanus, Abergavenny, Llandovery and Craig-y-nos Country Park.
National Park Authority, Plas y Ffynnon, Cambrian Way, Brecon, Powys LD3 7HP **T** 01874-624437
E enquiries@breconbeacons.org
W www.breconbeacons.org
Chief Executive, Christopher Gledhill

BROADS (1989), Norfolk/Suffolk, 303 sq. km/117 sq miles – The Broads are located between Norwich and Great Yarmouth on the flood plains of the six rivers flowing through the area to the sea. The area is one c fens, winding waterways, woodland and marsh. The 6 or so broads are man-made, and many are connected the rivers by dykes, providing over 200km of navigab waterways. There are information centres at Beccles, Hoveton, Potter Heigham, Ranworth, Whitlingham and Toad Hole Cottage at How Hill.
Broads Authority, 18 Colegate, Norwich NR3 1BQ
T 01603-610734 **E** broads@broads-authority.gov.uk
W www.broads-authority.gov.uk
Chief Executive, Dr John Packman

DARTMOOR (1951), Devon, 954 sq. km/368 sq. mile – The park consists of moorland and rocky granite to

and is rich in prehistoric remains. There are information centres at Haytor, Newbridge, Princetown (main visitor centre) and Postbridge.
National Park Authority, Parke, Bovey Tracey, Devon TQ13 9JQ **T** 01626-832093 **E** hq@dartmoor-npa.gov.uk **W** www.dartmoor-npa.gov.uk
Chief Executive, Kevin Bishop, PHD

EXMOOR (1954), Somerset (71 per cent)/Devon, 693 sq. km/267 sq. miles – Exmoor is a moorland plateau inhabited by wild Exmoor ponies and red deer. There are many ancient remains and burial mounds. There are national park centres at Dunster, Dulverton and Combe Martin.
National Park Authority, Exmoor House, Dulverton, Somerset TA22 9HL **T** 01398-323665 **E** info@exmoor-nationalpark.gov.uk **W** www.exmoor-nationalpark.gov.uk
Chief Executive/National Park Officer, Dr Nigel Stone

LAKE DISTRICT (1951), Cumbria, 2,292 sq. km/885 sq. miles – The Lake District includes England's highest mountains (Scafell Pike, Helvellyn and Skiddaw) but it is most famous for its glaciated lakes. There are national park information centres at Bowness Bay, Keswick, Glenridding and a visitor centre at Brockhole, Windermere.
National Park Authority, Murley Moss, Oxenholme Road, Kendal, Cumbria LA9 7RL **T** 01539-724555 **E** hq@lake-district.gov.uk **W** www.lake-district.gov.uk
National Park Officer, Richard Leafe

NEW FOREST (2005), Hampshire, 567 sq. km/219 sq. miles – The forest has been protected since 1079 when it was declared a royal hunting forest. The area consists of forest, ancient woodland and heathland. Much of the forest is managed by the Forestry Commission, which provides several campsites. The main villages are Brockenhurst, Burley and Lyndhurst, which has a visitor centre.
National Park Authority, South Efford House, Milford Road, Lymington, Hants SO41 0JD **T** 01590-646600 **E** enquiries@newforestnpa.gov.uk **W** www.newforestnpa.gov.uk
Chief Executive, Lindsay Cornish

NORTH YORK MOORS (1952), North Yorkshire (96 per cent)/Redcar and Cleveland, 1,432 sq. km/554 sq. miles – The park consists of woodland and moorland, and includes the Hambleton Hills and the Cleveland Way. There are information centres at Danby, Sutton Bank and at the Old Coastguard Station in Robin Hood's Bay.
National Park Authority, The Old Vicarage, Bondgate, Helmsley, York YO6 5BP **T** 01439-770657 **E** general@northyorkmoors-npa.gov.uk **W** www.moors.uk.net
Chief Executive/National Park Officer, Andrew Wilson

NORTHUMBERLAND (1956), Northumberland, 1,049 sq. km/405 sq. miles – The park is an area of hill country stretching from Hadrian's Wall to the Scottish border. There are information centres at Ingram, Once Brewed and Rothbury.
National Park Authority, Eastburn, South Park, Hexham, Northumberland NE46 1BS **T** 01434-605555 **E** admin@nnpa.org.uk **W** www.northumberlandnationalpark.org.uk
Chief Executive, Tony Gates

PEAK DISTRICT (1951), Derbyshire (64 per cent)/Staffordshire/South Yorkshire/Cheshire/West Yorkshire/Greater Manchester, 1,438 sq. km/555 sq. miles – The Peak District includes the gritstone moors of the 'Dark Peak' and the limestone dales of the 'White Peak'. There are information centres at Bakewell, Castleton, Edale and Upper Derwent.
National Park Authority, Aldern House, Baslow Road, Bakewell, Derbyshire DE45 1AE **T** 01629-816200 **E** customer.service@peakdistrict.gov.uk **W** www.peakdistrict.gov.uk
Chief Executive, Jim Dixon

PEMBROKESHIRE COAST (1952 and 1995), Pembrokeshire, 620 sq. km/240 sq. miles – The park includes cliffs, moorland and a number of islands, including Skomer. There are information centres at St David's, Newport and Tenby.
National Park Authority, Llanion Park, Pembroke Dock, Pembrokeshire SA72 6DY **T** 0845-345 7275 **E** info@pembrokeshirecoast.org.uk **W** www.pcnpa.org.uk
Chief Executive (National Park Officer), Nic Wheeler

SNOWDONIA/ERYRI (1951), Gwynedd/Conwy, 2,132 sq. km/823 sq. miles – Snowdonia is an area of deep valleys and rugged mountains. There are information centres at Aberdyfi, Beddgelert, Betws y Coed, Blaenau Ffestiniog, Dolgellau and Harlech.
National Park Authority, Penrhyndeudraeth, Gwynedd LL48 6LF **T** 01766-770274 **E** parc@eryri-npa.gov.uk **W** www.eryri-npa.gov.uk
Chief Executive, Aneurin Phillips

YORKSHIRE DALES (1954), North Yorkshire (88 per cent)/Cumbria, 1,762 sq. km/680 sq. miles – The Yorkshire Dales are composed primarily of limestone overlaid in places by millstone grit. The three peaks of Ingleborough, Whernside and Pen-y-Ghent are within the park. There are information centres at Grassington, Hawes, Aysgarth Falls, Malham and Reeth.
National Park Authority, Yoredale, Bainbridge, Leyburn, N. Yorks DL8 3EL **T** 0870-1666333 **E** info@yorkshiredales.org.uk **W** www.yorkshiredales.org.uk
Chief Executive, David Butterworth

In 1999 the Countryside Agency began the process of designating the South Downs (within the Sussex Downs and East Hampshire 'Areas of Outstanding Natural Beauty') as a national park. A designation order for a South Downs national park was submitted by the Countryside Agency to the Secretary of State on 27 January 2003. In February 2006 the designation process was indefinitely postponed following a high court judgement (the 'Meyrick' judgement) regarding part of the 2005 New Forest designation which changed the way in which criteria for national park status had generally been understood. The Department for Environment, Food and Rural Affairs (DEFRA) clarified the national parks legislation through the Natural Environment and Rural Communities Act 2006 and the South Downs designation process was restarted in March 2007.

THE SOUTH DOWNS, West Sussex/Hampshire,1,637 sq. km/632 sq. miles – The South Downs contains a diversity of natural habitats, including flower-studded chalk grassland, ancient woodland, flood meadow, lowland heath and rare chalk heathland.
South Downs Joint Committee, Victorian Barn, Victorian Business Centre, Ford Lane, Ford, Arundel, W. Sussex BN18 0EF **T** 01243-558700 **E** comms@southdowns-aonb.gov.uk
South Downs Officer, Martin Beaton

SCOTLAND

On 9 August 2000 the national parks (Scotland) bill received royal assent, giving parliament the ability to create national parks in Scotland. The first two Scottish national parks, Loch Lomond and the Trossachs and the Cairngorms, became operational in 2002 and 2003 respectively. The Act gives Scottish parks wider powers than in England and Wales, including statutory responsibilities for the economy and rural communities. The board of each Scottish NPA consists of 25 members, of which five are directly elected by a postal ballot of the local electorate. The remaining 20 members, ten of which are nominated by the constituent local authorities, are chosen by the Scottish ministers. In Scotland, the national parks are central government bodies and wholly funded by the Scottish Executive. Funding for 2007–8 totals £11.4m with £6.9m allocated to Loch Lomond and the Trossachs and £4.5m to the Cairngorms.

CAIRNGORMS (2003), Morayshire, 3,800 sq. km/1,466 sq. miles – The Cairngorms national park is the largest in the UK. It displays a vast collection of landforms and includes four of Scotland's highest mountains.
National Park Authority, 14 The Square, Grantown-on-Spey, Morayshire PH26 3HG **T** 01479-873535
E enquiries@cairngorms.co.uk **W** www.cairngorms.co.uk
Chief Executive, Jane Hope

LOCH LOMOND AND THE TROSSACHS (2002), Argyll and Bute/Perth and Kinross/Stirling/West Dunbartonshire, 1,865 sq. km/720 sq. miles – The park boundaries encompass lochs, rivers, forests, 20 mountains above 3,000ft including Ben More and a further 20 mountains between 2,500ft and 3,000ft.
National Park Authority, The Old Station, Balloch Road, Balloch G83 8BF **T** 01389-722600
E info@lochlomond-trossachs.org
W www.lochlomond-trossachs.org
Chief Executive, William Dalrymple

NORTHERN IRELAND

There is a power to designate national parks in Northern Ireland under the Nature Conservation and Amenity Lands Order (Northern Ireland) 1985, but there are currently no national parks in Northern Ireland.

AREAS OF OUTSTANDING NATURAL BEAUTY

ENGLAND AND WALES

Under the National Parks and Access to the Countryside Act 1949, provision was made for the designation of areas of outstanding natural beauty (AONBs). Natural England (formerly the Countryside Agency) is responsible for AONBs in England and the Countryside Council for Wales for the Welsh AONBs. Designations in England are confirmed by the Secretary of State for Environment, Food and Rural Affairs and those in Wales by the National Assembly for Wales. The Countryside and Rights of Way (CROW) Act 2000 placed greater responsibility on local authorities to protect AONBs and made it a statutory duty for relevant authorities to produce a management plan for their AONB area. The CROW Act also provided for the creation of conservation boards for larger and more complex AONBs. The first two conservation boards for the Cotswolds and Chilterns AONBs were established in July 2004 following confirmation by the secretary of state.

The primary objective of the AONB designation is to conserve and enhance the natural beauty of the area. Where an AONB has a conservation board, it has the additional purpose of increasing public understandin and enjoyment of the special qualities of the area, wit the first purpose having greater weight, if there should b a conflict of interests between the two. In addition to th above, the board is also required to foster the economi and social well-being of the local communities bu without incurring significant expenditure in doing sc Overall responsibility for AONBs lies with the relevan local authorities or conservation board. To coordinat planning and management responsibilities between loca authorities in whose area they fall, AONBs are oversee by a joint advisory committee (or similar body) whic includes representatives from the local authorities landowners, farmers, residents and conservation an recreation groups. In addition, an AONB officer i appointed to oversee matters. Core funding for AONBs i provided by central government through Natural Englan and the Countryside Council for Wales.

The 40 Areas of Outstanding Natural Beauty (wit date designation confirmed) are:

ARNSIDE AND SILVERDALE (1972), Cumbria/Lancashire, 75 sq. km/29 sq. miles
BLACKDOWN HILLS (1991), Devon/Somerset, 370 sc km/143 sq. miles
CANNOCK CHASE (1958), Staffordshire, 68 sq. km/2 sq. miles
CHICHESTER HARBOUR (1964), Hampshire/West Sussex, 74 sq. km/29 sq. miles
CHILTERNS (1965; extended 1990), Bedfordshire/Buckinghamshire/Herefordshire/Oxfordshire, 833 sc km/322 sq. miles
CLWYDIAN RANGE (1985), Denbighshire/Flintshire, 157 sq. km/61 sq. miles
CORNWALL (1959; Camel Estuary 1983), 958 sq. km/370 sq. miles
COTSWOLDS (1966; extended 1990), Gloucestershire/Oxfordshire/Warwickshire/Wiltshire/Worcestershire, 2,038 sq. km/787 sq. miles
CRANBORNE CHASE AND WEST WILTSHIRE DOWNS (1983), Dorset/Hampshire/Somerset/Wiltshire, 983 sq. km/380 sq. miles
DEDHAM VALE (1970; extended 1978, 1991), Essex/Suffolk, 90 sq. km/35 sq. miles
DORSET (1959), Dorset/Somerset, 1,129 sq. km/436 sq. miles
EAST DEVON (1963), 268 sq. km/103 sq. miles
EAST HAMPSHIRE (1962), 383 sq. km/148 sq. miles
FOREST OF BOWLAND (1964), Lancashire/North Yorkshire, 802 sq. km/310 sq. miles
GOWER (1956), Swansea, 188 sq. km/73 sq. miles
HIGH WEALD (1983), East Sussex/Kent/Surrey/West Sussex, 1,460 sq. km/564 sq. miles
HOWARDIAN HILLS (1987), North Yorkshire, 204 sq. km/79 sq. miles
ISLE OF WIGHT (1963), 189 sq. km/73 sq. miles
ISLES OF SCILLY (1976), 16 sq. km/6 sq. miles
KENT DOWNS (1968), 878 sq. km/339 sq. miles
LINCOLNSHIRE WOLDS (1973), 558 sq. km/215 sq miles
LLEYN (1957), Gwynedd, 161 sq. km/62 sq. miles
MALVERN HILLS (1959), Gloucestershire/Worcestershire, 150 sq. km/58 sq. miles
MENDIP HILLS (1972; extended 1989), Somerset, 19 sq. km/76 sq. miles
NIDDERDALE (1994), North Yorkshire, 603 sq. km/233 sq. miles

NORFOLK COAST (1968), 451 sq. km/174 sq. miles
NORTH DEVON (1960), 171 sq. km/66 sq. miles
NORTH PENNINES (1988), Cumbria/Durham/North Yorkshire/Northumberland, 1,983 sq. km/766 sq. miles
NORTH WESSEX DOWNS (1972), Hampshire/Oxfordshire/Wiltshire, 1,730 sq. km/668 sq. miles
NORTHUMBERLAND COAST (1958), 135 sq. km/52 sq. miles
QUANTOCK HILLS (1957), Somerset, 99 sq. km/38 sq. miles
SHROPSHIRE HILLS (1959), 804 sq. km/310 sq. miles
SOLWAY COAST (1964), Cumbria, 115 sq. km/44 sq. miles
SOUTH DEVON (1960), 337 sq. km/130 sq. miles
SUFFOLK COAST AND HEATHS (1970), 403 sq. km/156 sq. miles
SURREY HILLS (1958), 419 sq. km/162 sq. miles
SUSSEX DOWNS (1966), 983 sq. km/379 sq. miles
TAMAR VALLEY (1995), Cornwall/Devon, 195 sq. km/75 sq. miles
WYE VALLEY (1971), Gloucestershire/Herefordshire/Monmouthshire, 326 sq. km/126 sq. miles
YNYS MON (ISLE OF ANGLESEY) (1967), 221 sq. km/85 sq. miles

NORTHERN IRELAND

The Department of the Environment for Northern Ireland, with advice from the Council for Nature Conservation and the Countryside, designates Areas of Outstanding Natural Beauty in Northern Ireland. At present there are nine and these cover a total area of 2,849 sq. km (1,100 sq. miles). Dates given are those of designation.

ANTRIM COAST AND GLENS (1988), Co. Antrim, 706 sq. km/272 sq. miles
BINEVENAGH (2006), Co. Londonderry, 166 sq. km/64 sq. miles
CAUSEWAY COAST (1989), Co. Antrim, 42 sq. km/16 sq. miles
LAGAN VALLEY (1965), Co. Down, 21 sq. km/8 sq. miles
LECALE COAST (1967), Co. Down, 31 sq. km/12 sq. miles
MOURNE (1986), Co. Down, 570 sq. km/220 sq. miles
RING OF GULLION (1991), Co. Armagh, 154 sq. km/59 sq. miles
SPERRIN (1968), Co. Tyrone/Co. Londonderry, 1,010 sq. km/390 sq. miles
STRANGFORD LOUGH (1972), Co. Down, 186 sq. km/72 sq. miles

NATIONAL SCENIC AREAS

In Scotland, national scenic areas have a broadly equivalent status to AONBs. Scottish Natural Heritage recognises areas of national scenic significance. At the end of June 2007 there were 40, covering a total area of 1,001,800 hectares (2,475,443 acres).

Development within national scenic areas is dealt with by local authorities, who are required to consult Scottish Natural Heritage concerning certain categories of development. Disagreements between Scottish Natural Heritage and local authorities are referred to the Scottish Executive. Land management uses can also be modified in the interest of scenic conservation.

ASSYNT-COIGACH, Highland, 90,200 ha/222,884 acres
BEN NEVIS AND GLEN COE, Highland, 101,600 ha/251,053 acres
CAIRNGORM MOUNTAINS, Highland/Aberdeenshire/Moray, 67,200 ha/166,051 acres
CUILLIN HILLS, Highland, 21,900 ha/54,115 acres
DEESIDE AND LOCHNAGAR, Aberdeenshire, 40,000 ha/98,840 acres
DORNOCH FIRTH, Highland, 7,500 ha/18,532 acres
EAST STEWARTRY COAST, Dumfries and Galloway, 4,500 ha/11,119 acres
EILDON AND LEADERFOOT, Borders, 3,600 ha/8,896 acres
FLEET VALLEY, Dumfries and Galloway, 5,300 ha/13,096 acres
GLEN AFFRIC, Highland, 19,300 ha/47,690 acres
GLEN STRATHFARRAR, Highland, 3,800 ha/9,390 acres
HOY AND WEST MAINLAND, Orkney Islands, 14,800 ha/36,571 acres
JURA, Argyll and Bute, 21,800 ha/53,868 acres
KINTAIL, Highland, 15,500 ha/38,300 acres
KNAPDALE, Argyll and Bute, 19,800 ha/48,926 acres
KNOYDART, Highland, 39,500 ha/97,604 acres
KYLE OF TONGUE, Highland, 18,500 ha/45,713 acres
KYLES OF BUTE, Argyll and Bute, 4,400 ha/10,872 acres
LOCH NA KEAL, Mull, Argyll and Bute, 12,700 ha/31,382 acres
LOCH LOMOND, Argyll and Bute, 27,400 ha/67,705 acres
LOCH RANNOCH AND GLEN LYON, Perthshire and Kinross, 48,400 ha/119,596 acres
LOCH SHIEL, Highland, 13,400 ha/33,111 acres
LOCH TUMMEL, Perthshire and Kinross, 9,200 ha/22,733 acres
LYNN OF LORN, Argyll and Bute, 4,800 ha/11,861 acres
MORAR, MOIDART AND ARDNAMURCHAN, Highland, 13,500 ha/33,358 acres
NITH ESTUARY, Dumfries and Galloway, 9,300 ha/22,980 acres
NORTH ARRAN, North Ayrshire, 23,800 ha/58,810 acres
NORTH-WEST SUTHERLAND, Highland, 20,500 ha/50,655 acres
RIVER EARN, Perthshire and Kinross, 3,000 ha/7,413 acres
RIVER TAY, Perthshire and Kinross, 5,600 ha/13,838 acres
ST KILDA, Eilean Siar (Western Isles), 900 ha/2,224 acres
SCARBA, LUNGA AND THE GARVELLACHS, Argyll and Bute, 1,900 ha/4,695 acres
SHETLAND, Shetland Isles, 11,600 ha/28,664 acres
SMALL ISLANDS, Highland, 15,500 ha/38,300 acres
SOUTH LEWIS, HARRIS AND NORTH UIST, Eilean Siar (Western Isles), 109,600 ha/270,822 acres
SOUTH UIST MACHAIR, Eilean Siar (Western Isles), 6,100 ha/15,073 acres
THE TROSSACHS, Stirling, 4,600 ha/11,367 acres
TROTTERNISH, Highland, 5,000 ha/12,355 acres
UPPER TWEEDDALE, Borders, 10,500 ha/25,945 acres
WESTER ROSS, Highland, 145,300 ha/359,036 acres

THE NATIONAL FOREST

The National Forest is being planted across 517 sq. km (200 sq. miles) of Derbyshire, Leicestershire and Staffordshire. Seven million trees, of mixed species but mainly broadleaved, covering over 5,400 hectares (13,300 acres) have been planted. The aim is to eventually cover about one-third of the designated area.

The project was developed in 1992–5 by the Countryside Commission and is now run by the National Forest Company, which was established in April 1995. The National Forest Company is responsible for the delivery of the government-approved National Forest Strategy and is funded by the DEFRA.

NATIONAL FOREST COMPANY, Enterprise Glade, Bath Lane, Moira, Swadlincote, Derbyshire DE12 6BD
T 01283-551211 E enquiries@nationalforest.org
W www.nationalforest.org
Chief Executive, Sophie Churchill

SITES OF SPECIAL SCIENTIFIC INTEREST

Site of special scientific interest (SSSI) is a legal notification applied to land in England, Scotland or Wales which Natural England (NE) (formerly English Nature), Scottish Natural Heritage (SNH) or the Countryside Council for Wales (CCW) identifies as being of special interest because of its flora, fauna, geological, geomorphological or physiographical features. In some cases, SSSIs are managed as nature reserves.

NE, SNH and CCW must notify the designation of an SSSI to the local planning authority, every owner/occupier of the land, and the environment secretary, the Scottish ministers or the National Assembly for Wales. Forestry and agricultural departments and a number of other interested parties are also formally notified.

Objections to the notification of an SSSI can be made and ultimately considered at a full meeting of the Council of NE or CCW. In Scotland an objection will be dealt with by the main board of SNH or an appropriate subgroup, depending on the nature of the objection. Unresolved objections on scientific grounds from those with a legal interest in the land must be referred to the Advisory Committee on SSSI.

The protection of these sites depends on the cooperation of individual landowners and occupiers. Owner/occupiers must consult NE, SNH or CCW and gain written consent before they can undertake certain listed activities on the site. Funds are available through management agreements and grants to assist owners and occupiers in conserving sites' interests. As a last resort a site can be purchased.

The number and area of SSSIs in Britain as at May 2007 was:

	Number	*Hectares*	*Acres*
England	4,113	1,076,496	2,658,945
Scotland	1,455	1,036,577	2,561,347
Wales	1,016	264,531	653,682

NORTHERN IRELAND

In Northern Ireland 241 Areas of Special Scientific Interest (ASSIs) have been declared by the Department of the Environment for Northern Ireland.

NATIONAL NATURE RESERVES

National nature reserves are defined in the National Parks and Access to the Countryside Act 1949 as modified by the Natural Environment and Rural Communities Act (2006). National nature reserves may be managed solely for the purpose of conservation, or for both the purposes of conservation and recreation, providing this does not compromise the conservation purpose.

Natural England (NE), Scottish Natural Heritage (SNH) or the Countryside Council for Wales (CCW) can declare as a national nature reserve land which is held and managed as a nature reserve under an agreement; land held and managed by NE, SNH or CCW; or land held and managed as a nature reserve by an approved body. NE, SNH or CCW can make by-laws to protect reserves from undesirable activities; these are subject to confirmation by the Secretary of State for Environment, Food and Rural Affairs, the National Assembly for Wales or the Scottish ministers in Scotland.

The number and area of national nature reserves in Britain as at May 2007 was:

	Number	*Hectares*	*Acres*
England	222	93,001	229,80
Scotland	63	111,913	276,53
Wales	68	24,156	59,69

NORTHERN IRELAND

Nature reserves are established and managed by the Department of the Environment for Northern Ireland with advice from the Council for Nature Conservation and the Countryside. Nature reserves are declared under the Nature Conservation and Amenity Lands (Northern Ireland) order 1985; to date, 47 nature reserves have been declared.

LOCAL NATURE RESERVES

Local nature reserves are defined in the National Parks and Access to the Countryside Act 1949 as land designated for the study and preservation of flora and fauna, or of geological or physiographical features. The Act gives local authorities in England, Scotland and Wales the power to acquire, declare and manage reserves in consultation with Natural England (formerly English Nature), Scottish Natural Heritage and the Countryside Council for Wales. There is similar legislation in Northern Ireland where the consulting organisation is the Environment and Heritage Service.

Any organisation, such as water companies, educational trusts, local amenity groups and charitable nature conservation bodies, such as wildlife trusts, may manage local nature reserves, provided that a local authority has a legal interest in the land. This means that the local authority must either own it, lease it or have a management agreement with the landowner.

The number and area of designated local nature reserves in Britain as at May 2007 was:

	Number	*Hectares*	*Acres*
England	1,366	35,000	86,45
Scotland	48	9,791	24,19
Wales	69	4,999	12,35

FOREST NATURE RESERVES

The Forestry Commission is the government department responsible for forestry policy throughout Great Britain. Forestry is a devolved matter, with the separate Forestry Commissions for England, Scotland and Wales reporting directly to their appropriate minister. The Forestry Commission in each country is led by a director who is also a member of the GB Board of Commissioners. As at March 2006 Forestry Commission managed woodland amounted to 772,000 hectares: 204,000 hectares in England, 108,000 hectares in Wales and 460,000 hectares in Scotland.

NORTHERN IRELAND

There are 34 forest nature reserves in Northern Ireland, covering 1,512 hectares (3,736 acres). They are designated and administered by the Forest Service, an agency of the Department of Agriculture and Rural Development for Northern Ireland. There are also 16 national nature reserves on Forest Service-owned property.

MARINE NATURE RESERVES

The Secretary of State for Environment, Food and Rural Affairs, the National Assembly for Wales and the Scottish Executive have the power to designate marine nature reserves. Natural England, Scottish Natural Heritage and the Countryside Council for Wales select and manage these reserves. Marine nature reserves may be established in Northern Ireland under a 1985 Order.

Marine nature reserves provide protection for marine flora and fauna, and geological and physiographical features on land covered by tidal waters or parts of the sea in or adjacent to the UK. Reserves also provide opportunities for study and research.

The three statutory marine nature reserves are:

LUNDY (1986), Bristol Channel
SKOMER (1990), Dyfed
STRANGFORD LOUGH (1995), Northern Ireland

WORLD HERITAGE SITES

The Convention Concerning the Protection of the World Cultural and Natural Heritage was adopted by the United Nations Educational Scientific and Cultural Organisation (UNESCO) in 1972 and ratified by the UK in 1984. As at 25 October 2006 184 states were party to the convention. The convention provides for the identification, protection and conservation of cultural and natural sites of outstanding universal value.

Cultural sites may be:

- monuments
- groups of buildings
- sites of historic, aesthetic, archaeological, scientific, ethnologic or anthropologic value
- historic areas of towns
- 'cultural landscapes', ie sites whose characteristics are marked by significant interactions between human populations and their natural environment

Natural sites may be:

- those with remarkable physical, biological or geological formations
- those with outstanding universal value from the point of view of science, conservation or natural beauty
- the habitat of threatened species and plants

Governments which are party to the convention nominate sites in their country for inclusion in the World Cultural and Natural Heritage List. Nominations are considered by the World Heritage Committee, an inter-governmental committee composed of 21 representatives of the parties to the convention. The committee is advised by the International Council on Monuments and Sites (ICOMOS), the International Centre for the Study of the Preservation and Restoration of Cultural Property (ICCROM) and the World Conservation Union (IUCN). ICOMOS evaluates and reports on proposed cultural and mixed sites, ICCROM provides expert advice and training on how to conserve the listed sites and IUCN provides technical evaluations of natural sites and reports on the state of conservation of listed sites. The Department for Culture, Media and Sport represents the UK government in matters relating to the convention.

A prerequisite for inclusion in the World Cultural and Natural Heritage List is the existence of an effective legal protection system in the country in which the site is situated (eg listing, conservation areas and planning controls in the UK) and a detailed management plan to ensure the conservation of the site. Inclusion in the list does not confer any greater degree of protection on the site than that offered by the national protection framework.

If a site is considered to be in serious danger of decay or damage, the committee may add it to a complementary list, the World Heritage in Danger List. Sites on this list may benefit from particular attention or emergency measures.

Financial support for the conservation of sites on the World Cultural and Natural Heritage List is provided by the World Heritage Fund. This is administered by the World Heritage Committee, which determines the financial and technical aid to be allocated. The fund's income is derived from compulsory and voluntary contributions from the states party to the convention and from private donations.

DESIGNATED SITES

As at 2 July 2007, following the 31st session of the World Heritage Committee, 851 sites were inscribed on the World Cultural and Natural Heritage List. Of these, 24 are in the United Kingdom and three in British overseas territories; 22 are listed for their cultural significance (†), four for their natural significance (*) and one for both cultural and natural significance. The year in which sites were designated appears in parentheses. In 2005 Hadrian's Wall, a World Heritage Site in its own right since 1987, was joined by the upper German-Raetian Limes to form the first section of a trans-national world heritage site, Frontiers of the Roman Empire.

UNITED KINGDOM

†Bath – the city (1987)
†Blaenarvon industrial landscape, Wales (2000)
†Blenheim Palace and Park, Oxfordshire (1987)
†Canterbury Cathedral, St Augustine's Abbey, St Martin's Church, Kent (1988)
†Castle and town walls of King Edward I, north Wales – Beaumaris, Caernarfon Castle, Conwy Castle, Harlech Castle, Ynys Mon (Isle of Anglesey) (1986)
†Cornwall and west Devon mining landscape (2006)
†Derwent Valley Mills, Derbyshire (2001)
*Dorset and east Devon coast (2001)
†Durham Cathedral and Castle (1986)
†Edinburgh old and new towns (1995)
†Frontiers of the Roman Empire, Hadrian's Wall, northern England (1987, 2005)
*Giant's Causeway and Causeway coast, Co. Antrim (1986)
†Greenwich, London – maritime Greenwich, including the Royal Naval College, Old Royal Observatory, Queen's House, town centre (1997)
†Heart of Neolithic Orkney (1999)
†Ironbridge Gorge, Shropshire – the world's first iron bridge and other early industrial sites (1986)
†Liverpool – six areas of the maritime mercantile city (2004)
†New Lanark, South Lanarkshire, Scotland (2001)
†Royal Botanic Gardens, Kew (2003)
†*St Kilda, Eilean Siar (Western Isles) (1986)
†Saltaire, West Yorkshire (2001)
†Stonehenge, Avebury and related megalithic sites, Wiltshire (1986)
†Studley Royal Park, Fountains Abbey, St Mary's Church, N. Yorkshire (1986)
†Tower of London (1988)
†Westminster Abbey, Palace of Westminster, St Margaret's Church, London (1987)

BRITISH OVERSEAS TERRITORIES

*Henderson Island, Pitcairn Islands, South Pacific Ocean (1988)
*Gough Island and Inaccessible Island (part of Tristan da Cunha), South Atlantic Ocean (1995)
†St George town and related fortifications, Bermuda (2000)

WORLD HERITAGE CENTRE, UNESCO, 7 Place de Fontenoy, 75352 Paris 07 SP, France
W http://whc.unesco.org

CONSERVATION OF WILDLIFE AND HABITATS

The UK is party to a number of international conventions.

RAMSAR CONVENTION

The 1971 Ramsar Convention on Wetlands of International Importance especially as Waterfowl Habitat entered into force in the UK in May 1976. As at July 2007, 155 countries were party to the convention.

The aim of the convention is the conservation and wise use of wetlands and their resources. Governments that are party to the convention must designate wetlands and include wetland conservation considerations in their land-use planning. 1,671 wetland sites, totalling 151 million hectares, have been designated for inclusion in the list of wetlands of international importance. The UK currently has 165 designated sites covering 895,144 hectares. The member countries meet every three years to assess the progress of the convention and the next meeting is scheduled for November 2008.

The UK has set targets under the Ramsar Strategic Plan, 2003–8. Progress towards these is monitored by the UK Ramsar Committee, known as the Joint Working Party. The UK and the Republic of Ireland have established a formal protocol to ensure common monitoring standards for waterbirds in the two countries.

RAMSAR CONVENTION SECRETARIAT, rue Mauverney 28, CH-1196 Gland, Switzerland
T (+41) (22) 999 0170 W www.ramsar.org

BIODIVERSITY

The UK ratified the Convention on Biological Diversity in June 1994. As at July 2007 there were 190 parties to the convention.

The objectives are the conservation of biological diversity, the sustainable use of its components and the fair and equitable sharing of the benefits arising out of the use of genetic resources. There are seven thematic work programmes addressing agricultural biodiversity, marine and coastal biodiversity and the biodiversity of inland waters, dry and sub-humid lands, islands, mountains and forests. The Conference of the Parties to the Convention on Biological Diversity adopted a supplementary agreement to the convention known as the Cartagena Protocol on Biosafety on 29 January 2000. The protocol seeks to protect biological diversity from potential risks that may be posed by introducing modified living organisms, resulting from biotechnology, into the environment. As at July 2007, 141 countries were party to the protocol; the UK joined on 17 February 2004.

The UK Biodiversity Action Plan (UKBAP) is the UK government's response to the Convention on Biological Diversity and constitutes a record of UK biological resources and a detailed plan for their protection. UKBAP currently consists of 391 species action plans, 45 habitat action plans and 162 local biodiversity plans. The UK Biodiversity Partnership Standing Committee guides and supports the UK Biodiversity Partnership in implementing UKBAP; it also coordinates between the four UK country groups which form the partnership and are responsible for implementing UKBAP at a national level. In addition, the UK Biodiversity Partnership includes two support groups: the Biodiversity Research Advisory Group and the Biodiversity Reporting and Information Group.

BIODIVERSITY POLICY UNIT, Zone 1/10B, Temple Quay House, 2 The Square, Temple Quay, Bristol BS1 6EB
T 0117-372 6276 W www.ukbap.org.uk

CITES

The 1973 Convention on International Trade in Endangered Species of Wild Fauna and Flora (CITES) is an agreement between governments to ensure that international trade in specimens of wild animals and plants does not threaten their survival. The UK became party to the convention in July 1975 and there are currently 172 member countries. Countries party to the convention ban commercial international trade in an agreed list of endangered species and regulate and monitor trade in other species that might become endangered. The convention accords varying degrees of protection to more than 30,000 species of animals and plants whether they are traded as live specimens or as products derived from them, such as fur coats and dried herbs.

The Conference of the Parties to CITES meets every two to three years to review the convention's implementation. The Wildlife Species Conservation Division at the Department for Environment, Food and Rural Affairs in Bristol (*see* address above) carries out the government's responsibilities under CITES.

CITES SECRETARIAT, International Environment House, Chemin des Anémones, CH-1219 Châtelaine, Geneva, Switzerland T (+41) (22) 917 8139/8140 E info@cites.org
W www.cites.org

BONN CONVENTION

The 1979 Convention on Conservation of Migratory Species of Wild Animals came into force in the UK in October 1979. As at 1 January 2007, 101 countries were party to the convention.

It requires the protection of listed endangered migratory species and encourages international agreements covering these and other threatened species. International agreements can range from legally binding treaties to less formal memorandums of understanding.

Six agreements have been concluded to date under the convention. They aim to conserve seals in the Wadden Sea; bat populations in Europe; small cetaceans of the Baltic and North Seas; African-Eurasian migratory waterbirds; cetaceans of the Mediterranean Sea, Black Sea and contiguous Atlantic area; and albatrosses and petrels. A further ten memorandums of understanding have been agreed for the Siberian crane, slender-billed curlew, marine turtles of the Atlantic coast of Africa, Indian Ocean and South-East Asia, the middle-European population of the great bustard, bukhara deer, aquatic warbler, West African populations of the African elephant, the saiga antelope and cetaceans of the Pacific Islands.

UNEP/CMS SECRETARIAT, United Nations Premises, Hermann-Ehlers-Str. 10, 53113 Bonn, Germany
T (+49) (228) 815 2401/2 E secretariat@cms.int
W www.cms.int

BERN CONVENTION

The 1979 Bern Convention on the Conservation of European Wildlife and Natural Habitats came into force in the UK in June 1982. Currently there are 45 contracting parties and a number of other states attend meetings as observers.

The aims are to conserve wild flora and fauna and their natural habitats, especially where this requires the cooperation of several countries, and to promote such cooperation. The convention gives particular emphasis to endangered and vulnerable species.

All parties to the convention must promote national conservation policies and take account of the conservation of wild flora and fauna when setting planning and development policies. Reports on contracting parties' conservation policies must be submitted to the standing committee every four years.

SECRETARIAT OF THE BERN CONVENTION STANDING COMMITTEE, Council of Europe, Avenue de l'Europe, 67075 Strasbourg-Cedex, France
T (+33) (3) 8841 2000 **W** www.coe.int

EUROPEAN WILDLIFE TRADE REGULATION

The Council (EC) Regulation on the Protection of Species of Wild Fauna and Flora by Regulating Trade Therein came into force in the UK on 1 June 1997. It is intended to standardise wildlife trade regulations across Europe and to improve the application of CITES.

UK LEGISLATION

The Wildlife and Countryside Act 1981 gives legal protection to a wide range of wild animals and plants. Subject to parliamentary approval, the environment secretary may vary the animals and plants given legal protection. The most recent variation of schedules 5 and 8 came into effect in March and April 1998. The fourth quinquennial review of species listed in schedules 5 and 8 is ongoing.

Under section 9 of the act it is an offence to kill, injure, take, possess or sell (whether alive or dead) any wild animal included in schedule 5 of the act and to disturb its place of shelter and protection or to destroy that place. However certain species listed on schedule 5 are protected against some, but not all, of these activities.

Under section 13 of the act it is illegal without a licence to pick, uproot, sell or destroy plants listed in schedule 8. Since January 2001, under the Countryside and Rights of Way Act 2000, persons found guilty of an offence under part 1 of the Wildlife and Countryside Act 1981 face a maximum penalty of up to £5,000 and/or up to six months custodial sentence per specimen.

The act lays down a close season for birds (listed on Schedule 2, part 1) from 1 February to 31 August inclusive, each year. Exceptions to these dates are made for:

Capercaillie and (except Scotland) Woodcock – 1 February to 30 September
Snipe – 1 February to 11 August
Birds listed on schedule 2, part 1 (below high water mark) (*see* below) – 21 February to 31 August
Birds listed on schedule 2, part 1, which may be killed or taken outside the close season (except on Sundays and on Christmas Day in Scotland, and on Sundays in prescribed areas of England and Wales) are capercaillie, coot, certain wild duck (gadwall, goldeneye, mallard, pintail, pochard, shoveler, teal, tufted duck, wigeon), certain wild geese (Canada, greylag, pink-footed, white-fronted (in England and Wales only)), moorhen, golden plover and woodcock.

Section 16 of the 1981 act allows licences to be issued on either an individual or general basis, to allow the killing, taking and sale of certain birds for specified reasons such as public health and safety. All other wild birds are fully protected by law throughout the year.

ANIMALS PROTECTED BY SCHEDULE 5
Adder *(Vipera berus)**
Allis Shad *(Alosa alosa)**
Atlantic Stream Crayfish *(Austropotomobius pallipes)**
Anemone, Ivell's Sea *(Edwardsia ivelli)*
Anemone, Starlet Sea *(Nematosella vectensis)*
Bat, Horseshoe *(Rhinolophidae,* all species*)*
Bat, Typical *(Vespertilionidae,* all species*)*
Beetle *(Hypebaeus flavipes)*
Beetle, Lesser Silver Water *(Hydrochara caraboides)*
Beetle, Mire Pill *(Curimopsis nigrita)**
Beetle, Rainbow Leaf *(Chrysolina cerealis)*
Beetle, Spangled Water *(Graphoderus zonatus)*
Beetle, Stag *(Lucanus cervus)**
Beetle, Violet Click *(Limoniscus violaceus)*
Beetle, Water *(Paracymus aeneus)*
Burbot *(Lota lota)*
Butterfly, Adonis Blue *(Lysandra bellargus)*
Butterfly, Black Hairstreak *(Strymonidia pruni)*
Butterfly, Brown Hairstreak *(Thecla betulae)*
Butterfly, Chalkhill Blue *(Lysandra coridon)*
Butterfly, Chequered Skipper *(Carterocephalus palaemon)*
Butterfly, Duke of Burgundy Fritillary *(Hamearis lucina)*
Butterfly, Glanville Fritillary *(Melitaea cinxia)*
Butterfly, Heath Fritillary *(Mellicta athalia* or *Melitaea athalia)*
Butterfly, High Brown Fritillary *(Argynnis adippe)*
Butterfly, Large Blue *(Maculinea arion)*
Butterfly, Large Copper *(Lycaena dispar)*
Butterfly, Large Heath *(Coenonympha tullia)*
Butterfly, Large Tortoiseshell *(Nymphalis polychloros)*
Butterfly, Lulworth Skipper *(Thymelicus acteon)*
Butterfly, Marsh Fritillary *(Eurodryas aurinia)*
Butterfly, Mountain Ringlet *(Erebia epiphron)*
Butterfly, Northern Brown Argus *(Aricia artaxerxes)*
Butterfly, Pearl-bordered Fritillary *(Boloria euphrosyne)*
Butterfly, Purple Emperor *(Apatura iris)*
Butterfly, Silver Spotted Skipper *(Hesperia comma)*
Butterfly, Silver-studded Blue *(Plebejus argus)*
Butterfly, Small Blue *(Cupido minimus)*
Butterfly, Swallowtail *(Papilio machaon)*
Butterfly, White Letter Hairstreak *(Stymonida w-album)*
Butterfly, Wood White *(Leptidea sinapis)*
Cat, Wild *(Felis silvestris)*
Cicada, New Forest *(Cicadetta montana)*
Cricket, Field *(Gryllus campestris)*
Cricket, Mole *(Gryllotalpa gryllotalpa)*
Damselfly, Southern *(Coenagrion mercuriale)*
Dolphin, all species *(Cetacea)*
Dormouse *(Muscardinus avellanarius)*
Dragonfly, Norfolk Aeshna *(Aeshna isosceles)*
Frog, Common *(Rana temporaria)**
Goby, Couch's *(Gobius couchii)*
Goby, Giant *(Gobius cobitis)*
Grasshopper, Wart-biter *(Decticus verrucivorus)*
Hatchet Shell, Northern *(Thyasira gouldi)*
Hydroid, Marine *(Clavopsella navis)*

agoon Snail *(Paludinella littorina)*
agoon Snail, De Folin's *(Caecum armoricum)*
agoon Worm, Tentacled *(Alkmaria romijni)*
eech, Medicinal *(Hirudo medicinalis)*
izard, Sand *(Lacerta agilis)*
izard, Viviparous *(Lacerta vivipara)**
larten, Pine *(Martes martes)*
loth, Barberry Carpet *(Pareulype berberata)*
loth, Black-veined *(Siona lineata* or *Idaea lineata)*
loth, Essex Emerald *(Thetidia smaragdaria)*
loth, Fiery Clearwing *(Bembecia chrysidiformis)*
loth, Fisher's Estuarine *(Gortyna borelii)*
loth, New Forest Burnet *(Zygaena viciae)*
loth, Reddish Buff *(Acosmetia caliginosa)*
loth, Sussex Emerald *(Thalera fimbrialis)*
lussel, Fan *(Atrina fragilis)**
lussel, Pearl Freshwater *(Margaritifera margaritifera)*
ewt, Great Crested (or Warty) *(Triturus cristatus)*
ewt, Palmate *(Triturus helveticus)**
ewt, Smooth *(Triturus vulgaris)**
tter, Common *(Lutra lutra)*
orpoise, all species *(Phocaena Phocaena)*
andworm, Lagoon *(Armandia cirrhosa)*
a Fan, Pink *(Eunicella verrucosa)**
a Slug, Lagoon *(Tenellia adspersa)*
a-mat, Trembling *(Victorella pavida)*
ad, Twaite *(Alosa fallax)**
ark, Basking *(Cetorhinus maximus)*
rimp, Fairy *(Chirocephalus diaphanus)*
rimp, Lagoon Sand *(Gammarus insensibilis)*
rimp, Tadpole *(Triops cancriformis)*
ow-worm *(Anguis fragilis)**
ail, Glutinous *(Myxas glutinosa)*
ail, Sandbowl *(Catinella arenaria)*
ake, Grass *(Natrix natrix* or *Natrix helvetica)**
ake, Smooth *(Coronella austriaca)*
oider, Fen Raft *(Dolomedes plantarius)*
oider, Ladybird *(Eresus niger)*
quirrel, Red *(Sciurus vulgaris)*
urgeon *(Acipenser sturio)*
oad, Common *(Bufo bufo)**
oad, Natterjack *(Bufo calamita)*
ırtle, Marine *(Dermochelyidae* and *Cheloniidae,* all species)
ndace *(Coregonus albula)*
ole, Water *(Arvicola terrestris)**
alrus *(Odobenus rosmarus)*
hale, all species *(Cetacea)*
hitefish *(Coregonus lavaretus)*

These species are protected against some, but not all, of the activities listed under section 9 of the Wildlife and Countryside Act 1981

.ANTS PROTECTED BY SCHEDULE 8

dder's Tongue, Least *(Ophioglossum lusitanicum)*
ison, Small *(Alyssum alyssoides)*
nomodon, Long-leaved *(Anomodon longifolius)*
ech-lichen, New Forest *(Enterographa elaborata)*
ackwort *(Southbya nigrella)*
uebell *(Hyacinthoides non-scripta)**
olete, Royal *(Boletus regius)*
oomrape, Bedstraw *(Orobanche caryophyllacea)*
oomrape, Oxtongue *(Orobanche loricata)*
oomrape, Thistle *(Orobanche reticulata)*
abbage, Lundy *(Rhynchosinapis wrightii)*
lamint, Wood *(Calamintha sylvatica)*
aloplaca, Snow *(Caloplaca nivalis)*
tapyrenium, Tree *(Catapyrenium psoromoides)*
Catchfly, Alpine *(Lychnis alpina)*
Catillaria, Laurer's *(Catellaria laureri)*
Centaury, Slender *(Centaurium tenuiflorum)*
Cinquefoil, Rock *(Potentilla rupestris)*
Cladonia, Convoluted *(Cladonia convoluta)*
Cladonia, Upright Mountain *(Cladonia stricta)*
Clary, Meadow *(Salvia pratensis)*
Club-rush, Triangular *(Scirpus triquetrus)*
Colt's-foot, Purple *(Homogyne alpina)*
Cotoneaster, Wild *(Cotoneaster integerrimus)*
Cottongrass, Slender *(Eriophorum gracile)*
Cow-wheat, Field *(Melampyrum arvense)*
Crocus, Sand *(Romulea columnae)*
Crystalwort, Lizard *(Riccia bifurca)*
Cudweed, Broad-leaved *(Filago pyramidata)*
Cudweed, Jersey *(Gnaphalium luteoalbum)*
Cudweed, Red-tipped *(Filago lutescens)*
Cut-grass *(Leersia oryzoides)*
Diapensia *(Diapensia lapponica)*
Dock, Shore *(Rumex rupestris)*
Earwort, Marsh *(Jamesoniella undulifolia)*
Eryngo, Field *(Eryngium campestre)*
Fern, Dickie's Bladder *(Cystopteris dickieana)*
Fern, Killarney *(Trichomanes speciosum)*
Flapwort, Norfolk *(Leiocolea rutheana)*
Fleabane, Alpine *(Erigeron borealis)*
Fleabane, Small *(Pulicaria vulgaris)*
Fleawort, South Stack *(Tephroseris integrifolia ssp maritima)*
Frostwort, Pointed *(Gymnomitrion apiculatum)*
Fungus, Hedgehog *(Hericium erinaceum)*
Galingale, Brown *(Cyperus fuscus)*
Gentian, Alpine *(Gentiana nivalis)*
Gentian, Dune *(Gentianella uliginosa)*
Gentian, Early *(Gentianella anglica)*
Gentian, Fringed *(Gentianella ciliata)*
Gentian, Spring *(Gentiana verna)*
Germander, Cut-leaved *(Teucrium botrys)*
Germander, Water *(Teucrium scordium)*
Gladiolus, Wild *(Gladiolus illyricus)*
Goblin Lights *(Catolechia wahlenbergii)*
Goosefoot, Stinking *(Chenopodium vulvaria)*
Grass-poly *(Lythrum hyssopifolia)*
Grimmia, Blunt-leaved *(Grimmia unicolor)*
Gyalecta, Elm *(Gyalecta ulmi)*
Hare's-ear, Sickle-leaved *(Bupleurum falcatum)*
Hare's-ear, Small *(Bupleurum baldense)*
Hawk's-beard, Stinking *(Crepis foetida)*
Hawkweed, Northroe *(Hieracium northroense)*
Hawkweed, Shetland *(Hieracium zetlandicum)*
Hawkweed, Weak-leaved *(Hieracium attenuatifolium)*
Heath, Blue *(Phyllodoce caerulea)*
Helleborine, Red *(Cephalanthera rubra)*
Helleborine, Young's *(Epipactis youngiana)*
Horsetail, Branched *(Equisetum ramosissimum)*
Hound's-tongue, Green *(Cynoglossum germanicum)*
Knawel, Perennial *(Scleranthus perennis)*
Knotgrass, Sea *(Polygonum maritimum)*
Lady's-slipper *(Cypripedium calceolus)*
Lecanactis, Churchyard *(Lecanactis hemisphaerica)*
Lecanora, Tarn *(Lecanora archariana)*
Lecidea, Copper *(Lecidea inops)*
Leek, Round-headed *(Allium sphaerocephalon)*
Lettuce, Least *(Lactuca saligna)*
Lichen, Arctic Kidney *(Nephroma arcticum)*
Lichen, Ciliate Strap *(Heterodermia leucomelos)*
Lichen, Coralloid Rosette *(Heterodermia propagulifera)*
Lichen, Ear-lobed Dog *(Peltigera lepidophora)*
Lichen, Forked Hair *(Bryoria furcellata)*

Lichen, Golden Hair *(Teloschistes flavicans)*
Lichen, Orange-fruited Elm *(Caloplaca luteoalba)*
Lichen, River Jelly *(Collema dichotomum)*
Lichen, Scaly Breck *(Squamarina lentigera)*
Lichen, Stary Breck *(Buellia asterella)*
Lily, Snowdon *(Lloydia serotina)*
Liverwort, Lindenberg's Leafy *(Adelanthus lindenbergianus)*
Marsh-mallow, Rough *(Althaea hirsuta)*
Marshwort, Creeping *(Apium repens)*
Milk-parsley, Cambridge *(Selinum carvifolia)*
Moss, Alpine Copper *(Mielichoferia mielichoferi)*
Moss, Baltic Bog *(Sphagnum balticum)*
Moss, Blue Dew *(Saelania glaucescens)*
Moss, Blunt-leaved Bristle *(Orthotrichum obtusifolium)*
Moss, Bright Green Cave *(Cyclodictyon laetevirens)*
Moss, Cordate Beard *(Barbula cordata)*
Moss, Cornish Path *(Ditrichum cornubicum)*
Moss, Derbyshire Feather *(Thamnobryum angustifolium)*
Moss, Dune Thread *(Bryum mamillatum)*
Moss, Flamingo *(Desmatodon cernuus)*
Moss, Glaucous Beard *(Barbula glauca)*
Moss, Green Shield *(Buxbaumia viridis)*
Moss, Hair Silk *(Plagiothecium piliferum)*
Moss, Knothole *(Zygodon forsteri)*
Moss, Large Yellow Feather *(Scorpidium turgescens)*
Moss, Millimetre *(Micromitrium tenerum)*
Moss, Multi-fruited River *(Cryphaea lamyana)*
Moss, Nowell's Limestone *(Zygodon gracilis)*
Moss, Polar Feather *(Hygrohypnum polare)*
Moss, Rigid Apple *(Bartramia stricta)*
Moss, Round-leaved Feather *(Rhyncostegium rotundifolium)*
Moss, Schleicher's Thread *(Bryum schleicheri)*
Moss, Slender Green Feather *(Drepanocladus vernicosus)*
Moss, Triangular Pygmy *(Acaulon triquetrum)*
Moss, Vaucher's Feather *(Hypnum vaucheri)*
Mudwort, Welsh *(Limosella austeralis)*
Naiad, Holly-leaved *(Najas marina)*
Naiad, Slender *(Najas flexilis)*
Orache, Stalked *(Halimione pedunculata)*
Orchid, Early Spider *(Ophrys sphegodes)*
Orchid, Fen *(Liparis loeselii)*
Orchid, Ghost *(Epipogium aphyllum)*
Orchid, Lapland Marsh *(Dactylorhiza lapponica)*
Orchid, Late Spider *(Ophrys fuciflora)*
Orchid, Lizard *(Himantoglossum hircinum)*
Orchid, Military *(Orchis militaris)*
Orchid, Monkey *(Orchis simia)*
Pannaria, Caledonia *(Panneria ignobilis)*
Parmelia, New Forest *(Parmelia minarum)*
Parmentaria, Oil Stain *(Parmentaria chilensis)*
Pear, Plymouth *(Pyrus cordata)*
Penny-cress, Perfoliate *(Thlaspi perfoliatum)*
Pennyroyal *(Mentha pulegium)*
Pertusaria, Alpine Moss *(Pertusaria bryontha)*
Petalwort *(Petallophyllum ralfsi)*
Physcia, Southern Grey *(Physcia tribacioides)*
Pigmyweed *(Crassula aquatica)*
Pine, Ground *(Ajuga chamaepitys)*
Pink, Cheddar *(Dianthus gratianopolitanus)*
Pink, Childing *(Petroraghia nanteuilii)*
Pink, Deptford (England and Wales only) *(Dianthus armeria)*
Polypore, Oak *(Buglossoporus pulvinus)*
Pseudocyphellaria, Ragged *(Pseudocyphellaria lacerata)*
Psora, Rusty Alpine *(Psora rubiformis)*
Puffball, Sandy Stilt *(Battarraea phalloides)*
Ragwort, Fen *(Senecio paludosus)*
Ramping-fumitory, Martin's *(Fumaria martinii)*
Rampion, Spiked *(Phyteuma spicatum)*
Restharrow, Small *(Ononis reclinata)*
Rock-cress, Alpine *(Arabis alpina)*
Rock-cress, Bristol *(Arabis stricta)*
Rustwort, Western *(Marsupella profunda)*
Sandwort, Norwegian *(Arenaria norvegica)*
Sandwort, Teesdale *(Minuartia stricta)*
Saxifrage, Drooping *(Saxifraga cernua)*
Saxifrage, Yellow Marsh *(Saxifrage hirulus)*
Saxifrage, Tufted *(Saxifraga cespitosa)*
Solenopsora, Serpentine *(Solenopsora liparina)*
Solomon's-seal, Whorled *(Polygonatum verticillatum)*
Sow-thistle, Alpine *(Cicerbita alpina)*
Spearwort, Adder's-tongue *(Ranunculus ophioglossifolius)*
Speedwell, Fingered *(Veronica triphyllos)*
Speedwell, Spiked *(Veronica spicata)*
Spike-rush, Dwarf *(Eleocharis parvula)*
Star-of-Bethlehem, Early *(Gagea bohemica)*
Starfruit *(Damasonium alisma)*
Stonewort, Bearded *(Chara canescens)*
Stonewort, Foxtail *(Lamprothamnium papulosum)*
Strapwort *(Corrigiola litoralis)*
Sulphur-tresses, Alpine *(Alectoria ochroleuca)*
Threadmoss, Long-leaved *(Bryum neodamense)*
Turpswort *(Geocalyx graveolens)*
Violet, Fen *(Viola persicifolia)*
Viper's-grass *(Scorzonera humilis)*
Water-plantain, Floating *(Luronium natans)*
Water-plantain, Ribbon-leaved *(Alisma gramineum)*
Wood-sedge, Starved *(Carex depauperata)*
Woodsia, Alpine *(Woodsia alpina)*
Woodsia, Oblong *(Woodsia ilvenis)*
Wormwood, Field *(Artemisia campestris)*
Woundwort, Downy *(Stachys germanica)*
Woundwort, Limestone *(Stachys alpina)*
Yellow-rattle, Greater *(Rhinanthus serotinus)*

* Protected against some, but not all, of the activities listed under section 13 of the Wildlife and Countryside Act 1981

HISTORIC BUILDINGS AND MONUMENTS

:NGLAND

'nder the Planning (Listed Buildings and Conservation reas) Act 1990, the Secretary of State for Culture, Media nd Sport has a statutory duty to compile lists of uildings or groups of buildings in England which are of pecial architectural or historic interest. Under the ncient Monuments and Archaeological Areas Act 1979 ; amended by the National Heritage Act 1983, the ecretary of state is also responsible for compiling a hedule of ancient monuments. Decisions are taken on e advice of English Heritage. On 1 April 2005 esponsibility for the administration of the listing system as transferred from the secretary of state to English eritage. This marked the start of a programme of hanges designed to increase the involvement and wareness of the property owner and make the listing rocess more straightforward and more accountable.

ISTED BUILDINGS

isted buildings are classified into Grade I, Grade II* and rade II. There are currently around 372,000 individual sted buildings in England, of which approximately 92 er cent are Grade II listed. Almost all pre-1700 uildings are listed, as are most buildings of 1700 to 840. English Heritage carries out thematic surveys of articular types of buildings with a view to making commendations for listing, and members of the public ay propose a building for consideration. The main urpose of listing is to ensure that care is taken in eciding the future of a building. No changes which fect the architectural or historic character of a listed uilding can be made without listed building consent (in ddition to planning permission where relevant). pplications for listed building consent are normally ealt with by the local planning authority, although nglish Heritage is always consulted about proposals fecting Grade I and Grade II* properties. It is a criminal fence to demolish a listed building, or alter it in such a ay as to affect its character, without consent.

CHEDULED MONUMENTS

here are currently around 19,700 scheduled monuments England. English Heritage is carrying out a Monuments otection Programme assessing archaeological sites with view to making recommendations for scheduling, and embers of the public may propose a monument for nsideration. All monuments proposed for scheduling e considered to be of national importance. Where ildings are both scheduled and listed, ancient onuments legislation takes precedence. The main rpose of scheduling a monument is to preserve it for the ture and to protect it from damage, destruction or any necessary interference. Once a monument has been heduled, scheduled monument consent is required fore any works can be carried out. The scope of the ntrol is more extensive and more detailed than that plied to listed buildings, but certain minor works, as tailed in the Ancient Monuments (Class Consents) der 1994, may be carried out without consent. It is a minal offence to carry out unauthorised work to heduled monuments.

WALES

Under the Planning (Listed Buildings and Conservation Areas) Act 1990 and the Ancient Monuments and Archaeological Areas Act 1979, the Secretary of State for Wales is responsible for listing buildings and scheduling monuments in Wales on the advice of Cadw (the Welsh Assembly's historic environment division), the Historic Buildings Advisory Council for Wales, the Ancient Monuments Advisory Board for Wales and the Royal Commission on the Ancient and Historical Monuments of Wales (RCAHMW). The criteria for evaluating buildings are similar to those in England and the same listing system is used. There are approximately 29,900 listed buildings and approximately 3,900 scheduled monuments in Wales.

SCOTLAND

Under the Planning (Listed Buildings and Conservation Areas) (Scotland) Act 1997 and the Ancient Monuments and Archaeological Areas Act 1979, Scottish ministers are responsible for listing buildings and scheduling monuments in Scotland on the advice of Historic Scotland, the Historic Environment Advisory Council for Scotland (HEACS) and the Royal Commission on the Ancient and Historical Monuments of Scotland (RCAHMS). The criteria for evaluating buildings are similar to those in England but an A, B, C categorisation is used. There are approximately 46,900 listed buildings and 8,000 scheduled monuments in Scotland.

NORTHERN IRELAND

Under the Planning (Northern Ireland) Order 1991 and the Historic Monuments and Archaeological Objects (Northern Ireland) Order 1995, the Department of the Environment of the Northern Ireland Executive is responsible for listing buildings and scheduling monuments in Northern Ireland on the advice of the Historic Buildings Council for Northern Ireland and the Historic Monuments Council for Northern Ireland. The criteria for evaluating buildings are similar to those in England but an A, B+, B1 and B2 categorisation is used. There are approximately 8,500 listed buildings and 1,733 scheduled monuments in Northern Ireland.

ENGLAND

For more information on any of the English Heritage properties listed below, the official website is www.english-heritage.org.uk

For more information on any of the National Trust properties listed below, the official website is www.nationaltrust.org.uk

(EH) English Heritage property
(NT) National Trust property

A LA RONDE (NT), Exmouth, Devon EX8 5BD
T 01395-265514
Unique 16-sided house completed *c.*1796

ALNWICK CASTLE, Alnwick, Northumberland NE66 1NQ
T 01665-510777 W www.alnwickcastle.com
Seat of the Dukes of Northumberland since 1309; Italian Renaissance-style interior; gardens with spectacular water features

ALTHORP, Northants NN7 4HQ T 01604-770107
W www.althorp.com
Spencer family seat; Diana, Princess of Wales memorabilia

ANGLESEY ABBEY (NT), Lode, Cambs CB25 9EJ
T 01223-810080
House built *c.*1600; houses many paintings and a unique clock collection; gardens and Lode Mill

APSLEY HOUSE (EH), London W1J 7NT T 020-7499 5676
Built by Robert Adam 1771–8, home of the Dukes of Wellington since 1817 and known as 'No. 1 London'; collection of fine and decorative arts

ARUNDEL CASTLE, Arundel, W. Sussex BN18 9AB
T 01903-882173 W www.arundelcastle.org
Castle dating from the Norman Conquest; seat of the Dukes of Norfolk

AVEBURY (NT), Wilts SN8 1RF T 01672-539250
Remains of stone circles constructed 4,000 years ago surrounding the later village of Avebury

BANQUETING HOUSE, Whitehall, London SW1A 2ER
T 0870-751 5178 W www.hrp.org.uk
Designed by Inigo Jones; ceiling paintings by Rubens; site of the execution of Charles I

BASILDON PARK (NT), Reading, Berks RG8 9NR
T 0118-984 3040
Palladian house built in 1776–83 by John Carr

BATTLE ABBEY (EH), Battle, E. Sussex TN33 0AD
T 01424-773792
Remains of the abbey founded by William the Conqueror on the site of the Battle of Hastings

BEAULIEU, Brockenhurst, Hants SO42 7ZN T 01590-612345
W www.beaulieu.co.uk
House and gardens; Beaulieu Abbey and exhibition of monastic life; National Motor Museum

BEESTON CASTLE (EH), Cheshire CW6 9TX
T 01829-260464
13th-century inner ward with gatehouse and towers, and remains of outer ward built by Ranulf, sixth Earl of Chester

BELTON HOUSE (NT), Grantham, Lincs NG32 2LS
T 01476-566116
17th-century house; formal gardens in landscaped park

BELVOIR CASTLE, Grantham, Leics NG32 1PD
T 01476-871000 W www.belvoircastle.com
Seat of the Dukes of Rutland; 19th-century Gothic-style castle

BERKELEY CASTLE, Glos GL13 9BQ T 01453-810332
W www.berkeley-castle.com
Completed 1153; site of the murder of Edward II (1327)

BLENHEIM PALACE, Woodstock, Oxon OX20 1PX
T 0870-060 2080 W www.blenheimpalace.com
Seat of the Dukes of Marlborough and Winston Churchill's birthplace; designed by Vanbrugh

BLICKLING HALL (NT), Blickling, Norfolk NR11 6NF
T 01263-738030
Jacobean house with state rooms; temple and 18th-century orangery

BODIAM CASTLE (NT), Bodiam, E. Sussex TN32 5UA
T 01580-830436
Well-preserved medieval moated castle built in 1385

BOLSOVER CASTLE (EH), Bolsover, Derbys S44 6PR
T 01246-822844
17th-century buildings on site of medieval castle

BOSCOBEL HOUSE (EH), Bishops Wood, Shrops ST19 9AR T 01902-850244
Timber-framed 17th-century hunting lodge; refuge of fugitive Charles II

BOUGHTON HOUSE, Kettering, Northants NN14 1BJ
T 01536-515731 W www.boughtonhouse.org.uk
A 17th-century house with French-style additions; home of the Dukes of Buccleuch and Queensbury

BOWOOD HOUSE, Calne, Wilts SN11 0LZ
T 01249-812102 W www.bowood-house.co.uk
An 18th-century house in Capability Brown park, with lake, temple and arboretum

BROADLANDS, Romsey, Hants SO51 9ZD T 01794-505010
W www.broadlands.net
Palladian mansion in Capability Brown park; Mountbatten exhibition

BRONTË PARSONAGE, Haworth, W. Yorks BD22 8DR
T 01535-642323 W www.bronte.org.uk
Home of the Brontë sisters; museum and memorabilia

BUCKFAST ABBEY, Buckfastleigh, Devon TQ11 0EE
T 01364-645550 W www.buckfast.org.uk
Benedictine monastery on medieval foundations

BUCKINGHAM PALACE, London SW1A 1AA
T 020-7766 7300 W www.royal.gov.uk
Purchased by George III in 1761, and the Sovereign's official London residence since 1837; 18 state rooms, including the Throne Room, and Picture Gallery

BUCKLAND ABBEY (NT), Yelverton, Devon PL20 6EY
T 01822-853607
13th-century Cistercian monastery; home of Sir Francis Drake

BURGHLEY HOUSE, Stamford, Lincs PE9 3JY
T 01780-752451 W www.burghley.co.uk
Late Elizabethan house built by William Cecil, first Lord Burghley

CALKE ABBEY (NT), Ticknall, Derbys DE73 7LE
T 01332-863822
Baroque 18th-century mansion

CARISBROOKE CASTLE (EH), Newport, Isle of Wight PO30 1XY T 01983-522107
W www.carisbrookecastlemuseum.org.uk
Norman castle; prison of Charles I 1647–8

CARLISLE CASTLE (EH), Carlisle, Cumbria CA3 8UR
T 01228-591922
Medieval castle; prison of Mary Queen of Scots

CARLYLE'S HOUSE (NT), Cheyne Row, London SW3 5H
T 020-7352 7087
Home of Thomas Carlyle

CASTLE ACRE PRIORY (EH), Swaffham, Norfolk PE32 2XD T 01760-755394
Remains include 12th-century church and prior's lodgings

CASTLE DROGO (NT), Drewsteignton, Devon EX6 6PB
T 01647-433306
Granite castle designed by Lutyens
CASTLE HOWARD, N. Yorks YO60 7DA T 01653-648444
W www.castlehoward.co.uk
Designed by Vanbrugh 1699–1726; mausoleum designed by Hawksmoor
CASTLE RISING CASTLE (EH), King's Lynn, Norfolk PE31 6AH T 01553-631330
12th-century keep in a massive earthwork with gatehouse and bridge
CHARTWELL (NT), Westerham, Kent TN16 1PS
T 01732-868381
Home of Sir Winston Churchill
CHATSWORTH, Bakewell, Derbys DE45 1PP
T 01246-565300 W www.chatsworth.org
Tudor mansion in magnificent parkland
CHESTERS ROMAN FORT (EH), Chollerford, Northumberland NE46 3EU T 01434-681379
Roman cavalry fort
CHYSAUSTER ANCIENT VILLAGE (EH), Penzance, Cornwall TR20 8XA T 07831-757934
Remains of Celtic settlement; eight stone-walled homesteads
CLIFFORD'S TOWER (EH), York YO1 9SA
T 01904-646940
13th-century tower built on a mound
CLIVEDEN (NT), Taplow, Berks SL6 0JA
T 01628-605069
Former home of the Astors, now a hotel set in garden and woodland
CORBRIDGE ROMAN SITE (EH), Corbridge, Northumberland NE45 5NT T 01434-632349
Excavated central area of a Roman town and successive military bases
CORFE CASTLE (NT), Wareham, Dorset BH20 5EZ
T 01929-481294
Ruined former royal castle dating from the 11th century
CROFT CASTLE (NT), Herefordshire HR6 9PW
T 01568-780246
Pre-Conquest border castle with Georgian-Gothic interior
DEAL CASTLE (EH), Deal, Kent CT41 7BA
T 01304-372762
Largest of the coastal defence forts built by Henry VIII
DICKENS HOUSE, Doughty Street, London WC1N 2LX
T 020-7405 2127 W www.dickensmuseum.com
House occupied by Dickens 1837–9; manuscripts, furniture and portraits
DOVE COTTAGE, Grasmere, Cumbria LA22 9SH
T 01539-435544 W www.wordsworth.org.uk
Wordsworth's home 1799–1808; museum
DOVER CASTLE (EH), Dover, Kent CT16 1HU
T 01304-211067
Castle with Roman, Saxon and Norman features; wartime operations rooms
DR JOHNSON'S HOUSE, Gough Square, London EC4A 3DE T 020-7353 3745 W www.drjohnsonshouse.org
Home of Samuel Johnson
DUNSTANBURGH CASTLE (EH), Craster, nr Alnwick, Northumberland NE66 3TT T 01665-576231
14th-century castle on a cliff with a substantial gatehouse-keep
ELTHAM PALACE (EH), Eltham, London SE9 5QE
T 020-8294 2548
Combines an Art Deco country house and remains of medieval palace set in moated gardens

FARLEIGH HUNGERFORD CASTLE (EH), Somerset BA2 7RS T 01225-754026
Late 14th-century castle with two courts; chapel with tomb of Sir Thomas Hungerford
FARNHAM CASTLE KEEP (EH), Farnham, Surrey GU9 0JA T 01252-713393
Large 12th-century motte and bailey
FOUNTAINS ABBEY (NT), nr Ripon, N. Yorks HG4 3DY
T 01765-608888 W www.fountainsabbey.org.uk
Deer park; St Mary's Church; ruined Cistercian monastery; 18th-century landscaped gardens of Studley Royal estate
FRAMLINGHAM CASTLE (EH), Woodbridge, Suffolk IP13 9BP T 01728-724189
Castle (*c.*1200) with high curtain walls enclosing an almshouse (1639)
FURNESS ABBEY (EH), Barrow-in-Furness, Cumbria LA13 0PS T 01229-823420
Remains of church and conventual buildings founded in 1123
GLASTONBURY ABBEY, Glastonbury, Somerset BA6 9EL
T 01458-832267 W www.glastonburyabbey.com
Ruins of a 12th-century abbey rebuilt after fire; site of an early Christian settlement
GOODRICH CASTLE (EH), Ross-on-Wye, Herefordshire HR9 6HY T 01600-890538
Remains of 13th- and 14th-century castle with 12th-century keep
GREENWICH, London SE10 9NF T 020-8858 4422
W www.rog.nmm.ac.uk
Former Royal Observatory (founded 1675) housing the time ball and zero meridian of longitude; the Queen's House, designed for Queen Anne, wife of James I, by Inigo Jones; Painted Hall and Chapel (Royal Naval College)
GRIMES GRAVES (EH), Brandon, Norfolk IP26 5DE
T 01842-810656
Neolithic flint mines; one shaft can be descended
GUILDHALL, London EC2P 2EJ T 020-7606 3030
W www.cityoflondon.gov.uk
Centre of civic government of the City built *c.*1441; facade built 1788–9
HADDON HALL, Bakewell, Derbys DE45 1LA
T 01629-812855 W www.haddonhall.co.uk
Well-preserved 12th-century manor house
HAILES ABBEY (EH), Cheltenham, Glos GL54 5PB
T 01242-602398
Ruins of a 13th-century Cistercian monastery
HAM HOUSE (NT), Richmond-upon-Thames, Surrey TW10 7RS T 020-8940 1950
Stuart house with lavish interiors and formal gardens
HAMPTON COURT PALACE, East Molesey, Surrey KT8 9AU T 0870-751 5175
W www.hrp.org.uk
16th-century palace with additions by Wren; gardens with maze; Tudor tennis court
HARDWICK HALL (NT), Chesterfield, Derbys S44 5QJ
T 01246-850430
Built 1591–7 for Bess of Hardwick
HARDY'S COTTAGE (NT), Higher Bockhampton, Dorset DT2 8QJ T 01297-561900
Birthplace and home of Thomas Hardy
HAREWOOD HOUSE, Harewood, W. Yorks LS17 9LG
T 0113-218 1010 W www.harewood.org
18th-century house designed by John Carr and Robert Adam; park by Capability Brown

HATFIELD HOUSE, Hatfield, Herts AL9 5NQ
T 01707-287010 W www.hatfield-house.co.uk
Jacobean house built by Robert Cecil; surviving wing of Royal Palace of Hatfield (*c*.1485)

HELMSLEY CASTLE (EH), Helmsley, N. Yorks YO62 5AB
T 01439-770442
12th-century keep and curtain wall with 16th-century buildings; spectacular earthwork defences

HEVER CASTLE, nr Edenbridge, Kent TN8 7NG
T 01732-865224 W www.hever-castle.co.uk
13th-century double-moated castle; childhood home of Anne Boleyn

HOLKER HALL, Cumbria LA11 7PL T 01539-558328
W www.holker-hall.co.uk
Former home of the Dukes of Devonshire; award-winning gardens

HOLKHAM HALL, Wells-next-the-Sea, Norfolk NR23 1AB
T 01328-710227 W www.holkham.co.uk
Palladian mansion; notable fine art collection

HOUSESTEADS ROMAN FORT (EH), Hexham, Northumberland NE47 6NN T 01434-344363
Excavated infantry fort on Hadrian's Wall with extra-mural civilian settlement

HUGHENDEN MANOR (NT), High Wycombe, Bucks HP14 4LA T 01494-755573
Home of Disraeli; small formal garden

JANE AUSTEN'S HOUSE, Chawton, Hants GU34 1SD T 01420-83262
W www.jane-austens-house-museum.org.uk
Jane Austen's home from 1809 to 1817

KEDLESTON HALL (NT), Derbys DE22 5JH
T 01332-842191
Classical Palladian mansion built 1759–65; complete Robert Adam interiors

KELMSCOTT MANOR, nr Lechlade, Glos GL7 3HJ
T 01367-252486 W www.kelmscottmanor.org.uk
Summer home of William Morris, with products of Morris and Co.

KENILWORTH CASTLE (EH), Kenilworth, Warks CV8 1NE
T 01926-864152
Largest castle ruin in England

KENSINGTON PALACE, Kensington Gardens, London W8 4PX T 0870-751 5170 W www.hrp.org.uk
Built in 1605 and enlarged by Wren; birthplace of Queen Victoria; Royal Ceremonial Dress Collection

KENWOOD HOUSE (EH), Hampstead Lane, London NW3 7JR T 020-8348 1286
Adam villa housing the Iveagh bequest of paintings and furniture

KEW PALACE, Richmond-upon-Thames, Surrey TW9 3AB
T 0870-751 5179 W www.hrp.org.uk
Includes Queen Charlotte's Cottage, used by King George III and family as a summerhouse

KINGSTON LACY (NT), Wimborne Minster, Dorset BH21 4EA T 01202-883402
17th-century house with 19th-century alterations; important art collection

KNEBWORTH HOUSE, Knebworth, Herts SG3 6PY
T 01438-812661 W www.knebworthhouse.com
Tudor manor house concealed by 19th-century Gothic decoration; Lutyens gardens

KNOLE (NT), Sevenoaks, Kent TN15 0RP T 01732-462100
House dating from 1456 set in parkland; fine art collection

LAMBETH PALACE, London SE1 7JU T 020-7898 1200
W www.archbishopofcanterbury.org
Official residence of the Archbishop of Canterbury; partly dating from the 12th century

LANERCOST PRIORY (EH), Brampton, Cumbria CA8 2HQ T 01697-73030
The nave of the Augustinian priory church, *c*.1166, is still used; remains of other claustral buildings

LANHYDROCK (NT), Bodmin, Cornwall PL30 5AD
T 01208-265950
House dating from the 17th century; 45 rooms, including kitchen and nursery

LEEDS CASTLE, nr Maidstone, Kent ME17 1PL
T 01622-765400 W www.leeds-castle.com
Castle dating from 9th century, on two islands in lake

LEVENS HALL, Kendal, Cumbria LA8 0PD T 01539-560321
W www.levenshall.co.uk
Elizabethan house with unique topiary garden (1694) steam engine collection

LINCOLN CASTLE, Lincoln, Lincs LN1 3AA
T 01522-511068 W www.lincolnshire.gov.uk
Built by William the Conqueror in 1068

LINDISFARNE PRIORY (EH), Holy Island, Northumberland TD15 2RX T 01289-389200
Founded in AD 635; re-established in the 12th centur as a Benedictine priory, now ruined

LITTLE MORETON HALL (NT), Congleton, Cheshire CW12 4SD T 01260-272018
Timber-framed moated manor house with knot garden

LONGLEAT HOUSE, Warminster, Wilts BA12 7NW
T 01985-844400 W www.longleat.co.uk
Elizabethan house in Italian Renaissance style; safari park

LULLINGSTONE ROMAN VILLA (EH), Eynsford, Kent DA4 0JA T 01322-863467
Large villa occupied for much of the Roman period; fine mosaics

MANSION HOUSE, London EC4N 8BH
W www.cityoflondon.gov.uk
The official residence of the Lord Mayor of London

MARBLE HILL HOUSE (EH), Twickenham, Middx TW1 2NL T 020-8892 5115
English Palladian villa with Georgian paintings and furniture

MICHELHAM PRIORY, Hailsham, E. Sussex BN27 3QS
T 01323-844224 W www.sussexpast.co.uk
Tudor house built onto an Augustinian priory

MIDDLEHAM CASTLE (EH), Leyburn, N. Yorks DL8 4QR
T 01969-623899
12th-century keep within later fortifications; childhood home of Richard III

MONTACUTE HOUSE (NT), Montacute, Somerset TA15 6XP T 01935-823289
Elizabethan house with National Portrait Gallery collection of portraits from the period

MOUNT GRACE PRIORY (EH), Northallerton, N. Yorks DL6 3JG T 01609-883494
Carthusian priory with remains of monastic buildings

NETLEY ABBEY (EH), Hants T 01424-775705
Remains of Cistercian abbey; used as house in Tudor period

OLD SARUM (EH), Salisbury, Wilts SP1 3SD
T 01722-335398
Earthworks enclosing remains of castle and 11th-century cathedral

ORFORD CASTLE (EH), Orford, Suffolk IP12 2ND
T 01394-450472
Circular keep of *c*.1170 and remains of coastal defenc castle built by Henry II

OSBORNE HOUSE (EH), East Cowes, Isle of Wight PO32 6JY T 01983-200022
Queen Victoria's seaside residence

OSTERLEY PARK (NT), Isleworth, Middx TW7 4RB T 020-8232 5050 W www.osterleypark.org.uk
Elizabethan mansion set in parkland

PENDENNIS CASTLE (EH), Falmouth, Cornwall TR11 4LP T 01326-316594
Well-preserved 16th-century coastal defence castle

PENSHURST PLACE, Penshurst, Kent TN11 8DG T 01892-870307 W www.penshurstplace.com
House with medieval Baron's Hall and 14th-century gardens

PETWORTH HOUSE (NT), Petworth, W. Sussex GU28 0AE T 01798-342207
Late 17th-century house set in Capability Brown landscaped park

PEVENSEY CASTLE (EH), Pevensey, E. Sussex BN24 5LE T 01323-762604
Walls of a 4th-century Roman fort; remains of an 11th-century castle

EVERIL CASTLE (EH), Castleton, Derbys S33 8WQ T 01433-620613
12th-century castle defended on two sides by precipitous rocks

OLESDEN LACEY (NT), nr Dorking, Surrey RH5 6BD T 01372-452048
Regency villa remodelled in the Edwardian era; fine paintings and furnishings

ORTCHESTER CASTLE (EH), Portchester, Hants PO16 9QW T 02392-378291
Walls of a late Roman fort enclosing a Norman keep and an Augustinian priory church

POWDERHAM CASTLE, Kenton, Devon EX6 8JQ T 01626-890243 W www.powderham.co.uk
Medieval castle with 18th- and 19th-century alterations; historic home of the Earl of Devon

ABY CASTLE, Staindrop, Co. Durham DL2 3AH T 01833-660202 W www.rabycastle.com
14th-century castle with walled gardens

AGLEY HALL, Alcester, Warks B49 5NJ T 01789-762090 W www.ragleyhall.com
17th-century house with gardens, park and lake

ICHBOROUGH ROMAN FORT (EH), Richborough, Kent CT13 9JW T 01304-612013
Landing-site of the Claudian invasion in AD 43

RICHMOND CASTLE (EH), Richmond, N. Yorks DL10 4QW T 01748-822493
12th-century keep with 11th-century curtain wall

IEVAULX ABBEY (EH), nr Helmsley, N. Yorks YO62 5LB T 01439-798228
Remains of a Cistercian abbey founded *c.*1132

ROCHESTER CASTLE (EH), Rochester, Kent ME1 1SW T 01634-402276
11th-century castle partly on the Roman city wall, with a square keep of *c.*1130

ROCKINGHAM CASTLE, Market Harborough, Leics LE16 8TH T 01536-770240 W www.rockinghamcastle.com
Built by William the Conqueror

ROYAL PAVILION, Brighton BN1 1EE T 01273-290900 W www.royalpavilion.org.uk
Palace of George IV, in Chinese style with Indian exterior and Regency gardens

UFFORD OLD HALL (NT), nr Ormskirk, Lancs L40 1SG T 01704-821254
16th-century hall with unique screen

ST AUGUSTINE'S ABBEY (EH), Canterbury, Kent CT1 1TF T 01227-767345
Remains of Benedictine monastery on site of abbey founded AD 598

ST MAWES CASTLE (EH), St Mawes, Cornwall TR2 3AA T 01326-270526
Coastal defence castle built by Henry VIII

ST MICHAEL'S MOUNT (NT), Cornwall TR17 0HS T 01736-710507
12th-century castle with later additions, off the coast at Marazion

SANDRINGHAM, Norfolk PE35 6EN T 01553-612908 W www.sandringhamestate.co.uk
The Queen's private residence; a neo-Jacobean house built in 1870

SCARBOROUGH CASTLE (EH), Scarborough, N. Yorks YO11 1HY T 01723-372451
Remains of 12th-century keep and curtain walls

SHERBORNE CASTLE, Sherborne, Dorset DT9 3PY T 01935-813182 W www.sherbornecastle.com
16th-century castle built by Sir Walter Raleigh set in landscaped gardens

SHUGBOROUGH (NT), Milford, Staffs ST17 0XB T 01889-881388
House set in 18th-century park with monuments, temples and pavilions in the Greek Revival style; seat of the Earls of Lichfield

SKIPTON CASTLE, Skipton, N. Yorks BD23 1AW T 01756-792442 W www.skiptoncastle.co.uk
D-shaped castle, six round towers and inner courtyard

SMALLHYTHE PLACE (NT), Tenterden, Kent TN30 7NG T 01580-762334
Half-timbered 16th-century house; home of Ellen Terry 1899–1928; the Barn Theatre

STANFORD HALL, Lutterworth, Leics LE17 6DH T 01788-860250 W www.stanfordhall.co.uk
William and Mary house with Stuart portraits; motorcycle museum

STONEHENGE (EH), nr Amesbury, Wilts SP4 7DE T 0870-333 1181
Prehistoric monument consisting of concentric stone circles surrounded by a ditch and bank

STONOR PARK, Henley-on-Thames, Oxon RG9 6HF T 01491-638587 W www.stonor.com
Medieval house with Georgian facade; centre of Roman Catholicism after the Reformation

STOURHEAD (NT), Stourton, Wilts BA12 6QD T 01747-841152
English Palladian mansion with famous gardens

STRATFIELD SAYE HOUSE, Hants RG7 2BZ T 01256-882882 W www.stratfield-saye.co.uk
House built 1630–40; home of the Dukes of Wellington since 1817

STRATFORD-UPON-AVON, Warks T 01789-204016 W www.shakespeare.org.uk
Shakespeare's Birthplace Trust with Shakespeare Centre; Anne Hathaway's Cottage, home of Shakespeare's wife; Mary Arden's House, home of Shakespeare's mother; grammar school attended by Shakespeare; Holy Trinity Church, where Shakespeare is buried; Royal Shakespeare Theatre (burnt down 1926, rebuilt 1932) and Swan Theatre (opened 1986)

SUDELEY CASTLE, Winchcombe, Glos GL54 5JD T 01242-602308 W www.sudeleycastle.co.uk
Castle built in 1442; restored in the 19th century

SULGRAVE MANOR, nr Banbury, Oxon OX17 2SD T 01295-760205 W www.sulgravemanor.org.uk
Home of George Washington's family

SYON HOUSE, Brentford, Middx TW8 8JF T 020-8560 0881 W www.syonpark.co.uk
Built on the site of a former monastery; Adam interior; Capability Brown park

TILBURY FORT (EH), Tilbury, Essex RM18 7NR T 01375-858489
17th-century coastal fort

TINTAGEL CASTLE (EH), Tintagel, Cornwall PL34 0HE T 01840-770328
12th-century cliff-top castle and Dark Age settlement site; linked with Arthurian legend

TOWER OF LONDON, London EC3N 4AB T 0870-756 6060 W www.hrp.org.uk
Royal palace and fortress begun by William the Conqueror in 1078; houses the Crown Jewels

TRERICE (NT), nr Newquay, Cornwall TR8 4PG T 01637-875404
Elizabethan manor house

TYNEMOUTH PRIORY AND CASTLE (EH), Tyne and Wear NE30 4BZ T 0191-257 1090
Remains of a Benedictine priory, founded *c*.1090, on Saxon monastic site

UPPARK (NT), South Harting, W. Sussex GU31 5QR T 01730-825415
Late 17th-century house, completely restored after fire; Fetherstonhaugh art collection

WALMER CASTLE (EH), Walmer, Kent CT14 7LJ T 01304-364288
One of Henry VIII's coastal defence castles, now the residence of the Lord Warden of the Cinque Ports

WALTHAM ABBEY (EH), Waltham Abbey, Essex EN9 1DJ T 01992-702200
Ruined abbey including the nave of the abbey church, 'Harold's Bridge' and late 14th-century gatehouse; traditionally the burial place of Harold II (1066)

WARKWORTH CASTLE (EH), Warkworth, Northumberland NE65 0UJ T 01665-711423
15th-century keep amidst earlier ruins, with 14th-century hermitage upstream

WARWICK CASTLE, Warwick, Warks CV34 4QU T 0870-442 2000 W www.warwick-castle.co.uk
Medieval castle with Madame Tussaud's waxworks, in Capability Brown park

WHITBY ABBEY (EH), Whitby, N. Yorks YO22 4JT T 01947-603568
Remains of Norman church on the site of a monastery founded in AD 657

WILTON HOUSE, nr Salisbury, Wilts SP2 0BJ T 01722-746714 W www.wiltonhouse.co.uk
17th-century house on the site of a Tudor house and ninth-century nunnery

WINDSOR CASTLE, Windsor, Berks SL4 1NJ T 020-7766 7304 W www.royal.gov.uk
Official residence of the Queen; oldest royal residence still in regular use; largest inhabited castle in the world. Also St George's Chapel

WOBURN ABBEY, Woburn, Beds MK17 9WA T 01525-290333 W www.woburnabbey.co.uk
Built on the site of a Cistercian abbey; seat of the Dukes of Bedford; important art collection; antiques centre

WROXETER ROMAN CITY (EH), nr Shrewsbury, Shropshire SY5 6PH T 01743-761330
Second-century public baths and part of the forum of the Roman town of Viroconium

WALES

For more information on any of the Cadw properties listed below, the official website is www.cadw.wales.gov.uk

For more information on any of the National Trust properties listed below, the official website is www.nationaltrust.org.uk

(C) Property of Cadw: Welsh Historic Monuments
(NT) National Trust property

BEAUMARIS CASTLE (C), Anglesey LL58 8AP T 01248-810361
Concentrically planned castle, still virtually intact

CAERLEON ROMAN BATHS AND AMPHITHEATRE (C), nr Newport NP18 1AE T 01633-422518
Rare example of a legionary bath-house and late first-century arena surrounded by bank for spectators

CAERNARFON CASTLE (C), Gwynedd LL5 2AY T 01286-677617 W www.caernarfon.com
Important castle built between 1283 and 1330, initially for King Edward I of England

CAERPHILLY CASTLE (C), Caerphilly CF83 1JD T 029-2088 3143
Concentrically-planned castle (*c*.1270) notable for its scale and use of water defences

CARDIFF CASTLE, Cardiff CF10 3RB T 029-2087 8100 W www.cardiffcastle.com
Castle built on the site of a Roman fort; spectacular towers and rich interior

CASTELL COCH (C), nr Cardiff CF15 7JS T 029-2081 010[illegible]
'Fairytale castle' rebuilt 1875–90 on medieval foundations

CHEPSTOW CASTLE (C), Monmouthshire NP16 5EZ T 01291-624065
Rectangular keep amid extensive fortifications

CONWY CASTLE (C), Gwynedd LL32 8AY T 01492-592358
Built by Edward I, 1283–7

CRICCIETH CASTLE (C), Gwynedd LL55 0DP T 01766-522227
Native Welsh 13th-century castle, altered by Edward [illegible]

DENBIGH CASTLE (C), Denbighshire LL16 3NB T 01745-813385
Remains of the castle (begun 1282), including triple-towered gatehouse

HARLECH CASTLE (C), Gwynedd LL46 2YH T 01766-780552
Well-preserved Edwardian castle, constructed 1283–90, on an outcrop above the former shoreline

PEMBROKE CASTLE, Dyfed SA71 4LA T 01646-681510 W www.pembrokecastle.co.uk
Castle founded in 1093; Great Tower built 1200; birthplace of King Henry VII

PENRHYN CASTLE (NT), Bangor, Gwynedd LL57 4HN T 01248-353084
Neo-Norman castle built in the 19th-century; industrial railway museum

PORTMEIRION, Gwynedd LL48 6ET T 01766-770228 W www.portmeirion-village.com
Village in Italianate style

POWIS CASTLE (NT), nr Welshpool, Powys SY21 8RF T 01938-551929
Medieval castle with interior in variety of styles; 17th-century gardens; Clive of India museum

RAGLAN CASTLE (C), Monmouthshire NP15 2BT T 01291-690228
Remains of 15th-century castle with moated hexagon[illegible] keep

ST DAVIDS BISHOP'S PALACE (C), Dyfed SA62 6PE T 01437-720517
Remains of residence of Bishops of St Davids built 1328–47

TINTERN ABBEY (C), nr Chepstow, Monmouthshire NP16 6SE T 01291-689251
Remains of 13th-century church and conventual buildings of a Cistercian monastery

TRETOWER COURT AND CASTLE (C), nr Crickhowell, Powys NP8 1RF T 01874-730279
Medieval house with remains of 12th-century castle nearby

SCOTLAND

For more information on any of the Historic Scotland properties listed below, the official website is www.historic-scotland.gov.uk

For more information on any of the National Trust for Scotland properties listed below, the official website is www.nts.org.uk

(HS) Historic Scotland property
(NTS) National Trust for Scotland property

ABBOTSFORD HOUSE, Melrose, Roxburghshire TD6 9BQ T 01896-752043 W www.scottsabbotsford.co.uk
Home of Sir Walter Scott

ANTONINE WALL, between the Clyde and the Forth
Built around AD 142; consists of ditch, turf rampart, road and forts at regular intervals

BALMORAL CASTLE, nr Braemar, Aberdeenshire AB35 5TB T 01339-742534 W www.balmoralcastle.com
Baronial-style castle built for Victoria and Albert; the Queen's private residence

BLACK HOUSE, ARNOL (HS), Lewis, Western Isles HS2 9DB T 01851-710395
Traditional Lewis thatched house

BLAIR CASTLE, Blair Atholl, Perthshire PH18 5TL T 01796-481207 W www.blair-castle.co.uk
Mid-18th-century mansion with 13th-century tower; seat of the Dukes and Earls of Atholl

BONAWE IRON FURNACE (HS), Taynuilt, Argyll PA35 1JQ T 01866-822432
Charcoal-fuelled ironworks founded in 1753

BOWHILL, Selkirkshire TD7 5ET T 01750-22204
Seat of the Dukes of Buccleuch and Queensberry; fine collection of paintings, including portrait miniatures

BROUGH OF BIRSAY (HS), Orkney KW17 2NH T 01856-841815
Remains of Norse church and village on the tidal island of Birsay

CAERLAVEROCK CASTLE (HS), Glencaple, Dumfriesshire DG1 4RU T 01387-770244
Triangular 13th-century castle with classical Renaissance additions

CAIRNPAPPLE HILL (HS), Torphichen, West Lothian T 01506-634622
Neolithic and Bronze Age burial chambers and henge

CALANAIS STANDING STONES (HS), Lewis, Western Isles HS2 9DY T 01851-621422
Standing stones in a cross-shaped setting, dating from 2900–2600 BC

CATERTHUNS (BROWN AND WHITE) (HS), Menmuir, nr Brechin, Angus T 0131-668 8800
Two large Iron Age hill forts

CAWDOR CASTLE, Nairn, Moray IV12 5RD T 01667-404401 W www.cawdorcastle.com
14th-century keep with 15th- and 17th-century additions

CLAVA CAIRNS (HS), nr Inverness, Inverness-shire T 01667-460232
Late Neolithic or early Bronze Age cairns

CRATHES CASTLE (NTS), nr Banchory, Aberdeenshire AB31 5QJ T 01330-844525
16th-century baronial castle in woodland, fields and gardens

CULZEAN CASTLE (NTS), Maybole, Ayrshire KA19 8LE T 0870-118 1945 W www.culzeanexperience.org
18th-century Adam castle with oval staircase and circular saloon

DRYBURGH ABBEY (HS), nr Melrose, Roxburghshire TD6 0RQ T 01835-822381
12th-century abbey containing tomb of Sir Walter Scott

DUNVEGAN CASTLE, Skye IV55 8WF T 01470-521206 W www.dunvegancastle.com
13th-century castle with later additions; home of the chiefs of the Clan MacLeod; trips to seal colony

EDINBURGH CASTLE (HS) EH1 2NG T 0131-225 9846
Includes the Scottish Crown Jewels, Scottish National War Memorial, Scottish United Services Museum and historic apartments

EDZELL CASTLE (HS), nr Brechin, Angus DD9 7UE T 01356-648631
Medieval tower house; walled garden

EILEAN DONAN CASTLE, Dornie, Ross and Cromarty IV40 8DX T 01599-555202 W www.eileandonancastle.com
13th-century castle with Jacobite relics

ELGIN CATHEDRAL (HS), Moray IV30 1EL T 01343-547171
13th-century cathedral and chapterhouse

FLOORS CASTLE, Kelso, Roxburghshire TD5 7SF T 01573-223333 W www.floorscastle.com
Largest inhabited castle in Scotland; seat of the Dukes of Roxburghe; built 1721 by William Adam

FORT GEORGE (HS), Ardersier, Inverness-shire IV2 7TE T 01667-460232
18th-century fort

GLAMIS CASTLE, Forfar, Angus DD8 1RJ T 01307-840393 W www.glamis-castle.co.uk
Seat of the Lyon family (later Earls of Strathmore and Kinghorne) since 1372

GLASGOW CATHEDRAL (HS), Lanarkshire G4 0QZ T 0141-552 6891 W www.glasgowcathedral.org.uk
Medieval cathedral with elaborately vaulted crypt

GLENELG BROCHS (HS), Shielbridge, Ross and Cromarty T 01667-460232
Two broch towers with well-preserved structural features

HOPETOUN HOUSE, South Queensferry, W. Lothian EH30 9SL T 0131-331 2451 W www.hopetounhouse.com
House designed by Sir William Bruce, enlarged by William Adam

HUNTLY CASTLE (HS), Aberdeenshire AB54 4SH T 01466-793191
Ruin of a 16th- and 17th-century house

INVERARAY CASTLE, Argyll PA32 8XE T 01499-302203 W www.inveraray-castle.com
Gothic-style 18th-century castle; seat of the Dukes of Argyll

IONA ABBEY (HS), Iona, Inner Hebrides PA76 6SQ T 01681-700512
Monastery founded by St Columba in AD 563

JARLSHOF (HS), Sumburgh, Shetland ZE3 9JN
T 01950-460112
Prehistoric and Norse settlement

JEDBURGH ABBEY (HS), Scottish Borders TD8 6JQ
T 01835-863925
Romanesque and early Gothic church founded *c.*1138

KELSO ABBEY (HS), Kelso, Scottish Borders TD5 7JD
Remains of great abbey church founded 1128

KISIMUL CASTLE (HS), Castlebay, Barra, Western Isles
T 01871-810313
Medieval home of the Clan MacNeil

LINLITHGOW PALACE (HS), Kirkgate, Linlithgow, W. Lothian EH49 7AL T 01506-842896
Ruin of royal palace in park setting; birthplace of James V and Mary, Queen of Scots

MAES HOWE (HS), Stenness, Orkney KW16 3HA
T 01856-761606
Neolithic tomb

MEIGLE SCULPTURED STONES (HS), Meigle, Perthshire PH12 8SB T 01828-640612
Twenty-six Celtic Christian stones

MELROSE ABBEY (HS), Melrose, Roxburghshire TD6 9LG
T 01896-822562
Ruin of Cistercian abbey founded *c.*1136 by David I

MOUSA BROCH (HS), Mousa, Shetland T 01856-841815
Finest surviving Iron Age broch tower

NEW ABBEY CORN MILL (HS), Dumfriesshire DG2 8BX
T 01387-850260
Working water-powered mill

PALACE OF HOLYROODHOUSE, Edinburgh EH8 8DX
T 0131-556 5100 W www.royal.gov.uk
The Queen's official Scottish residence; main part of the palace built 1671–9

RING O' BRODGAR (HS), nr Stromness, Orkney
T 01856-841815
Neolithic circle of upright stones with an enclosing ditch

ROSSLYN CHAPEL, Roslin, Midlothian EH25 9PU
T 0131-440 2159 W www.rosslynchapel.org.uk
Historic church with unique stone carvings

RUTHWELL CROSS (HS), Ruthwell, Dumfriesshire
T 01387-870249
Seventh-century Anglian cross

ST ANDREWS CASTLE AND CATHEDRAL (HS), Fife KY16 9AR T 01334-477196 (castle); 01334-472563 (cathedral)
Ruins of 13th-century castle and remains of the largest cathedral in Scotland

SCONE PALACE, Perth, Perthshire PH2 6BD
T 01738-552300 W www.scone-palace.net
House built 1802–13 on the site of a medieval palace

SKARA BRAE (HS), nr Stromness, Orkney KW16 3LR
T 01856-841815
Stone Age village with adjacent 17th-century house

SMAILHOLM TOWER (HS), nr Kelso, Roxburghshire TD5 7PG T 01573-460365
Well-preserved 15th-century tower-house

STIRLING CASTLE (HS), Stirlingshire FK8 1EJ
T 01786-450000
Great Hall and gatehouse of James IV, palace of James V, Chapel Royal remodelled by James VI

TANTALLON CASTLE (HS), North Berwick, E. Lothian EH39 5PN T 01620-892727
Fortification with earthwork defences; and a 14th-century curtain wall with towers

THREAVE CASTLE (HS), Castle Douglas, Kirkcudbrightshire T 07711-223101
Late 14th-century tower on an island; accessible only by boat

URQUHART CASTLE (HS), Drumnadrochit, Inverness-shire IV63 6XJ T 01456-450551
13th-century castle remains on the banks of Loch Ness

NORTHERN IRELAND

For the Northern Ireland Environment and Heritage Service, the official website is www.ehsni.gov.uk

For more information on any of the National Trust properties listed below, the official website is www.nationaltrust.org.uk

(EHS) Property in the care of the Northern Ireland Environment and Heritage Service
(NT) National Trust property

CARRICKFERGUS CASTLE (EHS), Carrickfergus, Co. Antrim BT38 7BG T 028-9335 1273
Castle begun in 1180 and garrisoned until 1928

CASTLE COOLE (NT), Enniskillen, Co. Fermanagh BT74 6JY T 028-6632 2690
18th-century mansion by James Wyatt in parkland

CASTLE WARD (NT), Strangford, Co. Down BT30 7LS
T 028-4488 1204
18th-century house with Classical and Gothic facades

DEVENISH ISLAND (EHS), nr Enniskillen, Co. Fermanagh T 028-9054 6518
Island monastery founded in the sixth century by St Molaise

DOWNHILL DEMESNE (NT), Castlerock, Co. Londonderry BT51 4RP T 028-2073 1582
Ruins of palatial house in landscaped estate including Mussenden Temple

DUNLUCE CASTLE (EHS), Bushmills, Co. Antrim BT57 8QG T 028-2073 1938
Ruins of 16th-century stronghold of the MacDonnells

FLORENCE COURT (NT), Enniskillen, Co. Fermanagh BT92 1DB T 028-6634 8249
Mid-18th-century house with Rococo decoration

GREY ABBEY (EHS), Greyabbey, Co. Down
T 028-9054 6552
Substantial remains of a Cistercian abbey founded in 1193

HILLSBOROUGH FORT (EHS), Hillsborough, Co. Down BT26 6AG T 028-9054 6552
Square keep built in 1650

MOUNT STEWART (NT), Newtownards, Co. Down BT22 2AD T 028-4278 8387
18th century house; childhood home of Lord Castlereagh

NENDRUM MONASTERY (EHS), Mahee Island, Co. Down T 028-9181 1491
Founded in the fifth century by St Machaoi

TULLY CASTLE (EHS), Co. Fermanagh T 028-9054 6552
Fortified house and bawn built in 1613

WHITE ISLAND (EHS), Co. Fermanagh
Tenth-century monastery; 12th-century church featuring stone figures dating from the sixth century

MUSEUMS AND GALLERIES

There are approximately 2,500 museums and galleries in the United Kingdom. Around 1,800 are accredited by the Museums, Libraries and Archives Council (MLA), which indicates that they have an appropriate constitution, are soundly financed, have adequate collection management standards and public services, and have access to professional curatorial advice. Applications for accreditation are assessed by either the relevant regional agency in England, Museums Archives and Libraries Wales (CyMAL), the Scottish Museums Council or the Northern Ireland Museums Council.

The following is a selection of museums and art galleries in the United Kingdom. Opening hours and admission charges vary. Further information about museums and galleries in the UK is available from the Museums Association (T 020-7426 6970 W www.museumsassociation.org). W www.24hourmuseum.org.uk is the UK's national virtual museum and includes a database of all the museums and galleries in the UK.

ENGLAND

* Receives government funding directly from the DCMS. These institutions are deemed to have collections of national importance, and the government is able to call upon their staff for expert advice

BARNARD CASTLE, Co. Durham – *The Bowes Museum*, Newgate DL12 8NP T 01833-690606 W www.thebowesmuseum.org.uk
European art from the late medieval period to the 19th century; English period rooms from Elizabeth I to Victoria; local archaeology

BATH – *American Museum*, Claverton Manor BA2 7BD T 01225-460503 W www.americanmuseum.org
American decorative arts from the 17th to 19th century

Museum of Costume, Bennett Street BA1 2QH T 01225-477173 W www.museumofcostume.co.uk
Fashion from the 16th century to the present day

Roman Baths Museum, Pump Room, Stall Street BA1 1LZ T 01225-477785 W www.romanbaths.co.uk
Museum adjoins the remains of a Roman baths and temple complex

Victoria Art Gallery, Bridge Street BA2 4AT T 01225-477233 W www.victoriagal.org.uk
European Old Masters and British art since the 18th century

BEAMISH, Co. Durham – *Beamish, The North of England Open Air Museum*, DH9 0RG T 0191-370 4000 W www.beamish.org.uk
Recreated northern town *c.*1900, with rebuilt local buildings, colliery village, farm, railway station, tramway, Pockerley Manor and horse-yard (set *c.*1800)

BEAULIEU, Hants – *National Motor Museum*, SO42 7ZN T 01590-612345 W www.beaulieu.co.uk
Over 250 vehicles dating from 1895 to the present day

BIRMINGHAM – *Aston Hall*, Trinity Road B6 6JD T 0121-327 0062 W www.bmag.org.uk/aston_hall
Jacobean House containing paintings, furniture and tapestries from the 17th to 19th century

Barber Institute of Fine Arts, University of Birmingham, Edgbaston B15 2TS T 0121-414 7333 W www.barber.org.uk
Fine arts, including Old Masters

Birmingham Museum and Art Gallery, Chamberlain Square B3 3DH T 0121-303 2834 W www.bmag.org.uk
Includes notable collection of Pre-Raphaelite art

Museum of the Jewellery Quarter, Vyse Street, Hockley B18 6HA T 0121-554 3598 W www.bmag.org.uk
Built around a real jewellery workshop

BOVINGTON, Dorset – *Tank Museum*, BH20 6JG T 01929-405096 W www.tankmuseum.co.uk
Collection of 300 tanks from the earliest days of tank warfare to the present

BRADFORD – *Cartwright Hall Art Gallery*, Lister Park BD9 4NS T 01274-431212 W www.bradfordmuseums.org
British 19th- and 20th-century fine art

Bradford Industrial Museum and Horses at Work, Moorside Road, Eccleshill BD2 3HP T 01274-435900 W www.bradfordmuseums.org
Engineering, textiles, transport and social history exhibits, including recreated back-to-back cottages, shire horses and horse tram-rides

**National Museum of Photography, Film & Television*, Princes Way BD1 1NQ T 0870-7010200 W www.nationalmediamuseum.org.uk
Photography, film and television interactive exhibits; features the UK's first IMAX cinema and the only public Cinerama screen in the world

BRIGHTON – *Booth Museum of Natural History*, Dyke Road BN1 5AA T 01273-292777 W www.booth.virtualmuseum.info
Zoology, botany and geology collections; British birds in recreated habitats

Brighton Museum and Art Gallery, Royal Pavilion Gardens BN1 1EE T 01273-290900 W www.brighton.virtualmuseum.info
Includes fine art and design, fashion, non-Western art, Brighton history

BRISTOL – *Arnolfini*, Narrow Quay BS1 4QA T 0117-917 2300 W www.arnolfini.org.uk
Contemporary visual arts, dance, performance, music, talks and workshops

Blaise Castle House Museum, Henbury BS10 7QS T 0117-903 9818 W www.bristol-city.gov.uk/museums
Agricultural and social history collections in an 18th-century mansion

Bristol Industrial Museum, Princes Wharf, Wapping Road BS1 4RN T 0117-903 1569 W www.bristol-city.gov.uk/museums
Industrial, maritime and transport collections

City Museum and Art Gallery, Queen's Road BS8 1RL T 0117-922 3571 W www.bristol-city.gov.uk/museums
Includes fine and decorative art, oriental art, Egyptology and Bristol ceramics and paintings

CAMBRIDGE – *Fitzwilliam Museum*, Trumpington Street CB2 1RB T 01223-332900 W www.fitzmuseum.cam.ac.uk
Antiquities, fine and applied arts, clocks, ceramics, manuscripts, furniture, sculpture, coins and medals

**Imperial War Museum Duxford*, Duxford CB22 4QR T 01223-835000 W http://duxford.iwm.org.uk
Displays of military and civil aircraft, tanks, guns and naval exhibits

Sedgwick Museum of Earth Sciences, Downing Street CB2 3EQ T 01223-333456 W www.sedgwickmuseum.org
Extensive geological collection

University Museum of Archaeology and Anthropology, Downing Street CB2 3DZ **T** 01223-333516 **W** http://museum.archanth.cam.ac.uk
Archaeology and anthropology from all parts of the world

University Museum of Zoology, Downing Street CB2 3EJ **T** 01223-336600 **W** www.zoo.cam.ac.uk
Extensive zoological collection

Whipple Museum of the History of Science, Free School Lane CB2 3RH **T** 01223-330906 **W** www.hps.cam.ac.uk/whipple
Scientific instruments from the 14th century to the present

CARLISLE – *Tullie House Museum and Art Gallery,* Castle Street CA3 8TP **T** 01228-534781 **W** www.tulliehouse.co.uk
Prehistoric archaeology, Hadrian's Wall, Viking and medieval Cumbria, and the social history of Carlisle; British 19th- and 20th-century art; English porcelain

CHATHAM – *Dickens World,* Leviathan Way ME4 4LL **T** 0870-241 1415 **W** www.dickensworld.co.uk
Theme park based on the life, books and era of Charles Dickens

The Historic Dockyard, ME4 4TZ **T** 01634-823800 **W** www.chdt.org.uk
Maritime attractions including HMS *Cavalier,* the UK's last Second World War destroyer

Royal Engineers Museum of Military Engineering, Prince Arthur Road, Gillingham ME4 4UG **T** 01634-822839 **W** www.remuseum.org.uk
Regimental history, ethnography, decorative art and photography

CHELTENHAM – *Art Gallery and Museum,* Clarence Street GL50 3TJ **T** 01242-237431 **W** www.cheltenham.gov.uk
Paintings, arts and crafts

CHESTER – *Grosvenor Museum,* Grosvenor Street CH1 2DD **T** 01244-402008 **W** www.chester.gov.uk
Roman collections, natural history, art, Chester silver, local history and costume

CHICHESTER – *Weald and Downland Open Air Museum,* Singleton PO18 0EU **T** 01243-811363 **W** www.wealddown.co.uk
Rebuilt vernacular buildings from south-east England; includes medieval houses, agricultural and rural craft buildings and a working watermill

COLCHESTER – *Colchester Castle Museum,* Castle Park CO1 1TJ **T** 01206-282939 **W** www.colchestermuseums.org.uk
Largest Norman keep in Europe standing on foundations of the Roman Temple of Claudius; tours of the Roman vaults, castle walls and chapel

COVENTRY – *Coventry Transport Museum,* Hales Street CV1 1PN **T** 024-7623 4270 **W** www.transport-museum.com
Hundreds of motor vehicles and bicycles

Herbert Art Gallery and Museum, Jordan Well CV1 5QP **T** 024-7683 2386 **W** www.theherbert.org
Local history, archaeology and industry; fine and decorative art

DERBY – *Derby Museum and Art Gallery,* The Strand DE1 1BS **T** 01332-716659 **W** www.derby.gov.uk
Includes paintings by Joseph Wright of Derby and Derby porcelain

Pickford's House Museum, Friar Gate DE1 1DA **T** 01332-255363 **W** www.derby.gov.uk
Georgian town house by architect Joseph Pickford; reconstructed period rooms and garden

The Silk Mill, Derby's Museum of Industry and History, Full Street DE1 3AF **T** 01332-255308 **W** www.derby.gov.uk
Rolls-Royce aero engine collection and railway engineering gallery

DEVIZES – *Wiltshire Heritage Museum,* Long Street SN10 1NS **T** 01380-727369 **W** www.wiltshireheritage.org.uk
Natural and local history, art gallery, archaeological finds from Bronze Age, Iron Age, Roman and Saxon sites

DORCHESTER – *Dorset County Museum,* High West Street DT1 1XA **T** 01305-262735 **W** www.dorsetcountymuseum.org
Includes a collection of Thomas Hardy's manuscripts, books, notebooks and drawings

DOVER – *Dover Museum,* Market Square CT16 1PB **T** 01304-201066 **W** www.dovermuseum.co.uk
Contains Dover Bronze Age Boat Gallery and archaeological finds from Bronze Age, Roman and Saxon sites

EXETER – *Royal Albert Memorial Museum and Art Gallery,* Queen Street EX4 3RX **T** 01392-665858 **W** www.exeter.gov.uk/ramm
Natural history, archaeology, worldwide fine and decorative art including Exeter silver

GATESHEAD – *Baltic Centre for Contemporary Art,* South Shore Road NE8 3BA **T** 0191-478 1810 **W** www.balticmill.com
Contemporary art exhibitions and events

Shipley Art Gallery, Prince Consort Road NE8 4JB **T** 0191-477 1495 **W** www.twmuseums.org.uk/shipley
Contemporary crafts

GAYDON, Warks – *Heritage Motor Centre,* Banbury Road CV35 0BJ **T** 01926-641188 **W** www.heritage-motor-centre.co.uk
History of British motor industry from 1895 to present; classic vehicles; engineering gallery; Corgi and Lucas collections

GLOUCESTER – *National Waterways Museum,* Gloucester Docks GL1 2EH **T** 01452-318200 **W** www.nwm.org.uk
Two-hundred-year history of Britain's canals and inland waterways

GOSPORT, Hants – *Royal Navy Submarine Museum,* Haslar Jetty Road PO12 2AS **T** 023-9252 9217 **W** www.rnsubmus.co.uk
Underwater warfare, including the submarine *Alliance*; first Royal Navy submarine

GRASMERE, Cumbria – *Dove Cottage* and the *Wordsworth Museum,* LA22 9SH **T** 01539-435544 **W** www.wordsworth.org.uk
William Wordsworth's home and garden

HULL – *Ferens Art Gallery,* Queen Victoria Square HU1 3RA **T** 01482-300300 **W** www.hullcc.gov.uk/museums
European art, especially Dutch 17th-century paintings, British portraits from 17th to 20th century, and marine paintings

Hull Maritime Museum, Queen Victoria Square HU1 3DX **T** 01482-300300 **W** www.hullcc.gov.uk/museums
Whaling, fishing and navigation exhibits

HUNTINGDON – *The Cromwell Museum,* Grammar School Walk PE29 3LF **T** 01480-375830 **W** www.cambridgeshire.gov.uk/cromwell
Portraits and memorabilia relating to Oliver Cromwell

IPSWICH – *Christchurch Mansion* and *Wolsey Art Gallery,* Christchurch Park IP4 2BE **T** 01473-433554 **W** www.ipswich.gov.uk
Tudor house with paintings by Gainsborough, Constable and other Suffolk artists; furniture and 18th-century ceramics; temporary exhibitions

LEEDS – *Armley Mills, Leeds Industrial Museum,* Canal Road, Armley LS12 2QF **T** 0113-263 7861 **W** www.leeds.gov.uk/armleymills
World's largest woollen mill

Leeds City Art Gallery, The Headrow LS1 3AA
T 0113-247 8248 W www.leeds.gov.uk/artgallery
British and European paintings including English watercolours; modern sculpture; Henry Moore gallery; print room

Lotherton Hall, Aberford LS25 3EB T 0113-281 3259
W www.leeds.gov.uk/lothertonhall
Costume and oriental collections in furnished Edwardian house; deer park and bird garden

**Royal Armouries Museum,* Armouries Drive LS10 1LT
T 0113-220 1916 W www.royalarmouries.org
National collection of arms and armour from BC to present; demonstrations of foot combat in museum's five galleries; falconry and mounted combat in the tiltyard

Temple Newsam, LS15 0AE T 0113-264 5535
W www.leeds.gov.uk/templenewsam
Old Masters and 17th- and 18th-century decorative art in furnished Jacobean/Tudor house

LEICESTER – *Jewry Wall Museum,* St Nicholas Circle
LE1 4LB T 0116-225 4971 W www.leicestermuseums.ac.uk
Archaeology; Roman Jewry Wall and baths; mosaics

New Walk Museum and Art Gallery, New Walk LE1 7EA
T 0116-255 4900 W www.leicestermuseums.ac.uk
Natural history and geology; ancient Egypt gallery; European art and decorative arts

LINCOLN – *Museum of Lincolnshire Life,* Burton Road
LN1 3LY T 01522-528448 W www.lincolnshire.gov.uk
Social history and agricultural collection

Usher Gallery, Lindum Road LN2 1NN T 01522-527980
W www.lincolnshire.gov.uk
Watches, miniatures, porcelain, silver; collection of Peter de Wint works; Lincolnshire topography; Royal Lincs Regiment memorabilia

LIVERPOOL – **Lady Lever Art Gallery,* Wirral CH62 5EQ
T 0151-478 4136 W www.liverpoolmuseums.org/ladylever
Paintings, furniture and porcelain

**Merseyside Maritime Museum,* Albert Dock L3 4AQ
T 0151-478 4499
W www.liverpoolmuseums.org.uk/maritime
Floating exhibits, working displays and craft demonstrations; incorporates *HM Customs and Excise National Museum*

**Sudley House,* Mossley Hill Road L18 8BX T 0151-724 3245
W www.liverpoolmuseums.org/sudley
Late 18th- and 19th-century paintings in former shipowner's home

**Tate Liverpool,* Albert Dock L3 4BB T 0151-702 7400
W www.tate.org.uk/liverpool
Twentieth-century paintings and sculpture

**Walker Art Gallery,* William Brown Street L3 8EL
T 0151-478 4199 W www.liverpoolmuseums.org.uk/walker
Paintings from the 14th to 20th century

**World Museum Liverpool,* William Brown Street L3 8EN
T 0151-478 4393 W www.liverpoolmuseums.org.uk/wml
Includes Egyptian mummies, weapons and classical sculpture; planetarium, aquarium, vivarium and natural history centre

LONDON: GALLERIES – *Barbican Art Gallery,* Barbican Centre, Silk Street EC2Y 8DS T 020-7638 4141
W www.barbican.org.uk
Temporary exhibitions

Courtauld Institute of Art Gallery, Somerset House, Strand
WC2R 0RN T 020-7848 2777 W www.courtauld.ac.uk
Impressionist and Post-Impressionist paintings

Dulwich Picture Gallery, Gallery Road, Dulwich Village
SE21 7AD T 020-8693 5254
W www.dulwichpicturegallery.org.uk
England's first public art gallery; built by Sir John Soane to house 17th- and 18th-century paintings

Hayward Gallery, Belvedere Road SE1 8XZ T 0870-165 6000
W www.southbankcentre.co.uk
Temporary exhibitions

**National Gallery,* Trafalgar Square WC2N 5DN
T 020-7747 2885 W www.nationalgallery.org.uk
Western painting from the 13th to 20th century; early Renaissance collection in the Sainsbury Wing

**National Portrait Gallery,* St Martin's Place WC2H 0HE
T 020-7306 0055 W www.npg.org.uk
Portraits of eminent people in British history

Percival David Foundation of Chinese Art, Gordon Square
WC1H 0PD T 020-7387 3909 W www.pdfmuseum.org.uk
Chinese ceramics from 10th to 18th century

Photographers' Gallery, Great Newport Street WC2H 7HY
T 020-7831 1772 W www.photonet.org.uk
Temporary exhibitions

The Queen's Gallery, Buckingham Palace SW1A 1AA
T 020-7766 7301 W www.royal.gov.uk
Art from the Royal Collection

Royal Academy of Arts, Burlington House, Piccadilly W1J 0BD
T 020-7300 8000 W www.royalacademy.org.uk
British art since 1750 and temporary exhibitions; annual Summer Exhibition

Saatchi Gallery, Sloane Square SW3 4RY
T 020-7823 2363 W www.saatchi-gallery.co.uk
Contemporary art including paintings, photographs, sculpture and installations

Serpentine Gallery, Kensington Gardens W2 3XA
T 020-7402 6075 W www.serpentinegallery.org
Temporary exhibitions of British and international contemporary art

**Tate Britain,* Millbank SW1P 4RG T 020-7887 8888
W www.tate.org.uk/britain
British painting and 20th-century painting and sculpture

**Tate Modern,* Bankside SE1 9TG T 020-7887 8888
W www.tate.org.uk/modern
International modern art from 1900 to the present

**Wallace Collection,* Manchester Square W1U 3BN
T 020-7563 9500 W www.wallacecollection.org
Paintings and drawings, French 18th-century furniture, armour, porcelain, clocks and sculpture

Whitechapel Art Gallery, Whitechapel High Street E1 7QX
T 020-7522 7888 W www.whitechapel.org
Temporary exhibitions of modern art

LONDON: MUSEUMS – *Bank of England Museum,* Threadneedle Street EC2R 8AH (entrance on Bartholomew Lane) T 020-7601 5545
W www.bankofengland.co.uk/museum
History of the Bank of England since 1694

**British Museum,* Great Russell Street WC1B 3DG
T 020-7323 8000 W www.thebritishmuseum.ac.uk
Antiquities, coins, medals, prints and drawings

**Cabinet War Rooms,* King Charles Street SW1A 2AQ
T 020-7930 6961 W www.cwr.iwm.org.uk
Underground rooms used by Churchill and the government during the Second World War

Cutty Sark, Greenwich SE10 9HT T 020-8858 3445
W www.cuttysark.org.uk
Damaged by fire in May 2007; temporary exhibition next to the ship while closed

Design Museum, Shad Thames SE1 2YD T 0870-833 9955
W www.designmuseum.org
The development of design and the mass-production of consumer objects

Firepower, the Royal Artillery Museum, Royal Arsenal, Woolwich SE18 6ST **T** 020-8855 7755 **W** www.firepower.org.uk
The history and development of artillery over the last 700 years including the collections of the Royal Regiment of Artillery

Geffrye Museum, Kingsland Road E2 8EA **T** 020-7739 9893 **W** www.geffrye-museum.org.uk
English urban domestic interiors from 1600 to present day; also paintings, furniture, decorative arts, walled herb garden and period garden rooms

Gilbert Collection, Strand WC2R 1LA **T** 020-7420 9400 **W** www.gilbert-collection.org.uk
Collection comprising some 800 works of art including European silver, gold snuff boxes and Italian mosaics

HMS Belfast,* Morgan's Lane, Tooley Street SE1 2JH **T 020-7940 6300 **W** http://hmsbelfast.iwm.org.uk
Life on a Second World War cruiser

Horniman Museum, London Road SE23 3PQ **T** 020-8699 1872 **W** www.horniman.ac.uk
Museum of ethnography, musical instruments and natural history; aquarium; reference library; sunken, water and flower gardens

Imperial War Museum,* Lambeth Road SE1 6HZ **T 020-7416 5320 **W** http://london.iwm.org.uk
All aspects of the two world wars and other military operations involving Britain and the Commonwealth since 1914

Jewish Museum, Camden Town, Albert Street NW1 7NB **T** 020-7284 1997 **W** www.jewishmuseum.org.uk
Jewish life, history and religion

London's Transport Museum, Wellington Street WC2E 7BB **T** 020-7379 6344 **W** www.ltmuseum.co.uk
Vehicles, photographs and graphic art relating to the history of transport in London

MCC Museum, Lord's, St John's Wood NW8 8QN **T** 020-7616 8656 **W** www.lords.org
Cricket museum; conducted tours by appointment

Museum in Docklands,* West India Quay, Hertsmere Road E14 4AL **T 0870-444 3857 **W** www.museumindocklands.org.uk
Explores the story of London's river, port and people over 2,000 years, from Roman times through to the recent regeneration of London's Docklands

Museum of Childhood at Bethnal Green (V&A),* Cambridge Heath Road E2 9PA **T 020-8983 5200 **W** www.museumofchildhood.org.uk
Toys, games and exhibits relating to the social history of childhood

Museum of Garden History, Lambeth Palace Road SE1 7LB **T** 020-7401 8865 **W** www.museumgardenhistory.org
History and development of gardens and gardening; recreated 17th-century garden

Museum of London,* London Wall EC2Y 5HN **T 0870-444 3852 **W** www.museumoflondon.org.uk
History of London from prehistoric times to present day

National Army Museum, Royal Hospital Road SW3 4HT **T** 020-7730 0717 **W** www.national-army-museum.ac.uk
Five-hundred-year history of the British soldier; exhibits include model of the Battle of Waterloo and recreated First World War trench

National Maritime Museum,* Greenwich SE10 9NF **T 020-8858 4422 **W** www.nmm.ac.uk
Maritime history of Britain; collections include globes, clocks, telescopes and paintings; comprises the main building, the Royal Observatory and the Queen's House

Natural History Museum,* Cromwell Road SW7 5BD **T 020-7942 5000 **W** www.nhm.ac.uk
Natural history collections

Petrie Museum of Egyptian Archaeology, University College London, Malet Place WC1E 6BT **T** 020-7679 2884 **W** www.petrie.ucl.ac.uk
Egyptian archaeology collection

Royal Air Force Museum, Hendon NW9 5LL **T** 020-8205 2266 **W** www.rafmuseum.org.uk
Aviation from before the Wright brothers to the present-day RAF; features more than 70 full-size aircraft

Royal Mews, Buckingham Palace SW1A 1AA **T** 020-7766 7302 **W** www.royal.gov.uk
State vehicles, including the Queen's gold state coach; home to the Queen's horses

Science Museum,* Exhibition Road SW7 2DD **T 0870 870 4868 **W** www.sciencemuseum.org.uk
Science, technology, industry and medicine collections

Shakespeare's Globe Exhibition, Bankside SE1 9DT **T** 020-7902 1400 **W** www.shakespeares-globe.org
Recreation of Elizabethan theatre using 16th-century techniques; includes a tour of the theatre

Sir John Soane's Museum,* Lincoln's Inn Fields WC2A 3BP **T 020-7405 2107 **W** www.soane.org
Art and antiquities

Theatre Museum,* Russell Street WC2E 7PR **T 020-7943 4700 **W** www.theatremuseum.org.uk
History of the performing arts

Tower Bridge Experience, SE1 2UP **T** 020-7403 3761 **W** www.towerbridge.org.uk
History of the bridge and display of Victorian steam machinery; panoramic views from walkways

Victoria and Albert Museum,* Cromwell Road SW7 2RL **T 020-7942 2000 **W** www.vam.ac.uk
Includes National Art Library and Print Room; fine and applied art and design; furniture, glass, textiles and dress collections

Wimbledon Lawn Tennis Museum, Church Road SW19 5AE **T** 020-8946 6131 **W** www.wimbledon.org/museum
Tennis trophies, fashion and memorabilia; view of Centre Court

MALTON, N. Yorks – *Eden Camp,* YO17 6RT **T** 01653 697777 **W** www.edencamp.co.uk
Restored POW camp and Second World War memorabilia

MANCHESTER – *Gallery of Costume,* Platt Hall, Rusholme M14 5LL **T** 0161-224 5217 **W** www.manchestergalleries.org
Exhibits from the 16th to the 20th century

Imperial War Museum North,* Trafford Wharf, Trafford Park M17 1TZ **T 0161-836 4000 **W** http://north.iwm.org.uk

Manchester Art Gallery, Mosley Street M2 3JL **T** 0161-235 8888 **W** www.manchestergalleries.org
Six centuries of European fine and decorative art

Manchester Museum, Oxford Road M13 9PL **T** 0161-275 2634 **W** www.museum.man.ac.uk
Collections include archaeology, decorative arts, Egyptology, natural history and zoology

Museum of Science and Industry, Liverpool Road, Castlefield M3 4FP **T** 0161-832 2244 **W** www.msim.org.uk
On site of world's oldest passenger railway station; galleries relating to space, energy, power, transport, aviation, textiles and social history

People's History Museum, The Pump House, Bridge Street M3 3ER **T** 0161-839 6061 **W** www.phm.org.uk
Political and working life history

Whitworth Art Gallery, Oxford Road M15 6ER T 0161-275 7450 W www.whitworth.man.ac.uk
Watercolours, drawings, prints, textiles, wallpapers and 20th-century British art

MILTON KEYNES – *Bletchley Park National Codes Centre,* Bucks MK3 6EB T 01908-640404 W www.bletchleypark.org.uk
Home of British codebreaking during the Second World War; Enigma machine; computer museum; wartime toys and memorabilia

MONKWEARMOUTH, Sunderland – *Monkwearmouth Station Museum,* North Bridge Street SR5 1AP T 0191-567 7075 W www.twmuseums.org.uk/monkwearmouth
Victorian train station

NEWCASTLE UPON TYNE – *Discovery Museum,* Blandford Square NE1 4JA T 0191-232 6789 W www.twmuseums.org.uk/discovery
Science and industry, local history, fashion; Tyneside's maritime history; *Turbinia* (first steam-driven vessel) gallery

Laing Art Gallery, New Bridge Street NE1 8AG T 0191-232 7734 W www.twmuseums.org.uk/laing
British and European art, ceramics, glass, silver, textiles and costume; Art on Tyneside display

NEWMARKET – *National Horseracing Museum,* High Street CB8 8JL T 01638-667333 W www.nhrm.co.uk
Horseracing simulator, temporary exhibitions and tours of local trainers' yards and studs

NORTH SHIELDS – *Stephenson Railway Museum,* Middle Engine Lane NE29 8DX T 0191-200 7146 W www.twmuseums.org.uk/stephenson
Locomotive engines and rolling stock

NOTTINGHAM – *Brewhouse Yard Museum,* Castle Boulevard NG7 1FB T 0115-915 3600 W www.nottinghamcity.gov.uk
Daily life from the 17th to 20th century

Castle Museum and Art Gallery, Friar Lane NG1 6EL T 0115-915 3700 W www.nottinghamcity.gov.uk
Paintings, ceramics, silver and glass; history of Nottingham

Industrial Museum, Wollaton NG8 2AE T 0115-915 3900 W www.nottinghamcity.gov.uk
Lacemaking machinery, steam engines and transport exhibits

Natural History Museum, Wollaton NG8 2AE T 0115-915 3900 W www.nottinghamcity.gov.uk
Local natural history and wildlife dioramas

OXFORD – *Ashmolean Museum,* Beaumont Street OX1 2PH T 01865-278000 W www.ashmolean.org
European and oriental fine and applied arts, archaeology, Egyptology and numismatics

Museum of Modern Art, Pembroke Street OX1 1BP T 01865-722733 W www.modernartoxford.org.uk
Temporary exhibitions

Museum of the History of Science, Broad Street OX1 3AZ T 01865-277280 W www.mhs.ox.ac.uk
Displays include early scientific instruments, chemical apparatus, clocks and watches

Oxford University Museum of Natural History, Parks Road OX1 3PW T 01865-272950 W www.oum.ox.ac.uk
Entomology, geology, mineralogy and zoology

Pitt Rivers Museum, South Parks Road OX1 3PP T 01865-270927 W www.prm.ox.ac.uk
Ethnographic and archaeological artefacts

PLYMOUTH – *City Museum and Art Gallery,* Drake Circus PL4 8AJ T 01752-304774 W www.plymouthmuseum.gov.uk
Local and natural history; ceramics; silver; Old Masters; temporary exhibitions

Plymouth Dome, Hoe Road PL1 2NZ T 01752-603300 W www.plymouthdome.info
Maritime history museum

PORTSMOUTH – *Charles Dickens Birthplace,* Old Commercial Road PO1 4QL T 023-9282 7261 W www.charlesdickensbirthplace.co.uk
Dickens memorabilia

D-Day Museum, Clarence Esplanade, Southsea PO5 3NT T 023-9282 7261 W www.ddaymuseum.co.uk
Includes the Overlord embroidery

Portsmouth Historic Dockyard, HM Naval Base PO1 3LJ T 023-9283 9766 W www.historicdockyard.co.uk
Incorporates the *Royal Naval Museum* (PO1 3NH T 023-9272 7562 W www.royalnavalmuseum.org), HMS *Victory* (PO1 3NH T 023-9286 1533 W www.hms-victory.com), HMS *Warrior* (PO1 3QX T 023-9277 8609 W www.hmswarrior.org), the *Mary Rose* (PO1 3LX T 023-9281 2931 W www.maryrose.org) and *Action Stations* (PO1 3LJ T 023-9289 3316 W www.actionstations.org)
History of the Royal Navy and of the dockyard; warships and technology spanning 500 years

PRESTON – *Harris Museum and Art Gallery,* Market Square PR1 2PP T 01772-258248 W www.harrismuseum.org.uk
British art since the 18th century; ceramics, glass, costume and local history; contemporary exhibitions

National Football Museum, Deepdale PR1 6RU T 01772-908442 W www.nationalfootballmuseum.com
Home to the FIFA museum collection; FA, Football League and Wembley collections on long-term loan

ST ALBANS – *Verulamium Museum,* St Michael's Street AL3 4SW T 01727-751810 W www.verulamium.com
Remains of Iron Age settlement and the third-largest city in Roman Britain; exhibits include Roman wall plasters, jewellery, mosaics and room reconstructions

ST IVES, Cornwall – **Tate St Ives,* Porthmeor Beach TR26 1TG T 01736-796226 W www.tate.org.uk/stives
Modern art, much by artists associated with St Ives; includes the Barbara Hepworth Museum and Sculpture Garden

SALISBURY – *Salisbury & South Wiltshire Museum,* The Close SP1 2EN T 01722-332151 W www.salisburymuseum.org.uk
Archaeology collection

SHEFFIELD – *Graves Art Gallery,* Surrey Street S1 1XZ T 0114-278 2600 W www.sheffieldgalleries.org.uk
20th-century British art, Grice Collection of Chinese ivories

Millennium Galleries, Arundel Gate S1 2PP T 0114-278 2600 W www.sheffieldgalleries.org.uk
Incorporates four different galleries: the Special Exhibition Gallery, the Craft and Design Gallery, the Metalwork Gallery and the Ruskin Gallery, which houses John Ruskin's collection of paintings, drawings, books and medieval manuscripts

Weston Park Museum, Western Bank S10 2TP T 0114-278 2600 W www.sheffieldgalleries.org.uk
World history for families

SOUTHAMPTON – *City Art Gallery,* Commercial Road SO14 7LP T 023-8083 2277 W www.southampton.gov.uk/art
Fine art, especially 20th-century British

Maritime Museum, Town Quay Road SO14 2NY T 023-8063 5904 W www.southampton.gov.uk
Southampton maritime history

Museum of Archaeology, Winkle Street SO14 2NY T 023-8063 5904 W www.southampton.gov.uk
Roman, Saxon and medieval archaeology

SOUTH SHIELDS – *Arbeia Roman Fort,* Baring Street NE33 2BB **T** 0191-456 1369 **W** www.twmuseums.org.uk/arbeia
Excavated ruins

South Shields Museum and Art Gallery, Ocean Road NE33 2JA **T** 0191-456 8740 **W** www.twmuseums.org.uk/southshields
South Tyneside history, including reconstructed street

STOKE-ON-TRENT – *Etruria Industrial Museum,* Lower Bedford Street ST4 7AF **T** 01782-233144 **W** www.stoke.gov.uk/museums
Britain's sole surviving steam-powered potter's mill

Gladstone Pottery Museum, Longton ST3 1PQ **T** 01782-237777 **W** www.stoke.gov.uk/museums
A working Victorian pottery

Potteries Museum and Art Gallery, Hanley ST1 3DW **T** 01782-232323 **W** www.stoke.gov.uk/museums
Pottery, china and porcelain collections and a Mark XVI Spitfire

SUNDERLAND – *Sunderland Museum & Winter Gardens,* Burdon Road SR1 1PP **T** 0191-553 2323 **W** www.twmuseums.org.uk/sunderland
Fine and decorative art, local history and gardens

TELFORD – *Ironbridge Gorge Museums,* TF8 7DQ **T** 01952-884391 **W** www.ironbridge.org.uk
World's first iron bridge; Blists Hill (late Victorian working town); Museum of Iron; Jackfield Tile Museum; Coalport China Museum; Tar Tunnel; Broseley Pipeworks

WAKEFIELD – *National Coal Mining Museum for England,* Overton WF4 4RH **T** 01924-848806 **W** www.ncm.org.uk
Underground tours of one of Britain's oldest working mines

Yorkshire Sculpture Park, West Bretton WF4 4LG **T** 01924-832631 **W** www.ysp.co.uk
Open-air sculpture gallery including works by Moore, Hepworth, Frink and others in 121 hectares (300 acres) of parkland

WEYBRIDGE – *Brooklands Museum,* KT13 0QN **T** 01932-857381 **W** www.brooklandsmuseum.com
Birthplace of British motorsport; world's first purpose-built motor racing circuit

WILMSLOW – *Quarry Bank Mill,* Styal SK9 4LA **T** 01625-527468 **W** www.quarrybankmill.org.uk
Working mill owned by the National Trust illustrating history of cotton industry; costumed guides at restored Apprentice House

WORCESTER – *City Museum and Art Gallery,* Foregate Street WR1 1DT **T** 01905-25371 **W** www.worcestercitymuseums.org.uk
Includes a military museum, 19th-century chemist shop and changing art exhibitions

Museum of Worcester Porcelain, Severn Street WR1 2NE **T** 01905-746000 **W** www.worcesterporcelainmuseum.org.uk
Worcester porcelain from 1751 to the present day. Also the *Royal Worcester Visitor Centre* (**W** www.royal-worcester.co.uk)

WROUGHTON, nr Swindon, Wilts – **Science Museum,* SN4 9NS **T** 01793-846200 **W** www.sciencemuseum.org.uk/wroughton
Aircraft displays and some of the Science Museum's transport and agricultural collection

YEOVIL, Somerset – *Fleet Air Arm Museum,* Royal Naval Air Station, Yeovilton BA22 8HT **T** 01935-840565 **W** www.fleetairarm.com
History of naval aviation; historic aircraft, including Concorde 002

YORK – *Beningbrough Hall,* Beningbrough YO30 1DD **T** 01904-472027 **W** www.nationaltrust.org.uk
Portraits from the National Portrait Gallery

Jorvik – The Viking City, Coppergate YO1 9WT **T** 01904-543400 **W** www.jorvik-viking-centre.co.uk
Reconstruction of Viking York

National Railway Museum,* Leeman Road YO26 4XJ **T 01904-214001 **W** www.nrm.org.uk
Includes locomotives, rolling stock and carriages

York Castle Museum, Eye of York YO1 9RY **T** 01904-687687 **W** www.yorkcastlemuseum.org.uk
Reconstructed streets; costume and military collections

York Art Gallery, Exhibition Square YO1 7EW **T** 01904-687687 **W** www.yorkartgallery.org.uk
European and British painting spanning seven centuries; modern pottery

Yorkshire Museum & Gardens, Museum Gardens YO1 7FR **T** 01904-687687 **W** www.yorkshiremuseum.org.uk
Yorkshire life from Roman to medieval times; geology gallery

WALES

* Members of National Museum Wales, a public body that receives its funding through grant-in-aid from the Welsh Assembly

BLAENAFON, Torfaen – **Big Pit National Coal Museum,* NP4 9XP **T** 01495-790311 **W** www.museumwales.ac.uk
Colliery with underground tour

BODELWYDDAN, Denbighshire – *Bodelwyddan Castle,* LL18 5YA **T** 01745-584060 **W** www.bodelwyddan-castle.co.uk
Portraits from the National Portrait Gallery; furniture from the Victoria and Albert Museum; sculptures from the Royal Academy

CAERLEON – **National Roman Legion Museum,* NP18 1AE **T** 01633-423134 **W** www.museumwales.ac.uk
Material from the site of the Roman fortress of Isca and its suburbs

CARDIFF – **National Museum Cardiff,* Cathays Park CF10 3NP **T** 029-2039 7951 **W** www.museumwales.ac.uk
Includes natural sciences, archaeology and Impressionist paintings

St Fagans: National History Museum,* St Fagans CF5 6XB **T 029-2057 3500 **W** www.museumwales.ac.uk
Open-air museum with re-erected buildings, agricultural equipment and costume

DRE-FACH FELINDRE, nr Llandysul – **National Wool Museum,* SA44 5UP **T** 01559-370929 **W** www.museumwales.ac.uk
Exhibitions, a working woollen mill and craft workshops

LLANBERIS, nr Caernarfon – **National Slate Museum,* LL55 4TY **T** 01286-870630 **W** www.museumwales.ac.uk
Former slate quarry with original machinery and plant; slate crafts demonstrations

LLANDRINDOD WELLS – *National Cycle Collection,* Automobile Palace, Temple Street LD1 5DL **T** 01597-825531 **W** www.cyclemuseum.org.uk
Over 200 bicycles on display, from 1818 to the present day

SWANSEA – *Glynn Vivian Art Gallery,* Alexandra Road SA1 5DZ **T** 01792-516900 **W** www.swansea.gov.uk/glynnvivian
Paintings, ceramics, Swansea pottery and porcelain, clocks, glass and Welsh art

National Waterfront Museum,* Oystermouth Road SA1 3RD **T 01792-638950 **W** www.museumwales.ac.uk
Wales during the Industrial Revolution

vansea Museum, Victoria Road SA1 1SN T 01792-653763 W www.swansea.gov.uk
Archaeology, social history, Swansea pottery

COTLAND

Members of National Museums of Scotland or National Galleries of Scotland, which are non-departmental public bodies funded by, and accountable to, the Scottish Executive

BERDEEN – *Aberdeen Art Gallery,* Schoolhill AB10 1FQ T 01224-523700 W www.aagm.co.uk
Art from the 18th to 20th century

erdeen Maritime Museum, Shiprow AB11 5BY T 01224-337700 W www.aagm.co.uk
Maritime history, including shipbuilding and North Sea oil

DINBURGH – *Britannia,* Leith EH6 6JJ T 0131-555 5566 W www.royalyachtbritannia.co.uk
Former royal yacht with royal barge and royal family picture gallery

y Art Centre, Market Street EH1 1DE T 0131-529 3993 W www.cac.org.uk
Late 19th- and 20th-century art and temporary exhibitions

ean Gallery, Belford Road EH4 3DS T 0131-624 6200 W www.nationalgalleries.org
Dada, Surrealism and sculpture – particularly works by Sir Eduardo Paolozzi

useum of Childhood, High Street EH1 1TG T 0131-529 4142 W www.cac.org.uk
Toys, games, clothes and exhibits relating to the social history of childhood

useum of Edinburgh, Canongate EH8 8DD T 0131-529 4143 W www.cac.org.uk
Local history, silver, glass and Scottish pottery

Museum of Flight, East Fortune Airfield, East Lothian EH39 5LF T 01620-897240 W www.nms.ac.uk/flight
Display of aircraft

Museum of Scotland, Chambers Street EH1 1JF T 0131-247 4422 W www.nms.ac.uk/scotland
Scottish history from prehistoric times to the present

ational Gallery of Scotland, The Mound EH2 2EL T 0131-624 6200 W www.nationalgalleries.org
Paintings, drawings and prints from the 16th to the 20th century; the national collection of Scottish art

ational War Museum of Scotland, Edinburgh Castle EH1 2NG T 0131-247 4413 W www.nms.ac.uk/war
History of Scottish military and conflicts

oyal Museum, Chambers Street EH1 1JF T 0131-247 4422 W www.nms.ac.uk/royal
Decorative arts; natural history; science and industry; part of the museum will be closed from spring 2008

cottish National Gallery of Modern Art, Belford Road EH4 3DR T 0131-624 6200 W www.nationalgalleries.org
20th-century painting, sculpture and graphic art

cottish National Portrait Gallery, Queen Street EH2 1JD T 0131-624 6200 W www.nationalgalleries.org
Portraits of eminent people in Scottish history; the national collection of photography

e Writers' Museum, Lawnmarket EH1 2PA T 0131-529 4901 W www.cac.org.uk
Robert Louis Stevenson, Walter Scott and Robert Burns exhibits

FORT WILLIAM – *West Highland Museum,* Cameron Square PH33 6AJ T 01397-702169 W www.westhighlandmuseum.org.uk
Tartan collections; exhibits relating to 1745 uprising

GLASGOW – *Burrell Collection,* Pollokshaws Road G43 1AT T 0141-287 2550 W www.glasgowmuseums.com
Paintings, textiles, furniture, ceramics, stained glass and silver from classical times to the 19th century

Gallery of Modern Art, Royal Exchange Square G1 3AH T 0141-229 1996 W www.glasgowmuseums.com
Collection of contemporary Scottish and world art

Hunterian Museum & Art Gallery, University of Glasgow G12 8QQ T 0141-330 4221 W www.hunterian.gla.ac.uk
Rennie Mackintosh and Whistler collections; Old Masters; Scottish paintings; modern paintings; sculpture; prints

Kelvingrove Art Gallery & Museum, Argyle Street G3 8AG T 0141-287 2699 W www.glasgowmuseums.com
Old Masters; 19th-century French paintings; armour collection

**Museum of Piping,* McPhater Street G4 0HW T 0141-353 0220 W www.thepipingcentre.co.uk
The history and origins of bagpiping

**Museum of Rural Life,* East Kilbride G76 9HR T 0131-247 4377 W www.nms.ac.uk/museumofrurallife
History of rural life and work

Museum of Transport, Bunhouse Road G3 8DP T 0141-287 2720 W www.glasgowmuseums.com
Includes a reproduction of a 1938 Glasgow street, cars since the 1930s, trams and a Glasgow subway station

People's Palace and Winter Gardens, Glasgow Green G40 1AT T 0141-271 2962 W www.glasgowmuseums.com
History of Glasgow since 1175; objects from all the main world religions

NORTHERN IRELAND

* Members of National Museums Northern Ireland, a non-departmental public body of the Northern Ireland Office

ARMAGH – **Armagh County Museum,* The Mall East BT61 9BE T 028-3752 3070 W www.armaghcountymuseum.org.uk
Local history; archaeology; crafts

BELFAST – **WhoWhatWhenWhereWhy,* Odyssey, Queen's Quay BT3 9QQ T 028-9046 7700 W www.w5online.co.uk
Interactive science and technology centre

HOLYWOOD, Co. Down – **Ulster Folk and Transport Museum,* Cultra BT18 0EU T 028-9042 8428 W www.uftm.org.uk
Open-air museum with original buildings from Ulster town and rural life *c.*1900; indoor galleries including Irish rail and road transport and *Titanic* exhibitions

LONDONDERRY – *The Tower Museum,* Union Hall Place BT48 6LU T 028-7137 2411 W www.derrycity.gov.uk/museums
Tells the story of Ireland through the history of Londonderry

OMAGH, Co. Tyrone – **Ulster American Folk Park,* Castletown BT78 5QY T 028-8224 3292 W www.folkpark.com
Open-air museum telling the story of Ulster's emigrants to America; restored or recreated dwellings and workshops; ship and dockside gallery

SIGHTS OF LONDON

For historic buildings, museums and galleries in London, *see* the Historic Buildings and Monuments and Museums and Galleries sections.

BRIDGES

The bridges over the Thames in London, from east to west, are:

Queen Elizabeth II Bridge (2,872m/9423ft), designed by Sir William Halcrow and partners, opened 1991

Tower Bridge (268m/880ft by 18m/60ft), designed by John Wolfe Barry, opened 1894

London Bridge (262m/860ft by 32m/105ft), original 13th-century stone bridge rebuilt by John Rennie and opened 1831, reconstructed in Arizona when current London Bridge opened 1973

Cannon Street Railway Bridge (261m/855ft), designed by Sir John Hawkshaw and John Wolfe Barry, originally named the Alexandra Bridge, opened 1866; renovated 1979–82

Southwark Bridge (244m/800ft by 17m/55ft), designed by John Rennie opened 1819; rebuilt 1912–21 (Mott, Hay and Anderson)

Millennium Bridge (325m/1,066ft by 5m/14 ft), designed by Ove Arup and Partners, opened 2000; reopened after modification 2002

Blackfriars Railway Bridge (284m/933ft), designed by John Wolfe Barry and Henri Marc Brunel, opened 1886

(*London, Chatham and Dover Railway Bridge* (234m/933ft), designed by Joseph Cubitt and opened in 1864, only the columns remain; the rest of the structure was removed in 1985)

Blackfriars Bridge (294m/963ft by 32m/105ft), designed by Robert Mylne, opened 1769; rebuilt 1869 (Joseph Cubitt); widened 1909

Waterloo Bridge (366m/1,200ft by 24m/80ft), designed by John Rennie, opened 1817; rebuilt (Sir Giles Gilbert Scott) 1945

Golden Jubilee Bridges (325m/1,066ft by 4.7m/15ft), designed by WSP Group, opened 2002; commonly known as the Hungerford Footbridges

Hungerford Railway Bridge (366m/1,200ft), designed by Isambard Kingdom Brunel, suspension bridge opened 1845; present railway bridge (Sir John Hawkshaw) opened 1864; widened in 1886

Westminster Bridge (228m/748ft by 26m/85ft), designed by Charles Labelye, opened 1750; rebuilt 1862 by Thomas Page

Lambeth Bridge (237m/776ft by 18m/60ft), designed by Peter W. Barlow, original suspension bridge opened 1862; current structure by George W. Humphreys opened 1932

Vauxhall Bridge (231m/759ft by 24m/80ft), designed by James Walker, opened 1816; redesigned by Sir Alexander Binnie and opened 1906

Grosvenor Railway Bridge (213m/700ft), designed by John Fowler, opened 1860; rebuilt 1965; also known as the Victoria Railway Bridge

Chelsea Bridge (213m/698ft by 25m/83ft), original suspension bridge designed by Thomas Page opened 1858; rebuilt by Rendel, Palmer and Triton in 1937

Albert Bridge (216m/710ft, by 12m/40ft) designed by Rowland M. Ordish, opened 1873; restructured by S Joseph Bazalgette in 1884; strengthened 1971–3

Battersea Bridge (204m/670ft by 17m/55ft), designed b Henry Holland, opened 1771; rebuilt by Bazalgette 1890

Battersea Railway Bridge (204m/670ft), designed b William Baker, opened 1863

Wandsworth Bridge (189m/619ft by 18m/60ft), design by Julian Tolmé, opened 1873; rebuilt 1940 (Sir Peirson Frank)

Putney Railway Bridge (229m/750ft), also known as th Fulham Railway Bridge or the Iron Bridge – it has n official name, designed by William Jacomb and open 1889

Putney Bridge (213m/700ft by 23m/74ft), designed b Sir Jacob Ackworth, original wooden bridge opened 1729; current granite structure by Bazalget completed in 1886

Hammersmith Bridge (210m/688ft by 10m/33f designed by William Tierney Clarke, the fi suspension bridge in London, originally built 182 rebuilt by Bazalgette in 1887

Barnes Railway Bridge (also footbridge, 110m/360f designed by Joseph Locke and opened in 1849; rebu 1895 by Head, Wrightson and co.; the origin structure stands unused

Chiswick Bridge (137m/450ft by 21m/70ft), designed b Alfred Dryland, opened 1933

Kew Railway Bridge (175m/575ft), designed by W. Galbraith, opened 1869

Kew Bridge (110m/360ft by 17m/56ft), designed b Robert Tunstall, original timber bridge built 175 replaced by a Portland stone structure by James Pai in 1789. Current granite bridge designed by Sir Jo Wolfe Barry and Cuthbert Brereton and renamed Ki Edward VII Bridge in 1903, but still known as Ke Bridge

Richmond Lock (91m/300ft by 11m/36ft), designed FGM Stoney, lock and footbridge opened 1894

Twickenham Bridge (85m/280ft by 21m/70ft), design by Alfred Dryland, opened 1933

Richmond Railway Bridge (91m/300ft), designed Joseph Locke, opened 1848; restructured 1906–8

Richmond Bridge (85m/280ft by 9m/36ft), design by Kenton Couse, built 1777; widened 1939

Teddington Lock (198m/650ft), designed by G. Poole two footbridges opened 1889; marks the end of th tidal reach of the Thames

Kingston Railway Bridge, designed by J. E. Errington an W. R. Galbraith, opened 1863

Kingston Bridge (116m/382ft), designed by Edwa Lapidge, built 1825–8; widened 1911–14 (Mott an Hay) and 1999–2001

Hampton Court Bridge designed by Samuel Stevens an Benjamin Ludgator, built 1753; replaced by ir bridge 1865; present bridge by W. P. Robinson and S Edwin Lutyens opened in 1933

CEMETERIES

In 1832, in response to the overcrowding of buri grounds in London, the government authorised th establishment of seven non-denominational cemeteri ɩat would encircle the city. These large cemeteries, ɿown as the 'magnificent seven', were seen by many ictorian families as places in which to demonstrate their ealth and stature, and as a result there are some highly ·nate graves and tombs.

HE MAGNIFICENT SEVEN

bney Park, Stamford Hill, N16 (13 hectares/32 acres), established 1840; tomb of General Booth, founder of the Salvation Army, and memorials to many nonconformists and dissenters

ompton, Old Brompton Road, SW10 (16 hectares/40 acres), established 1840; graves of Sir Henry Cole, Emmeline Pankhurst, John Wisden

ighgate, Swains Lane, N6 (15 hectares/38 acres), established 1839; graves of Douglas Adams, George Eliot, Michael Faraday, Karl Marx, Christina Rossetti and Radclyffe Hall; western side only accessible as part of a guided tour

ensal Green, Harrow Road, W10 (31.5 hectares/79 acres), established 1832; tombs of William Makepeace Thackeray, Anthony Trollope, Sydney Smith, Wilkie Collins, Tom Hood, George Cruikshank, Leigh Hunt, Isambard Kingdom Brunel and Charles Kemble

unhead, Linden Grove, SE15 (21 hectares/52 acres), established 1840; closed in 1969, subsequently restored and opened for burials

ɔwer Hamlets, Southern Grove, E3 (11 hectares/27 acres), established 1841; bombed heavily during the Second World War and closed to burials in 1966; now a nature reserve

'est Norwood Cemetery and Crematorium, Norwood High Street, SE27 (17 hectares/42 acres), established 1837; tombs of Sir Henry Bessemer, Mrs Beeton, Sir Henry Tate and Joseph Whitaker *(Whitaker's Almanack)*

THER CEMETERIES

ɹnhill Fields, City Road, EC1 (1.6 hectares/4 acres), 17th-century nonconformist burial ground containing the graves of William Blake, John Bunyan and Daniel Defoe

'ty of London Cemetery and Crematorium, Aldersbrook Road, E12 (81 hectares/200 acres), established 1856

olders Green Crematorium, Hoop Lane, NW11 (5 hectares/12 acres), established 1902; retains the ashes of Kingsley Amis, Peter Sellers, Marc Bolan, Sigmund Freud, Ivor Novello, Bram Stoker, H. G. Wells, Anna Pavlova and Joe Orton

ampstead, Fortune Green Road, NW6 (10.5 hectares/26 acres), established 1876; graves of Kate Greenaway, Lord Lister, Marie Lloyd

ARKETS

'llingsgate (fish), a market site for over 1,000 years, with the Lower Thames Street site dating from 1876; moved to the Isle of Dogs (Trafalgar Way, E14) in 1982; owned and run by the Corporation of London.

rough, Southwark Street, SE1 (vegetables, fruit, flowers, etc), established on present site in 1756; privately owned and run.

amden Lock, NW1 (second-hand clothing, jewellery, alternative fashion, crafts), established in 1973

ɔlumbia Road, E2 (flowers), dates from 19th century; became dedicated flower market in the 20th century

ɔvent Garden (vegetables, fruit, flowers, etc), established in 1670 under a charter of Charles II; owned and run by the Covent Garden Market Authority, whose board is appointed by DEFRA; moved in 1974 to Nine Elms, SW8

Leadenhall, Leadenhall Street, EC3 (meat, poultry, fish, etc), site of market since 14th century; present hall built 1881; owned and run by the Corporation of London

Petticoat Lane, Middlesex Street, E1, a market has existed on the site for over 500 years, now a Sunday morning market selling almost anything

Portobello Road, W11, originally for herbs and horse-trading from 1870; became famous for antiques after the closure of the Caledonian Market in 1948

Smithfield, EC1 (meat, poultry), built 1866–8, refurbished 1993–4; the site of St Bartholomew's Fair from 12th to 19th century; owned and run by the Corporation of London

New Spitalfields, E10 (vegetables, fruit, etc), established 1682, modernised 1928, moved out of the City to Leyton in 1991

Old Spitalfields, E1, continues to trade on the original Spitalfields site on Commercial Street, selling arts, crafts, books, clothes, organic food and antiques on Sundays

MONUMENTS

CENOTAPH, Whitehall, SW1. The Cenotaph (from the Greek meaning 'empty tomb') was built to commemorate 'The Glorious Dead' and is a memorial to all ranks of the sea, land and air forces who gave their lives in the service of the Empire during the First World War. Designed by Sir Edwin Lutyens and constructed in plaster as a temporary memorial in 1919, it was replaced by a permanent structure of Portland stone and unveiled by George V on 11 November 1920, Armistice Day. An additional inscription was made in 1946 to commemorate those who gave their lives in the Second World War.

FOURTH PLINTH, Trafalgar Square, WC2. The fourth plinth (1841) was designed for an equestrian statue that was never built due to lack of funds. From 1999 temporary works have been displayed on the plinth including *Ecce Homo* (Mark Wallinger), *Regardless of History* (Bill Woodrow), *Monument* (Rachel Whiteread), and *Alison Lapper Pregnant* (Marc Quinn). *Hotel for the Birds* by Thomas Schütte was installed in 2007.

LONDON MONUMENT (commonly called the Monument), Monument Street, EC3. Built to designs by Sir Christopher Wren and Robert Hooke between 1671 and 1677, the Monument commemorates the Great Fire of London, which broke out in Pudding Lane on 2 September 1666. The fluted Doric column is 36.6m (120ft) high, the moulded cylinder above the balcony supporting a flaming vase of gilt bronze is an additional 12.8 m (42ft), and the column is based on a square plinth 12.2m (40ft) high (with fine carvings on the west face), making a total height of 61.6m (202ft) – the tallest isolated stone column in the world, with views of London from a gallery at the top (311 steps).

OTHER MONUMENTS (sculptor's name in parentheses):

Albert Memorial (Scott), Kensington Gore

Royal Air Force (Blomfield), Victoria Embankment

Viscount Alanbrooke (Roberts-Jones), Whitehall

Beatty (Wheeler), Trafalgar Square

Belgian Gratitude (setting by Blomfield, statue by Rousseau), Victoria Embankment

Boadicea (or Boudicca), *Queen of the Iceni* (Thornycroft), Westminster Bridge

Brunel (Marochetti), Victoria Embankment
Burghers of Calais (Rodin), Victoria Tower Gardens, Westminster
Burns (Steell), Embankment Gardens
Canada Memorial (Granche), Green Park
Carlyle (Boehm), Chelsea Embankment
Cavalry (Jones), Hyde Park
Edith Cavell (Frampton), St Martin's Place
Charles I (Le Sueur), Trafalgar Square
Charles II (Gibbons), Royal Hospital, Chelsea
Churchill (Roberts-Jones), Parliament Square
Cleopatra's Needle (20.9m/68.5ft high, *c.*1500 BC, erected in 1878; the sphinxes are Victorian), Thames Embankment
Clive (Tweed), King Charles Street
Captain Cook (Brock), The Mall
Oliver Cromwell (Thornycroft), outside Westminster Hall
Cunningham (Belsky), Trafalgar Square
Gen. Charles de Gaulle (Conner), Carlton Gardens
Disraeli, Earl of Beaconsfield (Raggi), Parliament Square
Lord Dowding (Winter), Strand
Duke of Cambridge (Jones), Whitehall
Duke of York (37.8m/124ft column, with statue by Westmacott), Carlton House Terrace
Edward VII (Mackennal), Waterloo Place
Elizabeth I (Kerwin, 1586, oldest outdoor statue in London; from Ludgate), Fleet Street
Eros (Shaftesbury Memorial) (Gilbert), Piccadilly Circus
Marechal/Marshall Foch (Mallisard, copy of one in Cassel, France), Grosvenor Gardens
Charles James Fox (Westmacott), Bloomsbury Square
George III (Cotes Wyatt), Cockspur Street
George IV (Chantrey), Trafalgar Square
George V (Reid Dick and Scott), Old Palace Yard
George VI (Macmillan), Carlton Gardens
Gladstone (Thornycroft), Strand
Guards' (Crimea) (Bell), Waterloo Place
Guards Division (Ledward, figures, Bradshaw, cenotaph), Horse Guards' Parade
Haig (Hardiman), Whitehall
Sir Arthur (Bomber) Harris (Winter), Strand
Gen. Henry Havelock (Behnes), Trafalgar Square
Irving (Brock), north side of National Portrait Gallery
James II (Gibbons), Trafalgar Square
Jellicoe (Macmillan), Trafalgar Square
Samuel Johnson (Fitzgerald), opposite St Clement Danes
Kitchener (Tweed), Horse Guards' Parade
Abraham Lincoln (Saint-Gaudens, copy of one in Chicago), Parliament Square
Milton (Montford), St Giles, Cripplegate
Mountbatten (Belsky), Foreign Office Green
Gen. Charles James Napier (Adams), Trafalgar Square
Nelson (Railton), Trafalgar Square, with Landseer's lions (cast from guns recovered from the wreck of the *Royal George*)
Florence Nightingale (Walker), Waterloo Place
Palmerston (Woolner), Parliament Square
Peel (Noble), Parliament Square
Pitt (Chantrey), Hanover Square
Portal (Nemon), Embankment Gardens
Prince Albert (Bacon), Holborn Circus
Queen Elizabeth Gate (Lund and Wynne), Hyde Park Corner
Raleigh (Macmillan), Greenwich
Richard I (Coeur de Lion) (Marochetti), Old Palace Yard
Roberts (Bates), Horse Guards' Parade
Franklin D. Roosevelt (Reid Dick), Grosvenor Square
Royal Artillery (Jagger and Pearson), Hyde Park Corner
Royal Artillery (South Africa) (Colton), The Mall
Captain Scott (Lady Scott), Waterloo Place
Shackleton (Jagger), Kensington Gore
Shakespeare (Fontana, copy of one by Scheemakers Westminster Abbey), Leicester Square
Smuts (Epstein), Parliament Square
Sullivan (Goscombe John), Victoria Embankment
Trenchard (Macmillan), Victoria Embankment
Victoria Memorial (Webb and Brock), in front Buckingham Palace
Raoul Wallenberg (Jackson), Great Cumberland Place
George Washington (Houdon copy), Trafalgar Square
Wellington (Boehm), Hyde Park Corner
Wellington (Chantrey), outside Royal Exchange
John Wesley (Adams Acton), City Road
Westminster School (Crimea) (Scott), Broad Sanctuary
William III (Bacon), St James's Square
Wolseley (Goscombe John), Horse Guards' Parade.

PARKS, GARDENS AND OPEN SPACES

CORPORATION OF LONDON OPEN SPACES

Ashtead Common (200 hectares/500 acres), Surrey
Burnham Beeches and *Fleet Wood* (220 hectares/540 acres Bucks. Purchased by the Corporation for the benefit the public in 1880, Fleet Wood (26 hectares/65 acre being presented in 1921
Coulsdon Common (51 hectares/127 acres), Surrey
Epping Forest (2,428 hectares/6,000 acres), Esse Purchased by the Corporation and opened to t public in 1882. The present forest is 19.3km (12 mile long by around 3km (2 miles) wide, approximate one-tenth of its original area
Farthing Downs and New Hill (95 hectares/235 acre Surrey
Hampstead Heath (319 hectares/791 acres), NW Including Golders Hill (15 hectares/36 acres) ar Parliament Hill (110 hectares/271 acres)
Highgate Wood (28 hectares/70 acres), N6/N10
Kenley Common (56 hectares/139 acres), Surrey
Queen's Park (12 hectares/30 acres), NW6
Riddlesdown (43 hectares/107 acres), Surrey
Spring Park (21 hectares/51 acres), Kent
West Ham Park (31 hectares/77 acres), E15
West Wickham Common (10 hectares/26 acres), Kent
Woodredon and Warlies Park Estate (299 hectares/74 acres), Waltham Abbey
Also over 150 smaller open spaces within the City London, including *Finsbury Circus* and *Dunstan-in-the-East*

OTHER PARKS AND GARDENS

CHELSEA PHYSIC GARDEN, 66 Royal Hospital Roa SW3 4HS T 020-7352 5646 W www.chelseaphysicgarden.co.uk A garden of gener botanical research and education, maintaining a wi range of rare and unusual plants; established in 167 by the Society of Apothecaries
HAMPTON COURT PARK AND GARDENS (303 hectares/750 acres), Surrey KT8 9AU T 0870-751 51 W www.hrp.org.uk Also known as Home Park, the pa lies beyond the palace's formal gardens. It contains herd of deer and a 1,000-year-old oak tree from t original park

ROYAL PARKS

W www.royalparks.gov.uk
Bushy Park (445 hectares/1,099 acres), Middx. Adjoi Hampton Court; contains avenue of horse-chestnu enclosed in a fourfold avenue of limes planted William III

reen Park (19 hectares/47 acres), W1 Between Piccadilly and St James's Park, with Constitution Hill leading to Hyde Park Corner

reenwich Park (74 hectares/183 acres), SE10

yde Park (142 hectares/350 acres), W1/W2 From Park Lane to Kensington Gardens and incorporating the Serpentine lake, Apsley House, the Achilles Statue, Rotten Row and the Ladies' Mile; fine gateway at Hyde Park Corner. To the north-east is Marble Arch, originally erected by George IV at the entrance to Buckingham Palace and re-erected in the present position in 1851

ensington Gardens (111 hectares/275 acres), W2/W8 From the western boundary of Hyde Park to Kensington Palace; contains the Albert Memorial, Serpentine Gallery and Peter Pan statue

ew, Royal Botanic Gardens, Richmond, Surrey TW9 3AB T 020-8332 5655 W www.rbgkew.org.uk Officially inscribed on the UNESCO list of World Heritage Sites

egent's Park and *Primrose Hill* (197 hectares/487 acres), NW1 From Marylebone Road to Primrose Hill surrounded by the Outer Circle; divided by the Broad Walk leading to the Zoological Gardens

ichmond Park (1,000 hectares/2,500 acres), Surrey

James's Park (23 hectares/58 acres), SW1 From Whitehall to Buckingham Palace; ornamental lake of 4.9 hectares (12 acres); the Mall leads from Admiralty Arch to Buckingham Palace, Birdcage Walk from Storey's Gate to Buckingham Palace

LACES OF HISTORICAL AND ULTURAL INTEREST

CANADA SQUARE, Canary Wharf, E14 5DY T 020-7418 2000 W www.canarywharf.com Also known as 'Canary Wharf', the steel and glass skyscraper is the tallest structure in London and the tallest habitable building in the UK

) ST MARY AXE, EC3A 8EP W www.30stmaryaxe.com Completed in 2004 and commonly known as the 'Gherkin', it is the second-tallest building in the City of London

LEXANDRA PALACE, Alexandra Palace Way, Wood Green, N22 7AY T 020-8365 2121 W www.alexandrapalace.com The Victorian palace was severely damaged by fire in 1980 but was restored, and reopened in 1988. Alexandra Palace now provides modern facilities for exhibitions, conferences, banquets and leisure activities. There is an ice rink, a boating lake, the Phoenix Bar and a conservation area

ARBICAN CENTRE, Silk Street, EC2Y 8DS T 020-7638 4141 W www.barbican.org.uk Owned, funded and managed by the Corporation of London, the Barbican Centre opened in 1982 and houses the Barbican Theatre, a studio theatre called The Pit and the Barbican Hall; it is also home to the London Symphony Orchestra. There are three cinemas, six conference rooms, two art galleries, a sculpture court, a lending library, trade and banqueting facilities, a conservatory, shops, restaurants, cafes and bars

ENTRAL CRIMINAL COURT, Old Bailey, EC4M 7EH T 020-7248 3277 W www.cityoflondon.gov.uk The highest criminal court in the UK, the 'Old Bailey' was built in 1907 on the site of the old Newgate Prison. Trials held there have included those of Oscar Wilde, Dr Crippen and the Yorkshire Ripper

CHARTERHOUSE, Charterhouse Square, EC1M 6AN T 020-7253 9503 A Carthusian monastery from 1371 to 1537, purchased in 1611 by Thomas Sutton, who endowed it as a residence for aged men 'of gentle birth' and a school for poor scholars (removed to Godalming in 1872)

DOWNING STREET, SW1 Number 10 Downing Street is the official town residence of the Prime Minister, number 11 of the Chancellor of the Exchequer and number 12 is the office of the Government Whips. The street was named after Sir George Downing, Bt., soldier and diplomat, who was MP for Morpeth from 1660 to 1684

GEORGE INN, Borough High Street, SE1 1NH T 020-7407 2056 W www.nationaltrust.org.uk The last galleried inn in London, built in 1677. Now owned by the National Trust and run as an ordinary public house

GREENWICH, SE10 *Royal Naval College* T 020-8269 4747 W www.greenwichfoundation.org.uk The building was the Greenwich Hospital until 1873. It was built by Charles II, largely from designs by John Webb, and by Queen Mary II and William III, from designs by Wren. It stands on the site of an ancient abbey, a royal house and Greenwich Palace, which was constructed by Henry VII. Henry VIII, Mary I and Elizabeth I were born in the royal palace and Edward VI died there

Greenwich Park (74 hectares/183 acres), T 020-8858 2608, W www.royalparks.gov.uk Enclosed by Humphrey, Duke of Gloucester, and laid out by Charles II from the designs of Le Nôtre. On a hill in Greenwich Park is the *Royal Observatory* (founded 1675). Its buildings are now managed by the *National Maritime Museum,* T 020-8858 4422 W www.nmm.ac.uk and the earliest building is named Flamsteed House, after John Flamsteed (1646–1719), the first Astronomer Royal

The Cutty Sark, T 020-8858 2698, W www.cuttysark.org.uk The last of the famous tea clippers, it was moved into a specially constructed dry dock in 1954 and opened to the public in 1957

HORSE GUARDS, Whitehall, SW1 Archway and offices built about 1753. The changing of the guard takes place daily at 11am (10am on Sundays) and the inspection at 4pm. Only those with the Queen's permission may drive through the gates and archway into *Horse Guards' Parade,* where the colour is 'trooped' on the Queen's official birthday

HOUSES OF PARLIAMENT

House of Commons, Westminster, SW1A 0AA T 020-7219 4272 E hcinfo@parliament.uk W www.parliament.uk

House of Lords, Westminster, SW1A 0PW T 020-7219 3107 E hlinfo@parliament.uk W www.parliament.uk

The royal palace of Westminster, originally built by Edward the Confessor, was the normal meeting place of Parliament from about 1340. St Stephen's Chapel was used from about 1550 for the meetings of the House of Commons, which had previously been held in the Chapter House or Refectory of Westminster Abbey. The House of Lords met in an apartment of the royal palace. The fire of 1834 destroyed much of the palace, and the present Houses of Parliament were erected on the site from the designs of Sir Charles Barry and Augustus Welby Pugin between 1840 and 1867. The chamber of the House of Commons was destroyed by bombing in 1941, and a new chamber designed by Sir Giles Gilbert Scott was used for the first time in 1950. *Westminster Hall and the Crypt Chapel* was the only part of the old palace of Westminster to survive the fire of 1834. It was built by William II from 1097 to 1099 and altered by Richard II between 1394 and 1399. The hammerbeam roof of carved oak dates from 1396–8. The Hall was the scene of the trial of Charles I. *The Victoria Tower* of the House of Lords is 98.5m (323ft) high, and when Parliament is sitting, the Union flag flies by day from its flagstaff. *The Clock Tower* of the House of Commons is 96.3m (316ft) high and contains 'Big Ben', the hour bell said to be named after Sir Benjamin Hall, First Commissioner of Works when the original bell was cast in 1856. This bell, which weighed 16 tons 11 cwt, was found to be cracked in 1857. The present bell (13.5 tons) is a recasting of the original and was first brought into use in 1859. The dials of the clock are 7m (23ft) in diameter, the hands being 2.7m (9ft) and 4.3m (14ft) long (including balance piece). A light is displayed from the Clock Tower at night when parliament is sitting

During session, tours of the Houses of Parliament are only available to UK residents who have made advance arrangements through an MP or peer. Overseas visitors are no longer provided with permits to tour the Houses of Parliament during session, although they can tour during the summer opening and attend debates for both houses in the Strangers' Galleries. During the summer recess tickets for tours of the Houses of Parliament can be booked by telephone (T 0870-906 3773) or bought on site at the ticket office on Abingdon Green opposite Parliament and the Victoria Tower Gardens. The Strangers' Gallery of the House of Commons is open to the public when the house is sitting. To acquire tickets in advance UK residents should write to their local MP and overseas visitors should apply to their embassy or high commission in the UK for a permit. If none of these arrangements have been made, visitors should join the public queue outside St Stephen's Entrance, where there is also a queue for entry to the House of Lords Gallery

INNS OF COURT

The Inns of Court are ancient unincorporated bodies of lawyers which for more than five centuries have had the power to call to the Bar those of their members who have qualified for the rank or degree of Barrister-at-Law. There are four Inns of Court as well as many lesser inns

Lincoln's Inn, Chancery Lane/Lincoln's Inn Fields, WC2A 3TL T 020-7405 1393 W www.lincolnsinn.org.uk The most ancient of the inns with records dating back to 1422. The hall and library buildings are of 1845, although the library is first mentioned in 1474; the old hall (late 15th century) and the chapel were rebuilt *c.*1619–23

Inner Temple, King's Bench Walk, EC4Y 7HL T 020-7797 8250 W www.innertemple.org.uk

Middle Temple, Middle Temple Lane, EC4Y 9AT T 020-7427 4800 W www.middletemple.org.uk Records for the Middle and Inner Temple date back to the beginning of the 16th century. The site was originally occupied by the Order of Knights Templar *c.*1160–1312. The two inns have separate halls thought to have been formed *c.*1350. The division between the two societies was formalised in 1732 with Temple Church and the Masters House remaining in common. The Inner Temple Garden is normally open to the public on weekdays between 12.30pm and 3pm

Temple Church, EC4Y 7BB T 020-7353 3470 W www.templechurch.com The nave forms one of fiv remaining round churches in England

Gray's Inn, South Square, WC1R 5ET T 020-7458 780 W www.graysinn.org.uk Founded early 14th centur Hall 1556–8 No other 'Inns' are active, but there a remains of *Staple Inn,* a gabled front on Holbor (opposite Gray's Inn Road). *Clement's Inn* (near S Clement Danes Church), *Clifford's Inn,* Fleet Street, an *Thavies Inn,* Holborn Circus, are all rebuilt. *Serjeants' In* Fleet Street, and another (demolished 1910) of the sam name in Chancery Lane, were composed c Serjeants-at-Law, the last of whom died in 1922

INSTITUTE OF CONTEMPORARY ARTS, The Ma SW1Y 5AH T 020-7930 3647 W www.ica.org.uk Exhibitions of modern art in the fields of film, theatr new media and the visual arts

LLOYD'S, Lime Street, EC3M 7HA T 020-7327 100 W www.lloydsoflondon.com International insuranc market which evolved during the 17th century fro Lloyd's Coffee House. The present building was opene for business in May 1986, and houses the Lutine Bel Underwriting is on three floors with a total area c 10,591 sq. m (114,000 sq. ft). The Lloyd's building not open to the general public

LONDON CENTRAL MOSQUE AND THE ISLAMI CULTURAL CENTRE, Park Road, NW8 7R T 020-7724 3363 W www.iccuk.org The focus fc London's Muslims; established in 1944 but nc completed until 1977, the mosque can accommoda about 5,000 worshippers; guided tours are available

LONDON EYE, South Bank, SE1 7PB T 0870-990 060 W www.londoneye.com Opened in February 2000 a London's millennium landmark, this 450ft observatio wheel is the capital's fourth-largest structure. The whe provides a 30-minute ride offering panoramic views the capital

LONDON ZOO, Regent's Park, NW1 4RY T 020-7722 333 W www.londonzoo.org

MADAME TUSSAUD'S AND THE LONDO PLANETARIUM, Marylebone Road, NW1 5L T 0870-400 3000 W www.madame-tussauds.co.uk Waxwork exhibition and interactive star show

MARLBOROUGH HOUSE, Pall Mall, SW1Y 5H T 020-7747 6491 Built by Wren for the first Duke c Marlborough and completed in 1711, the hous reverted to the Crown in 1835. In 1863 it became th London house of the Prince of Wales and was th London home of Queen Mary until her death in 195 In 1959 Marlborough House was given by the Queen a the headquarters for the Commonwealth Secretariat an it was opened as such in 1965. The Queen's Chape Marlborough Gate, was begun in 1623 from the design of Inigo Jones for the Infanta Maria of Spain, an completed for Queen Henrietta Maria. Marlboroug House is not open to the public

PORT OF LONDON, Port of London Authority, Baker Hall, 7 Harp Lane, EC3R 6LB T 020-7743 7900 W www.portoflondon.co.uk The Port of London cove the tidal section of the River Thames from Teddingto to the seaward limit (the outer Tongue buoy and th Sunk light vessel), a distance of 150km. The governin body is the Port of London Authority (PLA). Cargo handled at privately operated riverside termina between Fulham and Canvey Island, including th enclosed dock at Tilbury, 40km below London Bridg Passenger vessels and cruise liners can be handled a moorings at Greenwich, Tower Bridge and Tilbury

OMAN REMAINS
The city wall of Roman *Londinium* was largely rebuilt during the medieval period but sections may be seen near the White Tower in the Tower of London; at Tower Hill; at Coopers' Row; at All Hallows, London Wall, its vestry being built on the remains of a semi-circular Roman bastion; at St Alphage, London Wall, showing a succession of building repairs from the Roman until the late medieval period; and at St Giles, Cripplegate. Sections of the great forum and basilica, more than 165m^2, have been encountered during excavations in the area of Leadenhall, Gracechurch Street and Lombard Street. Traces of Roman activity along the river include a massive riverside wall built in the late Roman period, and a succession of Roman timber quays along Lower and Upper Thames Street. Finds from these sites can be seen at the Museum of London

Other major buildings are the amphitheatre at Guildhall, remains of bath-buildings in Upper and Lower Thames Street, and the temple of Mithras in Walbrook

OYAL ALBERT HALL, Kensington Gore, SW7 2AP T 020-7589 8212 W www.royalalberthall.com The elliptical hall, one of the largest in the world, was completed in 1871; since 1941 it has been the venue each summer for the Promenade Concerts founded in 1895 by Sir Henry Wood. Other events include pop and classical music concerts, dance, opera, sporting events, conferences and banquets

OYAL COURTS OF JUSTICE, Strand, WC2A 2LL T 020-7947 6000 Victorian Gothic building that is home to the High Court. Visitors are free to watch proceedings

OYAL HOSPITAL, CHELSEA, Royal Hospital Road, SW3 4SR T 020-7881 5200 W www.chelsea-pensioners.co.uk Founded by Charles II in 1682, and built by Wren; opened in 1692 for old and disabled soldiers. The extensive grounds include the former Ranelagh Gardens and are the venue for the Chelsea Flower Show each May

OYAL OPERA HOUSE, Covent Garden, WC2E 9DD T 020-7240 1200 W www.royalopera.org Home of The Royal Ballet (1931) and The Royal Opera (1946). The Royal Opera House is the third theatre to be built on the site, opening 1858; the first was opened in 1732

T JAMES'S PALACE, Pall Mall, SW1A 1BQ T 020-7930 4832 W www.royal.gov.uk Built by Henry VIII, only the Gatehouse and Presence Chamber remain; later alterations were made by Wren and Kent. Representatives of foreign powers are still accredited 'to the Court of St James's'. *Clarence House* (1825), the official London residence of the Prince of Wales and his sons, stands within the St James's Palace estate

T PAUL'S CATHEDRAL, St Paul's Churchyard, EC4M 8AD T 020-7236 4128 E chapter@stpaulscathedral.org.uk W www.stpauls.co.uk Built 1675–1710. The cross on the dome is 111m (365ft) above ground level, the inner cupola 66.4 m (218ft) above the floor. 'Great Paul' in the south-west tower weighs nearly 17 tons. The organ by Father Smith (enlarged by Willis and rebuilt by Mander) is in a case carved by Grinling Gibbons, who also carved the choir stalls

OMERSET HOUSE, Strand, WC2R 1LA T 020 7845 4600 W www.somerset-house.org.uk The river facade (183m/600ft long) was built in 1776–1801 from the designs of Sir William Chambers; the eastern extension, which houses part of King's College, was built by Smirke in 1829–35. Somerset House was the property of Lord Protector Somerset, at whose attainder in 1552 the palace passed to the Crown, and it was a royal residence until 1692. Somerset House has recently undergone extensive renovation and is home to the Gilbert Collection, Hermitage Rooms and the Courtauld Institute Gallery. Open-air concerts and ice-skating (Dec–Jan) are held in the courtyard

SOUTH BANK, SE1 Arts complex on the south bank of the River Thames which consists of

The *Royal Festival Hall* T 08703-600400 W www.southbankcentre.co.uk Opened in 1951 for the Festival of Britain, adjacent are the 917-seat *Queen Elizabeth Hall*, the *Purcell Room*, and the *Voice Box*.

The *National Film Theatre*, T 020-7928 3535 W www.bfi.org.uk Opened in 1952 and is administered by the British Film Institute, has three auditoria showing over 2,000 films a year. The London Film Festival is held here every November. There is also an IMAX cinema with 477 seats

The *Royal National Theatre*, T 020-7452 3000 W www.nationaltheatre.org.uk opened in 1976 and stages classical, modern, new and neglected plays in its three auditoria: the Olivier, the Lyttelton and the Cottesloe theatres

SOUTHWARK CATHEDRAL, London Bridge, SE1 9DA T 020-7367 6700 E cathedral@southwark.anglican.org W www.dswark.org Mainly 13th century, but the nave is largely rebuilt. The tomb of John Gower (1330–1408) is between the Bunyan and Chaucer memorial windows in the north aisle; Shakespeare's effigy, backed by a view of Southwark and the Globe Theatre, is in the south aisle; the tomb of Bishop Andrewes (died 1626) is near the screen. The Lady Chapel was the scene of the consistory courts of the reign of Mary (Gardiner and Bonner) and is still used as a consistory court. John Harvard, after whom Harvard University is named, was baptised here in 1607, and the chapel by the north choir aisle is his memorial chapel

THAMES EMBANKMENTS
Sir Joseph Bazalgette (1819–91) constructed the *Victoria Embankment*, on the north side from Westminster to Blackfriarsfor the Metropolitan Board of Works, 1864–70; (the seats, of which the supports of some are a kneeling camel, laden with spicery, and of others a winged sphinx, were presented by the Grocers' Company and by W. H. Smith, MP, in 1874); the *Albert Embankment*, on the south side from Westminster Bridge to Vauxhall, 1866–9, and the Chelsea Embankment, 1871–4. The total cost exceeded £2m. Bazalgette also inaugurated the London main drainage system, 1858–65. A medallion *(Flumini vincula posuit)* has been placed on a pier of the *Victoria Embankment* to commemorate the engineer

THAMES FLOOD BARRIER
Officially opened in May 1984, though first used in February 1983, the barrier consists of ten rising sector gates which span approximately 570 yards from bank to bank of the Thames at Woolwich Reach. When not in use the gates lie horizontally, allowing shipping to navigate the river normally; when the barrier is closed, the gates turn through 90 degrees to stand vertically more than 50 feet above the river bed. The barrier took eight years to complete and can be raised within about 30 minutes

WESTMINSTER ABBEY, Broad Sanctuary, SW1P 3PA T 0207-222 5152 E info@westminster-abbey.org W www.westminster-abbey.org Founded as a Benedictine monastery over 1,000 years ago, the church was rebuilt by Edward the Confessor in 1065 and again by Henry III in the 13th century. The abbey is the resting place for monarchs including Edward I, Henry III, Henry V, Henry VII, Elizabeth I, Mary I and Mary Queen of Scots, and has been the setting of coronations since that of William the Conqueror in 1066. In Poets' Corner there are memorials to many literary figures, and many scientists and musicians are also remembered here. The grave of the Unknown Warrior is to be found in the nave

WESTMINSTER CATHEDRAL, Francis Street, SW1P 1QW
T 020-7798 9090 W www.westminstercathedral.org.uk
Roman Catholic cathedral built 1895–1903 from the designs of J. F. Bentley. The campanile is 284 feet high

LONDON THEATRES

Adelphi Theatre, Strand, WC2E 7NA T 020-7344 0055 ⊖ Charing Cross
Aldwych Theatre, Aldwych, WC2B 4DF T 020-7379 3367 ⊖ Covent Garden/Holborn
Almeida Theatre, Almeida Street, N1 1TA T 020-7359 4404 ⊖ Angel/Highbury & Islington
Apollo Theatre, Shaftesbury Avenue, W1V 7DH T 020-7494 5700 ⊖ Piccadilly Circus
Apollo Victoria Theatre, Wilton Road, SW1V 1LL T 0207-834 63184 ⊖ Victoria
Barbican Theatre, Barbican Centre, EC2Y 8DS T 020-7638 8891 ⊖ Barbican/Moorgate
Cambridge Theatre, Earlham Street, WC2 9HU T 020-7850 8710 ⊖ Covent Garden/Leicester Square
Chelsea Theatre, World's End Place, SW10 0DR T 020-7352 1967 ⊖ Sloane Square
Comedy Theatre, Panton Street, SW1Y 4DN T 0870-060 6637 ⊖ Leicester Square/Piccadilly Circus
Criterion Theatre, Jermyn Street, SW1Y 4XA T 0870-060 2313 ⊖ Piccadilly Circus
Dominion Theatre, Tottenham Court Road, W1T 7AQ T 020-7636 2295 ⊖ Tottenham Court Road
Donmar Warehouse, Earlham Street, WC2H 9LX T 020-7240 4882 ⊖ Covent Garden
Duchess Theatre, Catherine Street, WC2B 5LA T 020-7494 5075 ⊖ Covent Garden
Duke Of York's Theatre, St Martin's Lane, WC2N 4BG T 0870-060 6623 ⊖ Leicester Square/Piccadilly Circus
Fortune Theatre, Russell Street, WC2B 5HH T 0870-060 6626 ⊖ Covent Garden
Garrick Theatre, Charing Cross Road, WC2H 0HH T 020-7520 5690 ⊖ Charing Cross/Leicester Square
Gielgud Theatre, Shaftesbury Avenue, W1D 6AR T 020-7494 5065 ⊖ Piccadilly Circus
Globe Theatre, New Globe Walk, SE1 9DT T 020-7902 1400 ⊖ Mansion House
Hackney Empire, Mare Street, E8 1EJ T 020-8510 4500 ⊖ Bethnal Green
Her Majesty's Theatre, Haymarket, SW1Y 4QL T 020-7494 5400 ⊖ Piccadilly Circus
Jermyn Street Theatre, Jermyn Street, SW1Y 6ST T 020-7287 2875 ⊖ Piccadilly Circus
London Coliseum, St Martin's Lane, WC2N 4ES T 020-7836 0111 ⊖ Charing Cross
London Palladium, Argyll Street, W1F 7TF T 020-7494 5020 ⊖ Oxford Circus
Lyceum Theatre, Wellington Street, WC2E 7RQ T 0870-243 9000 ⊖ Covent Garden
Lyric Theatre, Shaftesbury Avenue, W1D 7ES T 020-7494 5045 ⊖ Piccadilly Circus
Lyric Theatre Hammersmith, King Street, W6 0QL T 020-8741 2311 ⊖ Hammersmith
National Theatre, South Bank, SE1 9PX T 020-7452 3000 ⊖ Waterloo
New Ambassadors Theatre, West Street, WC2H 9ND T 0870-060 6627 ⊖ Leicester Square
New London Theatre, Drury Lane, WC2B 5PW T 020-7242 9802 ⊖ Holborn
Noël Coward (formerly Albery), St Martin's Lane, WC2N 4BW T 0870-950 0920 ⊖ Leicester Square
Novello Theatre, Aldwych, WC2B 4LD T 020-7759 9640 ⊖ Charing Cross
Old Vic Theatre, The Cut, SE1 8NB T 020-7928 2651 ⊖ Waterloo
Palace Theatre, Shaftesbury Avenue, W1V 8AY T 020-7434 0909 ⊖ Leicester Square/Piccadilly Circus
Phoenix Theatre, Charing Cross Road, WC2H 0JP T 0870-060 6629 ⊖ Tottenham Court Road
Piccadilly Theatre, Denman Street, W1D 7DY T 020-8544 7424 ⊖ Piccadilly Circus
Playhouse Theatre, Northumberland Avenue, WC2N 5DE T 0870-060 6631 ⊖ Embankment
Prince Edward Theatre, Old Compton Street, W1D 4HS T 0870-850 9191 ⊖ Leicester Square
Prince of Wales Theatre, Coventry Street, W1D 6AS T 0870-850 0393 ⊖ Piccadilly Circus
Queen's Theatre, Shaftesbury Avenue, W1D 6BA T 0870-950 0930 ⊖ Piccadilly Circus
Royal Albert Hall, Kensington Gore, SW7 2AP T 020-7589 8212 ⊖ South Kensington
Royal Court Theatre, Sloane Square, SW1W 8AS T 020-7565 5000 ⊖ Sloane Square
Royal Festival Hall, South Bank SE1 8XX T 0871-663 2500 ⊖ Waterloo
Sadler's Wells, Rosebery Avenue, EC1R 4TN T 020-7863 819 ⊖ Angel
St Martin's Theatre, West Street, WC2H 9NZ T 0870-162 8787 ⊖ Leicester Square
Savoy Theatre, Strand, WC2R 0ET T 0870-164 8787 ⊖ Charing Cross
Shaftesbury Theatre, Shaftesbury Avenue, WC2H 8DP T 020-7379 5399 ⊖ Holborn/Tottenham Court Road
Soho Theatre, Dean Street, W1D 3NE T 020-7287 5060 ⊖ Tottenham Court Road
Southwark Playhouse, Southwark Bridge Road, SE1 0BL T 020-7620 3494 ⊖ Southwark
Theatre Royal Drury Lane, Catherine Street, WC2B 5JF T 020-7494 5000 ⊖ Covent Garden
Theatre Royal Haymarket, Haymarket, SW1Y 4HT T 020-7930 8890 ⊖ Piccadilly Circus
Trafalgar Studios, Whitehall, SW1A 2DY T 020-8544 7424 ⊖ Charing Cross/Embankment
Tricycle Theatre, Kilburn High Road, NW6 7JR T 020-7372 6611 ⊖ Kilburn
Vaudeville Theatre, Strand, WC2R 0NH T 020-7836 3191 ⊖ Charing Cross
Venue Theatre, Leicester Place, WC2H 7BP T 020-7734 600 ⊖ Leicester Square
Victoria Palace Theatre, Victoria Street, SW1E 5EA T 020-7834 3034 ⊖ Victoria
Wyndham's Theatre, Charing Cross Road, WC2H 0DA T 0870-060 6633 ⊖ Leicester Square
Young Vic, The Cut, SE1 8LZ T 020-7922 2922 ⊖ Waterloo

HALLMARKS

Hallmarks are the symbols stamped on gold, silver or platinum articles to indicate that they have been tested at an official Assay Office and that they conform to one of the legal standards. With certain exceptions, all gold, silver or platinum articles are required by law to be hallmarked before they are offered for sale. The marking of gold and silver articles to identify the maker was instituted in England in 1363 under a statute of Edward III. In 1478 the Assay Office in Goldsmiths' Hall was established and all gold and silversmiths were required to bring their wares to be date-marked by the Hall, hence the term 'hallmarked'.

MODERN HALLMARKS

Since 1 January 1999, UK hallmarks have consisted of three compulsory symbols – the sponsor's mark, the fineness (purity) mark and the assay office mark. Traditional marks such as the year date letter, the Britannia for 958 silver, the lion passant for 925 silver (lion rampant in Scotland) and the orb for 950 platinum may be added voluntarily. The distinction between UK and foreign articles has been removed, and more finenesses are now legal, reflecting the more common finenesses elsewhere in Europe.

SPONSOR'S MARK

Instituted in England in 1363, the sponsor's mark was originally a device such as a bird or fleur-de-lis. Now it consists of the initial letters of the name or names of the manufacturer or firm. Where two or more sponsors have the same initials, there is a variation in the surrounding shield or style of letters.

FINENESS (PURITY) MARK

The fineness (purity) mark indicates that the content of the precious metal in the alloy, from which the article is made, is not less than the legal standard. The legal standard is the minimum content of precious metal by weight in parts per thousand, and the standards are:

Gold	999	
	990	
	916.6	(22 carat)
	750	(18 carat)
	585	(14 carat)
	375	(9 carat)
Silver	999	
	958.4	(Britannia)
	925	(sterling)
	800	
Platinum	999	
	950	
	900	
	850	

ASSAY OFFICE MARK

This mark identifies the particular assay office at which the article was tested and marked. The British assay offices are:

LONDON, Goldsmiths' Hall, Gutter Lane, London EC2V 8AQ **T** 020-7606 8971 **W** www.thegoldsmiths.co.uk

BIRMINGHAM, PO Box 151, Newhall Street, Birmingham B3 1SB **T** 0121-236 6951 **W** www.theassayoffice.co.uk

SHEFFIELD, Guardians' Hall, 137 Portobello Street, Sheffield S1 4DS **T** 0114-275 5111 **W** www.assayoffice.co.uk

EDINBURGH, Goldsmiths' Hall, 24a Broughton Street, Edinburgh EH1 3RH **T** 0131-556 1144 **W** www.assayofficescotland.com

Assay offices formerly existed in other towns, eg Chester, Exeter, Glasgow, Newcastle, Norwich and York, each having its own distinguishing mark.

DATE LETTER

The date letter shows the year in which an article was assayed and hallmarked. Each alphabetical cycle has a distinctive style of lettering or shape of shield. The date letters were different at the various assay offices and the particular office must be established from the assay office mark before reference is made to tables of date letters. Date letter marks became voluntary from 1 January 1999.

The table which follows shows one specimen shield and letter used by the London Assay Office on silver articles for each alphabetical cycle from 1498. The same letters are found on gold articles but the surrounding shield may differ. Until 1 January 1975 two calendar years are given for each specimen date letter as the letter changed annually in May on St Dunstan's Day (the patron saint of silversmiths). Since 1 January 1975, each date letter has indicated a calendar year from January to December and each office has used the same style of date letter and shield for all articles:

LONDON (GOLDSMITHS' HALL) DATE LETTERS FROM 1498

from	*to*
 1498–9	1517–8
 1518–9	1537–8
 1538–9	1557–8
 1558–9	1577–8
 1578–9	1597–8
 1598–9	1617–8
 1618–9	1637–8
 1638–9	1657–8
 1658–9	1677–8
 1678–9	1696–7
 1697	1715–6
 1716–7	1735–6
 1736–7	1738–9
 1739–40	1755–6

from	*to*
 1756–7	1775–6
 1776–7	1795–6
 1796–7	1815–6
 1816–7	1835–6
 1836–7	1855–6
 1856–7	1875–6
 1876–7 [A to M square shield, N to Z as shown]	1895–6
 1896–7	1915–6
 1916–7	1935–6
 1936–7	1955–6
 1956–7	1974
 1975	1999
 2000	

OTHER MARKS

FOREIGN GOODS

Foreign goods imported into the UK are required to be hallmarked before sale, unless they already bear a convention mark (*see* below) or a hallmark struck by an independent assay office in the European Economic Area which is deemed to be equivalent to a UK hallmark.

The following are the assay office marks used for gold until the end of 1998. For silver and platinum the symbols remain the same but the shields differ in shape.

 *London*  *Sheffield*

 *Birmingham* *Edinburgh*

CONVENTION HALLMARKS

Special marks at authorised assay offices of the signatory countries of the International Convention on Hallmarking (Austria, the Czech Republic, Denmark, Finland, Hungary, Ireland, Latvia, Lithuania, the Netherlands, Norway, Poland, Portugal, Sweden, Switzerland, UK and Ukraine) are legally recognised in the United Kingdom as approved hallmarks. These consist of a sponsor's mark, a common control mark, a fineness mark (arabic numerals showing the standard in parts per thousand), and an assay office mark. There is no date letter.

The common control marks are:

GOLD SILVER PLATINUM

COMMEMORATIVE MARKS

There are other marks to commemorate special events: the silver jubilee of King George V and Queen Mary in 1935, the coronation of Queen Elizabeth II in 1953, and her silver jubilee in 1977. During 1999 and 2000 there was a voluntary additional Millennium Mark. A mark to commemorate the golden jubilee of Queen Elizabeth II was available during 2002.

BRITISH CURRENCY

The unit of currency is the pound sterling (£) of 100 pence. The decimal system was introduced on 15 February 1971.

COIN

Gold Coins
One hundred pounds £100*
Fifty pounds £50*
Twenty-five pounds £25*
Ten pounds £10*
Five pounds £5
Two pounds £2
Sovereign £1
Half-sovereign 50p

Silver Coins
(Britannia coins)*
Two pounds £2
One pound £1
Fifty pence 50p
Twenty pence 20p

Maundy Money†
Fourpence 4p
Threepence 3p
Twopence 2p
Penny 1p

Bi-colour Coins‡
Two pounds £2

Nickel-Brass Coins
Two pounds £2 (pre-1997)§
One pound £1

Cupro-Nickel Coins
Crown £5 (since 1990)
Fifty pence 50p
Crown 25p (pre-1990)
Twenty pence 20p
Ten pence 10p
Five pence 5p

Bronze Coins
Two pence 2p
One penny 1p

Copper-plated Steel Coins¶
Two pence 2p
One penny 1p

* Britannia coins: gold bullion coins introduced 1987; silver coins introduced 1997
† Gifts of special money distributed by the sovereign annually on Maundy Thursday to the number of aged poor men and women corresponding to the sovereign's own age
‡ Cupro-nickel centre and nickel-brass outer ring
§ Commemorative coins; not intended for general circulation
¶ Since September 1992, although in 1998 the 2p was struck in both copper-plated steel and bronze

GOLD COIN

Gold ceased to circulate during the First World War. Since then controls on buying, selling and holding gold coin have been imposed at various times but have subsequently been revoked. Under the Exchange Control (Gold Coins Exemption) Order 1979, gold coins may now be imported and exported without restriction, except gold coins which are more than 50 years old and valued at a sum in excess of £8,000; these cannot be exported without specific authorisation from the Department for Business, Enterprise and Regulatory Reform.

Value Added Taxation on the sale of gold coins was revoked in 2000.

SILVER COIN

Prior to 1920 silver coins were struck from sterling silver, an alloy of which 925 parts in 1,000 were silver. In 1920 the proportion of silver was reduced to 500 parts. From 1 January 1947 all 'silver' coins, except Maundy money, have been struck from cupro-nickel, an alloy of 75 parts copper and 25 parts nickel, except for the 20p, composed of 84 parts copper, 16 parts nickel. Maundy coins continue to be struck from sterling silver.

BRONZE COIN

Bronze, introduced in 1860 to replace copper, is an alloy of 97 parts copper, 2.5 parts zinc and 0.5 part tin. Bronze was replaced by copper-plated steel in September 1992 with the exception of 1998 when the 2p was made in both copper-plated steel and bronze.

LEGAL TENDER

Gold (dated 1838 onwards, if not below least current weight)	to any amount
£5 (Crown since 1990)*	to any amount
£2	to any amount
£1	to any amount
50p	up to £10
25p (Crown pre-1990)	up to £10
20p	up to £10
10p	up to £5
5p	up to £5
2p	up to 20p
1p	up to 20p

* Only redeemable at the Post Office

The £1 coin was introduced in 1983 to replace the £1 note. The following coins have ceased to be legal tender:

Farthing	31 December 1960
Halfpenny (½d)	1 July 1969
Half-crown	1 January 1970
Threepence	31 August 1971
Penny (1d)	31 August 1971
Sixpence	30 June 1980
Halfpenny (½p)	31 December 1984
Old 5 pence	31 December 1990
Old 10 pence	30 June 1993
Old 50 pence	28 February 1998

The Channel Islands and the Isle of Man issue their own coinage, which are legal tender only in the island of issue.

	Metal	*Standard weight (g)*	*Standard diameter (mm)*
1p	bronze	3.564	20.3
1p	copper-plated steel	3.564	20.3
2p	bronze	7.128	25.9
2p	copper-plated steel	7.128	25.9
5p	cupro-nickel	3.25	18.0
10p	cupro-nickel	6.5	24.5
20p	cupro-nickel	5.0	21.4
25p Crown	cupro-nickel	28.28	38.6
50p	cupro-nickel	8.00	27.3
£1	nickel-brass	9.5	22.5
£2	nickel-brass	15.98	28.4
£2	cupro-nickel, nickel-brass	12.00	28.4
£5 Crown	cupro-nickel	28.28	38.6

The 'remedy' is the amount of variation from standard permitted in weight and fineness of coins when first issued from the Mint.

THE TRIAL OF THE PYX

The Trial of the Pyx is the examination by a jury to ascertain that coins made by the Royal Mint, which have been set aside in the pyx (or box), are of the proper weight, diameter and composition required by law. The trial is held annually, presided over by the Queen's Remembrancer (the Senior Master of the Supreme Court), with a jury of freemen of the Company of Goldsmiths.

BANKNOTES

Bank of England notes are currently issued in denominations of £5, £10, £20 and £50 for the amount of the fiduciary note issue, and are legal tender in England and Wales. No £1 notes have been issued since 1984 and in March 1998 the outstanding notes were written off in accordance with the provision of the Currency Act 1983.

The current E series of notes was introduced from June 1990, replacing the D series (*see* below). A new-style £20 note, the first in series F, was introduced on 13 March 2007. The historical figures portrayed in these series are:

£5	May 2002–date	Elizabeth Fry
£5	June 1990–2003	George Stephenson*
£10	November 2000–date	Charles Darwin*
£10	April 1992–2003	Charles Dickens*
£20	March 2007–date	Adam Smith
£20	June 1999–date	Sir Edward Elgar
£20	June 1991–2001	Michael Faraday*
£50	April 1994–date	Sir John Houblon

* These notes have been withdrawn from circulation: George Stephenson on 21 November 2003; Charles Dickens on 31 July 2003; Michael Faraday on 28 February 2001

NOTE CIRCULATION

Note circulation is highest at the two peak spending periods of the year, around Christmas and during the summer holiday period.

The value of notes in circulation (£million) at the end of February 2005 and 2006 was:

	2006	*2007*
£5	1,051	1,100
£10	5,591	5,886
£20	22,690	23,740
£50	6,510	6,705
Other notes*	1,071	1,108
TOTAL	36,914	38,449

* Includes higher value notes used internally in the Bank of England, eg as cover for the note issues of banks in Scotland and Northern Ireland in excess of their permitted issue

LEGAL TENDER

Banknotes which are no longer legal tender are payable when presented at the head office of the Bank of England in London.

The white notes for £10, £20, £50, £100, £500 and £1,000, which were issued until April 1943, ceased to be legal tender in May 1945, and the white £5 note in March 1946.

The white £5 note issued between October 1945 and September 1956, the £5 notes issued between 1957 and 1963 (bearing a portrait of Britannia) and the first series to bear a portrait of the queen, issued between 1963 and 1971, ceased to be legal tender in March 1961, June 1967 and September 1973 respectively.

The series of £1 notes issued during the years 1928 to 1960 and the 10 shilling notes issued from 1928 to 1961 (those without the royal portrait) ceased to be legal tender in May and October 1962 respectively. The £1 note first issued in March 1960 (bearing on the back a representation of Britannia) and the £10 note first issued in February 1964 (bearing a lion on the back), both bearing a portrait of the Queen on the front, ceased to be legal tender in June 1979. The £1 note first issued in 1978 ceased to be legal tender on 11 March 1988. The 10 shilling note was replaced by the 50p coin in October 1969, and ceased to be legal tender on 21 November 1970.

The D series of banknotes was introduced from 1970 and ceased to be legal tender from the dates shown below. The predominant identifying feature of each note was the portrayal on the back of a prominent figure from British history:

£1	Feb. 1978–March 1988	Sir Isaac Newton
£5	Nov. 1971–Nov. 1991	Duke of Wellington
£10	Feb. 1975–May 1994	Florence Nightingale
£20	July 1970–March 1993	William Shakespeare
£50	March 1981–Sept. 1996	Sir Christopher Wren

The £1 coin was introduced on 21 April 1983 to replace the £1 note.

OTHER BANKNOTES

SCOTLAND – Banknotes are issued by three Scottish banks. The Royal Bank of Scotland issues notes for £1, £5, £10, £20, £50 and £100. Bank of Scotland and the Clydesdale Bank issue notes for £5, £10, £20, £50 and £100. Scottish notes are not legal tender in the UK but they are an authorised currency.

NORTHERN IRELAND – Banknotes are issued by four banks in Northern Ireland. The Bank of Ireland, the Northern Bank and the Ulster Bank issue notes for £5, £10, £20, £50 and £100. The First Trust Bank issues notes for £10, £20, £50 and £100. Northern Ireland notes are not legal tender in Northern Ireland but they circulate widely and enjoy a status comparable to that of Bank of England notes.

CHANNEL ISLANDS – The States of Guernsey issues its own currency notes and coinage. The notes are for £1, £5, £10, £20 and £50, and the coins are for 1p, 2p, 5p, 10p, 20p, 50p, £1, £2 and £5. The States of Jersey issues its own currency notes and coinage. The notes are for £1, £5, £10, £20 and £50, and the coins are for 1p, 2p, 5p, 10p, 20p, 50p, £1 and £2.

THE ISLE OF MAN – The Isle of Man government issues notes for £1, £5, £10, £20 and £50. Although these notes are only legal tender in the Isle of Man, they are accepted at face value in branches of the clearing banks in the UK. The Isle of Man issues coins for 1p, 2p, 5p, 10p, 20p, 50p, £1, £2 and £5.

Although none of the series of notes specified above is legal tender in the UK, they are generally accepted by banks irrespective of their place of issue. At one time banks made a commission charge for handling Scottish and Irish notes but this was abolished some years ago.

BANKING AND PERSONAL FINANCE

There are two main types of deposit-taking institutions: banks and building societies, although National Savings and Investments also provides savings products. Banks and building societies are supervised by the Financial Services Authority and National Savings and Investments is accountable to the Treasury. As a result of the conversion of several building societies into banks in the 1990s, the size of the banking sector, which was already substantially greater than the non-bank deposit-taking sector, increased further.

The main institutions within the British banking system are the Bank of England (the central bank), retail banks, investment banks and overseas banks. In its role as the central bank, the Bank of England acts as banker to the government and as a note-issuing authority; it also oversees the efficient functioning of payment and settlement systems.

Since May 1997, the Bank of England has had operational responsibility for monetary policy. At monthly meetings of its monetary policy committee the bank sets the interest rate at which it will lend to the money markets.

OFFICIAL INTEREST RATES 2001–7

8 November 2001	4.00%
6 February 2003	3.75%
10 July 2003	3.50%
6 November 2003	3.75%
5 February 2004	4.00%
6 May 2004	4.25%
10 June 2004	4.50%
5 August 2004	4.75%
4 August 2005	4.50%
3 August 2006	4.75%
9 November 2006	5.00%
11 January 2007	5.25%
10 May 2007	5.50%
5 July 2007	5.75%

RETAIL BANKING

Retail banks offer a wide variety of financial services to individuals and companies, including current and deposit accounts, loan and overdraft facilities, automated teller (cash dispenser) machines, cheque guarantee cards, credit and debit cards, investment services, pensions, insurance and mortgages. All banks offer telephone and internet banking facilities in addition to traditional branch services.

The Financial Ombudsman Service provides independent and impartial arbitration in disputes between banks and their customers (*see* Financial Services Regulation).

PAYMENT CLEARINGS

The Association for Payment Clearing Services (APACS) is the UK trade association for payments and for those institutions that deliver payment services to customers. It is also the banking industry's voice on payment issues regarding plastic cards, card fraud, cheques, electronic payments and cash. Membership of APACS is open to any member of a payment scheme which is widely used or significant in the UK. As at April 2007 APACS had 31 members, comprising the major banks, one building society and Royal Mail Group.

There are three separate companies which manage the majority of payment clearings in the UK (and which are contactable through APACS):

- BACS Payment Schemes Ltd manages the schemes under which electronic payments are made, processing direct debits, direct credits and standing orders
- CHAPS Ltd provides electronic same-day clearing for sterling and euro payments
- Cheque and Credit Clearing Company Ltd oversees the clearing of cheques and paper credits in Great Britain

APACS, Mercury House, Triton Court, 14 Finsbury Square, London EC2A 1LQ **T** 020-7711 6200 **W** www.apacs.org.uk

MAJOR RETAIL BANKS' FINANCIAL RESULTS 2006

Bank group	*Profit before taxation £ million*	*Profit after taxation £ million*	*Total assets £ million*
Abbey	183	68	191,805
Alliance and Leicester	569	450	68,557
Barclays	7,136	5,195	996,787
HBOS	5,706	3,934	591,029
HSBC	11,993	9,161	947,126
Lloyds TSB	4,248	2,907	343,598
Northern Rock	627	443	101,011
RBS Group	9,186	6,497	871,432

GLOSSARY OF FINANCIAL TERMS

AER (ANNUAL EQUIVALENT RATE) – A notional rate quoted on savings and investment products which demonstrates the return on interest, when compounded and paid annually.

APR (ANNUAL PERCENTAGE RATE) – Calculates the total amount of interest payable over the whole term of a product (such as investment or loan), allowing consumers to compare rival products on a like-for-like basis. Companies offering loans, credit cards, mortgages or overdrafts are required by law to provide the APR rate. Where typical APR is shown, it refers to the company's typical borrower and so is given as a best example; rate and costs may vary depending on individual circumstances.

ANNUITY – A type of insurance policy that provides regular income in exchange for a lump sum. Everyone who has a pension and has built up a lump sum with their provider must buy an annuity by the time they reach 75. The annuity can be bought from a company other than the existing pension provider.

ASU – Accident, sickness and unemployment insurance taken out by a borrower to protect against being unable to work for these reasons. The policy will usually pay a percentage of the normal monthly mortgage repayment if the borrower is unable to work.

ATM (AUTOMATED TELLER MACHINE) – Commonly referred to as cash machines. Users can access their bank accounts using a card for simple transactions such as withdrawing and depositing cash. Some banks and independent ATM deployers charge for transactions.

BANKER'S DRAFT – A cheque drawn on a bank against a cash deposit. Considered to be a secure way of receiving money in instances where a cheque could 'bounce' or where it is not desirable to receive cash.

BASE RATE – The minimum rate at which banks are prepared to lend money. This acts as a benchmark for all other interest rates.

BASIS POINT – Unit of measure (usually one-hundredth of a percentage point) used to express movements in interest rates, foreign rates or bond yields.

BUY-TO-LET – The purchase of a residential property for the sole purpose of letting to a tenant. Not all lenders provide mortgage finance for this purpose. Buy-to-let mortgages typically require at least a 15–25 per cent deposit and the loan agreed is based on a combination of the borrower's income in addition to the rental value of the property. Because of the higher risks involved in letting property, buy-to-let mortgages are more expensive.

CAPITAL GAIN/LOSS – Increase/decrease in the value of a capital asset when it is sold or transferred compared to its initial worth.

CAPPED RATE MORTGAGE – The interest rate applied to a loan is guaranteed not to rise above a certain rate for a set period of time; the rate can therefore fall but will not rise above the capped rate. The level at which the cap is fixed is usually higher than for a fixed rate mortgage for a comparable period of time. The lender normally imposes early redemption penalties within the first few years.

CASH CARD – Issued by banks and building societies for withdrawing cash from ATMs.

CHARGE CARD – Charge cards, eg American Express and Diners Club, can be used in a similar way to credit cards but the debt must be settled in full each month.

CHIP AND PIN CARD – A credit/debit card which incorporates an embedded chip containing unique owner details. When used with a PIN number, such cards offer greater security as they are less prone to fraud. Since 14 February 2006, most card transactions in the UK have required the use of a chip and pin card.

CREDIT CARD – Normally issued with a credit limit, credit cards can be used for purchases until the limit is reached. There is normally an interest-free period on the outstanding balance of up to 56 days. Charges can be avoided if the balance is paid off in full within the interest-free period. Alternatively part of the balance can be paid and in most cases there is a minimum amount set by the issuer (normally a percentage of the outstanding balance) which must be paid on a monthly basis. Some card issuers charge an annual fee and most issuers belong to a least one major credit card network, eg Mastercard or Visa.

CREDIT RATING – Overall credit worthiness of a borrower based on information from a credit reference agency, such as Experian or Equifax, which holds details of credit agreements, payment records, county court judgements etc for all adults in the UK. This information is supplied to lenders who use it in their credit scoring or underwriting systems to calculate the risk of granting a loan to an individual and the probability that it will be repaid. Each lender sets their own criteria for credit worthiness and may accept or reject a credit application based on an individual's credit rating.

CRITICAL ILLNESS COVER – Insurance that covers borrowers against critical illnesses such as stroke, heart attack or cancer and is designed to protect mortgage or other loan payments.

DEBIT CARD – Debit cards were introduced on a large scale in the UK in the mid-1980s, replacing cash and cheques to purchase goods and services. They can be used to withdraw cash from ATMs in the UK and abroad and may also function as a cheque guarantee card. Funds are automatically withdrawn from an individual's bank account after making a purchase and no interest is charged.

DISCOUNTED MORTGAGE – Discounted mortgages guarantee an interest rate set at a margin below the standard variable rate for a period of time. The discounted rate will move up or down with the standard variable rate, but the payment rate will retain the agreed differential below the standard variable rate. The lender normally imposes early redemption penalties within the first few years.

EARLY REDEMPTION PENALTY – *see* Redemption Penalty

ENDOWMENT MORTGAGE – Only the interest on a property loan is paid back to the lender each month as long as an endowment life insurance policy is taken out for an agreed amount of time, typically 25 years. When the policy matures the lender will take repayment of the money owed on the property loan and any surplus goes to the policyholder. If the endowment policy shows a shortfall on projected returns, the policy holder must make further provision to pay off the mortgage.

EQUITY – When applied to real estate, equity is the difference between the value of a property and the amount outstanding on any loan secured against it. Negative equity occurs when the loan is greater than the market value of the property.

FIXED RATE MORTGAGE – A repayment mortgage

where the interest rate on the loan is fixed for a set amount of time, normally a period of between one and ten years. The interest rate does not vary with changes to the base rate resulting in the monthly mortgage payment remaining the same for the duration of the fixed period. The lender normally imposes early redemption penalties within the first few years.

INTEREST ONLY MORTGAGE – Only interest is paid by the borrower and capital remains constant for the term of the loan. The onus is on the borrower to make provision to repay the capital at the end of the term. This is usually achieved through an investment vehicle such as an endowment policy or pension.

ISA – The individual savings account is a means by which investors can save and invest without paying any tax on the proceeds. Money can be invested across three investment elements: cash, stocks and shares and life insurance products. There are limits on the amount that can be invested during any given tax year.

LOAN TO VALUE – This is the ratio between the size of a mortgage loan sought and the mortgage lender's valuation. On a loan of £55,000, for example, on a property valued at £100,000 the loan to value is 55 per cent. This means that there is sufficient equity in the property for the lender to be reassured that if interest or capital repayments were stopped, it could sell the property and recoup the money owed. Fewer options are available to borrowers requiring high LTV.

MIG (MORTGAGE INDEMNITY GUARANTEE) – An insurance policy designed to protect the lender against loss in the event of the borrower defaulting or ceasing to repay a mortgage. It offers no protection to the borrower. Not all lenders charge MIG premiums.

ONLINE BANKING – Also known as internet or e-banking, where a range of banking transactions from paying bills, transferring funds to arranging overdrafts can be carried out online.

PERSONAL PENSION PLAN (PPP) – Designed for the self-employed or those in non-pensionable employment. Contributions made to a PPP are exempt from tax and the retirement age may be selected at any time from age 50 to 75. Up to 25 per cent of the pension fund may be taken as a tax-free cash sum on retirement.

PHISHING – A fraudulent attempt to obtain bank account details and security codes through an email. The email purports to come from a *bona fide* bank or building society and attempts to steer the recipient, usually under the pretext that the banking institution is updating its security arrangements, to a website which requests personal details.

PIN (PERSONAL IDENTIFICATION NUMBER) – A PIN is issued alongside a cash card to allow the user to access a bank account via an ATM. PINs are also issued with smart, credit and debit cards and, since 14 February 2006, have been requested in the majority of shops and restaurants as a further security measure when making a purchase.

PORTABLE MORTGAGE – A mortgage product that can be transferred to a different property in the event of a house move. Preferable where early redemption penalties are charged.

REDEMPTION PENALTY – A charge levied for paying off a loan, debt balance or mortgage before a date agreed with the lender.

REPAYMENT MORTGAGE – In contrast to the interest only mortgage, the monthly repayment includes an element of the capital sum borrowed in addition to the interest charged.

SELF-CERTIFICATION – Several lenders allow borrowers to self-certify their income. This type of scheme is useful to the self-employed who may not have accounts available or any other person who has difficulty proving their regular income.

SHARE – A share is a divided-up unit of the value of a company. If a company is worth £100 million, and there are 50 million shares in issue, then each share is worth £2 (usually listed as pence). As the overall value of the company fluctuates so does the share price.

SMART CARD – A new generation of cashless payment system. They carry more information than debit cards including mortgage and health details and a fixed number of units of real money. The card is used in conjunction with a PIN and once the money on the card is spent, it must be loaded again by transferring money to it from a bank account via an ATM or telephone.

TELEPHONE BANKING – Banking facilities which can be accessed via the telephone.

UNIT TRUST – A 'pooled' fund of assets, usually shares, owned by a number of individuals. Managed by professional, authorised fund-management groups, unit trusts have traditionally delivered better returns than average cash deposits, but do rise and fall in value as their underlying investment varies in value.

WITH-PROFITS – Usually applies to pensions, endowments, savings schemes or bonds. The intention is to smooth out the rises and falls in the stock market for the benefit of the investor. Actuaries working for the insurance company, or fund managers, hold back some profits in good years in order to make up the difference in years when shares perform badly.

VARIABLE RATE MORTGAGE – Repayment mortgages where the interest rate set by the lender increases or decreases in relation to the base interest rate which can result in fluctuating monthly repayments.

FINANCIAL SERVICES REGULATION

·INANCIAL SERVICES AUTHORITY

'he FSA has been the single regulator for financial ervices in the UK since 1 December 2001, when the 'inancial Services and Markets Act 2000 (FSMA) came nto force. The FSA's aim is to promote efficient, orderly nd fair financial markets and help retail consumers to eceive a fair deal.

The FSA is required to pursue four statutory objectives:

maintaining market confidence
raising public awareness
protecting consumers
reducing financial crime

'he legislation also requires the FSA to have regard to ne following principles while carrying out its general ınctions:

using its resources in an economic and efficient way
the responsibilities of regulated firms' own management
being proportionate in imposing burdens or restrictions on the industry
facilitating innovation
the international character of financial services and the competitive position of the United Kingdom
not impeding or distorting competition unnecessarily

)RGANISATION AND STRUCTURE

he FSA is a company limited by guarantee and financed y levies on the industry. It receives no funds from the ublic purse. It is accountable to treasury ministers and, ırough them, to parliament. The FSA must report nnually on the achievement of its statutory objectives to ne Treasury, which is required to lay the report before arliament.

The FSA's budgeted costs for 2007–8 are £301.7m.

SA REGISTER OF AUTHORISED FIRMS AND ERSONS

he FSA maintains a register of all firms that are ıthorised to carry out regulated activities. The entry for ıch firm gives its name, address and telephone number; a ·ference number; its authorisation status (outlining ·actly what regulated activities the firm is authorised to ırry out), stating which organisation regulates it, and hether it can handle client money. In addition the FSA eeps a list of approved persons in the industry who are ıthorised to carry out functions regulated by the FSA. ach entry includes a list of controlled functions an dividual is authorised to perform and for which firms.

NANCIAL SERVICES AUTHORITY
25 the North Colonnade, Canary Wharf, London E14 5HS
T 020-7066 1000 **Helpline** 0845-606 1234
W www.fsa.gov.uk
Chair, Sir Callum McCarthy
Chief Executive, vacant

:OMPENSATION

INANCIAL SERVICES COMPENSATION SCHEME

he Financial Services Compensation Scheme (FSCS) is independent statutory body created under the FSMA. It provides compensation if a firm authorised by the FSA is unable or likely to be unable to pay claims against it. This is usually when a firm becomes insolvent. The FSCS covers deposits, insurance policies, insurance broking (for business on or after 14 January 2005), investment business and mortgage advice and arranging (for business on or after 31 October 2004). The FSCS is independent of the FSA, with separate staff and premises. However, the FSA appoints the board of the FSCS and sets its guidelines. The FSCS is funded by levies on authorised firms.

FINANCIAL SERVICES COMPENSATION SCHEME
7th Floor, Lloyds Chambers, Portsoken Street, London E1 8BN
T 020-7892 7300 **E** enquiries@fscs.org.uk
W www.fscs.org.uk
Chair, David Hall
Chief Executive, Loretta Minghella

PENSION PROTECTION FUND

The Pension Protection Fund (PPF) is a statutory fund established under the Pensions Act 2004 that became operational on 6 April 2005. The fund was set-up to pay compensation to members of eligible defined benefit pension schemes, where there is a qualifying insolvency event in relation to the employer and where there are insufficient assets in the pension scheme to cover PPF levels of compensation. Compulsory annual levies are charged on all eligible schemes to help fund the PPF, in addition to investment of PPF assets.

PENSION PROTECTION FUND
Knollys House, 17 Addiscombe Road, Croydon, Surrey CR0 6SR **T** 0845-600 2541 **E** information@ppf.gsi.gov.uk
W www.pensionprotectionfund.org.uk
Chair, Lawrence Churchill
Chief Executive, Partha Dasgupta

DESIGNATED PROFESSIONAL BODIES

Professional firms are exempt from requiring direct regulation by the FSA if they carry out only certain restricted activities that arise out of, or are complementary to, the provision of professional services, such as arranging the sale of shares on the instructions of executors or trustees or providing services to small, private companies. These firms are, however, supervised by designated professional bodies (DPBs). There are a number of safeguards to protect consumers dealing with firms that do not require direct regulation. These arrangements include:

- the FSA's power to ban a specific firm from taking advantage of the exemption and to restrict the regulated activities permitted to the firms
- rules which require professional firms to ensure that their clients are aware that they are not authorised persons
- a requirement for the DPBs to supervise and regulate the firms and inform the FSA on how the professional firms carry on their regulated activities

See Professional Education section for the contact details of the following DPBs:

Institute of Chartered Accountants in England and Wales
Institute of Chartered Accountants in Scotland
Institute of Chartered Accountants in Ireland
Association of Chartered Certified Accountants
Institute of Actuaries
Law Society of England and Wales
Law Society of Northern Ireland
Law Society of Scotland

RECOGNISED INVESTMENT EXCHANGES

The FSA currently supervises six recognised investment exchanges (RIEs); under the FSMA, recognition confers an exemption from the need to be authorised to carry out regulated activities in the UK. The RIEs are organised markets on which member firms can trade investments such as equities and derivatives. As a regulator the FSA must focus on the impact of changes brought about by the continued growth in electronic trading by exchanges and other organisations. Issues such as how these changes affect market quality, reliability and access are important and the FSA works with the exchanges to ensure that new systems meet regulatory requirements. The RIEs are listed with their year of recognition in parentheses:

EUROPEAN DERIVATIVES EXCHANGE (EDX) LONDON (2003), 10 Paternoster Square, London EC4M 7LS **T** 020-7797 1000
W www.londonstockexchange.com/edx
(*see also* London Stock Exchange)

INTERCONTINENTAL EXCHANGE (ICE) FUTURES (2001)*, International House, 1 St Katharine's Way, London E1W 1UY **T** 020-7265 3648 **W** www.theice.com

LONDON INTERNATIONAL FINANCIAL FUTURES (LIFFE) ADMINISTRATION AND MANAGEMENT (2001), Cannon Bridge House, 1 Cousin Lane, London EC4R 3XX **T** 020-7623 0444 **W** www.liffe.com

LONDON STOCK EXCHANGE (LSE) (2001), 10 Paternoster Square, London EC4M 7LS
T 020-7797 1000 **W** www.londonstockexchange.com

NEW YORK MERCANTILE EXCHANGE (NYMEX) EUROPE (2005), 131 Finsbury Pavement, London EC2A 1NT **T** 020-7131 3001 **W** www.nymex.com

LONDON METAL EXCHANGE (2001), 56 Leadenhall Street, London EC3A 2BJ
T 020-7264 5555 **W** www.lme.co.uk

VIRT-X EXCHANGE (2001), 34th Floor, One Canada Square, Canary Wharf, London E14 5AA **T** 020-7864 4310
W www.virt-x.com

* Formerly the International Petroleum Exchange (IPE)

RECOGNISED CLEARING HOUSES

The FSA is also responsible for recognising and supervising recognised clearing houses (RCHs), which organise the settlement of transactions on recognised investment exchanges. There are two RCHs:

CREST CO LTD (2001), Watling House, 33 Cannon Street, London EC4M 5SB **T** 020-7849 0000 **W** www.crestco.co.uk

LONDON CLEARING HOUSE CLEARNET LTD (LCH.CLEARNET) (2001), Aldgate House, 33 Aldgate High Street, London EC3N 1EA **T** 020-7426 7000
W www.lchclearnet.com

OMBUDSMAN SCHEMES

The Financial Ombudsman Service was set up by the Financial Services and Markets Act 2000 to provide consumers with a free, independent service for resolving disputes with authorised financial firms. The Financial Ombudsman Service can consider complaints about most financial matters including: banking; credit cards and store cards; financial advice; hire purchase and pawnbroking; insurance; loans and credit; mortgages; pensions; savings and investments; stocks, shares, unit trusts and bonds.

Complainants must first complain to the firm involved. They do not have to accept the ombudsman's decision and are free to go to court if they wish, but if a decision is accepted, it is binding for both the complainant and the firm.

The Pensions Ombudsman can investigate and decide complaints and disputes about the way that occupational and personal pension schemes are administered and managed. The Pensions Ombudsman is also the Ombudsman for the board of the Pension Protection Fund (PPF) and as such can deal with disputes regarding decisions made by the board of the actions of PPF staff.

FINANCIAL OMBUDSMAN SERVICE, South Quay Plaza, 183 Marsh Wall, London E14 9SR **Helpline:** 0845-080 1800
T 020-7964 1000
E complaint.info@financial-ombudsman.org.uk
W www.financial-ombudsman.org.uk
Chief Ombudsman, Walter Merricks
Principal Ombudsmen, Tony Boorman; David Thomas

PENSIONS OMBUDSMAN, 11 Belgrave Road, London SW1V 1RB **T** 020-7834 9144
E www.enquiries@pensions-ombudsman.org.uk
W www.pensions-ombudsman.org.uk
Pensions Ombudsman/Pension Protection Fund Ombudsman, David Laverick

PANEL ON TAKEOVERS AND MERGERS

The Panel on Takeovers and Mergers is an independent body, established in 1968, whose main functions are to issue and administer the City code on takeovers and mergers. Its principal objective is to ensure equality of treatment and opportunity for all shareholders in takeover bids and mergers.

The panel comprises up to 34 members drawn from major financial and business institutions. The chair, deputy chair and up to 20 independent members are nominated by the panel's own nomination committee. The remaining members are nominated by professional bodies representing the banking, insurance, investment, pension and accountancy industries and the CBI.

PANEL ON TAKEOVERS AND MERGERS, 10 Paternoster Square, London EC4M 7DY
T 020-7382 9026 **W** www.thetakeoverpanel.org.uk
Chair, Peter Scott, QC

NATIONAL SAVINGS AND INVESTMENTS

Vational Savings and Investments (formerly National Savings) is one of the largest savings organisations in the JK, and is an executive agency of HM Treasury. Savings and investment products are offered to personal savers and investors and the money is used to manage the national debt more effectively. When people invest in National Savings and Investments they are lending money o the government which pays them interest or prizes in eturn.

TAX-FREE PRODUCTS

NATIONAL SAVINGS AND INVESTMENT CERTIFICATES

NDEX-LINKED SAVING CERTIFICATES

)therwise known as inflation-beating savings, index-inked saving certificates are fixed rate investments that ay tax-free returns guaranteed to be above inflation. 'hey are available in three- and five-year terms and are sold n issues. The minimum investment for each issue is £100 nd the maximum £15,000.

'IXED INTEREST SAVING CERTIFICATES

'ixed interest saving certificates are fixed rate investments hat pay tax-free returns. They are available in two- and ve-year terms and are sold in issues for which the ninimum investment is £100 and the maximum £15,000.

'REMIUM BONDS

ntroduced in 1956, premium bonds are an integral part f the government's management of national debt. They nable savers to enter a regular draw for tax-free prizes, vhile retaining the right to get their money back. A sum quivalent to interest on each bond is put into a prize und and distributed by monthly prize draws. The prizes re drawn by ERNIE (electronic random number ıdicator equipment) and are free of all UK income tax nd capital gains tax. The top prize is £1m.

Bonds are in units of £1, with a minimum purchase of 100; above this, purchases must be in multiples of £10, p to a maximum holding limit of £30,000 per person. onds become eligible for prizes once they have been eld for one clear calendar month following the month of urchase. Each £1 unit can win only one prize per draw, ut it will be awarded the highest for which it is drawn. onds remain eligible for prizes until they are repaid. /hen a holder dies, bonds remain eligible for prizes up to nd including the twelfth monthly draw after the month which the holder dies.

The scheme offers a facility to reinvest prize wins utomatically. Upon completion of an automatic prize einvestment mandate, holders receive new bonds which re immediately eligible for future prize draws. Bonds can nly be held in the name of an individual and not by rganisations.

As at March 2007, 149.75 million prizes totalling 9.5bn had been distributed since the first prize draw in 957.

CHILDREN'S BONUS BONDS

Children's bonus bonds were introduced in 1991. They can be bought for any child under 16 and will go on growing in value until he or she is 21. The bonds are sold in five-year issues at multiples of £25. For each issue the minimum holding is £25 and the maximum holding is £3,000 per child. Bonds for children under 16 must be held by a parent or guardian. All returns are totally exempt from UK income tax and a bonus is payable if the bond is held for the full five years.

OTHER PRODUCTS

GUARANTEED EQUITY BONDS

Guaranteed equity bonds are five-year investments where the returns are linked to the performance of the FTSE-100 index with a guarantee that the original capital invested will be returned even if the FTSE-100 index falls over the five years. They are sold in limited issues with a minimum investment of £1,000 and a maximum of £1m. The returns are subject to income tax on maturity, unless they are held in a self-invested pension plan (SIPP).

SAVINGS AND INVESTMENT ACCOUNTS

The easy access savings account was launched in January 2004 replacing the ordinary account (also known as the Post Office savings account). The easy access savings account offers access to savings via Post Office counters, an ATM card, telephone and online. It can be opened with a minimum balance of £100 and has a maximum limit of £2m (£4m jointly). The interest is paid without deduction of tax at source. Holders of the ordinary account can no longer undertake transactions except for closing the account or transferring the funds to an easy access savings account or the investment account.

The investment account is a passbook account which pays tiered rates of interest and requires one month's notice for withdrawals. Repayments are made without notice or penalty. It can be opened with a minimum balance of £20 and has a maximum limit of £100,000. The interest is paid without deduction of tax at source.

Since April 1999 National Savings and Investments has offered cash mini individual savings accounts (ISAs). A cash mini ISA can be opened online, by post, telephone and in post offices with a minimum investment of £10. A direct ISA was launched in April 2006 which can be opened by telephone and online with a minimum investment of £1,000. Interest for both ISAs is calculated daily and is free of tax.

INCOME BONDS

National Savings and Investments income bonds were introduced in 1982. They are suitable for those who want to receive regular monthly payments of interest while preserving the full cash value of their capital. The bonds are sold in multiples of £500. The minimum holding is £500 and the maximum £1m (sole or joint holding). Interest is calculated on a day-to-day basis and paid monthly. Interest is taxable but is paid without deduction of tax at source. Since August 2005, there is no penalty or notice required for making withdrawals.

PENSIONERS GUARANTEED INCOME BONDS
Pensioners guaranteed income bonds were introduced in January 1994 and are designed for people aged 60 and over who wish to receive regular monthly payments with a rate of interest that is fixed for a period whilst preserving the full cash value of their investment. Five-, two- and one-year terms are available and are sold in issues. The minimum limit for each issue is £500. The maximum holding is £1m (sole or joint holding) with the rate of interest fixed and guaranteed for each bond purchased. Interest is taxable but is paid without deduction of tax at source. The original capital investment is repaid in full at the end of the term.

FIXED RATE SAVINGS BOND
Fixed rate savings bonds are investments that earn fixed rates of interest. Five-, three- and one-year terms are available and are sold in issues. The minimum investment is £500 and the maximum £1m. Interest, from which basic rate tax is deducted at source, can be paid out or reinvested into the bond monthly, annually or at the end of the term. Holders can also choose where the interest is paid. The original capital investment is repaid in full at the end of the term.

CAPITAL BONDS
National Savings and Investments capital bonds were introduced in 1989. Five-year capital bonds are sold in issues. The interest is taxable each year (for those who pay income tax) but is not deducted at source. For each issue the minimum investment is £100 and the maximum £1m Capital bonds are repaid in full with all interest gained at the end of five years.

TREASURER'S ACCOUNT
The treasurer's account, introduced in September 1996 offers attractive rates and security to non-profit making organisations such as charities, friendly societies and clubs. The minimum holding is £10,000 and the maximum is £2m.

FURTHER INFORMATION
Further information can be obtained from the Pos Office, by telephone (T 0845-964 5000) or online (W www.nsandi.com).

THE LONDON STOCK EXCHANGE

The London Stock Exchange serves the needs of industry and investors by providing facilities for raising capital and a central market place for securities trading. This market place covers government stocks (called gilts), UK and overseas company shares (called equities and fixed interest stocks), and other instruments such as covered warrants and exchange traded funds (ETFs).

PRIMARY MARKETS

The London Stock Exchange enables companies to raise capital for development and growth through the issue of securities. For a company entering the market for the first time there is a choice of exchange markets, depending upon the size, history and requirements of the company. The first is the main market. A company's securities are admitted to the official list by the Financial Services Authority (FSA), which acts as the UK Listing Authority.

The Alternative Investment Market (AIM) was established in June 1995. It enables small, young and growing companies to raise capital, widen their investor base and have their shares traded on a regulated market without the expense of a full London Stock Exchange listing. Many companies use AIM as a stepping-stone to a full listing.

A third market, the Professional Securities Market (PSM), was established in July 2005, to coincide with the introduction of the FSA's new listing rules. PSM provides a solution to issuers who want to list their debt securities or depository receipts in London without having to restate their financial information to conform with international financial reporting standards.

Once admitted, all companies are obliged to keep their shareholders informed of their progress, making announcements of a price-sensitive nature through a primary information provider approved by the FSA.

At 31 December 2006 there were 3,256 companies listed on the London Stock Exchange: 1,276 were main market UK-listed, with an equity market value of £1,931.9bn; 330 main market internationally listed, with an equity market value of £2,373.7bn; 1,634 listed on AIM, with a market value of £90.7bn; and 16 equity only companies listed on PSM.

UK equity turnover in 2006 was £3,210.5bn with a total number of 89.6 million equity bargains. International equity turnover in 2006 totalled £3,447.7bn with a total number of 21.8 million equity bargains.

'BIG BANG'

During 1986 the London Stock Exchange went through the greatest period of change in its 200-year history. In March 1986 it opened its doors for the first time to overseas and corporate membership, allowing banks, insurance companies and overseas securities houses to become members of the exchange and to buy existing member firms. On 27 October 1986, three major reforms took place and became known as Big Bang:

- the abolition of scales of minimum commissions, allowing clients to negotiate freely with their brokers about the charge for their services
- the abolition of the separation of member firms into brokers and jobbers: firms are now broker/dealers, able to act as agents on behalf of clients; to act as principals buying and selling shares for their own account; and to become registered market makers, making continuous buying and selling prices in specific securities
- the introduction of the Stock Exchange automated quotations system (SEAQ)

Since the introduction of SEAQ in 1986, dealing in stocks and shares has taken place by telephone in the firms' own dealing rooms, rather than face to face on the floor of the exchange. The Stock Exchange electronic trading service (SETS), launched in 1997, introduced order-driven trading in which deals are executed electronically on an electronic order book. SETS runs alongside SEAQ and allows remote access to the exchange. The new systems also provide increased investor protection. All deals taking place via the exchange systems are recorded on a database which can be used to resolve disputes or to carry out investigations.

Firms trading on the London Stock Exchange buy and sell shares on behalf of the public, as well as institutions such as pension funds or insurance companies. In return for transacting the deal, the broker will charge a commission, which is usually based upon the value of the transaction. The market makers, or wholesalers, in each security do not charge a commission for their services, but will quote the broker two prices, a price at which they will buy and a price at which they will sell. It is the middle of these two prices which is published in lists of share prices in newspapers.

REGULATION

The FSA has overall responsibility for regulating the UK's financial industry under the provisions of the Financial Services and Markets Act 2000. The Act compels business to be conducted through a recognised investment exchange (RIE). The London Stock Exchange is an RIE, regulating three main markets: UK equities, international equities and gilts.

DEVELOPMENTS

On 15 March 2000, the 298 members voted to become shareholders in a demutualised London Stock Exchange, making possible the further commercialisation of the company.

At the end of May 2001 the exchange announced its intention to list on its own main market. The exchange was listed on 20 July 2001 following an annual general meeting the previous day. The full listing is intended to enable the exchange to exploit business opportunities with greater flexibility.

In 2003 the London Stock Exchange created EDX London (European derivatives exchange), a recognised investment exchange for international equity derivatives.

LONDON STOCK EXCHANGE, 10 Paternoster Square, London EC4M 7LS **T** 020-7797 1000
W www.londonstockexchange.com
Chair, Chris Gibson-Smith
Chief Executive, Clara Furse

INSURANCE

AUTHORISATION AND REGULATION OF INSURANCE COMPANIES

Since 2001, the Financial Services Authority (FSA) has been the authorising, enforcement, supervisory and rule-making body of insurers. Since 2005, this has also included insurance brokers.

The FSA's powers are primarily conferred by the Financial Services and Markets Act 2000, which unified the previous sectoral arrangements and regulators.

AUTHORISATION

The FSA's role is to ensure that firms to which it grants authorisation satisfy the necessary financial criteria, that the senior management of the company are 'fit and proper persons' and that unauthorised firms are not permitted to trade. This part of the FSA's role was previously undertaken by HM Treasury under the Insurance Companies Act 1982, which was repealed when the Financial Services and Markets Act came fully into force. At the end of 2006 there were over 1,000 insurance organisations and friendly societies with authorisation from the FSA to transact one or more classes of insurance business in the UK. However, the single European insurance market, established in 1994, gave insurers authorised in any other European Union country automatic UK authorisation without further formality. This means a potential market of over 5,000 insurance companies.

REGULATION

All life insurers, general insurers, reinsurers, insurance and reinsurance brokers, and composite firms are statutorily regulated. This is achieved through the formulation (after consultation) by the FSA of rules and guidance for regulated organisations. The FSA is also responsible for consumer education and the reduction of financial crime, particularly money laundering.

FINANCIAL SERVICES AUTHORITY, 25 The North Colonnade, London E14 5HS **T** 020-7066 1000 **W** www.fsa.gov.uk

COMPLAINTS

Disputes between policyholders and insurers can be referred to the Financial Ombudsman Service (FOS). Policyholders with a complaint against their financial services provider must firstly take the matter to the highest level within the company. Thereafter, if it remains unresolved and it involves an amount below £100,000, they can refer, free of charge, to the Ombudsman Bureau, which examines the facts of a complaint and delivers a decision binding on the insurer (but not the policyholder). Small businesses with a turnover of up to £1m also have access to the scheme. The Financial Ombudsman Service also covers other areas of the financial services industry including banks, building societies and investment firms.

FINANCIAL SERVICES OMBUDSMAN SERVICE, South Quay Plaza, 183 Marsh Wall, London E14 9SR **T** 020-7964 1000 **F** 020-7964 1002 **W** www.financial-ombudsman.org.uk
Chief Ombudsman, Walter Merricks

ASSOCIATION OF BRITISH INSURERS

Over 94 per cent of the domestic business of UK insurance companies is transacted by the 380 members of the Association of British Insurers (ABI). ABI is a trade association which protects and promotes the interests of all its insurance company members. Only insurers authorised in EU countries are eligible for membership. Brokers, intermediaries and claims handlers may not join ABI but may have their own trade associations.

ASSOCIATION OF BRITISH INSURERS (ABI), 51 Gresham Street, London EC2V 7HQ **W** www.abi.org.uk
Chair, Archie Kane
Director-General, Stephen Haddrill

BALANCE OF PAYMENTS

The financial services industry contributes 8.5 per cent to the UK's gross domestic product (GDP). In 2005 insurance companies generated net exports of £1.6bn, a drop of two-thirds on 2004 caused largely by claims in the aftermath of Hurricane Katrina and a fall in reinsurance business.

TAKEOVERS AND MERGERS

2006 continued to be a very quiet period for takeovers and mergers in the insurance sector. The most significant development was the takeover of GE Insurance by Swiss Reinsurance.

GENERAL INSURANCE

In recent years, measures to combat fraud and guard against climate change have dominated every annual review of general insurance. After the heavy flooding in the UK in 1953, home and property insurers responded to consumer demand by offering flood insurance cover to all areas of the UK. At the time, the comparatively rare instance of flooding meant the average cost of such cover was minimal.

Times and circumstances have since changed and although insurers are still able to offer flood cover, they maintain they can only do so as long as the government is able to continue adequate funding for flood defences. During 2006 and 2007, it became clear that government funding for defences needed a ten per cent increase to prevent breaches by rising sea levels causing substantial damage. Managing risks relating to climate change remains a top priority for general insurers.

Insurance fraud also remains a problem. In 2005 insurers exposed and stopped frauds worth over £400m, an increase of 50 per cent on 2004. To tackle this, after a pilot period of six months, the Insurance Fraud Bureau (**W** www.insurancefraudbureau.org.uk) was launched in July 2006. This new body was designed to combat insurance fraud in all its forms, whether opportunist – policyholders who exaggerate claims – or organised – premeditated and planned by criminal gangs with proceeds used to fund other crimes. It is not clear how quickly the results of the Bureau's work can be quantified, but some early successes have been recorded.

With average premiums rising for all types of private motorists during the year, the spotlight fell on two types of driver most likely to face higher premiums: newly qualified and older drivers. Pressure groups such as Age Concern and Help the Aged argued that increased premiums may force older drivers to give up driving and rob them of much of their mobility. Insurers countered these concerns by citing statistical data demonstrating that the frequency of accidents increases heavily once a driver passes 70.

An report produced for ABI, published in July 2006, highlighted that younger drivers are ten times more likely to be involved in a serious or fatal accident than a driver aged 40. The report called for measures to reduce road deaths in this age group. These included limiting the times of day when a young driver can be on the road, restricting the number of passengers he or she can carry and creating a 12-month probationary period for newly qualified drivers. Although popular with media and road safety groups, there has been no sign the government is willing to introduce these proposals.

Claims figures were unremarkable with no striking rises of falls. The highest change was a 34.2 per cent increase in the cost of domestic subsidence claims.

LONDON INSURANCE MARKET

The London Insurance Market is a unique wholesale marketplace and a distinct, separate sector of the UK insurance and reinsurance industry. It is the world's leading market for internationally traded insurance and reinsurance, its business comprising mainly overseas non-life large and high-exposure risks. The market is centred on the City of London, which provides the required financial, banking, legal and other support services. Over 50 per cent of London market business is transacted at Lloyd's, 44 per cent through insurance companies and 3 per cent through protection and indemnity clubs. In 2005, the market had a written gross premium income of over £28bn. Around 150 Lloyd's brokers service the market.

The trade association for the international insurers and reinsurers writing primarily non-marine insurance and all classes of reinsurance business in the London market is the International Underwriting Association (IUA).

INTERNATIONAL UNDERWRITING ASSOCIATION, London Underwriting Centre, 3 Mincing Lane, London EC3R 7DD
W www.iua.co.uk

BRITISH INSURANCE COMPANIES

The following insurance company figures refer to members and certain non-members of the ABI.

WORLDWIDE GENERAL BUSINESS UNDERWRITING RESULTS *(£m)*

	2004			*2005*		
	UK	*Overseas*	*Total*	*UK*	*Overseas*	*Total*
Motor						
Premiums	10,154	3,326	13,480	10,397	3,412	13,809
Profit (loss)	(72)	(48)	(24)	(191)	221	30
Percentage of premiums	0.7	1.4	0.18	1.8	6.5	0.2
Non-motor						
Premiums	19,340	5,343	24,646	20,081	6,055	26,136
Profit (loss)	1,370	(139)	1,079	1,371	607	1,978
Percentage of premiums	7.1	2.6	4.4	6.8	10.0	7.6

CLAIMS STATISTICS *(£m)*

	2002	*2003*	*2004*	*2005*	*2006*
Theft	728	630	512	475	517
Fire	1,045	1,067	812	1,128	1,139
Weather	1,258	610	424	735	475
Domestic subsidence	183	390	199	225	302
Business interruption	236	92	108	267	168
Total	3,490	2,738	2,052	2,851	2,601

NET PREMIUM INCOME BY SECTOR 2005 *(£m)*

	UK	*Overseas*
Motor	10,397	3,412
Non-motor	20,081	6,055
Marine, aviation and transport	576	223
Reinsurance	910	204
Total general business	31,964	9,894
Ordinary long-term	99,270	24,984
Industrial long-term	303	–
Total long-term business	99,572	24,984

WORLDWIDE GENERAL BUSINESS TRADING RESULTS *(£m)*

	2004	*2005*
Net written premiums	40,204	42,103
Underwriting results	1,321	1,831
Investment income	4,133	6,198
Overall trading profit	5,454	8,029
Profit as percentage of premium income	13.6	19.1

LLOYD'S OF LONDON

Lloyd's of London is an international market for almost all types of general insurance. Lloyd's currently has a capacity to accept insurance premiums of around £13.7bn. Much of this business comes from outside Great Britain and makes a valuable contribution to the balance of payments.

A policy is underwritten at Lloyd's by a mixture of private and corporate members, corporate members having been admitted for the first time in 1992. Specialist underwriters accept insurance risks at Lloyd's on behalf of members (referred to as 'Names') grouped in syndicates. There are currently 62 syndicates of varying sizes, each managed by an underwriting agent approved by the Council of Lloyd's.

Individual members are still in the majority at Lloyd's with a total of 1,124 individuals as opposed to 1,017 corporate members. In 2006, the market capacity of the corporate sector was £14,989m (93.1 per cent) while individuals represented £1,111m (6.9 per cent) of capacity.

Lloyd's is incorporated by an act of parliament (Lloyd's Acts 1971 onwards) and is governed by an 18-person council, made up of six working, six external and six nominated members. The structure immediately below this changed when, in 2002, Lloyd's members voted at an extraordinary general meeting to implement a new franchise system for the market with the aim of improving profitability. The first move was the introduction of a new governance structure, replacing the Lloyd's Market Board and the Lloyd's Regulatory Board with a new 11-person Lloyd's Franchise Board. Four main committees report to this new board.

The corporation is a non-profit making body chiefly financed by its members' subscriptions. It provides the premises, administrative staff and services enabling Lloyd's underwriting syndicates to conduct their business. It does not, however, assume corporate liability for the risks accepted by its members. Individual members are responsible to the full extent of their personal means for their underwriting affairs unless they have converted to limited liability companies (known as NameCos).

Lloyd's syndicates have no direct contact with the public. All business is transacted through insurance brokers accredited by the Corporation of Lloyd's. In addition, non-Lloyd's brokers in the UK, when guaranteed by Lloyd's brokers, are able to deal directly with Lloyd's motor syndicates, a facility which has made the Lloyd's market more accessible to the insuring public.

The FSA has ultimate responsibility for the regulation of the Lloyd's market. However, in situations where Lloyd's internal regulatory and compensation arrangements are more far-reaching – as for example with the Lloyd's Central Fund which safeguards claim payments to policyholders – the regulatory role is delegated to the Council of Lloyd's.

Lloyd's also provides the most comprehensive shipping intelligence service in the world. The shipping and other information received from Lloyd's agents, shipowners, news agencies and other sources throughout the world is collated and distributed to the media as well as to the maritime and commercial sectors in general. *Lloyd's List* is London's oldest daily newspaper and contains news of general commercial interest as well as shipping information. It has been independent of Lloyd's since a management buy-out in 1992. *Lloyd's Shipping Index,* also published daily, lists some 25,000 ocean-going vessels in alphabetical order and gives the latest known report of each.

DEVELOPMENTS IN 2006

After the small loss of £103m in 2005, Lloyd's recorded a profit of £3,662m in 2006. This was largely due to the lack of serious losses during the hurricane season. The only reported major event was Hurricane Kyrill with estimates of £1.4–5.4bn. However, the loss to the Lloyd's market is estimated at only £200m.

Claims from damage caused by Hurricane Katrina in 2005 pushed up premium rates in the United States. Elsewhere there was evidence that the market was softening. Gross premiums rose by 9.6 per cent.

Despite the profits recorded in all segmental areas, increased capacity and new syndicates joining the market, some experts believe that increased hurricane activity and the ever-present terrorist threat could ensure that the 2006 result is the exception rather than the rule for the future.

LLOYD'S OF LONDON, One Lime Street, London EC3M 7HA
T 020-7327 1000 W www.lloydsoflondon.co.uk
Chair, Lord Levene of Portsoken
Chief Executive, Richard Ward

LLOYD'S MEMBERSHIP

	2005	*2006*
Individual	1,497	1,124
Corporate	714	1,017

TOTAL MARKET CAPACITY *(£m)*

	2005	*2006*
Individual (unlimited liability)	1,445	1,124
Individual (limited liability)	927	927
Corporate	11,328	12,427
Total	13,700	14,788

LLOYD'S SEGMENTAL RESULTS 2006 *(£m)*

	Gross premiums written	*Net earned premium*	*Result*
Reinsurance	5,547	4,186	802
Casualty	3,572	2,964	327
Property	3,638	2,730	495
Marine	1,153	921	105
Motor	923	829	30
Energy	1,125	737	9
Aviation	393	278	97
Life	50	40	2
Total from syndicate operations	16,411	12,685	1,867

LIFE AND LONG-TERM INSURANCE AND PENSIONS

Pensions and savings were the dominant issues for life and pensions insurers during 2006. April saw the publication of the final report from the Pensions Commission, a body set up to review pension provision in the UK. Although the report dealt mainly with state provision, there were some important proposals for the private sector. A delivery authority is to be responsible for introducing a new type of pension, which is designed to help those on lower incomes make adequate provision for their retirement.

Among the measures proposed by Lord Turner's reports were mandatory employer contributions and automatic enrolment for every person with no other form of pension provision. This latter proposal was widely welcomed but still faces some barriers as the EU distance marketing directive prohibits use of such measures. The test of success for personal accounts will not be the number of people who enrol into them but the amount of new money they attract, as many fear that investors may simply transfer their existing savings into these new accounts for a better deal.

A number of new regulatory initiatives were announced by the FSA during the year. These were designed to move the regulatory emphasis away from prescriptive rulebooks to a more principles-based approach, a move welcomed by the industry.

In June, the FSA announced a distribution review designed to examine the way the financial services industry markets and sells its products. Issues to be covered include the professionalism and reputation of the industry; access to financial products; the impact of insurers paying commission to sales staff and intermediaries; and the sustainability of the market. The results of the review were expected to be announced in June 2007.

Although the issues of genetic testing and insurance continued to be discussed in the media during 2006, no alteration to the existing moratorium between life insurers and the government's genetic and insurance advisory committee was sought. In February 2006, the ABI wrote to the government confirming that they would not be applying to use predictive genetic test results in underwriting during 2006 or 2007.

The year ended with a warning from life insurers for policyholders who had complaints about mis-sold endowment policies. A survey had revealed that policyholders who used claims management companies to help them with their claims received, on average, £1,400 in compensation after their fees were deducted. Customers who used the process without help received £3,200. The total amount of compensation paid to the 1.8 million customers that were mis-sold endowments had reached £2.7bn by the end of 2006. Overall, the industry had a better year in 2006 with increases recorded in both single premium and regular premium new business.

PAYMENTS TO POLICYHOLDERS *(£m)*

	2004	*2005*
Payments to UK policyholders	93,653	108,798
Payments to overseas policyholders	13,766	13,447
Total	107,301	122,245

WORLDWIDE LONG-TERM PREMIUM INCOME *(£m)*

	2001	*2002*	*2003*	*2004*	*2005*
UK Life Insurance					
Regular Premium	12,226	12,015	11,777	10,507	10,544
Single Premium	25,340	23,731	17,010	20,516	25,488
Total	37,566	35,746	28,787	31,023	36,032
Individual Pensions					
Regular Premium	7,821	8,547	8,059	8,973	7,959
Single Premium	17,702	19,443	14,278	12,036	11,642
Total	25,523	27,990	22,337	21,009	19,601
Other Pensions					
Regular Premium	3,563	3,744	4,239	4,183	4,717
Single Premium	24,981	26,682	29,052	25,836	34,822
Total	28,544	30,426	33,291	30,019	39,539
Other (eg Income protection, Annuities)	1,806	1,922	5,502	4,994	4,400
TOTAL UK PREMIUM INCOME	93,439	96,084	89,917	87,045	99,572
Overseas Premium Income					
Regular Premium	6,933	7,436	7,958	7,692	8,089
Single Premium	17,069	17,833	14,464	16,075	16,890
Total	24,002	25,269	22,422	23,767	24,979
TOTAL WORLDWIDE PREMIUM INCOME	117,441	121,353	112,339	110,812	124,551

PRIVATE MEDICAL INSURANCE

	2002	*2003*	*2004*	*2005*	*2006*
Number of people covered (thousand)	6,191	6,080	5,820	5,820	5,879
Corporate	4,304	4,207	4,084	4,125	4,188
Personal	1,887	1,873	1,736	1,695	1,691
Gross Earned Premiums (£m)	2,710	2,816	2,855	2,942	3,070
Corporate	1,341	1,394	1,433	1,493	1,561
Personal	1,369	1,422	1,422	1,449	1,509
Gross Claims Incurred (£m)	2,136	2,203	2,188	2,255	2,376

INVESTMENTS OF INSURANCE COMPANIES 2005

Investment of funds	*Long-term business (£m)*	*General business (£m)*
Index-linked British government securities	38,687	2,401
Non-index-linked British government securities	120,277	15,310
Other UK public sector debt securities	21,384	507
Overseas government, provincial and municipal securities	38,039	11,986
Debentures, loan shares, preference and guaranteed stocks and shares		
UK	137,666	11,885
Overseas	98,891	14,878
Ordinary stocks and shares UK	293,783	9,258
Overseas	164,578	3,552
Unit trusts		
Equities	107,290	1,759
Fixed interest	27,012	479
Loans secured on property	20,634	3,080
Real property and ground rents	66,564	1,623
Other invested assets	86,610	31,398
Total invested assets	1,221,414	108,116
NET INVESTMENT INCOME	62,744	6,198

NEW BUSINESS

	2002	*2003*	*2004*	*2005*	*2006*
New regular premiums					
Investment and savings	253	186	109	85	70
Collective investment schemes	417	337	463	535	620
Other stakeholder products	n/a	n/a	n/a	31	22
Individual protection	1,055	1,117	977	1,046	1,033
Group protection	284	273	385	387	314
Individual pension	2,233	1,859	1,864	2,127	3,023
Group pension	804	862	802	766	753
Offshore business	n/a	n/a	n/a	26	22
TOTAL REGULAR	5,047	4,633	4,599	5,004	5,858
New single premiums					
Investments and savings	22,894	16,372	20,150	23,957	30,326
Collective investment schemes	7,314	7,643	8,380	10,866	17,670
Other stakeholder products	n/a	n/a	n/a	164	201
Individual protection	1,001	1,264	1,606	1,698	1,634
Individual pension	11,766	10,551	10,621	12,164	18,757
Pension annuities and income drawdown	9,577	9,208	9,022	9,375	12,207
Group pension	7,609	5,760	4,385	6,544	8,428
Offshore business	n/a	n/a	n/a	4,804	7,150
TOTAL SINGLE	60,161	50,800	54,161	69,572	96,374

ECONOMIC STATISTICS

All data is for the UK unless otherwise stated.

ABBREVIATIONS

AAS	*Annual Abstract of Statistics*
ST	*Social Trends*

THE BUDGET (2007)

GOVERNMENT RECEIPTS

	Outturn 2005–6	*Estimate 2006–7*	*Projection 2007–8*
			£ billion
HM Revenue and Customs (HMRC)			
Income tax (gross of tax credits)	135.0	146.9	156.9
Income tax credits	–4.5	–4.7	–4.4
National insurance contributions (NIC)	85.5	88.0	95.1
Value added tax	72.9	77.3	80.0
Corporation tax[1]	42.4	44.9	50.0
Corporation tax credits[2]	–0.5	–0.5	–0.5
Petroleum revenue tax	2.0	2.2	1.6
Fuel duties	23.4	23.6	25.1
Capital gains tax	3.0	3.9	4.6
Inheritance tax	3.3	3.6	4.0
Stamp duties	10.9	13.4	14.3
Tobacco duties	8.0	8.1	8.1
Spirits duties	2.3	2.2	2.3
Wine duties	2.3	2.4	2.5
Beer and cider duties	3.2	3.3	3.4
Betting and gaming duties	1.4	1.4	1.4
Air passenger duty	0.9	1.0	2.1
Insurance premium tax	2.3	2.3	2.4
Landfill tax	0.7	0.8	0.9
Climate change levy	0.7	0.7	0.7
Aggregates levy	0.3	0.3	0.3
Customs duties and levies	2.3	2.3	2.4
TOTAL HMRC	398.0	423.6	453.4
Vehicle excise duties	5.0	5.1	5.6
Business rates	19.9	21.3	22.1
Council tax[3]	21.4	22.4	23.5
Other taxes and royalties[4]	12.7	13.4	14.5
NET TAXES AND NIC[5]	456.8	485.7	519.2
Accruals adjustments on taxes	1.4	3.4	2.4
Less own resources contribution to European Commission (EC) budget	–4.3	–4.7	–4.1
Less private company corporation tax payments	–0.2	–0.2	–0.2
Tax credits adjustment[6]	0.6	0.5	0.6
Interest and dividends	6.7	6.0	7.1
Other receipts[7]	24.7	26.5	28.0
CURRENT RECEIPTS	485.7	517.2	553.0
North Sea revenues[8]	9.7	9.1	8.1

1 National accounts measure: gross of enhanced and payable tax credits
2 Includes enhanced company tax credits
3 Council tax figures are projections based on stylised assumptions and are not government forecasts as increases are determined annually by local authorities
4 Includes VAT refunds and money paid into the National Lottery Distribution Fund
5 Includes VAT and 'traditional own resources' contributions to EC budget
6 Tax credits which are scored as negative tax in the calculation of net taxes and NIC but expenditure in the national accounts
7 Includes gross operating surplus and rent; net of oil royalties and business rate payments by local authorities
8 Consists of North Sea corporation tax, petroleum revenue tax and royalties

Source: HM Treasury – *Budget 2007* (Crown copyright)

GOVERNMENT EXPENDITURE

The Economic and Fiscal Strategy Report in June 1998 introduced changes to the public expenditure control regime. Three-year departmental expenditure limits (DELs) now apply to most government departments. Spending which cannot easily be subject to three-year planning is reviewed annually in the budget as annually managed expenditure (AME). Current and capital expenditure are treated separately.

DEPARTMENTAL EXPENDITURE LIMITS (DEL)

RESOURCE AND CAPITAL BUDGETS

	Outturn 2005–6	*Estimate 2006–7*	*Projection 2007–8*
			£ billion
Resource Budget			
Education and Skills[1]	25.1	53.6	57.4
Health	76.4	81.1	89.7
of which NHS	74.2	79.2	87.6
Transport	6.1	6.9	6.7
Department for Communities and Local Government	3.5	3.7	4.3
Local Government	46.2	22.5	22.8
Home Office	12.7	13.2	13.5
Department for Constitutional Affairs*	3.6	3.7	4.0
Law Officers' Departments	0.7	0.7	0.7
Defence	33.4	33.7	32.8
Foreign and Commonwealth Office	1.9	2.0	1.9
International Development	4.1	4.3	4.6
Trade and Industry*	5.2	5.8	6.2
Environment, Food and Rural Affairs	2.8	3.3	3.0
Culture, Media and Sport	1.4	1.6	1.6
Work and Pensions	7.8	7.7	7.7
Scotland[2]	20.8	22.3	23.5
Wales[2]	11.0	11.9	12.4
Northern Ireland Executive[2]	6.7	7.2	7.6
Northern Ireland Office	1.2	1.3	1.1

Chancellor's departments	4.9	5.2	5.0
Cabinet Office	2.2	2.4	2.4
Invest to Save Budget	0.0	0.0	0.0
Reserve	0.0	0.0	0.6
Unallocated special reserve[3]	0.0	0.0	0.4
Allowance for shortfall	0.0	–0.7	0.0
TOTAL RESOURCE BUDGET DEL	277.8	293.4	310.0
Capital Budget			
Education and Skills[1]	5.7	5.2	7.0
Health	2.2	3.8	4.3
of which NHS	2.2	3.7	4.2
Transport	5.0	6.5	6.6
Department for Communities and Local Government	5.5	5.4	5.9
Local Government	0.3	0.2	0.1
Home Office	1.0	1.3	1.3
Departments for Constitutional Affairs[1]	0.1	0.2	0.1
Law Officers' Departments	0.0	0.0	0.0
Defence	6.4	7.1	7.6
Foreign and Commonwealth Office	0.1	0.1	0.1
International Development	0.4	0.7	0.6
Trade and Industry[1]	1.2	1.2	1.2
Environment, Food and Rural Affairs	0.8	0.9	0.9
Culture, Media and Sport	0.1	0.2	0.4
Work and Pensions	0.4	0.2	0.1
Scotland[2]	2.4	3.1	3.1
Wales[2]	1.2	1.4	1.6
Northern Ireland Executive[2]	0.8	0.9	1.0
Northern Ireland Office	0.1	0.1	0.1
Chancellor's departments	0.4	0.3	0.3
Cabinet Office	0.3	0.4	0.3
Invest to Save Budget	0.0	0.0	0.0
Reserve	0.0	0.0	1.5
Allowance for shortfall	0.0	–0.4	0.0
TOTAL CAPITAL BUDGET DEL	34.6	38.8	44.3
Less depreciation	(9.5)	(10.5)	(10.6)
TOTAL DEL	302.9	321.7	343.7

[1] Due to changes announced as part of the government reshuffle on 28 June 2007, estimate and projection figures may no longer be accurate for the new departments

[2] For Scotland, Wales and Northern Ireland, the split between current and capital budgets is indicative and reflects the consequentials of the application of the Barnett formula to planned changes in UK departments' spending

[3] This represents provision for the costs of military operations in Iraq and Afghanistan, as well as the UK's other international obligations

Source: HM Treasury – *Budget 2007* (Crown copyright)

ANNUALLY MANAGED EXPENDITURE (AME) *£ billion*

	Outturn 2005–6	*Estimate 2006–7*	*Projection 2007–8*
Social security benefits[1]	127.4	132.0	139.2
Tax credits[1]	15.5	16.2	16.5
Net public service pensions[2]	0.2	1.1	1.7
National Lottery	1.8	1.7	1.6
BBC domestic services	3.2	3.3	3.3
Other departmental expenditure	3.3	3.6	3.1
Net expenditure transfers to EU institutions[3]	4.4	4.7	5.0
Locally financed expenditure[4]	25.8	25.9	27.8
Central government gross debt interest	25.8	27.4	29.1
Public corporations' own-financed capital expenditure	5.4	4.3	4.6
AME margin	0.0	0.0	1.0
Accounting adjustments[5]	7.6	10.4	10.0
AME	220.5	230.5	242.9

[1] Includes Income Support and Jobseekers' Allowance child allowances, which are paid as part of the Child Tax Credit

[2] Reported on a national accounts basis

[3] AME spending component only

[4] This expenditure is mainly financed by council tax revenues

[5] Excludes depreciation

Source: HM Treasury – *Budget 2007* (Crown copyright)

PUBLIC SECTOR FINANCES

PUBLIC SECTOR CAPITAL EXPENDITURE *£ billion*

	Outturn 2005–6	*Estimate 2006–7*	*Projection 2007–8*
Capital Budget DEL	34.6	38.8	44.3
Locally financed expenditure	1.2	2.0	1.9
National Lottery	1.0	1.0	0.8
Public corporations' own-financed capital expenditure	5.4	4.3	4.6
Other capital spending in AME	0.8	0.3	0.4
AME margin	0.0	0.0	0.1
Accounting adjustments	–3.8	–3.2	–4.2
PUBLIC SECTOR GROSS INVESTMENT[1]	39.2	43.2	48.0
Less depreciation	(16.5)	(17.7)	(18.7)
PUBLIC SECTOR NET INVESTMENT	22.7	25.5	29.4
Proceeds from the sale of fixed assets[2]	6.1	6.2	6.2

[1] This and previous lines are all net of sales of fixed assets

[2] Projections of total receipts from the sale of fixed assets by public sector

Source: HM Treasury – *Budget 2007* (Crown copyright)

SIZE OF THE ECONOMY

GNI	US$2,272.7bn (2005)
GNI, per capita	US$37,740 (2005)
GDP	US$2,198.8bn (2005)
GDP, annual growth	1.8 per cent (2004–5)

Source: The World Bank – *World Development Indicators 2007*

EMPLOYMENT

DISTRIBUTION OF THE WORKFORCE

Claimant count	944,100
Workforce jobs	31,409,000
HM forces	204,000
Self-employment jobs	4,073,000
Employees jobs	27,067,000
Government-supported trainees	66,000

Source: ONS – *AAS 2007* (Crown copyright)

EMPLOYMENT

	Thousands	
Age	*Male*	*Female*
16–17	263	300
18–24	1,867	1,699
25–34	3,408	2,853
35–49	5,819	5,121
50–64(m)/59(f)	3,830	2,616
65+(m)/60+(f)	392	763
All aged 16+	15,578	13,352

m = male, f = female
Source: ONS – *AAS 2007* (Crown copyright)

UNEMPLOYMENT

	Thousands	
Age	*Male*	*Female*
16–17	104	74
18–24	313	207
25–34	182	149
35–49	228	187
50–64(m)/59(f)	137	74
65+(m)/60+(f)	11	16
All aged 16+	975	708

Source: ONS – *AAS 2007* (Crown copyright)

DURATION OF UNEMPLOYMENT	*Thousands*
All unemployed	1,683
Duration of unemployment	
Less than 6 months	1,024
6 months–1 year	303
1 year +	356
1 year + as percentage of total	21.2

Source: ONS – *AAS 2007* (Crown copyright)

AVERAGE EARNINGS AND HOURS OF FULL-TIME EMPLOYEES

	All	*Male*	*Female*
Average weekly earnings (£)	537.4	591.6	453.6
Average hours	37.5	40.7	37.6
Average hourly earnings (£)			
Including overtime	13.62	14.54	12.08
Excluding overtime	13.67	14.62	12.11

Source: ONS – *AAS 2007* (Crown copyright)

LABOUR DISPUTES BY DURATION

Under 5 days	102
5–10 days	8
10–20 days	3
20–30 days	–
30–50 days	3
50+ days	–

Source: ONS – *AAS 2007* (Crown copyright)

WORKING DAYS LOST THROUGH LABOUR DISPUTES BY INDUSTRY

Mining, quarrying, electricity, gas and water	6,000
Manufacturing	16,000
Construction	2,000
Transport, storage and communications	33,000
Public administration and defence	23,000
Education	43,000
Health and social work	–
Other community, social and personal services	6,000
All other industries and services	29,000

Source: ONS – *AAS 2007* (Crown copyright)

TRADE UNIONS

Year	*No. of unions*	*Total membership*
1997	252	7,801,000
1998	238	7,851,904
1999	237	7,897,519
2000	226	7,779,393
2001	216	7,750,990
2002	210	7,735,983
2003	206	7,559,062
2004	193	7,473,000

Source: ONS – *AAS 2007* (Crown copyright)

TRADE

TRADE IN GOODS

			£ million
	Exports	*Imports*	*Balance*
1996	167,196	180,918	–13,722
1997	171,923	184,265	–12,342
1998	164,056	185,869	–21,813
1999	166,166	195,217	–29,051
2000	187,936	220,912	–32,976
2001	189,093	230,305	–41,212
2002	186,524	234,229	–47,705
2003	188,320	236,927	–48,607
2004	190,877	251,770	–60,893
2005	211,616	280,399	–68,783
2006	244,542	328,233	–83,691

Source: ONS – *AAS 2007* (Crown copyright)

BALANCE OF PAYMENTS	*£ million*
CURRENT ACCOUNT	
Trade in goods and services	
Trade in goods	–83,691
Trade in services	29,605
Total trade in goods and services	–54,086
Income	
Compensation of employees	58
Investment income	22,743
Total income	22,801
Current transfers	
Central government	–9,968
Other sectors	–2,136
Total current transfers	–12,104
TOTAL (CURRENT BALANCE)	–43,389

Source: ONS – *AAS 2007* (Crown copyright)

HOUSEHOLD INCOME AND EXPENDITURE

AVERAGE ANNUAL HOUSEHOLD INCOME

Number of households in the UK	24,431,000
Original income (before state benefits)	£27,569
Gross income (after state benefits)	£31,884
Disposable income	£25,360
Post-tax income	£20,627

Source: ONS – *AAS 2007* (Crown copyright)

AVERAGE WEEKLY HOUSEHOLD INCOME BY SOURCE

		Percentage of total
Wages and salaries	£414.80	67
Self-employment	£50.80	8
Investments	£19.50	3
Annuities and pensions (other than social security benefits)	£45.50	7
Social security benefits	£78.00	13
Other sources	£7.40	1
Total	£616.90	100

Source: ONS – *AAS 2007* (Crown copyright)

PERCEPTION OF ADEQUACY OF INCOME (GREAT BRITAIN)

Percentages

	1986	*1994*	*2004*
Living comfortably	24	29	40
Coping	50	49	46
Finding it difficult to manage	18	15	11
Finding it very difficult to manage	8	6	3

Source: ONS – *ST 2006* (Crown copyright)

NUMBER OF TAXPAYERS BY ANNUAL INCOME[1]

	Number of taxpayers (thousands)
£5,035[2]–£7,499	2,700
£7,500–£9,999	3,370
£10,000–£14,999	5,970
£15,000–£19,999	4,890
£20,000–£29,999	6,440
£30,000–£49,999	4,450
£50,000–£99,999	1,460
£100,000–£199,999	350
£200,000–£499,999	100
£500,000–£999,999	18
£1,000,000+	6
All incomes	29,700

[1] Includes investment income
[2] Basic personal tax-free allowance (*see* Taxation)
Source: ONS – *ST 2007* (Crown copyright)

HOUSEHOLD OWNERSHIP OF SELECTED DURABLE GOODS

Percentages

	2000–1	*2005–6*
Car	72	74
One	44	46
Two	22	23
Three+	6	5
Central heating, full or partial	91	94
Washing machine	92	95
Fridge/freezer or deep freezer	94	97
Dishwasher	25	35
Telephone	93	92
Mobile phone	47	79
Home computer	44	65
Video recorder	87	86
Digital television service[1]	40	65
Internet connection	32	55

[1] Includes digital, satelite and cable receivers
Source: ONS – *AAS 2007* (Crown copyright)

HOUSEHOLD EXPENDITURE *£ per week*

	Couple		*Single*				
	With children	*No children*	*With children*	*No children*	*Retired couple*	*Retired single*	*All households*
Food and non-alcoholic drink	62.80	46.70	38.60	22.50	46.00	23.70	45.30
Alcohol and tobacco	13.00	13.90	8.70	7.60	9.00	3.90	10.80
Clothing and footwear	33.60	24.50	23.30	11.50	14.00	6.10	22.70
Housing, fuel and power[1]	48.50	46.90	44.70	41.30	31.80	28.80	44.20
Household goods and services	39.00	38.80	25.50	15.00	31.40	14.50	30.00
Health	5.60	7.00	2.10	5.30	5.90	2.80	5.50
Transport	85.60	77.80	30.80	38.70	45.20	12.40	61.70
Communication	15.10	12.70	11.50	8.90	7.00	5.10	11.90
Recreation and culture	79.00	68.10	39.60	34.90	52.90	21.10	57.50
Education	14.30	3.90	6.10	2.40	–	–	6.60
Restaurants and hotels[2]	47.20	45.50	22.80	23.20	24.40	9.50	36.70
Miscellaneous goods and services	50.40	38.70	24.10	18.50	26.90	17.50	34.60
Other expenditure items	120.40	102.80	42.60	58.30	37.70	21.20	75.80
All household expenditure (=100%)	614.20	527.30	320.40	288.20	333.50	166.60	443.40

[1] Excludes mortgage payments, water charges and council tax (domestic rates in Northern Ireland) – these are included in *Other expenditure items*
[2] Includes purchases of alcoholic drink in restaurants and hotels
Source: ONS – *ST 2007* (Crown copyright)

SAVINGS AND WEALTH

	Men by age				Women by age				*Percentages* All individuals aged 16+
	16–24	*25–64*	*65+*	*All 16+*	*16–24*	*25–64*	*65+*	*All 16+*	
Current account	81.0	89.9	86.1	88.2	84.1	89.3	80.8	86.9	87.5
ISAs	10.2	26.8	35.1	26.3	13.5	29.0	30.5	27.6	26.9
Basic bank account	2.9	3.8	5.2	3.9	4.2	4.9	6.1	5.1	4.5
TESSA	0.1	4.1	9.2	4.5	–	4.2	7.7	4.5	4.5
Post Office account	2.3	2.5	3.3	2.6	2.8	3.3	4.6	3.5	3.1
Other bank/building society account	23.4	44.9	49.4	43.0	27.2	47.3	48.8	45.4	44.2
Stocks and shares	3.2	18.7	23.0	17.5	2.2	14.7	17.2	13.9	15.6
PEPs	0.3	5.4	10.0	5.6	0.1	4.7	7.0	4.7	5.2
Unit trusts	0.4	3.8	6.5	3.9	0.5	2.9	4.5	3.0	3.4
Endowment policy (not linked)	0.1	3.1	0.3	2.2	–	2.4	0.2	1.7	1.9
Gilts	–	0.3	1.3	0.4	–	0.3	1.4	0.5	0.5
Premium bonds	4.7	16.1	24.4	16.2	4.5	15.6	22.1	15.8	16.0
National Savings bonds	0.8	1.3	6.5	2.2	0.5	1.6	7.5	2.7	2.5
Guaranteed equity bonds	–	0.2	0.6	0.2	–	0.3	0.6	0.3	0.3
Company share scheme	0.6	4.7	0.4	3.4	0.6	2.7	0.1	1.9	2.6
Credit unions	0.3	0.7	0.1	0.5	0.4	0.8	0.1	0.6	0.5
Save as you earn	0.2	0.6	–	0.4	0.2	0.6	0.1	0.4	0.4
Any form of wealth	86.5	94.2	93.7	93.1	90.1	94.6	92.4	93.6	93.4
No form of wealth	13.5	5.9	6.3	6.9	9.9	5.4	7.7	6.4	6.6

Source: ONS – *ST 2007* (Crown copyright)

AVERAGE DWELLING PRICES BY REGION

	2003	*2005*
UK	£155,485	£183,966
England	£165,834	£193,097
North East	£94,950	£131,814
North West	£108,956	£146,111
Yorkshire and the Humber	£107,325	£143,281
East Midlands	£133,215	£159,249
West Midlands	£132,898	£163,945
East	£181,494	£204,215
London	£236,476	£266,328
South East	£213,115	£233,069
South West	£170,560	£199,230
Wales	£104,140	£145,825
Scotland	£92,006	£124,390
Northern Ireland	£102,348	£129,580

Source: ONS – *ST 2006 and 2007* (Crown copyright)

COST OF LIVING AND INFLATION RATES

The first cost of living index to be calculated took July 1914 as 100 and was based on the pattern of expenditure of working-class families in 1914. The cost of living index was superseded in 1947 by the general index of retail prices (RPI), although the older term is still popularly applied.

The Harmonised Index of Consumer Prices (HICP) was introduced in 1997 to enable comparisons within the European Union using an agreed methodology. In 2003 the National Statistician renamed the HICP as the Consumer Prices Index (CPI) to reflect its role as the main target measure of inflation for macroeconomic purposes. The RPI and indices based on it will continue to be published alongside the CPI. Pensions, benefits and index-linked gilts continue to be calculated with reference to RPI or its derivatives.

CPI AND RPI

The RPI and CPI measure the changes month by month in the average level of prices of goods and services purchased by households in the UK. The indices are compiled using a selection of around 650 goods and services, and the prices charged for these items are collected at regular intervals at about 150 locations throughout the country. The Office for National Statistics (ONS) reviews the components of the indices once every year to reflect changes in consumer preferences and the establishment of new products. The table below shows changes made by the ONS to the CPI 'shopping basket' in 2007.

CPI excludes a number of items that are included in RPI, mainly related to housing such as council tax and a range of owner-occupier housing costs, such as mortgage payments. The CPI covers all private households whereas RPI excludes the top 4 per cent by income and pensioner households who derive at least three-quarters of their income from state benefits. The two indices use different methodologies to combine the prices of goods and services, which means that since 1996 the CPI inflation measure is on average less than the RPI inflation measure.

'SHOPPING BASKET' OF GOODS AND SERVICES

Changes to the CPI* 2007 basket of goods and services include:

Goods and Services Group	*Removed items*	*New items*
Food and non-alcoholic beverages	vegetable oil; brie; Brussels sprouts; pre-packed fresh vegetables	olive oil; pro-biotic drink; courgettes; broccoli
Clothing and footwear	child's wellington boots; men's leather boots	–
Housing and household services	–	shower head
Furniture and household goods	–	portable or free-standing electric fan
Health	UV protection sunglasses (non-designer frames); designer spectacle frames	–
Transport	–	satellite navigation system
Communication	–	mobile downloads (eg ringtones)
Recreation and culture	portable colour television (CRT); VHS video recorder; portable CD radio cassette; car CD/radio auto-changer; widescreen (CRT) television; blank VHS cassette; pre-recorded video; 35mm compact camera; mail order develop and print photography services; digital television installation fee; decorative outdoor plant pot	flat panel television (14–25″); digital (DAB) radio; pre-recorded DVD (non-film) from chart; recordable DVD (price per DVD from pack of 5–25); digital photography processing (print of up to 50 photographs)
Restaurants and hotels (catering)	–	onboard catering (rail, sea and air); vending machine canned/bottled fizzy drink
Miscellaneous goods and services	gemstone cluster ring	diamond solitaire ring; credit card charges; mortgage fees; toothbrush

* RPI goods and services are grouped together under different classifications

NFLATION RATE

ne twelve-monthly percentage change in the 'all items' dex of the RPI or CPI is referred to as the rate of flation. As the most familiar measure of inflation, RPI is ten referred to as the 'headline rate of inflation'. CPI is e main measure of inflation for macroeconomic irposes and forms the basis for the government's flation target, which is currently 2 per cent. The rcentage change in prices between any two months/ ars can be obtained using the following formula:

$$\frac{\text{Later date RPI/CPI} - \text{Earlier date RPI/CPI}}{\text{Earlier date RPI/CPI}} \times 100$$

; to find the CPI rate of inflation for 2006, using the nual averages for 2005 and 2006:

$$\frac{102.3 - 100.0}{100.0} \times 100 = 2.3$$

om 14 February 2006 the reference year for CPI was -based to 2005=100 to improve price comparison irity across the EU. None of the underlying data, from hich the re-referenced series was calculated, was revised. istorical rates of change (such as annual inflation ;ures), calculated from the re-based rounded index vels, were revised due to the effect of rounding. The CPI e of inflation figure given in the table below may differ plus or minus 0.1 percentage points from the figure lculated by the above equation. The change of reference riod and revision due to rounding does not apply to the PI which remains unchanged.

The RPI and CPI figures are published by the Office for ational Statistics on either the second or third Tuesday of each month in an Indices bulletin and electronically on the National Statistics website (W www.statistics.gov.uk). They are also available as a recorded telephone message (T 020-7533 5866).

PURCHASING POWER OF THE POUND

Changes in the internal purchasing power of the pound may be defined as the 'inverse' of changes in the level of prices: when prices go up, the amount which can be purchased with a given sum of money goes down. To find the purchasing power of the pound in one month or year, given that it was 100p in a previous month or year, the calculation would be:

$$100\text{p} \times \frac{\text{Earlier month/year RPI}}{\text{Later month/year RPI}}$$

Thus, if the purchasing power of the pound is taken to be 100p in 1975, the comparable purchasing power in 2000 would be:

$$100\text{p} \times \frac{34.2}{170.3} = 20.1\text{p}$$

For longer term comparisons, it has been the practice to use an index which has been constructed by linking together the RPI for the period 1962 to date; an index derived from the consumers expenditure deflator for the period from 1938 to 1962; and the pre-war 'cost of living' index for the period 1914 to 1938. This long-term index enables the internal purchasing power of the pound to be calculated for any year from 1914 onwards. It should be noted that these figures can only be approximate.

	Annual average RPI (1987 = 100)	*Purchasing power of £ (1998 = 1.00)*	*Annual average CPI (2005 = 100)**	*Rate of inflation (RPI/CPI)*
14	2.8	58.18		
15	3.5	46.54		
20	7.0	23.27		
25	5.0	32.58		
30	4.5	36.20		
35	4.0	40.72		
38	4.4	37.02		
ere are no official figures for 1939–45				
46	7.4	22.01		
50	9.0	18.10		
55	11.2	14.54		
60	12.6	12.93		
65	14.8	11.00		
70	18.5	8.80		
75	34.2	4.76		
80	66.8	2.44	18.0	
85	94.6	1.72	6.1	
90	126.1	1.29	71.5	9.5/7.0
95	149.1	1.09	86.0	3.5/2.6
98	162.9	1.0	91.1	3.4/1.6
00	170.3	0.96	93.1	3.0/0.8
05	192.0	0.85	100	2.8/2.1
06	198.1	0.82	102.3	3.2/2.3

n accordance with an EU Commission regulation all published CPI figures were re-based to 2005 = 100 with effect from 14 bruary 2006, replacing the 1996 = 100 series

TAXATION

The government raises money to pay for public services such as education, health and the social security system through tax. Each year the Chancellor of the Exchequer's Budget sets out how much it will cost to provide these services and how much tax is therefore needed to pay for them. HM Revenue and Customs (HMRC) is the government department that collects it. There are several different types of tax. The varieties that individuals may have to pay include income tax payable on earnings, pensions, state benefits, savings and investments; capital gains tax (CGT) payable on the disposal of certain assets; inheritance tax (IHT) payable on estates upon death and certain lifetime gifts; stamp duty payable when purchasing property and shares; and value added tax (VAT) payable on goods and services, plus certain other duties such as fuel duty on petrol and excise duty on alcohol and tobacco. Government funds are also raised from companies and small businesses through corporation tax.

HELP AND INFORMATION ON TAXATION

For detailed information on any aspect of taxation individuals may contact their local tax office or enquiry centre. The HMRC website at www.hmrc.gov.uk provides a wide range of information online. All HMRC forms, leaflets and guides are listed on, and can be downloaded from, the website or ordered by telephone. A list of all HMRC telephone helplines can also be found on the website. Those most relevant to topics covered in this section on taxation have been included at pertinent points throughout. Information on taxation is also available in the Money, Tax and Benefits section of the government's public information website www.direct.gov.uk.

INCOME TAX

Income tax is a tax paid on different sorts of income. Not all types of income are taxable, however, and individuals are only taxed on their 'taxable income' above a certain level. Even then, there are other reliefs and allowances that can reduce or, in some cases, cancel out an individual's income tax bill.

An individual's taxable income is assessed each tax year, starting on 6 April one year and ending on 5 April the following year. The following information relates specifically to the year of assessment 2007–8 ending on 5 April 2008 and has only limited application to earlier years. Changes due to come into operation at a later date are briefly mentioned where information is available. Types of income that are taxable include:

- earnings from employment or self-employment
- most pensions income including state, company and personal pensions
- interest on most savings
- income (dividends) from shares and income from unit trusts
- income from property
- income received from a trust
- certain state benefits
- an individual's share of any joint income

There are certain sorts of income on which individuals never pay tax. These are ignored altogether when working out how much income tax an individual m need to pay. Types of income that are not taxable includ

- certain state benefits and tax credits such as workir tax credit and child tax credit, attendance allowan and disability living allowance, income support ar war widow(er)'s pension
- cold weather payments
- income from tax-free National Savings ar Investments, such as savings certificates
- interest and terminal bonuses under Save As You Ea schemes
- interest, dividends and other income from vario tax-free investments, notably individual savin accounts (ISAs)
- premium bond, national lottery and gambling prizes

PERSONAL ALLOWANCE

Every individual resident in the UK for tax purposes has personal allowance. This is an amount of taxable incom an individual is allowed to earn or receive each ye tax-free. This tax year (2007–8) the basic person allowance or tax-free amount is £5,225. Individuals m be entitled to a higher personal allowance if they are 6 or over. Income tax is only due on an individual's taxab income that is above his or her tax-free allowanc Husbands and wives are taxed separately, with ea entitled to his or her personal allowance. Each spouse m obtain other allowances and reliefs where the requir conditions are satisfied.

The amount of personal allowance depends on individual's age on 5 April 2007 and, if he or she is 65 over, the total income received from all taxable sourc There are three age-related levels of personal allowance *see* table below. If an individual turns 65 or 75 during t year to 5 April 2007, he or she is entitled to the allowan for that age group.

If an individual's income is over the income limit, th the age-related allowance reduces by half the amount (£ for every £2) he or she has over that limit, until the bas rate allowance is reached. For a 66-year-old with income of £21,300 (£400 over the limit), for example, t age-related allowance would reduce by £200 to £20,70

Individuals always receive the basic allowanc whatever the level of their income. The age-relat allowances mean that in 2007–8 no one aged 65 or ov need pay tax on income of up to £145 a week. Arou half of all pensioners pay no tax on their incom according to HMRC. Further information is available leaflet *IR121: Approaching Retirement – A Guide to Tax a National Insurance Contributions.*

LEVELS OF PERSONAL ALLOWANCE FOR 2007–8

	Personal allowance	*Income limit*
Basic rate	£5,225	none
Age 65-74	£7,550	£20,900
Age 75 and over	£7,690	£20,900

BLIND PERSON'S ALLOWANCE

If an individual is registered blind or is unable to perfor any work for which eyesight is essential, he or she c aim blind person's allowance, an extra amount of x-free income added to the personal allowance. In)07–8 the blind person's allowance is £1,730. It is the me for everyone who can claim it, whatever his or her e or level of income. If an individual is married or in a vil partnership and cannot use all of his or her blind rson's allowance because of insufficient income, the used part of the allowance can be passed to the spouse civil partner.

Other deductible allowances and reliefs that have the ect of reducing an income tax bill are available to tax yers in certain circumstances and will be explained in ore detail later in this section.

ALCULATING INCOME TAX DUE

dividuals' liability to pay income tax is determined by tablishing their level of taxable income for the year. For arried couples and civil partners income must be ocated between the couple by reference to the dividual who is beneficially entitled to that income. here income arises from jointly held assets, it is rmally apportioned equally between the partners. If, wever, the beneficial interests in jointly held assets are t equal, in most cases couples can make a special claration to have income apportioned by reference to e actual interests in that income.

To work out an individual's liability for tax, his or her xable income must be allocated between three different pes: earned income (excluding income from savings and vidends); income from savings; and company dividends om shares and other equity-based investments.

After the tax-free allowance plus any deductible owances and reliefs have been taken into account, the nount of tax an individual pays is calculated using fferent tax rates and a series of tax bands. The tax band plies to an individual's income after tax allowances and y reliefs have been taken into account. Individuals are t taxed on all of their income.

COME TAX RATES (PER CENT) FOR 2007–8

ncome tax band	*Income tax rate on earned income*	*Income tax rate on savings*	*Income tax rate on dividends*
tarting rate: :1–2,230	10	10	10
tarting rate: :2,231–34,600	22	20	10
Iigher rate: :34,601 and above	40	40	32.5

ie first calculation is applied to earned income which cludes income from employment or self-employment, ost pension income and rental income plus the value of wide range of employee fringe benefits such as mpany cars, living accommodation and private medical surance (for more information on fringe benefits, *see* er section on payment of income tax). In working out e amount of an individual's net taxable earnings, all penses incurred 'wholly, exclusively and necessarily' in e performance of his or her work duties, together with e cost of business travel, may be deducted. Fees and bscriptions to certain professional bodies may also be ducted. Redundancy payments and other sums paid on e termination of an employment are assessable to come tax, but the first £30,000 is normally tax-free provided the payment is not linked with the recipient's retirement or performance.

The first £2,230 of taxable income remaining is taxed at the starting rate of 10 per cent. The next £32,370 is taxed at the basic rate of 22 per cent. Any excess over £34,600 (£2,230 plus £32,370) is taxed at the higher rate of 40 per cent.

Savings and dividend income is added to an individual's other taxable income and taxed last. This means that tax on these sorts of income is based on an individual's highest income tax band.

The chancellor announced in the 2007 Budget that from April 2008 the basic rate of income tax will go down from 22 per cent to 20 per cent and the starting rate band of 10 per cent will be removed as part of the government's ongoing programme of reform to the UK tax and benefit system. This will create a simpler structure of two rates: a 20 pence (in the pound) basic rate and a 40 pence (in the pound) higher rate.

SAVINGS INCOME

The second calculation is applied to any income from savings received by an individual. The appropriate rate at which it must be taxed is determined by adding income from savings to an individual's other taxable income, excluding dividends. It is then taxed as follows:

- savings income that falls within the £2,230 starting rate income tax band is taxed at 10 per cent. In most cases it is likely to fall above this limit unless the individual has little or no other income
- savings income that falls above the £2,230 band but within the £34,600 basic rate band is taxable at 20 per cent
- savings income that falls above the £34,600 band is taxable at 40 per cent
- if it falls on both sides of a tax band, the relevant amounts are taxed at the rates for each tax band

Most savings income, such as interest paid on bank and building society accounts, already has tax at a rate of 20 per cent deducted from it 'at source' – that is, before it is paid out to individuals. This is confirmed by the entry 'net interest' on bank and building society statements.

Basic rate (22 per cent) taxpayers need to take no further action because they owe no extra tax on their savings income even though tax was only deducted at 20 per cent.

Higher rate taxpayers whose income is sufficient to pay 40 per cent tax on their savings income must let their tax office know what savings income they have received so that the extra tax they owe can be collected.

Non-taxpayers – that is, individuals, including most children, whose taxable income is less than their tax allowances – can register to have their savings interest paid 'gross' without any tax being deducted from it at source. To do this, they must complete Form R85, available at all banks and building societies. Parents or guardians need to fill in this form on behalf of those under 16.

Non-taxpayers who have already had tax deducted from their savings interest can claim it back from HMRC by filling in Form R40. Similarly, people whose level of taxable income is low enough for them to pay income tax only at the 10 per cent starting rate can use Form R40 to claim back the difference on savings interest already taxed at 20 per cent. For help or information about registering to get interest paid tax-free or to claim tax back on savings interest, individuals may call a dedicated helpline on 0845-980 0645. Further information is available in the leaflet *IR111: Bank and building society interest – Are you paying tax when you don't need to?*

DIVIDEND INCOME

The third and final income tax calculation is on UK dividends, which means income from shares in UK companies and other share-based investments including unit trusts and open-ended investment companies (OEICs).

Tax on dividends differs from tax on savings income. There are two different rates which depend on whether the individual's overall taxable income (after allowances) falls within or above the basic rate income tax limit, which is £34,600 for the 2007–8 tax year. All dividend income that falls within this limit is taxable at 10 per cent while any that falls above is taxable at 32.5 per cent.

When dividends are paid, a voucher is sent that shows the dividend paid and the amount of associated 'tax credit'. Companies pay dividends out of profits on which they have already paid or are due to pay tax. The tax credit takes account of this and is available to the shareholder to offset against any income tax that may be due on their dividend income. The dividend paid represents 90 per cent of their dividend income. The remaining 10 per cent is made up of the tax credit. In other words the tax credit represents 10 per cent of the dividend income.

Individuals who pay tax at or below the basic rate have no tax to pay on their dividend income because the tax liability is 10 per cent – the same amount as the tax credit. Higher rate taxpayers pay a total of 32.5 per cent tax on dividend income that falls above the £34,600 basic rate income tax limit, but because the first 10 per cent of the tax due on their dividend income is already covered by the tax credit, in practice they owe only 22.5 per cent.

Non-taxpayers cannot claim the 10 per cent tax credit. This is because income tax has not been deducted from the dividends paid to them. The view is that they have simply been given a 10 per cent credit against any income tax due.

If there is significant change to an individual's savings or other income, whatever his or her current tax bracket, it is the individual's responsibility to contact the relevant tax office immediately, even if he or she does not normally complete a tax return. This enables the tax office to work out whether extra or less tax should be paid.

INDIVIDUAL SAVINGS ACCOUNTS (ISAs)

There is a small selection of savings and investment products that are tax-free, meaning that there is no tax to pay on any income they generate in the form of interest or dividends nor on any increase in the value of the capital invested. Their tax-efficient status has been granted by the government in order to give people an incentive to save more. For this reason there are usually limits and restrictions on the amount of money that an individual may invest in such savings and investments. Individual savings accounts (ISAs) are the best known among tax-efficient savings and investments. They were introduced in 1999 to replace other similar schemes called PEPs and TESSAs. Individuals can use an ISA to save cash, or invest in stocks and shares. They may save up to £7,000 each tax year in an ISA and receive all profits free of tax provided that they are UK residents and are over 18 (over 16 for cash ISAs). An ISA must be in an individual's name and cannot be held jointly with another person.

ISAs can include one or more components:

- cash (bank and building society savings accoun National Savings and Investments)
- stocks and shares (unit trusts, shares, bonc investment-type life insurance and so on)

There are strict rules regarding the maximum amou allowed for each component and the overall amou individuals can invest in any one tax year.

At present, ISAs come in two types. Maxi ISAs m contain cash and stocks and shares, and all t investments in a maxi ISA must be with the san management company. Mini ISAs can contain eith stocks and shares or cash. Each tax year individuals m put money into either one maxi ISA or two mini ISA They may not have both. They may save up to £7,000 a maxi ISA invested only in stocks and shares or in a ma ISA with a maximum of £3,000 in cash and the remaind in stocks and shares. Alternatively, individuals can inve up to £3,000 in one cash mini ISA and up to £4,000 one stocks and shares mini ISA. They cannot invest more than one mini cash ISA, or more than one mi stocks and shares ISA in the same tax year.

The government has announced that new rules simplify ISAs will come into force in April 2008. T reforms will remove the distinction between maxi a mini ISAs and allow transfers from a previous year's ca ISA into a stocks and shares version. Also from April 20 the annual ISA investment limit will go up to £7,200 wi an increase in the cash limit to £3,600.

Further details are available via HMRC's ISA helpli on 0845-604 1701.

DEDUCTIBLE ALLOWANCES AND RELIEFS

Income tax payers may be entitled to certa tax-deductible allowances and reliefs as well as the personal allowances. Examples include the marri couple's allowance and maintenance payments relief, bo of which are explained below. Unlike the tax-fr allowances, these are not amounts of income that individual can receive tax-free but amounts by which the tax bill can be reduced.

MARRIED COUPLE'S ALLOWANCE

A married couple's allowance (MCA) is available taxpayers who are married or in a civil partnership on where one or other partner was born before 6 April 193 Eligible couples can start to claim the MCA from the ye of marriage or civil partnership registration.

The MCA is restricted to give relief at a fixed rate of 1 per cent which means that, unlike the personal allowanc it is not income that can be received without paying ta Instead, it reduces an individual's tax bill by up to a fix amount calculated as 10 per cent of the amount of t allowance to which they are entitled.

In 2007–8 there are two different levels of MCA:

- £6,285 at 10 per cent – if either partner was bo before 6 April 1935 but is aged under 75. This is wor up to £628.50 off their tax bill
- £6,365 at 10 per cent – if either partner is aged 75 over. This is worth up to £636.50 off their tax bill

The MCA is made up of two parts: a minimum amou (£2,440 in 2007–8); and a second amount dependent the age bracket of the individual or his or her partner. F a couple where one or other was born before 6 Ap 1935 but is under 75, this second amount is £3,84 Where one or the other is aged 75 or over, it is £3,925.

For married couples, the minimum amount will alwa be due whatever the level of the husband's income. Th ge-related amount can be reduced if the husband's come exceeds certain limits. Whatever the level of the lowance, it is normally reduced in the year of marriage take account of the months elapsed before the arriage.

The husband will normally receive the allowance but e couple can jointly decide which of them will get the inimum amount of the allowance. Alternatively, they can cide to have the minimum amount of the allowance lit equally between them. They must inform their tax fice of their decision by completing Form 18 before the art of the new tax year in which they want the decision become effective. Once this is done, the change will ply until the couple decides to alter it, so there is no ed to complete a new form every year. If there is no ch decision, the husband will normally get the owance. The remaining part of the allowance due cause of age must go to the husband unless he does not ve sufficient income to use it.

If an individual does not have enough income to use all s or her share of the married couple's allowance, the tax fice can transfer the unused part of it to his or her ouse or civil partner.

Like the personal allowance, the MCA can be gradually duced at the rate of £1 of the allowance for every £2 of come above the income limit (£20,900 in 2007–8). The nount of MCA can only be affected by the husband's come, and it only starts to be affected if his personal owance has already been reduced back to the basic vel for people under 65. The wife's income never affects e amount of the MCA. It does not matter whether all or rt of the minimum amount of the allowance has been ansferred to her. Whatever the level of the husband's come, the MCA can never be reduced below a minimum vel. In 2007–8 this minimum amount is £2,440 at 10 r cent.

The same system of allowance allocation applies to civil rtners based on the income of the highest earner. *See* aflets *FS1 (MCA): Married couple's allowance restrictions*; d *REV BN 28: Tax and civil partners.*

AINTENANCE PAYMENTS RELIEF

n allowance is available to reduce an individual's tax bill r maintenance payments he or she makes to his or her spouse or former civil partner in certain circumstances. be eligible one or other partner must have been born fore 6 April 1935; the couple must be legally separated divorced; the maintenance payments being made must under a court order; and the payments must be for the aintenance of an ex spouse or former civil partner rovided he or she is not now remarried or in a new civil rtnership) or for children who are under 21. This owance enables individuals to reduce their tax bill by e lower of 10 per cent of £2,350 (maximum £235) or per cent of the amount actually paid in maintenance yments.

To claim maintenance payments relief individuals ould contact their tax office and request Form IR41.

HARITABLE DONATIONS

number of charitable donations qualify for tax relief. dividuals can increase the value of regular or one-off aritable gifts, however small, by using the Gift Aid heme that allows charities to reclaim basic rate tax relief donations they receive. The gift is treated as being paid om net income – that is, after income tax at the basic rate 22 per cent has been deducted from it. The effect is at, for every £10 a donor gives, the charity actually receives £12.82 once it reclaims the tax at the basic rate. Higher rate taxpayers also benefit. They can reclaim the 18 per cent difference to give the full 40 per cent relief.

For gifts to qualify for Gift Aid, an individual must pay at least as much income tax as the recipient charities will reclaim on the gifts in the tax year in which they are made. Non-taxpayers should not use Gift Aid. The scheme is only for monetary gifts and there are rules limiting the value of benefits individuals may receive in return for their charitable donations.

For employees or those in receipt of an occupational pension, a tax-efficient way of making regular donations to charities is to make them straight from a salary or pension before income tax is deducted under the Payroll Giving scheme. This effectively increases the value of an individual's contributions, meaning more money for the recipient charity at less cost to the donor. For example, it costs a basic-rate taxpayer only £7.80 in take-home pay to give £10 to charity from their pre-tax pay. Higher rate taxpayers can claim an additional 18 per cent relief, reducing the cost of a £10 donation to £6. Anyone who pays tax through PAYE can give in this way, providing his or her employer or pension provider offers a payroll giving scheme, and there is no limit to the amount individuals can donate.

TAX RELIEF ON PENSION CONTRIBUTIONS

Pensions are long-term investments designed to help ensure that people have enough income in retirement. The government encourages individuals to save towards a pension by offering tax relief on their contributions.

For each pound individuals contribute to their scheme, whether it be an occupational pension or a private or stakeholder plan, the pension provider claims tax back from the government at the basic rate of 22 per cent and reinvests it on behalf of the individual into the scheme. In practice, this means that for every £78 taxpayers pay into their pension, they end up with £100 in their pension fund.

Higher rate taxpayers get 40 per cent tax relief on money they put into a pension, but the way that the money is given back is different. The first 22 per cent is claimed back from HMRC by the pension scheme in the same way as for a lower rate taxpayer. It is then up to individuals to claim back the other 18 per cent from their tax office, either when they fill in their annual tax return or by letter.

The most non-taxpayers can pay into a pension is £2,808 a year; since they receive basic rate 22 per cent tax relief on this sum, the government effectively tops up their contribution to make it £3,600.

Until April 2006 there were various restrictions – based on age and salary – limiting the amounts an individual could save and get tax relief on in personal and company pension schemes. But on 6 April 2006 a new, simplified pensions regime came into effect that included the introduction of just one, more generous annual allowance applied to all types of pension scheme.

In any one tax year, individuals can now get tax relief on pension contributions of 100 per cent of their annual earnings, irrespective of age, up to a maximum 'annual allowance' (£225,000 for 2007–8). Everyone now also has a 'lifetime allowance' (£1.6m for 2007–8) which means taxpayers can save up to this amount in their pension fund and still get tax relief at their highest income tax rate on all their contributions. Individuals may also now pay concurrently into as many different types of pension as they wish and get tax relief on all their contributions, provided they do not exceed the annual allowance.

For information and leaflets on pensions and tax relief, contact the government's Pensions Service on 0845-606 0265 or visit www.thepensionservice.gov.uk.

PAYMENT OF INCOME TAX

Employees have their income tax deducted from their wages throughout the year by their employer who sends it on to HMRC. Those in receipt of a company pension have their due tax deducted in the same way by their pension provider. This system of collecting income tax is known as 'pay as you earn' (PAYE).

BENEFITS IN KIND

The PAYE system is also used to collect tax on certain fringe benefits or 'benefits in kind' that employees or directors receive from their employer but that are not included in their salary cheque or wages. These include company cars, private medical insurance paid for by the employer or cheap or free loans from the employer. Some fringe benefits are tax-free, including employer-paid contributions into an employee's pension fund, cheap or free canteen meals, works buses, in-house sports facilities, relocation expenses up to £8,000, provision of a mobile phone, and workplace nursery places provided for the children of employees and certain other employer-supported childcare up to £50 per week.

For taxable fringe benefits tax is paid on the 'taxable value' of the benefit. The way this is worked out depends on whether or not the benefit is given to a director or 'higher-paid' employee defined as an individual earning £8,500 gross or more per year, including the value of his or her taxable fringe benefits. Company directors normally count as higher-paid, however much they earn.

Employers submit returns for individual employees to the tax office on the Form P11D, with details of any fringe benefits they have been given. Employees should get a copy of this form by 6 July following the end of the tax year and must enter the value of the fringe benefits they have received on their tax return for the relevant year, even if tax has already been paid on them under PAYE. Fringe benefits may be taxed under PAYE by being offset against personal tax allowances in an individual's PAYE code. Otherwise tax will be collected after the end of the tax year by the issue of an assessment on the fringe benefits.

SELF-ASSESSMENT

Individuals who are not on PAYE, notably the self-employed, need to complete a self-assessment tax return each year, in paper form or online at the HMRC website (W www.hmrc.gov.uk), and pay any income tax owed in twice-yearly instalments. Some individuals with more complex tax affairs such as those who earn money from rents or investments above a certain level, even if they are on PAYE, may also need to fill out a self-assessment return. HMRC uses the figures supplied on the tax return to work out the individual's tax bill, or they can choose to work it out themselves. It is called self-assessment because individuals are responsible for making sure the details they provide are correct.

Tax returns are usually sent out in early April, following the end of the tax year to which they apply. They may also go out at other times, for example if an individual wants to claim an allowance or repayment or to register for self-assessment for the first time.

Individuals with simple tax affairs, or with self-employment or rental income of less than £15,00 receive a short four-page return. Those with more compl affairs must fill out a full return that has 10 core pages pl extra pages, depending on the sorts of income received.

Central to the self-assessment system is the requireme for individuals to contact their tax office if they do n receive a self-assessment return but think they should or their financial circumstances change. Individuals have s months from when the tax year ends to report any ne income, for example, and three months to tell HMRC they become self-employed.

TAX RETURN FILING AND PAYMENT DEADLINE

There are also key deadlines for filing (sending i completed tax returns and paying the tax due. Failure do so can incur penalties, interest charges and surcharge The deadlines are more generous for individuals who d not want to calculate the tax due themselves and file the tax return online.

KEY FILING DATES FOR SELF-ASSESSMENT RETURNS

Date	*Why the deadline is important*
31 January*	Formal deadline for filing tax return received by the previous 31 October. Late filing incurs an automatic £100 penalty.
30 September†	Paper tax returns for tax year ended th previous 5 April must reach the HMRC by this date if the taxpayer wishes HMRC to: • calculate the tax • notify the taxpayer what to pay by th following 31 January • collect tax through the taxpayer's PAYE tax code (if possible) where th amount owed is less than £2,000.
29 December	Where a taxpayer's agent (eg an accountant) submits his or her tax retu via electronic lodgement service (ELS), must be sent back by this date if the taxpayer wants HMRC to collect tax through his or her tax code (if possible where the amount owed is less than £2,000.
30 December	Where a taxpayer files the return onlin he or she must do so by this date if HMRC is to collect tax through his or her tax code (if possible) where the amount owed is less than £2,000. Otherwise it can be filed up to 31 January.

* It was announced in the 2007 Budget that new filing dates f paper and online self-assessment tax returns will be introduc applying to tax returns that are issued on or after 6 April 20(and relate to the tax year 2007–8 and subsequent years. F paper returns, the date will be 31 October (for tax year 2007 8 that will be 31 October 2008). For returns filed online, t date will remain at 31 January (for tax year 2007–8 that w be 31 January 2009). For taxpayers filing paper returns wh want HMRC to calculate their tax liability for them, the ne cut off date will move from 30 September to 31 October align with the new paper return filing deadline.

† If HMRC receives the paper tax return after 30 September ar processes it by 30 December, it will still calculate the tax ow and try to collect it through the taxpayer's tax code but cannot guarantee to inform the taxpayer what to pay by 3 January. A calculation of tax liability is automatically provid when a return is filed online.

EY SELF-ASSESSMENT DATES

ate	*What payments or penalties are due?*
1 January	If a tax return was sent by the previous 31 October, this is the deadline for paying the balance of any tax owed – the 'balancing payment'. HMRC will charge daily interest after this date until it receives the payment. It is also the date by which a taxpayer must make any first 'payment on account' for the current tax year. For example on 31 January 2008 a taxpayer will have to pay both the balancing payment for the year 2006–7 and the first payment on account for 2007–8.
3 February	If the balancing payment is not paid by 31 January, there is an automatic 5 per cent surcharge incurred on top of the amount outstanding. This is in addition to any interest payments.
1 July	The deadline for making a second payment on account for tax owing for the preceding tax year. If tax is still owed that was due by the previous 31 January, there is a second automatic 5 per cent surcharge levied on top of the amount owed.

AX CREDITS

hild tax credit and working tax credit are paid to ıalifying individuals. Although the title of both credits corporates the word 'tax', neither affects the amount of come tax payable or repayable. Both are forms of social curity benefits. *See* Social Welfare

:APITAL GAINS TAX

apital gains tax (CGT) is a tax on increases in value of pital. When an individual disposes of an asset – that is, mething he or she owns such as shares, land or ıildings – by selling it or giving it away, CGT may have be paid on the gain or profit. An individual is otentially chargeable to CGT on gains that accrue from sposals made during a year of tax assessment. The llowing information relates to the year of assessment 007–8 ending on 5 April 2008 and has only limited levance to earlier years.

Liability extends to individuals who are either resident ordinarily resident in the UK for the tax year, but ecial rules apply where a person permanently leaves the K or comes to this country for the purpose of acquiring sidence. Non-residents are not usually liable to CGT less they carry on a business in the UK through a anch or agency. However, individuals who left the UK ter 16 March 1998 and who have been resident or dinarily resident in at least four of the seven years eceding departure may remain liable to CGT unless ey reside overseas over a period of five complete tax ars. Exceptions to this may apply where there is a sposal of assets acquired in the period of absence. dividuals should consult their tax office for details, hich are available in leaflet *IR20: Residents and on-residents: Liability to Tax in the United Kingdom.*

XAMPLES OF CAPITAL GAINS CHARGEABLE O CGT

ypically, individuals have made a gain if they sell an asset r more than they paid for it. It is the gain that is taxed, not the amount the individual receives for the asset. For example, a man buys shares for £1,000 and later sells them for £3,000. He has made a gain of £2,000. If someone gives an asset away, the gain will be based on the difference between what the asset was worth when originally acquired compared with its worth at the time of disposal. The same is true when an asset is sold for less than its full worth in order to give away part of the value. For example, a woman buys a property for £120,000 and three years later, when the property's market value has risen to £180,000, she gives it to her son. The son may pay nothing for the property or pay less than its true worth, eg £100,000. Either way, she has made a gain of £60,000.

If an individual disposes of an asset he or she received as a gift, the gain is worked out according to the market value of the asset when it was received. For example, a man gives his sister a painting worth £8,000. She pays nothing for it. Later she sells the painting for £10,000. For CGT purposes, she is treated as making a gain of £2,000. If an individual inherits an asset, the estate of the person who died does not pay CGT at the time. If the inheritor later disposes of the asset, the gain is worked out by looking at the market value at the time of the death. For example, a woman acquires some shares for £5,000 and leaves them to her niece when she dies. No CGT is payable at the time of death when the shares are worth £8,000. Later the niece sells the shares for £10,000. She has made a gain of £2,000 (£10,000 less £8,000). Individuals may also have to pay CGT if they dispose of part of an asset or exchange one asset for another. Similarly, CGT may be payable if an individual receives a capital sum of money from an asset without disposing of it, for example where he or she receives compensation when an asset is damaged.

Assets that may lead to a CGT charge when they are disposed of include:

- shares in a company
- units in a unit trust
- land and buildings (though not normally an individual's main home – *see* 'disposal of a home' section for details)
- higher value jewellery, paintings, antiques and other personal effects assets used in business such as goodwill

EXEMPT GAINS

Certain kinds of assets do not give rise to a chargeable gain when they are disposed of. Assets exempt from CGT include:

- an individual's private car
- an individual's main home, provided certain conditions are met
- tax-free investments such as assets held in an individual savings account (ISA) or personal equity plan (PEP)
- UK government gilts or 'bonds'
- personal belongings including jewellery, paintings, antiques individually worth £6,000 or less
- cash in sterling or foreign currency held for an individual or his/her family's own personal use
- betting, lottery or pools winnings
- personal injury compensation

DISPOSAL OF A HOME: PRIVATE RESIDENCE RELIEF

Individuals do not have to pay CGT when they sell their main home if all the following conditions are met:

- they bought it and made any expenditure on it, primarily for use as their home rather than with a view to making a profit

- the property was their only home throughout the period they owned it (ignoring the last three years of ownership)
- the property was actually used as their home all the time that they owned it and, throughout the period, it was not used for any purpose other than as a home for the individual, his or her family and no more than one lodger
- the garden and area of grounds sold with the property does not exceed 5,000 sq. m (1.24 acres) including the site of the property

Even if all these conditions are not met, individuals may still be entitled to CGT relief when they sell the home. They may, for example, qualify for relief if they lived away from home temporarily while working abroad. Married couples or couples in a civil partnership may have relief from CGT on only one home. There is a special exception, however, where the spouse or partner each had a qualifying home before marriage or civil partnership and both live together in one of these homes after marriage or civil partnership and sell the other. Provided that it is sold within three years of marriage or the civil partnership, they may not have to pay any CGT (subject to the normal rules for this relief). If they sell it after more than three years it may qualify for partial relief. There are special rules on divorce and separation. Further details are available in HMRC help sheet *IR283: Private Residence Relief.*

Certain other kinds of disposal similarly do not give rise to a chargeable gain. For example, individuals who are married or in a civil partnership and who live together may sell or give assets to their spouse or civil partner without having to pay CGT. Individuals may not, however, give or sell assets cheaply to their children without having to consider CGT. There is no CGT to pay on assets given to a registered charity. See HMRC help sheet *IR178: Giving Shares and Securities to Charity.*

CALCULATING CGT

CGT is worked out for each tax year and is charged on the total of an individual's taxable gains after taking into account certain costs and reliefs that can reduce or defer chargeable gains, allowable losses made on assets to which CGT normally applies and an annual exempt (tax-free) amount that applies to every individual. If the total of an individual's net gains in a tax year is less than the annual exempt amount (AEA), the individual will not have to pay CGT. For the tax year 2007–8 the AEA is £9,200. If an individual's net gains are more than the AEA, they pay CGT on the excess. Should any part of the exemption remain unused, this cannot be carried forward to a future year. A smaller exemption limit applies to most trusts. There are many reliefs available that may eliminate, reduce or defer CGT. Some reliefs are available to many people. For example, taper relief (*see* below) reduces the amount of a gain charged to tax the longer an asset has been held. Other reliefs are available only in special circumstances. Some reliefs are given automatically while others are given only if they are claimed. Some of the costs of buying, selling and improving assets may be deducted from total gains when working out an individual's chargeable gain.

RATES OF TAX

The net gains remaining, if any, calculated after deduction of costs, taking into account all CGT reliefs and subtracting the annual exemption, incur liability to capital gains tax. The rate of CGT individuals pay depends on their overall income. Their total taxable gains are added their taxable income for the year and treated as the t part of that total. The gains are then charged to CGT the following rates for the 2007–8 tax year:

- 10 per cent where they fall below the starting rate lin for income tax of £2,230
- 20 per cent where they fall between the starting ra and basic rate limits for income tax (£2,231 £34,600)
- 40 per cent where they fall above the basic rate lin for income tax (£34,600 and above)

Although income tax rates are used for this purpos liability arises only at the starting rate of 10 per cent, t lower rate of 20 per cent, the higher rate of 40 per cer or a combination of the three rates. Unlike some incon tax commitments, there is no liability at the basic rate 22 per cent. Despite the use of some income tax rat CGT remains an entirely separate tax. CGT for 2007– falls due for payment in full on 31 January 2009. payment is delayed, interest or surcharges may imposed. A husband and wife or registered civil partne who live together are separately assessed to CGT. Ea partner must independently calculate his or her gains an losses, with each entitled to the benefit of taper relief, any, and the AEA of £9,200 for 2007–8.

VALUATION OF ASSETS

The disposal proceeds – that is the amount received consideration for the disposal of an asset – are the su used to establish the gain or loss once certain allowab costs have been deducted. In most cases this straightforward because the disposal proceeds are t amount actually received for disposing of the asset. Th may include cash payable now or in the future and t value of any asset received in exchange for the ass disposed of. However, in certain circumstances, t disposal proceeds may not accurately reflect the value the asset and the individual may be treated as disposing an asset for an amount other than the actual amount any) that they received. This applies, in particular, whe an asset is transferred as a gift or sold for a price known be below market value. Disposal proceeds in su transactions are deemed to be equal to the market value the asset at the time it was disposed of rather than t actual amount (if any) received for it.

Market value represents the price that an asset mig reasonably be expected to fetch upon sale in the op market. In the case of unquoted shares or securities, it is be assumed that the hypothetical purchaser in the op market would have available all the information that prudent prospective purchaser of shares or securiti might reasonably require if that person were proposing purchase them from a willing vendor by private treaty an at arm's length. The market value of unquoted shares securities will often be established following negotiatio with the HM Revenue and Customs: Shares Valuatio The valuation of land and interests in land in the UK dealt with by District Valuer Services, part of t Valuation Office Agency. Special rules apply to determi the market value of shares quoted on the London Sto Exchange.

ALLOWABLE COSTS

When working out a chargeable gain, once the actual notional disposal proceeds have been determined, fi kinds of allowable costs may be deducted. There is general rule that no costs that could be taken into accou when working out income or losses for income t urposes may be deducted. Subject to this, allowable costs re:

- acquisition costs – the actual amount spent on acquiring the asset or, in certain circumstances, the equivalent market value
- incidental costs of acquiring the asset such as fees paid for professional advice, valuation costs, stamp duty and advertising costs to find a seller
- enhancement costs – incurred for the purpose of enhancing the value of the asset (not including normal maintenance and repair costs)
- expenditure on defending or establishing a person's rights over the asset
- incidental costs of disposing of the asset such as fees paid for professional advice, valuation costs, stamp duty and advertising costs to find a buyer

f an individual disposes of part of his or her interest in an sset, or part of a holding of shares of the same class in ne same company, or part of a holding of units in the ame unit trust, he or she can deduct part of the allowable osts of the asset or holding when working out the hargeable gain. Allowable costs may also be reduced by ome reliefs.

NDEXATION ALLOWANCE

or many years an indexation allowance could be inserted hen calculating a gain on the disposal of an asset. The llowance was based on percentage increases in the retail rices index between the month of March 1982, or the nonth in which expenditure was incurred if later, and the nonth of disposal.

Taper relief has largely replaced the indexation llowance for disposals made after 5 April 1998. owever, where an asset was acquired before this date, ne indexation allowance will be calculated to the month f April 1998 and frozen. The frozen allowance then nters into the calculation of chargeable gain, if any, when ne asset is disposed of at some later date. The adjustment or the indexation allowance must be made before alculating taper relief on the net sum remaining.

APER RELIEF

aper relief, an important and potentially valuable relief om CGT, was introduced with effect from 6 April 1998 replace the former indexation allowance and to ncourage long-term investment. It has been extended ubstantially since its introduction. The taper relief rules e potentially complex and individuals are advised to eek professional advice if uncertain.

Taper relief is available to individuals, partnerships, states and trusts but cannot be claimed by companies to hom other tax rules apply. This relief reduces the roportion of a capital gain charged to tax according to ne period of ownership since April 1998 and whether ne asset disposed of is a business or non-business asset. usiness assets, which have a higher rate of relief than on-business assets, are broadly identified as assets used or business purposes and shares in both trading and on-trading companies. The maximum abatement is chieved after a holding period of two years for business ssets and ten years for non-business assets. The holding eriod is normally the number of complete years (not tax ears) after 5 April 1998 that the asset is held. For on-business assets acquired before 17 March 1998, owever, the period is deemed to be increased by one onus year. For example, a non-business asset acquired on 6 March 1998 and sold on 6 April 2007 would have a olding period for taper relief of ten years – that is, nine years' ownership post 5 April 1998 plus the extra bonus year because the asset was held on 17 March 1998. Where an inter-spouse or inter-registered civil partner transfer is involved, the holding period is the combined ownership period of both spouses/partners.

Taper relief reduces the gains on non-business assets by 5 per cent per year, once the asset has been held for three years with a maximum reduction amounting to 40 per cent. Business assets attract a maximum taper relief of 75 per cent of the gain after two years of ownership. The percentages of gains remaining chargeable for disposals taking place on and after 6 April 2007 are shown in the table below .

	Percentage of gains chargeable	
No. of whole years of ownership	*Business assets* %	*Non-business assets* %
1	50	100
2	25	100
3	25	95
4	25	90
5	25	85
6	25	80
7	25	75
8	25	70
9	25	65
10 or more	25	60

If an asset has been used partly as a business asset and partly as a non-business asset (ie during different periods of ownership, and/or at the same time) during the 10 years of ownership leading up to disposal, the chargeable gain is calculated and apportioned between business and non-business use of the asset. Business asset taper relief is applied to the business element of the gain, and non-business asset taper relief to the remainder, as if two separate gains had arisen on the disposal of different assets. The two gains are then added together.

If only chargeable gains arise from disposals carried out in 2007–8 the taper relief, if any, must be calculated by reference to each disposal. The aggregate sum of taper relief will then be subtracted from the total chargeable gains to produce the net gains for the year. Where disposals made in 2007–8 give rise to both gains and losses, the losses must be subtracted from the gains and taper relief calculated on the net sum remaining. It is necessary to allocate the losses between the gains where there are two or more disposals producing gains. Losses brought forward from an earlier year must also be subtracted when calculating the net gains qualifying for taper relief. However, the losses brought forward are not to reduce the net gains below the annual exemption limit of £9,200 which applies for 2007–8.

BUSINESS ASSET ROLL-OVER RELIEF

A capital gain on the disposal of certain types of asset used in a person's business may be deferred or 'rolled over' if the proceeds are reinvested in new qualifying trading assets. The gain is deducted from the base cost of the new asset and only becomes chargeable to CGT on the eventual disposal of that replacement asset unless a further roll-over situation then develops. Full relief is available if all the proceeds from the original asset (the old asset) are reinvested in the qualifying replacement asset (the new asset). If only part of the proceeds is reinvested, the difference represents an immediately chargeable gain.

If the amount not reinvested is greater than the gain, no roll-over relief is due.

Relief is only available if the acquisition of the new asset takes place within a period commencing 12 months before, and ending three years after, the disposal of the old asset. However, HMRC may extend this time limit at their discretion where there is a clear intention to acquire a replacement asset. The most common types of business assets that qualify for roll-over relief are land, buildings occupied and used for the purposes of trade, fixed plant and machinery. Roll-over relief is also available for assets used for the commercial letting of furnished holiday accommodation if certain conditions are satisfied. For details, *see* help sheet *IR290: Business Asset Roll-over Relief.* Roll-over relief is also available where shares in a company are transferred to trustees administering an employees' share incentive plan for the benefit of persons employed by that company. For details, *see* help sheet *IR287: Employee Share Schemes and Capital Gains Tax.* A similar relief, known as business transfer relief or incorporation relief, is available to defer a gain where business people transfer their business to a company in return for shares.

GIFTS HOLD-OVER RELIEF

The gift of an asset is treated as a disposal made for a consideration equal to market value, with a corresponding acquisition by the transferee at an identical value. In the case of gifts made by individuals and a limited range of trustees to a transferee resident in the UK, a form of hold-over relief may be available. This relief, which must be claimed, in effect enables liability for CGT to be deferred and passed to the person to whom the gift is made. Relief is limited to the transfer of certain assets including the following:

- gifts of assets used for the purposes of a business carried on by the donor or his or her personal company
- gifts of shares in trading companies that are not listed on a stock exchange
- gifts of shares or securities in the donor's personal trading company
- gifts of agricultural land and buildings that would qualify for inheritance tax agricultural property relief
- gifts that are chargeable transfers for inheritance tax purposes
- certain types of gifts that are specifically exempted from inheritance tax

Hold-over relief is automatically due on certain sorts of gifts including gifts to charities and community amateur sports clubs, and gifts of works of art where certain undertakings have been given. There are certain rules to prevent gifts hold-over relief being used for tax-avoidance purposes. For example, restrictions may apply where an individual gifts assets to trustees administering a trust in which the individual retains an interest or where the assets transferred comprise a dwelling-house. Subject to these exceptions, the effect of a valid claim for hold-over relief is similar to that following a claim for roll-over relief on the disposal of business assets. Adjustments may be necessary where some consideration (less than market value) is given for a gift or where a gifted asset has not been used for business purposes throughout the period of ownership. Further information is available in help sheet *IR295: Relief for Gifts and Similar Transactions.*

OTHER CGT RELIEFS

Enterprise investment scheme (EIS) deferral relief allows the deferral of gains on the disposal of an asset when an individual subscribes for shares in an EIS company; *se* help sheet *IR297: Enterprise Investment Scheme and Capita Gains Tax.* Similarly, venture capital trust (VCT) deferra relief allows the deferral of gains on the disposal of a asset when an individual subscribes for shares in a VCT *see* help sheet *IR298: Venture Capital Trusts and Capita Gains Tax.* Halving relief reduces by half certain gain deferred from before April 1988; *see* help sheet *IR28(Rebasing – Assets Held at 31 March 1982.* For mor general guidance on CGT, *see* HMRC booklet *CGT Capital Gains Tax – An Introduction.*

INHERITANCE TAX

Inheritance tax (IHT) is a tax on the value of a person' estate on death and on certain gifts made by an individu during his or her lifetime, usually payable within si months of death. Broadly speaking, a person's estate i everything he or she owned at the time of death includin property, possessions, money and investments, less his o her debts. Not everyone pays IHT. It only applies if th taxable value of an estate is above the current inheritanc tax threshold. If an estate, including any assets held i trust and gifts made within seven years of death, is les than the threshold, no IHT will be due. See table for th lower threshold limit, known as the nil rate band.

2006–7	£285,000
2007–8	£300,000
2008–9	£312,000
2009–10	£325,000
2010–11	£350,000

IHT used to be something only very wealthy individual needed to consider. This is no longer the case. A dramati rise in house prices over recent years coupled with the fa that the IHT threshold has not kept pace with house pric inflation means that the estates of an increasing number c taxpayers who would not consider themselves wealthy, ar now becoming liable for IHT purely because of the valu of their home. However, there are a number of ways th individuals – while still alive – can legally reduce the IH bill that will apply to their estates on death. Sever valuable IHT exemptions are available (explained furthe below) which allow individuals to pass on assets durin their lifetime or in their will without any IHT being du IHT forms and information leaflets can be downloade from the HMRC website (W www.hmrc.gov.uk). Th main guide is entitled, *HMRC Inheritance Tax: Custom Guide.* Paper versions and further help are available fro the probate and IHT helpline on 0845-302 0900.

DOMICILE

Liability to IHT depends on an individual's domicile the time of any gift or on death. Domicile is a comple legal concept and what follows explains some of the mai issues. An individual is domiciled in the country where h or she has a permanent home. Domicile is different fro nationality or residence, and an individual can only hav one domicile at any given time.

A domicile of origin is normally acquired from th individual's father on birth, though this may not be th country in which he or she is born. For example, a chil born in Germany while his or her father is working ther but whose permanent home is in the UK, will have th UK as his or her domicile of origin. Until a person legall changes his or her domicile, it will be the same as that c the person on whom they are legally dependent.

Individuals can legally acquire a new domicile – a omicile of choice – from the age of 16 by leaving the urrent country of domicile and settling in another ountry and providing strong evidence of intention to live here permanently or indefinitely. Women who were narried before 1974 acquired their husband's domicile nd still retain it until they legally acquire a new domicile.

For IHT purposes, there is a concept of deemed omicile. This means that even if a person is not omiciled in the UK under general law, he or she is reated as domiciled in the UK at the time of a transfer (ie t the time of a lifetime gift or on death) if he or she (a) vas domiciled in the UK within the three years nmediately before the transfer, or (b) was resident in the JK in at least 17 of the 20 income tax years of assessment nding with the year in which a transfer is made. Where a erson is domiciled, or treated as domiciled, in the UK at he time of a gift or on death, the location of assets is nmaterial and full liability to IHT arises. A non-UK omiciled individual is also liable to IHT but only on hargeable property in the UK. The assets of husband and vife and registered civil partners are not merged for IHT urposes. Each spouse or partner is treated as a separate ndividual entitled to receive the benefit of his or her xemptions, reliefs and rates of tax.

HT EXEMPTIONS

here are some important exemptions that allow ndividuals to legally pass assets on to others, both before nd after their death – without being subject to IHT.

xempt beneficiaries

ssets can be given away to certain people and rganisations without any IHT having to be paid. These ifts, which are exempt whether individuals make them uring their lifetime or in their will, include gifts to:

- a husband, wife or civil partner, even if the couple is legally separated (but not if they are divorced or the civil partnership has dissolved), as long as both partners have a permanent home in the UK. Note that gifts to an unmarried partner or a partner with whom the donor has not formed a civil partnership are not exempt
- UK charities, including the National Trust
- some national institutions, including national museums and universities
- UK political parties

nnual exemption

he first £3,000 of gifts made each tax year by each ndividual is exempt from IHT. If this exemption is not sed, or not wholly used in any year, the balance may be arried forward to the following year only. A couple, herefore, may give away a total of £6,000 per tax year etween them or £12,000 if they haven't used their revious year's annual exemptions.

Vedding gifts/civil partnership ceremony gifts

ome gifts are exempt from IHT because of the type of ift or reason for making it. Wedding or civil partnership eremony gifts made to either of the couple are exempt om IHT up to certain amounts:

- gifts by a parent, £5,000
- gifts by a grandparent or other relative, £2,500
- gifts by anyone else, £1,000

he gift must be made on or shortly before the date of the edding or civil partnership ceremony. If it is called off nd the gift is still made, this exemption will not apply.

Small gifts

An individual can make small gifts, up to the value of £250, to any number of people in any one tax year without them being liable for IHT. However, a larger sum such as £500 cannot be given and exemption claimed for the first £250. In addition, this exemption cannot be used with any other exemption when giving to the same person. For example, a parent cannot combine a small gifts exemption with a wedding/civil partnership ceremony gift exemption to give a child £5,250 when he or she gets married or forms a civil partnership. Neither may an individual combine a small gifts exemption with the annual exemption to give someone £3,250. Note that it is possible to use the annual exemption with any other exemption, such as the wedding/civil partnership ceremony gift exemption. For example, if a child marries or forms a civil partnership, the parent can give him or her a total IHT-free gift of £8,000 by combining £5,000 under the wedding/civil partnership gift exemption and £3,000 under the annual exemption.

Normal expenditure

Any gifts made out of individuals' after-tax income (not capital) are exempt from IHT if they are part of their normal expenditure and do not result in a fall in their standard of living. These can include regular payments to someone, such as an allowance or gifts for Christmas or a birthday and regular premiums paid on a life insurance policy for someone else.

Maintenance gifts

An individual can make IHT-free maintenance payments to his or her spouse or registered civil partner, ex-spouse or former civil partner, relatives dependent because of old age or infirmity, and children (including adopted children and step-children) who are under 18 or in full-time education.

POTENTIALLY EXEMPT TRANSFERS

If an individual makes a gift to either another individual or certain types of trust and it is not covered by one of the above exemptions, it is known as a potentially exempt transfer (PET). A PET is only free of IHT on two strict conditions: (a) the gift must be made at least seven years before the donor's death. If the donor does not survive seven years after making the gift, it will be liable for IHT and (b) the gift must be made as a true gift with no strings attached (technically known as a gift with reservation of benefit). This means that the donor must give up all rights to the gift and stop benefiting from it in any way.

If a gift is made and the donor does retain some benefit from it then it will still count as part of his or her estate no matter how long he or she lives after making it. For example, a father could make a lifetime gift of his home to his child. HMRC would not accept this as a true gift, however, if the father continued to live in the home (unless he paid his child a full commercial rent to do so) because he would be considered to still have a material interest in the gifted home. Its value, therefore, would still be liable for IHT.

In some circumstances a gift with strings attached might give rise to an income tax charge on the donor based on the value of the benefit he or she retains. In this case the donor can choose whether to pay the income tax or have the gift treated as a gift with reservation.

CHARGEABLE TRANSFERS

Any remaining lifetime gifts that are not (potentially or otherwise) exempt transfers are chargeable transfers or 'chargeable gifts', meaning that they incur liability to IHT. Chargeable transfers comprise mainly gifts to or from companies and gifts to particular types of trust called discretionary trusts. There is an immediate claim for IHT on chargeable gifts, and additional tax may be payable if the donor dies within seven years of making a chargeable gift.

DEATH

Immediately before the time of death an individual is deemed to make a transfer of value. This transfer will comprise the value of assets forming part of the deceased's estate after subtracting most liabilities. Any exempt transfers may be excluded such as transfers for the benefit of a surviving spouse or civil partner, and charities. Death may also trigger three additional liabilities:

- a PET made within the seven years before the death loses its potential status and becomes chargeable to IHT
- the value of gifts made with reservation may incur liability if any benefit was enjoyed within the seven years before the death
- additional tax may become payable for chargeable lifetime transfers made within the seven years before the death

The personal representative (the person nominated to handle the affairs of the deceased person) arranges to value the estate and pay any IHT that is due. One or more personal representatives can be nominated in a person's will, in which case they are known as the executors. If a person dies without leaving a will a court can nominate the personal representative, who is then known as the administrator. Valuing the deceased person's estate is one of the first things his or her personal representative needs to do. The representative will not normally be able to take over management of the estate (called 'applying for probate') until all or some of any IHT that is due has been paid.

VALUATIONS

When valuing a deceased person's estate all assets (property, possessions and money) owned at the time of death and certain assets given away during the seven years before death must be included. The valuation must accurately reflect what those assets would reasonably fetch in the open market at the date of death. The value of all of the assets that the deceased owned should include:

- his or her share of any assets owned jointly with someone else, for example a house owned with a partner
- any assets that are held in a trust, from which the deceased had the right to benefit
- any assets given away, but in which he or she kept an interest (gifts with reservation)
- PETs given away within the last seven years

Most estate assets can be valued quite easily, for example money in bank accounts or stocks and shares. In other instances the help of a professional valuer may be needed. Advice on how to value different assets including joint or trust assets is available at www.hmrc.gov.uk. When valuing an estate, special relief is made available for certain assets. The two main reliefs are business relief and agricultural property relief outlined below. Once all assets have been valued, the next step is to deduct from the total assets everything that the deceased person owed such as unpaid bills, outstanding mortgages and other loans plus their funeral expenses. The value of all of the assets, less the deductible debts, is their estate. IHT is only payable on any value above £300,000 for the tax year 2007–8 at the current rate of 40 per cent.

RELIEF FOR SELECTED ASSETS

Agricultural Property

Relief from IHT is available on the agricultural value of agricultural property that is transferred. Agricultur property generally includes land or pasture used in th growing of crops or intensive rearing of animals fo food consumption. It can also include farmhouse and farm cottages. The agricultural property can b owner-occupied or let. Relief is only due if the transfero has owned the property and it has been occupied fo agricultural purposes for a minimum period.

The value transferred, either on a lifetime gift or o death, must be determined. This value may then b reduced by a percentage. Under current rates, a 100 pe cent deduction will be available if the transferor retaine vacant possession or could have obtained that possessio within a period of 12 months following the transfer. I other cases, notably including land let to tenants, a lowe deduction of 50 per cent is usually available. Howeve this lower deduction may be increased to 100 per cent the letting was made after 31 August 1995.

To qualify for the relief, the agricultural property mus either have been occupied by the transferor for th purposes of agriculture throughout a two-year perio ending on the date of the transfer, or have been owne by the transferor throughout a period of seven yea ending on that date and also occupied for agricultur purposes.

Business Relief

Business relief is available on transfers of certain types c business and of business assets if they qualify as relevar business property and the transferor has owned them for minimum period. The relief can be claimed for transfe made during the person's lifetime and on death and o chargeable occasions arising on relevant business propert held in trust. Where the value transferred is attributable t relevant business property, the business relief reduces th value by a percentage. Business relief may be claimed o relevant business property including:

- a business or an interest in a business such as partnership
- unquoted shares and securities
- shares or securities of a quoted company whic themselves or with other listed shares or securities gi the transferor control of a company
- any land, buildings, plant or machinery owned by partner or controlling shareholder and used wholly c mainly in the business of the partnership or compan immediately before the transfer; this applies only if th partnership interest or shareholding would itself, if were transferred, qualify for business relief
- any land, buildings, machinery or plant that were use wholly or mainly for the purpose of a business carrie on by the transferor

If an asset qualifies for business relief, the rat (percentage) at which it is currently allowed are as follow

A business or interest in a business	100
A holding of shares in an unquoted company	100
Control holding of shares in a quoted company (more than 50 of the voting rights)	50
Land, buildings or plant and machinery used in a business of which the deceased was a partner at the date of death or used by a company controlled by the deceased	50
Land, buildings, plant and machinery held in a trust where the deceased had the right to benefit from the trust and the asset was used in a business carried on by the deceased	50

t is a general requirement that the property must have een retained for a period of two years before the transfer r death, and restrictions may be necessary if the property as not been used wholly for business purposes. The same roperty cannot obtain both business property relief and he relief available for agricultural property.

ALCULATION OF TAX PAYABLE

The calculation of IHT payable adopts the use of a umulative or 'running' total. Looking back seven years rom the death the chargeable value of gifts in that period s added to the total value of the estate at death. The gifts vill use up all or part of the inheritance tax threshold (the nil rate band' above which IHT becomes payable) first.

ifetime Chargeable Transfers

The value transferred by lifetime chargeable transfers must e added to the seven-year running total to calculate vhether any IHT is due. If the nil rate band is exceeded, ax will be imposed on the excess at the rate of 20 per ent. However, if the donor dies within a period of seven ears from the date of the chargeable lifetime transfer, dditional tax may be due. This is calculated by applying ax at the full rate of 40 per cent in substitution for the ate of 20 per cent previously used. The amount of tax is hen reduced to a percentage by applying tapering relief. This percentage is governed by the number of years from he date of the lifetime gift to the date of death, as ollows:

ERIOD OF YEARS BEFORE DEATH

Not more than 3	100%
More than 3 but not more than 4	80%
More than 4 but not more than 5	60%
More than 5 but not more than 6	40%
More than 6 but not more than 7	20%

hould this exercise produce liability greater than that reviously paid at the 20 per cent rate on the lifetime ransfer, additional tax, representing the difference, must e paid. Where the calculation shows an amount falling elow tax paid on the lifetime transfer, no additional ability can arise nor will the shortfall become repayable.

Tapering relief is, of course, only available if the alculation discloses a liability to IHT. There is no liability f the lifetime transfer falls within the nil rate band.

otentially Exempt Transfers

Vhere a PET loses immunity from liability to IHT ecause the donor dies within seven years of making the ransfer, the value transferred by that transfer enters into he running total. Any liability to IHT will be calculated y applying the full rate of 40 per cent, reduced to the ercentage governed by tapering relief if the original ransfer occurred more than three years before death. Again, liability to IHT can only arise if the nil rate band is xceeded.

Death

On death, IHT is due on the value of the deceased's estate lus the running total of gifts made in the seven years efore death if they come to more than the nil-rate band. HT is then charged at the full rate of 40 per cent on the mount in excess of the nil rate band.

ettled Property and Trusts

Trusts are special legal arrangements that can be used by ndividuals to control how their assets are distributed to their beneficiaries and minimise their IHT liability. Complex rules apply to establish IHT liability on settled property which includes property held in trust, and individuals are advised to take expert legal advice when setting up trusts.

RATES OF TAX

In earlier times there were several rates of IHT that progressively increased as the value transferred grew in size. However, since 1988 there have been only three rates:

- a nil rate
- a lifetime rate of 20 per cent
- a full rate of 40 per cent

The nil rate band usually changes on an annual basis, and for events taking place after 5 April 2007 applies to the first £300,000. Any excess over this level is taxable at 20 per cent or 40 per cent as the case may be. The IHT threshold will be increased to £312,000 for 2008–9 and £325,000 for 2009–10.

PAYMENT OF TAX

IHT is normally due six months after the end of the month in which the death occurs or the chargeable transaction takes place. This is referred to as the due date. Tax on some assets such as business property, certain shares and securities and land and buildings (including the deceased person's home) can be deferred and paid in equal instalments over ten years, though interest will be charged in most cases. If IHT is due on lifetime gifts and transfers, the person or transferee who received the gift or assets is normally liable to pay the IHT, though any IHT already paid at the time of a transfer into a trust or company will be taken into account. If tax owed is not paid by the due date, interest is charged on any unpaid IHT, no matter what caused the delay in payment.

CORPORATION TAX

Corporation tax is a tax on a company's profits, including all its income and gains. This tax is payable by UK resident companies and by non-resident companies carrying on a trade in the UK through a permanent establishment. The following comments are confined to companies resident in the UK. The word company is also used to include:

- members' clubs, societies and associations
- trade associations
- housing associations
- groups of individuals carrying on a business but not as a partnership (for example, cooperatives)

A company's taxable income is charged by reference to income or gains arising in its accounting period, which is normally 12 months long. In some circumstances accounting periods can be shorter than 12 months, but never longer. The accounting period is also normally the period for which a company's accounts are drawn up, but the two periods do not have to coincide.

If a company is liable to pay corporation tax on its profits, several things must be done. HMRC must be informed that the company exists and is liable for tax. A self-assessment company tax return plus full accounts and calculation of tax liability must be filed by the statutory filing date, normally 12 months after the end of the accounting period. Companies have to work out their own tax liability and have to pay their tax without prior assessment by HMRC. Records of all company expenditure and income must be kept in order to work out the tax liability correctly. Companies are liable to penalties if they fail to carry out these obligations.

Measures to reform the business tax system were announced in the 2007 Budget with a staged introduction over the next few years. The major elements of the reform package will apply from 2008–9.

Extensive corporation tax information is available on the HMRC website and companies may file their company tax returns online at the HMRC's Corporation Tax Online service at www.hmrc.gov.uk/ctsa/ct-online.htm.

RATE OF TAX

The rate of corporation tax is fixed for a financial year starting on 1 April and ending on the following 31 March. If a company's accounting period does not coincide with the financial year, its profits must be apportioned between the financial years and the tax rates for each financial year applied to those profits. The corporation tax liability is the total tax for both financial years.

The main rate of corporation tax for 2007–8 is 30 per cent, as it has been for the past nine years. It has been announced in advance that the rate will go down to 28 per cent from April 2008 (North Sea oil and gas ring fence activities will retain a main corporation tax rate of 30 per cent).

SMALL COMPANIES' RATE

Where the profits of a company do not exceed stated limits, corporation tax becomes payable at the small companies' rate. It is the amount of profits and not the size of the company that governs the application of the small companies' rate.

For each of the three financial years ending on 31 March 2000, 31 March 2001 and 31 March 2002 the small companies' rate was 20 per cent. It was then reduced to 19 per cent for ensuing years but has been increased once again to 20 per cent from April 2007. It has been announced that there will be a staged increase in the small companies' rate from 20 per cent to 21 per cent from April 2008 and to 22 per cent from April 2009. (North Sea oil and gas ring activities will retain a small companies' rate of 19 per cent).

A company can make profits of up to £300,000 without losing the benefit of the small companies' rate. If, however, its profits exceed £300,000 but fall below £1,500,000, then marginal small companies' rate relief applies. The effect of marginal relief is that the average rate of corporation tax imposed on all profits steadily increases from the lower small companies' rate of 20 per cent to the main rate of 30 per cent, with tax being imposed on profits in the margin at an increased rate. Where a change in the rate of tax is introduced and the accounting period of a company overlaps 31 March, profits must be apportioned to establish the appropriate rate for each part of those profits.

The lower limit of £300,000 and the upper limit of £1,500,000 apply to a period of 12 months and must be proportionately reduced for shorter periods. Some restriction in the small companies' rate and the marginal rate may be necessary if there are two or more associated companies, namely companies under common control. Prior to 1 April 2006 there was a corporation tax starting rate of zero for very small companies where profits for a 12-month period were below £10,000, with marginal relief available where profits were between £10,001 and £50,000. There was also a non-corporate distribution rate (NCDR) set at 19 per cent for the financial year to 31 March 2006. This was a minimum rate of corporation tax that could apply to company profits distributed to persons who were not companies (ie individuals or trustees) if the company's underlying rate of tax on profits was less than the NCDR. From 1 April 2006, both the starting rate and non-corporate distribution rate were replaced with a single banding for small companies.

CORPORATION TAX ON PROFITS

£ per year	*2006–7*	*2007–8*
£0–£300,000	19%	20%
£300,001–£1,500,000	Marginal relief	Marginal relief
£1,500,000 or more	30%	30%

CAPITAL ALLOWANCES

Businesses can claim tax allowances, called capital allowances, on certain purchases or investments. This means that a proportion of these costs can be deducted from a business' taxable profits and reduce its tax bill. Capital allowances are currently available on plant and machinery, buildings and research and development. The amount of the allowance depends on what is being claimed for. As part of the staged business tax reform package announced in the 2007 Budget, changes to the capital allowances regime are to be introduced, mainly from April 2008.

Detailed information on capital allowances is available from the Enhanced Capital Allowances website (W www.eca.gov.uk).

PAYMENT OF TAX

Corporation tax liabilities are normally due and payable in a single lump sum not later than nine months and one day after the end of the accounting period. For large companies – those with profits over £1.5m which pay corporation tax at the main rate – there is a requirement to pay corporation tax in four quarterly instalments. Where a company is a member of a group, the profits of the entire group must be merged to establish whether the company is large.

CAPITAL GAINS

Chargeable gains arising to a company are calculated in a manner similar to that used for individuals. However, the withdrawal of the indexation allowance after April 1998 and the introduction of taper relief from the same date have no application to companies. Nor are companies entitled to the CGT annual exemption of £9,200. Companies do not suffer capital gains tax on chargeable gains but incur liability to corporation tax instead. Tax is due on the full chargeable gain of an accounting period after subtracting relief for losses, if any.

GROUPS OF COMPANIES

Each company within a group is separately charged to corporation tax on profits, gains and income. However where one group member realises a loss for which special rules apply, other than a capital loss, a claim may be made to offset the deficiency against profits of some other member of the same group. The transfer of capital assets from one member of a group to a fellow member will usually incur no liability to tax on chargeable gains.

SPORTS CLUBS

Though corporation tax is payable by unincorporated associations including most clubs, a substantial exemption from liability to corporation tax, introduced in April

2002, is available to qualifying registered community amateur sports clubs (CASCs). Sports clubs that are registered as CASCs are exempt from liability to corporation tax on:

- profits from trading where the turnover of the trade is less than £30,000 in a 12-month period (limit was £15,000 prior to 1 April 2004)
- income from property where gross rental income is less than £20,000 in a 12-month period (limit was £10,000 prior to 1 April 2004)
- bank and building society interest received
- chargeable gains

All of the exemptions depend upon the club having been a registered CASC for the whole of the relevant accounting period and the income or gains being used only for qualifying purposes. If the club has only been a registered CASC for part of an accounting period the exemption amounts of £30,000 (for trading) and £20,000 (for income from property) are reduced proportionately. Only interest and gains received after the club is registered are exempted.

Among other advantages available to registered clubs is that donations may be received under the Gift Aid arrangements. Charities are also generally exempt from corporation tax where they operate through a company structure.

VALUE ADDED TAX

Value added tax (VAT) is a tax on consumer expenditure charged when an individual buys goods and services in the European Union including the UK. It is normally included in the sale price of goods and services and paid at the point of purchase. Each EU country has its own rate of VAT. From a business point of view, VAT is charged on most business transactions involving the supply of goods and services by a registered trader in the UK and Isle of Man. It is also charged on goods, and some services, imported from places outside the EU and on goods and some services coming into the UK from the other EU countries. VAT is administered by HM Revenue and Customs. A wide range of information on VAT, including VAT forms, is available online (W www.hmrc.gov.uk). HMRC notice *700: The VAT Guide* is the main guide to VAT rules and procedures. HMRC runs a national advice service enquiry line dealing with VAT queries on 0845-010 9000.

RATES OF TAX

There are three rates of VAT in the UK. The standard rate – currently 17.5 per cent – is payable on most goods and services in the UK. The reduced rate – currently 5 per cent – is payable on certain goods and services including, for example, domestic fuel and power, children's car seats, women's sanitary products, contraceptive products and the installation of energy-saving materials such as wall insulation and solar panels. The 5 per cent rate will also be introduced on 'over the counter' sales of smoking cessation products. It will apply for one year and will take effect alongside the introduction of the ban on smoking in public places in England starting on 1 July 2007. A zero, or nil, rate applies to certain items including, for example, children's clothes, books, newspapers, most food and drink, and drugs and aids for disabled people. There are numerous exceptions to the zero-rated categories however. While most food and drink is zero-rated, items including ice creams, chocolates, sweets, potato crisps and alcoholic drinks are not. Neither are drinks or items sold for consumption in a restaurant or cafe. Takeaway cold items such as sandwiches are zero-rated, while takeaway hot foods like fish and chips are not.

REGISTRATION

All traders, including professional persons and companies, must register for VAT if they are making 'taxable supplies' of a value exceeding stated limits. All goods and services that are VAT-rated are defined as taxable supplies including zero-rated items which must be included when calculating the total value of a trader's taxable supplies – his or her taxable turnover. The limits that govern mandatory registration are amended periodically.

From 1 April 2007, an unregistered trader must register for VAT if:

- at the end of any month the total value of his or her taxable turnover (not just profit) for the past 12 months or less is more than the current VAT threshold of £64,000 – *and*
- at any time he or she has reasonable grounds to expect that his or her taxable turnover will be more than the current registration threshold of £64,000 in the next thirty days alone

To register for VAT, form VAT 1 must be completed and sent to HMRC within 30 days of any of the above. Traders who do not register at the correct time can be fined. Traders must charge VAT on their taxable supplies from the date they first need to be registered. Traders who only supply zero-rated goods may not have to register for VAT even if their taxable turnover goes above the registration threshold. However, a trader in this position must inform HMRC first and apply to be exempt from registration. A trader whose taxable turnover does not reach the mandatory registration limit may choose to register for VAT voluntarily if what he or she does counts as a business for VAT purposes. This step may be thought advisable to recover input tax (*see* below) or to compete with other registered traders. Registered traders may submit an application for deregistration if their taxable turnover subsequently falls. An application for deregistration can be made if the taxable turnover for the year beginning on the application date is not expected to exceed £62,000.

INPUT TAX

Registered traders suffer input tax when buying in goods or services for the purposes of their business. It is the VAT that traders pay out to their suppliers on goods and services coming *in* to their business. Relief can usually be obtained for input tax suffered, either by setting that tax against output tax due or by repayment. Most items of input tax can be relieved in this manner. Where a registered trader makes both exempt supplies and taxable supplies to his customers or clients, there may be some restriction in the amount of input tax that can be recovered.

OUTPUT TAX

When making a taxable supply of goods or services, registered traders must account for output tax, if any, on the value of that supply. Output tax is the term used to describe the VAT on the goods and services that they supply or sell – the VAT on supplies going *out* of the business and collected from customers on each sale made. Usually the price charged by the registered trader will be increased by adding VAT, but failure to make the required addition will not remove liability to account for output tax. The liability to account for output tax, and also relief for input tax, may be affected where a trader is using a special second-hand goods scheme.

EXEMPT SUPPLIES

VAT is not chargeable on certain goods and services because the law deems them exempt from VAT. These include the provision of burial and cremation facilities, insurance, loans of money, certain types of education and training and some property transactions. The granting of a lease to occupy land or the sale of land will usually comprise an exempt supply, for example, but there are numerous exceptions. Exempt supplies do not enter into the calculation of taxable turnover that governs liability to mandatory registration (*see* above). Such supplies made by a registered trader may, however, limit the amount of input tax that can be relieved. It is for this reason that the exemption may be useful.

COLLECTION OF TAX

Registered traders submit VAT returns for accounting periods usually of three months in duration, but arrangements can be made to submit returns on a monthly basis. Very large traders must account for tax on a monthly basis, but this does not affect the three-monthly return. The return will show both the output tax due for supplies made by the trader in the accounting period and also the input tax for which relief is claimed. If the output tax exceeds input tax the balance must be remitted with the VAT return. Where input tax suffered exceeds the output tax due, the registered trader may claim recovery of the excess from HMRC.

This basis for collecting tax explains the structure of VAT. Where supplies are made between registered traders the supplier will account for an amount of tax that will usually be identical to the tax recovered by the person to whom the supply is made. However, where the supply is made to a person who is not a registered trader there can be no recovery of input tax, and it is on this person that the final burden of VAT eventually falls. Where goods are acquired by a UK trader from a supplier within the EU, the trader must also account for the tax due on acquisition. There are a number of simplified arrangements to make VAT accounting easier for businesses, particularly small businesses:

Cash accounting

Since April 1 2004, if taxable turnover is under £660,000 a year, the trader has been able to arrange to account to HMRC for VAT on the basis of cash received and paid, rather than the invoice date or time of supply. If a trader opts to use this scheme, he or she has been able to do so until the taxable turnover reaches £825,000. From 1 April 2007 the threshold for the cash accounting scheme has more than doubled to £1.35m.

Annual accounting

If taxable turnover is under £1,350,000 a year, the trader may join the annual accounting scheme and send in just one return a year. Traders in the scheme must make nine interim payments of VAT on account throughout the year, with a final balancing payment accompanying submission of the return. The number of interim payments may be reduced if turnover is small. Once a trader has joined the annual accounting scheme, membership may continue until the annual taxable turnover reaches £1,600,000.

Flat rate scheme

Introduced in the 2002 Budget, this scheme allows small businesses with an annual taxable turnover under £150,000 excluding VAT (£187,500 including VAT) to save on administration by paying VAT as a set flat percentage of their annual turnover instead of accounting internally for VAT on each individual 'in and out'. The percentage rate used is governed by the trade sector into which the business falls. The scheme can no longer be used once VAT-inclusive turnover exceeds £225,000.

Retail schemes

There are special schemes that offer retailers an alternative if it is impractical for them to issue invoices for a large number of supplies direct to the public. These schemes include a provision to claim relief from VAT on bad debts where goods or services are supplied to a customer who does not pay for them.

VAT FACT SUMMARY
from 1 April 2007

Standard rate	17.5%
Reduced rate	5%
Registration (last 12 months or next 30 days)	£64,000
Deregistration (next 12 months under)	£62,000
Cash accounting scheme – up to	£660,000
Flat rate scheme – up to	£150,000*
Annual accounting scheme – up to	£1,350,000

* Excluding VAT

STAMP DUTY

For the majority of people, contact with stamp duty arises when they buy a property. Stamp duty is payable by the buyer as a way of raising revenue for the government based on the purchase price of a property, stocks and shares. This section aims to provide a broad overview of stamp duty as it may affect the average person.

STAMP DUTY LAND TAX

Stamp duty land tax was introduced on 1 December 2003 and covers the purchase of houses, flats and other land, buildings and certain leases in the UK.

Before 1 December 2003 property purchasers had to submit documents providing all details of the purchase to the Stamp Office for 'stamping'. The purchaser's solicitor or licensed conveyancer would then send the stamped documentation to the appropriate land registry to register ownership of the property. Under stamp duty land tax, purchasers do not have to send documents for stamping. Instead, a land transaction return form SDLT1, which contains all information regarding the purchase that is relevant to HMRC, is signed by the purchaser. Buyers of property are responsible for completing the land transaction return and payment of stamp duty, though the solicitor or licensed conveyancer acting for them in a land transaction will normally complete the relevant paperwork. Once HMRC has received the completed land transaction return and the payment of any stamp duty due, a certificate will be issued that enables a solicitor or licensed conveyancer to register the property in the new owner's name at the Land Registry.

RATES OF STAMP DUTY LAND TAX

The following table shows the rates of stamp duty that apply on a property purchase price. A change in 2005, welcomed by many first-time buyers, was the doubling of he threshold from £60,000 to £120,000, below which no stamp duty is payable on residential property purchases. The new threshold took effect from 17 March 2005. This was increased again to £125,000 from 23 March 2006:

Purchase price	*Rate of tax (% of purchase price)*
£125,000 or less*	0%
£125,001 to £250,000	1%
£250,001 to £500,000	3%
£500,001 or more	4%

For transactions of non-residential land and property, the zero per cent rate applies for purchases of up to £150,000. A 1 per cent rate is payable for transactions of £150,001–£250,000; thereafter, rates are as per residential property transactions. The zero per cent band for residential property transactions in certain designated disadvantaged areas is £150,000. A full list of these areas can be found at www.hmrc.gov.uk

When assessing how much stamp duty is payable, the entire purchase price must be taken into account so the relevant stamp duty rate is paid on the whole sum, not just on the amount over each tax threshold. For example, on a property bought for £250,000, 1 per cent – £2,500 – is payable in stamp duty. On a property bought for £250,001, however, 3 per cent of the whole price – £7,500 – is payable.

RELIEF FOR NEW ZERO CARBON HOMES

A new relief from stamp duty land tax was to be introduced on 1 October 2007 for the vast majority of new 'zero carbon' homes in the UK. The relief will be time limited for five years and will therefore expire on 30 September 2012. Qualifying criteria for the relief will require zero carbon emissions from all energy use in the home over a year. To achieve this, the fabric of the home will be required to reach a very high energy efficiency standard and to be able to provide onsite renewable heat and power. New homes which are liable to stamp duty land tax on the first will be eligible to qualify. The relief will provide complete removal of stamp duty liabilities for all homes up to a purchase price of £500,000. Where the purchase price is in excess of £500,000 then the stamp duty liability will be reduced by £15,000. The balance of the stamp duty will be due in the normal way. Relief will not be available on second and subsequent sales of new zero carbon homes.

FIXTURES AND CHATTELS

As well as buying a property a purchaser may buy items inside the property. Some things inside a property are, in law, part of the land. These are called fixtures. Examples are fitted kitchen units and bathroom suites. Because these fixtures are part of the land, any price paid for them must be taken into account for stamp duty purposes. Other items inside a property are not part of the land. These are called chattels. Examples are free-standing cookers, curtains and fitted carpets. The purchase of chattels is not chargeable to stamp duty. However, where both a property and chattels are purchased, the amount shown on the land transaction return as the purchase price of the property must be a just and reasonable apportionment of the total amount paid. As with other entries on the form, the purchaser is responsible for the accuracy of this information. HMRC pays especial attention to residential property purchases just below stamp duty thresholds to prevent arrangements between buyer and seller to hand over cash so that the purchase price on paper looks lower or to pay unreasonably high amounts to buy chattels.

STAMP DUTY RESERVE TAX

Stamp duty or stamp duty reserve tax (SDRT) is payable at the rate of 0.5 per cent when shares are purchased. Stamp duty is payable when the shares are transferred using a stock transfer form, whereas SDRT is payable on paperless share transactions where the shares are transferred electronically without using a stock transfer form. Most share transactions nowadays are paperless and settled by stockbrokers through CREST (the electronic settlement and registration system). SDRT therefore now accounts for the majority of taxation collected on share transactions effected through the London Stock Exchange.

The flat rate of 0.5 per cent is based on the amount paid for the shares, not what they are worth. If, for example, shares are bought for £1,000, £5 SDRT is payable, whatever the value of the shares themselves. If shares are transferred for free, no SDRT is payable.

A higher rate of 1.5 per cent is payable if shares are transferred into a depositary receipt scheme or a clearance service. These are special arrangements where the shares are held by a third party.

CREST automatically deducts the SDRT and sends it to the HMRC. A stockbroker will settle up with CREST for the cost of the shares and the SDRT and then bill the purchaser for these and the broker's fees. If shares are not purchased through CREST, the stamp duty must be paid by the purchaser to HMRC.

UK stamp duty or SDRT is not payable on the purchase of foreign shares, though there may be foreign taxes to pay. SDRT is already accounted for in the price paid for units in unit trusts or shares in open-ended investment companies.

HELP AND INFORMATION

Further information on stamp duty land tax is available via the stamp taxes helpline on 0845-603 0135 (open 8.30am to 5.00pm Monday to Friday) or the HMRC website at www.hmrc.gov.uk, where a stamp duty calculator for both shares and land and property can be found. For buyers wishing to undertake their own conveyancing, copies of the land transaction return (SDLT1) and guidance notes (SDLT6) can be obtained by calling 0845-302 1472.

LEGAL NOTES

These notes outline certain aspects of the law as they might affect the average person. They are intended only as a broad guideline and are by no means definitive. The law is constantly changing so expert advice should always be taken. In some cases, sources of further information are given in these notes.

It is always advisable to consult a solicitor without delay. Anyone who does not have a solicitor already can contact the following for assistance in finding one: Citizens Advice Bureau (W www.nacab.org.uk), the Community Legal Service (W www.legalservices.gov.uk), the Law Society of England and Wales For assistance in Scotland, contact the Scottish Citizens Advice Bureau (W www.cas.org.uk) or the Law Society of Scotland.

The community legal service fund and legal aid and assistance schemes exist to make the help of a lawyer available to those who would not otherwise be able to afford one. Entitlement depends on an individual's means but a solicitor or Citizens Advice Bureau will be able to advise about entitlement.

LAW SOCIETY OF ENGLAND AND WALES
113 Chancery Lane, London WC2A 1PL T 020-7242 1222 W www.lawsociety.co.uk

LAW SOCIETY OF SCOTLAND
26 Drumsheugh Gardens, Edinburgh EH3 7YR T 0131-1226 7411 W www.lawscot.org.uk

ABORTION

Abortion is governed by the Abortion Act 1967. This act is currently under review by the Common Select Committee on science and technology. The provisions below are accurate at the time of writing.

Under the provisions of the Abortion Act 1967, a legally induced abortion must be:

- performed by a registered medical practitioner
- carried out in an NHS hospital or other approved premises
- certified by two registered medical practitioners as justified on one or more of the following grounds:
  (a) that the pregnancy has not exceeded its twenty-fourth week and that the continuance of the pregnancy would involve risk, greater than if the pregnancy were terminated, of injury to the physical or mental health of the pregnant woman or any existing children of her family
  (b) that the termination is necessary to prevent grave permanent injury to the physical or mental health of the pregnant woman
  (c) that the continuance of the pregnancy would involve risk to the life of the pregnant woman, greater than if the pregnancy were terminated
  (d) that there is a substantial risk that if the child were born it would suffer from such physical or mental abnormalities as to be seriously handicapped.

In determining whether the continuance of a pregnancy would involve such risk of injury to health as is mentioned in grounds (a) or (b), account may be taken of the pregnant woman's actual or reasonably foreseeable environment.

The requirements relating to the opinion of two registered medical practitioners and to the performance of the abortion at an NHS hospital or other approved place cease to apply in circumstances where a registered medical practitioner is of the opinion, formed in good faith, that a termination is immediately necessary to save the life, or to prevent grave permanent injury to the physical or mental health, of the pregnant woman.

Further information and advice can be obtained from:

FAMILY PLANNING ASSOCIATION (UK)
50 Featherstone Street, London EC1Y 8QU T 0845 122 8690 W www.fpa.org.uk

FAMILY PLANNING ASSOCIATION (SCOTLAND)
Unit 10, Firhill Business Centre, 76 Firhill Road, Glasgow G20 7BA T 0141-576 5088 W www.fpa.org.uk

BRITISH PREGNANCY ADVISORY SERVICE (BPAS)
T 08457-304030 W www.bpas.org

ADOPTION OF CHILDREN

The Adoption and Children Act 2002 reforms the framework for domestic and intercountry adoption in England and Wales and some parts of it extend to Scotland and Northern Ireland.

WHO MAY APPLY FOR AN ADOPTION ORDER

A couple (whether married or two people living as partners in an enduring family relationship) may apply for an adoption order where both of them are over 21 or where one is only 18 but the natural parent and the other is 21. An adoption order may be made for one applicant where that person is 21 and: a) the court is satisfied that person is the partner of a parent of the person to be adopted; or b) they are not married and are not civil partners; or c) married or in a civil partnership but they are separated from their spouse or civil partner and living apart with the separation likely to be permanent; or d) their spouse/civil partner is either unable to be found, or their spouse/civil partner is incapable by reason of ill health of making an application. There are certain qualifying conditions an applicant must meet eg residency in the British Isles.

ARRANGING AN ADOPTION

Adoptions may generally only be arranged by an adoption agency or by way of an order from the high court; breach of the restrictions on who may arrange an adoption would constitute a criminal offence. When deciding whether a child should be placed for adoption the court or adoption agency must consider all the factors set out in the 'welfare checklist'. These factors include amongst other things the child's wishes, needs and any harm which the child has suffered or is likely to suffer and the interest of the child is paramount. The parent must consent to the adoption, although the need for consent can be dispensed with by the court.

ADOPTION ORDER

Once an adoption has been arranged, a court order is necessary to make it legal; this may be obtained from the high court, county court or magistrates court (including family proceedings court). An adoption order may not be given unless the court is either satisfied that the consent of the child's natural parents (or guardians) has correctly been given or that consent should be dispensed with, eg where the parent or guardian cannot be found or is incapable of giving consent or where the welfare of the child so demands.

An adoption order has the effect of extinguishing the parental responsibility that a person other than the adopters (or adopter) has for the child, although where an order is made on the application of the partner of the parent, that parent keeps parental responsibility. This means that once adopted the child has the same status as a child born to the adoptive parents and will be treated as such for the purposes of intestate succession, National Insurance, child benefit etc. In addition the child may lose ights to the estates of those losing their parental esponsibility.

REGISTRATION AND CERTIFICATES

All adoption orders made in England and Wales are equired to be registered in the Adopted Children Register which also contains particulars of children adopted under registrable foreign adoptions. The General Register Office keeps this register from which certificates may be obtained in a similar way to birth certificates. The General Register Office also has equivalents in Scotland nd Northern Ireland.

TRACING NATURAL PARENTS OR CHILDREN WHO HAVE BEEN ADOPTED

An adult adopted person may apply to the Registrar-General to obtain a certified copy of his/her birth ertificate. For those adopted before 12 November 1975 t is obligatory to receive counselling services before this nformation is given. In any event, adoption agencies and doption support agencies should provide services to dopted persons to assist them in obtaining information bout their adoption and facilitate contact with their elatives. There is an Adoption Contact Register which provides a safe and confidential way for birth parents and ther relatives to assure an adopted person that contact vould be welcome. The BAAF (*see* below) can provide ddresses of organisations which offer advice, information nd counselling to adopted people, adoptive parents and eople who have had their children adopted. Further nformation can be obtained from:

BRITISH ASSOCIATION FOR ADOPTION AND FOSTERING (BAAF)
Saffron House, 6–10 Kirkby Street, London EC1N 8TS
T 020-7421 2600 **W** www.baaf.org.uk

SCOTLAND

The relevant legislation is the Adoption (Scotland) Act 1978 (as amended by the Children Act 1995 and the Adoption and Children (Scotland) Act 2007) and the provisions are similar to those described above. In Scotland, petitions for adoption are made to the sheriff court or the court of session.

Further information can be obtained from:

BRITISH ASSOCIATION FOR ADOPTION AND FOSTERING (BAAF)
BAAF Scottish Centre, 40 Shandwick Place, Edinburgh EH2 4RT
T 0131-220 4749

SCOTTISH ADOPTION ADVICE SERVICE
Suite 5/3, Skypark SP5, 45 Finnieston Street, Glasgow G3 8JU
T 0141-248 7530

BIRTHS (REGISTRATION)

It is the duty of the parents of a child born in England or Wales to register the birth within 42 days of the date of birth at the register office in the district in which the baby was born. If it is inconvenient to go to the district where the birth took place, the information for the registration may be given to a registrar in another district. Failure to register the birth within 42 days without reasonable cause may leave the parents liable to a penalty. If a birth has not been registered within 12 months of its occurrence it is possible for the late registration of the birth to be authorised by the Registrar-General, provided certain requirements can be met.

If the parents of the child were married to each other at the time of the birth (or conception), either parent may register the birth. If the parents were not married to each other at the time of the child's birth (or conception), the father's particulars may be entered in the register only where he attends the register office with the mother and they sign the birth register together. Where an unmarried parent is unable to attend the register office either parent may submit to the registrar a statutory declaration acknowledging the father's paternity (this form may be obtained from any registrar in England or Wales); alternatively a parental responsibility agreement or appropriate court order may be produced to the registrar.

If the parents do not register the birth of their child the following people may do so:

- the occupier of the house or hospital where the child was born
- a person who was present at the birth
- a person who is responsible for the child

Upon registration of the birth a short certificate is issued.

BIRTHS ABROAD

There are certain countries where birth registrations may be made for British subjects overseas. The British consul or high commission may register the births and issue certificates which are then sent to the General Register Office. If a birth is registered by the British consul or high commission, the registration would show the person's claim to British citizenship, British dependent territories citizenship or British overseas citizenship.

SCOTLAND

In Scotland the birth of a child must be registered within 21 days at the register office of either the district in which the baby was born or the district in which the mother was resident at the time of the birth.

If the child is born, either in or out of Scotland, on a ship, aircraft or land vehicle that ends its journey at any place in Scotland, the child, in most cases, will be registered as if born in that place.

CERTIFICATES OF BIRTHS, DEATHS OR MARRIAGES

Certificates of births, deaths or marriages that have taken place in England and Wales since 1837 can be obtained from the General Register Office or the Family Records Centre.

Certificates of births, marriages and deaths may be obtained in any of the following ways:

- by a personal visit to the Family Records Centre
- by post, telephone, fax or online (details of which may be obtained by calling T 0845-603 7788 or visiting W www.gro.gov.uk)
- locally from the register office where the event was originally registered

Marriage or death certificates may be obtained from the minister of the church in which the marriage or funeral took place. Any register office can advise about the best way to obtain certificates.

The fees for certificates are:

By personal application:

- full certificate of birth, marriage, death or adoption, £7.00
- short certificate of birth, £7.00
- short certificate of adoption, £5.50

By postal/phone/fax application:

- full certificate of birth, marriage, death or adoption, £11.50
- full certificate of birth, marriage, death or adoption with GRO reference supplied, £8.50
- short certificate of birth, £11.50
- short certificate of adoption, £10.00
- extra copies of the same birth, marriage or death certificate issued at the same time, £7.00

A priority service is also available with certificates despatched on the working day following receipt of your application at an additional cost. Visit W www.gro.gov.uk or call T 0845-603 7788 for further information.

Indexes prepared from the registers are available for searching by the public at the Family Records Centre in London or at a Superintendent Registrar's Office; indexes at the latter relate only to births, deaths and marriages which occurred in that registration district. There is no charge for searching the indexes in the Public Search Room at the Family Records Centre but a general search fee is charged for searches at a Superintendent Registrar's Office. A fee is charged for verifying index references against the records.

The Society of Genealogists has many records of baptisms, marriages and deaths prior to 1837.

SCOTLAND

Certificates of births, deaths or marriages that have taken place in Scotland since 1855 can be obtained from the General Register Office for Scotland or from the appropriate local registrar. The General Register Office for Scotland also keeps the Register of Divorces (including decrees of declaration of nullity of marriage), and holds parish registers dating from before 1855.

Fee for each particular search is:

- personal application: £3.00
- postal, telephone or fax order: £5.00
- internet order: £6.00

Document fee for each extract or abbreviated certificate of birth, death, marriage or adoption:

- personal application: £8.00
- postal, telephone or fax order: £8.00
- internet order: £10.00

A priority service for a response within 24 hours is available for an additional fee of £10.00

General search in the indexes to the statutory registers and parochial registers, per day or part thereof:

- full day (ie 9am to 4.30pm) search, £17.00
- afternoon (ie 1pm to 4.30pm) search, £10.00
- one-week search, £65.00
- four-week search, £220.00
- one-quarter search, £500.00
- one-year search, £1,500.00

Online searching is also available. For more information, visit W www.scotlandspeople.gov.uk Further information can be obtained from:

THE GENERAL REGISTER OFFICE
General Register Office, Trafalgar Road, Southport PR8 2HH
T 0845-603 7788 W www.gro.gov.uk

FAMILY RECORDS CENTRE
1 Myddelton Street, London EC1R 1UW

THE GENERAL REGISTER OFFICE FOR SCOTLAND
New Register House, 3 West Register Street, Edinburgh EH1 3YT
T 0131-334 0380 W www.gro-scotland.gov.uk

THE SOCIETY OF GENEALOGISTS
14 Charterhouse Buildings, Goswell Road, London EC1M 7BA
T 020-7251 8799

BRITISH CITIZENSHIP

Almost everyone who was a citizen of the UK and colonies and had a right of abode in the UK prior to the British Nationality Act 1981 became British citizens when the act came into force. British citizens have the right to live permanently in the UK and are free to leave and re-enter the UK at any time.

A person born on or after 1 January 1983 in the UK (including, for this purpose, the Channel Islands and the Isle of Man) is entitled to British citizenship if he/she falls into one of the following categories:

- he/she has a parent who is a British citizen
- he/she has a parent who is settled in the UK
- he/she is a newborn infant found abandoned in the UK
- his/her parents subsequently settle in the UK or become British citizens and an application is made before he/she is 18
- he/she lives in the UK for the first ten years of his/her life and is not absent for more than 90 days in each of those years
- he/she is adopted in the UK and one of the adopters is a British citizen
- if he/she has always been stateless and lives in the UK for a period of five years before his/her 22nd birthday

A person born outside the UK may acquire British citizenship if he/she falls into one of the following categories:

- he/she has a parent who is a British citizen otherwise than by descent, eg a parent who was born in the UK
- he/she has a parent who is a British citizen serving the crown overseas
- the home secretary consents to his/her registration while he/she is a minor
- he/she is a British dependent territories citizen, a British overseas citizen, a British subject or a British protected person and has been lawfully resident in the UK for five years
- he/she is a British dependent territories citizen wh

acquired that citizenship from a connection with Gibraltar
- he/she is adopted or naturalised

Where parents are married, the status of either may confer citizenship on their child. If a child is illegitimate, the status of the mother determines the child's citizenship.

Under the 1981 act, Commonwealth citizens and citizens of the Republic of Ireland were entitled to registration as British citizens before 1 January 1988. In 1985, citizens of the Falkland Islands were granted British citizenship.

Renunciation of British citizenship must be registered with the home secretary and will be revoked if no new citizenship or nationality is acquired within six months. If the renunciation was required in order to retain or acquire another citizenship or nationality, the citizenship may be reacquired once. The secretary of state may deprive a person of a citizenship status if he or she is satisfied that the person has done anything seriously prejudicial to the vital interests of the United Kingdom, or a British overseas territory, unless making the order would have the effect of rendering a person stateless. A person may also be deprived of a citizenship status which results from his registration or naturalisation if the secretary of state is satisfied that the registration or naturalisation was obtained by means of fraud, false representation or concealment of a material fact.

BRITISH DEPENDENT TERRITORIES CITIZENSHIP

Under the 1981 act, this type of citizenship was conferred on citizens of the UK and colonies by birth, naturalisation or registration in British dependent territories. British dependent territories citizens may be entitled to registration as British citizens on completion of five years' legal residence in the UK.

On 1 July 1997 citizens of Hong Kong who did not qualify to register as British citizens under the British Nationality (Hong Kong) Act 1990 lost their British dependent territories citizenship on the handover of sovereignty to China; they may, however, have applied to register as British nationals (overseas).

BRITISH OVERSEAS CITIZENSHIP

Under the 1981 act, as amended by the British Overseas Territories Act 2002, this type of citizenship was conferred on any UK and colonies citizens who did not qualify for British citizenship or citizenship of the British dependent territories. British overseas citizenship may be acquired by the wife, civil partner and minor children of a British overseas citizen in certain circumstances. British overseas citizens may be entitled to registration as British citizens on completion of five years' legal residence in the UK.

RESIDUAL CATEGORIES

British subjects, British protected persons and British nationals (overseas) may be entitled to registration as British citizens on completion of five years' legal residence in the UK.

Citizens of the Republic of Ireland who were also British subjects before 1 January 1949 can retain that status if they fulfil certain conditions.

EUROPEAN UNION CITIZENSHIP

British citizens (including Gibraltarians who are registered as such) are also EU citizens and are entitled to travel freely to other EU countries to work, study, reside and set up a business. EU citizens have the same rights with respect to the United Kingdom.

NATURALISATION

Naturalisation is granted at the discretion of the home secretary. The basic requirements are five years' residence (three years if the applicant is married to, or is the civil partner of a British citizen), good character, adequate knowledge of the English, Welsh or Scottish Gaelic language, passing the UK citizenship test and an intention to reside permanently in the UK.

STATUS OF ALIENS

Aliens may not hold public office or vote in Britain and they may not own a British ship or aircraft. Citizens of the Republic of Ireland are not deemed to be aliens. Certain provisions of the Immigration and Asylum Act 1999 make provision about immigration and asylum and about procedures in connection with marriage by superintendent registrar's certificate.

CONSUMER LAW

SALE OF GOODS

A sale of goods contract is the most common type of contract. It is governed by the Sale of Goods Act 1979 (as amended by the Sale and Supply of Goods Act 1994). The act provides protection for buyers by implying terms into every sale of goods contract. These terms include:

- an implied term that the seller will pass good title to the buyer (unless the seller agrees to transfer only such title as he has)
- where the seller sells goods by reference to a description, an implied term that the goods will match that description and, where the sale is by sample and description, it will not be sufficient that the bulk of the goods corresponds with the sample if the goods do not also correspond with the description
- where goods are sold by a business seller, an implied term that the goods will be of satisfactory quality if they meet the standard that a reasonable person would regard as satisfactory, taking into account any description of the goods, the price, and all other relevant circumstances. The quality of the goods includes their state and condition, relevant aspects being whether they are fit for the purposes for which such goods are commonly supplied, their appearance and finish, freedom from minor defects and their safety and durability. This term will not be implied, however, if a buyer has examined the goods and should have noticed the defect or if the seller specifically drew the buyer's attention to the defect
- where goods are sold by a business seller, an implied term that the goods are reasonably fit for any purpose made known to the seller by the buyer (either expressly or by implication), unless it is shown that the buyer does not rely on the seller's judgement, or it is not reasonable for him/her to do so
- where goods are sold by sample, implied terms that the bulk of the sample will correspond with the sample in quality, and that the goods are free from any defect rendering them unsatisfactory which would have been apparent on a reasonable examination of the sample

Some of the above terms can be excluded from contracts by the seller. The seller's right to do this is, however, restricted by the Unfair Contract Terms Act 1977. The act offers more protection to a buyer who 'deals as a consumer', (that is where the seller is selling in the course of a business, the goods are of a type ordinarily bought for private use and the goods are bought by a buyer who is not a business buyer, though not allowing any liability for breach of the implied terms described above to be excluded). In a sale by auction or competitive tender, a buyer never deals as consumer. Also, a seller can never exclude the implied term as to title mentioned above.

HIRE-PURCHASE AGREEMENTS

Terms similar to those implied in contracts of sales of goods are implied into contracts of hire-purchase, under the Supply of Goods (Implied Terms) Act 1973. The 1977 act limits the exclusion of these implied terms as before.

SUPPLY OF GOODS AND SERVICES

Under the Supply of Goods and Services Act 1982, similar terms are also implied in other types of contract under which ownership of goods passes, eg a contract for 'work and materials' such as supplying new parts while servicing a car, and contracts for the hire of goods (though not hire-purchase agreements). These types of contracts have additional implied terms:

- that the supplier will use reasonable care and skill in carrying out the service
- that the supplier will carry out the service in a reasonable time (unless the time has been agreed)
- that the supplier will make a reasonable charge (unless the charge has already been agreed)

The 1977 act limits the exclusion of these implied terms in a similar manner as before.

UNFAIR TERMS

The Unfair Terms in Consumer Contracts Regulations 1999 apply to contracts between business sellers (or suppliers of goods and services) and consumers. Where the terms have not been individually negotiated, ie where the terms were drafted in advance so that the consumer was unable to influence those terms, there will be an unfair term where a term operates to the detriment of the consumer (ie carries a significant imbalance in the parties' rights and obligations arising under the contract). An unfair term does not bind the consumer but the contract will continue to bind the parties if it is capable of existing without the unfair term. The regulations contain a non-exhaustive list of terms which are regarded as unfair. Whether a term is regarded as fair or not will depend on many factors, including the nature of the goods or services, the surrounding circumstances (such as the bargaining strength of both parties) and the other terms in the contract.

TRADE DESCRIPTIONS

It is a criminal offence under the Trade Descriptions Act 1968 for a business seller to apply a false trade description of goods or to supply or offer to supply any goods to which a false description has been applied. A 'trade description' includes descriptions of quality, size, composition, fitness for purpose, performance, method of manufacture, and place and date of manufacture of the goods.

FAIR TRADING

The Fair Trading Act 1973 is designed to protect the consumer. It provides for the appointment of a Director-General of Fair Trading, one of whose duties is to review commercial activities in the UK relating to the supply of goods and services to consumers. An example of a practice which has been prohibited by a reference made under this act is that of business sellers posing in advertisements as private sellers.

CONSUMER PROTECTION

Under the Consumer Protection Act 1987, producers of goods are liable for any injury or for any damage exceeding £275 caused by a defect in their product (subject to certain defences).

The Consumer Protection (Cancellation of Contracts Concluded Away from Business Premises) Regulations 1987 allow consumers a seven-day period in which to cancel contracts for the supply of goods and services, where the contracts were made during an unsolicited visit by a trader to the consumer's home or workplace. A contract will not be enforceable at all in this situation unless the trader has written to the consumer to notify them of the right to cancel within seven days.

Consumers are also afforded protection under the Consumer Protection (Distance Selling) Regulations 2000 in relation to cancellation periods, for example.

CONSUMER CREDIT

In matters relating to the provision of credit (or the supply of goods on hire or hire-purchase), consumers are also protected by the Consumer Credit Act 1974. Under this act a licence, issued by the Director-General of Fair Trading, is required to conduct a consumer credit or consumer hire business or an ancillary credit business. Any 'fit' person as defined within the act may apply to the Director-General of Fair Trading for a licence, which is normally renewable after five years. A licence is not necessary if only exempt agreements are involved. The provisions of the act only apply to 'regulated' agreements, ie those that are with individuals or partnerships, those that are not exempt (certain local authority and building society loans will be exempt), and those where the total credit does not exceed £25,000. Provisions include:

- the terms of the regulated agreement can be altered by the creditor, provided the agreement gives him/her the right to do so; in such cases the debtor must be given proper notice of this
- in order for a creditor to enforce a regulated agreement, the agreement must comply with certain formalities and must be properly executed. The debtor must also be given specified information by the creditor or his/her broker or agent during the negotiations which take place before the signing of the agreement. The agreement must state certain information such as the amount of credit, the annual interest rate, and the amount and timing of repayments
- if an agreement is signed other than at the creditor's (or credit broker's or negotiator's) place of business and oral representations were made in the debtor's presence during discussions pre-agreement, the debtor has a right to cancel the agreement. Time for cancellation expires five clear days after the debtor receives a second copy of the agreement. The agreement must inform the debtor of his right to cancel and how to cancel
- if the debtor is in arrears (or otherwise in breach of the agreement), the creditor must serve a default notice before taking any action such as repossessing the goods
- if the agreement is a hire-purchase or conditional sale agreement, the creditor cannot repossess the goods without a court order if the debtor has paid one third of the total price of the goods
- in agreements where the debtor is required to make grossly exorbitant payments or where the agreemen grossly contravenes the ordinary principles of fai

trading, the debtor may request that the court alter or set aside some of the terms of the agreement. The agreement can also be reopened during enforcement proceedings by the court itself

Where a credit reference agency has been used to check the debtor's financial standing, the creditor must give the agency's name to the debtor, who is entitled to see the agency's file on him. A fee of £1 is payable to the agency.

SCOTLAND

The legislation governing the sale and supply of goods applies to Scotland as follows:

- the Sale of Goods Act 1979 applies with some modifications and it has been amended by the Sale and Supply of Goods Act 1994
- the Supply of Goods (Implied Terms) Act 1973 applies
- the Supply of Goods and Services Act 1982 does not extend to Scotland but some of its provisions were introduced by the Sale and Supply of Goods Act 1994
- only Parts II and III of the Unfair Contract Terms Act 1977 apply
- the Trade Descriptions Act 1968 applies with minor modifications
- the Consumer Credit Act 1974 applies
- the Consumer Protection Act 1987 applies
- the General Product Safety Regulations 2005 apply
- the Unfair Terms in Consumer Contracts Regulations 1999 apply
- the Unfair Terms in Consumer Contracts (Amendment) Regulations 2001 apply
- the Consumer Protection (Distance Selling) Regulations 2000 apply
- the Sale and Supply of Goods to Consumers Regulations 2002 apply

PROCEEDINGS AGAINST THE CROWN

Until 1947, proceedings against the crown were generally possible only by a procedure known as a petition of right, which put the litigant at a considerable disadvantage. The Crown Proceedings Act 1947 placed the crown (not the sovereign in his/her private capacity, but as the embodiment of the state) largely in the same position as a private individual. The act did not however, extinguish or limit the crown's prerogative or statutory powers, and it granted immunity to HM ships and aircraft. It also left certain crown privileges unaffected. The act largely abolished the special procedures which previously applied to civil proceedings by and against the crown. Civil proceedings may be instituted against the appropriate government department or if there is doubt regarding which is the appropriate department, then against the attorney-general.

In Scotland proceedings against the crown founded on breach of contract could be taken before the 1947 act and no special procedures applied. The crown could, however, claim certain special pleas. The 1947 act applies in part to Scotland and brings the practice of the two countries as closely together as the different legal systems permit. As a result of the Scotland Act 1998 actions against government departments should be raised against the Lord Advocate or the advocate-general. Actions should be raised against the Lord Advocate where the department involved administers a devolved matter. Devolved matters include agriculture, education, housing, local government, health and justice. Actions should be raised against the advocate-general where the department is dealing with a reserved matter. Reserved matters include defence, foreign affairs and social security.

DEATHS

WHEN A DEATH OCCURS

If the death (including stillbirth) was expected, the doctor who attended the deceased during their final illness should be contacted. If the death was sudden or unexpected, the family doctor (if known) and police should be contacted. If the cause of death is quite clear the doctor will provide:

- a medical certificate that shows the cause of death
- a formal notice that states that the doctor has signed the medical certificate and that explains how to get the death registered

If the death was known to be caused by a natural illness but the doctor wishes to know more about the cause of death, he/she may ask the relatives for permission to carry out a post–mortem examination.

In England and Wales a coroner is responsible for investigating deaths occurring in the following circumstances:

- where there is no doctor who can issue a medical certificate of cause of death
- when no doctor has treated the deceased during his or her last illness or when the doctor attending the patient did not see him or her within 14 days before death, or after death
- when the death occurred during an operation or before recovery from the effect of an anaesthetic
- when the death was sudden and unexplained or attended by suspicious circumstances
- when the death might be due to an industrial injury or disease, or to accident, violence, neglect or abortion, attended by suspicious circumstances
- the death occurred in prison or in police custody

The doctor will write on the formal notice that the death has been referred to the coroner; if the post-mortem shows that death was due to natural causes, the coroner may issue a notification which gives the cause of death so that the death can be registered. If the cause of death was violent or unnatural, the coroner is obliged to hold an inquest.

In Scotland the office of coroner does not exist. The local procurator fiscal inquires into sudden or suspicious deaths. A fatal accident inquiry will be held before the sheriff where the death has resulted from an accident during the course of the employment of the person who has died, or where the person who has died was in legal custody, or where the Lord Advocate deems it in the public interest that an inquiry be held.

REGISTERING A DEATH

In England and Wales the death must be registered by the registrar of births and deaths for the district in which it occurred; details can be obtained from the doctor or local council, or at a post office or police station. From April 1997, information concerning a death can be given before any registrar of births and deaths in England and Wales. The registrar will pass the relevant details to the registrar for the district where the death occurred, who will then register the death.

In England and Wales the death must normally be registered within five days; in Scotland it must be registered within eight days. If the death has been referred to the coroner/local procurator fiscal it cannot be registered until the registrar has received authority from the coroner/local procurator fiscal to do so. Failure to register a death involves a penalty in England and Wales and may lead to a court decree being granted by a sheriff in Scotland.

If the death occurred at a house or hospital, the death may be registered by:

- any relative of the deceased
- any person present at the death
- the occupier or any inmate of the house or hospital if he/she knew of the occurrence of the death
- any person making the funeral arrangements
- in Scotland, the deceased's executor or legal representative

For deaths that took place elsewhere, the death may be registered by:

- any relative of the deceased
- someone present at the death
- someone who found the body
- a person in charge of the body
- any person making the funeral arrangements

The majority of deaths are registered by a relative of the deceased. The registrar would normally allow one of the other listed persons to register the death only if there were no relatives available.

The person registering the death should take the medical certificate of the cause of death with them; it is also useful, though not essential, to take the deceased's birth and marriage certificates, NHS medical card (if possible), pension documents and life assurance details. The details given to the registrar must be absolutely correct, otherwise it may be difficult to change them later. The person registering the death should check the entry very carefully before it is signed. The registrar will issue a certificate for burial or cremation and a certificate of registration of death; both are free of charge. A death certificate is a certified copy of the entry in the death register; these can be provided on payment of a fee and may be required for the following purposes:

- the will
- bank and building society accounts
- savings bank certificates and premium bonds
- insurance policies
- pension claims
- certificate for applicable Social Security Benefits

If the death occurred abroad or on a foreign ship or aircraft, the death should be registered according to the local regulations of the relevant country and a death certificate should be obtained. The death can also be registered with the British consul in that country and a record will be kept at the General Register Office. This avoids the expense of bringing the body back.

After 12 months (three months in Scotland) of death or the finding of a dead body, no death can be registered without the consent of the registrar-general.

BURIAL AND CREMATION

In most circumstances in England and Wales a certificate for burial or cremation must be obtained from the registrar before the burial or cremation can take place. If the death has been referred to the coroner, an order for burial or a certificate for cremation must be obtained. In Scotland a body may be buried (but not cremated) before the death is registered.

Funeral costs can normally be repaid out of the deceased's estate and will be given priority over any other claims. If the deceased has left a will it may contain directions concerning the funeral; however, these directions need not be followed by the executor.

The deceased's papers should also indicate whether a grave space had already been arranged. This information will be contained in a document known as a 'Deed of Grant'. Most town churchyards and many suburban churchyards are no longer open for burial because they are full. Most cemeteries are non-denominational and may be owned by local authorities or private companies; fees vary.

If the body is to be cremated, an application form, two cremation certificates (for which there is a charge) or a certificate for cremation if the death was referred to the coroner, and a certificate signed by the medical referee must be completed in addition to the certificate for burial or cremation (the form is not required if the coroner has issued a certificate for cremation). All the forms are available from the funeral director or crematorium. Most crematoria are run by local authorities; the fees usually include the medical referee's fee and the use of the chapel. Ashes may be scattered, buried in a churchyard or cemetery, or kept.

The registrar must be notified of the date, place and means of disposal of the body within 96 hours (England and Wales) or three days (Scotland).

If the death occurred abroad or on a foreign ship or aircraft, a local burial or cremation may be arranged. If the body is to be brought back to England or Wales, a death certificate from the relevant country or an authorisation for the removal of the body from the country of death from the coroner or relevant authority will be required. To arrange a funeral in England or Wales, an authenticated translation of a foreign death certificate or a death certificate issued in Scotland or Northern Ireland which must show the cause of death, is needed, together with a certificate of no liability to register from the registrar in England and Wales in whose sub-district it is intended to bury or cremate the body. If it is intended to cremate the body, a cremation order will be required from the Home Office or a certificate for cremation.

Further information can be obtained from:

THE GENERAL REGISTER OFFICE
General Register Office, Trafalgar Road, Southport PR8 2HH
T 0845-603 7788 **W** www.gro.gov.uk

THE GENERAL REGISTER OFFICE FOR SCOTLAND
New Register House, 3 West Register Street, Edinburgh EH1 3YT
T 0131-314 4452

DIVORCE AND RELATED MATTERS

There are three types of matrimonial suit: annulment of marriage, judicial separation and divorce. To obtain an annulment, judicial separation or divorce in England and Wales (provided a European Union court (except Denmark) has jurisdiction) the one commencing the proceedings (the petitioner) and the one defending the proceedings (the respondent) must be habitually resident in England and Wales; or the petitioner and the respondent must have last been habitually resident in England and Wales and one of them must continue to reside there; or the respondent must be habitually resident in England and Wales; or the petitioner must have been habitually resident in England and Wales throughout the period of at least one year ending with the start of proceedings; or the petitioner must be domiciled in England and Wales and must have been habitually resident in England and Wales throughout the period of at least six months, ending with the start of the proceedings; or both parties must be domiciled in England and Wales. If no European Union court (except Denmark) ha urisdiction, one or both parties must be domiciled in England and Wales. All cases are commenced in a divorce county court or in the Principal Registry in London. If a suit is defended, it may be transferred to the high court.

NULLITY OF MARRIAGE

Various circumstances have the potential to render a marriage void or voidable in nullity proceedings including: if there has been wilful non-consummation of the marriage; one partner has a venereal disease at the time of the marriage and the other did not know about it; the female partner was pregnant at the time of the marriage with another person's child and the male partner did not know of the pregnancy; the parties were within prohibited degrees of consanguinity, affinity or adoption; the parties were not male and female; either of the parties was already married or had entered a civil partnership; either of the parties was under the age of 16; the formalities of the marriage were defective, eg the marriage did not take place in an authorised building and both parties knew of the defect.

SEPARATION

A couple may enter into a private agreement to separate by consent without getting divorced but for the agreement to be valid it must be followed by an immediate separation; a solicitor should be contacted.

Another form of separation is judicial separation. Judicial separation does not dissolve a marriage and it is not necessary to prove that the marriage has irretrievably broken down. Either party can petition for a judicial separation at any time; the grounds listed below as grounds for divorce are also grounds for judicial separation. To petition for judicial separation, the parties do not have to prove that they have been married for 12 months or more.

A financial settlement between spouses in a separation agreement or which accompanies a judicial separation is not binding on the court and will not necessarily be upheld by the court after the commencement of divorce proceedings.

DIVORCE

Neither party can petition for divorce until at least one year after the date of the marriage. The sole ground for divorce is the irretrievable breakdown of the marriage; this must be proved on one or more of the following facts:

- the respondent has committed adultery and the petitioner finds it intolerable to live with him/her; however, the petitioner cannot rely on an act of adultery by the respondent if they have lived together as husband and wife for more than six months after the discovery of the adultery
- the respondent has behaved in such a way that the petitioner cannot reasonably be expected to continue living with him/her
- the respondent has deserted the petitioner for two years immediately before the petition
- the petitioner and the respondent have lived separately for two years immediately before the petition and the respondent consents to the divorce
- the petitioner and the respondent have lived separately for five years immediately before the petition

A total period of less than six months during which the parties have resumed living together is disregarded in determining whether the prescribed period of separation or desertion has been continuous (but may not be included as part of the period of separation).

The Matrimonial Causes Act 1973 requires the solicitor for the petitioner to certify whether the possibility of a reconciliation has been discussed with the petitioner.

THE DECREE NISI

A decree nisi does not dissolve or annul the marriage, but must be obtained before a divorce or annulment can take place.

Where the suit is undefended, the evidence normally takes the form of a sworn written statement made by the petitioner which is considered by a district judge. If the judge is satisfied that the petitioner has proved the contents of the petition, a date will be set for the pronouncement of the decree nisi in open court: neither party need attend.

If the suit is defended, the petition will be heard in open court with parties giving oral evidence.

THE DECREE ABSOLUTE

The decree nisi is capable of being made absolute on the application of the petitioner six weeks after the decree nisi. If the petitioner does not apply, the respondent must wait for a further three months before application may be made. In exceptional circumstances the granting of the decree absolute may be delayed, for example if matters regarding children are not capable of resolution. A decree absolute is unlikely to be applied for until the financial matters have been resolved. The decree absolute dissolves or annuls the marriage. Where the couple have been married in accordance with Jewish or other religious usages, the court may require them to produce a declaration that they have taken such steps as are required to dissolve the marriage in accordance with those usages before the decree absolute is issued.

MAINTENANCE

Either party may be liable to pay maintenance to a spouse or former spouse. If there are any children of the marriage, both parties have a legal responsibility to support them financially if they can afford to do so.

The courts are responsible for assessing maintenance for a spouse or former spouse, taking into account each party's income and essential outgoings and other aspects of the case. The court also deals with any maintenance for a child that has been treated by the spouses as a child of the family, such as a step-child.

The law relating to child support is currently under review. The intention is to replace the Child Support Agency (CSA) with the Child Maintenance and Enforcement Commission (C-MEC). At the time of writing the CSA is still responsible for assessing the maintenance that non-resident parents shall pay for their natural or adopted children (whether or not a marriage has taken place).

The CSA accepts applications only when all the people involved are habitually resident in the UK; the courts will continue to deal with cases where one of the individuals lives abroad. The CSA deals with all new cases unless it is agreed by the spouses that the court may grant an order for child support (but even in agreed jurisdiction cases one parent may give the other 14 months' notice to have the case dealt with by the CSA).

A formula is used to work out how much child maintenance is payable under CSA jurisdiction. The formula requires the non-resident parent to pay 15 per cent net of post-tax, national insurance and pension contributions for one child, 20 per cent for two and 25 per cent for more than two. An earnings cap of £104,000 net a year applies. The parent with care's income is not taken into account. Deductions are applied for staying contact and for further children in the non-resident parent's household. In court jurisdiction cases, the CSA formula is adopted as a guideline only.

Some cases involving unusual circumstances are treated as special cases and the assessment is modified, and in some cases the court retains jurisdiction (for educational costs and high income cases, for example). Where there is financial need (eg because of disability or continual education) maintenance may be ordered by the court for children even beyond the age of 18.

CSA maintenance is reviewed automatically every two years. Either parent can report a change of circumstances and request a review at any time. An independent complaints examiner for the CSA has been appointed.

If the non-resident parent does not pay CSA maintenance, the CSA may make an order for payments to be deducted directly from his/her salary; if all other methods fail, the CSA may take court action to enforce payment.

OTHER FINANCIAL RELIEF

Unlike in some other jurisdictions, there is no algebraic formula for division of assets on divorce. The courts must exercise their powers so as to achieve an outcome which is fair between the parties. In determining what is 'fair' the court must have regard to all the circumstances of the case, first consideration being given to the welfare of any minor child(ren) of the family. Beyond this, the court must have particular regard to a prescribed list of statutory factors, being:

- the income, earning capacity, property and other financial resources which each of the parties to the marriage has or is likely to have in the foreseeable future, including in the case of earning capacity, any increase in that capacity which it would, in the opinion of the court, be reasonable to expect a party to the marriage to take steps to acquire
- the financial needs, obligations and responsibilities which each of the parties to the marriage has or is likely to have in the foreseeable future
- the standard of living enjoyed by the family before the breakdown of the marriage
- the age of each party to the marriage and the duration of the marriage
- any physical or mental disability of either of the parties to the marriage
- the contribution which each of the parties has made or is likely in the foreseeable future to make to the welfare of the family, including any contribution by looking after the home or caring for the family
- the conduct of each of the parties, if that conduct is such that it would, in the opinion of the court, be inequitable to disregard it
- in the case of proceedings for divorce or nullity of marriage, the value to each of the parties to the marriage of any benefit (for example a pension) which by reason of the dissolution of the marriage that party will lose the chance of acquiring.

The court also has a duty to consider making an order which will settle once and for all the parties financial responsibilities towards each other. This is known as a financial 'clean break'. Where a clean break is not possible, the court will combine provision of capital via a lump sum and/or property adjustment order and/or pension sharing/attachment order with an ongoing income order, known as maintenance (alimony).

Maintenance can be for a 'term' (ie for a limited period only) or it can be for the joint lives of the parties. In some cases, the courts use nominal maintenance to leave a party's income claims open. It is possible for either party to apply to court to vary the amount or duration of the maintenance at a future date.

Prior to 2000, in considering the above factors, the courts considered the 'reasonable financial requirements' of the applicant, usually the wife, and treated this as determinative of the extent of the applicant's award. In the landmark case of *White v White* in 2000 the House of Lords re-evaluated the court's approach to dividing assets on divorce. The law lords enunciated three key principles. Firstly, the outcome has to be as fair as possible in all the circumstances with each party being entitled to a fair share of the available property. Secondly, in seeking to achieve a fair outcome there is no space for discriminating between the breadwinner and the homemaker in their respective roles. Thirdly, having considered all the circumstances of the case, and the statutory checklist, the judge should consider his view against the 'yardstick of equality of division'.

More recently, the law lords have offered further guidance as to how to achieve a fair division of assets on divorce in the cases of *Miller* and *McFarlane*. In determining fairness, the court must now consider three strands or principles, being each party's respective needs, the possibility of compensating the financially weaker party for any 'relationship' generated disadvantage, which will be relevant where one party has given up a career, and 'equal sharing' of family assets, which is applicable as much to short marriages as to long marriages, and which will apply unless there is good reason to the contrary.

In assessing whether there is a good reason to depart from the concept of equal sharing, the court will consider the nature of property and whether the property was acquired during the marriage otherwise than by inheritance or gift, known as matrimonial property, such as the matrimonial home, or other property to which the other spouse has not contributed. Whilst the yardstick of equality will apply to matrimonial assets to give full effect to the sharing entitlement, it will apply less readily to non-matrimonial assets, particularly in short marriages. Additionally, conduct and special contributions will be relevant in assessing whether there should be a departure from equality, but only in exceptional cases, where such conduct or contribution is 'gross and obvious'.

COHABITING COUPLES

Rights of unmarried couples are not the same as for married couples. Agreements, whether express or inferred by conduct, often determine interests in money and property. Reliance upon inferences is problematic. By virtue of this, it is important to consider entering into a contract which establishes how money and property should be divided in the event of a relationship breakdown. These contracts are commonly known as 'separation deeds' or 'cohabitation contracts'. The law relating to cohabiting couples is under review. The Law Commission published its recommendations to parliament at the end of July 2007, which were expected to lead to legislative reform.

CIVIL PARTNERSHIP

The Civil Partnership Act 2004 came into force on 5 December 2005; it has UK-wide status. Same-sex couples, y registering as civil partners, are able to gain legal ecognition of their relationship and thereby obtain rights nd obligations broadly equivalent to those of married ouples. These rights and responsibilities include a duty to rovide reasonable maintenance for your civil partner and ny children of the family, equitable treatment in respect f life assurance and pension benefits, recognition under ntestacy rules and domestic violence protection. In ddition, inheritance tax is waived as with married ouples and there is a right of succession for tenancy. A ivil partnership which has irretrievably broken down nay be dissolved by the court on the application of either ivil partner. The irretrievable breakdown of the artnership must be proved on one of four facts. These acts are the same as those for divorce (*see* above), save for civil partner may not seek dissolution of the partnership n the basis of the other's adultery.

OMESTIC VIOLENCE

f one spouse has been subjected to violence at the hands f the other, it is possible to obtain a court order very uickly to restrain further violence and if necessary to ave the other spouse excluded from the home. Such rders may also relate to unmarried couples and to a ange of other relationships including parents and hildren.

COTLAND

lthough some provisions are similar to those for ngland and Wales, there is separate legislation for cotland covering nullity of marriage, judicial separation, ivorce and ancillary matters. The principal legislation in elation to family law in Scotland is the Family Law Scotland) Act 1985. The Family Law (Scotland) Act 006 came in to force on 4 May 2006, and introduced eforms to various aspects of Scottish family law. The ollowing is confined to major points on which the law in cotland differs from that of England and Wales.

An action for judicial separation or divorce may be aised in the court of session; it may also be raised in the heriff court if either party was resident in the sheriffdom or 40 days immediately before the date of the action or or 40 days ending not more than 40 days before the date f the action. The fee for starting a divorce petition in the heriff court is £81.

The grounds for raising an action of divorce in cotland have been subject to reform in terms of the 2006 ct. The current grounds for divorce are:

- the defender has committed adultery. When adultery is cited as proof that the marriage has broken down irretrievably, it is not necessary in Scotland to prove that it is also intolerable for the pursuer to live with the defender
- the defender's behaviour is such that the pursuer cannot reasonably be expected to cohabit with the defender
- there has been no cohabitation between the parties for one year prior to the raising of the action for divorce, and the defender consents to the granting of decree of divorce
- there has been no cohabitation between the parties for two years prior to the raising of the action for divorce

he previously available ground of desertion has been bolished by the 2006 act.

A simplified procedure for 'do-it-yourself divorce' was ntroduced in 1983 for certain divorces. If the action is ased on one or two years' separation and will not be pposed, and if there are no children under 16 and no financial claims, and there is no sign that the applicant's spouse is unable to manage his or her affairs through mental illness or handicap, the applicant can write directly to the local sheriff court or to the court of session for the appropriate forms to enable him or her to proceed. The fee is £62, unless the applicant receives income support, family credit or legal advice and assistance, in which case there is no fee.

Where a divorce action has been raised, it may be sisted or put on hold for a variety of reasons. In all actions for divorce an extract decree, which brings the marriage to an end, will be made available 14 days after the divorce has been granted. Unlike in England, there is no decree nisi, only a final decree of divorce. Parties must ensure that all financial issues have been resolved prior to divorce, as it is not possible to seek further financial provision after divorce has been granted.

FINANCIAL PROVISION

In relation to financial provision on divorce, the first, and most important, principle is fair sharing of the matrimonial property. In terms of Scots law matrimonial property is defined as all property acquired by either spouse from the date of marriage up to the date of separation. Property acquired before the marriage is not deemed to be matrimonial unless it was acquired for use by the parties as a family home or as furniture for that home. Property acquired after the date of separation is not matrimonial property. Any property acquired by either of the parties by way of gift or inheritance during the marriage is excluded and does not form part of the matrimonial property.

When considering whether to make an award of financial provision a court shall also take account of any economic advantage derived by either party to the marriage as a result of contributions, financial or otherwise, by the other, and of any economic disadvantage suffered by either party for the benefit of the other party. The court must also ensure that the economic burden of caring for a child under the age of 16 is shared fairly between the parties.

A court can also consider making an order requiring one party to pay the other party a periodical allowance for a certain period of time following divorce. Such an order may be appropriate in cases where there is insufficient capital to effect a fair sharing of the matrimonial property. Orders for periodical allowance are uncommon, as courts will favour a 'clean break' where possible.

CHILDREN

The court has the power to award a residence order in respect of any children of the marriage or to make an order regulating the child's contact with the non-resident parent. The court will only make such orders if it is deemed better for the child to do so than to make no order at all, and the welfare of the children is of paramount importance. The fact that a spouse has caused the breakdown of the marriage does not in itself preclude him/her from being awarded residence.

NULLITY

An action for 'declaration of nullity' can be brought if someone with a legitimate interest is able to show that the marriage is void or voidable. The action can only be brought in the court of session. Although the grounds on which a marriage may be void or voidable are similar to those on which a marriage can be declared invalid in England, there are some differences. Where a spouse is capable of sexual intercourse but refuses to consummate the marriage, this is not a ground for nullity in Scots law, though it could be a ground for divorce. Where a spouse was suffering from venereal disease at the time of marriage and the other spouse did not know, this is not a ground for nullity in Scots law, neither is the fact that a wife was pregnant by another man at the time of marriage without the knowledge of her husband.

COHABITING COUPLES

The law in Scotland now provides certain financial and property rights for cohabiting couples in terms of the Family Law (Scotland) Act 2006, or 'the 2006 act'. The relevant 2006 act provisions do not place cohabitants in Scotland on an equal footing with married couples or civil partners, but provide some rights for cohabitants in the event that the relationship is terminated by separation or death. The provisions relate to couples who cease to cohabit after 4 May 2006.

The legislation provides for a presumption that any contents of the home shared by the cohabitants are owned in equal shares. A former cohabitee can also seek financial provision on termination of the relationship in the form of a capital payment if they can successfully demonstrate that they have been financially disadvantaged, and that conversely the other cohabitant has been financially advantaged, as a consequence of contributions made (financial or otherwise).

The 2006 act also provides that a cohabitant may make a claim on their partner's estate in the event of that partner's death, providing that there is no will.

Further information can be obtained from:

THE PRINCIPAL REGISTRY
First Avenue House, 42-49 High Holborn, London WC2V 6NP

THE COURT OF SESSION
Parliament House, Parliament Square, Edinburgh EH1 1RQ
T 0131-225 2595

THE CHILD SUPPORT AGENCY
National Enquiry Line 08457-133133 **W** www.csa.gov.uk

EMPLOYMENT LAW

PAY AND CONDITIONS

The Employment Rights Act 1996 consolidates the statutory provisions relating to employees' rights. Employers must give each employee employed for one month or more a written statement containing the following information:

- names of employer and employee
- date when employment began and the date on which the employee's period of *continuous* employment began (taking into account any employment with a previous employer which counts towards that period)
- remuneration and intervals at which it will be paid
- job title or description of job
- hours and place(s) of work
- holiday entitlement and holiday pay
- provisions concerning incapacity for work due to sickness and injury, including provisions for sick pay
- details of pension scheme(s)
- length of notice period that employer and employee need to give to terminate employment
- if the employment is not intended to be permanent, the period for which it is expected to continue or, if it is for a fixed term, the end date of the contract
- details of any collective agreement which affects th terms of employment
- details of disciplinary and grievance procedures
- if the employee is to work outside the UK for mor than one month, the period of such work and th currency in which payment is made
- a note stating whether a contracting out certificate is i force

This must be given to the employee within two months o the start of their employment. The Working Tim Regulations 1998, the National Minimum Wage Ac 1998, the Employment Rights (Dispute Resolution) Ac 1998 and the Employment Relations Act 1999 nov supplement the 1996 act. If the employer does nc provide the written statement within two months then th employee can complain to an employment tribunal, whic can specify the information that the employer should hav given. The Employment Act 2002 provides that when, i the context of an employee's successful tribunal claim, th employer is also found to have been in breach of the dut to provide the written statement at the time proceeding were commenced, the tribunal must award the employe two weeks' pay, and may award four weeks' pay, unless i is unjust or inequitable to do so.

FLEXIBLE WORKING

The Employment Act 2002 (and regulations made unde it) gives employees who are responsible for th upbringing of a child the right to apply for a flexibl working pattern for the purpose of caring for that child The right was extended to carers of adults in 2006. If a application under the act is rejected, it is open to th employee to complain to an employment tribunal.

SICK PAY

Employees absent from work through illness or injury ar entitled to receive Statutory Sick Pay (SSP) from th employer for a maximum period of 28 weeks in any three year period. Where average earnings (before deduction such as tax and National Insurance) are £87 a week o more, the standard rate of SSP is £72.55 per week.

MATERNITY AND PARENTAL RIGHTS

Under the Employment Relations Act 1999, th Employment Act 2002 and the Maternity and Parenta Leave Regulations 1999 (as amended in 2002 and 2006) both men and women are entitled to take leave when the become a parent. Women are protected fron discrimination, detriment or dismissal by reason of thei pregnancy. Men are protected from suffering a detrimen or dismissal for taking paternity or parental leave.

All women are entitled to a maximum period c maternity leave of 52 weeks. This comprises 26 weeks ordinary maternity leave, followed immediately by 2 weeks' additional maternity leave. A woman who take ordinary maternity leave normally has the right to retur to the job in which she was employed before her absence If she takes additional maternity leave, she is entitled t return to the same job or, if that is not reasonabl practicable, to another job that is suitable and appropriat for her to do.

A woman will qualify for Statutory Maternity Pa (SMP), which is payable for up to 39 weeks, if she ha been continuously employed for not less than 26 weeks a the beginning of the 14th week before the expected wee of childbirth. The first six weeks of SMP are paid at 9 per cent of the employee's average weekly earnings, an the remaining 33 weeks are paid at the rate of £122.7

er week, or 90 per cent of weekly earnings, whichever is ower.

Employees are entitled to adoption leave and adoption ay subject to fulfillment of criteria similar (but not dentical) to those in relation to maternity leave and pay. Vhere a couple is adopting a child, one may take doption leave, and the other may take paternity leave.

Certain employees are entitled to paternity leave on the irth or adoption of a child. To be eligible, the employee ıust be the child's father, or the partner of the mother or dopter, and meet other conditions. One of those onditions is that they must have been continuously mployed for not less than 26 weeks at the beginning of he 14th week before the expected week of childbirth (or, n the case of adoptions, 26 weeks ending with the week n which notification of the adoption match is given). The mployee may take either one week's leave, or two onsecutive weeks' leave. This leave may be taken at any ime between the date of the child's birth (or placement of doption) and 56 days later. During paternity leave, most mployees will be entitled to Statutory Paternity Pay, vhich is paid at the same rate as the second stage rate of MP (ie £122.75 per week or 90 per cent of weekly arnings, whichever is lower).

Any employee with one year's service who has, or xpects to have, responsibility for a child may take arental leave to care for the child. Each parent is entitled o a total of 13 weeks' parental leave for each of their hildren (or 18 weeks if the child is disabled) but this eave must be taken (at the rate of no more than four veeks per year, and in blocks of whole weeks only) before he child's fifth birthday (or 18th birthday if the child is isabled).

n May 2007 the government issued a consultation paper n certain proposed modifications to statutory paternity eave and pay. The proposed scheme would allow a father o take some of the mother's statutory maternity leave and pay) where the mother wants to return to work efore the end of her ordinary or additional maternity eave entitlement. At the time of writing the consultation s still underway.

UNDAY TRADING

he Sunday Trading Act 1994 allows shops to open on unday for serving retail customers. The Employment Rights Act 1996 gives shop workers and betting workers he right not to be dismissed, selected for redundancy or o suffer any detriment (such as the denial of overtime, romotion or training) if they refuse to work on Sundays. his does not apply to those who, under their contracts, re employed to work on Sundays.

ERMINATION OF EMPLOYMENT

n employee may be dismissed without notice if guilty of ross misconduct but in other cases a period of notice nust be given by the employer. The minimum periods of otice specified in the Employment Rights Act 1996 are:

- one week if the employee has been continuously employed for one month or more but for less than two years
- two weeks if the employee has been continuously employed for at least two years
- a week is added for every additional complete year of continuous employment up to 12 years (making the maximum statutory notice period 12 weeks after 12 years' continuous employment)
- longer periods apply if these are specified in the contract of employment

If an employee is dismissed with less notice than he/she is entitled to by statute, or under their contract if longer, he/she will have a wrongful dismissal claim (unless the employer paid the employee in lieu of notice in accordance with a contractual provision entitling it to do so). This claim for wrongful dismissal can be brought by the employee either in the court system or the employment tribunal, but if brought in the tribunal the maximum amount that can be awarded is £25,000. This claim can also be brought by an employee whose fixed-term contract has been terminated prematurely, and without justification, by the employer.

REDUNDANCY

An employee dismissed because of redundancy may be entitled to redundancy pay. This applies if:

- the employee has at least two years' continuous service
- the employee is dismissed by the employer (this can include cases of voluntary redundancy)
- dismissal is due to redundancy. Redundancy can mean closure of the entire business, closure of a particular site of the business, or a reduction in the need for employees to carry out work of a particular kind (eg as a result of over-manning or a reduction in work).

An employee may not be entitled to a redundancy payment if offered a suitable alternative job by the same employer. The amount of statutory redundancy pay depends on the length of service, age, and their earnings, subject to a weekly maximum of (currently) £310. The maximum payment that can be awarded is £9,300. The redundancy payment is guaranteed by the State in cases where the employer becomes insolvent (subject to the conditions above).

UNFAIR DISMISSAL

Complaints of unfair dismissal are dealt with by an employment tribunal. Any employee with one year's continuous service (subject to exceptions, including in relation to whistleblowers – *see* below) can make a complaint to the tribunal. At the tribunal, it is for the employer to prove that the dismissal was due to one or more of the following six potentially fair reasons:

- the employee's capability or qualifications for the job he/she was employed to do
- the employee's conduct
- redundancy
- retirement
- a legal restriction preventing the continuation of the employee's contract
- some other substantial reason

If the employer succeeds in showing this, the tribunal must then decide whether the employer acted reasonably in dismissing the employee for that reason. If the employee is found to have been unfairly dismissed, the tribunal can order that he/she be reinstated, re-engaged or compensated. Any person believing that they may have been unfairly dismissed should contact their local Citizens Advice Bureau or seek legal advice. A claim must be brought within three months of the date of termination of employment.

The normal maximum compensatory award for unfair dismissal is £60,600 (as at 1 February 2007). Where an employer has failed to follow the statutory dismissal procedures which came into force on 1 October 2004, the tribunal must usually increase the compensatory award by 10 per cent and it may increase by up to 50 per cent.

WHISTLEBLOWING

Under the whistleblowing legislation (Public Interest Disclosure Act 1998, which inserted provisions into the Employment Rights Act 1996) dismissal of an employee is automatically unfair if the reason or principal reason for the dismissal is that the employee has made a protected disclosure. The legislation also makes it unlawful to subject workers (a broad category that includes employees and certain other individuals, such as agency workers) who have made a protected disclosure to any detriment on the ground that they have done so.

For a disclosure to qualify for protection, the claimant must show that he has disclosed information, which in his reasonable belief tends to show one or more of the following six categories of wrongdoing:

- criminal offences
- breach of any legal obligation
- miscarriages of justice
- danger to the health and safety of any individual
- damage to the environment
- the deliberate concealing of information about any of the above

The malpractices can be past, present, prospective or merely alleged.

A qualifying disclosure will only be protected if the manner of the disclosure fulfills certain conditions, including being made in good faith and being made to a defined category of persons, which varies according to the type of disclosure.

Any whistleblower claim in the employment tribunal must normally be brought within three months of the date of dismissal or other act leading to a detriment.

An individual does not need to have been working with the employer for any particular period of time to be able to bring such a claim and compensation is uncapped (and can include an amount for injury to feelings).

DISCRIMINATION

Discrimination in employment on the grounds of sex (including gender reassignment), sexual orientation, race, colour, nationality, ethnic or national origins, religion or belief, married status, age or (subject to wide exceptions) disability is unlawful. Discrimination legislation generally covers direct discrimination, indirect discrimination, harassment and victimisation. Only in limited circumstances can such discrimination be justified (rendering it lawful).

An individual does not need to be employed for any particular period of time to be able to claim discrimination, and discrimination compensation is uncapped (and can include an amount for injury to feelings). These features distinguish the discrimination laws from, for example, the unfair dismissal laws.

The following legislation applies to those employed in Great Britain but not to employees in Northern Ireland or (subject to EC exceptions) to those who work mainly abroad:

- the Equal Pay Act 1970 (as amended) entitles men and women to equality in matters related to their contracts of employment
- the Sex Discrimination Act 1975 (as amended) makes it unlawful to discriminate on grounds of sex or marital/civil partner status. This covers all aspects of employment (including advertising for recruits, terms offered, opportunities for promotion and training, and dismissal procedures) and protects job applicants, employees and other types of worker, as well as ex-workers
- the Race Relations Act 1976 gives individuals the right not to be discriminated against on the grounds of race, colour, nationality, or ethnic or national origins. It applies to all aspects of employment
- the Disability Discrimination Act 1995 makes discrimination against a disabled person in all aspects of employment unlawful. In certain circumstances, the employer may show that the less favourable treatment is justified. The act also imposes a duty on employers to make 'reasonable adjustments' to the arrangements and physical features of the workplace if these place disabled people at a substantial disadvantage compared with those who are not disabled. The definition of a 'disabled person' is wide and now includes people diagnosed with HIV, cancer and multiple sclerosis. Since early 2007 there has been a new positive duty on public bodies to promote equality of opportunity for disabled people
- the Employment Equality (Religion or Belief) Regulations 2003 make discrimination against a person on the grounds of religion or belief, in all aspects of employment, unlawful
- the Employment Equality (Sexual Orientation) Regulations 2003 make discrimination against an individual on the grounds of sexual orientation, in all aspects of employment, unlawful
- The Employment Equality (Age) Regulations 2006 outlaw age discrimination in the workplace. This legislation is having profound implications for employers' policies and practices and has required major changes to selection procedures, recruitment policies, terms and conditions, benefits, dismissals and retirements

The Equal Opportunities Commission, the Commission for Racial Equality and the Disability Rights Commission (which will soon all be merged into the new Commission for Equality and Human Rights) have, as part of their roles, the function of eliminating such discrimination in the workplace, and can provide further information and assistance.

In Northern Ireland similar provisions exist but are contained in separate legislation (although the Disability Discrimination Act does extend to Northern Ireland).

In Northern Ireland there is one combined body working towards equality and eliminating discrimination, the Equality Commission for Northern Ireland.

WORKING TIME

The Working Time Regulations 1998 impose rules that limit working hours and provide for rest breaks and holidays. The regulations apply to workers and so cover not only employees but also other individuals who undertake to perform personally any work or services (e.g. freelancers). The regulations are complex and subject to various exceptions and qualifications but the basic provisions relating to adult day workers are as follows:

No worker is permitted to work more than an average of 48 hours per week (unless they opt out of this limit) and a worker is entitled to the following breaks:

- 11 consecutive hours' rest in every 24-hour period
- an uninterrupted rest period of at least 24 hours in each 7 day period (in addition to the daily rest period)
- 20 minutes' rest break provided that the working day is longer than 6 hours
- 4 weeks' paid annual leave (this is to increase to 4.8 weeks (24 days full-time) on 1 October 2007 and 5.6 weeks (28 days full-time) on 1 April 2009). 5.6 weeks equates to 4 weeks plus public holidays

'here are specific provisions relating to night work and oung workers (ie those over school leaving age but under 8).

IUMAN RIGHTS

)n 2 October 2000 the Human Rights Act 1998 came nto force. This act incorporates the European Convention n Human Rights into the law of the United Kingdom. he main principles of the act are as follows:

- all legislation must be interpreted and given effect by the courts as compatible with the Convention so far as it is possible to do so. Before the second reading of a new bill the minister responsible for the bill must provide a statement regarding the compatibility of the bill with the Human Rights Act
- subordinate legislation (eg statutory instruments) which are incompatible with the Convention can be struck down by the courts
- primary legislation (eg acts of parliament) which is incompatible with the Convention cannot be struck down by a court, but the higher courts can make a declaration of incompatibility which is a signal to parliament to change the law
- all public authorities (including courts and tribunals) must not act in a way which is incompatible with the Convention
- individuals whose Convention rights have been infringed by a public authority may bring proceedings against that authority, but the act is not intended to create new rights as between individuals

he main human rights protected by the Convention are 1e right to life (article 2); protection from torture and ıhuman or degrading treatment (article 3); protection 'om slavery or forced labour (article 4); the right to berty and security of the person (article 5); the right to a ıir trial (article 6); the right not to be subject to etrospective criminal offences (article 7); the right to espect for private and family life (article 8); freedom of 1ought, conscience and religion (article 9); freedom of xpression (article 10); freedom of peaceful association nd assembly (article 11); the right to marry and found a ımily (article 12); protection from discrimination (article 4); the right to property (article 1 Protocol No.1); the ght to free election (article 3 Protocol No.1); and the ght to education (article 2 Protocol No.1). Most of the Convention rights are subject to limitations which deem 1e breach of the right acceptable on the basis it is ecessary in a democratic society'.

'ARENTAL RESPONSIBILITY

'he Children Act 1989 gives the mother parental esponsibility for the child. There are different rules for nmarried fathers obtaining parental responsibility epending on whether the child was born before or after December 2003. For babies born after 1 December 003, unmarried fathers can get parental responsibility y: (a) registering the child's birth jointly with the mother t the time of birth or (b) re-registering the birth if you are 1e natural father or (c) marrying the mother of their child r (d) by obtaining a parental responsibility order from 1e court or (e) registering with the court for parental esponsibility. The Adoption and Children Act 2002 also 1akes provision for a father who is not married to the hild's mother to acquire parental responsibility for the hild if he becomes registered as the child's father. The onsent of a father without parental responsibility is not required for adoption. However, adoption agencies and local authorities must be careful to establish if possible the identity of the father, as the father then has an opportunity to apply for parental responsibility within the proceedings.

In Scotland, the relevant legislation is the Children (Scotland) Act 1995, which also gives the mother parental responsibility for her child whether or not she is married to the child's father. A father who is married to the mother, either at the time of the child's conception or subsequently, will also have automatic parental rights. Section 23 of the 2006 act provides that an unmarried father will obtain automatic parental responsibilities and rights if he is registered as the father on the child's birth certificate. For unmarried fathers who are not named on the birth certificate, or whose children were born before the 2006 act came into force, it is possible to acquire parental responsibilities and rights by applying to the court or by entering into a parental responsibilities and rights agreement with the mother. The father of any child, regardless of parental rights, has a duty to aliment that child until he/she is 18 (25 if the child is still in full-time education).

LEGITIMATION

Under the Legitimacy Act 1976, an illegitimate person automatically becomes legitimate when his/her parents marry. This applies even where one of the parents was married to a third person at the time of the birth. In such cases it is necessary to re-register the birth of the child. In Scotland, the status of illegitimacy has finally been abolished by section 21 of the 2006 act. The Law Reform Act 1987 reformed the law so as to remove so far as possible the legal disadvantages of illegitimacy.

JURY SERVICE

In England and Wales a person charged with more serious criminal offences and more complex civil cases is entitled to be tried by jury. No such right exists in Scotland, although more serious offences are heard before a jury. In England and Wales there are 12 members of a jury in a criminal case and eight members in a civil case. In Scotland there are 12 members of a jury in a civil case in the court of session (the civil jury being confined to the court of session and a restricted number of actions), and 15 in a criminal trial in the high court of justiciary. Jurors are normally asked to serve for ten working days, although jurors selected for longer cases are expected to sit for the duration of the trial.

Every 'registered' parliamentary or local government elector between the ages of 18 and 70 who has lived in the UK (including, for this purpose, the Channel Islands and the Isle of Man) for any period of at least five years since reaching the age of 13 is qualified to serve on a jury unless he/she is 'mentally disordered' or disqualified.

Those disqualified from jury service include:

- those who have at any time been sentenced by a court in the UK (including, for this purpose, the Channel Islands and the Isle of Man) to a term of imprisonment or youth custody of five years or more
- those who have been imprisoned or detained for public protection
- those who have within the previous ten years served any part of a sentence of imprisonment, youth custody or detention, been detained in a young offenders' institution, received a suspended sentence of

imprisonment or order for detention, or received a community service order
- those who are on bail in criminal proceedings

The court has the discretion to excuse a juror from service, or defer the date of service, if the juror can show there is good reason why he/she should be excused from attending or good reason why his attendance should be deferred. It is an offence to fail to attend when summoned or to make false representations in an attempt to evade service. The defendant can object to any juror if he/she can show cause.

A juror may claim travelling expenses, a subsistence allowance and an allowance for other financial loss (eg loss of earnings or benefits, fees paid to carers or child-minders) up to a stated limit. It is a contempt of court for a juror to disclose what happened in the jury room even after the trial is over. A jury's verdict need not be unanimous. In criminal proceedings the agreement of ten jurors will suffice (when there are at least 11 jurors remaining). In civil proceedings the agreement of seven jurors will suffice. However the court must be satisfied that the jury had reasonable time to consider its verdict based on the nature and complexity of the case. In criminal proceedings this must be no less than two hours.

SCOTLAND

Qualification criteria for jury service in Scotland are similar to those in England and Wales, except that the maximum age for a juror is 65, members of the judiciary are ineligible for ten years after ceasing to hold their post, and others concerned with the administration of justice are only eligible for service five years after ceasing to hold office. Certain persons who have the right to be excused include full-time members of the medical, dental, nursing, veterinary and pharmaceutical professions, full-time members of the armed forces, ministers of religion, persons who have served on a jury within the previous five years, members of the Scottish parliament, members of the Scottish Executive and junior Scottish ministers. Those convicted of a serious crime are automatically disqualified. Those who are incapable by reason of a mental disorder may also be excused. The maximum fine for a person serving on a jury knowing himself/herself to be ineligible is £1,000. The maximum fine for failing to attend without good cause is also £1,000.

Further information can be obtained from:

THE COURT SERVICE
Southside, 105 Victoria Street, London SW1E 6QT
T 020-7210 2266

SCOTTISH COURTS SERVICE
Courts of Session, Parliament House, Parliament Square, Edinburgh EH1 1RQ T 0131-225 2595

THE CLERK OF JUSTICIARY
High Court of Justiciary, Lawnmarket, Edinburgh EH2 2NS
T 0131-240 6900

LANDLORD AND TENANT

RESIDENTIAL LETTINGS

The provisions outlined here apply only where the tenant lives in a separate dwelling from the landlord and where the dwelling is the tenant's only or main home. It does not apply to licensees such as lodgers, guests or service occupiers.

The 1996 Housing Act radically changed certain aspects of the legislation referred to below; in particular the grant of assured and assured shorthold tenancies under the Housing Act 1988.

ASSURED SHORTHOLD TENANCIES

If a tenancy was granted on or after 15 January 1989 and before 28 February 1997, the tenant would have an assured tenancy unless the landlord served notice under section 20 in the prescribed form prior to the commencement of the tenancy, stating that the tenancy is to be an assured shorthold tenancy and the tenancy is for a minimum fixed term period of six months (*see* below). An assured tenancy gives that tenant greater rights of security. The tenant could, for example, stay in possession of the dwelling for as long as the tenant observed the terms of the tenancy. The landlord cannot obtain possession from such a tenant unless the landlord can establish a specific ground for possession (set out in the Housing Act 1988) and obtains a court order. The rent payable is that agreed with the landlord at the start of the tenancy. The landlord has the right to increase the rent annually by serving a notice. If that happens the tenant can apply to have the rent fixed by the rent assessment committee of the local authority. The tenant or the landlord may request that the committee sets the rent in line with open market rents for that type of property.

Under the Housing Act 1996, all new lettings entered into on or after 28 February 1997 (for whatever term) will be assured shorthold tenancies unless the landlord serves a notice stating that the tenancy is not to be an assured shorthold tenancy. This means that the landlord is entitled to possession at the end of the tenancy provided he serves a notice under section 21 Housing Act 1988 and commences the proceedings in accordance with the correct procedure. The landlord must obtain a court order however, to obtain possession if the tenant refuses to vacate at the end of the tenancy. If the tenancy is an assured shorthold tenancy, the court must grant the order. For both assured and assured shorthold tenancies, if the tenant is more than eight weeks in arrears, the landlord can serve notice and, if the tenant is still in arrears at the date of the hearing, the court must make an order for possession.

REGULATED TENANCIES

Before the Housing Act 1988 came into force (15 January 1989) there were regulated tenancies; some are still in existence and are protected by the Rent Act 1977. Under this act it is possible for the landlord or the tenant to apply to the local rent officer to have a 'fair' rent registered. The fair rent is then the maximum rent payable.

SECURE TENANCIES

Secure tenancies are generally given to tenants of local authorities, housing associations (before 15 January 1989) and certain other bodies. This gives the tenant security of tenure unless the terms of the agreement are broken by the tenant and it is reasonable to make an order for possession. Those with secure tenancies may have the right to buy their property. In practice this right is generally only available to council tenants.

AGRICULTURAL PROPERTY

Tenancies in agricultural properties are governed by the Agricultural Holdings Act 1986, the Agricultural Tenancies Act 1995 (both amended by the Regulatory Reform (Agricultural Tenancies) (England and Wales) Order 2006) and the Rent (Agriculture) Act 1976, which ve similar protections to those described above, eg curity of tenure, right to compensation for disturbance, c. The Agricultural Holdings (Scotland) Act 1991 along ith Agricultural Holdings (Scotland) Act 2003 apply milar provisions to Scotland.

VICTION

he Protection from Eviction Act 1977 (as amended by e Housing Act 1988) sets out the procedure a landlord ust follow in order to obtain possession of property. It is nlawful for a landlord to evict a tenant otherwise than in cordance with the law. For common law tenancies and r Rent Act tenants a Notice to Quit in the prescribed rm giving 28 days is required. For secure and assured nancies a Notice Seeking Possession must be served. It is nlawful for the landlord to evict a person by putting eir belongings onto the street, by changing the locks d so on. It is also unlawful for a landlord to harass a nant in any way in order to persuade him/her to give up e tenancy. The tenant may be able to obtain an junction to restrain the actions of the landlord and get ck into the property and be awarded damages.

ANDLORD RESPONSIBILITIES

nder the Landlord and Tenant Act 1985, where the term the lease is less than seven years, the landlord is sponsible for maintaining the structure and exterior of e property, for sanitation, for heating and hot water, and installations for the supply of water, gas and electricity.

EASEHOLDERS

rictly speaking, leaseholders have bought a long lease ther than a property and in certain limited circumstances e landlord can end the tenancy. Under the Leasehold eform Act 1967 (as amended by the Housing Acts 969, 1974 and 1980), leaseholders of houses may have e right to buy the freehold or to take an extended lease r a term of 50 years. This applies to leases where the rm of the lease is over 21 years and where the aseholder has occupied the house as his/her main sidence for the last two years, or for a total of two years er the last ten.

The Leasehold Reform, Housing and Urban evelopment Act came into force in 1993 and allows the aseholders of flats in certain circumstances to buy the eehold of the building in which they live.

Responsibility for maintenance of the structure, terior and interior of the building should be set out in e lease. Usually the upkeep of the interior of his/her rt of the property is the responsibility of the aseholder, and responsibility for the structure, exterior d common interior areas is shared between the eeholder and the leaseholder(s).

If leaseholders are in any way dissatisfied with eatment from their landlord or with charges made in spect of lease extensions, they are entitled to have their uation evaluated by the Leasehold Valuation Tribunal.

The Commonhold and Leasehold Reform Act 2002 akes provision for the freehold estate in land to be gistered as commonhold land and for the legal interest the land to be vested in a 'commonhold association' ie a ivate limited company.

USINESS LETTINGS

ne Landlord and Tenant acts 1927 and 1954 (as nended) give security of tenure to the tenants of most isiness premises. The landlord can only evict the tenant n one of the grounds laid down in the 1954 act, and in some cases where the landlord repossesses the property the tenant may be entitled to compensation.

SCOTLAND

In Scotland assured and short assured tenancies exist for lettings after 2 January 1989 and are similar to assured tenancies in England and Wales. The relevant legislation is the Housing (Scotland) Act 1988.

Most tenancies created before 2 January 1989 were regulated tenancies and the Rent (Scotland) Act 1984 still applies where these exist. The act defines, among other things, the circumstances in which a landlord can increase the rent when improvements are made to the property. The provisions of the Rent Act do not apply to tenancies where the landlord is the Crown, a local authority or a housing corporation.

The Housing (Scotland) Acts of 1987 and 2001 relate to local authority responsibilities for housing, the right to buy, and local authority secured tenancies. The provisions are broadly similar to England and Wales.

In Scotland, business premises are not controlled by statute to the same extent as in England and Wales, although the Tenancy of Shops (Scotland) Act 1949 gives some security to tenants of shops. Tenants of shops can apply to the sheriff, within 21 days of being served a notice to quit, for a renewal of tenancy if threatened with eviction. This application may be dismissed on various grounds including where the landlord has offered to sell the property to the tenant at an agreed price or, in the absence of agreement as to price, at a price fixed by a single arbiter appointed by the parties or the sheriff. The act extends to properties where the Crown or government departments are the landlords or the tenants.

Under the Leases Act 1449 the landlord's successors (either purchasers or creditors) are bound by the agreement made with any tenants so long as the following conditions are met:

- the lease, if for more than one year, must be in writing
- there must be a rent
- there must be a term of expiry
- the tenant must have entered into possession
- the subjects of the lease must be land
- the landlord, if owner, must be the proprietor with a recorded title, ie the title deeds are recorded in the Register of Sasines or registered in the Land Register

The Antisocial Behaviour (Scotland) Act 2001 provides that all landlords letting property in Scotland must register with the local authority in which the let property is situated. It is a criminal offence to fail to do this. Exceptions apply to holiday lets, owner-occupied accommodation and agricultural holdings. The act applies to partnerships, trusts and companies as well as to individuals.

LEGAL AID

The Access to Justice Act 1999 has transformed what used to be known as the Legal Aid system. The Legal Aid Board has been replaced by the Legal Services Commission, which is responsible for the development and administration of two legal funding schemes in England and Wales, namely the Criminal Defence Service and the Community Legal Service fund. The Community Legal Service is designed to increase access to legal information and advice by involving a much wider network of funders and providers in giving publicly funded legal services. In Scotland, provision of legal aid is governed by the Legal Aid (Scotland) Act 1986 and administered by the Scottish Legal Aid Board.

LEGAL SERVICES COMMISSION
(85 Gray's Inn Road, London WC1X 8TX T 020-7759 000 W www.legalservices.gov.uk)

CIVIL LEGAL AID

From 1 January 2000, only organisations (such as solicitors or Citizens Advice Bureaux) with a contract with the Legal Services Commission have been able to give initial help in any civil matter. Moreover, from that date decisions about funding were devolved from the Legal Services Commission to contracted organisations in relation to any level of publicly funded service in family and immigration cases. For other types of case, applications for public funding are made through a solicitor (or other contracted legal services providers) in much the same way as the former Legal Aid. On 1 April 2001 the so-called civil contracting scheme was extended to cover all levels of service for all types of cases.

Under the new civil funding scheme there are broadly seven levels of service available:

- legal help
- help at court
- general family help
- legal representation – either investigative help or full representation
- help with mediation
- family mediation
- such other services as authorised by specific orders

ELIGIBILITY
Eligibility for funding from the Community Legal Service depends broadly on five factors:

- the level of service sought (*see* above)
- whether the applicant qualifies financially
- the merits of the applicant's case
- a costs-benefits analysis (if the costs are likely to outweigh any benefit that might be gained from the proceedings, funding may be refused)
- whether there is any public interest in the case being litigated (ie whether the case has a wider public interest beyond that of the parties involved – for example, a human rights case)

The limits on capital and income above which a person is not entitled to public funding vary with the type of service sought.

CONTRIBUTIONS
Some of those who qualify for Community Legal Service funding will have to contribute towards their legal costs. Contributions must be paid by anyone who has a disposable income or disposable capital exceeding a prescribed amount. The rules relating to applicable contributions are complex and detailed information can be obtained from the Legal Services Commission.

STATUTORY CHARGE
A statutory charge is made if a person keeps or gains money or property in a case for which they have received legal aid. This means that the amount paid by the Community Legal Service fund on their behalf is deducted from the amount that the person receives. This does not apply if the court has ordered that the costs be paid by the other party (unless the amount paid by the other party does not cover all of the costs). In certain circumstances, the Legal Services Commission may waive or postpone payment.

CONTINGENCY OR CONDITIONAL FEES
This system was introduced by the Courts and Leg Services Act 1990. It offers legal representation on a 'n win, no fee' basis. It provides an alternative form assistance, especially for those cases which are ineligib for funding by the Community Legal Service. The ma area for such work is in the field of personal injuries.

Not all solicitors offer such a scheme and differe solicitors may well have different terms. The effect of th agreement is that solicitors will not make any charg until the case is concluded successfully. If a case is wo then the losing party will usually have to pay towar costs, with the winning party contributing around or third.

SCOTLAND
Civil legal aid is available for cases in the following:

- the sheriff courts
- the court of session
- the House of Lords
- the lands valuation appeal court
- the Scottish land court
- the Lands Tribunal for Scotland
- the Employment Appeal Tribunals
- the Judicial Committee of the Privy Council
- the Proscribed Organisations Appeal Commissioner
- proceedings before the Social Security Commissioner
- proceedings before the Child Support Commissioners

Civil legal aid is not available for defamation action small claims or simplified divorce procedures or petitior by a debtor for his own sequestration.

Eligibility for civil legal aid is assessed in a similar wa to that in England and Wales, though the financial limi differ in some respects and are as follows:

- a person is eligible and will not have to pay contribution if his yearly disposable income is £2,99 or less and disposable capital is £6,640 or less
- if disposable income exceeds £9,781, the person is n eligible for legal aid
- if disposable income is between £2,995 and £9,78 contributions are payable
- if disposable capital exceeds £11,070, the person is n eligible for legal aid
- if disposable capital is between £6,640 and £11,07 contributions are payable
- those receiving income support or income-related jo seeker's allowance qualify automatically

CRIMINAL LEGAL AID

The Legal Services Commission provides defendan facing criminal charges with free legal representation they pass a merits test and a means test.

Criminal legal aid covers the cost of preparing a ca and legal representation in criminal proceedings. It is als available for appeals against verdicts or sentences magistrates' courts, the crown court or the court of appea It is not available for bringing a private prosecution in criminal court.

If granted criminal legal aid, either the person ma choose their own solicitor or the court will assign on Contributions to the legal costs may be required if th case proceeds to the crown court. The rules relating applicable contributions are complex and detaile information can be obtained from the Legal Servic Commission.

·UTY SOLICITORS

he Legal Aid Act 1988 also provides free advice and ›sistance to anyone questioned by the police (whether nder arrest or helping the police with their enquiries). o means test or contributions are required for this.

COTLAND

egal advice and assistance operates in a similar way in cotland. A person is eligible:

- if disposable income does not exceed £215 a week. If disposable income is between £91 and £215 a week, contributions are payable
- if disposable capital does not exceed £1,502 (if the person has dependent relatives, the savings allowance is higher)
- if receiving income support or income-related job seeker's allowance they qualify automatically provided they have no savings over the limit

he procedure for application for criminal legal aid epends on the circumstances of each case. In solemn ›ses (more serious cases, such as murder) heard before a ry, a person is automatically entitled to criminal legal aid ntil they are given bail or placed in custody. Thereafter, it for the court to decide whether to grant legal aid. The ›urt will do this if the person accused cannot meet the :penses of the case without undue hardship on him or s dependants. In less serious cases the procedure epends on whether the person is in custody:

- anyone taken into custody has the right to free legal aid from the duty solicitor up to and including the first court appearance
- if the person is not in custody and wishes to plead guilty, they are not entitled to criminal legal aid but may be entitled to legal advice and assistance, including assistance by way of representation
- if the person is not in custody and wishes to plead not guilty, they can apply for criminal legal aid. This must be done within 14 days of the first court appearance at which they made the plea

he criteria used to assess whether or not criminal legal d should be granted is similar to the criteria for England ›d Wales. When meeting with your solicitor, take ›idence of your financial position such as details of vings, bank statements, pay slips, pension book or enefits book.

ırther information can be obtained from:

HE SCOTTISH LEGAL AID BOARD
4 Drumsheugh Gardens, Edinburgh EH3 7SW
0131-226 7061 **W** www.slab.org.uk

1ARRIAGE

ny two persons may marry provided that:

- they are at least 16 years old on the day of the marriage (in England and Wales persons under the age of 18 must generally obtain the consent of their parents; if consent is refused an appeal may be made to the high court, the county court or a court of summary jurisdiction)
- they are not related to one another in a way which would prevent their marrying
- they are unmarried (a person who has already been married must produce documentary evidence that the previous marriage has been ended by death, divorce or annulment)
- they are not of the same sex (though same sex couples can register a civil partnership instead)
- they are capable of understanding the nature of a marriage ceremony and of consenting to marriage

The marriage may be valid in England and Wales and void by the law of the domicile of both or either of the parties. The parties should check the marriage will be recognised as valid in their home country if either is not a British citizen.

DEGREES OF RELATIONSHIP

A marriage between persons within the prohibited degrees of consanguinity, affinity or adoption is void.

A man may not marry his mother, daughter, grandmother, granddaughter, sister, aunt, niece, great-grandmother, adoptive mother, former adoptive mother, adopted daughter or former adopted daughter.

A woman may not marry her father, son, grandfather, grandson, brother, uncle, nephew, great-grandfather, adoptive father, former adoptive father, adopted son or former adopted son. Under the Marriage Act 1983, some exceptions to the law permit a man or a woman to marry certain step-relatives or in-laws.

ENGLAND AND WALES

TYPES OF MARRIAGE CEREMONY

It is possible to marry by either religious or civil ceremony. A religious ceremony can take place at a church or chapel of the Church of England or the Church in Wales, or at any other place of worship which has been formally registered by the Registrar-General.

A civil ceremony can take place at a register office, a registered building or any other premises approved by the local authority.

An application for an approved premises licence must be made by the owners or trustees of the building concerned; it cannot be made by the prospective marriage couple. Approved premises must be regularly open to the public so that the marriage can be witnessed; the venue must be deemed to be a permanent and immovable structure. Open-air ceremonies are prohibited.

Non-Anglican marriages may also be solemnised following the issue of a Registrar-General's licence in unregistered premises where one of the parties is seriously ill, is not expected to recover, and cannot be moved to registered premises. Detained and housebound persons may be married at their place of residence.

MARRIAGE IN THE CHURCH OF ENGLAND OR THE CHURCH IN WALES

Marriage by banns

The marriage must take place in a parish in which one of the parties lives, or in a church in another parish if it is the usual place of worship of either or both of the parties. The banns must be called in the parish in which the marriage is to take place on three Sundays before the day of the ceremony; if either or both of the parties lives in a different parish the banns must also be called there. After three months the banns are no longer valid. The minister will not perform the marriage unless he or she is satisfied that the banns have been properly called.

Marriage by common licence

The vicar who is to conduct the marriage will arrange for a common licence to be issued by the diocesan bishop; this dispenses with the necessity for banns. One of the parties must have lived in the parish for 15 days immediately before the issuing of the licence or must usually worship at the church. Eligibility requirements vary from diocese to diocese, but it is not normally required that the parties should have been baptised. The licence is valid for three months.

Marriage by special licence
A special licence is granted by the Archbishop of Canterbury in special circumstances for the marriage to take place at any place, with or without previous residence in the parish, or at any time. Application must be made to the registrar of the Faculty Office (1 The Sanctuary, London SW1P 3JT T 020-7222 5381).

Marriage by certificate
The marriage can be conducted on the authority of the superintendent registrar's certificate, provided that the vicar's consent is obtained (there is no obligation upon the vicar to accept the certificate). One of the parties must live in the parish or must usually worship at the church.

MARRIAGE BY OTHER RELIGIOUS CEREMONY
One of the parties must normally live in the registration district where the marriage is to take place. In addition to giving notice to the superintendent registrar it may also be necessary to book a registrar to be present at the ceremony.

CIVIL MARRIAGE
A marriage may be solemnised at any register office, registered building or approved premises in England and Wales. The superintendent registrar of the district should be contacted, and, if the marriage is to take place at approved premises, the necessary arrangements at the venue must also be made.

NOTICE OF MARRIAGE
Unless it is to take place by banns or under common or special licence in the Church of England or the Church in Wales, a notice of the marriage must be given in person to the superintendent registrar. Notice of marriage may be given in the following ways:

- by certificate. Both parties must have lived in a registration district in England or Wales for at least seven days immediately before giving notice at the local register office. If they live in different registration districts, notice must be given in both districts. The marriage can take place in any register office or other approved premises in England and Wales no sooner than 16 days after notice has been given, when the superintendent registrar issues a certificate.
- by licence (often known as 'special licence'). One of the parties must have lived in a registration district in England or Wales for at least 15 days before giving notice at the register office; the other party need only be a resident of, or be physically in, England and Wales on the day notice is given. The marriage can take place one clear day (other than a Sunday, Christmas Day or Good Friday) after notice has been given.

A notice of marriage is valid for 12 months, unless it is for the marriage of a detained or housebound person, when it will usually only be accepted within three months of publication. Notice for marriages taking place within the Church of England or Church of Wales should also only be valid within three months of publication. It should be possible to make an advance (provisional) booking 12 months before the ceremony. In this case it is still necessary to give formal notice three months before the marriage. When giving notice of the marriage it is necessary to produce official proof, if relevant, that any previous marriage has ended in divorce or death b producing a decree absolute or death certificate; it is als necessary to provide proof of age, identity and nationalit for each of the parties, for example, with a passport. either party is under 18 years old, evidence of consent b their parent or guardian is required. There are speci procedures for those wishing to get married in the U that are subject to immigration control; the register offi will be able to advise on these.

SOLEMNISATION OF THE MARRIAGE
On the day of the wedding there must be at least tw other people present who are prepared to act as witness and sign the marriage register. A registrar of marriag must be present at a marriage in a register office or approved premises, but an authorised person may act the capacity of registrar in a registered building.

If the marriage takes place at approved premises, th room must be separate from any other activity on th premises at the time of the ceremony, and no food drink can be sold or consumed in the room during th ceremony or for one hour beforehand.

The marriage must be solemnised between 8am an 6pm, with open doors. At some time during the ceremon the parties must make a declaration that they know of n legal impediment to the marriage and they must also sa the contracting words; the declaratory and contractin words may vary according to the form of service. A civ marriage cannot contain any religious aspects, but it ma be possible for non-religious music and/or readings to b included. It may also be possible to embellish th marriage vows taken by the couple.

CIVIL FEES
Marriage at a Register Office
By superintendent registrar's certificate, £30 per perso for the notice of the marriage (which is not refundable the marriage does not in fact take place) and £40 for th ceremony at the register office.

Marriage on Approved Premises
By superintendent registrar's certificate, £30 per perso for the ceremony at the register office.

An additional fee will also be payable for th superintendent registrar's and registrar's attendance at th marriage. This is set locally by the local authori responsible. A further charge is likely to be made by th owners of the building for the use of the premises. F marriages taking place in a religious building other tha the Church of England or Church of Wales, an addition fee of £47 is payable for the registrar's attendance at th marriage unless an 'Authorised Person' appointed by th trustees of the building has agreed to register th marriage. Additional fees may be charged by the truste of the building for the wedding and by the person wh performs the ceremony.

ECCLESIASTICAL FEES
(Church of England and Church in Wales*)

Marriage by banns
For publication of banns, £19
For certificate of banns issued at time of publicatio £12.00
For marriage service, £240
Marriage by common licence
Fee for licence, £70
Marriage by special licence

ee for licence, £140

These fees are revised from 1 April each calendar year. Some ay not apply to the Church in Wales

COTLAND

EGULAR MARRIAGES

regular marriage is one which is celebrated by a inister of religion or authorised registrar or other elebrant. Each of the parties must complete a marriage otice form and return it to the district registrar for the rea in which they are to be married, irrespective of where ey live, at least 15 days before the ceremony is due to ke place. The district registrar must then enter the date f receipt and certain details in a marriage book kept for is purpose, and must also enter the names of the parties nd the proposed date of marriage in a list which is isplayed in a conspicuous place at the registration office ntil the date of the marriage has passed. All persons ishing to enter into a regular marriage in Scotland must ollow the same preliminary procedure regardless of hether they intend to have a religious or civil ceremony. efore the marriage ceremony takes place any person may ubmit an objection in writing to the district registrar.

A marriage schedule, which is prepared by the registrar, ill be issued to one or both of the parties in person up to even days before a religious marriage; for a civil marriage e schedule will be available at the ceremony. The chedule must be handed to the celebrant before the eremony starts; it must be signed immediately after the edding and the marriage must be registered within three ays.

The authority to conduct a religious marriage is eemed to be vested in the authorised celebrant rather an the building in which it takes place; open-air eligious ceremonies are therefore permissible in Scotland.

From 10 June 2002 it has been possible, under the larriage (Scotland) Act 2002, for venues or couples to pply to the local council for a licence to allow a civil eremony to take place at a venue other than a registration ffice. To obtain further information, a venue or couple hould contact the district registrar in the area they wish o marry. A list of licensed venues is also available on the eneral Registers of Scotland website (W www.gro-cotland.gov.uk).

1ARRIAGE BY COHABITATION WITH HABIT ND REPUTE

rior to the enactment of the 2006 act, if two people had ved together constantly as husband and wife and were enerally held to be such by the neighbourhood and mong their friends and relations, a presumption could rise from which marriage could be inferred. Before such marriage could be registered, however, a decree of eclarator of marriage had to be obtained from the court f session. Section 3 of the 2006 act provides that it will o longer be possible for a marriage to be constituted by ohabitation with habit and repute, but it will still be ossible for couples whose period of cohabitation began efore commencement of the 2006 act to seek a eclarator under the old rule of law.

IVIL FEES

he fee for submitting a notice of marriage to the district egistrar is £25. Solemnisation of a civil marriage costs 45, whilst the extract of the entry in the register of arriages attracts a fee of £8.50. The costs of religious arriage ceremonies can vary.

Further information can be obtained from:

THE GENERAL REGISTER OFFICE
Trafalgar Road, Southport PR8 2HH
T 0845-603 7788 W www.gro.gov.uk

THE GENERAL REGISTER OFFICE FOR SCOTLAND
New Register House, 3 West Register Street, Edinburgh EH1 3YT
T 0131-314 4452

TOWN AND COUNTRY PLANNING

The planning system can help to protect the environment and assist individuals in assessing their land rights. There are a number of acts governing the development of land and buildings in England and Wales and advice should always be sought from a Citizens Advice Bureau or local planning authority before undertaking building works on any land or to property. If development takes place which requires planning permission without permission being given, enforcement action may take place and the situation may need to be rectified.

PLANNING PERMISSION

Planning permission is needed if the work involves:

- making a material change in use, such as dividing off part of the house so that it can be used as a separate home or dividing off part of the house for commercial use, eg for a workshop
- going against the terms of the original planning permission, eg there may be a restriction on fences in front gardens on an open-plan estate
- building, engineering for mining, except for the permissions below
- new or wider access to a main road
- additions or extensions to flats or maisonettes

Planning permission is not needed to carry out internal alterations or work which does not affect the external appearance of the building, and are not works for making good damage or works begun after 5 December 1968 for the alteration of a building by providing additional space in it underground.

There are certain types of development for which the Secretary of State for the Environment, Food and Rural Affairs has granted general permissions (permitted development rights). These include:

- house extensions and additions (including conservatories, loft conversions, garages and dormer windows). Up to 10 per cent or up to 50 cubic metres (whichever is the greater) can be added to the original house for terraced houses or houses on land designated as an area of outstanding natural beauty or in a conservation area. Up to 15 per cent or 70 cubic metres (whichever is the greater) to other kinds of houses. The maximum that can be added to any house is 115 cubic metres
- buildings such as garden sheds and greenhouses so long as they are no more than 3 metres high (or 4 metres if the roof is ridged), are no nearer to a highway than the house or 20 metres (whichever is nearer), and at least half the ground around the house remains uncovered by buildings
- adding a porch with a ground area of less than 3 square metres and that is less than 3 metres in height and not within 2 metres of any boundary of the curtilage of the dwelling house with a highway
- putting up fences, walls and gates of under 1 metre in height if next to a road and under 2 metres elsewhere
- laying patios, paths or driveways for domestic use

However, before carrying out any of the above permitted

developments you should contact your local authority to find out whether the general permission has been modified in your area.

OTHER RESTRICTIONS

It may be necessary to obtain other types of permissions before carrying out any development. These permissions are separate from planning permission and apply regardless of whether or not planning permission is needed, eg:

- building regulations will probably apply if a new building is to be erected, if an existing one is to be altered or extended, or if the work involves building over a drain or sewer. The building control department of the local authority will advise on this
- any alterations to a listed building or the grounds of a listed building must be approved by the local authority. Listing will include not only the main building but everything in the curtilage of the building
- local authority approval is necessary if a building (or, in some circumstances, gates, walls, fences or railings) in a conservation area is to be demolished; each local authority keeps a register of all local buildings that are in conservation areas
- many trees are protected by tree preservation orders and must not be pruned or taken down without local authority consent
- bats and many other species are protected, and Natural England, the Countryside Council for Wales or Scottish National Heritage must be notified before any work is carried out that will affect the habitat of protected species, eg timber treatment, renovation or extensions of lofts
- any development in areas designated as a national park, an area of outstanding national beauty, a national scenic area or in the Norfolk or Suffolk Broads is subject to greater restrictions. The local planning authority will advise or refer enquirers to the relevant authority

The local authority should be contacted if a planning permission is required. There may also be restriction on development contained in the title to the property which should be considered when works are planned.

VOTERS' QUALIFICATIONS

Those entitled to vote at parliamentary, and local government elections are those who are:

- on the electoral roll
- aged 18 years or older
- British citizens, Commonwealth citizens or citizens of the Irish Republic who are resident in the UK
- In Northern Ireland electors must have been resident in Northern Ireland during the whole of the three-month period prior to the relevant date

British citizens resident abroad are entitled to vote for 15 years after leaving Britain, as overseas electors in parliamentary and EU elections in the constituency in which they were last resident. Members of the armed forces, Crown servants and employees of the British Council who are overseas and their spouses are entitled to vote regardless of how long they have been abroad. British citizens who had never been registered as an elector in the UK are not eligible to register as an overseas voter unless they left the UK before they were 18, providing they left the country no more than 15 years ago.

The main categories of people who are not entitled to vote at general elections are:

- sitting peers in the House of Lords
- convicted persons detained in pursuance of thei sentences (though remand prisoners, unconvicte prisoners and civil prisoners can vote if on the electora register)
- those convicted within the previous five years c corrupt or illegal election practices
- EU citizens (who may only vote in EU and loca government elections)

Under the Representation of the Peoples Act 200C several new groups of people are permitted to vote for th first time. These include: people who live on barge people in mental health hospitals (other than those wit criminal convictions) and homeless people who hav made a 'declaration of local connection'.

REGISTERING TO VOTE

Voters must be entered on an electoral register. Th Electoral Registration Officer (ERO) for each council are is responsible for preparing and publishing the register fo his area by 1 December each year. Names may be adde to the register to reflect changes in people's circumstance as they occur and each month during December t August, the ERO publishes a list of alterations to th published register.

A registration form is sent to all households in th autumn of each year and the householder is required t provide details of all occupants who are eligible to vot including ones who will reach their 18th birthday in th year covered by the register. Anyone failing to suppl information to the ERO when requested, or supplyin false information, may be fined. Application forms an more information are available from the Electora Commission on W www.electoralcommision.org.uk.

VOTING

Voting is not compulsory in the UK. Those who wish t vote do so in person at the allotted polling station. Posta votes are now available to anyone on request. Those wh will be away at the time of the election, those who wi not be able to attend in person due to physical incapacit or the nature of their occupation, and those who hav changed address during the period for which the registe is valid, may apply for a postal vote or nominate a prox to vote for them. Overseas electors who wish to vote mus do so by proxy.

Further information can be obtained from the loca authority's ERO in England and Wales or the electora registration office in Scotland, or the Chief Electora Officer in Northern Ireland.

WILLS

In a will a person leaves instructions as to the disposal c their property after they die. A will is also used t appoint executors (who will administer the estate), giv directions as to the disposal of the body, appoir guardians for children and, for larger estates, can operat to reduce the level of inheritance tax. It is best to have will drawn up by a solicitor, but if a solicitor is nc employed the following points must be taken int account:

- if possible the will must not be prepared on behalf c another person by someone who is to benefit from it c who is a close relative of a major beneficiary
- the language used must be clear and unambiguous an it is better to avoid the use of legal terms where th same thing can be expressed in plain language

it is better to rewrite the whole document if a mistake is made. If necessary, alterations can be made by striking through the words with a pen, and the signature or initials of the testator and the witnesses must be put in the margin opposite the alteration. No alteration of any kind should be made after the will has been executed

if the person later wishes to change the will or part of it, it is better to write a new will revoking the old. The use of codicils (documents written as supplements or containing modifications to the will) should be left to a solicitor

the will should be typed or printed, or if handwritten be legible and preferably in ink. Commercial will forms can be obtained from some stationers

ıe form of a will varies to suit different cases – a solicitor ll be able to advise as to wording, however, 'DIY' will-·iting kits can be purchased from good stationery shops d many banks offer a will-writing service.

ᴀPSED LEGATEES

a person who has been left property in a will dies before e person who made the will, the gift fails and will pass the person entitled to everything not otherwise sposed of (the residuary estate).

If the person left the residuary estate dies before the rson who made the will, their share will generally pass the closest relative(s) of the person who made the will ; in intestacy), unless the will names a beneficiary such a charity who will take as a 'long stop' if this gift is ıable to take effect for any reason. It is always better to aw up a new will if a beneficiary predeceases the person ıo made the will.

‹ECUTORS

is usual to appoint two executors, although one is fficient. No more than four persons can deal with the tate of the person who has died. The name and address ʼeach executor should be given in full (the addresses are ›t essential but including them adds clarity to the ›cument). Executors should be 18 years of age or over. ı executor may be a beneficiary of the will.

ʼITNESSES

person who is a beneficiary of a will, or the spouse of a :neficiary at the time the will is signed, must not act as a itness or else he/she will be unable to take his/her gift. usband and wife can both act as witnesses provided ·ither benefits from the will.

It is better that a person does not act as an executor and a witness, as he/she can take no benefit under a will to hich he/she is witness. The identity of the witnesses ould be made as explicit as possible.

‹ECUTION OF A WILL

ıe person making the will should sign his/her name at e foot of the document, in the presence of the two itnesses. The witnesses must then sign their names while e person making the will looks on. If this procedure is ›t adhered to, the will will be considered invalid. There e certain exceptional circumstances where these rules are laxed, eg where the person may be too ill to sign.

APACITY TO MAKE A WILL

ıyone aged 18 or over can make a will. However, if ere is any suspicion that the person making the will is ›t, through reasons of infirmity or age, fully in command ʼhis/her faculties, it is advisable to arrange for a medical actitioner to examine the person making the will at the time it is to be executed (to verify his/her mental capacity and to record that medical opinion in writing), and to ask the examining practitioner to act as a witness. If a person is not mentally able to make a will, the court may do this for him/her by virtue of the Mental Health Act 1983.

REVOCATION

A will may be revoked or cancelled in a number of ways:

- a later will revokes an earlier one if it says so; otherwise the earlier will is by implication revoked by the later one to the extent that it contradicts or repeats the earlier one
- a will is also revoked if the physical document on which it is written is destroyed by the person whose will it is. There must be an intention to revoke the will and it may not be sufficient to obliterate the will with a pen
- a will is revoked when the person marries or forms a civil partnership, unless it is clear from the will that the person intended the will to stand after the marriage or civil partnership
- where a marriage or civil partnership ends in divorce or dissolution or is annulled or declared void, gifts to the spouse or civil partner and the appointment of the spouse or civil partner as executor fail unless the will says that this is not to happen. A former spouse or civil partner is treated as having predeceased the testator. A separation does not change the effect of a married person's will.

PROBATE AND LETTERS OF ADMINISTRATION

Probate is granted to the executors named in a will and once granted, the executors are obliged to carry out the instructions of the will. Letters of administration are granted where no executor is named in a will or is willing or able to act or where there is no will or no valid will; this gives a person, often the next of kin, similar powers and duties to those of an executor.

Applications for probate or for letters of administration can be made to the Principal Registry of the Family Division, to a district probate registry or to a probate sub-registry. Applicants will need the following documents: the original will (if any); a certificate of death; oath for executors or administrators; particulars of all property and assets left by the deceased; and a list of debts and funeral expenses. Certain property, up to the value of £5,000, may be disposed of without a grant of probate or letters of administration.

WHERE TO FIND A PROVED WILL

Since 1858 wills which have been proved, that is wills on which probate or letters of administration have been granted, must have been proved at the Principal Registry of the Family Division or at a district probate registry. The Lord Chancellor has power to direct where the original documents are kept but most are filed where they were proved and may be inspected there and a copy obtained. The Principal Registry also holds copies of all wills proved at district probate registries and these may be inspected at First Avenue House, High Holborn. An index of all grants, both of probate and of letters of administration, is compiled by the Principal Registry and may be seen either at the Principal Registry or at a district probate registry.

It is also possible to discover when a grant of probate or letters of administration is issued by requesting a standing search. In response to a request and for a small fee, a district probate registry will supply the names and addresses of executors or administrators and the registry in which the grant was made, of any grant in the estate of a specified person made in the previous 12 months or following six months. This is useful for applicants who may be beneficiaries to a will but who have lost contact with the deceased and for creditors of the deceased.

INTESTACY

Intestacy occurs when someone dies without leaving a will or leaves a will which is invalid or which does not take effect for some reason. Intestacy can be partial, for instance, if there is a will which disposes of some but not all of the testator's property. In such cases the person's estate (property, possessions, other assets following the payment of debts) passes to certain members of the family. The relevant legislation is the Administration of Estates Act 1925, as amended by various legislation including the Intestates Estates Act 1952, the Law Reform (Succession) Act 1995, and the Trusts of Land and Appointment of Trustees Act 1996 and Orders made thereunder. Some of the provisions of this legislation are described below. If a will has been written that disposes of only part of a person's property, these rules apply to the part which is undisposed of.

If the person (intestate) leaves a spouse or a civil partner who survives for 28 days and children (legitimate, illegitimate and adopted children and other descendants), the estate is divided as follows:

- the spouse or civil partner takes the 'personal chattels' (household articles, including cars, but nothing used for business purposes), £125,000 tax-free (with interest payable at six per cent from the time of the death until payment) and a life interest in half of the rest of the estate (which can be capitalised by the spouse or civil partner if he/she wishes)
- the rest of the estate goes to the children*

If the person leaves a spouse or civil partner who survives for 28 days but no children:

- the spouse or civil partner takes the personal chattels, £200,000 tax-free (interest payable as before) and full ownership of half of the rest of the estate
- the other half of the rest of the estate goes to the parents (equally, if both alive) or, if none, to the brothers and sisters of the whole blood*
- if there are no parents or brothers or sisters of the whole blood or their children, the spouse or civil partner takes the whole estate

If there is no surviving spouse or civil partner, the estate is distributed among those who survive the intestate as follows:

- to surviving children*, but if none to
- parents (equally, if both alive), but if none to
- brothers and sisters of the whole blood* (including issue of deceased ones), but if none to
- brothers and sisters of the half blood* (including issue of deceased ones), but if none to
- grandparents (equally, if more than one), but if none to
- aunts and uncles of the whole blood*, but if none to
- aunts and uncles of the half blood*, but if none to
- the crown, Duchy of Lancaster or the Duke of Cornwall (*bona vacantia*)

* To inherit, a member of these groups must survive the intestate and attain the age of 18, or marry under that age. If they die under the age of 18 (unless married under that age), their share goes to others, if any, in the same group. If any member of these groups predeceases the intestate leaving children, their share is divided equally among their children.

In England and Wales the provisions of the Inheritan (Provision for Family and Dependants) Act 1975 ma allow other people to claim provision from the deceased assets. This act also applies to cases where a will has bee made and allows a person to apply to the court if they fe that the will or rules of intestacy or both do not mak adequate provision for them. The court can order payme from the deceased's assets or the transfer of property fro them if the applicant's claim is accepted. The applicatic must be made within six months of the grant of proba or letters of administration and the following people ca make an application:

- the spouse or civil partner
- a former spouse or civil partner who has not remarrie or formed a subsequent civil partnership
- a child of the deceased
- someone treated as a child of the deceased's family
- someone maintained by the deceased
- someone who has cohabited for two years before th death in the same household as the deceased and as th husband or wife or civil partner of the deceased

SCOTLAND

In Scotland any person over 12 and of sound mind ca make a will. The person making the will can only free dispose of the heritage and what is known as the 'dead part' of the estate because:

- the spouse or civil partner has the right to inherit on third of the moveable estate if there are children other descendants, and one-half of it if there are not
- children are entitled to one-third of the moveable esta if there is a surviving spouse or civil partner, and on half of it if there is not

The remaining portion is the dead's part, and legacies an bequests are payable from this. Debts are payable out the whole estate before any division.

From August 1995, wills no longer needed to b 'holographed' and it is now only necessary to have or witness. The person making the will still needs to sig each page. It is better that the will is not witnessed by beneficiary although the attestation would still be sour and the beneficiary would not have to relinquish th gift.

Subsequent marriage or civil partnership does n revoke a will but the birth of a child who is not provide for may do so. A will may be revoked by a subseque will, either expressly or by implication, but in so far as th two can be read together both have effect. If a subseque will is revoked, the earlier will is revived.

Wills may be registered in the sheriff court Books the Sheriffdom in which the deceased lived or in th Books of Council and Session at the Registers Scotland.

CONFIRMATION

Confirmation (the Scottish equivalent of probate) obtained in the sheriff court of the sheriffdom in whic the deceased was resident at the time of death. Executiv are either 'nominate' (named by the deceased in the wi or 'dative' (appointed by the court in cases where n executor is named in a will or in cases of intestacy Applicants for confirmation must first provide a inventory of the deceased's estate and a schedule of deb with an affidavit. In estates under £30,000 gros confirmation can be obtained under a simplifie procedure at reduced fees, with no need for a solicitc The local sheriff clerk's office can provide assistance.

Further information can be obtained from:

ꞯINCIPAL REGISTRY (FAMILY DIVISION)
st Avenue House, 42–49 High Holborn, London WC2V 6NP
020-7947 6980

EGISTERS OF SCOTLAND
eadowbank House, 153 London Road, Edinburgh EH8 7AU
0131-659 6111

ꞮTESTACY

ıe rules of distribution are contained in the Succession cotland) Act 1964 and are extended to include civil ırtners by the Civil Partnership Act 2004.

A surviving spouse or civil partner is entitled to 'prior ghts'. This means that the spouse or civil partner has the ght to inherit:

the matrimonial or family home up to a value of £300,000, or one matrimonial or family home if there is more than one, or, in certain circumstances, the value of the home

the furnishings and contents of that home, up to the value of £24,000

a cash sum of £42,000 if the deceased left children or other descendants, or £75,000 if not

ıese figures are increased from time to time by gulations.

Once prior rights have been satisfied legal rights are ttled. Legal rights are:

s relicti(ae) and rights under the section 131 of the Civil Partnership Act 2004 – the right of a surviving spouse or civil partner to one-half of the net moveable estate, after satisfaction of prior rights, if there are no surviving children; if there are surviving children, the spouse or civil partner is entitled to one-third of the net moveable estate

Legitim and rights under the section 131 of the Civil Partnership Act 2004 – the right of surviving children to one-half of the net moveable estate if there is no surviving spouse or civil partner; if there is a surviving spouse or civil partner, the children are entitled to one-third of the net moveable estate after the satisfaction of prior rights

Where there is no surviving spouse, civil partner or children, half of the estate is taken by the parents and half by the brothers and sisters. Failing that, the lines of succession, in general, are:

- to descendants
- if no descendants, then to collaterals (ie brothers and sisters) and parents
- surviving spouse or civil partner
- if no collaterals, parents, spouse or civil partner, then to ascendants collaterals (ie aunts and uncles), and so on in an ascending scale
- if all lines of succession fail, the estate passes to the crown. Relatives of the whole blood are preferred to relatives of the half blood. The right of representation, ie the right of the issue of a person who would have succeeded if he/she had survived the intestate, also applies

INTELLECTUAL PROPERTY

Intellectual property is a broad term covering a number of legal rights provided by the government to help people protect their creative works and encourage further innovation. By using these legal rights people can own the things they create and control the way in which others use their innovations. Intellectual property owners can take legal action to stop others using their intellectual property, they can license their intellectual property to others or they can sell it on. Different types of intellectual property utilise different forms of protection including copyright, designs, patents and trademarks which are all covered below in more detail.

COPYRIGHT

Copyright protects all original literary, dramatic, musical and artistic works (including photographs, maps and plans), published editions of works, computer programs, sound recordings, films (including video and DVD) and broadcasts (including cable, radio, satellite broadcasts, and transmissions on the internet). Under copyright the creators of these works can control the various ways in which their material may be exploited, the rights broadly covering copying, adapting, issuing (including renting and lending) copies to the public, performing in public, and broadcasting the material. The transfer of copyright works to formats accessible to visually impaired persons without infringement of copyright was enacted in 2002.

Copyright protection in the United Kingdom is automatic and there is no official registration system. Steps can be taken by the work's creator to provide evidence that he/she had the work at a particular time (eg by depositing a copy with a bank or solicitor). The main legislation is the Copyright, Designs and Patents Act 1988, which has been amended by other acts and by statutory instrument to take account of EU directives. As a result of an EU directive effective from January 1996, the term of copyright protection for literary, dramatic, musical and artistic works lasts for 70 years after the death of the author. For film copyright lasts for 70 years after the death of the director, authors of the screenplay and dialogue or the composer of any music specially created for the film. Sound recordings are protected for 50 years after their publication, and broadcasts for 50 years from the end of the year in which the first broadcast/transmission was made. Published editions remain under copyright protection for 25 years from the end of the year in which the edition was published.

The main international treaties protecting copyright are the Berne Convention for the Protection of Literary and Artistic Works (administered by the World Intellectual Property Organisation (WIPO)), the Rome Convention for the Protection of Performers, Producers of Phonograms and Broadcasting Organisations (administered jointly by UNESCO and the International Labour Organisation), and the Universal Copyright Convention (developed by UNESCO); the UK is a signatory to these conventions. Copyright material created by UK nationals or residents is protected in each country that is a member of the conventions by the national law of that country. A list of participating countries may be obtained from the UK Intellectual Property Office, previously known as the UK Pate Office.

Two treaties which strengthen and update internatior standards of protection, particularly in relation to ne technologies, were agreed in December 1996: the WIP copyright treaty, and the WIPO performance a phonograms treaty. In May 2001 the European Uni passed a new directive (which in 2003 became law in t UK) aimed at harmonising copyright law throughout t EU to take account of the internet and other technologi More information can be found onli (W www.ipo.gov.uk).

LICENSING

Use of copyright material without seeking permission each instance may be permitted under 'blanket' licen available from copyright licensing agencies. T International Federation of Reproduction Rig Organisations facilitates agreements between its memb licensing agencies and on behalf of its members wi organisations such as the WIPO, UNESCO, the Europe Union and the Council of Europe.

DESIGN PROTECTION

Design protection covers the outward appearance of article and in the UK takes two forms: registered desi and design right, which are not mutually exclusi Registered design protects the aesthetic appearance of article, including shape, configuration, pattern ornament, although artistic works such as sculptures excluded, being generally protected by copyright. In ord to qualify for protection, a design must be new a materially different from earlier UK published desig The owner of the design must apply to the UK Intellect Property Office. Initial registration lasts for five years a can be extended in five-year increments to a maximum 25 years. The current legislation is the Registered Desig Act 1949 which has been amended several times, m recently by the Registered Designs Regulations 2003.

UK applicants wishing to protect their designs in t EU can do so by applying for a Registered Commun Design with the Office of Harmonisation in the Inter Market. Outside the EU separate applications must made in each country in which protection is sought.

Design right is an automatic right which applies to t shape or configuration of articles and does not requ registration. Unlike registered design, two-dimensior designs do not qualify for protection but designs semiconductor chips (topographies) are protected design right. Designs must be original a non-commonplace. The term of design right is ten ye from first marketing of the design and the right effective only in the UK. The current legislation is Par of the Copyright, Designs and Patents Act 198 amended on 9 December 2001 to incorporate t European Designs Directive.

ATENTS

patent is a document issued by the UK Intellectual ·operty Office relating to an invention and giving the ·oprietor the right for a limited period to stop others ›m making, using or selling the invention without the ventor's permission. In return the patentee pays a fee to ver the costs of processing the patent and publicly scloses details of the invention.

To qualify for a patent an invention must be new, must hibit an inventive step, and must be capable of industrial plication. The patent is valid for a maximum of 20 years ›m the date on which the application was filed, subject payment of annual fees from the end of the fourth year.

The UK Intellectual Property Office, established in 352, is responsible for ensuring that all stages of an plication comply with the Patents Act 1977, and that e invention meets the criteria for a patent.

The WIPO is responsible for administering many of e international conventions on intellectual property. The tent Cooperation Treaty allows inventors to file a single plication for patent rights in some or all of the ntracting states. This application is searched by an ternational Searching Authority and published by the ternational Bureau of WIPO. It may also be the subject an (optional) international preliminary examination. ›plicants must then deal directly with the patent offices the countries where they are seeking patent rights. The ıropean Patent Convention allows inventors to obtain tent rights in all the contracting states by filing a single plication with the European Patent Office. More formation can be found online (W www.ipo.gov.uk).

ESEARCH DISCLOSURES

:search disclosures are publicly disclosed details of ventions. Once published, an invention is considered no nger novel and becomes prior art. Publishing a sclosure is significantly cheaper than applying for a tent, however unlike a patent, it does not entitle the thor to exclusive rights to use or license the invention. stead, research disclosures are primarily published to sure the inventor freedom to use the invention. This ›rks because publishing legally prevents other parties ›m patenting the disclosed innovation and in the UK, tent law dictates that by disclosing, even the inventor inquishes their right to a patent.

In theory, publishing details of an invention anywhere ould be enough to make a research disclosure. However be effective a research disclosure really needs to be blished in a location which patent examiners will :lude in their prior art searches. To ensure global legal ecedent it must be included in a publication with a :ognised date stamp and made publicly available across e world.

The *Research Disclosure* journal established in 1960, blished by KMP Ltd, is the primary publisher of search disclosures. It is the only disclosure service :ognised by the Patent Cooperation Treaty as a ındatory search resource which must be consulted by e international search authorities. More information can found online (W www.researchdisclosure.com).

TRADE MARKS

Trade marks are a means of identification, whether a word or device or a combination of both, a logo, or the shape of goods or their packaging, which enable traders to make their goods or services readily distinguishable from those supplied by other traders. Registration prevents other traders using the same or similar trade marks for similar products or services for which the mark is registered.

In the UK trade marks are registered at the UK Intellectual Property Office. In order to qualify for registration a mark must be capable of distinguishing its proprietor's goods or services from those of other undertakings; it should be non-deceptive, should not be contrary to law or morality and should not be similar or identical to any earlier marks for the same or similar goods or services. The relevant current legislation is the Trade Marks Act 1994.

It is possible to obtain an international trade mark registration, effective in 80 countries, under the Madrid Agreement or the Madrid Protocol, to which the UK is party. British companies can obtain international trade mark registration through a single application to the WIPO in those countries party to the protocol.

EC trade mark regulation is now in force and is administered by the Office for Harmonisation in the Internal Market (Trade Marks and Designs) in Alicante, Spain. The office registers EC trade marks, which are valid throughout the European Union. The national registration of trade marks in member states continues in parallel with EC trade mark standards.

DOMAIN NAMES

A domain name is a name by which a company or organisation is known on the internet and is a shorthand way of identifying a company's website. A domain name has to be registered separately from a trade mark. Although there are many registrars prepared to register domain names, each country has a central registry to store unique names and addresses used on the internet. A list of accredited registrars can be found online (W www.icann.org).

CONTACTS

THE UK INTELLECTUAL PROPERTY OFFICE, Cardiff Road, Newport NP10 8QQ T 0845-950 0505 W www.ipo.gov.uk

COPYRIGHT LICENSING AGENCY LTD, 90 Tottenham Court Road, London W1T 0LP T 020-7631 5555 W www.cla.co.uk

EUROPEAN PATENT OFFICE, Headquarters, Erhardtstrasse 27, D-8000, Munich 2, Germany T (+49) 892 3990 W www.epo.org

WORLD INTELLECTUAL PROPERTY ORGANISATION, 34 chemin des Colombettes, CH-1211 Geneva 20, Switzerland T (+41) 22 338 9111 W www.wipo.int

BROADCASTING

CROSS-MEDIA OWNERSHIP

The Communications Act, which received royal assent on 17 July 2003, overhauled the rules surrounding cross-media ownership. They were simplified and relaxed to encourage dispersion of ownership and new market entry while preventing the most influential media in any community being controlled by too narrow a range of interests. However, transfers and mergers are not solely subject to examination on competition grounds by the competition authorities. The secretary of state has a broad remit to intervene and decide if a transaction is permissible on public interest grounds (relating both to newspapers and cross-media criteria, if broadcasting interests are also involved). The Office of Communications (OFCOM) has an advisory role. Government and parliamentary assurances were given that any intervention into local newspaper transfers would be rare and exceptional.

REGULATION

OFCOM is the regulator for the communication industries in the UK and has responsibility for television, radio, telecommunications and wireless communications services. It replaced the Broadcasting Standards Commission, the Independent Television Commission, the Radio Authority, the Radio Communications Agency and OFTEL. OFCOM is required to report annually to parliament and exists to further the interests of consumers by balancing choice and competition with the duty to foster plurality; protect viewers and listeners and promote cultural diversity in the media; and ensuring full and fair competition between communications providers.

OFFICE OF COMMUNICATIONS (OFCOM)
Riverside House, 2A Southwark Bridge Road, London SE1 9HA
T 020-7981 3000 E enquiries@ofcom.org.uk
W www.ofcom.org.uk
Chief Executive, Stephen Carter

COMPLAINTS

Under the Communications Act 2003 OFCOM's licensees are obliged to adhere to the provisions of its codes (including advertising, programme standards, fairness, privacy and sponsorship). OFCOM also inherited the Broadcasting Standards Commission's Standards Code and is transitionally applying it in respect of BBC/S4C programmes. Complainants should contact the broadcaster in the first instance (details can be found on OFCOM's website), however, if the complainant wishes the complaint to be considered by OFCOM, it will do so. Complaints should be made within a reasonable time as broadcasters are only required to keep recordings for the following periods of time: radio, 42 days; television, 90 days; and cable and satellite, 60 days.

TELEVISION

There are six major television broadcasters operating the UK. Four of these – the BBC, ITV, Channel 4 and Fi – are free-to-air analogue terrestrial networks. BSkyB ar Virgin Media Television provide satellite television servic

The BBC is the oldest broadcaster in the world. T corporation began a London-only television service fro Alexandra Palace in 1936 and achieved nationwi coverage 15 years later. A second station, BBC Two, w launched in 1964. The BBC's digital services compri BBC Three, BBC Four, BBC News 24 and BB Parliament; the children's channels, CBeebies and CBB and the interactive channel BBCi. The services are fund by the licence fee. The corporation also has a commerci arm, BBC Worldwide, which was formed in 1994 a exists to maximise the value of the BBC's programme ar publishing assets for the benefit of the licence payer. businesses include international programmi distribution, magazines, other licensed products, li events and media monitoring.

The ITV (Independent Television) network was set on a regional basis in 1955 to provide competition to t BBC. It comprised a number of independent licensees, t majority of which have now merged to form ITV plc. T network generates funds through broadcasting televisi advertisements. Its flagship analogue channel w renamed ITV1 in 2001 as part of a rebranding exercise coincide with the creation of a number of digital-on channels. These now include ITV2, ITV3, ITV4 a CITV. ITV Network Centre is wholly owned by the IT companies and undertakes commissioning and scheduli of programmes shown across the ITV network and, with the other terrestrial channels, 25 per cent programmes must come from independent producers.

Channel Four and S4C were launched in 1982 provide programmes with a distinctive character th appeal to interests not catered for by ITV. Although sta owned, Channel 4 receives no public funding and financed by commercial activities, including advertisin S4C has announced that after the digital switchover, it w become a Welsh-only channel. Channel 4 has expanded create the digital stations E4, More4 and Film4.

Channel 5 (later renamed Five) began broadcasting 1997. Despite initial problems with coverage, it no reaches about 80 per cent of the population. Digi stations Five US and Five Life were launched in Octob 2006.

BSkyB was formed after the merger in 1990 of S Television and British Sky Broadcasting. The compa operates a satellite television service and around television channels, including the Sky Sports and S Movies ranges. It is part-owned by Rupert Murdoc News Corporation. BSkyB's digital package, Sky Digit was launched in 1998 and offers access to 530 channe With the 2005 acquisition of Easynet, an internet acc provider and network operator, BSkyB now offers vo over IP (VoIP) telephony, video on demand and intern based TV.

Virgin Media Television was founded in Februa 2007 as the television production arm of Virgin Media.

as previously known as NTL:Telewest. It owns a ımber of channels available via satellite, digital and cable atforms, including Bravo, Trouble and Living and runs a ngle branded channel, Virgin Central.

HE TELEVISION LICENCE

the United Kingdom and its dependencies, a television cence is required to receive any publicly broadcast levision service, regardless of its source, including ommercial, satellite and cable programming.

The TV licence is classified as a tax, therefore non-ayment is a criminal offence. A fine of up to £1,000 can e imposed on those successfully prosecuted. The roadcasting Act 1990 made the BBC responsible for cence administration. TV Licensing is the name of the gent contracted to collect the licence fee on behalf of the BC. Total licence fee income for 2006 was £3,124.8m. 2007 an annual colour television licence cost £135.50 nd a black and white licence £45.50. Concessions are ailable for the elderly and the disabled. Further details n be found at W www.tvlicensing.co.uk/information

OW THE LICENCE FEE IS SPENT

	Percentage
Television (terrestrial and digital)	57.3
Local television and radio	16.3
Network radio	10.6
Transmission costs and licence fee collection	10.2
New media	3.4
BBC jam	1.3
Interactive TV	0.7

urce: BBC Online

IGITAL SWITCHOVER

he digital switchover involves the turning off of the nalogue terrestrial transmissions network that has been place since the 1930s and replacing it with an all-gital terrestrial network. Viewers who receive television rough an aerial will need to upgrade their sets with a t-top box (typically costing between £20 and £100) or se integrated digital television (iDTV), cable or satellite gital services. The switchover will take place between 008 and 2012. The old analogue frequencies are likely be sold to mobile telephone companies. For more formation, *see* W www.digitaluk.co.uk

Region	*Expected switchover date*
Border	2008–9
West Country, Granada	2009
Wales	2009–10
West, STV North	2010
STV Central	2010–11
Central, Yorkshire, Anglia	2011
Meridian, London, Tyne Tees, Ulster	2012

ource: Digital UK

IGITAL TELEVISION

igital broadcasting has dramatically increased the ımber and reception quality of television channels. ound and pictures are converted into a digital format and mpressed, using as few bits as possible to convey the formation on a digital signal. This technique enables veral television channels to be carried in the space used y the current analogue signals to carry one channel. igital signals can be received by standard aerials using Freeview (*see* below), satellite dishes or cable. The signals are decoded and turned back into sound and pictures by either a set-top box or a decoder built into the television set (iDTV). A basic package of channels is available without charge and services are also offered by cable and satellite companies.

The Broadcasting Act 1996 provided for the licensing of 20 or more digital terrestrial television channels (on six frequency channels or 'multiplexes'). The first digital services went on air in autumn 1998.

In June 2002, following the collapse of ITV Digital, the digital terrestrial television licence was awarded to a consortium made up of the BBC, BSkyB and transmitter company Crown Castle by the Independent Television Commission. Freeview, a new digital network, was launched on 30 October 2002. Freeview offers around 30 digital channels and requires the purchase of a set-top box, but is subsequently free of charge.

By 2006 70 per cent of British homes had access to multi-channel TV. Freeview, cable and satellite channels now account for over a third of all TV viewing. The digital channels combined have a greater share of viewing than any of the five main channels and continue to increase this lead.

The advent of digital television has coincided with the emergence of the internet as a viable alternative means of watching TV. Channel 4's 4oD (4 on Demand) service allows views to revisit and download programmes shown in the previous 28 days and access an archive of older footage using their PC. At the time of writing, the BBC was preparing to launch its iPlayer, which will provide a similar service to 4oD; viewers will be able to download most of the programmes broadcast in the previous week and store each episode for 30 days. Eventually, the iPlayer will be offered through Freeview and satellite. ITV dramas and soaps can also be viewed online through the ITV website and there are plans to extend this service to the sport, entertainment and news sectors.

ESTIMATED AUDIENCE SHARE

	Percentage of all homes		
	2004–5	*2005–6*	*2006–7*
BBC One	24.4	22.9	22.7
BBC Two	9.6	9.4	8.6
ITV1	22.3	21.1	19.4
Channel 4	9.8	9.8	9.6
five	6.5	6.3	5.6
BBC Three	0.5	0.6	0.8
BBC Four	0.2	0.2	0.3
BBC News 24	0.4	0.4	0.5
ITV2	1.2	1.5	1.7
ITV3	0.7	0.3	1.1
ITV4*	–	–	0.4
E4	0.6	1.4	1.5
More4†	–	–	0.5
Film4‡	–	–	0.8
Sky One	1.5	1.4	1.3
Sky News	0.4	0.4	0.4
All BBC channels (total)	36.2	34.9	34.3
All Sky channels (total)	6.5	6.3	6.8
Cable, satellite and digital channels (total)	27.3	30.5	34.1

* Commenced broadcasting in November 2005
† Commenced broadcasting in October 2005
‡ Launched on Freeview in July 2006
Source: BBC Annual Report and Accounts/BARB

CONTACTS

THE BRITISH BROADCASTING CORPORATION
BBC TV CENTRE, Wood Lane, London W12 7RJ
T 020-8743 8000 **W** www.bbc.co.uk
Chair, Sir Michael Lyons

BBC WORLDWIDE LTD, Woodlands, 80 Wood Lane, London W12 0TT **T** 020-8433 2000 **W** www.bbcworldwide.com

INDEPENDENT TELEVISION NETWORK
ITV NETWORK CENTRE/ITV ASSOCIATION, 200 Gray's Inn Road, London WC1X 8HF **T** 020-7843 8000 **W** www.itv.com
Chair, Michael Grade

INDEPENDENT TELEVISION NETWORK REGIONS AND COMPANIES

ANGLIA *(eastern England)*, Anglia House, Rose Lane, Norwich NR1 3JG **T** 01603-615151 **W** www.itvregions.com/anglia

BORDER *(Borders and the Isle of Man)*, The Television Centre, Carlisle CA1 3NT **T** 01228-525101 **W** www.itvregions.com/border

CENTRAL *(east, west and south Midlands)*, Gas Street, Birmingham B1 2JT **T** 0870-600 6766 **W** www.itvregions.com/central

CHANNEL *(Channel Islands)*, The Television Centre, St Helier, Jersey JE1 3ZD **T** 01534-816816 **W** www.channelonline.tv

GRANADA *(north-west England)*, Quay Street, Manchester M60 9EA **T** 0161-832 7211 **W** www.itvregions.com/granada

LONDON *(London)*, London Television Centre, Upper Ground, London SE1 9LT **T** 020-7261 8163 **W** www.itvregions.com/london

MERIDIAN *(south and south-east England)*, Solent Business Park, Whiteley, Hants PO15 7PA **T** 01489-442000 **W** www.meridiantv.com

STV *(Scotland)*, 200 Renfield Street, Glasgow G2 3PR **T** 0141-300 3000 **W** www.stv.tv

TYNE TEES *(north-east England)*, Television House, The Watermark, Gateshead, Tyne and Wear NE11 9SZ **T** 0191-404 8700 **W** www.itvregions.com/tyne_tees

ULSTER *(Northern Ireland)*, Havelock House, Belfast BT7 1EB **T** 02890-328122 **W** www.u.tv

WALES The Television Centre, Culverhouse Cross, Cardiff CF5 6XJ **T** 029-2059 0590 **W** www.itvregions.com/wales

WEST Television Centre, Bath Road, Bristol BS4 3HG **T** 0117-972 2722 **W** www.itvregions.com/west

WEST COUNTRY *(south-west England)*, Langage Science Park, Western Wood Way, Plymouth PL7 5BQ **T** 01752-333333 **W** www.itvregions.com/westcountry

YORKSHIRE *(Yorkshire)*, 96–104 Kirkstall Road, Leeds LS3 1JS **T** 0113-243 8283 **W** www.itvregions.com/yorkshire

OTHER TELEVISION COMPANIES

CHANNEL FOUR TELEVISION, 124 Horseferry Road, London SW1P 2TX **T** 020-7396 4444 **W** www.channel4.com

FIVE BROADCASTING LTD, 22 Long Acre, London WC2E 9LY **T** 0845-705 0505 **W** www.five.tv

GMTV, The London Television Centre, Upper Ground, London SE1 9TT **T** 020-7827 7000 **W** www.gm.tv
Owned by ITV and Disney, with 75 per cent and 25 per cent respectively, GMTV provides breakfast television and sells its own advertising.

INDEPENDENT TELEVISION NEWS, 200 Gray's Inn Road, London WC1X 8XZ **T** 020-7833 3000 **W** www.itn.co.uk

TELETEXT LTD, Building 10, Chiswick Park, 566 Chiswick High Road London W4 5TS **T** 0870-731 3000
Provides teletext services for the ITV companies an Channel 4 and offers holiday, car rental and mobi telecom services.

WELSH FOURTH CHANNEL AUTHORITY, (Sianel Pedwar Cymru/Channel Four Wales), Parc Ty Glas, Llanishen, Cardiff CF14 5DU **T** 029-2074 7444 **W** www.s4c.co.uk
S4C schedules Welsh language and most Channel programmes.

DIRECT BROADCASTING BY SATELLITE TELEVISION

BRITISH SKY BROADCASTING GROUP, Grant Way, Isleworth, Middx TW7 5QD **T** 020-7705 3000 **W** www.sky.com
Chair, Rupert Murdoch

VIRGIN MEDIA TELEVISION, 160 Great Portland Stree London W1W 5QA **T** 020-7299 5000 **W** www.virginmediatv.co.uk
Chair, Jim Mooney

RADIO

UK domestic radio services are broadcast across thre wavebands: FM, medium wave and long wave (used b BBC Radio 4). In the UK the FM waveband extends i frequency from 87.5MHz to 108MHz and the mediu waveband from 531kHz to 1602kHz. A number of radi stations are now being broadcast in both analogue an digital as well as a growing number in digital alone. As March 2007, the BBC Radio network controlled 56 p cent of the listening market (*see* BBC Radio section), wi the independent sector (*see* Independent Radio sectio recording 42 per cent.

ESTIMATED AUDIENCE SHARE

			Percentage
	Apr–Jun 2005	*Jan–Mar 2006*	*Jan–Mar 2007*
BBC Radio 1	9.2	9.1	10.1
BBC Radio 2	16.0	16.0	15.8
BBC Radio 3	1.1	1.3	1.2
BBC Radio 4	11.2	11.7	12.2
BBC Radio Five Live	4.4	4.6	4.2
Five Live Sports Extra	0.1	0.1	0.1
6 Music	0.1	0.2	0.3
BBC7	0.2	0.3	0.4
Asian Network	0.2	0.2	0.2
1Xtra	0.1	0.2	0.2
BBC Local/Regional	10.9	11.1	10.6
BBC World Service	0.5	0.6	0.7
All BBC	54.0	55.4	56.0
All independent	44.0	42.6	42.1
All national independent	10.2	10.5	10.7
All local independent	33.8	32.2	31.4
Other	2.0	2.0	1.8

Source: RAJAR/Ipsos-MORI

IGITAL RADIO

AB (Digital Audio Broadcasting) allows more services to e broadcast to a higher technical quality and provides ie data facility for text and pictures. It improves the bustness of high fidelity radio services, especially ompared with current FM and AM radio transmissions. It as developed in a collaborative research project under ie pan-European Eureka 147 initiative and has been dopted as a world standard by the International elecommunication Union for new digital radio systems. he frequencies allocated for terrestrial digital radio in the K are 217.5 to 230MHz. More spectrum (in the 'L-and' range: 1452–1467.5MHz) was planned for digital idio in the UK in 2007.

It is necessary to possess a digital radio set in order to ceive digital broadcasts. Digital radios are available in veral different forms: as standalone portable units, hi-fi acks, car radios and PC cards, and inbuilt within a obile phone. Newer DAB radios allow the listener to wind, pause and record broadcasts and can be uploaded a computer using a USB cable. Some portable sets now ombine MP3 playback with DAB. An alternative method to listen to digital radio through television sets via reeview, cable or satellite.

ICENSING

he Broadcasting Act 1996 provided for the licensing of igital radio services (on multiplexes, where a number of ations share one frequency to transmit their services). To locate the multiplexes, OFCOM advertises licences for hich interested parties can bid. Once the licence has een awarded, the new owner seeks out services to roadcast on the multiplex. There is one national ommercial multiplex owner (Digital One) operating ght services. The BBC has a separate national multiplex r its services. There are local multiplexes around the ountry, each broadcasting an average of seven services, us the local BBC station. There are also several regional ultiplexes covering a wider area and broadcasting up to 1 services each.

NOVATIONS

s with television, the opportunities offered by digital rvices and the internet have made important changes to dio. Programmes are now more readily available and ore interactive than ever before. Listeners can tune in to ny BBC radio station live on the internet or listen again nline for seven days after broadcast. Since 2005 creasing numbers of radio stations offer all or part of eir programmes as downloadable files to listen to on omputers or mobile devices such as MP3 players or hones. These files are known as podcasts.

Podcasting technology allows the listener to itomatically receive latest episodes of regularly ansmitted programmes as soon as they become available. he user usually needs to subscribe to receive the updates, the same way as a magazine. While some radio stations id newspapers charge for updates, all of the BBC's odcasts are free.

The relationship between a radio presenter and his or er audience is also undergoing change. Listeners have ng been given the opportunity to request songs to be ayed on air, but the quantity and easy availability of usic on the internet has led to the creation of shows edicated entirely to music sent in by listeners, much of hich can be previously unknown to the presenter.

BBC RADIO

BBC Radio broadcasts network services to the UK, Isle of Man and the Channel Islands. There is also a tier of national services in Wales, Scotland and Northern Ireland and 40 local radio stations in England and the Channel Islands. In Wales and Scotland there are also dedicated language services in Welsh and Gaelic respectively. The frequency allocated for digital BBC broadcasts is 225.648MHz.

BBC RADIO Broadcasting House, Portland Place, London W1A 1AA T 020-7580 4468

BBC NETWORK RADIO STATIONS

RADIO 1 (contemporary pop music and entertainment news) – 24 hours a day, *frequencies:* 97–99 FM

RADIO 2 (popular music, entertainment, comedy and the arts) – 24 hours a day, *frequencies:* 88–91 FM

RADIO 3 (classical music, classic drama, documentaries and features) – 24 hours a day, *frequencies:* 90–93 FM

RADIO 4 (news, documentaries, drama, entertainment and cricket on long wave in season) – 5.20am–1am daily, with BBC World Service overnight, *frequencies:* 92–95 FM and 198 LW

RADIO FIVE LIVE (news and sport) – 24 hours a day, *frequencies:* 693/909 MW

FIVE LIVE SPORTS EXTRA (live sport) – schedule varies, digital only

6 MUSIC (contemporary and classic pop and rock music) – 24 hours a day, digital only

BBC7 (comedy, drama and children's) – 24 hours a day, digital only

Asian Network (news, music and sport) – 5am–1am Monday–Friday and Sunday; 5am–2am Saturday, with Radio Five Live overnight

1Xtra (urban music: drum & bass, garage, hip hop, R&B) – 24 hours a day, digital only

BBC NATIONAL RADIO STATIONS

RADIO CYMRU (Welsh-language), *frequencies:* 93.6–96.8 FM and 103.5–105 FM, coverage 97 per cent

RADIO FOYLE, *frequencies:* 792 AM and 93.1 MW

RADIO NAN GAIDHEAL (Gaelic service), *frequencies:* 103.5–105 FM plus 990 MW, coverage 90 per cent

RADIO SCOTLAND, *frequencies:* 810/585 MW and 92.4–94.7 FM, coverage 99 per cent. Local programmes for: Highlands and Islands; North East; Borders; South West; Orkney; and Shetland

RADIO ULSTER, *frequencies:* 1341 MW and 92.4–95.4 FM, coverage 96 per cent. Local programmes on Radio Foyle

RADIO WALES, *frequencies:* 882 MW and 93.9–95.9 FM, coverage 97 per cent

BBC LOCAL RADIO STATIONS

There are 40 local stations serving England and the Channel Islands:

BERKSHIRE, PO Box 1044, Reading RG4 8FH T 08459-001041 *Frequencies:* 94.6/95.4/104.1/104.4 FM and digital

BRISTOL, Whiteladies Road, Bristol BS8 2LR T 0117-974 2211 *Frequencies:* 94.9/95.5 FM and 1548 MW and digital

CAMBRIDGESHIRE, 104 Hills Road, Cambridge CB2 1LD T 01223-259696 *Frequencies:* 95.7/96 FM

CLEVELAND, Broadcasting House, Newport Road, Middlesbrough TS1 5DG T 01642-225211 *Frequency:* 95 FM and digital

CORNWALL, Phoenix Wharf, Truro TR1 1UA T 01872-275421 *Frequencies:* 95.2/96.0/103.9 FM and digital
COVENTRY AND WARWICKSHIRE, Priory Place, Coventry CV1 5SQ T 024-7655 1000 *Frequencies:* 94.8/104/103.7 FM and digital
CUMBRIA, Annetwell Street, Carlisle CA3 8BB T 01228-592444 *Frequencies:* 95.2/95.6/96.1/104.1/104.2 FM, 756/837/1458 MW
DERBY, 56 St Helen's Street, Derby DE1 3HY T 01332-361111 *Frequencies:* 95.3/96.0/104.5 FM, 1116 MW
DEVON, Broadcasting House, Seymour Road, Plymouth PL3 5BD T 01752-260323 *Frequencies:* 94.8/95.7/95.8/96.0/103.4/104.3 FM, 801/855/990/1458 MW and digital
ESSEX, PO Box 765, Chelmsford CM2 9XB T 01245-616000 *Frequencies:* 95.3/103.5 FM, 729/765/1530 MW and digital
GLOUCESTERSHIRE, London Road, Gloucester GL1 1SW T 01452-308585 *Frequencies:* 95.0/95.8/104.7 FM, 1413 MW
GUERNSEY, Broadcasting House, Bulwer Avenue, St Sampson's GY2 4LA T 01481-200600 *Frequencies:* 93.2/99 FM, 1116 AM
HEREFORD AND WORCESTER, Hylton Road, Worcester WR2 5WW T 01905-748485 *Frequencies:* 94.7/104.0/104.6 FM, 738/1584 MW
HUMBERSIDE, Queen's Court, Hull HU1 3RH T 01482-323232 *Frequency:* 95.9 FM, 1485 MW and digital
JERSEY, 18 Parade Road, St Helier JE2 3PL T 01534-837228 *Frequency:* 88.8 FM and digital
KENT, The Great Hall, Mount Pleasant, Tunbridge Wells TN1 1QQ T 01892-670000 *Frequencies:* 96.7/97.6/104.2 FM, 774/1602 MW
LANCASHIRE, 20–26 Darwen Street, Blackburn BB2 2EA T 01254-262411 *Frequencies:* 95.5/103.9/104.5 FM, 855/1557 MW and digital
LEEDS, 2 St Peter's Square, Leeds LS9 8AH T 0113-244 2131 *Frequency:* 92.4 FM, 774 MW and digital
LEICESTER, 9 St Nicholas Place, Leicester LE1 5LB T 0116-251 6688 *Frequency:* 104.9 FM and digital
LINCOLNSHIRE, PO Box 219, Lincoln LN1 3XY T 01522-511411 *Frequencies:* 94.9/104.7 FM, 1368 MW and digital
LONDON, PO Box 949, Marylebone High Street, London W1A 6FL T 020-7224 2424 *Frequency:* 94.9 FM and digital
MANCHESTER, PO Box 951, Oxford Road, Manchester M60 1SD T 0161-200 2020 *Frequencies:* 95.1/104.6 FM and digital
MERSEYSIDE, 55 Paradise Street, Liverpool L1 3BP T 0151-708 5500 *Frequency:* 95.8 FM and digital
NEWCASTLE, Broadcasting Centre, Barrack Road, Newcastle upon Tyne NE99 1RN T 0191-232 4141 *Frequency:* 95.4 and digital
NORFOLK, The Forum, Millennium Plain, Norwich NR2 1BH T 01603-617411 *Frequencies:* 95.1/95.6/104.4 FM and digital
NORTHAMPTON, Broadcasting House, Abington Street, Northampton NN1 2BH T 01604-239100 *Frequencies:* 103.6/104.2 FM
NOTTINGHAM, London Road, Nottingham NG2 4UU T 0115-955 0500 *Frequencies:* 95.5/103.8 FM and digital
OXFORD, 269 Banbury Road, Oxford OX2 7DW T 08459-311 444 *Frequency:* 95.2 FM
SHEFFIELD, 54 Shoreham Street, Sheffield S1 4RS T 0114-273 1177 *Frequencies:* 88.6/94.7/104.1 FM and digital
SHROPSHIRE, 2–4 Boscobel Drive, Harlescott, Shrewsbury SY1 3TT T 01743-237019 *Frequency:* 96 FM and digital
SOLENT, Havelock Road, Southampton SO14 7PW T 0845-313 0961 *Frequencies:* 96.1/103.8 FM
SOMERSET SOUND, Broadcasting House, Park Street, Taunton TA1 4DA T 01823-323956 *Frequency:* 1566 MW
SOUTHERN COUNTIES, Broadcasting Centre, Guildford GU2 7AP T 01483-306306 *Frequencies:* 95–95.3/104–104.8 FM and digital
STOKE, Cheapside, Hanley, Stoke-on-Trent ST1 1JJ T 01782-208080 *Frequencies:* 94.6/104.1 FM, 1503 MW and digital
SUFFOLK, Broadcasting House, St Matthew's Street, Ipswic IP1 3EP T 01473-250000 *Frequencies:* 95.5/95.9/103.9/104.6 FM
SWINDON, Broadcasting House, 56–58 Prospect Place, Swindon SN1 3RW T 01793-513626 *Frequency:* 103.6 FM and digital
THREE COUNTIES, 1 Hastings Street, Luton LU1 5XL T 01582-637400 *Frequencies:* 94.7/95.5/98.0/103.8/104.5 FM, 630/1161 MW
WILTSHIRE, Broadcasting House, 56–58 Prospect Place, Swindon SN1 3RW T 01793-513626 *Frequencies:* 103.5/104.3/104.9 FM and digital
WM (WEST MIDLANDS), The Mailbox, Birmingham B1 1R T 0121-567 6000 *Frequency:* 95.6 FM and digital
YORK, 20 Bootham Row, York YO30 7BR T 01904-641351 *Frequencies:* 95.5/103.7/104.3 FM

BBC WORLD SERVICE

The BBC World Service broadcasts to an estimated weekl audience of 163 million worldwide, in 33 language including English, and is now available in 150 capit cities. It no longer broadcasts in Dutch, French for Europ German, Hebrew, Italian, Japanese or Malay because it wa found that most speakers of these languages preferred t listen to the English broadcasts. In 2006 services in te languages (Bulgarian, Croatian, Czech, Greek, Hungaria Kazakh, Polish, Slovak, Slovene, and Thai) wer terminated to provide funding for a new Arabic televisio channel, which was to be launched in late 2007. The BB World Service website offers interactive news services i English, Arabic, Chinese, Hindi, Persian, Portuguese fc Brazil, Russian, Spanish and Urdu with audiostreamin available in 33 languages:
Albanian, Arabic, Azeri, Bengali, Burmese, Caribbear English, Cantonese, French for Africa, Hausa, Hind Indonesian, Kinyarwanda/Kirundi, Kyrgyz, Macedonia Mandarin, Nepali, Pashto, Persian, Portuguese for Brazi Romanian, Russian, Serbian, Sinhala, Somali, Spanis Swahili, Tamil, Turkish, Ukrainian, Urdu, Uzbek an Vietnamese.

UK frequencies: 648 MW in southern England an overnight on BBC Radio 4, BBC Radio Ulster, BB Radio Wales or the Asian Network.

BBC LEARNING ENGLISH teaches English worldwid through radio, television and a wide range of publishe and online courses.
BBC MONITORING tracks the global media for th latest news reports emerging around the world.
BBC WORLD SERVICE TRUST is a registered charit established in 1999 by BBC World Service. It promote development through the innovative use of the medi in the developing world. The trust presently works i over 30 countries worldwide, tackling healt education and good governance.
BBC WORLD SERVICE Bush House, Strand, London WC2 4PH T 020-7557 2462

INDEPENDENT RADIO

Until 1973, the BBC had a legal monopoly on radio broadcasting in the UK. During this time, the corporation's only competition came from pirate stations located abroad, such as Radio Luxembourg. Christopher Chataway, Minister for Post and Telecommunications in Edward Heath's government, changed this by creating the first licences for commercial radio stations. The Independent Broadcasting Authority (IBA) awarded the first of these licences to the London Broadcasting Company (LBC) to provide London's news and information service. LBC was followed by Capital Radio, to offer the city's entertainment service, Radio Clyde in Glasgow and BRMB in Birmingham.

The IBA was dissolved when the Broadcasting Act of 1990 de-regulated broadcasting, to be succeeded by the less rigid Radio Authority (RA). The RA began advertising new licences for the development of independent radio in January 1991. It awarded national and local radio, satellite and cable services licences, and long-term restricted service licences for stations serving non-commercial establishments such as hospitals and universities. The first national commercial digital multiplex licence was awarded in October 1998 and a number of local digital multiplex licences followed.

At the end of 2003 the RA was replaced by OFCOM, which now carries out the licensing administration.

The RadioCentre was formed in July 2006 as a result of the merger between the Radio Advertising Bureau (RAB) and the Commercial Radio Companies Association (CRCA), the former non-profit trade body for commercial radio companies in the United Kingdom, to operate essentially as a union for commercial radio stations.

THE RADIOCENTRE, 77 Shaftesbury Avenue, London W1D 5DU T 020-7306 2603 W www.radiocentre.org
Chief Executive, Andrew Harrison

INDEPENDENT NATIONAL RADIO STATIONS

CLASSIC FM, 30 Leicester Square, London WC2H 7LA T 020-7343 9000 – 24 hours a day, *Frequencies:* 100–102 FM

TALK SPORT, 18 Hatfields, London SE1 8DJ T 020-7959 7800 – 24 hours a day, *Frequencies:* 1053/1071/1089/1107 AM

VIRGIN 1215, 1 Golden Square, London W1F 9DJ T 020-7434 1215 – 24 hours a day, *Frequencies:* 1197/1215/1233/1242/1260 AM

INDEPENDENT LOCAL RADIO STATIONS ENGLAND

2BR, Lomeshaye Business Village, Nelson, Lancs BB9 7DR T 01282-690000 *Frequency:* 99.8 FM

2CR FM, 5–7 Southcote Road, Bournemouth BH1 3LR T 01202-234900 *Frequency:* 102.3 FM

2-TEN FM, PO Box 2020, Reading, Berks RG31 7FG T 0118-945 4400 *Frequencies:* 97.0/102.9/103.4 FM

3FM, 45 Victoria Street, Douglas, IOM IM1 3RS T 01624-616333 *Frequencies:* 104–106 FM

3TR FM, Riverside Studios, Warminster, Wilts BA12 9HQ T 01985-211111 *Frequency:* 107.5 FM

95.8 CAPITAL RADIO, 30 Leicester Square, London WC2H 7LA T 020-7766 6000 *Frequency:* 95.8 FM

96 TRENT FM, Maid Marian Way, Nottingham NG1 6JR T 0115-873 1500 *Frequencies:* 96.2/96.5 FM

96.2 THE REVOLUTION, Sarah Moor Studios, Henshaw Street, Oldham OL1 3JF T 0161-621 6500 *Frequency:* 96.2 FM

96.2 TOUCH FM, Watch Close, Spon Street, Coventry CV1 3LN T 024-7652 5656 *Frequency:* 96.2 FM

96.3 RADIO AIRE, 51 Burley Road, Leeds LS3 1LR T 0113-283 5500 *Frequency:* 96.3 FM

96.4 FM BRMB, Nine Brindleyplace, 4 Oozells Square, Birmingham B1 2DJ T 0121-566 5200 *Frequency:* 96.4 FM

96.4 THE EAGLE, Dolphin House, North Street, Guildford, Surrey GU1 4AA T 01483-300964 *Frequency:* 96.4 FM

96.9 CHILTERN FM, 5 Abbey Court, Fraser Road, Priory Business Park, Bedford MK44 3WH T 01234-235010 *Frequency:* 96.9 FM

96.9 VIKING FM, The Boathouse, Commercial Road, Hull, E. Yorks HU1 2SG T 01482-325141 *Frequency:* 96.9 FM

97 FM PLYMOUTH SOUND, Earl's Acre, Plymouth PL3 4HX T 01752-275600 *Frequencies:* 96.6/97 FM

97.2 STRAY FM, The Hamlet, Hornbeam Park Avenue, Harrogate HG2 8RE T 01423-522972 *Frequency:* 97.2 FM

97.4 ROCK FM, PO Box 974, St. Paul's Square, Preston, Lancs PR1 1YE T 01772-477700 *Frequency:* 97.4 FM

97.6 CHILTERN FM, Chiltern Road, Dunstable LU6 1HQ T 01582-676200 *Frequency:* 97.6 FM

100–102 CENTURY FM, Century House, PO Box 100, Gateshead NE8 2YY T 0191-556 3000 *Frequencies:* 96.2/94.6/100.7/101.8 FM

100.7 HEART FM, 1 The Square, 111 Broad Street, Birmingham B15 1AS T 0121-695 0000 *Frequency:* 100.7 FM

102 TOUCH FM, The Guard House Studios, Banbury Road, Stratford-upon-Avon, Warks CV37 7HX T 01789-262636 *Frequency:* 102.0 FM

102.2 SMOOTH FM, 26–27 Castlereagh Street, London W1H 5DL T 020-7706 4100 *Frequency:* 102.2 FM

102.4 WISH FM, Orrell Lodge, Orrell Road, Wigan, Lancs WN5 8HJ T 01942-761024 *Frequency:* 102.4 FM

102.7 HEREWARD FM, PO Box 225, Queensgate Centre, Peterborough PE1 1XJ T 01733-460460 *Frequency:* 102.7 FM

102.7 MERCURY FM, 9 The Stanley Centre, Kelvin Way, Crawley, W. Sussex RH10 9SE T 01293-519161 *Frequencies:* 97.5/102.7 FM

103.2 ALPHA FM, Radio House, 11 Woodland Road, Darlington, Co. Durham DL3 7BJ T 01325-255552 *Frequency:* 103.2 FM

103.2 POWER FM, Radio House, Whittle Avenue, Segensworth West, Fareham, Hants PO15 5SH T 01489-579000 *Frequency:* 103.2 FM

103.4 SUN FM, PO Box 1034, Sunderland, Tyne and Wear SR5 2YL T 0191-548 1034 *Frequency:* 103.4 FM

105.4 CENTURY FM, Laser House, Waterfront Quays, Manchester M50 3XW T 0161-662 4701 *Frequency:* 105.4 FM

107.2 WIN FM, The Brooks, Winchester, Hants SO23 8FT T 01962-841071 *Frequency:* 107.2 FM

107.2 THE WYRE, Foley House, 123 Stourport Road, Kidderminster DY11 7BW T 01562-641072 *Frequency:* 107.2 FM

107.4 THE QUAY, Flagship Studios, PO Box 1074, Portsmouth PO2 8YG T 023-9236 4141 *Frequency:* 107.4 FM

107.5 SOVEREIGN RADIO, 14 St Mary's Walk, Hailsham, E. Sussex BN27 1AF T 01323-442700 *Frequency:* 107.5 FM

107.6 FM JUICE LIVERPOOL, 27 Fleet Street, Liverpool L1 4AR T 0151-707 3107 *Frequency:* 107.6 FM

107.6 TOUCH BANBURY, Unit 9A, Manor Park, Banbury, Oxfordshire OX16 3TB T 0129-566 1076 *Frequency:* 107.6 FM

107.7 SPLASH FM, The Guildbourne Centre, Worthing, W. Sussex BN11 1LZ T 01903-233005 *Frequency:* 107.7 FM

107.7 THE WOLF, 10th Floor, Mander House, Wolverhampton WV1 3NB T 01902-571070 *Frequency:* 107.7 FM

107.8 ARROW FM, Priory Meadow Centre, Hastings, E. Sussex TN34 1PJ T 01424-461177 *Frequency:* 107.8 FM

107.8 RADIO JACKIE, 110–112 Tolworth Broadway, Surbiton, Surrey KT6 7JD T 020-8288 1300 *Frequency:* 107.8 FM

107.9 DUNE FM, The Power Station, Victoria Way, Southport, Merseyside PR8 1RR T 01704-502500 *Frequency:* 107.9 FM

1548 AM CAPITAL GOLD, 30 Leicester Square, London WC2H 7LA T 020-7054 8000 *Frequency:* 1548 AM

ASIAN SOUND RADIO, Globe House, Southall Street, Manchester M3 1LG T 0161-288 1000 *Frequencies:* 963/1377 AM

ATLANTIC FM, Unit 10, Wheal Kitty Workshops, St Agnes, Cornwall TR5 0RD T 01872-554400 *Frequencies:* 105.1/107.0 FM

BATH FM, Station House, Ashley Avenue, Lower Weston, Bath BA1 3DS T 01225-471571 *Frequency:* 107.9 FM

THE BAY, PO Box 969, St George's Quay, Lancaster LA1 3LD T 01524-848747 *Frequencies:* 96.9/102.3/103.2 FM

THE BEACH, PO Box 103.4, Lowestoft, Suffolk NR32 2TL T 0845-345 1035 *Frequencies:* 97.4/103.4 FM

BEACON FM, 267 Tettenhall Road, Wolverhampton WV6 0DE T 01902-461300 *Frequencies:* 97.2/103.1 FM

THE BEAR 102, The Guard House Studios, Banbury Road, Stratford upon Avon, Warks CV37 7HX T 01789 262636 *Frequency:* 102.0 FM

BRIDGWATER'S 107.4 BCR FM, Royal Clarence House, High Street, Bridgwater, Somerset TA6 3AT T 01278-727701 *Frequency:* 107.4 FM

BRIGHT 106.4, 11A The Market Place Shopping Centre, Burgess Hill, W. Sussex RH15 9NP T 01444-248127 *Frequency:* 106.4 FM

CAPITAL GOLD (1152), Nine Brindleyplace, 4 Oozells Square, Birmingham B1 2DJ T 0121-245 5000 *Frequency:* 1152 AM

CAPITAL GOLD (1242/603), Radio House, John Wilson Business Park, Whitstable, Kent CT5 3QX T 01227-772004 *Frequencies:* 603/1242 AM

CAPITAL GOLD (1323/945), Radio House, PO Box 2000, Brighton BN41 2SS T 01273-430111 *Frequencies:* 945/1323 AM

CAPITAL GOLD 1458 AM, Laser House, Waterfront Quays, Manchester M5 2XW T 0161-662 4700 *Frequency:* 1458 AM

CAPITAL GOLD (1557/1170), Radio House, Whittle Avenue, Segensworth West, Farnham, Hants PO15 5SH T 01489-589911 *Frequencies:* 1170/1557 AM

CFM (CARLISLE AND WEST CUMBRIA), PO Box 964, Carlisle, Cumbria CA1 3NG T 01228-818964 *Frequencies:* 96.4/102.5 FM (Carlisle) (west Cumbria); 102.2/103.4 FM

CHESHIRE'S 106.9 SILK FM, Radio House, Bridge Street, Macclesfield, Cheshire SK11 6DJ T 01625-268000 *Frequency:* 106.9 FM

CHOICE 96.9/107.1 FM, 30 Leicester Square, London WC2H 7LA T 020-7766 6810 *Frequency:* 96.9/107.1 FM

CLASSIC GOLD (666/954), Hawthorn House, Exeter Business Park, Exeter EX1 3QS T 01392-444444 *Frequencies:* 666/954 AM

CLASSIC GOLD (774), Bridge Studios, Eastgate Centre, Gloucester GL1 1SS T 01452-572400 *Frequency:* 774 AM

CLASSIC GOLD (828), 5–7 Southcote Road, Bournemouth, Dorset BH1 3LR T 01202-234900 *Frequency:* 828 AM

CLASSIC GOLD (828/792), Chiltern Road, Dunstable, Beds LU6 1HQ T 01582-676200 *Frequencies:* 792/828 AM

CLASSIC GOLD (936/1161), 1st Floor, Chiseldon House, Stonehill Green, Westlea, Swindon, Wilts SN5 7HB T 01793-663000 *Frequencies:* 936/1161 AM

CLASSIC GOLD (990/1017), 267 Tettenhall Road, Wolverhampton WV6 0DQ T 01902-461200 *Frequencies:* 990/1017 AM

CLASSIC GOLD (1152), Earl's Acre, Plymouth PL3 4HX T 01752-275600 *Frequency:* 1152 AM

CLASSIC GOLD (1260), PO Box 2000, One Passage Street, Bristol BS99 7SN T 0117-984 3200 *Frequency:* 1260 AM

CLASSIC GOLD (1332), PO Box 225, Queensgate Centre, Peterborough, Cambridge PE1 1XJ T 01733-460460 *Frequency:* 1332 AM

CLASSIC GOLD (1359), Hertford Place, Coventry CV1 3TT T 024-7686 8200 *Frequency:* 1359 AM

CLASSIC GOLD (1359/1431), 31 Glebe Road, Chelmsford, Essex CM1 1QG T 01245-524549, *Frequencies:* 1359/1431 AM

CLASSIC GOLD (1431/1485), The Chase, Calcot, Reading, Berks RG3 7RB T 0118-945 4400 *Frequencies:* 1431/1485 AM

CLASSIC GOLD (1521), 9 The Stanley Centre, Kelvin Way, Crawley, W. Sussex RH10 9SE T 01293-519161 *Frequency:* 1521 AM

CLASSIC GOLD (1557), 19–21 St Edmunds Road, Northampton NN1 5DY T 01604-795600 *Frequency:* 1557 AM

CLASSIC GOLD AMBER (NORFOLK), St George's Plain, 47–49 Colegate, Norwich NR3 1DB T 01603-630621 *Frequency:* 1152 AM

CLASSIC GOLD AMBER (SUFFOLK), Alpha Business Park, 6–12 White House Road, Ipswich IP1 5LT T 01473-461000 *Frequency:* 1170/1251 AM

CLASSIC GOLD GEM, 29–31 Castle Gate, Nottingham NG1 7AP T 0115-873 1500 *Frequencies:* 945/999 AM

CLASSIC HITS (954/1530), PO Box 262, Worcester WR6 5ZE T 01905-740600 *Frequencies:* 954/1530 AM

CLUB ASIA, Asia House, 227–247 Gascoigne Road, Barking, Essex IG11 7LN T 020-8594 6662 *Frequencies:* 963/972 AM

COMPASS FM, 26A Wellowgate, Grimsby, Lincs DN32 0RA T 01472-346666 *Frequency:* 96.4 FM

CONNECT FM, Unit 1, Centre 2000, Robinson Close, Telford Way Industrial Estate, Kettering, Northants NN16 8PU T 01536-412413 *Frequencies:* 97.2/107.4 FM

COUNTY SOUND RADIO 1566 AM, Dolphin House, North Street, Guildford, Surrey GU1 4AA T 01483-300964 *Frequency:* 1566 AM

CTR FM, 6–8 Mill Street, Maidstone, Kent ME15 6XH T 01622-662500 *Frequency:* 105.6 FM

DEARNE FM, Unit 7, Network Centre, Zenith Park, Whaley Road, Barnsley S75 1HT T 01226-321733 *Frequencies:* 97.1/102.0 FM

DEE 106.3, 2 Chantry Court, Chester CH1 4QN T 01244-391000 *Frequency:* 106.3 FM

DELTA FM, Tindle House, High Street, Bordon, Hants GU35 0AY T 01420-473473 *Frequencies:* 97.1/101.6/101.8/102.0 FM

DREAM 100 FM, Northgate House, St Peter's Street, Colchester, Essex CO1 1HT T 01206-764466 *Frequency:* 100.2 FM

DREAM 107.7 FM, 12 Bentalls Shopping Centre, Colchester Road, Heybridge, Maldon, Essex CM9 4GD T 01473-836100 *Frequency:* 107.7 FM

EASY RADIO LONDON (1035), Radio House, Merrick Road, Southall, Middlesex UB2 4AU, T 020-8574 6666, *Frequency:* 1035 AM

ENERGY FM, 100 Market Street, Douglas, IOM IM1 2PH T 01624-611936 *Frequencies:* 91.2 FM (Laxey); 93.4 FM (north Isle of Man); 98.4 FM (Ramsey); 98.6 FM

ESSEX FM, Radio House, 31, Glebe House, Chelmsford, Essex CM1 1QG T 01245-524500 *Frequencies:* 96.3/97.5/102.6 FM

FEN RADIO 107.5, Quadrant Studios, Old Christchurch Road, Bournemouth BH1 2AD T 01202-318100 *Frequency:* 107.5 FM

FIRE 107.6 FM, Quadrant Studios, Old Christchurch Road, Bournemouth BH1 2AD T 01202-318100 *Frequency:* 107.6 FM

FOSSEWAY RADIO, Suite 1, 1 Castle Street, Hinckley, Leics LE10 1DA T 01455-614151 *Frequency:* 107.9 FM

FOX FM, Brush House, Pony Road, Oxford OX4 2XR T 01865-871000 *Frequencies:* 97.4/102.6 FM

FRESH RADIO, Firth Mill, Firth Street, Skipton, N. Yorks BD23 2PT T 01756-799991 *Frequencies:* 936/1413/1431 AM

GALAXY BIRMINGHAM, 1 The Square, 111 Broad Street, Birmingham, West Midlands B15 1AS T 0121-695 0000 *Frequency:* 102.2 FM

GALAXY MANCHESTER, 5th Floor, The Triangle, Hanging Ditch, Manchester M4 3TR T 0161-279 0300 *Frequency:* 102.0 FM

GALAXY NORTH EAST, Kingfisher Way, Silverlink Business Park, Wallsend, Tyne and Wear NE28 9NX T 0191-206 8000 *Frequencies:* 105.3/105.6/105.8/106.4 FM

GALAXY YORKSHIRE, Joseph's Well, Hanover Walk, Leeds LS3 1AB T 0113-213 0105 *Frequencies:* 105.1/105.6/105.8 FM

GEMINI FM, Hawthorn House, Exeter Business Park, Exeter EX1 3QS T 01392-444444 *Frequencies:* 96.4/97.0/103.0 FM

GWR FM (Bristol and Bath), PO Box 2000, One Passage Street, Bristol BS99 7SN T 0117-984 3200 *Frequencies:* 96.3/103.0 FM

GWR FM (Swindon and West Wiltshire), Chiseldon House, Stonehill Green, Westlea, Swindon, Wilts SN5 7HB T 01793-842600 *Frequencies:* 96.5/97.2/102.2 FM

HALLAM FM, Radio House, 900 Herries Road, Sheffield S6 1RH T 0114-209 1000 *Frequencies:* 97.4/102.9/103.4 FM

HEART 106, City Link, Nottingham NG2 4NG T 0115-910 6100 *Frequency:* 106 FM

HEART 106.2, The Chrysalis Building, Bramley Road, London W10 6SP T 020-7468 1062 *Frequency:* 106.2 FM

HERTBEAT FM, The Pump House, Knebworth Park, Herts SG3 6HQ T 01438-810900 *Frequencies:* 106.7/106.9 FM

HERTFORDSHIRE'S MERCURY 96.6, St Albans and Watford Broadcasting Company Ltd, 9 Nelson Street, Southend on Sea, Essex SS1 1EH; Unit 5, The Metro Centre, Dwight Road, Watford WD18 9UP T 01923-205470 *Frequency:* 96.9 FM

HIGH PEAK RADIO, The Studios, Smithbrook Close, Chapel-en-le-Frith, High Peak, Derbys SK23 0QD T 01298-813144 *Frequencies:* 103.3/106.4 FM

HOME 107.9, The Old Stable Block, Lockwood Park, Huddersfield HD1 3UR T 01484-321107 *Frequency:* 107.9 FM

HORIZON RADIO, 14 Vincent Avenue, Crowhill, Milton Keynes MK8 0AB, T 01908-269111 *Frequency:* 103.3 FM

IMAGINE FM, Regent House, Heaton Lane, Stockport, Cheshire SK4 1BX T 0161-609 1400 *Frequency:* 104.9 FM

INVICTA FM, Radio House, John Wilson Business Park, Whitstable, Kent CT5 3QX T 01227-772004 *Frequencies:* 95.9/96.1/97.0/102.8/103.1 FM

ISLE OF WIGHT RADIO, Dodnor Park, Newport, IOW PO30 5XE T 01983-822557 *Frequencies:* 102.0/107.0 FM

IVEL FM, The Studios, Middle Street, Yeovil, Somerset BA20 1DJ T 01935-848488 *Frequency:* 105.6/106.6 FM

KCR FM, The Studios, Cables Retail Park, Prescot, Merseyside LS4 5SW T 0151-290 1501 *Frequency:* 106.7 FM

KERRANG! 105.2 FM, Kerrang House, 20 Lionel Street, Birmingham B3 1AQ T 0845-053 1052 *Frequency:* 105.2 FM

KESTREL FM, 2nd Floor, Paddington House, Festival Place, Basingstoke, Hants RG21 7LJ T 01256-694000 *Frequency:* 107.6 FM

KEY 103, Castle Quay, Castlefield, Manchester M15 4PR T 0161-288 5000 *Frequency:* 103.0 FM

KICK FM, The Studios, 42 Bone Lane, Newbury, Berks RG14 5SD T 01635-841600 *Frequencies:* 105.6/107.4 FM

KISMAT, Radio House, Merrick Road, Southall, Middx UB2 4AU T 020-8843 5330 *Frequency:* 1035 AM

KISS 100 FM, Mappin House, 4 Winsley Street, London W1W 8HF T 020-7975 8100 *Frequency:* 100.0 FM

KISS 101 FM, 26 Baldwin Street, Bristol BS1 1SE T 0117-901 0101 *Frequency:* 97.2/101.0 FM

KISS FM 105–108, Reflection House, The Anderson Centre Olding Road, Bury St Edmunds IP33 3TA T 01284-715300 *Frequency:* 105.6/106.1/106.4/107.7 FM

KL.FM 96.7, 18 Blackfriars Street, King's Lynn, Norfolk PE30 1NN T 01553-772777 *Frequency:* 96.7 FM

KMFM FOR ASHFORD, Express House, 34–36 North Street, Ashford, Kent TN24 8JR T 01233-623232 *Frequency:* 107.7 FM

KMFM FOR CANTERBURY, 9 St George's Place, Canterbury, Kent CT1 1UU T 01227-475950 *Frequency:* 106.0 FM

KMFM FOR MEDWAY, Medway House, Ginsbury Close, Sir Thomas Longley Road, Medway City Estate, Strood, Rochester, Kent ME2 4DU T 01634-711079 *Frequencies:* 100.4/107.9 FM

KMFM FOR SHEPWAY AND WHITE CLIFFS COUNTRY, 93–95 Sandgate Road, Folkstone, Kent CT20 2BQ T 01303-220303 *Frequencies:* 96.4/106.8 FM

KMFM FOR THANET, 183 Northdown Road, Cliftonville, Margate, Kent CT9 2TA T 01843-220222 *Frequency:* 107.2 FM

KMFM FOR WEST KENT, 1 East Street, Tonbridge, Kent TN9 1AR T 01732-369200 *Frequencies:* 96.2/101.6 FM

LAKELAND RADIO, Unit 4, Lakelands Food Park, Plumgarths, Crook Road, Kendal, Cumbria LA8 8QJ T 01539-737390 *Frequencies:* 100.1/100.8 FM

LANTERN FM, Unit 2B, Lauder Lane, Roundswell Business Park, Barnstaple EX31 3TA T 01271-366350 *Frequencies:* 96.2/97.3 FM

LBC 97.3 FM, The Chrysalis Building, 13 Bramley Road, London W10 6SP T 020-7314 7300 *Frequency:* 97.3 FM

LBC NEWS 1152 AM, The Chrysalis Building, 13 Bramley Road, London W10 6SP T 020-7221 2213 *Frequency:* 1152 AM

LEICESTER SOUND, 6 Dominus Way, Meridian Business Park, Leicester LE19 1RP T 0116-256 1300 *Frequency:* 105.4 FM

LINCS FM, Witham Park, Waterside South, Lincoln LN5 7JN T 01522-549900 *Frequencies:* 96.7/102.2/97.6 FM

LITE FM, 2nd Floor, 5 Church Street, Peterborough PE1 1XB T 01733-898106 *Frequency:* 106.8/96.4 FM

LONDON GREEK RADIO, LGR House, 437 High Road, London N12 0AP T 020-8349 6950 *Frequency:* 103.3 FM

LONDON TURKISH RADIO, 185B High Road, Wood Green, London N22 6BA T 020-8881 0606 *Frequency:* 1584 AM

MAGIC 105.4 FM, Mappin House, 4 Winsley Street, London W1 8HF T 020-7182 8000 *Frequency:* 105.4 FM

MAGIC 828, 51 Burley Road, Leeds LS3 1LR T 0113-283 5500 *Frequency:* 828 AM

MAGIC 999, St Paul's Square, Preston, Lancs PR1 1YE T 01772-477700 *Frequency:* 999 AM

MAGIC 1152 (TYNE & WEAR), 50 Degrees North, Pilgrim Street, Newcastle upon Tyne NE1 6BF T 0191-230 6100 *Frequency:* 1152 AM

MAGIC 1161 AM, Commercial Road, Hull, E. Yorks HU1 2SG T 01482-325141 *Frequency:* 1161 AM

MAGIC 1170, Radio House, Yale Crescent, Thornaby, Stockton-on-Tees TS17 6AA T 01642-888222 *Frequency:* 1170 AM

MAGIC 1548 AM, St John's Beacon, 1 Houghton Street, Liverpool L1 1RL T 0151-472 6800 *Frequency:* 1548 AM

MAGIC AM, Radio House, 900 Herries Road, Sheffield S6 1RH T 0114-209 1000 *Frequencies:* 990/1305/1548 AM

MANCHESTER'S MAGIC 1152, Castle Quay, Castlefield, Manchester M1 4AW T 0161-288 5000 *Frequency:* 1152 AM

MANSFIELD 103.2 FM, The Media Suite, Brunts Business Centre, Samuel Brunts Way, Mansfield, Notts NG18 2AH T 01623-646666 *Frequency:* 103.2 FM

MANX RADIO, PO Box 1368, Broadcasting House, Douglas, IOM IM99 1SW T 01624-682600 *Frequencies:* 89.0/97.2/103.7 FM, 1368 AM

MERCIA FM, Hertford Place, Coventry CV1 3TT T 024-7686 8200 *Frequencies:* 97.0/102.9 FM

METRO RADIO, Longrigg, Swalwell, Newcastle upon Tyne NE99 1BB T 0191-420 0971 *Frequencies:* 97.1/102.6/103.0/103.2 FM

MINSTER FM, PO Box 123, Dunnington, York YO1 5ZX T 01904-488888 *Frequencies:* 102.3/104.7 FM

MIX 96, Friars Square Studios, 11 Bourbon Street, Aylesbury, Bucks HP20 2PZ T 01296-399396 *Frequency:* 96.2 FM

MIX 107, 11 Duke Street, High Wycombe, Bucks HP13 6EE T 01494-446611 *Frequencies:* 107.4/107.7 FM

NORTH NORFOLK RADIO, The Studio, Breck Farm, Stody, Norfolk NR24 2ER T 01263-860808 *Frequencies:* 96.2/103.2 FM

NORTHANTS 96, 19–21 St Edmunds Road, Northampton NN1 5DY T 01604-795600 *Frequency:* 96.6 FM

OAK 107, 7 Waldron Court, Prince William Road, Loughborough, Leics LE11 5GD T 01509-211711 *Frequency:* 107.0 FM

OCEAN FM, Radio House, Whittle Avenue, Segensworth West, Fareham, Hants PO15 5SH T 01489-589911 *Frequencies:* 96.7/97.5 FM

ORCHARD FM, Haygrove House, Shoreditch Road, Taunton, Somerset TA3 7BT T 01823-338448 *Frequencies:* 96.5/97.1/102.6 FM

OXFORD'S FM 1079, 270 Woodstock Road, Oxford OX2 7NW T 01865-315980 *Frequency:* 107.9 FM

PALM (105.5), Marble Court, Lymington Road, Torquay TQ1 4AU T 01803-321 055 *Frequency:* 105.5 FM

PEAK 107 FM, Radio House, Foxwood Road, Chesterfield, Derbys S41 9RF T 01246-269107 *Frequencies:* 102.0/107.4 FM

PIRATE FM, Carn Brea Studios, Wilson Way, Redruth, Cornwall TR15 3XX T 01209-314400 *Frequencies:* 102.2/102.8 FM

PREMIER CHRISTIAN RADIO, 22 Chapter Street, London SW1P 4NP T 020-7316 1300 *Frequencies:* 1305/1332/1413 AM

THE PULSE OF WEST YORKSHIRE, Forster Square, Bradford, W. Yorks BD1 5NE T 01274-203040 *Frequencies:* 97.5/102.5 FM

PULSE CLASSIC GOLD, Forster Square, Bradford, W. Yorks BD1 5NE T 01274-203040 *Frequencies:* 1278/1530 AM

Q103 FM, Enterprise House, The Vision Park, Chivers Way, Histon, Cambridge CB4 9WW T 01223-235255 *Frequencies:* 97.4/103.0 FM

QUAY 102.4 FM, Harbour Studios, The Esplanade, Watchet, Somerset TA23 0AJ T 01984-634900 *Frequencies:* 100.8/102.4 FM

RADIO BROADLAND 102.4, St George's Plain, 47–49 Colegate, Norwich NR3 1DB T 01603-630621 *Frequency:* 102.4 FM

RADIO CITY 96.7, St John's Beacon, 1 Houghton Street, Liverpool L1 1RL T 0151-472 6800 *Frequency:* 96.7 FM

RADIO WAVE 96.5 FM, 965 Mowbray Drive, Blackpool, Lancs FY3 7JR T 01253-304965 *Frequency:* 96.5 FM

RADIO XL 1296 AM, KMS House, Bradford Street, Birmingham B12 0JD T 0121-753 5353 *Frequency:* 1296 AM

RAM FM, 35/36 Irongate, Derby DE1 3GA T 01332-324000 *Frequency:* 102.8 FM

READING 107 FM, Radio House, Madejski Stadium, Reading, Berks RG2 0FN T 0118-986 2555 *Frequency:* 107.0 FM

REAL RADIO (YORKSHIRE), 1 Sterling Court, Capitol Park, Leeds WF3 1EL T 0113-238 1114 *Frequencies:* 106.2/107.6/107.7 FM

RIDINGS FM, 2 Thornes Office Park, Monckton Road, Wakefield WF2 7AN T 01924-367177 *Frequency:* 106.8 FM

ROTHER FM, Aspen Court, Bessemer Way, Rotherham S60 1FB T 01709-369993 *Frequency:* 96.1 FM

RUGBY FM, Suites 4–6, Dunsmore Business Centre, Spring Street, Rugby, Warks CV21 3HH T 01788-541100 *Frequency:* 107.1 FM

RUTLAND RADIO, 40 Melton Road, Oakham, Rutland, Leics LE15 6AY T 01572-757868 *Frequencies:* 97.4/107.2 FM

SABRAS RADIO, Radio House, 63 Melton Road, Leicester LE4 6PN T 0116-261 0666 *Frequency:* 1260 AM

THE SAINT, The Friends Provident, St. Mary's Stadium, Britannia Road, Southampton SO14 5FP T 023-8033 0300 *Frequency:* 107.8 FM

THE SEVERN, Abbey Studios, 13–14 Abbey Foregate, Shrewsbury SY2 6AE T 01743-284940 *Frequencies:* 106.5/ 107.1 FM

SEVERN SOUND, Bridge Studios, Eastgate Centre, Gloucester GL1 1SS T 01452-572400 *Frequencies:* 102.4/103.0 FM

SGR COLCHESTER, Abbeygate Two, 9 Whitewell Road, Colchester, Essex CO2 7DE T 01206-575859 *Frequency:* 96.1 FM

SGR-FM, Alpha Business Park, 6–12 White House Road, Ipswich, Suffolk IP1 5LT T 01473-461000 *Frequencies:* 96.4/97.1 FM

SIGNAL 1, Stoke Road, Stoke-on-Trent ST4 2SR T 01782-441300 *Frequencies:* 96.4/96.9/102.6 FM

SIGNAL 2, Stoke Road, Stoke-on-Trent ST4 2SR T 01782-441300 *Frequency:* 1170 AM

SMOOTH 100.4, 8 Exchange Quay, Manchester M5 3EJ T 0845-050 1004 *Frequency:* 100.4 FM

SMOOTH 105.7, 3rd Floor, Crown House, Beaufort Court 123 Hagley Road, Birmingham B16 8LD T 0121-452 1057, *Frequency:* 105.7 FM

SMOOTH 106.6, Saga Radio House, Unit 2, Alder Court, Rennie Hogg Road, Riverside Retail Park, Nottingham NG2 1RX T 0115-986 1066, *Frequencies:* 101.4/106.6 FM

SOUTH HAMS RADIO, Unit 1G, South Hams Business Park, Churchstow, Kingsbridge, Devon TQ7 3QH T 01548-854595 *Frequency:* 100.5/100.8/101.2/101.9 FM

SOUTHERN FM, PO Box 2000, Franklin Road, Brighton BN41 2SS T 01273-430111 *Frequencies:* 96.9/102.0/102.4/103.5 FM

SPECTRUM RADIO, 4 Ingate Place, Battersea, London SW8 3NS T 020-7627 4433 *Frequency:* 558 AM

SPIRE FM, City Hall Studios, Malthouse Lane, Salisbury, Wilts SP2 7QQ T 01722-416644 *Frequency:* 102.0 FM

SPIRIT FM, 9–10 Dukes Court, Bognor Road, Chichester,

W. Sussex PO19 8FX T 01243-773600 *Frequencies:* 96.6/102.3/106.6 FM

STAR 106.6, The Observatory, Slough, Berks SL1 1LH T 01753-551066 *Frequency:* 106.6 FM

STAR RADIO IN BRISTOL, Bristol Evening Post Building, Temple Way, Bristol BS99 7HD T 0117-910 6600 *Frequency:* 107.2 FM

STAR RADIO IN CAMBRIDGE, 20 Mercers Row, Cambridge CB5 8HY T 01223-722300 *Frequencies:* 107.1/107.9 FM

STAR RADIO IN CHELTENHAM, Cheltenham Film Studios, 1st Floor, West Suite, Arle Court, Cheltenham, Glos GL51 6PN T 01242-699555 *Frequency:* 107.5 FM

STAR RADIO IN SOMERSET, 11 Beaconsfield Road, Weston-super-Mare BS23 1YE T 01934-624455 *Frequency:* 107.7 FM

STAR RADIO IN STROUD, Brunel Mall, London Road, Stroud GL5 2BP T 01453-767369 *Frequencies:* 107.3/107.9 FM

SUNRISE FM, Sunrise House, 30 Chapel Street, Little Germany, Bradford BD1 5DN T 01274-735043 *Frequency:* 103.2 FM

SUNRISE RADIO, Sunrise House, Sunrise Road, Southall, Middx UB2 4AU T 020-8574 6666 *Frequency:* 1458 AM

SUNSHINE 855, Unit 11, Burway Trading Estate, Ludlow, Shropshire SY8 1EN T 01584-873795 *Frequency:* 855 AM

TELFORD FM, c/o The Shropshire Star, Waterloo Road, Ketley TF1 5HU T 01952-280011 *Frequency:* 107.4 FM

TEN 17, Latton Bush Centre, Southern Way, Harlow, Essex CM18 7BB T 01279-431017 *Frequency:* 101.7 FM

TFM, Radio House, Yale Crescent, Thornaby, Stockton-on-Tees TS17 6AA T 01642-888222 *Frequency:* 96.6 FM

TIME 106.6, The Observatory, Slough, Berks SL1 1LH T 01753-551066 *Frequency:* 106.6 FM

TIME 106.8, 2–6 Basildon Road, Abbey Wood, London SE2 0EW T 020-8311 3112 *Frequency:* 106.8 FM

TIME 107.3, 2–6 Basildon Road, Abbey Wood, London SE2 0EW T 020-8311 3112 *Frequency:* 107.3 FM

TIME 107.5, 7th Floor, Lambourne House, 7 Western Road, Romford, Essex RM1 3LD T 01708-731 643 *Frequency:* 107.5 FM

TOUCH FM, 5/6 Aldergate, Hamworth, Staffordshire B79 7DJ T 01827-318000 *Frequencies:* 101.6/ 102.4 FM

TOWER FM, The Mill, Brownlow Way, Bolton BL1 2RA T 01204-387000 *Frequency:* 107.4 FM

TOWN FM, First Floor, Radio House Prion Court, Great Blakenham, Ipswich, Suffolk IP6 0LW T 0845-3651102 *Frequency:* 102.0 FM

TRAX FM (BASSETLAW), White Hart Yard, Bridge Street, Worksop, Notts S80 1HR T 01909-500611 *Frequency:* 107.9 FM

TRAX FM (DONCASTER), 5 Sidings Court, White Rose Way, Doncaster DN4 5NU T 01302-341166 *Frequency:* 107.1 FM

VALE FM, Longmead Studios, Shaftesbury, Dorset SP7 8QQ T 01747-855711 *Frequencies:* 96.6/97.4 FM

VIRGIN RADIO 105.8 FM, 1 Golden Square, London W1F 9DJ T 020-7434 1215 *Frequency:* 105.8 FM

WAVE 105 FM, 5 Manor Court, Barnes Wallis Road, Segensworth East, Fareham, Hampshire PO15 5TH T 01489-481050 *Frequencies:* 105.2/105.8 FM

WESSEX FM, Radio House, Trinity Street, Dorchester, Dorset DT1 1DJ T 01305-250333 *Frequencies:* 96.0/97.2 FM

WIRE FM, Warrington Business Park, Long Lane, Warrington WA2 8TX T 01925-445545 *Frequency:* 107.2 FM

WYVERN FM, 5–6 Barbourne Terrace, Worcester WR1 3JZ T 01905-545500 *Frequencies:* 96.7/97.6/102.8 FM

XFM MANCHESTER, Laser House, Waterfront Quay, Salford Quays, Manchester M50 3XW T 0161-662 4701 *Frequency:* 97.7 FM

XFM UK, 30 Leicester Square, London WC2H 7LA T 020-7054 8000 *Frequency:* 104.9 FM

YORKSHIRE COAST RADIO (BRIDLINGTON), The Old Harbour Master's Office, Harbour Road, Bridlington, E. Yorks YO15 2NR T 01262-404400 *Frequency:* 102.4 FM

YORKSHIRE COAST RADIO (SCARBOROUGH), Unit 2B, Newchase Business Centre, Hopper Hill Road, Scarborough, N. Yorks YO11 3YS T 01723-581700 *Frequencies:* 96.2/103.1 FM

WALES

96.4 FM THE WAVE, PO Box 964, Victoria Road, Gowerton, Swansea SA4 3AB T 01792-511964 *Frequency:* 96.4 FM

97.1 RADIO CARMARTHENSHIRE, Unit 14, The Old School Estate, Station Road, Narberth, Pembrokeshire SA67 7DU T 0845-355 0570 *Frequencies:* 97.1/97.5 FM

97.5 SCARLET FM, Unit 14, The Old School Estate, Station Road, Narberth, Pembrokeshire SA67 7DU T 0845-355 0570 *Frequency:* 97.5 FM

106.3 BRIDGE FM, PO Box 1063, Bridgend CF35 6WF T 0845-890 4000 *Frequency:* 106.3 FM

102.5 RADIO PEMBROKESHIRE, Unit 14, The Old School Estate, Station Road, Narberth, Pembrokeshire SA67 7DU T 01834-869384 *Frequencies:* 102.5/107.5 FM

CAPITAL GOLD (1359/1305), Red Dragon Centre, Atlantic Wharf, Cardiff CF10 4DJ T 029-2066 2066 *Frequencies:* 1305/1359 AM

CHAMPION FM 103, Llys-Y-Dderwen, Parc Menai, Bangor, Gwynedd LL55 4BN T 01248-673400 *Frequency:* 103.0 FM

CLASSIC GOLD MARCHER (1260), The Studios, Mold Road Gwersyllt, Wrexham LL11 4AF T 01978-752202 *Frequency:* 1260 AM

COAST 96.3, PO Box 963, Bangor LL57 4ZR T 01248-673272 *Frequency:* 96.3 FM

MFM 103.4, The Studios, Mold Road, Gwersyllt, Wrexham LL11 4AF T 01978-752200 *Frequency:* 103.4 FM

RADIO CEREDIGION, Yr Hen Ysgol Gymraeg, Aberystwyth, Ceredigion SY23 1LF T 01970-627999 *Frequencies:* 96.6/97.4/103.3/FM

RADIO MALDWYN, The Studios, The Park, Newtown, Powys SY16 2NZ T 01686-623555 *Frequency:* 756 AM

REAL RADIO, Unit 1, Ty-Nant Court, Ty-Nant Road, Morganstown, Cardiff CF15 8LW T 029-2031 5100 *Frequencies:* 105.2/105.4/105.7/105.9/106/106.2 FM

RED DRAGON FM, Atlantic Wharf, Cardiff CF10 4DJ T 029-2066 2066 *Frequencies:* 97.4/103.2 FM

SWANSEA SOUND, Victoria Road, Gowerton, Swansea SA4 3AB T 01792-511170 *Frequency:* 1170 AM

VALLEYS RADIO, PO Box 1116, Ebbw Vale, Gwent NP23 8XW T 01495-301116 *Frequencies:* 999/1116 AM

SCOTLAND

ARGYLL FM, 27–29 Longrow, Campbelltown, Argyll PA28 8ER T 01586-551800 *Frequencies:* 106.5/107.1/107.7 FM

CENTRAL 103.1 FM, 201–203 High Street, Falkirk FK1 1DU T 01324-611164 *Frequency:* 103.1 FM

CLYDE 1, Clydebank Business Park, Clydebank, Glasgow G81 2RX T 0141-565 2200 *Frequencies:* 97/102.5/103.3 FM

CLYDE 2, Clydebank Business Park, Clydebank, Glasgow G81 2RX T 0141-565 2200 *Frequency:* 1152 AM

CUILLIN FM, Stormyhill Road, Portree, Isle of Skye IV51 9DY T 01478-611234 *Frequency:* 106.2 FM

FORTH ONE, Forth House, Forth Street, Edinburgh EH1 3LE T 0131-556 9255 *Frequencies:* 97.3/97.6/102.2 FM

FORTH 2, Forth House, Forth Street, Edinburgh EH1 3LE T 0131-556 9255 *Frequency:* 1548 AM

HEARTLAND FM, Atholl Curling Rink, Lower Oakfield, Pitlochry, Perthshire PH16 5HQ T 01796-474040 *Frequency:* 97.5 FM

ISLES FM, PO Box 333, Stornoway, Isle of Lewis HS1 2PU T 01851-703333 *Frequency:* 103.0 FM

KINGDOM FM, Haig House, Haig Business Park, Balgonie Road, Markinch, Fife KY7 6AQ T 01592-753753 *Frequencies:* 95.2/96.1/96.6/105.4/106.3 FM

LANARKSHIRE'S L107, Media Corp House, 2 Caird Park, Hamilton, Lanarkshire ML3 0EU T 01698-303420 *Frequencies:* 107.5/107.9 FM

LOCHBROOM FM, Radio House, Mill Street, Ullapool, Ross-shire IV26 2UN T 01854-613131 *Frequencies:* 96.8/102.2 FM

MORAY FIRTH RADIO (MFR), Scorguie Place, Inverness IV3 8UJ T 01463-224433 *Frequencies:* 97.4 FM, 1107 AM

NECR, The Shed, School Road, Kintore, Iveruie, Aberdeenshire AB51 0US T 01467-632909 *Frequencies:* 97.1/101.9/102.1/102.6/103.2/106.4 FM

NEVIS RADIO, Ben Nevis Estate, Claggan, Fort William PH33 6PR T 01397-700007 *Frequencies:* 96.6/97.0/102.3/102.4 FM

NORTHSOUND 1, Abbotswell Road, West Tullos, Aberdeen AB12 3AJ T 01224-337000 *Frequencies:* 96.9/97.6/103.0 FM

NORTHSOUND 2, Abbotswell Road, West Tullos, Aberdeen AB12 3AJ T 01224-337000 *Frequency:* 1035 AM

OBAN FM, 132 George Street, Oban, Argyll PA34 5NT T 01631-570057 *Frequency:* 103.3 FM

RADIO BORDERS, Tweedside Park, Galashiels TD1 3TD T 01896-759444 *Frequencies:* 96.8/97.5/103.1/103.4 FM

REAL RADIO (SCOTLAND), Parkway Court, Glasgow Business Park, Glasgow G69 6GA T 0141-781 1011 *Frequencies:* 100.3/101.1 FM

RIVER FM, Stadium House, Alderstone Road, Livingston EH54 7DN T 01506-410411 *Frequency:* 103.4/107.7 FM

RNA FM, Radio North Angus Ltd, Rosemount Road, Arbroath, Angus DD11 2AT T 01241-879660 *Frequencies:* 100.3 /101.1 FM

ROCK RADIO, 65 Sussex Street, Kinning Park, Glasgow, G41 1XD T 0141 429 9430 *Frequency:* 96.3 FM

SIBC, Market Street, Lerwick, Shetland ZE1 0JN T 01595-695299 *Frequencies:* 96.2/102.2 FM

SMOOTH 105.2, City Park Alexandra Parade, Glasgow G31 3AU T 0141-551 1052, *Frequency:* 105.2 FM

SOUTH WEST SOUND FM, Unit 40, The Loreburne Centre, High St, Dumfries DG1 4DA T 01387-250999 *Frequencies:* 96.5/97.0/103.0 FM

TALK 107, 9 South Gyle Crescent, Edinburgh EH12 9EB T 0131-316 3107 *Frequency:* 107.0 FM

TAY AM, 6 North Isla Street, Dundee DD3 7JQ T 01382-200800 *Frequencies:* 1161/1584 AM

TAY FM, 6 North Isla Street, Dundee DD3 7JQ T 01382-200800 *Frequencies:* 96.4/102.8 FM

TWO LOCHS RADIO, Gairloch, Ross-shire IV21 2BQ T 0870-741 4657 *Frequencies:* 106.0/106.6 FM

UCA, University Campus Ayr, Beech Grove, Ayr, S. Ayrshire KA8 0SR T 01292-886385 *Frequency:* 87.7 FM

WAVE 102, 8 South Tay Street, Dundee DD1 1PA T 01382-901000 *Frequency:* 102.0 FM

WAVES RADIO, 7 Blackhouse Circle, Blackhouse Industrial Estate, Peterhead, Aberdeenshire AB42 1BW T 01779-491012 *Frequency:* 101.2 FM

WEST FM, Radio House, 54A Holmston Road, Ayr KA7 3BE T 01292-283662 *Frequencies:* 96.7/97.5 FM

WEST SOUND AM, Radio House, 54A Holmston Road, Ayr KA7 3BE T 01292-283662 *Frequency:* 1035 AM

XFM SCOTLAND, Four Winds Pavilion, Pacific Quay, Glasgow G51 1EB T 0141-566 6109 *Frequencies:* 105.7/106.1 FM

YOURRADIO, Pioneer Park Studios, Unit 3, 80 Castlegreen Street, Dumbarton G82 1JB T 01389-734422 *Frequencies:* 103.0 (Dumbarton), 106.9 (Helensburgh) FM

NORTHERN IRELAND

CITY BEAT 96.7 FM, 46 Stranmillis Embankment, Belfast BT9 5FN T 028-9020 5967 *Frequency:* 96.7 FM

COOL FM, PO Box 974, Belfast BT1 1RT T 028-9181 7181 *Frequency:* 97.4 FM

DOWNTOWN RADIO, Newtownards, Co. Down BT23 4ES T 028-9181 5555 *Frequencies:* 96.4 FM (Limavady); 96.6 FM (Enniskillen); 97.1 FM (Larne); 102.3 FM (Ballymena); 102.4 FM (Londonderry)

Q97.2 FM, 24 Cloyfin Road, Coleraine, Co. Londonderry BT52 2NU T 028-7035 9100 *Frequency:* 97.2 FM

Q101.2 WEST FM, 42A Market Street, Omagh, Co. Tyrone BT78 1EH T 028-8224 5777 *Frequency:* 101.2 FM

Q102.9 FM, The Riverview Suite, 87 Rossdowney Road, Waterside, Londonderry BT47 5SU T 028-7134 4449/346666 *Frequency:* 102.9 FM

SEVEN FM, 1 Millenium Park, Woodside Industrial Estate, Woodside Road, Ballymena, Co. Antrim BT42 4QT T 028-2564 8777 *Frequency:* 107.0 FM

SIX FM, 2C Park Avenue, Cookstown, Co. Tyrone BT80 5AH T 028-8675 8696 *Frequencies:* 106.0/107.2 FM

U105, Ulster Television plc, Unit 105, Havelock House Ormeau Road, Belfast BT7 1EB T 028-9032 8122 / 028 9033 3105 *Frequency:* 105.8 FM

CHANNEL ISLANDS

CHANNEL 103 FM, 6 Tunnell Street, St Helier, Jersey JE2 4LU T 01534-888103 *Frequency:* 103.7 FM

ISLAND FM, 12 Westerbrook, St Sampsons, Guernsey GY2 4QQ T 01481-242000 *Frequencies:* 93.7/104.7 FM

THE PRESS

The newspaper and periodical press in the UK is large and diverse, catering for a wide variety of views and interests. There is no state control or censorship of the press; however, it is subject to the laws on publication, and the Press Complaints Commission (PCC) was set up by the industry as a means of self-regulation.

The press is not state-subsidised and receives few tax concessions. The income of most newspapers and periodicals is derived largely from sales and from advertising; the press is the largest advertising medium in Britain.

SELF-REGULATION

The PCC was founded by the newspaper and magazine industry in January 1991 to replace the Press Council (established in 1953). It is a voluntary, non-statutory body set up to operate the press' self-regulation system following the Calcutt report in 1990 on privacy and related matters, when the industry feared that failure to regulate itself might lead to statutory regulation of the press. The performance of the PCC was reviewed after 18 months of operation (the *Calcutt Review of Press Self-Regulation,* presented to parliament in January 1993) to determine whether statutory measures were required. No proposals for replacing the self-regulation system have been made to date. The commission is funded by the industry through the Press Standards Board of Finance.

COMPLAINTS

The PCC's aims are to consider, adjudicate, conciliate, and resolve complaints of unfair treatment by the press; and to ensure that the press maintains the highest professional standards and shows respect for generally recognised freedoms, including freedom of expression, the public's right to know, and the right of the press to operate free from improper pressure. The commission judges newspaper and magazine conduct by a code of practice drafted by editors, agreed by the industry and ratified by the commission.

Six of the commission's members are editors of national, regional and local newspapers and magazines, and ten, including the chair, are drawn from other fields. At the time of writing there was one vacancy for a 'press member' (working as an editor in newspaper or magazine publishing) on the commission. The PCC received 1,647 complaints in the six months to March 2007.

PRESS COMPLAINTS COMMISSION
Halton House, 20–23 Holborn, London EC1N 2JD
T 020-7831 0022 **F** 020-7831 0025
E complaints@pcc.org.uk
W www.pcc.org.uk
Chair, Sir Christopher Meyer, KCMG

NEWSPAPERS

Newspapers are mostly financially independent of any political party, though most adopt a political stance in their editorial comments, usually reflecting proprietorial influence. Ownership of the national and regional daily newspapers is concentrated in the hands of large corporations whose interests cover publishing and communications. The rules on cross-media ownership, as amended by the Broadcasting Act 1996, which limited the extent to which newspaper organisations may become involved in broadcasting, have been relaxed by the Communications Act 2003: newspapers with over 20 per cent share of national circulation may own national and/or local radio licences.

There are around 15 daily and 15 Sunday national papers and several hundred local papers that are published daily, weekly or twice-weekly. Scotland, Wales and Northern Ireland all have at least one daily and one Sunday national paper.

Newspapers are usually published in either broadsheet or smaller, tabloid format. The 'quality' daily papers, ie those providing detailed coverage of a wide range of public matters, have traditionally used a broadsheet format, while the tabloid papers typically take a more populist approach and are more illustrated. In 2004 this correlation between format and content was abandoned when three traditionally broadsheet newspapers, *The Times, The Independent* and *The Scotsman,* switched to tabloid-sized editions, while *The Guardian* launched a new 'Berliner' format in September 2005. In October 2005 *The Independent on Sunday* became the first Sunday broadsheet to be published in the tabloid (or 'compact') size, and *The Observer,* like its daily counterpart *The Guardian,* began publishing in the Berliner format in January 2006.

UK CIRCULATION *net average for June 2006/7*

National Daily Newspapers	*2006*	*2007*
The Sun	2,949,697	2,852,952
Daily Mail	2,157,567	2,123,008
Daily Mirror	1,499,404	1,433,954
The Daily Telegraph	847,959	841,555
Daily Express	782,749	720,386
Daily Star	667,012	666,343
The Times	612,998	597,899
Daily Record	416,152	389,152
The Guardian	330,496	314,519
The Independent	200,957	188,986
Financial Times	134,337	136,697
The Herald	71,510	69,218
The Scotsman	60,696	56,979

National Sunday Newspapers	*2006*	*2007*
News of the World	3,211,961	3,021,301
The Mail on Sunday	2,165,890	2,033,504
Sunday Mirror	1,311,578	1,312,198
The Sunday Times	1,132,118	1,008,168
Sunday Express	759,941	668,997
The People	740,366	669,056
The Sunday Telegraph	611,032	620,255
Sunday Mail	504,028	486,534
Sunday Post	—	411,317
The Observer	414,657	401,959
Daily Star Sunday	319,477	320,383
The Independent on Sunday	176,335	204,138
Sunday Sport	114,526	97,281
Scotland on Sunday	71,736	72,815
Sunday Herald	52,455	53,964

Source: Audit Bureau of Circulations Ltd. For further information see **W** www.abc.org.uk

NATIONAL DAILY NEWSPAPERS

DAILY EXPRESS
Northern & Shell Building, 10 Lower Thames Street, London EC3R 6EN **T** 0871-434 1010 **W** www.express.co.uk
Editor, Peter Hill

DAILY MAIL
Northcliffe House, 2 Derry Street, London W8 5TT
T 020-7938 6000 **W** www.dailymail.co.uk
Editor, Paul Dacre

DAILY MIRROR
1 Canada Square, Canary Wharf, London E14 5AP
T 020-7293 3000 **W** www.mirror.co.uk
Editor, Richard Wallace

DAILY RECORD
1 Central Quay, Glasgow G3 8DA **T** 0141-309 3000
W www.dailyrecord.co.uk
Editor, Bruce Waddell

DAILY SPORT
19 Great Ancoats Street, Manchester M60 4BT
T 0161-236 4466 **W** www.dailysport.co.uk
Editor, David Beevers

DAILY STAR
Northern & Shell Building, 10 Lower Thames Street, London EC3R 6EN **T** 0871-434 1010 **W** www.dailystar.co.uk
Editor, Dawn Neesom

THE DAILY TELEGRAPH
1 Canada Square, Canary Wharf, London E14 5DT
T 020-7931 2000 **W** www.telegraph.co.uk
Editor, John Bryant

FINANCIAL TIMES
1 Southwark Bridge, London SE1 9HL **T** 020-7873 3000
W www.ft.com
Editor, Lionel Barber

THE GUARDIAN
119 Farringdon Road, London EC1R 3ER **T** 020-7278 2332
W www.guardian.co.uk
Editor, Alan Rusbridger

THE HERALD
200 Renfield Street, Glasgow G2 3QB **T** 0141-302 7000
W www.theherald.co.uk
Editor, Charles McGhee

THE INDEPENDENT
Independent House, 191 Marsh Wall, London E14 9RS
T 020-7005 2000 **W** www.independent.co.uk
Editor-in-Chief, Simon Kelner

MORNING STAR
William Rust House, 52 Beachy Road, London E3 2NS
T 020-8510 0815 **W** www.morningstaronline.co.uk
Editor, John Haylett

THE SCOTSMAN
Barclay House, 108 Holyrood Road, Edinburgh EH8 8AS
T 0131-620 8620 **W** www.scotsman.com
Editor, Mike Gilson

THE SUN
1 Virginia Street, London E1 9XP **T** 020-7782 4000
W www.the-sun.co.uk
Editor, Rebekah Wade

THE TIMES
1 Pennington Street, London E98 1TT **T** 020-7782 5000
W www.timesonline.co.uk
Editor, Robert Thomson

WEEKLY NEWSPAPERS

DAILY STAR SUNDAY
Northern & Shell Building, 10 Lower Thames Street, London EC3R 6EN **T** 0871-434 1010
W www.dailystarsunday.co.uk
Editor, Gareth Morgan

THE INDEPENDENT ON SUNDAY
Independent House, 191 Marsh Wall, London E14 9RS
T 020-7005 2000 **W** www.independent.co.uk
Editor, Tristan Davies

THE MAIL ON SUNDAY
Northcliffe House, 2 Derry Street, London W8 5TS
T 020-7938 6000 **W** www.mailonsunday.co.uk
Editor, Peter Wright

NEWS OF THE WORLD
1 Virginia Street, London E98 1NW **T** 020-7782 4000
W www.newsoftheworld.co.uk
Editor, Colin Myler

THE OBSERVER
3–7 Herbal Hill, London EC1R 5EJ **T** 020-7278 2332
W www.observer.co.uk
Editor, Roger Alton

THE PEOPLE
1 Canada Square, Canary Wharf, London E14 5AP
T 020-7293 3000 **W** www.people.co.uk
Editor, Mark Thomas

SCOTLAND ON SUNDAY
108 Holyrood Road, Edinburgh EH8 8AS **T** 0131-620 8620
W www.scotlandonsunday.co.uk
Editor, Les Snowdon

SUNDAY EXPRESS
Northern & Shell Building, 10 Lower Thames Street, London EC3R 6EN **T** 0871-434 1010 **W** www.express.co.uk
Editor, Martin Townsend

SUNDAY HERALD
200 Renfield Street, Glasgow G2 3QB **T** 0141-302 7800
W www.sundayherald.com
Editor, Richard Walker

SUNDAY MAIL
1 Central Quay, Glasgow G3 8DA **T** 0141-309 3000
W www.sundaymail.com
Editor, Allan Rennie

SUNDAY MIRROR
1 Canada Square, Canary Wharf, London E14 5AP
T 020-7293 3000 **W** www.sundaymirror.co.uk
Editor, Tina Weaver

THE SUNDAY POST
144 Port Dundas Road, Glasgow G4 0HZ **T** 0141-332 9933
W www.sundaypost.com
Editor, David Pollington

THE SUNDAY TELEGRAPH
111 Buckingham Palace Road, London SW1W 0DT
T 020-7931 2000 **W** www.telegraph.co.uk
Editor, Patience Wheatcroft

THE SUNDAY TIMES
1 Pennington Street, London E98 1ST **T** 020-7782 5000
W www.timesonline.co.uk
Editor, John Witherow

THE SUNDAY TIMES SCOTLAND
124 Portman Street, Kinning Park, Glasgow G41 1EJ
T 0141-420 5100 **W** www.timesonline.co.uk
Editor, Carlos Alba

WALES ON SUNDAY
Thomson House, Havelock Street, Cardiff CF10 1XR
T 029-2058 3583 **W** www.icwales.co.uk
Editor, Tim Gordon

EGIONAL DAILY NEWSPAPERS

AST ANGLIA

AMBRIDGE EVENING NEWS
Winship Road, Milton, Cambs CB24 6PP **T** 01223-434437
W www.cambridge-news.co.uk
Editor, Murray Morse

AST ANGLIAN DAILY TIMES
30 Lower Brook Street, Ipswich, Suffolk IP4 1AN
T 01473-230023 **W** www.eadt.co.uk
Editor, Terry Hunt

ASTERN DAILY PRESS
Prospect House, Rouen Road, Norwich NR1 1RE
T 01603-628311 **W** www.edp24.co.uk
Editor, Peter Franzen, OBE

VENING STAR
Press House, 30 Lower Brook Street, Ipswich, Suffolk IP4 1AN
T 01473-230023 **W** www.eveningstar.co.uk
Editor, Jess Gallagher

HE EVENING TELEGRAPH
Telegraph House, 57 Priestgate, Peterborough PE1 1JW
T 01733-555111 **W** www.peterboroughtoday.co.uk
Editor, Rebecca Stephens

ORWICH EVENING NEWS
Prospect House, Rouen Road, Norwich NR1 1RE
T 01603-628311 **W** www.eveningnews24.co.uk
Editor (acting), Tim Williams

AST MIDLANDS

URTON MAIL
65–68 High Street, Burton on Trent DE14 1LE
T 01283-512345 **W** www.burtonmail.co.uk
Editor, Paul Hazeldine

VENING TELEGRAPH
Northcliffe House, Meadow Road, Derby DE1 2DW
T 01332-291111 **W** www.thisisderbyshire.co.uk
Editor, Steve Hall

EICESTER MERCURY
St George Street, Leicester LE1 9FQ **T** 0116-251 2512
W www.thisisleicestershire.co.uk
Editor, Nick Carter

INCOLNSHIRE ECHO
Brayford Wharf East, Lincoln LN5 7AT **T** 01522-820000
W www.thisislincolnshire.co.uk
Editor, Jon Grubb

ORTHAMPTON CHRONICLE & ECHO
Upper Mounts, Northampton NN1 3HR **T** 01604-467000
W www.northamptonchron.co.uk
Editor, Mark Edwards

OTTINGHAM EVENING POST
Castle Wharf House, Nottingham NG1 7EU
T 0115-948 2000 **W** www.thisisnottingham.co.uk
Editor, Malcolm Pheby

ONDON

VENING STANDARD
Northcliffe House, 2 Derry Street, London W8 5EE
T 020-7938 6000 **W** www.thisislondon.com
Editor, Veronica Wadley

ETRO
Northcliffe House, 2 Derry Street, London W8 5TT
T 020-7651 5200 **W** www.metro.co.uk
Editor, Kenny Campbell

ORTH EAST

VENING CHRONICLE
Groat Market, Newcastle upon Tyne NE1 1ED
T 0191-232 7500 **W** www.chroniclelive.co.uk
Editor, Paul Robertson

EVENING GAZETTE
Borough Road, 105–111 Middlesbrough TS1 3AZ
T 01642-245401 **W** www.gazettelive.co.uk
Editor, Darren Thwaites

HARTLEPOOL MAIL
New Clarence House, Wesley Square, Hartlepool TS24 8BX
T 01429-239333 **W** www.hartlepoolmail.co.uk
Editor, Joy Yates

THE JOURNAL
Groat Market, Newcastle upon Tyne NE1 1ED
T 0191-232 7500 **W** www.icnewcastle.co.uk
Editor, Brian Aitken

THE NORTHERN ECHO
Priestgate, Darlington, Co. Durham DL1 1NF
T 01325-381313 **W** www.thenorthernecho.co.uk
Editor, Peter Barron

THE SHIELDS GAZETTE
Chapter Row, South Shields, Tyne & Wear NE33 1BL
T 0191-455 4661 **W** www.shieldsgazette.com
Editor, John Szymanski

SUNDERLAND ECHO
Echo House, Pennywell, Sunderland, Tyne & Wear SR4 9ER
T 0191-501 5800 **W** www.sunderlandecho.com
Editor, Rob Lawson

NORTH WEST

THE BOLTON NEWS
Newspaper House, Churchgate, Bolton, Lancs BL1 1DE
T 01204-522345 **W** www.theboltonnews.co.uk
Editor-in-Chief, Steve Hughes

THE GAZETTE
Avroe House, Avroe Crescent, Blackpool Business Park, Squires Gate, Blackpool FY4 2DP **T** 01253-400888
W www.blackpoolgazette.co.uk
Editor, David Helliwell

LANCASHIRE EVENING POST
Unit 4, Fulwood Business Park, Caxton Road, Fulwood, Preston, Lancs PR2 9NZ **T** 01772-254841 **W** www.lep.co.uk
Editor, Simon Reynolds

LANCASHIRE TELEGRAPH
Newspaper House, High Street, Blackburn, Lancs BB1 1HT
T 01254-678678 **W** www.thisislancashire.co.uk
Editor, Kevin Young

LIVERPOOL DAILY POST
PO Box 48, Old Hall Street, Liverpool L69 3EB
T 0151-227 2000 **W** www.liverpooldailypost.co.uk
Editor, Mark Thomas

LIVERPOOL ECHO
PO Box 48, Old Hall Street, Liverpool L69 3EB
T 0151-227 2000 **W** www.icliverpool.co.uk
Editor, Alastair Machray

MANCHESTER EVENING NEWS
164 Deansgate, Manchester M60 2RD **T** 0161-832 7200
W www.manchesteronline.co.uk
Editor, Paul Horrocks

NEWS & STAR
Newspaper House, Dalston Road, Carlisle CA2 5UA
T 01228-612600 **W** www.news-and-star.co.uk
Editor, Neil Hodgkinson

NORTH-WEST EVENING MAIL
Newspaper House, Abbey Road, Barrow-in-Furness, Cumbria LA14 5QS **T** 01229-840150 **W** www.nwemail.co.uk
Editor, Steve Brauner

OLDHAM EVENING CHRONICLE
PO Box 47, Union Street, Oldham, Lancs OL1 1EQ
T 0161-633 2121 **W** www.oldham-chronicle.co.uk
Editor, Jim Williams

SOUTH

THE ARGUS
Argus House, Crowhurst Road, Hollingbury, Brighton BN1 8AR **T** 01273-544544 **W** www.theargus.co.uk
Editor, Michael Beard

ECHO
Newspaper House, Chester Hall Lane, Basildon, Essex SS14 3BL **T** 01268-522792 **W** www.echo-news.co.uk
Editor, Martin McNeill

MEDWAY MESSENGER
Medway House, Ginsbury Close, Sir Thomas Longley Road, Medway City Estate, Strood, Kent ME2 2DU
T 01634-227800 **W** www.kentonline.co.uk

THE NEWS
The News Centre, Hilsea, Portsmouth PO2 9SX
T 023-9266 4488 **W** www.portsmouth.co.uk
Editor (acting), Mark Acheson

OXFORD MAIL
Newspaper House, Osney Mead, Oxford OX2 0EJ
T 01865-425262 **W** www.oxfordmail.net
Editor, Simon O'Neill

READING EVENING POST
8 Tessa Road, Reading, Berks RG1 8NS **T** 0118-918 3000
W www.getreading.co.uk
Editor, Andy Murrill

SOUTHERN DAILY ECHO
Newspaper House, Test Lane, Redbridge, Southampton SO16 9JX **T** 023-8042 4777 **W** www.dailyecho.co.uk
Editor, Ian Murray

SWINDON ADVERTISER
100 Victoria Road, Old Town, Swindon SN1 3BE
T 01793-528144 **W** www.swindonadvertiser.co.uk
Editor, Mark Waldron

SOUTH WEST

THE CITIZEN
1 Clarence Parade, Cheltenham GL50 3NY **T** 01242-271900
W www.nng.co.uk
Editor, Ian Mean

DAILY ECHO
Richmond Hill, Bournemouth BH2 6HH **T** 01202-554601
W www.bournemouthecho.co.uk
Editor, Neal Butterworth

DORSET ECHO
Fleet House, Hampshire Road, Weymouth, Dorset DT4 9XD
T 01305-830930 **W** www.dorsetecho.co.uk
Editor, David Murdock

EVENING POST
Temple Way, Bristol BS99 7HD **T** 0117-934 3000
W www.thisisbristol.co.uk
Editor-in-chief, Mike Norton

EXPRESS & ECHO
Heron Road, Sowton, Exeter EX2 7NF **T** 01392-442211
W www.thisisexeter.co.uk
Editor, Marc Astley

GLOUCESTERSHIRE ECHO
1 Clarence Parade, Cheltenham, Glos GL50 3NY
T 01242-271900 **W** www.thisisgloucestershire.co.uk
Editor, Anita Syvret

THE HERALD
17 Brest Road, Derriford Business Park, Plymouth PL6 5AA
T 01752-765500 **W** www.thisisplymouth.co.uk
Editor, Bill Martin

HERALD EXPRESS
Harmsworth House, Barton Hill Road, Torquay, Devon TQ2 8JN **T** 01803-676000 **W** www.thisissouthdevon.co.uk
Editor, Andy Phelan

WESTERN DAILY PRESS
Temple Way, Bristol BS99 7HD **T** 0117-934 3000
W www.westpress.co.uk
Editor, Andy Wright

WESTERN MORNING NEWS
17 Brest Road, Derriford, Plymouth PL6 5AA
T 01752-765500 **W** www.westernmorningnews.co.uk
Editor, Alan Qualtrough

WEST MIDLANDS

BIRMINGHAM MAIL
PO Box 78, Weaman Street, Birmingham B4 6AY
T 0121-236 3366 **W** www.icbirmingham.co.uk
Editor, Steve Dyson

THE BIRMINGHAM POST
PO Box 78, Weaman Street, Birmingham B4 6AT
T 0121-236 3366 **W** www.icbirmingham.co.uk
Editor, Mark Reeves

COVENTRY EVENING TELEGRAPH
Corporation Street, Coventry CV1 1FP **T** 024-7663 3633
W www.iccoventry.co.uk
Editor, Alan Kirby

EXPRESS & STAR
Queen Street, Wolverhampton WV1 1ES **T** 01902-313131
W www.expressandstar.com
Editor, Adrian Faber

THE SENTINEL
Sentinel House, Etruria, Stoke-on-Trent ST1 5SS
T 01782-602525 **W** www.thisisthesentinel.co.uk
Editor, Michael Sassi

SHROPSHIRE STAR
Ketley, Telford TF1 5HU **T** 01952-242424
W www.shropshirestar.com
Editor, Sarah Jane Smith

WORCESTER NEWS
Berrows House, Hylton Road, Worcester WR2 5JX
T 01905-742244 **W** www.thisisworcester.co.uk
Editor, Stewart Gilbert

YORKSHIRE AND HUMBERSIDE

EVENING COURIER
PO Box 19, King Cross Street, Halifax HX1 2SF
T 01422-260200 **W** www.halifaxcourier.co.uk
Editor, John Furbisher

GRIMSBY TELEGRAPH
80 Cleethorpe Road, Grimsby, North East Lincolnshire DN31 3EH **T** 01472-360360 **W** www.thisisgrimsby.co.uk
Editor, Michelle Lalor

THE HUDDERSFIELD DAILY EXAMINER
PO Box A26, Queen Street South, Huddersfield HD1 2TD
T 01484-430000 **W** www.examiner.co.uk
Editor, Roy Wright

HULL DAILY MAIL
Blundell's Corner, Beverley Road, Hull HU3 1XS
T 01482-327111 **W** www.thisishullandeastriding.co.uk
Editor, John Meehan

THE PRESS
PO Box 29, 76–86 Walmgate, York YO1 9YN
T 01904-653051 **W** www.yorkpress.co.uk
Editor, Kevin Booth

SCARBOROUGH EVENING NEWS
17–23 Aberdeen Walk, Scarborough, North Yorkshire YO11 1BB **T** 01723-363636
W www.scarboroughneveningnews.co.uk
Editor, Ed Asquith

ꟷIE STAR
York Street, Sheffield S1 1PU T 0114-276 7676
W www.thestar.co.uk
Editor, Alan Powell

ELEGRAPH & ARGUS
Hall Ings, Bradford BD1 1JR T 01274-729511
W www.thisisbradford.co.uk
Editor, Perry Austin-Clarke

ORKSHIRE EVENING POST
PO Box 168, Wellington Street, Leeds LS1 1RF
T 0113-243 2701 W www.ypn.co.uk
Editor, Paul Napier

ORKSHIRE POST
Wellington Street, Leeds LS1 1RF T 0113-243 2701
W www.yorkshirepost.co.uk
Editor, Peter Charlton

COTLAND

IE COURIER
80 Kingsway East, Dundee DD4 8SL T 01382-223131
W www.thecourier.co.uk
Editor, Bill Hutchin

VENING TELEGRAPH AND POST
80 Kingsway East, Dundee DD4 8SL T 01382-223131
W www.eveningtelegraph.co.uk

VENING EXPRESS
PO Box 43, Lang Stracht, Mastrick, Aberdeen AB15 6DF
T 01224-690222 W www.thisisaberdeen.co.uk
Editor, Damian Bates

VENING NEWS
108 Holyrood Road, Edinburgh EH8 8AS T 0131-620 8620
W www.edinburghnews.com
Editor, John McLellan

VENING TIMES
200 Renfield Street, Glasgow G2 3PR T 0141-302 7000
W www.eveningtimes.co.uk
Editor, Donald Martin

HE INVERNESS COURIER
New Century House, Stadium Road, Inverness IV1 1FF
T 01463-732222 W www.inverness-courier.co.uk
Editor, Robert Taylor

AISLEY DAILY EXPRESS
14 New Street, Paisley, Renfrewshire PA1 1YA
T 0141-887 7911 W www.icrenfrewshire.co.uk
Editor, Anne Dalrymple

IE PRESS AND JOURNAL
Lang Stracht, Aberdeen AB15 6DF T 01224-690222
W www.thisisnorthscotland.co.uk
Editor, Derek Tucker

ALES

VENING LEADER
Centenary Buildings, King Street, Wrexham, Clwyd LL11 1PN
T 01978-355151 W www.eveningleader.co.uk
Editor, Barrie Jones

OUTH WALES ARGUS
Cardiff Road, Maesglas, Newport, Gwent NP20 3QN
T 01633-777219
Editor, Gerry Keighley

OUTH WALES ECHO
Thomson House, Havelock Street, Cardiff CF10 1XR
T 029-2058 3622 W www.icwales.co.uk
Editor, Richard Williams

OUTH WALES EVENING POST
PO Box 14, Adelaide Street, Swansea SA1 1QT
T 01792-510000 W www.thisissouthwales.co.uk
Editor-in-Chief, Spencer Feeney

WESTERN MAIL
Thomson House, Havelock Street, Cardiff CF10 1XR
T 029-2058 3583 W www.icwales.co.uk
Editor, Alan Edmunds

NORTHERN IRELAND

BELFAST TELEGRAPH
124–144 Royal Avenue, Belfast BT1 1EB T 028-9026 4000
W www.belfasttelegraph.co.uk
Editor, Martin Lindsay

THE IRISH NEWS
113–117 Donegall Street, Belfast BT1 2GE T 028-9032 2226
W www.irishnews.com
Editor, Noel Doran

NEWS LETTER
2 Esky Drive, Portadown, Craigaron, Belfast BT63 5WD
T 028-3839 3939 W www.newsletter.co.uk
Editor, Darwin Templeton

CHANNEL ISLANDS

THE GUERNSEY PRESS AND STAR
PO Box 57, Braye Road, Vale, Guernsey GY1 3BW
T 01481-240240 W www.guernseypress.com
Editor, Richard Digard

JERSEY EVENING POST
PO Box 582, Five Oaks, St Saviour, Jersey JE4 8XQ
T 01534-611611 W www.thisisjersey.com
Editor, Chris Bright

PERIODICALS

ACCOUNTANCY AGE
VNU Business Publications, VNU House, 32–34 Broadwick Street, London W1A 2HG T 020-7316 9236
W www.accountancyage.com
Editor, Gavin Hinks

AEROPLANE MONTHLY
The Blue Fin Building, 110 Southwark Street, London SE1 0SU T 020-7261 5849 W www.aeroplanemonthly.com
Editor, Michael Oakey

AMATEUR PHOTOGRAPHER
The Blue Fin Building, 110 Southwark Street, London SE1 0SU T 020-3148 5000
Editor, Damien Demolder

ANGLING TIMES
Bushfield House, Orton Centre, Peterborough PE2 5UW
T 01733-232600 W www.anglingtimes.co.uk
Editor, Richard Lee

THE ARCHITECTS' JOURNAL
151 Rosebery Avenue, London EC1R 4GB T 020-7505 6700
W www.ajplus.co.uk
Editor, Keiron Long

THE ARCHITECTURAL REVIEW
151 Rosebery Avenue, London EC1R 4GB T 020-7505 6725
W www.arplus.com
Editor, Paul Finch

ARCHITECTURE TODAY
161 Rosebery Avenue, London EC1R 4QX T 020-7837 0143
W www.architecturetoday.co.uk
Editor, Ian Latham

ARENA
Endeavour House, 189 Shaftesbury Avenue, London WC2H 8JG T 020-7437 9011
Editor, Giles Hattersley

ART MONTHLY
4th Floor, 28 Charing Cross Road, London WC2H 0DB
T 020-7240 0389 W www.artmonthly.co.uk
Editor, Patricia Bickers

THE ART NEWSPAPER
70 South Lambeth Road, London SW8 1RL **T** 020-7735 3331 **W** www.theartnewspaper.com
Editor, Christina Ruiz

ART REVIEW
1 Sekforde Street, 23–24 Smithfield Street, London EC1R 0BE **T** 020-7107 2760 **W** www.artreview.com
Editor, Mark Rappolt

ATTITUDE
Northern Shell Tower, City Harbour, London E14 9GL **T** 020-7308 5090 **W** www.attitude.co.uk
Editor, Adam Mattera

AUTO EXPRESS
30 Cleveland Street, London W1T 4JD **T** 020-7907 6200 **W** www.autoexpress.co.uk
Editor, David Johns

THE BANKER
1 Southwark Bridge, London SE1 9HL **T** 020-7775 6359 **W** www.thebanker.com
Editor-in-Chief, Stephen Timewell

THE BEANO
Albert Square, Dundee DD1 9QJ **T** 01382-223131
Editor, Alan Dogby

BELLA
Academic House, 24–28 Oval Road, London NW1 7DT **T** 020-7241 8000
Editor, Jayne Marsden

BEST
33 Broadwick Street, London W1F 0DQ **T** 020-7339 4500
Editor, Michelle Hather

THE BIG ISSUE
1–5 Wandsworth Road, London SW8 2LN **T** 020-7526 3200 **W** www.bigissue.com
Editor-in-Chief, John Bird

BIKE
Media House, Lynchwood, Peterborough PE2 6EA **T** 01733-468000 **W** www.emapbikes.com
Editor, John Westlake

BIRD WATCHING
Bretton Court, Bretton, Peterborough PE3 8DZ **T** 01733-264666 **W** www.birdwatchingmagazine.co.uk
Editor, Kevin Wilmott

BIZARRE
30 Cleveland Street, London W1T 4JD **T** 020-7907 6000 **W** www.bizarremag.com
Editor, Alex Godfrey

BLISS
Panini House, Coach and Horses Passage, The Pantiles, Tunbridge Wells, Kent TN2 5OT **T** 01892-500106 **W** www.blissmag.co.uk
Editor, Leslie Sinoway

THE BOOKSELLER
5th Floor, Endeavour House, 189 Shaftesbury Avenue, London WC2H 8TJ **T** 020-7420 6006 **W** www.thebookseller.com
Editor-in-Chief, Neill Denny

BRITISH MEDICAL JOURNAL
BMA House, Tavistock Square, London WC1H 9JR **T** 020-7387 4499 **W** www.bmj.com
Editor, Dr Fiona Godlee

BROADCAST
33–39 Bowling Green Lane, London EC1R 0DA **T** 020-7505 8014 **W** www.broadcastnow.co.uk
Editor, Lisa Campbell

BUILDING
8th Floor, 245 Blackfriars Road, London SE1 9UY **T** 020-7560 4000
Editor, Denise Chevin

THE BURLINGTON MAGAZINE
14–16 Duke's Road, London WC1H 9SZ **T** 020-7388 8157 **W** www.burlington.org.uk
Editor, Richard Shone

THE BUSINESS
22 Old Queen Street, London SW1H 9HP **T** 020-7961 0000 **W** www.thebusiness.co.uk
Editor, Andrew Neil

CAMPAIGN
174 Hammersmith Road, London W6 7JP **T** 020-8943 5000 **W** www.brandrepublic.com
Editor, Claire Beale

CAR
3rd Floor, Media House, Lynchwood, Peterborough PE2 6EA **T** 01733-468000
Editor, Greg Fountain

CARAVAN MAGAZINE
Leon House, 233 High Street, Croydon CR9 1HZ **T** 020-8726 8000 **W** www.caravanmagazine.co.uk
Editor, Victoria Heath

CATERER AND HOTELKEEPER
Quadrant House, The Quadrant, Sutton, Surrey SM2 5AS **T** 020-8652 3221
Editor, Mark Lewis

THE CATHOLIC HERALD
Herald House, Lambs Passage, Bunhill Row, London EC1Y 8TQ **T** 020-7448 3603 **W** www.catholicherald.co.uk
Editor, Luke Coppen

CATHOLIC TIMES
1st Floor, St James's Buildings, Oxford Street, Manchester M1 6FP **T** 0161-236 8856
Editor, Kevin Flaherty

CHAT
The Blue Fin Building, 110 Southwark Street, London SE1 0SU **T** 020-3148 5000 **W** www.ipcmedia.com
Editor, Gilly Sinclair

CHURCH TIMES
33 Upper Street, London N1 0PN **T** 020-7359 4570 **W** www.churchtimes.co.uk
Editor, Paul Handley

CLASSIC CARS
Media House, Lynchwood, Peterborough PE2 6EA **T** 01733-468219 **W** www.classiccarsmagazine.co.uk
Editor, Phil Bell

CLASSICAL MUSIC
241 Shaftesbury Avenue, London WC2H 8TF **T** 020-7333 1742 **W** www.rhinegold.co.uk
Editor, Keith Clarke

CLASSICS MONTHLY
30 Monmouth Street, Bath BA1 2BW **T** 01225-442244
Editor, Gary Streatham

CLOSER
Endeavour House, 189 Shaftesbury Avenue, London WC2H 8JG **T** 020-7437 9011 **W** www.closermag.co.uk
Editor, Jane Johnson

COMPANY
National Magazine House, 72 Broadwick Street, London W1V 2BP **T** 020-7439 5000 **W** www.company.co.uk
Editor, Victoria White

CONDÉ NAST TRAVELLER
Vogue House, Hanover Square, London W1S 1JU **T** 020-7499 9080 **W** www.cntraveller.com
Editor, Sarah Miller

COSMOPOLITAN
National Magazine House, 72 Broadwick Street, London W1F 9EP **T** 020-7439 5000
Editor-in-Chief, Louise Court

OUNTRY HOMES AND INTERIORS
The Blue Fin Building, 110 Southwark Street, London SE1 0SU T 020-3261 5000
Editor, Rhoda Parry

OUNTRY LIFE
The Blue Fin Building, 110 Southwark Street, London SE1 0SU T 020-3261 6400 W www.countrylife.co.uk
Editor, Mark Hedges

OUNTRY LIVING
National Magazine House, 72 Broadwick Street, London W1F 9EP T 020-7439 5000 W www.countryliving.co.uk
Editor, Susy Smith

YCLING WEEKLY
Leon House, 233 High Street, Croydon CR9 1HZ
T 020-8726 8463 W www.cyclingweekly.co.uk
Editor, Robert Garbutt

ANCING TIMES
45–47 Clerkenwell Green, London EC1R 0EB
T 020-7250 3006 W www.dancing-times.co.uk
Editor, Mary Clarke

HE DANDY
Albert Square, Dundee DD1 9QJ T 01382-223131

ECANTER
The Blue Fin Building, 110 Southwark Street, London SE1 0SU T 020-3148 5000 W www.decanter.com
Editor (acting), Guy Woodward

ASTERN EYE
Unit 2, 65 Whitechapel Road, London E1 1DU
T 020-7650 2000 W www.easterneyeonline.co.uk
Editor, Hamant Verma

HE ECOLOGIST
Unit 102, Lana House Studios, 116–118 Commercial Street, London E1 6NF T 020-7422 8100
Editor, Pat Thomas

HE ECONOMIST
25 St James's Street, London SW1A 1HG T 020-7830 7000
W www.economist.com
Editor, John Micklethwait

DINBURGH REVIEW
22A Buccleugh Place, Edinburgh EH8 9LN T 0131-651 1415
W www.edinburghreview.org.uk
Editor, Brian McCabe

LLE
64 North Row, London W1K 7LL T 020-7150 7000
W www.elleuk.com
Editor, Lorraine Candy

MPIRE
Mappin House, 4 Winsley Street, London W1W 8HF
T 020-7182 8781 W www.empireonline.com
Editor, Mark Dinning

HE ENGINEER
St Giles House, 50 Poland Street, London W1F 7AX
T 020-7970 4000 W www.theengineer.com
Editor, Andrew Lee

HE EROTIC REVIEW
1st Floor, 17 Harwood Road, London SW4 4QP
T 020-7736 5800 W www.eroticreviewmagazine.com
Editor, Jamie Maclean

SQUIRE
National Magazine House, 72 Broadwick Street, London W1F 9EP T 020-7439 5000 W www.esquire.co.uk
Editor, Jeremy Langmead

SSENTIALS
The Blue Fin Building, 110 Southwark Street, London SE1 0SU T 020-3148 7211
Editor, Julie Barton-Breck

EVE
174 Hammersmith Road, London W6 7JP
W www.evemagazine.co.uk

EVENTING
The Blue Fin Building, 110 Southwark Street, London SE1 0SU T 020-3148 5000
Editor, Julie Harding

FARMERS WEEKLY
Quadrant House, The Quadrant, Sutton, Surrey SM2 5AS
T 020-8652 4911 W www.fwi.co.uk
Editor, Jane King

FHM
Mappin House, 4 Winsley Street, London W1W 8HF
T 020-7182 8028 W www.fhm.com
Editor, Anthony Naguera

THE FIELD
The Blue Fin Building, 110 Southwark Street, London SE1 0SU T 020-3148 5000 W www.thefield.co.uk
Editor, Jonathan Young

FINANCIAL ADVISER
Tabernacle Court, 16–28 Tabernacle Street, London EC2A 4DD T 020-7382 8000 W www.ftadviser.com
Editor, Hal Austin

FISHING NEWS
Telephone House, 69–77 Paul Street, London EC2A 4LQ
T 020-7017 4531 W www.fishingnews.co.uk
Editor, Tim Oliver

FLIGHT INTERNATIONAL
Quadrant House, The Quadrant, Sutton, Surrey SM2 5AS
T 020-8652 3842 W www.flightglobal.com
Editor, Kieran Daly

FORTEAN TIMES
Box 2409, London NW5 4NP T 020-7907 6235
W www.forteantimes.com
Editor, David Sutton

FOURFOURTWO
38–42 Hampton Road, Teddington TW11 0JE
T 020-8267 5337 W www.fourfourtwo.co.uk
Editor, Hugh Sleight

THE FRIEND
173 Euston Road, London NW1 2BJ T 020-7663 1010
W www.thefriend.org
Editor, Judy Kirby

GARDEN NEWS
Bretton Court, Bretton Centre, Peterborough PE3 8DZ
T 01733-264666
Editor, Neil Pope

GAY TIMES
Spectrum House, 32–34 Gordon House Road, London NW5 1LP T 020-7424 7400 W www.gaytimes.co.uk
Editor, Joseph Galliano

GEOGRAPHICAL JOURNAL
Kensington Gore, London SW7 2AR T 020-7591 3026
Editor, Prof. John Briggs

GLAMOUR
Vogue House, Hanover Square, London W15 1JU
T 020-7499 9080 W www.glamourmagazine.com
Editor, Jo Elvin

GOLF WORLD
Bushfield House, Orton Centre, Peterborough PE2 5UW
T 01733-237111 W www.golfworld-magazine.com
Editor, Paul Hamblin

GOOD HOUSEKEEPING
National Magazine House, 72 Broadwick Street, London W1F 9EP T 020-7439 5000 W www.natmags.co.uk
Editor-in-Chief, Louise Chunn

GQ
Vogue House, Hanover Square, London W1S 1JU
T 020-7499 9080 W www.gq-magazine.co.uk
Editor, Dylan Jones

GRANTA
2–3 Hanover Yard, Noel Road, London N1 8BE
T 020-7704 9776 W www.granta.com
Editor, Jason Cowley

GRAZIA
Endeavour House, 189 Shaftesbury Avenue, London WC2H 8JG W www.graziamagazine.co.uk
Editor, Jane Bruton

THE GROCER
Broadfield Park, Crawley, West Sussex RH11 9RT
T 01293-613400 W www.thegrocer.co.uk
Editor, Adam Leyland

GUITARIST
30 Monmouth Street, Bath BA1 2BW T 01225-442244
W www.futurenet.co.uk
Editor, Michael Leonard

HARPER'S BAZAAR
National Magazine House, 72 Broadwick Street, London W1F 9EP T 020-7439 5000 W www.natmags.co.uk
Editor, Lucy Yeomans

HEALTH AND FITNESS MAGAZINE
2 Balcombe Street, London NW1 6NW T 020-7042 4000
W www.healthandfitnessonline.co.uk
Editor, Mary Comber

HEAT
Endeavour House, 189 Shaftesbury Avenue, London WC2H 8JG T 020-7859 8657
Editor, Mark Frith

HELLO!
Wellington House, 69–71 Upper Ground, London SE1 9PQ
T 020-7667 8700
Editor, Ronnie Whelan

HOMES AND GARDENS
The Blue Fin Building, 110 Southwark Street, London SE1 0SU T 020-3148 5000 W www.homesandgardens.com
Editor, Deborah Barker

HORSE AND HOUND
The Blue Fin Building, 110 Southwark Street, London SE1 0SU T 020-3148 4562 W www.horseandhound.co.uk
Editor, Lucy Higginson

HOUSE AND GARDEN
Vogue House, Hanover Square, London W1S 1JU
T 020-7499 9080
Editor, Susan Crewe

HOUSE BEAUTIFUL
National Magazine House, 72 Broadwick Street, London W1F 9EP T 020-7439 5000 W www.housebeautiful.co.uk
Editor, Julia Goodwin

HOUSEBUILDER
Byron House, 7–9 St James's Street, London SW1A 1DW
T 020-7960 1630 W www.house-builder.co.uk
Editor, Allison Heller

IDEAL HOME
The Blue Fin Building, 110 Southwark Street, London SE1 0SU T 020-3148 5000
Editor, Susan Rose

IN STYLE
The Blue Fin Building, 110 Southwark Street, London SE1 0SU T 020-3148 5000
Editor, Trish Halpin

INSURANCE AGE
Haymarket House, 28–29 Haymarket, London SW1Y 4RX
T 020-7484 9776 W www.insuranceage.com
Editor, Michelle Worvell

JANE'S DEFENCE WEEKLY
Sentinel House, 163 Brighton Road, Coulsdon, Surrey CR5 2YH T 020-8700 3700 W jdw.janes.com
Editor, Peter Felstead

THE JEWISH QUARTERLY
PO Box 37645, London NW7 1WB T 020-8343 4675
W www.jewishquarterly.org
Editor, Matthew Reisz

KERRANG!
Mappin House, 4 Winsley Street, London W1W 8HF
T 020-7436 1515 W www.kerrang.com
Editor, Paul Brannigan

THE LADY
39–40 Bedford Street, London WC2E 9ER T 020-7379 471
W www.lady.co.uk
Editor, Arline Usden

LANCET
32 Jamestown Road, London NW1 7BY T 020-7424 4910
W www.thelancet.com
Editor, Dr Richard Horton

LEGAL WEEK
28–29 Haymarket, London SW1Y 4RX T 020-7484 9700
W www.legalweek.com
Editor, John Malpas

LITERARY REVIEW
44 Lexington Street, London W1F 0LW T 020-7437 9392
W www.literaryreview.co
Editor, Nancy Sladek

LOADED
The Blue Fin Building, 110 Southwark Street, London SE1 0SU T 020-3148 5000 W www.loaded.co.uk
Editor, Martin Daubney

LONDON REVIEW OF BOOKS
28 Little Russell Street, London WC1A 2HN T 020-7209 11
Editor, Mary-Kay Wilmers

MACUSER
30 Cleveland Street, London W1T 4JD T 020-7907 6000
W www.macuser.co.uk
Editor, Nik Rawlinson

MARIE CLAIRE
7th Floor, The Blue Fin Building, 110 Southwark Street, London SE1 0LU T 020-3148 7513
Editor, Marie O'Riordan

MARKETING WEEK
50 Poland Street, London W1F 7AX T 020-7970 6328
W www.marketingweek.co.uk
Editor, Stuart Smith

MAXIM
30 Cleveland Street, London W1T 4JD T 020-7907 6410
W www.maxim-magazine.co.uk
Editor, Derek Harbinson

MEDIA WEEK
174 Hammersmith Road, London W6 7JP T 020-8267 802
Editor, Steve Barrett

MEN'S HEALTH
33 Broadwick Street, London W1F 9EP T 020-7339 4400
W www.menshealth.co.uk
Editor, Morgan Rees

MIXMAG
90–92 Pentonville Road, London N1 9HS T 020-7520 8625
W www.mixmag.net
Editor, Andrew Harrison

MOJO
Mappin House, 4 Winsley Street, London W1W 8HF
T 020-7436 1515 W www.mojo4music.com
Editor, Phil Alexander

ORE
Endeavour House, 189 Shaftesbury Avenue, London WC2H 8JG **T** 020-7208 3165 **W** www.moremagazine.co.uk
Editor, Lisa Smosarski

OTHER AND BABY
Greater London House, Hampstead Road, London NW1 7EJ **T** 020-7347 1869 **W** www.motherandbabymagazine.com
Editor, Elena Dalrymple

USIC WEEK
1st Floor, Ludgate House, 245 Blackfriars Road, London SE1 9UR **T** 020-7921 8348
Editor, Martin Talbot

IE NATIONAL TRUST MAGAZINE
Heelis, Kemble Drive, Swindon SN2 2NA **T** 01793-817400 **W** www.nationaltrust.org.uk
Editor, Sue Herdman

ATURE
The Macmillan Building, 4 Crinan Street, London N1 9XW **T** 020-7833 4000 **W** www.nature.com/nature
Editor, Philip Campbell

ME
The Blue Fin Building, 110 Southwark Street, London SE1 0SU **T** 020-3148 5000
Editor, Conor McNicholas

EW SCIENTIST
Lacon House, 84 Theobalds Road, London WC1X 8NS **T** 020-7611 1200 **W** www.newscientist.com
Editor, Jeremy Webb

EW STATESMAN
3rd Floor, 52 Grosvenor Gardens, London SW1W 0AU **T** 020-7730 3444 **W** www.newstatesman.com
Editor, John Kampfner

EW WOMAN
Endeavour House, 189 Shaftesbury Avenue, London WC2H 8JG **T** 020-7437 9011 **W** www.nwdaily.co.uk
Editor, Lauren Libbert

URSING TIMES
Greater London House, Hampstead Road, London NW1 7EJ **T** 020-7874 0500
Editor, Rachel Downey

K!
10 Lower Thames Street, London EC3R 6EN **T** 0871-434 1010
Editor, Lisa Byrne

IE OLDIE
65 Newman Street, London W1T 3EG **T** 020-7436 8801 **W** www.theoldie.co.uk
Editor, Richard Ingrams

PERA
36 Black Lion Lane, London W6 9BE **T** 020-8563 8893 **W** www.opera.co.uk
Editor, John Allison

C ADVISOR
99 Gray's Inn Road, London WC1X 8TY **T** 020-7071 3615 **W** www.pcadvisor.co.uk
Editor, Paul Trotter

RIOD LIVING
50 Poland Street, London W1F 7AX **T** 020-7970 4433
Editor, Sarah Whelan

RSONAL COMPUTER WORLD
32–34 Broadwick Street, London W1A 2HG **T** 020-7316 9000 **W** www.pcw.co.uk
Editor, Kelvyn Taylor

IE PINK PAPER
Spectrum House, 32–34 Gordon House Road, London NW5 1LP **T** 020-7424 7400 **W** www.pinkpaper.com
Editor, Tris Reid-Smith

POETRY REVIEW
22 Betterton Street, London WC2H 9BX **T** 020-7420 9883 **W** www.poetrysociety.org.uk
Editor, Fiona Sampson

PR WEEK
174 Hammersmith Road, London W6 7JP **T** 020-8267 5000 **W** www.prweek.com
Editor, Daniel Rogers

PRACTICAL FISHKEEPING
Bretton Court, Bretton, Peterborough PE3 8DZ **T** 01733-264666 **W** www.practicalfishkeeping.co.uk
Editor, Karen Youngs

PRACTICAL PHOTOGRAPHY
Bretton Court, Bretton, Peterborough PE3 8DZ **T** 01733-264666 **W** www.practicalphotography.co.uk
Editor, Andrew James

PRIMA
72 Broadwick Street, London W1F 9EP **T** 020-7439 5000
Editor, Maire Fahey

PRIVATE EYE
6 Carlisle Street, London W1D 3BN **T** 020-7437 4017 **W** www.private-eye.co.uk
Editor, Ian Hislop

PROSPECT MAGAZINE
2 Bloomsbury Place, London WC1A 2QA **T** 020-7255 1281 **W** www.prospect-magazine.co.uk
Editor, David Goodhart

PUBLISHING NEWS
7 John Street, London WC1N 2ES **T** 0870-870 2345 **W** www.publishingnews.co.uk
Editor, Liz Thomson

Q MAGAZINE
Mappin House, 4 Winsley Street, London W1W 8HF **T** 020-7182 8000 **W** www.q4music.com
Editor, Paul Rees

RA MAGAZINE
Royal Academy of Arts, Burlington House, Piccadilly, London W1J 0BD **T** 020-7300 5820 **W** www.ramagazine.org.uk
Editor, Sarah Greenberg

RACING POST
Floor 23, 1 Canada Square, Canary Wharf, London E14 5AP **T** 020-7293 3000 **W** www.racingpost.co.uk
Editor, Chris Smith

RADIO TIMES
80 Wood Lane, London W12 0TT **T** 020-8433 3400 **W** www.radiotimes.com
Editor, Gill Hudson

RAILWAY GAZETTE INTERNATIONAL
Quadrant House, The Quadrant, Sutton, Surrey SM2 5AS **T** 020-8652 8608 **W** www.railwaygazette.com
Editor, Chris Jackson

RAILWAY MAGAZINE
The Blue Fin Building, 110 Southwark Street, London SE1 0SU **T** 020-3148 5000
Editor, Nick Pigott

READER'S DIGEST
11 Westferry Circus, Canary Wharf, London E14 4HE **T** 020-7715 8000 **W** www.readersdigest.co.uk
Editor-in-Chief, Katherine Walker

RECORD COLLECTOR
Wales Farm Road, London W3 6UG **T** 0870-732 8080 **W** www.recordcollectormag.com
Editor-in-Chief, Alan Lewis

RED
64 North Row, London W1K 7LL **T** 020-7150 7000 **W** www.redmagazine.co.uk
Editor, Sam Baker

RUNNER'S WORLD
33 Broadwick Street, London W1F 0DG T 020-7339 4400 W www.runnersworld.co.uk
Editor, Andy Dixon

SAGA MAGAZINE
The Saga Building, Enbrook Park, Sandgate, Folkestone, Kent CT20 3SE T 01303-771523
Editor, Emma Soames

SCREEN INTERNATIONAL
33–39 Bowling Green Lane, London EC1R 0DA T 020-7505 8000 W www.screendaily.com
Editor, Michael Gubbins

SHE
National Magazine House, 72 Broadwick Street, London W1F 9EP T 020-7439 5000

SIGHT AND SOUND
British Film Institute, 21 Stephen Street, London W1T 1LN T 020-7255 1444 W www.bfi.org.uk/sightandsound
Editor, Nick James

SKI AND BOARD
The White House, 57–63 Church Road, London SW19 5SB T 0845-458 0780 W www.skiclub.co.uk
Editor, Arnie Wilson

THE SPECTATOR
22 Old Queen Street, London SW1H 9HP T 020-7961 0200 W www.spectator.co.uk
Editor, Matthew d'Ancona

THE STAGE
Stage House, 47 Bermondsey Street, London SE1 3XT T 020-7403 1818 W www.thestage.co.uk
Editor, Brian Attwood

STAMP MAGAZINE
Leon House, 233 High Street, Croydon CR9 1HZ T 020-8726 8241
Editor, Guy Thomas

STUFF
Teddington Studios, Broom Road, Teddington, Middlesex TW11 9BE T 020-8267 5036 W www.stuffmag.co.uk
Editor, Fraser MacDonald

THE TABLET
1 King Street Cloisters, Clifton Walk, London W6 0QZ T 020-8748 8484 W www.thetablet.co.uk
Editor, Catherine Pepinster

TAKE A BREAK
Academic House, 24–28 Oval Road, London NW1 7DT T 020-7241 8000 W www.bauer.com
Editor, John Dale

TATLER
Vogue House, Hanover Square, London W1S 1JU T 020-7499 9080 W www.tatler.co.uk
Editor, Geordie Greig

THAT'S LIFE!
Academic House, 24–28 Oval Road, London NW1 7DT T 020-7241 8000
Editor, Jo Checkley

TIME OUT
Universal House, 251 Tottenham Court Road, London W1T 7AB T 020-7813 3000 W www.timeout.com
Editor, Gordon Thomson

THE TIMES EDUCATIONAL SUPPLEMENT
Admiral House, 66–68 East Smithfield, London E1W 1BX T 020-7782 3000 W www.tes.co.uk
Editor, Gerard Kelly

THE TIMES LITERARY SUPPLEMENT
Times House, 1 Pennington Street, London E98 1BS T 020-7782 5000 W www.thetls.co.uk
Editor, Peter Stothard

TOTAL FILM
2 Balcombe Street, London NW1 6NW T 020-7042 4000 W www.futurenet.com
Editor, Nev Pierce

TRAVELLER
45 Brompton Road, London SW3 1DE T 020-7589 0500 W www.traveller.org.uk
Editor, Amy Sohanpaul

TVTIMES MAGAZINE
The Blue Fin Building, 110 Southwark Street, London SE1 0SU T 020-3148 5615 W www.tvtimes.co.uk
Editor, Ian Abbott

VANITY FAIR
Vogue House, Hanover Square, London W1S 1JU T 020-7499 9080 W www.vanityfair.co.uk
Editor-in-Chief, Graydon Carter

VIZ
30 Cleveland Street, London W1T 4JD T 020-7687 7000 W www.viz.co.uk
Editor, Simon Donald

VOGUE
Vogue House, Hanover Square, London W1S 1JU T 020-7499 9080 W www.vogue.co.uk
Editor, Alexandra Shulman

WALLPAPER
The Blue Fin Building, 110 Southwark Street, London SE1 0SU T 020-3148 5000 W www.wallpaper.com
Editor-in-Chief, Tony Chambers

WANDERLUST
PO Box 1832, Windsor SL4 1YT T 01753-620426 W www.wanderlust.co.uk
Editor, Dan Linstead

WHAT CAR?
Teddington Studios, Broom Road, Teddington, Middlesex TW11 9BE T 020-8267 5000 W www.whatcar.com
Group Editor, Steve Fowler

WOMAN'S OWN
The Blue Fin Building, 110 Southwark Street, London SE1 0SU T 020-3148 5000
Editor, Karen Livermore

THE WORLD OF INTERIORS
Vogue House, Hanover Square, London W1S 1JU T 020-7499 9080 W www.worldofinteriors.co.uk
Editor, Rupert Thomas

WORLD SOCCER
The Blue Fin Building, 110 Southwark Street, London SE1 0SU T 020-3148 5000 W www.worldsoccer.com
Editor, Gavin Hamilton

YACHTING MONTHLY
The Blue Fin Building, 110 Southwark Street, London SE1 0SU T 020-3261 6040
Editor, Paul Gelder

ZEST
72 Broadwick Street, London W1F 9EP T 020-7439 5000
Editor, Alison Pylkkanen

BOOK PUBLISHERS

IAN ALLAN PUBLISHING LTD
Riverdene Business Park, Molesey Road, Hersham, Surrey KT12 4RG **T** 01932-266600 **W** www.ianallanpublishing.com
Transport, military history, reference

ANDERSEN PRESS LTD
20 Vauxhall Bridge Road, London SW1V 2SA **T** 020-7840 8701 **W** www.andersenpress.co.uk
Children's picture books and junior and teenage fiction. Founded 1976.

ANOVA BOOKS
The Old Magistrate's Court, 10 Southcom Street, London W14 0RA **T** 020-7605 1400 **W** www.anovabooks.com
Art and design, biography, children's, fashion, fiction, food and drink, gardening, history, military, sport, travel. Founded 2005

ANVIL PRESS POETRY
Neptune House, 70 Royal Hill, London SE10 8RF **T** 020-8469 3033 **W** www.anvilpresspoetry.com
Poetry. Founded 1968

BAREFOOT BOOKS LTD
124 Walcot Street, Bath BA1 5BG **T** 01225-322400 **W** www.barefootbooks.co.uk
Children's picture books and audiobooks. Founded 1993

BIRLINN LTD
West Newington House, 10 Newington Road, Edinburgh H9 1QS **T** 0131-668 4371 **W** www.birlinn.co.uk
Adventure, archaeology, guides, history, military, Scottish history, Scottish humour, sport. Founded 1992

A&C BLACK PUBLISHERS LTD
38 Soho Square, London W1D 3HB **T** 020-7758 0200 **W** www.acblack.com
Art and craft, business, ceramics, children's, dictionaries, drama, nautical, ornithology, reference, sport, theatre, books for writers. Founded 1807

BLACKWELL PUBLISHING LTD
9600 Garsington Road, Oxford OX4 2DQ **T** 01865-776868 **W** www.blackwellpublishing.com
Books and journals in business, dentistry, humanities, medicine, science and veterinary science

BLOOMSBURY PUBLISHING PLC
6 Soho Square, London W1D 3QY **T** 020-7494 2111 **W** www.bloomsbury.com
Biography, children's, fiction, illustrated, travel. Founded 986

MARION BOYARS PUBLISHERS LTD
4 Lacy Road, London SW15 1NL **T** 020-8788 9522 **W** www.marionboyars.co.uk
Cultural studies, film, jazz, literary fiction, memoirs, music, travel. Founded 1975

CAMBRIDGE UNIVERSITY PRESS
The Edinburgh Building, Shaftesbury Road, Cambridge CB2 2RU **T** 01223-312393 **W** www.cambridge.org
Academic and reference books and journals. Founded 1534

CANONGATE BOOKS LTD
14 High Street, Edinburgh EH1 1TE **T** 0131-557 5111 **W** www.canongate.net
General fiction, literary fiction and non-fiction. Founded 1973

CHAMBERS HARRAP PUBLISHERS LTD
7 Hopetoun Crescent, Edinburgh EH7 4AY **T** 0131-556 5929 **W** www.chambersharrap.co.uk
Dictionaries, puzzles, reference, word games, writing guides

EDINBURGH UNIVERSITY PRESS
22 George Square, Edinburgh EH8 9LF **T** 0131-650 4218 **W** www.eup.ed.ac.uk
Academic books and journals

EGMONT BOOKS
239 Kensington High Street, London W8 6SA **T** 020-7761 3500 **W** www.egmont.co.uk
Children's fiction, non-fiction and annuals. Founded 1878

ELSEVIER LTD
The Boulevard, Langford Lane, Kidlington, Oxford OX5 1GB **T** 01865-843000 **W** www.elsevier.com
Academic and professional reference books and journals; science, technology, medicine

EVERYMAN'S LIBRARY
Northburgh House, 10 Northburgh Street, London EC1V 0AT **T** 020-7566 6350
Reprints of classic fiction and poetry. Founded 1929

FABER AND FABER LTD
3 Queen Square, London WC1N 3AU **T** 020-7465 0045 **W** www.faber.co.uk
General fiction and non-fiction, children's fiction and non-fiction, drama, film, music, poetry

SAMUEL FRENCH LTD
52 Fitzroy Street, London W1T 5JR **T** 020-7387 9373 **W** www.samuelfrench-london.co.uk
Plays. Founded 1830

GOMER PRESS
Llandysul, Ceredigion SA44 4JL **T** 01559-363090 **W** www.gomer.co.uk, www.pontbooks.co.uk
Biography, children's, fiction of relevance to Welsh culture, history, poetry and travel, in English and in Welsh. Founded 1892

GRANTA PUBLICATIONS
2–3 Hanover Yard, Noel Road, London N1 8BE **T** 020-7704 9776 **W** www.granta.com
History, literary fiction, memoir, political non-fiction, travel. Founded 1982

continued on page 636

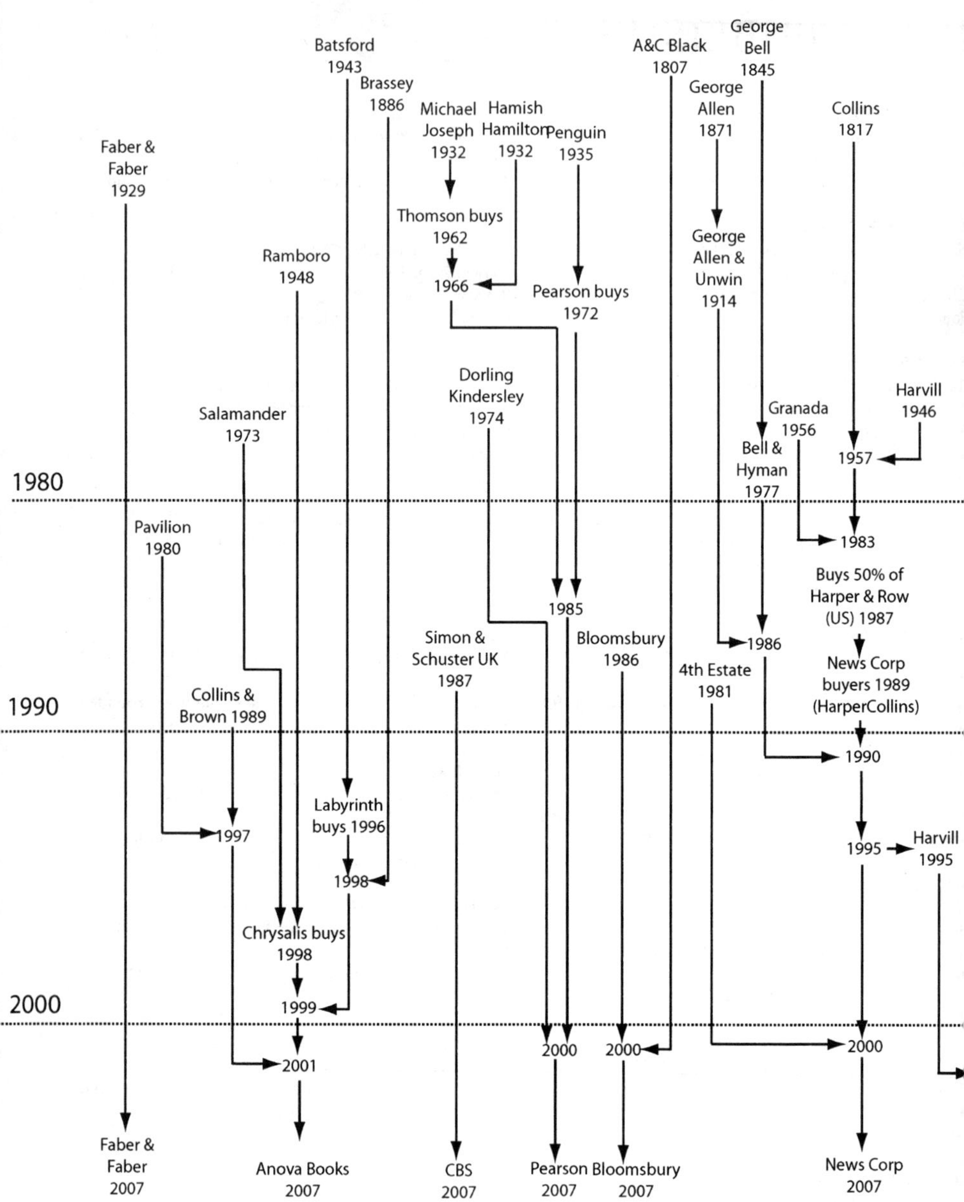
Batsford 1943
Brassey 1886
Michael Joseph 1932
Hamish Hamilton 1932
Penguin 1935
A&C Black 1807
George Bell 1845
George Allen 1871
Collins 1817
Faber & Faber 1929
Thomson buys 1962
1966
Ramboro 1948
Pearson buys 1972
George Allen & Unwin 1914
Dorling Kindersley 1974
Salamander 1973
Granada 1956
Harvill 1946
Bell & Hyman 1977
1957
1980
Pavilion 1980
1983
Buys 50% of Harper & Row (US) 1987
1985
Simon & Schuster UK 1987
Bloomsbury 1986
1986
4th Estate 1981
News Corp buyers 1989 (HarperCollins)
1990
Collins & Brown 1989
1990
Labyrinth buys 1996
1997
1995
Harvill 1995
1998
Chrysalis buys 1998
2000
1999
2000
2000
2000
2001
Faber & Faber 2007
Anova Books 2007
CBS 2007
Pearson 2007
Bloomsbury 2007
News Corp 2007

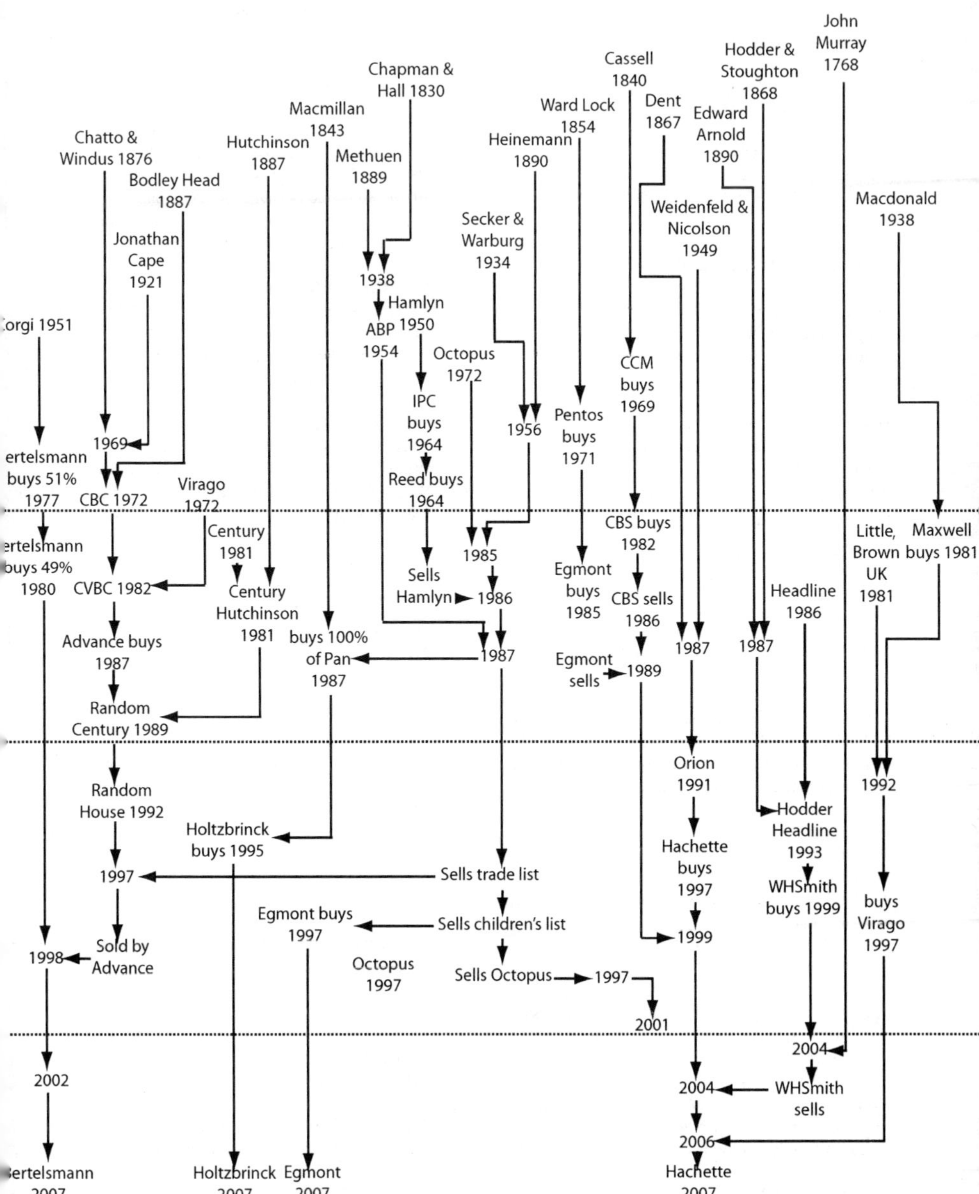

John Murray 1768
Hodder & Stoughton 1868
Cassell 1840
Chapman & Hall 1830
Ward Lock 1854
Dent 1867
Edward Arnold 1890
Macmillan 1843
Hutchinson 1887
Chatto & Windus 1876
Methuen 1889
Heinemann 1890
Bodley Head 1887
Weidenfeld & Nicolson 1949
Macdonald 1938
Secker & Warburg 1934
Jonathan Cape 1921
1938
Hamlyn 1950
orgi 1951
ABP 1954
Octopus 1972
CCM buys 1969
IPC buys 1964
1956
Pentos buys 1971
1969
ertelsmann buys 51% 1977
CBC 1972
Virago 1972
Reed buys 1964
CBS buys 1982
Little, Brown UK 1981
Maxwell buys 1981
ertelsmann buys 49% 1980
Century 1981
1985
Sells Hamlyn
1986
Egmont buys 1985
CBS sells 1986
Headline 1986
CVBC 1982
Century Hutchinson 1981
Advance buys 1987
buys 100% of Pan 1987
1987
Egmont sells
1989
1987
1987
Random Century 1989
Orion 1991
1992
Random House 1992
Holtzbrinck buys 1995
Hodder Headline 1993
Hachette buys 1997
1997
Sells trade list
WHSmith buys 1999
buys Virago 1997
Egmont buys 1997
Sells children's list
1999
1998
Sold by Advance
Octopus 1997
Sells Octopus
1997
2001
2004
2002
2004
WHSmith sells
2006
ertelsmann 2007
Holtzbrinck 2007
Egmont 2007
Hachette 2007

HACHETTE CHILDREN'S BOOKS
338 Euston Road, London NW1 3BH T 020-7873 6000
W www.hodderchildrens.co.uk
Children's fiction, gift, information, non-fiction, novelty, picture and reference books

HARLEQUIN MILLS & BOON LTD
Eton House, 18–24 Paradise Road, Richmond, Surrey TW9 1SR
T 020-8288 2800 W www.millsandboon.co.uk
Romantic fiction. Founded 1908

HARPERCOLLINS PUBLISHERS
77–85 Fulham Palace Road, London W6 8JB T 020-8741 7070
W www.harpercollins.co.uk
Biographies, celebrity memoirs, dictionaries, fiction, history, maps, popular science and reference. Founded 1819

HEADLINE PUBLISHING GROUP
338 Euston Road, London NW1 3BH T 020-7873 6000
W www.headline.co.uk
Autobiography, biography, fiction, food and wine, gardening, history, popular science, sport, TV tie-ins

HODDER & STOUGHTON
338 Euston Road, London NW1 3BH T 020-7873 6000
W www.hodder.co.uk, www.hachettelivreuk.co.uk
Autobiography, biography, fiction, cookery, history, humour, lifestyle, mind, body & spirit, travel

ICON BOOKS LTD
The Old Dairy, Brook Road, Thriplow, Cambridge SG8 7RG
T 01763-208008 W www.iconbooks.co.uk
Current affairs, history, philosophy, politics, psychology, religion, science, children's gamebooks

IRISH ACADEMIC PRESS LTD
44 Northumberland Road, Ballsbridge, Dublin 4, Republic of Ireland T 020–8952 9526 W www.iap.ie
Academic heritage and culture, history and literature

JESSICA KINGSLEY PUBLISHERS
116 Pentonville Road, London N1 9JB T 020-7833 2307
W www.jkp.com
Education, law, practical theology, psychiatry, psychology, social work, special needs. Founded 1987

LETTS EDUCATIONAL
4 Grosvenor Place, London SW1X 7DL T 020-7096 2900
W www.letts-educational.co.uk
Children's study and revision guides. Founded 1979

LION HUDSON PLC
Mayfield House, 256 Banbury Road, Oxford OX2 7DH
T 01865-302750 W www.lionhudson.com
Christianity (biography, contemporary issues, history, reference, spirituality) children's Bibles, fiction, illustrated non-fiction and prayer collections

LITTLE, BROWN BOOK GROUP
100 Victoria Embankment, London EC4Y 0DY
T 020-7911 8000 W www.littlebrown.co.uk
Fiction and general non-fiction. Founded 1988

LONELY PLANET PUBLICATIONS
72–82 Rosebery Avenue, London EC1R 4RW T 020-7841 9000
W www.lonelyplanet.com
Travel guidebooks

MCGRAW-HILL EDUCATION
McGraw-Hill House, Shoppenhangers Road, Maidenhead, Berks SL6 2QL T 01628-502500 W www.mcgraw-hill.co.uk
Higher education and professional academic and reference books

MACMILLAN PUBLISHERS LTD
The Macmillan Building, 4 Crinan Street, London N1 9XW
T 020-7833 4000 W www.macmillan.com
Arts, biography, business, cookery, fiction, gardening history, humour, politics, sport, travel

METHUEN PUBLISHING LTD
11–12 Buckingham Gate, London SW1E 6LB T 020-7798 1600
W www.methuen.co.uk
Autobiography, biography, film, history, humour, literary fiction, performing arts, sport, travel

JOHN MURRAY (PUBLISHERS)
338 Euston Road, London NW1 3BH T 020-7873 6000
W www.johnmurray.co.uk, www.hachettelivreuk.co.uk
Biography and memoir, entertainment, fiction, history travel, true stories

W. W. NORTON & COMPANY
Castle House, 75–76 Wells Street, London W1T 3QT
T 020-7323 1579 W www.wwnorton.co.uk
Economics, English and American literature, music psychology, science. Founded 1980

THE ORION PUBLISHING GROUP LTD
Orion House, 5 Upper St Martin's Lane, London WC2H 9EA
T 020-7240 3444 W www.orionbooks.co.uk
Fiction, non-fiction and audio. Founded 1992

OXFORD UNIVERSITY PRESS
Great Clarendon Street, Oxford OX2 6DP T 01865-556767
W www.oup.com
Academic, dictionaries, literature, reference. Founded 1478

PEARSON EDUCATION
Edinburgh Gate, Harlow, Essex CM20 2JE T 01279-623623
W www.pearsoned.co.uk
Educational and professional materials

PENGUIN GROUP (UK)
80 Strand, London WC2R 0RL T 020-7010 3000
W www.penguin.co.uk
Biography, children's, current affairs, fiction, health history, humour, literature, politics, sports, travel

PHAIDON PRESS LTD
Regent's Wharf, All Saints Street, London N1 9PA
T 020-7843 1000 W www.phaidon.com
Visual arts

PIATKUS BOOKS
5 Windmill Street, London W1T 2JA T 020-7631 0710
W www.piatkus.co.uk
Biography, business and careers, fiction, health, history self-help

PROFILE BOOKS LTD
3A Exmouth House, Pine Street, London EC1R 0JH
T 020-7841 6300 W www.profilebooks.com
Biography, business management, current affairs, history politics, popular science. Founded 1996

QUERCUS BOOKS LTD
21 Bloomsbury Square, London WC1A 2NS T 020-7291 7200
W www.quercusbooks.co.uk
Fiction and non-fiction. Founded 2005

THE RANDOM HOUSE GROUP LTD
20 Vauxhall Bridge Road, London SW1V 2SA T 020-7840 8400
W www.randomhouse.co.uk
Biography, drama, fiction, general non-fiction, poetry, translations

THE READER'S DIGEST ASSOCIATION LTD
11 Westferry Circus, Canary Wharf, London E14 4HE
T 020-7715 8000
Condensed and series books, cookery, computers, folklore, gardening, handicrafts, law, music, nature, puzzles

RYLAND PETERS & SMALL
20–21 Jockey's Fields, London WC1R 4BW T 020-7025 2200
W www.rylandpeters.com
Illustrated books: food and drink, gift books, home and garden and wellbeing. Founded 1995

SCHOLASTIC LTD
Villiers House, Clarendon Avenue, Leamington Spa CV32 5PR
T 01926-887799 W www.scholastic.co.uk
Children's fiction and non-fiction and education for primary schools. Founded 1964

SERPENT'S TAIL
3A Exmouth House, Pine Street, London EC1R 0JH
T 020-7841 6300 W www.serpentstail.com
Fiction and non-fiction, literary and non-mainstream work, and work in translation. Founded 1986

SIMON & SCHUSTER UK LTD
Africa House, 64–78 Kingsway, London WC2B 6AH
T 020-7316 1900 W www.simonsays.co.uk
Commercial and literary fiction, non-fiction, children's. Founded 1986

SPRINGER-VERLAG LONDON LTD
Ashbourne House, The Guildway, Old Portsmouth Road, Guildford GU3 1LP T 01483-734666 W www.springer.com
Astronomy, biosciences, chemistry, computing, engineering, mathematics, medicine. Founded 1972

SWEET & MAXWELL
100 Avenue Road, London NW3 3PF T 020-7393 7000
Law. Founded 1799

TASCHEN UK LTD
5th Floor, 1 Heathcock Court, 415 Strand, London WC2R 0NS
T 020-7845 8580 W www.taschen.com
Architecture, art, design, film, lifestyle, photography, popular culture. Founded 1980

TAYLOR AND FRANCIS GROUP
2 and 4 Park Square, Milton Park, Abingdon, Oxon OX14 4RN
T 01235-828600 W www.tandf.co.uk, www.tfinforma.com
Academic and reference books

THAMES & HUDSON LTD
181A High Holborn, London WC1V 7QX T 020-7845 5000
W www.thamesandhudson.com
Illustrated non-fiction: archaeology, architecture, art, ethnic arts, fashion, graphic design, history, photography, religion

TRANSWORLD PUBLISHERS
61–63 Uxbridge Road, London W5 5SA T 020-8579 2652
W www.booksattransworld.co.uk
Biography, children's, fiction, history, popular science, sport, travel

TSO (THE STATIONERY OFFICE)
St Crispins, Duke Street, Norwich NR3 1PD T 0870-600 5522
W www.tso.co.uk
Business, current affairs, directories, highway code and driving guides, professional, reference

USBORNE PUBLISHING LTD
Usborne House, 83–85 Saffron Hill, London EC1N 8RT
T 020-7430 2800 W www.usborne.com
Children's fiction, non-fiction and reference. Founded 1973

V&A PUBLICATIONS
V&A Museum, South Kensington, London SW7 2RL
T 020-7942 2966 W www.vandabooks.com
Architecture, fine and decorative arts, contemporary design, fashion and photography. Founded 1980

VERSO LTD
6 Meard Street, London W1F 0EG T 020-7437 3546
W www.versobooks.com
Cultural studies, economics, history, philosophy, politics, sociology. Founded 1970

VIRGIN BOOKS LTD
Thames Wharf Studios, Rainville Road, London W6 9HA
T 020-7386 3300 W www.virgin.com/books
Biography, children's computing, fiction, food and drink, health, history, literature, nature, sport, travel. Founded 1991

WALKER BOOKS LTD
87 Vauxhall Walk, London SE11 5HJ T 020-7793 0909
W www.walkerbooks.co.uk
Children's picture books, non-fiction and novelty titles, junior and teenage fiction. Founded 1980

WILEY EUROPE LTD
The Atrium, Southern Gate, Chichester, West Sussex PO19 8SQ
T 01243-779777 W www.wiley.com
Academic and reference books and journals. Founded 1807

WORDSWORTH EDITIONS LTD
8B East Street, Ware, Herts SG12 9HJ T 01920-465167
W www.wordsworth-editions.com
Reprints of classic books: children's, literary, poetry, reference. Founded 1987

YALE UNIVERSITY PRESS LONDON
47 Bedford Square, London WC1B 3DP T 020-7079 4900
W www.yalebooks.co.uk
Architecture, art, biography, current affairs, economics, history, music, political science, religion. Founded 1961

EMPLOYERS' AND TRADE ASSOCIATIONS

Most national employers' associations are members of the Confederation of British Industry (CBI).

CBI

Centre Point, 103 New Oxford Street, London WC1A 1DU
T 020-7379 7400 W www.cbi.org.uk

The CBI was founded in 1965 and is an independent non-party political body financed by industry and commerce. It exists primarily to ensure that the government understands the intentions, needs and problems of British business. It is the recognised spokesman for the business viewpoint and is consulted as such by the government.

The CBI speaks for some 240,000 businesses that together employ approximately one-third of the private sector workforce. Member companies, which decide all policy positions, include 80 of the FTSE 100 index, some 200,000 small and medium-size firms, more than 20,000 manufacturers and over 150 sectoral associations.

The governing body of the CBI is the Chairmen's Committee, which meets four times a year in London under the chairmanship of the president. It is assisted by 16 expert standing committees which advise on the main aspects of policy. There are 12 regional councils and offices, covering the administrative regions of England, Wales, Scotland and Northern Ireland. There are also offices in Beijing, Brussels and Washington.
President, Martin Broughton

WALES: 2 Caspian Point, Caspian Way, Cardiff Bay, Cardiff CF10 4DQ T 029-2045 3710
Regional Director, David Rosser

SCOTLAND: 16 Robertson Street, Glasgow G2 8DS T 0141-222 2184
Regional Director, Ian McMillan

NORTHERN IRELAND: Scottish Amicable Building, 11 Donegall Square, Belfast BT1 5JE T 028-9032 6658
Regional Director, Nigel Smyth

ASSOCIATIONS

ADVERTISING ASSOCIATION 7th Floor North, Artillery House, 11–19 Artillery Row, London SW1P 1RT T 020-7340 1100 E aa@adassoc.org.uk W www.adassoc.org.uk
Chief Executive, Baroness Peta Buscombe

ASSOCIATION OF BRITISH INSURERS 51 Gresham Street, London EC2V 7HQ T 020-7600 3333 E info@abi.org.uk W www.abi.org.uk
Director-General, Stephen Haddrill

ASSOCIATION OF PRIVATE MARKET OPERATORS 4 Worrygoose Lane, Rotherham S60 4AD T 01709-700072 E marketsman2@aol.com
General Secretary, David J. Glasby

BLC LEATHER TECHNOLOGY CENTRE LTD Leather Trade House, Kings Park Road, Moulton Park, Northampton NN3 6JD T 01604-679999 E info@blcleathertech.com W www.blcleathertech.com
Sales Director, Adam Hughes

BRITISH APPAREL AND TEXTILE CONFEDERATION 5 Portland Place, London W1B 1PW T 020-7636 7788 E batc@dial.pipex.com
Director-General, John Wilson, OBE

BRITISH BANKERS' ASSOCIATION Pinners Hall, 105–108 Old Broad Street, London EC2N 1EX T 020-7216 8800 E info@bba.org.uk W www.bba.org.uk
Chief Executive, Angela Knight

BRITISH BEER AND PUB ASSOCIATION Market Towers, 1 Nine Elms Lane, London SW8 5NQ T 020-7627 9191 E web@beerandpub.com W www.beerandpub.com
Chief Executive Officer, Rob Hayward, OBE

BRITISH CLOTHING INDUSTRY ASSOCIATION LTD 5 Portland Place, London W1B 1PW T 020-7636 7788 E bcia@dial.pipex.com
Director, John Wilson, OBE

BRITISH ELECTROTECHNICAL AND ALLIED MANUFACTURERS' ASSOCIATION (BEAMA) Westminster Tower, 3 Albert Embankment, London SE1 7SL T 020-7793 3000 E info@beama.org.uk W www.beama.org.uk
Chief Executive Officer, David Dossett

BRITISH MARINE FEDERATION Marine House, Thorpe Lea Road, Egham TW20 8BF T 01784-473377 E info@britishmarine.co.uk W www.britishmarine.co.uk
Chief Executive, Rob Stevens, CB

BRITISH OFFICE SUPPLIES AND SERVICES (BOSS) FEDERATION 12 Corporation Street, High Wycombe HP13 6TQ T 0845-450 1565 E info@bossfederation.co.uk W www.bossfederation.co.uk
Chief Executive, Keith Davies

BRITISH PLASTICS FEDERATION 6 Bath Place, Rivington Street, London EC2A 3JE T 020-7457 5000 E bpf@bpf.co.uk W www.bpf.co.uk
Director-General, Peter Davis, OBE

BRITISH PORTS ASSOCIATION Africa House, 64–78 Kingsway, London WC2B 6AH T 020-7242 1200 E info@britishports.org.uk W www.britishports.org.uk
Director, David Whitehead

BRITISH PRINTING INDUSTRIES FEDERATION Farringdon Point, 29–35 Farringdon Road, London EC1M 3JF T 0870-240 4085 E info@bpif.org.uk W www.britishprint.com
Chief Executive, Michael Johnson

BRITISH PROPERTY FEDERATION 7th Floor, 1 Warwick Row, London SW1E 5ER T 020-7828 0111 E info@bpf.org.uk W www.bpf.org.uk
Chief Executive, Liz Peace

BRITISH RETAIL CONSORTIUM 2nd Floor, 21 Dartmouth Street, London SW1H 9BP T 020-7854 8900 E info@brc.org.uk W www.brc.org.uk
Director-General, Dr Kevin Hawkins, OBE

BRITISH TYRE MANUFACTURERS' ASSOCIATION LTD 6 Bath Place, Rivington Street, London EC2A 3JE T 020-7457 5040 E mail@btmauk.com W www.btmauk.com
Chief Executive, John Dorken

CHAMBER OF SHIPPING LTD Carthusian Court, 12 Carthusian Street, London EC1M 6EZ T 020-7417 2800 E postmaster@british-shipping.org W www.british-shipping.org
Director-General, Mark Brownrigg

CHEMICAL INDUSTRIES ASSOCIATION Kings Buildings, Smith Square, London SW1P 3JJ T 020-7834 3399 E enquiries@cia.org.uk W www.cia.org.uk
Chief Executive, Steve Elliott

CONFEDERATION OF PAPER INDUSTRIES 1 Rivenhall Road, Swindon SN5 7BD T 01793-889600 E cpi@paper.org.uk W www.paper.org.uk
Director-General, Dr Martin Oldman

CONFEDERATION OF PASSENGER TRANSPORT UK Drury House, 34–43 Russell Street, London WC2B 5HA T 020-7240 3131 E admin@cpt-uk.org W www.cpt-uk.org
Chief Executive, Simon Posner

CONSTRUCTION CONFEDERATION 55 Tufton Street, London SW1P 3QL T 0870-898 9090 E enquiries@thecc.org.uk W www.thecc.org.uk
Chief Executive, Stephen Ratcliffe

CONSTRUCTION PRODUCTS ASSOCIATION 26 Store Street, London WC1E 7BT T 020-7323 3770 E enquiries@constprod.org.uk W www.constprod.org.uk
Chief Executive, Michael Ankers, FRSA

DAIRY UK 93 Baker Street, London W1U 6QQ T 020-7486 7244 E info@dairyuk.org W www.dairyuk.org
Director-General, J. Begg

ENGINEERING EMPLOYERS' FEDERATION (EEF) Broadway House, Tothill Street, London SW1H 9NQ T 020-7222 7777 E enquiries@eef-fed.org.uk W www.eef.org.uk
Director-General, Martin Temple, CBE

FEDERATION OF BAKERS 6 Catherine Street, London WC2B 5JW T 020-7420 7190 W www.bakersfederation.org.uk
Director, Gordon Polson

FEDERATION OF MASTER BUILDERS Gordon Fisher House, 14–15 Great James Street, London WC1N 3DP T 020-7242 7583 E central@fmb.org.uk W www.fmb.org.uk
Director-General, Richard Diment

FEDERATION OF SPORTS AND PLAY ASSOCIATIONS Federation House, Stoneleigh Park, CV8 2RF T 024-7641 4999 E admin@sportsandplay.com W www.sportsandplay.com
Operations Director, David Pomfret

FINANCE AND LEASING ASSOCIATION 2nd Floor, Imperial House, 15–19 Kingsway, London WC2B 6UN T 020-7836 6511 E info@fla.org.uk W www.fla.org.uk
Director-General, Stephen Sklaroff

FOOD AND DRINK FEDERATION 6 Catherine Street, London WC2B 5JJ T 020-7836 2460 E generalenquiries@fdf.org.uk W www.fdf.org.uk
Director-General, Melanie Leech

FREIGHT TRANSPORT ASSOCIATION LTD Hermes House, St John's Road, Tunbridge Wells TN4 9UZ T 01892-526171 E enquiries@fta.co.uk W www.fta.co.uk
Chief Executive, Theo de Pencier

INSTITUTE OF CHARTERED FORESTERS 7A St Colme Street, Edinburgh EH3 6AA T 0131-225 2705 E icf@charteredforesters.org W www.charteredforesters.org
Executive Director, Shireen Chambers

KNITTING INDUSTRIES' FEDERATION LTD 12 Beaumanor Road, Leicester LE4 5QA T 0116-266 3332 E directorate@knitfed.co.uk
Director, Anne Carvell

LEATHER PRODUCERS' ASSOCIATION 8 Queensberry Road, Kettering NN15 7HL T 01536-483668 E jakopo@btinternet.com
National Secretary, Jack Purvis

MANAGEMENT CONSULTANCIES ASSOCIATION 60 Trafalgar Square, London WC2N 5CS T 020-7321 3990 E mca@mca.org.uk W www.mca.org.uk
Chief Executive, Peter Hill

NATIONAL FARMERS' UNION (NFU) Stoneleigh Park, Stoneleigh CV8 2TZ T 024-7685 8500 E nfu@nfuonline.com W www.nfuonline.com
Director-General, Richard Macdonald

NATIONAL FEDERATION OF RETAIL NEWSAGENTS Yeoman House, Sekforde Street, London EC1R 0HF T 020-7253 4225 E info@nfrn.org.uk W www.nfrnonline.com
President, Sam Whiteside

NATIONAL LANDLORDS ASSOCIATION 3rd floor, 22–26 Albert Embankment, London SE1 7TJ T 020-7840 8900 W www.landlords.org.uk
Chair, David Salusbury

NATIONAL MARKET TRADERS' FEDERATION Hampton House, Hawshaw Lane, Hoyland, Barnsley S74 0HA T 01226-749021 E enquiries@nmtf.co.uk W www.nmtf.co.uk
Chief Executive, Joe Harrison

NEWSPAPER PUBLISHERS ASSOCIATION LTD St Andrews House, 18–20 St Andrews Street, London EC4A 3AY T 020-7632 7430
Director, David Newell

NEWSPAPER SOCIETY St Andrews House, 18–20 St Andrews Street, London EC4A 3AY T 020-7632 7400 E ns@newspapersoc.org.uk W www.newspapersoc.org.uk
Director, David Newell

OIL AND GAS UK Second Floor, 232–242 Vauxhall Bridge Road, London SW1V 1AY T 020-7802 2400 E info@oilandgasuk.co.uk W www.oilandgasuk.co.uk
Chief Executive, Malcolm Webb

PUBLISHERS ASSOCIATION 29B Montague Street, London WC1B 5BW T 020-7691 9191 E mail@publishers.org.uk W www.publishers.org.uk
Chief Executive, A. R. Williams, OBE

RADIOCENTRE 77 Shaftesbury Avenue, London W1D 5DU T 020-7306 2603 E info@radiocentre.org W www.radiocentre.org
Chief Executive, Andrew Harrison

ROAD HAULAGE ASSOCIATION LTD Roadway House, 35 Monument Hill, Weybridge KT13 8RN T 01932-841515 E weybridge@rha.net W www.rha.net
Chief Executive, Roger King

SOCIETY OF BRITISH AEROSPACE COMPANIES LTD Salamanca Square, 9 Albert Embankment, London SE1 7SP T 020-7091 4500 E post@sbac.co.uk W www.sbac.co.uk
Director-General, Dr Sally Howes

SOCIETY OF MOTOR MANUFACTURERS AND TRADERS LTD Forbes House, Halkin Street, London SW1X 7DS T 020-7235 7000 W www.smmt.co.uk
Chief Executive, Christopher Macgowan

TIMBER TRADE FEDERATION The Building Centre, 26 Store Street, London WC1E 7BT T 020-7839 1891 E ttf@ttf.co.uk W www.ttf.co.uk
Chief Executive, John White

TRADE MARKS, PATENTS & DESIGNS FEDERATION Fifth Floor, 63–66 Hatton Gardens, London EC1N 8LE T 020-7242 3923 E admin@tmpdf.org.uk W www.tmpdf.org.uk
President, Dr M. T. Barlow

UK PETROLEUM INDUSTRY ASSOCIATION LTD 9 Kingsway, London WC2B 6XF T 020-7240 0289 E info@ukpia.com W www.ukpia.com
Director-General, Chris Hunt

ULSTER FARMERS' UNION 475 Antrim Road, Belfast BT15 3DA T 028-9037 0222 E info@ufuhq.com W www.ufuni.org
Chief Executive, Clarke Black

TRADE UNIONS

A trade union is an organisation of workers formed (historically) for the purpose of collective bargaining over pay and working conditions. Today, trade unions may also provide legal and financial advice, sickness benefits and education facilities to their members. Legally any employee has the right to join a trade union, but not all employers recognise all or any trade unions. Conversely an employee also has the right not to join a trade union, in particular since the practice of a "closed shop" system where all employees have to join the employer's preferred union, is no longer permitted. Below is a list of key dates in the development of British trade unionist movement.

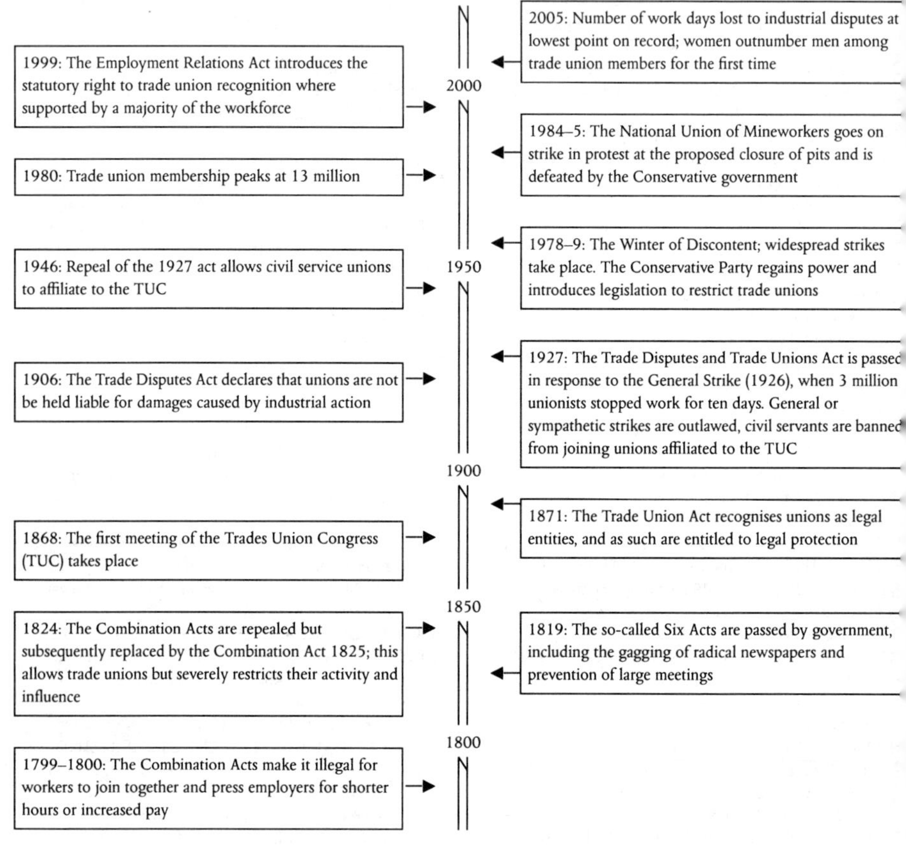

THE CENTRAL ARBITRATION COMMITTEE

PO Box 51547, London SE1 1ZG **T** 020-7904 2300
F 020-7904 2301 **E** enquiries@cac.gov.uk **W** www.cac.gov.uk

The Central Arbitration Committee deals with the following employment relations issues: arbitration in trade disputes; adjudication of complaints that an employer has failed to disclose information for collective bargaining purposes; determining claims for statutory recognition and derecognition; deciding on issues relating to the implementation of European Works Councils and the European Company Statute; and resolving applications and complaints under the Information and Consultation Regulations 2004, the European Public Limited Liability Company Regulations 2004, and the Transnational Information and Consultation of Employees Regulation 1999.

Chair, Sir Michael Burton
Chief Executive, Graeme Charles

TRADES UNION CONGRESS (TUC)

Congress House, 23–28 Great Russell Street, London WC1B 3LS **T** 020-7636 4030
E info@tuc.org.uk **W** www.tuc.org.uk

The Trades Union Congress, founded in 1868, is an independent association of trade unions. The TUC promotes the rights and welfare of those in work and helps the unemployed. It helps its member unions promote membership in new areas and industries, and campaigns for rights at work for all employees, including rt-time and temporary workers, whether union members not. TUC representatives sit on many public bodies at tional and international level such as government, litical parties, employers and the European Union.

The governing body of the TUC is the annual congress. tween congresses, business is conducted by a general uncil, which meets five times a year, and an executive mmittee, which meets monthly. The full-time staff is aded by the general secretary who is elected by con- ess and is a permanent member of the general council.

There are 63 affiliated unions, with a total membership nearly 6,500,000.

esident (2006–7), Alison Shepherd
neral Secretary, Brendan Barber

COTTISH TRADES UNION CONGRESS TUC)

3 Woodlands Road, Glasgow G3 6NG **T** 0141-337 8100
nfo@stuc.org.uk **W** www.stuc.org.uk

e congress was formed in 1897 and acts as a national ntre for the trade union movement in Scotland. The UC promotes the rights to welfare of those in work d helps the unemployed. It helps its member unions to omote membership in new areas and industries, and mpaigns for rights at work for all employees, including rt-time temporary workers, whether union members or t. It also makes representations to government and ployers. In March 2007 it consisted of 39 unions with otal membership of 633,462 and 24 directly affiliated des councils.

The annual congress in April elects a 36-member neral council on the basis of six sections.

air, Katrina Purcell
neral Secretary, Grahame Smith

ALES TUC

Cathedral Road, Cardiff CF11 9SD **T** 029-2034 7010
vtuc@tuc.org.uk **W** www.wtuc.org.uk

e Wales TUC was established in 1974 to ensure that role of the TUC was effectively undertaken in Wales. structure reflects the four economic regions of Wales d matches the regional committee areas of the National sembly of Wales. The regional committees oversee the livery of Wales TUC policy and campaigns in the evant regions, and liaise with local government, ining organisations and regional economic velopment bodies. The Wales TUC seeks to reduce employment, increase the levels of skill and pay, and minate discrimination.

The governing body of Wales TUC is the conference, ich meets annually in May and elects a general council ually of around 50 people) which oversees the work of TUC throughout the year.

There are over 50 affiliated unions, with a total mbership of around 500,000.

esident, Ruth Jones
neral Secretary, Felicity Williams

UC-AFFILIATED UNIONS

at April 2007

CORD Simmons House, 46 Old Bath Road, Charvil RG10 9QR **T** 0118-934 1808 **E** info@accordhq.org **W** www.accord-myunion.org
General Secretary, Ged Nichols *Membership:* 29,500

CM (ASSOCIATION FOR COLLEGE MANAGEMENT) 35 The Point, Market Harborough LE16 7QU **T** 01858-461110 **E** admin@acm.uk.com **W** www.acm.uk.com
General Secretary, Peter Pendle *Membership:* 3,894

AEP (ASSOCIATION OF EDUCATIONAL PSYCHOLOGISTS) 26 The Avenue, Durham DH1 4ED **T** 0191-384 9512 **E** sao@aep.org.uk **W** www.aep.org.uk
General Secretary, Charles Ward *Membership:* 3,118

AFA COUNCIL 7 (ASSOCIATION OF FLIGHT ATTENDANTS) United Airlines Cargo Centre, Shoreham Road East, Heathrow Airport TW6 3UA **T** 020-8276 6723 **E** afalhr@unitedafa.org **W** www.afalhr.org.uk
President, Saad Bhatkar *Membership:* 585

ANGU (ABBEY NATIONAL GROUP UNION) 2nd Floor, 16–17 High Street, Tring HP23 5AH **T** 01442-891122 **E** info@angu.org.uk **W** www.angu.org.uk
General Secretary, Linda Rolph *Membership:* 7,051

ASLEF (ASSOCIATED SOCIETY OF LOCOMOTIVE ENGINEERS AND FIREMEN) 9 Arkwright Road, London NW3 6AB **T** 020-7317 8600 **E** info@aslef.org.uk **W** www.aslef.org.uk
General Secretary, Keith Norman *Membership:* 18,500

ASPECT (FORMERLY NAEIAC) Woolley Hall, Woolley WF4 2JR **T** 01226-383428 **E** info@aspect.org.uk **W** www.aspect.org.uk
General Secretary, John Chowcat *Membership:* 4,000

ATL (ASSOCIATION OF TEACHERS AND LECTURERS) 7 Northumberland Street, London WC2N 5RD **T** 020-7930 6441 **E** info@atl.org.uk **W** www.atl.org.uk
President, Stuart Herdson *Membership:* 160,000

BACM-TEAM (BRITISH ASSOCIATION OF COLLIERY MANAGEMENT – TECHNICAL, ENERGY AND ADMINISTRATIVE MANAGEMENT) Daneham House, 6A South Parade, Doncaster DN1 2DY **T** 01302-815551 **E** enquiries@bacmteam.org.uk **W** www.bacmteam.org.uk
General Secretary, Patrick Carragher *Membership:* 2,908

BALPA (BRITISH AIR LINE PILOTS' ASSOCIATION) BALPA House, 5 Heathrow Boulevard, 278 Bath Road, West Drayton UB7 0DQ **T** 020-8476 4000 **E** balpa@balpa.org **W** www.balpa.org
Chair, Mervyn Granshaw *Membership:* 9,000

BDA (BRITISH DIETETIC ASSOCIATION) 5th Floor, Charles House, 148–149 Great Charles Street, Birmingham B3 3HT **T** 0121-200 8080 **E** info@bda.uk.com **W** www.bda.uk.com
President, Prof. Dame Barbara Clayton *Membership:* 5,000

BECTU (BROADCASTING, ENTERTAINMENT, CINEMATOGRAPH AND THEATRE UNION) 373–377 Clapham Road, London SW9 9BT **T** 020-7346 0900 **E** info@bectu.org.uk **W** www.bectu.org.uk
General Secretary, Gerry Morrisey *Membership:* 26,543

BFAWU (BAKERS, FOOD AND ALLIED WORKERS' UNION) Stanborough House, Great North Road, Stanborough, Welwyn Garden City AL8 7TA **T** 01707-260150 **E** bfawuho@aol.com **W** www.bfawu.org
General Secretary, Joe Marino *Membership:* 24,507

BIOS (BRITISH AND IRISH ORTHOPTIC SOCIETY) Tavistock House North, Tavistock Square, London WC1H 9HX **T** 020-7387 7992 **E** bios@orthoptics.org.uk **W** www.orthoptics.org.uk
Executive Officer, Denise Malone *Membership:* 999

BSU (BRITANNIA STAFF UNION) Court Lodge, Leonard Street, Leek ST13 5JP **T** 01538-399627 **E** staff.union@britannia.co.uk **W** www.britanniasu.org.uk
General Secretary, John Stoddard *Membership:* 3,200

CDNA (COMMUNITY AND DISTRICT NURSING ASSOCIATION) Thames Valley University, 18–22 Bond Street, London W5 5AA **T** 020-8231 0180 **E** info@cdnaonline.org **W** www.cdnaonline.org
Chief Executive, Anne Duffy *Membership:* 3,045

COMMUNITY Swinton House, 324 Gray's Inn Road, London WC1X 8DD **T** 020-7239 1200 **E** info@community-tu.org **W** www.community-tu.org
General Secretary, Michael Leahy, OBE *Membership:* 70,000

CONNECT (THE UNION FOR PROFESSIONALS IN COMMUNICATIONS) 30 St George's Road, London SW19 4BD **T** 020-8971 6000 **E** union@connectuk.org **W** www.connectuk.org
General Secretary, A. Askew *Membership:* 19,700

CSMTS (CARD SETTING MACHINE TENTERS' SOCIETY) 48 Scar End Lane, Staincliffe, Dewsbury WF13 4NY **T** 01924-400206
General Secretary, Anthony John Moorhouse *Membership:* 88

CSP (CHARTERED SOCIETY OF PHYSIOTHERAPY) 14 Bedford Row, London WC1R 4ED **T** 020-7306 6666 **E** enquiries@csp.org.uk **W** www.csp.org.uk
Chief Executive, Phil Gray *Membership:* 47,000

CWU (COMMUNICATION WORKERS UNION) 150 The Broadway, Wimbledon, London SW19 1RX **T** 020-8971 7200 **E** info@cwu.org **W** www.cwu.org
General Secretary, B. Hayes *Membership:* 247,042

DGSU (DERBYSHIRE GROUP STAFF UNION) The Lodge, Duffield Hall, DE56 1AG **T** 01332-844396 **E** deirdre.smith@dgsu.org.uk **W** www.dgsu.org.uk
Chair, Deirdre Smith *Membership:* 513

DSA (DIAGEO STAFF ASSOCIATION) Sun Works Cottage, Park Royal Brewery, London NW10 7RR **T** 020-8978 6069 **E** diageo.staff.association@diageo.com
Chair, Tara Kelly *Membership:* 408

EIS (EDUCATIONAL INSTITUTE OF SCOTLAND) 46 Moray Place, Edinburgh EH3 6BH **T** 0131-225 6244 **E** enquiries@eis.org.uk **W** www.eis.org.uk
President, Peter Quigley *Membership:* 59,000

EQUITY Guild House, Upper St Martin's Lane, London WC2H 9EG **T** 020-7379 6000 **E** info@equity.org.uk **W** www.equity.org.uk
General Secretary, Christine Payne *Membership:* 35,847

FBU (FIRE BRIGADES UNION) Bradley House, 68 Coombe Road, Kingston upon Thames KT2 7AE **T** 020-8541 1765 **E** office@fbu.org.uk **W** www.fbu.org.uk
President, Mick Shaw *Membership:* 47,000

FDA 8 Leake Street, London SE1 7NN **T** 020-7401 5555 **E** info@fda.org.uk **W** www.fda.org.uk
General Secretary, Jonathan Baume *Membership:* 18,175

GMB 22–24 Worple Road, London SW19 4DD **T** 020-8947 3131 **E** info@gmb.org.uk **W** www.gmb.org.uk
General Secretary, Paul Kenny *Membership:* 591,000

HCSA (HOSPITAL CONSULTANTS' AND SPECIALISTS' ASSOCIATION) 1 Kingsclere Road, Overton, Basingstoke RG25 3JA **T** 01256-771777 **E** conspec@hcsa.com **W** www.hcsa.com
Chief Executive, Stephen Campion *Membership:* 3,100

MU (MUSICIANS' UNION) 60–62 Clapham Road, London SW9 0JJ **T** 020-7582 5566 **E** info@musiciansunion.org.uk **W** www.musiciansunion.org.uk
General Secretary, John F. Smith *Membership:* 32,500

NACODS (NATIONAL ASSOCIATION OF COLLIERY OVERMEN, DEPUTIES AND SHOTFIRERS) Wadsworth House, 130–132 Doncaster Road, Barnsley S70 1TP **T** 01226-203743 **E** natnacods@aol.com **W** www.nacods.co.uk
General Secretary, Ian Parker *Membership:* 400

NACO (NATIONAL ASSOCIATION OF COOPERATIVE OFFICIALS) 6A Clarendon Place, Hyde, Cheshire SK14 2QZ **T** 0161-351 7900 **E** ndb@nacoco-op.org **W** www.naco.coop
President, Mark Craig *Membership:* 2,136

NAPO (TRADE UNION AND PROFESSIONAL ASSOCIATION FOR FAMILY COURT AND PROBATION STAFF) 4 Chivalry Road, London SW11 1HT **T** 020-7223 4887 **E** info@napo.org.uk **W** www.napo.org.uk
Chair, Mike McClelland *Membership:* 9,000

NASUWT (NATIONAL ASSOCIATION OF SCHOOLMASTERS/UNION OF WOMEN TEACHERS) Hillscourt Education Centre, Rose Hill, Rednal, Birmingham B45 8RS **T** 0121-453 6150 **E** nasuwt@mail.nasuwt.org.uk **W** www.teachersunion.org.uk
General Secretary, Chris Keates *Membership:* 251,763

NAUTILUS UK Oceanair House, 750–760 High Road, Leytonstone, London E11 3BB **T** 020-8989 6677 **E** enquiries@nautilusuk.org **W** www.nautilusuk.org
General Secretary, Brian Orrell *Membership:* 19,000

NGSU (NATIONWIDE GROUP STAFF UNION) Middleton Farmhouse, 37 Main Road, Middleton Cheney OX17 2QT **T** 01295-710767 **E** ngsu@ngsu.org.uk **W** www.ngsu.org.uk
President, Walter Wright *Membership:* 12,000

NUJ (NATIONAL UNION OF JOURNALISTS) Headland House, 308–312 Gray's Inn Road, London WC1X 8DP **T** 020-7278 7916 **E** info@nuj.org.uk **W** www.nuj.org.uk
General Secretary, Jeremy Dear *Membership:* 39,000

NUM (NATIONAL UNION OF MINEWORKERS) Miners' Offices, 2 Huddersfield Road, Barnsley S70 2LS **T** 01226-215555 **E** steve.kemp@nationalunionofmineworkers.com **W** www.num.org.uk
National Secretary, vacant *Membership:* 2,441

NUT (NATIONAL UNION OF TEACHERS) Hamilton House, Mabledon Place, London WC1H 9BD **T** 020-7388 6191 **W** www.teachers.org.uk
General Secretary, Steve Sinnott *Membership:* 368,06

PCS (PUBLIC AND COMMERCIAL SERVICES UNION) 160 Falcon Road, London SW11 2LN **T** 020-7924 2727 **E** editor@pcs.org.uk **W** www.pcs.org.uk
General Secretary, Mark Serwotka *Membership:* 325,0

PFA (PROFESSIONAL FOOTBALLERS' ASSOCIATION) 20 Oxford Court, Bishopsgate, Manchester M2 3WQ **T** 0161-236 0575 **E** info@thepfa.co.uk **W** www.givemefootball.com
Chief Executive, Gordon Taylor *Membership:* 2,435

POA (PRISON OFFICERS' ASSOCIATION) Cronin House, 245 Church Street, London N9 9HW **T** 020-8803 0255 **E** general@poauk.org.uk **W** www.poauk.org.uk
General Secretary, Brian Caton *Membership:* 35,806

PROSPECT New Prospect House, 8 Leake Street, London SE1 7NN **T** 020-7902 6600 **E** enquiries@prospect.org.uk **W** www.prospect.org.uk
President, Graeme Henderson *Membership:* 102,000

RMT (NATIONAL UNION OF RAIL, MARITIME AND TRANSPORT WORKERS) Unity House, 39 Chalton Street, London NW1 1JD **T** 020-7387 4771 **E** info@rmt.org.uk **W** www.rmt.org.uk
President, John Leach *Membership:* 75,000

SCP (SOCIETY OF CHIROPODISTS AND PODIATRISTS) 1 Fellmonger's Path, Tower Bridge Road, London SE1 3LY **T** 020-7234 8620 **E** enq@scpod.org **W** www.feetforlife.org
Chief Executive, Joanna Brown *Membership:* 10,000

SKISA (SKIPTON STAFF ASSOCIATION) 1 Providence Place, Skipton BD23 2HN **T** 01756-692000 **E** jennifer.tate@hml.co.uk
Chair, Jennifer A. Tate *Membership:* 1,400

SOR (SOCIETY OF RADIOGRAPHERS) 207 Providence Square, Mill Street, London SE1 2EW **T** 020-7740 7200 **E** info@sor.org **W** www.sor.org
Chief Executive, Richard Evans *Membership:* 18,300

TSSA (TRANSPORT SALARIED STAFFS' ASSOCIATION) Walkden House, 10 Melton Street, London NW1 2EJ **T** 020-7387 2101 **E** enquiries@tssa.org.uk **W** www.tssa.org.uk
President, Andy Bain *Membership:* 33,000

UBAC (UNION FOR BRADFORD AND BINGLEY STAFF AND STAFF IN ASSOCIATED COMPANIES) H13 PO Box 88, Croft Road, Croff Flats, W. Yorks BB16 2UA **T** 01653-697634 **E** ubac@btconnect.com
General Secretary, David Matthews *Membership:* 1,700

UCAC (UNDEB CENEDLAETHOL ATHRAWON CYMRU) (NATIONAL UNION OF THE TEACHERS OF WALES) Pen Roc, Rhodfa'r Môr, Aberystwyth SY23 2AZ **T** 01970-639950 **E** ucac@athrawon.com **W** www.athrawon.com
General Secretary, Gruff Hughes *Membership:* 4,000

UCATT (UNION OF CONSTRUCTION, ALLIED TRADES AND TECHNICIANS) UCATT House, 177 Abbeville Road, London SW4 9RL **T** 020-7622 2442 **E** info@ucatt.org.uk **W** www.ucatt.org.uk
General Secretary, Alan Ritchie *Membership:* 120,000

UCU (UNIVERSITY AND COLLEGE UNION) 27 Britannia Street, London WC1X 9JP **T** 020-7837 3636 **E** hq@ucu.org.uk **W** www.ucu.org.uk
Joint Presidents, Dr Dennis Hayes; Dr Steve Wharton *Membership:* 116,000

UNISON 1 Mabledon Place, London WC1H 9AJ **T** 0845-355 0845 **W** www.unison.org.uk
President, Malcolm Cantello *Membership:* 1,365,000

UNITE (FORMERLY AMICUS AND T&G)* 35 King Street, London WC2E 8JG **T** 0845-850 4242 **E** enquiries@amicustheunion.org **W** www.amicustheunion.org
General Secretaries, Derek Simpson; Tony Woodley *Membership:* 2,000,000

UNITY (FORMERLY CATU) Hillcrest House, Garth Street, Hanley, Stoke-on-Trent ST1 2AB **T** 01782-272755 **E** contact@unitytheunion.org.uk **W** www.unitytheunion.org.uk
General Secretary, Geoff Bagnall *Membership:* 9,000

URTU (UNITED ROAD TRANSPORT UNION) 76 High Lane, Chorlton-cum-Hardy, Manchester M21 9EF **T** 0800-526639 **E** info@urtu.com **W** www.urtu.com
President, Trevor Bray *Membership:* 16,500

USDAW (UNION OF SHOP, DISTRIBUTIVE AND ALLIED WORKERS) 188 Wilmslow Road, Manchester M14 6LJ **T** 0161-224 2804 **E** enquiries@usdaw.org.uk **W** www.usdaw.org.uk
General Secretary, John Hannett *Membership:* 341,000

WRITERS' GUILD OF GREAT BRITAIN (WGGB) 15 Britannia Street, London WC1X 9JN **T** 020-7833 0777 **E** admin@writersguild.org.uk **W** www.writersguild.org.uk
President, David Nobbs *Membership:* 2,000

YORKSHIRE INDEPENDENT STAFF ASSOCIATION (YISA) c/o Yorkshire Building Society, Yorkshire House, Yorkshire Drive, Rooley Lane, Bradford BD5 8LJ **T** 01274-472453 **E** kmwatson@ybs.co.uk
General Secretary, Yvonne Chapman *Membership:* 1,500

* Formed from the amalgamation of Amicus and T&G; an 18-month transitional period began on 1 May 2007. At the time of going to press, Unite agreed an accord with United Steeworkers (of the USA) to begin preparations for the creation of the first transatlantic trade union, which will represent over 3.4 million members in the UK, Ireland, USA and Canada

NON-AFFILIATED UNIONS

As at April 2007

ASCL (ASSOCIATION OF SCHOOL AND COLLEGE LEADERS) 130 Regent Road, Leicester LE1 7PG **T** 0116-299 1122 **E** info@ascl.org.uk **W** www.ascl.org.uk
General Secretary, Dr J. E. Dunford, OBE *Membership:* 13,200

BDA (BRITISH DENTAL ASSOCIATION) 64 Wimpole Street, London W1G 8YS **T** 020-7935 0875 **E** enquiries@bda.org **W** www.bda.org
President, Dr Sue Greening *Membership:* 18,000

CIOJ (CHARTERED INSTITUTE OF JOURNALISTS) 2 Dock Offices, Surrey Quays Road, London SE16 2XU **T** 020-7252 1187 **E** memberservices@cioj.co.uk **W** www.cioj.co.uk
President, Sangita Shah *Membership:* 2,000

NAHT (NATIONAL ASSOCIATION OF HEAD TEACHERS) 1 Heath Square, Boltro Road, Haywards Heath RH16 1BL **T** 01444-472472 **E** info@naht.org.uk **W** www.naht.org.uk
General Secretary, Mick Brookes *Membership:* 39,439

NSEAD (NATIONAL SOCIETY FOR EDUCATION IN ART AND DESIGN) The Gatehouse, Corsham Court, Corsham SN13 0BZ **T** 01249-714825 **E** bookshop@nsead.org **W** www.nsead.org
General Secretary, Dr J. M. Steers *Membership:* 2,500

PGA (PRISON GOVERNORS ASSOCIATION) Room 217, Cleland House, Page Street, London SW1P 4LN **T** 020-7217 8591 **E** charles.bushell@hmps.gsi.gov.uk
General Secretary, Charles Bushell *Membership:* 1,187

RBA (RETAIL BOOK ASSOCIATION) 22 Borough Fields Shopping Centre, Wootton Bassett, Swindon SN4 7AX **T** 01793-841414 **E** info@the-rba.org **W** www.the-rba.org
President, David Pickles *Membership:* 4,300

RCM (ROYAL COLLEGE OF MIDWIVES) 15 Mansfield Street, London W1G 9NH **T** 020-7312 3535 **E** info@rcm.org.uk **W** www.rcm.org.uk
General Secretary, Dame Karlene Davis, DBE *Membership:* 37,000

SOCIETY OF AUTHORS 84 Drayton Gardens, London SW10 9SB **T** 020-7373 6642 **E** info@societyofauthors.org **W** www.societyofauthors.org
General Secretary, Mark Le Fanu, OBE *Membership:* 8,000

SSTA (SCOTTISH SECONDARY TEACHERS' ASSOCIATION) 14 West End Place, Edinburgh EH11 2ED **T** 0131-313 7300 **E** info@ssta.org.uk **W** www.ssta.org.uk
General Secretary, David Eaglesham *Membership:* 9,500

SPORTS BODIES

SPORTS COUNCILS

CENTRAL COUNCIL OF PHYSICAL RECREATION 4th Floor, Burwood House, 14–16 Caxton Street, London SW1H 0QT **T** 020-7976 3900 **E** info@ccpr.org.uk **W** www.ccpr.org.uk
PA to Chief Executive, Tim Lamb

SPORT ENGLAND 3rd Floor, Victoria House, Bloomsbury Square, London WC1B 4SE **T** 0845-850 8508 **E** info@sportengland.org **W** www.sportengland.org
Chief Executive, Jennie Price

SPORTSCOTLAND Caledonia House, South Gyle, Edinburgh EH12 9DQ **T** 0131-317 7200 **E** library@sportscotland.org.uk **W** www.sportscotland.org.uk
Chief Executive, Stewart Harris

SPORTS COUNCIL FOR NORTHERN IRELAND House of Sport, Upper Malone Road, Belfast BT9 5LA **T** 028-9038 1222 **E** info@sportni.net **W** www.sportni.net
Chief Executive, Eamonn McCartan

SPORTS COUNCIL FOR WALES Sophia Gardens, Cardiff CF11 9SW **T** 0845-045 0904 **E** scw@scw.co.uk **W** www.sports-council-wales.org.uk
Chair, Philip Carling

UK SPORT 40 Bernard Street, London WC1N 1ST **T** 020-7211 5100 **E** info@uksport.gov.uk **W** www.uksport.gov.uk
Chair, Sue Campbell

AMERICAN FOOTBALL

BRITISH AMERICAN FOOTBALL ASSOCIATION West House, Hedley on the Hill, Stocksfield NE43 7SW **T** 01661-843179 **E** chairman@bafa.org.uk **W** www.bafa.org.uk
Chair, Gary Marshall

ANGLING

NATIONAL FEDERATION OF ANGLERS National Water Sports Centre, Adbolton Lane, Holme Pierrepoint, Nottingham NG12 2LU **T** 0115-981 3535 **E** office@nfadirect.com **W** www.nfadirect.com
Chief Executive Officer, Paul Baggaley

ARCHERY

GRAND NATIONAL ARCHERY SOCIETY Lilleshall National Sports Centre, Newport TF10 9AT **T** 01952-677888 **E** enquiries@gnas.org **W** www.gnas.org
Chief Executive, D. Sherratt

ASSOCIATION FOOTBALL

FOOTBALL ASSOCIATION 25 Soho Square, London W1D 4FA **T** 020-7745 4545 **W** www.thefa.com
Chief Executive, Brian Barwick

FOOTBALL ASSOCIATION OF WALES 11–12 Neptune Court, Vanguard Way, Cardiff CF24 5PJ **T** 029-2043 5830 **E** info@faw.org.uk **W** www.faw.org.uk
Secretary-General, David G. Collins

FOOTBALL LEAGUE 30 Gloucester Place, London W1U 8FL **T** 0870-4420 1888 **E** fl@football-league.co.uk **W** www.football-league.co.uk
Chair, Lord Mawhinney, PC

IRISH FOOTBALL ASSOCIATION 20 Windsor Avenue, Belfast BT9 6EG **T** 028-9066 9458 **E** info@irishfa.com **W** www.irishfa.com
President, Jim Boyce

IRISH PREMIER LEAGUE Benmore House, Unit 2, 343–353 Lisburn Road, Belfast BT9 7EN **T** 028-9066 9559 **E** enquiries@irishpremierleague.com **W** www.irishpremierleague.com
Secretary, Craig Stanfield

SCOTTISH FOOTBALL ASSOCIATION Hampden Park, Glasgow G42 9AY **T** 0141-616 6000 **E** info@scottishfa.co.uk **W** www.scottishfa.co.uk
Chief Executive, Gordon Smith

SCOTTISH FOOTBALL LEAGUE The National Stadium, Hampden Park, Glasgow G42 9EB **T** 0141-620 4160 **E** info@scottishfootballleague.com **W** www.scottishfootballleague.com
Secretary, Peter Donald

ATHLETICS

ATHLETICS ASSOCIATION OF WALES Cardiff Athletics Stadium, Leckwith Road, Cardiff CF11 8AZ **T** 0870-1622 530 **E** office@welshathletics.org **W** www.welshathletics.org
President, John Collins

NORTHERN IRELAND ATHLETIC FEDERATION Athletics House, Old Coach Road, Belfast BT9 5PR **T** 028-9060 2707 **E** info@niathletics.org **W** www.niathletics.org
Chair, David Seaton, MBE

SCOTTISH ATHLETICS 9A South Gyle Crescent, South Gyle, Edinburgh EH12 9EB **T** 0870-145 1500 **E** admin@scottishathletics.org.uk **W** www.scottishathletics.org.uk
Chief Executive, Geoff Wightman

UK ATHLETICS Athletics House, Central Boulevard, Blythe Valley Park, Solihull B90 8AJ **T** 0870-998 6800 **E** information@ukathletics.org.uk **W** www.ukathletics.net
President, Lynn Davies, CBE

BADMINTON

BADMINTON ASSOCIATION OF ENGLAND National Badminton Centre, Bradwell Road, Milton Keynes MK8 9LA **T** 01908-268400 **E** enquiries@badmintonengland.co.uk **W** www.badmintonengland.co.uk
President, John Havers

SCOTTISH BADMINTON UNION Cockburn Centre, 40 Bogmoor Place, Glasgow G51 4QT **T** 0141-445 1218 **E** enquiries@badmintonscotland.org.uk **W** www.badmintonscotland.org.uk
Chief Executive, Anne Smillie

WELSH BADMINTON UNION Unit E4, Southpoint Industrial Estate, Foreshore Road, Cardiff CF10 4SP **T** 029-2049 7225 **E** wbu@welshbadminton.net **W** www.welshbadminton.net
Chair, Robert Hall

BASEBALL

BASEBALLSOFTBALL UK Ariel House, 74A Charlotte Street, London W1T 4QJ **T** 020-7453 7055 **E** info@baseballsoftballuk.com **W** www.baseballsoftballuk.com
Head of Operations, Jenny Fromer

BASKETBALL

BASKETBALL SCOTLAND Caledonia House, 1 Redheughs Rigg, South Gyle, Edinburgh EH12 9DQ

T 0131-317 7260 E enquiries@basketball-scotland.com W www.basketball-scotland.com
Chief Executive Officer, Kevin Pringle

NGLAND BASKETBALL EIS Sheffield, Coleridge Road, Sheffield S9 5DA T 0870-774 4225 E info@englandbasketball.co.uk W www.englandbasketball.co.uk
Chief Executive, Keith Mair

ILLIARDS AND SNOOKER

ORLD LADIES BILLIARDS AND SNOOKER ASSOCIATION Richmond Lodge, 231 Ramnoth Road, Wisbech, PE13 2SN T 01945-588598 E admin@worldladiessnooker.co.uk W www.worldladiessnooker.co.uk
Chair, Mandy Fisher

ORLD PROFESSIONAL BILLIARDS AND SNOOKER ASSOCIATION 2nd Floor, Albert House, 111–117 Victoria Street, Bristol BS1 6AX T 0117-317 8200 E enq@worldsnooker.com W www.worldsnooker.com
Chair, Sir Rodney Walker

OBSLEIGH AND LUGE

RITISH BOB SKELETON ASSOCIATION 4–10 Barttelot Road, Horsham RH12 1DQ T 01403-221844 E hq@bobteamgb.org W www.bobteamgb.org
Chair, Peter Shakeshaft

RITISH BOBSLEIGH ASSOCIATION 4–10 Barttelot Road, Horsham RH12 1DQ T 01403-221844 E hq@bobteamgb.org W www.bobteamgb.org
Chair, Peter Shakeshaft

REAT BRITAIN LUGE ASSOCIATION 61 West Malvern Road, Malvern, Worcs WR14 4NF T 01684-576604 E markaluge@hotmail.com W www.gbla.org.uk
Chief Executive, Lt.-Col Mark Armstrong

OWLS

RITISH ISLES BOWLS COUNCIL 23 Leysland Avenue, Countesthorpe LE8 5XX T 0116-277 3234 E michaelswatland@btinternet.com W www.britishislesbowls.com
Hon. Secretary, Michael Swatland

RITISH ISLES WOMEN'S INDOOR BOWLS COUNCIL 19 Dinam Park Avenue, Ton Pentre CF41 7AT T 01443-439655 E secretary@wliba.com
Hon. Secretary, Hilary King

NGLISH BOWLING ASSOCIATION Lyndhurst Road, Worthing BN11 2AZ T 01903-820222 E ebaqueries@bowlsengland.com W www.bowlsengland.com
Chief Executive, A. Allcock, MBE

NGLISH INDOOR BOWLING ASSOCIATION David Cornwell House, Bowling Green, Leicester Road, Melton Mowbray LE13 0FA T 01664-481900 E enquiries@eiba.co.uk W www.eiba.co.uk
President, A. C. F. Turvey

NGLISH WOMEN'S BOWLING ASSOCIATION EWBA Office, Victoria Park, Archery Road, Royal Leamington Spa CV31 3PT T 01926-430686 E office@englishwomensbowling.net W www.englishwomensbowling.net
Chief Executive, Mrs P. A. Biddlecombe

NGLISH WOMEN'S INDOOR BOWLING ASSOCIATION 3 Moulton Business Park, Scirocco Close, Northampton NN3 6AP T 01604-494163 E ewiba@btconnect.com W www.ewiba.com
National Secretary, Tricia Thomas

BOXING

AMATEUR BOXING ASSOCIATION OF ENGLAND EIS Sheffield, Coleridge Road, Sheffield S9 5DA T 0114-223 5654 E info@abae.org.uk W www.abae.co.uk
Chief Executive, Paul King

BRITISH AMATEUR BOXING ASSOCIATION 96 High Street, Lochee, Dundee DD2 3AY T 01382-508261 E frankhendry@accnet.zzn.com
Chief Executive, Frank Hendry

BRITISH BOXING BOARD OF CONTROL The Old Library, Trinity Street, Cardiff CF10 1BH T 029-2036 7000 E info@bbbofc.com W www.bbbofc.com
General Secretary, Simon Block

CANOEING

BRITISH CANOE UNION John Dudderidge House, Adbolton Lane, West Bridgford, Nottingham NG2 5AS T 0845-370 9500 E info@bcu.org.uk W www.bcu.org.uk
Chief Executive, Paul Owen

CHESS

ENGLISH CHESS FEDERATION The Watch Oak, Chain Lane, Battle TN33 0YD T 01424-775222 E office@englishchess.org.uk W www.englishchess.org.uk
President, Gerry Walsh

CRICKET

ENGLAND AND WALES CRICKET BOARD Lord's Cricket Ground, London NW8 8QZ T 020-7432 1200 E reception@ecb.co.uk W www.ecb.co.uk
Chair, David Morgan

MCC Lord's Cricket Ground, St John's Wood, London NW8 8QZ T 020-7616 8500 E communications@mcc.org.uk W www.lords.org
Secretary and Chief Executive, Keith Bradshaw

CROQUET

CROQUET ASSOCIATION Cheltenham Croquet Club, Old Bath Road, Cheltenham GL53 7DF T 01242-242318 E caoffice@croquet.org.uk W www.croquet.org.uk
President, Bernard Neal

CURLING

BRITISH CURLING ASSOCIATION Scottish Institute of Sport, Airthrey Road, Stirling FK9 5PH T 01463-242922 W www.britishcurling.co.uk
Chair, Chris Hildrey

ROYAL CALEDONIAN CURLING CLUB Cairnie House, Avenue K, Ingliston Showground, Newbridge EH28 8NB T 0131-333 3003 E office@royalcaledoniancurlingclub.org W www.royalcaledoniancurlingclub.org
President, Alistair J. McCabe

CYCLING

BRITISH CYCLING FEDERATION National Cycling Centre, Stuart Street, Manchester M11 4DQ T 0870-871 2000 E info@britishcycling.org.uk W www.britishcycling.org.uk
President, Brian Cookson

CYCLING TIME TRIALS 77 Arlington Drive, Pennington, Leigh WN7 3QP T 01942-603976 E phil.heaton@cyclingtimetrials.org.uk W www.ctt.org.uk
National Secretary, Phil Heaton

DARTS

BRITISH DARTS ORGANISATION 2 Pages Lane, Muswell Hill, London N10 1PS T 020-8883 5544

E britishdartsorg@btconnect.com W www.bdodarts.com
Chair, Dave Alderman

EQUESTRIANISM

BRITISH EQUESTRIAN FEDERATION Stoneleigh Park, Kenilworth CV8 2RH T 024-7669 8871 E info@bef.co.uk W www.bef.co.uk
Chair, Hugh Thomas

BRITISH EVENTING Stoneleigh Park, Kenilworth CV8 2RN T 024-7669 8856 E info@britisheventing.com W www.britisheventing.com
Chief Executive, Peter Durrant

ETON FIVES

ETON FIVES ASSOCIATION 3 Bourchier Close, Sevenoaks TN13 1PD T 01732-458775 E efa@etonfives.co.uk W www.etonfives.co.uk
Chair, Richard Barber, OBE

FENCING

BRITISH FENCING ASSOCIATION 1 Baron's Gate, 33–35 Rothschild Road, London W4 5HT T 020-8742 3032 E enquiries@britishfencing.com W www.britishfencing.com
President, Keith A. Smith

GLIDING

BRITISH GLIDING ASSOCIATION 3rd Floor, Kimberley House, Vaughan Way, Leicester LE1 4SE T 0116-253 1051 E office@gliding.co.uk W www.gliding.co.uk
Chief Executive, Pete Stratten

GOLF

LADIES' GOLF UNION The Scores, St Andrews KY16 9AT T 01334-475811 E info@lgu.org W www.lgu.org
Chief Executive, Lesley Burn

THE ROYAL AND ANCIENT GOLF CLUB OF ST ANDREWS Golf Place, St Andrews KY16 9JD T 01334-460000 E thesecretary@randagc.org W www.randa.org
Secretary, Peter Dawson

GREYHOUND RACING

NATIONAL GREYHOUND RACING CLUB Twyman House, 16 Bonny Street, London NW1 9QD T 020-7267 9256 E mail@ngrc.org.uk W www.ngrc.org.uk
Chief Executive, Alistair McLean

GYMNASTICS

BRITISH GYMNASTICS Ford Hall, Lilleshall National Sports Centre, Newport TF10 9NB T 0845-129 7129 E information@british-gymnastics.org W www.british-gymnastics.org
Chief Executive, Alan Sommerville

HANDBALL

BRITISH HANDBALL ASSOCIATION 40 Newchurch Road, Rawtenstall, BB4 7QX T 01706-229354 E office@britishhandball.com W http://britishhandball.worldhandball.com
Chair, Stevie Neilson

HOCKEY

ENGLAND HOCKEY The National Hockey Stadium, Silbury Boulevard, Milton Keynes MK9 1HA T 01908-544644 E info@englandhockey.org W www.englandhockey.co.uk
Chair, Philip Kimberley

SCOTTISH HOCKEY UNION 589 Lanark Road, Edinburgh EH14 5DA T 0131-453 9070 E info@scottish-hockey.org.uk W www.scottish-hockey.org.uk
Chief Executive, Brent Deans

WELSH HOCKEY UNION Severn House, Station Terrace, Ely, Cardiff CF5 4AA T 029-2057 3940 E info@welsh-hockey.co.uk W www.welsh-hockey.co.uk
President, Anne Ellis, OBE

HORSERACING

BRITISH HORSERACING BOARD 151 Shaftesbury Avenue, London WC2H 8AL T 020-7152 0000 E info@bhb.co.uk W www.britishhorseracing.com
Chair, Martin Broughton

HORSERACING REGULATORY AUTHORITY 151 Shaftesbury Avenue, London WC2H 8AL T 020-7189 3800 E info@thehra.org W www.thehra.org
Chair, John Bridgeman, CBE, TD

THE JOCKEY CLUB 151 Shaftesbury Avenue, London WC2H 8AL T 020-7189 3800 E info@thejockeyclub.co.uk W www.thejockeyclub.co.uk
Senior Steward, Julian Richmond-Watson

ICE HOCKEY

ICE HOCKEY UK 19 Heather Avenue, Rise Park, Romford RM1 4SL T 07917-194264 E ihukoffice@yahoo.co.uk W www.icehockeyuk.co.uk
Chair, Bob Wilkinson

ICE SKATING

NATIONAL ICE SKATING ASSOCIATION OF THE UK National Ice Centre, Lower Parliament Street, Nottingham NG1 1LA T 0115-988 8060 E info@iceskating.org.uk W www.iceskating.org.uk
Chief Executive, Keith Horton

LACROSSE

ENGLISH LACROSSE ASSOCIATION 26 Wood Street, Manchester M3 3EF T 0161-834 4582 E info@englishlacrosse.co.uk W www.englishlacrosse.co.uk
Presidents, John Maynard; Romy Schofield

LAWN TENNIS

LAWN TENNIS ASSOCIATION 100 Priory Lane, London SW15 5JQ T 020-8487 7000 E info@lta.org.uk W www.lta.org.uk
President, Stuart Smith

MARTIAL ARTS

BRITISH JUDO ASSOCIATION Suite B, Loughborough Technology Park, Epinal Way, Loughborough LE11 3GE T 01509-631670 E bja@britishjudo.org.uk W www.britishjudo.org.uk
Chair, Densign White

BRITISH TAEKWONDO COUNCIL Yiewsley Leisure Centre, Otterfield Road, West Drayton UB7 8PE T 01895-427359 E admin@tkdcouncil.com W www.britishtaekwondocouncil.org
Chair, M. Prewett

MARTIAL ARTS DEVELOPMENT COMMISSION PO Box 416, Wembley, HA0 3WD T 0870-770 0461 E office@madec.org W www.madec.org
Chair, Richard Thomas

MODERN PENTATHLON

MODERN PENTATHLON ASSOCIATION OF GREAT BRITAIN Norwood House, University of Bath, Claverton Down, Bath BA2 7AY T 01225-386808

E enquiries@mpagb.org.uk W www.mpagb.org.uk
Chair, Anthony Temple, QC

MOTOR SPORTS

BRITISH SUPERBIKES RACE ORGANISATION MCRCB, PO Box 6450, Woodford Halse, Daventry NN11 3ZD T 01327-264010 E dougbarnfield@mcrcb.org W www.mcrcb-events.co.uk
General Manager, Doug Barnfield

MOTORCYCLE GREAT BRITAIN ACU House, Wood Street, Rugby CV21 2YX T 01788-566400 E admin@acu.org.uk W www.acu.org.uk
General Secretary, Gary Thompson, MBE, BEM

SCOTTISH AUTO CYCLE UNION 28 West Main Street, Uphall EH52 5DW T 01506-858354 E office@sacu.co.uk W www.sacu.co.uk
President, Andy Russell

THE MOTOR SPORTS ASSOCIATION Motor Sports House, Riverside Park, Colnbrook, SL3 0HG T 01753-765000 W www.msauk.org
Chief Executive, Colin Hilton

MOUNTAINEERING

BRITISH MOUNTAINEERING COUNCIL 177–179 Burton Road, Manchester M20 2BB T 0161-445 6111 E office@thebmc.co.uk W www.thebmc.co.uk
Chief Executive, Dave Turnbull

MULTI-SPORTS BODIES

BRITISH OLYMPIC ASSOCIATION 1 Wandsworth Plain, London SW18 1EH T 020-8871 2677 E boa@boa.org.uk W www.olympics.org.uk
Chief Executive, Simon Clegg, CBE

BRITISH UNIVERSITIES SPORTS ASSOCIATION 20–24 Kings Bench Street, London SE1 0QX T 020-7633 5080 E office@busa.org.uk W www.busa.org.uk
Chief Executive, Jenny Brown

COMMONWEALTH GAMES COUNCIL FOR ENGLAND PO Box 36288, London SE19 2YY T 020-8676 3543 E info@cgce.co.uk W www.cgce.co.uk
Chief Executive, Ann Hogbin

COMMONWEALTH GAMES FEDERATION Second Floor, 138 Piccadilly, London W1J 7NR T 020-7491 8801 E info@thecgf.com W www.thecgf.com
Chief Executive Officer, Michael Hooper

NETBALL

ALL ENGLAND NETBALL ASSOCIATION Netball House, 9 Paynes Park, Hitchin SG5 1EH T 01462-442344 E info@englandnetball.co.uk W www.englandnetball.co.uk
Chief Executive (acting), Paul Clark

NETBALL NORTHERN IRELAND House of Sport, Upper Malone Road, Belfast BT9 5LA T 028-9038 3806 E netballni@houseofsport.net
President (acting), Denise Prue

NETBALL SCOTLAND Suite 196, Second Floor, Central Chambers, 93 Hope Street, Glasgow G2 6LD T 0141-572 0114 E tellus@netballscotland.com W www.netballscotland.com
Chair, Brian McKelvie

WELSH NETBALL ASSOCIATION Second Floor, 33–35 Cathedral Rd, Cardiff CF11 9HB T 029-2023 7048 E welshnetball@welshnetball.com W www.welshnetball.co.uk
Chief Executive Officer, Mrs S. J. Holvey

ORIENTEERING

BRITISH ORIENTEERING FEDERATION 8A Stancliffe House, Whitworth Road, Darley Dale, Matlock DE4 2HJ T 01629-734042 E bof@britishorienteering.org.uk W www.britishorienteering.org.uk
Chair, Neil Cameron

POLO

THE HURLINGHAM POLO ASSOCIATION Manor Farm, Little Coxwell, Faringdon SN7 7LW T 01367-242828 E enquiries@hpa-polo.co.uk W www.hpa-polo.co.uk
Chair, Maj. C. O. P. Hanbury

RACKETS AND REAL TENNIS

TENNIS AND RACKETS ASSOCIATION c/o The Queen's Club, Palliser Road, London W14 9EQ T 020-7386 3447/8 E office@tennis-rackets.net W www.tennisandrackets.com
President, J. R. Greenwood

ROWING

AMATEUR ROWING ASSOCIATION The Priory, 6 Lower Mall, London W6 9DJ T 0870-060 7100 E info@ara-rowing.org W www.ara-rowing.org
National Manager, Rosemary Napp

HENLEY ROYAL REGATTA Regatta Headquarters, Henley-on-Thames RG9 2LY T 01491-572153 W www.hrr.co.uk
Secretary, D. G. M. Grist

RUGBY FIVES

THE RUGBY FIVES ASSOCIATION 32 Ashbourne Grove, East Dulwich, London SE22 8RL T 020-8693 0488 E ianfuller@lycos.com W www.rfa.org.uk
Director, Ian Fuller

RUGBY LEAGUE

BRITISH AMATEUR RUGBY LEAGUE ASSOCIATION West Yorkshire House, 4 New North Parade, Huddersfield HD1 5JP T 01484-544131 E info@barla.org.uk W www.barla.org.uk
President, Lord Lofthouse of Pontefract

THE RUGBY FOOTBALL LEAGUE Red Hall, Red Hall Lane, Leeds LS17 8NB T 0113-232 9111 E enquiries@rfl.uk.com W www.therfl.co.uk
Executive Chair, Richard Lewis

RUGBY UNION

IRISH RUGBY FOOTBALL UNION 62 Lansdowne Road, Ballsbridge, Dublin 4 T (+353) 1647 3800 E info@irishrugby.ie W www.irishrugby.ie
Chief Executive, P. R. Browne

RUGBY FOOTBALL UNION Rugby House, Rugby Road, Twickenham TW1 1DS T 0870-405 2000 E reception@rfu.com W www.rfu.com
Chief Executive, Frances Baron

RUGBY FOOTBALL UNION FOR WOMEN Rugby House, Rugby Road, Twickenham TW1 1DS T 020-8831 7996 E rfuw@therfu.com W www.rfu.com/rfuw.htm
President, Gill Burns, MBE

SCOTTISH RUGBY UNION Murrayfield, Roseburn Street, Edinburgh EH12 5PJ T 0131-346 5000 E feedback@sru.org.uk W www.scottishrugby.org
President, Andy Irvine

SCOTTISH WOMEN'S RUGBY UNION Scottish Rugby Union, Murrayfield, Edinburgh EH12 5PJ T 0131-346 5086 E jo.wells@sru.org.uk W www.scottishrugby.org
Chair, Sandra Kinnear

WELSH RUGBY UNION 1st Floor, Golate House, 101 St Mary Street, Cardiff CF10 1GE T 0870-013 8600 E info@wru.co.uk W www.wru.co.uk
Chief Executive, Roger Lewis

SHOOTING

CLAY PIGEON SHOOTING ASSOCIATION Edmonton House, Bisley Camp, Brookwood, Woking GU24 0NP **T** 01483-485400 **E** info@cpsa.co.uk **W** www.cpsa.co.uk
Chair, Terry Blaney

GREAT BRITAIN TARGET SHOOTING FEDERATION Edmonton House, Bisley Camp, Brookwood, Woking GU24 0NP **T** 01483-486948 **E** admin@gbtsf.org.uk **W** www.gbtsf.org.uk
Chair, P. J. Boakes

NATIONAL RIFLE ASSOCIATION Bisley, Brookwood, Woking GU24 0PB **T** 01483-797777 **E** info@nra.org.uk **W** www.nra.org.uk
Chair, John Jackman

NATIONAL SMALL-BORE RIFLE ASSOCIATION Lord Robert's Centre, Bisley Camp, Brookwood, Woking GU24 0NP **T** 0845-130 6772 **E** info@nsra.co.uk **W** www.nsra.co.uk
Chair (acting), Ken Nash

SKIING AND SNOWBOARDING

SNOWSPORT GB Hillend, Biggar Road, Midlothian EH10 7EF **T** 0131-445 7676 **E** info@snowsportgb.com **W** www.snowsportgb.com
President, Sir John Ritblat

SNOWSPORT SCOTLAND Hillend, Biggar Road, Midlothian, EH10 7EF **T** 0131-445 4151 **E** info@snowsportscotland.org **W** www.snowsportscotland.org
Chair, Craig McKillop

SPEEDWAY

SPEEDWAY CONTROL BUREAU ACU House, Wood Street, Rugby CV21 2YX **T** 01788-565603 **E** office@scbureau.plus.com
Chair, E. Bartlett

SQUASH RACKETS

ENGLAND SQUASH National Squash Centre, Rowsley Street, Manchester M11 3FF **T** 0161-231 4499 **E** enquiries@englandsquash.com **W** www.englandsquash.com
President, Jackie Robinson

SCOTTISH SQUASH Caledonia House, 1 Redheughs Rigg, South Gyle, Edinburgh EH12 9DQ **T** 0131-317 7343 **E** info@scottishsquash.org **W** www.scottishsquash.org
President, Rona McCraw

SQUASH WALES St Mellons Country Club, St Mellons, Cardiff CF3 2XR **T** 01633-682108 **E** squashwales@squashwales.co.uk **W** www.squashwales.co.uk
President, Alan James

SUB-AQUA

BRITISH SUB-AQUA CLUB Telford's Quay, South Pier Road, Ellesmere Port CH65 4FL **T** 0151-350 6200 **E** postmaster@bsac.com **W** www.bsac.com
Chair, M. Allen

SWIMMING

AMATEUR SWIMMING ASSOCIATION Harold Fern House, Derby Square, Loughborough LE11 5AL **T** 01509-618700 **E** customerservices@swimming.org **W** www.britishswimming.org
Chief Executive, D. Sparkes

SCOTTISH SWIMMING National Swimming Academy, University of Stirling, Stirling, FK9 4LA **T** 01786-466520 **E** info@scottishswimming.com **W** www.scottishswimming.com
Chair, Maureen Campbell

WELSH AMATEUR SWIMMING ASSOCIATION Wales National Pool, Sketty Lane, Swansea SA2 8QG **T** 01792-513636 **E** secretary@welshasa.co.uk **W** www.welshasa.co.uk
Chair, Vivian Perry

TABLE TENNIS

ENGLISH TABLE TENNIS ASSOCIATION Queensbury House, Havelock Road, Hastings TN34 1HF **T** 01424-722525 **E** admin@etta.co.uk **W** www.etta.co.uk
Chief Executive, R. Yule

SCOTTISH TABLE TENNIS ASSOCIATION Caledonia House, South Gyle, Edinburgh EH12 9DQ **T** 0131-317 8077 **E** sarah.moffat@ttscotland.com **W** www.ttscotland.com
Chair, Jonathan Whitaker

TABLE TENNIS ASSOCIATION OF WALES 8 Hopkins Close, Thornbury, Bristol BS35 2PX **T** 01454-417491 **E** ttaw@btinternet.com **W** www.ttaw.co.uk
Chair, Kim Johnson

VOLLEYBALL

ENGLISH VOLLEYBALL ASSOCIATION Suite B, Loughborough Technology Centre, Epinal Way, Loughborough LE11 3GE **T** 01509-631699 **E** general@eng-volleyball.demon.co.uk **W** www.volleyballengland.org
President, Richard Callicott

NORTHERN IRELAND VOLLEYBALL ASSOCIATION House of Sport, Upper Malone Road, Belfast BT9 5LA **T** 07966-056137 **E** nick@nivb.co.uk **W** www.nivb.co.uk
General Secretary, Nick Wright

SCOTTISH VOLLEYBALL ASSOCIATION 48 The Pleasance, Edinburgh EH8 9TJ **T** 0131-556 4633 **E** info@scottishvolleyball.org **W** www.scottishvolleyball.org
Chair, Margaret Ann Fleming

WALKING

RACE WALKING ASSOCIATION Hufflers, Heard's Lane, Shenfield, Brentwood CM15 0SF **T** 01277-220687 **E** racewalkingassociation@btinternet.com **W** www.racewalkingassociation.btinternet.co.uk
Hon. General Secretary, Peter Cassidy

WATER SKIING

BRITISH WATER SKI FEDERATION The Tower, Thorpe Road, Chertsey, KT16 8PH **T** 01932-570885 **E** info@bwsf.co.uk **W** www.britishwaterski.org.uk
Executive Officer, Patrick Donovan

WEIGHTLIFTING

BRITISH WEIGHTLIFTERS ASSOCIATION (BWLA) Lilleshall National Sports Centre, Nr. Newport TF10 9AT **T** 01952-604201 **E** lorraine.fleming@bwla.co.uk **W** www.bwla.co.uk
Chair, Bill Barton

WRESTLING

BRITISH WRESTLING ASSOCIATION 12 Westwood Lane, Chesterfield S43 1PA **T** 01246-236443 **E** admin@britishwrestling.org **W** www.britishwrestling.org
Chair, Malcolm Morley

YACHTING

ROYAL YACHTING ASSOCIATION RYA House, Ensign Way, Hamble, Southampton SO31 4YA **T** 0845-345 0400 **E** info@rya.org.uk **W** www.rya.org.uk
Chief Executive, Rod Carr, OBE

CLUBS

Originally called gentlemen's clubs, these organisations are permanent institutions with a fixed clubhouse, which usually includes restaurants, bars, a library and overnight accommodation. Members are fee-paying and typically vetted for their suitability.

Gentlemen's clubs were created for males of the English upper class and grew out of the seventeenth century fashion for coffee houses which enjoyed enormous popularity, despite opposition from Charles II, who believed they encouraged the spreading of royal disaffection. The first of the London clubs – White's – was founded in 1693 by Francesco Bianco in St James's Street, in the area that quickly became known as 'clubland' (*see* map below). Membership to the first of the clubs was a matter of hereditary privilege or special favour, a deliberately exclusionary measure which prompted an enormous growth in the number of clubs throughout the nineteenth century, fed by a burgeoning and aspirational middle class.

At the turn of the twentieth century, there were more than 200 gentlemen's clubs in London alone, half of which had been founded since 1870. Inevitably, this level of competition could not be sustained, particularly given the number of men killed in two world wars. Financial restrictions necessitated greater provision for women and the relaxation of the social qualifications needed for membership. Nevertheless, waiting lists still exist for the leading clubs and a recommendation from at least one current member is almost always required to join.

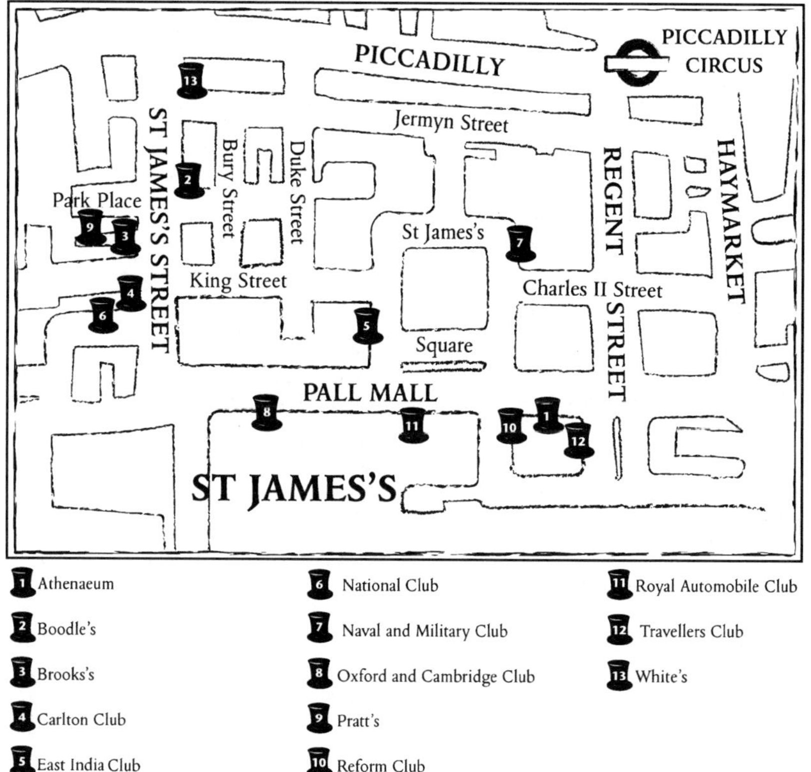

ARMY AND NAVY CLUB (1837), 36 Pall Mall, London SW1Y 5JN T 020-7930 9721 E secretary@therag.co.uk W www.armynavyclub.co.uk
Chief Executive and Secretary, Cdr. J. A. Holt, MBE, RN

ARTS CLUB (1863), 40 Dover Street, London W1S 4NP T 020-7499 8581 E secretary@theartsclub.co.uk W www.theartsclub.co.uk
Secretary, Brian Clivaz
Former members: Edgar Degas, Algernon Charles Swinburne, Ivan Turgenev

ATHENAEUM (1824), 107 Pall Mall, London SW1Y 5ER T 020-7930 4843 E library@hellenist.org.uk
Secretary, J. H. Ford
Former members: Matthew Arnold, Michael Faraday, Anthony Trollope

ATHENAEUM (1797), Church Alley, Liverpool L1 3DD T 0151-709 7770 E info@theathenaeum.org.uk W www.theathenaeum.org.uk
Honorary Secretary, H. Thompson

AUTHORS' CLUB (1892), 40 Dover Street, London W1S 4NP T 020-7408 5092 W www.theauthorsclub.co.uk
Secretary, Anna Drybala
Former members: E. M. Forster, Jerome K. Jerome, George Meredith

BATH AND COUNTY CLUB (1858), Queen's Parade, Bath BA1 2NJ T 01225-423732 E secretary@bathandcountyclub.com W www.bathandcountyclub.com
President, Sir Alec Morris, KBE, CB

BEEFSTEAK CLUB (1876) *(Men only)*, 9 Irving Street, London WC2H 7AH T 020-7930 5722 E beefsteakclub@tiscali.co.uk
Secretary, Maria Hibbert
Former members: John Betjeman, Rudyard Kipling, Harold Macmillan

BOODLE'S (1762), 28 St James's Street, London SW1A 1HJ T 020-7930 7166 E secretary@boodles.org
Secretary, Andrew Phillips
Former members: Winston Churchill, Ian Fleming

BROOKS'S (1764) *(Men only)*, St James's Street, London SW1A 1LN T 020-7493 4411 E secretary@brooksclub.org
Secretary, G. Snell
Former members: Edward Gibbon, Roy Jenkins, William Pitt

BUCK'S CLUB (1919) *(Men only)*, 18 Clifford Street, London W1S 3RF T 020-7734 2337
Secretary, Maj. Rupert Lendrum

CALEDONIAN CLUB (1891), 9 Halkin Street, London SW1X 7DR T 020-7235 5162 E admin@caledonianclub.com W www.caledonianclub.com
Secretary, P. J. Varney

CANNING CLUB (1910), 4 St James's Square, London SW1Y 4JU T 020-7827 5757 E canningclub@compuserve.com
Secretary, T. M. Harrington

CARLTON CLUB (1832), 69 St James's Street, London SW1A 1PJ T 020-7493 1164 E secretary@carltonclub.co.uk W www.carltonclub.co.uk
Secretary, A. E. Telfer
Former members: Stanley Baldwin, Benjamin Disraeli, William Gladstone

CAVALRY AND GUARDS CLUB (1890), 127 Piccadilly, London W1J 7PX T 020-7499 1261 E secretary@cavgds.co.uk W www.cavgds.co.uk
Secretary, D. Cowdery

CHELSEA ARTS CLUB (1891), 143 Old Church Street, London SW3 6EB T 020-7376 3311 E secretary@chelseaartsclub.com W www.chelseaartsclub.com
Secretary, D. Winterbottom

CITY LIVERY CLUB (1914), 38 St. Mary Axe, London EC3A 8EX T 020-7369 1672 E postbox@cityliveryclub.com W www.cityliveryclub.com
Hon. Secretary, P. Herbage

CITY OF LONDON CLUB (1832) *(Men only)*, 19 Old Broad Street, London EC2N 1DS T 020-7588 7991 E secretary@cityoflondonclub.com W www.cityoflondonclub.com
Secretary, Ian Faul
Former members: Robert Peel

CITY UNIVERSITY CLUB (1895), 50 Cornhill, London EC3V 3PD T 020-7626 8571 E secretary@cityuniversityclub.co.uk W www.cityuniversityclub.co.uk
Secretary, Miss R. C. Graham

THE COBDEN CLUB (1996), 170-172 Kensal Road, London W10 5BN T 020-8960 4222 W www.cobdenclub.co.uk
Membership Secretary, Lesley Young

THE COMMONWEALTH CLUB (1868), 25 Northumberland Avenue, London WC2N 5AP T 020-7766 9200 E info@rcsint.org W www.rcsint.org
Membership Secretary, Jamie Gould

DEN NORSKE KLUB LTD (1887), In & Out, 4 St James's Square, London SW1Y 4JU T 020-7839 6242 W www.dennorskeklub.co.uk
Secretary, Bjørg Tangen

DURHAM COUNTY CLUB (1890), 52 Old Elvet, Durham DH1 3HN T 0191-384 8156
Hon. Secretary, S. Smith

EAST INDIA CLUB (1849) *(Men only)*, 16 St James's Square, London SW1Y 4LH T 020-7930 1000 E secretary@eastindiaclub.co.uk W www.eastindiaclub.co.uk
Secretary, A. Bray

FARMERS CLUB (1842), 3 Whitehall Court, London SW1A 2EL T 020-7930 3751 W www.thefarmersclub.com
Secretary, Gp Capt. G. P. Carson

FOX CLUB 46 Clarges Street, London W1J 7ER T 020-7495 3656 E gerry@foxclublondon.com W www.foxclublondon.com
Secretary, Bethan Seaton

FREWEN CLUB (1869) *(Men only)*, 98 St Aldate's, Oxford OX1 1BT T 01865-243816
Hon. General Secretary, M. J. Dean

GARRICK CLUB (1831) *(Men only)*, 15 Garrick Street, London WC2E 9AY T 020-7379 6478 W www.garrickclub.co.uk
Secretary, Olaf Born
Former members: Charles Dickens, Henry Irving, William Thackeray

GROUCHO CLUB (1985), 45 Dean Street, London W1D 4QB T 020-7439 4685 E info@thegrouchoclub.com W www.thegrouchoclub.com
Secretary, Anna Hugo

HURLINGHAM CLUB (1869), Ranelagh Gardens, London SW6 3PR T 020-7736 8411
Chief Executive, Rear-Adm. Niall Kilgour
Former members: King Edward VII

LONDON PRESS CLUB (1882), St Bride Institute, 14 Bride Lane, London EC4Y 8EQ T 020-7353 7086 E info@londonpressclub.co.uk W www.londonpressclub.co.uk
Secretary, Dr Mark Bryant
Former members: Edgar Wallace, Lord Astor, Lord Rothermere

NATIONAL CLUB (1845), The National Club *(Men only)*, c/o 69 St James's Street, London SW1A 1PJ T 01225-463399 W www.thenationalclub.org.uk
Hon. Secretary, James Paice
Former members: Lord Coggan

NATIONAL LIBERAL CLUB (1882), Whitehall Place, London SW1A 2HE T 020-7930 9871 W www.nlc.org.uk
Secretary, S. J. Roberts
Former members: Ramsey MacDonald, George Bernard Shaw, H. G. Wells

NAVAL AND MILITARY CLUB (1862), 4 St James's Square, London SW1Y 4JU T 020-7827 5757 E club@navalandmilitaryclub.co.uk W www.navalandmilitaryclub.co.uk
Secretary, Ian Gregory

THE NEW CLUB (1874), 2 Montpellier Parade, Cheltenham GL50 1UD T 01242-541121 W www.thenewclub.co.uk
Hon. Secretary, Peter Chadwick

THE NEW CLUB (1787), 86 Princes Street, Edinburgh EH2 2BB T 0131-226 4881 E info@newclub.co.uk W www.newclub.co.uk
Secretary, Brig. Charles Ritchie

NEW CAVENDISH CLUB (1920), 44 Great Cumberland Place, London W1H 7BS T 020-7723 0391 E info@newcavendishclub.co.uk W www.newcavendishclub.co.uk
Chair, Christine Bird

NORTHERN COUNTIES CLUB (1829), 11 Hood Street, Newcastle upon Tyne NE1 6LH T 0191-232 2744 E secretary@northerncountiesclub.co.uk W www.northerncountiesclub.co.uk
Secretary, P. J. McCutcheon

ORIENTAL CLUB (1824), Stratford House, Stratford Place, London W1C 1ES T 020-7629 5126 W www.orientalclub.org.uk
Secretary, Capt. D. M. Swain, RN

OXFORD AND CAMBRIDGE CLUB (1836), 71 Pall Mall, London SW1Y 5HD T 020-7930 5151 E club@oandc.uk.com W www.oxfordandcambridgeclub.co.uk
Secretary, A. Telfer
Former members: Clement Attlee, William Gladstone, Duke of Wellington

PORTLAND CLUB (1816), 69 Brook Street, London W1Y 4ER T 020-7499 1523
Secretary, J. Burns, CBE

PRATT'S CLUB (1841) *(Men only)*, 14 Park Place, London SW1A 1LP T 020-7493 0397 E secretary@prattsclub.org
Secretary, Graham Snell
Former members: Winston Churchill

REFORM CLUB (1836), 104–105 Pall Mall, London SW1Y 5EW T 020-7930 9374 E generaloffice@reformclub.com W www.reformclub.com
Secretary, M. D. B. McKerchar
Former members: Isambard Kingdom Brunel, Guy Burgess, Henry James

ROYAL AIR FORCE CLUB (1918), 128 Piccadilly, London W1J 7PY T 020-7399 1000 E admin@rafclub.org.uk W www.rafclub.org.uk
Secretary, P. N. Owen

ROYAL ANGLO-BELGIAN CLUB (1955), 60 Knightsbridge, London SW1X 7LF T 020-7235 2121
Chairman, Jean Pierre Wellens

ROYAL AUTOMOBILE CLUB (1897), Pall Mall Clubhouse, 89 Pall Mall, London SW1Y 5HS T 020-7930 2345 W www.royalautomobileclub.co.uk
Secretary, A. I. G. Kennedy, CB, CBE
Former members: Winston Churchill, Charles Rolls

ROYAL NORTHERN & UNIVERSITY CLUB (1854), 9 Albyn Place, Aberdeen AB1 1YE T 01224-583292 W www.rnuc.org.uk
Secretary, Rosemary Black

ROYAL OVER-SEAS LEAGUE (1910), Over-Seas House, Park Place, St James's Street, London SW1A 1LR T 020-7408 0214 E info@rosl.org.uk W www.rosl.org.uk
Director-General, R. F. Newell, LVO

T STEPHEN'S CLUB (1870), 34 Queen Anne's Gate, London SW1H 9AB T 020-7222 1382 E info@ststephensclub.co.uk W www.ststephensclub.co.uk
Chief Executive, James M. Wilson
Former members: Benjamin Disraeli

SAVAGE CLUB (1857) *(Men only)*, 1 Whitehall Place, London SW1A 2HD T 020-7930 8118 E info@savageclub.com W www.savageclub.com
Hon. Secretary, Dr David Brown, CB
Former members: Edward Elgar, Dylan Thomas, Mark Twain

SAVILE CLUB (1868) *(Men only)*, 69 Brook Street, London W1K 4ER T 020-7629 5462 W www.savileclub.co.uk
Secretary, Julian Malone-Lee
Former members: Max Beerbohm, Thomas Hardy, Robert Louis Stevenson

SCOTTISH ARTS CLUB (1872), 24 Rutland Square, Edinburgh EH1 2BW T 0131-229 8157 E info@scottishartsclub.co.uk W www.scottishartsclub.co.uk
Club Master, Brian Stewart

SLOANE CLUB (1976), Lower Sloane Street, London SW1W 8BS T 020-7730 9131 W www.sloaneclub.co.uk
Secretary, Fran Bremner

SOHO HOUSE (1995), 40 Greek Street, London W1D 4EB T 020-7734 5188 W www.sohohouse.com

THREE ALBION PLACE (1849), 3 Albion Place, Leeds LS1 6JL T 0870-224 9333 W www.threealbionplace.co.uk
Sales Manager, M. Hirst

TRAVELLERS CLUB (1819) *(Men only)*, 106 Pall Mall, London SW1Y 5EP T 020-7930 8688 E secretary@thetravellersclub.org.uk W www.thetravellersclub.org.uk
Secretary, Malcolm S. Allcock
Former members: Arthur Balfour, Alec Douglas-Home, Anthony Powell

TURF CLUB (1868), 5 Carlton House Terrace, London SW1Y 5AQ T 020-7930 8555 E mail@turfclub.co.uk
Secretary, Lt.-Col. O. R. StJ. Breakwell, MBE

ULSTER REFORM CLUB (1885), 4 Royal Avenue, Belfast BT1 1DA T 028-9032 3411 E info@ulsterreformclub.com W www.ulsterreformclub.com
General Manager, A. W. Graham

UNIVERSITY WOMEN'S CLUB (1886) *(Women only)*, 2 Audley Square, London W1K 1DB T 020-7499 2268 E uwc@uwc-london.com W www.universitywomensclub.com
Secretary, Ms S. McCue *(acting)*

THE VICTORIA CLUB (1853), 8 Beresford Street, St Helier JE2 4WN T 01534-723381 E victoriaclub@jerseymail.co.uk W www.victoriaclubjersey.com
Manager, Martyn Styles

VINCENT'S (1863), 1A King Edward Street, Oxford OX1 4HS T 01865-722984 E vin5oxford@yahoo.co.uk W www.vincents.org
President, Doug Abbott
Former members: Roger Bannister, King Edward VIII

WESTERN CLUB (1825), 32 Royal Exchange Square, Glasgow G1 3AB T 0141-221 2016 E secretary@westernclub.co.uk W www.westernclub.co.uk
Secretary, Douglas Gifford

WHITE'S (1693) *(Men only)*, 37–38 St James's Street, London SW1A 1JG T 020-7493 6671
Secretary, D. A. Anderson
Former members: Beau Brummel, Horace Walpole, Evelyn Waugh

SOCIETIES AND INSTITUTIONS

ABBEYFIELD SOCIETY (1956), Abbeyfield House, 53 Victoria Street, St Albans AL1 3UW **T** 01727-857536 **E** post@abbeyfield.com **W** www.abbeyfield.com
Chief Executive, B. House

ACE STUDY TOURS (1958),Babraham, Cambridge CB22 3AP **T** 01223-835055 **E** ace@acestudytours.co.uk **W** www.acestudytours.co.uk
General Secretary, Paul Barnes

ACTION FOR BLIND PEOPLE (1857), 14–16 Verney Road, London SE16 3DZ **T** 020-7635 4800 **E** info@actionforblindpeople.org.uk **W** www.actionforblindpeople.org.uk
Chief Executive, Stephen Remington

ACTION MEDICAL RESEARCH (1952), Vincent House, Horsham RH12 2DP **T** 01403-210406 **E** info@action.org.uk **W** www.action.org.uk
Chief Executive, Simon Moore

ACTORS' BENEVOLENT FUND (1882), 6 Adam Street, London WC2N 6AD **T** 020-7836 6378 **E** office@abf.org.uk **W** www.actorsbenevolentfund.co.uk
General Secretary, Willie Bicket

ACTORS' CHARITABLE TRUST (1896), Africa House, 64–78 Kingsway, London WC2B 6BD **T** 020-7242 0111 **E** robert@tactactors.org **W** www.tactactors.org
General Secretary, Robert Ashby

ADAM SMITH INSTITUTE (1977), 23 Great Smith Street, London SW1P 3BL **T** 020-7222 4995 **W** www.adamsmith.org
President, Dr Madsen Pirie

ADVERTISING STANDARDS AUTHORITY (1962), Mid City Place, 71 High Holborn, London WC1V 6QT **T** 020-7492 2222 **E** enquiries@asa.org.uk **W** www.asa.org.uk
Director-General, Christopher Graham

AGE CONCERN (1940), Astral House, 1268 London Road, London SW16 4ER **T** 020-8765 7200, **Freephone** 0800-009 966 **W** www.ageconcern.org.uk
Director-General, Gordon Lishman, CBE

AGE CONCERN CYMRU, Ty John Pathy, 13–14 Neptune Court, Vanguard Way, Cardiff CF24 5PJ **T** 029-2043 1555 **E** enquiries@accymru.org.uk **W** www.accymru.org.uk
Director, R. W. Taylor

AGE CONCERN SCOTLAND (1943), Causewayside House, 160 Causewayside, Edinburgh EH9 1PR **T** 0845-833 0200 **E** enquiries@acscot.org.uk **W** www.ageconcernscotland.org.uk
Chair, Betty Bridgeford

AGRICULTURAL ENGINEERS ASSOCIATION (1875), Samuelson House, Paxton Road, Orton Centre, Peterborough PE2 5LT **T** 01733-362925 **E** ceo@aea.uk.com **W** www.aea.uk.com
Chief Executive Officer, Roger Lane-Nott

ALCOHOLICS ANONYMOUS (1947), PO Box 1, 10 Toft Green, York YO1 7NJ **T** 01904-644026 **W** www.alcoholics-anonymous.org.uk
General Secretary, Ann Napier

ALEXANDRA ROSE DAY (1912), 5 Mead Lane, Farnham GU9 7DY **T** 01252-726171 **E** enquiries@alexandraroseday.org.uk **W** www.alexandraroseday.org.uk
Operations Director, Diana le Clercq

ALZHEIMER'S SOCIETY (1979), Gordon House, 10 Greencoat Place, London SW1P 1PH **T** 020-7306 0606 **E** info@alzheimers.org.uk **W** www.alzheimers.org.uk
Chief Executive, Neil Hunt

AMNESTY INTERNATIONAL UNITED KINGDOM (1961), The Human Rights Action Centre, 17–25 New Inn Yard, London EC2A 3EA **T** 020-7033 1500 **E** information@amnesty.org.uk **W** www.amnesty.org.uk
UK Director, Kate Allen

AMREF UK (1957), Clifford's Inn, Fetter Lane, London EC4A 1BZ **T** 020-7400 0230 **E** info@amrefuk.org **W** www.amref.org/uk
Chief Executive, Jo Ensor

ANCIENT MONUMENTS SOCIETY (1924), St Ann's Vestry Hall, 2 Church Entry, London EC4V 5HB **T** 020-7236 3934 **E** office@ancientmonumentssociety.org.uk **W** www.ancientmonumentssociety.org.uk
Secretary, M. J. Saunders, MBE

ANGLO-BELGIAN SOCIETY (1982), 5 Hartley Close, Bickley BR1 2TP **T** 020-8467 8442 **E** secretary@anglo-belgiansoc.com **W** www.anglo-belgiansoc.com
Chair, David Colvin, CMG

ANGLO-DANISH SOCIETY (1924), 6 Keats Avenue, Littleover, Derby DE23 4ED **T** 01332-517160 **E** info@anglo-danishsociety.org.uk **W** www.anglo-danishsociety.org.uk
Chair, Simon Freeman

ANGLO-NORSE SOCIETY (1918), 25 Belgrave Square, London SW1X 8QD **T** 020-7235 9529 **E** secretariat@anglo-norse.org.uk **W** www.anglo-norse.org.uk
Chairman, Sir Richard Dales

ANIMAL CONCERN (1876), PO Box 5178, Dumbarton G82 5YJ T 01389-841639 E animals@jfrobins.force9.co.uk W www.animalconcern.com
Secretary, John F Robins

ANIMAL HEALTH TRUST (1942), Lanwades Park, Kentford, Newmarket CB8 7UU T 08700-502424 E info@aht.org.uk W www.aht.org.uk
Chief Executive Officer, Dr Peter Webbon

ANTHROPOSOPHICAL SOCIETY IN GREAT BRITAIN (1923), Rudolf Steiner House, 35 Park Road, London NW1 6XT T 020-7723 4400 E rsh-office@anth.org.uk W www.rsh.anth.org.uk
General Secretaries, Ann Druitt & Philip Martyn

ANTI-SLAVERY INTERNATIONAL (1839), Thomas Clarkson House, The Stableyard, Broomgrove Road, London SW9 9TL T 020-7501 8920 E antislavery@antislavery.org W www.antislavery.org
Director, Aidan McQuade

ARCHITECTS BENEVOLENT SOCIETY (1850), 43 Portland Place, London W1B 1QH T 020-7580 2823 E help@absnet.org.uk W www.absnet.org.uk
Company Secretary, Keith Robinson

ARCHITECTURAL HERITAGE FUND (1976), Clareville House, 26–27 Oxendon Street, London SW1Y 4EL T 020-7925 0199 E ahf@ahfund.org.uk W www.ahfund.org.uk
Chief Executive, I. Lush

ARLIS/UK AND IRELAND (1969), The Courtauld Institute of Art, Somerset House, The Strand, London WC2R 0RN T 020-7848 2703 E arlis@courtauld.ac.uk W www.arlis.org.uk
Chair, Vanessa Crane

ART FUND (1903), Millais House, 7 Cromwell Place, London SW7 2JN T 020-7225 4800 E info@artfund.org W www.artfund.org
Director, David Barrie

ARTHRITIS CARE (1947), 18 Stephenson Way, London NW1 2HD T 020-8800 4050 E helplines@arthritiscare.org.uk W www.arthritiscare.org.uk
Chief Executive, Neil Betteridge

ASLIB (1924), Holywell Centre, 1 Phipp Street, London EC2A 4PS T 020-7613 3031 E aslib@aslib.com W www.aslib.com
Managing Director, Roger Bowes

ASSOCIATION FOR LANGUAGE LEARNING (1990), 150 Railway Terrace, Rugby CV21 3HN T 01788-546443 E info@all-languages.org.uk W www.all-languages.co.uk
President, David Wilson

ASSOCIATION FOR THE PROTECTION OF RURAL SCOTLAND (1926), 3rd Floor, Gladstone's Land, 483 Lawnmarket, Edinburgh EH1 2NT T 0131-225 7012 E info@ruralscotland.org W www.ruralscotland.org
Director, Bill Wright

ASSOCIATION OF ACCOUNTING TECHNICIANS (1980), 154 Clerkenwell Road, London EC1R 5AD T 020-7837 8600 E aat@aat.org.uk W www.aat.org.uk
Chief Executive, Jane Scott Paul

ASSOCIATION OF ANAESTHETISTS OF GREAT BRITAIN AND IRELAND (1932), 21 Portland Place, London W1B 1PY T 020-7631 1650 E info@aagbi.org W www.aagbi.org
President, Dr David Whitaker

ASSOCIATION OF BRITISH DISPENSING OPTICIANS (1925), 199 Gloucester Terrace, London W2 6LD T 020-7298 5100 E general@abdo.org.uk W www.abdo.org.uk
General Secretary, Sir Anthony Garrett, CBE

ASSOCIATION OF BRITISH INSURERS (1985), 51 Gresham Street, London EC2V 7HQ T 020-7600 3333 E info@abi.org.uk W www.abi.org.uk
Director-General, Stephen Haddrill

ASSOCIATION OF BUILDING ENGINEERS (1925), Lutyens House, Billing Brook Road, Weston Favell, Northampton NN3 8NW T 01604-404121 E building.engineers@abe.org.uk W www.abe.org.uk
Chief Executive, D. Gibson

ASSOCIATION OF BUSINESS RECOVERY PROFESSIONALS (1990), 8th Floor, 120 Aldersgate Street, London EC1A 4JQ T 020-7566 4200 E association@r3.org.uk W www.r3.org.uk
Chief Operating Officer, Graham Rumney

ASSOCIATION OF CHARTERED CERTIFIED ACCOUNTANTS (1904), 29 Lincoln's Inn Fields, London WC2A 3EE T 020-7059 5000 E info@accaglobal.com W www.accaglobal.com
Chief Executive, Allen Blewitt

ASSOCIATION OF CONSULTING SCIENTISTS (1958), 14 Walnut Drive, Mile End, Colchester CO4 5ES T 01206-851755 E secretary@consultingscientists.co.uk W www.consultingscientists.co.uk
Secretary, Dr Diana Simpson

ASSOCIATION OF CONVENIENCE STORES LTD (1995), Federation House, 17 Farnborough Street, Farnborough GU14 8AG T 01252-515001 E acs@acs.org.uk W www.thelocalshop.com
Chief Executive, James Lowman

ASSOCIATION OF CORPORATE TREASURERS (1979), 51 Moorgate, London EC2R 6BH T 020-7847 2540 W www.treasurers.org
Chief Executive, Richard Raeburn

ASSOCIATION OF COUNTY CHIEF EXECUTIVES (1974), Chief Executive's Office, County Hall, Chester CH1 1SF T 01244-602174
Hon. Secretary, C. J. B. Taylor

ASSOCIATION OF DIRECTORS OF CHILDREN'S SERVICES (ADCS) (2007), Humanities Building, Devas Street, University of Manchester, Oxford Road, Manchester M13 9PL T 0161-275 8810 E info@adcs.org.uk W www.adcs.org.uk
Executive Director, Chris Waterman

ASSOCIATION OF DRAINAGE AUTHORITIES (1937), 12 Cranes Drive, Surbiton KT5 8AL
T 020-8399 7350 E admin@ada.org.uk W www.ada.org.uk
Chief Executive, Jean Venables, OBE

ASSOCIATION OF FRIENDLY SOCIETIES (1995), Denzell House, Dunham Road, Bowdon, Cheshire WA14 4PD T 0161-952 5051 E info@afs.org.uk
W www.afs.org.uk
General Secretary, Martin Shaw

ASSOCIATION OF GENEALOGISTS AND RESEARCHERS IN ARCHIVES (1968), 29 Badgers Close, Horsham RH12 5RU E agra@agra.org.uk
W www.agra.org.uk
Company Secretary, David R. Young

ASSOCIATION OF ROYAL NAVY OFFICERS (1920), 70 Porchester Terrace, London W2 3TP
T 020-7402 5231 E osec@arno.org.uk W www.arno.org.uk
Secretary, Cdr W. K. Ridley

ASSOCIATION OF SPEAKERS CLUBS (1971), 36 Pemberton Road, Winstanley, Wigan WN3 6DA
T 01942-222815 E natsec@tiscali.co.uk
W www.the-asc.org.uk
National President, Gwyn Redgers

ASTHMA UK (1989), Summit House, 70 Wilson Street, London EC2A 2DB T 020-7786 4900 E info@asthma.org.uk
W www.asthma.org.uk
Chief Executive, Donna Covey

AUTOMOBILE ASSOCIATION (1905), Southwood East, Apollo Rise, Farnborough GU14 0JW T 0800-085 2721
E customer.services@theaa.com W www.theaa.com
Managing Director, Tim Parker

BALTIC EXCHANGE (1744), 38 St Mary Axe, London EC3A 8BH T 020-7623 5501
E enquiries@balticexchange.com
W www.balticexchange.com
Chief Executive, Jeremy Penn

BALTIC EXCHANGE CHARITABLE SOCIETY (1978), 20 St Dunstans Hill, London EC3R 8HL
T 020-7283 6090
Secretary, R. J. M. Butler

BAR ASSOCIATION FOR LOCAL GOVERNMENT AND THE PUBLIC SERVICE (1945), c/o Birmingham City Council, Ingleby House, 11–14 Cannon Street, Birmingham B2 5EN T 0121-303 9991
E chairman@balgps.org.uk W www.balgps.org.uk
Chair, M. F. N. Ahmad

BARNARDO'S (1866), Tanners Lane, Barkingside, Ilford IG6 1QG T 020-8550 8822
E information@barnardos.org.uk W www.barnardos.org.uk
Chief Executive, Martin Narey

BARRISTERS' BENEVOLENT ASSOCIATION (1873), 14 Gray's Inn Square, London WC1R 5JP
T 020-7242 4761 E enquiries@the-bba.com
W www.the-bba.com
Director, Janet South

BEAT, Wensum House, 103 Prince of Wales Road, Norwich NR1 1DW T 0870-770 3256,
Helpline 0845-634 1414 **Youthline** 0845-634 7650
E info@b-eat.co.uk W www.b-eat.co.uk
Chief Executive, Mrs Susan Ringwood

BEVIN BOYS ASSOCIATION (1989), 1 Rundlestone Court, Poundbury, Dorchester DT1 3TN T 01305-261269
Vice-President and Public Relations, Warwick Taylor, MBE

BIBLIOGRAPHICAL SOCIETY (1892), c/o University of London, Institute of English Studies, Senate House, Malet Street, London WC1E 7HU T 020-7862 8679
E admin@bibsoc.org.uk W www.bibsoc.org.uk
Hon. Secretary, M. L. Ford

BIRMINGHAM AND WARWICKSHIRE ARCHAEOLOGICAL SOCIETY (1870), c/o Birmingham and Midland Institute, Margaret Street, Birmingham B3 3BS W www.bwas.org.uk
President, Mr P. Watson

BLUE CROSS (1897), Shilton Road, Burford OX18 4PF
T 01993-822651 E info@bluecross.org.uk
W www.bluecross.org.uk
Chief Executive, John Rutter

BOOK AID INTERNATIONAL (1954), 39–41 Coldharbour Lane, London SE5 9NR
T 020-7733 3577 E info@bookaid.org
W www.bookaid.org
Director, Sara Harrity, MBE

BOOKSELLERS ASSOCIATION OF THE UK & IRELAND LTD (1895), Minster House, 272 Vauxhall Bridge Road, London SW1V 1BA T 020-7802 0802
E mail@booksellers.org.uk W www.booksellers.org.uk
Chief Executive, T. E. Godfray

BOOKTRUST (1926), Book House, 45 East Hill, London SW18 2QZ T 020-8516 2977
E query@booktrust.org.uk W www.booktrust.org.uk
Director, Chris Meade

BOTANICAL SOCIETY OF SCOTLAND (1836), c/o Royal Botanic Garden Edinburgh, 20A Inverleith Row, Edinburgh EH3 5LR T 0131-552 7171
W www.botsocscot.org.uk
Hon. General Secretary, Dr M. P. Cochrane

BOTANICAL SOCIETY OF THE BRITISH ISLES (1836), c/o Department of Botany, The Natural History Museum, Cromwell Road, London SW7 5BD
T 020-7942 5002 E coordinator@bsbi.org.uk
W www.bsbi.org.uk
Director of Research and Development, K. Walker

BOYS' BRIGADE (1883), Felden Lodge, Felden, Hemel Hempstead HP3 0BL T 01442-231681
E enquiries@boys-brigade.org.uk
W www.boys-brigade.org.uk
Brigade Secretary, Steven Dickinson

BRISTOL AND GLOUCESTERSHIRE ARCHAEOLOGICAL SOCIETY (1876), Stonehatch, Oakridge Lynch, Stroud GL6 7NR T 01285-760460 E john@loosleyj.freeserve.co.uk W www.bgas.org.uk
Hon. General Secretary, John Loosley

BRITISH ACADEMY OF FORENSIC SCIENCES (1960), Haematology Department, ICMS, Barts and The London, 4 Newark Street, London E1 2AT T 020-7882 2276 E y.d.syndercombe-court@qmul.ac.uk W www.bafs.org.uk
Secretary-General, Dr Denise Syndercombe Court

BRITISH AND FOREIGN BIBLE SOCIETY (1804), Stonehill Green, Westlea, Swindon SN5 7DG T 01793-418100 E contactus@biblesociety.org.uk W www.biblesociety.org.uk
Chief Executive, James Catford

BRITISH ANTIQUE DEALERS' ASSOCIATION (1918), 20 Rutland Gate, London SW7 1BD T 020-7589 4128 E info@bada.org W www.bada.org
Secretary-General, Mrs E. J. Dean

BRITISH ASSOCIATION FOR EARLY CHILDHOOD EDUCATION (1923), 136 Cavell Street, London E1 2JA T 020-7539 5400 E office@early-education.org.uk W www.early-education.org.uk
Chief Executive, Anne Nelson

BRITISH ASSOCIATION FOR THE ADVANCEMENT OF SCIENCE (1831), Wellcome Wolfson Building, 165 Queen's Gate, London SW7 5HD T 0870-770 7101 E info@the-ba.net W www.the-ba.net
Chief Executive, Sir Roland Jackson

BRITISH ASSOCIATION OF COMMUNICATORS IN BUSINESS (1949), Suite GA2, Oak House, Woodlands Business Park, Breckland, Linford Wood West MK14 6EY T 01908-313755 E enquiries@cib.uk.com W www.cib.uk.com
Secretary-General, Kathie Jones

BRITISH ASSOCIATION OF SOCIAL WORKERS (1970), 16 Kent Street, Birmingham B5 6RD T 0121-622 3911 W www.basw.co.uk
Director, I. Johnston

BRITISH ASTRONOMICAL ASSOCIATION (1890), Burlington House, Piccadilly, London W1J 0DU T 020-7734 4145 E office@britastro.org W www.britastro.org
President, Dr Richard Miles

BRITISH BEEKEEPERS' ASSOCIATION (1874), National Beekeeping Centre, Stoneleigh Park, Kenilworth CV8 2LG T 024-7669 6679 E bbka@britishbeekeepers.com W www.britishbeekeepers.com
General Secretary, Martin Tovey

BRITISH BOARD OF FILM CLASSIFICATION (1912), 3 Soho Square, London W1D 3HD T 020-7440 1570 E contact_the_bbfc@bbfc.co.uk W www.bbfc.co.uk
Director, David Cooke

BRITISH CATTLE BREEDERS' CLUB LTD (1946), Lake Villa, Bradworthy, Holsworthy, Devon EX22 7SQ T 01409-241579 E lesley.lewin@cattlebreeders.org.uk W www.cattlebreeders.org.uk
Secretary, Mrs Lesley Lewin

BRITISH CHAMBERS OF COMMERCE, 65 Petty France, St James Park, London SW1H 9EU T 020-7654 5800 E info@britishchambers.org.uk W www.chamberonline.co.uk
Director-General, David Frost

BRITISH COPYRIGHT COUNCIL (1965), 29–33 Berners Street, London W1T 3AB T 01986-788122 E secretary@britishcopyright.org W www.britishcopyright.org
Secretary, Janet Ibbotson

BRITISH DEAF ASSOCIATION (1890), 1–3 Worship Street, London EC2A 2AB T 02476-550936 E midlands@signcommunity.org.uk W www.signcommunity.org.uk
Executive Chair, Francis P. Murphy

BRITISH DENTAL ASSOCIATION (1880), 64 Wimpole Street, London W1G 8YS T 020-7935 0875 E enquiries@bda.org W www.bda.org
Chief Executive, Peter Ward

BRITISH ECOLOGICAL SOCIETY (1913), 26 Blades Court, Putney, London SW15 2NU T 020-8871 9797 E info@britishecologicalsociety.org W www.britishecologicalsociety.org
Executive Secretary, Dr Hazel Norman

BRITISH EXPERTISE (1965), One Westminster Palace Gardens, 1–7 Artillery Row, London SW1P 1RJ T 020-7222 3651 E mail@britishexpertise.org W www.bccb.org.uk
Chief Executive, G. Hand

BRITISH FALSE MEMORY SOCIETY (1993),Bradford on Avon BA15 1NF T 01225-868682 E bfms@bfms.org.uk W www.bfms.org.uk
Director, M. Greenhalgh

BRITISH FEDERATION OF WOMEN GRADUATES (1907), 4 Mandeville Courtyard, 142 Battersea Park Road, London SW11 4NB T 020-7498 8037 E hq@bfwg.org.uk W www.bfwg.org.uk
Secretary, Mrs A. B. Stein

BRITISH HEART FOUNDATION (1961), 14 Fitzhardinge Street, London W1H 6DH T 020-7935 0185 E internet@bhf.org.uk W www.bhf.org.uk
Director-General, Peter Hollins

BRITISH HEDGEHOG PRESERVATION SOCIETY (1982), Hedgehog House, Dhustone, Ludlow SY8 3PL T 01584-890801 E info@britishhedgehogs.org.uk W www.britishhedgehogs.org.uk
Chief Executive, Fay Vass

BRITISH HERPETOLOGICAL SOCIETY (1947), c/o The Zoological Society of London, Regent's Park, London NW1 4RY T 01674-671676 E enquiries@thebhs.org W www.thebhs.org
President, Prof. Trevor J. C. Beebee

BRITISH HOROLOGICAL INSTITUTE (1858), Upton Hall, Upton, Newark NG23 5TE **T** 01636-813795 **E** info@bhi.co.uk **W** www.bhi.co.uk

BRITISH HUMANIST ASSOCIATION, 1 Gower Street, London WC1E 6HD **T** 020-7079 3580 **E** info@humanism.org.uk **W** www.humanism.org.uk
Chief Executive, Hanne Stinson

BRITISH INSTITUTE IN EASTERN AFRICA (1959), 10 Carlton House Terrace, London SW1Y 5AH **T** 020-7969 5201 **E** biea@britac.ac.uk **W** www.biea.ac.uk
Director, Dr Justin Willis

BRITISH INSTITUTE OF PROFESSIONAL PHOTOGRAPHY (1901), Fox Talbot House, Amwell End, Ware SG12 9HN **T** 01920-464011 **E** info@bipp.com **W** www.bipp.com
Chief Executive Officer, Chris Harper

BRITISH-ISRAEL-WORLD FEDERATION (1919), 121 Low Etherley, Bishop Auckland, Co Durham DL14 0HA **T** 01388-834395 **E** admin@britishisrael.co.uk **W** www.britishisrael.co.uk
President, M. A. Clark

BRITISH LUNG FOUNDATION (1985), 73–75 Goswell Road, London EC1V 7ER **T** 08458-505020 **W** www.lunguk.org
Chief Executive, Dame Helena Shovelton, DBE

BRITISH MANAGEMENT DATA FOUNDATION (1979), Highfield, Longridge, Sheepscombe GL6 7QU **T** 01452-812837 **E** bmdfstroud@aol.com **W** www.bmdf.co.uk
Director, Anthony Cowgill, MBE

BRITISH MEDICAL ASSOCIATION (1832), BMA House, Tavistock Square, London WC1H 9JP **T** 020-7387 4499 **W** www.bma.org.uk
Chief Executive, Tony Bourne

BRITISH MENSA LTD (1946), St John's House, St John's Square, Wolverhampton WV2 4AH **T** 01902-772771 **E** enquiries@mensa.org.uk **W** www.mensa.org.uk
Chief Executive and Company Secretary, John Stevenage

BRITISH MUSIC HALL SOCIETY (1963), 'Meander', 361 Watford Road, Chiswell Green, St Albans AL2 3DB **T** 01727-768878 **W** www.music-hall-society.com
President, Roy Hudd

BRITISH MUSIC INFORMATION CENTRE (1967), 1st Floor, Lincoln House, 75 Westminster Bridge Road, London SE1 7HS **T** 020-7928 1902 **E** info@bmic.co.uk **W** www.bmic.co.uk
Director, Matthew Greenall

BRITISH NATURALISTS' ASSOCIATION (1905), 1 Bracken Mews, London E4 7UT **W** www.bna-naturalists.org
Hon. Membership Secretary, Yvonne Griffiths

BRITISH NUCLEAR ENERGY SOCIETY (1962), 1 Great George Street, London SW1P 3AA **T** 020-7665 2241 **E** mark.askew@ice.org.uk **W** www.bnes.org.uk
Secretary, Mark Askew

BRITISH NUTRITION FOUNDATION (1967), High Holborn House, 52–54 High Holborn, London WC1V 6RQ **T** 020-7404 6504 **E** postbox@nutrition.org.uk **W** www.nutrition.org.uk
Director-General, Prof. R. S. Pickard, PHD

BRITISH PHARMACOLOGICAL SOCIETY (1931), 16 Angel Gate, City Road, London EC1V 2SG **T** 020-7417 0110 **E** ml@bps.ac.uk **W** www.bps.ac.uk
President, Prof. G. Henderson

BRITISH PSYCHOLOGICAL SOCIETY (1901), St Andrews House, 48 Princess Road East, Leicester LE1 7DR **T** 0116-254 9568 **E** enquiry@bps.org.uk **W** www.bps.org.uk
President, Pam Maras

BRITISH RED CROSS (1870), 44 Moorfields, London EC2Y 9AL **T** 0870-170 7000 **E** information@redcross.org.uk **W** www.redcross.org.uk
Chief Executive, Sir Nicholas Young

BRITISH TRUST FOR ORNITHOLOGY (1933), The Nunnery, Thetford IP24 2PU **T** 01842-750050 **E** info@bto.org **W** www.bto.org
Director, Prof. Jeremy Greenwood

BRITISH VETERINARY ASSOCIATION (1883), 7 Mansfield Street, London W1G 9NQ **T** 020-7636 6541 **E** bvahq@bva.co.uk **W** www.bva.co.uk
Company Secretary, Henrietta Alderman

BTBS THE BOOK TRADE CHARITY (1837), The Foyle Centre, The Retreat, Kings Langley WD4 8LT **T** 01923-263128 **E** btbs@booktradecharity.demon.co.uk **W** www.booktradecharity.demon.co.uk
Chief Executive, David Hicks

BUCKINGHAMSHIRE ARCHAEOLOGICAL SOCIETY (1847), County Museum, Church Street, Aylesbury HP20 2QP **T** 01296-678114 **E** bucksas@buckscc.gov.uk
Hon. Secretary, Maureen Brown

BUILDING SOCIETIES ASSOCIATION (1869), 23 Kingsway, London WC2B 6UJ **T** 020-7437 0655 **E** information@bsa.org.uk **W** www.bsa.org.uk
Director-General, A. Coles

CAFOD (CATHOLIC FUND FOR OVERSEAS DEVELOPMENT) (1962), Romero Close, Stockwell Road, London SW9 9TY **T** 020-7733 7900 **E** cafod@cafod.org.uk **W** www.cafod.org.uk
Director, Chris Bain

CALOUSTE GULBENKIAN FOUNDATION (1956), 98 Portland Place, London W1B 1ET **T** 020-7636 5313 **E** info@gulbenkian.org.uk **W** www.gulbenkian.org.uk
Director, Ms P. Ridley

CAMBRIAN ARCHAEOLOGICAL ASSOCIATION (1847), Halfway House, Pont y Pandy, Bangor LL57 3DG **T** 01248-364865 **E** f.m.lynch@btopenworld.com **W** www.cambrians.org.uk
General Secretary, Rev M. Coombe

:AMBRIDGE ANTIQUARIAN SOCIETY (1840), 21 High Street, West Wickham, Cambridge CB21 4RY **E** secretary@camantsoc.org **W** www.camantsoc.org
Hon. Secretary, Janet Morris

:AMERON FUND (1970), Tavistock House North, Tavistock Square, London WC1H 9HR **T** 020-7388 0796 **E** administrator@cameronfund.org.uk **W** www.cameronfund.org.uk
Chief Executive, David Harris

:AMPAIGN FOR COURTESY (1986), 16 Grice Road, Hartshill, Stoke-on-Trent ST4 7PJ **T** 01782-614407 **W** www.campaignforcourtesy.org
Secretary, Revd Ian Gregory

:AMPAIGN FOR FREEDOM OF INFORMATION (1984), Suite 102, 16 Baldwins Gardens, London EC1N 7RJ **T** 020-7831 7477 **E** katherine@cfoi.demon.co.uk **W** www.cfoi.org.uk
Director, Maurice Frankel

:AMPAIGN FOR NUCLEAR DISARMAMENT (CND) (1958), 162 Holloway Road, London N7 8DQ **T** 020-7700 2393 **E** enquiries@cnduk.org **W** www.cnduk.org
Chair, Kate Hudson

:AMPAIGN FOR THE PROTECTION OF RURAL WALES (1928), Ty Gwyn, 31 High Street, Welshpool SY21 7YD **T** 01938-552525 **E** gill@cprwmail.org.uk **W** www.cprw.org.uk
Director, Peter Ogden

:ANADA-UNITED KINGDOM CHAMBER OF COMMERCE (1921), 38 Grosvenor Street, London W1K 4DP **T** 020-7258 6576 **E** info@canada-uk.org **W** www.canada-uk.org
Executive Director, Nigel Bacon

:ANCER RESEARCH UK (2002), PO Box 123, Lincoln's Inn Fields, London WC2A 3PX **T** 020-7242 0200 **W** www.cancerresearchuk.org
Chief Executive, Harpal Kumar

:AREERS RESEARCH AND ADVISORY CENTRE, 2nd Floor, Sheraton House, Castle Park, Cambridge CB3 0AX **T** 01223-460277 **E** enquiries@crac.org.uk **W** www.crac.org.uk
Chief Executive, Jeffrey Defries

:ARERS UK (1965), 20–25 Glasshouse Yard, London EC1A 4JT **T** 020-7490 8818 **E** info@carersuk.org **W** www.carersuk.org
Chief Executive, Imelda Redmond

:ATHEDRALS FABRIC COMMISSION FOR ENGLAND (1991), Church House, Great Smith Street, London SW1P 3NZ **T** 020-7898 1863 **E** enquiries@ccb.c-of-e.org.uk
Secretary, Paula Griffiths

:ATHOLIC TRUTH SOCIETY (1868), 40–46 Harleyford Road, London SE11 5AY **T** 020-7640 0042 **E** info@cts-online.org.uk **W** www.cts-online.org.uk
General Secretary, Fergal Martin

CATHOLIC UNION OF GREAT BRITAIN (1872), St Maximillian Kolbe House, 63 Jeddo Road, London W12 9EE **T** 020-8749 1321 **E** phiggs@cathunion.fsnet.co.uk **W** www.catholicunion.org
President, Lord Brennan, QC

CENTRAL COUNCIL OF CHURCH BELL RINGERS (1891), The Cottage, School Hill, Warnham, Horsham RH12 3QN **T** 01403-269743 **W** www.cccbr.org.uk
Hon. Secretary, Ian H. Oram

CENTREPOINT (1969), Central House, 25 Clamperdown Street, London E1 8DZ **T** 0845-466 3400 **E** info@centrepoint.org **W** www.centrepoint.org.uk
Chief Executive, Anthony Lawton

CHARITIES AID FOUNDATION (1924), 25 Kings Hill Avenue, West Malling ME19 4TA **T** 01732-520000 **E** enquiries@cafonline.org **W** www.cafonline.org
Chief Executive, John Low, FRSA

CHARTERED INSTITUTE OF ARBITRATORS (1915), International Arbitration and Mediation Centre, 12–14 Bloomsbury Square, London WC1A 2LP **T** 020-7421 7444 **E** info@arbitrators.org **W** www.arbitrators.org
Director-General, Michael Forbes Smith

CHARTERED INSTITUTE OF ENVIRONMENTAL HEALTH (1883), Chadwick Court, 15 Hatfields, London SE1 8DJ **T** 020-7928 6006 **E** information@cieh.org **W** www.cieh.org.uk
Chief Executive, G. Jukes

CHARTERED INSTITUTE OF JOURNALISTS (1890), 2 Dock Offices, Surrey Quays Road, London SE16 2XU **T** 020-7252 1187 **E** memberservices@cioj.co.uk **W** www.cioj.co.uk
General Secretary, Dominic Cooper

CHARTERED INSTITUTE OF LINGUISTS (1910), Saxon House, 48 Southwark Street, London SE1 1UN **T** 020-7940 3100 **E** info@iol.org.uk **W** www.iol.org.uk
Chief Executive, D. John Hammond

CHARTERED INSTITUTE OF PURCHASING AND SUPPLY (1932), Easton House, Easton on the Hill, Stamford PE9 3NZ **T** 01780-756777 **E** info@cips.org **W** www.cips.org
Chief Executive, Ken James

CHARTERED INSTITUTE OF TAXATION (1930), 12 Upper Belgrave Street, London SW1X 8BB **T** 020-7235 9381 **E** post@ciot.org.uk **W** www.tax.org.uk
Secretary-General, R. A. Dommett

CHARTERED INSURANCE INSTITUTE (1897), 42-48 High Road, South Woodford, London E18 2JP **T** 020-8989 8464 **E** customer.serv@cii.co.uk **W** www.cii.co.uk
Director-General, Dr A. Scott

CHARTERED MANAGEMENT INSTITUTE (1947), Management House, Cottingham Road, Corby NN17 1TT **T** 01536-204222 **E** enquiries@managers.org.uk **W** www.managers.org.uk
Chief Executive, Mary Chapman

CHATHAM HOUSE (1920), Chatham House, 10 St James's Square, London SW1Y 4LE T 020-7957 5700 E contact@chathamhouse.org.uk W www.chathamhouse.org.uk
Director, Dr Robin Niblett

CHILDREN 1ST (1884), 83 Whitehouse Loan, Edinburgh EH9 1AT T 0131-446 2300 E info@children1st.org.uk W www.children1st.org.uk
Chief Executive, Anne Houston

CHRISTIAN AID (1945), 35 Lower Marsh, London SE1 7RL T 020-7620 2444 E info@christian-aid.org W www.christianaid.org.uk
Director, Dr Daljeep Mukarji

CHRISTIAN AID SCOTLAND (1945), 41 George IV Bridge, Edinburgh EH1 1EL T 0141-221 7475 E glasgow@christian-aid.org W www.christianaid.org.uk
National Secretary for Scotland, Gavin McLellan

CHRISTIAN EDUCATION, 1020 Bristol Road, Selly Oak, Birmingham B29 6LB T 0121-472 4242 E enquiries@christianeducation.org.uk W www.christianeducation.org.uk
Chief Executive, Peter Fishpool

CHURCHILL SOCIETY – LONDON (1990), Ivy House, 18 Grove Lane, Ipswich IP4 1NR T 01473-413533 E dutysecretary@churchill-society-london.org.uk W www.churchill-society-london.org.uk
General Secretary, J. H. Rogers

CHURCH LADS' AND CHURCH GIRLS' BRIGADE (1891), 2 Barnsley Road, Wath-upon-Dearne, Rotherham S63 6PY T 01709-876535 E brigadesecretary@clcgb.org.uk W www.clcgb.org.uk
Brigade Secretary, A. Millward

CHURCH MISSION SOCIETY (1799), PO Box 1799, Oxford OX4 9BN T 0845-620 1799 E info@cms-uk.org W www.cms-uk.org
General Secretary, Revd Canon T. Dakin

CHURCH MONUMENTS SOCIETY (1979), Moor View, Exbourne, Okehampton EX20 3SA T 01837-851483 E churchmonuments@aol.com W www.churchmonumentssociety.org
President, Philip Lindley

CHURCH UNION (1859), Faith House, 7 Tufton Street, London SW1P 3QN T 01371-830132 E secretary@churchunion.co.uk W www.churchunion.co.uk
Chair, David Llewelyn Morgan

CITIZENS ADVICE (1939), Myddelton House, 115–123 Pentonville Road, London N1 9LZ T 020-7833 2181 W www.citizensadvice.org.uk
Chief Executive, D. Harker

CITY BUSINESS LIBRARY (1970), Corporation of London, 1 Brewers' Hall Garden, London EC2V 5BX T 020-7332 1812 E cbl@corpoflondon.gov.uk W www.cityoflondon.gov.uk/citybusinesslibrary
Business Librarian, Goretti Considine

CITY OF COVENTRY FREEMEN'S GUILD (1946), 1 Trossachs Road, Coventry CV5 7BJ T 024-7646 3203 W www.coventryfreemensguild.co.uk
Hon. Clerk, George Wilkinson

CITY OF STOKE-ON-TRENT MUSEUM ARCHAEOLOGICAL SOCIETY (1959), The Potteries Museum and Art Gallery, Hanley, Stoke-on-Trent ST1 3DW T 01782-232323 E outrams@smartemail.co.uk W www.stokearchaeologysociety.org.uk
Chair, Mrs M Thomas

CIVIC TRUST (1957), Essex Hall, 1–6 Essex Street, London WC2R 3HU T 020-7539 7900 E info@civictrust.org.uk W www.civictrust.org.uk
Managing Director, Peter Bembridge

COLLEGE OF OPTOMETRISTS (1980), 42 Craven Street, London WC2N 5NG T 020-7839 6000 E optometry@college-optometrists.org W www.college-optometrists.org
Chief Executive, Bryony Pawinska

COMMONWEALTH SOCIETY FOR THE DEAF 'SOUND SEEKERS' (1959), 34 Buckingham Palace Road, London SW1W 0RE T 020-7233 5700 E sound.seekers@btinternet.com W www.sound-seekers.org.uk
Chief Executive, Gary Williams

CONSUMERS' ASSOCIATION (1957), 2 Marylebone Road, London NW1 4DF T 020-7770 7000 E which@which.co.uk W www.which.co.uk
Director, Peter Vicary-Smith, OBE

CONTEMPORARY APPLIED ARTS (1948), 2 Percy Street, London W1T 1DD T 020-7436 2344 E info@caa.org.uk W www.caa.org.uk

COOPERATIVES UK, Holyoake House, Hanover Street, Manchester M60 0AS T 0161-246 2900 E info@cooperatives-uk.coop W www.cooperatives-uk.coop
Chief Executive, Dame Pauline Green

CORONERS' SOCIETY OF ENGLAND AND WALES (1846), The Court House, Bewdley Road, Stourport on Severn, Worcs DY13 8XE T 0151-233 5708 W www.coroner.org.uk
Hon. Secretary, André Joseph Anthony Rebello

CORPORATION OF CHURCH HOUSE (1888), Church House, Great Smith Street, London SW1P 3AZ T 020-7898 1000 W www.churchhouse.org.uk
Secretary, Colin D. L. Menzies

COUNCIL FOR AWARDS OF ROYAL AGRICULTURAL SOCIETIES, 23 Queen's Road, Ryde, PO33 3BG T 01626-873159 E john@wibbs.fsnet.co.uk
Hon. Secretary, Dr John Wibberley

COUNCIL FOR BRITISH ARCHAEOLOGY (1944), St Mary's House, 66 Bootham, York YO30 7BZ T 01904-671417 E info@britarch.ac.uk W www.britarch.ac.uk
Director, Dr M. Heyworth

COUNCIL FOR THE CARE OF CHURCHES (1921), Church House, Great Smith Street, London SW1P 3NZ T 020-7898 1866 E enquiries@ccb.c-of-e.org.uk
Secretary, Paula Griffiths

COUNCIL FOR WORLD MISSION (1977), Ipalo House, 32–34 Great Peter Street, London SW1P 2DB T 020-7222 4214 E council@cwmission.org.uk W www.cwmission.org.uk
General Secretary, Revd Dr D. van der Water

COUNCIL OF CHRISTIANS AND JEWS (1942), 1st Floor, Camelford House, 87-89 Albert Embankment, London SE1 7TP T 020-7820 0090 E cjrelations@ccj.org.uk W www.ccj.org.uk
Chief Executive, David Gifford

COUNCIL OF UNIVERSITY CLASSICAL DEPARTMENTS (1972), Institute of Classical Studies, Senate House, Malet Street, London WC1E 7HU T 01223-331437 E ro225@cam.ac.uk W www.rhul.ac.uk/classics/cucd
Chair, Prof Robin G. Osborne, FSA

COUNSEL AND CARE (1954), Twyman House, 16 Bonny Street, London NW1 9PG T 020-7241 8555 E advice@counselandcare.org.uk W www.counselandcare.org.uk
Chief Executive, Stephen Burke

COUNTRY HOUSES FOUNDATION (2005), The Manor, Hasely Business Centre, Warwick CV35 7LS T 0845-402 4102 E info@countryhousesfoundation.org.uk W www.countryhousesfoundation.org.uk
Chief Executive, Amanda Witherall

COUNTRY LAND & BUSINESS ASSOCIATION (1907), 16 Belgrave Square, London SW1X 8PQ T 020-7235 0511 E mail@cla.org.uk W www.cla.org.uk
President, Sir Henry Aubrey-Fletcher

COUNTRYSIDE ALLIANCE (1997), Old Town Hall, 367 Kennington Road, London SE11 4PT T 020-7840 9200 E info@countryside-alliance.org W www.countryside-alliance.org.uk
Chair, Kate Hoey, MP

CPRE (CAMPAIGN TO PROTECT RURAL ENGLAND) (1926), 128 Southwark Street, London SE1 0SW T 020-7981 2800 E info@cpre.org.uk W www.cpre.org.uk
Chief Executive, Shaun Spiers

CRAFTS COUNCIL (1971), 44A Pentonville Road, London N1 9BY T 020-7278 7700 E reference@craftscouncil.org.uk W www.craftscouncil.org.uk
Chief Executive, Rosy Greenlees

CRISIS UK (1967), 66 Commercial Street, London E1 6LT T 0870-011 3335 E enquiries@crisis.org.uk W www.crisis.org.uk
Chief Executive, Leslie Morphy

CRUSE BEREAVEMENT CARE (1959), PO Box 800, Richmond TW9 2GW T 020-8939 9530 E info@cruse.org.uk W www.cruse.org.uk
Chief Executive, Anne Viney

CTC (THE UK'S NATIONAL CYCLISTS' ORGANISATION) (1878), Parklands, Railton Road, Guildford GU2 9JX 0870-873 0060 E cycling@ctc.org.uk W www.ctc.org.uk
Director, Kevin Mayne

CYSTIC FIBROSIS TRUST (1964), 11 London Road, Bromley BR1 1BY T 020-8464 7211 E enquiries@cftrust.org.uk W www.cftrust.org.uk
Chief Executive, Rosie Barnes

DATA PUBLISHERS ASSOCIATION (1970), PO Box 23034, London W6 0RJ T 020-7405 0836 E christine@dpassoc.org W www.dpa.org.uk
Director, Christine Scott

DEMOS, Third Floor, Magdalen House, 136 Tooley Street, London SE1 2TU T 0845-458 5949 E hello@demos.co.uk W www.demos.co.uk
Director, Catherine Fieschi

DEVON ARCHAEOLOGICAL SOCIETY (1929), Royal Albert Memorial Museum, Queen Street, Exeter EX4 3RX E dasonline@wanadoo.co.uk W www.ex.ac.uk/das
Hon. Secretary, Valerie Barns

DIABETES UK (1934), Macleod House, 10 Parkway, London NW1 7AA T 020-7424 1000 E info@diabetes.org.uk W www.diabetes.org.uk
Chief Executive, Douglas Smallwood

DIANA, PRINCESS OF WALES MEMORIAL FUND (1997), County Hall, Westminster Bridge Road, London SE1 7PB T 020-7902 5500 E memorial.fund@memfund.org.uk W www.theworkcontinues.org
Chief Executive, Dr Astrid Honeyman

DITCHLEY FOUNDATION (1958), Ditchley Park, Enstone, Chipping Norton OX7 4ER T 01608-677346 E mail@ditchley.co.uk W www.ditchley.co.uk
Director, Sir Jeremy Greenstock, GCMG

DOWN'S SYNDROME ASSOCIATION (1970), The Langdon Down Centre, 2A Langdon Park, Teddington TW11 9PS T 0845-230 0372 E info@downs-syndrome.org.uk W www.downs-syndrome.org.uk
Chief Executive Officer, Mrs C. Boys

DUKE OF EDINBURGH'S AWARD (1956), Gulliver House, Madeira Walk, Windsor SL4 1EU T 01753-727400 E info@theaward.org W www.theaward.org
Chief Executive, Peter Westgarth

DYSLEXIA ACTION (2006), Park House, Wick Road, Egham TW20 0HH T 01784-222300 E info@dyslexiaaction.org.uk W www.dyslexiaaction.org.uk
Chief Executive, Shirley Cramer

EAST HERTFORDSHIRE ARCHAEOLOGICAL SOCIETY (1898), 11 St Leonard's Close, Bengeo, Hertford SG14 3LL
President, Mr C. L. Lee

EAST OF ENGLAND AGRICULTURAL SOCIETY (1797), East of England Showground, Peterborough PE2 6XE **T** 01733-234451 **E** info@eastofengland.org.uk **W** www.eastofengland.org.uk
Chief Executive, Andrew Mercer

EDINBURGH CHAMBER OF COMMERCE (1785), Capital House, 2 Festival Square, Edinburgh EH3 9SU **T** 0131-221 2999 **E** reception@edinburghchamber.co.uk **W** www.edinburghchamber.co.uk
Chief Executive, Ron Hewitt

EGYPT EXPLORATION SOCIETY (1882), 3 Doughty Mews, London WC1N 2PG **T** 020-7242 1880 **W** www.ees.ac.uk
Secretary-General, Dr Patricia Spencer

ELECTORAL REFORM SOCIETY (1884), 6 Chancel Street, London SE1 0UU **T** 020-7928 1622 **E** ers@electoral-reform.org.uk **W** www.electoral-reform.org.uk
Chief Executive, Dr Ken Ritchie

ELGAR FOUNDATION (1935), The Elgar Birthplace Museum, Lower Broadheath, Worcester WR2 6RH **T** 01905-333224 **E** birthplace@elgarmuseum.org **W** www.elgarmuseum.org
Museum Director, Catherine Sloan

EMERGENCY PLANNING SOCIETY (1993), The Media Centre, Culverhouse Cross, Cardiff CF6 6XJ **T** 0845-600 9587 **E** manager@theeps.org **W** www.the-eps.org

ENABLE SCOTLAND (1954), 6th Floor, 7 Buchanan Street, Glasgow G1 3HL **T** 0141-226 4541 **E** enable@enable.org.uk **W** www.enable.org.uk
Chief Executive, Norman Dunning

ENERGY INSTITUTE (2003), 61 New Cavendish Street, London W1G 7AR **T** 020-7467 7100 **E** info@energyinst.org.uk **W** www.energyinst.org.uk
Chief Executive, Louise Kingham

ENGLISH ASSOCIATION (1906), University of Leicester, University Road, Leicester LE1 7RH **T** 0116-252 3982 **E** engassoc@le.ac.uk **W** www.le.ac.uk/engassoc
Chief Executive, Ms H. Lucas

ENGLISH CHESS FEDERATION (1904), The Watch Oak, Chain Lane, Battle TN33 0YD **T** 01424-775222 **E** office@englishchess.org.uk **W** www.englishchess.org.uk
Chief Executive, Martin Regan

ENGLISH FOLK DANCE AND SONG SOCIETY (1932), Cecil Sharp House, 2 Regent's Park Road, London NW1 7AY **T** 020-7485 2206 **E** info@efdss.org **W** www.efdss.org
Chief Executive, H. Miller

ENGLISH-SPEAKING UNION OF THE COMMONWEALTH (1918), Dartmouth House, 37 Charles Street, London W1J 5ED **T** 020-7529 1550 **E** esu@esu.org **W** www.esu.org
Director-General, Mrs V. Mitchell, OBE

ENVIRONMENT COUNCIL (1970), 212 High Holborn, London WC1V 7BF **T** 020-7836 2626 **E** info@envcouncil.org.uk **W** www.the-environment-council.org.uk
Chief Executive, Mike King

EPILEPSY ACTION (1950), New Anstey House, Gate Way Drive, Yeadon, Leeds LS19 7XY **T** 0113-210 8800 **E** helpline@epilepsy.org.uk **W** www.epilepsy.org.uk
Chief Executive, P. Lee

ESPERANTO ASSOCIATION OF BRITAIN (1976), Esperanto House, Station Road, Barlaston, Stoke-on-Trent ST12 9DE **T** 0845-230 1887 **E** eab@esperanto-gb.org **W** www.esperanto-gb.org
President, Prof. John Wells

EVANGELICAL LIBRARY, 78A Chiltern Street, London W1U 5HB **T** 020-7935 6997 **E** stlibrary@zen.co.uk **W** www.elib.org.uk
Librarian, S. J. Taylor

EX-SERVICES MENTAL WELFARE SOCIETY (1919), Hollybush House, Hollybush, nr Ayr KA6 7EA **T** 01292-560214 **E** contactus@combatstress.org.uk **W** www.combatstress.com
Clinical Manager, Garry Wacker

FABIAN SOCIETY (1884), 11 Dartmouth Street, London SW1H 9BN **T** 020-7227 4900 **E** info@fabian-society.org.uk **W** www.fabian-society.org.uk
General Secretary, S. Katwala

FACULTY OF ACTUARIES (1856), 18 Dublin Street, Edinburgh EH1 3PP **T** 0131-240 1300 **E** faculty@actuaries.org.uk **W** www.actuaries.org.uk
Secretary, Richard Maconachie

FAIR ISLE BIRD OBSERVATORY TRUST (1948), Fair Isle Bird Observatory, Fair Isle ZE2 9JU **T** 01595-760258 **E** fairisle.birdobs@zetnet.co.uk **W** www.fairislebirdobs.co.uk
Administrator, H. Shaw

FAITH AND THOUGHT (1865), 15 The Drive, Harlow, Essex CM20 3QD **E** j.buxton@virgin.net **W** www.faithandthought.org.uk
President, Sir John Houghton, FRS

FEDERATION OF BRITISH ARTISTS (1961), 17 Carlton House Terrace, London SW1Y 5BD **T** 020-7930 6844 **E** info@mallgalleries.com **W** www.mallgalleries.org.uk
Director, Lewis McNaught

FEDERATION OF FAMILY HISTORY SOCIETIES (1974), PO Box 2425, Coventry CV5 6YX **T** 07041-492032 **E** info@ffhs.org.uk **W** www.ffhs.org.uk
Administrator, Maggie Loughran

FEDERATION OF SMALL BUSINESSES (1974), Sir Frank Whittle Way, Blackpool Business Park, Blackpool FY4 2FE **T** 01253-336000 **E** membership@fsb.org.uk **W** www.fsb.org.uk
Head of Parliamentary Affairs, Stephen Alambritis

FIELD STUDIES COUNCIL (1943), Preston Montford, Montford Bridge, Shrewsbury SY4 1HW T 01743-852100 E headoffice@field-studies-council.org W www.field-studies-council.org
Chief Executive, A. D. Thomas

FIRE SERVICES NATIONAL BENEVOLENT FUND (1943), Second Floor, Copenhagen Court, 32 New Street, Basingstoke RG21 7DT T 01256-366566 E info@fsnbf.org.uk W www.fsnbf.org.uk
Chief Executive, Roy Lawrenson

FLAG INSTITUTE (1971), 38 Hill Street, Mayfair, London W1J 5NS E membership@flaginstitute.org W www.flaginstitute.org
President, Capt. Malcolm Farrow, OBE, FFI, RN

FLEET AIR ARM OFFICERS' ASSOCIATION (1957), 4 St James's Square, London SW1Y 4JU T 020-7930 7722 E faaoa@fleetairarmoa.org W www.fleetairarmoa.org
Chair, Rear-Adm. S. Lidbetter

FOOD FROM BRITAIN, 4th Floor, Manning House, 22 Carlisle Place, London SW1P 1JA T 020-7233 5111 E info@foodfrombritain.co.uk W www.foodfrombritain.com
Chief Executive, D. McNair

FOUNDATION FOR SPORT AND THE ARTS (1991), PO Box 20, Liverpool L13 1HB T 0151-259 5505 E contact@thefsa.net W www.thefsa.net
Secretary, R. Boardley

FOUNDATION FOR THE STUDY OF INFANT DEATHS (1971), Artillery House, 11–19 Artillery Row, London SW1P 1RT T 020-7222 8001 E office@fsid.org.uk W www.fsid.org.uk
Director, Mrs J. Epstein

FPA (1930), 50 Featherstone Street, London EC1Y 8QU T 020-7608 5240 E library&information@fpa.org.uk W www.fpa.org.uk
Chief Executive, Ms A. Weyman, OBE

FRIENDS OF CATHEDRAL MUSIC (1956), 21 Bradford Road, Trowbridge BA14 9AL T 0845-644 3721 E info@fcm.org.uk W www.fcm.org.uk
Secretary, Roger Bishton

FRIENDS OF FRIENDLESS CHURCHES (1957), St Ann's Vestry Hall, 2 Church Entry, London EC4V 5HB T 020-7236 3934 E office@friendsoffriendlesschurches.org.uk W www.friendsoffriendlesschurches.org.uk
Hon. Director, Matthew Saunders, MBE

FRIENDS OF THE BODLEIAN (1925), Bodleian Library, Oxford OX1 3BG T 01865-277234 E fob@bodley.ox.ac.uk W www.bodley.ox.ac.uk/friends
Chairman, Prof. Jon Stallworthy

FRIENDS OF THE EARTH SCOTLAND (1978), Lamb's House, Burgess Street, Edinburgh EH6 6RD T 0131-554 9977 W www.foe-scotland.org.uk
Chief Executive, Duncan McLaren

FRIENDS OF THE NATIONAL LIBRARIES (1931), c/o Department of Manuscripts, The British Library, 96 Euston Road, London NW1 2DB T 020-7412 7559 W www.friendsofnationallibraries.org.uk
Chair, Lord Egremont

FURNITURE HISTORY SOCIETY (1964), 1 Mercedes Cottages, St John's Road, Haywards Heath RH16 4EH T 01444-413845 E furniturehistorysociety@hotmail.com W www.furniturehistorysociety.org
Membership Secretary, Dr Brian Austen

GALLIPOLI ASSOCIATION (1969), Earleydene Orchard, Earleydene, Ascot SL5 9JY T 01344-626523 E webmaster@gallipoli-association.org W www.gallipoli-association.org
Hon. Secretary, J. C. Watson Smith

GAME CONSERVANCY TRUST (1969), Fordingbridge, Hants SP6 1EF T 01425-652381 E info@gct.org.uk W www.gct.org.uk
Chief Executive, Teresa Dent

GARDEN HISTORY SOCIETY (1965), 70 Cowcross Street, London EC1M 6EJ T 020-7608 2409 E enquiries@gardenhistorysociety.org W www.gardenhistorysociety.org
Chair, Dr Colin Treen

GEMMOLOGICAL ASSOCIATION AND GEM TESTING LABORATORY OF GREAT BRITAIN (1931), 27 Greville Street (Saffron Hill entrance), London EC1N 8TN T 020-7404 3334 E information@gem-a.info W www.gem-a.info
Chief Executive Officer, Dr Jack Ogden

GENERAL DENTAL COUNCIL (1956), 37 Wimpole Street, London W1G 8DQ T 020-7887 3800 E information@gdc-uk.org W www.gdc-uk.org
Chief Executive & Registrar, Duncan Rudkin

GENERAL MEDICAL COUNCIL (1858), Regent's Place, 350 Euston Road, London NW1 3JN T 0845-357 3456 E gmc@gmc-uk.org W www.gmc-uk.org
Chief Executive, Finlay Scott

GENERAL OPTICAL COUNCIL (1959), 41 Harley Street, London W1G 8DJ T 020-7580 3898 E goc@optical.org W www.optical.org
Chief Executive and Registrar, P. C. Coe

GENERAL OSTEOPATHIC COUNCIL (1997), Osteopathy House, 176 Tower Bridge Road, London SE1 3LU T 020-7357 6655 E info@osteopathy.org.uk W www.osteopathy.org.uk
Chief Executive and Registrar, Madeleine Craggs

GEOGRAPHICAL ASSOCIATION (1893), 160 Solly Street, Sheffield S1 4BF T 0114-296 0088 E info@geography.org.uk W www.geography.org.uk
Chief Executive, David Lambert

GEOLOGICAL SOCIETY OF LONDON (1807), Burlington House, Piccadilly, London W1J 0BG T 020-7434 9944 E enquiries@geolsoc.org.uk W www.geolsoc.org.uk
Executive Secretary, E. Nickless

GEORGIAN GROUP (1937), 6 Fitzroy Square, London W1T 5DX T 0871-750 2936 E info@georgiangroup.org.uk W www.georgiangroup.org.uk
Secretary, Robert Bargery

GIRLGUIDING UK (1910), 17–19 Buckingham Palace Road, London SW1W 0PT T 020-7834 6242 E chq@girlguiding.org.uk W www.girlguiding.org.uk
Chief Guide, Liz Burnley

GIRLS' BRIGADE ENGLAND AND WALES, PO Box 196, 129 The Broadway, Didcot OX11 8XN T 01235-510425 E admin@girlsbrigadeew.org.uk W www.girlsbrigadeew.org.uk
National Director, Ruth Gilson

GIRLS' VENTURE CORPS AIR CADETS (1964), 1 Bawtry Gate, Sheffield S9 1WD T 0114-244 8405 E gvcac@toucansurf.com W www.gvcac.org.uk
Corps Director, Mrs Brenda Layne, MBE

GLASGOW CHAMBER OF COMMERCE (1783), 30 George Square, Glasgow G2 1EQ T 0141-204 2121 E chamber@glasgowchamber.org W www.glasgowchamber.org
Chief Executive, Dr Lesley Sawers

GREEK INSTITUTE (1969), 34 Bush Hill Road, London N21 2DS T 020-8360 7968 E info@greekinstitute.co.uk W www.greekinstitute.co.uk
Director, Dr K. Tofallis

GREENPEACE UK (1979), Canonbury Villas, London N1 2PN T 020-7865 8100 E info@uk.greenpeace.org W www.greenpeace.org.uk
Executive Director (acting), John Sauven

GUIDE DOGS FOR THE BLIND ASSOCIATION (1934), Hillfields, Burghfield Common, Reading RG7 3YG T 0118-983 5555 E guidedogs@guidedogs.org.uk W www.guidedogs.org.uk
Chief Executive, Bridget Warr

GUILD OF AID FOR GENTLEPEOPLE (1904), 10 St Christopher's Place, London W1U 1HZ T 020-7935 0641 E admin@pcac.org.uk W www.pcac.uk
Secretary, N. E. Inkson

GUILD OF GLASS ENGRAVERS (1975), 87 Nether Street, Finchley, London N12 7NP T 020-8446 4050 E enquiries@gge.org.uk W www.gge.org.uk
Secretary, Christine Reyland

GURKHA WELFARE TRUST, PO Box 18215, 2nd Floor, 1 Old Street, London EC1V 9XB T 020-7251 5234 E secretary@gwt.org.uk W www.gwt.org.uk

HAEMOPHILIA SOCIETY (1950), First Floor, Petersham House, 57A Hatton Garden, London EC1N 8JG T 020-7831 1020, **Helpline** 0800-018 6068 E info@haemophilia.org.uk W www.haemophilia.org.uk

HAIG HOMES (1929), Alban Dobson House, Green Lane, Morden SM4 5NS T 020-8685 5777 E haig@haighomes.org.uk W www.haighomes.org.uk
Major-General, P. V. R. Besgrove, CBE

HAKLUYT SOCIETY (1846), c/o Map Library, The British Library, 96 Euston Road, London NW1 2DB T 01428-641850 E office@hakluyt.com W www.hakluyt.com
President, Prof. R. C. Bridges

HALIFAX ANTIQUARIAN SOCIETY (1900), 66 Drub Lane, Gomersal, Cleckheaton BD19 4BU T 01274-865418 W www.halifaxhistory.org.uk
Hon. Secretary, J. H. Patchett

HANSARD SOCIETY FOR PARLIAMENTARY GOVERNMENT (1944), 40–43 Chancery Lane, London WC2A 1JA T 020-7438 1222 E hansard@hansard.lse.ac.uk W www.hansardsociety.org.uk
Chief Executive, Clare Ettinghausen

HARVEIAN SOCIETY OF LONDON (1831), Lettsom House, 11 Chandos Street, London W1G 9EB T 020-7580 1043
Executive Secretary, Col. R. Kinsella-Bevan

HAWICK ARCHAEOLOGICAL SOCIETY (1856), Orrock House, Stirches Road, Hawick TD9 7HF T 01450-376220
President, Gerald M. Graham

HEARING CONCERN (1947), 95 Grays Inn Road, London WC1X 8TX T 020-7440 9871 E info@hearingconcern.org.uk W www.hearingconcern.org.uk
Director, Damian Barry

HELP THE AGED (1961), 207–221 Pentonville Road, London N1 9UZ T 020-7278 1114 E info@helptheaged.org.uk W www.helptheaged.org.uk
Director-General, C. M. Lake, CBE

HERALDRY SOCIETY (1947), PO Box 772, Guildford GU3 3ZX T 01483-237373 E memsec@theheraldrysociety.com W www.theheraldrysociety.com
Honorary Secretary, Melvyn Jeremiah

HIGH SHERIFFS' ASSOCIATION OF ENGLAND & WALES (1971), PO Box 198, Letchworth SG6 3ZQ T 01462-629914 E secretary@highsheriffs.com W www.highsheriffs.com
Chair, Gloria Oates, OBE

HISPANIC AND LUSO BRAZILIAN COUNCIL (1943), Canning House, 2 Belgrave Square, London SW1X 8PJ T 020-7235 2303 E enquiries@canninghouse.com W www.canninghouse.com
Director, Veronica Scott

HISTORICAL ASSOCIATION (1906), 59A Kennington Park Road, London SE11 4JH T 020-7735 3901 E enquiry@history.org.uk W www.history.org.uk
Chief Executive, Rebecca Sullivan

HISTORIC HOUSES ASSOCIATION (1973), 2 Chester Street, London SW1X 7BB T 020-7259 5688 E info@hha.org.uk W www.hha.org.uk
Director-General, Nick Way

ONOURABLE SOCIETY OF CYMMRODORION (1751), 30 Eastcastle Street, London W1W 8DJ T 020-7631 0502
E aelodau1751we@yahoo.co.uk
W www.cymmrodorion1751.org.uk

OSTELLING INTERNATIONAL NORTHERN IRELAND (1931), 22–32 Donegall Road, Belfast BT12 5JN T 028-9032 4733 E info@hini.org.uk
W www.hini.org.uk
Hon. Secretary, Kevin Butler

OUSING JUSTICE (1956), 209 Old Marylebone Road, London NW1 5QT T 020-7723 7273
E info@housingjustice.org.uk W www.housingjustice.org.uk
Chief Executive, Alison Gelder

UGUENOT SOCIETY OF GREAT BRITAIN AND IRELAND (1885), The Huguenot Library, University College, Gower Street, London WC1E 6BT T 020-7679 5199
E secretary@huguenotsociety.org.uk
W www.huguenotsociety.org.uk
Hon. Secretary, Barbara Julien

UMANE RESEARCH TRUST (1962), Brook House, 29 Bramhall Lane South, Bramhall, Stockport SK7 2DN
T 0161-439 8041 E info@humaneresearch.org.uk
W www.humaneresearch.org.uk
Chair, K. Cholerton

YMN SOCIETY OF GREAT BRITAIN AND IRELAND (1936), 99 Barton Road, Lancaster LA1 4EN
T 01524-66740 E robcanham@haystacks.fsnet.co.uk
W www.hymnsocietygbi.org.uk
Hon. Secretary, Revd Robert A. Canham

CAN (1888), 8 Wakely Street, London EC1V 7QE
T 0845-225 4071 E info@ican.org.uk
W www.talkingpoint.org.uk
Chief Executive, Virginia Beardshaw

S SCHOOL OF FINANCE (1879), IFS House, 4–9 Burgate Lane, Canterbury, Kent CT1 2XJ T 01227-818609
E customerservices@ifslearning.com
W www.ifslearning.com
Chief Executive, Gavin Shreeve

MMIGRATION ADVISORY SERVICE (1970), 3rd Floor, County House, 190 Great Dover Street, London SE1 4YB T 020-7967 1200 E advice@iasuk.org
W www.iasuk.org
Chief Executive, Keith Best

NCORPORATED COUNCIL OF LAW REPORTING FOR ENGLAND AND WALES (1865), Megarry House, 119 Chancery Lane, London WC2A 1PP
T 020-7242 6471 E postmaster@iclr.co.uk
W www.lawreports.co.uk
Secretary, J. Cobbett

NCORPORATED SOCIETY OF MUSICIANS (1882), 10 Stratford Place, London W1C 1AA
T 020-7629 4413 E membership@ism.org W www.ism.org
Chief Executive, N. Hoyle

INDEPENDENTAGE (1863), 6 Avonmore Road, London W14 8RL T 020-7605 4200
E charity@independentage.org.uk
W www.independentage.org.uk
Chief Executive, Janet Morrison

INDEPENDENT SCHOOLS' BURSARS ASSOCIATION (1932), Unit 11–12, Manor Farm, Cliddesden, Hants RG25 2JB T 01256-330369
E office@theisba.org.uk W www.theisba.org.uk
General Secretary, Jonathan Cook

INDEPENDENT SCHOOLS COUNCIL (1998), St Vincent House, 30 Orange Street, London WC2H 7HH
T 020-7766 7070 E office@isc.co.uk W www.isc.co.uk
General Secretary, Jonathan Shephard

INDUSTRY AND PARLIAMENT TRUST (1977), Suite 101, 3 Whitehall Court, London SW1A 2EL
T 020-7839 9400 E admin@ipt.org.uk W www.ipt.org.uk
Director and Chief Executive, Sally Muggeridge

INSTITUTE FOR PUBLIC POLICY RESEARCH (1988), 30–32 Southampton Street, London WC2E 7RA
T 020-7470 6100 W www.ippr.org.uk
Chairman, Chris Powell

INSTITUTE OF ACOUSTICS (1974), 77A St Peter's Street, St Albans AL1 3BN T 01727-848195
E ioa@ioa.org.uk W www.ioa.org.uk
Chief Executive, Kevin Macan-Lind

INSTITUTE OF ACTUARIES (1848), Staple Inn Hall, High Holborn, London WC1V 7QJ T 020-7632 2100
E institute@actuaries.org.uk W www.actuaries.org.uk
President, Nicholas John Dumbreck, FIA, FSAI, FRSA
Chief Executive, Caroline M. Instance

INSTITUTE OF ADMINISTRATIVE MANAGEMENT (1915), Caroline House, 55–57 High Holborn, London WC1V 6DX T 020-7841 1100
E info@instam.org W www.instam.org
Chief Executive, David Woodgate

INSTITUTE OF BIOLOGY (1950), 9 Red Lion Court, London EC4A 3EF T 020-7936 5900 E info@iob.org
W www.iob.org
Chief Executive, Prof. A. D. B. Malcolm

INSTITUTE OF BREWING AND DISTILLING (1886), 33 Clarges Street, London W1J 7EE
T 020-7499 8144 E enquiries@ibd.org.uk
W www.ibd.org.uk
Executive Director, Simon Jackson

INSTITUTE OF BRITISH ORGAN BUILDING (IBO), 13 Ryefields, Thurston, Bury St Edmunds IP31 3TD
T 01359-233433 W www.ibo.co.uk
President, Katherine Venning

INSTITUTE OF CANCER RESEARCH (1909), 123 Old Brompton Road, London SW7 3RP
T 020-7352 8133 W www.icr.ac.uk
Chief Executive, Prof. Peter Rigby

INSTITUTE OF CAST METAL ENGINEERS (1904), National Metalforming Centre, 47 Birmingham Road, West Bromwich B70 6PY T 0121-601 6979 E info@icme.org.uk W www.icme.org.uk
Manager, Dr Pam Murrell

INSTITUTE OF CHARTERED ACCOUNTANTS IN ENGLAND AND WALES (1880), Chartered Accountants' Hall, PO Box 433, Moorgate Place, London EC2P 2BJ T 020-7920 8100 W www.icaew.com
Chief Executive, Michael Izza

INSTITUTE OF CHARTERED SHIPBROKERS (1911), 85 Gracechurch Street, London EC3V 0AA T 020-7623 1111 E info@ics.org.uk W www.ics.org.uk
Director-General, Alan Phillips

INSTITUTE OF DIRECTORS (1903), 116 Pall Mall, London SW1Y 5ED T 020-7839 1233 E enquiries@iod.com W www.iod.com
Chief Operating Officer, A. Main Wilson

INSTITUTE OF ECONOMIC AFFAIRS (1955), 2 Lord North Street, London SW1P 3LB T 020-7799 8900 E iea@iea.org.uk W www.iea.org.uk
Director-General, John Blundell

INSTITUTE OF EXPORT (1935), Export House, Minerva Business Park, Lynch Wood, Peterborough PE2 6FT T 01733-404400 E institute@export.org.uk W www.export.org.uk
Chair, Andy Nemes

INSTITUTE OF FIELD ARCHAEOLOGISTS (1982), School of Human and Environmental Science, Whiteknights, University of Reading, PO Box 227 RG6 6AB T 0118-378 6446 E admin@archaeologists.net W www.archaeologists.net
Chief Executive, Peter Hinton

INSTITUTE OF FOOD SCIENCE AND TECHNOLOGY (1964), 5 Cambridge Court, 210 Shepherd's Bush Road, London W6 7NJ T 020-7603 6316 E info@ifst.org W www.ifst.org
President, Helen G. Wild

INSTITUTE OF HEALTH PROMOTION AND EDUCATION, School of Dentistry, University of Manchester, Higher Cambridge Street, Manchester M15 6FH T 0161-275 6610 E honsec@ihpe.org.uk W www.ihpe.org.uk
Hon. Secretary, Prof. A. S. Blinkhorn

INSTITUTE OF HERALDIC AND GENEALOGICAL STUDIES (1961), 79–82 Northgate, Canterbury CT1 1BA T 01227-768664 E ihgs@ihgs.ac.uk W www.ihgs.ac.uk
Principal, C. R. Humphery-Smith

INSTITUTE OF HOSPITALITY (1971), 34 West Street, Sutton, Surrey SM1 1SH T 020-8661 4902 E commdept@instituteofhospitality.org W www.hcima.org.uk
Chief Executive, Phillipe Rossiter

INSTITUTE OF MANAGEMENT SERVICES (1941), Brooke House, 24 Dam Street, Lichfield WS13 6A T 01543-266 909 E admin@ims-stowe.fsnet.co.uk W www.ims-productivity.com

INSTITUTE OF MARINE ENGINEERING, SCIENCE AND TECHNOLOGY (1889), 80 Coleman Street, London EC2R 5BJ T 020-7382 2600 E info@imarest.org W www.imarest.org
Chief Executive, Keith Read, CBE

INSTITUTE OF MASTERS OF WINE (1953), Mapfre House, 2/3 Philpot Lane, London EC3M 8AN T 020-7621 2830 E enquiries@masters-of-wine.org W www.masters-of-wine.org
Executive Director, Siobhan Turner

INSTITUTE OF MATERIALS, MINERALS AND MINING (2002), 1 Carlton House Terrace, London SW1Y 5DB T 020-7451 7300 E admin@iom3.org W www.iom3.org
Chief Executive, Dr Bernie Rickinson

INSTITUTE OF MATHEMATICS AND ITS APPLICATIONS (1964), Catherine Richards House, 16 Nelson Street, Southend-on-Sea SS1 1EF T 01702-354020 E post@ima.org.uk W www.ima.org.uk
Executive Director, David Youdan

INSTITUTE OF MEASUREMENT AND CONTROL (1944), 87 Gower Street, London WC1E 6A T 020-7387 4949 E records@instmc.org.uk W www.instmc.org.uk
Secretary, Michael Yates

INSTITUTE OF THE MOTOR INDUSTRY (IMI) (1920), Fanshaws, Brickendon, Hertford SG13 8PQ T 01992-511521 E imi@motor.org.uk W www.motor.org.uk
Chief Executive, Sarah Sillars

INSTITUTION OF CHEMICAL ENGINEERS (1922), Davis Building, 165–189 Railway Terrace, Rugby CV21 3HQ T 01788-578214 E icheme@icheme.org.uk W www.icheme.org
Chief Executive, Dr D. J. Brown

INSTITUTION OF ENGINEERING AND TECHNOLOGY (1871), Savoy Place, London WC2R 0B T 020-7240 1871 E postmaster@iet.org.uk W www.theiet.org
Chief Executive, Robin McGill

INSTITUTION OF ENGINEERING DESIGNERS (1945), Courtleigh, Westbury Leigh, Westbury BA13 3TA T 01373-822801 E ied@ied.org.uk W www.ied.org.uk
Chief Executive, E Brodhurst

INSTITUTION OF MECHANICAL ENGINEERS (1847), 1 Birdcage Walk, London SW1H 9JJ T 020-7222 7899 W www.imeche.org
Chief Executive, Ruth Spellman, OBE

INSTITUTION OF OCCUPATIONAL SAFETY AND HEALTH (IOSH) (1945), The Grange, Highfield Drive, Wigston LE18 1NN T 0116-257 3100 E techinfo@iosh.co.uk W www.iosh.co.uk
Chief Executive, R. W. H. Strange

NTERCONTINENTAL CHURCH SOCIETY (1823), 1 Athena Drive, Tachbrook Park CV34 6NL T 01926-430347 E enquiries@ics-uk.org W www.ics-uk.org
Communications Manager, David Healey

NTERNATIONAL AFRICAN INSTITUTE (1926), SOAS, Thornhaugh Street, Russell Square, London WC1H 0XG T 020-7898 4420 E iai@soas.ac.uk W www.iaionthe.net
Hon. Director, Prof. Philip Burnham

NTERNATIONAL CHURCHILL SOCIETY (1968), PO Box 1257, Melksham, Wilts SN12 6GQ T 01380-828609 E nigel.knocker@btinternet.com W www.winstonchurchill.org
UK Chairman, N. B. Knocker

NTERNATIONAL FEDERATION OF HYDROGRAPHIC SOCIETIES (1972), PO Box 103, Plymouth PL4 7YP T 01752-223512 E helen@hydrographicsociety.org W www.hydrographicsociety.org

NTERNATIONAL INSTITUTE FOR CONSERVATION OF HISTORIC AND ARTISTIC WORKS (1950), 6 Buckingham Street, London WC2N 6BA T 020-7839 5975 E iic@iiconservation.org W www.iiconservation.org
Secretary-General, David Leigh

NTERNATIONAL PEN (1921), Brownlow House, 50–51 High Holborn, London WC1V 6ER T 020-7405 0338 E info@internationalpen.org.uk W www.internationalpen.org.uk
Executive Director, Caroline McCormick

NTERNATIONAL POLICE ASSOCIATION (BRITISH SECTION) (1950), 1 Fox Road, West Bridgford, Nottingham NG2 6AJ T 0115-981 3638 E mail@ipa-uk.org W www.ipa-uk.org
Executive Officer, Elizabeth Jones

NTERNATIONAL TREE FOUNDATION (1924), Sandy Lane, Crawley Down RH10 4HS T 0870-774 4269 E info@internationaltreefoundation.org W www.internationaltreefoundation.org
Company Secretary, Lynne Witheyman

NTERSERVE (1852), 5–6 Walker Avenue, Walverton Hill MK12 5TW T 01908-552700 E enquiries@isewi.org W www.interserveonline.org.uk
National Director, Richard Clark

RAN SOCIETY (1935), 2 Belgrave Square, London SW1X 8PJ T 020-7235 5122 E info@iransociety.org W www.iransociety.org
Chair, Hugh Arbuthnott, CMG

SCO (1973), 12A Princess Way, Camberley GU15 3SP T 01276-21188 E admin@isco.org.uk W www.isco.org.uk
Chief Executive, Andrew Airey

SLE OF WIGHT NATURAL HISTORY AND ARCHAEOLOGICAL SOCIETY (1919), Salisbury Gardens, Dudley Road, Ventnor PO38 1EJ T 01983-855385 W www.iwnhas.org
President, Dr C. Pope

JERUSALEM AND THE MIDDLE EAST CHURCH ASSOCIATION (1929), 1 Hart House, The Hart, Farnham GU9 7HJ T 01252-726994 E secretary@eclipse.co.uk W www.jmeca.org.uk
Chief Executive, Richard Owens

JOHN STUART MILL INSTITUTE (1992), 1 Whitehall Place, London SW1A 2HE T 01749-675071 E alan@buttphilip.freeserve.co.uk W www.jsmillinstitute.org.uk
Convenor, Dr Alan Butt Philip

JUSTICE (1957), 59 Carter Lane, London EC4V 5AQ T 020-7329 5100 E admin@justice.org.uk W www.justice.org.uk
Director, Roger Smith

KENT ARCHAEOLOGICAL SOCIETY (1857), Maidstone Museum, St Faiths Street, Maidstone ME14 1LH T 01474-822280 E secretary@kentarchaeology.org.uk W www.kentarchaeology.org.uk
Hon. General Secretary, A. I. Moffat

KING'S FUND (1897), 11–13 Cavendish Square, London W1G 0AN T 020-7307 2400 E sales&infopoint@kingsfund.org.uk W www.kingsfund.org.uk
Chief Executive, Niall Dickson

KIPLING SOCIETY (1927), 6 Clifton Road, London W9 1SS T 020-7286 0194 E jane@keskar.fsworld.co.uk W www.kipling.org.uk
Hon. Secretary, Jane Keskar

LCIA (LONDON COURT OF INTERNATIONAL ARBITRATION) (1892), 70 Fleet Street, London EC4Y 1EU T 020-7936 7007 E lcia@lcia.org W www.lcia.org
Director-General, Adrian Winstanley

LEAGUE OF THE HELPING HAND (1908), PO Box 2548, Henfield, BN5 9WS T 01273-493551 E secretary@lhh.org.uk W www.lhh.org.uk
Executive Secretary, Moira Parrott

LEPROSY MISSION, ENGLAND, WALES, THE CHANNEL ISLANDS AND THE ISLE OF MAN (1874), Goldhay Way, Orton Goldhay, Peterborough PE2 5GZ T 01733-370505 E post@tlmew.org.uk W www.leprosymission.org.uk

LEUKAEMIA RESEARCH FUND (1960), 43 Great Ormond Street, London WC1N 3JJ T 020-7405 0101 E info@lrf.org.uk W www.lrf.org.uk
Chief Executive, Cathy Gilman

LIBERAL PARTY (1877), 1 Coningsby Road, Anfield, Liverpool L4 0RS E libparty@libparty.demon.co.uk W www.liberal.org.uk
Membership Secretary, Mike Butler

LIBERTY (NATIONAL COUNCIL FOR CIVIL LIBERTIES) (1934), 21 Tabard Street, London SE1 4LA T 020-7403 3888 W www.liberty-human-rights.org.uk
Director, Shami Chakrabarti

LIONS CLUBS INTERNATIONAL (BRITISH ISLES AND IRELAND) (1950), 257 Alcester Road South, Kings Heath, Birmingham B14 6DT T 0121-441 4544 E lionsmd105@lineone.net W www.lions.org.uk
Office Manager, Mrs J. Davis

LISTENING BOOKS (1959), 12 Lant Street, London SE1 1QH T 020-7407 9417 E info@listening-books.org.uk W www.listening-books.org.uk
Director, Bill Dee

LOCAL GOVERNMENT ASSOCIATION (1997), Local Government House, Smith Square, London SW1P 3HZ T 020-7664 3000 E info@lga.gov.uk W www.lga.gov.uk
Chief Executive, Paul Coen

LONDON AND MIDDLESEX ARCHAEOLOGICAL SOCIETY (1855), c/o Museum of London, 150 London Wall, London EC2Y 5HN E lamas@owlpost.plus.com W www.lamas.org.uk
Hon. Secretary, Jackie Keily

LONDON CATALYST (1873), 45 Westminster Bridge Road, London SE1 7JB T 020-7021 4004 E londoncatalyst@peabody.org.uk W www.londoncatalyst.org.uk
Director, Victor Willmott, OBE

LONDON COLLEGE OF OSTEOPATHIC MEDICINE (1946), 8–10 Boston Place, London NW1 6QH T 020-7262 1128 E lcom-bostonplace@btconnect.com W www.lcom.org.uk
Clinic Manager, Anne Dalby

LONDON COUNCILS (2000), 59½ Southwark Street, London SE1 0AL T 020-7934 9999 E info@londoncouncils.gov.uk W www.londoncouncils.gov.uk
Chief Executive, John O'Brien

LONDON LIBRARY (1841), 14 St James's Square, London SW1Y 4LG T 020-7930 7705 E membership@londonlibrary.co.uk W www.londonlibrary.co.uk
Librarian, Inez T. P. A. Lynn

LONDON PLAYING FIELDS FOUNDATION (1890), 73 Collier Street, London N1 9BE T 0845-026 2292 E enquiries@lpff.org.uk W www.lpff.org.uk
Chief Executive, Dr Charles Goodson-Wickes

LONDON SOCIETY (1912), Mortimer Wheeler House, 46 Eagle Wharf Road, London N1 7ED T 020-7253 9400 E info@londonsociety.org.uk W www.londonsociety.org.uk
Hon. Secretary, John D. Hill

MACMILLAN CANCER SUPPORT (1911), 89 Albert Embankment, London SE1 7UQ T 0808-808 2020 E cancerline@macmillan.org.uk W www.macmillan.org.uk
Chief Executive, Ciaran Devane

MAIL USERS' ASSOCIATION, 70 Main Road, Emsworth, Hants PO10 8AX T 01243-370840 W www.mailusers.co.uk
Chair, Alan Halfacre

MANORIAL SOCIETY OF GREAT BRITAIN (1906), 104 Kennington Road, London SE11 6RE T 020-7735 6633 W www.msgb.co.uk
Chairman, Robert Smith

MARIE CURIE CANCER CARE (1948), 89 Albert Embankment, London SE1 7TP T 020-7599 7777 W www.mariecurie.org.uk
Chief Executive, Thomas Hughes-Hallett

MARINE BIOLOGICAL ASSOCIATION OF THE UK (1884), Citadel Hill, Plymouth PL1 2PB T 01752-633207 E sec@mba.ac.uk W www.mba.ac.uk
President, Sir Neil Chalmers

MARRIAGE CARE (1946), 1 Blythe Mews, Blythe Road, London W14 0NW T 020-7371 1341 E info@marriagecare.org.uk W www.marriagecare.org.uk
Chief Executive, Terry Prendergast

MATHEMATICAL ASSOCIATION (1871), 259 London Road, Leicester LE2 3BE T 0116-221 0013 E office@m-a.org.uk W www.m-a.org.uk
Senior Administrator, Marcia Murray

MCPS-PRS ALLIANCE, 29–33 Berners Street, London W1T 3AB T 020-7580 5544 W www.mcps-prs-alliance.co.uk
Managing Director, Steve Porter

MDF THE BIPOLAR ORGANISATION (1983), Castle Works, 21 St George's Road, London SE1 6ES T 08456-340540 E mdf@mdf.org.uk W www.mdf.org.uk
Chief Executive, Kate Schroder

ME ASSOCIATION (1976), 4 Top Angel, Buckingham Industrial Park, Buckingham MK18 1TH T 0870-444 8233 E meconnect@meassociation.org.uk W www.meassociation.org.uk
Chair, Neil Riley

MEDIAWATCH-UK (1965), 3 Willow House, Kennington Road, Ashford TN24 0NR T 01233-633936 E info@mediawatchuk.org W www.mediawatchuk.org
Director, John C. Beyer

MEDICAL SOCIETY OF LONDON (1773), Lettsom House, 11 Chandos Street, London W1G 9EB T 020-7580 1043
Registrar, Col. R. Kinsella-Bevan

MEDICAL WOMEN'S FEDERATION (1917), Tavistock House North, Tavistock Square, London WC1H 9HX T 020-7387 7765 E admin.mwf@btconnect.com W www.medicalwomensfederation.org.uk
President, Dr Melanie Davies

MENCAP (ROYAL MENCAP SOCIETY) (1946), 7 Hammet Street, Taunton TA1 1RZ T 020-7454 0454 E information@mencap.org.uk W www.mencap.org.uk
Chief Executive, Jo Williams, CBE

MENTAL HEALTH FOUNDATION, Sea Containers House, 20 Upper Ground, London SE1 9QB T 020-7803 1100 E mhf@mhf.org.uk W www.mentalhealth.org.uk
Chief Executive, Andrew McCulloch

MERCHANT NAVY WELFARE BOARD (1948), 30 Palmerston Road, Southampton SO14 1LL
T 023-8033 7799 E enquiries@mnwb.org.uk
W www.mnwb.org
Chief Executive, Capt. D. A. Parsons

MIDDLE EAST ASSOCIATION (1961), Bury House, 33 Bury Street, London SW1Y 6AX T 020-7839 2137
E mail@the-mea.co.uk W www.the-mea.co.uk
Director-General, Michael Thomas

MIGRAINE ACTION ASSOCIATION (1958), Unit 6, Oakley Hay Lodge Business Park, Great Folds Road, Great Oakley NN18 9AS T 01536-461333 E info@migraine.org.uk
W www.migraine.org.uk
Director, Paul Jansen

MIND (NATIONAL ASSOCIATION FOR MENTAL HEALTH) (1946), 15–19 Broadway, London E15 4BQ
T 020-8519 2122, 0845-766 0163 E contact@mind.org.uk
W www.mind.org.uk
Chief Executive, Paul Farmer

MINERALOGICAL SOCIETY (1876), 12 Baylis Mews, Amyand Park Road, Twickenham TW1 3HQ
T 020-8891 6600 E info@minersoc.org
W www.minersoc.org
President, Prof. Ben Harte

MISSION TO SEAFARERS (1856), St Michael Paternoster Royal, College Hill, London EC4R 2RL
T 020-7248 5202 E general@missiontoseafarers.org
W www.missiontoseafarers.org
Secretary-General, The Revd Canon Bill Christianson

MULTIPLE SCLEROSIS SOCIETY (1953), MS National Centre, 372 Edgware Road, Staples Corner, London NW2 6ND T 020-8438 0700 E info@mssociety.org.uk
W www.mssociety.org.uk
Chief Executive, Simon Gillespie

MUSEUMS ASSOCIATION (1889), 24 Calvin Street, London E1 6NW T 020-7426 6910
E info@museumsassociation.org
W www.museumsassociation.org
Director, Mark Taylor

NATIONAL AIDS TRUST (1987), New City Cloisters, 196 Old Street, London EC1V 9FR T 020-7814 6767
E info@nat.org.uk W www.nat.org.uk
Chief Executive, Deborah Jack

NATIONAL ASSOCIATION OF ALMSHOUSES (1951), Billingbear Lodge, Maidenhead Road, Wokingham RG40 5RU T 01344-452922 E naa@almshouses.org
W www.almshouses.org
Director, A. P. De Ritter

NATIONAL ASSOCIATION OF PRISON VISITORS (1924), 32 Newnham Avenue, Bedford ME41 9PT E info@naopv.com W www.naopv.com
General Secretary, Mrs A. G. McKenna, MBE

NATIONAL BENEVOLENT INSTITUTION (1812), Peter Herve House, Eccles Court, Tetbury GL8 8EH
T 01666-505500 E office@nbl.org.uk
W www.nbicharity.org.uk

NATIONAL CATTLE ASSOCIATION (DAIRY) (1998), Brick House, Risbury, Leominster HR6 0NQ
T 01568-760632
Executive Secretary, Tim Brigstocke

NATIONAL CHILDBIRTH TRUST (1956), Alexandra House, Oldham Terrace, London W3 6NH
T 0870-770 3236
E enquiries@national-childbirth-trust.co.uk
W www.nctpregnancyandbabycare.co.uk
Chief Executive, Ms B. Phipps

NATIONAL COUNCIL OF WOMEN OF GREAT BRITAIN (1895), 72 Victoria Road, Darlington DL1 5JG
T 01325-367375
E ncwgb@danburystreet.freeserve.co.uk
W www.ncwgb.org
President, Monica Hall

NATIONAL EXTENSION COLLEGE (1963), Michael Young Centre, Purbeck Road, Cambridge CB2 2HN
T 01223-400200 E info@nec.ac.uk W www.nec.ac.uk
Chief Executive, Alison West

NATIONAL FOUNDATION FOR EDUCATIONAL RESEARCH IN ENGLAND AND WALES (1946), The Mere, Upton Park, Slough SL1 2DQ T 01753-574123
E enquiries@nfer.ac.uk W www.nfer.ac.uk
Chief Executive, Sue Rossiter

NATIONAL GARDENS SCHEME CHARITABLE TRUST (1927), Hatchlands Park, East Clandon, Guildford GU4 7RT T 01483-211535 E ngs@ngs.org.uk
W www.ngs.org.uk
Chief Executive, Julia Grant

NATIONAL MISSING PEOPLE (1992), PO Box 28908, London SW14 72U T 020-8392 4590
E enquiries@missingpeople.org.uk
W www.missingpeople.org.uk
Chief Executive, Paul Tuohy

NATIONAL OPERATIC AND DRAMATIC ASSOCIATION (1899), NODA House, 55–60 Lincoln Road, Peterborough PE1 2RZ T 0870-770 2480
E everyone@noda.org.uk W www.noda.org.uk
Chief Executive, M. Pemberton

NATIONAL OSTEOPOROSIS SOCIETY (1986), Camerton, Bath BA2 0PJ T 01761-471771
E info@nos.org.uk W www.nos.org.uk
Chief Executive, Claire Severgnini

NATIONAL SOCIETY FOR EPILEPSY (1892), Chesham Lane, Chalfont St Peter, Bucks SL9 0RJ
T 01494-601300 W www.epilepsynse.org.uk
Chief Executive, Graham Faulkner

NATIONAL SOCIETY FOR PROMOTING RELIGIOUS EDUCATION (1811), Church House, Great Smith Street, London SW1P 3AZ T 020-7898 1499
E info@natsoc.c-of-e.org.uk W www.natsoc.org.uk
General Secretary, Revd Jan Ainsworth

NATIONAL TRUST (1895), 36 Queen Anne's Gate, London SW1H 9AS T 0870-458 4000
E enquiries@thenationaltrust.org.uk
W www.nationaltrust.org.uk
Director-General, Fiona Reynolds

NATIONAL TRUST FOR SCOTLAND (1931), Wemyss House, 28 Charlotte Square, Edinburgh EH2 4ET
T 0844-493 2100 E information@nts.org.uk
W www.nts.org.uk
Chief Executive, Mark Adderley

NATIONAL UNION OF STUDENTS (1922), 2nd Floor, Centro 3, 19 Mandela Street, London NW1 0DU
T 0871-221 8221 E nusuk@nus.org.uk
W www.nusonline.co.uk
President, Kat Fletcher

NAVY RECORDS SOCIETY (1893), c/o Pangbourne College, Pangbourne, Berks RG8 8LA
W www.navyrecordssociety.com
Hon. Secretary, Robin Brodhurst

NCH (1869), 85 Highbury Park, London N5 1UD
T 020-7704 7000 W www.nch.org.uk
Chief Executive, Clare Tickell

NOISE ABATEMENT SOCIETY (1959), Flat 2, 26 Brunswick Terrace, Brighton, BN3 1HJ T 01273-823851
E nas@noiseabatementsociety.fsnet.co.uk
W www.noiseabatementsociety.com
Director, Peter Wakeham

NORFOLK AND NORWICH ARCHAEOLOGICAL SOCIETY (1846), 30 Brettingham Avenue, Norwich NR4 6XG T 01603-455913 W www.nnas.info
Secretary, Roger Bellinger

NORTHERN IRELAND TOURIST BOARD (1948), St Anne's Court, 59 North Street, Belfast BT1 1NB
T 028-9023 1221 E info@nitb.com
W www.discovernorthernireland.com
Chief Executive, Alan Clarke

NOTARIES SOCIETY (1882), PO Box 266 Melton, Woodbridge IP12 1WX T 01394-380436
E admin@thenotariessociety.org.uk
W www.thenotariessociety.org.uk
Secretary, C. J. Vaughan

NSPCC (NATIONAL SOCIETY FOR THE PREVENTION OF CRUELTY TO CHILDREN) (1884), Weston House, 42 Curtain Road, London EC2A 3NH T 020-7825 2500 E info@nspcc.org.uk
W www.nspcc.org.uk
Director and Chief Executive, Dame Mary Marsh

NUFFIELD FOUNDATION (1943), 28 Bedford Square, London WC1B 3JS T 020-7631 0566
W www.nuffieldfoundation.org
E cporter@nuffieldfoundation.org
Director, A. Tomei

NUFFIELD TRUST (1940), 59 New Cavendish Street, London W1G 7LP T 020-7631 8450
E mail@nuffieldtrust.org.uk W www.nuffieldtrust.org.uk
Chief Operating Officer, Kim Beazor

NURSE AID (1917), PO Box 223, Evesham WR11 4WB
T 01386-446023 E admin@nurseaid.org.uk
W www.nurseaid.org.uk
Director, Mrs A. M. Barnard

OMBUDSMAN FOR ESTATE AGENTS (1990), Beckett House, 4 Bridge Street, Salisbury SP1 2LX
T 01722-333306 E admin@oea.co.uk W www.oea.co.uk
Chair and Chief Operating Officer, Bill McClintock

OPEN-AIR MISSION (1853), 4 Harrier Court, Woodside Road, Slip End, Luton LU1 4DQ T 01582-841141
E info@oamission.com W www.oamission.com
General Secretary, Andy Banton

OPEN SPACES SOCIETY (1865), 25A Bell Street, Henley-on-Thames RG9 2BA T 01491-573535
E hq@oss.org.uk W www.oss.org.uk
General Secretary, Kate Ashbrook

OPSIS (1992), c/o Queen Alexandra College, Court Oak Road, Birmingham B17 9TG T 0121-428 5037
E opsis@dircon.co.uk W www.opsis.org.uk
Chief Executive, Mike Brace

ORDERS AND MEDALS RESEARCH SOCIETY (1942), PO Box 1233, High Wycombe HP11 9BW
T 01494-441207 E generalsecretary@omrs.org
W www.omrs.org.uk
General Secretary, P. M. R. Helmore

OVERSEAS DEVELOPMENT INSTITUTE (1960), 111 Westminster Bridge Road, London SE1 7JD
T 020-7922 0300 E odi@odi.org.uk W www.odi.org.uk
Director, S. Maxwell

OVERSEAS SERVICE PENSIONERS' ASSOCIATION (1960), 138 High Street, Tonbridge TN9 1AX T 01732-363836 E mail@ospa.org.uk
W www.ospa.org.uk
Secretary, D. F. B. Le Breton, CBE

OXFAM GREAT BRITAIN (1942), Oxfam House, John Smith Drive, Oxford OX4 2JY T 0870-333 2700
E enquiries@oxfam.org.uk W www.oxfam.org.uk
Director, Barbara Stocking, CBE

OXFORD PRESERVATION TRUST (1927), 10 Turn Again Lane, St Ebbes, Oxford OX1 1QL T 01865-242918
E info@oxfordpreservation.org.uk
W www.oxfordpreservation.org.uk
Director, Debbie Dance

OXFORDSHIRE ARCHITECTURAL AND HISTORICAL SOCIETY (1839), 28 Sadler Walk, Oxford OX1 1TX T 07865-723784 E secretary@oahs.org.uk
W www.oahs.org.uk
Hon. Secretary, Dr A. J. Dodd

OXFORD UNIVERSITY SOCIETY (1932), Oxenford House, Magdalen Street, Oxford OX1 3AB T 01865-288088
E enquiries@ousoc.ox.ac.uk W www.alumni.ox.ac.uk
Secretary, Lady Nancy Kenny

PARLIAMENTARY AND SCIENTIFIC COMMITTEE (1939), 3 Birdcage Walk, Westminster, London SW1H 9JJ **T** 020-7222 7085 **E** secretariat@pandsctte.demon.co.uk **W** www.scienceinparliament.org.uk
Scientific Secretary, Prof. Peter Simpson

PASSENGER FOCUS (2005), Freepost WA1521, Warrington WA4 6GP **T** 08453-022022 **E** info@passengerfocus.org.uk **W** www.passengerfocus.org.uk
Chief Executive, Anthony Smith

PENSIONS ADVISORY SERVICE (1983), 11 Belgrave Road, London SW1V 1RB **T** 0845-601 2923 **E** enquiries@pensionsadvisoryservice.org.uk **W** www.pensionsadvisoryservice.org.uk
Chief Executive, M. McLean, OBE

PERENNIAL (1839), Bridge House, 115–117 Kingston Road, Leatherhead KT22 7SU **T** 0845-230 1839 **E** info@perennial.org.uk **W** www.perennial.org.uk
Chief Executive, Richard Capewell

PHYSIOLOGICAL SOCIETY (1876), PO Box 11319, London WC1X 8WQ **T** 020-7269 5710 **E** admin@physoc.org **W** www.physoc.org
Chief Executive, Dr Michael Collis

PILGRIMS OF GREAT BRITAIN (1902), Allington Castle, Maidstone ME16 0NB **T** 01622-606404 **E** sec@pilgrimsociety.org
Chair, Sir Robert Worcester, KBE, DL

PILGRIM TRUST (1930), Cowley House, 9 Little College Street, London SW1P 3SH **T** 020-7222 4723 **E** jo@thepilgrimtrust.org.uk **W** www.thepilgrimtrust.org.uk
Director, Georgina Nayler

PLAIN ENGLISH CAMPAIGN (1979), PO Box 3, New Mills, High Peak SK22 4QP **T** 01663-744409 **E** info@plainenglish.co.uk **W** www.plainenglish.co.uk
Director, Ms C. Maher

POSTWATCH (2001), Freepost, Postwatch **T** 08456-013265 **E** info@postwatch.co.uk **W** www.postwatch.co.uk
Chief Executive, Howard Webber

POWYSLAND CLUB (1867), The Vicarage, Church Street, Welshpool SY21 7DP **T** 01938-533164 **W** www.powyslandclub.co.uk
Hon. Secretary, Revd Roger L. Brown

PRAYER BOOK SOCIETY (1975), The Studio, Copyhold Farm, Goring Heath, Reading RG8 7RT **T** 0118-984 2582 **E** pbs.admin@prayerbook.org.uk **W** www.prayerbook.org.uk
Chair, Prudence Dailey

PRINCESS ROYAL TRUST FOR CARERS, (1991), 142 Minories, London EC3N 1LB **T** 020-7480 7788 **E** info@carers.org **W** www.carers.org
Chief Executive, Ms S. Nicholas

PRINCE'S TRUST (1976), 18 Park Square East, London NW1 4LH **T** 0800-842842 **E** webinfops@princes-trust.org.uk **W** www.princes-trust.org.uk
Chief Executive, M. Milburn

PRISONERS ABROAD (1978), 89–93 Fonthill Road, London N4 3JH **T** 020-7561 6820 **E** info@prisonersabroad.org.uk **W** www.prisonersabroad.org.uk
Chief Executive, Pauline Crowe

PRIVATE LIBRARIES ASSOCIATION (1956), Ravelston, South View Road, Pinner HA5 3YD **E** dchambers@aol.com **W** http://plabooks.org

PROSTATE RESEARCH CAMPAIGN UK (1994), 10 Northfields Prospect, Putney Bridge Road, London SW18 1PE **T** 020-8877 5840 **E** info@prostate-research.org.uk **W** www.prostate-research.org.uk
Chief Executive, John Anderson

PSORIASIS ASSOCIATION (1968), 7 Milton Street, Northampton NN2 7JG **T** 0845-676 0076 **E** mail@psoriasis.demon.co.uk **W** www.psoriasis-association.org.uk
Chief Executive, Gladys Edwards

QUAKER PEACE AND SOCIAL WITNESS, Friends House, 173–177 Euston Road, London NW1 2BJ **T** 020-7663 1000 **E** qpsw@quaker.org.uk **W** www.quaker.org.uk
General Secretary, Kevin Franz

QUEEN ELIZABETH'S FOUNDATION FOR DISABLED PEOPLE (1934), Leatherhead Court, Leatherhead KT22 0BN **T** 01372-841100 **E** info@qef.org.uk **W** www.qef.org.uk
Chief Executive, Cynthia Robinson

QUEEN VICTORIA CLERGY FUND (1897), Church House, Great Smith Street, London SW1P 3AZ **T** 020-7898 1000
Secretary, Colin Menzies

QUIT (1926), 4th Floor, 211 Old Street, London EC1V 9NR **T** 020-7251 1551 **E** info@quit.org.uk **W** www.quit.org.uk
Chief Executive, Steve Crone

RADAR (ROYAL ASSOCIATION FOR DISABILITY AND REHABILITATION) (1977), 12 City Forum, 250 City Road, London EC1V 8AF **T** 020-7250 3222 **E** radar@radar.org.uk **W** www.radar.org.uk
Chief Executive, Liz Sayce

RAILWAY AND CANAL HISTORICAL SOCIETY (1954), 3 West Court, West Street, Oxford OX2 0NP **T** 01865-240514 **E** secretary@rchs.org.uk **W** www.rchs.org.uk
Hon. Secretary, M. Searle

RARE BREEDS SURVIVAL TRUST (1973), Stoneleigh Park, Nr. Kenilworth CV8 2LG T 024-7669 6551 E enquiries@rbst.org.uk W www.rbst.org.uk
Executive Director, Richard Clarke

REFUGEE COUNCIL (1981), 240–250 Ferndale Road, London SW9 8BB T 020-7346 6700 E info@refugeecouncil.org.uk W www.refugeecouncil.org.uk
Chief Executive, Donna Covey

REGIONAL STUDIES ASSOCIATION (1965), PO Box 2058, Seaford BN25 4QU T 01323-899698 E info@rsa-ls.ac.uk W www.regional-studies-assoc.ac.uk
Chief Executive, Sally Hardy

REGULAR FORCES EMPLOYMENT ASSOCIATION LTD (1885), 1st Floor, Mountbarrow House, 6–20 Elizabeth Street, London SW1W 9RB T 0845-873 7162 E adminrfea@ctp.org.uk W www.rfea.org.uk
Chief Executive, Air Cdre. Peter G. Johnson, OBE

RELATE (1938), 4th Floor, 24–32 Stephenson Way, London NW1 2HX T 0845-456 1310 E enquiries@relate.org.uk W www.relate.org.uk

RESEARCH DEFENCE SOCIETY (RDS) (1908), 25 Shaftesbury Avenue, London W1D 7EG T 020-7287 2818 E info@rds-net.org.uk W www.rds-net.org.uk
Executive Director, Dr S. Festing

RETHINK (1972), 30 Tabernacle Street, London EC2A 4DD T 0845-456 0455 E info@rethink.org W www.rethink.org
Chief Executive, Paul Jenkins

RETIRED NURSES' NATIONAL HOME (1934), Riverside Avenue, Bournemouth BH7 7EE T 01202-396418 E rnnhoffice@btconnect.com W www.rnnh.co.uk
Chair, Mrs S. Young

RNIB NATIONAL LIBRARY SERVICE (1868), Far Cromwell Road, Bredbury, Stockport SK6 2SG T 0161-406 2525 E reader.advice@rnib.org.uk W www.rnib.org.uk/reading
Head of National Library Service, Helen Brazier

RNIB (ROYAL NATIONAL INSTITUTE OF THE BLIND) (1868), 105 Judd Street, London WC1H 9NE T 0845-669999 E helpline@rnib.org.uk W www.rnib.org.uk
Chief Executive, Lesley-Anne Alexander

RNID (1911), 19–23 Featherstone Street, London EC1Y 8SL T 020-7296 8000, **Textphone** 020-7296 8001 E informationline@rnid.org.uk W www.rnid.org.uk
Chief Executive, Dr John Low

ROADS AND ROAD TRANSPORT HISTORY ASSOCIATION (1992), 124 Shenstone Avenue, Norton, Stourbridge DY8 3EJ T 01384-394832 E roadsandrtha@aol.com W www.rrtha.org.uk
Chair, Garry Turvey, CBE

ROTARY INTERNATIONAL IN GREAT BRITAIN AND IRELAND (1922), Kinwarton Road, Alcester B49 6PB T 01789-765411 E secretary@ribi.org W www.rotary-ribi.org
Secretary, Robin Freeman

ROYAL AERONAUTICAL SOCIETY (1866), 4 Hamilton Place, London W1J 7BQ T 020-7670 4300 W www.raes.org.uk
Chief Executive, Keith Mans

ROYAL AGRICULTURAL SOCIETY OF ENGLAND (1840), National Agricultural Centre, Stoneleigh Park, Warks CV8 2LZ T 024-7669 6969 E info@rase.org.uk W www.rase.org.uk
Chief Executive, Professor J. Moverley

ROYAL AGRICULTURAL SOCIETY OF THE COMMONWEALTH (1957), c/o Royal Highland Centre, Ingliston, Edinburgh EH28 8NF T 0131-335 6200 E rasc@commagshow.org W www.commagshow.org
Hon. Secretary, W. H. Yarr, OBE

ROYAL AIR FORCES ASSOCIATION (1943), 117½ Loughborough Road, Leicester LE4 5ND T 0116-266 5224 E enquiries@rafa.org.uk W www.rafa.org.uk
Secretary-General, E. Jarron

ROYAL ARTILLERY ASSOCIATION, Artillery House, Artillery Centre, Larkhill, Salisbury SP4 8QT T 01980-845698 E ac-rhqra-racf-raa-gensecpa@mod.uk W www.theraa.co.uk
General Secretary, Lt.-Col. I. A. Vere Nicoll, MBE

ROYAL ASIATIC SOCIETY (1823), 14 Stephenson Way, London N21 2HD T 020-7388 4539 E info@royalasiaticsociety.org W www.royalasiaticsociety.org
Curator, Alison Ohta

ROYAL ASSOCIATION FOR DEAF PEOPLE (1841), 18 Westside Centre, London Road, Stanway CO3 8PH T 0845-668 2525 E info@royaldeaf.org.uk W www.royaldeaf.org.uk
Chief Executive, Tom Fenton

ROYAL ASSOCIATION OF BRITISH DAIRY FARMERS (1876), Dairy House, Unit 31, Stoneleigh Deer Park, Stareton, Kenilworth CV8 2LY T 0845-458 2711 E office@rabdf.co.uk W www.rabdf.co.uk
Chief Executive, N. Everington

ROYAL BIRMINGHAM SOCIETY OF ARTISTS (1814), 4 Brook Street, Birmingham B3 1SA T 0121-236 4353 E secretary@rbsa.org.uk W www.rbsa.org.uk
Gallery Director, Marie Considine

ROYAL BRITISH LEGION (1921), 48 Pall Mall, London SW1Y 5JY T 0845-7725 725 E info@britishlegion.org.uk W www.britishlegion.org.uk
Director-General, Frances Done

ROYAL BRITISH LEGION SCOTLAND (1921), New Haig House, Logie Green Road, Edinburgh EH7 4HR E admin@rblscotland.org W www.rblscotland.org
General Secretary, Heather Nicholson

ROYAL CALEDONIAN SCHOOLS TRUST (1815), Unit 75, WENTA Business Park, Colne Way, Watford WD24 7ND T 01923-215 350 E admin@rsct.org.uk W www.rsct.org.uk
Chief Executive, John Horsfield

ROYAL CAMBRIAN ACADEMY (1882), Crown Lane, Conwy LL32 8AN T 01492-593413 E rca@rcaconwy.org W www.rcaconwy.org
President, Maurice Cockrill

ROYAL CELTIC SOCIETY (1820), 23 Rutland Street, Edinburgh EH1 2RN T 0131-228 6449 E gcameron@stuartandstuart.co.uk W www.royalcelticsociety.org.uk
Secretary, J. Gordon Cameron, WS

ROYAL COLLEGE OF OBSTETRICIANS AND GYNAECOLOGISTS (1929), 27 Sussex Place, Regent's Park, London NW1 4RG T 020-7772 6200 W www.rcog.org.uk
Chief Executive, Helen Moffatt

ROYAL COLLEGE OF PAEDIATRICS AND CHILD HEALTH (1996), 50 Hallam Street, London W1W 6DE T 020-7307 5600 E enquiries@rcpch.ac.uk W www.rcpch.ac.uk
President, Dr Patricia Hamilton

ROYAL COLLEGE OF PSYCHIATRISTS (1841), 17 Belgrave Square, London SW1X 8PG T 020-7235 2351 E rcpsych@rcpsych.ac.uk W www.rcpsych.ac.uk
President, Prof. S. Hollins

ROYAL COLLEGE OF RADIOLOGISTS (1975), 38 Portland Place, London W1B 1JQ T 020-7636 4432 E enquiries@rcr.ac.uk W www.rcr.ac.uk
Chief Executive, A. Hall

ROYAL COLLEGE OF VETERINARY SURGEONS (1844), Belgravia House, 62–64 Horseferry Road, London SW1P 2AF T 020-7222 2001 E admin@rcvs.org.uk W www.rcvs.org.uk
Registrar, Miss J. C. Hern

ROYAL COMMONWEALTH EX-SERVICES LEAGUE (1921), 48 Pall Mall, London SW1Y 5JG T 020-7973 7263 W www.commonwealthveterans.org.uk

ROYAL FACULTY OF PROCURATORS IN GLASGOW (*c*.1668), 12 Nelson Mandela Place, Glasgow G2 1BT T 0141-332 3593 E jmckenzie@rfpg.org W www.rfpg.org
Librarian, Iain C. Pearson

ROYAL GEOGRAPHICAL SOCIETY (with the INSTITUTE OF BRITISH GEOGRAPHERS) (1830), 1 Kensington Gore, London SW7 2AR T 020-7591 3000 W www.rgs.org
Director, Dr R. Gardner, CBE

ROYAL HIGHLAND AND AGRICULTURAL SOCIETY OF SCOTLAND (1784), Royal Highland Centre, Ingliston, Edinburgh EH28 8NF T 0131-335 6200 E info@rhass.org.uk W www.rhass.org.uk
Chief Executive, R. Jones

ROYAL HISTORICAL SOCIETY (1868), University College London, Gower Street, London WC1E 6BT T 020-7387 7532 E rhsinfo@rhs.ac.uk W www.rhs.ac.uk
President, Prof. Martin Daunton

ROYAL HORTICULTURAL SOCIETY (1804), 80 Vincent Square, London SW1P 2PE T 020-7834 4333 E info@rhs.org.uk W www.rhs.org.uk
Director-General, Inga Grimsey

ROYAL HOSPITAL FOR NEURO-DISABILITY (1854), West Hill, Putney, London SW15 3SW T 020-8780 4500 E info@rhn.org.uk W www.rhn.org.uk
Chief Executive, Peter Franklyn

ROYAL HUMANE SOCIETY (1774), Brettenham House, Lancaster Place, London WC2E 7EP T 020-7836 8155 E info@royalhumanesociety.org.uk W www.royalhumanesociety.org.uk
Secretary, Adrian Gilbert, MBE

ROYAL INCORPORATION OF ARCHITECTS IN SCOTLAND (1916), 15 Rutland Square, Edinburgh EH1 2BE T 0131-229 7545 E info@rias.org.uk W www.rias.org.uk
Chief Executive, Mary Wrenn

ROYAL INSTITUTE OF BRITISH ARCHITECTS (1837), 66 Portland Place, London W1B 1AD T 020-7580 5533, 0906-302 0400 E info@inst.riba.org W www.architecture.com
Chief Executive, Richard Hastilow, CBE

ROYAL INSTITUTE OF NAVIGATION (1947), 1 Kensington Gore, London SW7 2AT T 020-7591 3130 E info@rin.org.uk W www.rin.org.uk
Director, Gp Capt. D. W. Broughton, MBE

ROYAL INSTITUTE OF OIL PAINTERS (1882), 17 Carlton House Terrace, London SW1Y 5BD T 020-7930 6844 E info@mallgalleries.com W www.mallgalleries.org.uk
President, Dennis Syrett

ROYAL INSTITUTE OF PAINTERS IN WATER COLOURS (1831), 17 Carlton House Terrace, London SW1Y 5BD T 020-7930 6844 E info@mallgalleries.com W www.mallgalleries.org.uk
President, Ronald Maddox

ROYAL INSTITUTION OF CHARTERED SURVEYORS (1868), 12 Great George Street, Parliament Square, London SW1P 3AD T 020-7222 7000 E contactrics@rics.org W www.rics.org
Chief Executive, J. H. A. J. Armstrong

ROYAL INSTITUTION OF NAVAL ARCHITECTS (1860), 10 Upper Belgrave Street, London SW1X 8BQ T 020-7235 4622 E hq@rina.org.uk W www.rina.org.uk
Chief Executive, T. Blakeley

ROYAL LIFE SAVING SOCIETY UK (1891), River House, High Street, Broom B50 4HN T 01789-773994 E lifesavers@rlss.org.uk W www.lifesavers.org.uk
Chief Executive, D. Standley

ROYAL MASONIC BENEVOLENT INSTITUTION (1842), 20 Great Queen Street, London WC2B 5BG T 020-7596 2400 E enquiries@rmbi.org.uk W www.rmbi.org.uk
Chief Executive, Peter J. Gray

ROYAL MASONIC TRUST FOR GIRLS AND BOYS (1982), 31 Great Queen Street, London WC2B 5AG T 020-7405 2644 E info@rmtgb.org W www.rmtgb.org
Chief Executive, C. F. Andrews

ROYAL MICROSCOPICAL SOCIETY (1839), 37–38 St Clements, Oxford OX4 1AJ T 01865-254760 E info@rms.org.uk W www.rms.org.uk
Executive Director, R. Flavin

ROYAL NATIONAL COLLEGE FOR THE BLIND (1872), College Road, Hereford HR1 1EB T 01432-265725 E info@rncb.ac.uk W www.rncb.ac.uk
Principal, Mrs C. Steadman

ROYAL NATIONAL LIFEBOAT INSTITUTION (1824), West Quay Road, Poole BT15 1HZ T 0845-122 6999 E info@rnli.org.uk W www.rnli.org.uk
Chief Executive, A. Freemantle, MBE

ROYAL NAVAL ASSOCIATION (1949), 82 Chelsea Manor Street, London SW3 5QJ T 020-7352 6764 E rna@netcomuk.co.uk W www.royal-naval-association.co.uk
President, Vice-Adm. John McAnally, CB, LVO

ROYAL NAVAL BENEVOLENT SOCIETY FOR OFFICERS (1739), 70 Porchester Terrace, London W2 3TP T 020-7402 5231 E rnbso@lineone.net
Chair, Rear-Adm. D. J. Anthony, MBE

ROYAL NAVAL BENEVOLENT TRUST (1922), Castaway House, 311 Twyford Avenue, Portsmouth PO2 8RN T 023-9269 0112 E rnbt@rnbt.org.uk W www.rnbt.org.uk
Chief Executive, Cdr Stephen Farrington, QGM, RN

ROYAL PHILATELIC SOCIETY LONDON (1869), 41 Devonshire Place, London W1G 6JY T 020-7486 1044 E secretary@rpsl.org.uk W www.rpsl.org.uk
President, S. J. Sacher, CBE

ROYAL PHILHARMONIC SOCIETY (1813), 10 Stratford Place, London W1C 1BA T 020-7491 8110 E admin@royalphilharmonicsociety.org W www.royalphilharmonicsociety.org.uk
Chair, Graham Sheffield

ROYAL PHOTOGRAPHIC SOCIETY (1853), Fenton House, 122 Wells Road, Bath BA2 3AH T 01225-325733 E rps@rps.org W www.rps.org
President, Prof. R. Jacobson

ROYAL SCHOOL OF CHURCH MUSIC (1927), 19 The Close, Salisbury SP1 2EB T 01722-424848 E enquiries@rscm.com W www.rscm.com
Director-General, Prof. J. Harper

ROYAL SCHOOL OF NEEDLEWORK (1872), Apartment 12A, Hampton Court Palace, Surrey KT8 9AU T 020-8943 1432 E enquiries@royal-needlework.co.uk W www.royal-needlework.co.uk
Principal, Dr Thomas Cocke

ROYAL SOCIETY (1660), 6–9 Carlton House Terrace, London SW1Y 5AG T 020-7451 2500 E info@royalsoc.ac.uk W www.royalsoc.ac.uk
Executive Secretary, Stephen Cox, CVO

ROYAL SOCIETY FOR ASIAN AFFAIRS (1901), 2 Belgrave Square, London SW1X 8PJ T 020-7235 5122 E sec@rsaa.org.uk W www.rsaa.org.uk
Chairman of Council, Sir Harold Walker, KCMG

ROYAL SOCIETY FOR THE ENCOURAGEMENT OF ARTS, MANUFACTURES AND COMMERCE (1754), 8 John Adam Street, London WC2N 6EZ T 020-7930 5115 E general@rsa.org.uk W www.thersa.org
Executive Director, Penny Egan

ROYAL SOCIETY FOR THE PREVENTION OF ACCIDENTS (1917), RoSPA House, Edgbaston Park, 353 Bristol Road, Birmingham B5 7ST T 0121-248 2000 E help@rospa.com W www.rospa.com
Chief Executive, Tom Mullarkey, MBE

ROYAL SOCIETY FOR THE PREVENTION OF CRUELTY TO ANIMALS (1824), Wilberforce Way, Horsham RH13 9RS T 0870-333 5999 W www.rspca.org.uk
Director-General, Jackie Ballard

ROYAL SOCIETY FOR THE PROTECTION OF BIRDS (1889), The Lodge, Sandy SG19 2DL T 01767-680551 W www.rspb.org.uk
Chief Executive, G. R. Wynne

ROYAL SOCIETY OF LITERATURE (1820), Somerset House, Strand, London WC2R 1LA T 020-7845 4676 E info@rslit.org W www.rslit.org
President, Michael Holroyd

ROYAL SOCIETY OF MARINE ARTISTS (1939), 17 Carlton House Terrace, London SW1Y 5BD T 020-7930 6844 E info@mallgalleries.com W www.mallgalleries.org.uk
President, G. Hunt

ROYAL SOCIETY OF MEDICINE (1805), 1 Wimpole Street, London W1G 0AE T 020-7290 2900 E membership@rsm.ac.uk W www.rsm.ac.uk
Chief Executive, Stephen Dodd, MA, MBA

ROYAL SOCIETY OF MUSICIANS OF GREAT BRITAIN (1738), 10 Stratford Place, London W1C 1BA T 020-7629 6137 W www.royalsocietyofmusicians.co.uk
Secretary, Mrs M. Gibb

ROYAL SOCIETY OF PAINTER-PRINTMAKERS (1880), Bankside Gallery, 48 Hopton Street, London SE1 9JH T 020-7928 7521 E info@banksidegallery.com
President, Prof. Hilary Paynter

ROYAL SOCIETY OF PORTRAIT PAINTERS (1891), 17 Carlton House Terrace, London SW1Y 5BD T 020-7930 6844 E info@mallgalleries.com W www.mallgalleries.org.uk
President, Andrew Festing

ROYAL SOCIETY OF ST GEORGE (1894), 127 Sandgate Road, Folkstone CT20 2BH T 01303-241795 E info@rssg.u-net.com W www.royalsocietyofstgeorge.com
Chair, James E. Newton

ROYAL SOCIETY OF TROPICAL MEDICINE AND HYGIENE (1907), 50 Bedford Square, London WC1B 3DP T 020-7580 2127 E mail@rstmh.org W www.rstmh.org
Hon. Secretaries, Prof. G. Pasvol; Dr J. R. Stothard

.OYAL STAR AND GARTER HOME FOR DISABLED EX-SERVICE MEN AND WOMEN (1916), Richmond Hill, Richmond TW10 6RR
T 020-8439 8000 E generalenquiries@starandgarter.org
W www.starandgarter.org
Chief Executive, Lynn McDougall

.OYAL ULSTER AGRICULTURAL SOCIETY (1896), The King's Hall, Balmoral, Belfast BT9 6GW
T 028-9066 5225 E general@kingshall.co.uk
W www.balmoralshow.co.uk
Chief Executive, Colin McDonald

.OYAL WATERCOLOUR SOCIETY (1804), Bankside Gallery, 48 Hopton Street, London SE1 9JH
T 020-7928 7521 E info@banksidegallery.com
W www.royalwatercoloursociety.com
President, Richard Sorrell

.OYAL ZOOLOGICAL SOCIETY OF SCOTLAND (1909), 134 Corstorphine Road, Edinburgh EH12 6TS
T 0131-334 9171 W www.edinburghzoo.org.uk
Chief Executive, David Windmill

SABI (1897), The Rural Centre, West Mains of Ingliston, Newbridge, Edinburgh EH28 8LT T 0131-472 4166
E rsabi@rsabi.org.uk W www.rsabi.org.uk
Chief Executive, Dr Maurice S Hankey

T DEINIOL'S RESIDENTIAL LIBRARY (1894), Church Lane, Hawarden, Deeside CH5 3DF
T 01244-532350 E deiniol.visitors@btconnect.com
W www.st-deiniols.org
Warden and Chief Librarian, Revd Peter Francis

T JOHN AMBULANCE (1877), 27 St John's Lane, London EC1M 4BU T 020-7324 4000 E info@sja.org.uk
W www.sja.org.uk
Chief Executive, Roger Holmes

ALTIRE SOCIETY (1936), 9 Fountain Close, 22 High Street, Edinburgh EH1 1TF T 0131-556 1836
E saltire@saltiresociety.org.uk W www.saltiresociety.org.uk
Administrator, Mrs K. Munro

AMARITANS (1953), The Upper Mill, Kingston Road, Ewell KT17 2AF T 020-8394 8300 E admin@samaritans.org
W www.samaritans.org
Chief Executive, Dominic Rudd

ANE (1986), 1st Floor, Cityside House, 40 Adler Street, London E1 1EE T 020-7375 1002 E info@sane.org.uk
W www.sane.org.uk
Chief Executive, Ms M. Wallace, MBE

AVE BRITAIN'S HERITAGE (1975), 70 Cowcross Street, London EC1M 6EJ T 020-7253 3500
E save@btinternet.com W www.savebritainsheritage.org
President, Marcus Binney, OBE

AVE THE CHILDREN UK (1919), 1 St. John's Lane, London EC1M 4AR T 020-7012 6400
E supporter.care@savethechildren.org.uk
W www.savethechildren.org.uk
Chief Executive, Jasmine Whitbread

SCHOOL LIBRARY ASSOCIATION (1937), Unit 2, Lotmead Business Village, Lotmead Farm, Wanborough, nr Swindon SN4 0UY T 01793-791787 E info@sla.org.uk
W www.sla.org.uk
Chief Executive, Ms K. Lemaire

SCHOOL OF PUBLIC POLICY (1996), University College London, 29 Tavistock Square, London WC1H 9QU
T 020-7679 4999 E spp@ucl.ac.uk W www.ucl.ac.uk/spp
Director, Prof. Richard Bellamy

SCOPE (1952), 6 Market Road, London N7 9PW
T 0808-800 3333 E response@scope.org.uk
W www.scope.org.uk
Chief Executive, Jon Sparkes

SCOTTISH CHAMBERS OF COMMERCE (1948), 30 George Square, Glasgow G2 1EQ T 0141-204 8316
E admin@scottishchambers.org.uk
W www.scottishchambers.org.uk
Executive Director, Liz Cameron

SCOTTISH COUNCIL FOR VOLUNTARY ORGANISATIONS (1943), Mansfield Traquair Centre, 15 Mansfield Place, Edinburgh EH3 6BB T 0131-556 3882
E enquiries@scvo.org.uk W www.scvo.org.uk
Chief Executive, M. Sime

SCOTTISH GENEALOGY SOCIETY (1953), Library and Family History Centre, 15 Victoria Terrace, Edinburgh EH1 2JL T 0131-220 3677 E info@scotsgenealogy.com
W www.scotsgenealogy.com
Hon. Secretary, Kenneth A. M. Nisbet

SCOTTISH NATIONAL WAR MEMORIAL (1927), The Castle, Edinburgh EH1 2YT T 0131-226 7393
W www.snwm.org
Secretary to the Trustees, Lt.-Col. I. Shepherd

SCOTTISH NATURAL HISTORY LIBRARY (1970), Foremount House, Kilbarchan, RenfrewshirePA10 2EZ T 01505-702419
Director, Dr J. A. Gibson

SCOTTISH RURAL PROPERTY AND BUSINESS ASSOCIATION (SRPBA), Stuart House, Eskmills Business Park, Musselburgh EH21 7PB T 0131-653 5400
E info@srpba.com W www.srpba.com
Chief Executive, Douglas McAdam

SCOTTISH SOCIETY FOR THE PREVENTION OF CRUELTY TO ANIMALS (1839), Braehead Mains, 603 Queensferry Road, Edinburgh EH4 6EA
T 0131-339 0222 E enquiries@scottishspca.org
W www.scottishspca.org
Chief Executive, Stuart Earley

SCOTTISH SOCIETY FOR THE PROTECTION OF WILD BIRDS (1927), Foremount House, Kilbarchan PA10 2EZ T 01505-702419
Hon. Secretary, Dr J. A. Gibson

SCOTTISH WILDLIFE TRUST (1964), Cramond House, Cramond Glebe Road, Edinburgh EH4 6NS
T 0131-312 7765 E enquiries@swt.org.uk
W www.swt.org.uk
Chief Executive, Simon Milne

SCOUT ASSOCIATION (1907), Gilwell Park, Chingford, London E4 7QW T 020-8443 7100 E info.centre@scout.org.uk W www.scouts.org.uk
Chief Executive, D. M. Twine

SEEABILITY (1799), SeeAbility House, Hook Road, Epsom, Surrey KT19 8SQ T 01372-755000 E enquiries@seeability.org W www.seeability.org
Chief Executive, D. Scott-Ralphs

SELDEN SOCIETY (1887), Faculty of Laws, Queen Mary School of Law, Mile End Road, London E1 4NS T 020-7882 5136 E selden-society@qmul.ac.uk W www.selden-society.qmul.ac.uk
Secretary, V. Tunkel

SENSE (THE NATIONAL DEAFBLIND AND RUBELLA ASSOCIATION) (1955), 11–13 Clifton Terrace, London N4 3SR T 0845-127 0060 E enquiries@sense.org.uk W www.sense.org.uk
Chief Executive, A. Best

SHELTER (NATIONAL CAMPAIGN FOR HOMELESS PEOPLE), 88 Old Street, London EC1V 9HU T 0844-515 4699 E info@shelter.org.uk W www.shelter.org.uk
Director, Adam Sampson

SHIRE HORSE SOCIETY (1878), East of England Showground, Peterborough PE2 6XE T 01733-234451 E info@shire-horse.org.uk W www.shire-horse.org.uk
Chief Executive Officer, Andrew Mercer

SHROPSHIRE ARCHAEOLOGICAL AND HISTORICAL SOCIETY (1877), Lower Wallop Farm, Westbury SY5 9RT T 01743-891215 E walloparch@farming.co.uk W www.discovershropshire.org
President, Sir Neil Cossons, OBE

SIGHT SAVERS INTERNATIONAL (ROYAL COMMONWEALTH SOCIETY FOR THE BLIND) (1950), Grosvenor Hall, Bolnore Road, Haywards Heath RH16 4BX T 01444-446600 E info@sightsavers.org W www.sightsavers.org.uk
Chief Executive, Dr Caroline Harper, OBE

SOCIALIST PARTY OF GREAT BRITAIN (1904), 52 Clapham High Street, London SW4 7UN T 020-7622 3811 E spgb@worldsocialism.org W www.worldsocialism.org
General Secretary, John Bissett

SOCIÉTÉ JERSIAISE (1873), 7 Pier Road, St Helier, Jersey JE2 4XW T 01534-758314 E societe@societe-jersiaise.org W www.societe-jersiaise.org
Executive Director, Mrs P. Syvret

SOCIETY FOR NAUTICAL RESEARCH (1910), 6 Ashmeadow Road, Arnside, via Carnforth LA5 0AE T 01524-761616 E honsec@snr.org.uk W www.snr.org.uk
Hon. Secretary, Peter Winterbottom

SOCIETY FOR PROMOTING CHRISTIAN KNOWLEDGE (SPCK) (1698), 36 Causton Street, London SW1P 4ST T 020-7592 3900 E spck@spck.org.uk W www.spck.org.uk
General Secretary, Simon Kingston

SOCIETY FOR THE PROMOTION OF ROMAN STUDIES (1910), Senate House, Malet Street, London WC1E 7HU T 020-7862 8727 E office@romansociety.org W www.romansociety.org
Secretary, Dr Helen Cockle

SOCIETY FOR THE PROTECTION OF UNBORN CHILDREN (1967), 5–6 St Matthew Street, London SW1P 2JT T 020-7222 5845 E information@spuc.org.uk W www.spuc.org.uk
National Director, John Smeaton

SOCIETY OF ANTIQUARIES OF LONDON (1707), Burlington House, Piccadilly, London W1J 0BE E admin@sal.org.uk W www.sal.org.uk
General-Secretary, David Gaimster, PHD, FSA

SOCIETY OF ANTIQUARIES OF NEWCASTLE UPON TYNE (1813), The Black Gate, Castle Garth, Newcastle upon Tyne NE1 1RQ T 0191-261 5390 E admin@newcastle-antiquaries.org.uk W www.newcastle-antiquaries.org.uk
Hon. Secretary, Dr N. Hodgson

SOCIETY OF ANTIQUARIES OF SCOTLAND (1780), Royal Museum, Chambers Street, Edinburgh EH1 1JF T 0131-247 4115/4133 E director@socantscot.org W www.socantscot.org
Director, Simon Gilmour, PHD, FSA, SCOT

SOCIETY OF APOTHECARIES OF LONDON (1617), Black Friars Lane, London EC4V 6EJ T 020-7236 1189 E clerk@apothecaries.org W www.apothecaries.org
Clerk, A. M. Wallington-Smith

SOCIETY OF ARCHIVISTS (1947), Prioryfield House, 20 Canon Street, Taunton TA1 1SW T 01823-327030 E societyofarchivists@archives.org.uk W www.archives.org.uk
Executive Secretary, P. S. Cleary

SOCIETY OF AUTHORS (1884), 84 Drayton Gardens, London SW10 9SB T 020-7373 6642 E info@societyofauthors.org W www.societyofauthors.org
General Secretary, Mark Le Fanu, OBE

SOCIETY OF COUNTY TREASURERS, Warwickshire County Council, PO Box 3, Shire Hall, Warwi CV34 4RH T 020-8541 9200 E mjtaylor@surreycc.gov.uk W www.sctnet.org.uk
Hon. Secretary, Mike Taylor

SOCIETY OF EDITORS, University Centre, Granta Place, Mill Lane, Cambridge CB2 1RU T 01223-304080 E info@societyofeditors.org W www.societyofeditors.co.uk
Executive Director, Bob Satchwell

SOCIETY OF GENEALOGISTS (1911 and 1999), 14 Charterhouse Buildings, Goswell Road, London EC1M 7BA T 020-7251 8799 E library@sog.org.uk W www.sog.org.uk
Chief Executive, June Perrin

SOCIETY OF GLASS TECHNOLOGY (1917), Unit 9, Twelve O'Clock Court, 21 Attercliffe Road, Sheffield S4 7WW T 0114-263 4455 E info@sgt.org W www.sgt.org
Managing Editor, David Moore

SOCIETY OF INDEXERS, Woodbourn Business Centre, 10 Jessell Street, Sheffield S9 3HY T 0114-244 9561 E admin@indexers.org.uk W www.indexers.org.uk
Chair, Sue Lightfoot

SOCIETY OF LEGAL SCHOLARS (1908), School of Law, Southampton University, Southampton SO17 1BJ T 028-8059 4039 E s.j.thomson@soton.ac.uk W www.legalscholars.ac.uk
Hon. Secretary, Prof. Stephen Bailey

SOCIETY OF LOCAL AUTHORITY CHIEF EXECUTIVES AND SENIOR MANAGERS, Hope House, 45 Great Peter Street, London SW1P 3LT T 0845-601 0649 E hope.house@solace.org.uk W www.solace.org.uk
Director-General, David Clark

SOCIETY OF SCHOOLMASTERS AND SCHOOLMISTRESSES (1798), c/o L. I. Baggott, SGBI Office, Queen Mary House, Manor Park Road, Chistlehurst BR7 5PY T 020-8468 7997 E sgbi@sgbi.freeserve.co.uk
Secretary (acting), Laurence Baggott, FCA

SOCIETY OF SCRIBES AND ILLUMINATORS (1921), 6 Queen Square, London WC1N 3AT T 01524-251534 E scribe@calligraphyonline.org W www.calligraphyonline.org
Chairman, David Graham

SOCIETY OF SOLICITORS IN THE SUPREME COURT OF SCOTLAND (1784), SSC Library, Parliament House, 11 Parliament Square, Edinburgh EH1 1RF T 0131-225 6268 E enquiries@ssclibrary.co.uk W www.ssclibrary.co.uk
Secretary, I. L. S. Balfour

SOCIETY OF WRITERS TO HM SIGNET (1594), The Signet Library, Parliament Square, Edinburgh EH1 1RF T 0131-220 3249 E enquiries@wssociety.co.uk W www.wssociety.co.uk
Chief Executive, Robert Pirrie

SOIL ASSOCIATION (1946), Bristol House, 40–56 Victoria Street, Bristol BS1 6BY T 0117-314 5000 E info@soilassociation.org W www.soilassociation.org
Director, Patrick Holden

SOMERSET ARCHAEOLOGICAL AND NATURAL HISTORY SOCIETY (1849), Taunton Castle, Taunton TA1 4AA T 01823-272429 E office@sanhs.org W www.sanhs.org
Chairman, Dr Pat Hill-Cottingham

SOUTH AMERICAN MISSION SOCIETY (1844), Allen Gardiner Cottage, Pembury Road, Tunbridge Wells TN2 3QU T 01892-538647 E gensec@samsgb.org W www.samsgb.org
General Secretary, Revd Canon J. W. Sutton

SPORT HORSE BREEDING OF GREAT BRITAIN (1886), 96 High Street, Edenbridge TN8 5AR T 01732-866277 E office@sporthorsegb.co.uk W www.sporthorsegb.co.uk
General Secretary, Catherine Burdock

STANDING COUNCIL OF SCOTTISH CHIEFS, Hope Chambers, 52 Leith Walk, Edinburgh EH6 5HW T 0131-553 2232 E romilly.squire@virgin.net
Hon. Secretary, Romilly Squire of Rubislaw

STANDING COUNCIL OF THE BARONETAGE (1903), Forestside, Martin's Corner, Hambledon, Waterlooville PO7 4RA T 023-9263 2672 E secretary@baronetage.org W www.baronetage.org
Chair, Sir Ian Lowson, BT, OSTJ

STRATEGIC PLANNING SOCIETY (1967), Weston Street, London SE1 3ER T 020-7091 1310 E enquiries@sps.org.uk W www.sps.org.uk
Chairman, Jon Vyse

SUFFOLK INSTITUTE OF ARCHAEOLOGY AND HISTORY (1848), 56 Orford Street, Ipswich IP1 3PE T 01473-405622 E john.fairclough@ntlworld.com W www.suffolkarch.org.uk
Hon. Secretary, John Fairclough

SUNDERLAND ANTIQUARIAN SOCIETY (1900), c/o Southmoor Community School, Ryhope Road, Sunderland SR2 7TF T 0191-522 0517
President, D. W. Smith

SURREY ARCHAEOLOGICAL SOCIETY (1854), Castle Arch, Guildford GU1 3SX T 01483-532454 E info@surreyarchaeology.org.uk W www.surreyarchaeology.org.uk
Hon. Secretary, P. E. Youngs

SUSSEX ARCHAEOLOGICAL SOCIETY (1846), Bull House, 92 High Street, Lewes BN7 1XH T 01273-486260 E admin@sussexpast.co.uk W www.sussexpast.co.uk
Chief Executive, J. Manley

SUZY LAMPLUGH TRUST (1986), National Centre for Personal Safety, 20 Albert Embankment, London SE1 7TJ T 020-7091 0014 E info@suzylamplugh.org W www.suzylamplugh.org
Chief Executive, Julie Bentley

SWEDENBORG SOCIETY (1810), 20–21 Bloomsbury Way, London WC1A 2TH T 020-7405 7986 E swed.soc@netmatters.co.uk W www.swedenborg.org.uk
Secretary, Richard Lines

TERRENCE HIGGINS TRUST (1982), 314 Gray's Inn Road, London WC1X 8DP T 0845-122 1200 E info@tht.org.uk W www.tht.org.uk
Chief Executive, Nick Partridge

THEATRES TRUST (1976), 22 Charing Cross Road, London WC2H 0QL T 020-7836 8591 E info@theatrestrust.org.uk W www.theatrestrust.org.uk
Director, Mhora Samuel

THORESBY SOCIETY (1889), Claremont, 23 Clarendon Road, Leeds LS2 9NZ T 0113-247 0704 E president@thoresby.org.uk W www.thoresby.org.uk
President, C. J. Morgan

TOGETHER: WORKING FOR WELLBEING (1879), 1st Floor, Lincoln House, 296–302 High Holborn, London WC1V 7JH T 020-7780 7300 E contactus@together-uk.org W www.together-uk.org
Chief Executive, Liz Felton

TOWN AND COUNTRY PLANNING ASSOCIATION (1899), 17 Carlton House Terrace, London SW1Y 5AS T 020-7930 8903 W www.tcpa.org.uk
Chair, Gideon Amos

TRADING STANDARDS INSTITUTE (1881), 1st Floor, 1 Sylvan Court, Sylvan Way, Southfields Business Park, Basildon SS15 6TH T 0870-872 9000 E institute@tsi.org.uk W www.tsi.org.uk
Chief Executive, Ron Gainsford

TURNER SOCIETY (1975), BCM Box Turner, London WC1N 3XX W www.turnersociety.org.uk
Chair, Eric Shanes

UNIVERSITIES FEDERATION FOR ANIMAL WELFARE (1926), The Old School, Brewhouse Hill, Wheathampstead AL4 8AN T 01582-831818 E ufaw@ufaw.org.uk W www.ufaw.org.uk
Scientific Director, Dr J. K. Kirkwood

UNITED GRAND LODGE OF ENGLAND (1717), Freemasons' Hall, Great Queen Street, London WC2B 5AZ T 020-7831 9811 E ugle@ugle.org.uk W www.ugle.org.uk
Grand Master, HRH The Duke of Kent, KG, GCMG, GCVO

UNITED KINGDOM RESERVE FORCES ASSOCIATION (1972), Holderness House, 51–61 Clifton Street, London EC2A 4EY T 020-7426 8361 E co-rfa@co.rfca.mod.uk W www.ukrfa.org
President, Air Vice-Marshal B. H. Newton, CB, CVO, OBE

UNITED NATIONS ASSOCIATION OF GREAT BRITAIN AND NORTHERN IRELAND (1945), 3 Whitehall Court, London SW1A 2EL T 020-7766 3444 W www.una.org.uk
Executive Director, Sam Daws

UNITED REFORMED CHURCH HISTORY SOCIETY (1972), Westminster College, Madingley Road, Cambridge CB3 0AA T 01223-741300 E mt212@cam.ac.uk
Hon. Secretary, Revd E. J. Brown

UNIVERSITIES UK (2000), Woburn House, 20 Tavistock Square, London WC1H 9HQ T 020-7419 4111 E info@universitiesuk.ac.uk W www.universitiesuk.ac.uk
Chief Executive, Baroness Warwick

VEGAN SOCIETY (1944), Donald Watson House, 7 Battle Road, St Leonards-on-Sea TN37 7AA T 0845-458 8244 E info@vegansociety.com W www.vegansociety.com
General Managers, Dave Palmer and Rosamund Raha

VEGETARIAN SOCIETY OF THE UNITED KINGDOM LTD (1847), Parkdale, Dunham Road, Altrincham, Cheshire WA14 4QG T 0161-925 2000 E info@vegsoc.org W www.vegsoc.org
Chief Executive, Dr Annette Pinner

VERNACULAR ARCHITECTURE GROUP (1952), 'Ashley', Willows Green, Chelmsford CM3 1QD T 01245-361408 W www.vag.org.uk
Hon. Secretary, Mrs B. A. Watkin

VICTIM SUPPORT (NATIONAL ASSOCIATION OF VICTIM SUPPORT SCHEMES) (1979), National Office, Cranmer House, 39 Brixton Road, London SW9 6DZ T 020-7735 9166 E contact@victimsupport.org.uk W www.victimsupport.org.uk
Chief Executive, Gillian Guy

VICTORIA CROSS AND GEORGE CROSS ASSOCIATION (1956), Horse Guards, Whitehall, London SW1A 2AX T 020-7930 3506
Secretary, Mrs D. Grahame, MVO

VICTORIAN SOCIETY (1958), 1 Priory Gardens, Bedford Park, London W4 1TT T 020-8994 1019 E admin@victorian-society.org.uk W www.victorian-society.org.uk
Director, Dr Ian Dungavell

VSO (VOLUNTARY SERVICE OVERSEAS) (1958), 317 Putney Bridge Road, London SW15 2PN T 020-8780 7200 E enquiry@vso.org.uk W www.vso.org.uk
Chief Executive, Mark Goldring

WELLBEING OF WOMEN (1965), 27 Sussex Place, Regent's Park, London NW1 4SP T 020-7772 6400 E wellbeingofwomen@rcog.org.uk W www.wellbeingofwomen.org.uk
Directors, Liz Campbell

WESLEY HISTORICAL SOCIETY (1893), 7 Haugh Shaw Road, Halifax, West Yorkshire HX1 3AH T 01422-250780 E johnahargreaves@blueyonder.co.uk W www.wesleyhistoricalsociety.org.uk
General Secretary, Dr John A. Hargreaves

WESTMINSTER FOUNDATION FOR DEMOCRACY (1992), Artillery House, 11–19 Artillery Row, London SW1P 1RT T 020-7799 1311 E wfd@wfd.org W www.wfd.org
Chief Executive, David French

WILDFOWL AND WETLANDS TRUST (1946), Slimbridge GL2 7BT T 01453-891900 E info.slimbridge@wwt.org.uk W www.wwt.org.uk
Chief Executive, M. Spray

WILLIAM MORRIS SOCIETY AND KELMSCOTT FELLOWSHIP (1955), Kelmscott House, 26 Upper Mall London W6 9TA T 020-8741 3735 E williammorris@care4free.net W www.morrissociety.org
Hon. Secretary, P. Bennett

WILTSHIRE ARCHAEOLOGICAL AND NATURAL HISTORY SOCIETY (1853), Wiltshire Heritage Museum, 41 Long Street, Devizes SN10 1NS T 01380-727369 E wanhs@wiltshireheritage.org.uk W www.wiltshireheritage.org.uk
Curator, Dr P. H. Robinson

WOMEN'S ROYAL NAVAL SERVICE BENEVOLENT TRUST (1941), 311 Twyford Avenue, Portsmouth PO2 8RN **T** 023-9265 5301 **E** wrnsbt@care4free.net
General Secretary, Mrs S. Tarabella

WOODLAND TRUST (1972), Autumn Park, Dysart Road, Grantham NG31 6LL **T** 01476-581111 **E** enquiries@woodland-trust.org.uk **W** www.woodland-trust.org.uk
Chief Executive, Sue Holden

WORCESTERSHIRE ARCHAEOLOGICAL SOCIETY (1854), 26 Albert Park Road, Malvern WR14 1HN **T** 01299-250416 **E** museum@worcestershire.gov.uk **W** www.communigate.co.uk/worcs
Hon. Secretary, Dr J. W. Dunleavey

WRVS (1938), Garden House, Milton Hill, Abingdon OX13 6AD **T** 01235-442900 **E** enquiries@wrvs.org.uk **W** www.wrvs.org.uk
Chair, Ruth Markland

YORKSHIRE ARCHAEOLOGICAL SOCIETY (1863), Claremont, 23 Clarendon Road, Leeds LS2 9NZ **T** 0113-245 7910 **W** www.yas.org.uk
Hon. Secretary, Ms J. Heron

YOUNG MEN'S CHRISTIAN ASSOCIATION (YMCA) (1844), National Council of YMCAs, 640 Forest Road, London E17 3DZ **T** 0845-873 6633 **E** enquiries@ymca.org.uk **W** www.ymca.org.uk
National Secretary, Angela Sarkis

YOUTH HOSTELS ASSOCIATION (ENGLAND & WALES) (1930), Trevelyan House, Dimple Road, Matlock, Derbys DE4 3YH **T** 01629-592600 **E** customerservices@yha.org.uk **W** www.yha.org.uk
Chief Executive, Roger Clarke

YOUNG WOMEN'S CHRISTIAN ASSOCIATION ENGLAND & WALES (1855), Clarendon House, 52 Cornmarket Street, Oxford OX1 3EJ **T** 01865-304200 **E** info@ywca.org.uk **W** www.ywca.org.uk
Chief Executive, Gill Tishler

ZOOLOGICAL SOCIETY OF LONDON (1826), Regent's Park, London NW1 4RY **T** 020-7722 3333 **W** www.zsl.org
Director-General, Ralph Armond, FRS

THE WORLD

THE WORLD IN FIGURES

THE ANTARCTIC

AIR DISTANCES FROM LONDON

TIME ZONES

CURRENCIES AND EXCHANGE RATES

TRAVEL OVERSEAS

EUROPEAN UNION

INTERNATIONAL ORGANISATIONS

COUNTRIES OF THE WORLD A–Z

UK OVERSEAS TERRITORIES

THE WORLD IN FIGURES

THE EARTH

The shape of the Earth is that of an oblate spheroid or solid of revolution whose meridian sections are ellipses, whilst the sections at right angles are circles.

DIMENSIONS

Equatorial diameter = 12,756.27km (7,926.38 miles)
Polar diameter = 12,713.50km (7,899.80 miles)
Equatorial circumference = 40,075.01km (24,901.46 miles)
Polar circumference = 40,007.86km (24,859.73 miles)
Mass = 5,974,000,000,000,000,000,000 tonnes (5.879×10^{21} tons)

The equatorial circumference is divided into 360 degrees of longitude, which is measured in degrees, minutes and seconds east or west of the Greenwich meridian (0°) to 180°, the meridian 180° E. coinciding with 180° W. This dateline was internationally ratified on 13 October 1884. The position of the dateline has been modified on occasions, most recently on 1 January 1995 when it was moved to the east of Kiribati. *See also* Astronomy.

Distance north and south of the equator is measured in degrees, minutes and seconds of latitude. The equator is 0°, the North Pole is 90°N. and the South Pole is 90°S. The tropics lie at 23° 27′ N. (Tropic of Cancer) and 23° 27′ S. (Tropic of Capricorn). The Arctic Circle lies at 66° 33′ N. and the Antarctic Circle at 66° 33′ S. (Note the tropics and the Arctic and Antarctic circles are affected by the slow decrease in obliquity of the ecliptic, of about 0.47 arcseconds per year. The effect of this is that the Arctic and Antarctic circles are currently moving towards their respective poles by about 14m per annum, while the tropics move towards the equator by the same amount.)

AREA, ETC

The surface area of the Earth is 510,069,120km² (196,938,800 miles²), of which the water area is 70.92 per cent and the land area is 29.08 per cent.

The radial velocity on the Earth's surface at the equator is 1,669.79km per hour (1,037.56mph). The Earth's mean velocity in its orbit around the Sun is 107,229km per hour (66,629mph). The Earth's mean distance from the Sun is 149,597,870km (92,955,807 miles).

OCEANS

AREA

	km²	*miles²*
Pacific	155,557,000	59,270,000
Atlantic	76,762,000	29,638,000
Indian	68,556,000	26,467,000
Southern	20,327,000	7,848,300
Arctic	14,056,000	5,427,000

The equator divides the Pacific into the North and South Pacific and the Atlantic into the North and South Atlantic. In 2000 the International Hydrographic Organisation approved the description of the 20,327,000km² (7,848,300 miles²) of circum-Antarctic waters up to 60°S. as the Southern Ocean – a seventh ocean.

GREATEST OCEAN DEPTHS

Greatest depth	*Location*	*metres*	*feet*
Mariana Trench*	Pacific	10,911	35,798
Puerto Rico Trench	Atlantic	8,605	28,232
South Sandwich Trench	Southern	7,235	23,737
Java (Sunda) Trench	Indian	7,125	23,376
Molloy Deep	Arctic	5,680	18,400

* On 23 January 1960, Jacques Piccard (Swiss) and Don Walsh (USA) descended in the bathyscaphe *Trieste* to the floor of the Mariana Trench, a depth later calculated as 10,916m (25,831ft). The current depth was calculated by the Japanese remote-controlled probe *Kaiko* on 24 March 1995.

SEAS

LARGEST BY AREA

	km²	*miles²*
South China	2,974,600	1,148,500
Caribbean	2,515,900	971,400
Mediterranean	2,509,900	969,100
Bering	2,261,000	873,000
Gulf of Mexico	1,507,600	582,100
Okhotsk	1,392,000	537,500
Japan	1,012,900	391,100
Hudson Bay	730,100	281,900
East China	664,600	256,600
Andaman	564,880	218,100
Black Sea	507,900	196,100
Red Sea	453,000	174,900
North Sea	427,100	164,900

GREATEST DEPTHS

	metres	*feet*
Caribbean	8,605	28,232
East China (Ryu Kyu Trench)	7,507	24,629
South China	7,258	23,812
Mediterranean (Ionian Basin)	5,150	16,896
Andaman	4,267	14,000
Bering	3,936	12,913
Gulf of Mexico	3,504	11,496
Okhotsk	3,365	11,040
Japan	3,053	10,016
Red Sea	2,266	7,434
Black Sea	2,212	7,257
North Sea	439	1,440

THE CONTINENTS

There are six geographic continents, although America is often divided politically into North and Central America, and South America, so making seven.

AFRICA is surrounded by sea except for the narrow isthmus of Suez in the north-east, through which was cut the Suez Canal (opened 17 November 1869). Its extreme longitudes are 17° 20′ W. at Cape Verde, Senegal, and 51° 24′ E. at Raas Xaafunn, Somalia. The extreme latitudes are 37° 20′ N. at Cape Blanc, Tunisia, and 34° 50′ S. at Cape Agulhas, South Africa, about 7,081km (4,400 miles) apart. The Equator passes across Gabon, Republic of the Congo, Uganda, Kenya and Somalia in the middle of the continent.

NORTH AMERICA, including Mexico, is surrounded by ocean except in the south, where the isthmian states of Central America link North America with South America. Its extreme longitudes are 168° 5′ W. at Cape Prince of Wales, Alaska, and 55° 40′ W. at Cape Charles, Newfoundland. The extreme continental latitudes are the tip of the Boothia peninsula, NW Territories, Canada (71° 51′ N.) and 14° 22′ N. in southern Mexico near La Victoria, Guatemala.

SOUTH AMERICA lies mostly in the southern hemisphere, the equator passing across Ecuador, Colombia and Brazil in the north of the continent. It is surrounded by ocean except where it is joined to Central America in the north by the narrow isthmus through which was cut the Panama Canal (opened 15 August 1914). Its extreme longitudes are 34° 47′ W. at Cape Branco in Brazil and 81° 20′ W. at Punta Pariña, Peru. The extreme continental latitudes are 12° 25′ N. at Punta Gallinas, Colombia, and 53° 54′ S. at the southernmost tip of Peninsula de Brunswick, Chile. Cape Horn, on Cape Island, Chile, lies in 55° 59′ S.

ANTARCTICA lies almost entirely within the Antarctic Circle (66° 33′ S.) and is the largest of the world's glaciated areas. Ninety-eight per cent of the continent is permanently covered in ice. The ice amounts to some 30 million km^3 (7.2 million miles^3) and represents more than 70 per cent of the world's fresh water. The ice sheet is on average 1.6km (1 mile) thick; if it were to melt, the world's seas would rise by more than 60m (197ft). The environment is too hostile for unsupported human habitation.

ASIA is the largest continent and occupies 29.6 per cent of the world's land surface. The extreme longitudes are 26° 05′ E. at Baba Buran, Turkey, and 169° 40′ W. at Mys Dezhneva (East Cape), Russia, a distance of about 9,656km (6,000 miles). Its extreme northern latitude is 77° 45′ N. at Mys Chelyuskin, Russia, and it extends over 8,046km (5,000 miles) south to Tanjong Piai, Malaysia.

AUSTRALIA is the smallest of the continents and lies in the southern hemisphere. It is entirely surrounded by ocean. Its extreme longitudes are 113° 11′ E. at Steep Point, Western Australia, and 153° 11′ E. at Cape Byron, New South Wales. The extreme latitudes are 10° 42′ S. at Cape York, Queensland, and 39°S. at South East Point, Tasmania. Australia, together with New Zealand (Australasia), Papua New Guinea and the Pacific Islands, comprises Oceania.

EUROPE, including European Russia, is the smallest continent in the northern hemisphere. Its extreme latitudes are 71° 11′ N. at Nord Kapp in Norway, and 36° 23′ N. at Akra Tainaron (Matapas) in southern Greece, a distance of about 3,862km (2,400 miles). Its breadth from Cabo Carvoeiro in Portugal (9° 34′ W.) in the west to the Kara River, north of the Urals (66° 30′ E.) in the east is about 5,310km (3,300 miles). The division between Europe and Asia is generally regarded as the watershed of the Ural Mountains; down the Ural river to Atyrau, Kazakhstan; across the Caspian Sea to Apsheronskiy Poluostrov, near Baku; along the watershed of the Caucasus Mountains to Anapa and then across the Black Sea to the Bosporus in Turkey; across the Sea of Marmara to Canakkale Bogazi (Dardanelles).

Continent	*Area*	
	km^2	miles^2
Asia	43,998,000	16,988,000
America*	41,918,000	16,185,000
Africa	29,800,000	11,506,000
Antarctica	13,209,000	5,100,000
Europe†	9,699,000	3,745,000
Australia	7,618,493	2,941,526

* North and Central America has an area of 24,255,000km^2 (9,365,000 miles^2)

† Includes 5,571,000km^2 (2,151,000 miles^2) of former USSR territory, including the Baltic states, Belarus, Moldova, Ukraine and the part of Russia west of the Ural Mountains and Kazakhstan west of the Ural river. European Turkey (24,378km^2/9,412 miles^2) comprises territory to the west and north of the Bosporus and the Dardanelles

GLACIATED AREAS

It is estimated that 14,800,000km^2 (5,712,800 miles^2) or 10 per cent of the world's land surface is permanently covered with ice. Glacial retreat and thinning occurs where glaciers melt faster than they are created. The phenomenon has been observed since the mid-19th century but has accelerated since about 1980 as a result of global warming. It is most notable in the Antarctic: a 2005 report by the American Association for the Advancement of Science indicated that 87 per cent of the continent's 244 marine glaciers have retreated over the past 50 years. The largest glacier is the 515km (320 miles) long Lambert-Fisher Ice Passage, Mac Robertson Land, Eastern Antarctica.

Location	*Area*	
	km^2	miles^2
South Polar regions	13,830,000	5,340,000
North Polar regions (incl. Greenland)	1,965,000	758,500
Alaska-Canada	58,800	22,700
Asia	37,800	14,600
South America	11,900	4,600
Europe	10,700	4,128
New Zealand	1,015	391
Africa	238	92

PENINSULAS

Peninsula	*Area*	
	km^2	miles^2
Arabian	3,250,000	1,250,000
Southern Indian	2,072,000	800,000
Alaskan	1,500,000	580,000
Labradorian	1,300,000	500,000
Scandinavian	800,300	309,000
Iberian	584,000	225,500

LARGEST ISLANDS

Island and ocean	*Area*	
	km²	miles²
Greenland (Kalaallit Nunaat), Arctic	2,175,500	840,000
New Guinea, Pacific	792,500	306,000
Borneo, Pacific	725,450	280,100
Madagascar, Indian	587,041	226,674
Baffin Island, Arctic	507,451	195,928
Sumatra, Indian	427,350	165,000
Honshu, Pacific	227,413	87,805
Great Britain, Atlantic*	218,077	84,200
Victoria Island, Arctic	217,292	83,897
Ellesmere Island, Arctic	196,236	75,767

* Mainland only

LARGEST DESERTS

Desert and location	*Area (approx)*	
	km²	miles²
Sahara, N. Africa	9,000,000	3,500,000
Gobi, Mongolia/China	1,300,000	500,000
Arabian (Eastern) Desert, Egypt	1,000,000	385,000
Kalahari Desert, Botswana/ Namibia/S. Africa	570,000	220,000
Great Victoria, Australia	350,000	135,000
Taklimakan Shamo, Mongolia/ China	320,000	125,000
Kara Kum, Turkmenistan*	310,000	120,000
Great Sandy, Australia	270,000	100,000
Thar Desert, India/Pakistan	260,000	100,000
Somali Desert, Somalia	260,000	100,000

* Together with the Kyzyl Kum 259,000km² (100,000 miles²) known as the Turkestan Desert

DEEPEST DEPRESSIONS

Depression and location	*Maximum depth below sea level*	
	metres	feet
Dead Sea, Jordan/Israel	408	1,338
Lake Assal, Djibouti	156	511
Turfan Depression, Sinkiang, China	153	505
Qattara Depression, Egypt	132	436
Mangyshlak peninsula, Kazakhstan	131	433
Danakil Depression, Ethiopia	116	383
Death Valley, California, USA	86	282
Salton Sink, California, USA	71	235
West of Ustyurt plateau, Kazakhstan	70	230
Prikaspiyskaya Nizmennost', Russia/ Kazakhstan	67	220
Lake Sarykamysh, Uzbekistan/ Turkmenistan	45	148
El Faiyum, Egypt	44	147
Peninsula Valdes, Chubut, Argentina	40	131
Lake Eyre, South Australia	16	52

The world's largest exposed depression is the Prikaspiyskaya Nizmennost' covering the hinterland of the northern third of the Caspian Sea, which is itself 28m (92ft) below sea level.

Western Antarctica and central Greenland largely comprise crypto-depressions under ice burdens. The Antarctic Bentley subglacial trench has a bedrock 2,538m (8,326ft) below sea level. In Greenland (lat. 73° N., long. 39° W.) the bedrock is 365m (1,197ft) below sea level.

Nearly one quarter of the area of the Netherlands lies marginally below sea-level, an area of more than 10,000km² (3,860 miles²).

No part of the Maldives is higher than 2.4m (8ft) and nowhere in Lesotho is lower than 1,381m (4,531ft).

CAVES

DEEPEST CAVES

The world's deepest cave was discovered in January 2001 by a team of Ukrainian cave explorers in the Arabikskaya system in the western Caucasus mountains of the Georgian Republic. It is a branch of the Voronya or 'Crow's Cave'.

Cave system/location	*Depth*	
	metres	feet
Krubera (Voronya), Georgia	2,170	7,119
Lamprechtsofen Vogelschacht, Austria	1,632	5,354
Gouffre Mirolda, France	1,626	5,335
Réseau Jean Bernard, France	1,602	5,256
Torca del Cerro del Cuevon/Torca de las Saxifragas, Spain	1,589	5,213
Sarma, Georgia	1,543	5,062
Cehi 2, Slovenia	1,533	5,030
Shakta Vyacheslav, Georgia	1,508	4,947
Sistema Cheve (Cuicateco), Mexico	1,484	4,868
Sistema Huautla, Mexico	1,475	4,839

LONGEST CAVE SYSTEMS

Cave system/location	*Total known length*	
	km	miles
Mammoth Cave System, Kentucky, USA	590.6	367
Jewel Cave, South Dakota, USA	218.2	135
Optimisticheskaya, Ukraine	215.0	133
Wind Cave, South Dakota, USA	199.8	124
Hölloch, Switzerland	193.6	120
Lechuguilla Cave, New Mexico, USA	193.4	120
Fisher Ridge System, Kentucky, USA	177.3	110
Sistema Sac Actun, Mexico	155.4	97
Siebenhengste-hohgant, Switzerland	154.0	96
Gua Air Jernih, Malaysia	151.4	94

LONGEST MOUNTAIN RANGES

Range and location	*Length*	
	km	miles
Cordillera de Los Andes, W. South America	7,200	4,500
Rocky Mountains, W. North America	4,800	3,000
Himalaya-Karakoram-Hindu Kush, S. Central Asia	3,850	2,400
Great Dividing Range, E. Australia	3,620	2,250
Trans-Antarctic Mts, Antarctica	3,540	2,200
Atlantic Coast Range, E. Brazil	3,050	1,900
West Sumatran-Javan Range, Indonesia	2,900	1,800
Aleutian Range, Alaska and N.W. Pacific	2,650	1,650
Tien Shan, S. Central Asia	2,250	1,400
Central New Guinea Range, Irian Jaya/Papua New Guinea	2,010	1,250

HIGHEST MOUNTAINS

The world's twelve 8,000m (26,247ft) mountains (with five subsidiary peaks) are all in the Himalaya-Karakoram-Hindu Kush ranges.

Mountain (first ascent)	*Height*	
	metres	feet
Mt Everest* (Qomolangma) (29 May 1953)	8,850	29,035
K2 (Qogir)† (31 July 1954)	8,611	28,251
Kangchenjunga (25 May 1955)	8,597	28,208
Lhotse I (18 May 1956)	8,510	27,923
Makalu I (15 May 1955)	8,480	27,824
Lhotse Shar (II) (12 May 1979)	8,400	27,560
Dhaulagiri I (13 May 1960)	8,171	26,810
Manaslu I (Kutang I) (9 May 1956)	8,156	26,760
Cho Oyu (19 October 1954)	8,153	26,750
Nanga Parbat (Diamir) (3 July 1953)	8,125	26,660

* Named after Sir George Everest (1790–1866), Surveyor-General of India 1830–43, in 1863. He pronounced his name Eve-rest

† Formerly named after Col. Henry Haversham Godwin-Austen (1834–1923), who worked on the Trigonometrical Survey of India, which established the heights of the Himalayan peaks, including Everest

The culminating summits in the other major mountain ranges are:

Mountain, by range or country	*Height*	
	metres	feet
Pik Pobedy, Tien Shan	7,439	24,406
Cerro Aconcagua, Cordillera de Los Andes	6,960	22,834
Mt McKinley (S. Peak), Alaska Range	6,194	20,320
Kilimanjaro (Kibo), Tanzania	5,894	19,340
Hkakabo Razi, Myanmar	5,881	19,296
Citlaltépetl (Orizaba), Sierra Madre Oriental, Mexico	5,655	18,555
El'brus, (W. Peak), Caucasus	5,642	18,510
Vinson Massif, E. Antarctica	4,897	16,066
Puncak Jaya, Central New Guinea Range	4,884	16,023
Mt Blanc, Alps	4,807	15,771

HIGHEST ACTIVE VOLCANOES

Although it displays fumarolic activity, emitting steam and gas, no major eruption has ever been observed of the world's highest volcano and second highest peak in the western hemisphere, the 6,893m (22,615ft) Ojos del Salado, in the Andes on the Argentina/Chile border.

Volcano and location (most recent activity)	*Height*	
	metres	feet
Volcan Llullaillaco, Andes, Argentina/Chile (1877)	6,723	22,057
Volcan Guallatiri, Andes, Chile (1960)	6,069	19,882
Cotopaxi, Andes, Ecuador (1904)	5,897	19,347
Tupungatito, Andes, Chile (1987)	5,640	18,504
Lascar, Andes, Chile (2006)	5,591	18,346
Popocatepetl, Mexico (2006)	5,465	17,930
Nevado del Ruiz, Colombia (1991)	5,321	17,457
Sangay, Andes, Ecuador (2007)	5,188	17,021
Irruputuncu, Chile (1995)	5,163	16,939
Klyuchevskaya Sopka, Kamchatka peninsula, Russia (2005)	4,835	15,863

LAKES

LARGEST LAKES

The areas of some of the lakes listed are subject to seasonal variation. The most voluminous lakes are the Caspian Sea (saline) with 78,700km³ (18, 880 miles³) and Baikal (fresh water) with 23,000km³ (5,518 miles³). Baikal is also the world's deepest lake (*see* below). It is estimated that it contains as much water as the entire Great Lakes system – more than 20 per cent of the world's fresh water and some 90 per cent of all the fresh water in Russia.

The Aral was once the fifth largest in the world, with an area of 68,000km² (26,255 miles²), but since the 1960s its feeder rivers have been diverted for irrigation, as a result of which its area is now under 17,160km² (6,626 miles²) and continuing to contract.

Lake and location	*Area*		*Length*	
	km²	miles²	km	miles
Caspian Sea, Iran/Azerbaijan/Russia/Turkmenistan/Kazakhstan	371,000	143,000	1,171	728
Michigan–Huron, USA/Canada*	117,610	45,300	1,010	627
Superior, Canada/USA	82,100	31,700	563	350
Victoria, Uganda/Tanzania/Kenya	69,500	26,828	362	225
Tanganyika, Dem. Rep. of Congo/Tanzania/Zambia/Burundi	32,900	12,665	725	450
Great Bear, Canada	31,328	12,096	309	192
Baykal (Baikal), Russia†	30,500	11,776	620	385
Malawi (Nyasa), Tanzania/Malawi/Mozambique	28,900	11,150	580	360
Great Slave, Canada	28,570	11,031	480	298
Erie, Canada/USA	25,670	9,910	388	241

* Lakes Michigan and Huron may be regarded as lobes of the same lake. The Michigan lobe has an area of 57,750km² (22,300 miles²) and the Huron lobe an area of 59,570km² (23,000 miles²)

† World's deepest lake (1,637m/5,371ft)

UNITED KINGDOM (BY COUNTRY)

Lake and location	*Area*		*Length*	
	km²	miles²	km	miles
Lough Neagh, Northern Ireland	381.73	147.39	28.90	18.00
Loch Lomond, Scotland	71.12	27.46	36.44	22.64
Windermere, England	14.74	5.69	16.90	10.50
Lake Vyrnwy, Wales (artificial)	4.53	1.75	7.56	4.70
Llyn Tegid (Bala), Wales (natural)	4.38	1.69	5.80	3.65

LARGEST MANMADE LAKES

*Dam/lake**	*Volume*	
	km³	miles³
Owen Falls, Uganda/Kenya/Tanzania (1954)	204.80	49.13
Bratskoye, Russia (1967)	169.27	40.61
Nasser, Egypt (1970)	168.90	40.52
Kariba, Zimbabwe/Zambia (1959)	160.30	38.46
Volta, Ghana (1965)	148.00	35.51
Daniel Johnson, Canada (1968)	141.85	34.03
Guri (Raul Leoni), Venezuela (1986)	136.30	33.11
Krasnoyarskoye, Russia (1967)	73.30	17.58
Wadi-Tatar, Iraq (1967)	72.80	17.46
W.A.C. Bennett, Canada (1967)	70.31	16.87

* Formed as a result of dam construction

DEEPEST LAKES

Lake and location	*Greatest depth*	
	metres	feet
Baikal, Russia	1,637	5,371
Tanganyika, Burundi/Tanzania/Dem. Rep. of Congo/Zambia	1,470	4,825
Caspian Sea, Azerbaijan/Iran/Kazakhstan/Russia/Turkmenistan	1,025	3,363
Malawi, Malawi/Mozambique/Tanzania	706	2,316
Issyk Kul, Kyrgyzstan	702	2,303
Great Slave, Canada	614	2,015
Danau Toba, Indonesia	590	1,936
Hornindalsvastnet, Norway	514	1,686
Sarezskoye Ozero, Tajikistan	505	1,657
Tahoe, California/Nevada, USA	501	1,645
Lago Argentina, Argentina	500	1,640
Lac Kivu, Rwanda/Dem. Rep. of Congo	480	1,574
Quesnel, Canada	475	1,558

LONGEST RIVERS

River, source and outflow	*Length*	
	km	miles
Nile (Bahr-el-Nil), R. Luvironza, Burundi–E. Mediterranean Sea	6,725	4,180
Amazon (Amazonas), Lago Villafro, Peru–S. Atlantic Ocean	6,448	4,007
Yangtze-Kiang (Chang Jiang), Kunlun Mts, W. China–Yellow Sea	6,380	3,964
Mississippi-Missouri-Red Rock, Montana–Gulf of Mexico	5,970	3,710
Yenisey-Angara, W. Mongolia–Kara Sea	5,536	3,440
Huang He (Yellow River), Bayan Har Shan range, Central China–Yellow Sea	5,463	3,395
Ob'-Irtysh, W. Mongolia–Kara Sea	5,410	3,362
Zaire (Congo), R. Lualaba, Dem. Rep. of Congo-Zambia–S. Atlantic Ocean	4,665	2,900
Amur-Argun, R. Argun, Khingan Mts, N. China–Sea of Okhotsk	4,416	2,744
Lena-Kirenga, R. Kirenga, W. of Lake Baikal–Laptev Sea, Arctic Ocean	4,400	2,734

BRITISH ISLES

River, source and outflow	*Length*	
	km	miles
Shannon, Co. Cavan, Rep. of Ireland–Atlantic Ocean	386	240
Severn, Powys, Wales–Bristol Channel	354	220
Thames, Gloucestershire, England–North Sea	346	215
Tay, Perthshire, Scotland–North Sea	188	117
Clyde, Lanarkshire, Scotland–Firth of Clyde	158	98.5
Tweed, Scottish Borders–North Sea	155	96.5
Bann (Upper and Lower), Co. Down, N. Ireland–Atlantic Ocean	122	76

WATERFALLS

GREATEST BY HEIGHT

Waterfall, river and location	*Total drop*		*Greatest single leap*	
	metres	feet	metres	feet
Salto Angel, Carrao Auyan Tepui, Venezuela	979	3,212	807	2,648
Tugela, Tugela, Natal, S. Africa (5 leaps)	948	3,110	410	1,350
Ramnefjellsfossen, Jostedal Glacier, Norway	800	2,625	600	1,970
Mongefossen, Monge, Norway	773	2,535	—	—
Gocta, Cocahuayco, Peru	771	2,531	—	—
Mutarazi, Mutarazi, Zimbabwe	762	2,499	479	1,572
Yosemite, Yosemite Creek, USA	739	2,425	435	1,430
Østre Mardola Foss, Mardals, Norway*	655	2,149	296	974
Tyssestrengene, Tysso, Norway*	646	2,120	289	948
Cuquenan, Arabopo, Venezuela	610	2,000	—	—

* Volume much affected by hydroelectric harnessing

BRITISH ISLES, BY HEIGHT

Waterfall, river and location	*Total drop*	
	metres	feet
Eas a' Chual Aluinn, Glas Bheinn, Sutherland, Scotland	200	656
Powerscourt Falls, Dargle, Co. Wicklow, Rep. of Ireland	121	398
Pistyll-y-Llyn, Powys/Dyfed border, Wales (cascades)	91	300
Pistyll Rhyadr, Clwyd/Powys border, Wales (single leap)	71.5	235
Cauldron Snout, Tees, Cumbria/Durham, England (cascades)	61	200

GREATEST BY VOLUME

*Waterfall, river and location**	*Mean annual flow* m^3/sec
Khone, Mekong, Laos	11,610
Para, Caura, Venezuela	3,540
Paulo Afonso, Sao Francisco, Brazil	2,832
Niagara (Horseshoe), Niagara/Lake Erie–Lake Ontario, Canada	2,407
Salto de Iguaçu, Parana, Argentina/Brazil	1,746
Victoria (Mosi-oa-Tunya), Zambezi, Zimbabwe/Zambia	1,088
Virginia, Nahanni, Canada	1,000
Sivasamudram, Kaveri (Cauvery), India	934
Kongou, Ivindo, Gabon	900
Williamette, Williamette, Oregon, USA	874

* Excludes waterfalls that have been submerged as a result of dam construction or consist of rapids or cascades with individual vertical drops of less than 6m (20ft)

DAMS

TALLEST DAMS

Dam and location	Height metres	Height feet
Rogun, R. Vakhsh, Tajikistan	335	1,098
Nurek, R. Vakhsh, Tajikistan	300	984
Grande Dixence, Switzerland	285	935
Longtan, R. Hangshui, China	285	935
Inguri, Georgia	272	892
Borucu, Costa Rica	267	876
Vaiont, Italy	262	859
Manuel M. Torres, Chicoasén, Mexico	261	856
Tehri, R. Bhagivathi, India	261	856

GREATEST VOLUME* DAMS

Dam and location	Volume thousand m³	Volume thousand yd³
Three Gorges, China†	39,300,000	51,402,459
Syncrude Tailings, Canada (1992)	540,000	706,293
Chapetón , Argentina†	296,200	387,415
Pati, Argentina (1990)	238,180	311,528
New Cornelia Tailings, USA (1973)	209,500	274,016
Tarbela, Pakistan (1976)	121,720	159,204
Kambaratinsk, Kyrgyzstan†	112,200	146,752
Fort Peck, USA (1937)	96,050	125,629
Lower Usuma, Nigeria (1990)	93,049	121,703
Cipasang, Indonesia†	90,000	117,716

* Of material used in construction (earth, rocks, concrete, etc)
† Under construction

TALLEST ...

INHABITED BUILDINGS*

Building and location	Height metres	Height feet
Burj Dubai, UAE (2008)	643	2,111
Taipei 101, Taipei, Taiwan (2003)	509	1,671
Petronas Towers I and II, Kuala Lumpur, Malaysia (1998)	452	1,482
Sears Tower, Chicago† (1974)	443	1,454
Jin Mao, Shanghai, China (1998)	420	1,378
Two International Finance Centre, Hong Kong (2003)	412	1,352
CITIC Plaza, Guangzhou, China (1996)	391	1,283
Shun Hing Square, Shenzhen, China (1996)	384	1,260
Empire State Building, New York, USA (1931)‡	381	1,250
Central Plaza, Hong Kong, China (1992)	373	1,227

* The two World Trade Center towers, One (1972) 110 storeys, 417m (1,368ft) or 521m (1,716ft) with TV antennae; and Two (1973) 110 storeys, 415m (1,362ft), were destroyed by two terrorist-hijacked aircraft on 11 September 2001
† With TV antennae, 520m (1,707ft)
‡ With TV tower (added 1950–1), 430.9m (1,414ft)

STRUCTURES

Structure and location	Height metres	Height feet
Warszawa Radio Mast, Konstantynow, Poland (1974)*	646	2,120
KVLY (formerly KTHI)-TV Mast, Blanchard, North Dakota (guyed), USA (1963)†	629	2,063
Indosat Telkom Tower, Jakarta, Indonesia	558	1,831
CN Tower, Metro Centre, Toronto, Canada (1975)	555	1,822
Ostankino Tower, Moscow (1967)	540	1,772

* Collapsed during renovation, August 1991. New structure planned on site at Solkajawski
† The USA has eight other guyed TV towers above 555m (1,822ft)

TWIN TOWERS

Structure and location	Storeys	Height metres	Height feet
Petronas Towers, Malaysia (1997)	96	452	1,482
Al Fattan Towers, UAE (2006)	60	245	802
Grand Gateway, China (2005)	25	225	738
Atlantic Richfield Tower, USA (1972)	52	213	699
Huaxia Finance Square, China (2005)	42	202	670
Parque Central Offinicas, Venezuela (1986)	56	200	656
Murjan/Mesk Towers, UAE (2003)	40	185	607
Collins Place, Australia (1981)	50	185	607
101 California Plaza, USA (1986)	48	183	600
Exchange Square, Hong Kong (1982)	52	182	597
Destroyed			
World Trade Center One, USA (1972)	110	417	1,368
World Trade Center Two, USA (1973)	110	415	1,362

CHURCHES

Structure and location	Height metres	Height feet
Sagrada Família, Barcelona, Spain (2026*)	170	558
Ulm Cathedral, Ulm, Germany (1890)	162	530
Notre-Dame Cathedral, Rouen, France (1876)	158	518
Cologne Cathedral, Cologne, Germany (1880)	157	516
Our Lady of Peace Basilica, Yamoussoukro, Côte d'Ivoire (1990)	149	489
St Nicholas Church, Hamburg, Germany (1847)	147	482
Notre-Dame Cathedral, Strasbourg, France (1439)	144	472
Queen of Peace Shrine and Basilica, Lichen, Poland (2002)	140	459
Basilica of St Peter, Rome, Italy (1626)	138	452
St Stephen's Cathedral, Vienna, Austria (1570)	137	448

* Projected completion date

The Chicago Methodist Temple, Chicago, USA (completed 1924) is 173m (568ft) high, but is sited atop a 25-storey, 100m (328ft) building. Salisbury Cathedral (1521), at 123m (404ft), is the UK's tallest religious building. St Paul's Cathedral, London, and Liverpool Anglican Cathedral are the only others in the UK over 100m (328ft) tall.

TALLEST STRUCTURES — A CHRONOLOGY

Structure and location	*Year*	*Height*	
		metres	feet
Djoser's Step Pyramid, Saqqara, Egypt	c.2650 BC	61	200
Pyramid of Meidum, Egypt	c.2600 BC	92	302
Snefru's Bent Pyramid, Dahshur, Egypt	c.2600 BC	102	336
Red Pyramid, Dahshur, Egypt	c.2590 BC	105	345
Great Pyramid, Giza, Egypt*	c.2580 BC	146	479
Liuhe (Six Harmonies) Pagoda, Hangzhou, China†	AD 970	150	492
Lincoln Cathedral, Lincoln, England‡	1311–1400	160	525
St Paul's Cathedral, London, England§☾	1315	149	489
St Olaf's Church, Tallinn, Estonia**	1438–1519	159	522
Notre-Dame, Strasbourg, France§	1439	143	469
St Nicholas Church, Hamburg, Germany§	1847	147	482
Rouen Cathedral, Rouen, France	1876	148	485
Cologne Cathedral, Cologne, Germany	1880	157	515
Washington Monument, Washington DC, USA	1884	169	555
Eiffel Tower, Paris, France	1889	300	984
Chrysler Building, New York, USA	1930	319	1,046
Empire State Building, New York, USA	1930	381	1,250
KWTV Mast, Oklahoma City, USA	1954	479	1,572
KOBR-TV Tower, Caprock, USA	1960	490	1,608
KFVS TV Mast, Egypt Mills, USA	1960	511	1,677
Nexstar Broadcasting Tower Vivian, Vivian, USA	1961	534	1,752
KVLY (formerly KTHI)-TV Mast, Blanchard, USA§	1963	629	2,063
Warszawa Radio Mast, Konstantynow, Poland††	1974	646	2,118

* Later reduced through loss of topstone to 137m (449ft)
† Destroyed in 1121
‡ Destroyed in 1549
§ The collapse of taller structures enabled these runners-up to gain or re-gain the status of 'world's tallest'
☾ Destroyed in 1561
** Spire burned down in 1625; renovated in 1931 to present height of 123m (403ft)
†† Collapsed in 1991 during renovation

BRIDGES

The longest stretch of bridgings of any kind is that carrying the Interstate 55 and Interstate 10 highways at Manchac, Louisiana, USA (1979), on twin concrete trestles over 55.21km (34.31 miles). The 'floating' bridging at Evergreen Point, Seattle, Washington, USA (1963), is 3,839m (12,596ft) long, of which 2,310m (7,578ft) floats.

LONGEST SUSPENSION SPANS

Bridge and location	*Length*	
	metres	feet
Akashi-Kaikyo, Shikoku, Japan (1998)	1,990	6,529
Xihoumen, China (due in 2008)	1,650	5,413
Storebaelt East Bridge, Denmark (1998)	1,624	5,328
Runyang (Yangtze), China (2005)	1,490	4,888
Humber Estuary, England (1981)	1,410	4,626
Jiangyin (Yangtze), China (1999)	1,385	4,544
Tsing Ma, Hong Kong, China (1997)	1,377	4,518
Verrazano Narrows, NY, USA (1964)	1,298	4,260
Golden Gate, San Francisco Bay, USA (1937)	1,280	4,200
Yangluo, Wuhan, China (2007)	1,280	4,200

LONGEST CANTILEVER SPANS

Bridge and location	*Length*	
	metres	feet
Pont de Québec (rail-road), St Lawrence, Canada (1917)	548.6	1,800
Ravenswood, W. Virginia, USA (1981)	525.1	1,723
Firth of Forth (rail), Scotland (two spans of 1,710ft each) (1890)	521.2	1,710
Minato (Nanko), Osaka, Japan (1974)	510.0	1,673
Commodore Barry, Pennsylvania to New Jersey, USA (1974)	494.3	1,622
Greater New Orleans, Louisiana, USA (I 1958, II 1988)	480.0	1,575
Howrah (rail-road), Calcutta, India (1936–43)	457.2	1,500
Veterans Memorial, Louisiana, USA (1995)	445.0	1,460
Transbay, San Francisco, USA (1936)	426.7	1,400
Ikitsuki, Nagasaki, Japan (1991)	400.0	1,312

LONGEST STEEL ARCH SPANS

Bridge and location	*Length*	
	metres	feet
Lupu, Shanghai, China (2003)	550.0	1,804
New River Gorge, W. Virginia, USA (1977)	518.0	1,700
Bayonne (Kill van Kull), NY, USA (1931)	510.5	1,675
Sydney Harbour, Sydney, Australia (1932)	502.9	1,650
Chenab, Katra, India (due in 2008)	480.0	1,575
Wushan, Chongqing, China (2005)	460	1,509

Caiyuanba, Chongqing, China (2005)	420.0	1,378
Numata River Gorge, Hiroshima, Japan (due in 2007)	380.0	1,247
Port Mann, Vancouver, Canada (1964)	365.7	1,200

TALLEST BRIDGE TOWERS

Bridge and location	*Height*	
	metres	feet
Millau, Millau, France (2004)	343	1,125
Akashi-Kaikyo, Akashi, Japan (1998)	298	978
East Bridge, Great Belt Fixed Link, Sprogo, Denmark (1997)	254	833
Golden Gate, San Francisco, USA (1937)	227	754
Tatara, Onomichi, Japan (1999)	226	741
Jambatan Pulau Pinang, Penang Malaysia (1985)	225	739
Le Ponte de Normandie, Le Havre, France (1994)	215	705
Verrazano Narrows, New York, USA (1964)	211	692
Tsing Ma, Hong Kong, China (1997)	206	675
Mezcala-Solidaridad, Cuilapan, Mexico (1993)	205	673

LONGEST VEHICULAR TUNNELS

Tunnel and location	*Length*	
	km	miles
*Seikan (rail), Tsugaru Channel, Japan (1988)	53.85	33.46
*Channel Tunnel, (rail) Cheriton, Kent, UK–Sangatte, Calais, France (1994)	50.45	31.35
Moscow metro, Belyaevo–Bittsevsky, Moscow, Russia (1979)	37.90	23.50
Lötschberg (rail), Switzerland (2007)	34.58	21.49
Northern Line tube, East Finchley–Morden, London (1939)	27.84	17.30
Guadarrama (rail), Spain (2007)	28.38	17.63
Iwate (rail), Japan (2002)	25.81	16.03
Laerdal–Aurland Road Link, Norway (2000)	24.51	15.22
*Oshimizu (rail), Honshu, Japan (1982)	22.17	13.78
Simplon II (rail), Brigue, Switzerland–Iselle, Italy (1922)	19.82	12.31

* Sub-aqueous

The longest non-vehicular tunnelling in the world is the Delaware Aqueduct in New York State, USA, constructed in 1937–44 to a length of 168.9km (105 miles).

St Gotthard (rail) tunnel in Switzerland will be 57.07km (35.46 miles) long when completed in 2010.

BRITISH RAIL TUNNELS

	Length	
	km	miles
Severn, Bristol—Newport	6.88	4.28
Totley, Manchester—Sheffield	5.70	3.54
Standedge, Manchester—Huddersfield	4.89	3.04
Sodbury, Swindon—Bristol	4.06	2.53
Strood, Medway, Kent	3.61	2.24
Disley, Stockport—Sheffield	3.54	2.20
Ffestiniog, Llandudno—Blaenau Ffestiniog	3.53	2.19
Bramhope, Leeds—Harrogate	3.44	2.14
Cowburn, Manchester—Sheffield	3.39	2.10

The longest road tunnel in Britain is the Mersey Queensway Tunnel (1934), 3.42km (2 miles 228 yards) long. The longest canal tunnel, at Standedge, W. Yorks, is 5.03km/3.13 miles long; it was completed in 1811, closed in 1944 and reopened in 2001.

LONGEST SHIP CANALS

Canal	*Length*		*Min. depth*	
	km	miles	metres	feet
White Sea-Baltic (formerly Stalin) (1933), of which canalised river 51.5km (32 miles)	235	146.02	5.0	16.5
*Suez (1869) Links Red and Mediterranean Seas	162	100.60	12.9	42.3
V. I. Lenin Volga-Don (1952) Links Black and Caspian Seas	100	62.20	n/a	n/a
Kiel (or North Sea) (1895) Links North and Baltic Seas	98	60.90	13.7	45.0
*Houston (1940) Links inland city with Gulf of Mexico	91	56.70	10.4	34.0
Alphonse XIII (1926) Gives Seville access to Atlantic Ocean	85	53.00	7.6	25.0
Panama (1914) Links Pacific Ocean and Caribbean Sea; lake chain, 78.9km (49 miles) dug	82	50.71	12.5	41.0
Manchester Ship (1894) Links city with Irish Channel	64	39.70	8.5	28.0
Welland (1932) Circumvents Niagara Falls and Rapids	43.5	27.00	8.8	29.0
Brussels (Rupel Sea) (1922) Renders Brussels an inland port	32	19.80	6.4	21.0

* Has no locks

The first section of China's Grand Canal, running 1,782km (1,107 miles) from Beijing to Hangzhou, was opened in AD 610 and completed in 1283. Today it is limited to 2,000-tonne vessels.

The St Lawrence Seaway comprises the Beauharnois, Welland and Welland Bypass and Seaway 54-59 canals, and allows access to Duluth, Minnesota, USA via the Great Lakes from the Atlantic end of Canada's Gulf of St Lawrence, a distance of 3,769km (2,342 miles). The St Lawrence Canal, completed in 1959, is 293km (182 miles) long.

THE ANTARCTIC

ne Antarctic is generally defined as the area lying within e Antarctic Convergence, the zone where cold orthward-flowing Antarctic sea water sinks below armer southward-flowing water. This zone is pproximately at latitude 50° S. in the Atlantic Ocean and titude 55°– 62° S. in the Pacific Ocean. The continent self lies almost entirely within the Antarctic Circle, an ea of around 13,209,000 million sq. km, 99.4 per cent which is permanently ice-covered. The average ickness of the ice is 2,450m but in places exceeds 500m. The ice amounts to some 30 million cubic km nd represents almost 70 per cent of the world's fresh ater and 90 per cent of the world's ice. Much of the sea eezes in winter, forming fast ice which breaks up in mmer and drifts north as pack ice.

ISTORY AND DISCOVERY

he idea of Antarctica is much older than the proof of e continent's existence. The belief in *Terra Australis*, a st southern continent to balance the northern lands f Europe, Asia and North Africa, originated with ristotle and was commonly found on world maps until e end of the eighteenth century. The size of this land as corrected after the explorer James Cook rcumnavigated the globe in 1774. He travelled from ew Zealand to the Cape of Good Hope (via Tierra del uego) at a high southern latitude (between 53° and 0°), confirming that any landmass must be confined to e polar regions.

The date of the first sighting of Antarctica is unclear. In 820 three separate expeditions, from the UK, the USA nd Russia each claimed to have seen the continent within ays of each other and the argument has never been ttled. The golden age of Antarctic exploration was rompted by the discovery of the magnetic North Pole in 831, but it was not until the beginning of the twentieth entury that real progress was made. James Clark Ross as the first to identify the approximate location of the outh Pole, but he was unable to reach it. British explorers obert Scott in 1901–4 and Ernest Shackleton in 1907– got closer, but it was not until Norwegian adventurer oald Amundsen pioneered a new route, through the xel Heiberg Glacier, that the pole was reached in ecember 1911. Scott's second attempt was also ccessful, but he arrived a month later. Infamously, he nd all his team perished on their return journey.

By the 1930s aircraft had superseded ships as the rimary method to explore the continent, following US avy Rear Admiral Richard Evelyn Byrd's first flight over e South Pole in 1929. In 1957 US Navy Commander onrad Shinn became the first man to land an aeroplane n the continent; this enabled scientific study and polar abitation on a much larger scale.

LIMATE AND TERRAIN

ntarctica is the highest, coldest and driest continent on arth with average coastal temperatures ranging from just bove freezing in the summer (December–February) to 20°C (–4°F) in the winter. Conditions on the interior lateau are more severe with katabatic (gravity-driven) inds and frequent cyclonic storms pushing average winter temperatures down to –65°C (–85°F). The Vostok research station holds the current record for the lowest surface temperature ever recorded on earth at –89.5°C (–129°F).

Elevation extremes range from 4,897m (Vinson Massif) at the highest point to –2,540m (Bentley Subglacial Trench) at the lowest. The most conspicuous physical features of the Antarctic are the high inland plateau (much of which is 3,000m above sea level), the Transantarctic Mountains, the Antarctic Peninsula and off-lying islands that extend north towards South America.

CLIMATE CHANGE

Unlike in the Arctic, where there has been a significant and visible decline in the levels of sea ice, there have been only negligible changes in equivalent levels in the Antarctic. However, a number of other important changes to the ecosystem have been observed. The British Antarctic Survey have found that the west coast of the Antarctic Peninsula has become one of the fastest-warming areas on the planet, with annual mean temperatures rising by nearly 3°C in the last 50 years. This is approximately ten times the mean rate of global warming. Curiously, the temperatures recorded by the Amundsen-Scott station at the South Pole actually show a recent cooling. The precise cause of this is unknown, but scientists have proposed that the warming of the seas in the surrounding ocean has produced more precipitation, which has cooled the centre when it falls as snow.

This change in climate has already affected the continent's wildlife. The number of Adelie penguins – a species well adapted to sea ice conditions – has fallen, replaced by open-water species such as the chinstrap penguin. Similarly, there has been a substantial fall in the recorded levels of krill because of the reduction in sea ice that provides protection from predators.

The climate is evidently changing, but as yet, it cannot be conclusively proven that these changes are a result of human activity rather than natural variability. However, the collapse of the Larsen B ice shelf in 2002 indicates some human impact – records show it has been stable for much of the previous 10,000 years. Recent warm temperatures are exceptional within this context, making natural deviation alone unlikely.

FLORA AND FAUNA

The only land animals to survive on the Antarctic continent are tiny insects and mites, with nematodes, rotifers and tardigrades in the mosses. The largest land animal is the *Belgica antarctica*, a flightless midge just 12mm in size. The snow petrel is one of only three birds that breed exclusively in Antarctica and have been seen at the South Pole. Large numbers of seals, penguins and other sea-birds go ashore to breed in the summer; the emperor penguin is the only species that breeds ashore throughout the winter. By contrast, the Antarctic seas abound with life; recent expectations identified over 700 previously unknown species. Krill, which congregates in large schools containing millions of organisms, is the centre of the Antarctic ecosystem and provides a diet for whales (including killer, humpback and blue whales), a number of species of seal, penguins, albatrosses and other smaller birds. Four species of albatross breed in South Georgia during the summer, but their numbers are in serious decline due to the effects of longline fishing in the Southern Ocean region.

With almost all of the Antarctic continent permanently covered in ice, only a small number of flowering plants, ferns and clubmosses survive. Most of these are found on the sub-Antarctic islands, while only two species (a grass and a pearlwort) extend south of 60° S. Both of these species are thriving due to the warming temperatures. Antarctic vegetation is dominated by lichens and mosses, with a few liverworts, algae and fungi surviving in the cracks and pore spaces of sandstone and granite rocks.

The 1978 Antarctic Conservation Act introduced new measures to maintain the balance of the ecosystem in the face of rising numbers of human visits. The introduction of alien plant and animal species is illegal, as is the extraction of indigenous species.

ANTARCTIC LAW

The Antarctic Treaty was signed on 1 December 1959 when 12 states (Argentina, Australia, Belgium, Chile, France, Japan, New Zealand, Norway, South Africa, the Soviet Union, the UK and the USA) pledged themselves to promote scientific and technical cooperation unhampered by politics. The signatories agreed t establish free use of the Antarctic continent for peacefu scientific purposes; to freeze all territorial claims an disputes in the Antarctic; to ban all military activities i the area; and to prohibit nuclear explosions and th disposal of radioactive waste. The Antarctic Treaty wa defined as covering areas south of latitude 60° S. excluding the high seas but including the ice shelves, an came into force in 1961. The treaty provides that an member of the United Nations can accede to it. It ha since been signed by a further 34 states, 16 of which ar active in the Antarctic and have therefore been accorde consultative status, bringing the number of consultativ parties to 28. In 1998 an extension to the treaty came int effect, placing a 50-year ban on mining, oil exploratio and mineral extraction in Antarctica. Furthermore, a tourists, explorers and expeditions now need permissio to enter the Antarctic.

TERRITORIAL CLAIMS

Under the provisions of the Antarctic Treaty all territori claims and disputes were frozen.

The section of the continent between 90° W. an 150° W. is unclaimed by any state, the only such piece c land on Earth.

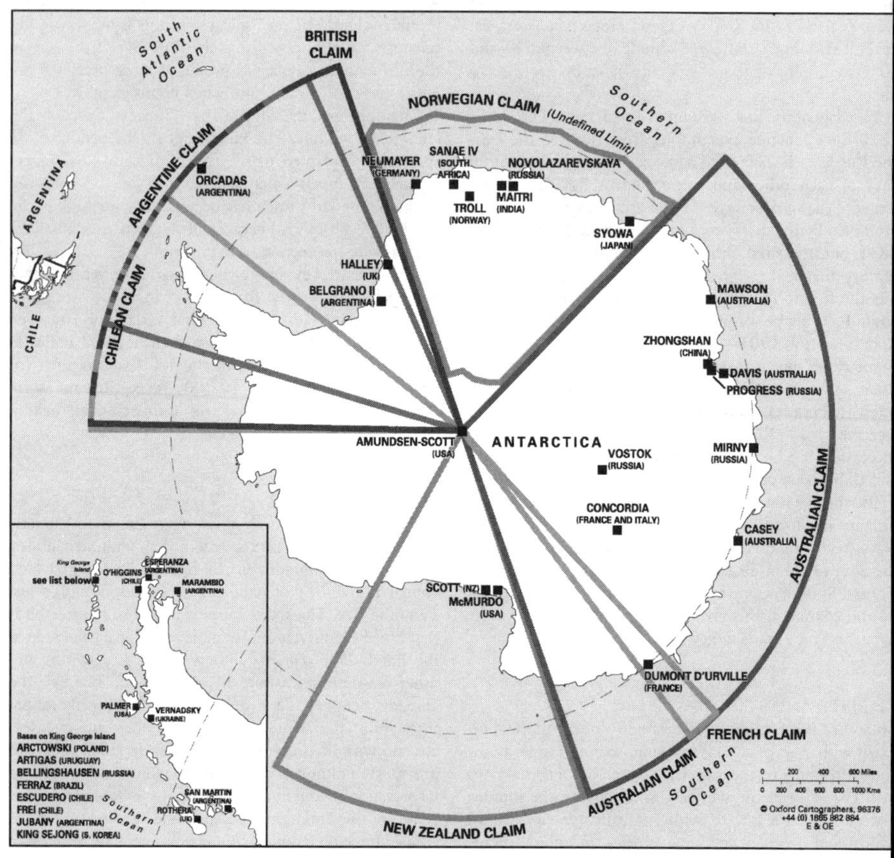

CIENTIFIC RESEARCH

here are some 20 nations with permanently manned search stations in Antarctica:

Country	*Number of research stations*
Argentina	6
Russian Federation	5
Australia	3
Chile	3
USA	3
France	2
UK	2

razil, China, Germany, India, Italy, Japan, New Zealand, orway, Poland, Republic of Korea, South Africa, kraine and Uruguay each have a single station.

OPULATION AND TOURISM

ntarctica has no indigenous inhabitants, although the ontinent maintains a population of tourists, scientists and search workers which peaks in the summer months, at pproximately 3,500.

Antarctic tourism is a growth industry. The first *Lonely lanet* guide to Antarctica was published in 2000 and nip-borne cruises now depart from Argentina, Chile, ustralia and New Zealand, lasting from two days to veral weeks. The continent has also become a popular enue for extreme sports enthusiasts: it is now possible to ky-dive, ski, ride a motorbike and fly a helicopter across ne continent, whilst the huts built by Scott and Shackleton are also popular attractions. The Antarctic and Southern Ocean Coalition recorded 4,698 tourists in the 1990–1 summer season, rising to over 28,000 by 2005–6.

In 1991 the International Association of Antarctica Tour Operators was founded with the objective of providing a self-regulating code of conduct for all operators to follow, but membership is not yet compulsory, raising fears about the environmental damage a booming tourist industry could create.

INTERNATIONAL POLAR YEAR

The first International Polar Year (IPY) since 1957 began on 1 March 2007. IPY is a large collaborative scientific programme focused on both the Arctic and Antarctic. The 'year' actually spans two full seasonal cycles on both poles, and so runs until March 2009. Four 'urgencies' have been identified for particular study in this period: the effects of changing levels of snow and ice within the polar regions; their tangential influence on the wider world; the changes facing northern communities and the further discovery and understanding of life under ice.

THE BRITISH ANTARCTIC SURVEY

The British Antarctic Survey (BAS) is part of the Natural Environment Research Council and carries out the majority of Britain's scientific research in Antarctica. Over 400 staff are employed by BAS and the organisation supports five research stations, two of which are staffed throughout the winter months. See BAS's website (W www.bas.ac.uk) for further information.

DISTANCES FROM LONDON BY AIR

The following list details the distances from Heathrow Airport in London to various airports abroad. International Air Transport Association (IATA) airport codes are given in brackets.

To	*Km*	*Miles*
Abu Dhabi (AUH)	5,512	3,425
Acapulco (Gen. Juan N Alvarez/ ACA)	9,177	5,702
Accra (Kotoka, ACC)	5,097	3,167
Addis Ababa (Bole, ADD)	5,915	3,675
Adelaide (ADL)	16,283	10,111
Aden (ADE)	5,907	3,670
Alexandria (ALY)	3,350	2,082
Algiers (Houari Boumediene, ALG)	1,666	1,035
Amman (Queen Alia, AMM)	3,681	2,287
Amsterdam (Schiphol, AMS)	370	230
Anchorage (Ted Stevens, ANC)	7,196	4,472
Ankara (Esenboga, ESB)	2,848	1,770
Atlanta (Hartsfield-Jackson, ATL)	6,756	4,198
Auckland (AKL)	18,353	11,404
Bali (Ngurah Rai, DPS)	12,518	7,779
Bangkok (Suvarnabhumi, BKK)	9,540	5,928
Barcelona (El Prat, BCN)	1,146	712
Beijing (Capital, PEK)	8,148	5,063
Beirut (Rafic Hariri, BEY)	3,478	2,161
Belfast (Aldergrove, BFS)	524	325
Belgrade (Nikola Tesla, BEG)	1,700	1,056
Belize City (Philip Goldson, BZE)	8,340	5,182
Benghazi (Benina, BEN)	2,734	1,699
Berlin (Tegel, TXL)	947	588
Bogotá (El Dorado, BOG)	8,468	5,262
Boston (Logan, BOS)	5,239	3,255
Brasília (Presidente Juscelino Kubitschek, BSB)	8,775	5,452
Bratislava (M. R. Stefanik, BTS)	1,315	817
Brazzaville (Maya Maya, BZV)	6,368	3,957
Bridgetown (Grantley Adams, BGI)	6,748	4,193
Brisbane (BNE)	16,533	10,273
Brussels (BRU)	349	217
Bucharest (Henri Coanda, OTP)	2,103	1,307
Budapest (Ferihegy, BUD)	1,486	923
Buenos Aires (Ezeiza, EZE)	11,129	6,915
Cairo (CAI)	3,531	2,194
Calgary (YYC)	7,012	4,357
Canberra (CBR)	16,999	10,563
Cape Town (CPT)	9,675	6,011
Caracas (Simón Bolívar, CCS)	7,466	4,639
Casablanca (Mohammed V, CMN)	2,092	1,300
Chennai/Madras (MAA)	8,229	5,113
Chicago (O'Hare, ORD)	6,343	3,941
Cologne/Bonn (CGN)	533	331
Colombo (Bandaranaike, CMB)	8,708	5,411
Copenhagen (CPH)	978	608
Dallas-Fort Worth (DFW)	7,622	4,736
Damascus (DAM)	3,577	2,223
Dar es Salaam (DAR)	7,502	4,662
Darwin (DRW)	13,861	8,613
Denver (DEN)	7,492	4,655
Dhaka (Zia, DAC)	8,008	4,976
Doha (DOH)	5,235	3,253
Douala (DLA)	5,356	3,32
Dresden (DRS)	987	61
Dubai (DXB)	5,494	3,41
Dublin (DUB)	449	27
Dubrovnik (DBV)	1,727	1,07
Dundee (DND)	579	35
Durban (DUR)	9,555	5,93
Düsseldorf (DUS)	500	31
Edmonton (YEG)	6,805	4,22
Frankfurt (FRA)	653	40
Gaborone (Sir Seretse Khama, GBE)	8,842	5,49
Geneva (GVA)	754	46
Glasgow (GLA)	555	34
Guatemala City (La Aurora, GUA)	8,745	5,43
Hamburg (HAM)	745	46
Hannover (HAJ)	703	43
Harare (HRE)	8,298	5,15
Havana (José Martí, HAV)	7,479	4,64
Helsinki (Vantaa, HEL)	1,847	1,14
Ho Chi Minh City (Tan Son Nhat, SGN)	10,211	6,34
Hong Kong (HKG)	9,640	5,99
Honolulu (HNL)	11,619	7,22
Houston (George Bush Intercontinental, IAH)	7,759	4,82
Islamabad (ISB)	6,062	3,76
Isle of Man (Ronaldsway, IOM)	403	25
Istanbul (Ataturk, IST)	2,510	1,56
Jakarta (Halim Perdanakusuma, HLP)	11,741	7,29
Jeddah (King Abdulaziz, JED)	4,743	2,94
Johannesburg (JNB)	9,068	5,63
Kabul (Khwadja Rawash, KBL)	5,726	3,55
Karachi (Jinnah, KHI)	6,334	3,93
Kathmandu (Tribhuvan, KTM)	7,354	4,57
Khartoum (KRT)	4,943	3,07
Kiev (Boryspil, KBP)	2,184	1,35
Kigali (KGL)	6,600	4,10
Kilimanjaro (JRO)	7,055	4,38
Kingston, Jamaica (Norman Manley, KIN)	7,513	4,66
Kinshasa (N'Djili, FIH)	6,387	3,96
Kolkata/Calcutta (Netaji Subhas Chandra Bose, CCU)	7,979	4,95
Kraków (John Paul II, KRK)	1,425	88
Kuala Lumpur (KUL)	10,552	6,55
Kuwait (KWI)	4,671	2,90
Lagos (Murtala Muhammed, LOS)	5,000	3,10
Larnaca (LCA)	3,276	2,03
Las Palmas (Gran Canaria, LPA)	2,897	1,80
Lisbon (Portela, LIS)	1,564	97
Ljubljana (Brnik, LJU)	1,233	76
Lomé (Tokoin, LFW)	5,036	3,12
Los Angeles (LAX)	8,753	5,43
Luanda (Quatro de Fevereiro, LAD)	6,830	4,24
Lusaka (LUN)	7,933	4,92
Luxor (LXR)	3,999	2,48
Lyon-Bron (LYN)	750	46
Madrid (Barajas, MAD)	1,244	77
Málaga (AGP)	1,675	1,04
Malé (MLE)	8,533	5,30
Malmö-Sturup (MMX)	1,017	63
Malta (Luqa, MLA)	2,100	1,30

anila (Ninoy Aquino, MNL)	10,758	6,685
aputo (MPM)	9,184	5,707
arrakech-Menara (RAK)	2,292	1,424
arseille (Provence, MRS)	988	614
elbourne (Tullamarine, MEL)	16,897	10,499
emphis (MEM)	7,005	4,353
enorca (MAH)	1,339	832
exico City (Benito Juarez, MEX)	8,899	5,529
iami (MIA)	7,104	4,414
ilan (Malpensa, MXP)	979	609
inneapolis-St Paul (MSP)	6,439	4,001
insk (Minsk 2, MSQ)	1,893	1,176
ombasa (Moi, MBA)	7,236	4,497
ontego Bay (Sangster, MBJ)	7,544	4,687
ontevideo (Carrasco, MVD)	11,010	6,841
ontréal (Pierre Elliott Trudeau, YUL)	5,213	3,239
oscow (Sheremetyevo, SVO)	2,506	1,557
umbai/Bombay (Chhatrapati Shivaji, BOM)	7,207	4,478
unich (MUC)	940	584
uscat (Seeb, MCT)	5,828	3,621
aples (NAP)	1,628	1,011
assau (NAS)	6,973	4,333
atal (Augusto Severo, NAT)	7,180	4,462
'Djamena (NDJ)	4,588	2,851
ewark (EWR)	5,558	3,454
ew Delhi (Indira Gandhi, DEL)	6,727	4,180
ew York (John F. Kennedy, JFK)	5,536	3,440
ice (Côte d'Azur, NCE)	1,039	645
ovosibirsk (Tolmachevo, OVB)	5,216	3,241
rlando (MCO)	6,954	4,321
saka (Itami, ITM)	9,498	5,901
slo (Gardermoen, OSL)	1,206	749
stend-Bruges (OST)	232	144
ttawa (YOW)	5,344	3,321
uagadougou (OUA)	4,348	2,702
alma de Mallorca (PMI)	1,347	836
anama City (Tocumen, PTY)	8,448	5,249
aris (Charles de Gaulle, CDG)	346	215
enang (PEN)	10,277	6,386
erth, Australia (PER)	14,497	9,008
hiladelphia (PHL)	5,686	3,533
isa (Galileo Galilei, PSA)	1,184	736
ort of Spain (Piarco, POS)	7,088	4,404
rague (Ruzyne, PRG)	1,043	649
uébec (Jean Lesage, YQB)	4,979	3,093
uito (Mariscal Sucre, UIO)	9,188	5,709
abat (Sale, RBA)	2,001	1,243
angoon/Yangon (RGN)	8,984	5,582
eykjavik (Keflavik, KEF)	1,895	1,177
Rhodes (Diagoras, RHO)	2,805	1,743
Riga (RIX)	1,695	1,054
Rimini (Federico Fellini, RMI)	1,275	793
Rio de Janeiro (Galeao, GIG)	9,245	5,745
Riyadh (King Khaled, RUH)	4,936	3,067
Rome (Fiumicino, FCO)	1,441	895
St Lucia (Hewanorra, UVF)	6,785	4,216
St Petersburg (Pulkovo, LED)	2,114	1,314
Salt Lake City (SLC)	7,806	4,850
Salzburg (W. A. Mozart, SZG)	1,048	651
San Diego (Lindbergh Field, SAN)	8,802	5,469
San Francisco (SFO)	8,610	5,351
São Paulo (Congonhas, CGH)	9,483	5,892
Sarajevo (SJJ)	1,636	1,017
Seoul (Gimpo, SEL)	8,863	5,507
Seychelles (SEZ)	8,169	5,076
Shannon (SNN)	594	369
Shetland Islands (Sumburgh, LSI)	936	582
Singapore (Changi, SIN)	10,873	6,756
Skopje (SKP)	1,963	1,220
Sofia (Vrazhdebna, SOF)	2,038	1,266
Split (SPU)	1,530	951
Stockholm (Arlanda, ARN)	1,461	908
Strasbourg (Entzheim, SXB)	663	412
Stuttgart (STR)	754	469
Suva (Nausori, SUV)	16,285	10,119
Sydney (Kingsford Smith, SYD)	17,008	10,568
Tahiti (Faa'a, PPT)	15,361	9,545
Taipei (Chiang Kai Shek, TPE)	9,775	6,074
Tbilisi (TBS)	3,571	2,219
Tehran (Mehrabad, THR)	4,411	2,741
Tel Aviv (Ben Gurion, TLV)	3,585	2,227
Thessaloniki (Makedonia, SKG)	2,164	1,345
Tokyo (Narita, NRT)	9,585	5,956
Toronto (Pearson, YYZ)	5,704	3,544
Treviso (St Angelo, TSF)	1,130	703
Tripoli (TIP)	2,362	1,468
Trondheim (Vaernes, TRD)	1,490	926
Tunis-Carthage (TUN)	1,830	1,137
Turin (TRN)	917	570
Ulaanbaatar (Buyant Uhaa, ULN)	6,984	4,340
Vancouver (YVR)	7,574	4,707
Venice (Marco Polo, VCE)	1,150	715
Vienna (VIE)	1,272	790
Vladivostok (VVO)	8,526	5,298
Warsaw (Frederic Chopin, WAW)	1,468	912
Washington (Dulles, IAD)	5,898	3,665
Wellington (WLG)	18,817	11,692
Zagreb (Pleso, ZAG)	1,365	848
Zürich (Unique, ZRH)	787	490

TIME ZONES

Standard time differences from the Greenwich meridian

+ hours ahead of GMT
– hours behind GMT
* may vary from standard time at some part of the year (Summer Time or Daylight Saving Time)
† some areas may keep another time zone
h hours
m minutes

	h	*m*
Afghanistan	+ 4	30
*Albania	+ 1	
Algeria	+ 1	
*Andorra	+ 1	
Angola	+ 1	
Antigua and Barbuda	– 4	
Argentina	– 3	
*Armenia	+ 4	
*Australia		
*ACT, NSW (except Broken Hill area), Tas, Vic, Whitsunday Islands	+10	
Northern Territory	+ 9	30
Queensland	+10	
*South Australia	+ 9	30
*Western Australia	+ 8	
Christmas Island (Indian Ocean)	+ 7	
Cocos (Keeling) Islands	+ 6	30
Norfolk Island	+11	30
*Austria	+ 1	
*Azerbaijan	+ 4	
*Bahamas	– 5	
Bahrain	+ 3	
Bangladesh	+ 6	
Barbados	– 4	
*Belarus	+ 2	
*Belgium	+ 1	
Belize	– 6	
Benin	+ 1	
Bhutan	+ 6	
Bolivia	– 4	
*Bosnia and Hercegovina	+ 1	
Botswana	+ 2	
*Brazil		
western states	– 5	
central states	– 4	
N. and N. E. coastal states	– 2	
*S. and E. coastal states, including Brasilia	– 3	
Fernando de Noronha Island	– 2	
Brunei	+ 8	
*Bulgaria	+ 2	
Burkina Faso	0	
Burundi	+ 2	
Cambodia	+ 7	

	h	*m*
Cameroon	+ 1	
*Canada		
*Alberta	– 7	
*†British Columbia	– 8	
*Manitoba	– 6	
*New Brunswick	– 4	
*†Newfoundland	– 3	30
*†Northwest Territories	– 7	
*Nova Scotia	– 4	
*Nunavut		
central	– 6	
eastern	– 5	
mountain	– 7	
*Ontario		
east of 90° W.	– 5	
west of 90° W.	– 6	
*Prince Edward Island	– 4	
*Québec		
east of 63° W.	– 4	
*west of 63° W.	– 5	
*†Saskatchewan	– 6	
*Yukon	– 8	
Cape Verde	– 1	
Central African Republic	+ 1	
Chad	+ 1	
*Chile	– 4	
China (inc. Hong Kong and Macao)	+ 8	
Colombia	– 5	
The Comoros	+ 3	
Congo, Dem. Rep. of		
Haut-Zaire, Kasai, Kivu, Shaba	+ 2	
Kinshasa, Mbandaka	+ 1	
Congo, Republic of	+ 1	
Costa Rica	– 6	
Côte d'Ivoire	0	
*Croatia	+ 1	
*Cuba	– 5	
*Cyprus	+ 2	
*Czech Republic	+ 1	
*Denmark	+ 1	
*Faeroe Islands	0	
*Greenland	– 3	
Danmarks Havn, Mesters Vig	0	
*Scoresby Sund	– 1	
*Thule area	– 4	
Djibouti	+ 3	
Dominica	– 4	
Dominican Republic	– 4	
East Timor	+ 9	
Ecuador	– 5	
Galápagos Islands	– 6	
*Egypt	+ 2	
El Salvador	– 6	
Equatorial Guinea	+ 1	
Eritrea	+ 3	
*Estonia	+ 2	
Ethiopia	+ 3	

	h	*m*
Fiji	+ 12	
*Finland	+ 2	
*France	+ 1	
French Guiana	– 3	
French Polynesia	–10	
Guadeloupe	– 4	
Marquesas Islands	– 9	30
Martinique	– 4	
New Caledonia	+11	
Réunion	+ 4	
*St Pierre and Miquelon	– 3	
Wallis and Futuna	+12	
Gabon	+ 1	
The Gambia	0	
Georgia	+ 4	
*Germany	+ 1	
Ghana	0	
*Greece	+ 2	
Grenada	– 4	
*Guatemala	– 6	
Guinea	0	
Guinea-Bissau	0	
Guyana	– 4	
*Haiti	– 5	
Honduras	– 6	
*Hungary	+ 1	
Iceland	0	
India	+ 5	30
Indonesia		
Java, Kalimantan (west and central), Madura, Sumatra	+ 7	
Bali, Flores, Kalimantan (south and east), Lombok, Sulawesi, Sumbawa, West Timor	+ 8	
Irian Jaya, Maluku	+ 9	
Iran	+ 3	30
*Iraq	+ 3	
*Ireland, Republic of	0	
*Israel	+ 2	
*Italy	+ 1	
Jamaica	– 5	
Japan	+ 9	
*Jordan	+ 2	
Kazakhstan		
western	+ 5	
eastern	+ 6	
Kenya	+ 3	
Kiribati	+12	
Line Islands	+14	
Phoenix Islands	+13	
Korea, Dem. People's Rep. of	+ 9	
Korea, Republic of	+ 9	
Kuwait	+ 3	
Kyrgyzstan	+ 6	
Laos	+ 7	
*Latvia	+ 2	
*Lebanon	+ 2	

	h	m
esotho	+ 2	
beria	0	
bya	+ 2	
iechtenstein	+ 1	
ithuania	+ 2	
uxembourg	+ 1	
Macedonia	+ 1	
adagascar	+ 3	
alawi	+ 2	
alaysia	+ 8	
aldives	+ 5	
ali	0	
Malta	+ 1	
arshall Islands	+12	
auritania	0	
auritius	+ 4	
Mexico	− 6	
*Nayarit, Sinaloa, S. Baja California	− 7	
*N. Baja California	− 8	
Sonora	− 7	
icronesia, Fed. States of		
Chuuk, Yap	+10	
Kosrae, Pingelap, Pohnpei	+11	
Moldova	+ 2	
Monaco	+ 1	
†Mongolia	+ 8	
Montenegro	+ 1	
orocco	0	
ozambique	+ 2	
yanmar	+ 6	30
Namibia	+ 1	
auru	+12	
epal	+ 5	45
The Netherlands	+ 1	
Aruba	− 4	
Netherlands Antilles	− 4	
New Zealand	+12	
Cook Islands	−10	
Niue	11	
Tokelau Island	−10	
icaragua	− 6	
iger	+ 1	
igeria	+ 1	
Norway	+ 1	
*Svalbard, Jan Mayen	+ 1	
man	+ 4	
akistan	+ 5	
alau	+ 9	
anama	− 5	
apua New Guinea	+10	
Paraguay	− 4	
eru	− 5	
he Philippines	+ 8	
Poland	+ 1	
Portugal	0	
*Azores	− 1	
*Madeira	0	
atar	+ 3	
Romania	+ 2	
Russia		
Zone 1	+ 2	
Zone 2	+ 3	
Zone 3	+ 4	
Zone 4	+ 5	
Zone 5	+ 6	

	h	m
Zone 6	+ 7	
Zone 7	+ 8	
Zone 8	+ 9	
Zone 9	+10	
Zone 10	+11	
Zone 11	+12	
Rwanda	+ 2	
St Christopher and Nevis	− 4	
St Lucia	− 4	
St Vincent and the Grenadines	− 4	
Samoa	−11	
*San Marino	+ 1	
São Tomé and Príncipe	0	
Saudi Arabia	+ 3	
Senegal	0	
*Serbia	+ 1	
Seychelles	+ 4	
Sierra Leone	0	
Singapore	+ 8	
*Slovakia	+ 1	
*Slovenia	+ 1	
Solomon Islands	+11	
Somalia	+ 3	
South Africa	+ 2	
*Spain	+ 1	
*Canary Islands	0	
Sri Lanka	+ 5	30
Sudan	+ 3	
Suriname	− 3	
Swaziland	+ 2	
*Sweden	+ 1	
*Switzerland	+ 1	
*Syria	+ 2	
Taiwan	+ 8	
Tajikistan	+ 5	
Tanzania	+ 3	
Thailand	+ 7	
Togo	0	
Tonga	+13	
Trinidad and Tobago	− 4	
*Tunisia	+ 1	
*Turkey	+ 2	
Turkmenistan	+ 5	
Tuvalu	+12	
Uganda	+ 3	
*Ukraine	+ 2	
United Arab Emirates	+ 4	
*United Kingdom	0	
Anguilla	− 4	
*Bermuda	− 4	
†British Antarctic Territory	− 3	
British Indian Ocean Territory	+ 5	
British Virgin Islands	− 4	
Cayman Islands	− 5	
*Falkland Islands	− 4	
*Gibraltar	+ 1	
Montserrat	− 4	
Pitcairn Islands	− 8	
St Helena and Dependencies	0	
South Georgia Islands	− 2	
*Turks and Caicos Islands	− 5	
*United States of America		

	h	m
*Alaska	− 9	
Aleutian Islands, east of 169° 30′ W.	− 9	
Aleutian Islands, west of 169° 30′ W.	−10	
*central time	− 6	
*eastern time	− 5	
Guam	+10	
Hawaii	−10	
*mountain time	− 7	
Northern Mariana Islands	+10	
*Pacific time	− 8	
Puerto Rico	− 4	
Samoa, American	−11	
Virgin Islands	− 4	
*Uruguay	− 3	
Uzbekistan	+ 5	
Vanuatu	+11	
*Vatican City State	+ 1	
Venezuela	− 4	
Vietnam	+ 7	
Yemen	+ 3	
Zambia	+ 2	
Zimbabwe	+ 2	

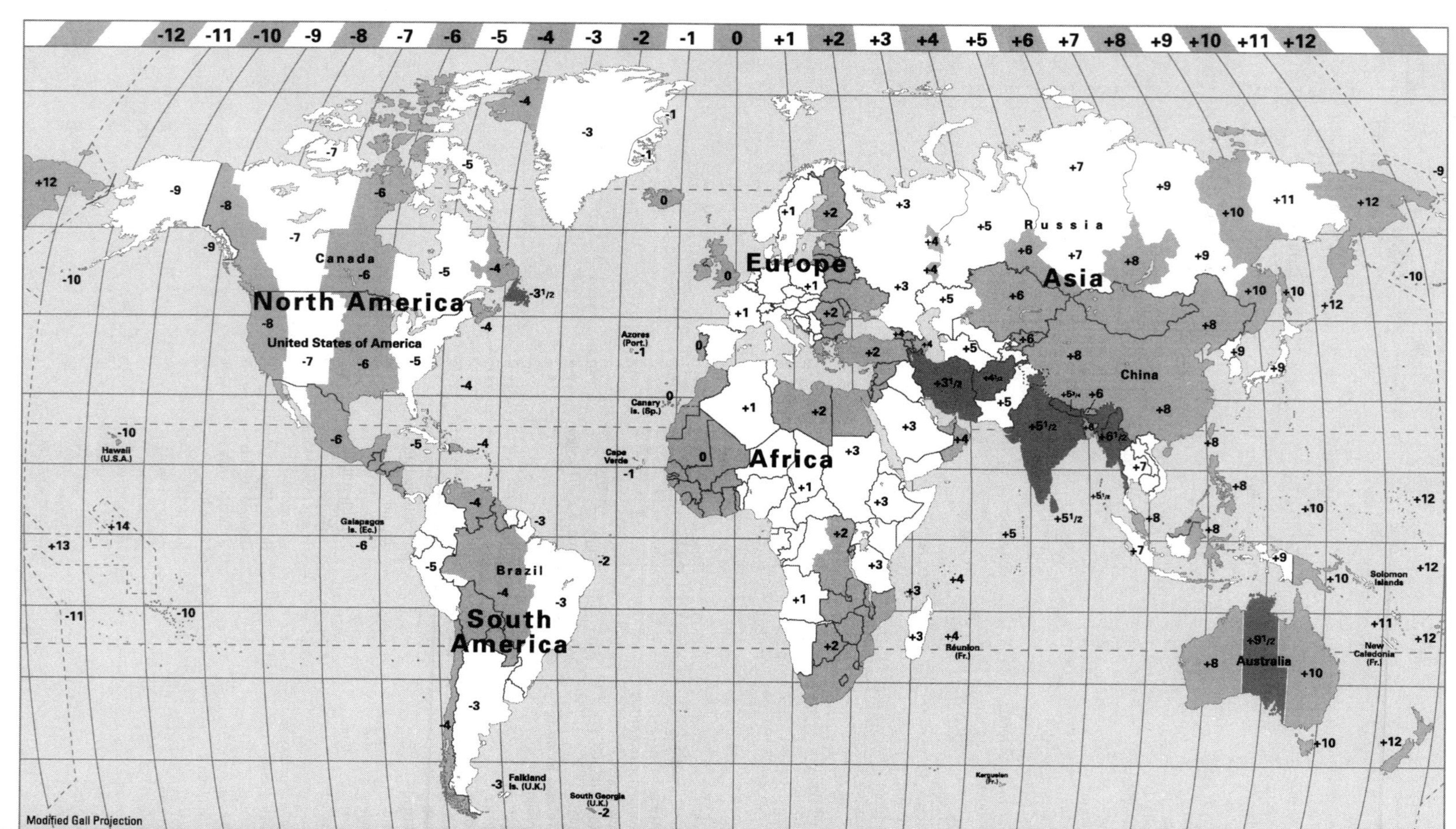

-12 -11 -10 -9 -8 -7 -6 -5 -4 -3 -2 -1 0 +1 +2 +3 +4 +5 +6 +7 +8 +9 +10 +11 +12
North America
Canada
United States of America
South America
Brazil
Europe
Africa
Asia
Russia
China
Australia
Hawaii (U.S.A.)
Galapagos Is. (Ec.)
Azores (Port.)
Canary Is. (Sp.)
Cape Verde
Falkland Is. (U.K.)
South Georgia (U.K.)
Réunion (Fr.)
Kerguelen (Fr.)
Solomon Islands
New Caledonia (Fr.)
Modified Gall Projection

CURRENCIES AND EXCHANGE RATES

AVERAGE RATE AGAINST £1 STERLING

COUNTRY/TERRITORY	CURRENCY	30 MARCH 2007
Afghanistan	Afghani (Af) of 100 puls	Af 77.75
Albania	Lek (Lk) of 100 qindraka	Lk 186.44
Algeria	Algerian dinar (DA) of 100 centimes	DA 141.38
American Samoa	Currency is that of the USA	US$1.98
Andorra	Euro (€) of 100 cents	€1.47
Angola	Readjusted kwanza (Krzl) of 100 lwei	Kzrl 158.16
Anguilla	East Caribbean dollar (EC$) of 100 cents	EC$5.34
Antigua and Barbuda	East Caribbean dollar (EC$) of 100 cents	EC$5.34
Argentina	Peso of 10,000 australes	Pesos 6.13
Armenia	Dram of 100 louma	Dram 714.12
Aruba	Aruban guilder	Guilder 3.54
Ascension Island	Currency is that of St Helena	—
Australia	Australian dollar ($A) of 100 cents	$A2.42
Austria	Euro (€) of 100 cents	€1.47
Azerbaijan	New manat of 100 gopik	New manat 1.71
The Bahamas	Bahamian dollar (B$) of 100 cents	B$1.98
Bahrain	Bahraini dinar (BD) of 1,000 fils	BD 0.73
Bangladesh	Taka (Tk) of 100 poisha	Tk 134.99
Barbados	Barbados dollar (BD$) of 100 cents	BD$3.92
Belarus	Belarusian rouble of 100 kopeks	BYR 4,206.12
Belgium	Euro (€) of 100 cents	€1.47
Belize	Belize dollar (BZ$) of 100 cents	BZ$3.86
Benin	Franc CFA	Francs 970.07
Bermuda	Bermuda dollar of 100 cents	$1.96
Bhutan	Ngultrum of 100 chetrum (Indian currency is also legal tender)	Ngultrum 85.97
Bolivia	Boliviano ($b) of 100 centavos	$b15.68
Bosnia-Hercegovina	Convertible marka	Marka 2.88
Botswana	Pula (P) of 100 thebe	P 12.26
Brazil	Real of 100 centavos	Real 4.01
Brunei	Brunei dollar (B$) of 100 sen	B$2.98
Bulgaria	Lev of 100 stotinki	Leva 2.89
Burkina Faso	Franc CFA	Francs 970.07
Burundi	Burundi franc of 100 centimes	Francs 2,042.95
Cambodia	Riel of 100 sen	Riel 7,875.23
Cameroon	Franc CFA	Francs 970.07
Canada	Canadian dollar (C$) 100 cents	C$2.26
Cape Verde	Escudo Caboverdiano of 100 centavos	Esc 162.96
Cayman Islands	Cayman Islands dollar (CI$) of 100 cents	CI$1.70
Central African Republic	Franc CFA	Francs 970.07
Chad	Franc CFA	Francs 970.07
Chile	Chilean peso of 100 centavos	Pesos 1,056.87
China	Renminbi Yuan of 10 jiao or 100 fen	Yuan 15.16
Colombia	Colombian peso of 100 centavos	Pesos 4,320.71
The Comoros	Comorian franc (KMF) of 100 centimes	Francs 727.55
Congo, Rep. of	Franc CFA	Francs 970.07
Congo, Dem. Rep. of	Congolese franc	CFr 1,112.09
Cook Islands	Currency is that of New Zealand	NZ$2.74
Costa Rica	Costa Rican colón (C) of 100 céntimos	C1,017.59
Côte d'Ivoire	Franc CFA	Francs 970.07
Croatia	Kuna of 100 lipa	Kuna 10.99
Cuba	Cuban peso of 100 centavos	Pesos 1.96
Cyprus	Cyprus pound (C£) of 100 cents	C£0.86
Czech Republic	Koruna (Kcs) of 100 haléru	Kcs 41.29
Denmark	Danish krone of 100 re	Kroner 10.98
Djibouti	Djibouti franc of 100 centimes	Francs 347.22
Dominica	East Caribbean dollar (EC$) of 100 cents	EC$5.34
Dominican Republic	Dominican Republic peso (RD$) of 100 centavos	RD$63.94
East Timor	Currency is that of the USA	US$1.98

Ecuador	Currency is that of the USA (formerly sucre of 100 centavos)	US$1.98
Egypt	Egyptian pound (£E) of 100 piastres or 1,000 millièmes	£E11.17
El Salvador	Currency is that of USA	US$1.98
Equatorial Guinea	Franc CFA	Francs 970.07
Eritrea	Nakfa	Nakfa 29.63
Estonia	Kroon of 100 sents	Kroons 23.05
Ethiopia	Ethiopian birr (EB) of 100 cents	EB 17.43
Faeroe Islands	Currency is that of Denmark	Kroner 10.98
Falkland Islands	Falkland pound of 100 pence	—
Fiji	Fiji dollar (F$) of 100 cents	F$3.23
Finland	Euro (€) of 100 cents	€1.47
France	Euro (€) of 100 cents	€1.47
French Guiana	Euro (€) of 100 cents	€1.47
French Polynesia	Franc CFP	Francs 175.71
Gabon	Franc CFA	Francs 970.07
Gambia	Dalasi (D) of 100 butut	D 53.74
Georgia	Laria of 100 tetri	Laria 3.33
Germany	Euro (€) of 100 cents	€1.47
Ghana	Cedi of 100 pesewas	Cedi 18,191.53
Gibraltar	Gibraltar pound of 100 pence	—
Greece	Euro (€) of 100 cents	€1.47
Greenland	Currency is that of Denmark	Kroner 10.98
Grenada	East Caribbean dollar (EC$) of 100 cents	EC$5.34
Guadeloupe	Euro (€) of 100 cents	€1.47
Guam	Currency is that of the USA	US$1.98
Guatemala	Quetzal (Q) of 100 centavos	Q 15.10
Guinea	Guinea franc of 100 centimes	Francs 11,768.11
Guinea-Bissau	Franc CFA	Francs 970.07
Guyana	Guyana dollar (G$) of 100 cents	G$397.97
Haiti	Gourde of 100 centimes	Gourdes 71.88
Honduras	Lempira of 100 centavos	Lempiras 37.05
Hong Kong	Hong Kong (HK$) of 100 cents	HK$15.32
Hungary	Forint of 100 fillér	Forints 364.43
Iceland	Icelandic króna (Kr) of 100 aurar	Kr 129.50
India	Indian rupee (Rs) of 100 paisa	Rs 85.25
Indonesia	Rupiah (Rp) of 100 sen	Rp 17,897.32
Iran	Rial	Rials 18,132.68
Iraq	New Iraqi dinar (NID)	NID 2,510.77
Ireland, Republic of	Euro (€) of 100 cents	€1.47
Israel	Shekel of 100 agora	Shekels 8.15
Italy	Euro (€) of 100 cents	€1.47
Jamaica	Jamaican dollar (J$) of 100 cents	J$132.83
Japan	Yen	Yen 231.59
Jordan	Jordanian dinar (JD) of 1,000 fils	JD 1.39
Kazakhstan	Tenge	Tenge 242.83
Kenya	Kenya shilling (Ksh) of 100 cents	Ksh 134.65
Kiribati	Australian dollar ($A) of 100 cents	$A2.42
Korea, Dem. People's Rep. Of	Won of 100 chon	Won 335.85
Korea, Republic of	Won	Won 1,844.85
Kuwait	Kuwaiti dinar (KD) of 1,000 fils	KD 0.57
Kyrgyzstan	Som	Som 74.65
Laos	Kip (K) of 100 at	K 19,044.55
Latvia	Lats of 100 santims	Lats 1.05
Lebanon	Lebanese pound (L£) of of 100 piastres	L£2,965.56
Lesotho	Loti (M) of 100 lisente	M 14.22
Liberia	Liberian dollar (L$) of 100 cents	L$119.53
Libya	Libyan dinar (LD) of 1,000 dirhams	LD 2.52
Liechtenstein	Swiss franc of 100 rappen (or centimes)	Francs 2.40
Lithuania	Litas of 100 centas	Litas 5.09
Luxembourg	Euro (€) of 100 cents	€1.47
Macao	Pataca of 100 avos	Pataca 15.78
Macedonia	Denar of 100 deni	Den 90.08
Madagascar	Ariary of 5 iraimbilanja	MGA 3,830.71
Malawi	Kwacha (K) of 100 tambala	MK 273.94
Malaysia	Malaysian dollar (ringgit) (M$) of 100 sen	M$6.78
Maldives	Rufiyaa of 100 laaris	Rufiyaa 25.32
Mali	Franc CFA	Francs 970.07

Malta	Maltese lira (LM) of 100 cents of 1,000 mils	LM 0.63
Marshall Islands	Currency is that of the USA	US$1.98
Martinique	Currency is that of France	€1.47
Mauritania	Ouguiya (UM) of 5 khoums	UM 531.91
Mauritius	Mauritius rupee of 100 cents	Rs 63.16
Mayotte	Currency is that of France	€1.47
Mexico	Peso of 100 centavos	Pesos 21.59
Micronesia, Federated States of	Currency is that of the USA	US$1.98
Moldova	Moldovan leu of 100 bani	MDL 24.55
Monaco	Euro (€) of 100 cents	€1.47
Mongolia	Tugrik of 100 möngö	Tugriks 2,284.97
Montenegro	Euro (€) of 100 cents	€1.47
Montserrat	East Caribbean dollar (EC$) of 100 cents	EC$5.34
Morocco	Dirham (DH) of 100 centimes	DH 16.45
Mozambique	New Metical (MT) of 100 centavos (?)	MT 51.94
Myanmar	Kyat (K) of 100 pyas	K 12.68
Namibia	Namibian dollar of 100 cents	—
Nauru	Australian dollar ($A) of 100 cents	$A2.42
Nepal	Nepalese rupee of 100 paisa	Rs 136.40
The Netherlands	Euro (€) of 100 cents	€1.47
Netherlands Antilles	Netherlands Antilles guilder of 100 cents	Guilders 3.54
New Caledonia	Franc CFP	Francs 175.71
New Zealand	New Zealand dollar (NZ$) of 100 cents	NZ$2.74
Nicaragua	Córdoba (C$) of 100 centavos	C$35.73
Niger	Franc CFA	Francs 970.07
Nigeria	Naira (N) of 100 kobo	N 250.95
Niue	Currency is that of New Zealand	NZ$2.74
Norfolk Island	Currency is that of Australia	$A2.42
Northern Mariana Islands	Currency is that of the USA	US$1.98
Norway	Krone of 100 ore	Kroner 11.97
Oman	Rial Omani (OR) of 1,000 baisas	OR 0.75
Pakistan	Pakistan rupee of 100 paisa	Rs 119.14
Palau	Currency is that of the USA	US$1.98
Panama	Balboa of 100 centésimos (US notes are in circulation)	Balboa 1.96
Papua New Guinea	Kina (K) of 100 toea	K 5.83
Paraguay	Guarani (Gs) of 100 céntimos	Gs 9,963.67
Peru	New Sol of 100 cénts	New Sol 6.24
The Philippines	Philippine peso (P) of 100 centavos	P 94.64
Pitcairn Islands	Currency is that of New Zealand	NZ$2.74
Poland	Zloty of 100 groszy	Zlotych 5.68
Portugal	Euro (€) of 100 cents	€1.47
Puerto Rico	Currency is that of the USA	US$1.98
Qatar	Qatar riyal of 100 dirhams	Riyals 7.14
Réunion	Currency is that of France	€1.47
Romania	New leu of 100 bani	Lei 4.94
Russian Federation	Rouble of 100 kopeks	Rbl 51.06
Rwanda	Rwanda franc of 100 centimes	Francs 1,071.78
t Christopher and Nevis	East Caribbean dollar (EC$) of 100 cents	EC$5.34
t Helena	St Helena pound (£) of 100 pence	—
t Lucia	East Caribbean dollar (EC$) of 100 cents	EC$5.34
t Pierre and Miquelon	Currency is that of France	€1.47
t Vincent and the Grenadines	East Caribbean dollar (EC$) of 100 cents	EC$5.34
amoa	Tala (S$) of 100 sene	S$5.17
an Marino	Euro (€) of 100 cents	€1.47
ão Tomé and Princípe	Dobra of 100 centavos	Dobra 13,368.98
audi Arabia	Saudi riyal (SR) of 20 qursh or 100 halala	SR 7.36
enegal	Franc CFA	Francs 970.07
erbia	New dinar of 100 paras	New dinars 118.89
eychelles	Seychelles rupee of 100 cents	Rs 12.01
ierra Leone	Leone (Le) of 100 cents	Le 5,875.92
ingapore	Singapore dollar (S$) of 100 cents (fully interchangeable with Brunei currency)	S$2.98
lovakia	Koruna (Sk) of 100 halierov	Kcs 48.92
lovenia	Euro (€) of 100 cents	€1.47
olomon Islands	Solomon Islands dollar (SI$) of 100 cents	SI$14.97
omalia	Somali shilling of 100 cents	Shillings 2,680.92
outh Africa	Rand (R) of 100 cents	R 14.40
pain	Euro (€) of 100 cents	€1.47

Sri Lanka	Sri Lankan rupee of 100 cents	Rs 215.5
Sudan	Sudanese pound of 100 piastres	SDG 3.9
Suriname	Surinam dollar of 100 cents	Dollar 5.3
Swaziland	Lilangeni (E) of 100 cents (South African currency is also in circulation)	—
Sweden	Swedish krona of 100 öre	Kronor 13.7
Switzerland	Swiss franc of 100 rappen (or centimes)	Francs 2.4
Syria	Syrian pound (S£) of 100 piastres	S£103.1
Taiwan	New Taiwan dollar (NT$) of 100 cents	NT$65.4
Tajikistan	Somoni (TJS) of 100 dirams	—
Tanzania	Tanzanian shilling of 100 cents	Shillings 2,430.1
Thailand	Baht of 100 satang	Baht 68.6
Togo	Franc CFA	Francs 970.0
Tokelau	Currency is that of New Zealand	NZ$2.7
Tonga	Pa'anga (T$) of 100 seniti	T$3.9
Trinidad and Tobago	Trinidad and Tobago dollar (TT$) of 100 cents	TT$12.4
Tristan da Cunha	Currency is that of the UK	—
Tunisia	Tunisian dinar of 1,000 millimes	Dinars 2.5
Turkey	New Turkish lira (TL) of 100 kurus	TL 2.7
Turkmenistan	Manat of 100 tenge	Manat 10,273.8
Turks and Caicos Islands	US dollar (US$) of 100 cents	US$1.9
Tuvalu	Australian dollar ($A) of 100 cents	$A2.4
Uganda	Uganda shilling of 100 cents	Shillings 3,431.3
Ukraine	Hryvna of 100 kopiykas	UAH 9.8
United Arab Emirates	UAE dirham (Dh) of 100 fils	Dirham 7.2
United States of America	US dollar (US$) of 100 cents	US$1.9
Uruguay	Uruguayan peso of 100 centésimos	Pesos 47.3
Uzbekistan	Sum of 100 tiyin	Sum 2,451.8
Vanuatu	Vatu of 100 centimes	Vatu 210.94
Vatican City State	Euro (€) of 100 cents	€1.47
Venezuela	Bolívar (Bs) of 100 céntimos	Bs 6,273.14
Vietnam	Dong of 10 hao or 100 xu	Dong 31,420.83
Virgin Islands, British	US dollar (US$) (£ sterling and EC$ also circulate)	US$1.98
Virgin Islands, US	Currency is that of the USA	US$1.98
Wallis and Futuna Islands	Franc CFP	Francs 175.71
Yemen	Riyal of 100 fils	Riyals 389.83
Zambia	Kwacha (K) of 100 ngwee	K 8,296.52
Zimbabwe	Zimbabwe dollar (Z$) of 100 cents	Z$490.34

Source: WM/Reuters Closing Spot Rates

TRAVEL OVERSEAS

PASSPORT REGULATIONS

Application forms for United Kingdom passports can be obtained from the UK Identity and Passport Service's (IPS) general telephone enquiry line or website, regional passport offices, or from main post offices and WorldChoice travel agents.

UK IDENTITY AND PASSPORT SERVICE
T 0870-521 0410 **W** www.passport.gov.uk

REGIONAL OFFICES

Hampton House, 47–53 High Street, Belfast BT1 2QS
Millburngate House, Durham DH97 1PA
3 Northgate, 96 Milton Street, Cowcaddens, Glasgow G4 0BT
101 Old Hall Street, Liverpool L3 9BD
Globe House, 89 Eccleston Square, London SW1V 1PN
Olympia House, Upper Dock Street, Newport, Gwent NP20 1XA
Aragon Court, Northminster Road, Peterborough PE1 1QG

The passport offices are open Monday–Saturday on an appointment-only basis (appointments should be arranged by calling the central telephone number listed above). For an additional fee, passport offices provide either a guaranteed same-day service (for renewals and minor amendments only) or a one-week fast-track service (all except new adult applications).

Standard postal applications are processed within three weeks. The completed application form should be posted, with the appropriate supporting documents and fee, to the regional passport office indicated on the addressed envelope which is provided with each application form. Accompanying cheques and postal orders should be crossed and made payable to 'UK Passport Service'. For online applications, the completed online form will be printed out by the Passport Office and posted to the applicant for them to sign and return. After the paper copy has been received, online applications are also returned within three weeks.

Applications can also be submitted through selected main post offices and WorldChoice travel agents ('partners'), who, for a small handling charge, will forward the application form to the relevant regional passport office after having checked that it has been completed correctly and has the appropriate documents attached. Applications through partners take a minimum of two weeks.

A passport cannot be issued or extended on behalf of a person already abroad; such persons should apply to the nearest British High Commission or Consulate.

UK passports are granted to:

British citizens
British dependent territories citizens
British nationals (overseas)
British overseas territories citizens
British subjects
British protected persons

UK passports are generally available for travel to all countries. The possession of a passport does not, however, exempt the holder from compliance with any immigration regulations in force in British or foreign countries, or from the necessity of obtaining a visa where required (*see* below for a list of countries for which UK citizens require a visa).

Biometric passports were introduced in 2006. The new design and security features, including a chip containing (the facial image and biographical data of the holder, are intended to render the passport more secure against forgery and aid border controls.

ADULTS

A passport granted to a person over 16 will normally be valid for ten years. Thereafter, or if at any time the passport contains no further space for visas, a new passport must be obtained.

The issue of passports including details of the holder's spouse has been discontinued, but existing family passports may be used until expiry. A spouse who is included in a family passport cannot travel on the passport without the holder.

British nationals born on or before 2 September 1929 are eligible for a free standard passport.

CHILDREN

Since 5 October 1998 all children under the age of 16 are required to have their own passport. This is primarily to help prevent child abductions. The passports are initially valid for five years, but can be renewed for a further five years at the end of this period.

Children included in their parents' passports when the new regulations came into force are not affected and can continue to travel on them until they reach the age of 16 or the passport expires or is amended.

COUNTERSIGNATURES

A countersignature is only needed if the application is for a first passport or to replace a lost, stolen or missing passport, though a countersignature is also needed for renewals if the applicant's appearance has significantly changed and the photograph in their previous passport is unrecognisable. The list of acceptable countersignatories includes: MP; justice of the peace; minister of religion; a professionally qualified person (eg doctor, engineer, lawyer, teacher); bank officer; military officer; established civil servant; police officer; or a person of similar standing who has known the applicant for at least two years, and who is either a British citizen, British dependent territories citizen, British national (overseas), British overseas territories citizen, British subject or a citizen of a Commonwealth country. A relative or partner must not countersign the application.

If the application is for a child under the age of 16, the countersignature should be by someone of relevant standing who has known the parent or person with parental responsibility who signs the declaration of consent, rather than the child.

PHOTOGRAPHS

Two identical, unmounted, recent photographs of the applicant must be sent. These photographs should measure 45mm by 35mm, be printed on normal thin photographic paper and should be taken full face against a white background. The photo must show the applicant's full face, looking straight at the camera, with a neutral expression and with their mouth closed. The person who countersigns the application form should certify one photograph as a true likeness of the applicant.

DOCUMENTATION

The applicant's birth certificate or previous British passport, and other documents in support of the statements made in the application, must be produced at the time of applying. Details of which documents are required are set out in the notes accompanying the application form.

If the passport applicant is a British national by naturalisation or registration, the certificate proving this must be produced with the application, unless the applicant holds a previous British passport issued after registration or naturalisation.

INTERVIEWS

Interviews for adults applying for their first passport (not including those who held their own passport as a child) were introduced on 1 June 2007 to combat passport fraud and forgery. After applying for a passport, applicants will be sent a letter asking them to book an interview at one of the 69 offices in the UK. Interviews last for approximately 30 minutes and applicants are asked to confirm facts about themselves that someone attempting to steal their identity would not know. The IPS recommends that new applicants now allow six weeks to receive their passport and has withdrawn the one-week fast-track service for first adult passports.

The scheme is being introduced gradually throughout 2007 and a limited number of UK offices are currently operating. While the scheme is being implemented, not all adults applying for their first passport will be called for an interview, although those that are will not be able to choose which office their interview will be held in.

48-PAGE PASSPORTS

The 48-page passport is intended to meet the needs of frequent travellers who fill standard passports well before the validity has expired. It is valid for ten years but is not available for children.

PASSPORT FEES*
from October 2007

First adult passport	£72
First child passport	£46
Renewal or amendment of adult passport	£72
Renewal or amendment of child passport	£46
48-page passport	£85.50

* Standard postal applications only. A charge is added for applications made in person at a partner office in the UK, currently £7 at a post office and £6 at a WorldChoice travel agent.

HEALTH ADVICE

Health Advice for Travellers, published by the Department of Health, contains information on health precautions, reciprocal health agreements with other countries and immunisation. It is available online, from some travel agents, local post offices or the Department of Health, Richmond House, 79 Whitehall, London SW1A 2NS
T 020-7210 4850 E dhmail@dh.gsi.gov.uk
W www.dh.gov.uk/travellers

IMMUNISATION

In very general terms immunisation against typhoid, polio and hepatitis A should be considered for all countries with lower standards of hygiene and sanitation. Protection against malaria, in the form of tablets, as well as measures to avoid mosquito bites, is advised for visits to malarious areas.

Immunisation against yellow fever is compulsory for entry into some countries, either for all travellers or for those arriving from a yellow fever-infected area, and is recommended for all travellers to infected areas.

A doctor should be consulted, preferably at least eight weeks before departure, and will advise travellers and arrange vaccinations. Most doctors will charge a fee for a course of vaccinations. If children will be travelling outside Europe, North America, Australia and New Zealand, the doctor should be informed, especially if they have not completed their full course of childhood immunisation. As a precaution, it is also recommended that all travellers are up to date with their tetanus and diptheria inoculations.

Country-by-country guidance is set out on the website www.fitfortravel.nhs.uk. Healthcare professionals can obtain information about immunisation recommendations from the Department of Health publication *Health Information for Overseas Travel* or from:

HEALTH PROTECTION AGENCY, 7th Floor, Holborn Gate, 330 High Holborn, London WC1V 7PP
T 020-7759 2700 E webteam@hpa.org.uk W www.hpa.org.uk

SCOTTISH EXECUTIVE HEALTH DEPARTMENT, St Andrew's House, Edinburgh EH1 3DG
T 0131-556 8400 W www.scotland.gov.uk

HEALTH PROTECTION SCOTLAND, Clifton House, Clifton Place, Glasgow G3 7LN
T 0141-300 1100 E hpsenquiries@hps.scot.nhs.uk
W www.hps.scot.nhs.uk

DEPARTMENT OF HEALTH, SOCIAL SERVICES AND PUBLIC SAFETY, Castle Buildings, Stormont, Belfast BT4 3SJ
T 028-9052 0500 E webmaster@dhsspsni.gov.uk
W www.dhsspsni.gov.uk

MEDICAL TREATMENT ABROAD

Details of free or reduced cost emergency medical treatment when visiting European countries, and countries with which the UK has reciprocal health arrangements, are set out in *Health Advice for Travellers* and on the website for the Department of Health (www.dh.gov.uk/travellers). They also contain guidance on applying for the European Health Insurance Card (EHIC), which was introduced in September 2005 as a replacement for the E111 form. EHIC entitles people to urgent medical treatment in the European Economic Area (EEA) and Switzerland. The booklet and website also explain changes to entitlement and the claims process.

For countries where the UK has no healthcare agreements, including Canada, the USA, India, the Far East, Africa and Latin America, it is advisable to take out medical insurance. A certain amount of insurance is also needed in countries with which the UK has healthcare agreements.

VISA REQUIREMENTS

The countries listed below require British citizens to hold a valid visa before arrival. The list only includes countries with diplomatic representation in the UK (*see* Countries of the World section for other foreign embassy contact details). It is advisable to check specific visa requirements with the appropriate embassy before making final travel arrangements.

Afghanistan
Algeria
Angola
Armenia
Australia
Azerbaijan
Bahrain
Bangladesh
Belarus
Benin
Burkina Faso
Burundi
Cambodia
Cameroon
Cape Verde
Central African Republic
Chad
China
Comoros
Dem. Rep. of Congo
Rep. of Congo
Côte d'Ivoire
Cuba
Djibouti
Egypt
Equatorial Guinea
Eritrea
Ethiopia
Gabon
Ghana
Guinea
Guinea-Bissau
India
Indonesia
Iran
Iraq
Jordan
Kazakhstan
Kenya
Dem. People's Republic of Korea
Kuwait
Kyrgyzstan
Laos
Lebanon
Liberia
Libya
Madagascar
Mali
Mauritania
Mongolia
Mozambique
Myanmar
Nauru
Nepal
Niger
Nigeria
Oman
Pakistan
Papua New Guinea
Qatar
Russian Federation
São Tomé and Príncipe
Saudi Arabia
Sierra Leone
Somalia
Sudan
Suriname
Syria
Tajikistan
Tanzania
Togo
Turkmenistan
Uganda
Uzbekistan
Venezuela (only for entry over land or by sea)
Vietnam
Yemen
Zambia
Zimbabwe.

THE EUROPEAN UNION

MEMBER STATE	ACCESSION DATE	POPULATION (2006)	COUNCIL VOTES	EP SEATS
Austria	1 Jan 1995	8,265,925	10	18
Belgium	1 Jan 1958	10,511,382	12	24
Bulgaria	1 Jan 2007	7,718,750	10	18
Cyprus	1 May 2004	766,414	4	6
Czech Republic	1 May 2004	10,251,079	12	24
Denmark	1 Jan 1973	5,427,459	7	14
Estonia	1 May 2004	1,344,684	4	6
Finland	1 Jan 1995	5,255,580	7	14
France	1 Jan 1958	62,886,171	29	78
Germany	1 Jan 1958	82,437,995	29	99
Greece	1 Jan 1981	11,125,205	12	24
Hungary	1 May 2004	10,076,581	12	24
Ireland	1 Jan 1973	4,209,019	7	13
Italy	1 Jan 1958	58,751,711	29	78
Latvia	1 May 2004	2,294,590	4	9
Lithuania	1 May 2004	3,403,284	7	13
Luxembourg	1 Jan 1958	459,500	4	6
Malta	1 May 2004	404,346	3	5
The Netherlands	1 Jan 1958	16,334,210	13	27
Poland	1 May 2004	38,157,055	27	54
Portugal	1 Jan 1986	10,569,592	12	24
Romania	1 Jan 2007	21,610,213	14	35
Slovakia	1 May 2004	5,389,180	7	14
Slovenia	1 May 2004	2,003,358	4	7
Spain	1 Jan 1986	43,758,250	27	54
Sweden	1 Jan 1995	9,047,752	10	19
UK	1 Jan 1973	60,393,100	29	78

Source: Eurostat

CHRONOLOGY

1950	Robert Schuman (French foreign minister) proposes that France and West Germany pool their coal and steel industries under a supranational authority (Schuman Plan)
1951	Paris treaty, signed by France, West Germany, Belgium, Italy, Luxembourg and the Netherlands, establishes the European Coal and Steel Community (ECSC)
1952	ECSC treaty enters into force
1957	25 March: treaty of Rome, signed by the six ECSC member countries, establishes the European Economic Community (EEC) and the European Atomic Energy Authority (EURATOM). Treaty aims to create a customs union; remove obstacles to free movement of capital, goods, people and services; establish common external trade policy and common agricultural and fisheries policies; coordinate economic policies; harmonise social policies; promote cooperation in nuclear research
1958	1 January: EEC and EURATOM begin operation. Joint parliament and court of justice established for all three communities, and the Commission, Council of Ministers, Economic and Social Committee and Investment Bank for the EEC established
1962	Common Agricultural Policy (CAP) agreed
1967	EEC, ECSC and EURATOM merge to form the European Communities (EC), with a single Council of Ministers and Commission
1968	EEC customs union completed Implementation of CAP completed
1974	Regular heads of governments summits begin
1975	'Own resources' funding of EC budget introduced UK renegotiates its terms of accession European Regional Development Fund created
1979	European Monetary System (EMS) comes into operation June: first direct elections to European Parliament (June)
1984	Fontainebleau summit settles UK annual budget rebate and agrees first major CAP reform
1986	Single European Act (SEA) signed European Political Cooperation (EPC) established
1988	Second major CAP reform
1991	Maastricht treaty agreed
1992	31 December: single internal market programme completed
1993	September: the exchange rate mechanism (ERM) of the EMS effectively suspended 1 November: Maastricht treaty enters into force, establishing the European Union (EU)
1994	1 January: European Economic Area (EEA) agreement comes into operation Norway rejects EU membership in referendum
1997	Amsterdam treaty agreed
1998	11 states chosen to enter first round of European Monetary Union (EMU)
1999	1 January: Euro launched 1 May: Amsterdam treaty enters into force
2000	9 December: treaty of Nice agreed 23 July: ECSC treaty expires following transfer of coal and steel sectors to the treaty of Rome
2004	1 May: Cyprus, Czech Republic, Estonia, Hungary, Latvia, Lithuania, Malta, Poland, Slovakia and Slovenia become members of the EU 29 October: The European constitution is signed in Rome. Before it can be adopted it must be ratified by all EU member states
2007	1 January: Bulgaria and Romania become members of the EU 25 March: The EU celebrates its 50th birthday 23 June: EU leaders agree on a new reform treaty to replace the constitution of 2004. At the time of going to press, the treaty was expected to be finalised in late 2007 and come into force mid-2009

RECENT LEGISLATION

MAASTRICHT TREATY

Agreed in Maastricht, the Netherlands, in 1991, the treaty came into effect in November 1993 following ratification by the member states.

Three pillars formed its basis:

- the European Community (removing Economic from its name) with its established institutions and decision-making processes
- a common foreign and security policy (*see* below) with the Western European Union as the potential defence component of the EU
- cooperation in justice and home affairs, with the Council of Ministers coordinating policies on asylum, immigration, conditions of entry, cross-border crime, drug trafficking and terrorism

The treaty established a common European citizenship for nationals of all member states and introduced the principle of subsidiarity, whereby decisions are taken at the most appropriate level (national, regional or local). It extended EC competency into the areas of environmental and industrial policies, consumer affairs, health, and education and training, and extended qualified majority voting in the Council of Ministers to some areas which had previously required a unanimous vote. The powers of the European parliament over the budget and over the European Commission were also enhanced, and a co-decision procedure enabled the parliament to override decisions made by the council in certain policy areas. A separate protocol to the Maastricht treaty on social policy was agreed by 11 states and was incorporated into the Amsterdam treaty in 1997 following adoption by the UK.

COMMON FOREIGN AND SECURITY POLICY

The common foreign and security policy (CFSP) was created as a pillar of the EU by the Maastricht treaty (*see* above). It adopted the machinery of the European political cooperation framework, which it replaced, and was charged with providing a forum for member states and EU institutions to consult on foreign affairs.

The CFSP system is headed by the Council of the European Union, which provides general lines of policy. Specific policy decisions are taken by the Council of Foreign Ministers, which meets at least four times a year to determine areas for joint action. The high representative of the CFSP initiates action, manages the CFSP and represents it abroad. The Council of Ministers is supported by the Political Committee, which meets monthly, or within 48 hours if there is a crisis, to prepare for ministerial discussions. A group of correspondents, designated diplomats in each member's foreign ministry, provides day-to-day contact.

As part of the CFSP the EU also created a European security and defence policy (ESDP) with the potential, if agreed later on, for creating a common defence structure. In the recent past, ESDP missions have been deployed in the former Yugoslavia, Lebanon and the Democratic Republic of Congo. The member states agreed at the Helsinki summit in 1999 to establish a capability for military crisis-management operations, known as the rapid reaction force, which would have a credible intervention capability and be able to undertake peacemaking missions independently of NATO. The force was declared operational at the Laeken summit in 2001.

The Amsterdam treaty introduced qualified majority voting for foreign affairs and created a high representative on CFSP to act as a spokesperson. It also established a new planning and early warning unit to monitor international developments and provide the opportunity for the EU to react to these developments with a cohesive response. The unit consists of specialists from the member states, the council and the commission, as well as from the Western European Union (WEU).

SCHENGEN AGREEMENT

The Schengen agreement was signed by France, Germany, Belgium, Luxembourg and the Netherlands in 1985. The agreement committed the five states to abolishing internal border controls, erecting external frontiers against illegal immigrants, drug traffickers, terrorists and organised crime, and implementing the Schengen Information System to enable police stations and consular agents from Schengen member states to access data on specific individuals or vehicles and objects which are lost or stolen.

Subsequently signed by Spain and Portugal, the agreement was ratified by the seven signatory states and entered into force in March 1995 with the removal of internal frontier, passport, customs and immigration controls. Provisional agreement was reached in 1995 between the signatory states and the Nordic Union on a merger of the two frontier-free zones – Denmark, Finland and Sweden in 1996 and Iceland and Norway in 2001. Italy and Austria became full members of the agreement in 1998; Greece in 2000; Switzerland in 2005. The UK and the Republic of Ireland have not signed the agreement and are only partial participants, since their border controls have been maintained.

The Schengen agreement originated as an intergovernmental agreement but became part of the EU following the signing of the Amsterdam treaty. A second generation Schengen Information System (SIS II), which will cater for the newest member states, is under development, but with delays due to legal and technical problems. The target dates for the phasing out of land and sea borders, for the ten member states that joined the EU in 2004, is 31 December 2007 with airports following before 29 March 2008.

AMSTERDAM TREATY

The treaties of Rome and Maastricht were amended through the Amsterdam treaty, which was signed in 1997 and came into effect on 1 May 1999. It extended the scope of qualified majority voting and the powers of the European parliament. It also included a formal commitment to fundamental human rights, gave additional powers to the European court of justice and provided for the reform of the CFSP.

ENLARGEMENT AND EXTERNAL RELATIONS

The procedure for accession to the EU is laid down in the treaty of Rome; states must be stable European democracies governed by the rule of law with free-market economies. A membership application is studied by the European Commission, which produces an 'opinion'. If the opinion is positive, negotiations may be opened leading to an accession treaty that must be approved by all member state governments and parliaments, the European Parliament, and the applicant state's government and parliament.

Cyprus, Czech Republic, Estonia, Hungary, Latvia, Lithuania, Malta, Poland, Slovakia and Slovenia became full members of the EU on 1 May 2004. Bulgaria and Romania joined the EU on 1 January 2007. The European Council recalled the offer of an accession partnership to Turkey in 2002, following the commission's conclusion that Turkey did not yet fully meet the required political criteria. However, at its December 2004 meeting in Brussels, the council decided that Turkey sufficiently met the Copenhagen political criteria, and accession negotiations began in October 2005. Accession talks with Croatia, originally due to start in March 2005 but postponed due to the lack of full cooperation with the UN war crimes tribunal, began in October 2005. Macedonia was granted candidate status in December 2005.

The EU has several types of agreements with other European and non-European states. Association agreements include a commitment to EU financial aid and to eventual membership; such an agreement has been signed with Turkey (1963). Partnership and cooperation agreements (PCAs) are legal frameworks, based on the respect of democratic principles and human rights, setting out the political, economic and trade relationship between the EU and its partner countries. Each PCA is a ten-year bilateral treaty signed and ratified by the EU and the individual state. Agreements have been implemented with Russia (1997), Ukraine and Moldova (1998), Armenia, Azerbaijan, Georgia, Kazakhstan, Kyrgyzstan and Uzbekistan (1999), and Tajikistan (2004). A PCA has been signed with Turkmenistan (1998) but is not yet in force. Negotiations to establish PCAs with Thailand and Singapore were launched in October 2004. In 2003 the PCA council summit decreed to strengthen EU cooperation with the Russian Federation by establishing a permanent partnership council (PPC). At the council's first meeting in April 2004 a protocol was signed, extending the PCA with the Russian Federation to the ten new member states of the EU; the agreement currently in place also covers Romania and Bulgaria. A trade and cooperation agreement with Mongolia entered into force in 1993, intended to foster trade and economic relations; the agreement also included a commitment to protect human rights. The European neighbourhood policy was developed in 2004 and applies to the enlarged EU's immediate neighbours. It aims to strengthen stability and security through economic integration and deeper political relationships based on a mutual commitment to common values (democracy, human rights, rule of law, good governance and market economy).

A stabilisation and association agreement (SAA) – which is tailored towards the western Balkan states and i similar to the earlier Europe agreements held with previous candidate countries, in that it provides the contractual framework for relations that will lead to accession to the EU – entered into force with Montenegro in March 2007, Croatia in February 2005, and with Macedonia in April 2004. SAA negotiations were launched with Bosnia and Hercegovina in November 2005, Serbia in October 2005; the SAA with Albania was signed in June 2006 and will enter into force following its ratification.

TREATY OF NICE

The treaty of Nice was signed in 2001 and came into effect in 2003. It aims to enable the EU to accommodate up to 13 new member states, and extends qualified majority voting to 30 further articles of the treaties that previously required unanimity. The weighting of votes in the EU Council was altered from 1 January 2005 in preparation for the new member states. To obtain a qualified majority, a decision requires a specified number of votes (to be reviewed following each accession); the decision has to be approved by a majority of member states and represent at least 62 per cent of the total population of the EU. The treaty also set the number of MEPs that both existing and new member states would have following enlargement.

The Maastricht treaty established the right of groups of member states to work together without requiring the participation of all members (enhanced cooperation); the treaty of Nice removes the right of individual member states to veto the launch of enhanced cooperation.

The European Commission has been limited to one member per member state since 2005, with a maximum of 27 commissioners; a rotation system is to be introduced once EU membership exceeds 27 states. The treaty also adds to the powers of the president of the commission and amends the rules of operation of the court of justice.

When the European reform treaty, currently under discussion enters into force it will replace the voting rights under the treaty of Nice.

ECONOMY

COMMUNITY BUDGET

The principles of funding the European Community budget were established by the treaty of Rome and remain, with modifications, to this day. There is a legally binding limit on the overall level of resources (known as 'own resources') that the community can raise from its member states; this limit is defined as a percentage of gross national product (GNP). Budget revenue and expenditure must balance, and there is therefore no deficit financing. The own resources decision, which came into effect in 1975 and has been regularly updated, states that there are four sources of community funding under which each member state makes contributions: levies charged on agricultural imports into the community from non-member states; customs duties on imports from non-member states; contributions based on member states' shares of a notional community-harmonised VAT base; and contributions based on member states' shares of community GNP. The latter is the budget-balancing item and covers the difference between total expenditure and the revenue from the other three sources.

The framework budget for 2007–13 (formally known as the Financial Perspective) was completed at the end of the UK's presidency of the EU in December 2005. A figure of €862.36bn (£584.57bn) was agreed, which is equal to 1.045 per cent of the EU's combined gross national income.

From 1984 up until 2005 the UK had received an annual rebate equivalent to 66 per cent of the difference between UK contributions to the budget and its receipts. This was introduced to compensate the UK for disproportionate contributions caused by its high share of agricultural and non-agricultural imports from non-member states and its relatively small receipts from the Common Agricultural Policy, the most important portion of community expenditure. Before the budget for 2007–13 was finalised, the UK conceded €10.5bn (£7.1bn) (approximately 20 per cent) of its rebate over the six-year period, in return for a wide-ranging review of EU spending; this is due to be held in 2008–9.

BUDGET 2007

	*Billion euro**
Natural resources	56.3
Sustainable growth	54.9
Global activities	6.8
Citizenship	0.6
Freedom, security and justice	0.6
Administration	6.9
Compensations	0.4
Total	126.5

Source: Office for Official Publications of the European Communities
* 1 euro = £0.68 as at 7 September 2007

SINGLE MARKET

Even after the removal of tariffs and quotas between member states in the 1970s and 1980s, the EC was still separated into a number of national markets by a series of non-tariff barriers. It was to overcome these internal barriers to trade that the concept of the single market was developed. The measures to be undertaken were codified in the commission's 1985 white paper on completing the internal market.

The white paper included articles removing obstacles distorting the internal market: the elimination of frontier controls; the mutual recognition of professional qualifications; the harmonisation of product specifications, largely by the mutual recognition of national standards; open tendering for public procurement contracts; the free movement of capital; the harmonisation of VAT and excise duties; and the reduction of state aid to particular industries. The Single European Act (SEA) aided the completion of the single market by changing the legislative process within the EC, particularly with the introduction of qualified majority voting in the Council of Ministers for some policy areas, and the introduction of the assent procedure in the European parliament. The SEA also extends EC competence into the fields of technology, the environment, regional policy, monetary policy and external policy. The single market came into effect on 1 January 1993, though full implementation of the elimination of frontier controls and the harmonisation of taxes have been repeatedly delayed. At the time of going to press, a fundamental review of the single market was in process with the aim of producing concrete proposals for further improvement.

EUROPEAN ECONOMIC AREA

The EC single market programme spurred European non-member states to open negotiations with the EC on preferential access for their goods, services, labour and capital to the single market. Principal among these states were European Free Trade Association (EFTA) members who opened negotiations on extending the single market to EFTA by the formation of the European Economic Area (EEA), encompassing all 19 EC and EFTA states. Agreement was reached in 1992, but the operation of the EEA was delayed by its rejection in a Swiss referendum, necessitating an additional protocol agreed by the remaining 18 states. The EEA came into effect in 1994 after ratification by 17 member states (Liechtenstein joined in 1995 after adapting its customs union with Switzerland).

Austria, Finland and Sweden joined the EU on 1 January 1995, leaving only Norway, Iceland and Liechtenstein as the non-EU EEA members. Under the EEA agreement, the three states are to adopt the EU's *acquis communautaire,* apart from in the fields of agriculture, fisheries, and coal and steel.

The EEA is controlled by regular ministerial meetings and by a joint EU-EFTA committee which extends relevant EU legislation to EEA states. Apart from single market measures, there is cooperation in several areas, including education, civil protection, research and development, consumer policy and tourism. An EFTA court of justice has been established in Luxembourg and an EFTA surveillance authority in Brussels to supervise the implementation of the EEA Agreement.

The EEA Enlargement Agreement came into force on 1 May 2004, which allowed the simultaneous expansion of both the EU and the EEA without disruption of the internal market.

EUROPEAN MONETARY SYSTEM AND THE SINGLE CURRENCY

The European Monetary System (EMS) began operation in March 1979 with three main purposes. The first was to establish monetary stability in Europe, initially in exchange rates between EC member state currencies through the Exchange Rate Mechanism (ERM), and in the longer term to be part of a wider stabilisation process, overcoming inflation and budget and trade deficits. The second purpose was to overcome the constraints resulting from the interdependence of EC economies, and the third was to aid the long-term process of European monetary integration.

The Maastricht treaty set in motion timetables for achieving economic and monetary union (EMU) and a single currency (the euro). At the Brussels summit in May 1998, 11 member states were judged to fulfil or be close to fulfilling the necessary convergence criteria for participation in the first stage of EMU: Austria, Belgium, Finland, France, Germany, Ireland, Italy, Luxembourg, the Netherlands, Portugal and Spain.

The criteria were that:

- the budget deficit should be 3 per cent or less of gross domestic product (GDP)
- total national debt must not exceed 60 per cent of GDP
- inflation should be no more than 1.5 per cent above the average rate of the three best performing economies in the EU
- long-term interest rates should be no more than 2 per cent above the average of the three best performing economies in the EU in the previous 12 months
- applicants must have been members of the ERM for two years without having realigned or devalued their currency

Under the terms of a stability and growth pact agreed in Dublin in December 1996, penalties may be imposed on EMU members with high budget deficits. Governments with deficits exceeding 3 per cent of GDP will receive a warning and will be obliged to pay up to 0.5 per cent of their GDP into a fund after ten months. This will become a fine if the budget deficit is not rectified within two years. A member state with negative growth will be allowed to apply for an exemption from the fine in 'exceptional circumstances', eg a recession whereby GDP had fallen by 0.75 per cent or more during one year.

On 1 January 1999 the qualifying member states adopted the euro at irrevocably fixed exchange rates, the European Central Bank (ECB) took charge of the single monetary policy, and the euro replaced the ecu on a one-for-one basis.

In 2000 Greece was judged to have fulfilled the criteria for participation and adopted the euro on 1 January 2001. Referendums on the adoption of the euro have been held in Denmark and Sweden, but participation was rejected. In June 2003 Britain announced that the euro would not be adopted at present on the grounds that the country was not economically ready to join the single currency, though a future joining of the eurozone was not ruled out.

The euro is now the legal currency in the participating states. Euro notes and coins were introduced on 1 January 2002 and circulated alongside national currencies for a period of up to two months, after which time national notes and coins ceased to be legal tender. The new EU member states are expected to adopt the euro when the necessary economic conditions have been met; Slovenia became the 13th member of the eurozone on 1 January 2007. At the time of going to press Cyprus, Estonia, Latvia and Malta had 1 January 2008 as their target date for adoption of the euro.

The ECB meets twice a month to set the following month's monetary policy applicable to the countries participating in the euro. Its governing council has 19 members, being the six members of the ECB's executive board and the 13 governors of the national central banks of the participating states.

COMMON AGRICULTURAL POLICY

The Common Agricultural Policy (CAP) was established to increase agricultural production, provide a fair standard of living for farmers and ensure the availability of food at reasonable prices. This aim was achieved by a number of mechanisms:

- import levies
- intervention purchase
- export subsidies

These measures stimulated production but also placed increasing demands on the EC budget which were exacerbated by the increase in EC members and yields enlarged by technological innovation; CAP now accounts for over 40 per cent of EC expenditure. To surmount these problems reforms were agreed in 1984, 1988, 1992, 1997, 1999 and 2003.

REFORMS

The 1984 reforms created the system of co-responsibility levies: farm payments to the EC by volume of product sold. This system was supplemented by national quotas for particular products, such as milk. The 1988 reforms emphasised 'set-aside', whereby farmers are given direct grants to take land out of production as a means of reducing surpluses. The set-aside reforms were extended in 1993 for another five years and to every farm in the EC. The 1999 reforms further reduced surpluses of cereals, beef and milk by cutting the intervention prices by up to 20 per cent and compensating producers by making area payments. Under the reforms, CAP rules were also simplified, eliminating inconsistencies between policies.

Under the Uruguay round agreement of General Agreement of Tariff and Trade (GATT) concluded in 1993, the EU was required, over a six-year period from 1 January 1995, to reduce its import levies by 36 per cent, reduce its domestic subsidies by 20 per cent, reduce its export subsidies by 36 per cent in value, and reduce its subsidised exports by 21 per cent in volume.

In June 2003, EU farm ministers adopted a fundamental reform of the CAP, which included the following provisions:

- a single farm payment for EU farmers, independent of production
- payment to be linked to the respect of environmental, food safety, animal and plant health and animal welfare standards, and the requirement to keep all farmland in good condition
- a strengthened rural development policy with more EU money to help farmers meet EU production standards (begun in 2005)
- a reduction in direct payments for bigger farms
- a mechanism for financial discipline to ensure that the farm budget fixed until 2013 is not exceeded

The single farm payment entered into force in 2005, although if a member state needs a transitional period due to its specific agricultural conditions, it may apply the single farm payment from 2007 at the latest. The ten newest EU members were also given access to a special €5.8bn (£3.9bn) three-year funding package. The 2007–13 EU budget stipulates that no extra money will be made available to pay farm subsidies to Romania and Bulgaria.

A review of EU agricultural policy is planned for 2008, and may lead to further reforms.

LEGISLATIVE PROCESS

The core of the EU policy-making process is a dialogue between the European Commission, which initiates and implements policy, and the Council of Ministers, which takes policy decisions. An increasing degree of democratic control is exercised by the European parliament.

The original legislative process is known as the consultative procedure. The commission drafts a proposal which it submits to the council and to the parliament. The council then consults the Economic and Social Committee (ESC), the parliament and the Committee of the Regions; the parliament may request that amendments are made. With or without these amendments, the proposal is then adopted by the council and becomes law.

Under the Single European Act (SEA), the role of the parliament was strengthened by the introduction of the cooperation procedure. The parliament now has a second reading of proposals in some fields, and after the second reading its rejection of a proposal can only be overturned by a unanimous decision of the council. The Maastricht treaty extended the scope of the cooperation procedure, which was applied to Single Market laws and harmonisation, trans-European networks, development policy, the social fund, and some aspects of transport, environment, research, social policy and competition policy.

The SEA introduced the assent procedure, whereby an absolute majority of the parliament must vote to approve laws in certain fields before they are passed. Issues covered by the assent procedure include foreign treaties, accession treaties, international agreements with budgetary implications, citizenship, residence rights, the CAP, and regional and structural funds.

The Maastricht treaty introduced the co-decision procedure; if, after the parliament's second reading of a proposal, the council and parliament fail to agree, a conciliation committee of the two will reach a compromise. If a compromise is not reached, the parliament can reject the legislation by the vote of an absolute majority of its members. The Amsterdam treaty extended the co-decision procedure to all areas covered by qualified majority voting, with the exception of measures related to European Monetary Union (EMU).

The council issues the following legislation:

- regulations, which are binding in their entirety and directly applicable to all member states; they do not need to be incorporated into national law to come into effect
- directives, which are less specific, binding as to the result to be achieved but leaving the method of implementation open to member states; a directive thus has no force until it is incorporated into national law
- decisions, which are also binding but are addressed solely to one or more member states or individuals in a member state
- recommendations
- opinions, which are merely persuasive

The council also has certain budgetary powers, including the power to reject the budget as a whole and to increase expenditure or redistribute money within sectors. However, the final decision on whether the budget should be adopted or rejected lies with the parliament.

The council may delegate legislative powers to the commission. These consist of implementing powers and technical updating of existing legislation.

The European Central Bank has legislative powers within its field of competence. The commission also has limited legislative powers, where it has been delegated the power to implement or revise legislation by the council.

EUROPEAN CONSTITUTION

At the European Council held in Laeken, Belgium, in December 2001, a declaration was agreed that established a convention to prepare for treaty reforms at the intergovernmental conference, which was held in July 2004. The convention, composed of representatives of national governments (15), national parliaments (30), the European parliament (16), the European Commission (2) and the applicant states (39), started work in February 2002, under the chairmanship of former French president Valéry Giscard d'Estaing.

At the intergovernmental conference in July 2004, the council produced a provisional consolidated version of the draft treaty establishing a constitution for Europe. It was signed by the heads of state on 29 October 2004 at a ceremony in Rome.

The European constitution, which can only come into force once it has been ratified by the 27 member states (either through a referendum or by vote in the national parliament), reorganises and codifies EU decision-making as well as replacing the main existing treaties with a single text designed to suit the needs of an expanding European Union. The constitution defines the relationships and functions of the European parliament, the European Commission, the European court of justice and the council of the European Union. It repeats existing EU agreements concerning the legal supremacy of EU law, economic cooperation and EU citizens' freedom of movement. It also introduces new legislation to establish the EU as a separate body in law; extends the powers of the European parliament; removes member states' right of veto currently applicable in over 30 areas; and incorporates the Charter of Fundamental Rights into the constitution itself.

After France and the Netherlands rejected the constitution in 2005, a period of reflection was deemed necessary; this was declared over during the German presidency of the EU in the first half of 2007, with EU leaders charged with finding a solution to the impasse by the next European parliament elections in 2009.

THE UK AND THE EU IN 2007

- The constitution: in April, Prime Minister Tony Blair stated that he did not intend to hold a referendum on a new EU constitution, instead proposing revisions to the EU treaty. In June, Germany – holder of the EU presidency in the first half of 2007 – with support from 17 other states, presented leaders of EU states with a roadmap for the adoption of a new constitutional treaty, though it stated its wish to preserve as much of the old constitution as possible.
- Freedom of speech: justice ministers from the 27 member states agreed to make incitement to racial hatred or violence a crime across the EU, but stopped short of singling out Holocaust denial as a criminal offence. The UK had resisted such a law concerning the Holocaust, so as not to compromise artistic or academic freedom of expression.
- Metric and imperial measurements: the EC's industry commissioner ruled in May that EU plans to enforce metrication by 2009 had been shelved; imperial weights and measures can be displayed indefinitely alongside metric measurements.
- The environment: the UK is committed to targets agreed by the EU in March to cut greenhouse gas emissions by 20 per cent by 2020 (compared to 1990 levels) and to generate 20 per cent of energy from renewable sources by 2020 (*see also* Environment).
- The UK's rebate: in April the Treasury finally began implementing the reduction in the UK's rebate from the EU budget that was agreed in December 2005, comprising a 20 per cent concession of the rebate (approximately €10.5bn (£7.1bn)) over a six-year period.

INSTITUTIONS

EUROPEAN PARLIAMENT

E eplondon@europarl.europa.eu **W** www.europarl.europa.eu

The European parliament (EP) originated as the Common Assembly of the ECSC, acquiring its present name in 1962. The parliament now comprises 785 seats. Members (MEPs), initially appointed from the membership of national parliaments, have been directly elected at five-year intervals since 1979. Elections to the parliament are held on differing bases throughout the EC; British MPs have been elected by a regional list system of proportional representation since June 1999. The most recent elections were held in June 2004, and the next elections are due to be held in June 2009.

MEPs serve on committees which scrutinise draft EC legislation and the activities of the European Commission. A minimum of 12 plenary sessions a year are held in Strasbourg and six additional shorter plenary sessions a year are held in Brussels; committees meet in Brussels, and the secretariat's headquarters is in Luxembourg.

The influence of the EP has gradually expanded within the EU since the Single European Act of 1985, which introduced the cooperation procedure; the Maastricht treaty, which extended the cooperation procedure and introduced the co-decision procedure (*see* Legislative Process); and the Amsterdam treaty, which effectively extended co-decision to all areas except economic and monetary union, and taxation. Parliament has general powers of supervision over the European Commission, and consultation and co-decision with the Council of Ministers; it votes to approve a newly appointed commission and can dismiss it at any time by a two-thirds majority (as it threatened to do in January 1999, bringing about the resignation of the Santer Commission). Under the Maastricht treaty it has the right to be consulted on the appointment of the new commission, and can also veto its appointment. The EP can reject the EU budget as a whole, alter non-compulsory expenditure not specified in the EU primary legislation, and can question the commission's management of the budget and call in the court of auditors. Although the EP cannot directly initiate legislation, its reports can spur the commission into action. In accordance with the Maastricht treaty the EP appoints the European Ombudsman, to provide citizens with redress against maladministration by EU institutions.

The EP's organisation is deliberately biased in favour of multinational political groupings; recognition of a political grouping in the parliament entitles it to offices, funding, representation on committees and influence in debates and legislation. A political group must be comprised of a minimum of 20 MEPs elected in at least six member states. For a list of UK MEPs, *see* European Parliament section.

PARLIAMENT, Palais de l'Europe, Allée du Printemps, BP 1024/F, F-67070 Strasbourg Cedex, France
T (+33) (3) 8817 4001 **F** (+33) (3) 8825 6501
Wiertzstraat, Postbus 1047, B-1047 Brussels, Belgium
T (+32) (2) 284 2111 **F** (+32) (2) 284 6974

SECRETARIAT, Centre Européen, Plateau du Kirchberg, BP 1601, L-2929 Luxembourg
T (+352) 43001 **F** (+352) 4300 29393/29292

President, Hans-Gert Poettering (Germany)

OMBUDSMAN, 1 Avenue du Président Robert Schuman, BP 403, F-67001, Strasbourg Cedex, France
E euro-ombudsman@europarl.europa.eu
W www.euro-ombudsman.europa.eu

Ombudsman, Nikiforos Diamandouros (Greece)

EUROPEAN PARLIAMENT UK OFFICE
2 Queen Anne's Gate, London SW1H 9AA
E eplondon@europarl.europa.eu **W** www.europarl.org.uk

EUROPEAN PARLIAMENT OFFICE IN SCOTLAND
The Tun, Holyrood Road, Edinburgh EH8 8PJ
E epedinburgh@europarl.europa.eu

COUNCIL OF THE EUROPEAN UNION

Wetstraat 175, B-1048 Brussels, Belgium

The Council of the European Union (Council of Ministers) formally comprises the foreign ministers of the member states but in practice the ministers attending depend on the subject under discussion. Council decisions are taken by qualified majority vote (in which members' votes are weighted), by a simple majority, or by unanimity. The council is assisted by a general secretariat, whose head has since 1999 been the High Representative for the Common Foreign and Security Policy.

Unanimity votes are taken on sensitive issues such as taxation and constitutional matters; in preparation for an expanded EU, the Amsterdam treaty extended areas where qualified majority votes may be taken, to areas such as single market laws and harmonisation, environment policy, health and safety, transport policy, overseas aid, research and development, culture, consumer protection, education and training, the development of a single currency and some aspects of social policy. Member states have weighted votes in the council loosely proportional to their relative population sizes (*see* introductory table), with a total of 321 votes. The acts of the council can take the form of regulations, directives, decisions, common actions or common positions, recommendations or opinions. The council can also adopt conclusions, declarations or resolutions. The number of votes each member state can cast is set by treaties. The treaties also define cases in which a simple majority, qualified majority or unanimity are required. Since 1 January 2007 a qualified majority will be reached if the following two conditions are met:

- a majority of member states approve (in some cases a two-thirds majority)
- a minimum of 255 votes is cast in favour of the proposal, ie 73.9 per cent of the total (roughly the same share as under the previous system)

In addition, a member state may ask for confirmation that the votes in favour represent at least 62 per cent of the total population of the EU. If this is found not to be the case, the decision will not be adopted.

The treaty of Nice agreed amendments to the treaties in relation to the size and composition of the European Commission, the weighting of votes and the extension of qualified majority voting in the Council of Ministers and other issues relating to the treaty of Amsterdam. The extension of qualified majority voting to external border controls, the EU budget, the composition of the European courts and certain committees, visa rules and structural funds, was also agreed.

The European Council, comprising the heads of state or government of the member states and the president of the European Commission, meets twice a year to provide overall policy direction. The presidency of the EC is held in rotation for six-month periods, setting the agenda for and chairing all council meetings. The European Council holds a summit in the country holding the presidency at the end of its period in office. The holders of the presidency for the years 2007–8 are:

2007 January–June, Germany
2007 July–December, Portugal
2008 January–June, Slovenia
2008 July–December, France

GENERAL SECRETARIAT OF THE COUNCIL OF THE EUROPEAN UNION
Wetstraat 175, B-1048 Brussels, Belgium
W www.consilium.europa.eu

Secretary-General of the Council of the European Union and High Representative for the Common Foreign and Security Policy, Javier Solana (Spain)
Deputy Secretary-General of the Council of the European Union, Pierre de Boissieu (France)

OFFICE OF THE UNITED KINGDOM PERMANENT REPRESENTATIVE TO THE EUROPEAN UNION
Ave d'Auderghem 10, B-1040 Brussels, Belgium

Ambassador and UK Permanent Representative, Kim Darroch, CMG, *apptd* 2007

EUROPEAN COMMISSION

Wetstraat 200, rue de la Loi, B-1049 Brussels, Belgium

The European Commission consists of 27 commissioners, one per member state. The members of the commission are appointed for five-year renewable terms by the agreement of the member states; the terms run concurrently with the terms of the European parliament. The president and the other commissioners are nominated by the governments of the member states, and, under the terms of the Nice treaty, the appointments are approved by the European parliament. The commissioners pledge sole allegiance to the EC. The commission initiates and implements EC legislation and is the guardian of the EC treaties. It is the exponent of community-wide interests rather than the national preoccupations of the council. Each commissioner is supported by advisers and oversees the departments assigned to them, known as directorates-general and services. Each directorate-general is headed by a director-general.

President José Manuel Barroso was nominated by the governments of the member states on 28 June 2004, and the European parliament confirmed his appointment with a secret ballot vote on 22 July 2004. He announced the finalised commission on 4 November 2004, which officially took office on 22 November.

The commission has a total staff of around 23,000 permanent civil servants.

COMMISSIONERS *as at May 2007*

President, José Manuel Barroso (Portugal)
Vice-President, Administrative Affairs, Audit and Anti-Fraud, Siim Kallas (Estonia)
Vice-President, Enterprise and Industry, Günter Verheugen (Germany)
Vice-President, Institutional Relations and Communication Strategy, Margot Wallstrom (Sweden)
Vice-President, Justice, Freedom and Security, Franco Frattini (Italy)
Vice-President, Transport, Jacques Barrot (France)
Agriculture and Rural Development, Marian Fischer Boel (Denmark)
Competition, Neelie Kroes (Netherlands)
Consumer Protection, Meglena Kuneva (Bulgaria)
Development and Humanitarian Aid, Louis Michel (Belgium)
Economic and Monetary Affairs, Joaquin Almunia (Spain)
Education, Training, Culture and Youth, Jan Figel (Slovakia)
Employment, Social Affairs and Equal Opportunities, Vladimir Spidla (Czech Republic)
Energy, Andris Piebalgs (Latvia)
Enlargement, Olli Rehn (Finland)
Environment, Stavros Dimas (Greece)
External Relations and European Neighbourhood Policy, Benita Ferrero-Waldner (Austria)
Financial Programming and Budget, Dalia Grybauskaite (Lithuania)
Fisheries and Maritime Affairs, Joe Borg (Malta)
Health, Markos Kyprianou (Cyprus)
Information, Society and Media, Viviane Reding (Luxembourg)

Internal Market and Services, Charlie McCreevy (Ireland)
Multilingualism, Leonard Orban (Romania)
Regional Policy, Danuta Hübner (Poland)
Science and Research, Janez Potocnik (Slovenia)
Taxation and Customs Union, Laszlo Kovacs (Hungary)
Trade, Peter Mandelson (UK)

COURT OF JUSTICE OF THE EUROPEAN COMMUNITIES

Boulevard Konrad Adenauer, Kirchberg, L-2925 Luxembourg
W www.curia.europa.eu

The court of justice is common to the two European Communities. It exists to safeguard the law in the interpretation and application of the community treaties, to decide on the legality of decisions of the Council of Ministers or the European Commission, and to determine infringements of the treaties. Cases may be brought to it by the member states, the community institutions, firms or individuals. Its decisions are directly binding in the member countries, and the Maastricht treaty enhanced the court's powers by permitting it to impose fines on member states. The 27 judges and eight advocates-general of the court are appointed for renewable six-year terms by the member governments in concert. During 2006, 537 new cases were lodged at the court and 546 cases were concluded.
President, Vassilios Skouris (Greece)
First Advocate-General, Juliane Kokott (Germany)

COURT OF FIRST INSTANCE

Palais de la Cour de Justice, Boulevard Konrad Adenauer, Kirchberg, L-2925 Luxembourg

Established under powers conferred by the Single European Act, the court of first instance has jurisdiction to hear and determine all actions brought by natural or legal persons, and all direct actions except those reserved for the court of justice. It is composed of 27 judges, appointed for renewable six-year terms by the governments of the member states. During 2006, 432 new cases were lodged at the court and 436 cases were concluded.
President, Bo Vesterdorf (Denmark)

EUROPEAN COURT OF AUDITORS

12 rue Alcide de Gasperi, L-1615 Luxembourg
E euraud@eca.europa.eu W www.eca.europa.eu

The European court of auditors, established in 1977, examines the accounts of all revenue and expenditure of the European Communities and community bodies. It evaluates whether all revenue has been received and all expenditure incurred in a lawful and regular manner and in accordance with the principles of sound financial management. The court issues an annual report and a statement of assurance as to the reliability of the accounts and the legality and regularity of the underlying transactions. It also publishes special reports on specific topics and delivers opinions on financial matters. The court has one member from each member state appointed for a six-year term by the Council of Ministers following consultation with the European parliament.
President, Hubert Weber (Austria)

FINANCIAL BODIES

EUROPEAN CENTRAL BANK

Kaiserstrasse 29, D-60311 Frankfurt am Main, Germany
E info@ecb.int W www.ecb.int

The European Central Bank (ECB), which superseded the European Monetary Institute, was established on 1 June 1998. Its governing bodies are the executive board, the governing council and the general council. The executive board consists of the president, the vice-president and four other members. All members are appointed by the governments of the states participating in the single currency, at the level of heads of state and government. The governing council, the main decision-making body of the ECB, comprises the six members of the executive board and the governors of the national central banks of the 13 euro area states. The general council comprises the president and vice-president and the 27 governors of the national central banks, the other members of the executive board being entitled to participate but not to vote. The ECB is independent of national governments and of all other EU institutions. It became fully operational on 1 January 1999, and defines and implements the single monetary policy for the euro area.
President, Jean-Claude Trichet (France)
Vice-President, Lucas Papademos (Greece)

EUROPEAN INVESTMENT BANK

100 Boulevard Konrad Adenauer, L-2950 Luxembourg
E info@eib.org W www.eib.org

The European Investment Bank (EIB) was set up in 1958 under the terms of the treaty of Rome and is the financing arm of the European Union. The EIB's main activity is to provide long-term loans in support of investments undertaken by private or public promoters, for projects furthering European integration. Six key operational areas have been set out in the bank's corporate operational plan for 2007–2009: cohesion and convergence; development of trans-European networks of transport and energy; environmental sutainability; implementation of the Innovation 2010 initiative; support for small and medium-sized enterprises; and sustainable, competitive and secure energy.

The EIB also operates outside the EU, in support of EU development and cooperation policies in partner countries including the enlargement area of Europe (both candidate and potential candidate countries), the Mediterranean, Africa, the Caribbean and the Pacific, Asia and Latin America.

The EIB assesses and selects the projects it finances independently and never finances over 50 per cent of the total cost of a project. Each EIB-financed project must be financially, technically and environmentally viable.

The bank is not dependent on the EU budget, and raises its own resources on the capital markets. It is the biggest supranational bond issuer and lender in the world with an AAA credit rating. In 2006 it borrowed €48bn (£32bn) and lent a total of €46bn (£31bn), of which €40bn (£27bn) was lent within the EU.

The shareholders of the EIB are the 27 member states, whose ministers of economy and finance constitute its board of governors. This body lays down general directives on the credit policy of the bank and appoints members to the board of directors. The board of directors consists of 27 members nominated by the member states, and one by the European Commission. It takes decisions

on the granting and raising of loans and the fixing of interest rates. A management committee, composed of the bank's president and eight vice-presidents and also appointed by the board of governors, is responsible for the day-to-day operations of the bank.
President, Philippe Maystadt (Belgium)

ADVISORY BODIES

COMMITTEE OF THE REGIONS

Bâtiment Jacques Delors, rue Belliard 99–101, B-1040 Brussels, Belgium
E pressecdr@cor.europa.eu **W** www.cor.europa.eu

The Committee of the Regions (CoR), established in 1994, is the political assembly which provides local and regional authorities with a voice within the European Union. The EU treaties oblige the European Commission and Council of Ministers to consult the Committee of the Regions whenever new proposals are made in areas which have repercussions at regional or local level. The CoR issues opinions on proposals for EU laws, which directly affect local and regional authorities. It can also draw up opinions on its own initiative, which enables it to put issues on the EU agenda, as well as resolutions on topical political issues.

The committee has 344 full members and the same number of alternate members. They are proposed by the member states to the Council of Ministers, which appoints them for a four-year renewable term of office. Members must hold a regional or local authority electoral mandate or be politically accountable to an elected assembly. They participate in the work of six specialist commissions which are responsible for drafting the CoR's opinions and resolutions on a wide range of topics.
President, Michel Delebarre (France)
Secretary-General, Gerhard Stahl (Germany)

EUROPEAN ECONOMIC AND SOCIAL COMMITTEE

Rue Belliard 99, B-1040 Brussels, Belgium
W www.eesc.europa.eu

The European Economic and Social Committee (EESC) is an advisory and consultative body, which has 344 members appointed by the governments of the 27 member states for a four-year renewable term. It is divided into three groups: employers, workers, and other interest groups such as consumers, farmers and the self-employed. Every two years the EESC elects a bureau made up of 39 members, and a president and two vice-presidents chosen from each of the three groups in rotation. The EESC issues opinions on draft EC legislation and can bring matters to the attention of the commission, council and parliament. The EESC's competencies have increased as a result of revisions to the treaty of Rome, and the treaty of Nice formally recognised the importance of the opinions of the EU's economic and social partners.
President, Dimitris Dimitriadis (Greece)

AGENCIES

EUROPEAN ENVIRONMENT AGENCY

Kongens Nytorv 6, DK-1050 Copenhagen K, Denmark
T (+45) 3336 7100 **W** www.eea.europa.eu

The European Environment Agency (EEA) aims to support sustainable development and to help achieve significant and measurable improvement in Europe's environment, through the provision of information to policy-making agents and the public. The EEA has been operational since 1994, and now has 32 member countries. It is a European Union body but is open to non-EU countries that share its objectives. The management board consists of representatives of the member countries, two representatives of the European Commission and two representatives designated by the European parliament.
Chair, Lars-Erik Liljelund (Sweden)

EUROPEAN JUDICIAL COOPERATION UNIT (EUROJUST)

Maanweg 174, 2516 AB The Hague, The Netherlands
E info@eurojust.europa.eu **W** www.eurojust.europa.eu

The European Union's Judicial Cooperation Unit (Eurojust), established in 2002, aims at enhancing the development of Europe-wide cooperation in criminal justice cases involving serious cross-border and organised crime. Eurojust improves cooperation between the authorities of member states, in particular by facilitating the execution of international mutual legal assistance and through the implementation of extradition requests. It is a key interlocutor with the European parliament, the Council of Ministers and the European Commission.

The college of Eurojust is composed of 27 national members, one nominated by each member state. The national members are experienced prosecutors or judges.
President of the College, Michael Kennedy (UK)

EUROPEAN POLICE OFFICE (EUROPOL)

PO Box 90850, NL-2509 LW, The Hague, The Netherlands
E info@europol.europa.eu **W** www.europol.europa.eu

The European Police Office (Europol) came into being on 1 October 1998 and assumed its full powers on 1 July 1999. It superseded the Europol Drugs Unit and exists to improve police cooperation between member states and to combat terrorism, illicit traffic in drugs and other serious forms of organised international crime. It is ultimately responsible to the Council of Ministers. Each member state has set up a national unit to liaise with Europol, and the units send at least one liaison officer to represent its interests at Europol headquarters. Europol maintains a computerised information system, designed to facilitate exchange of information between member states. It has a management board comprising one senior representative from each member state. All Europol activities are monitored by an independent joint supervisory body to ensure the rights of the individual are upheld.
Director, Max-Peter Ratzel (Germany)

EUROPEAN COMMUNITY INFORMATION

EUROPEAN COMMISSION REPRESENTATION OFFICES

ENGLAND, 8 Storey's Gate, London SW1P 3AT
T 020-7973 1992
WALES, 2 Caspian Point, Caspian Way, Cardiff CF10 4QQ
T 029-208 95020
SCOTLAND, 9 Alva Street, Edinburgh EH2 4PH
T 0131-225 2058
NORTHERN IRELAND, Windsor House, 9–15 Bedford Street, Belfast BT2 7EG **T** 028-9024 0708

EUROPEAN PARLIAMENT

POLITICAL GROUPINGS
as at May 2007

	EPP-ED	PES	ALDE	GUE/NGL	Green/EFA	UEN	Ind-Dem	ITS	Others	Total
Austria	6	7	1	–	2	–	–	–	1	18
Belgium	6	7	6	–	2	–	–	3	–	24
Bulgaria	4	6	7	–	–	–	–	1	–	18
Cyprus	3	–	1	2	–	–	–	–	–	6
Czech Republic	14	2	–	6	–	–	1	–	1	24
Denmark	1	5	4	1	1	1	1	–	–	14
Estonia	1	3	2	–	–	–	–	–	–	6
Finland	4	3	5	1	1	–	–	–	–	14
France	17	31	11	3	6	–	3	7	–	78
Germany	49	23	7	7	13	–	–	–	–	99
Greece	11	8	–	4	–	–	1	–	–	24
Hungary	13	9	2	–	–	–	–	–	–	24
Ireland	5	1	1	1	–	4	1	–	–	13
Italy	24	14	13	7	2	13		2	3	78
Latvia	3	–	1	–	1	4	–	–	–	9
Lithuania	2	2	7	–	–	2	–	–	–	13
Luxembourg	3	1	1	–	1	–	–	–	–	6
Malta	2	3	–	–	–	–	–	–	–	5
The Netherlands	7	7	5	2	4	–	2	–	–	27
Poland	15	9	5	–	–	20	3	–	2	54
Portugal	9	12	–	3	–	–	–	–	–	24
Romania	9	12	8	–	–	–	–	6	–	35
Slovakia	8	3	–	–	–	–	–	–	3	14
Slovenia	4	1	2	–	–	–	–	–	–	7
Spain	24	24	2	1	3	–	–	–	–	54
Sweden	6	5	3	2	1	–	2	–	–	19
UK	27	19	12	1	5	–	10	1	3	78
Total	277	217	106	41	42	44	24	21	13	785

EPP-ED – European People's Party and European Democrats
W www.epp-ed.eu

PES – Party of European Socialists
W www.socialistgroup.org

ALDE – Alliance of Liberals and Democrats for Europe
W www.alde.eu

GUE/NGL – Confederal Group of the European United Left/Nordic Green Left
W www.guengl.eu

Green/EFA – Greens/European Free Alliance
W www.greens-efa.org

UEN – Union for a Europe of Nations
W www.uengroup.org

Ind-Dem – Independence/Democracy Group
W www.indemgroup.org

ITS – Identity, Tradition and Sovereignty Group
W www.its-pe.eu

INTERNATIONAL ORGANISATIONS

International organisations are intergovernmental organisations, whose membership can only include either sovereign states or other international organisations. They are subject to international law and are capable of entering into agreements among themselves or with states. They do not include private non-governmental organisations with an international scope. International organisations are usually established by a treaty providing them with legal recognition, which distinguishes them from collections of states such as the G8.

AFRICAN UNION

PO Box 3243, Addis Ababa, Ethiopia
T (+251) (1) 1551 7700 **E** webmaster@africa-union.org
W www.africa-union.org

The African Union (AU), was launched in 2002 as a successor to the amalgamated Organisation of African Unity and the African Economic Community. It currently has 53 members, representing every African country except Mauritania, whose membership was suspended following a military coup in 2005, and Morocco, which left the AU in 1985 in protest at the Saharan Arab Democratic Republic, representing Western Sahara, being admitted as a member. The AU aims to further African unity and solidarity, to coordinate political, economic, social and defence policies, and eventually, to create an African single currency.

Chief AU governing organs include the assembly of heads of state or government, which coordinates the organisation's policies; the executive council, composed of ministers from member states; the African Commission, which is the AU secretariat and consists of ten commissioners, each with a separate portfolio; the peace and security council, modelled on that of the UN and capable of military intervention, and the pan-African parliament, established in 2004 to debate and advise heads of state.

Substantial budgetary arrears due to delays in the payment of national contributions have led to the AU continually facing difficulties in furthering its aims. Since 2004, the AU has deployed a peacekeeping force in the Darfur region of Sudan. The number of troops has steadily grown but it has not been able to contain the violence. The UN proposed the despatch of its own force to support the AU troops, but this resolution was declined by the Sudanese government.

Chair, John Kufuor (Ghana)

ANDEAN COMMUNITY

General Secretariat, Paseo de la Republica 3895, esq. Aramburs, San Isidro, Lima 27, Peru
T (+51) (1) 411 1400 **E** contacto@comunidadandina.org
W www.comunidadandina.org

The Andean Community began operating formally on 21 November 1969 with the establishment of its commission and was known as the Andean Pact until 1996. It comprises four member states – Bolivia, Colombia, Ecuador and Peru – and the bodies of the Andean Integrated System (AIS). Mexico and Panama hold observer status, while Argentina, Brazil, Chile, Paraguay and Uruguay are associated states.

The organisation's objectives are to facilitate economic growth, boost job availability and assist the creation of a Latin American common market. It also aims to reduce the differences in development that exist between the member states. It seeks to achieve its objectives through a programme of complete trade liberalisation, a common external tariff, the reduction of border controls, the coordination of national legislation and the promotion of industrial, agricultural and technological development.

The general secretariat of the Andean Community is its executive body, responsible for administration and dispute resolution. The general secretariat operates under the direction of the secretary-general, who is elected by the Andean council of foreign ministers (ACFM). It can propose decisions or suggestions to the ACFM. It also manages the integration process, ensures that community commitments are fulfilled and maintains relations with the member countries and the executive bodies of other international organisations.

The Andean presidential council is the highest-level body of the AIS and comprises the presidents of the member states. Its responsibilities include setting new policies, evaluating the integration process and communicating with other bodies. The chairmanship is rotated among the members of the council each calendar year.

In 2001, the organisation introduced Andean passports for member states and in 2005 created a policy of free flow of persons, enabling citizens to travel throughout the area without requiring a visa.

Secretary-General, Freddy Ehlers (Ecuador)

ARAB MAGHREB UNION

14 rue Zalagh, Agdal, Rabat, Morocco
T (+212) (3) 767 1274 **E** sg.uma@maghrebarabe.org
W www.maghrebarabe.org

The treaty establishing the Arab Maghreb Union (AMU) was signed on 17 February 1989 by the heads of state of the five member states: Algeria, Libya, Mauritania, Morocco and Tunisia. The AMU aims to strengthen ties between the member countries by developing agriculture and commerce, introducing the free circulation of goods and services, and establishing joint projects and economic cooperation programmes.

Decisions must be unanimous and are made by a council of heads of state briefed by a council of foreign affairs ministers. A consultative assembly – consisting of 30 representatives from each member state – is based in Algiers, the secretariat is in Rabat, and the court of justice, with two judges from each country, operates in Nouakchott, Mauritania.

Secretary-General, Habib Ben Yahia (Tunisia)

ARCTIC COUNCIL

Ministry of Foreign Affairs, PO Box 8114 Dep, N-0032 Oslo, Norway **T** (+47) 2224 3243 **W** www.arctic-council.org

The Arctic Council was founded in 1996 in Ottawa, Canada, and is a regional forum for socio-economic development and scientific research within the Arctic region. It comprises eight states: Canada, Denmark (including Greenland and the Faeroe Islands), Finland, Iceland, Norway, Russia, Sweden and the USA. A further six organisations representing indigenous peoples are granted permanent participatory status and include the Saami Council, Inuit Circumpolar Conference and the Arctic Athabaskan Council. Five states (France, Germany, the Netherlands, Poland and the UK) have observer status.

Decisions within the Arctic Council are taken at biennial ministerial meetings attended by foreign ministers or designates of the member states. The chairmanship of the council and secretariat also rotate on a biennial basis. Between these meetings, the operation of the council is administered by the Committee of Senior Arctic Officials.

The main scientific work of the Arctic Council is carried out in five working groups, each focusing on specific issues such as the monitoring and prevention of pollution, climate change, biodiversity and public health.

Chair, Norway

ASIA COOPERATION DIALOGUE

E acd@mfa.go.th W www.acddialogue.com

The Asia Cooperation Dialogue (ACD) was initiated by former Thailand prime minister, Thaksin Shinawatra, and inaugurated in June 2002. It currently has 30 members after Tajikistan and Uzbekistan joined in 2006.

Its purpose is to provide a continent-wide forum to assist development in every Asian nation, with the ultimate goal to create an Asian community capable of equal interaction with the rest of the world. It aims to achieve these objectives through promoting interdependence among Asian countries, improving quality of life and expanding the continent's trade and financial markets.

Representatives from each of the member states (typically foreign ministers) meet annually to discuss ACD developments, issues of regional cooperation and methods of enhancing Asian unity. In addition, ministers also meet following the annual UN general assembly to update policy and project progress.

ASIAN-AFRICAN LEGAL CONSULTATIVE ORGANISATION

E-66, Vasant Marg, Vasant Vihar, 110057 New Delhi, India T (+91) (11) 2615 2251
E mail@aalco.org W www.aalco.int

The Asian-African Legal Consultative Organisation (AALCO), founded as a result of the Bandung Conference of 1955, was previously known as both the Asian Legal Consultative Committee and the Asian-African Legal Consultative Committee before its name was changed again in 2001. It was initally established as a non permanent committee for a five-year term which was repeatedly extended until 1981, when its was granted permanent status. It has 48 member states.

The functions of the AALCO include serving as an advisory body to its member states in the field of international law, operating as a forum for common concerns among its members and making recommendations to governments and other international organisations.

Representatives from member states meet for the annual session which is hosted on a rotational basis and is attended by members of government, observers from other organisations and members of the International Court of Justice and International Law Commission.

The secretariat is located in New Delhi and is responsible for the day-to-day functioning of the organisation. It is headed by a secretary-general, elected to a three-year term. Other infrastructure includes four regional arbitration centres in Egypt, Iran, Malaysia and Nigeria.

Secretary-General, Dr Wafik Z. Kamil (Egypt)

ASIAN DEVELOPMENT BANK

PO Box 789, 0980 Manila, The Philippines
T (+632) 632 4444 E information@adb.org W www.adb.org

The Asian Development Bank (ADB) was founded in 1966 and is a multilateral financial institution dedicated to reducing poverty in Asia and the Pacific. It has 67 member countries from across the world. The ADB extends loans, equity investments and technical assistance to governments and public and private enterprises in its member countries and promotes the investment of public and private capital for development. The bank's programmes prioritise economic growth, human development, good governance, environmental protection, private sector growth and regional cooperation.

The ADB is controlled by its board of governors, which consists of a representative from each of the member states. Its powers are delegated to a board of directors which is responsible for administration and policy review.

The ADB raises funds through members' contributions and issuing bonds on the world's capital markets. In 2006, the ADB provided loans totalling US$6,820m (£3,412m) and technical assistance costing US$241.6m (£120.8m).

President, Haruhiko Kuroda (Japan)

ASIA-PACIFIC ECONOMIC COOPERATION

35 Heng Mui Keng Terrace, Singapore 119616
T (+65) 6775 6012 E info@apec.org W www.apec.org

Asia-Pacific Economic Cooperation (APEC) is an economic forum for Pacific Rim countries to discuss regional economy, cooperation, trade and investment. APEC was founded in 1989 in response to the growing interdependence among Asia-Pacific economies. The 1994 Declaration of Common Resolve envisaged a free trade zone, to be established by 2010 in industrialised economies and by 2020 in developing member economies. Members define and fund work programmes for APEC's four committees, 11 working groups and other task forces.

APEC's chairmanship rotates annually among member states and the chair is responsible for hosting the annual ministerial meeting of foreign affairs and trade ministers. The permanent secretariat, based in Singapore, is responsible for implementing policy.

Executive-Director, Colin S. Heseltine (Australia)

ASSOCIATION OF SOUTH-EAST ASIAN NATIONS

Jalan Sisingamangaraja 70a, Jakarta 12110, Indonesia
T (+62) (21) 726 2991/724 3372 E public@aseansec.org
W www.aseansec.org

The Association of South-East Asian Nations (ASEAN) is a geo-political and economic organisation formed in 1967 with the aim of accelerating economic growth, social progress and cultural development, and ensuring regional stability. It currently has ten member states.

The ASEAN summit, an annual meeting of the heads of government, is the organisation's highest authority. The ASEAN ministerial meeting is an annual meeting of foreign ministers of member states and is responsible for the formulation of policy guidelines and the coordination of ASEAN's activities. The ASEAN economic ministers meet annually to coordinate economic policy.

An ASEAN free trade area was implemented in 2003, while a common preferential tariff was introduced in 1993. At the ASEAN summit in 1995, a south-east Asia nuclear weapon-free zone was declared.

The secretary-general of ASEAN is appointed on merit by the heads of government and can initiate, advise, coordinate and implement ASEAN activities. In addition to the ASEAN secretariat based in Jakarta, each member state has a national secretariat in its foreign ministry which organises and implements activities at national level. The ASEAN region has a combined GDP of around US$1,875bn and a total trade value of approximately US$1,442bn.

Secretary-General, HE Ong Keng Yong (Singapore)

BALTIC ASSEMBLY

Tornu 4, Kazarmas III, Section C, Room 301, Riga, LV-1050, Latvia **T** (+371) 722 5178
E baltasam@baltasam.org **W** www.baltasam.org

Established in November 1991, the Baltic Assembly (BA) is an international organisation for cooperation between the parliaments of Estonia, Latvia and Lithuania. Each member state appoints 20 parliamentarians to the assembly, including a head and deputy head of the national delegation. The political allegiances of the appointments reflect party proportions in each of the domestic parliaments. The BA holds two sessions per year in each of the member states in rotation. In addition, there are permanent and *ad hoc* committees. The Baltic council of ministers, which comprises the heads of government and ministers of the member states, meets with the BA once a year and promotes intergovernmental and regional cooperation between the Baltic states; the joint sessions are known as the Baltic council.

President, Valerijus Simulik (Lithuania)

CAB INTERNATIONAL

Wallingford, Oxon OX10 8DE
T 01491-832111 **E** corporate@cabi.org **W** www.cabi.org

Founded in 1930, CAB International (CABI) (formerly the Commonwealth Agricultural Bureau) is a non-profit organisation specialising in scientific knowledge to assist sustainable development, with an emphasis on agriculture, forestry and natural resources and the needs of developing countries. The organisation consists of 40 countries and five British overseas territories; each is represented on an executive council. A governing board provides guidance on policy issues.

CABI has two divisions: bioscience and publishing. They undertake research and provide consultancy aimed at raising agricultural productivity, conserving biological resources, protecting the environment and controlling disease. Any country is eligible to apply for membership. Applications are by invitation from existing members and are authorised by a head of state or delegated authority.

Chief Executive Officer, Dr Trevor Nicholls (UK)

CARIBBEAN COMMUNITY AND COMMON MARKET

Turkeyen, PO Box 10827, Georgetown, Guyana
T (+592) 2220 0175 **E** doccentre@caricom.org
W www.caricom.org

The Caribbean Community and Common Market (CARICOM) was established in 1973 with the signing of the Treaty of Chaguaramas. The objectives of CARICOM are to improve member states' working and living standards, boost employment levels, promote economic development and competitiveness, coordinate foreign and economic policies and enhance cooperation in the delivery of services such as health and education.

The supreme organ is the conference of heads of government, which determines policy and resolves conflict. The community council of ministers consists of ministers of government assigned to CARICOM affairs and is responsible for economic and strategic planning. The principal administrative arm is the secretariat, based in Guyana. The Bureau of the Conference of Heads of Government is the executive body; it comprises the chairman of the conference, the outgoing chair and the secretary-general, who are all authorised to initiate proposals and to secure the implementation of decisions. In addition, there are four ministerial councils dealing with trade and economic development, foreign and community relations, human and social development, and finance and planning.

In 2005, Suriname became the first country to issue CARICOM passports. Seven other member states have introduced them since.

CARICOM has 15 member states, five associate members and seven states with observer status.

Secretary-General, Edwin W. Carrington (Trinidad and Tobago)

THE COMMONWEALTH

The Commonwealth is a voluntary association of 53 sovereign and independent states together with their associated states and dependencies. All of the states were formerly part of the British Empire or League of Nations (later the UN) mandated territories, except for Mozambique which was admitted as a unique case because of its history of cooperation with neighbouring Commonwealth nations.

The status and relationship of member nations were first defined by the inter-imperial relations committee of the 1926 Imperial Conference, when the six existing dominions (Australia, Canada, the Irish Free State, Newfoundland, New Zealand and South Africa) were described as 'autonomous communities within the British Empire, equal in status, in no way subordinate one to another in any aspect of their domestic or external affairs, though united by a common allegiance to the Crown and freely associated as members of the British Commonwealth of Nations'. This formula was given legal substance by the Statute of Westminster 1931.

This concept of a group of countries owing allegiance to a single crown changed in 1949 when India decided to become a republic. Her continued membership of the Commonwealth was agreed by the other members on the basis of her 'acceptance of the monarch as the symbol of the free association of its independent member nations and as such the head of the Commonwealth'. This paved the way for other republics to join the association in due course. Member nations agreed at the time of the accession of Queen Elizabeth II to recognise Her Majesty as the new head of the Commonwealth. However, the position is not vested in the British Crown.

THE MODERN COMMONWEALTH

As the UK's former colonies joined, after India and Pakistan in 1947, the Commonwealth was transformed from a grouping of all-white dominions into a multiracial association of equal, sovereign nations. It increasingly focused on promoting development and racial equality. South Africa withdrew in 1961 when it became clear that its reapplication for membership on becoming a republic would be rejected over its policy of apartheid.

The new goals of advocating democracy, the rule of law, good government and social justice were enshrined in the Harare Commonwealth Declaration (1991), which formed the basis of new membership guide-lines agreed in Cyprus in 1993. Following the adoption of measures at the New Zealand summit in 1995 against serious or persistent violations of these principles, Nigeria was suspended in 1995 and Sierra Leone was suspended in 1997 for anti-democratic behaviour. Sierra Leone's suspension was revoked in March 1998 when the legitimate government was returned to power. Similarly, Nigeria's suspension was lifted in May 1999, the day a newly elected civilian president took office. The heads of government meeting in Edinburgh in 1997 established a set of economic principles for the Commonwealth, promoting economic growth whilst protecting smaller member states from the negative effects of globalisation. Zimbabwe was suspended from the councils of the Commonwealth in March 2002 and, in December 2003, the Zimbabwean government officially confirmed its departure from the association.

MEMBERSHIP

Membership of the Commonwealth involves acceptance of the association's basic principles and is subject to the approval of existing members. There are 53 members at present, of which 16 have Queen Elizabeth II as head of state, 31 are republics and six have national monarchies. (The date of joining the Commonwealth is shown in parentheses.)

*Antigua and Barbuda (1981)
*Australia (1931)
*The Bahamas (1973)
Bangladesh (1972)
*Barbados (1966)
*Belize (1981)
Botswana (1966)
Brunei (1984)
Cameroon (1995)
*Canada (1931)
Cyprus (1961)
Dominica (1978)
§Fiji (1970)
The Gambia (1965)
Ghana (1957)
*Grenada (1974)
Guyana (1966)
India (1947)
*Jamaica (1962)
Kenya (1963)
Kiribati (1979)
Lesotho (1966)
Malawi (1964)
Malaysia (1957)
Maldives (1982)
Malta (1964)
Mauritius (1968)
Mozambique (1995)
Namibia (1990)
†Nauru (1968)
New Zealand (1931)
Nigeria (1960)
Pakistan (1947)
*Papua New Guinea (1975)
*St Kitts and Nevis (1983)
*St Lucia (1979)
*St Vincent and the Grenadines (1979)
Samoa (1970)
Seychelles (1976)
Sierra Leone (1961)
Singapore (1965)
*Solomon Islands (1978)
South Africa (1931)
Sri Lanka (1948)
Swaziland (1968)
Tanzania (1961)
Tonga (1970)
Trinidad and Tobago (1962)
‡Tuvalu (1978)
Uganda (1962)
*United Kingdom
Vanuatu (1980)
Zambia (1964)

* Realms of Queen Elizabeth II
† Nauru is a special member
‡ Originally a special member due to its small size, small economy and limited involvement in international affairs, Tuvalu became a full member in September 2000.
§ Fiji joined in 1970, rejoined in 1997; suspended in 2000 and again in 2006, following a military coup.

COUNTRIES WHICH HAVE LEFT THE COMMONWEALTH

Republic of Ireland (1949)
Pakistan (1972, rejoined 1989, suspended from the councils of the commonwealth 1999, suspension lifted May 2004)
South Africa (1961, rejoined 1994)
Zimbabwe (2003)

In each of the realms where Queen Elizabeth II is head of state (except for the UK), she is personally represented by a governor-general, who holds in all essential respects the same position in relation to the administration of public affairs in the realm as is held by Her Majesty in the UK. The governor-general is appointed by the Queen on the advice of the government of the state concerned.

INTERGOVERNMENTAL AND OTHER LINKS

The main forum for consultation is the Commonwealth heads of government meetings, held biennially to discuss international developments and to consider cooperation among members. Decisions are reached by consensus, and the views of the meeting are set out in a communiqué. There are also annual meetings of finance ministers and frequent meetings of ministers and officials in other fields, such as education, health, gender and youth affairs. Intergovernmental links are complemented by the activities of some 80 Commonwealth non-governmental organisations linking professionals, sportsmen and sportswomen, and interest groups, forming a people's Commonwealth. The Commonwealth Games take place every four years.

Assistance to other Commonwealth countries normally has priority in the bilateral aid programmes of the association's developed members (Australia, Britain, Canada and New Zealand), who direct about 30 per cent of their aid to other member countries. Developing Commonwealth nations also assist their poorer partners, and many Commonwealth voluntary organisations promote development.

COMMONWEALTH SECRETARIAT

The Commonwealth has a secretariat, established in 1965 in London, which is funded by member governments. This is the main agency for multilateral communication between member governments on issues relating to the Commonwealth as a whole. It promotes consultation and cooperation, disseminates information on matters of common concern, organises meetings including the biennial summits, coordinates Commonwealth activities, and provides technical assistance for economic and social development through the Commonwealth fund for technical cooperation.

The Commonwealth foundation was established by Commonwealth governments in 1966 as an autonomous body with a board of governors representing Commonwealth governments that fund the foundation. It promotes and funds exchanges and other activities aimed at strengthening the skills and effectiveness of professionals and non-governmental organisations. It also promotes culture, rural development, social welfare and the role of women.

COMMONWEALTH SECRETARIAT, Marlborough House, Pall Mall, London SW1Y 5HX T 020-7747 6500 E info@commonwealth.int W www.thecommonwealth.org
Secretary-General, Rt. Hon. Don McKinnon (New Zealand)

COMMONWEALTH FOUNDATION, Marlborough House, Pall Mall, London SW1Y 5HY T 020-7930 3783 E geninfo@commonwealth.int W www.commonwealthfoundation.com
Chair, Prof. Guido de Marco

COMMONWEALTH INSTITUTE, New Zealand House, 80 Haymarket, London SW1Y 4TQ T 020-7024 9822 E information@commonwealth-institute.org.uk W www.commonwealth.org.uk

COMMONWEALTH OF INDEPENDENT STATES

Ul. Kirova 17, Minsk 220030, Belarus
T (+375) (17) 222 3517 E postmaster@cis.minsk.by
W www.cis.minsk.by

The Commonwealth of Independent States (CIS) is a multilateral grouping of 12 former Soviet republics. It was formed in 1991 and its charter was signed by seven states in 1993, an event that established the functions of the organisation and the obligations of its members.

The CIS acts as a coordinating mechanism for foreign, defence and economic policies and is a forum for addressing problems arising from the break-up of the USSR. These matters are addressed in more than 70 inter-state, intergovernmental coordinating and consultative statutory bodies. However, member states have criticised the CIS for operating ineffectively and for failing to carry through decisions made by CIS organs.

STRUCTURE

The two supreme CIS bodies are the council of heads of state and the council of heads of government. The executive committee, based in Minsk and Moscow, provides administrative support. There are also numerous ministerial, parliamentary, economic and security councils.

DEFENCE COOPERATION

On becoming members of the CIS, the member states agreed to recognise their existing borders, respect one another's territorial integrity and reject the use of military force or other forms of coercion to settle disputes between them.

A treaty on collective security was signed in 1992 by six states and a joint peacemaking force, to intervene in CIS conflicts, was agreed upon by nine states. Russia concluded bilateral and multilateral agreements with other CIS states under the supervision of the council of heads of collective security (established 1993). These were gradually upgraded into CIS agreements under the umbrella of the collective security treaty, enabling Russia to station troops in eight of the other 11 CIS states (not Moldova, Turkmenistan or Ukraine), and giving Russian forces *de facto* control of virtually all of the former USSR's external borders. Only Ukraine and Moldova remained outside the defence cooperation framework and did not sign the treaty. In 1999, Azerbaijan, Georgia and Uzbekistan withdrew from the treaty and formed a new defensive grouping with Moldova and Ukraine.

ECONOMIC COOPERATION

In 1991, 11 republics signed a treaty forming an economic community. Members agreed to refrain from economic actions that would damage each other and to coordinate economic and monetary policies. A coordinating consultative committee, an economic arbitration court and an inter-state bank were established. A single monetary unit, the rouble, was originally agreed upon by all member states, and the members recognised that the basis of recovery for their economies was private ownership, free enterprise and competition.

The 11 CIS members who signed the Establishment of an Economic Union treaty in September 1993 (Ukraine is an associate member of the economic union) committed themselves to a common economic space with free movement of goods, services, capital and labour. Belarus, Kazakhstan, Kyrgyzstan and Russia signed a treaty on the establishment of a customs union in March 1996; the treaty was later signed by Tajikistan. On 10 October 2000, the presidents of the five countries approved a treaty establishing the Eurasian Economic Community. In 2006, Russia, Belarus and Kazakhstan announced the formation of a customs union.

Executive Secretary, Vladimir Rushaylo (Russian Federation)

COOPERATION COUNCIL FOR THE ARAB STATES OF THE GULF

PO Box 7153, Riyadh 11-462, Saudi Arabia
T (+966) (1) 482 7777 W www.gcc-sg.org

The Cooperation Council for the Arab States of the Gulf, or Gulf Cooperation Council (GCC), as it is informally known, was established on 25 May 1981. Its main objectives are increasing coordination and integration, harmonising economic, commercial, educational and social policies and promoting scientific and technical innovation among its member states. It also aims to establish a common currency by 2010. The GCC has six members: Bahrain, Kuwait, Oman, Qatar, Saudi Arabia and the United Arab Emirates.

The highest authority of the GCC is the supreme council, whose presidency rotates among members' heads of states. It holds one regular session every year, but extraordinary sessions may be convened if necessary.

The ministerial council, which ordinarily meets every three months, consists of the foreign ministers of the member states or other delegated ministers. It is authorised to propose policies and recommendations and ensure that resolutions are implemented.

Secretary-General, Abdul-Rahman bin Hamad al-Attiyah (Qatar)

COUNCIL OF EUROPE

Avenue de l'Europe, F-67075 Strasbourg, France
T (+33) (3) 8841 2033 E infopoint@coe.int W www.coe.int

The Council of Europe was founded in 1949. Its aim is to achieve greater unity between its members, to safeguard their European heritage and to facilitate their progress in economic, social, cultural, educational, scientific, legal and administrative matters, and to further pluralist democracy, human rights and fundamental freedoms. It has 46 members.

The organs are the committee of ministers, consisting of the foreign ministers of member countries, and the parliamentary assembly of 315 members (and 315 substitutes), elected or chosen by the national parliaments of member countries in proportion to the relative strength of political parties.

The committee of ministers is the executive organ. The majority of its conclusions take the form of international agreements (known as European conventions) or recommendations to governments. Decisions of the ministers may also be embodied in partial agreements to which a limited number of member governments are party.

One of the principal achievements of the Council of Europe is the European Convention on Human Rights (1950) under which the European Commission and the European Court of Human Rights was established. They merged in 1993. The reorganised European Court of Human Rights sits in chambers of seven judges, or exceptionally, as a grand chamber of 17 judges. Litigants must exhaust legal processes in their own country prior to bringing cases before the court.

Among other conventions and agreements are the European Social Charter, the European Cultural Convention, the European Code of Social Security, the European Convention on the Protection of National Minorities, and conventions on extradition, the legal status of migrant workers, torture prevention, conservation and the transfer of sentenced prisoners. Most recently, the specialised bodies of the Venice Commission and Demosthenes have been set up to assist in developing legislative, administrative and constitutional reforms in Central and Eastern Europe.

Non-member states take part in certain Council of Europe activities on a regular or *ad hoc* basis; thus the Holy See participates in all the educational, cultural and sports activities. The council's ordinary budget for 2007 totalled €270m (£184m).

Secretary-General, Rt. Hon. Terry Davis (UK)

COUNCIL OF THE BALTIC SEA STATES

Secretariat, Stromsborg, PO Box 2010, S-103 11 Stockholm, Sweden
T (+46) 8440 1920 E cbss@cbss.org W www.cbss.org

The Council of the Baltic Sea States was established in March 1992 with the aim of creating a regional forum to increase cooperation and coordination among the states which border on the Baltic Sea. The organisation focuses on assisting new democratic institutions, economic and technical development, humanitarian aid and health, energy and environmental issues, cultural programmes, education, tourism, transportation and communication. It currently has 12 members (11 countries and the European Commission).

The council consists of the foreign ministers of each member state and a member of the European Commission. Chairmanship of the council rotates on an annual basis, and the annual session is held in the country currently in the chair. The foreign minister of the presiding country is responsible for coordinating activities between the sessions. Since 1998 a permanent international secretariat has been established in Stockholm, Sweden.

Chair, Latvia (2007–8), Denmark (2008–9)

ECONOMIC COMMUNITY OF WEST AFRICAN STATES

Secretariat Building, 101 Yakubu Gowon Crescent, PMB 401, Abuja, Nigeria
T (+234) (9) 314 7647 E info@ecowas.int W www.ecowas.int

The Economic Community of West African States (ECOWAS) was founded in 1975 and came into operation in 1977. It aims to prevent and control regional conflicts and promote the cultural, economic and social development of West Africa through mutual cooperation.

The supreme authority of ECOWAS is vested in the annual summit of heads of government of all 15 member states. A council of ministers meets biannually to monitor the organisation and make recommendations to the summit. ECOWAS operates through a secretariat, headed by the executive secretary. In addition there are four deputy executive secretaries. The ECOWAS parliament was inaugurated in November 2000 and judges for the court of justice were sworn in in January 2001.

Five member states of ECOWAS (The Gambia, Ghana, Guinea, Nigeria and Sierra Leone) have announced plans to introduce the Eco as a single common currency on 1 December 2009. Eight other states currently use the CFA franc. These currencies are planned to eventually be amalgamated. An ECOWAS travel certificate is operational in seven countries and a common passport in a separate three.

An ECOWAS peacekeeping force has been involved in attempts to restore peace in Liberia (1990–6), in Guinea-Bissau (1998–9) and in Sierra Leone (1997–9).

Executive Secretary, Dr Mohamed ibn Chambas (Ghana)

EUROPEAN BANK FOR RECONSTRUCTION AND DEVELOPMENT

One Exchange Square, London EC2A 2JN
T 020-7338 6000 W www.ebrd.com

The European Bank for Reconstruction and Development (EBRD), established in 1991, is an international institution, whose membership comprises 61 member states, the European Community and the European Investment Bank.

The aim of EBRD is to build market economies and democracies in 29 countries across the world. EBRD provides project financing for banks, industries and businesses. It also works with publicly owned companies to support privatisation, restructuring state-owned firms and improving public services.

The main forms of EBRD financing are loans, equity investments and guarantees. No more than 40 per cent of the EBRD's investment can be made in state-owned concerns. The EBRD pays particular attention to strengthening the financial sector and to promoting small and medium-sized enterprises. It works in cooperation with national governments, private companies, and international organisations such as the OECD, the IMF, the World Bank and the UN specialised agencies. The EBRD is also able to borrow on world capital markets.

In 2005, the EBRD committed €4.3bn (£2.9bn) to 151 new projects. Net profit in 2005 reached €1.5bn (£1.02bn) while total assets were estimated at €28bn (£19bn).

The highest authority is the board of governors; each member appoints one governor and one alternate. The governors delegate most powers to a 23-member board of directors; the directors are responsible for the EBRD's

operations and budget, and are elected by the governors for three-year terms. The governors also elect the president of the board of directors, who acts as the bank's president for a four-year term.
President of the Board of Directors, Jean Lemierre (France)

EUROPEAN FREE TRADE ASSOCIATION

9–11 rue de Varembé, CH-1211 Geneva 20, Switzerland
T (+32) (2) 286 1711 E mail.gva@efta.int W www.efta.int

The European Free Trade Association (EFTA) was established in 1960 by Austria, Denmark, Norway, Portugal, Sweden, Switzerland and the UK, and was subsequently joined by Finland, Iceland and Liechtenstein. Six members have left to join the European Union: Denmark and the UK (1972), Portugal (1985), Austria, Finland and Sweden (1995). The existing members are Iceland, Liechtenstein, Norway and Switzerland.

The first objective of EFTA was to establish free trade in industrial products between members; this was achieved in 1966. Its second objective was the creation of a single market in Western Europe and in 1972 EFTA signed free trade agreements with the EC covering trade in industrial goods. The remaining tariffs on industrial products were abolished in 1977 and the Luxembourg Declaration on broader cooperation between EFTA and the EC was signed in 1984.

An agreement on the creation of the European Economic Area (EEA), an extension of the EC single market to the EFTA states, was signed in 1992 and entered into force in January 1994. Switzerland rejected EEA membership in a referendum in 1992 and Liechtenstein joined in May 1995 after adapting its customs union with Switzerland.

Since 2002, free trade area agreements have been signed between the EFTA states and Singapore, Chile, Lebanon and the Republic of Korea. With these agreements, the EFTA states will have concluded free trade agreements with 15 states and territories, representing a population of 340 million, in addition to the free trade relations with the EU. Negotiations on free trade agreements with Canada, Egypt, the Gulf Cooperation Council and Thailand are ongoing.

The EFTA council is the principal organ. It meets regularly at the level of ambassadors to the EFTA secretariat in Geneva.
Secretary-General, Kare Bryn (Norway)

EUROPEAN ORGANISATION FOR NUCLEAR RESEARCH (CERN)

CH-1211 Geneva 23, Switzerland
T (+41) (22) 767 6111 E cern.reception@cern.ch
W www.cern.ch

The convention establishing the European Organisation for Nuclear Research (CERN) came into force in 1954. CERN promotes European collaboration in high energy physics with scientific goals and no military implication. It has 20 member states and eight members with observer status, including the European Commission and UNESCO.

The council, which is the highest policy-making body, comprises two delegates from each member state and is chaired by the president, who is elected by the council in session. The council also elects a director-general, who is responsible for the internal organisation of CERN. The director-general heads a workforce of approximately 3,000, including physicists, craftsmen, technicians and administrative staff. At present over 8,500 physicists use CERN's facilities.

Scientists Tim Berners-Lee and Robert Cailliau developed the World Wide Web whilst working at CERN in 1989.
Director-General, Dr Robert Aymar (France)

EUROPEAN SPACE AGENCY

8–10 rue Mario Nikis, F-75738 Paris Cedex 15, France
T (+33) (1) 5369 7155 W www.esa.int

The European Space Agency (ESA) was created in 1975 by the merger of the European Space Research Organisation and the European Launcher Development Organisation. Its aims include the advancement of space research and technology and the implementation of a long-term European space policy. ESA has 17 member states and one cooperating state. ESA's mandatory activities are funded by contributions from all member states and calculated in accordance with each country's gross national income. In 2006, ESA's budget was €2,904m (£1,958m).

The agency is directed by a council composed of the representatives of the member states; its chief officer is the director-general who is elected by the council every four years. ESA has liaison offices in Belgium, the United States of America and Russia, while a launch base is stationed in French Guiana.
Director-General, Jean-Jacques Dordain (France)

EUROPEAN UNION

See European Union section

FOOD AND AGRICULTURE ORGANISATION OF THE UNITED NATIONS

Viale delle Terme di Caracalla, 00153 Rome, Italy
T (+39) (06) 57051 E fao-hq@fao.org W www.fao.org

The Food and Agriculture Organisation (FAO) is a specialised UN agency, established in 1945. It assists rural populations by raising levels of nutrition and living standards, and by encouraging greater efficiency in food production and distribution. It analyses and publishes information on agriculture and natural resources. The FAO also advises governments on national agricultural policy and planning through its investment centre and collaboration with the World Bank and other financial institutions. The FAO's field programme covers a range of activities, including strengthening crop production, rural and livestock development and conservation.

The FAO's top priorities are sustainable agriculture, rural development and food security. The organisation monitors potential famine areas, channels emergency aid from governments and other agencies, assists in rehabilitation, and responds to urgent or unforeseen requests for technical assistance.

The FAO has 190 members (189 states plus the EU). It is governed by a biennial conference of its members which sets a programme and budget. The budget for 2006–7 was US$765.7m (£382.9m), funded by member countries in proportion to their gross national income. The FAO is also funded by the UN development programme, donor governments and other institutions.

The conference elects a director-general and a 49-member council which governs between conferences. The regular and field programmes are administered by a

secretariat, headed by the director-general. Five regional, five sub-regional and 74 national offices help administer the field programme.
Director-General, Jacques Diouf (Senegal)

INTERNATIONAL ATOMIC ENERGY AGENCY

Vienna International Centre, Wagramer Strasse 5, PO Box 100, A-1400 Vienna, Austria
T (+43) (1) 26000 **E** official.mail@iaea.org **W** www.iaea.org

The International Atomic Energy Agency (IAEA) was established in 1957. It is an intergovernmental organisation that reports to, but is not a specialised agency of, the UN.

The IAEA aims to enhance the contribution of atomic energy to peace, health and prosperity. It does not advocate the use of atomic energy for military purposes. It establishes atomic energy safety standards and offers services to its member states for the safe operation of their nuclear facilities and for radiation protection. It is the focal point for international conventions on the early notification of a nuclear accident, accident assistance, civil liability for nuclear damage, physical protection of nuclear material, and the safety of spent fuel and radioactive waste management. The IAEA also encourages research and training in nuclear power. It is additionally charged with drawing up safeguards and verifying their use in accordance with several international nuclear weapons treaties.

The IAEA has 144 members that meet annually in a general conference. The conference decides policy, a programme and a budget – €283m (£192m) in 2007 – as well as electing a director-general and a 35-member board of governors. The board meets four times a year to formulate policy which is implemented by the secretariat.
Director-General, Mohamed ElBaradei (Egypt)

INTERNATIONAL CIVIL AVIATION ORGANISATION

999 University Street, Montréal, Québec, Canada H3C 5H7
T (+1) (514) 954 8219 **E** icaohq@icao.int **W** www.icao.int

The International Civil Aviation Organisation (ICAO) was founded with the signing of the Chicago Convention on International Civil Aviation in 1944 and became a specialised agency of the UN in 1947. It sets international technical standards and regulations for aviation safety, security and efficiency, as well as environmental protection.

ICAO has 190 members and is governed by an assembly. A council of 36 members is elected, which represents leading air transport nations as well as less developed countries. The council elects the president, appoints the secretary-general and supervises the organisation through subsidiary committees, serviced by a secretariat.
President of the Council, Roberto Kobeh González (Mexico)

INTERNATIONAL CONFEDERATION OF FREE TRADE UNIONS

Koning Albert II laan 5, Bus 1, B-1210 Brussels, Belgium
T (+32) (2) 224 0211 **E** internetpo@icftu.org **W** www.icftu.org

The International Confederation of Free Trade Unions (ICFTU) was created in 1949. It aims to establish, maintain and promote free trade unions, and to promote peace with economic security and social justice. In February 2007, the ICFTU had 155 million members in 241 affiliated organisations in 156 countries and territories.

The congress, the supreme authority of the ICFTU, is composed of delegates from the affiliated trade union organisations. The congress elects an executive board of 53 members, including five nominated by the women's committee and one by the youth committee. The board establishes the budget and receives suggestions and proposals from affiliates, as well as acting on behalf of the confederation. The congress also elects the general secretary. A steering committee of 17 members of the executive board plus the general secretary and the president meet twice a year to oversee ICFTU financial matters.
General Secretary, Guy Ryder (UK)

INTERNATIONAL CRIMINAL POLICE ORGANISATION (INTERPOL)

200 Quai Charles de Gaulle, F-69006 Lyon, France
E compr@interpol.int **W** www.interpol.int

Interpol was set up in 1923 to establish an international criminal records office and to harmonise extradition procedures. In 2007, the organisation comprised 186 member states. Interpol's aims are to promote cooperation between criminal police authorities and to support government agencies concerned with combating crime, while respecting national sovereignty. It is financed by annual contributions from the governments of member states.

Interpol's policy is decided by the general assembly which meets annually and is composed of delegates appointed by the member states. The 13-member executive committee is elected by the general assembly from the member states' delegates and is chaired by the president, who has a four-year term of office. The permanent administrative organ is the general secretariat, headed by the secretary-general, who is appointed by the general assembly.
Secretary-General, Ronald K. Noble (USA)

INTERNATIONAL ENERGY AGENCY

9 rue de la Fédération, F-75739 Paris, France
T (+33) (1) 4057 6500/01 **E** info@iea.org **W** www.iea.org

The International Energy Agency (IEA), founded in 1974, is an autonomous agency within the framework of the Organisation for Economic Cooperation and Development (OECD). The IEA's objectives include the improvement of energy cooperation worldwide, development of alternative energy sources and the promotion of relations between oil producing and oil consuming countries. The IEA also maintains an emergency system to alleviate the effects of severe oil supply disruptions.

The main decision-making body is the governing board, composed of senior energy officials from member countries. The IEA secretariat, with a staff of energy experts, carries out the work of the governing board and its subordinate bodies. The executive director is appointed by the board. The IEA has 26 member states.
Executive Director, Nobuo Tanaka (Japan)

INTERNATIONAL FRANCOPHONE ORGANISATION

Cabinet du Secrétaire général, 28 rue de Bourgogne, F-75007 Paris, France
T (+33) (1) 4411 1250 **W** www.francophonie.org

The International Francophone Organisation (known as La Francophonie) is an intergovernmental organisation founded in 1970 by 21 French-speaking countries. It aims to prevent conflict and promote development and cooperation, represent its member states internationally and promote French culture and language.

The conference of heads of state and heads of government of countries using French as a common language, also known as the Francophone summit, takes place biennially. Other institutions include the ministerial conference, the permanent council and the secretariat.

The ministerial conference, which consists of the foreign ministers or the ministers responsible for Francophone affairs of each member state, implements decisions made at the summits and puts forward prospective new members. The permanent council, which is chaired by the secretary-general and consists of representatives of the member states, oversees the execution of decisions made by the ministerial conference, allocates funds, and reviews and approves projects.

La Francophonie has 55 member states, two associate member states and 13 observers.

Secretary-General, Abdou Diouf (Senegal)

INTERNATIONAL FUND FOR AGRICULTURAL DEVELOPMENT

107 Via del Serafico, I-00142 Rome, Italy
T (+39) (06) 54591 **E** ifad@ifad.org **W** www.ifad.org

The International Fund for Agricultural Development (IFAD) began operations as a UN specialised agency in 1977. It aims to mobilise funds for agricultural and rural projects in developing countries, provide employment and additional income for poor farmers, reduce malnutrition and improve food security systems.

IFAD has 165 members and membership is divided into three lists: List A (OECD countries), List B (OPEC countries), and List C (developing countries) which is subdivided into C1 (Africa), C2 (Europe, Asia and the Pacific) and C3 (Latin America and the Caribbean). All powers are vested in a governing council of all member countries. It elects an 18-member executive board responsible for IFAD's operations. The council meets annually and elects a president who is also chair of the board. The president serves a four-year term that can be renewed once.

Since its establishment, IFAD has committed a total of $9.4bn (£4.7bn) in loans for 731 approved projects and programmes.

President, Lennart Bage (Sweden)

INTERNATIONAL HYDROGRAPHIC ORGANISATION

International Hydrographic Organisation, 4 Quai Antoine 1er, B.P. 445, 98011, Monaco
T (+377) 9310 8100 **E** info@ihb.mc **W** www.iho.shom.fr

The International Hydrographic Organisation began its activity in 1921 with 19 member states and, at the invitation of H.S.H. Prince Albert I, was provided with headquarters in the Principality of Monaco. In 1970, its name was changed from the International Hydrographic Bureau. The IHO is an intergovernmental organisation that has a purely consultative role and aims to support safety in international navigation and set policy for marine conservation. The IHO has a membership of 75 states that meet at five-yearly conferences to set policy, approve budget, review progress and adopt programmes of work. Each member is represented at these conferences by their most senior hydrographer. All member states have an opportunity to initiate new proposals for IHO consideration. Outside of its membership, the IHO acts to promote hydrography and facilitate the exchange of technology with developing countries. It is also the source that defines the boundaries between seas and oceans.

President, Vice-Adm. Alexandros Maratos (Greece)

INTERNATIONAL LABOUR ORGANISATION

4 route des Morillons, CH-1211 Geneva 22, Switzerland
T (+41) (22) 799 6111 **E** ilo@ilo.org **W** www.ilo.org

The International Labour Organisation (ILO) was established in 1919 as an autonomous body of the League of Nations and became the UN's first specialised agency in 1946. The ILO aims to increase employment, improve working conditions and living standards and encourage democratic development.

It sets minimum international labour standards through the drafting of international conventions. Member countries are obliged to submit these to their domestic authorities for ratification, and thus undertake to bring their domestic legislation in line with the conventions. Members must report to the ILO periodically on how these regulations are being implemented. The ILO plays a major role in helping developing countries achieve economic stability and job expansion through its wide-ranging programme of technical cooperation. The ILO is also the world's principal resource centre for information, analysis and guidance on labour and employment.

The ILO has 180 members and is composed of the International Labour Conference, the governing body and the International Labour Office. The conference of members meets annually, and is attended by national delegations comprising of two government delegates, one worker delegate and one employer delegate. It adopts international labour conventions and recommendations, provides a forum for discussion of world employment and social issues and approves the ILO's programme and budget.

The 56-member governing body is composed of 28 government, 14 worker and 14 employer members and acts as the ILO's executive council. Ten governments, including the UK, hold permanent seats on the governing body because of their industrial importance. There are also various regional conferences and advisory committees. The ILO acts as a secretariat and as a centre for operations, publishing and research.

Director-General, Juan Somavia (Chile)

INTERNATIONAL MARITIME ORGANISATION

4 Albert Embankment, London SE1 7SR
T 020-7735 7611 **E** media@imo.org **W** www.imo.org

Originally called the Inter-Governmental Maritime Consultative Organisation, the International Maritime

Organisation (IMO) was established as a UN specialised agency in 1948. Owing to delays in treaty ratification it did not commence operations until 1958.

The IMO fosters intergovernmental cooperation in technical matters relating to international shipping, particularly regarding safety and security at sea, efficiency in navigation and protecting the marine environment from pollution caused by shipping. The IMO is responsible for convening maritime conferences and drafting marine conventions. It also provides technical aid to countries wishing to develop their activities at sea.

In 2007, the IMO had 167 members and three associate members. It is governed by an assembly comprising delegates of all its members. It meets biennially to formulate policy, set a budget (£49.7m for 2006–7), to vote on specific recommendations on pollution, maritime safety and security, and to elect the council. The council, which meets twice a year, fulfils the functions of the assembly between sessions and appoints a secretary-general. It consists of 40 members: ten from the world's largest shipping nations, ten from the nations most dependent on seaborne trade, and 20 other members to ensure a fair geographical representation. The IMO acts as the secretariat for the London Convention (1972) which regulates the disposal of land-generated waste at sea.

Secretary-General, Efthimios E. Mitropoulos (Greece)

INTERNATIONAL MONETARY FUND

700 19th Street NW, Washington DC 20431, USA
T (+1) (202) 623 7300 E publicaffairs@imf.org W www.imf.org

The International Monetary Fund (IMF) was established at the UN Monetary and Financial Conference at Bretton Woods, New Hampshire, in 1944. Its articles of agreement entered into force in 1945 and it began operations in 1947.

The IMF exists to promote international monetary cooperation, the expansion of world trade and exchange stability. It advises members on their economic and financial policies; promotes policy coordination among the major industrial countries; and gives technical assistance in central banking, balance of payments accounting, taxation and other financial matters. The IMF serves as a forum for members to discuss monetary policy issues and seeks the balanced growth of international trade. It has 185 members.

Upon joining the IMF, a member is assigned a quota, based on the member's relative standing in the world economy and its balance of payments position. The quota determines the member's capital subscription to the fund, access to IMF resources, voting power and share in the allocation of special drawing rights (SDRs). Quotas are reviewed every five years and adjusted accordingly. The SDR, an international reserve asset issued by the IMF, is calculated daily on a basket of usable currencies and is the IMF's unit of account; on 23 April 2007, 1 SDR equalled US$1.52 (£0.76). SDRs are allocated at intervals to supplement members' reserves and thereby improve international financial liquidity. Total quotas as at March 2007 were US$327bn (£163bn).

The IMF is not a bank and does not lend money; it provides temporary financial assistance by selling a member's SDRs or other members' currencies in exchange for the member's own currency. The member can then use the purchased currency to alleviate its balance of payments difficulties. IMF financial resources derive primarily from members' capital subscriptions, which are equivalent to their quotas. In addition, the IMF is authorised to borrow from official lenders. It may also draw on a line of credit of SDR18.5bn from various countries under the so-called general arrangements to borrow (GAB). Periodic charges are also levied on financial assistance. In July 2006, total outstanding IMF credits amounted to US$34bn (£17bn).

The IMF supports long-term efforts at economic reform and transformation as well as medium-term programmes under the extended fund facility, which runs for three to four years and is aimed at overcoming balance of payments difficulties stemming from macroeconomic and structural problems. Members experiencing a temporary balance of payments shortfall have access to the compensatory and contingency financing facility.

The IMF is headed by a board of governors, comprising representatives of all members, which meets annually. The governors delegate powers to 24 executive directors, who are appointed or elected by member countries. The executive directors operate the fund on a daily basis under a managing director, whom they elect.

Managing Director, Rodrigo de Rato y Figaredo (Spain)

INTERNATIONAL ORGANISATION FOR MIGRATION

17, Route des Morillons, CH-1211 Geneva 19, Switzerland
T (+41) 22717 9111 E info@iom.int W www.iom.int

The International Organisation for Migration (IOM) was founded in 1951 to resettle European displaced persons and refugees. During the 1960s and 1970s the IOM developed links with the United Nations High Commissioner for Refugees (UNHCR) and began a programme of assistance and reintegration outside of Europe. There are currently 120 member states and 19 observers. Internally, the IOM is led by a director-general who is elected for a five-year term. The director-general's office has the constitutional authority to manage the organisation, carry out the activities within its mandate and develop current policies, procedures and strategies. The office of the inspector-general (OIG) incorporates the functions of evaluation, internal audit and assessment of projects. The OIG is also involved in investigations within the formal complaints procedure.

The role of the IOM has recently expanded to cover migration health services, counter-trafficking measures, emergency and post-crises management and assisted voluntary returns.

Director-General, Brunson McKinley (USA)

INTERNATIONAL RED CROSS AND RED CRESCENT MOVEMENT

19 avenue de la Paix, CH-1202 Geneva, Switzerland
T (+41) 2273 46001 W www.icrc.org

The International Red Cross and Red Crescent Movement is composed of three elements – the International Committee of the Red Cross, the International Federation of Red Cross and Red Crescent Societies, and the national Red Cross and Red Crescent societies.

The International Committee of the Red Cross (ICRC), the organisation's founding body, was formed in 1863. It aims to negotiate between warring factions and to protect and assist victims of armed conflict. It also seeks to ensure the application of the Geneva Conventions regarding prisoners of war and detainees.

The International Federation of Red Cross and Red

Crescent Societies was founded in 1919 to assist the humanitarian activities of national societies, coordinate their relief operations for victims of natural disasters and care for refugees outside areas of conflict. There are Red Cross and Red Crescent societies in 185 countries, with a total membership of over 250 million.

The international conference of the Red Cross and Red Crescent meets every four years, bringing together delegates of the ICRC, the International Federation and the national societies, as well as representatives of nations bound by the Geneva Conventions.

President of the ICRC, Jakob Kellenberger (Switzerland)

INTERNATIONAL TELECOMMUNICATION UNION

Place des Nations, CH-1211 Geneva 20, Switzerland
T (+41) (22) 730 5111 E itumail@itu.int W www.itu.int

The International Telecommunication Union (ITU) was founded in Paris in 1865 as the International Telegraph Union and became a UN specialised agency in 1947.

The ITU is an intergovernmental organisation for the development of telecommunications and the harmonisation of national telecommunication policies. It comprises 191 member states and some 700 sector members and 100 associates who represent public and private organisations involved in telecommunications. Its mission is to promote the development of information and communication technologies, and to offer technical assistance to developing countries.

ITU operates initiatives aimed at promoting the growth and expansion of electronic commerce. These include a programme of strategic workshops; the adoption of international regulations, treaties and technical standards to foster global interactivity; and the provision of policy advice and technical assistance. ITU also organises worldwide and regional exhibitions and forums to exchange ideas, knowledge and technology.

Secretary-General, Hamadoun Touré (Mali)

INTERNATIONAL WHALING COMMISSION

The Red House, 135 Station Road, Impington, Cambridge CB24 9NP T 01223-233971
E secretariat@iwcoffice.org W www.iwcoffice.org

The International Whaling Commission (IWC) was set up under the International Convention for the Regulation of Whaling, signed in Washington DC in 1946. It has 73 member states as of April 2007. The purpose of the IWC is to provide for the conservation of whale stocks, enabling the development of the whaling industry. The organisation reviews and revises the schedule to the convention which sets limits for when and where whaling can take place, coordinates and funds whale research and publishes and promotes scientific studies.

The IWC has four main committees, responsible for scientific, technical, conservation and finance matters. There are further sub-committees concerned with aboriginal subsistence whaling, infractions and working groups involved with whale-killing methods and animal welfare issues.

Chair, Dr William Hogarth (USA)

LATIN UNION

131 rue du Bac, F-75007 Paris, France
T (+33) (1) 4549 6060 E ulsg@unilat.org W www.unilat.org

The Latin Union is an international organisation whose member states use a Romance language. It was created in 1954 with the signing of a constituent agreement in Madrid and has existed as a functioning institution since 1983. The aims of the organisation are to protect, project and promote the common heritage and to unify identities of the Latin and Latin-influenced world. It has 37 member states and 3 members with observer status.

The congress is the senior body of the organisation. It consists of representatives from each of the member states and meets every two years. It is responsible for approving the budget and setting the agenda for the Union's activities. The executive council is made up of representatives from 12 member states who are elected for a four-year term by congress. The general secretariat is directed by a secretary-general who is elected by congress and instructed to implement policy.

The official languages of the Latin Union are French, Italian, Portuguese, Spanish and Romanian, though the latter is not used as a working language.

Secretary-General, Bernardino Osio

LEAGUE OF ARAB STATES

Maidan Al-Tahrir, Cairo, Egypt
T (+20) (2) 575 0511 W www.arableagueonline.org

The League of Arab States was founded in 1945 to protect the independence and sovereignty of its member states, supervise the affairs and interests of Arab countries and promote the process of integration among them. The organisation has 22 member states. The League itself has observer status at the United Nations.

The heads of member states meet annually at the Arab League summit, while foreign ministers convene every six months as part of the Arab League council. Member states participate in various specialised agencies which develop specific areas of cooperation between Arab states. These include: the Arab Organisation for Mineral Resources; the Arab Monetary Fund; the Arab Satellite Communications Organisation; the Arab Academy of Maritime Transport; the Arab Bank for Economic Development in Africa; the Arab League Educational, Cultural and Scientific Organisation and the Council of Arab Economic Unity.

Secretary-General, Amre Moussa (Egypt)

MERCOSUR

Luis Piera 1992, piso 1, 11200-Montevideo, Uruguay
T (+598) (2) 412 9024 E secretaria@mercosur.org.uy
W www.mercosur.org.uy

In 1988, Brazil and Argentina signed an integration, cooperation and development treaty which aimed to create a common market between the two countries within ten years, eliminating all tariff barriers and harmonising macroeconomic policies. The agreement was to be open to other Latin American countries. Paraguay and Uruguay expressed their interest and MERCOSUR (the Southern Common Market) was created by the treaty of Asunción, which was signed by the four countries on 26 March 1991. Venezuela became the fifth member in 2006. Five other countries have associate member status.

The Common Market Council (CMC) is the highest-level agency of MERCOSUR, with authority to conduct its policy and responsibility for compliance with the treaty of Asunción. The CMC comprises ministers of foreign affairs and economic ministers of the member states and meets at least once a year.

The Common Market Group is the executive body of MERCOSUR and is coordinated by the foreign ministries of the member states. Its function is to implement decisions made by the CMC and resolve disputes. It can establish subgroups to work on particular issues and comprises four permanent members and four substitutes from each country. Other bodies include a joint parliamentary committee, a trade commission and a socio-economic advisory forum.

In 2005, Argentina, Brazil, Paraguay and Uruguay became associate members of the Andean Community, reciprocating MERCOSUR's action to grant associate membership to all Andean Community nations. In December 2005, the Columbian president ratified a free trade agreement with MERCOSUR giving Columbian products preferential access to MERCOSUR countries.

President of the Commission of Permanent Representatives, Carlos Alvarez (Argentina)

NORDIC COUNCIL

Store Strandstræde 18, DK-1255 Copenhagen K, Denmark **T** (+45) 3396 0400
E nordisk-rad@norden.org **W** www.norden.org

The Nordic Council was established in March 1952 as an advisory body on economic and social cooperation, comprising of parliamentary delegates from Denmark, Iceland, Norway and Sweden. It was subsequently joined by Finland (1956), and representatives from the Faroes (1970), the Aland Islands (1970), and Greenland (1984).

Cooperation is regulated by the treaty of Helsinki signed in 1962. This was amended in 1971 to create a Nordic council of ministers, which discusses all matters except defence and foreign affairs. Decisions of the council of ministers, which are taken by consensus, are binding, although if ratification by member parliaments is required, decisions only become effective following parliamentary approval. The council of ministers is advised by the Nordic Council, to which it reports annually. There are ministers for Nordic cooperation in every member government.

The Nordic Council comprises 87 voting delegates nominated from member parliaments and about 80 non-voting government representatives. It meets at least once a year in plenary sessions. The full council chooses a 13-member praesidium, which conducts business between sessions. A secretariat, headed by a secretary-general provides administrative support. The presidency and chairmanship of the Nordic Council rotate between the five countries but the same country never holds the presidency and chair of both organisations for the same year.

*President,*Ole Stavad (Denmark)

NORTH AMERICAN FREE TRADE AGREEMENT

NAFTA Secretariat, Canadian Section, 90 Sparks Street, Suite 705, Ottawa, Ontario K1P 5B4, Canada
T (+1) (613) 992 9388 **E** canada@nafta-sec-alena.org

NAFTA Secretariat, Mexican Section, Blvd. Adolfo López Mateos 3025, 2° Piso, Col. Héroes de Padierna, C.P. 10700, Mexico, D.F. **T** (+52) (55) 629 9630
E mexico@nafta-sec-alena.org

NAFTA Secretariat, US Section, Room 2061, 14th Street and Constitution Avenue, NW, Washington DC, 20230, USA
T (+1) (202) 482 5438 **E** usa@nafta-sec-alena.org
W www.nafta-sec-alena.org

The leaders of Canada, Mexico and the USA signed the North American Free Trade Agreement (NAFTA) on 17 December 1992 in their respective capitals; it came into force in January 1994 after being ratified by the legislatures of the three member states.

NAFTA aims to eliminate barriers to trade in goods and services, promote fair competition within the free trade area, protect and enforce intellectual property rights and create a framework for further cooperation. To achieve these aims, import tariffs and quotas are being removed, with the aim of achieving a free trade zone by 2008 at the latest.

The NAFTA secretariat is composed of Canadian, Mexican and US sections. It is responsible for administering the dispute settlement provisions of the agreement, providing assistance to the Free Trade Commission and support for various committees and working groups, and facilitating the operation of the agreement.

NORTH ATLANTIC TREATY ORGANISATION

Leopold III laan, Brussels B-1110, Belgium
T (+32) (2) 707 4111 **E** natodoc@hq.nato.int **W** www.nato.int

NATO is the structural framework for a political and military alliance designed to provide common security for its members through cooperation and consultation in political, military and economic as well as scientific and other non-military fields.

The North Atlantic treaty (treaty of Washington) was signed in 1949 by Belgium, Canada, Denmark, France, Iceland, Italy, Luxembourg, the Netherlands, Norway, Portugal, the UK and the USA. Greece and Turkey acceded to the treaty in 1952, the Federal Republic of Germany in 1955 (the reunited Germany acceded in October 1990), Spain in 1982, and the Czech Republic, Hungary and Poland in 1999. Bulgaria, Estonia, Latvia, Lithuania, Romania, Slovakia and Slovenia signed membership protocols in March 2003 and officially joined the North Atlantic Treaty Organisation (NATO) in March 2004.

STRUCTURE

The North Atlantic council (NAC), chaired by the secretary-general, is the highest authority of the alliance and is composed of permanent representatives of the 26 member countries. It meets at ministerial level (foreign and/or defence ministers) at least twice a year. The permanent representatives (ambassadors) head national delegations of advisers and experts. The defence planning committee (DPC) and the nuclear planning group (NPG) are composed of representatives of all member countries except France (which does not participate in NATO's integrated military structure). Both the DPC and the NPG also meet at ministerial level at least twice a year. The NATO secretary-general chairs the council, the DPC and the NPG. Much of the NAC policy is prepared and drafted by the senior political committee, a group of deputy permanent representatives and policy advisers.

The senior military authority in NATO, under the council and DPC, is the military committee, composed of the chief of defence staffs of each member country except

Iceland, which has no military forces and is represented by a civilian. The military committee, which is assisted by an integrated international military staff, also meets in permanent session with permanent military representatives and is responsible for making recommendations to the council and DPC on measures considered necessary for the common defence of the NATO area and for supplying guidance on military matters to the NATO strategic commanders. The chair of the military committee, elected for a period of two to three years, represents the committee on the council.

The alliance's military command structure is divided between two functional strategic commands. The strategic commanders have responsibility for all NATO military operations (allied command operations or ACO) and for the further transformation of the alliance's military forces and capabilities (allied command transformation or ACT). There is also a regional planning group for Canada and the USA. The headquarters of ACO is at Mons, Belgium, and comes under the command of the Supreme Allied Commander Europe (SACEUR). The headquarters of ACT is at Norfolk, Virginia, USA, and is under the command of the Supreme Allied Commander, Transformation.

POST COLD WAR DEVELOPMENTS

The Euro-Atlantic partnership council (EAPC) was established in 1997 to develop closer security links with Eastern European and former Soviet states. Replacing the North Atlantic cooperation council (NACC) as the first institutional framework for cooperation between NATO member countries and former adversaries from Central and Eastern Europe, the EAPC focuses on defence planning, defence industry conversion, defence management and force structuring, and the democratic concepts of civilian-military relations. Its membership comprises the 26 NATO members and Albania, Armenia, Austria, Azerbaijan, Belarus, Croatia, Finland, Georgia, Ireland, Kazakhstan, Kyrgyzstan, Macedonia, Moldova, Russia, Sweden, Switzerland, Tajikistan, Turkmenistan, Ukraine and Uzbekistan. Its membership may in future be expanded to include Bosnia and Hercegovina, Montenegro and Serbia, once these countries have fulfilled the conditions for membership. The EAPC provides the multilateral, political framework for the partnership for peace programme (PFP) in which each of its member countries participates. The PFP is the basis for practical, bilateral security cooperation between NATO and individual partner countries in the fields of defence planning and budgeting, military exercises and civil emergency operations. It also works to improve interoperability between the forces of partner and member countries to enable them to undertake joint operations and has provided the context for cooperation by many of the partner countries in NATO-led peacekeeping and peace-support operations in Bosnia and Hercegovina, Kosovo and Afghanistan.

NATO and Russia committed themselves to helping build a stable, secure and undivided continent on the basis of partnership and mutual interest, when they signed the 1997 Founding Act on mutual relations, cooperation and security, which provided for the creation of a NATO-Russia permanent joint council (PJC). In May 2002 it was replaced by the NATO-Russia council which brought together the 27 participating countries for consultation and practical cooperation in fields of common interest and endeavour on the basis of equality. The NRC meets every month at ambassadorial level and twice each year at ministerial level to address issues of common concern such as the threat of global terrorism and bilateral programmes in other areas of security such as defence reform, search and rescue, and civil emergency planning. NATO and Ukraine pursue an annual programme of cooperation and consultation following the signing of a NATO-Ukraine charter in 1997. NATO's Mediterranean dialogue, launched in 1994, aims to improve trust and understanding of NATO's goals and objectives among the countries of the southern Mediterranean area: Algeria, Egypt, Israel, Jordan, Mauritania, Morocco and Tunisia. The dialogue brings together seven Mediterranean countries: Algeria, Egypt, Israel, Jordan, Mauritania, Morocco and Tunisia.

At its summit meeting in June 2004, the alliance launched the Istanbul cooperation initiative, inviting contacts and cooperation with interested countries in the broader Middle East region.

The development of a European security and defence identity, which would strengthen NATO's European pillar, was agreed at the 1999 NATO summit meeting in Washington. Since then further developments have served to strengthen cooperation between NATO and the European Union and to establish a strategic partnership. This has led *inter alia* to the transfer of responsibility from NATO to the European Union, for continuing peace-support operations in the Former Yugoslav Republic of Macedonia and in Bosnia and Hercegovina, in accordance with special arrangements providing for NATO support for EU-led military operations of this kind.

At the Washington summit a defence capabilities initiative was also launched. It aims to improve defence interoperability among NATO forces to ensure the effectiveness of future multinational operations. At the 2002 Prague summit, further measures to improve capabilities were taken on the basis of a new capabilities commitment, in which member countries agreed to specific targets and time frames for improvements. A military concept for defence against terrorism was also agreed, and additional initiatives taken in the areas of nuclear, biological and chemical weapons defence, and protection against cyber attacks. A missile defence feasibility study was initiated. The NATO response force, a rapid-reaction unit comprising land, sea and air special forces was officially launched at the Prague summit and became fully operational (approx. 25,000 troops) in 2006.

AFGHANISTAN

From January 2001, following the establishment of the Afghan Transitional Authority, an international security assistance force (ISAF) was created on the basis of a UN mandate to provide the security needed to allow infrastructure reconstruction and create a stable democratic government. A number of NATO member countries took on responsibility on a six-monthly rotational basis for the leadership of this force. In 2002, NATO began providing support for ISAF at the request of the lead nations and, in August 2003, assumed full responsibility for the leadership of ISAF. In accordance with decisions taken at the Istanbul summit meeting in June 2004, and at the request of President Karzai, ISAF extended its authority from the capital, Kabul, to provide security assistance for almost 50 per cent of the country. In 2006, there were approximately 9,000 ISAF troops serving in Afghanistan from over 35 NATO and non-NATO countries.

IRAQ

Following a summit meeting in Istanbul in 2004, NATO agreed to establish an Iraq training mission. This included the foundation of a joint staff college that was tasked with the training of Iraqi army officers and other senior defence staff. It is estimated that around 900 officers have graduated from the centre since its opening at Ar-Rustamiyah, near Baghdad, in September 2005.

Secretary-General and Chair of the North Atlantic Council, of the DPC and of the NPG, Jaap de Hoop Scheffer (The Netherlands)

ORGANISATION FOR ECONOMIC COOPERATION AND DEVELOPMENT

2 rue André-Pascal, F-75775 Paris, France
T (+33) (1) 4524 8200 E webmaster@oecd.org
W www.oecd.org

The Organisation for Economic Cooperation and Development (OECD) was formed in 1961 to replace the Organisation for European Economic Cooperation. It is the instrument for international cooperation among industrialised member countries on economic and social policies. Its objectives are to assist its member governments in creating policies designed to achieve high, sustained economic growth and maintaining financial stability; to contribute to world trade on a multilateral basis and to stimulate members' aid to developing countries. OECD has 30 members, the vast majority in Europe. The European Commission is involved in the work of the OECD but is not a member of the organisation.

The council is the supreme body of the organisation. It is composed of one representative for each member country and meets at permanent representative level under the chairmanship of the secretary-general, and at ministerial level (usually once a year) under the chair of a minister, elected annually. Decisions and recommendations are adopted by the unanimous agreement of all members. Most of the OECD's work is undertaken in over 150 specialised committees and working parties. These are serviced by an international secretariat headed by a secretary-general.

In May 2006, OECD revealed it is considering expansion, with a number of countries interested in gaining membership. Before this can take place, a new method for calculating member funding is required. Funding is currently divided according to a member states' economy and population size, but many of the proposed members may struggle to fund their participation.

Secretary-General, Angel Gurria (Mexico)

ORGANISATION FOR SECURITY AND COOPERATION IN EUROPE

Kärntner Ring 5–7, A-1010 Vienna, Austria
T (+43) (1) 5143 6180 E info@osce.org W www.osce.org

The Organisation for Security and Cooperation in Europe (OSCE) was launched in 1975 as the Conference on Security and Cooperation in Europe (CSCE) under the Helsinki Final Act. This established agreements between NATO members, Warsaw Pact members, and neutral and non-aligned European countries covering security, cooperation and human rights. It was renamed in 1995.

The Charter of Paris for a New Europe, signed in November 1990, committed members to support multiparty democracy, free-market economics, the rule of law and human rights. The signatories also agreed to regular meetings of heads of government, ministers and officials. The first CSCE summit was held in Helsinki in December 1992, at which the Helsinki Document was adopted. This declared the CSCE to be a regional organisation under the UN charter and defined the structures of the organisation.

Three structures have been established: the ministerial council, which comprises the foreign ministers of participating states and meets at least once a year; the permanent council, which is the main regular body for political consulation, meeting weekly in Vienna; and the forum for security cooperation, also meeting weekly. The chairmanship of the OSCE rotates annually and the post of chair-in-office is held by the foreign minister of a participating state.

The OSCE is also underpinned by four permanent institutions: a secretariat (Vienna); an office for democratic institutions and human rights (Warsaw), which is charged with furthering human rights, democracy and the rule of law; an office of the high commissioner on national minorities (The Hague), which identifies ethnic tensions that might endanger peace and promotes their resolution; and a representative on freedom of the media (Vienna), which is responsible for assisting governments in the furthering of free, independent and pluralistic media.

The OSCE has 19 field missions in 17 member countries. Since 1996, the OSCE has observed more than 150 elections and supervised all elections in Bosnia and Hercegovina between 1996 and 2000 and in Kosovo between 2000 and 2004. In November 1999, the charter on European security committed the OSCE to cooperating with other organisations and institutions concerned with the promotion of security within the OSCE area. The OSCE has 56 participating states and in 2006 its budget was €163m (£111m).

Chair, Spain (2007)

Chair-in-office, Miguel Angel Moratinos (Spain)

ORGANISATION OF AMERICAN STATES

17th Street and Constitution Avenue, NW, Washington DC 20006, USA T (+1) (202) 458 3000
E multimedia@oas.org W www.oas.org

Originally founded in 1890 for largely commercial purposes, the Organisation of American States (OAS) adopted its present name and charter in 1948. The charter entered into force in 1951 and was amended in 1967, 1985 and 1996; the 1992 Protocol of Washington, which gives the OAS the right to suspend a member state whose democratically elected government is overturned by force, was ratified in 1997. OAS has 35 member states. Cuba remains a member but has been excluded from participation since 1962. The European Union and 59 non-American states have permanent observer status.

The OAS aims to strengthen the peace and security of the continent; to promote and consolidate representative democracy; to prevent possible causes of difficulties and to ensure the peaceful resolution of disputes among member states; to seek the resolution of political, judicial and economic problems that may arise among them; to promote their economic, social and cultural development;

nd to achieve an effective limitation of conventional weapons.

The declaration of principles and the plan of action resulting from the 1994 Miami summit and signed by all the members except Cuba, envisage the establishment of a free trade area, in which barriers to trade and investment will be progressively eliminated.

Policy is determined by the annual general assembly, which is the supreme authority and elects the secretary-general for a five-year term. The meeting of consultation of ministers of foreign affairs considers urgent problems on an *ad hoc* basis. The permanent council, comprising one representative from each member state, promotes friendly relations, acts as an intermediary in case of disputes arising between states and oversees the general secretariat, the main administrative body. The Inter-American council for integral development was created in 1996 by the ratification of the protocol of Managua to promote sustainable development.

Secretary-General, Jose Miguel Insulza (Chile)

ORGANISATION OF ARAB PETROLEUM EXPORTING COUNTRIES

PO Box 20501, Safat 13066, Kuwait
T (+965) 484 4500 E oapec@oapec.org W www.oapecorg.org

The Organisation of Arab Petroleum Exporting Countries (OAPEC) was founded in 1968. Its objectives are to promote cooperation in economic activities, safeguard members' interests, unite efforts to ensure the flow of oil to consumer markets, and create a favourable climate for the investment of capital and expertise. OAPEC has 11 member states, although Tunisia's membership has been inactive since 1987.

The ministerial council is composed of oil ministers from the member countries and meets twice a year to determine policy and approve the budgets and accounts of the general secretariat and the judicial tribunal. The judicial tribunal is composed of seven part-time judges who rule on disputes between member countries and between countries and oil companies. The executive organ of OAPEC is the general secretariat.

The members are Algeria, Bahrain, Egypt, Iraq, Kuwait, Libya, Qatar, Saudi Arabia, Syria and the United Arab Emirates.

Secretary-General, Abdulaziz A. al-Turki (Saudi Arabia)

ORGANISATION OF THE BLACK SEA ECONOMIC COOPERATION

Permanent International Secretariat, Sakip Sabanci Caddesi, Musir Fuad Pasa Yalisi, Eski Tersane, 34460 Istinye-Istanbul, Turkey T (+90) (212) 229 6330/6335
E info@bsec-organization.org W www.bsec-organization.org

The Black Sea Economic Cooperation (BSEC) resulted from the Istanbul Summit Declaration and the adoption of the Bosporus Statement on 25 June 1992. BSEC acquired a permanent secretariat in 1994. A charter was inaugurated to found the Organisation of the Black Sea Economic Cooperation in May 1999, following the Yalta Summit of the heads of state or government in June 1998. It has 12 member states.

The organisation aims to promote closer political and economic cooperation between the countries in the Black Sea region and to foster security, regional initiatives, social justice, economic liberty and respect for human rights.

The council of the ministers of foreign affairs is the highest decision-making authority and meets twice--yearly. The meetings rotate among the member states and the chair is the foreign minister of the state in which the meeting is held. There is also a committee of senior officials and 16 working groups, which deal with specific areas of cooperation.

Secretary-General, Leonidas Chrysanthopoulos (Greece)

ORGANISATION OF THE ISLAMIC CONFERENCE

PO Box 178, Jeddah 21411, Saudi Arabia
T (+966) (2) 690 0001 E cabinet@oic-oci.org
W www.oic-oci.org

The Organisation of the Islamic Conference (OIC) was established in 1969 with the purpose of promoting solidarity and cooperation between Islamic countries. It also has the specific aims of coordinating efforts to safeguard Muslim holy places, supporting the formation of a Palestinian state, coordinating the views of member states in international forums such as the UN, and improving cooperation in the fields of economics, culture and science.

The OIC has three main bodies, the summit of the heads of state, the conference of foreign ministers and the general secretariat which is headed by a secretary-general, elected by the conference of foreign ministers for a four-year term.

In addition to this structure, the OIC has several subsidiary bodies, institutions, and standing committees. These include the Islamic Solidarity Fund, to aid Islamic institutions in member countries; the Islamic Development Bank, to finance development projects in poorer member states and the Islamic Educational, Scientific and Cultural Organisation.

The achievement of the OIC's aims has often been prevented by political rivalry and conflicts between member states, such as the Iran-Iraq war and the Iraqi invasion of Kuwait. Egypt's membership was suspended from 1979 to 1984 because of its peace treaty with Israel. Saudi Arabia, the main source of funding, exercises great influence within the OIC. Since 1991, the OIC has become more united and has spoken out in protest of violence against Muslims in India, the Occupied Territories and Bosnia-Hercegovina. From 1993 to 1995 the OIC coordinated the offering of troops to the UN by Muslim states to protect Muslim areas of Bosnia-Hercegovina.

The organisation has 57 members (56 sovereign Muslim states in Africa, the Middle East, central and south-east Asia and Europe, plus the Palestine Authority) and five observer states.

Secretary-General, Prof. Ekmeleddin Ihsanoglu (Turkey)

ORGANISATION OF THE PETROLEUM EXPORTING COUNTRIES

Obere Donaustrasse 93, A-1020 Vienna, Austria
T (+43) (1) 2111 2279 E prid@opec.org W www.opec.org

The Organisation of the Petroleum Exporting Countries (OPEC) was created in 1960 as a permanent intergovernmental organisation with the principal aims of unifying and coordinating the petroleum policies of its members, determining ways of protecting their interests, and ensuring the stabilisation of prices in international oil markets. Since 1982, OPEC has attempted to impose overall production limits and production quotas to maintain stable oil prices.

The supreme authority is the conference of ministers of oil, mining and energy of member countries, which meets at least twice a year. The board of governors, nominated by member countries, directs the management of OPEC and implements conference resolutions. The secretariat carries out executive functions under the direction of the board of governors.

OPEC's 12 member countries hold about two-thirds of the world's oil reserves. In 2005, OPEC accounted for 42.7 per cent of the world's oil production. The value of OPEC oil exports in 2005 was US$512bn (£256bn) and their proven crude oil reserves were 904 billion barrels.
Secretary-General, Abdalla Salem el-Badri (Libya)

PACIFIC ISLANDS FORUM

Secretariat, Private Mail Bag, Suva, Fiji
T (+679) 332 1600 **E** info@forumsec.org.fj
W www.forumsec.org.fj

The Pacific Islands Forum (PIF) was established in 1971 and represents heads of governments of 16 independent and self-governing Pacific island countries. It aims to foster cooperation between its governments and to represent the interests of the region in international organisations. The PIF meets annually, following which a dialogue is conducted at ministerial level with 12 forum partners.

The PIF secretariat comprises divisions dealing with development and economic policy, trade and investment, political and international affairs and services, and is responsible for implementing Forum decisions.

In 2006, French Polynesia and New Caledonia became associate members. Tokelau and East Timor currently hold observer status.
Secretary-General, Gregory Lawrence Urwin (Australia)

PARTNERS IN POPULATION AND DEVELOPMENT

IPH Building, Mohakhali, 1212 Dhaka, Bangladesh
T (+88) (2) 988 1882 **E** partners@ppdsec.org
W www.partners-popdev.org

Partners in Population and Development (PPD) is an inter-governmental organisation launched at the UN International Conference on Population and Development in Cairo in 1994. It has 21 member states. PPD is dedicated to forming partnerships between and among individuals, organisations and the governments of developing countries. It provides a platform for its members to share successful experiences in education, migration, sexual health and combating infant mortality.

PPD is controlled by a board of directors consisting of a single representative from each member state. The responsibilities of the board include setting policy, promoting cooperation among members and providing advice to the secretariat. The secretariat is based in Dhaka and is mandated to serve as the administrative centre of the organisation. It ensures policies are implemented and identifies new areas for collaboration. PPD also has an international advisory committee consisting mainly of scientists who advise the board and secretariat of current trends in population, development and reproductive health.

PPD is a permanent observer at the United Nations.
Chair, HE Zhang Weqing (China)

SECRETARIAT OF THE PACIFIC COMMUNITY

BP D5, 98848 Nouméa Cedex, 95 Promenade Roger Laroque, New Caledonia **T** (+687) 262 000
E spc@spc.int **W** www.spc.int

The Secretariat of the Pacific Community (SPC) (formerly the South Pacific Commission) was established in 1947 by Australia, France, the Netherlands, New Zealand, the UK and the USA with the aim of promoting the economic and social stability of the islands in the region. The community now numbers 26 member states and territories: the four remaining founder states (the Netherlands and the UK have withdrawn) and the other 22 states and territories of Melanesia, Micronesia and Polynesia.

The SPC is a technical assistance agency with programmes in marine and land development and social resources. The governing body is the conference of the Pacific community.
Director-General, Dr Jimmie Rodgers (Solomon Islands)

SHANGHAI COOPERATION ORGANISATION

41 Liangmaqiao Road, Chaoyang District, 100600 Beijing, China **T** (+86) (10) 6532 9806
E sco@sectsco.org **W** www.sectsco.org

The Shanghai Cooperation Organisation (SCO) is a permanent inter-governmental organisation. It was established in 1996 as the Shanghai Five, when China, Kazakhstan, Kyrgyzstan, Russia and Tajikistan signed an agreement on cooperating to resolve disputes along the former Sino-Soviet border. It was renamed in 2001 when Uzbekistan became an official member.

The main principle of the SCO is strengthening cooperation among member states across a range of fields including politics, economics, culture, energy, transportation, environment protection and tourism. The organisation encourages regional peace, security and stability, and the pursuit of democracy.

The council of heads of member states meets annually and is the organisation's supreme body responsible for policy. The council of heads of governments of SCO member states also holds annual meetings to discuss cooperation strategies and approve budget. The SCO has two permanent bodies, a secretariat based in Beijing and a regional anti-terrorist structure in Tashkent. The secretary-general and the director of the executive committee are appointed by the council of heads of state for a period of three years.

Since 2005, Iran, Mongolia and Pakistan have applied for full membership and India has gained observer status. In the same year, the SCO announced it would prioritise joint energy projects, including developments in the oil and gas sectors, the exploration of new hydrocarbon reserves and joint use of water resources. The creation of an inter-bank SCO council was also agreed in order to fund future joint projects.
Secretary-General, Bolat Nurgaliev (Kazakhstan)

SOUTH ASIAN ASSOCIATION FOR REGIONAL COOPERATION

PO Box 4222, Tridevi Marg, Kathmandu, Nepal
T (+977) (1) 422 1785/6350 **E** saarc@saarc-sec.org
W www.saarc-sec.org

The South Asian Association for Regional Cooperation (SAARC) was established in 1985 by Bangladesh,

[Bh]utan, India, the Maldives, Nepal, Pakistan and Sri [La]nka. Its primary objective is the acceleration of [ec]onomic and social development in member states [th]rough collective action in agreed areas of cooperation. [Th]ese include agricultural and environmental [de]velopment, science and technology and transport and [co]mmunications.

A SAARC preferential trading arrangement, which is [de]signed to reduce tariffs on trade between SAARC [m]ember states, was signed in 1993 and entered into force [in] December 1995. A committee of experts was [es]tablished in 1998 to draft a comprehensive treaty to [cr]eate a South Asian free trade area. Agreement was [re]ached in January 2002 to work towards the [es]tablishment of a South Asian economic union.

The highest authority rests with the heads of state or [go]vernment of each member state. The council of [m]inisters, which meets twice a year, is made up of the [fo]reign ministers of the member states and is responsible [fo]r formulating policy. The standing committee is [co]mposed of the foreign secretaries of the member states [an]d monitors and coordinates SAARC programmes; it [m]eets twice a year. Technical committees are assigned to [in]dividual areas of SAARC's activities. Its secretariat [m]onitors, facilitates and promotes SAARC's activities and [se]rves as a channel of communication between the [as]sociation and other regional and intergovernmental [in]stitutions.

In 2005, as the only country in South Asia not to be a [m]ember of SAARC, Iran declared its wish to join. Other [p]otential future members include Afghanistan and China. [I]n August 2006, the USA, South Korea and the European [U]nion were granted observer status.

[S]ecretary-General, Chenkyab Dorji (Bhutan)

[S]OUTHERN AFRICAN DEVELOPMENT [C]OMMUNITY

[P]rivate Bag 0095, Gaborone, Botswana
[T] (+267) 395 1863 **E** registry@sadc.int **W** www.sadc.int

[T]he Southern African Development Community (SADC) [w]as formed in 1992 by the members of its predecessor, [th]e Southern African Development Coordination [C]onference. The latter was founded in 1980 to harmonise [e]conomic development among the countries in southern [A]frica and reduce their dependence on South Africa. The [S]ADC now comprises 14 countries, including South [A]frica, and works on a regional basis to increase economic [in]tegration and regional security.

It aims to evolve common political values, promote [d]evelopment and economic growth, regional security, [s]elf-sustaining development and the interdependence of [m]ember states, maximise production and strengthen and [c]onsolidate the historical, social and cultural links among [t]he peoples of the region.

The headquarters of the SADC is in Gaborone, Botswana, but member states each have a responsibility for an area of economic activity.

Executive Secretary, Tomaz Augusto Salomao (Mozambique)

UNITED NATIONS

UN Plaza, New York, NY 10017, USA
T (+1) (212) 963 1234 **W** www.un.org

The United Nations (UN) is an intergovernmental organisation of member states, dedicated through signature of the UN charter to the maintenance of international peace and security and the solution of economic, social and political problems through international cooperation.

The UN was founded as a successor to the League of Nations and inherited many of its procedures and institutions. The name United Nations was first used in the Washington Declaration 1942 to describe the 26 states that had allied to fight the Axis powers. The UN charter developed from discussions at the Moscow conference of the foreign ministers of China, the Soviet Union, the UK and the USA in 1943. Further progress was made at Dumbarton Oaks, Washington, in 1944 during talks involving the same states. The role of the security council was formulated at the Yalta conference in 1945. The charter was formally drawn up by 50 allied nations at the San Francisco conference between April and June 1945, when it was signed. Following ratification the UN came into effect on 24 October 1945, which is celebrated annually as United Nations Day. The UN flag is light blue with the UN emblem centred in white.

The principal organs of the UN are the general assembly, the security council, the economic and social council, the trusteeship council, the secretariat and the International Court of Justice. The economic and social council and the trusteeship council are auxiliaries, charged with assisting and advising the general assembly and security council. The official languages used are Arabic, Chinese, English, French, Russian and Spanish. Deliberations at the International Court of Justice are in English and French only.

In March 2006, former secretary-general Kofi Annan published a report that proposed specific reforms to the UN's structure and role. These included greater responsibilites for the deputy secretary-general and the complete reorganisation of all departments directly answerable to the secretariat.

MEMBERSHIP

Membership is open to all countries which accept the charter and its principle of peaceful co-existence. New members are admitted by the general assembly on the recommendation of the security council. The original membership of 51 states has grown to 192.

[A]fghanistan
[A]lbania
[A]lgeria
[A]ndorra
[A]ngola
[A]ntigua and Barbuda
[A]rgentina*
[A]rmenia
[A]ustralia*
[A]ustria
[A]zerbaijan
Bahamas
Bahrain
Bangladesh
Barbados
Belarus*
Belgium*
Belize
Benin
Bhutan
Bolivia*
Bosnia and Hercegovina
Botswana
Brazil*
Brunei
Bulgaria
Burkina Faso
Burundi
Cambodia
Cameroon
Canada*
Cape Verde
Central African Republic
Chad
Chile*
China*
Colombia*
Comoros
Congo, Republic of the
Costa Rica*
Côte d'Ivoire
Croatia
Cuba*
Cyprus

Czech Republic
Congo, Dem. Rep of the
Denmark*
Djibouti
Dominica
Dominican Republic*
East Timor
Ecuador*
Egypt*
El Salvador*
Equatorial Guinea
Eritrea
Estonia
Ethiopia*
Fiji
Finland
France*
Gabon
The Gambia
Georgia
Germany
Ghana
Greece*
Grenada
Guatemala*
Guinea
Guinea-Bissau
Guyana
Haiti*
Honduras*
Hungary
Iceland
India*
Indonesia
Iran*
Iraq*
Ireland
Israel
Italy
Jamaica
Japan
Jordan
Kazakhstan
Kenya
Kiribati
Korea, Dem. People's Rep. of
Korea, Rep. of
Kuwait
Kyrgyzstan
Laos
Latvia
Lebanon*
Lesotho
Liberia*
Libya
Liechtenstein
Lithuania
Luxembourg*
FYR Macedonia
Madagascar
Malawi
Malaysia
Maldives
Mali
Malta
Marshall Islands
Mauritania
Mauritius
Mexico*
Micronesia, Federated States of
Moldova
Monaco
Mongolia
Montenegro
Morocco
Mozambique
Myanmar
Namibia
Nauru
Nepal
The Netherlands*
New Zealand*
Nicaragua*
Niger
Nigeria
Norway*
Oman
Pakistan
Palau
Panama*
Papua New Guinea
Paraguay*
Peru*
The Philippines*
Poland*
Portugal
Qatar
Romania
Russian Federation*
Rwanda
St Kitts and Nevis
St Lucia
St Vincent and the Grenadines
Samoa
San Marino
São Tomé and Princípe
Saudi Arabia*
Senegal
Serbia
Seychelles
Sierra Leone
Singapore
Slovakia
Slovenia
Solomon Islands
Somalia
South Africa*
Spain
Sri Lanka
Sudan
Suriname
Swaziland
Sweden
Switzerland
Syria
Tajikistan
Tanzania
Thailand
Togo
Tonga
Trinidad and Tobago
Tunisia
Turkey*
Turkmenistan
Tuvalu
Uganda
Ukraine*
United Arab Emirates
United Kingdom*
United States of America*
Uruguay*
Uzbekistan
Vanuatu
Venezuela
Vietnam
Yemen
Zambia
Zimbabwe

*Original member (ie from 1945). Czechoslovakia, Yugoslavia and the USSR were all original members until their dissolution.

OBSERVERS
Permanent observer status is held by the Holy See. The Palestine Authority has special observer status.

THE GENERAL ASSEMBLY
UN Plaza, New York, NY 10017, USA
The general assembly is the main deliberative organ of the UN. It consists of all members, each entitled to five representatives but having only one vote. The annual session begins on the third Tuesday of September, when the president is elected, and usually continues until mid-December. Special sessions are held on specific issues and emergency special sessions can be called within 24 hours.

The assembly is empowered to discuss any matter within the scope of the charter, except when it is under consideration by the security council, and to make recommendations. Under the peace resolution, adopted in 1950, the assembly may also take action to maintain international peace and security when the security council fails to do so because of a lack of unanimity of its permanent members. Important decisions, such as those on peace and security, the election of officers, the budget, etc, need a two-thirds majority. Others need a simple majority. The assembly has effective power only over the internal operations of the UN itself; external recommendations are not legally binding.

The work of the general assembly is divided among six main committees, on each of which every member has the right to be represented: disarmament and international security; economic and financial; social, humanitarian and cultural; special political issues and decolonisation (including non-self governing territories); administrative and budgetary; and legal. In addition, the general assembly appoints *ad hoc* committees to consider special issues, such as human rights, peacekeeping and international law. All committees consider items referred to them by the assembly and recommend draft resolutions to its plenary meeting.

The assembly is assisted by a number of functional committees. The general committee coordinates its proceedings and operations, while the credentials committee verifies the representatives. There are also two standing committees, the advisory committee on administration and budgetary questions and the committee on contributions, which suggests the scale of members' payments to the UN.

President of the General Assembly, HE Haya Rashed al-Khalifa (Bahrain)

SPECIALISED BODIES
The assembly has created a large number of specialised bodies, some of which are supervised jointly with the economic and social council. They are supported by UN

nd voluntary contributions from governments, on-governmental organisations and individuals. These rganisations include:

CONFERENCE ON DISARMAMENT
alais des Nations, CH-1211 Geneva 10, Switzerland

The Conference on Disarmament (CD) was established in 979 as the single multilateral disarmament negotiating orum of the international community. Originally omprising 40 member states, the CD has expanded to 65 nembers. The non-proliferation of nuclear weapons treaty ntered into force on 5 March 1970 and has so far been atified by 188 states. A chemical weapons convention vas agreed in Paris in 1993 and came into force in April 997 after being ratified by 87 countries. It bans the use, production, stockpiling and transfer of all chemical veapons. All US and Russian weapons must be destroyed within 15 years of the convention entering into force and ll other states' weapons must be destroyed within ten years.

UNITED NATIONS CHILDREN'S FUND (UNICEF)
3 UN Plaza, New York, NY 10017, USA T (+1) 212 326 7000
W www.unicef.org

Established in 1947 to assist children and mothers in the immediate post-war period, UNICEF now concentrates on developing countries. It provides primary healthcare and health education. In particular, UNICEF conducts programmes in oral hydration, immunisation against eading diseases, child growth monitoring and the encouragement of breast-feeding. Its operations are often conducted in cooperation with the World Health Organisation.

UNITED NATIONS DEVELOPMENT PROGRAMME (UNDP)
1 UN Plaza, New York, NY 10017, USA T (+1) 212 906 5000
W www.undp.org

Established in 1966 from the merger of the UN expanded programme of technical assistance and the UN special fund, UNDP is the central funding agency for economic and social development projects around the world. Much of its annual expenditure is channelled through UN specialised agencies, governments and non-governmental organisations.

UNITED NATIONS HIGH COMMISSIONER FOR REFUGEES (UNHCR)
Case Postale 2500, CH-1211 Geneve 2 Depot, Switzerland
T (+41) 22 739 8111 W www.unhcr.org

Established in 1951 to protect the rights and interests of refugees, UNHCR organises emergency relief and longer-term solutions, such as voluntary repatriation, local integration or resettlement.

UNITED NATIONS RELIEF AND WORKS AGENCY FOR PALESTINE REFUGEES IN THE NEAR EAST (UNRWA)
HQ Gaza PO Box 140157, Amman 11814, Jordan
T (+972)8 677 7333 W www.unrwa.org

Established in 1949 to bring relief to the Palestinians displaced by the Arab-Israeli conflict. The UN general assembly has repeatedly voted every three years to extend the mandate of the UNRWA, most recently until June 2008.

UNITED NATIONS HUMAN RIGHTS COUNCIL (UNHRC)
The UNHRC is a 47-member council, established in 2006, replacing the United Nations Commission on Human Rights (UNCHR). The UNHRC has a mandate to secure respect for, and prevent violations of human rights by engaging in dialogue with governments and international organisations. It is also responsible for the coordination of all UN human rights activities and reports to, and is directly elected by, the general assembly.

THE SECURITY COUNCIL
UN Plaza, New York, NY 10017, USA
T (+41) (22) 917 9000
W www.ohchr.org/english/bodies/hrcouncil

The security council is the senior arm of the UN and has the primary responsibility for maintaining world peace and security. It consists of 15 members, each with one representative and one vote. There are five permanent members – China, France, Russia, the UK and the USA – and ten non-permanent members. Each of the non-permanent members is elected for a two-year term by a two-thirds majority of the general assembly and is ineligible for immediate re-election. Five of the elective seats are allocated to Africa and Asia, one to eastern Europe, two to Latin America and two to western Europe and remaining countries. Procedural questions are determined by a majority vote. Other matters require a majority inclusive of the votes of the permanent members; they thus have a right of veto. The abstention of a permanent member does not constitute a veto. The presidency rotates each month by state in (English) alphabetical order. Parties in a dispute, other non-members and individuals can be invited to participate in security council debates but are not permitted to vote.

The security council is empowered to settle or adjudicate in disputes or situations which threaten international peace and security. It can adopt political, economic and military measures to achieve this end. Any matter considered to be a threat to or breach of the peace or an act of aggression can be brought to the security council's attention by any member state or by the secretary-general. The charter envisaged members placing at the disposal of the security council armed forces and other facilities which would be coordinated by the military staff committee, composed of military representatives of the five permanent members. The security council is also supported by a committee of experts, to advise on procedural and technical matters, and a committee on admission of new members.

Owing to superpower disunity, the security council has rarely played the decisive role set out in the charter; the military staff committee was effectively suspended from 1948 until 1990, when a meeting was convened during the Gulf crisis on the formation and control of UN-supervised armed forces. In 1992, heads of government laid plans to transform the UN in light of the changed post-Cold War world. The secretary-general produced *An Agenda for Peace,* a report which centred on the establishment of a UN army composed of national contingents on permanent standby, as envisaged at the time of the UN's formation. However, enthusiasm for UN intervention waned during the rest of the decade after a problematic mission in Somalia during which 42 UN personnel were killed. The security council has since been criticised for its failure to intervene in subsequent conflicts, including the genocide in Rwanda and the ongoing situation in Darfur.

The security council also has the power to elect judges to the International Court of Justice and to recommend to the general assembly the election of a secretary-general.

PEACEKEEPING FORCES

The security council has established a number of peacekeeping forces since its foundation, comprising contingents provided mainly by neutral and non-aligned UN members. As at 2006, current operations were: the UN Truce Supervision Organisation, Israel, 1948; the UN Military Observer Group in India and Pakistan, 1949; the UN Peacekeeping Force in Cyprus, 1964; the UN Disengagement Observer Force, Golan Heights, Syria, 1974; the UN Interim Force in Lebanon, 1978; the UN Mission for the Referendum in Western Sahara, 1991; the UN Observer Mission in Georgia, 1993; the UN Interim Administration Mission in Kosovo, 1999; the UN Organisation Mission in the Democratic Republic of the Congo, 1999; the UN Mission in Ethiopia and Eritrea, 2000; the UN Operations in Cote d'Ivoire, 2004; the UN Stabilization Mission in Haiti, 2004; UN Integrated Office in Burundi, 2007; UN Mission in the Sudan, 2005; UN Office in Timor-Leste, 2005; UN Integrated Office in Sierra Leone, 2006.

TOP FIVE CONTRIBUTORS TO UN PEACEKEEPING MISSIONS (*as at* March 2007)

Country	*Number of Troops*
Pakistan	10,173
Bangladesh	9,675
India	9,471
Nepal	3,626
Jordan	3,564

Source: UN Department of Public Information

INTERNATIONAL CRIMINAL TRIBUNAL FOR THE FORMER YUGOSLAVIA

Churchill Plein 1, PO Box 13888, NL-2501 EW The Hague, The Netherlands

In February 1993, the security council voted to establish the International Criminal Tribunal for the Former Yugoslavia (ICTFY) a war crimes tribunal to hear cases covering grave breaches of the Geneva Conventions and crimes against humanity during the Balkans conflict of the 1990s. The court was inaugurated in November 1993 in The Hague with 11 judges elected by the UN general assembly from 11 states, divided into two trial chambers of three judges each and an appeal chamber of five judges. The court is unable to force suspects to stand trial but is empowered to pass verdicts in the absence of suspects and can put suspects under an 'act of accusation' which prevents them from leaving their own country. As well as running and managing a detention unit based at The Hague and a witness protection and assistance programme, the ICTFY also has powers to interview witnesses and seize evidence. The total budget for 2006–7 was US$276m (£138m) and 1135 staff representing 79 nations are currently employed by the tribunal.

President, Fausto Pocar (Italy)

INTERNATIONAL CRIMINAL TRIBUNAL FOR RWANDA

Following serious violations of humanitarian law in Rwanda, the UN security council created the International Criminal Tribunal for Rwanda on 8 November 1994. The purpose of this measure was to contribute to the process of national reconciliation in Rwanda and to the maintenance of peace in the region. The tribunal was established for the prosecution of persons responsible for genocide and other serious violations of international humanitarian law committed in the territory of Rwanda between 1 January 1994 and 31 December 1994. It may also deal with the prosecution of Rwandan citizens responsible for genocide and other such violations of international law committed in the territory of neighbouring states during the same period. The total budget for 2006–7 was US$270m and 1,042 staff representing 85 nations are currently employed by the tribunal.

President, Judge Erik Mose (Norway)

UNITED NATIONS MONITORING, VERIFICATION AND INSPECTION COMMISSION (UNMOVIC)

ALCOA Building, 866 United Nations Plaza, Room A-610, 48th St., New York, NY 10017, USA

T (+1) (212) 963 3022 E info@unmovic.org

W www.unmovic.org

The United Nations Monitoring, Verification and Inspection Commission (UNMOVIC), was created by UN Security Council Resolution 1284, adopted in December 1999.

UNMOVIC is mandated to verify Iraq's compliance with its obligation not to possess or acquire weapons of mass destruction (biological or chemical, together with ballistic missiles with a target distance of more than 150km), to destroy all research, development and production facilities and to desist from the future development or acquisition of such weapons. It also operates a monitoring and verification programme to ensure that prohibited items and programmes are not reactivated.

In January 2003, chief weapons inspector Dr Hans Blix stated that Iraq had failed to disarm, greatly strengthening the American and British case for war. US president George W. Bush presented the deadline of 17 March 2003 for Iraq to disarm and despite no UN support, began air strikes against Baghdad on 19 March. In a report covering March to May 2003, Blix stated that the commission had at no point during the inspections in Iraq found evidence of the continuation or resumption of programmes of weapons of mass destruction or significant quantity of proscribed items – whether pre-1991 or after. He stressed that this did not mean that such items could not exist as there remained long lists of unaccounted items.

In Resolution 1483 (May 2003) lifting Iraqi economic sanctions, the security council declared its intention to revisit the mandate of UNMOVIC, which remains ready to resume its work in Iraq.

Executive Chair (acting), Demetrius Perricos (Greece)

THE ECONOMIC AND SOCIAL COUNCIL

UN Plaza, New York, NY 10017, USA

The economic and social council is responsible under the general assembly for the economic and social work of the UN and for the coordination of the activities of the 14 specialised agencies and other UN bodies. It makes reports and recommendations on economic, social, cultural, educational, health and related matters, often in consultation with non-governmental organisations, passing the reports to the general assembly and other UN bodies. It also drafts conventions for submission to the assembly and calls conferences on matters within its remit.

The council consists of 54 members, 18 of whom are

ected annually by the general assembly for a three-year rm. Each has one vote and can be immediately -elected on retirement. A president is elected annually nd is also eligible for re-election. One substantive session held annually and decisions are reached by a simple ajority vote of those present.

The council has established a number of standing ommittees on particular issues and several commissions. ommissions include statistical, human rights, social evelopment, sustainable development, status of women, rime prevention and criminal justice, narcotic drugs, cience and technology for development and population; nd regional economic commissions for Europe, Asia and ne Pacific, Western Asia, Latin America and Africa.

resident, Dalius Gekuolis (Lithuania)

HE SECRETARIAT

N Plaza, New York, NY 10017, USA

he secretariat services the other UN organs and is eaded by a secretary-general elected by a majority vote f the general assembly on the recommendation of the ecurity council. He is assisted by an international staff, hosen to represent the international character of the rganisation. The secretary-general is charged with ringing to the attention of the security council any natter which he considers poses a threat to international eace and security. He may also bring other matters to the ttention of the general assembly and other UN bodies nd may be entrusted by them with additional duties. As hief administrator to the UN, the secretary-general is resent in person or via representatives at all meetings of he other five main organs of the UN. He may also act as n impartial mediator in disputes between member states.

The power and influence of the secretary-general has een determined largely by the character of the ffice-holder and by the state of relations between the uperpowers. The thaw in these relations since the nid-1980s has increased the effectiveness of the UN, articularly in its attempts to intervene in international isputes. It helped to end the Iran-Iraq War and ponsored peace in Central America. Following Iraq's nvasion of Kuwait in 1990, the UN took its first ollective security action since the Korean War. Conflicts n Cyprus, East Timor, Libya, Nigeria and Western Sahara nave been successfully prevented from escalating or preading during Kofi Annan's time in office. In addition o maintenance of international security, ending poverty nd inequality, improving education, reducing HIV/AIDS nd safeguarding the environment were some of the issues utlined in the UN Millennium Report.

Secretary-General, Ban Ki-moon, *apptd* 2007 (South Korea)

Deputy Secretary-General, Asha-Rose Migiro (Tanzania)

FORMER SECRETARIES-GENERAL	
1946–53	Trygve Lie (Norway)
1953–61	Dag Hammarskjöld (Sweden)
1961–71	U Thant (Burma)
1971–81	Kurt Waldheim (Austria)
1981–91	Javier Pérez de Cuéllar (Peru)
1991–96	Boutros Boutros-Ghali (Egypt)
1997–2006	Kofi Annan (Ghana)

JK MISSION TO THE UN

Dag Hammarskjöld Plaza, 885 Second Avenue, New York, NY 0017, USA

T (+1) (212) 745 9200 **E** uk@un.int **W** www.ukun.org

Permanent Representative to the United Nations and Representative on the Security Council, Sir Emyr Jones Parry, *apptd* 2007

UK MISSION TO THE OFFICE OF THE UN AND OTHER INTERNATIONAL ORGANISATIONS IN GENEVA

37–39 rue de Vermont, CH-1211 Geneva 20, Switzerland

T (+41) (22) 918 2300 **E** mission.uk@ties.itu.int

Permanent UK Representative, Nicholas Thorne, CMG, *apptd* 2003

UK MISSION TO THE UN IN VIENNA

Jaurčsgasse 12, A-1030 Vienna, Austria

Permanent UK Representative, John Macgregor, *apptd* 2007

REGIONAL UN INFORMATION CENTRE

Block C, Level 5, Residence Palace, 155 rue de la Loi, Wetstraat 155, Brussels 1040, Belgium

T (+32) 2287 4019 **E** info@unric.org **W** www.unric.org

THE INTERNATIONAL COURT OF JUSTICE

The Peace Palace, NL-2517 KJ, The Hague, The Netherlands

The International Court of Justice is the principal judicial organ of the UN. The statute of the court is an integral part of the UN charter and all members of the UN are *ipso facto* parties to it. The court is composed of 15 judges, elected by both the general assembly and the security council for nine-year terms which are renewable. Judges may deliberate over cases in which their country is involved. If no judge on the bench is from a country which is a party to a dispute under consideration, that party may designate a judge to participate *ad hoc* in that particular deliberation. If any party to a case fails to adhere to the judgment of the court, the other party may have recourse to the security council.

President, Rosalyn Higgins (UK)

Vice-President, Awn Shawkat al-Khasawneh (Jordan)

Judges, Shi Jiuyong (China); Ronny Abraham (France); Bruno Simma (Germany); Hisashi Owada (Japan); Raymond Ranjeva (Madagascar); Bernado Sepulveda Amor (Mexico); Mohamed Bennouna (Morocco); Kenneth Keith (New Zealand); Leonid Skotnikov (Russian Federation); Abdul G. Koroma (Sierra Leone); Peter Tomka (Slovakia); Thomas Buergenthal (USA); Gonzalo Parra-Aranguren (Venezuela)

UNITED NATIONS EDUCATIONAL, SCIENTIFIC AND CULTURAL ORGANISATION

7 place de Fontenoy, F-75352 Paris, France

T (+33) (01) 4568 1000 **E** bpi@unesco.org **W** www.unesco.org

The United Nations Educational, Scientific and Cultural Organisation (UNESCO) was established in 1946. It promotes collaboration among its member states in education, science, culture and communication. It aims to further a universal respect for human rights, justice and the rule of law, without distinction of race, sex, language or religion, in accordance with the UN charter.

UNESCO runs a number of programmes to improve education and extend access to it. It provides assistance to ensure the free flow of information and its wider dissemination without any obstacle to freedom of expression, and to maintain cultural heritage in the face of development. It fosters research and study in social and environmental sciences. The UNESCO world heritage list includes more than 800 cultural and natural sites.

UNESCO has 192 member states and six associate

members. The general conference, consisting of representatives of all the members, meets biennially to decide the programme and the budget. It elects the 58-member executive board, which supervises operations, and appoints a director-general who heads a secretariat responsible for carrying out the organisation's programmes. In most member states national commissions liaise with UNESCO to execute its policies.
Director-General, Koichiro Matsuura (Japan)

UNITED NATIONS INDUSTRIAL DEVELOPMENT ORGANISATION

Vienna International Centre, Wagramerstrasse 5, PO Box 300, A-1400 Vienna, Austria
T (+43) (1) 260 260 E unido@unido.org W www.unido.org

The United Nations Industrial Development Organisation (UNIDO) was established in 1966 by the UN general assembly to act as the central coordinating body for industrial activities within the UN. It became a UN specialised agency in 1985. UNIDO aims to help developing countries and those with transitional economies to develop sustainable industrialisation by concentrating on economic competitiveness, environmental awareness and employment issues.

UNIDO has 172 members. It is funded by regular and operational budgets, together with contributions for technical cooperation activities. The regular budget is derived from member states' contributions. Technical cooperation is funded mainly through voluntary contributions from donor countries and institutions and by intergovernmental and non-governmental organisations. A general conference of all the members meets biennially to discuss strategy and policy, approve the budget – €150.8m (£102m) in 2006–7 – and elect the director-general. The industrial development board is composed of representatives from 53 member states and reviews the work programme and the budget, which is prepared by the programme and budget committee of 27 member states.
Director-General, Kandeh K. Yumkella (Sierra Leone)

UNIVERSAL POSTAL UNION

Weltpoststrasse 4, CH-3000 Bern 15, Switzerland
T (+41) (31) 350 3111 E info@upu.int W www.upu.int

The Universal Postal Union (UPU) was established by the treaty of Bern 1874, taking effect from 1875, and became a UN specialised agency in 1948. The UPU exists to form and regulate a single postal territory of all member countries for the reciprocal exchange of correspondence without discrimination. With a total of 191 members, it also assists and advises on the improvement of postal services.

The universal postal congress is the UPU's supreme authority and meets every four years. The council of administration meets annually to ensure continuity between congresses, to investigate regulatory developments and broad policy issues, to approve the budget and to examine proposed treaty changes. The consultative committee, set up in 2004 and consisting of customers, suppliers and printers, represents the interests of the wider international postal sector and provides a forum for dialogue between postal industry stakeholders. The three UPU bodies are served by the international bureau, a secretariat headed by a director-general.

Funding is provided by members according to a scale of contributions drawn up by the congress. The council of administration sets the budget which amounts to approximately SFr35m (£14.5m) per year.
Director-General, Edouard Dayan (France)

UNREPRESENTED NATIONS AND PEOPLES ORGANISATION

Paviljoensgracht 76, 2512 BR, The Hague, The Netherlands
T (+31) (70) 364 6504 E unpo@unpo.org W www.unpo.org

The Unrepresented Nations and Peoples Organisation (UNPO) was founded in 1991 to offer an international forum for occupied nations, indigenous peoples and national minorities who are not represented in other international organisations.

The UNPO does not aim to represent these nations and peoples, but rather to assist and empower them to represent themselves more effectively, and provide professional services and facilities as well as education and training in the fields of diplomacy, international and human rights law, democratic processes, institution building, conflict management and resolution, and environmental protection.

Participation is open to all nations and peoples who are inadequately represented at the UN and who declare allegiance to five principles relating to the right of self-determination of all peoples: human rights, democracy, non-violence and the rejection of terrorism, and protection of the natural environment. Applicants must show that they constitute a nation or people and that the organisation applying for membership is representative of that nation or people.

As at February 2007, there were 69 full members.
Director-General, Marino Busdachin (Italy)

WESTERN EUROPEAN UNION

15 rue de l'Association, 1000 Brussels, Belgium
T (+32) (2) 500 4412 E secretariatgeneral@weu.int
W www.weu.int

Western European Union (WEU) is a defence and security organisation. It began as the Brussels Treaty Organisation (BTO) and was formed in 1948 by Belgium, France, Luxembourg, the Netherlands and the UK. The BTO was designed to provide collective self-defence and economic and social collaboration amongst its signatories. It was modified to become the WEU in 1954 with the admission of West Germany and Italy.

In 1991, the EU Maastricht Treaty committed the European Community to the establishment of a common foreign and security policy. The WEU was designated as the future defence component of the European Union and member states of the EU who were not already members of the WEU were invited to join or become observers. In 1992, the WEU's role as the common security dimension of the EU was enhanced when WEU ministers signed a declaration with remaining European NATO members to give them various forms of WEU membership.

A council of ministers (foreign and defence) meets biannually in the presiding country and from 1999 the sequence of WEU presidencies has been harmonised with those of the EU. A council of the member states' permanent representatives meets in Brussels. It is chaired by the secretary-general and serviced by the secretariat.

In 1999, NATO and the EU decided to establish a direct relationship; the EU committed itself to ensuring that it was able to take decisions on conflict prevention and crisis management and NATO agreed to give the EU ccess to its collective assets and capabilities for perations in which NATO as a whole was not engaged. 'he WEU's crisis management functions were transferred o the EU in 2001.

The WEU currently has ten member states, six associate nembers, five observers and a further seven countries are ssociate partners.

'residency, Germany, Portugal (2007)
ecretary-General, Javier Solana Madariaga (Spain)

VORLD BANK GROUP

818 H Street NW, Washington DC 20433, USA
(+1) (202) 473 1000 **E** feedback@worldbank.org
V www.worldbank.org

The World Bank Group was founded in 1944 and is one of the world's largest sources of development assistance. It has 185 members. Originally directed towards post-war econstruction in Europe, the bank subsequently turned owards assisting less-developed countries and is currently vorking in more than 100. It works with government gencies, non-governmental organisations and the private ector to formulate assistance strategies. Its local offices mplement the bank's programme in each country.

The World Bank is owned by the governments of nember countries and its capital is subscribed by its nembers. It finances its lending primarily from borrowing n world capital markets, and derives a substantial contribution to its resources from its retained earnings and he repayment of loans. The interest rate on its loans is calculated in relation to its cost of borrowing. Loans generally have a grace period of five years and are epayable within 20 years.

The World Bank Group consists of five institutions. The International Bank for Reconstruction and Development (IBRD) has 185 members and provides oans and development assistance to middle-income countries and creditworthy poorer countries (total loans for 2006 US$14.1bn (£7bn)). The International Finance Corporation (IFC) has 179 members and promotes private sector investment in developing member countries by nobilising domestic and foreign capital. The International Development Association (IDA) has 165 members and performs the same function as the World Bank but primarily to less-developed countries and on terms that bear less heavily on their balance of payments than IBRD loans (total loans for 2006 US$9.5bn (£4.7bn)). The Multilateral Investment Guarantee Agency (MIGA) has 170 members and promotes foreign direct investment in developing states by providing guarantees to potential investors and advisory services to developing member countries. The International Centre for Settlement of Investment Disputes has 155 members (known as contracting states) and provides facilities for the settlement of investment disputes between foreign investors and their host countries.

The IBRD and its affiliates are financially and legally distinct but share headquarters. The IBRD is headed by a board of governors, consisting of one governor and one alternate governor appointed by each member country. Twenty-four executive directors exercise all powers of the World Bank except those reserved to the board of governors. The president, elected by the executive directors, conducts the business of the bank, assisted by an international staff. Membership in both the IFC and the IDA is open to all IBRD countries. The IDA is administered by the same staff as the bank; the IFC has its own personnel but draws on the IBRD for administrative and other support. All share the same president.

President, Robert Zoellick (USA)

WORLD CUSTOMS ORGANISATION

rue de Marche 30, B-1210, Brussels, Belgium
T (+32) 2209 9211 **E** information@wcoomd.org
W www.wcoomd.org

The World Customs Organisation (WCO) is an independent body that works to enhance the effectiveness and efficiency of customs administrations worldwide. By developing a harmonised commodity description and coding system, the WCO introduced a universal goods classification and revenue collection method. The WCO also administers the WTO valuation agreement.

With 171 member governments that process more than 98 per cent of international trade, the WCO is organised into a forum where each member has one representative and one vote. The WCO is directed by the council and a policy commission. Locally recruited staff are used to provide secretarial, translation, interpretation and general support services.

Council Chair, Tampani Erling (France)

WORLD HEALTH ORGANISATION

Avenue Appia 20, 1211 Geneva 27, Switzerland
T (+41) (22) 791 2111 **E** info@who.int **W** www.who.int

The UN International Health Conference, held in 1946, established the World Health Organisation (WHO) as a UN specialised agency, with effect from 1948. It is dedicated to attaining the highest possible level of health for all. It collaborates with member governments, UN agencies and other bodies to improve health standards, control communicable diseases and promote all aspects of family and environmental health. It seeks to raise the standards of health teaching and training, and promotes research through collaborating with research centres worldwide.

WHO has 193 members and is governed by the annual assembly of members which sets policy, approves the budget, appoints a director-general, and adopts health conventions and regulations. It also elects 32 members who designate one expert to serve on the executive board. The board effects the programme, suggests initiatives and is empowered to deal with emergencies. A secretariat, headed by the director-general, supervises the activities of six regional offices.

Director-General, Dr Margaret Chan (China)

WORLD INTELLECTUAL PROPERTY ORGANISATION

PO Box 18, CH-1211, Geneva 20, Switzerland
T (+41) (22) 338 9111 **E** information.centre@wipo.int
W www.wipo.int

The World Intellectual Property Organisation (WIPO) was established in 1967 by the Stockholm Convention, which entered into force in 1970. WIPO administers 24 treaties that deal with different legal and administrative aspects of intellectual property, notably the Paris Convention for the protection of industrial property and the Bern Convention for the protection of literary and artistic works. WIPO became a UN specialised agency in 1974.

Intellectual property falls into two main branches: industrial property (inventions, trademarks, industrial designs and geographical indications) and copyright (literary, musical, photographic, audiovisual and artistic works, etc). WIPO assists creative intellectual activity and facilitates technology transfer, particularly to developing countries.

WIPO's mission is to promote the protection of intellectual property rights worldwide. The organisation's activities fall into three broad categories, namely, the progressive development of interational intellectual property law, assistance to developing countries and services which facilitate the process of obtaining intellectual property rights in multiple countries.

WIPO had 184 members as at April 2007. The biennial session of all its governing bodies sets policy, a programme and a budget. A separate agency, the International Union for the Protection of New Varieties of Plants, established by convention in 1961, is linked to WIPO and has 63 members.

Director-General, Dr Kamil Idris (Sudan)

WORLD METEOROLOGICAL ORGANISATION

7 bis, avenue de la Paix, PO Box 2300, CH-1211 Geneva 2, Switzerland **T** (+41) (22) 730 8111
E wmo@wmo.int **W** www.wmo.int

The World Meteorological Organisation (WMO) was established in 1950 and became a UN specialised agency in 1951, succeeding the International Meteorological Organisation founded in 1873. It facilitates cooperation in the establishment of networks for making, processing and exchanging meteorological, climatological, hydrological and geophysical observations. It also fosters collaboration between meteorological and hydrological services, and furthers the application of meteorology to aviation, shipping, environment, water problems, agriculture and the mitigation of natural disasters.

In March 2007, the WMO had 182 member states and six member territories. Six regional associations are responsible for the coordination of activities within their own regions. There are also eight technical commissions, which study meteorological and hydrological problems, establish methodology and procedures, and make recommendations to the executive council and the congress. The supreme authority is the world meteorological congress, which meets every four years to determine general policy and set the budget (SFr253.8m (£105m) for 2004–7). It also elects 31 members of the 37-member executive council which supervises the implementation of congress decisions, initiates studies and makes recommendations on matters needing international action. The secretariat is headed by a secretary-general, appointed by the congress.

Secretary-General, Michel Jarraud (France)

WORLD TOURISM ORGANISATION

Capitán Haya 42, 28020 Madrid, Spain
T (+34) 9156 78100 **E** omt@unwto.org **W** www.unwto.org

Originally formed in 1925 as the International Congress of Official Tour Associations, the World Tourism Organisation (UNWTO) was officially launched in 1975 to act as an executing agency of the United Nations Development Programme. Primarily concerned with developing public and private sector partnerships, the UNWTO also promotes the global code of ethics for tourism, a framework of policy aimed at tour operators, governments, labour organisations and travellers. There are 150 member states and seven associate member states.

The general assembly is the principal gathering of the UNWTO and meets every two years in order to approve policy and budget. Every four years, the assembly elects a secretary-general. The executive council is UNWTO's governing board and meets twice a year to ensure the organisation adheres to policy and budget. It is composed of 27 members of the general assembly. As host country of UNWTO's headquarters, Spain has a permanent seat on the executive council.

Secretary-General, Francesco Frangialli (France)

WORLD TRADE ORGANISATION

Centre William Rappard, 154 rue de Lausanne, CH-1211 Geneva 21, Switzerland **T** (+41) (22) 739 5111
E enquiries@wto.org **W** www.wto.org

The World Trade Organisation was established on January 1995 as the successor to the General Agreement on Tariffs and Trade (GATT).

GATT was dedicated to the expansion of non-discriminatory international trade and progressively extended free trade via 'rounds' of multilateral negotiations. The final act of the Uruguay round was signed by trade ministers from the 128 GATT negotiating states and the EU in Marrakesh, Morocco, in April 1994. The implementation of the Uruguay round measures in 2002 resulted in a reduction on duties on manufactured goods from 40 per cent in the 1940s to per cent. New talks on agriculture and services began in 2000 and were incorporated into a broader agenda launched at the 2001 ministerial conference in Doha, Qatar.

The WTO is the legal and institutional foundation of the multilateral trading system. It provides the contractual obligations determining how governments frame and implement trade policy and provides the forum for the debate, negotiation and adjudication of trade problems. The WTO's principal aims are to liberalise world trade and place it on a secure basis, and it seeks to achieve this through a combination of an agreed set of trade rules and market access agreements and further trade liberalisation negotiations. The WTO also administers and implements multilateral agreements in fields such as agriculture, textiles and clothing, services, government procurement, rules of origin and intellectual property.

The highest authority of the WTO is the ministerial conference composed of all members, which meets at least once every two years. The general council meets as required and acts on behalf of the ministerial conference in regard to the regular working of the WTO. The general council also convenes in two particular forms: as the dispute settlement body, dealing with disagreements between members arising from the Uruguay round final act; and as the trade policy review body, conducting regular reviews of the trade policies of members. A secretariat of 635 staff headed by a director-general services WTO bodies and provides trade performance and trade policy analysis.

As at February 2007, there were 150 WTO members and 31 observers. The WTO budget for 2006 was SFr181m (£75m), with members' contributions calculated on the basis of their share of the total trade conducted by WTO members. The official languages of the WTO are English, French and Spanish.

Director-General, Pascal Lamy (France)

COUNTRIES OF THE WORLD A–Z

DEFINITIONS AND ABBREVIATIONS

est = estimate
(m) = male; (f) = female
BIRTH RATE – figures are per 1,000 population. The birth rate is usually the dominant factor in determining the rate of population growth. It depends on both the level of fertility and the age structure of the population
CAPITAL/MAJOR CITIES – figures represent the size of a city, excluding surrounding suburban areas; major cities are listed in order of population size. For the following countries, figures given under capital include surrounding suburban areas: Armenia, Canada, Cyprus, Finland, Indonesia, Nepal, the Netherlands, Norway, Oman, South Korea and Thailand
CPI SCORE – the perception of the degree of corruption as seen by business people and country analysts; ranging between 10 (highly clean) and 0 (highly corrupt)
DEATH PENALTY:
No – abolished for all crimes (year in which death penalty was abolished in parentheses)
No* – 'abolitionist in practice', ie countries that retain the death penalty but have not executed anybody in the last ten years
Yes* – abolished but retained for exceptional circumstances (ie crimes committed under military law)
Yes – used as a legal form of punishment
GROSS ENROLMENT RATIO – the ratio of total enrolment, regardless of age, to the total population of the relevant age group expressed as a percentage
HEALTH EXPENDITURE – where a period of years is given (eg 2000–5), data is for the most recent year available
HIV/AIDS ADULT PREVALENCE – estimate of the percentage of the total adult population (aged 15–49) living with HIV/AIDS
INFANT MORTALITY RATE – averages for male and female infants under one year old and per 1,000 live births
LIFE EXPECTANCY – averages for men and women aged between 15 and 49 years
MORTALITY RATE – figures are per 1,000 population. This indicator is significantly affected by age distribution, and most countries will eventually show a rise in the overall death rate, in spite of continued decline in mortality at all ages, as declining fertility results in an ageing population
PARAMILITARIES – not included in the total military personnel figure for each country
POPULATION BELOW POVERTY LINE – although strict definitions of poverty vary considerably between nations, this figure represents the percentage of the adult population whose income is under US$1 per day
TOTAL EXTERNAL DEBT – the total public and private debt owed to nonresidents repayable in foreign currency, goods, or services

AFGHANISTAN

Jomhuri-ye Eslami-ye Afghanestan – Islamic Republic of Afghanistan

AREA – 647,500 sq. km. Neighbours: Iran (west), Pakistan (east and south), Tajikistan, Uzbekistan and Turkmenistan (north), China (north-east)
CAPITAL – Kabul; population, 2,536,300 (2006 est)
MAJOR CITIES – Herat; Kandahar; Mazar-e-Sharif; Jalalabad
CURRENCY – Afghani (Af) of 100 puls
POPULATION – 31,056,997 rising at 2.67 per cent per year (2006 est); Pashtun (42 per cent), Tajik (27 per cent), Hazara (9 per cent), Uzbek (9 per cent), Aimak (4 per cent), Turkmen (3 per cent), Baloch (2 per cent) (est)
RELIGION – Islam (99 per cent) (est)
LANGUAGE – Dari, Pashto (both official), Uzbek, Turkmen
URBAN POPULATION – 24.3 per cent (2005 est)
MEDIAN AGE (years) – 17.6 (2006 est)
NATIONAL ANTHEM – 'Soroud-e-Melli' ['National Anthem']
NATIONAL DAY – 19 August (Independence Day)
LIFE EXPECTANCY (years) – 43.34 (2006 est)
MORTALITY RATE – 20.34 (2006 est)
BIRTH RATE – 46.6 (2006 est)
INFANT MORTALITY RATE – 160.23 (2006 est)
DEATH PENALTY – Yes
POPULATION BELOW POVERTY LINE – 53 per cent (2003)

CLIMATE AND TERRAIN

Mountains, chief among which are the Hindu Kush, cover three-quarters of the landlocked country, with plains in the north and south-west. Elevation extremes range from 7,485m at the highest point (Nowshak, in the Hindu Kush) to 258m at the lowest (Amu Dar'ya). There are three great river basins, the Amu Dar'ya (Oxus), Helmand, and Kabul. Natural hazards are flooding, drought and earthquakes. The climate is arid to semi-arid, with extreme temperatures. Summers are hot and dry and the winters cold with heavy snowfalls, particularly in the northern mountains. Annual rainfall varies between 101mm and 406mm per year. The temperatures in Kabul average −8 to 2°C in January and 16 to 33°C in July.

HISTORY AND POLITICS

Afghanistan first became a nation in 1747 under Ahmad Shah Durrani. Britain and Russia vied for influence over the country in the 19th and early 20th centuries, but it remained independent. The monarchy was overthrown in 1973 and a republic was formed. After a coup in 1978, a communist government took power, and Muslim guerrilla (mujahidin) resistance began. The government was overthrown in a further coup in 1979 that prompted an invasion by the Soviet Union, which installed a pro-Soviet government. The mujahidin, with US backing, fought against Soviet forces, which withdrew in 1989, and against Afghan government forces until the government collapsed in 1992. Mujahidin forces overran Kabul and declared an Islamic state. However, factionalism led to continued fighting until the rise from 1994 of the Taliban (armed Islamic students), which extended its power across more than 90 per cent of the country by 1998 and imposed strict Shariah law.

The Taliban allowed al-Qaida to base terrorist training camps in Afghanistan, and its refusal to hand over al-Qaida's leaders after the 11 September 2001 terrorist attacks on the USA led to the regime's overthrow in 2001 by a US-led international coalition and the Northern Alliance, a grouping of the four main mujahidin factions. A multi-ethnic interim government under Hamid Karzai was installed in December 2001 and, following a *Loya Jirga* (tribal council) in June 2002, a transitional government was installed until presidential and parliamentary elections were held in 2004 and 2005.

The government's control of areas outside Kabul is tenuous and dependent on the presence of foreign troops. The vacuum has been filled by ad hoc networks of drug traffickers, other criminals and, in some provinces, the Taliban. In the south and east in particular, Taliban-inspired violence against government forces and foreign troops has risen since 2005. Drug-eradication programmes and attempts to suppress trafficking elicit further violent opposition.

In 2004 Hamid Karzai was elected president for a five-year term with 55.4 per cent of the vote. Elections to the lower house of the legislature and to the provincial seats in the upper house were held in September 2005 and the new legislature was inaugurated in December. A new government was announced in March 2006.

POLITICAL SYSTEM

Under the constitution approved by a *Loya Jirga* in 2004, the executive president, who is directly elected for a five-year term, appoints the government, subject to the approval of the lower house of the legislature. The bicameral legislature, the *Jirga*, comprises a lower house, the *Wolesi Jirga* (House of the People), and the *Meshrano Jirga* (House of Elders). The *Wolesi Jirga* has 249 members directly elected for a five-year term; ten seats are reserved for the Kuchi ethnic group and at least 65 seats for women. The *Meshrano Jirga* has 102 members: 34 indirectly elected from provincial councils for a three-year term; 34 indirectly elected from district councils for a four-year term; and 34 appointed by the president for a five-year term. There are, at present, no formal political parties.

HEAD OF STATE

President, Hamid Karzai, *elected* 9 October 2004, *sworn in* 7 December 2004

Vice-Presidents, Ahmad Zia Massood; Karim Khalili

SELECTED GOVERNMENT MEMBERS *as at May 2007*

Defence, Gen. Abdul Raheem Wardak

Foreign Affairs, Rangeen Dadfar Spanta

Finance, Anwar-ul Haq Ahadi

Interior, Ahmad Moqbel Zarar

EMBASSY OF THE ISLAMIC REPUBLIC OF AFGHANISTAN

31 Prince's Gate, London SW7 1QQ

T 020-7589 8891 W www.afghanembassy.co.uk

Ambassador Extraordinary and Plenipotentiary, vacant

BRITISH EMBASSY

15th Street, Roundabout Wazir Akbar Khan

PO Box 334, Kabul

T (+93) (70) 102 000 E britishembassy.kabul@fco.gov.uk

W www.britishembassy.gov.uk/afghanistan

Ambassador Extraordinary and Plenipotentiary, HE Sir Sherard Cowper-Coles, KCMG, LVO, *apptd* 2007

BRITISH COUNCIL

House 15–17, Kart-e-Parwan, Kabul T (+93) (70) 000 0101

W www.britishcouncil.org/afghanistan

Director, Malcolm Jardine

ECONOMY AND TRADE

The economy has been devastated by the political upheavals of the last 30 years. Reconstruction is hampered by the lack of infrastructure and resources, the challenge to the government's authority from regional power bases and drug traffickers, and the continuing violence by militants. The return of many of the 4–6 million refugees who sheltered in Pakistan and Iran during the decades of unrest places a further burden on resources. Since 2001 reconstruction efforts have been supported by international aid, with over US$24bn (£12bn) pledged by over 60 countries and international financial institutions. The eradication of the illegal opium trade and the search for oil and gas resources in the northern region are two major long-term objectives.

FUNDING AFGHANISTAN'S RECONSTRUCTION

US$640m for health services
US$660m for mine clearance
US$1,100m for education
US$1,000m for the electricity industry
US$380m for the drug control programme

Source: UNDP; based on ten-year projected costs

Most of the labour force is engaged in agriculture, which saw a huge expansion in opium production, banned under the Taliban, from 185 tonnes in 2001 to 4,475 tonnes in 2005. Production has continued to increase and may account for 60 per cent of total national output. Less lucrative agricultural products are wheat, fruit, nuts, wool, meat, sheepskins and lambskins. There is a range of natural resources; at present, natural gas, coal and copper are exploited. Other industries include the manufacture of silk, woollen hair cloths and carpets, soap, shoes and fertilisers. These agricultural and manufactured products are the main exports. Imports are chiefly capital goods, food, textiles and petroleum products.

GNI – US$19,000m (2002); US$700 per capita (2002)
ANNUAL AVERAGE GROWTH OF GDP – 14 per cent (2005 est)
INFLATION RATE – 16.3 per cent (2005 est)
UNEMPLOYMENT – 40 per cent (2005 est)
IMPORTS – US$1,300m (2001)
EXPORTS – US$1,200m (2001)

Trade with UK	*2005*	*2006*
Imports from UK	£14,454,000	£22,428,000
Exports to UK	£734,000	£10,605,000

COMMUNICATIONS

There are two international airports, at Kabul and Kandahar, and a further four major and 16 smaller regional airports servicing internal flights. The Amu Dar'ya river makes up most of the 1,200km of inland waterways and carries barge traffic; the main river ports are Kheyrabad and Shir Khan. There is no railway system, although there are railheads on the Pakistan border and a railway is under construction from Mashhad, in Iran, to Herat. Much of the road system is in total disrepair, although most of the main highways from Kabul to Kandahar and Herat have been reconstructed. The fixed-line telephone network is very limited in extent, and connections are exceeded by mobile phone distribution, as the major cities now have coverage.

EDUCATION AND HEALTH

Education is free and nominally compulsory, elementary schools having been established in most centres. In March 2002, schools reopened to 1.5 million children, many of whom had not received schooling for six years under the Taliban.

GROSS ENROLMENT RATIO (percentage of relevant age group) – primary 87 per cent; secondary 16 per cent; tertiary 1 per cent (2005 est)
HEALTH EXPENDITURE (per capita) – US$14 (2004)
HOSPITAL BEDS (per 1,000 people) – 0.4 (2000–5)

MEDIA AND CULTURE

Afghanistan's media was seriously restricted under the Taliban, which banned television broadcasting. However, in late 2001 Radio Afghanistan returned to the air in Kabul after the Taliban deserted the capital, and within days Kabul TV also began broadcasting. Relays of foreign radio stations are available in Kabul, including the BBC, Radio France Internationale, Deutsche Welle, US-funded broadcasts from Radio Free Afghanistan and the Voice of America, and Radio Azadi run by the International Security Assistance Force. Local radio stations include Radio Afghanistan, Erat Radio Khilid Kabul and Arman FM. Television services are mainly provided by the state-run TV Afghanistan, but ownership of television sets is very limited. Afghanistan's press now enjoys considerable freedom of expression, although print runs are small. Titles include *Hewad, Anis* and the Northern Alliance organ *Payam-e Mojahed.*

Due to prolonged conflict, much of the cultural heritage has been destroyed. During the civil war the Kabul Museum was looted, and treasures such as the Kunduz Hoard (silver Greek-style coins) were stolen. This was followed during the Taliban regime by systematic ideological destruction. Most notably the giant Bamiyan Buddhas, carved by Buddhist monks in the fourth to sixth centuries, were demolished in March 2001.

ALBANIA

Republika e Shqiperise – Republic of Albania

AREA – 28,748 sq. km. Neighbours: Serbia, Montenegro (north), Kosovo, Macedonia (east), Greece (south)
CAPITAL – Tirana; population, 353,400 (2003)
MAJOR TOWNS – Durres; Elbasan; Shkoder
CURRENCY – Lek (Lk) of 100 qindarka
POPULATION – 3,581,655 rising at 0.52 per cent per year (2006 est); Albanian (95 per cent), Greek (3 per cent) (est)
RELIGION – Islam (65 per cent), Roman Catholicism (10 per cent), other Christian denominations (25 per cent) (est)
LANGUAGE – Albanian (official), Greek, Vlach, Romani, Slavic dialects
POPULATION DENSITY – 114 per sq. km (2005)
URBAN POPULATION – 45 per cent (2005 est)
MEDIAN AGE (years) – 28.9 (2006 est)
NATIONAL ANTHEM – 'Hymni i Flamurit' ['Hymn to the Flag']
NATIONAL DAY – 28 November (Independence Day)
LIFE EXPECTANCY (years) – 77.43 (2006 est)
MORTALITY RATE – 5.22 (2006 est)
BIRTH RATE – 15.11 (2006 est)
INFANT MORTALITY RATE – 20.75 (2006 est)
DEATH PENALTY – Yes*
CPI SCORE – 2.6 (2006)
POPULATION BELOW POVERTY LINE – 25 per cent (2004 est)

CLIMATE AND TERRAIN

Much of the country is mountainous, with the highest point at 2,764m (Maja e Korabit), and nearly half is covered by forest. The lowest point of elevation is 0m (Adriatic Sea). The climate is Mediterranean with frequent thunderstorms. The average daily temperature ranges from 2°C in January to 31°C in July.

HISTORY AND POLITICS

Albania was under Turkish suzerainty from 1468 until 1912, when independence was declared. After a period of unrest, a republic was unveiled in 1925 and in 1928 a monarchy. The king went into exile in 1939 when the country was occupied by the Italians; Albania was liberated in 1944. Elections in 1945 resulted in a communist-controlled assembly; the king was deposed *in absentia* and a republic declared in 1946.

From 1946 to 1990 Albania was a one-party, communist state, isolated from outside influence, particularly after breaking with the USSR in 1961 and China in 1978. Gradual moves towards democratic reform and westernisation began in the late 1980s, and between 1990 and 1992 democratic elections took place, the communists losing power in 1992. Economic decline and food shortages led to rioting in the early 1990s, and rioting broke out again in 1997 following the collapse of several investment schemes, with anti-government protests nationwide. The country experienced further political and economic pressure in 1999 when Serbian attacks on ethnic Albanians in Kosovo caused over 400,000 people to take refuge in Albania. The government supported NATO's moves to deal with the crisis and by the end of 1999 nearly all the refugees had left Albania.

In the July 2005 general election, the Democratic Alliance (DAP) defeated the Socialist Party in polls, the results of which were disputed; the DAP leader Sali Berisha was appointed prime minister at the head of a new government in September after re-runs in a number of constituencies. After four rounds of voting, Bamir Topi, formerly of the DAP, was elected president in July 2007.

Talks with the EU on an association agreement began in 2003 and, following progress on political and economic reform, a stabilisation and association agreement was signed in 2006.

POLITICAL SYSTEM

Under the 1998 constitution, the president is indirectly elected by the legislature for a five-year term, renewable only once. The unicameral legislature, the People's Assembly, has 140 members directly elected for a four-year term. The president appoints the prime minister, who must be approved by the People's Assembly. The Assembly elects the council of ministers.

HEAD OF STATE
President, Bamir Topi, *elected by the People's Assembly* 20 July 2007, *took office* 24 July 2007

SELECTED GOVERNMENT MEMBERS *as at May 2007*
Prime Minister, Sali Berisha
Deputy Prime Minister, Gazemend Oketa
Foreign Affairs, Lulzim Basha
Defence, Fatmir Mediu
Interior, Bujar Nishani
Finance, Ritvan Bode

EMBASSY OF THE REPUBLIC OF ALBANIA
2nd Floor, 24 Buckingham Gate, London SW1E 6LB
T 020-7828 8897 W www.albanianembassy.co.uk
Ambassador Extraordinary and Plenipotentiary, HE Kastriot Robo, *apptd* 2002

BRITISH EMBASSY
Rruga Skenderbeg 12, Tirana
T (+355) (4) 234 973 W www.uk.al
Ambassador Extraordinary and Plenipotentiary, HE Fraser Wilson, MBE, *apptd* 2006

BRITISH COUNCIL
Rruga Perlat Rexhepi, Pallati 197 Ana, Tirana
T (+355) (4) 240 856/7 W www.britishcouncil.org/albania
Director, Joan Barry

DEFENCE

The army has 40 main battle tanks and 123 armoured personnel carriers. The navy has 13 patrol and coastal combatant vessels at two bases. The air force has 10 helicopters.
MILITARY BUDGET – US$147m (2006)
MILITARY PERSONNEL – 11,020: army 6,200, navy 1,100, air force 1,370, joint staff 2,350; paramilitaries 500
CONSCRIPTION DURATION – 12 months

ECONOMY AND TRADE

Albania is one of the poorest countries in Europe. The communist isolationist policy left a dilapidated energy and transport infrastructure, antiquated equipment and practices, and widespread corruption. After years of liberalisation measures, the economy is showing signs of sustained growth and inflation is under control. Nevertheless, the economy is still heavily dependent on the US$600–800m (£300–400m) a year remitted by nationals working abroad and overseas aid of about US$350m (£175m), primarily from the EU and its member states. The problems with infrastructure and corruption have deterred foreign investment and tackling these is a government priority.

Agriculture accounts for nearly 60 per cent of employment but only about 23 per cent of GDP. The main crops are wheat, maize, vegetables, fruit, sugar beet and livestock products. The principal industries are food processing, textiles, timber, oil, cement, chemicals and mining (base metals).

Exports include textiles and footwear, crude oil, minerals (bitumen, chrome, nickel, copper), tobacco, fruit and vegetables. Imports include machinery and equipment, foodstuffs, textiles and chemicals.
GNI – US$8,000m; US$2,570 per capita (2005)
ANNUAL AVERAGE GROWTH OF GDP – 5.5 per cent (2005 est)
INFLATION RATE – 2.4 per cent (2005 est)
UNEMPLOYMENT – 14.3 per cent (2005 est)
TOTAL EXTERNAL DEBT – US$1,550m (2004)
IMPORTS – US$2,600m (2005)
EXPORTS – US$700m (2005)
BALANCE OF PAYMENTS
Trade – US$1,821m deficit (2005)
Current Account – US$571m deficit (2005)

Trade with UK	*2005*	*2006*
Imports from UK	£14,585,000	£17,149,000
Exports to UK	£1,628,000	£1,559,000

EDUCATION AND HEALTH

LITERACY RATE – 98.7 per cent (2004 est)
GROSS ENROLMENT RATIO (percentage of relevant age group) – primary 106 per cent; secondary 78 per cent; tertiary 19 per cent (2005 est)
HEALTH EXPENDITURE (per capita) – US$157 (2004)
HOSPITAL BEDS (per 1,000 people) – 3.1 (2000–5)

MEDIA

The public broadcaster Albanian Radio and TV (RTSh) faces increasing competition from around 75 private television channels, many of which were established less than ten years ago. There are approximately 30 private radio stations. Political parties, trade unions, religious groups and state bodies are prohibited from owning private television and radio stations but can own newspapers.

ALGERIA

Al-Jumhuriya al-Jaza'iriyah as Dimuqratiyah ash Sha'biyah – People's Democratic Republic of Algeria

AREA – 2,381,740 sq. km. Neighbours: Morocco and Western Sahara (west), Mauritania and Mali (south-west), Niger (south-east), Libya and Tunisia (east)
CAPITAL – Algiers (El Djazair, Al-Jaza'ir); population, 1,519,570 (1998 est). It is one of the principal ports of the Mediterranean
MAJOR CITIES – Annaba; Oran (Wahran); Constantine (Qacentina); Blida (El Boulaida)
CURRENCY – Algerian dinar (DA) of 100 centimes
POPULATION – 32,930,091, rising at 1.22 per cent per year (2006 est); Arab-Berber (99 per cent) (est)
RELIGION – Islam (99 per cent) (est)
LANGUAGE – Arabic (official), French, Berber dialects
POPULATION DENSITY – 14 per sq. km (2005)
URBAN POPULATION – 60 per cent (2005 est)
MEDIAN AGE (years) – 24.9 (2006 est)
NATIONAL ANTHEM – 'Kassaman' ['We Pledge']
NATIONAL DAY – 1 November (Revolution Day)
LIFE EXPECTANCY (years) – 73.26 (2006 est)
MORTALITY RATE – 4.61 (2006 est)
BIRTH RATE – 17.14 (2006 est)
INFANT MORTALITY RATE – 29.87 (2006 est)
DEATH PENALTY – No*
CPI SCORE – 3.1 (2006)
POPULATION BELOW POVERTY LINE – 25 per cent (2005 est)

CLIMATE AND TERRAIN

Algeria, the second largest country in Africa after Sudan, is dominated by the Sahara desert, which covers 80 per cent of its territory. The eastern part of the Atlas mountain range crosses the north of the country, separating the coastal plain, where the majority of the population lives, from the desert plateaux of the interior. The mountains are subject to earthquakes, flooding and mudslides during the rainy season (November to March). The highest point of elevation is 3,003m (Tahat) and the lowest is −40m (Chott Melrhir). Algeria has mild, wet winters and hot, dry summers. The climate is drier along the coastline, while the high plateaux experience cold winters.

HISTORY AND POLITICS

Algeria was a Roman province that came under Arabic and Islamic influence from the eighth century, and was part of the Ottoman Empire from the 16th century until its annexation by France in 1830. It gained its independence in 1962 following an eight-year guerrilla war by the socialist Front de Libération Nationale (FLN). Ben Bella was elected president in 1963, but was deposed in 1965 by Col. Houari Boumediene, who was formally elected president in 1976, when the FLN became the only permitted political party. Boumediene died in 1978 and was succeeded by Chadli Bendjedid.

A new constitution agreed by referendum in 1988 moved Algeria towards pluralism. However, the 1991 legislative elections were abandoned in anticipation of the success of the opposition Islamic Salvation Front (FIS), which had campaigned on a radical Islamist platform. The FIS was banned in 1991, triggering civil unrest and conflict between Islamic groups (the FIS-backed Islamic Salvation Army and the more extreme Armed Islamic Group) and the military. A state of emergency was declared in 1992 and the country suffered an insurgency that claimed an estimated 100,000 lives. The level of violence has fallen since 1999, when the newly elected president Abdelaziz Bouteflika initiated a policy of reconciliation with the Islamists, and despite a resurgence in 2003, his 'charter for peace and reconciliation' was approved by referendum in September 2005. In 2006 a second amnesty for militants was supported by the FIS leadership, but since December 2006 a group allying itself to al-Qaida has carried out a number of bombings.

Another divisive issue is the ethnic Berber population's campaign since 2001 for greater political and cultural recognition. Following occasionally violent demonstrations and a Berber boycott of the 2002 and 2004 elections, negotiations led to an agreement in 2005 that promised greater government investment in the Berber-populated Kabylie region and greater recognition for the Berber language Tamazight. The Berber protests also reflected a more widespread discontent with social conditions and living standards among the population.

In 2004, Bouteflika was elected for a second term as president with 85 per cent of the vote. In the legislative election in May 2007, the National Liberation Front gained the highest number of seats. The elections were blighted by violence, a low turnout and a high number of spoilt ballots, suggesting widespread political disaffection.

POLITICAL SYSTEM

The president is directly elected for a five-year term. The legislature *(Barlaman)* is bicameral. *Majlis al-Chaabi al-Watani* (national people' assembly) is the lower chamber and has 389 members, directly elected for a five-year term. The *Majlis al-Umma* (council of the nation) is the upper chamber, with a third of its 144 members appointed by the president; two-thirds are indirectly elected for six-year terms, of which half are re-elected every three years. Although Algeria is no longer a one-party state, parties based on religion, including the FIS, are banned.

HEAD OF STATE

President, Defence, Abdelaziz Bouteflika, *elected* 15 April 1999, *re-elected* April 2004

SELECTED GOVERMENT MEMBERS *as at May 2007*

Prime Minister, Abdelaziz Belkhadem
Finance, Mourad Medelci
Ministers of State, Mohammed Bedjaoui *(Foreign Affairs)*; Noureddine Yazid Zerhouni *(Interior and Local Authorities)*

ALGERIAN EMBASSY

54 Holland Park, London W11 3RS
T 020-7221 7800 W www.algerianembassy.org.uk
Ambassador Extraordinary and Plenipotentiary, HE Mohamed Salah Dembri, *apptd* 2005

BRITISH EMBASSY

7th Floor, Hilton Hotel Alger, Pins Maritimes, Palais des Expositions, El Mohammadia, Algiers
T (+213) (21) 230 068
Ambassador Extraordinary and Plenipotentiary, HE Andrew Tesoriere, *apptd* 2005

BRITISH COUNCIL

c/o The British Embassy
T (+213) (21) 480 947 E john.mitchell@britishcouncil.org
Director, John Mitchell

DEFENCE

The army has 920 main battle tanks, 1,084 armoured infantry fighting vehicles and 910 armoured personnel carriers. The navy has 2 submarines, 3 frigates and 22 patrol and coastal vessels. The air force has 204 combat aircraft and 33 armed helicopters.
MILITARY BUDGET – US$3,020m (2006)
MILITARY PERSONNEL – 137,500: army 120,000, navy 7,500, air force 10,000; paramilitaries 187,200
CONSCRIPTION DURATION – 18 months

ECONOMY AND TRADE

In 1994 the government embarked on the liberalisation of the economy, formerly centrally planned and state-controlled, and in 1997 initiated a privatisation programme. These reforms, combined with recent high oil prices, have resulted in trade surpluses, record foreign exchange reserves and the reduction of foreign debt. However, attempts to diversify away from the energy sector are progressing slowly due to the difficulty of attracting foreign and internal investment, often deterred by corruption and bureaucratic resistance, and the economic buoyancy has had little impact on the social ills of poverty and high unemployment.

Algeria has substantial oil and gas reserves and the hydrocarbon industry accounts for nearly 60 per cent of government revenue, 30 per cent of GDP and over 95 per cent of export earnings in 2006. Services provided 32 per cent of GDP and agriculture 9 per cent of GDP in 2006. Industries other than oil and gas production and processing include mining, electrical goods, food processing and light industries.

Algeria's main trading partners are Italy, France, the USA and Spain. The chief imports are capital goods, foodstuffs and consumer goods.
GNI – US$89,600m; US$2,730 per capita (2005)

ANNUAL AVERAGE GROWTH OF GDP – 5.5 per cent (2005 est)
INFLATION RATE – 1.9 per cent (2005 est)
UNEMPLOYMENT – 17.1 per cent (2005 est)
TOTAL EXTERNAL DEBT – US$19,450m (2005 est)
IMPORTS – US$20,000m (2005)
EXPORTS – US$46,500m (2005)

Trade with UK	*2005*	*2006*
Imports from UK	£145,096,000	£167,225,000
Exports to UK	£465,030,000	£962,297,000

EDUCATION AND HEALTH

LITERACY RATE – 69.8 per cent (2004 est)
GROSS ENROLMENT RATIO (percentage of relevant age group) – primary 112 per cent; secondary 83 per cent; tertiary 20 per cent (2005 est)
HEALTH EXPENDITURE (per capita) – US$94 (2004)
HOSPITAL BEDS (per 1,000 people) – 2.1 (2002)

MEDIA

The state controls the television (Entreprise Nationale de Télévision) and radio stations (Radio-Télévision Algérienne), but domestic satellite dishes are used by the population to receive French and European channels, some of which actively target Algerian viewers. There are five main daily newspapers, all of them published in French. There is no direct censorship but laws permit prison terms and fines for insulting or defaming the president, MPs, judges and the army. Daily newspapers mark the anniversary of the introduction of these laws with a day of suspended production.

ANDORRA

Principat d'Andorra – Principality of Andorra

AREA – 468 sq. km. Neighbours: Spain and France
CAPITAL – Andorra la Vella; population, 23,587 (2005 est)
CURRENCY – Euro (€) of 100 cents
POPULATION – 71,201, rising at 0.89 per cent per year (2006 est); Spanish (43 per cent), Andorran (33 per cent), Portuguese (11 per cent), French (7 per cent) (est)
RELIGION – Roman Catholicism (90 per cent), Islam (3 per cent) (est)
LANGUAGE – Catalan (official), French, Castilian, Portuguese
POPULATION DENSITY – 141 per sq. km (2005)
URBAN POPULATION – 91.3 per cent (2005 est)
MEDIAN AGE (years) – 40.9 years (2006 est)
NATIONAL ANTHEM – 'El Gran Carlemany' [The Great Charlemagne]
NATIONAL DAY – 8 September (Our Lady of Meritxell Day)
LIFE EXPECTANCY (years) – 83.51 (2006 est)
MORTALITY RATE – 6.25 (2006 est)
BIRTH RATE – 8.71 (2006 est)
INFANT MORTALITY RATE – 4.04 (2006 est)
DEATH PENALTY – No (abolished 1993)

CLIMATE AND TERRAIN

Located between the French and Spanish borders, Andorra is a landlocked country of dramatic mountains interspersed by narrow valleys. A third of the country is classified as forest. The highest point of elevation is 2,946m (Coma Pedrosa) and the lowest is 840m (Riu Runer). The climate is alpine, with heavy snowfall in winter and warm summers. The average temperature ranges from −1 to 6°C in January to 12 to 26°C in July.

HISTORY AND POLITICS

Liberated from Muslim rule by Charlemagne in 803, Andorra is a small, neutral principality that was formed by a *paréage* (a type of feudal treaty) in 1278 and since then has owed dual allegiance to two co-princes, the Spanish Bishop of Urgel and the president of the French Republic. Andorra became an independent democratic parliamentary co-principality in 1993. The first elections under the new constitution were held in 1993, and on 20 January 1994 the first sovereign government of Andorra took office. The country has subsequently formalised its links with the EU and joined the UN and the Council of Europe. Legislative elections in 2005 were won by the Liberal Party of Andorra (PLA) with 41.2 per cent of the vote and 14 seats in the general council. Albert Pintat Santolaria of the PLA was nominated as president of the executive council and confirmed in office on 27 May 2005.

POLITICAL SYSTEM

Under the 1993 constitution, Andorra's sovereignty is vested in the people rather than in the two co-princes. The constitution enables Andorra to establish an independent judiciary and to conduct its own foreign policy, whilst its people may now join political parties and trade unions. The two co-princes remain heads of state, represented in Andorra by the permanent delegates (the Spanish vicar-general of the diocese of Urgel and the French prefect of the Pyrénées Orientales department at Perpignan), but now only have the power to veto treaties with France and Spain that affect the state's borders and security.

Andorra has a unicameral legislature of 28 members known as the *Consell General de las Valls* (General Council of the Valleys), directly elected for a four-year term. 14 members are elected on a national list basis and 14 in seven dual-member constituencies based on Andorra's seven parishes. The council appoints the president of the executive council, who designates government members.
Permanent French Delegate, Philippe Massoni
Permanent Episcopal Delegate, Nemesi Marqués Oste

SELECTED GOVERNMENT MEMBERS *as at May 2007*
President of the Executive Council, Albert Pintat Santolaria
Finance, Ferran Mirapeix Lucas
Foreign Affairs, Juli Minoves Triquell
Justice and Interior, Josep Maria Cabanes Dalmau

EMBASSY OF THE PRINCIPALITY OF ANDORRA
63 Westover Road, Wandsworth, London SW18 2RF
T 020-8874 4806
Ambassador Extraordinary and Plenipotentiary, Maria Rosa Picart de Francis, *apptd* 2007

BRITISH CONSULATE-GENERAL
Ambassador, HE Stephen Wright, *apptd* 2007, resident at Madrid, Spain

ECONOMY AND TRADE

The economy is largely based on tourism, especially skiing (80 per cent of GDP, with 11 million visitors annually), banking and commerce (due in part to the principality's tax-free status), tobacco, forestry, furniture-making and sheep-farming. Andorra has been a member of the EU customs union since 1991.
ANNUAL AVERAGE GROWTH OF GDP – 4 per cent (2004 est)

INFLATION RATE – 3.4 per cent (2004)

Trade with UK	*2005*	*2006*
Imports from UK	£10,381,000	£7,349,00
Exports to UK	£406,000	£165,000

COMMUNICATIONS

There are 269km of roads but no railways, airports or waterways. A road into Andorra from Spain is open all year round, and that from France is closed only occasionally in winter. Mobile telephones are nearly twice as widespread as fixed-line connections.

MEDIA

The Andorran media is heavily influenced by France and Spain and Andorrans have access to broadcasts from both countries. There are two radio stations in Andorra, one is privately owned and one is operated by the government (Radio Andorra), as well as a state-owned television channel and two major daily newspapers *(Diari d'Andorra and El Periodic)*.

ANGOLA

Republica de Angola – Republic of Angola

AREA – 1,246,700 sq. km. Neighbours: Democratic Republic of the Congo (north and east), Zambia (east), Namibia (south). The enclave of Cabinda is separated from the rest of Angola by the Democratic Republic of the Congo and also borders the Republic of Congo
CAPITAL – Luanda; population, 2,644,000 (2005 est)
MAJOR CITIES – Huambo; Benguela; Lobito
CURRENCY – Readjusted kwanza (Kzrl) of 100 lwei
POPULATION – 12,127,071, rising at 2.45 per cent per year (2006 est); Ovimbundu (37 per cent), Kimbundu (25 per cent), Bakongo (13 per cent) (est)
RELIGION – Roman Catholicism 28 per cent (est). A small portion of the rural population practices animism or traditional indigenous religions
LANGUAGE – Portuguese (official), Bantu
POPULATION DENSITY – 13 per sq. km (2005)
URBAN POPULATION – 37.2 per cent (2005 est)
MEDIAN AGE (years) – 18 (2006 est)
NATIONAL ANTHEM – 'Angola Avante' ['Forward Angola']
NATIONAL DAY – 11 November (Independence Day)
LIFE EXPECTANCY (years) – 38.62 (2006 est)
MORTALITY RATE – 24.2 (2006 est)
BIRTH RATE – 45.11 (2006 est)
INFANT MORTALITY RATE – 185.36 (2006 est)
HIV/AIDS ADULT PREVALENCE – 3.9 per cent (2003 est)
DEATH PENALTY – No (abolished 1992)
CPI SCORE – 2.2 (2006)
POPULATION BELOW POVERTY LINE – 70 per cent (2003 est)
LITERACY RATE – 66.8 per cent (2004 est)
GROSS ENROLMENT RATIO (percentage of relevant age group) – secondary 19 per cent (2002); tertiary 1 per cent (2005 est)
HEALTH EXPENDITURE (per capita) – US$26 (2004)

CLIMATE AND TERRAIN

The land rises from a narrow coastal plain to a large interior plateau. On the plateau rise the Cunene, Cubango and Cuanza rivers and the headwaters of tributaries of the Zambezi and Congo rivers, although some of these are dry except in the rainy season, when flooding may occur. The south is desert. The highest point of elevation is 2,620m (Morro de Moco) and the lowest is 0m (Atlantic Ocean). The climate is tropical in the north, with a cool, dry season from May to October and a hot, rainy season from November to April, and sub-tropical in the south and along the coast to Luanda.

HISTORY AND POLITICS

A Portuguese colony was established in the region in the 15th century and its territory expanded over the centuries, the current boundaries being defined in the 19th century. An anti-colonial war began in 1961, and Angola became independent on 11 November 1975. Shortly afterwards, civil war broke out between the Popular Movement for the Liberation of Angola (MPLA) government and two factions, the National Union for the Total Independence of Angola (UNITA) led by Jonas Savimbi, and the Front for the Liberation of Angola (FNLA). The FNLA ceased operations in the 1980s and foreign support for the MPLA and UNITA was withdrawn after 1988, but the civil war between the government and UNITA continued. A peace agreement in 1991 was followed by multiparty elections in 1992 but UNITA refused to accept the results and fighting resumed. Another peace agreement (the Lusaka protocol) was signed in 1994 but UNITA appeared not to comply with its provisions and UN peacekeeping forces were dispatched to Angola.

In 1997 a government of national reconciliation was formed under the power-sharing provisions of the Lusaka protocol; although a nominal participant, UNITA prevented the restoration of central state administration in key areas. In spite of intervention by the UN security council, fighting continued until 2002, when, following the death of Jonas Savimbi in February, UNITA and the government signed a formal ceasefire agreement in April and pledged to adhere to the 1994 peace agreement. UNITA gradually demobilised its forces and transformed itself into a political party, electing Isaias Samakuva as leader in 2003.

In 2004 the government announced a timetable of voter registration in preparation for elections in 2006, but the elections have been delayed repeatedly, most recently to 2008 (legislative and presidential); the government cited the need to overcome the inaccessibility of many parts of the country due to transport infrastructure damage and landmines.

SECESSION

In the northern enclave of Cabinda, separatists have fought for independence since the mid-1970s. Following the end of the civil war, the government stepped up its military campaign against the separatists, destroying their military capability by 2004, although it was accused of serious infringements of human rights. A truce in 2006 led to talks and a peace agreement, although this was not accepted by all the separatist groups.

POLITICAL SYSTEM

The MPLA, formerly a Marxist-Leninist party, was the sole legal party until early 1991 when a multiparty system was adopted. The constitution provides for an executive president directly elected for a five-year term. The president appoints the council of ministers. The 223-member national assembly is directly elected for a four-year term. Neither presidential nor legislative elections have been held since 1992; in 1996 and in 2000, the national assembly adopted a constitutional amendment extending its own mandate.

HEAD OF STATE
President, José Eduardo dos Santos, *re-elected* 30 September 1992

SELECTED GOVERNMENT MEMBERS *as at May 2007*
Prime Minister, Interior, Fernando da Piedade Dias dos Santos ('Nando')
Deputy Prime Minister, Aguinaldo Jaime
Defence, Gen. Kundi Pahiama
Finance, José Pedro de Morais
Foreign Affairs, João Bernardo de Miranda
Interior, Gen. Roberto Leal Monteiro

EMBASSY OF THE REPUBLIC OF ANGOLA
22 Dorset Street, London W1U 6QY
T 020-7299 9850 E embassyo@angola.org.uk
Ambassador Extraordinary and Plenipotentiary, HE Ana Maria Teles Carreira, *apptd* 2005

BRITISH EMBASSY
Rua Diogo Cao 4 (Caixa Postal 1244), Luanda
T (+244) (22) 233 4582
Ambassador Extraordinary and Plenipotentiary, HE Ralph Publicover, *apptd* 2005

DEFENCE
The army has an estimated 300 main battle tanks, 250 armoured infantry fighting vehicles and 170 armoured personnel carriers. The navy has 9 patrol and coastal combatants. The air force has 90 combat aircraft and 16 armed helicopters.
MILITARY BUDGET – US$1,560m (2006)
MILITARY PERSONNEL – 107,000: army 100,000, navy 1,000, air force 6,000; paramilitaries 10,000

ECONOMY AND TRADE
Since the civil war ended, the government has made progress towards liberalising the economy and stabilising the exchange rate. Inflation has been brought down from 325 per cent in 2000 to 13.2 per cent in 2006. That this progress has been possible is largely due to high economic growth driven by the post-war increase in oil production, reconstruction and agricultural production. However, widespread corruption means that most of the population has seen little benefit and 70 per cent remained below the poverty line in 2003.

Angola and the Cabinda enclave are rich in natural resources that include oil, diamonds, gold, uranium and other minerals, forests and fisheries. In 2005, oil production accounted for nearly half of GDP and 90 per cent of exports. Since 2004, the government has clamped down on the illegal trade in diamonds that flourished during the civil war, and the gems are now the second largest export. Agriculture is mostly at subsistence level, although coffee, sisal and cotton are exported. Production has risen but the country still imports half its food; expansion is hampered by unexploded landmines in areas affected by the civil war. The main industrial activities are the processing of oil, mining of gems, metals and other minerals, forestry, fishing and fish processing, the manufacture of cement and tobacco products, and ship repair.
GNI – US$22,500m; US$1,410 per capita (2005)
ANNUAL AVERAGE GROWTH OF GDP – 19.9 per cent (2005 est)
INFLATION RATE – 13.2 per cent (2006 est)
TOTAL EXTERNAL DEBT – US$9,401m (2005 est)

Trade with UK	*2005*	*2006*
Imports from UK	£158,264,000	£206,322,000
Exports to UK	£15,011,000	£16,037,000

COMMUNICATIONS
The conflict of the past 30 years has left the road and rail systems in extremely poor condition. Land transport difficulties are compounded by the many uncleared landmines and security problems, which mean that most road travel is in convoys. Reconstruction began in 2005 with aid from China and several projects were completed in 2006. There are 51,429km of roads, 46,080km of which are unsurfaced, and 2,761km of railway. Most internal travel takes place by air between the country's 244 airports (31 of which have surfaced runways). The main ports are Luanda, Lobito and Benguela. The fixed-line telephone system is largely confined to business and administrative use; mobile telephone use is growing.

MEDIA
Angola's only news agency (Angop), the country's biggest broadcaster, Televisao Popular de Angola (TPA), and the country's only daily newspaper *(Jornal de Angola)* are all government-owned and rarely outspoken. There are several commercial radio stations and private newspapers, one private television station, and some subscription services (operated by Multichoice Angola) that include Brazilian and Portuguese channels. The private media is liable to harassment.

ANTIGUA AND BARBUDA

State of Antigua and Barbuda

AREA – 443 sq. km; Antigua 279 sq. km; Barbuda 160 sq. km; Redonda 1.2 sq. km
CAPITAL – St John's; population, 24,451 (2001 est)
CURRENCY – East Caribbean dollar (EC $) of 100 cents
POPULATION – 69,108 rising at 0.55 per cent per year (2006 est)
RELIGION – Christianity (70 per cent) (est)
LANGUAGE – English (official)
POPULATION DENSITY – 188 per sq. km (2005)
URBAN POPULATION – 38.4 per cent (2005 est)
MEDIAN AGE (years) – 30 (2006 est)
NATIONAL ANTHEM – 'Fair Antigua, We Salute Thee'
NATIONAL DAY – 1 November (Independence Day)
LIFE EXPECTANCY (years) – 72.16 (2006 est)
MORTALITY RATE – 5.37 (2006 est)
BIRTH RATE – 16.93 (2006 est)
INFANT MORTALITY RATE – 18.86 (2006 est)
DEATH PENALTY – Yes
MILITARY BUDGET – US$4.8m (2006 est)
MILITARY PERSONNEL – 170: army 125, navy 45

CLIMATE AND TERRAIN
The subtropical island of Antigua is part of the Leeward Islands in the eastern Caribbean. It is distinguished from the rest of the Leeward Islands by an absence of high hills and forest, and has a drier climate than most of the West Indies. The elevation extremes range from 402m at the highest point (Boggy Peak) to 0m sea level (Caribbean Sea).

Barbuda is 48km away from Antigua. It is a very flat coral island with a large lagoon. Both of the islands lie within the hurricane belt and are subject to tropical storms and hurricanes between June and November.

HISTORY AND POLITICS

Antigua was discovered by Columbus in 1493. Colonised by the English in 1632, it was granted to Lord Willoughby by Charles II. Barbuda was colonised from Antigua in 1661. Administered as part of the Leeward Islands Federation from 1871 to 1956, it became internally self-governing in 1967 and fully independent on 1 November 1981.

The United Progressive Party won the 2004 election with 13 seats to the Antigua Labour Party's (ALP) four, removing the ALP from power for the first time in three decades.

POLITICAL SYSTEM

The head of state is the British monarch, represented by the governor-general. There is a senate of 17 appointed members and a house of representatives of 17 members, elected every five years by proportional representation. The attorney-general may be appointed.

Governor-General, HE Sir James B. Carlisle, GCMG, *apptd* 1993

SELECTED GOVERNMENT MEMBERS *as at May 2007*

Prime Minister, Foreign Affairs and Foreign Trade, National Security, Barbuda Affairs, Ecclesiastical Affairs, Winston Baldwin Spencer

Deputy Prime Minister, Public Works, Transport; Energy and Environment, Wilmoth Daniel

Minister of Finance and Economy, Leon Errol Cort

HIGH COMMISSION FOR ANTIGUA AND BARBUDA

2nd Floor, 45 Crawford Place, London W1H 4LP

T 020-7258 0070 W www.antigua-barbuda.com

High Commissioner, HE Dr Carl Roberts, *apptd* 2004

BRITISH HIGH COMMISSION

High Commissioner, HE Duncan Taylor, *apptd* 2005, resident at Bridgetown, Barbados

ECONOMY AND TRADE

Antigua is one of the Caribbean's more prosperous nations. The economy is largely based on tourism and related services (contributing more than half of GDP), offshore financial services, construction and light manufacturing. To reduce its dependence on tourism, the government has encouraged the establishment of internet gambling sites. Agricultural production includes livestock, sea island cotton, mixed market gardening and fishing, mostly for local consumption.

GNI – US$855m; US$10,500 per capita (2005)

ANNUAL AVERAGE GROWTH OF GDP – 3.8 per cent (2005 est)

INFLATION RATE – 0.9 per cent (2005 est)

UNEMPLOYMENT – 11 per cent (2001 est)

BALANCE OF PAYMENTS

Trade – US$291m deficit (2002)

Current Account – US$103m deficit (2002)

Trade with UK	*2005*	*2006*
Imports from UK	£12,450,000	£30,816,000
Exports to UK	£5,428,000	£5,517,000

MEDIA AND CULTURE

Many of the television and radio stations are owned or controlled by the Antigua Labour Party. Antigua's first independent radio station, Observer Radio, began broadcasting in 2001.

Antiguan culture is dominated by cricket and the country has produced several of the sport's most illustrious names. Batsman Viv Richards (*b.* 1952) and Richie Richardson (*b.* 1962) both captained the West Indian team, while Curtly Ambrose (*b.* 1963) is one of only ten bowlers to have taken 400 Test wickets. The new Sir Vivian Richards Stadium in St John's hosted several matches during the 2007 Cricket World Cup.

ARGENTINA

República Argentina – Argentine Republic

AREA – 2,766,890 sq. km. Neighbours: Bolivia (north), Paraguay, Brazil and Uruguay (north-east), Chile (west) from which it is separated by the Cordillera de los Andes

CAPITAL – Buenos Aires; population, 2,776,138 (2001)

MAJOR CITIES – Córdoba; San Justo; Rosario; Lomas de Zamora; La Plata; Mar del Plata

CURRENCY – Peso of 10,000 australes

POPULATION – 39,921,833 rising at 0.96 per cent per year (2006 est)

RELIGION – Roman Catholicism (88 per cent), Protestantism (7 per cent), Islam (1 per cent), Judaism (1 per cent) (est)

LANGUAGE – Spanish (official), English, Italian, French, German

POPULATION DENSITY – 14 per sq. km (2005)

URBAN POPULATION – 90.6 per cent (2005 est)

MEDIAN AGE (years) – 29.7 (2006 est)

NATIONAL ANTHEM – 'Marcha de la Patria' ['March of the Fatherland']

NATIONAL DAY – 25 May (Revolution Day)

LIFE EXPECTANCY (years) – 76.12 (2006 est)

MORTALITY RATE – 7.55 (2006 est)

BIRTH RATE – 16.73 (2006 est)

INFANT MORTALITY RATE – 14.73 (2006 est)

DEATH PENALTY – Yes*

CPI SCORE – 2.9 (2006)

POPULATION BELOW POVERTY LINE – 38.5 per cent (2005)

CLIMATE AND TERRAIN

The Andes mountain range runs the full length of Argentina, a dramatic spine to the country's western border with Chile. Parts of the Andes are prone to earthquakes. East of the Andes, the north of the country is mostly subtropical forest and savanna, the east is rich, grassy pampas, and the southern Patagonian plateau has an arid, desert-like terrain. The highest point of elevation is 6,960m (Cerro Aconcagua) and the lowest is −40m (Peninsula Valdes). Temperatures range from subtropical to subantarctic, with an average annual temperature of 16°C.

HISTORY AND POLITICS

The estuary of La Plata was discovered in 1515 by Juan Díaz de Solís and the region was subsequently colonised by the Spanish. Spain ruled the territory from the 16th century until 1810. In 1816, after a long campaign of liberation, independence was declared by the congress of

Tucumán and during the following century, power swung between conservative and liberal factions, and between civil and military regimes.

A 1943 coup introduced a period of military rule before Juan Domingo Perón became president in 1946, establishing an authoritarian regime. His overthrow in 1955 was followed by 18 years of political instability until 1973, when he was recalled from exile. Perón died within a year and was succeeded by his widow, vice-president Maria Estela Martínez de Perón. A coup led to the establishment of a military junta in 1976; this conducted a so-called 'dirty war' in which over 8,000 people are alleged to have disappeared. The failure of Argentina's attempt to annex the Falkland Islands/Malvinas in 1982 discredited the junta and led to the restoration of civilian rule in 1983.

President Fernando de la Rúa, elected in 1999, resigned in 2001 in the face of violent public unrest caused by a severe economic crisis. Following a series of interim presidents, Néstor Kirchner was elected president in 2003. The next presidential and legislative elections are scheduled for October 2007.

POLITICAL SYSTEM

The 1853 constitution was amended in 1994. The executive president is directly elected for a four-year term, renewable only once. The bicameral legislature (national congress) consists of a 72-member senate (three members for each province and three for Buenos Aires) and a 257-member chamber of deputies. Half of the chamber is elected every two years, and deputies serve a four-year term. The senate is directly elected for a six-year term, with one-third renewable every two years.

HEAD OF STATE
President, Néstor Kirchner, *sworn in* 25 May 2003
Vice-President, Daniel Scioli

SELECTED GOVERNMENT MEMBERS *as at May 2007*
Cabinet Chief, Alberto Fernández
Defence, Nilda Garré
Economy, Production, Felisa Miceli
Foreign Relations, International Trade and Worship, Jorge Taiana
Interior, Anibal Fernández

EMBASSY OF THE ARGENTINE REPUBLIC
65 Brook Street, London W1K 4AH
T 020-7318 1300 W www.argentine-embassy-uk.org
Ambassador Extraordinary and Plenipotentiary, HE Federico Mirré, *apptd* 2003

BRITISH EMBASSY
Dr Luis Agote 2412/52, (Casilla de Correo 2050)
1425 Buenos Aires
T (+54) (11) 4808 2200
Ambassador Extraordinary and Plenipotentiary, HE Dr John Hughes, *apptd* 2004

BRITISH COUNCIL
Marcelo T. de Alvear 590, C1058AAF Buenos Aires
T (+54) (11) 4311 9814/7519
W www.britishcouncil.org/argentina
Director, Martin Fryer

FEDERAL STRUCTURE

The republic is divided into 22 provinces, each with an elected governor and legislature, the federal district of Buenos Aires, which has an elected mayor and autonomous government, and the national territory of Tierra del Fuego.

DEFENCE

The army has 230 main battle tanks, 123 armoured infantry fighting vehicles and 518 armoured personnel carriers. The navy has 3 submarines, 5 destroyers, 9 frigates, 15 patrol and coastal vessels and 28 combat aircraft. The air force has 121 combat aircraft.
MILITARY BUDGET – US$1,840m (2006)
MILITARY PERSONNEL – 71,655: army 41,400, navy 17,755, air force 12,500; paramilitaries 31,240

ECONOMY AND TRADE

The economy has been turned around since the economic collapse of 2001–2. Argentina has experienced strong growth since 2003, restructuring its defaulted debt in 2005 and repaying its IMF loan in 2006. The government budget is in surplus and exports are strong, although public debt (62 per cent of GDP in 2006) and unemployment remain high, and over 30 per cent of the population lives below the poverty line.

The country is rich in natural resources, particularly lead, zinc, tin, copper, iron ore, manganese, uranium, oil and coal. The fertile pampas supports a strong and export-orientated agricultural sector; the main crops are cereals, oil-bearing seeds, fruit, tea, tobacco and livestock products, especially beef, mutton and wool.

The main industrial activities are food processing (meat-packing, flour-milling, sugar-refining, wine production) and the production of motor vehicles, consumer durables, textiles, chemicals, petrochemicals, printing, metallurgy and steel.

The main trading partners are Brazil, USA, China and Chile. The main exports include edible oils, fuel and energy, cereals, feed and motor vehicles. The major imports are machinery and equipment, motor vehicles, chemicals, metal manufactures and plastics.
GNI – US$173,100m; US$4,470 per capita (2005)
ANNUAL AVERAGE GROWTH OF GDP – 9.2 per cent (2005 est)
INFLATION RATE – 9.6 per cent (2005 est)
UNEMPLOYMENT – 11.6 per cent (2005 est)
TOTAL EXTERNAL DEBT – US$118,200m (2005 est)
IMPORTS – US$29,000m (2005)
EXPORTS – US$40,000m (2005)

FOREIGN EXCHANGE RATE 1996–2005
(peso units per £ sterling)

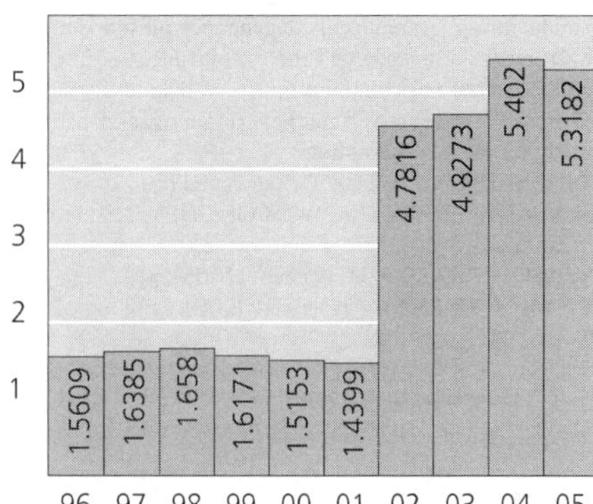

Source: HM Revenue and Customs

BALANCE OF PAYMENTS
Trade – US$13,239m surplus (2004)
Current Account – US$3,353m surplus (2004)

Trade with UK	*2005*	*2006*
Imports from UK	£168,902,000	£216,078,000
Exports to UK	£290,887,000	£359,126,000

COMMUNICATIONS

The road and rail networks are extensive in the north and centre of the country; in Patagonia, roads are fewer and there are no railways. The 34,902km of railway is state owned. The combined national and provincial road network totals approximately 229,144km, of which 68,809km are surfaced. A US$20bn (£10bn) programme of road-building and upgrading of existing road, rail and air infrastructure began in 2000. The main form of internal long-distance travel is by air and there are over 1,000 airports and airfields; the principal airports are at Buenos Aires, Cordoba, Salta and Rio Gallegos. There are many ports on the long coastline and the 11,000km of inland waterways formed by the major rivers; Buenos Aires, Ensenada (La Plata) and Bahia Blanca are the main seaports. The telecommunications system has modernised rapidly since the market was opened to competition and foreign investment in 1998, but fixed-line telephone density is still low at 9 million in 2005 compared to 22 million mobile phone users.

EDUCATION AND HEALTH

Education is compulsory and free from the age of six to 15.

LITERACY RATE – 97.2 per cent (2004 est)
GROSS ENROLMENT RATIO (percentage of relevant age group) – primary 112 per cent; secondary 86 per cent; tertiary 64 per cent (2005 est)
HEALTH EXPENDITURE (per capita) – US$383 (2004)
HOSPITAL BEDS (per 1,000 people) – 4.1 (2000–5)

MEDIA AND CULTURE

The media is well developed, with over 150 daily newspapers (published in both English and Spanish), including seven major dailies published in Buenos Aires. There are more than a thousand commercial radio stations (many unlicensed), over 40 television stations and widespread access to cable television.

The culture is primarily Latin American but has strong European influences, thanks to the country's large Italian and Spanish populations. Argentina's most notable writer is Jorge Luis Borges (1899–1986) whose short stories belong within the magical realist movement. The world's first animated films were made in Argentina by Quirino Cristani (1896–1984) and the country's filmmaking pedigree has been maintained by the success of composer Lalo Schiffrin (*b.* 1932), responsible for the themes to *Mission Impossible* and *Bullitt*.

Argentina has historically been a successful sporting country. Its football team is a double World Cup winner and has held the Copa America trophy 14 times. Two of football's greatest entertainers, Alfredo di Stefano (*b.* 1926) and Diego Maradona (*b.* 1960), are Argentinian. Juan Michael Fangio's (1911–95) record of five Formula One World Championships stood for 45 years until 2003.

ARGENTINE ANTARCTIC TERRITORY

The Argentine Antarctic Territory consists of the Antarctic Peninsula and a triangular section extending to the South Pole, defined as the area between 25°W and 74° W and 60°S. This overlaps with both Britain's and Chile's claim areas (*see* The Antarctic). Administratively, the territory is a department of the province of Tierra del Fuego, Antarctica, and South Atlantic Islands. The population varies from 150 to 300 people, all of whom are scientific researchers.

ARMENIA

Hayastani Hanrapetut'yun – Republic of Armenia

AREA – 29,800 sq. km. Neighbours: Azerbaijan (east and south-west), Georgia (north), Iran (south), Turkey (west)
CAPITAL – Yerevan; population, 1,102,900 (2005 est)
MAJOR CITIES – Gyumri; Vanadzor
CURRENCY – Dram of 100 louma
POPULATION – 2,976,372, falling at 0.19 per cent per year (2006 est); Armenian (97.9 per cent), Kurdish (1.3 per cent). The Armenian diaspora numbers some 5,300,000
RELIGION – Christianity (92 per cent), Islam (1 per cent) (est). Armenia adopted Christianity as its official religion in AD 301, the first state in the world to do so
LANGUAGE – Armenian, Yezidi, Russian
POPULATION DENSITY – 107 per sq. km (2005)
URBAN POPULATION – 64.1 per cent (2005 est)
MEDIAN AGE (years) – 30.4 (2006 est)
NATIONAL ANTHEM – 'Mer Hayrenik' ['Our Fatherland']
NATIONAL DAY – 21 September (Independence Day)
LIFE EXPECTANCY (years) – 71.84 (2006 est)
MORTALITY RATE – 8.23 (2006 est)
BIRTH RATE – 12.07 (2006 est)
INFANT MORTALITY RATE – 22.47 (2006 est)
DEATH PENALTY – No (abolished 2003)
CPI SCORE – 2.9 (2006)
POPULATION BELOW POVERTY LINE – 43 per cent (2003 est)

CLIMATE AND TERRAIN

A landlocked country lying between the Black and Caspian seas, Armenia occupies the south-western part of the Caucasus region of the former Soviet Union. It is very mountainous, consisting of several vast tablelands surrounded by ridges. The elevation extremes range from 4,090m at the highest point (Aragats Lerrnagagat) to 400m at the lowest (Debed River). The climate is continental, dry and cold, but the Ararat valley has a long, hot and dry summer. Armenia is in an active seismic zone, and the north of the country suffered an earthquake in 1988 that left an estimated 50,000 people dead.

HISTORY AND POLITICS

Armenia was first unified in 95 BC but was divided between the Persian and Byzantine empires in AD 387 and then conquered in the 11th century by the Seljuk Turks and the Mongols. In the 16th century most of Armenia was incorporated into the Ottoman Empire. In 1639 the country was divided again, the most easterly areas, now the Republic of Armenia, becoming part of the Persian Empire. In 1828 eastern Armenia became part of the Russian Empire while western Armenia remained under Ottoman rule. The Ottomans launched pogroms against the Armenians from 1894 onwards, and from 1915 to 1918 deported or killed over 1,500,000.

Armenia declared its independence on 28 May 1918, but was crushed and divided between Turkish and Soviet forces in 1920, with the area under Soviet control proclaimed a Soviet Socialist Republic. The Soviet government was overthrown by a nationalist revolt in 1921 but reinstated by the Red Army a few months later. In early 1922 Armenia acceded to the USSR.

An Armenian nationalist movement gained power in national elections in mid-1990. In a referendum in 1991, 99 per cent of the electorate voted for independence, which was declared on 21 September 1991. In 1992, a state of emergency was declared as a result of a worsening economic situation and the dispute with Azerbaijan over Nagorny-Karabakh. Prime Minister Vazgen Sarkisian and six other politicians were shot dead in the national assembly during an attempted coup in 1999.

In the 2003 presidential election, Robert Kocharian was re-elected for a second term in the second round of voting. In the legislative election in May 2007, the Republican Party of Armenia (HHK) remained the largest party in the legislature, with about 33 per cent of the vote, and its leader Serzh Sarkisian, prime minister since March 2007, continued in office.

FOREIGN RELATIONS

The longstanding dispute with Azerbaijan over the predominantly Armenian-populated Azeri enclave of Nagorny-Karabakh escalated in May 1992 into war, when ethnic Armenian Nagorno-Karabakh forces, supported by Armenia, breached Azerbaijan's defences to form a land bridge to Armenia. By the end of summer 1992, all of Nagorny-Karabakh was under Armenian control, and by the end of 1993 all Azeri territory that separated Nagorny-Karabakh from Armenia and all mountainous Azeri territory around Nagorny-Karabakh was under the control of the Armenians. Armenia claims this territory as historically native land arbitrarily given to Azerbaijan by Stalin in 1921–2. A ceasefire agreement between Armenia, Azerbaijan and Nagorny-Karabakh was reached in 1994, and talks mediated by the Organisation for Security and Cooperation in Europe continue to seek a peaceful resolution to the dispute.

POLITICAL SYSTEM

The 1995 constitution was amended by national referendum in November 2005. The president is directly elected for a five-year term, renewable only once. The unicameral *Azgayin Joghov* (national assembly) has 131 members who are directly elected for a four-year term.

HEAD OF STATE

President, Robert Kocharian, *elected* 30 March 1998, *re-elected* 5 March 2003

SELECTED GOVERNMENT MEMBERS *as at May 2007*

Prime Minister, Serzh Sarkisian
Defence, Col.-Gen. Mikael Arutyunyan
Finance and Economy, Vardan Khachatrian
Foreign Affairs, Vardan Oskanian

EMBASSY OF THE REPUBLIC OF ARMENIA
25A Cheniston Gardens, London W8 6TG
T 020-7938 5435 E armemb@armenianembassyuk.com
Ambassador Extraordinary and Plenipotentiary, HE Dr Vahe Gabrielyan, *apptd* 2003

BRITISH EMBASSY
Baghramyan Ave 24, Yerevan 0019
T (+374) (10) 264 301 E britemb@areminco.com
Ambassador Extraordinary and Plenipotentiary, HE Anthony Cantor, *apptd* 2006

BRITISH COUNCIL
c/o The British Embassy
T (+374) (56) 9923 W www.britishcouncil.org/armenia
Director (acting), Dr Nigel Townson

DEFENCE

The army has 110 main battle tanks, 104 armoured infantry fighting vehicles and 136 armoured personnel carriers. The air force has 16 combat aircraft and 8 armed helicopters.

Russia maintains 3,500 army personnel in Armenia. An agreement on military cooperation with Russia was signed in 1996 which paved the way for joint military exercises. A protocol was also signed on the establishment of coalition troops in Transcaucasia and the planned use of Russian and Armenian armed forces as part of coalition troops in cases of mutual interest. In 2001 Russian president Vladimir Putin signed a federal law relating to an agreement between the Russian Federation and the Republic of Armenia on the joint planning of the use of troops (forces) in the interests of joint security provision. This stipulates measures to prevent the use by third countries of the territory of Armenia for purposes that may inflict damage on Russian national interests.

MILITARY BUDGET – US$194m (2006)
MILITARY PERSONNEL – 43,641: army 40,421, air force 3,220; paramilitaries 4,748
CONSCRIPTION DURATION – 24 months

ECONOMY AND TRADE

The economy experienced a severe decline following the break-up of the USSR in 1991, adding to existing problems arising from the 1988 earthquake and subsequently exacerbated by the trade embargos imposed by Azerbaijan and Turkey over the Nagorny-Karabakh conflict, both of which are still in place. An economic liberalisation programme initiated in 1994 has brought some stability and sustained high growth rates, although unemployment and poverty are still widespread, resulting in high levels of emigration by younger adults.

Armenia has a strong agricultural sector, although this is in need of modernisation. It produces fruit, vegetables and livestock as cash crops, and grain. There are large mineral deposits, including copper ore and molybdenum. Industry is diversified and most small and medium-sized enterprises are now privatised. The main activities are diamond-processing; the production of chemicals, industrial machinery and vehicles, textiles and clothing; microelectronics and software development; and food processing. The constraining energy shortages of the mid-1990s were overcome by reopening the nuclear power plant at Metsamor. This has enabled Armenia to become an energy exporter, but there is international pressure to close the plant because of the earthquake risks in the area.

The trade deficit is partly offset by international aid and remittances from citizens working abroad. The main trading partners are Russia, Belgium, Israel and other EU and neighbouring states. Principal exports are diamonds, foodstuffs, mineral products and energy. The main imports are natural gas, petrol, tobacco products, foodstuffs and diamonds.

GNI – US$4,400m; US$1,470 per capita (2005)
ANNUAL AVERAGE GROWTH OF GDP – 13.9 per cent (2005 est)
INFLATION RATE – 0.6 per cent (2005 est)
UNEMPLOYMENT – 31.6 per cent (2004 est)
TOTAL EXTERNAL DEBT – US$1,819m (2005)
IMPORTS – US$1,770m (2005)
EXPORTS – US$950m (2005)

BALANCE OF PAYMENTS
Trade – US$588m deficit (2005)
Current Account – US$193m deficit (2005)

Trade with UK	*2005*	*2006*
Imports from UK	£5,104,000	£11,084,000
Exports to UK	£392,000	£2,622,000

EDUCATION AND HEALTH

State education is free and compulsory for all children aged seven to 14. Children attend primary school for three years, until the age of nine, then progress on to secondary school for five years, until the age of 14. At the end of intermediate school a certificate of basic education is awarded. Senior secondary school may be attended for two years from the ages of 14 to 16.
LITERACY RATE – 99.4 per cent (2004 est)
GROSS ENROLMENT RATIO (percentage of relevant age group) – primary 94 per cent; secondary 88 per cent; tertiary 28 per cent (2005 est)
HEALTH EXPENDITURE (per capita) – US$63 (2004)
HOSPITAL BEDS (per 1,000 people) – 4.4 (2000–5)

MEDIA

Armenia has more than 40 private television stations, which operate alongside two public networks. The main Russian television channels are also available. Television and radio are both controlled by the state and all print and broadcast media are obliged to register with the ministry of justice. Libel and defamation are punishable by prison terms. Newspapers have limited influence and tend to be owned by wealthy individuals and political parties.

AUSTRALIA

Commonwealth of Australia

AREA – 7,686,850 sq. km
CAPITAL – Canberra, in the Australian Capital Territory; population, 322,500 (2003 est). It has been the seat of government since 1927
MAJOR CITIES – Sydney; Melbourne; Brisbane; Perth, including Fremantle; Adelaide
CURRENCY – Australian dollar ($A) of 100 cents
POPULATION – 20,264,082 rising at 0.85 per cent per year (2006 est) of which 458,520 are of Aboriginal and Torres Strait Islander origin (2001 est)
RELIGION – Roman Catholicism (26 per cent), other Christian denominations (47 per cent), Buddhism (2 per cent), Islam (1 per cent) (est); 15 per cent is estimated to be atheist
LANGUAGE – English (official), Chinese, Italian
POPULATION DENSITY – 3 per sq. km (2005)
URBAN POPULATION – 92.7 per cent (2005 est)
MEDIAN AGE (years) – 36.9 (2006 est)
NATIONAL ANTHEM – 'Advance Australia Fair'
NATIONAL DAY – 26 January (Australia Day)
LIFE EXPECTANCY (years) – 80.5 (2006 est)
MORTALITY RATE – 7.51 (2006 est)
BIRTH RATE – 12.14 (2006 est)
INFANT MORTALITY RATE – 4.63 (2006 est)
DEATH PENALTY – No (abolished 1985)
CPI SCORE – 8.7 (2006)

CLIMATE AND TERRAIN

Australia is a continent, the world's sixth-largest country and home to a wide variety of landscapes and weather conditions. The interior is dominated by hot deserts and is only thinly populated. The eastern and south-eastern coastlines are the most densely populated areas and feature mountains, flat golden beaches and rainforests. The highest point of elevation is 2,229m (Mount Kosciuszko) and the lowest is −16m (Lake Eyre). The summer begins in December, the winter in June, the spring in September and the autumn in March. Average temperatures range from 0°C to 34°C.

HISTORY AND POLITICS

The Aboriginals are thought to have arrived in Australia from south-east Asia *c.*40,000 years ago. Europeans first discovered Australia in the 17th century. Its eastern coast was claimed by Capt. James Cook on behalf of Britain in 1770 and became a penal colony; Tasmania, Western Australia, South Australia, Victoria and Queensland were established as colonies between 1825 and 1859. The individual colonies became self-governing from the 1850s onwards and were federated as the Commonwealth of Australia on 1 January 1901, at which time Australia gained dominion status within the British Empire. Australia became independent within the British Commonwealth under the 1931 Statute of Westminster. Following a referendum in 1967, the Aboriginal population was granted full political rights. In 1986, the Australia Act was passed, which abolished the remaining legislative, executive and judicial links to the UK while retaining the British monarch as head of state. In 1998, the Constitutional Convention voted to sever constitutional links with the British monarchy, but a national referendum in 1999 on the proposal to make Australia a republic was defeated, with 45.3 per cent voting in favour and 54.7 per cent against.

The 2004 general election was won by the ruling Liberal Party/National Party coalition with 46.4 per cent of the vote and a total of 87 seats in the house of representatives.

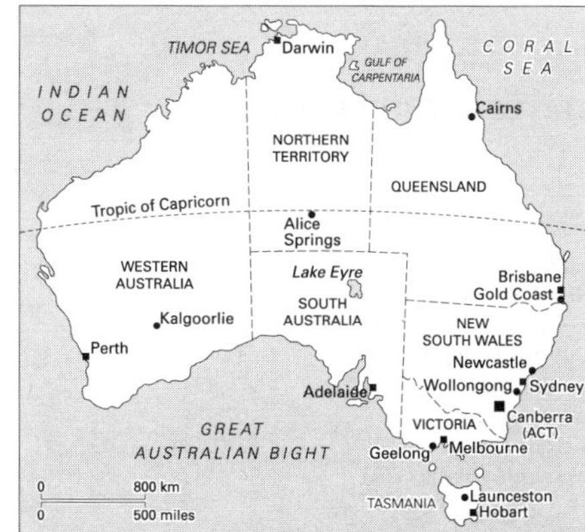

POLITICAL SYSTEM
The Commonwealth of Australia is a federation of six states and two territories. Executive power is vested in the sovereign, who is represented by the governor-general, assisted by a federal government. Under the constitution, the powers of the federal government are defined, and residuary legislative power remains with the states. The right of a state to legislate on any matter is not abrogated except in connection with matters exclusively under federal control, but where a state law is inconsistent with a law of the Commonwealth, the latter prevails to the extent of the inconsistency.

Parliament consists of Queen Elizabeth II, the senate and the house of representatives. The constitution provides that the number of members of the house of representatives shall be, as nearly as practicable, twice the number of senators. Members of the senate are elected for six years by universal suffrage, half the members retiring every third year, except in the Australian Capital Territory and the Northern Territory, where members are elected for a three-year term. Each of the six states returns 12 senators, and the Australian Capital Territory and the Northern Territory two each. The house of representatives, directly elected for a maximum of three years, contains members proportionate to the population, with a minimum of five members for each state. There are now 150 members in the house of representatives, including two members for the Northern Territory and two for the Australian Capital Territory.

The federal court of Australia has jurisdiction mainly in areas of civil law and as a court of appeal from state and territory courts in some cases. The high court of Australia has jurisdiction mainly in areas of constitutional law, inter-state cases and external relations, and hears appeals from the federal court and from the supreme courts of states and territories.
Governor-General, Maj.-Gen. Michael Jeffery (retd) AC, CVO, MC, *assumed office* 11 August 2003

SELECTED GOVERNMENT MEMBERS *as at May 2007*
Prime Minister, John Howard
Deputy Prime Minister, Mark Vaile
Defence, Brendan Nelson
Foreign Affairs, Alexander Downer
Treasurer, Peter Costello

AUSTRALIAN HIGH COMMISSION
Australia House, Strand, London WC2B 4LA
T 020-7379 4334 W www.uk.embassy.gov.au
High Commissioner, HE Hon. Richard Alston, *apptd* 2005

GOVERNMENT OFFICES
New South Wales, Australia Centre, Strand, London WC2B 4LG T 020-7887 5871 *Director,* Leanne Grogan
Queensland, 392 Strand, London WC2R 0LZ T 020-7836 1333 *Agent-General,* John Dawson
South Australia, Australia Centre, Strand, London WC2B 4LG T 020-7836 3455 *Agent-General,* Maurice de Rohan
Victoria, Australia Centre, Strand, London WC2B 4LG T 020-7836 2656 *Agent-General,* David Buckingham
Western Australia, Australia Centre, Strand, London WC2B 4LG T 020-7240 2881 *Agent-General,* Noel Ashcroft

BRITISH HIGH COMMISSION
Commonwealth Avenue, Yarralumla, Canberra, ACT 2600
T (+61) (2) 6270 6666 E bhc.canberra@uk.emb.gov.au
W www.uk.emb.gov.au
High Commissioner, HE Helen Liddell, *apptd* 2005

BRITISH COUNCIL
PO Box 88, Edgecliff, Sydney, NSW 2027
T (+61) (2) 9326 2022 W www.britishcouncil.org/au
Director, Christopher Wade

FEDERAL STRUCTURE
Each state has its own constitution, executive, legislature and judicature. Executive authority is vested in a governor (appointed by the crown), assisted by a council of ministers or executive council. Each state has a legislative council and a legislative assembly or house of assembly which are elected for four-year terms, except Queensland, the Northern Territory and the Australian Capital Territory which have a legislative assembly only.

DEFENCE
The army has 119 main battle tanks and 740 armoured personnel carriers. The navy has 6 submarines, 13 frigates, 13 patrol and coastal vessels and 46 armed helicopters. There are bases at Sydney, Stirling, Cairns, Darwin, Flinders, Jervis Bay and Nowra. The air force has 156 combat aircraft.
MILITARY EXPENDITURE – US$15,500m (2005)
MILITARY PERSONNEL – 51,610: army 25,259, navy 12,681, air force 13,670

ECONOMY AND TRADE
Australia has a highly diversified free-market economy that saw strong growth in the 1990s. The economy remains robust, with low inflation and a government budget surplus, although the trade deficit has grown in

STATES AND TERRITORIES

	Area (sq. km)	*Population (2004 est)*	*Capital*	*Governor (2006)*
Australian Capital Territory (ACT)	2,349	324,021	Canberra	–
New South Wales (NSW)	801,349	6,371,745	Sydney	Prof. Marie Bashir, AC
Northern Territory (NT)	1,352,158	199,913	Darwin*	Ted Egan, OAM†
Queensland (Qld)	1,734,157	3,882,037	Brisbane	Quentin Bryce, AC
South Australia (SA)	985,335	1,534,250	Adelaide	Rear Adm. Kevin Scarce, AC, MBE
Tasmania (Tas.)	67,914	482,128	Hobart	William Cox, AC
Victoria (Vic.)	227,594	4,972,779	Melbourne	David de Kretser, AC
Western Australia (WA)	2,534,483	1,982,204	Perth	Ken Michael, AC

* Seat of administration † Administrator

ecent years and agricultural output, a key export sector, dropped by about 20 per cent in 2006 owing to severe drought. In 2005, the service sector contributed 70 per cent of GDP and employed 75 per cent of the workforce; industry accounted for 26 per cent of GDP and 21 per cent of labour; and agriculture contributed 4 per cent of GDP and employed 3.6 per cent of the workforce.

A wide range of crops are grown owing to the diversity of climatic and soil conditions, although most are onfined to specific regions. Scant or erratic rainfall, limited scope for irrigation and unsuitable soils or opography have restricted intensive agriculture, although wheat is a major export. Cattle and sheep ranching is widespread and significant products include meat, meat derivatives, wool and dairy products.

Significant natural resources include bauxite, coal, opper, diamonds, gold, iron ore, lead, mineral salts, nickel, silver, tin, tungsten, uranium, zinc, oil and natural gas. The main industrial activities are mining, the production of industrial and transport equipment, hemicals and steel, and food processing. Production and processing of hydrocarbons are expected to increase once the exploitation of oil and gas fields in the Timor Sea begins.

Over the past 20 years, the focus of Australia's trade, ike its foreign policy, has shifted from Europe to the USA and, in particular, the Asia and Pacific region. It is a leading member of the Asia-Pacific Economic Co-operation Forum and is negotiating free-trade agreements with China and the ASEAN countries. Major trading partners include Japan, USA, China, South Korea, New Zealand, Singapore, Germany and India. The chief exports are coal, gold, meat, wool, alumina, iron ore, wheat, machinery and transport equipment. The main imports are machinery and transport equipment, computers, office and telecommunications equipment, crude oil and petroleum products.

GNI – US$673,200m; US$33,1205 per capita (2005)
ANNUAL AVERAGE GROWTH OF GDP – 2.7 per cent (2005 est)
INFLATION RATE – 2.7 per cent (2005 est)
UNEMPLOYMENT – 5.1 per cent (2005 est)
TOTAL EXTERNAL DEBT – US$323,400m (2005 est)
IMPORTS – US$125,000m (2005)
EXPORTS – US$106,000m (2005)

BALANCE OF PAYMENTS
Trade – US$13,672m deficit (2005)
Current Account – US$42,084m deficit (2005)

Trade with UK	*2005*	*2006*
Imports from UK	£2,520,790,000	£2,420,322,000
Exports to UK	£2,115,655,000	£2,141,266,000

COMMUNICATIONS

Most long-distance internal travel is by air or road. There are 455 airports and airfields. Road and rail networks are concentrated in the more densely populated areas of the east and south, and around Perth in the west. Elsewhere, roads are more usual than railways, and both skirt the deserts of the interior, apart from a few transcontinental routes. There are six government-owned railway systems, and in 2005 there was a total of 47,738km of railway track. Most heavy freight is moved by road trains (trucks hauling two or three trailers) which measure up to 45m in length. There are 810,641km of highways. The 11 major ports and terminals, including all the state capitals except Hobart, and there are private mining ports at Gove and Groote Eylandt in the Northern Territory. Mobile telephone distribution has grown rapidly to about 18 million in 2005, exceeding fixed-line usage. There were around 14.6 million internet users in 2006.

AREA AFFECTED BY FOREST FIRES (million ha)

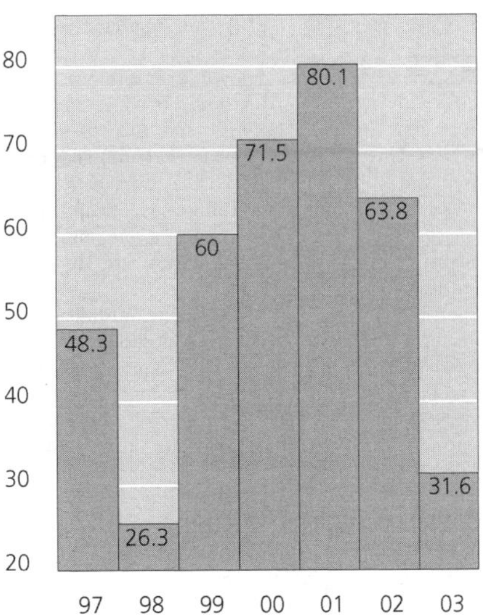

Source: UN Food and Agriculture Organisation

EDUCATION AND HEALTH

Education is administered by the state and is compulsory between the ages of six and 15 (16 in Tasmania). It is available at government schools controlled by the state education department and at private or independent schools, some of which are denominational.

GROSS ENROLMENT RATIO (percentage of relevant age group) – primary 103 per cent; secondary 149 per cent; tertiary 72 per cent (2005 est)
HEALTH EXPENDITURE (per capita) – US$3,123 (2005)
HOSPITAL BEDS (per 1,000 people) – 7.4 (2000–5)

MEDIA

Australia's leading newspapers are *The Sydney Morning Herald, Herald Sun, The Australian* and *The Daily Telegraph*. There is an established tradition of public service broadcasting (via the Australian Broadcasting Corporation and the Special Broadcasting Service) and of commercial television (Seven Network, Nine Network, Ten Network). Commercial broadcasters are required to transmit a minimum percentage of Australian programming. Media tycoon Rupert Murdoch owns News Corporation and a considerable subscription-based television empire.

CULTURE

Indigenous Aboriginal culture was superseded on colonisation by European culture and latterly by influences from the USA, but Australia has been very successful in exporting modern aspects of its culture.

Australia's most decorated authors are Nobel Prize winner Patrick White (1912–90) and double Booker Prize winner Peter Carey (*b.* 1943). Germaine Greer (*b.* 1939) and Clive James (*b.* 1939) are respected cultural commentators.

The country's cinema enjoyed a renaissance in the 1980s, with acclamation for both art-house and mass market films, eg the *Mad Max* and *Crocodile Dundee* franchises. Director Baz Luhrmann (*b.* 1962) and actors Russell Crowe (*b.* 1964) and Nicole Kidman (*b.* 1967) are established figures in Hollywood. Soap operas *Neighbours* and *Home and Away* and the programmes of naturalist Steve Irwin (1962–2006) are broadcast internationally.

Sport is an integral part of the culture. Australian rules football and cricket are the country's most popular sports, but it takes part at international level in most major team sports, in addition to producing individual participants such as swimmer Ian Thorpe (*b.* 1982), athlete Cathy Freeman (*b.* 1973) and tennis players Rod Laver (*b.* 1938) and Roy Emerson (*b.* 1936).

EXTERNAL TERRITORIES

ASHMORE AND CARTIER ISLANDS

Ashmore Islands (known as Middle, East and West Islands) and Cartier Island are situated in the Indian Ocean 850km and 790km west of Darwin respectively. The uninhabited islands are a nature and marine reserve. The islands became an Australian territory in 1933, and are administered through the Department of Transport and Regional Services.

THE AUSTRALIAN ANTARCTIC TERRITORY

The Australian Antarctic Territory was established in 1933 and comprises all the islands and territories, other than Adélie Land, that are situated south of latitude 60° S. and lying between 160° E. longitude and 45° E. longitude. The territory is administered by the Antarctic Division of the Department of the Environment and Water Resources. (*see also* The Antarctic.)

CHRISTMAS ISLAND

AREA – 135 sq. km
POPULATION – 1,493 (2006 est)

Christmas Island is situated in the Indian Ocean about 1,408 km north-west of North West Cape in Western Australia. The island was annexed by Britain in 1888, but sovereignty was transferred to Australia in 1958 and the island is administered through the Department of Transport and Regional Services. The Shire of Christmas Island (SOCI) is responsible for municipal functions and services on the island; it has nine members directly elected for a four-year term. The main industry is phosphate mining. A space satellite launching facility is currently being built on the island for the Asia Pacific Space Centre.

COCOS (KEELING) ISLANDS

AREA – 14 sq. km
POPULATION – 574 (2006 est)

The Cocos (Keeling) Islands are two separate atolls (North Keeling Island and, 24km to the south, the main atoll) comprising some 27 small coral islands, situated in the Indian Ocean, about 2,950km north-west of Perth. The main islands of the southern atoll are West Island (about 9km in length); Home Island, where 80 per cent of the population lives, including most of the Cocos Malay community; Direction Island; Horsburgh Island and South Island.

The islands were declared a British possession in 1857 and became an Australian territory in 1955. All land in the islands was granted to George Clunies-Ross and his heirs by Queen Victoria in 1886. The Australian government purchased most of the Clunies-Ross land and property in 1978, and the remainder in 1984 and 1993. The land is held in trust for the residents, with the local government body, the Shire of the Cocos (Keeling) Islands, as trustee. In 1984 the Cocos community, in a UN-supervised Act of Self-Determination, voted to integrate with Australia. The islands are administered by the Australian government through the Department of Transport and Regional Services.

CORAL SEA ISLANDS TERRITORY

The Coral Sea Islands Territory lies east of Queensland, between the Great Barrier Reef and longitude 156° 06′ E., and between latitudes 12° and 24° S. It comprises scattered islands, spread over a sea area of 780,000 sq. km. The islands are formed mainly of coral and sand, and most are extremely small. There is a manned meteorological station on Willis Island but the remaining islands are uninhabited. The Territory was established in 1969 and is administered through the Department of Transport and Regional Services.

HEARD ISLAND AND MCDONALD ISLANDS

The Territory of Heard Island and the McDonald Islands, about 4,100km south-west of Perth, comprises all the islands and rocks lying between 52° 30′ and 53° 30′ S. latitude and 72° and 74° 30′ E. longitude. The subantarctic islands were discovered in the 1850s and transferred from British to Australian administration in 1947; they are now administered by the Antarctic Division of the Department of the Environment and Water Resources.

NORFOLK ISLAND

AREA – 34.6 sq. km
POPULATION – 1,828 (2006 est)
SEAT OF GOVERNMENT – Kingston

Norfolk Island is situated in the South Pacific Ocean, about 1,600km north-east of Sydney. It is around 8km long by 5km wide. The climate is mild and subtropical.

Discovered by Captain Cook in 1774, the island served as a penal colony from 1788 to 1814 and from 1825 to 1855. In 1856, 194 descendants of the *Bounty* mutineers accepted an invitation to leave Pitcairn and settle on Norfolk Island.

The island has had a substantial degree of internal self-government since 1979, when the nine-member legislative assembly was established. The Administrator represents the federal government and reports to the Australian Minister for Territories, Local Government and Roads. The Australian government intended to change the governance arrangements, on the grounds of financial unsustainability. This was dropped after the island's assembly committed to generate more revenue in late 2006. The economy is heavily dependent on tourism.

AUSTRIA

Republik Österreich – Republic of Austria

AREA – 83,870 sq. km. Neighbours: Czech Republic and Slovakia (north), Italy and Slovenia (south), Hungary (east), Germany (north-west), Switzerland and Liechtenstein (west)
CAPITAL – Vienna; population, 1,651,365 (2006 est)
MAJOR CITIES – Graz; Linz; Salzburg; Innsbruck; Klagenfurt
CURRENCY – Euro (€) of 100 cents
POPULATION – 8,192,880 rising at 0.09 per cent per year (2006 est); Austrians (91.1 per cent), former Yugoslavs (4 per cent), Turks (1.6 per cent)
RELIGION – Roman Catholicism (74 per cent), Protestantism (4 per cent), Islam (4 per cent) (est). It is estimated 12 per cent of the population is atheist
LANGUAGE – German (official nationwide), Slovene, Croatian, Hungarian (each official in different regions)
POPULATION DENSITY – 100 per sq. km (2005)
URBAN POPULATION – 65.8 per cent (2005 est)
MEDIAN AGE (years) – 40.9 (2006 est)
NATIONAL ANTHEM – 'Bundeshymne' ['Federal Hymn']
NATIONAL DAY – 26 October
LIFE EXPECTANCY (years) – 79.07 (2006 est)
MORTALITY RATE – 9.76 (2006 est)
BIRTH RATE – 8.74 (2006 est)
INFANT MORTALITY RATE – 4.6 (2006 est)
DEATH PENALTY – No (abolished 1968)
CPI SCORE – 8.6 (2006)
POPULATION BELOW POVERTY LINE – 5.9 per cent (2004)

CLIMATE AND TERRAIN

The north and east of the landlocked country feature rolling hills, while the west and south contain the Austrian Alps, famous as a winter sports destination. The highest point of elevation is 3,798m (Grossglockner) and the lowest is 115m (Lake Neusiedl). Around 47 per cent of the land area is forested. There is a temperate climate, with temperature averages ranging from 2°C in January to 20°C in July.

HISTORY AND POLITICS

The Austrian state dates back to the eighth century AD when Charlemagne conquered the territory and founded the *Ostmark,* the eastern march of the Holy Roman Empire, which had been settled from the sixth century onwards by Germanic tribes. It became a duchy and in 1282 passed to the Habsburg dynasty, which established an empire that united much of central Europe, including present-day Austria and Hungary, and established hegemony over the other German states. Hegemony was lost to Prussia in the 19th century, when growing Hungarian nationalism also led to the establishment of the dual monarchy of Austria-Hungary. The assassination of the heir to the throne in 1914 triggered the First World War, towards the end of which the Austro-Hungarian Empire collapsed, and most of the German-speaking lands became the Republic of Austria in November 1918. In March 1938, Austria was incorporated into Nazi Germany (the *Anschluss*) under the name *Ostmark.* After the Second World War, the Republic of Austria was reconstituted within its 1937 frontiers and a freely elected government took office in December 1945. The country was divided into four zones, each occupied by the UK, USA, USSR or France, while Vienna was jointly occupied by the four powers.

In 1955 the occupying powers withdrew, recognising Austria as a sovereign, independent and democratic state with the same frontiers as on 1 January 1938. Austria joined the European Union in 1995. The national assembly ratified the EU constitution in May 2005.

The 2004 presidential election was won by Heinz Fischer of the Social Democrats (SPÖ). In the October 2006 legislative elections, the Social Democrats (SPÖ) became the largest party but without an outright majority. After weeks of negotiations, it formed a coalition in January 2007 with the Austrian People's Party (ÖVP), the main partner in the previous coalition government.

POLITICAL SYSTEM

Under the 1955 constitution, the federal president is directly elected for a six-year term, renewable only once. There is a bicameral legislature, the *Parlament,* consisting of the *Nationalrat* (national council), which has 183 members directly elected for a four-year term, and the *Bundesrat* (federal council), which has 62 members elected for terms of various lengths by the provincial assemblies. There is a 4 per cent qualification for parliamentary representation. Some powers may only be exercised by both houses acting together as the *Bundesversammlung* (federal assembly). The executive is headed by the federal chancellor, who is appointed by the president.

HEAD OF STATE

Federal President, Heinz Fischer, *took office* 8 July 2004

SELECTED GOVERNMENT MEMBERS *as at May 2007*

Chancellor, Alfred Gusenbauer
Vice-Chancellor, Minister for Finance, Wilhelm Molterer
Defence, Norbert Darabos
Foreign Affairs, Ursula Plassnik
Interior, Günter Platter

EMBASSY OF AUSTRIA

18 Belgrave Mews West, London SW1X 8HU
T 020-7344 3250 W www.bmaa.gv.at/london
Ambassador Extraordinary and Plenipotentiary, HE Gabriele Matzner-Holzer, *apptd* 2005

BRITISH EMBASSY

Jaurèsgasse 10, 1030 Vienna
T (+43) (1) 716 130 E britem@netway.at
W www.britishembassy.at
Ambassador Extraordinary and Plenipotentiary, HE John Macgregor, CVO, *apptd* 2003

BRITISH COUNCIL

Siebensterngasse 21, 1070 Vienna
T (+43) (1) 533 2616 W www.britishcouncil.org/austria
Regional Director, Terry Toney

FEDERAL STRUCTURE

There are nine provinces: Burgenland, Carinthia, Lower Austria, Salzburg, Styria, Tirol, Upper Austria, Vienna and Vorarlberg.

DEFENCE

The army has 114 main battle tanks, 112 armoured infantry fighting vehicles and 684 armoured personnel carriers. The air force has 40 combat aircraft.
MILITARY BUDGET – US$2,320m (2006)

MILITARY PERSONNEL – 39,600: army 32,900, air force 6,700
CONSCRIPTION DURATION – Eight months, or seven months plus refresher training

ECONOMY AND TRADE

Austria has a well-developed market economy which is closely linked to other EU states. Its proximity to the new EU members in central, east and south-east Europe makes for strong commercial links with those countries and is also an attraction for foreign investors. Rates of growth have been low in recent years, reflecting the trend for Europe as a whole, and a small budget deficit developed in 2006 owing to reductions in taxes.

The services sector contributes most to GDP (68 per cent in 2005), followed by industry (30 per cent) and the small but highly developed agricultural sector (2 per cent). The main industries include construction, manufacturing of machinery, vehicles and parts, food processing, timber and wood processing, production of metals and metal goods, chemicals, paper and cardboard and communications equipment, and tourism. Tourism makes a valuable contribution to foreign exchange receipts.

The main trading partners are other EU states, the USA and Switzerland. Principal exports include the goods produced by the main industries, iron and steel, textiles and clothing, other finished goods and raw materials. The main imports are machinery and equipment, motor vehicles, chemical products, metal goods, foodstuffs, oil and oil products.

GNI – US$306,200m; US$37,190 per capita (2005)
ANNUAL AVERAGE GROWTH OF GDP – 1.8 per cent (2005 est)
INFLATION RATE – 2.3 per cent (2005 est)
UNEMPLOYMENT – 5.2 per cent (2005 est)
TOTAL EXTERNAL DEBT – US$510,600m (2005 est)
IMPORTS – US$47,200m (2005)
EXPORTS – US$46,400m (2005)

BALANCE OF PAYMENTS
Trade – US$3,427m surplus (2005)
Current Account – US$3,848m surplus (2005)

Trade with UK	*2005*	*2006*
Imports from UK	£1,303,538,000	£1,615,600,000
Exports to UK	£2,086,087,000	£2,369,100,000

COMMUNICATIONS

Although landlocked, Austria is strategically located in central Europe because of the navigability of the Danube and the presence of traversable passes over the Alps. Of the 425km of waterways, 358km are navigable and there is considerable trade through the Danube ports (Vienna, Krems, Enns, Linz) from both local and foreign shipping. There are 133,718km of roads and a network of 1,677km of *Autobahn* between major cities that also links up with German and Italian networks. The railways are state-owned and comprised 6,011km of track in 2005. The main airports are at Vienna, Graz, Innsbruck, Klagenfurt, Linz and Salzburg. Mobile telephone distribution was over 8 million in 2005, and there were 4.6 million internet users.

EDUCATION AND HEALTH

Education is free and compulsory between the ages of six and 15 and there are good facilities for secondary, technical and professional education.

GROSS ENROLMENT RATIO (percentage of relevant age group) – primary 106 per cent; secondary 101 pe cent; tertiary 50 per cent (2005 est)
HEALTH EXPENDITURE (per capita) – US$3,683 (2004)
HOSPITAL BEDS (per 1,000 people) – 8.3 (2000–5)

MEDIA

The public broadcaster Österreichischer Rundfunk (ÖRF dominated Austrian television and radio for many year but the number of private broadcasters is now increasin By contrast, Austria's print media is largely privatel owned. There are five main daily titles, including *De Standard* and *Neue Kronenzeitung*.

CULTURE

During the 18th, 19th and 20th centuries, Vienna wa one of Europe's greatest cultural centres. Active musician included Haydn (1732–1809), Mozart (1756–91 Beethoven (1770–1827), Mahler (1860–1911 Schoenberg (1874–1951) and the Strauss family. The lat 19th century produced the writers Rilke (1875–1926 and Robert Musil (1880–1942), while notable scientis included psychoanalyst Sigmund Freud (1856–1939 Erwin Schrödinger (1887–1961), who contributed to th development of quantum mechanics, and Gregor Mende (1822–1884) whose experiments with pea plants ar widely believed to be the beginning of modern genetics.

In art, Gustav Klimt's (1862–1918) symbolis paintings are among the most recognisable works in A Nouveau and director Fritz Lang (1890–1976) produce two of the earliest film classics: *Metropolis* (1927) and *M* (1931).

AZERBAIJAN

Azerbaycan Respublikasi – Republic of Azerbaijan

AREA – 86,600 sq. km. Neighbours: Iran (south), Armenia (west), Georgia and Russia (north). The exclave of Naxcivan lies between Armenia and Iran; there is no land link with Azerbaijan.
CAPITAL – Baku (Baki); population, 1,132,800 (2006 est)
MAJOR CITIES – Ganca; Sumqayit
CURRENCY – New Manat of 100 gopik
POPULATION – 7,961,619 rising at 0.66 per cent per year (2006 est); Azeri (90.6 per cent), Dagestani (2.2 per cent). There are more Azeris in Iran than in Azerbaijan
RELIGION – Islam (96 per cent) (est)
LANGUAGE – Azeri (official), Russian, Armenian
POPULATION DENSITY – 101 per sq. km (2005)
URBAN POPULATION – 49.9 per cent (2005 est)
MEDIAN AGE – 27.7 years (2006 est)
NATIONAL ANTHEM – 'Azerbaijan Marsi' ['March of Azerbaijan']
NATIONAL DAY – 28 May (Founding of the Democratic Republic of Azerbaijan)
LIFE EXPECTANCY – 63.85 (2006 est)
MORTALITY RATE – 9.75 (2006 est)
BIRTH RATE – 20.74 (2006 est)
INFANT MORTALITY RATE – 79 (2006 est)
DEATH PENALTY – No (abolished 1998)
CPI SCORE – 2.4 (2006)
POPULATION BELOW POVERTY LINE – 49 per cent (2002 est)

:LIMATE AND TERRAIN

zerbaijan occupies the eastern part of the Caucasus gion of the former Soviet Union, on the western shore f the Caspian Sea. The highest point of elevation is ,485m (Bazarduzu Dagi) while the lowest is −28m :aspian Sea). The north-eastern part of the republic is ken up by the south-eastern end of the main Caucasus dge, its south-western part by the smaller Caucasus hills ıd its south-eastern corner by the spurs of the Talysh idge. Central Azerbaijan is formed by a depression rigated by the River Kura and the lower reaches of its ibutary the Araks. Azerbaijan has a continental climate.

IISTORY AND POLITICS

he Turkic Azeri people formed an independent state in ıe first century BC. By the seventh century AD, this recarious civilisation was invaded by Muslim Arabs who ıtroduced Islam and secured the region as a province of ıe Muslim caliphate. Azerbaijan was invaded by Persia in ıe 16th century. The country was divided during the usso-Persian wars of the early 19th century, the orthern portion (present-day Azerbaijan) becoming part f the Russian Empire and the southern portion emaining Persian and subsequently Iranian.

In 1918 the Azerbaijan Democratic Republic was stablished. It was subsequently overthrown by ommunists and Azerbaijan acceded to the USSR in 922.

In 1990, the Azeri Popular Front took power from the ocal communist party and declared independence from he Soviet Union. Soviet troops restored the communist egime, which declared Azerbaijan's independence in ugust 1991 after the failed coup in Moscow. President :lchibey, elected in 1992, was overthrown in a coup and eplaced by Heydar Aliyev, the former communist party eader, who retained power despite a number of coup ttempts in the mid-1990s. President Aliyev won the ›residential election in 1998, but withdrew from the 2003 presidential race owing to health problems (he died n December 2003) and endorsed the campaign of his on, Ilham, who was elected president. His regime is ›roving to be as authoritarian as that of his father. The 2005 legislative election was won by the ruling New Azerbaijan Party by a large margin; as with all other ›residential and legislative elections since independence, xternal monitors judged that the poll failed to meet nternational democratic standards.

;ECESSION

n 1988 the predominantly Armenian-populated region ›f Nagorny-Karabakh attempted to secede and unite with Armenia, leading to conflict between the separatists and Soviet Azeri forces. This escalated in 1992, when Nagorno-Karabakh forces breached Azeri defences to orm a land bridge between the enclave and Armenia, efore going on to capture all the Azeri territory between Nagorny-Karabakh and Armenia. Although Azeri forces ushed back the Nagorno-Karabakh forces in early 1994, ıbout 16 per cent of Azeri territory remains in separatist control, and Azerbaijan has had to absorb over half a million Azeris displaced from the territory. A ceasefire was agreed in 1994, and has held despite occasional infringements. Peace talks mediated by the OSCE continue to seek a peaceful resolution.

POLITICAL SYSTEM

The 1995 constitution was amended in 2002. The executive president is directly elected for a five-year term; under the 1995 constitution, this was not renewable but a 2002 referendum allowed this proviso to be waived. Legislative power is vested in the unicameral *Milli Majlis* (national assembly), which has 125 members directly elected for a five-year term. The president appoints the prime minister and the cabinet.

HEAD OF STATE
President, Ilham Aliyev, *assumed office* 31 October 2003

SELECTED GOVERNMENT MEMBERS *as at May 2007*
Prime Minister, Artur Rasizade
First Deputy Prime Ministers, Abbas Abbasov; Yakub Abdulla Eyyubov
Deputy Prime Ministers, Elchin Efendiyev; Ali Hasanov; Abid Sarifov
Defence, Lt.-Gen. Safar Abiyev
Finance, Samir Sharifov
Foreign Affairs, Elmar Mammadyarov

EMBASSY OF THE REPUBLIC OF AZERBAIJAN
4 Kensington Court, London W8 5DL
T 020-7938 3412 W www.azembassy.org.uk
Ambassador Extraordinary and Plenipotentiary, HE Rafael Ibrahimov, *apptd* 2001

BRITISH EMBASSY
45 Khagani Street, 1000 Baku 1
T (+994) (12) 497 51 88 E office@britemb.baku.az
W www.britishembassy.az
Ambassador Extraordinary and Plenipotentiary, HE Dr Lawrence Bristow, *apptd* 2004

BRITISH COUNCIL
1 Vali Mammadov Street, Icheri Sheher, Baku AZ1000
T (+994) (12) 497 1593/497 2013
W www.britishcouncil.org/azerbaijan
Director, Andy Williams

DEFENCE

The army has 220 main battle tanks, 127 armoured infantry fighting vehicles and 468 armoured personnel carriers. The navy is based at Baku, with a share of the former Soviet Caspian Fleet Flotilla, comprising six patrol and coastal vessels. The air force has 47 combat aircraft and 15 attack helicopters.
MILITARY EXPENDITURE – US$1,100m (2005 est)
MILITARY PERSONNEL – 66,740: army 56,840, navy 2,000, air force 7,900; paramilitaries 15,000
CONSCRIPTION DURATION – 17 months, but can be extended for ground forces

ECONOMY AND TRADE

Azerbaijan is making the transition from a command to a market economy, but the slow progress is exacerbated by its failure to attract foreign investment in sectors other than energy, and widespread corruption. The economy is dominated by oil and natural gas extraction and related industries, centred in Baku and Sumgait, and exploited with the aid of foreign investment. Oil pipelines (2,436km) link the Azeri oilfields to Black Sea ports in Russia and Georgia, and to the Turkish port of Ceyhan.

Although agriculture contributes only 14 per cent of GDP, it employs over 40 per cent of the workforce. The main crops are cotton, cereals, fruits, vegetables, tea, tobacco and livestock. Around 90 per cent of agricultural land has now been privatised. Industry produces petroleum products, oilfield equipment, steel, iron ore, cement, chemicals, petrochemicals and textiles.

Trade with Russia and other former Soviet republics is declining, while growing with Turkey, Italy and various European countries. Oil and gas constitute 90 per cent of exports, which also include machinery, cotton and foodstuffs. Principal imports are machinery and equipment, oil products, foodstuffs, metals and chemicals.

GNI – US$10,400m; US$1,240 per capita (2005)
ANNUAL AVERAGE GROWTH OF GDP – 26.4 per cent (2005 est)
INFLATION RATE – 9.6 per cent (2005 est)
UNEMPLOYMENT – 1.1 per cent (2005 est)
TOTAL EXTERNAL DEBT – US$1,873m (2005 est)
IMPORTS – US$4,200m (2005)
EXPORTS – US$4,300m (2005)

BALANCE OF PAYMENTS
Trade – US$3,299m surplus (2005)
Current Account – US$167m surplus (2005)

Trade with UK	*2005*	*2006*
Imports from UK	£212,834,000	£474,844,000
Exports to UK	£41,818,000	£232,950,000

COMMUNICATIONS

There are 2,957km of railway track, about half of it electrified, and over 59,000km of roads, though fewer than half are paved. Moscow has agreed to provide S$300m (£150m) for the construction of the Azeri section of the north-south highway between northern and central Europe and the Gulf states. There are 27 airports, of which three (at Baku, Ganca and Naxcivan) accepting international flights, with another two being extended to do so. Baku is the main port. There are ferry links to Turkmenistan.

The telephone system is largely confined to Baku and the main industrial centres, with only about 1,000 main lines in use. Mobile telephone distribution is about double that number, but internet users numbered fewer than 700,000 in 2005.

EDUCATION AND HEALTH

Education up to university level is free.
LITERACY RATE – 98.8 per cent (2004 est)
GROSS ENROLMENT RATIO (percentage of relevant age group) – primary 96 per cent; secondary 83 per cent; tertiary 15 per cent (2005 est)
HEALTH EXPENDITURE (per capita) – US$37 (2004)
HOSPITAL BEDS (per 1,000 people) – 8.3 (2000–5)

MEDIA

The state runs press, television and radio but there is an increasingly successful private sector, boosted by the issue of five new regional television licences in 2002. Media critical of the government have been subjected to harassment. As a requirement of the country's membership of the Council of Europe, a public television and radio service, iTV, was launched in 2005.

THE BAHAMAS

Commonwealth of the Bahamas

AREA – 13,940 sq. km
CAPITAL – Nassau; population, 210,832 (2000)
CURRENCY – Bahamian dollar (B $) of 100 cents
POPULATION – 303,770 rising at 0.64 per cent per year (2006 est)
RELIGION – Protestantism (52 per cent), Roman Catholicism (19 per cent) (est)
LANGUAGE – English (official), Creole
POPULATION DENSITY – 32 per sq. km (2005)
URBAN POPULATION – 90 per cent (2005 est)
MEDIAN AGE (years) – 27.8 (2006 est)
NATIONAL ANTHEM – 'March on, Bahamaland'
NATIONAL DAY – 10 July (Independence Day)
LIFE EXPECTANCY (years) – 65.6 (2006 est)
MORTALITY RATE – 9.05 (2006 est)
BIRTH RATE – 17.57 (2006 est)
INFANT MORTALITY RATE – 24.68 (2006 est)
HIV/AIDS ADULT PREVALENCE – 3 per cent (2003 est)
DEATH PENALTY – Yes
POPULATION BELOW POVERTY LINE – 9.3 per cent (2004)
MILITARY BUDGET – US$42m (2006 est)
MILITARY PERSONNEL – 860

CLIMATE AND TERRAIN

The Bahamas extend in a chain running from the coast of Florida in the north-west almost to Hispaniola in the south-east. The group consists of more than 700 islands and 2,400 cays, all low-lying; the highest point is 63m at Mount Alvernia, Cat Island. The principal islands include Abaco, Acklins, Andros, Berry Islands, Bimini, Cat Island, Crooked Island, Eleuthera, Exuma, Grand Bahama, Harbour Island, Inagua, Long Island, Mayaguana, New Providence (on which the capital, Nassau, is located), Ragged Island, Rum Cay, San Salvador and Spanish Wells. The 14 major islands are inhabited, as are a few of the smaller islands. The climate is semitropical. The hurricane season is June to November.

HISTORY AND POLITICS

The Bahamas was discovered by Columbus in 1492, settled by the British in the 17th century and became a crown colony in 1717. Taken over in 1782 by the Spanish, the treaty of Versailles in 1783 restored them to the British. The Bahamas became self-governing in 1964 and gained their independence on 10 July 1973.

The Progressive Liberal Party (PLP) held power for 25 years until the Free National Movement (FNM) won an absolute majority in the 1992 general election. Power has subsequently alternated between the two parties, and the PLP was defeated in the May 2007 legislative election, which the FNM won with 23 seats.

POLITICAL SYSTEM

The head of state is the British monarch, who is represented by a governor-general. The bicameral parliament has a senate of 16 appointed members and a house of assembly of 40 members, who are directly elected for a five-year term.

Governor-General, Arthur Dion Hanna, *apptd* 2006

SELECTED GOVERNMENT MEMBERS *as at May 2007*
Prime Minister, Finance, Hubert Ingraham
Deputy Prime Minister, Foreign Affairs, Brent Symonette
National Security and Immigration, Tommy Turnquest
Attorney-General, Claire Hepburn

BAHAMAS HIGH COMMISSION
10 Chesterfield Street, London W1J 5JL
T 020-7408 4488 E information@bahamashclondon.net

'igh Commissioner, HE Basil O'Brien, CMG, *apptd* 1999

RITISH HIGH COMMISSION
'igh Commissioner, Jeremy Michael Cresswell, *apptd* 005, resident in Kingston, Jamaica

CONOMY AND TRADE

he Bahamas have enjoyed sustained economic growth in cent decades owing to the development of tourism and ffshore financial services. The services sector contributes 0 per cent of GDP and employs about 55 per cent of the bour force. The lack of diversification makes the conomy vulnerable to fluctuations in these sectors, and e growth rate slowed in the period 2000–3, when ghter financial regulations were introduced, causing a umber of international businesses to relocate elsewhere, nd because of fewer visitors from the USA (over 80 per ent of all visitors) since 2001.

Manufacturing and agriculture account for 10 per cent f GDP and employment. Agricultural production is ainly of fresh vegetables, fruit, meat and eggs. Mineral eserves are exploited to produce aragonite and salt for xport. Other industrial products include cement, rum, harmaceuticals, steel pipes and the provision of oil trans-hipment services.

The main trading partners are Spain, the USA, South orea and Brazil. The chief exports are mineral products nd salt, animal products, rum, chemicals, fruit and egetables. Imports are chiefly machinery and transport quipment, manufactured articles, chemicals, fuel and oodstuffs.

NI – US$4,700m (2003); US$15,110 per capita (2003)
NNUAL AVERAGE GROWTH OF GDP – 3.7 per cent (2005 est)
NFLATION RATE – 1.2 per cent (2005 est)
JNEMPLOYMENT – 10.2 per cent (2005 est)
OTAL EXTERNAL DEBT – US$342.6m (2004 est)
MPORTS – US$2,100m (2005)
XPORTS – US$500m (2005)

BALANCE OF PAYMENTS
rade – US$1,340m deficit (2004)
urrent Account – US$203m deficit (2004)

Trade with UK	*2005*	*2006*
Imports from UK	£36,821,000	£61,671,000
Exports to UK	£44,608,000	£74,381,000

COMMUNICATIONS

The main ports are Nassau (New Providence), Freeport nd South Riding Point (Grand Bahama). International air ervices are operated from Andros, Chubb Cay, Eleuthera, xuma, Grand Bahama and New Providence. More than 0 smaller airports and landing strips facilitate services etween the islands, mainly provided by Bahamasair, the ational carrier. The Bahamas have some 2,693km of oads, 1,546km of which are paved. There are no ailways.

BAHRAIN

Mamlakat al-Bahrayn – Kingdom of Bahrain

AREA – 665 sq. km
CAPITAL – Manama; population, 143,035 (2001)
MAJOR TOWNS – Muharraq; Rifa; Hammad
CURRENCY – Bahraini dinar (BD) of 1,000 fils
POPULATION – 698,585 rising at 1.45 per cent per year (2006 est); Bahraini (62.4 per cent). The rest of the population consists of an expatriate minority, including large numbers of Europeans and South Asians
RELIGION – Islam (98 per cent) (est)
LANGUAGE – Arabic (official), English, Farsi, Urdu
POPULATION DENSITY – 1,023 per sq. km (2005)
URBAN POPULATION – 90.2 per cent (2005 est)
MEDIAN AGE (years) – 29.4 (2006 est)
NATIONAL ANTHEM – 'Bahrainona' ['Our Bahrain']
NATIONAL DAY – 16 December
LIFE EXPECTANCY (years) – 74.45 (2006 est)
MORTALITY RATE – 4.14 (2006 est)
BIRTH RATE – 17.8 (2006 est)
INFANT MORTALITY RATE – 16.8 (2006 est)
DEATH PENALTY – Yes
CPI SCORE – 5.7 (2006)
LITERACY RATE – 87.7 per cent (2004 est)

CLIMATE AND TERRAIN

Bahrain consists of a group of 33 low-lying islands situated approximately halfway down the Gulf, some 32km off the east coast of Saudi Arabia. The largest of these, Bahrain Island, is about 48km long and 16km wide at its broadest. The capital, Manama, is situated on the north shore. The elevation extremes range from 122m at the highest point (Jabal ad Dukhan) to 0m at the lowest (Persian Gulf). The climate is hot and humid, with average temperatures ranging from 20°C to 40°C and little rainfall.

HISTORY AND POLITICS

Bahrain was ruled by Persia (Iran) from 1602 until it was ousted in 1783 by the al-Khalifa family, who remain in power. It was under British political control from 1820 until 1971, when it became fully independent. In 1975 the national assembly was suspended and the amir assumed virtually absolute power after clashes between the Sunni and Shia communities. Moves to return to democratic rule were made only in response to civil agitation from the 1990s onwards, and a 40-member consultative council, the *Majlis al-Shura,* was appointed in 1996; although this is an advisory body with no legislative powers. A new constitution was introduced in 2002, which established Bahrain as a kingdom and a constitutional monarchy and legalised elections and political parties. There is a continuing campaign for political reform, including greater powers for the legislature.

The legislative election in 2002, the first since 1973, was boycotted by Shi'ite opposition groups, but in the 2006 election, a radical Shi'ite group won 17 of the 40 seats. Although some Shia ministers were appointed, the majority of the cabinet are Sunnis.

POLITICAL SYSTEM
Under the 2002 constitution, the country became a constitutional hereditary monarchy with the king as head of state. The king appoints the cabinet. There is a bicameral legislature consisting of a lower house, *Majlis al-Nuwab* (chamber of deputies), and an upper house, *Majlis al-Shura* (consultative council). The chamber of deputies has 40 members directly elected for a four-year term. The members of the consultative council are appointed by the king for a four-year term. The 2002 constitution granted women the right to vote.

HEAD OF STATE
HH The King of Bahrain, C.-in -C. of the Armed Forces, Shaikh Hamad bin Isa al-Khalifa, KCMG *succeeded as amir* 6 March 1999, *proclaimed king* 14 Feburary 2002
Crown Prince, Chair of the National Economic Development Council, Shaikh Salman bin Hamad al-Khalifa

SELECTED GOVERNMENT MEMBERS *as at May 2007*
Prime Minister, HH Shaikh Khalifa bin Salman al-Khalifa
Deputy Prime Ministers, Shaikh Mohammed bin Mubarak al-Khalifa; Shaikh Ali bin Khalifa al-Khalifa; Jawad bin Salem al Oraied
Defence, Lt.-Gen. Shaikh Khalifa bin Ahmed al-Khalifa
Finance, Shaikh Ahmed bin Mohammed al-Khalifa
Interior, Maj.-Gen. Shaikh Rashid bin Abdulla bin Ahmed al-Khalifa

EMBASSY OF THE KINGDOM OF BAHRAIN
30 Belgrave Square, London SW1X 8QB
T 020-7201 9170 W www.bahrainembassy.co.uk
Ambassador Extraordinary and Plenipotentiary, vacant

BRITISH EMBASSY
21 Government Avenue, Manama 306, PO Box 114
T (+973) 1757 4100 E britemb@batelco.com.bh
W www.ukembassy.gov.bh
Ambassador Extraordinary and Plenipotentiary, HE James Bowden, *apptd* 2007

BRITISH COUNCIL
PO Box 452, AMA Centre, 146 Shaikh Salman Highway, Manama 356
T (+973) 17 261 555 W www.britishcouncil.org/bahrain
Director, Sandra Hamrouni

DEFENCE

The army has 180 main battle tanks, 25 armoured infantry fighting vehicles and 235 armoured personnel carriers. The navy, based at Mina' Salman, has 1 frigate and 8 patrol and coastal vessels. The air force has 33 combat aircraft and 24 armed helicopters.
MILITARY BUDGET – US$478m (2006)
MILITARY PERSONNEL – 11,200: army 8,500, navy 1,200, air force 1,500; paramilitaries 11,260

ECONOMY AND TRADE

Bahrain was one of the first Gulf states to discover oil, in the 1930s, but reserves and production are lower than neighbouring countries and so it has sought to diversify its economy, developing particularly as an offshore financial centre and tourism destination. Petroleum production and refining accounted for an estimated 11 per cent of GDP, 70 per cent of government revenue and 60 per cent of total exports in 2005. Other industry includes aluminium smelting and ship repair.
GNI – US$10,288m; US$14,370 per capita (2005)
ANNUAL AVERAGE GROWTH OF GDP – 5.9 per cent (2005 est)
INFLATION RATE – 2.7 per cent (2005 est)
UNEMPLOYMENT – 15 per cent (2005 est)
TOTAL EXTERNAL DEBT – US$6,814m (2005 est)
IMPORTS – US$7,900m (2005)
EXPORTS – US$10,000m (2005)

BALANCE OF PAYMENTS
Trade – US$1,485m surplus (2004)
Current Account – US$415m surplus (2004)

Trade with UK	*2005*	*2006*
Imports from UK	£180,904,000	£263,644,000
Exports to UK	£164,592,000	£164,485,000

COMMUNICATIONS

Bahrain International airport is one of the main air traffic centres of the Gulf; it is the headquarters of Gulf Air, and a stopping point for other airlines on routes between Europe and Australia and the Far East. A 25-km causeway links Bahrain to Saudi Arabia; construction of its continuation, linking Bahrain to Qatar, was approved in 2005. Of the 3,498km of road, over three quarters (2,768km) is paved. There are no railways. The main ports and terminals are Mina' Salman and Sitrah. Mobile telephone distribution is close to 100 per cent.

MEDIA

Domestic television and radio is run by the state-controlled Bahrain Radio and Television Corporation (BRTC). The country's first private radio station – Sawt al-Ghad – was launched in 2005, but was closed down by the government a year later due to alleged irregularities. Bahrain has a free press but self-censorship is widely practised. There are four main daily newspapers, two of which are published in English.

BANGLADESH

Gana Prajatantri Banladesh – People's Republic of Bangladesh

AREA – 144,000 sq. km. Neighbours: India (west, north and east), Myanmar (south-east)
CAPITAL – Dhaka; population, 10,430,597 (2001)
MAJOR TOWNS – Chittagong; Khulna; Rajshahi; Narayanganj
CURRENCY – Taka (Tk) of 100 paisa
POPULATION – 147,365,352 rising at 2.09 per cent per year (2006 est); Bengali (98 per cent) (est)
RELIGION – Islam (88 per cent), Hinduism (10 per cent) (est)
LANGUAGE – Bengali (official), English
POPULATION DENSITY – 1,090 per sq. km (2005)
URBAN POPULATION – 25 per cent (2005 est)
MEDIAN AGE (years) – 22.2 (2006 est)
NATIONAL ANTHEM – 'Amar Shonar Bangla' ['My Golden Bengal']
NATIONAL DAY – 26 March (Independence Day)
LIFE EXPECTANCY (years) – 62.46 (2006 est)
MORTALITY RATE – 8.27 (2006 est)
BIRTH RATE – 29.8 (2006 est)
INFANT MORTALITY RATE – 60.83 (2006 est)
DEATH PENALTY – Yes
CPI SCORE – 2.0 (2006)
POPULATION BELOW POVERTY LINE – 45 per cent (2004 est)

CLIMATE AND TERRAIN

Although hilly in the south-east and north-east, over 75 per cent of the country is less than 3m above sea-level; the highest elevation is 1,230m (Keokradong). The south-west forms the delta of the Ganges (Padma) and Brahmaputra (Jamuna) rivers on the Bay of Bengal, the largest estuarine delta in the world; with annual rainfall of over 2,500mm, about one third of the country floods each year during the monsoon season. The climate is tropical: hot, wet and extremely humid during the summer, and mild and dry during the winter.

HISTORY AND POLITICS

In British India, Bangladesh was the region of East Bengal and the Sylhet district of Assam. On independence in 1947, these territories acceded to Pakistan, forming East Pakistan. Tensions between East and West Pakistan (separated by over 1,600km) caused East Pakistan to seek autonomy; fighting in 1970 developed into civil war in 1971. After several months of war, and with the support of India, Bangladesh achieved its independence from Pakistan on 16 December 1971.

The late 1970s and 1980s were marked by political instability, with a number of coups and attempted coups, the assassination of President Mujibar Rahman in 1975 and President Zia in 1981, and long periods of government under martial law (1975–8, 1982–6) or a state of emergency (1987–8). Mass anti-government protests forced the resignation in 1990 of Gen. Ershad (assumed power in 1982, elected president in 1986); and the Bangladesh Nationalist Party (BNP) won the subsequent parliamentary elections. In 1991 a constitutional amendment returned Bangladesh to parliamentary government.

Parliamentary government has remained in place since this date, despite a number of boycotts of parliament. The governments have been formed, or coalition governments have been led, by one of the two main parties: the BNP, led by Khaleda Zia (widow of President Zia), in 1991–6 and 2001–6; and the Awami League, led by Sheikh Hasina Wajed (daughter of President Mujibar Rahman), in 1996–2001.

A BNP-led four-party alliance led by Khaleda Zia held office after the 2001 election until its term of office expired in October 2006. Violent protests arose over the choice of a caretaker government and the impartiality of election preparations, leading President Iajuddin Ahmed (elected unopposed in 2002) to assume the leadership of a caretaker administration until the January 2007 legislative election. However, these elections were postponed and a state of emergency declared because of continuing protests and the opposition parties' threat to boycott the election unless electoral reforms were implemented. No new date has been set. Fakhruddin Ahmed took over from the president as head of the caretaker administration, which launched an anti-corruption drive against politicians and bureaucrats. A number of party leaders, including Sheikh Hasina, were arrested in April 2007 on charges relating to the 2006 violence, and Khaleda Zia was placed under virtual house arrest.

POLITICAL SYSTEM

The head of state is the president, elected by parliament for a five-year term. There is a unicameral parliament, *Jatiya Sangsad*, of 345 members directly elected for a five-year term; under a 2004 constitutional amendment, 45 seats are reserved for women. The parliament can amend the constitution by a two-thirds majority. The president appoints the prime minister and the cabinet, on the advice of the prime minister.

HEAD OF STATE

President, Iajuddin Ahmed, *elected* 6 September 2002

SELECTED GOVERNMENT MEMBERS *as at May 2007*

Chief Adviser for the Caretaker Government, Establishment, Home Affairs, Cabinet Division, Election Commission, Fakhruddin Ahmed
Finance, Planning, Mirza Azizul Islam
Foreign Affairs, Iftekhar Ahmed Chowdhury
Minister of Law, Justice and Parliamentary Affairs, Mainul Hosein

BANGLADESH HIGH COMMISSION

28 Queen's Gate, London SW7 5JA
T 020-7584 0081 W www.bangladeshhighcommission.org.uk
High Commissioner, HE Sabihuddin Ahmed, *apptd* 2005

BRITISH HIGH COMMISSION

PO Box 6079, United Nations Road, Baridhara, Dhaka-1212
T (+880) (2) 882 2705 E dhaka.consular@fco.gov.uk
W www.ukinbangladesh.org
High Commissioner, HE Anwar Choudhury, *apptd* 2004

BRITISH COUNCIL

PO Box 161, 5 Fuller Road, Dhaka 1000
T (+880) (2) 861 8905 W www.britishcouncil.org/bangladesh
Director, Dr June Rollinson

DEFENCE

The army has 180 main battle tanks and 180 armoured personnel carriers. The navy has 5 frigates and 44 patrol and coastal vessels. The air force has 62 combat aircraft.
MILITARY EXPENDITURE – US$840m (2005)
MILITARY PERSONNEL – 126,500: army 110,000, navy 10,000, air force 6,500; paramilitaries 63,200

ECONOMY AND TRADE

Bangladesh is a poor country, dependent on foreign aid and with nearly half its population living below the poverty line. Progress on economic reform is slow because of political infighting, corruption, the opposition of vested interests and an apparent lack of political will. However, there has been steady annual growth of around 5 per cent in recent years, primarily in the manufacturing and energy sectors, which have attracted foreign aid and investment. Despite this, the economy is unable to employ all the workforce and many emigrate in search of work, primarily to the Gulf states and south-east Asian countries. Remittances from these workers make a significant economic contribution of nearly US$2bn (£1bn) a year.

The service and industrial sectors account for 52.8 per cent and 26.7 per cent of GDP respectively. Although the smallest contributor to GDP, agriculture is the primary occupation of over 60 per cent of the population. The chief industries are based on processing agricultural products such as cotton, jute, tea and sugar, and the manufacture of garments, cement and fertiliser and light engineering.
GNI – US$66,700m; US$470 per capita (2005)
ANNUAL AVERAGE GROWTH OF GDP – 6.4 per cent (2005 est)
INFLATION RATE – 7 per cent (2005 est)
UNEMPLOYMENT – 2.5 per cent (2005 est)
TOTAL EXTERNAL DEBT – US$20,630m (2005 est)
IMPORTS – US$12,900m (2005)
EXPORTS – US$7,200m (2005)

BALANCE OF PAYMENTS

Trade – US$3,006m deficit (2004)
Current Account – US$279m deficit (2004)

Trade with UK	*2005*	*2006*
Imports from UK	£79,956,000	£75,995,000
Exports to UK	£596,272,000	£746,179,000

COMMUNICATIONS

The principal seaports are Chittagong and Mongla. A state enterprise, the Bangladesh Shipping Corporation, operates the Bangladesh merchant fleet. The 8,372km of internal waterways are a key element of the transport infrastructure, although the 5,635km of main cargo routes are reduced to 5,200km in the dry season. There are three international airports (at Dhaka, Chittagong and Sylhet) and five domestic airports, with a sixth under construction. The international airline, Bangladesh Biman, provides international and internal flights. There are 2,768km of rail track, and rail links with India. The country's 239,226km of roads includes only 22,726km which are paved. The telephone network is limited, with only 1 million main lines and has been overtaken by mobile telephone distribution, which was 9 million in 2005.

EDUCATION AND HEALTH

Primary education is compulsory and free.
LITERACY RATE – 41.1 per cent (2004 est)
GROSS ENROLMENT RATIO (percentage of relevant age group) – primary 109 per cent; secondary 46 per cent; tertiary 6 per cent (2005 est)
HEALTH EXPENDITURE (per capita) – US$14 (2004)

MEDIA

The main broadcast medium (Bangladesh Television (BTV)) is state-owned and subject to censorship. The main commercial stations are ATN Bangla TV and Channel i, but their influence is limited to urban areas. The four main newspapers are *The Daily Star, Dainik Ittefaq, Daily Prothom Alo* and *The New Nation*. The constitution promises press freedom, but journalists are regularly subjected to harassment.

BARBADOS

AREA – 431 sq. km
CAPITAL – Bridgetown, in the parish of St Michael; population, 6,720 (1990)
MAJOR TOWNS – Holetown, in St James; Oistins, in Christ Church; Speightstown, in St Peter
CURRENCY – Barbadosdollar (BD$) of 100 cents
POPULATION – 279,912, rising at 0.37 per cent per year (2006 est)
RELIGION – Christianity (95 per cent) (est)
LANGUAGE – English (official)
POPULATION DENSITY – 627 per sq. km (2005)
URBAN POPULATION – 52.9 per cent (2005)
MEDIAN AGE (years) – 34.6 (2006 est)
NATIONAL ANTHEM – 'In Plenty and in Time of Need'
NATIONAL DAY – 30 November (Independence Day)
LIFE EXPECTANCY (years) – 72.79 (2006 est)
MORTALITY RATE – 8.67 (2006 est)
BIRTH RATE – 12.71 (2006 est)
INFANT MORTALITY RATE – 11.77 (2006 est)
HIV/AIDS ADULT PREVALENCE RATE – 1.5 per cent (2003 est)
DEATH PENALTY – Yes
CPI SCORE – 6.7 (2006)
MILITARY BUDGET – US$25m (2006 est)
MILITARY PERSONNEL – 610: army 500, navy 110

CLIMATE AND TERRAIN

Barbados is the most easterly of the Caribbean islands. The land rises in a series of terraced tablelands, and elevation extremes range from 336m (Mt Hillaby) at the highest point to 0m (Atlantic Ocean) at the lowest. The climate is tropical with a wet season from June to October, and the island is subject to occasional hurricanes.

HISTORY AND POLITICS

The first inhabitants of Barbados were Amerindian nomads from South America who arrived on the islands *c*.350 AD. Arawak Indians and then Caribs followed. The island was uninhabited when settled by the British in 1627 and was a crown colony from 1652, achieving self-government in 1961. It became an independent state within the Commonwealth on 30 November 1966. Since independence, power has alternated between the two main political parties, the Barbados Labour Party (BLP) and the Democratic Labour Party (DLP). In the 2003 general election the governing BLP won 23 seats in the house of assembly and the DLP won 7 seats.

POLITICAL SYSTEM

The head of state is the British sovereign, represented by the governor-general. The bicameral parliament consists of a senate and a house of assembly. The senate comprises 21 senators appointed by the governor-general for a five-year term, of whom 12 are appointed on the advice of the prime minister, two on the advice of the leader of the opposition and seven at the governor-general's discretion to represent religious, economic and social interests. The house of assembly comprises 30 members directly elected for a five-year term.

There are 11 administrative areas (parishes): St Michael, Christ Church, St Andrew, St George, St James, St John, St Joseph, St Lucy, St Peter, St Philip and St Thomas.

Governor-General, HE Sir Clifford Husbands, GCMG, KA, *apptd* June 1996

SELECTED GOVERNMENT MEMBERS *as at May 2007*
Prime Minister, Defence and Security, Finance, Owen Arthur
Deputy Prime Minister, Economy, Mia Mottley
Commerce, Consumer Affairs and Business Development, Lynette Eastmond
Foreign Affairs, Foreign Trade, Billie Miller

BARBADOS HIGH COMMISSION
1 Great Russell Street, London WC1B 3ND
T 020-7631 4975 E london@foreign.gov.bb
High Commissioner, HE Edwin Pollard, OBE, *apptd* 2003

BRITISH HIGH COMMISSION
Lower Collymore Rock, PO Box 676, Bridgetown
T (+1) (246) 430 7800 E britishhc@sunbeach.net
High Commissioner, HE Duncan Taylor, *apptd* 2005

ECONOMY AND TRADE

Historically, Barbados' chief products were sugar, rum and molasses. Since independence, tourism and other service industries have become of greater significance. The economy has suffered as a result of the downturn in tourism in recent years, but offshore finance and information services remain a valuable source of foreign exchange earnings. Chief exports are sugar and molasses, rum, other food and beverages, chemicals, electronic components and clothing.
GNI – US$2,500m (2003); US$9,270 per capita (2003)
ANNUAL AVERAGE GROWTH OF GDP – 4.1 per cent (2005 est)
INFLATION RATE – –0.5 per cent (2003 est)

UNEMPLOYMENT – 10.7 per cent (2003 est)
TOTAL EXTERNAL DEBT – US$668m (2003)
IMPORTS – US$1,600m (2005)
EXPORTS – US$360m (2005)

BALANCE OF PAYMENTS
Trade – US$971m deficit (2004)
Current Account – US$337m deficit (2004)

Trade with UK	*2005*	*2006*
Imports from UK	£55,551,000	£46,989,000
Exports to UK	£16,556,000	£19,865,000

COMMUNICATIONS
Barbados has around 1,600km of roads, all of which are surfaced. The Grantley Adams International airport is situated at Seawell, 19km from Bridgetown, and is a hub for connections to other Caribbean islands. Bridgetown, the only port of entry, has a deep-water harbour with berths for eight ships; there are also four tanker terminals. Mobile phone ownership is high, at 206,200 in 2005.

EDUCATION
Education is free in government schools at primary (ages four to 11) and secondary (ages 11 to 18) levels.
LITERACY RATE – 99.7 per cent (2004 est)

MEDIA
Barbados has two daily newspapers, both privately-owned. The sole television station is run by the government-owned Caribbean Broadcasting Corporation. There are both public and privately owned radio stations. The media air a range of views and are free to criticise the authorities.

BELARUS

Respublika Byelarus – Republic of Belarus

AREA – 207,600 sq. km. Neighbours: Latvia and Lithuania (north), Russia (east), Ukraine (south), Poland (west)
CAPITAL – Minsk (the administrative centre of the CIS); population, 1,765,800 (2005 est)
MAJOR CITIES – Homyel'; Mahilyow; Vicebsk; Hrodna; Brest
CURRENCY – Belarusian rouble
POPULATION – 10,293,011 falling at 0.06 per cent per year (2006 est); Belarusian (81.2 per cent), Russian (11.4 per cent), Polish (3.9 per cent), Ukrainian (2.4 per cent)
RELIGION – Orthodox Christianity (80 per cent), Roman Catholicism (15 per cent) (est)
LANGUAGE – Belarusian, Russian (both official)
POPULATION DENSITY – 47 per sq. km (2005)
URBAN POPULATION – 71.6 per cent (2005 est)
MEDIAN AGE (years) – 37.2 (2006 est)
NATIONAL ANTHEM – 'My Belarusy' ['We, the Belarusians']
NATIONAL DAY – 3 July (Independence Day)
LIFE EXPECTANCY (years) – 69.08 (2006 est)
MORTALITY RATE – 14.02 (2006 est)
BIRTH RATE – 11.16 (2006 est)
INFANT MORTALITY RATE – 13 (2006 est)
DEATH PENALTY – Yes
CPI SCORE – 2.1 (2006)
POPULATION BELOW POVERTY LINE – 27.1 per cent (2003 est)

CLIMATE AND TERRAIN
Belarus is a landlocked country in eastern Europe, and was formerly part of the USSR. Its main rivers are the upper reaches of the Dnieper, the Nyoman and the Western Dvina. Much of the land is a plain, with many lakes, forests, swamps and marshy areas. The climate is continental, with mild, humid winters and relatively cool and rainy summers. Elevation extremes range from 346m (Dzyarzhynskaya Hara) at the highest point to 90m (Nyoman River) at the lowest.

HISTORY AND POLITICS
The area was absorbed into Lithuania in the 13th century, and came under Polish rule from the 1570s, but following the partitions of Poland in the late 18th century it came under the control of the expanding Russian Empire. It was the site of fierce fighting during the First World War, but its brief period of independence ended, after a war over the territory, in partition between Poland and the USSR. The Polish territory was largely regained after the Second World War, which devastated Belarus: 25 per cent of the population was killed and thousands were deported.

Belarus declared its independence from the USSR after a failed coup in Moscow in 1991. Stanislav Shuskevich became Belarusian leader at the head of a coalition of Communists and Democrats, but he was forced to resign in 1994 and was replaced by Gen. Mecheslav Grib who pursued closer political, economic and trade relations with Russia. The 1994 presidential election was won by Alexander Lukashenko.

President Lukashenko resisted privatisation and economic liberalisation in the late 1990s, precipitating economic collapse and public unrest. An attempt to impeach him in 1996 was countered by the suspension of parliament, and his regime has become increasingly repressive, with many allegations of human rights abuses, particularly concerning the imprisonment or disappearance of opposition leaders and the violent suppression of public demonstrations. The EU and USA have imposed travel restrictions and other sanctions several times in recent years because of the regime's poor human rights record and obstructiveness towards international election monitors. The 2000 and 2004 legislative elections and the 2001 and 2006 presidential elections were condemned as neither free nor fair by opposition groups and international observers. In the 2004 legislative election, opposition parties failed to win any seats; in the 2006 election, President Lukashenko was returned with 82.6 per cent of the vote. Popular protests at the outcome of these polls and subsequent public expressions of opposition to the regime were suppressed by the police.

FOREIGN RELATIONS
Belarus was a founder member of the Commonwealth of Independent States (CIS) in 1991. President Lukashenko, who opposed the break-up of the Soviet Union, has sought closer relations with Russia. In 1997 a treaty was signed with Russia providing for closer political and economic integration, and in 1999 the two countries signed a treaty on the creation of a union state, which committed them to eventually becoming a confederal state. However, there has been little real progress towards integration, and Russia has increasingly condemned Belarus' poor economic development.

POLITICAL SYSTEM
Under the 1994 constitution, the president is directly elected for a five-year term; this was renewable only once until a 2004 constitutional amendment removed the two-term limit. The president may appoint half the members of the constitutional court and the electoral commission. The legislature is the bicameral national assembly, comprising a 110-member house of representatives (lower chamber), directly elected for a four-year term, and a council of the republic, which has 56 members elected by local *soviets* (councils) and other members appointed by the president.

President Lukashenko's term of office was extended by two years in 1996, when his powers were increased at the expense of the legislature, and again in 1997.

HEAD OF STATE
President, Alexander Lukashenko, *elected* 10 July 1994, *re-elected* September 2001, March 2006

SELECTED GOVERNMENT MEMBERS *as at May 2007*
Prime Minister, Sergei Sidorsky
First Deputy Prime Minister, Vladimir Semashko
Defence, Col.-Gen. Leonid Maltsev
Finance, Nikolai Korbut
Foreign Affairs, Sergei Martynov
Internal Affairs, Maj.-Gen. Vladimir Naumov

EMBASSY OF THE REPUBLIC OF BELARUS
6 Kensington Court, London W8 5DL
T 020-7937 3288
W www.uk.belembassy.org
Ambassador Extraordinary and Plenipotentiary, HE Alexander Mikhnevich, *apptd* 2006

BRITISH EMBASSY
37 Karl Marx Street, 220030 Minsk
T (+375) (172) 105 920 E britinfo@nsys.by
Ambassador Extraordinary and Plenipotentiary, HE Brian Bennett, *apptd* 2002

DEFENCE
The army has 1,586 main battle tanks, 1,588 armoured infantry fighting vehicles and 916 armoured personnel carriers. The air force has 174 combat aircraft and 50 armed helicopters.
MILITARY BUDGET – US$270m (2005 est)
MILITARY PERSONNEL – 72,940: army 29,600, joint staff 25,170, air force 18,170; paramilitaries 110,000
CONSCRIPTION DURATION – Nine to 12 months

ECONOMY AND TRADE
Although very prosperous under the Soviet regime, the country experienced a dramatic economic decline after independence and over a quarter of the population now lives below the poverty line. Since 1994, President Lukashenko has resisted structural reform of the economy and reimposed state control of prices and currency exchange rates. Some privatised businesses were renationalised in 2005, and the small private sector is subject to pressure and intervention by the state, circumstances that continue to discourage foreign investment. Recent years have seen steady economic growth, largely based on the re-export at market prices of heavily discounted oil from Russia. This revenue stream will be reduced in future by a sharp increase in oil prices from early 2007 (increasing to world prices by 2011), Russia's introduction of an export duty on oil shipped to Belarus, and Belarus' obligation to share with Russia its duties on re-exported oil.

Industrial output has grown at nearly twice the rate of the economy as a whole. The main activities are the manufacture of machinery and equipment, vehicles, domestic appliances, chemicals and textiles. These commodities, along with oil, mineral products, metals and foodstuffs, form the main exports and the main imports. The main trading partner is Russia.
GNI – US$27,000m; US$2,760 per capita (2005)
AVERAGE ANNUAL GROWTH OF GDP – 9.2 per cent (2005 est)
INFLATION RATE – 10.3 per cent (2005 est)
UNEMPLOYMENT – 1.6 per cent (2005)
TOTAL EXTERNAL DEBT – US$4,662m (2005 est)
IMPORTS – US$17,000m (2005)
EXPORTS – US$16,000m (2005)

BALANCE OF PAYMENTS
Trade – US$527m deficit (2005)
Current Account – US$469m surplus (2005)

Trade with UK	*2005*	*2006*
Imports from UK	£56,961,000	£62,763,000
Exports to UK	£275,486,000	£726,243,000

COMMUNICATIONS
Belarus has an extensive 2,500km canal and river system but its use is limited by shallowness or location. There is an international airport at Minsk and seven other major domestic airports, plus over 70 smaller airports and airfields. Most of the 93,310km of roads are surfaced but many are in bad repair. There are 5,512km of railways. The telephone system is state-operated; the network is not extensive in rural areas. Land-line connections are exceeded by mobile phone distribution. There were 3.4 million internet users in 2005.

EDUCATION AND HEALTH
The national education system comprises pre-school, general secondary, out-of-school, vocational training and trade schools, secondary specialised and higher education. General secondary education begins at the age of six.
LITERACY RATE – 99.6 per cent (2004 est)
GROSS ENROLMENT RATIO (percentage of relevant age group) – primary 101 per cent; secondary 95 per cent; tertiary 62 per cent (2005 est)
HEALTH EXPENDITURE (per capita) – US$147 (2004)
HOSPITAL BEDS (per 1,000 people) – 11.3 (2000–5)

MEDIA
A Soviet-era attitude to press freedom remains; the government controls media content and the appointment of senior editors in the print and broadcast media. State-run newspapers and television channels receive large subsidies and support government policies. The most popular privately owned newspaper is *Belorusskaya Delovaya Gazeta.* The Belarusian National State Teleradio Company operates domestic radio and TV channels. Radio Baltic Waves (Baltijos Bangos) is a private broadcaster that targets Belarusian audiences but operates from Vilnius in Lithuania.

BELGIUM

Koninkrijk Belgie/Royaume de Belgique/Königreich Belgien – Kingdom of Belgium

AREA – 30,528 sq. km. Neighbours: the Netherlands (north), France (south), Germany and Luxembourg (east)
CAPITAL – Brussels; population, 978,384 (2002)
MAJOR CITIES – Antwerp, the chief port; Ghent; Charleroi; Liège; Bruges
CURRENCY – Euro (€) of 100 cents
POPULATION – 10,379,067 rising at 0.13 per cent per year (2006 est); Fleming (58 per cent), Walloon (31 per cent) (est)
RELIGION – Roman Catholicism (47 per cent), Islam (3 per cent) (est). In addition, 8 per cent of the population is estimated to be laic (belonging to a non-confessional philosophical organisation) and 15 per cent atheist
LANGUAGE – Dutch, French, German (all official)
POPULATION DENSITY – 347 per sq. km (2005)
URBAN POPULATION – 97.3 per cent (2005 est)
MEDIAN AGE (years) – 40.9 (2006 est)
NATIONAL ANTHEM – 'La Brabançonne' ['The Song of Brabant']
NATIONAL DAY – 21 July (Ascension of King Leopold I, 1831)
LIFE EXPECTANCY (years) – 78.77 (2006 est)
MORTALITY RATE – 10.27 (2006 est)
BIRTH RATE – 10.38 (2006 est)
INFANT MORTALITY RATE – 4.62 (2006 est)
DEATH PENALTY – No (abolished 1996)
CPI SCORE – 7.3 (2006)

CLIMATE AND TERRAIN

Belgium is divided into two distinct regions. The west is generally low-lying and fertile, while the east, the tableland of the Ardennes, is more rugged with poorer soil. Elevation extremes range from sea level on the North Sea coast to 694m at the highest point (Signal de Botrange). The polders near the coast, which are protected by dykes against floods, cover an area of 499 sq. km. The principal rivers are the Schelde and the Meuse (Maas). Average temperatures range from 2°C in January to 18°C in July.

HISTORY AND POLITICS

Part of the Roman Empire until the second century, after invasion by Germanic tribes it became part of the Frankish Empire until much of the area was absorbed by the duchy of Burgundy from 1385. Under the rule of the Spanish Habsburgs from 1477 until 1713 and the Austrian Habsburgs until 1794, the area was conquered and held by Revolutionary France until the collapse of the Napoleonic regime in 1814, when it united with the kingdom of the Netherlands. The Belgian Revolution in 1830 led to the declaration of independence on 14 October 1830, and in 1831 the country became a constitutional monarchy. In the 20th century Belgium was invaded and occupied by Germany in both world wars; Eupen and Malmédy were ceded to Belgium by Germany under the Versailles treaty of 1919.

Tensions between the Flemings (Flemish speakers in the north of the country) and the Walloons (French speakers in the south) caused political instability in the post-war period, and several governments collapsed. Inter-communal disputes led in 1980 to the establishment of regional assemblies, and in 1989 the country adopted a federal constitution. Belgium was a founder member of the EU in 1957 and joined the eurozone in 2002. In 2005, the federal parliament approved the EU constitution.

After the 2003 general election, liberal and socialist parties held the majority of seats in the chamber of representatives and Guy Verhofstadt, prime minister since 1999, formed a new liberal-socialist coalition government. This coalition was defeated in the June 2007 election, in which the Christian Democrats won the most seats. At the time of going to press, negotiations were under way to form a new coalition led by the Christian Democrats.

POLITICAL SYSTEM

Belgium is a constitutional monarchy with a bicameral legislature (the federal chambers) consisting of the senate and the chamber of representatives. The senate has 71 members, who serve a four-year term; 40 are directly elected and the rest are co-opted by the elected members. The chamber of representatives has 150 members, directly elected by proportional representation for a four-year term.

Amendments to the constitution since 1968 have devolved power to the regions. The national government retains competence only in foreign and defence policies, the national budget and monetary policy, social security, and the judicial, legal and penal systems.

HEAD OF STATE

HM The King of the Belgians, King Albert II, *born* 6 June 1934; *acceded* 9 August 1993
Heir, HRH Prince Philippe Léopold Louis Marie, *born* 15 April 1960

SELECTED GOVERNMENT MEMBERS *as at May 2007*

Prime Minister, Guy Verhofstadt
Deputy Prime Ministers; Freya Van den Bossche *(Budget);* Didier Reynders *(Finance);* Patrick Dewael *(Interior);* Laurette Onkelinx *(Justice);* Karel De Gucht *(Foreign Affairs)*

EMBASSY OF BELGIUM

17 Grosvenor Crescent, London SW1X 7EE
T 020-7470 3700 W www.diplomatie.be/london
Ambassador Extraordinary and Plenipotentiary, HE Jean-Michel Veranneman de Watervliet, *apptd* 2006

BRITISH EMBASSY

rue d'Arlon 85 , 1040 Brussels
T (+32) (2) 287 6211 E richard.kinchen@fco.gov.uk
W www.british-embassy.be
Ambassador Extraordinary and Plenipotentiary, HE Richard Kinchen, *apptd* 2003

BRITISH COUNCIL

Leopold Plaza, Rue de Trône 108/Troonstraat 108, 1050 Brussels
T (+32) (2) 227 0840 W www.britishcouncil.org/belgium
Regional Director, Stephen Roman

FEDERAL STRUCTURE

There are three communities: Flemish, Francophone and Germanophone. Each community has its own assembly, which elects the community government. At this level, Flanders is covered by the Flemish community assembly; most of Wallonia is covered by the Francophone community assembly, and the areas of Wallonia in the

German-speaking communities of Eupen and Malmédy are covered by the Germanophone community assembly; Brussels is covered by a joint community commission of the Flemish and Francophone community assemblies.

At regional level, Belgium is divided into the three regions of Wallonia, Brussels and Flanders. Each region has its own directly elected assembly and government.

The ten provinces of Belgium are: Antwerp, East Flanders, Flemish Brabant, Hainaut, Liege, Limburg, Luxembourg, Namur, Walloon Brabant and West Flanders. In addition, 589 communes form the lowest level of local government.

Minister-President of the Flemish Community and Flemish Region, Yves Leterme
Minister-President of the Walloon Region, Jean-Claude Van Cauwenberghe
Minister-President of the French Community, Hervé Hasquin
Minister-President of the German-Speaking Community, Karl-Heinz Lambertz
Minister-President of the Brussels Capital Government, Jacques Simonet

DEFENCE

The army has 40 main battle tanks, 224 armoured personnel carriers, 95 armoured infantry fighting vehicles. The navy is based at Zeebrugge and has 3 frigates. The air force has 71 combat aircraft and 6 air bases.

The headquarters of NATO, Supreme Headquarters Allied Powers Europe, and the Western European Union Military Planning Cell are in Belgium; 1,327 US personnel (EUCOM) are stationed in the country.

MILITARY EXPENDITURE – US$4,620 million (2005)
MILITARY PERSONNEL – 39,690: army 12,571, navy 1,605, air force 7,470, medical and joint services 18,044

ECONOMY AND TRADE

Belgium has a free-market economy with highly diversified industrial and commercial sectors. With no natural resources except coal (production of which has now ceased), industry is based largely on the processing of imported raw materials for export. This makes the economy dependent on the state of world markets, and rates of growth have recently been low. Principal industries are engineering and metal products, vehicle assembly, transport equipment, scientific instruments, food processing and beverages, chemicals, base metals, textiles, glass and petroleum.

Industry accounts for about one quarter of GDP and one quarter of employment. There is a large service sector, largely owing to the location in Brussels of EU institutions, NATO headquarters and a number of other international organisations, as well as the multinational companies attracted by them. The service sector accounts for three-quarters of GDP and the same proportion of employment. There is a small agricultural sector (1 per cent of GDP and employment). The government has succeeded in balancing the budget recently but public debt is high (90 per cent of GDP in 2006).

About 75 per cent of trade is with other EU states, especially Germany, France and the Netherlands. External trade statistics relate to Luxembourg as well as Belgium as the two countries formed an economic union in 1921.

GNI – US$378,700m; US$37,140 per capita (2005)
ANNUAL AVERAGE GROWTH OF GDP – 1.5 per cent (2005 est)
INFLATION RATE – 2.8 per cent (2005 est)
UNEMPLOYMENT – 8.4 per cent (2005 est)
TOTAL EXTERNAL DEBT – US$980,100m (2005 est)
IMPORTS – US$319,000m (2005)
EXPORTS – US$336,000m (2005)

BALANCE OF PAYMENTS
Trade – US$1,978m surplus (2005)
Current Account – US$6,563m surplus (2005)

Trade with UK	*2005*	*200*
Imports from UK	£10,898,748,000	£12,751,800,00
Exports to UK	£13,114,614,000	£13,863,900,00

COMMUNICATIONS

There are 2,043km of inland waterways, of which 1,528km are in regular commercial use; ship canals link Ostend and Zeebrugge with Bruges and Ghent, Ghent with Terneuzen in the Netherlands, Brussels with Charleroi and Willebroek Rupel, and Liège with Antwerp. The rivers Meuse (Maas), Sambre and Schelde form an integral part of the network. The main seaports are Antwerp, Ghent, Ostend and Zeebrugge, with inland ports at Brussels and Liège. The major airports are at Antwerp, Brussels, Liège and Ostend. The rail system is run by Belgian National Railways and at 3,521km the network is one of the densest in the world. There are 150,567km of roads, including 1,747km of motorways. In 2005, mobile phone ownership was 9.5 million, representing over 90 per cent of the population, and there were 5.1 million internet users.

EDUCATION AND HEALTH

Nursery schools provide free education for children from two-and-a-half to six years of age. There are over 4,000 primary schools (six to 12 years) and more than 1,000 secondary schools offering a general academic education, slightly over half of which are free institutions (predominantly Roman Catholic and subsidised by the state) and the remainder state-run institutions. The official school-leaving age is 18.

GROSS ENROLMENT RATIO (percentage of relevant age group) – primary 104 per cent; secondary 109 per cent (2005 est); tertiary 63 per cent (2002 est)
HEALTH EXPENDITURE (per capita) – US$3,363 (2004)
HOSPITAL BEDS (per 1,000 people) – 6.9 (2000–5)

MEDIA AND CULTURE

The media reflects the multilingual nature of the population. There are two broadcasting authorities with programming priorities in radio, TV and external broadcasting. RTBF is the French-language broadcaster. VRT is the Flemish broadcaster. There are also French and Flemish commercial television channels and Belgischer Rundfunk (BRF), a German-language radio broadcaster. Cable television is very popular, with 95 per cent of the population subscribing to domestic and foreign channels. A small number of media groups own and run the main news publications.

Belgium has contributed a number of significant names to the history of art. Peter Paul Rubens (1577–1640) commands a room of his own in the Louvre, while Flemish painters Bruegel (1525–69) and Anthony van Dyck (1599–1641) are found in galleries worldwide. Notable modern artists include James Ensor (1860–1949) and surrealist René Magritte (1898–1967), and those behind comic creations Tintin (Hergé) and the Smurfs (Peyo). The prolific novelist Georges Simenon (1903–89) achieved notable success writing in French. The country's beer is considered to be among the world's finest. Six of the seven Trappist breweries are based in Belgium, as is the world's largest brewery, InBev, producers of Stella Artois and Leffe.

BELIZE

AREA – 22,966 sq. km. Neighbours: Mexico (north and north-west), Guatemala (west and south)
CAPITAL – Belmopan; population, 13,500 (2005 est)
MAJOR CITIES – Belize City, the former capital; San Ignacio; Orange Walk
CURRENCY – Belize dollar (BZ $) of 100 cents. The Belize dollar is tied to the US dollar
POPULATION – 287,730 rising at 2.31 per cent per year (2006 est); *mestizo* (48.7 per cent), Creole (24.9 per cent), Maya (10.6 per cent), Garifuna (6.1 per cent) (est)
RELIGION – Roman Catholicism (58 per cent), Protestantism (21 per cent), Mennonitism (4 per cent) (est)
LANGUAGE – English (official), Spanish, Mayan, Creole, Garifuna
POPULATION DENSITY – 13 per sq. km (2005)
URBAN POPULATION – 48.6 per cent (2005 est)
MEDIAN AGE (years) – 19.6 (2006 est)
NATIONAL ANTHEM – 'Land of the Free'
NATIONAL DAY – 21 September (Independence Day)
LIFE EXPECTANCY (years) – 68.3 (2006 est)
MORTALITY RATE – 5.72 (2006 est)
BIRTH RATE – 28.84 (2006 est)
INFANT MORTALITY RATE – 24.89 (2006 est)
HIV/AIDS ADULT PREVALENCE RATE – 2.4 per cent (2003 est)
DEATH PENALTY – Yes
CPI SCORE – 3.5 (2006)
POPULATION BELOW POVERTY LINE – 33 per cent (1999)
MILITARY BUDGET – US$16m (2006 est)
MILITARY PERSONNEL – army 1,050 (est)

CLIMATE AND TERRAIN

Belize comprises a large coastal plain, swamps in the north, fertile land in the south, and the Maya Mountains. The highest point of elevation is 1,160m (Victoria Peak), the lowest is at 0m (Caribbean Sea). The climate is subtropical but is cooled by trade winds. There are frequent hurricanes (the hurricane season is June to November). Belize's inner coastal waters are protected by the world's second-largest barrier reef.

HISTORY AND POLITICS

Numerous ruins in the area indicate that Belize was heavily populated by the Maya Indians. The first British settlement was established in 1638 but was subject to repeated attacks by the Spanish, who claimed sovereignty until their defeat by the British navy and settlers in 1798. In 1862 the area was recognised by Britain as a colony and called British Honduras. The colony became self-governing in 1964. In 1973 it was renamed Belize, and it was granted independence on 21 September 1981. Since independence, power has alternated between the two main politicial parties, the People's United Party (PUP) and the United Democratic Party (UDP).

The 2003 general election was won by the ruling People's United Party, which took 22 of the 29 seats in the house of representatives.

FOREIGN RELATIONS

There is a longstanding territorial dispute with Guatemala, which claims half of the territory of Belize. In 2002 Belize and Guatemala agreed a draft settlement brokered by the the Organisation of American States (OAS), but Guatemala rejected the terms of the settlement in 2003. The OAS continues to work with Guatemala and Belize to resolve the dispute.

POLITICAL SYSTEM

The head of state is the British sovereign, represented by a governor-general. There is a bicameral national assembly, comprising a house of representatives (29 members directly elected for a five-year term) and a senate (13 members appointed by the governor-general, including six on the advice of the prime minister, three on the advice of the opposition leader, and one each representing various sectors of society). Executive power is vested in the cabinet, which is responsible to the national assembly.
Governor-General, HE Sir Colville Young, GCMG, *apptd* 17 November 1993

SELECTED GOVERNMENT MEMBERS *as at May 2007*
Prime Minister, Finance, Defence, Said Musa
Deputy Prime Minister, Natural Resources, Environment, John Briceno
Foreign Affairs, Foreign Trade, Eamon Courtenay
Home Affairs, Ralph Fonseca

BELIZE HIGH COMMISSION
3rd Floor, 45 Crawford Place, London W1H 4LP
T 020-7723 3603 W www.belizehighcommission.com
High Commissioner, HE Lawrence Sylvester, *apptd* 2006

BRITISH HIGH COMMISSION
PO Box 91, Belmopan
T (+501) 822 2146 E brithicom@btl.net
W www.britishhighbze.com
High Commissioner, HE Alan Jones, *apptd* 2004

ECONOMY AND TRADE

The economy has grown steadily since 1999, although the rate of growth has slowed slightly in recent years. This is partly owing to the downturn in tourism, which now dominates the economy. The government introduced an austerity budget in 2005 to deal with the budget and trade deficits and the high level of foreign debt, provoking widespread protests. About one-third of the population lives below the poverty line.

The services sector, primarily tourism, accounts for around 62 per cent of GDP; industry contributes about 14 per cent, and agriculture and fisheries contribute about 23 per cent. The main industries apart from tourism are garment manufacturing and food processing, construction and oil production; commercial exploitation of oil reserves began in 2006. The main crops are also major export items: sugar, bananas, citrus fruits and juice, fish products, molasses and timber (mostly mahogany). The UK and the USA account for over 55 per cent of export revenue. Imports are primarily machinery and transport equipment, manufactured goods, fuel, chemicals, pharmaceuticals, food, beverages and tobacco.
GNI – US$1,042m; US$3,570 per capita (2005)
ANNUAL AVERAGE GROWTH OF GDP – 3.8 per cent (2005)

INFLATION RATE – 3 per cent (2005 est)
UNEMPLOYMENT – 12.9 per cent (2003)
TOTAL EXTERNAL DEBT – US$1,362m (2004 est)
IMPORTS – US$590m (2005)
EXPORTS – US$210m (2005)

BALANCE OF PAYMENTS
Trade – US$174m deficit (2004)
Current Account – US$182m deficit (2004)

Trade with UK	*2005*	*2006*
Imports from UK	£9,279,000	£8,244,000
Exports to UK	£46,855,000	£86,503,000

COMMUNICATIONS

Although there are 825km of waterways, these are only accessible to small craft. The main port is Belize City, which has deep water quays. There are about 17 major airports and airfields, including the international airport is at Belize City. There are 2,872km of roads, including 488km of paved highways, but no railway system. Mobile phone distribution is growing, and exceeds land-line connections.

EDUCATION

Education is free and compulsory from six to 14 years of age. The government maintains some schools but most are run by churches.
LITERACY RATE – 76.9 per cent (2004 est)

MEDIA

The government-operated radio service was privatised in 1998 and there is now a variety of commercial radio stations. There are no daily newspapers but there are a number of privately owned weekly news publications. There are three main television stations (Channels 5, 7 and 9), all of which are commercial.

BENIN

République du Bénin – Republic of Benin

AREA – 112,620 sq. km. Neighbours: Togo (west), Burkina Faso and Niger (north), Nigeria (east)
CAPITAL – Porto Novo; population, 223,552 (2002)
MAJOR TOWNS – Cotonou is the principal commercial town and port; Godomey; Parakou
CURRENCY – Franc CFA of 100 centimes
POPULATION – 7,862,944 rising at 2.73 per cent per year (2006 est)
RELIGION – Indigenous beliefs (50 per cent), Christianity (30 per cent), Islam (20 per cent) (est). Among the most commonly practised indigenous religions is voodoo, which originated in this region of Africa.
LANGUAGE – French (official), Fon, Yoruba
POPULATION DENSITY – 76 per sq. km (2005)
URBAN POPULATION – 46.1 per cent (2005 est)
MEDIAN AGE (years) – 17.6 (2006 est)
NATIONAL ANTHEM – 'L'Aube Nouvelle' ['The Dawn of a New Day']
NATIONAL DAY – 1 August
LIFE EXPECTANCY – 53.04 (2006 est)
MORTALITY RATE – 12.22 (2006 est)
BIRTH RATE – 38.85 (2006 est)
INFANT MORTALITY RATE – 79.56 (2006 est)
HIV/AIDS ADULT PREVALENCE – 1.9 per cent (2003 est)
DEATH PENALTY – No*
CPI SCORE – 2.5 (2006)
POPULATION BELOW POVERTY LINE – 33 per cent (2001 est)
MILITARY BUDGET – US$71m (2005 est)
MILITARY PERSONNEL – 4,750: army 4,300, navy 100, air force 350; paramilitaries 2,500
CONSCRIPTION DURATION – 18 months (selective)
LITERACY RATE – 33.6 per cent (2004 est)
GROSS ENROLMENT RATIO (percentage of relevant age group) – primary 96 per cent; secondary 33 per cent (2005 est)
HEALTH EXPENDITURE (per capita) – US$24 (2004)

CLIMATE AND TERRAIN

Benin has a short coastline of 124km on the Gulf of Guinea but extends northwards inland for 699km. The coast is a sandbar backed by lagoons that are fed by rivers. Elevation extremes range from 658m (Mt Sokbaro) at the highest point to 0m (Atlantic Ocean) at the lowest. Benin has a tropical climate.

HISTORY AND POLITICS

Dahomey, on the site of modern-day Benin, was a west African kingdom founded in the 11th and 12th centuries that rose to prominence during the 15th and 16th centuries. The first Europeans to visit the country were the Portuguese in 1472. Slavery became the region's primary trade, hence the area's historical name of the Slave Coast.

After a war between the French and the Dahomey kingdom in 1892–4, the French established a protectorate and this was incorporated into the federation of French West Africa in 1899. Dahomey became an independent republic within the French Community in 1958; full independence was proclaimed on 1 August 1960. Between 1960 and 1972 there was acute political instability, with frequent switches from civil to military rule and regional ethnic conflicts, until a coup d'état in 1972 brought to power a Marxist-Leninist military government headed by Lt.-Col. Mathieu Kérékou. The name of the country was changed to Benin in 1975.

The country became more stable and moved gradually towards democratic government; civil rule was restored in 1977 (though Kérékou remained president), Marxist-Leninism was abandoned in 1989 for economic liberalisation, a pluralistic constitution was adopted in 1990, and legislative and presidential elections were held in 1991. The transition to fully democratic government was effected smoothly and has operated successfully, making Benin one of the most stable countries in Africa.

The 2006 presidential election was won in the second round by Yayi Boni, an independent candidate, who received 74.5 per cent of the vote. In the 2007 legislative election, the Cauri Forces for an Emerging Benin party, which supports the president, won the most seats.

POLITICAL SYSTEM

Under the 1990 constitution, the executive president is directly elected for a five-year term. The unicameral legislature, the national assembly, has 83 members, directly elected for a four-year term. The president appoints and chairs the council of ministers.

HEAD OF STATE

President and Head of the Armed Forces, Yayi Boni, *elected* 19 March 2006

ELECTED GOVERNMENT MEMBERS *AS AT MAY 2007*
conomic Development and Finance, Pascal Koukpaki
oreign Affairs, Mariam Aladji Boni Diallo
Vational Defence, Issifou Koguidro

MBASSY OF THE REPUBLIC OF BENIN
7 Avenue Victor Hugo, F-75116 Paris, France
(+33) (1) 4500 9882 E ambassade.benin@gofornet.com
mbassador Extraordinary and Plenipotentiary, HE Edgar-Yves Monnou, *apptd* 2004

RITISH AMBASSADOR
IE Richard Gozney, *apptd* 2004, resident at Abuja, Nigeria

CONOMY AND TRADE

'he economy is underdeveloped, with a third of the opulation below the poverty line, and Benin has a high rade deficit and massive foreign debt. Restructuring of he economy to meet the criteria of international aid onors secured a US$460m (£230m) debt reduction ackage in 2000, G8 debt relief in 2005 and a US$307m £153m) grant in 2006. Economic growth has been teady since 2000 but its effects have been outweighed by ven more rapid population growth and continuing Vigerian trade protection. Plans for further economic xpansion include the development of tourism, new gricultural products and food processing systems and nformation and communications technology together vith attracting more foreign investment. Privatisation of ndustries, including utilities, began in 2001.

The contribution of agriculture to GDP has recently leclined as industry and services have developed. The nain cash crops are cotton, palm products, cashew nuts, hea butter and seafood, and the principal industrial ctivities are textiles and food processing. Main trading artners include China, France and Asian and eighbouring countries, to which textiles and some of the ash crops are exported.

GNI – US$4,300m; US$510 per capita (2005)
ANNUAL AVERAGE GROWTH OF GDP – 3.5 per cent (2005 est)
NFLATION RATE – 3.5 per cent (2005 est)
TOTAL EXTERNAL DEBT – US$1,600m (2000)
MPORTS – US$890m (2005)
EXPORTS – US$290m (2005)

BALANCE OF PAYMENTS
Trade – US$278m deficit (2003)
Current Account – US$349m deficit (2003)

Trade with UK	*2005*	*2006*
Imports from UK	£33,276,000	£37,644,000
Exports to UK	£38,000	£291,000

MEDIA

The media in Benin is mostly free of interference. Free peech is guaranteed by the constitution, although ournalists are wary of stringent libel laws. There are over 50 newspapers and periodicals, including five daily ewspapers, four of which are privately-owned. The state uns a single television station and there are a handful of ther commercial broadcasters. Radio stations are also a nixture of state, commercial and local.

BHUTAN

Druk Gyalkhap – Kingdom of Bhutan

AREA – 47,000 sq. km. Neighbours: Tibet (north), India (west, south and east)
CAPITAL – Thimphu; population, 98,676 (2005)
CURRENCY – Ngultrum of 100 chetrum (Indian currency is also legal tender)
POPULATION – 2,279,723 rising at 2.1 per cent per year (2006 est); Bhote (50 per cent), ethnic Nepalese (35 per cent), indigenous or migrant tribes (15 per cent) (est)
RELIGION – Buddhism (75 per cent), Hinduism (25 per cent) (est)
LANGUAGE – Dzongkha, English (both official)
POPULATION DENSITY – 14 per sq. km (2005)
URBAN POPULATION – 9.1 per cent (2005 est)
MEDIAN AGE (years) – 20.4 (2006 est)
NATIONAL ANTHEM – 'Druk Tsendhen' ['In the Thunder Dragon Kingdom]
NATIONAL DAY – 17 December
LIFE EXPECTANCY (years) – 54.78 (2006 est)
MORTALITY RATE – 12.7 (2006 est)
BIRTH RATE – 33.65 (2006 est)
INFANT MORTALITY RATE – 98.41 (2006 est)
DEATH PENALTY – No (abolished 2004)
CPI SCORE – 6.0 (2006)

CLIMATE AND TERRAIN

Bhutan is a landlocked Himalayan country lying between China and India. There is a mountainous northern region which is infertile and sparsely populated, a central zone of upland valleys, where most of the population and cultivated land is found, and densely forested foothills in the south, which are mainly inhabited by Nepalese settlers and indigenous tribespeople. Extremes of elevation range from 7,553m (K'ula Shan) at the highest point to 97m (Drangme Chhu) at the lowest. The climate is dependent on altitude and average temperatures range from 4°C in January to 17°C in July. There is heavy annual rainfall of around 1,000mm in the central valleys and 5,000mm in the south.

HISTORY AND POLITICS

Bhutan's remoteness limited outside contact until modern times, although it signed a treaty of cooperation with Britain in 1774. A trade treaty was signed with Britain in 1865 after Britain had annexed the south of the country. A 1910 treaty placed foreign relations under the guidance of the British government in India, and in 1949 Bhutan signed a similar treaty with India under which it is guided by India in its external relations; a 2007 agreement revising this relationship gave Bhutan more say over its foreign and defence policies. It has its own diplomatic representatives and is a member of the UN.

Although the country has opened up since the 1970s, the king has taken measures to preserve its indigenous culture, language and the environment, including the introduction of a code of national etiquette in 1989, compulsory national dress and restrictions on tourism. The emphasis on the majority culture, together with the granting of citizenship only to Nepalis settled in Bhutan before 1958, led to tension with the sizeable Nepali minority which resulted in an exodus to Nepal, where they remain living in refugee camps. In 2001 Bhutan and Nepal began an agreed process of refugee repatriation.

Since the 1950s Bhutan has been moving towards the

establishment of more formal political institutions. An elected legislature was established in 1953, and in 1969 the absolute monarchy was replaced by a form of democratic monarchy with the king as head of a cabinet. However, popular agitation in the 1990s for greater democracy led the king to transfer some of his powers to the national assembly. Democratisation was taken further with the king's endorsement of a draft constitution in 2005; a referendum on the constitution is expected in late 2007, followed by the first fully democratic elections to a bicameral legislature in spring 2008. The king had announced that he would abdicate at the time of the election, allowing the Crown Prince to accede to the throne as a constitutional monarch, but instead abdicated in December 2006.

POLITICAL SYSTEM

Bhutan has no formal constitution at present; institutions and roles are defined mainly by a royal edict of 1998. The head of state is the hereditary monarch, whose position is confirmed by a two-thirds majority in a vote in the legislature every three years. The unicameral legislature, the *Tshogdu Chhenmo* (national assembly), has 155 members, 105 directly elected for a three-year term, 37 members nominated by the government, and 12 members representing religious bodies. The *Lhengyal Shungtshog* (council of ministers) is headed by an annually rotating chairman. Ministers are elected by the national assembly for a five-year term, after which time they must face a vote of confidence. Political parties are being established to coincide with the introduction of democracy.

HEAD OF STATE

HM The King of Bhutan, Jigme Khesar Namgyal Wangchuk, *born* 21 February 1980, *succeeded his father* 14 December 2006

SELECTED GOVERNMENT MEMBERS *as at May 2007*

Chair of the Cabinet, Foreign Affairs, Khandu Wangchuk
Finance, Wangdi Norbu
Home and Cultural Affairs, Jigme Thinley
Attorney-General, Damcho Dorji

HONORARY CONSULATE

2 Windacres, Warren Road, Guildford GU1 2HG
T 01483-538189 E mrutland@aol.com
Honorary Consul, Michael R. Rutland

ECONOMY AND TRADE

The economy is based on industry (37 per cent of GDP in 2005), and agriculture (25 per cent of GDP). The services sector is growing, accounting for 38 per cent of GDP. Agriculture and animal husbandry engage around 63 per cent of the workforce in what is largely a self-sufficient rural society, although the country's mountainous topography and 60 per cent forest cover limit the area under cultivation. The principal food crops are rice and cereals. Vegetables and fruit are also produced. Bhutan is the world's largest producer of cardamom, which forms its principal export to countries other than India.

Industries include mining (limestone, gypsum, dolomite, graphite, coal), cement, chemicals, food processing, distilling and forestry. Tourism and postage stamps are increasingly important sources of foreign exchange. Principal exports are electricity (to India), cardemom, gypsum, timber, handicrafts, cement, fruit, precious stones and spices; main imports are fuel and lubricants, grain, aircraft, machinery and parts, vehicles fabrics and rice.

GNI – US$798m; US$1,250 per capita (2005)
ANNUAL AVERAGE GROWTH OF GDP – 5.9 per cent (2005 est)
INFLATION RATE – 7 per cent (2005 est)
TOTAL EXTERNAL DEBT – US$593m (2004)
IMPORTS – US$400m (2004)
EXPORTS – US$200m (2004)

Trade with UK	*2005*	*2006*
Imports from UK	£794,000	£513,000
Exports to UK	£243,000	£58,000

MEDIA

Television was introduced as recently as 1999 owing to fears that outside influences would undermine the country's culture and institutions. Services are controlled by the state's Bhutan Broadcasting Service (BBS). Radio broadcasting was introduced in 1973 and internet access in 1999. Media freedom is heavily restricted by the government, ensuring there are no private broadcasters.

BOLIVIA

República de Bolivia – Republic of Bolivia

AREA – 1,098,580 sq. km. Neighbours: Brazil (north and east), Paraguay and Argentina (south), Chile and Peru (west)
CAPITAL – La Paz, the seat of government; population, 835,200 (2006 est). Sucre is the legal centre and seat of the judiciary.
MAJOR CITIES – Santa Cruz; El Alto; Cochabamba; Sucre; Oruro
CURRENCY – Boliviano ($b) of 100 centavos
POPULATION – 8,989,046 rising at 1.45 per cent per year (2006 est); Quechua (30 per cent), *mestizo* (30 per cent), Aymara (25 per cent) (est)
RELIGION – Roman Catholicism (78 per cent), Protestantism (16 per cent) (est)
LANGUAGE – Spanish, Quecha, Aymara (all official)
POPULATION DENSITY – 8 per sq. km (2005)
URBAN POPULATION – 64.4 per cent (2005 est)
MEDIAN AGE (years) – 21.8 (2006 est)
NATIONAL ANTHEM – 'Cançion Patriótica' ['Patriotic Song']
NATIONAL DAY – 6 August (Independence Day)
LIFE EXPECTANCY (years) – 65.84 (2006 est)
MORTALITY RATE – 7.53 (2006 est)
BIRTH RATE – 23.3 (2006 est)
INFANT MORTALITY RATE – 51.77 (2006 est)
DEATH PENALTY – Yes*
CPI SCORE – 2.7 (2006)
POPULATION BELOW POVERTY LINE – 64 per cent (2004 est)

CLIMATE AND TERRAIN

A landlocked country, Bolivia's chief topographical feature is its great central plateau. Over 800km in length, at an average altitude of 3,750m above sea level, this plateau lies between the two great chains of the Andes which traverse the country from south to north. Elevation extremes range from 6,542m (Nevado Sajama) at the highest point to 90m (Rio Paraguay) at the lowest. The and falls from the Andean ridges in the west through forested foothills to the plains of the north and east. These are drained by the principal rivers, the Itenez, Beni, Mamore and Madre de Dios. The wet season is November to March. There is an average temperature of 26°C in most of the country but the south is prone to droughts and temperatures become subpolar at an altitude of 500m.

HISTORY AND POLITICS

The area of present-day Bolivia was assimilated into the Inca Empire in 1450. The Inca Empire was conquered by the Spanish in 1525. Bolivia won its independence from Spain in 1825 after a war of liberation led by Simón Bolívar (1783–1830), from whom the country derives its name. Much territory was lost after wars with neighbouring countries, including a devastating defeat in the Chaco War (1932–5) against Paraguay.

Bolivia was ruled by military juntas from 1936 to 1952 and from 1964 to 1982, when civilian rule was restored amid worsening economic conditions as the tin market collapsed and inflation rose dramatically. Austerity measures introduced in 1983 succeeded over the next decade in curbing inflation and attracting foreign investment, but the measures widened social divisions and created great social unrest. The unrest centred on coca crop eradication programmes, which were essential to attract overseas aid but caused economic hardship amongst the poor, and plans to exploit and export natural gas. Civil unrest over the latter resulted in the resignations of two successive presidents: Gonzalo Sánchez de Lozada in 2002 (after only three months in office) and his successor Carlos Mesa in 2005.

Evo Morales, the country's first indigenous president and a former coca growers' leader, has dealt with these issues by renationalising the energy industry and promising to relax restrictions on coca cultivation and seek alternative uses for the crop. There are plans to renationalise other industries, including utilities.

President Morales, leader of the Movement Towards Socialism (MAS), took office in 2006 after winning the 2005 presidential elections. In the simultaneous legislative elections, the MAS won an outright majority in the chamber of deputies but the Social and Democratic Power party became the largest party in the senate.

POLITICAL SYSTEM

The 1967 constitution was revised in 1994. It provides for an executive president who is directly elected for a five-year term, which is not renewable; the president is chosen by the congress if no candidate wins the majority of the vote. The bicameral national congress consists of a 27-member senate and a 130-member chamber of deputies; members of both chambers are directly elected for a five-year term.

An assembly was elected in June 2006 to consider a new constitution.

HEAD OF STATE

President, Evo Morales Ayma, *elected* 18 December 2005, *sworn in* 22 January 2006

President of the Senate, Vice-President, Alvaro Garcia

SELECTED GOVERNMENT MEMBERS *as at May 2007*

Defence, Walker Rodriguez San Miguel

Finance, Luis Alberto Arce Catacora

Foreign Affairs, David Choquehuanca Cespedes

Interior, Alfredo Rada Velez

BOLIVIAN EMBASSY

106 Eaton Square, London SW1W 9AD

T 020-7235 2257 W www.embassyofbolivia.co.uk

Ambassador Extraordinary and Plenipotentiary, HE Beatriz Souviron, *apptd* 2007

BRITISH EMBASSY

Avenida Arce 2732, PO Box 694, La Paz

T (+591) (2) 243 2397 E ppa@megalink.com

W www.britishembassy.gov.uk/bolivia

Ambassador Extraordinary and Plenipotentiary, HE Peter Bateman, *apptd* 2005

BRITISH COUNCIL

Avenida Arce 2732 (esq. Campos), Casilla 694, La Paz

T (+591) (2) 2431240 E information@britishcouncil.org.bo

Director, Eric Lawrie

DEFENCE

The army has 115 armoured personnel carriers and 54 light tanks. The navy has 54 patrol and coastal vessels. The air force has 33 combat aircraft.

MILITARY BUDGET – US$155m (2006)

MILITARY PERSONNEL – 46,100: army 34,800, navy 4,800, air force 6,500; paramilitaries 37,100

ECONOMY AND TRADE

The country is one of the poorest and least developed in South America. Economic reform from 1983 turned around the 1980s economic crisis, creating steady growth in the 1990s, although this slowed from 1999 to 2006. Despite this growth, over 60 per cent of the population lives below the poverty line. Debt cancellation by the G8 countries and international institutions, and budget and trade surpluses have relieved fiscal pressures on the government, but foreign investment has dropped as a result of the renationalisation of the energy industry.

Mining (principally for zinc, tin and gold) and smelting, natural gas and oil production and agriculture are the principal industries. Exporting of natural gas has contributed to higher economic growth since 2003; production in 2004 was 10,050m cubic metres, of which 7,910m cubic metres was exported.

In 1996 Bolivia joined MERCOSUR, which aims to create a free trade zone. Bolivia's main trading partners are other South American countries, particularly Brazil and Argentina, and the USA. Principal exports are natural gas, soya beans and soya products, crude oil, zinc ore and tin. The main imports are petroleum products, plastics, papers, transport equipment, vehicles and processed foods.

GNI – US$9,300m; US$1,010 per capita (2005)

ANNUAL AVERAGE GROWTH OF GDP – 4.1 per cent (2005 est)

INFLATION RATE – 5.4 per cent (2005 est)

TOTAL EXTERNAL DEBT – US$6,309m (2005)

IMPORTS – US$2,300m (2005)

EXPORTS – US$2,700m (2005)

BALANCE OF PAYMENTS

Trade – US$479m surplus (2005)

Current Account – US$467m surplus (2005)

Trade with UK	*2005*	*2006*
Imports from UK	£11,150,000	£6,081,000
Exports to UK	£14,272,000	£10,170,000

COMMUNICATIONS

Although landlocked, Bolivia has 10,000km of commercially navigable waterways, with an inland port on the River Paraguay at the border with Brazil. It has free port privileges at seaports in Argentina, Brazil, Chile and Paraguay, and a lease on a free-trade zone at the Peruvian port of Ilo. Bolivia has 1,084 airports and airfields, including four international airports serving the major cities. The 3,519km of railways form an eastern network and an Andean network; plans to link the two were initiated in 2004, and the link would complete a transcontinental railway line between the Brazilian and Chilean coasts. Of the 62,479km of roads, fewer than 4,000km are surfaced. The land-line telephone system is largely confined to the cities. Mobile phone use is growing rapidly.

EDUCATION AND HEALTH

Elementary education is compulsory and free from the ages of six to 11. There are secondary schools in urban centres but only about a third of children of secondary school age attend.

LITERACY RATE – 86.5 per cent (2004 est)
GROSS ENROLMENT RATIO (percentage of relevant age group) – primary 113 per cent; secondary 88 per cent; tertiary 41 per cent (2005 est)
HEALTH EXPENDITURE (per capita) – US$66 (2004)
HOSPITAL BEDS (per 1,000 people) – 1 (2000–5)

MEDIA

Radio is the most important news medium in Bolivia owing to low literacy levels, particularly in rural areas. The media is largely privately owned and operated. Journalists practise self-censorship, avoiding sensitive topics such as drug-trafficking and political corruption. There are six daily newspapers, each with limited influence. Television is mostly commercial, with only one government-run channel.

BOSNIA AND HERCEGOVINA

Bosna i Hercegovina – Bosnia and Hercegovina

AREA – 51,129 sq. km. Neighbours: Serbia, Montenegro (east), Croatia (north and west)
CAPITAL – Sarajevo; population, 380,000 (2005 est)
MAJOR CITIES – Banja Luka; Zenica; Tuzla; Mostar
CURRENCY – Convertible marka
POPULATION – 4,498,976 rising at 1.35 per cent per year (2006 est); Bosniak (48 per cent), Serb (37.1 per cent), Croat (14.3 per cent) (est)
RELIGION – Islam (40 per cent), Orthodox Christianity (31 per cent), Roman Catholicism (15 per cent), other Christian denominations (10 per cent) (est)
LANGUAGE – Bosnian, Croatian, Serbian (all official)
POPULATION DENSITY – 76 per sq. km (2005)
URBAN POPULATION – 45.3 per cent (2005 est)
MEDIAN AGE (years) – 38.4 (2006 est)
NATIONAL ANTHEM – 'Intermeco'
NATIONAL DAY – 25 November
LIFE EXPECTANCY (years) – 78 (2006 est)
MORTALITY RATE – 8.27 (2006 est)
BIRTH RATE – 8.77 (2006 est)
INFANT MORTALITY RATE – 9.82 (2006 est)
DEATH PENALTY – No (abolished 2001)
CPI SCORE – 2.9 (2006)
POPULATION BELOW POVERTY LINE – 25 per cent (2004 est)
LITERACY RATE – 94.6 per cent (2004 est)
MILITARY BUDGET – US$144m (2006)
MILITARY PERSONNEL – 11,865: State Joint Operational Command 21, State Joint Staff 19, AFBiH 11,825
HEALTH EXPENDITURE (per capita) – US$198 (2004)

CLIMATE AND TERRAIN

Lying in the Balkan peninsula, the country includes the Dinaric Alps in the west. The mountainous centre is split by gorges, while the north is lower-lying, falling to the valley of the River Sava, which forms the northern border with Croatia. There is 20km of Adriatic coastline. The highest point of elevation is 2,386m (Maglic), the lowest point is 0m (Adriatic Sea). Average temperatures in Sarajevo range from 0°C in January to 25°C in July.

HISTORY AND POLITICS

The country was settled by Slavs in the seventh century and conquered by the Ottoman Turks in 1463. Ruled by the Turks for over 400 years, the country came under Austro-Hungarian control in 1878. The assassination of Franz Ferdinand, the heir to the Austro-Hungarian throne by Gavrilo Princip, an ethnic Serb, precipitated the First World War, after which Bosnia-Hercegovina became part of the Kingdom of Serbs, Croats and Slovenes (renamed Yugoslavia in 1929). It was occupied by German and Axis forces between 1941 and 1945. At the end of the war, Bosnia-Hercegovina became part of the Socialist Federal Republic of Yugoslavia, which eventually collapsed with the secession of Slovenia and Croatia in 1991.

In October 1991 the government of Bosnia-Hercegovina outlined plans for a referendum on independence. In response, the Serbian Democratic Party, led by Radovan Karadzic, pulled out of the coalition government and founded what would become the Republic of Serbia. This state included of a number of Serb autonomous regions within Bosnia, which the government ruled as unconstitutional. The referendum, though boycotted by Bosnian Serbs, showed 99.43 per cent in favour and independence was declared on 5 March 1992. Despite the turnout failing to match the two-thirds required by constitution to make the result legal, Bosnia-Hercegovina was recognised as an independent state and granted UN membership in May 1992.

In March 1992 Republic of Serbia forces, which included the Federal Yugoslav Army (JNA) of Ratko Mladic, began a military campaign in the eastern Bosnian-held area of the country, expelling Bosniaks and Croats. The military firepower of the JNA ensured 70 per cent of the country fell by May. The Serbs also instituted a complete blockade of the capital, Sarajevo, which led to the deployment of a UN protection force whose role was quickly expanded to provide aid across the country.

Meanwhile, the government of Bosnia-Hercegovina splintered further as the Croatian Democratic Union proclaimed the creation of the Croatian Republic of Herceg-Bosnia as a third separate territory. Tensions between the Bosniaks and the Croats were aggravated by the 1993 joint UN-EC plan (the Vance-Owen plan), which proposed to divide the country into ten autonomous areas on ethnic lines, and further conflicts broke out. Croat forces were able to take control of much of the Bosniak infrastructure and imposed Croatian language, propaganda and currency. The Bosniak-Croat conflict was officially ended by the Washington agreement in 1994, which united the two forces against the Serbs.

The Vance-Owen plan was also rejected by the Serbs. In July 1995 JNA forces moved into the UN designated safe area of Srebrenica and killed 8,000 Bosniak men, in an event later ruled as genocide by the International Criminal Tribunal for the Former Yugoslavia. In August NATO intervened in the siege of Sarajevo following months of escalating bloodshed. A sustained bombing campaign was launched aimed at weakening Serb forces, the impact of which forced the Serb leader Slobodan Milosevic to negotiate the Dayton agreement, which brought the war to an end in December 1995. It is estimated 100,000 died between 1992 and 1995.

The Dayton agreement preserved Bosnia as a single state with an almost equal division of territory between two self-governing entities, the Federation of Bosnia-Hercegovina (Bosniak/Croat) and the Republic of Serbia (Bosnian Serbs), with a national government, presidency and democratically elected institutions.

The latest legislative and collective presidental elections and elections for the presidency of the Republic of Serbia were held in 2006. In the federal parliamentary assembly, the largest party remained the Bosniak Party of Democratic Action (SDA). It became a partner in a coalition government with five other parties. The SDA also prevailed in the Federation of Bosnia and Hercegovina and formed a new government under Nedzad Brankovic. In the Republic of Serbia, Milan Jelic was elected president, the Alliance of Independent Social Democrats won most seats in the people's assembly and formed a government under Milorad Dodik. The 2007 presidential election in the Bosniak-Croat Federation was won by Borjana Kristo.

POLITICAL SYSTEM

Under the Dayton Peace Accord, the Bosnian republican (national) government is responsible for foreign affairs, currency, citizenship and immigration. The head of state is a collective presidency comprising a representative from each of the three ethnic groups, all directly elected for a four-year term; the chairmanship of the presidency rotates among its members every eight months. Legislative authority is vested in the bicameral parliamentary assembly of Bosnia and Hercegovina, comprising a house of peoples and a house of representatives. Both houses have four-year terms. The house of peoples has 15 members, ten from the Federation and five from the Republika Srpska, who are selected by the house of representatives. The house of representatives has 42 members who are directly elected to the two constituent chambers, the chamber of deputies of the Federation, which has 28 members, and the chamber of deputies of the Republika Srpska, which has 14 members.

In the Bosniac-Croat Federation, the president and vice-president are elected by the Bosniac and Croat members of the house of peoples for a four-year term; a second vice-president is elected to represent the Serb population. There is a bicameral assembly comprising a 58-member house of peoples elected on an ethnic basis and a house of representatives with 98 directly elected members.

In the Republika Srpska, the president is directly elected for a four-year term. There is a unicameral people's assembly with 83 members directly elected for a four-year term.

There is a national council of ministers and each of the entities also has its own executive. All appointments to the executives are in consultation with the UN High Representative and may be vetoed by him.

REPUBLIC OF BOSNIA AND HERCEGOVINA
HEADS OF STATE
Presidency Members, Nebojsa Radmanovic, Zeljko Komsic, Haris Silajdzic

SELECTED GOVERNMENT MEMBERS *as at May 2007*
Prime Minister, European Integration, Nikola Spiric
Deputy Prime Minister, Treasury and Finance, Dragan Vrankic
Foreign Affairs, Sven Alkalaj
Defence, Selmo Cikotic

FEDERATION OF BOSNIA AND HERCEGOVINA
HEAD
President, Borjana Kristo
Vice-Presidents, Mirsad Kebo, Spomenka Micic

SELECTED GOVERNMENT MEMBERS *as at May 2007*
Prime Minister, Nedzad Brankovic
Deputy Prime Minister, Culture and Sport, Gavrilo Grahovac
Deputy Prime Minister, Finance, Vjekoslav Bevanda
Interior, Muhidin Alic

REPUBLIKA SRPSKA
HEAD
President, Milan Jelic
Vice-Presidents, Adil Osmanovic; Davor Cordas

SELECTED GOVERNMENT MEMBERS *as at May 2007*
Prime Minister, Milorad Dodik
Finance, Aleksandar Dzombic
Interior, Stanislav Cadjo

OFFICE OF THE UN HIGH REPRESENTATIVE / EU SPECIAL REPRESENTATIVE
UN High Representative, Christian Schwarz-Schilling, *apptd* 2006

EMBASSY OF BOSNIA AND HERCEGOVINA
5–7 Lexham Gardens, London W8 5JJ
T 020-7373 0867 E bhembassylondon@yahoo.com
Ambassador Extraordinary and Plenipotentiary, HE Dr Tanja Milasinovic, *apptd* 2005

BRITISH EMBASSY
Tina Ujevica 8, 71000 Sarajevo
T (+387) (33) 282 200 E britemb@bih.net.ba
W www.britishembassy.ba
Ambassador Extraordinary and Plenipotentiary, HE Matthew Rycroft, CBE, *apptd* 2005

BRITISH COUNCIL
Ljubljanska 9, 71000 Sarajevo
T (+387) (033) 250 220 W www.britishcouncil.org/bih
Director, Chris Rawlings

ECONOMY AND TRADE

When the civil war broke out, the structure of the economy (dominated by state-owned industries, mainly of a military nature) still reflected the central planning of the Communist era. Industrial recovery after the war has been hampered by this lack of diversity and commercial potential. Privatisation of industry has been slow, and although most agriculture is now in the private sector, it suffers from inefficiency. The economic growth rate has slowed in recent years and there is a considerable trade deficit and high unemployment; the latter was officially 45.4 per cent in 2004. Unofficial economic activity could represent output equivalent to half of the official GDP. The difficulties inherent in tackling these problems is exacerbated by the uneasy relations and reluctant co-operation between the different national and local political and administrative entities.

Most agricultural products are for domestic consumption and foodstuffs also have to be imported. There are a variety of natural resources and the main industrial activities include mining (metals, minerals and coal), production of steel, textiles, tobacco products, wooden furniture and domestic appliances, assembly of vehicles, tanks and aircraft, and oil refining. The country has enough hydroelectric power for its needs and is an exporter of electricity, but an importer of natural gas. The main trading partners are Croatia, Italy, Slovenia and other EU states. Principal exports are metals, clothing and wood products, and the main imports are machinery and equipment, chemicals, fuels and foodstuffs.

GNI – US$10,500m; US$2,700 per capita (2005)
ANNUAL AVERAGE GROWTH OF GDP – 5 per cent (2005 est)
INFLATION RATE – 4.4 per cent (2005 est)
UNEMPLOYMENT – 45.5 per cent (2004 est)
TOTAL EXTERNAL DEBT – US$3,116m (2005)

BALANCE OF PAYMENTS
Trade – US$4,954m deficit (2005)
Current Account – US$2,087m deficit (2005)

Trade with UK	*2005*	*2006*
Imports from UK	£24,330,000	£18,905,000
Exports to UK	£5,381,000	£7,933,000

COMMUNICATIONS

Although the country has 20km of coastline on the Adriatic Sea, there are no seaports. There are four river ports on the River Sava, which is navigable by shipping but its use is limited. The 28 airports and airfields include international airports at Sarajevo, Banja Luka, Mostar and Tuzla. There are 608km of railways and 21,846km of roads, 11,425km of which are paved. The telephone network is in need of modernisation. Mobile phone distribution is greater than main line use.

MEDIA

Since the 1995 peace accord, efforts have been made to reintroduce a balanced press that crosses ethnic divides. These efforts have not been entirely successful because of the pressure placed on the media by governments and political parties. A national broadcasting service is being developed under the aegis of the Office of the High Representative. There are more than 200 commercial television and radio stations.

BOTSWANA

Republic of Botswana

AREA – 600,370 sq. km. Neighbours: South Africa (south and east), Zimbabwe (north and north-east), Namibia (west), Zambia (north)
CAPITAL – Gaborone; population, 186,007 (2001)
MAJOR CITIES – Francistown; Molepolole; Selebi-Phikwe
CURRENCY – Pula (P) of 100 thebe
POPULATION – 1,639,833 falling at 0.04 per cent per year (2006 est); Motswana (79 per cent), Bakalanga (11 per cent), Basarwa (3 per cent) (est)
RELIGION – Christianity (50 per cent), Islam (1 per cent), Hinduism (1 per cent) (est)
LANGUAGE – English (official), Setswana, Kalanga, Sekgalagadi
POPULATION DENSITY – 3 per sq. km (2005)
URBAN POPULATION – 52.5 per cent (2005 est)
MEDIAN AGE (years) – 19.4 (2006 est)
NATIONAL ANTHEM – 'Fatshe Leno La Rona' ['Blessed be this Noble Land']
NATIONAL DAY – 30 September (Botswana Day)
LIFE EXPECTANCY (years) – 33.74 (2006 est)
MORTALITY RATE – 29.5 (2006 est)
BIRTH RATE – 23.08 (2006 est)
INFANT MORTALITY RATE – 53.7 (2006 est)
HIV/AIDS ADULT PREVALENCE – 37.3 per cent (2003 est)
DEATH PENALTY – Yes
CPI SCORE – 5.6 (2006)
POPULATION BELOW POVERTY LINE – 30.3 per cent (2003)
MILITARY BUDGET – US$262m (2006 est)
MILITARY PERSONNEL – 9,000: army 8,500, air force 500; Paramilitary 1,500

CLIMATE AND TERRAIN

A landlocked country in southern Africa, Botswana has two main topographical regions divided by a plateau with an average height of around 1,200m. To the east of the plateau, streams run into the Marico, Notwani and Limpopo rivers; to the west lies a flat region comprising the Bakgalagadi Desert, the Okavango swamps and the Northern State Lands area. Elevation extremes range from 1,489m (Tsodilo Hills) at the highest point to 513m (junction of the Limpopo and Shashe rivers) at the lowest. The climate is subtropical in the north (Okavango Delta, including the Central Kalahari game reserve), arid in the south and west (Kalahari Desert), and temperate in the east (arable farming land). Average temperatures range from 26°C in January to 13°C in July.

HISTORY AND POLITICS

The Tswana people were dominant in the area from the 17th century. In 1885, at the request of indigenous chiefs fearing invasion by the Boers, Britain formally took control of Bechuanaland, and the northern part of the territory was declared the Bechuanaland Protectorate, while land to the south of the Molopo River became British Bechuanaland, which was later incorporated into the Cape Colony. In 1964, the British Protectorate of Bechuanaland became self-governing, and on 30 September 1966 it became an independent republic under the name Botswana. Since independence, Botswana has been stable and relatively prosperous owing to the diamond mining industry, but the high level of HIV/AIDS among the population means that despite an advanced treatment programme in place since 2001, it is facing serious demographic and social problems.

The 2004 general election was won by the Botswana Democratic Party, with 51.7 per cent of the vote. In the presidential election the following day, Festus Mogae was re-elected for a second term.

POLITICAL SYSTEM
Under the 1966 constitution, the executive president is elected by the national assembly for a five-year term, renewable only once. He appoints the vice-president and the cabinet. The national assembly has 57 members directly elected for a five-year term, plus a variable number of co-opted members (currently four). A 15-member house of chiefs advises on tribal matters and constitutional changes.

HEAD OF STATE
President, C.-in-C. of the Armed Forces, HE Festus Mogae, *sworn in* 2 April 1998, *re-elected* 1 November 2004
Vice-President, Lt.-Gen. Ian Khama

SELECTED GOVERNMENT MEMBERS *as at May 2007*
Finance and Development Planning, Baledzi Gaolathe
Foreign Affairs, Lt.-Gen. Mompati Merafhe
Labour and Home Affairs, Charles Tibone
Health, Sheila Tlou

BOTSWANA HIGH COMMISSION
6 Stratford Place, London W1C 1AY
T 020-7499 0031 E bohico@govbw.com
High Commissioner, HE Roy Blackbeard, *apptd* 1998

BRITISH HIGH COMMISSION
Private Bag 0023, Gaborone
T (+267) 395 2841 E bhc@botsnet.bw
W www.britishhighcommission.gov.uk/botswana
High Commissioner, HE Francis Martin, *apptd* 2005

BRITISH COUNCIL
PO Box 439, British High Commission Building, Queen's Road, The Mall, Gaborone
T (+267) 395 3602 W www.britishcouncil.org/botswana
Director, Stephen Forbes

ECONOMY AND TRADE
Botswana has been relatively prosperous since independence because of its mining industry, political stability and sound economic management. Despite this, about 30 per cent of the population lives below the poverty line and there are high levels of unemployment. Longer-term problems are the economic and social impact of the high levels of HIV/AIDS among the workforce, and the levelling off of diamond production. The government has sought to reduce the economy's dependence on the diamond industry by diversifying; safari tourism and financial services in particular have grown in recent years, and the services sector now contributes 51 per cent of GDP. The industrial sector contributes 47 per cent of GDP, of which 36 per cent is from mining diamonds, copper, nickel, salt, soda ash, potash and coal. Agriculture is predominantly pastoral and accounts for 2 per cent of GDP. Cattle-rearing represents over 80 per cent of agricultural production.

The main trading partners are European and other southern African countries. Principal exports are diamonds, copper, nickel, soda ash, meat and textiles. The main imports are foodstuffs, machinery, electrical goods, transport equipment, textiles, energy and fuel.
GNI – US$9,900m; US$5,590 per capita (2005)
ANNUAL AVERAGE GROWTH OF GDP – 5.5 per cent (2005 est)
INFLATION RATE – 8.6 per cent (2005 est)
UNEMPLOYMENT – 23.8 per cent (2004 est)
TOTAL EXTERNAL DEBT – US$519m (2005 est)
IMPORTS – US$4,000m (2005)
EXPORTS – US$4,290m (2005)

BALANCE OF PAYMENTS
Trade – US$897m surplus (2003)
Current Account – US$483m surplus (2003)

Trade with UK	*2005*	*2006*
Imports from UK	£15,637,000	£13,942,000
Exports to UK	£1,157,199,000	£1,204,906,000

COMMUNICATIONS
Because of its landlocked position, Botswana's trade is dependent on its international rail and road links. The only railway line is the link from Zimbabwe to South Africa, which passes through eastern Botswana. There are 24,355km of roads, of which 8,914km are paved. These include a highway connecting all the main towns and district capitals. The network links at the borders with the road networks of South Africa and Namibia. A major link is the 595km Trans-Kalahari Highway, completed in 1998, which connects Botswana with Namibia's capital (Windhoek) and its port of Walvis Bay. There are over 80 airports and airfields, including the international airport at Gaborone. The land-line telephone system is limited in extent. Mobile phone distribution is growing rapidly.

EDUCATION AND HEALTH
Botswana does not have a compulsory education policy. Many children receive ten years of education, though the government announced in 2004 that efforts would be made to increase this to 12 years (seven years of primary education, three years of junior secondary, and two years of senior secondary).
LITERACY RATE – 78.9 per cent (2004 est)
GROSS ENROLMENT RATIO (percentage of relevant age group) – primary 105 per cent (2005 est); secondary 75 per cent (2002 est); tertiary 5 per cent (2005 est)
HEALTH EXPENDITURE (per capita) – US$329 (2004)

MEDIA
Botswana has a good record on press transparency, though newspaper circulation is almost entirely limited to urban areas. In rural communities radio is the most important news medium; there are state-run and private commercial stations, and programmes are broadcast in both English and Setswana. State-run television (Botswana Television) was established in 2000.

BRAZIL

República Federativa do Brasil – Federative Republic of Brazil

AREA – 8,511,965 sq. km. Neighbours: Guyana, Suriname, French Guiana, Colombia and Venezuela (north), Peru, Bolivia, Paraguay and Argentina (west), Uruguay (south)
CAPITAL – Brasília; population, 2,231,100 (2005 est)
MAJOR CITIES – Sao Paulo; Rio de Janeiro, the former capital; Salvador; Belo Horizonte; Fortaleza; Curitiba; Manaus; Recife
CURRENCY – Real of 100 centavos
POPULATION – 188,078,227 rising at 1.04 per cent per year (2006 est)

RELIGION – Roman Catholicism (74 per cent), Protestantism (15 per cent) (est)
LANGUAGE – Portuguese (official), English, French, Spanish
POPULATION DENSITY – 22 per sq. km (2005)
URBAN POPULATION – 84.2 per cent (2005 est)
MEDIAN AGE (years) – 28.2 (2006 est)
NATIONAL ANTHEM – 'Hino Nacional Brasileiro' ['Brazilian National Anthem']
NATIONAL DAY – 7 September (Independence Day)
LIFE EXPECTANCY (years) – 71.97 (2006 est)
MORTALITY RATE – 6.17 (2006 est)
BIRTH RATE – 16.56 (2006 est)
INFANT MORTALITY RATE – 28.6 (2006 est)
DEATH PENALTY – Yes*
CPI SCORE – 3.3 (2006)

CLIMATE AND TERRAIN

Brazil is South America's biggest country, taking up almost half of the continent. There are five distinct topographical areas: the Amazon basin (north and west, taking up nearly a third of the country), the River Plate basin (south), the Guyanan Highlands (north of the Amazon), the Brazilian Highlands (south of the Amazon), and the coastal strip. Brazil is mostly tropical, with the equator passing through the north and the Tropic of Capricorn through the south-east. It is the location of the world's biggest rainforest. The Amazon basin sees annual rainfall of up to 2,000mm a year and there is no dry season (average temperature 17°C). The north-east is the driest area of the country and can experience long periods of drought (average temperature 40°C). The southern states have a seasonal temperate climate (the average temperature is between 17°C and 19°C). Elevation extremes range from 3,014m (Pico da Neblina) at the highest point to 0m (Atlantic Ocean) at the lowest.

HISTORY AND POLITICS

Brazil was claimed by the Portuguese navigator Pedro lvares Cabral in 1500 and colonised by Portugal in the early 16th century, becoming a viceroyalty in 1572. During the Napoleonic Wars the Portuguese court transferred to Brazil. In 1822 it became an independent monarchy under Pedro I, son of King João VI of Portugal. In 1889, Pedro II was dethroned in a coup, and a republic was proclaimed in 1891. Brazil was a dictatorship from 1930 to 1945 and under military rule from 1964 to 1985, when civilian rule was restored after several years of gradual democratisation. Governments since then have faced difficult economic conditions, and exploitation of the Amazon basin has attracted controversy because it threatens the environmentally important rainforest.

In the 2006 legislative election, the Party of the Brazilian Democratic Movement (PMDB) became the largest party in the chamber of deputies and increased its seats in the senate, although the largest party in that house was the Liberal Front Party. President Luis ('Lula') da Silva of the Workers' Party (PT) was elected to a second term in the simultaneous presidential election. After the elections, the 11-party coalition government, dominated by the PT and including the PMDB, continued in office.

POLITICAL SYSTEM

Under the 1988 constitution, the executive president is directly elected for a four-year term; in 1997 the constitution was amended to allow the president to stand for a second term. The national congress consists of an 81-member federal senate (three senators per state, directly elected for an eight-year term) and a 513-member chamber of deputies which is directly elected every four years; the number of deputies per state depends upon the state's population. The republic's 26 states each has a governor and a legislative assembly with a four-year term.

HEAD OF STATE

President, Luis Inácio 'Lula' da Silva, *sworn in* 1 January 2003, *re-elected* October 2006
Vice-President, José Alencar Gomes da Silva

SELECTED GOVERNMENT MEMBERS *as at May 2007*

Defence, Waldir Pires
Foreign Affairs, Celso Amorim
Finance, Guido Mantega

EMBASSY OF BRAZIL

32 Green Street, London W1K 7AT
T 020-7399 9000 W www.brazil.org.uk
Ambassador Extraordinary and Plenipotentiary, HE José Maurício Bustani, *apptd* 2003

BRITISH EMBASSY

Setor de Embaixadas Sul, Quadra 801, Conjunto K, 70408, Brasília DF
T (+55) (61) 3325 2710 E contact@uk.org.br
W www.uk.org.br
Ambassador Extraordinary and Plenipotentiary, HE Dr Peter Collecot, CMG, *apptd* 2004

BRITISH COUNCIL

Edificio Centro Empresarial Varig, SCN Quadra 04, Bloco B, Torre Oeste Conjunto 202, 70710-926 Brasília DF
T (+55) (61) 2106 7500 W www.britishcouncil.org.br
Director, David Cordingley

FEDERAL STRUCTURE

The Federative Republic of Brazil is composed of the federal district in which the capital lies and 26 states: Acre, Alagoas, Amapá, Amazonas, Bahia, Ceará, Distrito Federal, Espírito Santo, Goiás, Maranhão, Mato Grosso, Mato Grosso do Sul, Minas Gerais, Pará, Paraíba, Paraná, Pernambuco, Piauí, Rio de Janeiro Rio Grande de Norte, Rio Grande de Sul, Rondônia, Roraima, Santa Catarina, São Paulo, Sergipe and Tocantins.

DEFENCE

The army has 219 main battle tanks, 803 armoured personnel carriers and 63 armed helicopters. The navy is equipped with 5 submarines, 1 aircraft carrier, 10 frigates and 32 patrol and coastal vessels. Naval aviation consists of 26 combat aircraft and 26 armed helicopters; the Marines have 45 armoured personnel carriers and 17 light tanks. The air force has 276 combat aircraft.
MILITARY BUDGET – US$16,400m (2006)
MILITARY PERSONNEL – 287,870: army 189,000, navy 32,850, air force 66,020; paramilitaries 385,600
CONSCRIPTION DURATION – 12 months (can be extended to 18)

ECONOMY AND TRADE

Historically subject to severe boom and bust cycles, the economy was stabilised by reforms in the 1990s that included privatisation and the removal of trade barriers. Tight fiscal management, IMF programmes, a growth in output and an expanding export base have produced steady growth in recent years, achieving trade surpluses and current account surpluses each year since 2003.

AREA OF DEFORESTATION IN BRAZILIAN AMAZON (sq. km)

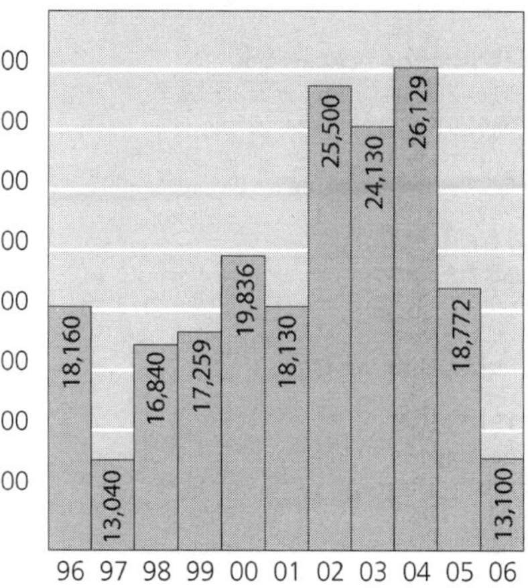

Source: W http://mongabay.com

Inflation and unemployment have both declined from their 2003 peak. However, public debt and foreign debt remain high, and poverty is still widespread.

The country is rich in mineral deposits, including iron ore (hematite), bauxite, diamonds, gold, nickel, lead and zirconium. It also produces oil, natural gas and hydroelectricity, although it is a net importer of all three. Brazil is the world's largest producer of coffee; the other main agricultural products being soya beans, wheat, rice, maize, sugar cane, cocoa, citrus fruits and beef. The expansion of agriculture and forestry threaten the rainforest, despite recent governments' attempts to prevent further depredations by loggers and farmers. Tourism is a growing industry. In 2006 services generated 54 per cent of GDP, industry 38 per cent and agriculture 8 per cent.

The main trading partners are the USA and Argentina, although trade with, and inward investment from, China are growing rapidly. Principal exports are transport equipment, iron ore, soya beans, footwear, coffee and vehicles. The main imports are machinery, electrical and transport equipment, chemicals and fuel.

GNI – US$662,000m; US$3,550 per capita (2005)
ANNUAL AVERAGE GROWTH OF GDP – 2.3 per cent (2005 est)
INFLATION RATE – 6.9 per cent (2005 est)
UNEMPLOYMENT – 9.8 per cent (2005 est)
TOTAL EXTERNAL DEBT – US$188,000m (2005 est)
IMPORTS – US$78,000m (2005)
EXPORTS – US$118,000m (2005)

BALANCE OF PAYMENTS
Trade – US$44,757m surplus (2005)
Current Account – US$14,199m surplus (2005)

Trade with UK	*2005*	*2006*
Imports from UK	£840,115,000	£920,759,000
Exports to UK	£1,771,469,000	£1,931,748,000

COMMUNICATIONS

The 1,751,868km road network and 29,252km rail network are concentrated in the more densely populated south and east of the country. The railways are used primarily for transporting minerals to the ports; most passenger and freight traffic is on the roads. The Trans-Amazonian Highway connects the Amazon region with the rest of the country, although being unpaved it is often impassable in the rainy season. In the remoter regions, transport is primarily by air or water, utilising the 50,000km of navigable waterways and the 4,276 airports and airfields; international flights operate to the major cities. Rio de Janeiro and Santos are the two leading seaports but there are also another 14 fully equipped ports. The land-line telephone system is extensive. Mobile phone distribution has grown rapidly to 86 million in 2005. In the same year, there were 26 million internet users.

EDUCATION AND HEALTH

The education system includes both public and private institutions. Public education is free at all levels. Brazil has 42 million students (2002) and 30.5 million of these are enrolled in primary education.

LITERACY RATE – 88.4 per cent (2004 est)
GROSS ENROLMENT RATIO (percentage of relevant age group) – primary 141 per cent; secondary 102 per cent (2005 est); tertiary 22 per cent (2005 est)
HEALTH EXPENDITURE (per capita) – US$290 (2004)
HOSPITAL BEDS (per 1,000 people) – 2.7 (2000–5)

MEDIA AND CULTURE

Brazilian television is South America's biggest media industry, with Brazilian-made soap operas, game shows and dramas exported all over the world. There are thousands of radio stations and hundreds of television channels. Globo, Brazil's most successful broadcasting conglomerate, dominates the market and owns television and radio networks, newspapers and subscription television stations. The country is heavily promoting digital television and aims to cut off the analogue signal in 2016.

Paolo Coelho (*b.* 1947) is Brazil's most commercially successful author and his novel *The Alchemist* is estimated to have sold 50 million copies worldwide. The film industry is currently thriving, with two directors, Walter Salles *(The Motorcycle Diaries)* and Fernando Meirelles *(City of God)*, achieving international recognition.

Football is central to contemporary Brazil. The country has produced some of the world's most technically gifted players, including Pele (*b.* 1940), Zico (*b.* 1953) and Ronaldinho (*b.* 1980). The yellow jersey of the national team is widely recognised due to a record five World Cup victories.

BRUNEI

Negara Brunei Darussalam – State of Brunei Darussalam

AREA – 5,770 sq. km. Neighbour: Malaysian state of Sarawak
CAPITAL – Bandar Seri Begawan; population, 46,000 (2001 est)
MAJOR TOWNS – Kuala Belait; Seria
CURRENCY – Brunei dollar (B $) of 100 sen (fully interchangeable with Singapore currency)
POPULATION – 379,444 rising at 1.87 per cent per year (2006 est); Malay (67 per cent), Chinese (15 per cent) (est)
RELIGION – Islam (67 per cent), Buddhism (13 per

cent), Christianity (10 per cent), indigenous religions (10 per cent) (est)
LANGUAGE – Malay (official), English, Chinese
POPULATION DENSITY – 71 per sq. km (2005)
URBAN POPULATION – 77.6 per cent (2005 est)
MEDIAN AGE (years) – 27.4 (2006 est)
NATIONAL ANTHEM – 'Allah Peliharakan Sultan' ['God Bless the Sultan']
NATIONAL DAY – 23 February
LIFE EXPECTANCY (years) – 75.01 (2006 est)
MORTALITY RATE – 3.45 (2006 est)
BIRTH RATE – 18.79 (2006 est)
INFANT MORTALITY RATE – 12.25 (2006 est)
DEATH PENALTY – No*

CLIMATE AND TERRAIN

Lying in the north-east of the island of Borneo, the country is divided into two sections by the Limbang River valley in Sarawak (Malaysia). The terrain is mostly rainforest (75 per cent), with extensive mangrove swamps along the coastal plain. There are mountains on the border with Sarawak. Elevation extremes range from 1,850m (Bukit Pagon) at the highest point to 0m (South China Sea) at the lowest. The climate is tropical, with high levels of humidity and an average daily temperature of between 24°C and 30°C.

HISTORY AND POLITICS

Formerly a powerful Muslim sultanate that controlled Borneo and parts of the Philippines, Brunei was reduced to its present size by the mid-19th century and became a British protectorate in 1888. In 1963 the sultanate chose to remain a British dependency rather than joining the Federation of Malaysia, and on 1 January 1984 Brunei gained full independence from Britain.

The first written constitution was promulgated in 1959, but in 1962 the legislative election was annulled after it was won by a party that sought to remove the sultan; a state of emergency was declared and the sultan has ruled by decree since. A ministerial system of government was introduced in 1984. Some political liberalisation and modernisation has taken place since 2004, but no date has been set for a legislative election.

POLITICAL SYSTEM

The 1959 constitution vests supreme executive authority in the sultan, who presides over and is advised by the privy council, the religious council and the council of ministers. The 21-member appointed legislative council was reconvened in 2004 and passed constitutional amendments that will increase its size to 45 members, one-third of whom will be directly elected. There are now three legal political groupings.

HEAD OF STATE
HM The Sultan of Brunei; Defence; Prime Minister; Finance, HM Sir Hassanal Bolkiah, GCB, *acceded* 1967, *crowned* 1 August 1968
HM Crown Prince; Senior Minister in the Prime Minister's Office, Prince Al-Muhtadee Billah

SELECTED GOVERNMENT MEMBERS *as at May 2007*
Foreign Affairs, Prince Mohamed Bolkiah
Home Affairs, Pehin Dato Adanan Yussof

BRUNEI DARUSSALAM HIGH COMMISSION
19–20 Belgrave Square, London SW1X 8PG
T 020-7581 0521
E bhcl@brunei-high-commission.co.uk
High Commissioner, HE Pengiran Dato Maidin Hashim, *apptd* 2006

BRITISH HIGH COMMISSION
PO Box 2197, Bandar Seri Begawan 8674
T (+673) (2) 222 231 E brithc@brunet.bn
W www.britishhighcommission.gov.uk/brunei
High Commissioner, John Saville, *apptd* 2005

BRITISH COUNCIL
Level 2, Block D, Yayasan Sultan Hj Hassanal Bolkiah, Jl Pretty, Bandar Seri Begawan B58711 T (+673) (2) 237742
E all.enquiries@bn.britishcouncil.org
Director, Amanda Griffiths

DEFENCE

The army has 20 light tanks and 39 armoured personnel carriers. The navy, based in Muara, has 6 patrol and coastal vessels. The air force has 5 support helicopters. There are around 1,120 UK troops currently stationed in Brunei.
MILITARY BUDGET – US$343m (2006)
MILITARY PERSONNEL – 7,000: army 4,900, navy 1,000, air force 1,100; paramilitaries 3,750

ECONOMY AND TRADE

The economy is based on the production of oil and natural gas and the income from overseas investments. Royalties and taxes from these operations form the bulk of government revenue and have enabled the construction of free health, education and welfare services. However, oil and gas reserves are declining and Brunei is diversifying its economy, developing financial services and tourism.

In 2005 agriculture accounted for 1 per cent of GDP, industry accounted for 72 per cent and services for 27 per cent. The main trading partners are other countries in the Pacific Rim region and the UK. Principal exports are crude oil, natural gas, refined products and clothing. The main imports are machinery and transport equipment, manufactured goods, foodstuffs (over 80 per cent of domestic requirements is imported) and chemicals.
ANNUAL AVERAGE GROWTH OF GDP – 1.7 per cent (2004 est)
INFLATION RATE – 0.9 per cent (2004)
UNEMPLOYMENT – 4.8 per cent (2004)

Trade with UK	*2005*	*2006*
Imports from UK	£44,087,000	£79,306,000
Exports to UK	£28,103,000	£75,319,000

COMMUNICATIONS

There are five ports at Kuala Belait, Muara and Tanjong Salirong, and terminals at Lumut and Seria. Seria is the location of one of Brunei's two airports, the other being the international airport at Bandar Seri Begawan. The 209km of waterways is navigable only by shallow craft. There is a road network of 3,650km, most of which is paved, but no railway service. The telephone system is extensive and modern. Mobile phone distribution is very high.

EDUCATION

All levels of education are free. Children undertake seven years of primary education, three of lower secondary and two years of upper secondary which can be in a secondary school, a vocational school or technical college.
LITERACY RATE – 92.7 per cent (2004 est)

MEDIA

The media is privately owned but very tightly controlled; laws against reporting 'false news' carry heavy punishments, and criticism of the government is therefore rare. The only broadcast media organisation, Radio Television Brunei (RTB), is state-owned and controlled. It broadcasts television in Malay and English and radio in Malay, English, Mandarin Chinese and Gurkhali.

BULGARIA

Republika Balgariya – Republic of Bulgaria

AREA – 110,910 sq. km. Neighbours: Romania (north), Serbia, Macedonia (west), Greece and Turkey (south)
CAPITAL – Sofia; population, 1,138,950 (2004 est)
MAJOR CITIES – Plovdiv; Varna; Burgas
CURRENCY – Lev of 100 stotinki
POPULATION – 7,385,367 falling at 0.86 per cent per year (2006 est); Bulgarian (83.9 per cent), Turkish (9.4 per cent), Romani (4.7 per cent)
RELIGION – Christianity (82 per cent), Islam (12 per cent) (est)
LANGUAGE – Bulgarian (official), Turkish, Romani
POPULATION DENSITY – 71 per sq. km (2005)
URBAN POPULATION – 70.5 per cent (2005 est)
MEDIAN AGE (years) – 40.8 (2006 est)
NATIONAL ANTHEM – 'Milo Rodino' ['Dear Native Land']
NATIONAL DAY – 3 March (Liberation Day)
LIFE EXPECTANCY (years) – 72.3 (2006 est)
MORTALITY RATE – 14.27 (2006 est)
BIRTH RATE – 9.65 (2006 est)
INFANT MORTALITY RATE – 19.85 (2006 est)
DEATH PENALTY – No (abolished 1998)
CPI SCORE – 4.0 (2006)
POPULATION BELOW POVERTY LINE – 4 per cent (2003)

CLIMATE AND TERRAIN

The country is dominated by mountains: the Balkan Mountains cross the country from west to east, averaging 2,000m in height; and the Rhodope Mountains are found in the south-west, climbing to almost 3,000m. Elevation extremes range from 2,925m (Musala) at the highest point to 0m (Black Sea) at the lowest. The lowland plains of the north and south-east are in the basins of the main rivers: the Danube in the north, which forms much of the border with Romania, and the Maritsa, which divides the Balkan and Rhodope Mountains, and follows the Black Sea coast. The climate is transitional between the Mediterranean and the southern planes of the Russian Federation. Temperatures in Sofia range from 0°C in January to 25°C in July.

HISTORY AND POLITICS

Bulgarians are descended from Slavs who came to the area of modern-day Bulgaria in the fifth century AD. The Bulgarian state can trace its foundation back to AD 680. Bulgaria was part of the Ottoman Empire from 1390 until 1877, when Turkish rule was brought to an end with the aid of Russia. A principality of Bulgaria was created by the Treaty of Berlin in 1878, and in 1908 the country was declared an independent kingdom.

Bulgaria was allied with Germany in both world wars and was occupied in 1944 by the Soviet Union. A coup d'état in September 1944 gave power to the Fatherland Front, a coalition of Communists, Agrarians and Social Democrats, which came to be dominated by the Communists. A referendum in 1946 led to the abolition of the monarchy and the establishment of a republic dominated by the Communist Party (BCP), which in 1947 resulted in a one-party state and a centralised economy. From the mid-1980s cautious reforms were introduced in line with the Soviet policies of *perestroika* and *glasnost,* and Bulgaria became a multiparty democracy in 1990. Political and economic liberalisation progressed slowly in the early 1990s, causing economic difficulties and political unrest. The political volatility had calmed by the late 1990s, when more radical economic reforms were introduced. Since then progress has been sufficient for Bulgaria to become a member of the EU in 2007.

In the 2005 general election, the Coalition for Bulgaria (led by the BSP) won the most seats but not an outright majority. After a month of negotiation, the BSP leader Sergei Stanishev succeeded in forming a coalition government with the National Movement for Simeon II and the Turkish Movement for Rights and Freedoms. Georgi Parvanov, president since 2002, was elected to a second term of office in 2006.

POLITICAL SYSTEM

Under the 1991 constitution, the president is directly elected for a five-year term, renewable once only. The head of government is the prime minister, who is appointed by the president, and is usually the leader of the largest party in the legislature. There is a unicameral national assembly of 240 members who are directly elected by proportional representation for a four-year term.

HEAD OF STATE

President, Georgi Parvanov (BSP), *elected* 18 November 2001, *re-elected* 29 October 2006
Vice-President, Angel Marin (BSP)

SELECTED GOVERNMENT MEMBERS *as at May 2007*

Prime Minister, Sergey Stanishev
Deputy Prime Ministers, Emel Etem; Ivailo Kalfin; Daniel Vulchev
Defence, Vesselin Bliznakov
Finance, Plamen Oresharski
Internal Affairs, Roumen Petkov

EMBASSY OF THE REPUBLIC OF BULGARIA

186–188 Queen's Gate, London SW7 5HL
T 0870-060 2350
W www.bulgarianembassy.org.uk
Ambassador Extraordinary and Plenipotentiary, HE Dr Lachezar Matev, *apptd* 2005

BRITISH EMBASSY

9 Moskovska Street, Sofia 1000
T (+359) (2) 933 9222 **E** britembsof@mbox.cit.bg
W www.british-embassy.bg
Ambassador Extraordinary and Plenipotentiary, HE Jeremy Hill

BRITISH COUNCIL

7 Krakra Street, 1504 Sofia
T (+359) 2942 4344 **W** www.britishcouncil.org/bulgaria
Director, Ian Stewart

DEFENCE

The army has 1,474 main battle tanks, 214 armoured infantry fighting vehicles and 1,643 armoured personnel carriers. The navy has 1 submarine, 2 frigates, 19 patrol and coastal vessels, and 10 armed helicopters. The air force has 70 combat aircraft and 24 armed helicopters.

MILITARY EXPENDITURE – US$652m (2005)
MILITARY PERSONNEL – 51,000: army 25,000, navy 4,370, air force 13,100, central staff 8,530; paramilitaries 34,000
CONSCRIPTION DURATION – Nine months

ECONOMY AND TRADE

The government adopted a radical economic reform package in 1996 and the economy has achieved stability and steady growth over the past decade. This was reinforced by the imposition of a fixed exchange rate against the Deutsche Mark in 1997 (the currency is now fixed against the euro), and a US$300m (£150m) agreement with the IMF in 2001. Inflation has dropped and unemployment is also declining. As a result, foreign investment is growing, although administrative corruption and organised crime remain potential deterrents.

Natural resources include copper, lead, zinc, other minerals, coal and timber. Fertile arable land produces crops that include vegetables, fruits, tobacco, wine, wheat, barley, sunflowers and livestock. Around 8 per cent of the population is engaged in agriculture, which accounted for 14 per cent of GDP in 2006. Industries include energy generation, food processing, beverages, machinery and equipment, base metals, chemicals, mining and oil refining. Tourism is growing. One of Bulgaria's main exports is electricity generated at its controversial Kozloduy nuclear power plant. It has decommissioned two reactors in response to EU concerns about safety.

The main trading partners are EU countries, Turkey and Russia. Principal exports are clothing and footwear, iron and steel, machinery and equipment, and fuels. The main imports are predominantly raw materials for the industrial sector.

GNI – US$26,700m; US$3,450 per capita (2005)
ANNUAL AVERAGE GROWTH OF GDP – 5.5 per cent (2005 est)
INFLATION RATE – 5 per cent (2005 est)
UNEMPLOYMENT – 9.9 per cent (2005)
TOTAL EXTERNAL DEBT – US$15,320m (2005 est)
IMPORTS – US$18,000m (2005)
EXPORTS – US$12,000m (2005)

BALANCE OF PAYMENTS
Trade – US$5,399m deficit (2005)
Current Account – US$3,133m deficit (2005)

Trade with UK	*2005*	*2006*
Imports from UK	£219,918,000	£224,343,000
Exports to UK	£164,397,000	£197,643,000

EDUCATION AND HEALTH

Education is free and compulsory for children from six to 16 years.

LITERACY RATE – 98.2 per cent (2004 est)
GROSS ENROLMENT RATIO (percentage of relevant age group) – primary 105 per cent; secondary 102 per cent; tertiary 41 per cent (2005 est)
HEALTH EXPENDITURE (per capita) – US$251 (2004)
HOSPITAL BEDS (per 1,000 people) – 6.3 (2000–5)

COMMUNICATIONS

The main ports are Burgas, Varna and Nesebur on the Black Sea. There are 470km of waterways, and inland ports include Vidin, Lom and Ruse on the River Danube. The main airports are at Sofia, Plovdiv, Burgas and Varna. There are 4,294km of railways and 44,033km of roads, including 333km of motorways. The telephone system is extensive but needs modernising. Mobile phone distribution is high.

MEDIA AND CULTURE

In 1996 Bulgaria gave national radio and television the status of public services and granted them independence. The first national commercial channels were launched in 2003.

Bulgaria is still a country in transition: some rural areas are virtually unchanged since the Communist era while urban centres are now radically Western in character and outlook. Bulgaria's Roman and Byzantine ruins are culturally significant, as are its churches and monasteries. Notable Bulgarian writers include Stoyan Mikhaylovski (1856–1927) and Iordan Iovkov (1884–1938).

BURKINA FASO

AREA – 274,200 sq. km. Neighbours: Mali (west and north), Niger (north-east), Benin (south-east), Togo, Ghana and Côte d'Ivoire (south)
CAPITAL – Ouagadougou; population, 1,000,000 (2000 est)
MAJOR TOWNS – Bobo-Dioulasso; Koudougou
CURRENCY – Franc CFA of 100 centimes
POPULATION – 13,902,972 rising at 3 per cent per year (2006 est)
RELIGION – Islam (55 per cent), indigenous religions (20 per cent), Roman Catholicism (15 per cent) (est). Atheism is virtually non-existent
LANGUAGE – French (official)
POPULATION DENSITY – 48 per sq. km (2005)
URBAN POPULATION – 18.6 per cent (2005 est)
MEDIAN AGE (years) – 16.5 (2006 est)
NATIONAL ANTHEM – 'Une Seule Nuit' ['One Single Night']
NATIONAL DAY – 11 December (Republic Day)
LIFE EXPECTANCY – 48.85 (2006 est)
MORTALITY RATE – 15.6 (2006 est)
BIRTH RATE – 46.62 (2006 est)
INFANT MORTALITY RATE – 91.35 (2006 est)
HIV/AIDS ADULT PREVALENCE – 4.2 per cent (2004 est)
DEATH PENALTY – No*
CPI SCORE – 3.2 (2006)
POPULATION BELOW POVERTY LINE – 45 per cent (2003 est)
MILITARY BUDGET – US$87m (2006 est)
MILITARY PERSONNEL – 10,800: army 6,400, air force 200, Gendarmerie 4,200; paramilitaries 250

CLIMATE AND TERRAIN

Burkina Faso is a landlocked state occupying a plateau in west Africa. There are wooded savannahs in the south and the north is semi-desert. Elevation extremes range from 749m (Tena Kourou) at the highest point to 200m (Mouhoun River) at the lowest. The wet season runs from June to October and the dry season from December to May; there are recurring droughts. Average temperatures range from 24°C in January to 28°C in July.

HISTORY AND POLITICS

Burkina Faso (Upper Volta until 1983) was part of the Mossi Empire in the 18th and 19th centuries. It was annexed by France in 1896 and between 1932 and 1947 was administered as part of the colony of the Ivory Coast. In 1947 its original borders were reconstituted, and in 1958 became autonomous within the French Community; full independence was achieved on 5 August 1960.

In the following three decades there were several military coups, the latest of which in 1987 brought to power Capt. Blaise Compaoré. Military power ended in 1991 when a new constitution was adopted, and multiparty elections were held in 1992. Despite the constitutional restriction on the number of terms a president may serve, President Compaoré was re-elected for a third term in 2005. The May 2007 legislative election was won by the governing Congress for Democracy and Progress (CDP) with an overall majority.

POLITICAL SYSTEM

Under the 1991 constitution, the president is directly elected; in 2000 the presidential term was reduced from seven to five years, renewable only once. The unicameral legislature, the national assembly *(Assemblée Nationale)* has 111 deputies, who are directly elected for a five-year term. Executive power is jointly vested in the president and the council of ministers, both responsible to the national assembly.

HEAD OF STATE
President, Capt. Blaise Compaoré, *assumed office* October 1987, *elected* December 1991, *re-elected* November 1998

SELECTED GOVERNMENT MEMBERS *as at May 2007*
Prime Minister, Paramanga Ernest Yonli
Defence, Yero Boli
Finance and Budget, Jean-Baptiste Compaoré
Foreign Affairs and Regional Cooperation, Youssouf Ouédraogo

EMBASSY OF THE REPUBLIC OF BURKINA FASO
16 Place Guy d'Arezzo, 1180 Brussels, Belgium
T (+32) (2) 345 9912 W www.ambassadeduburkina.be
Ambassador Extraordinary and Plenipotentiary, HE Kadré Désiré Ouedraogo, *apptd* 2001

BRITISH HIGH COMMISSIONER
HE Dr Nicholas Westcott, CMG, *apptd* 2007, resident at Accra, Ghana

ECONOMY AND TRADE

Despite economic reforms introduced in the 1990s and international aid, the country is very poor, with a high level of foreign debt and 45 per cent of the population below the poverty line. Around 90 per cent of the population is engaged in subsistence agriculture, which is vulnerable to the harsh climatic conditions, while the economy is heavily dependent on cotton exports and therefore exposed to the vagaries of global price fluctuations. The situation in neighbouring Cote d'Ivoire continues to harm trade and industry.

Agriculture contributes 32 per cent of GDP; the principal cash crop apart from cotton is livestock. Although there are few natural resources, small quantities of gold are mined. The processing of cotton and other agricultural products, gold mining and manufacturing of soap, cigarettes and textiles are the main industries, contributing 20 per cent to GDP. Services account for 48 per cent of GDP. The main trading partners are China, France, neighbouring countries and Singapore. Principal exports are cotton, livestock and gold. The chief imports are capital goods, foodstuffs and fuel.

GNI – US$5,200m; US$400 per capita (2005)
ANNUAL AVERAGE GROWTH OF GDP – 3.5 per cent (2005 est)
INFLATION RATE – 6.4 per cent (2005 est)
TOTAL EXTERNAL DEBT – US$1,850m (2003)
IMPORTS – US$1,290m (2005)
EXPORTS – US$590m (2005)

BALANCE OF PAYMENTS
Trade – US$286m deficit (2001)
Current Account – US$381m deficit (2001)

Trade with UK	*2005*	*2006*
Imports from UK	£4,243,000	£2,730,000
Exports to UK	£548,000	£540,000

COMMUNICATIONS

There are over 30 airports and airfields; the two main airports are at Ouagadougou, which receives international flights, and Bobo Dioulasso. There are 15,272km of roads, of which 4,766km are surfaced; an estimated 60 per cent of the country's villages are further than 3km from a main road, and the predominantly unpaved roads are often impassable during the wet season. There is 622km of railway track in operation.

EDUCATION AND HEALTH

LITERACY RATE – 12.8 per cent (2004 est)
GROSS ENROLMENT RATIO (percentage of relevant age group) – primary 58 per cent; secondary 14 per cent; tertiary 2 per cent (2005 est)
HEALTH EXPENDITURE (per capita) – US$24 (2004)
HOSPITAL BEDS (per 1,000 people) – 1.4 (2002)

MEDIA

Radio is the country's most popular medium. Tens of private and community radio stations and several private television channels operate alongside their state-run counterparts. All media outlets are regulated by the Ministry of Communication and Culture but some dissent is still expressed.

BURUNDI

République du Burundi – Republic of Burundi

AREA – 27,830 sq. km. Neighbours: Rwanda (north), Tanzania (east and south), Democratic Republic of the Congo (west)
CAPITAL – Bujumbura; population, 319,098 (1999 est)
MAJOR TOWN – Gitega
CURRENCY – Burundi franc of 100 centimes
POPULATION – 8,090,068 rising at 3.7 per cent per year (2006 est); Hutu (85 per cent), Tutsi (14 per cent), Twa (1 per cent) (est)
RELIGION – Roman Catholicism (60 per cent), Islam (10 per cent) (est). The remainder of the population belongs to other Christian denominations, practices indigenous religions or has no religious affiliation
LANGUAGE – Kirundi, French (both official), Swahili
POPULATION DENSITY – 294 per sq. km (2005)

URBAN POPULATION – 10.6 per cent (2005 est)
MEDIAN AGE (years) – 16.6 (2006 est)
NATIONAL DAY – 1 July (Independence Day)
NATIONAL ANTHEM – 'Burundi Bwacu' ['Our Burundi']
MORTALITY RATE – 13.46 (2006 est)
BIRTH RATE – 42.22 (2006 est)
INFANT MORTALITY RATE – 63.13 (2006 est)
LIFE EXPECTANCY – 50.81 (2006 est)
HIV/AIDS ADULT PREVALENCE – 6 per cent (2003 est)
DEATH PENALTY – Yes
CPI SCORE – 2.4 (2006)
POPULATION BELOW POVERTY LINE – 68 per cent (2002 est)
MILITARY BUDGET – US$51m (2006)
MILITARY PERSONNEL – 35,000: army 35,000; paramilitaries 31,050
LITERACY RATE – 58.9 per cent (2004 est)
GROSS ENROLMENT RATIO (percentage of relevant age group) – primary 85 per cent; secondary 13 per cent; tertiary 2 per cent (2005 est)
HEALTH EXPENDITURE (per capita) – US$3 (2004)

CLIMATE AND TERRAIN

The landlocked country lies across the Nile–Congo watershed in central Africa. An interior plateau rises 1,500m to the country's highest point at 2,670m (Heha). The River Ruzizi forms part of the north-western border with the Democratic Republic of the Congo, along with Lake Tanganyika (the lowest elevation in the country at 772m) in the south-west. The climate is equatorial. The dry season runs from June to September. The average daily temperature is 23°C.

HISTORY AND POLITICS

From the 16th century the area was ruled by Tutsi kings who dominated a predominantly Hutu population. Germany annexed the area in 1890 and included it in German East Africa, which after the First World War was administered by Belgium. In 1946 it was joined with Rwanda as a UN Trust Territory but broke the union when it became independent as a constitutional monarchy on 1 July 1962. The monarchy was overthrown in 1966 and the country became a republic and a one-party state.

The majority of the population remains Hutu but since independence political and military power tended to lie with the Tutsi minority, leading to intercommunal tensions that have often resulted in ethnic conflict. The first multiparty elections in 1993 ended Tutsi political dominance with the election of a Hutu president and a Hutu majority in the national assembly. The president was killed shortly afterwards in a coup by the Tutsi-dominated army; although the coup was suppressed, inter-racial fighting left more than 100,000 dead. The following year the new (Hutu) president was killed when the plane in which he was travelling with the Rwandan president was shot down. These deaths sparked off fierce ethnic conflict which degenerated into a civil war that lasted over a decade.

Two years of talks between Burundi's 19 political parties resulted in a peace accord at Arusha (Tanzania) in July 2000; the accord was ratified by the transitional assembly in November 2000. In October 2001 a transitional constitution was adopted and institutions set up; legislative elections took place in July 2005. The National Council for the Defence of Democracy-Forces for the Defence of Democracy (CNDD-FDD), a Hutu party, won a majority of seats in both chambers of the legislature. Pierre Nkurunziz of the CNDD-FDD was elected president by members of the newly elected legislature in August 2005. A government was formed of a coalition of six parties dominated by the CNDD-FDD; one party, Frodebu, withdrew in 2006.

Since 2000, the government has signed ceasefire agreements with most of the rebel groups; the last active group signed a such an agreement with the government in September 2006. The UN ended its peacekeeping mission in February 2007 and redirected its operations to helping with reconstruction.

POLITICAL SYSTEM

Although President Nkurunziza was elected by the legislature in 2005, under the 2004 constitution future presidents will be directly elected; the executive president serves a five-year term, renewable only once.

The bicameral *Parlement* comprises the national assembly and the senate; members of both serve a five-year term. The national assembly has 100 directly elected members; up to 21 co-opted members (currently 15) to ensure a 60 per cent Hutu and 40 per cent Tutsi split and that 30 per cent of the total are women; and three co-opted members from the Twa ethnic group. The senate has 49 members: 34 directly elected members (one Hutu and one Tutsi from each province); three co-opted Twa members; all former presidents (currently four); and enough women (currently eight) to make the number of women senators up to 30 per cent of the total. The constitution also specifies the proportion of Hutu, Tutsi and female members of the council of ministers.

HEAD OF STATE

President, Pierre Nkurunziza, *sworn in* 26 August 2005
First Vice-President, Martin Nduwimana
Second Vice-President, Gabriel Ntisezerana

SELECTED GOVERNMENT MEMBERS *as at May 2007*

Defence, Maj.-Gen. Germain Niyoyankana
External Relations and International Co-operation, Antoinette Batumubwira
Finance, Denise Sinankwa
Interior and Public Security, Brig.-Gen. Evariste Ndayishimiye

EMBASSY OF THE REPUBLIC OF BURUNDI

46 Sq. Marie Louise, 1000 Brussels, Belgium
T (+32) (2) 230 4535 W www.ambassade-burundi.be
Ambassador Extraordinary and Plenipotentiary, vacant

BRITISH AMBASSADOR

HE Jeremy Macadie, *apptd* 2004, resident at Kigali, Rwanda

ECONOMY AND TRADE

Economic activity has increased since fighting ended, but reform and reconstruction are hampered by a lack of administrative capacity and a poorly educated workforce. At present, exports of coffee and tea account for over 90 per cent of foreign exchange earnings, leaving the economy vulnerable to the effects of weather conditions and global price fluctuations. Agriculture sustained over 90 per cent of the population in 2002, accounting for 45 per cent of GDP in 2006 and producing the main exports: coffee, tea, sugar, cotton and hides. Industry is relatively small-scale and employs only about 3 per cent of the workforce but contributes 21 per cent of GDP. The main activities are light manufacturing, food processing, the assembly of imported components and public sector construction. The service sector contributes 34 per cent of GDP and employs 4 per cent of the workforce. Most trade is with European countries and neighbouring states, but is constrained by the poor transport infrastructure and limited connections with neighbouring countries and the coast.

GNI – US$700m; US$100 per capita (2005)
ANNUAL AVERAGE GROWTH OF GDP – 1.1 per cent (2005 est)
INFLATION RATE – 16 per cent (2005 est)
TOTAL EXTERNAL DEBT – US$1,200m (2003)
IMPORTS – US$270m (2005)
EXPORTS – US$90m (2005)

BALANCE OF PAYMENTS
Trade – US$93m deficit (2003)
Current Account – US$37m deficit (2003)

Trade with UK	*2005*	*2006*
Imports from UK	£1,822,000	£1,085,000
Exports to UK	£675,000	£688,000

COMMUNICATIONS

There are no railways at present, but in late 2006 a feasibility study was planned into the possibility of including Burundi in a project to expand the rail network in this region of central Africa. Rail links to neighbouring countries and to Tanzanian seaports would facilitate trade. Movement is currently either by water, on Lake Tanganyika, by road or by air. Bujumbura is the only port, the location of the only airport with a surfaced runway, and the main focus of the limited road network of 12,322km, only 1,286km of which are paved. The telephone system is rudimentary and limited. Mobile phone distribution is growing.

MEDIA

La Radiodiffusion et Télévision Nationale du Burundi (RTNB) is the main TV station and is government-controlled. Low literacy levels mean that the dominant news medium is radio. Radio Burundi (RTNB) broadcasts in Kirundi, Swahili, French and English and is state-controlled. There are several newspapers published sporadically due to government interference.

CAMBODIA

Preahreacheanachakr Kampuchea – Kingdom of Cambodia

AREA – 181,040 sq. km. Neighbours: Laos (north), Thailand (north and west), Vietnam (east and south)
CAPITAL – Phnom Penh; population, 1,200,000 (2003 est)
MAJOR TOWNS – Battambang; Siem Reap; Sihanoukville
CURRENCY – Riel of 100 sen
POPULATION – 13,881,427 rising at 1.78 per cent per year (2006 est); Khmer (90 per cent), Vietnamese (5 per cent) (est)
RELIGION – Buddhism (93 per cent) (est)
LANGUAGE – Khmer (official), French, English
POPULATION DENSITY – 80 per sq. km (2005)
URBAN POPULATION – 19.7 per cent (2005 est)
MEDIAN AGE (years) – 20.6 (2006 est)
NATIONAL ANTHEM – 'Nokoreach' ['Royal Kingdom']
NATIONAL DAY – 9 November (Independence Day)
LIFE EXPECTANCY (years) – 59.29 (2006 est)
MORTALITY RATE – 9.06 (2006 est)
BIRTH RATE – 26.9 (2006 est)
INFANT MORTALITY RATE – 68.78 (2006 est)
HIV/AIDS ADULT PREVALENCE – 2.6 per cent (2003 est)
DEATH PENALTY – No (abolished 1997)
CPI SCORE – 2.1 (2006)
POPULATION BELOW POVERTY LINE – 40 per cent (2004 est)
LITERACY RATE – 73.6 per cent (2004 est)
GROSS ENROLMENT RATIO (percentage of relevant age group) – primary 134 per cent; secondary 29 per cent; tertiary 3 per cent (2005 est)
HEALTH EXPENDITURE (per capita) – US$24 (2004)
HOSPITAL BEDS (per 1,000 people) – 0.6 (2000–5)

CLIMATE AND TERRAIN

Cambodia is a mostly flat country, apart from the Cardamom Mountains in the south-west and the uplands of the north-east. Dominated by the Mekong River, Cambodia is also home to Tonle Sap, the largest lake in south-east Asia. The highest point of elevation is at 1,810m (Phnum Aoral) while the lowest is 0m (Gulf of Thailand). The monsoon season is from May to November and is accompanied by very high humidity. Temperatures range from 25°C in January to 32°C in July.

HISTORY AND POLITICS

Although the Khmer people have inhabited the region for almost 2,000 years, the Khmer kingdom was at its strongest during the 11th century, its territory covering modern-day Laos, Thailand and Vietnam. The kingdom lost power and territory from 1432 onwards.

Cambodia became a French protectorate in 1863 and part of Indochina in 1887. It became an associate state within the French Union in 1949, and gained full independence in 1953 as the Kingdom of Cambodia. From the late 1960s there was a growing insurgency led by the Khmer Rouge, and in 1970 the monarchy was overthrown in a right-wing coup and the country was renamed the Khmer Republic. Fighting throughout the country involved forces from North and South Vietnam and the USA. In 1975, Phnom Penh fell to the North Vietnamese-backed Khmer Rouge. During Khmer Rouge rule under Pol Pot (1975–8), extreme Marxist policies were brutally implemented and famine, disease and maltreatment caused the deaths of an estimated 2.5 million people. In 1978, Vietnamese troops invaded Cambodia and in 1979 established a government in Phnom Penh. Fighting continued between the Vietnamese-backed government and guerrilla resistance from the Khmer Rouge and Sihanouk's nationalist forces until the Vietnamese withdrawal in 1987–9.

Under a UN peace plan agreed in 1991 and after a period of transitional government, multiparty elections were held in May 1993. In the following September a new constitution was adopted and Prince Sihanouk was elected king. The premiership was shared between the two main parties, the Cambodian People's Party (CPP), headed by former leaders of the Vietnamese-backed regime, and Funcinpec, formed by supporters of the king and led by Prince Ranariddh. Ranariddh was ousted as co-prime minister in 1997 in an effective coup by Hun Sen, who became the sole prime minister. His CPP party has won the 1998 and 2003 elections but without the two-thirds majority needed to form a government on its own, and the coalition with Funcinpec has continued.

King Sihanouk abdicated in October 2004 and was succeeded by one of his sons, Prince Norodom Sihamoni.

INSURGENCIES

The Khmer Rouge was outlawed in 1994 but continued with guerrilla warfare until 1996, when it was weakened by internal divisions. Pol Pot was seized in 1997 and died in captivity in 1998. The remaining Khmer Rouge soldiers surrendered in 1999. After years of talks, in 2006 an international tribunal was given a mandate to prosecute former leaders of the Khmer Rouge regime for atrocities committed during its rule.

POLITICAL SYSTEM

Under the 1993 constitution, Cambodia is a pluralist liberal democracy with a hereditary constitutional monarchy. Executive power rests with the government, with the king having the power only to make appointments and declare a state of emergency, in consultation with the government. Legislative power is vested in the bicameral parliament, comprising the national assembly, which has 123 members directly elected for a five-year term, and the senate, which has 57 members elected for a six-year term by the national assembly, and commune councils, two members appointed by the king and two appointed by the national assembly.

HEAD OF STATE

HM The King of Cambodia, Supreme Commander of the Cambodian National Armed Forces, Norodom Sihamoni, *elected by the Council of the Throne* 29 October 2004

President of the National Assembly, Heng Samrin

SELECTED GOVERNMENT MEMBERS *as at May 2007*

Prime Minister, Hun Sen

Deputy Prime Ministers, Hor Namhong *(Foreign Affairs and International Co-operation);* Sar Kheng *(Interior);* Gen. Tea Banh *(National Defence);* Sok An

ROYAL EMBASSY OF CAMBODIA

28–32 Wellington Road, London NW8 9SP

T 020-7483 9063

W www.cambodianembassy.org.uk

Ambassador Extraordinary and Plenipotentiary, HE Hor Nambora, *apptd* 2004

BRITISH EMBASSY

29 Street 75, Phnom Penh

T (+855) (23) 427 124 E britemb@bigpond.com.kh

W www.britishembassy.gov.uk/cambodia

Ambassador Extraordinary and Plenipotentiary, HE David Reader, *apptd* 2005

DEFENCE

The army has 150 main battle tanks, 70 armoured infantry fighting vehicles and 190 armoured personnel carriers. The navy has 10 patrol and coastal vessels. The air force has 24 combat aircraft.

MILITARY BUDGET – US$123m (2006)

MILITARY PERSONNEL – 124,300: army 75,000, navy 2,800, air force 1,500, provincial forces 45,000; paramilitaries 67,000

ECONOMY AND TRADE

Since the Khmer Rouge insurgency ended in 1999 the government has made progress with economic reform and development. But the country remains very poor, with 40 per cent of the population below the poverty line and an absence of basic infrastructure in rural areas. Economic growth has been driven by the expansion of garment manufacturing and tourism, and the discovery of oil and gas deposits in territorial waters promises additional revenue once exploitation begins. Recent international aid has been made conditional on the government tackling the widespread corruption.

The agricultural, industrial and service sectors each contribute about one-third of GDP at present, although the industrial sector and tourism are growing more rapidly than the economy as a whole. Agriculture still employs over 75 per cent of the workforce; the main crops are rice, rubber, maize, vegetables, cashew nuts, livestock, fresh and dried fish and tobacco. The main industrial activities are tourism, garment and footwear manufacturing, processing of agricultural and forestry products and mining gemstones. Exports go mostly to western countries; imports come mainly from other countries in the region.

GNI – US$6,100m; US$430 per capita (2005)

ANNUAL AVERAGE GROWTH OF GDP – 13.4 per cent (2005 est)

INFLATION RATE – 5.8 per cent (2005 est)

UNEMPLOYMENT – 2.5 per cent (2000)

TOTAL EXTERNAL DEBT – US$800m (2003 est)

IMPORTS – US$1,000m (2005)

EXPORTS – US$1,000m (2005)

BALANCE OF PAYMENTS

Trade – US$718m deficit (2004)

Current Account – US$240m deficit (2004)

Trade with UK	*2005*	*2006*
Imports from UK	£3,526,000	£2,646,000
Exports to UK	£73,012,000	£91,805,000

COMMUNICATIONS

There are 2,400km of navigable waterways, mostly on the Mekong River, and ships of up to 2,500 tons can sail as far as Phnom Penh all year round. The deep-water port at Sihanoukville (Kompong Som) on the Gulf of Thailand can receive ships of up to 10,000 tons. The port is linked to Phnom Penh by a modern highway. The main airports are at Phnom Penh, Angkor and Sihanoukville, the latter two having been upgraded recently to deal with the increasing tourist traffic. The country has about 38,257km of roads, although only 2,406km are surfaced and most are in a state of disrepair. There are two railway lines, one from Phnom Penh to the Thai border, the other from Phnom Penh to Kampot and Sihanoukville.

Land-line and mobile telephone systems operate in the cities and major towns, and mobile phone distribution is expanding rapidly in rural areas.

MEDIA

Much of the media is owned by political parties but the prime minister, Hun Sen, has expressed his support for press freedom. The state broadcaster is National Television of Cambodia (TVK) and there are five other major commercial and privately owned channels. There are no restrictions on the ownership and use of private satellite dishes, and foreign radio is also easily received and widely accessed.

CAMEROON

République du Cameroun – Republic of Cameroon

AREA – 475,440 sq. km. Neighbours: Nigeria (north and west), Chad and Central African Republic (east), Republic of Congo, Gabon and Equatorial Guinea (south)
CAPITAL – Yaoundé; population, 1,248,200 (2001 est)
MAJOR CITIES – Douala is the commercial centre; Garoua; Bamenda
CURRENCY – Franc CFA of 100 centimes
POPULATION – 17,340,702 rising at 2.04 per cent per year (2006 est); Cameroon Highlanders (31 per cent), Equatorial Bantu (19 per cent), Kirdi (11 per cent), Fulani (10 per cent), Northwestern Bantu (8 per cent), Eastern Nigritic (7 per cent) (est)
RELIGION – Christianity (40 per cent), indigenous religions (40 per cent), Islam (20 per cent) (est)
LANGUAGE – English, French (official)
POPULATION DENSITY – 35 per sq. km (2005)
URBAN POPULATION – 52.9 per cent (2005 est)
MEDIAN AGE (years) – 18.9 (2006 est)
NATIONAL ANTHEM – 'Chant de Ralliement' ['Rallying Song']
NATIONAL DAY – 20 May (Republic Day)
LIFE EXPECTANCY (years) – 51.16 (2006 est)
MORTALITY RATE – 13.47 (2006 est)
BIRTH RATE – 33.89 (2006 est)
INFANT MORTALITY RATE – 63.52 (2006 est)
HIV/AIDS ADULT PREVALENCE – 6.9 per cent (2003 est)
DEATH PENALTY – Yes
CPI SCORE – 2.3 (2006)
POPULATION BELOW POVERTY LINE – 48 per cent (2000 est)
MILITARY BUDGET – US$262m (2006)
MILITARY PERSONNEL – 14,100: army 12,500, navy 1,300, air force 300; paramilitaries 9,000
LITERACY RATE – 67.9 per cent (2004 est)
GROSS ENROLMENT RATIO (percentage of relevant age group) – primary 117 per cent; secondary 44 per cent; tertiary 6 per cent (2005 est)
HEALTH EXPENDITURE (per capita) – US$51 (2004)

CLIMATE AND TERRAIN

There are three main geographic zones: desert plains in the north (the Lake Chad basin), mountains and savannah plateau in the central region, and tropical rainforests in the south and east. Elevation extremes range from 4,095m (Mt Cameroun) at the highest point to 0m (Atlantic Ocean) at the lowest. The wet season runs from June to September in the north and from May to November in the south.

HISTORY AND POLITICS

The Bakas (Pygmies) and Bantu speakers of the Cameroonian highlands were probably the country's earliest inhabitants. Cameroon was explored by the Portuguese from 1472 and later by Spanish, Dutch and English traders. The Fulani people of the western Sahel conquered northern Cameroon between the 1770s and the early 1800s.

The German protectorate of Kamerun was established in 1884. After the First World War it was divided into the League of Nations-mandated territories (later UN trusteeships) of East (French) and West (British) Cameroon. On 1 January 1960 East Cameroon became independent as the Republic of Cameroon. This was joined on 1 October 1961 by the southern part of West Cameroon after a plebiscite held under the auspices of the UN; the northern part voted to join Nigeria. Cameroon became a federal republic with separate East and West Cameroon state governments; the federal system was abolished in 1972. From 1972 to 1992, Cameroon was ruled by one party, the Cameroon People's Democratic Movement (RDPC), with Paul Biya as president from 1982.

Economic decline in 1990 provoked widespread civil unrest and agitation for political pluralism. In the 1992 multiparty elections, the ruling RDPC won the legislative election, and Paul Biya the presidential. The result was challenged by the opposition, which protested vote-rigging; similar allegations have been made after all subsequent elections, to the extent that in 1997 the opposition boycotted the presidential election altogether. In the 2004 presidential election, Paul Biya was returned to office with 70.8 per cent of the vote. In the July 2007 legaslative election, the RDCP retained its majority with 140 of 180 seats in the national assembly, though the supreme court annulled the results of several districts on suspicion of fraud.

INTERNATIONAL RELATIONS

A long-running dispute with Nigeria over the oil-rich Bakassi peninsula was referred to the international court of justice and in 2002 the court ruled in favour of Cameroon. In August 2005, the peninsula was officially handed over to Cameroon.

Cameroon joined the Commonwealth in 1995, becoming the first member that had never been entirely under British rule at any point in its history.

POLITICAL SYSTEM

The 1972 constitution was amended in 1990 to enable a return to multiparty rule. It was amended again in 1996 to extend the president's term of office and to provide for the establishment of a second legislative chamber, but this has not yet been implemented.

The president is directly elected for a seven-year term, and appoints the prime minister and cabinet. The unicameral national assembly has 180 members, directly elected for a five-year term.

President, Paul Biya, *took power* 6 November 1982, *elected* 14 January 1984, *re-elected* 1988, 1992, 1997, 2004

SELECTED GOVERNMENT MEMBERS *as at May 2007*
Prime Minister, Ephraim Inoni
Deputy Prime Minister, Justice, Keeper of the Seals, Ali Amadou
Economy and Finance, Polycarpe Abah Abah
Foreign Affairs, Jean-Marie Atangana Mebara

HIGH COMMISSION FOR THE REPUBLIC OF CAMEROON
84 Holland Park, London W11 3SB
T 020-7727 0771
Ambassador Extraordinary and Plenipotentiary, HE Samuel Libock Mbei, *apptd* 1995

BRITISH HIGH COMMISSION
PO Box 547 Avenue Winston Churchill, Yaoundé
T (+237) (2) 220 545 E bhc.yaounde@fco.gov.uk
W www.britcam.org
High Commissioner, HE Syd Maddicott, *apptd* 2006

BRITISH COUNCIL
Immeuble Christo, Avenue Charles de Gaulle, BP 818, Yaoundé
T (+237) (2) 211 696/203 172
W www.britishcouncil.org/cameroon
Director, Jenny Scott

ECONOMY AND TRADE

Cameroon's political stability and natural resources such as oil and timber have enabled agricultural, industrial and infrastructure development. But progress is hampered by a large and top-heavy public sector and endemic corruption. Recent IMF funding has been conditional on reforms such as greater budget transparency and privatisation.

Agriculture contributes 45 per cent to GDP, industry 16 per cent and services 39 per cent. About 70 per cent of the workforce is engaged in agriculture. The main industrial activity is oil production and refining. Revenue is also earned from the oil pipeline passing through the country from Chad. The main trading partners are EU countries, Nigeria, the USA, South Korea and China. Principal exports are crude oil and petroleum products, timber, cocoa, aluminium, coffee and cotton. Imports are chiefly machinery, electrical equipment, transport equipment, fuel and foodstuffs.

GNI – US$16,400m; US$1,000 per capita (2005)
ANNUAL AVERAGE GROWTH OF GDP – 2.4 per cent (2005 est)
INFLATION RATE – 2 per cent (2005 est)
UNEMPLOYMENT – 30 per cent (2001 est)
TOTAL EXTERNAL DEBT – US$9,168m (2005 est)
IMPORTS – US$2,500m (2005)
EXPORTS – US$2,500m (2005)

Trade with UK	*2005*	*2006*
Imports from UK	£26,066,000	£22,828,000
Exports to UK	£176,431,000	£70,500,000

COMMUNICATIONS

The main seaports are at Douala and the Limboh terminal. Some inland navigation is also possible on the River Benue. There are 47 airports and airfields; of these, the main ones are at Yaoundé, Douala and Garoua. The 50,000km of roads include 5,000km of surfaced roads linking the main population centres. A rail network of 987km links the coast with the capital and the central highlands.

The telephone service is very restricted, with only 99,500 main lines in 2004, and it is available only to government and business. Mobile phone distribution is growing and there were 2.3 million subscribers in 2005.

MEDIA

The government controls the media via the state-run Cameroon Radio-Television Corporation (CRTV), which operates national television and radio networks as well as provincial stations. Newspapers are also subject to government control. The first private television station – TV Max – was launched in 2001. Dozens of private radio stations were set up following a liberalisation of telecommunications in 2000.

CANADA

AREA – 9,984,670 sq. km. Neighbours: USA (south), Alaska (USA) (west)
CAPITAL – Ottawa; population, 1,145,500 (2004 est)
MAJOR CITIES – Toronto; Montréal; Vancouver; Calgary; Edmonton; Quebec; Hamilton; Winnipeg
CURRENCY – Canadian dollar (C $) of 100 cents
POPULATION – 33,098,932 rising at 0.88 per cent per year (2006 est)
RELIGION – Roman Catholicism (43 per cent), Protestantism (29 per cent), Islam (2 per cent), Judaism (1 per cent), Buddhism (1 per cent), Hinduism (1 per cent), Sikhism (1 per cent) (est)
LANGUAGE – English, French (official)
POPULATION DENSITY – 4 per sq. km (2005)
URBAN POPULATION – 81.1 per cent (2005 est)
MEDIAN AGE (years) – 38.9 (2006 est)
NATIONAL ANTHEM – 'O Canada'
NATIONAL DAY – 1 July (Canada Day)
LIFE EXPECTANCY (years) – 80.22 (2006 est)
MORTALITY RATE – 7.8 (2006 est)
BIRTH RATE – 10.78 (2006 est)
INFANT MORTALITY RATE – 4.69 (2006 est)
DEATH PENALTY – No (abolished 1998)
CPI SCORE – 8.5 (2006)

CLIMATE AND TERRAIN

Canada occupies the entire northern part of the North American continent except for Alaska. In eastern Canada the most southerly point is Middle Island in Lake Erie. The six main physiographic divisions are: the Appalachian-Acadian region, the Canadian shield, which comprises more than half the country, the St Lawrence-Great Lakes lowland, the interior plains, the Cordilleran region and the Arctic archipelago. Elevation extremes range from 5,959m (Mt Logan) at the highest point to 0m (Atlantic Ocean) at the lowest. The climate of the eastern and central portions presents greater extremes than in corresponding latitudes in Europe, but the climate is milder in the south-western part of the prairie region and the southern parts of the Pacific slope. The tornado season is May to September, peaking in June and early July in Ontario, Alberta, Québec, Saskatchewan and Manitoba through to Thunder Bay. The interior of British Columbia and western New Brunswick are also tornado zones.

HISTORY AND POLITICS

St John's, Newfoundland, was established as a shore base for English fisheries in 1504 and claimed for England in 1583. The French explored the St Lawrence Seaway from the 1530s, and founded Québec in 1608. The Hudson's Bay Company, founded in 1670, was significant in exploring and opening up the interior. From the 17th century the territory was a pawn in the power struggles of the main colonial powers. Britain gained large areas of the country under the treaty of Utrecht (1713), and after the Seven Years' War, the treaty of Paris (1763) awarded almost all of France's North American possessions to Britain. The American War of Independence caused many British loyalists to migrate to southern Canada, exacerbating existing tensions between British and French colonists. In the mid-19th century, Canadian territory still under Hudson's Bay Company control was brought under government rule.

The British North America Act of 1867 formed a dominion under the name of Canada, comprising four provinces – Ontario, Québec, New Brunswick and Nova Scotia. To this federation the other provinces and territories were subsequently admitted: Manitoba and Northwest Territories (1870), British Columbia (1871), Prince Edward Island (1873), Yukon (1898), Alberta and Saskatchewan (1905) and Newfoundland (1949). In

1982, the constitution was patriated (severed from the British parliament).

In 1985, following French-Canadian separatist agitation, the federal prime minister and the provincial premiers concluded the Meech Lake accord which provided for Québec to be recognised as a distinct society within Canada. However, two provincial legislatures withheld approval and the accord did not come into force. A referendum in Québec calling for sovereignty and a new political and economic partnership was defeated in 1995, and support for independence has declined. In 1997, Québec was recognised as having a 'unique character' by leaders of the other provinces and territories, and in 2006 the federal parliament passed a motion recognising the Québecois as a nation within a united Canada.

An autonomous territory for the Inuit people, Nunavut ('our land'), was created by partitioning the Northwest Territories and was inaugurated on 1 April 1999.

A parliamentary vote of no confidence ended 12 years of Liberal government in November 2005. A snap general election in January 2006 was won by the Conservative Party of Canada with 124 seats; the Liberal party won 103 seats, the Bloc Quebecois 51 seats and the New Democratic Party 29 seats. The Conservative Party formed a minority government under Stephen Harper.

POLITICAL SYSTEM

Under the 1982 constitution, the head of state is the British monarch, represented by a governor-general appointed on the advice of the Canadian prime minister.

The bicameral parliament consists of a senate and a house of commons. The senate comprises 105 members, appointed by the governor-general on the advice of the prime minister, the seats being distributed between the various provinces. The house of commons has 308 members, directly elected for a five-year term. Representation is proportional to the population of each province.

Civil law is followed in Québec and common law in the other provinces. The supreme court of Canada exercises general appellate jurisdiction throughout Canada in civil and criminal cases. The federal court of Canada has jurisdiction on appeals from its trial division, from federal tribunals and reviews of decisions and references by federal boards.

GOVERNOR-GENERAL

Governor-General, HE Michaëlle Jean

SELECTED GOVERNMENT MEMBERS *as at May 2007*

Prime Minister, Stephen Harper
Finance, James Michael Flaherty
Foreign Affairs, Peter Gordon MacKay
National Defence, Gordon O'Connor

CANADIAN HIGH COMMISSION

Macdonald House, 1 Grosvenor Square, London W1K 4AB
T 020-7258 6600 W www.london.gc.ca
High Commissioner, HE James R. Wright, *apptd* 2006

BRITISH HIGH COMMISSION

80 Elgin Street, Ottawa, Ontario K1P 5K7
T (+1) (613) 237 1530 E bhc@fco.gov.uk
W www.britainincanada.org
High Commissioner, HE Anthony Cary, CMG, *apptd* 2007

BRITISH COUNCIL

c/o British High Commission
T (+1) (613) 364 6233/6236 W www.britishcouncil.org/canada
Director, Martin Rose

DEFENCE

The Canadian armed forces are unified and organised into three functional commands: land force command, maritime command and air command.

The army (land forces) has 114 main battle tanks and 1,551 armoured personnel carriers. The navy (maritime forces) has four submarines, 3 destroyers, 12 frigates and 12 patrol and coastal vessels. The air force has 120 combat aircraft.

FEDERAL STRUCTURE

Provinces or Territories (with official contractions)	*Population (2001)*	*Capital*	*Lieutenant-Governor*	*Premier*
Alberta (AB)	3,022,861	Edmonton	Normie Kwong	Ed Stelmach
British Columbia (BC)	4,077,369	Victoria	Iona Campagnolo	Gordon Campbell
Manitoba (MB)	1,149,220	Winnipeg	John Harvard	Gary Doer
New Brunswick (NB)	757,267	Fredericton	Herménégilde Chiasson	Shawn Graham
Newfoundland and Labrador (NF)	537,797	St John's	Edward Roberts	Danny Williams
Northwest Territories (NT)	42,105	Yellowknife	†Tony Whitford	Joe Handley
Nova Scotia (NS)	942,322	Halifax	Mayann E. Francis	Rodney MacDonald
§Nunavut (NT)	27,978	Iqaluit	†Ann Meekitjuk Hanson	Paul Okalik
Ontario (ON)	11,741,793	Toronto	James K. Bartleman	Dalton McGinley
Prince Edward Island (PE)	139,078	Charlottetown	Barbara Hagerman	Pat Binns
Québec (QC)	7,383,300	Québec	Lise Thibeault	Jean Charest
Saskatchewan (SK)	1,020,650	Regina	Gordon Barnhart	Lorne Calvert
Yukon Territory (YT)	30,194	Whitehorse	†Geraldine Van Bibber	Dennis Fentie

† Commissioner
§ Nunavut was created in 1999 from the Northwest Territories

MILITARY EXPENDITURE – US$12,800m (2005)
MILITARY PERSONNEL – 62,500: army 21,000, navy 10,000, air force 13,500, special forces 18,000; paramilitaries 9,350

ECONOMY AND TRADE

Canada has a highly developed, industrialised and diversified market economy, which developed in the second half of the 20th century when mining, manufacturing and services transformed it from predominantly rural to industrial. Abundant natural resources, a skilled workforce and modern equipment provide a solid basis for further strong growth. Tight management of government finances has resulted in balanced budgets since the late 1990s, and free-trade agreements with the USA in 1989 and 1994 have stimulated trade.

Canada's wealth of natural resources make it the world's largest exporter of timber, pulp and newsprint (nearly half the land is forested), and it is one of the world's largest exporters of minerals, particularly uranium (of which it is the world's largest single producer) and diamonds (of which it is the world's third largest producer). About 5.3 per cent of the land area is farmed, of which 4.6 per cent is under cultivation, mostly in the prairie region of western Canada. The country is one of the world's leading food producers, particularly of wheat, barley, oilseed, fruit, vegetables and dairy products. The fishing industry is also significant but has declined in recent years because of the restrictions introduced to protect stocks after decades of overfishing. Oil, natural gas and hydroelectricity production is high enough for Canada to be a net exporter of energy. The shrinking of the Arctic ice cap is opening up access to offshore oil and gas reserves, new fishing grounds and shipping routes in the region. The government has development plans for the area but the assertion of its sovereignty has attracted criticism from other Arctic countries and is complicated by the lack of international agreement on countries' territorial claims.

In 2005, the services sector contributed 68.5 per cent of GDP, industry 29.2 per cent and agriculture 2.3 per cent. Finance and real estate generated most revenue in the services sector, and tourism is growing. However, most tourists are from the USA and it is feared that planned security measures at the US border might reduce visitor numbers.

The USA is the main trading partner, taking 84 per cent of exports and providing 57 per cent of imports. The main exports are motor vehicles and parts, industrial machinery, aircraft, telecommunications equipment, chemicals, plastics, fertilisers, forestry products (including wood, wood pulp and paper products), energy products (including crude oil, natural gas and electricity) and aluminium.

GNI – US$1,052,600m; US$32,590 per capita (2005)
ANNUAL AVERAGE GROWTH OF GDP – 2.9 per cent (2005 est)
INFLATION RATE – 2.2 per cent (2005 est)
UNEMPLOYMENT – 6.8 per cent (2005)
TOTAL EXTERNAL DEBT – US$439,800m (2005)
IMPORTS – US$332,000m (2005)
EXPORTS – US$359,000m (2005)

BALANCE OF PAYMENTS
Trade – US$53,791m surplus (2005)
Current Account – US$26,555m surplus (2005)

Trade with UK	*2005*	*2006*
Imports from UK	£3,283,781,000	£3,863,464,000
Exports to UK	£4,242,134,000	£5,040,027,000

COMMUNICATIONS

Canada has coastline on three oceans, the Atlantic, the Arctic and the Pacific. In addition, the Great Lakes/St Lawrence Seaway system, the world's longest inland waterway, provides ocean-going shipping with access to the North American interior. There are over 300 ports, the most significant of which are Vancouver and Prince Rupert on the Pacific coast and Montreal, Halifax, Port Cartier, Sept-Iles/Pointe Noire, Saint John and Québec in the east. Most deep-water ports are open all year, and Churchill, on Hudson's Bay, is ice-free for longer periods as a result of global warming.

There are over 300 airports, of which 26 serve national and provincial capitals and other major cities. The national carriers are Air Canada and Canadian Airlines International. The 48,467km railway network transports over 270 million tonnes of freight a year; the main service providers are Canadian National Railways and Canadian Pacific Railways, which also own several US lines. There are 1.04 million km of roads. The 7,300km Trans-Canadian Highway links all ten provinces.

The telephone system has 18 million main lines in use. There were 16 million mobile phone subscribers in 2005, and nearly 22 million internet users.

EDUCATION AND HEALTH

Education is under the control of the provincial governments, the cost of the publicly controlled schools being met by local taxation and aided by provincial grants. Education is compulsory between the ages of six and 15 or seven and 16.

GROSS ENROLMENT RATIO (percentage of relevant age group) – primary 100 per cent; secondary 109 per cent; tertiary 60 per cent (2005 est)
HEALTH EXPENDITURE (per capita) – US$3,038 (2004)
HOSPITAL BEDS (per 1,000 people) – 3.7 (2000–5)

MEDIA

The public broadcaster, the Canadian Broadcasting Corporation (CBC), was established in the 1930s and transmits programmes in English and French. Société Radio Canada is the French-language public broadcast service. There are several commercial TV channels. The CBC also operates four radio networks, and television channels and radio services for indigenous peoples in the north of the country. There are 2,000 licensed radio stations in Canada. The broadcasting regulator enforces quotas of Canadian material (30–35 per cent) on Canadian radio and television.

CULTURE

Canadian culture has traditionally been influenced by the British and French colonialists, but is now dominated by the neighbouring USA. Canada has produced a long list of actors, directors and comedians who have achieved success in film and television, including Jim Carrey (*b.* 1962), David Cronenberg (*b.* 1943), Mike Myers (*b.* 1963) and the Sutherlands, Donald (*b.* 1935) and Kiefer (*b.* 1966).

The country is also one of the world's largest exporters of popular music. Leonard Cohen (*b.* 1934), Joni Mitchell (*b.* 1943), Neil Young (*b.* 1945), and Céline Dion (*b.* 1968) are all internationally successful, while the Montreal International Jazz Festival is the largest of its kind in the world. Among Canada's many award-winning writers are Nobel laureate Saul Bellow (1915–2005), Booker Prize winner Margaret Atwood (*b.* 1939) and Carol Shields (1935–2003).

CAPE VERDE

Republica de Cabo Verde – Republic of Cape Verde

AREA – 4,033 sq. km. Comprising the Windward Islands (Santo Antão, São Vicente, Santa Luzia, São Nicolau, Bõa Vista and Sal) and Leeward Islands (Maio, São Tiago, Fogo and Brava)
CAPITAL – Praia; population, 95,200 (2000), on São Tiago
MAJOR TOWN – Mindelo
CURRENCY – Escudo Caboverdiano of 100 centavos
POPULATION – 420,979 rising at 0.64 per cent per year (2006 est); Kriolus (71 per cent) (est)
RELIGION – Roman Catholicism (85 per cent) (est). Less than 1 per cent is atheist
LANGUAGE – Creole (official), Portuguese, French
POPULATION DENSITY – 126 per sq. km (2005)
URBAN POPULATION – 57.6 per cent (2005 est)
MEDIAN AGE (years) – 19.8 (2006 est)
NATIONAL ANTHEM – 'Cântico da Liberdade' ['Song of Liberty']
NATIONAL DAY – 5 July (Independence Day)
LIFE EXPECTANCY – 70.73 (2006 est)
MORTALITY RATE – 6.55 (2006 est)
BIRTH RATE – 24.87 (2006 est)
INFANT MORTALITY RATE – 46.52 (2006 est)
DEATH PENALTY – No (abolished 1981)
POPULATION LIVING BELOW POVERTY LINE – 30 per cent (2000)
MILITARY BUDGET – US$7.4m (2006)
MILITARY PERSONNEL – 1,200: army 1,000, air force 100, coast guard 100
CONSCRIPTION DURATION – Selective conscription
LITERACY RATE – 75.7 per cent (2004)

CLIMATE AND TERRAIN

The republic consists of a group of islands of volcanic origin lying 600km off the west African coast. Elevation extremes range from 2,829m (Mt Fogo) at the highest point to 0m (Atlantic Ocean) at the lowest. The climate is hot and dry.

HISTORY AND POLITICS

The islands were uninhabited when they were first discovered and colonised *c.*1460 by Portugal. Administered with Portuguese Guinea until 1879, they became an overseas province in 1951. The country achieved independence on 5 July 1975 after a campaign by the African Party for the Independence of Guinea Bissau and Cape Verde (PAIGC).

The republic was a one-party state under the African Party for the Independence of Cape Verde (PAICV) until 1990. Multiparty elections in 1991 were won by the opposition Movement for Democracy (MPD), and the MPD candidate António Mascarenhas Monteiro was elected president. The MPD and President Monteiro served two terms until the 2001 legislative elections returned the PAICV to power, with Pedro Pires as its candidate, who narrowly won the second round of the presidential election. In the 2006 elections, the PAICV retained its overall majority in the national assembly with 41 seats, and President Pires was re-elected with 51 per cent of the vote.

POLITICAL SYSTEM

Under the 1992 constitution, the head of state is the president, who is directly elected for a five-year term. There is a unicameral national assembly *(Assembleia Nacional)* with 72 members directly elected for a five-year term. The prime minister, who is responsible to the national assembly, appoints the council of ministers.

HEAD OF STATE

President, Pedro Pires, *elected* 25 February 2001, *re-elected* 12 February 2006

SELECTED GOVERNMENT MEMBERS *as at May 2007*

Prime Minister, José Maria Neves
Economy, Growth and Competitiveness, Joao Pereira Silva
Finance and Planning, Cristina Duarte
Foreign Affairs, Co-operation and Communities, Victor Borges
Defence, State Reform, Christina Fontes Lima

EMBASSY OF THE REPUBLIC OF CAPE VERDE

Avenue Jeane 29, 1050 Brussels, Belgium
T (+32) (2) 643 6270
Ambassador Extraordinary and Plenipotentiary, vacant

BRITISH AMBASSADOR
HE Peter Newall, *apptd* 2004, resident at Dakar, Senegal

ECONOMY AND TRADE

The islands have few natural resources, little fresh water and are subject to periods of prolonged drought. The economy is dependent on foreign aid; reforms are intended to attract foreign investment to finance diversification and develop the private sector. The expatriate population is larger than the resident one and remittances are an important source of revenue. The service sector dominates, with commerce, tourism, transport and public services accounting for 66 per cent of GDP in 2004. Industry contributed 22 per cent and agriculture 12 per cent; fishing, which accounts for about 1.5 per cent of GDP, is not fully exploited.

The main industries are the production of food, beverages, garments and footwear, fishing and fish processing, salt mining and ship repair. The main trading partners are Portugal, other EU countries and the USA. Exports are footwear, garments, fish and hides. Imports include foodstuffs (over 80 per cent of food is imported), industrial products, transport equipment and fuels.

GNI – US$976m; US$1,930 per capita (2005)
ANNUAL AVERAGE GROWTH OF GDP – 5.5 per cent (2005 est)
INFLATION RATE – 0.4 per cent (2005 est)
UNEMPLOYMENT – 21 per cent (2000 est)
TOTAL EXTERNAL DEBT – US$325m (2002)
IMPORTS – US$440m (2005)
EXPORTS – US$20m (2005)

BALANCE OF PAYMENTS
Trade – US$291m deficit (2003)
Current Account – US$77m deficit (2003)

Trade with UK	*2005*	*2006*
Imports from UK	£4,345,000	£4,121,000
Exports to UK	£538,000	£635,000

COMMUNICATIONS

The main ports are Praia, Mindelo and Tarrafal. Ferry services operate between the islands. There are seven operational airports, including international airports on Sal and Santiago islands, and regular internal flights between the islands. The national carrier, Cape Verde Airlines, is being privatised. The islands have no railways. There are over 5,000km of roads, most of which is paved with cobbles.

Since privatisation in 1995 the telephone system has been modernised and extends to all the islands. Mobile phone services were introduced in 1998 and there were 81,700 subscribers in 2005.

MEDIA

Freedom of the media is guaranteed in the constitution and this is generally upheld. Much of the media is state-run, but there is a growing private sector in both print and broadcast journalism. Portuguese African services and Radio France Internationale are both available, as are a range of Portuguese and Brazilian newspapers.

CENTRAL AFRICAN REPUBLIC

République Centrafricaine – Central African Republic

AREA – 622,984 sq. km. Neighbours: Chad (north), Sudan (east), Democratic Republic of the Congo and Republic of Congo (south), Cameroon (west)
CAPITAL – Bangui; population, 622,771 (2003)
MAJOR CITIES – Bimbo; Berbérati
CURRENCY – Franc CFA of 100 centimes
POPULATION – 4,303,356 rising at 1.53 per cent per year (2006 est); Baya (33 per cent), Banda (27 per cent), Mandjia (13 per cent), Sara (10 per cent), Mboum (7 per ent), M'Baka (4 per cent), Yakoma (4 per cent) (est)
RELIGION – Christianity (50 per cent), indigenous religions (35 per cent), Islam (15 per cent) (est)
LANGUAGE – French (official), Sangho
POPULATION DENSITY – 6 per sq. km (2005)
URBAN POPULATION – 43.8 per cent (2005 est)
MEDIAN AGE (years) – 18.4 (2006 est)
NATIONAL ANTHEM – 'La Renaissance' ['The Revival']
NATIONAL DAY – 1 December (Republic Day)
LIFE EXPECTANCY – 43.54 (2006 est)
MORTALITY RATE – 18.65 (2006 est)
BIRTH RATE – 33.91 (2006 est)
INFANT MORTALITY RATE – 85.63 (2006 est)
HIV/AIDS ADULT PREVALENCE – 13.5 per cent (2003 est)
DEATH PENALTY – No*
CPI SCORE – 2.4 (2006)
MILITARY BUDGET – US$16m (2006 est)
MILITARY PERSONNEL – 3,150: army 2,000, air force 150, Gendarmerie 1,000
CONSCRIPTION DURATION – 24 months (selective)
LITERACY RATE – 48.6 per cent (2004 est)
GROSS ENROLMENT RATIO (percentage of relevant age group) – primary 56 per cent; secondary 12 per cent; tertiary 2 per cent (2005 est)
HEALTH EXPENDITURE (per capita) – US$13 (2004)

CLIMATE AND TERRAIN

This landlocked central African state is a plateau between the Chad and Congo river basins, with hills in the north-east and the west. The main river is the Oubangui and is the lowest point of elevation (335m). At 1,420m, Mount Ngaoui is the highest. The climate is tropical with a wet season in the north from June to September and from May to October in the south. The north can reach a temperature of 40°C between February and May and the humidity can be extreme. The south has a more equatorial climate.

HISTORY AND POLITICS

The area was annexed by France in the 1880s and the colony of Ubanghi Chari became part of French Equatorial Africa. In 1958 it elected to remain within the French Community and adopted the title of the Central African Republic. The country became fully independent on 17 August 1960. Since independence it has been politically unstable, experiencing several coups. Jean-Bedel Bokassa, who took power in 1966, proclaimed himself emperor in 1976 and renamed the country the Central African Empire. In 1979 Bokassa was deposed in a bloodless coup and the country reverted to a republic. Gen. André Kolingba seized power in 1981 and instituted military rule until 1985, when a civilian-dominated cabinet was appointed. In 1986 a referendum was held which approved a new constitution and the establishment of a one-party state.

President Kolingba permitted multiparty elections in 1992 but these were annulled because of irregularities. In rerun elections in 1993, Ange-Félix Patassé of the Central African People's Liberation Party (MLPC) was elected president. President Patassé was deposed in 2003 in a coup led by Gen. François Bozizé, who declared himself president and appointed a transitional government.

There has been an insurgency in the north since 2003, causing thousands to seek refuge from the violence in Chad and Cameroon. The government signed a peace accord with one rebel group in February 2007.

In the 2005 elections, François Bozizé was elected president in the second round of voting. The National Convergence–Kwa Na Kwa won most seats in the national assembly and became the main party in the seven-party coalition government.

POLITICAL SYSTEM

Under the 2004 constitution, the president is elected for a five-year term, renewable only once. There is a unicameral legislature, the national assembly, which has 105 members, directly elected for a five-year term. The prime minister is appointed by the president and appoints the ministers.

HEAD OF STATE

President, Minister of Defence, Gen. François Bozizé, *took power* 15 March 2003

SELECTED GOVERNMENT MEMBERS *as at May 2007*

Prime Minister, Finance and Budget, Elie Dote

Foreign Affairs, Regional Integration and Francophone Affairs, Come Zoumara

Interior and Public Security, Lt.-Col. Michel Sallé

EMBASSY OF THE CENTRAL AFRICAN REPUBLIC

30 rue des Perchamps, F-75016, Paris

T (+33) (1) 4224 4256

Ambassador Extraordinary and Plenipotentiary, vacant

BRITISH AMBASSADOR

HE Syd Maddicott, *apptd* 2006, resident at Yaoundé, Cameroon

ECONOMY AND TRADE

The economy is largely undeveloped owing to decades of instability and misrule. Development is still hindered by political factionalism, a landlocked location, poor transport infrastructure, an unskilled workforce and corruption. The country is dependent on international aid. Natural resources include diamonds, gold, uranium, timber and oil; diamond and gold mining and forestry are among the main industrial activities but the economy still rests on agriculture, which accounts for over 50 per cent of GDP. Most production is at subsistence level but cotton, coffee and tobacco form the main exports along with diamonds and timber. The main imports are food, textiles, fuels and machinery. Trade is mainly with EU countries, the USA, Cameroon and China.

GNI – US$1,400m; US$350 per capita (2005)
ANNUAL AVERAGE GROWTH OF GDP – 2.2 per cent (2005 est)
INFLATION RATE – 3.6 per cent (2001 est)
UNEMPLOYMENT – 8 per cent (2001 est)
TOTAL EXTERNAL DEBT – US$1,060m (2002 est)
IMPORTS – US$160m (2005)
EXPORTS – US$140m (2005)

Trade with UK	*2005*	*2006*
Imports from UK	£508,000	£626,000
Exports to UK	£161,000	£100,000

COMMUNICATIONS

The infrastructure is poor, with no railway system and little of the 23,810km road network is surfaced, making many roads unusable in the wet season. There are 2,800km of waterways, mostly on the Oubangui and Sangha rivers, which are navigable all year and are used for passenger and freight transport. The principal airport is at Bangui, and there are about 50 other airports and airfields. The telephone system had 10,000 main lines in use in 2004. Mobile phone distribution is much more widespread, at 60,000 in 2004.

MEDIA

The most balanced media output is from the UN-sponsored radio broadcaster Radio Ndeke Luka. The other radio and television stations are operated by the state via Télévision Centrafricaine (TVCA). There are a number of privately owned newspapers but relatively low literacy levels mean that they have little influence. Legislation passed in 2004 abolished prison terms for press offences.

CHAD

République du Tchad – Republic of Chad

AREA – 1,284,000 sq. km. Neighbours: Niger, Nigeria and Cameroon (west), Libya (north), Sudan (east), Central African Republic (south)
CAPITAL – N'Djaména; population, 639,000 (2000)
MAJOR CITIES – Moundou; Sarh; Abéché
CURRENCY – Franc CFA of 100 centimes
POPULATION – 9,944,201 rising at 2.93 per cent per year (2006 est)
RELIGION – Islam (54 per cent), Christianity (33 per cent) (est). Most Muslims adhere to a moderate branch of mystical Islam known locally as Tidjani, which incorporates some indigenous religious elements.
LANGUAGE – French, Arabic (official), Sara
POPULATION DENSITY – 8 per sq. km (2005)
URBAN POPULATION – 25.8 per cent (2005 est)
MEDIAN AGE (years) – 16 (2006 est)
NATIONAL ANTHEM – 'La' Tchadienne'
NATIONAL DAY – 11 August (Independence Day)
LIFE EXPECTANCY – 47.52 (2006 est)
MORTALITY RATE – 16.38 (2006 est)
BIRTH RATE – 45.73 (2006 est)
INFANT MORTALITY RATE – 91.45 (2006 est)
HIV/AIDS ADULT PREVALENCE – 4.8 per cent (2004 est)
DEATH PENALTY – Yes
CPI SCORE – 2.0 (2006)
POPULATION LIVING BELOW POVERTY LINE – 80 per cent (2001 est)
MILITARY BUDGET – US$60m (2006)
MILITARY PERSONNEL – 25,350: army 17,000–20,000, air force 350, Republican Guard 5,000; paramilitaries 9,500

LITERACY RATE – 25.5 per cent (2004 est)
GROSS ENROLMENT RATIO (percentage of relevant age group) – primary 77 per cent; secondary 16 per cent; tertiary 1 per cent (2005 est)
HEALTH EXPENDITURE (per capita) – US$20 (2004)

CLIMATE AND TERRAIN

The population of this landlocked country is concentrated in the fertile lowlands of the south, away from the arid central and northern desert areas. The highest point of elevation is 3,415m (Emi Koussi) and the lowest is at 160m (the Djourab Depression). The north is almost rainless, the south is tropical and the central plain is hot and dry with a wet season from June to September.

HISTORY AND POLITICS

Chad was colonised by France from the 1890s and became part of French Equatorial Africa. It became self-governing after the Second World War and fully independent on 11 August 1960. Since independence the country has been politically unstable due to tension between the Muslim Arab north and the Christian and animist African south; different factions have attracted support from Libya and France. After a number of coups in the 1960s and 1970s, fighting led to civil war. In 1982 French-supported rebels captured the capital and formed a government under Hissène Habré, but fighting with Libyan-backed factions continued until a ceasefire was agreed in 1987 by all three countries. Habré was deposed in 1990 in a Libyan-backed coup led by Idriss Déby. Under Déby, there was a gradual move towards democracy. A new constitution establishing a unified, democratic state, was introduced in 1996. Despite a decade of greater stability, violence continues, with insurgencies and refugee problems, and Déby's regime looked vulnerable in 2006 but has managed to retain control of the capital.

Déby won the first multiparty presidential election in 1996 and was re-elected in 2001 and 2006, despite doubts over the integrity of the polls. The 2002 legislative election was won by Déby's Patriotic Salvation Movement (MPS); the election due in April 2006 was postponed until 2007, but no date was set at the time of publication.

INSURGENCIES

There are armed insurgencies in the north and in the east, although one rebel group, the United Front for Change, signed a peace agreement with the government in December 2006. The east of the country has also been destabilised by the overspill of fighting in Sudan's Darfur region and has seen the influx of an estimated 200,000 refugees.

POLITICAL SYSTEM

The 1996 constitution was amended in 2005 to remove the limit on the number of terms a president may serve. The executive president is directly elected for a five-year term. The unicameral legislature is *Assemblée Nationale* (national assembly) of 155 members directly elected for a four-year term. The prime minister is appointed by the president.

HEAD OF STATE

President, Idriss Déby, *took power* December 1990, *elected* 3 July 1996, *re-elected* 2001, 2006

SELECTED GOVERNMENT MEMBERS *as at May 2007*

Prime Minister, Nouradine Delwa Kassire Coumakoye
Economy and Planning, Ousmane Matar Breme
Finance, Abbas Mahamat Tolli
Foreign Affairs and African Integration, Ahmad Allam-mi

EMBASSY OF THE REPUBLIC OF CHAD

Boulevard Lambermont 52, 1030 Brussels, Belgium
T (+32) (2) 215 1975 E ambassade.tchad@chello.be
Ambassador Extraordinary and Plenipotentiary, HE Ahmat Abderaman Hagger

BRITISH AMBASSADOR

HE Syd Maddicott, *apptd* 2006, resident at Yaoundé, Cameroon

ECONOMY AND TRADE

Economic development has been limited by political instability, a landlocked position and poor transport infrastructure. About 80 per cent of the workforce is occupied in subsistence agriculture, herding and fishing, which contribute about 32 per cent of GDP. The main development, funded by foreign investment and international aid, is the exploitation of oil deposits in the Doba basin in the south, which came into production in 2003; the oil is exported via a pipeline through Cameroon. The use of the oil revenue is subject to restrictions imposed by the World Bank. The government's failure to comply with these led the World Bank to freeze the account and suspend loans in 2006; the government is now close to insolvency.

Chad's main trading partners are the USA, China, France, other EU countries and Cameroon. Principal exports are cotton, cattle, gum arabic and oil. The main imports are machinery and transport equipment, industrial goods, food and textiles.

GNI – US$3,900m; US$400 per capita (2005)
ANNUAL AVERAGE GROWTH OF GDP – 6 per cent (2005 est)
INFLATION RATE – 3 per cent (2005 est)
TOTAL EXTERNAL DEBT – US$1,500m (2003 est)
IMPORTS – US$850m (2005)
EXPORTS – US$3,230m (2005)

Trade with UK	*2005*	*2006*
Imports from UK	£4,940,000	£3,063,000
Exports to UK	£361,000	£243,000

COMMUNICATIONS

There are over 4,000km of waterways, although only 2,000km is navigable all year round. Of the 33,400km of roads, only 267km are surfaced, so many are unusable in the wet season. The principal airport is at N'Djaména and there are 50 other airports and airfields. There are no railways. The telephone system is primitive; mobile phone distribution is growing rapidly.

MEDIA

Low levels of literacy make radio the most important news medium. Radiodiffusion Nationale Tchadienne is the state-controlled radio station. There are private radio stations but they are closely monitored by the government. There is only one television station, Télétchad, and it is state-owned and controlled. Privately owned opposition newspapers circulate in the capital.

CHILE

República de Chile – Republic of Chile

AREA – 756,950 sq. km. Neighbours: Peru (north), Bolivia and Argentina (east)
CAPITAL – Santiago; population, 4,656,690 (2002)
MAJOR CITIES – Puente Alto; Vina del Mar; Antofagasta; Valparaíso; San Bernado
CURRENCY – Chilean peso of 100 centavos
POPULATION – 16,134,219 rising at 0.94 per cent per year (2006 est)
RELIGION – Roman Catholicism (70 per cent), other Christian denominations (15 per cent) (est). An estimated 8 per cent of the population is atheist
LANGUAGE – Spanish (official)
POPULATION DENSITY – 22 per sq. km (2005)
URBAN POPULATION – 87.7 per cent (2005 est)
MEDIAN AGE (years) – 30.4 (2006 est)
NATIONAL ANTHEM – 'Canción Nacional de Chile' ['National Anthem of Chile']
NATIONAL DAY – 18 September (Independence Day)
LIFE EXPECTANCY (years) – 76.77 (2006 est)
MORTALITY RATE – 5.81 (2006 est)
BIRTH RATE – 15.23 (2006 est)
INFANT MORTALITY RATE – 8.58 (2006 est)
DEATH PENALTY – Yes*
CPI SCORE – 7.3 (2006)
POPULATION LIVING BELOW POVERTY LINE – 18.2 per cent (2005)

CLIMATE AND TERRAIN

Chile lies between the shores of the South Pacific Ocean and the Andes (1,524m to 4,572m above sea level), extending from the arid north around Arica to Cape Horn. The length of the country is about 4,480km, with an average breadth, north of 41°, of 160km. In the central zone there is a fertile valley between the Andes and the coastal range of mountains. Elevation extremes range from 6,880m (Nevado Ojos del Salado) at the highest point to 0m (Pacific Ocean) at the lowest. The north is arid desert, the centre has a Mediterranean climate, and the south is cool and has high precipitation.

HISTORY AND POLITICS

Chile was discovered by Spanish adventurers in the 16th century and remained under Spanish rule until 1810, when the first autonomous government was established. Full independence was consolidated in 1818 after a revolutionary war.

A military coup in 1973 overthrew the Marxist president Salvador Allende. General Augusto Pinochet, who led the coup, assumed the presidency until elections were held in 1989, beginning the transition to full democracy. Between 1998 and his death in 2006, various attempts were made to bring Gen. Pinochet to trial for human rights atrocities committed during his time in office.

In the 2005 legislative elections, the ruling Coalition of Parties for Democracy (CPD) won an overall majority in the chamber of deputies and the senate. The CPD candidate, Michelle Bachelet, became the country's first female president in 2006 after winning the second round of the presidential election.

POLITICAL SYSTEM

The 1981 constitution was amended in 1989 and 2005. The executive president is directly elected for a four-year term that is not renewable. The bicameral legislature, the national congress, comprises of a senate of 38 members elected for an eight-year term (half renewed every four years) and a chamber of deputies of 118 members directly elected for a four-year term.

HEAD OF STATE

President, Michelle Bachelet, *elected* 15 January 2006, *sworn in* 11 March 2006

SELECTED GOVERNMENT MEMBERS *as at May 2007*

Defence, José Goñi Carrasco
Economy, Alejandro Ferreiro
Finance, Andres Velasco
Foreign Affairs, Alejandro Foxley
Interior, Belisario Velasco

EMBASSY OF CHILE

12 Devonshire Street, London W1G 7DS
T 020-7580 6392
W www.echileuk.demon.co.uk
Ambassador Extraordinary and Plenipotentiary, HE Rafael Moreno, *apptd* 2006

BRITISH EMBASSY

PO Box 72-D, Av. El Bosque Norte 0125, Santiago 9 ()
T (+56) (2) 370 4100 E chancery.santiago@fco.gov.uk
W www.britemb.cl
Ambassador Extraordinary and Plenipotentiary, HE Howard Drake, *apptd* 2005

BRITISH COUNCIL

Eliodoro Yáñez 832, 750-0651 Providencia, Casilla 115 Correo 55, Santiago
T (+56) (2) 410 6900 W www.britishcouncil.cl
Director, John W. Knagg, OBE

DEFENCE

The army has 260 main battle tanks, 20 armoured infantry fighting vehicles and 1,066 armoured personnel carriers. The navy has 4 submarines, 7 frigates, 22 patrol and coastal vessels, 18 combat aircraft and 8 armed helicopters. The air force has 87 combat aircraft.
MILITARY EXPENDITURE – US$4,590m (2006)
MILITARY PERSONNEL – 75,698: army 47,700, navy 19,398, air force 8,600; paramilitaries 38,000

ECONOMY AND TRADE

Economic reforms in the late 1970s and the 1980s and sound management of government finances and financial institutions have made Chile one of the most successful economies in Latin America. But wealth distribution is uneven, with over 18 per cent of the population still below the poverty line, and tackling poverty is a priority of President Bachelet.

Chile is the world's largest producer of copper, and the world's only commercial producer of nitrate of soda (Chile saltpetre) from natural resources. The chief industries are mining, forestry, fishing, food and fish processing, and wine-making. Agriculture, which contributes 6 per cent of GDP, produces fruit, vegetables, cereals, meat and wool.

The main trading partners are the USA, Japan, other Latin American states, South Korea, the EU and, increasingly, China. Principal exports are copper, fruit, fish products, paper and pulp, chemicals and wine. The main imports are petrol and petroleum products,

chemicals, electrical and telecommunications equipment, industrial machinery, vehicles and natural gas.
GNI – US$95,700m; US$5,870 per capita (2005)
ANNUAL AVERAGE GROWTH OF GDP – 6.3 per cent (2005 est)
INFLATION RATE – 3.1 per cent (2005 est)
UNEMPLOYMENT – 8.1 per cent (2005 est)
TOTAL EXTERNAL DEBT – US$47,450m (2005 est)
IMPORTS – US$32,600m (2005)
EXPORTS – US$40,600m (2005)

BALANCE OF PAYMENTS
Trade – US$10,180m surplus (2005)
Current Account – US$703m surplus (2005)

Trade with UK	*2005*	*2006*
Imports from UK	£151,922,000	£186,624,000
Exports to UK	£485,249,000	£530,386,000

COMMUNICATIONS
The main ports are Valparaíso, Antofagasta, Arica, Iquique and Punta Arenas. There is a 6,585km railway system, but lines in some areas are not in use as rail travel is increasingly superseded by road and air travel. Services are run by a state-owned company. The road network is about 80,000km in length, of which 16,000km is surfaced. There are over 300 airports and airfields; the principal airport is at Santiago. The national air carrier is LAN Airlines, with Sky Airline and Aerolíneas del Sur also providing domestic flights. Mobile phone distribution is growing rapidly. There were 6.7 million internet users in 2005.

EDUCATION AND HEALTH
Elementary education is free and compulsory, although the education system has suffered from years of under-investment and mismanagement. Following student demonstrations and strikes in May 2006, the government announced plans to reorganise the ministry of education and make further investments in education infrastructure.
LITERACY RATE – 95.7 per cent (2004 est)
GROSS ENROLMENT RATIO (percentage of relevant age group) – primary 104 per cent; secondary 89 per cent; tertiary 43 per cent (2005 est)
HEALTH EXPENDITURE (per capita) – US$359 (2004)
HOSPITAL BEDS (per 1,000 people) – 2.6 (2000–5)

MEDIA AND CULTURE
Television is a combination of national and local, private and state-run, cable and terrestrial channels. Radio is the country's most important news medium, with 800 stations country-wide. Chile has a good record for press freedom and a 2004 media reform bill abolished several media restrictions remaining from the Pinochet era.

Chile has a vibrant arts culture and is considered the most 'European' of the Latin American countries. Chilean Nobel Prize winners for literature include the writers Gabriela Mistral (1889–1957), in 1945, and poet Pablo Neruda (1904–73), in 1971.

Chile's island possessions include the Juan Fernández group about 576km from Valparaíso; one of these islands is the reputed scene of Alexander Selkirk's shipwreck (the inspiration for Daniel Defoe's novel *Robinson Crusoe).* Easter Island, about 3,200km away in the South Pacific Ocean, contains stone platforms and hundreds of mysterious stone figures, *moai,* thought to be carved from volcanic ash by Polynesian colonizers between 1100 and 1600.

CHILEAN ANTARCTIC TERRITORY
The Chilean Antarctic Territory covers the Antarctic peninsula and an area of the landmass that extends from 53°W to 90°W along a latitude of 60°S. This area is also claimed by the UK and Argentina, although the Antarctic treaty has frozen all disputes over territory. (*see also* The Antartic.)

CHINA

Zhonghua Renmin Gongheguo – People's Republic of China

AREA – 9,596,960 sq. km. Neighbours: Russia and Mongolia (north), North Korea (east), Vietnam, Laos, Myanmar, India, Bhutan and Nepal (south), India, Pakistan, Afghanistan, Tajikistan, Kyrgyzstan and Kazakhstan (west)
CAPITAL – Beijing; population, 7,441,000 (2001 est)
MAJOR CITIES – Shanghai; Tianjin; Wuhan; Guangzhou; Shenyang; Chongqing; Nanjing; Harbin; Xi'an; Chengdu; Changchun; Dalian
CURRENCY – Renminbi yuan of 10 jiao or 100 fen
POPULATION – 1,313,973,713 rising at 0.59 per cent per year (2006 est); Han Chinese (91.9 per cent) (est). The remainder of the population belongs to around 55 ethnic minorities
RELIGION – Buddhism (8 per cent), Christianity (3 per cent), Islam (1 per cent) (est). Most of the country's population does not subscribe to any religious faith
LANGUAGE – Mandarin (official), English, Cantonese, Fuzhou, Mongolian, Tibetan, Korean, Taiwanese
POPULATION DENSITY – 140 per sq. km (2005)
URBAN POPULATION – 40.5 per cent (2005 est)
MEDIAN AGE (years) – 32.7 (2006 est)
NATIONAL ANTHEM – 'Yiyongjun Jinxingqu' ['March of the Volunteers']
NATIONAL DAY – 1 October (Founding of People's Republic)
LIFE EXPECTANCY (years) – 72.58 (2006 est)
MORTALITY RATE – 6.97 (2006 est)
BIRTH RATE – 13.25 (2006 est)
INFANT MORTALITY RATE – 22.12 (2006 est)
DEATH PENALTY – Yes
CPI SCORE – 3.3 (2006)
POPULATION BELOW POVERTY LINE – 10 per cent (2001 est)

CLIMATE AND TERRAIN
China is twice the size of western Europe and contains a vast range of landscapes and climates. Two-thirds of the country is hilly or mountainous. The highest mountains are on the Tibetan plateau, in the west of the country, where the highest elevation is 8,850m (Mt Everest). To the north of the Tibetan plateau, the land drops to the arid, semi-desert steppes bisected by the Tian Shan mountains; the country's lowest elevation is −153m at Turfan Pendi. The southern plains and east coast have the most fertile land, irrigated by the Huang He (Yellow), Chang Jiang (Yangtze) and Xi Jiang (West) rivers, and therefore are the most heavily populated areas.

There are seven climate zones. The north-east has cold winters, fierce winds, hot and humid summers and erratic rainfall. The south-west has mild winters and warm summers. Inner Mongolia has cold winters and hot

ummers. Central China has hot and humid summers with he occasional tropical cyclone. South China is partly ropical with heavy rainfall. Xizang is a high plateau urrounded by mountains that is subject to harsh winters. Xinjiang and the west have a desert climate, cold winters nd year-round rain.

HISTORY AND POLITICS

China was ruled by imperial dynasties from the second millennium BC. The last emperor of the Qing dynasty abdicated in 1912 after a revolution broke out in 1911. Central authority collapsed, leading to a period of chaos and regional warlord domination as neither the Guomindang, led by Sun Yat-sen, nor the Chinese Communist Party (CCP), founded in 1921, were able to unify China. The conflict between them also hindered heir individual and joint efforts to resist Japanese encroachment; Japan occupied Manchuria in 1932, and most northern and coastal areas of China by 1939. Japan's occupation was ended by its defeat by the allies in 1945. Despite allied support after 1941 for the Guomindang, now led by Chiang Kai-shek, the Communists established control over large areas of China n the early 1940s, seizing the territory abandoned by Japan in 1945. Following a civil war (1946–9) the uccessful CCP inaugurated the People's Republic of China (PRC), and the Guomindang went into exile in Taiwan. The USA continued to recognise the Chiang Kai-hek regime as the rightful government of China until 1971, when the PRC took over China's membership of he UN from Taiwan.

Under Mao Zedong, China was ruled on the basis of four 'cardinal principles': Marxist-Leninist-Maoist thought, the Socialist Road, the dictatorship of the proletariat, and the leadership of the CCP. Mao's 'Great Leap Forward' (1958–61) was an attempt to industrialise rural areas that resulted in a famine in which 30–40 million people died. China was plunged into chaos during the Cultural Revolution (1966–70) when the Red Guards were used to rid the country of 'rightist elements'.

Following Mao Zedong's death in 1976, the disgraced Deng Xiaoping was recalled and he became the dominant force within the party, eliminating leftist influence, rehabilitating fallen leaders and promoting an 'open door' policy of economic liberalisation. The Party Congresses of 1982 and 1987 reaffirmed Deng's policies, and in 1987 most of the revolutionary generation was replaced in the most senior posts by younger, more liberal supporters of reform.

Liberalisation suffered a setback in 1989, when student-led pro-democracy demonstrations in April and May, centred on Tiananmen Square in Beijing, were brutally repressed by the army. Over 2,000 protesters died. The events strengthened the position of hardliners within the leadership, who readopted policies of centralisation based on Marxist ideology.

Although Deng retired from his last official post in 1989, he retained effective control until late 1994, and at his instigation, the emphasis switched back to economic reform in 1992 and the power of the hardliners waned. The 1992 party congress endorsed Deng's calls for faster, bolder economic reforms and a socialist market economy. Following Deng's death in 1997, Jiang Zemin became leader and continued the economic reforms. He also sought to improve China's standing in the international community. In 2003 Hu Jintao was elected by the national people's congress as the new state president and Wen Jaibao was elected as premier the following day.

INSURGENCIES

Separatists from the Uighur Muslim minority group in Xinjiang Autonomous Region have demonstrated against Han rule, and have claimed responsibility for bomb attacks in the provincial capital, Urumqi, and in Beijing. Two Muslim separatists were executed in 1999 as part of an effort to tighten control of the region, and in 2001 the founder of an underground Islamic party was sentenced to death. In 1999 the government banned the Falun Gong spiritual sect, which had claimed to have 70 million followers, after it was revealed that a large number of party officials and senior army officers had joined the cult. Tens of thousands of Falun Gong members have been arrested since the ban.

POLITICAL SYSTEM

Under the 1982 constitution, the national people's congress is the highest organ of state power. It has 2,979 members indirectly elected for a five-year term and it is supposed to hold one session a year. It is empowered to amend the constitution, make laws, select the president and vice-president and other leading state officials, approve the national economic plan, the state budget and the final state accounts, and to decide on questions of war and peace. The state council is the highest organ of the state administration and is elected by the national people's congress on the nomination of the premier. It is composed of the premier, the vice-premiers, the state councillors, heads of ministries and commissions, the auditor-general and the secretary-general. Command over the armed forces is vested in the central military commission. The president's term of office is five years, renewable only once.

Deputies to congresses at the primary level are directly elected by the voters through a secret ballot after democratic consultation. This is now extended to county level. These congresses elect the deputies to the congress at the next higher level. Deputies to the national people's congress are elected by the people's congresses of the provinces, autonomous regions and municipalities directly under the central government, and by the armed forces.

Local government is conducted through people's governments at provincial, municipal and county levels. Autonomous regions, prefectures and counties exist for national minorities and are described as self-governing.

HEAD OF STATE

President of the Republic, Hu Jintao, *elected* 15 March 2003
Vice-President, Zeng Qinghong

STATE COUNCIL *as at May 2007*

Premier, Wen Jiabao
Vice-Premiers, Huang Ju; Wu Yi; Zeng Peiyan; Hui Liangyu
State Councillors, Zhou Yongkang *(Public Security)*; Gen. Cao Gangchuan *(National Defence)*; Tang Jiaxuan; Hua Jianmin *(Secretary-General of the State Council)*; Chen Zhili

SELECTED GOVERNMENT MEMBERS *as at May 2007*

Civil Affairs, Li Xueju
Finance, Xie Xuren
Foreign Affairs, Yang Jiechi
State Security, Xu Yongyue

EMBASSY OF THE PEOPLE'S REPUBLIC OF CHINA
49–51 Portland Place, London W1B 1JL
T 020-7299 4049 **W** www.chinese-embassy.org.uk
Ambassador Extraordinary and Plenipotentiary, HE Zha Peixin, *apptd* 2002

BRITISH EMBASSY
11 Guang Hua Lu, Jian Guo Men Wai, Beijing 100600
T (+86) (10) 5192 4000
E commercialmail.beijing@fco.gov.uk
Ambassador, HE Sir William Ehrman, *apptd* 2006

BRITISH COUNCIL
Cultural and Education Section, British Embassy, 4th Floor Landmark Building Tower 1, 8 North Dongsanhuan Road, Chaoyang District, Beijing 100004
T (+86) (10) 6590 6903 **W** www.britishcouncil.org/china
Regional Director, Michael O'Sullivan

DEFENCE

All three military arms are parts of the People's Liberation army (PLA). China has at least 46 intercontinental, 72[illegible] short range and 35 intermediate ballistic missiles, and 12 submarine-launched nuclear ballistic missiles. The army has over 7,580 main battle tanks, over 3,500 armoured personnel carriers and 31 attack helicopters.

The navy has 58 submarines (one strategic), 28 destroyers, 48 frigates, 242 patrol and coastal vessels, 792 combat aircraft and 35 armed helicopters. The air force has 2,643 combat aircraft.

MILITARY EXPENDITURE – US$122,000m (2006 est)
MILITARY PERSONNEL – 2,255,000: army 1,600,000 navy 255,000, air force 400,000; paramilitaries 1,500,000
CONSCRIPTION DURATION – 24 months (selective)

ECONOMY AND TRADE

Liberalisation since the 1980s has transformed the economy from centrally planned to a more market-orientated one with a rapidly growing private sector that saw a record trade surplus and record inward investment in 2006. A significant industrial base and transport infrastructure have been constructed, especially in the coastal regions, where the economy has become a free market in all but name, with several stock markets and Shanghai's emergence as a financial centre.

The economy has grown more than five-fold since 1980, but is slowing now, partly in response to government measures to prevent overheating and partly because it is becoming a victim of its success: there are skills shortages, although some managerial expertise is being provided by foreign investors, and labour shortages, particularly in the southern cities, which are causing industrial activity to move further inland to find workers.

The effects of the rapid transformation have been unevenly distributed, with rural incomes rising only 6.2 per cent in 2005 compared to a 9.6 per cent increase in urban areas. This has caused social unrest and in 2005 officials recorded 87,000 protests by those who have so far missed out on the benefits or been adversely affected by the effects of economic growth. A serious downside of industrialisation is the effect on the environment: officials estimate that pollution costs China between 8 per cent and 15 per cent of GDP, adversely affecting land and water as well as air quality. The latest five-year plan approved in March 2006, makes environmental protection a priority.

AVERAGE WAGE 1991–2004 *(yuan)*

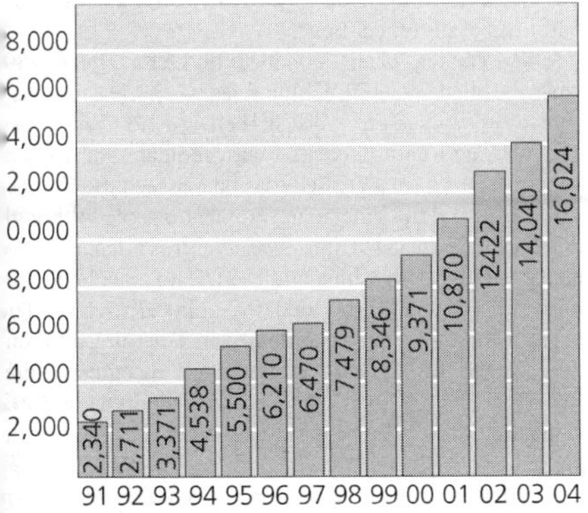

Source: National Bureau of Statistics of the People's Republic of China

Tensions are also arising from China's effects on world trade; the cheapness of its exports, especially garments, has provoked protective measures by the EU and USA. It has also had a desperate need for greater supplies of oil, putting it into competition with countries such as Japan for supplies. The urgency of this need may decline, however, as the increasing availability of domestic coal and oil help to reduce energy imports. Energy supplies will also be boosted as the amount of hydroelectric power generated by the Three Gorges Dam increases; the reservoir began filling in 2003, construction was completed in 2006, and by 2011 the power station will be capable of generating 18.2 million kilowatts per hour.

Although rural areas have seen few benefits and often some drawbacks from the economic transformation, agriculture remains of great importance: it contributes 12 per cent of GDP but employs 45 per cent of the working population. Cereals, with peas and beans, are grown in the northern provinces, and rice and sugar in the south. Cotton (mostly in valleys of the Yangtze and Yellow rivers), tea (in the west and south), with hemp, jute and flax, are the most important crops. Livestock is raised in large numbers. Sericulture is one of the oldest industries. Cottons, woollens and silks are manufactured in large quantities.

The highly diversified industrial sector, encompassing heavy industry, manufacturing and construction, contributes 48 per cent of GDP and employs 24 per cent of the workforce. The services sector accounts for 40 per cent of GDP and 31 per cent of employment. Tourism has become a major industry, with over 91 million foreign visitors in 2003. Foreign trade and external economic relations have grown enormously since 1978, and particularly since China joined the World Trade Organisation in 2001. China is the world's fifth largest exporter of goods, which include machinery and equipment, plastics, optical and medical equipment, iron and steel, and clothing. The principal imports are machinery and equipment, oil and mineral fuels, plastics, organic chemicals, iron and steel. The main trading partners are the USA, Japan, South Korea, Germany and Taiwan, although trade with Latin America and Africa is growing rapidly. China is also investing heavily in Latin America, particularly in joint ventures in oil and gas exploration, and in Africa.

GNI – US$2,269,700m; US$1,740 per capita (2005)
ANNUAL AVERAGE GROWTH OF GDP – 10.2 per cent (2005 est)
INFLATION RATE – 1.8 per cent (2005 est)
UNEMPLOYMENT – 9 per cent 2004 est)
TOTAL EXTERNAL DEBT – US$252,800m (2005 est)
IMPORTS – US$660,000m (2005)
EXPORTS – US$762,000m (2005)

BALANCE OF PAYMENTS
Trade – US$134,189m surplus (2005)
Current Account – US$160,818m surplus (2005)

Trade with UK	*2005*	*2006*
Imports from UK	£2,823,652,000	£3,278,879,000
Exports to UK	£13,194,496,000	£15,559,074,000

COMMUNICATIONS

The infrastructure was created after the civil war and has been expanded and modernised considerably since liberalisation began. In the past the principal means of internal communication was by river, the most important of which are the Huang He (Yellow), Chang Jiang (Yangtze) and Xi Jiang (West). These, together with the network of canals connecting them, are still much used, but their overall importance has declined. Coastal port facilities are being improved and the merchant fleet expanded. The main seaports are Shanghai and Dalian in the north, and Guangzhou (Canton) in the south; Nanjing is the largest river port.

Nowadays, long-distance internal travel is mostly by air and rail. The length of civil air routes has more than tripled in the past two decades. There are 486 airports and airfields and several national air carriers. The rail system has 74,408km of track, although only 19,303km is electrified; the Qinghai-Tibet railway opened in 2006, opening up the remote western provinces. The road network has been expanded to over 1.8 million km, making all towns and villages accessible, and the major cities are linked by 34,000km of modern highways. Motor vehicle ownership is growing rapidly, leading to rising problems of congestion, road safety and pollution.

The telecommunications system is also expanding, although facilities for personal subscribers are unevenly distributed, concentrated in the cities, industrial centres and major towns. Mobile phone distribution is growing rapidly and, at 437 million, has overtaken land-line subscriptions. There were 123 million internet users in 2006.

EDUCATION AND HEALTH

Primary education lasts six years and secondary education six years (three years in junior middle school and three years in senior middle school).
LITERACY RATE – 90.9 per cent (2004 est)
GROSS ENROLMENT RATIO (percentage of relevant age group) – primary 118 per cent; secondary 73 per cent (2005 est); tertiary 19 per cent (2002 est)
HEALTH EXPENDITURE (per capita) – US$71 (2004)
HOSPITAL BEDS (per 1,000 people) – 2.5 (2000–5)

MEDIA

China's media industry is huge – it has 25,000 newspapers and magazines, 750,000 journalists and 12,000 radio and television stations. In 2002 Communist

Party officials stated that China has a domestic television audience of 1.1 billion. Subscription services are expected to have a market of 128 million by the year 2010. The Communist Party has always maintained a firm grip on the nation's news reporting but with the installation as president of Hu Jintao, a more liberal approach was adopted, and since December 2006 foreign journalists have been allowed to travel freely and interview people without official permission. Market reforms are also being introduced into the media with the closure in 2004 of hundreds of state-funded publications that relied on government departments for their readership. Despite these reforms, journalists still exercise a significant degree of self-censorship and the Communist Party still attempts to restrict access to foreign news media by blocking websites and radio broadcasts and limiting the distribution of overseas newspapers. Several bloggers have found themselves the target of Beijing officials.

CULTURE

The Chinese language has many dialects, notably Cantonese, Hakka, Amoy, Foochow, Changsha, Nanchang, Wu (Shanghai) and the northern dialect. The common speech or *putonghua* (often referred to as Mandarin) is based on the northern dialect. The Communists have promoted it as the national language and it is taught throughout the country. As *putonghua* encourages the use of the spoken language in writing, the old literary style and ideographic form of writing has fallen into disuse. Since 1956 simplified characters have been introduced to make reading and writing easier. In 1958 the National People's Congress adopted a system of romanisation known as *pinyin.*

Chinese literature is one of the oldest in the world. Paper has been employed for writing and printing for nearly 2,000 years. The Confucian classics, which formed the basis of traditional Chinese culture, date from the Warring States period (fourth to third centuries BC), as do the earliest texts of Taoism. Histories, philosophical and scientific works, poetry, literary and art criticism, novels and romances survive from most periods.

TIBET

AREA – 1,199,164 sq. km
POPULATION – 2,610,000 (2001 est)
CAPITAL – Lhasa

Tibet is a plateau, seldom lower than 3,000m, in south-west China which forms the frontier with India (boundary imperfectly demarcated), from Kashmir to Myanmar, from which it is separated by the Himalayas. The Indus, Brahmaputra, Mekong and Yangtze rivers all rise on the Tibet plateau.

Tibet was under Mongol rule almost continuously from the 13th to the 17th century. Chinese control grew from the 18th century and direct rule began in 1910, but with the collapse of the Chinese Empire in 1911 Tibet declared its independence and the Dalai Lama ruled undisturbed until Communist rule was established in China. In 1950 Chinese Communist forces invaded Tibet, and in 1951 the Tibetan authorities signed a treaty agreeing joint Chinese-Tibetan rule. A series of revolts against Chinese rule culminated in a 1959 uprising in the capital, which was crushed after several days of fighting and military rule was imposed. The Dalai Lama fled to India where he and his followers were granted political asylum and established a government in exile. Tibet became an Autonomous Region of China in 1965. Martial law was declared in Tibet in 1989, and sporadic outbursts of unrest continue.

The Panchen Lama remained in Lhasa after 1959; when he died in 1989, China rejected the Dalai Lama's choice of successor, who is believed to have been executed, and enthroned its own candidate. Subsequent appointments have increased tension between the Chinese authorities and the Tibetan government in exile. Although the 17th Karmapa Lama was the first lama to be recognised by both China and the Dalai Lama, he fled to India in 1999 and appealed for political asylum. The seventh Reting Lama was ordained in Tibet in 2000, but the Dalai Lama has refused to recognise him. Representatives of the Dalai Lama visited China in 2002 in an attempt to improve the situation but relations remain poor.

Another source of tension has been the number of Chinese migrants settling in Tibet. Since the 1980s, large numbers of Chinese have been encouraged to move to Tibet, a development that the Tibetan government-in-exile regards as an attempt to eradicate the culture of the Tibetan people.

In 1997, the International Commission of Jurists issued a report declaring that Tibet was 'under alien subjugation' and called for a UN-managed referendum to decide its future status. China contested that the report failed to acknowledge its historical claims to the region.

In 2001, the Chinese government published details of a modernisation programme for Tibet which is intended to improve the low standard of living by promoting market reforms and extensive public construction projects.

SPECIAL ADMINISTRATIVE REGIONS

HONG KONG

AREA – 1,092 sq. km
CURRENCY – Hong Kong dollar (HK $) of 100 cents
POPULATION – 6,940,432 (2006 est), rising at 0.59 per cent per year (2006 est)
POPULATION DENSITY – 6,664 per sq. km (2005)
URBAN POPULATION – 93.1 per cent (2000 est)
FLAG – Red, with a white bauhinia flower of five petals each containing a red star
LIFE EXPECTANCY (years) – 81.59 (2006 est)
BIRTH RATE – 7.29 (2006 est)
MORTALITY RATE – 6.29 (2006 est)
INFANT MORTALITY RATE – 2.95 (2006 est)
HIV/AIDS ADULT PREVALENCE – 0.1 per cent (2003 est)
CPI SCORE – 8.3 (2006)

CLIMATE AND TERRAIN

Hong Kong consists of more than 230 islands and a portion of the mainland (Kowloon and the New Territories, a peninsula in the southern part of Guangdong province and adjacent islands) on the south-east coast of China, situated on the eastern side of the mouth of the Pearl River. Hong Kong Island is about 18km long and 3–8km broad. It is separated from the mainland by a narrow strait. The highest point is Tai Mo Shan (958m). The climate is subtropical, tending towards the temperate for nearly half the year. Mean monthly temperatures range from 16°C to 29°C. Tropical cyclones occur between May and November, and nearly 80 per cent of the average annual rainfall of 2,214mm falls between May and September.

HISTORY AND POLITICS

Hong Kong Island was first occupied by Britain in 1841 and formally ceded to Britain in 1842. Kowloon was acquired in 1860 and the New Territories by a 99-year lease signed in 1898.

In 1984, the UK and China agreed that China would resume sovereignty over Hong Kong in 1997. In the run-up to the handover, the Chinese government's insistence on a greater say in the running of the colony and the governor's plan for an extension of democracy prompted acrimonious disputes. On 1 July 1997, Hong Kong became a Special Administrative Region (SAR) of the People's Republic of China.

The 1984 joint declaration, which took effect in May 1985, contains guarantees to preserve Hong Kong's free-market economy, its autonomy in the conduct of its external commercial relations and its own monetary and financial policies, and preserve judicial independence. Hong Kong's constitution is the Basic Law, which was passed by China's national people's congress in 1990 and guarantees that the SAR's social and economic systems will remain unchanged for 50 years.

After the 2004 legislative council elections, pro-China parties held 34 of the 60 elected seats and pro-democracy parties 25. Tung Chee-hwa resigned in March 2005 and in June, Donald Tsang was elected as chief executive to serve out the rest of the term of office. He was re-elected in March 2007.

POLITICAL SYSTEM

Hong Kong is administered by the Hong Kong SAR government, headed by the chief executive, who is elected by a 800-strong election committee and aided by an executive council and a legislative council. The chief executive serves a five-year term. The executive council consists of the chief executive, 14 official members, who are the heads of administrative departments, and 15 non-official members. The legislative council consists of 60 members, 30 directly elected by geographic constituencies, and 30 elected by functional constituencies composed of professional and business groups. They serve a four-year term.

Chief Executive, Donald Tsang, *sworn in* 24 June 2005, *re-elected* 25 March 2007

SELECTED GOVERNMENT MEMBERS *as at May 2007*

Chief Secretary for Administration, Rafeal Hui

Economy and Finance, Henry Tang

CONSULATE-GENERAL

PO Box 528,1 Supreme Court Road, Central Hong Kong

T (+852) 2901 3000 E consular@britishconsulate.org.hk

Consul-General, Stephen Bradley, *apptd* 2002

BRITISH COUNCIL

3 Supreme Court Road, Admiralty, Hong Kong

T (+852) 2913 5100 W www.britishcouncil.org/hongkong

Director, Ruth Gee

ECONOMY AND TRADE

Hong Kong's free-market economy has experienced strong growth in recent years, partly derived from closer integration with China as it has become more open to international trade. Diversification of products and markets continues to be the main feature of industrial development, as are industrial partnerships with overseas companies. The economy is based on export rather than the domestic market.

The economy is dominated by the service sector, which accounted for 91 per cent of GDP in 2006. The main contributors to this were tourism, banking and shipping; wholesale and retail trade, restaurants and hotels and financial services. Industry contributed 9 per cent of GDP, and manufacturing occupied 7.5 per cent of the workforce. Principal products are textiles, clothing, electrical machinery and appliances, plastics, toys, and clocks and watches.

The principal export markets are China, the USA and Japan. China is Hong Kong's principal supplier of imported goods.

GNI – US$192,100m; US$27,670 per capita (2005)

ANNUAL AVERAGE GROWTH OF GDP – 7.3 per cent (2005 est)

INFLATION RATE – 0.9 per cent (2005)

UNEMPLOYMENT – 5.5 per cent (2005 est)

IMPORTS – US$300,000m (2005)

EXPORTS – US$289,000m (2005)

BALANCE OF PAYMENTS

Trade – US$7,627m deficit (2005)

Current Account – US$20,284m surplus (2005)

Trade with UK	*2005*	*2006*
Imports from UK	£3,104,307,000	£2,869,960,000
Exports to UK	£6,718,751,000	£7,494,492,000

COMMUNICATIONS

Hong Kong has one of the world's finest natural harbours, and is the busiest container port in the world. Dockyard facilities include eight floating drydocks, the largest being capable of docking vessels up to 150,000 tonnes deadweight. There are three airports, one accommodating international flights.

286.7	**WORLD HIGHEST**
	vehicles per km of road

Source: Economist Intelligence Unit

EDUCATION

Education is free of charge and compulsory for children up to the age of 15.

GROSS ENROLMENT RATIO (percentage of age group) – primary 105 per cent; secondary 87 per cent; tertiary 31 per cent (2005 est)

MACAO (AOMEN)

AREA – 28.2 sq. km

CURRENCY – Pataca of 100 avos

POPULATION – 453,125 (2006 est)

FLAG – Green, with a white lotus flower above a white stylised bridge and water, under a large gold five-point star and four gold stars in crescent

CLIMATE AND TERRAIN

Macao consists of a peninsula and the islands of Coloane and Taipa, situated at the mouth of the Pearl River. It is 64km from Hong Kong. The highest point is Coloane Alto (172.4m). The climate is subtropical.

HISTORY AND POLITICS

The first Portuguese ship arrived at Macao in 1513 and trade with China commenced in 1553. Macao became a Portuguese colony in 1557; China recognised Portugal's sovereignty over Macao by treaty in 1887. An agreement to transfer the administration of Macao to the Chinese authorities was signed in 1987, and Macao became the Macao Special Administrative Region (MSAR) of China on 19 December 1999. Edmund Ho Hao Wah, elected as the first chief executive in 1999, was re-elected in 2004. The last legislative election was in 2005; various parties won one or two seats each.

The Basic Law, approved in 1993, has served as Macao's constitution since 1999. The chief executive is elected by a 300-member election committee and serves a five-year term of office; the election of the next chief executive must take place no more than 60 days before the incumbent office-holder's term expires. The chief executive is assisted in policy-making by the ten-member executive council. The legislative council has 29 members, who serve for four years; 12 are directly elected, ten are indirectly elected by corporate constituencies and seven are appointed by the chief executive.

Chief Executive, Edmund Ho Hao Wah

SELECTED GOVERNMENT MEMBERS *as at May 2007*

Economy and Finance, Francis Tam Pak Yuen

Secretary for Administration and Justice, Florida Rosa Silver Chan

CONSUL-GENERAL

Stephen Bradley, resident at Hong Kong

ECONOMY AND TRADE

The economy is based on tourism, gambling and garment manufacturing. The service sector contributes about 93 per cent of GDP and industry 7 per cent. Gambling is the largest employer, occupying 18 per cent of the workforce in 2005; restaurants and hotels employed 10 per cent, wholesale and retail trade 15 per cent and manufacturing 14 per cent. The principal products and exports are clothing, textiles, electronics, footwear and toys. The main trading partners are China, the USA, Hong Kong and Japan.

IMPORTS – US$3,910 million (2005)
EXPORTS – US$2,480 million (2005)

BALANCE OF PAYMENTS

Trade – US$1,841m deficit (2004)
Current Account – US$4,163m surplus (2004)

Trade with UK	*2005*	*2006*
Imports from UK	£17,258,000	£20,993,000
Exports to UK	£23,534,000	£23,644,000

COLOMBIA

República de Colombia – Republic of Colombia

AREA – 1,138,910 sq. km. Neighbours: Venezuela (north and east), Brazil (south-east), Peru (south), Ecuador (south-west), Panama (north-west)
CAPITAL – Bogotá; population, 6,763,325 (2005 est)
MAJOR CITIES – Medellin; Cali; Barranquilla, the major port on the Caribbean; Cartagena; Cuctua; Bucaramanga
CURRENCY – Colombian peso of 100 centavos
POPULATION – 43,593,035 rising at 1.46 per cent per year (2006 est)
RELIGION – Roman Catholicism (81 per cent), Protestantism (13 per cent) (est)
LANGUAGE – Spanish (official)
POPULATION DENSITY – 41 per sq. km (2005)
URBAN POPULATION – 77.4 per cent (2005 est)
MEDIAN AGE (years) – 26.3 (2006 est)
NATIONAL ANTHEM – 'Himno Nacional de la República de Columbia' ['National Anthem of the Republic of Columbia']
NATIONAL DAY – 20 July (Independence Day)
LIFE EXPECTANCY (years) – 71.99 (2006 est)
MORTALITY RATE – 5.58 (2006 est)
BIRTH RATE – 20.48 (2006 est)
INFANT MORTALITY RATE – 20.35 (2006 est)
DEATH PENALTY – No (abolished 1910)
CPI SCORE – 3.9 (2006)
POPULATION BELOW POVERTY LINE – 49.2 per cent (2005)

CLIMATE AND TERRAIN

Colombia lies in the extreme north-west of South America, having a coastline on both the Caribbean Sea and the Pacific Ocean. Elevation extremes range from 5,775m (Pico Cristobal Colon) at the highest point to 0m (Pacific Ocean) at the lowest. The country is divided by the Cordillera de los Andes into a coastal region in the north and west and extensive plains in the east. The eastern range of the Colombian Andes is a series of vast tablelands. This temperate region is the most densely populated portion of the country. The principal rivers are the Magdalena, Guaviare, Cauca, Caquetá, Putumayo and Patia. The climate is predominantly tropical but the Caribbean coastline is typically drier than the rest of the country.

HISTORY AND POLITICS

The Colombian coast was visited in 1502 by Columbus, and in 1536 a Spanish expedition penetrated the interior and established a government. The country remained under Spanish rule until 1819 when Simón Bolivar established the Republic of Gran Colombia, consisting of the territories now known as Colombia, Panama, Venezuela and Ecuador. In 1829–30 Venezuela and Ecuador withdrew, and in 1831 the remaining territories formed a separate state. The name of Colombia was adopted in 1866. Panama seceded in 1903.

In 1949, a civil war broke out which lasted until 1957 when the Conservative and Liberal parties formed a coalition government known as the National Front. This arrangement continued until 1974 and was revived in 1978 in an attempt to maintain the rule of law in the face of violence by drugs cartels, a left-wing insurgency and counter-attacks by right-wing paramilitaries. Despite foreign assistance and increased military spending, drugs trafficking continues to be widespread, although less of a threat to civil order than hitherto, but the government has been unable to suppress or reach a negotiated settlement with insurgents' leaders despite peace talks.

In the 2006 legislative elections, the Liberal Party (PL) remained the largest party in the house of representatives, but was only the third largest in the senate. President Uribe, seen by many as a key ally of US president George Bush, was re-elected in 2006 with 62.2 per cent of the vote.

INSURGENCIES

Since the 1960s Colombia has been dogged by insurgency by several guerrilla groups, mainly the Revolutionary Armed Forces of Colombia (FARC), the National Liberation army (ELN) and the right-wing United Self-Defence Forces of Colombia (AUC), which is suspected of having links with the security forces. All the groups are known to be involved in drugs trafficking and other crime, and now act to protect these sources of funding as much as to further their political aims. Talks between the government and the FARC began in 1998 but were broken off by the government in 2002 after further violence. The AUC declared an indefinite ceasefire in 2002 and peace talks from 2004 led to the start of demobilisation, which continued despite some AUC leaders pulling out of further talks in 2006. Talks with the ELN began in December 2005.

Action against the insurgents was a key election pledge of President Uribe in 2002 and the government's increased efforts since then have extended government control so that it now has a presence in every municipality. The level of violence has dropped but drug-eradication programmes are aggressively resisted. It is estimated that since 2000 the US government has contributed some US$3bn (£1.5bn) to drug-eradication and military training programmes in Colombia.

POLITICAL SYSTEM

Under the 1991 constitution, the executive president is directly elected for a single four-year term; a 2005 amendment allows an incumbent president to stand for a second term. The legislature, the congress, is bicameral. The lower house (the house of representatives) has 166 members directly elected for a four-year term. The upper house (the senate) has 102 members directly elected for four years; two seats are reserved for representatives of indigenous people. The president appoints the cabinet.

HEAD OF STATE

President, Álvaro Uribe Vélez, *elected* 26 May 2002, *re-elected* 28 May 2006

Vice-President, Francisco Santos Calderon

SELECTED GOVERNMENT MEMBERS *as at May 2007*

Defence, Juan Manuel Santos

Finance and Public Credit, Oscar Ivan Zuluaga

Foreign Affairs, Fernando Araujo

Interior, Justice, Carlos Holguin Sardi

EMBASSY OF COLOMBIA

3 Hans Crescent, London SW1X 0LN

T 020-7589 9177 **E** mail@colombianembassy.co.uk

Ambassador Extraordinary and Plenipotentiary, HE Alfonso Lopez-Caballero, *apptd* 2002

BRITISH EMBASSY

Edificio Ing Barings, Carrera 9, No 76–49, Piso 5, Santafe de Bogotá D.C.

T (+57) (1) 317 6690 **E** britain@cable.net.co

Ambassador Extraordinary and Plenipotentiary, HE Haydon Warren-Gash, *apptd* 2005

BRITISH COUNCIL

c/o British Embassy

T (+57) (1) 325 9090 **W** www.britishcouncil.org/colombia

Director, Charles Nuttall

DEFENCE

The army has 368 armoured personnel carriers. The navy has 4 submarines, 4 corvettes, 96 patrol and coastal vessels, 11 aircraft and 2 helicopters at 9 bases. The air force has 90 combat aircraft.

MILITARY EXPENDITURE – US$5,290m (2006)

MILITARY PERSONNEL – 208,600: army 178,000, navy 22,000, air force 8,600; paramilitaries 129,000

ECONOMY AND TRADE

The improving security situation, government austerity budgets and international funding have aided economic growth. Public sector debt has been reduced and inflation and unemployment levels are declining, although nearly half the population is still below the poverty line. The government has encouraged diversification to reduce dependence on coffee as the major export and this has led to the growth of new export-orientated industries, particularly textiles, paper products and leather goods.

Services accounted for around 53 per cent of GDP, industry 35 per cent and agriculture 12 per cent in 2006. Coal, oil, natural gas and hydroelectricity resources are being exploited, and Colombia is a net exporter of electricity and oil. Hydrocarbons account for half of mining output, precious metals (gold, platinum and silver), emeralds, nickel and other minerals for the remainder. Major cash crops are coffee, bananas and cut flowers. Cattle are raised in large numbers, and forestry is also important.

The principal trading partners are the USA, other Latin American countries and China. Principal exports are oil, coffee, coal, nickel, emeralds, garments, bananas and cut flowers. The main imports are industrial and transport equipment, consumer goods, chemicals, paper products and fuels.

GNI – US$104,5m; US$2,290 per capita (2005)

ANNUAL AVERAGE GROWTH OF GDP – 5.2 per cent (2005 est)

INFLATION RATE – 5 per cent (2005 est)

UNEMPLOYMENT – 11.8 per cent (2005 est)

TOTAL EXTERNAL DEBT – US$32,330m (2005 est)

IMPORTS – US$21,200m (2005)

EXPORTS – US$21,100m (2005)

BALANCE OF PAYMENTS

Trade – US$1,594m surplus (2005)

Current Account – US$1,930m deficit (2005)

Trade with UK	*2005*	*2006*
Imports from UK	£117,858,000	£133,040,000
Exports to UK	£303,418,000	£305,628,000

COMMUNICATIONS

The terrain has always hampered internal transport, and historically travel was largely along the rivers, especially the River Magdalena. This is still used for some bulk cargo but most long-distance internal travel is now by air, although the growing road network (113,000km) is the main means of freight transport, superseding the 3,304km rail system as well as the waterways. There are 981 airports and airstrips, although only 100 have surfaced runways. The principal airports are at Bogotá, Barranquilla and Cali. The main seaports are Barranquilla, Cartagena and Santa Marta on the Caribbean Sea and Buenaventura on the Pacific coast. A modern telephone system covers the whole of the country but with only 7.7 million main lines in 2005; mobile phone distribution is three times higher, with 21.8 million in 2005.

EDUCATION AND HEALTH

Elementary education is free of charge and compulsory for five years. Most primary schools are run by the Roman Catholic church and courses in Roman Catholicism are compulsory. There are some Protestant church schools (mainly in the capital). The government finances secondary and university level education.

LITERACY RATE – 94.2 per cent (2004 est)
GROSS ENROLMENT RATIO (percentage of relevant age group) – primary 113 per cent; secondary 79 per cent; tertiary 28 per cent (2005 est)
HEALTH EXPENDITURE (per capita) – US$168 (2004)
HOSPITAL BEDS (per 1,000 people) – 1.1 (2000–5)

MEDIA

There are state-owned television (Inravision) and radio stations (Radiodifusora Nacional de Colombia) as well as private commercial networks. There are five main daily newspapers, but television remains the most popular medium. Colombia is one of the most dangerous countries in the world for journalists, who are often targeted by drug-traffickers, guerrillas and paramilitary groups. More than 120 Colombian journalists were killed during the 1990s.

THE COMOROS

L'Union des Comores – Union of the Comoros

AREA – 2,170 sq. km. The Comoros includes the islands of Ngazidja (formerly Grande Comore), Anjouan (also known as Nzwani), Moheli (also known as Mwali) and certain islets in the Indian Ocean. The easternmost island of the archipelago, Mayotte, is a French dependency.
CAPITAL – Moroni; population, 40,275 (2002 est), on Ngazidja
MAJOR TOWNS – Mutsamudu; Domoni; Fomboni
CURRENCY – Comorian franc (KMF) of 100 centimes. The Franc CFA of 100 centimes is also used
POPULATION – 690,948 rising at 2.87 per cent per year (2006 est)
RELIGION – Islam (99 per cent) (est). There are no known atheists
LANGUAGE – Arabic, French (both official), Shikomoro
POPULATION DENSITY – 269 per sq. km (2005)
URBAN POPULATION – 36.3 per cent (2005 est)
MEDIAN AGE (years) – 18.6 (2006 est)
NATIONAL ANTHEM – 'Udzima wa ya Masiwa' ['The Union of the Islands']
NATIONAL DAY – 6 July (Independence Day)
LIFE EXPECTANCY (years) – 62.33 (2006 est)
MORTALITY RATE – 8.2 (2006 est)
BIRTH RATE – 36.93 (2006 est)
INFANT MORTALITY RATE – 72.85 (2006 est)
DEATH PENALTY – Yes
POPULATION BELOW POVERTY LINE – 60 per cent (2002 est)
LITERACY RATE – 56.2 per cent (2004 est)

CLIMATE AND TERRAIN

Located in the Mozambique Channel between Africa and Madagascar, Njazidja, Anjouan and Moheli are volcanic islands in the Comoros archipelago. The highest point is Karthala (2,360m) on Njazidja, an active volcano that last erupted in 2005, and the lowest is 0m (Indian Ocean). There is a tropical climate with a dry season from May to October and a hot season from November to April. The average temperature ranges from 20°C to 28°C. Cyclones afflict the islands between January and April.

HISTORY AND POLITICS

The islands became a French protectorate in the late 19th century, and achieved internal self-government in 1961. In 1974, the islanders voted on independence from France and three main islands became independent on 6 July 1975; Mayotte voted to remain part of France. The republic experienced political instability after independence, with a number of coups between 1976 and 1999, some supported by European mercenaries. Anjouan and Moheli seceded in 1997 but after the president was deposed in a military coup by Col. Assoumani Azali in April 1999, the military took control of the other islands' governments and reunited them with the Comoros. Talks on the secessionist crisis produced a new constitution, which was approved by referendum in 2002 (though not initially in Ngazidha), and a federal structure with greater autonomy for the individual islands was introduced.

The first elections of the union president and the islands' presidents were held in spring 2002; Col. Azali was elected president of the union. Elections to the union parliament and the islands' legislatures were held in 2004; the union government is a coalition. The federal presidential election in May 2006 was won by Ahmed Abdallah Sambi from Anjouan with 58 per cent of the vote.

POLITICAL SYSTEM

The 2002 constitution created a federal structure. Under this, the union president is elected from each of the three islands in turn and serves a four-year term. The executive president appoints the union ministers. The union legislature, the assembly, has 33 members; five are appointed by each of the three local parliaments and 18 are directly elected for a five-year term. Each island has its own president and legislative assembly, and each island president appoints the island's eight ministers. The islands' governments deal with local issues; foreign affairs, finance, defence, judicial and religious matters remain the responsibility of the union government. There are still areas of dispute, principally over security, budget control and customs revenue.

HEAD OF STATE
President of the union, Ahmed Abdallah Sambi, *elected* 14 May 2006, *sworn in* 25 May 2006

SELECTED GOVERNMENT MEMBERS *as at May 2007*
Vice-President, Transport, Tourism, Post and Communications, Nadhoim Idi
Vice-President, Health, Solidarity and Gender Equality, Ikililou Dhoinine
Foreign Relations and Cooperation, Francophone and Arab Affairs, Ahmed ben Said Jaffar
Finance, Budget and Planning, Mohamed Ali Soilihi

EMBASSY OF THE FEDERAL ISLAMIC REPUBLIC OF THE COMOROS
20 rue Marbeau, F-75016 Paris, France

BRITISH AMBASSADOR
HE Anthony Godson, *apptd* 2005, resident at Port Louis, Mauritius

ECONOMY AND TRADE

The Comoros is very poor and heavily dependent on foreign aid and technical assistance. It has few natural resources, an uneducated workforce and a poor transport infrastructure. Continuing political tensions hinder government attempts to reform and develop the economy and social welfare provision. Unemployment is high and over 20 per cent of the workforce is employed abroad; remittances are a valuable contribution to the economy. Agriculture, fishing and forestry account for about 40 per cent of GDP and employ 80 per cent of the population; service industries account for 56 per cent and the manufacturing industry 4 per cent. The principal exports are vanilla, copra, cloves and perfume essence; coconuts, bananas and cassava are also cultivated. The main industries are fishing, tourism and perfume distillation.

GNI – US$389m; US$650 per capita (2005)
ANNUAL AVERAGE GROWTH OF GDP – 3 per cent (2005 est)
INFLATION RATE – 3 per cent (2005 est)
TOTAL EXTERNAL DEBT – US$177m (2001)

Trade with UK	*2005*	*2006*
Imports from UK	£305,000	£87,000
Exports to UK	£127,000	£65,000

MEDIA

Radio is the country's primary source of information and there is healthy competition between state and privately-owned radio broadcasters. Television Nationale Comorienne is the state-run television channel, which exists alongside programmes broadcast from Mayotte, which can be received on several of the islands. Most newspapers are published weekly and have small circulations owing to a weak advertising market and poor distribution. Much of their content is restricted by self-censorship, practised because of the government's willingness to close down media who broadcast material deemed offensive.

DEMOCRATIC REPUBLIC OF CONGO

République Démocratique du Congo – Democratic Republic of the Congo

AREA – 2,345,410 sq. km. Neighbours: Central African Republic (north), Sudan (north-east), Uganda, Rwanda, Burundi and Tanzania (east), Zambia (south), Angola (south-west), Republic of Congo (north-west)
CAPITAL – Kinshasa; population, 7,273,947 (2004 est)
MAJOR CITIES – Lubumbashi; Mbuji-Mayi; Kananga; Kisangani; Bukavu; Kolwezi
CURRENCY – Congolese franc
POPULATION – 62,660,551 rising at 3.07 per cent per year (2006 est). The population is composed of Bantu, Hamitic, Nilotic, Sudanese and Pygmoid groups, divided into more than 200 tribes
RELIGION – Roman Catholicism (50 per cent), Protestantism (20 per cent), Kimbanguism (10 per cent), Islam (10 per cent) (est)
LANGUAGE – French (official), Lingala, Kingwana, Kikongo, Tshiluba
POPULATION DENSITY – 25 per sq. km (2005)
URBAN POPULATION – 32.7 per cent (2005 est)
MEDIAN AGE (years) – 16.2 (2006 est)
NATIONAL ANTHEM – 'Debout Congolais' ['Stand Up, Congolese']
NATIONAL DAY – 30 June (Independence Day)
LIFE EXPECTANCY (years) – 51.46 (2006 est)
MORTALITY RATE – 13.27 (2006 est)
BIRTH RATE – 43.69 (2006 est)
INFANT MORTALITY RATE – 88.62 (2006 est)
HIV/AIDS ADULT PREVALENCE – 4.2 per cent (2003 est)
DEATH PENALTY – Yes
CPI SCORE – 2.0 (2006)
MILITARY BUDGET – US$163m (2006)
MILITARY PERSONNEL – 51,000: army 46,000, navy 1,000, air force 4,000
LITERACY RATE – 65.3 per cent (2004 est)
GROSS ENROLMENT RATIO (percentage of relevant age group) – primary 62 per cent; secondary 22 per cent (2005 est)
HEALTH EXPENDITURE (per capita)– US$5 (2004)

CLIMATE AND TERRAIN

The Democratic Republic of the Congo is Africa's third largest country. Most of the state lies in the basin of the River Congo and its principal tributaries, the Lualaba and the Kasai. A chain of mountains and lakes (Albert, Edward, Kivu and Tanganyika) run along the eastern border. Elevation extremes range from 5,110m (Mt Ngaliema, also known as Mt Stanley) at the highest point to 0m (Atlantic Ocean) at the lowest. The central region has an equatorial climate with high humidity and an average temperature of 26°C. The equator passes through the north of the country and there are different climatic cycles either side of it, with a dry season in the north from December to February and in the south from May to September.

HISTORY AND POLITICS

The state of the Congo, founded in 1885, became a Belgian colony in 1908 and gained its independence in 1960. Mobutu Sésé Seko came to power in a coup in 1965 and was elected president in 1970. Legislative power was vested in a unicameral national legislative council, with candidates proposed by the sole legal political party, Mouvement Populaire de la Révolution (MPR). The regime began moves towards a multiparty system from the late 1980s, but progress was hindered by army revolts and political disagreements.

In 1996 ethnic conflict, largely resulting from the influx of refugees from the Rwandan genocide, sparked a civil war in which the army found itself outgunned by anti-Mobutu rebels, backed by the Rwandan and Ugandan governments. Under the leadership of Laurent Kabila, the Alliance of Democratic Forces for the Liberation of Congo-Zaire (AFDL) captured Kinshasa in May 1997 and President Mobutu fled. Zaire was then renamed the Democratic Republic of the Congo.

In August 1998, a rebellion against Kabila's government began in the east, initiating further years of fighting between government forces and a shifting alliance of rebel groups, with neighbouring countries lending support to either the government (Angola, Chad, Kenya, Namibia, Zimbabwe) or the rebels (Rwanda, Uganda). All parties to the conflict plundered the country's rich natural resources and left an estimated 3.5 million dead from violence, famine and disease. A number of ceasefires were negotiated and broken, but by December 2000 the government and rebel groups had signed a disengagement agreement and withdrew their troops 15km from their frontline positions by the end of March 2001. UN-sponsored peace talks the following year concluded with the signing of a power-sharing agreement between the government and the main rebel groups.

In July 2003, a transitional government was established under the incumbent president, Maj.-Gen. Joseph Kabila (who had succeeded his father Laurent Kabila, assassinated in January 2001) and an interim legislature was inaugurated in August 2003. Despite a number of coup attempts and occasional clashes with renegade rebels, a fragile peace has held, but the government has no real control over large areas of the country and the eastern provinces remain very tense. There are still 15,000 UN peacekeeping troops in the country.

A new constitution was adopted in February 2006 and came into effect with presidential and legislative elections on 30 July 2006. The presidential election was won in the second round in October 2006 by the incumbent, Joseph Kabila. His People's Party for Reconstruction and Development (PPRD) won the largest number of seats in the national assembly but not an overall majority; the party became the major partner in the coalition government formed in February 2007.

POLITICAL SYSTEM

Under the 2006 constitution, the executive president is directly elected for a five-year term, renewable only once. The bicameral legislature, the *Parlement*, consists of the national assembly, which has 500 members directly elected for a five-year term, and the senate, which has 120 members indirectly elected by provincial assemblies to serve a five-year term. Former elected presidents are senators for life.

There are 10 provinces: Bas-Congo (provincial capital, Matadi); Bandundu (Bandundu); Equateur (Mbandaka); Kasai East (Mbuji-Mayi); Kasai West (Kananga), Katanga (Lubumbashi); Kivu North (Goma); Kivu South (Bukavu); Maniema (Kindu); and Western (Kisangani). The capital, Kinshasa, has the status of a 'neutral city'. The constitution provides for these to be replaced by 26 provinces by 2009.

HEAD OF STATE

President, Maj.-Gen. Joseph Kabila, *sworn in* 26 January 2001, *sworn in as president of the transitional government* 7 April 2003, *elected* 29 October 2006

Vice-President, Abdoulaye Yerodia Ndombasi

SELECTED GOVERNMENT MEMBERS *as at May 2007*

Prime Minister, Antonie Gizenga

Defence, Chikez Diemu

Finance, Athanase Matenda Kyelu

Foreign Affairs and International Co-operation, Antipas Mbusa Nyamwisi

Interior, Gen. Denis Kalume Numbi

EMBASSY OF THE DEMOCRATIC REPUBLIC OF CONGO

281 Gray's Inn Road, London WC1X 8QF

T 020-7278 9825

Ambassador Extraordinary and Plenipotentiary, HE Eugénie Tshiela Compton, *apptd* 2005

BRITISH EMBASSY

83 Avenue du Roi Baudouin, Kinshasa

T (+243) 98 169 100 E ambrit@ic.cd

Ambassador Extraordinary and Plenipotentiary, HE Andrew Sparkes, *apptd* 2004

ECONOMY AND TRADE

The country has immense natural resources, including copper, diamonds, gold, silver, uranium, other minerals, coal, oil, timber and hydroelectric power, and so great potential wealth. But the years of civil war have devastated the economy and the country now has a huge external debt, little infrastructure, widespread corruption and an operating environment that discourages foreign investment. Improved stability since 2003 has allowed some economic growth. The transitional government has obtained financing from international organisations and donors and begun reforms. It was also granted US$10bn (£5bn) of debt relief by the IMF in 2003.

Renewed economic activity, especially in the revenue-generating mining sector, boosted GDP by an estimated 50 per cent in 2005. Over half of GDP was contributed by agriculture, about 35 per cent by the services sector and 11 per cent by industry. Apart from mining and mineral processing, the main industrial activities are the production of textiles, footwear, food, beverages, cigarettes and cement, and ship repair. Oil deposits are exploited off the Congo estuary, and hydroelectric schemes on the River Congo supply power to the major cities.

The main trading partners are Belgium, which takes 38 per cent of exports, Finland, South Africa, the USA, France and China. Principal exports are diamonds, copper, crude oil, coffee and cobalt. The main imports are foodstuffs, mining and other machinery, transport equipment and fuels.

GNI – US$7,000m; US$120 per capita (2005)

ANNUAL AVERAGE GROWTH OF GDP – 7.1 per cent (2005 est)

INFLATION RATE – 9 per cent (2004 est)

TOTAL EXTERNAL DEBT – US$10,600m (2003 est)

Trade with UK	*2005*	*2006*
Imports from UK	£11,592,000	£16,912,000
Exports to UK	£6,083,000	£786,000

COMMUNICATIONS

The transport infrastructure is undeveloped owing to the terrain, poverty and warfare. The River Congo and its main tributaries provide 15,000km of waterways, and the 5,138k rail system links the interior to the rivers and to the great lakes in the east. The system also connects with neighbouring states, through which east and south African ports can be accessed. There are approximately 153,000km of roads, of which 3,000km are surfaced. The country has over 230 airports and airfields, the principal airports being at Kinshasa, Kananga, Goma, Gemena and Mbandaka. The principal seaports are at Matadi and Boma.

The telecommunications infrastructure is also poor with limited coverage in and between urban areas; only 10,600 main lines were in use in 2005 and there were 140,600 internet users. Mobile phone distribution is growing rapidly, with 2.7 million subscribers in 2005.

MEDIA

The state-controlled Radio-Télévision Nationale Congolaise (RTNC) and La Voix du Congo have the greatest influence and broadcast reach. There are some eight other private and commercial television stations and ten radio stations (some run by the Roman Catholic Church, some by the UN). Around 15 newspapers are published regularly in Kinshasa.

REPUBLIC OF CONGO

République du Congo – Republic of the Congo

AREA – 342,000 sq. km. Neighbours: Gabon (west), Cameroon and Central African Republic (north), Angola (Cabinda) (south-west), Democratic Republic of the Congo (east and south)
CAPITAL – Brazzaville; population, 1,174,000 (2005 est)
MAJOR CITIES – Pointe Noire, the main commercial centre; Louborno
CURRENCY – Franc CFA of 100 centimes
POPULATION – 3,702,314 rising at 2.6 per cent per year (2006 est); Bakongo (48 per cent), Sangha (20 per cent), Bateke (17 per cent), M'Bochi (12 per cent) (est)
RELIGION – Christianity (45 per cent), Islam (2 per cent) (est)
LANGUAGE – French (official), Lingala, Monokutuba, Kikongo
POPULATION DENSITY – 12 per sq. km (2005)
URBAN POPULATION – 54.4 per cent (2005 est)
MEDIAN AGE (years) – 16.6 (2006 est)
NATIONAL ANTHEM – 'La Congolaise' ['The Congolese']
NATIONAL DAY – 15 August (Independence Day)
LIFE EXPECTANCY (years) – 52.8 (2006 est)
MORTALITY RATE – 12.93 (2006 est)
BIRTH RATE – 42.57 (2006 est)
INFANT MORTALITY RATE – 85.29 (2006 est)
HIV/AIDS ADULT PREVALENCE – 4.9 per cent (2003 est)
DEATH PENALTY – No*
CPI SCORE – 2.2 (2006)
MILITARY BUDGET – US$66m (2006 est)
MILITARY PERSONNEL – 10,000: army 8,000, navy 800, air force 1,200; paramilitaries 2,000

CLIMATE AND TERRAIN

The republic is covered by grassland, mangrove and dense rainforest. The land rises from sea level on the narrow Atlantic coastal plain to a central plateau, and then falls to the northern part of the River Congo basin, which forms part of the border with the Democratic Republic of the Congo. In the north, the main rivers are the Sangha and Alima. Elevation extremes range from 903m (Mt Berongou) at the highest point to 0m at the lowest (Atlantic Ocean). The climate is equatorial. The annual daily temperature in Brazzaville is between 28°C and 33°C. The dry season is June to September but the country is prone to flooding during the wet season (March to June).

HISTORY AND POLITICS

The first European visitors to the area were the Portuguese, who established slave trading in the 16th century. The French established a colonial presence in the area in the 1880s and, as Middle Congo, it was part of French Equatorial Africa from 1908. It became independent as the Republic of Congo on 17 August 1960.

In 1968, a military coup created the first Marxist state in Africa, under the Congolese Labour Party (PCT). Marxism was renounced and, after popular pressure, the PCT abandoned its monopoly of power in 1990. The following decade was a period of ethnically-derived political instability, with factional fighting after the 1993 election and a civil war between 1997 and 2003, incited by Denis Sassou-Nguesso's deposition of the elected president. A peace accord ended the civil war in 2003 but the peace is fragile and remnants of the rebel militias are still active in the south of the country, where many have turned to banditry.

In the 2002 presidential election, Sassou-Nguesso was elected legitimately with nearly 90 per cent of the vote, although his victory was criticised after his candidature was unopposed owing to the barring of his main rivals. A prime minister was appointed in 2005, the first time the post had been filled since 1997. In the 2007 legislative elections the PCT and its allies won a comfortable majority, but the election was heavily criticised by the African Union.

POLITICAL SYSTEM

Under the 2002 constitution, the head of state is a president, directly elected for a seven-year term, who heads the government and appoints the cabinet. The parliament is bicameral. The *Assemblée Nationale* (national assembly), the lower chamber, has 137 members directly elected for a five-year term. The *Sénat* (senate) has 66 members indirectly elected for a six-term term, half of the members retiring every three years.

HEAD OF STATE

President, Defence, Denis Sassou-Nguesso, *took power* October 1997, *elected* 10 March 2002

SELECTED GOVERNMENT MEMBERS *as at May 2007*

Prime Minister, Isidore Mvouba
Economy, Finance and Budget, Pacifique Issoibeka
Foreign and Francophone Affairs, Rodolphe Adada
Security and Public Order, Gen. Paul Mbot
Defence, Brig.-Gen. Jacques Yvon Ndolou

EMBASSY OF THE REPUBLIC OF CONGO

37 bis rue Paul Valéry, 75116 Paris, France
T (+33) (1) 4500 6057
Ambassador Extraordinary and Plenipotentiary, HE Henri Lopes, *apptd* 1999

BRITISH AMBASSADOR

HE Andrew Sparkes, *apptd* 2004, resident at Kinshasa, Dem. Rep. of Congo

ECONOMY AND TRADE

Oil revenues enabled the government to embark on development schemes in the 1980s but the slump in oil prices in the late 1990s and a decade of civil conflict have left the country with a high external debt, a budget deficit and widespread poverty. Since 2003 the government has made efforts to address these problems and in 2006 qualified for debt relief under the IMF-World Bank heavily indebted poor countries initiative.

Oil production is the backbone of the economy and the recovery in oil prices has boosted GDP. Mining, especially diamonds, forestry, brewing, agricultural processing and cement production are the other main industries. Agriculture accounts for about 6 per cent of GDP, industry for 55 per cent and services for 39 per cent.

The main markets are China, the USA, France and Taiwan. Principal exports are oil, timber, plywood, sugar, cocoa, coffee and diamonds. Imports are mainly capital equipment, construction materials and foodstuffs.
GNI – US$3,800m; US$950 per capita (2005)

ANNUAL AVERAGE GROWTH OF GDP – 8.2 per cent (2005 est)
INFLATION RATE – 2.2 per cent (2005 est)
TOTAL EXTERNAL DEBT – US$5,000m (2000)
IMPORTS – US$2,040m (2005)
EXPORTS – US$5,000m (2005)

BALANCE OF PAYMENTS
Trade – US$1,011m surplus (2003)
Current Account – US$3m deficit (2003)

Trade with UK	*2005*	*2006*
Imports from UK	£20,494,000	£26,892,000
Exports to UK	£7,980,000	£9,747,000

COMMUNICATIONS

Pointe Noire is the main seaport and is the centre of the offshore oil industry. It is linked to Brazzaville by rail and road. Brazzaville is the main river port, lying on the River Congo, which, with the Ubango river, provides 4,385km of commercially navigable waterways. There are 894km of railways and 17,289km of roads, 864km of which are surfaced. Four of the 32 airports and airfields have surfaced runways. Telecommunications are poor and frequently out of order. Mobile phone distribution was 490,000 in 2005.

EDUCATION AND HEALTH

LITERACY RATE – 82.8 per cent (2004 est)
GROSS ENROLMENT RATIO (percentage of relevant age group) – primary 88 per cent; secondary 39 per cent; tertiary 4 per cent (2005 est)
HEALTH EXPENDITURE (per capita) – US$28 (2004)
HIV/AIDS ADULT PREVALENCE – 4.9 per cent (2003 est)

MEDIA

Brazzaville is the centre of the country's print media industry with five privately owned newspapers regularly published there. TV Congo is the only television station and it is state-owned and controlled by Radiodiffusion Télévision Congolaise. Radio Congo is also state-controlled. A 2001 media reform law abolished jail sentences for libel and insult but retained punishments for incitement to violence and racism.

COSTA RICA

República de Costa Rica – Republic of Costa Rica

AREA – 51,100 sq. km. Neighbours: Nicaragua (north), Panama (south)
CAPITAL – San José; population, 336,829 (2004 est)
MAJOR CITIES – Limón; Alajuela
CURRENCY – Costa Rican colón of 100 céntimos
POPULATION – 4,075,261 rising at 1.45 per cent per year (2006 est)
RELIGION – Roman Catholicism (69 per cent), other Christian denominations (18 per cent) (est)
LANGUAGE – Spanish (official), English
POPULATION DENSITY – 85 per sq. km (2005)
URBAN POPULATION – 61.7 per cent (2005 est)
MEDIAN AGE (years) – 26.4 (2006 est)
NATIONAL ANTHEM – 'Noble Patria, Tu Hermosa Bandera' ['Noble Fatherland, Your Beautiful Flag']
NATIONAL DAY – 15 September (Independence Day)
LIFE EXPECTANCY (years) – 77.02 (2006 est)
MORTALITY RATE – 4.36 (2006 est)
BIRTH RATE – 18.32 (2006 est)
INFANT MORTALITY RATE – 9.7 (2006 est)
DEATH PENALTY – No (abolished 1877)
CPI SCORE – 4.1 (2006)
POPULATION BELOW POVERTY LINE – 18 per cent (2004 est)
MILITARY BUDGET – US$98m (2006)
MILITARY PERSONNEL – 8,400 paramilitaries
LITERACY RATE – 95.8 per cent (2004 est)
GROSS ENROLMENT RATIO (percentage of relevant age group) – primary 110 per cent; secondary 79 per cent; tertiary 25 per cent (2005 est)
HEALTH EXPENDITURE (per capita) – US$290 (2004)

CLIMATE AND TERRAIN

The Cordillera de Guanacaste (north-west), Cordillera Central and Cordillera de Talamanca (south-east) form a chain of volcanic mountain ranges that traverse the country from north to south. Elevation extremes range from 3,810m (Chirripó Grande) to 0m (Pacific Ocean) at the lowest. The climate is tropical, with an average annual temperature of 26°C. The wet season runs from May to November. The area is subject to occasional earthquakes, hurricanes, flooding and landslides.

HISTORY AND POLITICS

Visited by Columbus in 1502, for nearly three centuries (1530–1821) Costa Rica was under Spanish rule. In 1821 the country gained its independence from Spain, and was a member of the United Provinces (Federation) of Central America from 1824 until its secession in 1839. Political unrest in the mid-20th century led to a brief civil war in 1948, after which the army was abolished and replaced with a national guard. Since then power has alternated between the two main political parties, the Social Christian Unity Party (PUSC) and the National Liberation Party (PLN).

In the 2006 legislative elections, the PLN became the largest party, with 25 seats, but without an outright majority. The simultaneous presidential election was won narrowly by the PLN candidate Oscar Arias Sanchez, president in 1986–90 and the winner of the Nobel Peace Prize in 1987 for devising the peace plan that ended the civil wars in Nicaragua and El Salvador; he received 40.92 per cent of the vote.

POLITICAL SYSTEM
Under the 1949 constitution, the executive president is directly elected for a four-year term. Legislative power is vested in the unicameral *Asamblea Legislativa* (legislative assembly), which has 57 members directly elected for a four-year term.

HEAD OF STATE
President, Oscar Arias, *elected* 5 February 2006, *sworn-in* 9 May 2006
First Vice-President, Minister of Justice, Justice, Laura Chinchilla
Second Vice-President, Planning, Kevin Casas

SELECTED GOVERNMENT MEMBERS *as at May 2007*
Finance, Guillermo Zuniga
Foreign Affairs, Bruno Stagno
Foreign Trade, Marco Vinicio Ruiz

EMBASSY OF COSTA RICA
14 Lancaster Gate, London W2 3LH
T 020-7706 8844 E costaricanembassy@btconnect.com
Ambassador Extraordinary and Plenipotentiary, vacant

BRITISH EMBASSY
Apartado 815, Edificio Centro Colón (11th Floor), San José 1007
T (+506) 258 2025 E britemb@racsa.co.cr
W www.britishembassycr.com
Ambassador Extraordinary and Plenipotentiary, HE Tom Kennedy

ECONOMY AND TRADE

Sixty years of political stability has allowed economic growth, the creation of a social welfare system and a reduction in poverty; less than 20 per cent of the population is below the poverty line. The economic problems of the 1990s were overcome by diversification, but budget and trade imbalances have created large internal and external debt and inflation is high. Economic reforms are difficult because of inflexibilities in the labour market and the last administration's reform attempts provoked widespread public protests.

Tourism is the largest single industry, and with one-third of the country now national parkland or nature reserve, eco-tourism is on the increase. The manufacturing industry accounts for around 31 per cent of GDP, the principal products being computer components, foodstuffs, textiles, clothing, construction materials and plastic goods. The agricultural sector contributes 9 per cent of GDP; the principal products are bananas, pineapples, coffee, melons, ornamental plants, sugar, beef and timber.

The USA is Costa Rica's largest trading partner, accounting for over 40 per cent of imports and exports. Other major trading partners are Japan, the Netherlands, Mexico, Guatemala and Brazil. The chief exports are agricultural products, textiles, electrical components and medical equipment. The chief imports are raw materials, consumer goods, capital equipment and fuel and petroleum.

GNI – US$20,300m; US$4,700 per capita (2005)
ANNUAL AVERAGE GROWTH OF GDP – 5.9 per cent (2005 est)
INFLATION RATE – 13.8 per cent (2005 est)
UNEMPLOYMENT – 6.6 per cent (2005 est)
TOTAL EXTERNAL DEBT – US$5,049m (2005 est)
IMPORTS – US$9,800m (2005)
EXPORTS – US$7,000m (2005)

BALANCE OF PAYMENTS
Trade – US$1,463m deficit (2004)
Current Account – US$831m deficit (2004)

Trade with UK	*2005*	*2006*
Imports from UK	£40,044,000	£33,643,000
Exports to UK	£562,481,000	£501,352,000

COMMUNICATIONS

The chief seaports are Limón on the Atlantic coast, through which passes most of the coffee exported, and Puntarenas on the Pacific coast. There are 156 airports, 31 of which have surfaced runways; the principal ones are at San José and Limón. The national air carrier is LACSA. There are 278km of railways and 35,889km of roads, 8,075km of which are surfaced. The telephone system is modern and efficient, although mobile phone coverage is restricted.

CÔTE D'IVOIRE

République de la Côte d'Ivoire – Republic of Côte d'Ivoire

AREA – 322,460 sq. km. Neighbours: Guinea and Liberia (west), Mali and Burkina Faso (north), Ghana (east)
CAPITAL – Yamoussoukro; population, 299,243 (1998), the political and administrative capital since 1983
MAJOR CITIES – Abidjan, the economic and financial centre; Bouaké; Daloa; Korhogo
CURRENCY – Franc CFA of 100 centimes
POPULATION – 17,654,843 rising at 2.03 per cent per year (2006 est); Akan (42.1 per cent), Voltaiques or Gur (17.6 per cent), Northern Mandes (16.5 per cent), Krous (11 per cent), Southern Mandes (10 per cent) (est)
RELIGION – Islam (38 per cent), Roman Catholicism (19 per cent), indigenous religions (11 per cent), Protestantism (6 per cent), other Christian denominations (3 per cent) (est)
LANGUAGE – French (official)
POPULATION DENSITY – 57 per sq. km (2005)
URBAN POPULATION – 45.8 per cent (2005 est)
MEDIAN AGE (years) – 19.2 (2006 est)
NATIONAL ANTHEM – 'L'Abidjanaise' ['Song of Abidjan']
NATIONAL DAY – 7 August (Independence Day)
LIFE EXPECTANCY (years) – 48.82 (2006 est)
MORTALITY RATE – 14.84 (2006 est)
BIRTH RATE – 35.11 (2006 est)
INFANT MORTALITY RATE – 89.11 (2006 est)
HIV/AIDS ADULT PREVALENCE – 7 per cent (2003 est)
DEATH PENALTY – No (abolished 2000)
CPI SCORE – 2.1 (2006)
MILITARY BUDGET – US$192m (2005 est)
MILITARY PERSONNEL – 17,050: army 6,500, navy 900, air force 700, Presidential Guard 1,350, Gendarmerie 7,600; paramilitaries 1,500
CONSCRIPTION DURATION – 18 months (selective)
LITERACY RATE – 48.1 per cent (2004 est)
GROSS ENROLMENT RATIO (percentage of relevant age group) – primary 72 per cent; secondary 25 per cent (2005 est)
HEALTH EXPENDITURE (per capita) – US$33 (2004)

CLIMATE AND TERRAIN

The climate is equatorial in the southern and western rainforest areas, tropical in the central and eastern savannah regions, and dry and tropical in the north. Elevation extremes range from 1,752m (Mt Nimba) at the highest point to 0m (Gulf of Guinea) at the lowest. Average temperatures range from 24°C in August to 27°C in March.

HISTORY AND POLITICS

The first European visitors were Portuguese navigators in the 1460s, and Europeans established the ivory trade and some slave trading in the 16th century. The area came under French influence from 1842, and Côte d'Ivoire became a protectorate in 1889 and a colony in 1893, although it was not pacified until 1912. It achieved self-government in 1958, and became independent on 7 August 1960 as a one-party state with Felix Houphouët-Boigny as president.

A multiparty system was introduced in 1990. President Houphouët-Boigny died in 1993 and was succeeded by

Henri Konan-Bédié. The post-independence period of stability ended and President Konan-Bédié was deposed in 1999 in a military coup led by Gen. Robert Guëi, who became president. He was ousted when he tried to claim victory in the 2000 presidential election and was replaced by Laurent Gbagbo of the Ivorian Popular Front (FPI), who was believed to be the winning candidate.

Religious and ethnic divisions that had been kept in check by the stability of the Houphouët-Boigny regime opened up as xenophobia was adopted as a political tool, exposing divisions between the Muslim north and Christian south and west of the country. A civil war in 2002–3 ended with a ceasefire that left the country divided between the government-controlled south and the rebel-held north, with international peacekeeping troops deployed in 2003 to maintain a buffer zone between the two. Despite the ceasefire, clashes continued, drawing in UN peacekeepers in late 2004. Further talks between the government and rebels in 2006–7 resulted in a power-sharing peace agreement in March 2006 and the rebel leader Guillaume Soro became prime minister of the transitional government. Elections are expected in late 2007.

POLITICAL SYSTEM

Under the 2000 constitution, the executive president is directly elected for a five-year term, renewable only once. The president appoints the prime minister. The legislature is the unicameral *Assemblée Nationale* (national assembly) of 225 members, directly elected for a five-year term.

HEAD OF STATE

President, Laurent Gbagbo, *elected* 22 October 2000, *sworn in* 26 October 2000

SELECTED GOVERNMENT MEMBERS *as at May 2007*

Prime Minister, Guillaume Soro
Defence, Michel Amani N'guessan
Interior, Desire Tagro Assegnini
Foreign Affairs, Youssouf Bakayoko

EMBASSY OF THE REPUBLIC OF CÔTE D'IVOIRE

2 Upper Belgrave Street, London SW1X 8BJ
T 020-7235 6991
Ambassador Extraordinary and Plenipotentiary, HE Youssoufou Bamba, *apptd* 2001

BRITISH HIGH COMISSIONER

HE Dr Nicholas Westcott, CMG, *apptd* 2007, resident at Accra, Ghana

ECONOMY AND TRADE

Political instability has damaged an economy that was performing well. It is vulnerable to weather conditions and fluctuations in world prices of its key exports but diversification has been hampered by the civil war and the decline in foreign investment.

Agriculture accounts for 27 per cent of GDP, industry for 18.5 per cent and services for 54.5 per cent. Agriculture employs around 68 per cent of the workforce, producing cocoa (which accounts for about 90 per cent of export earnings), coffee, cotton, bananas, pineapples and palm oil for export. The principal industries are food processing, forestry, oil refining, vehicle assembly, textiles, fishing and the production of oil, natural gas and hydroelectric power; the country is a net exporter of electricity. The main trading partners are France and Nigeria.

GNI – US$15,700m; US$870 per capita (2005)
ANNUAL AVERAGE GROWTH OF GDP – 1 per cent (2005 est)
INFLATION RATE – 3.9 per cent (2005 est)
TOTAL EXTERNAL DEBT – US$13,430m (2005 est)
IMPORTS – US$4,700m (2005)
EXPORTS – US$7,200m (2005)

BALANCE OF PAYMENTS

Trade – US$2,734m surplus (2004)
Current Account – US$303m surplus (2004)

Trade	*2005*	*2006*
Imports from UK	£54,022,000	£39,841,000
Exports to UK	£74,919,000	£83,252,000

COMMUNICATIONS

Côte d'Ivoire has 660km of railways and 80,000km of roads, 6,500km of which are surfaced. There are 980km of navigable rivers, canals and lagoons. The main seaports are Abidjan and San Pedro. There are 35 airports and airfields, the principal international airport being at Abidjan. Although well developed, the telephone system operates below capacity. Mobile phone distribution was 2.2 million in 2005, and internet users numbered 160,000.

MEDIA

The state broadcaster is Radiodiffusion Télévision Ivoirienne (RTI). RTI operates two national radio stations and two television channels, all of which have frequently been used as propaganda tools by the government. There are no private terrestrial television stations although subscription services are available.

Radio is the most popular medium for news, with around 30 non-commercial community radio stations located throughout the country. In August 2004, UN peacekeepers launched their own radio station, ONUCI FM. Initially available only in Abidjan, the station now covers rebel-held towns in the north.

The print media is represented by two government-owned and around 20 privately owned daily newspapers. Several opposition newspapers have been raided by government officials and ceased publication.

CROATIA

Republika Hrvatska – Republic of Croatia

AREA – 56,542 sq. km. Neighbours: Slovenia, Hungary (north), Serbia, Montenegro (east), Bosnia and Hercegovina (south, and east of Adriatic coastal strip)
CAPITAL – Zagreb; population, 867,717 (2001)
MAJOR CITIES – Split; Rijeka; Osijek
CURRENCY – Kuna of 100 lipa
POPULATION – 4,494,749 falling at 0.03 per cent per year (2006 est); Croat (89.6 per cent), Serb (4.5 per cent)
RELIGION – Roman Catholicism (85 per cent), other Christian denominations (6 per cent), Islam (1 per cent) (est); 2 per cent of the population is thought to be atheist
LANGUAGE – Croatian (official), Serbian, Italian, Hungarian, Czech, Slovak, German

POPULATION DENSITY – 79 per sq. km (2005)
URBAN POPULATION – 59.9 per cent (2005 est)
MEDIAN AGE (years) – 40.3 (2006 est)
NATIONAL ANTHEM – 'Lijepa Nasa Domovina' ['Our Beautiful Homeland']
NATIONAL DAY – 8 October (Independence Day)
LIFE EXPECTANCY (years) – 74.68 (2006 est)
MORTALITY RATE – 11.48 (2006 est)
BIRTH RATE – 9.61 (2006 est)
INFANT MORTALITY RATE – 6.72 (2006 est)
DEATH PENALTY – No (abolished 1990)
CPI SCORE – 3.4 (2006)
POPULATION BELOW POVERTY LINE – 11 per cent (2003)

CLIMATE AND TERRAIN

There are three major geographic areas: the Pannonian region in the north, the central mountain belt, and the Adriatic coast region of Istria and Dalmatia, which has 1,185 islands and islets and 1,778km of coastline. Elevation extremes range from 1,830m (Dinara) at the highest point to 0m (Adriatic Sea) at the lowest. The climate varies significantly between the Dalmatian coast, where the winters are mild and the summers hot, and inland areas, which are more typical of eastern Europe with colder temperatures and rain in the summer. Average temperatures in Zagreb, away from the coast, range from 2°C in January to 26°C in July.

HISTORY AND POLITICS

Croatia was ruled by the Habsburgs from 1526 to 1918. With the collapse of the Austro-Hungarian Empire at the end of the First World War, Croatia declared its independence on 29 October 1918 and soon after joined with Slovenia, Bosnia-Hercegovina, Serbia and Montenegro to form the Kingdom of Serbs, Croats and Slovenes (renamed Yugoslavia in 1929). From 1941 to 1945, Yugoslavia was occupied by the Axis powers; Italy and Hungary annexed parts of Croatia and a pro-Nazi Croat puppet state was established in the remainder of Croatia and Bosnia-Hercegovina. The armed extremists of this state (the Ustae) engaged in fierce fighting with Serbian royalists, communist partisans and pro-allied Croat partisans. At the end of the Second World War, Yugoslavia was re-established as a federal republic under Communist rule, but gradually disintegrated following the death of President Tito in 1980.

In 1991 Croatia declared its independence from the Yugoslav federation. The efforts of the Federal Yugoslav Army (JNA) and ethnic Serbs in Croatia to prevent Croatia's secession led to civil war until January 1992, when a ceasefire was declared. Fighting restarted the following year as Croatian forces set out to retake the ethnic Serb areas of the country that had seceded; Krajina and Western Slavonia were recaptured in 1995, and Eastern Slavonia agreed in 1995 to re-integration by 1998. From 1992 to 1995 Croatian forces were also involved in the war in Bosnia-Hercegovina. Croatia signed the Dayton Accord in 1995.

Post-independence politics was dominated by the authoritarian President Franjo Tudjman, a former partisan first elected president in 1990. Since his death in 1999, Croatia has become more outward-looking, and applied to join the EU in 2003; its expected accession date is 2010.

In the 2003 legislative election, the Croatian Democratic Union (HDZ) regained its position as the largest party in the legislature but without an overall majority, and formed a minority government with the Democratic Centre party. President Stipe Mesic, first elected in 2000, was re-elected in the 2005 presidential election, winning 66 per cent of the second round vote.

POLITICAL SYSTEM

The 1990 constitution was amended in 2000 to increase the powers of the legislature, making the presidency a largely ceremonial role, and in 2001 to abolish the upper house of the legislature. The head of state is a president, who is directly elected for a five-year term. Executive power is vested in the prime minister, who is appointed by the legislature, and government. Legislative power is vested in the unicameral chamber of representatives, which has 152 members directly elected for a four-year term.

HEAD OF STATE

President, Stipe Mesic, *elected* 7 February 2000, *re-elected* 17 January 2005

SELECTED GOVERNMENT MEMBERS *as at May 2007*
Prime Minister, Ivo Sanader
Deputy Prime Ministers, Jadranka Kosor; Damir Polancec
Defence, Berislav Roncevic
Finance, Ivan Suker
Foreign Affairs, Kolinda Grabar Kitarovic
Interior, Ivica Kirin

EMBASSY OF THE REPUBLIC OF CROATIA
21 Conway Street, London W1T 6BN
T 020-7387 2022 W http://uk.mvp.hr
Ambassador Extraordinary and Plenipotentiary, HE Josip Paro, *apptd* 2002

BRITISH EMBASSY
ul Ivana Lucica 4, 10000 Zagreb
T (+385) 6009 100 E british.embassyzagreb@fco.gov.uk
Ambassador Extraordinary and Plenipotentiary, HE Sir John Ramsden, Bt., *apptd* 2000.

BRITISH COUNCIL
Illica 12, PP 55, 10001 Zagreb
T (+385) 1489 9500 W www.britishcouncil.org/croatia
Director, Adrian Chadwick

DEFENCE

The armed forces are subject to an arms limitation regime established under the Dayton Peace Accord. The army has 291 main battle tanks, 53 armoured personnel carriers and 104 armoured infantry fighting vehicles. The air force has 27 combat aircraft and 9 armed helicopters. The navy has 2 submarines and 9 patrol and coastal combatants at five major bases.
MILITARY BUDGET – US$712m (2006)
MILITARY PERSONNEL – 20,800: army 14,050, navy 2,500, air force 2,300, joint staff 1,950; paramilitaries 10,000
CONSCRIPTION DURATION – Six months

ECONOMY AND TRADE

As part of Yugoslavia, Croatia was a prosperous and industrialised area but the conflict in 1991–5 damaged the infrastructure, large areas of farmland, industrial production and the tourist industry. Since 2000 there has been steady economic growth, led by a recovery in tourism, banking and public investment. However, there are budget and trade deficits, a large public sector and a lack of political will to remedy these problems, although structural reform will be necessary to meet the criteria for EU membership.

The service sector accounts for 62 per cent of GDP, industry for 31 per cent, and agriculture for 7 per cent. Industry produces chemicals and plastics, machine tools, metal and metals, electronics, wood products and textiles, and includes food processing, shipbuilding and oil refining. Agricultural production includes grains, fruit and vegetables, livestock and dairy products. Most trade is with neighbouring countries.

GNI – US$36,900m; US$8,290 per capita (2005)
ANNUAL AVERAGE GROWTH OF GDP – 4.3 per cent (2005 est)
INFLATION RATE – 3.3 per cent (2005 est)
UNEMPLOYMENT – 18 per cent (2005 est)
TOTAL EXTERNAL DEBT – US$30,620m (2005 est)
IMPORTS – US$18,600m (2005)
EXPORTS – US$8,800m (2005)

BALANCE OF PAYMENTS
Trade – US$9,291m deficit (2005)
Current Account – US$2,541m deficit (2005)

Trade with UK	*2005*	*2006*
Imports from UK	£117,985,000	£146,557,000
Exports to UK	£55,041,000	£68,769,000

COMMUNICATIONS

Those parts of the transport infrastructure destroyed in fighting in the 1990s have mostly been reconstructed, and parts of the rail and road networks have been modernised and expanded. There are 2,726km of railways and 28,588km of roads, most of which are surfaced. The principal airports are at Zagreb and Split. The national carrier is Croatia Airlines. There are 785km of inland waterways, including a stretch of the River Danube, and frequent ferry services to the many Adriatic islands. The main seaports are Rijeka (Fiume), Zadar, Split, Sibenik and Dubrovnik. The telephone system is being modernised and extended. There were 2.9 million mobile phone subscribers in 2005, compared to 1.9 million main line users.

EDUCATION AND HEALTH

LITERACY RATE – 98.1 per cent (2004 est)
GROSS ENROLMENT RATIO (percentage of relevant age group) – primary 96 per cent; secondary 88 per cent; tertiary 42 per cent (2005 est)
HEALTH EXPENDITURE (per capita) – US$609 (2004)
HOSPITAL BEDS (per 1,000 people) – 5.5 (2000–5)

MEDIA

The constitution guarantees freedom of the press. Croatian Radio-Television (HRT) is the national state-owned broadcaster and is the main source of news. Nove TV is the country's first national private network. There are three main news publications: *Vecernji List* (daily), *Feral Tribune* (weekly), *Nacional* (weekly).

CUBA

República de Cuba – Republic of Cuba

AREA – 110,860 sq. km
CAPITAL – Havana; population, 2,201,610 (2002)
MAJOR CITIES – Santiago; Camagüey; Holguín; Santa Clara
CURRENCY – Cuban peso of 100 centavos
POPULATION – 11,382,820 rising at 0.31 per cent per year (2006 est)
RELIGION – Christianity (93 per cent) (est)
LANGUAGE – Spanish (official)
POPULATION DENSITY – 103 per sq. km (2005)
URBAN POPULATION – 76 per cent (2005 est)
MEDIAN AGE (years) – 35.9 (2006 est)
NATIONAL ANTHEM – 'La Bayamesa' ['The Bayamo Song']
NATIONAL DAY – 1 December (Independence Day)
LIFE EXPECTANCY (years) – 77.41 (2006 est)
MORTALITY RATE – 7.22 (2006 est)
BIRTH RATE – 11.89 (2006 est)
INFANT MORTALITY RATE – 6.22 (2006 est)
DEATH PENALTY – Yes
CPI SCORE – 3.4 (2006)

CLIMATE AND TERRAIN

Cuba, the largest island in the Caribbean, is part of an archipelago that also includes Isla de la Juventud and 1,600 other islets and cays. The island of Cuba has three mountainous ranges running from east to west. Elevation extremes range from 2,005m (Pico Turquino) at the highest point to 0m (Caribbean Sea) at the lowest. The climate is subtropical, with an average annual temperature of 25°C.

HISTORY AND POLITICS

The island was visited by Columbus in 1492. In the early 16th century the island was settled by the Spanish and remained under rule until 1898, when power was transferred to the USA as part of the spoils of the Spanish-American War. Cuba became independent in 1902, albeit with a condition allowing the USA to retain naval bases on the island. The dictatorship of Gen. Batista (1933–44, 1952–9) was overthrown in 1959 in a revolution led by Fidel Castro. He established a communist state was in 1961 which quickly became allied with the USSR. This alliance and the regime's policies on the one hand, and the USA's support of exiled Cuban opponents on the other, created great friction in US–Cuban relations, to the extent that the USA has maintained an economic and trade embargo since 1961.

When the USSR collapsed in 1991, Cuba lost the economic, commercial and military support it had enjoyed since 1960. Faced with severe economic deterioration, the government introduced rationing and relaxed state controls on economic activity. The latter resulted in increased overseas investment and a growing tourist sector, although state control has been reasserted in recent years. Since 2003 the EU has restricted its political and cultural contacts with Cuba over its poor human rights record.

In the 2003 legislative election, all 609 unopposed candidates received the required 50 per cent of the vote. The national assembly re-elected Fidel Castro as president in March 2003. Castro underwent surgery in July 2006 and his brother Raúl became acting president.

POLITICAL SYSTEM
The Communist Party of Cuba (PCC), formed in 1965, is the only authorised political party. The 1976 constitution was amended in 1991 to allow direct election of the national assembly by secret ballot, and in 2002 to enshrine socialism in the constitution. The president is

indirectly elected by the national assembly for a five-year term. The assembly has 609 members directly elected for a five-year term; all candidates are approved by the PCC and stand unopposed. Between its sessions, the assembly is represented by the council of state, whose members the assembly elects.

HEAD OF STATE
President of Council of State and Council of Ministers, Fidel Castro Ruz, since 1959, *appointed* 2 November 1976, *re-elected* 1993, 1998, 2003

COUNCIL OF STATE *as at May 2007*
President, Fidel Castro Ruz
First Vice-President, Gen. Raúl Castro Ruz
Secretary, Jose Miyar Barrueco

SELECTED GOVERNMENT MEMBERS *as at May 2007*
Acting President, First Vice President, Minister of the Revolutionary Armed Forces, Gen. Raúl Castro Ruz
Finance and Prices, Georgina Barreiro Fajardo
Foreign Relations, Felipe Pérez Roque
Interior, Gen. Abelardo Colomé Ibarra

EMBASSY OF THE REPUBLIC OF CUBA
167 High Holborn, London WC1 6PA
T 020-7240 2488 W www.cubaldn.com
Ambassador Extraordinary and Plenipotentiary, HE René Juan Mujica Cantelar, *apptd* 2005

BRITISH EMBASSY
Calle 34, No 704 e/ 7ma y 17, Miramar, Havana
T (+53) (0) 7204 1771 E embrit@ceniai.inf.cu
Ambassador Extraordinary and Plenipotentiary, HE John Dew, *apptd* 2001

BRITISH COUNCIL
c/o British Embassy
T (+53) (0) 7204 1771/2 W www.britishcouncil.org/cuba
Director, Jenny White

DEFENCE

The army has about 900 main battle tanks and 700 armoured personnel carriers. The navy has 7 patrol and coastal vessels and bases. The air force has 179 combat aircraft (of which only some 31 are operational) and 4 armed helicopters.

The USA has 1,016 joint task force personnel at Guantánamo Bay Naval Base, which has been leased since before the 1959 revolution.

MILITARY PERSONNEL – 49,000: army 38,000, navy 3,000, air force 8,000; paramilitaries 26,500
CONSCRIPTION DURATION – 24 months

ECONOMY AND TRADE

After the revolution virtually all land and industrial and commercial enterprises were nationalised. With the collapse of communism in Europe in 1989–91, the economy deteriorated sharply, necessitating rationing of energy, food and consumer goods, and obliging the government to introduce reforms. Since 1993, the government has permitted private enterprise, cut subsidies to loss-making state industries, allowed prices for some goods and services to rise, and introduced income tax. Since ownership of property and business enterprises was opened to foreign investors in 1995, foreign companies have started to operate here, especially in the oil and mining industries. The reforms, some now reversed, resulted in steady growth but the standard of living for most Cubans is still below the pre-1991 level. There are government budget and trade deficits.

State farms have been transformed into privately run cooperatives and are permitted to sell 20 per cent of their produce on the open market. Agriculture contributes 5 per cent of GDP but employs about 20 per cent of the workforce. The main crop is sugar, one of the mainstays of the economy although it is subject to fluctuating world prices. Industrial activities include sugar refining, oil production, tobacco processing, nickel mining and construction. Industry contributes 27 per cent of GDP, and the service sector 68 per cent. About 78 per cent of the workforce is employed in the state sector.

The main trading partners are Canada, the Netherlands, China and Spain; Venezuela provides oil at preferential terms. Principal exports are sugar, nickel, tobacco, fish, medical products, citrus fruits and coffee. The main imports are oil, food, machinery and equipment and chemicals.

ANNUAL AVERAGE GROWTH OF GDP – 8 per cent (2005 est)
INFLATION RATE – 7 per cent (2005 est)
UNEMPLOYMENT – 1.9 per cent (2005 est)
TOTAL EXTERNAL DEBT – US$12,560m (2005 est)

Trade with UK	*2005*	*2006*
Imports from UK	£15,686,000	£20,533,000
Exports to UK	£8,871,000	£8,050,000

COMMUNICATIONS

The transport system has suffered as a result of recent economic difficulties, although the growth in tourism has stimulated and paid for some remedies. Even so, road and rail services are subject to cancellation owing to breakdowns or fuel shortages. There are 4,226km of railways, with an additional 7,742km of track used exclusively by the sugar plantations. There are 60,858km of roads, 29,820km of which are surfaced, including 638km of motorway. Air services link the major cities and offshore islands; the islands are also served by ferries. There are 170 airports and airfields, of which 78 are surfaced; the main international airport is at Havana. The main ports are Havana, Cienfuegos and Matanzas.

The telephone system has been improved since 2000 but land-line density is low, with fewer than 10 lines per 100 residents. Mobile phone distribution is low but expanding. Internet access is largely restricted to foreigners and the government elite; ownership of computers and access to the internet is prohibited for private citizens.

EDUCATION AND HEALTH

Education is free of charge and compulsory at all levels. In some rural areas children attend boarding schools where agricultural tasks are compulsory in addition to schoolwork. After basic education students can choose to go to a pre-collegiate school or a technical school. The pre-collegiate school is free to graduates.

LITERACY RATE – 99.8 per cent (2004 est)
GROSS ENROLMENT RATIO (percentage of relevant age group) – primary 102 per cent; secondary 94 per cent; tertiary 61 per cent (2005 est)
HEALTH EXPENDITURE (per capita) – US$230 (2004)
HOSPITAL BEDS (per 1,000 people) – 4.9 (2000–5)

170	WORLD LOWEST
	people per doctor

Source: Economist Intelligence Unit

MEDIA

The Cuban media is tightly controlled by the government so journalists practice self-censorship. Conviction for libel or insulting officials can result in a three-year prison term. Private ownership of electronic media is prohibited and foreign news agencies are permitted only to hire local journalists through government offices. The official Communist Party newspaper is *Granma*. The main television stations are Cubavision, Tele-Rebelde and CHTV. The main radio stations are Radio Rebelde and Radio Reloj. Radio-TV Marti is a US government-backed station that transmits from Florida.

CULTURE

Cubans are perhaps most famous for their music, a vibrant mix of Spanish traditional guitar melodies and African rhythms. Rumba, mambo, bolero, salsa and cha-cha-cha all evolved from *son,* a type of Cuban music that originated in the hills of Oriente at the turn of the 20th century. Cuban music returned to the world stage with the success of the Buena Vista Social Club (publicised by the Wim Wenders film of the same name) in the late 1990s. Writers of international standing include Cirilo Villaverde y de la Paz (1812–94), José Martí (1853–95), Alejo Carpentier (1904–80), Nicolás Guillén (1902–89) and Guillermo Cabrera Infante (1929–2005).

CYPRUS

Kypriaki Dimokratía/Kibris Cumhuriyeti – Republic of Cyprus

AREA – 9,250 sq. km: of which 3,355 sq. km are in Turkish Republic of Northern Cyprus
CAPITAL – Nicosia; population 47,832 (2001 est)
MAJOR CITIES – Limassol; Larnaca; Famagusta
CURRENCY – Cyprus pound (C£) of 100 cents
POPULATION – 784,301 rising at 0.53 per cent per year (2006 est); Greek (77 per cent), Turkish (18 per cent)
RELIGION – 96 per cent Greek Orthodox south of the partition; 99 per cent Muslim north of the partition
LANGUAGE – Greek, Turkish (both official), English
POPULATION DENSITY – 82 per sq. km (2005)
URBAN POPULATION – 69.5 per cent (2005 est)
MEDIAN AGE (years) – 34.9 (2006 est)
NATIONAL ANTHEM – 'Ymnos eis tin Eleftherian' ['Ode to Freedom']
NATIONAL DAY – 1 October (Independence Day)
LIFE EXPECTANCY (years) – 77.82 (2006 est)
MORTALITY RATE – 7.68 (2006 est)
BIRTH RATE – 12.56 (2006 est)
INFANT MORTALITY RATE – 7.04 (2006 est)
DEATH PENALTY – No (abolished 2002)
CPI SCORE – 5.6 (2006)
LITERACY RATE – 96.8 per cent (2004 est)

CLIMATE AND TERRAIN

Cyprus is the third largest island in the Mediterranean. It has two mountain ranges, the Pentadaktylos range along the north coast, and the Troodos range (which includes Mt Olympus) in the centre and west. Elevation extremes range from 1,951m (Mt Olympus) at the highest point to 0m (Mediterranean Sea) at the lowest. The climate is Mediterranean with very warm summers.

HISTORY AND POLITICS

Cyprus has a recorded history of over 4,000 years, and its rulers have included the Greeks, Phoenicians, Ptolemaic Egyptians, Romans, Byzantines, Arabs, Franks, Venetians, Turks and British. Cyprus was ceded to Britain by Turkey in 1878, then formally annexed by Britain in 1914, and became a crown colony in 1925. Greek Cypriot demands for union with Greece *(enosis)* led to guerrilla warfare against the British administration in the 1950s and a four-year state of emergency (1955–9). An agreement was signed in 1959 between Britain, Greece, Turkey and the Greek and Turkish Cypriots which stipulated that Cyprus would become an independent republic; the island became independent on 16 August 1960, with Britain retaining sovereignty over the military bases at Akrotiri and Dhekelia.

The constitution provided for power-sharing between the Greek and Turkish Cypriots but this proved unworkable and led to intercommunal trouble throughout the 1960s and in 1971. The UN Peacekeeping Force in Cyprus was deployed in 1964. In 1974, a coup by mainland Greek officers in the Cypriot National Guard led Turkey, which feared *enosis,* to invade and occupy the northern third of the island, partitioning the island and displacing over 160,000 Greek Cypriots. Talks on reunification in the 1980s and 1990s were unsuccessful, and there were further sporadic outbreaks of intercommunal violence, but the approach of Cyprus' admission to the EU gave added impetus to the search for a settlement. UN-sponsored talks from 1999 resulted in a reunification plan which was approved in a referendum in April 2004 by Turkish Cypriots (64.9 per cent in favour) but rejected by Greek Cypriots (75.8 per cent against), and only the southern part of the island joined the EU in May 2004. The legislature ratified the EU constitution in 2005.

Tassos Papadopoulos of the Democratic Party (DIKO) won the 2003 presidential election. In the 2006 legislative election, the Progressive Party of the Working People (AKEL) and the Democratic Rally (DISY) each won 18 seats. AKEL formed a coalition government with DIKO and another smaller party.

HEAD OF STATE
President, Tassos Papadopoulos, *elected* 16 February 2003 *sworn in* 1 March 2003

SELECTED GOVERNMENT MEMBERS *AS AT MAY 2007*
Defence, Christodoulos Pasiardis
Finance, Michalis Sarris
Foreign Affairs, Yiorgos Lillikas
Interior, Neoklis Silikiotis

HIGH COMMISSION FOR THE REPUBLIC OF CYPRUS
93 Park Street, London W1K 7ET
T 020-7499 8272 E cyphclondon@dial.pipex.com
High Commissioner, HE George Iacovou, *apptd* 2006

BRITISH HIGH COMMISSION
Alexander Pallis Street (PO Box 21978), 1587 Nicosia
T (+357) (22) 861100 E infobhc@cylink.cy
W www.britain.org.cy
High Commissioner, HE Peter Millett, *apptd* 2005

BRITISH COUNCIL
1–3 Aristotelous Street, 1011 Nicosia
T (+357) 2258 5000 W www.britishcouncil.org/cyprus
Director, Richard Walker

BRITISH SOVEREIGN BASE AREAS
The Sovereign Base Areas (SBAs) of Akrotiri and Dhekelia are those parts of the island which remained under British sovereignty and jurisdiction when Cyprus became independent in 1960. They have the status of a British overseas territory and are around 253 sq. km in size. There are approximately 15,700 residents: 7,700 Cypriots, 3,900 service and UKBC personnel, of whom 3,600 live in the SBAs, and nearly 5,000 dependants, of whom over 4,400 live in the SBAs. There are also nearly 2,700 locally employed civilians.
Administrator of the British Sovereign Base Areas, Air Vice Adm. Richard Lacey, *apptd* 2006

DEFENCE

The National Guard has 154 main battle tanks, 43 armoured infantry fighting vehicles and 310 armoured personnel carriers. Turkey has around 36,000 troops in northern Cyprus.

A military airfield in Paphos provides a base for Greek military aircraft, as Cyprus does not possess its own air force.

MILITARY BUDGET – US$440m (2006)
MILITARY PERSONNEL – National Guard 10,000; paramilitaries 750; Northern Cyprus Army 5,000, paramilitaries 150
CONSCRIPTION DURATION – 25 months

ECONOMY AND TRADE

The Greek Cypriot economy is dominated by the service sector, which accounted for 77 per cent of GDP in 2005; this was derived mainly from tourism and financial services. With about 2.5 million visitors each year, tourism represents around 20 per cent of GDP. Shipping services are also important; about 20 per cent of the world's shipping is Cypriot-registered. Industry contributes 19 per cent of GDP and agriculture 4 per cent. The main products for export are citrus fruits, potatoes, pharmaceuticals, cement, clothing and cigarettes. Imports are primarily consumer goods, fuel and lubricants, intermediate goods and machinery. Over 50 per cent of trade is with other EU countries. Cyprus is expected to adopt the euro in 2008.

The Turkish Cypriot economy suffers from a small domestic market, international isolation and a large public sector. It is heavily dependent on financial support from the Turkish government. Services accounted for about 69 per cent of GDP in 2003, industry for 20 per cent and agriculture for 11 per cent. The main products for export are citrus fruits, potatoes and textiles. The main imports are vehicles, fuel, cigarettes, food, minerals, chemicals and machinery. The tourist industry is small because the only international transport links are via Turkey.

GNI – US$13,633m; US$18,430 per capita (2005)
ANNUAL AVERAGE GROWTH OF GDP – 3.8 per cent (2005 est)
INFLATION RATE – 2.6 per cent (2005 est)
UNEMPLOYMENT – 4 per cent (2005 est)
TOTAL EXTERNAL DEBT – US$10,530m (2005 est)
IMPORTS – US$6,280m (2005)
EXPORTS – US$1,300m (2005)

BALANCE OF PAYMENTS
Trade – US$4,292m deficit (2005)
Current Account – US$962m deficit (2005)

Trade with UK	*2005*	*2006*
Imports from UK	£346,403,000	£995,300,000
Exports to UK	£217,885,000	£1,246,800,000

COMMUNICATIONS

There are no railways. The road network (12,146km in the Greek part of the island and 2,350km in the Turkish part) serves the main population centres, although crossings between the Greek and Turkish parts of the island are closed or controlled. In the Greek area, the main airports are at Larnaca and Paphos, and the principal ports are Limassol, Larnaca and Paphos. In the Turkish area, the main ports are Famagusta and Kyrenia; there is an airport but flight connections are with Turkey only.

MEDIA

The division of the country is mirrored in the media, with the Turkish north operating its own services and broadcasts. There is competition between state and privately owned television and radio stations. Newspapers on both sides of the divide are free to criticise the authorities.

TURKISH REPUBLIC OF NORTHERN CYPRUS

In 1974, a coup by mainland Greek officers in the Cypriot National Guard, led Turkey, fearing the coup was a precursor to the union of Cyprus with Greece, to invade northern Cyprus and occupy over a third of the island. The next year, a Turkish Federated State of Cyprus under Rauf Denktash was declared and in 1983 a declaration of statehood was issued which purported to establish the Turkish Republic of Northern Cyprus. The declaration was condemned by the UN security council and only Turkey has recognised the new state. In 1985 Denktash was elected president and a general election was held. Denktash was re-elected in 1990, 1995 and 2000, retiring at the 2005 election. A UN plan for the re-unification of the island was approved by the Turkish Cypriot population in a 2004 referendum, but the plan's rejection by the Greek Cypriots has left the status of northern Cyprus unchanged. Recent confidence-building measures instituted by both governments have improved relations between the two communities.

The legislative election in February 2005 was won by the party of the incumbent prime minister, Mehmet Ali Talat, and his allies. Talat also won the presidential election in April 2005.

DE FACTO HEAD OF STATE
President, Mehmet Ali Talat, *sworn in* 24 April 2005
Prime Minister, Ferdi Sabit Soyer

CZECH REPUBLIC

Ceska Republika – Czech Republic

AREA – 78,866 sq. km. Neighbours: Poland (north-east), Germany (west and north-west), Austria (south), Slovakia (east)
CAPITAL – Prague (Praha) on the Vltava (Moldau); population, 1,181,610 (2006 est)

MAJOR CITIES – Brno (Brünn); Ostrava; Plzen (Pilsen)
CURRENCY – Koruna (Kcs) of 100 haleru
POPULATION – 10,235,455 falling at 0.06 per cent per year (2006 est); Czech (90.4 per cent), Moravian (3.7 per cent), Slovak (1.9 per cent) (est)
RELIGION – Roman Catholicism (26 per cent), Protestantism (2 per cent). The majority of the population has no religious beliefs
LANGUAGE – Czech (official)
POPULATION DENSITY – 132 per sq. km (2005)
URBAN POPULATION – 74.5 per cent (2005 est)
MEDIAN AGE (years) – 39.3 (2006 est)
NATIONAL ANTHEM – 'Kde Domov Muj?' ['Where is My Motherland?']
NATIONAL DAY – 28 October (Founding Day)
LIFE EXPECTANCY (years) – 76.22 (2006 est)
MORTALITY RATE – 10.59 (2006 est)
BIRTH RATE – 9.02 (2006 est)
INFANT MORTALITY RATE – 3.89 (2006 est)
DEATH PENALTY – No (abolished 1990)
CPI SCORE – 4.8 (2006)

CLIMATE AND TERRAIN

The landlocked republic is composed of Bohemia (the west and centre) and Moravia (the east). Bohemia is a fertile plain surrounded by mountain ranges, while Moravia extends to the Danubian basin. Roughly a third of the country is covered by forest. Elevation extremes range from 1,602m (Snezka) at the highest point to 115m (Elbe River) at the lowest. The climate is continental, with warm, humid summers and cold, dry winters. The average temperature in Prague ranges from 2°C in January to 19°C in July.

HISTORY AND POLITICS

The area came under the rule of the Habsburg dynasty in 1526 and remained part of the Austro-Hungarian Empire until 1918. The rise of Czech nationalism in the late 19th century led to Czechoslovakia's independence on 28 October 1918 following an amalgamation of Bohemia, Moravia, Slovakia and Ruthenia. It was officially confirmed at the Versailles Peace Conference of 1919.

Czechoslovakia was forced to cede the ethnic German Sudetenland to Nazi Germany in 1938 after the Munich agreement. German forces invaded the Czech lands in 1939 and incorporated them into Germany while Slovakia became a puppet state. The republic was liberated by Soviet and US forces in 1945. The pre-war democratic Czechoslovak state was re-established in 1945, having ceded Ruthenia to the Soviet Union. Communists took power in a coup in 1948 and remained until 1989.

In 1968, the Communist Party under Alexander Dubcek embarked on a political and economic reform programme (known as the Prague Spring). The reforms were suppressed following an invasion by Warsaw Pact troops on 20 August 1968, and were abandoned when Gustav Husak became leader of the Communist Party in 1969.

After mass protests in November 1989, the Communist Party central committee resigned, and the party was forced to concede its monopoly of power. On 10 December a new government was appointed in which only half the ministers were Communists. Husak resigned as president and was replaced by the dissident writer Vaclav Havel. Free elections were held in 1990 in which the Communist Party was defeated.

In late 1992, the leaders of the Czech and Slovak republics agreed to dissolve the federation and form two sovereign states; this took effect on 1 January 1993. The Czech Republic joined the EU in 2004.

President Havel left office in February 2003 but parliament was unable to agree on a successor until, at the third attempt, Vaclav Klaus of the Civic Democrat Party (ODS) was elected on 28 February and took office in March. The 2006 elections to the chamber of deputies were inconclusive and after a minority ODS government lost a vote of confidence in October 2006, the ODS formed a three-party centre-right coalition government with the Christian Democrats and the Green Party in January 2007.

POLITICAL SYSTEM

The 1992 constitution provided for the separation of the Czech Republic and Slovakia; federal laws remain in place unless superseded by Czech ones. The president is elected by parliament for a five-year term, with a maximum of two consecutive terms. The bicameral parliament comprises a 200-member chamber of deputies directly elected for a four-year term, and an 81-member senate directly elected for a six-year term, one-third being elected every two years. Executive power is held by the prime minister and council of ministers, appointed by the president on the recommendation of the prime minister.

HEAD OF STATE

President, Vaclav Klaus, *elected by parliament* 28 February 2003, *sworn in* 7 March 2003

SELECTED GOVERNMENT MEMBERS *as at May 2007*

Prime Minister, Mirek Topolanek
Minister of Vice-Premiers, Finance, Bohuslav Sabotka
Vice-Premiers, Jiri Havel; Pavel Nemec; Zdenek Skromach
Defence, Vlasta Parkanova
Interior, Ivan Langer
Foreign Affairs, Karel Schwarzenberg

EMBASSY OF THE CZECH REPUBLIC

26 Kensington Palace Gardens, London W8 4QY
T 020-7243 1115
W www.czechembassy.org.uk
Ambassador Extraordinary and Plenipotentiary, HE Jan Winkler, *apptd* 2005

BRITISH EMBASSY

Thunovska 14, 11800 Prague 1
T (+420) (2) 5740 2111 E info@britain.cz W www.britain.cz
Ambassador Extraordinary and Plenipotentiary, HE Linda Duffield, *apptd* 2004

BRITISH COUNCIL

Bredovsky dvur, Politickych veznu 13, 11000 Prague 1
T (+420) 221 991 111 W www.britishcouncil.org/czechrepublic
Director, Mandy Johnson

DEFENCE

The army has 244 main battle tanks, 561 armoured infantry fighting vehicles and 79 armoured personnel carriers. The air force has 38 combat aircraft and 24 attack helicopters.
MILITARY EXPENDITURE – US$2,230m (2005)
MILITARY PERSONNEL – 24,752: joint staff 19,050, MoD staff 5,702; paramilitaries 54,600

ECONOMY AND TRADE

Economic reforms since 1990 have produced a stable and prosperous market economy. Accession to the EU has encouraged further reform and restructuring, as well as contributing to the continuing steady growth by expanding export markets and encouraging investment. A customs union between the Czech and Slovak republics is in place but separate currencies were introduced in 1993 following speculation.

Services account for 59 per cent of GDP, industry for 38 per cent and agriculture for 3 per cent. The principal agricultural products are sugar beet, potatoes and cereal crops; the timber industry is also very important. Having been the major industrial area of the Austro-Hungarian Empire, the country has long been industrialised, and metals, machinery, vehicles, glass and armaments are major products. The principal trading partners are EU countries, especially Germany as well as Russia and China.

GNI – US$114,800m; US$11,220 per capita (2005)
ANNUAL AVERAGE GROWTH OF GDP – 6.1 per cent (2005 est)
INFLATION RATE – 1.9 per cent (2005 est)
UNEMPLOYMENT – 7.9 per cent (2005)
TOTAL EXTERNAL DEBT – US$49,140m (2005 est)
IMPORTS – US$77,000m (2005)
EXPORTS – US$78,000m (2005)

BALANCE OF PAYMENTS
Trade – US$1,735m surplus (2005)
Current Account – US$2,495m deficit (2005)

Trade with UK	*2005*	*2006*
Imports from UK	£994,928,000	£1,503,100,000
Exports to UK	£1,586,528,000	£2,151,400,000

COMMUNICATIONS

There are extensive road (127,747km) and rail (9,572km) networks linking the main population centres. Navigable inland waterways include 664km on the Elbe, Vltava and Oder rivers. The principal airport is at Prague and the national carrier is Czech Airlines, which operates international and domestic services. The telecommunications system was privatised recently and is being modernised. Mobile phone distribution is growing rapidly.

EDUCATION AND HEALTH

Education is free of charge and compulsory for all children from the age of six to 15. Primary education lasts for nine years, divided into two stages of five and four years respectively. Secondary education comprises three main types of school: general schools, technical schools and vocational schools.

GROSS ENROLMENT RATIO (percentage of relevant age group) – primary 102 per cent; secondary 96 per cent; tertiary 43 per cent (2005 est)
HEALTH EXPENDITURE (per capita) – US$771 (2004)
HOSPITAL BEDS (per 1,000 people) – 8.8 (2000–5)

MEDIA AND CULTURE

The public broadcaster is Ceska Televize (CT) and it runs two channels. There are several private television stations. Czech public radio, Cesky Rozhlas (CRo), operates three national networks and local services alongside over 70 private radio stations throughout the country. The country is at the forefront of television digitalisation and plans to switch off its analogue signal in 2012.

Prague is famous for its art nouveau architecture, cobbled streets and squares and thriving cultural life (particularly its contemporary jazz scene). Best-known Czech composers include Antonin Dvorak (1841–1904), Bedrich Smetana (1824–84) and Leos Janacek (1854–1928). Among its important writers are Franz Kafka (1883–1924), Milan Kundera (*b.* 1929), Ivan Klima (*b.* 1931) and Vaclav Havel (*b.* 1936).

DENMARK

Kongeriget Danmark – Kingdom of Denmark

AREA – 43,094 sq. km. Neighbour: Germany (south)
CAPITAL – Copenhagen; population, 1,086,762 (2004 est)
MAJOR CITIES – Arhus; Odense; Alborg
CURRENCY – Danish krone of 100 Ore
POPULATION – 5,450,661 rising at 0.33 per cent per year (2006 est)
RELIGION – Lutheran (84 per cent), Islam (3 per cent) (est)
LANGUAGE – Danish (official), English, German, Faroese
POPULATION DENSITY – 128 per sq. km (2005)
URBAN POPULATION – 85.5 per cent (2005 est)
MEDIAN AGE (years) – 39.8 (2006 est)
NATIONAL ANTHEMS – 'Det er et Yndigt Land' ['There is a Lovely Land']
NATIONAL DAY – 5 June (Constitution Day)
LIFE EXPECTANCY (years) – 77.79 (2006 est)
MORTALITY RATE – 10.36 (2006 est)
BIRTH RATE – 11.13 (2006 est)
INFANT MORTALITY RATE – 4.51 (2006 est)
DEATH PENALTY – No (abolished 1978)
CPI SCORE – 9.5 (2006)

CLIMATE AND TERRAIN

Denmark consists of most of the Jutland peninsula and 406 islands, mainly in the Baltic Sea or part of the northern Frisian Islands in the North Sea. The largest islands are Sjælland (Zealand), Fyn, Lolland, Faister and Bornholm. It is a low-lying country, indented by fjords on its east coast and with lagoons and sand dunes along the west coast. Elevation extremes range from 173m (Yding Skovhoej) at the highest point to –7m (Lammefjord) at the lowest. There are cold winters and warm summers. Temperatures range from 0°C in January to 17°C in July.

HISTORY AND POLITICS

The Danes were at the forefront of Viking expansionism from the eighth century. Denmark was unified in the 10th century and was the centre of the short-lived empire, also including Norway and England, created by Cnut (Canute) in the 11th century. The Union of Kalmar (1397) brought Norway and Sweden (including Finland) under Danish rule. Danish power waned during the 16th century, enabling Sweden to re-establish its independence in 1523. In 1814 Norway was ceded to Sweden under the Treaty of Kiel, and in 1864 Schleswig and Holstein, which had been subsumed in 1460, were lost to Germany. Northern Schleswig was returned in 1919 after a plebiscite. Denmark was neutral during the First World War, but in the Second World War it was invaded and occupied by Germany.

Iceland declared its independence from Denmark in 1944 and the Faeroe Islands were granted home rule in 1948. Greenland, which previously had the status of a colony, was integrated into Denmark in 1953 and granted home rule in 1979.

Denmark joined the European Community in 1973. In a referendum in 2000, it rejected membership of the European single currency. A 2005 referendum on the EU constitution was postponed without a new date being set.

Social Democrat-led coalitions dominated the post-war era, creating a welfare state. They lost the 1982 election but were in power again from 1993 to 2001. In the 2001 legislative election, the Liberal Party became the largest party in parliament, and formed a coalition government with the Conservative People's Party. This coalition government retained power in the 2005 general election, winning 94 of the 179 seats.

POLITICAL SYSTEM

The country is a constitutional monarchy, with the hereditary monarch as head of state. The head of government is the prime minister, who appoints the cabinet. The unicameral legislature, the *Folketing*, has 179 members, including two for the Faeroes and two for Greenland, who are elected for a four-year term. The voting age is 18 with an electoral system based on proportional representation and a 2 per cent threshold for parliamentary representation.

HEAD OF STATE

HM The Queen of Denmark, Queen Margrethe II, KG, *born* 16 April 1940, *acceded* 14 January 1972

Heir, HRH Crown Prince Frederik, *born* 26 May 1968

SELECTED GOVERNMENT MEMBERS *as at May 2007*

Prime Minister, Anders Fogh Rasmussen

Defence, Soeren Gade Jensen

Finance, Thor Pedersen

Foreign Affairs, Per Stig Moeller

Interior and Health, Lars Loekke Rasmussen

ROYAL DANISH EMBASSY

55 Sloane Street, London SW1X 9SR

T 020-7333 0200 W www.denmark.org.uk

Ambassador Extraordinary and Plenipotentiary, HE Birger Riis-Jorgensen, *apptd* 2006

BRITISH EMBASSY

Kastelsvej 36/38/40, 2100 Copenhagen

T (+45) 3544 5200 E brit-emb@post6.tele.dk

W www.britishembassy.dk

Ambassador Extraordinary and Plenipotentiary, HE David Frost, *apptd* 2006

BRITISH COUNCIL

Gammel Mont 12.3, DK-1117 Copenhagen K

T (+45) (33) 369 400 W www.britishcouncil.org/denmark

Director, Dr Michael Sorensen-Jones

DEFENCE

The army has 231 main battle tanks, 310 armoured personnel carriers and 12 attack helicopters. The navy has 62 patrol and coastal vessels at three bases. The air force has 48 combat aircraft.

MILITARY EXPENDITURE – US$3,350m (2005)

MILITARY PERSONNEL – 21,620: army 13,580, navy 3,450, air force 3,910, joint staff 680

CONSCRIPTION DURATION – Four to ten months

ECONOMY AND TRADE

As with the rest of Scandinavia, Denmark enjoys a diversified and industrialised market economy. Sound management of public finances means the budget and balance of trade are in surplus. It is a net exporter of food and energy – oil, natural gas and electricity. The service sector contributes 74 per cent of GDP, industry 25 per cent and the highly efficient agricultural sector 1 per cent.

The main trading partners are other EU countries, especially Germany and Sweden. Principal exports are machinery and instruments, meat and meat products, dairy products, fish, pharmaceuticals, furniture and windmills. The main imports are machinery and equipment, industrial raw materials and semi-manufactures, chemicals, grain and foodstuffs, and consumer goods.

GNI – US$261,800m; US$48,330 per capita (2005)

ANNUAL AVERAGE GROWTH OF GDP – 3.2 per cent (2005 est)

INFLATION RATE – 1.8 per cent (2005 est)

UNEMPLOYMENT – 5.7 per cent (2005 est)

TOTAL EXTERNAL DEBT – US$352,900m (2005)

IMPORTS – US$74,500m (2005)

EXPORTS – US$83,700m (2005)

BALANCE OF PAYMENTS

Trade – US$9,527m surplus (2004)

Current Account – US$5,941m surplus (2004)

Trade with UK	*2005*	*2006*
Imports from UK	£2,256,120,000	£3,711,700,000
Exports to UK	£3,753,962,000	£4,258,800,000

COMMUNICATIONS

The main ports are Arhus, Odense, Copenhagen, Alborg and Esbjerg. The principal airports are at Copenhagen, Arhus, Alborg and near Vejle. There are 2,673km of railway, of which 601km is electrified. A rail tunnel and a bridge link the islands of Sjælland (Zealand) and Fyn, and a road and rail tunnel and a bridge across the Oresund links Copenhagen with Malmo (Sweden). There are 72,257km of roads, including 1,032km of motorways. The telecommunications network is modern and extensive; mobile phone distribution is, at 5.4 million in 2005, nearly 100 per cent.

EDUCATION AND HEALTH

Education is free of charge and compulsory. Specialist schools are numerous, with commercial, technical and agricultural predominating.

GROSS ENROLMENT RATIO (percentage of relevant age group) – primary 101 per cent; secondary 124 per cent; tertiary 74 per cent (2005 est)

HEALTH EXPENDITURE (per capita) – US$3,897 (2004)

HOSPITAL BEDS (per 1,000 people) – 4.0 (2000–5)

MEDIA

The public broadcaster is Danmarks Radio, which operates two television networks and national and regional radio stations. Private television stations can be obtained via satellite and cable. There are some 250 local commercial and community radio stations in operation. The country's commitment to a free press was reiterated in 2006 following the publication of satirical cartoons of the Prophet Muhammad in the *Jyllands-Posten* daily newspaper, which led to violent protests and unofficial boycotts of Danish products.

CULTURE

Denmark has made significant contributions to science and its Nobel laureates include atomic physicist Niels Bohr (1885–1962), who collaborated on the Manhattan project to develop nuclear power during Second World War, and medical researcher Niels Finsen (1860–1904). Notable contributions have been made in music: by Carl Nielsen (1865–1931); design: by Arne Jacobsen (1902–71) and Georg Jensen (1866–1935); philosophy: by Soren Kierkegaard (1813–55); and literature: by Hans Christian Andersen (1805–75) and Karen Blixen (1885–1962), author *Out of Africa*. Perhaps the most famous Dane of all remains William Shakespeare's Prince Hamlet.

THE FAEROE ISLANDS

AREA – 1,399 sq. km
POPULATION – 47,000 (2001)
CAPITAL – Torshavn; population, 16,511 (2001)

The Faeroe (Sheep) Islands are a group of 18 islands (17 inhabited) and a few islets in the North Atlantic Ocean, between the Shetland Islands and Iceland. First settled in the ninth century, the islands were a Norwegian province and, with Norway, came under Danish rule in the 14th century. Since 1948 the Faeroes have been self-governing. The islands are not part of the EU.

The sovereign is represented in the islands by a high commissioner. The government *(Landsstryrid)* of three to six members deals with internal affairs. The parliament *(Logting)* has 32 members, elected for a four-year term. The islands send two representatives to the *Folketing* at Copenhagen. After the 2004 election to the *Logting*, the Social Democrats, Union Party and People's Party formed a coalition government.
Prime Minister, Joannes Eidesgaard (Social Democrat)

ECONOMY AND TRADE

The economy has grown steadily in recent years, but remains highly dependent on fishing and fish processing; fish and fish products account for 94 per cent of exports. Offshore oil discoveries raise the possibility of future diversification.

BALANCE OF PAYMENTS
Trade – US$90m deficit (2003)
Current Account – US$7m deficit (2003)

Trade with UK	*2005*	*2006*
Imports from UK	£6,706,000	£11,558,000
Exports to UK	£99,502,000	£103,851,000

BRITISH CONSULATE
P/F Damfar, PO Box 1154, Niels Finsengota 5, FR-110 Torshavn
T (+298) 35 99 77
Hon. Consul, Tummas H. Dam

GREENLAND (KALAALLIT NUNAAT)

AREA – 2,166,086 sq. km
POPULATION – 56,361 (2006 est)
CAPITAL – Godthab (Nuuk); population 14,5012 (2005 est)

Greenland, the world's largest island, lies between the Atlantic and Arctic oceans, to the east of Canada and to the west of Iceland. Most of Greenland is within the Arctic Circle, with permafrost covering around 81 per cent of the island. Elevation extremes range from 3,700m (Gunnbjorn) at the highest point to 0m (Atlantic Ocean) at the lowest. Natural resources include zinc, lead, iron ore, coal, molybdenum, gold, platinum and uranium, some of which are mined, but fish and fish products comprise 94 per cent of exports.

Greenland was first discovered by small groups of hunters and nomadic groups who travelled from Canada *c.*500 BC. In the late 10th century, Viking invaders began establishing settlements along the south-eastern coast and started subsistence farming and trading with northern Europe. These colonies came under Norwegian rule in 1261 and had died out by the 16th century, though some Inuit settlements continued. Greenland became a Danish colony in the 18th century, and was granted internal autonomy in 1979. Greenland negotiated its withdrawal from the EU, without discontinuing relations with Denmark, and left in 1985. The USA has acquired the right to maintain air bases in Greenland.

The sovereign is represented by a high commissioner. The government *(Landsstyre)* is elected by parliament. The parliament *(Landsting)* has 31 members, elected for a four-year term. Greenland sends two representatives to the *Folketing* at Copenhagen. In the 2002 parliamentary election, the Siumut ('forward') party won ten seats and formed a coalition government with the Inuit Brotherhood and Atassut parties.
Prime Minister, Hans Enoksen (Siumut)

Trade with UK	*2005*	*2006*
Imports from UK	£464,000	£856,000
Exports to UK	£65,000	£578,000

DJIBOUTI

Jumhuriyya Jibuti/République du Djibouti – Republic of Djibouti

AREA – 23,000 sq. km. Neighbours: Eritrea (north), Ethiopia (west and south), Somalia (south-east)
CAPITAL – Djibouti; population, 430,000 (1998 est)
MAJOR TOWNS – Dikhil; Ali-Sabieh
CURRENCY – Djibouti franc of 100 centimes
POPULATION – 486,530 rising at 2.02 per cent per year (2006 est); Somali (60 per cent), Afar (35 per cent) (est)
RELIGION – Islam (99 per cent) (est)
LANGUAGE – French, Arabic (official), Somali, Afar
POPULATION DENSITY – 34 per sq. km (2005)
URBAN POPULATION – 84.6 per cent (2005 est)
MEDIAN AGE (years) – 18.2 (2006 est)
NATIONAL ANTHEM – 'Djibouti'
NATIONAL DAY – 27 June (Independence Day)
LIFE EXPECTANCY – 43.17 (2006 est)
MORTALITY RATE – 19.31 (2006 est)
BIRTH RATE – 39.53 (2006 est)
INFANT MORTALITY RATE – 102.44 (2006 est)
HIV/AIDS ADULT PREVALENCE – 2.9 per cent (2003 est)
DEATH PENALTY – No (abolished 1995)
POPULATION BELOW POVERTY LINE – 50 per cent (2001 est)
MILITARY BUDGET – US$26m (2006 est)
MILITARY PERSONNEL – 10,950: army 8,000, navy 200, air force 250, National Security Force 2,500; paramilitaries 1,400

CLIMATE AND TERRAIN

Djibouti is situated on the east coast of Africa, at the point where the Gulf of Aden and the Red Sea meet. Elevation extremes range from 2,028m (Moussa Ali) at the highest point to −156m (Lake Abbé) at the lowest. The country is prone to flash floods as well as cyclones, droughts and earthquakes. The climate is semi-arid with a hot season between May and September.

HISTORY AND POLITICS

Settled by the Afars (Ethiopian) and Issas (Somali) about 2,000 years ago, the area was annexed by the French in 1888 and became French Somaliland; in 1967 it was renamed the French Territory of the Afars and the Issas. The territory became independent as Djibouti on 27 June 1977, under President Hassan Gouled Aptidon (an Issa), the leader of the *Rassemblement Populaire pour le Progrès* (RPP) party, which became the only legal political party in 1981.

In 1991, Afar discontent with Issa domination of government under one-party rule led to civil war between the government and the *Front pour la Restauration de L'Unité et de la Democratie* (FRUD), an alliance of rebel groups. A multiparty constitution was introduced and multiparty elections were held in 1992, but fighting continued until a power-sharing agreement was reached in 1994. The civil war ended with the signing of a peace accord in 1996, although a breakaway faction of the FRUD continued its armed opposition to the government until 2001.

In the 2003 legislative election, for the first time since independence the number of parties allowed to contest an election was not limited. The Union for Presidential Majority (UMP), an alliance of the RPP, FRUD and two other parties supporting President Guelleh, won all 65 seats in the national assembly. In the 2005 presidential election President Guelleh was re-elected unopposed.

POLITICAL SYSTEM

Under the 1992 constitution, the president is directly elected for a six-year term, renewable only once. The unicameral legislature, the *Assemblée Nationale* (national assembly) has 65 members, directly elected for a five-year term. The president appoints the council of ministers.

HEAD OF STATE

President, C.-in-C. of the Armed Forces, Ismail Omar Guelleh, *elected* 9 April 1999, *re-elected* 8 April 2005

SELECTED GOVERNMENT MEMBERS *as at May 2007*

Prime Minister, National and Regional Development, Dileita Muhammad Dileita
Defence, Ougoureh Kifleh Ahmed
Interior, Yacin Elmi Bouh
Economy, Finance Ali Farah Assoweh
Foreign Affairs and International Co-operation, Mahamoud Ali Youssouf

EMBASSY OF THE REPUBLIC OF DJIBOUTI

26 rue Emile Ménier, F-75116 Paris, France
T (+33) (1) 4727 4922 W www.ambdjibouti.org
Ambassador Extraordinary and Plenipotentiary, HE Rachad Farah, *apptd* 2005

BRITISH AMBASSADOR

HE Robert Dewar, *apptd* 2004, resident at Addis Ababa, Ethiopia

ECONOMY AND TRADE

A barren country with few natural resources and little industry, Djibouti's chief asset is its location. It is a transit port for neighbouring landlocked countries, a transshipment and refuelling centre, and a military base for US and EU forces because of its strategic position. The service sector accounts for 60 per cent of GDP, agriculture for 18 per cent, and industry for 22 per cent. The country is highly dependent on foreign aid and has fallen behind with external debt servicing in recent years. The main trading partners are Somalia, Yemen, Saudi Arabia, Ethiopia, India and China. Principal exports are re-exports, hides and skins, and coffee (in transit). The main imports are foodstuffs, transport equipment, chemicals and petroleum products.

GNI – US$803m; US$1,010 per capita (2005)
ANNUAL AVERAGE GROWTH OF GDP – 3.2 per cent (2005 est)
INFLATION RATE – 3 per cent (2005 est)
UNEMPLOYMENT – 50 per cent (2004 est)
TOTAL EXTERNAL DEBT – US$394m (2004 est)

Trade with UK	*2005*	*2006*
Imports from UK	£5,617,000	£5,183,000
Exports to UK	£1,311,000	£2,172,000

COMMUNICATIONS

There is 100km of railway, the Djibouti section of the Addis Ababa–Djibouti railway, controlled by both Djibouti and Ethiopia. The government is keen to expand the rail network into neighbouring countries to improve trade. Of the 2,890km of roads, 364km are surfaced. Djibouti is the main port, and the location of the principal airport. Three of the country's 13 airports and airfields have surfaced runways. The telephone system in Djibouti city, home to much of the population, is adequate but mobile phone distribution is now three times greater than land-line density.

MEDIA

The government owns *La Nation,* the main newspaper, as well as Radiodiffusion-Télévision de Djibouti (RTD), the company which operates national radio and television stations. There are a number of privately owned newspapers including *Al Qarn, La République,* and *Le Renouveau.* Independent newspapers are generally allowed to circulate freely, but journalists exercise self-censorship.

DOMINICA

Commonwealth of Dominica

AREA – 754 sq. km
CAPITAL – Roseau; population, 16,038 (1991)
CURRENCY – East Caribbean dollar (EC $) of 100 cents
POPULATION – 68,910 falling at 0.08 per cent per year (2006 est)
RELIGION – Roman Catholicism (61 per cent), other Christian denominations (27 per cent) (est)
LANGUAGE – English (official), French patois
POPULATION DENSITY – 96 per sq. km (2005)
URBAN POPULATION – 72.7 per cent (2005 est)
MEDIAN AGE (years) – 30.1 (2006 est)
NATIONAL ANTHEM – 'Isle of Beauty, Isle of Splendour'

NATIONAL DAY – 3 November (Independence Day)
LIFE EXPECTANCY – 74.87 (2006 est)
MORTALITY RATE – 6.73 (2006 est)
BIRTH RATE – 15.27 (2006 est)
INFANT MORTALITY RATE – 13.71 (2006 est)
DEATH PENALTY – Yes
CPI SCORE – 4.5 (2006)
POPULATION BELOW POVERTY LINE – 30 per cent (2002 est)

CLIMATE AND TERRAIN

Dominica, in the Lesser Antilles, lies in the Windward Islands group 95 miles south of Antigua. It is about 46km long and 25km wide, with a mountainous central ridge. Elevation extremes range from 1,447m (Morne Diablatins) at the highest point to 0m (Caribbean Sea) at the lowest. The climate is tropical with average daily temperatures ranging from 25°C to 32°C. The island is located within a hurricane zone.

HISTORY AND POLITICS

Dominica was discovered by Columbus in 1493, when it was a stronghold of the Caribs, the sole inhabitants of the island until the French founded settlements in the 18th century. It was captured by the British in 1759 but passed back and forth between France and Britain until 1805, after which British possession was unchallenged. From 1871 to 1939 Dominica was part of the Leeward Islands federation, then from 1940 part of the Windward Islands federation, and from 1958 part of the West Indies. Internal self-government from 1967 was followed on 3 November 1978 by independence as a republic. In 1980 Eugenia Charles of the Dominica Freedom Party (DFP) became the first woman prime minister in the Caribbean. She held office until 1995, when the United Workers' Party (UWP) won the legislative elections. The UWP lost the 2000 election to the Dominica Labour Party (DLP), which formed a coalition government with the DFP. The DLP remained the largest party after the 2005 election and continued in government in coalition with the DFP.

POLITICAL SYSTEM

Under the 1978 constitution, the president is elected by the house of assembly for a five-year term, renewable only once. The unicameral legislature, the house of assembly, has 21 members, who are directly elected, and nine senators, five appointed on the advice of the prime minister and the other four on the advice of the leader of the opposition; all members sit for a five-year term.

HEAD OF STATE

President, Nicholas Liverpool, *elected* 2 October 2003, *took office* 6 October 2003

SELECTED GOVERNMENT MEMBERS *as at May 2007*

Prime Minister, Finance, Roosevelt Skerrit
Foreign Affairs, Trade, Charles Savarin
Attorney-General, Ian Douglas

HIGH COMMISSION FOR THE COMMONWEALTH OF DOMINICA

1 Collingham Gardens, London SW5 0HW
T 020-7370 5194 E dominicahighcom@btconnect.com
High Commissioner (acting), Agnes Adonis

BRITISH HIGH COMMISSIONER

High Commissioner, HE Duncan Taylor, *apptd* 2005, resident at Bridgetown, Barbados

ECONOMY AND TRADE

Traditionally dependent on banana exports, the economy suffered a negative growth rate in 2003 after EU preferential treatment for this trade ended. Tourism is growing but is limited by poor facilities, including the lack of an international airport. The government is encouraging diversification into offshore financial services, fishing, forestry and light industry. An IMF-funded economic restructuring programme began in 2003 and the economy is starting to grow again but at the expense of jobs; the unemployment rate is 23 per cent.

Agriculture is the principal occupation, employing 40 per cent of the workforce but producing only 18 per cent of GDP. Services now contribute 49 per cent of GDP and industry 33 per cent. Principal exports are bananas, soap, bay oil, vegetables and citrus fruits. The main imports are manufactured goods, machinery, food and chemicals. The main trading partners are the UK, the USA, China, South Korea and other Caribbean countries.

GNI – US$271m; US$3,800 per capita (2005)
ANNUAL AVERAGE GROWTH OF GDP – 3.1 per cent (2005 est)
INFLATION RATE – –0.1 per cent (2005 est)
UNEMPLOYMENT – 23 per cent (2000 est)
TOTAL EXTERNAL DEBT – US$213m (2004)
IMPORTS – US$200m (2005)
EXPORTS – US$100m (2000)

BALANCE OF PAYMENTS
Trade – US$71m deficit (2002)
Current Account – US$49m deficit (2002)

Trade with UK	*2005*	*2006*
Imports from UK	£5,796,000	£5,698,000
Exports to UK	£14,001,000	£13,866,000

MEDIA

Although there is no national television service, a private cable network covers part of the island. There are no daily newspapers but there are weekly publications. Private and public radio stations are in operation throughout the country. All media are free of government interference.

DOMINICAN REPUBLIC

República Dominicana – Dominican Republic

AREA – 48,730 sq. km. Neighbour: Haiti (west)
CAPITAL – Santo Domingo; population, 1,887,586 (2002 est)
MAJOR CITIES – Santiago de los Caballeros; San Pedro de Macoris; La Romana; Los Alcarrizos
CURRENCY – Dominican Republic peso (RD $) of 100 centavos
POPULATION – 9,183,984 rising at 1.47 per cent per year (2006 est)
RELIGION – Roman Catholicism (68 per cent), Protestantism (11 per cent) (est). Many Catholics also practice a combination of Christianity and Afro-Caribbean beliefs (Santería) or witchcraft (brujería), but because these practices are rarely admitted, the number of adherents is impossible to estimate
LANGUAGE – Spanish (official)
POPULATION DENSITY – 184 per sq. km (2005)
URBAN POPULATION – 60.1 per cent (2005 est)
MEDIAN AGE (years) – 24.1 (2006 est)

NATIONAL ANTHEM – 'Quisqueyanos Valientes' ['Valiant Sons of Quisqueya']
NATIONAL DAY – 27 February (Independence Day)
LIFE EXPECTANCY (years) – 71.73 (2006 est)
MORTALITY RATE – 5.73 (2006 est)
BIRTH RATE – 23.22 (2006 est)
INFANT MORTALITY RATE – 28.25 (2006 est)
HIV/AIDS ADULT PREVALENCE – 1.7 per cent (2003 est)
DEATH PENALTY – No (abolished 1966)
CPI SCORE – 2.8 (2006)
POPULATION BELOW POVERTY LINE – 25 per cent (2002)
MILITARY BUDGET – US$191m (2005 est)
MILITARY PERSONNEL – 24,500: army 15,000, navy 4,000, air force 5,500; paramilitaries 15,000
LITERACY RATE – 87.7 per cent (2004 est)
GROSS ENROLMENT RATIO (percentage of relevant age group) – primary 113 per cent; secondary 71 per cent; tertiary 33 per cent (2005 est)
HEALTH EXPENDITURE (per capita) – US$148 (2004)

CLIMATE AND TERRAIN

The republic forms the eastern two-thirds of the island of Hispaniola (the remainder is Haiti) and is crossed from the north-west to the south-east by the Cordillera Central mountain range. Many of the mountains are over 3,000m. Elevation extremes range from 3,175m (Pico Duarte) at the highest point to –46m (Lake Enriquillo) at the lowest. The climate is maritime tropical with average temperatures of between 23°C and 27°C.

HISTORY AND POLITICS

The island was discovered by Columbus in 1492, and became a Spanish colony. The eastern province of Santo Domingo remained Spanish after the partition of Hispaniola in 1697, but was ceded to France in 1795. It was restored to Spanish rule in 1809. Independence was declared in 1821, but in 1822 it was subjugated by the neighbouring Haitians who remained in control until 1844, when the Dominican Republic was proclaimed. Under Spanish occupation for a third time in 1861–5, a long dictatorship at the end of the 19th century was followed by revolution and bankruptcy, which led to occupation by US forces from 1916 until 1924. A military coup in 1930 established the dictatorship of Gen. Rafael Trujillo, who ruled until his assassination in 1961. After a period of political instability, a new constitution was adopted in 1966 and democracy was restored.

The 2004 presidential election was won by Leonel Fernandez (president 1996–2000) of the Dominican Liberation Party (PLD). The 2006 legislative elections were won in both houses by the PLD, which defeated the ruling Dominican Revolutionary Party.

POLITICAL SYSTEM

Under the 1966 constitution (amended in 2002), the executive president is directly elected for a four-year term, renewable only once. Legislative power is exercised by the bicameral national congress. The lower chamber, the chamber of deputies, has 178 members directly elected for a four-year term, and the upper chamber, the senate, has 30 members, one for each province and one for Santo Domingo, directly elected for a four-year term.

HEAD OF STATE

President, Leonel Fernández Reyna, *elected* May 2004, *sworn in* August 2004
Vice-President, Rafael Alburquerque

SELECTED GOVERNMENT MEMBERS *as at May 2007*

Foreign Affairs, Carlos Morales Troncoso
Armed Forces, Gen. Ramon Aquino Garcia
Finance, Vincente Bengoa
Interior and Police, Franklin Almeyda

EMBASSY OF THE DOMINICAN REPUBLIC

139 Inverness Terrace, London W2 6JF
T 020-7727 7091 W www.dominicanembassy.org.uk
Ambassador Extraordinary and Plenipotentiary, HE Anibal de Castro, *apptd* 2005

BRITISH EMBASSY

Edificio Corominas Pepín, Ave 27 de Febrero No 233, Santo Domingo
T (+1) (829) 472 7111 E brit.emb.sadom@codetel.net.do
Ambassador Extraordinary and Plenipotentiary, HE Ian Worthington, *apptd* 2006

ECONOMY AND TRADE

The economy is recovering well from a downturn in 2003 but unemployment and inflation remain problematic. In recent years, tourism and the free trade zones have overtaken agriculture as the mainstay of the economy, and services now account for 58 per cent of GDP. Agriculture accounts for 11 per cent of GDP, and industry for 31 per cent. The main crops are sugar, coffee, cotton, cocoa, tobacco, rice, vegetables and bananas, and the main industrial activities are sugar processing, mining of ferro-nickel, gold and silver, and the production of textiles, cement and tobacco products. Remittances from expatriate workers are a valuable supplement to GDP.

The main trading partner is the USA, which takes 79 per cent of exports and provides half of imports. Principal exports are ferro-nickel, sugar, gold, silver, coffee, cocoa, tobacco, meats and consumer goods. The chief imports are foodstuffs, fuel, cotton and fabrics, chemicals and pharmaceuticals.

GNI – US$21,900m; US$2,460 per capita (2005)
ANNUAL AVERAGE GROWTH OF GDP – 9.3 per cent (2005 est)
INFLATION RATE – 4.2 per cent (2005 est)
UNEMPLOYMENT – 17 per cent (2005 est)
TOTAL EXTERNAL DEBT – US$7,687m (2005 est)
IMPORTS – US$8,300m (2005)
EXPORTS – US$1,400m (2005)

BALANCE OF PAYMENTS

Trade – US$3,481m deficit (2005)
Current Account – US$143m deficit (2005)

Trade with UK	*2005*	*2006*
Imports from UK	£51,820,000	£51,449,000
Exports to UK	£52,881,000	£113,994,000

COMMUNICATIONS

Santo Domingo and Rio Haina are the main seaports. There are 32 airports and airfields, seven of which handle international flights; the principal airport is at Santo Domingo. There are over 12,600km of roads, 6,224km of which are surfaced. There is 57km of railway, plus a further 1,226km operated by private companies. A metro system is under construction in Santo Domingo. Mobile phone distribution, at 3.6 milion in 2005, is over three times greater than main line use, which was 894,500 in the same year.

MEDIA

There are several terrestrial commercial broadcasting stations and 30 multi-channel cable TV operators. The government-owned channel is Radio Television Dominicana (Canal 4). There are more than 200 commercial radio stations as well as two government stations. Press freedom is guaranteed by law.

EAST TIMOR

Republika Demokratika Timor Lorosa'e' – Democratic Republic of Timor-Leste

AREA – 15,007 sq. km. Neighbour: Indonesia (west). The enclave of Oekussi is separated from the rest of East Timor by the Indonesian province of West Timor
CAPITAL – Dili; population, 56,000 (2001 est)
CURRENCY – Currency is that of the USA
POPULATION – 1,062,777 rising at 2.08 per cent per year (2006 est): Timorese (78 per cent), Indonesian (20 per cent) (est)
RELIGION – Christianity (93 per cent), Islam (4 per cent), Hinduism (1 per cent) (est)
LANGUAGE – Tetum, Portuguese (both official), Indonesian, English
POPULATION DENSITY – 66 per sq. km (2005)
URBAN POPULATION – 7.8 per cent (2005 est)
MEDIAN AGE (years) – 20.8 (2006 est)
NATIONAL ANTHEM – 'Patria' ['Fatherland']
NATIONAL DAY – 28 November (Independence Day)
LIFE EXPECTANCY – 66.26 (2006 est)
MORTALITY RATE – 6.24 (2006 est)
BIRTH RATE – 26.99 (2006 est)
INFANT MORTALITY RATE – 45.89 (2006 est)
DEATH PENALTY – No (abolished 1999)
CPI SCORE – 2.6 (2006)
POPULATION BELOW POVERTY LINE – 42 per cent (2003 est)
MILITARY PERSONNEL – 1,286: army 1,250, naval element 36

CLIMATE AND TERRAIN

The republic comprises the eastern half of the island of Timor, plus the enclave of Oekussi on the northern coast. The island, about 296km long and 72km wide, lies at the eastern end of the Indonesian archipelago. The interior is covered in forests and mountains. Elevation extremes range from 2,963m (Mt Tatamailau) at the highest point to 0m (Timor Sea) at the lowest. The climate is tropical.

HISTORY AND POLITICS

East Timor was a Portuguese colony from 1702 until 1975, when Portuguese rule was withdrawn following the 1974 coup in Portugal, but without a formal handover of power. The Revolutionary Front for an Independent East Timor (Fretilin), which supported independence, emerged as the strongest party in the 1975 election, but opposition by supporters of the integration of the territory into Indonesia led to civil war. Despite Fretilin's success in suppressing opposition, Indonesia used the civil war as an excuse to invade in December 1975 and declared East Timor Indonesia's 27th province in July 1976. By 1979, most of East Timor was under Indonesia's control, although Fretlin continued to engage in guerrilla warfare until the 1990s. The UN never recognised the annexation.

Following the fall of the Suharto regime in Indonesia, a plebiscite was held in August 1999 offering East Timor autonomy within Indonesia or independence; in a turnout of 98.5 per cent, 78.5 per cent voted for independence; the Indonesian consultative assembly unanimously ratified the result in October. This result provoked violence by pro-Indonesian militias and Indonesian troops, who murdered hundreds of people and devasted towns, and Indonesia agreed to the deployment in September 1999 of UN peacekeeping troops. The UN security council set up a transitional administration. This was succeeded by the UN Mission of Support in East Timor, whose peacekeeping duties ended in 2005. Peacekeeping troops returned to the country in May 2006 to re-establish law and order after widespread violence broke out following the dismissal in April of almost half the army for going on strike. A non-military UN peacekeeping mission was set up in August.

A legislative election was held in 2001; Fretilin, with 55 seats, was the largest party but did not hold an overall majority. The presidential election in 2002 was won by the former Fretilin leader Jose Xanana Gusmao, who stood as an independent. East Timor became independent on 20 May 2002. The post-independence government was a coalition of Fretilin and Democratic Party members and independents.

A presidential election took place in April and May 2007, and was won in the second round by Jose Ramos-Horta. Fretilin won the largest number of seats in the June 2007 legislative elections, but did not win an overall majority. A coalition was formed lead by the National Congress for Timorese Reconstruction (CNRT) resulting in violent protests by Fretilin supporters.

POLITICAL SYSTEM

The 2002 constitution established a parliamentary democracy. The president is directly elected for a five-year term, renewable only once. The pre-independence constitutent assembly voted to convert itself into the unicameral national parliament without further elections in January 2002. It has 88 members, one from each of the 13 districts elected by a first-past-the-post system and 75 nationally elected by proportional representation; members serve a five-year term. The council of ministers is nominated by the prime minister.

HEAD OF STATE

President, Jose Ramos Horta, *elected* 9 May 2007, *took office* 20 May 2007

SELECTED GOVERNMENT MEMBERS *as at May 2007*

Prime Minister; Defence, Jose Xanana Gusmao
Deputy Prime Minister, Jose Louis Guterres
Finance and Planning, Emilia Pires
Foreign Affairs, Zacarias da Costa

BRITISH EMBASSY

Ambassador Extraordinary and Plenipotentiary, HE Charles Humfrey, *apptd* 2006, resident at Jakarta, Indonesia

ECONOMY AND TRADE

In the post-referendum violence in 1999, an estimated 70 per cent of the infrastructure was destroyed, and 300,000 people fled the country. An internationally funded programme in 2002–5 achieved substantial reconstruction and most refugees had returned by the end of this period, although there were setbacks in 2003 owing to drought and in 2006 due to civil violence and looting. The economy has grown since independence, but over 40 per cent of the population is below the poverty line and unemployment is at a similar level. Exploitation of offshore oil and natural gas deposits generates considerable revenue, but few jobs, as there are no production facilities in East Timor so the oil is piped to Australia. In 2005, the parliament set up a fund to hold all oil revenues for use to benefit future generations.

Services contribute 68 per cent of GDP, industry 23 per cent and agriculture 8 per cent. The main commercial crops are timber, coffee, rice, corn, vegetables, tropical fruits and vanilla. There are some light manufacturing industries and quarrying. Principal exports are oil, coffee, sandalwood and marble. The main imports are food, fuels and machinery. The main trading partner is Indonesia.

GNI – US$588m; US$600 per capita (2005)
ANNUAL AVERAGE GROWTH OF GDP – 1.8 per cent (2005 est)
INFLATION RATE – 1.4 per cent (2005)
UNEMPLOYMENT – 50 per cent (2001 est)

Trade with UK	*2005*	*2006*
Imports from UK	£138,000	£503,000
Exports to UK	£52,000	£18,000

COMMUNICATIONS

There are no railways or waterways, and Dili is the only port. There is one major road, which links the main townships along the northern coast to the east of Dili. There are 5,000km of roads in total, 2,500km of which are surfaced. There are eight airports and airfields; the only international airport is at Dili.

MEDIA

East Timor's national public radio and television services began broadcasting in May 2002. Radio coverage extends to around 90 per cent of the country, but access to television broadcasts is roughly limited to the capital, Dili. Two newspapers are published daily.

ECUADOR

República del Ecuador – Republic of Ecuador

AREA – 283,560 sq. km. Neighbours: Colombia (north-east), Peru (east and south)
CAPITAL – Quito; population, 1,482,447 (2003 est)
MAJOR CITIES – Guayaquil, the chief port; Cuenca; Machala
CURRENCY – Currency is that of the USA
POPULATION – 13,547,510 rising at 1.5 per cent per year (2006 est)
RELIGION – Christianity (95 per cent) (est)
LANGUAGE – Spanish (official), Quechua
POPULATION DENSITY – 48 per sq. km (2005)
URBAN POPULATION – 62.8 per cent (2005 est)
MEDIAN AGE (years) – 23.6 (2006 est)
NATIONAL ANTHEM – 'Salve, Oh Patria' ['We Salute You Our Homeland']
NATIONAL DAY – 10 August (Independence Day)
LIFE EXPECTANCY (years) – 76.42 (2006 est)
MORTALITY RATE – 4.23 (2006 est)
BIRTH RATE – 22.29 (2006 est)
INFANT MORTALITY RATE – 22.87 (2006 est)
DEATH PENALTY – No (abolished 1906)
CPI SCORE – 2.3 (2006)
POPULATION BELOW POVERTY LINE – 41 per cent (2003)

CLIMATE AND TERRAIN

Ecuador is an equatorial state lying on the north-west coast of South America. Its territory includes the Galápagos Islands in the Pacific Ocean. It has five different climatic zones and is one of the most bio-diverse countries on earth. The Andes run north to south through the centre of the country, dividing the coastal plain in the west from the low-lying rainforest in the east. Elevation extremes range from 0m (Pacific Ocean) at the lowest point to 6,267m (Chimborazo) at the highest. Other Andean peaks include Cotopaxi (5,896m) and Cayambe (5,790m) in the Eastern Cordillera. Ecuador is located in an earthquake zone and has two active volcanoes (Pichincha, only 12km away from the capital, and Tungurahua). The average annual temperature in Quito is 15°C.

HISTORY AND POLITICS

The former kingdom of Quito was conquered by the Incas of Peru in the 15th century. In 1534, Francisco Pizarro's (1475–1541) acquisitions led to the inclusion of the present territory of Ecuador in the Spanish viceroyalty of Quito. Independence from Spain was achieved in a revolutionary war that culminated in the battle of Mount Pichincha (1822). Ecuador then formed part of Gran Colombia with Colombia, Panama and Venezuela but left this union to become a fully independent state in 1830. Since then, the country has experienced periods of political instability interspersed with dictatorships or military rule. The country has been a democracy since 1979.

The oil-generated economic and social transformation from the 1970s onwards also caused rapid inflation and increased foreign debt, and the austerity measures introduced by various governments in the 1980s and 1990s caused widespread civil unrest. In recent years, these problems have worsened due to economic recession, provoking strikes and demonstrations. The most notable of these were by indigenous people, who have benefited least from the oil boom but been hardest hit by the economic downturn. Civil unrest has forced three presidents from office in eight years.

In the October 2006 legislative election, the Institutional Renewal Party of Democratic Action (PRIAN) was the largest party with 28 seats, but without an overall majority. The presidential election was won in the second round by the Country Alliance candidate Rafael Correa. President Correa's proposal of constitutional reform was approved by referendum in April 2007 and elections to a 130-member constituent national assembly were scheduled for 30 September.

POLITICAL SYSTEM

The 1998 constitution provides for an executive president who is directly elected for a single four-year term. There is a unicameral national congress which has 121 members, 101 elected on a provincial basis and 20 elected on a national basis, all for a four-year term. The republic is divided into 22 provinces.

HEAD OF STATE
President, Rafael Correa *took office* 15 January 2007
Vice-President, Lenin Moreno

SELECTED GOVERNMENT MEMBERS *as at May 2007*
Finance and Economy, Ricardo Patino
Foreign Relations, Maria Fernanda Espinosa
National Defence, Lorena Escudero Durán

EMBASSY OF ECUADOR
lat 3B, 3 Hans Crescent, London SW1X 0LS
T 020-7584 1367 E eecugranbretania@mmrree.gov.ec
Ambassador Extraordinary and Plenipotentiary, HE Dr Teodoro Maldonado Riera, *apptd* 2006

BRITISH EMBASSY
Citiplaza Building, Av. Naciones Unidas y Republica de El alvador, Piso 14, , Quito
T (+593) (2) 2970 800 britembq@interactive.net.ec
W www.britembquito.org.ec
Ambassador Extraordinary and Plenipotentiary, HE Bernard Whiteside, *apptd* 2006

DEFENCE

The army has over 30 main battle tanks, 113 armoured personnel carriers and 20 attack helicopters. The navy has 2 submarines, 2 frigates, 6 corvettes, and 15 patrol and coastal combatant vessels at two bases. The air force has 3 combat aircraft.
MILITARY BUDGET – US$653m (2006)
MILITARY PERSONNEL – 56,500: army 47,000, navy 5,500, air force 4,000; paramilitaries 270
CONSCRIPTION DURATION – 12 months (selective)

ECONOMY AND TRADE

Oil is Ecuador's principal export, accounting for pproximately 40 per cent of export earnings and over 30 per cent of government revenue in recent years. The conomy is vulnerable to oil price fluctuations, however, nd a sharp drop in prices helped to plunge the country into a severe economic crisis in 1999. Structural reforms in 2000, including the adoption of the US dollar in place of the sucre, stabilised the economy; growth has resumed nd inflation has dropped in recent years. However, the government in office from 2005–6 reversed policies intended to cushion the economy from oil price fluctuations, using the funds released for social relief programmes, as nearly half the population is below the poverty line.

After oil, agriculture is the most important sector of the conomy, providing products both for export and for the food and timber processing industries. The main products for export are oil, bananas, cut flowers and fish (shrimp). The main imports are vehicles, medicines, telecommunications equipment and electricity. Principal trading partners are the USA, other Latin American ountries, China and Germany.
GNI – US$34,700m; US$2,620 per capita (2005)
ANNUAL AVERAGE GROWTH OF GDP – 4.7 per cent (2005 est)
INFLATION RATE – 2.1 per cent (2005 est)
UNEMPLOYMENT – 10.7 per cent (2005 est)
TOTAL EXTERNAL DEBT – US$18,090m (2005 est)
IMPORTS – US$10,300m (2005)
EXPORTS – US$10,100m (2005)

BALANCE OF PAYMENTS
Trade – US$321m surplus (2004)
Current Account – US$157m deficit (2004)

Trade with UK	*2005*	*2006*
Imports from UK	£30,763,000	£41,052,000
Exports to UK	£41,980,000	£43,705,000

COMMUNICATIONS

There are 43,197km of permanent roads, 6,467km of which are surfaced, and there are 966km of railways. The road and rail networks are largely to the west of the Andes. Travel to the east is mostly by air, with internal services between all major towns. There are 285 airports and airfields, of which 85 have surfaced runways, and international flights operate to Quito and Guayaquil. The main ports are Guayaquil and Esmeraldas. The land-line telephone system is being expanded but the service is unreliable. Mobile phone distribution, at 6.2 million subscribers in 2005, encompasses nearly half the population.

EDUCATION AND HEALTH

Elementary education is free of charge and compulsory.
LITERACY RATE – 91 per cent (2004 est)
GROSS ENROLMENT RATIO (percentage of relevant age group) – primary 117 per cent; secondary 61 per cent (2005 est)
HEALTH EXPENDITURE (per capita) – US$127 (2004)
HOSPITAL BEDS (per 1,000 people) – 1.5 (2000–5)

MEDIA AND CULTURE

Newspapers include *El Mercurio, El Universo* and *Diario Hoy.* There are four commercial television stations, including Ecuavision, Teleamazon, ETV Telerama and TC Television. Radio Nacional del Ecuador is the government-owned radio station. By law, the media is required to accede to government demands for free space or air time so programmes by the state are occasionally broadcast.

The capital Quito has been a UNESCO World Heritage Site since 1978, while South America's most famous market, which pre-dates Inca times, can be found in the small town of Otavalo.

The most popular sport is football, which reflects the growing success of the country's national team, which reached the second round of the World Cup for the first time in 2006. Tennis also attracts a lot of support, since the success of former world number one Pancho Segura (*b.* 1921).

GALÁPAGOS ISLANDS

The Galápagos (Giant Tortoise) Islands, forming the province of the Archipelago de Colón, were annexed by Ecuador in 1832. The archipelago lies in the Pacific, about 800km from the mainland. There are 12 large and several hundred smaller islands with a total area of about 7,769 sq. km and an estimated population of 18,640. The capital is Puerto Barquerizo Moreno, on San Cristóbal Island. Although the archipelago lies on the equator, the temperature of the surrounding water is well below equatorial average owing to the Humboldt current. The province consists for the most part of national park territory, where unique marine birds, iguanas, and the giant tortoises are conserved. The islands' wildlife provided naturalist Charles Darwin (1809–82) with inspiration and research material for his landmark theory of natural selection, explained in *The Origin of the Species* (1859). There is some local subsistence farming; the main industry, apart from tourism, is tuna and lobster fishing.

EGYPT

Jumhuriyat Misr al-Arabiyah – Arab Republic of Egypt

AREA – 1,001,450 sq. km. Neighbours: Sudan (south), Libya (west), Gaza Strip and Israel (east)
CAPITAL – Cairo; population, 7,500,000 (2006 est), stands on the Nile about 14 miles from the head of the delta
MAJOR CITIES – Alexandria, founded 332 BC by Alexander the Great, was the capital for over 1,000 years; Giza; Shubra el-Khayma; Port Said; Suez
CURRENCY – Egyptian pound (£E) of 100 piastres or 1,000 millièmes
POPULATION – 78,887,007 rising at 1.75 per cent per year (2006 est); Egyptian (98 per cent) (est). The remainder includes the Bedouin, or nomadic Arabs of the Western and Eastern deserts, who are now mainly demi-sedentary tent-dwellers. Another element is the Nubian of the Nile Valley, of mixed Arab and African blood
RELIGION – Islam (91 per cent), Christianity (8 per cent) (est)
LANGUAGE – Arabic (official), English, French
POPULATION DENSITY – 74 per sq. km (2005)
URBAN POPULATION – 42.3 per cent (2005 est)
MEDIAN AGE (years) – 24 (2006 est)
NATIONAL ANTHEM – 'Biladi' ['My Homeland']
NATIONAL DAY – 23 July (Revolution Day)
LIFE EXPECTANCY (years) – 71.29 (2006 est)
MORTALITY RATE – 5.23 (2006 est)
BIRTH RATE – 22.94 (2006 est)
INFANT MORTALITY RATE – 31.33 (2006 est)
DEATH PENALTY – Yes
CPI SCORE – 3.3 (2006)
POPULATION BELOW POVERTY LINE – 20 per cent (2005 est)
LITERACY RATE – 55.6 per cent (2004 est)
GROSS ENROLMENT RATIO (percentage of relevant age group) – primary 101 per cent; secondary 87 per cent; tertiary 33 per cent (2005 est)
HEALTH EXPENDITURE (per capita) – US$64 (2004)
HOSPITAL BEDS (per 1,000 people) – 2.2 (2000–5)

CLIMATE AND TERRAIN

The country is mainly flat but there are mountainous areas in the south-west, along the Red Sea coast and in the south of the Sinai peninsula. Elevation extremes range from 2,629m (Mt Catherine, Sinai) at the highest point to −132m (Qattara Depression) at the lowest. Most of the land is desert and the Nile valley and delta were the only fertile areas until the construction of the Aswan Dam allowed areas of desert to be reclaimed. West of the Nile Valley is the Western Desert, containing some depressions whose springs irrigate oases. The Eastern Desert between the Nile and the mountains along the Red Sea coast is mostly plateaux dissected by wadis (dry watercourses). The average daily temperature ranges from 18°C to 30°C.

HISTORY AND POLITICS

The unification of the kingdoms of Lower Egypt and Upper Egypt *c.*3100 BC marked the establishment of the Egyptian state, with Memphis as its capital. Egypt was ruled for nearly 2,800 years by a succession of 31 pharaonic dynasties, which built the pyramids at Giza. Egypt's independence was lost to the Assyrians in 666 BC, and it was conquered by the Persians in 525 BC and by Alexander the Great in 332 BC. Subsequently ruled by Alexander's general Ptolemy and his descendants, it wa conquered and ruled by Rome (30 BC to AD 324) an then by the Byzantine Empire. In AD 640 Egypt wa subjugated by Arab Muslim invaders. In 1517 the countr was incorporated into the Ottoman Empire, under whic it remained until the early 19th century. Britain occupie Egypt in 1882, and a British protectorate over Egyp lasted from 1914 to 1922, when Sultan Ahmed Fuad wa proclaimed King of Egypt. Full independence wa achieved in 1936. In 1953 the monarchy was depose and Egypt became a republic.

Egypt was involved in the Arab-Israeli wars in 1948 1967 and 1973. In the 1967 war (the June War/the Si Day War), the Sinai peninsula was lost to Israel. Sinai wa returned to Egypt in 1982 under the 1979 treaty tha resulted from the Camp David talks (1978–9) an formally terminated the 31-year-old state of war betwee the two countries. The treaty led to strained relations wit other Arab nations until the mid-1980s.

President Hosni Mubarak, who took office after th assassination of President Sadat in 1981, played an activ part in the Middle East peace process in the 1990s bu was unable to suppress internal terrorism by Islami fundamentalists. Frustration and resentment at the lack o political freedom has found expression in publi demonstrations in recent years. President Mubarak was re elected for a fifth term in September 2005. In th legislative elections of the same year, the ruling Nationa Democratic Party (NDP) won an overall majority; 88 seat (20 per cent of the total) were won by members of th Muslim Brotherhood standing as independents because o the ban on religious political parties.

INSURGENCIES

Militant Islamic fundamentalists emerged in the 1980s Their campaign against the government becam increasingly violent from the early 1990s, and wa eventually directed against foreign tourists as well a domestic targets. Although the largest fundamentalis organisation, Gamaat-i-Islamiya, renounced violence i 1999, attacks continue, often aimed at foreign tourists.

POLITICAL SYSTEM

The 1971 constitution was amended in 2005 to allow fo direct elections to the presidency and in 2007 t introduce changes increasing the president's powers. I provides for an executive president who appoints th council of ministers and determines government polic The president is directly elected from multiple candidate (who must meet strict criteria) and serves a six-year term The unicameral legislature is the *Majlis al-Sha'ab* (people' assembly) which has 454 members, 444 directly electe and ten appointed by the president to increase the ethni or religious diversity of the representatives; all serve five-year term. The *Majlis al-Shura* (consultative counci has an advisory role; its 264 members include 176 wh are directly elected and 88 presidential appointees, all serv ing a six-year term. Religious political parties are banned

HEAD OF STATE
President, Mohammed Hosni Mubarak, *elected* 1981, *re-elected* 1987, 1993, 1999, 2005

SELECTED GOVERNMENT MEMBERS *as at May 2007*
Prime Minister, Economy, Ahmed Nazif
Defence and Military Production, Field Marshal Mohammad Hussein Tantawi
Finance, Youssef Boutros Ghali

oreign Affairs, Ahmed Ali abu el-Ghait
nterior, Maj.-Gen. Habib al-Adli

MBASSY OF THE ARAB REPUBLIC OF EGYPT
6 South Street, London W1K 1DW
020-7499 2401 E embassy@embassyofegypt.co.uk
mbassador Extraordinary and Plenipotentiary, HE Gehad Madi, *apptd* 2004

RITISH EMBASSY
Ahmed Ragheb Street, Garden City, Cairo
(+20) (2) 794 0852 E info@britishembassy.org.eg
V www.britishembassy.org.eg
mbassador Extraordinary and Plenipotentiary, HE Sir Derek Plumbly, *apptd* 2003

RITISH COUNCIL
92 El Nil Street, Agouza, Cairo
(+20) (2) 300 1666 W www.britishcouncil.org/egypt
irector, Paul Smith

EFENCE

he army has 3,855 main battle tanks, 520 armoured nfantry fighting vehicles and 4,750 armoured personnel arriers. The navy has 1 destroyer, 10 frigates, 4 ubmarines and 41 patrol and coastal vessels at eight ases. The air force has 471 combat aircraft and 115 rmed helicopters.

ILITARY EXPENDITURE – US$4,200m (2006 est)
ILITARY PERSONNEL – 468,500: army 340,000, navy 18,500, air force 30,000, Air Defence Command 80,000; paramilitaries 330,000
ONSCRIPTION DURATION – 12 months to three years (selective)

CONOMY AND TRADE

conomic liberalisation in recent years has promoted rowth in GDP but living standards for most of the opulation remain low, with nearly a quarter below the overty line. There is a growing budget deficit, partly wing to price subsidies on basic necessities, and public ebt was more than 100 per cent of GDP in 2006. lthough the dams on the Nile have expanded the area of nd under cultivation, other factors, such as population rowth, are putting resources under pressure.

The services sector contributes 50 per cent to GDP and mploys 51 per cent of the workforce; tourism is the rgest component of this sector, visitor numbers having ncreased by over 50 per cent since the late 1990s. ndustry accounts for 35 per cent of GDP and 17 per cent f employment, but despite increasing industrialisation, griculture still employs 32 per cent of the workforce, lthough it contributes only 15 per cent of GDP. Egypt is net importer of foodstuffs, especially grain, and a food ecurity programme has been set up with the aim of chieving self-sufficiency. The main cash crop is cotton, of hich Egypt is one of the world's main producers. Other nportant crops are rice, maize, wheat, vegetables, fruit nd livestock. Industry is centred on processing oil, cotton nd other agricultural products. Oil is the backbone of the conomy and, alongside considerable reserves of natural as and the hydroelectric power produced by the Aswan nd High dams, helps to make Egypt self-sufficient in nergy.

The main trading partners are the USA, EU countries, audi Arabia, China and Syria. Principal exports are crude il and petroleum products, cotton, textiles, metal roducts and chemicals. The main imports are machinery and equipment, foodstuffs, chemicals, wood products and fuels.

GNI – US$93,000m; US$1,260 per capita (2005)
ANNUAL AVERAGE GROWTH OF GDP – 4.9 per cent (2005 est)
INFLATION RATE – 4.9 per cent (2005 est)
UNEMPLOYMENT – 9.5 per cent (2005 est)
TOTAL EXTERNAL DEBT – US$35,260m (2005 est)
IMPORTS – US$19,900m (2005)
EXPORTS – US$10,700m (2005)

BALANCE OF PAYMENTS
Trade – US$6,576m deficit (2004)
Current Account – US$3,922m surplus (2004)

Trade with UK	*2005*	*2006*
Imports from UK	£546,785,000	£579,169,000
Exports to UK	£373,535,000	£676,744,000

COMMUNICATIONS

Egypt has 5,063km of railways and 92,000km of roads, 75,000km of which are surfaced. Road and rail networks link the Nile valley and delta with the main development areas east and west of the river, but there are few routes in the interior. There are 88 airports and airfields; the principal airports are at Cairo, Luxor, Alexandria, Aswan and Hurgadah. Egypt has 3,500km of waterways, including the River Nile, the Alexandra-Cairo waterway, numerous small canals in the Nile delta, and the Suez Canal, which was re-opened in 1975. The main seaports are Alexandria, Damietta and Port Said on the Mediterranean Sea and Suez on the Red Sea. The telephone system was modernised in the 1990s; there were 10 million main-line, 14 million mobile phone and 5 million internet subscribers in 2005.

MEDIA

The Egyptian media takes a central role in the Arab world and its newspapers are some of the most influential in the region. There are two state-run national television channels and six regional channels. Egypt has an important satellite television industry (Egypt was the first Arab country to have its own satellite, Nilesat 101) that is watched all over the Arab-speaking world. In 2001, the country's first three private television stations went on air. The state has a monopoly on all radio broadcasting. The government has actively encouraged foreign media to base themselves in Egypt by setting up a free media zone in 2000 that offers economic incentives and access to its media infrastructure.

CULTURE

Egyptian culture dates back five thousand years to one of the earliest-known civilisations on Earth; ancient Egyptian hieroglyphic scripts provide some of the world's oldest records of written communication. The country has experienced ages of Hellenism, Christianity, Arab and Islamic culture and remains most famous for the Pyramids of Giza, Library of Alexandria and the art and architecture of its ancient periods (beginning in the fourth millennium BC and waning around 31 BC when Greece fell to the Romans). The modern-day Egyptian state retains cultural significance. The country has the highest number of Nobel laureates in Africa, including author Naguib Mahfouz (1911–2006) and politician Boutros Boutros-Ghali (*b.* 1922); actor Omar Sharif (*b.* 1932) is an Academy Award winner, while Cairo is home to Al-Ahly, the most widely supported football club in Africa.

EL SALVADOR

República de El Salvador – Republic of El Salvador

AREA – 21,040 sq. km. Neighbours: Guatemala (north-west), Honduras (north-east and east)
CAPITAL – San Salvador; population, 2,198,200 (2005 est)
MAJOR CITIES – Soyapango; Mejicanos; San Miguel; Santa Ana
CURRENCY – US dollar (US$) of 100 cents
POPULATION – 6,822,378 rising at 1.72 per cent per year (2006 est)
RELIGION – Roman Catholicism (57 per cent), Protestantism (21 per cent) (est)
LANGUAGE – Spanish (official), Nahua
POPULATION DENSITY – 332 per sq. km (2005)
URBAN POPULATION – 60.1 per cent (2005 est)
MEDIAN AGE (years) – 21.8 (2006 est)
NATIONAL ANTHEM – 'Himno Nacional de El Salvador' ['National Anthem of El Salvador']
NATIONAL DAY – 15 September (Independence Day)
LIFE EXPECTANCY (years) – 71.49 (2006 est)
MORTALITY RATE – 5.78 (2006 est)
BIRTH RATE – 26.61 (2006 est)
INFANT MORTALITY RATE – 24.39 (2006 est)
DEATH PENALTY – Yes*
CPI SCORE – 4.0 (2006)
POPULATION BELOW POVERTY LINE – 36.1 per cent (2003 est)
MILITARY PERSONNEL – 15,500: army 13,850, navy 700, air force 950; paramilitaries 12,000
CONSCRIPTION DURATION – 12 months (selective)

CLIMATE AND TERRAIN

El Salvador extends along the Pacific coast of Central America for 307km. The country is very mountainous (much of the interior has an average altitude of 600m) and many of its peaks are volcanoes; most are extinct, but Ilamatepec (or Santa Ana) erupted in 2005. There are also numerous volcanic lakes. Elevation extremes range from 2,730m (Cerro El Pital) at the highest point to 0m (Pacific Ocean) at the lowest. Average temperatures vary with altitude, with coastal areas tending to be hotter. The average annual temperature in San Salvador is 23°C. Earthquakes and volcanic activity are common, and the country is susceptible to hurricanes and tropical storms.

HISTORY AND POLITICS

El Salvador was part of the Aztec kingdom conquered in 1524 by Pedro de Alvarado, and formed part of the Spanish viceroyalty of Guatemala until 1821. It became part of the United Provinces of Central America in 1823 until the federation's dissolution, and became fully independent in 1841.

There was political unrest in the 1970s, and guerrilla activity by the left-wing Farabundo Martí National Liberation Front (FMLN), which intensified from 1977 amid reports of human rights abuses by government-backed militias. Decades of military rule ended in 1979, but elections in 1982 were boycotted by left-wing parties and the right-wing National Republican Alliance (ARENA) took office. The civil war between the FMLN and the US-backed government lasted throughout the 1980s, until a UN-sponsored peace agreement was signed in 1991. The FMLN was recognised as a political party, and it won a few seats in the 1994 election, which returned ARENA to power. Since then, the FMLN has increased its vote, often being the largest party in parliament, but it has never held office, as ARENA has always formed coalition governments with smaller right-wing parties.

In 2004, Antonio Saca of ARENA won the presidential election with 57 per cent of the vote. Following the 2006 legislative elections, ARENA was the largest party in the legislative assembly and continued its coalition with the National Conciliation Party to create a conservative majority.

POLITICAL SYSTEM
Under the 1983 constitution, the executive president is directly elected for a five-year term. The unicameral legislative assembly has 84 members, who are directly elected for a three-year term. The country is divided into 14 departments.

HEAD OF STATE
President, Elias Antonio Saca, *elected* 21 March 2004, *took office* 1 June 2004
Vice-President, Ana Vilma Albanez de Escobar

SELECTED GOVERNMENT MEMBERS *as at May 2007*
Defence, Gen. Otto Romero Orellana
Economy, Yolanda Mayora de Gavidia
Foreign Affairs, Francisco Lainez
Interior, Rene Figueroa

EMBASSY OF EL SALVADOR
8 Dorset Square, London NW1 6PU
T 020-7224 9800
E embajadalondres@rree.gob.sv
Ambassador Extraordinary and Plenipotentiary, HE Dr Vladimiro P. Villalta, *apptd* 2005

BRITISH AMBASSADOR
HE Ian Hughes, resident at Guatemala City, Guatemala

DEFENCE

The army has 51 armoured personnel carriers and 1[illegible] reconnaissance vehicles. The navy has 39 patrol and coastal combatant vessels. The air force has 21 combat aircraft.
MILITARY BUDGET – US$106m (2006)
MILITARY PERSONNEL – 15,500: army 13,850, navy 700, air force 950; paramilitaries 12,000
CONSCRIPTION DURATION – 12 months (selective)

ECONOMY AND TRADE

The country is one of the most industrialised in Central America and has the third largest economy despite being the smallest country and having few natural resources. Recovery after the civil war has been set back by a series of natural disasters since the late 1990s, resulting in a sluggish economy and 35 per cent of the population living below the poverty line. Remittances from El Salvadoreans working abroad (equivalent to over 16 per cent of GDP) and foreign aid help to offset the large trade deficit. The free trade agreement with the USA and other Central American states that came into effect in 2006 is strengthening exports and government diversification efforts have promoted textile production, international port services and tourism.

Agriculture contributes 10 per cent to GDP and employs 17 per cent of the workforce. The principal agricultural products are coffee, sugar, maize, rice, beans, oilseed, cotton, beef, dairy products and shrimps. Industr ontributes 29 per cent of GDP, mostly through food rocessing, beverages, petroleum, chemicals, fertilizer, extiles, furniture and light metals. Services contribute 61 er cent of GDP.

The main trading partners are the USA, Guatemala, Honduras and Mexico. Principal exports are offshore ssembly products, coffee, sugar, shrimps, textiles, hemicals and electricity. The chief imports are raw naterials, consumer goods, capital goods, fuels, foodstuffs, etroleum and electricity.

GNI – US$16,800m; US$2,450 per capita (2005)
ANNUAL AVERAGE GROWTH OF GDP – 2.8 per cent (2005 est)
INFLATION RATE – 4.7 per cent (2005 est)
UNEMPLOYMENT – 6.5 per cent (2005 est)
TOTAL EXTERNAL DEBT – US$8,087m (2005 est)
IMPORTS – US$5,400m (2005)
EXPORTS – US$1,600m (2005)

BALANCE OF PAYMENTS
Trade – US$2,619m deficit (2004)
Current Account – US$612m deficit (2004)

Trade with UK	*2005*	*2006*
Imports from UK	£34,517,000	£25,813,000
Exports to UK	£5,614,000	£4,331,000

COMMUNICATIONS

he principal ports are Cutuco and Acajutla, and ports in Honduras and Guatemala are also used. There are 0,886km of roads, of which 2,827km are surfaced. The an-American Highway from the Guatemalan frontier asses through Santa Ana and San Salvador, continuing to he Honduran frontier. The rail network has not been in peration since 2005 because of lack of maintenance. here are 75 airports and airfields, although only four ave surfaced runways. There is an international airport at an Salvador.

EDUCATION AND HEALTH

rimary education is state-run and is compulsory and free f charge.

LITERACY RATE – 79.7 per cent (2004 est)
GROSS ENROLMENT RATIO (percentage of relevant age group) – primary 113 per cent; secondary 63 per cent; tertiary 19 per cent (2005 est)
HEALTH EXPENDITURE (per capita) – US$184 (2004)
HOSPITAL BEDS (per 1,000 people) – 1.6 (2002)

MEDIA

here are three major commercial television channels perating in El Salvador: Teledos, Canal Seis and TV oce. There are hundreds of private radio stations (70 perate in San Salvador alone). Press freedom is uaranteed by the country's constitution.

EQUATORIAL GUINEA

epública de Guinea Ecuatorial – Republic of Equatorial Guinea

AREA – 28,051 sq. km. Neighbours: Cameroon (north), Gabon (east and south); comprises a mainland area (Río Muni) and several islands in the Gulf of Guinea, principally Bioko (40km off the coast of Cameroon) and Annabón.
CAPITAL – Malabo; population, 60,065 (1994) on Bioko Island
MAJOR TOWNS – Bata is the principal town and port of Río Muni; Ebeblyln
CURRENCY – Franc CFA of 100 centimes
POPULATION – 540,109 rising at 2.05 per cent per year (2006 est)
RELIGION – Christianity (93 per cent), indigenous religions (5 per cent) (est)
LANGUAGE – Spanish (official), French (official), Fang, Bubi, Ibo
POPULATION DENSITY – 18 per sq. km (2005)
URBAN POPULATION – 50 per cent (2005 est)
MEDIAN AGE (years) – 18.8 (2006 est)
NATIONAL ANTHEM – 'Caminemos Pisando la Senda' ['Let's Walk Down the Path']
NATIONAL DAY – 12 October (Independence Day)
LIFE EXPECTANCY – 49.54 (2006 est)
MORTALITY RATE – 15.06 (2006 est)
BIRTH RATE – 35.59 (2006 est)
INFANT MORTALITY RATE – 89.21 (2006 est)
HIV/AIDS ADULT PREVALENCE – 3.4 per cent (2001 est)
DEATH PENALTY – Yes
CPI SCORE – 2.1 (2006)
MILITARY BUDGET – US$7m (2005 est)
MILITARY PERSONNEL – 1,320: army 1,100, navy 120, air force 100
LITERACY RATE – 84.2 per cent (2004 est)

CLIMATE AND TERRAIN

There are two provinces: Bioko Island and the mainland, where 80 per cent of the population lives. Bioko is of volcanic origin. The mainland rises from a narrow coastal plain to a mountainous interior plateau, and is covered in dense vegetation. The climate is tropical, with a rainy season from July to January on Bioko and from April to May and October to December on the mainland. Elevation extremes range from 3,008m (Pico Basile) at the highest point to 0m (Atlantic Ocean) at the lowest.

HISTORY AND POLITICS

The island of Fernando Po (Bioko) was claimed by the Portuguese in 1494 and held until 1778, when it was ceded to Spain. The mainland territory of Río Muni came under Spanish rule in 1885, and the whole colony became known as Spanish Guinea. Constituted as two provinces of metropolitan Spain in 1959, the colony became autonomous in 1963, and fully independent in 1968 under its present name.

Francisco Macias Nguema won the first multiparty elections but in 1970 established a one-party state. His regime was brutal and he was overthrown in 1979 in a military coup led by his nephew, Col. Obiang Nguema. A military regime was established after the coup and only presidential nominees could stand in the 1983 and 1988 elections. Constitutional amendments were introduced in 1991 to allow multiparty elections, and ten opposition parties were legalised, operating alongside the ruling Equatorial Guinea Democratic Party (PDGE). However, President Obiang Nguema and the PDGE have retained power since 1992; most elections have been boycotted by the opposition parties because of election irregularities and intimidation. The regime has been accused of human rights abuses and the suppression of political opposition, and in 2003 opposition leaders set up a government-in-exile in Spain.

President Obiang Nguema won the 2002 presidential election unopposed, opposition candidates having withdrawn after voting began, alleging irregularities. In the 2004 legislative election, the PDGE and its allies took 98 out of 100 seats in parliament. In August 2006 the government resigned en masse after being accused of corruption and poor leadership by the president; it was replaced a few days later.

POLITICAL SYSTEM
The 1991 constitution introduced a multiparty system. The president is directly elected for a seven-year term. The unicameral legislature, the house of representatives of the people, has 100 members, who are directly elected for a five-year term.

HEAD OF STATE
President, Brig.-Gen. Teodoro Obiang Nguema Mbasogo, *took office* August 1979, *re-elected* 1989, 1996, 2002

SELECTED GOVERNMENT MEMBERS *as at May 2007*
Prime Minister, Ricardo Mangue Obama Nfubea
Economy, Jaime Ela Ndong
Foreign Affairs, International Cooperation and Francophone Affairs, Pastor Micha Ondo Bile
Interior and Local Corporations, Clemente Engonga Nguema Onguene
Defence, Gen. Antonio Mba Nguema Mikwe

EMBASSY OF THE REPUBLIC OF EQUATORIAL GUINEA
13 Park Place, London SW1A 1LP
T 020-7499 6867 W www.embarege-londres.org
Ambassador Extraordinary and Plenipotentiary, Agustin Nze Nfumu, *apptd* 2003

BRITISH AMBASSADOR
HE Richard Gozney, *apptd* 2005, resident at Abuja, Nigeria

ECONOMY AND TRADE
Large oil and natural gas deposits discovered off Bioko in the 1990s have transformed the economy, which enjoyed a growth rate of 18 per cent in 2005; the country is the third largest oil exporter in sub-Saharan Africa. It also has the reputation of being one of the most corrupt countries in the world; oil exploitation have not benefited much of the population as most businesses are owned by government officials or their families and, despite the oil revenues, the country has external debt.

Industry contributes 93 per cent of GDP, agriculture 3 per cent and services 4 per cent. Agriculture, once the mainstay of the economy, has declined to subsistence level owing to neglect and lack of investment. The main crops are coffee, cocoa, rice, fruit, nuts, livestock and timber. Industrial activities include oil and natural gas production, fishing and timber processing. The main trading partners are the USA, Spain, China and Italy. Principal exports are petroleum, methanol, timber and cocoa. The main imports are oil industry equipment and other industrial equipment.

GNI – US$400m (2003); US$930 per capita (2003)
ANNUAL AVERAGE GROWTH OF GDP – 18.6 per cent (2005 est)
INFLATION RATE – 5 per cent (2005 est)
TOTAL EXTERNAL DEBT – US$353m (2005 est)
IMPORTS – US$2,050m (2005)
EXPORTS – US$6,950m (2005)

Trade with UK	*2005*	*2006*
Imports from UK	£38,878,000	£45,434,000
Exports to UK	£16,691,000	£17,183,000

0.6	WORLD LOWEST
	per cent of GDP spent on education

Source: Economist Intelligence Unit

MEDIA
Television and radio broadcasts are state-controlled an the government owns the only television and radi stations, Television Nacional and Radio Nacional d Guinea Ecuatorial. The main newspaper, *Ebano,* is state owned. A few privately owned publications appe sporadically.

ERITREA

Hagere Eretra – State of Eritrea

AREA – 121,320 sq. km. Neighbours: Sudan (north an west), Ethiopia (south), Djibouti (south-east)
CAPITAL – Asmara; population, 500,600 (2002 est)
MAJOR TOWNS – Keren; Mendefera; Dek'emhare
CURRENCY – Nakfa
POPULATION – 4,786,994 rising at 2.47 per cent per year (2006 est); Tigray-Tigrinya (50 per cent), Tigre and Kunama (40 per cent), Afar (4 per cent), Saho (3 per cent), other (3 per cent) (est)
RELIGION – Islam (50 per cent), Coptic Christianity (4 per cent), indigenous religions (2 per cent) (est)
LANGUAGE – Arabic, English, Tigrinya
POPULATION DENSITY – 44 per sq. km (2005)
URBAN POPULATION – 20.8 per cent (2005 est)
MEDIAN AGE (years) – 17.8 (2006 est)
NATIONAL ANTHEM – 'Ertra, Ertra, Ertra' ['Eritrea, Eritrea, Eritrea']
NATIONAL DAY – 24 May (Independence Day)
LIFE EXPECTANCY – 59.03 (2006 est)
MORTALITY RATE – 9.6 (2006 est)
BIRTH RATE – 34.33 (2006 est)
INFANT MORTALITY RATE – 46.3 (2006 est)
HIV/AIDS ADULT PREVALENCE – 2.7 per cent (200 est)
DEATH PENALTY – Yes
CPI SCORE – 2.9 (2006)
POPULATION BELOW POVERTY LINE – 50 per cen (2004 est)
GROSS ENROLMENT RATIO (percentage of relevant age group) – primary 64 per cent; secondary 31 per cent; tertiary 1 per cent (2005 est)
HEALTH EXPENDITURE (per capita) – US$10 (2004)

CLIMATE AND TERRAIN
The northern end of the Ethiopian Highlands exten into central Eritrea, where the average altitude is ov 2,000m. The mountains fall in the west to a plateau, the rise to the hills on the Sudan border. To the east of th mountains, the land falls to the narrow coastal plain. Th coastal strip extending to the Djibouti border is lov lying, the border with Ethiopia running along the edge the Denakil Desert. Elevation extremes range fro

,018m (Soira) at the highest point to –75m (Denakil)epression) at the lowest. The climate changes with the ountry's varying altitudes, from temperatures averaging 6°C in the mountains and 30°C on the arid coastal lain.

IISTORY AND POLITICS

'rom the mid-16th century, the area was under the ontrol of the Ottoman Empire. It was occupied by Italy ı the late 19th century and was the base for the 1936 talian invasion of Abyssinia (now Ethiopia). After the :alian defeat in North Africa in 1941, Eritrea became a 3ritish protectorate until 15 September 1952, when a ederation with Ethiopia was created by the UN. In 1962, :thiopia annexed Eritrea.

The Eritrean Liberation Front (ELF) began a campaign or independence in 1961, fighting a guerrilla war from ıe 1960s. The Eritrean People's Liberation Front (a reakaway faction of the ELF) emerged as the dominant ebel group in the 1980s and joined with Ethiopian esistance groups, including the People's Front for)emocracy and Justice (PFDJ), to help overthrow the Aengistu regime in 1991. The EPLF secured the whole f Eritrea and formed a provisional government. The new 'FDJ-led government in Ethiopia agreed to an Eritrean eferendum on independence, which was held in April 993 and recorded a 99.89 per cent vote in favour. ndependence was declared on 24 May 1993.

Following independence, a transitional government for four-year period was formed under Issaias Afwerki, and ıe EPLF became the ruling political party, renaming self the People's Front for Democracy and Justice (PFDJ) ı 1994. The post-independence regime has become ıcreasingly authoritarian; although a new constitution /as introduced in 1997, no presidential election has ıken place since independence, and legislative elections :heduled for 2001 did not take place and have not been escheduled.

OREIGN RELATIONS

ince independence, Eritrea has been involved in disputes /ith Yemen over the Hanish and Mohabaka islands in the .ed Sea (possession divided between Yemen and Eritrea y international arbitration), and with Djibouti over their ommon border. Sudan has accused Eritrea of supporting ebels in eastern Sudan.

There has been fighting with Ethiopia in disputes over order territory, especially in Tigray, since 1998. Though sually sporadic, fighting escalated in 1999–2000 into a /ar that left thousands of people dead. The independent ritrea-Ethiopia Boundary Commission (EEBC) defined ıe international border between the two countries in 002 but both countries have failed to abide by the riginal demarcation or a revised ruling in 2006. The UN, 'hich deployed peacekeeping troops in 2000, continues monitor the disputed area despite obstructiveness by ıe Eritrean government, which has also violated the easefire agreement.

'OLITICAL SYSTEM

'nder the 1997 constitution, the head of state is the resident, elected for a five-year term by the legislature, ıd the 150-member unicameral *Hagerawi Baito* (national ssembly) is directly elected for a four-year term; however, residential and legislative elections have yet to be held ıd the transitional president, state council (cabinet) and gislature remain in place. The People's Front for emocracy and Justice (PFDJ) is the only legal political arty.

HEAD OF STATE

President, Chairman of the National Assembly, C.-in-C. of the Armed Forces, Issaias Afewerki, *elected by the national assembly* 22 May 1993

SELECTED GOVERNMENT MEMBERS *as at May 2007*

Defence, Gen. Sebhat Ephrem
Foreign Affairs, Osman Saleh
Finance and Development, Berhane Abrehe
Health, Saleh Meki

EMBASSY OF THE STATE OF ERITREA

96 White Lion Street, London N1 9PF
T 020-7713 0096 **E** eriemba@eriembauk.com
Ambassador Extraordinary and Plenipotentiary, HE Negassi Sengal, *apptd* 2003

BRITISH EMBASSY

66–68 Mariam Ghimbi Street, PO Box 5584, Asmara
T (+291) (1) 120 145 **E** asmara.enquiries@fco.gov.uk
Ambassador Extraordinary and Plenipotentiary, HE Nick Astbury, *apptd* 2006

BRITISH COUNCIL

PO Box 997, 175 – 11 Street No 23, Asmara
T (+291) (1) 123 415/120 529
W www.britishcouncil.org/eritrea
Director, Dr Negusse Araya

DEFENCE

The army has 150 main battle tanks and 40 armoured infantry fighting vehicles and armoured personnel carriers. The navy has 13 patrol and coastal combatants. The air force has 8 combat aircraft and 1 attack helicopter.
MILITARY BUDGET – US$65m (2005 est)
MILITARY PERSONNEL – 201,750: army 200,000, navy 1,400, air force 350
CONSCRIPTION DURATION – 16 months

ECONOMY AND TRADE

Over 30 years of conflict left the country's economy devastated. The government hopes to base the rebuilding of the economy on the return of well-educated exiles, international aid and investment, the development of tourism along the coast and the diversification of the economy away from subsistence agriculture. Although it is pushing through a development programme that has seen much of the transport infrastructure reconstructed, the concentration of business ownership in party hands and the reduction of the workforce because of the failure to demobilise the large army is restricting economic growth. Other problems include the effect on agricultural output of the conflict with Ethiopia, which has affected the most productive agricultural regions, and the frequent droughts and ensuing famines; currently agriculture is the means of subsistence of around 80 per cent of the population, and emergency food programmes have been needed to help over 840,000 people.

Mineral reserves include zinc, potash, gold, copper and possibly oil, but they are not fully exploited. Industries include food processing, beverages, clothing and textiles, salt, cement and light manufacturing. The main trade partners are Italy, the USA, France and Germany. Principal exports are livestock, sorghum, textiles, food and light manufactures. The main imports are machinery, petroleum products, food and manufactured goods. The largest source of foreign exchange is remittances from Eritreans overseas.

GNI – US$800m; US$170 per capita (2005)
ANNUAL AVERAGE GROWTH OF GDP – 2 per cent (2005 est)
INFLATION RATE – 15 per cent (2005 est)
TOTAL EXTERNAL DEBT – US$311m (2000 est)

Trade with UK	*2005*	*2006*
Imports from UK	£5,678,000	£2,011,000
Exports to UK	£274,000	£189,000

COMMUNICATIONS
Infrastructure reconstruction has focused on the ports of Massawa and Assab, the roads from these ports to Ethiopia, and the railway from Massawa to Sudan via Asmara. There are 306km of railways and 4,010km of roads, of which 874km are surfaced. There are 17 airports and airfields, of which four have surfaced runways; the international airport is at Asmara. The land-line telephone system is poor and largely confined to Asmara; mobile phone subscriptions are nearly double the number of main-line subscribers, at 58,000 in 2006.

MEDIA
Eritrea is the only country in Africa to have no privately owned news media. Existing organisations were closed down by the government in 2001, making Eritrea the third worst country in the world for press freedom according to Reporters Without Borders. Eri TV is the state-run television station. There are no private networks or radio stations.

ESTONIA

Eesti Vabariik – Republic of Estonia

AREA – 45,226 sq. km. Neighbours: Russia (east), Latvia (south)
CAPITAL – Tallinn; population, 396,193 (2006 est)
MAJOR TOWNS AND CITIES – Tartu; Narva; Kohtla-Jarve; Parnu
CURRENCY – Kroon of 100 sents
POPULATION – 1,324,333 falling at 0.64 per cent per year (2006 est); Estonian (67.9 per cent), Russian (25.6 per cent), Ukrainian (2.1 per cent)
RELIGION – Christianity (25 per cent) (est). Fifty years of Soviet occupation has diminished the role of religion in society
LANGUAGE – Estonian (official), Russian
POPULATION DENSITY – 32 per sq. km (2005)
URBAN POPULATION – 69.6 per cent (2005 est)
MEDIAN AGE (years) – 39.3 (2006 est)
NATIONAL ANTHEM – 'Mu Isamaa, Mu Onn Ja Room' ['My Native Land, My Joy, Delight']
NATIONAL DAY – 24 February (Independence Day)
LIFE EXPECTANCY (years) – 72.04 (2006 est)
MORTALITY RATE – 13.25 (2006 est)
BIRTH RATE – 10.04 (2006 est)
INFANT MORTALITY RATE – 7.73 (2006 est)
HIV/AIDS ADULT PREVALENCE – 4.4 per cent (2003)
DEATH PENALTY – No (abolished 1998)
CPI SCORE – 6.7 (2006)
POPULATION BELOW POVERTY LINE – 5 per cent (2003)
MILITARY EXPENDITURE – US$215 million (2005)
MILITARY PERSONNEL – 4,100: army 3,600, navy 300, air force 200; paramilitaries 2,600
CONSCRIPTION DURATION – Eight to 11 months

CLIMATE AND TERRAIN
The country is mostly a plain of lakes, marshes an forests, with a low range of hills in the south-eas Elevation extremes range from 318m (Munamagi) at th highest point to 0m (Baltic Sea) at the lowest. Part of th border with Russia runs through the large Lake Peipu The climate is mild, with average temperatures rangin from −6°C in January to 17°C in July.

HISTORY AND POLITICS
Estonia came under Swedish control between 1561 an 1629, and was ceded in 1721 to the Russian Empire. A Estonian nationalist movement developed in the late 19t century and fought against occupying German force during the First World War. Estonia declared i independence in February 1918 and defended it agains Soviet forces until 1920, when independence wa recognised by the USSR. However, the USSR annexe Estonia in 1940, and the country was subsequentl occupied by German forces when they invaded the USS in 1941. In 1944 the USSR expelled the Germans an reannexed the country, beginning a process c 'Sovietisation'.

There was a resurgence of nationalist feeling in th 1980s, and in 1989 the Estonian Supreme Soviet declare the republic to be sovereign and its 1940 annexation b the USSR to be illegal. In 1990, the Communist Party monopoly of power was abolished and, followin multiparty elections in which pro-independenc candidates won the majority of seats, a period c transition to independence was inaugurated, culminatin in its declaration on 20 August 1991. The last Russia troops withdrew in 1994. Since independence, Estoni has pursued pro-Western policies. It joined NATO and th EU in 2004 and its parliament ratified the EU constitutio in May 2006.

In 2006 Toomas Hendrik Ilves was elected president b an electoral assembly. In the March 2007 legislativ election, the Reform Party (RE), the main partner in th coalition government since 2005, became the large party and formed a new coalition with the Union of Pr Patria and Res Publica (IRL) and the Estonian Soci Democratic Party (SDE).

POLITICAL SYSTEM
Under the 1992 constitution, the president is elected for five-year term by the legislature by a two-thirds majori or, if no candidate receives this majority after three round of voting, by an electoral assembly composed of th legislature members and local government representative The unicameral legislature, the *Riigikogu,* has 10 members, directly elected for a four-year term. The prim minister is appointed by the president and nominates th government. Members of the government need not b members of the *Riigikogu.*

HEAD OF STATE
President, Toomas Hendrik Ilves, *elected by electoral assembly* 23 September 2006, *sworn in* 9 October 200

SELECTED GOVERNMENT MEMBERS *as at May 2007*
Prime Minister, Andrus Ansip
Defence, Jaak Aaviksoo
Finance, Ivari Padar
Foreign Affairs, Urmas Paet
Internal Affairs, Juri Pihl

EMBASSY OF THE REPUBLIC OF ESTONIA
16 Hyde Park Gate, London SW7 5DG
T 020-7589 3428 W www.estonia.gov.uk
Ambassador Extraordinary and Plenipotentiary, HE Dr Margus Laidre, *apptd* 2006

BRITISH EMBASSY
Wismari 6, Tallinn 10136
T (+372) 677 4700 E information@britishembassy.ee
W www.britishembassy.ee
Ambassador Extraordinary and Plenipotentiary, HE Nigel Haywood, *apptd* 2003

BRITISH COUNCIL
Vana–Posti 7, Tallinn 10146
T (+372) 625 7788 W www.britishcouncil.org/estonia
Director, Kyllike Tohver

ECONOMY AND TRADE

Economic reforms and restructuring since 1992 have resulted in a market economy. Estonia's ties to Western Europe were strengthened by accession to the EU, which has also boosted economic growth, and it aims to join the eurozone in 2008, although this might be delayed if inflation continues to rise. There is a high trade deficit, but the government budget is in balance and public debt is low.

Agriculture engages 11 per cent of the workforce and accounts for 3 per cent of GDP, the main products being potatoes, vegetables, livestock and dairy products, and fish. Industry accounts for 20 per cent of employment and 28 per cent of GDP, concentrating on engineering, electronics, wood and wood products, textiles, information technology and telecommunications; electronics and telecommunications are particularly strong at present. The services sector accounts for 69 per cent of both employment and GDP.

Estonia's main trading partners are Finland, Sweden and Germany. Principal exports are machinery and equipment, wood and paper, textiles and clothing, foodstuffs, furniture, metals and chemicals. The main imports are machinery and equipment, chemicals, textiles, foodstuffs and vehicles. Estonia is still dependent on Russian natural gas supplies, although it is a net exporter of electricity.

GNI – US$12,200m; US$9,060 per capita (2005)
ANNUAL AVERAGE GROWTH OF GDP – 10.5 per cent (2005 est)
INFLATION RATE – 4.1 per cent (2005 est)
UNEMPLOYMENT – 7.8 per cent (2005)
TOTAL EXTERNAL DEBT – US$11,030m (2005 est)
IMPORTS – US$10,100m (2005)
EXPORTS – US$7,700m (2005)

BALANCE OF PAYMENTS
Trade – US$1,845m deficit (2005)
Current Account – US$1,445m deficit (2005)

Trade with UK	*2005*	*2006*
Imports from UK	£113,435,000	£456,700,000
Exports to UK	£348,077,000	£467,400,000

EDUCATION AND HEALTH

Estonia has a three-tier education system, consisting of primary level (four years), secondary level (six years) and university level (four to six years). Primary and secondary level education is compulsory between the ages of seven and 17. The country's best known university is Tartu, founded in 1632.

LITERACY RATE – 99.8 per cent (2004 est)
GROSS ENROLMENT RATIO (percentage of relevant age group) – primary 100 per cent; secondary 98 per cent; tertiary 65 per cent (2005 est)
HEALTH EXPENDITURE (per capita) – US$463 (2004)
HOSPITAL BEDS (per 1,000 people) – 6 (2000–5)

MEDIA AND CULTURE

Freedom of the press is guaranteed in the constitution, and the state monopoly on television and radio ended soon after independence. All newspapers have been privatised and broadcasting channels are in the process of being privatised. Russian-language news and programmes are provided on Estonian television.

The old town area of Tallinn is a UNESCO World Heritage Site. The city has suffered many occupations but apart from a Soviet bombing raid in 1944, its medieval and 18th-century architecture has never been harmed. Like its Scandinavian neighbours, Estonia's heritage is rich in traditional folk songs and poetry, which influences much of its contemporary culture. Estonia is particularly distinguished in the field of classical music and has produced many well-known conductors, such as Neeme Jarvi (*b.* 1937) and Tonu Kaljuste (*b.* 1953), and composers Arvo Part (*b.* 1935), and Veljo Tormis (*b.* 1930).

ETHIOPIA

Ityop'iya Federalawi Demokrasyawi Repeblik – Federal Democratic Republic of Ethiopia

AREA – 1,127,127 sq. km. Neighbours: Sudan (west), Kenya (south), Somalia (east), Djibouti (north-east), Eritrea (north)
CAPITAL – Addis Ababa; population, 2,973,000 (2006 est)
MAJOR CITY – Dire Dawa; Nazret; Gondar; Mekele; Dese
CURRENCY – Ethiopian birr (EB) of 100 cents
POPULATION – 74,777,981, rising at 2.31 per cent per year (2006 est); Oromo (40 per cent), Amhara and Tigre (32 per cent), Sidamo (9 per cent), Shankella (6 per cent), Somali (6 per cent), Afar (4 per cent), Gurage (2 per cent) (est)
RELIGION – Coptic Christianity (45 per cent), Islam (45 per cent), other Christian denominations (10 per cent) (est)
LANGUAGE – Amharic (official), Tigrinya, Oromigna, Somali, Arabic, English, Guaragigna
POPULATION DENSITY – 71 per sq. km (2005)
URBAN POPULATION – 16.2 per cent (2005 est)
MEDIAN AGE (years) – 17.8 (2006 est)
NATIONAL ANTHEM – 'Wodefit' Gesgeshi Widd Innat Ityopp'ya' ['March Forward Dear Mother Ethiopia']
NATIONAL DAY – 28 May
LIFE EXPECTANCY (years) – 49.03 (2006 est)
MORTALITY RATE – 14.86 (2006 est)
BIRTH RATE – 37.98 (2006 est)
INFANT MORTALITY RATE – 93.62 (2006 est)
HIV/AIDS ADULT PREVALENCE – 4.4 per cent (2003 est)
DEATH PENALTY – Yes
CPI SCORE – 2.4 (2006)
POPULATION BELOW POVERTY LINE – 50 per cent (2004 est)

CLIMATE AND TERRAIN

Ethiopia is a landlocked country dominated by a central plateau, rising to the central mountains of the Ethiopian Highlands, which are divided by the Great Rift Valley. The western mountains are the source of the Blue Nile. The land drops to desert plains in the east (Ogaden) and north-east (Denakil Desert). Elevation extremes range from 4,620m (Ras Dejen) at the highest point to −116m (Denakil Depression) at the lowest. There is a tropical monsoon climate that varies according to altitude. The wet season is April to September.

HISTORY AND POLITICS

The Hamitic culture was heavily influenced by Semitic immigration from Arabia around the time of Christ, and Coptic Christianity was introduced in the fourth century. The empire attained its zenith in the sixth century under the Axum rulers but was checked by Islamic expansion from the east. The independent kingdom of Abyssinia emerged in the 11th century. Modern Ethiopia dates from 1855 when Theodros established supremacy over the various tribes. Menelik II repulsed an Italian invasion in 1896, but Italy conquered Abyssinia in 1936 and occupied the country until its liberation and the return of the emperor, Haile Selassie, in 1941. Ethiopia was federated with Eritrea in 1952 and annexed the area in 1962.

Following a severe famine in 1973–4, Emperor Haile Selassie was deposed in a military coup in 1974 and a military government was installed. By 1977 Lt.-Col. Mengistu Haile Mariam had become head of state and his single-party Marxist regime initiated reforms based on the Soviet model, brutally suppressing opposition. War with Somalia over the Ogaden (1977–8), internal conflict with Ethiopian resistence and Eritrean separatist forces, drought and severe famine (1984–5), and government mismanagement and corruption undermined the Mengistu regime. Under pressure from the Ethiopian People's Revolutionary Democratic Front (EPRDF) and the allied Eritrean People's Liberation Front (EPLF), the regime collapsed in 1991. A transitional administration comprising the EPRDF and other opposition groups governed until a new federal constitution was adopted in 1994. The Federal Democratic Republic of Ethiopia was proclaimed on 22 August 1995.

The 2001 presidential election was won by Lt. Girma Wolde Giorgis, the EPRDF candidate. In the 2005 legislative election, the EPRDF retained an overall but reduced majority in parliament; opposition parties accused the EPRDF of electoral fraud and there were reruns of polls in over 30 seats. Popular protests against the irregularities were violently suppressed amid a crackdown on the opposition and the media, provoking foreign aid donors to cut direct aid. A presidential election was due in October 2007.

FOREIGN RELATIONS

There has been fighting with Eritrea in disputes over border territory, especially in Tigray, since 1998. Though usually sporadic, fighting escalated in 1999–2000 into a war in which thousands of people died. The independent Eritrea–Ethiopia Boundary Commission (EEBC) defined the international border between the two countries in 2002 but both countries have failed to abide by the original demarcation or a revised ruling in 2006. Relations remain strained. The UN, which deployed peacekeeping troops in 2000, continues to monitor the disputed area.

Ethiopia intervened in Somalia from July 2006 in support of the Somali transitional government, based in Baidoa. Ethiopian forces joined with those loyal to the transitional government to push back an Islamist offensive towards Baidoa and then went on to capture Mogadishu in December and Kismaayo in January 2007. Ethiopia subsequently began a three-phase withdrawal of its troops.

POLITICAL SYSTEM

The 1994 constitution provides for a federal government responsible for foreign affairs, defence and economic policy, and nine ethnically based states. The president is elected by both houses of the legislature for a six-year term, renewable only once. The prime minister is appointed by the house of people's representatives and appoints the government. The federal parliamentary assembly, *Yememakirtoch Mekir Bet,* is bicameral. The lower house, the *Yehizb Tewokayoch Mekir Bet* (house of people's representatives), has 547 members, directly elected for a five-year term. The *Yefedereshn Mekir Bet* (house of the federation) has 110 members, indirectly elected for a five-year term by the government councils of the nine states in the federation. These regional administrations have considerable autonomy and the right to secede.

HEAD OF STATE

President, Lt Girma Wolde Giorgis, *elected by parliament* 8 October 2001

SELECTED GOVERNMENT MEMBERS *as at May 2007*

Prime Minister, C.-in-C. of the National Armed Forces, Meles Zenawi
Deputy Prime Minister, Addisu Legesse
Finance and Economic Development, Sufian Ahmed
Foreign Affairs, Seyoum Mesfin
National Defence, Kuma Demekesa

EMBASSY OF THE FEDERAL DEMOCRATIC REPUBLIC OF ETHIOPIA

17 Princes Gate, London SW7 1PZ
T 020-7589 7212 **E** info@ethioembassy.org.uk
Ambassador Extraordinary and Plenipotentiary, HE Berhanu Kebede, *apptd* 2002

BRITISH EMBASSY

PO Box 858, Fikre Mariam Abatechan Street, Addis Ababa
T (+251) (11) 661 2354
E britishembassy.addisababa@fco.gov.uk
W www.britishembassy.gov.uk/ethiopia
Ambassador Extraordinary and Plenipotentiary, HE Robert Dewar, *apptd* 2004

BRITISH COUNCIL

PO Box 1043, Artistic Building, Adwa Avenue, Addis Ababa
T (+251) (11) 155 0022 **W** www.britishcouncil.org/ethiopia
Director, Michael Moore, MBE

DEFENCE

The army has over 250 main battle tanks and around 400 armoured infantry fighting vehicles and armoured personnel carriers. The air force has 48 combat aircraft and 25 armed helicopters.
MILITARY BUDGET – US$345m (2006)
MILITARY PERSONNEL – 152,500: army 150,000, air force 2,500

ECONOMY AND TRADE

Since 1993 the government has implemented a programme of economic reforms. The economy is highly dependent on agriculture, and therefore on the rains; recurring droughts led to famine conditions in 1984–5, 1992, 1997, 2000 and 2002, and much of the population is dependent on food aid. In 2004, a government resettlement programme began to move more than two million people away from the drought-stricken and overworked highlands in the east of the country; the government claimed this would be a long-term solution to food shortages. There is a high level of foreign debt, but in 2001 Ethiopia met the criteria of the IMF-World Bank heavily indebted poor countries initiative, and in 2005 it was promised 100 per cent debt relief by the G8 countries and the IMF.

Agriculture and herding account for approximately 48 per cent of GDP, and around 80 per cent of the population is dependent upon the land for a living. The main crops are cereals, pulses, coffee, oilseed, cotton, sugar, potatoes, qat, cut flowers, livestock products and fish. Natural resources, including gold, platinum, copper, potash, oil and natural gas, are largely unexploited and most industrial activity involves the processing of agricultural products. The main trade partners are Saudi Arabia, China, the USA and Germany. Principal exports are coffee (which normally provides over 20 per cent of foreign exchange earnings), qat, gold, leather products, livestock and oilseeds. The main imports are food, livestock, petroleum and petroleum products, chemicals, machinery, vehicles, cereals and textiles.

GNI – US$11,100m; US$160 per capita (2005)
ANNUAL AVERAGE GROWTH OF GDP – 8.9 per cent (2005 est)
INFLATION RATE – 11.6 per cent (2005 est)
TOTAL EXTERNAL DEBT – US$5,101m (2005 est)
IMPORTS – US$4,130m (2005)
EXPORTS – US$880m (2005)

BALANCE OF PAYMENTS
Trade – US$2,090m deficit (2004)
Current Account – US$668m deficit (2004)

Trade with UK	*2005*	*2006*
Imports from UK	£31,497,000	£38,273,000
Exports to UK	£20,723,000	£21,615,000

COMMUNICATIONS

A network of roads in rural areas links the major cities with each other, with the Sudanese and Kenyan borders and through Eritrea to the Red Sea coast. There are 36,469km of roads, 6,980km of which are surfaced. The only railway line, 681km in length, links Addis Ababa to Djibouti City. There are over 80 airports and airfields, including the international airport at Addis Ababa. Ethiopian Airlines maintains regular services throughout Africa and to Europe. There is a limited telephone service, with only 610,300 main lines in use in 2005. Mobile phone distribution was lower, at 410,600 subscribers in 2005.

EDUCATION AND HEALTH

Elementary and secondary education are provided by government schools in the main centres of population; there are also mission schools. The National University (founded 1961) coordinates the institutions of higher education.

LITERACY RATE – 41.5 per cent (2004 est)
GROSS ENROLMENT RATIO (percentage of relevant age group) – primary 93 per cent; secondary 31 per cent; tertiary 3 per cent (2005 est)
HEALTH EXPENDITURE (per capita) – US$6 (2004)

MEDIA

There are over 50 privately owned newspapers in addition to the state-owned daily *Addis Zemen*. There is only one television station, the state-owned Ethiopian Television (ETV). Radio Ethiopia is state-owned but several private stations were given licences in 2004.

FIJI

Matanitu ko Viti – Republic of the Fiji Islands

AREA – 18,270 sq. km
CAPITAL – Suva; population, 77,366 (1996), on Viti Levu Island
CURRENCY – Fiji dollar (F $) of 100 cents
POPULATION – 905,949 rising at 1.4 per cent per year (2006 est); Fijian (51 per cent), Indian (44 per cent) (est). After the 1987 coup many Indians left, and by 1994 Melanesian Fijians formed the largest population group
RELIGION – Christianity (52 per cent), Hinduism (33 per cent), Islam (7 per cent) (est)
LANGUAGE – English, Fijian (both official), Hindustani
POPULATION DENSITY – 46 per sq. km (2005)
URBAN POPULATION – 53.2 per cent (2005 est)
MEDIAN AGE (years) – 24.6 (2006 est)
NATIONAL ANTHEM – 'God Bless Fiji'
NATIONAL DAY – second Monday of October (Independence Day)
LIFE EXPECTANCY (years) – 69.82 (2006 est)
MORTALITY RATE – 5.65 (2006 est)
BIRTH RATE – 22.55 (2006 est)
INFANT MORTALITY RATE – 12.3 (2006 est)
DEATH PENALTY – Yes*
MILITARY BUDGET – US$44m (2006)
MILITARY PERSONNEL – 3,500: army 3,200, navy 300
LITERACY RATE – 92.9 per cent (2004 est)

CLIMATE AND TERRAIN

Fiji is a Melanesian island group of roughly 332 islands (around 100 are permanently inhabited) and over 500 islets in the South Pacific, about 1,760km north of New Zealand. The group extends 480km from east to west and 480km north to south. The International Date Line has been diverted to the east of the island group. The largest islands are Viti Levu and Vanua Levu. The terrain is mountainous and volcanic, with tropical rainforest and grassland, and most islands are surrounded by coral reefs. Elevation extremes range from 1,324m (Tomaniivi, on Viti Levu) at the highest point to 0m (Pacific Ocean) at the lowest. Fiji has a tropical oceanic climate with high humidity and an average annual temperature of 27°C.

HISTORY AND POLITICS

The islands were visited by Dutch explorer Abel Tasman in 1643, and by Captain Cook in 1774. They became a British colony in 1874, and sugar plantations, employing more than 60,000 indentured Indian labourers, were established. Fiji became independent as a constitutional monarchy within the Commonwealth on 10 October 1970, and became a republic after the 1987 coups.

Racial and political tension between the native Melanesians and the growing ethnic Indian population has caused political instability since the 1980s. There have been four coups in 20 years: two in 1987 and one in 2000 as ethnic Fijians attempted to reassert their political dominance; and one in 2006 over the government's proposed amnesty for those involved in the 2000 coup.

Vice-president Josefa Iliolo, appointed interim president after the 2000 coup, was confirmed in office in March 2001 and was re-appointed for a second term in March 2006. In the May 2006 legislative election, the Fijian People's Party (SDL) remained the largest party in the house of representatives, with the predominantly Indian Fijian Labour Party (FLP) a close second. Tension between the prime minister, Laisenia Qarase, and Commodore Frank Bainimarama escalated in autumn 2006 and in December Commodore Bainimarama overthrew the government and assumed executive authority. President Iloilo was reinstated in January 2007, when Commodore Bainimarama became interim prime minister. He announced that elections would be held in 2010.

POLITICAL SYSTEM
Under the 1997 constitution, the head of state is the president, appointed for a five-year term by the Great Council of Chiefs. The lower house of the bicameral parliament is the house of representatives, which has 71 members directly elected for a five-year term. Of the 71 seats, 25 are open to all races and elected in single-member constituencies, while the other 46 are allocated for election by the country's various ethnic communities. The upper house, the senate, has 32 members, who are appointed for a five-year term by the president on the recommendation of the political parties (in proportion to their representation in the lower house) and by the Great Council of Chiefs.

HEAD OF STATE
President, Ratu Josefa Iloilo, *appointed* 13 July 2000, *reappointed* 13 March 2001, *sworn in* 15 March 2001

SELECTED GOVERNMENT MEMBERS *as at May 2007*
Prime Minister, Commodore Frank Voreqe Bainimarama
Finance and National Planning, Mahendra Chaudhry
Foreign Affairs, Ratu Epeli Nailatikau
Attorney-General, Justice, Aiyaz Sayed-Khaiyum

HIGH COMMISSION OF THE REPUBLIC OF THE FIJI ISLANDS
34 Hyde Park Gate, London SW7 5DN
T 020-7584 3661 W www.fijihighcommission.org.uk
High Commissioner, HE Emitai Lausiki Boladuadua, *apptd* 2002

BRITISH HIGH COMMISSION
PO Box 1355, Victoria House, 47 Gladstone Road, Suva
T (+679) 322 9100 E publicdiplomacysuva@fco.gov.uk
W www.britishhighcommission.gov.uk/fiji
High Commissioner, HE Roger Sykes, *apptd* 2006

ECONOMY AND TRADE
Fiji has abundant natural resources and a developed and diverse economy. However, economic problems arose after the 1987 coup because of the large-scale emigration of Indian Fijians and the impact of continuing political instability on the tourist industry. Tourism has overtaken the sugar industry as the mainstay of the economy. Budget and trade deficits are long-term problems, and remittances from Fijians working abroad are important.

Agriculture accounts for 9 per cent of GDP and employs approximately 70 per cent of the workforce. The principal cash crop is sugar cane; in 2002 the government announced the privatisation of the industry, threatened with collapse by the withdrawal of EU subsidies. The other main crops are coconuts, cassava, rice, sweet potatoes, bananas, livestock and fish. Light industry is being encouraged in order to diversify the economy. The main industries are tourism, sugar processing, manufacturing of clothing, copra, gold and silver mining, forestry and small cottage industries. The main trade partners are Australia, Singapore, the USA, New Zealand and the UK. Principal exports are sugar, garments, gold, timber, fish, molasses and coconut oil. The chief imports are manufactured goods, machinery and transport equipment, petroleum products, food and chemicals.

GNI – US$2,684m; US$3,170 per capita (2005)
ANNUAL AVERAGE GROWTH OF GDP – 1.7 per cent (2005 est)
INFLATION RATE – 3 per cent (2005)
TOTAL EXTERNAL DEBT – US$127m (2004 est)
IMPORTS – US$1,610m (2005)
EXPORTS – US$720m (2005)

Trade with UK	*2005*	*2006*
Imports from UK	£4,694,000	£5,143,000
Exports to UK	£64,382,000	£74,616,000

COMMUNICATIONS
Fiji is one of the main aerial crossroads in the Pacific, providing services to New Zealand, Australia and other Pacific states; the 28 airports and airfields include international airports at Suva and Nadi. The main seaports are Suva and Lautoka. There are 3,440km of roads, 1,692km of which are surfaced. There are 597km of railway track, principally used by the sugar industry. The telephone system is modern and covers all the islands.

MEDIA
Fiji's privately owned newspapers are published in English, Fijian and Hindi. Government-owned newspapers are also multilingual. Radio (both public and private) is the main source of news, particularly on the more remote outer islands. There are two main television networks, operated by Fiji Television Ltd: Fiji 1, a national channel, and Sky Fiji, accessed via subscription.

FINLAND

Suomen Tasavalta/Republiken Finland – Republic of Finland

AREA – 338,145 sq. km. Neighbours: Norway (north-west and north), Russia (east), Sweden (west)
CAPITAL – Helsinki (Helsingfors); population, 560,905 (2005 est)
MAJOR CITIES – Espoo (Esbo); Tampere (Tammerfors); Vantaa (Vanda); Turku (Abo); Oulu (Uleaborg)
CURRENCY – Euro (€) of 100 cents
POPULATION – 5,231,372 rising at 0.14 per cent per year (2006 est); Finnish (93.4 per cent), Swedish (5.7 per cent) (est)

RELIGION – Christianity (85 per cent) (est)
LANGUAGE – Finnish, Swedish (both official)
POPULATION DENSITY – 17 per sq. km (2005)
URBAN POPULATION – 60.9 per cent (2005 est)
MEDIAN AGE (years) – 41.3 (2006 est)
NATIONAL ANTHEM – 'Maamme'/'Vart Land' ['Our Land']
NATIONAL DAY – 6 December (Independence Day)
LIFE EXPECTANCY (years) – 78.5 (2006 est)
MORTALITY RATE – 9.86 (2006 est)
BIRTH RATE – 10.45 (2006 est)
INFANT MORTALITY RATE – 3.55 (2006 est)
DEATH PENALTY – No (abolished 1972)
CPI SCORE – 9.6 (2006)

CLIMATE AND TERRAIN

Most of the country is a glaciated plain of forests (over 65 per cent of the land area) and over 60,000 lakes, with low hills along the eastern border with Russia and in the far north. Elevation extremes range from 1,328m (Haltaitunturi) at the highest point to 0m (Baltic Sea) at the lowest.

Owing to the isostatic uplift, a name given to the vertical movement of post-glaciated land masses, the surface area of Finland is growing by an estimated 7 sq. km a year. A third of the country is north of the Arctic Circle and temperatures there can range from −20°C in January to 10°C in July. Temperatures in Helsinki range from −6°C in January to 17°C in July.

HISTORY AND POLITICS

Finland was part of the Swedish Empire from the Middle Ages until it was ceded to Russia in 1809 and became an autonomous grand duchy of the Russian Empire. After the Russian Revolution in 1917, Finland declared its independence. An attempted coup by Finnish Bolsheviks led to a short civil war that ended in their defeat in 1918, and in 1919 a republic was set up. It resisted the 1939 invasion by the USSR but was defeated in 1940 and forced to cede territory; in the hope of recovering this territory it joined Germany's attack on the USSR in 1941. After agreeing an armistice with the USSR in 1944, Finland concluded a peace treaty in 1947 that conceded further territory to the USSR and obliged it to pay reparations. A Soviet-Finnish cooperation treaty in 1948 forced Finland to demilitarise its Soviet border and to adopt a stance of neutrality; these terms lasted until the demise of the USSR in 1991.

Since the mid-1960s the majority of Finnish governments have been coalitions of centre and moderate left-wing parties, with the Social Democratic Party (SDP) or the Centre Party (KESK) the leading parties in the coalitions. Finland joined the EU in 1995 and the European Monetary Union in 1998; its parliament voted in favour of ratifying the EU constitution in May 2006.

In the 2006 presidential election, Tarja Halonen of the SDP was re-elected with 51.8 per cent of the vote. Following the March 2007 legislative election, KESK remained the largest party and formed a new coalition government with the National Coalition Party, the Greens and the Swedish People's Party.

POLITICAL SYSTEM

Under the 2000 constitution, the president is directly elected for a six-year term. There is a unicameral legislature, the *Eduskunta,* with 200 members directly elected for a four-year term. The prime minister is elected by the *Eduskunta* and appointed by the president.

HEAD OF STATE
President, Tarja Halonen, *elected* 6 February 2000, *inaugurated* 1 March 2000, *re-elected* January 2006

SELECTED GOVERNMENT MEMBERS *as at May 2007*
Prime Minister, Matti Vanhanen
Deputy Prime Minister; Finance, Jyrki Katainen
Defence, Jyri Hakamies
Foreign Affairs, Ilkka Kanerva
Interior, Anne Holmlund

EMBASSY OF FINLAND
38 Chesham Place, London SW1X 8HW
T 020-7838 6200 W www.finemb.org.uk
Ambassador Extraordinary and Plenipotentiary, HE Jaakko Laajava, *apptd* 2005

BRITISH EMBASSY
Itainen Puistotie 17, 00140 Helsinki
T (+358) (9) 2286 5100 E info@ukembassy.fi
W www.ukembassy.fi
Ambassador Extraordinary and Plenipotentiary, HE Valerie Caton, *apptd* 2006

BRITISH COUNCIL
Urho Kekkosen Katu 2 C 00100 Helsinki
T (+358) (9) 774 3330 W www.britishcouncil.fi
Director, Tuija Talvitie

DEFENCE

The army has 163 main battle tanks, 182 armoured infantry fighting vehicles and 538 armoured personnel carriers. The navy has 10 patrol and coastal vessels. The air force has 61 combat aircraft.
MILITARY EXPENDITURE – US$2,750m (2006)
MILITARY PERSONNEL – 29,300: army 20,500, navy 4,100, air force 4,700; paramilitaries 3,100
CONSCRIPTION DURATION – Six to 12 months

ECONOMY AND TRADE

The country has a highly industrialised market economy which is thriving as a result of the cutting-edge telecommunications and electronics industries, particularly the manufacture of mobile phones, as well as its traditional timber and metals industries. Most trade is with other EU countries and Russia. Principal exports are machinery and equipment (especially electronic and electrical goods), chemicals, metals, timber, paper and wood pulp. The main imports are foodstuffs (especially grain), petroleum and petroleum products, chemicals, transport equipment, iron and steel, machinery, textile yarn and fabrics, and components for manufactured goods. Finland is a net importer of energy.

GNI – US$196,900m; US$37,530 per capita (2005)
ANNUAL AVERAGE GROWTH OF GDP – 3 per cent (2005 est)
INFLATION RATE – 0.9 per cent (2005 est)
UNEMPLOYMENT – 8.4 per cent (2005 est)
TOTAL EXTERNAL DEBT – US$211,700m (2005)
IMPORTS – US$58,200m (2005)
EXPORTS – US$65,200m (2005)

BALANCE OF PAYMENTS
Trade – US$10,145m surplus (2005)
Current Account – US$4,983m surplus (2005)

Trade with UK	*2005*	*2006*
Imports from UK	£1,468,302,000	£1,772,700,000
Exports to UK	£2,272,854,000	£2,713,400,000

COMMUNICATIONS

The road and rail networks are concentrated in the southern half of the country, where most of the population and industry are located. There are 78,189km of roads, 50,633km of which are surfaced. There are 5,741km of railways. The main seaports are Helsinki, Kotka, Rauma and Turku, and there are passenger services with Sweden, Estonia and Germany as well as countries outside the Baltic. There are 29 major airports; the principal ones are at Helsinki, Turku and Vaasa. Mobile phone distribution, at 5.2 million subscribers in 2005, matches the size of the population.

EDUCATION AND HEALTH

Primary education is free of charge and compulsory for children from seven to 16 years.

GROSS ENROLMENT RATIO (percentage of relevant age group) – primary 101 per cent; secondary 109 per cent; tertiary 90 per cent (2005 est)
HEALTH EXPENDITURE (per capita) – US$2,664 (2004)
HOSPITAL BEDS (per 1,000 people) – 7.2 (2000–5)

MEDIA

Finnish law gives every citizen the right to publish printed material, and guarantees the right of reply. It was rated as the best country in the world for press freedom by Reporters Without Borders in 2006. Newspapers are privately owned and offer a wide spectrum of political views. There are both commercial and state-owned broadcasters; the state broadcaster is Yleisradio Oy (YLE). The analogue television signal was scheduled to be switched off during 2007. Newspapers, books, plays and films appear in both Finnish and Swedish.

FRANCE

République Française – French Republic

AREA – 547,030 sq. km. Neighbours: Belgium and Luxembourg (north-east), Germany, Switzerland and Italy (east), Monaco (south), Spain and Andorra (south-west)
CAPITAL – Paris; population, 2,144,700 (2004 est)
MAJOR CITIES – Marseille; Lyon; Toulouse; Nice; Nantes; Strasbourg; Montpellier; Bordeaux; Lille; Rennes. The chief towns of Corsica are Ajaccio and Bastia
CURRENCY – Euro (€) of 100 cents
POPULATION – 60,876,136 rising at 0.35 per cent per year (2006 est)
RELIGION – Christianity (90 per cent), Islam (7 per cent), Judaism (1 per cent), Buddhism (1 per cent) (est). Although the majority of the population is nominally Roman Catholic, only about 8 per cent of Catholics practice their religion
LANGUAGE – French (official)
POPULATION DENSITY – 111 per sq. km (2005)
URBAN POPULATION – 76.7 per cent (2005 est)
MEDIAN AGE (years) – 39.1 (2006 est)
NATIONAL ANTHEM – 'La Marseillaise' ['Song of Marseille']
NATIONAL DAY – 14 July (Fete de la Federation)
LIFE EXPECTANCY (years) – 79.73 (2006 est)
MORTALITY RATE – 9.14 (2006 est)
BIRTH RATE – 11.99 (2006 est)
INFANT MORTALITY RATE – 4.21 (2006 est)
HIV/AIDS ADULT PREVALENCE – 0.4 per cent (2003 est)
DEATH PENALTY – No (abolished 1981)
CPI SCORE – 7.4 (2006)
POPULATION BELOW POVERTY LINE – 6.5 per cent (2000)

CLIMATE AND TERRAIN

The north and west are flat plains, especially in the basin of the Somme, Seine, Loire and Garonne rivers, with some low hills. The centre of the south is occupied by the Massif Central plateau, which is divided by the valley of the Rhone and Soane rivers from the French Alps and the Jura mountains on the eastern border with Switzerland. The Pyrenees range lies along the southern border with Spain. Elevation extremes range from 4,807m (Mt Blanc

Alps) at the highest point to –2m (Rhone delta) at the lowest. The south has a Mediterranean climate with warm winters and hot, arid summers. The east has a continental climate.

HISTORY AND POLITICS

The area that is now France was conquered by the Romans in the first century BC and, as the province of Gaul, remained part of the Roman Empire until the Frankish invasions of the fifth and sixth centuries. The Treaty of Verdun (AD 843) divided the Frankish Empire created by Charlemagne into three parts, of which the western part, *Francia Occidentalis,* became the basis for modern France. Weak central government allowed the great nobles to form virtually independent duchies, and the assertion of royal power over these nobles was not completed until the 16th century. France's attempts to establish itself as the supreme European power from the 16th century were hindered by civil and religious wars (1562–98), but by the early 18th century France was the leading power in Europe and had a large overseas empire.

The *ancien régime* was overthrown in the French Revolution (1789), a republic was declared in 1792 and the king, Louis XVI, was executed. The republic was overthrown by Napoléon Bonaparte, who established the first French Empire (1804–14). After Bonaparte's defeat, the congress of Vienna restored the monarchy, but in 1848 the Second Republic was declared, which lasted only until 1852, when the Second Empire was proclaimed under Napoléon III. He was forced to abdicate following the defeat of France in the Franco-Prussian war (1870–71), after which the Third Republic (1870–1940) was established.

France was one of the victors in the First World War (1914–18), when German offensives in the north and east of the country were held and eventually defeated. However, the country was invaded in the Second World War and the north was occupied by Germany from 1940 until 1944, with a pro-German government in the south. The Fourth Republic was declared in 1946, but collapsed in 1958, when a new constitution was adopted and the Fifth Republic was proclaimed. France granted most of its colonies independence between 1954 and 1962.

France was a founder member of the EEC in 1958, and joined the European Monetary Union in 1999. In a referendum in May 2005, the population rejected the EU constitution.

The largest party in the senate is the Socialist Party. The presidential election in May 2007 was won in the second round by Nicolas Sarkozy, the Union for a Popular Movement (UMP) candidate. In the national assembly elections in June 2007, the UMP party won 313 of 577 seats, with the Socialists prevailing with 185.

INSURGENCIES

Corsican separatists began a campaign of bombings and shootings in the mid-1970s. The French government's proposals to combine the island's two departments and to give the Corsican regional parliament a degree of autonomy by 2004 were accepted by the regional parliament in 2000 and narrowly passed by the national assembly in 2001. But the constitutional council rejected the legislation as unconstitutional in 2002, and a referendum in 2003 voted narrowly against the proposals. In spring 2005 the main separatist faction announced an end of its 2003 ceasefire and the resumption of its campaign.

POLITICAL SYSTEM

Under the 1958 constitution, the head of state is a president directly elected for a five-year term. The legislature, the *Parlement,* consists of the national assembly and the senate. The national assembly has 577 deputies, 555 for metropolitan France and 22 for the overseas departments and territories; members are directly elected for a five-year term. The senate currently has 331 senators, elected by an electoral college to serve a nine-year term, with a third being elected every three years. By 2010, 25 new seats will be added to the senate to make a total of 346 senators (326 for metropolitan France and the overseas departments, two for New Caledonia, two for Mayotte, one for St-Pierre and Miquelon, three for overseas territories and 12 for French nationals living abroad), and members will serve for a six-year term, with one half of the seats being renewed every three years.

The prime minister is nominated by the national assembly and appointed by the president, as is the council of ministers. They are responsible to the legislature, but as the executive is constitutionally separate from the legislature, ministers may not sit in the legislature and must hand over their seats to a substitute.

A government plan for decentralisation of power from Paris was initiated in 2002, and constitutional amendments in 2003 paved the way for the devolution to the 22 regions and 96 departments of powers over economic development, transport, tourism, culture and further education.

HEAD OF STATE

President of the French Republic, Nicolas Sarkozy, *elected* 6 May 2007

SELECTED GOVERNMENT MEMBERS *as at May 2007*

Prime Minister, Francois Fillon
Defence, Herve Morin
Economy, Finance and Employment, Christine Lagarde
Foreign, Bernard Kouchner
Interior, Michele Alliot-Marie

EMBASSY OF FRANCE

58 Knightsbridge, London SW1X 7JT
T 020-7073 1000 E presse.londres-amba@diplomatie.fr
W www.ambafrance-uk.org
Ambassador Extraordinary and Plenipotentiary, HE Gérard Errera, *apptd* 2002

BRITISH EMBASSY

35 rue du Faubourg St Honoré, 75383 Paris Cédex 08
T (+33) (1) 4451 3100 W www.amb-grandebretagne.fr
Ambassador Extraordinary and Plenipotentiary, HE Sir Peter Westmacott, KCMG, LVO, *apptd* 2007

BRITISH COUNCIL

9 rue de Constantine, 75340 Paris Cédex 07
T (+33) (1) 4955 7300 W www.britishcouncil.org/france
Director, Paul de Quincey

DEFENCE

The army has 926 main battle tanks, 4,413 armoured personnel carriers and 601 armoured infantry fighting vehicles.

The navy has 10 submarines including 4 strategic submarines, 2 aircraft carriers, 1 cruiser, 13 destroyers, 20 frigates and 36 patrol and coastal vessels, 60 combat aircraft and 77 armed helicopters. The navy has 4 domestic and 5 overseas bases. The air force has 303

combat aircraft. There are currently 2 military satellites in service.
MILITARY EXPENDITURE – US$53,100m (2005)
MILITARY PERSONNEL – 254,895: army 133,500, navy 43,995, air force 63,600, central staff 5,200, Service de Santé 8,600; paramilitaries 104,275

ECONOMY AND TRADE

The economy is in transition from a state of extensive government ownership and intervention to one of greater market orientation. Reform was begun because of poor performance, to stimulate growth and reduce government expenditure. Implementation has been difficult because of the constraints of eurozone membership and the strong resistance to the government's privatisation and labour, pension and welfare reform plans, particularly by the trade unions and the large public sector, provoking demonstrations and strikes.

Nearly 40 per cent of the land area of metropolitan France is utilised for agricultural production and a further quarter is accounted for by forests. Viniculture is extensive, though France has lost market share to other countries in recent years. Cognac, liqueurs and cider are also produced. Other important agricultural products include cereals, sugar beet, potatoes, beef, dairy products and fish. Agriculture employs 4 per cent of the workforce but contributes only 2 per cent of GDP.

Oil is produced from fields in the Landes area, but France is a net importer of crude oil, for processing by its oil-refining industry. Natural gas is produced in the foothills of the Pyrenees.

Industry contributes 21 per cent of GDP, employing 24 per cent of the workforce. The sector is highly diversified and includes the production of machinery, iron, steel, aluminium, chemicals, vehicles, aircraft, electronic goods, textiles and food processing. The services sector contributes 77 per cent of GDP and employs 72 per cent of the workforce; tourism is an important part of this sector.

The main trading partners are other EU countries. Principal exports are machinery, vehicles, aircraft, plastics, chemicals, pharmaceutical products, iron and steel, and beverages. The main imports are raw materials for industry (eg crude oil, chemicals, plastics), machinery and equipment, vehicles and aircraft.
GNI – US$2,169,200m; US$34,600 per capita (2005)
ANNUAL AVERAGE GROWTH OF GDP – 1.2 per cent (2005 est)
INFLATION RATE – 1.7 per cent (2005 est)
UNEMPLOYMENT – 9.9 per cent (2005 est)
TOTAL EXTERNAL DEBT – US$2,826,000m (2005)
IMPORTS – US$483,000m (2005)
EXPORTS – US$440,000m (2005)

BALANCE OF PAYMENTS
Trade – US$32,144m deficit (2005)
Current Account – US$33,289m deficit (2005)

Trade with UK	*2005*	*2006*
Imports from UK	£19,442,987,000	£28,314,000,000
Exports to UK	£19,883,549,000	£20,746,100,000

COMMUNICATIONS

There are extensive road and rail networks covering the whole country, with approximately 900,000km of roads, including 11,000km of motorways, and around 30,000km of railways. The world's tallest road bridge was opened at Millau in 2004.

The principal seaports are Marseille on the Mediterranean Sea, Bordeaux and Nantes on the Atlantic coast, and Le Havre, Calais, Dunkirk on the Channel coast. There are 8,500km of navigable inland waterways, 1,686km navigable by large vessels, and Paris, Rouen and Strasbourg are significant river ports. The French mercantile marine consisted in 2006 of 215 ships of 1,000 gross tonnage or over, 154 of which are registered overseas. There are two international airports serving Paris, and many regional airports capable of accepting international flights.

In 2005, there were 35.7 million main telephone lines in use and 48 million mobile phone users. There were 29.5 million internet users in 2006.

ASYLUM APPLICATIONS

Year	*New applications*	*Year*	*New applications*
1996	17,405	2001	54,291
1997	21,416	2002	58,971
1998	22,375	2003	59,768
1999	30,907	2004	58,545
2000	38,747	2005	49,733

Source: UNHCR

EDUCATION AND HEALTH

Education is compulsory, free of charge and secular from the ages of six to 16. Schools may be single-sex or co-educational. Primary education is given in nursery schools, primary schools and *collèges d'enseignement général* (four-year secondary modern course), and secondary education in *collèges d'enseignement technique, collèges d'enseignement secondaire* and *lycées* (a seven-year course leading to one of the five *baccalauréats*). Specialist schools are numerous.

There are many *grandes écoles* in France which award diplomas in subjects not taught at university, especially applied science and engineering. Most of these are state institutions but have a competitive system of entry, unlike the universities.
GROSS ENROLMENT RATIO (percentage of relevant age group) – primary 105 per cent; secondary 111 per cent; tertiary 56 per cent (2005 est)
HEALTH EXPENDITURE (per capita) – US$3,464 (2004)
HOSPITAL BEDS (per 1,000 people) – 7.7 (2000–5)

MEDIA

There are over 100 daily newspapers in France including *Le Monde, Le Figaro* and *Libération*. The press is mostly privately owned and not linked to political parties. State radio broadcasting caters for both domestic (Radio France) and overseas (Radio France Internationale) audiences. TV5 is an international French-language television channel co-financed by Belgium, Canada, France and Switzerland. The main domestic channel, TF1, was privatised in 1987. A global news channel, France 24, was launched in 2006 and broadcasts in both French and English.

CULTURE

French literature contains two of the masterpieces of the Middle Ages, the anonymous *Song of Roland* and *The Romance of the Rose* by Guillaume de Lorris, later lengthened by Jean de Meun. Philosophers Voltaire (1694–1778) and Rousseau (1712–78) also used fiction to illustrate their thought and created *Candide* (1759) and *Julie* (1761). The 19th century saw a flowering of French literature in novels of Victor Hugo (1802–85), Alexandre Dumas (1802–70), Jules Verne (1828–1905), Gustave Flaubert (1821–80) and Émile Zola (1840–1902). Marcel Proust's (1871–1922) *Remembrance of Things Past* remains the heaviest of French literary heavyweights.

14	WORLD HIGHEST
	Nobel prize for literature laureates

France's many artistic movements have inspired generations of artists all over the world. The first significant French painter is commonly believed to be classicist Nicholas Poussin (1594–1665). The works of Édouard Manet (1832–83) represent the change from the Romanticism characterised by Eugène Delacroix (1798–1863) to Impressionism, one of France's most productive artistic periods as demonstrated by Edgar Degas (1834–1917), Pierre-Auguste Renoir (1841–1919), Paul Cézanne (1839–1906), along with sculptors Auguste Rodin (1840–1917) and Marcel Duchamp (1887–1968).

French cinema is characterised by the experimental auteurs such as Jean-Luc Godard (*b.* 1930) and François Truffaut (1932–1984). Actresses to succeed in Hollywood include Brigitte Bardot (*b.* 1934), Catherine Deneuve (*b.* 1943) and Juliette Binoche (*b.* 1964). In music, *chansons* is a uniquely French popular form of entertainment of which Edith Piaf (1915–63) and Serge Gainsbourg (1928–91) are cultural icons. In classical music, Hector Berlioz (1803–69), Georges Bizet (1838–75) and Claude Debussy (1862–1918) are among the country's best-known composers.

OVERSEAS DEPARTMENTS

Greater powers of self-government were granted to French Guiana, Guadeloupe, Martinique and Réunion in 1982. These former colonies had enjoyed departmental status since 1946. Their directly elected assemblies operate in parallel with the existing, indirectly constituted regional councils. The French government is represented by a *prefect* in each.

FRENCH GUIANA

AREA – 83,534 sq. km
CAPITAL – Cayenne; population, 50,675 (1999)
POPULATION – 199,000 (2006 est)

Situated on the north-eastern coast of South America, French Guiana is flanked by Suriname on the west and by Brazil on the south and east. Under the administration of French Guiana is the Îles du Salut group of islands (St Joseph, Île Royal and Île du Diable). The European Space Agency rocket launch site is situated at Kourou, and accounts for 25 per cent of GDP. Fishing and forestry are the main activities, and the main exports are timber, shrimp and gold. Tourism is restricted by the lack of infrastructure, as much of the interior is accessible only by river.
Prefect, Ange Mancini

GUADELOUPE

AREA – 1,780 sq. km
CAPITAL – Basse-Terre; population 12,410 (1999), on Guadeloupe
POPULATION – 452,000 (2006 est)

Consists of a number of islands in the Leeward Islands group of the West Indies, including Guadeloupe (or Basse-Terre), Grande-Terre, Marie-Galante, La Désirade and the Îles des Saintes; under the administration of Guadeloupe are the islands of St-Barthélemy and the French part of St-Martin, which lie over 240km to the north-west. The main towns are Les Abymes; St-Martin; Pointe-à-Pitre (Grande-Terre) and Grand Bourg (Marie-Galante). The main industries are tourism, sugar refining, rum distilling, and bananas are the main export.
Prefect, Paul Girot de Langlade

MARTINIQUE

AREA – 1,128 sq. km
CAPITAL – Fort-de-France; population, 94,778 (1999)
POPULATION – 436,000 (2006 est)

An island in the Windward Islands group of the West Indies, between Dominica in the north and St Lucia in the south. Mount Pelée (1,397m) is an active volcano that last erupted in 1902. Tourism is a major industry. The main products are bananas, rum and petroleum products.
Prefect, Yves Dassonville

RÉUNION

AREA – 2,547 sq. km
CAPITAL – St-Denis; 158,139 (1999)
POPULATION – 787,000 (2006 est)

A French possession since 1638, Réunion lies in the Indian Ocean, about 650km east of Madagascar and 180km south-west of Mauritius. The smaller, uninhabited islands of Bassas da India, Europa, les Glorieuses, Juan de Nova and Tromelin are administered from Réunion. The main industries are tourism, and sugar and rum production.
Prefect, Gonthier Friederici

TERRITORIAL COLLECTIVITIES

MAYOTTE

AREA – 374 sq. km
POPULATION – 201,234 (2006 est)
CAPITAL – Mamoudzou; population, 45,458 (2004 est)

Part of the Comoros archipelago, Mayotte remained a French dependency when the other three islands became independent as the Comoros Republic in 1975. Since 1976 the island has been a *collectivité territoriale,* an intermediate status between Overseas Department and Overseas Territory. The main products are vanilla, ylang-ylang (perfume essence), coffee and copra. Lobster and shrimp fishing is being established.
Prefect, Jean-Paul Kihl

Trade with UK	*2005*	*2006*
Imports from UK	£511,000	£1,900,000
Exports to UK	—	—

ST PIERRE AND MIQUELON

AREA – 242 sq. km
POPULATION – 7,026 (2006 est)
CAPITAL – St-Pierre; population, 5,618 (1999)

These two small groups of eight islands off the south coast of Newfoundland became a *collectivité territoriale* in 1985. There is a French-appointed commissioner and an elected local council. The main industry of fishing and servicing fishing fleets has declined in step with the

decline in cod stocks, and fish farming, crab fishing and agriculture are being developed. Tourism is of growing importance.
Prefect, Albert Dupuy

Trade with UK	*2005*	*2006*
Imports from UK	£58,000	£113,000
Exports to UK	—	£4,000

OVERSEAS TERRITORIES

FRENCH POLYNESIA

AREA – 4,167 sq. km
CAPITAL – Papeete; population, 26,181 (2002), in Tahiti
POPULATION – 274,578 (2006 est)

French Polynesia consists of over 118 volcanic and coral islands and atolls in the South Pacific. There are five archipelagos: the Society Islands (Windward Islands group includes Tahiti, Moorea, Makatea, Mehetia, Tetiaroa, Tubuai Manu; Leeward Islands group includes Huahine, Raiatea, Tahaa, Bora-Bora, Maupiti), the Tuamotu Islands (Rangiroa, Hao, Turéia, etc), the Gambier Islands (Mangareva, etc), the Tubuai Islands (Rimatara, Rurutu, Tubuai, Raivavae, Rapa, etc) and the Marquesas Islands (Nuku-Hiva, Hiva-Oa, Fatu-Hiva, Tahuata, Ua Huka, etc). Some of the atolls were used by France for testing nuclear weapons between 1966 and 1996. The territory has considerable autonomy, with its own parliament and president, as well as the French-appointed High Commissioner. The main industries are tourism, pearl-farming, fishing, coconut products and vanilla production.
High Commissioner, Anne Boquet

Trade with UK	*2005*	*2006*
Imports from UK	£9,022,000	£6,062,000
Exports to UK	£436,000	£1,205,000

NEW CALEDONIA

AREA – 19,060 sq. km
CAPITAL – Nouméa; population, 91,386 (2004 est)
POPULATION – 219,246 (2006 est)

New Caledonia is a large island in the western Pacific, 1,120km off the eastern coast of Australia. Dependencies are the Isles of Pines, the Loyalty Islands (Mahé, Lifou, Urea, etc), the Bélep Archipelago, the Chesterfield Islands, the Huon Islands and Walpole. New Caledonia was discovered in 1774 and annexed by France in 1853. Agitation for independence from the 1980s ended with the Nouméa accord in 1998, under which an increasing degree of autonomy will be transferred to the territory up to 2018, with three referendums on independence to be held between 2013 and 2018. The territory is divided into three provinces, each with a provincial assembly; these combine to form the territorial assembly.

A quarter of the world's nickel deposits are found in the territory, and nickel, ferronickel and fish are the main exports.
High Commissioner, Michel Mathieu

Trade with UK	*2005*	*2006*
Imports from UK	£10,113,000	£9,600,000
Exports to UK	£522,000	£808,000

SOUTHERN AND ANTARCTIC TERRITORIES
Created in 1955 from former Réunion dependencies, the territory comprises the islands of Amsterdam (64 sq. km) and St Paul (7 sq. km), the Kerguelen Islands (6,992 sq. km) and Crozet Islands (300 sq. km) archipelagos and Adélie Land (302,500 sq. km) in the Antarctic continent. The population consists only of members of staff of the scientific stations.
Administrator, Michel Champon

WALLIS AND FUTUNA ISLANDS
AREA – 274 sq. km
CAPITAL – Mata-Utu; population, 1,191 (2003 est), on Uvea, the main island of the Wallis group
POPULATION – 16,025 (2006 est)

The two groups of islands (the Wallis Archipelago and the Îles de Horne) lie in the South Pacific, north-east of Fiji. The main products are copra, vegetables, bananas, livestock products and fish.
Administrator, Xavier de Furst

THE FRENCH COMMUNITY OF STATES
The 1958 constitution envisaged the establishment of a French Community of States. A number of the former French states in Africa have seceded from the community but for all practical purposes continue to enjoy the same close links with France as those that remain formal members. Most former French African colonies are closely linked to France by financial, technical and economic agreements.

GABON

République Gabonaise – Gabonese Republic

AREA – 267,667 sq. km. Neighbours: Equatorial Guinea and Cameroon (north), Republic of Congo (east and south)
CAPITAL – Libreville; population, 419,596 (1993)
MAJOR TOWNS – Port-Gentil; Franceville; Oyem; Moanda
CURRENCY – Franc CFA of 100 centimes
POPULATION – 1,424,906 rising at 2.13 per cent per year (2006 est)
RELIGION – Christianity (73 per cent), Islam (12 per cent), indigenous religions (10 per cent) (est). It is estimated that 5 per cent of the population is atheist
LANGUAGE – French (official), Fang, Myene, Nzebi
POPULATION DENSITY – 5 per sq. km (2005)
URBAN POPULATION – 85.2 per cent (2005 est)
MEDIAN AGE (years) – 18.6 (2006 est)
NATIONAL ANTHEM – 'La Concorde' ['Concord']
NATIONAL DAY – 12 March (Founding of the Gabonese Democratic Party)
LIFE EXPECTANCY (years) – 54.49 (2006 est)
MORTALITY RATE – 12.25 (2006 est)
BIRTH RATE – 36.16 (2006 est)
INFANT MORTALITY RATE – 54.51 (2006 est)
HIV/AIDS ADULT PREVALENCE – 8.1 per cent (2003 est)
DEATH PENALTY – No*
CPI SCORE – 3.0 (2006)
MILITARY BUDGET – US$19m (2005 est)
MILITARY PERSONNEL – 4,700: army 3,200, navy 500, air force 1,000; paramilitaries 2,000
GROSS ENROLMENT RATIO (percentage of relevant

age group) – primary 130 per cent; secondary 50 per cent (2005 est)
HEALTH EXPENDITURE (per capita) – US$231 (2004)

CLIMATE AND TERRAIN

The terrain rises from a narrow coastal plain to a hilly interior; approximately 85 per cent of the land is rainforest, with savannah in the east and south. Elevation extremes range from 1,575m (Mt Iboundji) at the highest point to 0m (Atlantic Ocean) at the lowest. The climate is hot and humid with an average temperature of 27°C. There are two wet seasons each year, from February to May, and from October to December.

HISTORY AND POLITICS

The first Europeans to visit the region were the Portuguese in the 15th century; Dutch, French and English traders arrived soon after. Sovereignty was signed over to the French in 1839 by a local Mpongwe ruler. In 1849, a slave ship was captured by the French and the freed slaves formed a settlement which they called Libreville, the current capital. The country was occupied by the French in 1885 and became part of French Equatorial Africa in 1910. Gabon became autonomous within the French Community in 1958 and gained full independence on 17 August 1960.

President Bongo came to power in 1967, and in 1968 a one-party state was established with the *Parti Démocratique Gabonais* (PDG) as the only party. By the late 1980s, the deteriorating economy was provoking unrest, and in 1991 a multiparty system was reintroduced.

Under the multiparty system, the PDG has remained in power (amid allegations of electoral fraud) although it has included opposition party members in coalition governments since 1994. President Bongo was re-elected for a sixth term of office in November 2005 with nearly 80 per cent of the vote. The last elections to the national assembly in December 2006 were won by the PDG, which formed a coalition government with two smaller parties.

POLITICAL SYSTEM

The 1991 constitution, amended in 1995, 1997 and 2003, provides for a president, who is directly elected for a seven-year term; since 2003, there has been no limit on the number of terms a president may serve. The prime minister is appointed by the president, and then appoints the council of ministers in consultation with the president. There is a bicameral parliament; the national assembly has 120 members, 111 directly elected and nine appointed by the president for a five-year term, and the senate has 91 members elected for a six-year term by municipal and regional councillors.

HEAD OF STATE

President, Omar Bongo, *assumed office* December 1967, *re-elected* 1973, 1979, 1986, 1993, 1998, 2005
Vice-President, Didjob Divungi di Ndinge

SELECTED GOVERNMENT MEMBERS *as at May 2007*

Prime Minister, Jean Eyeghe Ndong
Deputy Prime Minister, Foreign Affairs, Jean Ping
Defence, Ali Bongo Ondimba
Finance, Economy, Budget and Privatisation, Paul Toungui
Interior, André Mba Obame

EMBASSY OF THE GABONESE REPUBLIC

27 Elvaston Place, London SW7 5NL
T 020-7823 9986 **W** www.gaboneseembassy.org

Ambassador Extraordinary and Plenipotentiary, HE Alain Mensah Zoguelet, *apptd* 2003

BRITISH AMBASSADOR

HE Syd Maddicott, *apptd* 2005, resident at Yaoundé, Cameroon

ECONOMY AND TRADE

Gabon is one of the most stable and prosperous countries in Africa, largely owing to its small population and abundance of oil and mineral resources. The economy is heavily dependent on oil (which contributes 50 per cent of GDP) and on other mineral resources, including manganese and uranium, and timber, all of which can be subject to fluctuating prices. Despite the country's wealth, a large proportion of the population remains poor, and weak fiscal management has resulted in a high foreign debt which has had to be rescheduled several times.

Agriculture is largely at subsistence level, employing 60 per cent of the workforce but contributing only 6 per cent of GDP. The main products include cocoa, coffee, sugar, palm oil, rubber, cattle, timber and fish. Industry contributes 60 per cent of GDP and employs 15 per cent of the workforce, mainly in oil and mineral extraction. The service sector contributes 34 per cent of GDP and employs 25 per cent of the workforce. The main trading partners are the USA, France and China. Principal exports are crude oil (77 per cent), timber, manganese and uranium. The main imports are machinery and equipment, food, chemicals and construction materials.

GNI – US$6,900m; US$5,010 per capita (2005)
ANNUAL AVERAGE GROWTH OF GDP – 2.9 per cent (2005 est)
INFLATION RATE – –0.1 per cent (2005 est)
TOTAL EXTERNAL DEBT – US$3,903m (20005 est)
IMPORTS – US$1,400m (2005)
EXPORTS – US$4,700m (2005)

Trade with UK	*2005*	*2006*
Imports from UK	£29,335,000	£28,415,000
Exports to UK	£10,091,000	£6,350,000

MEDIA

The biggest broadcaster, Radiodiffusion-Télévision Gabonaise, is state controlled and operates two stations. There are two other main channels: TéléAfrica, which is privately owned, and TV Sat, a subscription operator. There are several privately owned newspapers that usually publish on a weekly basis. The only daily newspaper, *L'Union,* is government-run. Radio is an important news medium because of rural illiteracy. Africa No1, a pan-African broadcaster based in Gabon, is partly French-owned.

THE GAMBIA

Republic of the Gambia

AREA – 11,300 sq. km. Neighbour: Senegal, which surrounds the Gambia except at the coast
CAPITAL – Banjul; population, 34,828 (2003)
MAJOR TOWNS – Kanifeng; Brikama
CURRENCY – Dalasi (D) of 100 butut
POPULATION – 1,641,564 rising at 2.84 per cent per year (2006 est); Mandinka (42 per cent per year), Fula (18 per cent), Wolof (16 per cent), Jola (10 per cent), Soninke (9 per cent) (est)
RELIGION – Islam (90 per cent), Christianity (9 per cent), indigenous religions (1 per cent) (est)
LANGUAGE – English (official), Mandinka, Wolof, Fula

POPULATION DENSITY – 152 per sq. km (2005)
URBAN POPULATION – 26.1 per cent (2005 est)
MEDIAN AGE (years) – 17.7 (2006 est)
NATIONAL ANTHEM – 'For The Gambia Our Homeland'
NATIONAL DAY – 18 February (Independence Day)
LIFE EXPECTANCY (years) – 54.14 (2006 est)
MORTALITY RATE – 12.25 (2006 est)
BIRTH RATE – 39.37 (2006 est)
INFANT MORTALITY RATE – 71.58 (2006 est)
HIV/AIDS ADULT PREVALENCE – 1.2 per cent (2003 est)
DEATH PENALTY – No*
CPI SCORE – 2.5 (2006)
MILITARY BUDGET – US$1.6m (2006 est)
MILITARY PERSONNEL – army 800

CLIMATE AND TERRAIN

The Gambia consists of a narrow strip of land along the Gambia River; the low-lying land is mostly a flood plain flanked by hills. Elevation extremes range from 53m at the highest point to 0m (Atlantic Ocean) at the lowest. The climate is tropical, with an average temperature of between 23°C and 40°C. The wet season runs from June to September.

HISTORY AND POLITICS

The Gambia river basin was part of a region dominated from the 10th to 16th centuries by the Mali and Songhai kingdoms. The Portuguese reached the Gambia river in 1447; English merchants began to trade along the river from 1588. Merchants from France, Courland (now Latvia) and the Netherlands also established trading posts there. In 1816, the British stationed a garrison on an island at the river mouth that became the capital of a small British-administered colony; this became a crown colony in 1843. In 1889, France agreed that the British rights along the upper river should extend to 10km from the river on either bank. The Gambia became independent within the Commonwealth on 18 February 1965 and a republic on 24 April 1970.

The post-independence prime minister, Sir Dawda Jawara, was president from 1970 until he was overthrown in 1994, in a coup by junior army officers. The coup leader, Lt. (later Capt.) Jammeh, assumed the presidency, the constitution was suspended and a civilian-military government was formed to rule in conjunction with the ruling military council. A referendum approved a new constitution in August 1996, Jammeh was elected president the following month and the military council was dissolved.

In the 2006 presidential election, Jammeh was re-elected with 67 per cent of the vote. The January 2007 legislative election was won by President Jammeh's party, the Alliance for Patriotic Reorientation and Construction (APRC), with an overwhelming majority.

POLITICAL SYSTEM

Under the 1996 constitution, the executive president is directly elected for a five-year term; there is no limit on re-election. The unicameral legislature, the national assembly, has 53 members, of whom 48 are directly elected and five are appointed by the president, for a five-year term.

HEAD OF STATE

President, Defence, Col. Yahya A. Jammeh, *took power* 23 July 1994, *elected* 26 September 1996, *re-elected* 2001, 2006

Vice-President, Women and Social Affairs, Ajaratou Isatou Njie-Saidy

SELECTED GOVERNMENT MEMBERS *as at May 2007*

External Affairs, Bala Garba-Jahumpa
Finance and Economic Affairs, Musa Gibril-Bala Gaye
Interior, Col. Baboucarr Jatta

GAMBIA HIGH COMMISSION

57 Kensington Court, London W8 5DG
T 020-7937 6316 E gambia@gamhighcom.wanadoo.co.uk
High Commissioner, HE Tamsir Jallow, *apptd* 2006

BRITISH HIGH COMMISSION

PO Box 507, 48 Atlantic Road, Fajara, Banjul
T (+220) 449 5133 E bhcbanjul@gamtel.gm
High Commissioner, HE Philip Sinkinson, *apptd* 2006

ECONOMY AND TRADE

The country has limited natural resources and agricultural land and, historically, the mainstay of the economy was re-export trade with neighbouring countries. This has declined owing to the government's imposition of pre-shipment inspection plans in 1999 and the instability of the currency. Although the discovery of offshore oil deposits was announced in 2004, none are currently exploited. There are high levels of public and foreign debt and the country is dependent on financial and technical aid from foreign donors. An important revenue source is remittances from Gambians working abroad.

Most of the population is dependent on subsistence agriculture, which employs 75 per cent of the workforce and contributes 30 per cent of GDP. The chief product, peanuts, is the basis of the main industrial activity and the main export, leaving the economy vulnerable to market fluctuations. Industry contributes 14 per cent to GDP and employs 19 per cent of the workforce, chiefly in light manufacturing: processing peanuts, fish and hides, assembling agricultural machinery, metalworking, woodworking and production of beverages and clothing. The services sector employs only 6 per cent of the workforce but contributes 56 per cent of GDP, largely owing to the growing tourism industry.

The main trade partners are India, the UK, China and Senegal. Principal exports are peanut products, fish, cotton lint, palm kernels and re-exports. The main imports are foodstuffs, manufactures, fuel and machinery and transport equipment.

GNI – US$400m; US$290 per capita (2005)
ANNUAL AVERAGE GROWTH OF GDP – 5.5 per cent (2005 est)
INFLATION RATE – 8.8 per cent (2005 est)
TOTAL EXTERNAL DEBT – US$628.8m (2003 est)
IMPORTS – US$240m (2005)
EXPORTS – US$9m (2005)

Trade with UK	*2005*	*2006*
Imports from UK	£16,468,000	£14,042,000
Exports to UK	£3,055,000	£3,513,000

EDUCATION AND HEALTH

There are four types of school in the Gambia: primary school (ages four to 10); junior school (ages 11–14), secondary school (ages 14–15) and Islamic school.

GROSS ENROLMENT RATIO (percentage of relevant age group) – primary 81 per cent; secondary 47 per cent; tertiary 1 per cent (2005 est)
HEALTH EXPENDITURE (per capita) – US$19 (2004)

MEDIA

Since 2002 private newspapers and radio stations have been regulated by a government-run commission that has the power to suspend publication or transmission licences and imprison journalists. The state operates the only national television station, Gambia Television. There is one private satellite channel, Premium TV Network. State-run Radio Gambia produces tightly controlled news broadcasts, which are relayed by private radio stations.

GEORGIA

Sak'art'velo – Georgia

AREA – 69,700 sq. km. Neighbours: Russia (north), Azerbaijan (east and south), Armenia (south), Turkey (south-west). It includes the autonomous republics of Abkhazia and Ajaria and the disputed region of South Ossetia (Tskhinvali)
CAPITAL – Tbilisi; population, 1,095,000 (2006 est)
MAJOR CITIES – Kutaisi; Batumi; Rustavi
CURRENCY – Lari of 100 tetri
POPULATION – 4,661,473, falling at 0.34 per cent per year (2006 est): Georgian (83.8 per cent), Azeri (6.5 per cent), Armenian (5.7 per cent)
RELIGION – Christianity (70 per cent), Islam (9 per cent) (est)
LANGUAGE – Georgian (official), Russian, Armenian, Azeri
POPULATION DENSITY – 64 per sq. km (2005)
URBAN POPULATION – 51.5 per cent (2005 est)
MEDIAN AGE (years) – 37.7 (2006 est)
NATIONAL ANTHEM – 'Tavisupleba' ['Freedom']
NATIONAL DAY – 26 May (Independence Day)
LIFE EXPECTANCY (years) – 76.09 (2006 est)
MORTALITY RATE – 9.23 (2006 est)
BIRTH RATE – 10.41 (2006 est)
INFANT MORTALITY RATE – 17.97 (2006 est)
DEATH PENALTY – No (abolished 1997)
CPI SCORE – 2.8 (2006)
POPULATION BELOW POVERTY LINE – 54 per cent (2001 est)
GROSS ENROLMENT RATIO (percentage of relevant age group) – primary 94 per cent; secondary 83 per cent; tertiary 46 per cent (2005 est)
HEALTH EXPENDITURE (per capita) – US$60 (2004)

CLIMATE AND TERRAIN

Georgia lies in the western part of the Caucasus region, with the Black Sea to the west. It is mountainous, with the Great Caucasus mountain range in the north and the Lesser Caucasus in the south, divided by the valleys of the Kura and Rioni rivers. Elevation extremes range from 5,201m (Mt Shkhara) at the highest point to 0m (Black Sea) at the lowest. The climate is almost tropical in the summer, whilst cold winters affect both the mountains and valleys. Average temperatures in Tbilisi range from 3°C in January to 28°C in July.

HISTORY AND POLITICS

The Georgians formed two states, Colchis and Iberia, on the edge of the Black Sea around 1000 BC. After several centuries of Arab rule, Georgia was liberated and entered a period of prosperity in the 12th century AD, when trade, irrigation and communications were developed. Invasions by the Khazars and Mongols led to the division of Georgia into several states. These precarious states struggled against the Turkish and the Persian empires from the 16th to the 18th centuries, gradually turning to the Russian Empire for protection and support. Eastern Georgia signed a treaty of alliance with Russia which recognised Russian supremacy in 1783 and joined the Russian Empire in 1801, followed soon after by western Georgia.

In the late 19th century, nationalist and Marxist movements competed for limited political influence under autocratic Russian rule. One of the most prominent Marxist activists was Iosif Dzhugashvili (Joseph Stalin). After the Russian Revolution of 1917, an independent nationalist government came to power in Georgia supported by allied intervention forces. In 1921 Soviet forces occupied Tbilisi, and in 1922 Georgia joined the USSR as part of the Transcaucasian Soviet Socialist Republic, becoming a separate republic in 1936.

In the 1980s there were growing demands for autonomy, and in 1990 the Communist Party's monopoly on power was abolished. In multiparty elections held in autumn 1990, the nationalist leader Zviad Gamsakhurdia was elected president. Georgia declared its independence from the USSR in May 1991.

Demonstrations against Gamsakhurdia's increasingly dictatorial government in 1991 developed into civil war that resulted in Gamsakhurdia's overthrow and replacement by Eduard Shevardnadze in 1992. The war continued until 1993, when, with most government forces engaged in Abkhazia, Georgia was forced to accept Russian armaments and troops to defeat the rebels and in return agreed to join the Commonwealth of Independent States.

President Shevardnadze was re-elected in 2000, but resigned in November 2003 after mass demonstrations against alleged electoral fraud in the 2003 parliamentary elections. Mikhail Saakashvili, leader of the National Movement, was elected president in a landslide victory in January 2004. In rerun elections in the disputed parliamentary seats in March 2004, the National Movement Democrats won 67 per cent of the vote.

Russia agreed in 2005 to withdraw from its two remaining military bases, in Ajaria and southern Georgia, by 2008. However, relations between the two countries remain fraught owing to Russia's support for the secessionists in South Ossetia and Abkhazia, Georgia's increasingly pro-Western stance and ties with the US government (including joint military exercises), and Russia's use of trade embargos and disruption of energy supplies.

SECESSION

The growth of Georgian nationalism and demands for autonomy from the USSR in the 1980s led to unilateral declarations of independence by the regions of South Ossetia (1991) and Abkhazia (1992). The Georgian government resisted these moves and there was conflict with both regions, which received support from Russia. Fighting ended in South Ossetia in 1992, while in Abkhazia, Georgian forces were forced to withdraw in 1993 and a ceasefire was signed the following year. In both cases, the peace is fragile and there have been subsequent sporadic clashes. Both regions remain outside government control, under de facto unrecognised governments, and continue to assert their independence. In both regions the economy and infrastructure are in ruins and the secessionists are increasingly influenced by and dependent on Russia. Russian peacekeeping forces remain in both areas, but the Georgian government is trying to have them replaced by international forces.

In 2004, relations between Georgia and Ajaria, a semi-autonomous region on the Black Sea coast bordering Turkey, deteriorated. Aslan Abashidze, Ajaria's leader from 1991, refused to recognise the authority of the newly elected Georgian president Mikhail Saakashvili, and in 2004 accused Georgia of planning to invade Ajaria and ordered the destruction of connecting bridges. Public demonstrations against Abashidze followed and he was forced to resign. In parliamentary elections of 2004, the pro-Georgian Saakashvili-Victorious Ajaria (SUA) party won 28 of the 30 seats in the Ajarian parliament, which has powers over local affairs.

POLITICAL SYSTEM

The 1995 constitution provides for a federal republic with a unicameral legislature, to become bicameral 'following the creation of appropriate conditions'. There is a president who is directly elected for a five-year term, renewable only once. The present parliament has 235 members, 85 elected in single-member constitutencies and the rest from party lists by proportional representation, who serve for a four-year term.

HEAD OF STATE

President, Mikhail Saakashvili, *elected* 4 January 2004, *sworn in* 25 January 2004

SELECTED GOVERNMENT MEMBERS *as at May 2007*

Prime Minister, Zurab Noghaideli

Deputy Prime Ministers, Ivane Merabishvili; Giorgi Baramidze

Defence, Davit Kezerashvili

Finance and Tax Revenue, Aleksi Aleksishvili

Foreign Affairs, Gela Bezhuashvili

EMBASSY OF GEORGIA

4 Russell Gardens, London W14 8EZ

T 020-7603 7799 W www.geoemb.org.uk

Ambassador Extraordinary and Plenipotentiary, HE Gela Charkviani, *apptd* 2006

BRITISH EMBASSY

GMT Plaza, 4 Freedom Square, 0105 Tbilisi

T (+995) (32) 274 747 E british.embassy.tbilisi@fco.gov.uk

Ambassador Extraordinary and Plenipotentiary, HE Denis Keefe, *apptd* 2007

BRITISH COUNCIL

34 Rustaveli Avenue, 380008 Tbilisi

T (+995) (32) 250 407/ 988 014 W www.britishcouncil.org.ge

Director, Lena Milosevic

DEFENCE

The army has 86 main battle tanks, 91 armoured personnel carriers and 89 armoured infantry fighting vehicles. The navy has 14 patrol and coastal combatants. The Air force has 7 combat aircraft and 3 attack helicopters.

MILITARY EXPENDITURE – US$380m (2005 est)

MILITARY PERSONNEL – 11,320: army 7,042, navy 1,350, air force 1,350, National Guard 1,578; paramilitaries 11,700

CONSCRIPTION DURATION – 18 months

ECONOMY AND TRADE

The economy is making good progress towards recovery from the near-collapse of the 1990s, particularly under the post-Shevardnadze government, which has reformed the tax system, started to collect tax revenues, given added impetus to the privatisation programme and cracked down on corruption. Although Georgia has coal and oil deposits and considerable hydroelectric power potential, they are not being fully exploited and the country is dependent on energy supplies from Russia; the fuel crises of 2005–6 and the massive increases in Russian fuel prices have added urgency to the search for alternatives and prompted repair of the pipeline from Azerbaijan. The government hopes Georgia's position as a transit state for oil and gas pipelines and for trade between central Asia and Europe will provide economic growth.

The most productive sector of the economy is agriculture, which employs 40 per cent of the workforce and generates 18 per cent of GDP, with a concentration on viniculture, tea growing, and citrus fruits. Industry, which contributes 27 per cent of GDP, produces steel, aircraft, machine tools, electrical appliances, manganese, copper, chemicals, wood products and wine. The main trading partners are Russia, Turkey, Azerbaijan, Ukraine, Turkmenistan and Armenia. Principal exports are scrap metal, machinery, chemicals, fuel re-exports, citrus fruits, tea and wine. The main imports are fuels, machinery and parts, vehicles, food (especially grain) and pharmaceuticals.

GNI – US$5,900m; US$1,320 per capita (2005)

ANNUAL AVERAGE GROWTH OF GDP – 9.3 per cent (2005 est)

INFLATION RATE – 8.2 per cent (2005 est)

UNEMPLOYMENT – 12.6 per cent (2004 est)

TOTAL EXTERNAL DEBT – US$2,040m (2004)

IMPORTS – US$2,000m (2005)

EXPORTS – US$1,000m (2005)

BALANCE OF PAYMENTS

Trade – US$1,214m deficit (2005)

Current Account – US$751m deficit (2005)

Trade with UK	*2005*	*2006*
Imports from UK	£26,705,000	£37,771,000
Exports to UK	£19,493,000	£230,961,000

MEDIA

A government-funded public broadcaster, Georgian State TV, has replaced former state television and radio networks. The state has also relinquished control of newspapers and news agencies, and there are over 200 privately owned newspapers, although readership is generally low. A 2004 law decriminalised slander and libel.

GERMANY

Bundesrepublik Deutschland – Federal Republic of Germany

AREA – 357,021 sq. km. Neighbours: Denmark (north), Poland and Czech Republic (east), Austria and Switzerland (south), France, Luxembourg, Belgium and the Netherlands (west)

CAPITAL – Berlin; population, 3,388,477 (2004 est).

MAJOR CITIES – Hamburg; Munich; Cologne; Frankfurt; Dortmund; Essen; Stuttgart; Düsseldorf; Bremen; Hannover; Duisberg

CURRENCY – Euro (€) of 100 cents

POPULATION – 82,422,299 falling at 0.02 per cent pe

year (2006 est); German (91.5 per cent), Turkish (2.4 per cent) (est)
RELIGION – Christianity (68 per cent; includes Roman Catholicism, 33 per cent), Islam (3 per cent) (est)
LANGUAGE – German (official)
POPULATION DENSITY – 236 per sq. km (2005)
URBAN POPULATION – 88.5 per cent (2005 est)
MEDIAN AGE (years) – 42.6 (2006 est)
NATIONAL ANTHEM – 'Einigkeit und Recht und Freiheit' ['Unity and Right and Freedom']
NATIONAL DAY – 3 October (Unity Day)
LIFE EXPECTANCY (years) – 78.8 (2006 est)
MORTALITY RATE – 10.62 (2006 est)
BIRTH RATE – 8.25 (2006 est)
INFANT MORTALITY RATE – 4.12 (2006 est)
DEATH PENALTY – No (abolished 1949 in FRG and 1987 in GDR)
CPI SCORE – 8.0 (2006)

CLIMATE AND TERRAIN

The north of the country is low-lying, rising in the central region to uplands, Alpine foothills and then to the Bavarian Alps in the south. Elevation extremes range from 2,963m (Zugspitze, Bavaria) at the highest point to −3.5m (Neuendorf bei Wilster) at the lowest. The Rhine, Weser and Elbe rivers flow from the south to the North Sea, the Oder and Neisse rivers flow north to the Baltic Sea, and the River Danube flows east from its source in the south of the country to the Austrian border. More than a third of the land is covered by forest. The climate is temperate, with average temperatures ranging from −5°C in January to 19°C in July.

HISTORY AND POLITICS

Charlemagne extended Frankish authority over the Germanic tribes in the eighth century, and took the title of Holy Roman Emperor. The treaty of Verdun (843) divided this empire into three, the eastern part (corresponding to modern Germany) comprising hundreds of small dukedoms and principalities that enjoyed virtual independence under the hegemony of a nominally elective Holy Roman Emperor. Although a succession of dynasties succeeded at times in centralising power between 962 and 1806, shifting allegiances and alliances enabled the states to challenge the authority of the emperor, which was never sufficient to overcome the fragmentation and achieve unification into a nation state.

The empire was replaced in 1806 by a loose association of sovereign states known as the German Confederation, which was dissolved in 1866 and replaced by the Prussian-dominated North German Federation. The south German principalities united with the northern federation to form a second German Empire in 1871 and the King of Prussia was proclaimed emperor.

Defeat in the First World War led to the abdication of the emperor, and the country became a republic. The treaty of Versailles (1919) ceded Alsace-Lorraine to France, and large areas in the east were lost to Poland. The world economic crisis of 1929 contributed to the collapse of the Weimar Republic and the subsequent rise to power of the National Socialist movement of Adolf Hitler, who became chancellor in 1933.

After concluding a treaty of non-aggression with the Soviet Union in August 1939, Germany invaded Poland (1 September 1939), precipitating the Second World War, which lasted until 1945. Hitler committed suicide on 30 April 1945. On 8 May 1945, Germany unconditionally surrendered.

Germany was divided into American, French, British and Soviet zones of occupation. The Federal Republic of Germany (FRG) was created out of the three Western zones in 1949. A Communist government was established in the Soviet zone (henceforth the German Democratic Republic (GDR)). In 1961 the Soviet zone of Berlin was sealed off, and the Berlin Wall was built along the zonal boundary, partitioning the western sectors of the city from the eastern.

Soviet-initiated reform in eastern Europe during the late 1980s led to unrest in the GDR, culminating in the opening of the Berlin Wall in November 1989 and the collapse of the Communist government. The 'treaty on the final settlement with respect to Germany' concluded between the FRG, GDR and the four former occupying powers in September 1990, unified Germany with effect from 3 October 1990 as a fully sovereign state. Economic and monetary union preceded formal union on 1 July 1990. Constitutionally, unification was the accession of Berlin and the five reformed *Länder* (states) of the GDR to the FRG, which remains in being. Berlin was declared the capital of the unified Germany and parliament and government departments were transferred from Bonn.

Germany was a founder member of the EEC in 1958 and joined the eurozone in 1999. Its parliament ratified the EU constitution in May 2005.

Horst Köhler was elected federal president in 2004. An early legislative election was held in September 2005 after Chancellor Gerhard Schröder's Social Democratic Party (SPD) lost control of several *Länder* governments in the May 2005 regional elections and Schröder lost a parliamentary vote of no confidence in July. In the general election, the opposition Christian Democratic Union/Christian Social Union (CDU/CSU) coalition won four more seats than the SDP, but Chancellor Schröder refused to concede defeat. To break the political deadlock, a grand coalition of the SDP and CDU/CSU was formed under the CDU/CSU leader Angela Merkel, who became Germany's first female chancellor in November 2005.

POLITICAL SYSTEM

The Basic Law (constitution) provides for a president, elected by the *Bundesversammlung* (an electoral college comprising the members of the Bundestag and an equal number of representatives elected by the state legislatures) for a five-year term, and a bicameral legislature. The lower house, *Bundestag,* has 603 members directly elected by proportional representation for a four-year term. The upper house, *Bundesrat,* has 69 members appointed by the governments of the states *(Länder)* in proportion to *Länder* populations, without a fixed term of office. The head of government is the chancellor, who is proposed by the president and elected by the *Bundestag.*

HEAD OF STATE

Federal President, Horst Köhler, *elected* 23 May, *sworn in* 1 July 2004

SELECTED GOVERNMENT MEMBERS *as at May 2007*

Federal Chancellor, Angela Merkel
Federal Vice-Chancellor; Labour and Social Affairs, Franz Müntefering
Foreign Affairs, Frank-Walter Steinmeier
Defence, Franz Josef Jung
Interior, Wolfgang Schäuble
Finance, Peer Steinbrück

EMBASSY OF THE FEDERAL REPUBLIC OF GERMANY

23 Belgrave Square/Chesham Place, London SW1X 8PZ
T 020-7824 1300 **W** www.german-embassy.org.uk
Ambassador Extraordinary and Plenipotentiary, HE Wolfgang Ischinger, *apptd* 2002

BRITISH EMBASSY

Wilhelmstrasse 70, D-10117 Berlin
T (+49) (30) 204 570 **W** www.britischebotschaft.de
Ambassador Extraordinary and Plenipotentiary, HE Sir Michael Arthur, KCMG, *apptd* 2007

BRITISH COUNCIL

Hackescher Markt 1, D-10178 Berlin
T (+49) (30) 311 0990 **W** www.britishcouncil.de/e
Director, Michael Bird OBE

FEDERAL STRUCTURE

Germany is a federal republic composed of 16 states *(Länder)* (ten from the former FRG, five from the former GDR, and Berlin). Each *Land* has its own directly elected legislature and government led by Minister-Presidents (prime ministers) or equivalents. The 1949 Basic Law vests executive power in the *Länder* governments except in those areas reserved for the federal government.

State	*Capital*	*Population (millions) (2005 est)*
Baden-Württemberg	Stuttgart	10.7
Bavaria	Munich	12.5
Berlin	—	3.4
Brandenburg	Potsdam	2.6
Bremen	—	0.7
Hamburg	—	1.7
Hesse	Wiesbaden	6.1
Lower Saxony	Hannover	8.0
Mecklenburg-West Pomerania	Schwerin	1.7
North Rhine-Westphalia	Düsseldorf	18.1
Rhineland-Palatinate	Mainz	4.1
Saarland	Saarbrücken	1.1
Saxony	Dresden	4.3
Saxony-Anhalt	Magdeburg	2.5
Schleswig-Holstein	Kiel	2.8
Thuringia	Erfurt	2.3

DEFENCE

The army has 2,035 main battle tanks, 2,300 armoured personnel carriers, 2,218 armoured infantry fighting vehicles and 192 attack helicopters. The navy has 13 submarines, 15 frigates, 10 patrol and coastal vessels and 22 armed helicopters. The air force has 295 combat aircraft.

MILITARY EXPENDITURE – US$38,000m (2005)
MILITARY PERSONNEL – 245,702: army 160,794, navy 24,328, air force 60,580.
CONSCRIPTION DURATION – Nine months

ECONOMY AND TRADE

Germany has one of the world's largest economies but decades of strong economic performance gave way in the 1990s to Germany's most severe post-war recession, largely an aftermath of reunification and of macroeconomic stagnation. The economy in the east remains weak despite costly modernisation and integration measures. However, an overall revival began in 2006, with growth in GDP exceeding 2 per cent for the first time since 2001, a drop in unemployment and the budget deficit being reduced to less than 3 per cent. Government reforms to the labour and welfare systems contributed to the improvement.

The country has a modern, diverse, highly industrialised and technologically advanced market economy. The services sector contributes 70 per cent of GDP, industry 29 per cent and agriculture 1 per cent. The industrial sector is among the world's largest producers of iron, steel, coal, cement, chemicals, machinery, vehicles, machine tools, electronics, food and beverages, ships and textiles. Germany depends on imports to meet its oil and natural gas needs but is a net exporter of electricity; this may change, though, as all 19 of its nuclear power stations, which supply over 30 per cent of its energy, are to be closed down by 2032.

The main trading partners are other EU countries, the USA and China. Machinery, vehicles, chemicals, footstuff and textiles are all principal imports and exports.

GNI – US$2,875,600m; US$34,870 per capita (2005)
ANNUAL AVERAGE GROWTH OF GDP – 0.9 per cent (2005 est)
INFLATION RATE – 2 per cent (2005 est)
UNEMPLOYMENT – 11.7 per cent (2005 est)
TOTAL EXTERNAL DEBT – US$3,626,000m (2005)
IMPORTS – US$777,000m (2005)
EXPORTS – US$978,000m (2005)

BALANCE OF PAYMENTS

Trade – US$189,241m surplus (2005)
Current Account – US$115,519m surplus (2005)

Trade with UK	*2005*	*200*
Imports from UK	£22,545,081,000	£26,366,500,00
Exports to UK	£36,367,941,000	£38,882,800,0

COMMUNICATIONS

There is an extensive road network of aroun 232,000km, including 12,000km of motorway *(autobahn).* There are 47,000km of railways. Around 2 per cent of domestic freight is carried on the 7,500km o inland waterways. The Rhine and the Danube are linke by the Rhine-Maine-Danube Canal, creating a through route from the North Sea to the Black Sea. The Kiel Canal links the North Sea and the Baltic Sea. The main river ports are Duisburg, Frankfurt, Karlsruhe and Mainz; the main seaports are Hamburg, Kiel, Bremen, Bremerhaven, Rostock and Wilhemshaven. The busiest airport is at Frankfurt, other principal airports include Berlin, Munich and Bonn. The telephone system in the east has been modernised and integrated with the rest of the country. Mobile phone distribution is widespread, with 79 million subscribers in 2005. There were 51 million internet users in 2006.

EDUCATION AND HEALTH

Education is free of charge and compulsory between the ages of six and 18 and comprises nine years of full-time education at primary and main schools and three years of vocational education on a part-time basis. The secondary school leaving examination *(Abitur)* entitles the holder to a place at a university or another institution of higher education.

Children below the age of 18 who are not attending a general secondary or a full-time vocational school have compulsory day-release at a vocational school.

The largest universities are in Munich, Berlin, Hamburg, Bonn, Frankfurt and Cologne. Germany's oldest university is Heidelberg, founded in 1386.

GROSS ENROLMENT RATIO (percentage of relevant age group) – primary 100 per cent; secondary 100 per cent (2005 est)
HEALTH EXPENDITURE (per capita) – US$3,521 (2004)
HOSPITAL BEDS (per 1,000 people) – 8.9 (2000–5)

MEDIA

Each of the country's 16 states operates its own television stations, both private and public. Germany is implementing digital radio and television and will cease analogue services in 2010. Over 90 per cent of households receive cable or satellite television. Germany also has a considerable press industry and is home to many international media companies. It is hoped digital television and radio will replace analogue services by 2010.

CULTURE

Germany has produced a wealth of classical composers, among them Bach (1685–1750), Beethoven (1770–1827), Schubert (1797–1828), Wagner (1813–83) and Brahms (1833–97). Philosophers include Immanuel Kant (1724–1804), Karl Marx (1818–83), Friedrich Engels (1820–95) and Friedrich Nietzsche (1844–1900). The work of playwrights Goethe (1749–1832) and Friedrich Schiller (1759–1805) had a European-wide influence. Novelists Thomas Mann (1875–1955), Hermann Hesse (1877–1962) and Günter Grass (*b.* 1927) have all received the Nobel prize for literature.

Key figures in the visual arts are Hans Holbein the Younger (1497–1543), who achieved success in England as a court painter in the Renaissance, surrealist Max Ernst (1891–1976) and Joseph Beuys (1921–86), and in film-making directors Friedrich Murnau (1888–1931), Leni Riefenstahl (1902–2003), Werner Herzog (*b.* 1942) and Wim Wenders (*b.* 1945), and actor Klaus Kinski (1926–1) all gained Hollywood recognition.

Physicist Albert Einstein (1879–1955) is perhaps the world's most recognisable scientist, having introduced theory of relativity to the wider world in 1905. Other notable German scientists include Max Planck (1858–1947), Hans Geiger (1882–1945) and Wilhelm Röntgen (1845–1923).

GHANA

Republic of Ghana

AREA – 239,460 sq. km. Neighbours: Burkina Faso (north), Côte d'Ivoire (west), Togo (east)
CAPITAL – Accra; population, 1,658,937 (2000)
MAJOR CITIES – Kumasi; Sekondi-Takoradi; Tamale
CURRENCY – Cedi of 100 pesewas
POPULATION – 22,409,572 rising at 2.07 per cent per year (2006 est); Akan (49 per cent), Moshi-Dagomba (16 per cent), Ewe (13 per cent), Ga (8 per cent)
RELIGION – Christianity (69 per cent), Islam (15 per cent), indigenous religions (15 per cent) (est)
LANGUAGE – English (official), Akan, Moshi-Dagomba, Ewe, Ga
POPULATION DENSITY – 97 per sq. km (2005)
URBAN POPULATION – 46.3 per cent (2005 est)
MEDIAN AGE (years) – 19.9 (2006 est)
NATIONAL ANTHEM – 'God Bless Our Homeland Ghana'
NATIONAL DAY – 6 March (Independence Day)
LIFE EXPECTANCY (years) – 58.87 (2006 est)
MORTALITY RATE – 9.72 (2006 est)
BIRTH RATE – 30.52 (2006 est)
INFANT MORTALITY RATE – 55.02 (2006 est)
HIV/AIDS ADULT PREVALENCE – 3.1 per cent (2003 est)
DEATH PENALTY – No*
CPI SCORE – 3.3 (2006)
MILITARY BUDGET – US$72m (2006)
MILITARY PERSONNEL – 13,500: army 10,000, navy 2,000, air force 1,500

CLIMATE AND TERRAIN

Ghana consists mostly of tropical interior plains bisected by the Volta River basin and the great central Lake Volta, and rising to the Ashanti plateau in the west. Elevation extremes range from 880m (Mt Afadjato) at the highest point to 0m (Atlantic Ocean) at the lowest. The climate is tropical but there is also a warm and dry coastal area in the south-east. The average temperature in Accra is 30°C.

HISTORY AND POLITICS

First reached by Europeans in the 15th century, after which it became a centre for gold and slave trading, the constituent parts of Ghana came under British administration at various times. The original Gold Coast colony was constituted in 1874 and Ashanti and the Northern Territories Protectorate in 1901. Trans-Volta-Togoland, part of the former German colony of Togo, was mandated to Britain by the League of Nations after the First World War and was integrated with the Gold Coast colony in 1956 following a plebiscite. The colony became independent on 6 March 1957 and was proclaimed a republic in 1960.

Since 1966, Ghana has experienced long periods of military rule interspersed with short-lived civilian governments. A coup in 1978 led to the formation of an Armed Forces Revolutionary Council chaired by Flt. Lt. Jerry Rawlings. Civilian rule was restored in 1979 but another coup in 1981 brought Rawlings back to power. Civilian rule was restored again in 1992 after a referendum approved a new multiparty constitution and the legalisation of political parties. A reconciliation commission was set up in 2002 to investigate human rights violations during military rule. Recommendations included reparations and rehabilitation for victims, particularly of sexual violence and a formal presidential apology.

Since the mid-1990s there have been intermittent clashes over land ownership between different ethnic groups in the Northern Region. A two-year state of emergency was imposed after the latest ethnic violence in 2002.

In the 2004 elections, President John Kufuor was re-elected with 52.75 per cent of the vote, and the New Patriotic Party retained its parliamentary majority.

POLITICAL SYSTEM
Under the 1993 constitution, the executive president is directly elected for a four-year term, renewable only once. The president nominates members of the council of ministers subject to approval by parliament. The unicameral legislature, the parliament, has 230 members, who are directly elected for a four-year term.

HEAD OF STATE
President, John Kufuor, *elected* 28 December 2000, *sworn in* 7 January 2001, *re-elected* 7 December 2004
Vice-President, Aliu Mahama

SELECTED GOVERNMENT MEMBERS *as at May 2007*
Defence, Kwame Addo-Kufuor
Finance and Economic Planning, Kwadwo Baah Wiredu
Foreign Affairs, Nana Akufo Addo
Interior, Albert Kan Dapaah

OFFICE OF THE HIGH COMMISSION OF GHANA
13 Belgrave Square, London SW1X 8PN
T 020-7201 5900 W www.ghana-com.co.uk
High Commissioner, HE Annan Arkyin Cato, *apptd* 2006

BRITISH HIGH COMMISSION
PO Box 296, Osu Link, off Gamel Abdul Nasser Avenue, Accra
T (+233) (21) 221 665 E high.commission.accra@fco.gov.uk
W www.britishhighcommission.gov.uk/ghana
High Commissioner, HE Dr Nicholas Westcott, CMG, *apptd* 2007

BRITISH COUNCIL
PO Box GP 771, Liberia Road, Accra
T (+233) (21) 683 068/663 979
W www.britishcouncil.org/ghana
Director, Moses Anibaba

ECONOMY AND TRADE

Ghana has abundant natural resources, but high foreign debt, and budget and trade deficits make it dependent on international financial and technical aid. It qualified for the IMF/World Bank heavily indebted poor countries intitiative in 2002 and was promised 100 per cent debt relief by the G8 in 2005. Economic priorities include tighter management of government finances, further privatisation and reduction of inflation.

Subsistence agriculture forms the basis of the economy, along with forestry and fishing. The sector employs 60 per cent of the workforce and generates 37 per cent of GDP. The main cash crops are cocoa, timber and tuna. Industry employs 15 per cent of the workforce and contributes 25 per cent of GDP, mainly from mining (manganese, gold, bauxite, diamonds), light manufacturing, aluminium smelting and food processing. Services employ 25 per cent and account for 38 per cent of GDP. Hydroelectric power is generated at dams on the Volta and is fed into a power transmission network for most of Ghana, Togo and Benin.

The main export markets are EU countries, the USA and Japan. Principal exports are gold, cocoa, timber, tuna, metals, minerals and diamonds. Imports are provided mainly by Nigeria, China, EU countries and the USA. The main imports are capital equipment, fuel and foodstuffs.

GNI – US$10,000m; US$450 per capita (2005)
ANNUAL AVERAGE GROWTH OF GDP – 5.9 per cent (2005 est)
INFLATION RATE – 15.1 per cent (2005 est)
TOTAL EXTERNAL DEBT – US$6,999m (2005 est)
IMPORTS – US$5,100m (2005)
EXPORTS – US$2,500m (2005)

BALANCE OF PAYMENTS
Trade – US$1,513m deficit (2004)
Current Account – US$236m deficit (2004)

Trade with UK	*2005*	*2006*
Imports from UK	£155,043,000	£189,834,000
Exports to UK	£117,690,000	£148,788,000

EDUCATION AND HEALTH

The government provides compulsory basic education for all children free of charge. In 2003, investment in education constituted 25 per cent of all government spending. Ghana has one of Africa's oldest universities, at Legon in Accra (established in 1948).

LITERACY RATE – 54.1 per cent (2004 est)
GROSS ENROLMENT RATIO (percentage of relevant age group) – primary 94 per cent; secondary 45 per cent; tertiary 5 per cent (2006)
HEALTH EXPENDITURE (per capita) – US$27 (2004)

MEDIA

The Ghana Broadcasting Corporation (GBC) is the state-owned broadcaster. GBC operates a television network and various radio stations that transmit in English and Ghanaian dialects. TV3 is a private television channel. Multichoice is a cable television operator and Metro TV is jointly owned by the government and private backers. Radio is the country's most popular medium and there are hundreds of private stations. Ghana's private press and broadcasters operate without major restrictions.

GREECE

Elliniki Dhimokratia – Hellenic Republic

AREA – 131,940 sq. km. Neighbours: Albania, Macedonia and Bulgaria (north), Turkey (east)
CAPITAL – Athens; population, 745,514 (2001)
MAJOR CITIES – Thessaloniki (Salonika); Patrai (Patras); Iraklion (Heraklion); Volos; Larissa
CURRENCY – Euro (€) of 100 cents
POPULATION – 10,688,058 rising at 0.18 per cent per year (2006 est)
RELIGION – Greek Orthodox Christianity (97 per cent), Islam (2 per cent) (est)
LANGUAGE – Greek (official), English, French
POPULATION DENSITY – 86 per sq. km (2005)

URBAN POPULATION – 61.4 per cent (2005 est)
MEDIAN AGE (years) – 40.8 (2006 est)
NATIONAL ANTHEM – 'Imnos eis tin Eleftherian' ['Hymn to Freedom']
NATIONAL DAY – 25 March (Independence Day)
LIFE EXPECTANCY (years) – 79.24 (2006 est)
MORTALITY RATE – 10.24 (2006 est)
BIRTH RATE – 9.68 (2006 est)
INFANT MORTALITY RATE – 5.43 (2006 est)
DEATH PENALTY – No (abolished 2004)
CPI SCORE – 4.4 (2006)

CLIMATE AND TERRAIN

The main areas of Greece are: Macedonia, Thrace, Epirus, Thessaly, Continental Greece, the Peloponnese and the island of Crete. The main island groups are the Sporades, the Dodecanese or Southern Sporades, the Cyclades, the Aegean and Ionian islands and Corfu. Low-lying coastal areas rise to a hilly or mountainous interior on the mainland and the islands. The Pindos mountains form a spine down the centre of the mainland, continuing down the Peloponnese, which is divided from the mainland by the Gulf of Corinth, the largest of the gulfs and bays indenting the coast. Elevation extremes range from 2,917m (Mt Olympus) at the highest point to 0m (Mediterranean Sea) at the lowest. The coastline and islands have a Mediterranean climate with hot, dry summers and mild, wet winters. The average temperature in Athens ranges from 9°C in January to 28°C in July.

HISTORY AND POLITICS

Successive civilizations flourished in ancient Greece from the second millennium BC until it was conquered by Philip II of Macedon in the fourth century BC and the Romans in 146 BC. When the western Roman Empire fell, the eastern part continued as the Byzantine Empire until it was conquered by the Turks in the mid-15th century. Turkish rule began to be overthrown in a war of independence (1821–7) that led to the establishment of a Greek kingdom in the Peloponnese in 1829. Other islands and territories were added gradually over the next century, culminating in the return of the Dodecanese by Italy in 1947.

After the German Nazi occupation of 1941–4, a civil war broke out between monarchist and communist groups that lasted from 1946 to 1949, and although it resulted in the restoration of democracy, tension between right-wing and radical groups continued. In 1967, right-wing elements in the army seized power and established a military regime (the Greek Colonels). The king went into voluntary exile in 1967. Unrest in Athens intensified after the government was involved in the overthrow of President Makarios of Cyprus in July 1974 and led the Colonels to surrender power. Konstantinos Karamanlis (prime minister 1955–63) returned from exile to form a provisional government, and the first elections for ten years were held in 1974. The restoration of the monarchy was rejected by referendum in December 1974 and Greece became a republic. The restored democracy has proved stable, with political life dominated for the next two decades by Karamanlis, founder of the conservative New Democracy (ND) party, and Andreas Papandreou, who founded the left-wing Panhellenic Socialist Party (PASOK). Greece joined the European Community in 1981 and the eurozone in 2000. The parliament ratified the EU constitution in April 2005.

In the 2004 legislative election, ND won an overall majority in parliament, with 165 seats, and PASOK, which had been in power since 1994, won 117 seats. The 2005 presidential election was won by Karolos Papoulias.

POLITICAL SYSTEM
Under the 1975 constitution, the head of state is the president, elected by parliament for a five-year term, renewable only once. The unicameral parliament *(Vouli)* has 300 members directly elected for a four-year term by proportional representation, with a 3 per cent threshold for parliamentary representation.

HEAD OF STATE
President of the Hellenic Republic, Karolos Papoulias, *elected by parliament* 8 February 2005, *sworn in* 12 March 2005

SELECTED GOVERNMENT MEMBERS *as at May 2007*
Prime Minister; Minister for Culture, Costas Karamanlis
Foreign Affairs, Theodora Bakoyiannis
Internal Affairs, Public Administration and Decentralisation, Prokopis Pavlopoulos
Defence, Evangelos Meimarakis
Economy and Finance, Georgios Alogoskoufis

EMBASSY OF GREECE
1A Holland Park, London W11 3TP
T 020-7229 3850 W www.greekembassy.org.uk
Ambassador Extraordinary and Plenipotentiary, Vassilis-Achilleas Pispinis, *apptd* 2007

BRITISH EMBASSY
1 Ploutarchou Street, 106 75 Athens
T (+30) (210) 727 2600 E information.athens@fco.gov.uk
W www.british-embassy.gr
Ambassador Extraordinary and Plenipotentiary, HE Simon Gass, CMG, CVO, *apptd* 2004

BRITISH COUNCIL
17 Kolonaki Square (Plateia Philikis Etairias), 106 73, Athens
T (+30) (210) 369 2333 W www.britishcouncil.org/greece
Director, Desmond Lauder

DEFENCE

The army has 1,434 main battle tanks, 1,797 armoured personnel carriers, 378 armoured infantry fighting vehicles and 20 attack helicopters. The navy has 9 submarines, 17 principal surface combatants, 37 patrol and coastal vessels and 11 armed helicopters. The air force has a total of 278 combat aircraft.

Greece maintains 1,100 army personnel in Cyprus.
MILITARY EXPENDITURE – US$6,860m (2005)
MILITARY PERSONNEL – 147,100: army 93,500, navy 19,000, air force 23,000, joint staff 11,600; paramilitaries 4,000
CONSCRIPTION DURATION – Up to 15 months

ECONOMY AND TRADE

Greece experienced rapid economic growth in the final quarter of the 20th century, partly through revenues from tourism and partly through accession to the EC. It has a capitalist economy, though with a large public sector. The construction boom and infrastructure improvements before the 2004 Olympic Games in Athens caused a boom, but growth subsequently slowed, exacerbating the problems of high unemployment and rising inflation. Government measures to tackle these problems and the budget deficit include spending cuts, reduction of the public sector, and pension and labour reforms; these proposals have provoked strikes and demonstrations.

Though there has been substantial industrialisation, agriculture still employs 12 per cent of the workforce and contributes 5 per cent of GDP. The most important agricultural products are cereals, vegetables, olives, tomatoes, fruit, tobacco, beef and dairy products. Industrial activities, which contribute 21 per cent of GDP, include food and tobacco processing, textiles, chemicals, metal products, mining and petroleum production. The service sector employs 68 per cent of the workforce and generates 74 per cent of GDP; much of this is derived from tourism, which accounts for about 15 per cent of GDP, and shipping. Greece is a net importer of energy, including oil for refining and re-export.

The main trading partners are other EU countries (especially Germany and Italy), the USA, Bulgaria, Russia and Turkey. Principal exports are food and wine, manufactured goods, petroleum products, chemicals and textiles. The main imports are machinery, transport equipment, fuels and chemicals.

GNI – US$220,300m; US$19,840 per capita (2005)
ANNUAL AVERAGE GROWTH OF GDP – 3.7 per cent (2005 est)
INFLATION RATE – 3.5 per cent (2005 est)
UNEMPLOYMENT – 9.9 per cent (2005 est)
TOTAL EXTERNAL DEBT – US$78,180m (2005 est)
IMPORTS – US$49,800m (2005)
EXPORTS – US$15,500m (2005)

BALANCE OF PAYMENTS
Trade – US$34,253m deficit (2005)
Current Account – US$17,879m deficit (2005)

Trade with UK	*2005*	*2006*
Imports from UK	£1,348,123,000	£1,403,300,000
Exports to UK	£679,325,000	£640,400,000

COMMUNICATIONS

There are extensive rail and road networks. The 2,500km of railways are state-owned, with the exception of the Athens–Piraeus Electric Railway. There are 115,000km of roads, including 880km of motorways. The main seaports are Piraeus, Thessaloniki and Patrai on the mainland and Iraklion on Crete. An extensive ferry system connects the islands to one another and to the mainland. The 6km Corinth canal across the Corinth isthmus shortens the sea journey by 325km. There are 82 airports and airfields, of which 66 have surfaced runways; the main airports are at Athens, Thessaloniki, Iraklion (Crete) and Corfu town (Corfu), although several other islands, especially tourist destinations, have airports. The land-line and mobile telephone systems cover the whole country. There were 3.8 million internet users in 2005.

EDUCATION AND HEALTH

Education is free of charge and compulsory between the ages of six and 15, and is maintained by state grants.

LITERACY RATE – 91 per cent (2004 est)
GROSS ENROLMENT RATIO (percentage of relevant age group) – primary 102 per cent; secondary 96 per cent; tertiary 79 per cent (2005 est)
HEALTH EXPENDITURE (per capita) – US$1,879 (2004)
HOSPITAL BEDS (per 1,000 people) – 4.7 (2000–5)

8.5	WORLD HIGHEST
	cigarettes smoked per head per day

Source: Economist Intelligence Unit

MEDIA

Although the Greek media is largely free from regulation, editors and publishers risk prosecution should their material be deemed offensive to religious beliefs or the president. A sizeable proportion of the country's 1,700 private radio and television stations are unlicensed. State-run broadcasters have lost a large segment of the market to commercial services in recent years.

CULTURE

Greek civilisation emerged *c.*1300 BC and underpins the philosophy, politics, literature, art and mathematics of the Western world. The epic poems of Homer, the *Iliad* and *Odyssey*, are thought to date from *c.*800 BC, making them the earliest recorded works in Western literature. Aeschylus (*c.*525 BC–*c.*456 BC) is credited with inventing modern drama through the use of dialogue; prior to this, actors could only communicate through the chorus. Other dramatists whose work has survived include Euripedes (480–406 BC) and Aristophanes (446–388 BC), author of the earliest known comedies. Socrates (470–399 BC), Plato (*c.*428–*c.*348 BC) and Aristotle (384–322 BC), whose *Poetics* is the earliest work of literary criticism, are considered the founders of philosophy. Hippocrates (*c.*460 –370 BC) was the first to separate medicine from philosophy and religion; his theory of the body ruled by four humours persisted until late medieval times.

The spoken language of modern Greece is descended from the common Greek of Alexander the Great's empire. *Katharevousa,* a conservative literary dialect evolved by Adamantios Korais (1748–1833), which was used for official and technical matters, has been phased out. Novels and poetry are mostly written in *dimotiki,* a progressive literary dialect which owes much to Yannis Psycharis (1854–1929). Giorgos Seferis (1900–71) and Odysseus Elytis (1911–96) both won the Nobel prize for literature, in 1963 and 1979 respectively.

GRENADA

State of Grenada

AREA – 344 sq. km
CAPITAL – St George's; population, 3,908 (2001)
CURRENCY – East Caribbean dollar (EC $) of 100 cents
POPULATION – 89,703 rising at 0.26 per cent per year (2006 est)
RELIGION – Roman Catholicism (64 per cent), Protestantism (28 per cent) (est)
LANGUAGE – English (official), French patois
POPULATION DENSITY – 313 per sq. km (2005)
URBAN POPULATION – 42.4 per cent (2005 est)
MEDIAN AGE (years) – 21.7 (2006 est)
NATIONAL ANTHEM – 'Hail Grenada'
NATIONAL DAY – 7 February (Independence Day)
LIFE EXPECTANCY (years) – 64.87 (2006 est)
MORTALITY RATE – 6.88 (2006 est)

BIRTH RATE – 22.08 (2006 est)
INFANT MORTALITY RATE – 14.27 (2006 est)
DEATH PENALTY – No*
CPI SCORE – 3.5 (2006)
POPULATION BELOW POVERTY LINE – 32 per cent (2000)

CLIMATE AND TERRAIN

The most southerly of the Windward Islands, Grenada comprises three islands: Grenada (the largest at 18km in length and 34km in width), Carriacou and Petite Martinique. Elevation extremes range from 840m (Mt St Catherine) at the highest point to 0m (Caribbean Sea) at the lowest. The climate is subtropical with a wet season running from June to December. Grenada is in a hurricane zone.

HISTORY AND POLITICS

Discovered by Columbus in 1498 and named Concepción, Grenada was originally colonised by France and was ceded to Great Britain in 1763. It became a crown colony in 1877, an associated state in 1967 and an independent nation within the Commonwealth on 7 February 1974.

The government was overthrown in 1979 by the New Jewel Movement led by Maurice Bishop, and a People's Revolutionary Government (PRG) was set up with Bishop as prime minister. In 1983, disagreements within the PRG led to the deposition and execution of Bishop, whose government was replaced by a revolutionary military council. These events prompted the intervention of Caribbean and US forces. The governor-general installed an advisory council to act as an interim government until a general election was held in 1984. A phased withdrawal of US forces was completed by the following June. Since the restoration of democracy, power has alternated between the New National Party (NNP) and the National Democratic Congress (NDC).

In the 2003 general election, the New National Party, led by Keith Mitchell, was narrowly re-elected to a third successive term of office, winning eight seats.

POLITICAL SYSTEM

Under the 1974 constitution, reinstated in 1984, the British monarch is head of state and is represented locally by a governor-general. Legislative power is vested in a bicameral parliament consisting of a lower house, the house of representatives, with 15 members directly elected for a five-year term, and a senate with 13 members appointed by the governor-general on the advice of the prime minister and the leader of the opposition.

Governor-General, HE Sir Daniel Williams, GCMG, QC, *apptd* 1996

SELECTED GOVERNMENT MEMBERS *as at May 2007*
Prime Minister, National Security and Information, Keith Mitchell
Deputy Prime Minister, Gregory Bowen
Economic Development and Planning, Anthony Boatswain
Foreign Affairs and International Trade, Attorney-General, Elvin Nimrod

HIGH COMMISSION FOR GRENADA
The Chapel, Archel Road, London W14 9QH
T 020-7385 4277 E grenada@high-commission.demon.co.uk
High Commissioner, HE Joseph Stephen Charter, *apptd* 2005

BRITISH HIGH COMMISSION
High Commissioner, Duncan Taylor, *apptd* 2005, resident at Bridgetown, Barbados

ECONOMY AND TRADE

Grenada's economy has grown considerably in recent decades owing to the development of tourism and offshore financial services. However, poverty is still widespread (32 per cent of the population is below the poverty line), there are budget and trade deficits as well as foreign debt and a need for overseas aid, and severe damage was sustained in Hurricanes Ivan (2004) and Emily (2005).

The economy was principally agrarian, but agriculture now employs only 24 per cent of the workforce and produces 5 per cent of GDP. Industry consists of processing agricultural products, textiles manufacturing, light assembly operations and construction, and contributes 18 per cent of GDP. The service sector, including tourism and financial services, accounts for 62 per cent of employment and 77 per cent of GDP.

The main trading partners are the USA, Trinidad and Tobago, other Caribbean countries and EU countries. Principal exports are bananas, cocoa, nutmeg, fruit and vegetables, clothing and mace. Imports include foodstuffs, manufactured goods, machinery, chemicals and fuels.

GNI – US$408m; US$3,860 per capita (2005)
ANNUAL AVERAGE GROWTH OF GDP – 0.9 per cent (2005 est)
INFLATION RATE – 3 per cent (2005 est)
UNEMPLOYMENT – 12.5 per cent (2004 est)
TOTAL EXTERNAL DEBT – US$347m (2004)
IMPORTS – US$280m (2004)
EXPORTS – US$30m (2004)

BALANCE OF PAYMENTS
Trade – US$136m deficit (2000)
Current Account – US$79m deficit (2000)

Trade with UK	*2005*	*2006*
Imports from UK	£10,033,000	£7,250,000
Exports to UK	£1,914,000	£165,000

MEDIA

There are no daily newspapers but several private weekly publications which enjoy a considerable amount of independence. There are two television stations: GBN TV, which is operated by the public broadcaster Grenada Broadcasting Network, and MTV, which is US-owned. There are several radio stations jointly owned by the public and private sector.

GUATEMALA

República de Guatemala – Republic of Guatemala

AREA – 108,890 sq. km. Neighbours: Mexico (north and west), El Salvador, Honduras and Belize (east)
CAPITAL – Guatemala City; population, 942,348 (2002 est)
MAJOR CITIES – Mixco; Villa Neuva; Quetzaltenango
CURRENCY – Quetzal (Q) of 100 centavos
POPULATION – 12,293,545 rising at 2.27 per cent per year (2006 est); *mestizo* and European (59.4 per cent), K'iche (9.1 per cent), Kaqchikel (8.4 per cent), Mam (7.9 per cent)

RELIGION – Roman Catholicism (50 per cent), Protestantism (40 per cent) (est)
LANGUAGE – Spanish (official)
POPULATION DENSITY – 116 per sq. km (2005)
URBAN POPULATION – 47.2 per cent (2005 est)
MEDIAN AGE (years) – 18.9 (2006 est)
NATIONAL ANTHEM – 'Himno Nacional de Guatemala' ['Guatemala National Anthem']
NATIONAL DAY – 15 September (Independence Day)
LIFE EXPECTANCY (years) – 69.38 (2006 est)
MORTALITY RATE – 5.2 (2006 est)
BIRTH RATE – 29.88 (2006 est)
INFANT MORTALITY RATE – 30.94 (2006 est)
HIV/AIDS ADULT PREVALENCE – 1.1 per cent (2003 est)
DEATH PENALTY – Yes
CPI SCORE – 2.6 (2006)
POPULATION BELOW POVERTY LINE – 75 per cent (2004 est)
MILITARY BUDGET – US$146m (2006)
MILITARY PERSONNEL – 15,500: army 13,444, navy 986, air force 1,070; paramilitaries 19,000

CLIMATE AND TERRAIN

Narrow plains on both the north (Caribbean) and south (Pacific) coasts rise to a mountainous interior in the centre and south. The mountains fall in the north to a plateau, which drops further to low-lying marshland. Elevation extremes range from 4,211m (Volcan Tajumulco) at the highest point to 0m (Pacific Ocean) at the lowest. There are 33 volcanoes. The climate is tropical but is cooler in the highlands. The wet season runs from May to October, when mudslides and hurricanes can occur. There are also frequent minor earth tremors and some earthquakes.

HISTORY AND POLITICS

Mayan civilization flourished in the area until the Spanish conquest in 1523, when the area became a Spanish colony. It gained its independence in 1821, and formed part of the United Provinces of Central America from 1823 to 1835. After independence, the country was ruled by a series of dictatorships and military regimes, interspersed with periods of democratic government. The latest restoration of civilian rule in 1984 has survived an attempted coup in 1989 and the mass protests and military intervention that ousted President Serrano in 1993 when he attempted to introduce rule by decree.

Alvaro Alvarez, elected president in 1996, concluded a peace agreement with the left-wing Guatemalan Revolutionary National Unity guerrillas in 1996 that ended the 36-year civil war, in which over 200,000 died or disappeared, and began a reduction in the size and political influence of the army that has been continued by his successors. In 1999, an independent commission found that 93 per cent of human rights abuses during the war had been instigated by the security forces, and in 2000 and 2004 the state formally admitted guilt in several human rights crimes, paying damages to the victims. Only a small number of the military personnel found to be responsible for the atrocities have been prosecuted so far.

In the 2003 legislative election, the *Gran Alianza Nacional* (GANA) was the largest party, with 49 seats. The 2003 presidential election was won by Oscar Berger, the GANA candidate, with 54 per cent of the vote. Presidential and legislative elections were scheduled for September 2007.

POLITICAL SYSTEM

Under the 1986 constitution, the executive president is directly elected for a single four-year term, which is not renewable. He is responsible to congress and appoints the cabinet. Legislative authority is vested in the unicameral congress of the republic, whose 158 members are directly elected for a four-year term.

HEAD OF STATE

President, Oscar Berger, *elected* December 2003, *sworn in* 14 January 2004
Vice-President, Eduardo Stein Barillas

SELECTED GOVERNMENT MEMBERS *as at May 2007*
Defence, Gen. Francisco Bermudez
Economy, Marcio Ronaldo Cuevas Quezada
Foreign Affairs, Gert Rozenthal
Interior, Adela de Torrebiarte

EMBASSY OF GUATEMALA
13A Fawcett Street, London SW10 9HN
T 020-7351 3042 E embassy.gtm@btconnect.com
Ambassador Extraordinary and Plenipotentiary, Edmundo Urrutia, *apptd* 2006

BRITISH EMBASSY
Edificio Torre Internacional, Nivel 11 16 Calle 00-55, Zona 10, Guatemala City
T (+502) 2367 5425 E embassy@intelnett.com
Ambassador Extraordinary and Plenipotentiary, Ian Hughes, *apptd* 2006

ECONOMY AND TRADE

The country suffers from a huge imbalance in wealth, and a civic structure and infrastructure damaged by the civil war. IMF funding and foreign aid have underpinned the government's economic reforms and stabilisation programmes, but the government needs to reduce the trade deficit and deal with high levels of corruption and violence. Remittances from expatriates are vital to the economy, exceeding the combined foreign revenue from exports and tourism. Around 56 per cent of the population is below the poverty line and 50 per cent depends on agriculture, which contributes 22 per cent of GDP. Industry accounts for 19 per cent of GDP and 15 per cent of employment, and the services sector, which includes tourism, for 59 per cent of GDP and 35 per cent of employment.

The main trading partners are the USA, El Salvador, Mexico and Honduras. The principal exports are coffee, sugar, oil, clothing, bananas, fruit, vegetables and cardamom. The chief imports are fuels, machinery and transport equipment, construction materials, grain, fertilisers and electricity.

GNI – US$30,300m; US$2,400 per capita (2005)
ANNUAL AVERAGE GROWTH OF GDP – 3.2 per cent (2005 est)
INFLATION RATE – 9.1 per cent (2005 est)
UNEMPLOYMENT – 7.5 per cent (2003 est)
TOTAL EXTERNAL DEBT – US$5,503m (2005 est)
IMPORTS – US$8,800m (2005)
EXPORTS – US$3,500m (2005)
BALANCE OF PAYMENTS

Trade – US$3,760m deficit (2004)
Current Account – US$1,188m deficit (2004)

Trade with UK	*2005*	*2006*
Imports from UK	£25,628,000	£28,852,000
Exports to UK	£14,127,000	£18,923,000

EDUCATION AND HEALTH

LITERACY RATE – 69.1 per cent (2004 est)
GROSS ENROLMENT RATIO (percentage of relevant age group) – primary 114 per cent; secondary 51 per cent; tertiary 10 per cent (2005 est)
HEALTH EXPENDITURE (per capita) – US$127 (2004)
HOSPITAL BEDS (per 1,000 people) – 0.5 (2000–5)

MEDIA AND CULTURE

Freedom of the press is enshrined in the constitution, but journalists who pursue controversial stories are often subjected to threats. There are four major daily newspapers, including *Prensa Libre* and *El Periodico*. Four privately run channels are under the same ownership and monopolise Guatemalan television.

Guatemala enjoys a rich and varied cultural history. The ruins of the Mayan civilisation (AD *c*.300–900) dot the country while the influences of African culture are evident along the Caribbean coast. Distinguished Guatemalans include the writers Miguel Angel Asturias (1899–1974), who won the Nobel prize for literature in 1967; Luis Cardoza y Aragon (1901–92), who edited the influential periodical *Revista de Guatemala* after the 1944 revolution; and Rigoberta Menchu (*b*. 1959), who won the Nobel peace prize in 1992.

GUINEA

République de Guinée – Republic of Guinea

AREA – 245,857 sq. km. Neighbours: Guinea-Bissau (west), Senegal and Mali (north), Côte d'Ivoire (east), Liberia and Sierra Leone (south)
CAPITAL – Conakry; population, 1,092,936 (1996)
MAJOR CITIES – N'Zérékoré; Kankan; Kindia; Guéckédougou; Kissidougou
CURRENCY – Guinea franc of 100 centimes
POPULATION – 9,690,222 rising at 2.63 per cent per year (2006 est); Fula (40 per cent), Malinke (30 per cent), Susu (20 per cent) (est)
RELIGION – Islam (85 per cent), Christianity (10 per cent), indigenous religions (5 per cent) (est)
LANGUAGE – French (official)
POPULATION DENSITY – 38 per sq. km (2005)
URBAN POPULATION – 36.5 per cent (2005 est)
MEDIAN AGE (years) – 17.7 (2006 est)
NATIONAL ANTHEM – 'Liberté' ['Liberty']
NATIONAL DAY – 2 October (Independence Day)
LIFE EXPECTANCY – 49.5 (2006 est)
MORTALITY RATE – 15.48 (2006 est)
BIRTH RATE – 41.76 (2006 est)
INFANT MORTALITY RATE – 90 (2006 est)
HIV/AIDS ADULT PREVALENCE – 3.2 per cent (2003 est)
DEATH PENALTY – Yes
CPI SCORE – 1.9 (2006)
POPULATION BELOW POVERTY LINE – 40 per cent (2003 est)
MILITARY BUDGET – US$36m (2006 est)
MILITARY PERSONNEL – 12,300: army 8,500, navy 400, air force 800, Gendarmerie 1,000, Republican Guard 1,600; paramilitaries 7,000
CONSCRIPTION DURATION – 24 months
GROSS ENROLMENT RATIO (percentage of relevant age group) – primary 81 per cent; secondary 30 per cent; tertiary 3 per cent (2005 est)
HEALTH EXPENDITURE (per capita) – US$22 (2004)

CLIMATE AND TERRAIN

Guinea has a flat coastal plain that rises to a mountainous interior, where the Senegal and Niger rivers rise. The River Gambia rises on the Fouta Djallon plateau in the north-west of the country. Elevation extremes range from 1,752m (Mt Nimba) at the highest point to 0m at the lowest (Atlantic Ocean). The south-east is forested. There is a wet season from June to November and the average daily temperature is 27°C.

HISTORY AND POLITICS

Susi kingdoms were established in the area by the 13th century, and in the 16th century the north-east of the country was part of the Mali Empire. The Portuguese established ivory and slave trading from the mid-15th century. In 1849 the French established a protectorate over the coastal areas, and the country was governed with Senegal until the 1890s, when it was renamed French Guinea, becoming part of French West Africa in 1904. Guinea became independent on 2 October 1958 under President Ahmed Sekou Touré, who established a one-party state pursuing Marxist policies in the 1960s and 1970s. Decades of economic stagnation followed as Sekou Touré attempted first to ally Guinea to the USSR, and then, when the relationship with the USSR soured, imposed a series of socialist reforms. Touré died in 1984, shortly after introducing limited economic liberalisation in response to strong opposition to his policies, and his death was followed by a military coup that brought Lansana Conté to power. As president, Conté introduced greater economic liberalisation and, following strikes and mass protests in 1991, reintroduced a multiparty system. President Conté narrowly won the presidential election in 1993, was re-elected in 1998 with 54 per cent of the vote, and again in 2003 with 95 per cent of the vote after several opposition parties boycotted the election.

The civil wars in neighbouring Sierra Leone and Liberia caused an influx of nearly half a million refugees in 2000 that has severely strained the economy, exacerbating the poor conditions which have contributed to the growing unpopularity of the government and created ethnic tension.

The 2002 legislative election was won by President Conté's Party of Unity and Progress (PUP), which gained 85 of the 114 national assembly seats. In May 2004, Prime Minister François Fall resigned and went into exile after just two months in the job, protesting that President Conté was blocking his attempts at political and economic reform, and he was replaced in December by Cellou Dalein Diallo. President Conté reshuffled the cabinet following the dismissal of Diallo in April 2006 but did not appoint a new prime minister until February 2007, after a two-week general strike and violent demonstrations protesting against the regime. The new prime minister, Lansana Kouyaté, nominated a new government which included only one member of the outgoing administration. The legislative election due in June has been postponed until late 2007.

POLITICAL SYSTEM

Under the 1991 constitution, the executive president is directly elected for a five-year term, renewable only once;

a 2001 referendum approved an amendment allowing the president to stand for a third term, lasting seven years, in 2003. The unicameral legislature, the national assembly, has 114 members, who are directly elected for a five-year term. The president appoints the council of ministers.

HEAD OF STATE
President, Maj.-Gen. Lansana Conté, *took power* 3 April 1984, *elected* 19 December 1993, *re-elected* 1998, 2003

SELECTED GOVERNMENT MEMBERS *as at May 2007*
Prime Minister, Lansana Kouyaté
Economy, Finance and Planning Ousmane Dorè
Foreign Affairs, Abdoul Kabèlè Camara
Defence, Gen. Bailo Diallo
Interior and Security, M'Boh Keita

EMBASSY OF THE REPUBLIC OF GUINEA
48 Onslow Gardens, London SW7 3PY
T 020-7594 4809 E ambaguineeuk@yahoo.co.uk
Ambassador Extraordinary and Plenipotentiary, Lansana Keita, *apptd* 2005

BRITISH CONSULATE GENERAL
BP 834 Conakry, Guinea
T (+224) 455 807/456 020/452 959

BRITISH EMBASSY
Ambassador Extraordinary and Plenipotentiary, HE John McManus, *appt d* 2004, resident at Freetown, Sierra Leone

ECONOMY AND TRADE

Despite an abundance of natural resources, including over 40 per cent of the world's bauxite reserves, decades of mismanagement have left Guinea's economy undeveloped, and 47 per cent of the population is below the poverty line. There is a large foreign debt, budget and trade deficits and inflation reached 29 per cent in 2006, but little foreign aid as most IMF and World Bank aid was suspended in 2003. Agriculture, much of it at subsistence level, employs 76 per cent of the population but contributes only 24 per cent of GDP. Industry accounts for 36 per cent of GDP, mostly through mining and the processing of minerals and agricultural produce.

The main trading partners are Russia, France, South Korea, Spain, Belgium and China. Principal exports are bauxite, alumina, gold, diamonds, coffee, fish and other agricultural products. The main imports are petroleum products, metals, machinery, transport equipment, textiles, grain and other foodstuffs.

GNI – US$3,900m; US$420 per capita (2005)
ANNUAL AVERAGE GROWTH OF GDP – 2 per cent (2005 est)
INFLATION RATE – 25 per cent (2005 est)
TOTAL EXTERNAL DEBT – US$3,460m (2003 est)
EXPORTS – US$910m (2005)

BALANCE OF PAYMENTS
Trade – US$37m surplus (2004)
Current Account – US$175m deficit (2004)

Trade with UK	*2005*	*2006*
Imports from UK	£22,186,000	£33,252,000
Exports to UK	£4,426,000	£1,728,000

COMMUNICATIONS

Guinea has over 837km of railways, 44,348km of roads (only 10 per cent of which are surfaced) and 1,300km of inland waterways navigable by shallow-draught craft. The major seaports are Conakry and Kamsar. Guinea has 16 airports, including five with surfaced runways; the principal airport is at Conakry. The fixed-line telephone system is small in scope, with 26,200 main line subscribers, but mobile phone distribution is more extensive, with 189,000 subscribers in 2005. There were 46,000 internet users in 2005.

MEDIA

Government control over the media has tightened considerably in 2007 and many private radio stations and cybercafes have been closed. Criticism of the government is rare in the five national newspapers. There is a single state-run television broadcaster, Radiodiffusion-Television Guineenne (RTG).

GUINEA-BISSAU

Republica da Guine-Bissau – Republic of Guinea-Bissau

AREA – 36,120 sq. km. Neighbours: Senegal (north), Guinea (east and south)
CAPITAL – Bissau; population, 203,000 (1990 est)
CURRENCY – Franc CFA
POPULATION – 1,442,029 rising at 2.07 per cent per year (2006 est)
RELIGION – Indigenous religions (49 per cent), Islam (38 per cent), Christianity (5 per cent) (est)
LANGUAGE – Portuguese (official), Crioulo
POPULATION DENSITY – 56 per sq. km (2005)
URBAN POPULATION – 35.6 per cent (2005 est)
MEDIAN AGE (years) – 19 (2006 est)
NATIONAL ANTHEM – 'Esta e a Nossa Patria Ben Amada' ['This is Our Beloved Country']
NATIONAL DAY – 24 September (Independence Day)
LIFE EXPECTANCY (years) – 46.87 (2006 est)
MORTALITY RATE – 16.53 (2006 est)
BIRTH RATE – 37.22 (2006 est)
INFANT MORTALITY RATE – 105.21 (2006 est)
HIV/AIDS ADULT PREVALENCE – 10 per cent (2003 est)
DEATH PENALTY – No (abolished 1993)
MILITARY EXPENDITURE – US$14m (2006 est)
MILITARY PERSONNEL – 9,250: army 6,800, navy 350, air force 100, Gendarmerie 2,000
CONSCRIPTION DURATION – Selective conscription
GROSS ENROLMENT RATIO (percentage of relevant age group) – primary 70 per cent (2002); secondary 18 per cent (2002)
HEALTH EXPENDITURE (per capita) US$9 (2004)

CLIMATE AND TERRAIN

Guinea-Bissau has a low coastal plain that rises to savannah in the east. Elevation extremes range from 300m (in the north-east) at the highest point to 0m (Atlantic Ocean) at the lowest. Average temperatures range from 24°C in January to 27°C in October, with a wet season from June to November.

HISTORY AND POLITICS

A part of the ancient African empire of Mali, Guinea-Bissau was once the kingdom of Gabu, which became independent of the empire in 1546 and survived until

1867. In 1446, Portuguese traders discovered the coast and established slave trading there, subsequently administering Guinea-Bissau with the Cape Verde islands. After becoming a separate colony in 1879, Guinea-Bissau achieved independence in 1974 after a guerrilla war led by the left-wing African Party for the Independence of Guinea and Cape Verde (PAIGC).

Since independence, Guinea-Bissau has suffered periods of political instability interspersed with military rule. From 1981 until 1994, the country was under military and one-party rule by the PAIGC. A multiparty system was introduced in 1991 after popular agitation. The first multiparty elections in 1994 were won by the PAIGC, and General Joao Vieira was confirmed as president. An army mutiny against President Vieira in 1998 developed into a civil war that ended in May 1999 with Vieira's deposition, and a military junta appointed an interim president. In 2000 Kumba Yala was elected president, but his increasingly erratic behaviour and the worsening economic situation led to his overthrow in a military coup in 2003. Under ECOWAS influence, the military accepted the formation of a civilian-led transitional government.

In the 2004 legislative election, the PAIGC won 45 seats, the Party for Social Renewal (PSR) won 35 seats and the United Social Democratic Party (USDP) won 27. The 2005 presidential election was won in the second round by Joao Vieira (president 1980–99) with 52 per cent of the vote. The PAIGC did not accept Vieira's election initially, and objected to his choice of prime minister in November 2005; it refused to participate in the coalition government and expelled party members who remained in their ministerial posts. The government was defeated in a vote of no confidence in March 2007 and a new coalition government was formed under PAIGC leadership.

POLITICAL SYSTEM

Under the 1999 constitution, the executive president is directly elected for a five-year term, which is renewable only once. The president appoints the council of ministers. There is a unicameral legislature, the *Assembleia Nacional Popular* (national people's assembly), composed of 102 members who are directly elected for a four-year term.

HEAD OF STATE

President, Brig.-Gen. Joao Vieira, *elected* June 2005, *took office* October 2005

SELECTED GOVERNMENT MEMBERS *as at May 2007*

Prime Minister, Martinho N'Dafa Cabi
Economy, Abubcar Demba Dahahba
Foreign Affairs, Maria de Concicao Nobre Cabral
Defence, Marciano Silva Berbeiro
Interior, Baciro Dabo

EMBASSY OF THE REPUBLIC OF GUINEA-BISSAU
94 rue St Lazare, Paris F-75009, France
T (+33) (1) 4526 1851
Ambassador Extraordinary and Plenipotentiary, vacant

BRITISH CONSULATE
Ambassador Extraordinary and Plenipotentiary, HE Peter Newall, *apptd* 2004, resident in Dakar, Senegal

ECONOMY AND TRADE

The economy is in a poor state, with one of the world's greatest extremes of wealth distribution, after decades of mismanagement and corruption and the devastating effects of the 1998–9 civil war. There is a massive foreign debt and the country is heavily dependent on foreign aid, which provided over 80 per cent of the national budget in 2004.

Although Guinea-Bissau has mineral resources, including oil, the high cost of exploiting these has prevented development and the economy is based almost exclusively on agriculture and fishing. This sector employs 82 per cent of the population and contributes 62 per cent of GDP. The small industrial sector generates 12 per cent of GDP through the processing of agricultural products and beer and soft drink production.

The main trading partners are India, Italy, Senegal, Nigeria and Portugal. Principal exports include cashew nuts, fish, peanuts, palm kernels and timber. The main imports are foodstuffs, machinery and transport equipment, and fuels.

GNI – US$300m; US$180 per capita (2005)
ANNUAL AVERAGE GROWTH OF GDP – 2.3 per cent (2005 est)
INFLATION RATE – 4 per cent (2002 est)
TOTAL EXTERNAL DEBT – US$941.5m (2000 est)
IMPORTS – US$120m (2005)
EXPORTS – US$80m (2005)

BALANCE OF PAYMENTS
Trade – US$4m deficit (2002)
Current Account – US$6m deficit (2003)

Trade with UK	*2005*	*2006*
Imports from UK	£389,000	£672,000
Exports to UK	£1,000	£91,000

COMMUNICATIONS

Guinea-Bissau has 3,455km of roads, of which only 965km are surfaced, but no railways. There are 28 airports and airfields, three of which have surfaced runways; the principal airport is at Bissau. The main rivers are navigable for part of their lengths, and shallow-draught craft can access much of the interior through creeks, etc. Bissau is the main seaport. The land-line telephone system is small, with only 10,600 main lines in use; mobile phone distribution was 67,000 in 2005. There were 26,000 internet users in 2005.

MEDIA

Following the 2003 military coup, media organisations have been able to operate with greater freedom. Government interference is often less of an concern than reliable power supplies, although RTP Africa, a television broadcaster set up by Portugal in its former colonies, has been taken off the air. Of the four national newspapers, three are privately owned. Guinea-Bissau's single television station, Radio Televisao de Guinea-Bissau (RTGB), is state-run. Radio consists of the national broadcaster, Radio Nacional, and three commercial stations.

GUYANA

Cooperative Republic of Guyana

AREA – 214,970 sq. km. Neighbours: Venezuela (west), Brazil (west and south), Suriname (east)
CAPITAL – Georgetown; population, 35,440 (2002)

MAJOR TOWNS – Linden; New Amsterdam; Anna Regina
CURRENCY – Guyana dollar (G $) of 100 cents
POPULATION – 767,245 rising at 0.25 per cent per year (2006 est)
RELIGION – Christianity (50 per cent), Hinduism (35 per cent), Islam (10 per cent) (est)
LANGUAGE – English (official), Creole, Hindi, Urdu
POPULATION DENSITY – 4 per sq. km (2005)
URBAN POPULATION – 38.5 per cent (2005 est)
MEDIAN AGE (years) – 27.4 (2006 est)
NATIONAL ANTHEM – 'Dear Land of Guyana'
NATIONAL DAY – 23 February (Republic Day)
LIFE EXPECTANCY (years) – 65.86 (2005 est)
MORTALITY RATE – 8.28 (2006 est)
BIRTH RATE – 18.28 (2006 est)
INFANT MORTALITY – 32.19 (2006 est)
HIV/AIDS ADULT PREVALENCE – 2.5 per cent (2003 est)
DEATH PENALTY – Yes
CPI SCORE – 2.5 (2006)
MILITARY PERSONNEL – 1,100: army 900, navy 100, air force 100; paramilitaries 1,500

CLIMATE AND TERRAIN

The land rises from a coastal plain to highlands in the west and savannah in the south. Much of the interior is covered in rainforest, with elevation extremes ranging from 2,835m (Mt Roraima) at the highest point to 0m (Atlantic Ocean) at the lowest. The average daily temperature is 28°C.

HISTORY AND POLITICS

Carib and Arawak Indians inhabited the coastal region of Guyana and began trading with the Dutch merchants who founded the first European settlement in 1615. Guyana became an important producer of sugar, grown on plantations worked first by African slaves and then, after the abolition of slavery, by indentured Indian labourers. Several areas were ceded to Britain in 1815, and were consolidated as British Guiana before coming formally under British rule in 1831. The country became independent, as Guyana, on 26 May 1966, and became a republic in 1970.

Guyana's first political party, the People's Progressive Party (PPP), divided along ethnic lines in 1957; the PPP continued as a predominantly Indian party under Cheddi Jagan while those of African descent formed the People's National Congress (PNC), led by Forbes Burnham. Burnham dominated political life after independence, as prime minister from 1966 until 1980 and then as executive president until his death in 1985. Under his autocratic rule, politics became characterised by suspect elections and the disregard of civil liberties and human rights. The PPP's electoral victory in 1992 ended the PNC's monopoly of power but the persistent ethnic tension continues to destabilise politics.

Bharrat Jagdeo of the PPP was elected president in 2001. His presidency has seen attempts to encourage joint action between the government and the private sector, and soon after the 2001 elections he called for reconciliation between the PPP and Guyana's other political parties in order to prevent further political violence.

The 2006 legislative election was won by the PPP, with 54.6 per cent of the vote, securing its fourth consecutive term of office. President Jagdeo was confirmed in office for a further five-year term.

POLITICAL SYSTEM

The 1980 constitution provides for an executive president who is nominated by the majority party in the national assembly after legislative elections and serves a five-year term. The unicameral national assembly has 65 members, of whom 53 are elected by proportional representation and 12 are regional representatives; they serve a five-year term.

HEAD OF STATE

President, Bharrat Jagdeo, *succeeded* 11 August 1999, *elected* 2001, *re-elected* 28 August 2006

SELECTED GOVERNMENT MEMBERS *as at May 2007*
Prime Minister, Samuel Hinds
Finance, Asni Kumar Singh
Foreign Affairs, Rudolph Insanally
Home Affairs, Clement Rohee

HIGH COMMISSION FOR GUYANA
3 Palace Court, Bayswater Road, London W2 4LP
T 020-7229 7684 E ghc.1@ic24.net
High Commissioner, HE Laleshwar Singh, *apptd* 1993

BRITISH HIGH COMMISSION
44 Main Street (PO Box 10849), Georgetown
T (+592) (226) 5881 E consular@georgetown.mail.fsc.gov.uk
High Commissioner, HE Fraser Wheeler, *apptd* 2006

ECONOMY AND TRADE

Serious economic problems arose in the late 1980s because of mismanagement of the largely state-owned industries and falling commodity prices. In the 1990s the government privatised many industries but in 1998 the economy suffered growth of −1.8 per cent and recovery has been slow and fitful. There is a high level of foreign debt, although nearly US$400m (£200m) was cancelled in 2006, and Guyana has received funding under the IMF/World Bank highly indebted poor countries initiative as well as from donor agencies and the World Bank.

Agriculture is the principal economic activity, accounting for 36 per cent of GDP and providing the raw materials for the major industries of sugar processing and rice milling. Industry accounts for 19 per cent of GDP, non-agricultural activities including bauxite and gold mining. Oil deposits have been found, but these are mainly in offshore areas disputed with neighbouring Suriname. Attempts are being made to develop tourism, especially eco-tourism, but these are constrained by the poor infrastructure. The main trading partners are the USA, Trinidad and Tobago, Canada and the UK. Principal exports include sugar, gold, bauxite, alumnia, rice, shrimps, molasses, rum and timber. The main imports are manufactured goods, machinery, fuel and food.
GNI – US$770m; US$1,020 per capita (2005)
ANNUAL AVERAGE GROWTH OF GDP – −3 per cent (2005 est)
INFLATION RATE – 6.9 per cent (2005 est)
TOTAL EXTERNAL DEBT – US$1,200m (2002)
IMPORTS – US$790m (2005)
EXPORTS – US$550m (2005)

BALANCE OF PAYMENTS
Trade – US$14m deficit (2004)
Current Account – US$30m deficit (2004)

Trade with UK	*2005*	*2006*
Imports from UK	£18,189,000	£20,329,000
Exports to UK	£45,881,000	£35,379,000

COMMUNICATIONS

Roads and navigable waterways (the Berbice, Demerara and Essequibo rivers) form the main arteries of communication in the country, though only 590km of roads, out of a total of 7,970km, are surfaced. The railway system is only 187km in length and is used only for transporting minerals. Georgetown is the main seaport and the location of the principal airport. There are 90 airports and airfields in total, though only nine have surfaced runways. In 2005, main-line telephone subscribers numbered 110,100, mobile phone subscribers 281,400 and internet users 160,000.

MEDIA

Guyana has six radio and three television stations. One television station is state-run and the remaining two are privately owned. Journalists operate freely but practise self-censorship.

HAITI

République d'Haïti – Republic of Haiti

AREA – 27,750 sq. km. Neighbour: Dominican Republic (east)
CAPITAL – Port-au-Prince; population, 990,558 (1999 est)
MAJOR CITIES – Carrefour; Delmas; Cap Haitien
CURRENCY – Gourde of 100 centimes
POPULATION – 8,308,504 rising at 2.3 per cent per year (2006 est)
RELIGION – Roman Catholicism (63 per cent). At least half of the country is believed to practise voodoo, which was recognised as an official religion in 2003
LANGUAGE – French, Creole (both official)
POPULATION DENSITY – 309 per sq. km (2005)
URBAN POPULATION – 38.8 per cent (2005 est)
MEDIAN AGE (years) – 18.2 (2006 est)
NATIONAL ANTHEM – 'La Dessalinienne' ['Song of Dessalines']
NATIONAL DAY – 1 January (Independence Day)
LIFE EXPECTANCY (years) – 53.23 (2006 est)
MORTALITY RATE – 12.17 (2006 est)
BIRTH RATE – 36.44 (2006 est)
INFANT MORTALITY RATE – 71.65 (2006 est)
HIV/AIDS ADULT PREVALENCE – 5.6 per cent (2003 est)
DEATH PENALTY – No (abolished 1987)
CPI SCORE – 1.8 (2006)
POPULATION BELOW POVERTY LINE – 80 per cent (2003 est)
LITERACY RATE – 51.9 per cent (2004 est)
HEALTH EXPENDITURE (per capita) – US$33 (2004)

CLIMATE AND TERRAIN

The country occupies the western third of the island of Hispaniola (the remainder is the Dominican Republic). The terrain is mountainous, with lower-lying coastal areas in the north. Elevation extremes range from 2,680m (Chaîne de la Selle) at the highest point to 0m (Caribbean Sea) at the lowest. The climate is tropical.

HISTORY AND POLITICS

Haiti was ceded to France by Spain in 1697. It was named Saint Domingue and was popularly known as the pearl of the Antilles, as it became the richest colony in the French empire. This wealth was generated by African slaves working in the sugar and coffee plantations. In 1791, a slave rebellion expelled the French from the northern part of the colony and instigated a long war between freed slaves and colonists. By 1804 the Republic of Haiti was founded, marking the inception of the world's first black republic and, after the USA, the oldest republic in the western hemisphere.

Haiti has experienced very little stability since. The country endured 22 changes of government between 1843 and 1915. The resulting upheaval led the USA to intervene in 1915, marking the beginning of 19 years of US occupation. Haiti was restored to sovereign rule in 1934.

In 1957, the Duvalier family gained control of the country and began a dictatorial rule which lasted 29 years. A series of transitional governments followed before Jean-Bertrand Aristide won the 1990 presidential election. Aristide was deposed in a coup the following year which instigated a period of military rule. The severity of the military's repression prompted the UN to authorise US-led intervention in 1994. Though re-elected in 2000, Aristide's administration became the focus of mounting opposition. An armed rebellion broke out in January 2004 and by late February the rebels controlled most of the country. Under pressure from the USA and France, Aristide resigned and went into exile. An interim government was sworn in and a UN-led multinational stabilisation force was deployed, although its presence has done little to counteract the widespread violence, lawlessness and corruption. The presidential election in February 2006 was won by René Préval (president 1996–2000) of the Front for Hope (Lespwa) party, with 51.21 per cent of the vote. In the legislative election, held in two rounds in February and April 2006, the Lespwa party won most seats but not an overall majority. A six-party coalition government was formed under Lespwa leadership.

POLITICAL SYSTEM

Under the 1987 constitution, the head of state is the president, directly elected for a five-year term that may not be renewed immediately. The bicameral legislature is the national assembly; the lower house, the chamber of deputies, has 99 members directly elected for a four-year term. The upper house, the senate, has 30 members directly elected for a six-year term; one-third of the senators is elected every two years. The president appoints the prime minister, who must be approved by the national assembly.

HEAD OF STATE

President, René Préval, *elected* February 2006, *sworn in* 14 May 2006

SELECTED GOVERNMENT MEMBERS *as at May 2007*

Prime Minister, Jacques-Édouard Alexis
Foreign Affairs, Renald Clerisme
Finance and Economy, Daniel Dorsainvil
Interior, Paul Antoine Bien-Aime

BRITISH AMBASSADOR

HE Ian Worthington, *apptd* 2006, resident at Santo Domingo, Dominican Republic

ECONOMY AND TRADE

The country is the poorest in the western hemisphere, with a huge imbalance in wealth, a devastated infrastructure, and high levels of violence and corruption;

around 80 per cent of the population lives below the poverty line. Remittances from the estimated one in six Haitians living abroad, principally in the USA, are the main source of foreign revenue, worth nearly a quarter of GDP in 2005. The government is completely dependent on international economic aid; an IMF-assisted programme has stimulated moderate economic growth since 2005, and Haiti should benefit from foreign aid pledged in 2006 and the resumption of relations with the World Bank. Two-thirds of the population depends on agriculture – predominantly small-scale subsistence farming – but this is vulnerable to natural disasters. Industrial activities include sugar refining, flour milling, textiles and assembly of goods, using imported parts, for re-export.

The main trading partners are the USA, Netherlands Antilles, Dominican Republic, Canada and Brazil. Principal exports are manufactured goods, coffee, oils, cocoa and mangoes. The main imports are foodstuffs, manufactured goods, machinery and transport equipment, fuels and raw materials.

GNI – US$3,900m; US$450 per capita (2005)
ANNUAL AVERAGE GROWTH OF GDP – 1.8 per cent (2005 est)
INFLATION RATE – 15.7 per cent (2005 est)
TOTAL EXTERNAL DEBT – US$1,313m (2005 est)
IMPORTS – US$1,454m (2005)
EXPORTS – US$470m (2005)

BALANCE OF PAYMENTS
Trade – US$783m deficit (2003)
Current Account – US$13m deficit (2003)

Trade with UK	*2005*	*2006*
Imports from UK	£4,635,000	£7,102,000
Exports to UK	£559,000	£401,000

COMMUNICATIONS

Less than a quarter of the country's 4,160km of highways are surfaced. There are 12 airports, four of which have surfaced runways; the international airports are at Port-au-Prince and Cap-Haitien. Cap-Haitien is the main port. The telephone system is poor, with only 140,000 main lines in use; mobile phone distribution is greater, with 400,000 subscribers in 2004, but still scarcely 5 per cent of the population. There were 500,000 internet users in 2005.

MEDIA

Radio is the most important medium due to low literacy levels and there are more than 250 radio stations, broadcasting in French and Creole. A single state broadcaster, Télévision Nationale d'Haiti, provides four television channels and these have been joined by two privately owned French-language stations. Press freedom is reported to have improved significantly since the fall of Jean-Bertrand Aristide.

HONDURAS

República de Honduras – Republic of Honduras

AREA – 112,090 sq. km. Neighbours: Guatemala (north-west), El Salvador (south-west), Nicaragua (south)
CAPITAL – Tegucigalpa; population, 769,061 (2001)
MAJOR CITIES – San Pedro Sula; La Ceiba; Choloma
CURRENCY – Lempira of 100 centavos
POPULATION – 7,326,496 rising at 2.16 per cent per year (2006 est) of mixed Spanish and Indian descent. The Garinagu in the north are of West Indian origin.
RELIGION – Roman Catholicism (63 per cent), other Christian denominations (23 per cent) (est)
LANGUAGE – Spanish (official)
POPULATION DENSITY – 64 per sq. km (2005)
URBAN POPULATION – 46.4 per cent (2005 est)
MEDIAN AGE (years) – 19.5 (2006 est)
NATIONAL ANTHEM – 'Tu Bandera es un Lampo de Cielo ['Your Flag is a Heavenly Light']
NATIONAL DAY – 15 September (Independence Day)
LIFE EXPECTANCY – 69.33 (2006 est)
MORTALITY RATE – 5.28 (2006 est)
BIRTH RATE – 28.24 (2006 est)
INFANT MORTALITY RATE – 25.82 (2006 est)
HIV/AIDS ADULT PREVALENCE – 1.8 per cent (2003 est)
DEATH PENALTY – No (abolished 1956)
CPI SCORE – 2.5 (2006)
MILITARY BUDGET – US$55.6m (2006)
MILITARY PERSONNEL – 12,000: army 8,300, navy 1,400, air force 2,300; paramilitaries 8,000

CLIMATE AND TERRAIN

Honduras has a mountainous interior, falling to narro coastal plains. Elevation extremes range from 2,870r (Cerro Las Minas) at the highest point to 0m (Caribbea Sea) at the lowest. The climate is subtropical in th lowlands and temperate in the mountains. Averag temperatures range from 19°C in January to 23°C in Jun

HISTORY AND POLITICS

Honduras was home to part of the Mayan civilisatio between the fourth and ninth centuries AD. Christophe Columbus first set foot on the American mainland a Trujillo in Honduras in 1502, but it was 1525 befor Spanish colonisation began. In 1821, the country becam independent of Spain and was part of the Unite Provinces of Central America from 1823 until it becam fully independent in 1838. Thereafter the countr underwent periods of political instability intersperse with military rule until 1981, when a civilian governmer was elected. It became embroiled in the civil wars Nicaragua and El Salvador as a base for US forces an anti-Sandinista Contras. The ending of the civil wa meant a decline in the power of the army, which w brought under civilian control in 1999.

The presidential election in November 2005 was wo by Manuel Zelaya of the Liberal Party (PLH). In th simultaneous legislative election, the PLH won the mo seats, though not an overall majority, and formed government after the inauguration of President Zelaya.

POLITICAL SYSTEM
Under the 1982 constitution, the executive president directly elected for a four-year term, which is n renewable, and appoints the government. The unicamer legislature, the national congress, has 128 member elected for a four-year term.

HEAD OF STATE
President, C.-in-C. of the Armed Forces, Manuel Zelaya Rosales, *elected* 27 November 2005, *took office* 27 January 2006
Vice-President, Elvin Santos Ordonez

;ELECTED GOVERNMENT MEMBERS *as at May 2007*
Defence, Aristides Mejia
Finance, Rebeca Santos
Foreign Relations, Milton Jimenez Puerto
Interior and Justice, Jorge Arturo Reina

:MBASSY OF HONDURAS
15 Gloucester Place, London W1U 6JT
020-7486 4880 E hondurasuk@lineone.net
Ambassador Extraordinary and Plenipotentiary, vacant

BRITISH AMBASSADOR
HE Ian Hughes, *apptd* 2006, resident at Guatemala City, Guatemala

:CONOMY AND TRADE

The country has a huge imbalance in wealth and high evels of corruption and violent crime, often connected with drug-trafficking. Honduras began a three-year IMF-sponsored poverty reduction and economic growth rogramme in 2004 and is working towards qualifying or debt relief under the IMF/World Bank heavily ndebted poor countries initiative; its public debt is 67 per ent of GDP.

The economy is dependent on agriculture, fishing and orestry, whose products form the basis of industrial ctivity and are the main exports. Agriculture employs 4 per cent of the workforce and contributes 14 per ent of GDP. Industry accounts for 31 per cent of GDP nd 23 per cent of employment, and the services sector or 55 per cent of GDP and 43 per cent of mployment.

The main trading partners are the USA, Guatemala and l Salvador. Principal exports are coffee, shrimps, ananas, gold, palm oil, fruit, lobster and timber. The nain imports are machinery and transport equipment, ndustrial raw materials, chemical products, fuels and oodstuffs.

GNI – US$8,000m; US$1,120 per capita (2005)
ANNUAL AVERAGE GROWTH OF GDP – 4.2 per cent (2005 est)
NFLATION RATE – 8.8 per cent (2005 est)
NEMPLOYMENT – 28 per cent (2005 est)
OTAL EXTERNAL DEBT – US$5,795m (2005 est)
MPORTS – US$4,600m (2005)
XPORTS – US$1,700m (2005)

ALANCE OF PAYMENTS
rade – US$1,267m deficit (2004)
urrent Account – US$413m deficit (2004)

Trade with UK	*2005*	*2006*
Imports from UK	£9,548,000	£7,750,000
Exports to UK	£23,270,000	£17,897,000

:OMMUNICATIONS

Honduras has ports on its Caribbean (Puerto Castilla, uerto Cortes, Tela) and Pacific (San Lorenzo) coasts. here are 699km of railway and 13,603km of roads, 775km of which are surfaced. The mountainous interior as led to the development of a large number of airports, ough only 11 of the 116 have surfaced runways; the rincipal airports are at Tegucigalpa, La Ceiba and San edro Sula. The land-line telephone system is poor and obile phone distribution has grown rapidly, to 1.3 illion in 2005. Internet usage is low, at 223,000 users in 005.

EDUCATION AND HEALTH

Primary and secondary education is free of charge and primary education is compulsory between the ages of seven and 12. The government has launched a campaign to eradicate illiteracy.

LITERACY RATE – 80 per cent (2004 est)
GROSS ENROLMENT RATIO (percentage of relevant age group) – primary 113 per cent; secondary 65 per cent; tertiary 16 per cent (2005 est)
HEALTH EXPENDITURE (per capita) – US$77 (2004)
HOSPITAL BEDS (per 1,000 people) – 1 (2000–5)

MEDIA

Honduras has a state-owned radio station as well as several privately run broadcasters and newspapers. Televicentro operates several television channels. Journalists are known to restrict their coverage of controversial events.

HUNGARY

Magyar Koztarsasag – Republic of Hungary

AREA – 92,030 sq. km. Neighbours: Slovakia (north), Ukraine and Romania (east), Serbia and Croatia (south), Slovenia and Austria (west)
CAPITAL – Budapest; population, 1,697,343 (2005 est)
MAJOR CITIES – Debrecen; Miskolc; Szeged; Pecs
CURRENCY – Forint of 100 filler
POPULATION – 9,981,334 falling at 0.25 per cent per year (2006 est); there are minorities of Romanies, ethnic Germans, Serbs, Romanians and Slovaks
RELIGION – Roman Catholicism (55 per cent), other Christian denominations (18 per cent), Judaism (1 per cent) (est). An estimated 15 per cent of the population is atheist
LANGUAGE – Hungarian (official)
POPULATION DENSITY – 113 per sq. km (2005)
URBAN POPULATION – 65.9 per cent (2005 est)
MEDIAN AGE (years) – 38.7 (2006 est)
NATIONAL ANTHEM – 'Himnusz' ['Hymn']
NATIONAL DAY – 20 August (Saint Stephen's Day)
LIFE EXPECTANCY (years) – 72.66 (2006 est)
MORTALITY RATE – 13.11 (2006 est)
BIRTH RATE – 9.72 (2006 est)
INFANT MORTALITY RATE – 8.39 (2006 est)
DEATH PENALTY – No (abolished 1990)
CPI SCORE – 5.2 (2006)

CLIMATE AND TERRAIN

A landlocked state in central Europe, Hungary is mostly low-lying with a mountainous region in the north. Elevation extremes range from 1,014m (Kekes) at the highest point to 78m (Tisza River) at the lowest. The main rivers are the Danube and the Tisza, and Lake Balaton lies in the west. Average temperatures range from −1°C in January to 21°C in July.

HISTORY AND POLITICS

Hungary became a Christian kingdom in 1000 but had been settled by Magyar tribes (the ancestors of modern Hungarians) since 896. Between 1699 and 1867, Hungary was ruled as a province of the Austrian Habsburg Empire. Following years of Hungarian agitation, a dual monarchy was created in 1867, giving Hungary control of its internal affairs in return for the continued union of the Austrian and Hungarian crowns. The Austro-Hungarian Empire is remembered as a time of great cultural achievement and economic success. Nevertheless, the union took the country into the First World War on the side of Germany, resulting in defeat for the Hungarians and the fall of the Habsburg dynasty. Initially a communist republic after the war, in 1920 a kingdom was established, with Admiral Horthy as regent. Hungary signed the Anti-Comintern Pact with Germany, Italy and Japan in 1939 but remained neutral when the Second World War began, joining the conflict in 1941 on the side of the Axis powers. Horthy was deposed in 1944 after seeking an armistice with advancing Soviet troops, who drove out German forces in 1945.

The Communists came to power in the 1947 elections, and in 1949 Hungary became a communist state aligned with the Soviet Union. A national uprising broke out in 1956, with protesters demanding the withdrawal of Soviet forces from the country, but this was brutally suppressed. In the 1960s Janos Kadar introduced limited liberalisation, which encouraged the development of the most wealthy and permissive regime in the Soviet bloc.

The opening of Hungary's border with Austria in 1989 triggered the developments that led to the fall of communism throughout eastern Europe. Communist rule ended in Hungary, which began the transition to a free-market democracy. The country became a member of NATO in 1999 and joined the EU in 2004. Its parliament ratified the EU constitution in the same year.

The national assembly elected Laszlo Solyom president in 2005. In the 2006 legislative election, the Hungarian Socialist Party (MSzP) remained the largest party in the legislature and continued its coalition with the Free Democrats.

POLITICAL SYSTEM

The 1949 constitution has been amended several times, most radically in 1989 to allow a return to a multiparty democracy. The president is elected by the national assembly for a five-year term, renewable only once; the post is largely ceremonial but powers include the appointment of the prime minister. The unicameral national assembly has 386 members directly elected for a four-year term.

HEAD OF STATE

President, Laszlo Solyom, *elected* June 2005, *sworn in* 5 August 2005

SELECTED GOVERNMENT MEMBERS *as at May 2007*

Prime Minister, Ferenc Gyurcsany
Defence, Imre Szekeres
Finance, Janos Veres
Foreign Affairs, Kinga Goencz

EMBASSY OF THE REPUBLIC OF HUNGARY
35 Eaton Place, London SW1X 8BY
T 020-7201 3440 W www.huemblon.org.uk
Ambassador Extraordinary and Plenipotentiary, HE Bela Szombati, *apptd* 2002

BRITISH EMBASSY
Harmincad Utca 6, 1051 Budapest
T (+36) (1) 266 2888 E info@britemb.hu
W www.britishembassy.hu
Ambassador Extraordinary and Plenipotentiary, HE John Nichols, *apptd* 2003

BRITISH COUNCIL
Benczur Utca 26, 1068 Budapest
T (+36) (1) 478 4700 W www.britishcouncil.org/hungary
Director, David Martin

DEFENCE

The army has 238 main battle tanks, 178 armoured infantry fighting vehicles and 458 armoured personnel carriers. The air force has 19 combat aircraft and 12 attack helicopters.

MILITARY EXPENDITURE – US$1,430m (2005)
MILITARY PERSONNEL – 32,300: army 23,950, air force 7,500, joint staff 850; paramilitaries 12,000
CONSCRIPTION DURATION – Six months

ECONOMY AND TRADE

Hungary has made a successful transition to a market economy since 1989, with 80 per cent of enterprises now in the private sector, and it has attracted high levels of foreign direct investment. There has been strong and sustained economic growth and inflation has been brought down to single figures, but the growing budget and trade deficits are a concern and public debt is 69 per cent of GDP.

Nearly half the land is under cultivation, but agriculture accounts for only 3 per cent of GDP; the main crops are cereals, sunflower seeds, vegetables, livestock, dairy products and grapes for wine. Industry contributes 32 per cent of GDP; the main activities include mining, metallurgy, construction materials, food processing, textiles, chemicals (especially pharmaceuticals) and motor vehicles. The main trading partners are other EU countries, Russia and China. Machinery and manufactured goods account for 90 per cent of exports and 87 per cent of imports. The country is a net importer of fuels and electricity.

GNI – US$101,600m; US$10,070 per capita (2005)
ANNUAL AVERAGE GROWTH OF GDP – 4.1 per cent (2005 est)
INFLATION RATE – 3.6 per cent (2005 est)
UNEMPLOYMENT – 7.2 per cent (2005)
TOTAL EXTERNAL DEBT – US$66,220m (2005 est)
IMPORTS – US$65,300m (2005)
EXPORTS – US$61,800m (2005)

BALANCE OF PAYMENTS
Trade – US$1,917m deficit (2005)
Current Account – US$7,962m deficit (2005)

Trade with UK	*2005*	*2006*
Imports from UK	£806,650,000	£807,000,000
Exports to UK	£1,772,454,000	£2,028,400,000

COMMUNICATIONS

Hungary has 159,600km of highways, about 40 per cent of which is surfaced, and 7,900km of railways (including a cross-border line to Austria, jointly managed by the two countries). There are 1,622km of permanently navigable waterways, mainly on the River Danube, and several major river ports and harbours on the Danube, including Budapest. There are 46 airports and airfields, 20 of which have surfaced runways; the principal airport is Budapest. The land-line telephone system has been modernised since 2003. Mobile phone distribution is very widespread, at 9 million subscribers in 2005. There were 3 million internet users in 2005.

EDUCATION AND HEALTH

Hungarians have ten years of compulsory education, though a further two years at secondary level is optional.

LITERACY RATE – 99.3 per cent (2004 est)
GROSS ENROLMENT RATIO (percentage of relevant age group) – primary 98 per cent; secondary 97 per cent; tertiary 60 per cent (2005 est)
HEALTH EXPENDITURE (per capita) – US$800 (2004)
HOSPITAL BEDS (per 1,000 people) – 7.8 (2000–5)

MEDIA AND CULTURE

The state-run broadcaster, Magyar Televizo, has recently lost ground in competition with privately owned television and radio stations. Hungary has a wide range of weekly and daily newspapers, many of which are owned by foreign investors.

The strong folk music culture has influenced a powerful musical tradition, including the composers Franz Liszt (1811–86), Bela Bartok (1881–1945), Zoltan Kodaly (1882–1967) and Gyorgy Ligeti (1923–2006). Hungary's best known author is Imre Kertesz (*b.* 1929), who won the Nobel prize for literature in 2002.

ICELAND

Lydveldid Island – Republic of Iceland

AREA – 103,000 sq. km
CAPITAL – Reykjavik; population, 113,387 (2004)
MAJOR CITIES – Kopavogur; Hafnarfjordur; Akureyri; Reykjanesbaer
CURRENCY – Icelandic krona (Kr) of 100 aurar
POPULATION – 299,388 rising at 0.87 per cent per year (2006 est)
RELIGION – Christianity (88 per cent) (est)
LANGUAGE – Icelandic (official), English, German
POPULATION DENSITY – 3 per sq. km (2005)
URBAN POPULATION – 93 per cent (2005 est)
MEDIAN AGE (years) – 34.2 (2006 est)
NATIONAL ANTHEM – 'Lofsongur' ['Hymn']
NATIONAL DAY – 17 June (Independence Day)
LIFE EXPECTANCY (years) – 80.31 (2006 est)
MORTALITY RATE – 6.72 (2006 est)
BIRTH RATE – 13.64 (2006 est)
INFANT MORTALITY RATE – 3.29 (2006 est)
DEATH PENALTY – No (abolished 1928)
CPI SCORE – 9.6 (2006)
MILITARY BUDGET – US$42.9m (2005) (spent mostly on coast guard)
MILITARY PERSONNEL – paramilitaries 130
GROSS ENROLMENT RATIO (percentage of relevant age group) – primary 101 per cent (2002)

CLIMATE AND TERRAIN

Iceland is located in the North Atlantic Ocean, to the east of Greenland and to the west of Norway, and its northernmost coasts reach the Arctic Circle. Some coasts have narrow strips of low-lying land, others sheer cliffs. An inland plateau of glaciers, lakes and lava fields covers 79 per cent of the interior, with mountainous areas in the north and at the four glaciers in the centre and south. Elevation extremes range from 2,110m (Hvannadalshnukur) at the highest point to 0m (North Atlantic Ocean) at the lowest. There are geysers and hot springs owing to the numerous active volcanoes, which can create new islands, such as Surtsey in 1963. It is estimated that over the past 500 years, Iceland has emitted a third of the earth's total lava flow. The climate is influenced by the Gulf Stream and is therefore temperate, in spite of the country's location. Average temperature ranges from −3°C in January to 11°C in July.

HISTORY AND POLITICS

The first major settlements occurred from around AD 870 onwards, as turmoil in Scandinavia drove migrants to seek new homelands. Iceland hosted a flourishing Viking culture in the ninth and tenth centuries, becoming a fully Christian country in 999. Iceland recognised Norwegian sovereignty in 1263, and along with Norway, came under Danish rule in 1397. When Norway was ceded to Sweden in 1814, Iceland remained Danish territory, achieving autonomy in domestic affairs in 1874. Though it became an independent state with the same sovereign as Denmark in 1918, Copenhagen continued to control its foreign policy and defence. The treaty of union with Denmark expired in 1943, while Denmark was under German occupation, and in a referendum Icelanders voted to become a fully independent republic, proclaimed on 17 June 1944.

The country's dependence on the fishing industry has led occasionally to fraught foreign relations. The introduction and extensions of an exclusive fishing limit around Iceland in 1958, 1972 and 1975 caused the so-called 'Cod War' disputes with the UK with clashes between Icelandic patrol boats and British trawlers and navy vessels. Subsequent restrictions on fishing in Icelandic waters in the 1990s were less controversial.

In the 2004 presidential election, the incumbent president Olafur Grimsson was returned to office for a third term. In the 2007 legislative election, the governing coalition of the Conservative Independence Party (SSF) and the Progressive Party (FSF) retained its parliamentary majority by one seat.

POLITICAL SYSTEM

Under the 1944 constitution, the head of state is the president, who is directly elected for a four-year term, which is renewable. The unicameral legislature, the *Althing*, has 63 members, who are directly elected for a four-year term. Founded in AD 930, the *Althing* is the world's oldest parliament.

HEAD OF STATE

President, Olafur Ragnar Grimsson, *elected* 29 June 1996, *re-elected* 2000 and 2004

SELECTED GOVERNMENT MEMBERS *As at June 2007*

Prime Minister, Geir Hilmar Haarde
Finance, Arni M. Mathiesen
Foreign Affairs, Ingibjorg Solrun Gisladottir
Social Affairs, Johanna Sigurdardottir

EMBASSY OF ICELAND

2A Hans Street, London SW1X 0JE
T 020-7259 3999 **W** www.iceland.org/uk
Ambassador Extraordinary and Plenipotentiary, HE Sverrir Haukur Gunnlaugsson, *apptd* 2003

BRITISH EMBASSY

PO Box 460, Laufasvegur 31, IS-101 Reykjavik
T (+354) 550 5100 **E** britemb@centrum.is
Ambassador Extraordinary and Plenipotentiary and Consul-General, HE Alp Mehmet, MVO, *apptd* 2004

ECONOMY AND TRADE

Iceland has a market economy with an extensive welfare system. The economy is heavily dependent on the fishing industry; although fishing contributes only about 10 per cent of GDP, it accounts for 70 per cent of exports. Careful management of the industry has allowed stocks to recover from the over-fishing of the 1980s, when declining catches adversely affected the economy. However, Iceland resumed whaling on a commercial level in October 2006. The government has encouraged economic diversification, and aluminium smelting, ferrosilicon production, geothermal power, financial services and tourism now account for industry's 16 per cent contribution to GDP and the service sector's 76 per cent. Owing to the plentiful supply of geothermal power, which runs industrial complexes and provides most of the island's heating, the island is self-sufficient in energy apart from vehicle fuels.

The main trading partners are EU countries, especially Germany and the UK, and the USA. Principal exports are fish and fish products, aluminium, animal products, ferrosilicon and diatomite. The main imports are machinery, petroleum products, foodstuffs and textiles.

GNI – US$14,414,000m; US$48,570 per capita (2005)
ANNUAL AVERAGE GROWTH OF GDP – 5.6 per cent (2005 est)
INFLATION RATE – 4 per cent (2005 est)
UNEMPLOYMENT – 2.1 per cent (2005 est)
TOTAL EXTERNAL DEBT – US$3,073m (2002)
IMPORTS – US$4,560m (2005)
EXPORTS – US$2,940m (2005)

BALANCE OF PAYMENTS
Trade – US$1,480m deficit (2005)
Current Account – US$2,617m deficit (2005)

Trade with UK	*2005*	*2006*
Imports from UK	£183,852,000	£190,067,000
Exports to UK	£358,464,000	£411,776,000

COMMUNICATIONS

Iceland has no railways and no navigable waterways. Although the country has about 13,000km of roads, about two-thirds are unsurfaced and in winter these are often blocked by snow. Consequently much internal travel is by air or sea. Iceland has 98 airports and airfields, the principal ones being at Keflavik, near Reykjavik, in the south and Akureyri in the north. The national carrier, Icelandair, is a major employer. There are nine major ports and the capital, Reykjavik, operates shipping services to the USA and Europe. The land-line telephone system has 194,000 main lines in use; mobile phone subscribers numbered 304,000 and there were 258,000 internet users in 2005.

MEDIA AND CULTURE

The state provides public service broadcasting on television and radio via the Icelandic National Broadcasting Service (RUV), which is mandated to promote Icelandic culture and history. There are several commercial stations and a wide variety of newspapers. Reporters Without Borders ranks the country the joint highest for press freedom in 2006.

Iceland enjoys a rich literary tradition. The anonymous Icelandic prose sagas, dating from the 12th to the 14th centuries, are among the most important works of medieval European literature. One of Iceland's best known modern writers is Halldor Laxness (1902–98), winner of the Nobel prize for literature in 1955. The country has also become a successful exporter of popular music through groups including the Sugarcubes (whose singer Bjork has enjoyed worldwide recognition) and Sigur Ros.

INDIA

Bharatiya Ganarajya – The Republic of India

AREA – 3,287,590 sq. km. Neighbours: Pakistan (north-west), China, Tibet, Nepal and Bhutan (north), Myanmar and Bangladesh (east)
CAPITAL – New Delhi; population, 12,877,470 including Delhi/Dilli (2001)
MAJOR CITIES – Bombay/Mumbai; Calcutta/Kolkata; Madras/Chennai; Hyderabad; Bengaluru; Ahmadabad; Pune; Surat; Kanpur; Jaipur
CURRENCY – Indian rupee (Rs) of 100 paise
POPULATION – 1,095,351,995 rising at 1.38 per cent per year (2006 est); Indo-Aryan (72 per cent), Dravidian (25 per cent) (est)
RELIGION – Hinduism (82 per cent), Islam (12 per cent), Christianity (2 per cent), Sikhism (2 per cent) (est)
LANGUAGE – English, Hindi, Bengali, Bodo, Dogri, Kannada, Konkani, Maithili, Manipuri, Nepali, Telugu, Marathi, Tamil, Urdu, Gujurati, Malayalam, Santhali, Oriya, Punjabi, Assamese, Kashmiri, Sindhi, Sanskrit (all official)
POPULATION DENSITY – 368 per sq. km (2005)
URBAN POPULATION – 28.7 per cent (2005 est)
MEDIAN AGE (years) – 24.9 (2006 est)
NATIONAL ANTHEM – 'Jana Gana Manag' ['Thou art the Ruler of the Minds of all People']
NATIONAL DAY – 26 January (Republic Day)
LIFE EXPECTANCY (years) – 64.71 (2006 est)
MORTALITY RATE – 8.18 (2006 est)
BIRTH RATE – 22.01 (2006 est)
INFANT MORTALITY RATE – 54.63 (2006 est)
DEATH PENALTY – Yes
CPI SCORE – 3.3 (2006)
POPULATION BELOW POVERTY LINE – 25 per cent (2002 est)

CLIMATE AND TERRAIN

India has three well-defined regions: the mountain range of the Himalayas, the Indo-Gangetic plain, and the southern peninsula. The Himalayas along the northern border reach 8,597m (Kanchenjunga) at the highest point of elevation, then drop to the northern plains formed by the basins of the Indus, Ganges and Brahmaputra river before rising to low hills running east to west that mark the division with the southern, Deccan peninsula. The peninsula has narrow coastal plains rising to a central plateau, with the Western Ghats and Eastern Ghats range of hills lying along the west and east coasts respectively. The Thar Desert lies in the north-west. The averag temperature in New Delhi ranges from 14°C in January to 34°C in June.

HISTORY AND POLITICS

The Indus civilisation emerged in the Indus river valley region *c.*2500 BC, and the beginnings of Hinduism dat from this period. This civilisation was destroyed by Arya tribes from central Asia between 1500 and 200 BC Buddhism emerged in India from *c.*500 BC and wa mbraced by the Emperor Ashoka; it spread to the rest of astern Asia via trade routes, but a Hindu revival from AD 0 onwards pushed Buddhism into decline in the sub-ontinent.

The first Muslim advances into India occurred in the 0th and 11th centuries. Incursions swept across the orth of the country, where large Muslim communities vere established. India thus became a country with two reat religious traditions: a Muslim-dominated north and largely Hindu south. Europeans arrived in India in the 5th century and had established territorial holdings by ne 18th century, though it was not until 1803, when the ritish East India Company consolidated its influence, hat a single power came to dominate the entire ubcontinent. In 1857 rule passed to the British overnment. From the late 19th century, opposition to ritish rule, led by the Indian National Congress (INC), atterly under the leadership of Mahatma Gandhi, became concerted nationwide movement, and India achieved its ndependence in 1947. Against a backdrop of violence, ndia's predominantly Muslim regions were partitioned ff to became the separate state of Pakistan. India became republic in 1950.

The INC has been the dominant party in Indian olitics in the decades since independence, holding ower almost continuously for four decades, with periods opposition in 1977–80, 1989–91 and 1996–2004. awaharlal Nehru's appointment as prime minister at ndependence began the rise of the Gandhi family, which as dominated the INC. Nehru was succeeded by his aughter, Indira Gandhi, who was succeeded after her ssassination in 1984 by her son Rajiv until he too vas assassinated in 1991; Rajiv's widow Sonia became resident of the party in 1998. The INC's dominance ppeared to be over in the early 1990s when the Hindu ationalist Bharatiya Janata Party (BJP) began to beat the NC at the polls and formed a series of coalition overnments. The INC returned to power with a surprise ictory in the 2004 parliamentary election, winning 217 ats in the *Lok Sabha*. Sonia Gandhi was nominated as rime minister but declined the office, and Manmohan ingh became India's first Sikh prime minister at the head f an INC-dominated coalition government called the nited Progressive Alliance. A presidential election in July 007 was won by Pratibha Patil, who became the ountry's first female head of state.

OMMUNALISM

ensions between India's Hindu majority and large uslim minority have never been fully resolved. Violence etween the two at the time of partition in 1947 is ought to have cost up to one million lives. The rise of indu nationalism in the 1990s accompanied a rise in mmunal clashes. In 1992, a mosque in the town of yodhya was destroyed by Hindus who claimed it was ilt on the site of the Hindu god Rama's birth. Anti-uslim mobs rampaged through many parts of India and e army was called upon to restore order. Intercommunal olence flared up again in 2002 when the massacre of lgrims returning from Ayodhya prompted revenge llings.

Sikh separatist agitation for an independent state in the njab became increasingly violent in the 1980s. The ppression of militant Sikh separatism, and particularly e Indian army offensive at the Golden Temple at mritsar, led to the assassination of Indira Gandhi by her kh bodyguards in 1984.

FOREIGN RELATIONS

Since partition, sovereignty over the predominantly Muslim state of Jammu and Kashmir has been disputed by India and Pakistan. A short war in 1947–8 resulted in the state being partitioned between the two countries; its status remained unresolved, leading to another war in 1965, low-level conflict for control of the Siachen glacier since 1985 and occasional increases in military exchanges, most recently in 1999–2002 and 2003. Tension was exacerbated by Pakistan's support of the Muslim insurgency in the Indian part of the state, which began in the 1980s and has included terrorist attacks in Indian cities, and both countries' acquisition of nuclear weapons. Moves towards a peaceful settlement began in 2003, when diplomatic missions were reopened and the resumption of transport links was initiated (a bus service across the line of control began in 2005). Formal diplomatic talks began in 2004 and have achieved several accords intended to reduce tension between the two countries, but the issue of Kashmir has yet to be addressed.

In the Sino-Indian war in 1962, India lost territory to China. In addition, China claims Arunachal Pradesh and does not recognise Indian sovereignty over Sikkim. Talks between India and China in 2003 resulted in India's formal recognition of the Tibetan Autonomous Region as a part of China and a cross-border trade agreement on Sikkim.

POLITICAL SYSTEM

Under the 1950 constitution, executive power is vested in the president, who is elected for a five-year term by an electoral college consisting of members of the upper and lower houses of the legislature. The president appoints the prime minister, who is responsible to the parliament. The vice-president, who is elected by both houses of parliament for a five-year term, is *ex-officio* chair of the upper house. The legislature, the *Sansad*, consists of two chambers. The upper house, the *Rajya Sabha* (house of the states) has up to 250 members serving a six-year term, with one-third of seats contested every two years; up to 238 members are elected by the state legislative assemblies and the rest are nominated by the president. In the lower house, the *Lok Sabha* (house of the people), there are 545 members; 543, representing the states and union territories, are directly elected for a five-year term, and two representatives of the Anglo-Indian community are nominated by the president.

HEAD OF STATE

President of the Republic of India, Pratibha Patil, *elected* 19 July 2007, *took office* 25 July 2007
Vice-President, Bhairon Singh Shekhawat

SELECTED GOVERNMENT MEMBERS *as at June 2007*

Prime Minister, Manmohan Singh
Defence, A. K. Antony
Finance, Palaniappan Chidambaram
Home Affairs, Shivraj V. Patil
External Affairs, Pranab Mukherjee

HIGH COMMISSION OF INDIA

India House, London WC2B 4NA
T 020-7836 8484 W www.hcilondon.net
High Commissioner, HE Kamalesh Sharma, *apptd* 2004

BRITISH HIGH COMMISSION
Chanakyapuri, New Delhi 21 1100-21
T (+91) (11) 2687 2161 E postmaster.newdelhi@fco.gov.uk
W www.ukinindia.org
High Commissioner, Richard Stagg, CMG, *apptd* 2007

BRITISH COUNCIL
17 Kasturba Gandhi Marg, New Delhi 110001
T (+91) (11) 2371 1401/2371 0111
W www.britishcouncil.org/india
Minister and Regional Director, Rod Pryde

FEDERAL STRUCTURE
There are 28 states and six union territories and the national capital territory. Each state is headed by a governor, who is appointed by the president and holds office for five years, and by a council of ministers. All states have a legislative assembly, and some also have a legislative council, elected directly for a maximum period of five years. The union territories are administered, except where otherwise provided by parliament, by the president acting through an administrator or lieutenant-governor, or other authority appointed by him. The states have considerable autonomy, although the union government controls such matters as foreign policy, defence and external trade.

DEFENCE

The army has 3,978 main battle tanks, over 1,700 armoured infantry fighting vehicles, 12 combat helicopters and more than 817 armoured personnel carriers. The navy has 16 submarines, 1 aircraft carrier, 8 destroyers, 24 frigates, 19 patrol and coastal vessels, 34 combat aircraft and 9 armed helicopters. The air force has 849 combat aircraft and 60 armed helicopters.

India has had nuclear weapon technology since the mid-1970s, and by the mid-1990s had also successfully developed intermediate-range ballistic missiles.

MILITARY EXPENDITURE – US$21,700m (2005)
MILITARY PERSONNEL – 1,316,000: army 1,100,000, navy 55,000, air force 161,000; paramilitaries 1,300,586

ECONOMY AND TRADE

The economy was closed for three decades after independence, with high import tariffs and limits on foreign investment to stimulate domestic growth. Since the late 1980s, economic liberalisation and more foreign investment have generated the rapid expansion of the past decade, when GDP has grown by an average 7 per cent a year. India's large skilled workforce, especially its pool of English-speaking graduates, has enabled it to develop knowledge-based industries, such as IT and telecommunications, becoming a global centre for manufacturing and services. Pharmaceuticals is another area of growth, as are tourism and the provision of services to the burgeoning urban middle class. The service sector now accounts for 61 per cent of GDP and industry for 19 per cent, employing 28 per cent and 12 per cent of the workforce respectively. The government's plans to set up over 600 special economic zones to stimulate the growth of manufacturing industries has met with opposition in the mainly agricultural areas earmarked for development.

Rural areas have benefited little from this growth, with an estimated 60 million living in poverty. Since 2004 the government has initiated schemes intended to reduce rural poverty, which has been exacerbated by prolonged drought in some areas and the displacement of 600,000 from coastal areas by the Indian Ocean tsunami of 2004. Agriculture, forestry and fishing support 60 per cent of the population and contribute 20 per cent of GDP. The main food crops are rice, cereals (principally wheat) and pulses. The major cash crops include sugar cane, jute, cotton and tea. Agriculture and forestry are threatened by deforestation, soil erosion, over-grazing and desertification.

Despite the economic growth, there is a high trade deficit and growing inflation. Problems that threaten to constrain continued growth include the halting of the privatisation of state enterprises, under-investment in the infrastructure (especially transport and power supply), excessive regulation and corruption.

The main trading partners are the USA, China, the UAE, EU and ASEAN countries. Principal exports include textiles and garments, gemstones and jewellery, engineering goods, chemicals and leather manufactures. Its main imports are crude oil, machinery, gemstones, fertiliser and chemicals.

GNI – US$840,100m; US$730 per capita (2005)
ANNUAL AVERAGE GROWTH OF GDP – 8.4 per cent (2005 est)
INFLATION RATE – 4.2 per cent (2005 est)
UNEMPLOYMENT – 8.9 per cent (2005 est)
TOTAL EXTERNAL DEBT – US$125,500m (2005 est)
IMPORTS – US$134,600m (2005)
EXPORTS – US$95,200m (2005)

BALANCE OF PAYMENTS
Trade – US$8,870m deficit (2003)
Current Account – US$6,853m surplus (2003)

Trade with UK	*2005*	*2006*
Imports from UK	£2,812,957,000	£2,703,856,000
Exports to UK	£2,828,618,000	£3,187,831,000

COMMUNICATIONS

India has over 63,230km of railway and 3.38 million km of roads, however less than half are surfaced. There are 341 airports and airfields, the principal ones being at Delhi, Bombay/Mumbai, Madras/Chennai and Calcutta/Kolkata. The chief seaports are Bombay/Mumbai, Calcutta/Kolkata, Haldia, Madras/Chennai, Cochin, Visakhapatnam, Mangalore and Tuticorin. The merchant fleet includes 316 ships of over 1,000 tonnes. There is 485km of canals and the great rivers provide over 5,200km of navigable waterways.

Deregulation and liberalisation has enabled the telephone system to expand rapidly. Services are still concentrated in urban areas. Mobile phone distribution is expanding even more quickly; there were 69 million subscribers in 2006 compared to 50 million main-line subscribers. There were 60 million internet users in 2005 and 1.5 million internet hosts.

EDUCATION AND HEALTH

Education is free of charge and compulsory until the age of 14.

LITERACY RATE – 61 per cent (2004 est)
GROSS ENROLMENT RATIO (percentage of relevant age group) – primary 116 per cent; secondary 54 per cent; tertiary 12 per cent (2005 est)
HEALTH EXPENDITURE (per capita) – US$31 (2004)
HOSPITAL BEDS (per 1,000 people) – 0.9 (2000–5)

MEDIA

The state's monopoly of television broadcasting ended in 1992, since when the number of channels available has increased rapidly; Doordarshan and Zee TV are major broadcasters, while satellite and cable channels are also popular. The private press is a thriving and diverse industry, often outspoken and critical of the government; in 2004 some 142 million newspapers were sold throughout the country.

CULTURE

Contemporary writers of international standing include Vikram Seth (*b.* 1952), Salman Rushdie (*b.* 1947) and Arundhati Roy (*b.* 1961). Bollywood is the common name for the Mumbai-based Indian film industry which produces over 800 films a year. The influence of Bollywood in the West is growing rapidly, as shown by the success of collaborative efforts such as *Bride and Prejudice* (2004) and Andrew Lloyd Webber's 2004 musical *Bombay Dreams*.

Cricket, the most popular sport in India, was introduced by the British and matches have been played in the country since 1721. Notable players include spin bowlers Bishan Singh Bedi (*b.* 1946) and Anil Kumble (*b.* 1970) and *Wisden*'s Indian Cricketer of the Century, Kapil Dev (*b.* 1959).

NDONESIA

epublik Indonesia – Republic of Indonesia

REA – 1,919,440 sq. km. Indonesia shares borders with Malaysia (on Borneo), Papua New Guinea (on New Guinea) and East Timor (on Timor)
APITAL – Jakarta; population, 8,603,349 (2003)
AJOR CITIES – Surabaya; (Java) Bandung; Medan; Bekasi; Tangerang; Semarang
URRENCY – Rupiah (Rp) of 100 sen
OPULATION – 245,452,739 rising at 1.41 per cent per year (2006 est); Javanese (45 per cent), Sundanese (14 per cent), Madurese (7.5 per cent), Malay (7.5 per cent) (est)
ELIGION – Islam (88 per cent), Christianity (9 per cent), Hinduism (2 per cent), Buddhism (1 per cent) (est)
ANGUAGE – Bahasa Indonesian (official), English, Dutch, Javanese
OPULATION DENSITY – 122 per sq. km (2005)
RBAN POPULATION – 47.9 per cent (2005 est)
EDIAN AGE (years) – 26.8 (2006 est)
ATIONAL ANTHEM – 'Indonesia Raya' ['Great Indonesia']
ATIONAL DAY – 17 August (Independence Day)
FE EXPECTANCY (years) – 69.87 (2006 est)
ORTALITY RATE – 6.25 (2006 est)
IRTH RATE – 20.34 (2006 est)
NFANT MORTALITY RATE – 34.39 (2006 est)
EATH PENALTY – Yes
PI SCORE – 2.4 (2006)
OPULATION BELOW POVERTY LINE – 16.7 per cent (2004)
TERACY RATE – 87.9 per cent (2004 est)
ROSS ENROLMENT RATIO (percentage of relevant age group) – primary 117 per cent; secondary 64 per cent; tertiary 17 per cent (2005 est)
EALTH EXPENDITURE (per capita) – US$33 (2004)

CLIMATE AND TERRAIN

Indonesia comprises over 13,000 islands, of which over 6,000 are inhabited. They include the islands of Java, Madura, Sumatra, the Riouw-Lingga archipelago, Bangka and Billiton, part of the island of Borneo (Kalimantan), Sulawesi (formerly Celebes), Maluku (formerly Moluccas), the islands of Bali, Lombok, Sumbawa, Sumba, Flores and others comprising the provinces of East and West Nusa Tenggara, and the western half of the islands of New Guinea (Papua; formerly Irian Jaya) and Timor. Elevation extremes range from 4,884m (Puncak Jaya, in Papua) at the highest point to 0m (Indian Ocean) at the lowest. Many of the islands have narrow coastal plains with hilly or mountainous interiors, and over half of the country is covered by tropical rainforest. Average temperatures in Jakarta range from 23°C in January to 32°C in August.

HISTORY AND POLITICS

Hindu and Buddhist kingdoms existed in some parts of the Indonesian islands until the 14th century. Islam was introduced in the 13th century and spread over the next three centuries. Trading by the Portuguese began in the 16th century, but the Portuguese were displaced by the Dutch who, lured by the rich spice trade, came to dominate Indonesia by the early 20th century. Opposition to Dutch rule grew in the 1920s and the Japanese occupation of Indonesia during the Second World War strengthened nationalism, leading to a declaration of independence after liberation in 1945. This was not recognised by the Dutch, who attempted to reassert control, but after four years of guerrilla warfare they granted independence to the Netherlands Indies in 1949 and Irian Jaya in 1963. East Timor was invaded and annexed in 1975 but gained independence in 2002.

Achmed Soekarno, the foremost proponent of self-rule since the 1920s, became president in 1949 but was deposed in 1966 in a military coup that brought General Suharto to power. Suharto remained in power until 1998 when, amidst economic and social upheaval, he was succeeded by his deputy B. J. Habibie. Habibie's cautious introduction of social and economic reforms led to him being defeated in 1999, in the first democratically held elections for 44 years, which brought Abdurrahman Wahid to power. President Wahid was impeached for alleged financial corruption and in 2001 the people's consultative assembly appointed Megawati Soekarnoputri (daughter of Achmed Soekarno) to replace him.

In the 2004 legislative elections, the greatest number of seats was won by Golkar, the former ruling party. The 2004 presidential election was won by Susilo Bambang Yudhoyono of the Democratic Party, who defeated Megawati Soekarnoputri in the second round; Yudhoyono appointed a coalition government that included two Golkar ministers.

INSURGENCIES

Separatist movements developed in several parts of Indonesia after independence, including Maluku, which fought an unsuccessful separatist war in the 1950s; Irian Jaya (now Papua), which was granted greater autonomy in 2001, although separatist agitation continues; East Timor, from its annexation in 1975 until independence in 2002; and Aceh province in Sumatra, granted a degree of autonomy after a peace accord between the separatist movement and the government in August 2005.

Since the fall of Suharto in 1998, tensions between different racial or religious groups have surfaced, and there has been intercommunal violence in Kalimantan

(1996–7, 1999 and 2001), Sulawesi (1998–2000 and 2001) and Maluku (1999–2002).

At least two Muslim extremist groups are based in Indonesia and claim links with al-Qaida. They have been held responsible for bombings in Bali in 2002, 2003 and 2005.

POLITICAL SYSTEM

The 1959 constitution was amended in 2001 to provide for the establishment of the upper chamber of the legislature, and in 2002 to provide for the direct election of the president and the abolition of parliamentary seats reserved for the armed forces. The executive president, who is directly elected for a five-year term of office, appoints the prime minister and the cabinet. The bicameral legislature, the people's consultative assembly, is the state's highest authority, with powers to alter the constitution. The lower house, the house of representatives, has 550 members directly elected for a five-year term. The upper house, the house of representatives of the regions, was created in 2001 to deal with regional matters; it has 128 members, four for each province, directly elected on a non-partisan basis for a five-year term.

HEAD OF STATE

President, Susilo Bambang Yudhoyono, *sworn in* 20 October 2004

Vice-President, Muhammad Jusuf Kalla

SELECTED GOVERNMENT MEMBERS *as at June 2007*

Defence, Juwono Sudarsono

Economy, Boediono

Foreign Affairs, Hasan Wirayuda

Home Affairs, Lt.-Gen. Muhammad Ma'aruf (retd)

EMBASSY OF THE REPUBLIC OF INDONESIA

38 Grosvenor Square, London W1K 2HW

T 020-7499 7661 W www.indonesianembassy.org.uk

Ambassador Extraordinary and Plenipotentiary, Dr R. M. Marty M. Natalegawa, *apptd* 2006

BRITISH EMBASSY

Jalan M. H. Thamrin 75, Jakarta 10310

T (+62) (21) 315 6264 E consulate.jakarta@fco.gov.uk

W www.british-emb-jakarta.or.id

Ambassador Extraordinary and Plenipotentiary, HE Charles Humfrey

BRITISH COUNCIL

Jakarta Stock Exchange, Tower II, 16th Floor, Jalan Jenderal Sudirman Kav. 52–53, Jakarta 12190

T (+62) (021) 515 5561 W www.britishcouncil.org/indonesia

Director, Prof. Mike Hardy, OBE

DEFENCE

The army has 356 armoured personnel carriers, 11 armoured infantry fighting vehicles and 2 attack helicopters. The navy has 2 submarines, 12 frigates, 37 patrol and coastal vessels and 9 armed helicopters. There are 5 principal naval bases. The air force has 94 combat aircraft.

MILITARY EXPENDITURE – US$10,300m (2006 est)

MILITARY PERSONNEL – 302,000: army 233,000, navy 45,000, air force 24,000; paramilitaries 280,000

CONSCRIPTION DURATION – 24 months (selective)

ECONOMY AND TRADE

The economy has struggled since the late 1990s, when the Asian financial crisis coincided with the fall of Suharto and the ensuing period of political upheaval. Owing to the caution, corruption and indecision of subsequent governments, the economy has drifted, its recovery hit by a downturn in tourism following the Bali bombings and the devastation caused by a succession of natural disasters since 2004. Unemployment and inflation levels are rising and the fragile currency, poor infrastructure and endemic corruption have discouraged foreign investment. Public debt has been reduced to 4[illegible] per cent of GDP, however, and there is a trade surplus.

Natural resources include oil, tin, natural gas, nickel, timber, bauxite, copper, coal, gold and silver. However, lack of investment in finding new sources of oil has led to a decline in oil production that has made Indonesia a net importer since 2004. The exploitation and processing of mineral assets, production of textiles, clothing, timber, chemicals and rubber, and tourism are the main industrial activities; industry accounts for 46 per cent of GDP and services 41 per cent, employing 18 per cent and 39 per cent of the workforce respectively. Agriculture contributes only 13 per cent of GDP but employs 43 per cent of the workforce. The main crops are rice, cassava, peanuts, rubber, cocoa, coffee, palm oil, copra and livestock products.

The main trading partners are Japan, Singapore, the USA, China, South Korea, other Pacific Rim nations and Saudi Arabia. Principal exports are oil and natural gas, electrical appliances, plywood, textiles and rubber. The main imports are machinery and equipment, chemicals, fuel and foodstuffs.

GNI – US$282,200m; US$1,280 per capita (2005)

ANNUAL AVERAGE GROWTH OF GDP – 5.6 per cent (2005 est)

INFLATION RATE – 10.5 per cent (2005 est)

UNEMPLOYMENT – 11.8 per cent (2005 est)

TOTAL EXTERNAL DEBT – US$135,000m (2005 est)

IMPORTS – US$38,900m (2005)

EXPORTS – US$47,900m (2005)

BALANCE OF PAYMENTS

Trade – US$22,368m surplus (2005)

Current Account – US$929m surplus (2005)

Trade with UK	*2005*	*2006*
Imports from UK	£374,283,000	£318,173,000
Exports to UK	£911,995,000	£1,021,567,000

COMMUNICATIONS

Indonesia has 368,400km of highways, 6,458km of railways and 21,579km of navigable waterways. An extensive network of ferry services links the islands. There are 662 airports and airfields, of which 159 have surfaced runways; each of the main islands has a major airport, most capable of accepting international flights. There are nine major ports, usually the chief towns of the major islands, and the merchant fleet contains 825 ships of over 1,000 tonnes. Although the telephone system covers the whole country, density is low, with 13 million main-line subscribers, 47 million mobile phone subscribers and 1[illegible] million internet users in 2005.

MEDIA

A state-run television broadcaster, Televisi Republik Indonesia (TVRI), competes with several commerci[illegible]

stations. There are several newspapers and many radio stations with national coverage. In 2003 more than 2,000 unlicensed radio and television stations were given the chance to apply for licences.

IRAN

Jomhuri-ye-Eslami-ye-Iran – Islamic Republic of Iran

AREA – 1,648,000 sq. km. Neighbours: Armenia, Azerbaijan, Turkmenistan (north), Afghanistan and Pakistan (east), Iraq and Turkey (west)
CAPITAL – Tehran; population 7,797,520 (2006 est)
MAJOR CITIES – Mashhad; Esfahan; Tabriz; Shiraz; Karaj
CURRENCY – Rial
POPULATION – 68,688,433 rising at 1.1 per cent per year (2006 est); Persian (51 per cent), Azeri (24 per cent) Mazandarani (8 per cent), Kurdish (7 per cent), Arab (3 per cent), Lurs (2 per cent), Baloch (2 per cent), Turkmen (2 per cent) (est)
RELIGION – Islam (99 per cent) (est), almost all Muslims practice Shia Islam
LANGUAGE – Persian (official), Turkic, Kurdish, Arabic
POPULATION DENSITY – 42 per sq. km (2005)
URBAN POPULATION – 68.1 per cent (2005 est)
MEDIAN AGE (years) – 24.8 (2006 est)
NATIONAL ANTHEM – 'Sorud-e Melli-e Iran' ['Anthem of the Islamic Republic of Iran']
NATIONAL DAY – 1 April (Republic Day)
LIFE EXPECTANCY (years) – 70.26 (2006 est)
MORTALITY RATE – 5.55 (2006 est)
BIRTH RATE – 17 (2006 est)
INFANT MORTALITY RATE – 40.3 (2006 est)
DEATH PENALTY – Yes
CPI SCORE – 2.7 (2006)
POPULATION BELOW POVERTY LINE – 40 per cent (2002 est)

CLIMATE AND TERRAIN

Apart from narrow coastal strips at sea-level on the Gulf coasts and the shores of the Caspian Sea, the interior is a plateau rising to mountains in the north, west and east. The western and eastern ranges are divided by the Dasht-e Kavir desert. Elevation extremes range from 5,671m (Qolleh-ye Damavand) at the highest point to −28m (Caspian Sea) at the lowest. Earthquakes are frequent. Average temperatures in Tehran are 3°C in January and 30°C in July.

HISTORY AND POLITICS

Iran is part of the Middle East's so-called fertile crescent, an area associated with the development of sophisticated agriculture. In the sixth century BC, the Achaemenian king Cyrus the Great developed his control over the area. This dynasty founded the Persian Empire under the Zoroastrian religion. Two hundred years later, Persia was conquered by Alexander the Great. Alexander's death led to a period of economic turbulence, civil conflict and foreign invasion until the Sassanian Persian Empire was founded in the second century AD. This was destroyed in AD 637 by Arab conquerors who introduced Islam, converting the majority of the population and creating a cultural revolution. The area was ruled by the Arabs, Turks and Mongols until the accession of the Safavid dynasty, which ruled between the 16th and 18th centuries, a time recognised as one of great cultural production; it was followed by the Qajar dynasty in the 19th and 20th centuries.

The Qajar dynasty was overthrown in 1921 by Reza Khan, who became prime minister in 1923 and was crowned Shah in 1925. He was succeeded in 1941 by his son, Mohammad Reza Shah Pahlavi, who began a programme of economic modernisation, Westernisation and secularisation in the 1960s. Opposition to reform and popular protests against the Shah's regime in the 1970s led to a revolution in 1978. The Shah went into exile and in 1979 a non-party theocratic Islamic republic was proclaimed under Ayatollah Khomeini.

Since Ayatollah Khomeini's death in 1989, there has been a struggle for political dominance between conservatives and more liberal reformers. Although the reformists were generally in the ascendancy until 2004, liberalisation has been blocked by the religious authorities and the conservative judiciary, which also constitutes the membership of the council of guardians and so is able to influence the selection of parliamentary candidates. There is a vocal popular pro-democracy movement.

In the 2004 legislative election, conservative candidates won the majority of seats; over 2,500 reformist candidates were disqualified from standing by the council of guardians. The 2005 presidential election was won in the second round by a conservative, Mahmoud Ahmadinejad, with 61.6 per cent of the vote. The assembly of experts was last elected in December 2006.

FOREIGN RELATIONS
Between 1980 and 1988, Iran was engaged in a bitter war with Iraq, that was ostensibly a boundary dispute over the Shatt-al-Arab waterway, fuelled by Iran's fear that Iraq was encouraging demands for autonomy by Arabs in its westernmost province. Fighting ended in 1988 and a peace settlement was agreed in 1990. Iran remained neutral in the Gulf War (1991) and the Iraq War (2003).

Since the 1978 revolution, Iran's relations with the West, and especially the USA, have been strained. It has not cooperated with international efforts to achieve peace in the Middle East, and has long been suspected of sponsoring terrorism by Islamic fundamentalists; since 2003 it has been accused of subverting Western efforts at reconstruction in Iraq by arming insurgents. Relations with the West have deteriorated further in the last five years over concerns surrounding Iran's nuclear power programme (for which Russia provides technical support and equipment), especially its acquisition of the ability to enrich uranium. Iran denies that this is a precursor to developing nuclear weapons, but refuses to halt its programme or cooperate with nuclear inspectors. In February 2006, the IAEA reported Iran to the UN security council, and in December the security council voted to impose sanctions on trade in nuclear materials and technology.

POLITICAL SYSTEM
Under the 1979 constitution, overall authority rests with the spiritual leader of the republic, who is elected by the *Majlis-e Khobregan* (assembly of experts); this consists of 83 clerics who are directly elected every eight years and decide on religious and spiritual matters. The executive president is directly elected for a four-year term, renewable only once. Ministers are nominated by the president but must be approved by the legislature. The unicameral legislature, the *Majlis al-Shoura,* has 290 members who are directly elected for a four-year term on a non-party basis. Laws passed by the *Majlis* must be

approved by the council of guardians of the constitution, a 12-member judicial body elected by the Majlis for an eight-year term, which also has a supervisory role in elections. In 1997, a committee for the implementation and supervision of the constitution, a five-member body, was established to supervise the proper implementation of constitutional laws.

Spiritual Leader of the Islamic Republic and C.-in-C. of Armed Forces, Ayatollah Seyed Ali Khamenei, *appointed* June 1989
President, Mahmoud Ahmadinejad, *elected* 24 June 2005
First Vice-President, Parviz Dawoodi

SELECTED GOVERNMENT MEMBERS *as at June 2007*
Defence and Logistics, Brig.-Gen. Mohammad Mostafa Najjar
Economic Affairs and Finance, Davoud Danesh-Jafari
Foreign Affairs, Manouchehr Mottaki
Interior, Chair of State Security Council, Mostafa Pourmohammadi

EMBASSY OF THE ISLAMIC REPUBLIC OF IRAN
16 Prince's Gate, London SW7 1PT
T 020-7225 3000 **W** www.iran-embassy.org.uk
Ambassador Extraordinary and Plenipotentiary, HE Rasoul Movahedian Attar, *apptd* 2006

BRITISH EMBASSY
PO Box 11365–4474, 198 Ferdowsi Avenue, Tehran 11344
T (+98) (21) 6670 5018 **E** britishembassytehran@fco.gov.uk
W www.britishembassy.gov.uk/iran
Ambassador Extraordinary and Plenipotentiary, HE Geoffrey Adams, *apptd* 2006

BRITISH COUNCIL
North Entrance, British Embassy Compound, Shariati Street, Qolhak 19396 13661
T (+98) (21) 2200 1222 **W** www.britishcouncil.org/iran
Director, Neville McBain

DEFENCE

The army has over 1,613 main battle tanks, 640 armoured personnel carriers, 610 armoured infantry fighting vehicles and 50 attack helicopters. The navy has 3 submarines, 3 frigates, 140 patrol and coastal vessels, 3 combat aircraft and 10 armed helicopters. There are 7 naval bases. The air force has some 286 combat aircraft, of which about 60–80 per cent are serviceable.

MILITARY BUDGET – US$6,600m (2006)
MILITARY PERSONNEL – 545,000: army 350,000, Islamic Revolutionary Guard Corps 125,000, navy 18,000, air force 52,000; paramilitaries 40,000

ECONOMY AND TRADE

Iran has one of the best-performing economies in the Middle East owing to its vast reserves of oil and natural gas and the buoyancy of oil prices in recent years, which have sustained strong growth in GDP. But despite high revenues, unemployment and inflation are serious problems and the predominantly state-controlled economy is inefficient. The ongoing programme of economic liberalisation and diversification has made only limited progress with privatisation, deregulation and the abolition of subsidies, and fears of UN sanctions led to some foreign disinvestment and a paralysing degree of uncertainty.

Oil and gas extraction and processing dominate the economy, but Iran also produces textiles, construction materials, metals and armaments. Agricultural productio includes wheat, rice, other grains, sugar beets, fruits, nut cotton, dairy products, wool and caviar. The main tradin partners are China, Japan, Germany, Italy, South Kore and the UAE. Principal exports are oil (80 per cent chemical and petrochemical products, fruit and nuts, an carpets. The main imports are industrial raw materials an intermediate goods, capital goods, foodstuffs, consume goods, technical services and military supplies.

GNI – US$177,300m; US$2,600 per capita (2005)
ANNUAL AVERAGE GROWTH OF GDP – 6.9 per cen (2005 est)
INFLATION RATE – 13.5 per cent (2005 est)
UNEMPLOYMENT – 11.2 per cent (2004 est)
TOTAL EXTERNAL DEBT – US$19,060m (2005 est)
IMPORTS – US$42,000m (2005)
EXPORTS – US$58,000m (2005)

BALANCE OF PAYMENTS
Trade – US$13,138m surplus (2000)
Current Account – US$12,481m surplus (2000)

Trade with UK	*2005*	*2006*
Imports from UK	£463,944,000	£431,404,000
Exports to UK	£38,789,000	£71,689,000

COMMUNICATIONS

Iran's seaports include Asaluyeh, Bushehr and Abada (largely destroyed in the 1980–8 war with Iraq) on th Persian Gulf and Bandar Abbas on the Strait of Hormu Its merchant fleet includes 141 ships of over 1,00 tonnes. The 850km of navigable waterways are mainly o the River Karun and Lake Urmia. There are a total c 179,388km of roads, of which 120,782km are surface and 7,256km of railways. There are over 300 airports an airfields; the principal airports are at Tehran and Shiraz.

The state-owned telephone system is being modernise and expanded to include rural as well as urban areas. Th land-line network doubled in capacity, to over 19 millio between 1995 and 2005. Mobile phone distribution ha grown dramatically and there were 8.5 million subscribe in 2005. Internet users numbered 7.5 million in 2005.

EDUCATION AND HEALTH

Since 1943 primary education has been compulsory an free of charge.

LITERACY RATE – 77 per cent (2004 est)
GROSS ENROLMENT RATIO (percentage of relevant age group) – primary 111 per cent; secondary 81 per cent; tertiary 24 per cent (2005 est)
HEALTH EXPENDITURE (per capita) – US$158 (2004)
HOSPITAL BEDS (per 1,000 people) – 1.6 (2000–5)

MEDIA

The relative freedom of the press under previous reformi governments is now being challenged by th conservatives and a number of more liberal publicatio have been closed down. The Islamic Republic of Ira Broadcasting (IRIB) is a state-run national televisio broadcaster which is supplemented by regional channe Viewing of satellite television channels is widespread an tolerated by the authorities despite the ban on receive Internet usage is the most common method circumventing censorship, although several bloggers hav attracted the attention of the authorities by publishir controversial views.

CULTURE

Iran is rich in Islamic and pre-Islamic architecture. Persepolis, constructed by Darius in the sixth century BC and the capital of the Achaemenian Empire, lies 644km south of the present capital city of Tehran. It was declared a UNESCO World Heritage Site in 1979.

000Since the Iranian revolution of 1978, the film industry in Iran has flourished and was boosted in 1998 by the government's decision to subsidise productions. Director Abbas Kiarostami (*b.* 1940), whose films include Palme d'Or winner *Taste of Cherry* and *Ten*, has received much critical acclaim.

IRAQ

Al-Jumhuriyah al-Iraqiyah – Republic of Iraq

AREA – 437,072 sq. km. Neighbours: Iran (east), Saudi Arabia, Kuwait (south), Jordan and Syria (west), Turkey (north)
CAPITAL – Baghdad; population, 5,750,000 (2003 est)
MAJOR CITIES – Mosul; Basra; Arbil; Kirkuk
CURRENCY – New Iraqi dinar (NID) of 1,000 fils
POPULATION – 26,783,383 rising at 2.66 per cent per year (2006 est); Arab (75 per cent), Kurdish (15 per cent) (est)
RELIGION – Islam (97 per cent) (est); the majority of Muslims practice Shia Islam
LANGUAGE – Arabic (official), Kurdish (official in Kurdish Autonomous Region), Assiryan, Armenian
POPULATION DENSITY – 55 per sq. km (2001 est)
URBAN POPULATION – 66.8 per cent (2005 est)
MEDIAN AGE (years) – 19.7 (2006 est)
NATIONAL ANTHEM – 'Mawtini' ['My Homeland']
NATIONAL DAY – 7 July
LIFE EXPECTANCY (years) – 69.01 (2006 est)
MORTALITY RATE – 5.37 (2006 est)
BIRTH RATE – 31.98 (2006 est)
INFANT MORTALITY RATE – 48.64 (2006 est)
DEATH PENALTY – Yes
CPI SCORE – 1.9 (2006)
GROSS ENROLMENT RATIO (percentage of relevant age group) – primary 99 per cent; secondary 38 per cent; tertiary 14 per cent (2002)

CLIMATE AND TERRAIN

Iraq is mostly desert with mountainous areas in the north. The wide valley of the Euphrates and Tigris rivers runs across the country from north-west to south-east, discharging into the Persian Gulf. Elevation extremes range from 3,595m (Haji Ibrahim) at the highest point to 0m (Persian Gulf) at the lowest. Average temperatures in Baghdad range from 9°C in January to 35°C in July.

HISTORY AND POLITICS

The Sumerians, the world's oldest civilisation, were the first people to populate the areas around the Tigris and Euphrates rivers. They began to build city-states from around 3000 BC of which Ur, Lagash and Eridu are the earliest examples; the city-states were unified into an empire *c.*2350 BC. In the seventh century BC, the area became part of the Assyrian Empire until this was destroyed by the Babylonians and the Medes. Apart from 150 years of Roman rule (AD 114–266), Iraq was under Persian rule from the mid-sixth century BC until the Persian defeat and conquest by Arab Muslims in AD 637. The Battle of Karbala in AD 680 marked a decisive moment in Islamic history: the split between Sunnis and Shias was created when the Shi'ite leader Hussein was killed attempting to claim the Caliphate. Iraq came under the control of the Ottoman Empire from 1533 until 1916, when the Ottomans, weakened by the First World War, ceded control to the British. A provisional government was set up in 1920, and in 1921 the Emir Faisal was elected king of Iraq. King Faisal II was assassinated in 1958 in a military-led revolution, following which a left-wing military regime assumed power. Iraq briefly came under the control of the socialist Ba'ath Party after a coup in 1963 and then from 1968. In 1979, Saddam Hussein deposed President Bakr and became president.

Iraq fought a bitter war with Iran from 1980–8. Ostensibly a border dispute over the Shatt-al-Arab waterway, it arose from Iraq's fear that Iran was encouraging a Shi'ite majority uprising against its predominantly Sunni regime. Fighting ended with a ceasefire in 1988 and a peace settlement in 1990. In August 1990, Iraq invaded and annexed Kuwait, ignoring international and UN demands for it to withdraw. In January 1991, a US-led alliance of NATO and Middle East countries launched a military offensive against Iraq that liberated Kuwait the following month. UN sanctions, imposed after Kuwait's annexation, remained in place owing to Iraq's obstruction of attempts to verify the destruction of its weapons of mass destruction. It was Iraq's failure to comply with the latest attempts at inspection in 2002 that led to the invasion in March 2003 by US-led military forces. Saddam Hussein was captured in December 2003, and was executed in December 2006, after being convicted of crimes against humanity.

Following the invasion and occupation in March–May 2003, a coalition provisional authority became the occupying authority in Iraq before handing over sovereignty in June 2004 to the Iraqi interim governing council, despite deteriorating internal security.

Elections to the transitional national assembly took place in January 2005; the turnout was high generally, but low among Sunni Muslims, who won only 17 seats. Elections for a permanent legislature took place on 15 December 2005. The United Iraqi Alliance (Shia) won 128 seats, Kurdish Alliance 53 seats, National Accord Front (Sunni) 44 seats, Iraqi National List (secular) 25 seats, Iraqi Front for National Dialogue (Sunni) 11 seats, Kurdish Islamic Union five seats, and six other parties took nine seats between them. With no party or bloc commanding an outright majority, there were four months of political deadlock before Jalal Talabani, the Kurdish president of the transitional government since April 2005, was re-elected president in April 2006 and asked Nouri Jawad al-Maliki (leader of one of the parties in the UIA) to form a government after the UIA's preferred candidate, former prime minister Ibrahim al-Jaafari, was rejected by the Kurdish, Sunni and secular parties. Maliki's coalition government, including the four main parliamentary blocs and one minor party, was sworn in on 20 May. The issues of federalism and regional distribution of oil revenues, favoured by the Shias and Kurds but strongly opposed by the Sunnis, remain major issues.

INSURGENCIES

There are about four million Kurds in north-east Iraq, in areas adjoining the predominantly Kurdish areas in Iran and Turkey. Iraq's Kurdish nationalists have demanded an autonomous homeland, Kurdistan, since the 1960s, and turned to militant tactics in the 1970s. Their demands were opposed by Saddam Hussein's regime with great brutality. An uprising after the Gulf War (1991) was suppressed by Iraqi troops, prompting the creation of UN safe havens which enabled the Kurds to set up a semi-autonomous region in the north. An air exclusion zone was also provided, but there was further conflict with Iraqi forces and between the two main Kurdish parties in the 1990s. During the war of 2003, Kurdish fighters fought alongside US troops in the north, taking control of the northern cities and establishing a relatively stable administration in the area, which is now autonomous. The Kurdish Alliance, made up of the two main Kurdish parties, is the second largest party in the Iraqi legislature, holds the presidency and participates in the government.

The Shi'ites in southern Iraq also rebelled after the Gulf War and were brutally suppressed. The UN established an air exclusion zone over southern Iraq in 1992 to protect the population, but persecution continued until the Iraq War.

Since the end of the Iraq War in May 2003, there has been insurgent activity throughout the country, though it is particularly marked in the Baghdad area and the 'Sunni triangle', ie the predominantly Sunni-populated towns in the centre and west of the country. Initially the targets were foreign troops, Iraqi military and police, and foreign aid and reconstruction workers. In the last two years the attacks have become increasingly sectarian in nature, displacing large numbers of people, especially from Baghdad. The approximate number of deaths as at June 2007 is estimated at: Iraqi civilians 64,776, US troops 3,497, other coalition troops 276.

POLITICAL SYSTEM

A new constitution was approved by referendum in 2005. Under this, the president serves a four-year term, renewable only once. The legislature elects the president and two vice-presidents (by a two-thirds majority) to form the presidency council, which nominates a prime minister to form a government; this must be approved by the legislature. The unicameral legislature, the *Majlis al-Nuwab* (council of representatives) has 275 members, of whom 69 must be women, directly elected for a four-year term.

HEAD OF STATE

President, Jalal Talabani, *elected* 6 April 2005, *re-elected* 22 April 2006

Vice-Presidents, Tariq al-Hashimi; Adil Abd al-Mahdi

SELECTED GOVERNMENT MEMBERS *as at June 2007*

Prime Minister, Nouri Jawad al-Maliki

Deputy Prime Minister, Economic Affairs, Barham Salih

Deputy Prime Minister, Salam Zaubai

Foreign Affairs, Hoshyar al-Zebari

Defence, Gen. Abdel Qader Jassim

Interior, Jawad Kadem al-Bolani

EMBASSY OF THE REPUBLIC OF IRAQ

9 Holland Villas Road, London W14 8BP

T 020-7602 8456

E lonemb@iraqmofamail.net

Ambassador Extraordinary and Plenipotentiary, HE Dr Salah al-Shaikhly *apptd* 2004

BRITISH EMBASSY

International Zone, Baghdad

T (+964) 790 192 6280 E britishconsulbaghdad@gtnet.gov.uk

Ambassador Extraordinary and Plenipotentiary, HE Dominic Asquith, *apptd* 2006

BRITISH COUNCIL

c/o British Embassy, International Zone, Baghdad *(no postal service available)*

T (+962) 790 191 1971 W www.britishcouncil.org/iraq

Director, David Alderdice

DEFENCE

Iraq's armed forces were officially disbanded by the coalition provisional authority in May 2003. Since then new Iraqi security forces have been recruited and trained by coalition troops. As at May 2007 the Iraqi security forces numbered 347,800: army 152,500, navy 1,100, air 900, police 161,300 and other Ministry of Interior forces 32,000.

ECONOMY AND TRADE

The economy declined dramatically after the 1991 Gulf War because of damage sustained in the conflict and subsequent UN sanctions. Although the UN oil-for-food programme improved conditions from the mid-1990s productivity and standards of living in 2003 ere still well below pre-1991 standards. The allied invasion in May 2003 damaged relatively little of the infrastructure but subsequent looting, insurgency and sabotage have undermined reconstruction and restricted productivity and foreign exchange earnings. Unemployment (25–30 per cent) and inflation are very high. However government revenue has been higher than expected owing to high oil prices, the institutions needed to implement economic policy are now in place and a debt reduction programme has been arranged. In 200[illegible] international donors pledged over US$33bn (£16.5bn) in aid for 2004–7.

Oil is Iraq's main resource and export, and production returned to pre-war levels in 2005. Other industries include textiles, chemicals and construction materials. The main market for exports is the USA (50 per cent in 2005) and the main sources of imports were Syria (23 per cent) and Turkey (23 per cent). Principal exports are crude oil (84 per cent), other crude materials, food and livestock. The main imports are food, medicine and manufactured goods.

ANNUAL AVERAGE GROWTH OF GDP – –3 per cent (2005 est)

INFLATION RATE – 33 per cent (2005 est)

TOTAL EXTERNAL DEBT – US$92,330m (2005 est)

Trade with UK	*2005*	*2006*
Imports from UK	£126,886,000	£77,449,000
Exports to UK	£1,359,000	£1,768,000

COMMUNICATIONS

The transport infrastructure was severely damaged during the wars in 1991 and 2003 and reconstruction is slow. There are 2,200km of railways and 45,550km of roads, the majority surfaced. There are 5,279km of waterways, primarily on the Tigris and Euphrates rivers. The main seaport is Basra, and the principal airport is at Baghdad.

The telephone system was badly disrupted in the aftermath of the 2003 invasion but has been repaired and now has a greater capacity than previously, but is still subject to sabotage. Mobile phone services are available i the major cities and are expanding. There were 1.5 million main lines in use and 36,000 internet users in 2005, and 8.7 million mobile phone subscribers in 2006.

EDUCATION AND HEALTH

Since May 2003 the country's education system has been reviewed, and over 2,500 schools have been refurbished.

GROSS ENROLMENT RATIO (percentage of relevant age group) – primary 98 per cent; secondary 45 per cent; tertiary 15 per cent (2005 est)
HEALTH EXPENDITURE (per capita) – US$58 (2004)
HOSPITAL BEDS (per 1,000 people) – 1.3 (2000–5)

MEDIA

Once strictly controlled, the media has begun to flourish since May 2003, although media workers have fallen victim to the insurgency. There are more than 200 newspapers and periodicals, many with an ethnic or religious affiliation, and private radio and television stations have also begun to thrive. The television and radio stations set up by the coalition provisional authority now form part of the publicly-funded Iraqi Public Broadcasting Service. The Iraqi Media Network (IMN) operates the *Al-Iraqiya* television station and publishes the *Al-Sabah* newspaper. The *Al-Zaman* daily newspaper is based in London but printed in Baghdad and Basra. In the autonomous Kurdish areas, rival factions operate their own media.

IRELAND

Eire – Ireland

AREA – 70,280 sq. km. Neighbour: Northern Ireland (north)
CAPITAL – Dublin *(Baile Átha Cliath)*; population, 560,905 (2006)
MAJOR CITIES – Cork *(Corcaigh)*; Galway *(Gaillimh)*
CURRENCY – Euro (€) of 100 cents
POPULATION – 4,062,235 rising at 1.15 per cent per year (2006 est)
RELIGION – Roman Catholicism (88 per cent), Protestantism (2 per cent) (est)
LANGUAGE – English, Irish (both official), Scots, Gaelic
POPULATION DENSITY – 60 per sq. km (2005)
URBAN POPULATION – 60.4 per cent (2005 est)
MEDIAN AGE (years) – 34 (2006 est)
NATIONAL ANTHEM – 'Amhran na bhFiann' ['The Soldier's Song']
NATIONAL DAY – 17 March (St Patrick's Day)
LIFE EXPECTANCY (years) – 77.73 (2006 est)
MORTALITY RATE – 7.82 (2006 est)
BIRTH RATE – 14.45 (2006 est)
INFANT MORTALITY RATE – 5.31 (2006 est)
DEATH PENALTY – No (abolished 1990)
CPI SCORE – 7.4 (2006)
MILITARY BUDGET – US$970m (2006)
MILITARY PERSONNEL – 10,470: army 8,500, navy 1,100, air force 860

CLIMATE AND TERRAIN

The greatest length of the island is 486km, from Torr Head in the north-east to Mizen Head in the south-west, and the greatest breadth is 280km, from Dundrum Bay in the east to Annagh Head in the west. The republic has a central plain surrounded by hills and low mountains, including the Wicklow, Knockmealdown, Galty and Boggeragh mountains, and drained by the principal river, the Shannon (386km), which flows into the Atlantic Ocean. On the north coast of Achill Island (Co. Mayo) are the highest cliffs in the British Isles, 609m above sea level. Elevation extremes range from 1,040m (Carrantoohill, Co. Kerry) at the highest point to 0m (Irish Sea) at the lowest.

HISTORY AND POLITICS

Settled by the Celts around 300 BC, Ireland developed a flourishing and distinct culture that remained largely intact until Christianity was introduced in the fifth century AD, after which Christian Ireland established itself as a centre of learning and high culture, a place of intellectual thought and spiritual refuge. Viking raiders began sustained attacks *c.*800 and established settlements from the mid-ninth century. In the 12th century, Anglo-Norman barons, invited to Ireland by a Gaelic king seeking allies, brought much of the south of the island under their own control, and Henry II of England declared himself Lord of Ireland in 1171. The island was unified under English control under Elizabeth I. From the early 17th century, England began to promote the settlement of Protestant Scots in the north-eastern kingdom of Ulster, the final stronghold of Celtic power. This policy produced a long-standing antagonism between the north's Protestant and Catholic populations.

In the mid-17th century, widespread support in Ireland for the royalist side in the English Civil War prompted bloody reprisals from Oliver Cromwell, who invaded Ireland and reasserted English control in 1649–50. Catholic Irish support for the deposed Catholic king James II was defeated by William III at the Battle of the Boyne (1690) and penal laws passed in 1695 suppressed Catholic wealth and power. Popular discontent in the late 18th century and a rebellion in 1798 led to the abolition of the Irish parliament by the Act of Union (1800), which united Britain and Ireland. Simultaneously, Catholic opposition to English rule became increasingly organised with the formation of the Catholic Association, but agitation for home rule failed until 1912, when legislation was passed but did not come into effect because of the First World War.

By 1916, demands in some quarters had shifted from home rule to independence from Britain, and a rebellion broke out in Dublin. Known as the Easter Uprising, it was eventually repressed by the British but served to inspire Irish nationalists to contest the 1918 elections and, on gaining a majority of the Irish seats, to declare Irish independence under the leadership of Eamon de Valera. The British response was an attempt at violent suppression of the nationalists. The ensuing Anglo-Irish War lasted from 1919 to 1921 when the two sides negotiated the Anglo-Irish treaty, giving Ireland internal self-government as the Irish Free State, with dominion status within the Commonwealth, but leaving the six predominantly Protestant counties in the north part of the UK. This partition was not accepted by all nationalists and opposition developed into civil war in 1922–3. In 1937, the Irish Free State declared itself independent and sovereign, and in 1948 it left the Commonwealth and became a republic.

The status of Northern Ireland remained divisive with the partition unacknowledged by the Irish constitution of 1937. The Anglo-Irish agreement in 1985 gave the Irish government a consultative role in the government of Northern Ireland, and in 1993 the Downing Street Declaration set out a joint Anglo-Irish peace proposal to end the conflict in the north. The Irish government was involved in the negotiation of the 1998 Good Friday agreement; its proposals, including Irish recognition of the partition and the right of the north to self-determination, were approved in a referendum by 94 per cent of voters in the Irish Republic.

Ireland joined the EEC in 1973 and the eurozone in 1999; it has yet to schedule a referendum on the EU constitution.

The 1997 presidential election was won by Mary McAleese, and she was confirmed in office unopposed in 2004. In the 2007 elections to the house of representatives, Fianna Fail (FF), led by Bertie Ahern (prime minister since 1997), remained the largest party but without an overall majority. The coalition government of the FF and the Progressive Democrats (PD) was expanded to include the Green Party.

POLITICAL SYSTEM

Under the 1937 constitution the president, *Uachtaran na Eireann,* is directly elected for a term of seven years, renewable only once. The bicameral national parliament, *Oireachtas,* consists of the *Dail Eireann* (house of representatives) and the *Seanad Eireann* (senate). *Dail Eireann* is composed of 166 members elected for a five-year term on a basis of proportional representation by means of the single transferable vote. *Seanad Eireann* is composed of 60 members, who serve a five-year term; of these, 11 are nominated by the *Taoiseach* (prime minister) and 49 are elected, six by institutions of higher education and 43 from panels of candidates representing various sectoral interests.

Executive power is vested in the government, which is responsible to the *Dail Eireann.* The *Taoiseach* is appointed by the president on the nomination of the *Dail Eireann,* while other members of the government are appointed by the president on the nomination of the *Taoiseach* with the previous approval of the *Dail Eireann.* The *Taoiseach* appoints a member of the government to be the *Tanaiste* (deputy prime minister).

HEAD OF STATE

President, Mary McAleese, *elected* 30 October 1997, *confirmed in office* 1 October 2004, *sworn in* 11 November 2004

SELECTED GOVERNMENT MEMBERS *as at June 2007*

Taoiseach (Prime Minister), Bertie Ahern
Tánaiste (Deputy PM), Mary Harney
Defence, Willie O'Dea
Finance, Brian Cowen
Foreign Affairs, Dermot Ahern

EMBASSY OF IRELAND

17 Grosvenor Place, London SW1X 7HR
T 020-7235 2171
Ambassador Extraordinary and Plenipotentiary, HE Daithi O'Ceallaigh, *apptd* 2001

BRITISH EMBASSY

29 Merrion Road, Ballsbridge, Dublin 4
T (+353) (1) 205 3700 E dubembassy@internet-ireland.ie
W www.britishembassy.ie
Ambassador Extraordinary and Plenipotentiary, HE David Reddaway, *apptd* 2006

BRITISH COUNCIL

Newmount House, 22/24 Lower Mount Street, Dublin 2
T (+353) (1) 676 4088 W www.britishcouncil.org/ireland
Director, Tony Reilly, MBE

ECONOMY AND TRADE

In the past few decades Ireland's economy has been transformed from mainly agricultural to a modern, export-led economy which has experienced strong growth since the mid-1990s; GDP per head is now the second highest in the EU. Government action to keep inflation low, improve labour skills and attract foreign investment means that light industry and services have overtaken agriculture, which now accounts for only 5 per cent of GDP and 8 per cent of employment; services contributes 49 per cent and industry 46 per cent of GDP, and the sectors account for 64 per cent and 29 per cent of employment respectively. The major industries are computer software, information technology, food and drink production, chemicals, pharmaceuticals and tourism. Although the Kinsale gas field off the south coast provides for some of its gas needs, and hydroelectric power is generated from the Shannon barrage and other schemes, Ireland still imports nearly half the fuel needed for power generation.

The main trading partners are other EU countries and the USA. Principal exports are machinery, computers, chemicals, pharmaceuticals, livestock and livestock products. The main imports are data processing equipment, other machinery, chemicals, petroleum and petroleum products, textiles and clothing.

GNI – US$171,100m; US$41,140 per capita (2005)
ANNUAL AVERAGE GROWTH OF GDP – 5.5 per cent (2005 est)
INFLATION RATE – 2.4 per cent (2005 est)
UNEMPLOYMENT – 4.3 per cent (2005 est)
TOTAL EXTERNAL DEBT – US$1,049,000m (2005)
IMPORTS – US$69,100m (2005)
EXPORTS – US$109,600m (2005)

BALANCE OF PAYMENTS

Trade – US$37,649m surplus (2005)
Current Account – US$3,954m deficit (2005)

Trade with UK	*2005*	*200*
Imports from UK	£16,018,666,000	£15,941,700,00
Exports to UK	£9,998,649,000	£10,001,100,00

COMMUNICATIONS

Ireland has 96,600km of roads and 3,312km of railways. There are over 700km of waterways, although these are used only by leisure craft. The main ports are Cork, Dun Laoghaire, Galway, Limerick and Waterford. The principal airport is at Dublin, with others at Shannon, Waterford, Cork, Killarney, Galway and Knock. There were 2 million main telephone lines in use, 4.2 million mobile subscribers and 2 million internet users in 2005.

EDUCATION AND HEALTH

Primary education is directed by the state, with the exception of several private primary schools.

GROSS ENROLMENT RATIO (percentage of relevant age group) – primary 106 per cent; secondary 112 per cent; tertiary 59 per cent (2005 est)
HEALTH EXPENDITURE (per capita) – US$3,234 (2004)
HOSPITAL BEDS (per 1,000 people) – 4.3 (2000–5)

MEDIA

Irish broadcasting is regulated by a commission appointed by the Department of Communications. The main Irish broadcaster is the state-run Radio Telefis Eireann (RTE) and the British satellite broadcaster BSkyB is widely available. There are three national newspapers: the *Irish Times, Irish Independent* and *Irish Examiner*. Reporters Without Borders ranked the country the equal highest for press freedom in 2006.

CULTURE

Ireland has a disproportionately rich literary history given the size of the country. Irish poetry is the oldest in Europe, with extracts dating back to the 6th century. Jonathan Swift (1667–1745) created one of the English language's finest satires in *Gulliver's Travels*, and Bram Stoker (1847–1912) one of the most enduring horror stories when he wrote *Dracula*. Ireland has produced four Nobel prize-winning writers: poets W. B. Yeats (1865–1939) and Seamus Heaney (*b.* 1939) and dramatists George Bernard Shaw (1856–1950) and Samuel Beckett (1906–89). The country's greatest literary icons remain Oscar Wilde (1854–1900) and James Joyce (1882–1941), one of the 20th century's most influential, if often inscrutable, novelists.

In the fields of sport and music, Ireland has maintained a strong interest in traditional forms. Hurling and Gaelic football attract passionate support, as do the more recently introduced rugby and football. Similarly, musicians adopting and adapting musical folklore, such as Van Morrison (*b.* 1945), Clannad and Enya (*b.* 1961), have achieved international success, alongside rock groups U2 and Thin Lizzy and boybands Westlife and Boyzone.

ISRAEL AND PALESTINIAN TERRITORIES

Medinat Yisra'el/Dawlat Isra'il – State of Israel

AREA – 20,770 sq. km. Neighbours: Lebanon (north), Syria (north-east), Jordan and the West Bank (east), the Gaza Strip and the Egyptian province of Sinai (south-west)

CAPITAL – Most of the government departments are in Jerusalem; population 729,100 (2006 est). A resolution proclaiming Jerusalem as the capital of Israel was adopted by the *Knesset* in 1950. It is not, however, recognised as the capital by the UN because East Jerusalem is part of the Occupied Territories captured in 1967. The UN and international law continues to reject the Israeli annexation of East Jerusalem and considers the pre-1950 capital Tel Aviv (population, 382,500) to be the capital.

MAJOR CITIES – Haifa; Rishon Le'Zion

CURRENCY – Shekel of 100 agora

POPULATION – 6,352,117 rising at 1.18 per cent per year (2006 est). Since independence Israel has had a policy of granting an immigration visa to every Jew who expresses a desire to settle in the country. Between 1948 and 1992, 2.3 million immigrants entered Israel from over 100 different countries.

RELIGION – Judaism (80 per cent), Islam (4 per cent), Christianity (2 per cent) (est)

LANGUAGE – Hebrew (official), Arabic, English

POPULATION DENSITY – 320 per sq. km (2005)

URBAN POPULATION – 91.7 per cent (2005 est)

MEDIAN AGE (years) – 29.6 (2006 est)

NATIONAL ANTHEM – 'Hatikvah' ['The Hope']

NATIONAL DAY – 14 May (Independence Day)

LIFE EXPECTANCY (years) – 79.46 (2006 est)

MORTALITY RATE – 6.18 (2006 est)

BIRTH RATE – 17.97 (2006 est)

INFANT MORTALITY RATE – 6.89 (2006 est)

DEATH PENALTY – Yes*

CPI SCORE – 5.9 (2006)

POPULATION BELOW POVERTY LINE – 21 per cent (2005)

CLIMATE AND TERRAIN

Israel comprises the hill country of Galilee and parts of Judea and Samaria, the coastal plain from the Gaza Strip to north of Acre (including the plain of Esdraelon running from Haifa Bay to the south-east); the Negev, a semi-desert triangular-shaped region, and parts of the Jordan valley, including the Hula region, Tiberias and the south-western extremity of the Dead Sea. Elevation extremes range from 1,208m (Mt Hermon) at the highest point to –408m (Dead Sea) at the lowest, which is the Earth's deepest depression. Average temperatures in Tel Aviv range from 14°C in January to 27°C in August.

HISTORY AND POLITICS

Regarded by Jews as their homeland since the Israelite settlement in Old Testament times, Palestine was conquered by the Babylonians, the Greeks and the Romans between the sixth and first centuries BC, beginning the diaspora. Conquered by Muslim Arabs in the seventh century AD, the area was contested between Muslims and Christians during the Crusades before becoming part of the Turkish Ottoman Empire in the 16th century. Zionist settlement in Palestine began in the 1880s and the British declared support for a Jewish homeland there in 1917 after capturing much of the Middle East from the Ottoman Empire during the First World War. Britain administered the area under a League of Nations mandate from 1918 to 1947, during which period Jewish immigration from Europe was encouraged, but this resulted in tension with the Arab population of Palestine, who had also been promised recognition for an Arab state by the British.

After the Second World War, the British mandate became increasingly untenable and they withdrew in 1947. The UN voted to partition Palestine, creating a Jewish and an Arab state, but the proposal was rejected by the Arabs, prompting the Jews to announce the creation of the independent State of Israel on 14 May 1948. This led to the first of a series of conflicts between Israel and neighbouring Arab states, creating a large number of Palestinian refugees. Further conflict occurred in 1956, when Israel attacked the Suez Canal zone; in 1967 (the Six-Day War) when Israel gained control of the Gaza Strip, the Sinai peninsula, the West Bank and east Jerusalem, and the Golan Heights in Syria (the 'Occupied Territories'); in 1973, when Egypt and Syria attempted to regain their lost territory; and in 1982, when Israel invaded Lebanon to drive Palestinian guerrillas out of Beirut, occupying a buffer zone in the south until 2000. A peace agreement with Egypt was reached in 1979, as a result of which Israel withdrew from Sinai, and a similar agreement with Jordan in 1994.

From the 1960s, the Palestine Liberation Organisation (PLO), under Yasser Arafat, fought a guerrilla war against

Israeli occupation of the territories taken in 1967, and in 1974 the PLO was recognised by the Arab League as the official representative of the Palestinian people. Talks between Israel and the PLO resulted in the Oslo accords (1993–5), which led to the establishment of the Palestinian Autonomous Areas in 1994. This appeared to end the popular Palestinian uprising *(intifada)* in the Gaza Strip and West Bank but the situation deteriorated from the mid-1990s, with further violence in the West Bank and suicide bombings in Israeli cities. These attacks evoked an increasingly hard line from a new Israeli government already critical of the peace agreement. Implementation of the Oslo accords stalled and negotiations on outstanding issues reached deadlock. Palestinian frustration was inflamed by the visit of Israeli opposition leader Ariel Sharon to the Temple Mount in Jerusalem, triggering a second *intifada*. In 2002, Israel began building a security wall between Jewish and Palestinian areas to prevent suicide bombings despite international diplomatic and legal opposition to a *de facto* partitioning of the country.

In 2003, the USA, Russia, the EU and the UN proposed a 'road map' for peace which envisioned a two-state solution to the conflict. Progress stalled until the death of Arafat in 2004. Despite the Israeli goverment's commitment on a key issue – the evacuation and dismantling of Jewish settlements in, and military disengagement from, the Gaza Strip (achieved by September 2005) – no further progress has been made owing to the Israeli refusal to deal with the militant Palestinian government elected in January 2006, and the announcement in March 2006 of Israel's unilateral plans to impose a permanent border and to retain control of areas of the West Bank. This situation worsened further in the summer of 2006 with the kidnapping of Israeli soldiers by Hamas guerrillas in Gaza and by Hezbollah guerrillas on the Lebanese border; Hezbollah also launched rocket attacks on northern Israel. Israel retaliated with military strikes on Gaza and airstrikes and a ground offensive in southern Lebanon.

In the March 2006 legislative election, the largest number of seats was won by Kadima, a centrist party set up in autumn 2005 by Ariel Sharon, the prime minister and former leader of the Likud party; after his incapacitation by a series of strokes in early 2007, Ehud Olmert became acting prime minister and leader of Kadima. As it lacked an overall majority, Kadima formed a coalition government with Labour, Shas and the Gil; the Yisrael Beitenu party joined the coalition in October 2006. The July 2007 presidential election was won by Shimon Peres.

POLITICAL SYSTEM

There is no written constitution; most constitutional provision is set out in the basic law on government; this was amended in 2001 to end the system of separate prime ministerial elections. The unicameral legislature, the *Knesset*, has 120 members elected by proportional representation for a four-year term. The president is head of state and is elected by the *Knesset* to serve for a seven-year term which is not renewable. The prime minister is head of the executive and responsible to the *Knesset*, and is formally appointed by the president.

HEAD OF STATE

President of Israel, Shimon Peres, *elected* 13 June 2007, *sworn in* 15 July 2007

SELECTED GOVERNMENT MEMBERS *as at August 2007*

Vice Prime Ministers, Haim Ramon; Tzipi Livni (Foreign Affairs)
Deputy Prime Ministers, Eliyahi Yishai; Aviqdor Lieberman; Gen. Shaul Mofaz
Defence, Ehud Barak

EMBASSY OF ISRAEL
2 Palace Green, London W8 4QB
T 020-7957 9500 W www.israel-embassy.org.uk
Ambassador Extraordinary and Plenipotentiary, HE Zvi Heifetz, *apptd* 2004

BRITISH EMBASSY
192 Hayarkon Street, Tel Aviv 63405
T (+972) (3) 725 1222 E webmaster.telaviv@fco.gov.uk
W www.britemb.org.il
Ambassador Extraordinary and Plenipotentiary, HE Tom Phillips CMG, *apptd* 2006

BRITISH COUNCIL
PO Box 3302, Crystal House, 12 Hahilazon Street, Ramat Gan 52136
T (+972) (3) 611 3600 W www.britishcouncil.org/israel
Director, Jim Buttery

DEFENCE

Israel is believed to have a nuclear capacity of around 200 warheads which could be delivered by aircraft or Jericho I and II missiles. The army has 3,657 main battle tanks and around 10,419 armoured personnel carriers. The navy has 3 submarines and 52 patrol and coastal vessels at 3 bases. The air force has 402 combat aircraft and over 95 armed helicopters.

MILITARY EXPENDITURE – US$9,820m (2005)
MILITARY PERSONNEL – 168,000: army 125,000, navy 8,000, air force 35,000; paramilitaries 8,050
CONSCRIPTION DURATION – 24–48 months (Jews and Druze only; Christians, Circassians and Muslims may volunteer)

ECONOMY AND TRADE

Israel has a technically advanced market economy, having developed its agriculture and industry intensively since the 1970s despite limited natural resources. After a short recession in the early 2000s, structural reforms and tighter fiscal control were implemented, resulting in steady growth since 2003 and rising confidence as well as increased demand for exports. However, there is a high level of public debt (89 per cent of GDP) and budget and trade deficits. These are covered by foreign aid and loans; the USA is the main source of economic and military aid and is Israel's main creditor, owed about half of its external debt.

Israel has developed a strong technology sector, central to which are the aviation, electronics, biotechnology and software industries. Other important industries include timber and paper, mineral and metal products, cement, chemicals, plastics, diamond cutting and tourism, which is reviving. The country is also an important producer of citrus fruits, vegetables, cotton, beef, poultry and dairy products. In 2003, service industries accounted for 66 per cent of GDP, industry for 31 per cent and agriculture for 3 per cent.

The main trading partners are the USA, accounting for 37 per cent of exports, Belgium and other EU states. Principal exports are high-technology machinery and equipment, software, cut diamonds, agricultural products

chemicals, textiles and clothing. The main imports are raw materials, military equipment, investment goods, rough diamonds, fuels, grain and consumer goods.
GNI – US$128,700m; US$18,580 per capita (2005)
ANNUAL AVERAGE GROWTH OF GDP – 5.2 per cent (2005 est)
INFLATION RATE – 1.3 per cent (2005 est)
UNEMPLOYMENT – 9 per cent (2005 est)
TOTAL EXTERNAL DEBT – US$75,550m (2005 est)
IMPORTS – US$47,100m (2005)
EXPORTS – US$43,000m (2005)

BALANCE OF PAYMENTS
Trade – US$4,034m deficit (2005)
Current Account – US$2,385m surplus (2005)

Trade with UK	*2005*	*2006*
Imports from UK	£1,357,233,000	£1,293,047,000
Exports to UK	£1,022,604,000	£985,634,000

COMMUNICATIONS

Israel State Railways operates a network of 853km, serving Haifa, Tel Aviv, Jerusalem, Lod, Nahariya, Beersheba, Dimona, Ashdod and intermediate stations. There are 17,446km of roads, including 144km of motorway. A major road-building programme has been under way in the West Bank since 1992. The chief seaports are Haifa and Ashdod on the Mediterranean, and Eilat on the Red Sea; Acre has an anchorage for small vessels. There are 53 airports and airfields; the chief international airport is Ben Gurion between Tel Aviv and Jerusalem. The highly developed telephone system provides services for 2.9 million main-line users, 7.7 million mobile phone subscribers and 3.7 million internet users.

EDUCATION AND HEALTH

Education is compulsory between the ages of five and 16 and is free of charge. Youths aged 16–18 who are in work but have not completed their education can be given time off to finish their studies.
LITERACY RATE – 96.9 per cent (2004 est)
GROSS ENROLMENT RATIO (percentage of relevant age group) – primary 110 per cent; secondary 93 per cent; tertiary 56 per cent (2005 est)
HEALTH EXPENDITURE (per capita) – US$1,534 (2004)
HOSPITAL BEDS (per 1,000 people) – 6.1 (2000–5)

MEDIA AND CULTURE

The Israeli Broadcasting Authority (IBA) is a public broadcaster operating television and radio services funded largely by a licence fee. It competes with two main terrestrial commercial channels and a number of satellite and cable stations. The radio sector features a number of commercial stations, but there are also a large number of unlicensed radio stations. There are five national daily newspapers.

The Israel Museum in Jerusalem houses the Dead Sea Scrolls along with an extensive collection of Jewish religious and folk art. Jerusalem has a vast number of historic sites, including the Church of the Holy Sepulchre, sacred to Christians, and the al-Aqsa Mosque, which stands on the remains of the Temple Mount.

PALESTINIAN AUTONOMOUS AREAS

AREA – The total area is 6,231 sq. km. The area which is fully autonomous is 412 sq. km, of which the Gaza Strip is 352 sq. km and the Jericho enclave 60 sq. km.
POPULATION – 3,634,585 (2003 est)
CAPITAL – Although Palestinians claim East Jerusalem as their capital, the administrative capital has been established in Gaza City; population 479,400 (2005 est)
MAJOR TOWNS – Khan Yunis, Rafah in the Gaza Strip; Nablus, Hebron, Jericho, Ramallah and Bethlehem on the West Bank
FLAG – Three horizontal stripes of black, white, green with a red triangle based on the hoist (the PLO flag)
NATIONAL ANTHEM – 'Fidai, Fidai' ['Freedom Fighter, Freedom Fighter']
DEATH PENALTY – Yes

HISTORY AND POLITICS

Since 1967 the West Bank and Gaza Strip have been under Israeli occupation and until 1994 were administered by the Israeli ministry of defence. Frustration at continued Israeli occupation led to the start of a popular Palestinian uprising, the *intifada,* in 1987. Negotiations between Israel and the Palestinian Liberation Organisation (PLO) led to the signing of the Oslo accords in 1993. The accords established self-government in the Palestinian areas and set a timetable for progress towards a final settlement; the 1993 provisions were intended to be for a five-year interim period during which the final status of the West Bank, Gaza and Jerusalem was to be resolved.

The Oslo B or Taba accord, signed in 1995, provided for Israeli withdrawal from six West Bank towns and 85 per cent of Hebron; the extension of self-rule to most of the West Bank by 1998; the release of 5,300 Palestinian prisoners and the striking out of the demand for Israel's destruction from the PLO's charter. On 29 December 1995 an agreement was reached on the transfer of 17 areas of civilian power to the Palestinian National Authority (PNA) in Hebron.

The first areas, the Gaza Strip and the town of Jericho on the West Bank, were handed over to the PNA in 1994, and the six West Bank towns in 1995. The final status talks opened in 1996, but stalled in the late 1990s and broke down in 2001. Efforts to restart negotiations were hindered by the election of Israeli governments critical of the peace accords and the outbreak of the second *intifada.*

In 2003, the USA, Russia, the EU and the UN proposed the road map peace plan, a staged process leading to the establishment of an autonomous Palestinian state by 2005, which also sought political reforms in the PNA. The plan was endorsed by the Palestinian and Israeli prime ministers, while the three main groups responsible for violent attacks on Israelis, Hamas, Islamic Jihad and Fatah, announced a three-month truce, and Israeli forces withdrew from some key areas in the West Bank and the Gaza Strip. However, implementation of the peace plan made little progress because of the continuing *intifada,* internal power struggles within the Palestinian administration and the refusal of Israel and the USA to negotiate with the Palestinian president Yasser Arafat. This stalemate was broken only by the death of Arafat in November 2004 and the election of a moderate as his successor. Talks with Israel resumed but the peace process continued to be jeopardised by the Palestinian authorities' inability to rein in the violence of extremists, and it stalled in early 2006 with the victory of the extremist group Hamas in the Palestinian legislative election. Relations with Israel worsened dramatically in summer 2006 with the kidnapping of an Israeli soldier by Hamas guerrillas and Israeli military retaliation against Gaza.

The 2005 presidential election was won by the Fatah candidate Mahmoud Abbas, who secured 67.4 per cent of the vote. In the January 2006 legislative election, the Hamas movement, regarded internationally as a terrorist organisation, received 44.45 per cent of the vote and won 76 seats, forming the new government. The organisation's post-election refusal to renounce violence, to recognise Israel's right to exist or to abide by existing peace agreements with Israel led international donors to cut off funding, which caused severe economic hardship. Relations between Hamas and the more moderate Fatah, always tense, were often violent in 2006–7 and the power struggle between the two descended into a near civil war in June 2007 that left Hamas in control of the Gaza Strip and Fatah in control of the West Bank areas. President Abbas declared a state of emergency and dissolved the unity government, appointed in March 2007, on 14 June and subsequently appointed a new government; Hamas politicians refused to accept the dissolution of the unity government and claimed its continued legitimacy.

POLITICAL SYSTEM

The president is directly elected for a five-year term. Legislative authority is vested in the unicameral Palestinian legislative council, which has one seat reserved for the president and 132 seats for members who are directly elected in single-member constituencies by a first past the post system. The president appoints the prime minister, who appoints the council of ministers, which must be approved by the legislature.

SELECTED GOVERNMENT MEMBERS *as at June 2007*
President, Mahmoud Abbas
Prime Minister, Interior, Ismail Haniyeh
Economy, Ziyad al-Thatha
Foreign Affairs, Ziad abu Amr

PALESTINIAN GENERAL DELEGATION
5 Galena Road, London W6 0LT
T 020-8563 0008
General Delegate, Afif Safieh

BRITISH CONSULATE-GENERAL
PO Box 19690, 19 Nashashibi Street, East Jerusalem 97200
T (+972) (2) 541 4100 E british.jerusalem@fco.gov.uk
W www.britishconsulate.org
Consul-General, Richard Makepeace, *apptd* 2006

BRITISH COUNCIL
31 Nablus Road, PO Box 19136, East Jerusalem 97200
T (+972) (2) 626 7111 W www.britishcouncil.org/ps
Director, Dr Ken Churchill, OBE

ECONOMY AND TRADE

The economy of the Palestinian areas has been severely affected in recent years by the *intifada* and Israeli security restrictions. The authority's main sources of revenue are the customs dues collected on its behalf by Israel and funding from the EU, the USA, Russia and the UN. These funds have been withheld since Hamas came to power in January 2006, causing severe hardship and prompting fears of a humanitarian crisis; emergency aid, provided through channels that bypass the government, was resumed in late 2006, while the Hamas government sought alternative funding from other, predominantly Muslim, countries.

Most economic activity consists of small family businesses producing construction materials, textiles, metal goods and agricultural produce. The main export is citrus fruits and the main trading partners are Israel and Jordan.

ANNUAL AVERAGE GROWTH OF GDP – 19.1 per cent (2002 est)
INFLATION RATE – 23.6 per cent (2002 est)
POPULATION BELOW POVERTY LINE – 59 per cent (2002 est)

Trade with UK	*2005*	*2006*
Imports from UK	£2,130,000	£1,096,000
Exports to UK	£665,000	£882,000

ITALY

Repubblica Italiana – Italian Republic

AREA – 301,230 sq. km. Neighbours: Switzerland and Austria (north), Slovenia (east), France (west)
CAPITAL – Rome; population, 2,547,677 (2006 est). The Eternal City was founded, according to legend, by Romulus in 753 BC. It was the centre of Latin civilisation and capital of the Roman Republic and Roman Empire
MAJOR CITIES – Milan; Naples; Turin; Palermo; Genoa; Bologna; Florence; Bari
CURRENCY – Euro (€) of 100 cents
POPULATION – 58,133,509 rising at 0.04 per cent per year (2006 est)
RELIGION – Roman Catholicism (87 per cent), Islam (1 per cent) (est)
LANGUAGE – Italian (official), German, French, Slovene, English
POPULATION DENSITY – 199 per sq. km (2005)
URBAN POPULATION – 67.5 per cent (2005 est)
MEDIAN AGE (years) – 42.2 (2006 est)
NATIONAL ANTHEM – 'Inno di Mameli' ['Song of the Italians']
NATIONAL DAY – 2 June (Republic Day)
LIFE EXPECTANCY (years) – 79.81 (2006 est)
MORTALITY RATE – 10.4 (2006 est)
BIRTH RATE – 8.72 (2006 est)
INFANT MORTALITY RATE – 5.83 (2006 est)
DEATH PENALTY – No (abolished 1994)
CPI SCORE – 4.9 (2006)

CLIMATE AND TERRAIN

Italy consists of a peninsula, the islands of Sicily, Sardinia Elba and about 70 smaller islands. The smaller islands include Pantelleria, the Pelagian islands, the Aeolian islands, Capri, the Flegrean islands, the Pontine archipelago, the Tremiti islands and the Tuscan archipelago. Most of the islands are mountainous.

The peninsula is also largely mountainous, but between the spine of the Apennines and the eastern coastline are two large fertile plains: Emilia-Romagna in the north and Apulia in the south. Italy is divided from France and Switzerland by the Alps, and from Austria and Slovenia by both the Alps and the Dolomites. Three volcanoes Vesuvius, Etna and Stromboli, are still active. Elevation

extremes range from 4,807m (Mt Bianco di Courmayeur) at the highest point to 0m (Mediterranean Sea) at the lowest. At the foot of the Alps lie the great lakes of Como, Maggiore and Garda. The chief rivers are the Po (651km) and the Adige, flowing through the northern plain to the Adriatic Sea, and the Arno (Florentine plain) and the Tiber (flowing through Rome to Ostia), which flow to the west coast. The climate is Mediterranean, with warm dry summers and mild winters.

HISTORY AND POLITICS

The Etruscans were the first people to control the Italian peninsula. Their empire flourished between the 12th and 8th centuries BC, but was eventually overtaken by the Romans. At the height of its power, the Roman Empire spread from Italy across Europe, Asia Minor and North Africa. Conquered and settled by a variety of invaders throughout the Dark Ages, Italy began to develop into a number of competing city states. These, with their powerful and wealthy merchant classes, became the locations (and provided the capital) for the Renaissance. Italian nationalists began to agitate for a unified Italy in the 19th century, culminating in the declaration of the Kingdom of Italy in 1861; unification was achieved by 1870. The major figures in Italian unification were Mazzini (1805–72), Garibaldi (1807–82) and Cavour (1810–61).

In 1923, the fascist leader Benito Mussolini seized power and promised a firm rule to end political instability. He tied Italy into an alliance with Nazi Germany and thus led Italy into the Second World War on the Axis side. The Allied invasion of Sicily in 1943 led to a coup to depose Mussolini, who was eventually captured and killed by partisans in April 1945. Italy became a republic after the war; the king abdicated when the country's new constitution came into force and the monarchy was abolished.

A post-war economic boom lasted until the late 1970s, when high inflation and unemployment ensued. This was a time of serious civil unrest, with unions opposed to often corrupt governments, and extreme right- and left-wing groups conducting violent campaigns. In the early 1990s, there was a drive to reform the political establishment after links were exposed between the government and organised crime; many politicians were arrested. In 1993, the electoral system was changed from proportional representation to majority voting in 75 per cent of the seats, helping to remedy the political instability that had resulted in 45 governments in 47 years. Although governments have continued to be coalitions, those of the past ten years have generally lasted longer. Corruption in public administration and business remains a problem.

Italy was a founding member of the EEC in 1957 and of the eurozone in 1999. Its parliament ratified the EU constitution in April 2005.

The April 2006 legislative election was so closely fought that a recount and a final decision by the supreme court were needed to establish that Romano Prodi's centre-left Union coalition was the winner, with 348 seats in the lower house and 158 (a majority of only two) in the senate. The presidential election of May 2006 was won, after four rounds of voting, by Giorgio Napolitano.

POLITICAL SYSTEM

The 1948 constitution has been amended several times, notably in 2001 to provide for greater autonomy for the 20 regions in tax, education and environment matters. The president, who must be over 50 years of age, is elected for a seven-year term by an electoral college which consists of both chambers of the legislature and 58 regional representatives. The bicameral legislature, *Parlamento,* comprises the chamber of deputies and the senate. The chamber of deputies has 630 members, 75 per cent (472) elected on a first past the post basis, and 25 per cent (158) by proportional representation, with a 4 per cent threshold for parliamentary representation; deputies serve for five years. The senate has 315 elected members, of whom 75 per cent (232) are elected for a five-year term on a first-past-the-post basis and the remainder are elected by proportional representation; there is also a variable number of life senators, who are past presidents and senators appointed by incumbent presidents.

HEAD OF STATE

President, Giorgio Napolitano, *elected* 11 May 2006, *took office* 15 May 2006

SELECTED GOVERNMENT MEMBERS *as at June 2007*

Prime Minister, Romano Prodi
Deputy Prime Minister; Foreign Affairs, Massimo D'Alema
Defence, Arturo Parisi
Economy and Finance, Tomasso Padoa Schioppa
Interior, Giuliano Amato

ITALIAN EMBASSY

14 Three Kings Yard, Davies Street, London W1K 4EH
T 020-7312 2200 E emblondon@embitaly.org.uk
Ambassador Extraordinary and Plenipotentiary, HE Giancarlo Aragona, *apptd* 2004

BRITISH EMBASSY

Via XX Settembre 80A, 00187 Rome
T (+39) (6) 4220 0001 E info@rome.mail.foc.gov.uk
W www.britain.it
Ambassador Extraordinary and Plenipotentiary, HE Edward Chaplin, *apptd* 2006

BRITISH COUNCIL

Palazzo del Drago, Via Quattro Fontane 20, 00184 Rome
T (+39) (6) 478 141 W www.britishcouncil.org/italy
Director, Paul Docherty

DEFENCE

The army has 320 main battle tanks, 200 armoured infantry fighting vehicles and 2,036 armoured personnel carriers. The navy has 7 submarines, 2 aircraft carriers, 5 destroyers, 12 frigates, 14 patrol and coastal vessels, 15 combat aircraft and 63 armed helicopters. The air force has 258 combat aircraft and 2 armed helicopters.

MILITARY EXPENDITURE – US$31,300m (2005)
MILITARY PERSONNEL – 191,152: army 112,000, navy 34,000, air force 45,152; paramilitaries 254,300
CONSCRIPTION DURATION – 10 months

ECONOMY AND TRADE

Italy has a diversified industrial economy, divided between a prosperous and industrially developed north and a largely agricultural and welfare-dependent south that has high unemployment levels. The growth rate has been low in recent years, with a budget deficit that has now breached the 3 per cent limit set by eurozone rules. Inflation and unemployment rates are high and public debt is 107 per cent of GDP. The Prodi government was elected on a platform of improving the economy and has introduced short-term measures to promote growth but economic restructuring is expected to meet with opposition, as has been the case in the past.

Tourism is the main industry. Other industries centre around manufactured goods, including motor vehicles, chemicals, electrical goods, textiles, clothing, footwear and ceramics. The services sector contributes 69 per cent of GDP, industry 29 per cent and agriculture 2 per cent. The main trading partners are other EU states, especially Germany. Principal exports are the products of the main industries, plus foodstuffs, beverages, minerals and non-ferrous metals. The main imports are industrial raw materials and energy.

GNI – US$1,772,900m; US$30,250 per capita (2005)
ANNUAL AVERAGE GROWTH OF GDP – 0.1 per cent (2005 est)
INFLATION RATE – 2 per cent (2005 est)
UNEMPLOYMENT – 7.7 per cent (2005 est)
TOTAL EXTERNAL DEBT – US$922,500m (2005 est)
IMPORTS – US$385,000m (2005)
EXPORTS – US$373,000m (2005)

BALANCE OF PAYMENTS
Trade – US$405m surplus (2005)
Current Account – US$26,814m deficit (2005)

Trade with UK	*2005*	*2006*
Imports from UK	£8,524,682,000	£9,194,100,000
Exports to UK	£11,729,057,000	£11,801,500,000

COMMUNICATIONS

A 6,620km network of motorways *(autostrade)* covers the country but there are 484,688km of roads in total. There are 19,485km of railways; the main railway system is state-run by the *Ferrovia dello Stato*. In 2001, Italy and France agreed plans to build a 52km rail tunnel through the Alps as part of a high-speed rail link between Turin and Lyons; commissioning of the project is scheduled for 2012. Alitalia is the principal international and domestic airline. There are 133 airports and airfields, the major ones being at Rome, Milan, Naples and Venice, Palermo and Catania (Sicily) and Cagliari (Sardinia). The main seaports are Naples, Genoa, Livorno, Trieste, Venice, Palermo and Catania. In 2005, there were 25 million main telephone lines in use, 72 million mobile phone subscribers and 29 million internet users.

EDUCATION AND HEALTH

Education is free of charge and compulsory between the ages of six and 16. Pupils who obtain a middle school certificate may seek admission to any senior secondary school, which may be a lyceum with a classical or scientific or artistic bias, or an institute directed at technology, trade or industry, or teacher training. Courses at the lyceums and technical institutes usually last five years and success in the final examination qualifies for admission to university. The universities at Bologna, Modena, Parma and Padua were established in the 12th century.

GROSS ENROLMENT RATIO (percentage of relevant age group) – primary 101 per cent; secondary 99 per cent; tertiary 63 per cent (2005 est)
HEALTH EXPENDITURE (per capita) – US$2,580 (2004)
HOSPITAL BEDS (per 1,000 people) – 4.4 (2000–5)

MEDIA

Rai is Italy's public broadcaster and competes with a number of private broadcasters, including Mediaset, part of the media empire of former prime minister Silvio Berlusconi. The press includes many regional publications, as well as five national dailies, including *La Stampa* and *La Repubblica*, however readership is generally low, with television the primary source of news.

CULTURE

Florence, the capital of Tuscany, was one of the greatest cities in Europe from the 11th to the 16th centuries, and the 'cradle' of the Renaissance. Under the Medici family in the 15th century flourished many of the greatest names in Italian art, including Donatello (1386–1466) and Botticelli (1445–1510) and, in the 16th century, Michelangelo (1475–1564) and Leonardo da Vinci (1452–1519). Significant non-Florentine artists include Titian (*c.*1490–1576), Caravaggio (1571–1610) and Modigliani (1884–1920).

In music, Italy has produced a wealth of composers, including Monteverdi (1567–1643), whose *Orfeo* (1607) is the oldest opera still regularly performed, Vivaldi (1678–1741), Verdi (1813–1901) and Puccini (1858–1924).

Dante Alighieri (1265–1321) and Boccaccio (1313–75) were two of the earliest writers to compose works in vernacular languages. The works of the poet Petrarch (1304–74) and diplomat Baldassare Castiglione (1478–1529) had a strong influence on the writers of the English Renaissance. Notable contemporary writers include Dario Fo (*b.* 1926), winner of the Nobel prize for literature in 1997, and Umberto Eco (*b.* 1932).

Italian cinema produced world-renowned auteurs such as Luchino Visconti (1906–76), Federico Fellini (1920–33) and Michelangelo Antonioni (1912–2007). Director Sergio Leone (1929–89) and composer Ennio Morricone (*b.* 1928) are famed for their work on spaghetti westerns.

Sport has been an integral part of Italian life since the gladiators of the Roman Empire. Football is now the most popular sport and the country's national team have won the World Cup four times, including victory in 2006. Formula 1 motor racing also attracts significant interest and Ferrari has won more World Championships than any other constructor.

JAMAICA

AREA – 10,991 sq. km
CAPITAL – Kingston; population, 579,006 (2001)
MAJOR CITIES – Portmore; Spanish Town; Montego Bay
CURRENCY – Jamaican dollar (J $) of 100 cents
POPULATION – 2,758,124 rising at 0.8 per cent per year (2006 est)
RELIGION – Protestantism (63 per cent), Roman Catholicism (2 per cent) (est)
LANGUAGE – English (official)
POPULATION DENSITY – 245 per sq. km (2005)
URBAN POPULATION – 52.2 per cent (2005 est)
MEDIAN AGE (years) – 23 (2006 est)
NATIONAL ANTHEM – 'Jamaica, Land We Love'
NATIONAL DAY – 6 August (Independence Day)
LIFE EXPECTANCY (years) – 73.24 (2006 est)
MORTALITY RATE – 6.52 (2006 est)
INFANT MORTALITY RATE – 15.98 (2006 est)
BIRTH RATE – 20.82 (2006 est)
HIV/AIDS ADULT PREVALENCE – 1.2 per cent (2003 est)
DEATH PENALTY – Yes
CPI SCORE – 3.7 (2006)
POPULATION BELOW POVERTY LINE – 19.1 per cent (2003 est)
MILITARY BUDGET – US$56.9m (2006)
MILITARY PERSONNEL – 2,830: army 2,500, coast guard 190, air wing 140

CLIMATE AND TERRAIN

An island in the Caribbean Sea, south of Cuba and west of Hispaniola, Jamaica is mountainous, with tropical vegetation. Elevation extremes range from 2,256m (Blue Mountain Peak) at the highest point to 0m (Caribbean Sea) at the lowest. The climate is hot and humid, with average temperatures ranging from 25°C in January to 29°C in July.

HISTORY AND POLITICS

Jamaica was visited by Columbus in 1494 and settled by the Spanish from 1509. Captured by the British in 1655, it became a crown colony in 1865. Autonomy was achieved in 1947 and independence in 1962.

Post-independence politics has been dominated by the conservative Jamaican Labour Party (JLP) and social-democratic People's National Party (PNP). Relations between the two parties, often fraught, degenerated in the 1970s into violence that marred elections and political life for some years. Despite the current political stability, there is widespread poverty and lawlessness that is often connected to drug-trafficking.

The PNP has been in power since 1989, retaining its overall majority at the 2002 general election to secure its fourth term in office. After three terms as prime minister, Percival Patterson stood down in February 2006 and was replaced as PNP party leader and prime minister by Portia Simpson Miller.

According to early exit polls, the opposition JLP won a narrow majority in the September 2007 general election.

POLITICAL SYSTEM

Under the 1962 constitution, the head of state is the British monarch, represented locally by a governor-general. The bicameral legislature consists of the house of representatives, with 60 members directly elected for a five-year term, and the senate of 21 appointed members, 13 nominated by the prime minister and eight by the leader of the opposition. The prime minister is the leader of the majority party in the house of representatives.
Governor-General, HE Kenneth Hall, *apptd* 2006

SELECTED GOVERNMENT MEMBERS *as at June 2007*
Prime Minister, Defence, Portia Simpson Miller
Finance and Planning, Omar Davies
Foreign Affairs and Foreign Trade, Anthony Hilton
National Security, Peter Phillips

JAMAICAN HIGH COMMISSION
1–2 Prince Consort Road, London SW7 2BZ
T 020-7823 9911 **W** www.jhcuk.com
High Commissioner, HE the Hon. Burchell Whiteman, OJ, *apptd* 2007

BRITISH HIGH COMMISSION
PO Box 575, 28 Trafalgar Road, Kingston 10
T (+1) (876) 510 9050 **E** bhckingston@cw.com
W www.britishhighcommission.gov.uk/jamaica
High Commissioner, HE Jeremy Cresswell, CVO, *apptd* 2005

BRITISH COUNCIL
c/o British High Commission
T (+1) (876) 929 7090 **W** www.britishcouncil.org/jamaica
Manager, Pauline Samuels

ECONOMY AND TRADE

Tight fiscal and monetary policies have slowed inflation and reduced public debt to 133 per cent of GDP, but the economy remains weak owing to high interest rates, increased foreign competition, unemployment and growing internal and external debt, and the devastation caused by Hurricane Ivan in 2004. Economic growth is hindered by the high level of violent crime. Tourism, the main foreign exchange earner, is particularly vulnerable. The economy depends on foreign aid and remittances from expatriates.

The economy is dominated by the service sector, which makes up 68 per cent of GDP; industry accounts for 27 per cent, and agriculture for 5 per cent. Natural resources include alumina and bauxite (extraction of which is the main industry after tourism), processing of agricultural produce and light manufacturing.

The main trading partners are the USA, Canada, Trinidad and Tobago, EU countries and China. Principal exports are alumina, bauxite, sugar, bananas, rum, coffee, yams, beverages, chemicals and clothing. The main imports are food, consumer goods, industrial supplies, fuel, and parts and accessories for capital goods.
GNI – US$9,000m; US$3,390 per capita (2005)
ANNUAL AVERAGE GROWTH OF GDP – 1.8 per cent (2005 est)
INFLATION RATE – 15.3 per cent (2005 est)
UNEMPLOYMENT – 11.5 per cent (2005 est)
TOTAL EXTERNAL DEBT – US$7,162m (2005 est)
IMPORTS – US$4,460m (2005)
EXPORTS – US$1,500m (2005)

BALANCE OF PAYMENTS
Trade – US$1,945m deficit (2004)
Current Account – US$509m deficit (2004)

Trade with UK	*2005*	*2006*
Imports from UK	£59,067,000	£71,727,000
Exports to UK	£101,755,000	£131,481,000

COMMUNICATIONS

There are several harbours, Kingston being the main seaport. The principal airports are at Kingston and Montego Bay. The island has 20,996km of roads, of which 15,386km are surfaced. Most of the rail network is no longer in use, apart from 57km of privately owned track used to transport bauxite. In 2005, there were 342,000 main telephone lines in use, 2.7 million mobile phone subscribers and 1 million internet users.

EDUCATION AND HEALTH

LITERACY RATE – 87.6 per cent (2004 est)
GROSS ENROLMENT RATIO (percentage of relevant age group) – primary 95 per cent; secondary 88 per cent; tertiary 19 per cent (2005 est)
HEALTH EXPENDITURE (per capita) – US$176 (2004)
HOSPITAL BEDS (per 1,000 people) – 1.4 (2000–5)

MEDIA

The state broadcaster was privatised in 1997 and now operates as Television Jamaica Ltd (TVJ). It competes with a commercial and a religious broadcaster. The press operates independently and freely criticises the establishment.

CULTURE

Jamaica's cultural heritage includes a vibrant music scene. Kingston is widely regarded as the birthplace of reggae, and Jamaica is also the home of ska, dub and dancehall. The most significant Jamaican musician is reggae pioneer Bob Marley (1945–81); others include Jimmy Cliff (*b.* 1948), Desmond Dekker (1941–2006). Closely connected to reggae is the Rastafari religious movement, which originated in the 1930s among descendants of slaves brought from Africa.

The most widely recognised literary figures are the Nobel prize winning poet Derek Walcott (*b.* 1930) and the novelist Jean Rhys (1890–1979).

JAPAN

Nihon-koku – Japan

AREA – 377,835 sq. km
CAPITAL – Tokyo; population, 8,535,792 (2006 est)
MAJOR CITIES – Yokohama; Osaka; Nagoya; Sapporo; Kobe; Kyoto
CURRENCY – Yen
POPULATION – 127,463,611 rising at 0.02 per cent per year (2006 est)
RELIGION – Shintoism (49 per cent), Buddhism (44 per cent), Christianity (1 per cent) (est)
LANGUAGE – Japanese (official)
POPULATION DENSITY – 351 per sq. km (2005)
URBAN POPULATION – 65.7 per cent (2005 est)
MEDIAN AGE (years) – 42.9 (2006 est)
NATIONAL ANTHEM – 'Kimi Ga Yo' ['His Majesty's Reign']
NATIONAL DAY – 23 December (Birthday of Emperor Akihito)
LIFE EXPECTANCY (years) – 81.25 (2006 est)
MORTALITY RATE – 9.16 (2006 est)
BIRTH RATE – 9.37 (2006 est)
INFANT MORTALITY RATE – 3.24 (2006 est)
DEATH PENALTY – Yes
CPI SCORE – 7.6 (2006)

CLIMATE AND TERRAIN

Japan consists of four large islands: Honshu (or Mainland), 230,448 sq. km; Shikoku, 18,757 sq. km; Kyushu, 42,079 sq. km; Hokkaido, 78,508 sq. km and many smaller islands. Typically, the islands have coastal plains and wooded, mountainous interiors. The mountains running across the mainland from the Sea of Japan to the Pacific Ocean include a number of volcanoes, mainly extinct or dormant. Elevation extremes range from 3,776m (Mt Fuji) at the highest point to –4m (Hachirogata) at the lowest. Average temperatures in Tokyo range from 3°C in January to 27°C in August.

The islands are located on the boundaries of three tectonic plates and are prone to earthquakes; 20 per cent of the world's earthquakes occur in this area.

HISTORY AND POLITICS

By the ninth century AD, a single empire had been established in what is now Japan. In the 12th century, the country was plunged into centuries of rivalry and aggression between different *samurai* (feudal warrior class) families, who were subdued and ruled by successive dynasties of *shoguns* (military overlords) nominally appointed by the emperor. Imperial control was re-established in 1868 after long periods of civil warfare.

Contact with the West was severely restricted until the 19th century, when the visit of a US naval officer, Commodore Perry, led to the Japanese opening up to foreign trade. Industrialisation followed and Japan adopted a Western-style constitution in 1889. Policies became more outward-looking and, in the case of foreign policy, more aggressive, with successful wars against imperial China (1894–5) and Russia (1904–5), and the annexation of Korea in 1910.

Emperor Hirohito's accession in 1926 ushered in a period of intense nationalism accompanied by a rise in militarism, leading to Japan's invasion of China in 1931 and a pact with Germany and Italy in 1940. Japan entered the Second World War in 1941 with an attack on the US naval base at Pearl Harbor, Hawaii, and occupied British, French and Dutch colonial possessions in south-east Asia in 1941–2. Pushed back by Allied Forces in 1943–5, Japan surrendered after atomic bombs were dropped on Hiroshima and Nagasaki in 1945.

The Liberal Democrat Party (LDP) has dominated post-war politics, holding power continuously from 1955 until 1993. It returned to power in 1995, though usually as the main party in coalition governments. Following a year dominated by scandals, elections to the upper house of the legislature in July 2007 saw the LDP lose its majority to the Democratic Party of Japan.

POLITICAL SYSTEM

The 1947 constitution established Japan as a constitutional monarchy with the emperor as head of state. Legislative authority rests with the bicameral *Kokkai* (Diet), which comprises the *Shugi-in* (house of representatives) and the *Sangi-in* (house of councillors). The house of representatives has 480 members directly elected for a four-year term; 180 by proportional representation in 11 regional blocks, and 300 in single-member, first-past-the-post constituencies. It elects the prime minister from among its ranks. The house of councillors has 242 members who serve for six years, with half elected every three years. Unlike the lower house it cannot be dissolved by the prime minister. Executive authority is vested in the cabinet which is responsible to the legislature.

HEAD OF STATE
His Imperial Majesty the Emperor of Japan, Emperor Akihito, *born* 23 December 1933, *succeeded* 8 January 1989, *enthroned* 12 November 1990
Heir, HRH Crown Prince Naruhito Hironomiya, *born* 23 February 1960

SELECTED GOVERNMENT MEMBERS *as at June 2007*
Prime Minister, Shinzo Abe
Finance, Koji Omi
Foreign Affairs, Taro Aso
Defence, Fumio Kyuma
Internal Affairs, Yoshihide Suga

EMBASSY OF JAPAN
101–104 Piccadilly, London W1J 7JT
T 020-7465 6500
W www.uk-emb-japan.go.jp
Ambassador Extraordinary and Plenipotentiary, HE Yoshiji Nogami, *apptd* 2004

BRITISH EMBASSY
No. 1 Ichiban-cho, Chiyoda-ku, Tokyo 102–8381
T (+81) (3) 5211 1100 E embassy.tokyo@fco.gov.uk
W www.uknow.or.jp
Ambassador Extraordinary and Plenipotentiary, HE Sir Graham Fry, KCMG, *apptd* 2004

BRITISH COUNCIL
1–2 Kagurazaka, Shinjuku-ku, Tokyo 162–0825
T (+81) (3) 3235 8031 W www.britishcouncil.org/japan
Director, Joanna Burke

DEFENCE

The constitution prohibits the maintenance of armed forces, although internal security forces were created in the 1950s and their mission was extended in 1954 to include the defence of Japan against aggression. In the 1990s, legislation was passed permitting limited participation by the armed forces in UN peacekeeping missions and allowing them to enter foreign conflicts in order to rescue Japanese nationals. A revision to the USA–Japan defence cooperation guidelines agreed in 1997 permits Japan to play a supporting role in US military operations in areas surrounding Japan. In 2003, the Japanese parliament passed legislation approving the deployment of Japanese troops in Iraq to assist with post-war reconstruction; it withdrew its troops in 2006.

The Ground Self-Defence Force (GSDF) has some 980 main battle tanks, 730 armoured personnel carriers, 70 armoured infantry fighting vehicles, 20 aircraft and 90 attack helicopters. The Maritime Self-Defence Force (MSDF) has 16 submarines, 44 destroyers, 9 frigates, 9 patrol and coastal vessels, 80 combat aircraft and 92 armed helicopters at five bases. The Air Self-Defence Force (ASDF) has 280 combat aircraft.
MILITARY BUDGET – US$41,100m (2006)
MILITARY PERSONNEL – 240,400: GSDF 148,300, MSDF 44,500, ASDF 45,900, central staff 1,700; paramilitaries 12,250

ECONOMY AND TRADE

Japan is the third-largest economy in the world after the USA and China. Its rapid post-war economic growth, based largely on car and consumer electronics manufacturing, experienced a marked contraction in the early 1990s. Exacerbated by the 1997 Asian economic crisis, the recession lasted 14 years, causing unprecedented levels of bankruptcy, unemployment and homelessness and leaving the government with a huge public debt (176 per cent of GDP in 2006). Reforms introduced since 2001, particularly to the financial sector, public spending and private sector have improved economic growth since 2002. This has been boosted by the buoyancy of export markets and domestic business, and improved consumer confidence.

High-technology industries remain the mainstay of the economy, producing vehicles, electronic equipment, machine tools, steel and other metals, ships, chemicals, textiles and processed food. Financial services is also a major sector, supplying a global market. Agriculture is constrained by the mountainous terrain but intensive cultivation produces high yields, and there is a large fishing industry. The service sector contributes 73 per cent of GDP, industry 25 per cent and agriculture 2 per cent.

The main trading partners are the USA, China, South Korea, other Pacific Rim countries and the Gulf states. Principal exports include transport equipment, motor vehicles, semiconductors, electrical machinery and chemicals. The main imports are machinery and equipment, fuels, foodstuffs, chemicals, textiles and raw materials.
GNI – US$4,976,500m; US$38,950 per capita (2005)
ANNUAL AVERAGE GROWTH OF GDP – 2.6 per cent (2005 est)
INFLATION RATE – –0.3 per cent (2005 est)
UNEMPLOYMENT – 4.4 per cent (2005 est)
TOTAL EXTERNAL DEBT – US$1,545,000m (2004)
IMPORTS – US$515,000m (2005)
EXPORTS – US$595,000m (2005)

BALANCE OF PAYMENTS
Trade – US$93,958m surplus (2005)
Current Account – US$165,783m surplus (2005)

Trade with UK	*2005*	*2006*
Imports from UK	£3,811,798,000	£4,014,803,000
Exports to UK	£8,731,370,000	£7,983,607,000

110,053	WORLD HIGHEST
	patents issued per year

Source: Economist Intelligence Unit

COMMUNICATIONS

Japan has a large merchant fleet, with 683 ships of over 1,000 tonnes. The main seaports are Tokyo, Osaka, Nagoya, Yokohama, Kobe and Kawasaki. There are 175 airports and airfields; the principals airports are at Tokyo, Hiroshima, Nagoya, Osaka and Sendai. There are 23,556km of railway track and 1,183,000km of roads. *Shinkansen* (bullet train) tracks are currently being expanded. The Seikan rail tunnel and the Seto Ohashi rail bridge link the four major islands. In 2005, there were 58.8 million main telephone lines in use, 94.7 million mobile phone subscribers and 86.3 million internet users.

EDUCATION AND HEALTH

Elementary education is free of charge and compulsory at elementary level (six-year course) and lower secondary (three-year course).

GROSS ENROLMENT RATIO (percentage of relevant age group) – primary 100 per cent; secondary 102 per cent; tertiary 54 per cent (2005 est)
HEALTH EXPENDITURE (per capita) – US$2,831 (2004)
HOSPITAL BEDS (per 1,000 people) – 14.3 (2000–5)

MEDIA

A public broadcaster, NHK, competes with four national terrestrial television companies and a growing number of satellite and cable providers. NHK also runs national radio networks. Satellite and cable television is widespread and digital broadcasting is increasingly significant. Around 80 per cent of the population reads a newspaper, creating huge markets for dailies such as *Asahi Shimbun, Nikkei Net* and the English language title *The Japan Times*.

CULTURE

The popularity of technology in Japan has not obliterated traditional culture, instead creating a unique mix between the old and new. The indigenous art of woodblock printing and imported Western cartoons have been combined into Manga, a form of comic book illustration. Animated Manga, known as 'anime' are broadcast on television, included in computer games and have spawned a number of internationally successful films, most notably *Spirited Away* (2002), the first anime film to win an Academy Award. Akira Kurosawa (1910–98), awarded an Oscar for Lifetime Achievement, directed *Rashomon* (1950) and *Seven Samurai* (1954).

Japan has responded with enthusiasm to imported sports such as football and baseball. The country co-hosted the 2002 football World Cup with South Korea, while the national baseball league has existed since 1936. However, sumo remains the perennial Japanese sport. Its roots are lost, but references to its earlier name, Sumai, exist in texts from the eighth century. The sport is immersed in ceremony, which has largely survived despite the its huge commercial success.

JORDAN

Al-Mamlakah al-Urduniyah al-Hashimiyah – Hashemite Kingdom of Jordan

AREA – 92,300 sq. km. Neighbours: Syria (north), Israel and the West Bank (west), Saudi Arabia (south and east), Iraq (east)
CAPITAL – Amman; population, 1,036,330 (2004)
MAJOR CITIES – Az Zarqa; Irbid; Ar Rusayfah
CURRENCY – Jordanian dinar (JD) of 1,000 fils
POPULATION – 5,906,760 rising at 2.49 per cent per year (2006 est); Arab (98 per cent), Circassian (1 per cent), Armenian (1 per cent) (est)
RELIGION – Islam (95 per cent), Christianity (4 per cent) (est)
LANGUAGE – Arabic (official), English
POPULATION DENSITY – 62 per sq. km (2005)
URBAN POPULATION – 79.3 per cent (2005 est)
MEDIAN AGE (years) – 23 (2006 est)
NATIONAL ANTHEM – 'As-Salam a-Malaki al-Urdoni' ['Long Live the King']
NATIONAL DAY – 25 May (Independence Day)
LIFE EXPECTANCY (years) – 78.4 (2006 est)
MORTALITY RATE – 2.65 (2006 est)
BIRTH RATE – 21.25 (2006 est)
INFANT MORTALITY RATE – 16.76 (2006 est)
DEATH PENALTY – Yes
CPI SCORE – 5.3 (2006)
POPULATION BELOW POVERTY LINE – 30 per cent (2002)

CLIMATE AND TERRAIN

Most of the country is a desert plateau, with a range of hills in the south along the edge of the Great Rift Valley and a hilly outcrop in the centre of the desert. The Great Rift Valley is an important topographical feature that separates the east and west banks of the River Jordan. Elevation extremes range from 1,734m (Jabal Ram) at the highest point to –408m (Dead Sea) at the lowest. Average temperatures in Amman range from 7°C in January to 26°C in August, although temperatures in the Jordan Valley have been known to reach an oppressive 49°C.

HISTORY AND POLITICS

The area was part of the Roman Empire and subsequently of the Byzantine Empire. It came under Arab control in the seventh century, and in the 16th century became part of the Turkish Ottoman Empire. With the collapse of the latter in 1918, the state of Transjordan was created and administered by the British under a League of Nations mandate. Transjordan became independent in 1946 and changed its name to Jordan. During the first Arab–Israeli War of 1948, Jordan seized the West Bank and part of Jerusalem, but these areas were recaptured by Israel in the Six Day War of 1967, resulting in an influx of Palestinian refugees into Jordan; the descendants of these refugees now constitute the majority of the Jordanian population. Jordan attempted to expel Palestinian guerrillas from the West Bank in 1970–1, causing a civil war until 1973. Jordan recognised the Palestinian Liberation Organisation (PLO) as the sole representative of the Palestinian people in the Occupied Territories in 1974, but severed links with the PLO and expelled its personnel in 1986. Jordan formally renounced sovereignty over the West Bank and East Jerusalem in 1999, having signed a peace agreement with Israel in 1994.

The economy declined in the 1980s and internal stability became increasingly precarious. Riots in 1989 forced the government to initiate a process of political, social and economic reform. The country's first free elections under universal suffrage took place in 1989. A ban on political parties was lifted in 1992; Islamist parties have gained increasing support, but the system favours people's tribal loyalties over their religious affiliation. Real power, however, effectively rests with the king, with parliament amending or approving legislation originating with the monarch.

In the 2003 legislative election, a quota for women resulted, for the first time in Jordan's history, in the election of six female candidates. In November 2005, Marouf al-Bakhet was appointed prime minister with the remit of increasing the pace of the national agenda reform programme, which had made little progress under previous governments. The legislative election was due in November 2007.

POLITICAL SYSTEM

The 1952 constitution provides for a constitutional monarchy with the king as head of state. The bicameral national assembly comprises the house of deputies and the senate. The house of deputies has 110 members, directly elected for a four-year term; six seats are reserved for women. The senate has 55 members, who are appointed by the king for a four-year term. The king appoints the prime minister, who chooses the council of ministers.

HEAD OF STATE
His Majesty The King of Jordan, Abdullah II, *born* 30 January 1962, *succeeded* 7 February 1999
Crown Prince, Hamzeh ibn al-Hussein, *born* 29 March 1982

SELECTED GOVERNMENT MEMBERS *as at June 2007*
Prime Minister, Defence, Marouf al-Bakhet
Deputy Prime Minister, Finance, Ziad Fareiz
Foreign Affairs, Abdul Ilah Khatib
Interior, Eid al-Fayez

EMBASSY OF THE HASHEMITE KINGDOM OF JORDAN
6 Upper Phillimore Gardens, London W8 7HA
T 020-7937 3685 **W** www.jordanembassyuk.org
Ambassador Extraordinary and Plenipotentiary, HE Dr Alia Bouran, *apptd* 2006

BRITISH EMBASSY
PO Box 87, Abdoun, Amman 11118
T (+962) (6) 592 3100 **E** becommercial@nets.com.jo
W www.britain.org.jo
Ambassador Extraordinary and Plenipotentiary, HE James Watt, *apptd* 2006

BRITISH COUNCIL
PO Box 634, First Circle, Jebel Amman, Amman 11118
T (+962) (6) 463 6147 **W** www.britishcouncil.org/jordan
Director, Charles Walker

DEFENCE

The army has 1,120 main battle tanks, 1,350 armoured personnel carriers and 226 armoured infantry fighting vehicles. The navy has 20 patrol and coastal vessels at its base at Aqaba. The air force has 100 combat aircraft and over 20 armed helicopters.
MILITARY BUDGET – US$1,000m (2006)
MILITARY PERSONNEL – 100,500: army 85,000, navy 500, air force 15,000; paramilitaries 10,000

ECONOMY AND TRADE

High levels of poverty, unemployment and government and foreign debt are long-term problems. In recent years these have been exacerbated by the conflict between Israel and Palestine and the impact of the 2003 war and post-war insurgency in Iraq, which is normally a significant export market. Since his accession in 1999, King Abdullah has implemented economic reforms, including a reduction of the public sector, privatisation and trade liberalisation. These measures have increased productivity and exports, started to attract foreign direct investment and won agreement to debt rescheduling from international donors. Even so, the economy is still dependent on foreign aid, of which the USA is the largest provider.

Jordan has no oil reserves of its own and few natural resources. Since 2003, several Gulf states have temporarily extended aid to Jordan in order to compensate for the loss of its usual oil supplies from Iraq. The country imports natural gas as well as oil but is a net exporter of electricity via its national grid's links with those of Syria and Egypt. Jordan has also begun joint ventures with Israel and Syria to guarantee water supplies.

The service sector, including tourism, accounts for 66 per cent of GDP. Industry generates 30 per cent, from activities that include phosphate mining, fertilisers, pharmaceuticals, oil refining, cement, potash, clothing and light manufacturing. Agriculture, which accounts for 4 per cent of GDP, produces citrus and other fruit, tomatoes, cucumbers, olives, sheep, poultry and dairy products.

The main export markets are the USA and Iraq, and the main sources of imports are Saudi Arabia, China, Germany and the USA. Principal exports are clothing, phosphates, fertilisers, potash, vegetables, manufactured goods and pharmaceuticals. The main imports are crude oil, fabrics, machinery, transport equipment and manufactured goods.
GNI – US$13,500m; US$2,460 per capita (2005)
ANNUAL AVERAGE GROWTH OF GDP – 5.8 per cent (2005 est)
INFLATION RATE – 4.5 per cent (2005 est)
UNEMPLOYMENT – 12.5 per cent (2004 est)
TOTAL EXTERNAL DEBT – US$8,528m (2005 est)
IMPORTS – US$10,500m (2005)
EXPORTS – US$4,300m (2005)

BALANCE OF PAYMENTS
Trade – US$3,378m deficit (2004)
Current Account – US$18m deficit (2004)

Trade with UK	*2005*	*2006*
Imports from UK	£186,270,000	£159,536,000
Exports to UK	£21,801,000	£19,796,000

COMMUNICATIONS

Jordan has 7,500km of roads; Amman is linked to Jordan's seaport at Aqaba, the Saudi Arabian port of Jeddah and the Syrian and Iraqi capitals by roads which are of considerable importance in the overland trade of the Middle East. The 505km of rail track includes the former Hejaz Railway, used mainly for freight between Amman and Damascus, and the railway carrying phosphate rock from the mines of al-Hasa and al-Abiad to Aqaba. There are 17 airports and airfields; the principal airports are at Amman and Aqaba. The telephone system is modern but does not extend yet to all rural areas. Mobile phone subscribers numbered 3 million in 2005, and there were 629,500 internet users.

EDUCATION AND HEALTH

LITERACY RATE – 89.9 per cent (2004 est)
GROSS ENROLMENT RATIO (percentage of relevant age group) – primary 98 per cent; secondary 87 per cent; tertiary 39 per cent (2005 est)
HEALTH EXPENDITURE (per capita) – US$200 (2004)
HOSPITAL BEDS (per 1,000 people) – 1.7 (2000–5)

MEDIA

There is strict media censorship, but legislation permitting imprisonment for anyone criticising the king or harming the country's reputation was repealed in 2003. Jordan Radio and Television, the state-run broadcaster, operates three terrestrial channels and a satellite channel. There are radio services in Arabic, English and French. Radio Fann is an entertainment station run by the armed forces.

KAZAKHSTAN

Qazaqstan Respublikasy – Republic of Kazakhstan

AREA – 2,717,300 sq. km. Neighbours: Russia (north and west), Turkmenistan, Uzbekistan and Kyrgyzstan (south), China (east)
CAPITAL – Astana; population, 510,533 (2004 est); previously known as Akmola and Tselinograd. The capital was moved from Almaty in 1997
MAJOR CITIES – Almaty; Shymkent; Qaraghandy; Taraz
CURRENCY – Tenge of 100 tiyn
POPULATION – 15,233,244 rising at 0.33 per cent per year (2006 est); Kazakh (53.4 per cent), Russian (30 per cent), Ukrainian (3.7 per cent), Uzbek (2.5 per cent), German (2.4 per cent). The Russian population is concentrated in the north of the country, where it forms a significant majority, and in Almaty
RELIGION – Islam (60 per cent), Christianity (37 per cent) (est)
LANGUAGE – Kazakh, Russian (both official)
POPULATION DENSITY – 6 per sq. km (2005)
URBAN POPULATION – 55.9 per cent (2005 est)
MEDIAN AGE (years) – 28.8 (2006 est)
NATIONAL ANTHEM – 'Menin Qazaqstanym' ['My Kazakhstan']
NATIONAL DAY – 16 December (Independence Day)
LIFE EXPECTANCY (years) – 66.89 (2006 est)
MORTALITY RATE – 9.42 (2006 est)
BIRTH RATE – 16 (2006 est)
INFANT MORTALITY RATE – 28.3 (2006 est)
DEATH PENALTY – Yes
CPI SCORE – 2.6 (2006)
POPULATION BELOW POVERTY LINE – 19 per cent (2004 est)
GROSS ENROLMENT RATIO (percentage of relevant age group) – primary 109 per cent; secondary 99 per cent; tertiary 53 per cent (2005 est)
LITERACY RATE – 99.5 per cent (2004 est)
HEALTH EXPENDITURE (per capita) – US$109 (2004)

CLIMATE AND TERRAIN

Kazakhstan stretches from the basin of the River Volga and the Caspian Sea in the west to the Altai and Tien Shan mountains in the east. The terrain consists of arid steppes and semi-deserts, flat in the west, hilly in the east and mountainous in the south-east (southern Altai and Tien Shan mountains). Elevation extremes range from 6,995m (Khan Tangiri Shyngy) at the highest point to −131m (Vpadina Kaundy) at the lowest. It includes the northern part of the Aral Sea in the west, and Lake Balkhash and Lake Zaysan in the east. The climate is warm and dry in much of the country, but can be Siberian in the north. Average yearly temperatures in the capital Astana range from −16°C in January to 24°C in July.

HISTORY AND POLITICS

Kazakhstan was inhabited by nomadic tribes before being invaded by Ghenghis Khan and incorporated into his empire in 1218. After this empire disintegrated, feudal towns emerged based on large oases and the nomadic tribes formed federations led by khans. The towns affiliated and established a Kazakh state in the late 15th century which engaged in almost continuous warfare with the marauding khanates on its southern border. After turning to Russia for protection in the 1730s, the Kazakh khanates formally acceded to the Russian Empire, with tsarist rule replacing that of the khans in the early 19th century.

The 1917 Bolshevik revolution in Russia was followed by civil war in Kazakhstan, which became an autonomous republic in the USSR in 1920 and a full union republic in 1936. Kazakhstan suffered severely under Stalin's policies of agricultural collectivisation and 'sedentarisation', which forced nomadic tribes to become farmers; around 1.5 million people died of famine or disease. Later Soviet rule saw the country used as a testing ground for nuclear weapons.

Growing nationalism in the 1980s and a reformist leader led to economic and cultural reforms in 1989 and a declaration of sovereignty in 1990. Kazakhstan declared its independence in December 1991, and became a founding member of the Commonwealth of Independent States. It entered an economic, social and military union with Kyrgyzstan and Uzbekistan in 1994, and an economic and military pact with Russia in 1995, when it achieved nuclear-free status. Privatisation and other economic reforms began in 1993, but despite these and considerable foreign investment, the country has serious economic, social and environmental problems, while its international standing is tarnished by political illiberalism and corruption.

Nursultan Nazarbayev, the reformist communist leader from 1989, became head of state in 1990 and was re-elected in 1991, 1999 and 2005; the 2005 election, in which he received over 90 per cent of the vote, was considered seriously flawed by the Organisation for Security and Cooperation in Europe (OSCE). In 2007, a constitutional reform passed through parliament allowed him to serve for an unlimited number of terms. He has been criticised for concentrating power in the presidency and suppressing political and media freedom.

The 2004 elections to the *Majlis* (lower house) were won by the pro-Nazarbayev Fatherland Republican Party (Otan), which won a majority of seats in the first round of voting. Monitors from the OSCE criticised the elections as flawed, and the speaker of the *Majlis* resigned in protest at the conduct of voting. One of the main opposition parties, Democratic Choice, called for popular protests against the result, but in January 2005 a court ordered its dissolution for breaching state security. The following March, opposition parties joined together to form the For a Just Kazakhstan movement, led by Zharmakhan Tuyakbai, the former parliamentary speaker. In 2006, three pro-government parties merged with Otan, which subsequently changed its name to Nur Otan. The party won all of the seats in the lower house at the August 2007 legislative elections and 88 per cent of the total vote.

POLITICAL SYSTEM

The 1995 constitution was amended in 1998 to extend the presidential term from five to seven years. The president is directly elected. The bicameral legislature, the *Parlament,* is composed of a lower house, the *Majlis,* and the senate. The *Majlis* has 107 members directly elected on a single constituency basis. Nine seats are reserved for ethnic groups and all serve a five-year term. The senate has 39 members, of whom 32 are indirectly elected and seven are appointed for a six-year term, with half elected every three years. At the next renewal, the senate is to be expanded to 47 members. The president appoints the prime minister and other senior ministers.

HEAD OF STATE

President, Commander-in-Chief of the Armed Forces, Nursultan Nazarbayev, *elected* 1 December 1991, *confirmed in office by referendum* 1995, *re-elected* 1999, 2005

SELECTED GOVERNMENT MEMBERS *as at June 2007*
Prime Minister, Karim Masimov
Deputy Prime Minister; Economy, Aslan Musin
Defence, Daniyal Akhmetov
Foreign Affairs, Marat Tazhin
Interior, Baurzhan Mukhamedzhanov

EMBASSY OF THE REPUBLIC OF KAZAKHSTAN
33 Thurloe Square, London SW7 2SD
T 020-7581 4646 W www.kazakhstanembassy.org.uk
Ambassador Extraordinary and Plenipotentiary, Yerlan Idrissov, *apptd* 2002

BRITISH EMBASSY
173 Furmanova Street, Almaty
T (+7) (327) 250 6191 E british-embassy@kaznet.kz
Ambassador Extraordinary and Plenipotentiary, HE Paul Brummell, *apptd* 2005

BRITISH COUNCIL
13 Republic Square, 050013 Almaty
T (+7) (327) 272 0111 W www.britishcouncil.org/kazakhstan
Director, Christopher Baxter

DEFENCE

The CIS mutual defence treaty of 1993, to which Kazakhstan is a signatory, retains a common air defence force, and Kazakh forces also take part in the CIS peacekeeping force along the Tajikistan–Afghanistan border. An agreement signed with Russia in 1995 provides for eventual reunification of the two states' armed forces. By 1996, all nuclear warheads had been returned to Russia, although Kazakhstan retained 48 SS-18 intercontinental ballistic missiles. Kazakhstan participates in the NATO partnership for peace programme. The army has 930 main battle tanks, 770 armoured personnel carriers and 573 armoured infantry fighting vehicles. The Caspian Sea Flotilla, which Kazakhstan shares with Russia and Turkmenistan, operates under Russian command. The air force has 164 combat aircraft.

MILITARY EXPENDITURE – US$1,700m (2005)
MILITARY PERSONNEL – 65,800: army 46,800, air force 19,000; paramilitaries 34,500
CONSCRIPTION DURATION – 24 months

ECONOMY AND TRADE

Economic reforms and privatisation in the 1990s have enabled GDP to grow by at least 8 per cent a year since 2002. This has largely been achieved through exploitation of the vast oil and natural gas reserves, particularly since the opening of export pipelines to Black Sea ports in 2001 and to China in 2005. As a result of the boom, the government has eliminated the budget deficit, but it is also trying to stimulate growth in other industries to reduce dependency on oil. A fund was set up in 2001 to manage state finances and protect the economy from volatile oil prices. Despite these revenues, poverty is widespread, with 19 per cent living below the poverty line in 2004.

Other economic sectors are also performing well. Mineral resources are considerable and there is a significant industry mining coal, iron ore, manganese, chrome, lead, zinc, copper, titanium, bauxite, silver, gold and phosphates. A large and well-developed agricultural industry produces grain, wool, cotton and livestock as cash crops. The main industries are mineral extraction and processing and machine-building, especially construction equipment, tractors, agricultural machinery and electric motors. Services contribute 53 per cent of GDP, industry 41 per cent and agriculture 6 per cent, although agriculture employs 20 per cent of the workforce.

The main trading partners are Russia, China, Germany and other EU states. Principal exports are oil and oil products (58 per cent), ferrous metals, chemicals, machinery, grain, wool, meat and coal. The main imports are machinery and equipment, metal products and foodstuffs.

GNI – US$44,600m; US$2,940 per capita (2005)
ANNUAL AVERAGE GROWTH OF GDP – 9.5 per cent (2005 est)
INFLATION RATE – 7.6 per cent (2005 est)
UNEMPLOYMENT – 8.1 per cent (2005 est)
TOTAL EXTERNAL DEBT – US$41,660m (2005 est)
IMPORTS – US$17,400m (2005)
EXPORTS – US$27,800m (2005)

BALANCE OF PAYMENTS
Trade – US$10,322m surplus (2005)
Current Account – US$486m deficit (2005)

Trade with UK	*2005*	*2006*
Imports from UK	£154,311,000	£208,754,000
Exports to UK	£45,244,000	£81,726,000

COMMUNICATIONS

Because of Kazakhstan's size, long-distance internal travel is usually by air, and the country has 150 airports and airfields; the principal airports are at Astana, Almaty and Atyrau. There are extensive rail and road networks (13,700km of railways and 90,018km of roads), although the roads are concentrated in the more populous east. There are important ports on the Caspian and Aral seas which permit international trade while the Syr Darya and Irtysh rivers provide 3,900km of navigable waterways.

The telephone system is antiquated and services are poor. Mobile phone services cover most of the country and subscribers numbered 5 million in 2005. In the same year, there were 400,000 internet users.

MEDIA

There are several public television broadcasters, including Kazakh Television and Khabar TV (which is broadcast in Russian), the latter headed by the president's daughter Dariga Nazarbayeva. Popular newspapers include the government-backed *Kazakhstanskaya Pravda, Yegemen Qazaqstan* and the private *Karavan* and *Vremya.* There is also the English language *Almaty Herald.* Although freedom of the press is protected by the constitution, opposition and privately owned media are subject to censorship.

KENYA

Jamhuri y Kenya – Republic of Kenya

AREA – 582,650 sq. km. Neighbours: Somalia (east), Ethiopia (north), Sudan (north-west), Uganda (west), Tanzania (south)
CAPITAL – Nairobi; population, 2,845,400 (2006 est)
MAJOR CITIES – Mombasa; Kisumu; Nakuru
CURRENCY – Kenya shilling (Ksh) of 100 cents
POPULATION – 34,707,817, rising at 2.57 per cent per

year (2006 est); Kikuyu (22 per cent), Luhya (14 per cent), Luo (13 per cent), Kalenjin (12 per cent), Mukamba (11 per cent), Kisii (6 per cent), Ameru (6 per cent) (est)
RELIGION – Protestantism (38 per cent), Roman Catholicism (28 per cent), Islam (7 per cent), Hinduism (1 per cent) (est)
LANGUAGE – English, Swahili (both official)
POPULATION DENSITY – 60 per sq. km (2005)
URBAN POPULATION – 41.6 per cent (2005 est)
MEDIAN AGE (years) – 18.2 (2006 est)
NATIONAL ANTHEM – 'Ee Mungu Nguvu Yetu' ['Oh God of all Creation']
NATIONAL DAY – 12 December (Independence Day)
LIFE EXPECTANCY (years) – 48.93 (2006 est)
MORTALITY RATE – 14.02 (2006 est)
BIRTH RATE – 39.72 (2006 est)
INFANT MORTALITY RATE – 59.26 (2006 est)
HIV/AIDS ADULT PREVALENCE – 6.7 per cent (2003 est)
DEATH PENALTY – No*
CPI SCORE – 2.2 (2006)
POPULATION BELOW POVERTY LINE – 50 per cent (2001 est)

CLIMATE AND TERRAIN

The coastal plain in the south-east and semi-desert terrain in the east rise to an arid interior of highlands and mountains in the centre and west. Elevation extremes range from 5,199m (Mt Kenya) at the highest point to 0m (Indian Ocean) at the lowest. The country includes part of Lake Victoria in the south-west and Lake Turkana (Rudolph) in the north. As an equatorial country, the climate is tropical, with average temperatures reaching 27°C in February and 22°C in June.

HISTORY AND POLITICS

Fossils of early hominids found in the Lake Turkana region suggest that the area was inhabited some 2.6 million years ago. Arabs and Persians settled on the Kenyan coast from the eighth century AD. The Portuguese gained control of coastal areas in the 16th century but Arab overlordship was reasserted in the 18th century. European exploration of the interior began in the 19th century and in 1895, Kenya became part of Britain's East African Protectorate, becoming a colony in 1920. Demands for internal self-government by white settlers were rejected in 1923, but from 1944 a nationalist group, the Kenya African Union (KAU), was founded to campaign for African rights. The Mau Mau rebellion of 1952–6, intended to drive white settlers from African tribal lands, resulted in a state of emergency that lasted until 1960, when preparations for majority African rule began. Kenya became independent in 1963, with Jomo Kenyatta, who had spent seven years in prison for managing the Mau Mau rebellion, as prime minister. In 1964 it declared itself a republic and Kenyatta became president. On his death in 1978, Daniel arap Moi became president, remaining in power (amid allegations of electoral fraud) until 2002, when he was barred from standing for re-election.

Kenya was a one-party state ruled by the Kenya African National Union (KANU) from 1964 (in effect, though not formally declared until 1982) until 1991. A multiparty system was reintroduced after violent agitation and international pressure in the early 1990s but KANU maintained its grip on power until the 2002 elections, which were won by the National Rainbow Coalition (NARC). After decades of stability, intercommunal violence and conflict over land and water rights have become more frequent since the 1990s, exacerbated by a rural food crisis since 2004 following persistant drought.

In the 2002 elections, the NARC gained control of the legislature, with 125 out of 210 seats. Mwai Kibaki of the NARC won the simultaneous presidential election with 62.2 per cent of the vote. The government has tried to tackle the problems of extreme poverty, high levels of unemployment and crime, and endemic official corruption but has made little headway; constitutional changes intended to tackle corruption and nepotism were rejected in a referendum in 2005. A corruption scandal in 2006 implicated several current and former government ministers and three cabinet members subsequently resigned; it is estimated that up to US$1,000m (£500m) of official funds have been misappropriated since 2002. Some aid donors have suspended funding to pressurise the government into addressing the problem. Presidential and legislative elections are due in late 2007.

POLITICAL SYSTEM

The 1963 constitution is still in effect, after a proposed new constitution was rejected in a national referendum in 2005.

The head of state is the president, directly elected for a five-year term, who is also head of government and appoints the cabinet. The unicameral national assembly, the *Bunge*, has 224 members, of whom 210 are directly elected for a five-year term, 12 are nominated by the president, and two, the attorney-general and the speaker, are *ex-officio* members.

HEAD OF STATE

President and C.-in-C. Armed Forces, Mwai Kibaki, *elected* 27 December 2002, *took office* 30 December 2002
Vice-President, Arthur Moody Awori

SELECTED GOVERNMENT MEMBERS *as at June 2007*

Finance, Amos Kimunya
Foreign Affairs and International Cooperation, Raphael Tuju
Defence, Njenga Karume

KENYA HIGH COMMISSION

45 Portland Place, London W1B 1AS
T 020-7636 2371 W www.kenyahighcommission.net
High Commissioner, HE Joseph Muchemi, *apptd* 2003

BRITISH HIGH COMMISSION

PO Box 30465, Upper Hill Road, Nairobi
T (+254) (20) 284 4000 E nairobi-chancery@fco.gov.uk
W www.britishhighcommission.gov.uk/kenya
High Commissioner, HE Adam Wood, *apptd* 2004

BRITISH COUNCIL

Upper Hill Road, Nairobi
T (+254) (020) 283 6000 W www.britishcouncil.org.uk/kenya
Director, David Higgs

DEFENCE

The army has 78 main battle tanks and 62 armoured personnel carriers. The navy has 10 patrol and coastal combatant vessels. The air force has 29 combat aircraft and 11 attack helicopters.
MILITARY BUDGET – US$455m (2006 est)
MILITARY PERSONNEL – 24,120: army 20,000, navy 1,620, air force 2,500; paramilitaries 5,000

ECONOMY AND TRADE

Kenya acts as a regional trade and finance hub for its landlocked neighbours. However, its own economy is weak owing to endemic corruption, low commodity prices, low investor confidence and the frequent suspension of international aid because of successive governments' failure to tackle corruption. These problems are exacerbated by occasional severe droughts. There are high budget and trade deficits, a huge foreign debt, widespread unemployment and, with 50 per cent of the population living below the poverty line, the country is one of the poorest in Africa.

The country is overwhelmingly agricultural, with 75 per cent of the population engaged in agricultural and horticultural production; this sector contributes 16 per cent of GDP. The world's fourth largest producer of tea, it also grows coffee, maize, sugarcane, fruit and vegetables. Natural resources include gold, limestone, soda ash, salt, rubies, garnets and hydroelectric power, which makes it self-sufficient in energy.

The industrial sector has grown over the past two decades, developing a manufacturing base in consumer goods (such as textiles) and agricultural products (such as dehydrated vegetables), as well as oil refining, commercial ship repair and the production of steel, aluminium, lead and cement. Tourism generates some US$400m (£200m) a year and has now recovered from the slump following terrorist bombings in 1998 and 2002. Industry contributes 19 per cent to GDP and the service sector 65 per cent.

The main export markets are Uganda, the UK, the USA, the Netherlands, Tanzania and Pakistan, while imports come mainly from the UAE, the USA, India, Saudi Arabia, South Africa, the UK, China and Japan. Principal exports are tea, horticultural products, coffee, petroleum products, fish and cement. The main imports are machinery and transport equipment, petroleum products, vehicles, iron and steel, resins and plastics.

GNI – US$18,400m; US$540 per capita (2005)
ANNUAL AVERAGE GROWTH OF GDP – 5.8 per cent (2005 est)
INFLATION RATE – 10.3 per cent (2005 est)
UNEMPLOYMENT – 40 per cent (2001 est)
TOTAL EXTERNAL DEBT – US$7,391m (2005 est)
IMPORTS – US$6,100m (2005)
EXPORTS – US$3,300m (2005)

BALANCE OF PAYMENTS
Trade – US$1,598m deficit (2004)
Current Account – US$378m deficit (2004)

Trade with UK	*2005*	*2006*
Imports from UK	£192,299,000	£214,977,000
Exports to UK	£223,411,000	£255,875,000

COMMUNICATIONS

The Kenya Railways Corporation operates 2,778km of railways. There are 177,765km of roads, of which 63,265km connect the urban areas. The principal seaport is Mombasa, operated by the Kenya Ports Authority, and Lake Victoria also provides transport and trade routes. There are 225 airports and airfields; the international airports are at Nairobi, Mombasa and Eldoret.

The telephone system is antiquated and domestic services are unreliable, although business fares better. Mobile phone distribution has grown rapidly and subscribers numbered 6.5 million in 2006. There were 1 million internet users in 2005.

EDUCATION AND HEALTH

LITERACY RATE – 73.6 per cent (2004 est)
GROSS ENROLMENT RATIO (percentage of relevant age group) – primary 114 per cent; secondary 49 per cent; tertiary 3 per cent (2005 est)
HIV/AIDS ADULT PREVALENCE – 6.7 per cent (2003 est)
HEALTH EXPENDITURE – US$20 per capita (2004)

MEDIA

There are a number of television channels, including the state-run Kenya Broadcasting Corporation (KBC). Radio is a popular medium outside urban areas. There are six national newspapers that report a range of political views, including *The Daily Nation, The East African Standard* and *The East African*. Kenya has a more relaxed attitude towards press freedom than many of its neighbours and the Kibaki government came to power on the promise of further media liberalisation. However, several recent incidents, such as the storming of the Standard Press offices by police, have caused concern.

KIRIBATI

AREA – 811 sq. km
CAPITAL – Tarawa; population, 40,311 (2005 est)
CURRENCY – Australian dollar ($A) of 100 cents
POPULATION – 105,432 rising at 2.24 per cent per year (2006 est)
RELIGION – Roman Catholicism (55 per cent), Protestantism (37 per cent), Mormonism (3 per cent), Baha'i (2 per cent) (est). An estimated 5 per cent of the population is atheist
LANGUAGE – English, I-Kiribati (both official)
POPULATION DENSITY – 136 per sq. km (2005)
URBAN POPULATION – 50.2 per cent (2005 est)
MEDIAN AGE (years) – 20.2 (2006 est)
NATIONAL ANTHEM – 'Teirake kain Kiribati' ['Stand Kiribati']
NATIONAL DAY – 12 July (Independence Day)
LIFE EXPECTANCY (years) – 62.08 (2006 est)
MORTALITY RATE – 8.26 (2006 est)
BIRTH RATE – 30.65 (2006 est)
INFANT MORTALITY RATE – 47.27 (2006 est)
DEATH PENALTY – No (abolished 1979)

CLIMATE AND TERRAIN

Kiribati (pronounced Kiri-bas) comprises 36 islands, of which about 20 are inhabited: the Kiribati (Gilbert) group (17), including Banaba; the Rawaki (Phoenix) islands (8); and some of the Line Islands (11), including Kiritimati (Christmas Island). They are situated in the southern central Pacific Ocean, crossed by the Equator; the area was also crossed by the international date line until 1995, when the government unilaterally moved the date line eastwards so that the whole country shared the same day. The atolls are coral, and few are more than 800m wide or more than 3m high, making the the country particular vulnerable to rising sea levels. The climate is tropical.

HISTORY AND POLITICS

The islands were settled by Austronesian-speaking peoples in the first millennium BC and Samoans, Fijians and Tongans migrated there in the 11th to 14th centuries. British seafarers visited the islands in the 18th century. In 1892, the Gilbert (Kiribati) and Ellice (Tuvalu) Islands were proclaimed a British protectorate and in 1916 became a British colony, which subsequently incorporated the Line Islands and Phoenix Islands. During the Second World War, the islands were occupied by the Japanese and were the scene of fierce fighting between Japanese and US troops. Kiritimati (Christmas) Island became the site of British nuclear weapons tests in the 1950s and 1960s. In 1975, the territories separated and the Gilbert, Phoenix and Line Islands became independent as the Republic of Kiribati in 1979.

The republic faces a number of environmental problems. Open-cast phosphate mining left Banaba unfit for human habitation and the population was evacuated in 1945, now living on Rabi Island, Fiji; they have since been compensated for the environmental damage. The rise in the sea level owing to global warming threatens low-lying countries such as Kiribati, which reported in 1999 that two uninhabited atolls were completely submerged. In 2002, along with Tuvalu and the Maldives, Kiribati began legal action against the USA over its refusal to sign the Kyoto Protocol.

At the time of going to press the results of the August legislative election were being counted. A presidential election was set for October 2007.

POLITICAL SYSTEM

Under the 1979 constitution, the president is head of state and head of government, and is directly elected for a four-year term, with a maximum of three terms; presidential candidates are selected by and from members of the legislature. The unicameral legislature, the house of assembly, has 42 members: 40 members directly elected for a four-year term, an appointed representative of the Banaban community on Rabi Island, and the attorney-general. There are no formal political parties but some associations of politicians formed for elections have proved durable enough to be given names.

HEAD OF STATE

President, Foreign Affairs, Anote Tong, *elected* 4 July 2003, *sworn in* 6 July 2003

Vice-President, Teima Onorio

SELECTED GOVERNMENT MEMBERS *as at June 2007*

Internal Affairs, Amberoti Nikora

Finance and Economic Development, Nabuti Mwemwenikarawa

KIRIBATI HIGH COMMISSION

c/o Office of the President, PO Box 68, Bairiki, Tarawa, Kiribati

High Commissioner, vacant

BRITISH HIGH COMMISSIONER

HE Roger Sykes, *apptd* 2006, resident at Suva, Fiji

ECONOMY AND TRADE

Since the phosphate deposits on Banaba ran out in 1979, the economy has been weak, dependent on coconuts, fish and tourism (over 20 per cent of GDP) as the main economic activities. Additional revenue comes from international aid (over 10 per cent of GDP), remittances from expatriates and monies from the trust fund established with phosphate mining revenues. A financial sector is being developed. The main trading partners are Pacific Rim countries and EU states. The principal exports are copra (62 per cent), coconuts, seaweed and fish. The principal imports are foodstuffs, manufactured goods, machinery and transport equipment, and fuel.

GNI – US$119m; US$1,210 per capita (2005)

ANNUAL AVERAGE GROWTH OF GDP – 0.3 per cent (2005 est)

INFLATION RATE – 0.5 per cent (2005 est)

Trade with UK	*2005*	*2006*
Imports from UK	£42,000	£177,000
Exports to UK	£8,000	£8,000

COMMUNICATIONS

Air communication exists between most of the islands and is operated by Air Kiribati, a statutory corporation. Flights to other Pacific states are provided by Air Marshall Islands and Air Nauru. There are 19 airports and airfields on the islands; the international airport is on Tarawa. Inter-island shipping is operated by another statutory corporation, the Shipping Corporation of Kiribati. The main seaport is Betio, on Tarawa. There are no railways, and only *c.*670km of roads.

The telephone system provides good national and international services. Mobile phones are not widespread.

MEDIA

Kiribati has no domestic television, so radio forms the islands' main source of communication. There is one state-run and one private weekly newspaper.

KOREA

The independent kingdoms in the Korean peninsula were united by the Buddhist Silla dynasty in AD 668, and a distinct culture developed. The Silla were succeeded by the Koryo dynasty in 935 and the Yi dynasty from 1395 to 1910, during which period Korea became a vassal of China and Confucianism replaced Buddhism. Contact with outside cultures was discouraged by successive Korean rulers until 1876, when Japan forced the country to open up to foreign trade. Subsequently, Japan, China and Russia competed for influence, with Japan emerging as the dominant state, formally annexing Korea in 1910.

Japanese rule ended with its Second World War defeat in 1945, when Korea was divided along the 38th parallel by the occupying armies of liberation: US troops in the south and Soviet troops in the north. The Republic of Korea was founded in the south on 15 August 1948, following a general election and the adoption of a constitution. The Democratic People's Republic of Korea was established in the north on 9 September 1948, a Supreme People's Soviet was elected and a Soviet-style constitution was adopted.

UN plans to reunify the country after nationwide elections in 1950 were defied by North Korea. After elections in the south, South Korea declared its independence, which prompted its invasion by North Korea. A multinational UN force, with a large US contingent, intervened and pushed the North Korean troops back to the Chinese frontier. This brought China into the war in support of North Korea and their combined forces pushed back the UN troops, occupying Seoul. A UN counter-attack retook all territory south of the 28th parallel by the time an armistice was signed in 1953; a demilitarised border zone was established. The war devastated the entire peninsula, and particularly North Korea, and left over two million people dead.

Reunification talks between North and South Korea have taken place intermittently; they were broken off by North Korea in 1980 but further talks took place in 1990, 1997–9 and 2000. A non-aggression pact was signed in 1991 and an agreement on mutual inspection of nuclear facilities in 1992. The 2000 talks ended with a joint declaration under which both sides agreed to work independently for reunification and to recognise the common elements in each side's proposals for federation-confederation. Since the declaration, meetings have become more frequent, although tensions remain, primarily over North Korea's nuclear programme; high-level talks were suspended in 2006–7 over North Korea's testing of a nuclear missile. South Korea is concerned about the prospect of a reduction in US troop numbers in the demilitarised zone.

DEMOCRATIC PEOPLE'S REPUBLIC OF KOREA

Choson-Minjujuui-Inmin-Konghwaguk – Democratic People's Republic of Korea

AREA – 120,540 sq. km. Neighbours: China, Russia (north), Republic of Korea (south)
CAPITAL – Pyongyang; population, 2,741,260 (1993)
MAJOR CITIES – Nampo; Hamhung-Hungnam; Chongjin
CURRENCY – Won of 100 chon
POPULATION – 23,113,019 rising at 0.84 per cent per year (2006 est)
RELIGION – Religious activity is almost non-existent outside government-sponsored religious groups. Historically, the main religions were Buddhism and Confucianism
LANGUAGE – Korean (official)
POPULATION DENSITY – 187 per sq. km (2005)
URBAN POPULATION – 61.7 per cent (2005 est)
MEDIAN AGE (years) – 32 (2006 est)
NATIONAL ANTHEM – 'Aegukka' ['The Patriotic Song']
NATIONAL DAY – 9 September (Founding of the Democratic People's Republic of Korea)
LIFE EXPECTANCY (years) – 71.65 (2006 est)
MORTALITY RATE – 7.13 (2006 est)
BIRTH RATE – 15.54 (2006 est)
INFANT MORTALITY RATE – 23.29 (2006 est)
DEATH PENALTY – Yes

CLIMATE AND TERRAIN

The republic occupies the northern half of the Korean peninsula. A wide coastal plain in the west rises to mountains divided by deep valleys in the interior. Elevation extremes range from 2,744m (Paektu-san) at the highest point to 0m (Sea of Japan) at the lowest. The climate is more extreme than in South Korea. Temperatures in January can fall as far as −10°C in Pyongyang. The average July temperature is 25°C.

HISTORY AND POLITICS

After the Korean war ended in 1953, Kim Il-sung continued the process of Soviet-style reform that began with land reform and nationalisation in 1946. He also developed *Juche* (self-reliance), an ideology demanding total economic independence. North Korea pursued an isolationist foreign policy for several decades, only signing a mutual assistance treaty with China in 1961 and improving relations with the USSR in 1985. It established diplomatic contacts with South Korea and Japan in 1990, raising hopes that it was abandoning its isolationism, but it remains a secretive, closed country under tight Communist Party control, rejecting outside influences.

This situation has had serious consequences domestically and internationally. The economy has suffered a long decline under Communist rule, and a series of natural disasters in the 1990s caused severe famine, obliging the government to request international aid. It is estimated that two million people have died since the 1990s as a result of the acute food shortages, which continue despite international food and fuel aid.

There has been international concern since the 1990s over North Korea's attempts to develop a nuclear capability. In 1994, North Korea agreed to freeze its nuclear development programme in return for US oil shipments and assistance in building two nuclear power stations. However, in 2002 it became clear that it had reactivated the programme, and it subsequently expelled international nuclear inspectors. The following year North Korea withdrew from the treaty on the non-proliferation of nuclear weapons and announced that it had enough material to produce nuclear weapons. In July 2006 it test-fired several ballistic missiles, and in October claimed to have tested a nuclear weapon. Six-nation talks to resolve the nuclear issue began in 2003 but have failed to achieve a lasting resolution; North Korea has agreed to give up its nuclear weapons and nuclear programme in return for aid and security guarantees on a number of occasions, most recently in February 2007, but has rescinded its agreement after further demands were not met. The UN security council voted to impose weapons and financial sanctions on the country in October 2006.

Kim Il-sung died in 1994. His son, Kim Jong-il, became chairman of the National Defence Commission, designated as the highest post of the state, and general secretary of the Korean Workers' Party in 1997. The most recent legislative elections were held in 2003.

POLITICAL SYSTEM
The (communist) Korean Workers' Party, which was founded in 1946 by Kim Il-sung, is the only permitted political party. However, political control and leadership is maintained by the cult of personality created by Kim Il-sung and continued by his son and successor Kim Jong-il.

The 1972 constitution was amended in 1998 to designate leading state posts; it made Kim Il-sung the Eternal President and the chairmanship of the National Defence Commission, held by Kim Jong-il, the highest post in the state, while providing that the chairman of the Presidium of the Supreme People's Assembly would represent the state on formal occasions. There is a unicameral legislature, the Supreme People's Assembly, which has 687 members directly elected from a single list of candidates for a five-year term. The assembly elects a presidium and the premier, appointing the government on the recommendation of the premier. The Central People's Committee, which is also elected by the assembly, directs the administrative council (government), which implements the policy formulated by the committee.

HEAD OF STATE
Eternal President, Kim Il-sung (deceased)
Chair of the National Defence Commission, Kim Jong-il
Chair of the Presidium of the Supreme People's Assembly, Kim Yong-nam

SELECTED GOVERNMENT MEMBERS *as at June 2007*
Premier, Kim Yong-il
Deputy Premiers, Kwak Pon-ki, Ro Tu-chol, Chon Sung-hun

Finance, Mun Il-bong
Foreign Affairs, Pak Ui-chun

EMBASSY OF THE DEMOCRATIC PEOPLE'S REPUBLIC OF KOREA
73 Gunnersbury Avenue, London W5 4LP
T 020-8992 4965
Ambassador Extraordinary and Plenipotentiary, HE Ri Yong-ho, *apptd* 2003

BRITISH EMBASSY
Munsu Dong, Pyongyang
T (+850) (2) 381 7980
Ambassador Extraordinary and Plenipotentiary, HE John Everard, *apptd* 2006

DEFENCE

The army has about 3,500 main battle tanks and over 2,500 armoured personnel carriers. The navy has 63 submarines, 3 frigates and over 335 patrol and coastal vessels at 15 bases. The air force has 590 combat aircraft and 24 armed helicopters.
MILITARY BUDGET – US$2,300m (2006 est)
MILITARY PERSONNEL – 1,106,000: army 950,000, navy 46,000, air force 110,000; paramilitaries 189,000
CONSCRIPTION DURATION – Three to 12 years

25	WORLD HIGHEST
	per cent of GDP spent on defence

Source: Economist Intelligence Unit

ECONOMY AND TRADE

Although North Korea is rich in natural resources and Japan developed heavy industry during its years of occupation at the beginning of the 20th century, the economy is in a disastrous state. Internal mismanagement and underinvestment, low export levels and increasing debt sent the economy into a long decline that was compounded by the collapse of Soviet communism in the 1990s.

Severe floods and a series of disastrous harvests in the 1990s brought famine, and the centrally planned economy has not been able to pull North Korea out of its desperate condition. Lack of arable land, collective farming and chronic shortages of fuel and fertilisers hamper food production even with better weather conditions. Massive amounts of food aid since the mid-1990s from bilateral donors and international agencies have averted famine but malnutrition is widespread. A relaxation of restrictions on farmers' markets and private farming in 2003 reduced shortages but these measures were partially rescinded in 2005 and a centralised rationing system was reinstated. Industrial output is centred on coal, steel, chemicals and machine tools, but antiquated machinery and fuel shortages have limited capacity to a fraction of pre-1989 levels.

The main trading partners are China, South Korea, Thailand and Japan. Principal exports are minerals, metallurgical products, textiles, and agricultural and fish products. The main imports are petroleum, coal, machinery and equipment, textiles and grain.
ANNUAL AVERAGE GROWTH OF GDP – 1 per cent (2005 est)
IMPORTS – US$431m (2002)
EXPORTS – US$298m (2002)

BALANCE OF PAYMENTS
Trade – US$217m deficit (2002)
Current Account – US$82m deficit (2002)

Trade with UK	*2005*	*2006*
Imports from UK	£276,000	£343,000
Exports to UK	£737,000	£9,278,000

COMMUNICATIONS

North Korea has 5,214km of railways and 31,200km of roads. There are some 2,250km of waterways but these are navigable only by small craft. The main seaports are Chongjin, Nampo and Wonsan. There are 77 airports and airfields; the principal airport is at Pyongyang.

MEDIA

There is no independent media in North Korea. All televisions and radios are pre-tuned to government stations which broadcast state propaganda. Anyone found listening to foreign broadcasts is harshly punished. Reporters Without Borders rates the country as the worst in the world for press freedom. There are five national papers in circulation, including *Rodong Sinmun* and *Minju Choson.*

REPUBLIC OF KOREA

Taehan Min'guk – Republic of Korea

AREA – 98,480 sq. km. Neighbour: Democratic People's Republic of Korea (north)
CAPITAL – Seoul; population, 9,820,171 (2005)
MAJOR CITIES – Busan; Inchon; Daegu; Daejeon; Gwangju, Ulsan; Suwon; Pusan
CURRENCY – Won
POPULATION – 48,846,823 rising at 0.42 per cent per year (2006 est)
RELIGION – Buddhism (23 per cent), Protestantism (19 per cent), Roman Catholicism (6 per cent) (est). An estimated 48 per cent of the population is atheist
LANGUAGE – Korean (official), English
POPULATION DENSITY – 489 per sq. km (2005)
URBAN POPULATION – 80.8 per cent (2005 est)
MEDIAN AGE (years) – 35.2 (2006 est)
NATIONAL ANTHEM – 'Aegukka' ['The Patriotic Song']
NATIONAL DAY – 15 August (Liberation Day)
LIFE EXPECTANCY (years) – 77.04 (2006 est)
MORTALITY RATE – 5.85 (2006 est)
BIRTH RATE – 10 (2006 est)
INFANT MORTALITY RATE – 6.16 (2006 est)
DEATH PENALTY – Yes
CPI SCORE – 5.1 (2006)
POPULATION BELOW POVERTY LINE – 15 per cent (2003)

CLIMATE AND TERRAIN

The country occupies the southern part of the mountainous Korean peninsula, with highlands and mountains accounting for around 70 per cent of the land area. Elevation extremes range from 1,950m (Halla-san) at the highest point to 0m (Sea of Japan) at the lowest. The climate is temperate, although winters are very cold for the country's latitude. Temperatures in Seoul range from from −5°C in January to 29°C in July. The rainy season runs from June to September.

HISTORY AND POLITICS

Since 1948, South Korea has experienced mostly authoritarian, often military, rule and great industrial development. Syngman Rhee, president since 1948, resigned in 1960 in the face of popular protests at corruption and electoral fraud. A military coup in 1961 brought General Park Chung-hee to power and he instigated a programme of industrial development; by 1979 Korea was a leading shipbuilding nation and producer of electronic goods. Park's repressive regime introduced military law in 1972, and he was assassinated in 1979.

Following riots against the interim government, General Chun Do-hwan assumed power. Pro-democracy agitation in the mid-1980s led to constitutional changes in 1987 and the first multiparty elections in 1988, but despite the anti-corruption campaign of the new democratically elected president Roh Tae-woo, politics continued to be plagued by allegations of corruption and electoral fraud, and was subject to military influence. The first civilian president and the first wholly civilian government since 1961 were appointed as recently as 1993. Kim Dae-jung's inauguration as president in 1998 saw the adoption of the 'sunshine policy' of engagement with North Korea.

Roh Moo-hyun was elected president in 2002 and took office in February 2003. He was suspended from March until May 2004 after the legislature voted to impeach him for breaching his political neutrality in advance of the April 2004 legislative election; the constitutional court rejected the move and he was reinstated. In the 2004 election, the pro-presidential Uri party won an overall majority and formed a government. Han Myeong-sook was appointed prime minister in April 2006, the first woman to hold the office; she resigned after less than a year in office and was replaced by Han Duck-soo. A presidential election was due in December 2007.

POLITICAL SYSTEM

A new constitution was adopted when the Sixth Republic was inaugurated in 1988. Under this, the president is directly elected for a five-year term, which is not renewable. He appoints the prime minister with the approval of the national assembly and members of the state council (cabinet) on the recommendation of the prime minister. The president is also empowered to take wide-ranging measures in an emergency, including the declaration of martial law, but must obtain the agreement of the national assembly. The unicameral assembly, *Kuk Hoe*, has 299 members who are directly elected for a four-year term.

HEAD OF STATE

President, Roh Moo-hyun, *elected* 19 December 2002, *sworn in* 25 February 2003

SELECTED GOVERNMENT MEMBERS *as at June 2007*

Prime Minister, Han Duck-soo
Deputy Prime Minister, Finance and Economy, Kwon O-kyu
Defence, Gen. Kim Jang-soo (retd)
Foreign Affairs and Trade, Song Min-soon
Government Administration and Home Affairs, Park Myung-jae

EMBASSY OF THE REPUBLIC OF KOREA

60 Buckingham Gate, London SW1E 6AJ
T 020-7227 5500
Ambassador Extraordinary and Plenipotentiary, HE Dr Yoon-Je Cho, *apptd* 2005

BRITISH EMBASSY

Taepyeongno 40, 4 Jeong-dong, Jung-gu, Seoul 100-120
T (+82) (2) 3210 5500 E postmaster.seoul@fco.gov.uk
W www.uk.or.kr
Ambassador Extraordinary and Plenipotentiary, HE Warwick Morris, *apptd* 2003

BRITISH COUNCIL

4F Hungkook Life Insurance Building, 226 Shinmunro 1-ga, Jongro-gu, Seoul 110-786
T (+82) (2) 3702 0600 W www.britishcouncil.org/korea
Director, Gavin Anderson

DEFENCE

The army has 2,330 main battle tanks, 2,480 armoured personnel carriers, 2,040 armoured infantry fighting vehicles and 60 armed helicopters. The navy has 20 submarines, 6 destroyers, 9 frigates, around 75 patrol and coastal vessels, 16 combat aircraft, 24 armed helicopters and 60 main battle tanks. There are 8 naval bases. The air force has 518 combat aircraft.

MILITARY BUDGET – US$23,700m (2006)
MILITARY PERSONNEL – 687,700: army 560,000, navy 63,000, air force 64,700; paramilitaries 4,500
CONSCRIPTION DURATION – 26–30 months

ECONOMY AND TRADE

Industrialisation from the 1960s transformed South Korea from a predominantly agrarian country into one of the Asian 'miracle' economies by the 1980s. Initially based on shipbuilding and electrical goods, production shifted towards electronics and IT goods in the 1980s. By 1997 South Korea was the world's eleventh largest economy, with an annual GDP growth rate of 8 per cent. However, the Asian financial crisis in 1997 caused severe financial difficulties for the dominating conglomerates *(chaebols)* that and a number collapsed in the late 1990s, causing a 6.9 per cent drop in GDP in 1998. Despite a speedy recovery in 1999, it was clear that corporate and financial reforms were needed and these have since been introduced. Growth in GDP has been more modest since the early 2000s, but the economy is stable owing to sound fiscal management, budget and trade surpluses, and low rates of unemployment and inflation.

Services contribute 52 per cent to GDP, industry 45 per cent and agriculture 3 per cent. Major manufacturing industries include electronics, telecommunications, motor vehicles, chemicals, shipbuilding and steel. Tourism is of growing importance.

The main trading partners are China, Japan, the USA, Hong Kong and Saudi Arabia. Principal exports are semiconductors, telecommunications equipment, motor vehicles, computers, steel, ships and petrochemicals. The main imports are machinery, electronics and electronic equipment, oil, steel, transport equipment, organic chemicals and plastics.

GNI – US$765,000m; US$15,840 per capita (2005)
ANNUAL AVERAGE GROWTH OF GDP – 4 per cent (2005 est)
INFLATION RATE – 2.8 per cent (2005 est)
UNEMPLOYMENT – 3.5 per cent (2005 est)
TOTAL EXTERNAL DEBT – US$153,900m (2005 est)
IMPORTS – US$261,000m (2005)
EXPORTS – US$284,000m (2005)

BALANCE OF PAYMENTS
Trade – US$33,473m surplus (2005)
Current Account – US$16,559m surplus (2005)

Trade with UK	*2005*	*2006*
Imports from UK	£1,640,479,000	£1,702,036,000
Exports to UK	£3,084,466,000	£3,116,358,000

COMMUNICATIONS

There are 3,472km of railway in commercial operation, of which 1,361km are electrified. A high-speed railway line is being constructed between Seoul and Pusan and there are plans to build high-speed rail links from Seoul to Mokp'o and to Kangnung. There are 100,279km of roads, of which 3,060km are motorways. There are 107 airports and airfields and there are international airports at Seoul (Kimpo), Kimhae (near Pusan), Taegu, Cheju city and Inch'on. Pusan, Inch'on and P'ohang are the major ports, although development and operation at Inch'on is hampered by tidal variations of 9–10m.

A modern telephone system provides 23.7 million main lines. In 2005, there were 38 million mobile phone subscribers and 34 million internet users.

EDUCATION AND HEALTH

Primary education is free of charge and compulsory for six years from the age of six. Secondary and higher education is extensive, with the option of middle school to age 15 and high school to age 18.

GROSS ENROLMENT RATIO (percentage of relevant age group) – primary 105 per cent; secondary 93 per cent; tertiary 90 per cent (2005 est)
HEALTH EXPENDITURE (per capita) – US$787 (2004)
HOSPITAL BEDS (per 1,000 people) – 7.1 (2000–5)

MEDIA

Korea has a number of public broadcasters, such as Korea Broadcasting System (KBS), Munhwa Broadcasting Corporation (MBC) and Education Broadcasting System (EBS). RTV, South Korea's first public-access television channel, is run by the Citizen's Broadcast Foundation. Newspaper readership is very high. Popular publications include *Hangyore Sinmun,* and the English language title *Korea Daily News.*

KUWAIT

Dawlat al-Kuwayt – State of Kuwait

AREA – 17,820 sq. km. Neighbours: Iraq (north and west); Saudi Arabia (south and west)
CAPITAL – Kuwait City (Al-Kuwayt); population, 261,013 (2005 est)
MAJOR TOWNS – Jaleeb; Salmiya; Hawalli
CURRENCY – Kuwaiti dinar (KD) of 1,000 fils
POPULATION – 2,418,393 rising at 3.52 per cent per year (2006 est); 45 per cent are Kuwaiti citizens, the remainder being other Arabs, Iranians, Indians, Pakistanis and Westerners
RELIGION – Islam (64 per cent), Christianity (10 per cent), Hinduism (5 per cent) (est)
LANGUAGE – Arabic (official), English
POPULATION DENSITY – 142 per sq. km (2005)
URBAN POPULATION – 96.4 per cent (2005 est)
MEDIAN AGE (years) – 25.9 (2006 est)
NATIONAL ANTHEM – 'Al-Nashid al-Watani' ['National Anthem']
NATIONAL DAY – 25 February
LIFE EXPECTANCY (years) – 77.2 (2006 est)
MORTALITY RATE – 2.41 (2006 est)
BIRTH RATE – 21.94 (2006 est)
INFANT MORTALITY RATE – 9.71 (2006 est)
DEATH PENALTY – Yes
CPI SCORE – 4.8 (2006)

CLIMATE AND TERRAIN

Kuwait is an almost entirely flat and arid country with elevation extremes ranging from 306m at the highest point to 0m (Persian Gulf) at the lowest. Its territory includes the island of Bubiyan and others at the head of the Persian Gulf. Average temperatures range from 10°C in January to 37°C in July. High levels of humidity often compound the summer temperatures.

HISTORY AND POLITICS

The area was under the nominal control of the Ottoman Empire from the late 16th century, but in 1756 an autonomous sheikdom was founded that has been ruled by the al-Sabah family ever since. Kuwait entered into a treaty of friendship with Britain in 1899, in order to protect itself from Ottoman and Saudi domination, and it became a British protectorate in 1914. The borders with Saudi Arabia and Iraq were agreed between 1922 and 1933. Full independence was achieved in 1961, although Britain retained a military presence in the country until 1971.

An attempted Iraqi invasion shortly after independence in 1961 was discouraged by British troops in the Gulf. However, in August 1990 Iraq invaded and occupied Kuwait, proclaiming it a province of Iraq. In 1991, a short military campaign by a US-led coalition force expelled the Iraqi forces, although there were further Iraqi incursions in 1993 before Iraq renounced its claim a year later and acknowledged the new UN-demarcated border. Extensive damage was caused to the country's infrastructure and environment during the Iraqi occupation and the liberation campaign and reconstruction was a priority throughout the 1990s. In 2003, Kuwait was a base for the build-up of forces for the Iraq War, and it remains an important transit route for military and civilian traffic into and out of Iraq.

In recent years, there have been clashes between security forces and militant Islamists, some of whom are alleged to have links to al-Qaida.

Although Kuwait was the first Arab country in the Gulf to have an elected parliament, the national assembly was suspended from 1977 to 1981 and again from 1986 to 1992. Despite a brief suspension in 1999 because of a dispute between members and the government, it has since sat regularly, with regular democratic elections. After parliamentary disputes over the number of constituencies, the emir dissolved the national assembly ahead of schedule in May 2006 and an election was held in June. This was won by the opposition, a loose alliance of liberals, reformers and Islamists, which secured 21 of the 50 seats. The government resigned in March 2007 in advance of a vote of no confidence in the health minister. The prime minister was reappointed and formed a new cabinet.

POLITICAL SYSTEM

The 1962 constitution was amended in 2005 to extend the franchise to women, who are now allowed to vote and to stand for election. The head of state is the emir, chosen from among the ruling family. He exercises executive power through the council of ministers. In 2003, the post of prime minister was separated from the role of heir to the throne for the first time. The unicameral legislature is the national assembly, which has 50 members directly elected for a four-year term. There are no political parties. There are six governorates: Capital, Hawalli, Ahmadi, Al-Jahrah, Al-Farwaniya and Al-Asimah.

HEAD OF STATE
HH The Emir of Kuwait, Shaikh Sabah al-Ahmad al-Jaber al-Sabah, *born* 1929, *acceded* 29 January 2006
Crown Prince, HH Shaikh Nawaf al-Ahmad al-Jaber al-Sabah

SELECTED GOVERNMENT MEMBERS *as at June 2007*
Prime Minister, Shaikh Nasser al-Muhammad al-Ahmad al-Sabah
First Deputy Prime Minister; Interior; Defence, Shaikh Jaber al-Mubarak al-Hamad al-Sabah
Deputy Prime Minister; Foreign Affairs, Shaikh Muhammad Sabah al-Salem al-Sabah
Finance, Bader Mishari al-Humaidi

EMBASSY OF THE STATE OF KUWAIT
2 Albert Gate, London SW1X 7JU
T 020-7590 3400
Ambassador Extraordinary and Plenipotentiary, HE Khaled Al-Duwaisan, GCVO, *apptd* 1993

BRITISH EMBASSY
PO Box 13001, Arabian Gulf Street, Safat 13001
T (+965) 240 3334 E britemb@qualitynet.net
Ambassador Extraordinary and Plenipotentiary, HE Stuart Laing, *apptd* 2005

BRITISH COUNCIL
PO Box 345, 2 Al Arabi Street, Block 2, Mansouriya, Safat 13004, Kuwait City
T (+965) 251 5512 W www.britishcouncil.org/kuwait
Director, Jo Maher

DEFENCE

The army has 368 main battle tanks, 321 armoured personnel carriers and up to 450 armoured infantry fighting vehicles. The navy has 10 patrol and coastal vessels, based at Ras al-Qalaya. The air force has 50 combat aircraft and 32 armed helicopters.
MILITARY BUDGET – US$4,510m (2006 est)
MILITARY PERSONNEL – 15,500: army 11,000, navy 2,000, air force 2,500; paramilitaries 6,600

ECONOMY AND TRADE

Oil was discovered in 1938 and the development of the oil industry after 1945 transformed the country from one of the poorest in the world to one of the richest. Kuwait has oil reserves of around 96 billion barrels, about 10 per cent of the world's reserves. Petroleum accounts for 95 per cent of export revenues and 80 per cent of government income. Income from foreign reserves and investment is also high.

The climate and terrain limit agriculture and, with the exception of fish, all food is imported; the primary sector contributes only 0.4 per cent of GDP. Services account for 51.3 per cent of GDP and industry for 48.3 per cent. Apart from the oil and petrochemical industries, other activities include production of cement and construction materials, shipbuilding and repair, water desalination and food processing. Immigrant labour, mainly from Pakistan, India and Iran makes up about 80 per cent of the 1.14 million-strong workforce.

The main export markets are Japan, South Korea, the USA, Singapore and Taiwan, and the main sources of imports are the USA, Germany and other EU countries, Japan, Saudi Arabia and China. Principal exports are oil and refined products, and fertilisers. The main imports are food, construction materials, vehicles and vehicle parts, and clothing.
GNI – US$77,700m; US$30,630 per capita (2005)
ANNUAL AVERAGE GROWTH OF GDP – 8.3 per cent (2005 est)
INFLATION RATE – 4.1 per cent (2005 est)
UNEMPLOYMENT – 2.2 per cent (2004 est)
TOTAL EXTERNAL DEBT – US$16,120m (2005 est)
IMPORTS – US$17,500m (2005)
EXPORTS – US$44,900m (2005)

BALANCE OF PAYMENTS
Trade – US$19,301m surplus (2004)
Current Account – US$18,884m surplus (2004)

Trade with UK	*2005*	*2006*
Imports from UK	£436,649,000	£446,530,000
Exports to UK	£395,705,000	£789,549,000

COMMUNICATIONS

Kuwait has 5,749km of roads, most of which are surfaced, but no railway or internal waterways. There are seven airports and airstrips; the international airport is at Kuwait City. The main seaports are Ash Shu'aybah, Ash Shuwaykh, Kuwait City, Mina' 'Abd Allah, Mina' al Ahmadi and Mina' Su'ud. A modern telephone system provides 510,300 main lines; there were 2.5 million mobile phone subscribers in 2006 and 700,000 internet users in 2005.

EDUCATION AND HEALTH

Education is free of charge and compulsory from six to 14 years.
LITERACY RATE – 82.9 per cent (2004 est)
GROSS ENROLMENT RATIO (percentage of relevant age group) – primary 98 per cent; secondary 95 per cent; tertiary 18 per cent (2005 est)
HEALTH EXPENDITURE (per capita) – US$633 (2004)
HOSPITAL BEDS (per 1,000 people) – 2.2 (2000–5)

MEDIA

Kuwaiti newspapers are far more outspoken in their coverage of politics than newspapers in neighbouring Arab nations, although coverage of the emir and the royal family is often restrained and insulting references to God are banned. KUNA (Kuwaiti News Agency) is the official media agency; *Kuwait Times* is the English language daily newspaper and Radio Kuwait is the state radio broadcaster.

KYRGYZSTAN

Kyrgyz Respublikasy – Kyrgyz Republic

AREA – 198,000 sq. km. Neighbours: Kazakhstan (north), China (east), Tajikistan (south and west), Uzbekistan (west)
CAPITAL – Bishkek; population, 750,327 (1999)

MAJOR TOWNS – Osh; Jalal-Abad; Karakol
CURRENCY – Som of 100 tyin
POPULATION – 5,213,898 rising at 1.32 per cent per year (2006 est); Kyrgyz (64.9 per cent), Uzbek (13.8 per cent), Russian (12.5 per cent)
RELIGION – Islam (80 per cent), Christianity (14 per cent) (est)
LANGUAGE – Kyrgyz, Russian (both official)
POPULATION DENSITY – 27 per sq. km (2005)
URBAN POPULATION – 33.7 per cent (2005 est)
MEDIAN AGE (years) – 23.6 (2006 est)
NATIONAL ANTHEM – 'Mamlekettik Gimni' ['National Anthem of the Kyrgyz Republic']
NATIONAL DAY – 31 August (Independence Day)
LIFE EXPECTANCY (years) – 68.49 (2006 est)
MORTALITY RATE – 7.08 (2006 est)
BIRTH RATE – 22.8 (2006 est)
INFANT MORTALITY RATE – 34.49 (2006 est)
DEATH PENALTY – No*
CPI SCORE – 2.2 (2006)
POPULATION BELOW POVERTY LINE – 40 per cent (2004 est)
GROSS ENROLMENT RATIO (percentage of relevant age group) – primary 98 per cent; secondary 86 per cent; tertiary 41 per cent (2005 est)
LITERACY RATE – 98.7 per cent (2004 est)
HEALTH EXPENDITURE (per capita) – US$24 (2004)

CLIMATE AND TERRAIN

Kyrgyzstan (formerly Kyrgyzia) is a landlocked and mountainous country lying in the Tien Shan mountain range, with the Pamirs in the extreme south. Elevation extremes range from 7,439m (Pik Pobedy) at the highest point to 132m (Kara-Darya) at the lowest, though most of the country lies at over 1,000m. The principal rivers are the Naryn and the Chu, and the vast Issyk-Kul lake lies in the north-east. For its height, Kyrgyzstan is dry country due to its distance from the sea. Typical temperatures in the valleys range from 0°C in January to 25°C in July.

HISTORY AND POLITICS

After a long period under Turkic, Mongol and Chinese rule, the Kyrgyz became part of the Russian Empire in the 1860s and 1870s. After the October 1917 revolution in Russia, the area became part of the Turkestan autonomous republic within the USSR until 1924, when the Kirgiz Autonomous Region was formed; it became an autonomous republic in 1926 and a constituent republic of the USSR in 1936. Soviet rule brought land reforms in the 1920s that resulted in the settlement of many of the nomadic Kyrgyz.

Reform in the USSR in the 1980s provoked an upsurge in nationalism in Kyrgyzstan and agitation for independence. Following the attempted coup in Moscow in 1991, Kyrgyzstan became an independent republic and joined the Commonwealth of Independent States. Economic reforms were introduced from 1992, although privatisation of state assets was suspended between 1997 and 1998 because of fears that they were being sold too cheaply. Kyrgyzstan formed the Central Asian Union with Kazakhstan and Uzbekistan in 1994, agreeing to create a single economic market in 1996.

Since independence, there has been tension between Kyrgyz and ethnic Uzbeks, concentrated around Osh, and this has flared into intercommunal violence on occasions. There have also been clashes between security forces and militant Islamists, active near the border with Tajikistan. Both the USA and Russia have troops stationed in the country as part of the international fight against terrorism.

Askar Akayev, a pro-reform communist, was elected president in 1990 and re-elected 1991, 1995 and 2000, although the 2000 election was considered flawed. After growing unrest since 2002 over political and media suppression, persistent economic problems and corruption, Akayev was deposed in March 2005 in a popular uprising over alleged government interference in the 2005 legislative election. The opposition leader Kurmanbek Bakiyev was elected president in July 2005 but throughout 2006 he faced mass protests demanding action against corruption and crime after several politicians were murdered. President Bakiyev signed a new constitution limiting his powers in November 2006 but pushed through legislation restoring some of these powers in December. Renewed protests and calls for his resignation and early elections have continued in 2007.

POLITICAL SYSTEM

The 1994 constitution was replaced in November 2006 by a constitution that reduced the president's powers; revisions to this constitution were enacted the following month. The head of state is the president, who is directly elected for a five-year term, renewable only once. Since the 2005 legislative election the legislature has been the unicameral supreme council, which has 75 members directly elected for a five-year term; at the next election the number of seats will rise to 90. Under the 2006 constitution, the largest party in the legislature nominates the prime minister, subject to the approval of the supreme council; under the revised constitution, the president's right to appoint the government was restored. The Assembly of the People of Kyrgyzstan, which comprises the leaders of the republic's ethnic communities, was designated a consultative body in 1997.

HEAD OF STATE

President, Kurmanbek Bakiyev, *elected* 10 July 2005

SELECTED GOVERNMENT MEMBERS *as at June 2007*
Prime Minister, Almazbek Atambayev
Defence, Maj.-Gen. Ismail Isakov
Finance, Akylbek Zhaparov
Foreign Affairs, Ednan Karabayev
Interior, Maj.-Gen. Bolobek Nogoybaev

EMBASSY OF THE KYRGYZ REPUBLIC
119 Crawford Street, London W1U 6BJ
T 020-7935 1462 W www.kyrgyz-embassy.org.uk
Ambassador Extraordinary and Plenipotentiary, HE Kuban Mambetaliev, *apptd* 2006

BRITISH AMBASSADOR
HE Paul Brummell, *apptd* 2005, resident at Almaty, Kazakhstan

BRITISH COUNCIL
Director, Christopher Baxter, resident at Almaty, Kazakhstan

DEFENCE

The army has 215 main battle tanks, 63 armoured personnel carriers and 387 armoured infantry fighting vehicles. The air force has 52 combat aircraft and 9 attack helicopters.
MILITARY EXPENDITURE – US$275m (2005)

MILITARY PERSONNEL – 12,500: army 8,500, air force 4,000; paramilitaries 5,000
CONSCRIPTION DURATION – 18 months (selective)

ECONOMY AND TRADE

Economic reforms in the early 1990s caused severe hardship, with inflation of over 700 per cent in 1993, high levels of unemployment and poverty, and malnutrition. Inflation was brought under control in the late 1990s, most enterprises are now privatised and productivity and exports have grown, but the benefits of the transition to a market economy have yet to filter through to much of the population. The government has reduced its fiscal deficit and, with international support, is pursuing poverty reduction and economic growth programmes. These will require further economic restructuring and greater foreign direct investment, though the latter may be deterred by the recent political instability.

The economy is predominantly agrarian, with agriculture accounting for 34 per cent of GDP and employing 55 per cent of the workforce. There are deposits of gold, uranium, mercury and natural gas, and hydroelectric potential. Apart from mining and energy, industry consists of light manufacturing and contributes 20 per cent of GDP; services contribute 46 per cent.

The main trading partners are Russia, China, the UAE and Kazakhstan. Principal exports are cotton, wool, meat, tobacco, gold, mercury, uranium, natural gas, electricity, machinery and shoes. The main imports are oil, gas, machinery and equipment, chemicals and foodstuffs.

GNI – US$2,300m; US$450 per capita (2005)
ANNUAL AVERAGE GROWTH OF GDP – –0.6 per cent (2005 est)
INFLATION RATE – 5.2 per cent (2005 est)
UNEMPLOYMENT – 18 per cent (2005 est)
TOTAL EXTERNAL DEBT – US$2,428m (2004 est)
IMPORTS – US$1,100m (2005)
EXPORTS – US$700m (2005)

BALANCE OF PAYMENTS
Trade – US$171m deficit (2004)
Current Account – US$101m deficit (2004)

Trade with UK	*2005*	*2006*
Imports from UK	£2,638,000	£3,160,000
Exports to UK	£240,000	£5,473,000

COMMUNICATIONS

Kyrgyzstan has 18,500km of highways, 470km of railways and 600km of waterways. There are 37 airports and airfields; the international airport is at Bishkek.

Both fixed-line and mobile telephone systems are expanding, though density is currently low and, for fixed lines, concentrated in urban areas. In 2005, there were 438,200 main lines in use, 541,700 mobile phone subscribers and 280,000 internet users.

MEDIA

There is a large number of newspapers currently in circulation, several of which have affiliations to particular political parties. There are also a number of private and independent television and radio broadcasters. While still enjoying greater freedom than in neighbouring countries, the media has come under increasing pressure in recent years. Publications by Islamist fundamentalists are banned.

LAOS

Sathalanarat Paxathipatai Paxaxon Lao – Lao People's Democratic Republic

AREA – 236,800 sq. km. Neighbours: China (north), Vietnam (east), Cambodia (south), Thailand (west), Myanmar (north-west)
CAPITAL – Vientiane; population, 570,000 (2005 est)
MAJOR TOWNS – Savannakhet; Louandphrabang
CURRENCY – Kip (K) of 100 at
POPULATION – 6,368,481 rising at 2.39 per cent per year (2006 est); Lao Loum (68 per cent), Lao Theung (22 per cent), Lao Soung (9 per cent) (est)
RELIGION – Buddhism (40 per cent), Protestantism (1 per cent) (est). It is believed the majority of the population is animist
LANGUAGE – Lao (official), French, English
POPULATION DENSITY – 26 per sq. km (2005)
URBAN POPULATION – 21.6 per cent (2005 est)
MEDIAN AGE (years) – 18.9 (2006 est)
NATIONAL ANTHEM – 'Pheng Xat Lao' ['Hymn of the Lao People']
NATIONAL DAY – 2 December (Republic Day)
LIFE EXPECTANCY – 55.49 (2006 est)
BIRTH RATE – 35.49 (2006 est)
MORTALITY RATE – 11.55 (2006 est)
INFANT MORTALITY RATE – 83.31 (2006 est)
DEATH PENALTY – Yes
CPI SCORE – 2.6 (2006)
POPULATION BELOW POVERTY LINE – 34 per cent (2005 est)
MILITARY BUDGET – US$13.4m (2006)
MILITARY PERSONNEL – 29,100: army 25,600, air force 3,500; paramilitaries 100,000
CONSCRIPTION DURATION – 18 months minimum
LITERACY RATE – 68.7 per cent (2004 est)
GROSS ENROLMENT RATIO (percentage of age group) – primary 116 per cent; secondary 47 per cent; tertiary 8 per cent (2005 est)
HEALTH EXPENDITURE (per capita) – US$17 (2004)

CLIMATE AND TERRAIN

Laos is landlocked, the land rising from the Mekong River basin in the west to a range of hills in the east of the country and mountains in the north. Elevation extremes range from 2,817m (Phon Bia) at the highest point to 70m (Mekong River) at the lowest. Much of the land is covered by rainforest. The climate is tropical, with a wet season from May to November, during which humidity levels are very high. Average temperatures in Vientiane range from 14°C in January to 34°C in July.

HISTORY AND POLITICS

From the 9th to 13th centuries, Laos was part of the Khmer Empire centred on Angkor in Cambodia. Small principalities developed from the 12th century and were united in the 14th century into the kingdom of Lan Xang ('the land of a million elephants'), which dominated until 1713, when it split into the separate kingdoms of Luang Prabang, Vientiane and Champassac, which became tributaries of Siam (Thailand) in the late 18th century and then a protectorate of France from 1893.

Japanese occupation during the Second World War inspired a Lao nationalist movement, which proclaimed independence in 1945, but the French regained control of the country in 1946. Independence as a constitutional monarchy was granted in 1953, but much of the following 20 years was spent in civil war between the communist Pathet Lao, backed first by China and then by North Vietnam, and royalists, who attracted US support from the early 1960s. A ceasefire in 1973 partitioned the country between the two sides, but in 1975 the Pathet Lao seized power and proclaimed a republic, introducing a one-party state and initiating socialist policies. Greater economic liberalisation was introduced from the mid-1980s, and the first elections to the national assembly since 1975 were held in 1989.

The Hmong ethnic minority people have maintained a low-level insurgency against the communist regime since 1975. In 2000 and 2003, Laos suffered some serious civil disturbances, including bombings and armed attacks on buses. These were variously attributed to Hmong insurgents and anti-government groups based abroad.

In the April 2006 election to the national assembly, party candidates won all but one of the seats, the remaining seat being taken by an approved non-partisan candidate. In June 2006, the national assembly elected Choummaly Sayasone as president and approved a reshuffled council of ministers.

POLITICAL SYSTEM

Under the 1991 constitution, the head of state is a president elected by the national assembly for a five-year term. The unicameral legislature, the national assembly, has 115 members, who are party-approved candidates directly elected for a five-year term. The Lao People's Revolutionary Party (LPRP) is the only legal political party, although non-partisan candidates for the national assembly have been approved by it. Party congresses are held every five years.

HEAD OF STATE

President, Lt.-Gen. Choummaly Sayasone, *elected by the national assembly* 8 June 2006
Vice-President, Bounnhang Vorachit

SELECTED GOVERNMENT MEMBERS *as at June 2007*

Prime Minister, Bouasone Bouphavanh
Deputy Prime Minister, Somsavat Lengsavad
Deputy Prime Minister, Foreign Affairs, Thongloun Sisoulit
Deputy Prime Minister, Maj.-Gen. Asang Laoly
Finance, Chansy Phosikham
National Defence, Maj.-Gen. Douangchay Phichit

EMBASSY OF THE LAO PEOPLE'S DEMOCRATIC REPUBLIC

74 avenue Raymond-Poincaré, 75116 Paris, France
T (+33) (1) 4553 0298 W www.laoparis.com
Ambassador Extraordinary and Plenipotentiary, HE Soutsakhone Pathammavong, *apptd* 2003

BRITISH AMBASSADOR

HE Quinton Quayle, *apptd* 2007, resident at Bangkok, Thailand

ECONOMY AND TRADE

Economic liberalisation and a measure of private enterprise were permitted from the mid-1980s, producing growth averaging 6 per cent a year since 1988, except during the 1997 Asian financial crisis. Economic growth is currently being driven by dam and road construction projects and foreign investment in food processing and mining. Despite this, the country remains very poor, with only a rudimentary transport and energy infrastructure, and is dependent on international aid.

Subsistence agriculture, principally rice, accounts for 43 per cent of GDP and about 80 per cent of employment. Deposits of copper, tin and gypsum are exploited, as is the abundance of timber in the rainforests. Other activities include food processing, manufacture of garments and cement, and tourism. A hydro-electric dam under construction on the Mekong will export electricity to Thailand, earning valuable additional revenue.

The main trading partners are Thailand, Vietnam and China. Principal exports are garments, timber products, coffee, electricity and tin. The main imports are machinery and equipment, vehicles, fuel and consumer goods.

GNI – US$2,600m; US$430 per capita (2005)
ANNUAL AVERAGE GROWTH OF GDP – 7.3 per cent (2005 est)
INFLATION RATE – 7 per cent (2005 est)
UNEMPLOYMENT – 2.4 per cent (2005 est)
TOTAL EXTERNAL DEBT – US$2,490m (2001)
IMPORTS – US$800m (2005)
EXPORTS – US$500m (2005)

BALANCE OF PAYMENTS

Trade – US$217m deficit (2001)
Current Account – US$82m deficit (2001)

Trade with UK	*2005*	*2006*
Imports from UK	£1,564,000	£911,000
Exports to UK	£4,939,000	£816,000

COMMUNICATIONS

There are no railways and only a limited road network (31,210km), although expansion of the road system is under way. The Friendship Bridge over the River Mekong connects Laos with Thailand, and links up the road routes from Singapore to China. There are around 4,600km of navigable waterways, principally on the Mekong and its tributaries. There are 44 airports and airfields; the principal airports are at Vientiane and Luang Prabang.

The telephone system is poor and limited in extent but services are improving. Mobile phone distribution is growing rapidly and subscribers numbered 520,546 in 2006, compared to 90,067 main lines. There were 25,000 internet users in 2005.

MEDIA

All media is strictly controlled by the government. Slandering the state, distorting party policies and spreading false rumours are all criminal offences, which deters an objective media. There are three state-run newspapers, although circulation is very low, and also state-run television and radio broadcasters.

LATVIA

Latvijas Republika – Republic of Latvia

AREA – 64,589 sq. km. Neighbours: Estonia (north), Russia (east), Lithuania and Belarus (south)
CAPITAL – Riga; population, 727,578 (2006 est)
MAJOR CITIES – Daugavpils; Liepaja; Jelgava
CURRENCY – Lats of 100 santims
POPULATION – 2,274,735 falling at 0.67 per cent per year (2006 est); Latvian (57.7 per cent), Russian (29.6

per cent), Belarusian (4.1 per cent), Ukrainian (2.7 per cent), Polish (2.5 per cent) (est)
RELIGION – Protestantism (24 per cent), Roman Catholicism (18 per cent), Orthodox Christianity (15 per cent) (est)
LANGUAGE – Latvian (official), Russian, Lithuanian
POPULATION DENSITY – 37 per sq. km (2005)
URBAN POPULATION – 65.9 per cent (2005 est)
MEDIAN AGE (years) – 39.4 (2006 est)
NATIONAL ANTHEM – 'Dievs, Sveti Latviju' ['God Bless Latvia']
NATIONAL DAY – 18 November (Independence Day)
LIFE EXPECTANCY (years) – 71.33 (2006 est)
MORTALITY RATE – 13.66 (2006 est)
BIRTH RATE – 9.24 (2006 est)
INFANT MORTALITY RATE – 9.35 (2006 est)
DEATH PENALTY – Yes*
CPI SCORE – 4.7 (2006)

CLIMATE AND TERRAIN

Latvia is a flat, low-lying country with a coastline on the eastern shores of the Baltic Sea. Elevation extremes range from 312m (Gaizinkalns) at the highest point to 0m (Baltic Sea) at the lowest. Average temperatures in Riga range from −4°C in January to 18°C in July.

HISTORY AND POLITICS

Conquered and Christianised in the 13th century by the German Teutonic Knights, Latvia was successively under Polish, Lithuanian and Swedish rule in the 16th and 17th centuries, until it was incorporated into the Russian Empire in 1721. Under partial German occupation during the First World War, it declared its independence in 1918 and successfully defended this against the Bolsheviks in 1918–20. A dictatorship was established in 1934, following political instability and economic depression. The USSR invaded and annexed Latvia in 1940, and regained control in 1944 after ousting the German forces that had invaded in 1941. Latvia suffered huge civilian losses during the Second World War, including the destruction of its large Jewish community. Many more Latvians died after the war in purges and deportations ordered by Stalin.

Agitation by nationalist groups grew from the mid-1980s and in 1990 talks on independence began with the USSR. Following the failed coup in Moscow in 1991, the Latvian parliament declared the country's independence and this was internationally recognised. The last Russian troops left in 1994 but a large Russian minority remains and there are intercommunal tensions. Since the first post-Soviet elections in 1993, there has been a succession of centre-right coalition governments.

Latvia joined the EU in 2004. Its parliament ratified the EU constitution in June 2005.

In the 2006 legislative election, the People's Party (TP) won the most seats and continued in coalition with its previous government partners, the Latvia's First Party-Latvia's Way (LPP-LC) and Farmers' Union (ZZS) parties, plus the For Fatherland and Freedom party (TB/LNNK). The presidential election in May 2007 was won by Valdis Zatlers.

POLITICAL SYSTEM

The 1922 constitution was restored in 1993. The head of state is a president, who is elected by the legislature for a four-year term which may be renewed only once. The president appoints the prime minister, who appoints the cabinet subject to approval by the legislature. The unicameral legislature, the *Saeima*, has 100 deputies who are elected for a four-year term by proportional representation, with a five per cent threshold for parliamentary representation.

HEAD OF STATE

President, Valdis Zatlers, *elected* 31 May 2007, *sworn in* 7 July 2007

SELECTED GOVERNMENT MEMBERS *as at June 2007*

Prime Minister, Aigars Kalvitis
Defence, Atis Slakteris
Finance, Oskars Spurdzins
Foreign Affairs, Artis Pabriks
Interior, Ivars Godmanis

EMBASSY OF THE REPUBLIC OF LATVIA

45 Nottingham Place, London W1U 5LY
T 020-7312 0040 W www.london.mfa.gov.lv
Ambassador Extraordinary and Plenipotentiary, HE Indulis Berzins, *apptd* 2005

BRITISH EMBASSY

5 J. Alunana Street, Riga LV-1010
T (+371) 777 4700 E british.embassy@apollo.lv
Ambassador Extraordinary and Plenipotentiary, HE Ian Bond, *apptd* 2004

BRITISH COUNCIL

5A Blaumana Street, Riga LV-1011
T (+371) 728 1730 W www.britishcouncil.org/latvia
Director, Agita Kalvina

DEFENCE

The army has 3 main battle tanks, the navy has 4 patrol and coastal vessels and the air force has 19 aircraft and 6 helicopters. Latvia, Lithuania and Estonia operate a joint naval unit, BALTRON, which is located at 5 naval bases: Liepaja, Riga, Ventspils, Tallinn and Klaipeda.
MILITARY EXPENDITURE – US$204m (2005)
MILITARY PERSONNEL – 5,339: army 985, navy 614, air force 322, administration, central support and other forces 3,418

ECONOMY AND TRADE

The country has made the transition from a planned to a market economy, although a few large enterprises remain in state ownership. There are budget and trade deficits, and a low GDP per capita compared to other EU countries, which may postpone adoption of the euro, planned for 2008.

The economy has shifted towards service industries since independence. Transit, services and banking are large sectors, with services contributing 70 per cent of GDP. Industry contributes 26 per cent of GDP and include the manufacture of vehicles, synthetic fibres, agricultural machinery, fertilisers, washing machines, electronics, pharmaceuticals, processed foods and textiles. The agricultural sector accounts for 4 per cent of GDP, employs 13 per cent of the workforce and specialises in cattle and pig breeding, dairy farming and crop cultivation including sugar beet, flax, cereals and potatoes.

The main trading partners are other EU states and Russia. Principal exports are timber and wood products, machinery and equipment, metals, textiles and foodstuffs. The main imports are machinery and equipment, chemicals, fuel and vehicles.

GNI – US$15,600m; US$6,770 per capita (2005)
ANNUAL AVERAGE GROWTH OF GDP – 10.2 per cent (2005 est)
INFLATION RATE – 6.8 per cent (2005 est)
UNEMPLOYMENT – 7.5 per cent (2005 est)
TOTAL EXTERNAL DEBT – US$10,800m (2006)
IMPORTS – US$9,000m (2005)
EXPORTS – US$5,000m (2005)

BALANCE OF PAYMENTS
Trade – US$2,966m deficit (2005)
Current Account – US$1,959m deficit (2005)

Trade with UK	*2005*	*2006*
Imports from UK	£97,247,000	£339,300,000
Exports to UK	£675,445,000	£861,400,000

COMMUNICATIONS

Latvia has 2,303km of railway track and some 69,600km of roads. There are two major ports, Riga and Ventspils, which are warm-water ports. The main airports are at Riga, Ventspils and Liepaja. The telephone system has become increasingly competitive since 2003. In 2005, there were 731,000 main lines in use, 1.8 million mobile phone subscribers and 1 million internet users.

EDUCATION AND HEALTH

Education is compulsory from the age of seven until 16 years, after which there is the option for a further three years of either secondary or vocational study.
LITERACY RATE – 99.7 per cent (2004 est)
GROSS ENROLMENT RATIO (percentage of relevant age group) – primary 93 per cent; secondary 97 per cent; tertiary 74 per cent (2005 est)
HEALTH EXPENDITURE (per capita) – US$418 (2004)
HOSPITAL BEDS (per 1,000 people) – 7.8 (2000–5)

MEDIA

There are around 140 newspapers in circulation, including 24 national dailies. The most popular include *Diena Panorama, Latvii* and *Neatkariga RA*. Latvian Television is a public service broadcaster that has two channels, and Latvijas Neatkariga Televizija is the biggest private broadcaster.

LEBANON

Al-Jumhuriyah al-Lubnaniyah – Republic of Lebanon

AREA – 10,400 sq. km. Neighbours: Syria (north and east), Israel (south)
CAPITAL – Beirut (Bayrut); population, 1,171,000 (2003 est)
MAJOR CITIES – Tarabulus (Tripoli); Sayda (Sidon); Sur (Tyre)
CURRENCY – Lebanese pound (L£) of 100 piastres
POPULATION – 3,874,050 rising at 1.23 per cent per year (2006 est); Arab (95 per cent), Armenian (4 per cent) (est)
RELIGION – Islam (70 per cent), Christianity (23 per cent) (est)
LANGUAGE – Arabic (official), French, English, Armenian
POPULATION DENSITY – 350 per sq. km (2005)
URBAN POPULATION – 88 per cent (2005 est)
MEDIAN AGE (years) – 27.8 (2006 est)
NATIONAL ANTHEM – 'Koullouna Liloutaan Lil Oula Lil Alam' ['All of Us! For our Country, For our Flag and Glory']
NATIONAL DAY – 22 November (Independence Day)
LIFE EXPECTANCY (years) – 72.88 (2006 est)
MORTALITY RATE – 6.21 (2006 est)
BIRTH RATE – 18.52 (2006 est)
INFANT MORTALITY RATE – 23.72 (2006 est)
DEATH PENALTY – Yes
CPI SCORE – 3.6 (2006)

CLIMATE AND TERRAIN

There is a narrow plain on the Mediterranean Sea coast, and the fertile Bekaa valley runs from north to south between the Lebanon and Anti-Lebanon mountain ranges. Elevation extremes range from 3,088m (Qurnat as Sawda') at the highest point to 0m (Mediterranean Sea) at the lowest. The climate is Mediterranean, with average temperatures of 13°C in January and 29°C in August.

HISTORY AND POLITICS

Lebanon was part of the Phoenician Empire from the fifth century BC until the first century AD, when it came under Roman rule and Christianity was introduced. Islam was introduced by Arabs in the seventh century AD, and the Druze faith was developed by local Muslims in the 11th century. The area was contested between Muslims and Christians during the Crusades before becoming part of the Turkish Ottoman Empire in the 16th century. Following the Ottoman collapse at the end of the First World War, Lebanon became a French-administered mandated territory, achieving independence in 1943 with a constitution that enshrined power-sharing by all the country's religions.

The complicated system of government established by the constitution created tensions between Christians and Muslims that in 1975 erupted into a civil war that pitted a coalition of Christian groups against Druze and Muslim militias. Conflict continued for 15 years, drawing in the Palestine Liberation Organisation (PLO), then based in Beirut, and Syrian forces in support of the Muslim factions, and Israel, which invaded in 1978 and 1982 in response to PLO guerrilla raids on Israel; Israel forced the PLO to withdraw from Lebanon in 1982. By 1985, the country was close to partition as rival political and religious factions sought to gain control.

An Arab League-sponsored ceasefire came into effect in 1989 and a peace plan, the Ta'if Accord, proposed revisions to the constitution that would reduce Christian Maronite dominance. This was rejected by some Christian factions and fighting continued until this opposition was crushed by Syrian forces. A fragile peace was achieved in 1991, and elections in 1992 were peaceful, although they were boycotted by some Christian parties. In the security zones established by Israel in south Lebanon in 1985, clashes continued between occupying Israeli troops, or the Israeli-backed South Lebanon Army (SLA), and Hezbollah guerrillas throughout the 1990s. The SLA collapsed after Israel withdrew its forces in 2000.

Syria exerted a strong influence on Lebanese politics during and after the civil war; most Lebanese governments were pro-Syrian, and Syrian troops remained in the country. However, popular opposition to Syria's influence was inflamed by the assassination in 2005 of former prime minister Rafik Hariri, for which Syria was blamed. Huge rallies in Beirut brought down the pro-Syrian government and obliged Syria to withdraw its troops and intelligence agents, which it claimed to have completed in May 2005.

Despite the withdrawal of Syria, the government's control of the country was weak, especially in the pro-Syria south. In July 2006, Hezbollah guerrillas kidnapped two Israeli soldiers in northern Israel and in retaliation Israel launched air and sea attacks on Lebanon and, in August, sent ground troops over the border to destroy Hezbollah artillery positions. Over 1,000 Lebanese civilians were killed, thousands were displaced and infrastructure was severely damaged. Following a truce in mid-August, a UN peacekeeping force began to deploy along the border with Israel and in September, Lebanese troops were deployed along this border for the first time in decades. Lebanese forces also began an offensive against militants sheltering in refugee camps in northern Lebanon in May 2007.

In the 2005 legislative elections, an alliance of anti-Syrian parties led by Saad Hariri (son of Rafik Hariri) won an overall majority of seats in the national assembly (although pro-Syrian groups won the majority in south Lebanon), and the parliament appointed Fouad Siniora, an ally of Hariri, as prime minister. Although predominantly composed of Hariri supporters, Siniora's coalition government also included supporters of pro-Syrian President Emile Lahoud and Shia parties, including Hezbollah. The Hezbollah and pro-Lahoud ministers resigned in November 2006 in protest at their number of alloted seats in the national assembly and in response to a draft UN plan for the trial of those suspected of Rafik Hariri's murder. The Hezbollah-led opposition has since organised mass protests, including demonstrations and a general strike, demanding the resignation of the government. A presidential election was scheduled for 25 September 2007.

POLITICAL SYSTEM

The constitution dates from 1926 but has been heavily amended, most significantly in 1943, when the National Covenant set out the division of power between the religious communities, and in 1989 to incorporate the provisions of the Ta'if accord. By convention, the presidency is held by a Maronite Christian, the prime minister is a Sunni Muslim and the speaker is a Shia Muslim. The executive comprises the president, prime minister and cabinet. The president is elected by the national assembly for a six-year term, which is not renewable. The unicameral national assembly has 128 members, directly elected for a four-year term; seats are divided equally between Christians and Muslims. The prime minister is appointed by the president following consultation with the national assembly.

HEAD OF STATE

President of the Republic of Lebanon, Gen. Emile Lahoud, *elected* 15 October 1998, *sworn in* 24 November 1998

SELECTED GOVERNMENT MEMBERS *as at June 2007*

Prime Minister, Fouad Siniora

Deputy Prime Minister, Defence, Elias Murr

Finance, Jihad Azour

Foreign Affairs, Fawzi Salloukh

EMBASSY OF LEBANON

21 Palace Gardens Mews, London W8 4RB

T 020-7727 6696

Ambassador Extraordinary and Plenipotentiary, vacant

BRITISH EMBASSY

PO Box 11, 471 Serail Hill, Beirut Centre-Ville, Beirut

T (+961) (1) 990 400 E britemb@cyberia.net.lb

W www.britishembassy.org.lb

Ambassador Extraordinary and Plenipotentiary, HE Frances Guy, *apptd* 2006

BRITISH COUNCIL

Berytech Technology and Health, Sodeco Street, Damascus Road, 2064 1509 Beirut

T (+961) (1) 740 123 W www.britishcouncil.org/lebanon

Director, Amanda Burrell

DEFENCE

The army has 310 main battle tanks and 1,257 armoured personnel carriers. The navy has 32 patrol and coastal vessels at 2 bases. The air force has 14 aircraft and 2 armed helicopters.

MILITARY BUDGET – US$663m (2006 est)

MILITARY PERSONNEL – 72,100: army 70,000, navy 1,100, air force 1,000; paramilitaries 13,000

CONSCRIPTION DURATION – 12 months

ECONOMY AND TRADE

The civil war devastated Lebanon's economy and infrastructure, and its role as an entrepôt and financial services centre for the region. A government reconstruction programme launched in 1993 succeeded in stimulating economic growth and reducing inflation as well as rebuilding the infrastructure and financial systems. This was financed by heavy borrowing and debt has now reached 209 per cent of GDP. Austerity measures, foreign debt rescheduling and international aid had begun to stabilise government finances, but economic and financial reforms stalled, and the Israeli attacks in 2006 caused an estimated US$3.6bn (£1.8bn) of damage to the country's infrastructure. Internal political tensions are hindering economic activity and recovery.

In 2005, the service sector contributed 72 per cent of GDP, largely through banking and tourism, which are the two main economic activities. Industry accounted for 21 per cent, through food processing and the manufacture of jewellery, cement, textiles, mineral and chemical products, timber and furniture, oil refining and metal fabrication. Agriculture contributed 7 per cent of GDP, producing fruit, vegetables, tobacco and livestock.

The main export markets are Syria, the UAE, Turkey, Switzerland and Saudi Arabia, while imports come mainly from EU countries, Syria, China and the USA. Principal exports include jewellery, chemicals, consumer goods, fruit, tobacco and construction materials. The main imports are petroleum products, cars, medicines, clothing, foodstuffs and consumer products.

GNI – US$22,600m; US$6,320 per capita (2005)

ANNUAL AVERAGE GROWTH OF GDP – 0.1 per cent (2005 est)

INFLATION RATE – 2.4 per cent (2005 est)

TOTAL EXTERNAL DEBT – US$26,000m (2005 est)

IMPORTS – US$9,400m (2005)

EXPORTS – US$1,800m (2005)

BALANCE OF PAYMENTS

Trade – US$7,105m deficit (2004)

Current Account – US$4,805m deficit (2004)

Trade with UK	*2005*	*2006*
Imports from UK	£212,065,000	£207,737,000
Exports to UK	£20,169,000	£20,414,000

COMMUNICATIONS

The Israeli attacks in 2006 destroyed much of the country's infrastructure, including about 80 per cent of the major roads. The 401km railway system, some still not usable following the civil war, was rendered completely inoperable. There are seven airports and airfields, although the international airport at Beirut was damaged by airstrikes in 2006. The principal seaports are Tripoli, Tyre, Sidon and Jounieh.

The telephone system was repaired after the civil war but modernisation has been hampered by political tensions. In 2005, there were 990,000 main lines in use, 1.2 million mobile phone subscribers and 700,000 internet users.

EDUCATION AND HEALTH

There is a good provision throughout the country of primary and secondary schools, among which are a large number of private schools.

GROSS ENROLMENT RATIO (percentage of relevant age group) – primary 106 per cent; secondary 89 per cent; tertiary 51 per cent (2005 est)
HEALTH EXPENDITURE (per capita) – US$670 (2004)
HOSPITAL BEDS (per 1,000 people) – 3 (2000–5)

MEDIA

Lebanon was the first Arab country to permit private radio and television stations. There are a number of daily newspapers in circulation, including French and English language publications. Tele-Liban is the state-run broadcaster that competes with several commercial stations, including the pro-Hezbollah al-Manar TV, targeted by Israeli air raids during the conflict in 2006.

LESOTHO

Kingdom of Lesotho

AREA – 30,355 sq. km. Neighbour: South Africa, which completely surrounds Lesotho
CAPITAL – Maseru; population, 137,837 (1996)
MAJOR TOWN – Teyateyaneng
CURRENCY – Loti (M) of 100 lisente. The South African rand is also legal tender
POPULATION – 2,022,331 falling at 0.46 per cent per year (2006 est); Basotho (99.7 per cent) (est)
RELIGION – Christianity (90 per cent) (est)
LANGUAGE – English (official), Sesotho, Zulu, Xhosa
POPULATION DENSITY – 59 per sq. km (2005)
URBAN POPULATION – 18.2 per cent (2005 est)
MEDIAN AGE (years) – 20.3 (2006 est)
NATIONAL ANTHEM – 'Lesotho, Fatse la Bontata Rona' ['Lesotho, Land of Our Fathers']
NATIONAL DAY – 4 October (Independence Day)
LIFE EXPECTANCY – 34.4 (2006 est)
MORTALITY RATE – 28.71 (2006 est)
BIRTH RATE – 24.75 (2006 est)
INFANT MORTALITY RATE – 87.24 (2006 est)
HIV/AIDS ADULT PREVALENCE – 28.9 per cent (2003 est)
DEATH PENALTY – Yes
CPI SCORE – 3.2 (2006)
MILITARY BUDGET – US$30m (2006 est)
MILITARY PERSONNEL – army 2,000

CLIMATE AND TERRAIN

Lesotho is a landlocked country consisting of a highland plateau with hilly and mountainous areas. Elevation extremes range from 3,482m (Thabana Ntlenyana) at the highest point to 1,400m (the junction of the Orange and Makhaleng rivers) at the lowest. Due to the country's elevation, the climate is temperate. Average temperatures range from 25°C in January to 8°C in July.

HISTORY AND POLITICS

The area was organised into a single territory by Moshoeshoe the Great around 1820. Later in the 19th century, the Sotho people came under pressure from both the expanding Zulu nation and Europeans (the Boers) to give up land. In 1868, after fighting two wars with the Europeans, pressure from the Boers forced the Sotho to seek protection from the British government, and Basutoland became first a British territory in 1868, and then a crown colony in 1884.

The country gained independence in 1966 as the kingdom of Lesotho, under Moshoeshoe II and with Chief Lebua Jonathan as prime minister. The post-independence period has been one of political instability, with a number of coups and mutinies as rival political parties, army factions and the royal family competed for power. Chief Jonathan declared a state of emergency in 1970, fearing defeat in the elections. Although the constitution was restored in 1973, Jonathan was overthrown in a military coup in 1986, and another military coup in 1990 forced King Moshoeshoe II into exile, his son then ruling as Letsie III. Military rule ended with multiparty elections in 1993, although serious civil unrest followed the ousting of the military rulers; democratic rule was restored in 1994 and King Moshoeshoe II was reinstated in 1995. He died in a car accident in 1996 and King Letsie III returned to the throne.

Lesotho continued to be troubled by civil violence, and the 1998 elections were followed by particularly severe disturbances, which were quelled by an intervention force from neighbouring countries at the government's request. An interim political authority set up to review the constitution introduced a more representative electoral system in time for the 2002 election. In the legislative election in February 2007, the Lesotho Congress for Democracy remained the largest party, with 61 seats, and formed a new government.

POLITICAL SYSTEM

Under the 1993 constitution, subsequently amended, the head of state is a hereditary monarch, with ceremonial but no executive or legislative powers. The bicameral legislature comprises the national assembly, with 120 members elected for a five-year term using a voting system that incorporates a degree of proportional representation, and the senate, consisting of 22 principal chiefs and 11 members nominated by the king. The prime minister is the leader of the majority party in the legislature and appoints the council of ministers.

HEAD OF STATE

HM The King of Lesotho, King Letsie III, *acceded* February 1996, *crowned* 31 October 1997

SELECTED GOVERNMENT MEMBERS *as at June 2007*

Prime Minister; Defence, Bethuel Pakalitha Mosisili
Deputy Prime Minister; Home Affairs, Archibald Lesao Lehohla

Finance, Timothy Thahane
Foreign Affairs, Mohlabi Tsekoa

HIGH COMMISSION OF THE KINGDOM OF LESOTHO
7 Chesham Place, London SW1X 8HN
T 020-7235 5686 W www.lesotholondon.org.uk
High Commissioner, HE HRH Prince Seeiso Bereng Seeiso, *apptd* 2005

BRITISH HIGH COMMISSION
High Commissioner, HE Paul Boateng, *apptd* 2005, resident at Pretoria (Tshwane), South Africa

ECONOMY AND TRADE

The country is one of the poorest in the world, with 49 per cent of the population living below the poverty line, and the situation worsened with three years of drought in 2001–4; in 2004 the prime minister requested international food aid. With few natural resources apart from water, the main sources of government revenue are customs dues from the South African customs union and, since 1998, the export of water and electricity to South Africa from the hydroelectric facilities created by the Lesotho Highlands Water Project. A traditional source of revenue, remittances from miners employed in South Africa (35 per cent of the male workforce), is declining as the mines become exhausted. This decline is partially compensated for by the development of a small manufacturing base processing agricultural products, producing textiles and assembling garments, and the development of tourism, especially in the highlands. Even so, nearly half of the population is unemployed.

The economy has always been dependent on subsistance agriculture, which engages 86 per cent of the population, although productivity has declined in recent years because of drought, erosion and the loss of labour as farmers succumb to AIDS; over a quarter of the adult population is infected with HIV or AIDS. The main market for exports is the USA (84 per cent); imports come mainly from Hong Kong, China and Taiwan. Principal exports are clothing, footwear, road vehicles, wool and mohair, food and livestock. The main imports are food, construction materials, vehicles, machinery, medicines and petroleum products.

GNI – US$1,700m; US$950 per capita (2005)
ANNUAL AVERAGE GROWTH OF GDP – 1.2 per cent (2005 est)
INFLATION RATE – 4.7 per cent (2005 est)
UNEMPLOYMENT – 45 per cent (2002 est)
TOTAL EXTERNAL DEBT – US$735m (2002)
IMPORTS – US$1,410m (2005)
EXPORTS – US$680m (2005)

BALANCE OF PAYMENTS
Trade – US$595m deficit (2004)
Current Account – US$76m deficit (2004)

Trade with UK	*2005*	*2006*
Imports from UK	£511,000	£1,303,000
Exports to UK	£304,000	£363,000

COMMUNICATIONS

Most travel is by foot or by air, as there is little transport infrastructure other than to link the main towns to each other and to South Africa, and to access the highland hydroelectric facilities. Of the 5,940km of roads, 1,087km are surfaced. There are 28 airports and airfields; the international airport is at Maseru.

The telephone system is rudimentary but expanding. Mobile phone distribution is growing rapidly. In 2005, there were 48,000 main lines in use, 245,100 mobile phone subscribers and 43,000 internet users.

EDUCATION AND HEALTH

LITERACY RATE – 81.4 per cent (2004 est)
GROSS ENROLMENT RATIO (percentage of relevant age group) – primary 132 per cent; secondary 39 per cent; tertiary 3 per cent (2005 est)
HEALTH EXPENDITURE (per capita) – US$49 (2004)

MEDIA

Lesotho has a mixture of state-run and private media. Radio is the most important medium and reforms in 1998 prompted the growth of a number of commercial stations. State-run Radio Lesotho is the only national station. South African broadcasts can also be received. The press publishes a range of weekly papers in both Sesotho and English.

LIBERIA

Republic of Liberia

AREA – 111,370 sq. km. Neighbours: Guinea (north), Côte d'Ivoire (east), Sierra Leone (north-west)
CAPITAL – Monrovia; population, 572,000 (2003 est)
MAJOR TOWN – Buchanan (Grand Bassa)
CURRENCY – Liberian dollar (L $) of 100 cents
POPULATION – 3,042,004 rising at 4.91 per cent per year (2006 est); indigenous African (95 per cent), Americo-Liberians (descendents of free immigrants from the US) (2.5 per cent), Congo People (descendents of free immigrants from the Caribbean) (2.5 per cent) (est)
RELIGION – Indigenous religions (40 per cent), Christianity (40 per cent), Islam (20 per cent) (est)
LANGUAGE – English (official)
POPULATION DENSITY – 34 per sq. km (2005)
URBAN POPULATION – 47.9 per cent (2005 est)
MEDIAN AGE (years) – 18.1 (2006 est)
NATIONAL ANTHEM – 'All Hail, Liberia, Hail!'
NATIONAL DAY – 26 July (Independence Day)
LIFE EXPECTANCY (years) – 39.65 (2006 est)
MORTALITY RATE – 23.1 (2006 est)
BIRTH RATE – 44.77 (2006 est)
INFANT MORTALITY RATE – 155.76 (2006 est)
HIV/AIDS ADULT PREVALENCE – 5.9 per cent (2003 est)
DEATH PENALTY – No (abolished 2005)
MILITARY PERSONNEL – 2,400
LITERACY RATE – 55.9 per cent (2004 est)
HEALTH EXPENDITURE (per capita) – US$9 (2004)

CLIMATE AND TERRAIN

Liberia lies on the west African coast, just north of the equator. There are forested highlands in the interior and swampy plains on the coast, where several rivers enter the ocean. Elevation extremes range from 1,380m (Mt Wuteve) at the highest point to 0m (Atlantic Ocean) at the lowest. The climate is tropical and average annual temperature is consistently around 28°C.

HISTORY AND POLITICS

The land was purchased by the American Colonisation Society in 1821 and turned into a settlement for liberated black slaves from the USA, gaining recognition as an independent state in 1847; it is the only west African country never to be colonised.

Much of the first century of statehood was dominated by the True Whig Party, but political stability ended in 1980 when a coup installed a military government under Samuel Doe. When civilian rule was restored in 1985, Doe became president, but his regime's arbitrary, corrupt rule and an economic collapse led to a revolt in 1990 by the National Patriotic Forces of Liberia (NPFL), led by Charles Taylor, and the Armed Forces of Liberia (AFL). Liberia swiftly descended into a civil war that lasted, despite various peace initiatives and ceasefires, until 2003. Around 250,000 people were killed and thousands were displaced. Following mediation by a number of African and European countries, all factions in the conflict signed a peace agreement in 2003 and a UN peacekeeping force was deployed. The disarming of militias was completed in late 2004 but the situation remains volatile.

A transitional government was implemented until presidential and legislative elections were held at the end of 2005. In the legislative election, the Congress for Democratic Change (CDC) won the most seats but without an overall majority. The CDC leader Ellen Johnson-Sirleaf was elected president in the second round of voting and took office in January 2006, nominating a new government. In the same year, a commission was set up to investigate human rights abuses between 1979 and 2003.

POLITICAL SYSTEM
Under the 1986 constitution, the head of state is an executive president who is directly elected for a six-year term, renewable only once. There is a bicameral legislature: the national assembly, consisting of a lower chamber, the house of representatives, with 64 members directly elected for a six-year term, and a senate, with 30 members (two from each of the 15 counties) normally elected for a nine-year term, although half of this reconvened senate will serve for only six years. The president appoints the cabinet, which must be approved by the national assembly.

HEAD OF STATE
President, Ellen Johnson-Sirleaf, *elected* 8 November 2005, *sworn in* 16 January 2006
Vice-President, Joseph N. Boakai

SELECTED GOVERNMENT MEMBERS, *as at June 2007*
Defence, Brownie J. Samukai
Finance, Antoinette M. Sayeh
Foreign Affairs, George Wallace
Internal Affairs, Ambullai B. Johnson

EMBASSY OF THE REPUBLIC OF LIBERIA
23 Fitzroy Square, London W1T 6EW
T 020-7388 5489 W www.embassyofliberia.org.uk
Ambassador Extraordinary and Plenipotentiary, vacant

BRITISH AMBASSADOR
HE John Mitchiner, *apptd* 2003, resident at Freetown, Sierra Leone

ECONOMY AND TRADE

The civil war devastated an economy already weakened by government mismanagement and corruption, and drove those with expertise and capital into exile. In response, over US$500m (£250m) of foreign aid has been pledged to finance reconstruction, conditional on the adoption of anti-corruption measures, and economic activity has revived since the war ended. UN sanctions on timber and diamond exports, used by civil war factions as a source of finance, were lifted in 2006 and 2007 respectively, opening up new sources of revenue.

Natural resources include iron ore, timber, gold, diamonds and hydroelectric power potential, and Liberia benefits from reliable water resources and a climate suited to agriculture. Agriculture is the main economic activity, engaging 70 per cent of the workforce and generating 77 per cent of GDP. Industry centres on the processing of rubber and palm oil, forestry and diamond mining.

The main export markets are EU countries, the USA, Malaysia and Thailand, while imports come mainly from South Korea, Japan, Singapore and Croatia. Principal exports are rubber, timber, iron, diamonds, cocoa and coffee. The main imports are fuels, chemicals, machinery, transport equipment, manufactured goods and foodstuffs.

GNI – US$400m; US$130 per capita (2005)
ANNUAL AVERAGE GROWTH OF GDP – 9.8 per cent (2005 est)
INFLATION RATE – 15 per cent (2003 est)
UNEMPLOYMENT – 85 per cent (2003 est)
TOTAL EXTERNAL DEBT – US$3,200m (2005 est)

Trade with UK	*2005*	*2006*
Imports from UK	£11,355,000	£11,920,000
Exports to UK	£2,859,000	£9,882,000

COMMUNICATIONS

The main seaports are Monrovia and Buchanan, and there is a merchant fleet of 1,687 ships of over 1,000 tonnes, as well as 1,611 foreign-owned ships registered in Liberia. There are 10,600km of roads, of which only 657km are surfaced, and 490km of railway track, although little of this is operational due to war damage. There are 53 airports and airfields; the international airports, Robertsfield and Spriggs Payne, are at Monrovia.

Telephone services are limited and confined mostly to Monrovia. Mobile phone distribution is low, at 160,000 subscribers in 2005.

MEDIA

Liberia has no television service so radio is the main medium for news. The state-run broadcaster runs one station but does not provide national coverage. Many private radio stations were shut down under President Taylor's regime, but there is now a growing number of community radio stations, often supported by international agencies.

LIBYA

Al-Jumahiriyah al-Arabiya al-Libiyah ash Shabiyah al-Ishtirakiyah al-Uzma – Great Socialist People's Libyan Arab Jamahiriya

AREA – 1,759,500 sq. km. Neighbours: Egypt and Sudan (east), Chad and Niger (south), Algeria and Tunisia (west)
CAPITAL – Tripoli (Tarabulus); population, 1,150,000 (2003 est)
MAJOR CITIES – Benghazi; Misratah;
CURRENCY – Libyan dinar (LD) of 1,000 dirhams
POPULATION – 5,900,754 rising at 2.3 per cent per year (2006 est); the people are principally Arab, with

some Berbers in the west and some Tuareg tribesmen in the Fezzan
RELIGION – Islam (97 per cent), Christianity (2 per cent) (est)
LANGUAGE – Arabic (official), Italian, English
POPULATION DENSITY – 3 per sq. km (2005)
URBAN POPULATION – 86.9 per cent (2005 est)
MEDIAN AGE (years) – 23 (2006 est)
NATIONAL ANTHEM – 'Allahu Akbar' ['God is Great']
NATIONAL DAY – 1 September (Revolution Day)
LIFE EXPECTANCY (years) – 76.69 (2006 est)
MORTALITY RATE – 3.48 (2006 est)
BIRTH RATE – 26.49 (2006 est)
INFANT MORTALITY RATE – 23.71 (2006 est)
HIV/AIDS ADULT PREVALENCE – 0.2 per cent (2001 est)
DEATH PENALTY – Yes
CPI SCORE – 2.7 (2006)

CLIMATE AND TERRAIN

Plains in the north rise to plateaus and depressions in the centre and south, with some hills on the north-west and north-east coasts and in the far south. The terrain is arid, and much of it is desert. Elevation extremes range from 2,267m (Bikku Bitti) at the highest point to −47m (Sabkhat Guzayyil) at the lowest. The climate is Mediterranean on the coast and hot and dry in the interior. Average temperatures in Tripoli range from 13°C in January to 31°C in August.

HISTORY AND POLITICS

Libya comprises the three ancient regions of Tripolitania, Cyrenaica and Phazzania (Fezzan). Tripolitania was settled by the Phoenicians in the seventh century BC and then became the eastern part of the kingdom of Carthage. Cyrenaica was colonised by the Greeks in the fourth century BC. All three regions became provinces of the Roman Empire in the first century BC, and subsequently were under the control of the Byzantine Empire until conquered by the Arabs in the seventh century AD, when Islam was introduced. Libya was part of the Turkish Ottoman Empire from the mid-16th century until 1911, when the country was conquered and colonised by Italy. Libya suffered heavy fighting in the Second World War, and then came under British and French control until 24 December 1951, when it achieved independence as the Kingdom of Libya through a UN resolution.

The discovery of oil in 1959 made the country wealthy but created social problems. In 1969 the king was deposed in a military coup led by Col. Muammar al-Gaddafi and a Revolutionary Command Council was installed that proclaimed the country a republic. Economic activity, including the oil industry, was nationalised in the 1970s, but a degree of liberalisation was introduced in the late 1980s.

FOREIGN RELATIONS

After the 1969 revolution, Col. Gaddafi developed a brand of Islamic socialism and sought to promote pan-Arab unity and Islam abroad. This led Libya to support militant and revolutionary groups and to become involved in international terrorism. Relationships with Western governments became increasingly strained, bringing US military reprisals for terrorist activities in the 1980s and UN sanctions from 1992 after Libya refused to extradite the two men suspected of the the 1988 bombing of a Pan Am aircraft over Lockerbie, Scotland. Sanctions were suspended in 1999 after the suspects were handed over for trial, and were lifted in 2003 after Libya admitted responsibility for the bombing and paid compensation.

Since 2003, Col. Gaddafi has made further moves to end Libya's isolation and normalise relations with the West, such as abandoning its development of weapons of mass destruction and a promise in 2004 to allow UN nuclear weapons inspections.

POLITICAL SYSTEM

Under the 1977 constitution, the head of state is the 'Leader of the Revolution', Col. Muammar al-Gaddafi. The legislature is the General People's Congress, which has 750 members appointed by local basic and municipal people's congresses for a three-year term, together with representatives from unions and other organisations. The General People's Congress is the highest policy-making body in the country. It appoints the General People's Committee, which exercises executive power; the secretary-general of the General People's Committee is in effect the prime minister. The General People's Congress also has its own administrative secretariat. The Arab Socialist Union is the only legal political party.

HEAD OF STATE
Leader of the Revolution, Col. Muammar al-Gaddafi

SELECTED GOVERNMENT MEMBERS *as at June 2007*
Secretary-General of the People's Congress, Zanati Mohammad al-Zanati
Secretary-General of the General People's Committee; Prime Minister, Al-Baghdadi Ali al-Mahmudi
Secretary, Economy and Trade, Ali Abd-al-Aziz al-Isawi
Secretary, Finance, Muhammad al-Huwayj
Secretary, Foreign Liaison and International Cooperation, Abdel Rahman Muhammad Shalqam

LIBYAN PEOPLE'S BUREAU
15 Knightsbridge, London SW1X 7LY
T 020-7201 8280
Ambassador Extraordinary and Plenipotentiary, vacant

BRITISH EMBASSY
PO Box 4206, Sharia Uahran 1, Tripoli
T (+218) (21) 340 3644
Ambassador Extraordinary and Plenipotentiary, HE Sir Vincent Fean, *apptd* 2006

BRITISH COUNCIL
PO Box 6797, Casablanca Street, Siyahia, Tripoli
T (+218) (21) 483 2541 W www.britishcouncil.org/libya
Director, Carl Reuter

DEFENCE

The army has around 2,025 main battle tanks, over 1,000 armoured infantry fighting vehicles and 945 armoured personnel carriers. The navy has 2 submarines, 2 frigates, 14 patrol and coastal vessels, and 7 armed helicopters at 4 major bases. The air force has 374 combat aircraft and 60 armed helicopters.
MILITARY EXPENDITURE – US$793m (2006)
MILITARY PERSONNEL – 76,000: army 45,000, navy 8,000, air force 23,000
CONSCRIPTION DURATION – 1 to 2 years (selective)

ECONOMY AND TRADE

Normalisation of relations with the West has stimulated economic liberalisation and a slow transition towards a more market-orientated economy; some subsidies have been reduced and some privatisation is planned. Libya has also attracted more foreign direct investment, mainly in the energy sector, since UN sanctions ended. The substantial revenues from the energy sector mean that the budget and trade are in surplus, but unemployment is high and the country is in receipt of foreign aid.

The oil industry, which is state-controlled, dominates the economy, accounting for 95 per cent of total exports and about 25 per cent of GDP; as the population is small, this gives the country a relatively high per capita GDP. Oil and natural gas reserves are considerable and relatively undeveloped, and Libya licensed further exploration in 2005 in an auction open to foreign companies. Attempts to diversify the economy away from such heavy reliance on oil have led to expansion of the manufacturing and construction sectors, which account for 20 per cent of GDP, to include the production of petrochemicals, iron, steel and aluminium as well as food processing. Owing to the terrain and climate, agriculture is a small sector, contributing only 7.3 per cent of GDP, and Libya imports about 75 per cent of its food.

The main trading partners are Italy, Germany and other EU countries, Turkey and Tunisia. Prinicipal exports are crude oil, refined petroleum products, natural gas and chemicals. The main imports are machinery, semi-finished goods, food, transport equipment and consumer products.

GNI – US$32,400m; US$5,530 per capita (2005)
ANNUAL AVERAGE GROWTH OF GDP – 8.4 per cent (2005 est)
INFLATION RATE – 3.4 per cent (2005 est)
UNEMPLOYMENT – 30 per cent (2004 est)
TOTAL EXTERNAL DEBT – US$4,267m (2005 est)
IMPORTS – US$7,200m (2005)
EXPORTS – US$30,000m (2005)

BALANCE OF PAYMENTS
Trade – US$8,657m surplus (2004)
Current Account – US$3,705m surplus (2004)

Trade with UK	*2005*	*2006*
Imports from UK	£210,643,000	£203,493,000
Exports to UK	£355,903,000	£592,042,000

COMMUNICATIONS

There are about 83,200km of roads; the coastal road running from the Tunisian frontier through Tripoli, Benghazi and Tubruq to the Egyptian border, serves the main population centres. Main roads also link the provincial centres, and the oil-producing areas of the south with the coastal towns. Libya has had no railway services since 1965, but seven lines with a total of 2,757km of track are undergoing work with a view to resuming services from 2008. There are 141 airports and airfields; the principal airports are at Tripoli, Benghazi and Sebha. The main seaports are Benghazi, Tripoli, Misurata and Tobruq.

The telephone system is being modernised. Mobile phone distribution is low, at 234,800 subscribers in 2004, compared to 750,000 main fixed lines. There were 205,000 internet users in 2005.

EDUCATION AND HEALTH

There are nine years of compulsory education. The education system allows for six years each at primary and secondary level.

LITERACY RATE – 81.7 per cent (2004 est)
GROSS ENROLMENT RATIO (percentage of relevant age group) – primary 107 per cent; secondary 104 per cent; tertiary 56 per cent (2005 est)
HEALTH EXPENDITURE (per capita) – US$195 (2004)
HOSPITAL BEDS (per 1,000 people) – 3.9 (2000–5)

MEDIA

The state maintains strict control over the media. Great Jamahiriya TV is the state-run television broadcaster. Pan-Arab satellite television stations are available and internet access is free from disruption. Some international publications are available, but are routinely censored by the authorities.

LIECHTENSTEIN

Fürstentum Liechtenstein – Principality of Liechtenstein

AREA – 160 sq. km. Neighbours: Austria, Switzerland
CAPITAL – Vaduz; population, 5,050 (2006 est)
CURRENCY – Swiss franc of 100 rappen (or centimes)
POPULATION – 33,987 rising at 0.78 per cent per year (2006 est)
RELIGION – Roman Catholicism (78 per cent), Protestantism (7 per cent), Islam (4 per cent) (est)
LANGUAGE – German (official)
POPULATION DENSITY – 217 per sq. km (2005)
MEDIAN AGE (years) – 39.6 (2006 est)
NATIONAL ANTHEM – 'Oben am Jungen Rhein' ['Up on the Young Rhine']
NATIONAL DAY – 15 August (Assumption Day)
LIFE EXPECTANCY (years) – 79.68 (2006 est)
MORTALITY RATE – 7.18 (2006 est)
BIRTH RATE – 10.21 (2006 est)
INFANT MORTALITY RATE – 4.64 (2006 est)
DEATH PENALTY – No (abolished 1987)

CLIMATE AND TERRAIN

Liechtenstein is a small landlocked principality in the Alps, with part of the Rhine river valley running through the west of the country. Elevation extremes range from 2,599m (Garauspitz) at the highest point to 430m (Ruggeller Riet) at the lowest. There is heavy snowfall in winter and average temperatures range from 0°C in January to 21°C in July.

HISTORY AND POLITICS

Although there was a sovereign state within the present boundaries from the 14th century, the present state of Liechtenstein was formed from the lordships of Schellenberg and Vaduz in 1719. Part of the Holy Roman Empire, the principality became a member of the Confederation of the Rhine that succeeded the Empire in 1806, and then of the German Confederation from 1815 until 1866. It was the only German principality to remain outside the German Empire when it was formed in 1871. The country abolished its armed forces and declared permanent neutrality in 1868. The country's neutrality was not violated in either of the World Wars.

Economic decline in the years following the First World War led Liechtenstein to adopt the Swiss currency in 1921 and to enter into a Swiss customs union in 1923. The country became extremely prosperous as an international finance centre after the Second World War. However, it has faced criticism in recent years about the laxness of its financial regulation, and in 2000 tightened its laws to prevent money laundering. Nevertheless, it was threatened with sanctions by the OECD in 2002 for failing to meet international financial transparency and information exchange standards

Governments in the 20th century have been formed by the two main parties, each dominating at different periods: the northern-based Progressive Citizens' Party (FBP) from 1938 to 1970, and the southern-based Patriotic Union (VU) from 1970 to 2001, except for 1974–8. In the 2001 legislative election, the FBP returned to power for the first time since 1978, but although it remained the largest party after the 2005 election, it did not have an overall majority and formed a coalition government with the VU. However, the government's power is limited by the role and power of the monarchy, which has resisted attempts at reform. Prince Hans Adam II threatened to step down as head of state when the government suggested a reduction in his powers in 1995, and a referendum in 2003 approved constitutional changes that give the monarchy greater powers over the government and judiciary. Prince Hans Adam remains head of state but in 2004 he handed over day-to-day responsibility for running the principality to his son and heir, Prince Alois.

POLITICAL SYSTEM

Under the 1921 constitution, Liechtenstein is a constitutional monarchy, with the hereditary prince as head of state. Constitutional reforms approved in 2003 increase the prince's powers over the government and the judiciary, giving him the authority to dismiss the government and to appoint judges. The unicameral legislature, the *Landtag*, has 25 members directly elected for a four-year term. There is a threshold of 8 per cent for parties to gain representation. The cabinet is appointed by the prince on the advice of the *Landtag* and consists of the head of government and four ministers.

HEAD OF STATE

HSH The Prince of Liechtenstein, Hans Adam II, *born* 14 February 1945; *succeeded* 13 November 1989

Heir, HSH Prince Alois, *born* 11 June 1968

SELECTED GOVERNMENT MEMBERS *as at June 2007*

Head of Government, Finance, Otmar Hasler

Deputy Head of Government, Economy, Klaus Tschütscher

Foreign Affairs, Rita Kieber-Beck

Home Affairs, Martin Meyer

Education, Hugo Quaderer

BRITISH AMBASSADOR

HE Simon Featherstone, resident at Bern, Switzerland

ECONOMY AND TRADE

Liechtenstein has a prosperous, highly industrialised and diversified economy. Its mainstay is the financial services sector, which, with other service industries such as tourism, employs over half of the workforce. A light industrial base produces electronics, metal manufactures, dental products, ceramics, pharmaceuticals, food products, precision instruments and optical instruments, and employs 47 per cent of the workforce. Almost half the workforce commutes daily from Austria, Switzerland and Germany.

Liechtenstein became a member of the European Free Trade Association in 1991, and joined the European Economic Area in 1995. Most of its trade is with EU countries and Switzerland. The principal exports are its industrial products. The main imports are agricultural products, industrial raw materials, energy, machinery, metal goods, textiles, foodstuffs and vehicles.

INFLATION RATE – 1 per cent (2001)

UNEMPLOYMENT – 1.3 per cent (2002)

Trade with UK	*2005*	*2006*
Imports from UK	£3,776,000	£23,322,000
Exports to UK	£13,690,000	£39,076,000

COMMUNICATIONS

Liechtenstein has no airports and only 380km of highways, 28km of waterways, and 9km of rail track which is part of the Austrian system and connects Austria and Switzerland. In 2002, there were 19,900 main telephone lines in use, 11,400 mobile phone subscribers and 20,000 internet users. Liechtenstein relies on foreign broadcasters for television. Circulation for its two newspapers, *Liechtenstein News* and *Liechtensteiner Vaterland,* is under 10,000.

LITHUANIA

Lietuvos Respublika – Republic of Lithuania

AREA – 65,200 sq. km. Neighbours: Latvia (north), Belarus (east and south), Poland and the Kaliningrad region of Russia (south-west)

CAPITAL – Vilnius; population, 541,824 (2006 est)

MAJOR CITIES – Kaunas; Klaipeda

CURRENCY – Litas of 100 centas, pegged to the euro

POPULATION – 3,585,906 falling at 0.3 (2006 est); Lithuanian (83.4 per cent per year), Polish (6.7 per cent), Russian (6.3 per cent)

RELIGION – Roman Catholicism (79 per cent), Orthodox Christianity (4 per cent) (est)

LANGUAGE – Lithuanian (official), Russian, Polish

POPULATION DENSITY – 54 per sq. km (2005)

URBAN POPULATION – 66.6 per cent (2005 est)

MEDIAN AGE (years) – 38.2 (2006 est)

NATIONAL ANTHEM – 'Tautiska Giesme' ['The National Song']

NATIONAL DAY – 16 February (Independence Day)

LIFE EXPECTANCY (years) – 74.2 (2006 est)

MORTALITY RATE – 10.98 (2006 est)

BIRTH RATE – 8.75 (2006 est)

INFANT MORTALITY RATE – 6.78 (2006 est)

DEATH PENALTY – No (abolished 1998)

CPI SCORE – 4.8 (2006)

CLIMATE AND TERRAIN

Lithuania is a low-lying country with low hills in the west and south-east. It contains over 2,800 lakes, many of which lie in the east of the country. Elevation extremes range from 293m (Kalnas) at the highest point to 0m (Baltic Sea) at the lowest. The climate is mainly continental and average temperatures range from −3°C in January to 17°C in July.

HISTORY AND POLITICS

Lithuania became a nation in the late 12th century. It remained pagan for far longer than any other European country and only became fully Christian in the 15th century, when the Samogitians and the Aukstaitiai, the two main ethnic groups in the region, were converted. In the 14th century, a strong grand duchy was formed that stretched from the Baltic to the Black Sea and eastwards almost to Moscow. It confederated with Poland in the 16th century, before coming under Russian rule in 1795. The country joined Poland in rebelling against Russian domination twice in the 19th century.

Occupied by Germany during the First World War, Lithuania declared its independence in 1918 and successfully defended its autonomy against the Bolsheviks in 1918–19. However, the province and city of Vilnius were occupied by the newly independent Poland from 1920 until 1939. The USSR invaded and annexed Lithuania in 1940, but the country revolted in 1941 and briefly established its own government before being invaded and occupied by the Germans in their 1941 offensive against the USSR. Around 210,000 Lithuanians, mainly Jews, were killed during the German occupation. Soviet troops ousted the Germans in 1944 and re-established Soviet control, against which Lithuanians carried on a guerrilla war until 1952.

Growing nationalist sentiment led to the formation of the pro-democracy *Sajudis* ('The Movement') in 1988 to campaign for greater autonomy. A unilateral declaration of independence in 1990 was blocked by the USSR but following the failed August coup in Moscow in 1991, Lithuania declared its independence a second time, and this was internationally recognised. The last Russian troops left the country in 1993. Lithuania joined the EU and ratified its constitution in 2004.

Rolandas Paksas was elected president in 2003 but was impeached and dismissed the following year. He was succeeded by Valdus Adamkus (previously president 1998–2003), elected in June 2004. In the October 2004 legislative elections, the Labour Party became the largest party but without a majority, and in November the ruling coalition of the Social Democratic Party (SD) and New Union (Social Liberals) (NS(SL)) was widened to include the Labour Party and the Union of Farmers Democracy Party. This coalition collapsed in 2006 with the withdrawal of the NS(SL) in April and the Labour Party in May, when the government resigned. Gediminas Kirkilas of the SD party formed a coalition government that was approved by the *Seimas* in July. A legislative election is due in autumn 2007.

POLITICAL SYSTEM

Under the 1992 constitution, the head of state is a president, who is directly elected for a five-year term, renewable only once. The unicameral parliament, the *Seimas*, has 141 members who are directly elected for a four-year term; 71 members are elected in first past the post constituencies and 70 by proportional representation, with a 5 per cent threshold for representation. Executive authority is vested in the prime minister, who is appointed by the president with the approval of the *Seimas*, and ministers, who are appointed upon the recommendation of the prime minister.

HEAD OF STATE

President, Valdas Adamkus, *sworn in* 12 July 2004

SELECTED GOVERNMENT MEMBERS *as at June 2007*

Prime Minister, Gediminas Kirkilas
Defence, Juozas Olekas
Foreign Affairs, Petras Vaitiekunas
Interior, Raimondas Sukys
Economy, Vytas Navickas
Finance, Rimantas Sadzius

EMBASSY OF THE REPUBLIC OF LITHUANIA
84 Gloucester Place, London W1U 6AU
T 020-7486 6401
W http://uk.mfa.lt
Ambassador Extraordinary and Plenipotentiary, HE Vygaudas Usackas, *apptd* 2002

BRITISH EMBASSY
2 Antakalnio, Vilnius 10308
T (+370) (5) 246 2900 W www.britain.lt
Ambassador Extraordinary and Plenipotentiary, HE Colin Roberts, *apptd* 2004

BRITISH COUNCIL
Jogailos 4, LT 01116 Vilnius
T (+370) (5) 264 4890 W www.britishcouncil.org/lithuania
Director, Lina Balenaite

DEFENCE

The army has 137 armoured personnel carriers; the navy has 2 frigates and 3 patrol and coastal vessels based at Klaipeda; the air force has 17 aircraft and 12 helicopters.
MILITARY EXPENDITURE – US$310m (2005)
MILITARY PERSONNEL – 12,010: army 10,100, navy 710, air force 1,200; paramilitaries 14,600
CONSCRIPTION DURATION – 12 months

ECONOMY AND TRADE

Lithuania's transition to a market economy is mostly complete, with over 80 per cent of enterprises now privatised. The transition initially caused a deep recession exacerbated by the 1998 Russian financial crisis, but the economy has recovered and growth has been steady and sustained in the period up to and since Lithuania's accession to the EU, helping to halve unemployment since 2003. However, the inflation rate is high, causing the rejection of its application to join the eurozone from January 2007.

The economy is diverse, industries including amber extraction and jewellery-making, metal-cutting machine tools, electric motors, domestic appliances, oil refining, shipbuilding, furniture-making, textiles, food processing, fertilizers, agricultural machinery, optical equipment, electronic components and computers. Industry contributes 33 per cent to GDP, services 61 per cent and agriculture 6 per cent.

The main trading partners are other EU countries and Russia. Principal exports are mineral products, textiles and clothing, machinery and equipment, chemicals, timber and wood products, and foodstuffs. The main imports are mineral products, machinery, transport equipment, chemicals, textiles and clothing, and metals.
GNI – US$24,600m; US$7,210 per capita (2005)
ANNUAL AVERAGE GROWTH OF GDP – 7.5 per cent (2005 est)
INFLATION RATE – 2.7 per cent (2005)
UNEMPLOYMENT – 8.2 per cent (2005)
TOTAL EXTERNAL DEBT – US$11,700m (2006)
IMPORTS – US$15,000m (2005)
EXPORTS – US$12,000m (2005)

BALANCE OF PAYMENTS
Trade – US$2,843m deficit (2005)
Current Account – US$1,771m deficit (2005)

Trade with UK	*2005*	*2006*
Imports from UK	£163,816,000	£219,000,000
Exports to UK	£249,717,000	£282,500,000

COMMUNICATIONS

There are 79,479km of roads, and a railway system of 1,771km linking the major towns with Vilnius and Klaipeda, the main seaport. The 91 airports and airfields include major airports at Vilnius, Kaunas and Palanga.

The telephone system is being modernised and the mobile phone system is being expanded. In 2005 there were 801,000 main lines in use, 4.4 million mobile phone subscribers and 1.2 million internet users.

EDUCATION AND HEALTH

Education is free of charge and compulsory from seven to 16 years, with the system comprising elementary schools (four years), nine-year schools (five years), and secondary schools (three years). The language of instruction is predominantly Lithuanian, but there are also Russian and Polish schools. Vilnius University, founded in 1579, is one of the oldest universities in eastern Europe.

LITERACY RATE – 99.6 per cent (2004 est)
GROSS ENROLMENT RATIO (percentage of relevant age group) – primary 97 per cent; secondary 102 per cent; tertiary 73 per cent (2005 est)
HEALTH EXPENDITURE (per capita) – US$424 (2004)
HOSPITAL BEDS (per 1,000 people) – 8.7 (2000–5)

MEDIA

The daily newspapers operate independently of the state and are free to criticise the government. A mix of public and private television broadcasters operate; BTV is the largest commercial company while LTV is the publicly run station.

LUXEMBOURG

Groussherzogtom Lëtzebuerg/Grand-Duché de Luxembourg/Großherzogtum Luxembourg – Grand Duchy of Luxembourg

AREA – 2,586 sq. km. Neighbours: Germany (east), Belgium (west and north), France (south)
CAPITAL – Luxembourg; population, 76,420 (2005 est)
CURRENCY – Euro (€) of 100 cents
POPULATION – 474,413 rising at 1.23 per cent per year (2006 est)
RELIGION – Roman Catholicism (91 per cent), Islam (1 per cent) (est)
LANGUAGE – German, French (both official), Luxembourgish
POPULATION DENSITY – 176 per sq. km (2005)
URBAN POPULATION – 92.4 per cent (2005 est)
MEDIAN AGE (years) – 38.7 (2006 est)
NATIONAL ANTHEM – 'Ons Hemecht' ['Our Homeland']
NATIONAL DAY – 23 June
LIFE EXPECTANCY (years) – 78.89 (2006 est)
MORTALITY RATE – 8.41 (2006 est)
BIRTH RATE – 11.94 (2006 est)
INFANT MORTALITY RATE – 4.74 (2006 est)
DEATH PENALTY – No (abolished 1979)
CPI SCORE – 8.6 (2006)
MILITARY EXPENDITURE – US$264m (2005)
MILITARY PERSONNEL – army 900; paramilitaries 612

CLIMATE AND TERRAIN

landlocked principality, Luxembourg has the forested ateau of the Ardennes in the north, forming part of the Natural Germano-Luxembourg Park which extends east into Germany. The south of the country is mainly fertile farmland and in the east is the wine-growing region of the Moselle valley. Elevation extremes range from 559m (Buurgplaatz) at the highest point to 133m (Moselle River) at the lowest. The climate is mild and average temperatures range from 1°C in January to 22°C in July.

HISTORY AND POLITICS

The area was part of the Roman Empire and then became part of the Frankish Empire in the fifth century AD. It became autonomous within the Holy Roman Empire under Siegfried, Count of Ardennes and was given the status of a duchy in 1354. Controlled by a succession of European powers after 1437, when the House of Luxembourg died out, Luxembourg was made a grand duchy after the Napoleonic wars and passed to the Netherlands. Much of Luxembourg joined the Belgians in their revolt against the Netherlands in 1830; in 1838 the western, French-speaking region was assigned to Belgium, and the remainder of the grand duchy was granted autonomy. The treaty of London in 1867 confirmed its independence and neutrality. Occupation by Germany in both world wars prompted Luxembourg to give up its neutrality and it was a founding member of NATO in 1949.

Luxembourg entered into economic union with Belgium in 1921 and joined the Benelux economic union in 1948. It was a founder member of the European Economic Community in 1958 and joined the eurozone in 1999. A referendum in 2005 approved ratification of the EU constitution.

In the 2004 legislative election, the Christian Social Party (CSV) won the largest number of seats but without an overall majority. It formed a new coalition government with the Luxembourg Socialist Workers' Party, the second largest party, under the leadership of Jean-Claude Juncker of the CSV, who has been prime minister since 1995.

POLITICAL SYSTEM

Under the 1868 constitution, the head of state is a hereditary grand duke. There is a unicameral legislature, the chamber of deputies, which has 60 members directly elected for a five-year term. There is also a council of state, which has 21 members nominated by the grand duke; this acts as the supreme administrative tribunal and has some legislative functions. The prime minister is appointed by the grand duke on the basis of the election results and appoints the cabinet.

HEAD OF STATE

HRH The Grand Duke of Luxembourg, HRH Grand Duke Henri, *born* 16 April 1955; *succeeded* 7 October 2000
Heir, HRH Prince Guillaume, *born* 11 November 1981

SELECTED GOVERNMENT MEMBERS *as at June 2007*

Prime Minister, Finance, Jean-Claude Juncker
Deputy Prime Minister, Foreign Affairs, Jean Asselborn
Home Affairs, Jean-Marie Halsdorf

EMBASSY OF LUXEMBOURG

27 Wilton Crescent, London SW1X 8SD
T 020-7235 6961 E londres.amb@mae.etat.lu
Ambassador Extraordinary and Plenipotentiary, HE Jean-Louis Wolzfeld, *apptd* 2002

BRITISH EMBASSY
14 Boulevard Roosevelt, L-2450 Luxembourg
T (+352) 229 864 E britemb@pt.lu
W www.webplaza.pt.lu/public/britemb
Ambassador Extraordinary and Plenipotentiary, HE Peter Bateman, *apptd* 2007

ECONOMY AND TRADE

The economy is stable, with steady growth, low unemployment and low inflation providing an exceptionally high standard of living. Banking and financial services are the dominant sector, contributing 28 per cent of GDP. These have taken over from steel production, which still comprises a quarter of the country's exports, while the industrial sector has also diversified to include IT, telecommunications, freight transport, food processing, chemicals and metal products. Tourism is also important. The small agricultural sector consists mainly of family-owned farms. Services account for 86 per cent of GDP, industry for 13 per cent and agriculture for 1 per cent. Over 50 per cent of the workforce are foreign residents or commute daily from France, Belgium and Germany.

The main trading partners are other EU countries and China. Principal exports are the products of industrial activities. The main imports are minerals, metals, foodstuffs and quality consumer goods.

GNI – US$26,315m; US$58,050 per capita (2005)
ANNUAL AVERAGE GROWTH OF GDP – 4 per cent (2005 est)
INFLATION RATE – 2.5 per cent (2005 est)
UNEMPLOYMENT – 4.5 per cent (2005 est)
IMPORTS – US$17,000m (2005)
EXPORTS – US$13,000m (2005)

BALANCE OF PAYMENTS
Trade – US$4,181m deficit (2005)
Current Account – US$3,560m surplus (2005)

Trade with UK	*2005*	*2006*
Imports from UK	£210,183,000	£1,621,900,000
Exports to UK	£833,265,000	£1,512,400,000

COMMUNICATIONS

Luxembourg has one airport. There are 5,227km of highways (including 147km of motorways), and 274km of railways. The River Moselle provides 37km of navigable waterway. In 2005, there were 244,500 main telephone lines in use, 720,000 mobile phone subscribers and 315,000 internet users.

MEDIA

Despite its size, Luxembourg has significant international media influence. Media group RTL broadcasts to audiences in France, Germany and the UK as well as serving the domestic market. Luxembourg also hosts the Société Européenne des Satellites (SES), which operates the Astra satellite fleet, Europe's largest satellite operation. The two best-selling daily newspapers are *Luxembuger Wort* and *Tageblatt*.

MACEDONIA

Republika Makedonija – Republic of Macedonia

AREA – 25,333 sq. km. Neighbours: Serbia (north), Bulgaria (east), Greece (south), Albania (west)
CAPITAL – Skopje; population, 467,257 (2002)
MAJOR CITIES – Kumanovo; Bitola; Prilep
CURRENCY – Denar of 100 deni
POPULATION – 2,050,554 rising at 0.26 per cent per year (2006 est); Macedonian (64.2 per cent), Albanian (25.2 per cent), Turkish (3.9 per cent), Romani (2.7 per cent), Serb (1.8 per cent)
RELIGION – Macedonian Orthodox Christianity (66 per cent), Islam (30 per cent) (est)
LANGUAGE – Macedonian (official), Albanian, Turkish, Romani, Serbian (each official in different regions)
POPULATION DENSITY – 80 per sq. km (2005)
URBAN POPULATION – 59.7 per cent (2005 est)
MEDIAN AGE (years) – 34.1 (2006 est)
NATIONAL ANTHEM – 'Denes Nad Makedonija' ['Today Over Macedonia']
NATIONAL DAY – 2 August (Uprising Day)
LIFE EXPECTANCY (years) – 73.97 (2006 est)
MORTALITY RATE – 8.77 (2006 est)
BIRTH RATE – 12.02 (2006 est)
INFANT MORTALITY RATE – 9.81 (2006 est)
DEATH PENALTY – No (abolished 1991)
CPI SCORE – 2.7 (2006)
POPULATION BELOW POVERTY LINE – 29.6 per cent (2004 est)
MILITARY BUDGET – US$139m (2006)
MILITARY PERSONNEL – 10,890: army 9,760, air force 1,130; paramilitaries 7,600
CONSCRIPTION DURATION – Six months
GROSS ENROLMENT RATIO (percentage of relevant age group) – primary 98 per cent; secondary 84 per cent; tertiary 28 per cent (2005 est)
LITERACY RATE – 96.1 per cent (2004 est)
HEALTH EXPENDITURE (per capita) – US$212 (2004)

CLIMATE AND TERRAIN

The landlocked country is a mountainous plateau divided by the valleys of the rivers Struma and Vardar. Elevation extremes range from 2,764m (Golem Korab) at the highest point to 50m (Vardar River) at the lowest. Lakes Ohrid and Prespa lie on the south-west border with Albania. The climate is Mediterranean, with average temperatures ranging from 1°C in January to 23°C in July.

HISTORY AND POLITICS

The area of the former Yugoslav republic was part of the ancient kingdom of Macedonia, which also included northern Greece and south-west Bulgaria, in the fourth century BC. Macedonia became a province of the Roman Empire in the second century BC, coming under the control of the Byzantine Empire from the fourth century AD. Slav peoples settled the area in the seventh century and mixed with the Greek, Illyrian, Thracian, Scythian and Turkish peoples. From the ninth to the 14th centuries it was under the rule successively of the Bulgars, Byzantium and Serbs, and became part of the Turkish Ottoman Empire in the late 14th century. Following th Balkan wars of 1912 and 1913 the country wa partitioned between Bulgaria, Serbia and Greece. Th Serbian part was awarded to the newly created state tha became Yugoslavia after the First World War. During th Second World War, this area was occupied by Bulgari from 1941 to 1944, and after liberation became republic within the communist Federal Republic c Yugoslavia.

Nationalist sentiment grew after the death of th Yugoslav leader Josip Tito in 1980, and Macedoni formally seceded from Yugoslavia in 1992. International recognition was initially delayed by Greece's objections to the republic's name (Greece claims that its region of Macedonia is the only one entitled to the name), but the country joined the UN in 1993 as the Former Yugoslav Republic of Macedonia; Greece recognised it under this name and lifted its trade blockade in 1995.

Throughout the 1990s there was tension and sporadic violence between the ethnic Albanians and Macedonians. Instability in neighbouring Kosovo spilled over into Macedonia in 2001, sparking off a two-month uprising by ethnic Albanian separatists aggrieved at their lack of civil rights. Peace talks facilitated by international bodies resulted in the Ohrid framework agreement, giving Albanians greater recognition within Macedonia and making Albanian an official language.

The prime minister Branko Crvenkovski was elected president in 2004 after President Trajkovski died in an air crash. In the 2006 legislative election, the main opposition party, the Internal Macedonian Revolutionary Organisation-Democratic Party for Macedonian National Unity (VMRO–DPMNE), won the most seats but without an overall majority. A five-party, multi-ethnic coalition government was formed with the VMRO–DPMNE leader Nikola Gruevski as prime minister.

POLITICAL SYSTEM

The 1991 constitution was amended in 2001 in accordance with the Ohrid agreement to incorporate provisions relating to ethnic Albanian rights, and in 2004 to give ethnic Albanians greater local autonomy in areas where they predominate. The head of state is a president, who is directly elected for a five-year term. The unicameral assembly, *Sobranie,* has 120 members directly elected for a four-year term. The prime minister is appointed by the president. Government ministers are elected by the assembly but are not members of it.

HEAD OF STATE
President, Branko Crvenkovski, *elected* 28 April 2004, *sworn in* 12 May 2004

SELECTED GOVERNMENT MEMBERS *AS AT JUNE 2007*
Prime Minister, Nikola Gruevski
Deputy Prime Minister, Economic Affairs, Zoran Stavrevski
Foreign Affairs, Antonio Milososki
Interior, Gordana Jankulovska
Finance, Trajko Slavevski

EMBASSY OF THE REPUBLIC OF MACEDONIA
Suites 2.1/2.2, Buckingham Court, 75–83 Buckingham Gate, London SW1E 6PE
T 020-7976 0535 W www.macedonianembassy.org.uk
Ambassador Extraordinary and Plenipotentiary, HE Gjorgji Spasov, *apptd* 2003

BRITISH EMBASSY
Dimitrija Chupovski 4/26, Skopje 1000
T (+389) (2) 329 9299 E britishembassyskopje@fco.gov.uk
W www.britishembassy.org.mk
Ambassador Extraordinary and Plenipotentiary, HE Andrew Key, *apptd* 2007

BRITISH COUNCIL
PO Box 562, Bulevar Goce Delcev 6, 1000 Skopje
T (+389) (2) 313 5035 W www.britishcouncil.org/macedonia
Director, Frank Fitzpatrick

ECONOMY AND TRADE

Macedonia was the least developed republic in the former Yugoslavia before 1991 and progress towards a market economy was hindered by the trade embargo by Greece (1993–5) and the 2001 ethnic Albanian uprising. Although economic growth has recovered and is steady, the number of jobs has not risen and an estimated 36 per cent of the workforce is unemployed, although the grey economy is estimated to be more than 20 per cent of GDP. The country remains poor, with 30 per cent of the population living below the poverty line. Crime and corruption are other factors deterring foreign investment.

In 2006, 62 per cent of GDP was produced by the service industries, 29 per cent by industry and 9 per cent by agriculture. The main crops are grapes, tobacco, vegetables and dairy products. Food processing and wine-making are major industries, along with textiles, chemicals, iron, steel, cement, energy and pharmaceuticals. The main trading partners are Montenegro, Germany, Greece, Italy, Russia, Serbia and other Balkan states. Principal exports are food, wine, tobacco, textiles, manufactured goods, iron and steel. The main imports are machinery and equipment, cars, chemicals, fuels and foodstuffs.

GNI – US$5,800m; US$2,830 per capita (2005)
ANNUAL AVERAGE GROWTH OF GDP – 4 per cent (2005 est)
INFLATION RATE – 0 per cent (2005 est)
TOTAL EXTERNAL DEBT – US$2,190m (2005 est)
UNEMPLOYMENT – 37.3 per cent (2005 est)
IMPORTS – US$3,200m (2005)
EXPORTS – US$2,000m (2005)

BALANCE OF PAYMENTS
Trade – US$1,112m deficit (2004)
Current Account – US$415m deficit (2004)

Trade with UK	*2005*	*2006*
Imports from UK	£20,177,000	£17,610,000
Exports to UK	£24,825,000	£25,538,000

COMMUNICATIONS

Macedonia has 8,684km of roads, of which 5,500km are surfaced. There are 699km of railways, of which 233km are electrified. A 53km railway line from Beljakovci to the Bulgarian border was scheduled for completion in 2005 but is still under construction. The principal airports are at Skopje and Ohrid, and there are a further 15 airports and airfields around the country.

In 2005, there were 533,200 main telephone lines in use, 1.3 million mobile phone subscribers and 393,000 internet users.

MEDIA

The three channels of the state-run television broadcaster compete with a growing number of commercial stations. Broadcasters are loosely regulated and many are unlicensed. There are 11 major daily and weekly press publications, reflecting a range of views. Partially government-owned *Nova Makedonija* is the leading newspaper.

MADAGASCAR

Repoblikan'i Madagasikara/République de Madagascar – Republic of Madagascar

AREA – 587,040 sq. km.
CAPITAL – Antananarivo; population, 1,403,449 (2001 est)
MAJOR CITIES – Toamasina, the chief port; Antsirabe; Fianarantsoa; Mahajanga
CURRENCY – Ariary (MGA) of five iraimbilanja
POPULATION – 18,595,469 rising at 3.03 per cent per year (2006 est); the people are of mixed Malayo-Polynesian, Arab and African origin. There are sizeable French, Chinese and Indian communities
RELIGION – Christianity (50 per cent), Islam (9 per cent) (est)
LANGUAGE – English, French, Malagasy (all official)
POPULATION DENSITY– 32 per sq. km (2005)
URBAN POPULATION – 27 per cent (2005 est)
MEDIAN AGE (years) – 17.5 (2006 est)
NATIONAL ANTHEM – 'Ry Tanindraza nay Malala o' ['Oh, Our Beloved Country']
NATIONAL DAY – 26 June (Independence Day)
LIFE EXPECTANCY (years) – 57.34 (2006 est)
MORTALITY RATE – 11.11 (2006 est)
BIRTH RATE – 41.41 (2006 est)
INFANT MORTALITY RATE – 75.21 (2006 est)
HIV/AIDS ADULT PREVALENCE – 1.7 per cent (2003 est)
DEATH PENALTY – No*
CPI SCORE – 3.1 (2006)
POPULATION BELOW POVERTY LINE – 50 per cent (2004 est)
MILITARY BUDGET – US$300m (2006)
MILITARY PERSONNEL – 13,500: army 12,500, navy 500, air force 500; paramilitaries 8,100
CONSCRIPTION DURATION – 18 months

CLIMATE AND TERRAIN

Madagascar, the fourth-largest island in the world, lies 386km off the south-east coast of Africa, from which it is separated by the Mozambique Channel. Coastal plains rise to central highlands indented with river valleys. The terrain is arid in the south. Elevation extremes range from 2,876m (Maromokotro) at the highest point to 0m (Indian Ocean) at the lowest. Because of its isolation, most mammals and plants and half of its bird species are unique to the island. The climate is tropical along the coastline and temperate in the highlands. Average temperatures range from 9°C in July to 29°C in January. Madagascar is subject to tropical cyclones, which cause torrential rain and flooding.

HISTORY AND POLITICS

The island was settled by Indonesians from the first century AD and by African traders from the eighth century. Although first visited by Europeans *c.*1500, local kingdoms ruled until 1885, when the island became a French protectorate; it became a colony in 1895 after the last indigenous resistance was defeated. During the Second World War, the British invaded to replace the pro-Vichy government with a Free French government. At the end of the war Madagascar was returned to France, which suppressed a nationalist uprising in 1947–8. Nationalist agitation continued throughout the 1950s and resulted in independence in 1960.

The military took control in 1972 following civil disturbances, and in 1975 martial law was imposed after a coup. A Marxist one-party state was created with Lt-Com. Didier Ratsiraka as president. Marxism was abandoned in 1980 and – following pro-democracy agitation throughout the 1980s and early 1990s – other political parties were legalised in 1990 and a new constitution, adopted in 1992, made Madagascar a parliamentary democracy.

Didier Ratsiraka was defeated in the 1993 presidential elections but returned to office in 1997 after winning the 1996 election. He refused to accept the result of the 2001 presidential election and the six-month struggle between his supporters and those of Marc Ravalomanana, the successful candidate, brought the country close to civil war until, in July 2002, Ratsiraka went into exile and his supporters surrendered.

In the first senate elections in 2001 the majority of seats were won by the I Love Madagascar party (TIM), which supports President Ravalomanana. TIM also won the majority of seats in the 2002 election to the national assembly. President Ravalomanana won the presidential election in December 2006 and appointed a new government the following month. The next elections to the national assembly were due in September 2007.

POLITICAL SYSTEM

The 1992 constitution was amended in 1998 to create an upper chamber in the legislature, increase the powers of the presidency and increase the autonomy of the six provinces; amendments approved in a 2007 referendum further increased the powers of the president. The president is directly elected and serves a five-year term. The legislature is bicameral, comprising the national assembly, which has 127 members (reduced from 160 in July 2007) directly elected for a five-year term, and the senate, which has 90 members, of whom two-thirds are elected by an electoral college and one-third are nominated by the president; they serve a six-year term. The prime minister is appointed by the president, and appoints the ministers.

HEAD OF STATE

President, Marc Ravalomanana, *elected* 29 April 2002, *sworn in* 6 May 2002, *accepted* 5 July 2002

SELECTED GOVERNMENT MEMBERS *as at June 2007*
Prime Minister, Gen. Charles Rabemananjara
Defence, Maj.-Gen. Petera Behajaina
Foreign Affairs, Gen. Marcel Ranjeva
Economy, Harison Edmond Randriarimanana

EMBASSY OF THE REPUBLIC OF MADAGASCAR
8–10 Hallam Street, London W1W 6JE
T 020-3008 4550 W www.embassy-madagascar-uk.com
Ambassador Plenipotentiary and Extraordinary, vacant

BRITISH AMBASSADOR
Ambassador Extraordinary and Plenipotentiary, HE Anthony Godson, resident in Port Louis, Mauritius

ECONOMY AND TRADE

Economic liberalisation and privatisation since the mid 1990s have resulted in slow but steady growth, although the political disturbances in 2002 and cyclone devastation in 2000 and 2004 were serious setbacks. President Ravalomanana's reforms and anti-corruption measures attracted increased international aid and in 2004 half of the country's foreign debt was written off. Even so poverty remains endemic, with half the population living below the poverty line, and unemployment is widespread. For his second term the president has set out the Madagascar action plan, which aims to cut poverty levels by 50 per cent over five years.

Agriculture is the mainstay of the economy, accounting for 27 per cent of GDP and employing 80 per cent of the workforce. The main cash crops include coffee, vanilla, fish, sugar cane, cocoa and spices. The industrial sector contributes 16 per cent of GDP, producing processed meat, soap, beer, leather, sugar, textiles, glassware, cement and paper, assembling cars and extracting oil. Tourism is of growing importance. The main trading partners are the USA and France. Principal exports are agricultural products, cotton cloth, chromite and petroleum products. The main imports are capital goods, petroleum, consumer goods and food.

GNI – US$5,400m; US$290 per capita (2005)
ANNUAL AVERAGE GROWTH OF GDP – 5.1 per cent (2005 est)
INFLATION RATE – 15 per cent (2005 est)
TOTAL EXTERNAL DEBT – US$4,600m (2002)
IMPORTS – US$1,550m (2005)
EXPORTS – US$750m (2005)

BALANCE OF PAYMENTS
Trade – US$254m deficit (2003)
Current Account – US$439m deficit (2003)

Trade with UK	*2005*	*2006*
Imports from UK	£6,582,000	£4,223,000
Exports to UK	£15,466,000	£25,771,000

COMMUNICATIONS

The main seaports are Toamasina, Antsiranana, Mahajanga and Toliara. There are 116 airports and irfields, of which the major airports are at Antananarivo nd Mahajanga. Surface transport is by the 49,827km of ighways and 854km of railways.

In 2005, there were 67,000 main telephone lines in se, 505,000 mobile phone subscribers and 90,000 nternet users.

DUCATION AND HEALTH

ducation is free of charge and compulsory for eight ears; primary education (five years) is followed by a ossible seven years of secondary education.

ITERACY RATE – 70.6 per cent (2004 est)
ROSS ENROLMENT RATIO (percentage of relevant age group) – primary 138 per cent; tertiary 3 per cent (2005 est)
IEALTH EXPENDITURE (per capita) – US$7 (2004)
IOSPITAL BEDS (per 1,000 people) – 0.4 (2000–5)

MEDIA

n increasing number of private local radio stations are hallenging the monopoly of state-run national roadcasting. A wide range of press publications print a iverse range of opinions. The independence of the press as been protected by law since 1990.

MALAWI

ziko la Malawi – Republic of Malawi

REA – 118,480 sq. km. Neighbours: Tanzania (north-east), Zambia (west), Mozambique (west, south and east)
CAPITAL – Lilongwe; population, 597,619 (2003)
MAJOR CITIES – Blantyre, incorporating Blantyre and Limbe, the major commercial and industrial centre; Mzuzu; Zomba, the former capital
CURRENCY – Kwacha (K) of 100 tambala
POPULATION – 13,013,926 rising at 2.38 per cent per year (2006 est)
RELIGION – Christianity (70 per cent), Islam (20 per cent) (est)
LANGUAGE – Chichewa, English (both official), Chinyanja, Chiyao, Chitumbuka
POPULATION DENSITY – 137 per sq. km (2005)
URBAN POPULATION – 17.2 per cent (2005 est)
MEDIAN AGE (years) – 16.5 (2006 est)
NATIONAL ANTHEM – 'Mlungu Dalitsani Malawi' ['Oh God Bless Our Land of Malawi']
NATIONAL DAY – 6 July (Independence Day)
LIFE EXPECTANCY (years) – 41.7 (2006 est)
MORTALITY RATE – 19.33 (2006 est)
BIRTH RATE – 43.13 (2006 est)
INFANT MORTALITY RATE – 94.37 (2006 est)
HIV/AIDS ADULT PREVALENCE – 14.2 per cent (2004 est)
DEATH PENALTY – No*
CPI SCORE – 2.7 (2006)
POPULATION BELOW POVERTY LINE – 55 per cent (2004 est)
MILITARY BUDGET – US$21m (2006)
MILITARY PERSONNEL – army 5,300; paramilitaries 1,500

CLIMATE AND TERRAIN

Malawi is a landlocked state lying along the western and southern shores of Lake Nyasa (Malawi). The northern and central regions are plateaux with rolling terrain, and the south is mainly highlands. Elevation extremes range from 3,002m (Sapitwa) at the highest point to 37m (Shire River) at the lowest. There is a wet season from November to May and average temperatures range from 9°C in June to 30°C in January.

HISTORY AND POLITICS

Until contact was made with European missionaries in the mid-19th century, Malawi was dominated by a succession of powerful tribes that included the Maravi, the Yao and the Nogni. In 1891, the area was claimed as the Nyasaland and District Protectorate, renamed the British Central Africa Protectorate in 1893, before becoming the British colony of Nyasaland in 1907. The country was joined with Northern and Southern Rhodesia (now Zambia and Zimbabwe) between 1953 and 1963. It became independent, as Malawi, in 1964, with Dr Hastings Banda as prime minister.

In 1966, the country became a one-party state ruled by the Malawi Congress Party (MCP) and Dr Banda became president, declaring himself president for life in 1971. In the early 1990s, there was increasing pro-democracy agitation at home, and civil disturbances and pressure from abroad forced Banda to introduce multiparty democracy in 1994.

Bakili Muluzi won the 1994 presidential election and served until 2004, when he was replaced by Bingu wa Mutharika, elected as the United Democratic Front (UDF) candidate. In the 2004 legislative election, the MCP became the largest party with 60 seats, but without an overall majority. The UDF won 49 seats and remained in government by forming a coalition with smaller parties.

In 2005, President Mutharika resigned from the UDF

over its apparent hostility to his anti-corruption campaign and founded a new party, the Democratic Progressive Party. Vice-president Cassim Chilumpha was arrested on charges of treason in April 2006; his trial was ongoing at the time of going to press.

POLITICAL SYSTEM
Under the 1995 constitution, the head of state and government is the president, who is directly elected for a five-year term, renewable only once. The unicameral national assembly consists of 193 members directly elected for a five-year term.

HEAD OF STATE
President, Commander-in-Chief of the Armed Forces, Bingu wa Mutharika, *elected* 20 May 2004

SELECTED GOVERNMENT MEMBERS *as at June 2007*
Finance, Goodall Gondwe
Foreign Affairs, Joyce Banda
Home Affairs, Ernest Malenga
Defence, Bob Khamisa

HIGH COMMISSION OF THE REPUBLIC OF MALAWI
70 Winnington Road, Hampstead, London N2 0TX
T 020-8455 5624 W www.malawihighcom.org.uk
High Commissioner, HE Dr Francis Moto, *apptd* 2006

BRITISH HIGH COMMISSION
PO Box 30042, Lingadzi House, Lilongwe 3
T (+265) (1) 772 400 E bhclilongwe@fco.gov.uk
High Commissioner, Richard Wildash, LVO, *apptd* 2006

BRITISH COUNCIL
PO Box 30222, Plot No. 13/20 City Centre, Lilongwe 3
T (+265) (1) 773 244 W www.britishcouncil.org/malawi
Director, Marc Jessel

ECONOMY AND TRADE

The economy has suffered from years of mismanagement and corruption and Malawi is one of the poorest countries in Africa. These problems and the vulnerability of agricultural production to both drought and severe flooding make the country heavily dependent on food and economic aid from international agencies and donor nations. Debt relief under the IMF's heavily indebted poor countries programme and tighter fiscal control have reduced public debt from over 200 per cent of GDP to 68 per cent.

The economy is primarily agricultural, with 90 per cent of the workforce engaged in agriculture, which accounts for 35 per cent of GDP and 80 per cent of export revenue. Tobacco is the most important cash crop, providing over half of export earnings, along with tea, sugar, cotton, coffee and peanuts. A number of light manufacturing industries have been established, mainly in agricultural processing, sawmill products, cement, clothing/textiles and consumer goods. The main export markets are the USA, South Africa and Germany. The main sources of imports are South Africa, India and neighbouring countries. Apart from tobacco and other agricultural products, wood products and clothing are principal exports. The main imports are food, fuels, semi-manufactures, consumer goods and transport equipment.

GNI – US$2,100m; US$160 per capita (2005)
ANNUAL AVERAGE GROWTH OF GDP – 1.9 per cent (2005 est)
INFLATION RATE – 15.4 per cent (2005 est)
TOTAL EXTERNAL DEBT – US$3,287 (2005 est)
IMPORTS – US$1,100m (2005)
EXPORTS – US$500m (2005)

BALANCE OF PAYMENTS
Trade – US$151m deficit (2002)
Current Account – US$201m deficit (2002)

Trade with UK	*2005*	*2006*
Imports from UK	£11,667,000	£10,485,000
Exports to UK	£15,774,000	£11,461,000

COMMUNICATIONS

Much internal transport is by water; there are 700km of navigable waterways on Lake Nyasa (Malawi) and the River Shire. Communication with the Indian Ocean coast is by rail through Mozambique; the route to the port of Beira was severed during Mozambique's civil war but the route to Nacala reopened in 2002. There are 797km of railways, including a single-track line linking Blantyre with the Zambian border, via Lilongwe and Salima. There are 15,451km of roads, of which 6,956km are surfaced. The main airports are at Blantyre and Lilongwe, with 40 smaller airports and airstrips around the country.

In 2005, there were 102,700 main telephone lines in use, 429,300 mobile phone subscribers and 52,500 internet users.

EDUCATION AND HEALTH

The government is responsible for primary and secondary schools, technical education and primary teacher training.

LITERACY RATE – 64.1 per cent (2004 est)
GROSS ENROLMENT RATIO (percentage of relevant age group) – primary 122 per cent; secondary 28 per cent (2005 est)
HEALTH EXPENDITURE (per capita) – US$19 (2004)
HOSPITAL BEDS (per 1,000 people) – 1.3 (2002)

MEDIA

There are four national newspapers. Television Malawi is state-run, and the Malawi Broadcasting Corporation which is the chief provider of information for the country is a state-run radio network that competes with a number of private channels.

MALAYSIA

AREA – 329,750 sq. km. Peninsular Malaysia is bordered by Thailand to the north. On Borneo, the Malaysian states of Sarawak and Sabah are bordered by Indonesia to the south, and enclose Brunei to the north
CAPITAL – Kuala Lumpur; population, 1,297,526 (2000); Putrajaya is the administrative capital
MAJOR CITIES – Ipoh; Kelang; Petaling Jaya; Johore Bharu
CURRENCY – Malaysian dollar (M$) (ringgit) of 100 sen
POPULATION – 24,385,858 rising at 1.78 per cent per year (2006 est); Malay (50.4 per cent), Chinese (23.7 per cent), Indian (7.1 per cent) (est)
RELIGION – Islam (60 per cent), Buddhism (19 per cent), Christianity (9 per cent), Hinduism (6 per cent), Chinese traditional religions (2 per cent) (est)
LANGUAGE – Bahasa Melayu (official), English, Cantonese, Mandarin, Tamil, Telugu, Malayalam, Punjabi, Thai
POPULATION DENSITY – 77 per sq. km (2005)

URBAN POPULATION – 65.1 per cent (2005 est)
MEDIAN AGE (years) – 24.1 (2006 est)
NATIONAL ANTHEM – 'Negara-Ku' ['My Country']
NATIONAL DAY – 31 August (Malaysia Day)
LIFE EXPECTANCY (years) – 72.5 (2006 est)
MORTALITY RATE – 5.05 (2006 est)
BIRTH RATE – 22.86 (2006 est)
INFANT MORTALITY RATE – 17.16 (2006 est)
DEATH PENALTY – Yes
CPI SCORE – 5.0 (2006)

CLIMATE AND TERRAIN

Malaysia comprises the 11 states of peninsular Malaya plus Sabah and Sarawak on the island of Borneo. Each is separated from the other by 1,029km of the South China Sea. The Malay peninsula, which extends from the isthmus of Kra to the Singapore Strait, is a plain with two highland areas in the north. The Malaysian part of Borneo is mostly high plateau, rising to mountains in western Sabah and eastern Sarawak, while Sarawak also has lower-lying land along the coast and in the Rajang river valley. Elevation extremes range from 4,100m (Gunung Kinabalu, Sabah) at the highest point to 0m (Indian Ocean) at the lowest. There are monsoon seasons from April to October in the south-west of the country and from October to February in the north-east. Average temperatures in Kuala Lumpur range from 22°C in January to 31°C in September.

HISTORY AND POLITICS

Malaysia formed part of the Srivijaya Empire in the 9th to 14th centuries. From the 16th century, the Portuguese, Dutch and British vied for control in the region. The British possessions of Singapore, Penang and Malacca were formed in 1826 into the Straits Settlement, which became a crown colony in 1867. British protection was extended over four Malay states, which federated in 1896, and protection treaties were agreed with several other states between 1885 and 1930. Following occupation by the Japanese from 1941 to 1945, the United Malay National Organisation (UMNO) was founded in 1946 to oppose plans for centralisation. The nine peninsular states were federated as the Federation of Malaya in 1948. The Federation of Malaya became independent in 1957, and in 1963 it combined with Singapore, Sarawak and Sabah to form the Federation of Malaysia; Singapore withdrew from the federation in 1965.

UMNO has dominated post-independence political life, initially as the governing party and since 1971 as the dominant partner in the Barisan Nasional (National Front) coalition governments. Mahathir bin Muhammad became prime minister in 1981 and his 22-year tenure of office saw increasingly authoritarian rule, particularly as opposition to Malay dominance of political life grew in the 1980s and 1990s. There is considerable tension between the ethnic groups in Malaysia; Malay resentment of the large Chinese minority's economic dominance led to the adoption in 1971 of policies that favour ethnic Malays in education and employment, although the Chinese remain the wealthiest section of society. In recent years there has been intercommunal violence between ethnic Indians, the poorest group, and Malays.

In the 2004 legislative election, the Barisan Nasional coalition retained its large majority in the house of representatives, with 198 seats, and prime minister Abdullah Ahmed Badawi, appointed in 2003, formed a new coalition government.

POLITICAL SYSTEM

The 1957 constitution provides for a federal government and a degree of autonomy for the state governments. The head of state is the *Yang di-Pertuan Agong* (supreme head of state) who is elected by the state rulers from among their number and serves a five-year term.

The federal legislature has two houses, the house of representatives and the senate. The house of representatives, *Dewan Rakyat*, is the lower house and has 219 members, directly elected for a five-year term. The senate, *Dewan Negara*, has 70 members who serve a six-year term; the legislative assembly of each state elects two members to the senate, and 44 are nominated by the head of state.

HEAD OF STATE

Supreme Head of State, HM Sultan Mizan Zainal Abidin ibni al-Marhum Sultan Mahmud, *sworn in* 13 December 2006
Deputy Head of State, Abdul Halim Mu'adzam Shah

SELECTED GOVERNMENT MEMBERS *as at June 2007*

Prime Minister, Finance, Abdullah Ahmed Badawi
Deputy Prime Minister, Defence, Najib Tun Abdul Razak
Foreign Affairs, Hamid bin Jaafer Albar
Home Affairs, Mohamed Radzi bin Sheikh Ahmad

MALAYSIAN HIGH COMMISSION

45 Belgrave Square, London SW1X 8QT
T 020-7235 8033 E mwlon@btconnect.com
High Commissioner, HE Datuk Abd Aziz Mohammed, *apptd* 2003

BRITISH HIGH COMMISSION

PO Box 11030, 185 Jalan Ampang, 50450 Kuala Lumpur
T (+60) (3) 2170 2200 E consular.kualalumpur@fco.gov.uk
W www.britain.org.my
High Commissioner, HE Boyd McCleary, CVO, *apptd* 2006

BRITISH COUNCIL

Ground Floor, West Block, Wisma Selangor Dredging, 142 C Jalan Ampang, 50450 Kuala Lumpur
T (+60) (3) 2723 7900 W www.britishcouncil.org/malaysia
Director, Gerry Liston, CMG

FEDERAL STRUCTURE

Each state has its own constitution, which must not be inconsistent with the federal constitution. The Malay rulers are either chosen or succeed to their position in accordance with the custom of their particular state; in other states of Malaysia, choice of the head of state is at the discretion of the *Yang di-Pertuan Agong* after consultation with the chief minister of the state. The ruler or governor acts on the advice of an executive council appointed on the advice of the chief minister and a single-chamber legislative assembly. The legislative assemblies are elected on the same basis as the federal house of representatives.

DEFENCE

The army has 111 armoured infantry fighting vehicles, 1,020 armoured personnel carriers. The navy has 4 frigates, 35 patrol and coastal vessels and 6 armed helicopters at 7 bases. The air force has 63 combat aircraft.

MILITARY BUDGET – US$3,080m (2006)
MILITARY PERSONNEL – 109,000: army 80,000, navy 14,000, air force 15,000; paramilitaries 24,600

ECONOMY AND TRADE

The economy has grown vigorously since the 1970s, transforming the country into a diversified emerging economy; the government's goal is to achieve developed nation status by 2020. Growth has been largely export-driven and the economy depends on continued buoyancy in its key export markets. The agricultural sector produces the raw materials for its highly developed industries. Industrial production includes rubber manufacturing, palm oil processing, electronics, tin mining and smelting, and logging and timber processing; oil and timber are produced in Sabah and Sarawak, and oil is refined in Sarawak, which also processes agricultural and forestry products. Tourism is a major service industry. The services sector contributed 44 per cent of GDP, industry 48 per cent and agriculture 8 per cent in 2006.

The main trading partners are the USA, Japan, Singapore, China and other south-east Asian countries. Principal exports are electronic equipment, oil and liquefied natural gas, timber and wood products, palm oil, rubber, textiles and chemicals. The main imports are electronics, machinery, petroleum products, plastics, vehicles, iron and steel products, and chemicals.

GNI – US$125,900m; US$4,970 per capita (2005)
ANNUAL AVERAGE GROWTH OF GDP – 5.2 per cent (2005 est)
INFLATION RATE – 3 per cent (2005 est)
UNEMPLOYMENT – 3.6 per cent (2005 est)
TOTAL EXTERNAL DEBT – US$52,000m (2005 est)
IMPORTS – US$114,400m (2005)
EXPORTS – US$140,900m (2005)

BALANCE OF PAYMENTS
Trade – US$27,493m surplus (2004)
Current Account – US$14,871m surplus (2004)

Trade with UK	*2005*	*2006*
Imports from UK	£1,092,260,000	£881,626,000
Exports to UK	£1,847,085,000	£1,935,419,000

COMMUNICATIONS

There are six main seaports in peninsular Malaysia, plus Kita Kinabalu (Sabah) and Kuching (Sarawak), and a merchant fleet of 312 ships of over 1,000 tonnes, as well as 7,200km of navigable waterways. There are 98,721km of roads, and in peninsular Malaysia 1,890km of railways. The main airports are at Kuala Lumpur, Kuala Terengganu and Penang, with over 110 smaller airports and airfields around the country.

A modern telephone system provides services nationwide. In 2005, there were 4.4 million main telephone lines in use, 19.5 million mobile phone subscribers and 11 million internet users.

EDUCATION AND HEALTH

LITERACY RATE – 88.7 per cent (2004 est)
GROSS ENROLMENT RATIO (percentage of relevant age group) – primary 93 per cent; secondary 76 per cent; tertiary 32 per cent (2005 est)
HEALTH EXPENDITURE (per capita) – US$180 (2004)
HOSPITAL BEDS (per 1,000 people) – 1.9 (2000–5)

MEDIA

The government operates extremely strict censorship of all media outlets and newspapers must renew their licences annually; a renewal is granted subject to the opinion of the home minister. Scenes including kissing or swearing are routinely censored. Controversial political websites and blogs have begun to attract the attention of the government.

The four main national daily newspapers are English-language and include *The Star*, *Business Times* and *The Malay Mail*. Radio Television Malaysia is the state-run broadcaster and competes with two main commercial broadcasters.

MALDIVES

Divehi Raajjeyge ge Jumhooriyyaa – Republic of Maldives

AREA – 300 sq. km
CAPITAL – Male; population, 91,484 (2006)
CURRENCY – Rufiyaa of 100 laaris
POPULATION – 359,008 rising at 2.78 per cent per year (2006 est)
LANGUAGE – Dhivehi (official), English
POPULATION DENSITY – 1,097 per sq. km (2005)
URBAN POPULATION – 29.7 per cent (2005 est)
MEDIAN AGE (years) – 17.9 (2006 est)
NATIONAL ANTHEM – 'Gavmii mi Ekuverikan Matii Tibegen Kuriime Salaam' ['In National Unity We Salute Our Nation']
NATIONAL DAY – 26 July (Independence Day)
LIFE EXPECTANCY (years) – 64.41 (2006 est)
MORTALITY RATE – 7.06 (2006 est)
BIRTH RATE – 34.81 (2006 est)
INFANT MORTALITY RATE – 54.89 (2006 est)
DEATH PENALTY – No*
LITERACY RATE – 96.3 per cent (2004 est)

CLIMATE AND TERRAIN

The republic is a chain of coral atolls in the Indian Ocean, 643km to the south-west of Sri Lanka. There are about 1,196 coral islands grouped into 12 clusters of atolls, about 198 of which are inhabited. The islands are all flat and low-lying; none is more than 2.4m above sea-level. There is a tropical climate and daytime temperatures rarely drop below 28°C.

HISTORY AND POLITICS

The Maldives converted to Islam in 1153 and came under Portuguese rule in the 16th century. After becoming a dependency of Ceylon in 1645, the islands were under Dutch and then British rule until 1887, when they became an internally self-governing British protectorate. Full independence was achieved in 1968, when the Maldives became a republic under President Ibrahim Nasir. The autocratic Nasir retired in 1978 and was succeeded by Maumoon Abdul Gayoom. Despite attempted coups in the 1980s, his tenure has ensured political stability and allowed economic development, although he has been accused of authoritarianism and human rights abuses. Unprecedented violence during anti-government demonstrations in 2003 and 2004 led to the introduction of constitutional reforms in 2005. The 2004 Indian Ocean tsunami devastated the islands, destroying many homes and tourist resorts; the number of dead and missing was low compared to other countries in the region, but over 21,000 people were displaced.

In the 2003 presidential election, President Gayoom was re-elected for a sixth term. In the 2005 legislative election, all candidates for the elected seats ran as independents, although some were backed by the Maldivian Democratic Party, based in Sri Lanka.

Following the legalisation of political parties, President Gayoom became leader of the Dhivehi Raiyyithunge Party. The first multiparty elections are to be held in 2008.

POLITICAL SYSTEM
The 1998 constitution was amended in 2005 to legalise political parties. The executive president, who serves a five-year term, is elected by the legislature and confirmed by national referendum. The legislature is the unicameral *Majlis* (people's assembly) which has 50 members, two elected from each of the 21 provinces and eight appointed by the president, to serve a five-year term.

HEAD OF STATE
President, Commander-in-Chief of the Armed Forces, Maumoon Abdul Gayoom, *elected* 1978, *re-elected* 1983, 1989, 1993, 1998, 2003

SELECTED GOVERNMENT MEMBERS *as at June 2007*
Defence and National Security, Ismail Shafeeu
Foreign Affairs, Ahmed Shaheed
Finance, Qasim Ibrahim
Home Affairs, Ahmed Thasmeen Ali

HIGH COMMISSION OF THE REPUBLIC OF MALDIVES
22 Nottingham Place, London W1U 5NJ
T 020-7224 2135 W www.maldiveshighcommission.org
High Commissioner, HE Hassan Sobir, *apptd* 2004

BRITISH HIGH COMMISSIONER
HE Dominick Chilcott, CMG, *apptd* 2006, resident at Colombo, Sri Lanka

ECONOMY AND TRADE
Political stability and economic liberalisation have produced steady economic growth since the 1980s, although the economy contracted severely in 2005 owing to the devastation caused by the 2004 Indian Ocean tsunami. This destroyed tourist resorts, affecting an industry on which the economy is heavily dependent; tourism accounts for 28 per cent of GDP and 60 per cent of foreign exchange receipts. Import duties and tourism-related taxes provide over 90 per cent of government tax revenue. Fishing is the second largest activity. Agriculture and manufacturing are constrained by a shortage of cultivatable land and domestic labour, and so most food must be imported. Industry concentrates on the manufacture of clothes, boat-building and handicrafts, contributing 7 per cent to GDP.
GNI – US$762m; US$2,320 per capita (2005)
ANNUAL AVERAGE GROWTH OF GDP – –3.6 per cent (2005 est)
INFLATION RATE – 6 per cent (2005 est)
TOTAL EXTERNAL DEBT – US$304m (2004 est)
IMPORTS – US$700m (2005)
EXPORTS – US$100m (2005)

BALANCE OF PAYMENTS
Trade – US$386m deficit (2004)
Current Account – US$134m deficit (2004)

Trade with UK	*2005*	*2006*
Imports from UK	£8,858,000	£6,187,000
Exports to UK	£11,667,000	£14,342,000

COMMUNICATIONS
None of the islands is more than 13 sq. km in area. The larger islands have some roads. Transport between islands is by water or air, and the country's five airports handle 6,000 departures a year. The main port is Male. Telephone services are available on the majority of the inhabited islands and mobile phone distribution is expanding rapidly. The three daily newspapers are *Haveeru Daily, Aafathis News* and *Miadhu News.*

MEDIA
The government controls the only television station. Minivan Radio, the country's only independent radio station, broadcasts from overseas as the government has failed to honour its promise to give licences to proposed private stations.

MALI

République du Mali – Republic of Mali

AREA – 1,240,000 sq. km. Neighbours: Senegal (west), Mauritania (north-west), Algeria (north-east), Niger (east), Burkina Faso and Côte d'Ivoire (south), Guinea (south-west)
CAPITAL – Bamako; population, 1,016,167 (1998)
MAJOR CITIES – Sikasso; Ségou; Mopti; Koutiala
CURRENCY – Franc CFA of 100 centimes
POPULATION – 11,716,829 rising at 2.63 per cent per year (2006 est); Mandé (50 per cent), Fula (17 per cent), Voltaic (12 per cent), Songhai (6 per cent), Tuareg and Moor (10 per cent) (est)
RELIGION – Islam (90 per cent), Christianity (5 per cent) (est)
LANGUAGE – French (official), Bambara
POPULATION DENSITY – 11 per sq. km (2005)
URBAN POPULATION – 33.7 per cent (2005 est)
MEDIAN AGE (years) – 15.8 (2006 est)
NATIONAL ANTHEM – 'Pour l'Afrique et Pour Toi, Mali' ['For Africa and For You, Mali']
NATIONAL DAY – 22 September (Independence Day)
LIFE EXPECTANCY – 49 (2006 est)
MORTALITY RATE – 16.89 (2006 est)
BIRTH RATE – 49.82 (2006 est)
INFANT MORTALITY RATE – 107.58 (2006 est)
HIV/AIDS ADULT PREVALENCE – 1.9 per cent (2003 est)
DEATH PENALTY – No*
CPI SCORE – 2.8 (2006)
POPULATION BELOW POVERTY LINE – 64 per cent (2001 est)
MILITARY BUDGET – US$136m (2006 est)
MILITARY PERSONNEL – army 7,350; paramilitaries 4,800, inactive militia 3,000

CLIMATE AND TERRAIN
A landlocked state, the terrain is mainly savannah in the south and arid desert in the north, with some hills in the north-east. The centre is drained by the River Niger and the south-west by the River Senegal. Elevation extremes range from 1,155m (Hombori Tondo) at the highest point to 23m (Senegal River) at the lowest. Average temperatures range from 17°C in January to 31°C in September.

HISTORY AND POLITICS

Mali was successively part of the empire of the Malinke people from the 13th to 15th centuries, and the Songhai Empire in the 15th to 16th centuries. With the fall of the Songhai Empire, it was divided between the Tuareg and the Fulani and Bambara kingdoms, and then the Tukolor and Samori kingdoms. It was conquered by the French in 1880–95 and became a French colony. In 1959, it formed the Federation of Mali with Senegal before becoming a separate state in 1960 under a socialist regime. A military coup in 1968 resulted in Lt. Moussa Traoré becoming president, and in 1974 Mali became a one-party state. Traoré was ousted in 1991 in a military coup led by Gen. Amadou Toumani Touré. Multiparty elections were held in 1992, returning the country to civilian government.

In the early 1990s there was a rebellion in the north by the Tuareg, who were seeking greater land, linguistic and cultural rights. Unrest in 2006 raised fears of another rebellion by the Tuareg seeking greater autonomy for their region, but this was averted by an Algerian-brokered agreement.

Amadou Toumani Touré, standing as an independent candidate, won the 2002 presidential elections, and was re-elected in April 2007 in the first round of voting. In the 2002 legislative elections, the Alliance for Democracy in Mali (ADEMA), which had dominated government coalitions since 1992, was initially thought to have retained the majority of seats after a low turnout with many void votes; a month after the election this result was overturned by the constitutional court, which declared that the Hope 2002 coalition had won the largest number of seats. In the July 2007 legislative elections, ADEMA returned to power in a broad coalition with eleven other parties.

POLITICAL SYSTEM

Under the 1992 constitution, the president is directly elected for a five-year term. The unicameral legislature, the national assembly, has 147 members directly elected for a five-year term. The president appoints the prime minister and other ministers.

HEAD OF STATE

President, Amadou Toumani Touré, *elected* 12 May 2002, *took office* 8 June 2002

SELECTED GOVERNMENT MEMBERS *as at June 2007*

Prime Minister, Ousmane Issoufi Maiga
Defence, Mamadou Clazie Cissouma
Economy and Finance, Abou-Bacar Traore
Foreign Affairs, Bien Moctar Ouane

EMBASSY OF THE REPUBLIC OF MALI

Avenue Molière 487, 1050 Brussels, Belgium
T (+32) (2) 345 7432
Ambassador Extraordinary and Plenipotentiary, HE Ibrahim Bocar Ba, *apptd* 2003

BRITISH AMBASSADOR

HE Peter Newall, *apptd* 2004, resident at Dakar, Senegal

ECONOMY AND TRADE

Mali is one of the world's poorest countries, with over 60 per cent of the population living below the poverty line. Economic reform since the mid-1990s has produced steady growth, but Mali is heavily dependent on foreign aid and remittances from expatriates. There is a severe foreign trade deficit and high foreign debt; in 2003 Mali qualified for debt relief under the IMF heavily indebted poor countries initiative, and in 2005 it was promised 100 per cent debt relief by the G8 countries. The economy is based primarily on subsistence farming and animal husbandry, which contribute 45 per cent of GDP and occupy 80 per cent of the population.

Although usually self-sufficient in food, the country faced severe shortages in 2004–5 owing to drought and locust infestation. Gold and phosphate mining, and cotton and food processing are also important; industry accounts for 17 per cent of GDP. The main export markets are China, other Asian countries and the EU; imports come mainly from France, Senegal and Côte d'Ivoire. Principal exports are cotton, gold and livestock. The main imports are fuel, machinery and equipment, construction materials, foodstuffs and textiles.

GNI – US$5,200m; US$380 per capita (2005)
ANNUAL AVERAGE GROWTH OF GDP – 6.1 per cent (2005 est)
INFLATION RATE – 4.5 per cent (2002 est)
UNEMPLOYMENT – 14.6 per cent (2001 est)
TOTAL EXTERNAL DEBT – US$2,800m (2002)
IMPORTS – US$1,550m (2005)
EXPORTS – US$1,150m (2005)

BALANCE OF PAYMENTS

Trade – US$60m deficit (2003)
Current Account – US$271m deficit (2003)

Trade with UK	*2005*	*2006*
Imports from UK	£5,443,000	£4,304,000
Exports to UK	£1,204,000	£279,000

COMMUNICATIONS

Mali has 15,100km of roads, 729km of railway line and 1,815km of waterways. Bamako is the centre of the transport network and the main shipping point for freight, with links to ports in Côte d'Ivoire, where civil war has disrupted trade routes, Guinea and Senegal. The main port is Koulikoro on the River Niger, and the principal airport is at Bamako.

The telephone system is limited in extent and services are unreliable, though improving. Mobile phone distribution is growing rapidly. In 2005, there were 75,000 main telephone lines in use, 870,000 mobile phone subscribers and 60,000 internet users.

EDUCATION AND HEALTH

LITERACY RATE – 19 per cent (2004 est)
GROSS ENROLMENT RATIO (percentage of relevant age group) – primary 66 per cent; secondary 24 per cent; tertiary 3 per cent (2005 est)
HEALTH EXPENDITURE (per capita) – US$24 (2004)
HOSPITAL BEDS (per 1,000 people) – 0.2 (2002)

MEDIA

The media is among the most free-spoken in Africa. Laws exist to punish the slandering of public officials but these are rarely invoked. The print media consists of 40 privately owned newspapers, and there are a further 50 private television and radio stations. The state operates its own daily newspaper, *L'Essor.*

MALTA

Repubblika ta' Malta – Republic of Malta

AREA – 316 sq. km
CAPITAL – Valletta; population, 6,315 (2005)
MAJOR TOWNS – Birkikara; Mosta; Qormi
CURRENCY – Maltese lira (LM) of 100 cents or 1,000 mils
POPULATION – 400,214 rising at 0.42 per cent per year (2006 est)
RELIGION – Roman Catholicism (95 per cent), Islam (1 per cent)
LANGUAGE – Maltese, English (both official)
POPULATION DENSITY – 1,261 per sq. km (2005)
URBAN POPULATION – 92.1 per cent (2005 est)
MEDIAN AGE (years) – 38.7 (2006 est)
NATIONAL ANTHEM – 'L-Innu Malti' ['Hymn of Malta']
NATIONAL DAY – 21 September (Independence Day)
LIFE EXPECTANCY (years) – 79.01 (2005 est)
MORTALITY RATE – 8.1 (2006 est)
BIRTH RATE – 10.22 (2006 est)
INFANT MORTALITY RATE – 3.86 (2006 est)
DEATH PENALTY – No (abolished 2000)
CPI SCORE – 6.4 (2006)
MILITARY BUDGET – US$42m (2006)
MILITARY PERSONNEL – 1,609

CLIMATE AND TERRAIN

Malta is an archipelago of six islands in the Mediterranean Sea; Malta, Gozo and Comino are the largest. The island of Malta has a coastal plain in the north-east, rising to low hills on the south-west. Elevation extremes range from 253m (Ta'Dmejrek) at the highest point to 0m (Mediterranean Sea) at the lowest. The climate is warm and temperate with average summer temperatures reaching 30°C.

HISTORY AND POLITICS

The islands were controlled at various times by the Phoenicians, Greeks, Carthaginians, Romans, Arabs and the Spanish. Spain gave them to the Sovereign Military Order of Malta (known as the Knights of St John), which held them from 1530 until 1798. Recaptured from the French by Britain during the Napoleonic wars, the island became a British colony in 1814, and was developed into a substantial naval base and dockyard. Malta was strategically important in both world wars – particularly the second – when it was blockaded and subjected to aerial bombardment for five months. Its resistance led to the people of Malta being awarded the George Cross, the UK's highest award for civilian bravery, in 1942.

Malta gained independence in 1964 and became a republic in 1974. In the 1970s it developed close links with communist and Arab states, but more pro-European and pro-US policies were adopted after the election of the Nationalist Party in 1987. Malta became a member of the EU in 2004, and its legislature ratified the EU constitution in 2005.

The Nationalist Party was returned to power in the 2003 legislative election with an outright majority. Edward Fenech Adami, prime minister in 1987–96 and 1998–2004, stood down to contest the 2004 presidential election, which he won.

POLITICAL SYSTEM

Under the 1974 constitution, the president is elected by the house of representatives for a five-year term, renewable only once. The unicameral legislature, the house of representatives, has 65 members directly elected for a five-year term; if a party wins the majority of votes in a general election without winning a majority of seats, new seats are created until that party holds a majority of one seat. The prime minister is appointed by the president and nominates the other ministers.

HEAD OF STATE
President, Edward Fenech Adami, *took office* 15 April 2004

SELECTED GOVERNMENT MEMBERS *as at June 2007*
Prime Minister, Finance, Lawrence Gonzi
Deputy Prime Minister, Justice and Home Affairs, Tonio Borg
Foreign Affairs, Michael Frendo

MALTA HIGH COMMISSION
Malta House, 36–38 Piccadilly, London W1J 0LE
T 020-7292 4800 W www.foreign.gov.mt
High Commissioner, HE Dr Michael Refalo, *apptd* 2005

BRITISH HIGH COMMISSION
Whitehall Mansions, Ta'Xbiex Seafront, Msida 11
T (+356) 2323 0000 E bhccomm@vol.net.mt
W www.britishhighcommission.gov.uk/malta
High Commissioner, HE Nicholas Archer, MVO, *apptd* 2006

BRITISH COUNCIL
Exchange Buildings, Republic Street, Valletta VLT 05
T (+356) 2122 6377 W www.britishcouncil.org/malta
Director, Ronnie Micallef

ECONOMY AND TRADE

The mainstay of the economy for over a century was the dockyard, and ship-building and ship repairs remain significant industries, but since the 1980s Malta has developed into a tourist destination, financial services centre and freight trans-shipment point. Tourism is now the main source of income, followed by foreign trade and manufacturing, especially of electronics and pharmaceuticals. The service sector accounts for 74 per cent of GDP, industry for 23 per cent and agriculture for 3 per cent; Malta produces only about 20 per cent of its own food. The main trading partners are other EU states, the USA and Singapore. Principal exports are electronics, processed food and beverages, textiles and other manufactures. The main imports are machinery and transport equipment, manufactured goods, foodstuffs, beverages and tobacco.
GNI – US$5,491m; US$13,610 per capita (2005)
ANNUAL AVERAGE GROWTH OF GDP – 1 per cent (2005 est)
INFLATION RATE – 3 per cent (2005 est)
UNEMPLOYMENT – 7.8 per cent (2005 est)
TOTAL EXTERNAL DEBT – US$188.8m (2005)
IMPORTS – US$3,730m (2005)
EXPORTS – US$2,330m (2005)

BALANCE OF PAYMENTS
Trade – US$1,108m deficit (2005)
Current Account – US$725m deficit (2005)

Trade with UK	*2005*	*2006*
Imports from UK	£232,201,000	£293,300,000
Exports to UK	£168,118,000	£150,600,000

EDUCATION

Education is free at all levels and compulsory between the ages of five and 16.
LITERACY RATE – 87.9 per cent (2004 est)

COMMUNICATIONS

The main ports are Marsaxlokk and Valletta, and there is a large merchant fleet of 1,220 ships of over 1,000 tonnes. There are 2,227km of roads, but no railways. The only airport is at Valletta.

The telephone system extends to all the islands. In 2005, there were 202,000 main telephone lines in use, 324,000 mobile phone subscribers and 127,000 internet users.

MEDIA

Radio broadcasting began in the 1930s, partly to counter the fascist broadcasts from Italy. Malta Television, the public broadcaster, was set up in 1963. There are seven major daily and weekly news publications, which include *Malta Independent* and *It-Torca*. The newspapers usually have strong political affiliations.

MARSHALL ISLANDS

Republic of the Marshall Islands

AREA – 11,854 sq. km
CAPITAL – Dalap-Uliga-Darrit, on Majuro Atoll; population, 7,103 (1999)
MAJOR TOWN – Ebeye
CURRENCY – Currency is that of the USA
POPULATION – 60,422 rising at 2.25 per cent per year (2006 est); Micronesian (99 per cent) (est). About 60 per cent of the population is concentrated on the two atolls of Majuro and Kawjalein
RELIGION – Protestantism (80 per cent), Roman Catholicism (8 per cent), Mormonism (2 per cent) (est)
LANGUAGE – Marshallese, English (both official)
POPULATION DENSITY – 351 per sq. km (2005)
URBAN POPULATION – 66.7 per cent (2005 est)
MEDIAN AGE (years) – 20.3 (2006 est)
NATIONAL ANTHEM – 'Forever Marshall Islands'
NATIONAL DAY – 1 May (Constitution Day)
LIFE EXPECTANCY (years) – 70.31 (2006 est)
MORTALITY RATE – 4.78 (2006 est)
BIRTH RATE – 33.05 (2006 est)
INFANT MORTALITY RATE – 28.43 (2006 est)
DEATH PENALTY – No (abolished 1986)

CLIMATE AND TERRAIN

The republic consists of an archipelago of 29 coral atolls, five islands and over 1,000 islets in the west Pacific Ocean. All of the islands are low-lying and a 1989 UN report warned that a rise in sea level could submerge them all by 2030. There is a wet season from May to November and average temperatures range from 25°C in January to 31°C in August.

HISTORY AND POLITICS

The Marshall Islands were first claimed by Spain in 1592 but were left largely undisturbed. Consequently they were seized by Germany and formally became a protectorate in 1886. Japan took control of the islands in 1914 on behalf of the Allied powers and administered them from 1920 until 1944, when they were seized by US forces. In 1947 the islands became part of the UN Trust Territory of the Pacific Islands, administered by the USA. Between 1946 and 1962, US nuclear weapon tests were held on Bikini and Enewetak atolls. Enewetak has been partially decontaminated but Bikini is uninhabitable; the USA paid compensation to the test victims in the 1980s but the government is seeking US$2.7bn (£1.37bn) in further compensation to cover the medical care of radiation victims and rectify environmental damage.

The islands became internally self-governing in 1979, and the US–UN trusteeship administration came to an end in 1986, when a free association agreement between the USA and the Republic of the Marshall Islands came into effect. Under this agreement, the USA recognised the republic as a fully sovereign and independent state but retained control of external security and defence as well as giving financial help; the USA controls the Kwajalein Atoll, where it has a military base and missile test site. UN trust territory status was terminated in 1990 and full independence was granted in December 1990. A renegotiated compact with the USA was signed in 2003.

The United Democratic Party (UDP) won the legislative elections in 1999 and 2003. The UDP supported the candidacy of Kessai Note, who was elected president in 2000 and re-elected in 2004. A legislative election was due in November 2007.

POLITICAL SYSTEM

Under the 1979 constitution, the executive president is elected by the legislature from among its members to serve a four-year term. The unicameral legislature, the *Nitijela*, has 33 members, directly elected for a four-year term. There is also a 12-member *Iroij* (Council of Chiefs) who are traditional leaders with a consultative and advisory role.

HEAD OF STATE

President, Kessai Note, *elected* 3 January 2000, *re-elected* 14 January 2004

SELECTED GOVERNMENT MEMBERS *as at June 2007*

Finance, Brenson Wase
Foreign Affairs, Gerald Zackios
Internal Affairs, Rien Morris

BRITISH AMBASSADOR

HE Peter Beckingham, *apptd* 2005, resident at Manila, the Philippines

ECONOMY AND TRADE

The Marshall Islands has few natural resources, apart from possible seabed mineral deposits, and the economy is dependent on aid from the USA, supplemented by ship registration fees and the sale of fishing licences. Most islanders live by subsistence farming and fishing, with coconuts, breadfruit and fish the main commercial crops. A small-scale industrial sector produces copra and handicrafts and processes tuna. Tourism is being encouraged, but as yet employs less than 10 per cent of the workforce. The government is the largest employer. The main trading partners are the USA, Japan, Australia and China. Principal exports are copra and coconut products, handicrafts and fish. The main imports include foodstuffs and fuel.

GNI – US$185m; US$2,930 per capita (2005)
ANNUAL AVERAGE GROWTH OF GDP – 3.5 per cent (2005 est)
INFLATION RATE – 3 per cent (2005 est)
UNEMPLOYMENT – 30.9 per cent (2000 est)

Trade with UK	*2005*	*2006*
Imports from UK	£2,698,000	£2,733,000
Exports to UK	£1,809,000	£560,000

COMMUNICATIONS

Air transport provides the main means of internal travel, and there are 15 airports and airfields throughout the islands, with internal and international flights operated by Air Marshall Islands and Continental Air Micronesia. Majuro is the main airport as well as the main port, with a merchant fleet of 795 ships of over 1,000 tonnes; a further 730 foreign-owned ships are registered in the republic. There are 65km of surfaced roads on the two main islands. The modern telephone system extends to most of the islands. Mobile phone distribution in 2004 was still lower than main-line density, at 1,198 and 5,510 in 2004 respectively.

MEDIA

The media operates freely, although occasionally it practises self-censorship over controversial issues. US forces' radio and television broadcasts can be received. The print media consists of the *Marshall Islands Journal*, a private weekly newspaper, and the *Marshall Islands Gazette*, a government-owned monthly publication.

MAURITANIA

Al-Jumhuriyah al-Islamiyah al-Muritaniyah – Islamic Republic of Mauritania

AREA – 1,030,700 sq. km. Neighbours: Senegal (south-west), Mali (east and south), Algeria and Western Sahara (north)
CAPITAL – Nouakchott; population, 558,195 (2000 est)
MAJOR TOWNS – Nouadhibou; Rosso; Bogue
CURRENCY – Ouguiya (UM) of 5 khoums
POPULATION – 3,177,388 rising at 2.88 per cent per year (2006 est)
RELIGION – Islam (99 per cent) (est). Almost all Muslims practice Shia Islam
LANGUAGE – Arabic (official), Pulaar, Soninke, French, Hassaniya, Wolof
POPULATION DENSITY – 3 per sq. km (2005)
URBAN POPULATION – 64.3 per cent (2005 est)
MEDIAN AGE (years) – 17 (2006 est)
NATIONAL ANTHEM – 'National Anthem of Mauritania'
NATIONAL DAY – 28 November (Independence Day)
LIFE EXPECTANCY (years) – 53.12 (2006 est)
MORTALITY RATE – 12.16 (2006 est)
BIRTH RATE – 40.99 (2006 est)
INFANT MORTALITY RATE – 69.48 (2006 est)
DEATH PENALTY – No*
CPI SCORE – 3.1 (2006)
POPULATION BELOW POVERTY LINE – 40 per cent (2004 est)
MILITARY BUDGET – US$17.7m (2006)
MILITARY PERSONNEL – 15,870: army 15,000, navy 620, air force 250; paramilitaries 5,000
CONSCRIPTION DURATION – 24 months
LITERACY RATE – 51.2 per cent (2004 est)
GROSS ENROLMENT RATIO (percentage of relevant age group) – primary 93 per cent; secondary 21 per cent; tertiary 3 per cent (2005 est)
HEALTH EXPENDITURE (per capita) – US$15 (2004)

CLIMATE AND TERRAIN

The terrain is arid, apart from in the Senegal river valley, and flat, with some hilly regions in the centre of the country. Elevation extremes range from Kediet Ijill (915m) at the highest point to −5m (Sebkhet Te-n-Dghamcha) at the lowest. The climate is hot and dry; the north of the country is virtually rainless, while the south receives some unreliable rainfall between June and October. Humidity during the summer period is very high. Average temperatures range from 16°C in January to 34°C in July.

HISTORY AND POLITICS

Eastern Mauritania was part of the Ghana Empire and then the Mali and Songhai empires from the seventh to the 16th century. The area came under French influence in the 19th century, becoming first a protectorate in 1903 and then a colony in 1920. The country achieved independent as the Islamic Republic of Mauritania on 28 November 1960. There were military coups in 1978 and 1984, the latter bringing to power Col. Maaouya ould Sid Ahmed Taya. Civilian rule was restored after multiparty elections in 1992; the presidential election was won by Col. Taya.

In the 1990s and early 2000s, ethnic tension between the Arab north and African south and internal unrest by opposition groups was exacerbated by several years of drought. This led to serious civil disturbances and several attempted coups.

The 2001 legislative election was won by the Republican Democratic and Social Party (PRDS), which gained 64 seats. In the 2003 presidential election, President Taya was re-elected for a fourth term of office with 67 per cent of the vote, amid opposition allegations of fraud and intimidation. In 2005 a military coup, led by the former head of national security Col. Ely ould Mohamed Vall, took place when President Taya was out of the country.

Constitutional changes were approved by referendum in June 2006 and legislative elections were held in late 2006 and early 2007. The national assembly election was won by the Coalition of the Forces for Democratic Change, led by the Rally of Democratic Forces, with 41 seats; the senate election was won by independents grouped into the Al-Mithaq coalition, with 36 seats. The presidential election in March 2007 was won by Sidi ould Cheikh Abdallahi, who became the country's first democratically elected president since independence. He later appointed Zeine ould Zeidane as prime minister.

POLITICAL SYSTEM

The 1991 constitution was amended in 2006 to reduce the term of office of the president from six to five years and to limit the number of terms to two. The bicameral parliament comprises the national assembly, the lower house, and the senate. The national assembly has 95 members who are directly elected for a five-year term. The senate has 56 members who are indirectly elected for a six-year term; one-third is elected every two years.

HEAD OF STATE
President, Sidi ould Cheikh Abdallahi, *elected* 25 March 2007, *sworn in* 19 April 2007

SELECTED GOVERNMENT MEMBERS *as at June 2007*
Prime Minister, Zeine ould Zeidane
Finance, Abderrahmane ould Hamma Vezzaz
Foreign Affairs, Mohamed Saleck ould Mohamed Lemine
Interior, Yall Zakaria
Defence, Mohamed Mahmoud ould Mohamed Lemine

EMBASSY OF THE ISLAMIC REPUBLIC OF MAURITANIA
8 Carlos Place, Mayfair, London W1K 3AS
T 020-7478 9323 E ambarim@aol.com
Ambassador Extraordinary and Plenipotentiary, HE Mealainine ould Moctar Neche, *apptd* 2005

BRITISH AMBASSADOR
HE Charles Gray, *apptd* 2005, resident at Rabat, Morocco

ECONOMY AND TRADE

Mauritania is one of the poorer countries in the region, with 40 per cent of the population living below the poverty line and unemployment at 20 per cent. Past economic mismanagement and droughts created a huge foreign debt, although the country qualified for debt relief under the IMF heavily indebted poor country initiative in 2002, and in 2005 it was promised 100 per cent debt relief by the G8 countries.

Natural resources include iron ore, gypsum, gold, oil (off-shore production began in 2006) and rich fishing waters, although the latter are threatened by over-exploitation. Agriculture and animal husbandry, mainly at subsistence level, are the mainstay of the economy, accounting for 25 per cent of GDP and engaging 50 per cent of the population. However, food aid became necessary in 2005 after locust infestations in 2004 obliterated arable production.

The main trading partners are EU countries, Japan, the USA and China. Principal exports are iron ore (nearly 40 per cent), fish and fish products, and gold. The main imports are machinery, petroleum products, capital goods, food and consumer goods.

GNI – US$1,800m; US$580 per capita (2005)
ANNUAL AVERAGE GROWTH OF GDP – 5.5 per cent (2005 est)
INFLATION RATE – 7 per cent (2003 est)
UNEMPLOYMENT – 20 per cent (2004 est)
TOTAL EXTERNAL DEBT – US$2,500m (2000)

Trade with UK	*2005*	*2006*
Imports from UK	£47,989,000	£22,699,000
Exports to UK	£11,438,000	£13,952,000

COMMUNICATIONS

The main seaports are Nouakchott and Nouadhibou. There are 717km of railways and 7,660km of roads. Mauritania operates ferry services on the Senegal River. There are 25 airports and airfields. The telephone system is limited but improvements are being made. Mobile phone distribution is growing rapidly, with 746,000 subscribers in 2005, compared to 41,000 main lines in use.

MEDIA

The media is forbidden by law to publish opinions or information that undermine Islam or threaten national security. Television and radio services are state-owned. A five-year ban on Radio France Internationale was lifted in 2005 after it was accused of negative reporting. There are seven main national press publications, including the state-run dailies *Chaab* and *Horizon.*

MAURITIUS

Republic of Mauritius

AREA – 2,040 sq. km
CAPITAL – Port Louis; population, 147,688 (2003 est)
MAJOR TOWNS – Beau Bassin-Rose Hill; Vacoas-Phoenix; Curepipe; Quatre Bornes
CURRENCY – Mauritius rupee of 100 cents
POPULATION – 1,240,827 rising at 0.82 per cent per year (2006 est); Indo-Mauritian (68 per cent), Creole (27 per cent), Sino-Mauritian (3 per cent), Franco-Mauritian (2 per cent) (est)
RELIGION – Hinduism (50 per cent), Christianity (32 per cent), Islam (16 per cent) (est)
LANGUAGE – English, French (both official), Creole, Bhojpuri
POPULATION DENSITY – 612 per sq. km (2005)
URBAN POPULATION – 43.8 per cent (2005 est)
MEDIAN AGE (years) – 30.8 (2006 est)
NATIONAL ANTHEM – 'Motherland'
NATIONAL DAY – 12 March (Independence Day)
LIFE EXPECTANCY (years) – 72.63 (2006 est)
MORTALITY RATE – 6.86 (2006 est)
BIRTH RATE – 15.43 (2006 est)
INFANT MORTALITY RATE – 14.59 (2006 est)
DEATH PENALTY – No (abolished 1995)
CPI SCORE – 5.1 (2006)
POPULATION BELOW POVERTY LINE – 10 per cent (2001 est)
MILITARY BUDGET – US$18m (2006)
MILITARY PERSONNEL – paramilitaries 2,000

CLIMATE AND TERRAIN

The republic is an island group in the Indian Ocean, approximately 885km east of Madagascar. The mountainous volcanic island of Mauritius is mainly low-lying and surrounded by coral reefs. Elevation extremes range from 828m (Mt Piton) at the highest point to 0m (Indian Ocean) at the lowest. The island of Rodrigues, formerly a dependency but now part of Mauritius, is about 563km east of Mauritius, with an area of 64km; the population is 36,907 (2005 est). The islands of Agalega and St Brandon are dependencies of Mauritius; the total population is 289 (2002).

There is a tropical climate, modified by south-east trade winds, and average temperatures range from 25°C in July to 31°C in January.

HISTORY AND POLITICS

The island was discovered by the Dutch in 1598; the colonists withdrew in 1710. A decade later they were replaced by the French, who established plantations that were worked by African slaves. In 1814 Mauritius was ceded to the British, who had occupied it in 1810. The British abolished slavery in 1835 and so instead imported indentured Indian and Chinese labourers to work on the plantations. Independence was achieved on 12 March 1968 and the state became a republic in 1992.

The Mauritian Socialist Party (MSM) under Sir Anerood Jugnauth held power from 1982 until 1995, and hen returned to power in the 2000 election in coalition vith the Mouvement Militant Mauricien (MMM). ugnauth stood down as party leader and prime minister 1 2003 and was elected president later in the same year. he MSM-MMM coalition lost the 2005 election to the pposition Socialist Alliance led by Navinchandra amgoolam, who became prime minister.

OLITICAL SYSTEM
he 1968 constitution was amended in 1992 to introduce republican form of government, and in 2001 to give the land of Rodrigues a degree of autonomy. The head of ate is a president elected by the national assembly for a ve-year term. The unicameral legislature, the national ssembly, has 62 elected members (Mauritius has 20 hree-member constituencies and Rodrigues returns two embers) and eight specially elected members, who serve five-year term; of the latter, four seats go to the 'best oser' of whichever communities on the island are under-epresented in the assembly after the election, and the ther four seats are allocated on the basis of both party nd community. The prime minister is the member of the ational assembly who appears best able to command the upport of the majority of assembly members. Other inisters are appointed by the president on the advice of ne prime minister.

Rodrigues has an 18-member regional assembly, naugurated in 2002, when a chief commissioner and hief executive were appointed.

EAD OF STATE
resident, Sir Anerood Jugnauth, *took office* 7 October 2003
'ice-President, Abdoul Raouf Bundhun

ELECTED GOVERNMENT MEMBERS *as at June 2007*
rime Minister, Defence and Home Affairs, Navinchandra Ramgoolam
eputy Prime Minister, Finance, Rama Sithanen
oreign Affairs, Madan Murlidhar Dulloo

AURITIUS HIGH COMMISSION
2–33 Elvaston Place, London SW7 5NW
020-7581 0294
igh Commissioner, HE Abhimanu Kundasamy, *apptd* 2006

RITISH HIGH COMMISSION
) Box 1063, Les Cascades Building, Edith Cavell Street, rt Louis
(+230) 202 9400 **E** bhc@intnet.mu
igh Commissioner, HE Anthony Godson, *apptd* 2004

RITISH COUNCIL
) Box 111, Royal Road, Rose Hill
(+230) 403 0200 **W** www.britishcouncil.org/mauritius
irector, Simon Ingram-Hill

CONOMY AND TRADE

nce independence Mauritius has diversified its economy m a predominantly agricultural base into one ncentrating on the industrial, financial and tourism ctors. Agriculture continues to play a part, producing gar cane, tea, corn, potatoes, bananas, pulses and fish. gar cane is grown on 90 per cent of cultivated land and oduces 25 per cent of the island's export earnings. dustrial activity is centred on food processing, mining d manufacturing textiles, clothing, chemicals, metal products and transport equipment. Information technology, telecommunications and offshore banking services are priorities for development. Economic growth has slowed recently because of downturns in sugar and textile exports. The services sector accounts for 70 per cent of GDP, industry for 25 per cent and agriculture for 5 per cent.

The main trading partners are the UK, France, China, the USA, South Africa and the UAE. Principal exports are clothing, textiles, sugar, cut flowers and molasses. The main imports are manufactured goods, capitals equipment, food, fuels and chemicals.

GNI – US$6,500m; US$5,250 per capita (2005)
ANNUAL AVERAGE GROWTH OF GDP – 2.5 per cent (2005 est)
INFLATION RATE – 5 per cent (2005 est)
UNEMPLOYMENT – 9.6 per cent (2005 est)
TOTAL EXTERNAL DEBT – US$3,246m (2005 est)
IMPORTS – US$3,160m (2005)
EXPORTS – US$2,140m (2005)

BALANCE OF PAYMENTS
Trade – US$575m deficit (2004)
Current Account – US$107m deficit (2004)

Trade with UK	*2005*	*2006*
Imports from UK	£47,426,000	£45,144,000
Exports to UK	£354,402,000	£368,768,000

COMMUNICATIONS

Port Louis handles the bulk of the island's external trade. The international airport is located at Plaisance. The 2,020km of roads are all surfaced. There are no railways. The telephone system offers a good service; mobile phone distribution, at 713,300 subscribers, was nearly double the density of main telephone lines, recorded at 359,000 in 2005.

EDUCATION AND HEALTH

Primary education is free of charge and compulsory. There are a number of facilities offering vocational training. The Institute of Education is responsible for training primary and secondary school teachers and for curriculum development.

LITERACY RATE – 84.3 per cent (2004 est)
GROSS ENROLMENT RATIO (percentage of relevant age group) – primary 102 per cent; secondary 89 per cent; tertiary 17 per cent (2005 est)
HEALTH EXPENDITURE (per capita) – US$222 (2004)

MEDIA

Freedom of expression is guaranteed by the constitution and four daily newspapers and eight weekly publications offer a range of political viewpoints. The Mauritius Broadcasting Corporation is state-owned and runs television and radio services funded through advertising and a licence fee. Satellite television is available and private radio stations began broadcasting in 2002.

MEXICO

Estados Unidos Mexicanos – United Mexican States

AREA – 1,972,550 sq. km. Neighbours: USA (north), Guatemala and Belize (south-east)
CAPITAL – Mexico City; population, 8,591,309 (2000)

MAJOR CITIES – Guadalajara; Monterrey; Puebla; Toluca; Tijuana; León; Ciudad Juárez; Torreón
CURRENCY – Peso of 100 centavos
POPULATION – 107,449,525 rising at 1.16 per cent per year (2006 est)
RELIGION – Roman Catholicism (88 per cent), Protestantism (8 per cent) (est). An estimated 3 per cent of the population is atheist
LANGUAGE – Spanish
POPULATION DENSITY – 54 per sq. km (2005)
URBAN POPULATION – 76 per cent (2005 est)
MEDIAN AGE (years) – 25.3 (2006 est)
NATIONAL ANTHEM – 'Himno Nacional Mexicano' ['Mexican National Anthem']
NATIONAL DAY – 16 September (Independence Day)
LIFE EXPECTANCY (years) – 75.41 (2006 est)
MORTALITY RATE – 4.74 (2006 est)
BIRTH RATE – 20.69 (2006 est)
INFANT MORTALITY RATE – 20.26 (2006 est)
DEATH PENALTY – No (abolished 2005)
CPI SCORE – 3.3 (2006)
POPULATION BELOW POVERTY LINE – 40 per cent (2003 est)

CLIMATE AND TERRAIN

Coastal plains rise to a central plateau and then to a spine of high mountains, the Sierra Madre, running from the north-west to south-east. The Yucatán peninsula in the south-east is low-lying, and marshy on the coast. The narrow Lower California peninsula, separated from the rest of the country by the Gulf of California, has a range of hills running along it. The mountains include volcanoes such as Popocatepetl. Elevation extremes range from 5,655m (Volcan Pico de Orizaba) at the highest point to −10m (Laguna Salada) at the lowest. The Rio Grande forms the eastern part of the northern border with the USA. Average temperatures in Mexico City range from 10°C in January to 23°C in July.

HISTORY AND POLITICS

Mexico was the centre of Mesoamerican civilisations for over 2,500 years: the Olmecs (*c.*1200–600 BC), based on the Mexican Gulf Coast; the Zapotecs (*c.*300 BC to 300 AD) in the Oaxaca valley; the Mayas (*c.*300–900 AD) in southern Mexico and the Yucatán peninsula; the Mixtecs (*c.*800–1300) in the Oaxaca valley; and the Toltecs (*c.*900–1170) in central Mexico and the Yucatán peninsula. The Aztecs, who came to the region in the 13th century, subjugated these peoples and ruled until their civilisation fell to the Spanish under Hernán Cortés in 1519–21. As the viceroyalty of New Spain, Mexico remained under Spanish rule until the 19th century. In the first century of Spanish occupation, the indigenous population fell from around 21 million to one million, largely through lack of resistance to European diseases, such as Bubonic plague, smallpox and influenza.

After an unsuccessful revolt in 1810, independence was declared in 1821 and a federal republic was instituted in 1824. Mexico suffered extreme instability, civil war and invasion throughout much of the 19th century. War with the USA in 1836 and 1846–8 led to the loss of about one-third of its territory. There was civil war in 1858–61 between liberals and conservatives, and in 1862–7 war with Britain, France and Spain after Mexico defaulted on its foreign debt. Porfirio Díaz ruled as a dictator between 1876 and 1911, until his repressive regime was overthrown in a revolution that introduced radical land and labour reforms, but instability continued.

The National Revolutionary Party, founded in 192 came to dominate political life. Renamed the Institution Revolutionary Party (PRI) in 1946, it formed a successio of authoritarian governments. Although unrest was no eliminated under its regime, the 1960s saw rapi industrialisation and the 1970s an oil-fuelled economi boom. Falling oil prices led to a serious financial crisis i 1982 and Mexico defaulted on its debt. Economi difficulties were eased in the 1990s with the introductio of market reforms and privatisation, and membership o the North American Free Trade Agreement (NAFTA) fro 1994.

These reforms led to a degree of social upheava Fearing for the status of the already marginalise indigenous peoples, the Zapatista National Liberatio Front (EZLN) led revolts in the south of the country i 1994 and 1995. Although violence tailed off in the lat 1990s, civil campaigning continued, culminating in mass march from Chiapas to Mexico City in 2001 i support of a bill of indigenous rights. The bill was enacte later that year but the Zapatistas claimed its provisior had been watered down and vowed to continue the insurgency. The government also faces problems wit corruption and violent crime, often drug-relate former president Vicente Fox said in 2005 that drug cartels were trying to infiltrate state institutions.

The PRI's political dominance ended at the 199 election, when it lost its absolute majority in the lowe house of the legislature, although it continued i government until 2000 and was again in power fro 2003 until 2006. However, in the July 2006 legislativ election the Partido de Accion Nacional (PAN) becam the largest party in the chamber of deputies. In th simultaneous presidential election, the result was so clos that recounts were necessary in 9 per cent of pollin districts and the federal electoral tribunal confirmed onl in September that the winning candidate was Felip Calderón of the PAN, with 35.88 per cent of the vote; th result was contested with mass demonstrations in Mexic City by his rival Lopez Obrador and his supporters, wh alleged voting irregularities.

POLITICAL SYSTEM

Under the 1917 constitution, the federal republic consis of 31 states and the federal capital. The head of state is a executive president, directly elected for a six-year ter that may not be renewed. The bicameral legislature is th congress of the union, the lower house of which is th chamber of deputies and the upper house is the senat The chamber of deputies has 500 members, directl elected for a three-year term. The senate has 12 members, directly elected for a six-year term. Th president appoints the cabinet. Each of the states has i own constitution and is administered by a governo elected for a six-year term, and a state chamber deputies, elected for a three-year term.

HEAD OF STATE

President, Felipe Calderón, *elected* 2 July 2006, *sworn in* 1 December 2006

SELECTED GOVERNMENT MEMBERS *as at June 2007*

Defence, Gen. Guillermo Galván Galván
Economy, Eduardo Sojo Garza-Aldape
Foreign Affairs, Patricia Espinosa Cantellano
Interior, Francisco Javier Ramirez Acuna

EMBASSY OF MEXICO
16 St George Street, London W1S 1FD
T 020-7499 8586 W www.embamex.co.uk
Ambassador Extraordinary and Plenipotentiary, HE Juan José Bremer de Martino, CVO, *apptd* 2004

BRITISH EMBASSY
Calle Río Lerma 71, Col. Cuauhtémoc, 06500 Mexico City
T (+52) (55) 5242 8500 E ukinmex@att.net.mx
W www.embajadabritanica.com.mx
Ambassador Extraordinary and Plenipotentiary, HE Giles Paxman, *apptd* 2005

BRITISH COUNCIL
Lope de Vega 316, Col. Chapultepec Morales, 11570 Mexico City
T (+52) (55) 5263 1900 W www.britishcouncil.org/mexico
Director, Clive Bruton

DEFENCE

The army has over 757 armoured personnel carriers. The navy has 1 destroyer, 6 frigates, around 180 patrol and coastal vessels, and 8 combat aircraft. There are 18 naval bases. The air force has 84 combat aircraft and 123 helicopters.

MILITARY BUDGET – US$3,200m (2006)
MILITARY PERSONNEL – 237,800: army 183,700, navy 42,400, air force 11,700; paramilitaries 30,700

ECONOMY AND TRADE

Economic liberalisation and privatisation in the 1990s and membership of NAFTA (since 1994) have stimulated economic growth and development. This is especially true in the industrial sector, as Mexico's cheap labour has led US companies to establish factories in the north to assemble goods for the US market. But despite this and its prevalent oil, natural gas and mineral resources, Mexico remains a poor country with 40 per cent of the population living below the poverty line. A large proportion of the male population works overseas, predominantly in the USA, and much of the remaining population, especially in poor and rural areas, is dependent on their remittances. Further economic growth and poverty reduction measures are needed, but the success of President Calderón's economic programme will depend on the support of the opposition.

Agriculture is diverse and productive; major crops include maize, wheat, soya beans, rice, beans, cotton, coffee, fruit, tomatoes, beef, poultry and dairy products. Agriculture accounts for 4 per cent of GDP and 18 per cent of the labour force. The main industry is oil production, which generates nearly one-third of government revenue. Other industries include production of food, beverages, tobacco, chemicals, iron and steel, textiles, clothing, motor vehicles, consumer durables, mining and tourism. The services sector accounts for 70 per cent of GDP and industry for 26 per cent.

Mexico has free trade agreements with over 40 countries, covering 90 per cent of its trade. The main trading partner is the USA (86 per cent of exports; 53 per cent of imports). Canada is the other main export market, and China and Japan the other main sources of imports. Principal exports include manufactured goods, oil and oil products, silver, fruit, vegetables, coffee and cotton. The main imports include metal-working machines, steel mill products, agricultural machinery, electrical equipment, car parts for assembly, vehicle repair parts, aircraft and aircraft parts.

GNI – US$753,400m; US$7,310 per capita (2005)
ANNUAL AVERAGE GROWTH OF GDP – 3 per cent (2005 est)
INFLATION RATE – 41 per cent (2005 est)
UNEMPLOYMENT – 3.6 per cent (2005 est)
TOTAL EXTERNAL DEBT – US$137,200m (2005 est)
IMPORTS – US$232,000m (2005)
EXPORTS – US$214,000m (2005)

BALANCE OF PAYMENTS
Trade – US$7,559m deficit (2005)
Current Account – US$5,723m deficit (2005)

Trade with UK	*2005*	*2006*
Imports from UK	£637,866,000	£743,227,000
Exports to UK	£455,602,000	£454,803,000

COMMUNICATIONS

Veracruz, Tampico and Coatzacoalcos are the chief seaports on the Atlantic coast, and Guaymas, Mazatlán, Lázaro Cárdenas and Salina Cruz on the Pacific. There are 17,634km of railways; the rail network is currently undergoing reorganisation. There are 235,670km of roads, of which 116,751km are surfaced, and 2,900km of navigable rivers and coastal canals. The main international airport is at Mexico City, with 20 others across the country.

The telephone system is limited in scope, with a low density of provision for domestic users, and mobile phone distribution has grown rapidly. In 2005 there were 19.5 million main telephone lines in use, 47.5 million mobile phone subscribers and 18.6 million internet users.

EDUCATION AND HEALTH

Although Mexico allows for ten years of free and compulsory education, on average adults have only completed 7.2 years. The country's largest university is the National Autonomous University of Mexico, situated in Mexico City.

LITERACY RATE – 90.3 per cent (2004 est)
GROSS ENROLMENT RATIO (percentage of relevant age group) – primary 109 per cent; secondary 80 per cent; tertiary 23 per cent (2005 est)
HEALTH EXPENDITURE (per capita) – US$424 (2004)
HOSPITAL BEDS (per 1,000 people) – 1 (2000–5)

MEDIA

The Televisa group used to control all Mexican broadcasting but now competes with other channels and a huge number of independent radio stations, some of which broadcast to Mexicans working in the USA. There are six national newspapers, which represent a variety of political opinions.

CULTURE

The dominant figures in Mexican art are husband and wife Diego Rivera (1886–1957) and Frida Kahlo (1907–1954). In literature, essayist and poet Octavio Paz (1914–98) won the Nobel prize in 1990, while Carlos Fuentes (*b.* 1928) is a respected political commentator and novelist.

As in other Latin American countries, football has a huge following, and the country has hosted the World Cup twice, in 1970 and 1986. Bullfighting is also very popular and Mexico City is home to the largest ring in the world, seating 55,000.

FEDERATED STATES OF MICRONESIA

AREA – 702 sq. km
FEDERAL CAPITAL – Palikir; population, 6,444 (2000), on Pohnpei
CURRENCY – US dollar
POPULATION – 108,004 falling at 0.11 per cent per year (2006 est)
RELIGION – Protestantism (40 per cent), Roman Catholicism (40 per cent) (est)
LANGUAGE – English (official), Trukese, Pohnpeian, Yapese, Kosrean, Ulithian
POPULATION DENSITY – 158 per sq. km (2005)
URBAN POPULATION – 30 per cent (2005 est)
MEDIAN AGE (years) – 20.9 (2006 est)
NATIONAL ANTHEM – 'Patriots of Micronesia'
NATIONAL DAY – 10 May (Constitution Day)
LIFE EXPECTANCY (years) – 70.05 (2006 est)
MORTALITY RATE – 4.75 (2006 est)
BIRTH RATE – 24.68 (2006 est)
INFANT MORTALITY RATE – 29.16 (2006 est)
DEATH PENALTY – No (abolished 1986)
POPULATION BELOW POVERTY LINE – 26.7 per cent (2001 est)

CLIMATE AND TERRAIN

The republic consists of more than 600 volcanic islands extending 2,900km across the archipelago of the Caroline Islands in the western Pacific Ocean. Elevation extremes range from 791m (Totolom) at the highest point to 0m (Pacific Ocean) at the lowest. The islands lie to the north of the Equator; the climate is tropical, with only slight variations in temperatures, which are usually between 20°C and 30°C.

HISTORY AND POLITICS

Inhabited since around 4,000 BC by migrants from the Philippines and Indonesia, Micronesia came into contact with Europeans in the 1520s and the islands were colonised by Spain from the 16th century. German encroachment in the 1870s and 1880s was resisted until 1899, when Germany purchased the islands from Spain. The islands were occupied by Japan on behalf of the Allies during the First World War, and administered as a League of Nations mandated territory by Japan from 1920 until the Japanese defeat in the Second World War. In 1947 the islands became part of the UN Trust Territory of the Pacific, administered by the USA.

A constitution was adopted in 1979 and the islands became independent in 1986 under a free association agreement with the USA by which the USA retains responsibility for defence and provides substantial financial aid; a renegotiated agreement was signed in 2003. The UN trusteeship was formally terminated in 1990. The most recent presidential and legislative elections were in spring 2007. Emmanuel ('Manny') Mori was elected president in May.

The republic is threatened by the effects of global warming, particularly an increase in the frequency and intensity of storms in the region. A typhoon in 2004 devastated the island of Yap, badly damaging nearly all its infrastructure.

POLITICAL SYSTEM

The 1979 constitution established a federal republic of four states: Chuuk, Kosrae, Pohnpei and Yap. The federal head of state is an executive president, who is elected by the congress for a four-year term. The unicamera congress has 14 members, ten senators directly electec for a two-year term and four senators at large (one from each state) elected for a four-year term; the president anc vice-president must be selected from among the senators The federal cabinet is appointed by the president anc approved by the congress. There are no political parties Each state has its own government and legislative system.

HEAD OF STATE
President, Emmanuel Mori, *elected* 11 May 2007
Vice-President, Alik L. Alik

SELECTED GOVERNMENT MEMBERS *as at June 2007*
Economic Affairs, Akillino H. Susaia
Finance, Nick L. Andon
Foreign Affairs, Lorin Robert
Health, Nena S. Nena

BRITISH AMBASSADOR
HE Peter Beckingham, *apptd* 2005, resident at Manila the Philippines

ECONOMY AND TRADE

Micronesia has few natural resources apart from phosphate, which is not exploited, and is highly dependent on aid from the USA, which constitutes over quarter of GDP. The main economic activities ar subsistence farming and fishing, which nearly 30 per cen of GDP, but both are threatened by climate change an over-fishing. The islands' remoteness and lack of facilitie and air links has constrained the development of tourism the main industry; other industries include constructior fish processing, specialised aquaculture and handicrafts Two-thirds of the workforce is employed by th government.
GNI – US$254m; US$2,300 per capita (2005)
ANNUAL AVERAGE GROWTH OF GDP – 0.3 per cen (2005 est)
INFLATION RATE – 2.2 per cent (2005)
UNEMPLOYMENT – 22 per cent (2000 est)

Trade with UK	*2005*	*2006*
Imports from UK	£21,000	£17,000
Exports to UK	£4,000	£15,000

COMMUNICATIONS

Most transport is by air or sea. There are six airports an airfields, with major airports on the four main islands, an the main seaports are Colonia (Yap), Kolonia (Pohnpei Lele and Moen. There are 240km of roads. The islands a all connected to the telephone system. In 2005 there wer 12,400 main telephone lines in use, 14,100 mobi phone subscribers and 14,000 internet users.

MEDIA

There are no daily newspapers; the federal governmer produces a fortnightly information bulletin and sta governments produce weekly news publications. On government television channel competes with tw commercial channels, and there are several radi stations.

MOLDOVA

Republica Moldova – Republic of Moldova

AREA – 33,843 sq. km. Neighbours: Ukraine (north, east and south-east), Romania (west)
CAPITAL – Chisinau; population, 593,800 (2006 est)
MAJOR TOWNS – Tiraspol; Balti; Tighina
CURRENCY – Moldovan leu (plural lei) of 100 bani
POPULATION – 4,466,706 rising at 0.28 per cent per year (2006 est); Moldovan (78.2 per cent), Ukrainian (8.4 per cent), Russian (5.8 per cent), Gagauz (4.4 per cent)
RELIGION – Christianity (90 per cent) (est)
LANGUAGE – Moldovan (official), Russian, Gagauz
POPULATION DENSITY – 128 per sq. km (2005)
URBAN POPULATION – 46.3 per cent (2005 est)
MEDIAN AGE (years) – 32.3 (2006 est)
NATIONAL ANTHEM – 'Limba Noastra' ['Our Language']
NATIONAL DAY – 27 August (Independence Day)
LIFE EXPECTANCY (years) – 65.65 (2006 est)
MORTALITY RATE – 12.64 (2006 est)
BIRTH RATE – 15.7 (2006 est)
INFANT MORTALITY RATE – 38.38 (2006 est)
DEATH PENALTY – No (abolished 1995)
CPI SCORE – 3.2 (2006)
POPULATION BELOW POVERTY LINE – 80 per cent (2001 est)
MILITARY EXPENDITURE – US$180m (2005 est)
MILITARY PERSONNEL – 6,750: army 5,710, air force 1,040; paramilitaries 3,279
CONSCRIPTION DURATION – 12 months

CLIMATE AND TERRAIN

A landlocked country to the north-west of the Black Sea, Moldova is a hilly plain lying mostly between the Prut and Dniester rivers. Elevation extremes range from 430m (Dealul Bulanesti) at the highest point to 2m (Dniester River) at the lowest. The climate is continental and average temperatures range from −4°C in January to 20°C in August.

HISTORY AND POLITICS

Part of the Roman province of Dacia from AD 106, Moldova saw centuries of invasion and occupation after the fall of the Roman Empire but formed part of an independent Moldovan state from the mid-14th century. The principality was absorbed into the Ottoman Empire in the 16th century, then came under Russian protection in the 18th century. Partition saw the west (Bukovina) lost to Austria in the 18th century and the east (Bessarabia) to Russia in 1812. The remainder became independent of Turkish overlordship in 1856 and in 1859 joined with Wallachia to form the principality of Romania.

After the Russian revolution in 1917, Bessarabia was seized and incorporated into Romania in 1918, and the area east of the River Dniester formed the Moldovan autonomous republic in the USSR from 1924. Romania was forced to return Bessarabia to the USSR in 1940 but, with the help of its German allies, invaded and occupied the Soviet republic of Moldova in 1941 until its reconquest by Soviet forces in 1944.

Moldovan nationalism grew in the late 1980s and the parliament declared political and economic sovereignty in 1990, achieving independence and joining the Commonwealth of Independent States (CIS) in 1991 after the collapse of the USSR. Nationalist advocacy of unification with Romania was defeated in a plebiscite in 1994.

The rise in Moldovan nationalism was matched by the growing demands for autonomy by the republic's Russian and Ukrainian ethnic minorities in the Transdniestria region (east of the River Dniester) and the Gagauz in the south-west. Both areas declared their independence in 1990, though this was not recognised. Both regions were granted special autonomy status by the 1994 constitution, and the Gagauz exercise a degree of autonomy over political, economic and cultural affairs.

A stalemate has developed over the status of Transdniestria. Fighting between separatists and government forces in 1991 was followed by a fragile peace settlement in 1992, maintained by Russian peacekeeping troops. Despite talks sponsored by the OSCE, EU, Russia and Ukraine since the late 1990s, the situation has not been resolved. In 2005 the Moldovan parliament backed a Ukrainian settlement proposal, but the failure of Russia to withdraw its peacekeepers remains an obstacle to progress. Relations with Russia became tense in 2006 owing to Russia's suspension of gas exports to Moldova and of wine imports from the country.

The governments in the first decade after independence were made up of moderate reformists, but their ineffectiveness led to a resurgence in support for the Communist Party of Moldova (PCM), which won the majority of seats in the 1998, 2001 and 2005 legislative elections. After the 2005 election, the PCM leader Vladimir Voronin was re-elected president and Vasile Tarlev, an independent member of parliament and prime minister since 2001, was reappointed prime minister.

POLITICAL SYSTEM

The 1997 constitution was amended in 2000 to increase the powers of the legislature and the executive. The head of state is a president who (since 2000) is elected by the legislature for a four-year term. The unicameral legislature, the *Parlamentul*, has 101 members, who are directly elected for a four-year term. The prime minister and government are nominated by the president.

HEAD OF STATE

President, Vladimir Voronin, *elected* 4 April 2001, *re-elected* 4 April 2005

SELECTED GOVERNMENT MEMBERS *as at June 2007*

Prime Minister, Vasile Tarlev
Deputy Prime Minister, Foreign, Andrei Stratan
Defence, Valeriu Plesca
Finance, Mihai Pop
Interior, Col. Gheorghe Papuc

EMBASSY OF THE REPUBLIC OF MOLDOVA

5 Dolphin Square, Edensor Road, London W4 2ST
T 020-8995 6818 W www.moldovanembassy.org.uk
Ambassador Extraordinary and Plenipotentiary, HE Mariana Durlesteanu, *apptd* 2005

BRITISH EMBASSY

18 Nicolae Iorga str., Chisinau MD2012
T (+373) 222 225902 E enquiries.chisinau@fco.gov.uk
W www.britishembassy.gov.uk/moldova
Ambassador Extraordinary and Plenipotentiary, HE John C. Beyer, *apptd* 2006

ECONOMY AND TRADE

Moldova moved steadily towards a market economy after independence and from 2000 to 2005 experienced sustained growth. But with the most industrialised areas lying in the breakaway Transdniestria region, it has struggled to reduce poverty or its large foreign debt. About 30 per cent of the population lives below the poverty line, and although unemployment is only about 8 per cent, an estimated 25 per cent of the workforce is employed abroad. Its dependence on Russia, as an export market and main energy supplier, caused an economic downturn in 2006 owing to Russia's trade embargo.

The agricultural sector is the mainstay of the economy, accounting for 21.5 per cent of GDP. Principal crops include vegetables, fruit, wine, grain, sugar beet, sunflower seed, tobacco, beef and milk. Major industrial activities include food processing and production of sugar, vegetable oil, agricultural machinery, foundry equipment, domestic appliances and textiles. Industry accounts for 22 per cent of GDP and services for 56.5 per cent.

The main trading partners are Russia, Ukraine, Romania, Italy and Germany. Principal exports are foodstuffs, textiles and machinery. The main imports are fuel and energy, machinery and equipment, chemicals and textiles.

GNI – US$3,200m; US$930 per capita (2005)
ANNUAL AVERAGE GROWTH OF GDP – 7.1 per cent (2005 est)
INFLATION RATE – 11.9 per cent (2005 est)
UNEMPLOYMENT – 8 per cent (2002 est)
TOTAL EXTERNAL DEBT – US$1,986m (2005 est)
IMPORTS – US$2,000m (2005)
EXPORTS – US$1,000m (2005)

BALANCE OF PAYMENTS
Trade – US$1,191m deficit (2005)
Current Account – US$308m deficit (2005)

Trade with UK	*2005*	*2006*
Imports from UK	£9,834,000	£18,205,000
Exports to UK	£6,578,000	£12,358,000

COMMUNICATIONS

Moldova has 12,730km of roads and 1,130km of railways. There are 15 airports and airstrips; the principal airport is at Chisinau. There are 424km of navigable waterways on the River Dniester.

The telephone system is antiquated and service is poor outside the capital, although some modernisation is under way. In 2005 there were 929,400 main telephone lines in use, 1 million mobile phone subscribers and 406,000 internet users.

EDUCATION AND HEALTH

LITERACY RATE – 96.2 per cent (2004 est)
GROSS ENROLMENT RATIO (percentage of relevant age group) – primary 92 per cent; secondary 82 per cent; tertiary 34 per cent (2005 est)
HEALTH EXPENDITURE (per capita) – US$46 (2004)
HOSPITAL BEDS (per 1,000 people) – 6.7 (2000–5)

MEDIA

Freedom of media expression is guaranteed by the constitution. There are five main newspapers. State-run television and radio stations compete with a single commercial channel. The authorities in the breakaway Transdniestria region operate their own television and radio stations.

MONACO

Principaute de Monaco – Principality of Monaco

AREA – 1.95 sq. km. Neighbour: France
CAPITAL – Monaco
CURRENCY – Euro (€) of 100 cents
POPULATION – 32,543 rising at 0.4 per cent per year (2006 est); French (47 per cent), Monegasque (16 per cent), Italian (16 per cent) (est)
RELIGION – Roman Catholicism (90 per cent) (est)
LANGUAGE – French (official), English, Italian, Monegasque
POPULATION DENSITY – 17,128 per sq. km (2005)
URBAN POPULATION – 100 per cent (2005 est)
MEDIAN AGE (years) – 45.4 (2006 est)
NATIONAL ANTHEM – 'Hymne Monégasque' ['Hymn of Monaco']
NATIONAL DAY – 19 November
LIFE EXPECTANCY (years) – 79.69 (2006 est)
MORTALITY RATE – 12.91 (2006 est)
BIRTH RATE – 9.19 (2006 est)
INFANT MORTALITY RATE – 5.35 (2006 est)
DEATH PENALTY – No (abolished 1962)

CLIMATE AND TERRAIN

Monaco has a steep, rugged terrain on the Mediterranean coast; Fontvieille, a district in the south of the country, has been expanded into the sea by infilling. Elevation extremes range from 140m (Mt Agel) at the highest point to 0m (Mediterranean Sea) at the lowest. The climate is Mediterranean, with average temperatures that range from 10°C in January to 23°C in July.

HISTORY AND POLITICS

Monaco has been ruled by the Grimaldi family since the 13th century. Monarchical France recognised Monaco's independence in the 15th century, but Revolutionary France annexed it in the 18th century. Monaco did not regain its independence until 1861 and the principality remains under French protection. It was occupied by the Italians and subsequently by the Germans in the Second World War.

The 1962 constitution was amended in 2002 to allow the throne to pass in the female line in the absence of male heirs. Legislative power is held jointly by the prince and a 24-member national council directly elected for a five-year term. Executive power is exercised by the prince and a six-member council of government headed by a minister of state who is nominated by the prince from a list of three French diplomats submitted by the French government. The judicial code is based on that of France.

In the 2003 legislative election, the National and Democratic Union, which had been in power for most of the previous 40 years, was defeated by the Union for Monaco (UPM), which won 21 seats.

HEAD OF STATE
HSH The Prince of Monaco, Prince Albert II Alexandre Louis Pierre, *born* 14 March 1958, *succeeded* 6 April 2005
Heir, HSH Princess Caroline Louise Marguerite von Hannover, *born* 23 January 1957

SELECTED GOVERNMENT MEMBERS *as at June 2007*
Minister of State, Jean-Paul Proust
Finance and Economy, Franck Biancheri

nterior, Philippe Deslandes
oreign Affairs, Henri Fissori

:ONSULATE-GENERAL OF MONACO
' Upper Grosvenor Street, London W1K 2LY
' 020-7823 1771 W www.monacoconsulate.uk.com
:onsul-General, Evelyne Genta, *apptd* 2006

BRITISH CONSULATE-GENERAL
O Box 265, 33 Boulevard Princesse Charlotte, 98005 Monaco
' (+377) 9350 9966
Ion. Consul-General, Simon Lever, resident in Marseille, France

:CONOMY AND TRADE

'he economy has diversified away from its historic lependence on tourism and gambling to benefit from nancial services, real estate revenue and some light ndustry. A large floating jetty, installed in 2002, has xtended the harbour facilities, doubling the capacity of he port to handle cruise ships. Since the state collects no axes from individuals or businesses, it has become a tax aven for the wealthy, and non-Monegasques make up 84 er cent of the population. The state retains monopolies n a number of sectors, including tobacco, the telephone etwork, and the postal service.

NNUAL AVERAGE GROWTH OF GDP – 0.9 per cent (2000 est)
NFLATION RATE – 1.9 per cent (2000)
'OTAL EXTERNAL DEBT – US$18,000m (2000 est)

AEDIA

adio Monte-Carlo started broadcasting across France in ne 1960s and Italy in the 1970s. Monaco does not have n indigenous daily press (French newspapers are widely vailable) but does publish two weekly journals.

AONGOLIA

Iongol Uls – Mongolia

REA – 1,564,116 sq. km. Neighbours: Russia (north), China (south)
APITAL – Ulaanbaatar; population, 846,500 (2002 est)
IAJOR TOWNS – Erdenet; Darhan
'URRENCY – Tugrik of 100 mongo
OPULATION – 2,832,224 rising at 1.46 per cent per year (2006 est); Mongol (94.9 per cent), Turkic (5 per cent) (est)
ELIGION – Buddhism (93 per cent) (est)
ANGUAGE – Mongolian (official), Turkic, Russian
OPULATION DENSITY – 2 per sq. km (2005)
RBAN POPULATION – 57 per cent (2005 est)
IEDIAN AGE (years) – 24.6 (2006 est)
'ATIONAL ANTHEM – 'Bugd Nairamdakh Mongol' ['United Mongolia']
ATIONAL DAY – 11 July (Revolution Day)
'FE EXPECTANCY (years) – 64.89 (2006 est)
ORTALITY RATE – 6.95 (2006 est)
IRTH RATE – 21.59 (2006 est)
NFANT MORTALITY RATE – 52.12 (2006 est)
EATH PENALTY – Yes
PI SCORE – 2.8 (2006)
OPULATION BELOW POVERTY LINE – 36.1 per cent (2004 est)
'TERACY RATE – 97.8 per cent (2004 est)
ROSS ENROLMENT RATIO (percentage of relevant age group) – primary 118 per cent; secondary 94 per cent; tertiary 41 per cent (2005 est)
EALTH EXPENDITURE (per capita) – US$37 (2004)

CLIMATE AND TERRAIN

Landlocked Mongolia lies on part of the central Asiatic plateau, with steppes rising to the Mongolian Altai and Hangai mountain ranges in the west. The Gobi desert covers much of the southern half of the country. Elevation extremes range from 4,374m (Nayramadlin Orgil) at the highest point to 518m (Hoh Nuur) at the lowest. The country includes the world's northernmost desert and its southernmost permafrost. The country has long, very cold Siberian winters, which quickly turn into a short and warm summer. The wet season runs from June to September. Average temperatures in Ulaanbaatar range from −27°C in January to 19°C in July.

HISTORY AND POLITICS

The nomadic tribes of Mongolia, mostly Turks and Uighurs, were united in the early 13th century by Genghis Khan, forming the nucleus of a Mongol Empire that reached its zenith under Kublai Khan, Genghis' grandson, when it stretched from Hungary to China and as far south as Vietnam. After Kublai's death in 1294, the empire declined. Many of the khanates formed under Genghis survived as increasingly independent petty kingdoms, but Mongolia itself was conquered by China in the late 17th century and became the provinces of Inner and Outer Mongolia.

When imperial rule in China collapsed in 1911, Outer Mongolia declared itself an independent monarchy under a Buddhist lama king. Chinese rule was reasserted in 1915, but in 1921 Mongolian revolutionaries supported by the Soviets, overthrew Chinese rule and the Mongolian People's Revolutionary Party (MPRP) formed a government. When the king died in 1924, the monarchy was abolished and the ensuing republic introduced communist-inspired defeudalisation and collectivisation programmes and suppressed Buddhism. With the assistance of Soviet troops, Mongolia resisted Japanese attacks in the late 1930s and after the Second World War, Mongolia seemed likely to remain under Soviet control but in a 1946 UN plebiscite, the people voted for independence.

Mongolia became more open to external contacts from the mid-1980s and, influenced by events in eastern Europe, a democratisation campaign led to the first multiparty elections in 1990 and a massive privatisation programme, which began in 1991. The MPRP, which had eschewed communism, continued to dominate political life until 1996, when an alliance of nationalists and social democrats displaced it. The alliance quickly became the subject of corruption scandals and its transition to a market economy caused widespread social disruption and poverty. The MPRP returned to power in the 2001 election, having already regained the presidency in 1997, but lost nearly half of its seats in the legislature in the 2004 election.

In 2004 the MPRP won 36 seats and the Motherland Democratic Coalition (MDC) 34 seats; the two parties formed a coalition government with the MDC leader, Tsakhiagiin Elbegdorj, as prime minister. The coalition collapsed in 2006 after the MPRP members withdrew. Subsequently, the MPRP leader Miyeegombo Enkhbold was appointed prime minister and he formed a predominantly MPRP coalition. The 2005 presidential election was won by the MPRP candidate, Nambariyn Enkhbayar.

POLITICAL SYSTEM

The 1992 constitution established a parliamentary democracy. It was amended in 2000 to give the president the right to dissolve the legislature if it is unable to reach agreement on appointing a prime minister. The president is directly elected for a four-year term, which is renewable. The unicameral legislature is the *Ulsyn Ikh Khural* (State Great Hural) which has 76 members directly elected for a four-year term. The prime minister is elected by the Hural and appoints the cabinet.

HEAD OF STATE
President, Nambariyn Enkhbayar, *elected* 22 May 2005, *sworn in* 24 June 2005

SELECTED GOVERNMENT MEMBERS *as at June 2007*
Prime Minister, Miyeegombo Enkhbold
Defence, Mishigiyn Sonompil
Finance and Economy, Nadmidyn Bayartsaikhan
Foreign Affairs, Nyamaa Enkhbold
Justice and Internal Affairs, Dorjiyn Odbayar

EMBASSY OF MONGOLIA
7 Kensington Court, London W8 5DL
T 020-7937 0150 W www.embassyofmongolia.co.uk
Ambassador Extraordinary and Plenipotentiary, HE Dalrain Davaasambuu, *apptd* 2001

BRITISH EMBASSY
PO Box 703, 30 Enkh Taivny Gudamzh, Ulaanbaatar 13
T (+976) (11) 458 133 E britemb@mongol.net
Ambassador Extraordinary and Plenipotentiary, HE Christopher Osborne, *apptd* 2006

DEFENCE

The army has 370 main battle tanks, 150 armoured personnel carriers and 310 armoured infantry fighting vehicles. The air force has 11 attack helicopters.
MILITARY BUDGET – US$17m (2005)
MILITARY PERSONNEL – 8,600: army 7,500, air force 800, construction troops 300; paramilitaries 7,200
CONSCRIPTION DURATION – 12 months

ECONOMY AND TRADE

The economy suffered after the withdrawal of Soviet support and during the transition to a market economy, though in recent years it has shown signs of growth. Mongolia has been successful in attracting foreign investment and since 1990 foreign companies have invested more than US$800m (£406m) in mining, agricultural processing and infrastructure. However, economic growth is hindered by administrative corruption, the country's dependency on imported energy supplies (mostly from Russia) and the vulnerability of the agrarian sector to climate extremes, which decimated herds in 2000–2. About 36 per cent of the population lives below the poverty line.

Deposits of copper, coal, molybdenum, fluorspar, tin, tungsten and oil are being exploited, and gold mining has increased steadily since 1990. The agrarian sector, which makes up 22 per cent of GDP, engages 40 per cent of the workforce in agriculture and herding. The main products are grains, vegetables, forage crops, sheep, goats and other livestock. The main industries are construction, mining and the production of oil, food and beverages, cashmere and natural yarns.

The main export markets are China, the USA and Canada; the main import providers are Russia and China. Principal exports are copper, clothing, livestock, animal products, cashmere, wool and metals. The main imports are machinery and equipment, fuels, cars, foodstuffs, industrial goods, chemicals and construction materials.

GNI – US$1,800m; US$690 per capita (2005)
ANNUAL AVERAGE GROWTH OF GDP – 6.2 per cent (2005 est)
INFLATION RATE – 9.5 per cent (2005 est)
UNEMPLOYMENT – 6.7 per cent (2003)
TOTAL EXTERNAL DEBT – US$1,360m (2004)
IMPORTS – US$1,200m (2005)
EXPORTS – US$1,100m (2005)

BALANCE OF PAYMENTS
Trade – US$29m deficit (2004)
Current Account – US$25m deficit (2004)

Trade with UK	*2005*	*2006*
Imports from UK	£4,854,000	£3,593,000
Exports to UK	£1,772,000	£4,621,000

COMMUNICATIONS

Mongolia has 1,810km of railways and 49,250km of roads, though only about 4 per cent of the roads are surfaced. The main airport is at Ulaanbaatar, although there are over 40 other airports and airfields around the country. The lakes and main rivers are navigable in the summer months but ice-bound in winter. International trade is via Russia and China.

The telephone system is improving but there is a very low density of provision of land-lines. Mobile phone distribution has risen rapidly. In 2005 there were 156,000 main telephone lines in use, 557,200 mobile phone subscribers and 268,300 internet users.

MEDIA

There are five daily newspapers, including *Onoodor* which has the biggest circulation, and *Unen,* the organ of the Mongolian People's Revolutionary Party and the country's oldest newspaper. In 2005, the state-run radio and television was transformed into a public-service broadcaster. Violations of press freedom are rare.

MONTENEGRO

Republika Crna Gora – Republic of Montenegro

AREA – 14,026 sq. km. Neighbours: Bosnia and Hercegovina (north-west), Serbia (north-east) and the Serbian region of Kosovo (east), Albania (south), Croatia (south-west)
CAPITAL – Podgorica; population, 136,473 (2003)
MAJOR CITIES – Niksic
CURRENCY – Euro (€) of 100 cents
POPULATION – 630,548, rising at 3.5 per cent per year (2004); Montenegrin (43 per cent), Serbian (32 per cent), Bosniak (8 per cent), Albanian (5 per cent) (est)
LANGUAGE – Serbian (official), Bosnian, Albanian, Croatian
NATIONAL ANTHEM – 'Oj, Svijetla Majska Zoro' ['O, Bright Dawn of May']
NATIONAL DAY – 13 July
LIFE EXPECTANCY (years) – 74.73 (2005 est)
MORTALITY RATE – 10.49 (2005 est)
BIRTH RATE – 12.12 (2005 est)
INFANT MORTALITY RATE – 12.89 (2005 est)
DEATH PENALTY – No (abolished 2002)
POPULATION BELOW POVERTY LINE – 12.2 per cent (2003)
MILITARY PERSONNEL – army 4,000, navy 3,300

World Physical

40°W
30°W
20°W
70°N
10°W
0°
10°E
60°N
50°N
40°N
Arctic Circle
ICELAND
Reykjavík
Norwegian
Sea
0 100 200 300 400 Miles
0 100 200 300 400 500 600 Kms
Conical Orthomorphic Projection
© Oxford Cartographers, 96375
+44 (0) 1865 882 884
E & OE
Faroe Is.
(Denmark)
Shetland Is.
Trondheim
Bergen
Oslo
Stavanger
Kristiansand
Skagerrak
Gothenb
Orkney Is.
Hebrides
ATLANTIC
OCEAN
Inverness
Aberdeen
Dundee
Glasgow
Edinburgh
North
Sea
Londonderry
Belfast
UNITED
KINGDOM
Newcastle
upon Tyne
Galway
Dublin
REP. OF
IRELAND
Cork
Liverpool
Leeds
Manchester
Sheffield
Stoke-
on-Trent
Birmingham
Norwich
Swansea
Cardiff
Bristol
London
Plymouth
Southampton
English Channel
Alborg
Arhus
DENMARK
Odense
Kiel
Rostock
Hamburg
Bremen
Elbe
Amsterdam
NETHERLANDS
Rotterdam
Antwerp
Brussels
Osnabrück
Hanover
Munster
Essen
Düsseldorf
Cologne
Leipzig
Chemnitz
Lille
BELGIUM
LUX.
Luxembourg
GERMANY
Frankfurt
Cherbourg
Le Havre
Amiens
Rouen
Caen
Seine
Paris
Reims
Brest
Rennes
Metz
Mannheim
Nuremberg
Plzeň
Regensburg
Strasbourg
Nancy
Rhine
Stuttgart
Nantes
Loire
Orléans
Tours
Bay of
Biscay
FRANCE
Dijon
Munich
Salzbur
Zurich
Innsbruck
LIECH.
Bern
SWITZERLAND
Geneva
Mt. Blanc
4808
Limoges
Lyon
Clermont-
Ferrand
Grenoble
Rhône
Bordeaux
Milan
Trento
Verona
Trieste
Venice
Turin
Po
Parma
Genoa
Bologne
SAN
MARINO
La Spezia
La Coruña
Gijón
Vigo
León
Bilbao
San Sebastian
Pamplona
Burgos
Valladolid
Pyrenees
Toulouse
Montpellier
Nimes
Nice
MONACO
Marseille
ANDORRA
Livorno
Florence
Ancona
ITALY
Oporto
Douro
Coimbra
PORTUGAL
Salamanca
Zaragoza
Lerida
Lisbon
Setúbal
Tagus
Madrid
SPAIN
Barcelona
Corsica
(Fr.)
Ajaccio
Rome
Badajoz
Valencia
Balearic Is.
(Sp.)
Sassari
Naples
Faro
Huelva
Córdoba
Seville
Palma
Mallorca
Sardinia
(It.)
Granada
Murcia
Cartagena
Cadiz
Málaga
Almeria
Mediterrane
Cagliari
Tangier
Gibraltar(U.K.)
Ceuta(Sp.)
Tétouan
Palermo
Algiers
Rabat
Melilla(Sp.)
Oran
Blida
Bejaia
Skikda
Annaba
Aryanah
Tunis
Casablanca
Fès
Meknès
Oujda
Sidi Bel Abbès
Constantine
MOROCCO
Atlas
Mountains
ALGERIA
TUNISIA
Sousse
10°W
0°
10°E
Sfax

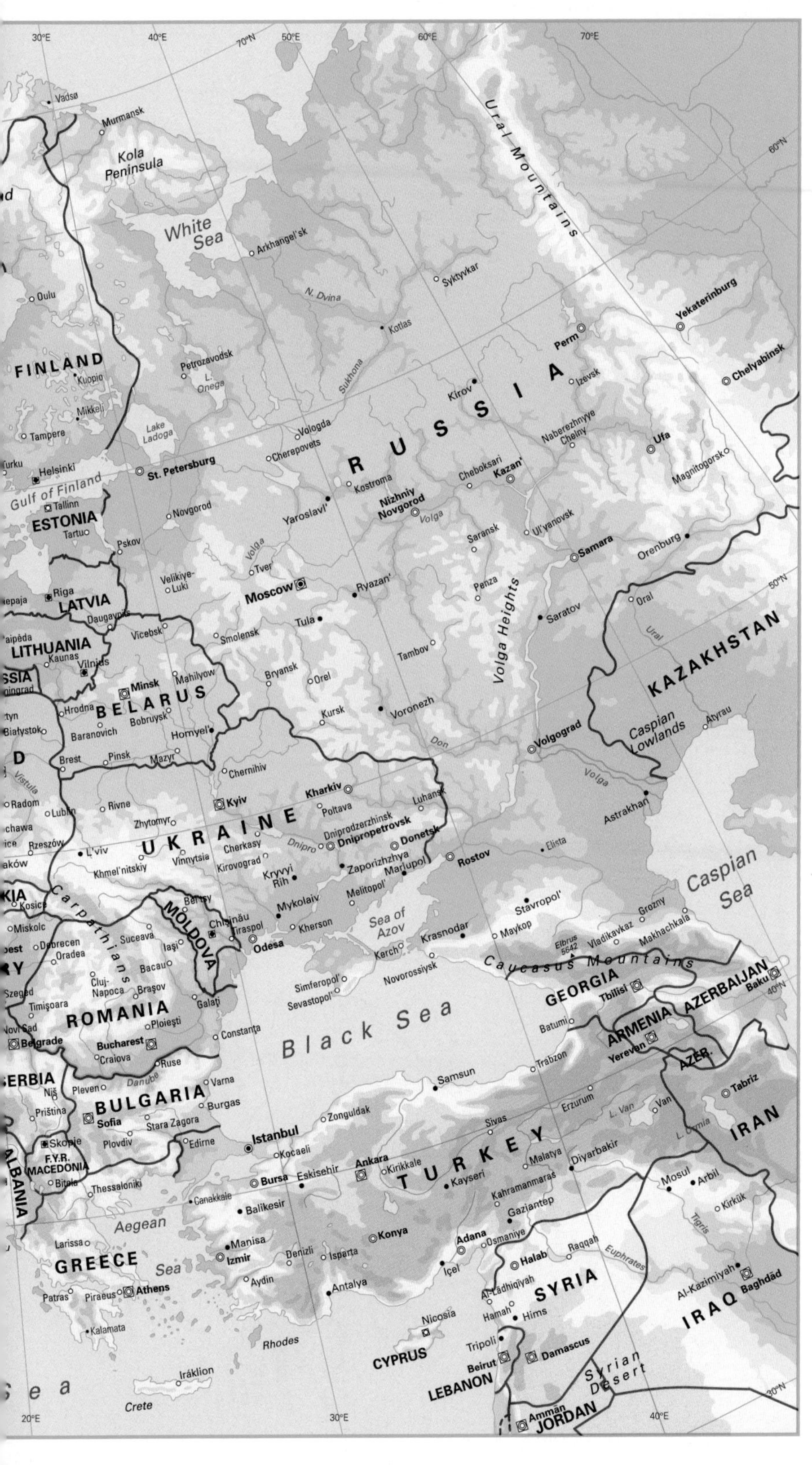

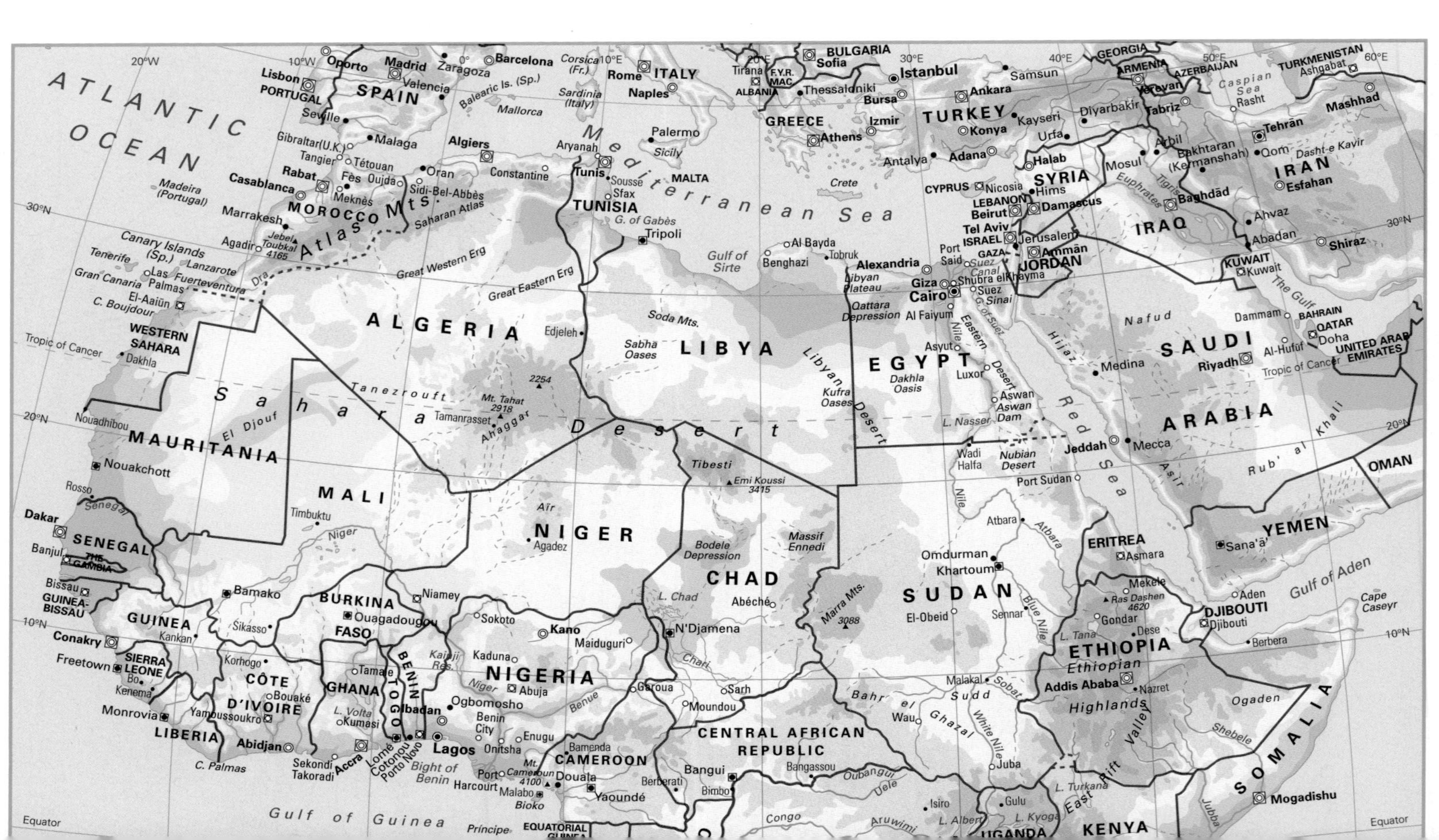

ATLANTIC OCEAN
Mediterranean Sea
Red Sea
Gulf of Guinea
Gulf of Aden
The Gulf
Caspian Sea
Sahara Desert
Libyan Desert
Eastern Desert
Nubian Desert
PORTUGAL
Lisbon
Oporto
SPAIN
Madrid
Zaragoza
Barcelona
Valencia
Seville
Malaga
Gibraltar(U.K.)
Balearic Is. (Sp.)
Mallorca
Corsica (Fr.)
Sardinia (Italy)
ITALY
Rome
Naples
Palermo
Sicily
MALTA
ALBANIA
Tirana
F.Y.R. MAC
GREECE
Thessaloniki
Athens
Crete
BULGARIA
Sofia
TURKEY
Istanbul
Bursa
Izmir
Ankara
Samsun
Konya
Kayseri
Antalya
Adana
Diyarbakir
Urfa
GEORGIA
ARMENIA
Yerevan
AZERBAIJAN
TURKMENISTAN
Ashgabat
IRAN
Tehrān
Tabriz
Rasht
Mashhad
Qom
Dasht-e Kavir
Esfahan
Bakhtaran (Kermanshah)
Ahvaz
Abadan
Shiraz
IRAQ
Baghdād
Mosul
Arbil
Euphrates
Tigris
SYRIA
Halab
Hims
Damascus
CYPRUS
Nicosia
LEBANON
Beirut
ISRAEL
Tel Aviv
Jerusalem
GAZA
JORDAN
Ammān
KUWAIT
Kuwait
SAUDI ARABIA
Riyadh
Medina
Mecca
Jeddah
Dammam
Al-Hufūf
Nafud
Hijaz
Asir
Rub' al Khali
BAHRAIN
QATAR
Doha
UNITED ARAB EMIRATES
OMAN
YEMEN
Sana'ā'
Aden
Cape Caseyr
Tropic of Cancer
Equator
MOROCCO
Rabat
Casablanca
Marrakesh
Agadir
Tangier
Tétouan
Fès
Meknès
Oujda
Atlas Mts
Jebel Toubkal 4165
Saharan Atlas
Madeira (Portugal)
Canary Islands (Sp.)
Tenerife
Gran Canaria
Las Palmas
Lanzarote
Fuerteventura
Dra
WESTERN SAHARA
El-Aaiūn
C. Boujdour
Dakhla
ALGERIA
Algiers
Oran
Sidi-Bel-Abbès
Constantine
Great Western Erg
Great Eastern Erg
Tanezrouft
Tamanrasset
Mt. Tahat 2918
Ahaggar
2254
Edjeleh
TUNISIA
Tunis
Aryanah
Sousse
Sfax
G. of Gabès
LIBYA
Tripoli
Gulf of Sirte
Benghazi
Al Bayda
Tobruk
Soda Mts.
Sabha Oases
Kufra Oases
EGYPT
Cairo
Alexandria
Giza
Shubra el Khayma
Port Said
Suez
Suez Canal
Sinai
G. of Suez
Al Faiyum
Asyut
Luxor
Aswan
Aswan Dam
L. Nasser
Nile
Qattara Depression
Libyan Plateau
Dakhla Oasis
MAURITANIA
Nouakchott
Nouadhibou
El Djouf
Rosso
MALI
Timbuktu
Bamako
Niger
NIGER
Niamey
Aïr
Agadez
CHAD
N'Djamena
L. Chad
Abéché
Tibesti
Emi Koussi 3415
Bodele Depression
Massif Ennedi
Chari
SUDAN
Khartoum
Omdurman
Port Sudan
Atbara
Wadi Halfa
El-Obeid
Sennar
Malakal
Sudd
Wau
Juba
Marra Mts. 3088
Blue Nile
White Nile
Sobat
Bahr el Ghazal
ERITREA
Asmara
ETHIOPIA
Addis Ababa
Mekele
Ras Dashen 4620
Gondar
Dese
Nazret
L. Tana
Ethiopian Highlands
East Rift Valley
DJIBOUTI
Djibouti
SOMALIA
Mogadishu
Berbera
Ogaden
Shebele
Jubba
KENYA
L. Turkana
UGANDA
Gulu
L. Kyoga
L. Albert
Isiro
Aruwimi
Uele
Oubangui
Congo
SENEGAL
Dakar
Senegal
THE GAMBIA
Banjul
GUINEA-BISSAU
Bissau
GUINEA
Conakry
Kankan
SIERRA LEONE
Freetown
Bo
Kenema
LIBERIA
Monrovia
C. Palmas
CÔTE D'IVOIRE
Yamoussoukro
Abidjan
Bouaké
Korhogo
Sikasso
BURKINA FASO
Ouagadougou
GHANA
Accra
Kumasi
Tamale
L. Volta
Sekondi Takoradi
TOGO
Lomé
BENIN
Cotonou
Porto Novo
NIGERIA
Lagos
Abuja
Ibadan
Ogbomosho
Kano
Kaduna
Sokoto
Maiduguri
Benin City
Onitsha
Enugu
Port Harcourt
Kainji Res.
Benue
Bight of Benin
CAMEROON
Yaoundé
Douala
Bamenda
Garoua
Mt. Cameroun 4100
EQUATORIAL GUINEA
Malabo
Bioko
Príncipe
CENTRAL AFRICAN REPUBLIC
Bangui
Bangassou
Berberati
Bimbo
Sarh
Moundou
10°W
0°
10°E
20°E
30°E
40°E
50°E
60°E
20°W
30°N
20°N
10°N

GROSS ENROLMENT RATIO (percentage of relevant age group) – primary 99 per cent; secondary 89 per cent; tertiary 36 per cent (2002)

CLIMATE AND TERRAIN

The terrain is mountainous in the north and centre of the country, intersected by the deep canyon of the Tara river valley, and falls to low-lying plains on the Adriatic coast. About half of the country is forested. Elevation extremes range from 2,522m (Bobotov Kuk) at the highest point to 0m (Adriatic Sea) at the lowest. The main rivers are the Piva (Drina), the Tara and the Lim. Lake Skadarsko straddles the border with Albania. The climate inland is moderate and continental, while along the coast a Mediterranean-Adriatic climate prevails. Average temperatures in Podgorica range from 5°C in January to 31°C in July.

HISTORY AND POLITICS

The area was part of the Roman province of Illyria, and then was settled by Slavs in the seventh century. In the late 12th century it was incorporated into the medieval kingdom of Serbia and so became part of the Ottoman Empire after Serbia's defeat by the Turks in 1389. When Serbia became independent in 1878, Montenegro followed and remained an independent monarchy until the end of the First World War. In 1918, Montenegro joined with Serbia and the former Austro-Hungarian provinces of Slovenia, Croatia and Bosnia-Hercegovina to form the Kingdom of Serbs, Croats and Slovenes, which was renamed Yugoslavia in 1929. Yugoslavia was occupied by Axis forces in 1941 and reformed as a communist federal republic under the presidency of partisan leader Josip Tito in 1945. When the federation disintegrated in 1991, Serbia and Montenegro formed the Federal Republic of Yugoslavia, which was declared on 27 April 1992.

Montenegro's desire for independence led in 2002 to an EU-brokered agreement between the leaders of Serbia, Montenegro and the Federal Republic of Yugoslavia to restructure the republic into a union of two semi-independent states; the union was renamed Serbia and Montenegro. The constitutional charter for the new union, which came into effect in March 2003, provided for the two republics to hold referendums on whether to retain or end the union after a minimum of three years. A referendum was held in Montenegro on 21 May 2006 and 55.5 per cent voted in favour of independence, which was declared on 3 June and acknowledged by the Serbian legislature on 5 June. Montenegro was admitted as a member of the UN on 26 June. Negotiations on separating the two states' assets are in progress.

The May 2002 presidential election in Montenegro failed to elect a president because of low turnout and President Milo Djukanovic remained in office. The minimum turnout rule was subsequently altered and in May 2003 the former prime minister Filip Vujanovic was elected president. The 2006 legislative election was won by the For a European Montenegro coalition. A coalition government was formed by the Democratic Party of Socialists, Social Democratic Party and Democratic Union of Albanians.

POLITICAL SYSTEM

The head of state is a president, who is directly elected for a five-year term. The unicameral legislature, the assembly, has 81 members directly elected for a four-year term; five members are elected from the ethnic Albanian community. The prime minister appoints the cabinet, subject to the approval of the assembly.

HEAD OF STATE
President, Filip Vujanovic, *elected* 11 May 2003

SELECTED GOVERNMENT MEMBERS *as at June 2007*
Prime Minister, Zeljko Sturanovic
Deputy Prime Ministers, Gordana Djurovic; Vujica Lazovic
Finance, Igor Luksic
Foreign Affairs, Milan Rocen
Defence, Boro Vucinic

BRITISH HONORARY CONSUL
First Floor, No. 3, Bulevar Svetog Petra Cetinjskog nn, 81000 Podgorica
T (+381) (81) 205 460 E britishoffice@cg.yu
Ambassador Extraordinary and Plenipotentiary, John Dyson, MVO, *apptd* 2006

ECONOMY AND TRADE

Montenegro achieved fiscal autonomy from the Yugoslav federation in the 1990s, managing its own budget, collecting customs tariffs on its own account, maintaining its own central bank and adopting the euro in place of the dinar. However, it faced the same problems as Serbia – slow growth, foreign debt, lack of foreign investment, high unemployment, corruption and organised crime – as well as having more limited health and educational facilities and a poor administrative capacity. It has privatised its aluminium industry and financial sector, and is beginning to attract foreign direct investment in tourism.

Since independence, it has pursued international integration, and especially its bid for EU membership, which is a priority of the post-independence government. The main agricultural products are grain, tobacco, fruit and vegetables. Major industrial activities include production of steel, aluminium and consumer goods, processing of agricultural products and tourism. The main trading partners are Switzerland, Italy, Bosnia and Hercegovina, Greece and Germany.

*GDP – US$15,500m (2003); US$1,910 per capita (2003)
*ANNUAL AVERAGE GROWTH OF GDP – 4 per cent (2005 est)
*INFLATION RATE – 15.5 per cent (2005 est)
*UNEMPLOYMENT – 27.7 per cent (2005)
*TOTAL EXTERNAL DEBT – US$11,960m (2000 est)
* Figures are for Serbia and Montenegro

Trade with UK	*2006*
Imports from UK	£1,583,000
Exports to UK	£1,154,000

COMMUNICATIONS

Montenegro's independence leaves Serbia landlocked, although access to the Adriatic ports of Bar and Kotor is expected to be negotiated. There is 250km of rail track, part of the European system linking Bar with Belgrade, via Podgorica. The 7,300km of roads include major roads linking Podgorica and the coastal ports with the hinterland and neighbouring countries. There are five airports, including international airports at Podgorica and Tivat. Modernised telecommunications systems provide services to 178,000 main-line subscribers, 543,000 mobile phone subscribers and 50,000 internet users.

MEDIA

Freedom of the press is guaranteed and media laws passed in 2002 provide for the transformation of the state-funded RCTG into a public broadcaster. Overseas donors and organisations have contributed funds to stimulate private media growth, but this has been limited by small advertising revenue.

MOROCCO

Al-Mamlakah al-Maghribiyah – Kingdom of Morocco

AREA – 446,550 sq. km. Neighbours: Algeria (east and south-east), Western Sahara (south-west)
CAPITAL – Rabat; population, 1,622,860 (2004)
MAJOR CITIES – Casablanca; Fez; Marrakesh; Agadir; Tangier; Meknes
CURRENCY – Dirham (DH) of 100 centimes
POPULATION – 33,241,259 rising at 1.55 per cent per year (2006 est)
RELIGION – Islam (99 per cent); almost all Muslims practice Sunni Islam
LANGUAGE – Arabic (official), French, Berber dialects
POPULATION DENSITY – 68 per sq. km (2005)
URBAN POPULATION – 58.8 per cent (2005 est)
MEDIAN AGE (years) – 23.9 (2006 est)
NATIONAL ANTHEM – 'Hymne Cherifien' ['Kingdom of Morocco']
NATIONAL DAY – 30 July (Throne Day)
LIFE EXPECTANCY (years) – 70.94 (2006 est)
MORTALITY RATE – 5.58 (2006 est)
BIRTH RATE – 21.98 (2006 est)
INFANT MORTALITY RATE – 40.24 (2006 est)
DEATH PENALTY – No*
CPI SCORE – 3.2 (2006)
POPULATION BELOW POVERTY LINE – 19 per cent (2005 est)

CLIMATE AND TERRAIN

Fertile coastal plains in the west rise to a mountainous centre, with ranges, including the Atlas range, running north-east to south-west. The Rif mountains lie along the northern, Mediterranean coast. Elevation extremes range from 4,165m (Jbel Toubkal) at the highest point to −55m (Sebkha Tah) at the lowest. Average temperatures in Rabat range from 7°C in January to 29°C in July, although summer temperatures in the desert interior can reach as high as 41°C.

HISTORY AND POLITICS

From the tenth century BC, the northern coast was settled by the Phoenicians. In the first century AD, Morocco became part of the Roman Empire until it was invaded by first the Vandals and then the Visigoths in the fifth and sixth centuries. Arab conquest of the area began in the seventh century and Morocco was part of a succession of Arab empires, but successfully resisted inclusion in the Turkish Ottoman Empire in the 16th century. The current Alawite dynasty was founded in the mid-17th century and under its rule Morocco remained independent but isolated until the mid-19th century, when the country opened up to European trade. The subsequent growth in Spanish and French influence resulted in its partition into two protectorates. In the Second World War, Morocco was a base for the Allied offensives that drove German forces out of North Africa.

Nationalist campaigning for independence began in the 1940s. French and Spanish forces withdrew in 1956, leaving Morocco independent under Sultan Mohammed V, who adopted the title of king in 1957; the coastal towns of Ceuta and Melilla remain under Spanish control. King Hassan II, who ruled from 1961 to 1999, annexed the mineral-rich Western Sahara region in 1975.

Since the accession of King Mohammed VI in 1999, Morocco has been moving away from absolute monarchy, increasing civil liberties and addressing human rights issues. The 2002 election to the house of representatives, seen by many to be the most democratic the country has ever held, was won by the Socialist Union of Popular Forces (USFP). They formed a coalition government with the Independence Party led by prime minister Driss Jettou. The next legislative elections were due in September 2007.

POLITICAL SYSTEM

The 1992 constitution was amended in 1996 to introduce a bicameral legislature. The head of state is a hereditary constitutional monarch. The king appoints the prime minister and, on the latter's recommendation, appoints the members of the council of ministers. There is a bicameral legislature. The lower house, the *Majlis al-Nuwab* (house of representatives) has 325 members who are directly elected for a five-year term. The *Majlis al-Mustashareen* (house of councillors) has 270 members, elected by local councils, professional organisations and the 'salaried classes'. One-third of its members is elected every three years, to serve a nine-year term.

HEAD OF STATE

HM The King of Morocco, King Mohammed VI (Sidi Mohammed Ben Hassan), *born* 21 August 1963, *acceded* 23 July 1999
Heir, HRH Crown Prince Moulay Hassan, *born* 2003

SELECTED GOVERNMENT MEMBERS *as at June 2007*

Prime Minister, Driss Jettou
Finance and Privatisation, Fathallah Oualalou
Foreign Affairs and Cooperation, Mohammed Benaissa
Interior Affairs, Chakib Benmoussa

EMBASSY OF THE KINGDOM OF MOROCCO

49 Queen's Gate Gardens, London SW7 5NE
T 020-7581 5001 E ihilan@yahoo.co.uk
Ambassador Extraordinary and Plenipotentiary, HE Mohammed Belmahi, *apptd* 1999

BRITISH EMBASSY

PO Box 45, 17 Boulevard de la Tour Hassan, Rabat
T (+212) (37) 729696 E consular.rabat@fco.gov.uk
W www.britain.org.ma
Ambassador Extraordinary and Plenipotentiary, HE Charles Gray, *apptd* 2005

BRITISH COUNCIL

36 rue de Tanger, BP 427, Rabat
T (+212) (37) 760 836 W www.britishcouncil.org/morocco
Director, Adam Ladbury

DEFENCE

The army has 540 main battle tanks, 70 armoured infantry fighting vehicles, and 765 armoured personnel carriers. The navy has 3 frigates and 27 patrol and coastal combatant vessels at five bases. The air force has 89 combat aircraft and 19 armed helicopters.
MILITARY BUDGET – US$2,190m (2006)

MILITARY PERSONNEL – 200,800: army 180,000, navy 7,800, air force 13,000; paramilitaries 50,000
CONSCRIPTION DURATION – 18 months

ECONOMY AND TRADE

Economic liberalisation since 1999 has attracted foreign direct investment, but private-sector enterprises are few, the financial system is rudimentary and the country is dependent on foreign energy imports, factors which inhibit growth. Morocco remains a poor country, with 19 per cent of the population living below the poverty line and unemployment averaging 11 per cent, though it is often nearly twice this level in urban areas; the remittances of expatriate workers are crucial to the domestic economy.

The large agrarian sector generates 13 per cent of GDP and engages 40 per cent of the workforce, producing cereals, citrus fruits, vegetables, wine, olives and livestock. It faces environmental problems such as desertification and soil erosion. Another major sector is the exploitation of mineral reserves, especially phosphate. Other industries include food processing, textiles, leather goods, construction and tourism, which the government wishes to expand. Industry accounts for 31 per cent of GDP and services for 56 per cent.

The main trading partners are EU countries and, increasingly, the USA, with which Morocco has trade agreements. Principal exports are clothing, inorganic chemicals, crude minerals, fertilisers, petroleum products and foodstuffs. The main imports are crude petroleum, fabrics, telecommunications equipment, wheat, gas and electricity.

GNI – US$52,600m; US$1,740 per capita (2005)
ANNUAL AVERAGE GROWTH OF GDP – 1.7 per cent (2005 est)
INFLATION RATE – 1 per cent (2005 est)
UNEMPLOYMENT – 11 per cent (2005 est)
TOTAL EXTERNAL DEBT – US$15,610m (2005 est)
IMPORTS – US$20,300m (2005)
EXPORTS – US$10,500m (2005)

BALANCE OF PAYMENTS
Trade – US$6,487m deficit (2004)
Current Account – US$922m surplus (2004)

Trade with UK	*2005*	*2006*
Imports from UK	£262,882,000	£290,102,000
Exports to UK	£472,289,000	£380,820,000

COMMUNICATIONS

There are 1,907km of railways linking the major towns and there are 57,500km of roads; a 32,700km network of surfaced roads connects the main towns. The main ports are Tangier, Casablanca and Agadir, on the Atlantic coast. The principal airports are at Rabat, Agadir, Casablanca and Marrakesh; Royal Air Maroc is the national airline. There is a modern telephone system, although main-line density is low. In 2005 there were 1.3 million main-line subscribers, 12.4 million mobile phone subscribers and 4.6 million internet users; internet access is expensive.

EDUCATION AND HEALTH

Education is compulsory between the ages of seven and 16. There are government primary, secondary and technical schools. At Fez there is a theological university. Schools for special denominations, Jewish and Catholic, are permitted and may receive government grants.

LITERACY RATE – 50.7 per cent (2004 est)
GROSS ENROLMENT RATIO (percentage of relevant age group) – primary 105 per cent; secondary 50 per cent; tertiary 11 per cent (2005 est)
HEALTH EXPENDITURE (per capita) – US$82 (2004)
HOSPITAL BEDS (per 1,000 people) – 0.8 (2000–5)

MEDIA

State control of the media has eased since the accession of King Mohammad VI, although its freedom to cover some topics is limited. There are three daily newspapers, one of which is state-owned. State-owned television and radio compete with a private broadcaster.

WESTERN SAHARA

Al-Jumhuriyya al-'Arabiyya as-Sahrawiyya ad-Dimuqratiyya – Sahrawi Arab Democratic Republic

AREA – 266,000 sq. km. Neighbours: Morocco (north), Algeria (north-east), Mauritania (east and south)
POPULATION – 273,008 (2006 est)
ADMINISTRATIVE CENTRE – El-Aaiun (Laayoune)
RELIGION – Islam (99 per cent) (est)
LANGUAGE – Arabic, Hassaniya, Spanish
FLAG – Three horizontal stripes of black, white and green with a red crescent and a five-pointed star in the centre and a red triangle based on the hoist

Western Sahara came under Spanish rule in 1884, and became a province in 1934. Following Spain's withdrawal in 1975, Morocco and Mauritania annexed the territory and divided it between them. The Polisario Front began a guerrilla war to secure the Western Sahara's independence as the Sahrawi Arab Democratic Republic, which they declared in 1976, setting up a government in exile. In 1979, Mauritania withdrew from its part of the territory, which was annexed by Morocco. Fighting between Polisario and Moroccan forces continued at varying levels of intensity until 1991, when a UN-brokered ceasefire came into effect. Around 180,000 Sahrawis were driven into exile, some to Algeria and some to Mauritania.

The 1991 ceasefire was established following both sides' agreement in 1988 to UN proposals for a peace settlement, which included the holding of a referendum on the future status of Western Sahara. But the precise terms of the referendum have proved a sticking point and an impasse was reached that has still not been overcome despite further proposals in the period 2001–4; Polisario agreed to a referendum offering the options of independence, semi-autonomy or integration for Western Sahara, but Morocco is only prepared to accept semi-autonomy or integration. The UN suspended the process of preparing for the referendum in 1996 because of disagreements over voter registration; the ceasefire remains in place.

MOZAMBIQUE

República de Moçambique – Republic of Mozambique

AREA – 801,590 sq. km. Neighbours: Swaziland (south), South Africa (south and west), Zimbabwe (west), Zambia and Malawi (north-west), Tanzania (north)
CAPITAL – Maputo; population, 1,074,800 (2004 est)
MAJOR CITIES – Matola; Beira; Nampula
CURRENCY – Metical (MT) of 100 centavos
POPULATION – 19,686,505 rising at 1.38 per cent per year (2006 est)

RELIGION – Roman Catholicism (10 per cent), Protestantism (9 per cent), Islam (8 per cent) (est). Indigenous practices are present in most Christian and Muslim worship. The majority of the population does not practice an organised religion
LANGUAGE – Portuguese (official), Emakhuwa, Xichangana, Elomwe
POPULATION DENSITY – 25 per sq. km (2005)
URBAN POPULATION – 38 per cent (2005 est)
MEDIAN AGE (years) – 18.3 (2006 est)
NATIONAL ANTHEM – 'Patria Amada' ['Beloved Fatherland']
NATIONAL DAY – 25 June (Independence Day)
LIFE EXPECTANCY (years) – 39.82 (2006 est)
MORTALITY RATE – 21.35 (2006 est)
BIRTH RATE – 35.18 (2006 est)
INFANT MORTALITY RATE – 129.24 (2006 est)
HIV/AIDS ADULT PREVALENCE – 12.2 per cent (2003 est)
DEATH PENALTY – No (abolished 1990)
CPI SCORE – 2.8 (2006)
POPULATION BELOW POVERTY LINE – 70 per cent (2001 est)
MILITARY BUDGET – US$58m (2006 est)
MILITARY PERSONNEL – 11,200: army 10,000, navy 200, air force 1,000
CONSCRIPTION DURATION – 24 months
LITERACY RATE – 46.5 per cent (2004 est)
GROSS ENROLMENT RATIO (percentage of relevant age group) – primary 105 per cent; secondary 14 per cent; tertiary 1 per cent (2005 est)
HEALTH EXPENDITURE (per capita) – US$12 (2004)

CLIMATE AND TERRAIN

Coastal plains rise to plateaux in the centre and west, with mountains on the western borders. Elevation extremes range from 2,436m (Mt Binga) at the highest point to 0m (Indian Ocean) at the lowest. A number of rivers run from the western highlands to the Indian Ocean coast, including the Zambezi, Limpopo, Sava and Ruvuma. The climate is tropical, with average temperatures in the capital an almost constant 28°C.

HISTORY AND POLITICS

Between the first and fourth centuries Mozambique was settled by Bantu peoples. Trade with India and the Arabian peninsula grew and migrants from both these regions settled in the coastal areas. The first European contact was with the Portuguese explorer Vasco de Gama, who arrived in 1498. Over the next three centuries the Portuguese exploited Mozambique for gold, ivory, spices and slaves. Proximity to the South African gold mines led to Mozambique's development as an important trading post from the late 19th century, and also as a source of cheap labour. It was administered as part of Portuguese India from 1751, becoming a separate colony in the late 19th century and an overseas province of Portugal in 1951. Concessions to private companies that had operated as *de facto* rulers over much of the country were ended in 1930.

The *Frente de Libertacao de Mocambique* (Frelimo) was founded in 1962 to fight for independence and a ten-year guerrilla war against Portuguese forces began in 1964. Independence was achieved in 1975, when a one-party socialist republic was set up. Opposition to this was led from 1977 by the *Resistencia Nacional de Mocambique* (Renamo) and a brutal civil war broke out that lasted until 1992. It was ended by a peace settlement that gave Renamo political party status. Mozambique joined the Commonwealth in 1996, becoming the only member country never to have been under British rule. Reconstruction of the economy and infrastructure progressed quickly after the civil war, although a series of natural catastrophes since 2000 have been major setbacks. An additional problem is the large number of remaining landmines, and the resulting amputees. The level of HIV/AIDS infection is also high.

In 1990 Frelimo abandoned Marxist-Leninism and ended one-party rule, introducing a multiparty system. The first elections under the new constitution were held in 1994 and won by Frelimo. Frelimo retained power in the 1999 and 2004 legislative and presidential elections, prompting allegations of vote-rigging by Renamo, though monitors believe that any irregularities were minor. In the December 2004 elections, the Frelimo candidate, Armando Guebuza, was elected president with 63.7 per cent of the vote, and Frelimo won 160 seats in the legislature, retaining its overall majority.

POLITICAL SYSTEM

Under the 2004 constitution, the executive president is directly elected and serves for a five-year term, which is renewable only once. The unicameral legislature, the *Assembleia da Republica* (assembly of the republic), has 250 members, who are directly elected for a five-year term. The president appoints the prime minister and the council of ministers.

HEAD OF STATE

President, Armando Emilio Guebuza, *elected* 22 December 2004, *sworn in* 2 February 2005

SELECTED GOVERNMENT MEMBERS *as at June 2007*

Prime Minister, Minister of Planning and Finance, Luisa Dias Diogo
Foreign Affairs, Alcinda Abreu
Interior, Jose Pacheco
National Defence, Tobias Joaquim Dai

HIGH COMMISSION FOR THE REPUBLIC OF MOZAMBIQUE

21 Fitzroy Square, London W1T 6EL
T 020-7383 3800 W www.mozambiquehc.org.uk
High Commissioner, HE Antonio Gumende, *apptd* 2002

BRITISH HIGH COMMISSION

PO Box 55, Av. Vladimir I Lenine 310, Maputo
T (+258) (21) 420 111 E info.maputo@fco.gov.uk
High Commissioner, HE Andrew Soper, *apptd* 2007

BRITISH COUNCIL

PO Box 4178, Rua John Issa 226, Maputo
T (+258) (1) 355 000 W www.britishcouncil.org/mozambique
Director, Peter Brown

ECONOMY AND TRADE

Political stability and economic liberalisation have attracted foreign direct investment and donor support, and achieved economic growth despite setbacks from devastating flooding (2000, 2001), droughts (2002, 2003) and an earthquake (2006). The country remains poor, with 70 per cent of the population living below the poverty line, and is dependent on foreign aid. The huge foreign debt has been reduced to a more manageable size by debt cancellation and rescheduling, but there is a substantial ongoing trade imbalance.

Agriculture is the mainstay of the economy, accounting for 21 per cent of GDP and engaging 81 per cent of the workforce; shellfish, cotton, cashew nuts, sugar and citrus fruits are important exports. There are considerable oil, gas, mineral and hydroelectric power resources, which are increasingly being exploited. Industries include aluminium extraction and smelting, food processing, production of beverages, fertiliser and petroleum. There are plans to expand titanium extraction and processing, and garment-manufacturing. Industry generates 31 per cent of GDP and services 48 per cent.

The main trading partners are the Netherlands and South Africa. Principal exports are aluminium, agricultural products, timber and electricity. The main imports are machinery, vehicles, fuel, chemicals, metal products, foodstuffs and textiles.

GNI – US$6,200m; US$310 per capita (2005)
ANNUAL AVERAGE GROWTH OF GDP – 7.5 per cent (2005 est)
INFLATION RATE – 6.5 per cent (2005 est)
TOTAL EXTERNAL DEBT – US$5,456m (2005 est)
IMPORTS US$2,000m (2005)

BALANCE OF PAYMENTS
Trade – US$497m deficit (2005)
Current Account – US$761m deficit (2005)

Trade with UK	*2005*	*2006*
Imports from UK	£11,271,000	£11,364,000
Exports to UK	£8,760,000	£5,754,000

COMMUNICATIONS

The main seaports are Maputo, Beira and Nacala; these handle trade also for landlocked countries such as Malawi and Zimbabwe, to which they are linked by rail. A new rail link to South Africa has been commissioned, and there are plans to develop rail and road links to Malawi and Zambia. There is currently a total of 3,123km of railways. Of the 30,400km of roads, only about one sixth is surfaced. The 460km of navigable waterways are on Cahora Bassa Lake and the lower reaches of the Zambezi. The principal airports are at Maputo and Beira, with over 150 smaller airports and airstrips around the country.

The telephone system is efficient but availability is limited and mobile phone distribution is much higher than land-line density. There were 70,000 main lines in use in 2004, and 1.2 million mobile phone subscribers and 138,000 internet users in 2005.

MEDIA

Freedom of speech is guaranteed in the constitution. There are two daily newspapers and three weekly publications, which have little influence outside urban areas due to low literacy levels, plus two television stations. Radio is the main medium for most people, with UNESCO and the government funding around 40 stations.

MYANMAR

Pyidaungzu Myanma Naingngandaw – Union of Myanmar

AREA – 676,500 sq. km. Neighbours: Bangladesh and India (west), China (north), Laos and Thailand (east)
CAPITAL – Naypyidaw
MAJOR CITIES – Yangon (Rangoon); Mandalay; Mawlamyine (Moulmein); Bago
CURRENCY – Kyat (K) of 100 pyas
POPULATION – 47,382,633 rising at 0.81 per cent per year (2006 est); Burman (68 per cent), Shan (9 per cent), Karen (7 per cent), Rakhine (4 per cent), Chinese (3 per cent), Indian (2 per cent), Mon (2 per cent) (est)
RELIGION – Buddhism (90 per cent), Christianity (4 per cent), Islam (4 per cent) (est)
LANGUAGE – Burmese (official)
POPULATION DENSITY – 77 per sq. km (2005)
URBAN POPULATION – 30.6 per cent (2005 est)
MEDIAN AGE (years) – 27 (2006 est)
NATIONAL ANTHEM – 'Kaba Ma Kyei' ['Till the End of the World, Myanmar']
NATIONAL DAY – 4 January (Independence Day)
LIFE EXPECTANCY (years) – 60.97 (2006 est)
MORTALITY RATE – 9.83 (2006 est)
BIRTH RATE – 17.91 (2006 est)
INFANT MORTALITY RATE – 61.85 (2006 est)
HIV/AIDS ADULT PREVALENCE – 1.2 per cent (2003 est)
DEATH PENALTY – No*
CPI SCORE – 1.8 (2006)
POPULATION BELOW POVERTY LINE – 25 per cent (2000 est)

CLIMATE AND TERRAIN

Central lowlands are ringed by mountains in the west, north (part of the foothills of the Himalayas) and east, and running down the Kra isthmus that Myanmar shares with Thailand. Elevation extremes range from 5,881m (Hkakabo Razi) at the highest point to 0m (Andaman Sea) at the lowest. The lowlands are drained by the Irrawaddy River and its chief tributary, the Chindwin, and the eastern mountains by the Salween. The climate is tropical, with a wet season from May to October. Average temperatures range from 16°C in January to 36°C in July, although summer temperatures in the interior can reach 43°C.

HISTORY AND POLITICS

Myanmar (also known as Burma) was first unified in the 11th century by King Anawrahta, who adopted Theravada Buddhism. The Mongols under Kublai Khan invaded in 1287. The country was reunified in the 15th century but was weakened by internal dissension and wars with Siam (Thailand). King Alaunghpaya reunited the nation in the 18th century. In the first half of the 19th century, border disputes with British India spiralled into a series of wars. Following the third Anglo-Burmese war, Burma was annexed as part of British India in 1885. It became a separate crown colony in 1937, and was occupied by the Japanese during the Second World War. Following liberation by British troops and Burmese nationalists, the country gained its independence as the quasi-federal Union of Burma in 1948.

Following a left-wing military coup led by Gen. Ne Win in 1962, the federal system was abolished and the economy nationalised. In 1974, a one-party socialist republic was formally established. Another coup in 1988 brought to power Gen. Saw Maung, who replaced all existing state institutions with the State Law and Order Council (SLORC), imposed martial law and changed the country's name to Myanmar; the SLORC was replaced by the State Peace and Development Council in 1997.

Pro-democracy forces, notably the National League for Democracy (NLD) under Aung San Suu Kyi, oppose military rule. In 1990 the NLD won a landslide victory in the first multiparty elections for 30 years. The military ignored the election results, prevented the constituent assembly from convening, and have continued to rule by diktat, suppressing and persecuting pro-democracy campaigners. Aung San Suu Kyi was under house arrest from 1989 to 1995 and almost continuously from 2000 to date. The NLD took part in UN-brokered talks with the government in 2000 but these stalled in 2003 and the NLD boycotted a constitutional convention that began in May 2004.

The constitutional convention was called by the then prime minister Khin Nyut, who was perceived to be a moderate; he was dismissed amid rumours of a power struggle in 2004 and placed under house arrest on charges of corruption. Lt.-Gen. Soe Win was immediately named as his replacement. The constitutional convention resumed the following year, but without the participation of the leading opposition and ethnic groups, and concluded in January 2006 without any clear outcome.

INSURGENCIES

Since independence in 1948 the government has fought various insurgencies, mostly by ethnic groups. These have included the Kachin, Kayin (Karen) National Union (KNU), Karenni, Wa, Shan, Mon, Arakan and Chin ethnic minorities. Since 1992, 15 ethnic groups have signed ceasefire agreements following government offensives against them; the most significant group, the KNU, began talks about a ceasefire in 2004. Many governments and non-governmental organisations believe that abuse of Myanmar's ethnic minorities continues. The UN commission for human rights passed a resolution in 2004, co-sponsored by the EU, that expressed concern over human rights abuses.

POLITICAL SYSTEM

The constitution was effectively abrogated in 1988 when the executive and legislature were abolished and replaced by the State Law and Order Restoration Council (SLORC); the SLORC was replaced by the State Peace and Development Council (SPDC) in 1997. The *de facto* head of state is the chair of the SPDC. A unicameral 485-member constituent assembly was elected in 1990 but has not been allowed to convene. There are no permitted political parties.

STATE PEACE AND DEVELOPMENT COUNCIL *as at June 2007*
Chair, Defence, Senior Gen. Than Shwe
Vice-Chair, Gen. Maung Aye

SELECTED GOVERNMENT MEMBERS *as at June 2007*
Prime Minister, Lt.-Gen. Soe Win
Finance and Revenue, Maj.-Gen. Hla Tun
Foreign Affairs, Maj.-Gen. U Nyan Win
Home Affairs, Maj.-Gen. Maung Oo

EMBASSY OF THE UNION OF MYANMAR
19A Charles Street, London W1J 5DX
T 020-7499 7043 E melondon@btconnect.com
Ambassador Extraordinary and Plenipotentiary, HE Nay Win, *apptd* 2005

BRITISH EMBASSY
PO Box 638, 80 Strand Road, Rangoon
T (+95) (1) 256 918 E consular.rangoon@fco.gov.uk
Ambassador Extraordinary and Plenipotentiary, HE Mark Canning, *apptd* 2006

BRITISH COUNCIL
PO Box 638, 78 Kanna Road, Rangoon
T (+95) (1) 254 658/256 290 W www.britishcouncil.org/burma
Director, Alan Smart

DEFENCE

The army has 150 main battle tanks and 325 armoured personnel carriers. The navy has 59 patrol and coastal vessels at 6 bases. The air force has 125 combat aircraft.
MILITARY BUDGET – US$6,230m (2005 est)
MILITARY PERSONNEL – 375,000: army 350,000, navy 13,000, air force 12,000; paramilitaries 107,250

ECONOMY AND TRADE

Myanmar has fertile soil and an abundance of natural resources such as timber (it is the world's largest exporter of teak), precious gems (jade, pearls, rubies and sapphires), oil and natural gas, but the economy is characterised by corruption, mismanagement and human rights abuses. The country has become increasingly poverty-stricken under military rule and around a quarter of the population lives below the poverty line. The economy suffers from fiscal and currency instability, and inflation and foreign debt are very high. The regime's suppression of the pro-democracy movement has lost it development aid and attracted economic and trade sanctions since the late 1990s. There is a large grey economy and considerable unofficial cross-border trade.

Agriculture is the dominant economic activity, accounting for 50 per cent of GDP and engaging 70 per cent of the workforce; the most important export crops are rice, beans, pulses and fish. The main industries are forestry and the extraction of minerals, gemstones, oil and gas; manufacturing and services are struggling, although tourism is growing. Industry contributes 15 per cent of GDP and services 35 per cent.

The main trading partners are Thailand, China, Singapore and India. Principal exports are gas, wood products, agricultural produce, clothing and gems. The main imports are fabric, petroleum products, fertiliser, plastics, machinery, transport equipment and construction materials.
ANNUAL AVERAGE GROWTH OF GDP – 5.2 per cent (2005 est)
INFLATION RATE – 20.2 per cent (2005 est)
UNEMPLOYMENT – 5 per cent (2005 est)
TOTAL EXTERNAL DEBT – US$6,990m (2005 est)
IMPORTS – US$1,930m (2005)
EXPORTS – US$3,810m (2005)

BALANCE OF PAYMENTS
Trade – US$928m surplus (2004)
Current Account – US$112m surplus (2004)

Trade with UK	*2005*	*2006*
Imports from UK	£9,964,000	£3,653,000
Exports to UK	£34,589,000	£26,676,000

COMMUNICATIONS

The 12,800km of navigable waterways includes the Irrawaddy and Chindwin rivers; the main stream of the Irrawaddy is navigable for 1,440km and carries most of the country's traffic. The chief seaports are Rangoon, Mawlamyine (Moulmein) and Akyab (Sittwe). The railway network of 3,955km covers most of the country. There are 27,000km of roads. The main airports are at Rangoon, Mandalay and Tavoy.

The telephone system is rudimentary and domestic services are poor. In 2005 there were 476,200 main telephone lines in use, 183,400 mobile phone subscribers and 78,000 internet users.

EDUCATION AND HEALTH

Most children attend primary school, attendance at secondary level is much more variable.

LITERACY RATE – 89.7 per cent (2004 est)
GROSS ENROLMENT RATIO (percentage of relevant age group) – primary 100 per cent; secondary 40 per cent; tertiary 11 per cent (2005 est)
HEALTH EXPENDITURE (per capita) – US$5 (2004)
HOSPITAL BEDS (per 1,000 people) – 0.6 (2000–5)

MEDIA

The government controls and censors nearly all the media outlets, including the four national newspapers and two television stations. Editors and journalists are answerable to the military authorities, ensuring that self-censorship is widespread. The English-language daily newspaper *New Light of Myanmar* publishes many heavily edited versions of foreign news reports from international agencies, but its domestic news strictly adheres to the government line. An opposition radio station, Democratic Voice of Myanmar, broadcasts on short-wave from Norway.

NAMIBIA

Republic of Namibia

AREA – 825,418 sq. km. Neighbours: Angola (north), South Africa (south), Botswana (east), Zambia and Zimbabwe (north-east)
CAPITAL – Windhoek; population, 233,529 (2001)
MAJOR TOWNS – Rundu; Walvis Bay
CURRENCY – Namibian dollar of 100 cents, at parity to South African rand
POPULATION – 2,044,147 rising at 0.59 per cent per year (2006 est); Ovambo (50 per cent), Kavangos (9 per cent), Herero (7 per cent), Damara (7 per cent), Nama (5 per cent) (est)
RELIGION – Christianity (90 per cent), indigenous religions (4 per cent) (est)
LANGUAGE – English (official), German
POPULATION DENSITY – 2 per sq. km (2005)
URBAN POPULATION – 33.5 per cent (2005 est)
MEDIAN AGE (years) – 20 (2006 est)
NATIONAL ANTHEM – 'Namibia, Land of the Brave'
NATIONAL DAY – 21 March (Independence Day)
LIFE EXPECTANCY (years) – 43.39 (2006 est)
MORTALITY RATE – 18.86 (2006 est)
BIRTH RATE – 24.32 (2006 est)
INFANT MORTALITY RATE – 48.1 (2006 est)
HIV/AIDS ADULT PREVALENCE – 21.3 per cent (2003 est)
DEATH PENALTY – No (abolished 1990)
CPI SCORE – 4.1 (2006)
POPULATION BELOW POVERTY LINE – 50 per cent (2002 est)
MILITARY BUDGET – US$184m (2006)
MILITARY PERSONNEL – 9,200: army 9,000, navy 200; paramilitaries 6,000
LITERACY RATE – 85 per cent (2004 est)
GROSS ENROLMENT RATIO (percentage of relevant age group) – primary 99 per cent; secondary 61 per cent; tertiary 6 per cent (2005 est)
HEALTH EXPENDITURE (per capita) – US$190 (2004)

CLIMATE AND TERRAIN

The Namib desert runs along the Atlantic coast and the Kalahari desert covers south-eastern Namibia, with veld in the north-east. The interior and coastal desert areas are divided by a line of hills and higher land. The terrain is almost completely arid and dry. Elevation extremes range from 2,606m (Konigstein) at the highest point to 0m (Atlantic Ocean) at the lowest. The only rivers not dependent on rains are the Orange River, which forms the southern border with South Africa, and the Zambezi, which is reached via the Caprivi Strip in the extreme north-east of the country. Average temperatures range from 21°C in July to 36°C in January.

HISTORY AND POLITICS

Pre-colonial Namibia was inhabited by Bantu tribes and San (Bushmen). It was annexed by Germany in 1884 and named South West Africa. From 1904, the Germans brutally suppressed indigenous uprisings, killing over half of some tribes and an estimated 80 per cent of the Herero. The territory was occupied by South Africa on behalf of the Allies in 1914 and after the First World War it became a League of Nations mandated territory, administered by South Africa.

After the Second World War, South Africa continued to administer the country, but its control became over-arching – extending representation in South Africa's parliament to the white population in 1949, and applying apartheid in 1966. These policies were applied despite the UN's refusal to permit the country's incorporation into South Africa in 1946 and a vote to end the mandate in 1964. In 1968, the UN general assembly changed the country's name to Namibia, and the South West Africa People's Organisation (SWAPO), which had campaigned for racial equality and independence since the late 1950s, began a guerrilla war against South Africa.

In 1978, South Africa accepted and then rescinded its acceptance of UN security council Resolution 435 for the granting of full independence to Namibia. South Africa's peace talks with Angola in 1988 led to agreement on independence for Namibia, and this was achieved on 21 March 1990; South Africa's Walvis Bay enclave was returned to Namibia in 1994.

The country has enjoyed stability since independence, apart from a brief period of secessionist violence in the Caprivi Strip in the late 1990s. In recent years there has been agitation for an acceleration of land reform, and the government programme moved from voluntary sales to expropriation of white-owned farms in 2005. The country's main problems arise from the demographic, economic and social impact of the high level of HIV/AIDS infection amongst the population.

SWAPO has been the dominant party since independence, holding the presidency and commanding a parliamentary majority without interruption. The 2004 presidential election was won by Hifikepunye Pohamba, who replaced Sam Nujoma, the president since independence. In the 2004 legislative elections, SWAPO retained its majority in both houses of parliament.

POLITICAL SYSTEM

Under the 1990 constitution, the executive president is directly elected for a five-year term, renewable only once. There is a bicameral legislature consisting of the national assembly, with 72 members directly elected for a five-year term and up to six additional non-voting members appointed by the president, and the national council, whose 26 members are indirectly elected by the regional councils from among their own members; the national council is elected for a six-year term, and its main function is to review and consider legislation from the national assembly. The president appoints the prime minister and the other ministers.

HEAD OF STATE
President, Hifikepunye Pohamba, *elected* 16 November 2004, *sworn in* 21 March 2005

SELECTED GOVERNMENT MEMBERS *as at June 2007*
Prime Minister, Nahas Angula
Deputy Prime Minister, Libertina Amathila
Defence, Maj-Gen.Charles Namoloh
Finance, Saarah Kuugongelwa-Amathila
Foreign Affairs, Marco Hausiku
Home Affairs, Rosalia Nghidinwa

HIGH COMMISSION OF THE REPUBLIC OF NAMIBIA
6 Chandos Street, London W1G 9LU
T 020-7636 6244 E namibia-highcomm@btconnect.com
High Commissioner, HE George Mbanga Liswaniso, *apptd* 2006

BRITISH HIGH COMMISSION
PO Box 22202, 116 Robert Mugabe Avenue, Windhoek
T (+264) (61) 274 800 E bhc@mweb.com.na
W www.britishhighcommission.gov.uk/namibia
High Commissioner, HE Alasdair MacDermott, *apptd* 2002

BRITISH COUNCIL
1–5 Fidel Castro Street, Windhoek
T (+264) (61) 226 776 W www.britishcouncil.org/namibia
Director, Patience Mahlalela

ECONOMY AND TRADE

Namibia is a poor country, with much of the population living below the poverty line. Its arid terrain limits agriculture, but the emphasis on environmental protection (enshrined in the constitution) is helping the development of tourism. The country has rich mineral deposits; extraction of these is the main industrial activity and minerals account for 54 per cent of exports. Other industries process the meat, fish and dairy products of the agricultural and fisheries sector. This operates mostly at subsistence level, accounting for 12 per cent of GDP but engaging nearly half the workforce.

The main trading partners are South Africa (33 per cent of exports; 85 per cent of imports) and the USA. Principal exports are diamonds, copper, gold, zinc, lead, uranium, cattle, processed fish and skins. The main imports are foodstuffs, petroleum products and fuel, machinery and equipment, and chemicals.

GNI – US$6,100m; US$2,990 per capita (2005)
ANNUAL AVERAGE GROWTH OF GDP – 3.2 per cent (2005 est)
INFLATION RATE – 2.3 per cent (2005 est)
TOTAL EXTERNAL DEBT – US$712.9m (2005 est)
IMPORTS – US$2,450m (2005)
EXPORTS – US$1,990m (2005)

BALANCE OF PAYMENTS
Trade – US$283m deficit (2004)
Current Account – US$573m surplus (2004)

Trade with UK	*2005*	*2006*
Imports from UK	£17,317,000	£13,191,000
Exports to UK	£283,940,000	£346,552,000

COMMUNICATIONS

Namibia has 2,382km of railways and 42,237km of roads. In 2002, a road bridge across the Zambezi opened, linking Namibia with Zambia and raising hopes of an increase in regional trade. The main airports are at Windhoek and Odangwa, with over 130 smaller airports and airfields around the country. The two main seaports are Luderitz and Walvis Bay.

Telephone services are good in both urban and rural areas. There were 128,000 main telephone lines in use in 2004, and 495,000 mobile phone subscribers in 2005.

MEDIA

Namibia is one of Africa's more liberal countries and the freedom of its press is guaranteed by the constitution. Government interference in reportage is rare. There are six national newspapers, including *The Namibian* and the Afrikaans language title *Die Republikein.* The state-administered Namibian Broadcasting Corporation runs alongside Desert TV, a private network based at Windhoek.

NAURU

Republic of Nauru

AREA – 21 sq. km
CAPITAL – Yaren District (unofficial); population, 1,100 (2003 est)
CURRENCY – Australian dollar ($A) of 100 cents
POPULATION – 13,287 rising at 1.81 per cent per year (2006 est); Nauruan (58 per cent), other Pacific Islander (26 per cent), Chinese (8 per cent) (est)
RELIGION – Protestantism (67 per cent), Roman Catholicism (33 per cent) (est)
LANGUAGE – Nauruan, English (both official)
POPULATION DENSITY – 609.9 per sq. km (2004 est)
URBAN POPULATION – 100 per cent (2005 est)
MEDIAN AGE (years) – 20.6 (2006 est)
NATIONAL ANTHEM – 'Nauru Bwiema' ('Nauru, Our Homeland')
NATIONAL DAY – 31 January (Independence Day)
LIFE EXPECTANCY (years) – 63.08 (2006 est)
MORTALITY RATE – 6.7 (2006 est)
BIRTH RATE – 24.76 (2006 est)
INFANT MORTALITY RATE – 9.78 (2006 est)
DEATH PENALTY – No*

CLIMATE AND TERRAIN

Nauru is a low-lying coral island in the Pacific Ocean 42km south of the Equator and 4,000km north-east of Sydney, Australia. The climate is tropical, with daily temperatures an almost constant 29°C.

HISTORY AND POLITICS

Nauru was first settled by Polynesian and Melanesian groups. The first Europeans to visit the island were British whalers in 1798 and by 1888 Nauru was annexed by Germany. At the outbreak of the First World War, Nauru was occupied by Australia, which continued to administer the island under a League of Nations mandate from 1920. During the Second World War, the island was occupied by the Japanese in 1942–3. UN trusteeship status superseded the mandate in 1947 and Nauru continued to be administered by Australia until it became independent on 31 January 1968.

The prospect of a financial crisis led to four successive presidents between January and May 2003. Ludwig Scotty, elected president in May 2003, was dismissed following a vote of no confidence and replaced by Rene Harris in August 2003. However, Harris's government lost a vote of no confidence in June 2004 and Scotty returned to office. Scotty dismissed parliament in September 2004 after it failed to pass a reform budget. In the ensuing general election in October, his supporters won a majority of seats and Scotty was re-elected president unopposed.

POLITICAL SYSTEM

Under the 1968 constitution, the executive president is elected by the legislature from among its members for a three-year term. The unicameral parliament has 18 members, who are directly elected for a three-year term. The president appoints the cabinet, which comprises no fewer than five nor more than six members including the president.

HEAD OF STATE

President, Ludwig Scotty, *elected* 26 October 2004

SELECTED GOVERNMENT MEMBERS *AS AT JUNE 2007*

Foreign Affairs, Finance, Internal Affairs, David Adeang

Justice, Godfrey Thoma

HONORARY CONSULATE

Romshed Courtyard, Underriver, Sevenoaks, Kent TN15 0SD

T 01732-746061 E nauru@weald.co.uk

Honorary Consul, Martin W. L. Weston

BRITISH HIGH COMMISSIONER

HE Roger Sykes, *apptd* 2006, resident at Suva, Fiji

ECONOMY AND TRADE

The economy is almost entirely dependent on phosphate extraction, but reserves are nearing exhaustion. Using profits derived from the mining industry, the government created trust funds in order to provide for the post-mining future. Heavy spending from the funds has left the country virtually bankrupt and caused it to default on loans and have assets seized in 2004. In response, Australian officials took charge of the state's finances, and Nauru is now dependent on international aid. The future is very uncertain as phosphate is the island's only resource and all other goods, including food and water, have to be imported. Diversification efforts includes offshore banking and small-scale tourism.

Most of the phosphate is exported to South Africa (64 per cent), South Korea and Canada. Imports come mainly from South Korea, Australia, the USA and Germany.

UNEMPLOYMENT – 90 per cent (2004 est)

TOTAL EXTERNAL DEBT – US$33.3m (2002)

Trade with UK	*2005*	*2006*
Imports from UK	£114,000	£186,000
Exports to UK	£51,000	£48,000

EDUCATION AND MEDIA

Education is free of charge and compulsory between the ages of six and 17.

Nauru has no daily press but there are three weekly or fortnightly publications. A domestic radio service broadcasts material from the BBC and Radio Australia, and is supplemented by Nauru Television (NTV), which broadcasts programmes from New Zealand.

NEPAL

State of Nepal

AREA – 147,181 sq. km. Neighbours: China (north), India (west, south and east)

CAPITAL – Kathmandu; population, 671,826 (2001)

MAJOR CITIES – Biratnagar; Lalitpur; Pokhara

CURRENCY – Nepalese rupee of 100 paisa

POPULATION – 28,287,147 rising at 2.17 per cent per year (2006 est); Chhettri (15.5 per cent), Brahman-Hill (12.5 per cent), Magar (7 per cent), Tharu (6.6 per cent), Tamang (5.5 per cent), Newar (5.4 per cent), Kami (3.9 per cent), Yadav (3.9 per cent)

RELIGION – Hinduism (81 per cent), Buddhism (11 per cent), Islam (4 per cent), indigenous religions (3 per cent) (est)

LANGUAGE – Nepali (official), Maithali, Bhojpuri, Tamang, English, Tharu

POPULATION DENSITY – 190 per sq. km (2005)

URBAN POPULATION – 15.8 per cent (2005 est)

MEDIAN AGE (years) – 20.3 (2006 est)

NATIONAL ANTHEM – 'Sayaun Thunga Phool Ka' ['Hundreds of Flowers']

NATIONAL DAY – 7 July (The King's Birthday)

LIFE EXPECTANCY (years) – 60.18 (2006 est)

MORTALITY RATE – 9.31 (2006 est)

BIRTH RATE – 30.98 (2006 est)

INFANT MORTALITY RATE – 65.32 (2006 est)

DEATH PENALTY – No (abolished 1997)

CPI SCORE – 2.5 (2006)

MILITARY BUDGET – US$139m (2006)

MILITARY PERSONNEL – army 69,000; paramilitaries 62,000

CLIMATE AND TERRAIN

The north of landlocked Nepal lies in the Himalayas, with the snowline at about 4,880m. The terrain descends from the mountains through a hilly central belt with fertile valleys to a southern region, the Terai, that lies in the valley of the River Ganges. Elevation extremes range from 8,850m (Mt Everest) at the highest point, to 70m (Kanchan Kalan) at the lowest. Average temperatures in Kathmandu range from 2°C in January to 29°C in July. The rainy season runs from June to September.

HISTORY AND POLITICS

Modern Nepal was formed from a number of hill states that were unified in the 18th century by the Gurkha ruler Prithvi Naryan Shah. After war with the British in 1815–16, Nepal became a British-dependent buffer state; its independence was formally recognised in 1923.

Power was seized by Jung Bahdur in 1846. He assumed the title Rana and his family became hereditary chief ministers, reducing the monarchy to a purely ceremonial role and keeping the country isolated. In 1950–1, the Ranas were overthrown in the so-called 'palace revolution' and the monarchy was restored to power. Apart from the period 1959–60, when a parliamentary system of government was in place, the kings ruled as absolute monarchs until 1990, when major constitutional reforms were introduced after violent pro-democracy demonstrations.

Under the reforms, the monarchy's powers were restricted and a multiparty parliamentary system was reintroduced. However, factionalism led to frequent changes of government, causing political and social instability, which was exacerbated by a Maoist insurgency led by the Nepal Communist Party from 1996. The insurgency began in the west and quickly spread, despite the government's often brutal attempts at suppression. King Gyanendra, who succeeded to the throne in 2001 after Crown Prince Dipendra killed King Birendra and eight other members of the royal family before fatally injuring himself, assumed direct control of the government in 2005–6 in an attempt to defeat the insurgents.

The king found himself increasingly isolated from November 2005 as politicians from seven opposition parties allied themselves with the Maoists to achieve the restoration of democracy, and in April 2006 the king agreed to reinstate the legislature after three months of violent pro-democracy protests. The legislature voted to curtail the king's powers, to hold elections to a constituent assembly to draft a new constitution and to open peace talks with the Maoists, who controlled 80 per cent of the country. In June talks began and a peace accord was signed in November. An interim constitution was approved in January 2007 and 83 Maoists became members of the interim legislature. In April a multiparty government was sworn in. Elections to the constituent assembly, expected by June 2007, have been delayed until November.

POLITICAL SYSTEM

The 1990 constitution was modified by a parliamentary proclamation in May 2006 curtailing the king's powers; the interim constitution transfers all the king's powers to the prime minister. At present, the head of state is a hereditary constitutional monarch. The bicameral legislature consists of a 205-member house of representatives, directly elected for a five-year term, and a 60-member national council comprising ten royal nominees and 50 members indirectly elected for a six-year term, with one-third elected every two years.

HEAD OF STATE

HM The King of Nepal, King Gyanendra Bir Bikram Shah Dev, *acceded* 4 June 2001

Heir, Crown Prince Paras Bir Bikram Shah Dev

SELECTED GOVERNMENT MEMBERS *as at June 2007*

Chair of the Council of Ministers, Defence, Girija Prasad Koirala

Vice-Chair, Khadga Prasad Sharma Oli

Finance, Ram Sharan Mahat

Home Affairs, Krishna Sitaula

Foreign Affairs, Sahana Pradhan

ROYAL NEPALESE EMBASSY

12A Kensington Palace Gardens, London W8 4QU

T 020-7229 1594 W www.nepembassy.org.uk

Ambassador Extraordinary and Plenipotentiary, vacant

BRITISH EMBASSY

PO Box 106 Lainchaur, Kathmandu

T (+977) (1) 441 0583 E britemb@wlink.com.np

W www.britishembassy.gov.uk/nepal

Ambassador Extraordinary and Plenipotentiary, HE Andrew Hall, *apptd* 2006

BRITISH COUNCIL

PO Box 640, Lainchaur, Kathmandu

T (+977) (1) 4410 798 W www.britishcouncil.org/nepal

Country Manager, John Fry

ECONOMY AND TRADE

The country is very poor, with about one-third of the population living below the poverty line, and is dependent on foreign aid and trade with India. Agriculture is the main economic sector, generating 38 per cent of GDP and engaging about 76 per cent of the workforce; principal crops are rice, corn, wheat, sugar cane, jute, root crops and milk. The main industry is tourism; other industries manufacture carpets, textiles, cigarettes, cement and bricks, and process rice, jute, sugar and oilseed. Industry accounts for 20 per cent of GDP and services for 42 per cent. Tourism's contribution has decreased recently because of the Maoist insurgency in much of the country but has potential for development, although this might compound environmental problems.

The main export markets are India (54 per cent) and the USA; the main import providers are India (48 per cent), the UAE and China. Principal exports are carpets, clothing, leather goods, jute goods and grain. The main imports are gold, machinery and equipment, petroleum products and fertilisers.

GNI – US$7,300m; US$270 per capita (2005)

ANNUAL AVERAGE GROWTH OF GDP – 2.7 per cent (2005 est)

INFLATION RATE – 7.8 per cent (2005 est)

UNEMPLOYMENT – 42 per cent (2004 est)

TOTAL EXTERNAL DEBT – US$3,340m (2005)

IMPORTS – US$1,860m (2005)

EXPORTS – US$830m (2005)

BALANCE OF PAYMENTS

Trade – US$1,049m deficit (2004)

Current Account – US$52m surplus (2004)

Trade with UK	*2005*	*2006*
Imports from UK	£5,780,000	£4,597,000
Exports to UK	£9,896,000	£10,354,000

COMMUNICATIONS

There is a total of 17,380km of roads, of which 9,886km are surfaced. A major highway runs the length of the country through the Terai, linking the main lowland centres and extending into the hills to Kathmandu and Pokhara. Other highways connect Kathmandu with India and Tibet. There are 59km of railways. The principal airport is at Kathmandu, and there are over 40 smaller airports and airfields around the country.

The telephone system is extensive but services are poor and mobile phone distribution is expanding rapidly. In 2005 there were 448,600 main telephone lines in use, 248,800 mobile phone subscribers and 175,000 internet users.

EDUCATION AND HEALTH

LITERACY RATE – 48.6 per cent (2004 est)

GROSS ENROLMENT RATIO (percentage of relevant age group) – primary 126 per cent; secondary 43 per cent; tertiary 6 per cent (2005 est)

HEALTH EXPENDITURE (per capita) – US$14 (2004)

HOSPITAL BEDS (per 1,000 people) – 0.2 (2002)

MEDIA

Nepal has had notoriously strict media laws for many years and is responsible for a large proportion of world censorship cases. These laws have been eased since the appointment of a multiparty government in 2006 but remain comparatively draconian. The two most widely circulated newspapers are the *Kathmandu Post* and *Rising Nepal*. The government-run Radio Nepal is the most influential media outlet.

THE NETHERLANDS

Koninkrijk der Nederlanden – Kingdom of the Netherlands

AREA – 41,526 sq. km. Neighbours: Belgium (south), Germany (east)
CAPITAL – Amsterdam; population, 1,021,245 (2006 est)
SEAT OF GOVERNMENT – The Hague (Den Haag or, in full, 's-Gravenhage), population 443,745 (2001)
MAJOR CITIES – Rotterdam; Utrecht; Eindhoven; Leiden; Tilburg
CURRENCY – Euro (€) of 100 cents
POPULATION – 16,491,461 rising at 0.49 per cent per year (2006 est)
RELIGION – Roman Catholicism (31 per cent), other Christian denominations (20 per cent), Islam (6 per cent) (est). An estimated 40 per cent of the population is atheist
LANGUAGE – Dutch, Frisian (both official), English
POPULATION DENSITY – 482 per sq. km (2005)
URBAN POPULATION – 66.8 per cent (2005 est)
MEDIAN AGE (years) – 39.4 (2006 est)
NATIONAL ANTHEM – 'Het Wilhelmus' ['The William']
NATIONAL DAY – 30 April (Queen's Day)
LIFE EXPECTANCY (years) – 78.96 (2006 est)
MORTALITY RATE – 8.68 (2006 est)
BIRTH RATE – 10.9 (2006 est)
INFANT MORTALITY RATE – 4.96 (2006 est)
DEATH PENALTY – No (abolished 1982)
CPI SCORE – 8.7 (2006)

CLIMATE AND TERRAIN

The Netherlands is a low-lying country, below sea level in many places, making it susceptible to flooding despite the coastal defences and a network of dykes and canals. Its land area has been extended over the centuries by land reclamation (polders), found especially in the west around the huge freshwater lake of Yssel, created in the 1930s by damming the Zuider Zee. The country is crossed by three major European rivers, the Rhine, Mass and Scheldt, whose estuaries are in the south-west. Elevation extremes range from 322m (Vaalserberg) at the highest point to −7m (Zuidplaspolder) at the lowest point. The climate is temperate with average temperatures ranging from 0°C in January to 23°C in July.

HISTORY AND POLITICS

The area was part of the Frankish Empire by the eighth century and was subsequently part of the Holy Roman Empire. From the 12th century the mercantile towns of the Low Countries became virtually independent principalities. In the 15th century these came under the influence of the dukes of Burgundy and then of the Habsburgs from 1477, passing to the Spanish branch of the Habsburgs in 1555. The northern provinces, led by William, Prince of Orange, rebelled against Spanish rule in 1568. The war of independence ended with the seven northern provinces forming the Union of Utrecht in 1579, and in 1581 independence was declared; the United Provinces were formally recognised as an independent republic in 1648.

The 17th century was a golden age in which the Dutch led the world in trade, art and science, founding colonies in the East and West Indies. Commercial and colonial rivalries led to three wars with Britain in the late 17th century, and resisting French attempts at domination exhausted the country in the 18th century. In 1795, French revolutionary armies overran the country and it remained under French rule until 1814. In 1815, the northern and southern provinces were reunited into one kingdom, with the hereditary stadtholder of the northern provinces becoming King William I of the Netherlands and grand duke of Luxembourg; the southern provinces seceded to form Belgium in 1830 and the Duchy of Luxembourg was made an independent state in 1867. The Netherlands was neutral during the First World War, but during the Second World War the country was invaded and occupied by Germany from 1940 until 1945.

The post-war period was marked by economic expansion and the construction of a liberal welfare state. The Netherlands formed the Benelux economic union with Belgium and Luxembourg in 1948, was a founder member of the EEC in 1958 and joined the eurozone in 1999. In a referendum in June 2005, its population rejected ratification of the EU constitution.

Although a stable democracy, one party has rarely commanded a sufficient parliamentary majority to govern alone and post-war governments have usually been coalitions of two or more parties. Following the legislative election in November 2006, the Christian Democratic Appeal (CDA) remained the largest party, but without an overall majority. After three months of negotiation, a new coalition comprising members of the CDA, the Labour Party (PvdA) and the Christian Union (CU) was sworn into office in February 2007 and led by Jan Peter Balkenende, prime minister since 2002.

POLITICAL SYSTEM

Under the 1983 constitution, the kingdom consists of three autonomous elements: the Netherlands, the Netherlands Antilles and Aruba. The head of state is a hereditary constitutional monarch. The legislature, the *Staten-Generaal* (parliament), consists of the *Eerste Kamer* (first chamber) of 75 members, elected for a four-year term by provincial councillors; and the *Tweede Kamer* (second chamber) of 150 members, directly elected for a four-year term. The head of government is the prime minister, who is responsible to parliament.

HEAD OF STATE

HM The Queen of the Netherlands, Queen Beatrix Wilhelmina Armgard, KG, GCVO, *born* 31 January 1938; *succeeded* 30 April 1980
Heir, HRH Prince Willem Alexander, *born* 27 April 1967

SELECTED GOVERNMENT MEMBERS *as at June 2007*

Prime Minister, General Affairs, Jan Peter Balkenende
Deputy Prime Minister, Finance, Wouter Bos
Defence, Eimert van Middelkoop
Economic Affairs, Maria van der Hoeven
Foreign Affairs, Maxime Verhagen
Interior, Guusje ter Horst

ROYAL NETHERLANDS EMBASSY

38 Hyde Park Gate, London SW7 5DP
T 020-7590 3200 E london@netherlands-embassy.org.uk
W www.netherlands-embassy.org.uk
Ambassador Extraordinary and Plenipotentiary, HE Count Jan M. V. A. de Marchant et d'Ansembourg, *apptd* 2003

BRITISH EMBASSY
Lange Voorhout 10, The Hague, NL-2514 ED
T (+31) (70) 427 0427 W www.britain.nl
Ambassador Extraordinary and Plenipotentiary, HE Lyn Parker, *apptd* 2005

BRITISH COUNCIL
Weteringschans 85A, Amsterdam, NL-1017 RZ
T (+31) (20) 550 6060 W www.britishcouncil.org/netherlands
Director, Ben Harris

DEFENCE

The army has 170 main battle tanks, 224 armoured infantry fighting vehicles and 94 armoured personnel carriers. The navy has 4 submarines, 4 destroyers and 6 frigates. The air force has 137 combat aircraft and 30 armed helicopters.
MILITARY EXPENDITURE – US$9,940m (2005)
MILITARY PERSONNEL – 53,130: army 23,150, navy 12,130, air force 11,050, paramilitaries 6,800

ECONOMY AND TRADE

The Netherlands has a highly industrialised and diversified market economy, and a European transport hub. The economy depends heavily on foreign trade. Economic growth slowed in 2001–5, coinciding with the slowdown in the global economy, causing a sharp rise in unemployment and the government budget deficit. Public spending cuts and welfare reforms were introduced in 2004, provoking demonstrations.

The highly mechanised agricultural sector employs only 2 per cent of the workforce but output supplies the food processing industries and the export as well as the domestic market. Flower bulbs and cut flowers are a major contributor to this sector, as is the fishing industry. The industrial sector contributes 24 per cent of GDP; major industries include food processing, and the manufacture of electrical machinery and equipment, metal and engineering products, chemicals, oil refining, construction and micro-electronics. The service industries represent 74 per cent of the economy. Other EU countries account for most overseas trade. Principal exports are machinery and equipment, chemicals, fuels and foodstuffs. The main imports are machinery and transport equipment, chemicals, fuels, foodstuffs and clothing.
GNI – US$642,000m; US$39,340 per capita (2005)
ANNUAL AVERAGE GROWTH OF GDP – 1.5 per cent (2005 est)
INFLATION RATE – 1.7 per cent (2005 est)
UNEMPLOYMENT – 6.6 per cent (2005 est)
TOTAL EXTERNAL DEBT – US$1,645,000m (2005)
IMPORTS – US$309,000m (2005)
EXPORTS – US$346,000m (2005)

BALANCE OF PAYMENTS
Trade – US$44,324m surplus (2005)
Current Account – US$40,187m surplus (2005)

Trade with UK	*2005*	*2006*
Imports from UK	£12,344,793,000	£16,063,200,000
Exports to UK	£18,849,308,000	£20,024,700,000

COMMUNICATIONS

The main seaport is Rotterdam, although there are a number of other ports on the river estuaries or linked to the coast by the canals; 6,183km of inland waterways, including canals, are navigable by ships of up to 50 tonnes. The large merchant fleet includes 558 ships of over 1,000 tonnes. There are 134,000km of roads and 2,808km of railways, of which 2,061km are electrified. The principal airports are at Amsterdam, Rotterdam, Eindhoven and Maastricht with a further 23 smaller airports and airfields around the country.

There is a modern telephone system and a very high density of mobile phone ownership. In 2005 there were 7.6 million main telephone lines in use, 15.8 million mobile phone subscribers and 10.8 million internet users.

EDUCATION AND HEALTH

Primary and secondary education is available at both denominational and state schools and is compulsory. The principal universities are at Leiden, Utrecht, Groningen, Amsterdam, Nijmegen, Maastricht and Rotterdam.
GROSS ENROLMENT RATIO (percentage of relevant age group) – primary 107 per cent; secondary 119 per cent; tertiary 59 per cent (2005 est)
HEALTH EXPENDITURE (per capita) – US$3,442 (2004)
HOSPITAL BEDS (per 1,000 people) – 4.7 (2004)

MEDIA

Ownership of the five national newspapers is highly concentrated. A competitive television sector includes Nederlandse Omroep Stichting (NOS), which oversees the country's three public networks and a large number of commercial stations. Freedom of the press is guaranteed by the constitution and the country is rated equal highest by Reporters Without Borders.

CULTURE

The Netherlands has produced many of the world's major artists, particularly in the period 1580–1700 which has become known as the Dutch Golden Age. Rembrandt (1606–69) and Johannes Vermeer (1632–75) have become the most enduring artists from the period, while mathematician and physicist Christiaan Huygens (1629–95) created the first pendulum clock, rendering time-keeping accurate for the first time and Baruch Spinoza (1632–77) wrote *Ethics*, a ground-breaking work in rationalist philosophy.

After the Golden Age, the works of Vincent van Gogh (1853–90), Piet Mondrian (1872–1944) and M. C. Escher (1898–1972) ensured that Dutch art remained inventive. Less celebrated is the life of Han van Meegeren (1889–1947), an expert forger of Golden Age painters until his confession in 1945.

In film, director Paul Verhoeven (*b.* 1938) is the country's most fiscally successful export and is known for the violence and explicit sexual content of his films, which include *RoboCop* (1987), *Total Recall* (1990) and *Basic Instinct* (1992). Fellow director Jan de Bont shot the action film *Speed* (1994).

OVERSEAS TERRITORIES

ARUBA

AREA – 193 sq. km
CAPITAL – Oranjestad; population, 26,355 (2000)
MAJOR TOWN – Sint Nicolaas
CURRENCY – Aruban florin of 100 cents
POPULATION – 71,891 (2006 est)
LANGUAGE – Dutch (official), Papiamento

The Caribbean island became part of the Dutch West Indies from 1828 and part of the Netherlands Antilles

from 1845. On 1 January 1986 it became a separate territory with full internal autonomy; plans to achieve independence by 1996 were dropped in 1994. The principal economic activities are tourism, oil refining and offshore financial services.
Governor, Fredis Refunjol
Prime Minister, Nelson O. Oduber

NETHERLANDS ANTILLES

AREA – 960 sq. km
CAPITAL – Willemstad; population, 125,000 (2006 est), on Curaçao
CURRENCY – Netherlands Antilles guilder of 100 cents
POPULATION – 221,736 (2006 est)
LANGUAGE – Dutch (official), Papiamento

The Netherlands Antilles comprise the Caribbean islands of Curaçao, Bonaire, part of St Maarten, St Eustatius and Saba. The islands were colonised by the Dutch in the 17th century and became a self-governing federation in 1954. Following referendums on the future status of the federation the islands' leaders agreed with the Dutch government to dissolve the federation by December 2008; Curaçao and St Maarten will become autonomous and the other three islands will become 'kingdom islands'. The principal economic activities are tourism, oil refining and offshore financial services.
Governor, Frits Goedgedrag
Prime Minister, Emily de Jongh-Elhage

NEW ZEALAND

Aotearoa – New Zealand

AREA – 268,680 sq. km
CAPITAL – Wellington; population, 370,000 (2005 est)
MAJOR CITIES – Auckland; Christchurch; Hamilton; Napier
CURRENCY – New Zealand dollar (NZ$) of 100 cents
POPULATION – 4,076,140 rising at 0.99 per cent per year (2006 est); 7.9 per cent are Maori (2001)
RELIGION – Protestantism (28 per cent), Roman Catholicism (12 per cent), Buddhism (1 per cent), Mormonism (1 per cent), Hinduism (1 per cent) (est)
LANGUAGE – English, Maori, sign language (all official)
POPULATION DENSITY – 15 per sq. km (2005)
URBAN POPULATION – 86 per cent (2005 est)
MEDIAN AGE (years) – 33.9 (2006 est)
NATIONAL ANTHEM – 'God Save the Queen'/'God Defend New Zealand'
NATIONAL DAY – 6 February (Waitangi Day)
LIFE EXPECTANCY (years) – 78.81 (2006 est)
MORTALITY RATE – 7.53 (2006 est)
BIRTH RATE – 13.76 (2006 est)
INFANT MORTALITY RATE – 5.76 (2006 est)
DEATH PENALTY – No (abolished 1989)
CPI SCORE – 9.6 (2006)

CLIMATE AND TERRAIN

New Zealand consists of a number of islands in the South Pacific Ocean, and also administers a number of territories and associated states in the region. The two larger islands, North Island and South Island, are separated by the relatively narrow Cook Strait. The remaining islands are much smaller and more widely dispersed.

Much of the North and South Islands is mountainous. The North Island mountains include several volcanoes, three of which are active. The principal range is the Southern Alps, extending the entire length of the South Island to the west of the Canterbury Plains. There are geysers and hot springs in the Rotorua district and glaciers in the Southern Alps. Elevation extremes range from 3,764m (Aoraki/Mt Cook) at the highest point to 0m (Pacific Ocean) at the lowest. The climate is temperate and average temperatures in Christchurch (South Island) range from 1°C in July to 24°C in January.

HISTORY AND POLITICS

Settled by Polynesian tribes since the ninth century, New Zealand was sighted by the Dutch navigator Abel Tasman in 1642 but he did not land. The British explorer James Cook surveyed the coastline in 1769, the year in which the islands were claimed by the British. In 1840, under the treaty of Waitangi, the Maoris accepted British sovereignty, with Maoris retaining some territorial rights. The Maoris attempted to resist the loss of their land in the 1840s and 1860s; their resistance was defeated but concessions such as parliamentary representation were won. New Zealand was administered as part of the New South Wales colony until 1841, when it became a separate colony. In 1907 it was granted dominion status; in 1931 the Statute of Westminster tacitly acknowledged its independence, which was formally confirmed in 1947.

New Zealand forces took part in the First and Second World Wars, the Korean War and the Vietnam War (1965–72). The UK's entry into the EEC in 1973 forced New Zealand to form closer trade links with Australia; the two countries entered into a free-trade agreement in 1988. In the 1990s, Maori demands for compensation for land lost to European settlers were settled either by compensation payments or grants of land.

Post-war politics has been dominated by the National Party and the Labour Party, forming governments on their own or in coalition with smaller parties. In the 2005 legislative election, the Labour Party won the most seats (50 to the National Party's 48) and formed a government with the Progressive Coalition, with additional support from the United Future, New Zealand First and Green parties.

POLITICAL SYSTEM

There is no written constitution. The head of state is the British sovereign, represented by the governor-general, who is appointed on the advice of the New Zealand government. The unicameral legislature, the house of representatives, has 121 members, elected for a three-year term; there are 69 members from single-member constituencies, which include seven Maori constituencies, and 52 allocated from party lists. A non-binding referendum in 1999 approved a reduction in the number of members to 100 in future parliaments. The prime minister and the cabinet are appointed by the governor-general on the advice of the house of representatives.

GOVERNOR-GENERAL
Governor-General and Commander-in-Chief, HE Anand Satyanand, *sworn in* August 2006

SELECTED GOVERNMENT MEMBERS *as at June 2007*
Prime Minister, Helen Clark
Deputy Prime Minister, Finance and Revenue, Michael Cullen
Defence, Phil Goff
Economic Development, Trevor Mallard

Internal Affairs, Rick Barker
Foreign Affairs, Winston Peters

NEW ZEALAND HIGH COMMISSION
2nd Floor, New Zealand House, 80 Haymarket, London SW1Y 4TQ
T 020-7930 8422 W www.nzembassy.com/uk
High Commissioner, HE Rt. Hon. Jonathan Hunt, ONZ, *apptd* 2005

BRITISH HIGH COMMISSION
PO Box 1812, 44 Hill Street, Wellington 1
T (+64) (4) 924 2888 E bhc.wel@xtra.co.nz
W www.britain.org.nz
High Commissioner, HE George Fergusson, *apptd* 2006

BRITISH COUNCIL
PO Box 1812, 44 Hill Street, Wellington 1
T (+64) (4) 924 2880 W www.britishcouncil.org/nz
Director, Paula Middleton

DEFENCE

With Australia and the USA, New Zealand formed the ANZUS Pacific security treaty in 1951, but its non-nuclear military policy led to disagreements with the USA and France in 1985, and in 1986 the USA suspended its ANZUS obligations towards New Zealand.

The army has 105 armoured personnel carriers. The navy has 2 frigates and 6 patrol and coastal vessels. The air force has 6 combat aircraft.

MILITARY BUDGET – US$1,310m (2006)
MILITARY PERSONNEL – 8,951: army 4,563, navy 1,998, air force 2,390

ECONOMY AND TRADE

The economy is based largely on agriculture, although since the 1980s it has become more industrialised. Growth is driven by trade, particularly in agricultural products. The agricultural sector contributes 4.3 per cent of GDP, employs 10 per cent of the workforce and provides 70–80 per cent of exports. The main products are wheat, barley, potatoes, pulses, fruits, vegetables, wool, meat, dairy products and fish. The major industries are food processing, wood and paper products, textiles, machinery, transport equipment, financial services and tourism, which is growing steadily. Non-metallic minerals such as coal, limestone and dolomite are heavily exploited, while gold and iron production is economically important. Natural gas deposits in offshore and onshore fields are used for electricity generation, though a significant amount of the country's energy is derived from sustainable sources such as hydroelectric power. Industry contributes 26.9 per cent of GDP and services 68.8 per cent.

The main trading partners are Australia, the USA, Japan and China. Principal exports are dairy products, meat, wood, fish and machinery. The main imports are machinery and equipment, vehicles and aircraft, petroleum, electronics, textiles and plastics.

GNI – US$106,300m; US$25,920 per capita (2005)
ANNUAL AVERAGE GROWTH OF GDP – 2.3 per cent (2005 est)
INFLATION RATE – 3 per cent (2005 est)
UNEMPLOYMENT – 3.7 per cent (2005 est)
TOTAL EXTERNAL DEBT – US$42.84m (2005 est)
IMPORTS – US$26,200m (2005)
EXPORTS – US$21,700m (2005)

BALANCE OF PAYMENTS
Trade – US$1,427m deficit (2004)
Current Account – US$6,456m deficit (2004)

*Trade with UK**	*2005*	*2006*
Imports from UK	£438,586,000	£364,334,000
Exports to UK	£596,546,000	£610,229,000

* Includes Niue, Tokelau and Cook Islands

COMMUNICATIONS

The national railway system is owned and operated by Tranz Rail Ltd; there is 4,128km of railway track. There are 92,931km of roads, of which about 64 per cent are surfaced. The principal airports are at Auckland, Wellington (North Island), Christchurch and Dunedin (South Island) and there are over 110 smaller airports and airfields around the country; the government holds an 83 per cent stake in Air New Zealand. Tauranga, Auckland, Christchurch, Dunedin and Napier are the main seaports.

The telephone system provided 1.8 million main lines in 2004. In 2005 there were 3.5 million mobile phone subscribers and 3.2 million internet users.

EDUCATION AND HEALTH

Education is free of charge and compulsory between the ages of six and 15.

GROSS ENROLMENT RATIO (percentage of relevant age group) – primary 102 per cent; secondary 118 per cent; tertiary 86 per cent (2005 est)
HEALTH EXPENDITURE (per capita) – US$2,040 (2004)
HOSPITAL BEDS (per 1,000 people) – 6.1 (2000–5)

MEDIA AND CULTURE

The broadcasting sector was deregulated in 1988. Two public networks, Television New Zealand and Maori TV, compete with four main private networks. There are four main national daily papers, including *The Press* and the *New Zealand Herald,* and a large number of radio stations, including Ruai Mai, a Maori-owned and operated broadcaster.

New Zealand's cultural history stretches back to the first Maori settlers, who brought the artform *Whakapapa,* a type of oral genealogy, to the islands. Notable cultural figures include the writer Katherine Mansfield (1888–1923), poet Sam Hunt (*b.* 1946), filmmakers Jane Campion (*b.* 1954) and Peter Jackson (*b.* 1961), singer Kiri Te Kanawa (*b.* 1944) and musicians Tim and Neil Finn (*b.* 1952 and 1958) who achieved international success under the names Split Enz and Crowded House.

TERRITORIES

TOKELAU

Tokelau is a group of three atolls: Fakaofo, Nukunonu and Atafu. Formerly part of Britain's Gilbert and Ellis Islands colony, they were transferred to New Zealand administration in 1926 and proclaimed part of New Zealand in 1949.

The Council of Ongoing Government (cabinet) comprises three *Faipule* (village leaders) and three *Pulenuku* (village mayors), one from each atoll; the position of *Ulu-o-Tokelau* (leader) is rotated among the three *Faipule* members annually. The *General Fono,* which has 21 members elected for a three-year term, has legislative powers. Each atoll has a *Taupulega* (council of elders). In a 2006 referendum, the islanders voted to

maintain Tokelau's current status, rejecting self-government or independence from New Zealand. The principal economic activities are subsistence farming, copra, handicrafts and the sale of postage stamps and coins.
Administrator, David Payton, *apptd* 2006

THE ROSS DEPENDENCY

New Zealand has administrative responsibility for the Ross Dependency. This is defined as all the Antarctic islands and territories between 160° E. and 150° W. longitude which are situated south of the 60° S. parallel, including Edward VII Land and portions of Victoria Land. (*See also* The Antarctic.)

ASSOCIATED STATES

COOK ISLANDS

The Cook Islands consist of the 15 volcanic islands and coral atolls of Rarotonga, Aitutaki, Mangaia, Atiu, Mauke, Mitiaro, Manuae, Takutea, Palmerston, Penrhyn (or Tongareva), Manihiki, Rakahanga, Suwarrow, Pukapuka (or Danger), and Nassau in the south Pacific Ocean. A former British protectorate, since 1965 the islands have been in free association with New Zealand and enjoy complete internal self-government. Queen Elizabeth II has a representative on the islands, and there is a New Zealand high commissioner. There is a 25-member legislative assembly, and executive power is exercised by a prime minister and a cabinet of five other ministers. The main economic activities are tourism, agriculture (especially fresh and canned tropical fruits), fishing, manufacture of clothing and handicrafts, and pearl-fishing.
HM Representative, Sir Frederick Goodwin, KBE
Prime Minister, Jim Marurai

NIUE

Niue was part of the Cook Islands group but was administered separately after 1903. Since 1974 the island has been self-governing in free association with New Zealand. A New Zealand high commissioner represents both the Queen and the New Zealand government. There is a 20-member legislative assembly, and executive power is exercised by a prime minister and a three-member cabinet drawn from the assembly's members. The principal economic activities are agriculture and fishing, tourism, handicrafts, food processing and the sale of postage stamps.
New Zealand High Commissioner, Anton Ojala, *apptd* 2005

NICARAGUA

República de Nicaragua – Republic of Nicaragua

AREA – 129,494 sq. km. Neighbours: Honduras (north), Costa Rica (south)
CAPITAL – Managua; population, 908,892 (2005)
MAJOR CITIES – León; Chinandega; Masaya
CURRENCY – Córdoba (C$) of 100 centavos
POPULATION – 5,570,129 rising at 1.89 per cent per year (2006 est). Three quarters are of mixed race, around 15 per cent are white and the remaining 10 per cent are West Indian or Indian
RELIGION – Roman Catholicism (72 per cent), other Christian denominations (19 per cent) (est). An estimated 8 per cent of the population is atheist
LANGUAGE – Spanish (official), English, Miskito
POPULATION DENSITY – 42 per sq. km (2005)
URBAN POPULATION – 58.1 per cent (2005 est)
MEDIAN AGE (years) – 20.9 (2006 est)
NATIONAL ANTHEM – 'Salve a ti Nicaragua' ['Hail to You, Nicaragua']
NATIONAL DAY – 15 September (Independence Day)
LIFE EXPECTANCY (years) – 70.63 (2006 est)
MORTALITY RATE – 4.45 (2006 est)
BIRTH RATE – 24.51 (2006 est)
INFANT MORTALITY RATE – 28.11 (2006 est)
DEATH PENALTY – No (abolished 1979)
CPI SCORE – 2.6 (2006)
POPULATION BELOW POVERTY LINE – 50 per cent (2001 est)

CLIMATE AND TERRAIN

The narrow Pacific coastal plain is separated from the broad Atlantic coastal plain by volcanic mountains and lakes Managua and Nicaragua. Elevation extremes range from 2,438m (Mogoton) at the highest point to 0m (Pacific Ocean) at the lowest. The climate is generally tropical near the coast, with average temperatures in Managua ranging from 20°C in January to 34°C in August. The country is subject to frequent earthquakes.

HISTORY AND POLITICS

The area was settled by Indians from Mexico and Mesoamerica from the tenth century AD. Spanish colonisation began in 1523 but in the 17th and 18th centuries the British were the dominant presence on the Caribbean coast, with the Spanish controlling the Pacific plain. Independence from Spain was achieved in 1821 and the area was initially part of Mexico. In 1823 it became part of the United Provinces of Central America but seceded from the federation and became fully independent in 1838. British control of the Caribbean coast was ceded to Nicaragua in 1860. In 1893, José Santos Zelaya established a dictatorship that lasted until 1909, when he was overthrown by US marines. Anastasio Somoza established a dictatorship in 1938 and ruled until his assassination in 1956, when he was succeeded by his sons Luis Somoza and Anastasio Somoza Debayle. The family amassed a huge fortune in its 44 years in power, until it was overthrown in 1979 by a popular revolt led by the *Frente Sandinista de Liberacíon Nacional* (FSLN), popularly known as the Sandinistas.

The Sandinistas' socialist government redistributed land and promoted education and health services, but was opposed by US-backed right-wing guerrillas (the Contras). The civil war lasted until the Sandinistas were unexpectedly defeated in the 1990 elections by a coalition of opposition parties. Ceasefires and disarmament were agreed with different Contra factions in 1990 and 1994. The country has struggled to recover from the effects of the civil war. Although some foreign debt has been cancelled, poverty is widespread and rises in fuel prices and the cost of living provoked protests, some violent, in 2005.

After the civil war, governments were liberal or liberal-dominated coalitions, keeping the FSLN from power even though it was often the largest party in the national assembly. However, in the 2006 presidential and legislative elections, the FSLN candidate, Daniel Ortega (president 1984–90) was elected president and the FSLN became the largest party in the assembly, with 38 seats.

POLITICAL SYSTEM
The 1987 constitution was amended in 1995 to reduce the presidential term; further changes reducing the power of the presidency came into effect in early 2007. The executive president is directly elected for a five-year term; a second term may be served, but terms may not be consecutive. There is a unicameral legislature, the national assembly, with 90 members directly elected for a five-year term; unsuccessful presidential and vice-presidential candidates may be awarded a seat if they receive more than the average percentage of the vote in each electoral district. The cabinet is appointed by the president.

HEAD OF STATE
President, Daniel Ortega, *elected* 5 November 2006, *sworn in* 11 January 2007
Vice-President, Jaime Morales

SELECTED GOVERNMENT MEMBERS *as at June 2007*
Defence, Ruth Tapia Roa
Finance and Public Credit, Alberto Guevara
Foreign Affairs, Samuel Santos
Interior, Ana Isabel Morales Mazún

EMBASSY OF NICARAGUA
Suite 31, Vicarage House, 58–60 Kensington Church Street, London W8 4DP
T 020-7938 2373
Ambassador Extraordinary and Plenipotentiary, HE Piero P. Coen Ubilla, *apptd* 2005

BRITISH AMBASSADOR
HE Tom Kennedy, resident at San José, Costa Rica

DEFENCE
The army has 127 main battle tanks and 166 armoured personnel carriers. The navy has 24 patrol and coastal vessels at 3 bases. The air force has 16 helicopters.
MILITARY BUDGET – US$33.9m (2005)
MILITARY PERSONNEL – 14,000: army 12,000, navy 800, air force 1,200
CONSCRIPTION DURATION – 18–36 months

ECONOMY AND TRADE
Progress towards economic recovery and reconstruction after the civil war was reversed in 1998 by Hurricane Mitch, which caused widespread devastation and left 20 per cent of the population homeless. Some debt relief was provided in 2004 and 2006, but the country remains very poor. Nearly half the population lives below the poverty line, and unemployment and underemployment are widespread. Ratification of the US-Central America Free Trade Agreement in 2005 should make Nicaragua more able to attract investment, create jobs and stimulate economic growth.

Agriculture is the mainstay of the economy, accounting for 17 per cent of GDP and 29 per cent of employment. The main commercial crops are coffee, beef, prawns, lobsters, tobacco, sugar and peanuts. Industry includes food and timber processing, mining, oil refining, the manufacture of chemicals, machinery and metal products and tourism. Industry contributes 26 per cent of GDP and services 57 per cent. The main trading partners are the USA, El Salvador, Costa Rica and other Central and South American countries. Principal exports are the main commercial crops and gold. The main imports are consumer goods, machinery and equipment, raw materials and petroleum products.
GNI – US$4,900m; US$950 per capita (2005)
ANNUAL AVERAGE GROWTH OF GDP – 4 per cent (2005 est)
INFLATION RATE – 9.6 per cent (2005 est)
UNEMPLOYMENT – 5.6 per cent (2005 est)
TOTAL EXTERNAL DEBT – US$3,188m (2005 est)
IMPORTS – US$2,600m (2005)
EXPORTS – US$900m (2005)

BALANCE OF PAYMENTS
Trade – US$1,089m deficit (2004)
Current Account – US$772m deficit (2004)

Trade with UK	*2005*	*2006*
Imports from UK	£2,291,000	£3,124,000
Exports to UK	£6,694,000	£11,584,000

COMMUNICATIONS
The Inter-American Highway runs between Nicaragua's Honduran and Costa Rican borders while the Inter-Oceanic Highway runs from Corinto on the Pacific coast via Managua to Rama, where there is a natural waterway to Bluefields on the Atlantic. There are 19,036km of roads and 6km of operable railway. The main airport is at Managua, and there are a further 175 airports and airfields around the country. The chief ports are Corinto (Pacific) and Bluefields and El Bluff (Caribbean Sea). There are 2,220km of inland waterways, mostly on lakes Managua and Nicaragua, and Lake Nicaragua is the chief element in a 2006 proposal to construct a canal linking the Pacific and Caribbean coasts.

The telephone system is being expanded and upgraded with the help of foreign investment. In 2005 there were 221,000 main telephone lines in use, 1.2 million mobile phone subscribers, and 140,000 internet users.

EDUCATION AND HEALTH
LITERACY RATE – 76.7 per cent (2004 est)
GROSS ENROLMENT RATIO (percentage of relevant age group) – primary 112 per cent; secondary 66 per cent; tertiary 18 per cent (2005 est)
HEALTH EXPENDITURE (per capita) – US$67 (2004)
HOSPITAL BEDS (per 1,000 people) – 0.9 (2000–5)

MEDIA
There are three daily newspapers, including the pro-Sandinista *El Nuevo Diario.* Canal 6, the state-owned broadcaster, competes with three commercial networks to provide television services. There are a large number of radio stations.

NIGER

République du Niger – Republic of Niger

AREA – 1,267,000 sq. km. Neighbours: Algeria and Libya (north), Chad (east), Nigeria and Benin (south), Mali and Burkina Faso (west)
CAPITAL – Niamey; population, 707,951 (2001)
CURRENCY – Franc CFA of 100 centimes
POPULATION – 12,525,094 rising at 2.92 per cent per year (2006 est); Hausa (56 per cent), Djerma (22 per cent), Fula (8.5 per cent), Tuareg (8 per cent) (est)
RELIGION – Islam (90 per cent), Christianity (5 per cent) (est)

LANGUAGE – French (official), Hausa, Djerma
POPULATION DENSITY – 11 per sq. km (2005)
URBAN POPULATION – 23.3 per cent (2005 est)
MEDIAN AGE (years) – 16.5 (2006 est)
NATIONAL ANTHEM – 'La Nigerienne'
NATIONAL DAY – 18 December (Republic Day)
LIFE EXPECTANCY (years) – 43.76 (2006 est)
MORTALITY RATE – 20.91 (2006 est)
BIRTH RATE – 50.73 (2006 est)
INFANT MORTALITY RATE – 118.25 (2006 est)
HIV/AIDS ADULT PREVALENCE – 1.2 per cent (2003 est)
DEATH PENALTY – No*
CPI SCORE – 2.3 (2006)
MILITARY BUDGET – US$43m (2006 est)
MILITARY PERSONNEL – 5,300: army 5,200, air force 100; paramilitaries 5,400
CONSCRIPTION DURATION – 24 months (selective)
HEALTH EXPENDITURE (per capita) – US$9 (2004)
LITERACY RATE – 14.4 per cent (2004 est)
GROSS ENROLMENT RATIO (percentage of relevant age group) – primary 47 per cent; secondary 9 per cent; tertiary 1 per cent (2005 est)

7.91	WORLD HIGHEST
	children per woman

Source: Economist Intelligence Unit

CLIMATE AND TERRAIN

A landlocked state, much of the country is desert, with low hills in the north and savannah in the south. Elevation extremes range from 2,022m (Mt Bagzane) at the highest point to 200m (River Niger) at the lowest. The Niger valley in the south-west and the seasonal part of Lake Chad in the south-east are the only well-watered areas. Average temperatures range from 24°C in January to 34°C in May.

HISTORY AND POLITICS

The area was divided between several kingdoms formed by different tribes (Tuareg, Songhai, Hausa, Fulani) from the 10th to 19th centuries. French colonial expansion from the 1880s brought the whole area under control in 1898 and in 1904 it became part of French West Africa. The country became autonomous in 1958 and achieved full independence in 1960. Widespread drought and perceived political corruption precipitated a military coup under Col. Seyni Kountché in 1974, who ruled until his death in 1987. His cousin and successor, Col. Ali Saibou, was unable to resist pressure for a multiparty democracy, despite the release of political prisoners and the drafting of a new constitution.

Civilian government was re-introduced in 1989 but Niger remained under a one-party system until other parties were legalised in 1990 following further civil unrest. In 1992, a multiparty constitution was introduced. Elections in 1993 produced a left-of-centre government that was overthrown in 1996 by the military under the leadership of Brig. Ibrahim Barre Mainassara. He was assassinated during a coup in 1999, and another new constitution was approved.

In presidential and legislative elections in November 1999, Mamadou Tandja of the National Movement for Society in Development (MNSD) was elected president and the MNSD won an overall majority in the national assembly. In the 2004 elections, President Tandja was re-elected president, and the MNSD remained the largest party in parliament but lost its overall majority.

POLITICAL SYSTEM
Under the 1999 constitution, the head of state is a president directly elected for a five-year term, renewable only once. The unicameral legislature, the national assembly, has 83 members, who are directly elected for a five-year term. The prime minister is appointed from the party with the parliamentary majority.

HEAD OF STATE
President, Mamadou Tandja, *elected* 24 November 1999, *sworn in* 22 December 1999, *re-elected* 4 December 2004

SELECTED GOVERNMENT MEMBERS *as at June 2007*
Prime Minister, Seyni Oumarou
Finance and Economy, Ali Mahamane Lamine Zène
Foreign Affairs, Aissatou Mindaoudou
Interior, Albade Abouba
National Defence, Djida Hamadou

EMBASSY OF THE REPUBLIC OF NIGER
154 rue de Longchamp, 75116 Paris, France
T (+33) (1) 4504 8060
Ambassador Extraordinary and Plenipotentiary, HE Adamou Seydou, *apptd* 2003

BRITISH AMBASSADOR
HE Dr Nicholas Westcott, CMG, *apptd* 2007, resident at Accra, Ghana

ECONOMY AND TRADE

Niger is one of the poorest countries in the world, with the majority of the population living below the poverty line. Economic progress has been constrained by political instability, recurrent droughts, over-grazing, desertification and rapid population growth, leaving the country dependent on foreign aid. Its huge foreign debt burden was much reduced by debt relief and cancellation in 2000 and 2005.

The mainstay of the economy is subsistence agriculture and herding, which account for 39 per cent of GDP and engage 90 per cent of the population; the main crops are cowpeas, cotton, peanuts, millet, sorghum, cassava, rice and livestock. Locust infestation in 2004 and drought since 2005 have caused serious shortages of food and fodder and in 2005 and 2006 the UN warned of the risk of famine. The main industry and most lucrative export is uranium, but dependency upon this makes the economy vulnerable to fluctuations in global prices. Efforts are being made to diversify into exploitation of oil, gold, coal and other mineral resources. The other industries are food processing and manufacturing of cement, bricks, soap, textiles and chemicals. Industry contributes 17 per cent of GDP and services 44 per cent. Of the salaried workforce, 60 per cent is employed in the public sector.

The main trading partners are France, the USA and Nigeria. Principal exports are uranium ore, livestock and cowpeas. The main imports are foodstuffs, machinery, vehicles and parts, petroleum and cereals.
GNI – US$3,300m; US$240 per capita (2005)
ANNUAL AVERAGE GROWTH OF GDP – 7 per cent (2005 est)

INFLATION RATE – 0.2 per cent (2004 est)
TOTAL EXTERNAL DEBT – US$2,100m (2003 est)
IMPORTS – US$920m (2005)
EXPORTS – US$410m (2005)

Trade with UK	*2005*	*2006*
Imports from UK	£6,257,000	£4,649,000
Exports to UK	£202,000	£261,000

COMMUNICATIONS

Niger has no railways. Of the 14,500km of roads, less than 4,000km are surfaced. The River Niger is navigable between September and March for 300km from Niamey to the Benin frontier. The principal airport is at Niamey; there are a further 27 airports and airfields around the country.

The telephone system is limited in extent, concentrated mainly in the south-west, and mobile phone distribution has grown rapidly. In 2005 there were 24,000 main lines in use, 300,000 mobile phone subscribers and 24,000 internet users.

MEDIA

Radio is the most important form of communication, and a growing sector; the state-owned broadcaster competes with a number of private stations. A single state-owned daily newspaper, *Le Sahel,* competes with a proliferating number of private publications.

NIGERIA

Federal Republic of Nigeria

AREA – 923,768 sq. km. Neighbours: Benin (west), Niger (north), Chad (north-east), Cameroon (east)
CAPITAL – Abuja (declared the federal capital in 1991); population, 107,069 (1991)
MAJOR CITIES – Lagos; Kano; Ibadan; Kaduna; Benin City; Port Harcourt
CURRENCY – Naira (N) of 100 kobo
POPULATION – 131,859,731 rising at 2.38 per cent per year (2006 est); Hausa and Fula (29 per cent), Yoruba (21 per cent), Igbo (18 per cent), Ijaw (10 per cent), Kanuri (4 per cent), Ibibio (3.5 per cent), Tiv (2.5 per cent) (est)
RELIGION – Islam (50 per cent), Christianity (40 per cent) (est)
LANGUAGE – English (official), Hausa, Yoruba, Igbo, Fulani
POPULATION DENSITY – 144 per sq. km (2005)
URBAN POPULATION – 48.3 per cent (2005 est)
MEDIAN AGE (years) – 18.7 (2006 est)
NATIONAL ANTHEM – 'Arise, O Compatriots, Nigeria's Call Obey'
NATIONAL DAY – 1 October (Independence Day)
LIFE EXPECTANCY (years) – 47.08 (2006 est)
MORTALITY RATE – 16.94 (2006 est)
BIRTH RATE – 40.43 (2006 est)
INFANT MORTALITY RATE – 97.14 (2006 est)
HIV/AIDS ADULT PREVALENCE – 5.4 per cent (2003 est)
DEATH PENALTY – Yes
CPI SCORE – 2.2 (2006)
POPULATION BELOW POVERTY LINE – 60 per cent (2000 est)
LITERACY RATE – 66.8 per cent (2004 est)
GROSS ENROLMENT RATIO (percentage of relevant age group) – primary 103 per cent; secondary 34 per cent; tertiary 10 per cent (2005 est)
HEALTH EXPENDITURE (per capita) – US$23 (2004)

CLIMATE AND TERRAIN

The north is arid savannah and semi-desert. The south is tropical rainforest, with mangrove swamps along the coast. The Niger River forms a broad delta in the south, and there are mountains in the south-east. Elevation extremes range from 2,419m (Chappal Waddis) at the highest point to 0m (Atlantic Ocean) at the lowest. The climate varies across the country, with the north experiencing a single rainy season and colder winter temperatures; by contrast the south has two rainy seasons (in the spring and autumn) and an average temperature between 20°C and 30°C all year round.

HISTORY AND POLITICS

Nigeria was at the centre of the Nok culture from 500 BC to AD 200. Various kingdoms flourished in the area in the Middle Ages, and Islam was introduced to the north in the 13th century. The Oyo Empire was dominant in the south in the 17th century and the Muslim Sokoto Empire in the north in the 19th century. European traders had arrived on the coast in the 15th century and participated in the gold and slave trades. After Britain abolished slavery, several other powers attempted to exploit the slave trade in Nigeria, which led Britain to annex Lagos in 1861. Britain occupied the rest of Nigeria in stages during the late 19th century, uniting the whole of modern Nigeria into a single political and administrative unit by 1914. The country became a federation in 1954, and increasing degrees of internal self-government were introduced until the country became fully independent in 1960.

Independence unleashed ethnic and regional tensions, and there were two military coups in 1966; the first coup was led by the eastern Igbo tribe, under the command of General Ironsi. His belief in a united, Igbo-led Nigeria led to a counter-coup from the north, which killed Ironsi and scores of other Igbos. Playing on the fear of imminent genocide, Igbo Lt-Col. Emeka Ojukwu argued that the east should secede, aware that the country's richest oilfields all belonged to this region. The following year, the east set up the state of Biafra, and in doing so instigated a civil war. The region quickly became surrounded and lost both territory and infrastructure to bombing campaigns. Despite an international relief effort, the conflict, which lasted until Ojukwu's surrender in 1970, killed around one million people.

In the 30 years after 1967 there were several military coups and the governments during most of the period were military or military-dominated. Some of the regimes made efforts to reintroduce civilian government, legalise political parties and restore democracy but invariably suspended these when the results were unfavourable to them. Nigeria was suspended from the Commonwealth in 1995 because of human rights abuses against pro-democracy campaigners (most notably the hanging of activist Ken Saro-Wiwa) but was readmitted in 1999 after moves towards civilian rule began. Following presidential and legislative elections in 1999, a civilian president and government took office and military rule ended. 2003 saw the first civilian-run elections in 20 years.

Ethnic and regional tensions have been more openly and violently expressed since 1999, including calls for secession by various groups. The main source of tension is the religious divide between the predominantly Muslim north, where Shariah law has been introduced, and the predominantly Christian south. There have been sporadic violent clashes in which thousands have died, leading to internal migration of Christians from the north. The latest trouble spot is the Niger delta, where militants have attacked oil facilities and kidnapped foreign oil workers, demanding greater local control over oil revenues.

Heavily criticised presidential and legislative elections were held in April 2007 amid reports of violence, intimidation and ballot-rigging. The presidential election was won by Umaru Musa Yar'Adua of the People's Democratic Party (PDP), which also retained its majority in both houses of parliament.

POLITICAL SYSTEM

The country is a federal democratic republic. Under the 1999 constitution, the executive president is directly elected for a four-year term, renewable only once. As head of the government, the president appoints the federal executive council, which must be approved by the senate. The national assembly is bicameral; the house of representatives has 360 members and the senate has 109 members, both elected for a four-year term. There are 36 states and the Federal Capital Territory.

HEAD OF STATE

President, Umaru Musa Yar'Adua, *elected* 21 April 2007, *re-elected* 29 May 2007
Vice-President, Goodluck Jonathan

SELECTED GOVERNMENT MEMBERS *as at June 2007*

Defence, Thomas I. Aguiyi-Ironsi
Finance, Esther Nenadi Usman
Foreign Affairs, Joy Ogwu
Internal Affairs, Oluyemi Adeniji

HIGH COMMISSION FOR THE FEDERAL REPUBLIC OF NIGERIA

Nigeria House, 9 Northumberland Avenue, London WC2N 5BX
T 020-7839 1244 W www.nigeria.org.uk
High Commissioner, HE Dr Christopher Olusola Kolade, *apptd* 2002

BRITISH HIGH COMMISSION

Shehu Shagari Way (North), Maitama, Abuja
T (+234) (1) 523 2010 E chancery@abuja.mail.fco.gov.uk
High Commissioner, HE Richard Gozney, *apptd* 2004

BRITISH COUNCIL

Plot 3645, IBB Way, Maitama, PMB 550, Garki, Abuja
T (+234) (9) 4137 8707 W www.britishcouncil.org/nigeria
Director, Peter Upton

FEDERAL STRUCTURE

The federal republic is divided into 36 states and the Federal Capital Territory: Abia, Adamawa, Akwa Ibom, Anambra, Bauchi, Bayelsa, Benue, Borno, Cross River, Delta, Ebonyi, Edo, Ekiti, Enugu, Gombe, Imo, Jigawa, Kaduna, Kano, Katsina, Kebbi, Kogi, Kwara, Lagos, Nassarawa, Niger, Ogun, Ondo, Osun, Oyo, Plateau, Rivers, Sokoto, Taraba, Yobe and Zamfara.

DEFENCE

The army has 270 main battle tanks, 150 light tanks and over 427 armoured personnel carriers. The navy has 1 frigate and 20 patrol and coastal vessels at 3 bases. The air force has 84 combat aircraft and 5 armed helicopters.
MILITARY BUDGET – US$768m (2006)
MILITARY PERSONNEL – 85,000: army 67,000, navy 8,000, air force 10,000; paramilitaries 82,000

ECONOMY AND TRADE

Nigeria is the leading sub-Saharan oil producer, enjoying an oil boom in the 1970s and currently benefiting again from high oil prices. The profits from the 1970s boom were dissipated by mismanagement and corruption. The majority of the population received little benefit, and 60 per cent still live below the poverty line. Past governments also failed to diversify the economy away from its dependence on the oil industry, which accounts for 20 per cent of GDP, 65 per cent of budgetary revenues and 95 per cent of foreign exchange earnings. However, the current government is showing the political will to introduce market-oriented reforms that will improve fiscal and monetary management, curb inflation and address regional agitation for wider distribution of oil revenues. To attract the maximum foreign investment, factors such as security and the inadequate infrastructure still need to be addressed. The recent high oil revenues have, however, freed Nigeria from much of its foreign debt, enabling it to pay off US$30bn (£15bn) in 2006.

Apart from crude oil, Nigeria exploits its reserves of coal, tin and columbite. The mainstay of the economy is agriculture, mostly at subsistence level, which generates 17 per cent of GDP and engages 70 per cent of the population. The main crops include cocoa, peanuts, palm oil, corn, rice, sorghum and millet. In addition to its main activities of oil production, mining and processing agricultural products, the industrial sector produces textiles, cement and other construction materials and footwear. Industry contributes 53 per cent of GDP and services 30 per cent.

The main trading partners are the USA (52 per cent of exports), Brazil, China and EU countries. Principal exports are oil and oil products, cocoa and rubber. The main imports are machinery, chemicals, transport equipment, manufactured goods, food and live animals. Agricultural output has failed to keep pace with rapid population growth, changing Nigeria from a net food exporter to a food importer.
GNI – US$74,000m; US$560 per capita (2005)
ANNUAL AVERAGE GROWTH OF GDP – 6.9 per cent (2005 est)
INFLATION RATE – 13.5 per cent (2005 est)
UNEMPLOYMENT – 2.9 per cent (2005 est)
TOTAL EXTERNAL DEBT – US$37,450m (2005 est)
IMPORTS – US$15,200m (2005)
EXPORTS – US$31,000m (2004)

BALANCE OF PAYMENTS

Trade – US$12,561m surplus (2004)
Current Account – US$12,264m surplus (2004)

Trade with UK	*2005*	*2006*
Imports from UK	£817,813,000	£836,230,000
Exports to UK	£163,000,000	£217,960,000

COMMUNICATIONS

Internal long-distance travel is mostly by air; there are 69 airports and airfields, including the principal airports at Lagos, Kano and Port Harcourt. The Nigerian railway network, which is controlled by the Nigerian Railway Corporation, has 3,505km of track. There are 194,394km of roads, and 8,600km of waterways, mostly on the Niger and Benue rivers. The main seaports are Lagos, Port Harcourt, Warri and Calabar.

The telephone system is being expanded and modernised, but slowly, and mobile phone distribution has grown rapidly. In 2005 there were 1.2 million main lines in use and 5 million internet users; by 2006 there were 21.6 million mobile phone subscribers.

MEDIA

There are nine main daily newspapers, supplemented by weekly publications, and popular titles include *The Guardian* and *Punch*. The Nigerian Television Authority (NTA) is a state-run broadcaster operating alongside a large number of private and commercial networks. Radio provides Nigerians with their main access to the media, and international broadcasters such as the BBC are popular.

CULTURE

Nigerians are responsible for several key post-colonial works of literature, most notably *Things Fall Apart* (1958) by Chinua Achebe (*b.* 1930), a historical novel examining the effects of British colonialism on the native Igbo tribe. It has been translated into 50 languages, making Achebe the most translated author in Africa. Other significant writers include Nobel prize winner Wole Soyinka (*b.* 1934) and Ken Saro-Wiwa (1941–1995), whose political activism resulted in his death at the hands of the military government.

'Nollywood' is the colloquial name for the Nigerian film industry, reported by *Time* magazine to be the third biggest in the world, behind the USA and India and worth around US$250m (£125m) a year. It is estimated that up to 2,000 films a year are produced, many of which outsell even the biggest Hollywood blockbusters across Africa. Most films go straight to DVD or VCD (video CD) and are sold at low prices, helping to spread popularity and increase demand.

Fela Kuti (1938–97) is Nigeria's most famous musician. He pioneered a style he called Afrobeat, combining traditional Yoruba rhythms with jazz and funk. The movement became inextricably linked with Kuti's personal politics, which saw him embrace black power, campaign against suppression of human rights in Africa and later twice run (unsuccessfully) for the Nigerian presidency.

NORWAY

Kongeriket Norge – Kingdom of Norway

AREA – 323,802 sq. km, of which Svalbard and Jan Mayen have a combined area of 63,080 sq. km. Neighbours: Sweden, Finland, Russia (east)
CAPITAL – Oslo; population, 538,411 (2006 est)
MAJOR CITIES – Bergen; Trondheim; Stavanger
CURRENCY – Krone of 100 re
POPULATION – 4,610,820 rising at 0.38 per cent per year (2006 est)
RELIGION – Protestantism (89 per cent), Islam (1 per cent), Roman Catholicism (1 per cent) (est). An estimated 1 per cent of the population is atheist
LANGUAGE – Bokmal and Nynorsk Norwegian (both official), Sami (official in six municipalities)
POPULATION DENSITY – 15 per sq. km (2005)
URBAN POPULATION – 80.5 per cent (2005 est)
MEDIAN AGE (years) – 38.4 (2006 est)
NATIONAL ANTHEM – 'Ja, Vi Elsker Dette Landet' ['Yes, We Love this Country']
NATIONAL DAY – 17 May (Constitution Day)
LIFE EXPECTANCY (years) – 79.54 (2006 est)
MORTALITY RATE – 9.4 (2006 est)
BIRTH RATE – 11.46 (2006 est)
INFANT MORTALITY RATE – 3.67 (2006 est)
DEATH PENALTY – No (abolished 1979)
CPI SCORE – 8.8 (2006)

CLIMATE AND TERRAIN

The terrain is mountainous, with elevated, barren tablelands separated by deep, narrow valleys. The coastline is deeply indented with numerous fjords and fringed with rocky islands; in 2005 Geirangerfjord and Naeroyfjord in the west were awarded UNESCO World Heritage status. Elevation extremes range from 2,469m (Galdhopiggen) at the highest point to 0m (Norwegian Sea) at the lowest.

Part of the country lies north of the Arctic Circle, and at the North Cape the sun does not appear to set between about 14 May and 29 July, causing the phenomenon known as the midnight sun; conversely, there is no apparent sunrise from about 18 November to 24 January. Average temperatures in Oslo range between −7°C in February to 22°C in August, though winter temperatures in the north can drop to −15°C.

HISTORY AND POLITICS

Norway became a unified country under rule of King Harald Fairhair in *c.*900 but dissolved after his death and was reunified by Olav II in *c.*1016–28. Canute brought Norway under Danish rule in 1028 but the throne reverted on his death to Magnus I. When the royal house died out in the 14th century, the Danish monarch was the nearest heir and in 1397 Norway, Denmark and Sweden were united under a single monarch under the Kalmar Union. Sweden seceded from the union in 1523, but Norway continued to be ruled by the Danish monarch until the end of the Napoleonic wars. In 1814 Norway was ceded to Sweden; it continued to have its own parliament although the cabinet was appointed by the king of Sweden. Internal self-government was achieved in 1884, but growing tension over the government's lack of control led to the union being dissolved and Norway became independent in 1905. The first king of the newly independent country was a Danish prince who took the throne as King Haakon VII.

The country was neutral in the First World War, but in the Second World War Norway was invaded and occupied by Germany from 1940 until 1945. Norway joined NATO in 1949 and was a founder member of the European Free Trade Association in 1960. Despite this integration with Europe, the Norwegians rejected opportunities to join the EU in referendums in 1972 and 1994. Since 1945 the Labour Party has held office for long periods, either on its own or in coalition with smaller parties, and pursued policies of economic planning and an extensive welfare state. After a period in opposition, the Labour Party returned to power in 2005 after winning a majority of seats in the legislative election, forming a coalition government with the Socialist Left and Centre parties.

POLITICAL SYSTEM

Norway is a constitutional monarchy with a hereditary monarch as head of state. Under the 1814 constitution, the unicameral *Storting* has 169 members who are directly elected for a four-year term. When legislative matters are under discussion, the *Storting* divides into two chambers.

It elects one-quarter of its members to constitute the *Lagting* (upper chamber), the other three-quarters forming the *Odelsting* (lower chamber). The prime minister, who is responsible to parliament, appoints the other ministers.

HEAD OF STATE
HM The King of Norway, King Harald V, KG, GCVO, *born* 21 February 1937, *succeeded* 17 January 1991
Heir, HRH Crown Prince Haakon Magnus, *born* 20 July 1973

SELECTED GOVERNMENT MEMBERS *as at June 2007*
Prime Minister, Jens Stoltenberg
Defence, Anne-Grete Strom-Erichsen
Finance, Kristin Halvorsen
Foreign Affairs, Jonas Gahr Store

ROYAL NORWEGIAN EMBASSY
25 Belgrave Square, London SW1X 8QD
T 020-7591 5500 **E** emb.london@mfa.no
W www.norway.org.uk
Ambassador Extraordinary and Plenipotentiary, HE Bjarne Lindstrom, *apptd* 2005

BRITISH EMBASSY
Thomas Heftyesgate 8, 0244 Oslo
T (+47) 2313 2700 **W** www.britain.no
Ambassador Extraordinary and Plenipotentiary, HE David Powell, *apptd* 2006

BRITISH COUNCIL
Fridtjof Nansens Plass 5, N-0160 Oslo
T (+47) (22) 396 190
W www.britishcouncil.org/norway
Director, Simon Giverin

DEFENCE

The army has 165 main battle tanks, 157 armoured infantry fighting vehicles and 189 armoured personnel carriers. The navy has 6 submarines, 5 frigates and 15 patrol and coastal vessels at three bases. The air force has 61 combat aircraft.
MILITARY EXPENDITURE – US$4,840m (2005)
MILITARY PERSONNEL – 23,400: army 14,700, navy 3,700, air force 5,000
CONSCRIPTION DURATION – 12 months plus refresher training

ECONOMY AND TRADE

Norway's prosperity depends primarily upon its oil and gas sectors and fisheries. The third largest oil exporter after Saudi Arabia and Russia, oil and gas account for one-third of net exports. Reserves in currently operating fields will be exhausted in the next 20 years but there are plans, opposed by environmentalists, to explore for oil and gas in the Barents Sea and other areas that are becoming more accessible as the Arctic ice cap retreats. Norway has planned for the time when current oil and gas reserves are exhausted by investing its budget surpluses in a government petroleum fund, now valued at US$250bn (£125bn).

The nature of the terrain restricts agriculture, which generates 2.3 per cent of GDP. The main industries apart from oil and gas are fishing, forestry, food processing, shipbuilding, pulp and paper products, metals, chemicals, mining and textiles. Shipping freight services are also significant, with Norwegian companies controlling 10 per cent of the world's shipping fleet. Industry contributes 41.4 per cent of GDP and services 56.3 per cent.

The main trading partners are EU countries, the USA and China. Principal exports are oil, machinery and equipment, metals, chemicals, ships and fish. The main imports are machinery and equipment, chemicals, metals and foodstuffs.
GNI – US$281,500m; US$60,890 per capita (2005)
ANNUAL AVERAGE GROWTH OF GDP – 4 per cent (2005 est)
INFLATION RATE – 1.6 per cent (2005 est)
UNEMPLOYMENT – 4.6 per cent (2005 est)
TOTAL EXTERNAL DEBT – US$281,000m (2005)
IMPORTS – US$54,800m (2005)
EXPORTS – US$101,900m (2005)

BALANCE OF PAYMENTS
Trade – US$50,138m surplus (2005)
Current Account – US$49,488m surplus (2005)

Trade with UK	*2005*	*2006*
Imports from UK	£2,276,274,000	£2,123,700,000
Exports to UK	£12,428,412,000	£14,755,152,000

COMMUNICATIONS

There are 4,077km of railways and 92,513km of roads. The rail network stops at Bodo, a little way north of the Arctic Circle, and there are few roads in the far north, to which the main means of transport is by sea; the state ferries operating between Bergen and Kirkenes carry freight, vehicles and passengers. There are 99 airports and airfields, including the principal airports at Oslo, Bergen, Kristiansand and Stavanger. The main ports are Oslo, Bergen, Kristiansand, Tonsberg, Stavanger and Narvik, and there is a large merchant fleet, with 724 ships of over 1,000 tonnes registered in Norway and 861 registered abroad.

The fixed-line telephone system serves all parts of the country and mobile phone distribution has grown rapidly. In 2005 there were 2.1 million main lines in use, 4.7 million mobile phone subscribers and 3.1 million internet users.

EDUCATION AND HEALTH

Education from six to 16 is free of charge and compulsory in the basic schools, and free from 16 to 19 years. The majority of pupils receive post-compulsory schooling at upper secondary schools, regional colleges, and universities and specialist colleges.
GROSS ENROLMENT RATIO (percentage of relevant age group) – primary 99 per cent; secondary 116 per cent; tertiary 80 per cent (2005 est)
HEALTH EXPENDITURE (per capita) – US$5,405 (2004)
HOSPITAL BEDS (per 1,000 people) – 3.8 (2000–5)

MEDIA AND CULTURE

Broadcasting is deregulated and there are a number of commercial channels, with satellite networks becoming increasingly popular. There are five widely read national daily newspapers and a single national weekly newspaper, *Morgenbladet.*

Celebrated cultural figures include the artist Edvard Munch (1863–1944), responsible for one of the world's most recognisable paintings, *The Scream* (1893); writer Knut Hamsun (1859–1952), winner of the Nobel prize for literature in 1920; dramatist Henrik Ibsen (1828–1906); the composer Edvard Grieg (1843–1907) and the 1980s pop group A-ha, which has sold over 30 million albums worldwide.

TERRITORIES

SVALBARD, area 61,020 sq. km; population 2,701 (2006 est)

The Svalbard archipelago consists of Spitsbergen, the main island, North East Land, the Wiche Islands, Barents Island, Edge Island, Prince Charles Foreland, Hope Island and Bear Island. Around 60 per cent of the islands in the archipelago are covered by ice. Over half of the Svalbard archipelago has been designated as a national park, such is the diversity of its wildlife, and a global seed repository is under construction. Norway's sovereignty was recognised by treaty in 1920 but the other signatories were granted equal rights to exploit mineral deposits, although this right is now only exercised by Russia. The main economic activity is coal mining, with some hunting of seal, reindeer and arctic fox.

JAN MAYEN ISLAND was joined to Norway in 1930.

NORWEGIAN ANTARCTIC TERRITORIES

The Norwegian Antarctic Territory consists of Queen Maud Land, Bouvet Island and Peter the First Island. Claimed in 1938, Queen Maud Land is a sector of the Antarctic content which extends from 45° E. to 20° E. Peter the First Island was formally claimed in 1931 and is the only claimed area covered under the Antarctic treaty that is not part of the main land mass. Bouvet Island was claimed in 1930. (*See also* The Antarctic.)

OMAN

Saltanat Uman – Sultanate of Oman

AREA – 212,460 sq. km. Neighbours: Yemen (south-west), Saudi Arabia (west) and the UAE (north-west)
CAPITAL – Muscat (Masqat); population, 540,000 (2001 est)
MAJOR CITIES – Salalah (the main town of Dhofar); Sohar; Ibra
CURRENCY – Rial Omani (OR) of 1,000 baisas
POPULATION – 3,102,229 rising at 3.28 per cent per year (2006 est)
RELIGION – Islam (59 per cent), Hinduism (25 per cent), Christianity (16 per cent) (est)
LANGUAGE – Arabic (official), English, Baluchi, Urdu
POPULATION DENSITY – 8 per sq. km (2005)
URBAN POPULATION – 78.6 per cent (2005 est)
MEDIAN AGE (years) – 19 (2006 est)
NATIONAL ANTHEM – 'Nashid as-Salaam as-Sultani' ['The Sultan's Anthem']
NATIONAL DAY – 18 November (Birthday of Sultan Qaboos)
LIFE EXPECTANCY (years) – 73.37 (2006 est)
MORTALITY RATE – 3.81 (2006 est)
BIRTH RATE – 36.24 (2006 est)
INFANT MORTALITY RATE – 18.89 (2006 est)
DEATH PENALTY – Yes
CPI SCORE – 5.4 (2006)

CLIMATE AND TERRAIN

Oman lies at the south-eastern corner of the Arabian peninsula. There are mountains in the north and the south-west of the country, divided by nearly 643km of high desert plateau. This descends to a fertile plain on the Arabian Sea coast. Elevation extremes range from 2,980m (Jabal Shams) at the highest point to 0m (Arabian Sea) at the lowest. Temperatures and humidity are high throughout the year; the highest temperatures are recorded inland, but the high humidity often makes coastal areas the most inhospitable. Rainfall is low and the majority of precipitation falls during December and January. Average temperatures in Muscat range from 20°C in January to 40°C in July.

HISTORY AND POLITICS

Oman began to build an empire in the Middle East from the eighth century AD and remained largely unchallenged until the arrival in 1507 of the Portuguese, who were ousted in 1650. Following a civil war in the early 18th century, an independent sultanate was established in 1749 by the founder of the dynasty that still rules the country. By the early 19th century, Omani rule extended to the east African coast and parts of Persia and Baluchistan (in modern Pakistan). The kingdom came under British influence in the late 19th century, where it remained until independence was declared in 1951.

Clashes between the sultan and religious leaders flared up again in the 1950s but by 1959 the sultan had established his control over the whole country. An insurrection in the south by left-wing rebels supported by South Yemen began in 1965 and was defeated with British military assistance in 1975. The discovery and subsequent exploitation of oil in the mid-1960s led to the steady economic transformation of Oman and, in 1970, Sultan Qaboos bin Said al-Said overthrew his father, Sultan Said bin Taimur, in a bloodless coup and initiated a modernisation programme.

A degree of political liberalisation has occurred in the past 20 years but the country is still essentially an absolute monarchy. In 1996 a succession mechanism was established and the system of government codified. Universal adult suffrage was introduced in 2002; the franchise was previously restricted to an electoral college of tribal leaders, intellectuals and businessmen (including some women) from 1997. The first direct election to the consultative council was held in 2000 and the first by universal adult suffrage in 2003. The 2003 election produced little change in the composition of the council; two women had been elected in 2000, and the first female ministers were appointed in 2004. Elections were expected in autumn 2007.

POLITICAL SYSTEM

In 1996 the sultan issued the basic statute of the state, which decreed Oman to be a hereditary absolute monarchy. There is no legislature; legislation is by decree of the sultan, and is implemented by the cabinet of ministers, which the sultan appoints. The sultan is advised by the *Majlis al-Shura* (consultative council) which has 83 members directly elected for a three-year term. The council has the right to review legislation, question ministers and make policy proposals. In 1997 the sultan set up the *Majlis al-Dawlah* (council of state) which has 41 members appointed by him; it is intended to facilitate 'constructive cooperation' between the sultan and the people. There are no political parties.

HEAD OF STATE

HM The Sultan of Oman, Sultan Qaboos bin Said al-Said, *succeeded following a coup,* 23 July 1970

SELECTED GOVERNMENT MEMBERS *as at June 2007*
Prime Minister, The Sultan
Deputy Prime Minister, Fahd bin Mamud al-Said
Defence, Badr bin Saud bin Hareb al-Busaidi

Foreign Affairs, Yusuf bin Alawi bin Abdullah
Interior, Saud bin Ibrahim al-Busaidi
Economy, Ahmed bin Abdul Nabi Makki

EMBASSY OF THE SULTANATE OF OMAN
167 Queens Gate, London SW7 5HE
T 020-7225 0001
Ambassador Extraordinary and Plenipotentiary, HE Hussain Ali Abdullatif, *apptd* 1995

BRITISH EMBASSY
PO Box 185, Mina al Fahal, 113 Muscat
T (+968) (24) 609 000 E enquiries.muscat@fco.gov.uk
W www.britishembassy.gov.uk/oman
Ambassador Extraordinary and Plenipotentiary, HE Noel Guckian, *apptd* 2005

BRITISH COUNCIL
PO Box 73, Road One, Madinat al Sultan, Qaboos West, 115 Muscat
T (+968) (24) 681 000 W www.britishcouncil.org/oman
Director, Steve McNulty

DEFENCE

The army has 117 main battle tanks and 191 armoured personnel carriers. The navy has 11 patrol and coastal vessels at 6 bases. The air force has 64 combat aircraft.
MILITARY BUDGET – US$3,270m (2006)
MILITARY PERSONNEL – 41,700: army 25,000, navy 4,200, air force 4,100, Royal Household 6,400, foreign forces 2,000; paramilitaries 4,400

ECONOMY AND TRADE

Although its production is more modest than other Gulf states, oil is the mainstay of Oman's economy and accounts for 80 per cent of government revenue. Economic liberalisation, including privatisation, began *c*.2000, when Oman joined the World Trade Organisation. Development plans centre on gas production, metal manufacturing, petrochemicals and trans-shipment ports, and improved training in IT and business skills to enable the local population to replace expatriate workers.

Agriculture and fishing remain important, accounting for 2 per cent of GDP and producing dates, limes, bananas, alfalfa and vegetables as well as fish. The natural gas industry is being developed, as are tourism and communication technology industries. The main industries apart from oil and natural gas extraction are oil refining, liquefied natural gas production, construction and production of cement, copper, steel, chemicals and optic fibre. Industry accounts for 39 per cent of GDP and services for 59 per cent.

The main trading partners are Japan, the UAE, China, South Korea, Thailand, the UK, Germany and the USA. Principal exports are petroleum, re-exports, fish, metals and textiles. The main imports are machinery and transport equipment, manufactured goods, food and livestock.
GNI – US$23,000m; US$9,070 per capita (2005)
ANNUAL AVERAGE GROWTH OF GDP – 5.6 per cent (2005 est)
INFLATION RATE – 1.2 per cent (2005 est)
UNEMPLOYMENT – 15 per cent (2004 est)
TOTAL EXTERNAL DEBT – US$4,361m (2005 est)
IMPORTS – US$8,830m (2005)
EXPORTS – US$18,700m (2005)

BALANCE OF PAYMENTS
Trade – US$5,472m surplus (2004)
Current Account – US$443m surplus (2004)

Trade with UK	*2005*	*2006*
Imports from UK	£376,410,000	£211,023,000
Exports to UK	£69,134,000	£83,778,000

COMMUNICATIONS

There are some 34,900km of roads, of which 9,700km are surfaced, but there are no railways. The main airports are at Muscat and Salalah, with some 130 other airports and airfields around the country. The main ports are Salalah and Port Qaboos at Mutrah, which has eight deep-water berths.

The modern telephone system served 265,200 main-line subscribers, 1.3 million mobile phone subscribers and 245,000 internet users in 2005.

EDUCATION AND HEALTH

LITERACY RATE – 74.4 per cent (2004 est)
GROSS ENROLMENT RATIO (percentage of relevant age group) – primary 84 per cent; secondary 87 per cent; tertiary 15 per cent (2005 est)
HEALTH EXPENDITURE (per capita) – US$295 (2004)
HOSPITAL BEDS (per 1,000 people) – 2 (2000–5)

MEDIA

The only television and radio broadcasters are state-controlled but private-sector Omani-owned stations are to be permitted and satellite services can be received. There are a large number of newspapers, including four national dailies. The press can be subject to political and cultural censorship by the government.

PAKISTAN

Jamhuryat Islami Pakistan – Islamic Republic of Pakistan

AREA – 803,940 sq. km. Neighbours: Iran (west), Afghanistan (north and north-west), China (north-east), the disputed territory of Kashmir, India (east)
CAPITAL – Islamabad; population, 529,180 (1998)
MAJOR CITIES – Karachi; Lahore; Faisalabad; Rawalpindi; Multan; Hyderabad; Gujranwala; Peshawar
CURRENCY – Pakistan rupee of 100 paisa
POPULATION – 165,803,560, rising at 2.09 per cent per year (2006 est)
RELIGION – Islam (96 per cent), Hinduism (2 per cent), Christianity (1 per cent) (est)
LANGUAGE – Urdu, English (both official), Punjabi, Sindhi, Siraiki, Pashto
POPULATION DENSITY – 202 per sq. km (2005)
URBAN POPULATION – 34.8 per cent (2005 est)
MEDIAN AGE (years) – 19.8 (2006 est)
NATIONAL ANTHEM – 'Pak Sarzmin Shaid Bad' ['Stay Prosperous Sacred Land']
NATIONAL DAY – 23 March (Republic Day)
LIFE EXPECTANCY (years) – 63.39 (2006 est)
MORTALITY RATE – 8.23 (2006 est)
BIRTH RATE – 29.74 (2006 est)
INFANT MORTALITY RATE – 70.45 (2006 est)
DEATH PENALTY – Yes
CPI SCORE – 2.2 (2006)
POPULATION BELOW POVERTY LINE – 35 per cent (2001 est)

CLIMATE AND TERRAIN

The arid Thar desert in the east gives way to the fertile Indus valley in the centre of the country. The terrain then rises to the Makran, Kirthar and Sulaiman mountain ranges in the west and the Karakoram and Himalayan ranges in the north. Elevation extremes range from 8,611m (K2) at the highest point to 0m (Indian Ocean) at the lowest. The climate varies greatly across the country. For the majority, the rainy season runs from June to October and is accompanied by very high humidity. Average temperatures in Islamabad range from 5°C in January to 38°C in June.

HISTORY AND POLITICS

Islam was introduced to the area from the eighth century onwards. From the 12th century, the territory formed part of successive empires covering northern India, including the Delhi sultanate and the Mughal Empire, and came under British control by the mid-19th century, when it formed part of the Empire of British India.

In 1940, Muslim leaders in British India signed the Lahore Resolution, which began a campaign for a separate Muslim state. The two predominantly Muslim areas were partitioned at independence in 1947, forming the state of Pakistan, comprising of two wings on the east and west sides of India. East Pakistan soon agitated for separation and relations between the two halves of the country deteriorated in civil war in March 1971, amid a process of military pacification initiated by West Pakistan. The eastern half gained independence after military assistance from India in December.

Pakistan became an Islamic republic in 1956. A coup in 1958 led to military rule until 1971, when Zulfiqar Ali Bhutto became head of a civilian government following Bangladesh's secession. He was overthrown and eventually sentenced to death after another military coup in 1977 which brought General Zia ul-Haq to power. Gen. ul-Haq's government abandoned the country's secular policies and initiated an Islamisation programme, which included the adoption of Shariah law. Following Zia's death in 1988, civilian government was again restored but proved unstable, with several rapid changes of government in the 1990s amid allegations of corruption.

In 1999 the government was overthrown in a military coup led by General Pervez Musharraf, who became head of government and, in 2001, president. A 2002 referendum confirmed his tenure of the presidency for a five-year term following an agreement, which he did not keep, to resign his army post at the end of 2004 and become a civilian president. A bill passed in 2004 allowed General Musharraf to continue as president and head of the military until 2007.

Since September 2001 President Musharraf has aligned Pakistan with the West in its war on terror, providing support to the allies in the Afghan War. This policy has angered militant factions, who are believed to be responsible for terrorist attacks in the country. Political opponents used procedural disruption to prevent the national assembly from functioning properly in 2002–3. President Musharraf's attempted dismissal of the chief justice in March 2007 triggered months of violent demonstrations.

In the 2002 elections to the national assembly, the Pakistan Muslim League (Qaid-i-Azam–PML-Q) won 77 seats, making it the largest single party but without an overall majority, and a coalition government was formed. Legislative and presidential elections were due in late 2007.

INSURGENCIES

Factional violence between Shia and Sunni fundamentalists has been a problem in Balochistan, Punjab and Sindh provinces since the 1980s, and has led to thousands of deaths. The government has banned several extremist groups. Government troops are also fighting in Balochistan against guerrilla forces seeking greater autonomy and financial resources for the province.

Since the early 1990s there has been civil disorder in Sindh province, especially in Karachi, where armed militants of the Mohajir Qaumi Movement (MQM), which represents Urdu-speaking Indian Muslims who fled India at partition and their descendants, are fighting for an autonomous Karachi province.

FOREIGN RELATIONS

Since partition, sovereignty over the predominantly Muslim state of Jammu and Kashmir has been disputed between Pakistan and India. A short war in 1947–8 resulted in the state being partitioned between the two countries; its status remained unresolved, leading to further outbreaks of war in 1965 and 1971, low-level conflict at altitude for control of the Siachen glacier since 1985 and occasional increases in military exchanges, most recently in 1999–2002 and 2003. Tension was exacerbated by Pakistan's support of the Muslim insurgency in the Indian part of the state, which began in the 1980s, and both countries' acquisition of nuclear weapons.

Moves towards a peaceful settlement began in 2003, when diplomatic missions were reopened and the resumption of transport links was initiated; a bus service across the line of control began in 2005. Formal diplomatic talks resumed in 2004 and have achieved several accords intended to reduce tension between the two countries, but the issue of Kashmir has yet to be addressed.

International concern was raised in 2004 by disclosures that Pakistan has sold its nuclear technology to other countries, but Musharraf continues to receive Western support.

POLITICAL SYSTEM

Pakistan is a federal republic. The 1973 constitution was suspended following the 1999 coup and was amended in 2002 by a legal framework order that increased the size of the legislature, and by other amendments that extended the powers of the presidency. Under the constitution, the head of state is a president elected by parliament for a five-year term; President Musharraf's term as president was extended for a further five years by a national referendum in 2002 and confirmed by the parliament and provincial assemblies in 2004. The legislature was suspended following the 1999 coup but new elections took place under the legal framework order in 2002 and 2003.

Under the 1973 constitution, the *Majlis as-Shura* (national assembly) had 237 members; this total was increased in 2002 to 342 members, of whom 60 are women and ten are elected by non-Muslim minorities; members serve for a five-year term. The senate has 100 members, 88 elected by provincial assemblies, eight chosen by tribal agencies and four elected by the national assembly; they serve a six-year term. General Musharraf was 'chief executive' from 1999 until 2002, when a new prime minister was appointed to lead the cabinet. The prime minister is nominated by and is responsible to the legislature.

There are four provinces: Balochistan, North-West Frontier Province, Punjab and Sindh. Each has a provincial assembly and government. In addition, there is the Federal Capital Territory and the Federally Administered Tribal Areas.

HEAD OF STATE
President, Chief of Army Staff, Gen. Pervez Musharraf, *assumed office* 20 June 2001, *confirmed in office by referendum* 30 April 2002

SELECTED GOVERNMENT MEMBERS *as at June 2007*
Prime Minister, Finance, Shaukat Aziz
Defence, Rao Sikandar Iqbal
Foreign Affairs, Mian Khurshid Kasuri
Interior, Aftab Ahmad Khan Sherpao

HIGH COMMISSION FOR THE ISLAMIC REPUBLIC OF PAKISTAN
35–36 Lowndes Square, London SW1X 9JN
T 020-7664 9200
W www.pakmissionuk.gov.pk
High Commissioner, HE Dr Maleeha Lodhi, *apptd* 2003

BRITISH HIGH COMMISSION
PO Box 1122, Diplomatic Enclave, Ramna 5, Islamabad
T (+92) (51) 282 2131 E bhctrade@isb.comsats.net.pk
High Commissioner, HE Robert Brinkley, *apptd* 2006

BRITISH COUNCIL
PO Box 1135, Islamabad
T (+92) (51) 111 424 424 W www.britishcouncil.org/pakistan
Director, Sue Beaumont

DEFENCE

The army has over 2,461 main battle tanks, 1,266 armoured personnel carriers and 22 attack helicopters. The navy has 8 submarines, 6 frigates, 6 patrol and coastal vessels, 16 combat aircraft and 12 armed helicopters at three bases. The air force has 352 combat aircraft.
MILITARY EXPENDITURE – US$4,000m (2005)
MILITARY PERSONNEL – 619,000: army 550,000, navy 24,000, air force 45,000; paramilitaries 302,000

ECONOMY AND TRADE

Political instability, confrontations between political institutions, inefficiency, corruption and high military expenditure have inhibited the development of the economy. About one-quarter of the population lives below the poverty line and a high proportion of its labour force works abroad, especially in the Middle East, providing valuable remittances, but also causing a growth in the use of child labour within Pakistan. Since 2000, economic reforms and international aid have helped to produce steady growth, although inflation remains a problem.

Agriculture employs 42 per cent of the labour force, producing cotton, wheat, rice, sugar cane, fruits, vegetables, milk, beef, mutton and eggs, and contributing 22 per cent to GDP. Significant manufacturing industries include textiles and clothing, food processing, pharmaceuticals, construction materials, paper products, fertiliser and seafood. Industry accounts for 26 per cent of GDP and services for 52 per cent. The main trading partners are the USA, the UAE, Saudi Arabia, China, Germany and Afghanistan. Principal exports are textiles (clothing, bed linen, cotton yarn and cloth), rice, leather goods, sports goods, chemicals and carpets. The main imports are petroleum and petroleum products, machinery, plastics, transport equipment, paper, iron, steel and tea.

GNI – US$107,300m; US$690 per capita (2005)
ANNUAL AVERAGE GROWTH OF GDP – 6.6 per cent (2005 est)
INFLATION RATE – 9.1 per cent (2005 est)
UNEMPLOYMENT – 6.6 per cent (2005 est)
TOTAL EXTERNAL DEBT – US$38,800m (2005 est)
IMPORTS – US$25,400m (2005)
EXPORTS – US$16,100m (2005)

BALANCE OF PAYMENTS
Trade – US$6,178m deficit (2005)
Current Account – US$3,463m deficit (2005)

Trade with UK	*2005*	*2006*
Imports from UK	£463,586,000	£489,948,000
Exports to UK	£469,159,000	£523,353,000

COMMUNICATIONS

There are some 258,000km of roads and 8,163km of railways. The principal airports are at Karachi, Islamabad, Lahore, Peshawar and Sialkot. Pakistan International Airlines operates domestic air services between the principal cities as well as international services. The main seaports are Karachi and Port Qasim. The government is planning to build a deepwater port at Gwadar in Balochistan, and a road link from there to Afghanistan and central Asia.

Recent investment has resulted in dramatic improvements in the fixed-line and mobile telephone networks. Since 2000 main-line availability has risen gradually but mobile phone distribution has rocketed; in 2006 there were 5.1 million main lines in use and 48.2 million mobile phone subscribers. In 2005 there were 10.5 million internet users.

EDUCATION AND HEALTH

Education is free of charge to upper secondary level. The system consists of five years of primary education (five to nine years), three years of middle or lower secondary (general or vocational), two years of upper secondary, two years of higher secondary (intermediate) and two to five years of higher education in colleges and universities.
LITERACY RATE – 48.7 per cent (2004 est)
GROSS ENROLMENT RATIO (percentage of relevant age group) – primary 87 per cent; secondary 27 per cent; tertiary 5 per cent (2005 est)
HEALTH EXPENDITURE (per capita) – US$14 (2004)
HOSPITAL BEDS (per 1,000 people) – 0.7 (2000–5)

MEDIA

There are eight national newspapers, and the state-owned broadcaster, Pakistan Television Corporation Ltd, competes with several private networks. In keeping with the liberalisation of the media under President Musharraf, the government has granted licences for a number of satellite television and radio stations since 2004. A number of unlicensed broadcasters are believed to exist in the north of the country. A notable characteristic of the Pakistani media is its willingness to criticise neighbouring India, which frequently responds in kind.

PALAU

Beluu er a Belau – Republic of Palau

AREA – 458 sq. km
CAPITAL – Melekeok; population, 581 (2005)
CURRENCY – Currency is that of the USA
POPULATION – 20,579 rising at 1.31 per cent per year (2006 est)
RELIGION – Roman Catholicism (65 per cent), other Christian denominations (16 per cent), Modekngei (4 per cent) (est). Modekngei is unique to Palau and combines elements of animism and Christian beliefs
LANGUAGE – Palauan, English, Tobi, Sonsoralese, Japanese, Angaur (all official)
POPULATION DENSITY – 44 per sq. km (2005)
URBAN POPULATION – 68.2 per cent (2005 est)
MEDIAN AGE (years) – 31.7 (2006 est)
NATIONAL ANTHEM – 'Belau Rekid' ['Our Palau']
NATIONAL DAY – 9 July (Constitution Day)
LIFE EXPECTANCY (years) – 70.42 (2006 est)
MORTALITY RATE – 6.8 (2006 est)
BIRTH RATE – 18.03 (2006 est)
INFANT MORTALITY RATE – 14.46 (2006 est)
DEATH PENALTY – No (abolished 1994)

CLIMATE AND TERRAIN

The republic consists of 340 volcanic and coral islands and islets in the western Pacific Ocean, of which only eight are inhabited. The islands are mainly low-lying, with elevation extremes ranging from 242m (Mt Ngerchelchauus) at the highest point to 0m (Pacific Ocean) at the lowest. The climate is tropical, with a wet season from May to November. Average daily temperatures are an almost constant 27°C.

HISTORY AND POLITICS

Britain became Palau's main trading partner in the 18th century, but did not colonise the islands. In 1889 control of the islands passed from Spain to Germany, which exploited the country for its phosphate deposits and coconut plantations. Japan occupied the islands on behalf of the Allies in 1914 and administered them after the First World War under a League of Nations mandate. Japanese forces were ousted by the USA during the Second World War.

In 1947 the islands became part of the UN Trust Territory of the Pacific, administered by the USA. In 1982 a compact of free association was signed with the USA under which the USA retained responsibility for defence and foreign policy in return for providing economic aid; the compact was implemented in 1993. Palau became independent on 1 October 1994.

In the 2004 presidential and legislative elections, President Remengesau was re-elected president and Elias Camsek Chin was elected vice-president. Presidential and legislative elections were due in November 2007.

POLITICAL SYSTEM

Under the 1981 constitution, the executive president is directly elected for a four-year term, renewable only once. The president appoints the cabinet. The bicameral legislature, the *Olbiil era Kelulau* (national congress), is composed of the house of delegates, which is the lower house, and the senate. The house of delegates has 16 members (one member from each of the 16 constituent states), directly elected for a four-year term. The senate has 14 members elected for a four-year term. Members of both houses stand for election as independents. A counci of indigenous chiefs, composed of the paramount chie from each of the 16 constituent states, acts as an advisory body to the president on matters concerning traditiona law and customs. Each of the 16 component states has its own elected governor and legislature.

HEAD OF STATE

President, Tommy Remengesau, *elected* 7 November 2000, *took office* 19 January 2001, *re-elected* 2 November 2004
Vice-President, Elias Camsek Chin

SELECTED GOVERNMENT MEMBERS *as at June 2007*

Commerce and Trade, Otoichi Besebes
Finance, Elbuchel Sadang
Justice, Michael Rosenthal

BRITISH AMBASSADOR

HE Peter Beckingham, *apptd* 2005, resident at Manila, the Philippines

ECONOMY AND TRADE

The economy is reliant on economic aid from the USA and so the government is keen to diversify. Tourism i growing and now caters for around 60,000 people a year but the government is limiting development to protect the environment. Subsistence agriculture and fishing remain important, engaging 20 per cent of the workforce and producing crops such as coconuts, copra, cassava and sweet potatoes as well as fish. Aside from tourism, th main industries are handicrafts, construction and clothing manufacturing. Revenue is also derived from the sale c licences to fishing fleets.

The main trading partners are the USA, Japan Singapore and South Korea. Principal exports ar shellfish, tuna, copra and clothing. The main imports ar machinery and equipment, fuels, metals and foodstuffs.
GNI – US$154m; US$7,670 per capita (2005)
ANNUAL AVERAGE GROWTH OF GDP – 5.5 per cen (2005 est)
INFLATION RATE – 2.7 per cent (2005 est)
UNEMPLOYMENT – 4.2 per cent (2005 est)

Trade with UK	*2005*	*2006*
Imports from UK	£273,000	£59,000
Exports to UK	–	–

COMMUNICATIONS

There are 61km of roads, but no railways. There are thre airports, on Koror, Peleliu and Angaur, which have dail flights from Guam operated by Continental Micronesia Koror is also the main seaport.

MEDIA

Most Palauans rely on satellite and cable services from th USA. T8AA Eco Paradise is the government-run radi station. There are a further two commercial stations. Pala has three weekly news publications and including *Ti Belau* and *Palau Horizon.*

PANAMA

República de Panamá – Republic of Panama

AREA – 78,200 sq. km. Neighbours: Colombia (east), Costa Rica (west)
CAPITAL – Panama City; population, 415,964 (2000)
MAJOR CITIES – San Miguelito; Las Cumbres
CURRENCY – Balboa of 100 centésimos (the US dollar is also in circulation)
POPULATION – 3,191,319 rising at 1.6 per cent per year (2006 est)
RELIGION – Roman Catholicism (82 per cent), Protestantism (10 per cent) (est)
LANGUAGE – Spanish (official), English
POPULATION DENSITY – 43 per sq. km (2005 est)
URBAN POPULATION – 57.8 per cent (2005 est)
MEDIAN AGE (years) – 26.1 (2006 est)
NATIONAL ANTHEM – 'Himno Istmeño' ['Isthmus Hymn']
NATIONAL DAY – 3 November (Independence Day)
LIFE EXPECTANCY (years) – 75.22 (2006 est)
MORTALITY RATE – 5.36 (2006 est)
BIRTH RATE – 21.47 (2006 est)
INFANT MORTALITY RATE – 16.37 (2006 est)
DEATH PENALTY – No (abolished 1903)
CPI SCORE – 3.1 (2006)
MILITARY BUDGET – US$171m (2006)
MILITARY PERSONNEL – paramilitaries 12,000

CLIMATE AND TERRAIN

Coastal plains on the Pacific and Atlantic coasts rise to a mountainous interior. There is rainforest in the north-west and the east. Elevation extremes range from 3,475m (Volcan de Chiriqui) at the highest point to 0m (Pacific Ocean) at the lowest. The climate is tropical, with a prolonged wet season from May to January. Average temperatures range from 20°C in January to 31°C in June.

HISTORY AND POLITICS

Panama was visited by Spanish explorers in 1502 and subsequently became part of the Viceroyalty of New Andalucia, later New Grenada. It became a strategically important centre of trade. When it gained its independence from Spain in 1821, Panama joined the Confederacy of Gran Colombia (comprising Colombia, Venezuela, Ecuador, Peru and Bolivia). The confederacy split up in 1830 and Panama became part of Colombia until 1903, when it achieved its independence.

In the 1880s, France attempted to construct a canal across Panama to link the Atlantic and Pacific oceans in order to enhance trade. Before the canal was constructed, ships travelling from New York to San Francisco had to travel via Cape Horn. The attempt failed, but the lucrative trade possibilities persuaded the USA to buy the rights to build the canal, which it completed in 1914. The USA was also given control of the canal and a ten-mile strip of land to either side of it, known as the Canal Zone, in perpetuity. In 1979, Panama and the USA agreed that sovereignty over the Canal Zone would transfer to Panama from 2000, with the USA guaranteeing the zone's protection and providing an annual payment.

Panama was under the military rule of General Omar Torrijos from 1968 until his death in a plane crash in 1981. In 1983, General Noriega seized power and instigated a period of military rule, supported by the USA until 1987, when, following an attack on an US embassy, the American authorities ordered his arrest for money laundering and drug trafficking. An internal coup to unseat Noriega was unsuccessful in 1988, but in 1989 US forces invaded and deposed him. Noriega surrendered in 1990 and was tried and sentenced in the USA in 1992. In 1991, Panama abolished its armed forces.

The 2004 presidential election was won by Martín Torrijos of the Partido Revolucionario Democrática (PRD), who gained 47.4 per cent of the vote. In the 2004 legislative election, the PRD won 41 seats in the legislative assembly.

POLITICAL SYSTEM

Under the 1972 constitution, as amended, the executive president is directly elected for a five-year term, which is not renewable. The unicameral legislative assembly has 78 members, who are directly elected for a five-year term. The president, who is responsible to the legislative assembly, appoints the cabinet.

HEAD OF STATE

President, Martín Torrijos, *elected* 2 May 2004, *sworn in* 14 September 2004
First Vice-President, Foreign Affairs, Samuel Lewis Navarro
Second Vice-President, Rubén Arosemena

SELECTED GOVERNMENT MEMBERS*As at June 2007*

Interior, Héctor Alemán
Economy and Finance, Ricaurte Vásquez
Health, Camilo Alleyne

EMBASSY OF PANAMA

40 Hertford Street, London W1J 7SH
T 020-7493 4646 E panama1@btconnect.com
Ambassador Extraordinary and Plenipotentiary, HE Liliana Fernandez, *apptd* 2005

BRITISH EMBASSY

Swiss Tower, Calle 53 (Apartado 889) Zona 1, Panama City
T (+507) 269 0866 E britemb@cwpanama.net
Ambassador Extraordinary and Plenipotentiary, HE Richard Austen, MBE, *apptd* 2006

ECONOMY AND TRADE

The economy is based on a large service sector and has experienced steady growth in recent years. However, the distribution of wealth is very uneven and about one-third of the population lives below the poverty line. Reform of the social welfare system, which was close to bankruptcy, and the tax system have been implemented despite widespread protests in 2005.

The service sector accounts for 76.4 per cent of GDP, derived from the operation of the Panama Canal and the Colón free trade zone, financial services and ship registry. Plans to enlarge the canal to take more and larger vessels were approved in a 2006 referendum, and work is expected to begin in 2008. Industry, which contributes 16.4 per cent of GDP, includes construction, brewing, the manufacture of cement and other construction materials and sugar refining. Agriculture, which accounts for 7.2 per cent of GDP, is centred on bananas, rice, coffee, maize, sugar cane, vegetables, livestock and prawns.

The main trading partners are the USA, Netherlands Antilles, Costa Rica, EU countries, Japan and other Central and South American countries. Principal exports are bananas, prawns, sugar, coffee and clothing. The main

imports are capital goods, foodstuffs, consumer goods and chemicals.
GNI – US$15,000m; US$4,630 per capita (2005)
ANNUAL AVERAGE GROWTH OF GDP – 6.4 per cent (2005 est)
INFLATION RATE – 2.9 per cent (2005 est)
UNEMPLOYMENT – 9.8 per cent (2005 est)
TOTAL EXTERNAL DEBT – US$9,758m (2005 est)
IMPORTS – US$4,180m (2005)
EXPORTS – US$1,080m (2005)

BALANCE OF PAYMENTS
Trade – US$1,358m deficit (2005)
Current Account – US$818m deficit (2005)

Trade with UK	*2005*	*2006*
Imports from UK	£78,891,000	£108,297,000
Exports to UK	£19,870,000	£17,638,000

COMMUNICATIONS

The Panama Canal was built between 1903 and 1914 to connect the Pacific and Atlantic oceans, shortening sea journeys significantly. Each year the canal handles over 14,000 transits, containing 200 million tonnes of cargo; this represents about 5 per cent of world trade and over 40 per cent of trade between Asia and the east coast of the USA. The chief ports are Colón, Cristóbal and Balboa, at either end of the canal.

Apart from the 82km of the canal, there are over 700km of navigable waterways. These are supplemented by 355km of railways and 11,600km of roads. There are 117 airports and airfields; the principal airport is at Panama City. Modern telephone systems serve 440,000 main-line subscribers, 1.3 million mobile phone subscribers and 300,000 internet users.

EDUCATION AND HEALTH

LITERACY RATE – 91.9 per cent (2004 est)
GROSS ENROLMENT RATIO (percentage of relevant age group) – primary 111 per cent; secondary 70 per cent; tertiary 44 per cent (2005 est)
HEALTH EXPENDITURE (per capita) – US$343 (2004)
HOSPITAL BEDS (per 1,000 people) – 2.5 (2000–5)

MEDIA

The freedom of the media has improved markedly in recent years due to reform laws. Four television and five radio networks, all commercial, and six daily newspapers constitute the news media. *La Prensa*, *Panama News* and *El Siglo* are popular newspapers.

PAPUA NEW GUINEA

Gau Hedinarai ai Papua-Matamata Guinea – Independent State of Papua New Guinea

AREA – 462,840 sq. km. Neighbour: Indonesia (west, on New Guinea)
CAPITAL – Port Moresby; population, 254,158 (2000 est)
MAJOR CITIES – Lae; Arawa; Mount Hagen; Madang
CURRENCY – Kina (K) of 100 toea
POPULATION – 5,670,544 rising at 2.21 per cent per year (2006 est)
RELIGION – Christianity (96 per cent) (est)
LANGUAGE – English, Motu (both official); 820 indigenous languages are spoken, representing over ten per cent of the world total
POPULATION DENSITY – 13 per sq. km (2005)
URBAN POPULATION – 13.2 per cent (2005 est)
MEDIAN AGE (years) – 21.2 (2006 est)
NATIONAL ANTHEM – 'Arise All You Sons'
NATIONAL DAY – 16 September (Independence Day)
LIFE EXPECTANCY (years) – 65.28 (2006 est)
MORTALITY RATE – 7.25 (2006 est)
BIRTH RATE – 29.36 (2006 est)
INFANT MORTALITY RATE – 49.96 (2006 est)
DEATH PENALTY – No*
CPI SCORE – 2.4 (2006)
POPULATION BELOW POVERTY LINE – 37 per cent (2002 est)
MILITARY BUDGET – US$30.2m (2006)
MILITARY PERSONNEL – 3,100: army 2,500, navy 400, air force 200
LITERACY RATE – 57.3 per cent (2004 est)
GROSS ENROLMENT RATIO (percentage of relevant age group) – primary 75 per cent; secondary 26 per cent (2005 est)
HEALTH EXPENDITURE (per capita) – US$30 (2004)

CLIMATE AND TERRAIN

Papua New Guinea lies in the south-west Pacific Ocean and consists of the eastern half of the island of New Guinea, the islands of Bougainville, New Britain and New Ireland, the Admiralty Islands, the D'Entrecasteaux Islands and the Louisiade archipelago. A range of densely forested mountains runs across the centre of the Papuan part of New Guinea, descending to coastal plains. Elevation extremes range from 4,509m (Mt Wilhelm) at the highest point to 0m (Pacific Ocean) at the lowest. The climate is tropical and temperatures in Port Moresby are around 26°C throughout the year.

HISTORY AND POLITICS

New Guinea was visited by the Portuguese and Spanish in the 16th century before being colonised by the British and Dutch in the late 19th century. The western part of the island (now Papua province, Indonesia) was incorporated into the Netherlands East Indies in 1828. In 1884 a British protectorate, British New Guinea, was proclaimed over south-eastern New Guinea and the adjacent islands, which were annexed outright in 1888. The territory was placed under Australian administration in 1906. The north-east of the island was claimed by Germany in 1884 and became a colony in 1899. It was occupied by Australia in the First World War and both the British territory and the German-mandated territory were administered by Australia from 1920 until 1942. The territories were occupied by Japan between 1942 and 1945. After the Second World War the territories were combined and administered by Australia before becoming independent on 16 September 1975.

In 1989 fighting began on Bougainville island between separatists led by the Bougainville Revolutionary Army and government forces. A ceasefire came into effect in 1998 and further talks led to a peace agreement in 2001 which provided for autonomy for the island and guaranteed a referendum on independence in 2009. The first elections for an autonomous government were held in 2005.

Border areas are sometimes affected by the overspill from fighting between separatists and Indonesian forces in the Indonesian province of Papua. Thousands of refugees from this conflict live in camps on the border.

Following the 2007 legislative election, the National Alliance Party (NAP) remained the largest party in parliament, and the NAP leader Sir Michael Somare was elected prime minister for the fourth time and formed a coalition cabinet. The make-up of the coalition has changed several times since 2002 and it currently has a substantial majority.

POLITICAL SYSTEM

The 1975 constitution was amended in 1998 to permit greater autonomy for Bougainville. The head of state is the British sovereign, represented by a governor-general who is elected by parliament for a six-year term. The unicameral legislature, the national parliament, has 109 members, 20 from provincial electorates and the remainder from open electorates, who are directly elected for a five-year term. The prime minister is nominated by the national parliament and appointed by the governor-general.

Governor-General, Sir Paulias Matane, *sworn in* 29 June 2004

SELECTED GOVERNMENT MEMBERS *as at June 2007*
Prime Minister; Defence, Sir Michael Somare
Treasury, Sir Rabbie Namaliu
Foreign Affairs, Paul Tiensten

PAPUA NEW GUINEA HIGH COMMISSION
14 Waterloo Place, London SW1Y 4AR
T 020-7930 0922 W www.pnghighcomm.org.uk
High Commissioner, HE Jean L. Kekedo, OBE, *apptd* 2002

BRITISH HIGH COMMISSION
PO Box 212, Waigani NCD 131, Port Moresby
T (+675) 325 1643 E bhcpng@datec.com.pg
High Commissioner, HE David Dunn, *apptd* 2007

ECONOMY AND TRADE

Political instability, corruption, a weak economy and high unemployment and crime levels have brought the economy to a parlous state, with an Australian report in 2004 warning that the country was in imminent danger of economic and social collapse. The economy has grown slightly since, owing to higher commodity prices and tight control of the national budget, but the country remains poor and underdeveloped, with about one-third of the population living below the poverty line and unemployment in some urban areas as high as 80 per cent. It continues to struggle to attract foreign investment and is dependent on foreign aid, mostly from Australia, which accounts for nearly 20 per cent of the budget.

Only about 1 per cent of the land area is suitable for commercial crops. Over 80 per cent of the population practises subsistence farming, including some tribes in the interior so isolated from the outside world that they live within an unmonetised economy. Mineral deposits, including copper, gold, silver, oil and natural gas, are abundant and constitute the main sources of revenue, although exploitation is hampered by the terrain and poor infrastructure. The main industries are mining, oil extraction and refining, forestry, processing of agricultural products, construction and tourism. Industry contributes 37 per cent of GDP and services 27 per cent.

The main trading partners are Australia, Singapore and Japan. Principal exports are oil, gold, copper ore, logs, palm oil, coffee, cocoa and shellfish. The main imports are machinery and transport equipment, manufactured goods, food, fuels and chemicals.

GNI – US$2,800m; US$500 per capita (2005)
ANNUAL AVERAGE GROWTH OF GDP – 3 per cent (2005 est)
INFLATION RATE – 1.7 per cent (2005 est)
UNEMPLOYMENT – 2.8 per cent (2004)
TOTAL EXTERNAL DEBT – US$1,882m (2005 est)
IMPORTS – US$1,730m (2005)
EXPORTS – US$3,200m (2005)

BALANCE OF PAYMENTS
Trade – US$881m surplus (2001)
Current Account – US$282m surplus (2001)

Trade with UK	*2005*	*2006*
Imports from UK	£4,664,000	£4,881,000
Exports to UK	£59,337,000	£40,275,000

COMMUNICATIONS

There are 19,600km of roads, of which less than 700km are surfaced; the most important road links Lae with the populous highlands. There are over 580 airports and airstrips, the principal airports being at Port Moresby, Lae and Rabaui. Air Niugini operates regular flights internally and to other countries in the region. The main seaports are Port Moresby, Lae and Madang on New Guinea and Rabaul on New Britain. Several shipping companies operate cargo services around the world, but cargo and passenger services between the main ports and outports are very limited.

The main-line telephone system provides an adequate service and mobile phones are not yet widespread. There were 62,000 main lines in use in 2002, and 26,000 mobile phone subscribers and 170,000 internet users in 2005.

MEDIA

Radio is the most important medium owing to the widely scattered population and low levels of literacy. The state-run National Broadcasting Corporation operates a radio network which competes with the commercial NAU FM. EMTV is the sole television broadcaster. There are two foreign-owned daily newspapers, *The National* and *The Post-Courier,* and a number of weekly publications.

PARAGUAY

República del Paraguay – Republic of Paraguay

AREA – 406,750 sq. km. Neighbours: Bolivia (north-west), Brazil (north-east and east), Argentina (south)
CAPITAL – Asunción; population, 512,122 (2002 est)
MAJOR CITIES – Ciudad del Este; San Lorenzo; Luque
CURRENCY – Guaraní (Gs) of 100 céntimos
POPULATION – 6,506,464 rising at 2.45 per cent per year (2006 est)
RELIGION – Roman Catholicism (90 per cent) (est)
LANGUAGE – Spanish, Guarani (both official)
POPULATION DENSITY – 15 per sq. km (2005)
URBAN POPULATION – 58.5 per cent (2005 est)
MEDIAN AGE (years) – 21.3 (2006 est)
NATIONAL ANTHEM – 'Paraguayos, República o Muerte' ['Paraguayans, Republic or Death']

NATIONAL DAY – 15 May (Independence Day)
LIFE EXPECTANCY (years) – 75.1 (2006 est)
MORTALITY RATE – 4.49 (2006 est)
BIRTH RATE – 29.1 (2006 est)
INFANT MORTALITY RATE – 24.78 (2006 est)
DEATH PENALTY – No (abolished 1992)
CPI SCORE – 2.6 (2006)
POPULATION BELOW POVERTY LINE – 32 per cent (2005 est)

CLIMATE AND TERRAIN

The country is landlocked and lies in the grassy and occasionally marshy plains of the River Paraguay, which divides the country, and the rivers Parana and Pilcomayo. Elevation extremes range from 842m (Cerro Pero) at the highest point to 46m (the junction of the Paraguay and Parana rivers) at the lowest. Average temperatures in Asunción range from 23°C in June to 34°C in January.

HISTORY AND POLITICS

Spanish colonisation of Paraguay began in the early 16th century and Asunción was founded in 1537. Paraguay became independent from Spain in 1811 under the dictator José Gaspar Rodriguez de Francia, who ruled until his death in 1840. His successors instigated a period of reform and modernisation which ended in 1865–70 with the catastrophic War of the Triple Alliance against Brazil, Uruguay and Argentina over access to the sea. The war resulted in the loss of over half the population as well as 150,000 sq. km of territory, and initiated a period of political instability that lasted until 1912. In the Chaco War of 1932–5, Paraguay gained territory in the west from Bolivia.

Political instability and conflict after the Second World War ended with a coup in 1954 in which General Alfredo Stroessner seized power. His rule was autocratic and increasingly repressive, marked by corruption and human rights abuses. He was ousted in a coup in 1989 that paved the way for free multiparty elections to the presidency and legislature in 1993. These were won by the National Republican Association-Colorado Party (ANR-PC) and its presidential candidate. The ANR-PC has won the subsequent elections but splits in the party have contributed to the instability that has prevailed since the 1990s, with the assassination of a vice-president, an attempted coup, widespread corruption and the growth of organised crime.

In the 2003 presidential and legislative elections, the ANR-PC remained the largest party in congress, winning 16 out of the 45 seats; its candidate, Nicanor Duarte Frutos, won the presidential election with 37.1 per cent of the vote.

POLITICAL SYSTEM

Under the 1992 constitution, the executive president is directly elected for a five-year term, which is not renewable. The bicameral legislature, the congress, consists of a 45-member senate and an 80-member chamber of deputies, both directly elected for a five-year term. Deputies are elected on a regional basis, the number of seats allocated to each regional department being directly proportional to the department's population. Voting is compulsory for all citizens over 18. The president, who is responsible to congress, appoints the council of ministers.

HEAD OF STATE

President, Nicanor Duarte Frutos, *elected* 27 April 2002, *sworn in* 15 August 2003
Vice-President, Luis Alberto Castiglioni

SELECTED GOVERNMENT MEMBERS *as at June 2007*

Defence, Roberto Eudez González Segovia
Finance and Economy, Ernst Ferdinand Bergen Schmidt
Foreign Affairs, Ruben Ramirez Lezcano
Interior, Rogelio Raimundo Benítez Vargas

EMBASSY OF THE REPUBLIC OF PARAGUAY

3rd Floor, 344 High Street Kensington, London W14 8NS
T 020-7610 4180 W www.paraguayembassy.co.uk
Ambassador Extraordinary and Plenipotentiary, vacant

BRITISH AMBASSADOR

HE Dr John Hughes, *apptd* 2004, resident in Buenos Aires, Argentina

DEFENCE

The army has 12 main battle tanks and 10 armoured personnel carriers. The navy has 28 patrol and coastal combatant vessels at 3 bases. The air force has 12 combat aircraft.

MILITARY BUDGET – US$58.2m (2005)
MILITARY PERSONNEL – 10,100: army 7,600, navy 1,400, air force 1,100; paramilitaries 14,800
CONSCRIPTION DURATION – 12 to 24 months

ECONOMY AND TRADE

The economy contracted in 2002, partly owing to the financial crisis in Argentina, but has made a modest recovery since 2003. Economic reforms, a condition of IMF loans in 2002, have not progressed owing to popular and parliamentary resistance. Political instability, corruption, national and foreign debt, an inadequate infrastructure and high crime levels have resulted in poor economic performance and the existence of a large unofficial economy. About one-third of the population lives below the poverty line, although this is higher in the cities because of migration from the countryside by families made landless by the increasing commercialisation of agriculture and forest clearances.

The country has few mineral resources and the economy is largely agricultural, much of it at subsistence level. Agricultural production, which accounts for 22.4 per cent of GDP and engages 45 per cent of the workforce, is centred on cotton, sugar cane, soya beans, maize, wheat, tobacco, cassava, timber and other foodstuffs. The main industries are sugar refining and manufacturing of cement, textiles, beverages, wood products, steel and electric power. Industry accounts for 18.4 per cent of GDP and services for 59.2 per cent. The main trading partners are Brazil, Argentina, Uruguay and China. Principal exports are soya beans, feed, cotton, meat, edible oils, electricity and wood. The main imports are vehicles, consumer goods, tobacco and petroleum products.

GNI – US$6,100m; US$1,040 per capita (2005)
ANNUAL AVERAGE GROWTH OF GDP – 2.7 per cent (2005 est)
INFLATION RATE – 6.8 per cent (2005 est)
UNEMPLOYMENT – 16 per cent (2005 est)
TOTAL EXTERNAL DEBT – US$3,450m (2005 est)
IMPORTS – US$2,900m (2005)
EXPORTS – US$1,700m (2005)

BALANCE OF PAYMENTS
Trade – US$391m deficit (2004)
Current Account – US$20m surplus (2004)

Trade with UK	*2005*	*2006*
Imports from UK	£12,684,000	£13,649,000
Exports to UK	£777,000	£1,371,000

COMMUNICATIONS

Although landlocked, Paraguay has 3,100km of navigable waterways on its rivers. Direct shipping services operate between Asunción and Europe and the USA, and river steamer services provide internal transport. There are 29,500km of roads, including connections with São Paulo and Buenos Aires, but many are impassable in severe weather. Paraguay has 36km of railways. There are about 12 airports, including the principal airport at Asunción, and around 860 airfields and airstrips around the country.

The fixed-line telephone system is not extensive and mobile phone distribution has risen rapidly. In 2005 there were 320,300 main lines in use, 1.9 million mobile phone subscribers and 200,000 internet users.

EDUCATION AND HEALTH

Basic education is free of charge and compulsory for nine years.
LITERACY RATE – 91.6 per cent (2004 est)
GROSS ENROLMENT RATIO (percentage of relevant age group) – primary 106 per cent; secondary 63 per cent; tertiary 24 per cent (2005 est)
HEALTH EXPENDITURE (per capita) – US$88 (2004)
HOSPITAL BEDS (per 1,000 people) – 1.2 (2000–5)

MEDIA

Paraguay has three daily newspapers, *ABC Color, La Nacion* and *Ultima Hora,* as well as three commercial television channels and a range of radio broadcasters. Intimidation of journalists covering politically sensitive issues is common.

PERU

Republica del Peru – Republic of Peru

AREA – 1,285,220 sq. km. Neighbours: Ecuador and Colombia (north), Brazil and Bolivia (east), Chile (south)
CAPITAL – Lima; including Callao, population, 7,712,000 (2005 est)
MAJOR CITIES – Arequipa; Trujillo; Chiclayo; Piura; Iquitos
CURRENCY – New sol of 100 cénts
POPULATION – 28,302,603 rising at 1.32 per cent per year (2006 est)
RELIGION – Roman Catholicism (80 per cent), Protestantism (7 per cent) (est)
LANGUAGE – Spanish, Quechua (official), Ayemara
POPULATION DENSITY – 22 per sq. km (2005)
URBAN POPULATION – 74.6 per cent (2005 est)
MEDIAN AGE (years) – 25.3 (2006 est)
NATIONAL ANTHEM – 'Somos Libres, Seámoslo Siempre' ['We are Free, Let Us Remain So Forever']
NATIONAL DAY – 28 July (Independence Day)
LIFE EXPECTANCY (years) – 69.84 (2006 est)
MORTALITY RATE – 6.23 (2006 est)
BIRTH RATE – 20.48 (2006 est)
INFANT MORTALITY RATE – 30.94 (2006 est)
DEATH PENALTY – Yes*
CPI SCORE – 3.3 (2006)
POPULATION BELOW POVERTY LINE – 54 per cent (2003 est)

CLIMATE AND TERRAIN

Peru has three main regions: the Costa, the coastal plain west of the Andes; the Sierra or mountain range of the Andes, which runs parallel to the Pacific coast; and the Montaña (or Selva), a vast area of jungle stretching from the eastern foothills of the Andes to the country's eastern and north-eastern borders. Elevation extremes range from 6,768m (Nevado Huascaran) at the highest point to 0m (Pacific Ocean) at the lowest. The country typically receives very little rain, but occasionally due to the El Niño weather system, the northern districts receive several days of higher temperatures accompanied by torrential rain. Average temperatures in Lima range from 16°C in July to 26°C in January.

HISTORY AND POLITICS

The Inca Empire centred on Cuzco had superseded earlier civilisations in Peru by the 15th century, when the Empire reached its zenith before falling to Spanish conquistadores led by Francisco Pizarro in 1532–3. The territory formed the Viceroyalty of Peru and its gold and silver mines made Peru the principal source of wealth in Spain's American empire. After 1810, Peru became the centre for the Spanish government as its other colonies rebelled. Although it declared its independence in 1821, this was achieved only with the final defeat of Spanish forces in 1824.

Peru entered into several border disputes with its neighbours in the 19th and 20th centuries, including the Pacific War (1879–83) in which it lost three southern coastal provinces to Chile. A border dispute with Ecuador was renewed in 1981, leading to a short, inconclusive war in 1995, but was resolved in 1998 following adjudication. A border dispute with Chile ended in 1999 with the implementation of accords first agreed in 1929.

Following independence, Peru alternated between military dictatorships and periods of democratic rule. The last military dictator was General Francisco Morales Bermundez, who guided the country to democracy in 1980. Civilian rule has not brought greater political stability or improved economic and social equality. Two left-wing insurgencies, by the Maoist *Sendero Luminoso* (Shining Path) and the *Movimento Revolucionario Tupac Amaru* (MRTA), began in the 1980s. The activities of the *Sendero Luminoso* in particular destabilised the government and the economy; the conflict caused about 69,000 deaths and provoked human rights abuses by both the security forces and the guerrillas. By the late 1990s both insurgencies had been overcome, although a few Maoists remain active. The conflict has left a legacy of criminal violence, much of it related to drug trafficking.

The economy deteriorated badly in the late 1980s and by 1990 inflation had reached 400 per cent. Alberto Fujimori was elected president in 1990 on a platform of economic reform. Within two years he had dismantled the existing order in Peru by dismissing congress, sacking senior judges, imposing order through a so-called Emergency National Reconstruction Government and changing the constitution. He fled to Japan in 2000 to escape corruption charges, and was succeeded by Alejandro Toledo, the candidate of the Possible Peru (PP) party. Toledo who won the 2001 presidential election, becoming the country's first president of Quechan descent.

In the 2006 legislative election, the Union for Peru (UPP) party won the most seats, but although the UPP candidate was leading in the first round of the presidential election, the second round in June was won by the Peruvian Aprista Party (APRA) candidate Alan Garcia (president 1985–90). In April 2007 the congress granted President Garcia emergency powers allowing him to rule by decree on issues related to organised crime and drug trafficking.

POLITICAL SYSTEM

Under the 1993 constitution, the executive president is directly elected for a five-year term, renewable only once. The unicameral legislature, the congress of the republic, has 120 members, directly elected for a five-year term. The president, who is responsible to the congress, appoints the council of ministers.

HEAD OF STATE

President of the Republic, Alan Garcia, *elected* 4 June 2006, *sworn in* 28 July 2006

Vice-Presidents, Jose Vega; Fabiola Morales; Luisa Cuculiza

SELECTED GOVERNMENT MEMBERS *as at July 2007*

President of the Council of Ministers, Jorge Del Castillo

Defence, Allan Wagner

Economy and Finance, Luis Carranza

Foreign Affairs, José Antonio García Belaunde

Interior, Luis Alva Castro

EMBASSY OF PERU

52 Sloane Street, London SW1X 9SP

T 020-7235 1917 W www.peruembassy-uk.com

Ambassador Extraordinary and Plenipotentiary, vacant

BRITISH EMBASSY

PO Box 854, Torre Parque Mar (Piso 22), Avenida José Larco 1301, Lima

T (+51) (1) 617 3000 E britemb@terra.com.pe

W www.britemb.org.pe

Ambassador Extraordinary and Plenipotentiary, HE Catherine Nettleton, *apptd* 2006

BRITISH COUNCIL

c/o British Embassy, Lima

T (+51) (1) 617 3060 W www.britishcouncil.org/peru

Director, Frank Fitzpatrick

DEFENCE

The army has 275 main battle tanks and over 276 armoured personnel carriers. The navy has 6 submarines, 1 cruiser, 8 frigates and 13 patrol and coastal combatant vessels at seven bases. The air force has 102 combat aircraft and 16 attack helicopters.

MILITARY BUDGET – US$1,100m (2006)

MILITARY PERSONNEL – 80,000: army 40,000, navy 25,000, air force 15,000; paramilitaries 78,000

ECONOMY AND TRADE

Following severe problems in the late 1980s, the economy underwent radical market-oriented restructuring after 1990; this reduced inflation, freed interest rates and privatised most state companies. Foreign investment increased, although the inadequate infrastructure remains an obstacle to development. The economy has grown steadily since 2002 but poverty remains widespread, with over half the population living below the poverty line and over a third of the wealth in the hands of 10 per cent of society.

Mineral resources, including copper, silver, gold, oil and natural gas, are abundant, and extracting and refining these is the mainstay of the economy, although this makes it vulnerable to global price fluctuations. Other industries include steel and metal fabrication, fishing and fish processing, textiles and clothes manufacture and food processing. Agriculture is centred on coffee, cotton, sugar cane, rice, maize, vegetables, fruit, coca, meat and dairy products. Services contribute 65 per cent to GDP, industry 26.5 per cent and agriculture 8.5 per cent.

The main trading partners are the USA, China, Chile other South American countries, Canada and Switzerland Principal exports are copper, gold, zinc, crude oil and petroleum products, coffee, vegetables and textiles. The main imports are petroleum and petroleum products plastics, machinery, vehicles, iron and steel, wheat and paper.

GNI – US$74,000m; US$2,650 per capita (2005)

ANNUAL AVERAGE GROWTH OF GDP – 6.4 per cent (2005 est)

INFLATION RATE – 1.6 per cent (2005 est)

UNEMPLOYMENT – 7.4 per cent (2000 est)

TOTAL EXTERNAL DEBT – US$30,940m (2005 est)

IMPORTS – US$8,900m (2000)

EXPORTS – US$17,200m (2005)

BALANCE OF PAYMENTS

Trade – US$5,163m surplus (2005)

Current Account – US$1,030m surplus (2005)

Trade with UK	*2005*	*2006*
Imports from UK	£46,432,000	£52,831,000
Exports to UK	£126,516,000	£199,564,000

COMMUNICATIONS

There are 78,829km of roads, of which 11,351km are surfaced. These include sections of two transnational highways: the east-west Andean Highway, linking the Pacific and Atlantic coasts, and the north-south Pan American Highway running along the Pacific coast. The state-run railways have 3,462km of track, and 8,600km of inland waterways are navigable, on tributaries of the River Amazon and Lake Titicaca. The main seaports are Callao and Matarani. There are over 260 airports and airstrips, including the international airport at Lima.

In 2005 there were 2.6 million main telephone lines in use, 5.6 million mobile phone subscribers and 4.6 million internet users.

EDUCATION AND HEALTH

Education is free of charge and compulsory between seven and 16.

LITERACY RATE – 87.7 per cent (2004 est)

GROSS ENROLMENT RATIO (percentage of relevant age group) – primary 114 per cent; secondary 92 per cent; tertiary 33 per cent (2005 est)

HEALTH EXPENDITURE (per capita) – US$104 (2004)

HOSPITAL BEDS (per 1,000 people) – 1.4 (2000–5)

MEDIA

Media freedom has greatly improved since the end of the Fujimori administration in 2000. There are six national daily newspapers and a host of commercial radi broadcasters. The state-owned Television Nacional de Peru competes with four commercial broadcasters, including America TV and Panamericana.

THE PHILIPPINES

Repúblika ng Pilipinas – Republic of the Philippines

AREA – 300,000 sq. km
CAPITAL – Manila; population, 1,581,082 (2005 est)
MAJOR CITIES – Quezon City; Kalookan; Davao; Cebu
CURRENCY – Philippine peso (P) of 100 centavos
POPULATION – 89,468,677 rising at 1.8 per cent per year (2006 est); Tagalog (28.1 per cent), Cebuano (13.1 per cent), Ilocano (9 per cent), Bisaya (7.6 per cent)
RELIGION – Roman Catholicism (81 per cent), other Christian denominations (11 per cent), Islam (5 per cent) (est)
LANGUAGE – Filipino, English (both official)
POPULATION DENSITY – 279 per sq. km (2005)
URBAN POPULATION – 62.6 per cent (2005 est)
MEDIAN AGE (years) – 22.5 (2006 est)
NATIONAL ANTHEM – 'Lupang Hinirang' ['Beloved Land']
NATIONAL DAY – 12 June (Independence Day)
LIFE EXPECTANCY (years) – 70.21 (2006 est)
MORTALITY RATE – 5.41 (2006 est)
BIRTH RATE – 24.89 (2006 est)
INFANT MORTALITY RATE – 22.81 (2006 est)
DEATH PENALTY – No (abolished 2006)
CPI SCORE – 2.5 (2006)
POPULATION BELOW POVERTY LINE – 40 per cent (2001 est)

CLIMATE AND TERRAIN

The Philippines comprises over 7,000 islands in the western Pacific Ocean. The principal islands are Luzon, Mindanao, Samar, Negros, Palawan, Panay and Leyte. Other groups include the Sulu islands (capital, Jolo), Babuyanes and Batanes, Calamian and Kalayaan islands. The larger islands are traversed by volcanic mountain ranges; some volcanoes are still active. Elevation extremes range from 2,954m (Mt Apo) at the highest point to 0m (Philippine Sea) at the lowest. The climate is tropical with temperatures fairly constant between 23°C in January and 31°C in June. The country is particular susceptible to typhoons during the rainy season from August to October, which cause widespread damage and frequent loss of life. Humidity is often oppressive, particularly in June and July.

HISTORY AND POLITICS

The Philippines was conquered by Spain in 1565 and colonial rule lasted until 1898, when Spain ceded the colony to the USA following the Spanish-American War. The country became internally self-governing in 1935, was occupied by Japan from 1942 to 1944, and achieved independence from the USA in 1946.

Ferdinand Marcos seized power in 1965, imposing martial law in 1972. His regime became increasingly repressive, corrupt and violent, and when he falsified election results in 1986 to prevent Corazon Aquino from taking office as president, mass protests forced him to flee the country. Aquino survived political unrest and six attempted military coups to introduce a new constitution and entrench democratic politics.

Fidel Ramos, Aquino's successor in 1992, built on her work by instigating peace talks with the communist and Muslim rebels involved in long-running insurgencies; a peace agreement with one Muslim group, the Moro National Liberation Front, was reached in 1996. Ramos was succeeded in 1998 by Joseph Estrada. Under Estrada, the peace process with the communist insurgents and the main Muslim insurgent group, the Moro Islamic Liberation Front (MILF), began to stall. Popular dissatisfaction with Estrada grew and he was forced out of office in January 2001. His term was completed by Vice-President Gloria Arroyo. She re-established peace talks with the MILF and the National Democratic Front (NDF), a front organisation for the communist insurgents. The talks with the MILF, though often interrupted by violence, achieved a ceasefire in 2003 and a breakthrough on key issues in 2005. Progress with the NDF has proved more problematic and clashes have continued despite six months of peace talks in 2004. Since the 11 September 2001 attacks, Abu Sayyaf, a Muslim group suspected of links with al-Qaida, has emerged on the island of Jolo, undertaking a spate of violent kidnappings.

Gloria Arroyo was elected president in 2004. Since the election, her popularity has plummeted. Her anti-corruption measures and economic reforms have been undermined by a series of corruption scandals and she came under intense pressure to resign in 2005 over accusations that she tried to influence the 2004 presidential election result. Despite these setbacks, Arroyo's administration won 200 seats in the May 2007 legislative election to the house of representatives. Her continued unpopularity was confirmed by the election of Lieutenant Antonio Trillanes to the senate. Trillanes led an attempted coup against Arroyo in 2003.

POLITICAL SYSTEM

Under the 1987 constitution, the executive president is directly elected for a six-year term, which is not renewable. There is a bicameral congress. The lower house, the house of representatives, has 236 members, of whom 212 are directly elected and the rest are appointed from party and minority group lists by the president; all serve a three-year term. The senate has 24 members directly elected for a six-year term, with half re-elected every three years. The president appoints the cabinet.

The autonomous region of Mindanao consists of four provinces: Lanao del Sur, Maguinadanao, Sulu and Tawi-Tawi. There is a 24-member regional assembly and a governor.

HEAD OF STATE

President, Gloria Macapagal Arroyo, *assumed office* 20 January 2001
Vice-President, Manuel Noli de Castro

SELECTED GOVERNMENT MEMBERS *as at June 2007*
Finance, Margarito Teves
Interior, Ronaldo Puno
Foreign, Alberto Romulo
Defence, Hermogenes Ebdane

EMBASSY OF THE REPUBLIC OF THE PHILIPPINES
9A Palace Green, London W8 4QE
T 020-7937 1600 E embassy@philemb.co.uk
W www.philemb.org.uk
Ambassador Extraordinary and Plenipotentiary, HE Edgardo Espiritu, *apptd* 2003

BRITISH EMBASSY
PO Box 2927 MCPO, Floors 15–17, LV Locsin Building, 6752 Ayala Avenue, Corner of Makati Avenue, 1226 Makati, Manila
T (+63) (2) 816 7116 E uk@info.com.ph
W www.britishembassy.gov.uk/philippines
Ambassador Extraordinary and Plenipotentiary, HE Peter Beckingham, *apptd* 2005

BRITISH COUNCIL
10th Floor, Taipan Place, Emerald Avenue, Ortigas Centre, Pasig City 1605
T (+63) (2) 914 1011 E britishcouncil@britishcouncil.org.ph
Director, Andrew Picken

DEFENCE

The army has 85 armoured infantry fighting vehicles and 370 armoured personnel carriers. The navy has 1 frigate and 59 patrol and coastal vessels at 3 bases. The air force has 21 combat aircraft and 25 armed helicopters.
MILITARY BUDGET – US$909m (2006)
MILITARY PERSONNEL – 106,000: army 66,000, navy 24,000, air force 16,000; paramilitaries 40,500

ECONOMY AND TRADE

The economy was one of the best-performing in the region until the Asian economic crisis of 1997, but it has steadily recovered since 2002 owing to growth in exports, agricultural output and the service industries. Greater and more rapid economic expansion is needed to offset the high rate of population growth, but this is hampered by the high level of public debt (61.6 per cent of GDP) produced by persistently large budget deficits and the inefficient performance of state enterprises. The government is attempting to introduce market reforms but investor confidence has suffered from recent political turmoil. About 40 per cent of the population is below the poverty line, and remittances from the millions of Filipinos working abroad are vital to the economy.

Major industries include electronics assembly, manufacture of clothing, footwear, production of pharmaceuticals, chemicals and wood products, food processing, oil refining and fishing. The large agricultural sector employs 36 per cent of the workforce, producing sugar cane, coconuts, rice, maize and tropical fruits. Agriculture accounts for 14 per cent of GDP, industry for 32 per cent and services for 54 per cent. The main trading partners are the USA, Japan, China, Singapore, Taiwan and Hong Kong. Principal exports are semiconductors and electronic products, transport equipment, clothing, copper products, petroleum products, coconut oil and fruit. The main imports are electronic products, fuels, machinery and transport equipment, iron and steel, fabrics, grains, chemicals and plastics.

GNI – US$109,700m; US$1,320 per capita (2005)
ANNUAL AVERAGE GROWTH OF GDP – 4.8 per cent (2005 est)
INFLATION RATE – 7.6 per cent (2005 est)
UNEMPLOYMENT – 8.7 per cent (2005 est)
TOTAL EXTERNAL DEBT – US$65,710m (2005 est)
IMPORTS – US$47,000m (2005)
EXPORTS – US$39,900m (2005)

BALANCE OF PAYMENTS
Trade – US$6,381m deficit (2004)
Current Account – US$2,080m surplus (2004)

Trade with UK	*2005*	*2006*
Imports from UK	£279,627,000	£243,583,000
Exports to UK	£724,430,000	£755,698,000

COMMUNICATIONS

There are about 200,000km of roads, and Philippine National Railway operates 897km of railways. The main ports are Manila (Luzon), Cebu, Davao, Iloilo and Zamboanga (Mindanao), and there are over 400 smaller ports. There are 256 airports and airfields, including international airports at Manila, Cebu and Davao City.

There is a good telephone system, and mobile phone distribution has grown rapidly. There were 3.4 million main-line subscribers in 2004, and 32.8 million mobile phone subscribers and 7.8 million internet users in 2005.

EDUCATION AND HEALTH

Secondary and higher education is extensive and the public and private universities are recognised by the government.
LITERACY RATE – 92.6 per cent (2004 est)
GROSS ENROLMENT RATIO (percentage of relevant age group) – primary 112 per cent; secondary 86 per cent; tertiary 29 per cent (2005 est)
HEALTH EXPENDITURE (per capita) – US$36 (2004)
HOSPITAL BEDS (per 1,000 people) – 1 (2000–5)

MEDIA

The government-owned IBC television network competes with two commercial broadcasters. There is a large number of radio stations and four main national publications that include *The Daily Tribune* and *Malaya.*

POLAND

Rzeczpospolita Polska – Republic of Poland

AREA – 312,685 sq. km. Neighbours: Russia (Kaliningrad) (north), Germany (west), the Czech Republic and Slovakia (south), Belarus and Ukraine (east) and Lithuania (north-east)
CAPITAL – Warsaw; population, 1,692,854 (2005 est)
MAJOR CITIES – Lodz; Krakow; Wroclaw (Breslau); Poznan; Gdansk (Danzig); Szczecin (Stettin); Bydgoszcz
CURRENCY – Zloty of 100 groszy
POPULATION – 38,536,869 falling at 0.05 per cent per year (2006 est)
RELIGION – Roman Catholicism (96 per cent), Orthodox Christianity (1 per cent) (est)
LANGUAGE – Polish (official)
POPULATION DENSITY – 125 per sq. km (2005)
URBAN POPULATION – 62 per cent (2005 est)
MEDIAN AGE (years) – 37 (2006 est)
NATIONAL ANTHEM – 'Mazurek Dabrowskiego' ['Poland is not yet Lost']
NATIONAL DAY – 3 May (Constitution Day)
LIFE EXPECTANCY (years) – 74.97 (2006 est)
MORTALITY RATE – 9.89 (2006 est)
BIRTH RATE – 9.85 (2006 est)
INFANT MORTALITY RATE – 7.22 (2006 est)
DEATH PENALTY – No (abolished 1997)
CPI SCORE – 3.7 (2006)
POPULATION BELOW POVERTY LINE – 17 per cent (2003 est)

CLIMATE AND TERRAIN

Poland lies mostly in a great plain crossed by the Oder, Neisse and Vistula rivers. The land rises to the Carpathian, Tatra and Sudeten mountains along the southern border. Elevation extremes range from 2,499m (Rysy) at the highest point to −2m (Raczki Elblaskie) at the lowest. The climate is continental and average temperatures in Warsaw range from −5°C in January to 24°C in July.

HISTORY AND POLITICS

Poland emerged as an independent kingdom in the ninth century. It formed a union with Lithuania in 1569 that stretched from the Baltic to the Black Sea. This commonwealth was weakened by attacks by its neighbours and in 1772, 1793 and 1795 its territory was partitioned between Russia, Prussia and Austria. Following the congress of Vienna in 1815, eastern Poland became a semi-independent kingdom within the Russian Empire.

After the First World War, Poland became independent for a second time with the signing of the treaty of Versailles. The Second World War began with the German invasion of western Poland on 1 September 1939; on 17 September, Soviet forces invaded eastern Poland, and on 21 September Germany and the USSR declared that Poland had ceased to exist. In 1941 the rest of Poland was occupied by Germany. After the USSR aligned with the Allies, the country was liberated by Soviet forces in 1944–5. Once the war was over, its boundaries were redrawn. Eastern Poland was ceded to the USSR but the country gained German territory in Silesia along the Oder and Neisse rivers, effectively shifting the state 240km westwards.

The post-war coalition government was Soviet-influenced and in 1947 a communist republic was proclaimed. Nationalisation and agricultural collectivisation programmes were introduced and the Roman Catholic Church was persecuted. By the 1970s attempts to boost the economy had failed and the country had a large foreign debt. In 1980, following a strike at the Gdansk shipyard prompted by economic crisis and popular discontent, a mass movement for civil and national rights coalesced around the newly formed independent Solidarity trade union, led by Lech Walesa. The following year, the demoralised Communist government declared martial law and interned Walesa and other leaders, driving Solidarity underground. Economic decline and continuing unrest in the 1980s eventually resulted in talks between Solidarity, the government and the Roman Catholic Church in 1989. In multiparty parliamentary elections later that year, the Communists lost power and Solidarity helped to form a coalition government. In 1990 Walesa was elected president. The Communist Party subsequently dissolved and reformed as the Democratic Left Alliance (SLD).

The post-communist governments introduced economic reforms from 1990 but the transition to a market economy caused unemployment and a sharp drop in living standards. Popular discontent and a fragmented parliament led to a succession of short-lived governments. In 1997 a new constitution was adopted that eradicated all signs of the former communist system. Poland joined NATO in 1999 and the EU in 2004. No date has yet been set for a referendum on the EU constitution.

In the September 2005 legislative election, the conservative Law and Justice Party (PiS) became the largest party in both chambers of the Diet, but without an outright majority in either. After the PiS candidate, Lech Kaczynski, won the presidential election in October, the PiS formed a minority government under Kazimierz Marcinkiewicz. The government entered into a coalition with the Self-Defence party and the League of Polish Families in April 2006 in order to have a parliamentary majority. Disagreements between the coalition partners led to Marcinkiewicz's resignation and a new government was formed by Jaroslaw Kaczynski, chair of the PiS and twin brother of the president.

POLITICAL SYSTEM

Under the 1997 constitution, the head of state is the president, who is directly elected for a five-year term, renewable only once. The president nominates the prime minister and has the right to be consulted over the appointment of the foreign, defence and interior ministers. There is a bicameral legislature, the national assembly. The lower house, the *Sejm* (Diet), has 460 members directly elected for a four-year term. The senate has 100 members elected on a provincial basis for a four-year term.

HEAD OF STATE

President, Lech Kaczynski, *elected* 23 October 2005, *sworn in* 23 December 2005

SELECTED GOVERNMENT MEMBERS *as at June 2007*

Prime Minister, Jaroslaw Kaczynski
Defence, Aleksander Szczyglo
Foreign Affairs, Anna Fotyga
Economy, Piotr Grzegorz Wozniak
Finance, Zyta Gilowska

EMBASSY OF THE REPUBLIC OF POLAND

47 Portland Place, London W1B 1JH
T 0870-774 2700 W www.polishembassy.org.uk
Ambassador Extraordinary and Plenipotentiary, vacant

BRITISH EMBASSY

Aleje Roz No. 1, 00-556 Warsaw
T (+48) (22) 628 1001 E britemb@it.com.pl
W www.britishembassy.pl
Ambassador Extraordinary and Plenipotentiary, HE Charles Crawford, *apptd* 2003

BRITISH COUNCIL

Al. Jerozolimskie 59, PL-00-697 Warsaw
T (+48) (22) 695 5900 W www.britishcouncil.org/poland
Director, Tony O'Brien

DEFENCE

The army has 947 main battle tanks, 1,281 armoured infantry fighting vehicles, 33 armoured personnel carriers and 65 attack helicopters. The navy has 5 submarines, 3 frigates, 6 patrol and coastal vessels, 18 combat aircraft and 17 armed helicopters at five bases. The air force has 187 combat aircraft.

MILITARY EXPENDITURE – US$5,500m (2005)
MILITARY PERSONNEL – 141,500: army 89,000, navy 14,300, air force 30,000, joint staff 8,200; paramilitaries 21,400
CONSCRIPTION DURATION – 9 months

ECONOMY AND TRADE

Poland made a successful transition to a market economy in the 1990s, encouraging the development of a private business sector, but at the cost of high levels of public debt, unemployment and inflation. Recent governments have tried to reduce these, but the current government favours state intervention, and so privatisation of loss-making state enterprises has halted and its predecessor's tight fiscal and monetary policies may be watered down.

The country has benefited from accession to the EU, with growing exports, higher food prices and agricultural subsidies, but further economic development is hindered by legal and bureaucratic obstacles, the inefficiency of agriculture and the large state sector, and corruption. About 17 per cent of the population lives below the poverty line, especially in rural areas, and high unemployment has encouraged large numbers to migrate to work in other parts of the EU.

Poland has vast mineral resources, especially of coal. The main industries are machine-building, iron and steel production, coal-mining, chemicals, shipbuilding, food processing, glass, beverages and textiles. Industry accounts for 31.2 per cent of GDP. The large agricultural sector has been modernised but remains inefficient; it employs 16 per cent of the workforce but contributes only 4.8 per cent of GDP. The main crops are vegetables, fruit, wheat, meat, eggs and dairy products.

The main trading partners are other EU countries (especially Germany) and Russia. Principal exports include machinery and vehicles, manufactured goods, foodstuffs and livestock. The main imports are machinery and vehicles, chemicals, fuels and lubricants.

GNI – US$273,100m; US$7,160 per capita (2005)
ANNUAL AVERAGE GROWTH OF GDP – 3.4 per cent (2005 est)
INFLATION RATE – 2.2 per cent (2005 est)
UNEMPLOYMENT – 18.2 per cent (2005 est)
TOTAL EXTERNAL DEBT – US$101,500m (2005 est)
IMPORTS – US$101,000m (2005)
EXPORTS – US$89,000m (2005)

BALANCE OF PAYMENTS
Trade – US$2,694m deficit (2005)
Current Account – US$4,364m deficit (2005)

Trade with UK	*2005*	*2006*
Imports from UK	£1,540,595,000	£2,677,500,000
Exports to UK	£2,130,265,000	£3,083,400,000

COMMUNICATIONS

The country has a total of 23,072km of railways, 423,997km of roads, and 3,997km of navigable rivers and canals. Around 122 airports and airfields are in use; the principal airports are at Warsaw, Gdansk, Krakow and Szczecin. The principal seaports are Gdansk, Gdynia, Szczecin and Swinoujscie.

The fixed-line telephone system is being modernised but progress has been slow, especially in rural areas. Mobile phone distribution has, by contrast, grown very rapidly. In 2005 there were 11.8 million main lines in use, 29.2 million mobile phone subscribers and 10.6 million internet users.

EDUCATION AND HEALTH

Elementary education (ages seven to 15) is free of charge and compulsory. Secondary education is also free, but optional.

GROSS ENROLMENT RATIO (percentage of relevant age group) – primary 99 per cent; secondary 97 per cent; tertiary 61 per cent (2005 est)
HEALTH EXPENDITURE (per capita) – US$411 (2004)
HOSPITAL BEDS (per 1,000 people) – 5.6 (2000–5)

MEDIA

Poland's broadcasting network is the largest in eastern and central Europe, and there is freedom and diversity of information in the media, although laws against criticism of the political system are still in force. State-owned television (TVP) still has the largest audience share for its two national channels. State-owned radio reaches just over half the population and there are more than 200 other commercial local and regional stations on air. Poland has over 300 newspapers, most of them local or regional, and popular titles include *Polityka* and *Rzeczpospolita*.

CULTURE

Polish literature dates from before the 14th century. Major writers include Nobel Prize winners Henryk Sienkiewicz (1846–1916), Wladyslaw Stanislaw Reymont (1867–1925), Czeslaw Milosz (1911–2004) and Wislawa Szymborska (*b.* 1923).

Other notable cultural figures include the pianist and composer Frédéric Chopin (1810–49); film directors Krzysztof Kieslowski (1941–1996) and Academy Award winner Roman Polanski (*b.* 1933); astronomer Nicolaus Copernicus (1473–1543), who formulated the first heliocentric theory of the solar system, and physicist Marie Curie (1867–1934), the first woman to win a Nobel prize.

PORTUGAL

República Portuguesa – Portuguese Republic

AREA – 92,391 sq. km. Neighbour: Spain (north and east)
CAPITAL – Lisbon; population, 556,797 (2001)
MAJOR CITIES – Vila Nova de Gaia; Oporto; Amadora
CURRENCY – Euro (€) of 100 cents
POPULATION – 10,605,870 rising at 0.36 per cent per year (2006 est)
RELIGION – Roman Catholicism (80 per cent), other Christian denominations (4 per cent) (est)
LANGUAGE – Portuguese, Mirandese (both official)
POPULATION DENSITY – 115 per sq. km (2005)
URBAN POPULATION – 55.6 per cent (2005 est)
MEDIAN AGE (years) – 38.5 (2006 est)
NATIONAL ANTHEM – 'A Portuguesa' ['The Portuguese']
NATIONAL DAY – 10 June (Portugal Day)
LIFE EXPECTANCY (years) – 77.7 (2006 est)
MORTALITY RATE – 10.5 (2006 est)
BIRTH RATE – 10.72 (2006 est)
INFANT MORTALITY RATE – 4.98 (2006 est)
DEATH PENALTY – No (abolished 1976)
CPI SCORE – 6.6 (2006)

CLIMATE AND TERRAIN

The terrain is mountainous north of the River Tagus, with rolling plains in the south. Elevation extremes range from 2,351m (Ponta do Pico) at the highest point to 0m (Atlantic Ocean) at the lowest. Forests of pine, cork and eucalyptus cover about 38 per cent of the country. The climate is mild, with average temperatures in Lisbon ranging from 8°C in January to 28°C in July.

HISTORY AND POLITICS

Part of the Roman Empire from the second century BC the country was overrun by Vandals and Visigoths in the fifth century AD. The Visigoths were ousted by Muslim from north Africa in the eighth century but Christian reconquest began in the tenth century and an independent Christian kingdom was established in the 12th century.

Portuguese navigators led the 15th-century European age of exploration and the country soon became a major commercial and colonial power; its empire expanding to cover Brazil, parts of China and vast areas of Africa. In 1807 Portugal was invaded by Napoleonic France and then became the base from which allied forces liberated Portugal and Spain in the Peninsular War. The 19th century was politically turbulent, with power struggles between conservative and liberal politicians and between different factions of the royal family. In 1910 an armed uprising in Lisbon drove King Manuel II into exile and a republic was declared.

A period of political instability ensued until the military intervened in 1926. The constitution of 1933 gave formal expression to the authoritarian *Estado Novo* (New State) introduced by Dr Antonio Salazar, prime minister from 1932 until 1968. Marcello Caetano succeeded Salazar in 1968 but the regime's failure to liberalise at home or to conclude wars in the African colonies resulted in the government's overthrow by a military coup in 1974. Great political turmoil followed in 1974–5, a period in which most of the colonies gained their independence. Elections in 1976 stabilised the situation and full civilian government was restored in 1982. Portugal joined the EEC in 1986 and the eurozone in 1999.

The Socialist Party won the 2005 legislative election with 120 seats, giving them their first absolute majority in the assembly since Portugal returned to democracy in 1974. The 2006 presidential election was won by the Social Democrat candidate, Anibal Cavaco Silva (prime minister 1985–95), with 50.6 per cent of the vote.

POLITICAL SYSTEM

Under the 1976 constitution, amended in 1982 and 1989, the head of state is a president who is elected for a five-year term, renewable only once. Legislative authority is vested in the unicameral assembly of the republic, which has 230 members directly elected by proportional representation for a four-year term. The prime minister, appointed by the president, is usually the leader of the largest party in the assembly.

HEAD OF STATE

President of the Republic, Anibal Cavaco Silva, *elected* 22 January 2006, *sworn in* 9 March 2006

SELECTED GOVERNMENT MEMBERS *As at June 2007*

Prime Minister, Jose Socrates
Foreign Affairs, Luis Amado
Interior, Antonio Costa
Finance, Fernando Teixeira dos Santos
Defence, Nuno Severiano Teixeira

EMBASSY OF PORTUGAL

11 Belgrave Square, London SW1X 8PP
T 020-7235 5331 E london@portembassy.co.uk
Ambassador Extraordinary and Plenipotentiary, HE Antonio Santana-Carlos, *apptd* 2006

BRITISH EMBASSY

Rua de São Bernardo 33, 1249-082 Lisbon
T (+351) (21) 392 4000 E britembassy@mail.telepac.pt
W www.uk-embassy.pt
Ambassador Extraordinary and Plenipotentiary, HE John Buck, *apptd* 2005

BRITISH COUNCIL

1–3 Rua Luís Fernandes, 1249-062 Lisbon
T (+351) (21) 321 4500 W www.pt.britishcouncil.org
Director, Rosemary Hilhorst, OBE

DEFENCE

The army has 187 main battle tanks and 353 armoured personnel carriers. The navy has 1 submarine, 5 frigates and 24 patrol and coastal vessels at six bases. The air force has 46 combat aircraft.

MILITARY EXPENDITURE – US$2,960m (2005)
MILITARY PERSONNEL – 43,960: army 26,700, navy 10,010, air force 7,250; paramilitaries 47,700

ECONOMY AND TRADE

Portugal has experienced rapid economic growth since joining the EU in 1986, developing a diversified and increasingly service-based economy. Since the mid-1990s, much of the economy has been liberalised and many state enterprises privatised. More recently economic growth has dropped, leading to a large budget deficit (exceeding the eurozone's 3 per cent limit) and rising unemployment. Scope to boost growth is limited by a shortage of foreign direct investment and a poor education system.

Around 10 per cent of the workforce is engaged in agriculture, contributing 6.6 per cent of GDP. The chief products are grain, fruit and vegetables, livestock, fish, dairy products and timber and cork from the forests. The main industries are manufacturing, oil refining, metalworking, shipbuilding and repair, wine-making and tourism. Manufactures include textiles and footwear, pulp and paper, cork, metals, chemicals, rubber and plastic products and rail and aerospace equipment. Natural resources are being exploited to generate electricity from hydroelectric and solar sources, to reduce Portugal's dependence on imported fuel and energy. Industry accounts for 28.6 per cent of GDP and services for 64.9 per cent.

The main trading partners are other EU countries, especially Spain, and the USA. Principal exports are clothing and footwear, machinery, chemicals, cork and paper products and hides. The main imports include machinery, vehicles, chemicals, oil, textiles and agricultural products.

GNI – US$181,300m; US$17,190 per capita (2005)
ANNUAL AVERAGE GROWTH OF GDP – 0.4 per cent (2005 est)
INFLATION RATE – 2.3 per cent (2005 est)
UNEMPLOYMENT – 7.6 per cent (2005 est)
TOTAL EXTERNAL DEBT – US$287,800m (2005 est)
IMPORTS – US$53,400m (2005)
EXPORTS – US$32,200m (2005)

BALANCE OF PAYMENTS

Trade – US$20,855m deficit (2005)
Current Account – US$17,007m deficit (2005)

Trade with UK	*2005*	*2006*
Imports from UK	£1,648,370,000	£2,271,500,000
Exports to UK	£1,786,973,000	£2,742,300,000

COMMUNICATIONS

There are 2,850km of railways, of which 623km are electrified, and 78,470km of roads. There are 66 airports and airfields, including international airports at Lisbon, Oporto, Faro and Santa Maria (Azores) and Funchal (Madeira). The main ports are Lisbon, Porto and Setubal.

Modern telephone systems serve 4.2 million main-line subscribers, 11.4 million mobile phone subscribers and 7.8 million internet users.

EDUCATION AND HEALTH

Education is free of charge and compulsory for nine years from the age of six. Secondary education is mainly conducted in state general unified schools, lyceums, technical and professional schools and private schools. There are also military, naval, polytechnic and other specialist schools. The university at Coimbra was founded in 1290.

GROSS ENROLMENT RATIO (percentage of relevant age group) – primary 116 per cent; secondary 97 per cent; tertiary 57 per cent (2005 est)
HEALTH EXPENDITURE (per capita) – US$1,665 (2004)
HOSPITAL BEDS (per 1,000 people) – 3.6 (2000–5)

MEDIA

The monopoly of the public broadcaster RTP ended in 1992 with the launch of commercial television. Public radio networks are operated by RTP, while the Roman Catholic Church owns Radio Renascenca. There are some 300 other local and regional commercial radio stations. Principal national newspapers include the daily titles *Diario de Noticias, Publico, Correio da Manha* and *Jornal de Noticias*.

AUTONOMOUS REGIONS

Madeira and the Azores are both autonomous regions, each with its own locally elected assembly and government.

MADEIRA is a group of islands in the Atlantic Ocean about 990km south-west of Lisbon, and consists of Madeira, Porto, Santo and three uninhabited islands. Total area is 779 sq. km; population, 243,007 (2003 est). Funchal in Madeira, the largest island, is the capital.

THE AZORES is an archipelago of nine islands in the Atlantic Ocean 1,400–1,800km west of Lisbon, and consists of Flores, Corvo, Terceira, Sao Jorge, Pico, Faial, Graciosa, Sao Miguel and Santa Maria. Total area 2,330 sq. km; population, 240,042 (2003 est). Ponta Delgada, on Sao Miguel, is the capital.

QATAR

Dawlat Qatar – State of Qatar

AREA – 11,437 sq. km. Neighbours: United Arab Emirates (south), Saudi Arabia (south-west)
CAPITAL – Doha (Al-Dawhah); population, 339,847 (2004)
MAJOR CITIES – Ar Rayyan; Al-Wakrah; Umm Salal Muhamma'd
CURRENCY – Qatar riyal of 100 dirhams
POPULATION – 885,359 rising at 2.5 per cent per year (2006 est); Arab (40 per cent), Indian (18 per cent), Pakistani (18 per cent), Iranian (10 per cent) (est)
RELIGION – Islam (75 per cent) (est)
LANGUAGE – Arabic (official), English
POPULATION DENSITY – 74 per sq. km (2005)
URBAN POPULATION – 92.3 per cent (2005 est)
MEDIAN AGE (years) – 31.7 (2006 est)
NATIONAL ANTHEM – 'As-Salam al-Amiri' ['The Peace of the Amir']
NATIONAL DAY – 3 September (Independence Day)
LIFE EXPECTANCY (years) – 73.9 (2006 est)
MORTALITY RATE – 4.72 (2006 est)
BIRTH RATE – 15.56 (2006 est)
INFANT MORTALITY RATE – 18.04 (2006 est)
DEATH PENALTY – Yes
CPI SCORE – 6.0 (2006)
LITERACY RATE – 89.2 per cent (2004 est)

CLIMATE AND TERRAIN

The terrain is mostly flat desert, with salt flats in the south. Elevation extremes range from 103m (Qurayn Abu al-Bawl) at the highest point to 0m (Persian Gulf) at the lowest. The country has a desert climate and average temperatures range from 23°C in January to 35°C in July. Humidity along the coast often reaches 90 per cent during the summer. Average annual rainfall is below 75mm.

HISTORY AND POLITICS

Qatar developed into an important trading centre from the eighth century. It came under the rule of the al-Khalifa family, which in the 18th century moved its base to Bahrain island. A revolt against al-Khalifa rule in the 1860s was suppressed but Britain intervened in 1867, at the behest of the Qatari nobles. The al-Khalifas were removed and replaced by the al-Thani family. Nominally under the rule of the Ottoman Empire from 1871 until the outbreak of the First World War, Qatar became a British protectorate in 1916. It became independent in 1971.

In 1972 Shaikh Ahmad was overthrown by the crown prince and prime minister, Shaikh Khalifa. Another coup followed in 1995 when Khalifa was overthrown by his son and heir, Shaikh Hamad, who has since introduced liberal reforms. Municipal elections, the first democratic polls since independence, were held in 1999. A referendum in 2003 approved a new constitution, which was promulgated in 2004. Elections to the partially elected consultative council established by the constitution are expected to take place in late 2007.

POLITICAL SYSTEM

A new constitution was promulgated in 2004. The head of state is a hereditary absolute monarch, the amir. There is no legislature at present, although the 2004 constitution provides for a *Shura* council with 45 members, 30 directly elected and 15 appointed by the amir, and this will have legislative powers. At present there is an advisory council with 35 members appointed by the amir. There are no political parties. Women have been permitted to vote and stand for election since 1999; the first female cabinet member was appointed in 2003.

HEAD OF STATE

HH Amir of Qatar, Minister of Defence and Commander-in-Chief of Armed Forces, Shaikh Hamad bin Khalifa al-Thani, KCMG, *assumed power* 27 June 1995
Crown Prince, HH Shaikh Tamim bin Hamad al-Thani

SELECTED GOVERNMENT MEMBERS *as at July 2007*

Prime Minister, Foreign Affairs, HH Shaikh Hamad bin Jassem bin Jabr al-Thani
Deputy Prime Minister, Abdullah bin Hamad al-Attiyah
Internal Affairs, Shaikh Abdulla bin Khalid al-Thani
Finance, Yousef bin Hussain Kamal

EMBASSY OF THE STATE OF QATAR
1 South Audley Street, London W1K 1NB
T 020-7493 2200
Ambassador Extraordinary and Plenipotentiary, HE Khalid Rashid al-Hamoudi al-Mansouri, *apptd* 2005

BRITISH EMBASSY
PO Box 3, Doha
T (+974) 442 1991 E bembcomm@qatar.net.qa
Ambassador Extraordinary and Plenipotentiary, HE Simon Collis, *apptd* 2005

BRITISH COUNCIL
PO Box 2992, 93 Al Sadd Street, Doha
T (+974) 425 1888 W www.britishcouncil.org/qatar
Director, Tony Jones

DEFENCE

The army has 30 main battle tanks, 226 armoured personnel carriers and 40 armoured infantry fighting vehicles. The navy has 21 patrol and coastal combatant vessels. The air force has 18 combat aircraft and 11 attack helicopters.

MILITARY BUDGET – US$2,330m (2006 est)
MILITARY PERSONNEL – 12,400: army 8,500, navy 1,800, air force 2,100

ECONOMY AND TRADE

The economy is based largely on the production of oil and gas, which account for more than 60 per cent of GDP, about 85 per cent of export earnings and 70 per cent of government revenues. The state-owned Qatar General Petroleum Corporation controls the industry, and is responsible for oil production onshore and offshore. There has been substantial foreign investment in exploitation of the large gasfields, and Qatar was expected to become the world's leading export of liquefied natural gas in 2007.

Other industries include oil refining, production of ammonia, fertilisers, petrochemicals, steel and cement, and ship repairing. Industry contributes 77.2 per cent of GDP, services 22.6 per cent and agriculture, which is constrained by the terrain and climate, just 0.2 per cent. The economy depends on foreign workers, who outnumber the indigenous population.

The main export markets are Japan, South Korea and Singapore. Principal exports are liquefied natural gas, petroleum products, fertilisers and steel. The chief sources of imports are France, Japan, the USA, Germany, Saudi Arabia, the UK and Italy. The main imports are machinery and transport equipment, foodstuffs and chemicals.

ANNUAL AVERAGE GROWTH OF GDP – 8.8 per cent (2005 est)
INFLATION RATE – 8.8 per cent (2005 est)
UNEMPLOYMENT – 2.7 per cent (2001)
TOTAL EXTERNAL DEBT – US$21,130m (2005 est)
IMPORTS – US$8,040m (2005)
EXPORTS – US$26,5000m (2005)

Trade with UK	*2005*	*2006*
Imports from UK	£362,589,000	£488,809,000
Exports to UK	£97,456,000	£199,329,000

COMMUNICATIONS

There are 1,230km of roads, of which 1,107km are surfaced, but no railways. There are five airports, of which Doha is the principal one, as well as being the main seaport. Gulf Air and Qatar Airways provide regular international air services. Halul is the terminal for offshore oilfields. There is a modern telephone system, which served 205,400 main lines and 219,000 internet users in 2005; mobile phone subscriptions numbered 855,000 in 2006.

MEDIA

Qatar officially lifted media censorship in 1995 and since then the press has essentially been free from government interference, although some self-censorship is practiced. The Qatari satellite station Al Jazeera, launched in 1997, has become one of the most important broadcasters in the Middle East. It launched an English-language network, Al-Jazeera International, in 2006. Radio is state-run by the Qatar Broadcasting Service (QBS), and the BBC World Service is available in Doha. The most popular newspapers are *Al-Watan* and the English-language *Gulf Times*.

ROMANIA

AREA – 237,500 sq. km. Neighbours: Ukraine (north and east), Moldova (east), Bulgaria (south), Serbia (south-west), Hungary (north-west)
CAPITAL – Bucharest; population, 1,921,751 (2002)
MAJOR CITIES – Iasi; Cluj-Napoca; Timisoara; Constanta; Craiova; Galati; Brasov
CURRENCY – New leu (Lei) of 100 bani
POPULATION – 22,303,552 falling at 0.12 per cent per year (2006 est); Romanian (89.5 per cent), Hungarian (6.6 per cent), Romani (2.5 per cent). There are German, Russian, Turkish and Ukrainian minorities
RELIGION – Orthodox Christianity (86 per cent), Roman Catholicism (5 per cent), Protestantism (3 per cent) (est)
LANGUAGE – Romanian (official), Hungarian, German
POPULATION DENSITY – 94 per sq. km (2005)
URBAN POPULATION – 54.7 per cent (2005 est)
MEDIAN AGE (years) – 36.6 (2006 est)
NATIONAL ANTHEM – 'Desteapta-te, Romane' ['Awake Thee, Romanian']
NATIONAL DAY – 1 December (Unification Day)
LIFE EXPECTANCY (years) – 71.63 (2006 est)
MORTALITY RATE – 11.77 (2006 est)
BIRTH RATE – 10.7 (2006 est)
INFANT MORTALITY RATE – 25.5 (2006 est)
DEATH PENALTY – No (abolished 1989)
CPI SCORE – 3.1 (2006)
POPULATION BELOW POVERTY LINE – 44.56 per cent (2000 est)

CLIMATE AND TERRAIN

The Carpathian mountains, running south into the centre of the country and then turning west, and the Transylvanian Alps, enclose a central plateau, which falls towards the basin of the River Tisa. To the south lies the plain of the River Danube, which forms part of the southern border, and to the east the plain of the River Siret and the Black Sea coast. The mountains are thickly forested. Elevation extremes range from 2,544m (Moldoveanu) at the highest point to 0m (Black Sea) at the lowest. The climate is continental, with average temperatures in Bucharest ranging from −2°C in January to 22°C in July.

HISTORY AND POLITICS

Romania was incorporated into the Roman Empire in the early part of the second century AD but was abandoned 200 years later when the power of Rome started to decline. After centuries of rule by invading and often disparate tribal forces, Romania was absorbed into the Ottoman Empire during the 15th century. The principalities of Moldavia and Wallachia were unified under a single native ruler in 1859, and independence was recognised by the Congress of Berlin in 1878. Romania joined the Allies in the First World War, and in the post-war peace settlement acquired Transylvania, Bukovina and Bessarabia.

In 1940 Romania was forced to cede territory to the USSR and Hungary, and power was seized by the Romanian fascists, who took the country into the Second World War on the side of the Axis. When its leaders were overthrown in 1944, Romania changed sides. It was occupied in 1945 by Soviet forces and a Communist-dominated government was installed. In 1947 King Michael abdicated, the monarchy was abolished and Romania became a communist republic. In 1965 Nicolae Ceausescu became leader of the Romanian Communist Party and pursued a foreign policy increasingly independent of the USSR, forming relationships with China and several Western countries. Ceausescu's regime was brutal and corrupt, and when the rest of eastern Europe threw off communist rule in 1989, violent suppression of reformers provoked an uprising in December 1989 that deposed and executed the dictator and his wife. A provisional government led by Ion Iliescu abolished the leading role of the Communist Party and held elections in 1990.

Although Romania became a multiparty democracy in 1991, governments continued to be dominated by former Communists until 1996. Popular unrest and demonstrations have persisted throughout the post-communist period, as most of the population has yet to benefit much from the transition to a market economy. Further economic (and constitutional) changes were introduced to prepare for EU membership and Romania joined the EU in 2007.

Presidential and legislative elections were held in November and December 2004. Traian Basescu, the candidate of a coalition of the Democratic and National Liberal parties, won the presidential election with 51.2 per cent of the vote. In the legislative election, the Social Democratic Party of Romania (PSDR) remained the largest party, with 189 seats, but without an overall majority. It formed a coalition government with three other centre parties under Calin Tariceanu. The Democratic Party left the government in April 2007, prompting a cabinet reshuffle. The president survived a referendum on his impeachment in May and resumed his powers, which had been temporarily exercised by the chair of the senate.

POLITICAL SYSTEM

The 1991 constitution was amended in 2003 to bring it into line with EU requirements. The head of state is a president who is directly elected for a five-year term, renewable only once. The bicameral parliament comprises the chamber of deputies with 345 seats, of which 18 are reserved for ethnic minorities, and the senate with 140 seats. Both houses are directly elected for a four-year term. The prime minister is appointed by the president.

HEAD OF STATE

President of the Republic, Traian Basescu, *elected* 12 December 2004

SELECTED GOVERNMENT MEMBERS *as at July 2007*

Prime Minister, Calin Tariceanu
Defence, Teodor Melescanu
Finance, Varujan Vosganian
Foreign Affairs, Adrian Cioroianu
Interior, Cristian David

EMBASSY OF ROMANIA

Arundel House, 4 Palace Green, London W8 4QD
T 020-7937 9666 W www.roemb.co.uk
Ambassador Extraordinary and Plenipotentiary, vacant

BRITISH EMBASSY

24 Strada Jules Michelet, 70154 Bucharest
T (+40) (21) 201 7200
Ambassador Extraordinary and Plenipotentiary, HE Robin Barnett, *apptd* 2006

BRITISH COUNCIL

Calea Dorobantilor 14, 010572 Bucharest
T (+40) (21) 307 9600 W www.britishcouncil.org/romania
Director (acting), Liliana Biglou

DEFENCE

The army has 473 main battle tanks, 1,081 armoured personnel carriers and 105 armoured infantry fighting vehicles. The navy has 3 frigates, 17 patrol and coastal vessels at four bases. The air force has 62 combat aircraft.

Under an agreement signed in December 2005, the USA is allowed to use military bases in Romania.

MILITARY EXPENDITURE – US$1,940m (2005)
MILITARY PERSONNEL – 69,600: army 41,300, navy 7,300, air force 10,500, joint staff 10,500; paramilitaries 79,900

ECONOMY AND TRADE

Transition to a market economy was slow to begin and has made sluggish progress. The president and government elected in 2004 accelerated reform and the campaign against corruption to meet the requirements for accession to the EU. Although the economy has grown steadily since 2000, it was from a low base and the effects have only recently started to have an impact on the country's widespread poverty; about 25 per cent of the population lives below the poverty line. Corruption and red tape continue to deter foreign investment. The high inflation of past years has been reduced, and the currency was revalued in 2005.

Agriculture employed 31.6 per cent of the workforce in 2004 and contributed 10.1 per cent of GDP in 2006. The principal crops are cereals, sugar beet, vegetables, sunflower seeds and livestock products. Vines and fruits are grown, and extensive forests in the mountains support an important timber industry. There are reserves of natural gas and oil, but Romania is a net importer of fossil fuels, although it exports electricity. Mineral deposits including coal, iron ore, bauxite, chromium and uranium support a mining industry. Other industries include manufacturing, machinery and car assembly, food processing and oil refining.

The main trading partners are EU states (especially Italy and Germany), Russia and Turkey. Principal exports include textiles, footwear, metallurgical products, machinery components, minerals and fuels, chemicals and

agricultural products. The main imports are machines and equipment, fuels, minerals, chemicals, textiles, base metals and agricultural products.
GNI – US$84,600m; US$3,910 per capita (2005)
ANNUAL AVERAGE GROWTH OF GDP – 4.1 per cent (2005 est)
INFLATION RATE – 9 per cent (2005)
UNEMPLOYMENT – 7.7 per cent (2005 est)
TOTAL EXTERNAL DEBT – US$35,680m (2005 est)
IMPORTS – US$40,500m (2005)
EXPORTS – US$27,700m (2005)

BALANCE OF PAYMENTS
Trade – US$6,665m deficit (2004)
Current Account – US$6,382m deficit (2004)

Trade with UK	*2005*	*2006*
Imports from UK	£643,739,000	£606,466,000
Exports to UK	£775,399,000	£827,115,000

COMMUNICATIONS

There are 11,385km of railways, over one-third of which are electrified. There are 198,817km of roads, of which 60,043km are surfaced and 228km are motorway. Navigable waterways include 1,599km on the River Danube and its tributaries and 132km of canals, principally the canal linking the Danube to the Black Sea. The principal ports are Braila, Constanta, Galati and Tulcea. The main airports are at Bucharest and Timisoara.

Liberalisation of telecommunications in 2003 has led to rapid growth, and 58 per cent of households now have access to a fixed line. In 2005 there were 4.4 million main lines in use, 13 million mobile phone subscribers and 5 million internet users.

EDUCATION AND HEALTH

Primary and secondary education is free of charge and compulsory.
LITERACY RATE – 97.3 per cent (2004 est)
GROSS ENROLMENT RATIO (percentage of relevant age group) – primary 107 per cent; secondary 85 per cent; tertiary 40 per cent (2005 est)
HEALTH EXPENDITURE (per capita) – US$178 (2004)
HOSPITAL BEDS (per 1,000 people) – 6.6 (2000–5)

MEDIA

Romania has a dynamic media network with television audiences predominantly shared between the state-owned Romania 1 and the private commercial stations Pro TV and Antena 1. Most households in Bucharest have cable TV. There are more than 100 private radio stations. State-run Radio Romania operates four national networks and regional and local stations. There are four main daily newspapers.

RUSSIAN FEDERATION

Rossiyskaya Federatsiya – Russian Federation

AREA – 17,075,200 sq. km. Neighbours: Norway, Finland, Estonia, Latvia, Belarus and Ukraine (west), Georgia, Azerbaijan, Kazakhstan, China, Mongolia and North Korea (south). The Kaliningrad enclave borders Lithuania and Poland
CAPITAL – Moscow; population, 10,406,578 (2005 est). Founded about 1147, it became the centre of the rising Moscow principality and in the 15th century the capital of the whole of Russia (Muscovy). In 1703 Peter the Great transferred the capital to St Petersburg, but on 14 March 1918 Moscow was again designated the capital
MAJOR CITIES – St Petersburg (Petrograd 1914–24; Leningrad 1924–91); Novosibirsk/Novonikolayevsk; Yekaterinburg; Nizhniy-Novgorod/Gorky; Samara/Kuibyshev; Omsk; Kazan; Chelyabinsk; Rostov; Ufa; Volgograd
CURRENCY – Rouble of 100 kopeks
POPULATION – 142,893,540 falling at 0.37 per cent per year (2006 est); Russian (79.8 per cent), Tatar (3.8 per cent), Ukrainian (2 per cent). There are a further 150 nationalities living in the country
RELIGION – Orthodox Christianity (50 per cent), Islam (10 per cent), other Christian denominations (2 per cent) (est)
LANGUAGE – Russian (official)
POPULATION DENSITY – 9 per sq. km (2005)
URBAN POPULATION – 73.3 per cent (2005 est)
MEDIAN AGE (years) – 38.4 (2006 est)
NATIONAL ANTHEM – 'Russia, Sacred Our Empire' (the former Soviet national anthem, with new lyrics)
NATIONAL DAY – 12 June (Independence Day)
LIFE EXPECTANCY (years) – 67.08 (2006 est)
MORTALITY RATE – 14.65 (2006 est)
BIRTH RATE – 9.95 (2006 est)
INFANT MORTALITY RATE – 15.13 (2006 est)
HIV/AIDS ADULT PREVALENCE – 1.1 per cent (2003 est)
DEATH PENALTY – No*
CPI SCORE – 2.5 (2006)
POPULATION BELOW POVERTY LINE – 17.8 per cent (2004 est)

CLIMATE AND TERRAIN

The Russian Federation includes the easternmost areas of Europe and the whole of northern Asia. There are three principal geographic areas: a low-lying flat western area stretching eastwards up to the Yenisei River and divided in two by the Ural mountain range; the eastern area between the Yenisei and the Pacific, consisting of plateaux and mountain ranges; and a southern mountainous area. The Kuril Islands form an archipelago in the north Pacific Ocean and are under Russian administration as part of the Sakhalin *oblast*. Elevation extremes range from 5,633m (Mt El'brus, Caucasus) at the highest point to −70m (Prikaspiyskaya Nizmennost') at the lowest. Russia has the longest Arctic coastline in the world (over 27,000km).

The most important rivers are the Volga, the Northern Dvina, the Neva, the Don and the Kuban in the European part, and in the Asiatic part, the Ob, the Irtysh, the Yenisei, the Lena, the Amur and, further north, the Khatanga, Olenek, Yana, Indigirka and Kolyma. Lake Baikal in eastern Siberia is the deepest lake in the world.

The climate varies dramatically, from the frozen tundra of the north Siberian plain to the temperate regions of the far east. Throughout the country, winters are cold, while summers are hot in the south and relatively warm elsewhere. Rainfall is highest in the westerly mountain regions, which have an average annual precipitation of up to 2,000mm. Average temperatures in Moscow range from −16°C in January to 23°C in July.

HISTORY AND POLITICS

Russia was settled by many ethnic groups, including Slavs, Turks and Bulgars in the third to seventh centuries AD, and in the 13th century came under the overlordship of the Mongols. In the 15th century the grand duke of Muscovy threw off Mongol overlordship and began a process of unification and territorial expansion continued by his successors. Internal disorder and war with neighbouring countries held back Russian development until the reign of Peter I (The Great) (1682–1725), who introduced Western ideas of government, modernised the army and founded the navy. Under Catherine II (The Great) (1762–96) Russia became a great power, extending its territory further. Russian expansion in Asia led to a war with Japan in 1904–5 that ended in an unexpected Russian defeat. This provoked a revolution in 1905 which, though suppressed, forced the emperor to establish Russia's first parliament *(Duma)*.

The *Duma's* powers were limited and it was unable to ameliorate the Tsarist regime's endemic misgovernment or the conditions of the increasingly militant urban working class. During the First World War discontent caused by autocratic rule, the poor military conduct of the war and wartime privation led to a revolution which broke out in March 1917. The emperor abdicated and a power struggle ensued between the provisional government and the Bolshevik Party. This led to a second revolution in November 1917 in which the Bolsheviks, led by Lenin, seized power.

Civil war between 'red' Bolshevik forces and 'white' monarchist and anti-communist forces, the latter supported by foreign powers, lasted until the end of 1922. During the civil war, Russia was declared a Soviet republic and other Soviet republics were formed in Ukraine, Belorussia and Transcaucasia. These four republics merged to form the Union of Soviet Socialist Republics (USSR) on 30 December 1922.

During the 1930s Joseph Stalin introduced a policy of rapid industrialisation under a series of five-year plans, brought all sectors of industry under government control, abolished private ownership and enforced the collectivisation of agriculture, causing considerable famine. Many ethnic minority groups suffered under Stalin's regime and it is estimated that up to 1.5 million people were deported to the Gulags of Siberia and the central Asian republics. After being attacked by Nazi Germany in 1941, the USSR joined the Second World War on the side of the Allies. In 1944–5 Soviet forces liberated much of eastern Europe and the post-war Communist regimes in these countries were closely tied to the Soviet government.

The death of Stalin in 1953 brought Nikita Khrushchev to power. Plans to modernise the economy were hampered by the difficulties of post-war reconstruction and his attempt to install nuclear missiles in Cuba in 1962 in response to a similar American deployment in Turkey, brought the country to the brink of war with the USA. The administration of Khrushchev's successor, Leon Brezhnev, saw the economy stagnate further and foreign policy become more aggressive. The 1968 Brezhnev Doctrine, which advocated military invention to prop up ailing Communist regimes, was the justification behind action in Czechoslovakia and Afghanistan.

Mikhail Gorbachev became Soviet leader in 1985 and introduced the policies of *perestroika* (complete restructuring) and *glasnost* (openness) in order to revamp the economy, which had stagnated since the 1970s, to root out corruption and inefficiency, and to end the Cold War. The retreat from total control by the Communist Party unleashed ethnic and nationalist tensions.

Following the defeat of an attempted coup by hardline Communists in August 1991, effective political power was in the hands of the republican leaders, especially Russian President Yeltsin, and the USSR began to break up as the constituent republics declared their independence. Gorbachev resigned as Soviet president on 25 December 1991 and the following day the USSR formally ceased to exist. The Russian Federation took over the USSR's seat at the UN in December 1991, was recognised as an independent state by the EC and USA in January 1992, and joined the G7 group of industrialised countries in 1996.

A new Russian Federal Treaty was signed in 1992 between the central government and the autonomous republics within Russia. Tatarstan and Bashkortostan signed the treaty in 1994 after securing considerable legislative and economic autonomy.

Vladimir Putin was elected president in 2000, and re-elected in 2004 with 71.2 per cent of the vote. His presidency has seen an increasing degree of centralisation, the partial renationalisation of industry (especially oil and gas), the re-assertion of state control over the media and an increasingly authoritarian stance on democracy. In the 2003 legislative elections, the pro-Putin United Russia party retained its majority in the *Duma*. In February 2004 President Putin dismissed Prime Minister Mikhail Kasyanov and the entire council of ministers. The president named Mikhail Fradkov as prime minister and he took office in March 2004 at the head of a smaller, restructured council of ministers.

INSURGENCIES

Chechnya's attempt to achieve independence has led to two wars with the Russian federal government, in 1994–6 and another ongoing since 1999. The area is strategically important to Russia because routes from central Russia to the Black and Caspian seas, and oil and gas pipelines from neighbouring countries pass through it.

The Chechen republic declared its independence in November 1991 and refused to sign the Russian Federal Treaty in 1992. Civil war began in early 1994 between the Chechen government and armed opposition forces tacitly supported by the Russian government. The Russian military invaded Chechnya in December 1994, meeting strong opposition from the Chechen army, guerrillas and civilians. The conflict became unpopular in Russia but the federal government was reluctant to withdraw for fear of encouraging other separatist movements in the Russian Federation. Peace negotiations in 1996 resulted in the signing of the Khasavyurt accords and Russian troops withdrew in January 1997.

The accords left the issue of Chechen independence unresolved and the uneasy peace broke down in September 1999 when Russian forces invaded Chechnya again. This followed bombings in Russia that were blamed on Chechen extremists and an incursion by Chechen forces into neighbouring Dagestan in August 1999. The Russians captured Grozny in February 2000. Refusing to negotiate with the Chechen government, President Putin imposed direct rule from Moscow in May 2000. Violent unrest has continued in Chechnya, and there have been reports of human rights violations by Russian troops. Chechen separatists have carried out suicide bombings and other attacks in Russia, such as the Moscow theatre siege in 2002 and the Beslan school siege in 2004.

In a referendum in Chechnya in March 2003, the majority voted in favour of a new constitution promising autonomy for the republic but also stating that Chechnya was an integral part of the Russian Federation. The election of a Russian-backed candidate, Alu Alkhanov, as president of Chechnya in August 2004 (following the assassination of his predecessor, Akhmad Kadyrov, in May) has helped reduce the level of violence; Alkhanov was succeeded in 2007 by Ramzan Kadyrov, son of Akhmad Kadyrov. Violence has spilled over into other parts of the northern Caucasus as Russian forces attempt to capture Chechen separatists based in the republics neighbouring Chechnya.

POLITICAL SYSTEM

The 1993 constitution introduced multiparty democracy and enshrines various human rights and civil liberties. The head of state is a president, who is directly elected for a four-year term, renewable only once consecutively. Legislative power is vested in the federal assembly, comprising the council of the federation (upper house) of 172 members, two elected by each member of the Russian Federation with terms of varying length; and the State *Duma* (lower house) of 450 members, all elected by proportional representation for a four-year term. The president appoints the chairman of the council of ministers (prime minister) but is also entitled to chair sessions of the council.

A constitutional court of 19 members appointed for a 12-year term protects and interprets the constitution and decides whether laws are compatible with it.

HEAD OF STATE

President, Vladimir Putin, *elected* 26 March 2000, *inaugurated* 7 May 2000, *re-elected* 14 March 2004

SELECTED GOVERNMENT MEMBERS *as at July 2007*

Chair, Mikhail Fradkov
First Deputy Chair, Dmitry Medvedev
First Deputy Chair, Sergei Ivanov
Foreign Affairs, Sergey Lavrov
Interior, Rashid Nurgaliyev
Finance, Alexei Kudrin
Defence, Anatoly Serdyukov

EMBASSY OF THE RUSSIAN FEDERATION

13 Kensington Palace Gardens, London W8 4QX
T 020-7229 2666
Ambassador Extraordinary and Plenipotentiary, HE Yury Fedotov, *apptd* 2005

BRITISH EMBASSY

Smolenskaya Naberezhnaya 10, 121099 Moscow
T (+7) (495) 956 7200 E moscow@britishembassy.ru
W www.britemb.msk.ru
Ambassador Extraordinary and Plenipotentiary, HE Anthony Brenton, *apptd* 2005

BRITISH COUNCIL

Ulitsa Nikoloyamskaya 1, 109189 Moscow
T (+7) (495) 782 0200 W www.britishcouncil.org/russia
Director, James Kennedy

FEDERAL STRUCTURE

The Russian Federation comprises 48 *oblasti* (regions), 7 *krai* (autonomous territories), 21 *respubliki* (republics), 9 *okrugi* (autonomous areas), 2 cities of federal status (Moscow and St Petersburg) and one autonomous Jewish region, Birobijan. The *oblasti* are Amur, Arkhangelsk, Astrakhan, Belgorod, Bryansk, Chelyabinsk, Chita, Irkutsk, Ivanovo, Kaliningrad, Kaluga, Kamchatka, Kemerovo, Kirov, Kostroma, Kurgan, Kursk, Leningrad, Lipetsk, Magadan, Moscow, Murmansk, Nizhny-Novgorod, Novgorod, Novosibirsk, Omsk, Orel, Orenburg, Penza, Pskov, Rostov, Ryazan, Sakhalin, Samara, Saratov, Smolensk, Sverdlovsk, Tambov, Tomsk, Tula, Tver, Tyumen, Ulyanovsk, Vladimir, Volgograd, Vologda, Voronezh and Yaroslavl. The *krai* are Altai, Khabarovsk, Krasnodar, Krasnoyarsk, Perm, Primorye and Stavropol. The *respubliki* are Adygeia, Altai, Bashkortostan, Buryatia, Chechnya, Chuvashia, Daghestan, Ingushetia, Kabardino-Balkaria, Kalmykia, Karachai-Cherkessia, Karelia, Khakassia, Komi, Mari-El, Mordovia, North Ossetia (Alania), Sakha, Tatarstan, Tyva and Udmurtia. The *okrugi* are Aga-Buryat, Chuckchi, Evenki, Khanty-Mansi, Koryak, Nenets, Taimyr, Ust-Orda-Buryat and Yamal-Nenets.

DEFENCE

Since the demise of the USSR, Russia's armed forces have been considerably reduced. Major army reform is planned for the period 2004–10, including transition from conscription to voluntary service.

A joint CIS air defence system covers Russia, Armenia, Belarus, Georgia, Kazakhstan, Kyrgyzstan, Tajikistan, Turkmenistan, Ukraine and Uzbekistan. The Black Sea fleet was divided between Russian and Ukraine under an agreement signed in 1997.

The Strategic Deterrent Forces have 15 nuclear-powered ballistic missile submarines and 570 intercontinental ballistic missiles equipped with some 2,035 nuclear warheads. Russia also has 80 long-range strike aircraft capable of carrying strategic missiles.

The army has about 22,831 main battle tanks, 9,900 armoured personnel carriers and 15,090 armoured infantry fighting vehicles. The navy has 112 submarines, 2 aircraft carriers, 9 cruisers, 24 destroyers, 30 frigates, 186 patrol and coastal vessels, 245 combat aircraft and 165 armed helicopters. The air force has 1,650 combat aircraft.

Russia deploys forces in Armenia (3,500), Georgia (3,000), Moldova (1,400) and Tajikistan (7,800).

MILITARY EXPENDITURE – US$59,100m (2005)
MILITARY PERSONNEL – 1,027,000: Strategic Deterrent Forces 80,000, army 395,000, navy 142,000, air force 160,000; paramilitaries 418,000

ECONOMY AND TRADE

Under the Soviet regime, an essentially agrarian economy in 1917 was transformed by the early 1960s into the second-greatest industrial power in the world. However, by the early 1970s the concentration of resources on the military-industrial complex had caused the civilian economy to deteriorate. Economic reforms were introduced by President Gorbachev, including the legalisation of small private businesses, the reduction of state control over the economy, and denationalisation and privatisation. The first stage of mass privatisation of state industries began in 1992 and by February 1996, 80 per cent of the economy had been privatised. The largest and most economically significant industries, oil and gas, have been partially renationalised since President Putin took office, although Rosneft, the state oil company, was floated on the London stock exchange in July 2006.

The transition to a market economy caused a severe economic crisis in 1993 and again in 1998, when the rouble collapsed. But since 1999, the economy has sustained growth averaging 6.7 per cent a year, and average incomes have grown by more than 12 per cent a year since 2002; the middle class is expanding and poverty is declining, with only 17.8 per cent still living below the poverty line. Investment and consumer demand have both increased significantly since 2000. Foreign debt now stands at around 39 per cent of GDP (down from 90 per cent), inflation has been reduced, the budget has been in surplus every year since 2001 and there is a healthy trade surplus.

Nevertheless, considerable problems remain: the country's manufacturing base is dilapidated, its banking system is weak and widespread corruption has led to a lack of trust in institutions. The economy is also vulnerable to fluctuations in global commodity prices for its main exports.

Russia has some of the world's richest natural resources, especially mineral deposits, and oil, natural gas, timber and minerals account for 80 per cent of its exports (and 32 per cent of government revenue). The recent growth in the economy is founded on the exploitation and export of its oil and natural gas reserves, and Russia is becoming the leading supplier to European countries and China, a position that has led the country into some dispute with its neighbours; Ukraine, Georgia and Belarus have all had gas supplies cut for short periods during negotiations over cutting price subsidies. Oil is produced in the northern Caucasus, between the Volga and the Urals, and in western Siberia, which also has large deposits of natural gas. Coal is mined in the Kuznetsk area, in the Urals, south of Moscow, in the Donets basin and in the Pechora area in the north. Coal and gas deposits in Siberia and the far east (especially Yakutia) are being developed, and Russia is keen to exploit the shrinking of the Arctic ice-cap to prospect for previously inaccessible deposits under the Arctic Sea. The Ural mountains contain many valuable natural resources, including high-quality iron ore, coal and oil. Iron ore is also mined near Kursk, Tula, Lipetsk, in several areas in Siberia and in the Kola Peninsula. Non-ferrous metals are found in the Altai, eastern Siberia, the northern Caucasus, the Kuznetsk basin, and the far east and north.

The vast area and the great variety in climatic conditions are reflected in the structure of agriculture. In the far north reindeer breeding, hunting and fishing are predominant. Further south, the timber industry is combined with grain growing. In the southern half of the forest zone and in the adjacent forest-steppe zone, the acreage under grain crops is larger and agriculture more complex. The southern part of the western Siberian plain is an important grain-growing and stock-breeding area. In the extreme south cotton is cultivated. Vine, tobacco and other southern crops are grown on the Black Sea shore of the Caucasus.

The service sector is the largest, accounting for 58 per cent of GDP and employing 60 per cent of the workforce; industry contributes 37 per cent of GDP and employs 29 per cent; and agriculture accounts for 5 per cent of GDP and 11 per cent of employment. Moscow and St Petersburg are still the two largest industrial centres, but new industrial areas have been developed in the Urals, the Kuznetsk basin, Siberia and the far east.

Russia's main trading partners are EU countries (especially Germany), Ukraine, China, Japan, the USA, Belarus, Turkey and Switzerland. Principal exports are oil and petroleum products, natural gas, timber and timber products, metals, chemicals, manufactured goods, military vehicles and defence equipment. The main imports are machinery and equipment, consumer goods, medicines, meat and sugar.

GNI – US$638,100m (2005); US$4,460 per capita (2005)
ANNUAL AVERAGE GROWTH OF GDP – 6.4 per cent (2005 est)
INFLATION RATE – 12.7 per cent (2005 est)
UNEMPLOYMENT – 7.6 per cent (2005 est)
TOTAL EXTERNAL DEBT – US$215,300m (2005 est)
IMPORTS – US$138,000m (2005)
EXPORTS – US$244,000m (2005)

BALANCE OF PAYMENTS
Trade – US$118,266m surplus (2005)
Current Account – US$84,249m surplus (2005)

Trade with UK	*2005*	*2006*
Imports from UK	£1,874,506,000	£2,057,506,000
Exports to UK	£5,221,894,000	£5,819,732,000

COMMUNICATIONS

The European area of Russia is well served by railways, which are state-run, but there are still large areas, notably in the far north and Siberia, with few or no railways. In 2004 there were 117,000km of railways, of which 87,000km were used for passenger transport and the rest by industry. The road system is similarly concentrated in the more densely populated European part of the country, and in the southernmost parts of Asian Russia. There are 871,000km of roads, 730,000km of which are surfaced.

The most important ports include Taganrog, Rostov and Novorossiysk around the Black Sea and the Sea of Azov. Two of the three northern ports, St Petersburg and Arkhangelsk, are icebound during winter; only Murmansk is accessible. Several ports have been built along the Arctic Sea route between Murmansk and Vladivostok and are in regular use in summer. The far eastern port of Vladivostok, Russia's Pacific naval base, is kept open by icebreakers all the year round.

There are 95,900km of waterways. The great rivers of European Russia flow outwards from the centre, linking all parts of the plain with the chief ports. They are supplemented by a 72,000km system of canals which provides a through route between the White Sea and Baltic Sea in the north and the Black Sea, Caspian Sea and the Sea of Azov in the south; the most notable are the White Sea–Baltic Canal, the Moscow–Volga Canal and the Volga–Don Canal.

Because of the vast distances, the terrain and the harsh winter climate, air transport is the quickest form of long-distance internal travel. There are over 1,620 airports and airfields, although only about 616 have paved runways. The principal international airports are at Moscow, St Petersburg and Novosibirsk. The main national carriers are Aeroflot and Sibir Airlines.

The telecommunications infrastructure is expanding and improving, although less quickly for fixed lines than for mobile phones, and rural services are still inadequate. In 2005 there were 40 million main lines in use, 120 million mobile phone subscribers and 23.7 million internet users.

EDUCATION AND HEALTH

There are 11 years of compulsory education: nine at basic school level and a further two at senior secondary level. Higher education is provided by public and private accredited higher education institutions.
LITERACY RATE – 99.4 per cent (2004 est)
GROSS ENROLMENT RATIO (percentage of relevant

age group) – primary 123 per cent; secondary 93 per cent; tertiary 68 per cent (2005 est)
HEALTH EXPENDITURE (per capita) – US$245 (2004)
HOSPITAL BEDS (per 1,000 people) – 10.5 (2000–5)

MEDIA

The main national television networks, Channel One, Radio Broadcasting company (RTR) and NTV, are state-run, ensuring the government controls media content. Many newspapers are privately owned and popular titles include *Kommersant, Komsomolskaya Pravda, Izvestia* and the English-language *Moscow Times*. The principal radio network is run by Russian State Television and RTR, alongside numerous regional and external services.

CULTURE

Russian is a branch of the Slavonic family of languages and is written in the Cyrillic script.

Before the westernisation of Russia under Peter the Great (1672–1725), Russian literature consisted mainly of *byliny* (folk songs), epic songs, chronicles and works of moral theology. The 19th century proved to be the most fertile period for Russian writing: poetry reached its zenith with Alexander Pushkin (1799–1837) and Mikhail Lermontov (1814–41), while novelists Nikolai Gogol (1809–52), Ivan Turgenev (1818–83), Fyodor Dostoyevsky (1821–81) and Leo Tolstoy (1828–1910) created masterpieces such as *Dead Souls, Fathers and Sons, Crime and Punishment* and *War and Peace* respectively. In the 20th century, Mikhail Bulgakov (1891–1940), Vladimir Nabokov (1899–1977) and Nobel laureate Alexander Solzhenitsyn (*b.* 1918) have been especially acclaimed. Anton Chekhov (1860–1904) is best-known as a playwright but also produced short stories.

Russia has made an equally impressive contribution to classical music. Mikhail Glinka (1804–57) was an innovator to match Pushkin, while those that followed him include Mussorgsky (1839–81), Rimsky-Korsakov (1844–1908), Tchaikovsky (1840–93) – arguably the most internationally successful Russian composer whose ballets include *Swan Lake* and *The Nutcracker* – Rachmaninov (1873–1943), Prokofiev (1891–1953), Stravinsky (1882–1971) and Shostakovich (1906–75).

Directors Sergey Eisenstein (1898–1948), Andrei Tarkovsky (1932–86) and Nikita Mikhalkov (*b.* 1945) are celebrated figures in Russian cinema.

RWANDA

Republika y'u Rwanda/République Rwandaise – Republic of Rwanda

AREA – 26,338 sq. km. Neighbours: Burundi (south), Democratic Republic of the Congo (west), Uganda (north), Tanzania (east)
CAPITAL – Kigali; population, 603,049 (2002)
MAJOR TOWNS – Gitarama; Butare; Ruhengeri
CURRENCY – Rwanda franc of 100 centimes
POPULATION – 8,648,248 rising at 2.43 per cent per year (2006 est); Hutu (84 per cent), Tutsi (15 per cent) (est)
RELIGION – Roman Catholicism (49 per cent), Protestantism (43 per cent), Islam (4 per cent) (est). A very small minority practises indigenous religions; an estimated 1 per cent of the population is atheist
LANGUAGE – Kinyarwanda, French, English (all official), Swahili
POPULATION DENSITY – 366 per sq. km (2005)
URBAN POPULATION – 21.8 per cent (2005 est)
MEDIAN AGE (years) – 18.6 (2006 est)
NATIONAL ANTHEM – 'Rwanda Nziza' ['Rwanda, Our Beautiful Country']
NATIONAL DAY – 1 July (Independence Day)
LIFE EXPECTANCY (years) – 47.3(2006 est)
MORTALITY RATE – 16.09 (2006 est)
BIRTH RATE – 40.37 (2006 est)
INFANT MORTALITY RATE – 89.61 (2006 est)
HIV/AIDS ADULT PREVALENCE – 5.1 per cent (2003 est)
DEATH PENALTY – Yes
CPI SCORE – 2.5 (2006)
POPULATION BELOW POVERTY LINE – 60 per cent (2001 est)
MILITARY BUDGET – US$71m (2006)
MILITARY PERSONNEL – 33,000: army 32,000, air force 1,000; paramilitaries 2,000
LITERACY RATE – 64 per cent (2004 est)
GROSS ENROLMENT RATIO (percentage of relevant age group) – primary 120 per cent; secondary 14 per cent; tertiary 3 per cent (2005 est)
HEALTH EXPENDITURE (per capita) – US$16 (2004)

CLIMATE AND TERRAIN

Landlocked Rwanda's terrain is mostly savannah uplands and mountains, including the volcanic Virunga range in the north-west. Elevation extremes range from 4,519m (Volcan Karisimbi) at the highest point to 950m (River Rusizi) at the lowest. Rwanda's western border runs through Lake Kivu. The climate is tropical, with two wet seasons, from February to April and November to January. Average daily temperatures range from 15°C in January to 35°C in July.

HISTORY AND POLITICS

Rwanda was settled by Hutu peoples from the tenth century. From the 14th century, they came under the dominance of Tutsi migrants, who established a monarchy in the 15th century and a unified state in the late 19th century. The historic dominance of the majority Hutus by the minority Tutsis is the source of the conflict between the two ethnic groups that has overshadowed the country's history.

Rwanda became a German protectorate in the 1890s and was occupied by Belgium when the First World War broke out. After the war, it became a mandated territory administered by Belgium. In 1959, the Hutu population rebelled against Tutsi domination, causing the king and some 150,000 Tutsis to flee the country. Rwanda became a republic in 1961 and independence was achieved in July 1962 under a Hutu president, Gregorie Kayibanda. He was overthrown in 1973 in a military coup led by Maj.-Gen. Juvenal Habyarimana, whose National Revolutionary Development Movement (MRND) was the only legal party until 1991.

Armed Tutsi exiles in Uganda repeatedly attempted to invade Rwanda in the 1960s and 1970s but were defeated by the predominantly Hutu army. Continued conflict left thousands dead over a period of 30 years. The exiles and opponents of the MRND regime eventually formed the Tutsi-led Rwandan Patriotic Front (FPR), and in 1990 they again invaded the country, winning control of parts of the north. After the government reneged on a 1992 peace agreement, the FPR advanced on Kigali and forced the government to restart negotiations, which led to the Arusha peace accord in August 1993.

In April 1994, President Habyarimana, who had retained the interim presidency, died in a plane crash blamed variously on extremist sections of the Hutu army and the FPR. His death was the trigger for the army and militia *(interahamwe)* to massacre the Tutsi minority and moderate Hutus; 800,000 people were systematically killed in three months and millions escaped to neighbouring countries. The FPR military response spread quickly southwards, causing millions of Hutus and the forces of the defeated government to flee.

In July 1994 the FPR established a broad-based government of national unity in which moderate Hutus were given the presidency and premiership and the FPR took eight of the 22 seats. An International Criminal Tribunal for Rwanda was established in 1995 to bring to trial those directly responsible for the 1994 genocide; so far, 27 people have been convicted. A government report in 2002 stated that 1,074,017 people, more than 93 per cent of them Tutsis, were killed between 1990 and 1994.

Despite continuing attacks by extremist Hutu insurgents and Rwandan involvement in the civil war in the neighbouring Democratic Republic of the Congo from 1996 until 2002, reconciliation efforts and political reforms have been introduced since 1994 in an attempt to stabilise the country. Local elections were held in 1999, and presidential and legislative elections took place in 2003 following the approval of a new constitution. In the 2003 presidential election, the FPR leader Paul Kagame was elected with 95.1 per cent of the vote. In the legislative elections, the FPR won 40 of the 53 directly elected seats and formed a coalition government with the Social Democratic Party, the Christian Democratic Party, the Islamic Democratic Party, the Liberal Party and a number of independent members. The FPR is regarded as authoritarian, suppressing dissent, but the country has achieved relative stability under its rule.

POLITICAL SYSTEM

Under the 2003 constitution, the head of state is a president directly elected for a seven-year term, renewable only once. The bicameral legislature consists of a chamber of deputies, the lower house, and a senate. The chamber of deputies has 80 members, of whom 53 are directly elected, 24 are women members elected by the provinces, two represent youth organisations and one represents organisations of disabled people; all serve a five-year term. The senate, has 26 members indirectly elected for an eight-year term.

In 2006 the 12 provinces were replaced by five provinces, North, East, South, West and Kigali, with the aim of creating more ethnically diverse administrative areas.

HEAD OF STATE

President, Maj-Gen. Paul Kagame, *appointed* 17 April 2000, *sworn in* 22 April 2000, *elected* 25 August 2003

SELECTED GOVERNMENT MEMBERS *as at July 2007*

Prime Minister, Bernard Makuza
Defence and National Security, Maj.-Gen. Marcel Gatsinzi
Finance and Economic Planning, James Musoni
Foreign Affairs, Charles Muligande
Internal Affairs, Sheikh Fazil Musa Harerimana

EMBASSY OF THE REPUBLIC OF RWANDA
120–122 Seymour Place, London W1H 1NR
T 020-7224 9832 W www.ambarwanda.org.uk
Ambassador Extraordinary and Plenipotentiary, HE Claver Gatete, *apptd* 2005

BRITISH EMBASSY
Parcelle No. 1131, Blvd de l'Umuganda, Kacyira-Sud, BP 576 Kigali
T (+250) 584 098 E ppao@rwanda1.com
W www.britishembassykigali.org.rw
Ambassador Extraordinary and Plenipotentiary, HE Jeremy Macadie, *apptd* 2004

ECONOMY AND TRADE

Rwanda is the most densely populated country in Africa, with few natural resources and minimal industry. Reconstruction efforts have restored the economy to pre-1994 levels, but 60 per cent of the population lives below the poverty line and Rwanda struggles to attract direct investment. IMF/World Bank heavily indebted poor country status has afforded some debt relief, and it was promised 100 per cent debt relief and additional development aid from the G8 countries in 2005. Around 90 per cent of the population is engaged in agriculture, mainly at subsistence level, but population growth is outpacing production, which contributes 39 per cent of GDP. There is a small industrial sector, processing agricultural products and producing small-scale manufactured goods. Primary foreign exchange earners are coffee, tea, tin and hides; the lack of adequate transport infrastructure handicaps export growth. The main trading partners are Germany, Belgium, Kenya, Uganda and China. The principal imports are foodstuffs, machinery, steel and petroleum products.

GNI – US$2,100m (2005); US$230 per capita (2005)
ANNUAL AVERAGE GROWTH OF GDP – 5.2 per cent (2005 est)
INFLATION RATE – 8 per cent (2005 est)
TOTAL EXTERNAL DEBT – US$1,400m (2004 est)
IMPORTS – US$430m (2005)
EXPORTS – US$130m (2005)

BALANCE OF PAYMENTS
Trade – US$160m deficit (2005)
Current Account – US$6m deficit (2005)

Trade with UK	*2005*	*2006*
Imports from UK	£4,568,000	£3,632,000
Exports to UK	£491,000	£279,000

COMMUNICATIONS

Rwanda has received considerable foreign aid to upgrade its transport infrastructure since the 1994 genocide. The main internal transport system is the 14,000km road network, which links with those of neighbouring countries to provide access to Kenyan and Tanzanian ports for international trade. There are no railways, but in late 2006 a feasibility study was planned into the possibility of including Rwanda in a project to expand the rail network in this region of central Africa. Lake Kivu is navigable by shallow boats, and provides the access, but no regular services, to the Democratic Republic of the Congo. The principal airport is at Kigali.

The fixed-line telephone system mostly serves government and business, and mobile phone distribution has grown rapidly. In 2004 there were 23,000 main lines in use, with 290,000 mobile phone subscribers and 38,000 internet users in 2005.

MEDIA

Rwanda's broadcast media is mainly government-controlled, and before and during the 1994 genocide Radio Tele Libre Mille Collines (RTLM) became a medium for anti-Tutsi propaganda. The first private radio station to open since the genocide began broadcasting in 2004. The BBC World Service, Voice of America and Deutsche Welle all broadcast in Kigali. There is a growing number of newspapers but they face government restrictions and generally exercise self-censorship.

ST CHRISTOPHER AND NEVIS

Federation of St Christopher and Nevis

AREA – 261 sq. km
CAPITAL – Basseterre; population, 11,500 (2001)
MAJOR TOWN – Charlestown, the chief town of Nevis
CURRENCY – East Caribbean dollar (EC$) of 100 cents
POPULATION – 39,129 rising at 0.5 per cent per year (2006 est)
RELIGION – Protestantism (50 per cent), Roman Catholicism (25 per cent) (est)
LANGUAGE – English (official)
POPULATION DENSITY – 133 per sq. km (2005)
URBAN POPULATION – 31.9 per cent (2005 est)
MEDIAN AGE (years) – 27.8 (2006 est)
NATIONAL ANTHEM – 'Oh Land of Beauty!'
NATIONAL DAY – 19 September (Independence Day)
MORTALITY RATE – 8.33 (2006 est)
BIRTH RATE – 18.02 (2006 est)
LIFE EXPECTANCY (years) – 72.4 (2006 est)
INFANT MORTALITY RATE – 14.12 (2006 est)
DEATH PENALTY – Yes

CLIMATE AND TERRAIN

The volcanic islands of St Christopher (St Kitts) (109.5 sq. km) and Nevis (58 sq. km) are part of the Leeward group in the eastern Caribbean Sea. The central area of St Christopher is forest-clad and mountainous, rising to 1,156m (Mount Liamuiga) at the highest point. Nevis, separated from the southern tip of St Christopher by a strait 3km wide, is dominated by Nevis Peak (985m). The climate is tropical and influenced by north-east trade winds. The average annual rainfall, principally during May to September, is 1,375mm, with average daily temperatures of 24°C.

HISTORY AND POLITICS

The islands were visited in 1493 by Christopher Columbus, who named St Christopher. It was settled by the British, becoming the first British colony in the West Indies in 1623; Nevis was settled from 1628. Control was disputed between the British and French in the 17th and 18th centuries, until France dropped its claims in 1783. The islands of St Christopher and Nevis were united in the late 19th century, and in 1967 became a state in association with Britain with internal self-government. Independence was achieved in September 1983.

A separatist movement was formed on Nevis in 1970, and in 1997 the Nevis government voted to secede. A referendum on the issue in 1998 resulted in a 61.8 per cent vote in favour of secession, which fell short of the two-thirds majority required.

In the 2004 legislative election the Labour Party retained its overall majority and began its third consecutive term of office.

POLITICAL SYSTEM

Under the 1983 constitution, the head of state is the British monarch, represented in the islands by a governor-general appointed on the advice of the prime minister. The unicameral national assembly has 15 members: 11 directly elected for a five-year term, a speaker, and three appointed by the governor-general on the advice of the prime minister and the leader of the opposition. The prime minister, who is responsible to the national assembly, and the cabinet are appointed by the governor-general. Nevis is responsible for its own internal affairs, has an eight-member Nevis island assembly and is governed by the Nevis island administration, headed by the premier.
Governor-General, HE Sir Cuthbert Montraville Sebastian, GCMG, OBE, *apptd* 1996

SELECTED GOVERNMENT MEMBERS *as at July 2007*

Prime Minister, Finance, Denzil Douglas
Deputy Prime Minister, Sam Condor
Foreign Affairs, Timothy Harris
National Security, Gerald Astaphan

HIGH COMMISSION FOR ST CHRISTOPHER AND NEVIS

10 Kensington Court, London W8 5DL
T 020-7937 9718
E sknhighcomm@btconnect.com
High Commissioner, HE James Ernest Williams, *apptd* 2001

BRITISH HIGH COMMISSIONER

HE Duncan Taylor, *apptd* 2005, resident at Bridgetown, Barbados

ECONOMY AND TRADE

The sugar industry was the mainstay of the economy for over 300 years but was closed down in 2005 after decades of losses at the state-run sugar company. Tourism (the chief source of foreign exchange), offshore financial services and light manufacturing – concentrating on distilling, food processing, clothing and electronics – are being developed; services now account for 71 per cent of GDP, industry for 26 per cent and agriculture for 3 per cent. The economy of Nevis relies on farming, but a sea-island cotton industry is being developed for export. The main trading partners are the USA, Trinidad and Tobago and the UK. Principal exports are machinery, foodstuffs, electronic equipment, beverages and tobacco. The main imports are machinery, manufactured goods, foodstuffs and fuels.
GNI – US$369m; US$7,840 per capita (2005)
ANNUAL AVERAGE GROWTH OF GDP – 4.9 per cent (2005 est)
INFLATION RATE – 8.7 per cent (2005 est)
TOTAL EXTERNAL DEBT – US$314m (2004)

BALANCE OF PAYMENTS

Trade – US$113m deficit (2002)
Current Account – US$124m deficit (2002)

Trade with UK	*2005*	*2006*
Imports from UK	£6,784,000	£7,217,000
Exports to UK	£2,804,000	£383,000

COMMUNICATIONS

The islands have a total of 320km of roads, of which 138km are surfaced, and 50km of narrow-gauge railways on St Christopher that served the sugar cane plantations. Basseterre is a port of registry and has deep-water harbour facilities. There are two airports; that on St Christopher can take most large jet aircraft, and Nevis' airport can take small aircraft and has night-time landing facilities. The sea ferry route from Basseterre to Charlestown is 18km. There are modern telecommunications systems.

ST LUCIA

AREA – 616 sq. km
CAPITAL – Castries; population, 37,963 (2001)
CURRENCY – East Caribbean dollar (EC$) of 100 cents
POPULATION – 168,458 rising at 1.29 per cent per year (2006 est)
RELIGION – Roman Catholicism (67 per cent) (est)
LANGUAGE – English (official), French patois
POPULATION DENSITY – 270 per sq. km (2005)
URBAN POPULATION – 31.3 per cent (2005 est)
MEDIAN AGE (years) – 25.7 (2006 est)
NATIONAL ANTHEM – 'Sons and Daughters of Saint Lucia'
NATIONAL DAY – 22 February (Independence Day)
LIFE EXPECTANCY (years) – 73.84 (2006 est)
MORTALITY RATE – 5.08 (2006 est)
BIRTH RATE – 19.68 (2006 est)
INFANT MORTALITY RATE – 13.17 (2006 est)
DEATH PENALTY – Yes
LITERACY RATE – 90.1 per cent (2004 est)

CLIMATE AND TERRAIN

St Lucia, the second largest of the Windward group, is 43.5km in length, with an extreme breadth of 22.5km. The terrain is mountainous, with elevation extremes that range from 950m (Mt Gimie) at the highest point to 0m (Caribbean Sea) at the lowest. The volcanic peaks of Gros Piton and Petit Piton were declared a UNESCO World Heritage Site in 2004. The climate is tropical and there is a wet season from June to September. The average daily temperature is 25°C.

HISTORY AND POLITICS

Originally inhabited by Arawak Indians and then settled by Carib Indians from AD 800, the island was sighted by Columbus in 1502. French settlement began in 1635 but control was disputed with Britain from 1659 until 1814, when the island was ceded to Britain. It achieved internal self-government in 1967 and became independent within the Commonwealth on 22 February 1979.

The St Lucia Labour Party, in power since 1997, lost the 2006 general election to the United Workers Party, which formed a government under Sir John Compton; he became ill in May 2007 and Stephenson King became acting prime minister.

POLITICAL SYSTEM

Under the 1979 constitution, the head of state is the British monarch, represented by a governor-general appointed on the advice of the prime minister. The bicameral parliament consists of the house of assembly and the senate. The senate has 11 members, six appointed by the government, three by the opposition and two by the governor-general. The house of assembly, which serves for a five-year term, has 17 elected members and an appointed speaker. The prime minister, who is responsible to parliament, and the cabinet are appointed by the governor-general.
Governor-General, HE Dame Pearlette Louisy, *apptd* 1997

SELECTED GOVERNMENT MEMBERS *as at July 2007*
Prime Minister, Sir John Compton
Finance, External Affairs, Home Affairs, Stephenson King
Economic Affairs, Ausbert d'Auvergne

HIGH COMMISSION FOR ST LUCIA
1 Collingham Gardens, London SW5 0HW
T 020-7370 7123 E hcslu@btconnect.com
High Commissioner, HE Emmanuel Cotter, MBE, *apptd* 1998

BRITISH HIGH COMMISSIONER
HE Duncan Taylor, *apptd* 2005, resident at Bridgetown, Barbados

ECONOMY AND TRADE

The economy was dependent on bananas (which still account for about 40 per cent of export earnings), but has been diversified to compensate for the ending of preferential access to EU markets in 1999. Offshore financial services and tourism have developed, and the manufacturing sector is the most diverse in the Caribbean, processing agricultural products, assembling electronic components and producing clothing, beverages and corrugated cardboard boxes. Services now account for 80 per cent of GDP, industry for 15 per cent and agriculture for 5 per cent.

The main trading partners are the USA, France, the UK and China. Principal exports are bananas, clothing, cocoa, vegetables, fruit and coconut oil. The main imports are foodstuffs, manufactured goods, machinery, transport equipment, chemicals and fuels.
GNI – US$744m (2005); US$4,580 per capita (2005)
ANNUAL AVERAGE GROWTH OF GDP – 5.1 per cent (2005 est)
INFLATION RATE – 2.9 per cent (2005 est)
UNEMPLOYMENT – 20 per cent (2003 est)
TOTAL EXTERNAL DEBT – US$257m (2004)
IMPORTS – US$600m (2005)
EXPORTS – US$100m (2003)

BALANCE OF PAYMENTS
Trade – US$207m deficit (2002)
Current Account – US$104m deficit (2002)

Trade with UK	*2005*	*2006*
Imports from UK	£17,153,000	£27,166,000
Exports to UK	£13,837,000	£16,678,000

COMMUNICATIONS

St Lucia contains around 910km of roads, of which 48km are surfaced. The island has two airports, at Castries and Vieux Fort. Castries also has a deep-water harbour. There are modern telecommunications systems.

MEDIA

The television and radio outlets are mainly privately owned. The government operates a radio network, which broadcasts in English and Creole. The island has two main newspapers, *The Star* and *The Voice,* both published three times a week.

ST VINCENT AND THE GRENADINES

AREA – 389 sq. km
CAPITAL – Kingstown; population, 26,097 (2003 est)
CURRENCY – East Caribbean dollar (EC$) of 100 cents
POPULATION – 117,848 rising at 0.26 per cent per year (2006 est)
RELIGION – Protestantism (30 per cent), Roman Catholicism (9 per cent) (est)
LANGUAGE – English (official), French patois
POPULATION DENSITY – 305 per sq. km (2005)
URBAN POPULATION – 60.5 per cent (2005 est)
MEDIAN AGE (years) – 26.9 (2006 est)
NATIONAL ANTHEM – 'St Vincent, Land So Beautiful'
NATIONAL DAY – 27 October (Independence Day)
LIFE EXPECTANCY (years) – 73.85 (2006 est)
MORTALITY RATE – 5.98 (2006 est)
BIRTH RATE – 16.18 (20065 est)
INFANT MORTALITY RATE – 14.4 (2006 est)
DEATH PENALTY – Yes

CLIMATE AND TERRAIN

The state, which lies in the Windward group, includes some of the northern Grenadines, a chain of small islands stretching 64km across the eastern Caribbean Sea between Grenada and St Vincent; the larger of these include Bequia, Canouan, Mayreau, Mustique, Union Island, Petit St Vincent and Prune Island. St Vincent itself has volcanic mountains, which are densely forested. Elevation extremes range from 1,234m (La Soufriére volcano) at the highest point to 0m (Caribbean Sea) at the lowest. The climate is tropical with an average daily temperature of 28°C.

HISTORY AND POLITICS

St Vincent was discovered by Christopher Columbus in 1498. It was granted by Charles I to the Earl of Carlisle in 1627 but British settlement did not begin until 1762, and was resisted by the French and the native Caribs. It was recognised as a British colony by the French in 1783. A Carib uprising in 1795–7 resulted in thousands of Caribs being deported. It became internally self-governing in 1969 and achieved full independence as St Vincent and the Grenadines on 27 October 1979.

An early election was called in 2001 after anti-government protests and strikes in 2000 over proposals to increase the pensions of parliamentarians. It was won decisively by the opposition Unity Labour Party (ULP); the ULP was returned for a second term in the 2005 general election.

POLITICAL SYSTEM

Under the 1979 constitution, the head of state is the British monarch, represented by a governor-general appointed on the advice of the prime minister. The unicameral house of assembly has 21 members: 15 directly elected for a five-year term and six senators appointed by the governor-general (four on the advice of the government and two on the advice of the opposition). The prime minister, who is responsible to the house of assembly, and the cabinet are appointed by the governor-general.

Governor-General, Sir Frederic Ballantyne, GCMG, *apptd* 2002

SELECTED GOVERNMENT MEMBERS *as at July 2007*
Prime Minister, Finance, Economy, National Security, Ralph Gonsalves
Deputy Prime Minister, Foreign Affairs, Louis Straker

HIGH COMMISSION FOR ST VINCENT AND THE GRENADINES
10 Kensington Court, London W8 5DL
T 020-7565 2874
E info@svghighcom.co.uk
High Commissioner, HE Cenio E. Lewis, *apptd* 1998

BRITISH HIGH COMMISSIONER
HE Duncan Taylor, *apptd* 2005, resident at Bridgetown, Barbados

ECONOMY AND TRADE

The economy was based on bananas (which still account for 39 per cent of exports) but since the ending of preferential access to EU markets in 1999, efforts have been made to diversify. Tourism, the development of which has been hampered by drug-related crime, manufacturing and offshore banking services have all expanded. Services now account for 64 per cent of GDP, industry for 26 per cent and agriculture for 10 per cent.

The main trading partners are the USA, the UK, Trinidad and Tobago and other Caribbean countries. Principal exports are bananas, vegetables, starch and tennis racquets. The main imports are foodstuffs, machinery and equipment, chemicals, fertilisers, minerals and fuel.

GNI – US$421m (2005); US$3,530 per capita (2005)
ANNUAL AVERAGE GROWTH OF GDP – 4.9 per cent (2005 est)
INFLATION RATE – 1 per cent (2005 est)
UNEMPLOYMENT – 15 per cent (2001 est)
TOTAL EXTERNAL DEBT – US$223m (2004)
IMPORTS – US$240m (2005)
EXPORTS – US$40m (2005)

BALANCE OF PAYMENTS
Trade – US$117m deficit (2002)
Current Account – US$42m deficit (2002)

Trade with UK	*2005*	*2006*
Imports from UK	£7,396,000	£8,863,000
Exports to UK	£7,958,000	£7,902,000

COMMUNICATIONS

The islands have around 829km of roads, of which 580km are surfaced. The main harbour is at Kingstown, which is a port of registry for shipping. There are six airports, although none can accommodate international flights.

MEDIA

The press is privately owned, and its freedom to criticise the government is guaranteed by the constitution. Most newspapers are published weekly. There are several private radio stations and a national radio service which is partly government-funded. Television broadcasting is operated by the St Vincent and the Grenadines Broadcasting Corporation.

SAMOA

Malo Sa'oloto Tuto'atasi o Samoa – Independent State of Samoa

AREA – 2,944 sq. km
CAPITAL – Apia; population, 38,836 (2001), on Upolu.
MAJOR TOWNS – Vaitele; Faleeasl'u; Vallele

CURRENCY – Tala (S$) of 100 sene
POPULATION – 176,908 falling at 0.2 per cent per year (2006 est). Samoans are a Polynesian people, though the population also includes other Pacific Islanders, Euronesians, Chinese and Europeans
RELIGION – Christianity (99 per cent) (est)
LANGUAGE – English (official), Samoan
POPULATION DENSITY – 65 per sq. km (2005)
URBAN POPULATION – 22.5 per cent (2005 est)
MEDIAN AGE (years) – 25.2 (2006 est)
NATIONAL ANTHEM – 'The Banner of Freedom'
NATIONAL DAY – 1 June (Independence Day)
LIFE EXPECTANCY (years) – 71 (2006 est)
MORTALITY RATE – 6.62 (2006 est)
BIRTH RATE – 16.43 (2006 est)
INFANT MORTALITY RATE – 26.85 (2006 est)
DEATH PENALTY – No (abolished 2004)
LITERACY RATE – 98.7 per cent (2004 est)

CLIMATE AND TERRAIN

Samoa consists of the islands of Savai'i, Upolu, Apolima, Manono, Fanuatapu, Namua, Nuutele, Nuulua and Nuusafee in the south Pacific Ocean. All the islands are mountainous and volcanic, with elevation extremes ranging from 1,857m (Mauga Silisili) at the highest point to 0m (Pacific Ocean) at the lowest. The climate is tropical with a wet season from November to April. Average temperatures range between 22 and 30°C all year round.

HISTORY AND POLITICS

Inhabited since *c.*1000 BC, Samoa was visited by Dutch traders and French explorers in the 18th century. In 1889, Germany took control of the nine western islands (Western Samoa) and the USA of the other Samoan islands (American Samoa). Western Samoa was occupied by New Zealand on the outbreak of the First World War and became a mandated territory administered by New Zealand from 1920. Internal self-government was established in 1959, and Western Samoa became fully independent on 1 June 1962. The state was treated as a member country of the Commonwealth until its formal admission in 1970. In 1997 the state changed its name to the Independent State of Samoa.

The Human Rights Protection Party, which has been in power since 1981, remained the largest party in the legislature after the 2006 election; it won 35 seats, the Samoan National Development Party won 10 seats and independents won four. The head of state for life, Malietoa Tanumafili, died in May 2007; his successor, the former prime minister Tuiatua Tupua Tamasese Efi, was elected the following month.

POLITICAL SYSTEM

Under the 1962 constitution, the head of state is an elected monarch whose functions are analogous to those of a constitutional monarch. Initially two of the four paramount chiefs held the office jointly for life and when one died in 1963, Malietoa Tanumafili II became head of state for life until his death in May 2007. In future, the monarch will be elected by the legislative assembly for a five-year term. The unicameral legislative assembly, *Fono,* has 49 members elected for a five-year term; only selected clan leaders, the Matai, may stand for election. The prime minister is appointed by the monarch on the recommendation of the legislative assembly and appoints the cabinet.

HEAD OF STATE

Head of State, Tuiatua Tupua Tamasese Efi, *elected* 16 June 2007, *sworn* in 20 June 2007

SELECTED GOVERNMENT MEMBERS *as at July 2007*

Prime Minister, Foreign Affairs, Tuilaepa Sailele Malielegaoi
Deputy Prime Minister, Finance, Misa Telefoni Retzlaff
Revenue, Tuuu Anasii Leota

HIGH COMMISSION FOR THE INDEPENDENT STATE OF SAMOA

20 avenue de l'Oree, 1000 Brussels, Belgium
T (+32) (2) 660 8454
E samoanembassy@skynet.be
High Commissioner, HE Tuala Falani Chan Tung, *apptd* 2006

BRITISH HIGH COMMISSIONER

HE George Fergusson, CVO, *apptd* 2006, resident at Wellington, New Zealand

ECONOMY AND TRADE

The economy is underdeveloped and dependent on fishing, agriculture (which is vulnerable to cyclones), remittances from migrant workers and international aid. Agriculture generates 11 per cent of GDP, employing about two-thirds of the labour force and supplying about 90 per cent of exports. Attempts at diversification are proving successful: manufacturing is branching out from small-scale processing of agricultural products into light manufacturing, and tourism and offshore financial services are being developed. Tourism has grown rapidly and now accounts for about 25 per cent of GDP. The main trading partners are Australia, New Zealand, the USA and American Samoa. Principal exports are fish, coconut oil and cream, copra, taro, vehicle parts, garments and beer. The main imports are machinery, industrial supplies and foodstuffs.

GNI – US$373m (2005); US$2,020 per capita (2005)
ANNUAL AVERAGE GROWTH OF GDP – 5.5 per cent (2005 est)
INFLATION RATE – 3.3 per cent (2005)
TOTAL EXTERNAL DEBT – US$177m (2004)
IMPORTS – US$187m (2005)
EXPORTS – US$12m (2005)

BALANCE OF PAYMENTS

Trade – US$175m deficit (2005)
Current Account – US$29m deficit (2005)

Trade with UK	*2005*	*2006*
Imports from UK	£534,000	£64,000
Exports to UK	£858,000	£453,000

COMMUNICATIONS

There are 2,300km of roads, of which 332km are surfaced. Upolu contains the harbours of Apia and Mulifanua, and Savai'i the harbour of Salelologa. There are four airports, including an international airport 35km west of Apia on Upolu.

MEDIA

There are two daily papers, one weekly and one fortnightly. The press is generally free to report as it chooses, although the *Samoa Observer* has been sued by the government for reporting about alleged corruption. The government operates the sole TV service, Televise

Samoa, and there are three FM radio stations and one state-run commercial radio service.

SAN MARINO

Repubblica di San Marino – Republic of San Marino

AREA – 61.2 sq. km. Neighbour: Italy
CAPITAL – San Marino; population, 2,294 (1996 est), on the slope of Monte Titano
CURRENCY – Euro (€) of 100 cents
POPULATION – 29,251 rising at 1.26 per cent per year (2006 est)
RELIGION – Roman Catholicism (95 per cent) (est)
LANGUAGE – Italian (official)
POPULATION DENSITY – 470 per sq. km (2005)
URBAN POPULATION – 88.7 per cent (2005 est)
MEDIAN AGE (years) – 40.6 (2006 est)
NATIONAL ANTHEM – 'Inno Nazionale della Repubblica' ['National Anthem']
NATIONAL DAY – 3 September (Republic Day)
LIFE EXPECTANCY (years) – 81.71 (2006 est)
MORTALITY RATE – 8.17 (2006 est)
BIRTH RATE – 10.02 (2006 est)
INFANT MORTALITY RATE – 5.63 (2006 est)
DEATH PENALTY – No (abolished 1865)

CLIMATE AND TERRAIN

A landlocked enclave in central Italy, the republic lies in the foothills of the Apennines, 20km from the Adriatic Sea. Elevation extremes range from 755m (Mt Titano) at the highest point to 55m (Torrente Aussa) at the lowest. The climate is Mediterranean, characterised by cool winters and warm summers. Average annual rainfall is 762mm, while average temperatures range between -6°C in January to 25°C in June.

HISTORY AND POLITICS

The republic is said to have been founded in the fourth century by a Christian stonecutter seeking refuge from religious persecution. By the 12th century a self-governing commune was established, and a parliamentary constitution was adopted in 1600. The republic resisted papal claims and those of neighbouring dukedoms from the 15th to 18th centuries, and the papacy recognised its independence in 1631. In 1862 it signed a treaty with the newly united kingdom of Italy which recognised its integrity and sovereignty and accorded it the protection of Italy. San Marino became a member of the UN in 1992.

The Socialist Party (PSS) and the Party of Democrats (PdD), partners at various times in a number of coalition governments that have held office since 2001, merged to form the Party of Socialists and Democrats (PSD) in 2005. Following the 2006 election to the Grand and General Council, the Christian Democratic Party (PDCS) remained the largest party in the legislature, but a coalition government was formed by the PSD, United Left and Popular Alliance parties.

POLITICAL SYSTEM

The 1600 constitution has been amended several times. The joint heads of state are two captains-regent who are elected at six-monthly intervals (March and September) by the Great and General Council, taking office the month after the election. Executive power is vested in the captains-regent and the Congress of State (cabinet), which is also elected by the Great and General Council. The latter, a unicameral legislature, has 60 members, directly elected for a five-year term. The Council of Twelve forms in certain cases a supreme court of justice.

HEADS OF STATE *as at July 2007*
Captain-Regent, Alessandro Mancini
Captain-Regent, Alessandro Rossi

SELECTED GOVERNMENT MEMBERS *as at July 2007*
Finance, Budget, Stefano Macina
Foreign and Political Affairs, Fiorenzo Stolfi
Internal Affairs, Valeria Ciavatta (AP)

EMBASSY OF THE REPUBLIC OF SAN MARINO
c/o Consulate of the Republic of San Marino,
Flat 51, 162 Sloane Street, London SW1X 9BS
T 020-7823 4762
Ambassador Extraordinary and Plenipotentiary, HE Countess Marina Meneghetti de Camillo, *apptd* 2002, resident at Rome, Italy

BRITISH AMBASSADOR
HE Sir Ivor Roberts, KCMG, *apptd* 2003, resident at Rome, Italy

BRITISH CONSULATE-GENERAL FOR SAN MARINO
Lungarno Corsini 2, 50123 Florence
T (+39) (55) 284 133
Consul-General, Moira Macfarlane

ECONOMY AND TRADE

Tourism is the basis of the economy, contributing over 50 per cent of GDP. Postage stamps and coins also generate significant revenue. The principal agricultural products are wine, cheeses, cereals and fruits, and the other main industries are banking and the manufacture of clothing, electronics and ceramics. The enclave is in a customs union with the EU.

ANNUAL AVERAGE GROWTH OF GDP – 2.3 per cent (2002 est)
INFLATION RATE – −1.7 per cent (2001)
UNEMPLOYMENT – 2.6 per cent (2001)

Trade with UK	*2005*	*2006*
Imports from UK	£9,991,000	£6,818,000
Exports to UK	£5,168,000	£5,085,000

MEDIA

San Marino has one state-run radio and television station. The two daily newspapers are *La Tribuna Sammarinese* and *San Marino Oggi.*

SAO TOME AND PRINCIPE

Republica Democratica de Sao Tome e Principe – Democratic Republic of Sao Tome and Principe

AREA – 1,001 sq. km
CAPITAL – Sao Tome; population, 49,957 (2001)
CURRENCY – Dobra of 100 centavos
POPULATION – 193,413 rising at 3.15 per cent per year (2006 est)
RELIGION – Roman Catholicism (80 per cent), Protestantism (15 per cent), Islam (3 per cent) (est). An estimated 2 per cent of the population is atheist.
LANGUAGE – Portuguese (official)

POPULATION DENSITY – 163 per sq. km (2005)
URBAN POPULATION – 37.9 per cent (2005 est)
MEDIAN AGE (years) – 16.2 (2006 est)
NATIONAL ANTHEM – 'Independencia Total' ['Total Independence']
NATIONAL DAY – 12 July (Independence Day)
LIFE EXPECTANCY (years) – 67.31 (2006 est)
MORTALITY RATE – 6.47 (2006 est)
BIRTH RATE – 40.25 (2006 est)
INFANT MORTALITY RATE – 41.83 (2006 est)
DEATH PENALTY – No (abolished 1990)
POPULATION BELOW POVERTY LINE – 54 per cent (2004 est)

CLIMATE AND TERRAIN

The republic consists of the islands of Sao Tome, Principe and several smaller islands in the Gulf of Guinea, off the west coast of Africa. All the islands are volcanic, thickly forested and fertile. Elevation extremes range from 2,024m (Pico de Sao Tome) at the highest point to 0m (Atlantic Ocean) at the lowest. The climate is tropical with a wet season from October to May. Average daily temperatures are an almost constant 30°C.

HISTORY AND POLITICS

The uninhabited islands were discovered by the Portuguese between 1469 and 1472, and settlement began in 1493. Plantations were established that became important producers of sugar cane, cocoa and coffee in the 18th and 19th centuries. Resistance to Portuguese rule began in the 1950s. The islands gained independence from Portugal in July 1975 and became a one-party state under the rule of the Movement for the Liberation of São Tomé and Príncipe (MLSTP). The government nationalised the plantations and formed close links with the communist bloc. These were scaled down in the 1980s as the economy deteriorated and in 1990 the MLSTP abandoned Marxism and introduced a democratic constitution. The first multiparty elections were held in 1991. Democracy has brought a degree of political instability, and tensions have been heightened recently by disagreements over how to use the expected revenue from exploitation of offshore oil reserves.

President Fradique de Menezes was deposed briefly in July 2003 in a military coup that occurred while he was out of the country. He was reinstated a week later following negotiations and in September 2003 appointed a new prime minister and a government comprising members of the MLSTP-PSD and the Force for Change Democratic Movement-Democratic Convergence Party (MDFM-PCD) coalition. In the 2006 legislative election, the MDFM-PCD became the largest party in the legislature, with 23 seats, and formed a government. President de Menezes won the presidential election with 60 per cent of the vote.

POLITICAL SYSTEM

Under the 1990 constitution, the head of state is the president, who is directly elected for a five-year term, renewable only once. The unicameral *Assembleia Nacional* (national assembly) has 55 members, directly elected for a four-year term. The prime minister is appointed by the president and appoints the cabinet. Since 1995 Principe has been internally self-governing, with an eight-member regional council.

HEAD OF STATE

President and Commander-in-Chief of the Armed Forces, Fradique de Menezes, *elected* 29 July 2001, *sworn in* 3 September 2001, *re-elected* July 2006

SELECTED GOVERNMENT MEMBERS *as at July 2007*

Prime Minister, Tomé Vera Cruz
Defence, Lt-Col. Oscar Aguiar Sacramento Sousa
Economy, Cristina Maria Fernandes Dias
Foreign Affairs, Carlos Gustavo dos Anjos

EMBASSY OF SÃO TOMÉ AND PRÍNCIPE

175 avenue de Tervuren, 1150 Brussels, Belgium
T (+32) (2) 734 8966
E ambassade@saotomeeprincipe.be
Ambassador Extraordinary and Plenipotentiary, vacant

BRITISH AMBASSADOR

HE Ralph Publicover, *apptd* 2005, resident at Luanda, Angola

ECONOMY AND TRADE

Economic mismanagement and over-dependency on cocoa have contributed to a large foreign debt that stood at about US$318m (£159m) in 2002. A debt-reduction package worth about US$200m (£100m) was agreed with the IMF and World Bank in 2000, and further support under the heavily indebted poor countries programme was received in 2006. The government is encouraging diversification away from cocoa: tourism is being promoted, and the exploitation of recently discovered offshore oil reserves in the Gulf of Guinea is expected to generate considerable revenue in the future. Most of the population is engaged in subsistence farming and fishing, and 54 per cent live below the poverty line. The principal trading partners are the Netherlands, Portugal and the USA. Principal exports are cocoa (80 per cent), copra, coffee and palm oil. The main imports are machinery and electrical equipment, foodstuffs and fuels.
GNI – US$68m; US$440 per capita (2005)
ANNUAL AVERAGE GROWTH OF GDP – 6 per cent (2004 est)
INFLATION RATE – 15.2 per cent (2005 est)
TOTAL EXTERNAL DEBT – US$318m (2002)

Trade with UK	*2005*	*2006*
Imports from UK	£697,000	£319,000
Exports to UK	£100,000	£133,000

COMMUNICATIONS

There are 320km of roads, 218km of which are surfaced but in poor condition. There are two airports, and the ports are Santo Antonio and Sao Tome. The telephone system is minimal in extent; in 2004 there were 7,000 main lines in use, and in 2005 there were 12,000 mobile phone subscribers and 20,000 internet users.

MEDIA

Freedom of expression is guaranteed by the constitution. The islands' only radio and television stations are state-run, but opposition parties are given free airtime. There are three privately owned newspapers and one which is published by the government.

SAUDI ARABIA

Al-Mamlakah al-Arabiyah as Suuddiyah – Kingdom of Saudi Arabia

AREA – 1,960,582 sq. km. Neighbours: the UAE and Qatar (east), Jordan, Iraq and Kuwait (north), Yemen and Oman (south)
CAPITAL – Riyadh (Ar-Riyad); population, 4,087,152 (2004)
MAJOR CITIES – Jeddah; Mecca; Medina; Dammam; At-Taif
CURRENCY – Saudi riyal (SR) of 20 qursh or 100 halala
POPULATION – 27,019,731 rising at 2.18 per cent per year (2006 est); includes some 5,576,076 non-nationals (2006 est)
RELIGION – Islam (100 per cent) (est)
LANGUAGE – Arabic (official)
POPULATION DENSITY – 12 per sq. km (2005)
URBAN POPULATION – 88.5 per cent (2005 est)
MEDIAN AGE (years) – 21.4 (2006 est)
NATIONAL ANTHEM – 'Aash al Maleek' ['The Royal Saudi Salut']
NATIONAL DAY – 23 September (Unification Day)
LIFE EXPECTANCY (years) – 75.67 (2006 est)
MORTALITY RATE – 2.58 (2006 est)
BIRTH RATE – 29.34 (2006 est)
INFANT MORTALITY RATE – 12.81 (2006 est)
DEATH PENALTY – Yes
CPI SCORE – 3.3 (2006)

CLIMATE AND TERRAIN

Saudi Arabia comprises most of the Arabian peninsula. The Nejd ('plateau') extends over the centre, including the Nafud and Dahna deserts. The Hejaz ('boundary') province runs along the Red Sea coast to Asir and contains the holy towns of Mecca and Medina. The Asir ('inaccessible') area is so named for its mountainous terrain, and, with the coastal plain of the Tihama, lies along the southern Red Sea coast from the Hejaz to the border with Yemen. The east and south-east of the country are low-lying and largely desert. Elevation extremes range from 3,133m (Jabal Sawda) at the highest point to 0m (Persian Gulf) at the lowest. The climate is hot, dry and extremely humid during the summer between May and September. Average temperatures in Riyadh range from 21°C in January to 42°C in July.

HISTORY AND POLITICS

The Arabian peninsula was the birthplace of the Muslim faith in the seventh century and the base from which the religion and a Muslim Empire expanded, eventually stretching from India to Spain. When this empire declined in the 12th century, Arabia became isolated and internally divided. The rise of the al-Saud family began in the 18th century, when it united the Nejd in support of the Wahhabi religious movement. The modern state was formed in 1932 when the head of the dynasty, Abd-al Aziz al-Saud (often known as Ibn Saud), united the four tribal provinces of the Hejaz, Asir, Najd and Al Hasa; the Kingdom of Saudi Arabia was proclaimed on 23 September 1932.

The ruling family preserved stability for many years by suppressing dissent and resisting calls for greater democracy, with some of its actions raising international concerns over human rights abuses. Internal tension grew in the 1990s because of the continuing presence of foreign, particularly US, troops in the country after the 1991 Gulf War who then became terrorist targets. Despite the redeployment of the troops to Qatar in early 2003, the frequency of attacks increased following the start of the Iraq war in 2003 and included Saudi as well as foreign victims. Some dissident groups are believed to have links with al-Qaida. Since 2003 demand for political reform has grown and become more militant. In 2005, the country's first nationwide elections were held for half the seats on municipal councils, with voting by universal male suffrage.

King Abdullah acceded after the death of his half-brother King Fahd in August 2005; he had carried out many of the king's official functions after King Fahd suffered a debilitating stroke in 1996.

POLITICAL SYSTEM

There is no written constitution; constitutional practice is provided for by articles of government based on the Koran *(Qur'an)* and the teachings and sayings of the Prophet Muhammad *(Sunnah)* and issued by royal decree. In 1992 the king announced a new system of government based on Shariah law and including rules to protect personal freedoms.

Saudi Arabia is a hereditary monarchy. The line of succession passes from brother to brother in the al-Saud family according to age; all sons and grandsons of Abd-al Aziz al-Saud must be consulted before a new king accedes to the throne. The king is head of government and appoints the council of ministers (established in 1953), whose term of office was fixed in 1993 at four years.

There is no legislature; the *Majlis-al-Shura* (consulative council) was established in 1993. It debates policy in the areas of the budget, defence, foreign and social affairs, and makes recommendations to the king; in 2003 its powers were widened and it is now permitted to propose legislation without the king's permission. The council's 150 members are appointed by the king and serve a four-year term. Its decisions are taken by majority vote. There are no political parties.

In 1993 the country was reorganised into 13 provinces: Al-Jawf, Asir, Al-Madinah, Al Qassim, Baha, Eastern, Ha'il, Al-Hududash Shamaliyah Jizan, Makkah, Najran, Riyadh and Tabuk. Each province has a governor appointed by the king and a council of prominent local citizens to advise the governor on local government, budgetary and planning issues.

HEAD OF STATE

HM The King of Saudi Arabia, Custodian of the Two Holy Mosques, Prime Minister, Commander of the National Guard, King Abdullah ibn Abdul Aziz al-Saud, *born* 1923, *succeeded* 2 August 2005
HRH Crown Prince, Deputy Prime Minister, Defence, Prince Sultan ibn Abdul Aziz al-Saud

SELECTED GOVERNMENT MEMBERS *as at July 2007*

Interior, HRH Prince Nayef ibn Abdul Aziz al-Saud
Finance, Ibrahim ibn Abdel Aziz al-Assaf
Foreign Affairs, HRH Prince Saud al-Faisal ibn Abdul Aziz al-Saud
Economy, Khaled ibn Mohammad al-Qussaibi

ROYAL EMBASSY OF SAUDI ARABIA

30 Charles Street, London W1J 5DZ
T 020-7917 3000
Ambassador Extraordinary and Plenipotentiary, HE HRH Prince Mohamed bin Nawaf bin Abdulaziz, *apptd* 2005

BRITISH EMBASSY
PO Box 94351, Diplomatic Quarter, Riyadh 11693
T (+966) (1) 488 0077
Ambassador Extraordinary and Plenipotentiary, HE William Patey, CMG, *apptd* 2007

BRITISH COUNCIL
PO Box 58012, C-14, 3rd Floor, Al-Fazari Square, Diplomatic Quarter, Riyadh 11594
T (+966) (1) 483 1818 W www.britishcouncil.org/saudiarabia
Director, Jim Scarth

DEFENCE

The army has 910 main battle tanks, 3,190 armoured personnel carriers, over 970 armoured infantry fighting vehicles and 12 attack helicopters. The navy has 7 frigates, 65 patrol and coastal vessels and 19 armed helicopters at eight bases. The air force has 278 combat aircraft.

MILITARY BUDGET – US$25,400m (2005)
MILITARY PERSONNEL – 244,500: army 75,000, navy 15,500, air force 18,000, Air Defence Force 16,000; National Guard 100,000; paramilitaries 15,500

ECONOMY AND TRADE

The economy is based on oil extraction and processing, but since 1970 the government has used a series of five-year development plans to encourage diversification, and the non-oil sector now accounts for around 60 per cent of GDP. The 2000–5 development plan encouraged the growth of the private sector (now responsible for about 40 per cent of GDP) and an increase in the proportion of Saudi Arabian citizens in the workforce (over 35 per cent of workers are foreign nationals). The 2005–9 plan extends privatisation further, covering a wide range of infrastructure and services, including the development of mineral industries, housing and transport schemes, petrochemical plants, electricity generation, water supplies and desalination, telecommunications and ports. To promote diversification and foreign investment, Saudi Arabia joined the World Trade Organisation in 2005.

Oil extraction since the 1940s has brought great wealth. Proven oil reserves of 262 billion barrels account for about one-quarter of the world total, and recoverable gas reserves are estimated at over 6.5 trillion cubic metres. Depending on world prices, the oil and gas industry contributes around 45 per cent of GDP and about 75 per cent of government revenue. The main industries apart from oil extraction and refining include minerals (especially gold, iron ore and copper), production of ammonia, industrial gases, caustic soda, cement, fertiliser and plastics, commercial ship and aircraft repair and construction. Industry accounts for 67 per cent of GDP and the service sector for 30 per cent. Agriculture contributes 3 per cent but is limited by the terrain, although productivity has been increased by extensive irrigation, desalination and the use of aquifers. The main products are cereals, fruit, meat and dairy products.

The main export markets are the USA, Japan, South Korea and China; the leading suppliers of imports are the USA, Japan, Germany, China and the UK. Oil and petroleum products constitute 90 per cent of exports. The main imports are machinery and equipment, foodstuffs, chemicals, motor vehicles and textiles. Importation of alcohol, pork products and other items regarded as non-Islamic is banned.

GNI – US$289,200m (2005); US$12,510 per capita (2005)
ANNUAL AVERAGE GROWTH OF GDP – 6.5 per cent (2005 est)
INFLATION RATE – 0.4 per cent (2005 est)
TOTAL EXTERNAL DEBT – US$36,780m (2005 est)
IMPORTS – US$56,000m (2005)
EXPORTS – US$181,000m (2005)

BALANCE OF PAYMENTS
Trade – US$123,308m surplus (2005)
Current Account – US$87,131m surplus (2005)

Trade with UK	*2005*	*2006*
Imports from UK	£1,598,400,000	£1,676,209,000
Exports to UK	£1,838,558,000	£1,309,707,000

COMMUNICATIONS

Jeddah is the main cargo seaport on the Red Sea coast and Dammam on the Gulf coast. The main oil port (the world's largest) is Ras Tanura. There are 1,392km of railways, operated by the Saudi Government Railway Organisation, which link Riyadh with the Gulf ports; there are plans to build a railway from Jeddah to Damman. In 2000 the road network totalled 152,044km (of which 45,461km were surfaced), including a motorway system connecting all the cities and main towns. The 25km-long King Fahd Causeway connects the Eastern Province to Bahrain and is the world's second longest causeway. There are over 200 airports and airfields; the three international airports are at Riyadh, Jeddah (serving Mecca) and Damman. There is a modern telecommunications system; there were 4.5 million main telephone lines in use and 3.2 million internet users in 2006, and 13.3 million mobile phone subscribers in 2005.

EDUCATION AND HEALTH

With the exception of a few schools for expatriate children, all schools are supervised by the government and are segregated. There are universities in Jeddah, Mecca, Riyadh (branches in Abha and Qassim), Dammam (branch at Al-Hufuf) and Az-Zahran, and Islamic universities in Medina and Riyadh. There is great emphasis on vocational training, provided at literacy and artisan skill training centres and more advanced industrial, commercial and agricultural education institutes.

LITERACY RATE – 79.4 per cent (2004 est)
GROSS ENROLMENT RATIO (percentage of relevant age group) – primary 91 per cent; secondary 88 per cent; tertiary 28 per cent (2005 est)
HEALTH EXPENDITURE (per capita) – US$348 (2004)
HOSPITAL BEDS (per 1,000 people) – 2.2 (2000–5)

MEDIA AND CULTURE

Saudi Arabia's media is one of the most tightly controlled in the Middle East. Criticism of the government and royal family and the questioning of religious tenets are not tolerated.

The state-run Broadcasting Service of the Kingdom of Saudi Arabia (BSKSA) is responsible for all broadcasting, operating four TV networks. Private radio and TV stations cannot operate from Saudi soil, but the country is a key market for pan-Arab satellite and subscription-based broadcasters. Saudi newspapers are created by royal decree. There are 10 dailies and many magazines. Pan-Arab newspapers, subject to censorship, are also available. The government has invested heavily in creating security systems to block websites with material deemed unsuitable.

Saudi culture revolves around Islam – two of Islam's holiest sites are situated there and it considers itself the birthplace of the religion. Mecca was the site of the Prophet Muhammad's birth, and contains the Great Mosque, within which is the *Ka'abah* or sacred shrine of the Muslim religion. This is the focus of the annual *Hajj* ('pilgrimage'). Medina ('city of light'), some 300km north of Mecca, is celebrated as the first city to embrace Islam and as the burial place of the Prophet Muhammad.

SENEGAL

République du Sénégal – Republic of Senegal

AREA – 196,190 sq. km. Neighbours: Mauritania (north), Mali (east), Guinea-Bissau and Guinea (south), the Gambia (surrounded by Senegal)
CAPITAL – Dakar; population, 2,243,400 (2007 est)
MAJOR CITIES – Rufisque; Thiés; Kaoleck
CURRENCY – Franc CFA of 100 centimes
POPULATION – 11,987,121 rising at 2.34 per cent per year (2006 est); Wolof (43.3 per cent), Fula (23.8 per cent), Serer (14.7 per cent), Jola (3.7 per cent), Mandinka (3 per cent) (est)
RELIGION – Islam (94 per cent), Christianity (4 per cent) (est)
LANGUAGE – French (official), Wolof, Pulaar, Jola, Mandinka
POPULATION DENSITY – 61 per sq. km (2005)
URBAN POPULATION – 51 per cent (2005 est)
MEDIAN AGE (years) – 19.1 (2006 est)
NATIONAL ANTHEM – 'Pincez Tous vos Koras, Frappez les Balafons' ['All Pluck Your Koras, Strike the Balafons']
NATIONAL DAY – 4 April (Independence Day)
LIFE EXPECTANCY (years) – 59.25 (2006 est)
MORTALITY RATE – 9.42 (2006 est)
BIRTH RATE – 32.78 (2006 est)
INFANT MORTALITY RATE – 52.94 (2006 est)
HIV/AIDS ADULT PREVALENCE – 0.8 per cent (2003 est)
DEATH PENALTY – No (abolished 1967)
CPI SCORE – 3.3 (2006)
POPULATION BELOW POVERTY LINE – 54 per cent (2001 est)
MILITARY BUDGET – US$136m (2006 est)
MILITARY PERSONNEL – 13,620: army 11,900, navy 950, air force 770; paramilitaries 5,000
CONSCRIPTION DURATION – 24 months (selective)

CLIMATE AND TERRAIN

The terrain is generally low and rolling, with plains rising to foothills in the south-east. There is desert in the north and tropical forest in the south. Elevation extremes range from 581m (Nepen Diakha) at the highest point to 0m (Atlantic Ocean) at the lowest. The River Senegal runs close to the northern border and the River Gambia flows through the south-east of the county. The climate is tropical, with a wet season from June to September. Average temperatures in Dakar range from 18°C in January to 32°C in July.

HISTORY AND POLITICS

Senegal was part of the Mali Empire in the 14th to 15th centuries. The first European visitors were the Portuguese in 1445. The French established a fort at Saint-Louis in 1659 and European traders exported slaves, ivory, gold and other commodities from there in the 17th and 18th centuries. The interior was occupied by the French in the mid-19th century and the territory became part of French West Africa in 1902. It became an autonomous state in 1958 and achieved independence as part of the Federation of Mali in June 1960, seceding to form the Republic of Senegal in September 1960. In 1966 the country became a one-party state under the rule of the Senegalese Progressive Union (UPS), which changed its name to the Socialist Party (PS) in 1976. Although a three-party system was introduced in 1978, the PS dominated political life until 2000. In 1980 President Léopold Senghor, who had been in power since 1960, achieved the distinction of becoming the first African leader since independence to surrender power voluntarily, when he resigned in favour of his protege Abdou Diouf. Senegal joined with Gambia to form the Confederation of Senegambia from 1982 to 1989.

In the early 1980s a violent separatist insurgency began in the southern Casamance region led by the Movement of Democratic Forces of Casamance (MFDC). A 2001 peace agreement was not implemented because of splits and leadership changes among the separatists. Violence in the region increased during the 2001 election campaign, but subsequently declined. In 2003 the MFDC leader said that the secessionist war was over, and a peace agreement with the government was signed in 2004 after two years of relative calm.

The Socialist Party's 40 years of political domination ended in 2000 with the election of Abdoulaye Wade, leader of the Senegalese Democratic Party (PDS), as president. The 2001 legislative election was won by an alliance of 40 parties, the *Sopi* (Change) coalition, led by the PDS; the PS retained only ten seats. President Wade was re-elected in the first round of the presidential election in February 2007. The Sopi coalition retained its majority in the legislative election in June 2007.

POLITICAL SYSTEM

Under the 2001 constitution, the executive president is directly elected for a five-year term, renewable only once; President Wade's first term was seven years, the duration of the presidential term when he was elected in 2000. The national assembly, which has 120 members, directly elected for a five-year term. The legislature has been unicameral since the abolition of the senate in 2001, although in 2007 the national assembly voted to re-establish an upper chamber of 100 members elected for a five-year term; no date has been set for an election. The president appoints the prime minister, who nominates the other ministers.

HEAD OF STATE

President, Abdoulaye Wade, *elected* 19 March 2000, *sworn in* 1 April 2000, *re-elected* 25 February 2007

SELECTED GOVERNMENT MEMBERS *as at July 2007*

Prime Minister, Cheikh Hadjibou Soumare
Defence, Becaye Diop
Finance and Economy, Abdoulaye Diop
Interior, Ousmane Ngom
Foreign Affairs, Cheikh Tidiane Gadio

EMBASSY OF THE REPUBLIC OF SENEGAL

39 Marloes Road, London W8 6LA
T 020-7938 4048 W www.senegalembassy.com

Ambassador Extraordinary and Plenipotentiary, HE Gen. Mamadou Niang, *apptd* 2004

BRITISH EMBASSY
PO Box 6025, 20 rue du Docteur Guillet, Dakar
T (+221) 823 7392 E britemb@sentoo.sn
Ambassador Extraordinary and Plenipotentiary, HE Christopher Trott, *apptd* 2005

BRITISH COUNCIL
34–36 Blvd de la République, BP 6232, Dakar
T (+221) 822 2015/48 W www.britishcouncil.org/senegal
Director, Andrew McNab

ECONOMY AND TRADE

An economic reform programme begun in 1994 has resulted in growth in GDP averaging over 5 per cent a year since 1995 and the reduction of inflation. Even so, the country is poor, with over half the population living below the poverty line and unemployment at over 40 per cent. The country is dependent on foreign aid and had high foreign debt, although the IMF/World Bank heavily indebted poor countries programme has provided some debt relief, and Senegal was promised 100 per cent debt relief by the G8 countries in 2005.

Agriculture is the mainstay of the economy, engaging around 60 per cent of the workforce and contributing 18 per cent of GDP. The main industries are food and fish processing, phosphate mining, oil refining, production of fertiliser and construction materials, ship construction and repair, and tourism. Services account for 63 per cent of GDP and industry for 19 per cent. The export markets are Mali, India, EU countries and neighbouring states; imports come from France, Nigeria, Brazil and Thailand. The principal exports are fish, groundnuts (raw and processed), petroleum products, phosphates and cotton. Principal imports are foodstuffs, capital goods and fuels.
GNI – US$8,200m (2005); US$700 per capita (2005)
ANNUAL AVERAGE GROWTH OF GDP – 6.1 per cent (2005 est)
INFLATION RATE – 1.7 per cent (2005 est)
UNEMPLOYMENT – 48 per cent (2001 est)
TOTAL EXTERNAL DEBT – US$3,529m (2005 est)
IMPORTS – US$3,330m (2005)
EXPORTS – US$1,600m (2005)

BALANCE OF PAYMENTS
Trade – US$809m deficit (2003)
Current Account – US$437m deficit (2003)

Trade with UK	*2005*	*2006*
Imports from UK	£102,990,000	£190,924,000
Exports to UK	£7,974,000	£7,446,000

COMMUNICATIONS

Senegal has a road network of some 13,576km, of which 3,972km are surfaced. There are also 906km of railways and 1,000km of navigable waterways, mainly on the Senegal, Saloum and Casamance rivers. Dakar is the main port and the location of the principal airport; there are around 20 other airports and airfields. The telephone system is good although not extensive; in 2005 there were 267,000 main lines in use, 1.7 million mobile phone subscribers and 540,000 internet users.

EDUCATION AND HEALTH

LITERACY RATE – 39.3 per cent (2004 est)
GROSS ENROLMENT RATIO (percentage of relevant age group) – primary 88 per cent; secondary 26 per cent; tertiary 5 per cent (2005 est)
HEALTH EXPENDITURE (per capita) – US$39 (2004)
HOSPITAL BEDS (per 1,000 people) – 0.4 (2002)

MEDIA

The constitution guarantees media freedom, though some newspapers and radio stations have been penalised for featuring separatist leaders. RTS is the state-run broadcaster and produces two channels. There are many private radio stations, and subscription-based television is readily available. Publications must be registered as a formality, but foreign media circulate freely. There are at least five daily newspapers, of which one is state-owned.

SERBIA

Republika Srbija – Republic of Serbia

AREA – 88,361 sq. km. Neighbours: Hungary (north), Romania and Bulgaria (east), Macedonia and Albania (south), Montenegro, Bosnia and Hercegovina and Croatia (west)
CAPITAL – Belgrade; population, 1,574,050 (2004 est)
MAJOR CITIES – Novi Sad; Nis; Kragujevac
CURRENCY – Dinar of 100 paras
POPULATION – 9,396,411 rising at 0.03 per cent per year (2002); Serb (66 per cent), Albanian (17 per cent), Hungarian (3.5 per cent) (est)
RELIGION – Orthodox Christianity (78 per cent), Islam (5 per cent), Roman Catholicism (4 per cent), other Christian denominations (1 per cent) (est)
LANGUAGE – Serbian (official), Romanian, Hungarian, Slovak, Ukrainian, Croatian, Albanian (official in different regions)
POPULATION DENSITY – 79 per sq. km (2005)
MEDIAN AGE (years) – 40.4 (2006 est)
NATIONAL ANTHEM – 'Boze Pravde' ['God the Righteous']
NATIONAL DAY – 27 April (National Day)
LIFE EXPECTANCY (years) – 74.73 (2005 est)
MORTALITY RATE – 10.49 (2005 est)
BIRTH RATE – 12.12 (2005 est)
INFANT MORTALITY RATE – 12.89 (2005 est)
DEATH PENALTY – No (abolished 2002)
CPI SCORE – 3.0 (2006)
GROSS ENROLMENT RATIO (percentage of relevant age group) – primary 99 per cent; secondary 89 per cent; tertiary 36 per cent (2002 est)
HEALTH EXPENDITURE (per capita) – US$219 (2004)
HOSPITAL BEDS (per 1,000 people) – 6 (2004)

CLIMATE AND TERRAIN

The landlocked country has an extremely mountainous south, while the north is dominated by the low-lying plains of the Danube. The highest point is 2,656m (Daravica). The major rivers are the Danube, the Sava, the Tisa and the Morava. The climate is moderate and continental. Average temperatures in Belgrade range from 2°C in January to 18°C in July.

HISTORY AND POLITICS

The medieval kingdom of Serbia emerged from the rule of the Byzantine Empire in the 13th century to form a large and prosperous state in the Balkans. Defeat by the Turks in 1389 led to almost 500 years of Turkish rule. After gaining autonomy within the Ottoman Empire in 1815, Serbia became fully independent in 1878 and a kingdom in 1881. At the end of the First World War Serbia joined with the former Austro-Hungarian provinces of Slovenia, Croatia and Bosnia-Hercegovina and the kingdom of Montenegro to form the Kingdom of Serbs, Croats and Slovenes, which was renamed Yugoslavia in 1929. Yugoslavia was occupied by Axis forces in 1941 and reformed after liberation as a communist federal republic under the presidency of partisan leader Josip Tito in 1945. When the federation disintegrated in 1991–2, Serbia and Montenegro were left to form the rump Federal Republic of Yugoslavia (FRY), which was declared on 27 April 1992.

Slobodan Milosevic, president of Serbia from 1989 until 1996, supported various military and militia efforts to unite ethnic Serbs in neighbouring republics into a Greater Serbia. All of these efforts were ultimately unsuccessful. Milosevic dominated Serbian and federal politics in the 1990s, becoming president of the Federal Republic in 1997. His corrupt and repressive regime was ended by the 2000 federal elections, in which the Democratic Opposition of Serbia became the largest party in both chambers of the parliament and the Democratic Party of Serbia presidential candidate, Vojislav Kostunica, won the most votes. Milosevic's attempts to pervert the outcome of the presidential election and remain in power were met with mass demonstrations and strikes, forcing him to stand down. He was arrested in 2001 and extradited to the UN International Criminal Tribunal for the Former Yugoslavia, where his trial began in 2002; he died unexpectedly in 2006 while still on trial.

In March 2003 the Federal Republic of Yugoslavia was restructured into a union of Serbia and Montenegro, each with semi-independent status. After three years either republic could hold a referendum on whether to retain or end the union; Montenegro voted to become independent in May 2006 and the union was dissolved in June, with Serbia succeeding to the union's membership of international bodies.

The 2004 presidential election was invalidated owing to a low turnout and the chair of the parliament became acting president. In February 2004 the parliament voted to abolish the 50 per cent turnout needed to elect a president, and in June 2004 Boris Tadic, leader of the Democratic Party (DS), was elected president with 53 per cent of the vote. In the January 2007 legislative election, the nationalist Serbian Radical Party remained the largest party but without an overall majority. A new coalition government was formed by the DS, the Democratic Party of Serbia (DSS), the New Serbia and Serbian Renewal Movement alliance and the G-17 party, under the incumbent prime minister, Vojislav Kostunica of the DSS, in May.

INSURGENCY

The provinces of Vojvodina (population, 2 million, of whom 21 per cent are Hungarian) and Kosovo (population, 1.6 million, of whom 90 per cent are Albanian) were stripped of their autonomy in 1990. Following the break-up of Yugoslavia in 1991–2, many Hungarians and Croats fled or were expelled from Vojvodina and their homes allocated to Serb refugees from Croatia.

In Kosovo the loss of autonomy resulted in the progressive exclusion of the Albanian majority from public life. The Kosovars' decisive vote in a 1991 referendum for independence from both Serbia and Yugoslavia was declared illegal by the Serbian government, which tightened its control. Fighting between Kosovar nationalists and Serb forces peaked in the late 1990s, the Serbs beginning a renewed crackdown in 1998 which developed into a brutal and systematic process of ethnic cleansing. Over 800,000 people sought refuge in Albania, Macedonia or Montenegro (which, although part of the FRY, refused to become involved in the fighting), and over 500,000 were internally displaced. Despite international condemnation, the attacks continued until NATO intervened in March 1999, bombing military targets in Kosovo and Serbia. Serbia accepted a peace plan proposed by NATO and Russia in June 1999 and its forces withdrew. A NATO-led peacekeeping force was deployed and facilitated the disarming of the Kosovo Liberation Army and the return of over 850,000 refugees, but over 200,000 Kosovar Serbs have fled the province for fear of reprisals.

The ethnic Albanian Liberation Army of Precevo, Medvedja and Bujanovac launched attacks on Serbs in Albanian-populated areas of southern Serbia in November 2000. Their aim was to annex these areas to Kosovo. A ceasefire was signed in March 2001 after NATO agreed to permit federal forces to enter the demilitarised buffer zone which had been established on the Serbian side of the border with Kosovo in 1999.

Since June 1999, Kosovo has been under the administration of the UN's Interim Administration Mission in Kosovo (UNMIK). UNMIK established democratic institutions in 2001, when a 120-member legislative assembly for Kosovo was elected; the first presidential election was held in 2002. Fatmir Sejdiu was elected president in February 2006, in place of Ibrahim Rugova, who had died in office. Agim Ceku was appointed prime minister in March 2006 after the resignation of his predecessor.

In February 2007 the UN plan for Kosovo's eventual independence was announced. Independence is strongly opposed by the Serbian government.

POLITICAL SYSTEM

A new constitution was approved by referendum in October 2006. Under this, the president is directly elected for a five-year term, renewable only once. The unicameral national assembly has 250 members, directly elected for a four-year term. The prime minister is appointed by the president.

SELECTED GOVERNMENT MEMBERS *as at July 2007*

President, Boris Tadic, *elected* 27 June 2004, *took office* 11 July 2004
Prime Minister, Vojislav Kostunica
Deputy Prime Minister, Bozidar Djelic
Economy, Mladjan Dinkic
Interior, Dragan Jocic
Foreign Affairs, Vuk Jeremic

EMBASSY OF THE REPUBLIC OF SERBIA
28 Belgrave Square, London SW1X 8QB
T 020-7235 9049 W www.serbianembassy.org.uk
Ambassador Extraordinary and Plenipotentiary, vacant

BRITISH EMBASSY
Resavska 46, YU-11000 Belgrade
T (+381) (11) 264 5055
Ambassador Extraordinary and Plenipotentiary, HE Stephen Wordsworth, *apptd* 2006

BRITISH COUNCIL
Terazije 8/1, YU-11000 Belgrade
T (+381) (11) 302 3800 W www.britishcouncil.org/yugoslavia
Director, Andrew Glass

DEFENCE

The army has 962 main battle tanks, 288 armoured personnel carriers and 525 armoured infantry fighting vehicles. The air force has 101 combat aircraft and 45 armed helicopters.

MILITARY BUDGET – US$736m (2006)
MILITARY PERSONNEL – 39,686: army 33,186, air force 6,500; paramilitaries 35,000
CONSCRIPTION DURATION – Nine months

ECONOMY AND TRADE

Economic mismanagement, UN sanctions in the 1990s and damage to infrastructure and industry from NATO bombing in 1999 had reduced the economy to about 40 per cent of its 1990 size by 2000. Since 2000 governments have pursued economic reforms and international reintegration, obtained international support for economic restructuring and rescheduled payments or received debt relief on much of its foreign debt. Progress remains slow, and only the country's agricultural self-sufficiency has kept it afloat. Industrial production remains extremely low and there is high unemployment, estimated to be around 32 per cent. EU aid and negotiations on accession were suspended in 2005 because of Serbia's failure to surrender alleged war criminals for trial; the resumption of negotiations was announced in June 2007.

Agriculture accounts for 17 per cent of GDP and employs 30 per cent of the workforce. The main agricultural products are cereals, sugar beet, sunflowers, meat and milk. Industry includes production of sugar, paper and pulp, lead and agricultural, transport and electrical and communications equipment. Industry contributes 25 per cent of GDP and services 58 per cent. Principal exports are manufactured goods, food and livestock, machinery and transport equipment.

GDP – US$26,300m (2005); US$3,220 per capita (2005)
ANNUAL AVERAGE GROWTH OF GDP – 5.9 per cent (2005 est)
*INFLATION RATE – 15.5 per cent (2005 est)
UNEMPLOYMENT – 31.6 per cent (2005 est)
*TOTAL EXTERNAL DEBT – US$11,960m (2000 est)

Trade with UK	*2005*	*2006*
Imports from UK	£24,332,000*	£85,285,000
Exports to UK	£18,300,000*	£63,629,000

* Figures are for Serbia and Montenegro

COMMUNICATIONS

Serbia has some 37,887km of roads, around 23,937km of which are surfaced. There are also 4,135km of railways, linking Belgrade directly to Athens, Bucharest, Budapest, Istanbul, Ljubljana, Munich, Skopje, Sofia, Thessaloniki, Vienna and Zagreb. There are 587km of navigable waterways on the Danube and Sava rivers; the principal ports include Belgrade and Novi Sad on the Danube. The main international airport is at Belgrade.

Modernisation of the telephone system has been slow and rural services are not as good as those in urban areas. There were 2.7 million main lines in use in 2004, 5.2 million mobile phone subscribers in 2005 and 1.4 million internet users in 2006.

MEDIA

The ousting of Milosevic allowed the media much greater freedom and outlets proliferated. A media regulatory system is in operation and issues licences to the hundreds of private-sector radio and television broadcasters. The state-funded national broadcaster, RTS, aims to develop into a public service, and state-funded local and regional media outlets are to be privatised. Newspapers include the daily *Danas,* the weekly *Vreme* and *NIN.*

In Kosovo, a Temporary Media Commission (TMC), set up by the UN, has set out a code of conduct for journalists which aims to prevent incitement to hatred in the media.

SEYCHELLES

République des Seychelles/Repiblik Sesel – Republic of Seychelles

AREA – 455 sq. km
CAPITAL – Victoria; population, 24,970 (2002), on Mahé
CURRENCY – Seychelles rupee of 100 cents
POPULATION – 81,541 rising at 0.43 per cent per year (2006 est)
RELIGION – Roman Catholicism (77 per cent), Protestantism (7 per cent) (est)
LANGUAGE – English (official), Creole
POPULATION DENSITY – 184 per sq. km (2005)
URBAN POPULATION – 50.2 per cent (2005 est)
MEDIAN AGE (years) – 28.1 (2006 est)
NATIONAL ANTHEM – 'Koste Seselwa' ['Seychelles Unite']
NATIONAL DAY – 18 June (Constitution Day)
LIFE EXPECTANCY (years) – 72.08 (2006 est)
MORTALITY RATE – 6.29 (2006 est)
BIRTH RATE – 16.03 (2006 est)
INFANT MORTALITY RATE – 15.14 (2006 est)
DEATH PENALTY – No (abolished 1993)
CPI SCORE – 3.6 (2006)
MILITARY BUDGET – US$13m (2006 est)
MILITARY PERSONNEL – 200: army 200; paramilitaries 250
LITERACY RATE – 91.9 per cent (2004 est)

CLIMATE AND TERRAIN

Seychelles consists of 115 islands spread over 643,737 sq. km of the south-west Indian Ocean, north of Madagascar. There is a relatively compact granitic group of 32 islands, with high hills and mountains, of which Mahé is the largest and most populated (90 per cent of the population lives on Mahé), and an outlying coralline group, for the most part only a little above sea-level. Elevation extremes range from 905m (Morne Seychellois) at the highest point to 0m (Indian Ocean) at the lowest. The climate is tropical, with an average temperature of 26°C.

HISTORY AND POLITICS

The islands were first sighted by European navigators in the early 15th century and were proclaimed French territory in 1756. The Mahé group was settled as a dependency of Mauritius from 1770, but was captured by the British in 1794 and ceded to Britain in 1814. In 1903 these islands, together with the coralline group, were formed into a colony separate from Mauritius. On 29 June 1976, the islands became an independent republic. Following a coup d'état in 1977, when France-Albert

René became president, Seychelles became a one-party state ruled by the Seychelles People's Progressive Front (SPPF) in 1979. Opposition parties were permitted from 1991 and in 1993 President René reintroduced a multiparty democratic system. Power has remained with the SPPF under the pluralist system as it dominates the parliament and holds the presidency, although opposition parties are beginning to achieve a greater share of the vote.

In the 2001 presidential election, President René was re-elected with 54 per cent of the vote. He stepped down in 2004 and the rest of his term was served by the vice-president James Michel, who was elected president in July 2006 with 53.73 per cent of the vote. In the May 2007 legislative election, the SPPF retained its majority.

POLITICAL SYSTEM

Under the 1993 constitution, the executive president is directly elected for a five-year term, with a maximum of three consecutive terms. The unicameral national assembly has up to 34 members: 23 directly elected by constituencies and up to 11 allocated by proportional representation; members serve a five-year term. The council of ministers is appointed by the president.

HEAD OF STATE

President, Head of Government, Defence, Interior, Economy, James Michel, *assumed office* 14 April 2004
Vice-President, Joseph Belmont

SELECTED GOVERNMENT MEMBERS *As at July 2007*
Foreign Affairs, Patrick Pillay
Health and Social Affairs, MacSuzy Mondon

SEYCHELLES HIGH COMMISSION
51 avenue Mozart, F-75016 Paris, France
T (+33) (1) 4230 5747
High Commissioner, HE Callixte D'Offay, *apptd* 2004

BRITISH HIGH COMMISSION
PO Box 161, Oliaji Trade Centre, Victoria, Mahé
T (+248) 283 666 E bhcvictoria@fco.gov.uk
High Commissioner, HE Diana Skingle, *apptd* 2005

ECONOMY AND TRADE

Seychelles has prospered since independence owing to the development of the tuna fishing and tourism industries. Tourism now provides 70 per cent of foreign exchange earnings, making the economy vulnerable to downturns in this sector, the latest of which occurred in 2005 following the devastation of the 2004 Indian Ocean tsunami. Agriculture, fishing and small-scale manufacturing industries have been developed to diversify the economy, and the government is promoting offshore financial services. Public debt is very high, at 166 per cent of GDP. Apart from tourism and fishing, the main industries involve processing agricultural products and fish. The principal exports are canned tuna, frozen fish, cinnamon bark and copra. The principal imports are machinery and transport equipment, foodstuffs, petroleum products and chemicals.

GNI – US$691m (2005); US$8,180 per capita (2005)
ANNUAL AVERAGE GROWTH OF GDP – −3 per cent (2005 est)
TOTAL EXTERNAL DEBT – US$508m (2005 est)
IMPORTS – US$550m (2005)
EXPORTS – US$400m (2005)

BALANCE OF PAYMENTS
Trade – US$116m deficit (2004)
Current Account – US$28m deficit (2004)

Trade with UK	*2005*	*2006*
Imports from UK	£13,375,000	£16,522,000
Exports to UK	£59,341,000	£52,837,000

COMMUNICATIONS

There are around 458km of roads, most of which are surfaced. The main port is Victoria, and ferries run regularly between Mahé, Praslin and la Digue. Some 15 airports, eight with surfaced runways, serve the islands; the principal airport is at Mahé.

The telephone system serves all the islands. In 2005 there were 21,400 main lines in use, 57,000 mobile phone subscribers and 20,000 internet users.

MEDIA

Freedom of speech has improved since one-party rule was abolished in 1993, but the government continues to control most of the media and operates the only radio and television stations and the sole daily newspaper. Expensive licensing fees have discouraged the development of privately owned broadcast media, and the opposition weekly newspaper, *Regar,* has been sued regularly by the government. The BBC World Service and Radio France Internationale broadcast in the area.

SIERRA LEONE

Republic of Sierra Leone

AREA – 71,740 sq. km. Neighbours: Guinea (north, north-east), Liberia (south-east)
CAPITAL – Freetown; population, 772,873 (2004)
MAJOR TOWNS – Bo; Kenema
CURRENCY – Leone (Le) of 100 cents
POPULATION – 6,005,250 rising at 2.3 per cent per year (2006 est); Temne (30 per cent), Mende (30 per cent) (est)
RELIGION – Islam (60 per cent), Christianity (30 per cent), indigenous religions (10 per cent) (est)
LANGUAGE – English (official), Mende, Temne, Krio
POPULATION DENSITY – 77 per sq. km (2005)
URBAN POPULATION – 40.2 per cent (2005 est)
MEDIAN AGE (years) – 17.4 (2006 est)
NATIONAL ANTHEM – 'High We Exalt Thee, Realm of the Free'
NATIONAL DAY – 27 April (Independence Day)
LIFE EXPECTANCY (years) – 40.22 (2006 est)
MORTALITY RATE – 23.03 (2006 est)
BIRTH RATE – 45.76 (2006 est)
INFANT MORTALITY RATE – 160.39 (2006 est)
HIV/AIDS ADULT PREVALENCE – 7 per cent (2001 est)
DEATH PENALTY – Yes
CPI SCORE – 2.2 (2006)
POPULATION BELOW POVERTY LINE – 68 per cent (2001 est)
MILITARY BUDGET – US$27m (2006 est)
MILITARY PERSONNEL – 10,500

CLIMATE AND TERRAIN

The terrain rises from coastal mangrove swamps to wooded hill country, upland plateau and mountains in the east. Elevation extremes range from 1,948m (Bintimani) at the highest point to 0m (Atlantic Ocean) at the lowest. The climate is tropical, with a wet season from May to October. Average daily temperatures in Freetown are 30°C all year round.

HISTORY AND POLITICS

Coastal trading posts were established by the Portuguese in the 15th century and the British in the 17th century. In the late 18th century British philanthropists bought land to establish a settlement for liberated and escaped African slaves on the Freetown peninsula. In 1808 the settlement was declared a crown colony and became the main base in West Africa for enforcing the 1807 Act outlawing the slave trade. Africans from North America and the West Indies and Africans rescued from slave ships also settled there. In 1896 a protectorate was declared over the hinterland. In 1951 the colony of Freetown and the protectorate were united and on 27 April 1961 Sierra Leone became a fully independent state.

The country became a republic in 1971 with Siaka Stevens as its first president. Under Stevens it became a one-party state until 1991 when a multiparty democracy was enshrined in a new constitution under Joseph Momoh. This was aborted by a military coup in 1992. Civilian rule returned in 1996 with the election of Ahmad Tejan Kabbah as president, but his administration lasted only months before another short-lived coup in May 1997 required military intervention from the ECOWAS Monitoring Group, which eventually ousted the military regime. Kabbah returned as president in 1998 after international intervention drove out the rebels.

The transition to multiparty and civilian rule was complicated by the civil war with the Revolutionary United Front (RUF), which began in 1991. The Lomé peace accord, signed in 1999, created a power-sharing structure that gave the RUF amnesty and brought it into government. However, violence continued and the ceasefire collapsed in May 2000 despite the presence of the UN Mission to Sierra Leone. Further international intervention in 2000 led to the capture of Foday Sankoh, the RUF leader in Sierra Leone and Kabbah finally declared an end to the war in January 2002. An estimated 50,000 people were killed and thousands mutilated between 1991 and 2002. A UN-supported war crimes tribunal was set up in 2002 to try senior militia leaders from both sides in the civil war.

In the 2002 presidential election, President Kabbah was re-elected with 70 per cent of the vote. The simultaneous legislative election was won by the Sierra Leone People's Party (SLPP), with 83 seats. At the time of going to press, second rounds of voting were required in both the 2007 presidential and legislative elections.

POLITICAL SYSTEM

Under the 1991 constitution, the head of state is an executive president who is directly elected for a five-year term, renewable only once. The unicameral parliament has 124 members: 112 directly elected for a five-year term and 12 indirectly elected to represent the 12 provincial districts. The president appoints and chairs the cabinet.

HEAD OF STATE

President, Defence, Ahmad Tejan Kabbah, *elected* 15 March 1996, *re-elected* 14 May 2002
Vice-President, Solomon Berewa

SELECTED GOVERNMENT MEMBERS *as at July 2007*

Finance, John O. Benjamin
Foreign Affairs, Momodu Koroma
Internal Affairs, Pascal Egbenda
Economic Planning, Mohamed B. Daramy

SIERRA LEONE HIGH COMMISSION

41 Eagle Street, London WC1R 4TL
T 020-7404 0140
E info@slhc-uk.org.uk
High Commissioner, HE Melvin Humpah Chalobah, *apptd* 2006

BRITISH HIGH COMMISSION

Spur Road, Freetown
T (+232) (22) 232 961 E bhc@sierratel.sl
High Commissioner, HE Sarah MacIntosh, *apptd* 2006

BRITISH COUNCIL

PO Box 124, Tower Hill, Freetown
T (+232) (22) 222 223 W www.britishcouncil.org/sierraleone
Director, Tom Walsh

ECONOMY AND TRADE

The country has been devastated by a decade of civil war, and unemployment has increased with the demobilisation of former combatants. Economic activity has grown since the end of the war but the country depends on substantial foreign aid to offset its trade imbalance and support reconstruction. It benefited from having around 90 per cent of foreign debt written off in 2006.

There are significant mineral deposits, mainly diamonds, bauxite, rutile, iron and gold, and agricultural and fishery resources, although the lack of infrastructure hampers development. Diamonds account for about half of export earnings, but nearly 50 per cent of GDP is generated by agriculture, much of which is at subsistence level. Industry consists mainly of diamond mining, processing agricultural products, light manufacturing for the domestic market, oil refining and ship repair. The main export market is Belgium (over 60 per cent); the chief import suppliers are EU countries, Côte d'Ivoire, the USA and China. Principal exports are diamonds, rutile, cocoa, coffee and fish. The main imports are foodstuffs, machinery and equipment, fuels and lubricants and chemicals.

GNI – US$1,200m (2005); US$220 per capita (2005)
ANNUAL AVERAGE GROWTH OF GDP – 7.5 per cent (2005 est)
INFLATION RATE – 1 per cent (2002 est)
TOTAL EXTERNAL DEBT – US$1,610m (2003 est)
IMPORTS – US$340m (2005)
EXPORTS – US$160m (2005)

BALANCE OF PAYMENTS

Trade – US$98m deficit (2004)
Current Account – US$74m deficit (2004)

Trade with UK	*2005*	*2006*
Imports from UK	£26,141,000	£18,553,000
Exports to UK	£1,244,000	£4,374,000

COMMUNICATIONS

The railway system was phased out in 1974, but an extensive road network has been developed since; there are now 11,300km of roads in the country, although only 904km is surfaced. A bridge over the Mano river links Sierra Leone and Liberia. There is an international airport at Freetown and nine airfields around the country. Freetown, which has one of the world's largest natural harbours, is the main port and there are smaller ports at Pepel, Bonthe and Niti.

The fixed-line telephone system is poor and mobile phone distribution has grown rapidly. In 2002–5, there were about 24,000 main lines in use, 113,000 mobile phone subscriptions and 10,000 internet users.

EDUCATION AND HEALTH

Technical education is provided in the two government technical institutes, situated in Freetown and Kenema, in two trade centres and in the technical training establishments of the mining companies.

LITERACY RATE – 29.6 per cent (2004 est)
GROSS ENROLMENT RATIO (percentage of relevant age group) – primary 155 per cent; secondary 30 per cent; tertiary 2 per cent (2005 est)
HEALTH EXPENDITURE (per capita) – US$7 (2004)

MEDIA

Media freedom is limited by the government's use of the libel laws to restrict coverage of politically sensitive issues. Broadcasters also face the problem of unreliable electricity supplies and lack of advertising revenue. The UN Mission in Sierra Leone operates a number of radio services, and the BBC World Service and Radio France Internationale are broadcast from Freetown. Dozens of privately run newspapers are published in Freetown, despite low literacy levels.

SINGAPORE

Repablik Singapura/Xinjiapo Gongheguo – Republic of Singapore

AREA – 692.7 sq. km
CAPITAL – Singapore; population, 4,163,700 (2004)
CURRENCY – Singapore dollar (S$) of 100 cents
POPULATION – 4,492,150 rising at 1.42 per cent per year (2006 est); Chinese (76.8 per cent), Malay (13.9 per cent), Indian (7.9 per cent)
RELIGION – Buddhism (43 per cent), Islam (12 per cent), Christianity (12 per cent), Hinduism (3 per cent) (est). An estimated 15 per cent of the population is atheist
LANGUAGE – English, Mandarian, Tamil (all official), Malay, Hokkien, Teochew, Cantonese
POPULATION DENSITY – 6,302 per sq. km (2005)
URBAN POPULATION – 100 per cent (2005 est)
MEDIAN AGE (years) – 37.3 (2006 est)
NATIONAL ANTHEM – 'Majulah Singapura' ['May Singapore Progress']
NATIONAL DAY – 9 August (Independence Day)
LIFE EXPECTANCY (years) – 81.71 (2006 est)
MORTALITY RATE – 4.28 (2006 est)
BIRTH RATE – 9.34 (2006 est)
INFANT MORTALITY RATE – 2.29 (2006 est)
DEATH PENALTY – Yes
CPI SCORE – 9.4 (2006)
LITERACY RATE – 92.5 per cent (2004 est)
HEALTH EXPENDITURE (per capita) – US$943 (2004)

CLIMATE AND TERRAIN

Singapore consists of the island of Singapore and 63 islets. Singapore island is 42km long and 22.5km wide and is situated just north of the Equator off the southern extremity of the Malay peninsula, from which it is separated by the Straits of Johore. A causeway crosses the 1.21km to the mainland. Elevation extremes range from 166m (Bukit Timah) at the highest point to 0m (Singapore Strait) at the lowest. The average temperature is 29°C all year round. Average annual rainfall is high at 2,410mm and flooding is common during the monsoon seasons of December and June.

HISTORY AND POLITICS

Singapore, a trading site since the 12th century, was leased from the Sultan of Johore by the British East India Company in 1819. In 1826 it was incorporated with Penang and Malacca to form the Straits Settlements and they became a crown colony in 1867. Singapore became the principal British military base in the Far East in the 1920s and in 1942, during the Second World War, fell to Japanese forces. Liberated in 1945, it became a separate colony in 1946. Internal self-government was introduced in 1959 and it became part of the Federation of Malaysia in 1963, before withdrawing to become an independent sovereign state on 9 August 1965.

Although Singapore is a multiparty state, the People's Action Party (PAP) has dominated politics since 1959; opposition candidates were elected to parliament for the first time in 1984. The PAP leader, Lee Kuan Yew, was prime minister from 1959 until he retired in 1990.

Sellapan Rama Nathan became president in September 1999 and was declared re-elected in August 2005, although no election was held on either occasion as he was the sole eligible candidate. In the 2006 general election, the PAP won 82 seats in parliament and opposition parties two. Lee Hsien Loong, the son of Lee Kuan Yew, continued in office as prime minister, a post he has held since 2004.

POLITICAL SYSTEM

The 1959 constitution was amended in 1965 to enable Singapore to become a republic, and in 1991 to make the presidency directly elective with increased responsibilites. The head of state is the president, directly elected for a six-year term, who has the power to veto government decisions relating to internal security, the budget, financial reserves and the appointment of senior civil servants. The president appoints the prime minister and, on his advice, the members of the cabinet. There is a unicameral parliament with 84 directly elected members and up to three extra members from opposition parties (NCMPs), depending on their share of the vote; they serve a five-year term. Up to nine members can also be nominated by the government for a two-year term (NMPs).

HEAD OF STATE

President, Sellapan Rama Nathan, *took office* 1 September 1999, *re-elected* 17 August 2005

SELECTED GOVERNMENT MEMBERS *as at July 2007*

Prime Minister, Lee Hsien Loong
Senior Minister, Prime Minister's Office, Goh Chok Tong
Deputy Prime Ministers, Shanmugam Jayakumar; Wong Kan Seng
Foreign Affairs, George Yong Boon Yeo
Defence, Rear Adm. Teo Chee Hean

HIGH COMMISSION FOR THE REPUBLIC OF SINGAPORE

9 Wilton Crescent, London SW1X 8SP
T 020-7235 8315 W http://mfa.gov.sg/london
High Commissioner, HE Michael Eng Cheng Teo, *apptd* 2002

BRITISH HIGH COMMISSION
100 Tanglin Road, Singapore 247919
T (+65) 6424 4200 E commercial.singapore@fco.gov.uk
W www.britain.org/sg
High Commissioner, HE Paul Madden, *apptd* 2007

BRITISH COUNCIL
30 Napier Road, Singapore 258509
T (+65) 6473 1111 W www.britishcouncil.org/sg
Director, Eunice Crook

DEFENCE

The army has 100 main battle tanks, over 1,280 armoured personnel carriers and 294 armoured infantry fighting vehicles. The navy has 4 submarines, 1 frigate and 17 patrol and coastal combatant vessels at 2 bases. The air force has 102 combat aircraft and 12 attack helicopters.
MILITARY BUDGET – US$6,400m (2006)
MILITARY PERSONNEL – 72,500: army 50,000, navy 9,000, air force 13,500; paramilitaries 93,800
CONSCRIPTION DURATION – 24 months

ECONOMY AND TRADE

Historically based on the sale and distribution of raw materials from surrounding countries and on entrepot trade in finished products, the economy has been diversified and industrialised since independence. Singapore has also developed as a financial centre for the region, with significant insurance and foreign exchange markets, a stock exchange, and a large commercial and merchant banking sector. Agriculture is limited and contributes little to GDP. Industries include the manufacture of electronic, electrical, telecommunications and oil-drilling equipment, and chemicals, oil refining, rubber processing, food processing, ship repair, offshore oil platform construction and life sciences; industry contributes 34 per cent of GDP. The service sector, which includes tourism as well as financial and business services and the entrepot trade, accounts for 66 per cent of GDP and employs 39 per cent of the workforce.

The main trading partners are Malaysia, the USA, China, Japan, Indonesia, Hong Kong and Taiwan. Principal exports are machinery and equipment (especially electronic), consumer goods, chemicals and mineral fuels. The main imports are machinery and equipment, mineral fuels, chemicals and foodstuffs.
GNI – US$119,800m (2005); US$27,580 per capita (2005)
ANNUAL AVERAGE GROWTH OF GDP – 6.4 per cent (2005 est)
INFLATION RATE – 0.4 per cent (2005 est)
UNEMPLOYMENT – 3.1 per cent (2005 est)
TOTAL EXTERNAL DEBT – US$23,760m (2005 est)
IMPORTS – US$200,000m (2005)
EXPORTS – US$229,600m (2005)

BALANCE OF PAYMENTS
Trade – US$31,239m surplus (2004)
Current Account – US$27,897m surplus (2004)

Trade with UK	*2005*	*2006*
Imports from UK	£2,089,013,000	£2,325,114,000
Exports to UK	£3,897,660,000	£3,834,344,000

COMMUNICATIONS

There are 30km of railway, connected to the Malaysian rail system by a causeway across the Straits of Johore, and an extensive light rail system on the island. There are 3,234km of roads, all surfaced. Singapore is one of the largest and busiest seaports in the world, with deep-water wharves and six terminals. It has a large merchant fleet of 1,063 ships of over 1,000 tonnes registered in Singapore and a further 285 ships registered in other countries, while 592 foreign-owned ships are registered in Singapore. There is one international airport, at Changi.

There is a modern telecommunications system. In 2005 there were 1.8 million main telephone lines in use, 4.4 million mobile phone subscribers and 2.4 million internet users.

MEDIA

Singapore's media is highly regulated by the government. Private satellite dishes are outlawed and internet access is controlled, although the government sees the country as a digital media pioneer and plans to create thousands of new jobs in this sector. The television sector is dominated by MediaCorp, owned by a state investment agency. Singapore Press Holdings, which has close links to the ruling party, has a virtual monopoly of the newspaper industry, and publishes 15 newspapers and six periodicals.

SLOVAKIA

Slovenska Republika – Slovak Republic

AREA – 48,845 sq. km. Neighbours: Poland (north), Ukraine (east), Hungary (south), Austria (west), the Czech Republic (north-west)
CAPITAL – Bratislava; population, 425,155 (2004 est), on the Danube
MAJOR CITY – Kosice
CURRENCY – Koruna (Sk) of 100 halierov
POPULATION – 5,439,448 rising at 0.15 per cent per year (2006 est); Slovak (85.8 per cent), Hungarian (9.7 per cent)
RELIGION – Roman Catholicism (68 per cent), other Christian denominations (14 per cent) (est)
LANGUAGE – Slovak (official), Hungarian, Romani, Ukrainian
POPULATION DENSITY – 112 per sq. km (2005)
URBAN POPULATION – 58 per cent (2005 est)
MEDIAN AGE (years) – 35.8 (2006 est)
NATIONAL ANTHEM – 'Nad Tatrou sa Blyska' ['Storm Over the Tatras']
NATIONAL DAY – 1 September (Constitution Day)
LIFE EXPECTANCY (years) – 74.73 (2006 est)
MORTALITY RATE – 9.45 (2006 est)
BIRTH RATE – 10.65 (2006 est)
INFANT MORTALITY RATE – 7.26 (2006 est)
DEATH PENALTY – No (abolished 1990)
CPI SCORE – 4.7 (2006)
LITERACY RATE – 99.6 per cent (2004 est)
GROSS ENROLMENT RATIO (percentage of relevant age group) – primary 99 per cent; secondary 94 per cent; tertiary 36 per cent (2005 est)
HEALTH EXPENDITURE (per capita) – US$565 (2004)

CLIMATE AND TERRAIN

Slovakia is landlocked and mostly mountainous, lying in the western Carpathian range and including the Tatra and Beskid mountains to the north. The lower-lying plain of the River Danube is in the south-west. Elevation extremes range from 2,655m (Gerlachorsky Stit) at the highest point to 94m (Bodrock River) at the lowest. The climate is continental, with warm humid summers and cold dry winters. Average temperatures range from 1°C in January to 21°C in July.

HISTORY AND POLITICS

The area was part of the kingdom of Greater Moravia in the ninth century, became part of the Hungarian Magyar Empire in the tenth century and came under Austrian Habsburg rule from the 16th century.

After the dissolution of the Austro-Hungarian Empire, Slovakia became part of Czechoslovakia in 1918. Following the German annexation of Czechoslovakia in 1939, Slovakia became a nominally independent state but was exploited as part of the German war effort. After an abortive uprising in 1944, Slovakia was liberated by Soviet forces in 1945 and returned to Czechoslovakia, where a communist regime assumed power in 1948. The formation of a federal republic between the Czech lands and Slovakia was the only Prague Spring reform to survive the Soviet invasion of 1968. Following the collapse of Communist rule in 1989, the Slovak separatist movement gained ground and the Czech and Slovak republics negotiated the dissolution of the federation into two sovereign states in 1992. Dissolution took effect on 1 January 1993.

The Movement for a Democratic Slovakia (HZDS), led by the authoritarian Vladimir Meciar, dominated the coalition governments that held office in the 1990s, pursuing populist nationalist policies. It was ousted at the 1998 election by an alliance of liberals, centrists, left-wingers and ethnic Hungarians, which formed a coalition government under Mikulas Dzurinda of the Slovak Democratic and Christian Union (SDKU). This government, which was re-elected in 2002, introduced the constitutional and economic reforms necessary to meet the requirements for membership of the EU. Slovakia joined NATO and the EU in 2004. Its parliament ratified the EU constitution in 2005.

The 2004 presidential election was won by Ivan Gasporovic, with 59.9 per cent of the vote; he was chair of the HZDS but resigned from this position after his election. After the 2006 legislative election, the Smer ('Direction') party became the largest party in the national council, with 50 seats. It formed a coalition government with the HZDS and the Slovak National Party, led by Smer leader Robert Fico.

POLITICAL SYSTEM

The 1993 constitution has been amended several times, most recently in 1999 to allow direct elections to the presidency. The head of state is the president, directly elected for a five-year term, renewable only once. The unicameral National Council of the Slovak Republic has 150 members, who are directly elected for a four-year term by proportional representation with a 5 per cent threshold for parliamentary representation. The prime minister, who is appointed by the president, nominates the cabinet.

HEAD OF STATE
President, Ivan Gasparovic, *elected* 17 April 2004, *sworn in* 15 June 2004

SELECTED GOVERNMENT MEMBERS *as at July 2007*
Prime Minister, Robert Fico
Deputy Prime Minister, Interior, Robert Kalinak
Deputy Prime Minister, Justice, Stefan Harabin
Defence, Frantisek Kasicky
Foreign Affairs, Jan Kubis
Finance, Jan Pociatek

EMBASSY OF THE SLOVAK REPUBLIC
25 Kensington Palace Gardens, London W8 4QY
T 020-7243 0803 W www.slovakembassy.co.uk
Ambassador Extraordinary and Plenipotentiary, vacant

BRITISH EMBASSY
Panska 16, Bratislava 811 01
T (+421) (2) 5998 2000 E bebra@internet.sk
W www.britemb.sk
Ambassador Extraordinary and Plenipotentiary, HE Judith Macgregor, *apptd* 2005

BRITISH COUNCIL
PO Box 68, Panska 17, 814 99 Bratislava
T (+421) (2) 5443 1074 W www.britishcouncil.org/slovakia
Director, Huw Jones

DEFENCE

The army has 247 main battle tanks, 132 armoured personnel carriers and 389 armoured infantry fighting vehicles. The air force has 71 combat aircraft and 16 attack helicopters.

MILITARY EXPENDITURE – US$830m (2005)
MILITARY PERSONNEL – 15,223: army 6,038, air force 3,660, central staff 2,621, support and training 2,904
CONSCRIPTION DURATION – Six months

ECONOMY AND TRADE

Slovakia has nearly completed the transition from a centrally planned to a free-market economy, following structural reforms and privatisation begun after 1998. As a result, foreign investment has risen, especially in the vehicle industry, and since 2000 the GDP has steadily grown. The transition caused some hardship, although unemployment has fallen from the 2003 peak of 20 per cent.

Natural resources include brown coal and lignite, natural gas, oil, iron ore, copper and manganese. Major industries include production of metal and metal products, food and beverages, fuel and energy (electricity, gas, coke, oil and nuclear), chemicals and synthetic fibres, machinery, paper and printing, ceramics, transport vehicles, textiles and electrical and optical equipment. Industry accounts for 31 per cent of GDP, services 65 per cent and agriculture 4 per cent. The main trading partners are other EU countries (especially Germany and the Czech Republic) and Russia. Principal exports are vehicles, machinery and electrical equipment, base metals, chemicals, minerals and plastics. The main imports are machinery and transport equipment, intermediate manufactured goods and fuels.

GNI – US$42,800m (2005); US$7,950 per capita (2005)
ANNUAL AVERAGE GROWTH OF GDP – 6 per cent (2005 est)
INFLATION RATE – 2.7 per cent (2005 est)
UNEMPLOYMENT – 16.4 per cent (2005 est)
TOTAL EXTERNAL DEBT – US$26,940m (2005 est)
IMPORTS – US$36,000m (2005)
EXPORTS – US$32,000m (2005)

BALANCE OF PAYMENTS
Trade – US$649m deficit (2003)
Current Account – US$282m deficit (2003)

Trade with UK	*2005*	*2006*
Imports from UK	£251,481,000	£260,300,000
Exports to UK	£346,450,000	£636,300,000

COMMUNICATIONS

Slovakia has a total of 42,993km of roads, including 313km of motorways. There are 3,662km of railways, and 172km of navigable waterways on the River Danube. The main Danube ports are Bratislava and Komarno, and the principal airport is at Bratislava.

The modern telecommunications system has expanded rapidly in recent years, especially for mobile phones. In 2005 there were 1.2 million main telephone lines in use, 4.5 million mobile phone subscribers and 2.5 million internet users.

MEDIA

Since the collapse of communism the public broadcaster Slovak TV has lost much of its audience share to the private sector TV Markiza. Cable and satellite television channels are also popular. All three major daily newspapers are privately owned and there are more than 20 private radio stations in addition to the public broadcaster Slovak Radio, which operates five national networks and an external service.

SLOVENIA

Republika Slovenija – Republic of Slovenia

AREA – 20,273 sq. km. Neighbours: Austria (north), Hungary (north-east), Croatia (east and south), Italy (west)
CAPITAL – Ljubljana; population, 247,772 (2005 est)
MAJOR CITY – Maribor
CURRENCY – Euro (€) of 100 cents
POPULATION – 2,010,347 falling at 0.05 per cent per year (2006 est); Slovene (83.1 per cent), Serb (2 per cent), Croat (1.8 per cent), Bosniak (1.1 per cent)
RELIGION – Roman Catholicism (57 per cent), Islam (2 per cent), Orthodox Christianity (2 per cent) (est). An estimated 10 per cent of the population is atheist
LANGUAGE – Slovene (official), Serbian, Croatian
POPULATION DENSITY – 99 per sq. km (2005)
URBAN POPULATION – 50.8 per cent (2005 est)
MEDIAN AGE (years) – 40.6 (2006 est)
NATIONAL ANTHEM – 'Zdravljica' ['A Toast']
NATIONAL DAY – 25 June (Statehood Day)
LIFE EXPECTANCY (years) – 76.33 (2006 est)
MORTALITY RATE – 10.31 (2006 est)
BIRTH RATE – 8.98 (2006 est)
INFANT MORTALITY RATE – 4.4 (2006 est)
DEATH PENALTY – No (abolished 1989)
CPI SCORE – 6.4 (2006)

CLIMATE AND TERRAIN

The terrain is mountainous, the only low-lying areas being the valleys of the rivers Sava and Drava and the short Adriatic coastline. Elevation extremes range from 2,864m (Triglav) at the highest point to 0m (Adriatic Sea) at the lowest. The majority of the country has an Eastern European climate; the exception is the stretch of Adriatic coastline, which has milder winters and more hours of sunshine. Average temperatures in Ljubljana range from 0°C in January to 25°C in July.

HISTORY AND POLITICS

Settled by Slovenes in the sixth century, the area was later controlled by Slavs, Franks and Hungarians before coming under the control of the Austrian Habsburg Empire in the 14th century. Following the collapse of the Austro-Hungarian Empire in 1918, Slovenia became part of the Kingdom of the Serbs, Croats and Slovenes (later Yugoslavia). German forces invaded Yugoslavia in 1941 and Slovenia was divided between Germany, Italy and Hungary. In 1945 it was reformed as a constituent republic of Yugoslavia, which became a communist state in 1946. After a dispute with Italy and nine years of international administration, the Adriatic coast and hinterland were returned to Slovenia in 1954, while Italy retained Trieste.

Slovenia's fears of Serbian dominance led the Slovene Assembly in 1989 to amend the republican constitution to allow secession. The first multiparty elections, held in April 1990, were won by the pro-independence 'Demos' coalition. In a referendum in December 1990, 88 per cent of the electorate voted for independence, which was declared on 25 June 1991. A ten-day war with the Yugoslav National Army followed before the army withdrew under the terms of an EU-brokered ceasefire. Slovenia became a member of NATO and the EU in 2004, and joined the eurozone in January 2007. The national assembly ratified the EU constitution in 2005.

The Liberal Democracy of Slovenia party (LDS) was the major party in every government from 1991 to 2004, when the Slovenian Democratic Party became the largest party in the national assembly following the legislative election; its leader, Janez Jansa, formed a four-party coalition government. Janez Drnovsek, the LDS candidate, was elected president in 2002, with 56.5 per cent of the vote.

POLITICAL SYSTEM
Under the 1991 constitution, the head of state is the president, directly elected for a five-year term. The unicameral legislature, the national assembly, has 90 members directly elected for a four-year term. The national council, which has 40 members indirectly elected for a five-year term, has an advisory role. The prime minister, who is nominated by the president and elected by the national assembly, appoints the cabinet.

HEAD OF STATE
President, Janez Drnovsek, *elected* 1 December 2002

SELECTED GOVERNMENT MEMBERS *as at July 2007*
Prime Minister, Janez Jansa
Defence, Karl Erjavec
Finance, Andrej Bajuk
Foreign Affairs, Dimitrij Rupel
Internal Affairs, Dragutin Mate

EMBASSY OF THE REPUBLIC OF SLOVENIA
10 Little College Street, London SW1P 3SH
T 020-7222 5700 E vlo@gov.si
Ambassador Extraordinary and Plenipotentiary, HE Iztok Mirosic, *apptd* 2004

BRITISH EMBASSY
4th Floor, Trg Republike 3, 1000 Ljubljana
T (+386) (1) 200 3910 E info@british-embassy.si

W www.british-embassy.si
Ambassador Extraordinary and Plenipotentiary, HE Timothy Simmons, *apptd* 2004

BRITISH COUNCIL
Tivoli Center, Tivolska 30, 1000 Ljubljana
T (+386) (1) 300 2030 W www.britishcouncil.org/slovenia
Director, Robert Munro

DEFENCE

The army has 70 main battle tanks, 64 armoured personnel carriers and 26 armoured infantry fighting vehicles. The army Maritime Element has one patrol and coastal combatant.

MILITARY EXPENDITURE – US$574m (2005)
MILITARY PERSONNEL – army 6,550; paramilitaries 4,500

ECONOMY AND TRADE

Always the most prosperous republic of the former Yugoslavia, Slovenia's transition to a market economy has been relatively smooth. It has a good infrastructure and a well-educated workforce, and it has successfully re-orientated its exports towards Western markets. Much of the economy remains in state ownership but privatisation and economic liberalisation are being accelerated by the current government.

Agriculture contributes 2 per cent of GDP, industry 34 per cent and the service sector 64 per cent. The main agricultural products are potatoes, hops, wheat, sugar beet, maize and grapes. Industries include metal extraction and processing, electronics, vehicles, electric power equipment, wood products, textiles, chemicals, machine tools and tourism.

The main trading partners are other EU countries and Croatia. Principal exports are manufactured goods, machinery and transport equipment, chemicals and food. These items, along with fuels and lubricants, are also the main imports.

GNI – US$34,900m (2005); US$17,440 per capita (2005)
ANNUAL AVERAGE GROWTH OF GDP – 4 per cent (2005 est)
INFLATION RATE – 2.5 per cent (2005 est)
UNEMPLOYMENT – 6.3 per cent (2005 est)
TOTAL EXTERNAL DEBT – US$18,970m (2005 est)
IMPORTS – US$20,000m (2005)
EXPORTS – US$18,000m (2005)

BALANCE OF PAYMENTS
Trade – US$1,270m deficit (2005)
Current Account – US$362m deficit (2005)

Trade with UK	*2005*	*2006*
Imports from UK	£164,890,000	£187,600,000
Exports to UK	£190,948,000	£267,300,000

COMMUNICATIONS

There are 38,400km of roads and 1,229km of railways, of which 483km are electrified. Major international road and rail routes cross the country. There are 14 airports and airfields, with international airports at Ljubljana, Maribor and Portoroz. Koper is the main port, receiving shipments from landlocked central European countries.

In 2005 there were 816,400 main telephone lines in use, 1.7 millon mobile phone subscribers and 1 million internet users.

EDUCATION AND HEALTH

Education is free of charge and compulsory between the ages of six and 14.

LITERACY RATE – 99.7 per cent (2004 est)
GROSS ENROLMENT RATIO (percentage of relevant age group) – primary 99 per cent; secondary 100 per cent; tertiary 74 per cent (2005 est)
HEALTH EXPENDITURE (per capita) – US$1,438 (2004)
HOSPITAL BEDS (per 1,000 people) – 5 (2000–5)

MEDIA

Slovenia saw a rapid development of its media market after the fall of communism. The main newspapers are privately owned, and the broadcasting sector is a mix of public and private ownership. The television market is mainly shared between the public service, RTV Slovenia, and the private stations Pop TV and Kanal A. About two-thirds of households are connected to cable or satellite.

SOLOMON ISLANDS

AREA – 28,450 sq. km
CAPITAL – Honiara, on Guadalcanal; population, 49,107 (1999)
CURRENCY – Solomon Islands dollar (SI$) of 100 cents
POPULATION – 552,438 rising at 2.61 per cent per year (2006 est); Melanesian (94.5 per cent), Polynesian (3 per cent), Micronesian (1.2 per cent)
RELIGION – Protestantism (73 per cent), Roman Catholicism (19 per cent), other Christian denominations (4 per cent) (est)
LANGUAGE – English (official), Melanesian pidgin
POPULATION DENSITY – 17 per sq. km (205)
URBAN POPULATION – 17.1 per cent (2005 est)
MEDIAN AGE (years) – 18.9 (2006 est)
NATIONAL ANTHEM – 'God Save Our Solomon Islands'
NATIONAL DAY – 7 July (Independence Day)
LIFE EXPECTANCY (years) – 72.91 (2006 est)
MORTALITY RATE – 3.92 (2006 est)
BIRTH RATE – 30.01 (2006 est)
INFANT MORTALITY RATE – 20.63 (2006 est)
DEATH PENALTY – No (abolished 1966)

CLIMATE AND TERRAIN

Forming a scattered archipelago of mountainous islands and low-lying coral atolls in the south-west Pacific Ocean, the Solomon Islands stretch about 1,448km in a south-easterly direction from the Shortland Islands to the Santa Cruz islands. The six biggest islands are Choiseul, New Georgia, Santa Isabel, Guadalcanal, Malaita and Makira (San Cristobal). They are characterised by thickly forested mountain ranges intersected by deep, narrow valleys. Elevation extremes range from 2,447m (Mt Makarakomburu) at the highest point to 0m (Pacific Ocean) at the lowest. The climate is tropical and the average temperature in Honiara is 27°C. The islands are occasionally prone to earthquakes, tsunamis and volcanic activity.

HISTORY AND POLITICS

The islands were discovered by the Spanish in 1568 and visited by Europeans intermittently for about 300 years. Following the inauguration of sugar plantations in Queensland and Fiji (which created a need for labour) and the arrival of missionaries and traders, Britain declared a protectorate in 1893 over the southern Solomons, adding the Santa Cruz group in 1898. The Shortland Islands were transferred from Germany to Britain by treaty in 1900. The islands were occupied by the Japanese in 1942, and recaptured by US forces in 1943 after fierce fighting, especially on Guadalcanal. Campaigns for self-government, which was achieved in 1976, began after the Second World War; independence followed in July 1978.

Ethnic tension on Guadalcanal between the native population and migrants from the island of Malaita began in 1998 and descended into conflict between two rival militias. A fragile peace began with an agreement signed in October 2000, allowing elections to be held in 2001. Escalating economic and social problems in early 2002 led to growing lawlessness throughout the country. In June 2003 the government requested military assistance from neighbouring countries and an Australian-led peacekeeping force was deployed, restoring order and disarming the militias.

In the April 2006 legislative election, the governing People's Alliance Party (PAP) and the opposition won an equal number of seats. Snyder Ridi of the PAP was elected prime minister on 20 April but resigned six days later after rioting in protest at his appointment. Manasseh Sogavare (prime minister 2000–1) of the Social Credit Party was elected to replace him and formed a government in May.

POLITICAL SYSTEM

Under the 1978 constitution, the Solomon Islands is a constitutional monarchy. The head of state is the British monarch, represented by a governor-general, who is chosen by the national parliament. The unicameral national parliament has 50 members who are directly elected for a four-year term. The prime minister is elected by the parliament from among its members, and nominates the cabinet, which is formally appointed by the governor-general.

Governor-General, Sir Nathaniel Waena, *apptd* 2004

SELECTED GOVERNMENT MEMBERS *as at July 2007*

Prime Minister, Manasseh Sogavare
Deputy Prime Minister, Toswel Kauwa
Foreign Affairs and Trade Relations, Patteson Oti
Home Affairs, Bernard Giro
Finance, Gordon Darcy Lilo

BRITISH HIGH COMMISSION

PO Box 676, Telekom House, Mendana Avenue, Honiara
T (+677) 21705 E bhc@welkam.solomon.com.sb
High Commissioner, HE Richard Lyne, *apptd* 2005

ECONOMY AND TRADE

The civil conflict of 1998–2003 left the country virtually bankrupt but the restoration of law and order has enabled the economy to recover and it has grown slightly, although rioting and looting in April 2006 has wiped out some advances. Owing to recent events, the country's dependency on foreign aid, principally from Australia, has increased.

Abundant mineral resources are largely undeveloped, although there is some gold mining. Agriculture, much at subsistence level, is the largest economic sector, accounting for over 40 per cent of GDP and engaging 75 per cent of the population. The main industries are fishing, mining, forestry and processing agricultural products; industry contributes 11 per cent of GDP. The main export markets are China, South Korea and Thailand; most imports come from Australia and Singapore. Principal exports are timber, fish, palm oil, copra and cocoa. The main imports are foodstuffs, machinery and equipment, manufactured goods, fuels and chemicals.

GNI – US$297m (2005); US$620 per capita (2005)
ANNUAL AVERAGE GROWTH OF GDP – 4.4 per cent (2005 est)
INFLATION RATE – 6.6 per cent (2005 est)
TOTAL EXTERNAL DEBT – US$166m (2004)
IMPORTS – US$144m (2005)
EXPORTS – US$102m (2005)

Trade with UK	*2005*	*2006*
Imports from UK	£982,000	£1,440,000
Exports to UK	£419,000	£442,000

COMMUNICATIONS

There are 1,360km of roads, of which only 34km are surfaced. The main ports are Honiara and Yandina. There are 35 airports and airfields, the main one being at Honiara. Solomon Airlines operates international services to other Pacific states and Australia. Air Niugini flies from Papua New Guinea to Honiara. Telephone services are limited; in 2005 there were 7,400 main telephone lines in use, 6,000 mobile phone subscribers and 8,400 internet users.

MEDIA

The Solomon Islands Broadcasting Corporation (SIBC) operates a public radio service; there are no television services on the islands, although external satellite services can be received. Low literacy levels mean that SIBC has greater influence than the press, which consists of one daily, two weekly and two monthly newspapers. Australia and Taiwan have donated funds and equipment to develop the domestic media.

SOMALIA

Jamhuuriyada Demuqraadiga Soomaaliyeed – Somalia

AREA – 637,657 sq. km. Neighbours: Djibouti (north-west), Ethiopia (west), Kenya (south-west)
CAPITAL – Mogadishu; population, 1,257,000 (2005 est)
MAJOR CITIES – Hargeysa; Berbera; Kismaayo
CURRENCY – Somali shilling of 100 cents
POPULATION – 8,863,338 rising at 2.85 per cent per year (2006 est)
RELIGION – Islam (90 per cent) (est)
LANGUAGE – Somali (official), Arabic, Italian, English
POPULATION DENSITY – 13 per sq. km (2005)
URBAN POPULATION – 35.9 per cent (2005 est)
MEDIAN AGE (years) – 17.6 (2006 est)
NATIONAL ANTHEM – 'Somaliyaay Toosoo' ['Somalia Wake Up']
NATIONAL DAY – 1 July (Foundation Day)
LIFE EXPECTANCY (years) – 48.47 (2006 est)
MORTALITY RATE – 16.63 (2006 est)
BIRTH RATE – 45.13 (2006 est)
INFANT MORTALITY RATE – 114.89 (2006 est)
HIV/AIDS ADULT PREVALENCE – 1 per cent (2001 est)
DEATH PENALTY – Yes

GROSS ENROLMENT RATIO (percentage of relevant age group) – primary 17 per cent (2005 est)

CLIMATE AND TERRAIN

The terrain is mostly arid, flat or undulating plateau, rising to hills in the north. Elevation extremes range from 2,416m (Shimbiris) at the highest point to 0m (Indian Ocean) at the lowest. The climate is tropical, influenced by the north-east and south-west monsoons. There are two wet seasons, from March to May and October to November. Temperatures in Mogadishu are an almost constant 30°C.

HISTORY AND POLITICS

Arab settlement from the eighth century onwards introduced Islam and established coastal trading towns that developed into sultanates. European contact began in the early 16th century, with Italian, French and British interest intensifying after the Suez Canal opened in 1869. Protectorates were established in the north by the British and in the centre (subsequently taking in the south) by the Italians in the 1880s. Italian Somalia was returned to Italian administration as a UN Trust Territory in 1950. The two protectorates became independent and merged to form the United Republic of Somalia in July 1960.

In 1969 the armed forces seized power in a coup led by Maj.-Gen. Muhammad Siad Barre, and established a socialist Islamic regime which became a one-party state in 1979. Insurrection in the north began in 1978, following a disastrous military campaign to regain territory from Ethiopia, and by the late 1980s opposition to the government had developed into a civil war. In January 1991 the rebels captured Mogadishu, forcing Siad Barre to flee. Attempts to establish a new central government failed as political and clan rivalries split the former rebels. Part of northern Somalia seceded in 1991 as Somaliland, and part of the north-east followed in 1998 (*see* below).

The fighting devastated large areas of the south, exacerbating famine conditions in 1992. A flawed UN intervention only increased the tension and provoked gun battles between foreign troops and rebel militias. All foreigners were withdrawn following a failed operation by US forces to capture rebel leaders, which cost the lives of nineteen US soldiers and hundreds of Somalis. The fighting, famines and disease resulted in an estimated one million deaths.

A transitional government, created under a 1999 peace plan, failed to assert its authority over the warlords and fighting continued. Internationally sponsored peace talks between 2002 and 2004 led to the establishment of a federal government and a new transitional legislature, which elected Col. Abdullahi Yusuf Ahmed as president in 2004 and an interim government in January 2005. Members of this administration only began to return to Somalia in mid-2005 because of the security situation; for this reason the assembly and the government are based in the central town of Baidoa. In August 2006 a new cabinet was nominated after a series of ministerial resignations led to the collapse of the government.

Early 2006 saw the rise in the south of Muslim militias loyal to the Union of Islamic Courts (UIC). These militias defeated the warlords, taking control of Mogadishu in June 2006, presenting a threat to the transitional government. A UIC advance in the direction of Baidoa was countered by government troops, supported by Ethiopian armed forces, forcing the UIC to abandon the capital to the transitional government. African Union peacekeeping forces were deployed in March 2007 as fighting with UIC supporters continued.

POLITICAL SYSTEM

Somalia has been without a recognised central government authority since the military overthrow of Siad Barre in 1991. The UN-backed Transitional Federal Institutions (TFI), consisting of a legislative branch, the parliament (TFP), an executive branch, the government (TFG) and a charter (TFC) was introduced as a result of peace talks in 2004. It has a five-year mandate. There is no constitution, but the government's powers are outlined in the charter. The unicameral legislature, the TFP, has 275 seats; 244 members are appointed by each of the country's four major clans (61 per clan) and 31 seats are allocated to an assortment of smaller groups. The parliament elects the president, who serves a four-year term. The president appoints the members of the TFG and the prime minister, who is also approved by the TFP.

HEAD OF STATE

President, Col. Abdullahi Yusuf Ahmed, *sworn in* 10 October 2004

SELECTED GOVERNMENT MEMBERS *as at July 2007*

Prime Minister, Ali Muhammed Ghedi
Deputy Prime Minister, Salim Aliyow Ibrow
Defence, Col. Abdirisak Isaq Bihi
Foreign Affairs, Hussein Elebe Fahiye
Finance, Hassan Mohammed Nuur
Interior, Mohamed Mohamoud Guled

SECESSION

The northern-based Somali National Movement (SNM) took control of the north-west (the former British Somaliland protectorate) after Siad Barre's deposition and in May 1991 declared unilateral independence as the 'Somaliland Republic'. A 2001 referendum on a new constitution, which confirmed the independence of Somaliland, was approved by 97.09 per cent of the voters. The leaders of the regime have refused to take part in the peace process since 1999 and have not signed the 2004 peace agreement; they are seeking international recognition of Somaliland's independence.

The north-east of the country proclaimed its autonomy as the region of Puntland in July 1998. Puntland does not seek independence but participation in a federal Somalia. Its leaders have taken part in the peace process, signing the 2004 peace agreement; its former leader, Col. Abdullahi Yusuf Ahmed, was elected national president in October 2004.

There has been sporadic fighting between Somaliland and Puntland over ownership of Somaliland's Sool and Sanaag regions, which Puntland claims on the grounds of ethnicity.

ECONOMY AND TRADE

The infrastructure, education and health services have suffered badly from the fighting and the years without a central government. These circumstances have prevented broad-based economic development and assistance from international aid. Many people are dependent on remittances from relatives working abroad. Natural resources are not exploited and industry is virtually non-existent but the lack of regulation has led to a thriving entrepreneurial economy in some sectors, especially money exchange services and telecommunications; the three main telecommunications companies are cooperating to fund the internet infrastructure. Businesses have also built small airfields and use natural harbours to trade with overseas countries. The main factor inhibiting trade is the lack of a central bank.

Agriculture, primarily livestock-raising by nomads or semi-nomads, is the most important economic sector. It accounts for about 40 per cent of GDP and 65 per cent of export earnings. The main export markets are the Gulf states, especially the UAE; imports come mainly from Djibouti, Kenya, India and Brazil. Principal exports are livestock, bananas, hides, fish, charcoal and scrap metal. The main imports are manufactures, petroleum products, foodstuffs and construction materials.

ANNUAL AVERAGE GROWTH OF GDP – 2.4 per cent (2005 est)
TOTAL EXTERNAL DEBT – US$3,000m (2001 est)

Trade with UK	*2005*	*2006*
Imports from UK	£1,893,000	£772,000
Exports to UK	£109,000	£71,000

COMMUNICATIONS

The main ports are Mogadishu, Kismaayo and Merca in the south, and Berber (within Somaliland) in the north, although these have all been damaged in the war. The international airports are at Mogadishu and Hargeisa (also within Somaliland).

Little of the public telephone system has survived the civil wars, but mobile phone services are available in most major population centres; in 2005 there were 100,000 main lines in use, 500,000 mobile phone subscribers and 90,000 internet users.

MEDIA

Many new print and broadcast outlets emerged after Siad Barre was ousted in 1991, but most were tied to one or another of the country's warring factions. Even though recent years have seen the emergence of stronger regional media, broadcasters and journalists operate in a dangerous environment, limiting their ability to report freely and objectively. Many Somalis rely on foreign broadcasts for their news.

SOUTH AFRICA

Republic of South Africa

AREA – 1,219,912 sq. km. Neighbours: Namibia (north-west), Botswana and Zimbabwe (north), Mozambique and Swaziland (north-east), Lesotho (surrounded by South Africa)
CAPITAL – The seat of the government is Pretoria (Tshwane): population 1,800,000 (1999 est); the seat of the legislature is Cape Town: population, 3,088,028 (1999 est) and the seat of the judiciary is Bloemfontein (467,400) (1999 est)
MAJOR CITIES – Durban; Johannesburg; Port Elizabeth; Pietermaritzburg
CURRENCY – Rand (R) of 100 cents
POPULATION – 44,187,637 falling at 0.4 per cent per year (2005 est)
RELIGION – Christianity (80 per cent), Hinduism (1 per cent), Islam (1 per cent) (est). An estimated 15 per cent of the population is atheist
LANGUAGE – Sesotho sa Leboa, Sesotho, Setswana, siSwati, Tshivenda, Xitsonga, Afrikaans, English, isiNdebele, isiXhosa, isiZulu (all official)
POPULATION DENSITY – 39 per sq. km (2005)
URBAN POPULATION – 57.9 per cent (2005 est)
MEDIAN AGE (years) – 24.1 (2006 est)
NATIONAL ANTHEMS – 'Nkosi Sikelel' iAfrika' ['God Bless Africa']; 'Die Stem van Suid-Afrika' ['The Call of South Africa']
NATIONAL DAY – 27 April (Freedom Day)
LIFE EXPECTANCY (years) – 42.73 (2006 est)
MORTALITY RATE – 22 (2006 est)
BIRTH RATE – 18.2 (2006 est)
INFANT MORTALITY RATE – 60.66 (2006 est)
HIV/AIDS ADULT PREVALENCE – 21.5 per cent (2004 est)
DEATH PENALTY – No (abolished 1997)
CPI SCORE – 4.6 (2006)
POPULATION BELOW POVERTY LINE – 50 per cent (2000 est)

CLIMATE AND TERRAIN

South Africa occupies the southernmost part of the African continent from the courses of the Limpopo, Marico, Molopo, Nosop and Orange rivers to the Cape of Good Hope, with the exception of Lesotho, Swaziland and the extreme south of Mozambique. To the west, south and east lie the south Atlantic and southern Indian oceans. Some 1,920km to the south-east of Cape Town lie Prince Edward and Marion Islands, part of South Africa since 1947. The country lies mostly on a high plateau fringed by mountains, including the Drakensberg range, with lower-lying strips along the coast. Elevation extremes range from 3,408m (Njesuthi) at the highest point to 0m (Atlantic Ocean) at the lowest. The climate is temperate and is influenced by the warm Agulhas current from Mozambique. Average temperatures in Pretoria (Tshwane) range from 3°C in June to 29°C in January.

HISTORY AND POLITICS

Hunter-gatherers, the San (Bushmen) and Khoikhoi (Hottentots), inhabited southern Africa from *c.*8000 BC. By the eighth century AD, Bantu-speaking peoples had arrived from the north and settled. The Portuguese navigator Bartolomeu Días charted the coast in 1488 and the Dutch founded the colony of the Cape of Good Hope in 1652. The British occupied the Cape in 1795 after Revolutionary France had conquered the Netherlands, and the colony was ceded to Britain in 1806. From 1836 the Boers (descendants of Dutch settlers) migrated north-east in the Great Trek to escape British rule, and founded the republic of Natal in 1839; the British annexed Natal in 1844, made it a colony in 1856 and added Zululand to it in 1897 after victory in the Zulu wars. The Boer republics of Transvaal (founded 1852) and Orange Free State (founded 1854) were recognised by Britain in 1853–4.

The discovery of diamonds (1866) and gold (1886), and the Boers' need for British assistance in defeating the Zulus in the 1870s, led to disputes and political tension that eventually resulted in the Boer Wars of 1880–1 and 1899–1902. After the British victory in the Second Boer War, Transvaal and the Orange Free State became British colonies. The four self-governing colonies were united in 1910 to form the Union of South Africa, with dominion status. It became a sovereign state within the Commonwealth in 1931. South Africa left the Commonwealth and became a republic on 31 May 1961, largely as a result of international condemnation of the Sharpeville massacre, in which 67 protesters were killed by police.

The Afrikaner National Party came to power in 1948 and adopted a policy of apartheid ('separateness'), which it pursued until 1991. As a result, South Africa's social and political structure came to be based on racial segregation, with separate institutions and facilities for different racial groups. The African National Congress (ANC) and other opposition groups mounted a civil disobedience campaign, following which most opposition groups were banned. Internal opposition continued, with strikes and violence in the 1980s leading to the declaration of a state of emergency in 1985. Internationally, the country became isolated as economic and cultural sanctions were imposed.

In 1984, a new constitution extended the franchise to mixed race and Asian people, but the progressive dismantling of apartheid began with the desegregation of public facilities in 1989. This was followed by the lifting of the bans on the ANC and other anti-apartheid groups, the release from prison of ANC leader Nelson Mandela (1990) and the effective abolition of the laws implementing apartheid in 1991 under the leadership of F. W. de Klerk. Negotiations between the government, the ANC and other political and civic groups reached agreement in 1991 on the establishment of an interracial administration and the formation of a five-year coalition government following multiracial elections. In 1993 the franchise was extended to all adults, and elections took place in April 1994. The ANC won a majority in both houses of parliament, and Nelson Mandela was elected president. South Africa rejoined the Commonwealth and took its UN seat again in 1994.

The parliament passed two significant pieces of legislation to settle the legacy of the apartheid era. The first, in November 1994, restored the rights of those dispossessed of their land, and the second, in June 1995, established the Truth and Reconciliation Commission, designed to assess confessions, grant amnesties for political crimes and set compensation for victims.

In 2003, after years of refusing to admit the scale of the epidemic, and the credibility of the science behind it, the government approved a programme to tackle the high levels of HIV/AIDS infection in the country. Other problems include a very high crime rate, social disruption and lack of education resulting from apartheid and opposition to it. Despite these social problems, South Africa is widely regarded as the dominant political, economic and diplomatic force in the region.

The ANC has won both the legislative elections held since 1994, increasing its majority each time. In the 2004 election, it won 279 seats in the national assembly and majorities in all the provincial assemblies. As a result, the ANC's candidate holds the presidency; Thabo Mbeki was elected to succeed Nelson Mandela in 1999 and was re-elected in 2004.

POLITICAL SYSTEM

Under the 1997 constitution, the executive president is elected by the national assembly for a five-year term, renewable only once. The president, who is responsible to parliament, appoints the cabinet. The bicameral parliament consists of the national assembly, the lower house, and the National Council of Provinces. The national assembly has 400 members directly elected by proportional representation for a five-year term. The National Council of Provinces has 90 members, ten for each province, elected by the provincial legislatures for a five-year term.

South Africa is divided into nine provinces (Eastern Cape, Free State, Gauteng, KwaZulu-Natal, Limpopo, Mpumalanga, North-West, Northern Cape, Western Cape). Each province has its own premier, legislature and constitution.

HEAD OF STATE

President, Commander-in-Chief of the Armed Forces, Thabo Mbeki, *elected by parliament* 14 June 1999, *sworn in* 16 June 1999, *re-elected* 24 April 2004

Executive Deputy President, Phumzile Mlambo-Ngcuka

SELECTED GOVERNMENT MEMBERS *as at July 2007*

Defence, Mosiuoa Lekota

Finance, Trevor Manuel

Foreign Affairs, Nkosazana Dlamini-Zuma

Home Affairs, Nosiviwe Mapisa-Ngakula

SOUTH AFRICAN HIGH COMMISSION

South Africa House, Trafalgar Square, London WC2N 5DP

T 020-7451 7299

High Commissioner, HE Dr Lindiwe Mabuza, *apptd* 2001

BRITISH HIGH COMMISSION

255 Hill Street, Arcadia 0002, Pretoria (Tshwane)

T (+27) (12) 405 2400 E media.pretoria@fco.gov.uk

W www.britain.org.za

High Commissioner, HE Rt. Hon. Paul Boateng, *apptd* 2005

BRITISH COUNCIL

Ground Floor, Forum 1, Braampark, 33 Hoofd Street, Braamfontein, Johannesburg 2001

T (+27) (8) 6001 2233 W www.britishcouncil.org/southafrica

Director, Shoba Ponnappa, OBE

DEFENCE

The new South African National Defence Force (SANDF) was created from the merger of the South African Defence Forces (SADF), the Umkhonto we Sizwe (MK) armed wing of the ANC, the Azanian People's Liberation army (APLA) of the Pan Africanist Congress of Azania, and the defence forces of the four former independent homelands.

The army has 167 main battle tanks, 810 armoured personnel carriers and 1,200 armoured infantry fighting vehicles. The navy has 2 submarines and 22 patrol and coastal vessels at 3 bases. The air force has 45 combat aircraft and 11 armed helicopters.

MILITARY BUDGET – US$3,300m (2006)

MILITARY PERSONNEL – 62,334: army 41,350, navy 5,801, air force 9,183, military health service 6,000

ECONOMY AND TRADE

South Africa is rich in natural resources and has well-developed financial, legal, energy and transport sectors and a modern infrastructure. Its industries and agriculture thrived despite the sanctions of the apartheid era. However, legacies of apartheid remain and widespread poverty (50 per cent of the population lives below the poverty line) and the high level of unemployment (48 per cent in some township areas) are a problem for the government.

Agriculture, forestry and fishing account for 3 per cent of GDP and employ nearly one-third of the workforce. Principal crops are maize, wheat, sugar cane, fruits and vegetables. Livestock farming and cotton and viticulture are also widespread.

The largest industry is mining, exploiting the abundant mineral resources. South Africa is the world's largest producer of gold, platinum and chromium, as well as producing diamonds, manganese, coal, copper, iron ore, tin, uranium and titanium. Other industries include car assembly, metalworking, food processing, ship repair and production of machinery, textiles, iron and steel, chemicals and fertiliser; manufacturing is concentrated most heavily around Johannesburg, Pretoria (Tshwane) and the major ports. Tourism is a significant industry, attracting nearly six million visitors in 2000. Industry contributes 30 per cent of GDP.

Energy production is based upon coal and natural gas and the production of synthetic liquid fuel from coal. One nuclear power station is in operation and others are planned. South Africa exports electricity through its electricity grid connections to all states in southern Africa. Water resources are inadequate to meet demand and so water is imported from the highlands of Lesotho.

The main trading partners are Germany, the USA, Japan, the UK and China. Principal exports are gold, diamonds, platinum, other metals and minerals, and machinery and equipment. Principal imports are machinery, chemicals, petroleum products, scientific instruments and foodstuffs.

GNI – US$223,500m (2005); US$4,770 per capita (2005)
ANNUAL AVERAGE GROWTH OF GDP – 4.9 per cent (2005 est)
INFLATION RATE – 4 per cent (2005 est)
UNEMPLOYMENT – 26.6 per cent (2005 est)
TOTAL EXTERNAL DEBT – US$29,970m (2005 est)
IMPORTS – US$62,000m (2005)
EXPORTS – US$51,700m (2005)

BALANCE OF PAYMENTS
Trade – US$1,878m deficit (2005)
Current Account – US$10,079m deficit (2005)

Trade with UK	*2005*	*2006*
Imports from UK	£2,083,893,000	£2,187,910,000
Exports to UK	£4,012,328,000	£3,988,533,000

COMMUNICATIONS
The country has 20,872km of railways and 362,099km of roads, of which 73,506km are surfaced. There are over 700 airports and airfields, with international airports at Johannesburg, Durban and Cape Town. South African Airways operates international services worldwide and it is the principal operator of domestic flights. Durban is the largest seaport. Other major ports are Cape Town, Port Elizabeth, East London, Saldanha Mossel Bay and Richards Bay.

The telephone system is the best developed in Africa, and there is a high level of mobile phone ownership. In 2005 there were 4.7 million main lines in use, 34 million mobile phone subscribers and 5.1 million internet users.

EDUCATION AND HEALTH
The national education system is provided by the state and organised into three levels: general education and training, further education and training, and higher education. The constitution allows for the nine provincial legislatures to manage education facilities, subject to a national policy framework.

LITERACY RATE – 82.4 per cent (2004 est)
GROSS ENROLMENT RATIO (percentage of relevant age group) – primary 104 per cent; secondary 93 per cent; tertiary 16 per cent (2005 est)
HEALTH EXPENDITURE (per capita) – US$390 (2004)

MEDIA AND CULTURE
South Africa's media industry is the largest and most influential in Africa. The South African Broadcasting Corporation (SABC) is a major state-owned television and radio broadcaster, while Channel Africa (owned by SABC) is an external radio service that reaches the entire continent. Deregulation in 1996 saw a large number of new radio stations. *The Star* is Johannesburg's oldest daily newspaper, while the *Sunday Times* is the longest running weekly title. *Beeld* is a popular Afrikaans daily title. Press freedom is generally respected, with little evidence of repressive measures against journalists.

South Africa is home to a diversity of cultures, and black cultures – such as Zulu, Xhosa and Ndebele – are reviving after suppression during the apartheid years. Celebrated figures include the writers Nadine Gordimer (*b.* 1923), winner of the Nobel prize for literature in 1991 and J. M. Coetzee (*b.* 1940), who won the same award in 2003. Archbishop Desmond Tutu (*b.* 1931) was awarded the Nobel peace prize in 1984.

SPAIN

Reino de España – Kingdom of Spain

AREA – 504,782 sq. km. Neighbours: Portugal (west), France and Andorra (north-east)
CAPITAL – Madrid; population, 3,128,600 (2006 est)
MAJOR CITIES – Barcelona; Valencia; Sevilla; Zaragoza; Málaga
CURRENCY – Euro (€) of 100 cents
POPULATION – 40,397,842 rising at 0.13 per cent per year (2006 est)
RELIGION – Roman Catholicism (81 per cent), Protestantism (2 per cent), Islam (2 per cent) (est). An estimated 4 per cent of the population is atheist
LANGUAGE – Spanish (official), Catalan, Galician, Basque (all are official in certain regions)
POPULATION DENSITY – 87 per sq. km (2005)
URBAN POPULATION – 76.7 per cent (2005 est)
MEDIAN AGE (years) – 39.9 (2006 est)
NATIONAL ANTHEM – 'Marcha Real Española' ['Spanish Royal March']
NATIONAL DAY – 12 October
LIFE EXPECTANCY (years) – 79.65 (2006 est)
MORTALITY RATE – 9.72 (2006 est)
BIRTH RATE – 10.06 (2006 est)
INFANT MORTALITY RATE – 4.37 (2006 est)
DEATH PENALTY – No (abolished 1995)
CPI SCORE – 6.8 (2006)

CLIMATE AND TERRAIN
The interior consists of an elevated tableland surrounded and traversed by mountain ranges: the Pyrenees on the border with France, the Cantabrian Mountains (north-west), the Sierra de Guadarrama, Sierra Morena, Montes de Toledo (centre) and the Sierra Nevada (south). The principal rivers are the Duero, the Tajo (Tagus), the Guadiana, the Guadalquivir, the Ebro and the Miño. Elevation extremes range from 3,718m (Pico de Teide) at the highest point to 0m (Mediterranean Sea) at the lowest. The climate is Mediterranean in the southern and eastern coastal areas, and temperate further inland. Average

temperatures in Madrid range from 1°C in January to 31°C in July.

HISTORY AND POLITICS

The Romans conquered the Iberian peninsula in the second century BC. It was overrun by Vandals and Visigoths in the fifth century AD, and invaded and occupied by Muslims from Africa in the eighth century. Christians in the north formed small kingdoms which reconquered the peninsula by 1492. Spain's modern form derives from the dynastic union of the kingdoms of Castile and Aragón in 1479. In the 16th century, Spain's exploration and colonisation of the New World made it one of the richest and most powerful nations in Europe, with an empire that covered most of central and southern America. However, a succession of costly wars and revolts in the 17th and 18th centuries saw this empire go into steady decline. Its central and southern American possessions declared independence in the early 19th century and most other overseas possessions had been lost by 1900.

The restoration of the Bourbon monarchy after the Napoleonic occupation of 1808–14 initiated over a century of political instability, with power struggles between conservative and liberal factions in royal, political and military circles. The dictatorship of Gen. Primo de Rivera (1923–30) ended with the exiling of King Alfonso XIII and the declaration of the Second Republic in 1931. The success of moderate and religious candidates in the 1933 elections provoked a socialist and Catalan insurrection in 1934. A narrow victory by the left-wing Popular Front (PF) in fresh elections in 1936 led to an army revolt in military garrisons in Spanish Morocco and this spread throughout Spain, led by Gen. Francisco Franco. Civil war ensued until March 1939, when the PF governments in Madrid and Barcelona surrendered to the Nationalists (as Gen. Franco's followers were then called). Gen. Franco became president and ruled the country until his death in 1975. His death was followed, according to his wishes, by the restoration of the monarchy, and Prince Juan Carlos of Bourbon (grandson of Alfonso XIII) became head of state as King Juan Carlos I. The first free election was held in 1977, and a referendum in 1978 endorsed a democratic constitution.

Spain joined NATO in 1982 and the EEC in 1986, becoming a member of the eurozone in 1999. A referendum in 2005 approved the ratification of the EU constitution.

There was strong opposition in Spain to its involvement in the 2003 Iraq war. Polling in March 2004 was overshadowed by a series of explosions on commuter trains in Madrid days earlier, which killed 191 people. Responsibility for the attack was attributed to Islamic militants with links to al-Qaida. The election resulted in an unexpected victory for the Spanish Socialist Workers' Party (PSOE), with 164 seats in the congress of deputies and 81 seats in the senate. José Luis Rodríguez Zapatero, a socialist, became prime minister and formed a minority PSOE government, which has the support of five small parties.

INSURGENCIES

The Basque separatist organisation ETA (*Euzkadi ta Azkatasuna* – Basque Nation and Liberty), formed in 1959, has carried out a terrorist campaign of bombings, shootings and kidnappings in an attempt to gain independence for the Basque country. ETA rejected regional autonomy for the Basque country in 1979 as insufficient and continued its campaign, but was greatly weakened in the early 1990s by increased cooperation between French and Spanish security forces. The Basque political party *Herri Batasuna*, regarded as ETA's political wing, was banned in 2003 because of its links with ETA. In May 2005, the PSOE government offered to hold peace talks with ETA if it would disarm; ETA announced a ceasefire in March 2006 but called this off in June 2007 after the collapse of the peace process.

POLITICAL SYSTEM

The 1978 constitution has been amended at various times to devolve powers to the 19 autonomous regions. The head of state is a hereditary constitutional monarch. There is a bicameral legislature, the *Cortes Generales*, comprising a 350-member *Congreso de los Diputados* (congress of deputies) directly elected for a four-year term, and a *Senado* (senate) with 259 members, 208 directly elected and 51 appointed by the assemblies of the autonomous regions, for a four-year term. There are 19 autonomous regions: Andalucía, Aragón, Asturias, Balearic Islands, the Basque Country, Canary Islands, Cantabria, Castilla-La Mancha, Castilla y León, Catalonia, Ceuta, Extremadura, Galicia, Madrid, Melilla, Murcia, Navarra, La Rioja and Valencia. Each has its own elected legislature and government. In June 2006 a referendum endorsed the *Cortes*' approval of greater autonomy for Catalonia.

HEAD OF STATE

HM The King of Spain, King Juan Carlos I de Borbón, KG, GCVO, *born* 5 January 1938, *acceded to the throne* 22 November 1975

Heir, HRH The Prince of the Asturias (Prince Felipe Juan Pablo Alfonso y Todos los Santos), *born* 30 January 1968

SELECTED GOVERNMENT MEMBERS *as at July 2007*

Prime Minister, José Luis Rodríguez Zapatero
First Deputy Prime Minister, Maria Teresa Fernandez de la Vega
Second Deputy Prime Minister, Economy, Pedro Solbes
Foreign Affairs, Miguel Ángel Moratinos
Interior, Alfredo Pérez Rubalcaba
Defence, José Antonio Alonso

EMBASSY OF SPAIN

39 Chesham Place, London SW1X 8SB
T 020-7235 5555
Ambassador Extraordinary and Plenipotentiary, Count Carlos Miranda, *apptd* 2004

BRITISH EMBASSY

Calle de Fernando el Santo 16, 28010 Madrid
T (+34) (91) 700 8200 E madridconsulate@ukinspain.com
W www.ukinspain.com
Ambassador Extraordinary and Plenipotentiary, HE Denise Holt, CMG, *apptd* 2007

BRITISH COUNCIL

Paseo del General Martínez, Campos 31, E-28010 Madrid
T (+34) (91) 337 3500 W www.britishcouncil.org/spain
Director, Chris Hickey

DEFENCE

The army has 323 main battle tanks, 144 armoured infantry fighting vehicles and 2,022 armoured personnel carriers. The navy has 4 submarines, 1 aircraft carrier, 11 frigates, 33 patrol and coastal vessels, 16 combat aircraft and 23 armed helicopters at 6 bases. The air force has 182 combat aircraft.

MILITARY EXPENDITURE – US$13,100m (2005)

MILITARY PERSONNEL – 147,255: army 95,600, navy 19,455, air force 22,750, joint staff 9,450; paramilitaries 73,360

ECONOMY AND TRADE

The conservatism and isolation of Franco's regime initially held back economic development in the mid-20th century, but the economy improved from the 1950s with industrialisation and the development of tourism. Since the mid-1990s the mixed capitalist economy has shown steady moderate growth, stimulated by liberalisation, privatisation and deregulation, although unemployment remains high.

The generally fertile country produces cereals, vegetables, olives, sugar beets, citrus and other fruits, meat and dairy products. Viticulture is widespread. Spain also has one of Europe's largest fishing industries. The agricultural sector contributes 3.9 per cent of GDP and employs 5.3 per cent of the workforce. Abundant mineral resources include coal, iron ore, copper, zinc, lead, uranium and tungsten. Metal extraction and the manufacture of metal products, including steel, are major industries. A diverse industrial sector includes manufacturing (principally textiles, clothing, footwear, beverages, chemicals, cars, machine tools, clay products, pharmaceuticals and medical equipment), food processing, shipbuilding and tourism; the tourist industry caters for over 52 million visitors a year. Industry accounts for 29.4 per cent of GDP and the service sector for 66.7 per cent.

The main trading partners are other EU countries, especially Germany and France. Principal exports include machinery, vehicles, foodstuffs, pharmaceuticals, medicines and other consumer goods. The main imports are manufactures and equipment, fuels, chemicals, semi-manufactures, foodstuffs, consumer goods, and measuring and medical instruments.

GNI – US$1,095,900m (2005); US$25,250 per capita (2005)

ANNUAL AVERAGE GROWTH OF GDP – 3.5 per cent (2005 est)

INFLATION RATE – 3.4 per cent (2005 est)

UNEMPLOYMENT – 9.2 per cent (2005 est)

TOTAL EXTERNAL DEBT – US$970,700m (2005 est)

IMPORTS – US$287,600m (2005)

EXPORTS – US$191,000m (2005)

BALANCE OF PAYMENTS

Trade – US$85,592m deficit (2005)

Current Account – US$83,136m deficit (2005)

Trade with UK	*2005*	*2006*
Imports from UK	£10,144,225,000	£12,156,000,000
Exports to UK	£9,352,297,000	£10,194,100,000

COMMUNICATIONS

Spain has a total of 666,292km of roads, nearly all of which are surfaced (including 12,009km of motorways). Railways total 14,873km. The main ports are Algeciras, Alicante, Barcelona, Bilbao, Cádiz, Santander and Valencia and Las Palmas in the Canary Islands, and there are 1,000km of navigable inland waterways. The principal airports are at Madrid, Barcelona, Alicante, Málaga, Valencia and Bilbao, and there are over 100 other airports and airfields around the country.

The modern telephone system has a density of less than 50 per cent but mobile phone distribution is very high. There were 18.3 million main telephone lines in use and 41.3 million mobile phone subscribers in 2005, and 19.2 million internet users in 2006.

EDUCATION AND HEALTH

Education is free from age six to 18, and compulsory to the age of 16. Private schools (30 per cent of primary and 60 per cent of secondary schools) have to fulfil certain criteria to receive government maintenance grants. There are 73 universities, the oldest of which, Salamanca, was founded in 1218. Other historic foundations are Valladolid (1346), Barcelona (1430), Zaragoza (1474), Santiago (1495), Valencia (1500), Seville (1505) and Madrid (1508).

LITERACY RATE – 97.1 per cent (2004 est)

GROSS ENROLMENT RATIO (percentage of relevant age group) – primary 108 per cent; secondary 119 per cent; tertiary 66 per cent (2005 est)

HEALTH EXPENDITURE (per capita) – US$1,971 (2004)

HOSPITAL BEDS (per 1,000 people) – 3.8 (2000–5)

MEDIA

Broadcasting has expanded in recent years and digital services are increasingly popular. Public radio and TV services are run by RadioTelevision Espanola (RTVE), which is funded by advertising and state subsidies. Many private radio and TV stations operate alongside, on both a national and regional level. There are plans to switch off the analogue signal in 2010. There are four Madrid-based daily newspapers and another two based in Barcelona. Popular titles include *El Mundo, ABC, La Razon* and *El Periodico de Catalunya.*

CULTURE

Spain's literature is one of the oldest in the world. The *Poem of the Cid,* the earliest of Spain's heroic songs, was written *c.*1140. The outstanding writers of Spain's Golden Age are Miguel de Cervantes (1547–1616), Lope Felix de Vega Carpio (1562–1635) and Pedro Calderón de la Barca (1600–81). The Nobel prize for literature has been awarded to five Spanish authors: J. Echegaray (1832–1916), J. Benavente (1866–1954), Juan Ramón Jiménez (1881–1958), Vicente Aleixandre (1898–1984) and Camilo José Cela (1916–2002). Federico Garciá Lorca (1898–1936) is the most significant modern dramatist.

Spain's long tradition in fine art includes the work of El Greco (1541–1614), Velázquez (1599–1660), Goya (1746–1828), Picasso (1881–1973), Miró (1893–1983) and Dali (1904–89).

ISLANDS AND ENCLAVES

THE BALEARIC ISLES form an archipelago off the east coast of Spain. There are four large islands (Majorca, Minorca, Ibiza and Formentera) and seven smaller ones (Aire, Aucanada, Botafoch, Cabrera, Dragonera, Pinto and El Rey). Area 5,014 sq. km; population 1,001,062. The archipelago forms a province of Spain. The capital is Palma on Majorca.

THE CANARY ISLANDS are an archipelago in the Atlantic off the African coast, consisting of seven islands and six islets. Area 7,270 sq. km; population 1,995,833 (2006 est). The Canary Islands form two provinces of Spain: Las Palmas, comprising Gran

Canaria, Lanzarote, Fuerteventura and the islets of Alegranza, Roque del Este, Roque del Oeste, Graciosa, Montaña Clara and Lobos, with the seat of administration at Las Palmas in Gran Canaria; and Santa Cruz de Tenerife, comprising Tenerife, La Palma, Gomera, and Hierro, with the seat of administration at Santa Cruz in Tenerife

ISLA DE FAISANES is an uninhabited Franco-Spanish condominium, at the mouth of the Bidassoa in La Higuera bay

CEUTA is a fortified post on the Moroccan coast, opposite Gibraltar. Area 13 sq. km; population 75,861 (2006 est)

MELILLA is a town on a rocky promontory of the Moroccan coast, connected with the mainland by a narrow isthmus. Population 66,871 (2006 est). Ceuta and Melilla are autonomous regions of Spain

OVERSEAS TERRITORIES

The following territories, which are Spanish settlements on the Moroccan seaboard, come under direct Spanish administration.

PENON DE ALHUCEMAS is a bay including six islands; population 366

PENON DE LA GOMERA (or Peñón de Velez) is a fortified rocky islet; population 450

THE CHAFFARINAS (or Zaffarines) is a group of three islands near the Algerian frontier; population 610

SRI LANKA

Shri Lamka Prajatantrika Samajaya di Janarajaya/Ilankai Jananayaka Choshalichak Kutiyarachu – Democratic Socialist Republic of Sri Lanka

AREA – 65,610 sq. km
CAPITAL – Colombo; population, 642,163 (2000), Sri Jayewardenepura Kotte is the administrative capital
MAJOR CITIES – Dehlwala-Mount Lavinia; Moratuwa; Jaffna
CURRENCY – Sri Lankan rupee of 100 cents
POPULATION – 20,222,240 rising at 0.78 per cent per year (2006 est); Sinhalese (73.8 per cent), Tamil (8.1 per cent), Sri Lankan Moor (7.2 per cent) (est)
RELIGION – Buddhism (70 per cent), Hinduism (15 per cent), Christianity (8 per cent), Islam (7 per cent) (est)
LANGUAGE – Sinhala (official), Tamil, English
POPULATION DENSITY – 304 per sq. km (2005)
URBAN POPULATION – 21 per cent (2005 est)
MEDIAN AGE (years) – 29.8 (2006 est)
NATIONAL ANTHEM – 'Sri Lanka Matha' ['Mother Lanka']
NATIONAL DAY – 4 February (Independence Day)
LIFE EXPECTANCY (years) – 73.41 (2006 est)
MORTALITY RATE – 6.52 (2006 est)
BIRTH RATE – 15.51 (2006 est)
INFANT MORTALITY RATE – 13.97 (2006 est)
DEATH PENALTY – No*
CPI SCORE – 3.1 (2006)
LITERACY RATE – 90.4 per cent (2004 est)
GROSS ENROLMENT RATIO (percentage of relevant age group) – primary 98 per cent; secondary 83 per cent (2005 est)
HEALTH EXPENDITURE (per capita) – US$43 (2004)

CLIMATE AND TERRAIN

Sri Lanka (formerly Ceylon) is an island in the Indian Ocean, off the southern tip of India and separated from it by the narrow Palk Strait. The land is low-lying in the north and along the coasts, with hills and mountains in the south and centre of the interior. Forests, jungle and scrub cover the greater part of the island. In areas over 600m above sea level, grasslands *(patanas* or *talawas)* are found. Elevation extremes range from 2,524m (Pidurutalagala) at the highest point to 0m (Indian Ocean) at the lowest. The climate is tropical with little seasonal variation in conditions and humidity, which often reaches around 90 per cent. The island experiences the south-west monsoon in May and the north-east monsoon in November. Average temperature in Colombo is 29°C all year round.

HISTORY AND POLITICS

Modern Sri Lanka is a product of its long history of occupation, which began with the arrival of the Sinhalese late in the sixth century BC. They settled the north, but gradually moved southwards under pressure from Tamil invasions from southern India, which began in the third century BC. These Tamils settled in the northern and eastern coastal areas. The Portuguese landed in the early 16th century and established control over most of the island by 1618. These territories were conquered by the Dutch in 1658 and held until 1798, when they were ceded to the British, becoming a British crown colony in 1802. With the annexation of the kingdom of Kandy in 1815, all Ceylon came under British rule, and was subsequently used as a front-line base for British forces fighting the Japanese in the Second World War. Ceylon achieved independence on 4 February 1948. A republican constitution was adopted in 1972 and the country was renamed Sri Lanka (meaning 'Resplendent Island').

Tension between the Buddhist Sinhalese majority and the Hindu Tamil minority dates from the early 20th century, and policies discriminating against Tamils were introduced after independence. Separatist movements developed in the 1970s to campaign for an independent Tamil state in the north and east of the island, and in the early 1980s the Liberation Tigers of Tamil Eelam (LTTE) began a guerrilla war against government forces for control of these areas. Although fighting has tended to be confined to the north, especially the Jaffna peninsula, bombings have occurred throughout the island. The LTTE controls areas in the north and east, and succeeded in capturing the Elephant Pass, the only land link to the Jaffna peninsula, in 2000.

Various attempts at peace talks in the 1980s and 1990s were unsuccessful, and LTTE ceasefires in 2000 and 2001 were not reciprocated by the government. In 2002, however, a ceasefire was arranged in January, peace talks began in May and the first formal direct negotiations in seven years began in September. Agreement was reached on a power-sharing arrangement providing for a federal system of government with substantial regional autonomy for the northern and eastern areas held by the LTTE. Talks stalled in 2003 and several times since and, although the 2002 ceasefire is still formally in place, conflict between Tamil and government forces has escalated since early 2006. In June 2007, the government attempted to forcibly move 400 Tamils from the capital, Colombo, to the north and east of the country, but were prevented by a parliamentary outcry and a supreme court order against the resettlement. Months earlier, both the UK and USA suspended aid to the country due to suspected human rights abuses.

In the 2004 legislative election, the United People's Freedom Alliance won 105 seats in the national assembly, the United National Party won 82 and the Sri Lanka Tamil Government Party secured 22. Mahinda Rajapakse became prime minister and formed a coalition government. The government lost its parliamentary majority in February 2005 after one coalition partner withdrew; another partner, the nationalist Sinhalese JVP, withdrew from the coalition four months later over the inclusion of Tamil separatist organisations in the arrangements for distributing foreign aid to tsunami victims. The 2005 presidential election was won by Mahinda Rajapakse, who was replaced as prime minister by Ratnasiri Wickremanayake (prime minister 2000–1).

POLITICAL SYSTEM

The 1978 constitution was amended in 1983 to ban parties advocating separatism and in 1987 to create provincial councils. The president is head of state and government, and is directly elected for a six-year term which may be renewed. The unicameral parliament has 225 members directly elected by proportional representation for a six-year term. The president appoints the cabinet.

Under the Indo-Sri Lankan peace accord in 1987, eight elected provincial councils were set up in an attempt to defuse ethnic tensions. Since 1988 all provinces, except for the temporarily merged North-East province, have elected provincial councils.

HEAD OF STATE

President, Defence, Finance, Mahinda Rajapakse, *elected* 17 November 2005 *took office* 19 November 2005

SELECTED GOVERNMENT MEMBERS *as at July 2007*

Prime Minister, Ratnasiri Wickremanayake
Home Affairs, Karu Jayasuriya
Foreign Affairs, Rohitha Bogollagama

HIGH COMMISSION OF THE DEMOCRATIC SOCIALIST REPUBLIC OF SRI LANKA

13 Hyde Park Gardens, London W2 2LU
T 020-7262 1841
W www.slhclondon.org
High Commissioner, HE Kshenuka Senewiratne, *apptd* 2005

BRITISH HIGH COMMISSION

PO Box 1433, 190 Galle Road, Kollupitiya, Colombo 3
T (+94) (11) 243 7336 E bhc@eureka.lk
High Commissioner, HE Dominick Chilcott, CMG, *apptd* 2006

BRITISH COUNCIL

PO Box 753, 49 Alfred House Gardens, Colombo 3
T (+94) (1) 1258 1171 W www.britishcouncil.org/srilanka
Director, Gill Westaway

DEFENCE

The army has 62 main battle tanks, 217 armoured personnel carriers and 62 armoured infantry fighting vehicles. The navy has 123 patrol and coastal vessels at 5 bases. The air force has 18 combat aircraft and 14 armed helicopters.

MILITARY BUDGET – US$686m (2006)
MILITARY PERSONNEL – 150,900: army 117,900, navy 15,000, air force 18,000; paramilitaries 58,200

ECONOMY AND TRADE

The economy, already damaged by decades of violence, was devastated by the Indian Ocean tsunami in December 2004. The central highlands, the centre of most cash crop production, were unscathed but the damage to the coastal areas wiped out cultivation there, destroyed the fishing industry and tourist resorts. Reconstruction boosted the economic growth rate in 2005 and 2006, but renewed conflict between the government and the LTTE since early 2006 has caused a slump in tourism, an important source of revenue which attracted over 400,000 visitors a year.

In recent decades the importance of agriculture has declined as manufacturing and service industries have grown, but it still accounts for 17 per cent of GDP and about one-third of employment. The main crops are rice, sugar cane, grains, pulses, oilseed, spices, tea, rubber, coconuts and fish. Manufacturing is based on processing the main cash crops of rubber, tea, coconuts, tobacco and other commodities, as well as clothing, textiles and cement; other industries include mining and oil refining. Service industries such as telecommunications, banking and insurance and tourism are also important; the sector accounts for 55 per cent of GDP and industry for 27 per cent. Remittances from expatriate workers are economically significant.

The main trading partners are the USA, India, the UK and Singapore. Principal exports are textiles and clothing, tea, spices, diamonds, emeralds, rubies, coconut products, rubber manufactures and fish. The main imports are textile fabrics, mineral products, oil, foodstuffs, machinery and transport equipment.

GNI – US$22,800m (2005); US$1,160 per capita (2005)
ANNUAL AVERAGE GROWTH OF GDP – 6 per cent (2005 est)
INFLATION RATE – 11.6 per cent (2005 est)
UNEMPLOYMENT – 7.7 per cent (2005 est)
TOTAL EXTERNAL DEBT – US$11,050m (2005 est)
IMPORTS – US$8,830m (2005)
EXPORTS – US$6,350m (2005)

BALANCE OF PAYMENTS

Trade – US$1,443m deficit (2004)
Current Account – US$6770m deficit (2004)

Trade with UK	*2005*	*2006*
Imports from UK	£112,917,000	£104,675,000
Exports to UK	£458,900,000	£508,230,000

COMMUNICATIONS

There are 97,287km of roads, of which 78,802km are surfaced. The rail network is government-run and there are 1,449km of railway. Colombo is the main port, and the principal airport is Bandaranaike International, to the north of the capital.

Fixed-line telephone services now extend to most of the country, although density remains low. Mobile phone distribution is expanding rapidly. There were 1.5 million main lines in use and 4.3 million mobile phone users in 2006, and 280,000 internet users in 2005.

MEDIA

Many of the main media outlets are government-controlled, including two major TV stations and radio networks operated by the Sri Lanka Broadcasting Corporation (SLBC). There are also privately owned broadcast media and newspapers. As part of the peace process, in 2002 the government permitted the Tamil Tigers to broadcast their Voice of Tigers radio station in the north of the island. The escalation in violence during 2006–7 increased the dangers faced by journalists, with threats and arrests occurring frequently.

SUDAN

Jumhuriyat as-Sudan – Republic of the Sudan

AREA – 2,505,810 sq. km. Neighbours: Egypt (north), Eritrea and Ethiopia (east), Kenya, Uganda and the Democratic Republic of the Congo (south), Central African Republic, Chad and Libya (west)
CAPITAL – Khartoum (Al-Khartum); population, 2,207,794 (2007 est)
MAJOR CITIES – Omdurman; Port Sudan (Bur Sudan); Kassala; El Obeid; Nyala
CURRENCY – Sudanese pound (SDP) of 100 piastres
POPULATION – 41,236,378 rising at 2.55 per cent per year (2006 est); Arab and Nubian peoples populate the north and centre with Nilotic and black African peoples in the south
RELIGION – Islam (65 per cent), indigenous religons (25 per cent), Christianity (10 per cent) (est)
LANGUAGE – Arabic (official), Nubian, Ta Bedawie, English
POPULATION DENSITY – 15 per sq. km (2005)
URBAN POPULATION – 40.8 per cent (2005 est)
MEDIAN AGE (years) – 18.3 (2006 est)
NATIONAL ANTHEM – 'Nahnu Djundulla Djundulwatan' ['We are the Army of God and of Our Land']
NATIONAL DAY – 1 January (Independence Day)
LIFE EXPECTANCY (years) – 58.92 (2006 est)
MORTALITY RATE – 8.97 (2006 est)
BIRTH RATE – 34.53 (2006 est)
INFANT MORTALITY RATE – 61.05 (2006 est)
HIV/AIDS ADULT PREVALENCE – 2.3 per cent (2003 est)
DEATH PENALTY – Yes
CPI SCORE – 2.0 (2006)
POPULATION BELOW POVERTY LINE – 40 per cent (2004 est)
MILITARY PERSONNEL – 104,800: army 100,000, navy 1,800, air force 3,000; paramilitaries 17,500
CONSCRIPTION DURATION – Two years

CLIMATE AND TERRAIN

Sudan is the largest country in Africa and is predominately desert. The Libyan Desert in the west is separated from the high rocky Nubian Desert in the east by the fertile valley of the River Nile and its tributaries. There are mountains in the west and along the Red Sea coast in the east. Elevation extremes range from 3,187m (Kinyeti) at the highest point to 0m (Red Sea) at the lowest. The climate is as varied as the terrain, with arid conditions in the desert, tropical conditions in the lower land and cooler conditions in the highlands. There is a wet season from April to October. Average temperatures in Khartoum, in the north of the country, range from 15°C in January to 38°C in July.

HISTORY AND POLITICS

Parts of northern Sudan formed part of the Egyptian Empire from 1900 BC and of the Nubian Empire from the sixth century BC. The country was converted to Coptic Christianity in the sixth century AD, and Islam was introduced in the seventh century by Arab invaders, but did not become widespread until the 15th century. From the eighth century onwards, northern Sudan was conquered and occupied by several Arab and Arab-African powers. The south remained independent. Egypt established its control over the north in the early 19th century but the Mahdi revolt in the 1880s led to a joint Anglo-Egyptian campaign to subdue the country. It was administered as an Anglo-Egyptian condominium from 1899. On 19 December 1955 the Sudan house of representatives declared Sudan an independent sovereign state, and on 1 January 1956 a republic was proclaimed and was recognised by Britain and Egypt.

The dominant Arab Muslim north and the black African Christian and animist south had been administered separately by the British, and unification created problems which have dominated the entire post-independence period. The first civil war in the south began in 1955 and persisted through a number of military coups, until 1972 when the south was given greater autonomy. In 1983, Gaafar Numeiri, who had been in power since 1969, attempted to turn the whole country into an Islamic state and impose Shariah law, a plan which ignited a second civil war. Further coups took place in 1985 and 1989 which eventually bought incumbent Omar Hassan al-Bashir to power, whose National Islamic Front military junta successfully implemented Numeiri's ideas, with only limited tolerance for those in the non-Muslim south.

A peace process began in 2000 and the parties to it – Bashir's government, the Sudan People's Liberation Army (SPLA) and their allies, the southern opposition National Democratic Alliance – finalised a peace agreement in 2004. Under this, a largely autonomous administration (installed in October 2005) governs in the south, and a referendum on independence will be held after six years. The war caused an estimated 1.5 million deaths, including over 300,000 in the 1988 and 1994 war-induced famines, and displaced some three million people. Large areas of the south are now desolate and uninhabitable.

Following the conclusion of the 2004 peace agreement, a new constitution was approved in July 2005. The president was sworn into office under this constitution and John Garang, the leader of the SPLM (the renamed SPLA), was sworn in as vice-president; Garang died almost immediately and was succeeded as SPLM leader, president of the government of southern Sudan and national vice-president by Salva Kiir Mayardit. Presidential and legislative elections scheduled for late 2005 were postponed and a power-sharing government took office in September 2005; elections are scheduled to take place within three years.

INSURGENCIES

The western region of Darfur has two main Muslim ethnic groupings: Arabs, who tend to be nomadic livestock herders, and black African peoples, who tend to be farmers. There has long been competition over resources, but prolonged drought and increasing desertification exacerbated tensions from the late 1990s, leading to increased intercommunal violence.

In 2003, black African rebels began to attack government targets, demanding more state resources for the region and an end to discrimination. The government responded with severe reprisals, operating through Arab militia *(Janjaweed)* which carried out mass executions and forcible depopulation, leading to accusations of ethnic cleansing. Over two million people have been displaced since 2003, fleeing to other parts of the region and across the border into Chad and the Central African Republic. Aid agencies have struggled to prevent starvation in the refugee camps inside Darfur, and in some cases even to gain access to certain areas, because of continuing violence and government obstructiveness.

Although the government acceded to settlements brokered by the African Union (AU) and the UN in 2004, it has not acted upon them and continues to resist international pressure to disarm the militias. It has also resisted pressure to increase the numbers of AU peacekeeping troops, and only agreed, conditionally, to their replacement by UN peacekeepers in April 2007. In May 2006 the government and the largest of the three main rebel groups signed a peace agreement, but the government has not met the implementation deadlines. Rebel forces supporting the agreement are at loggerheads with those opposing it, and violence and displacement have increased dramatically since the agreement was signed.

POLITICAL SYSTEM

Under the 2005 constitution, the executive president is directly elected for a five-year term. The unicameral national assembly has been replaced by a bicameral legislature and in August 2005 a transitional national legislature was established that comprises a 450-member national assembly and a council of states with two members from each of the 26 states. The president appoints the cabinet.

The south has a largely autonomous government. The president of the south is also the national vice-president.

HEAD OF STATE

President, Prime Minister, Lt.-Gen. Omar Hassan Ahmed al-Bashir, *seized power* 1989, *elected* 1996, *re-elected* 2000, *sworn in under new constitution* 9 July 2005
First Vice-President, Salva Kiir Mayardit
Second Vice-President, Ali Osman Mohammed Taha

SELECTED GOVERNMENT MEMBERS *as at July 2007*

Defence, Lt.-Gen. Abdel-Rahim Hussein
Finance and National Economy, Al-Zubeir Ahmed al-Hassan
Foreign Affairs, Lam Akol
Interior, Zubair Beshir Taha

EMBASSY OF THE REPUBLIC OF THE SUDAN

3 Cleveland Row, London SW1A 1DD
T 020-7839 8080 W www.sudanembassy.co.uk
Ambassador Extraordinary and Plenipotentiary, Omar Mohammed Ahmed Siddig, *apptd* 2007

BRITISH EMBASSY

PO Box 801, Off Sharia Al Baladiya, Khartoum East
T (+249) (1) 8377 7105 E british@sudanmail.net
W www.britishembassy.gov.uk/sudan
Ambassador Extraordinary and Plenipotentiary, HE Rosalind Marsden, CMG, *apptd* 2007

BRITISH COUNCIL

House 2, Street 65, Block 5, YE, Khartoum 2 *(temporary office)*
T (+249) 183 780817 W www.britishcouncil.org/sudan
Director, David Codling

DEFENCE

The army has 270 tanks, 241 armoured personnel carriers and 75 armoured infantry fighting vehicles. The navy has 15 patrol and coastal combatant vessels at 3 bases. The air force has 36 combat aircraft and 10 attack helicopters.
MILITARY BUDGET – US$535m (2006)
MILITARY PERSONNEL – 104,800: army 100,000, navy 1,800, air force 3,000; paramilitaries 17,500
CONSCRIPTION DURATION – 24 months

ECONOMY AND TRADE

Since 1997 Sudan has been implementing IMF economic reforms which, despite the country's political instability and vulnerability to drought, have stabilised the economy and enabled infrastructure improvements. In 1999 Sudan began exporting crude oil, and increases in oil production, light industry and exports have resulted in growth in GDP in recent years. However, development is operating from a low base and about 40 per cent of the population lives below the poverty line.

Agriculture provides employment for around 80 per cent of the workforce and contributes 35 per cent of GDP. The industry is based on large and medium-sized public sector irrigation projects; mechanised and traditional agriculture is practised in areas with sufficient rainfall. Much is at subsistence level; the principal crops include cotton, groundnuts, sorghum *(dura),* wheat, gum arabic and sugar cane. Industry consists of oil extraction and refining, cotton ginning, manufacture of cement, edible oils, sugar, soap, shoes and pharmaceuticals and armaments. Industry contributes 25 per cent of GDP and services 40 per cent.

The main trading partners are China (over 70 per cent of exports), Japan and Saudi Arabia. Principal exports are oil and petroleum products, cotton, sesame, livestock, groundnuts, gum arabic and sugar. The main imports are foodstuffs, manufactured goods, refinery and transport equipment, medicines, chemicals, textiles and wheat.
GNI – US$23,100m (2005); US$640 per capita (2005)
ANNUAL AVERAGE GROWTH OF GDP – 8 per cent (2005 est)
INFLATION RATE – 9 per cent (2005 est)
UNEMPLOYMENT – 18.7 per cent (2002 est)
TOTAL EXTERNAL DEBT – US$27,340m (2005 est)
IMPORTS – US$6,800m (2005)
EXPORTS – US$4,800m (2005)

BALANCE OF PAYMENTS

Trade – US$1,122m deficit (2005)
Current Account – US$3,013m deficit (2005)

Trade with UK	*2005*	*2006*
Imports from UK	£139,710,000	£155,148,000
Exports to UK	£18,149,000	£10,021,000

COMMUNICATIONS

The railway network is about 5,995km in length. There are 11,610km of roads, of which 4,320km are surfaced, and there are over 4,000km of navigable waterways, including 1,700km on the White and Blue Nile rivers. Port Sudan, on the Red Sea, is the main seaport. The principal airports are at Khartoum and Juba, and there are over 80 other airports and aifields. Sudan Airways provides domestic and international flights.

The fixed-line telephone system is being upgraded; mobile phone services are growing rapidly. In 2005 there were 670,000 main lines in use, 1.8 million mobile phone subscribers and 2.8 million internet users.

EDUCATION AND HEALTH

Education is free of charge for most children but not compulsory. Six years of primary education is followed by three years of secondary education; there are three types of secondary school: general, academic and vocational. The language of instruction is Arabic.

LITERACY RATE – 59 per cent (2004)
GROSS ENROLMENT RATIO (percentage of relevant age group) – primary 60 per cent; secondary 34 per cent (2005 est)
HEALTH EXPENDITURE (per capita) – US$25 (2004)
HOSPITAL BEDS (per 1,000 people) – 0.7 (2000–5)

MEDIA

Radio and television are controlled by the government, and a permanent military censor ensures that the news reflects official views. There are no privately owned television or radio stations. Satellite dishes are becoming common in affluent areas and pan-Arab TV stations are popular, as are foreign radio stations such as the BBC World Service and Paris-based Radio Monte Carlo, which broadcast in Khartoum. There are several privately owned newspapers.

SURINAME

Republiek Suriname – Republic of Suriname

AREA – 163,270 sq. km. Neighbours: French Guiana (east), Brazil (south), Guyana (west)
CAPITAL – Paramaribo; population, 212,840 (2000 est)
MAJOR TOWNS – Lelydorp; Nieuw Nickerie
CURRENCY – Suriname dollar of 100 cents
POPULATION – 439,117 rising at 0.2 per cent per year (2006 est); Hindustani (37 per cent), Creole (31 per cent), Javanese (15 per cent) (est)
RELIGION – Christianity (40 per cent), Hinduism (27 per cent), Islam (18 per cent), indigenous religions (8 per cent) (est)
LANGUAGE – Dutch (official), English, Surinamese, Hindustani, Javanese
POPULATION DENSITY – 3 per sq. km (2005)
URBAN POPULATION – 77.2 per cent (2005 est)
MEDIAN AGE (years) – 26.5 (2006 est)
NATIONAL ANTHEM – 'God Zij Met Ons Suriname' ['God Be With Our Suriname']
NATIONAL DAY – 25 November (Independence Day)
LIFE EXPECTANCY (years) – 69.01 (2006 est)
MORTALITY RATE – 7.27 (2006 est)
BIRTH RATE – 18.02 (2006 est)
INFANT MORTALITY RATE – 23.02 (2006 est)
HIV/AIDS ADULT PREVALENCE – 1.7 per cent (2003 est)
DEATH PENALTY – No*
CPI SCORE – 3.0 (2006)
POPULATION BELOW POVERTY LINE – 70 per cent (2002 est)
MILITARY BUDGET – US$20.5m (2006)
MILITARY PERSONNEL – 1,840: army 1,400, navy 240, air force 200
LITERACY RATE – 88 per cent (2004 est)

CLIMATE AND TERRAIN

A narrow coastal plain rises to a hilly, forested interior. Elevation extremes range from 1,230m (Juliana Top) at the highest point to –2m (Atlantic coastal plain) at the lowest. The climate is tropical, with high rainfall, high humidity and high temperatures which are tempered by the north-east trade winds. There are two wet seasons, from April to August and November to February. Average annual precipitation in Paramaribo is 2,200mm and average temperatures are an almost constant 27°C.

94.7	WORLD HIGHEST
	per cent of land is covered by forest

Source: Economist Intelligence Unit

HISTORY AND POLITICS

Although visited and claimed by Spanish explorers in 1593, the first European settlement was by the Dutch in 1602. A British colony was founded in 1651 but this was ceded to the Dutch in 1667. Dutch rule was interrupted by British occupation during the French Revolutionary and Napoleonic wars, but was restored in 1816. The colony, known as Dutch Guiana, remained part of the Netherlands West Indies until 25 November 1975, when it achieved independence as Suriname. At independence, about 40 per cent of the population emigrated to the Netherlands.

The early years of independence were politically unstable, with coups in 1980, 1982 and 1990. A guerrilla campaign for the restoration of democracy began in 1986. A peace accord with the guerrillas in 1989, following the return to civilian rule in 1988, was opposed by the military leader and former dictator Desi Bouterse, who engineered a coup in 1990 that deposed the president. Elections in 1991 were won by the New Front for Democracy and Development alliance, led by Ronald Venetiaan, who became president. President Venetiaan introduced an unpopular austerity programme, which improved the economy but lost him the 1996 election.

Suriname has a long-running dispute with its neighbour, Guyana, over the ownership of a potentially oil-rich offshore area. The matter was referred for settlement to a UN tribunal set up in 2004.

After the 2005 legislative election the New Front for Democracy, a four-party alliance, remained the largest bloc in the national assembly, but lost its overall majority. Two rounds of voting in the July 2005 presidential election failed to produce the required majority, requiring a third round of voting by a United People's Conference (UPC); this re-elected President Venetiaan to another term in office.

POLITICAL SYSTEM

Under the 1987 constitution, the executive president is elected for a five-year term by a two-thirds majority in the national assembly or, if the required majority cannot be achieved, by a specially convened United Peoples' Assembly including district and local council representatives. The vice-president is elected in the same way. The unicameral legislature, the national assembly, has 51 members directly elected for a five-year term.

HEAD OF STATE

President, Ronald Venetiaan, *sworn in* August 12, 2005
Vice-President, Ram Sardjoe

SELECTED GOVERNMENT MEMBERS *as at July 2007*

Defence, Ivan Fernald
Finance, Humphrey Hildenberg

Foreign Affairs, Lygia Kraag-Keteldijk
Internal Affairs, Trade and Industry, Maurits Hassankhan

EMBASSY OF THE REPUBLIC OF SURINAME
Alexander Gogelweg 2, 2517 JH The Hague, The Netherlands
T (+31) (70) 365 0844 E ambassade.suriname@wxs.nl
Ambassador Extraordinary and Plenipotentiary, vacant

BRITISH AMBASSADOR
HE Fraser Wheeler, *apptd* 2006, resident at Georgetown, Guyana

ECONOMY AND TRADE

Although an austerity programme in the mid-1990s achieved economic stability, this was undermined by the expansion of the public sector in the late 1990s. Since 2000 public spending cuts and other measures have stabilised the currency and are reducing inflation. The mainstays of the economy are mining, especially of bauxite and gold, and alumina production, although these make the economy vulnerable to global price fluctuations. Bauxite reserves are declining, but oil production is increasing from existing offshore fields and onshore exploration has begun. Agriculture employs only 8 per cent of the population but produces 13 per cent of GDP. Industries other than mining and oil production are forestry, food processing and fishing. Industry accounts for 22 per cent of GDP and services for 65 per cent.

The main trading partners are the the USA, Norway, the Netherlands, Canada and Trinidad and Tobago. Principal exports are alumina, crude oil, timber, fish and prawns, rice and bananas. The main imports are capital equipment, oil, foodstuffs, cotton and consumer goods.

GNI – US$1,141m (2005); US$2,540 per capita (2005)
ANNUAL AVERAGE GROWTH OF GDP – 5 per cent (2005 est)
INFLATION RATE – 9.5 per cent (2005 est)
UNEMPLOYMENT – 9.5 per cent (2004)
TOTAL EXTERNAL DEBT – US$504.3m (2005 est)
IMPORTS – US$280m (2005)
EXPORTS – US$270m (2005)

BALANCE OF PAYMENTS
Trade – US$22m surplus (2005)
Current Account – US$144m deficit (2005)

Trade with UK	*2005*	*2006*
Imports from UK	£9,167,000	£9,666,000
Exports to UK	£530,000	£540,000

COMMUNICATIONS

There are 4,300km of roads in total, of which approximately one-quarter is surfaced. There are no railways. The 1,200km of inland waterways provide the most effective means of transport. The main seaport is Paramaribo. There are over 40 airports and airfields, the principal airport being at Paramaribo.

The telephone system is good and mobile phone services have expanded rapidly. There were 81,000 main lines in use in 2004, and 232,800 mobile phone subscribers and 30,000 internet users in 2005.

MEDIA

State broadcast media offer a range of views, and operate alongside commercial radio and TV stations. The two daily newspapers, *De West* and *De Ware Tijd,* are privately owned. The government is tolerant of freedom of expression.

SWAZILAND

Umbuso we Swatini – Kingdom of Swaziland

AREA – 17,363 sq. km. Neighbours: South Africa (north, west and south), Mozambique (east)
CAPITAL – Mbabane; population, 67,200 (2002 est)
MAJOR TOWNS – Manzini; Big Bend
CURRENCY – Lilangeni (E) of 100 cents; South African currency is also in circulation. Swaziland is a member of the Common Monetary Area and its unit of currency *Emalangeni* (singular *Lilangeni*) has a par value with the South African rand
POPULATION – 1,136,334 rising at 0.23 per cent per year (2006 est)
RELIGION – Christianity (60 per cent), Islam (1 per cent) (est). The vast majority of Christians practice Zionism, a blend of Christianity and indigenous ancestral worship
LANGUAGE – English, siSwati (both official)
POPULATION DENSITY – 66 per sq. km (2005)
URBAN POPULATION – 23.9 per cent (2005 est)
MEDIAN AGE (years) – 18.5 (2006 est)
NATIONAL ANTHEM – 'Nkulunkulu Mnikati Wetibuiso temaSwati' ['Oh God, Bestower of Blessings on the Swazi']
NATIONAL DAY – 6 September (Independence Day)
LIFE EXPECTANCY (years) – 32.62 (2006 est)
MORTALITY RATE – 29.74 (2006 est)
BIRTH RATE – 27.41 (2006 est)
INFANT MORTALITY RATE – 71.85 (2006 est)
HIV/AIDS ADULT PREVALENCE – 38.8 per cent (2003 est)
DEATH PENALTY – No*
CPI SCORE – 2.5 (2006)
POPULATION BELOW POVERTY LINE – 69 per cent (2005)
LITERACY RATE – 79.2 per cent (2004 est)
GROSS ENROLMENT RATIO (percentage of relevant age group) – primary 107 per cent; secondary 45 per cent; tertiary 4 per cent (2005 est)
HEALTH EXPENDITURE (per capita) – US$146 (2004)

CLIMATE AND TERRAIN

The three regions of the landlocked country are the densely forested and mountainous Highveld along the western border, with an average altitude of 1,219m; the Middleveld, averaging about 609m, which is a mixed farming area; and the Lowveld in the east, which was mainly scrubland until the introduction of sugar cane plantations. Four rivers, the Komati, Usutu, Mbuluzi and Ngwavuma, flow from west to east. Elevation extremes range from 1,862m (Emlembe) at the highest point to 21m (Great Usutu River) at the lowest.

The climate varies from region to region. The Highveld is humid and temperate, the Middleveld and Lebombo range are subtropical and the Lowveld is tropical and semi-arid. Average temperatures in Mbabane, in the Highveld, range from 6°C in June to 25°C in January.

HISTORY AND POLITICS

The Swazi people are believed to have arrived in the area in the 16th century. They developed a strong kingdom which by the mid-19th century was three times the size of the present country. It became a protectorate of the Transvaal in 1884, of the Transvaal and Britain jointly in 1894 and of Britain solely in 1903. The Kingdom of

Swaziland became independent on 6 September 1968. In 1973 King Sobhuza II suspended the constitution, banned political parties and assumed absolute power. The parliamentary system was replaced by traditional tribal communities *(tinkhundla)*. Sobhuza II died in 1982, but as his son was a minor he did not succeed until 1986 at the age of 18 as King Mswati III. The regency between 1982 and 1986 led to power struggles within the royal family, but the real power passed to the Dlamini family, which dominates the government.

Demands for democratisation of the constitution have grown over the past 20 years, with the campaigning of trade unions and political movements supported by popular demonstrations, general strikes and blockades of the border with South Africa.

Swaziland has one of the highest levels of HIV/AIDS infection in the world and faces severe demographic, economic and social problems as a consequence. Three years of erratic rainfall compounded food shortages and over a quarter of the population needed food aid in 2004–5.

POLITICAL SYSTEM
The 2005 constitution retains the wide extent of the king's powers and the ban on political parties. The head of state is a hereditary king who is effectively an absolute monarch. There is a bicameral parliament comprising a 30-member senate and a 65-member house of assembly; members of both serve a five-year term. Each of the country's 55 administrative districts *(tinkhundla)* directly elects one member to the house of assembly and the king appoints ten members. The members of the house of assembly elect ten of their own number to the senate and a further 20 senators are appointed by the king.

HEAD OF STATE
King of Swaziland, HM King Mswati III, *inaugurated* 25 April 1986

SELECTED GOVERNMENT MEMBERS *as at July 2007*
Prime Minister, Absalom Themba Dlamini
Deputy Prime Minister, Constance Simelane
Finance, Majozi Sithole
Foreign Affairs and Trade, Mathendele Moses Dlamini
Home Affairs, Prince Gabheni Dlamini

KINGDOM OF SWAZILAND HIGH COMMISSION
20 Buckingham Gate, London SW1E 6LB
T 020-7630 6611 E swaziland@btinternet.com
High Commissioner, Mary Kanya, *apptd* 2005

BRITISH HIGH COMMISSIONER
HE Paul Boateng, apptd 2005, resident at Pretoria (Tshwane), South Africa

ECONOMY AND TRADE

The country is very poor, with 69 per cent of the population living below the poverty line. Customs dues from the South African Customs Union and remittances from expatriates working in South Africa are a vital supplement to the domestic economy. Subsistence agriculture supports about 80 per cent of the population and contributes 8 per cent of GDP. Sugar cane, cotton, citrus fruits and pineapples are the main cash crops and the basis of industries producing sugar, canned fruit and soft drink concentrates. The mining industry has scaled back in recent years but still produces some coal and asbestos. Other industries produce wood pulp, textiles and clothing, although a shift in global trading concessions has devastated sugar and clothing exports, making thousands unemployed. Industry contributes 50 per cent of GDP and services 42 per cent.

South Africa accounts for about 60 per cent of exports and provides about 95 per cent of imports. Principal exports are the products of agriculture and manufacturing. The main imports are vehicles, machinery, transport equipment, foodstuffs, petroleum products and chemicals.

GNI – US$2,600m (2005); US$2,280 per capita (2005)
ANNUAL AVERAGE GROWTH OF GDP – 1.8 per cent (2005 est)
INFLATION RATE – 4 per cent (2005 est)
UNEMPLOYMENT – 40 per cent (2005 est)
TOTAL EXTERNAL DEBT – US$357m (2003 est)
IMPORTS – US$210m (2005)
EXPORTS – US$201m (2005)

BALANCE OF PAYMENTS
Trade – US$24m surplus (2004)
Current Account – US$114m surplus (2004)

Trade with UK	*2005*	*2006*
Imports from UK	£6,511,000	£5,925,000
Exports to UK	£33,564,000	£35,113,000

COMMUNICATIONS

The railway network is 301km long and connects with the Mozambique port of Maputo and the South African railway to Richards Bay and Durban. There are 3,600km of roads, of which 1,078km are surfaced. There is an international airport at Manzini. Royal Swazi National Airways provides scheduled air services to southern and eastern Africa.

Although modern, the fixed-line telephone system is not extensive and mobile phone services have grown rapidly. In 2005 there were 35,000 main lines in use, 200,000 mobile phone subscribers and 36,000 internet users.

MEDIA

The state controls the media; all radio and TV stations, with the exception of a Christian radio station, are under government control and the country's only private daily newspaper, *The Times of Swaziland*, is strictly monitored. Criticism of the monarchy is banned.

SWEDEN

Konungariket Sverige – Kingdom of Sweden

AREA – 449,964 sq. km. Neighbours: Norway (west), Finland (east)
CAPITAL – Stockholm; population, 765,044 (2004 est)
MAJOR CITIES – Gothenburg (Goteborg); Malmo; Uppsala
CURRENCY – Swedish krona of 100 ore
POPULATION – 9,016,596 rising at 0.16 per cent per year (2006 est)
RELIGION – Christianity (81 per cent) (est). An estimated 15 per cent of the population is atheist
LANGUAGE – Swedish (official)
POPULATION DENSITY – 22 per sq. km (2005)
URBAN POPULATION – 83.4 per cent (2005 est)
MEDIAN AGE (years) – 40.9 (2006 est)
NATIONAL ANTHEM – 'Du Gamla, du Fria' ['Thou Ancient, Thou Freeborn']

NATIONAL DAY – 6 June (Flag Day)
LIFE EXPECTANCY (years) – 80.51 (2006 est)
MORTALITY RATE – 10.31 (2006 est)
BIRTH RATE – 10.27 (2006 est)
INFANT MORTALITY RATE – 2.76 (2006 est)
DEATH PENALTY – No (abolished 1972)
CPI SCORE – 9.2 (2006)

CLIMATE AND TERRAIN

The terrain is mostly flat or rolling lowlands in the south and along the east coast, with mountains in the west. Elevation extremes range from 2,111m (Kebnekaise) at the highest point to 0m (Baltic Sea) at the lowest. There are many lakes, including Vanern, Vattern, Malaren and Hjalmaren in the south, and over 20,000 islands off the coast near Stockholm. The climate is continental, with average temperatures in Stockholm ranging from −5°C in January to 22°C in July.

HISTORY AND POLITICS

Sweden takes its name from the Svear people who inhabited the region during the seventh century AD. The country was united *c.*1000, apart from the south and west, which remained under Danish rule until conquered in the 17th century. The Swedes participated in the Viking expansion from the ninth to 11th centuries and established sovereignty over Finland in the 13th century. The Union of Kalmar (1397) brought Sweden and Norway under Danish rule. Sweden regained its independence following a rebellion by noblemen in 1521 which resulted in the election of Gustav I to the Swedish throne.

Sweden's power reached its zenith in the 17th century under Gustavus II. The Danes were driven out of southern Sweden, the Baltic coast of Russia was seized and the Swedish army pushed into Germany after vanquishing the Catholic League. Swedish power waned in the late 17th and 18th centuries. Finland was lost to Russia in 1809; Norway was ceded to Sweden by the congress of Vienna (1814–15) but gained independence in 1905.

Sweden remained neutral during both world wars. Post-war governments have been dominated by Social Democrat-led coalitions which established a mixed economy and a generous welfare state between 1946 and 1969. Right-wing and centrist parties held power in 1976–82 and 1991–4. Sweden joined the EU in 1995, but decided against membership of the eurozone in 1997, a decision confirmed in a 2003 national referendum. It has yet to ratify the EU constitution.

After the 2006 general election, the Swedish Social Democratic Labour Party (SAP) remained the largest party in the legislature but a larger number of seats were won by a coalition led by the Moderate Party. A four-party coalition government comprising the Moderate Party, Centre Party, Liberal Party and Christian Democrat Party took office in October 2006. Several ministries were reorganised with effect from January 2007.

POLITICAL SYSTEM

Sweden is a constitutional hereditary monarchy. The constitution is based upon the Instrument of Government 1974, which removed from the monarch the roles of appointing the prime minister and signing parliamentary bills into law. A 1979 amendment vested the succession in the monarch's eldest child irrespective of sex.

The *Riksdag* is the unicameral legislature of 349 members directly elected by proportional representation (with a 4 per cent threshold for representation) for a four-year term. The prime minister appoints the council of ministers; the cabinet is responsible to the *Riksdag.* Sweden is divided into 21 counties *(län)* and 290 municipalities *(kommun).*

HEAD OF STATE

HM The King of Sweden, Carl XVI Gustaf, KG, *born* 30 April 1946, *succeeded* 15 September 1973
Heir, HRH Crown Princess Victoria Ingrid Alice Desiree, Duchess of Vastergotland, *born* 14 July 1977

SELECTED GOVERNMENT MEMBERS *as at July 2007*

Prime Minister, Fredrik Reinfeldt
Deputy Prime Minister, Maud Olofsson
Defence, Mikael Odenberg
Finance, Anders Borg
Foreign Affairs, Carl Bildt

EMBASSY OF SWEDEN

11 Montagu Place, London W1H 2AL
T 020-7917 6400 W www.swedenabroad.com/london
Ambassador Extraordinary and Plenipotentiary, HE Staffan Carlson, *apptd* 2004

BRITISH EMBASSY

PO Box 27819, Skarpogatan 6–8, 115 93 Stockholm
T (+46) (8) 671 3000 E info@britishembassy.se
W www.britishembassy.se
Ambassador Extraordinary and Plenipotentiary, HE Andrew Mitchell, *apptd* 2006

BRITISH COUNCIL

c/o British Embassy
T (+46) (8) 671 3110 W www.britishcouncil.org/sweden
Country Manager, Roger Budd

DEFENCE

The army has 280 main battle tanks, 475 armoured personnel carriers and 355 armoured infantry fighting vehicles. The navy has 5 submarines and 18 patrol and coastal vessels at 3 bases. The air force has 157 combat aircraft.

Sweden has a policy of non-alignment in peace and neutrality in war and has declined to become a member of NATO.

MILITARY BUDGET – US$5,900m (2006)
MILITARY PERSONNEL – 27,600: army 13,800, navy 7,900, air force 5,900; paramilitaries 600
CONSCRIPTION DURATION – Seven to 15 months

ECONOMY AND TRADE

Sweden developed from an agricultural to an industrial economy in the early 20th century. The prosperity that had funded the generous welfare state after 1946 ended in the early 1990s, when Sweden experienced a deep recession. Austerity measures and free-market reforms enabled an economic recovery.

Industrial prosperity is based on natural resources including forests, mineral deposits and water power. The forests cover about half the total land surface and sustain the timber, finished wood products, pulp and paper milling industries. Mineral resources include iron ore, lead, zinc, sulphur, granite, marble, precious and heavy metals (the latter not exploited) and extensive deposits of low-grade uranium ore. Industries based on mining are important but it is the general engineering industry that provides 50 per cent of exports, particularly specialised machinery and systems, motor vehicles, aircraft, electrical and electronic equipment, pharmaceuticals, plastics and chemical industries.

Hydroelectricity supplies 15 per cent of energy needs. Sweden has no significant indigenous resources of conventional hydrocarbon fuels and relies upon imported oil, gas and coal for 50 per cent of its energy needs. Less than 10 per cent of the land area is farmland and only 2 per cent of the labour force is employed in farming. Agriculture contributes 1 per cent of GDP, industry 28 per cent and services 71 per cent.

The main trading partners are other EU states, Norway and the USA. Principal exports include machinery, cars, trucks, paper products, pulp and wood, iron and steel products, and chemicals. The main imports are machinery, oil and petroleum products, chemicals, vehicles, iron and steel, foodstuffs and clothing.

GNI – US$369,100m (2005); US$40,910 per capita (2005)
ANNUAL AVERAGE GROWTH OF GDP – 2.7 per cent (2005 est)
INFLATION RATE – 0.5 per cent (2005 est)
UNEMPLOYMENT – 5.8 per cent (2005 est)
TOTAL EXTERNAL DEBT – US$516,100m (2005)
IMPORTS – US$111,200m (2005)
EXPORTS – US$130,200m (2005)

BALANCE OF PAYMENTS
Trade – US$19,701m surplus (2005)
Current Account – US$23,643m surplus (2005)

Trade with UK	*2005*	*2006*
Imports from UK	£4,400,028,000	£4,972,300,000
Exports to UK	£5,029,677,000	£5,547,500,000

COMMUNICATIONS

The railway network is 11,481km in length. There are 424,900km of roads, of which 130,000km are surfaced (including 1,500km of motorways). There are also 2,052km of waterways, navigable for small steamers and barges. The main ports are Gothenburg, Helsingborg, Malmo and Stockholm. The principal airports are at Stockholm, Gothenburg, Kalmar, Linkoping, Malmo, Norrkoping and Orebro. Scandinavian Airlines System provides international and domestic flights, and domestic flights are also provided by Malmo Aviation. The Oresund Bridge connects Sweden to Denmark.

The modern telecommunications systems provided services to 6.4 million main-line subscribers in 2004, and 8.4 million mobile phone subscribers and 6.8 million internet users in 2005.

EDUCATION AND HEALTH

The state education system provides nine years of free and compulsory schooling from the age of seven to 16 in the comprehensive elementary schools. Around 95 per cent continue into further education of two to four years' duration in the upper secondary schools and a unified higher education system administered in six regional areas containing one of the universities: Uppsala (founded 1477); Lund (1668); Stockholm (1878); Gothenburg (1887); Umea (1963) and Linkoping (1967).

GROSS ENROLMENT RATIO (percentage of relevant age group) – primary 99 per cent; secondary 103 per cent; tertiary 84 per cent (2005 est)
HEALTH EXPENDITURE (per capita) – US$3,532 (2004)
HOSPITAL BEDS (per 1,000 people) – 3.6 (2000–5)

MEDIA

Public television is run by Sveriges Television (SVT). There are a number of commercial stations and around two-thirds of households have cable or satellite television. The switch from analogue to digital services is expected to be completed in 2008. Commercial radio began in 1993, and some of the main stations now have near-national networks, in competition with public broadcaster Sveriges Radio. The country is among the world's top consumers of newspapers and the government provides subsidies to newspapers regardless of their political affiliation. There are four Stockholm-based daily newspapers and one based in Gothenburg.

CULTURE

Several Swedish writers have become globally successful, among them crime fiction writer Henning Mankel (*b.* 1948) and Astrid Lindgren (1907–2002), the creator of *Pippi Longstocking*. A number of Swedes have received Academy awards, including directors Ingmar Bergman (1918–2007), and Lasse Hallstrom (*b.* 1946) and actors Greta Garbo (1905–90) and Ingrid Bergman (1915–82). ABBA is the country's most recognisable musical export and has sold over 370 million albums. Founders Bjorn Ulvaeus and Benny Andersson have repeated their success in musical theatre, writing the international hits *Mamma Mia!* and *Chess*. In science, astronomer Anders Celsius (1701–44) invented the eponymous temperature scale and the polymath Alfred Nobel (1833–96) invented dynamite and founded the Nobel prizes for physics, chemistry, medicine, literature and world peace.

SWITZERLAND

Schweizerische Eidgenossenschaft/Confédération Suisse/ Confederazione Svizzera/Confederaziun Svizra – Swiss Confederation

AREA – 41,290 sq. km. Neighbours: France (west and north-west), Germany (north), Austria and Liechtenstein (east), Italy (south)
CAPITAL – Bern; population, 122,178 (2006 est)
MAJOR CITIES – Zurich; Geneva; Basel; Lausanne
CURRENCY – Swiss franc of 100 rappen (or centimes)
POPULATION – 7,523,934 rising at 0.43 per cent per year (2006 est); German (65 per cent), French (18 per cent), Italian (10 per cent), Romansch (1 per cent) (est)
RELIGION – Roman Catholicism (41 per cent), Protestantism (33 per cent), Islam (4 per cent), Orthodox Christianity (1 per cent) (est)
LANGUAGE – German, French, Italian (all official), Serbian, Croatian, English, Albanian, Portuguese, Spanish, Romansch
POPULATION DENSITY – 186 per sq. km (2005)
URBAN POPULATION – 67.5 per cent (2005 est)
MEDIAN AGE (years) – 40.1 (2006 est)
NATIONAL ANTHEM – 'Schweizerpsalm' ['Swiss Psalm']
NATIONAL DAY – 1 August (Confederation Day)
LIFE EXPECTANCY (years) – 80.51 (2006 est)
MORTALITY RATE – 8.49 (2006 est)
BIRTH RATE – 9.71 (2006 est)
INFANT MORTALITY RATE – 4.34 (2006 est)
DEATH PENALTY – No (abolished 1992)
CPI SCORE – 9.1 (2006)

CLIMATE AND TERRAIN

Landlocked Switzerland is the most mountainous country in Europe. The Alps, at no point lower than 1,700m, occupy the south and east, and include peaks such as Dufourspitze (4,634m), Matterhorn (4,478m), Finsteraarhorn (4,274m), Aletschhorn (4,195m) and Jungfrau (4,158m). The Jura mountains lie in the north-west, and the area between these and the Alps is a plateau of hills, flatland and lakes. Elevation extremes range from 4,634m (Dufourspitze) at the highest to 195m (Lake Maggiore) at the lowest. The climate is temperate, with conditions that vary with altitude. Average temperatures in Zurich range from −3°C in January to 24°C in July.

HISTORY AND POLITICS

The area was conquered by the Romans in 58 BC and then overrun by Germanic tribes in the fourth century AD. It was a province of the medieval Holy Roman Empire from 1033. The Swiss confederation began in 1291 as an alliance of three cantons to resist Habsburg control, and expanded during the 14th century when it became independent of the Habsburgs. Its independence was recognised under the Treaty of Westphalia in 1648. French revolutionary forces seized Switzerland in 1789 and named it the Helvetic Republic. Independence was restored in 1814, and the congress of Vienna (1815) joined Geneva, Neuchatel and Valais to the confederation and recognised the country's perpetual neutrality in international affairs. In 1847 a brief civil war between the federal government and seven Roman Catholic cantons over centralisation ended in the latter's defeat. A new constitution was adopted in 1848 which enhanced the powers of the central government.

Many policy decisions are submitted to national referendums. Although the federal government has pursued a policy of gradual integration with the EU and applied for membership in 1992, referendums have rejected membership of the European Economic Area (1992), approved bilateral trade agreements with the EU (2000), and rejected EU membership (2001).

Proportional representation, introduced in 1919, resulted in coalition governments throughout the 20th and into the 21st century. Since 1959 the federal government has been a coalition of four parties: the Swiss People's Party, the Social Democratic Party, the Christian Democratic People's Party and the Radical Democratic Party. Following the 2003 legislative election, the Swiss People's Party was the largest party in the legislature, with 55 seats.

POLITICAL SYSTEM

Under the 1998 constitution, the head of state is a president elected annually (along with the vice-president) for a one-year term by the federal assembly from the members of the federal council. The federal legislature, the federal assembly, has two chambers: the *Nationalrat* (national council) has 200 members, directly elected for a four-year term; the *Standerat* (council of states) has 46 members (two from each canton and one from each half-canton) directly elected within each canton for a four-year term.

Executive power is in the hands of a *Bundesrat* (federal council) of seven members, elected for a four-year term by the federal assembly after every legislative election. The federal council is chaired by the president. Not more than one person from the same canton may be elected a member of the federal council; however, there is a tradition that Italian- and French-speaking areas should between them be represented on the council by at least two members.

Any citizen able to obtain 100,000 voters' signatures in support of holding a referendum on a given issue can initiate a national referendum.

SELECTED GOVERNMENT MEMBERS *as at July 2007*

President of the Swiss Confederation, Foreign Affairs, Micheline Calmy-Rey
Vice-President, Interior, Pascal Couchepin
Federal Chancellor, Annemarie Huber-Hotz
Finance, Hans-Rudolf Merz

SWISS EMBASSY

16–18 Montagu Place, London W1H 2BQ
T 020-7616 6000 W www.swissembassy.org.uk
Ambassador Extraordinary and Plenipotentiary, HE Alexis Lautenburg, *apptd* 2004

BRITISH EMBASSY

Thunstrasse 50, 3005 Bern
T (+41) (31) 359 7700 W www.britain-in-switzerland.ch
Ambassador Extraordinary and Plenipotentiary, HE Simon Featherstone, *apptd* 2003

BRITISH COUNCIL

PO Box 532, Sennweg 2, 3000 Bern 9
T (+41) (31) 301 1473 W www.britishcouncil.org/switzerland
Director, Caroline Morrissey

CONFEDERAL STRUCTURE

There are 23 cantons, three of which are subdivided, making 20 cantons and six half-cantons, or 26 in all. Each canton and half-canton has its own government and a substantial degree of autonomy. The main language in 19 of the cantons is German; in the others it is French (*) or Italian (†).

The confederation consists of: Aargau, Appenzell-Ausserrhoden, Appenzell-Innerrhoden, Basel-Country, Basel-Town, Bern, *Fribourg, *Geneva, Glarus, Graubünden/Grischun, *Jura, Lucerne, *Neuchatel, Nidwalden, Obwalden, St Gallen, Schaffhausen, Schwyz, Solothurn, Thurgau, †Ticino, Uri, *Valais, *Vaud, Zug and Zurich.

DEFENCE

The army has 224 main battle tanks, 1,123 armoured personnel carriers and 186 armoured infantry fighting vehicles. The air force has 90 combat aircraft.

MILITARY BUDGET – US$3,600m (2006)
MILITARY PERSONNEL – 4,200 active (210,000 to be mobilised: army 191,600, air force 32,900, joint staff 10,000, command support 14,000); paramilitaries 105,000
CONSCRIPTION DURATION – 18 weeks, then 6–7 refresher courses

ECONOMY AND TRADE

Switzerland has a prosperous and stable market economy with low unemployment and a highly skilled labour force. Although it has rejected EU membership, it has brought many of its practices into line with EU members to maintain its competitiveness. GDP per capita is higher than in the EU and unemployment is much lower.

Agriculture is practised chiefly in the valleys and the central plateau, where cereals, fruits and vegetables are grown. Dairy farming and stock-raising are also important. The chief manufacturing industries comprise engineering and electrical engineering, metalworking, chemicals and pharmaceuticals, watchmaking, textiles, precision instruments, woodworking, foodstuffs and footwear. Banking, insurance and tourism are also major industries. Agriculture contributes 1.5 per cent of GDP, industry 34 per cent and services 64.5 per cent.

The main trading partners are the EU countries (especially Germany) and the USA. Principal exports are machinery, chemicals, metals, watches and agricultural products. The main imports are machinery, chemicals, vehicles, metals, agricultural products and textiles.

GNI – US$411,400m (2005); US$55,320 per capita (2005)
ANNUAL AVERAGE GROWTH OF GDP – 1.9 per cent (2005 est)
INFLATION RATE – 1.2 per cent (2005 est)
UNEMPLOYMENT – 3.8 per cent (2005 est)
TOTAL EXTERNAL DEBT – US$856,000m (2005)
IMPORTS – US$120,000m (2005)
EXPORTS – US$126,000m (2005)

BALANCE OF PAYMENTS
Trade – US$4,850m surplus (2005)
Current Account – US$49,710m surplus (2005)

Trade with UK	*2005*	*2006*
Imports from UK	£5,128,507,000	£4,204,719,000
Exports to UK	£3,999,478,000	£4,475,953,000

COMMUNICATIONS

There are 71,300km of roads, including 1,728km of motorways. Railway track totals 4,600km, almost all of which is electrified. Transnational Alpine routes are served by all-weather road and rail tunnels. The Rhine carries heavy shipping traffic on the 65km of the Basel-Rheinfelden and Schaffhausen-Bodensee stretches, and there are 12 navigable lakes. The principal airports are at Zurich, Basel, Bern and Geneva.

Modern telecommunications systems provided services to 5.1 million main-line subscribers, 6.8 million mobile phone subscribers and 5.1 million internet users in 2005.

EDUCATION AND HEALTH

Education is controlled by cantonal and communal authorities and is free and compulsory from age seven to 16. Special schools make a feature of commercial and technical instruction. Universities are Basel (founded 1460), Bern (1834), Fribourg (1889), Geneva (1873), Lausanne (1890), Zurich (1832), and Neuchatel (1909), the technical universities of Lausanne and Zurich and the economics university of St Gall.

GROSS ENROLMENT RATIO (percentage of relevant age group) – primary 102 per cent; secondary 93 per cent; tertiary 47 per cent (2005 est)
HEALTH EXPENDITURE (per capita) – US$5,572 (2004)
HOSPITAL BEDS (per 1,000 people) – 6 (2000–5)

MEDIA AND CULTURE

Broadcasting is dominated by the public service Swiss Broadcasting Corporation (SRG/SSR), which operates seven TV networks and 18 radio stations, mainly funded through licence fees. Private radio and TV stations operate at regional level, and television stations from France, Germany and Italy are widely available through multi-channel cable and satellite television. The press has full editorial freedom and operates mainly along regional lines, reflecting linguistic divisions: there are two German-language dailies based in Zurich, two French-language dailies in Geneva and an Italian-language daily in Lugano.

Important cultural figures include the writer and philosopher Jean-Jacques Rousseau (1712–78), the psychoanalyst Carl Gustav Jung (1875–1961), the poet Carl Spitteler (1845–1924), who won the Nobel prize for literature in 1919, and the writer and founder of modern structural linguistics Ferdinand de Saussure (1857–1913).

SYRIA

Al-Jumhuriyah al-Arabiyah as Suriyah – Syrian Arab Republic

AREA – 185,180 sq. km. Neighbours: Lebanon (west), Israel and Jordan (south-west), Iraq (east), Turkey (north)
CAPITAL – Damascus (Dimashq); population, 1,545,598 (2003 est)
MAJOR CITIES – Halab (Aleppo); Hims; Al-Ladhiqiyah, the principal port; Hamah
CURRENCY – Syrian pound (S£) of 100 piastres
POPULATION – 18,881,361 rising at 2.3 per cent per year (2006 est)
RELIGION – Islam (90 per cent), Christianity (10 per cent) (est)
LANGUAGE – Arabic (official), Kurdish, Armenian, Aramaic, Circassian, French
POPULATION DENSITY – 104 per sq. km (2005)
URBAN POPULATION – 50.3 per cent (2005 est)
MEDIAN AGE (years) – 20.7 (2006 est)
NATIONAL ANTHEM – 'Homat el Diyar' ['Guardians of the Homeland']
NATIONAL DAY – 17 April (Independence Day)
LIFE EXPECTANCY (years) – 70.32 (2006 est)
MORTALITY RATES – 4.81 (200 est)
BIRTH RATE – 27.76 (2006 est)
INFANT MORTALITY RATE – 28.61 (2006 est)
DEATH PENALTY – Yes
CPI SCORE – 2.9 (2006)
POPULATION BELOW POVERTY LINE – 20 per cent (2004 est)

CLIMATE AND TERRAIN

The terrain is primarily semi-arid and desert plateaux in the interior, with a narrow coastal plain and mountains in the west, and the fertile basin of the River Euphrates in the east. Elevation extremes range from 2,814m (Mt Hermon) at the highest point to −200m (Lake Tiberias) at the lowest. The climate varies; the coast has a Mediterranean climate, the mountains have moderate summers, the interior plateaux have very hot summers and cold winters, and the Hamad region has a desert climate. Average temperatures in Damascus range from 0°C in January to 37°C in August.

HISTORY AND POLITICS

The country was successively part of the Phoenician, Persian, Roman and Byzantine empires. It was conquered by Muslim Arabs in the seventh century, and was subsequently ruled by foreign dynasties before being defeated by the Turks in the 11th century. The location of many battles during the medieval Crusades, Syria became part of the Ottoman Empire in 1516 until its collapse after the First World War. It then became a mandated territory in 1920, administered by France with Lebanon as 'Greater Lebanon'. Syria's declaration of independence in 1944 was resisted by the French, but was effectively achieved in 1946 when French forces withdrew. Syria formed part of the United Arab Republic with Egypt from 1958 until 1961, when it seceded. It was involved in the Arab-Israeli wars in 1948, 1967 and 1973, losing the Golan Heights to Israel in 1967.

Syrian intervention in Lebanon began in 1976, its military presence influencing politics there after the civil war ended. Forces remained until 2005, when they were withdrawn in response to massive popular protests in Lebanon and intense international pressure following the assassination of a Lebanese politician. However, following the withdrawal, many Western states continued to accuse Syria of supporting and arming Lebanese militants. Relations with the USA, already strained by Syria's attempts to develop weapons of mass destruction, deteriorated in 2006 following the conflict between Israel and Lebanon. However, relations improved in 2007, with meetings with top-level US politicians in April and May.

The Arab Socialist Renaissance (Ba'ath) Party has been the ruling party since 1963. Hafez al-Assad seized power in a coup in 1970 and was elected president in 1971. He remained president until his death in 2000, when he was succeeded by his son, Bashar al-Assad, who was re-elected unopposed in 2007 with 96 per cent of the vote. Following the 2007 legislative election, the Ba'ath Party and its allies retained a large majority in the legislature.

POLITICAL SYSTEM

The 1973 constitution declares that the Arab Socialist Renaissance (Ba'ath) Party is the leading party in the state and society. The president is head of state and head of government. He is elected for a seven-year term by the *Majlis al-Sha'ab* (people's council) and confirmed in office by a national referendum. The president appoints the council of ministers. The unicameral legislature, the people's council has 250 members directly elected for a four-year term. The only candidates permitted to stand in elections are those from the Ba'ath Party and parties allied with it or independents.

HEAD OF STATE

President, Lt-Gen. Bashar al-Assad, *elected by parliament* 27 June 2000, *approved by referendum* 10 July 2000, *re-elected* May 2007

Vice-Presidents, Farouk al-Shara; Najah al-Attar

SELECTED GOVERNMENT MEMBERS *As at July 2007*

Prime Minister, Mohammed Naji al-Otari

Foreign Affairs, Waleed al-Muallem

Defence, Lt.-Gen. Hassan Turkmani

Interior, Gen. Bassam Abdel Majeed

Finance, Mohammad al-Husayn

EMBASSY OF THE SYRIAN ARAB REPUBLIC

8 Belgrave Square, London SW1X 8PH

T 020-7245 9012 W www.syrianembassy.co.uk

Ambassador Extraordinary and Plenipotentiary, Dr Sami Khiyami, *apptd* 2004

BRITISH EMBASSY

PO Box 37, Kotob Building, 11 Mohammad Kurd Ali Street, Malki, Damascus

T (+963) (11) 373 9241

Ambassador Extraordinary and Plenipotentiary, HE Dr John Jenkins, CMG, LVO, *apptd* 2007

BRITISH COUNCIL

PO Box 33105, Maysaloun Street, Shalaan, Damascus

T (+963) (11) 331 0631 W www.britishcouncil.org/syria

Director, Paul Doubleday

DEFENCE

The army has 4,950 main battle tanks, 1,500 armoured personnel carriers and up to 2,450 armoured infantry fighting vehicles. The navy has 2 frigates, 18 patrol and coastal vessels and 15 armed helicopters at 3 bases. The air force has 584 combat aircraft and 71 armed helicopters.

MILITARY BUDGET – US$1,360m (2006)

MILITARY PERSONNEL – 307,600: army 200,000, navy 7,600, air force 100,000; paramilitaries 108,000

CONSCRIPTION DURATION – 30 months

ECONOMY AND TRADE

The economy is state-controlled and predominantly state-owned, although recent modest economic reforms included some privatisation. Oil and agriculture account for nearly half of GDP; recent high oil prices have cushioned the impact of declining production and exports on government revenue. Gas is also produced, for domestic use, and phosphate is mined. An industrialisation programme is developing steadily; the main manufactures are textiles, processed food, beverages and tobacco. Agriculture contributes 24 per cent of GDP, industry 18 per cent and services 58 per cent.

The main export markets are Iraq, Italy, Germany and Lebanon; imports come chiefly from Saudi Arabia, China, Egypt and Italy. Principal exports are crude oil, petroleum products, fruits and vegetables, cotton fibre, clothing, meat, livestock and wheat. The main imports are machinery and transport equipment, food and livestock, metals and metal products, chemicals, plastics, yarn and paper.

GNI – US$26,300m (2005); US$1,380 per capita (2005)

ANNUAL AVERAGE GROWTH OF GDP – 2.8 per cent (2005 est)

INFLATION RATE – 5 per cent (2005 est)

UNEMPLOYMENT RATE – 12.3 per cent (2004 est)

TOTAL EXTERNAL DEBT – US$8,566m (2005 est)

IMPORTS – US$29,100m (2004)

EXPORTS – US$22,200m (2004)

BALANCE OF PAYMENTS

Trade – US$374m deficit (2004)

Current Account – US$205m surplus (2004)

Trade with UK	*2005*	*2006*
Imports from UK	£104,391,000	£81,594,000
Exports to UK	£132,032,000	£272,693,000

COMMUNICATIONS

There are 2,711km of railways, which link with the networks of neighbouring countries. The country has 94,890km of roads, 19,000km of which are surfaced. The principal airports are at Aleppo and Damascus; internal air services operate between all major cities. The main port is Latakia.

Telecommunications systems are being improved. In 2005 there were 2.9 million main telephone lines in use, 3.1 million mobile phone subscribers and 1.1 million internet users.

EDUCATION AND HEALTH

Education is under state control. Elementary education is free at state schools and is compulsory from the age of seven. Secondary education is not compulsory and is free only at the state schools. There are universities at Damascus, Halab, Tishrin, Latakia and the Ba'ath University at Hims.

LITERACY RATE – 82.9 per cent (2004 est)
GROSS ENROLMENT RATIO (percentage of relevant age group) – primary 124 per cent; secondary 68 per cent (2005 est)
HEALTH EXPENDITURE (per capita) – US$58 (2004)
HOSPITAL BEDS (per 1,000 people) – 1.5 (2000–5)

MEDIA

There was a brief period of press freedom when Bashar al-Assad became president in 2000 and instigated the first licensing of private publications in almost 40 years, but restrictions have since been imposed. It is now illegal to criticise the president or his family, and reportage of both foreign and domestic events is heavily censored. Most of the print and broadcast media are owned by the government and the Ba'ath Party. There are three state-run television networks, but satellite receivers are permitted so many viewers have access to foreign television broadcasts. Conditions were set out in 2002 for the licensing of private and commercial radio stations.

TAIWAN

T'ai-wan – Taiwan

AREA – 35,980 sq. km
CAPITAL – Taipei; population, 2,646,474 (2001 est)
MAJOR CITIES – Kaohsiung; Taichung; Tainan
CURRENCY – New Taiwan dollar (NT$) of 100 cents
POPULATION – 23,036,087 rising at 0.61 per cent per year (2006 est); Hoklo (70 per cent), Hakka (14 per cent), mainland Chinese (14 per cent), aborigine (2 per cent) (est)
RELIGION – Taoism (33 per cent), Buddhism (24 per cent), I Kuan Taoism (3 per cent), Christianity (2 per cent) (est). Many also practise Chinese folk beliefs, among which are shamanism, ancestor worship, magic and aspects of animism
LANGUAGE – Mandarin (official), Taiwanese
POPULATION DENSITY – 618 per sq. km (2001)
MEDIAN AGE – 34.6 (2006 est)
NATIONAL ANTHEM – 'San Min Chu-i' ['Three Principles of the People']
NATIONAL DAY – 10 October (Republic Day)
LIFE EXPECTANCY (years) – 77.43 (2006 est)
MORTALITY RATE – 6.48 (2006 est)
BIRTH RATE – 12.56 (2006 est)
INFANT MORTALITY RATE – 6.29 (2006 est)
DEATH PENALTY – Yes
CPI SCORE – 5.9 (2006)
POPULATION BELOW POVERTY LINE – 0.9 per cent (2005)

CLIMATE AND TERRAIN

An island in the China Sea, Taiwan (formerly Formosa) lies 145km east of the Chinese mainland. The island is mountainous and forested in the east, with lowlands in the west. Elevation extremes range from 3,952m (Yu Shan) at the highest point to 0m (South China Sea) at the lowest. The climate is tropical and influenced by the monsoons. Typhoons from the South China Sea bring heavy rains between July and September. Average temperatures in Taipei range from 12°C in January to 34°C in July.

Territories include the Penghu (Pescadores) islands (80.47 sq. km), some 56km west of Taiwan, as well as Kinmen (Quemoy) (109 sq. km) and Matsu (7 sq. km), which are only a few kilometres from mainland China.

HISTORY AND POLITICS

Settled for centuries by the Chinese, the island was annexed by China in the 17th century, and ceded to Japan in 1895 at the end of the Sino-Japanese War. It was returned to China after Japan's defeat in the Second World War. The Kuomintang (KMT) government, led by Gen. Chiang Kai-shek, withdrew to Taiwan in 1949 after being defeated by the Communists in mainland China. The territory remained under Chiang Kai-shek's presidency until his death in 1975. He was succeeded as president by his son, Gen. Chiang Ching-kuo, who ruled until his death in 1988. Martial law was lifted in 1987 after 38 years. In 1991 the Taiwanese government declared an end to the state of war with China, officially recognising the People's Republic of China for the first time, and ended emergency measures that had frozen political life in Taiwan since 1949.

Demands for democratisation of the authoritarian one-party state in the late 1980s led to the first multiparty elections in 1992. The 'Senior Parliamentarians' who had retained their seats since being elected on the mainland in 1948 were forcibly retired in 1991–2. From this point, power has shifted away from the mainlanders to the native Taiwanese, and 50 years of KMT rule ended when the Democratic Progressive Party (DPP), which favours self-determination, won the presidency in 2000 and the 2001 legislative election.

President Chen Shui-bian of the DPP, first elected in 2000, was re-elected in 2004 with 51.1 per cent of the vote. In the 2004 legislative election, the DPP won 89 seats, remaining the largest party in the Legislative Yuan and forming the government, although an alliance of opposition parties led by the KMT commands 114 seats. The prime minister, Su Tseng-chang, and his government resigned in May 2007; Chang Chun-hsiung (prime minister 2000–2) was re-appointed prime minister and a new government was sworn in. A legislative election was due in late 2007.

FOREIGN RELATIONS

Legally, most nations acknowledge the position of the Chinese government that Taiwan is a province of the People's Republic of China, and as a result Taiwan has formal diplomatic relations with only 25 countries and no seat at the UN. China has sanctioned the use of force to prevent Taiwan declaring itself independent.

Direct tourism, trade and communications links between mainland China and the Taiwanese islands of Kinmen and Matsu were inaugurated in 2001, the first direct links between Taiwan and China since 1949.

POLITICAL SYSTEM

The 1947 constitution (which originally applied to the whole of China) has been amended a number of times since 1991; reforms in 2005 disbanded the national assembly and will halve the number of seats in the Legislative Yuan. The head of state is a president directly elected for a four-year term, renewable only once. The Legislative Yuan has 225 members, 176 directly elected and 49 elected proportionately by party, and serves a three-year term. The national assembly, formerly an elected upper chamber, in 2000 became a largely ceremonial body convened *ad hoc* to consider constitutional amendments; in future, proposed amendments to the constitution will be put to a referendum.

HEAD OF STATE
President, Chen Shui-bian, *elected* 18 March 2000, *re-elected* 20 March 2004
Vice-President, Annette Lu

SELECTED GOVERNMENT MEMBERS *as at July 2007*
Premier, Chang Chun-hsiung
Finance, Henry Ho Chih-chin
Foreign Affairs, James Huang Chih-fang
Interior, Lee Yi-yang
Defence, Lee Tien-yu

BRITISH COUNCIL
2F-1, 106 XinYi Rd, Sec. 5, Taipei 110
T (+886) (2) 8722 1000 W www.britishcouncil.org/taiwan
Director, Christine Skinner

DEFENCE

The army has over 926 main battle tanks, 950 armoured personnel carriers, 225 armoured infantry fighting vehicles and 101 attack helicopters. The navy has 4 submarines, 11 destroyers, 22 frigates, 71 patrol and coastal vessels, 32 combat aircraft and 20 armed helicopters at 5 bases. The air force has 479 combat aircraft.
MILITARY BUDGET – US$7,730m (2006)
MILITARY PERSONNEL – 290,000: army 200,000, navy 45,000, air force 45,000; paramilitaries 26,650
CONSCRIPTION DURATION – 20 months

ECONOMY AND TRADE

Since the 1950s Taiwan has transformed itself from a mainly agricultural country into a highly developed industrial economy. This transition was driven by exports, and the trade surplus and foreign reserves are very high. There has been a gradual shift away from state domination of the economy, with a reduction in government influence on investment and foreign trade, and privatisation in the financial and industrial sectors.

The soil is very fertile and a quarter of the land area is used for agriculture, producing rice, corn, vegetables, fruit, meat and dairy products. The industrial base includes electronics, oil refining, armaments, chemicals, textiles, iron and steel, machinery and cement. Agriculture contributes 1.5 per cent of GDP, industry 25.2 per cent and services 73.3 per cent.

The main trading partners are China, the USA, Japan, Hong Kong and South Korea. Principal exports are computer products and electrical equipment, metals, textiles, plastics, rubber products and chemicals. The main imports are machinery and electrical equipment and minerals.
AVERAGE ANNUAL GROWTH OF GDP – 4 per cent (2005 est)
INFLATION RATE – 2.3 per cent (2005 est)
UNEMPLOYMENT – 4.1 per cent (2005 est)
TOTAL EXTERNAL DEBT – US$87,500m (2005 est)
IMPORTS – US$182,600m (2005)
EXPORTS – US$197,800m (2005)

BALANCE OF PAYMENTS
Trade – US$17,932m surplus (2005)
Current Account – US$16,116m surplus (2005)

Trade with UK	*2005*	*2006*
Imports from UK	£944,892,000	£912,853,000
Exports to UK	£2,267,258,000	£2,390,453,000

COMMUNICATIONS

Taiwan has 2,497km of railways and a total road network of 37,299km, most of which is surfaced (including 789km of motorways). The main ports are Keelung, Kaohsiung and Taichung, and there are international airports at Taoyuan (near Taipei) and Kaohsiung. There are internal flights between all the major cities.

Modern, digital telecommunications systems provided services to 13.6 million main-line telephone subscribers, 22.2 million mobile phone subscribers and 13.2 million internet users in 2005.

MEDIA

The media is among the most liberal and competitive in Asia. There are some 350 newspapers, all privately owned and reflecting a wide range of views. There are two main Chinese-language dailies, and three published in English. The broadcast media, especially television, has a high level of ownership by the government, the military and political parties; the government is taking steps to end this. Both terrestrial and cable television services operate, and cable subscription is the highest in the region. There are over 170 radio stations.

TAJIKISTAN

Jumhurii Tojikiston – Republic of Tajikistan

AREA – 143,100 sq. km. Neighbours: Uzbekistan (north and west), Kyrgyzstan (north), China (east), Afghanistan (south)
CAPITAL – Dushanbe; population, 575,900 (2002 est)
MAJOR TOWNS – Khujand; Kulob; Qurghonteppa
CURRENCY – Somoni of 100 dirams
POPULATION – 7,320,815 rising at 2.19 per cent per year (2006 est); Tajik (79.9 per cent), Uzbek (15.3 per cent). There are also Russian, Tatar, Kyrgyz, German and Ukrainian minorities
RELIGION – Islam (95 per cent)
LANGUAGE – Tajik (official), Russian
POPULATION DENSITY – 46 per sq. km (2005)
URBAN POPULATION – 24.2 per cent (2005 est)
MEDIAN AGE (years) – 20 (2006 est)
NATIONAL ANTHEM – 'Surudi Milli' ['Tajik National Anthem']
NATIONAL DAY – 9 September (Independence Day)
LIFE EXPECTANCY (years) – 64.94 (2006 est)
MORTALITY RATE – 8.25 (2006 est)
BIRTH RATE – 32.65 (2006 est)
INFANT MORTALITY RATE – 106.49 (2006 est)
DEATH PENALTY – Yes
CPI SCORE – 2.2 (2006)
POPULATION BELOW POVERTY LINE – 64 per cent (2004 est)
MILITARY EXPENDITURE – US$170m (2006)
MILITARY PERSONNEL – army 7,600; paramilitaries 5,300
CONSCRIPTION DURATION – 24 months
LITERACY RATE – 99.5 per cent (2004 est)

GROSS ENROLMENT RATIO (percentage of relevant age group) – primary 101 per cent; secondary 82 per cent; tertiary 17 per cent (2005 est)
HEALTH EXPENDITURE (per capita) – US$14 (2004)

CLIMATE AND TERRAIN

The landlocked country is mountainous, with the Pamir highlands in the east and the high ridges of the Pamir-Altai system in the centre. Plains are formed by wide stretches of the Syr-Darya valley in the north and of the Amu-Darya in the south. Elevation extremes range from 7,495m (Pik Imeni Ismail Samani) at the highest point to 300m (Syr-Darya) at the lowest. The climate is continental, with average temperatures ranging from –4°C in January to 18°C in July.

HISTORY AND POLITICS

The area that is now Tajikistan was conquered by Alexander the Great in the fourth century BC and remained under Greek and Greco-Persian rule for 200 years, until the kingdom of Kusha was established, based on Bacharia (Bukhara). Tajikistan was invaded by both the Arabs and the Samanid Persians between the seventh and ninth centuries AD. The cities of Bukhara and Samarkand (now in Uzbekistan) were two of the most important cultural and educational centres in the Islamic world. The area became part of the Mongol Empire in the 13th century, and remained under the control of various feudal emirates until the 19th century. In 1868, the northern part was subsumed within the Russian Empire, while the south was annexed by the Emirate of Bukhara. At the time of the Russian revolution in 1917 the Central Asian emirates attempted to establish their independence. Bolshevik power was established in northern Tajikistan by 1 April 1918, when the Turkestan Soviet Socialist Republic was formed, and the Bukhara emirate was overthrown by Soviet forces in 1920. In 1924 the Tajikistan Autonomous Soviet Socialist Republic was formed as part of the Uzbek Republic, before Tajikistan was given full republican status within the USSR in 1929.

Tajikistan declared its independence on 9 September 1991, and Rahmon Nabiyev, Communist leader in 1982–5, was elected president. In 1992, anti-government demonstrations escalated into a five-year civil war between pro-government forces and Islamic and pro-democracy groups. A four-part peace accord signed in 1997 was implemented by a National Reconciliation Commission in 2000. There have been several assassinations and bombings, targeted at government ministers and buildings, since the end of the civil war.

Former Communists have dominated the presidency and the governments since 1991. Some elections have been boycotted by opposition parties, and most have been deemed by international observers not to meet international standards of fairness. A number of opposition leaders have been arrested on criminal charges, moves that their supporters claim are politically motivated.

President Rakhmonov was re-elected in 1999 and in 2006. The 2005 legislative elections were won by the incumbent (former Communist) People's Democratic Party of Tajikistan (HDKT), which continued in office. The government was reshuffled after the 2006 presidential election.

POLITICAL SYSTEM

The 1994 constitution was amended in 1999 and 2003, following referendums, to introduce changes to the presidential term of office and the legislative structure. The executive president is directly elected for a single seven-year term, although the 2003 amendment permits the current incumbent to stand for two further terms. The bicameral legislature consists of the *Majlisi Namoyandogan* (assembly of representatives), which has 63 members directly elected for a five-year term, and the *Majlisi Milli* (national assembly), which has 33 members, 25 elected by five regional assemblies and eight appointed by the president, to serve a five-year term. Administratively Tajikistan is divided into two regions and the Gorno-Badakhstan autonomous region.

HEAD OF STATE
President, Emomali Rakhmonov, *elected by Supreme Soviet* 19 November 1992, *elected* 6 November 1994, *re-elected* 1999, 2006

SELECTED GOVERNMENT MEMBERS *as at July 2007*
Prime Minister, Akil Akilov
First Deputy Prime Minister, Asadullo Ghulomov
Defence, Col.-Gen. Sherali Khayrulloyev
Finance, Safarali Najmiddinov
Foreign Affairs, Hamrokhon Zaripov
Interior, Col.-Gen. Mahmadnazar Solehov

HONORARY CONSULATE
33 Ovington Square, London SW3 1LJ
T 020-7584 5111
Honorary Consul, Benjamin Brahms

BRITISH EMBASSY
65 Tursunzade Street, Dushanbe 734002
T (+992) 372 42221 E dushanbe.reception@fco.gov.uk
W www.britishembassy.gov.uk/tajikistan
Ambassador Extraordinary and Plenipotentiary, HE Graeme Loten, *apptd* 2004

ECONOMY AND TRADE

Since the civil war, there has been steady economic growth but the economy remains fragile due to inconsistent implementation of structural reforms, weak industrial infrastructure, widespread unemployment and high foreign debt. A debt restructuring and write-off agreement was reached with Russia in 2002, and the country has received US$67m (£34m) in aid from the USA. However, around 64 per cent of the population lives below the poverty line.

Agriculture is the major sector of the economy, accounting for 23 per cent of GDP but 67 per cent of employment. Cotton-growing and cattle-raising predominate; other crops are cereals, fruit, grapes and vegetables. Abundant mineral deposits are not fully exploited. Industry consists of aluminium and hydro-electric power production, zinc and lead extraction, food processing and light industries making chemicals and fertilisers, cement, metal-cutting machine tools, refrigerators and freezers. The sector contributes 28 per cent of GDP and employs 7.5 per cent of the workforce.

The main export markets are the Netherlands and Turkey; imports come chiefly from Russia, Uzbekistan and Kazakhstan. Principal exports are aluminium, electricity, cotton, fruits, vegetable oil and textiles. The main imports are electricity, petroleum products, aluminium oxide, machinery and equipment, and foodstuffs.

GNI – US$2,200m (2005); US$330 per capita (2005)
ANNUAL AVERAGE GROWTH OF GDP – 6.7 per cent (2005 est)

INFLATION RATE – 7.1 per cent (2005 est)
UNEMPLOYMENT – 12 per cent (2004 est)
TOTAL EXTERNAL DEBT – US$888m (2004 est)

BALANCE OF PAYMENTS
Trade – US$323m deficit (2005)
Current Account – US$19m deficit (2005)

Trade with UK	*2005*	*2006*
Imports from UK	£4,787,000	£5,016,000
Exports to UK	£680,000	£511,000

COMMUNICATIONS

There are 482km of railway and 27,767km of roads; many roads, including the main highways, are only open in the summer months. About 200km of the River Vakhsh is navigable. The main airport is at Dushanbe, and there are 40 other airports and airfields around the country.

Telecommunications systems are poor, with many towns not linked to the main-line network and very limited mobile phone coverage. There were 245,200 main telephone lines in use in 2005, and 265,000 mobile phone subscribers and 5,000 internet users in 2005.

MEDIA

Broadcasting is dominated by state-run radio and television, alongside more than 30 local and regional private television stations and a few private radio stations. There are more than 200 registered newspapers, some government-owned and others linked to political parties and movements. Journalists regularly come under pressure from the authorities, who control printing presses.

TANZANIA

Jamhuri ya Muungano wa Tanzania – United Republic of Tanzania

AREA – 945,087 sq. km. Neighbours: Kenya and Uganda (north), Mozambique (south), Malawi and Zambia (south-west), Rwanda, Burundi and the Democratic Republic of the Congo (west)
CAPITAL – Dodoma; population, 149,180 (2002)
MAJOR CITIES – Dar es Salaam, the economic and administrative centre; Arusha; Mbeya; Mwanza; Morogoro; Zanzibar
CURRENCY – Tanzanian shilling of 100 cents
POPULATION – 37,445,392 rising at 1.83 per cent per year (2006 est); Africans form a large majority, with European, Asian and other non-African minorities
RELIGION – Christianity (30 per cent), Islam (30 per cent) (est)
LANGUAGE – Swahili, English (both official), Arabic
POPULATION DENSITY – 43 per sq. km (2005)
URBAN POPULATION – 37.5 per cent (2005 est)
MEDIAN AGE (years) – 17.7 (2006 est)
NATIONAL ANTHEM – 'Mungu Ibariki Afrika' ['God Bless Africa']
NATIONAL DAY – 26 April (Union Day)
LIFE EXPECTANCY (years) – 45.64 (2006 est)
MORTALITY RATE – 16.39 (2006 est)
BIRTH RATE – 37.71 (2006 est)
INFANT MORTALITY RATE – 96.48 (2006 est)
HIV/AIDS ADULT PREVALENCE – 8.8 per cent (2003 est)
DEATH PENALTY – Yes
CPI SCORE – 2.9 (2006)
POPULATION BELOW POVERTY LINE – 36 per cent (2002 est)
MILITARY BUDGET – US$137m (2006 est)
MILITARY PERSONNEL – 27,000: army 23,000, navy 1,000, air force 3,000; paramilitaries 1,400
CONSCRIPTION DURATION – 24 months

CLIMATE AND TERRAIN

Tanzania comprises the former Tanganyika, on the mainland of east Africa, and the islands of Zanzibar, Pemba and Mafia. Most of the country lies on the central African plateau, from which rise mountains that run across the centre of the country from north-east to south-west. Peaks include Mt Kilimanjaro (5,894m), the highest point on the continent of Africa, and Mt Meru (4,564m). The land falls to plains in the south-east and along the coast, and to swamps in the west. Large areas of lakes Victoria, Tanganyika and Nyasa lie on the northern and western borders, and there are smaller lakes in the north-east and south-west. The Serengeti National Park covers an area of 9,656 sq. km in the north of the country. The climate is tropical equatorial, modified by altitude. The north has two wet seasons, from March to May and from November to December, while the rest of the country has one wet season from November to May. The average temperature in Dar es Salaam is 29°C all year round.

HISTORY AND POLITICS

The area was settled by Bantu people from the fifth century AD, and city states developed along the coast from the eighth century, trading with Arab, Indian and Persian merchants. Portuguese explorers arrived in the 15th century, and in the 16th century the Portuguese conquered Zanzibar, periodically controlling the coastal states on the mainland. They were ousted from Zanzibar in 1699 by Arabs from Oman, and Oman exercised overlordship over the east African coast from Zanzibar until 1861, when the sultanates of Oman and Zanzibar were separated. The sultanate of Zanzibar became a British protectorate in 1890 and Germany established the colony of German East Africa on the mainland in the 1890s. After the First World War, Tanganyika became a mandated territory under British administration, and achieved its independence on 9 December 1961. It became a republic in 1962. Zanzibar, comprising the islands of Zanzibar, Pemba and Mafia, became independent as a constitutional monarchy on 10 December 1963. The sultan was overthrown in a revolution in 1964 and Zanzibar united with Tanganyika on 26 April 1964 to form the United Republic of Tanzania.

The sole legal political party from 1977 to 1992 was the Revolutionary Party of Tanzania (CCM). The constitution was amended in 1992 to allow multiparty politics, with the stipulation that all parties must be active in both the mainland and Zanzibar and that parties must not be formed on regional, religious, tribal or racial grounds. The first multiparty presidential and parliamentary elections were held in 1995 and were won by the CCM, which has continued to dominate politics.

In the 2005 elections, the CCM candidate Jakaya Mrisho Kikwete was elected president with 80.3 per cent of the vote, and the CCM retained its overwhelming majority in the national assembly.

In Zanzibar's 2005 presidential and legislative elections, Amani Abeid Karume was re-elected president with 53 per cent of the vote, and the CCM won a majority in the national assembly. The elections were characterised by violence and accusations of electoral fraud.

POLITICAL SYSTEM

The 1977 constitution was amended in 1992 to introduce multiparty elections and in 2000 to allow the president to nominate some members of parliament. The executive president is directly elected for a five-year term, renewable only once. The president is always from Tanganyika and the vice-president is always from Zanzibar. The unicameral legislature *Bunge* (national assembly) has 323 members: 232 directly elected, 75 seats reserved for women, five chosen by Zanzibar's house of representatives, and the attorney-general; up to ten further members may be appointed by the president. All serve a five-year term. The national assembly enacts laws that apply to the whole of the United Republic of Tanzania and those that apply only to the mainland; laws that apply specifically to Zanzibar are enacted by the island's own legislature, the 50-member house of representatives. Zanzibar also has its own directly elected president, who is a member of the national assembly, and government.

HEAD OF STATE

President of the United Republic, Jakaya Mrisho Kikwete, *elected* 14 December 2005 *took office* 21 December 2005

Vice-President, Ali Mohamed Shein

President of Zanzibar, Amani Abeid Karume

SELECTED GOVERNMENT MEMBERS *as at July 2007*

Prime Minister, Edward Lowassa

Defence, Juma Kapuya

Finance, Zakia Meghji

Foreign Affairs, Bernard Membe

Home Affairs, Joseph Mungai

HIGH COMMISSION FOR THE UNITED REPUBLIC OF TANZANIA

3 Stratford Place, London W1C 1AS

T 020-7569 1470 W www.tanzania-online.gov.uk

High Commissioner, HE Mwanaidi Sinare Maajar, *apptd* 2006

BRITISH HIGH COMMISSION

PO Box 9200, Umoja House, Garden Avenue, Dar es Salaam

T (+255) (22) 211 0101 E bhc.dar@dar.mail.foc.gov.uk

W www.britishhighcommission.gov.uk/tanzania

High Commissioner, HE Philip Parham, *apptd* 2006

BRITISH COUNCIL

PO Box 9100, Samora Avenue/Ohio Street, Dar es Salaam

T (+255) (22) 211 6574 W www.britishcouncil.org/tanzania

Director, Kate Ewart-Biggs

ECONOMY AND TRADE

State control has been dismantled gradually since the mid-1980s. Liberalisation and modernisation policies have been supported by the World Bank, IMF and aid donors, increasing private-sector growth and investment and producing steady growth in GDP in recent years, but around one-third of the population still lives below the poverty line.

Agriculture is the mainstay of the economy, accounting for 43 per cent of GDP, about 80 per cent of employment and 85 per cent of exports. It provides coffee, tea, cotton, pyrethrum, cashew nuts, cereals, fruit and vegetables as well as the raw materials for industries producing sugar, beer, and cigarettes. Zanzibar and Pemba produce cloves and clove oil, and coconuts and their derivatives. Output of minerals (chiefly diamonds, gold and iron) has increased substantially, and soda ash, cement, petroleum products, footwear, clothing, wood products and fertiliser are also produced. Tourism is a major source of revenue. Industry accounts for 18 per cent of GDP and services for 39 per cent.

The main trading partners are China, India, South Africa, Canada, Kenya and EU countries. Principal exports are gold, coffee, cashew nuts, manufactures and cotton. The main imports are consumer goods, machinery and transport equipment, industrial raw materials and crude oil.

GNI – US$12,700m (2005); US$340 per capita (2005)

ANNUAL AVERAGE GROWTH OF GDP – 6.8 per cent (2005 est)

INFLATION RATE – 4.3 per cent (2005 est)

TOTAL EXTERNAL DEBT – US$8,178m (2005 est)

IMPORTS – US$2,700m (2005)

EXPORTS – US$1,480m (2005)

BALANCE OF PAYMENTS

Trade – US$906m deficit (2004)

Current Account – US$437m deficit (2004)

Trade with UK	*2005*	*2006*
Imports from UK	£71,492,000	£85,748,000
Exports to UK	£36,267,000	£29,490,000

COMMUNICATIONS

There are 78,900km of roads, only 6,808km of which are surfaced. The 3,690km of railways connect Dar es Salaam with Zambia, northern Tanzania and Kenya, and lakes Tanganyika and Victoria. The three major lakes in the east are major trade routes, via ports at Mwanza, Musoma, Bukoba (Lake Victoria) and Kigoma (Lake Tanganyika). The main seaports are Dar es Salaam, Tanga, Mtwara, Zanzibar, Mkoani and Wete (Pemba). Coastal shipping services connect the mainland to Zanzibar, and lake services to neighbouring countries are operated on Lake Tanganyika and Lake Nyasa. The principal international airports are Dar es Salaam, Kilimanjaro and Zanzibar.

The fixed-line telephone system is being modernised; mobile phone distribution has grown rapidly. There were 148,500 main lines in use in 2004, and 1.9 million mobile phone subscribers and 333,000 internet users in 2005.

EDUCATION AND HEALTH

The school system is administered in Swahili but the government is making efforts to improve English standards for the purposes of secondary and higher education.

LITERACY RATE – 69.4 per cent (2004 est)

GROSS ENROLMENT RATIO (percentage of relevant age group) – primary 106 per cent; secondary 6 per cent; tertiary 1 per cent (2005 est)

HEALTH EXPENDITURE (per capita) – US$12 (2004)

MEDIA

There are many state-owned and private newspapers available and popular titles include *Daily News, The Express* and *Uhuru.* Radio is prevalent in urban areas and channels include Radio Free Africa and Radio Tanzania Dar es Salaam. Television was not officially launched until 1994 as President Nyerere believed it was a luxury that would widen the gap between the rich and poor. It does not yet have national coverage. Zanzibar has a less liberal media policy and there are no private broadcasters or newspapers on the island, although locals can access mainland media.

THAILAND

Ratcha Anachak Thai – Kingdom of Thailand

AREA – 514,000 sq. km. Neighbours: Malaysia (south), Myanmar (west and north), Laos (north and east) and Cambodia (east)
CAPITAL – Bangkok; population, 6,355,144 (2000)
MAJOR CITIES – Samut Prakan; Nanthanburi; Udon Thani; Nakhon Ratchasima; Hat Yai
CURRENCY – Baht of 100 satang
POPULATION – 64,631,595 rising at 0.68 per cent per year (2006 est); Thai, including Lao (75 per cent), Chinese (14 per cent) (est)
RELIGION – Buddhism (94 per cent), Islam (5 per cent) (est)
LANGUAGE – Thai (official), English
POPULATION DENSITY – 126 per sq. km (2005)
URBAN POPULATION – 32.5 per cent (2005 est)
MEDIAN AGE (years) – 31.9 (2006 est)
NATIONAL ANTHEM – 'Phleng Chat' ['National Song']
NATIONAL DAY – 5 December (The King's Birthday)
LIFE EXPECTANCY (years) – 72.25 (2006 est)
MORTALITY RATE – 7.04 (2006 est)
BIRTH RATE – 13.87 (2006 est)
INFANT MORTALITY RATE – 19.49 (2006 est)
HIV/AIDS ADULT PREVALENCE – 1.5 per cent (2003 est)
DEATH PENALTY – Yes
CPI SCORE – 3.6 (2006)
POPULATION BELOW POVERTY LINE – 10 per cent (2004 est)

CLIMATE AND TERRAIN

Thailand is divided geographically into four regions: the centre is a fertile plain; to the north-east there is a semi-arid plateau; to the north-west, mountains; and the south is a narrow tropical isthmus with a spine of mountains. Extremes of elevation range from 2,576m (Doi Inthanon) at the highest point to 0m (Gulf of Thailand) at the lowest. The principal rivers are the Chao Phraya in the central plains and the Mekong on the northern and north-eastern borders. The climate is tropical, with high humidity all year round and average temperatures in Bangkok range from 20°C in January to 35°C in July.

HISTORY AND POLITICS

The Thai nation was founded in the 13th century and expanded in the following centuries at the expense of the declining Khmer Empire. Although trade with China, Japan and Europe developed in the 17th century, in 1699 an isolationist policy was adopted. Burma invaded in the 18th century, leaving the country in a state of anarchy until reunification in 1782 under the first king of the present Chakri dynasty. From the late 19th century, Thailand opened up to European contact and trade under a series of modernising kings who reformed the country's administration and commerce. It was the only country in the region to escape colonisation by a European power.

Following a revolution in 1932, Thailand became a constitutional monarchy with parliamentary government. It was occupied by Japan from 1941 until 1945, after which it was under military or military-controlled governments for most of the following 50 years. In 1992, mass demonstrations in Bangkok supported by the king, forced from power the military-aligned government which had won the 1992 election. Military power was curbed, the 1978 constitution was restored and the interim government sacked military chiefs. Another election in September 1992 resulted in a majority for parties not allied with the military. A new constitution was introduced in 1997.

The Thai Rak Thai (TRT) party, which had headed coalition governments since 2001, merged with its coalition partners, the New Aspiration Party and the National Development Party, before the 2005 legislative election. The enlarged party won 375 seats, an overall majority, and formed the country's first democratically elected single-party government. However, a snap election was held on 2 April 2006 after public protests at alleged abuse of power by the prime minister, Thaksin Shinawatra. The main opposition parties boycotted the poll, leading the constitutional court to annul the results and order a rerun, which was scheduled for October but was not held owing to a military coup in September 2006 while Shinawatra was out of the country. An interim government was appointed, and elections are scheduled for December 2007.

INSURGENCY

The Muslim minority is concentrated in the southern provinces of Narathiwat, Pattani, Songhkla and Yala. A separatist campaign in the region began in the 1970s but died down in the 1990s following promises of increased government resources and political representation. Violence resumed in early 2004 and has since claimed over 1,000 lives. In 2005 the prime minister was granted emergency powers in the region, which included allowing the government to monitor telephone calls and censor newspapers.

POLITICAL SYSTEM

Thailand is a constitutional monarchy with a hereditary monarch as head of state. The 1997 constitution provided for a bicameral national assembly comprising a 500-member house of representatives and a 200-member senate. An interim constitution promulgated in October 2006 appointed a non-political 242-member national legislative assembly and a 1,982-member national people's assembly; 100 members of the people's assembly form the council drafting a new constitution. Since the 2006 coup, the appointment of a prime minister has had to be approved by the chair of the national security council as well as the king.

HEAD OF STATE

HM The King of Thailand, King Bhumibol Adulyadej (Rama IX), *born* 5 December 1927, *succeeded* 9 June 1946
Heir, HRH Crown Prince Maha Vajiralongkorn, *born* 28 July 1952

SELECTED GOVERNMENT MEMBERS *as at July 2007*
Prime Minister, Gen. Surayud Chulanont (retd)
Defence, Gen. Boonrod Somtad (retd)
Finance, Chalongphob Sussangkarn
Foreign Affairs, Nitya Pibulsonggram
Interior, Aree Wongsearaya

ROYAL THAI EMBASSY
29–30 Queen's Gate, London SW7 5JB
T 020-7589 2944 W www.thaiembassyuk.org.uk
Ambassador Extraordinary and Plenipotentiary, vacant

BRITISH EMBASSY
14 Wireless Road, Lumpini, Pathumwan, Bangkok 10330
T (+662) 305 8333
Ambassador Extraordinary and Plenipotentiary, HE Quinton Quayle, *apptd* 2007

BRITISH COUNCIL
254 Chulalongkorn Soi 64, Siam Square, Phayathai Road, Pathumwan, Bangkok 10330
T (+662) 652 5480 W www.britishcouncil.org/thailand
Director, James Shipton

DEFENCE

The army has 333 main battle tanks, 950 armoured personnel carriers and 5 attack helicopters. The navy has 1 aircraft carrier, 10 frigates, 89 patrol and coastal vessels, 17 combat aircraft and 8 armed helicopters at 5 bases. The air force has 165 combat aircraft.
MILITARY BUDGET – US$2,130m (2006)
MILITARY PERSONNEL – 306,600: army 190,000, navy 70,600, air force 46,000; paramilitaries 113,700
CONSCRIPTION DURATION – 24 months

ECONOMY AND TRADE

With emergency financial reforms and IMF assistance, Thailand made a quick recovery from the 1997 economic crisis in south-east Asia and in 2002–4 was one of its best performing economies. Growth slowed in 2005 owing to higher oil prices, weaker export performance, a tsunami-related decline in tourism and drought in rural areas. In 2006 investors were deterred by the political climate prior to the coup.

The agricultural sector generates 10 per cent of GDP and employs nearly half the workforce. The main crops are rice, cassava, rubber, maize, sugar cane, coconuts, soya beans and rubber. In recent years fishing and livestock production have gained importance. There are reserves of natural gas, lignite, tin, tungsten and lead; Thailand is a leading producer of both tin and tungsten.

The main industry is tourism, which has been the chief foreign exchange earner since the 1980s. Other industries include textiles and clothing, agricultural processing, beverages, tobacco, cement, tin and tungsten extraction and light manufacturing, which produces jewellery, electrical appliances, computers and parts and cars. Industry contributes 45 per cent of GDP and services 45 per cent.

The main trading partners are Japan, the USA, China, Malaysia and Singapore. Principal exports are textiles and footwear, fish products, rice, rubber, jewellery, cars, computers and electrical appliances. The main imports are capital goods, intermediate goods and raw materials, consumer goods and fuels.
GNI – US$175,000m (2005); US$2,720 per capita (2005)
ANNUAL AVERAGE GROWTH OF GDP – 4.5 per cent (2005 est)
INFLATION RATE – 4.5 per cent (2005 est)
UNEMPLOYMENT – 1.8 per cent (2005 est)
TOTAL EXTERNAL DEBT – US$52,460m (2005 est)
IMPORTS – US$118,000m (2005)
EXPORTS – US$110,000m (2005)

BALANCE OF PAYMENTS
Trade – US$3,162m surplus (2005)
Current Account – US$3,719m deficit (2005)

Trade with UK	*2005*	*2006*
Imports from UK	£641,577,000	£567,654,000
Exports to UK	£1,750,053,000	£1,963,844,000

COMMUNICATIONS

There are 57,403km of roads, almost all of which are surfaced, and 4,071km of railways. Bangkok is the international airport, though airports at Chiang Mai, Phuket and Hat Yai also receive international flights. The main ports are Bangkok and Sattahip, and there are 3,701km of inland waterways navigable by small boats.

A competitive telecommunications sector has seen a rapid growth in mobile phone take-up. In 2005 there were 7 million main lines in use, 27.3 million mobile phone subscribers and 8.4 million internet users.

EDUCATION AND HEALTH

Primary education is compulsory and free, and secondary education in government schools is free. Private universities and colleges are playing an increasing role in higher education.
LITERACY RATE – 92.6 per cent (2004 est)
GROSS ENROLMENT RATIO (percentage of relevant age group) – primary 97 per cent; secondary 73 per cent; tertiary 43 per cent (2005 est)
HEALTH EXPENDITURE (per capita) – US$88 (2004)
HOSPITAL BEDS (per 1,000 people) – 2 (2002)

MEDIA

22.4	WORLD HIGHEST
	hours a week per head spent watching TV

Source: Economist Intelligence Unit

Nearly all the national terrestrial television networks and many of the country's radio networks are controlled by the government and the military. Media reforms are currently in progress, aimed at reducing military interest and opening up more opportunities to the private sector. Although free to criticise policy and uncover abuses, the media tends towards self-censorship regarding the monarchy and judiciary. Newspapers are largely privately run, with popular titles including *Bangkok Post* and *Thairath*.

TOGO

République Togolaise – Togolese Republic

AREA – 56,785 sq. km. Neighbours: Ghana (west), Burkina Faso (north), Benin (east)
CAPITAL – Lomé; population, 839,000 (2003 est)
MAJOR CITIES – Sodoké; Kara; Kpalimé; Atakpamé
CURRENCY – Franc CFA of 100 centimes
POPULATION – 5,548,702 rising at 2.72 per cent per year (2006 est)
RELIGION – Christianity (47 per cent), Animism (33 per cent), Islam (13 per cent) (est). An estimated 5 per cent of the population is atheist

LANGUAGE – French (official), Ewe, Mina, Kabye, Dagomba
POPULATION DENSITY – 113 per sq. km (2005)
URBAN POPULATION – 36.3 per cent (2005 est)
MEDIAN AGE (years) – 18.3 (2006 est)
NATIONAL ANTHEM – 'Salut à Toi, Pays de Nos Aïeux' ['Hail to Thee, Land of Our Forefathers']
NATIONAL DAY – 27 April (Independence Day)
LIFE EXPECTANCY (years) – 57.42 (2006 est)
MORTALITY RATE – 9.83 (2006 est)
BIRTH RATE – 37.01 (2006 est)
INFANT MORTALITY RATE – 60.63 (2006 est)
HIV/AIDS ADULT PREVALENCE – 4.1 per cent (2003 est)
DEATH PENALTY – No*
CPI SCORE – 2.4 (2006)
MILITARY BUDGET – US$35m (2006 est)
MILITARY PERSONNEL – 8,550: army 8,100, navy 200, air force 250; paramilitaries 750
CONSCRIPTION DURATION – 24 months (selective)
LITERACY RATE – 53 per cent (2004 est)
GROSS ENROLMENT RATIO (percentage of relevant age group) – primary 100 per cent; secondary 40 per cent (2005 est); tertiary 4 per cent (2002)
HEALTH EXPENDITURE (per capita) – US$18 (2004)

CLIMATE AND TERRAIN

From hills in the centre of the country, the terrain flattens out to savannah in the north and a plateau leading to a marshy coastal plain in the south. Elevation extremes range from 986m (Mt Agou) at the highest point to 0m (Atlantic Ocean) at the lowest. The climate is tropical, with two wet seasons (March to July and September to November). The average temperature in Lomé is 27°C all year round.

HISTORY AND POLITICS

Formerly part of the kingdom of Togoland, the territory became a German protectorate in 1884 but was occupied on the outbreak of the First World War by Britain and France. The country was divided between Britain and France as a League of Nations mandate after the war and the mandate was renewed by the UN in 1946. In 1957, following a plebiscite, British Togoland integrated with Ghana when it became independent. French Togoland achieved independence as the Republic of Togo in 1960.

There were military coups in 1963 and 1967, the latter bringing to power the army commander Lt.-Col. (later Gen.) Gnassingbé Eyadéma, who proclaimed himself president. Political parties were banned, and in 1969 the president's *Rassemblement du peuple togolais* (RPT) became the sole legal political party. Violent anti-government demonstrations in 1990 forced the government to legalise other political parties and introduce a multiparty constitution in 1992. Eyadéma and the RPT were returned to power in the first multiparty elections in 1993 and in two subsequent elections. President Eyadéma remained in power until his death in February 2005. His regime continued its brutal suppression of opposition, particularly before and after the 1998 elections, when an international inquiry concluded there was systematic abuse of human rights.

Following President Eyadéma's death, the military attempted to install his son, Faure Gnassingbé, as president but this attracted domestic and international condemnation. Gnassingbé resigned, only to be elected to the presidency in April 2005. Following reconciliation talks in 2006, the government and opposition leaders signed an accord providing for the participation of opposition parties in a transitional government, and a national unity government was appointed until elections, scheduled for October 2007, could be held.

POLITICAL SYSTEM
Under the 1993 constitution, the head of state is a president directly elected for a five-year term. The unicameral legislature, the national assembly, has 81 members who are directly elected for a five-year term. The prime minister, who is appointed by the president, is head of government and appoints the cabinet in consultation with the president.

HEAD OF STATE
President, Faure Gnassingbé, *elected* 24 April 2005, *sworn in* 4 May 2005

SELECTED GOVERNMENT MEMBERS *as at July 2007*
Prime Minister, Yawovi Madji Agboyibo
Economic Affairs, Adji Otheth Ayassor
Foreign Affairs, Zarifou Ayeva
Defence, Kpatcha Gnassingbé

EMBASSY OF THE REPUBLIC OF TOGO
8 rue Alfred-Roll, 75017 Paris, France
T (+33) (1) 4380 1213
Ambassador Extraordinary and Plenipotentiary, HE Tchao Sotou Bere, *apptd* 2003

BRITISH AMBASSADOR
HE Dr Nicholas Westcott, CMG, *apptd* 2007, resident at Accra, Ghana

ECONOMY AND TRADE

Progress on economic reform, intended to attract foreign investment and balance the budget, is slow; greater impetus is needed on privatisation, financial transparency and electoral fairness. Aid to Togo, mostly suspended in the 1990s because of its human rights record, has been partially resumed recently, and the country is working with donors on a debt reduction scheme.

The economy is predominantly based on agriculture accounting for 39 per cent of GDP, engaging 65 per cent of the workforce and providing most of the country's exports as well as the raw materials for industry. Industrial activity centres on phosphate mining agricultural processing and manufacture of cement handicrafts, textiles and beverages. Industry accounts for 20 per cent of GDP and 5 per cent of employment. The main export markets are Ghana, Burkina Faso and Benin imports come mainly from France, China and Côte d'Ivoire. Principal exports are re-exports, cotton phosphates, coffee and cocoa. The main imports are machinery and equipment, foodstuffs and petroleum products.

GNI – US$2,200m (2005); US$350 per capita (2005)
ANNUAL AVERAGE GROWTH OF GDP – 1 per cent (2005 est)
INFLATION RATE – 6 per cent (2005 est)
TOTAL EXTERNAL DEBT – US$2,000m (2005)
IMPORTS – US$590m (2005)
EXPORTS – US$360m (2005)

BALANCE OF PAYMENTS
Trade – US$157m deficit (2003)
Current Account – US$162m deficit (2003)

Trade with UK	*2005*	*2006*
Imports from UK	£97,525,000	£140,196,000
Exports to UK	£443,000	£489,000

COMMUNICATIONS

Togo has about 7,500km of roads, of which approximately one-third is surfaced. There are about 500km of railways. The chief waterway is the Mono River, depending on rainfall, and the main ports are Lomé and Kpeme. The principal airport is at Lomé.

The adequate telephone system served 58,600 main telephone lines, 443,600 mobile phone subscribers and 300,000 internet users in 2005.

MEDIA

The government owns Television Togolaise, the sole national television station, and the national radio station, Radiodiffusion Togolaise, and, in association with the ruling party RPT, some of the private radio stations. Togo's only daily newspaper, the *Togo-Presse,* is also government-owned. The constitution promises freedom of expression but this right is regularly abused, with journalists subject to harassment and law suits.

TONGA

Pule'anga Tonga – Kingdom of Tonga

AREA – 748 sq. km
CAPITAL – Nuku'alofa on Tongatapu; population, 23,854 (2006 est)
CURRENCY – Pa'anga (T$) of 100 seniti
POPULATION – 114,689 rising at 2.01 per cent per year (2006 est)
RELIGION – Roman Catholicism (16 per cent), Mormonism (14 per cent), other Christian denominations (70 per cent) (est)
LANGUAGE – English (official), Tongan
POPULATION DENSITY – 142 per sq. km (2005)
URBAN POPULATION – 34 per cent (2005 est)
MEDIAN AGE (years) – 20.7 (2006 est)
NATIONAL ANTHEM – 'E, Otua Mafimafi' ['Oh, Almighty God Above']
NATIONAL DAY – 4 June (Emancipation Day)
LIFE EXPECTANCY (years) – 69.82 (2006 est)
MORTALITY RATE – 5.28 (2006 est)
BIRTH RATE – 25.37 (2006 est)
INFANT MORTALITY RATE – 12.3 (2006 est)
DEATH PENALTY – No*
LITERACY RATE – 98.9 per cent (2004 est)

CLIMATE AND TERRAIN

Tonga comprises over 170 islands in three groups, situated in the south Pacific Ocean some 724km east-south-east of Fiji. Most of the islands are of coral formation, but some are volcanic (Tofua, Kao and Niuafoou or 'Tin Can' Island). Elevation extremes range from 1,033m (unnamed location on Kao island) at the highest point to 0m (Pacific Ocean) at the lowest. The climate is subtropical, influenced by prevailing south-west trade winds with average temperatures of 26°C all year round.

HISTORY AND POLITICS

The islands were settled by Polynesians from *c.*1000 AD. They were visited by Dutch explorers in 1643 and by Captain Cook in 1773. The country was reunited in 1845 after a civil war and a modern constitution adopted in 1875. Tonga became a British protectorate in 1900, and gained its independence on 4 June 1970.

A pro-democracy movement began in 1992 and gathered momentum throughout the 1990s, with the first political party being established in 1994. In the 2005 legislative election, the Human Rights and Democracy Movement won seven of the popularly elected seats, and following the election, some ministers were appointed from among the elected representatives in the legislative assembly for the first time. In February 2006, Prince Ulukalala resigned as prime minister and was replaced in March by Feleti (Fred) Sevele, the first elected commoner to hold the office. Rioting broke out in the capital, apparently in protest at the lack of democratic reform, in November 2006 and a state of emergency was declared. The government has agreed to hold elections in 2008 in which at least 21 seats in the legislature will be directly elected by popular vote.

POLITICAL SYSTEM

The 1875 constitution was amended in 2003 to give greater powers to the king, limit judicial review of royal decisions and increase state control of the media. The head of state is a hereditary monarch. The unicameral legislative assembly, *Fale Alea,* consists of the king, the 16-member privy council, nine hereditary nobles elected by their peers, and nine popularly elected representatives; the elected representatives serve a three-year term. The privy council acts as a cabinet. The prime minister is head of government.

HEAD OF STATE

King of Tonga, HM King Siaosi (George) Tupou V, *born* 4 May 1948, *acceded* 11 September 2006
Heir, HRH Crown Prince Tupouto'a Lavaka, *born* 12 July 1959

SELECTED GOVERNMENT MEMBERS *as at July 2007*

Prime Minister, Feleti (Fred) Sevele
Deputy Prime Minister, Villiami Tau Tangi
Finance, Siosiua Tu'italukua Tupou 'Utoikamanu
Foreign Affairs, Sonatane Tu'a Taumoepeau Tupou

TONGA HIGH COMMISSION

36 Molyneux Street, London W1H 5BQ
T 020-7724 5828 E snkioa@tongahighcom.co.uk
High Commissioner, HE Dr Sione Ngongo Kioa, *apptd* 2006

BRITISH HIGH COMMISSIONER

HE Roger Sykes, resident at Suva, Fiji, *apptd* 2006

ECONOMY AND TRADE

There are few natural resources and the country is dependent on foreign aid and remittances from Tongans working abroad, which are the greatest source of foreign exchange revenue. The government is encouraging the development of a private sector. Unemployment is high and inflation is rising.

Agriculture, fishing and tourism are the main economic activities. The main crops are squashes, coconuts, bananas, vanilla beans, cocoa, coffee, ginger and black pepper. Fish is an important staple food, though recent shortfalls have led to canned fish being imported. A small light industry sector processes agricultural produce.

The main export markets are Japan and the USA; imports come chiefly from New Zealand and Fiji. Principal exports are squashes, fish and vanilla beans. The main imports are foodstuffs, machinery and transport equipment, fuels and chemicals.

GNI – US$178m (2005); US$1,750 per capita (2005)
ANNUAL AVERAGE GROWTH OF GDP – 2.4 per cent (2005 est)
INFLATION RATE – 11.1 per cent (2005 est)
UNEMPLOYMENT – 13 per cent (2004 est)
TOTAL EXTERNAL DEBT – US$80.7m (2004)
IMPORTS – US$110m (2005)
EXPORTS – US$130m (2005)

BALANCE OF PAYMENTS
Trade – US$55m deficit (2002)
Current Account – US$3m deficit (2002)

Trade with UK	*2005*	*2006*
Imports from UK	£2,329,000	£3,228,000
Exports to UK	£92,000	£3,000

COMMUNICATIONS

There are 680km of roads in Tonga, 184km of which are surfaced. Its principal port is Nuku'alofa. There are six airfields on the islands; one has a surfaced runway.

Competition between providers has stimulated rapid expansion of telecommunications services. There were 11,200 main telephone lines in use in 2002, and 16,400 mobile phone subscribers and 3,000 internet users in 2004.

MEDIA

An amendment to the constitution in 2003 increased state control of the media. The primary television and radio broadcasters, Television Tonga and A3Z Radio Tonga, and the weekly newspaper, *Tonga Chronicle*, are all government-run. The private television station OBN TV7 ceased broadcasting in 2006 after a march originating at its headquarters ended in riots in the capital.

TRINIDAD AND TOBAGO

Republic of Trinidad and Tobago

AREA – 5,128 sq. km
CAPITAL – Port of Spain; population, 37,965 (2000)
MAJOR CITIES – Chaguanas; Scarborough, the main town of Tobago; San Fernando
CURRENCY – Trinidad and Tobago dollar (TT$) of 100 cents
POPULATION – 1,065,842 falling at 0.87 per cent per year (2006 est)
RELIGION – Roman Catholicism (26 per cent), Protestantism (24 per cent), Hinduism (22 per cent), Islam (5 per cent), indigenous religions (5 per cent) (est). An estimated 2 per cent of the population is atheist
LANGUAGE – English (official), Hindi, French, Spanish, Chinese
POPULATION DENSITY – 254 per sq. km (2005)
URBAN POPULATION – 76.2 per cent (2005 est)
MEDIAN AGE (years) – 31.2 (2006 est)
NATIONAL ANTHEM – 'Forged From the Love of Liberty'
NATIONAL DAY – 31 August (Independence Day)
LIFE EXPECTANCY (years) – 66.76 (2006 est)
MORTALITY RATE – 10.57 (2006 est)
BIRTH RATE – 12.9 (2006 est)
INFANT MORTALITY RATE – 25.05 (2006 est)
HIV/AIDS ADULT PREVALENCE – 3.2 per cent (2003 est)
DEATH PENALTY – Yes
CPI SCORE – 3.2 (2006)
MILITARY PERSONNEL – 2,700: army 2,000, coast guard 700

CLIMATE AND TERRAIN

Trinidad, the most southerly of the West Indian islands, lies 11km off the north coast of Venezuela. The island is mostly flat, with low mountains, the Northern Range across almost its entire northern width and some low hills in the centre. Elevation extremes range from 940m (Mt Aripo) at the highest point to 0m (Caribbean Sea) at the lowest. Pitch Lake on the south-west coast is one of the world's largest natural sources of asphalt.

Tobago lies 30km north-east of Trinidad. The island has a range of hills, Main Ridge, running along its length, the highest point is 565m. Several islands, of which Chacachacare, Huevos, Monos and Gaspar Grande are the most important, lie west of Corozal Point, the north-west extremity of Trinidad. There is a wet season from June to December. The average temperature in the coastal regions is 27°C all year round.

HISTORY AND POLITICS

Trinidad is assumed to be the oldest site of human habitation in the Caribbean archipelago, with excavated human remains dating back 7,200 years. For much of its history, the islands were home to a number of indigenous peoples, including the Nepuyo, Yaio and Carib peoples.

Trinidad and Tobago were discovered by Columbus in 1498. Trinidad was colonised in 1532 by Spain capitulated to the British in 1797, and was ceded to Britain in 1802. Tobago was colonised by the Dutch from 1632 but subsequently changed hands numerous times until it was ceded to Britain by France in 1814. The two islands were amalgamated as a British colony in 1889 The Territory of Trinidad and Tobago became independent on 31 August 1962, and became a republic in 1976.

The republic has been politically stable since independence, with power passing between the People's National Movement (PNM), principally supported by those of African descent, and the United National Congress (UNC), most of whose supporters are of Asian descent. The 2001 legislative election was inconclusive the two main parties each winning half of the seats. After political deadlock prevented the election of a speaker for parliament and of the president, fresh elections were held in October 2002. These were won by the PNM, with 20 seats, and its leader Patrick Manning became prime minister. The PNM also won the January 2005 election for the Tobago house of assembly.

POLITICAL SYSTEM

Under the 1976 constitution, the head of state is a president elected for a five-year term by an electoral college consisting of all members of the parliament. The bicameral parliament comprises the house of representatives, the lower house, and the senate. The house of representatives has 36 members, directly elected for a five-year term. The senate has 31 members, of whom 16 are appointed on the advice of the prime minister, six on the advice of the leader of the opposition and nine at the discretion of the president, to serve a five-year term. Since 1980 Tobago has had internal self-government through its house of assembly, which has 15 members, 12 directly elected and three chosen by the house for a four-year term.

HEAD OF STATE
President, George Maxwell Richards, *elected* 14 February 2003, *took office* 17 March 2003

SELECTED GOVERNMENT MEMBERS *as at July 2007*
Prime Minister, Finance, Patrick Manning
Attorney-General, John Jeremie
Foreign Affairs, Arnold Piggott
National Security, Martin Joseph

HIGH COMMISSION OF THE REPUBLIC OF TRINIDAD AND TOBAGO
42 Belgrave Square, London SW1X 8NT
T 020-7245 9351 E tthc@btconnect.com
High Commissioner, HE Glenda P. Morean-Phillip, *apptd* 2003

BRITISH HIGH COMMISSION
PO Box 778, 19 St Clair Avenue, St Clair, Port of Spain
T (+1 868) 622 2748 W http://britain-in-trinidad.org
High Commissioner, HE Eric Jenkinson OBE, *apptd* 2007

BRITISH COUNCIL
c/o British High Commission
T (+1) 868 628 0565 W www.britishcouncil.org/tt.htm
Manager, Peredur Evans

ECONOMY AND TRADE

The country is the most prosperous in the Caribbean owing largely to its oil and natural gas reserves. This dependence makes the economy vulnerable to fluctuations in global prices; low prices in the 1980s and 1990s led to the build-up of a large foreign debt, but the high prices of recent years have led to a growing trade surplus. The agricultural sector is small, accounting for 0.7 per cent of GDP and 9.5 per cent of employment; the main products are cocoa, rice, citrus fruits, coffee, vegetables and poultry. Sugar production decreased in 2003 when the state-owned sugar company was closed. Apart from oil and gas extraction, the main industries are tourism, food processing, production of chemicals, cement, beverages, cotton textiles, and car and appliance assembly. The main trading partners are the USA (69 per cent of exports; 27 per cent of imports), Venezuela, Brazil, Japan and Jamaica. Principal exports are oil and petroleum products, chemicals, steel products, fertiliser, cocoa, coffee, citrus fruits and flowers. The main imports are machinery, transport equipment, manufactured goods, food and livestock.

GNI – US$13,400m (2005); US$10,300 per capita (2005)
ANNUAL AVERAGE GROWTH OF GDP – 7 per cent (2005 est)
INFLATION RATE – 6.9 per cent (2005 est)
UNEMPLOYMENT – 8 per cent (2005 est)
TOTAL EXTERNAL DEBT – US$2,767m (2005 est)
IMPORTS – US$5,100m (2005)
EXPORTS – US$8,500m (2005)

BALANCE OF PAYMENTS
Trade – US$1,293m surplus (2003)
Current Account – US$985m surplus (2003)

Trade with UK	*2005*	*2006*
Imports from UK	£103,402,000	£102,138,000
Exports to UK	£70,048,000	£184,339,000

COMMUNICATIONS

The two islands have about 8,300km of roads, of which about half are surfaced. The three main ports are Scarborough (Tobago), Port of Spain and Point Lisas, where new industries powered by local natural gas are located. The international airport is at Port of Spain on Trinidad, and Tobago is served by Crown Point airport.

Modern telecommunications systems provided services to 323,500 main-line subscribers, 800,000 mobile phone subscribers and 160,000 internet users in 2005.

EDUCATION AND HEALTH

Education is free at all state-owned and government-assisted denominational schools, as are certain faculties at the University of the West Indies. Attendance is compulsory for children aged six to 12 years, after which attendance at free secondary schools is determined by success in the secondary school entrance examination at 11 years.

LITERACY RATE – 98.5 per cent (2004 est)
GROSS ENROLMENT RATIO (percentage of relevant age group) – primary 106 per cent; secondary 88 per cent; tertiary 12 per cent (2005 est)
HEALTH EXPENDITURE (per capita) – US$329 (2004)
HOSPITAL BEDS (per 1,000 people) – 3.4 (2000–5)

MEDIA

There are both private and state-run media organisations. Private television and radio stations predominate and the freedom of the press is constitutionally protected. *Newsday* and *Trinidad Guardian* are popular newspapers.

TUNISIA

Al-Jumhuriyah at Tunisiyah – Republic of Tunisia

AREA – 163,610 sq. km. Neighbours: Algeria (west), Libya (south)
CAPITAL – Tunis; population, 728,453 (2004)
MAJOR CITIES – Sfax; Aryanah; Sousse
CURRENCY – Tunisian dinar of 1,000 millimes
POPULATION – 10,175,014 rising at 0.99 per cent per year (2006 est)
RELIGION – Islam (99 per cent) (est)
LANGUAGE – Arabic (official), French
POPULATION DENSITY – 65 per sq. km (2005)
URBAN POPULATION – 64.4 per cent (2005 est)
MEDIAN AGE (years) – 27.8 (2006 est)
NATIONAL ANTHEM – 'Himat al-Hima' ['Defenders of the Homeland']
NATIONAL DAY – 20 March (Independence Day)
LIFE EXPECTANCY (years) – 75.12 (2006 est)
MORTALITY RATE – 5.13 (2006 est)
BIRTH RATE – 15.52 (2006 est)
INFANT MORTALITY RATE – 23.84 (2006 est)
DEATH PENALTY – No*
CPI SCORE – 4.6 (2006)
POPULATION BELOW POVERTY LINE – 7.4 per cent (2005 est)

CLIMATE AND TERRAIN

The north is mountainous with a central plateau that gives way to the semi-arid desert plains of the south. There are salt lakes in the west. Elevation extremes range from 1,544m (Jebel ech Chambi) at the highest point to –17m (Shatt al Gharsah) at the lowest. The climate varies considerably from north to south; the northern coastal regions have a Mediterranean climate with fine and hot summers, while the south is both drier and hotter. Average temperatures in Tunis, on the northern tip of the country, range from 11°C in January to 34°C in June.

HISTORY AND POLITICS

The area was ruled successively by the Phoenicians, Carthaginians, Romans, Byzantines, Arabs, Turks and French before formally becoming a French protectorate in 1883. It was briefly occupied by Germany during the Second World War (1942–3), and became independent as a monarchy under the bey in 1956. In 1957 the bey was deposed and the country became a republic under one-party rule with Habib Bourguiba as president.

There was a growing demand throughout the 1970s for the legalisation of other political parties and the government's resistance to these led to serious unrest. Multiparty legislative elections were held in 1981, but the ruling party (now known as the Constitutional Democratic Rally (RCD)) has retained its grip on power over the past two decades. Although proclaimed president for life in 1975, President Bourguiba was deposed in 1987 on the grounds of senility by the prime minister Zine el-Abidine Ben Ali. Ben Ali was subsequently elected president in unopposed elections in 1989 and 1994, and in multiparty elections in 1999 and 2004.

The main opposition party pulled out of the 2004 presidential election beforehand, claiming that its participation would only legitimise a show of democracy. The simultaneous legislative election was won by the ruling RCD, again with an overwhelming majority of seats after capturing 87.7 per cent of the vote. The new upper house of the legislature, the Chamber of Councillors, was elected for the first time in July 2005; membership is dominated by the RCD.

POLITICAL SYSTEM

The 1959 constitution has been amended a number of times, most recently in 2002 to allow the president to seek a fourth term and to establish a second parliamentary chamber. The president is head of state and head of government. He is directly elected for a five-year term. The legislature, the *Barlaman* (parliament), comprises the *Majlis al-Nuwaab* (chamber of deputies), with 189 members directly elected for a five-year term, and the *Majlis al-Mustasharin* (chamber of councillors), which has 126 members, (85 indirectly elected by regions and professional organisations and 41 appointed by the president) who serve a six-year term with half elected every three years.

HEAD OF STATE

President, Gen. Zine el-Abidine Ben Ali, *took office* 7 November 1987, *elected* 2 April 1989, *re-elected* 1994, 1999, 2004

SELECTED GOVERNMENT MEMBERS *as at July 2007*

Prime Minister, Mohammed Ghannouchi
Finance, Mohamed Rachid Kechiche
Foreign Affairs, Abdelwahab Abdallah
Interior, Rafik Belhaj Kacem
Defence, Kamel Morjane

EMBASSY OF TUNISIA

29 Prince's Gate, London SW7 1QG
T 020-7584 8117
Ambassador Extraordinary and Plenipotentiary, HE Mohamed Ghariani, *apptd* 2005

BRITISH EMBASSY

Rue du Lac Windemere, 1053 Tunis
T (+216) (71) 108 703 E british.emb@planet.tn
W www.britishembassy.gov.uk/tunisia
Ambassador Extraordinary and Plenipotentiary, HE Alan Goulty, CMG, *apptd* 2004

BRITISH COUNCIL

87 Avenue Mohamed V, 1002 Tunis Belvédère
T (+216) 7184 8588 W www.britishcouncil.org/tunisia
Director, Peter Skelton

DEFENCE

The army has 84 main battle tanks and 268 armoured personnel carriers. The navy has 25 patrol and coastal combatant vessels at 3 bases. The air force has 27 combat aircraft.

MILITARY BUDGET – US$443m (2006)
MILITARY PERSONNEL – 35,300: army 27,000, navy 4,800, air force 3,500; paramilitaries 12,000
CONSCRIPTION DURATION – 12 months (selective)

ECONOMY AND TRADE

The economy is diverse and transferral from state to private ownership is on the increase. Further liberalisation is planned to attract foreign investment and barriers to trade with the EU are being removed with the aim of creating a free trade zone by 2008. Agriculture and fisheries account for 13 per cent of GDP; the main products are olives, cereals, tomatoes, citrus fruits, sugar beets, dates, almonds, meat and dairy products. The main industries are oil production, mining (principally phosphate and iron ore), tourism, processing agricultural products and manufacture of textiles, footwear and beverages. Tourism is the chief foreign exchange earner.

The main trading partners are EU countries, especially France and Italy. Principal exports are clothing, semi-finished goods, textiles, agricultural products, mechanical goods, phosphates and chemicals and hydrocarbons. The main imports are textiles, machinery and equipment, hydrocarbons, chemicals and food.

GNI – US$28,800m (2005); US$2,880 per capita (2005)
ANNUAL AVERAGE GROWTH OF GDP – 4.2 per cent (2005 est)
INFLATION RATE – 2.1 per cent (2005 est)
UNEMPLOYMENT – 14.2 per cent (2005 est)
TOTAL EXTERNAL DEBT – US$16,090m (2005 est)
IMPORTS – US$13,200m (2005)
EXPORTS – US$10,500m (2005)

BALANCE OF PAYMENTS

Trade – US$2,434m deficit (2004)
Current Account – US$555m deficit (2004)

Trade with UK	*2005*	*2006*
Imports from UK	£133,220,000	£128,883,000
Exports to UK	£176,961,000	£160,857,000

COMMUNICATIONS

Tunisia has 19,000km of roads, over 12,000km of which are surfaced. There are 2,100km of railways. The main ports include Bizerte, Sfax, Sousse and Tunis-La Goulette. The principal airports are at Tunis, Monastir and Djerba.

The telephone system is being upgraded. In 2005 there were 1.3 million main lines in use, 5.7 million mobile phone subscribers and 950,000 internet users.

EDUCATION AND HEALTH

LITERACY RATE – 74.3 per cent (2004 est)
GROSS ENROLMENT RATIO (percentage of relevant age group) – primary 110 per cent; secondary 81 per cent; tertiary 29 per cent (2005 est)
HEALTH EXPENDITURE (per capita) – US$126 (2004)
HOSPITAL BEDS (per 1,000 people) – 1.7 (2000–5)

MEDIA

Alongside the state-run radio and television stations, many satellite television channels are available and a private radio station has recently been founded, ending the state monopoly on radio broadcasting. An independent press exists but its coverage of local political issues is monitored by the government. Self-censorship is common as breaches of the press code are punishable with a prison sentence. Editions of foreign publications are frequently seized.

TURKEY

Turkiye Cumhuriyeti – Republic of Turkey

AREA – 780,580 sq. km. Neighbours: Greece (west) and Bulgaria (north) in Europe; Georgia, Armenia, Azerbaijan and Iran (east), Syria and Iraq (south) in Asia
CAPITAL – Ankara (Angora), in Asia; population, 3,641,931 (2006 est)
MAJOR CITIES – Istanbul; Izmir; Bursa; Adana; Gaziantep; Konya; Antalya
CURRENCY – New Turkish lira (TL) of 100 kurus
POPULATION – 70,413,958 rising at 1.06 per cent per year (2006 est): Turkish (80 per cent), Kurdish (20 per cent) (est)
RELIGION – Islam (99 per cent) (est)
LANGUAGE – Turkish (official), Kurdish, Dimli, Azeri, Kabardian
POPULATION DENSITY – 94 per sq. km (2005)
URBAN POPULATION – 67.3 per cent (2005 est)
MEDIAN AGE (years) – 28.1 (2006 est)
NATIONAL ANTHEM – 'Istiklal Marsi' ['The Independence March']
NATIONAL DAY – 29 October (Republic Day)
LIFE EXPECTANCY (years) – 72.62 (2006 est)
MORTALITY RATE – 5.97 (2006 est)
BIRTH RATE – 16.62 (2006 est)
INFANT MORTALITY RATE – 39.69 (2006 est)
DEATH PENALTY – No (abolished 2004)
CPI SCORE – 3.8 (2006)
POPULATION BELOW POVERTY LINE – 20 per cent (2002)

CLIMATE AND TERRAIN

Turkey in Europe consists of the relatively low-lying area of Eastern Thrace, including the cities of Istanbul and Edirne, and is separated from Asia by the Bosporus at Istanbul and by the Sea of Marmara and the Dardanelles (about 64km in length, with a width varying from 1.6km to 6.4km).

Turkey in Asia comprises the whole of Asia Minor or Anatolia. The western part of Anatolia is a central plateau with narrow coastal plains fringed by mountains in the north and south. The eastern part is mountainous, the land falling to a plateau lying between the mountains and the Syrian border. Elevation extremes range from 5,166m (Mt Ararat) at the highest point to 0m (Mediterranean Sea) at the lowest. There are many lakes in the eastern mountains, where the Euphrates and Tigris rivers rise.

Climate varies greatly from region to region. The coastal areas and the mountains (except in the east) have fairly hot summers and wet, mild winters. Average temperatures in Ankara range from −4°C in January to 31°C in June.

HISTORY AND POLITICS

Part of the empire of Alexander the Great and then of the Roman and Byzantine empires, Anatolia came under Turkish rule in the 11th century. The Ottoman Turkish Empire was founded in the 13th century and reached its zenith in the 16th century, its rule encompassing much of western Asia, northern Africa and south-eastern Europe. In the 17th century it began a steady decline, and after defeat in the First World War the Empire's remaining territory was partitioned. Following a revolution and the expulsion of foreign forces, the sultanate was abolished and Turkey was proclaimed a republic on 29 October 1923, under Gazi Mustafa Kemal (later known as Kemal Atatürk), who was elected president. Policies of secularism, rapid modernisation, economic development and neutrality were introduced. Turkey was neutral for much of the Second World War, but joined the Allies in 1945. It joined NATO in 1952.

In 1945 a multiparty system was introduced but in 1960 the government was overthrown by the armed forces. A new constitution was adopted in 1961 and a civilian government took office. Civilian governments remained in power until 1980 when mounting problems with the economy and terrorism resulted in another military coup. After the 1983 general election the military leadership handed power to a civilian government.

Since becoming a candidate for EU membership in 1999, Turkey has introduced a number of human and civil rights reforms to meet the preconditions for membership negotiations. These include abolition of the death penalty and reform of the penal code, easing restrictions on freedom of speech, improving rights for women and Kurds, and reducing the political role of the military. Formal EU membership talks began in 2005.

Following elections in 2002, the Islamic-based Justice and Development Party (AKP), led by Recep Tayyip Erdogan, won an overall majority in parliament with 363 seats. Initially the deputy leader of the AKP, Abdullah Gul, was appointed prime minister, but Erdogan became prime minister in March 2003 after being elected to parliament in a by-election.

Tension between secularists and Islamists has grown in recent years and prevented the election of a new president by the legislature in May 2007. Amendments to the constitution that would, amongst other measures, make the president directly elected, have been blocked by President Sezer, as have moves to hold a national referendum on the proposed changes. Early legislative elections took place in July 2007 and the AKP achieved a resounding victory with 47 per cent of the vote, 13 percentage points points more than in 2002. As a result of increased confidence in the government, Abdullah Gul, a former Islamist, was elected president in August.

INSURGENCIES

From 1984 until 1999, government forces fought armed guerrillas of the secessionist Kurdistan Workers' Party (PKK) in the south and east of the country, where Turkey's 12 million Kurds are the majority population. The PKK seeks greater political and cultural rights for the Kurds. In 2004 it suspended its 1999 ceasefire because of what it called 'annihilation' attacks against its forces by the government. There were subsequently several armed clashes in south-east Turkey, and tensions mounted there again in summer 2007. The government has blamed bombings in 2004 and 2005 on the PKK, which has mostly denied responsibility for the attacks and which unilaterally reinstated its ceasefire in September 2006.

Pro-Islamic parties have become increasingly popular since the 1990s, and a number have been banned since 1998 for acting as a focus for anti-secular activities. A number of bombings, attributed to Muslim extremists, occurred in Istanbul in 2003 and 2004.

POLITICAL SYSTEM

The 1982 constitution has been amended several times. The head of state is a president elected by the legislature for a single seven-year term. The unicameral legislature, the Turkish Grand National Assembly, has 550 members who are directly elected for a five-year term. The prime minister, who is appointed by the president, is head of government and appoints the cabinet.

Constitutional changes proposed in 2007 would make the president directly elected, allow presidents to serve a second term, and reduce the presidential term to five years and the parliamentary term to four years.

HEAD OF STATE

President, Abdullah Gul, *elected* 27 August 2007

SELECTED GOVERNMENT MEMBERS *as at August 2007*

Prime Minister, Recep Tayyip Erdogan

Deputy Prime Ministers, Cemil Cicek; Hayati Yazici; Nazim Ekren

Finance, Kemal Unakitan

Interior, Besir Atalay

National Defence, Vecdi Gonul

EMBASSY OF THE REPUBLIC OF TURKEY

43 Belgrave Square, London SW1X 8PA

T 020-7393 0202 W www.turkishembassylondon.org

Ambassador Extraordinary and Plenipotentiary, HE Akin Alptuna, *apptd* 2003

BRITISH EMBASSY

Sehit Ersan Caddesi 46/A, Cankaya, Ankara

T (+90) (312) 455 3344 E britembinf@turk.net

W www.britishembassy.org.tr

Ambassador Extraordinary and Plenipotentiary, HE Nicholas Baird *apptd* 2006

BRITISH COUNCIL

Karum Is Merkezi, C Blok 437 Kat 5, Kavalklidere, Ankara

T (+90) (312) 455 3600 W www.britishcouncil.org.tr

Director, Chris Brown, OBE

DEFENCE

The army has 4,205 main battle tanks, 3,643 armoured personnel carriers, 650 armoured infantry fighting vehicles and 37 attack helicopters. The navy has 12 submarines, 26 frigates, 36 patrol and coastal vessels and 10 armed helicopters at 12 bases. The air force has 445 combat aircraft. Since its invasion of Cyprus in 1974, Turkey has maintained forces in the north of the island and at present has about 36,000 personnel stationed there.

As a member of NATO, Turkey is host to the Headquarters Joint Command South East and the Sixth Allied Tactical Air Force Headquarters. US air force detachments (1,650 personnel) are based at Incirlik in southern Turkey.

MILITARY EXPENDITURE – US$11,720m (2005)

MILITARY PERSONNEL – 514,850: army 402,000, navy 52,750, air force 60,100; paramilitaries 102,200

CONSCRIPTION DURATION – 15 months

ECONOMY AND TRADE

After years of economic difficulty, a stringent recovery programme was agreed with the IMF in 2002. Growth since has averaged over 5 per cent a year and inflation has fallen considerably, although there are still large foreign and public debts. The government's main priorities are to make progress with tax reforms and privatisation and to reduce employment in the public sector.

The agricultural sector accounts for 11.2 per cent of GDP and employs 36 per cent of the workforce. The principal crops are tobacco, cotton, cereals, olives, sugar beets, pulses, citrus and other fruits, and livestock products. A diverse industrial sector is dominated by textiles and clothing (which employ one-third of the industrial workforce), food processing, vehicle assembly, electronics, mining, iron and steel, oil, construction, timber and paper. Turkey is also a destination and a transit route for oil and gas from central Asian countries. Tourism is a major industry and source of foreign revenue. Industry contributes 29.4 per cent of GDP and services 59.4 per cent.

The main trading partners are EU countries (especially Germany), Russia, the USA and China. Principal exports are clothing, foodstuffs, textiles, metal manufactures and transport equipment. The main imports are machinery, chemicals, semi-finished manufactures, fuels and transport equipment.

GNI – US$342,000m (2005); US$4,750 per capita (2005)

ANNUAL AVERAGE GROWTH OF GDP – 7.4 per cent (2005 est)

INFLATION RATE – 8.2 per cent (2005 est)

UNEMPLOYMENT – 10.2 per cent (2005 est)

TOTAL EXTERNAL DEBT – US$170,100m (2005 est)

IMPORTS – US$99,000m (2005)

EXPORTS – US$72,000m (2005)

BALANCE OF PAYMENTS

Trade – US$23,924m deficit (2004)

Current Account – US$15,543m deficit (2004)

Trade with UK	*2005*	*2006*
Imports from UK	£2,224,628,000	£2,480,948,000
Exports to UK	£3,616,894,000	£4,038,493,000

COMMUNICATIONS

Turkey has nearly 430,000km of roads, of which about a third are surfaced. There are over 8,500km of railways, and 1,200km of navigable waterways. The principal ports are Istanbul (Europe) and Izmir (Asia). There is a large merchant fleet, with 545 ships of 1,000 tonnes or over registered in Turkey and 411 Turkish-owned ships registered overseas. The principal airports are at Istanbul and Ankara.

Telecommunications systems are being modernised and expanded, especially the mobile phone network. In 2005 there were 18.9 million main lines in use, 43.6 million mobile phone subscribers and 16 million internet users.

EDUCATION AND HEALTH

Education is free, secular and compulsory from the ages of six to 14. There are elementary, secondary and vocational schools.

LITERACY RATE – 88.3 per cent (2004 est)
GROSS ENROLMENT RATIO (percentage of relevant age group) – primary 93 per cent; secondary 79 per cent; tertiary 29 per cent (2005 est)
HEALTH EXPENDITURE (per capita) – US$325 (2004)
HOSPITAL BEDS (per 1,000 people) – 2.6 (2000–5)

MEDIA

The authorities monitor and censor broadcasts that cover sensitive political subjects, and the press is also subject to some censorship, although many of the restrictions have been lifted to comply with EU requirements. Turkey has one state television and radio station, TRT, over 300 private television channels and more than 1,000 private radio stations. TRT has begun to broadcast Kurdish-language programmes, to conform with the EU criteria on minority rights. There are several daily newspapers, including the titles *Hurriyet, Milliyet* and *Cumhuriyet*, and the English-language *Turkish Daily News.*

CULTURE

Turkey is rich in archaeological remains, including Ephesus, the cultural centre of the Greek Empire, which features in the Bible; Troy, the Homeric city of Ilium; and a wealth of sites from Roman, Byzantine, early Christian and Ottoman periods. Ankara (or Ancyra as it was known in Roman times) was the capital of the Roman province of *Galatia Prima,* and a marble temple (now in ruins), dedicated to Augustus, contains the *Monumentum (Marmor) Ancyranum,* inscribed with a record of the reign of Augustus Caesar.

The Roman city of Byzantium was selected by Constantine the Great as the capital of the Roman Empire in AD 328 and renamed Constantinople. Now Istanbul, it contains the celebrated church of St Sophia, which, after becoming a mosque, was made a museum in 1934, and Topkapi, the former palace of the Ottoman sultans. In 2006 author Orhan Pamuk (*b.* 1952) became the first Turkish Nobel laureate.

TURKMENISTAN

Turkmenostan Respublikasy – Republic of Turkmenistan

AREA – 488,100 sq. km. Neighbours: Iran and Afghanistan (south), Uzbekistan (east and north), Kazakhstan (north-west)
CAPITAL – Ashgabat; population, 695,300 (2001 est)
MAJOR CITIES – Turkmenabat; Dashhowuz
CURRENCY – Manat of 100 tenge
POPULATION – 5,042,920 rising at 1.83 per cent per year (2006 est): Turkmen (85 per cent), Uzbek (5 per cent), Russian (4 per cent) (est)
RELIGION – Islam (89 per cent) (est)
LANGUAGE – Turkmen (official), Russian, Uzbek
POPULATION DENSITY – 10 per sq. km (2005)
URBAN POPULATION – 45.8 per cent (2005 est)
MEDIAN AGE (years) – 21.8 (2006 est)
NATIONAL ANTHEM – 'Garashciiz Bitarap Turkmenistaniin Devlet Gimni' ['Independent Neutral Turkmenistan State Anthem']
NATIONAL DAY – 27 October (Independence Day)
LIFE EXPECTANCY (years) – 61.83 (2006 est)
MORTALITY RATE – 8.6 (2006 est)
BIRTH RATE – 27.61 (2006 est)
INFANT MORTALITY RATE – 72.56 (2006 est)
DEATH PENALTY – No (abolished 1999)
CPI SCORE – 2.2 (2006)
POPULATION BELOW POVERTY LINE – 58 per cent (2003 est)
LITERACY RATE – 98.8 per cent (2004 est)
HEALTH EXPENDITURE (per capita) – US$124 (2004)

CLIMATE AND TERRAIN

Over 80 per cent of the country is taken up by the Kara Kum (Black Sands) desert. There are mountains in the south, and areas below sea level along the edges of the Caspian Sea. Elevation extremes range from 3,139m (Gora Ayribaba) at the highest point to −45m (Lake Sarykamysh) at the lowest. Average temperatures in Ashgabat range from 0°C in January to 34°C in July. The heat of the summers is tempered by low humidity.

HISTORY AND POLITICS

Turkmenistan has been invaded and occupied by many empires, including the Persian, Greek (under Alexander the Great), Parthian and Mongol. From the early 19th century until 1886 Turkmenistan was gradually incorporated into the Russian Empire. A Turkmen revolt against Russian rule in 1916 brought a period of autonomy until 1921, when Soviet control over Turkmenistan was established and it became an Autonomous Soviet Socialist Republic. Turkmenistan became a full republic of the USSR in 1925. It declared its independence from the USSR on 27 October 1991 and joined the Commonwealth of Independent States in 1991 and the UN in 1992.

Saparmurat Niyazov became leader of the Turkmen Communist Party in 1985, and was elected president in 1990 and re-elected in 1992. After extending his term of office to 2002 the legislature removed it altogether and elected him president for life in 2004. His autocratic regime, through harassment and authoritarianism, prevented the development of any effective political opposition or press freedom, rejecting political pluralism in favour of a cult of personality.

The Democratic Party of Turkmenistan (DP), the renamed Communist Party, is the only legal political party, and held all the seats in the parliament after the elections of 1998 and 2004–5. President Niyazov died in December 2006 and Kurbanguly Berdymukhamedov became interim president before being elected to the post in February 2007.

POLITICAL SYSTEM

The 1992 constitution was amended in 1999 to remove restrictions on the number of terms a president can serve, and in 2003 to alter the status, powers and composition of the people's council. The president is head of state and head of government, directly elected for a five-year term. The *Majlis* (parliament) has 50 members directly elected for a five-year term. The *Khalk Maslakhaty* (people's council) is the supreme representative, legislative and supervisory body. It has 2,507 members: the president, the council of ministers, the 50 members of the parliament, regional governors, 50 elected and 10 appointed members from each region, and ethnic and regional representatives.

The country is divided into five regions: Ahal, Balkan, Dashowuz, Lebap and Mary.

HEAD OF STATE
President, Head of Government, Chair of the Council of Ministers, Kurbanguly Berdymukhamedov, *elected* 14 February 2007

SELECTED GOVERNMENT MEMBERS *as at July 2007*
First Deputy Chair, Foreign Affairs, Rashid Meredov
Defence, Col.-Gen. Agageldy Mamedgeldiyev
Economy and Finance, Hojamyrat Geldimyradow
Interior, Hojamyrat Annagurbanow

EMBASSY OF TURKMENISTAN
2nd Floor, St George's House, 14–17 Wells Street, London W1T 3PD
T 020-7255 1071
Ambassador Extraordinary and Plenipotentiary, HE Yazmurad Seryayev, *apptd* 2003

BRITISH EMBASSY
3rd floor, Office Building, Four Points Ak Altin Hotel, Ashgabat
T (+993) (12) 363 462 E beasb@online.tm
W www.britishembassy.gov.uk/turkmenistan
Ambassador Extraordinary and Plenipotentiary, HE Peter Butcher, *apptd* 2005

DEFENCE

The army has 702 main battle tanks, 829 armoured personnel carriers and 942 armoured infantry fighting vehicles. The navy has 6 patrol and coastal combatant vessels. The air force has 94 combat aircraft and 10 attack helicopters.

MILITARY EXPENDITURE – US$450m (2005)
MILITARY PERSONNEL – 26,000: army 21,000, navy 700, air force 4,300
CONSCRIPTION DURATION – 24 months

ECONOMY AND TRADE

The post-independence regime has been reluctant to adopt market reforms; most economic activity remains in state control and inefficient. Although Turkmenistan has large reserves of natural gas and oil, exports have hitherto been restricted by the lack of export routes. However, new gas pipelines are being built westwards to Turkey and eastwards to China. Russia is also becoming a major customer for gas following a 2003 agreement. Use of the revenues from these commodities is erratic and over half of the population lives below the poverty line.

Agriculture is intensive around the irrigated oases, with half the irrigated land used to grow cotton, although exports of this commodity have halved in recent years owing to poor harvests. Agriculture accounts for 24 per cent of GDP and 48 per cent of employment; grain and livestock are the other main products. The principal industries are gas and oil production, petroleum products, mineral extraction, the silk industry and food processing. The main export markets are Ukraine and Iran; imports come chiefly from the UAE, Azerbaijan, the USA, Russia, Ukraine and Turkey. Principal exports are gas, crude oil, petrochemicals, cotton fibre and textiles. The main imports are machinery and equipment, chemicals and foodstuffs.

GNI – US$5,400m (2003); US$1,120 per capita (2003)
ANNUAL AVERAGE GROWTH OF GDP – 6 per cent (2005 est)
INFLATION RATE – 10.5 per cent (2005 est)
UNEMPLOYMENT – 60 per cent (2004 est)
TOTAL EXTERNAL DEBT – US$2,259m (2000)

Trade with UK	*2005*	*2006*
Imports from UK	£13,810,000	£15,591,000
Exports to UK	£4,036,000	£26,613,000

COMMUNICATIONS

Turkmenistan has 24,000km of roads, nearly 20,000km of which are surfaced. There are 2,440km of railways. There are two important waterways, the Amudarya River in the north-east and the Niyazov (formerly Kara Kum) canal running across the Kara Kum desert from the Amudarya to the Caspian Sea, providing 1,300km of transport routes. The main port is Turkmenbashi, on the Caspian Sea, and the main airport is at Ashgabat.

Telecommunications networks are underdeveloped but are to be upgraded. There were 495,000 main lines in use in 2006, 52,000 mobile phone subscribers in 2004 and 36,000 internet users in 2005.

MEDIA

The government has total control of broadcast and print media. Newspapers are produced on government-owned presses, programmes from broadcasters other than the state channels are censored before airing in Turkmenistan, and internet access is controlled by the country's communication authorities. The country is ranked the second worst in the world for press freedom by Reporters Without Borders.

TUVALU

AREA – 26 sq. km
CAPITAL – Funafuti; population, 4,492 (2002)
CURRENCY – The Australian dollar (A$) of 100 cents is legal tender. In addition there are Tuvalu dollar and cent coins in circulation
POPULATION – 11,810 rising at 1.51 per cent per year (2006 est): Polynesian (96 per cent), Micronesian (4 per cent) (est)
RELIGION – Christianity (97 per cent), Baha'i (3 per cent (est)
LANGUAGE – English (official), Tuvaluan, Samoan, I-Kiribati
POPULATION DENSITY – 423 per sq. km (1999)
URBAN POPULATION – 57 per cent (2005 est)
MEDIAN AGE (years) – 24.6 (2006 est)
NATIONAL ANTHEM – 'Tuvalu mo te Atua' ['Tuvalu for the Almighty']
NATIONAL DAY – 1 October (Independence Day)
LIFE EXPECTANCY (years) – 68.32 (2006 est)
MORTALITY RATE – 7.11 (2006 est)
BIRTH RATE – 21.18 (2006 est)
INFANT MORTALITY RATE – 19.47 (2006 est)
DEATH PENALTY – No (abolished 1978)

CLIMATE AND TERRAIN

Tuvalu comprises nine low-lying islands, five of them coral atolls, in the south-west Pacific Ocean. The highest elevation is 5m and the climate is tropical, with average temperatures of 26°C all year round.

HISTORY AND POLITICS

The islands were discovered by Europeans in the 18th century and, as the Ellice Islands, came under the control of the British in 1877. They formed part of the Gilbert and Ellice Islands protectorate (later a colony) from 1892, but were granted separate status from the Gilbert Islands in 1975. Tuvalu became a fully independent state on 1 October 1978. It became a full member of the UN in 2000. Tuvalu is threatened by rising sea levels, and in 2002 it joined with Kiribati and the Maldives to begin legal action against the USA over its refusal to sign the Kyoto Protocol.

There are no political parties; allegiances are influenced by geography and personalities. Although politically stable as a democracy, there are frequent changes in government as support in parliament shifts. Following the 2002 legislative election, Saufatu Sopanga was elected prime minister by parliament in August 2002. He lost a vote of confidence in August 2004 and resigned; his deputy Maatia Toafa took over as acting prime minister and was elected to the post in October 2004. Most of the government lost their seats in the 2006 legislative election and a new cabinet was appointed following the election of Apisai Ielemia as prime minister.

POLITICAL SYSTEM

Under the 1978 constitution, Tuvalu is a constitutional monarchy with the British monarch as head of state, represented by a governor-general who is appointed on the advice of the prime minister. The unicameral legislature, the parliament of Tuvalu, has 15 members who are directly elected for a four-year term. The prime minister is elected by the legislature from among its members, and appoints the cabinet, who must be members of parliament. Local government services are provided by elected island councils.

Governor-General, HE Revd Filoimea Telito, GCMG, MBE

SELECTED GOVERNMENT MEMBERS *as at July 2007*

Prime Minister, Foreign Affairs, Apisai Ielemia
Deputy Prime Minister, Taavau Teii
Finance, Lotoala Metia
Home Affairs, Willy Telavi

HONORARY CONSULATE OF TUVALU

Tuvalu House, 230 Worple Road, London SW20 8RH
T 020-8879 0985 E tuvaluconsulate@netscape.net
Honorary Consul, Dr Iftikhar A. Ayaz

BRITISH HIGH COMMISSIONER

HE Roger Sykes, *apptd* 2006, resident at Suva, Fiji

ECONOMY AND TRADE

Tuvalu raises revenue through the sale of fishing licences, postage stamps and coins, and the leasing of its 900 telephone code and .tv internet suffix. The government also receives annual income from a trust fund set up in 1987, but the country is dependent on foreign aid and many people rely on remittances from expatriate workers. The main economic activities are subsistence agriculture and fishing; agriculture is threatened by the increasing salination of the soil as the sea level rises. The only cash crop is coconuts. Tourism is small-scale. The main trading partners are Fiji and Germany. The only exports are copra and fish. The main imports are foodstuffs, livestock, fuels, machinery and manufactured goods.

ANNUAL AVERAGE GROWTH OF GDP – 1.2 per cent (2002 est)
INFLATION RATE – 3.7 per cent (2003 est)

Trade with UK	*2005*	*2006*
Imports from UK	£78,000	£174,000
Exports to UK	£3,000	—

COMMUNICATIONS

Funafuti has an airfield, from which a service operates regularly to Fiji and Kiribati, and it is also the main port. There are 8km of roads on the islands. The telephone system provides an adequate service, with 700 main lines in use and 1,300 internet users in 2002. There are no mobile phone services.

MEDIA

The government runs Radio Tuvalu, the primary source of information. There is no domestic television, although many islanders watch foreign programming via satellite. The state-owned Tuvalu Media Corporation publishes a newspaper in both Tuvaluan and English. Press freedom is respected.

UGANDA

Republic of Uganda

AREA – 236,040 sq. km. Neighbours: Democratic Republic of the Congo (west), Sudan (north), Kenya (east), Tanzania and Rwanda (south)
CAPITAL – Kampala; population, 1,189,142 (2002)
MAJOR CITIES – Gulu; Lira; Jinja; Mbale; Mbarara
CURRENCY – Uganda shilling of 100 cents
POPULATION – 28,195,754 rising at 3.37 per cent per year (2006 est); Baganda (17 per cent), Bayankole (8 per cent), Basoga (8 per cent), Iteso (8 per cent), Bakiga (7 per cent), Lango (6 per cent), Bagisu (5 per cent), Acholi (4 per cent), Lugbara (4 per cent), Batoro (3 per cent) (est)
RELIGION – Christianity (75 per cent), Islam (15 per cent) (est). In many areas, indigenous beliefs are blended into or are observed alongside recognized religions
LANGUAGE – English (official), Ganda, Swahili, Arabic
POPULATION DENSITY – 146 per sq. km (2005)
URBAN POPULATION – 12.4 per cent (2005 est)
MEDIAN AGE (years) – 15 (2006 est)
NATIONAL ANTHEM – 'O Uganda'
NATIONAL DAY – 9 October (Independence Day)
LIFE EXPECTANCY (years) – 52.67 (2006 est)
MORTALITY RATE – 12.24 (2006 est)
BIRTH RATE – 47.35 (2006 est)
INFANT MORTALITY RATE – 66.15 (2006 est)
HIV/AIDS ADULT PREVALENCE – 4.1 per cent (2004 est)
DEATH PENALTY – Yes
CPI SCORE – 2.7 (2006)
POPULATION BELOW POVERTY LINE – 35 per cent (2001 est)
MILITARY EXPENDITURE – US$189m (2006)
MILITARY PERSONNEL – Ugandan People's Defence Force 45,000; paramilitaries 1,800
HEALTH EXPENDITURE (per capita) – US$19 (2004)

CLIMATE AND TERRAIN

The landlocked country lies on a high plateau with mountain ranges in the south and along the north-eastern border. Elevation extremes range from 5,110m (Mt Stanley) at the highest point to 621m (Lake Albert) at the lowest. Nearly 20 per cent of Uganda's area is covered by lakes, rivers and wetlands, and it contains about half of lakes Victoria, Edward and Albert (Mobuto), as well as lakes Kyoga, Kwania, George and Bisina (formerly Salisbury) and the course of the River Nile from its outlet from Lake Victoria to the Sudan border at Nimule. There is a wet season from December to February. The average temperature in Kampala is an almost constant 24°C.

HISTORY AND POLITICS

Indigenous people had formed several kingdoms in the area by the 14th century. External contact began in the early 19th century with Arab traders and then European explorers. A British protectorate was established over the kingdom of Buganda in 1893 and gradually extended to other territory by 1903. Uganda became an independent state on 9 October 1962, as a federation of the kingdoms of Ankole, Buganda, Bunyoro, Busoga and Toro.

In 1963 it was proclaimed a federal republic but in 1966 prime minister Milton Obote overthrew the president, ended the federal status and became executive president. In 1971 President Obote was deposed in an army coup led by Maj.-Gen. Idi Amin, who proclaimed himself head of state. His repressive dictatorship was characterised by human rights abuses, racial prejudice and the use of death squads. Amin was in power for only eight years, but in that time 250,000 people are believed to have died. He was overthrown in 1979 after a failed attempt to invade northern Tanzania.

Milton Obote was re-elected president in 1980 but political instability and human rights abuses continued. He was ousted by a military coup in 1985 amid a civil war with the rebel National Resistance army led by Yoweri Museveni. A military council was installed but the National Resistance army captured Kampala in January 1986, securing control of the rest of the country in the following few months. Museveni began a process of reconstruction which has resulted in Uganda becoming relatively peaceful and stable, and restored a degree of prosperity.

Museveni was sworn in as president in January 1986, and won the first direct presidential election in May 1996. In the subsequent legislative election, the majority of seats were won by supporters of his 'Movement' system of government, under which political parties are allowed to exist but not to contest elections. President Museveni was re-elected in 2001, and in the 2001 legislative election most of the seats were won by his supporters. A 2005 referendum resulted in an overwhelming vote in favour of a return to multiparty politics, suspended since 1986, and also abolished the restriction on the number of terms a president may serve. In multiparty elections held in 2006, President Museveni was re-elected in the second round of the presidential election with 59 per cent of the vote, and the National Resistance Movement retained its majority in parliament.

INSURGENCIES

The Lord's Resistance Army (LRA) is an insurgent group whose aims have never been specified. In the LRA's low-level insurgency since the late 1980s, thousands have been massacred and mutilated, an estimated 20,000 children abducted to serve in its forces, and over 1.6 million displaced into camps. Originally confined to the north of the country, in 2003 LRA attacks also started to occur in the east. Peace talks between the government and the LRA began in July 2006 and a ceasefire agreement was signed in August, however, peace lasted only until October 2006 when the Ugandan military announced the LRA failed to comply with the conditions of the peace agreement.

POLITICAL SYSTEM

The 1995 constitution was amended in 2005 to allow multiparty elections and to remove the restriction on the number of terms a president can serve. The president is directly elected for a five-year term. The unicameral legislature, the parliament, has 215 members directly elected by constituencies and 94 (including 69 women) elected indirectly to represent particular groups; all serve a five-year term. The prime minister is appointed by the president, subject to the approval of parliament.

HEAD OF STATE

President, Commander-in-Chief of the Armed Forces, Yoweri Museveni, *sworn in* 29 January 1986, *elected* 9 May 1996, *re-elected* 2001, 2006
Vice-President, Gilbert Balibaseka Bukenya

SELECTED GOVERNMENT MEMBERS *as at July 2007*

Prime Minister, Apolo Nsibambi
Deputy Prime Ministers, Henry Muganwa Kajura; Eriya Kategaya; Ali Kirunda Kivejinja
Defence, Crispus W. C. B. Kiyonga
Finance, Ezra Sumura
Internal Affairs, Ruhakana Rugunda
Foreign Affairs, Sam Kutesa

UGANDA HIGH COMMISSION

Uganda House, 58–59 Trafalgar Square, London WC2N 5DX
T 020-7839 5783 W www.ugandahighcommission.co.uk
High Commissioner, HE Joan Kakima Rwabyomere, *apptd* 2006

BRITISH HIGH COMMISSION

PO Box 7070, 10–12 Parliament Avenue, Kampala
T (+256) (31) 312 000 E bhcinfo@starcom.co.ug
W www.britain.or.ug
High Commissioner, HE Francois Gordon, CMG, *apptd* 2005

BRITISH COUNCIL

PO Box 7070, Rwenzori Courts, Plot 2 and 4A, Nakasero Road, Kampala
T (+256) (41) 423 4737 W www.britishcouncil.org/uganda
Director, Richard Weyers

ECONOMY AND TRADE

Economic reforms introduced after 1986 have produced steady economic growth and the reduction of inflation since 1990, but there has been little industrialisation and the economy is vulnerable to fluctuations in the global price of coffee, its main export. Uganda's debt burden has been reduced by the US$2bn (£1bn) debt relief received since 2000 but it is still dependent on foreign aid; some of this has been withheld recently because of donors' concerns about the regime's increasing autocracy.

Agriculture is the most important economic sector, contributing 29 per cent of GDP and engaging about 80 per cent of the workforce. The principal crops are coffee, tea, cotton, tobacco, cassava, potatoes, maize, millet, pulses, cut flowers and livestock products. Industrial activity centres on production of sugar, tobacco, cotton textiles, cement and steel, brewing and fishing. The main export markets are EU countries; imports come chiefly from Kenya and the UAE. Principal exports are coffee, fish and fish products, tea, cotton, cut flowers, horticultural products and gold. Hydroelectricity is exported to Kenya, Tanzania and Rwanda. The main imports are capital equipment, vehicles, petroleum, medical supplies and cereals.

GNI – US$8,000m (2005); US$280 per capita (2005)
ANNUAL AVERAGE GROWTH OF GDP – 4 per cent (2005 est)
INFLATION RATE – 8.1 per cent (2005 est)
TOTAL EXTERNAL DEBT – US$4,973m (2005 est)
IMPORTS – US$1,900m (2005)
EXPORTS – US$820m (2005)

BALANCE OF PAYMENTS
Trade – US$921m deficit (2005)
Current Account – US$267m deficit (2005)

Trade with UK	*2005*	*2006*
Imports from UK	£37,225,000	£38,978,000
Exports to UK	£11,633,000	£12,946,000

COMMUNICATIONS

There is over 1,200km of rail track, and 70,700km of roads, of which 16,300km are surfaced. Having no coast, Uganda is dependent upon rail and road links to Mombasa in Kenya and Dar es Salaam in Tanzania for much of its trade, although the lakes and the River Nile provide navigable routes internally and with neighbouring countries. There is an international airport at Entebbe, and 30 other airports and airfields around the country.

The fixed-line telephone system is inadequate. Two mobile phone systems are in place and subscribers numbered 1.5 million in 2005, compared to 100,800 main-line subscribers. There were 500,000 internet users.

EDUCATION AND HEALTH

Education is a joint undertaking by the government, local authorities and voluntary agencies. In 1996, the Universal Primary Programme was launched, under which four children per family are entitled to receive free primary education.

LITERACY RATE – 68.9 per cent (2004 est)
GROSS ENROLMENT RATIO (percentage of relevant age group) – primary 118 per cent; secondary 16 per cent; tertiary 3 per cent (2005 est)
HEALTH EXPENDITURE (per capita) – US$18 (2002)

MEDIA

Alongside the one state-owned television broadcaster and one radio station, there are more than 100 private radio and television stations, most of which have appeared after the loosening of media laws in 1993. There are two main newspapers, *New Vision* and *The Monitor*. The state has been known to interfere when reporting is perceived to encourage racial tension.

UKRAINE

Ukrayina – Ukraine

AREA – 603,700 sq. km. Neighbours: Belarus (north), Russia (north and east), Romania and Moldova (south-west), Hungary, Slovakia and Poland (west)
CAPITAL – Kyiv (Kiev); population, 2,660,401 (2005 est)
MAJOR CITIES – Kharkiv; Dnipropetrovsk; Odessa; Donetsk; Zaporizhzhia; Lviv
CURRENCY – Hryvna of 100 kopiykas
POPULATION – 46,710,816 falling at 0.6 per cent per year (2006 est); Ukrainian (77.8 per cent), Russian (17.3 per cent). There are smaller Belarusian, Molodovan, Tatar, Polish, Hungarian and Greek communities
RELIGION – Christianity (90 per cent) (est)
LANGUAGE – Ukrainian (official), Russian
POPULATION DENSITY – 81 per sq. km (2005)
URBAN POPULATION – 67.3 per cent (2005 est)
MEDIAN AGE (years) – 39.2 (2006 est)
NATIONAL ANTHEM – 'Shche ne Vmerla, Ukrainy' ['Thou Hast Not Perished, Ukraine']
NATIONAL DAY – 24 August (Independence Day)
LIFE EXPECTANCY (years) – 69.98 (2006 est)
MORTALITY RATE – 14.39 (2006 est)
BIRTH RATE – 8.82 (2006 est)
INFANT MORTALITY RATE – 9.9 (2006 est)
HIV/AIDS ADULT PREVALENCE – 1.4 per cent (2003 est)
DEATH PENALTY – No (abolished 1999)
CPI SCORE – 2.8 (2006)
POPULATION BELOW POVERTY LINE – 29 per cent (2003 est)

CLIMATE AND TERRAIN

Much of the country lies in a plain, rising to steppes and then to the Carpathian mountains in the west, and the mountains in the south of the Crimean peninsula. Elevation extremes range from 2,061m (Hora Hoverla) at the highest point to 0m (Black Sea) at the lowest. The main rivers are the Dnieper, which runs through the centre of the country, the Southern Buh and the Northern Donets (a tributary of the Don). Despite cold winters, the climate in Ukraine is more temperate than neighbouring Russia. Average temperatures in Kyiv, in the colder north of the country, range from −8°C in January to 28°C in June.

HISTORY AND POLITICS

The earliest Slavic state was formed in the middle reaches of the River Dnieper with its capital at Kyiv in the ninth century AD. The area was invaded successively by the Goths, Huns and Khazars, and then by the Tatar-Mongols in the 13th century. It came under Lithuanian rule in the 14th to 15th centuries, Polish rule in the 16th century, and gradually became part of Russia in the 17th to 18th centuries.

Ukraine declared its independence in 1918, and a civil war ensued between Ukrainian nationalists, Bolsheviks, anarchists, Russian monarchists and the Poles, which ended in 1921 with the partitioning of Ukraine between the USSR and Poland. In 1922 Ukraine became a constituent republic of the USSR. Germany invaded and occupied Ukraine from 1941 until forced to withdraw by the Red Army in 1944. Ukraine gained territory in the west in the aftermath of the Second World War, and in 1954 the Crimea was transferred from Russia to Ukraine.

In 1986 Ukraine was the scene of the world's worst nuclear disaster, when a reactor at the Chernobyl nuclear plant exploded. At least 10,000 people have died from radiation poisoning, the long-term health of millions more has been affected and a large area of the country is permanently contaminated.

Ukraine declared itself independent of the USSR on 24 August 1991. Independence was confirmed by a referendum in December 1991 and Leonid Kravchuk was elected to the presidency. In the 1994 presidential election Leonid Kuchma defeated President Kravchuk and won a further term of office in 1999. His resignation was demanded in mass protests after the 2002 legislative election resulted in a hung parliament amid allegations of electoral fraud. The Our Ukraine bloc, an alliance of parties opposed to President Kuchma, was the largest party but a coalition government was formed by supporters of the president and a number of independents.

The 2004 presidential election illustrated Ukraine's divide between the Russian-influenced and industrial east and the pro-European west. The announcement of a victory for Viktor Yanukovych, despite observers' reports of widespread vote-rigging, triggered mass demonstrations and civil disobedience by supporters of rival Viktor Yushchenko, with counter-demonstrations by Yanukovych's followers. The supreme court annulled the result and ordered a rerun, which was held in December 2004 and won by Viktor Yushchenko, with 52 per cent of the vote. President Yushchenko appointed Yuliya Tymoshenko as prime minister in January 2005 and she formed a coalition government led by the Our Ukraine bloc. However, serious divisions emerged within the coalition government, and in September 2005 the entire cabinet was sacked and Tymoshenko was replaced by Yuri Yekhanurov. His government lost a vote of confidence in early 2006 but continued as a caretaker government until the next round of legislative elections in March.

In the March election, the Party of Regions (led by Viktor Yanukovych) won 186 seats, the Yuliya Tymoshenko bloc 129 seats, Our Ukraine 81 seats, the Socialist Party 33 seats and the Communist Party 21 seats. President Yushchenko nominated Viktor Yanukovych as prime minister in July 2006. A power struggle developed between the president and prime minister, and amid a deepening political crisis, in April 2007 President Yushchenko called a snap legislative election for 30 September.

SECESSION

The predominantly Russian Crimea was transferred to Ukrainian rule in 1954. In September 1991 the Crimean parliament voted to make Crimea an autonomous republic, a vote that was accepted by the newly independent Ukraine. However, when the Crimean parliament voted in favour of independence in 1992, Ukraine did not accept the decision and the parliament was suspended. In 1994 the parliament attempted to restore the declaration of sovereignty, leading eventually to Ukraine imposing direct presidential rule over Crimea that ended only after parliamentary elections in 1995 saw a dramatic drop in support for pro-Russian parties. Since 1999 Crimea has had considerable autonomy.

FOREIGN RELATIONS

In the aftermath of the USSR's disintegration in 1991, relations between Ukraine and Russia were strained by disputes over the status of the Black Sea fleet and the status of Crimea. Agreement over the division of the fleet was reached in 1997. Disputes over Crimea have flared up intermittently, most recently in 2003 over a border in the region. The main causes of tension are the pro-Western policies pursued by recent governments, and the economic interdependence of the two countries; Ukraine is heavily dependent on Russia for gas supplies, and the pipelines carrying Russia's gas exports to Europe pass through Ukraine. In January 2006 Russia briefly cut Ukraine's supplies in a price dispute; in Ukraine the move was perceived to be politically motivated.

Ukraine signed a partnership and cooperation agreement with the EU in 1994, and EU membership is a declared long-term objective of the current president. Ukraine was involved in NATO's Partnership for Peace programme in the 1990s, and announced in 2002 that it was abandoning neutrality and applying for NATO membership.

POLITICAL SYSTEM

The 1996 constitution was amended in 2006 to transfer some powers from the president to the legislature. The head of state is a president, directly elected for a five-year term. The unicameral legislature, the Supreme Council, has 450 members, who are directly elected for a five-year term; half of the members are elected from single-seat constituencies by a simple majority, and the other 225 are filled by proportional representation from party lists, with a 4 per cent threshold for representation. A member may only be elected if the turnout in the electoral district is above 50 per cent.

The country is divided into 24 regions and the autonomous republic of Crimea.

HEAD OF STATE

President, Viktor Yushchenko, *elected* 26 December 2004, *sworn in* 23 January 2005

SELECTED GOVERNMENT MEMBERS *as at July 2007*

Prime Minister, Viktor Yanukovych
First Deputy Prime Minister, Mykola Azarov
Deputy Prime Ministers, Andriy Kliuyev; Oleksandr Kuzmuk; Volodymyr Rybak; Viktor Slauta; Dmytro Tabachnyk
Interior, Vasyl Tsushko
Foreign Affairs, Arseniy Yatsenyuk
Economy, Anatoliy Kinakh

EMBASSY OF UKRAINE

60 Holland Park, London W11 3SJ
T 020-7727 6312 W www.ukremb.org.uk
Ambassador Extraordinary and Plenipotentiary, Dr Ihor Kharchenko, *apptd* 2005

BRITISH EMBASSY

Desyatinna 9, 01025 Kyiv
T (+380) (44) 462 0011 E ukembinf@sovamua.com
W www.britemb-ukraine.net
Ambassador Extraordinary and Plenipotentiary, HE Timothy Barrow, CMG, *apptd* 2006

BRITISH COUNCIL

4/12 Vul. Hryhoriya Skovorody, Kyiv 04070
T (+380) (44) 490 5600 W www.britishcouncil.org/ukraine
Director, Terry Sandell, OBE, FRSA

DEFENCE

The army has 3,784 main battle tanks, 8,492 armoured personnel carriers, 3,043 armoured infantry fighting vehicles and 205 attack helicopters. The navy has 1 submarine, 5 principal surface combat vessels and 5 patrol and coastal vessels at 6 bases. The air force has 373 combat aircraft.

MILITARY EXPENDITURE – US$6,000m (2005 est)

MILITARY PERSONNEL – 187,600: army 125,000, navy 13,500, air force 49,100; paramilitaries 84,900
CONSCRIPTION DURATION – 18 to 24 months

ECONOMY AND TRADE

The first decade of independence was characterised by economic mismanagement and opposition to economic restructuring. Reform began in the late 1990s and brought economic growth, with rises in output and exports and a reduction in inflation. However, the slow progress of reform is proving a drag on the economy, leaving it vulnerable to external factors, and corruption remains a major problem, discouraging overseas investors.

Ukraine's agricultural sector is large and productive, with over half the land under cultivation. The main crops are wheat, sugar beet, sunflowers and vegetables; stock-raising is also important. Agriculture accounts for 17 per cent of GDP and nearly a quarter of employment. There are large deposits of coal and iron ore, and other minerals are mined. Metal processing, the manufacture of machinery, and chemical and petrochemical industries are major contributors to Ukraine's GDP; mining and metallurgy account for more than 40 per cent of exports. Industrial activities also include ship-building, engineering and food processing, especially of sugar.

The main trading partner is Russia (22 per cent of exports; 35 per cent of imports), Germany, Turkmenistan, Turkey, Italy and China. Principal exports are ferrous and non-ferrous metals, fuel and petroleum products, chemicals, machinery and transport equipment, and foodstuffs. The main imports are energy (primarily gas), machinery and equipment, and chemicals.

GNI – US$71,700m (2005); US$1,520 per capita (2005)
ANNUAL AVERAGE GROWTH OF GDP – 2.6 per cent (2005 est)
INFLATION RATE – 13.5 per cent (2003 est)
UNEMPLOYMENT – 3.1 per cent (2005 est)
TOTAL EXTERNAL DEBT – US$23,930m (2005 est)
IMPORTS – US$36,000m (2005)
EXPORTS – US$34,000m (2005)

BALANCE OF PAYMENTS
Trade – US$1,135m deficit (2005)
Current Account – US$2,531m surplus (2005)

Trade with UK	*2005*	*2006*
Imports from UK	£279,797,000	£337,863,000
Exports to UK	£93,076,000	£128,552,000

COMMUNICATIONS

Ukraine has a total of 170,000km of roads, 164,000km of which are surfaced. It has 22,500km of railways, and ,200km of waterways, mostly on the River Dnieper. Its main seaports are Mariupol on the Sea of Azov, and Kherson, Mykolayiv, Odessa and Sevastopol on the Black Sea. There is a large merchant fleet of 202 ships of 1,000 tonnes and over, with a further 160 Ukrainian-owned ships registered in other countries. The principal airports are at Kyiv and Odessa.

The fixed-line telephone system was antiquated and is being improved, although telephone density is still low and mobile phone distribution is rising rapidly. There were 12.1 million main lines in use in 2004, and 17.2 million mobile phone subscribers and 5.3 million internet users in 2005.

EDUCATION AND HEALTH

LITERACY RATE – 99.4 per cent (2004 est)
GROSS ENROLMENT RATIO (percentage of relevant age group) – primary 107 per cent; secondary 89 per cent; tertiary 69 per cent (2005 est)
HEALTH EXPENDITURE (per capita) – US$90 (2004)
HOSPITAL BEDS (per 1,000 people) – 8.8 (2000–5)

MEDIA

There are several private and state-owned television and radio networks. Ukraine has eight daily newspapers, many of which are mass-circulation publications; titles include *Silski Visti* and *Segodnya*. The independence of the press has become much more apparent since the disputed presidential election of 2004, and has been encouraged by President Yushchenko.

UNITED ARAB EMIRATES

Al-Imarat al-Arabiyah al-Muttahidah – United Arab Emirates

AREA – 82,880 sq. km approximately. Neighbours: Oman (north-east and east), Saudi Arabia (south and west), Qatar (north-west)
CAPITAL – Abu Dhabi; population, 578,000 (2004 est)
MAJOR CITIES – Dubai; Ash Shariqah; Al-Ain; Ajman
CURRENCY – UAE dirham (Dh) of 100 fils
POPULATION – 2,602,713 rising at 1.52 per cent per year (2006 est); South Asian (50 per cent), Arab and Iranian (23 per cent), Emirati (local Arabs) (19 per cent) (est)
RELIGION – Islam (76 per cent), Christianity (9 per cent) (est)
LANGUAGE – Arabic (official), Persian, English, Hindi, Urdu
POPULATION DENSITY – 54 per sq. km (2005)
URBAN POPULATION – 85.5 per cent (2005 est)
MEDIAN AGE (years) – 28.1 (2006 est)
NATIONAL ANTHEM – 'Ishy Bilady' ['Long Live My Homeland']
NATIONAL DAY – 2 December (Independence Day)
LIFE EXPECTANCY (years) – 75.44 (2006 est)
MORTALITY RATE – 4.4 (2006 est)
BIRTH RATE – 18.96 (2006 est)
INFANT MORTALITY RATE – 14.09 (2006 est)
DEATH PENALTY – Yes
CPI SCORE – 6.2 (2006)

CLIMATE AND TERRAIN

The United Arab Emirates (UAE) is situated in the south-east of the Arabian peninsula. Six of the emirates lie on the shore of the Gulf, between the Musandam peninsula in the east and the Qatar peninsula in the west, while the seventh, Fujairah, lies on the Gulf of Oman. Much of the inland terrain is desert, leading to a flat coastal plain, and there are mountains in the east. Elevation extremes range from 1,527m (Jabal Yibir) at the highest point to 0m (Persian Gulf) at the lowest. Average temperatures in Sharjah range between 12°C in January to 38°C in August. Humidity is very high between May and September.

HISTORY AND POLITICS

The United Arab Emirates (formerly the Trucial States) is composed of seven emirates. Six of these came together as an independent state on 2 December 1971 when they ended their individual special treaty relationships with the British government, and they were joined by Ras al-Khaimah on 10 February 1972. On independence, the union government assumed full responsibility for all internal and external affairs apart from some internal matters that remained the prerogative of the individual emirates.

Sheikh Zayed of Abu Dhabi was president from independence until his death in 2004. He was succeeded as Sultan of Abu Dhabi by his son, Sheikh Khalifa, who was also elected president of the UAE. The first national elections were held in 2006, when half the members of the Federal National Council were elected by a small electoral college.

FEDERAL STRUCTURE

The emirates are: Abu Dhabi, Ajman, Dubai, Fujairah, Ras al-Khaimah, Sharjah and Umm al-Qaiwain. Each emirate has its own government, court system and penal code. Abu Dhabi has an executive council chaired by the crown prince.

POLITICAL SYSTEM

The provisional constitution in use since 1971 was finally approved in 1996. Overall authority lies with the Supreme Council of the seven hereditary rulers of the emirates, each of whom also governs in his own territory. The president and vice-president are elected every five years by the Supreme Council from among its members. The president appoints the prime minister and the council of ministers. The unicameral Federal National Council is a consultative body which considers draft legislation proposed by the council of ministers. It has 40 members, eight members each from Abu Dhabi and Dubai, six each from Sharjah and Ras al-Khaimah and four each for Fujairah, Umm al-Qaiwain and Ajman, who serve a two-year term; half are elected and half are appointed by the rulers of each emirate.

HEAD OF STATE

President, HH Sheikh Khalifa bin Zayed al-Nahyan *(Abu Dhabi), elected* 3 November 2004

Vice-President, Prime Minister, Defence, HH Sheikh Mohammed bin Rashid al-Maktoum *(Dubai)*

SELECTED GOVERNMENT MEMBERS *as at July 2007*

Deputy Prime Ministers, Sheikh Sultan bin Zayed al-Nahyan; Sheikh Hamdan bin Zayed al-Nahyan

Finance, HH Sheikh Hamdan bin Rashid al-Maktoum

Foreign Affairs, Sheikh Abdullah bin Zayed al-Nahyan

Interior, Lt.-Gen. Sheikh Said bin Zayed al-Nahyan

EMBASSY OF THE UNITED ARAB EMIRATES

30 Princes Gate, London SW7 1PT

T 020-7581 1281 E information@uaeembassyuk.net

Ambassador Extraordinary and Plenipotentiary, HE Easa Saleh al-Gurg, CBE, *apptd* 1991

BRITISH EMBASSY

PO Box 248, Abu Dhabi

T (+971) (2) 610 1100 E chancery.abudhabi@fco.gov.uk

W www.britain-uae.org

Ambassador Extraordinary and Plenipotentiary, HE Edward Oakden, CMG, *apptd* 2006

BRITISH COUNCIL

PO Box 46523, Villa No. 7, Al-Nasr Street, Khalidiya, Abu Dhabi

T (+971) (2) 691 0600 W www.britishcouncil.org/uae

Director, Paul Sellers

DEFENCE

The army has 471 main battle tanks, 860 armoured personnel carriers and 430 armoured infantry fighting vehicles. The navy has 2 frigates and 14 patrol and coastal vessels at 8 bases. The air force has 184 combat aircraft and over 40 armed helicopters.

MILITARY BUDGET – US$2,580m (2006 est)

MILITARY PERSONNEL – 50,500: army 44,000, navy 2,500, air force 4,000

ECONOMY AND TRADE

Exploitation of the territories' oil reserves began in the 1960s and have transformed the UAE from poor rural principalities into modern states. Oil revenues have been invested in the transport and communications infrastructure and agriculture as well as education, health and social systems. The government is expanding infrastructure and job creation, and encouraging foreign investment. Oil and gas production dominate the economy, although diversification means that the hydrocarbon sector now accounts for only 30 per cent of GDP. Other industries include fishing, manufacturing (aluminium, cement, petrochemicals, fertilisers, construction materials, handicrafts, textiles), commercial ship repair, boat-building, financial services and tourism.

There is no personal or corporate taxation, apart from on oil companies and foreign banks. There are several zones where overseas companies can trade tax-free. Agriculture is limited by the terrain but the area under cultivation has been extended by irrigation and water desalination projects. The main products are dates, vegetables, watermelons, poultry, eggs and dairy products.

The main export markets are Japan, South Korea, India and Thailand; imports come chiefly from China, India, Japan, EU countries and the USA. Principal exports are crude oil (45 per cent), natural gas, re-exports, dried fish and dates. The main imports are machinery and transport equipment, chemicals and food.

GNI – US$103,500m; US$23,950 per capita (2005)

ANNUAL AVERAGE GROWTH OF GDP – 8.8 per cent (2005 est)

INFLATION RATE – 10.5 per cent (2005 est)

UNEMPLOYMENT – 2.4 per cent (2001)

TOTAL EXTERNAL DEBT – US$34,470m (2005 est)

IMPORTS – US$77,000m (2005)

EXPORTS – US$113,000m (2005)

Trade with UK	*2005*	*2006*
Imports from UK	£5,574,525,000	£3,637,426,000
Exports to UK	£1,425,074,000	£1,101,024,000

COMMUNICATIONS

Roads total 1,088km, all of which are surfaced, but there is no railway system. There are 15 ports, of which Abu Dhabi, Dubai and Sharjah are the most significant, and an international airport in every emirate except Ajman.

Modern telecommunications systems provide service to 1.2 million main-line subscribers, 4.5 million mobile phone subscribers and 1.4 million internet users.

EDUCATION AND HEALTH

Education is free in state schools.

LITERACY RATE – 77.3 per cent (2004 est)

GROSS ENROLMENT RATIO (percentage of relevant age group) – primary 83 per cent; secondary 64 per cent; tertiary 22 per cent (2005 est)

HEALTH EXPENDITURE (per capita) – US$711 (2004)
HOSPITAL BEDS (per 1,000 people) – 2.2 (2000–5)

MEDIA

Dubai is an important media hub and is home to pan-Arab satellite television channels and other international media organisations, including Reuters and Sony. Residents can receive several local and pan-Arab television and radio stations. There are three national newspapers, *Al-Bayan*, *Gulf News* and *Khaleej Times*. A 1988 law requires the licensing of publications and outlines acceptable subjects for coverage. Self-censorship is common, despite the guarantee of freedom of speech in the constitution.

UNITED STATES OF AMERICA

AREA – 9,631,420 sq. km. Neighbours: Canada (north), Mexico (south)
CAPITAL – Washington DC; population, 550,521 (2000). The area of the District of Columbia (with which the City of Washington is considered co-extensive) is 98.2 sq. km
MAJOR CITIES – New York; Los Angeles; Chicago; Philadelphia; Miami; Dallas; Boston; Detroit
CURRENCY – US dollar (US$) of 100 cents
POPULATION – 298,444,215 rising at 0.91 per cent per year (2006 est)
RELIGION – Protestantism (52 per cent), Roman Catholicism (24 per cent), Mormonism (2 per cent), Judaism (2 per cent), Islam (1 per cent) (est). An estimated 10 per cent of the population is atheist
LANGUAGE – English, Spanish, Hawaiian (official in Hawaii)
POPULATION DENSITY – 32 per sq. km (2005)
URBAN POPULATION – 80.8 per cent (2005 est)
MEDIAN AGE (years) – 36.5 (2006 est)
NATIONAL ANTHEM – 'The Star-Spangled Banner'
NATIONAL DAY – 4 July (Independence Day)
LIFE EXPECTANCY (years) – 77.85 (2006 est)
MORTALITY RATE – 8.26 (2006 est)
BIRTH RATE – 14.14 (2006 est)
INFANT MORTALITY RATE – 6.43 (2006 est)
DEATH PENALTY – Yes
CPI SCORE – 7.3 (2006)
POPULATION BELOW POVERTY LINE – 12 per cent (2004 est)

CLIMATE AND TERRAIN

The coastline has a length of about 3,329km on the Atlantic Ocean, 12,268km on the Pacific, 1,705km on the Arctic, and 2,624km on the Gulf of Mexico. The principal river is the Mississippi-Missouri-Red (5,970km long), traversing the whole country to its mouth in the Gulf of Mexico. The chain of the Rocky Mountains separates the western portion of the country from the remainder. West of these, bordering the Pacific coast, the Cascade Mountains and Sierra Nevada form the outer edge of a high tableland, consisting partly of stony and sandy desert and partly of grazing land and forested mountains, and including the Great Salt Lake, which extends to the Rocky Mountains. In the eastern states large forests still exist, the remnants of the forests which formerly extended over the entire Atlantic slope. The highest point is Mount McKinley (6,194m) in Alaska, and the lowest point is in Death Valley (Inyo, California), 86m below sea level. Temperatures vary dramatically throughout the country; average temperatures in Washington DC range from 6°C in January to 27°C in June.

Two states are detached: Alaska and Hawaii. Alaska occupies the north-western extremity of North America, separated from the rest of the USA by the Canadian province of British Columbia. The terrain is arctic tundra with mountain ranges, and the climate is arctic. The state of Hawaii is a chain of about 20 volcanic islands in the north Pacific Ocean, of which the chief islands are Hawaii, Maui, Oahu, Kauai and Molokai. The climate there is tropical.

HISTORY AND POLITICS

The area which is now the USA was first inhabited by nomadic hunters who probably arrived from Asia *c.*30,000 BC. The continent was explored by the Norse in the ninth century and, in 1492, by European explorer Christopher Columbus, whose first contact with the natives ushered in an age of widespread European colonisation. Between 1520 and 1620, diseases brought over by Europeans, such as smallpox, diptheria and measles killed up to 98 per cent of the native population. Of the early colonisers, the Spanish settled in the south, and British, Dutch, French, German and Swedish established strongholds in the east. Many black Africans were introduced as slaves to work on the plantations in the Caribbean and southern US states.

By 1733 there were 13 British colonies, composed mostly of religious non-conformists who had left Britain to escape persecution. A rebellion broke out in these colonies in 1775, largely because of the colonists' objection to being taxed by, but having no representation in, the British parliament. The British government's forces were defeated with French, Spanish and Dutch assistance. The Declaration of Independence which inaugurated the United States of America was signed on 4 July 1776; Britain recognised American sovereignty in 1783. The first federal constitution was drawn up in 1787; ten amendments, termed the Bill of Rights, were added in 1791. The 13 original states of the Union ratified the constitution between 1787 and 1790. Vermont, Kentucky and Tennessee were admitted in the 1790s, but most of the states acceded in the 19th century, as the opening up of the centre and west led to the creation of new states, and European or neighbouring countries ceded or sold their territories to the USA.

The Civil War (1861–5) was fought over the issue of slavery, which was integral to the economy of the southern states but was opposed by the northern states. The northern states defeated the Confederacy of 11 southern states (Virginia, North Carolina, South Carolina, Georgia, Alabama, Florida, Tennessee, Mississippi, Louisiana, Texas, Arkansas) after they seceded in 1860–1.

The USA industrialised rapidly in the late 19th century. It emerged as a world economic and military superpower in the 20th century and played a decisive role in the two world wars. Its economic and military (including nuclear) supremacy has given the USA a key role in shaping the post-war world. The Cold War with the USSR after the Second World War ended in 1990. Following terrorist attacks in New York and Washington DC on 11 September 2001, President George W. Bush declared a 'war on terror'. As part of this, the USA led multi-national forces into conflicts in Afghanistan in 2001 (*see*

Afghanistan) and Iraq in 2003 (*see* Iraq); US troops remain in both countries to help stabilise internal security. In response to the threat of terrorist attacks on US territory, the Department of Homeland Security was created in 2002.

The 2000 presidential election was won by the Republican candidate, George W. Bush, with 47.9 per cent of the vote. In 2004, President Bush was re-elected, with 51 per cent of the vote. In the simultaneous legislative election, the Republican Party retained its majorities in both houses of Congress. Control of both houses was lost to the Democratic Party in the mid-term elections in 2006.

POLITICAL SYSTEM

By the constitution of 17 September 1787 (last amended in 1992), the government of the USA is entrusted to three separate authorities: the federal executive (the president and cabinet), the legislature (congress – which is comprised of the senate and the house of representatives) and the judicature. The president is indirectly elected by an electoral college to serve a four-year term, and may serve a maximum of two consecutive terms. If a president dies in office, the vice-president serves the remainder of his term. The president appoints the cabinet officers and all the chief officials, subject to confirmation by the senate. He makes recommendations of a general nature to congress, and when laws are passed, he may return them to congress with a veto. But, if a measure so vetoed is again passed by both houses of congress by a two-thirds majority in each house, it becomes law, notwithstanding the objection of the president.

Each of the 50 states has its own executive, legislature and judiciary. In theory, they are sovereign, but in practice their autonomy is increasingly circumscribed.

PRESIDENTIAL ELECTIONS

Candidates for the presidency must be at least 35 years of age and a native citizen of the USA. The electoral college for each state is directly elected by universal adult suffrage in the November preceding the January in which the presidential term expires. The number of members of the electoral college is equal to the whole number of senators and representatives to which the state is entitled in the congress. The electoral college for each state meets in its state in December and each member votes for a presidential candidate by ballot. The ballots are sent to Washington, and opened on 6 January by the president of the senate in the presence of congress. The candidate who has received a majority of the whole number of electoral votes cast is declared president for the ensuing term. If no one has a majority, then from the highest on the list (not exceeding three) the house of pepresentatives elects a president, the votes being taken by states, the representation from each state having one vote. A presidential term begins at noon on 20 January.

HEAD OF STATE

President of the United States, George Walker Bush, *elected* 2000, *re-elected* 2 November 2004, *sworn in* 20 January 2005

Vice-President, Dick Cheney

SELECTED GOVERNMENT MEMBERS *as at August 2007*

Secretary of State, Condoleezza Rice

Defence, Robert Gates

Interior, Dirk Kempthorne

Treasury, Henry M. Paulson

Secretary for Homeland Security, Michael Chertoff

Attorney-General (acting), Paul Clement

Health, Mike Leavitt

Chief of Staff, Joshua Bolten

THE CONGRESS

Legislative power is vested in the bicameral congress, comprising the senate and the house of representatives. The senate has 100 members, two from each state, elected for a six-year term, with one-third elected every two years. The house of representatives has 435 members directly elected in each state for a two-year term; a resident commissioner from Puerto Rico and a delegate each from American Samoa, the District of Columbia, Guam and the Virgin Islands serve as non-voting members of the house. Members of the 110th congress were elected on 7 November 2006. As at August 2007, the 110th congress is constituted as follows:

Senate: Democrats 49; Republicans 49; Independent 1; Independent Democrat 1; total 100

House of Representatives: Democrats 231; Republicans 202; vacancies 2; total 435

President of the Senate, The Vice-President

Senate Majority Leader, Harry Reid *(D), Nevada*

Speaker of the House of Representatives, Nancy Pelosi *(D), California*

THE JUDICATURE

The federal judiciary consists of three sets of federal courts: the supreme court at Washington DC, consisting of a Chief Justice and eight Associate Justices, the United States courts of appeals, consisting of 168 circuit judges within 13 regional circuits, and the 94 United States district courts served by 575 district court judges.

THE SUPREME COURT

US Supreme Court Building, Washington DC 20543

Chief Justice, John Roberts, *apptd* 2005

UNITED STATES EMBASSY

24 Grosvenor Square, London W1A 1AE

T 020-7499 9000 W www.usembassy.org.uk

Ambassador Extraordinary and Plenipotentiary, HE Robert H. Tuttle, *apptd* 2005

BRITISH EMBASSY

3100 Massachusetts Avenue NW, Washington DC 20008

T (+1) (202) 588 6500 E washi@fco.gov.uk

W www.britainusa.com

Ambassador Extraordinary and Plenipotentiary, Sir Nigel Sheinwald, KCMG, *apptd* 2006

BRITISH COUNCIL

c/o The British Embassy

T (+1) (202) 588 6500 W www.britishcouncil.org/usa

Director, Sharon Memis

THE STATES OF THE UNION

The USA is a federal republic consisting of 50 states and the federal District of Columbia, and also of organised territories. Of the present 50 states, 13 are original states, seven were admitted without previous organisation as territories, and 30 were admitted after such organisation.

§ The 13 original states
(D) Democratic Party; (I) Independent; (R) Republican Party; (PDP) Popular Democratic Party; (C) Covenant

State (with date and order of admission)	*Area sq. km*	*Population (2006 est)*	*Capital*	*Governor (end of term in office)*
Alabama (AL) (1819, 22)	133,915	4,599,030	Montgomery	Bob Riley (R), Jan. 2011
Alaska (AK) (1959, 49)	1,530,694	670,053	Juneau	Sarah Palin (R), Dec. 2010
Arizona (AZ) (1912, 48)	295,259	6,166,318	Phoenix	Janet Napolitano (D), Jan. 2011
Arkansas (AR) (1836, 25)	137,754	2,810,872	Little Rock	Mike Beebe (D), Jan. 2011
California (CA) (1850, 31)	411,047	36,457,549	Sacramento	Arnold Schwarzenegger (R), Jan. 2011
Colorado (CO) (1876, 38)	269,595	4,753,377	Denver	Bill Ritter (D), Jan. 2011
Connecticut (CT) § (1788, 5)	12,997	3,504,809	Hartford	M. Jodi Rell (R), Jan. 2011
Delaware (DE) § (1787, 1)	5,297	853,476	Dover	Ruth Ann Minner (D), Jan. 2009
Florida (FL) (1845, 27)	151,939	18,089,888	Tallahassee	Charlie Crist (R), Jan. 2011
Georgia (GA) § (1788, 4)	152,576	9,363,941	Atlanta	Sonny Perdue (R), Jan. 2011
Hawaii (HI) (1959, 50)	16,760	1,285,498	Honolulu	Linda Lingle (R), Dec. 2010
Idaho (ID) (1890, 43)	216,430	1,466,465	Boise	C. L. Otter (R), Jan. 2011
Illinois (IL) (1818, 21)	145,933	12,831,970	Springfield	Rod R. Blagojevich (D), Jan. 2011
Indiana (IN) (1816, 19)	93,719	6,313,520	Indianapolis	Mitchell E. Daniels (R), Jan. 2009
Iowa (IA) (1846, 29)	145,752	2,982,085	Des Moines	Chet Culver (D), Jan. 2011
Kansas (KS) (1861, 34)	213,097	2,764,075	Topeka	Kathleen Sebelius (D), Jan. 2011
Kentucky (KY) (1792, 15)	104,661	4,206,074	Frankfort	Ernie Fletcher (R), Dec. 2007
Louisiana (LA) (1812, 18)	123,677	4,287,768	Baton Rouge	Kathleen Babineaux Blanco (D), Jan. 2008
Maine (ME) (1820, 23)	86,156	1,321,574	Augusta	John Baldacci (D), Jan. 2011
Maryland (MD) § (1788, 7)	27,091	5,615,727	Annapolis	Martin O'Malley (D), Jan. 2011
Massachusetts (MA) § (1788, 6)	21,455	6,437,193	Boston	Deval Patrick (D), Jan. 2011
Michigan (MI) (1837, 26)	151,584	10,095,643	Lansing	Jennifer Granholm (D), Jan. 2011
Minnesota (MN) (1858, 32)	218,600	5,167,101	St Paul	Tim Pawlenty (R), Jan. 2011
Mississippi (MS) (1817, 20)	123,514	2,910,540	Jackson	Haley Barbour (R), Jan. 2008
Missouri (MO) (1821, 24)	180,514	5,842,713	Jefferson City	Matt Blunt (R), Jan. 2009
Montana (MT) (1889, 41)	380,848	944,632	Helena	Brian Schweitzer (D), Jan. 2009
Nebraska (NE) (1867, 37)	200,349	1,768,331	Lincoln	Dave Heineman (R), Jan. 2011
Nevada (NV) (1864, 36)	286,352	2,495,529	Carson City	Jim Gibbons (R), Jan. 2011
New Hampshire (NH) § (1788, 9)	24,033	1,314,895	Concord	John Lynch (D), Jan. 2009
New Jersey (NJ) § (1787, 3)	20,168	8,724,560	Trenton	Jon Corzine (D), Jan. 2010
New Mexico (NM) (1912, 47)	314,925	1,954,599	Santa Fé	Bill Richardson (D), Jan. 2011
New York (NY) § (1788, 11)	127,189	19,306,183	Albany	Eliot Spitzer (D), Jan. 2011
North Carolina (NC) § (1789, 12)	136,412	8,856,505	Raleigh	Mike Easley (D), Jan. 2009
North Dakota (ND) (1889, 39)	183,117	635,867	Bismarck	John Hoeven (R), Dec. 2008
Ohio (OH) (1803, 17)	107,044	11,478,006	Columbus	Ted Strickland (D), Jan. 2011
Oklahoma (OK) (1907, 46)	181,185	3,579,212	Oklahoma City	Brad Henry (D), Jan. 2011
Oregon (OR) (1859, 33)	251,418	3,700,758	Salem	Ted R. Kulongoski (D), Jan. 2011
Pennsylvania (PA) § (1787, 2)	117,347	12,440,621	Harrisburg	Edward G. Rendell (D), Jan. 2011
Rhode Island (RI) § (1790, 13)	3,139	1,067,610	Providence	Don Carcieri (R), Jan. 2011
South Carolina (SC) § (1788, 8)	80,582	4,321,249	Columbia	Mark Sanford (R), Jan. 2011
South Dakota (SD) (1889, 40)	199,730	781,919	Pierre	Mike Rounds (R), Jan. 2011
Tennessee (TN) (1796, 16)	109,153	6,038,803	Nashville	Phil Bredesen (D), Jan. 2011
Texas (TX) (1845, 28)	691,027	23,507,783	Austin	Rick Perry (R), Jan. 2011
Utah (UT) (1896, 45)	219,888	2,550,063	Salt Lake City	Jon Huntsman Jr (R), Jan. 2009
Vermont (VT) (1791, 14)	24,900	623,908	Montpelier	James Douglas (R), Jan. 2009
Virginia (VA) § (1788, 10)	105,586	7,642,884	Richmond	Tim Kaine (D), Jan. 2010
Washington (WA) (1889, 42)	176,479	6,395,798	Olympia	Christine Gregoire (D), Jan. 2009
West Virginia (WV) (1863, 35)	62,761	1,818,470	Charleston	Joe Manchin III (D), Jan. 2009
Wisconsin (WI) (1848, 30)	145,436	5,556,506	Madison	Jim Doyle (D), Jan. 2011
Wyoming (WY) (1890, 44)	253,324	515,004	Cheyenne	Dave Freudenthal (D), Jan. 2011
Dist. of Columbia (DC, 1791)	179	581,530	–	Adrian M. Fenty (D), *(Mayor)*

OUTLYING TERRITORIES AND POSSESSIONS

	Area sq. km	*Population (2007 est)*	*Capital*	*Governor (end of term in office)*
American Samoa	199	57,663	Pago Pago	Togiola Tulafono (D), Jan. 2009
Guam	541	173,456	Hagatna	Felix Perez Camacho (R), Jan. 2011
Northern Mariana Islands	477	84,546	Saipan	Benigno Fitial (C), Jan. 2010
Puerto Rico	13,790	3,944,259	San Juan	Anibal Acevedo Vila (PDP), Jan. 2009
US Virgin Islands	363	108,448	Charlotte Amalie	John Percy De Jongh Jr (D), Jan. 2011

RESIDENT POPULATION BY RACE (2005 EST)

White	237,854,954
Black	37,909,341
Asian	12,687,472
American Indian and Alaska Native	2,863,001
Native Hawaiian and other Pacific Islanders	516,612
† Hispanic origin	42,687,224
Two or more races	4,579,024

† Persons of Hispanic origin may be of any race

IMMIGRATION
From 1820 to 2004, 69,869,450 migrants were admitted to the USA. The total number of migrants in 2004 was 946,142.

DEFENCE

Each military department is separately organised and functions under the direction, authority and control of the Secretary of Defence. The air force has primary responsibility for the Department of Defence space development programmes and projects. Under US strategic command the USA has 384 submarine-launched ballistic missiles, 1,050 laser-guided nuclear missiles *(Peacekeeper* and *Minuteman III)* and 256 heavy nuclear-capable bombers. There are currently 4 space-based early warning satellites in orbit and the USA operates land-based early warning systems throughout the world. The army has over 7,620 main battle tanks, 6,719 armoured infantry fighting vehicles, 16,008 armoured personnel carriers and 1,107 armed helicopters.

The navy has 14 strategic submarines, 58 tactical submarines, 12 aircraft carriers, 22 cruisers, 50 destroyers, 31 frigates, 16 patrol and coastal vessels, 35 amphibious and support ships, 1,154 combat aircraft and 224 armed helicopters. The Marine Corps has 403 main battle tanks, 387 combat aircraft and 176 attack helicopters. The air force has 2,658 combat aircraft.

MILITARY EXPENDITURE – US$535,000m (2006)

MILITARY PERSONNEL – 1,506,757: army 595,946, navy 376,750, Marine Corps 186,661, air force 347,400, coast guard 40,500

ECONOMY AND TRADE

The USA is one of the world's leading industrial nations, with a sophisticated market economy that saw huge growth during the 20th century. This economic development was due in part to an industrial revolution that mechanised the agrarian economy, the expansion of the country's transport infrastructure and large amounts of relatively cheap migrant labour. More recently, the economy has shifted reliance from industry to services, and government involvement in the economy has steadily reduced. Airlines were deregulated in 1978, telecommunications in 1996 and the electric utility companies were opened up to competition in 2001. In recent years, the economy has experienced steady growth, low unemployment and inflation, and rapid advances in technology, but there are large budget and trade deficits and an increasingly uneven distribution of wealth; an estimated 12 per cent of the population lives below the poverty line.

Most economic activity is in the private sector, so the main feature of government economic policy is the annual budget proposal, which is put forward by the president, and drafted into a budget resolution by the house and senate committees before being debated in congress. The 2007 budget estimate totalled US$870.7bn. The largest areas of expenditure were defence (US$439.3bn), health and human services (US$67.6bn), education (US$54.4bn), state and international assistance programmes (US$33.9bn), veterans' affairs (US$35.7bn), homeland security (US$30.9bn) and housing and urban development (US$33.6bn).

Agriculture is a major industry in the USA, with about 18 per cent of the land under cultivation. Principal crops are wheat, maize, other grains, fruit, vegetables, cotton, soya beans, meat and dairy products. Agriculture, fishing and forestry contribute 1 per cent of GDP and employ 0.7 per cent of the workforce.

Mining and extraction are also central to the economy. Large quantities of iron ore, phosphate rock, copper, zinc and lead are mined. About one-third of its oil requirements are supplied by domestic production, principally from fields in the Gulf of Mexico; production in 2005 was 7.61 million barrels per day. Most oil refining capacity is located on the Gulf coast; the damage caused by Hurricane Katrina in August 2005 reduced capacity by an estimated 10 per cent. Natural gas is also produced. Despite its domestic oil and natural gas resources and its electricity generating capacity, the USA is a net importer of energy; the largest exporters of oil to the USA are Canada (782.5 million barrels in 2005) and Mexico (609 million barrels in 2005).

The industrial sector is highly diversified and technologically advanced. The main manufacturing industries produce steel, vehicles, aircraft and aerospace equipment, telecommunications equipment, chemicals, electronic equipment and consumer goods, and process food. Industry contributes 20.4 per cent of GDP and employs about 22.9 per cent of the workforce; services account for 78.6 per cent of GDP and 76.4 per cent of employment.

The main trading partners are Canada, Mexico, China, Japan, Germany and the UK. Principal exports are capital goods (chiefly transistors, aircraft, vehicle parts, computers, telecommunications equipment), industrial supplies, consumer goods (cars, medicines) and agricultural produce (soya beans, fruit, maize). The main imports are consumer goods (cars, clothing, medicines, furniture, toys), capital goods (computers, telecommunications equipment, vehicle parts, office machines, electric power machinery), industrial goods (especially crude oil) and agricultural products.

GNI – US$12,912,900m (2005); US$43,560 per capita (2005)
ANNUAL AVERAGE GROWTH OF GDP – 3.2 per cent (2005 est)
INFLATION RATE – 3.2 per cent (2005 est)
UNEMPLOYMENT – 5.1 per cent (2005 est)
TOTAL EXTERNAL DEBT – US$8,837,000m (2005 est)
IMPORTS – US$1,732,000m (2005)
EXPORTS – US$907,000m (2005)

BALANCE OF PAYMENTS
Trade – US$777,861m deficit (2005)
Current Account – US$804,961m deficit (2005)

Trade with UK	*2005*	*2006*
Imports from UK	£30,735,419,000	£31,800,605,000
Exports to UK	£22,641,916,000	£26,088,161,000

GDP BY INDUSTRY (2005)

	US$bn
Private industries	20,256.0
Agriculture, forestry, fisheries	312.4
Mining	396.3
Construction	1,175.0
Manufacturing	4,501.8
Transportation and warehousing	712.1
Wholesale trade	1,073.6
Retail trade	1,288.7
Finance, insurance and real estate	3,990.9
Information	1,161.1

Source: Bureau of Economic Analysis

COMMUNICATIONS

There are approximately 6.4 million km of roads, with surfaced roads accounting for 64.7 per cent of the total. There are 226,600km of railways, and more than 41,000km of navigable waterways, of which 19,300km are used for commerce. The main seaports are at Anchorage, Baltimore, Boston, Charleston, Chicago, Corpus Christi, Duluth, Hampton Roads, Honolulu (Hawaii), Houston, Jacksonville, Long Beach, Los Angeles, New Orleans, New York, Philadelphia, Port Canaveral, Portland (Oregon), Prudhoe Bay, San Francisco, Savannah, Seattle, Tampa and Toledo. There are over 14,800 airports and airfields; nearly 200 are capable of handling international flights, but the rest cater for the high domestic demand as air travel is the main form of transport for long-distance internal journeys.

Technologically advanced systems provide multi-purpose telecommunications facilities, and the mobile phone network is growing rapidly. There were 268 million main-line subscribers in 2003, and 219.4 million mobile phone subscribers in 2005. The internet had 205.3 million users in 2005.

EDUCATION AND HEALTH

All the states have compulsory school attendance laws. In general, children are obliged to attend school from seven to 16 years of age. Most of the revenue for public elementary and secondary school purposes comes from federal, state and local governments. Less than 3 per cent comes from gifts and from tuition and transportation fees. Among the better-known universities are Harvard (founded in 1636), Yale (1701) and Princeton (1746).

GROSS ENROLMENT RATIO (percentage of relevant age group) – primary 99 per cent; secondary 95 per cent; tertiary 82 per cent (2005 est)
HEALTH EXPENDITURE (per capita) – US$6,096 (2004)
HOSPITAL BEDS (per 1,000 people) – 3.3 (2000–5)

MEDIA

The media industry is the largest and most influential in the world. Both television and radio are regulated by the Federal Communications Commission and are exported across the world (via the major networks of ABC, CBS, NBC, CNN, Fox, MTV, HBO and PBS). There are around 10,000 commercial radio stations and more than 1,500 daily newspapers, including *The Wall Street Journal, USA Today, The Washington Post* and *The New York Times. Time, Newsweek* and *US News and World Report* are influential current affairs magazines, while *Rolling Stone* and *Vanity Fair* are popular entertainment titles.

CULTURE

The culture of the USA is rooted in immigration and enjoys strong European, African, Central and South American influences. Often at the forefront of philosophical, literary or artistic movements (such as feminism, postmodernism or postcolonialism), the USA can boast many important writers, film-makers and artists.

The best-known early novelists include Nathaniel Hawthorne (1804–64) and Mark Twain (1835–1910), and poets Walt Whitman (1819–92) and Emily Dickinson (1830–86). The 20th century saw the emergence of writers such as William Faulkner (1897–1962), Ernest Hemingway (1899–1961) and John Steinbeck (1902–68); postwar US literature was personified by the 'beat poet' generation of writers that included Jack Kerouac (1922–69), William Burroughs (1914–97) and Allen Ginsberg (1926–1997). African American literature has been assimiliated into the literary canon in the last 50 years due to the works of Ralph Ellison (1913–94), Toni Morrison (*b.* 1931) and Alice Walker (*b.* 1944).

The Hollywood film industry is the most wide-reaching in the world and celebrated directors include Orson Welles (1915–85), Frank Capra (1897–1991), Stanley Kubrick (1928–99), Francis Ford Coppola (*b.* 1939) and Martin Scorsese (*b.* 1942).

Modern art found a spiritual home on the east coast and the Guggenheim and Metropolitan museums in New York both house vast collections of famous works. Renowned artists include Edward Hopper (1882–1967), Jackson Pollock (1912–56), Roy Lichtenstein (1923–97) and Andy Warhol (1928–87).

The music of the USA reflects the country's ethnic diversity, with superior recording and distribution methods ensuring that rock and roll, country, blues, jazz and hip-hop became known worldwide. Musical icons include Elvis Presley (1935–77) and Bob Dylan (*b.* 1941) in rock, Hank Williams (1923–53) and Johnny Cash (1932–2003) in country music, Leadbelly (1888–1949) and Muddy Waters (1915–83) in blues, and Louis Armstrong (1901–71), Miles Davis (1926–91) and John Coltrane (1926–67) in jazz.

US TERRITORIES, ETC

Responsibility within the federal government for the US insular areas other than Puerto Rico and Kingman Reef lies with the US Department of the Interior: the Office of Insular Affairs deals with American Samoa, Guam, the Northern Mariana Islands, the US Virgin Islands, Navassa Island (7.8 sq. km), Palmyra Atoll (4 sq. km) and Wake Atoll (6.4 sq. km), shared with the US army Space and Missile Defence Command; and the US Fish and Wildlife Service deals with Baker Island (1.5 sq. km), Howland Island (2.5 sq. km) and Jarvis Island (4.2 sq. km), Midway Atoll (5.2 sq. km) and Johnston Atoll (2.5 sq. km), shared with the Defence Special Weapons Agency. The Aleutian Islands (17,666 sq. km) form part of the Alaskan archipelago.

Four of the eight populated insular areas are represented in the house of representatives: Puerto Rico by a resident commissioner, and American Samoa, Guam and the US Virgin Islands by one non-voting delegate each. Although represented in the house of representatives by a delegate, the District of Columbia was an incorporated territory for only three years (1871–4).

THE COMMONWEALTH OF PUERTO RICO

AREA – 13,790 sq. km
POPULATION – 3,944,259 (2007 est). The majority of the inhabitants are of Spanish descent; Spanish and English are the official languages
CAPITAL – San Juan; population of the municipality 433,412 (2002 est). Other major towns are: Bayamón; Carolina; Ponce

Puerto Rico (Rich Port) is an island of the Greater Antilles group in the West Indies and was discovered in 1493 by Columbus. It was a Spanish possession until 1898, when it was ceded to the USA after the Spanish–American War. Residents of Puerto Rico are US citizens and Puerto Rico is represented in congress by a resident commissioner, elected for a four-year term, who is a non-voting member of the house of representatives. Under its 1952 constitution, the Commonwealth of Puerto Rico has full powers of internal self-government. The governor is directly elected for a four-year term. The bicameral legislative assembly consists of the 29-member senate and the 51-member house of representatives, whose members serve a four-year term; proposals to replace these bodies with a one-chamber legislature were approved by referendum in July 2005. Tourism, pharmaceuticals, electronics, clothing and food processing are the main economic activities.

Governor, Anibal Acevedo Vila (PDP)

Trade with UK	*2005*	*2006*
Imports from UK	£179,136,000	£187,164,000
Exports to UK	£349,402,000	£283,688,000

GUAM

AREA – 541.3 sq. km
POPULATION – 173,456 (2007 est); Chamorro (37 per cent), Filipino (26 per cent), other Pacific islander (11 per cent). Chamorro (a language of the Malayo-Polynesian family with admixtures of Spanish) and English are the official languages; most Chamorro residents are bilingual
CAPITAL – Hagatna (also known as Agana); population, 154,805 (2000), port of entry, Apra

Guam is the largest of the Mariana Islands, in the north Pacific Ocean. A Spanish colony for centuries, it was ceded to the USA in 1898 after the Spanish–American War. Guam was occupied by the Japanese in 1941 but was recaptured by US forces in 1944. Any person born in Guam is a US citizen. Guam is represented in congress by a delegate directly elected for a two-year term who is a non-voting member of the house of representatives. Under the Organic Act of Guam 1950, Guam has statutory powers of self-government. The governor and lieutenant-governor are directly elected for a four-year term. A 15-member unicameral legislature is directly elected every two years. The two main sources of revenue are tourism (particularly from Japan) and US military spending.

Governor, Felix Perez Camacho (R)

Trade with UK	*2005*	*2006*
Imports from UK	£3,922	£6,912,000
Exports to UK	£1,247	£351,000

AMERICAN SAMOA
AREA – 199 sq. km
POPULATION – 57,663 (2007 est)
CAPITAL – Pago Pago; population, 3,519
NATIONAL DAY – 17 April (Flag Day)

American Samoa consists of the islands of Tutuila, Aunu'u, Ofu, Olesega, Ta'u, Rose and Swains Islands. The islands were discovered by Europeans in the 18th century and the USA took possession in 1900. Those born in American Samoa are US non-citizen nationals, but some have acquired citizenship through service in the US armed forces or other naturalisation procedures. American Samoa is represented in congress by a delegate directly elected for a two-year term who is a non-voting member of the house of representatives. Its 1966 constitution grants American Samoa a measure of self-government, with certain powers reserved to the US Secretary of the Interior. The governor and deputy governor are directly elected for a four-year term. The bicameral legislature is a 21-member house of representatives (one appointed member and 20 members directly elected for a two-year term) and an 18-seat senate with members elected from among the traditional chiefs for a four-year term. Tuna fishing and canning are the principal economic activities.
Governor, Togiola Tulafono (D)

THE UNITED STATES VIRGIN ISLANDS
AREA – 363 sq. km
POPULATION – 108,448 (2007 est)
CAPITAL – Charlotte Amalie; population, 11,004 (2000), on St Thomas

There are three main islands, St Thomas, St Croix and St John, and about 50 small islets or cays. These constituted the Danish part of the Virgin Islands from the 17th century until purchased by the USA in 1917. Those born in the US Virgin Islands are US nationals. The Virgin Islands are represented in congress by a representative directly elected for a two-year term who is a non-voting member of the house of representatives. Under the provisions of the Revised Organic Act of the Virgin Islands 1954, the islands have powers of self-government. The governor is directly elected for a four-year term. The unicameral legislature is composed of 15 senators directly elected for a two-year term. Tourism, oil refining and manufacturing are the main industries.
Governor, John Percy De Jongh Jr (D)

NORTHERN MARIANA ISLANDS
AREA – 477 sq. km
POPULATION – 84,546 (2007 est)
SEAT OF GOVERNMENT – Saipan; population, 62,392 (2000)

The USA administered the Northern Mariana Islands, in the north-west Pacific Ocean, as part of a UN Trusteeship until the trusteeship agreement was terminated in 1986, bringing fully into effect a 1976 congressional law establishing the Northern Mariana Islands as a Commonwealth under US sovereignty. Those resident in 1976 and those subsequently born in the islands are US citizens. The islands are not represented in congress but have a resident representative in Washington DC. Under the 1978 constitution, the islands are self-governing. The governor is directly elected for a four-year term. The bicameral legislature comprises an 18-member house of representatives and a nine-member Senate; members are directly elected, representatives for two years and senators for four years. Tourism and manufacturing, especially of clothing, are the main industries.
Governor, Benigno Fitial (C)

URUGUAY

República Oriental del Uruguay – Oriential Republic of Uruguay

AREA – 176,220 sq. km. Neighbours: Argentina (west), Brazil (north and east)
CAPITAL – Montevideo; population, 1,269,552 (2004)
MAJOR CITIES – Salto; Paysandú; Las Piedras; Rivera
CURRENCY – Uruguayan peso of 100 centésimos
POPULATION – 3,431,932 rising at 0.46 per cent per year (2006 est)
RELIGION – Roman Catholicism (58 per cent), Protestantism (7 per cent) (est). An estimated 14 per cent of the population is atheist
LANGUAGE – Spanish (official), Portunol
POPULATION DENSITY – 20 per sq. km (2005)
URBAN POPULATION – 93 per cent (2005 est)
MEDIAN AGE (years) – 32.7 (2006 est)
NATIONAL ANTHEM – 'Orientales, la Patria o la Tumba' ['Uruguayans, the Fatherland or Death']
NATIONAL DAY – 25 August (Independence Day)
LIFE EXPECTANCY (years) – 76.33 (2006 est)
MORTALITY RATE – 9.05 (2006 est)
BIRTH RATE – 13.91 (2006 est)
INFANT MORTALITY RATE – 11.61 (2006 est)
DEATH PENALTY – No (abolished 1907)
CPI SCORE – 6.4 (2006)

CLIMATE AND TERRAIN

The country consists mainly of undulating grassy plains, with low hills. Elevation extremes range from 514m (Cerro Catedral) at the highest point to 0m (Atlantic Ocean) at the lowest. The principal river is the Rio Negro (with its tributary, the Yi), flowing from north-east to south-west into the Rio Uruguay. Average temperatures in Montevideo range from 6°C in July to 28°C in January.

HISTORY AND POLITICS

Originally populated by the Charras Amerindians, the Rio de la Plata was first visited by the Spanish in 1515. Although initially colonised by the Portuguese, the *Banda Oriental,* as the territory lying on the eastern bank of the River Uruguay was then called, formed part of Spanish South America from 1726 to 1814. Briefly independent, it became a province of Brazil in 1820, throwing off Brazilian rule in 1825. Its independence was recognised in 1828, and a republic was inaugurated in 1830. In the mid-19th century there was a power struggle, descending into civil war, between the conservatives *(Blancos)* and liberals *(Colorados)* which ended when the latter took office in the 1860s and governed until 1958.

The period from 1962 until 1973 saw unrest caused by the Marxist Tupamaros guerrillas. They were crushed by a military dictatorship that held power from 1973 until 1985, when a return to civilian rule was agreed after violent anti-government protests at the regime's repressive rule and the deteriorating economy. The presidential and general elections returned the Colorado Party to power and Julio Sanguinetti became president. The first fully free presidential and legislative elections since 1971 were held in 1989, and were won by the National *(Blanco)* Party.

The Colorado and National parties now both occupy the centre ground, but their dominance of politics has been eroded by left-wing parties such as New Space and coalitions such as the Progressive Encounter-Broad Front (EP-FA). The EP-FA won the most seats in both houses of the general assembly in the 1999 elections but lacked an overall majority in either, and a coalition government was formed by the Colorado Party and the National Party. In the 2004 legislative election, the EP-FA won outright majorities in both houses. The 2004 presidential election was won by Tabaré Vázquez of the EP-FA, the first left-wing president to hold office, and he appointed an EP-FA coalition government including other left-wing parties.

POLITICAL SYSTEM

Under the 1997 constitution, the executive president is directly elected for a five-year term; a president cannot serve two consecutive terms. The president, who appoints the council of ministers, is responsible to the legislature. The bicameral legislature, the general assembly, consists of a chamber of representatives, the lower house, and a chamber of senators. The chamber of representatives has 99 members directly elected for a five-year term. The chamber of senators has 31 members, 30 directly elected for five years by proportional representation and the vice-president as an *ex officio* member.

The republic is divided into 19 departments, each with an elected governor and legislature.

HEAD OF STATE

President, Tabaré Vázquez, *elected* October 2004, *took office* 1 March 2005

Vice-President, Rodolfo Nin Novoa

SELECTED GOVERNMENT MEMBERS *as at July 2007*

Economy and Finance, Danilo Astori

Foreign Relations, Reinaldo Gargano

Interior, Daisy Tourne

Defence, Azucena Berruti

EMBASSY OF URUGUAY

140 Brompton Road, London SW3 1HY

T 020-7589 8835 E emburuguay@emburuguay.org.uk

Ambassador Extraordinary and Plenipotentiary, HE Ricardo Varela, *apptd* 2004

BRITISH EMBASSY

PO Box 16024, Calle Marco Bruto 1073, 11300 Montevideo

T (+598) (2) 622 3630

E postmaster@montevideo.mail.fco.gov.uk

Ambassador Extraordinary and Plenipotentiary, HE Dr Hugh Salvesen, *apptd* 2005

DEFENCE

The army has 15 main battle tanks, 104 armoured personnel carriers and 18 armoured infantry fighting vehicles. The navy has 18 patrol and coastal combatant vessels and 3 aircraft. The air force has 19 combat aircraft.

MILITARY BUDGET – US$5,400m (2006)

MILITARY PERSONNEL – 25,100: army 17,000, navy 5,000, air force 3,100; paramilitaries 920

ECONOMY AND TRADE

After years of steady growth, Uruguay suffered a recession in 1999–2002 largely owing to the economic problems of Brazil and Argentina, its main export markets and sources of tourists. GDP dropped by 20 per cent and unemployment rose by 20 per cent over the four years, and the recession culminated in a banking crisis in 2002. IMF loans and the rescheduling of foreign debt repayments, along with the government's emergency measures, helped to achieve a fragile recovery. However, the recession reduced many to poverty in what had previously been a moderately prosperous society; 27 per cent of households still lived below the poverty line in 2006.

Ranching and livestock products (beef, mutton, wool) have been the mainstay of the economy since the mid-19th century, generating the prosperity that enabled Uruguay to develop an extensive welfare system in the early 20th century. Dependence on these products leaves the economy vulnerable to price fluctuations, a factor contributing to the recent recession. Other crops include rice, grains, citrus fruits, wine grapes, linseed and sunflower seed. Agricultural produce is the basis of the food processing and beverages industries. Other industries include fishing, forestry and the manufacture of electrical machinery, transport equipment, petroleum products, textiles and chemicals. Exploited minerals include clinker, dolomite, marble and granite. Tourism and offshore financial services also contribute substantially to revenue. Agriculture contributes 9 per cent of GDP, industry 34 per cent and services 57 per cent.

The main trading partners are Brazil, the USA, Argentina, Russia and Venezuela. Principal exports are meat, rice, leather products, wool, fish and dairy products. The main imports are machinery, chemicals, vehicles and crude oil.

GNI – US$15,100m (2005); US$4,360 per capita (2005)

ANNUAL AVERAGE GROWTH OF GDP – 6.8 per cent (2005 est)

INFLATION RATE – 4.7 per cent (2005 est)

UNEMPLOYMENT – 12.2 per cent (2005 est)

TOTAL EXTERNAL DEBT – US$13,240m (2005 est)

IMPORTS – US$3,900m (2005)

EXPORTS – US$3,400m (2005)

BALANCE OF PAYMENTS

Trade – US$31m surplus (2004)

Current Account – US$103m deficit (2005)

Trade with UK	*2005*	*2006*
Imports from UK	£37,504,000	£40,112,000
Exports to UK	£59,346,000	£65,239,000

COMMUNICATIONS

There are nearly 78,000km of roads, 8,000km of which are surfaced, and over 2,000km of railway, of which 1,500km is in full or partial use. There are 1,600km of navigable waterways, mainly on the Uruguay and Negro rivers. A bridge across the River Plate links Uruguay and Argentina. The main ports are Montevideo and Colonia on the coast, and Fray Bentos and Paysandú on the River Uruguay. There is an international airport near Montevideo, and over 60 smaller airports and airfields around the country.

Modernised telephone systems provided services to 1 million main-line subscribers and 600,000 mobile phone subscribers in 2004, and 680,000 internet users in 2005.

EDUCATION AND HEALTH

Primary and secondary education is compulsory and free, and technical and trade schools and evening courses for adult education are state-controlled. The university at Montevideo was founded in 1849.

LITERACY RATE – 97.7 per cent (2004 est)

GROSS ENROLMENT RATIO (percentage of relevant age group) – primary 109 per cent; secondary 108 per cent; tertiary 39 per cent (2005 est)
HEALTH EXPENDITURE (per capita) – US$315 (2004)
HOSPITAL BEDS (per 1,000 people) – 1.9 (2000–5)

MEDIA

The constitution enshrines freedom of expression. There are more than 100 daily and weekly newspapers, all privately owned, and more than 100 radio stations, as well as 20 television channels. The government runs one television and one radio station.

UZBEKISTAN

Osbekiston Respublikasi – Republic of Uzbekistan

AREA – 447,400 sq. km. Neighbours: Kazakhstan (north and west), Kyrgyzstan and Tajikistan (east), Afghanistan and Turkmenistan (south)
CAPITAL – Tashkent; population, 1,959,190 (2006 est)
MAJOR CITIES – Namangan; Samarkand; Andijon; Bukhara
CURRENCY – Sum of 100 tiyin
POPULATION – 27,307,134 rising at 1.7 per cent per year (2006 est); Uzbek (80 per cent), Russian (5.5 per cent), Tajik (5 per cent), Kazakh (3 per cent), Karakalpak (2.5 per cent) (est)
RELIGION – Islam (88 per cent) (est)
LANGUAGE – Uzbek (official), Russian, Tajik
POPULATION DENSITY – 62 per sq. km (2005)
URBAN POPULATION – 36.4 per cent (2005 est)
MEDIAN AGE (years) – 22.7 (2006 est)
NATIONAL ANTHEM – 'Osbekistan Respublikasining Davlat Madhiyasi' ['National Anthem of the Republic of Uzbekistan']
NATIONAL DAY – 1 September (Independence Day)
LIFE EXPECTANCY (years) – 64.58 (2006 est)
MORTALITY RATE – 7.84 (2006 est)
BIRTH RATE – 26.36 (2006 est)
INFANT MORTALITY RATE – 69.99 (2006 est)
DEATH PENALTY – Yes
CPI SCORE – 2.1 (2006)
POPULATION BELOW POVERTY LINE – 28 per cent (2004 est)
MILITARY EXPENDITURE – US$2,500m (2005)
MILITARY PERSONNEL – 55,000: army 40,000, air force 15,000; paramilitaries 20,000
CONSCRIPTION DURATION – 12 months

CLIMATE AND TERRAIN

The terrain of landlocked Uzbekistan falls from the Tien Shan mountains and the Pamir highlands in the east and south-east to the desert lowlands in the west and north-west, in the basin of the Amudarya River and the southern part of the Aral Sea. Elevation extremes range from 4,301m (Adelunga Toghi) at the highest point to −12m (Sariqarnish Kuli) at the lowest. Average temperatures in Tashkent range from −2°C in January to 33°C in June.

HISTORY AND POLITICS

Part of the Persian Empire and then the empire of Alexander the Great, Samarkand developed as an important transit point on the ancient 'Silk Road' in the first century BC. In the 13th century the area became part of the Mongol Empire, with Samarkand as its capital during the reign of Amir Timur (Tamerlane). With the decline of the Mongol Empire, independent emirates and khanates emerged. The three khanates in what is now Uzbekistan, Khiva, Kokand and Bukhara, were annexed by the Russian Empire in the second half of the 19th century. In 1917 a Bolshevik revolution broke out in Tashkent and by 1921 all of Uzbekistan had been absorbed into the USSR. Under Soviet rule a massive land irrigation programme was implemented to allow the cultivation of cotton, but this also led to the drying up of the Aral Sea.

Uzbekistan declared its independence from the USSR on 1 September 1991 but post-independence political life has been dominated by the former Communists. The main opposition parties, *Erk* (Freedom) and *Birlik* (Unity), have been banned since 1992, other forms of opposition are suppressed and the government has been accused of human rights abuses, including the systematic use of torture. The former Communist leader Islam Karimov, who came to power in 1990, was elected president in 1991 and has retained the presidency since, in unopposed elections or through the extension of his term of office in referendums. All legislative elections since independence have been won by the People's Democratic Party (the former Communist Party) or its allies.

After the latest legislative election in December 2004 and January 2005, the largest party in the legislative chamber was the pro-Karimov Liberal Democratic Party; opposition parties were barred from contesting the election. Most elections have been reported by observers to be neither free nor fair and have attracted international criticism.

INSURGENCIES

The Islamic Movement of Uzbekistan (IMU), which seeks to establish an Islamic state, was founded in 1996. Whilst it has carried out car bombings in Tashkent, its activities have centred on the Fergana valley, where it has clashed with Kyrgyz armed forces. The government has used the insurgency as an excuse to curtail human rights and suppress political opposition and protests such as those in Andijan in May 2005.

POLITICAL SYSTEM

The 1992 constitution was amended in 2002 to create a bicameral legislature and extend the president's term of office. The president is directly elected; his term of office was five years, renewable only once, but was extended in 2002 to seven years. The legislature, the Supreme Assembly, became bicameral after the 2004–5 elections. The lower house, the legislative assembly, has 120 members directly elected for a five-year term. The senate has 100 members, 16 appointed by the president and the rest elected by regional deputies to represent the regions and the capital; they serve a five-year term. The president appoints the cabinet, which is chaired by the prime minister.

The country is divided into the autonomous republic of Karakalpakstan, 12 provinces (Andijan, Bukhara, Fergana, Jizak, Kashka-Darya, Khorezm, Namanghan, Navoi, Samarkand, Surhan-Darya, Syr-Darya, Tashkent) and the city of Tashkent.

HEAD OF STATE
President, Islam Karimov, *elected* 29 December 1991, *elected by referendum for a five-year term* 26 March 1995, *re-elected* 9 January 2000

SELECTED GOVERNMENT MEMBERS *as at July 2007*
Prime Minister, Shavkat Mirziyaev
Deputy Prime Ministers, Abdulla Aripov; Rustam Azimov;

Svetlana Inamova; Rustam Kasymov; Nordirkhon Khanov; Ergash Shoismatov
Defence, Ruslan Mirzayev
Foreign Affairs, Vladimir Norov
Interior, Bahodir Matlubov

EMBASSY OF THE REPUBLIC OF UZBEKISTAN
41 Holland Park, London W11 3RP
T 020-7229 7679 W www.uzbekembassy.org
Ambassador Extraordinary and Plenipotentiary, HE Tukhtapulat Riskiev, *apptd* 2003

BRITISH EMBASSY
Ul. Gulyamova 67, UZ-700000 Tashkent
T (+998) (71) 120 6451 E brit@emb.uz
Ambassador Extraordinary and Plenipotentiary, HE Iain Kelly, *apptd* 2007

BRITISH COUNCIL
University of World Languages Building, 11 Mirobod St, Tashkent 700031
T (+998) (71) 140 0660/61/62/63
W www.britishcouncil.org.uk/uzbekistan
Director, Jeremy Jacobson

ECONOMY AND TRADE

The economy remains centrally planned and control has increased in some areas, stifling economic activity. Economic growth and living standards are among the worst in the former Soviet republics, with 33 per cent of the population living below the poverty level. Much foreign aid has been cut or withdrawn in protest at the country's poor human rights record.

The economy is based on intensive agricultural production, particularly of cotton, made possible by extensive irrigation schemes. Vegetables, fruit, grains and livestock are also produced. The main industries are textile manufacture, food processing, mineral mining (especially for gold), oil and natural gas production, machine building, metallurgy and chemicals. Oil and gas exports offer potential for economic growth and may attract foreign investment, possibly from Russia and China, but this is unlikely in the immediate future owing to a basic lack of modern oil pipelines and infrastructure. Agriculture contributes 31 per cent of GDP, industry 26 per cent and services 43 per cent.

The main trading partners are Russia, China, South Korea, Kazakhstan and Turkey. Principal exports are cotton (41 per cent), gold, oil and natural gas, mineral fertilisers, metals, textiles, food products and motor vehicles. The main imports are machinery and equipment, foodstuffs, chemicals and metals.

GNI – US$13,600m (2005); US$520 per capita (2005)
ANNUAL AVERAGE GROWTH OF GDP – 7 per cent (2005 est)
INFLATION RATE – 6.9 per cent (2005 est)
UNEMPLOYMENT – 0.7 per cent (2005 est)
TOTAL EXTERNAL DEBT – US$5,032m (2005 est)

Trade with UK	*2005*	*2006*
Imports from UK	£21,448,000	£28,419,000
Exports to UK	£29,107,000	£18,520,000

COMMUNICATIONS

Uzbekistan has 81,600km of roads, 71,000km of which are paved. It has nearly 4,000km of railway, and 1,100km of waterways. The principal airport is at Tashkent.

The fixed-line telephone system is antiquated and mobile phone distribution is growing rapidly, doubling in 2005. There were 1.7 million main lines in use in 2004, and 1.1 million mobile phone subscribers and 880,000 internet users in 2005.

EDUCATION AND HEALTH

LITERACY RATE – 99.3 per cent (2004 est)
GROSS ENROLMENT RATIO (percentage of relevant age group) – primary 100 per cent; secondary 95 per cent; tertiary 15 per cent (2005 est)
HEALTH EXPENDITURE (per capita) – US$23 (2004)
HOSPITAL BEDS (per 1,000 people) – 5.5 (2000–5)

MEDIA

Despite constitutional protection of free speech, the government strictly controls the political content of the media and much of the population relies on foreign broadcasts. Self-censorship is a way of life because of the frequent harassment of journalists. There is a mix of government-run and private television and radio stations in Uzbekistan. Almost all newspapers are produced by the state or by pro-government organisations. *Khalq Sozi* is a popular daily newspaper.

VANUATU

Ripablik blong Vanuatu/République de Vanuatu – Republic of Vanuatu

AREA – 12,200 sq. km
CAPITAL – Port Vila; population, 29,356 (1999), on Efate
MAJOR TOWN – Luganville, on Espiritu Santo
CURRENCY – Vatu of 100 centimes
POPULATION – 208,869 rising at 1.49 per cent per year (2006 est). About 95 per cent are Melanesian, the rest being mostly Micronesian, Polynesian and European.
RELIGION – Protestantism (60 per cent), Roman Catholicism (15 per cent), other Christian denominations (25 per cent) (est)
LANGUAGE – English, French (official), Bislama, over 100 local languages exist
POPULATION DENSITY – 17 per sq. km (2005)
URBAN POPULATION – 23.7 per cent (2005 est)
MEDIAN AGE (years) – 23 (2006 est)
NATIONAL ANTHEM – 'Yumi, Yumi, Yumi' ['We, We, We']
NATIONAL DAY – 30 July (Independence Day)
LIFE EXPECTANCY (years) – 62.85 (2006 est)
MORTALITY RATE – 7.82 (2006 est)
BIRTH RATE – 22.72 (2006 est)
INFANT MORTALITY RATE – 53.8 (2006 est)
DEATH PENALTY – No (abolished 1980)
LITERACY RATE – 74 per cent (2004 est)

CLIMATE AND TERRAIN

Situated in the south Pacific Ocean, Vanuatu includes 13 large and some 70 small islands, of coral and volcanic origin, including the Banks and Torres Islands in the north. The principal islands are Vanua Lava, Espiritu Santo, Maewo, Pentecost, Ambae, Malekula, Ambrym, Epi, Efate, Erromango, Tanna and Aneityum. Most islands are mountainous and there are active volcanoes on several. Elevation extremes range from 1,877m (Tabwemasana) at the highest point to 0m (Pacific Ocean) at the lowest. The climate is tropical, and the average temperature in Tana is around 29°C all year round.

HISTORY AND POLITICS

Some of the islands of Vanuatu have been inhabited for over 4,000 years. Europeans first visited in the early 17th century, and Captain Cook named the islands the New Hebrides in 1774. The islands were settled in the 19th century by the British and the French, who established plantations, and from 1906 were jointly administered as the Condominium of the New Hebrides. This became independent as the Republic of Vanuatu in 1980.

In the July 2004 legislative elections, the National United Party (NUP) won 10 seats, becoming the largest party in parliament. Serge Vohor of the Union of Moderate Parties (UMP) was elected prime minister and formed a six-party coalition government. Vohor lost a vote of confidence in December 2004 and was replaced by Ham Lini, who formed a nine-party coalition government. Alfred Maseng was elected president in April 2004 but was removed from office on 10 May because he was ineligible to stand for election. His successor, Kalkot Mataskelekele, was elected on 17 August 2004.

POLITICAL SYSTEM
Under the 1980 constitution, the head of state is a president who is elected for a five-year term by an electoral college consisting of the presidents of the six provincial governments and the members of parliament. The unicameral parliament has 52 members, directly elected for a four-year term. The executive is the prime minister, who is elected by parliament from among its members, and the council of ministers. A Council of Chiefs advises on matters of custom.

HEAD OF STATE
President, Kalkot Mataskelekele, *elected* 17 August 2004

SELECTED GOVERNMENT MEMBERS *AT JULY 2007*
Prime Minister, Ham Lini
Deputy Prime Minister, Foreign Affairs, Sato Kilman
Finance and Economic Development, Willie Jimmy Tapangararua
Internal Affairs, Keasipai Song

BRITISH HIGH COMMISSIONER
HE Roger Sykes, *apptd* 2006, resident at Suva, Fiji

ECONOMY AND TRADE

The economy is based on small-scale agriculture, with 65 per cent of the population employed on plantations or in subsistence agriculture. Subsistence crops include yams, taro, fruit and vegetables; the principal cash crops are coconuts, cocoa and coffee. Cattle are kept on the plantations. There is a small light industrial sector producing frozen food and fish, canned meat and processing wood. Eco-tourism and offshore financial services are of growing importance. The main export markets are Thailand (46 per cent), India, Poland, Turkey and Japan; imports come chiefly from Australia, Japan and Singapore. Principal exports are copra, beef, cocoa, timber, kava and coffee. The main imports are machinery and equipment, foodstuffs and fuels.
GNI – US$331m (2005); US$1,560 per capita (2005)
ANNUAL AVERAGE GROWTH OF GDP – 6.8 per cent (2005 est)
INFLATION RATE – –1.6 per cent (2005 est)
TOTAL EXTERNAL DEBT – US$81.2m (2004)
IMPORTS – US$140m (2005)
EXPORTS – US$40m (2005)

BALANCE OF PAYMENTS
Trade – US$93m deficit (2005)
Current Account – US$464m deficit (2005)

Trade with UK	*2005*	*2006*
Imports from UK	£1,519,000	£802,000
Exports to UK	£915,000	£894,000

COMMUNICATIONS

Vanuatu has just over 1,000km of roads, of which about one quarter is surfaced. The islands have no waterways or railways. The main ports are Forari, Port Vila and Santo. There are about 30 airports and airfields on the islands; the international airport is at Port Vila.

There were 6,800 main telephone lines in use and 7,500 internet users in 2004, and 12,700 mobile phone subscribers in 2005.

VATICAN CITY STATE

Status Civitatis Vaticanae/Stato della Città del Vaticano – State of the Vatican City

AREA – 0.44 sq. km. Neighbour: Rome (Italy)
CAPITAL – Vatican City; population, 780 (2005 est)
CURRENCY – Euro (€) of 100 cents
POPULATION – 921 (2005 est)
RELIGION – Roman Catholicism
LANGUAGE – Italian, Latin, French
POPULATION DENSITY – 2,273 per sq. km (1997)
NATIONAL ANTHEM – 'Inno e Marcia Pontificale' ('Hymn and Pontifical March')
NATIONAL DAY – 24 April (Inauguration of present Pontiff)
DEATH PENALTY – No (abolished 1969)
ANNUAL AVERAGE GROWTH OF GDP – 1.3 per cent (1998)

HISTORY

The Vatican City is surrounded on all sides by Rome. The head of the Roman Catholic Church became a temporal ruler in the eighth century. The Papal States were annexed in 1860 by the newly unified kingdom of Italy and Rome was captured by Italian troops in 1870–1, when the pope withdrew into the Vatican Palace. In the Lateran treaties (1929), Italy recognised the pope's sovereignty over the city of the Vatican, and declared the state to be neutral and inviolable territory. The Vatican City State has special observer status at the United Nations.

The head of state is the the Pope, the Sovereign Pontiff. He is elected for life by a conclave consisting of members of the Sacred College of Cardinals. Administration of the Vatican City State is carried out by the Pontifical Commission, which is appointed by the pope. All Vatican officials vacate their offices on the death of a pope. Pope Benedict XVI confirmed in office the president of the Pontifical Commission and the members of the secretariat of state in April 2005.
Sovereign Pontiff, His Holiness Pope Benedict XVI (Joseph Ratzinger), *born* 16 April 1927, *elected* 19 April 2005, *inaugurated* 24 April 2005

SECRETARIAT OF STATE *as at July 2007*
Secretary of State, Cardinal Tarcisio Bertone

Substitute for General Affairs, Archbishop Leonardo Sandri
Secretary for Relations with States, Archbishop Dominique Mamberti

PONTIFICAL COMMISSION
President, Archbishop Giovanni Lajolo

APOSTOLIC NUNCIATURE
54 Parkside, London SW19 5NE
T 020-8944 7189
Apostolic Nuncio, HE Archbishop Faustino Sainz Munoz, *apptd* 2005

BRITISH EMBASSY TO THE HOLY SEE
Via XX Settembre 80/A, 00187 Rome
T (+39) (6) 4220 4000 E holysee@fco.gov.uk
W www.britishembassy.gov.uk/holysee
Ambassador Extraordinary and Plenipotentiary, HE Francis Campbell, *apptd* 2005

ECONOMY

The Vatican City is unique in having a non-commercial economy. It is supported by financial contributions by Roman Catholic dioceses worldwide. Revenue is also generated by the sale of postage stamps, coins, medals and tourist mementoes, and from income from investments and property.

MEDIA AND CULTURE

There is one official television channel in the Vatican City, and one official radio station (Vatican Radio), broadcasting seven channels. The Vatican Information Service is the state's official news service. The city is a World Heritage Site. Its architectural masterpiece, St Peter's Basilica, is famed for its domed roof and the Sistine Chapel ceiling, respectively designed and painted by Michelangelo. Much of the state's wealth is in a vast art collection.

VENEZUELA

República Bolivariana de Venezuela – Bolivarian Republic of Venezuela

AREA – 912,050 sq. km. Neighbours: Colombia (west), Guyana (east), Brazil (south)
CAPITAL – Caracas; population, 3,435,795 (2002 est)
MAJOR CITIES – Maracaibo; Valencia; Barquisimeto
CURRENCY – Bolívar (Bs) of 100 céntimos
POPULATION – 25,730,435 rising at 1.38 per cent per year (2006 est)
RELIGION – Roman Catholicism (70 per cent), Protestantism (29 per cent) (est)
LANGUAGE – Spanish (official)
POPULATION DENSITY – 30 per sq. km (2005)
URBAN POPULATION – 88.1 per cent (2005 est)
MEDIAN AGE (years) – 26 (2006 est)
NATIONAL ANTHEM – 'Gloria al Bravo Pueblo' ['Glory to the Brave People']
NATIONAL DAY – 5 July (Independence Day)
LIFE EXPECTANCY (years) – 74.54 (2006 est)
MORTALITY RATE – 4.92 (2006 est)
BIRTH RATE – 8.711 (2006 est)
INFANT MORTALITY RATE – 21.54 (2006 est)
DEATH PENALTY – No (abolished 1863)
CPI SCORE – 2.3 (2006)

CLIMATE AND TERRAIN

The Andean mountains, of which the main range is the Sierra Nevada de Mérida, run across the north-west of the country, separating the northern coast from the central plains. The Guiana Highlands occupy the south-east of the country. Elevation extremes range from 5,007m (Pico Bolivar) at the highest point to 0m (Caribbean Sea) at the lowest. The River Orinoco flows across the centre of the country to its delta on the Atlantic coast. Its upper waters are united with those of the Rio Negro (a Brazilian tributary of the Amazon) by a natural river or canal, known as the Brazo Casiquiare. The coastal regions contain many lagoons and lakes, including Maracaibo (area 13,351 sq. km), the largest lake in South America. The wet season lasts from May to November. Average temperatures in Caracas range from 16°C in January to 29°C in June.

HISTORY AND POLITICS

The first Spanish settlement was established at Cumaná in 1520 and Venezuela became part of the Viceroyalty of New Granada in the early 18th century. There were several revolts against Spanish colonial rule, and a declaration of independence in 1811 was followed by several years of struggle until troops led by Simón Bolivar defeated the Spanish at the battle of Carabobo in 1821. Venezuela became part of Gran Colombia (with Colombia, Ecuador and Panama), and then an independent republic in 1830 under the first of a series of *caudillos* (military leaders). The first truly democratic elections were held in 1947 but the government was overthrown by the military within months. An enduring civilian democracy was established in 1958 and introduced a period of relative political stability.

Oil revenues supported a buoyant economy in the 1970s but economic difficulties since the mid-1980s, and the austerity measures adopted since 1989 to address these, have caused social unrest and a number of attempted coups. President Hugo Chávez's economic reforms and his authoritarian style have polarised domestic opinion, provoking strikes and demonstrations, an attempted military coup in 2002 and a recall referendum in 2004, which he won.

President Chávez was originally elected in 1998 under the 1961 constitution but in 2000 successfully sought re-election under the 1999 constitution; he was elected for a third term in December 2006. In the 2005 legislative election, the president's Fifth Republic Movement won an overall majority in the national assembly and parties allied to it took the remaining seats because of an opposition boycott of the election; international observers declared the polls fair. In January 2007 the legislature granted the president the power to rule by decree for 18 months.

POLITICAL SYSTEM

Under the 1999 constitution, the executive president is directly elected for a six-year term, renewable only once. The unicameral legislature, the *Asamblea Nacional* (national assembly), has 165 members, directly elected for a five-year term. The president appoints the vice-president and the council of ministers.

The country is divided into 22 states, two federal territories, one federal district (around the capital) and 72 federal dependencies. The states have considerable autonomy and each has its own legislature and elected governor.

HEAD OF STATE
President, Col. Hugo Chávez Frías (retd), *elected* 6 December 1998, *sworn in* 2 February 1999, *re-elected* 2000, 2006
Vice-President, Jorge Rodriguez

SELECTED GOVERNMENT MEMBERS *as at July 2007*
Interior and Justice, Pedro Carreno
Defence, Gen. Gustavo Rangel Briceno
Economy, Pedro Morejon
Foreign Relations, Nicholas Maduro

EMBASSY OF THE BOLIVARIAN REPUBLIC OF VENEZUELA
1 Cromwell Road, London SW7 2HW
T 020-7584 4206 E info@venezlon.co.uk
Ambassador Extraordinary and Plenipotentiary, HE Alfredo Toro-Hardy, *apptd* 2001

BRITISH EMBASSY
Edificio Torre la Castellana, Piso 11, Avenida la Principal de la Castellana, Caracas 1601
T (+58) (212) 263 8411 E britishembassy@internet.ve
W www.britain.org.ve
Ambassador Extraordinary and Plenipotentiary, HE Catherine Royle, *apptd* 2007

BRITISH COUNCIL
Torre Credicard, Piso 3, Avenida Principal El Bosque, Chacaito, Caracas
T (+58) (212) 952 9965 W www.britishcouncil.org/es/venezuela
Director, Barbara Wickham

DEFENCE

The army has 81 main battle tanks, 71 armoured personnel carriers and 13 helicopters. The navy has 2 submarines, 6 frigates, 6 patrol and coastal vessels and 3 combat aircraft at 9 bases. The air force has 56 combat aircraft and 25 helicopters.
MILITARY BUDGET – US$1,680m (2006)
MILITARY PERSONNEL – 82,300: army 34,000, navy 18,300, air force 7,000, National Guard 23,000
CONSCRIPTION DURATION – 30 months (selective)

ECONOMY AND TRADE

Much of industry is state-owned, and since President Chávez came to power a number of private assets, some foreign-owned, have been nationalised; nationalisation of key energy and telecommunications companies was announced in January 2007. The oil and gas industries are the mainstays of the economy, providing 90 per cent of exports and over 50 per cent of government revenue, but the heavy dependence on them makes the economy vulnerable to global price fluctuations. Tax collection has increased, and is now the largest source of non-oil revenue for the government.

Agriculture comprises large-scale commercial farms and subsistence farming. Land distribution is uneven, with 1 per cent of farms occupying 46 per cent of arable land and 250,000 smallholdings occupying less than 2 per cent of arable land; a land reform decree passed in 2005 will redistribute land to the rural poor, breaking up the larger estates. Agricultural products include maize, sorghum, sugar cane, rice, bananas, vegetables and coffee. There is an extensive beef and dairy farming industry. Products of the tropical forest region include orchids, wild rubber and timber, mangrove bark, balata gum and tonka beans. Agriculture provides 4 per cent of GDP and engages over 10 per cent of the workforce.

There are very large deposits of minerals, especially coal, iron ore, bauxite and gold, which are being mined. Apart from oil and gas extraction, the main industries are production of construction materials, textiles, steel and aluminium, food processing and vehicle assembly. Industry contributes 41 per cent of GDP and services 55 per cent.

The main trading partners are the USA (51 per cent of exports; 32 per cent of imports) and neighbouring countries. Principal exports are oil, bauxite and aluminium, steel, chemicals, agricultural products and basic manufactures. The main imports are raw materials, machinery, transport equipment and construction materials.
GNI – US$123,100m; US$4,820 per capita (2005)
ANNUAL AVERAGE GROWTH OF GDP – 9.3 per cent (2005 est)
INFLATION RATE – 16 per cent (2005 est)
UNEMPLOYMENT – 12.2 per cent (2005 est)
TOTAL EXTERNAL DEBT – US$41,510m (2005 est)
IMPORTS – US$24,000m (2005)
EXPORTS – US$52,000m (2005)

BALANCE OF PAYMENTS
Trade – US$31,532m surplus (2005)
Current Account – US$25,359m surplus (2005)

Trade with UK	*2005*	*2006*
Imports from UK	£236,172,000	£235,951,000
Exports to UK	£394,735,000	£604,960,000

COMMUNICATIONS

There are 96,155km of roads, some 32,308km of them surfaced. Road and river communications have made railways of negligible importance, except for carrying iron ore in the south-east, although the government is expanding the network and there are now some 682km of lines. The 7,500km of inland waterways include 400km on the River Orinoco which, with Lake Maracaibo, is navigable for ocean-going ships. The main ports are Maracaibo, Puerto Cabello and Caracas-La Guaira. There are over 300 airports and airfields, the principal airports being at Caracas and Maracaibo.

Telecommunications are being modernised and expanded. In 2005 there were 3.6 million main lines in use, 12.5 million mobile phone subscribers and 3 million internet users.

EDUCATION AND HEALTH

LITERACY RATE – 93 per cent (2004 est)
GROSS ENROLMENT RATIO (percentage of relevant age group) – primary 105 per cent; secondary 74 per cent; tertiary 41 per cent (2005 est)
HEALTH EXPENDITURE (per capita) – US$196 (2004)
HOSPITAL BEDS (per 1,000 people) – 0.8 (2000–5)

MEDIA

Media watchdogs have accused President Chávez of creating a climate of fear amongst journalists; in May 2007 Radio Caracas Television, the country's most influential private network and an outspoken critic of the president, was closed after the government refused to renew its licence. There are six daily newspapers, including *El Mundo* and *El Nacional.*

VIETNAM

Cong Hoa Xa Hoi Chu Nghia Viet Nam – Socialist Republic of Vietnam

AREA – 329,560 sq. km. Neighbours: China (north), Laos and Cambodia (west)
CAPITAL – Hanoi; population, 1,834,300 (2003 est)
MAJOR CITIES – Ho Chi Minh City, Haiphong; Da Nang
CURRENCY – Dong of 10 ho or 100 xu
POPULATION – 84,402,966 rising at 1.02 per cent per year (2006 est)
RELIGION – Buddhism (50 per cent), Roman Catholicism (8 per cent), Cao Dai (2 per cent), Hoa Hao (2 per cent) (est). Cao Dai is a syncretistic religion which combines elements of several faiths. Hoa Hao is a branch of Buddhism that focuses on private acts of worship and devotion
LANGUAGE – Vietnamese (official), English, French, Khmer
POPULATION DENSITY – 268 per sq. km (2005)
URBAN POPULATION – 26.7 per cent (2005 est)
MEDIAN AGE (years) – 25.9 (2006 est)
NATIONAL ANTHEM – 'Tien Quaan Ca' ['The March to the Front']
NATIONAL DAY – 2 September (Independence Day)
LIFE EXPECTANCY (years) – 70.85 (2006 est)
MORTALITY RATE – 6.22 (2006 est)
BIRTH RATE – 16.86 (2006 est)
INFANT MORTALITY RATE – 25.14 (2006 est)
DEATH PENALTY – Yes
CPI SCORE – 2.6 (2006)
POPULATION BELOW POVERTY LINE – 19.5 per cent (2004 est)

CLIMATE AND TERRAIN

The terrain consists of flat river deltas, of the Hong (Red) in the north and of the Mekong in the south, divided by central highlands. The country is mountainous in the far north and north-west. Elevation extremes range from 3,144m (Ngoc Linh) at the highest point to 0m (South China Sea) at the lowest. The climate is tropical, dominated by a monsoon season that lasts from May to September in the north of the country, and from September to January in the south. Average temperatures in Hanoi range from 17°C in January to 29°C in June.

HISTORY AND POLITICS

Independent kingdoms in Vietnam were unified in the 15th century but power became decentralised until the early 19th century, when central power was reasserted with the assistance of France. From 1858 to 1884 France conquered Vietnam, establishing three protectorates which in 1887 became part of France's Indo-Chinese Union with Cambodia and Laos. Vietnam was under Japanese occupation from 1940 to 1945; Vietnamese Communists fought a guerrilla war of resistance against the occupiers and, controlling most of the country when the Second World War ended, declared independence. France's attempts to reassert its control led to the Indo-China War (1946–54) that ended with France's withdrawal and an armistice dividing the country into communist North Vietnam and non-communist South Vietnam. In 1957 a communist insurgency that began in South Vietnam escalated into war between the Communist north and the US-backed south. A ceasefire and peace talks led to the withdrawal of US troops in 1973, but not before millions had been killed. North Vietnam violated the peace agreements to capture Saigon and took control of the south in 1975. North and South Vietnam were reunified in 1976 as the Socialist Republic of Vietnam.

A degree of economic liberalisation was introduced from 1986 and was enshrined in a new constitution in 1992 which approved many economic and political reforms, but power remains with the ruling Communist Party. The party leadership's request in early 2006 for comments on its political platform prompted a public debate about the party's role, criticism of government and some calls for political pluralism.

At its five-yearly meeting in June 2006, the Communist Party Congress elected a new Politburo and secretariat. Nguyen Minh Triet was confirmed as leader of the Communist Party and was then elected president by the national assembly. In the May 2007 national assembly elections, the Communist Party won 449 of the 500 seats.

POLITICAL SYSTEM

The 1992 constitution was amended in 2001 to allow small-scale capitalism greater freedom. The head of state is a president elected by the national assembly to serve a five-year term. The unicameral national assembly *(Quoc-Hoi)* has 500 members, who are directly elected for a five-year term, and appoints the council of ministers. The head of government is the prime minister, who is responsible to the national assembly. However, effective power lies with the Vietnamese Communist Party. Its highest executive body is the central committee, elected by the national party congress held every five years. The Politburo and the secretariat of the central committee, which exercise the real power, are elected at the party congress.

HEAD OF STATE

President, Nguyen Minh Triet, *elected* 27 June 2006
Vice-President, Truong My Hoa

SELECTED GOVERNMENT MEMBERS *as at July 2007*

Prime Minister, Nguyen Tan Dung
Deputy Prime Ministers, Pham Gia Khiem; Troung Vinh Trong; Nguyen Sinh Hung
Finance, Vu Van Ninh
Internal Affairs, Do Quang Trung
National Defence, Gen. Phung Quang Thanh

EMBASSY OF THE SOCIALIST REPUBLIC OF VIETNAM

12–14 Victoria Road, London W8 5RD
T 020-7937 1912 W www.vietnamembassy.org.uk
Ambassador Extraordinary and Plenipotentiary, HE Trinh Duc Du, *apptd* 2003

BRITISH EMBASSY

Central Building, 31 Hai Ba Trung, Hanoi
T (+84) (4) 936 0500 E bcghcmc@hcm.vnn.vn W www.uk-vietnam.org
Ambassador Extraordinary and Plenipotentiary, HE Robert Gordon, *apptd* 2003

BRITISH COUNCIL

40 Cat Linh Street, Dong Da, Hanoi
T (+84) (4) 843 6780 W www.britishcouncil.org/vietnam
Director, Keith Davies

DEFENCE

The army has 1,315 main battle tanks, 1,380 armoured personnel carriers and 300 armoured infantry fighting

ehicles. The navy has 2 submarines, 6 frigates and 39 atrol and coastal vessels at 7 principal bases. The air orce has 221 combat aircraft and 26 armed helicopters.
MILITARY BUDGET – US$3,430m (2006)
MILITARY PERSONNEL – 455,000: army 412,000, navy 13,000, air force 30,000; paramilitaries 40,000
CONSCRIPTION DURATION – 24 to 36 months

ECONOMY AND TRADE

The economy struggled for a decade after 1975 owing to he devastation of war and the imposition of a centrally lanned economy. Since economic liberalisation and nternational integration were adopted in 1986, the conomy has grown substantially, albeit from a low base, nd competitive, export-driven industries are being leveloped, attracting foreign investment and international id. Poverty has been reduced, although rural areas have enefited less, so there is a disparity in wealth distribution etween the urban and rural populations. The government ims to turn Vietnam into an industrialised country by 2020.

Agriculture is still a mainstay of the economy, ccounting for 20 per cent of GDP and employing 57 per ent of the workforce. The main industries are food rocessing, machine building, coal mining, manufacture f clothing, footwear, steel, cement, chemical fertiliser, glass, tyres and paper, and oil and gas production from arge offshore reserves. Industry now contributes 42 per ent of GDP and services 38 per cent. The main trading artners are Japan, China, the USA and Singapore. Principal exports are crude oil, fish and seafood, rice, offee, rubber, tea, clothing and footwear. The main mports are machinery and equipment, petroleum roducts, fertiliser, steel products, raw cotton, grain, ement and motorcycles.

GNI – US$51,300m (2005); US$620 per capita (2005)
ANNUAL AVERAGE GROWTH OF GDP – 8.5 per cent (2005 est)
INFLATION RATE – 8.3 per cent (2005 est)
UNEMPLOYMENT – 2.4 per cent (2005 est)
TOTAL EXTERNAL DEBT – US$20,160m (2005 est)
IMPORTS – US$36,000m (2005)
EXPORTS – US$32,000m (2005)

BALANCE OF PAYMENTS
Trade – US$2,256m deficit (2004)
Current Account – US$926m deficit (2004)

Trade with UK	*2005*	*2005*
Imports from UK	£81,704,000	£95,701,000
Exports to UK	£721,059,000	£809,500,000

COMMUNICATIONS

Vietnam has 222,000km of roads, 180,000km of which re unsurfaced. It has 2,600km of railways and 17,700km f navigable waterways. The main ports are Haiphong and Ho Chi Minh City. The principal airports are at Ho Chi Minh City, Hanoi and Da Nang.

92	WORLD HIGHEST
	per cent of business software pirated in 2004

Source: Economist Intelligence Unit

Telecommunications systems are being modernised and expanded, and mobile phone distribution is growing rapidly. There were 15.8 million main lines in use and 9.6 million mobile phone subscribers in 2005, and 13.1 million internet users in 2006.

EDUCATION AND HEALTH

LITERACY RATE – 90.3 per cent (2004 est)
GROSS ENROLMENT RATIO (percentage of relevant age group) – primary 95 per cent; secondary 76 per cent; tertiary 16 per cent (2005 est)
HEALTH EXPENDITURE (per capita) – US$30 (2004)
HOSPITAL BEDS (per 1,000 people) – 2.4 (2000–5)

MEDIA

The Communist Party has a firm grip on the media and has closed down television and radio stations which have expressed dissent from the party line. There is one national television station and many local stations; some satellite channels are also available. The state-run radio network operates several national stations. The Communist Party and the People's Army both publish a daily newspaper and there are also newspapers published in English and French.

YEMEN

Al-Jumhuriyah alYamaniyah – Republic of Yemen

AREA – 527,970 sq. km. Neighbours: Saudi Arabia (north), Oman (east)
CAPITAL – Sana'a; population, 1,707,586 (2004)
MAJOR CITIES – Aden (Adan), the former capital of South Yemen; Al-Hudaydah
CURRENCY – Riyal of 100 fils
POPULATION – 21,456,188 rising at 3.46 per cent per year (2006 est)
RELIGION – Islam (99 per cent) (est)
LANGUAGE – Arabic (official)
POPULATION DENSITY – 40 per sq. km (2005)
URBAN POPULATION – 26.3 per cent (2005 est)
MEDIAN AGE (years) – 16.6 (2006 est)
NATIONAL ANTHEM – 'United Republic'
NATIONAL DAY – 22 May (Unification Day)
LIFE EXPECTANCY (years) – 62.12 (2006 est)
MORTALITY RATE – 8.3 (2006 est)
BIRTH RATE – 42.89 (2006 est)
INFANT MORTALITY RATE – 59.88 (2006 est)
DEATH PENALTY – Yes
CPI SCORE – 2.6 (2006)
POPULATION BELOW POVERTY LINE – 45.2 per cent (2003)

Included in the state of Yemen are the offshore islands of Perim and Kamaran in the Red Sea, and Suqutra in the Gulf of Aden. The border with Saudi Arabia, except for the north-west corner, is unclear and is being delineated following an agreement between the two countries in 2000.

CLIMATE AND TERRAIN

A mountainous region in the west and south divides the desert interior from the coastal regions. Elevation extremes range from 3,760m (Jabal an Nabi Shu'ayb) at the highest point to 0m (Arabian Sea) at the lowest. The coastal area has high humidity, but rainfall throughout the country is unpredictable, resulting in droughts and severe floods. Average temperatures in Aden range from 22°C in January to 37°C in June.

HISTORY AND POLITICS

Northern Yemen became part of the Ottoman Empire in the early 16th century and although it achieved some independence in the 17th century, Ottoman control was re-established in the 1870s and the area remained part of the Empire until it collapsed at the end of the First World War. In 1918 north Yemen became an independent kingdom under the rule of the Hamid al-Din dynasty. A revolution in 1962 overthrew the monarchy and the Yemen Arab Republic was declared. Fighting between royalists and republicans continued until 1967, when the republican regime was recognised internationally.

Aden, on the south coast, came under British rule in 1839, and a protectorate was gradually established over the sultanates of the southern hinterland in the second half of the 19th century. An armed rebellion against British rule began in 1963. After British troops withdrew in 1967, power was seized by the National Liberation Front, which established a repressive communist regime in the People's Republic of South Yemen (later renamed the People's Democratic Republic of Yemen).

There were border clashes between the two Yemeni states in 1971–2 and again in 1978, when a ceasefire agreement included a commitment to merging the two states. Negotiations began in 1979 and the two countries united as the Republic of Yemen on 22 May 1990. A power struggle between the former northern and southern elites led to a three-month civil war in 1994 in which a southern attempt to secede was crushed by northern government forces. Tensions remain between the north and south with some southerners believing that they are being marginalised. Tourists have been kidnapped on several occasions by groups seeking concessions from the government.

Fighting occurred in the north-west in 2004–5 as government forces suppressed an uprising by some members of the Zaidi sect, a Shia group in the predominantly Sunni country. There was a resurgence in fighting in early 2007.

Lt.-Gen. Ali Abdullah Saleh, president of North Yemen from 1978, became president of the united country in 1990. He was elected president for a five-year term by the House of Representatives in 1994 and, following constitutional changes, re-elected for a seven-year term in the first direct presidential election in 1999; he was re-elected again in 2006. In the 2003 legislative election, the ruling General People's Congress (GPC) won 228 seats and formed a coalition goverment with the Yemeni Alliance for Reform (YAR or al-Islah) led by Abd al-Qadir Abd al-Rahman Bajammal. Bajammal was replaced as prime minister by Ali Mohammad Mujawar in March 2007.

POLITICAL SYSTEM

The 1991 constitution was amended following a referendum in 2001. The head of state is a president who is directly elected for a seven-year term, renewable once only. The unicameral legislature, the *Majlis al-Nowab* (house of representatives), has 301 members directly elected for a six-year term. In addition, there is an advisory Shura council, whose 111 members are appointed by the president. The prime minister is appointed by the president.

HEAD OF STATE

President, Field Marshal Ali Abdullah Saleh, *took office* 22 May 1990, *elected* 1 October 1994, *re-elected* 23 September 1999
Vice-President, Gen. Abd Rabbah Mansur Hadi

SELECTED GOVERNMENT MEMBERS *as at July 2007*

Prime Minister, Ali Mohammad Mujawar
Deputy Prime Ministers, Gen. Rashad Mohammad al-Alimi; Abdul-Karim Ismail al-Arhabi
Defence, Gen. Mohammad Nasser Ahmed Ali
Foreign Affairs, Abu-Bakr Abdallah al-Qirbi

EMBASSY OF THE REPUBLIC OF YEMEN

57 Cromwell Road, London SW7 2ED
T 020-7584 6607
Ambassador Extraordinary and Plenipotentiary, HE Mohamed Taha Mustafa, *apptd* 2005

BRITISH EMBASSY

PO Box 1287, 129 Haddah Road, Sana
T (+967) (1) 264 081
Ambassador Extraordinary and Plenipotentiary, HE Tim Torlot, *apptd* 2007

BRITISH COUNCIL

PO Box 2157, 3rd Floor, Administrative Tower, Sana'a Trade Centre, Algiers Street, Sana'a
T (+967) (1) 448 356/7 W www.britishcouncil.org/yemen
Director, Elizabeth White

DEFENCE

The army has 790 main battle tanks, 710 armoured personnel carriers and 200 armoured infantry fighting vehicles. The navy has 22 patrol and coastal vessels at 2 bases. The air force has 75 combat aircraft and 8 attack helicopters.

MILITARY BUDGET – US$823m (2006)
MILITARY PERSONNEL – 66,700: army 60,000, navy 1,700, air force 5,000; paramilitaries 71,200
CONSCRIPTION DURATION – 24 months

ECONOMY AND TRADE

Despite its oil industry, the mainstay of the economy, Yemen is the poorest country in the Arab world. It has received IMF support for restructuring and modernising the economy, though the political will to implement the programme has flagged in recent years and the government is also struggling to rein in high spending and corruption. Agriculture is largely of a subsistence nature, and, with herding and fishing, engages about 7[illegible] per cent of the population, contributing 12 per cent of GDP. Apart from oil producing and refining, industry consists of small-scale manufacturing of cotton textiles, leather goods, handicrafts, aluminium products and cement, food processing and ship repair. The main trading partners are China, the UAE, India, Thailand and Saudi Arabia. Principal exports are crude oil, coffee, and dried and salted fish. The main imports are food and livestock, machinery and equipment, and chemicals.

GNI – US$12,600m (2005); US$600 per capita (2005)
ANNUAL AVERAGE GROWTH OF GDP – 2.8 per cent (2005 est)
INFLATION RATE – 11.8 per cent (2005 est)
UNEMPLOYMENT – 35 per cent (2003 est)
TOTAL EXTERNAL DEBT – US$5,347m (2005 est)
IMPORTS – US$4,000m (2003)
EXPORTS – US$4,000m (2003)

BALANCE OF PAYMENTS
Trade – US$2,256m surplus (2005)
Current Account – US$1,215m surplus (2005)

Trade with UK	*2005*	*2006*
Imports from UK	£62,190,000	£61,876,000
Exports to UK	£19,930,000	£16,206,000

COMMUNICATIONS

Yemen has 71,000km of roads, of which 6,000km are surfaced. Its main ports are at Aden, Al-Hudaydah and Al-Mukalla. The principal airports are at Sana'a and Aden.

Since unification a national telephone network has been created. Mobile phone distribution is expanding rapidly. There were 900,000 main lines in use and 2 million mobile phone users in 2006, and 220,000 internet users in 2005.

EDUCATION AND HEALTH

LITERACY RATE – 49 per cent (2004 est)
GROSS ENROLMENT RATIO (percentage of relevant age group) – primary 87 per cent; secondary 48 per cent; tertiary 9 per cent (2005 est)
HEALTH EXPENDITURE (per capita) – US$34 (2004)
HOSPITAL BEDS (per 1,000 people) – 0.6 (2000–5)

MEDIA

All broadcasting is state-run and television and radio are the main means of communication owing to low levels of literacy. The government also funds some newspapers and controls most of the printing. There are four main newspapers: *Al-Thawrah, Yemen Times, Yemen Observer* and *Al-Ayyam.*

ZAMBIA

Republic of Zambia

AREA – 754,614 sq. km. Neighbours: Democratic Republic of the Congo and Tanzania (north), Malawi (east), Mozambique, Zimbabwe and Namibia (south), Angola (west)
CAPITAL – Lusaka; population, 1,084,703 (2000 est)
MAJOR CITIES – Ndola; Kitwe; Kabwe; Chingola
CURRENCY – Kwacha (K) of 100 ngwee
POPULATION – 11,502,010 rising at 2.11 per cent per year (2006 est)
RELIGION – Christianity (87 per cent), Hinduism and Islam (1 per cent) (est)
LANGUAGE – English (official); over 70 indigenous languages are spoken
POPULATION DENSITY – 16 per sq. km (2005)
URBAN POPULATION – 36.5 per cent (2005 est)
MEDIAN AGE (years) – 16.5 (2006 est)
NATIONAL ANTHEM – 'Stand and Sing of Zambia, Proud and Free'
NATIONAL DAY – 24 October (Independence Day)
LIFE EXPECTANCY (years) – 40.03 (2006 est)
MORTALITY RATE – 19.93 (2006 est)
BIRTH RATE – 41 (2006 est)
INFANT MORTALITY RATE – 86.84 (2006 est)
HIV/AIDS ADULT PREVALENCE – 16.5 per cent (2003 est)
DEATH PENALTY – Yes
CPI SCORE – 2.6 (2006)
LITERACY RATE – 67.9 per cent (2004 est)
GROSS ENROLMENT RATIO (percentage of relevant age group) – primary 111 per cent; secondary 28 per cent (2005 est); tertiary 2 per cent (2002)
MILITARY BUDGET – US$231m (2006 est)
MILITARY PERSONNEL – 15,100: army 13,500, air force 1,600; paramilitaries 1,400
HEALTH EXPENDITURE (per capita) US$30 (2004)

CLIMATE AND TERRAIN

Landlocked Zambia lies in central Africa on a forested plateau cut through by river valleys and with higher land in the north and north-east. Elevation extremes range from 2,301m (Mafinga Hills) at the highest point to 329m (Zambezi River) at the lowest. Lake Bangweulu and parts of Lakes Tanganyika, Mweru and Kariba lie within its boundaries. The climate is tropical, with an average temperature of 28°C all year.

HISTORY AND POLITICS

Most of the ethnic groups in Zambia migrated there between the 16th and the 18th centuries. Portuguese explorers arrived in the late 18th century and, with Arab traders, began slave-trading in the 19th century. The area came under British administration as Barotseland in 1889, was named Northern Rhodesia in 1911 and became a British protectorate in 1924. It was part of the Central African Federation with South Rhodesia (Zimbabwe) and Nyasaland (Malawi) from 1953 to 1963, when the federation was dissolved and Northern Rhodesia achieved internal self-government. It became an independent republic on 24 October 1964 under the name of Zambia. Kenneth Kaunda of the United National Independence Party (UNIP) became president at independence and remained in power until 1991.

Zambia was a one-party state ruled by the UNIP from 1972 until 1990, when pressure from opposition groups led to a new constitution, under which multiparty legislative and presidential elections were held in 1991. The Movement for Multiparty Democracy (MMD) won a majority of seats in the parliament, and the MMD candidate Frederick Chiluba defeated Kenneth Kaunda in the presidential election. President Chiluba was re-elected in 1996, surviving coup attempts in 1993 and 1997.

Serious food shortages have occurred in recent years owing to floods and drought. In 2001 the government appealed for international food aid, and the appeal was repeated in 2005 after another drought. The country also faces serious demographic, economic and social problems because of the high levels of HIV/AIDS infection.

The 2001 presidential election was won by MMD candidate Levy Mwanawasa. In the simultaneous legislative election, the MMD won 69 seats, the United Party for National Development (UPND) won 49 seats, other parties and independents won 32 seats. In the 2006 presidential and legislative elections, President Mwanawasa was re-elected and the MMD remained the largest party in the legislature, although it commands a majority only because of the appointed members.

POLITICAL SYSTEM

Under the 1991 constitution, the executive president is directly elected for a five-year term, renewable only once. The unicameral legislature, the national assembly, has 150 directly elected members, up to eight appointed by the president and a speaker; all serve a five-year term. The president appoints the cabinet.

HEAD OF STATE
President, Defence, Levy Mwanawasa, *elected* 27 December 2001, *sworn in* 2 January 2002, *re-elected* 2 October 2006
Vice-President, Rupiah Banda

SELECTED GOVERNMENT MEMBERS *as at July 2007*
Home Affairs, Lt.-Gen. Ronnie Shikapwasha
Foreign Affairs, Mundia Sikatana
Finance, Peter Ng'andu Magande

HIGH COMMISSION FOR THE REPUBLIC OF ZAMBIA
Zambia House, 2 Palace Gate, London W8 5NG
T 020-7589 6655 E zhal@btconnect.com
High Commissioner, HE Anderson K. Chibwa, *apptd* 2003

BRITISH HIGH COMMISSION
PO Box 50050, 5210 Independence Avenue, 15101 Ridgeway, Lusaka
T (+260) (1) 251 133 E bhc-lusaka@fco.gov.uk
High Commissioner, HE Alastair Harrison, CVO, *apptd* 2005

BRITISH COUNCIL
PO Box 34571, Heroes Place, Cairo Road, Lusaka
T (+260) (1) 223 602/228 332
W www.britishcouncil.org/zambia
Director, Paul Clementson

ECONOMY AND TRADE

Although prosperous at independence, the economy was devastated by the drop in world copper prices in the 1970s and Zambia remains one of the world's poorest countries, with about three-quarters of the population living below the poverty line. The transition in the 1990s from a state-controlled to a free-market system improved productivity, especially in the now privatised copper industry, which is the mainstay of the economy. Despite budgetary reform, foreign debt is high, but a 2005 World Bank debt relief package wrote off more than 50 per cent, and the G8 promised 100 per cent debt relief.

Copper is the main source of foreign earnings and increased demand in recent years, owing to the needs of the electronics industries, has spurred investment and greater output, increasing revenue and making the industry a potential driver of economic growth. However, 85 per cent of the workforce is engaged in agriculture, mostly at subsistence level, which accounts for 20 per cent of GDP. The main industries are copper mining and processing, construction, food processing, manufacture of beverages, chemicals, textiles and fertiliser, and horticulture. The main trading partners are South Africa, Switzerland, the UK and Zimbabwe. Principal exports are copper, cobalt, electricity, tobacco, cut flowers and cotton. The main imports are machinery, transport equipment, petroleum products, electricity, fertiliser, foodstuffs and clothing.

GNI – US$5,800m (2005); US$500 per capita (2005)
ANNUAL AVERAGE GROWTH OF GDP – 5 per cent (2005 est)
INFLATION RATE – 18.3 per cent (2005 est)
UNEMPLOYMENT – 50 per cent (2000 est)
TOTAL EXTERNAL DEBT – US$4,641m (2005 est)
IMPORTS – US$2,750m (2005)
EXPORTS – US$1,720m (2005)

Trade with UK	*2005*	*2006*
Imports from UK	£29,877,000	£35,323,000
Exports to UK	£12,470,000	£17,772,000

MEDIA

The broadcast media is dominated by the government-run television and radio networks. The only television service is provided by the state-run Zambia National Broadcasting Association. There are private radio stations but they do not provide much political content. Three of the four newspapers are state-owned.

ZIMBABWE

Republic of Zimbabwe

AREA – 390,580 sq. km. Neighbours: Zambia (north), Mozambique (north and east), South Africa (south), Botswana and Namibia (west)
CAPITAL – Harare; population, 1,444,534 (2002 est)
MAJOR CITIES – Bulawayo, the largest town in Matabeleland; Chitungwiza; Mutare; Gweru
CURRENCY – Zimbabwe dollar (Z$) of 100 cents
POPULATION – 12,236,805 rising at 0.62 per cent per year (2006 est); Shona (82 per cent), Ndebele (14 per cent) (est)
RELIGION – Christianity (60 per cent), Islam (1 per cent) (est). Indigenous religions are popular and are often combined with recognised faiths
LANGUAGE – English (official), Shona, Sinbebele
POPULATION DENSITY – 34 per sq. km (2005)
URBAN POPULATION – 35.9 per cent (2005 est)
MEDIAN AGE (years) – 19.9 (2006 est)
NATIONAL ANTHEM – 'Simudzai Mureza We Zimbabwe' ['Blessed Be the Land of Zimbabwe']
NATIONAL DAY – 18 April (Independence Day)
LIFE EXPECTANCY (years) – 39.29 (2006 est)
MORTALITY RATE – 21.84 (2006 est)
BIRTH RATE – 28.01 (2006 est)
INFANT MORTALITY RATE – 51.71 (2006 est)
HIV/AIDS ADULT PREVALENCE – 24.6 per cent (2003 est)
DEATH PENALTY – Yes
CPI SCORE – 2.4 (2006)
POPULATION BELOW POVERTY LINE – 80 per cent (2004 est)
MILITARY BUDGET – US$60m (2006)
MILITARY PERSONNEL – 29,000: army 25,000, air force 4,000; paramilitaries 21,800

CLIMATE AND TERRAIN

A landlocked country, Zimbabwe's terrain is mainly high plateau with a central high veld and mountains in the east. Elevation extremes range from 2,592m (Inyangani) at the highest point to 162m (Runde River) at the lowest. The wet season coincides with the summer, which runs from November to March. Average temperatures in Harare range from 7°C in June to 29°C in November.

HISTORY AND POLITICS

Organised settlement of the region began at least 20,000 years ago and culminated in the establishment of a powerful settlement at Great Zimbabwe in the 12th century AD. In the 19th century this was taken over by the Nbebele people and became the kingdom of Matabeleland, which was often in dispute with the people of Mashonaland to the north. The area came under British influence from the 1880s, when the British started to exploit the mineral resources. Britain invaded Mashonaland in 1890 and seized Matabeleland in 1893. The two areas became a British protectorate as Southern

Rhodesia in 1898, which became a self-governing colony in 1923. It was part of the Central African Federation from 1953 until 1963, when Northern Rhodesia (Zambia) and Nyasaland (Malawi) became independent. Opposition to independence under black majority rule in Southern Rhodesia prompted a unilateral declaration of independence (UDI) by the white-dominated colonial government in 1965. Economic sanctions and guerrilla warfare by African nationalist groups forced the government to negotiate, and UDI was terminated in 1979. Power was transferred to the majority population and the country became independent as the Republic of Zimbabwe on 18 April 1980.

Robert Mugabe became prime minister at independence and executive president in 1987. He was re-elected in 1990, 1996 and 2002, when he won 56.2 per cent of the vote. Since then, President Mugabe's regime has become increasingly autocratic, brutally suppressing opposition and dissent, and rejecting international criticism of human rights and other abuses; Zimbabwe left the Commonwealth in 2003 because its membership had been suspended indefinitely over the political situation. The appropriation of white-owned farms, which began in 2000, was accompanied by intimidation and violence. The seizures caused an agricultural collapse that, combined with a long drought, led to widespread food shortages in 2001, and a state of disaster was declared in 2002. Mass anti-government protests, including a general strike in 2003, provoked a brutal crackdown by the authorities; opposition leaders were arrested and allegedly tortured for holding demonstrations in 2006 and 2007. Government and opposition representatives began talks in South Africa in June 2007 aimed at solving the country's political and economic crises.

The 2002 election was criticised as seriously flawed by the opposition and international observers, including reports of President Mugabe's party using food handouts to garner votes. The March 2005 legislative election was won by President Mugabe's party, the Zimbabwe African National Union – Patriotic Front (ZANU-PF), which won 78 of the elective seats, giving it an overall majority. The results were disputed by the main opposition party, the Movement for Democratic Change (MDC) and many international observers. Elections to the re-introduced second chamber, the senate, in November 2005 were won by ZANU-PF after an opposition boycott that caused a split in the MDC.

POLITICAL SYSTEM

The 1980 constitution was amended in 1987 to create an executive presidency, in 1990 to make the legislature unicameral and provide for direct elections to the presidency, and in 2005 to re-introduce a second legislative chamber. The executive president is directly elected for a six-year term. The bicameral legislature, the parliament, comprises the house of assembly and the senate. The house of assembly has 150 members, 120 directly elected, 12 appointed by the president, ten provincial governors and eight traditional chiefs; all serve a five-year term. The senate has 66 members, 50 elected (five from each province), six appointed by the president and ten traditional chiefs (one from each province), who serve a five-year term. The president appoints the cabinet.

The country is divided into eight provinces and two cities (Bulawayo, Harare) with provincial status. The provinces are: Manicaland, Mashonaland Central, Mashonaland East, Mashonaland West, Masvingo, Matabeleland North, Matabeleland South and Midlands.

HEAD OF STATE

President, C.-in-C. of the Defence Forces, Robert Gabriel Mugabe, *elected* 30 December 1987, *re-elected* 1990, 1996, 2002

Vice-Presidents, Joseph Msika; Joyce Mujuru

SELECTED GOVERNMENT MEMBERS *as at July 2007*

Defence, Sidney Tigere Sekeramayi

Finance, Samuel Mumbengegw

Foreign Affairs, Simbarashe Mumbengegwi

Home Affairs, Kembo Mohadi

EMBASSY OF THE REPUBLIC OF ZIMBABWE

Zimbabwe House, 429 Strand, London WC2R 0JR

T 020-7836 7755 E zimlondon@yahoo.co.uk

Ambassador Extraordinary and Plenipotentiary, HE Gabriel Mharadze Machinga, *apptd* 2005

BRITISH EMBASSY

PO Box 4490, Corner House, Samora Machel Avenue/Leopold Takawira Street, Harare

T (+263) (4) 772 990 E british.info@fco.gov.uk

W www.britainzw.org

Ambassador Extraordinary and Plenipotentiary, HE Dr Andrew Pocock, *apptd* 2006

BRITISH COUNCIL

PO Box 664, Corner House, Samora Machel Avenue, Harare

T (+263) (4) 775 313-4/756 668

W www.britishcouncil.org/zimbabwe

Director, Louisa Waddingham

ECONOMY AND TRADE

The seizure of almost all the white-owned commercial farms has caused a devastating drop in production and the agriculture-based economy has collapsed. Unemployment was 80 per cent in 2005 and rampant inflation, officially 976 per cent in 2006 but unofficially estimated at over 4,000 per cent, has caused huge rises in the prices of basic commodities and fuel; about 80 per cent of the population is living below the poverty line and many are dependent on food aid. Other forms of international aid have been suspended because repayment of past loans had fallen into arrears, although government repayments started again in 2005. In August 2006 the government revalued the currency, and in June 2007 forcibly lowered goods prices to attempt to control inflation. The economy and social services have been badly hit by the migration of professional and skilled labour in recent years.

Agriculture accounted for 28 per cent of GDP in 1998 and engaged two-thirds of the workforce, but in 2006 accounted for only 18 per cent of GDP. The most important crops are cotton and tobacco for export and maize for domestic consumption. Other crops include wheat, coffee, sugar cane, peanuts and livestock.

The mining sector, although contributing a relatively small portion to GDP, is important to the economy as a foreign exchange earner. Almost all mineral production is exported. Gold is the most important product; others are coal, platinum, copper, nickel, tin, iron ore and other metal and non-metal ores. Mining is now the largest industrial activity and supports a ferro-alloy industry and a steel works. Manufacturing, traditionally highly dependent on the agricultural sector for raw materials, produces wood products, cement, chemicals, fertiliser, clothing, footwear, foodstuffs and beverages; output has dropped in some industries because of transport difficulties and power rationing. The main trading partners are South Africa and China. Principal exports are cotton, tobacco, gold, ferro-alloys, textiles and clothing. The main imports are machinery and transport equipment, other manufactures, chemicals and fuels.

GNI – US$4,500m (2005); US$350 per capita (2005)
ANNUAL AVERAGE GROWTH OF GDP – 7.7 per cent (2005 est)
UNEMPLOYMENT – 80 per cent (2005 est)
TOTAL EXTERNAL DEBT – US$5,216m (2005 est)
IMPORTS – US$2,750m (2005)
EXPORTS – US$1,490m (2005)

Trade with UK	*2005*	*2006*
Imports from UK	£22,113,000	£19,609,000
Exports to UK	£43,565,000	£26,661,000

ANNUAL AVERAGE INFLATION *(per cent)*

1998	31	2003	365
1999	58	2004	350
2000	56	2005	238
2001	73	2006	1,216*
2002	133	2007	4,279*

* estimated
Source: IMF, World Economic Outlook

COMMUNICATIONS

Zimbabwe has 97,400km of roads, over 18,500km of which are surfaced. There are 3,000km of railways but services have become increasingly restricted by lack of diesel and spare parts, leading to the reintroduction into service of steam locomotives. It relies on rail connections through Mozambique and South Africa for access to seaports. The main airports are at Harare and Bulawayo.

The telephone system, once one of the best in Africa, is now badly maintained. Mobile phone distribution is growing quickly, but internet access is limited to Harare and some of the major towns. In 2005 there were 328,000 main lines in use, 699,000 mobile phone subscribers and 1 million internet users.

EDUCATION AND HEALTH

Education is compulsory, and the language of instruction is English. Over 80 per cent of schools are government-aided.

LITERACY RATE – 90 per cent (2004 est)
GROSS ENROLMENT RATIO (percentage of relevant age group) – primary 96 per cent; secondary 36 per cent; tertiary 4 per cent (2005 est)
HEALTH EXPENDITURE (per capita) – US$27 (2004)

MEDIA

The government exercises strict control over the print and broadcast media, and some foreign correspondents are prevented from reporting from within the country. The only television and radio stations are state-run, but overseas radio stations can be received. Two of the main daily newspapers, *The Herald* and *The Chronicle*, are run by the government. Readership of newspapers has been badly hit by rising inflation as their price often exceeds daily wages. Journalists who write anti-government reports face imprisonment.

UK OVERSEAS TERRITORIES

ANGUILLA

AREA – 102 sq. km
CAPITAL – The Valley; population, 1,169 (2001)
CURRENCY – East Caribbean dollar (EC $) of 100 cents
POPULATION – 13,477 rising at 1.57 per cent per year (2006 est)
RELIGION – Protestantism (83 per cent), Roman Catholicism (5 per cent), other Christian denominations (1 per cent) (est)
LANGUAGE – English (official)
POPULATION DENSITY – 134 per sq. km (1999)
POPULATION BELOW POVERTY LINE – 23 per cent (2002)
FLAG – British blue ensign with the coat of arms and three dolphins in the fly
NATIONAL DAY – 30 May (Anguilla Day)
LIFE EXPECTANCY (years) – 77.28 (2006 est)
MORTALITY RATE – 5.34 (2006 est)
BIRTH RATE – 14.17 (2006 est)
INFANT MORTALITY RATE – 20.32 (2006 est)

CLIMATE AND TERRAIN

Anguilla is a flat coralline island in the Caribbean, and is the most northerly of the Leeward Islands. The climate is tropical, modified by north-east trade winds, with temperatures ranging from 24°C to 30°C throughout the year. Elevation extremes range from 65m (Crocus Hill) at the highest point to 0m (Caribbean Sea) at the lowest.

HISTORY AND POLITICS

Anguilla has been a British colony since 1650. For much of its history it was linked administratively with St Kitts, but three months after the Associated State of Saint Christopher (St Kitts)-Nevis-Anguilla came into being in 1967, the Anguillans repudiated government from St Kitts. A commissioner was installed in 1969 and in 1976 Anguilla was given a new status and separate constitution. Final separation from St Kitts and Nevis was effected in December 1980 and Anguilla reverted to a British dependency.

A new constitution was introduced in 1982, providing for a governor, an executive council comprising four elected ministers and two ex-officio members (the attorney-general and deputy governor), and a 12-member legislative House of Assembly, consisting of seven elected members, two nominated members, two ex-officio members (the attorney-general and deputy governor) and presided over by a speaker. The last general election was held in February 2005 and was won by the Anguilla United Front with 38.9 per cent of the vote.

Governor, HE Andrew George, *apptd* 2006
Chief Minister, Hon. Osbourne Fleming

ECONOMY

Low rainfall limits agricultural output and export earnings are mainly from sales of fish and lobsters. Tourism is the main economic activity; the offshore financial services sector is growing in importance.

IMPORTS – US $1,299m (2005)
EXPORTS – US $147m (2005)

BALANCE OF PAYMENTS
Trade – US $57m deficit (2002)
Current Account – US $35m deficit (2002)

Trade with UK	*2005*	*2006*
Imports from UK	£1,193,000	£1,236,000
Exports to UK	£51,000	£33,000

COMMUNICATIONS

The road network is gradually expanding but less than half is paved. Ports and harbours include Blowing Point and Road Bay, and the island is served by Wallblake Airport near The Valley and two airfields.

BERMUDA

AREA – 53.3 sq. km
CAPITAL – Hamilton; population, 5,270 (2000)
CURRENCY – Bermuda dollar of 100 cents
POPULATION – 65,773 rising at 0.61 per cent per year (2006 est)
RELIGION – Protestantism (52 per cent), Roman Catholicism (15 per cent) (est)
LANGUAGE – English (official), Portuguese
POPULATION DENSITY – 1,231 per sq. km (2001)
POPULATION BELOW POVERTY LINE – 19 per cent (2000)
FLAG – British red ensign with the shield of the arms in the fly
NATIONAL DAY – 24 May (Bermuda Day)
LIFE EXPECTANCY (years) – 77.96 (2006 est)
MORTALITY RATE – 7.74 (2006 est)
BIRTH RATE – 11.4 (2006 est)
INFANT MORTALITY RATE – 8.3 (2006 est)

CLIMATE AND TERRAIN

Bermuda is a group of over 100 small islands, of which about 20 are inhabited, in the North Atlantic Ocean. All the islands are volcanic in origin, with hilly interiors, surrounded by coral reefs. Elevation extremes range from 76m (Town Hill) at the highest point to 0m (Atlantic Ocean) at the lowest. The climate is subtropical, regulated by the Gulf Stream, with an average temperature of 23°C.

HISTORY AND POLITICS

Bermuda was discovered by the Spanish *c.*1503 but colonised by the British in the 17th century, becoming a colony in 1684. Internal self-government was introduced in 1968; independence from the UK was rejected in a 1995 referendum. There is a senate of 11 members and an elected house of assembly of 36 members. The governor retains responsibility for external affairs, defence, internal security and the police, although administrative matters for the police service have been delegated to the minister of labour, home affairs and public safety. In the last general election, in 2003, the Progressive Labour Party won 22 of the 36 seats. The next election is due by August 2008.

Governor and Commander-in-Chief, HE Sir Richard Gozney, KCMG, *apptd* 2007
Premier, Hon. Ewart Brown

ECONOMY

The economy is based on offshore financial services, which attract international business with a low level of corporate taxation and a sophisticated telecommunications system, and tourism. Pharmaceuticals and cut flowers are the leading exports.

Trade with UK	*2005*	*2006*
Imports from UK	£20,255,000	£19,580,000
Exports to UK	£16,042,000	£73,687,000

COMMUNICATIONS

There are 447km of roads, all of which are paved, and one airport, near Ferry Reach on St David's Island. The main ports are at Hamilton and St George. The telephone system is extensive, and mobile telephone distribution is widespread.

BRITISH ANTARCTIC TERRITORY

AREA – 1,709,340 sq. km. The British Antarctic Territory (BAT) consists of the areas south of 60°S. latitude between longitudes 20°W. and 80°W. The territory includes the South Orkney Islands, the South Shetland Islands, the mountainous Antarctic Peninsula and all adjacent islands, and the land mass extending to the South Pole

POPULATION – There is no indigenous population; the British Antarctic Survey maintains two permanently staffed research stations at Halley and Rothera, and two part-time (summer only) stations at Fossil Bluff (Alexander Island) and Signy (South Orkney Islands)

FLAG – British white ensign, without the cross of St George, with the coat of arms of the territory in the fly

CLIMATE AND TERRAIN

Only around 0.7 per cent of the British Antarctic Territory remains ice-free and the ice sheet that permanently covers the remainder is, in places, 5km thick. The climate is polar desert with very little precipitation, and the annual average temperature at the South Pole is −49°C. The highest point of elevation is 3,184m (Mt Jackson).

HISTORY AND POLITICS

Britain made its first territorial claim to part of the Antarctic in 1908. Since 1943, a permanent presence has been maintained which became the British Antarctic Survey (BAS) in 1962. In the same year, the territory, originally administered as a dependency of the Falkland Islands, became a UK overseas territory in its own right.

GOVERNMENT

The BAT is administered by the Foreign and Commonwealth Office, and has a full suite of laws, and legal and postal administrations. All activities are governed by the Antarctic Treaty of 1961, which has the objectives of keeping Antarctica demilitarised and promoting international scientific cooperation.

GOVERNMENT OF THE BRITISH ANTARCTIC TERRITORY
Polar Regions Unit, Overseas Territory Department, Foreign and Commonwealth Office, London SW1A 2AH
T 020-7008 3543
Commissioner (non-resident), Leigh Turner, *apptd* 2006
Administrator, Dr Michael Richardson

BRITISH INDIAN OCEAN TERRITORY

AREA – 54,400 sq. km, of which 60 sq. km is land

POPULATION – No indigenous population now lives in the archipelago; in 2004, around 4,000 military personnel and civilian contract employees were based at the joint UK–US naval support facility on Diego Garcia

FLAG – Divided horizontally into blue and white wavy stripes, with the Union Flag in the canton and a crowned palm-tree over all in the fly

CLIMATE AND TERRAIN

The British Indian Ocean Territory (BIOT) comprises the Chagos Archipelago of 55 islands in six main groups, situated on the Great Chagos Bank in the Indian Ocean about 1,900km north-east of Mauritius. The flat and low terrain rarely rises more than 2m above sea level, while the climate is hot and humid.

HISTORY AND POLITICS

The British Indian Ocean Territory was established in 1965 and included islands formerly administered from Mauritius and the Seychelles. The islands of Farquhar, Desroches and Aldabra became part of the Seychelles when it became independent in 1976; since then the territory has consisted of the Chagos Archipelago only. Successive Mauritian governments have asserted a sovereignty claim to the islands, arguing that they were annexed illegally.

The largest and most southerly of the Chagos Archipelago is Diego Garcia, a sand cay with a land area of about 44 sq. km, used as a joint naval support facility by Britain and the USA. The other main island groups of the archipelago are Peros Banhos (29 islands with a total land area of 6.5 sq. km) and Salamon (11 islands with a total land area of 3.2 sq. km).

The islands' former inhabitants (the Ilois) were expelled between 1967 and 1973 to allow for the construction of the naval base, most being resettled in Mauritius. Since the 1990s the Ilois have taken legal action to obtain the right to return to and settle in the islands; the first visit by former residents took place in March 2006, on a trip funded by the Foreign Office and the government of Mauritius. Two months later, the Ilois won a case before the high court allowing them to return home to the archipelago, but not to Diego Garcia. The British government turned to the court of appeal, but in May 2007 the Ilois' victory was upheld.

Commissioner, Leigh Turner, *apptd* 2006
Administrator, Tony Humphries, *apptd* 2005

BRITISH VIRGIN ISLANDS

AREA – 153 sq. km
CAPITAL – Road Town; population, 3,983 (2001 est)
CURRENCY – US dollar (US $)
POPULATION – 23,098 rising at 1.97 per cent per year (2006 est)
RELIGION – Protestantism (86 per cent), Roman Catholicism (10 per cent) (est)
LANGUAGE – English (official)
POPULATION DENSITY – 134 per sq. km (2001)
FLAG – British blue ensign with the shield of arms in the fly
NATIONAL DAY – 1 July (Territory Day)

LIFE EXPECTANCY (years) – 76.68 (2006 est)
MORTALITY RATE – 4.42 (2006 est)
BIRTH RATE – 14.89 (2006 est)
INFANT MORTALITY RATE – 18.72 (2006 est)

CLIMATE AND TERRAIN

Part of the Virgin Islands archipelago, the northernmost of the Leeward Islands in the Caribbean Sea, the British Virgin Islands comprise Tortola, Virgin Gorda, Anegada, Jost Van Dyke and about 40 islets. Apart from Anegada, which is a flat coral island, the British Virgin Islands are hilly. The highest point of elevation is 521m (Sage Mountain). The climate is sub-tropical and there is little variation in temperature; typically 25°C in January and 29°C in July. The hurricane season runs from June to October.

HISTORY AND POLITICS

Initially settled by Arawak Indians from South America, the islands were named by Christopher Columbus on his second voyage to the New World and annexed by the British in 1672. Under the 1977 constitution, amended in 2000, the islands have a large measure of self-government. The governor, appointed by the crown, is responsible for defence, security, external affairs and the civil service but in other matters acts in accordance with the advice of the executive council. This consists of the governor as chair, one ex-officio member (the attorney-general), the chief minister and four other ministers. The legislative council consists of a speaker chosen from outside the council, one ex-officio member (the attorney-general), and 13 elected members returned from ten electoral districts. The 2003 election was won by the National Democratic Party with a majority of eight seats in the legislative council. The next election is due in 2007.

Governor, HE David Pearey *apptd* 2006
Chief Minister, Hon. Dr Orlando Smith *apptd* 2003

ECONOMY

Tourism is the main industry but offshore financial services are of growing importance. Other industries include a rum distillery, three stone-crushing plants, and factories manufacturing concrete blocks and paint. The major export items are rum, fruit, livestock, gravel and sand. Chief imports are building materials, machinery, cars and beverages.

Trade with UK	*2005*	*2006*
Imports from UK	£16,556,000	£15,011,000
Exports to UK	£52,734,000	£23,656,000

COMMUNICATIONS

The principal airport is on Beef Island, linked by bridge to Tortola, and there are also airfields on Anegada and Virgin Gorda. Road Harbour, at Road Town, is the main port, and ferry services connect the main islands.

CAYMAN ISLANDS

AREA – 262 sq. km
CAPITAL – George Town; population, 20,626 (1999 census)
CURRENCY – Cayman Islands dollar (CI $) of 100 cents
POPULATION – 45,436 rising at 2.56 per cent per year (2006 est)
LANGUAGE – English (official)
POPULATION DENSITY – 163 per sq. km (2002)
FLAG – British blue ensign with the arms on a white disc in the fly
NATIONAL DAY – first Monday in July (Constitution Day)
LIFE EXPECTANCY (years) – 80.07 (2006 est)
MORTALITY RATE – 4.89 (2006 est)
BIRTH RATE – 12.74 (2006 est)
INFANT MORTALITY RATE – 8 (2006 est)
GNI – US $43,703 per capita (2002)
ANNUAL AVERAGE GROWTH OF GDP – 1.7 per cent (2002)

CLIMATE AND TERRAIN

The Cayman Islands comprise Grand Cayman, Cayman Brac, and Little Cayman. Situated about 241km south of Cuba, the low-lying islands are divided from Jamaica, 289km to the south-east, by the Cayman Trench, the deepest part of the Caribbean Sea. Typical temperatures range from 20°C in January to 30°C in July.

HISTORY AND POLITICS

The territory derives its name from the Carib word *caymanas* (crocodile). Permanent settlement followed the first land grant by Britain in 1734 and the islands were placed under direct control of Jamaica in 1863. When Jamaica became independent in 1962, the islands opted to remain under the British crown.

The constitution provides for a governor, a legislative assembly and a cabinet, and allows a large measure of self-government, the governor acting on the advice of the cabinet. This comprises three appointed official members and five ministers elected by the legislative assembly from among its elected members. The assembly has 18 members, 15 elected by popular vote and the three appointed official members of the cabinet. The governor has responsibility for the police, civil service, defence and external affairs. The normal life of the assembly is four years; a general election took place in May 2005 and was won by the People's Progressive Movement, which won nine seats in the assembly.

Following a modernisation review in 2002, a new constitution was drafted but has yet to be implemented owing to disagreements.

Governor, HE Stuart Jack, *apptd* 2005
Leader of Government Business, Hon. Kurt Tibbetts

CAYMAN ISLANDS GOVERNMENT OFFICE
6 Arlington Street, London SW1A 1RE T 020-7491 7772

ECONOMY

The mainstays of the economy are offshore financial services, largely owing to the absence of direct taxation, tourism, with an emphasis on scuba diving, and real estate. Government revenue is derived from fees and duties. Reconstruction, especially of housing, is still in progress after the devastation of Hurricane Ivan in September 2004.

Trade with UK	*2005*	*2006*
Imports from UK	£11,532,000	£14,662,000
Exports to UK	£35,305,000	£31,226,000

COMMUNICATIONS

The Cayman Islands are served by airports at George Town and on Cayman Brac and by an airfield on Little Cayman. George Town is the main port and there are 785km of surfaced roads.

FALKLAND ISLANDS

AREA – 12,173 sq. km
CAPITAL – Stanley; population, 1,989 (2001 census)
CURRENCY – Falkland pound of 100 pence
POPULATION – 2,967 rising at 2.44 per cent per year (2006 est)
URBAN POPULATION – 84 per cent (2001)
FLAG – British blue ensign with the arms on a white disc in the fly
NATIONAL DAY – 14 June (Liberation Day)

CLIMATE AND TERRAIN

The Falkland Islands consist of East Falkland (6,759 sq. km), West Falkland (5,413 sq. km) and over 700 small islands. Elevation extremes range from 705m (Mount Usbourne) at the highest point to 0m (Atlantic Ocean) at the lowest. Average annual temperatures in Stanley range from −1–5°C in winter to 6–13°C in summer, and annual rainfall is low (around 626mm per year).

HISTORY AND POLITICS

The Falkland Islands have a long history of occupation by European countries, including France, Spain and the UK, which established its first settlement in 1766.

After Argentina declared independence from Spain, the Argentine government in 1820 proclaimed its sovereignty over the Falklands and a settlement was founded in 1826 but was subsequently destroyed by the USA in 1831. In 1833 occupation was resumed by the British for the protection of the seal-fisheries, and the islands were permanently colonised. Argentina continued to claim sovereignty over the islands (known to them as *las Islas Malvinas*), and invaded the islands on 2 April 1982. A British naval and military task force recaptured the islands on 14 June 1982. A naval and military garrison of 1,265 personnel remains in the area.

Under the 1985 constitution, the governor is advised by an executive council consisting of three elected members of the legislative council and two ex-officio members, the chief executive and the financial secretary. The legislative council consists of eight elected members and the same two ex-officio members. The last election was held in November 2005; there are no political parties and all members sit as independents.

Governor and Chair of the Executive Council, HE Alan Huckle, *apptd* 2006
Chief Executive, Chris Simpkins

FALKLAND ISLANDS GOVERNMENT OFFICE
Falkland House, 14 Broadway, London SW1H 0BH
T 020-7222 2542

ECONOMY

Since the establishment of a conservation and managed fishing zone around the islands in 1987, the economy has been transformed, with revenue from fishing and related activities replacing sheep-farming as the main industry. Fishing licence fees now provide over half of government revenue, making the islands self-supporting in all but defence costs and funding the provision of good health, education and welfare facilities. Tourism, especially wildlife tourism, is growing. Fish, meat, wool and hides are the principal exports. Chief imports are fuel, provisions, alcoholic beverages, timber, clothing and hardware.

There are known to be substantial reserves of oil offshore and the Falkland Islands government is encouraging exploration for exploitable sites. Onshore, exploration is under way for gold.

Trade with UK	*2005*	*2006*
Imports from UK	£24,272,000	£26,560,000
Exports to UK	£3,820,000	£8,335,000

COMMUNICATIONS

There is an international airport at Mount Pleasant, served by charter flights to the UK (carrying civilian as well as military passengers) and commercial flights to Chile. The main port is Stanley Harbour and a regular shipping service operates to the UK. The road network is gradually expanding but only roads in and around Stanley are paved, and most longer internal journeys are by light aircraft. Telecommunications are possible through a satellite link and about half of the households have internet access.

GIBRALTAR

AREA – 6.5 sq. km
CAPITAL – Gibraltar; population 27,495 (2001)
CURRENCY – Gibraltar pound of 100 pence
POPULATION – 27,928 rising at 0.14 per cent per year (2006 est)
POPULATION GROWTH RATE – 0.14 per cent (2006 est)
RELIGION – Roman Catholicism (78 per cent), other Christian denominations (10 per cent), Islam (4 per cent), Judaism (2 per cent), Hinduism (1 per cent) (est)
LANGUAGE – English (official), Spanish, Italian, Portuguese
POPULATION DENSITY – 4,338 per sq. km (2001)
FLAG – White with a red stripe along the lower edge; over all a red castle with a key hanging from its gateway
NATIONAL DAY – 10 September
LIFE EXPECTANCY (years) – 79.8 (2006 est)
MORTALITY RATE – 9.31 (2006 est)
BIRTH RATE – 10.74 (2006 est)
INFANT MORTALITY RATE – 4.06 (2006 est)
GNI – US $5,000 per capita (2001)

CLIMATE AND TERRAIN

Gibraltar is a rocky promontory, 426m at its highest point, that juts southwards from the south-east coast of Spain, with which it is connected by a low isthmus. It is about 32km from the opposite coast of Africa.

HISTORY AND POLITICS

Gibraltar was captured in 1704, during the War of the Spanish Succession, by a combined Dutch and English force, and was ceded to Great Britain by the treaty of Utrecht (1713). This treaty stipulates that if Britain ever relinquishes colonial rights over Gibraltar, the colony would return to Spain.

Gibraltar is part of the EU (with the UK government responsible for enforcing EU directives affecting Gibraltar), but is not a full member and is exempt from the Common Customs Tariff and the Common Agricultural Policy. Spanish claims to the territory have been a source of tension for many years but after the overwhelming rejection of a joint sovereignty arrangement in a referendum in 2002, Spain moderated its attitude and the previously bilateral Anglo-Spanish talks about the territory became tripartite with the inclusion of Gibraltar from December 2003.

The 1969 constitution made provision for self-government in respect of certain domestic matters, but full internal autonomy came into effect with the constitution introduced in January 2007. This limited the governor's responsibilities to external affairs, defence, internal security and public service. The house of assembly was restyled as the parliament, and may determine its own size; at present, it consists of an independent speaker, 15 elected members, the attorney-general and the financial and development secretary. The government is formed by ministers appointed by the elected members of the assembly.

The 2003 elections were won by the Gibraltar Social Democrats with 51.5 per cent of the vote, securing the party eight seats, while a coalition of the Gibraltar Socialist Labour Party and the Liberal Party won 39.7 per cent of the vote and seven seats in the house of assembly. The next elections are due to be held in 2008.

Governor and Commander-in-Chief, HE Sir Robert Fulton, KBE, *apptd* 2006
Chief Minister, Hon. Peter Caruana

GOVERNMENT OF GIBRALTAR
Arundel Great Court, 178–179 The Strand, London WC2R 1EL
T 020-7836 0777

ECONOMY

Gibraltar has an extensive shipping trade, a strong offshore financial services sector and is a popular tourist and retail destination; these three sectors account for nearly 70 per cent of GDP. Telecommunications is a growing industry as the territory has become a centre for internet businesses, especially internet gaming. A shift from a predominantly public-sector to a private-sector economy has occurred in recent years, although government spending still has a significant impact on the local economy. The chief sources of government revenue are port dues, the rent of the crown estate in the town, and duties on consumer items (although value added tax is not applied in the territory).

Trade with UK	*2005*	*2006*
Imports from UK	£173,514,000	£254,586,000
Exports to UK	£68,455,000	£30,045,000

COMMUNICATIONS

Gibraltar has one international airport; in December 2006 air links to Spain and through Spanish air space reopened. The 29km road network is all paved; road links to Spain reopened in the 1980s. The port services the large shipping industry, cruise liners and a regular ferry service to Tangiers (Morocco).

MONTSERRAT

AREA – 102 sq. km
CAPITAL – Plymouth (abandoned 1997); the government's administrative headquarters is now at Brades, in the north-west of the island
CURRENCY – East Caribbean dollar (EC $) of 100 cents
POPULATION – 4,483 rising at 1.05 per cent per year (2006 est)
LANGUAGE – English (official)
POPULATION DENSITY – 108 per sq. km (1999)
FLAG – British blue ensign with the shield of arms in the fly
NATIONAL DAY – second Saturday in June (Queen's birthday)
LIFE EXPECTANCY (years) – 78.85 (2006 est)
MORTALITY RATE – 7.1 (2006 est)
BIRTH RATE – 17.59 (2006 est)
INFANT MORTALITY RATE – 7.19 (2006 est)

CLIMATE AND TERRAIN

Montserrat is a mountainous volcanic island in the Leeward group in the Caribbean Sea, with elevation extremes ranging from 914m (Chances Peak) at the highest point to 0m (Caribbean Sea) at the lowest. Volcanic activity since 1995 has left over half of the island devastated by lava flows and ash. The climate is tropical and the average temperature is 29°C.

HISTORY AND POLITICS

Discovered by Columbus in 1493, Montserrat became a British colony in 1632. The first settlers were predominantly Irish indentured servants from St Kitts. France and Britain fought over the island during the 17th and 18th centuries but Montserrat was finally assigned to Great Britain in 1783.

The present constitution came into force in 1990; talks are in progress about modernisation measures proposed by the Montserrat government in 2005, but some modifications were made in 1999 as over half of the constituencies were unoccupied owing to volcanic activity. The executive council is presided over by the governor and is composed of four elected members (the chief minister and three other ministers) and two ex-officio members (the attorney-general and the financial secretary). The four ministers are appointed from the members of the political party or coalition holding the majority in the legislative council. The legislative council consists of the speaker, two ex-officio members (the attorney-general and the financial secretary) and nine elected members. Following the 2006 general election the Movement for Change and Prosperity held four seats, the New People's Liberation Movement held three seats, the Montserrat Democratic Party held one seat and one seat was won by an independent candidate.

Volcanic activity by the Chances Peak and Soufrière Hills volcanoes, and particularly the severe 1997 eruption, have left over half of the island uninhabitable, and prompted the migration of two-thirds of the population in the late 1990s. Reconstruction and the return of migrants is hampered by the restriction of agriculture, industry and communications by the continuing volcanic activity.

Governor, HE Deborah Barnes-Jones, *apptd* May 2004
Chief Minister, Hon. Lowell Lewis

ECONOMY

The 1997 volcanic eruption buried agricultural land and the capital, destroyed buildings and closed the only airport. Much of the island's economic activity, especially the main activity of tourism, has been moribund since and reconstruction efforts are heavily dependent on British and EU aid. Gerald's airport opened in the north in 2005, allowing regular commercial air services to resume. There are port facilities at Little Bay.

Trade with UK	*2005*	*2006*
Imports from UK	£792,000	£664,000
Exports to UK	£53,000	£121,000

PITCAIRN ISLANDS

AREA – 47 sq. km
CAPITAL – Adamstown
CURRENCY – Currency is that of New Zealand
POPULATION – 45 falling at 0.01 per cent per year (2006 est)
LANGUAGE – English (official), Pitkern (official)
FLAG – British blue ensign with the arms in the fly
NATIONAL DAY – second Saturday in June (Queen's birthday)

CLIMATE AND TERRAIN

Pitcairn is the chief of a group of islands situated about midway between New Zealand and Panama in the South Pacific Ocean. The other three islands of the group are Henderson, lying 168km east-north-east of Pitcairn; Oeno, lying 120km north-west; and Ducie, lying 470km east; all are uninhabited. The climate is tropical, and the average temperature is 29°C.

HISTORY AND POLITICS

Pitcairn was settled in 1790 by the Bounty mutineers and their Tahitian companions. It became a British settlement under the British Settlement Act 1887 and was administered by the governor of Fiji from 1952 until 1970, when administration was transferred to the British High Commission in New Zealand and the British high commissioner was appointed governor. The Local Government Ordinance of 1964 provides for an island council, which manages internal affairs. It has ten members, of whom six are elected; elections are held yearly in December.

Governor (non-resident), George Fergusson (British High Commissioner to New Zealand) *apptd* 2006
Commissioner, Leslie Jaques

ECONOMY

The islanders live by subsistence fishing and gardening and the sale of handicrafts. Apart from small fees charged for licences there are no taxes and government revenue is derived almost solely from the sale of postage stamps and .pn internet domain names, and income from investments. Henderson Island, the largest of the islands in the group, was declared a UNESCO World Heritage Site in 1988.

Trade with UK	*2005*	*2006*
Imports from UK	£58,000	£203,000
Exports to UK	£5,000	£11,000

COMMUNICATIONS

There is no airfield and the only means of communication with the outside world is by sea; cruise and container ships stop irregularly but a regular shipping supply route to French Polynesia was established in 2006. There are 6.4km of roads on the islands, none of which are paved.

SOUTH GEORGIA AND THE SOUTH SANDWICH ISLANDS

AREA – 3,903 sq. km
CAPITAL – King Edward Point (administrative centre)
CURRENCY – Pound Sterling
POPULATION – There is no indigenous population. The British Antarctic Survey maintains two permanently staffed research stations, at King Edward Point and on Bird Island, to the north-west of South Georgia; in addition, there is the government's marine officer and the curators of the museum at Grytviken, South Georgia
FLAG – British blue ensign, with the shield of arms in the fly

CLIMATE AND TERRAIN

South Georgia is an island 1,390km east-south-east of the Falkland Islands. More than half of the island is covered by permanent ice with many large glaciers reaching the sea at the head of fjords. The main mountain range is the Allardyce and elevation extremes range from 2,934m (M Paget) at the highest point to 0m (Atlantic Ocean) at the lowest. The South Sandwich Islands, lying some 750km miles south-east of South Georgia, consist of a chain of 11 uninhabited volcanic islands some 350km long. Some of these volcanoes are still active.

HISTORY AND POLITICS

South Georgia was used by whalers and sealers of many nationalities following its discovery by Captain Cook in the 18th century. Britain annexed South Georgia and the South Sandwich Islands in 1908 and since then they have been under continuous British occupation apart from a brief period during the Falklands war in 1982. Following the conflict, a small British army garrison was maintained at King Edward Point on South Georgia, but this was withdrawn in 2001.

The present constitution came into effect in 1985. It provides for a commissioner who, for the time being, is the officer administering the government of the Falkland Islands.

Commissioner (non-resident), HE Alan Huckle *apptd* 2006

ECONOMY

A conservation and management fishing zone was established around the islands in 1993 and a licensing regime introduced for fishing vessels. Sale of fishing licences, postage stamps and commemorative coins, customs and harbour dues, and harbour and landing fees are the main sources of revenue. Tourism, especially wildlife tourism, is growing, but prior permission to land on the islands must be sought and is subject to environmental impact assessments.

ST HELENA AND DEPENDENCIES

ST HELENA

AREA – 122 sq. km
CAPITAL – Jamestown; population, 864 (1998)
CURRENCY – St Helena pound (£) of 100 pence
POPULATION – 5,008 rising at 0.56 per cent per year (2006 est)
LANGUAGE – English (official)
POPULATION DENSITY – 40 per sq. km (1998)
URBAN POPULATION – 39.2 per cent (1998)
FLAG – British blue ensign with the shield of arms in the fly
NATIONAL DAY – second Saturday in June (Queen's birthday)
LIFE EXPECTANCY (years) – 77.93 (2006 est)
MORTALITY RATE – 6.53 (2006 est)
BIRTH RATE – 12.13 (2006 est)
INFANT MORTALITY RATE – 18.35 (2006 est)

CLIMATE AND TERRAIN

St Helena is situated in the South Atlantic Ocean, 1,500km south of the Equator and about 1,900km west of Africa. The island is rugged and volcanic, with sheer cliffs rising to a central plateau. The climate is tropical but mild, tempered by trade winds, and the annual average temperature is 27°C.

HISTORY AND POLITICS

St Helena is believed to have been discovered by the Portuguese navigator João da Nova in 1502. It was used as a port of call for vessels of all nations trading to the East until it was annexed by the Dutch in 1633. It was never occupied by them, however, and the English East India Company seized it in 1659.

From 1815 to 1821 the island was lent to the British government as a place of exile for the Emperor Napoleon Bonaparte, who died in St Helena on 5 May 1821, and in 1834 it was annexed to the British crown. The Zulu chief Dinizulu was exiled to the island in 1890, and up to 6,000 Boer prisoners were held there between 1900 and 1903.

Government is administered by a governor, with the aid of an executive council comprising three ex-officio members (the chief secretary, financial secretary and attorney-general) and five elected members of the legislative council. The legislative council consists of a speaker, the three ex-officio members of the executive council, and 12 elected members.

Governor, HE Michael Clancy, *apptd* 2004

ECONOMY AND TRADE

St Helena was intended as a maritime base, with an economy dedicated to the provision of supplies for shipping and the local garrison, rather than as a self-sufficient colony. Its importance as a port of call declined after the opening of the Suez Canal reduced the amount of shipping on passing routes. Consequently, its economy is dependent on an annual grant from the UK. The main economic activities are agriculture, the sale of fishing licences and tourism, and the only significant exports are frozen fish and coffee.

Trade with UK	*2005*	*2006*
Imports from UK	£16,744,000	£8,946,000
Exports to UK	£874,000	£972,000

COMMUNICATIONS

Regular access is by sea at present, but plans are progressing for the establishment of an airport by 2010, when the regular supply ship is due to be withdrawn from scheduled service. Jamestown is the only port. St Helena has 138km of roads, most of which are single track. Telecommunication services are provided via satellite links, which also enable television programmes to be received for distribution by cable. There is a local radio station and two weekly newspapers.

ASCENSION ISLAND

AREA – 90 sq. km
CAPITAL – Georgetown; population, 560 (2003 est)
CURRENCY – Currency is that of St Helena or the UK
POPULATION – 1,100 (2003 est)

CLIMATE AND TERRAIN

The island lies in the South Atlantic Ocean some 1,200km north-west of St Helena. It is a rocky peak of purely volcanic origin. The highest point (Green Mountain), some 860m, is covered with lush vegetation.

HISTORY AND POLITICS

Ascension is said to have been discovered by João da Nova in 1501 and two years later was visited on Ascension Day by Alphonse d'Albuquerque, who gave the island its present name. It was uninhabited until the arrival of Napoleon in St Helena in 1815 when a small British naval garrison was stationed on the island. As HMS Ascension it remained under the supervision of the Board of Admiralty until 1922, when it was made a dependency of St Helena.

New constitutional arrangements introduced democratic self-government in 2002. The governor, who is resident in St Helena, retains responsibility for defence, external affairs, internal security and public service. The governor, represented locally by the island administrator, chairs the island council, which consists of seven elected members and two ex-officio members (the director of financial services and the attorney-general).

Administrator, Michael Hill, *apptd* 2005

ECONOMY AND TRANSPORT

Before 2002 the island was governed and financed by the main commercial users (the BBC and Cable and Wireless) and the military. With the change in governance in 2002, a fiscal regime was introduced to finance public services through taxation. This funds a school, a hospital, police and judicial services. A private sector is developing following the sale of previously government-owned concerns to commercial operators and the establishment of a sports fishing industry.

Communications with the outside world are by sea and air. Georgetown is the only port and there are regular scheduled shipping services, as well as regular air links to the UK, because of the transit stops by RAF aircraft en route to the Falkland Islands, and to the USA. Ascension has 40km of roads. Telecommunication services are provided via satellite links.

TRISTAN DA CUNHA

AREA – 98 sq. km
CAPITAL – Edinburgh of the Seven Seas
CURRENCY – Currency is that of the UK
POPULATION – 277 (2003 est)
FLAG – British blue ensign with the shield of arms in the fly

CLIMATE AND TERRAIN

Tristan da Cunha is the chief of a group of islands in the South Atlantic Ocean which lie some 2,333km south-south-west of St Helena. All of the islands are volcanic and steep-sided with cliffs or narrow beaches. The highest point of elevation is 2,060m (Queen Mary's Peak) while the lowest is 0m (Atlantic Ocean). Gough and Inaccessible islands are UNESCO World Heritage sites.

HISTORY AND POLITICS

Tristan da Cunha was discovered in 1506 by the Portuguese navigator Tristão da Cunha. In 1760 a British naval officer visited the islands and gave his name to Nightingale Island. In 1816 the group was annexed to the British crown and a garrison was placed on Tristan da Cunha, but this force was withdrawn in 1817. Corporal William Glass remained at his own request with his wife and two children and this party, with two others, formed a settlement. In 1827 five women from St Helena, and afterwards others from Cape Colony, joined the party.

Due to its position on a main sailing route the colony thrived, with an economy based on trading with passing ships, until the late 19th century, when the opening of the Suez Canal led to decline.

In 1961 a volcano, believed to have been extinct for thousands of years, erupted and the danger of further volcanic activity led to the evacuation of inhabitants to the UK until 1963.

In 1938 Tristan da Cunha and the neighbouring islands of Inaccessible, Nightingale (both uninhabited) and Gough were made dependencies of St Helena. They are administered by the governor of St Helena through a resident administrator. Under a constitution introduced in 1985, the administrator is advised by an island council of eight elected members, of whom one must be a woman, and three appointed members. Elections are held every three years.

Administrator, Mike Hentley, *apptd* 2004

ECONOMY

The island is almost financially self-sufficient; UK government aid finances training scholarships and a resident medical officer at the hospital. The main activities are crayfish fishing, fish-processing, agriculture and the sale of postage stamps and coins.

COMMUNICATIONS

Communications with the outside world are by sea as there is no airport. Scheduled visits to the island are restricted to about six calls a year by fishing vessels from Cape Town and annual calls by the St Helena supply ship and a South African research vessel. Tristan da Cunha has 20km of roads.

TURKS AND CAICOS ISLANDS

AREA – 430 sq. km
CAPITAL – Cockburn Town, on Grand Turk; population, 3,976 (2001)
CURRENCY – US dollar (US $)
POPULATION – 21,152 rising at 2.82 per cent per year (2006 est)
RELIGION – Protestantism (86 per cent) (est)
LANGUAGE – English (official)
POPULATION DENSITY – 37 per sq. km (2001)
FLAG – British blue ensign with the shield of arms in the fly
NATIONAL DAY – 30 August (Constitution Day)
LIFE EXPECTANCY (years) – 74.73 (2006 est)
MORTALITY RATE – 4.21 (2006 est)
BIRTH RATE – 21.84 (2006 est)
INFANT MORTALITY RATE – 15.18 (2006 est)

CLIMATE AND TERRAIN

The Turks and Caicos Islands are about 80km south-east of the Bahamas, of which they are geographically an extension. There are over 30 islands, of which six are permanently inhabited. The climate is marine tropical, moderated by trade winds; the average annual temperature is 27°C.

HISTORY AND POLITICS

The islands were settled by Bermudans in the 17th century. They were administered from Jamaica between 1872 and 1962, and from the Bahamas between 1965 and 1973. Since the Bahamas' independence in 1973, the territory has had its own governor.

Internal self-government was introduced in the 1970s, and a new constitution was introduced in 2006. The governor is responsible for defence, external affairs, internal security and the regulation of financial services. The cabinet is presided over by the governor and comprises the premier and six elected ministers, together with an ex-officio member (the attorney-general). The house of assembly comprises the speaker, 15 elected members, four appointed members and the attorney-general.

The general election of 9 February 2007 was won by the Progressive National Party, with 13 seats.

Governor, HE Richard Tauwhare, *apptd* 2005
Premier, Michael Misick

ECONOMY

The most important industries are tourism, offshore financial services and fishing.

COMMUNICATIONS

The principal airports are on the islands of Grand Turk and Providenciales and provide international air links. There are smaller airports on the other main islands, and regular internal air services between them. The main seaports are on Grand Turk and Providenciales. The islands also have a total of 121km of roads, 24km of which are surfaced.

THE YEAR 2006–7

EVENTS OF THE YEAR 2006–7

UK AFFAIRS

AUGUST 2006

10. Home secretary John Reid raised UK security alert status to 'critical' after receiving intelligence from MI5 of an imminent terrorist attack, with the plot allegedly involving mid-air detonation of bombs on board five transatlantic flights; chaos ensued at most UK airports as many flights were cancelled and delayed, and all passenger hand luggage was banned with a few restricted items allowed, provided they were carried in a transparent plastic bag. **11.** A total of 24 arrests relating to the alleged airline terrorist plot were made during dawn raids in Birmingham, High Wycombe and Walthamstow, London. **14.** UK security alert level was downgraded to 'severe' and some aircraft passenger hand luggage restrictions were lifted. **16.** In Northern Ireland, a partially detonated bomb that was found in a house being built for the Ulster Unionist peer Lord Ballyedmond was blamed on dissident republican groups. **18.** Police found a suitcase containing chemicals and equipment that could be used to make a home-made bomb in High Wycombe, close to the homes of some of those arrested on 11 August. **21.** Eleven of the 24 suspects arrested for their alleged involvement in the plot to blow up transatlantic passenger planes were charged: eight with conspiracy to murder and preparing acts of terrorism and the remaining three with offences under the Terrorism Act 2000. **23.** The Electoral Commission criticised both the Labour and Conservative parties for their continuing failure to voluntarily declare all party loans in the light of the approaching deadline – 11 September – when all political parties were to become legally obliged to disclose all financial aid received. **25.** Figures released by the ONS showed that the estimated population of the UK exceeded 60 million for the first time in June 2005. **31.** In an interview with *The Times*, Prime Minister Tony Blair refused to name a date for his departure to try to head off recently escalated demands by the media and his party members for him to set out a broad timetable for his exit.

SEPTEMBER 2006

2. A Nimrod aircraft flying at 6,100m (20,000ft) above the southern Kandahar province in Afghanistan crashed, killing all 14 RAF personnel on board; the MoD set up a board of inquiry to investigate the incident stating that enemy involvement was unlikely. **7.** During a visit to a London school Tony Blair announced that the forthcoming 2006 Labour party conference would be his last as prime minister. The European court of justice ruled that employers in the UK must ensure that all staff have at least 11 hours off between working days, a minimum of one day off a week and a 20-minute rest after every six hours of work; the ruling replaced the 1998 DTI guidelines that employers merely advise staff that they were entitled to certain rest breaks. **11.** Speaking at the launch of the government's social exclusion programme, minister for children Beverley Hughes called on the 21 councils with the highest or fastest-rising rates of teenage pregnancy to implement joint action plans to target vulnerable groups; government figures showed that Lambeth, London, had the highest rate with 84 conceptions per 1,000 girls aged 15 to 17. **20.** It was revealed that an Irish diplomat, Aine de Baroid, was forced to leave Northern Ireland as a result of death threats from loyalist paramilitaries. **21.** At the Liberal Democrat party conference Sir Menzies Campbell gave his first major speech as leader stating his party can aim for government. The Department for Transport relaxed the rules introduced after the 10 August security alert on in-flight passenger hand luggage allowances. **25.** In his address to the Labour Party conference, Chancellor Gordon Brown announced that he would 'relish the chance to take on David Cameron and the Conservative Party'. **26.** In his farewell speech at the Labour Party conference Prime Minister Tony Blair outlined the Labour policies he planned to pursue for his remaining time in office, which included further reforms to the NHS and welfare system.

OCTOBER 2006

3. The trustees of Canterbury Cathedral announced that the 900-year-old building needed £50m of restoration and modernisation if it was to be preserved for the nation; a programme of works costing £30m had been drawn up with a completion date of 2016. **4.** The inhabitants of the Channel Island of Sark, the last feudal state in Europe, voted by 234 to 184 to abolish Sark's 450-year-old system of governance and replace it with a 28-member elected assembly. David Cameron used his first conference speech as Conservative Party leader to outline his plans on modernising the party; he praised some of the Labour government's achievements, backed the institution of marriage – including same-sex unions within his policies – and emphasised his support for the NHS. The Independent Monitoring Commission for Northern Ireland reported that the IRA, including Sinn Fein, had ceased all criminal and paramilitary activities. **6.** The Leader of the House of Commons, Jack Straw, angered Muslim groups when he said in a BBC interview that he personally objected to Muslim women wearing the *niqab* veil; the statement followed comments made a day earlier when he admitted that he asked women visiting his Blackburn constituency surgery to consider removing it. **11.** The high court ruled that a London-based finance company owned by Michael Brown, which donated £2.4m to the Liberal Democrat Party, was an entirely fraudulent concern and had never traded; the Electoral Commission stated that it would study the judgement in detail to establish whether the party needed to return the gift. **13.** Three-day talks between Tony Blair, Irish Prime Minister Bertie Ahern, the DUP and Sinn Fein at St Andrews in Scotland ended with the publication of a draft agreement for a timetable to restore devolution in Northern Ireland; 24 November was set as the final date for nominations of the first minister and the deputy first minister and 26 March 2007 as the deadline for the formation of an operating power-sharing executive: the DUP and Sinn Fein had until 10 November to agree to the draft. **16.** The 875-mile Langeled gas pipeline from Norway was officially opened by Tony Blair at the Easington gas terminal in Yorkshire *(see also* Business and

Economic Affairs, 3 October). **17.** In Northern Ireland, the first session of the Programme for Government Committee, established on the 13 October by the St Andrews Agreement, was postponed when Ian Paisley refused to attend until he could be assured that Sinn Fein would support the rule of law and the police. **20.** Claire Short, MP for Birmingham Ladywood and former international development secretary, resigned as the Labour whip in parliament and announced she would sit as an independent for her remaining time in parliament, although she did not intend to resign from the Labour Party. **27.** The Archbishop of Canterbury, Rowan Williams, warned politicians against interfering with Muslim women's right to wear the veil, cautioning against a move towards secularism in British society. **30.** Sir Nicholas Stern, head of the government's Economic Service, published his report *The Economics of Climate Change,* commissioned by the Treasury; the report concluded that climate change was underway but argued that by making international policy changes it would be possible to stabilise greenhouse-gas levels in the atmosphere without halting economic growth. In Northern Ireland, the first public housing estate to be built for both Protestants and Catholics for 40 years was officially opened in County Fermanagh by Peter Hain, the Northern Ireland Secretary.

NOVEMBER 2006

2. A report by the National Audit Office concluded that the Armed Forces were operating with at least 5,000 fewer personnel than needed to maintain Britain's international defence commitments and had been operating beyond planned levels of defence for the past five years in order to keep the necessary levels of troops in Iraq and Afghanistan. **3.** A study by the Institute for Public Policy Research found that solvent abuse in young teenagers aged 11 to 15 years had increased from 28,000 in 1995 to 168,000 in 2005, though the use of cannabis and class A drugs within this age group had only risen slightly in the same time period. **6.** Sinn Fein and the DUP indicated they would support the St Andrews Agreement to restore devolution in Northern Ireland. **10.** Lord Sainsbury of Turville resigned from the government after eight years, citing personal reasons; energy minister Malcolm Wicks replaced him as science minister. **11.** A survey of 200,000 people by the Civil Aviation Authority showed that the social profiles of air passengers had remained constant in the past 10 years despite the increase in budget airlines, concluding that cheaper flights had not resulted in an increase in travel by lower-income groups. **13.** The Office of Rail Regulation criticised Network Rail's delivery of small investment schemes for the rail network; figures showed that Network Rail spent only £4m of its £50m annual budget for small schemes. **17.** British citizen Mirza-Tahir Hussain arrived in the UK after being released from prison in Pakistan where he had been detained for 18 years for allegedly murdering a taxi driver; his release came after President Musharraf of Pakistan granted clemency following an earlier decision to revoke Mr Hussain's death sentence. **18.** The Metropolitan Police announced it was investigating the alleged poisoning of Alexander Litvinenko, a former member of the Russian security services who came to the UK in 2001; preliminary toxicology tests indicated that Mr Litvinenko may have been poisoned with a potentially lethal dose of thallium. **19.** Oleg Gordievsky, a former KGB officer and double agent who defected to Britain in 1985, claimed that Mr Litvinenko's poisoning had been carried out by someone working for the Russian security services; the Foreign and Commonwealth Office stated it was going to wait for the outcome of the police investigation before making any approach to the Russian authorities. **21.** The culture secretary Tessa Jowell told the House of Commons' Culture, Media and Sport Committee that there had been a 40 per cent (£900m) increase to the core budget for the construction of the 2012 Olympic Park in East London. **23.** Alexander Litvinenko died at University College Hospital; the following day toxicologists confirmed that he had a large dose of alpha-radiation in his body believed to be polonium-210; police confirmed they had found traces of radioactive material at the sushi bar and the hotel where Mr Litvinenko had meetings on 1 November, as well as at his north London home. **24.** The Foreign and Commonwealth Office formally asked the Russian Ambassador to provide any information that could help with the Metropolitan Police's investigation into the death of Mr Litvinenko. The inaugural meeting of the transitional Northern Ireland assembly at Stormont was interrupted when loyalist paramilitary Michael Stone stormed the building armed with a knife, a handgun and a bag of explosive devices; Stone had been convicted for the murder of three mourners at an IRA funeral in 1988 but was released from prison under the Good Friday Agreement. **27.** The Metropolitan Police announced that traces of the radioactive isotope polonium-210 had also been found at seven locations in London that had been visited by Alexander Litvinenko; three people linked to these locations were referred for radiological tests. **28.** The Sinn Fein leadership indicated the party was prepared to support the police and court systems for a devolved Northern Ireland. **29.** The Chancellor Gordon Brown confirmed that his second son Fraser, born in July, had been diagnosed with cystic fibrosis. Police investigating Alexander Litvinenko's death discovered traces of polonium-210 aboard two British Airways aircraft that had flown to or from Moscow between the end of October and the beginning of November. **30.** Islanders on three of the Outer Hebrides Islands – Benbecula, South Ulst and Eriskay – bought the 93,000-acre South Ulst Estate for £4.5m, in the biggest community buyout in Scotland.

DECEMBER 2006

3. An explosion at a fireworks warehouse in Lewes, East Sussex, killed two firefighters and injured several others. **5.** Nine British counter-terrorism detectives arrived in Moscow as part of the investigation by the Metropolitan Police into the death of Alexander Litvinenko. **7.** A tornado struck Kensal Rise in West London injuring six people and leaving many people homeless; a number of residential houses were seriously damaged. Police investigating the death of Alexander Litvinenko announced that they suspected he had been poisoned in the bar of the Millennium Hotel in London on the evening of 1 November, following an earlier failed attempt at the Itsu sushi bar in Piccadilly; all seven hotel staff who had been working that evening had tested positive for polonium-210. **13.** A performance review of all government departments carried out at the behest of Cabinet Secretary Sir Gus O'Donnell called for the urgent review of the Cabinet Office, claiming that there were inconsistencies in operating procedures between its departments and its various units often worked at cross-purposes. **14.** The inquiry into the death of Diana, Princess of Wales, conducted by Lord Stevens of

Kirkwhelpington, concluded that her death in a car crash in Paris in 1997 alongside that of Dodi Fayed, son of Mohamed Al Fayed, and Henri Paul, their chauffeur, was a tragic accident. Prime Minister Tony Blair was questioned by the Metropolitan Police as part of its ongoing investigation into the legality and propriety of nominating people who had provided financial support to the Labour Party for honours. Alistair Darling, the trade and industry secretary, announced that 2,500 post offices would close. **21.** Thousands of people were stranded at UK airports as freezing fog grounded hundreds of flights. **22.** The Archbishop of Canterbury, Dr Rowan Williams, called on British churches to take action to raise the profile of Christians in the Middle East, stating that the UK government's policy in Iraq was endangering thousands of Christians in the region. **23.** Norfolk and Norwich University Hospital announced a bacterium outbreak at its baby ward may have affected six premature babies and contributed to the death of one of them. **26.** The Food Standards Agency announced a pilot scheme to test the viability of making the hygiene ratings of all places serving food in London available online and on the premises with a view to extending the scheme nationwide. **27.** Air Chief Marshal Sir Glenn Torpy, Chief of the Air Staff, stated that since the 9/11 terrorist attacks there had been at least one incident a month requiring an RAF fighter jet to be scrambled as a counter-hijacking measure. A pilot, co-pilot and five gas workers died in a helicopter crash off the Lancashire coast during a routine flight between gas platforms owned and operated by Centrica.

JANUARY 2007

1. The Parliamentary Commissioner for Standards, Sir Philip Mawer, called for the rules on MPs' allowable expenses to be reviewed, recommending that receipts should be provided for claims above £50, rather than £250, and that ministers with grace-and-favour homes in London should no longer be able to claim additional expenses for their constituency homes. **4.** National Express withdrew all its double-deck coaches from service after a late-night service from Heathrow to Aberdeen overturned on an M25 slip road killing two people and injuring 67. **5.** The MoD confirmed that the maximum age of new recruits for the Army had been raised from 26 to 33 to encourage more people to join the service and to bring it into line with the Royal Navy and the RAF. **8.** The Department of Health's director of immunisation, David Salisbury, announced that all poultry workers would be eligible for free human flu vaccinations in an attempt to reduce the likelihood of strains of avian and human flu crossing to create a new virus. **9.** It emerged that around six years worth of paper records on UK citizens convicted of criminal offences abroad, including information on 525 serious offenders, had not been processed and entered onto the national police database by the Home Office; police officers were making urgent enquiries to establish if any serious offenders had managed to secure jobs working with children or vulnerable people. Prime Minister Tony Blair issued a public denunciation of the manner of Saddam Hussein's execution in Iraq but qualified that this did not mean he excused the crimes the former Iraqi dictator had committed while in power. **15.** The trial of six men accused of plotting to blow up parts of London's transport system on 21 July 2005 began at Woolwich Crown Court in London. **18.** Eleven people died in the worst storms since 1990 to hit the UK; winds of up to 99mph wrecked transport infrastructure, damaged property and left thousands of households without electricity. **19.** Ruth Turner, director of government relations at Downing Street, was arrested in relation to the Metropolitan Police's ongoing 'cash-for-honours' investigation on suspicion of perverting the course of justice; she was released without charge *(see* 14 December). **21.** Experts attempted to salvage the *MSC Napoli* container ship which had been deliberately grounded a mile from the Devon coast after her crew had to abandon ship when the engine room was flooded in the 18 January storms; an estimated 200 containers had already fallen from the vessel, which was in danger of breaking apart due to a damaged hull. **22.** A report by Nuala O'Loan, the Northern Ireland Police Ombudsman, concluded that there had been extensive collusion during the 1990s between the Royal Ulster Constabulary (RUC) and a north Belfast unit of the loyalist Ulster Volunteer Force (UVF) when members of the UVF unit, responsible for a series of murders, also acted as paid RUC informants. **23.** The process of siphoning off 3,000 tonnes of heavy fuel oil from the main tank of the grounded *MSC Napoli* began; around 2,000 seabirds were believed to have been contaminated by oil which had already leaked from the ship's smaller fuel tank. **25.** Figures released by the Department for Transport showed that vehicle owners had failed to pay excise duty on 2,193,000 vehicles in 2006 compared with 1,240,000 vehicles in 2004. **30.** The transitional assembly in Northern Ireland was dissolved in preparation for elections to be held on 7 March. **31.** An alleged plot to kidnap and behead a British Muslim who had served in the armed forces in Iraq or Afghanistan was foiled in a joint counter-terrorism operation between MI5 and local police forces in the West Midlands; nine arrests were made in a series of dawn raids in Birmingham. Lord Levy was arrested for the second time in relation to the Metropolitan Police's 'cash-for-honours' investigation; he had originally been arrested in July 2006 in connection with alleged offences under the 1925 Honours (Prevention of Abuses) Act.

FEBRUARY 2007

1. An official Downing Street spokesperson revealed that Prime Minister Tony Blair had been interviewed for a second time in relation to the 'cash-for-honours' investigation prior to Lord Levy's arrest on 31 January. **5.** A woman suffered minor injuries after a letter bomb exploded at Capita's headquarters in Central London. **6.** Following a letter bomb explosion in Berkshire, Assistant Chief Constable Anton Setchell, the national coordinator for domestic extremism, revealed that it has been the sixth letter bomb to have been sent to a business or organisation providing services or technology to law enforcement agencies, within the past three weeks. **7.** A seventh letter bomb exploded at the DVLA in Swansea injuring four people; mail sorting offices were placed on alert. **8.** Britain awoke to the heaviest snowfalls in 11 years; between three and seven centimetres of snow fell overnight across much of England and Wales with some areas of central and south Wales recording depths of 20cm. The Department for Environment, Food and Rural Affairs announced that it was investigating whether the H5N1 strain of avian flu found in poultry at the Bernard Matthews farm in Suffolk *(see* Environment and Science, 3 February) had come from poultry imported from the company's slaughterhouse in Hungary. **9.** The millionth person registered their support by email for an online petition against government plans for a nationwide road charging scheme. **12.** It emerged that Bernard Matthews had transported 140 tonnes of raw turkey meat to Hungary since the presence of the H5N1 strain of avian flu had been confirmed at its Suffolk plant on 3 February. **19.** Miles Cooper, 26, of Cherry Hinton, Cambridge, was arrested in connection with the seven letter bombs which arrived at companies connected to law enforcement agencies between 18 January and 7 February. **23.** A woman died and five people were seriously injured when a Virgin train en route to Glasgow from London crashed at Grayrigg in Cumbria; the *Pendolino* train was reportedly travelling at 95mph when it derailed causing four of the nine carriages to overturn. A preliminary investigation by Network Rail concluded that a faulty set of points which the train passed prior to derailing was highly likely to have caused the accident; a visual examination revealed key parts responsible for keeping the rails secured at a set distance apart to be missing.

MARCH 2007

1. Around 1,000 motorists in the South East and the Midlands broke down after filling their vehicles with contaminated fuel; investigators traced the source of the fuel to the Vorpak terminal in Thurrock. **2.** The attorney-general, Lord Goldsmith, was granted an injunction which prevented the BBC from broadcasting a report into the cash-for-honours inquiry on the *Ten O'Clock News* on the grounds that the broadcast would prejudice the investigation. The foreign secretary Margaret Beckett announced that five Britons, all connected to the British embassy in Ethiopia, were among 14 people kidnapped during a geological tourist trip to the Afar desert on 1 March. **7.** Proposed reforms to the UK's bicameral parliamentary system took an unexpected step forward when MPs voted in favour of a fully or mainly (80 per cent) elected second chamber to replace the House of Lords. Elections to establish a new 108-member Stormont Assembly took place in Northern Ireland: the Democratic Unionist Party (DUP) emerged as the largest party winning 36 seats, followed by Sinn Fein, which won 28 seats. **12.** The BBC Gaza correspondent, Alan Johnston, was kidnapped on his way home from his Gaza City office. **13.** The five Britons kidnapped in Ethiopia on 1 March were freed unharmed in neighbouring Eritrea; the fate of nine Ethiopians captured with the group remained unknown. **15.** A report by Sir Hayden Phillips on the financing of political parties – ordered by the prime minister in response to the cash-for-honours inquiry – recommended that a limit of £50,000 should be imposed on political donations from individuals or organisations and that trade union members' affiliation fees should only be exempt from this cap as long as they were traceable to individual union members. **16.** Sally Clark, who was cleared of the murders of her two baby sons by the high court in 2003 after a wrongful conviction in 1999, was found dead at her home. **22.** Counter-terrorism police arrested three men suspected of providing behind-the-scenes support to the four suicide bombers who carried out the 7 July 2005 London terrorist attacks; two of the suspects were arrested at Manchester airport as they attempted to board a flight to Pakistan, a third man was arrested at his home in Leeds. **23.** Fifteen British naval personnel aboard *HMS Cornwall* in the Shatt al-Arab waterway bordering Iraq and Iran were taken captive by the Iranian Revolutionary Guard claiming that they had strayed into Iranian territorial waters; the Foreign and Commonwealth Office appealed for their immediate return, stating that the ship was patrolling Iraqi waters in accordance with a UN mandate. **26.** In their first joint news conference, DUP leader Ian Paisley and Sinn Fein leader Gerry Adams confirmed their commitment to forming a power-sharing government in Northern Ireland. A service at Westminster Abbey to commemorate the bicentenary of the abolition of slavery in Britain, and attended by the Queen, was interrupted when Toyin Agbetu, an invited member of the congregation, demanded a formal apology from the Queen; police escorted him from the Abbey. **28.** Faye Turney, one of 15 British sailors taken hostage on 23 March, admitted to trespassing in Iranian waters during an interview aired on Iranian television.

APRIL 2007

2. In Northern Ireland, the four main parties announced the ministerial portfolios in the new executive due to be formed on 8 May 2007: the DUP assumed responsibility for finance, economy, environment and culture, Sinn Fein for education, regional development and agriculture, the UUP for health and employment and learning, and the SDLP took responsibility for social development. Smoking in public places became illegal throughout Wales. **3.** *Maternity Matters,* a report published by the Department of Health, stated that women are to receive more options throughout pregnancy and outlined a 'minimum guarantee' regarding the service that women can expect from the NHS. **4.** The 15 British naval personnel taken hostage by Iran were released after a surprise announcement by the Iranian president Mahmoud Ahmadinejad. **6.** A report by the Mental Health Act Commission revealed that more than 1,300 children with mental health issues were placed on adult psychiatric wards between April 2003 and October 2006; the report called on the government to take urgent action, stating that hospital mental health provision for children was generally inadequate. **7.** The MoD allowed the 15 freed naval personnel captured in Iran to sell their stories to the newspapers; the decision was later reversed on 9 May by defence secretary Des Browne, but not before two of the personnel had completed deals with the media. **12.** A Norwegian tug boat *Bourbon Dolphin* capsized off the coast of the Shetland Islands while on a routine operation at the Transocean Rather drilling rig; seven men from the 15-strong crew and a 14-year old boy drowned. **16.** Following a request submitted to the British Nuclear Group to re-analyse data from body parts removed from deceased former employees of the Sellafield nuclear plant between 1962 and 1992, it emerged that there was no evidence that the families of the deceased workers had consented to the removal of the organs. **20.** A health alert was issued for ten miles of Scottish coastline after a pump failed at the Seafield sewage treatment plant in Leith and an estimated 100 million litres (22 million gallons) of untreated sewage was discharged into the Firth of Forth near Edinburgh. **28.** An earthquake registering 4.3 on the Richter scale hit Folkestone in Kent; nobody was seriously injured, although around 200 properties were structurally damaged. **30.** The Chief of the General Staff Gen. Sir Richard Dannatt confirmed that Prince Harry would go to Iraq as a reconnaissance troop leader with a squadron of the Blues and Royals. Northern Ireland banned smoking in most public places, workplaces and on public transport.

MAY 2007

3. Regional government elections took place in Scotland and Wales and local elections in England and Scotland;

the Labour Party lost its majority in the Scottish Parliament by one seat to the Scottish National Party but remained the largest party in the Welsh Assembly with 26 seats; in the English local elections the Conservative Party made gains of 911 seats while the Labour Party lost 505 seats. **8.** Ian Paisley and Martin McGuinness were sworn in as first minister and deputy first minister respectively of the Northern Ireland Assembly. **10.** Tony Blair announced his decision to stand down as prime minister on 27 June. **15.** Bertie Ahern became the first Irish prime minister to address both houses of parliament; in his address, Mr Ahern spoke of looking ahead to a 'partnership of peace' between Britain and Ireland. **16.** Chief of the General Staff Gen. Sir Richard Dannatt reversed his earlier decision (*see* 30 April) to send Prince Harry to Iraq, concluding that due to a number of specific threats the prince and his squadron would be exposed to an unacceptable level of risk. **17.** Gordon Brown became prime minister elect after 313 of 353 Labour MPs supported his nomination; Mr Brown was set to take over as prime minister on 27 June 2007. The Food Standards Agency recommended that the government should implement mandatory fortification of bread or flour with folic acid in order to reduce neural tube birth defects. **21.** The *Cutty Sark,* a 19th-century sailing ship, which was undergoing a £25m restoration in Greenwich, London, was damaged in a fire; the cause was undetermined. **22.** The Russian foreign ministry refused to comply with a request submitted by the British ambassador to Russia for the extradition of Andrei Lugovoy; the request was made following a decision by the Crown Prosecution Service that there was enough evidence to charge him with the deliberate poisoning of Alexander Litvinenko (*see* 23 November). **29.** Four British bodyguards and a British expert working for Iraqi finance ministry were kidnapped in Baghdad.

JUNE 2007

1. A video showing the first pictures of BBC journalist Alan Johnston since his abduction in the Gaza Strip on 12 March appeared on the internet; the date of its recording was unclear. **2.** Deputy Prime Minister John Prescott was admitted to hospital with a suspected chest infection; his office later confirmed he was suffering from pneumonia. **7.** New government statistics revealed that almost half of NHS patients requiring a stay in hospital were treated within 18 weeks, but one in eight patients was still waiting for more than a year: the figures were based on waiting time from the point of diagnosis rather than first referral for treatment by a GP. **8.** The first of four 7,800-tonne Astute Class nuclear-powered submarines was launched at BAE Systems' shipyard in Barrow-in-Furness. **17.** Figures published by the Healthcare Commission showed that in 2006–7 25 per cent of NHS trusts failed one or more aspects of 11 compulsory hygiene duties, introduced in 2006 to prevent or cope with hospital superbugs. **22.** European leaders agreed that the proposed European charter of rights would contain a clause preventing the European court of justice from using the charter to change UK law. Bashir Maan, Scottish representative on the Muslim Council of Britain, criticised the decision to award a knighthood to author Salman Rushdie in the Queen's Birthday Honours. **24.** In a second video released by the kidnappers of Alan Johnston (*see* 1 June), the reporter appealed to the British government and Hamas not to use force in an effort to free him. **25.** Torrential rain caused severe flooding and tornadoes across the UK; the worst-affected areas, where up to four inches of rain fell over 24 hours, were Lincolnshire, the Midlands and Yorkshire. **26.** Conservative MP for Grantham and Stamford, Quentin Davies, announced his defection to the Labour Party. **27.** Gordon Brown officially became prime minister following Tony Blair's formal resignation; the new cabinet included Jacqui Smith as home secretary, Alistair Darling as chancellor and David Miliband as foreign secretary. **29.** Police successfully defused two car bombs planted in London's West End. **30.** The UK was put on its highest level of security alert after two men attempted a fire-bombing at Glasgow airport by crashing a burning car into the main terminal building; four men were later arrested.

JULY 2007

1. Peter Clarke, head of the Counter Terrorism Command at the Metropolitan Police, confirmed that the two car bombs discovered in London and the incident at Glasgow airport were linked. England joined the rest of the UK in making smoking illegal in virtually all enclosed public places. **2.** Bilal Talal Samad Abdulla, an Iraqi doctor working at the Royal Alexandra Hospital in Paisley, and Mohammed Asha, a Jordanian of Palestinian descent working as a neurologist at the University of North Staffordshire, were named as suspects in the plot to bomb central London and Glasgow airport. **4.** After 114 days in captivity, BBC journalist Alan Johnston was released unharmed by his kidnappers in Gaza City. **8.** The Healthcare Commission served its first improvement notice, the recipient was Chase Farm Hospital in Enfield. **11.** Prime Minister Gordon Brown announced a new programme of house building with the annual target increased to 240,000 homes a year by 2016, he also said most would be built on previously developed brownfield land. **16.** In response to the Russian government's refusal to comply with the UK government's request to extradite Andrei Lugovoy (*see* 22 May), the foreign secretary David Miliband ordered punitive measures, expelling four Russian diplomats from the UK and tightening visa requirements for visiting Russian officials. **20.** Torrential downpours caused widespread flooding across the UK for the second time in two months; three people died after the River Severn burst its banks, flooding Gloucester and completely cutting-off the town of Tewkesbury; parts of Hereford and Worcestershire were under 1.82m (6ft) of water and around 900 homes were flooded in Oxfordshire. The 'cash-for-honours' investigation was closed after the Crown Prosecution Service ruled there was not enough evidence to bring charges against any individual.

ARTS AND MEDIA

AUGUST 2006

3. Figures released by RAJAR, the radio industry's audience research bureau, showed that during the second quarter of 2006 BBC Radio One DJ Chris Moyles had attracted the highest number of listeners to his breakfast show since 2004. **4.** The *Domesday Book,* commissioned by William the Conqueror in 1085 to catalogue every item of agricultural property in England, was made available on the internet. **6.** Figures from PACT, the television industry body, showed that foreign networks spent a record £632m on acquiring British television programmes in 2005. **15.** *The Sun* newspaper was forced to apologise to princes William and Harry for publishing three-year-old candid photographs of them on a night out and claiming that they were recently taken. **16.** A 16th-century painting of Mary Queen of Scots, one of only two thought to have been painted in her lifetime, was discovered in a National Portrait Gallery storeroom; the portrait had been bought in 1916 and later dismissed as a fake. **24.** The Kerrang! rock music awards named Lostprophets the best British group, and Muse the best live group. **27.** The Edinburgh Festival's if.comeddies prize (previously the Perrier comedy awards) went to the Canadian comic Phil Nichol for his one-hour show *The Naked Racist;* the best newcomer prize was awarded to 24-year-old Josie Long for her show *Kindness and Exuberance.* **28.** At the Emmy television awards in Los Angeles, *The Office* was named best comedy series and Dame Helen Mirren was named best lead actress in a mini series for her part in *Elizabeth I,* which also won the award for best mini series. **31.** Two years after they were stolen from the Munch Museum in Oslo, Edvard Munch's *The Scream* and *Madonna* were returned to the gallery.

SEPTEMBER 2006

6. Sony admitted that its long-awaited PlayStation 3 games console would not be available in Europe, Africa, Asia or Australasia until March 2007 because the company was focusing on delivering it to the US and Japanese markets in November 2006, six months behind the original schedule. **7.** The first *Dandy* annual, published in 1939, was sold for a record price for any comic annual on general sale; it raised £6,230 at auction in London. **8.** Sean Combs, the rapper also known as Puff Daddy, lost the right to use a new name he chose – Diddy – in the UK after Richard Dearlove, a music producer from London, who has used the name since 1992, sued and received an out-of-court settlement. **9.** Dame Helen Mirren was named best actress at the Venice International Film Festival for her performance in *The Queen;* Ben Affleck was named best actor for *Hollywoodland* and the Golden Lion award for best film was given to *Sanxia Haoren* (Still Life) by Chinese director Jia Zhang-Ke. **18.** The Tate made its accounts public for the first time, showing that in the course of two years it had spent a total of £12.6m on new works of art. **20.** At the 11th annual MOBO Awards, the Black Eyed Peas were named best group, Corinne Bailey Rae best UK female, and Lemar best UK male. **26.** The Advertising Standards Authority banned two adverts for alcopops because they were deemed likely to appeal to under-18s; the adverts for WKD and Smirnoff Ice were the first television adverts to fall foul of stricter rules on the promotion of alcohol that came into force in 2005. **29.** Three paintings by L. S. Lowry and two by Helen Bradley with a total worth of £300,000 were stolen from an art gallery in Hale, Cheshire.

OCTOBER 2006

3. Lily Allen was voted best pop artist, Muse best rock artist and Lemar best urban artist at the BT Digital Music Awards. **4.** *Swithering* by Robin Robertson won the £10,000 Forward Prize for best poetry collection; the poetry editor for the publisher Jonathan Cape beat the Nobel Laureate Seamus Heaney to the prize. The Swiss architects Jacques Herzog and Pierre de Meuron, who were responsible for Tate Modern, won the annual Royal Gold Medal for Architecture awarded by the Royal Institute of British Architects (RIBA) on behalf of the Queen. **7.** *Les Misérables* became the world's longest-running musical, with 21 years on stage in London and more than 38,000 performances worldwide. **10.** *The Inheritance of Loss* by Kiran Desai won the Booker prize; the novelist, whose mother Anita Desai was shortlisted for the prize three times, became the youngest female winner. **13.** *ArtReview* magazine's annual list of the contemporary art scene's 100 most powerful people was topped by Francois Pinault, the French owner of Christie's and Gucci who is also one of the world's leading art buyers; Sir Nicholas Serota, the director of Tate Modern, came second. RIBA's £20,000 Stirling prize was awarded to Richard Rogers' £1.2bn terminal at Madrid's Barajas airport. **20.** *The Periodic Table,* Primo Levi's 1975 memoir of life as a Jew in Mussolini's Italy, which uses chemistry as a metaphor, was named the best science book of all time at an event at the Royal Institution. **26.** Figures from RAJAR showed that the digital radio station BBC 6 Music had increased its audience by 40 per cent between 2005 and 2006. **27.** The first Dylan Thomas award for writers under the age of 30 went to Rachel Trezise for her novel *Fresh Apples;* the 28-year-old from Rhondda Valley in South Wales won £60,000. **30.** At the 2006 Q Music Awards, Corinne Bailey Rae was named best new act and 'Crazy' by Gnarls Barkley won the award for best track.

NOVEMBER 2006

2. Kate Moss was named model of the year and Giles Deacon designer of the year at the British Fashion Awards. Jackson Pollock's *No. 5, 1948* became the world's most expensive painting when it was sold by the entertainment mogul David Geffen for a reported $140m (£73m). **21.** At the International Emmy Awards, the BBC's *Life on Mars* was named best drama, *Little Britain* best comedy and *Ramsay's Kitchen Nightmares* best non-scripted entertainment. **23.** Figures published by the Art Fund showed that in 2004–5 British museums and galleries spent considerably less on new works of art than those in other countries; the National Gallery, which spent more than any other British institution, spent £6.3m, while New York's Metropolitan Museum of Art and the Louvre in Paris spent £53.4m and £16.8m respectively. **28.** Michael Grade announced that he was resigning his post as chairman of the BBC to become the executive chairman of ITV. **29.** At the British Independent Film Awards, Shane Meadows' *This is England* was named best film, and Kevin Macdonald was named best director for *The Last King of Scotland.*

DECEMBER 2006

1. Government figures released on the fifth anniversary of free entry into England's museums and galleries showed that, at the institutions which had previously charged for entry, visits had increased by 83 per cent; visits to National Museums Liverpool and the V&A increased by 138 per cent and 122 per cent respectively. **4.** The £25,000 Turner Prize was awarded to Tomma Abts, making her the first female painter to win the prize since it was founded in 1984. **5.** The 'little black dress' worn by Audrey Hepburn in *Breakfast at Tiffany's* sold for £467,200 at Christie's in London; the price – more than six times the estimate – made it the most expensive dress made for a film ever to be sold at auction. **6.** Channel 4 launched a service that allowed viewers to download most of its programmes for 30 days after transmission, with costs from 99p per show. **14.** Steven Merchant beat his co-star Ricky Gervais to win best actor at the British Comedy Awards; best actress was won by Catherine Tate, and best TV comedy award was won by Mitchell and Webb's *Peep Show.* **31.** Kylie Minogue's held her first major performance since her recovery from breast cancer at Wembley Arena.

JANUARY 2007

4. British choreographer Christopher Wheeldon left his job at the New York City Ballet to set up his own international dance company. **5.** Independent publisher Profile Books announced its acquisition of the imprint Serpent's Tail. **7.** New rules were introduced in UK singles charts incorporating sales of music downloaded from the internet. **9.** The category winners of the Costa Book Awards were announced: Stef Penney received the first novel award, John Haynes – the poetry award, Brian Thompson – the biography award, Linda Newberry – the children's book award, and William Boyd won novel of the year. **12.** Protesters targeted English National Ballet dancer Simone Clarke in her matinee performance after her membership of the far-right British National Party was exposed by *The Guardian*. **14.** Arts Council England and Penguin UK revised the rules of the selection process for the Decibel Penguin Prize to accept writers of all skin colours after the Commission for Racial Equality advised that the competition could breach Section 29 of the Race Relations Act and discriminate against white writers. Seamus Heaney won the T. S. Eliot poetry prize for his collection *District and Circle*. **16.** Britons won nine out of the 15 Golden Globes awarded, including two awards for Dame Helen Mirren for *The Queen* and *Elizabeth I*. **22.** The total number of viewers' complaints to OFCOM over alleged racial abuse in the fifth series of *Celebrity Big Brother* reached around 40,000. **26.** Clive Goodman, the royal editor of the *News of the World*, was jailed for four months for intercepting phone messages left for officials in the royal household; the editor Andy Coulson accepted responsibility and resigned.

FEBRUARY 2007

5. Sotheby's in London hosted the most successful art sale ever put on in Europe, the auction made almost £95m. The ICA announced that it was cancelling the Beck's Futures arts prize, awarded for the past seven years; it would be replaced with a new award from 2008. **7.** Stef Penney was named as the overall winner of the Costa book award chosen from the five category winners announced on 9 January. Peter Doig's painting *White Canoe* sold for £5.73m at Sotheby's, the highest amount for a work by a living European artist. **11.** The BAFTAs were announced: Dame Helen Mirren received the best actress award, *The Queen* best film, and Forest Whitaker best actor. **14.** At the Brit Awards Amy Winehouse won best female solo artist and the Arctic Monkeys received the best album award. **18.** Stephen Sondheim's *Sunday in the Park with George* won five Lawrence Olivier awards, Monty Python's *Spamalot* was nominated for seven awards but failed to win any. **19.** Television presenters Richard and Judy apologised on their Channel 4 show over claims that callers were charged in phone-in competitions after the winners had been chosen. **25.** The Academy Awards were announced: *The Departed* was named best film, Forest Whitaker received the best actor award and Dame Helen Mirren won best actress. **28.** Two paintings by Picasso worth £33m were stolen from his granddaughter's house in Paris; they were recovered in good condition in August 2007 and three people were arrested.

MARCH 2007

1. The Tate raised £4.9m, including £550,000 of public donations, to keep Turner's painting *The Blue Rigi*, which was originally won at auction by an overseas buyer. Muse was named best British band at the NME Awards. **5.** ITV suspended all its competitions and votes that used a premium-rate phone line after an investigation by independent auditors showed that programmes including *X Factor* were overcharging viewers and others, such as GMTV, kept phone lines open after the winner had been chosen. **8.** Antony Gormley was granted planning permission by Sefton council for his work *Another Place*; the collection of 100 cast-iron sculptures of naked men would be installed permanently on a beach at Crosby. Channel Five suspended all its premium-rate quizzes and votes after admitting to inventing names of some of the winners on quiz show *Brainteaser*. **16.** A high court judge ruled that Anish Kapoor should receive £350,000 in damages from a fine art storage firm, after it was found that one of his sculptures that disappeared from storage had been put in a skip by accident and crushed. **23.** The Sony PlayStation 3 games console went on sale in Europe (*see* 6 September 2006). **25.** Trustees of the Tate announced a decision to buy more works by female artists in order to address the gender imbalance at the galleries (where just 348 out of nearly 3,000 artists were women). The Courtauld Institute of Art received a surprise bequest of 51 important watercolours, including eight by Turner, from a previously unknown female collector. **28.** At the Galaxy British Book Awards John Grisham won the lifetime achievement award; Conn and Hal Iggulden received the Borders' book of the year award for *The Dangerous Book For Boys*, and Jed Rubenfeld's *The Interpretation of Murder* was named as the Richard and Judy best read of the year. Charles Saumarez Smith, the director of the National Gallery in London, announced that he would leave in Autumn 2007 to become secretary and chief executive of the Royal Academy of Arts.

APRIL 2007

3. The charity Art Fund pledged £5m to British museums and galleries to change 'insular collecting habits' and encourage the display of more work from overseas. **9.** Vaughan Williams' *The Lark Ascending* came top in a Classic FM poll to find Britain's favourite piece of classical music. **15.** Culture secretary Tessa Jowell announced that the budget for the 2012 Olympic Games would be increased; as a result £112.5m would be diverted from Arts Council England over four years from 2009 to help pay for the games. **19.** Two missing panels from a San Marco altarpiece by Fra Angelico that were discovered in a pensioner's spare room after her death sold for £1.7m at auction. **25.** A collection of 45 paintings and other items by Francis Bacon that were rescued by a friend when Bacon tried to throw them away raised over £1m at an auction house in Surrey.

MAY 2007

2. The House of Lords ruled that *OK!* magazine would be awarded £1m in damages from *Hello!* magazine, after the latter published photographs of the wedding of Michael Douglas and Catherine Zeta-Jones in 2000 despite the exclusive rights being granted to *OK!*. **3.** Paintings and drawings by L. S. Lowry worth £2m were stolen from an art dealer near Manchester. **9.** The Paul Hamlyn Foundation announced that it would donate £10m to the Royal Opera House, the joint-largest donation it had ever received. **12.** Serbia won the Eurovision Song Contest with Molitva ('Prayer') by Marija Serifovic. Seventy miniature sculptures by Willard Wigan that can all fit into a single matchbox were bought for over £11m. **20.** At the BAFTA Television Awards, Jim Broadbent received the award for best actor and Victoria Wood was named best actress. **27.** At the Cannes film festival the Palme d'Or was awarded to Cristian Mungui's Romanian film *4 Months, 3 Weeks and 2 Days*. New Zealand author Lloyd Jones won the Commonwealth writers' prize for his novel *Mister Pip*.

JUNE 2007

3. Damien Hirst's work *For the Love of God* went on display at the White Cube gallery; the diamond-encrusted skull was priced at £50m, the most expensive piece of contemporary art to date. **4.** The logo for the London 2012 Olympics was revealed to a mixed reaction. **6.** Nigerian writer Chimamanda Ngozi Adichie won the Orange prize for fiction for the novel *Half of a Yellow Sun*. **13.** The Booker international prize was awarded to Nigerian author Chinua Achebe. **15.** The Indian-born author Salman Rushdie was awarded a knighthood in the honours list. **18.** The Samuel Johnson non-fiction prize was awarded to American author Rajiv Chandrasekaran for *Imperial Life in the Emerald City*, a book about life in Baghdad's Green Zone. **21.** Philip Pullman's *Northern Lights* won the Carnegie of Carnegies medal for children's literature in a readers' poll, in celebration of the award's seventieth anniversary. **23.** Sotheby's and Christie's revealed they had raised a combined £414m for artwork sold in four days over the previous week, breaking London sales records. **27.** The British Library raised £635,000 to save a rare 15th-century manuscript for the public after it had been sold to a private overseas dealer in December 2006.

JULY 2007

5. Eckoh UK, the company responsible for overcharging viewers in the Richard and Judy television phone quiz (*see* 19 February) was fined £150,000 by ICSTIS, the premium rate phone-line regulator. **7.** Live Earth concerts were held in eight locations worldwide, including Wembley Stadium in the UK, to help draw attention to the causes of global warming. **9.** For the first time in the BBC's history OFCOM fined the broadcaster £50,000 for its part in the deception of callers taking part in television competitions. **11.** The Commission for Racial Equality advised high street book stores that it was unacceptable to sell *Tintin in the Congo*, a comic book written in 1930, as it featured racist stereotypes. **12.** The BBC apologised for portraying the Queen incorrectly in a documentary; the clip shown to journalists erroneously implied that she walked out of a photo shoot because she was angry with the photographer. **17.** A painting on auction in Leicestershire that was expected to fetch around £300 sold for £205,000 – with a potential future market value of more than £5m – when it was discovered that it may have been painted by Titian in the 1500s. **18.** The BBC admitted serious editorial breaches in six shows including *Children in Need* and *Comic Relief*; all BBC competitions were suspended. **23.** *Harry Potter and the Deathly Hallows* by J.K. Rowling sold 11m copies worldwide in the first 24 hours, it overtook the previous instalment *Harry Potter and the Half-Blood Prince* as the fastest-selling book in history. **25.** The managing director of GMTV, Paul Corley, resigned accepting responsibility for phone-in competitions that continued to charge viewers after winners had been chosen (*see* 8 March).

BUSINESS AND ECONOMIC AFFAIRS

AUGUST 2006

3. The Bank of England raised interest rates to 4.75 per cent, the first increase since August 2004. **7.** BP shut down crude oil production at its Prudhoe Bay complex in Alaska after discovering severe corrosion in a transit pipeline; the anticipated loss of 400,000 barrels-a-day from the indefinite closure increased the price of Brent crude oil to $78.64 per barrel. **9.** A survey by the global investment bank UBS, which compared the prices of 122 goods and services from 71 cities around from the world, concluded that London was the most expensive city to live in. **16.** The Council of Mortgage Lenders published figures showing that buy-to-let mortgage advances for the first half of 2006 reached 152,500, a 56 per cent increase from the first half of 2005.

SEPTEMBER 2006

5. John Armitt, chief executive of Network Rail, announced a ten-year freight strategy which included creating room for an extra 120 freight trains per day by 2015 with trains expected to carry up to 2,000 tonnes, the equivalent to 100 lorry loads. **7.** The Office of Fair Trading (OFT) announced an investigation into the default charges that are levied on current accounts when customers go overdrawn without prior arrangement; the charges were estimated to generate £4.7bn for the banking industry annually. **12.** Figures released by the Office for National Statistics showed that consumer price index (CPI) inflation rose to 2.5 per cent in August 2006, exceeding the government's target of 2.0 per cent for the fourth consecutive month. **15.** The 180m-high Swiss Re tower (also known as the Gherkin), which stands in the heart of the City of London, went up for sale for an estimated £600m. **18.** BP announced a further 18-month deferral of oil and gas production from its Thunder Horse offshore platform in the Gulf of Mexico after discovering cracks in equipment on the seabed; the company had originally planned to begin operations at the end of 2005 but the platform was damaged during the passage of Hurricane Katrina. **26.** Andrew Fastow, the former chief financial officer of Enron, was sentenced to six years in prison followed by two years of probation. **29.** British Airways announced that its pension deficit stood at £2.1bn.

OCTOBER 2006

3. The wholesale price of natural gas momentarily dropped to −5p per therm after the new Langeled pipeline from Norway was successfully tested by engineers, so much gas flooded the national grid that shippers were paid to take gas out to reduce the pressure; as the sudden surge was a technical fault there was no immediate commercial significance for consumers with the January forward price pegged at 74p per therm (*see* British Affairs 16 October). **9.** In a surprise announcement the chair of Gazprom, Russia's largest gas producer, revealed that the Shtokman Artic gasfield would be developed without international partners and gas would be exported via a pipeline to European customers rather than liquefied and shipped to the USA; five American and European oil and gas multinationals had been bidding for membership of the Shtokman consortium. **13.** Farepak, owned by European Home Retail (EHR), announced it had gone into administration with immediate effect and would be unable to honour commitments to its estimated 150,000 investors, who had paid money towards Christmas hampers and shopping tokens; the company employed 35,000 agents across the UK and had been trading since 1969. **16.** November baseload electricity prices increased from £43.50 per megawatt/hour to £45.00 and December forward prices increased from £52.90 to £54.00 after British Energy closed two of its nuclear reactors at Hunterston and Hinkley and revealed maintenance and outage problems with five of its remaining six reactors. **17.** The Treasury announced a review of hedge fund regulation after concerns were voiced by the Bank of England over excessive risk-taking within the sector. **31.** The Land Registry launched its own house price index; its figures showed that overall house prices in England and Wales increased by 1.3 per cent in September, bringing annual growth to 6.3 per cent.

NOVEMBER 2006

3. Figures from Standard and Poor's showed that the average quantity of debt held on a private equity-owned company's balance sheet had increased from four times the company's gross earnings in 2002 to nearly six times in the third quarter of 2006. **7.** The government announced that it would set up a charitable fund to help investors in Farepak, which collapsed without repaying £40m worth of investments on 13 October; three of Britain's retailers – Sainsbury's, Tesco and Marks and Spencer – also pledged donations to the fund. **9.** The Bank of England raised interest rates to 5.0 per cent. **14.** First Direct bank, the online arm of HSBC, announced that from February 2007 it would start levying a £10 monthly fee to hold a current account, though only some of its customers would be liable for the fee. **15.** A group of seven global investment banks announced that they had agreed to establish a pan-European electronic equities exchange to compete with Europe's domestic stock exchanges, following the introduction of the EU markets in financial instruments directive in November 2007. **30.** The pound reached a 14-year high against the dollar, closing at 1.9670 by the end of the day.

DECEMBER 2006

4. The energy market regulator OFGEM approved plans for UK gas and electricity distributors to spend £5bn on upgrading transmission systems; the average household energy bill for 2007 was expected to increase by £12 in order for energy distributors to meet the cost of these improvements. **6.** In the pre-Budget report Chancellor Gordon Brown announced a 1.25p per litre rise in petrol duty and an increase in air passenger duty from £5 to £10 for short-haul flights and up to £80 for some long-haul flights; he predicted the economy would continue to grow at between 2.75 and 3.25 per cent in 2007. **15.** British Gas revealed that due to losses incurred early in 2006, price cuts for its 16 million customers would be delayed for at least three months despite a rapid fall in the price of wholesale gas. **21.** Figures published by the Office for National Statistics showed that income tax and national insurance amounted to 23.6 per cent of the average UK wage or salary; the highest average tax burden since records began in 1987. **22.** BAE Systems won a £947m contract with the MoD to ensure that sufficient *Tornado* fighter jets are available to meet RAF's requirements. **28.** Nationwide released figures showing that the average house price in Britain had increased 10.5 per cent to £174,000 in 2006.

JANUARY 2007

1. A German utility company RWE npower announced it had abandoned plans to convert the Littlebrook power plant in Dartford, Kent, to run on palm oil, after concluding that sustainable palm plantations in Malaysia would be unable to meet demand. **2.** Rail fares across the UK increased on average by more than 1 per cent above inflation for the fourth consecutive year, with ticket prices on some routes rising by as much as 11 per cent. **8.** Germany and Poland were forced to use their emergency oil reserves for one night after Belarus blocked Russian oil supplies to Europe following Russia's refusal to pay customs duties to Belarus for use of the Druzhba pipeline (*see also* Europe, 10 January). **11.** The Bank of England raised interest rates for the third time in five months to 5.25 per cent. **16.** Figures published by the Office for National Statistics showed that the consumer price index (CPI) measure of inflation reached 3 per cent in December 2006, on level with the upper limit predicted by the chancellor Gordon Brown, but 1 per cent above the Bank of England's 2 per cent target. **23.** Sterling reached its highest level against the dollar for 14 years at $1.9917 to the pound. **24.** Trade and industry secretary Alistair Darling rejected Royal Mail's plans for a 20 per cent employee share ownership scheme stating that the impact on public finances would be too great. The German chancellor Angela Merkel used her keynote address at the opening of the World Economic Forum in Davos to urge all countries, including developing nations, to commit to an agreement to reduce greenhouse gas emissions. **30.** In its final report to culture secretary Tessa Jowell the Casino Advisory Panel recommended that UK's first regional casino licence should be awarded to Manchester City Council.

FEBRUARY 2007

2. The Insolvency Service reported that a total of 107,288 personal bankruptcies, insolvencies or individual voluntary arrangements (IVAs) were taken out in England and Wales in 2006, a 59 per cent increase from 2005. **7.** Mark Longford, former chair of the Accident Group, which went into administration in 2003 with debts of £100m, was issued with a court summons and a writ for £4.1m in unpaid tax by HM Revenue and Customs. **8.** British Gas announced its first reduction in consumer utility prices for six years – from March 2007 gas prices would decrease by 17 per cent and electricity prices by 11 per cent. **21.** Four pensioners whose occupational pension schemes collapsed won a landmark case at the high court when the judge ruled in favour of the Parliamentary Ombudsman's findings that by distributing misleading information regarding the security of such schemes, the government was guilty of maladministration and should provide compensation. **22.** The European Commission began an investigation to determine whether £2.6bn of government-guaranteed loans granted to Royal Mail since 2001 breached laws governing state subsidies after receiving complaints from rival postal operators. **27.** Accounts published by the National Health Pension Scheme showed that the liabilities of the scheme worsened from £128bn to £165bn in 2005–6.

MARCH 2007

5. British bank HSBC issued the first profit-warning in its 142-year history after unveiling bad debts of £5.51bn, of which 60 per cent was due to defaults on second-lien mortgages in the USA. **7.** The DTI announced that from October 2007 the hourly minimum wage for adults would increase to £5.52, the rate for those aged 18 to 21 would increase to £4.60 and the rate for 16 to 17-year-olds would rise to £3.40. **13.** Figures published by APACS, the UK trade body for payment clearing, showed that 14,156 fraudulent 'phishing' cons, each typically targeting 200,000 email addresses, had been carried out in 2006; money stolen through such fraud totalled £33.5m, an increase of 44 per cent from 2005. **21.** In the 2007 budget, Chancellor Gordon Brown announced that the basic rate of income tax would fall from 22 to 20 per cent from April 2008 and the lower rate of income tax of 10 per cent, currently applicable to the first £2,150 of taxable income, would be discontinued. **26.** Figures from the Department for Communities and Local Government showed that in 2006 there was a reduction in the number of home-owners in England for the first time since the 1950s; the number of owner-occupied dwellings decreased by 25,000 to 14.6 million and the number of households with mortgages fell by 96,000 to 8.2 million. **28.** The House of Lords rejected by 123 to 120 votes government proposals to introduce 17 casinos, including a regional or 'supercasino' in Manchester, to the UK (*see* 30 January). **29.** The OFT announced it would extend its six-month inquiry into overdraft fees levied by retail banks to cover all aspects of retail bank pricing.

APRIL 2007

3. Network Rail announced a £2.4bn railway expansion programme covering the installation of new tracks and signalling schemes and the lengthening of platforms; work is due to be completed by March 2009. **8.** Due to delays in production, the spot price of uranium reached $95 a pound, its highest price since the 1970s and an increase of 45 per cent from January. **9.** The Gas Exporting Countries Forum, whose members include Algeria, Iran, Nigeria, Russia and Qatar, announced that the countries had agreed to set up a study group to evaluate gas pricing, infrastructure and cooperation between gas-exporting nations. **17.** Official figures showed that CPI inflation reached 3.1 per cent in March 2007; the governor of the Bank of England, Mervyn King, wrote a letter to Chancellor Gordon Brown outlining measures that would be taken to bring inflation down to its 2 per cent target.

MAY 2007

1. The chief executive of BP, Lord Browne of Madingley, resigned his position after the House of Lords refused him permission to appeal against an earlier high court ruling permitting Associated Newspapers to publish details of his private life; Lord Browne admitted that he had lied under oath in order to suppress details of his four-year relationship with a former boyfriend. **10.** The Bank of England raised the base interest rate to 5.5 per cent. **18.** British Airways admitted that its staff had breached competition rules by colluding with rival airlines in setting fuel surcharge prices and announced that it had set aside £350m for settling regulatory fines and criminal and civil cases resulting from the regulatory breach. **30.** The government announced its decision to sell 25 per cent of its stake in the nuclear generator British Energy, reducing its holding to 39 per cent; the announcement was made as British Energy reported a 44 per cent increase in annual profits to £1.2bn.

JUNE 2007

17. EDF Energy won a four-year tender to supply energy to 300 government departments and public bodies on the condition that a third of the energy supplied would come from renewable sources. **21.** A survey by the accountancy firm Ernst and Young showed that disposable income for a typical family household had fallen by a sixth over the past four years, from 28 per cent in 2003–4 to 22 per cent in 2006–7. **22.** The OFT launched an investigation into the UK house building industry amid concerns over the quality and time taken to build housing stock. **23.** In a joint statement the London Stock Exchange and Borsa Italiana confirmed they had agreed an all-share takeover of the Milan stock exchange for £1.1bn. **26.** BAE issued a statement confirming it was the subject of an investigation by the US Department of Justice in relation to payments made to Saudi Arabia in a deal worth £50bn for the supply of Tornado jets. **29.** *The Times* reported that the average price of an acre of farmland in the UK had reached £3,500, an increase of 15 per cent in 12 months and an increase of 50 per cent compared with 2004 values. Fopp, one of the UK's largest music store groups with about 100 shops and 700 staff, went onto receivership; HMV bought the brand and six of its shops on 31 July. Postal workers went on strike for 24 hours after 77 per cent of members of the Communications Workers Union voted in favour of industrial action in a dispute over pay and conditions at the Royal Mail.

JULY 2007

6. The base interest rate was raised to 5.75 per cent; its highest level since February 2001. **5.** The price of lead reached $2,912 per tonne on London's Metal Exchange; a 70 per cent increase since January. **12.** The CWU launched a second one-day postal strike after Royal Mail refused to negotiate with its employees on pay and working conditions. **19.** The London Underground (LU) contractor Metronet filed for administration; Transport for London set aside £700m to ensure that the nine tube lines under Metronet's control would run smoothly for the rest of the year, although LU said that a programme of station upgrades planned by Metronet could be delayed for months. The chair of the US Federal Reserve, Ben Bernanke, issued a warning that the total loss from defaults on American sub-prime mortgages could total $100bn (£48bn) and indicated that banks should further devalue bonds backed by second-lien mortgages. **23.** In one of the country's largest foreign investments, the China Development Bank agreed to buy a £6.6bn share in Barclays. **25.** After two one-day walkouts failed to resolve a pay dispute between Royal Mail and its employees, the CWU launched a rolling two-week programme of strike action for Royal Mail postal workers. Geoff and Diana Jones, a couple pursued for back-dated taxes by HM Revenue and Customs, won a landmark ruling at the House of Lords which agreed that the couple's structuring of their IT company to minimise their combined tax bill was legitimate. **26.** The FTSE 100 index dropped by more than 200 points and £48.5bn was wiped off the value of the UK's leading shares; similar downward trends occurred on stock markets worldwide as investor anxiety grew over US sub-prime mortgage losses.

CRIMES AND LEGAL AFFAIRS

AUGUST 2006

1. A high court judge awarded more than £800,000 in damages to Helen Green, an employee at Deutsche Bank in London; the judge ruled that the two nervous breakdowns suffered by Ms Green were a result of a campaign of bullying by her colleagues. **4.** The former leader of the Scottish Socialist Party, Tommy Sheridan, was awarded £200,000 after winning a libel action against the *News of the World;* the newspaper had claimed that Mr Sheridan was a serial adulterer who had taken part in alcohol-fuelled orgies. A professional huntsman became the first person in England and Wales to be convicted for illegal hunting with dogs; Tony Wright was fined £500 and ordered to pay £250 costs as a result of the private prosecution brought by the League Against Cruel Sports. **8.** The British Crime Survey showed that robberies that involved the use of knives rose by 72 per cent in 2005–6. **9.** Two brothers, Ricky and Danny Preddie, were found guilty of the manslaughter of Damilola Taylor in November 2000; the ten-year-old bled to death in a stairwell in South London after being stabbed in the thigh with a broken bottle. **14.** Police in Northern Ireland issued a statement apologising for delaying the investigation into the disappearance of Jean McConville, who was abducted from her home in west Belfast in 1972; her body was recovered from a beach in County Louth, south of the border, in 2003. **24.** Following the murder of 22-year-old Peter Woodhams in East London, the Metropolitan Police Authority requested a report from the Metropolitan Police commissioner, Sir Ian Blair, on the handling of a previous incident, in which Mr Woodhams was stabbed in the neck after confronting a group of youths.

SEPTEMBER 2006

6. Statistics released under the Freedom of Information Act showed that a speed camera on the M5 near Bristol had caught more than 20,000 speeding motorists in seven months, raising £1.2m in fines. **7.** A report by Home Office watchdogs revealed that four out of ten criminals were being released from prison before the completion of assessments designed to establish whether they were a risk to the public. **10.** A man who had twice been acquitted of the murder of Julie Hogg in 1990 pleaded guilty to the crime in Britain's first double-jeopardy trial since the law was changed in 2005; he was sentenced to life in prison, with a minimum term of 17 years. **13.** In one of its biggest weapons seizures the Metropolitan Police recovered hundreds of firearms from a semi-detached house in Dartford, Kent. **15.** Lucy Braham, the 25-year-old daughter of a Harrow School teacher, was found stabbed to death in her parents' home; William Jaggs, the son of another Harrow teacher and a student at the University of Oxford, was also found with stab wounds and was taken to hospital. **17.** A study by the Metropolitan Police of the enforcement of the laws on cannabis possession that were changed in 2004 showed that 19 per cent of black people found to be in possession of the drug and only 14 per cent of white people were arrested and charged. **18.** A senior official at Wandsworth council, who had sexually assaulted six girls while disguised as a tramp, was jailed for 13 years and placed on the sex offenders register for life; Anthony De Boise's disguise was uncovered when samples of his DNA were taken for an unrelated matter. **19.** Corporal Donald Payne became the first British soldier to admit to a war crime; Payne pleaded guilty to the inhumane treatment of Iraqi civilians who were in British military custody at a detention centre in Basra, Iraq. **25.** Sean Hoey, an electrician from South Armagh, Northern Ireland, went on trial accused of the murder of 29 people in the Omagh bombing of 1998. **28.** Figures from the Department for Transport showed that drivers who broke the speed limit caused five per cent of all collisions and 12 per cent of fatal accidents in 2005.

OCTOBER 2006

2. The police opened the country's first national unit for victims of people-trafficking in Sheffield. Scotland Yard announced the merger of its Special Branch and Anti-Terrorism Branch to form a new unit designed to fight global terrorism called the Counter-Terrorism Command. **3.** The European court of justice ruled that employers cannot lawfully pay an employee a higher salary solely on the grounds of long service; it would only be justified if the employer could prove that longer service increased the employee's experience and that it improved his or her ability to do the job. **4.** The ringleader of one of the biggest people-smuggling networks in Europe, Ramazan Zorlu, was jailed for eight-and-a-half years. **9.** In response to the overcrowding of jails, the home secretary revealed that prisoners from outside the European Economic Area would be offered money to return home instead of being detained in UK prisons while awaiting deportation; John Reid also announced that police cells would be used to house up to 500 prisoners and that 200 prison places would be created from a converted army barracks. The brothers convicted of the manslaughter of Damilola Taylor (*see* 9 August) were sentenced to eight years in prison. **11.** A House of Commons report revealed that since 1999 more than 1,000 violent crimes had been committed by offenders who, in an attempt to reduce overcrowding, were released from jail early and were wearing electronic tags. **16.** Fifteen-year-old Michael Hamer was sentenced to a minimum of 12 years in prison after pleading guilty to the murder of Joe Geeling; Hamer, who was 14 at the time, lured the 11-year-old cystic fibrosis sufferer to his home and stabbed him repeatedly. **19.** Home Office figures showed that although recorded crime fell by two per cent during the second quarter of 2006, robberies increased by five per cent and drug offences rose by 16 per cent. **26.** Charles Fletcher, a Nottinghamshire police officer, was jailed for seven years for leaking information about investigations to suspected criminals in exchange for discounted designer suits.

NOVEMBER 2006

1. A study by the Youth Justice Board found that antisocial behaviour orders (ASBOs) were regarded by teenagers as a 'badge of honour' and that 49 per cent of those issued to under-18s had been breached since their introduction in 1999. **7.** A British Hindu who converted to Islam was jailed for a minimum of 40 years for planning terrorist atrocities in the UK and the USA; Dhiren Barot, 34, spent time at al-Qaida training camps in Pakistan and the Philippines and advocated 'worldwide jihad'. **8.** Three Asian gang members were jailed for life for the racially motivated murder of a white schoolboy in Glasgow; Kriss Donald, 15, was abducted, stabbed, covered in petrol and burned to death. More than 300 soldiers who were executed for desertion, cowardice, disobedience, mutiny and other offences during the First World War were pardoned when the Armed Forces Act gained royal assent. **9.** Figures from the Home Office showed that two-thirds of men returned to jail within two years of their release, with more than a third having reoffended within six months. **10.** A jury at Leeds crown court cleared the leader and the publicity chief of the British National Party of inciting racial hatred; Nick Griffin and Mark Collett had been secretly filmed at BNP meetings describing Islam as 'a wicked, vicious faith' and asylum seekers as 'cockroaches'. **14.** The high court awarded record damages of £250,000 in a civil claim for kidnapping and rape; Amanda Lawson was drugged and held prisoner for three days by Chris Dawes, a computer millionaire who died in 1999. **17.** An independent review of crime statistics condemned the official definition of violent crime as 'nonsensical', since half of the 1.05 million violent offences against individuals recorded in 2005–6 involved no injury. **19.** The family division of the high court ruled that a woman in a vegetative state should be given a 'miracle' drug that could help her to wake up, in spite of her family's objection that she should be allowed to die with dignity. **23.** Nine members of a gang of counterfeiters that was responsible for two-thirds of all the fake £20 notes in circulation in 2005 were jailed for up to seven years; the Bank of England recovered more than £14m in notes that had been manufactured in Essex and East London.

DECEMBER 2006

2. A naked female body was found in a brook at Hintlesham, Suffolk by a member of the public; the body was later identified as that of missing prostitute Gemma Adams. The Independent Police Complaints Commission was given the power to make disciplinary hearings for police officers public. **5.** Home Office figures showed that criminals on probation were convicted of 98 murders and more than 500 other serious violent and sexual offences between 2004 and 2006. **6.** The high court gave permission to an NHS trust responsible for the care of a woman in a persistent vegetative state to withdraw life-sustaining treatment after she failed to respond to a drug sanctioned for use by the high court on 19 November; the patient's family supported the decision. **8.** Police in Suffolk found a second body in a brook at Copdock Mill, near Ipswich, in the same stretch of water and only two miles away from where the body of Gemma Adams was found on 2 December; the body was later identified as that of a second missing prostitute Tania Nicol. **10.** Suffolk Constabulary discovered of the body of a third young woman, later identified as Anneli Alderton, in woodland close to the village of Nacton. **12.** The bodies of two more women, later confirmed to be those of missing sex workers Paula Clennell and Annette Nicholls, were discovered on scrubland near the village of Levington in Suffolk. **13.** Chief Superintendent Stewart Gull of Suffolk Police announced that 100 specialist detectives had been seconded from across the country to help with the investigation into the Suffolk murders. **14.** Ian Gilbert, a director at the Royal Bank of Scotland and the father of Jessica Gilbert, a 19-year-old chess prodigy who committed suicide in the Czech Republic in July 2006, was cleared of raping his daughter when she was a child; Miss Gilbert had made the allegations to her mother prior to her death and after her relationship with her father had disintegrated. The Serious Fraud Office (SFO) announced that it was dropping an ongoing investigation into an arms deal between BAE systems and Saudi Arabia in the 1980s; Tony Blair later said it ended due to national security concerns. **15.** Eighteen-year-old Natalie Connor was convicted of manslaughter and her parents Jane and Michael Connor were convicted of murder after an 18-month campaign of harassment against another family culminated in an arson attack on their home, which killed Alex and Maureen Cochrane and severely injured their 16-year-old daughter, Lucy. **21.** Steve Wright, aged 48, was formally charged with the murders of the five women who had worked as prostitutes in Ipswich; the first suspect Tom Stephens, arrested on 18 December, was released on police bail.

JANUARY 2007

1. The government announced that the minimum age for buying cigarettes would rise to 18 in October 2007. Ellie Lawrenson, aged five, was killed by a pitbull terrier owned by her uncle. **4.** The driver of a double-decker National Express coach that crashed on 3 January near Heathrow (*see* UK Affairs), was arrested on suspicion of dangerous driving. **9.** The chairman of the Parole Board revealed that the indeterminate life sentence, introduced in April 2005, had been used far more than expected, and that the number of prisoners sentenced for life could reach 12,500 within five years. **11.** A police recruitment drive in Northern Ireland resulted in nearly 1,000 Polish people living in Britain applying for jobs in the force. The court of appeal cleared Andrew Adams of murdering a man in an alleged revenge killing in 1990 after he had served 14 years of a life sentence for the crime; it was ruled that the defence at his trial was not properly prepared. **12.** The SFO confirmed an investigation of BAE systems had been underway for two years concerning allegations of bribery of members of the South African government in order to secure an arms contract. **29.** David Bradley, a Gulf war veteran, pleaded guilty to the charge of killing four members of his family in July 2006; his psychiatrists told the court that he was mentally ill at the time of the shootings. Tony Blair announced that Roman Catholic adoption agencies would have until the end of 2008 to prepare for the new anti-discrimination laws that would allow gay couples to adopt children.

FEBRUARY 2007

3. A 16-year-old boy was shot dead at an ice rink in Streatham, South London. **5.** The European Crime and Safety Survey for the UN revealed that Britain had the highest burglary rates in Europe, and that London was Europe's most dangerous city. Three men were given indeterminate life sentences for conspiracy to rape; they were convicted on the basis of exchanges in an internet chatroom. **6.** A 15-year-old boy was shot dead in Peckham, South London. Foster parents Elizabeth and Walter Roe were sentenced to four and three years in prison respectively; Elizabeth for cruelty to the children in their care and Walter for indecent assault. **14.** Roberto Malasi was sentenced to a minimum of 30 years in prison for shooting a woman at a christening and stabbing an 18-year-old girl in 2005. A 15-year-old boy was shot dead at his home in South London. **21.** The Association of Chief Police Officers asked all police forces in England and Wales to carry out an urgent review of over 2,000 criminal cases after the Forensic Science Service admitted that some tests on 'low copy number' DNA might not have been carried out properly and important evidence could have been missed. **23.** John Laidlaw, aged 24, was jailed for life for attempted murder; he shot at passers by in racially motivated attacks in North London in May 2006, injuring two. **26.** The immigration appeals commission ruled that Abu Qatada, a radical Muslim cleric, could be deported to Jordan because a memorandum of understanding existed between Jordan and Britain ensuring that deported foreign nationals would not face ill-treatment or torture. **27.** The fine for using a hand-held mobile phone while driving was doubled to £60, and a three point licence penalty was introduced.

MARCH 2007

2. Ian and Angela Gay were cleared of the manslaughter of their three-year-old son in a retrial after they had served 15 months of a prison sentence; with new medical evidence the jury decided that the boy had not been poisoned with salt by his parents, he had a rare medical condition. The high court ruled that a jury would be present at the inquest into the deaths of Princess Diana and Dodi Al Fayed, overruling all previous decisions taken over the inquest, including Lady Butler-Sloss' decision to hear the case alone as a coroner of the Queen's Household. **9.** Terry Adams, suspected to be the head of a criminal gang, was sentenced to seven years in prison for money laundering. **13.** A taxi driver from Manchester was found guilty of killing his wife and three children with a baseball bat and was sentenced to life in prison. **14.** Chief Petty Officer Philip Coates was convicted of the rape of a female sailor; he was sentenced to five years in prison and dismissed from the Royal Navy. **15.** The Home Office published a four-year-old report by academics from Oxford Brookes University, asserting that over 45,000 asylum seekers had been placed in deprived parts of the country, and police had concerns about their safety. **16.** A coroner reached a verdict of unlawful killing by US troops in the case of the death of Lance Corporal Matty Hull in Iraq in 2003. **26.** The body of Lindsay Ann Hawker, a 22-year-old female British teacher, was found buried in a bathtub of sand Tokyo, Japan. **29.** The British government secured the release of Bisher al-Rawi, a British resident who was detained as an alleged terrorist at Guantanamo Bay for four years, revealing that Mr Rawi had provided information about Abu Qatada for MI5. **30.** Kevin Brown and Jonathan McAvoy were sentenced to life in prison for armed robbery following a trial with the highest security ever seen in a UK court.

APRIL 2007

2. Brian Wright, a cocaine smuggler known as 'The Milkman', was found guilty of conspiracy to import and supply drugs and was expected to spend the rest of his life in prison. **3.** The grandmother of Ellie Lawrenson, the five-year-old who was killed by a pitbull terrier, (*see* 1 January) was charged with manslaughter. **8.** Daisy Angus, a 26-year-old British backpacker, had her conviction for drug smuggling quashed after spending nearly five years in prison in India. **10.** The European court of human rights ruled that Natallie Evans, a British woman left infertile by cancer treatment, could not use frozen embryos created with her ex-fiancé to have a child. **17.** An 81-year-old woman was sentenced to six months in prison for repeatedly breaching an antisocial behaviour order by harassing and verbally abusing her neighbours. **19.** Eunice Spry was jailed for 14 years for the abuse of three children in her care; the foster mother rubbed their skin with sandpaper and made them eat bleach. **24.** Lady Butler-Sloss announced that she would step down as coroner for the inquests into the death of Princess Diana and Dodi Al Fayed as she did not have enough experience in dealing with jury cases; her replacement was named as Lord Justice Scott Baker, who would take over in June 2007. In the case of Lucie Blackman, a British bar hostess working in Japan whose dismembered body was found buried in Miura near Tokyo in 2001, the chief suspect was acquitted of both rape and murder due to lack of evidence, but received a life sentence on eight other counts of rape and murder. **25.** The Home Office released statistics demonstrating that Asian people are twice as likely to be fatally stabbed in the UK than they were ten years ago. **30.** Five British men with connections to al-Qaida in Pakistan, including a man that trained with the ringleader of the London bombings in July 2005, received life sentences in the longest and most expensive criminal case in Britain for plotting to make bombs and target busy shopping centres and nightclubs; the police discovered enough ammonium nitrate fertiliser in storage to cover five football pitches. Corporal Donald Payne, the first British soldier to be convicted of war crimes was sentenced to a year in prison and dismissed from the army; he pleaded guilty on 19 September 2006.

MAY 2007

1. Police raided 32 addresses in the UK and Europe and arrested 15 men and 15 women who were thought to be animal rights extremists. **3.** A three-year-old British girl, Madeleine McCann, went missing from a holiday apartment at a resort in Portugal while her parents were dining 150 yards away. The Home Office released figures showing that innocent members of ethnic minorities were three times as likely to have their DNA samples on the national database than white people. **4.** A student was found beaten to death in her halls of residence at the University of Hull. Peter Tobin was jailed for at least 21 years for the murder of Polish student Angelika Kluk in Glasgow in September 2006; Tobin was a church handyman with a past history of violence. **6.** A police officer was shot dead in Shropshire by a man who was holding his partner and a friend at gunpoint; the man then turned the gun on himself. **8.** Ian Macleod, a gangster from Manchester, and his accomplice Constance Howarth were jailed for life after ordering a contract killing that led to the deaths of the hitmen. **15.** Robert Murat, a British man living in Portugal, was named as a suspect in the investigation into the disappearance of Madeleine McCann on 3 May. **23.** Three men were reported missing after breaching control orders imposed under the Prevention of Terrorism Act. **24.** A divorce settlement of £48m was awarded to the wife of an insurance magnate, the biggest payout ever awarded by the British courts. **25.** The widow of the 10th Earl of Shaftesbury and her brother were both sentenced to 25 years for the earl's murder. **31.** Government legislation came into effect allowing security guards to search school pupils for weapons without their consent.

JUNE 2007

11. A woman was shot dead by armed police in Kent after waving a firearm at the officers and refusing to drop the weapon. Jonathan Charles Henry, a newly qualified police officer, was stabbed to death in Luton while trying to restrain his attacker. **12.** Research commissioned by the Ministry of Justice revealed that black and ethnic minority jurors tended to be more lenient to defendants of the same race in court, where race was not an explicit element of the case. **13.** The high court ruled that the family of an Iraqi man who was assaulted and died while being held by British troops would be allowed to sue the Ministry of Defence for damages. John Reid announced new child protection measures that required all convicted sex offenders to give the police information, including whether they were living with children. **14.** It was revealed that over 50,000 under-18s that had been arrested but not convicted or cautioned had DNA records on the national database, including over 100 children under ten. **15.** Seven members of a terror cell linked to al-Qaida were given sentences ranging from 15 to 26 years for conspiracy to murder and cause explosions. **18.** Police discovered an online paedophile ring that was operating in 35 countries and took 31 children into care. **19.** The government announced an emergency scheme to release up to 25,000 prisoners early, in order to reduce prison overcrowding. **20.** The Criminal Cases Review Commission announced that Barry George, convicted of killing the television presenter Jill Dando in 1999, would be allowed a second appeal. **21.** A police officer that monitored sex offenders was sentenced to two years in prison and put on the sex offenders list for ten years for grooming a 13-year-old girl. The government announced that a seventh terrorist suspect had disappeared while under a control order (*see* 23 May). **22.** Philip Coates, the Navy officer who was convicted of the rape of a female colleague (*see* 14 March), was cleared of the crime by the court of appeal. **25.** The prosecution service decided that no-one would be charged for the murder of Pat Finucane due to insufficient evidence; Finucane was killed by Ulster Defence Association members in 1989. **29.** The European court of human rights ruled that car owners had to reveal who was behind the wheel when speed cameras recorded an offence.

JULY 2007

2. Eight people were being held in connection with bomb plots in London's West End and Glasgow airport on 29 and 30 June (*see* UK Affairs section); all of them were doctors or had a link to the National Health Service. A man was jailed for a minimum of 35 years for raping and strangling his two-year-old niece. Two 16-year-old British girls were arrested in Ghana for trying to smuggle cocaine into Britain, they claimed that they were tricked into carrying the drugs. **5.** Three Islamist extremists were imprisoned for up to ten years for using the internet to incite terrorism. **9.** Four men born in Eritrea, Somalia and Ethiopia and living in Britain were found guilty of conspiracy to murder for their attempt to detonate bombs on the London Underground on 21 July 2005; they were expected to spend the rest of their lives in prison. Three people were jailed for up to ten years for keeping a man locked in a garden shed for four months and repeatedly assaulting him; 29-year-old Kevin Davis died but murder charges could not be brought as his death could have been caused by epilepsy. **11.** The General Medical Council (GMC) cleared a consultant at Aberdeen community hospital who injected two terminally ill premature babies with muscle relaxant to ease their pain; the babies died but the GMC ruled that the consultant acted in their best interest. **12.** The Lord Chief Justice announced that judges in civil courts would no longer wear wigs, and high court judges would have two different robes instead of five. Former Oxford University student William Jaggs was detained indefinitely at Broadmoor secure hospital for murdering Lucy Braham, the daughter of a Harrow schoolmaster (*see* 15 September 2006). **13.** A jury in Chicago found life peer Conrad Black guilty on three charges of fraud and one of obstructing justice; the former owner of the Daily Telegraph Group was accused of stealing $60m (£29.5m) from investors. **16.** The high court ruled that a teenage girl would not be allowed to wear her 'purity ring' to school; the ring was an expression of her Christian faith and belief in sexual abstinence before marriage. The Ministry of Justice revealed that six prisoners released early under the government scheme to ease prison overcrowding had reoffended and a further 18 were on the run. **19.** An official analysis in the British Crime Survey of the first year of 24-hour licensing laws revealed that public disorder had increased, and crimes had increased by 22 per cent between the hours of 3am to 6am. **20.** The father, uncle and cousin of 20-year-old Banaz Mahmod were given life sentences for murdering her in an 'honour killing' after she left an arranged marriage and was seen with a boyfriend. **24.** James Oyebola, a former British heavyweight boxing champion, was shot in the face and left in a critical condition after he asked two men to stop smoking in a club; his life support machine was switched off three days later. **26.** A teenage boy shot dead in South London became the tenth to be killed by gang violence in London in less than six months. A schoolboy and four university students were found guilty of possessing terrorist material; the boy was sentenced to two years in a young offender institution and the students were given jail terms. **29.** A man was shot dead in a drive-by shooting while attending the wake of a victim of a similar shooting in Manchester. **31.** The high court ruled that prisoners serving indeterminate public protection sentences were unlawfully left in overcrowded conditions with no means of rehabilitation; as a result, prisoners may have to be released after their minimum term. A former candidate for the British National Party was jailed for two-and-a-half years for stockpiling explosive chemicals in anticipation of a civil war.

ENVIRONMENT AND SCIENCE

AUGUST 2006

2. The Medicines and Healthcare Regulatory Agency recalled Lipitor, a statin used to treat cardiovascular conditions, after 320 counterfeit packets of the drug were found in the NHS supply chain. **23.** A team of scientists at Advanced Cell Technology, a private American company, announced it had successfully cultivated human stem cells in a procedure which did not damage the embryo; the cells were generated from a single cell harvested at the early stages of embryonic development. **24.** Scientists at the general assembly of the International Astronomical Union in Prague voted in favour of re-classifying Pluto as a dwarf planet; in addition Ceres, Xena and Charon were also given dwarf planet status, resulting in a new two-tier solar system model consisting of eight classical planets and four dwarf planets.

SEPTEMBER 2006

1. Two men dying of the most aggressive form of skin cancer were successfully treated with their own genetically modified white blood cells in a trial carried out by a team at the US National Cancer Institute. **4.** The results from further trials of a vaccine for cervical cancer – Cervarix – showed that in addition to immunising against the two most common strains of the human papilloma virus, HPV 16 and 18, Cervarix was also effective against HPV 45 and 31 (the third and fourth most common strains). **5.** The US space agency NASA announced its plans to start work on a permanently occupied base on the Moon. **8.** Two Sowerby's beaked whales *(Mesoplodon bidens)* were sighted in the Moray Firth off the north coast of Scotland, the first healthy specimens of this sub-species to be sighted in the area since 1890. **21.** The initial results from a study of the fossilised remains of a three-year-old female hominin child named Selam, dating 3.3 million years ago, were published in the journal *Nature;* the *Australopithecus afarensis* species that Selam belonged to were thought to be accomplished bipeds.

OCTOBER 2006

4. Trials for Lucentis, a treatment for age-related macular degeneration, the most common cause of blindness, showed that the drug appeared to not only prevent further loss of vision but also reversed sight damage already caused by the disease. **20.** The Food Standards Agency ordered the reform of hygiene practices in the dairy industry and banned the use of milk contaminated with antibiotics, following the initiation of legal action by the European Commission against the government for allowing unsafe food to enter the food chain. **25.** *Nature* reported that a 15 million-year-old avian skull, measuring 60cm (2ft), had been found in Argentina; the bird was estimated to be at least 10 per cent bigger than the largest known *phorusrhacid*, or 'terror bird'. **31.** A study into the cause of cot death carried out in the USA suggested that defects in the serotonin system may impair a baby's ability to control its oxygen levels.

NOVEMBER 2006

1. A trial of a new medical procedure for patients suffering from life-threatening cardiomyopathy, conducted at the Royal Brompton and Harefield Hospital, resulted in 75 per cent of the 15 patients involved making a complete recovery; the patients, aged between 15 and 56, were fitted with an artificial device to assist the left ventricle (which was later removed) and then treated with a combination of drugs to encourage the heart muscle to regenerate. **7.** A two-year double-blind clinical trial using stem cells and a placebo to treat 100 heart attack patients began at two London hospitals; researchers hoped that the stem cells, taken from the patient's own bone marrow and administered directly to the heart, would delay the onset of heart failure by repairing tissue damage caused by cardiac arrest. **28.** The journal *Biology Letters* published research showing that *Dunkleosteus terrelli* – an armour-plated prehistoric fish that was capable of growing up to 10m (33ft) – had the most powerful bite of any creature yet known, with a force of 5,600kg per sq. cm (80,000lb per sq. in). **29.** A herd of wild Konik horses imported from Norway was released into a nature reserve on marshland meadows near the river Stour in Kent, as part of a project to restore vegetation through grazing and make the land suitable for a wider range of wildlife.

DECEMBER 2006

7. NASA scientists reported in the journal *Science* that some of the last images transmitted by the *Mars Global Surveyor,* which lost contact with mission control in November, indicated that water had flowed on the surface of Mars within the last decade. Research published in *The Lancet* showed that variant Creutzfeld-Jacob disease (vCJD) can be transmitted through infected blood; the study was carried out when a third person died after receiving a transfusion of blood from a donor who later developed vCJD. **11.** A team of scientists at the University of Cambridge announced that the gene responsible for pain perception had been isolated. **27.** The *Corot* spacecraft blasted off from Baikonur, Kazakhstan, at 2.23pm GMT on a planet-hunting mission; the probe is to monitor 120,000 stars for signs of exo-planets in addition to studying the asteroseismology of distant stars. **29.** Clinical trials in Denmark showed that a new fertility technique for extracting undeveloped eggs directly from the ovaries, known as in-vitro maturation (IVM), had a similar success rate to standard IVF procedures, but eliminated the need for patients to take expensive hormones to stimulate the release of mature eggs. **31.** The Institute of Cancer Research published findings in *Nature Genetics* of a newly discovered gene – PALB2 – which doubles the risk of breast cancer in women who inherit a damaged copy.

JANUARY 2007

8. Scientists in the USA claimed to have discovered a new source of stem cells that could eventually repair damaged human organs; researchers successfully extracted the cells from the fluid that fills the womb in pregnancy and then grew them in laboratory experiments. **11.** An EU-wide ban was agreed on the importation of wild birds after a vote by veterinary officers from the member states. **18.** The *British Medical Journal* named the advent of public sanitation as the greatest medical breakthrough since 1840, after conducting an international poll. **22.** Merck Research Laboratories announced a study which found that vaccinating boys as well as girls against cervical cancer would mean that over 90 per cent of cases of the disease caused by the four most common strains of HPV could be eliminated. **25.** An assessment published in *Nature* estimated that scrapping Greenwich Mean Time and synchronising clocks in Britain with the rest of Europe would result in a £485m saving and trim carbon dioxide emissions by 170,000 tonnes. **26.** Research published online by *The Lancet* linked permanent lung damage to traffic pollution for the first time; findings showed that young people who lived within 500m of a motorway grew up with a significantly reduced lung capacity. **30.** The Worldwide Fund for Nature (WWF) published a report stating that the UK was the world's third largest importer of illegal timber (3.2m hectares per year) behind China and Japan.

FEBRUARY 2007

2. The UN International Panel on Climate Change released a report predicting that the average global temperature would rise by 4°C by 2100 and that this was likely to be caused by human activity. **3.** An outbreak of the H5N1 strain of avian flu at a Bernard Matthews farm in Suffolk killed 2,500 turkeys; as a result, all 159,000 turkeys were culled. **5.** The biggest science facility to be built in the UK for 30 years opened; the Diamond Light Source synchrotron generates intense light beams to probe matter down to the molecular and atomic scale. **20.** The Scottish Executive announced plans to construct the world's largest commercial wave farm, capable of generating 3MW of electricity, off the west coast of the Orkney Islands. **21.** The Department of Trade and Industry said it would cut planned spending on scientific research by £98m over two years, to cover unexpected costs and the collapse of the Rover car manufacturer. **28.** Researchers reported in *Nature* that they had manufactured graphene – the world's thinnest material, at one atom thick – into an independent membrane.

MARCH 2007

3. The first total eclipse of the moon for three years was visible across the UK. **7.** *Nature* published the results of the largest-ever cancer genome study, identifying 500 per cent more genes than were previously known with the ability to mutate and cause cancer. **12.** Tayside Flow Technologies announced findings that showed its revolutionary artificial vein – which is 'rifled' internally to encourage the blood to spiral as it flows – had achieved a 100 per cent success rate after six months of human trials. **13.** The government published its draft climate change bill outlining its aim to reduce carbon dioxide emission levels by 60 per cent by 2050. **14.** The WWF announced that it had identified the first new species of big cat in almost 200 years: clouded leopards found in Sumatra and Borneo were declared distinct from those found in mainland Asia and have been reclassified as *Neofelis diardi*. **19.** The *Proceedings of the National Academy of Sciences* journal published research detailing the engineering of a genetically modified species of mosquito which is resistant to the malaria infection.

APRIL 2007

1. The journal *Nature Biotechnology* detailed the results of a breakthrough that alters blood from one group to another; the process uses bacterial enzymes to cut sugar molecules from the surface of red blood cells, converting blood from the A, B or AB groups to the sought-after O negative, which can be given to all patients. **2.** The European Commission released figures showing a 30 million tonne increase in carbon dioxide emissions in the EU over the past year. **4.** The government announced plans to allow homeowners to install microgeneration devices (such as wind turbines and solar panels) without obtaining planning permission. **10.** The *Journal of the American Medical Association* revealed results of a breakthrough trial in which 13 from 15 patients with type 1 diabetes were cured of the condition after receiving transfusions of stem cells drawn from their own blood. **20.** Norway pledged to become the first carbon-neutral country in the world by 2050. **24.** The journal *Astronomy and Astrophysics* reported the discovery of the first planet in another solar system that orbits in the 'Goldilocks zone' – where the conditions for life are just right; Gliese 581c is approximately 20.5 light years away. **27.** The Met Office revealed that the preceding 12 months were England's warmest-ever, beating the previous record by more than 2°C.

MAY 2007

2. The *New England Journal of Medicine* published trial results of a once-a-year treatment to prevent osteoporosis; the new drug, Aclasta, was found to cut the risk of fractures by almost 40 per cent. **8.** Scientists released details of the brightest supernova ever observed – NASA's orbiting Chandra x-ray telescope showed that the SN 2006gy released about 100 times more energy than a typical supernova. **9.** A consortium of scientific institutions launched a ten-year plan to document every one of Earth's 1.8 million known species; the project is known as the Encyclopaedia of Life, and will be made freely available on the internet when complete. **16.** *Nature* published the findings of an experiment using laboratory mice, which demonstrated that it is possible to create new hair follicles. *Nature* also published results of an extensive Antarctic survey that had, to date, identified over 700 previously unknown marine creatures. **17.** The company Farm Energy released the details of plans, subject to government approval, to build the world's biggest wind farm – at 370 turbines – in the Bristol Channel. **22.** Researchers announced that a hammerhead shark pup had been born asexually; it was the first time any species of cartilaginous fish had been proved capable of reproducing without a mate.

JUNE 2007

4. The *Public Library of Science: Biology* journal published research stating that a combination of climate change and habitat destruction will significantly threaten between 400 and 900 bird species by 2050. **6.** *Nature* published the results of the most comprehensive study of the human genome to date; it identified 24 genetic variants that influence six common conditions, which together affect tens of millions of people. **12.** The Wildlife Conservation Society announced that a study of southern Sudan's fauna had revealed potentially the biggest migration of large mammals, estimated at 1.3 million, on Earth; scientists observed a column from the air that was 80km long and 48km across. **19.** Researchers from the Netherlands Environmental Assessment Agency released estimates indicating that China had overtaken the USA as the world's biggest producer of carbon dioxide. **21.** *Science* published research indicating a substantial increase in wildlife around icebergs in the Antarctic as a result of global warming; nutrients released into the water by the melting ice promote the growth of phytoplankton, which attract krill and subsequently larger animals. **28.** *Science* reported that a team of researchers led by Dr Craig Venter converted a bacterium of one species into a bacterium of an entirely different species after performing the world's first genome transplant.

JULY 2007

1. Scientists in Israel revealed that they had successfully removed and frozen immature eggs from the ovaries of girls as young as five, allowing pre-pubescent girls with cancer to achieve fertility after treatment that would normally leave them sterile. **10.** The Royal Society's *Proceedings A* journal published research showing that the sun's output has decreased over the past 25 years, dispelling the theory that global warming is caused by the changes in the sun's activity, rather than carbon monoxide emissions. **16.** The journal *Proceedings of the National Academy of Sciences* published a study that suggested a link between obesity and asthma; scientists found that cells that control inflammation in the lungs and contribute to asthma also produce an appetite-increasing protein. **19.** After 18 years of research, Dr Jonathan Schaefer, of the University of Alberta in Canada, completed the first computer program that is unbeatable at the game of draughts – the most complicated game to be solved by artificial intelligence due to the 500 quadrillion possible arrangements of draughts on a board. **25.** The journal *Environmental Health Perspectives* published research suggesting that mobile phone masts, and consequently low-level electromagnetic fields, do not cause harmful short-term health problems. **26.** The Met Office stated that average rainfall between May and July was, at 382.4mm (15.1in), the heaviest since records began and double the seasonal average.

SPORT

AUGUST 2006

2. The England and Wales Cricket Board (ECB) stated that from the start of the 2008 season, participating counties will be allowed to register only one overseas player instead of two. **6.** Jenson Button won his first Formula One grand prix in Hungary. In swimming, Great Britain finished the European Championships with 13 medals, two more than the previous record set in 1958. **9.** The Lawn Tennis Association (LTA) appointed John Lloyd as Great Britain's Davis Cup captain. **10.** The Chelsea centre-back John Terry was named as the new captain of the England football team. **12.** In horse racing, the Great Britain and Ireland team won the Dubai Duty Free Shergar Cup after beating the Rest of the World team 158–95. **13.** The Great Britain athletics team finished the European Championships with 11 medals, the lowest total in the competition since 1978. **16.** Harry Aikines-Aryeetey won the 100m gold medal with a time of 10.37sec at the World Junior Athletics Championships. **18.** The Rugby Football Union (RFU) appointed Rob Andrew as its elite rugby director, a new position created to oversee all aspects of representative rugby in England. **20.** In cricket, the fourth Test between England and Pakistan was abandoned, with Pakistan deemed to have forfeited and England awarded the win; Pakistan had refused to take the field in protest at being penalised for ball-tampering earlier in the day. **24.** David Moorcroft resigned as chief executive of UK Athletics after nine years in the role. **25.** The London Stock Exchange announced that the American entrepreneur Randy Lerner had secured 59.69 per cent of Aston Villa FC shares; Lerner was officially installed as chairman on 19 September. The Football Association (FA) charged Manchester City defender Ben Thatcher with serious foul play following a violent tackle on Portsmouth's Pedro Mendes; Thatcher was banned for eight games on 12 September. **26.** In cricket, Sussex beat Lancashire by 15 runs to win the final of the Cheltenham & Gloucester Trophy. Great Britain's coxless four rowing team won its second successive World Championship gold medal. St Helens won the rugby league Powergen Challenge Cup final after beating Huddersfield 42–12. **27.** Zara Phillips, daughter of the Princess Royal, won the individual gold medal in the three-day eventing competition at the World Equestrian Games; she was also awarded the equestrian of the year award on 29 September.

SEPTEMBER 2006

3. Tim Don won the gold medal at the triathlon World Championship in Lausanne, Switzerland. **6.** The British Olympic Association (BOA) appointed Sir Clive Woodward as its director of elite performance. **13.** In sailing, Nic Asher and Elliot Willis won the 470 World Championships and became the first Great Britain crew to win the title in 18 years. **15.** UK Athletics banned Christine Ohuruogu, the Commonwealth 400m champion, for one year for missing three drugs tests; under a bylaw of the BOA, the ban also precludes her from future Olympic Games. Junior Witter won the World Boxing Council (WBC) light-welterweight title after a points win over DeMarcus Corley of the USA. FIFA (the international governing body for football) appointed Lord Coe, chairman of the London 2012 Olympic Games, as head of its ethics commission. **16.** The England men's hockey team won the fifth-place playoff against Pakistan to secure its highest World Cup placing for 16 years. Great Britain's women's recurve team defeated Ukraine 195–194 to win gold at the European Archery Championships. **17.** In cricket, Essex Eagles won the NatWest Pro40 League. **18.** The Lancashire Cricket Board banned the Zimbabwean cricketer Mark Vermeulen from all first-class and league cricket in England for one year (with a further two years suspended) in response to the player throwing a ball at a section of the crowd during a game on 10 September. The England women's rugby union team lost 25–17 to New Zealand in the World Cup final. **19.** The BBC screened a *Panorama* documentary that implicated the Bolton Wanderers FC manager Sam Allardyce, among others, in corrupt transfer dealings; Allardyce denied all allegations made against him. **21.** The British Basketball League signed a £2.5m ten-year television coverage deal with the cable channel MKTV. **22.** In cricket, Sussex won the Liverpool Victoria County Championship. **24.** Europe won golf's Ryder Cup for an unprecedented third time in succession after beating the USA 18½–9½. Gail Emms and Nathan Robertson became the first all-English pair to win a gold medal at the badminton World Championships. **26.** The FA fined football agent Jonathan Barnett £100,000 and suspended his licence for nine months as a result of malpractice in the transfer of one of his clients, the England and Chelsea full-back Ashley Cole; Barnett lost his appeal against the ruling on 1 December. **30.** The England women's football team qualified for the 2007 World Cup finals after a 1–1 draw with France.

OCTOBER 2006

4. The Union of European Football Associations (UEFA) selected the City of Manchester Stadium to host the its 2008 Cup final. **6.** Scott Harrison, the World Boxing Organisation (WBO) featherweight champion, was arrested in Spain and charged with attempted car theft and assault; he was granted bail on 11 November and vacated his title on 7 December. **8.** James Toseland finished as runner-up in the World Superbike championship after a victory and a third-place finish in the final round at Magny-Cours, France. **9.** The snooker player Paul Hunter, winner of five major titles, died of cancer at the age of 27. The St Helens full-back Paul Wellens won rugby league's highest individual accolade, the Man of Steel award. Paul Roy was appointed as the inaugural chairman of the British Horseracing Authority. **13.** Tim Don, the triathlon World Championship gold-medal winner (*see* 3 September), was banned for three months for missing three drugs tests. **14.** In rugby league, St Helens won the Engage Super League Grand Final after beating Hull 26–4. **20.** Beth Tweddle became the first Briton to win a gold medal at the World Gymnastics Championships for her routine on the asymmetric bars. **23.** England Netball signed a contract with Sky Sports to broadcast Superleague games for the first time. **25.** The International Volleyball Federation sanctioned a unified British volleyball team to compete at the 2012 Olympics. UEFA charged the English and Croatian football associations over the behaviour of a number of fans in and around Zagreb at the Euro 2008 qualifying match on 11 October; both associations were fined on 9 November. **29.** Irish golfer Padraig Harrington won the European Tour Order of Merit, with Englishmen Paul Casey and David Howell finishing second and third respectively. **31.** Npower announced a three-year extension to its present sponsorship deal with the ECB, worth around £15m, until the end of the Ashes in 2009. UK Sport, the non-departmental public body responsible for funding

Olympic athletes, set British competitors the target of winning 35 medals at the 2008 Games in Beijing.

NOVEMBER 2006

2. Richard Caborn, the sports minister, announced that the government will back England's bid to host football's 2018 World Cup finals. The rugby league club, Salford City Reds, received government approval for a new £130m, 20,000-seater stadium in Barton, near Manchester. **3.** Ian Bell won the International Cricket Council (ICC) emerging player of the year award. **5.** In bowls, Greg Harlow won the International Open; he became the first player to win a World Bowls Tour ranking event three times in succession. **6.** Channel 4 announced that it had agreed a £12m, three-year extension to its horse racing coverage with the sport's major stakeholders (the Tote, Racing UK, the Racecourse Holdings Trust and the Levy Board). **13.** The racehorse Desert Orchid, winner of 34 races during his career including a record four King George VI Chase titles, died at the age of 27. **14.** Edinburgh was chosen to host the 2008 World Cross Country Championships. Richard Guest, the former Grand National-winning jockey turned trainer, was conditionally discharged for two years after his admission of animal cruelty in the case of a racehorse that died after being incorrectly treated. **18.** The England rugby union team beat South Africa 23–21 to avoid its eighth successive defeat, preventing its worst ever sequence of results. The Commonwealth Games Federation announced that tennis and archery would be added to the programme of sports for the 2010 event in New Delhi, India. The Great Britain women's modern pentathlon squad won the silver medal at the World Championships in Guatemala City. **19.** Andy Priaulx retained his World Touring Car Championship title by one point. Bella Comerford became the first British woman to win the International Triathlon Union world long-distance title. **21.** In football, a consortium fronted by Icelandic businessman Eggert Magnusson completed the takeover of West Ham for £107.5m. **24.** The ECB awarded provisional Test match status to the Rose Bowl, the home ground of Hampshire Cricket Club, upon completion of its £35m development. **29.** Andy Robinson resigned as coach of the England rugby union team. The French horse racing authority, France Galop, implemented a worldwide six-month ban on the Irish jockey Kieren Fallon after he tested positive for a prohibited substance on 9 July. **31.** The LTA appointed Paul Hutchins as head of men's tennis.

DECEMBER 2006

4. UK Sport announced its sponsorship of British Cycling's under-23 academy. **6.** The FA charged Mike Newell, the Luton Town manager, with improper conduct following sexist comments he made regarding Amy Rayner, a female assistant referee; Newell was fined £6,500 on 13 February. The International Rugby Board announced changes to the rules of scrum engagement, in an effort to reduce the risk of serious injuries. The BOA announced that it had named Crista Cullen, the England and Leicester defender, as the Great Britain hockey athlete of the year. **8.** Kirsty Balfour won the gold medal for the 200m breaststroke in the European Championships, setting a new British record time of 2min 21.82sec; the BOA named Balfour as athlete of the year for aquatics on 29 December. **10.** Zara Phillips was voted the BBC sports personality of the year; she also became the first senior royal to receive an award in the New Year's Honours List when she was appointed MBE on 29 December. Arsenal striker Theo Walcott won the BBC young sports personality of the year award. Mo Farah won the senior men's title in the European Cross Country Championships. **12.** Paul Casey was named as the European Tour's golfer of the year. **13.** Ascot racecourse announced a £10m programme of development to remedy restricted sightlines. **14.** The LTA agreed to sell the Queen's Club to its members for £35m. David Morgan was re-elected as chairman of the ECB for a further two-year term, beginning in April 2007. **16.** Beth Tweddle won gold on the uneven bars event at the gymnastics World Cup final in Sao Paolo, Brazil; she won a silver in the floor final on 18 December. **20.** The RFU appointed Brian Ashton as the England team's new head coach. Lord Stevens of Kirkwhelpington delivered his final report into impropriety involving FA Premier League transfers and made 39 recommendations; 17 transfers were not signed off and were identified as suspect. **26.** Australian cricketer Shane Warne became the first bowler to claim 700 Test wickets, during England's fourth Test defeat in Melbourne; Warne retired on 5 January 2007 with a total of 706 wickets. **29.** The Queen appointed boxer Ricky Hatton, Faye White, the England women's football captain, and Steven Gerrard, the Liverpool FC captain, as MBEs in the New Year's Honours List; the golfer Ian Woosnam, captain of Europe's victorious Ryder Cup team, received an OBE.

JANUARY 2007

2. Phil Vickery was named as the new captain of the England rugby union team. **5.** In cricket, Australia secured a 5–0 series victory to regain the Ashes and complete the first whitewash since England's loss in 1920–21. **9.** UK Athletics named City businessman and financial commentator Edmond Warner as its first chair; Niels de Vos was appointed chief executive on 30 January. The Raymarine/Yachting Journalists' Association named Dee Caffari, the first woman to sail solo around the world against the prevailing winds and currents, as 2006 yachtsman of the year. **11.** In football, David Beckham agreed to leave Real Madrid for Los Angeles Galaxy in the summer; the deal – estimated to be worth £128m – made him the highest-paid footballer in the world. **16.** Tessa Jowell, the Secretary of State for Culture, Media and Sport, opened the £16m Picketts Lock indoor training and competition venue in north-east London. **19.** The Rugby Football League (RFL) agreed a £6m sponsorship deal with Leeds Metropolitan University for the Challenge Cup until 2012. Cyclist David Millar was acquitted of doping charges, after a two-year ban, by a French court because his cooperation helped in the fight against drug use in the sport. **21.** Ricky Hatton won the International Boxing Federation (IBF) light-welterweight title, his fourth consecutive world-title, from Juan Urango on a unanimous points decision. **22.** The Australian Youth Olympics ended; British competitors won 13 gold medals. **23.** An independent report commissioned by the Horseracing Regulatory Authority (HRA) cleared Wolverhampton racecourse of any wrongdoing concerning the state of the track; the report was instigated after seven horses died between November 2006 and January 2007. **25.** Peter Taylor resigned as manager of the England under-21 football team; the FA appointed Stuart Pearce as acting manager on 1 February. **26.** Michel Platini was elected as the new president of UEFA. **28.** British sailors finished the Miami Olympic Classes Regatta with nine medals, more than any other nation

29. The Scottish Football Association appointed Alex McLeish as the manager of the national side following the resignation of Walter Smith on 10 January. **30.** In snooker, Stephen Hendry became the first player to compile 700 centuries in professional competition.

FEBRUARY 2007
2. The National Football League (NFL) announced that Wembley stadium will host the first regular season NFL match to be held outside North America, between Miami Dolphins and New York Giants, on 28 October. **5.** FIFA announced that John McBeth, the Scottish FA president, was voted as the next British vice-president of the organisation; his nomination was subsequently withdrawn after McBeth made derogatory comments about African football in an interview and FA chairman Geoff Thompson took his place on 30 May. **6.** Liverpool FC agreed to a £174m takeover by the American businessmen George Gillett Jr and Tom Hicks. **7.** In football, a mass brawl took place involving players and officials in a friendly match between Queen's Park Rangers and the Chinese Olympic team. **10.** In rugby union, England's Jonny Wilkinson became the highest points scorer in Five- and Six Nations history after taking his total to 421 points during the 20–7 victory over Italy. **11.** The England cricket team won the Commonwealth Bank Series after beating Australia 2–0 in the best-of-three final; it was the team's first limited-overs series victory in Austalia since 1987. **13.** Milan Mandaric, the former Portsmouth FC owner, completed the takeover of Leicester City FC. **14.** Mitsubishi Motors announced a three-year extension to its sponsorship of the Badminton Horse Trials. **16.** The HRA found four jockeys guilty of passing information for reward; Robert Winston was banned from riding for a year, Robbie Fitzpatrick and Luke Fletcher were 'warned off' – a disqualification from all work in racing – for three years and Fran Ferris for two. **21.** The House of Commons Select Committee on Science and Technology produced a report that accused UK Sport of 'unacceptable complacency' in its drug-testing procedures, and recommended that the government consider making drug-taking in sport a criminal offence. **22.** In tennis, the All England Club announced that the 2007 Wimbledon Championships would pay equal prize money to women and men for the first time. **25.** Chelsea won the Carling Cup after beating Arsenal 2–1 in the final. The Swiss tennis player Roger Federer became the longest-running world number one in the history of the men's game after reaching 161 consecutive weeks at the top of the rankings.

MARCH 2007
2. In football, the Premier League charged West Ham United with fielding the players Javier Mascherano and Carlos Tevez illegally, due to the fact that they were part-owned by a third party, Media Sports Investment; the FA fined the club a record £5.5m on 27 April. **4.** In athletics, Great Britain finished top of the medals table for the first time in the 37-year history of the European Indoor Championships; the team won four gold, three silver and three bronze medals. **7.** The European Athletics Association announced that competitors who are given two-year mandatory bans for doping offences will also be barred from indoor and outdoor European championships for a further two years. **16.** The South African cricketer Herschelle Gibbs became the first player to hit six sixes in an over in international cricket, in the World Cup group match against the Netherlands. The European Rugby Cup (ERC) authorities banned the former Ireland lock Trevor Brennan from playing rugby for life and fined him £25,000, after finding him guilty of seriously assaulting a spectator during a Heineken Cup match. **18.** Bob Woolmer, the Pakistan cricket coach and former England player, was found dead in his hotel room in Jamaica the day after his side was knocked out of the World Cup by Ireland; Jamaican police initially suspected Woolmer was murdered but later announced that he died of natural causes. **24.** The new Wembley stadium hosted its first competitive fixture with a world-record attendance for an under-21 football match; 55,700 watched England draw 3–3 with Italy. **26.** In rugby league, the RFL appointed Tony Smith as head coach of the Great Britain team. **27.** The FA fined Chelsea and Arsenal £100,000 each for the brawl that took place between some players during the Carling Cup final on 25 February. **30.** The FA announced that the broadcasters ITV and Setanta Sports had submitted a successful joint bid for the rights to FA Cup and England home international games, among other matches; the four-year deal begins in August 2008 and is worth £425m.

APRIL 2007
1. In cycling, Great Britain finished top of the medal table at its most successful World Track Championships; the team won seven gold, two silver and two bronze medals in 17 events. In swimming, the Great Britain team finished the World Championships with two silver and three bronze medals; the USA's Michael Phelps won a record seven gold medals while setting five world records. **7.** Joe Calzaghe retained his WBO super-middleweight title for the 20th time following his fight against Peter Manfredo Jr. Cambridge won the University Boat Race to secure their 79th victory in the event. **14.** Silver Birch, a 33–1 outsider ridden by Robbie Power, won the Grand National. **17.** England exited the cricket World Cup at the super eights stage after defeat to South Africa. **18.** In rugby union, New Zealand tight-head prop Carl Hayman signed a deal worth £1m with Newcastle Falcons, becoming the best-paid player in the world. UEFA announced that the 2012 European Championship would be co-hosted by Poland and Ukraine. **19.** In cricket, Duncan Fletcher resigned as England head coach; the following day, the ECB announced that Peter Moores would take up the post from 1 May. **22.** The Professional Football Association named Manchester United's Cristiano Ronaldo as the player of the year; the Portuguese midfielder also won the young player award. **24.** The RFU banned Dylan Hartley, the Northampton hooker, for six months for eye-gouging players during a match with Wasps. **25.** In football, Alan Ball died of a heart attack; Ball was the youngest member of the England team that won the World Cup in 1966. The International Olympic Committee issued the heaviest-ever anti-doping penalties; six Austrian Nordic skiers were banned for life after evidence of systematic blood-doping was discovered. **29.** Surrey recorded a world-record score in limited-overs cricket after reaching 496 for four in a match against Gloucestershire. Arsenal Ladies became the first British club to win the UEFA Women's Cup after a two-legged victory over Sweden's Umea IK; the team completed an unprecedented quadruple of titles on 7 May after winning the FA Women's Cup.

MAY 2007

2. The MCC announced the appointment of Mike Brearley, the former England captain, as its president from October 2007. **4.** Sir Robin Knox-Johnston became the oldest person to complete a solo round-the-world ocean race. **6.** In football, Manchester United won their ninth Premier League title, with two games to spare. Floyd Mayweather Jr beat Oscar de La Hoya, both of the USA, to win the WBC super-middleweight title and become only the second boxer after Sugar Ray Leonard to win WBC titles at five different weights. **8.** In snooker, John Higgins won the World Championship for the second time after beating Mark Selby 18–13. **12.** In rugby union, Leicester Tigers won the Guinness Premiership final after beating Gloucester 44–16. **13.** Twenty-two-year-old Lewis Hamilton became the youngest championship leader in Formula One history after finishing second in the Spanish grand prix; he went on to win his first two grand prix in Canada and the USA on 10 June and 17 June. Dame Tanni Grey-Thompson, Great Britain's most successful Paralympian, retired; Grey-Thompson won 16 Paralympic medals, including 11 golds, and won the London Marathon six times. **14.** In cycling, Chris Hoy beat the 500m world record by more than a second, recording a time of 24.758sec. **19.** Chelsea won the first FA Cup final to be played at the new Wembley stadium, after beating Manchester United 1–0. **20.** In rugby union, London Wasps won the Heineken Cup after beating Leicester Tigers 25–9; the match at Twickenham set a world record attendance for a club game of 81,076. **23.** AC Milan beat Liverpool 2–1 to win the Champions League final in Athens. **26.** In rugby union, Gareth Thomas broke the Welsh appearance record after winning his 93rd cap against Australia. **27.** FIFA announced that no international matches would be allowed to take place above an altitude of 2,500m; it modified the limit to 3,000m on 27 June. Percy Sonn, the South African president of the ICC, died; David Morgan, the chair of the ECB, was elected as the next president on 27 June. **28.** In football, Derby County won the Coca-Cola Championship play-off final to become the third club – alongside Sunderland and Birmingham City – to achieve promotion to the Barclays Premiership, worth an estimated £52m.

JUNE 2007

1. A friendly against Brazil, the England football team's first full international match to be held at the new Wembley stadium, ended in a 1–1 draw. **2.** In horse racing, Frankie Dettori rode Authorized to victory in the 228th Derby; Dettori won the French Derby on Lawman the following day. **4.** The London Olympic Games Organising Committee unveiled the logo for the 2012 event; the angular £400,000 design was met with a mixed reaction. **8.** A motorbike racer, a steward and a bystander were killed in a crash at the Isle of Man TT. **10.** Rafael Nadal, the Spanish tennis player, won his third successive title at the French Open; he became only the second player, after Bjorn Borg, to achieve the feat in the modern era. **11.** In cricket, Michael Vaughan became England's most successful test captain after England beat West Indies in the third Test; it was Vaughan's 21st victory in 35 tests. **15.** Former England cricket all-rounder Ian Botham received a knighthood in the Queen's birthday honours list. **20.** The England under-21 football team were knocked out of the European Championship semi-final after a 32-penalty shoot-out loss against the Netherlands. **21.** Thaksin Shinawatra, the former prime minister of Thailand, bought a controlling interest of 55.9 per cent in Manchester City FC for £81.6m. **22.** Paul Collingwood was named as England's new one-day cricket captain following Michael Vaughan's resignation. **24.** In athletics, Britain's men finished fourth in the Super League of the European Cup; Craig Pickering, the 100m sprinter, was named male athlete of the competition. Ricky Hatton successfully defended his IBO welterweight title – and unbeaten professional record – after stopping Jose Luis Castillo in the fourth round. **26.** In football, Mike Ashley completed his £133m acquisition of Newcastle United.

JULY 2007

3. In sailing, Alinghi – the Switzerland-based crew – retained the America's Cup after the closest finish in the event's 156-year history; the team won by one second over Emirates Team New Zealand to seal a 5–2 victory. **7.** In cycling, the Tour de France began in London; it was the first time a portion of the race had been in the UK for 13 years. The American tennis player Venus Williams won the Wimbledon women's single final for the fourth time. **8.** Roger Federer won the Wimbledon men's title for the fifth successive time, equalling Bjorn Borg's record, set in 1980. Jamie Murray became the first Briton to win a senior Wimbledon title for 20 years when he won the final of the mixed doubles with his Serbian partner, Jelena Jankovic. Lewis Hamilton finished third in his debut British grand prix; it was his ninth consecutive top-three placing and the third-best ever sequence of podium finishes in Formula One. **14.** In boxing, Amir Khan beat Willie Limond after eight rounds to win the Commonwealth lightweight title. **15.** Great Britain became the overall rowing World Cup winners for the first time since the series was introduced in 1997, after beating Germany by 49 points. **19.** The FA appointed Stuart Pearce as full-time manager of the England under-21 team. **22.** The Irish golfer Padraig Harrington became the first European to win a major championship since 1999 after securing the Open Championship at Carnoustie. **26.** The International Automobile Association announced it would not penalise the McLaren-Mercedes Formula One team for possessing a large dossier of secret technical information belonging to their rival Ferrari, because there was insufficient evidence that the data had been used in McLaren's race cars. Michael Rasmussen, the Danish cyclist leading the Tour de France was sacked by his team for lying about his whereabouts in the build-up to the race; over the course of the event, four other riders were ejected for doping or drug offences. **27.** John Terry – the England and Chelsea captain – became the highest-paid footballer in British history after signing a five-year deal equating to £135,000 per week.

INTERNATIONAL EVENTS

AFRICA

AUGUST 2006

1. In Uganda, Joseph Kony, leader of the rebel group the Lord's Resistance Army, held peace talks with the government; a ceasefire was signed in Juba, Sudan, on 26 August. **12.** The river Omo in Kenya burst its banks following heavy rains in the area, killing 256 people. **20.** A presidential election was held in DR Congo and officials announced that a second-round run-off would take place after incumbent President Joseph Kabila failed to secure an outright majority; Kabila won the run-off with Vice-President Jean-Pierre Bemba on 16 November with 58 per cent of the vote. **21.** In an attempt to combat inflation running close to 1,000 per cent, the Zimbabwean government revalued its currency, effectively removing three zeroes from all of the country's bank notes. **22.** Three days of clashes between supporters of President Kabila and election rival Jean-Pierre Bemba in Kinshasa, DR Congo, killed at least 22 people. **30.** Ange-Felix Patasse, the former president of the Central African Republic, was sentenced in absentia to 20 years' imprisonment for fraud. **31.** Sudanese president Omar Hassan Ahmed al-Bashir rejected a UN security council resolution which authorised the creation of a UN peacekeeping force for the Darfur region.

SEPTEMBER 2006

1. The International Monetary Fund (IMF) announced that Malawi was eligible for \$3.1bn (£1.5bn) of debt relief through the heavily indebted poor countries initiative. **5.** Mohammed Taha Mohammed Ahmed, the editor of an independent newspaper in Khartoum, Sudan, was kidnapped and murdered. **6.** In Burundi, the last remaining Hutu rebel faction opposing the government signed a ceasefire agreement. **7.** A group of 81 scientists studying HIV and AIDS sent a petition to South African president Thabo Mbeki demanding the resignation of his health minister Mantombazana Tshabalala-Msimang after she told an international conference that garlic, beetroot and potatoes were effective treatments for the disease. **11.** The government of Côte d'Ivoire resigned following accusations that it had failed to sufficiently clean a toxic waste spillage that killed three people and injured hundreds more, near the capital Abijan. **18.** In Baidoa, Somalia, President Abdullahi Yusuf survived an assassination attempt when a car bomb exploded close to his convoy. **20.** The former deputy-president of South Africa, Jacob Zuma, was cleared of corruption charges by the South African high court. **22.** In the Gambia, Yahya Jammeh was re-elected for a third term as president. **25.** The Islamic Courts Union alliance in Somalia captured the port of Kismaayo, the country's third largest city; the advance triggered Ethiopia to send more troops in support of Somalia's transitional government. **28.** Presidential and legislative elections were held in Zambia; President Levy Mwanawasa easily defeated his two main challengers.

OCTOBER 2006

1. After talks with José Manuel Barroso, chair of the European Commission, Sudanese president Omar Hassan Ahmed al-Bashir reiterated his decision to refuse the replacement of the African Union (AU) peacekeepers in Darfur with an expanded UN force. **3.** The Ugandan army announced that military operations against the Lord's Resistance Army had resumed after the rebels failed to meet conditions of the ceasefire agreement (*see* 1 August); around 38 people died in a series of clashes in Juba, Sudan, where the peace deal was signed, on 18 October. **24.** Dahir Riyale Kahin, president of the self-declared republic of Somaliland, announced the introduction of Shariah law to the area. **29.** Ninety-six people were killed when a passenger jet crashed shortly after takeoff from Abuja airport in Nigeria; it was the country's third major civilian air disaster in a year and among the dead was Sultan Ibrahim Maccido, the head of Nigeria's Muslim faith. **30.** Fighting between rebel forces and government troops in Chad killed around 100 people at Marche Borgo. **31.** Former South African president P. W. Botha died, aged 90. In Ethiopia, floods caused by a burst river in the south-east of the country killed more than 60 people and displaced tens of thousands from their homes.

NOVEMBER 2006

2. Islamist fighters and government forces exchanged artillery fire in Somalia after peace talks collapsed. The UN security council voted to extend the mandate of Côte d'Ivoire's interim government for one year. **3.** African peacekeepers claimed that militias backing the Sudanese government killed over 60 people, including 27 children, during the preceding week in the town of Jebel Moon. **5.** At a forum in China, the leaders of 48 African countries signed trade agreements worth around £1bn, as well as a package of loans and credits designed to improve China's ties with the continent. **9.** The UN reported that up to 300 people were killed in ethnic clashes along Chad's border with the Darfur region of Sudan. **13.** In Darfur, Sudan, up to 30 people were allegedly killed by the pro-government Janjaweed militia; the AU claimed further attacks took place on 18 November with around 70 people killed. **19.** The UN and aid agencies launched a relief operation in Kenya, Ethiopia and Somalia to assist more than 1.8 million people affected by severe flooding. **23.** In the Rwandan capital Kigali, 25,000 people took part in a demonstration against France after a French judge issued arrest warrants against nine aides of President Paul Kagame in relation to the 1994 genocide; Rwanda cut diplomatic ties with France on 24 November. **30.** In the town of Malakal in Sudan, aid workers reported that over 300 soldiers and civilians had been killed in clashes between the army and former rebels, the Sudan People's Liberation Army. The AU extended the mandate of its peacekeeping force in the Sudanese region of Darfur for a further six months from January 2007.

DECEMBER 2006

1. South Africa became the first African nation to legally recognise same-sex partnerships. **3.** Marc Ravalomanana won a second term as president of Madagascar, with 54.8 per cent of the vote; he appointed General Charles Rabemananjara as prime minister on 20 January 2007. **9.** In Darfur, Sudan, about 30 civilians were killed in an attack by Janjaweed gunmen on a convoy carrying medical and relief supplies. **13.** Bushmen from the Kalahari desert won a court case in which they accused Botswana's government of illegally moving them from their land. **18.** At least 80 African migrants sailing to the Canary Islands drowned after their boat capsized off the Senegalese coast. The IMF announced that Sierra Leone's progress under the heavily indebted poor countries initiative had qualified the country for US\$994m (£488m) of nominal debt relief. **19.** In Libya, five Bulgarian nurses and a Palestinian doctor, held since 1999, were sentenced to death after being found guilty of deliberately infecting 426 children with HIV (*see* 17 July). Up to 40 people were reported to have been killed in clashes between Chad's security forces and rebel militias; a peace deal between President Idriss Déby and the rebel United Front for Democratic Change was signed in the Libyan capital Tripoli on 24 December. **26.** In Lagos, Nigeria, at least 265 people were killed after the explosion of a vandalised oil pipeline. **28.** Somali government forces and their Ethiopian allies reclaimed the capital Mogadishu from Islamic militias; thousands of people protested in the city at the presence of Ethiopian forces on the following day.

JANUARY 2007

1. Angola was formally admitted as the twelfth member of the Organisation of Petroleum Exporting Countries **5.** Tanzanian foreign minister, Asha-Rose Migiro, became the first female deputy secretary-general of the UN. **8.** The USA launched a series of airstrikes aimed at suspected al-Qaida leaders in Somalia, the first since the Battle of Mogadishu in 1993. A general strike was called in Guinea in protest at President Lansana Conté's authority as head of both state and government following accusations of economic mismanagement. **11.** Former Ethiopian leader Mengistu Haile Mariam – now living in exile in Zimbabwe – was sentenced to life imprisonment for genocide and crimes against humanity following a 12-year trial; he is unlikely to ever be extradited. **13.** Somalia's interim government announced that Ras Kamboni, the last stronghold of the Islamic movement, had been captured by Ethiopian and US troops. **25.** More than 70 people died in Angola following a week of storms and heavy rains that caused flash-floods in the capital, Luanda. In the Gambia, legislative elections gave the ruling Alliance for Patriotic Reorientation and Construction party an overwhelming majority. **27.** The general strike in Guinea ended after President Conté agreed to appoint a prime minister; over 60 people died in violent clashes during the strikes. In the KwaZulu-Natal province of South Africa, David Rattray, a leading Zulu historian, was shot dead by a six-strong gang. **29.** Ghana's John Kufuor was elected chair of the AU. **31.** In DR Congo, 90 people died after violent clashes between police and Bundu dia Kongo, an anti-government religious sect, who claimed that the election on 27 January for the governor of the Bas-Congo region was rigged. In Senegal, parliament agreed to re-introduce the senate – the country's government – after its abandonment in 2001.

FEBRUARY 2007

12. In Guinea, 23 people were shot dead by security forces after protesting against President Lansana Conté's choice of ally Eugene Camara as prime minister on 9 February. Floods in Mozambique left 68,000 people homeless after rains from Zimbabwe, Zambia and Malawi poured into an overflowing dam. **14.** Dutch-based oil trading firm Trafigura struck a deal with the government of Côte d'Ivoire to donate $198m (£102m) to clean areas damaged by toxic waste left by the company in the capital Abidjan in August 2006 (*see also* 11 September). **21.** The UN approved the deployment of an AU peacekeeping force to Somalia. **22.** The prime minister of Chad, Pascal Yoadimnadji, died in Paris, France, after suffering a heart attack, aged 56; Nouradine Coumakoye was appointed as his successor on 27 February. **25.** Senegalese president Abdoulaye Wade won a second term in office in the country's presidential election with over 50 per cent of the vote. **27.** After weeks of unrest and strikes, Guinean president Lansana Conté replaced ally Eugene Camara with the union-approved Lansana Kouyate as prime minister.

MARCH 2007

2. In DR Congo, the government acknowledged that the abrupt resignation of foreign trade minister Andre Kasongo Ilunga was due to the fact he was fictitious; he was allegedly created by fellow minister Kisimba Ngoy to boost his own chances of election to the cabinet. **3.** King Mohammed VI of Morocco announced the release of almost 9,000 prisoners under a pardon granted to mark the birth of his daughter. **4.** In Côte d'Ivoire, President Laurent Gbagbo and rebel leader Guillaume Soro signed a peace deal; Soro was appointed prime minister on 29 March. **6.** Ghana celebrated 50 years of independence from British rule. **11.** Zimbabwean opposition leaders Morgan Tsvangirai and Arthur Mutambara were among 40 people arrested as they tried to attend a rally in a Harare township; Tsvangirai was badly beaten in police custody. **12.** UN human rights investigators accused the Sudanese government of 'gross and systematic' abuse of human rights in the Darfur region and labelled the international response 'inadequate and ineffective'. **23.** An explosion at an arms depot on the outskirts of Maputo, Mozambique, killed 101 people. **25.** In DR Congo, more than 150 people were killed during two days of fighting between the army and forces loyal to former vice-president Jean-Pierre Bemba. Former cabinet minister Sidi ould Cheikh Abdallahi was elected president of Mauritania after winning 52.85 per cent of the vote in the first democratic election since the country gained independence in 1960. **26.** In Nigeria, an overturned oil tanker caught fire killing 89 people. **28.** The UN urged all countries with AIDS epidemics to launch mass male circumcision programmes following evidence from three trials in Africa which suggested the procedure could protect against HIV infection. **29.** At a summit of the Southern African Development Committee, 14 country leaders showed their support for Zimbabwean president Robert Mugabe by demanding the West lift all sanctions on the country. **30.** Mugabe's ruling Zanu-PF party announced he would stand as their candidate in next year's presidential elections.

APRIL 2007

3. Zimbabwe's trade unions launched a two-day national strike in protest at the plummeting value of wages in the country. A further 400 people died in Mogadishu, Somalia, after a week of increased fighting between Islamic insurgents and Ethiopian-backed troops. **10.** The UN announced that 380 people had been murdered as Janjaweed militia attacked villages in eastern Chad. **11.** Bombers affiliated to al-Qaida claimed responsibility for two blasts that killed at least 33 people in the Algerian capital Algiers. **16.** Sudan agreed to allow UN helicopters to patrol the Darfur region in support of the AU peacekeeping force; meanwhile a UN report on 19 April accused the Sudanese government of flouting an arms embargo by disguising aeroplanes carrying weapons into Darfur. **17.** Zimbabwe cancelled licences to all aid groups accusing them of working with the opposition to undermine President Mugabe. **18.** Over 200 people were killed as Nigeria suffered a week of violent clashes in the build-up to the country's first democratic handover of power; incumbent Umaru Yar'Adua of the People's Democratic Party was declared the winner of the residential election on 24 April with 70 per cent of the ote. **21.** Another surge in violence in the Somalian apital Mogadishu killed 186 people over four days. **24.** Rebels from an ethnic Somali group attacked a Chinese-un oilfield in Ethiopia, killing 74 people and destroying he facility. **29.** Incumbent Amadou Toumani Toure won Mali's presidential election with over 71 per cent of the ote.

MAY 2007

. The international criminal court issued arrest warrants or Ahmed Haroun, Sudan's minister for humanitarian ffairs and Ali Kosheib, a leader of the Janjaweed militia; oth men are suspected of war crimes in Darfur. **3.** The overnments of Chad and Sudan signed a cooperation eal with the AU and UN to stabilise the Darfur region; he agreement includes a joint border force and the guarantee not to work with rebels from the opposing ountry. **4.** In a civil case, Frederick Chiluba, the former resident of Zambia, was found guilty of stealing £23m rom the country, the majority of which he spent on uxury clothes, cars and jewellery. A Kenyan Airways light crashed into forests in southern Cameroon, killing ll 114 people on board. **9.** New restrictions on electricity vere implemented in Zimbabwe, limiting households to nly four hours of power per day. The government of Chad announced an agreement with UNICEF for the emoval of child soldiers from the national army; the overnment had previously repeatedly insisted no hildren were ever recruited. **10.** In response to nternational accusations of breaking an arms embargo, China appointed a special envoy to Sudan, the site of major Chinese oil interests; previously more than 100 US ongressmen sent a letter to President Hu Jintao uggesting the Beijing Olympics may be interrupted by rotests if China fails to intervene in Darfur. **12.** Zimbabwe was elected chair of the UN's commission on ustainable development. **14.** More than 40 people were illed across Algeria after fighting broke out between the military and al-Qaida members ahead of the arliamentary elections on 17 May. **17.** Inflation in Zimbabwe reached an unprecedented 3,700 per cent. **28.** Nigerian trade unions began a two-day general strike in rotest at the perceived corruption of April's elections. The Zimbabwean government arrested 200 opposition upporters in connection with a series of petrol bomb ttacks on police stations. **29.** The USA imposed fresh anctions on Sudan, targeting 31 state-run companies nvolved in the country's oil industry. **31.** The overnment of Niger was dissolved amid accusations of mbezzling education grants from foreign donors; President Tandja Mamadou appointed a new prime ninister, Seyni Oumarou, and a new cabinet on 9 June.

UNE 2007

. The trial of Charles Taylor, the former president of iberia began at the international court of justice; Taylor aces 11 counts of crimes against humanity relating to the ivil war in Sierra Leone. **5.** In a Nairobi shanty town, Kenyan police killed 21 suspected members of the utlawed Mungiki sect, following the deaths of two ellow officers. The Nigerian government announced a 3.5bn legal action against Pfizer, the world's largest drug nanufacturer, for allegedly carrying out illegal trials of an nti-meningitis drug on 200 children, 11 of whom later ied. **6.** Edinburgh University stripped Zimbabwean president Robert Mugabe of his honorary degree; it was awarded in 1984 for services to education in Africa. **13.** Thousands of public sector workers in Johannesburg, South Africa, took part in a general strike to demand higher salaries. **14.** African countries agreed a one-off sale of ivory, to allow countries with legally acquired stocks to raise capital, before extending the 18-year-old export ban for a further nine years. **20.** The first verdicts of the UN-backed Sierra Leone war crimes tribunal found three members of the Armed Forces Revolutionary Council militia group guilty of crimes against humanity, including the forced conscription of children; the three were jailed for between 45 and 50 years each. **21.** Twelve people were killed in the Niger Delta region of Nigeria after the army regained control of an oil platform captured by militants four days previously. **22.** The UN published a report arguing that climate change may have been a catalyst in the Darfur conflict in Sudan, with the deserts in the north of the country advancing southwards and causing displacement of people. **27.** Nigeria's main opposition party, the ANPP, announced it would participate in President Yar'Adua's new government despite reservations about the credibility of April's presidential election. **29.** Guillaume Soro, the prime minister of Côte d'Ivoire, escaped unhurt after his aircraft was hit by rockets as it landed in Bouaké; four members of his entourage were killed. An abandoned boat containing 1.2 million tonnes of cocaine was discovered off the coast of Senegal; six men were arrested, which led to the unearthing of an even bigger haul, worth \$100m (£50m), in the seaside town of Nianing on 2 July.

JULY 2007

1. In a progress report marking the halfway stage of the Millennium Development Goals programme, the UN warned that the whole of sub-Saharan Africa will fail to meet the agreed goals on poverty, education, gender equality, child mortality, health and environmental sustainability. **2.** French police launched a murder enquiry after the eldest son of President Déby of Chad was found dead in Paris; Brahim Déby was believed to be the president's political heir. **4.** Bernard Ntuyahaga, a former Rwandan army major, was found guilty of manslaughter for his involvement in the deaths of ten Belgian UN peacekeepers in 1994 in an incident that, as it led to Belgium withdrawing its troops, may have helped to trigger the subsequent genocide; he was sentenced to 20 years' imprisonment. **5.** Zimbabwean president Robert Mugabe ordered that prices of goods were to be halved in an attempt to solve the country's hyperinflationary crisis; over 1,000 businessmen and women were subsequently arrested for breaking price controls. **17.** Families of more than 400 Libyan children infected with the HIV virus (*see* 19 December) accepted compensation payments of up to \$1m (£488,000) each, enabling the six foreign medics initially sentenced to death for infecting them to be freed on 24 July. **28.** Kenya's MPs provoked ire in the country's media with a parliamentary proposal to reward themselves with severance pay of up to £45,000 each when their terms end in December. **31.** The UN security council voted to create a joint AU-UN peacekeeping force of 26,000 troops to be deployed in Darfur from October; the mission will have the jurisdiction to prevent armed attacks and defend civilians and aid workers.

THE AMERICAS

AUGUST 2006

10. Seven thousand public health workers in Guatemala commenced strike action in protest against the government's failure to resolve shortages of medical supplies. **16.** The former military dictator of Paraguay, Alfredo Stroessner, died aged 93 during surgery in Brazil. **17.** The president of Ecuador, Alfredo Palacio, declared two provinces to be disaster areas after a volcano erupted to the south of Quito, forcing 100,000 to flee their homes. In the USA, David Passaro, a former CIA contractor, became the first US civilian to be convicted of mistreating a detainee during the hostilities in Iraq and Afghanistan; he was sentenced to eight years imprisonment on 13 February for his part in the death of Adbul Wali, an Afghan farmer. **24.** In Brazil, military policeman Jorge Carvalho was sentenced to a total of 543 years in prison after he was found guilty of being part of a death squad that carried out 29 killings in a Rio de Janeiro slum in March 2005. **25.** The first legal abortion in Columbia was performed on an 11-year-old girl who had been raped by her stepfather. **28.** The ruling People's Progressive Party of Guyana returned to power for its fourth consecutive term after winning national assembly elections.

SEPTEMBER 2006

8. The supreme court in Santiago, Chile, stripped General Augusto Pinochet of his immunity from prosecution in connection to crimes committed at a detention centre during his dictatorship. **21.** In Brazil, President Lula da Silva's election campaign manager was arrested in connection with an alleged attempt to discredit the opposition candidate, Geraldo Alckmin. **29.** In the USA, Republican congressman Mark Foley resigned after he admitted sending sexually explicit emails to members of his staff. **30.** A Brazilian passenger jet crashed in the Amazon rainforest, killing all 155 people on board.

OCTOBER 2006

2. In the USA, a gunman entered an Amish school and killed three girls before turning the gun on himself; the following morning, a further two girls died of injuries sustained during the attack. **6.** Sixteen people were killed in Bolivia during violent clashes between state-employed and independent miners fighting over control of the country's mineral resources. **13.** In New York, the UN general assembly voted in favour of naming Ban Ki-moon as the organisation's next secretary-general. **29.** Thousands of protesters clashed with riot police in the Mexican city of Oaxaca following weeks of unrest over Governor Ulises Ruiz's refusal to stand in response to accusations of corruption from union leaders; further violent protests took place on 5 and 25 November. In Brazil, a second-round run-off presidential election was won by incumbent Lula da Silva; initial results gave da Silva 60 per cent of the vote.

NOVEMBER 2006

7. Panama won a non-permanent seat on the UN security council after gaining 164 of the 192 general assembly members' votes. **8.** In mid-term polls in the USA, the Democrats won control of the house of representatives from the Republicans for the first time in 12 years; on 9 November the Democrats also secured control of the senate. The US defence secretary, Donald Rumsfeld, announced his resignation in the wake of the poll losses; Robert Gates was sworn in as his successor on 19 December. Daniel Ortega won Nicaragua's presidential election, despite polling only 38 per cent of the vote. **11.** Two UN peacekeepers were shot dead in the Haitian capital Port-au-Prince amid increasing opposition to the UN presence. **17.** James Barker, a US soldier, was sentenced to 90 years in prison for the gang-rape of a 14-year-old Iraqi and the murder of her and her family; a second soldier was sentenced to 100 years on 23 February. **18.** The Nicaraguan government passed a law banning all forms of abortion. **28.** Rafael Correa won Ecuador's presidential election, polling 57 per cent of the vote after a second-round run-off. **29.** The Bolivian senate approved a reform bill proposed by President Evo Morales to redistribute under-used land to rural communities.

DECEMBER 2006

4. President Hugo Chávez of Venezuela won a third term in office after securing more than 60 per cent of the vote. **9.** The USA approved legislation to normalise trade ties with Vietnam. **10.** The former dictator of Chile, Augusto Pinochet, died of heart failure aged 91; thousands of his supporters and opponents clashed in Santiago the following day. **15.** Same-sex civil unions were legalised in the US state of New Jersey, giving gay and lesbian couples the same rights as heterosexual couples. The governor of Florida, Jeb Bush, halted executions in the state after a flawed death by lethal injection; Mr Bush said he needed to be sure that the method of death did not constitute 'cruel and unusual punishment'. **18.** President George W. Bush signed cooperative legislation committing the USA to sharing its nuclear technology and fuel with India. **28.** Eighteen people were killed in Rio de Janeiro, Brazil, after drug gangs set fire to buses and opened fire on police stations. **29.** In the US state of California, an anonymous individual delivered $200m (£98.5m) in unpaid taxes, writing off the revenue shortfall for the entire state.

JANUARY 2007

2. Sixteen inmates died in Venezuela after rival gangs rioted inside one of the country's most overcrowded prisons. **4.** Nancy Pelosi became the USA's first female speaker of the house of representatives. **6.** In El Salvador 21 inmates died after a prison riot. **10.** US president George W. Bush announced plans for a troop surge of 21,500 soldiers to Iraq in a national television broadcast. **12.** Spanish police arrested Isabel Perón, the former president of Argentina, following an investigation into a state terror network that operated during her time in power. Police in the USA searching for Ben Ownby, a missing 13-year-old boy, found both him and another boy, Shawn Hornbeck, who had been missing since 2002, in the same apartment in Missouri; Michael Devlin, the occupant, was arrested and later charged with attempted murder. **16.** Forty-two people were killed as a huge winter storm bringing snow, sleet and ice swept across the USA. **20.** In the USA, former first lady Hillary Clinton announced her intention to run for the Democratic Party presidential nomination at the 2008 elections. **24.** Guadalupe Larriva, Ecuador's first female defence minister, died in a helicopter collision which also killed her daughter and five military officials. **26.** Businesses and schools throughout Trinidad closed in protest against the country's rising crime rates and a spate of recent kidnappings. **31.** Venezuela's congress extended the power of President Hugo Chávez by passing a measure allowing him to rule by decree.

FEBRUARY 2007

1. The Travel Industry Association of America revealed a drop of 7.6 per cent in the number of tourists visiting the country between 2001 and 2005; the fall was blamed on concerns over tighter passport and customs control. **2.** Severe thunderstorms killed 19 people and destroyed over 500 homes in Florida, USA. **4.** Thirty-two workers died after explosions in a coal mine in the Columbian province of Norte de Santander. **9.** The USA announced it is to help fund efforts in Vietnam to cleanse soils stained by Agent Orange, a defoliant used for ten years during the Vietnam War. **16.** In the USA, the house of representatives passed a non-binding motion of disapproval of President George W. Bush's plan to deploy more troops to Iraq, the first congressional censure of the war. **20.** At least 35 people died in Bolivia following floods caused by months of heavy rain.

MARCH 2007

1. In the USA, police arrested 400 people and seized 18 tonnes of drugs after breaking a Mexican trafficking network. Tornadoes killed 17 people in the southern states of Alabama, Georgia and Missouri. **2.** The city of New Orleans filed a claim worth $77bn (£39bn) against the US army engineer corps for failing to build levees capable of withstanding the flood waters generated by Hurricane Katrina. The government in Paraguay declared a 60-day state of emergency after an outbreak of dengue fever. **4.** Cherokees in the USA voted to expel the descendants of black slaves they once owned, ensuring that fewer people receive tribal revenue, housing and medical support from the government. **6.** Lewis Libby, a senior White House aide, was convicted of four charges of perjury, obstructing justice and making false statements following the leak of the identity of a CIA agent; he was sentenced to 30 months in jail on 5 June. **11.** Daylight saving time began three weeks earlier than usual in the USA in a bid to cut energy consumption. **12.** The US army surgeon-general, Lieutenant-General Kevin Kiley, resigned over the growing criticism of the hospital treatment of soldiers returning from Iraq and Afghanistan. **14.** Hundreds of people demonstrated outside the US embassy in Mexico City in protest against a tour of Latin America by US President George W. Bush. **15.** The Pentagon claimed that during a closed hearing at Guantanamo Bay, Khalid Sheikh Mohammed, a Pakistani national held by the USA since 2003, confessed responsibility for the 9/11 attacks, the murder of US journalist Daniel Pearl and the plotting of 30 other terrorist acts.

APRIL 2007

2. The USA and North Korea agreed a landmark free trade agreement after ten months of negotiations. **3.** Joshua Wolf, a Californian reporter, was released from prison after serving 226 days, the longest sentence in US history for failing to hand over information; police demanded video footage he shot in San Francisco of violent protests against a G8 summit. **16.** Thirty-three people died at Virginia Tech University in the USA, after a single gunman committed the country's deadliest mass shooting and ended the spree by taking his own life; the following day he was identified as South Korean Cho Seung-hui, who had a history of mental illness. **23.** The Canadian government faced heavy criticism following the publication of a report suggesting members were aware of regular abuse suffered by Taliban militants captured by Canadian forces in Afghanistan and handed over to Afghan security forces. **24.** The legislative assembly in Mexico City passed a new law permitting abortion on demand during the first 12 weeks of pregnancy.

MAY 2007

1. The US president George W. Bush issued the second veto of his presidency, rejecting a military-spending bill passed to him by congress because of the inclusion of a timetable for the withdrawal of troops from Iraq; Democrats then abandoned their demand that a war-funding bill should contain a withdrawal date on 24 May, enabling the $95bn (£46bn) bill to pass the following day. The Venezuelan government announced it had taken control of four refineries in the substantial Orinoco oil belt from multinationals as part of President Hugo Chávez's drive towards nationalisation. **4.** Sixty-one Haitian migrants died after their boat sank in the Atlantic Ocean, en route to the USA. **9.** Nine Colombian policemen on a mission to destroy bushes used to produce cocaine were killed by a roadside bomb. **16.** In a trial widely seen as a test case for future policy, a Brazilian rancher was jailed for 30 years for ordering the murder of a US nun who campaigned for the rights of poor farmers targeted by loggers and ranchers in the Amazon rainforest. Twenty-two people died in a gun battle between gangsters and police in the Mexican town of Cananea. **17.** The US president of the World Bank, Paul Wolfowitz, resigned after an investigation into the pay-rise awarded to his girlfriend, also a World Bank employee. A Colombian police officer held hostage for nine years by the FARC rebel group escaped captivity after a 17-day trek through the jungle. **27.** Police in Caracas, Venezuela, used tear gas and water cannons to break up a demonstration against President Chávez's decision to revoke the licence of RCTV, an opposition television channel. The US government announced plans to spend $30bn (£15bn) over a five-year period to combat HIV and AIDS in Africa.

JUNE 2007

1. Anti-terrorism agents in the USA foiled an attempt to blow up the fuel tanks serving New York's JFK airport; four men were arrested by 5 June. **4.** US prosecutors arrested ten people in California on charges of plotting a violent coup in Laos; among them was General Vang Pao who led CIA-backed forces against communist guerrillas in the 1970s. **7.** At a G8 summit in Heiligendamm, Germany, the US president George W. Bush agreed to 'seriously consider' a post-Kyoto proposal to cut carbon emissions by 50 per cent by 2050, provided similar deals can be struck with India and China. **8.** A Council of Europe report confirmed that Polish and Romanian prisons were secretly used to hold suspects for the CIA as part of its extraordinary rendition programme; detainees were subject to what George W. Bush described as 'enhanced' interrogation. **14.** James Seale, allegedly a former member of the Ku Klux Klan, was found guilty of kidnapping and conspiracy relating to a 1964 case in which two black men were beaten and drowned in the Mississippi river; he was sentenced to three life terms in prison on 24 August. **15.** The government of Peru declared a 60-day state of emergency following severe cold weather which led to the deaths of at least 200 people. **22.** In a bid to cut reliance on oil, the US senate imposed the first increase in fuel efficiency standards for car manufacturers in 20 years; new cars must meet a benchmark of 35 miles per gallon by 2020. **25.** Three hundred high-ranking members of the Mexican police force were suspended after the government launched a probe into corruption. **28.** In Brazil, armed clashes between drug traffickers and police killed 19 people in a Rio de Janeiro slum. Eleven Colombian MPs who were abducted by the FARC rebel group in April 2002 were killed during an unidentified military raid on their camp.

JULY 2007

3. During a visit to Tehran, Venezuelan president Hugo Chávez pledged to sell petrol to Iran and to bolster cooperation between the two countries. Police officers in Brazil freed more than 1,000 workers from a sugar cane plantation hidden in the Amazon rainforest, where they were subjected to subhuman living and working conditions. **5.** At least 30 people died in the Mexican state of Puebla after a bus was buried underneath a landslide. **10.** Independence Day in Argentina was greeted by the first snowfall in the capital, Buenos Aires, for 90 years. **16.** The Roman Catholic Church in Los Angeles, USA, apologised to hundreds of people abused by its priests and agreed a $660m (£324m) pay-out to 508 victims. **17.** In Sao Paulo, Brazil, heavy rain caused a passenger plane to career off its runway and hit a fuel depot, bursting into flames and killing up to 200 people. Parts of Peru were paralysed by widespread street protests and workers strikes against food, water and electricity shortages. **18.** After an all-night debate in the senate, Republicans easily defeated Democrats who proposed that US troops should be withdrawn from Iraq by April 2008. **23.** On his weekly television show Venezuelan president Hugo Chávez threatened to expel foreigners who criticise his regime. **24.** US television network CNN staged an experimental debate between the eight Democrat presidential candidates who faced questions posted by voters on the website YouTube. **25.** A report by Human Rights Watch named Columbia as the country with the highest number of landmine victims in 2006. **26.** US president George W. Bush's long-standing plan to establish a missile defence system in Europe suffered a setback when a congressional committee cut $139m (£69.5m) from its funding for the most controversial aspect of the programme – the building of an interception system in Poland.

ASIA

AUGUST 2006

10. Typhoon Saomai struck the west coast of China, causing 1.5 million people to evacuate their homes in the Zhejiang province. **14.** In the Sri Lankan city of Colombo, seven people were killed by an explosion, thought to be an assassination attempt on Pakistan's high commissioner Bashir Wali Mohammed, who escaped unhurt. **18.** In the Philippines, an oil tanker sank near the southern Guimaras Islands, spilling around 350,000 litres of oil into the sea. **20.** South Korea shipped 100,000 tonnes of emergency supplies to assist North Koreans in the aftermath of heavy floods in July. **26.** In Pakistan, Baluch tribal leader Nawab Akbar Khan Bugti and 80 of his supporters were killed by government troops following an attack on his mountain hideout.

SEPTEMBER 2006

6. In Japan, Princess Akishino gave birth to a son, Hisahito, who became third in line to the throne. **7.** In Bhutan, foreign minister Lyonpo Khandu Wangchuk became the new prime minister after the annual rotation of the post. **14.** A court in Bali convicted and sentenced four men for their part in the suicide bombings that killed 20 people on the island in 2005. **15.** In Taiwan, around 250,000 protesters gathered outside the presidential office building in Taipei, demanding the resignation of President Shui-ban following allegations of corruption. **19.** Army officers backed by tanks and troops staged a military coup in Thailand, deposing Prime Minister Thaksin Shinawatra who was attending a UN conference in New York; former army general Surayud Chulanont was sworn in as interim prime minister on 1 October. **25.** In China, Chen Liangyu, the Communist Party leader in Shanghai, was sacked for misappropriating funds during his term of office. **26.** In Japan, Shinzo Abe was confirmed by parliament as the new prime minister. **28.** Typhoon Xangsene killed 63 people in the Philippines and caused widespread damage to the capital, Manila.

OCTOBER 2006

9. The North Korean government announced that it had successfully conducted an underground nuclear test. **10.** The Indian government passed legislation banning businesses and private individuals from employing children under the age of 14. **11.** Japan imposed trade sanctions on North Korea in response to the country's nuclear weapons test. **13.** Muhammad Yunus, the Bangladeshi economist who founded the Grameen bank and pioneered the use of microcredit in poor regions of the country, was awarded the Nobel peace prize for his work. **27.** Former Pakistani president Ghulam Ishaq Khan died aged 91. **30.** The Pakistani military launched an airstrike on a purported terrorist training camp in Bajaur province, near the border with Afghanistan, killing around 80 people; an estimated 20,000 armed tribesmen gathered a day later to protest against the government. **31.** China announced an amendment to its capital punishment law that would require its supreme court to endorse all executions.

NOVEMBER 2006

2. In Kyrgyzstan, an estimated 10,000 people gathered in the capital Bishkek to put pressure on the president, Kurmanbek Bakiyev, to agree to political reforms; on 9 November the parliament adopted a new constitution curbing presidential authority and boosting its legislative powers. **3.** Sultan Mizan Zainal Abidin was named as the new king of Malaysia; he was appointed to serve a five-year term with effect from 13 December. In Taiwan, first lady Wu Shu-jen was indicted on forgery and corruption charges. **6.** The president of Tajikistan, Emomali Rakhmonov, won a third term in office after gaining 76 per cent of the vote; the country's three main opposition parties either boycotted the vote or refused to field candidates. **15.** An earthquake with a preliminary magnitude of 8.1 on the Richter scale occurred in the Pacific Ocean; thousands of people were evacuated from Japan's northernmost island, Hokkaido. **16.** Pakistan claimed that it had successfully tested a nuclear-capable missile with a range of 1,300km (800 miles). **21.** The Nepalese government and Maoist rebels agreed a peace deal aimed at ending the country's decade-long civil war. **24.** China and Pakistan signed a free trade agreement; the countries also agreed new defence and energy deals and pledged to continue nuclear cooperation. **30.** In Bangladesh, protesters gathered in the capital, Dhaka, to call for Iajuddin Ahmed to step down as caretaker ruler; on 10 December, troops were deployed across the country to curb unrest ahead of the January elections.

DECEMBER 2006

5. At least 1,000 people died and thousands of houses were destroyed after the tropical storm Durian hit the Philippines causing floods and landslides; a further 100 people died in Vietnam. **10.** Around 110 people, including 41 civilians, were killed in Sri Lanka during heavy artillery exchanges between the Tamil Tiger rebels and government troops. **14.** Prime Minister Shinzo Abe of Japan agreed to forfeit three months of his pay after admitting helping to rig town meetings in order to improve the public's perception of official policy. King Jigme Singye Wangchuck of Bhutan abdicated the throne to make way for his son, Jigme Khesar Namgyal Wangchuck, who became the country's fifth monarch. **17.** In the Philippines, an estimated 50,000 people attended a peaceful rally in Manila to protest against President Gloria Arroyo. **18.** North Korean government anounced it would not consider halting its nuclear programme unless UN sanctions imposed after it tested a nuclear device in October were lifted. **19.** Felix Kulov resigned as prime minister of Kyrgyzstan. **21.** The president of Turkmenistan, Saparmurat Niyazov, died from a heart attack at the age of 66. **25.** Flooding in the Aceh and North Sumatra provinces of Indonesia killed 122 people. **29.** The remains of more than 20 women and children were found in a sewer underneath a house in Delhi, India; the owner and his servant reportedly pleaded guilty to several counts of rape and murder.

JANUARY 2007

3. The military government in Myanmar released 2,831 prisoners in an amnesty to mark the country's Independence Day. **7.** In the Indian state of Assam, the separatist group the United Liberation Front of Assam killed 57 people, the majority of whom were immigrant workers. **8.** The prime minister of Kazakhstan, Daniyal Akhmetov, resigned without explanation; he was replaced by Karim Masimov. **11.** China launched a successful missile strike against one of the country's orbiting weather satellites in the first known use of an anti-satellite weapon since 1985. **12.** In Bangladesh, President Iajuddin Ahmed declared a state of emergency, indefinitely postponed legislative elections and stood down as head of the interim government; he was replaced by Fakhruddin Ahmed. **13.** A Cambodian girl who disappeared in 1989 was reunited with her father after 19 years spent living in the jungle. **26.** In Thailand, the partial lifting of marshal law began following a bloodless coup in September (*see* 19 September). President Kurmanbek Bakiyev of Kyrgyzstan appointed former agriculture minister Azimbek Isabekov as the country's new prime minister.

FEBRUARY 2007

2. Fifty people were killed in the Philippines after a tanker carrying compressed carbon dioxide crashed and exploded. **5.** More than 100 Bangladeshi politicians went into hiding after the military-backed caretaker government arrested eight former ministers as part of a crackdown on corruption. **6.** Twenty-three politicians in South Korea defected from the ruling Uri party to form a new organisation ahead of December's presidential elections; the move left the conservative opposition Grand National Party as the largest in parliament. **13.** North Korea agreed to close down its nuclear reactor and re-admit international inspectors in exchange for millions of dollars of oil, following six-party talks in Beijing. **14.** In Turkmenistan, acting president Kurbanguly Berdymukhamedov was announced as the country's new president after winning 89 per cent of the vote in the election on 11 February. **17.** Police in the Indian province of Madhya Pradesh discovered 390 body parts from foetuses and newborn babies buried outside a hospital; on the same day, the government announced plans to build a series of girls-only orphanages to stem the practice of female foeticide; it is currently illegal but very common to identify a baby's sex before birth. **19.** Sixty-seven people were killed when two bombs exploded on an Indian train to Pakistan. **23.** The Pakistani military announced that it successfully tested a nuclear missile with a range of 2,000km (1,250 miles).

MARCH 2007

4. The Chinese government announced its annual defence budget would rise by 17.8 per cent, with extra spending on missile systems and electronic warfare. **9.** Roh Moo-hyun, the president of South Korea, named Han Myung-sook as the country's new prime minister. **13.** Japan signed a security agreement with Australia – its first with a country other than the USA – focusing on border security, disaster relief and the prevention of terrorism. **15.** Maoist rebels killed 55 police officers at a security post in central India. **16.** In Pakistan, police and protestors clashed over President Musharraf's attempts to sack the country's chief justice, Iftikhar Muhammad Chaudhry, on misconduct charges. The Chinese government announced new legislation to help protect the individual's right to own property and prevent land seizures. **18.** The government of West Bengal in India abandoned plans for a low-tax industrial zone following protests on 14 March in which police shot dead 14 farmers who refused to sell their land. **25.** Donald Tsang, the Chinese government's nominated candidate, comfortably won a second term as chief executive of Hong Kong in the territory's first contested election. **26.** The Sri Lankan separatist group Tamil Tigers launched their first ever airstrike, targeting the government's main air base and killing three people. After weeks of mounting pressure, Japan's prime minister Shinzo Abe apologised for the country's use of thousands of Chinese and Korean women as sex slaves during the Second World War, but did not acknowledge they had been forcibly recruited by the Japanese military. **27.** General Than Shwe, the leader of Myanmar, unveiled the purpose-built city of Naypyidaw as the country's new capital. **29.** In Kyrgyzstan, Prime Minister Azimbek Isabekov resigned after only two months in the job, following President Bakiyev's refusal to accept his cabinet reshuffle; he was replaced by Almazbek Atambayev, the first opposition prime minister in Central Asian history.

APRIL 2007

1. In Nepal, five ex-Maoist rebels were sworn into the interim government. **4.** Two weeks of fighting in the Waziristan region of Pakistan between local tribesmen and Uzbeks, who fled from Afghanistan after the fall of the Taliban in 2001, left 250 people dead. **9.** The government of Kazakhstan secured a US$126m (£63m) loan from the World Bank to continue the restoration of the Aral Sea, the disappearance of which has been described by the UN as the world's worst man-made environmental disaster. **12.** India tested its longest-range (over 3,000km (1,865 miles)) nuclear-capable ballistic missile. **15.** North Korea missed its self-imposed deadline to close down its main nuclear reactor at Yongbyon. An estimated 100,000 people protested in the Pakistani city of Karachi against the building of a radical mosque and associated schools in Islamabad. **26.** Myanmar and North

Korea agreed to restore diplomatic relations after a break of over 20 years. **30.** Gloria Arroyo, the president of the Philippines, ordered the military to assist the police to prevent escalating violence, which had so far claimed 30 lives, ahead of parliamentary elections in May.

MAY 2007

3. Britain suspended aid payments to Sri Lanka due to growing concerns about the government's involvement in human rights abuses relating to the ongoing conflict with Tamil Tiger rebels. **12.** Clashes between pro-government and opposition groups, inflamed by the ongoing suspension of chief justice Iftikhar Muhammad Chaudhry, killed 41 people in Karachi, Pakistan; further strikes across the country occurred two days later. The Taiwanese prime minister, Su Tseng-chang, resigned after failing to secure his party's nomination for the presidency; he was replaced by Chang Chun-hsiung. **17.** Trains from North and South Korea crossed the military demarcation line between the two countries for the first time in over 50 years. **18.** The parliament of Kazakhstan passed a constitutional reform allowing President Nazarbayev to stand for an unlimited number of terms in office. **21.** Thousands of villagers in south-west China rioted in response to a crackdown from the local government on families that break the state's one-child policy. **28.** Japan's minister for agriculture, forestry and fisheries, Toshikatsu Matsuoka, hanged himself in his home following months of corruption allegations. **29.** Zheng Xiaoyu, the former head of the Chinese Food and Drug Administration, was sentenced to death for corruption; he admitted accepting a number of bribes in exchange for allowing drugs companies to circumvent approval standards, killing dozens of patients; he was executed on 10 July. **30.** A state government in India announced plans to demolish its biggest slum and replace it with free homes for the current residents; the Dharavi shanty town in Mumbai occupies one square mile and houses 600,000 people. In Thailand, a tribunal ordered that Thai Rak Thai, the country's biggest political party, be disbanded after upholding charges of electoral fraud; meanwhile a bomb attack killed 12 soldiers in the south of the country in the single deadliest attack on security forces since the separatist insurgency of 2004.

JUNE 2007

5. A ban on political party activities, in place since September's coup, was lifted by Thailand's military-backed interim government. Police in Pakistan arrested Atta ur Rehman and Faisal Bhatti, two Islamic militants linked to the 2002 kidnap and murder of US journalist Daniel Pearl. **7.** Sri Lankan police forcibly removed almost 400 ethnic Tamils from the capital Colombo and drove them to the war-torn north and east regions of the country in an apparent bid to clear the city of terrorists; the country's supreme court called a halt to the process the following day. **11.** In Chittagong, Bangladesh, flooding and mudslides killed over 100 people as a hill partially collapsed onto a shanty town. **15.** An investigation by the Chinese police into illegal labour camps in the Shanxi and Henan provinces freed over 450 slave workers, including 109 children, from brick factories. **20.** The Sri Lankan army announced that they were close to eliminating Tamil Tiger rebels from the east of the country after 30 militants were killed in a series of skirmishes. Nursultan Nazarbayev dissolved parliament in Kazakhstan and called early elections; on 18 August the ruling Nur Otan party, supportive of President Nazarbayev, won all contested seats. **21.** Amanullah Aman, the former state minister for labour and employment in Bangladesh, became the first government minister to be sentenced as a result of the country's crackdown on corruption (*see* 5 February); he received a 13-year prison term. **24.** At least 228 people were killed by storms in Karachi, Pakistan, which caused houses to collapse and severed electricity cables – a further 140 people were killed in widespread flooding across neighbouring India; by 4 July, the death toll from floods in South Asia reached 700. **29.** Up to one million people were made homeless in the Baluchistan region of Pakistan after the country was struck by Cyclone Yemyin.

JULY 2007

1. Chinese and British representatives marked the tenth anniversary of the handover of Hong Kong. **3.** A radical Islamic cleric, Abdul Rashid, and thousands of his supporters began a week-long siege of the Red Mosque in Islamabad, Pakistan (*see* 15 April); on 4 July, 1,200 of the rebels surrendered before President Pervez Musharraf ordered government troops to storm the building on 10 July, killing at least 75 extremists and 11 soldiers. **6.** President Musharraf of Pakistan survived an assassination attempt when a gunman attempted to shoot down his plane as it took off in Rawalpindi. **11.** Sri Lankan troops captured the last Tamil Tiger base in the east of the country, claiming control of the area for the first time since 1994. **13.** Typhoon Man-Yi caused thousands of people to flee their homes in southern Japan after wind speeds reached 234km/h (145mph); the centre of the country was hit by an earthquake measuring 6.8 on the Richter scale, killing ten people and causing leaks from the nearby Kashiwazaki-Kariwa nuclear power plant, on 15 July. **15.** North Korea announced that it had closed down its only operating nuclear reactor. **16.** Bangladesh's former prime minister, Sheikh Hasina Wajed, became the most high-profile victim of the country's crackdown on corruption; she was arrested on charges of extortion. **17.** In China, one man was sentenced to death and another 28 received prison terms for their roles in a slave labour case at two brick factories in northern China (*see* 15 June). **20.** Pakistan's supreme court ruled that President Musharraf's suspension of chief justice Iftikhar Muhammad Chaudhry was illegal and ordered his immediate reinstatement. **21.** Former lawyer Prathibha Patel was elected as Indian's first female president by the country's MPs and state legislators. **23.** Police in India discovered the remains of dozens of female foetuses and newborn babies in an abandoned well in the Nayagahr district. **27.** In Islamabad, Pakistan, a suicide bomber killed 13 people in an explosion 300m away from the city's Red Mosque. **29.** In elections to Japan's upper house, the ruling Liberal Democrat Party led by prime minister Shinzo Abe – whose popularity had fallen dramatically since his appointment in September – lost control of the legislature for the first time since 1956. **31.** Kang Kek Ieu, a former Khmer Rouge prison guard, became the first person to be charged with crimes against humanity under a UN-supported Cambodian tribunal.

AUSTRALASIA AND THE PACIFIC

AUGUST 2006

3. In Tuvalu, the general election resulted in changes to eight of the 15 seats in parliament; Prime Minister Maatia Toafa was the only surviving cabinet member. **14.** The Australian government dropped a controversial bill to detain asylum seekers in camps on the pacific island of Nauru. **23.** In Indonesia, over 11,000 people were forced to leave their homes after liquid sediment, disturbed during an oil-drilling operation in East Java, buried four villages and destroyed 19 factories.

SEPTEMBER 2006

11. The king of Tonga, Taufa'ahau Tupou IV, died in hospital in New Zealand; his son, George Tupou V, was named as his successor.

OCTOBER 2006

11. Manasseh Sogavare, the prime minister of the Solomon Islands, survived a vote of no confidence. **16.** Australia announced that it would bar all North Korean ships from its ports following the country's nuclear test (*see* Asia, 9 October). **22.** The Australian Bureau of Statistics revealed that the country would lose around 35 per cent of its income from grain following a severe drought.

NOVEMBER 2006

16. The Tongan government agreed to far-reaching political reforms after pro-democracy riots in the capital of Nuku'alofa. **17.** Indonesia announced a deal to buy weaponry worth £530m from Russia over the next five years.

DECEMBER 2006

5. Fiji's military commander, Commodore Frank Bainimarama, seized control of the country and declared a state of emergency, sparking the fourth coup in two decades; Fiji was indefinitely suspended from the Commonwealth on 8 December. **18.** The Marshall Islands nuclear claims tribunal awarded islanders US$307m (£150m) in compensation for the radioactive contamination of their homes during a period of US nuclear testing between 1946–58; however, they are unlikely to receive any money as the tribunal's funds are exhausted and the US government maintains it has fulfilled its obligations to the islanders. **28.** Thirteen thousand homes were washed away and over 120 people were killed after severe flooding in Banda Aceh, Indonesia; meanwhile, President Yudhoyono ordered Lapindo Brantas – a gas company blamed for continuing toxic mudslides near Surabaya that left 10,000 people homeless – to pay £214m to victims. **30.** Nearly 400 people drowned after a ferry travelling between the Indonesian islands of Borneo and Java sank during a storm; 245 survivors were found over the next nine days.

JANUARY 2007

1. In Indonesia, an aeroplane carrying 102 passengers disappeared; ten days later wreckage was discovered washed ashore in the north-east of the country. **2.** After ten years of negotiations, an agreement was struck in Australia allowing Aborigines to help run national parks and rainforests in New South Wales; the land includes areas the natives believe house ancestral spirits. **3.** A month after leading a coup in Fiji, Commodore Frank Bainimarama became interim prime minister of the country. **25.** Australian prime minister John Howard announced plans to spend A$10bn (£4bn) on irrigation and repair work to restore the country's rivers following six years of drought. **29.** The New Zealand government refused a financial reward offered by Greenpeace to reveal the location of Japanese whalers hunting near Antarctica, fearing the information could lead to violent clashes.

FEBRUARY 2007

5. In Indonesia, 340,000 people were made homeless after heavy rain caused rivers to burst their banks resulting in widespread flooding. **20.** Australia's environment minister announced the country is to phase out incandescent light bulbs in favour of energy efficient fluorescent alternatives, cutting four million tonnes a year from the country's carbon emissions. **22.** An Indonesian ferry travelling from Jakarta to the island of Bangka caught fire, killing 48 people.

MARCH 2007

6. An earthquake measuring 6.3 on the Richter scale killed 74 people on the Indonesian island of Sumatra. **7.** An aeroplane landing in Java, Indonesia, overshot its runway and exploded in a nearby field killing 22 of the 140 people on board. **9.** Jurors on Norfolk Island found Glenn McNeill guilty of the first murder on the island for 151 years; he was sentenced to 24 years in prison on 25 July. **30.** A military tribunal at Guantanamo Bay sentenced Australian David Hicks to seven years in prison for assisting al-Qaida; he will serve the remaining nine months of his sentence in his native country.

APRIL 2007

1. A tsunami triggered by an undersea earthquake with a magnitude of 8.0 killed 52 people in the Solomon Islands; waves up to 10m (32ft) high were reported.

MAY 2007

9. Current prime minister Jose Ramos-Horta won East Timor's presidential elections with 70 per cent of the vote. Malietoa Tanumafili II, the head of state of Samoa and the world's third-longest serving ruler, died at the age of 95; he was replaced by Tuiatua Tupua Tamasese Efi on 15 June.

JUNE 2007

5. A collision between a passenger train and a truck at a level-crossing in the state of Victoria in Australia killed 11 people. **13.** Indonesian police captured Abu Dujana, a suspected Islamic terrorist believed to have participated in the 2002 Bali bombings; he and seven other men were arrested in raids across Java. **21.** Australian prime minister John Howard announced plans to ban alcohol and pornography and tighten control of welfare benefits in Aboriginal areas of the Northern Territories in an attempt to curb a rising rate of child abuse.

JULY 2007

9. Prosecutors in Indonesia launched a civil lawsuit against former president Suharto to recover £219m of state funds that allegedly disappeared during his administration. **10.** Julian Moti, a lawyer wanted in Australia on child sex charges was sworn in as the new attorney-general of the Solomon Islands, causing an angry response from the Australian government. **24.** At least 65 people were killed on the Indonesian island of Sulawesi following heavy flooding and landslides.

EUROPE

AUGUST 2006

4. Ukraine elected a new government, headed by Prime Minister Viktor Yanukovych, leader of the Party of Regions. **16.** Jiri Paroubek, the prime minister of the Czech Republic, resigned after attempts to form a coalition government with the opposition Civic Democrat party failed; Mirek Topolanek was named as his successor. **18.** The Dutch ministry of agriculture announced that it was banning all live exports of sheep, cows and goats after an outbreak of bluetongue disease. **20.** Seventy illegal immigrants drowned after two boats sank off the Mediterranean island of Lampedusa, situated between Sicily and Libya. **21.** In Moscow, two bombs exploded in a busy market killing ten people and injuring 41; two students with links to far-right groups were later arrested and charged. **22.** A Russian airliner crashed in Donetsk, Ukraine, killing all 170 passengers and crew onboard; the accident was blamed on severe weather. **25.** In Austria, police revealed that Natascha Kampusch, an 18-year-old girl from Vienna, had escaped from a cell after being kidnapped on her way to school and held captive for eight years; the kidnapper, a local man Wolfgang Priklopil, committed suicide soon after Kampusch's escape. The EU pledged around 7,000 troops for a UN peacekeeping mission in southern Lebanon.

SEPTEMBER 2006

10. Montenegro held its first parliamentary elections since the country's separation from Serbia; the coalition led by Prime Minister Milo Djukanovic achieved a comfortable victory. **17.** Hundreds of protesters gathered outside the parliament building in Budapest, Hungary, after a taped conversation between Prime Minister Ferenc Gyurcsany and his cabinet was leaked to a national radio station; on the tape he described how his party had misled voters and lied about the state of the economy during the April 2006 election campaign. A legislative election was held in Sweden and was won by the four-party coalition Alliance for Sweden with 48.1 per cent of the vote. **22.** In Germany, 23 people were killed when a high-speed monorail crashed into a maintenance vehicle. **23.** Toomas Hendrick Ilves was elected president of Estonia. **25.** President Chirac of France announced that full state pensions would be restored to African and Arab former service personnel who fought for France during the Second World War. **27.** Momcilo Krajisnik, the former speaker of the Bosnian-Serb parliament on trial in the Hague, was found guilty on five counts of war crimes and sentenced to 27 years in prison.

OCTOBER 2006

1. Bosnian general elections resulted in a new three-man presidency, consisting of Haris Silajdzic, Nebojsa Radmanovic and Zeljko Komsic. **2.** A general election was held in Austria and won by the opposition coalition Social and Christian Democrat Party with 35.7 per cent of the vote. **3.** Two men hijacked a Turkish airliner after taking off from Tirana in Albania; the plane landed in Italy where the two hijackers were arrested. **6.** It was announced that personal information on passengers flying from Europe to the USA would be shared between European and US intelligence agencies. **7.** The Russian journalist and writer Anna Politkovskaya was shot dead near her apartment in Moscow. **11.** The newly formed government of the Czech Republic resigned after losing a vote of no confidence; Prime Minister Mirek Topolanek announced he would remain in power until local and senate elections could be held. **12.** France adopted a bill making it illegal to deny that Armenians had suffered genocide at the hands of the Turkish in 1915; as a result, the commander of the Turkish army, General Ilker Basbug, announced that his country had suspended all military ties with France on 16 November. **29.** In Serbia, a referendum on whether to amend the national constitution was held and approved by 51.5 per cent of voters; proposed amendments included the abolition of the death penalty and the assertion that Kosovo would remain an integral part of the country. In Bulgaria, President Georgi Parvanov won a second five-year term in office following a second-round run-off.

NOVEMBER 2006

2. Romano Prodi, the Italian prime minister, met local leaders in Naples to discuss a solution to the recent increase in mafia-related murders in the town; 75 had taken place in 2006 to date. **6.** A leading suspect in the 2004 Madrid train bombings, Rabei Osman Sayed Ahmed, was sentenced to ten years' imprisonment by an Italian court. **8.** The EC stated that unless Turkey opened its ports and airports to Cypriot traffic within one month, accession negotiations would be suspended; Turkey introduced a new cooperative accession strategy on 25 December. **9.** The international criminal court – the only permanent international war crimes court – opened its first hearing in the Hague. Eighty per cent of workers in Portugal's public sector began a two-day strike to protest against government cost-cutting. **10.** In the north-east of Bosnia and Hercegovina, a mass grave was discovered containing more than 100 victims of the 1995 Srebrenica massacre. **13.** Officials in the Georgian separatist region of South Ossetia said that over 90 per cent of voters in a referendum backed independence. Romanian prosecutors indicted former prime minister Adrian Nastase, charging him with blackmail and accepting bribes worth £920,000. **17.** Ségolène Royal was elected as the Socialist candidate for the French presidency after she gained 60.6 per cent of her party's vote. **20.** In Germany, male nurse Stephan Letter was jailed for life for killing 28 patients, and performing illegal euthanasia on another, making him the country's most prolific serial killer since the Second World War. **21.** An international consortium – consisting of South Korea, Russia, China, the EU, the USA, India and Japan – signed a formal agreement to build an experimental nuclear fusion reactor in France. An underground explosion at a coal mine in Ruda Slaska, Poland, killed 23 miners. **22.** At the Dutch parliamentary elections, the governing Christian Democratic Appeal party retained their position as the largest in the chamber, but without a majority significant enough to prevent the formation of a coalition government. **23.** The European court of justice ruled against allowing consumers in the EU to purchase cigarettes and alcohol via the internet from countries with low excise duties. **28.** Pope Benedict XVI arrived in Turkey on a four-day tour, his first visit to a predominantly Muslim country. **30.** The UN Yugoslav war crimes tribunal sentenced Stanislav Galic, a Bosnian Serb general, to life imprisonment for commanding the siege of Sarajevo in the 1990s.

DECEMBER 2006

2. Thousands of people marched in the Serbian capital, Belgrade, in support of nationalist leader Vojislav Seselj, on trial in the Hague for war crimes. **5.** Spain and Senegal agreed a series of measures to curb illegal migration to the Canary Islands. **7.** In Bulgaria, 18 people were killed and ten were injured when a bus veered off a bridge into the Yantra river. **9.** Forty-five women died after a fire broke out at a drug rehabilitation clinic in Moscow, Russia. **10.** The breakaway Moldovan region of Transdniestria re-elected leader Igor Smirnov, who has been in power since 1990. **13.** The European parliament agreed a landmark law controlling toxic chemicals, which obliges companies to prove that substances in everyday products are safe. **14.** The European parliament approved the introduction of an EU-wide driving licence to be issued by governments in 2012. **20.** In Greece, around one million students protested in Athens against government plans to create private universities. **22.** French prime minister Dominique de Villepin was questioned by judges for 17 hours relating to his involvement in a bribes scandal. **30.** In Spain, two people were killed by an 800kg bomb which exploded at Barajas airport in Madrid after a warning call from the Basque separatist group ETA; the government suspended peace talks with the group as a result. **31.** In Belarus, Prime Minister Sergei Sidorsky signed an agreement with Russian energy firm Gazprom hours before a deadline that threatened to cut the supplies of ten million people. A Spanish woman became the oldest new mother in the world at the age of 67 after delivering twins; she later admitted she lied about her age to receive IVF treatment.

JANUARY 2007

1. Romania and Bulgaria joined the EU, Slovenia adopted the euro as its national currency and Germany took over the rotating EU presidency. **3.** Serbia's tripartite presidency nominated social democrat Nikola Spiric as prime minister. **7.** In Poland, Stanislaw Wielgus, newly appointed as archbishop of Warsaw, bowed to political pressure and resigned from his position after admitting his former involvement with the Polish communist secret service. **9.** Austria's two main political parties agreed to form a coalition government; Social Democrat leader Alfred Gusenbauer became chancellor. **10.** Belarus scrapped a controversial transit tax on Russian oil, ending the threat of a trade war. **12.** In France, Nicholas Sarkozy was appointed as the governing UMP party's candidate for the presidency. **13.** An Italian military court convicted ten former members of the Nazi SS for their part in the Marzabotto massacre of 1944. **19.** In Turkey, Hrant Dink, a newspaper editor who wrote frequently about the Armenian genocide at the beginning of the 20th century, was assassinated in Istanbul; a 17-year-old boy later confessed to the murder. At least 43 people were killed as storms and high winds swept across northern Europe. **21.** Seven members of the radical group Ansar al-Islam were jailed in Turkey for their part in a plot to assassinate US President George W. Bush during a 2004 NATO summit. **24.** More than 2,000 arrests were made across Italy as a result of an investigation into people trafficking. The Russian parliament unanimously approved a bill to relocate the constitutional court from Moscow to St Petersburg in 2008. **30.** The German chancellor Angela Merkel announced the end of state subsidies for the coal industry, a measure that will lead to the closure of the country's eight remaining pits.

FEBRUARY 2007

1. In France, a bill preventing smoking in workplaces came into force. **2.** A UN-backed draft proposal recommended that Kosovo be allowed to establish its own constitution, national flag and anthem and negotiate membership of the UN and other international organisations; the Serbian parliament voted overwhelmingly against the proposal on 14 February. Fifty-two people were convicted in France after police discovered 22 Bulgarian infants had been sold to French couples. **5.** Six people were discovered bound and shot dead in a Chinese restaurant near Hamburg, Germany; a seventh victim died and two Vietnamese men were arrested the following day. **7.** The EC announced plans to force vehicle manufacturers to cut greenhouse gas emissions from new cars by 20 per cent by 2012. Spanish police arrested 52 people accused of stealing 300,000 ancient artefacts from sites across Andalucia. Police in Vienna, Austria, uncovered a huge child pornography network extending to more than 2,360 suspects in 77 countries. **8.** Russia announced a major increase in military spending by committing $189bn (£97bn) over the next eight years to overhaul its infrastructure. **11.** Portuguese prime minister Jose Socrates announced that the country will legalise abortion during the first ten weeks of pregnancy; he upheld the result of a referendum despite the turnout being too low for the result to be legally binding. **12.** A German court announced that Baader-Meinhoff gang leader Brigitte Mohnhaupt will be freed on probation after serving 24 years in prison; she was released on 25 March. **15.** In Germany, a neo-Nazi publisher was jailed for five years – the maximum possible sentence – for denying the existence of the Holocaust. **16.** A judge in Italy ordered 26 Americans and five Italians to stand trial for the kidnapping and torture of Abu Omar, a Muslim cleric, the first criminal court case to arise from the CIA's controversial extraordinary rendition programme; the start of the trial was later adjourned until October. In Turkey, a court sentenced seven members of an al-Qaida cell to life imprisonment for plotting a series of suicide bombings in Istanbul which killed 58 people in 2003. **21.** The Italian prime minister Romano Prodi resigned after losing a key parliamentary vote on his commitment of foreign troops to Afghanistan; he was reinstated following President Giorgio Napolitano's refusal to accept his resignation on 28 February. **26.** The international court of justice rejected claims that Serbia was guilty of genocide in Bosnia, but ruled that the country had violated its obligation to prevent the 1995 Srebrenica massacre and bring those responsible to justice.

MARCH 2007

1. The Spanish government announced that Iñaki de Juana Chaos, a member of the ETA terrorist group, who was convicted of killing 25 people in 1987, was to be released to serve the remaining year of his sentence under police guard at home; tens of thousands of people marched in protest at the decision in Madrid on 11 March. **2.** Estonia became the first country to allow voters in a general election to cast their ballots online; the centre-right Reform Party of Prime Minister Andrus Ansip extended its majority. Ramzan Kadyrov was appointed president of the separatist republic of Chechnya. **4.** Over 600 people were arrested in Copenhagen, Denmark, following rioting against the eviction of anti-capitalist squatters from a building in the city, which was demolished the next day. Georgian president Mikhail Saakashvili dismissed elections held in the rebel Abkhazia region on 4 March as illegal, despite a strong turnout. **9.** All 27 EU countries agreed to cut greenhouse gas emissions by a fifth and generate 20 per cent of energy through renewable sources by 2020. **15.** Russia, Bulgaria and Greece announced plans for a new $1.2bn (£619m) oil pipeline, enabling Russian oil to reach the EU directly for the first time. **19.** In Russia, 108 miners died in a methane gas explosion in a Siberian coal mine, while another 62 people died in a fire at an old people's home in the Krasnodar region. **20.** A Polish woman was awarded damages after the European court of human rights ruled that Poland was in violation of a Council of Europe statute that requires guaranteed access to lawful abortions. **23.** The Russian supreme court liquidated the Republican and National Bolshevik parties, two of the few opposition parties remaining in the country, on the grounds that they violated electoral law by having too few members. **25.** Andranik Markarian, the prime minister of Armenia since 2000, died of heart failure; Serzh Sarkisian was confirmed as his successor on 4 April. European leaders celebrated 50 years since the inception of the EU.

APRIL 2007

2. In Ukraine, President Viktor Yushchenko signed a decree dissolving parliament and calling for new elections on 27 May; the decree was rejected by Yushchenko's main political rival, Prime Minister Viktor Yanukovych. **7.** A Slovenian man became the first person to swim the length of the Amazon river; the 5,265km (3,272 mile) journey took Martin Strel 66 days. **10.** A Serbian tribunal sentenced four members of the Scorpions – a paramilitary police unit – to between five and 20 years in prison for the killings of six Bosnian Muslims at the time of the Srebrenica genocide of 1995. **12.** Russia's chief public health officer revealed that the country's alcohol consumption per head had tripled since 1991. The government in Bosnia and Hercegovina stripped almost 400 people of their citizenship in a bid to crack down on foreign fighters who settled in the country after the wars of the 1990s. **14.** Former world chess champion Garry Kasparov was among 170 people arrested by police in Moscow following a pro-democracy demonstration. **19.** The Romanian parliament voted to suspend President Basescu amid accusations of spying on fellow politicians and blackmailing the judiciary; a public referendum on 19 May overwhelmingly rejected the chance to impeach him. Russia announced plans to build the world's longest tunnel under the Bering Strait as part of a large transport network connecting Europe and America via Siberia and Alaska. EU interior ministers agreed to make incitement-to-racism an EU-wide crime, but stopped short of banning all forms of Holocaust denial. **20.** Norway declared its intention to become the first carbon neutral country in the world by 2050. **23.** Boris Yeltsin, Russia's first democratically elected leader, died from heart failure aged 76. **26.** A diplomatic row broke out between Russia and Estonia after the Baltic country removed a statue in Tallinn commemorating the Red Army soldiers who died defending the country from the Nazis; subsequent clashes between ethnic Russians and police injured 100 people. Eighteen Russian soldiers and air crew died when their helicopter was shot down by insurgents in Chechnya. **29.** An estimated 700,000 people gathered in Istanbul, Turkey, to demand the government withdraw foreign minister Abdullah Gul as its presidential candidate because of his Islamist leanings; Gul abandoned his bid on 6 May.

MAY 2007

6. Nicholas Sarkozy was elected as president of France after victory in a second-round run-off with Ségolène Royal in which he received 53 per cent of the vote; thousands of people in several French cities rioted in protest. **11.** After months of negotiations, Serbia's nationalist prime minister Vojislav Kostunica and pro-western president Boris Tadic reached an agreement to form a coalition government. **13.** One-and-a-half million secular Turks gathered in the city of Izmir to protest at the perceived Islamisation of the country. **16.** Estonia's infrastructure experienced a wave of cyber-attacks in the wake of the diplomatic breakdown with Russia (*see* 27 April); hackers disabled the websites of the president, parliament, news organisations and banks. The Russian government announced a deal to supply Myanmar with its first nuclear reactor, despite the country remaining under international sanctions. **17.** The French president Nicholas Sarkozy appointed the former social affairs minister François Fillon as prime minister; other members of his politically mixed 15-member cabinet include Bernard Kouchner, the founder of Médecins sans Frontières and seven women. **18.** Garry Kasparov was one of 27 people banned by the Russian government from flying to Samara, the site of an EU-Russia summit. **20.** Eight reporters from a state-controlled Russian news service resigned en masse in protest against censorship from the Kremlin; new rules stated that they could not mention opposition leaders and were to ensure 50 per cent of news was 'positive'. **23.** A Serbian court found 12 men guilty of assassinating former prime minister Zoran Djindjic in 2003, they were jailed for between eight and 40 years. **24.** Thirty-eight people were killed by a methane blast in a Russian mine in Siberia. Bertie Ahern secured a third term as taoiseach in the Republic of Ireland; his Fianna Fail party remained the largest in parliament, but without an overall majority. **27.** The political stand-off in Ukraine between President Yushchenko and his prime minister, Viktor Yanukovych, ended with an agreement to hold parliamentary elections on 30 September. **29.** Russia unveiled a new intercontinental missile capable of breaching American defences.

JUNE 2007

1. Finland became the latest European country to introduce a smoking ban in public places. **2.** Rioting in Rostock, Germany, ahead of the G8 summit injured more than 1,000 people. **5.** ETA, the Spanish separatist group, announced an official end to the ceasefire, in place since March 2006, and blamed the government for the failed peace process. Austria became the first EU country to let 16-year-olds vote in national elections. **6.** After a 20-month trial in Rome, Italy, five people accused of conspiring to kill Roberto Calvi, an Italian banker murdered in London in 1982, were all acquitted. **8.** G8 leaders in Heiligendamm, Germany, pledged £30bn to tackle AIDS, malaria and tuberculosis in Africa. **12.** EU member states agreed to merge much of their criminal databases to give police automatic access to information such as DNA, fingerprints and car registrations anywhere within the union. A former policeman who led the Serbian insurgency in Croatia during the 1991–5 war was found guilty of 16 counts of war crimes during a trial at the Hague; Milan Martic was sentenced to 35 years in prison. **17.** In the French parliamentary elections, President Nicholas Sarkozy's UMP party failed to gain a widely predicted landslide victory, but still won 313 of the 577 seats to the Socialist Party's 185; his reshuffled cabinet also included the country's first female chancellor, Christine Lagarde.

JULY 2007

4. Sergei Ivanov, Russia's first deputy prime minister, said that the country could deploy missiles in the Kaliningrad area, in retaliation to US plans to install a missile defence shield in Eastern Europe. **10.** Cyprus and Malta gained approval from the International Monetary Fund to join the euro on 1 January 2008. **12.** The headquarters of a Swiss assisted-suicide organisation, where over 700 people died in its nine-year existence, was closed following a protest by local residents. **15.** Spanish police working with Interpol arrested 66 people in a child pornography operation and seized computers containing 48 million images and videos. **18.** Tuncay Seyranlioglu, a Turk running in the country's general election as an independent candidate, was shot dead in Istanbul. **19.** Former French president Jacques Chirac, now stripped of immunity, was quizzed by a judge over claims that, while mayor of Paris, he siphoned money from the city budget to pay workers at his political party. More than 50 African migrants travelling to Europe drowned off of the coast of Spain as their boat capsized. **22.** At least 26 people died in the French Alps when a coach carrying Polish pilgrims missed a tight bend and fell 40m (130ft) from a bridge. Turkey's incumbent prime minister Recep Erdogan won a second term in the country's general election, despite fears he would gradually introduce Islamisation into the country; his AK party won 46.9 per cent of the vote. **24.** Areas of Europe's Balkan peninsula experienced their highest temperatures for 120 years; the heatwave reached 43°C in Serbia, 44°C in Bulgaria and 45°C in Bosnia and Macedonia, while 500 heat-related deaths were reported in Hungary.

MIDDLE EAST

AUGUST 2006

1. A NATO-led force took military control of Afghanistan from the USA. **3.** A car bomb killed 21 people at a market in Panjwayi, southern Afghanistan. **4.** An Israeli airstrike on a farm in the Bekaa Valley region of Lebanon killed 33 people; in Israel, eight civilians and three soldiers were killed following Hezbollah missile strikes. More than 100,000 people gathered in Baghdad, Iraq, to show their support for Hezbollah in its conflict with Israel. **6.** Twelve Israeli soldiers were killed in a Hezbollah rocket attack on a kibbutz in northern Israel, while 16 Lebanese soldiers were killed by Israeli airstrikes; a further 15 were killed in Beirut the following day. **11.** The UN security council passed a draft resolution calling for the immediate cessation of hostilities between Israel and Hezbollah fighters in Lebanon and proposed that Israeli troops should withdraw from southern Lebanon to be replaced by a multinational UN peacekeeping force. **13.** Iraqi forces took full control of a province from foreign troops for the first time; the Muthana province in the south was largely untroubled by violence. **14.** Two days of continued fighting before the implementation of UN-brokered ceasefire killed 51 Israeli and Lebanese soldiers. **21.** A second trial against former Iraqi president Saddam Hussein, relating to the Anfal campaign of 1988-90, began in Baghdad. In Egypt, 51 people were killed and over 140 injured when two trains collided north of Cairo. **22.** In Israel, police raided the home of the president, Moshe Katsav, as part of an ongoing sexual harassment case against him. **27.** At least 34 people died in gun battles between Iraqi security troops and Mahdi militiamen in the town of Diwaniya. **30.** Naguib Mahfouz, the only Arab writer to win the Nobel prize for literature, died in Cairo aged 94. **31.** Representatives from 51 countries met in Stockholm, Sweden, and pledged \$940m (£475m) to finance relief efforts in Lebanon.

SEPTEMBER 2006

1. In Iran, 29 people were killed when a passenger jet crash-landed in the north-eastern city of Mashhad. **8.** The Israeli government lifted the air and sea blockade of Lebanon, handing control to a UN military force. **11.** Palestinian president Mahmoud Abbas announced an agreement with governing party Hamas to form a national unity government. The Iranian government banned a leading reformist newspaper following the publication of a cartoon that depicted President Ahmadinejad as a braying donkey. **12.** In Yemen, around 51 people were killed during a pre-election rally in the southern province of Ibb; the presidential election, held on 20 September, was won by incumbent president Ali Abdallah Saleh with 77 per cent of the vote. The chief judge in charge of the trial against Saddam Hussein was sacked by the Iraqi government for allegedly showing bias towards the former dictator. **13.** Over 100 members of Iraq's council of representatives signed a resolution demanding a timetable for the withdrawal of foreign troops. **17.** Six bombs in the Iraqi town of Kirkuk killed 24 people. **22.** Hezbollah held a rally of 500,000 people in Beirut to celebrate victory over Israel.

OCTOBER 2006

1. Gun battles between rival Palestinian factions Hamas and Fatah in the Gaza Strip killed eight people in the most intense fighting since January. Israel withdrew the last of its troops from Lebanon in accordance with the terms of the ceasefire signed in August. **4.** Palestinian president Mahmoud Abbas abandoned plans to include Hamas in a national unity coalition following four days of violence. **5.** NATO formally assumed military control of the east of Afghanistan from the US-led alliance. The government of Iraq suspended 700 policemen for suspected complicity with death squads operating in Baghdad. **11.** A controversial bill was passed in Iraq allowing the country's 18 provinces to hold referendums on amalgamating into federal regions; critics argued the law would hasten the disintegration of the country on sectarian lines. **15.** Three days of Israeli assaults on the Gaza Strip, launched in response to the kidnap of an Israeli soldier, killed 23 Palestinians. **17.** The Iraqi government sacked around 3,000 police officers after accusing them of human rights abuses, corruption and complicity with insurgents and local militia forces. **24.** A NATO bombing raid on the Kandahar province of Afghanistan killed 85 civilians, causing the organisation's supreme commander, General James Jones, to issue a public apology. **30.** In Iraq, 33 people were killed in a bomb attack in a Shia area of Baghdad.

NOVEMBER 2006

1. Israeli tanks and Apache helicopters launched a six-day operation into the Gaza town of Beit Hanoun in which over 50 Palestinians, including 16 civilians, were killed. **3.** The International Atomic Energy Agency announced that Algeria, Egypt, Morocco, Saudi Arabia, Tunisia and the United Arab Emirates had declared interest in embarking on civilian nuclear energy programmes. **5.** Saddam Hussein, the former Iraqi dictator on trial for crimes against humanity, was sentenced to death by hanging. **8.** Israeli tank fire killed 18 Palestinians in Beit Hanoun. At least 30 people died in renewed violence across Iraq, following the lifting of a curfew imposed for the sentencing of Saddam Hussein. **12.** In Baghdad, two suicide bombers killed 35 people and wounded over 60 others at a police recruiting centre. All five Shia Muslim ministers, including two from Hezbollah, resigned from the Lebanese cabinet after power-sharing talks ended. **19.** Israel called off a planned air strike on a house in the Gaza refugee camp of Jabaliya after hundreds of Palestinians formed a human shield around it. In Iraq, a suicide bomber killed 22 people and injured over 40 more in the town of Hilla. **21.** Pierre Gemayel, a Lebanese government minister, was assassinated in Beirut. Syria and Iraq agreed to restore diplomatic relations, which had been suspended since 1982. **23.** In Iraq, three car bombs exploded in the Shia Muslim district of Sadr City in Baghdad, killing at least 215 people and injuring over 250 others; 31 people died on 24 November following arson attacks on four Sunni mosques. **26.** The Palestinian Authority and Israel announced a ceasefire. **27.** Thirty-six people were killed when an Iranian military aircraft crashed while taking off from an airport in Tehran.

DECEMBER 2006

1. In Lebanon, an estimated 800,000 pro-Syrian and pro-Hezbollah protesters gathered in central Beirut to call for the government's resignation; another similar-sized demonstration took place on 10 December. **2.** More than 50 people were killed after three car bombs exploded in the centre of Baghdad. **3.** NATO forces in southern Afghanistan killed about 70 Taliban fighters following an ambush; troops fought a four-hour battle after a large-scale insurgent attack near the town of Musa Qala in the Helmand Province. **12.** At least 70 Shia labourers were killed, and over 230 injured, when a suicide bomber detonated a truck filled with explosives in Baghdad. **14.** The supreme court in Israel ruled that the targeted executions of Palestinian militants should not be banned. **16.** Armed supporters of Fatah and Hamas exchanged gunfire in the southern Gaza Strip; sporadic clashes continued until 19 December. **23.** In Afghanistan, Taliban commander Mullah Akhtar Mohammed Osmani was killed by a US airstrike, ending a five-year manhunt. **25.** British soldiers captured and destroyed an Iraqi police unit headquarters, releasing 100 prisoners who had allegedly been tortured and were awaiting execution. **26.** Three car-bomb blasts killed 47 people in Baghdad. **27.** Saddam Hussein lost his appeal against execution; he was hanged on 30 December at a secure facility in a northern Baghdad suburb. Israel announced it would resume retaliation against rocket attacks by Palestinian militants, but insisted it remained committed to the ceasefire announced on 26 November. **31.** Gunmen took to the streets of Saddam Hussein's hometown of Tikrit, Iraq, in response to his death.

JANUARY 2007

9. Fierce fighting in the centre of Baghdad killed around 50 Sunni insurgents. **15.** Two of Saddam Hussein's aides, his half-brother Barzan al-Tikriti and judge Awad Hamad al-Bandar, were hanged in Baghdad. **16.** In Iraq, more than 85 people were killed by two bombs that exploded outside Baghdad's al-Mustansiriya university. **17.** In Israel, the head of the armed forces, Lieutenant-General Dan Halutz, resigned amid inquiries into the 2006 conflict with Hezbollah in southern Lebanon. **22.** A double bomb blast in a Baghdad marketplace killed 88 people. **23.** The justice ministry of Israel announced that President Moshe Katsav would be charged with rape and abuse of power following a string of allegations made against him in 2006; he took a leave of absence to fight the charges the following day. In Lebanon, opposition supporters enforced a nationwide general strike in an attempt to destabilise the government of Prime Minister Fouad Siniora. **26.** The US national security council announced new rules of engagement to kill or capture members of the Iranian Revolutionary Guard operating in Iraq. **28.** Over 300 people died following a day-long battle between US and Iraqi forces and a Shi'ite millenarian cult on the outskirts of Najaf. A bomb exploded in Ramadi, west of Baghdad, killing 16 people; it contained chlorine, the first use of makeshift chemical weapons recorded during the current Iraq conflict. In Kuwait, Sheikh Salem al-Ali, dean of the ruling family, donated 100m dinars (£170m) to charities representing the poor and the families of those killed defending the country. Ghaleb Majadleh became the first Muslim government minister in Israel's history. In Gaza City, 25 people were killed after three days of violence between Hamas and Fatah, prompted by an explosion which killed a Hamas official. **29.** Three people died in Eilat, Israel, after a Palestinian suicide bomber blew himself up, the first attack of its kind in the country for eight months; a ceasefire between Fatah and Hamas was announced the following day. **30.** Thirty-six Iraqi pilgrims commemorating Ashura, the holiest day in the Shia calendar, were killed by bomb and gun attacks in Karbala.

FEBRUARY 2007

1. Two suicide bombers killed 45 people in the Shia city of Hilla, Iraq. In Afghanistan, parliament approved a bill offering immunity to anyone who fought against the Soviet Army in the 1980s; the bill will become law if approved by President Karzai and the Upper House. **2.** Musa Qala, a town in Afghanistan abandoned by British troops in September after a peace deal had been signed with local elders, was stormed by the Taliban; the leader of the insurrection, Mullah Ghafour, was killed by a NATO airstrike on 4 February. **3.** A suicide truck bomber killed 135 people at a food market in a Shia area of Baghdad. **4.** Gunmen dressed in Iraqi army uniforms kidnapped Jalal Sharafi, an Iranian diplomat, in Baghdad; the Iranian government suggested that the attack was conducted under US supervision; Sharafi was released on 3 April and claimed he had been repeatedly tortured by US CIA agents. **7.** A confrontation between the army and the al-Huthi militant group in Yemen killed 42 soldiers. **8.** The Iraqi deputy health minister Hakim al-Zamili was arrested on suspicion of aiding death-squads and passing millions of dollars of government funds to cleric Moqtada al-Sadr's Mahdi militia. Rival Palestinian factions Fatah and Hamas signed a deal agreeing to form a national unity government. **12.** More than 70 people died after three bombs exploded in marketplaces in Baghdad. **14.** In Beirut, Lebanon, 300,000 people took part in a rally to mark the second anniversary of the death of former prime minister Rafik Hariri, who was killed in a car bomb attack. **16.** A boat carrying Somali and Ethiopian migrants to Yemen capsized in the Gulf of Aden, drowning at least 107 people. **17.** A UN report revealed that Syria and Libya transported and trained suspected al-Qaida recruits to fight for the Islamic Courts Union, which deposed the government of Somalia in 2006. **18.** A twin car bombing in Baghdad killed at least 60 people. In Afghanistan, eight US soldiers were killed when their helicopter crashed due to engine failure. **22.** In Egypt, a law student was jailed for four years on charges of incitement, insulting the president and disrupting public order after posting controversial views on his blog. **25.** A suicide bomber killed 40 people at a Baghdad business college. **27.** A suicide bomber in Afghanistan killed 22 people at a US military base during a visit by vice-president Dick Cheney.

MARCH 2007

4. The Kuwaiti cabinet resigned to avoid a no-confidence vote against a senior minister, despite only holding office for eight months. A NATO airstrike killed nine members of a family in Afghanistan when two bombs hit their home. **6.** A twin suicide bombing in Hilla, south of Baghdad, killed 118 people. The UAE's tourist board announced it would pay €400m (£272m) to the Louvre for the use of its brand and the loan of some of its works for its Universal Museum in Abu Dhabi. **7.** A further 55 people were killed in bomb and shooting attacks in Iraq, including 30 who died after a suicide bomber attacked a restaurant in the town of Baladrouz. **20.** Taha Yasin Ramadan al-Jizrawi, Saddam Hussein's vice-president in Iraq, was hanged for his part in the killing of 143 people in Dujali in 1982. The Afghan government admitted that it released five Taliban militants from prison in exchange for Daniele Mastrogiacomo, an Italian journalist taken hostage. **21.** US commanders in Baghdad announced that two children had died whilst acting as decoys to allow a car bomb to pass through a US checkpoint, the first reported incident of children used in this manner. **22.** A live television broadcast in Baghdad by the UN secretary-general Ban Ki-moon was interrupted by a rocket landing 100m away from the building. **23.** Iraq's deputy prime minister Salam al-Zubaie was wounded when he was hit by several shards of shrapnel from a bomb attack at a prayer hall which killed nine people. **26.** In Egypt, 75.9 per cent of the voters in a referendum approved a series of constitutional changes which attracted widespread criticism for allegedly limiting democracy. **27.** Gunmen killed 40 Sunnis in the Iraqi town of Tall 'Afar in a revenge attack following the deaths of 63 Shias in a double truck bombing earlier in the day. **29.** Violence continued to escalate in Iraq as more than 110 people died after a number of suicide bomb attacks. Following a summit of the Arab League in Saudi Arabia, Palestinian president Mahmoud Abbas presented a land-for-peace deal to Israel, guaranteeing the resumption of normal relations if the country withdraws from all occupied territories and recognises Palestinian statehood; a similar deal was rejected five years ago by the then-prime minister, Ariel Sharon.

APRIL 2007

2. A suicide bomber killed 12 people when he detonated a truck laden with explosives outside a primary school in Kirkuk, Iraq; another 27 people died at a police checkpoint near Ramadi in a similar incident on 6 April. **7.** Australian prime minister John Howard announced that the country would double its number of troops in Afghanistan by the middle of 2008 to combat renewed Taliban insurgencies. **9.** An estimated 100,000 Iraqi Shias protested in Najaf against the occupation of the country by coalition forces. **10.** The US military in Baghdad started building a 4.8km (3 mile) long concrete wall around the largest remaining Sunni enclave in the city in a bid to prevent further clashes with Shias, despite opposition from the Iraqi government. A court in Jordan sentenced six men to between 40 months and five years in prison for conspiring to carry out terrorist attacks in coordination with al-Qaida, including an attack on the airport in the capital, Amman. **12.** A suicide bomber evaded security checks and blew himself up in the cafe of the Iraqi parliament building in the heart of the city's Green Zone, killing one person. A truck bomb partially destroyed the Sarafiya bridge in Baghdad, killing ten people and sending several vehicles into the River Tigris below. **14.** A car bomb outside a bus station in the Iraqi city of Karbala killed at least 65 people. **16.** Six Iraqi cabinet members resigned from the country's national unity government after Prime Minister Nouri al-Maliki refused to commit to a timetable for the withdrawal of foreign troops. **18.** A string of suicide bombings killed almost 200 people in Baghdad; in the worst of the attacks 122 died when a car bomb exploded in a Shia marketplace. **23.** Nine US soldiers died in a suicide bomb blast on a military base north of Baghdad, the deadliest attack on US troops for 18 months. **24.** Hamas announced a sudden end to their ceasefire with Israel by firing a series of rockets as Israelis celebrated their independence day. **27.** In Saudi Arabia, 172 suspected terrorists linked to al-Qaida were arrested; on the same day, Abd al-Hadi al-Iraqi, a former member of Saddam Hussein's army and a key figure in al-Qaida, was captured by US forces as he tried to enter Iraq and was transferred to Guantanamo Bay. **28.** A car bomb killed 60 people in Karbala, Iraq. **30.** NATO coalition forces in Afghanistan killed 136 Taliban militants in the Helmand province in a bid to secure the country's most volatile area. A suicide bomb at a Shia funeral in Khalis, Iraq, killed 30 people.

MAY 2007

3. Over 100,000 protesters filled Rabin Square in Tel Aviv, Israel, demanding the resignation of Prime Minister Ehud Olmert, following the publication of a government report criticising his handling of the war with Lebanon. **4.** US soldiers in Iraq discovered that a girls school under construction near Baghdad had been rigged with explosives; artillery shells were built into walls and giant propane tanks hidden under the floors. **9.** A US airstrike in southern Afghanistan killed 21 civilians, while further skirmishes on 12 May killed the Taliban's leading military commander, Mullah Dadullah. **13.** More than 50 people were killed in the north of Iraq when a suicide truck bomber crashed into the offices of a Kurdish political party. **14.** Hani al-Qawasmi, the Palestinian interior minister, resigned as street fighting between Hamas and Fatah returned to Gaza, killing nine people; another 16 died on 16 May. A chlorine bomb killed 45 people in the Iraqi town of Abu Sayda. **17.** Israel launched three air strikes against Hamas targets in Gaza. **20.** The Lebanese army attacked a refugee camp used as a base by Fatah, causing at least 40 deaths and forcing thousands of people to flee. **21.** Sheikh Mohammed bin Rashid al-Maktoum, the prime minister of the UAE, launched a charitable foundation with an endowment of $10bn (£5bn) to raise standards of education in the Middle East. **23.** Iranian president Mahmoud Ahmadinejad announced plans to introduce petrol rationing – despite the country being the world's third-largest petrol exporter – to reduce the economic burden of providing subsidised fuel; drivers will be limited to 100 litres a month. **28.** In Baghdad, diplomats from Iran and the USA met officially for the first time in almost 30 years. **29.** President Assad of Syria won a second seven-year term in a poll in which he was the only candidate.

JUNE 2007

2. Around 60 people, including members of the Taliban, died in the Helmand province of Afghanistan when their boat sank. **7.** Forty-nine people were killed by Cyclone Gonu in Oman. **10.** Afghan president Hamid Karzai survived a Taliban assassination attempt as he gave a speech in the Ghazni province; witnesses saw between three and six rockets land 150m from the president. **12.** Eight Afghan policemen were killed by an airstrike after US troops mistook them for members of the Taliban. **13.** Four days of gun battles between Hamas and Fatah killed 65 people in Gaza City. Shimon Peres, an 83-year-old veteran, was elected president of Israel after two secret ballots by MPs. Walid Eido, an anti-Syrian Lebanese MP, was among ten people killed by a car bomb in Beirut. Political and religious leaders from across Iraq condemned the destruction of two minarets at a sacred Shia shrine in Samarra by suspected Sunni militants. **14.** Hamas militants captured the whole of Gaza from their Fatah rivals and declared Islamic rule; Mahmoud Abbas, the Palestinian president, announced a state of emergency and dissolved the national unity government. Salam Fayyad, the former finance minister and a political independent, was appointed as prime minister the following day. **17.** A suicide bomber killed 35 people – including a number of police recruits – in Kabul, Afghanistan. **18.** The USA responded to Palestinian president Mahmoud Abbas' sacking of the Hamas-led government by lifting the economic and political embargo on the Palestinian National Authority and pledging $40m (£20m) of humanitarian aid to the Gaza and West Bank areas. Seven children died when coalition jets bombed a religious school in south-east Afghanistan. **19.** At least 75 people were killed by a truck bomb at a Shia mosque in the centre of Baghdad. The US military announced the beginning of a major operation involving 10,000 American and Iraqi soldiers against al-Qaida militants based north of Baghdad. **24.** Ali Hassan al-Majid, Saddam Hussein's cousin and cohort and the man dubbed 'Chemical Ali' by the West, was sentenced to death by an Iraqi tribunal for his role in the genocide against the Kurds in the 1980s. Ehud Olmert, the Israeli prime minister, agreed to free £175m in tax revenues to Palestine – withheld during 2006 because of the Hamas presence in the government – to stiffen the Fatah-led administration of Mahmoud Abbas in the West Bank. **26.** A UN report warned that the Helmand province of Afghanistan is on the verge of becoming the world's largest drugs supplier, with a substantial opium poppy harvest expected in 2007. **27.** A dozen petrol stations were set alight by protesters in Tehran, Iran, amid anger at President Ahmedinejad's fuel rationing policy (*see* 23 May). **28.** The president of Israel, Moshe Katsav, who had been under investigation for sex crimes (*see* 23 January), struck a plea bargain with prosecutors; under the agreement he resigned and pleaded guilty to charges of sexual harassment and abuse of authority in return for avoiding a prison sentence for rape. Floods caused by days of heavy rain in eastern Afghanistan killed 56 people. **28.** Egypt banned all forms of female circumcision after a 12-year-old girl died during the procedure.

JULY 2007

5. Forty-five Afghan civilians were killed in a NATO-led airstrike in the Helmand province. **7.** In the town of Tuz Khurmatu in northern Iraq, 105 people were killed as a truck bomb detonated in an outdoor market. **8.** Israel agreed to release 250 Fatah prisoners in a goodwill gesture towards Palestinian president Mahmoud Abbas' emergency government in the West Bank. The recent upsurge of violence in Iraq continued with the death of 23 army recruits in Haswa after a suicide truck bomb attack. **11.** Hamas members failed to attend a meeting of the Palestinian parliament called by Mahmoud Abbas, preventing the ratification of the emergency government appointed by Abbas in June. **16.** In Iraq, three bomb blasts in Kirkuk killed 85 people. **17.** Taliban militants operating in Afghanistan kidnapped 23 South Korean Christian aid workers; two of the hostages were killed by 30 July after the Afghan government failed to comply with the captors' deadlines for the release of Taliban members from the country's prisons. **21.** The half-completed Burj Dubai tower in the UAE became the world's tallest building at 512m (1,680ft), surpassing the Taipei 101 Tower in Taiwan (509m, 1,670ft); its eventual height is expected to be over 643m (2,111ft). **22.** Hamas announced their willingness to meet with former British prime minister Tony Blair in his new role as the international community's Middle East peace envoy. **23.** Zahir Shah, the former king of Afghanistan, died at the age of 92. **24.** A suicide bomber killed at least 22 people in the Iraqi market town of Hilla. **25.** Around 50 people died when two car bombs exploded in a Baghdad suburb as Iraqis celebrated their national football team's progress to the final of the Asian Cup. Foreign ministers from Jordan and Egypt proposed Arab League plans for an independent Palestinian state with Israeli representatives; under the deal all Arab nations would offer diplomatic recognition to Israel in exchange for the establishment of an independent Palestine in the occupied territories. **26.** Following recent developments, Palestinian president Mahmoud Abbas said he hoped to reach a final peace deal with Israel within a year. **30.** A damning report by Oxfam revealed that almost a third of Iraqis are in need of emergency aid and highlighted the government's failure to provide basic food and shelter amid conditions that have worsened since the 2003 invasion. **31.** US secretary of state Condoleezza Rice proposed a $63bn (£31bn) arms package to its Middle Eastern allies in an attempt to firm up opposition against Iran.

OBITUARIES

Akehurst, Gen. Sir John, KCB, CBE, Deputy Supreme Allied Commander, NATO Europe (1987–90), aged 77 – *d.* 20 February 2007, *b.* 12 February 1930

Altman, Robert, American film director, aged 81 – *d.* 20 November 2006, *b.* 20 February 1925

Andrews, Lucilla, novelist, aged 86 – *d.* 3 October 2006, *b.* 21 November 1919

Arnold, Sir Malcolm, composer, aged 84 – *d.* 23 September 2006, *b.* 21 October 1921

Backus, John, American computer programmer and mathematician, developed the Fortran programming language in the 1950s, aged 82 – *d.* 17 March 2007, *b.* 3 December 1924

Baird, Lt.-Gen. Sir James, KBE, director-general of the Army Medical Services (1973–7), aged 92 – *d.* 26 May 2007, *b.* 12 May 1915

Ball, Alan, MBE, footballer, aged 61 – *d.* 24 April 2007, *b.* 12 May 1945

Barbera, Joseph, American animator, formed one half of Hanna-Barbera Productions, aged 95 – *d.* 18 December 2006, *b.* 24 March 1911

Baudrillard, Jean, French postmodern cultural theorist, aged 77 – *d.* 6 March 2007, *b.* 20 June 1929

Baxter, Raymond, OBE, broadcaster and presenter of BBC television's popular science programme *Tomorrow's World* (1965–77), aged 84 – *d.* 15 September 2006, *b.* 25 January 1922

Benedict, Ed, American animator responsible for, amongst others, the original drawings of *The Flintstones* and *Yogi Bear*, aged 94 – *d.* 28 August 2006, *b.* 23 August 1912

Bennett-Coverley, Louise, MBE, Jamaican folk poet, comedian and entertainer, aged 86 – *d.* 26 July 2006, *b.* 7 September 1919

Bergman, Ingmar, Swedish film and theatre director, aged 89 – *d.* 30 July 2007, *b.* 14 July 1918

Bergne, Paul, CBE, Secret Intelligence Service officer (1959–92), diplomat (1992–6), linguist, scholar and broadcaster, aged 70 – *d.* 5 April 2007, *b.* 9 January 1937

Berthon, Vice-Adm. Sir Stephen, KCB, Deputy Chief of Defence Staff (Operational Requirements) (1978–91), aged 84 – *d.* 31 January 2007, *b.* 24 August 1922

Blow, Isabella, fashion journalist and stylist, aged 48 – *d.* 7 May 2007, *b.* 19 November 1958

Blow, Sandra, artist, aged 80 – *d.* 22 August 2006, *b.* 14 September 1925

Bracewell, Dame Joyanne, DBE, high court judge (1990–2006), aged 72 – *d.* 9 January 2007, *b.* 5 July 1934

Brecker, Michael, American jazz saxophonist, aged 57 – *d.* 13 January 2007, *b.* 29 March 1949

Bridge, Lt.-Cdr John, GC, GM and Bar, Second World War bomb-disposal officer, aged 91 – *d.* 14 December 2006, *b.* 5 February 1915

Brown, James, American soul singer, aged 78 – *d.* 25 December 2006, *b.* 3 May 1928

Browne-Evans, Dame Lois, DBE, lawyer and Bermudan politician, aged 79 – *d.* 29 May 2007, *b.* 1 June 1927

Bury, Capt. John, Master Mariner and Elder Brother of Trinity House, aged 91 – *d.* 17 October 2006, *b.* 28 July 1915

Butcher, John, Conservative MP for West Midlands (1979–97), aged 60 – *d.* 25 December 2006, *b.* 13 February 1946

Carter, Lord, PC, politician, farmer and campaigner for the disabled, aged 74 – *d.* 18 December 2006, *b.* 17 January 1932

Claiborne, Liz, Belgian-born American fashion designer, aged 78 – *d.* 26 June 2007, *b.* 31 March 1929

Clarke, Nick, journalist and presenter of the BBC news programme *The World at One* (1994–2006), aged 58 – *d.* 23 November 2006, *b.* 9 June 1948

Clarke, Peter, Children's Commissioner for Wales (2001–7), aged 58 – *d.* 21 January 2007, *b.* 7 October 1948

Clay, Dame Marie, DBE, educationist, aged 81 – *d.* 13 April 2007, *b.* 3 January 1926

Cockfield, Lord, PC, vice-president of the Commission of the European Communities (1985–8), aged 90 – *d.* 8 January 2007, *b.* 28 September 1916

Cooke of Thorndon, Lord, PC, New Zealand jurist and member of the British House of Lords since 1996, aged 80 – *d.* 30 August 2006, *b.* 9 May 1926

Corner, Dr Beryl, paediatrician, set up the UK's first special care baby unit at Southmead Hospital, Bristol, in 1946, aged 96 – *d.* 4 March 2007, *b.* 9 December 1910

Courtin-Clarins, Jacques, French beauty products entrepreneur, aged 85 – *d.* 23 March 2007, *b.* 6 August 1921

Cox, Vice-Adm. Sir John, KCB, Flag Officer Naval Air Command (1982–3), on retirement from the navy, director of the Spastics Society (later re-named as SCOPE) (1983–8), aged 77 – *d.* 3 October 2006, *b.* 27 October 1928

Cramphorn, Colin, QPM, chief constable of West Yorkshire Police (2002–6), aged 50 – *d.* 30 November 2006, *b.* 1 April 1956

Cronin, Jim, MBE, founder of the Monkey World sanctuary in Dorset who campaigned against the illegal trade in primates, aged 55 – *d.* 17 March 2007, *b.* 15 November 1951

Davies, Sir Michael, high court judge (1973–91), aged 85 – *d.* 5 September 2006, *b.* 29 July 1921

Denison, John, CBE, director of the Arts Council (1948–65) and the South Bank concert halls (1965–76), aged 95 – *d.* 31 December 2006, *b.* 21 January 1911

Dewhurst, Sir John, Professor of Obstetrics and Gynaecology, University of London, Queen Charlotte's Hospital for Women (1967–85), aged 86 – *d.* 1 December 2006, *b.* 2 July 1920

Diggory, Elizabeth, High Mistress of St Paul's Girls' School (1998–2006), aged 61 – *d.* 18 March 2007, *b.* 22 December 1945

Dodds-Parker, Sir Douglas, Conservative MP for Banbury (1945–59) and Cheltenham (1964–74), Parliamentary Under-Secretary of State for Foreign

Affairs (1953–4, 1955–7) and for the Commonwealth Relations Office (1954–5), aged 97 – *d.* 13 September 2006, *b.* 5 July 1909

Douglas, Prof. Dame Mary, DBE, anthropologist, aged 86 – *d.* 16 May 2007, *b.* 25 March 1921

Drummond, Sir John, CBE, broadcaster and director of the Edinburgh Festival (1979–83), aged 71 – *d.* 6 September 2006, *b.* 25 November 1934

Duvall, Richard, co-founder of Egg bank, aged 44 – *d.* 16 October 2006, *b.* 24 January 1962

Emery, Eleanor, CMG, high commissioner to Botswana (1973–7), aged 88 – *d.* 22 June 2007, *b.* 23 December 1918

Engel, Andi, founder of *Artificial Eye* film distributor, aged 64 – *d.* 26 December 2006, *b.* 11 November 1942

Evans, Sir Vincent, GCMG, MBE, QC, judge at the European court of human rights (1980–91), aged 91 – *d.* 18 May 2007, *b.* 20 October 1915

Ewing of Kirkford, Lord, Labour MP for Stirling and Falkirk (1971–4), Stirling, Falkirk and Grangemouth (1974–83) and Falkirk East (1983–92), Scottish Office Parliamentary Under-Secretary of State with responsibility for devolution (1974–9), aged 76 – *d.* 9 June 2007, *b.* 20 January 1931

Fabro, Luciano, Italian artist, aged 70 – *d.* 23 June 2007, *b.* 20 November 1936

Farrow, Kenneth, GC, police officer, aged 82 – *d.* 30 March 2007, *b.* 29 May 1924

Fearn, Sir Robin, KCMG, diplomat, aged 71 – *d.* 26 August 2006, *b.* 5 September 1934

Figures, Sir Colin, KCMG, OBE, chief of the Secret Intelligence Service (1981–5) and Intelligence Coordinator, Cabinet Office (1985–9), aged 81 – *d.* 8 December 2006, *b.* 1 July 1925

Fletcher, Alan, graphic designer, aged 74 – *d.* 21 September 2006, *b.* 27 September 1931

Ford, Air Marshal Sir Geoffrey, KBE, CB, Chief Engineer, RAF (1978–81), aged 83 – *d.* 1 April 2007, *b.* 6 August 1923

Ford, Gerald, President of the USA (1974–7), aged 93 – *d.* 26 December 2006, *b.* 14 July 1913

Forte, Lord, entrepreneur, aged 98 – *d.* 28 February 2007, *b.* 26 November 1908

Fox, Sir Michael, Lord Justice of Appeal (1981–92), aged 85 – *d.* 9 April 2007, *b.* 8 October 1921

Franca, Celia, ballet dancer and founding artistic director of the National Ballet of Canada (1951–74), aged 85 – *d.* 19 February 2007, *b.* 25 June 1921

Francis, Freddie, Oscar-winning cinematographer and film director, aged 89 – *d.* 17 March 2007, *b.* 22 December 1917

Freeman, Alan, MBE, radio DJ, aged 79 – *d.* 27 November 2006, *b.* 6 July 1927

Friedman, Milton, economist, aged 94 – *d.* 16 November 2006, *b.* 31 July 1912

Gadsden, Sir Peter, GBE, AC, Lord Mayor of London (1979–80), aged 77 – *d.* 4 December 2006, *b.* 28 June 1929

Gallo, Ernest, American winemaker, aged 97 – *d.* 6 March 2007, *b.* 18 March 1909

Ghoussoub, Mai, Lebanese writer and artist who founded Saqi, London's first Arabic bookshop and publishing house, aged 54 – *d.* 17 February 2007, *b.* 2 November 1952

Gilmour, Sir John, DSO, Conservative MP for East Fife (1961–79), lord-lieutenant of Fife (1980–7), lord high commissioner, General Assembly of the Church of Scotland (1982 and 1983), aged 94 – *d.* 1 June 2007, *b.* 24 October 1912

Goodhew, Sir Victor, Conservative MP for St Albans (1959–83), aged 86 – *d.* 11 October 2006, *b.* 30 November 1919

Hamilton of Dalzell (4th), Lord, aged 68 – *d.* 28 September 2006, *b.* 11 February 1938

Harington, Gen. Sir Charles, GCB, CBE, DSO, MC, Chief of Personnel and Logistics, MoD (1968–71), aged 97 – *d.* 13 February 2007, *b.* 30 January 1910

Harris of High Cross, Lord, general director of the Institute of Economic Affairs (1957–87), aged 81 – *d.* 19 October 2006, *b.* 10 December 1924

Hart, Sir Michael, high court judge, aged 58 – *d.* 20 February 2007, *b.* 7 May 1948

Hastings (22nd), Lord, aged 95 – *d.* 25 April 2007, *b.* 14 April 1912

Hatch, Sir David, CBE, managing director of BBC Radio (1987–93) and chair of the Parole Board of England and Wales (2000–4), aged 68 – *d.* 13 June 2007, *b.* 7 May 1939

Heath-Stubbs, John, OBE, poet, aged 88 – *d.* 26 December 2006, *b.* 9 July 1918

Helm, Christopher, publisher and ornithologist, aged 69 – *d.* 20 January 2007, *b.* 1 February 1937

Hepple, Peter, drama critic and editor of *The Stage* (1972–92), aged 79 – *d.* 12 October 2006, *b.* 2 January 1927

Hetherington, Sir Thomas, KCB, CBE, Director of Public Prosecutions (1977–87), aged 80 – *d.* 28 March 2007, *b.* 18 September 1926

Hodder-Williams, Paul, OBE, TD, publisher and chair of Hodder and Stoughton (1961–75), aged 97 – *d.* 17 June 2007, *b.* 29 January 1910

Hodges, Air Chief Marshal Sir Lewis, KCB, CBE, DSO and Bar, DFC and Bar, aged 88 – *d.* 4 January 2007, *b.* 1 March 1918

Hoffenberg, Sir Raymond, KBE, president of the Royal College of Physicians (1983–9), aged 84 – *d.* 22 April 2007, *b.* 6 March 1923

Hunt, Sir James, high court judge, aged 63 – *d.* 8 November 2006, *b.* 26 January 1943

Hunter, Paul, snooker player, aged 27 – *d.* 9 October 2006, *b.* 14 October 1978

Hussein, Saddam, former president of Iraq (1979–2003), aged 69 – *d.* 30 December 2006, *b.* 28 April 1937

Hussey of North Bradley, Lord, chair of the BBC (1986–96), aged 86 – *d.* 27 December 2006, *b.* 29 August 1923

Inman, John, comic actor, aged 71 – *d.* 8 March 2007, *b.* 28 June 1935

Jauncey of Tullichettle, Lord, PC, Lord of Appeal in Ordinary (1988–96), aged 82 – *d.* 18 July 2007, *b.* 8 May 1925

Jeger, Baroness, Labour MP for Holborn and St Pancras South (1953–9) and Camden, Holborn and St Pancras South (1974–9), aged 91 – *d.* 26 February 2007, *b.* 19 November 1915

Jellicoe (2nd), Earl, KBE, PC (*also* Lord Jellicoe of Southampton, life peerage), Lord Privy Seal and Leader of the House of Lords (1970–3), aged 88 – *d.* 22 February 2007, *b.* 4 April 1918

Johns, Hugh, football commentator, aged 84 – *d.* 27 June 2007, *b.* 6 September 1922

Jolley, Elizabeth, novelist, aged 83 – *d.* 13 February 2007, *b.* 4 June 1923

Jones, Gen. Sir Edward, KCB, CVO, CBE, Gentleman

Usher of the Black Rod (1995–2001), aged 72 – *d.* 14 May 2007, *b.* 25 September 1936

Jones, Air Marshal Sir Edward Gordon, KCB, CBE, DSO, DFC, aged 92 – *d.* 20 February 2007, *b.* 31 August 1914

Jones, Robert, Conservative MP for West Hertfordshire (1983–97), construction and planning minister (1995–7), aged 56 – *d.* 16 April 2007, *b.* 26 September 1950

Jordan, Armin, Swiss conductor, aged 74 – *d.* 20 September 2006, *b.* 9 April 1932

Kelvedon, Lord, PC, Conservative MP for Southend West (1959–97), Secretary of State for Trade and Industry (1986–7) and Transport (1987–9), aged 71 – *d.* 27 January 2007, *b.* 9 October 1935

Khabra, Piara, Labour MP for Ealing Southall (1992–2007), aged 82 – *d.* 19 June 2007, *b.* 20 November 1924

Kilbracken (3rd), Lord, aged 85 – *d.* 14 August 2006, *b.* 17 October 1920

King, Angela, special adviser on gender issues and the advancement of women to the UN Secretary-General (1997–2004), aged 68 – *d.* 5 February 2007, *b.* 28 August 1938

King, Dame Thea, DBE, clarinettist, aged 81 – *d.* 26 June 2007, *b.* 26 December 1925

Lambton, Viscount (styled *Lord Lambton*; disclaimed his right to the Earldom of Durham in 1970), Conservative MP for Berwick-upon-Tweed (1951–73) and Parliamentary Under-Secretary of State, MoD (1970–3), aged 84 – *d.* 30 December 2006, *b.* 10 July 1922

Le Fanu, Sir Victor, KCVO, Serjeant-at-Arms, House of Commons (1982–9), aged 82 – *d.* 5 February 2007, *b.* 24 January 1925

Lloyd, Sir Ian, Conservative MP for Portsmouth Langstone, later Havant (1964–92), aged 85 – *d.* 26 September 2006, *b.* 5 September 1934

Lloyd, Peter, CMG, CVO, governor of the Cayman Islands (1982–7), aged 80 – *d.* 24 June 2007, *b.* 23 September 1926

MacDiarmid, Prof. Alan, New Zealand-born winner of the Nobel prize in chemistry (2000) with Alan J. Heeger and Hideki Shirakawa for his work on plastics that conduct electricity, aged 79 – *d.* 7 February 2007, *b.* 14 April 1927

McGregor, Sir Ian, CBE, FRS, malariologist, president of the Royal Society for Tropical Medicine (1983–5), aged 84 – *d.* 1 February 2007, *b.* 26 August 1922

MacLeod of MacLeod, John, 29th chief of clan MacLeod, aged 71 – *d.* 12 February 2007, *b.* 10 August 1935

Magnusson, Magnus, Icelandic-born journalist and broadcaster, aged 77 – *d.* 7 January 2007, *b.* 12 October 1929

Marshall, Sir Arthur, OBE, engineer and life president of the motor and aeronautical engineering company Marshall of Cambridge, since 1990; chair (1942–90), aged 103 – *d.* 16 March 2007, *b.* 4 December 1903

Marshall, Sir Michael, Conservative MP for Arundel (1974–97), aged 76 – *d.* 6 September 2006, *b.* 21 June 1930

Marshall, Peter, QPM, commissioner of City of London police (1978–85), aged 76 – *d.* 20 February 2007, *b.* 21 June 1930

Mayne, Very Revd Michael, KCVO, Dean of Westminster (1986–96), aged 77 – *d.* 22 October 2006, *b.* 10 September 1929

Megarry, Sir Robert, PC, Vice-Chancellor of the supreme court (1982–5), aged 96 – *d.* 11 October 2006, *b.* 1 June 1910

Melly, George, jazz singer, critic and author, aged 80 – *d.* 5 July 2007, *b.* 17 August 1926

Menzies, John, businessman, aged 80 – *d.* 21 February 2007, *b.* 13 October 1926

Middlemass, Frank, actor, aged 87 – *d.* 8 September 2006, *b.* 28 May 1919

Millar, Sir Oliver, GCVO, FSA, FBA, Surveyor of the Queen's Pictures (1972–88), aged 84 – *d.* 10 May 2007, *b.* 26 April 1923

Miscampbell, Norman, Conservative MP for Blackpool North (1962–92), aged 81 – *d.* 16 February 2007, *b.* 20 February 1925

Moray Williams, Ursula, children's author, aged 95 – *d.* 17 October 2006, *b.* 19 April 1911

Mostyn, Gen. Sir David, KCB, CBE, Adjutant-General of the Army (1986–8), aged 78 – *d.* 20 January 2007, *b.* 28 November 1928

Mowbray (26th), Segrave (27th) and Stourton (23rd), Lord, CBE, one of the 92 hereditary peers elected to remain in the House of Lords in 1999, aged 83 – *d.* 12 December 2006, *b.* 11 March 1923

Nelson of Stafford (3rd), Lord, aged 62 – *d.* 22 September 2006, *b.* 26 October 1943

Newlin, Dika, American composer and musicologist, aged 82 – *d.* 22 July 2006, *b.* 22 November 1923

Nicholls, Air Marshal Sir John, KCB, CBE, DFC, AFC, Vice-Chief of the Air Staff (1979–80), aged 80 – *d.* 17 May 2007, *b.* 25 July 1926

Noiret, Philippe, French actor, aged 76 – *d.* 23 November 2006, *b.* 1 October 1930

Nolan, Lord, PC, Lord of Appeal in Ordinary (1994–8), aged 78 – *d.* 22 January 2007, *b.* 10 September 1928

Nykvist, Sven, Swedish cinematographer, aged 83 – *d.* 20 September 2006, *b.* 3 December 1922

Odell, Jack, OBE, engineer and co-founder of matchbox toys manufacturer Lesney Products, aged 87 – *d.* 7 July 2007, *b.* 19 March 1920

Pattinson, Revd Sir Derek, secretary-general of the General Synod of the Church of England (1972–90), aged 76 – *d.* 10 October 2006, *b.* 31 March 1930

Pearce, Bryan, painter, aged 77 – *d.* 11 January 2007, *b.* 25 July 1929

Pearce, Philippa, OBE, children's writer, author of *Tom's Midnight Garden* (1958), aged 86 – *d.* 21 December 2006, *b.* 23 January 1920

Pedersen, Carl-Henning, Danish artist, aged 93 – *d.* 20 February 2007, *b.* 23 September 1913

Peyton of Yeovil, Lord, PC, politician, Conservative MP for Yeovil (1951–83), aged 87 – *d.* 22 November 2006, *b.* 13 February 1919

Pinker, Sir George, KCVO, Surgeon-Gynaecologist to the Queen (1973–90), aged 82 – *d.* 29 April 2007, *b.* 6 December 1924

Pinochet, Gen. Augusto, president of Chile (1974–90), aged 91 – *d.* 10 December 2006, *b.* 25 November 1915

Pocock, Tom, journalist and historian, aged 81 – *d.* 7 May 2007, *b.* 18 August 1925

Pollock, Sir Michael, GCB, LVO, DSC, Admiral of the Fleet (1974–2006), First Sea Lord (1971–4), aged 89 – *d.* 27 September 2006, *b.* 19 October 1916

Prendergast, Peter, artist, aged 60 – *d.* 14 January 2007, *b.* 27 October 1946

Prentice, Dame Winifred, DBE, president of the Royal

College of Nursing, aged – *d.* 17 March 2007, *b.* 2 December 1910

Randle, Prof. Sir Philip, FRS, biochemist, aged 80 – *d.* 27 September 2006, *b.* 16 July 1926

Reid, Mike, comedian and actor, aged 67 – *d.* 29 July 2007, *b.* 19 January 1940

Renton, Lord, KBE, TD, PC, QC, politician and lawyer, aged 98 – *d.* 24 May 2007, *b.* 12 August 1908

Richardson, Ian, CBE, actor, aged 72 – *d.* 9 February 2007, *b.* 7 April 1934

Rivers-Bulkeley, Elisabeth, stockbroker, financial columnist and broadcaster, aged 82 – *d.* 19 December 2006, *b.* 30 April 1924

Roberts, Prof. Sir Gareth, FRS, FRENG, physicist, president of Wolfson College, Oxford (2001–7), aged 66 – *d.* 6 February 2007, *b.* 16 May 1940

Roth, Prof. Sir Martin, FRS, psychiatrist, aged 88 – *d.* 26 September 2006, *b.* 6 November 1917

Rowlands, Keith, president of the Welsh Rugby Union (2004–6), aged 70 – *d.* 18 November 2006, *b.* 7 February 1936

Ruttley, Eric, secretary-general World Energy Council (1966–86), aged 90 – *d.* 5 March 2007, *b.* 4 September 1916

Sainsbury, Simon, businessman and philanthropist, aged 76 – *d.* 27 September 2006, *b.* 1 March 1930

Schwarzkopf, Dame Elizabeth, soprano, aged 90 – *d.* 3 August 2006, *b.* 9 December 1915

Scott, Dr Olive, paediatric cardiologist, aged 82 – *d.* 4 March 2007, *b.* 25 June 1924

Singer, Aubrey, CBE, television executive and producer, aged 80 – *d.* 26 May 2007, *b.* 21 January 1927

Smedley, Sir Brian, high court judge (1995–2000), aged 72 – *d.* 6 April 2007, *b.* 28 November 1934

Smith, Sir John, CH, CBE, financier who founded the Landmark Trust building preservation charity, aged 83 – *d.* 28 February 2007, *b.* 3 April 1923

Smith, Dame Margot, chair of the National Association of Conservative and Unionist Associations (1973–4), aged 88 – *d.* 8 May 2007, *b.* 5 September 1918

Strathcarron (2nd), Lord, aged 82 – *d.* 31 August 2006, *b.* 23 January 1924

Tanumafili II, HH Susuga Malietoa, GCMG, CBE, head of state of Samoa, aged 95 – *d.* 11 May 2007, *b.* 4 January 1912

Taufa'ahau Tupou IV, king of Tonga, aged 88 – *d.* 10 September 2006, *b.* 4 July 1918

Tennant, Sir Iain, KT, lord-lieutenant of Morayshire (1963–94), Crown Estate Commissioner (1970–90), high commissioner, Church of Scotland (1988–9) and chair Grampian Television (1968–89), aged 87 – *d.* 25 September 2006, *b.* 11 March 1919

Tippet, Vice-Adm. Sir Anthony, KCB, Chief of Fleet Support (1983–6), aged 78 – *d.* 13 October 2006, *b.* 2 October 1928

Train, Christopher, CB, director-general of the Prison Service (1983-91), aged 75 – *d.* 7 May 2007, *b.* 12 March 1932

Vonnegut, Kurt, American writer, aged 84 – *d.* 11 April 2007, *b.* 11 November 1922

Wakeford, Sir Richard, KCB, LVO, OBE, AFC, Deputy Chief of Defence Staff (Intelligence) (1975–8), aged 84 – *d.* 13 February 2007, *b.* 22 April 1922

Waldheim, Kurt, secretary-general of the United Nations (1972–81), President of Austria (1986–92), aged 88 – *d.* 14 June 2007, *b.* 21 December 1918

Walker, Sir Cecil, Ulster Unionist MP for North Belfast (1983–2001), aged 82 – *d.* 3 January 2007, *b.* 17 December 1924

Weatherill, Lord, PC, speaker of the House of Commons (1983–92), aged 86 – *d.* 6 May 2007, *b.* 25 November 1920

Webster, Harry, CBE, automotive engineer, technical director of Standard-Triumph (1955–68), aged 89 – *d.* 6 February 2007, *b.* 27 May 1917

Williams, Sir Kyffin, OBE, artist, aged 88 – *d.* 1 September 2006, *b.* 9 May 1918

Wilson, Prof. Sir Colin St John, architect, designed the new British Library, aged 85 – *d.* 14 May 2007, *b.* 14 March 1922

Wolpe, Margaret, artist, aged 87 – *d.* 16 July 2006, *b.* 23 April 1919

Wooderson, Sydney, MBE, athlete, aged 92 – *d.* 21 December 2006, *b.* 30 August 1914

Woolmer, Bob, cricketer and international cricket coach, aged 58 – *d.* 18 March 2007, *b.* 14 May 1948

Yeltsin, Boris, former president of the Russian Federation (1991–9), aged 76 – *d.* 23 April 2007, *b.* 1 February 1931

Young, John, CBE, chair of Young & Co brewery (1962–2006), aged 85 – *d.* 17 September 2006, *b.* 7 August 1921

ARCHAEOLOGY

Dr Nadia Durrani and Dr Neil Faulkner

LOST WORLD OF THE MESOLITHIC HUNTERS

Beneath the southern North Sea, across an area the size of Wales, lie the hills, plains and valleys of a Stone Age landscape submerged by floods in an epoch of global warming thousands of years ago. It is likely to contain the most extensive and best-preserved prehistoric archaeology in Europe. Now, for the first time, archaeologists are mapping this lost world of the Mesolithic.

It has long been known that Britain was once joined to the Continent, and that great floods and inundations over thousands of years gradually eroded away the land bridge until it was finally broken around 6400 BC. The putative lost world beneath the sea, dubbed 'Doggerland', yielded occasional finds, such as a worked antler point dredged up from peat beds in 1931 by a fishing trawler. So though Doggerland was known to exist, it was *terra incognita*: the technical difficulty of exploration 50m beneath the sea, the vastness of the submerged area, the potential cost of investigation, and the uncertainty about whether anything useful would be learned, all combined to prevent systematic research.

Recently, however, because the southern North Sea is an economic asset, maritime geophysics has been applied on a massive scale to map the seabed and what lies beneath it. Petroleum Geo-Services has now donated to a team of archaeological specialists at Birmingham University, led by Professor Vince Gaffney, more than 22,000 sq. km of marine seismic data collected and analysed over decades at a cost of many millions of pounds. The archaeologists are able to explore the rivers, streams, lakes and coastlines of an entire European country that has not been seen for 8,000 years. The world revealed, undisturbed throughout this time, its remains pickled in brine, represents something akin to a Mesolithic Pompeii. Its secrets are only just beginning to emerge.

The data was created by equipment carried on ships that generated acoustic pulses capable of passing through different strata and returning with distinct signals. The data was then processed into 3D maps of the geology, accurate to within 12.5m. Traditional deep-sea recording measures only the sea-floor, the result of recent scouring and deposition that obscure the prehistoric landscape. The crucial advantage of seismic data is the view through recent sediments to the underlying geology and the sequence of superimposed past landscapes represented. Work so far has concentrated on mapping the upper land-surface representing Early Mesolithic Doggerland, dated *c.*8000–6400 BC. But the possibility arises that early landscapes might also be mapped, such as that inhabited by the Late Palaeolithic hunters of *c.*20000 BC.

The team has used the seismic data to create virtual reality images of the landscape, brought to life by 'seeding' with probable vegetation using an 'artificial life engine'. In the first 6,000 sq. km area studied, for example, it has identified a major river – dubbed the 'Shotton' – with a width of 600m, an observed length of 27.5km, and an associated network of tributaries and wetlands. They went on to map a series of distinct zones over some 22,000 sq. km, ranging from marine estuaries and salt marshes, through regions dominated by freshwater river systems and wetlands, to coastal plains and areas of rolling hills.

Rich in flora and teeming with game, Doggerland before the great flood may have been Mesolithic Europe's Garden of Eden. Systematic survey around the Danish coast – on the edge of Doggerland – has identified no less than 2,300 prehistoric sites. How many more must lie beneath the vastness of the southern North Sea?

THE NEW RADIOCARBON REVOLUTION

The exploration of Doggerland – only just beginning – may one day revolutionise our understanding of the Mesolithic, the last phase of hunter-gatherer life before the development of farming. However, new radiocarbon-based dating techniques are already revolutionising our understanding of the Early Neolithic, the epoch of the first cultivators and stock-raisers.

Until now, because of imprecise dates and long timescales, prehistory has been dominated by processes rather than events. Long barrows have been dated vaguely between 4000 and 3000 BC. Different phases of construction work have been attributed to successive generations. Jumbles of disarticulated bone found scattered in chambers and passageways have conjured images of communal mausolea in use for centuries and of complex rituals of ancestor worship involving the movement back and forth of ancient bone. Everything in the Neolithic has seemed slow and gradual, without sudden events and sharp breaks: part of the *longue durée* of prehistory. The problem has always been the vagueness of traditional radiocarbon dates.

Radiocarbon dating was developed just after the Second World War by the American physical chemist Willard Frank Libby and his colleagues. It relied on the fact that all living things absorb carbon dioxide, including carbon-14 or 'radiocarbon', which is atomically unstable and gradually decays. Because living organisms stop absorbing carbon dioxide when they die, and because radiocarbon decays at a known rate, measuring the amount of radiocarbon remaining in, say, human bone recovered from a prehistoric burial chamber, allows scientists to estimate the age.

The so-called first radiocarbon revolution involved the development and application of a technique for measuring the amount of radiocarbon remaining in dead organic matter. A second radiocarbon revolution occurred when it was realised that atmospheric carbon had varied over time, so that it was necessary to calibrate radiocarbon dates by comparing them with tree-ring chronologies.

Radiocarbon dates became more accurate, but not more precise. Regardless of calibration, there remains a wide margin of error in all radiocarbon dates, traditionally expressed in terms of two standard deviations. Thus, a radiocarbon date might be given as 3780–3380 cal BC (95 per cent) probability. This means that there is a 95 per cent probability that the date lies within this 400 year period! The uncertainty is due principally to counting errors and variations in the radiocarbon calibration curve.

The result is 'fuzzy' prehistory: vague date-ranges leading to perceptions of prehistory in terms of the *longue durée* rather than a sequence of discrete events.

Now a third revolution has begun, and a consortium of specialists are involved in a major project to re-date the British Neolithic. Long-held views on the chronology of England's prehistoric monuments are being overturned by a ground-breaking new dating programme. The first phase of the new programme – for five Early Neolithic long barrows – is now complete. The result is an academic bombshell that reveals the extraordinary potential of a new approach which combines Bayesian statistical methods and the processing power of modern computers.

It hinges on a 250-year-old mathematical formula of inverse probability: (Probability of A) × (Probability of B given A) = Probability of A and B. Given an archaeological sequence in which relative chronological relationships are known and a series of radiocarbon dates has been obtained, Bayesian statistics involve creating a mathematical relationship between the probabilities for each radiocarbon date and those of every other date within the sequence. This allows any particular date to be constrained and 'squeezed' by all the other probabilities in the sequence. With enough data and enough processing power – the programme being repeatedly re-run with newly squeezed dates – centuries can become decades and specific events suddenly punctuate the *longue durée* of prehistory.

The new dating for the construction, use and abandonment of West Kennett long barrow, for example, involved 31 separate radiocarbon dates, 30 million separate calculations, and 11 hours of computer processing. But it is now known that the sequence of 40-odd interments of men, women and children probably began in the 3640s BC and ended within 30 years. Comparable results have been obtained for Wayland's Smithy I, Ascott-under-Wychwood, Fussell's Lodge, and Hazleton North: the barrows were in use for three or four generations at the most, and in one case at least all 14 interments may represent a single mass burial.

Old ideas about the ritual manipulation of ancient bones and ancestor worship now look threadbare. In the brief period when a long barrow was in use, the people interred within were known to living or recent memory. Indeed, long-barrow burial as a whole may have been a relatively brief fashion. Four of the five barrows studied went out of use around 3625 cal BC. But each one ended in a different way. At Ascott-under-Wychwood the entrances were blocked. At Fussell's Lodge the timber chamber was consumed by fire. At Hazleton North burial ended but people kept returning to place offerings in passages. At West Kennett, burial just stopped and people went away. The Early Neolithic has suddenly become dynamic, with geographical diversity, rapid change, and sharply defined events.

It is also beginning to look more violent. As well as four Early Neolithic sites with clear evidence for some sort of armed clash – Carn Brea, Crickley Hill, Hambledon Hill and Hembury – the number of burials where evidence for violent death has been detected is increasing, often through careful re-examination of old excavation records and conserved human bone from barrows. Altogether at least 136 Early or Middle Neolithic burials associated with leaf-shaped arrowheads have been excavated. Traditionally these have been interpreted as ritual, but the discovery of one or two actually embedded in bone, and many others closely associated with skeletal material, make this interpretation questionable. In addition, among some 350 Early Neolithic skulls examined, 2 per cent revealed evidence of fatal injury, and a further 4 or 5 per cent evidence of healed injury. Many of the observed injuries resulted from the blows of blunt instruments such as clubs, picks, polished axes, or hand-thrown stones.

Not only does the Neolithic now look more episodic and dynamic; it also looks more violent and dangerous. Were long barrows attempts to substantiate claims to territory in an increasingly divided and competitive world? Were they short-lived because the communities they served were unstable? Are they evidence of an era of storm and stress in the first half of the 37th century BC? Or was occasional violence endemic throughout the period, breaking out in different places at different times?

With new dates for other monuments soon forthcoming, prehistory is now on a rollercoaster of new data – statistics-driven and computer-aided – that promises to transform our thinking.

WILD PARTIES AT STONEHENGE

The Neolithic Christmas seems to have been a matter of wild parties, with feasts of barbecued pig, half-eaten joints tossed to the floor, and much deliberate smashing of crockery – with no-one bothering to clear up the mess.

That is the picture that emerged when a team of archaeologists led by Professor Mike Parker Pearson uncovered the remains of the largest Neolithic village ever discovered in Britain. They found it outside Durrington Walls, part of the great ritual complex around Stonehenge in Wiltshire. Of around 25 houses identified in magnetometer survey, eight were excavated, in six of which the clay floors were intact. Each house was about 5m square, with a central hearth, and post-holes and slots that had once anchored wooden furniture. Strewn about were the remains of raucous feasts – heaps of broken pots and piles of pig and cow bone on a scale unprecedented in Neolithic archaeology. Some of the sherds contained chemical traces of a milk and meat stew. Study of pigs' teeth has shown that most animals were killed at around nine months, dating the feasts to the midwinter solstice.

Most of the houses were clustered on both sides of an imposing stone-surfaced avenue some 27m wide and 170m long which linked Durrington Walls with the River Avon. Durrington Walls was a huge henge monument with a ditch and external bank enclosing 12ha and containing two large timber structures. Now two more buildings have been found in the interior. The interior buildings were clean, and the speculation is that they may have been accommodation for priests or other functionaries. The houses lining the avenue, on the other hand, were perhaps only used on special ritual occasions, providing accommodation and feasting halls for visitors.

Parker Pearson argues that Durrington Walls represents the domain of the living, in contrast to Stonehenge itself, the realm of the ancestors. One reconstruction of how the complex was used is to imagine a body lying in state within Durrington Walls while the living conducted a wake in the houses along the avenue. Perhaps it was then conveyed along the avenue to the river, down the river by boat, and then along the other, more famous avenue to Stonehenge. The use of timber posts at Durrington Walls may have symbolised life, the gradual rotting of the posts the passage from life to death. The grey, silent monoliths of Stonehenge were a memorial to the dead, the final destination on life's journey, the place where the ancestors dwelt forever. That is why no-one feasted at Stonehenge: there are no houses, no discarded joints of meat, no smashed crockery, but some 250 cremations are known or suspected.

The new evidence fits with new interpretations more generally, which argue that in all sorts of ways the complex symbolises the dichotomy between life and death. The Stonehenge avenue is aligned on the midsummer solstice sunrise, and its giant stone trilithon frames the midwinter solstice sunset. The Durrington Walls is aligned on the midsummer solstice sunset, while its main timber circle lines up with the midwinter solstice sunrise. The movements of the sun; the cycle of the seasons; the contrast between day and night, summer and winter, light and darkness: these are all symbols of the transition from one state of being to another, of life and death.

The national headlines claimed that the settlement at Durrington Walls was 'the wild town next to Stonehenge where the builders partied'. This is true in a sense, but misleading: it conjures images of construction gangs like those on a modern building-site. More likely, the work of construction was itself a ceremony, or part of one. Perhaps it was done seasonally, and was a work of collective communal labour. It is doubtful that anything happened at Stonehenge that was not richly symbolic and ritually charged. The process of creating the monuments was perhaps as important as the finished result. The effort was an act of propitiation, dedication and respect for the dead. Thus the excavators find offerings of food and pottery in many of the post-holes at Durrington Walls – as if the erection of each post was itself a ceremony.

So the village discovered by Parker Pearson's team may indeed belong to the builders of Stonehenge. But the builders are likely to have been people of all ranks from the region 4,500 years ago, coming together perhaps twice a year, midwinter and midsummer, to bury the dead, honour the ancestors, and worship the forces of Nature on which their lives depended.

IRON AGE CHIEFTAINS AND ROMAN CONQUERORS

Metal-detector finds, now that they are being systematically recorded by the Portable Antiquities Scheme, are transforming British archaeology. Among recent discoveries is the identification of two hitherto unknown Celtic rulers of Late Iron Age Britain. The first is represented by the discovery of a silver-alloy coin of the Dobunni tribe of previously unknown type near Cirencester in Gloucestershire. Careful reading of the inscription seems to give the letters *INAMN*, which may correspond to *Inamnuetoutos*, a Dobunnic ruler who perhaps reigned at some point in the first half of the 1st century AD.

A second discovery concerns *ALE SCA*-inscribed coins, the first of which was recorded during excavations at the Roman town of Caistor St Edmund in 1929. A new type has recently been found with a fuller inscription, which might be read as *ALIFF SCAVO*, the most likely translation of which would be 'Scavo(s), son of Alef-', or perhaps *AL(II) FE SCAVO*, meaning 'Ale made [it for] Scavo'. In this case, because of close similarities in coin designs, it is very likely that Scavo was a contemporary of Prasutagus, the client-king of the Norfolk-based Iceni tribe and the husband of the rebel queen Boudica (whose coins are inscribed *SUB ESV PRASTO ESICO FECIT*: 'Esico made [it] under Lord Prasto'). He would therefore date to the middle years of the 1st century AD.

In both classes of coin, interpretation had proved difficult because elements of the inscription had been incorporated into the main design, respectively of a triple-tailed horse and of a wild boar. These and other similar discoveries have rendered the royal genealogies of the Late Iron Age tribes of Britain proposed in the past untenable, leaving us with a much more complex pattern of reigns, quite probably including sub-kings, and often perhaps with rapid changes of authority in a period of political turmoil.

Another historical scheme recently undermined concerns Julius Caesar. As every schoolboy used to know, Caesar stormed the British chieftain Cassivellaunus' stronghold somewhere north of the Thames in 54 BC. The great archaeologist Sir Mortimer Wheeler, in one of his characteristically flamboyant announcements, declared the Iron Age *oppidum* at Wheathampsted near St Albans to be the place. A number of other sites have also been proposed: Ravensburgh, Wallbury, Braughing, and The Aubreys. Now Philip Crummy, director of the Colchester Archaeological Trust, has proposed his own site: Iron Age Camulodunun, the precursor of Roman Colchester.

Recent excavations have shown that Camulodunun may have emerged as a high-status Iron Age centre earlier than previously thought. Certainly it was occupied from at least the 2nd century BC. Excavations at three sites – Stanway, Abbotstone and Colchester Garrison – have revealed evidence for roundhouses, enclosures and trackways of Middle Iron Age and later dates, some clearly associated with the corralling and movement of stock.

Old evidence, argues Crummy – such as that of the Lexden Tumulus, a princely burial of *c.* 15–10 BC, and coins mint-marked *CAM*, dating from *c.* 25 BC – should be re-evaluated in the context of this new excavation evidence. So, too, he suggests, should Caesar's famous account in his *Gallic War*, where Cassivellaunus' *oppidum* is described as 'defended by woods and marshes', 'fortified by a rampart and ditch', and as containing 'a great number of men and cattle'. Camulodunun has rivers on two sides, no doubt marshy and wooded in many places in antiquity, and was defended on the third side by giant dykes, the earliest of which was probably in place by the time of Caesar. And the field systems recorded in recent excavations imply that stock-raising was central to the Iron Age economy.

COMPUTERISING THE ANGLO-SAXON DEAD

A lot of modern archaeology – as the Doggerland and prehistoric dating projects described above indicate – is concerned with the application of new scientific methods to old problems. Another example is the Early Anglo-Saxon cemetery in Cleatham in Lincolnshire, the third largest in the country, which was fully excavated in the 1980s but is only now being published by excavator Kevin Leahy after exhaustive computer-aided analysis of the finds.

Cleatham yielded 1,204 funerary urns containing cremated remains (compared with 2,700 at Spong Hill in Norfolk, and 1,700 at Loveden Hill in Lincolnshire). During the excavation there was no sampling: every fragment, if it could be seen, was excavated and recorded, on the basis that even a few crumbly sherds in the fill of a grave might yield vital clues about the sequencing of the burials. But such vast amounts of data – thousands of potsherds and thousands of fragments of beads and brooches – could only be analysed using a computer database.

What has the analysis revealed? First, it has provided a chronological sequence for decorated urns, since on some parts of the site as many as seven urns had been placed one on top of the other at different periods between the 5th and 7th centuries AD, while elsewhere as many as five pots had been placed in the ground side-by-side at the same time. Such stratigraphic relationships between pots bearing contrasting designs are the very essence of chronological sequencing. Secondly, because of the relationships between the stratigraphic sequence, the pots containing burnt bone, and grave-goods (bone combs, bronze brooches, glass beads), it was also possible to organise the latter into a tight chronological sequence.

Third, it was found that many of both the decorated pots and other artefacts were similar to objects found elsewhere in Anglo-Saxon England, indicating the extent to which ideas travelled, artistic concepts were shared, and a single cultural *koine* existed across large areas of the country in this period. Some of the links were remarkable. Urns were found that had direct parallels up to 140km away – ie they had actually been made by the same potter. Other contacts implicit in the grave assemblages were more wide-ranging. Fragments of ivory bag-rings were found, the ivory probably coming from Africa. Cowrie shells and coral were being brought from the Indian Ocean. These exotic objects must have been passed from trader to trader across Europe to reach darkest Lincolnshire. The Anglo-Saxon inhabitants were part of an international trading system.

BIG DIGS IN OLD CITIES

Some big urban digs have been making waves. Cambridge has a poor track record in relation to its own archaeology – somewhat ironically, since the university has one of the strongest archaeology departments in the country. The problem is partly that, as serious academic sub-disciplines, medieval archaeology is relatively new, and post-medieval very new. Matters have now been put right with the excavation of an entire hectare of archaeology on the edge of the historic town, as part of the biggest city-centre redevelopment project in Cambridge's history involving Robert Sayles department store and surrounding properties.

Central to the archaeological plan was treating the entire site as a single entity: everything was dug and recorded in the same way, to the same standards, right across the site. A substantial proportion of 12 properties was investigated, and in each case, from the laying out of the suburb and the construction of the earliest buildings in the Norman period, to the still-standing buildings constructed in the late 19th or even late 20th century, a full archaeological record was created.

The Grand Arcade site straddled the medieval boundary of the city – the so-called King's Ditch – two substantial lengths of which were excavated. Around 10m across and 2m or more deep, it was a massive monument. It was also well-constructed, with a narrow drainage-channel in the base, and in places steps built into the sides, presumably to permit access for dredging, cleaning and repairs. The history of the ditch was long and complex. The details of re-cuts and repairs could be very different in one place compared with another, and modifications were frequent.

The earliest documentary reference to the ditch is in 1215, but it probably dates from the 11th century, and possibly earlier. It soon lost its original defensive purpose and became a commercial boundary, but Craig Cessford's Cambridge Archaeological Unit team found clear evidence that tolls were not always paid: a 15th-century timber bridge and a 16th or 17th brick one were presumably unofficial entrances into the city – and an obvious way in for smugglers. At this time the ditch was choked with rubbish and sewage, with latrines discharging directly into it. Bit by bit, stretches were infilled and built over, though some were still open into the 19th century.

The King's Ditch was the dominant feature on the site, but a more detailed picture of everyday life through the ages was obtained from the dozen properties excavated, each one apparently laid out in the 11th century, and forming long strips extending back from the street front. Many of these boundaries have remained fossilised in the city layout up to the present day. Each property had its own well – or rather, a series of wells spanning the many centuries between the time the plot was laid out and the advent of piped water in the 19th century.

Medieval wells were generally of timber, usually with walls of wattle, while those from the 16th century were often of stone (sometimes using stone cannibalised from dissolved monastic houses), while those from the 17th–19th century tended to be brick-built. Wooden structures and numerous datable artefacts were found within the deep, waterlogged fills of the wells. Discoveries included the wickerwork, barrel staves and timber planking used in the construction of wells, and also wooden water-tanks, timber linings, 16th-century wooden ladders, a wooden jug, a wooden bowl, and a leather tankard. The waterlogged conditions also preserved plant and insect remains that can be studied to reconstruct the environment, diet and living conditions of the old city.

The archaeologists paid unusual attention to post-medieval deposits – even recording a 1970s multi-storey car-park! A particular characteristic of the later assemblages is that they are very revealing of household activities and everyday life because there is so much material in the ground – like personalised plates with people's names on that can be linked with documentary records for those very individuals. This focus on the post-medieval evidence has highlighted the degree to which Cambridge remained an essentially modest settlement with extensive open space behind the street-frontages until well into the 19th century. The big change – with infilling of plots in the historic core and a rapid spread of new suburbs around it – did not come until enclosures and the railways, when land became available for development and the city was networked into a wider, growing, industrial economy.

The other big urban project was in Leicester. Leicester has problems associated with the decline of its traditional industries, and the Leicester Regeneration Company was set up to oversee a series of redevelopment schemes, one of which involves work in the historic core covering some 10 per cent of the former Roman and medieval walled towns. Developers Hammersons funded major excavations undertaken by Richard Buckley and University of Leicester Archaeological Services.

On the Vine Street site, 60 per cent of a complete Roman *insula* (city-block) was excavated, exposing a very rare example of an urban courtyard house. Roman town-houses usually comprised one, two, at the most three, ranges of rooms, yet this had four full ranges of rooms linked by corridors which opened onto an ornamental garden. The luxuries included a bath-suite represented by a hypocaust and a plunge-pool, an apsidal room which was probably a *triclinium* or dining-room, and underfloor heating in a number of other reception-rooms. Oddly, however, industrial activity, beginning in the 2nd century AD before the plot was developed into a grand house, seems to have continued, with evidence for iron smithing and bone-working. Another oddity was the discovery in the vicinity of two lead curse-tablets, which are usually only ever found in association with temples.

Nearby was a large rectangular building of 3rd century AD date that was almost certainly some sort of public building. The walls – the stone from which had all been robbed out – had originally been a massive 1.2m wide, and inside was a series of superimposed mortar floors. Three lead seals of the kind used for documents or consignments of goods were found nearby, identified as those of the 6th, the 20th, and possibly the 2nd legion. Presumably the building was associated with military supply.

Roman remains were also found on the High Cross Street site. After excavating medieval levels, archaeologists discovered the *in-situ* remains of a collapsed Roman wall 3m below the modern ground-level. The Roman *macellum* or market-building had once stood on the opposite side of the street, and it seems that the entire wall had fallen in one piece, covering the road and part of the plot opposite. The wall proved that the *macellum* had originally been two-storey: a rare example in Romano-British archaeology, most of which survives only at foundation level, of direct evidence for this.

New information about medieval Leicester was also found. As well as locating the former St Peter's Church, one of four 'lost' churches in the city that did not survive the Dissolution – along with some 1,340 associated burials – crucial evidence was recovered for the 'missing' Anglo-Saxon and Viking centuries of the city's history. It is known, for example, that Leicester was one of the five boroughs of the Danelaw, but until recently archaeological evidence for this period was virtually zero. Immediately beneath the later medieval layers on the High Cross Street site, however, archaeologists found the fragmentary remains of timber buildings of 'Saxo-Norman' date. Accumulations nearby of 'dark earth' – which probably represents rubbish dumping on waste-ground – yielded 9th–10th century AD pottery.

Equally important is the evidence for Early Anglo-Saxon occupation within the walls. Under the dark earth, and cutting into Roman walling beneath, was evidence for both a large, post-built hall and a sunken-featured building (SFB) – the two standard types of Anglo-Saxon building, often found together, the assumption being that the hall provided a main residence and one or more SFBs ancillary rooms. Two other SFBs were found nearby. Artefacts recovered at these levels imply a 5th–7th century AD date.

METAL-DETECTING CONTROVERSY FLARES AGAIN

Just when you thought it was safe to go out with your metal-detector, a one-liner from a government minister reveals that a lot of archaeologists remain hostile!

The culture minister, David Lammy, championed metal-detectorists 'the unsung heroes of the UK's heritage'. The occasion was the launch of the Portable Antiquities Scheme (PAS) and Treasure Annual Reports in January.

The PAS goes from strength to strength. Finds reporting is up again, from 426 to 506 objects in the case of treasure, and by 45 per cent in the case of antiquities generally, with some 57,566 objects recorded altogether last year. 'We now have a situation without parallel in Europe,' said British Museum director Neil MacGregor. 'Without doubt, these finds are rewriting history.'

The overwhelming majority of PAS-recorded finds are metal-detected. It is this that has produced an extraordinary turnaround in attitudes to metal-detecting among many archaeologists in the last few years. But Lammy's encomium obviously went too far for many, provoking an especially tetchy response from RESCUE, the highly respected lobby group that champions archaeology and heritage in the face of development threats. Lammy was the recipient of an open letter which expressed irritation that metal-detectorists had been praised and that 'amateur and professional archaeologists whose work is contributing in a significant way to our understanding of the past' had been slighted. Metal-detectors alone 'are only capable of recovering a tiny part of the rich and diverse archaeological record that forms part of our shared heritage'. Lammy, it seems, had failed to recognise that. As the open letter states, 'we long ago abandoned an antiquarian concern for individual artefacts *per se* in favour of an interest in the nature and structure of human society as revealed through the study of all aspects of material culture and landscape'.

But as one correspondent writing in the popular magazine *Current Archaeology* pointed out, the rumpus seemed out of proportion beside the rather more serious problem that £200m was being cut from the Heritage Lottery Fund budget to help cover a massive increase in the projected cost of the 2012 London Olympics. The implication is that the relatively minor but endlessly controversial issue of metal-detectors in archaeology has become something of a head-in-the-sand obsession on the part of some professional archaeologists.

ARCHITECTURE

John Hitchman

NATIONAL FOOTBALL STADIUM, WEMBLEY, NORTH LONDON

Architect: World Stadium Team (Foster & Partners and HOK Sport Architecture)

Few construction projects in recent years have occupied the media spotlight to quite the extent of the rebuilding of Wembley Stadium, not least because of its place in the nation's collective memory as the site of the country's sole World Cup success in 1966 or its familiarity as the backdrop to the annual season's ending showpiece, the FA Cup Final. Famous for its iconic twin towers, the original Empire Stadium was built for the British Empire Exhibition of 1924 and, while still unfinished, staged its first FA Cup Final in 1923. It continued in use until its closure in October 2000 and was finally demolished in the autumn of 2002.

Since then, the task of creating a world-class replacement has generated more than its fair share of pitfalls, and a significant amount of public controversy with rapidly escalating costs and repeated delays to the completion date. Finally, in 2007, it has taken shape and after a short series of preparatory matches, the new Wembley staged its first FA Cup Final on 19 May 2007.

The numbers alone are impressive. The stadium has a seating capacity of 90,000 and is a kilometre in circumference; there are 2,500 rooms in the spaces below the seating tiers, together with 2,600 lavatories, allegedly more than in any other building in the world. It is also claimed to be the world's largest all-covered football stadium (all the seats are covered, though not the pitch itself, so in theory if it rains all the spectators at least can remain dry). With the pitch surface laid at four metres below the ground level, 320,000 cubic metres of soil was excavated for the new structure, which was re-used to raise the ground levels around the perimeter of the site.

Given the public's emotional attachment to Wembley's predecessor and its position as the spiritual home of English football, a memorable, instantly recognisable eye-catching concept was a necessity. Inevitably a number of interesting structural options were proposed, including several multi-masted designs reminiscent of the ill-fated Millennium Dome. The chosen structural concept comprises an enormous single arch spanning the entire stadium from east to west, leaning over at an angle to the vertical and held in position by counter-balancing tension cables at either side (*Fig. 1*). A statement of dramatic simplicity, it is a powerful signpost to the stadium's location and rises to such a height that it is visible on the horizon throughout the length and breadth of Greater London.

The arch is not only a dominant visual feature, it is also an important component of the roof support structure and carries approximately 70 per cent of the total roof load. It is constructed as an open lattice, circular in cross-section, divided at 10m intervals by a series of open circular diaphragms, to which the diagonal latticework of steel struts is connected. The overall span of the arch is 315m, and it reaches a height of 133m, the whole construction having been assembled horizontally at ground level before being slowly hoisted into position. From regular points along the arch, pairs of cables are suspended and these provide support to the leading edge of the north side of the roof. As the arch is tilted outwards at an angle of 112°, there is the distinct feeling that it is pulling the edge of the roof upwards. The tension imposed by both sets of cables puts the arch structure into compression and aids the stability of the whole construction in conditions of wind uplift or downward pressure.

The dynamic of the opposing tensile forces can best be appreciated when the arch is seen from a lateral viewpoint, either to the east or west. The process of erection was a complex and delicate operation that

Fig. 1 Wembley Stadium

demanded total control of a dynamic loading pattern during the hoisting sequence in order to eliminate the potential for buckling of arch members or excessive creep in the supporting network of cables.

The arch also supports four large trusses aligned north to south that, in turn, support the tracks upon which the stadium's retractable sections of roof at the east and west ends can be moved. To reduce their visual impact these bowstring trusses employ tensile cables for the bottom cords of the trusses. The need for sunshine and air movement to ensure healthy turf was a critical design factor and has been catered for by the inclusion of substantial sections of retractable roof on three sides. In addition to the east and west sections of roof, the southern section has also been designed to be retracted so that on sunny days the whole of the pitch area can be in sunlight. This is not just to assist the grass, but an attempt to avoid also the disruptive glare for television viewers, noticeable when the playing action switches from areas in bright sunshine to parts of the field that are in shade, by eliminating as far as possible any shadows from overhead structural elements or areas of roofing falling over the pitch.

Though primarily intended for football, the number of matches that will be played during a year is limited and commercial pressures demand that flexibility is built in to enable other events to be staged. The stadium can be adapted for large concerts with relative ease, with sections of the stand permitting concert stages to be erected at either end and to one side, as demonstrated during the recent Princess Diana Memorial and Planet Earth concerts. Furthermore, the lowest 15 rows of seating can be removed from around the entire circumference of the pitch, clearing the way for the installation of a temporary Olympic standard running track and athletics field.

The traditional approach from Wembley Park station, the main point of arrival for most spectators, has been retained, as the new stadium is centred on the previous north–south axis and the approach framed dramatically by the soaring curve of the arch, like an enormous white rainbow. A symmetrical arrangement of ramped walkways brings people up to the main podium level at a considerable elevation above surrounding ground levels, and from here access can be gained to all parts of the stadium. The tiers of seating are arranged as a continuous curved bowl, avoiding sharp corners and thus providing clear sightlines to the pitch from every seat. 90,000 seats take a lot of housing and in order to retain a close proximity to the pitch the stadium bowl extends to a considerable height, with the seating arranged into three tiers.

Special attention has been paid to the acoustics of the space to ensure that audibility during the loudest rock concerts is guaranteed through the inbuilt loudspeaker systems, which also ensure that the famous 'Wembley roar' remains, in the hope it inspires play on the pitch.

Internal finishes are by necessity robust, and the design uses a palette of neutral whites and greys to enable individual events to impose their own identity. The theme of the diamond lattice, a geometric *leitmotif* derived directly from the stadium's principal structural elements, informs the design of many of the internal finishes, from wall panels to suspended ceilings and carpets. While the bowels of the stadium incorporate many hundreds of different spaces, including the players' changing rooms and media facilities, two major atrium spaces have been carved into both the north and south sides of the stadium to reveal the full height of the seating, providing useful pointers for way-finding and opening up dramatic views across the space and out over the hinterland.

The reported building cost is put at £352m, but substantial extras including design and legal fees, demolition costs, fitting out, project management and financing costs have all contributed to a total cost in excess of £750m. The contract delays will soon be a thing of the past, as will in all probability the cost. All that remains is for 11 Englishmen to bring home some long-awaited silverware and the ever-patient England fans to their feet. That's not too much to ask, is it?

PALLANT HOUSE GALLERY EXTENSION, CHICHESTER, WEST SUSSEX

Architects: Long and Kentish, with Professor Sir Colin St John Wilson

Chichester's Roman foundation is still evident in the physical survival of its street plan, with North, South, East and West streets meeting at the celebrated central Cross, and substantial stretches of the city wall that once enclosed the four quarters still intact. While the south-

Fig. 2 Pallant House

west quadrant is dominated by the medieval cathedral, the south-east quadrant, known as the Pallants, is distinguished by the survival of a number of fine Georgian houses, including the Grade 1 listed Pallant House, a handsome Queen Anne building dating from 1712.

Pallant House started life as the home of a successful wine merchant, and remained a private residence until 1919, when Chichester Council, who used it for offices, bought it. A number of unsympathetic additions were made and a neo-Georgian style building was erected immediately adjacent. In 1982, in response to an offer of a collection of artworks from the Dean of Chichester, the building became an art gallery and through various donations and bequests has built up an internationally significant collection of British Modern art.

It was the prospect of the acquisition of over 400 pieces from the Wilson Collection, built up over a lifetime by the architect Professor Sir Colin St John Wilson and his wife that led to a reappraisal of the gallery's potential. Rather than simply extend the existing building, a more ambitious plan was decided upon to secure the long-term future of the gallery.

The removal of the 1930s neo-Georgian office block immediately opened up the potential for a substantial increase in the gallery floor area. This demolition enabled the designers to plan the insertion of a new L-shaped building wrapping around the rear of the site to create a new courtyard at the back of the old house. This move brought the rear elevation of the house, with its central stair and tall round-headed central window, into a much more significant role in the defining of internal and external spaces, and ensured the house retains its stand-alone integrity.

The key elevation is the west facing façade along North Pallant, featuring the front façade of the old house, a fine seven-bay composition in warm red brick with tall well-proportioned windows and decorative quoins and mouldings. The new gallery extension is placed adjacent to the old house and finds expression as a relatively simple brick box, separated from the façade of Pallant House by a wide slot, into which is set the principal staircase and lift core of the new extension (*Fig. 2*). The external façade of this vertical circulation core is recessed behind the restored brick quoins of the old house and is clad in a modular system of dark red glazed terracotta and clear glass panels. The two principal elements, the old house and new extension, are therefore expressed as separate stand-alone volumes, though linked by a commonality of material, texture and colour.

The new gallery accommodation is set out on two main floor levels, with the public entrance and reception foyer, shop, restaurant, library and print gallery and other ancillary areas at ground floor level, the first floor being devoted to the principal gallery spaces and meeting rooms. This division is expressed in the main street elevation, with the upper façade being almost entirely blank, while the ground storey is expressed as a series of openings between substantial brick piers. The potentially blank upper part of the elevation, constructed with a red Sussex brick, is relieved by a sequence of narrow vertical recessed slots rising from the first floor level right up to the parapet, dividing the elevation into seven tall panels that pick up the rhythm of the repeated window bays of Pallant House.

On passing through the entrance, with the shop to the left and the stair and lift core to the right, the visitor is eased into a generous central area of informal layout, called the garden gallery, dominated as it is by a series of tall glazed openings with doors opening onto the new courtyard garden. Accessed from this core space at ground level are a studio space, a library, a prints and drawings gallery, and the restaurant, which occupies the return leg of the L-shape plan.

The landscaping of the courtyard has been designed by Christopher Bradley-Hole, and incorporates a reflecting pool and fountain, some carefully orchestrated planting and paved areas featuring sections of Italian marble. A short staircase leads up from the courtyard back into the central stairway of the old house. The upper parts of the courtyard elevations are finished simply, with an off-white lime render finish. This provides a clean and fresh counterpoint to the rich red brickwork of the old house.

The first floor offers a series of largely introspective gallery spaces, top-lit through canted concrete roof-lights with sections of suspended ceiling acting as central baffles reflecting and diffusing daylight. Light levels can be controlled by means of externally mounted louvres. A long galleria, with a single large recess incorporating windows overlooking the courtyard, provides access to all the subsidiary gallery spaces. These are designed to be small intimate spaces, imbued with an air of permanence and on a domestic scale akin to the gallery rooms in the old house matching the original environments for which many of the works of art were originally conceived.

The largest gallery is a tripartite space and backs onto the blank façade over the main entrance. Three smaller gallery spaces form an interconnected enfilade of rooms parallel to the central galleria, at the far end of which are an anteroom to gallery five and the entrance to gallery six, their entrances located on the main and cross axis points. The gallery sequence ends at the far side of gallery six in a burst of daylight, as the courtyard elevation is terminated by a tall fully glazed conservatory-like projecting bay, overlooking and centred on the central staircase of Pallant House opposite. It is a stimulating release from the concentration of the galleries and a good vantage point, providing views over the courtyard, the new extension, the rear of the old house and out over the surrounding streets.

The galleries are densely hung with works that have been donated over the years, so that a large percentage of the overall collection remains on display. The gallery holds what is now recognised as one of the most important small collections of British Modern art, and the pictures can now be viewed in ideal surroundings that have been thoughtfully designed and beautifully crafted by the very people who have spent half a lifetime collecting them.

The £8.6m extension has received many plaudits since its opening in the autumn of 2006, and in May 2007 it was awarded the annual Gulbenkian Prize for Museums and Galleries, one of the biggest prizes in the arts field, worth £100,000. Sadly this announcement came too late to be appreciated by Prof. Sir Colin St John Wilson, who in a long and successful career could list, among his many other achievements, the design of the new British Library. Sadly he died, aged 84, just two weeks before the announcement.

PETER HARRISON PLANETARIUM, ROYAL OBSERVATORY, GREENWICH, LONDON

Architect: Allies & Morrison

The name of Greenwich is firmly embedded into the history of time, global navigation and astronomy, and the historic site of the observatory that marks the point of zero degrees longitude is still a popular visitor attraction. Although the groundbreaking instruments of scientific observation that once operated from the site have long since departed, the site retains its magic and has been developed into a valuable educational facility.

This function has been greatly enhanced following the completion of the new planetarium in May 2007. Constructed in the area of the site between the Victorian South Building and the smaller Altazimuth Pavilion, the new building is the final phase of the £15m Time and Space Project carried out by the National Maritime Museum, and follows the improvement work to the Time Galleries in Flamsteed House, Wren's original observatory building, completed in 2006.

The recent work has included not only the new planetarium but also extensive refurbishment of the Grade 2 listed South Building, an 1890s cruciform brick and terracotta structure capped by a central dome. In this building the original massive masonry core, that previously provided a stable anchorage for the Thompson equatorial telescope, has been removed, permitting a new helical staircase to be inserted into the central well, linking all the floor levels and facilitating a direct access at the lowest level into the foyer area of the new Planetarium.

The heart of the new planetarium is a 118-seat circular auditorium, which has been located in the centre of the site at lower ground level, accessed through a new foyer space that looks out through a glazed wall onto the small courtyard area created in front of the South Building. The foyer, planetarium hall and supporting ancillary accommodation are all concealed beneath an open paved public terrace that provides a strong visual and physical link between the South Building and the Altazimuth Pavilion, and through which the domed upper part of the planetarium protrudes. Finding an appropriate physical expression for this protrusion was of critical importance for the designers and its treatment has been handled in a highly imaginative and symbolic manner.

Deciding that, given the existing domes of both the South Building and the Altazimuth Pavilion, a third dome was not the answer, the architect has instead chosen to create a form that, while to some extent echoing the earlier designs nevertheless speaks entirely of the 21st century and in its precise geometrical characteristics reflects a number of salient astronomical concepts.

Instead of a dome, the visible form takes the shape of a tilted and truncated conical outer skin concealing the internal hemispherical volume. The tilted profile of the cone is derived from two key angles, one at right angles to the earth's surface (ie vertical), the other tilted at an angle of 51.5° (the angle of latitude of Greenwich) and on an axis directly aligned with the North (Pole) Star. At a point above the terrace level, as the resulting cone narrows towards its apex, it is sliced off at an angle to reveal its circular internal plan shape. This plane is angled to be parallel with the 'celestial equator', in other words it is parallel to a similar plane taken as a section through the earth's equator, and it is clad in sheets of reflective glass designed to act as a 'mirror to the heavens'.

The expressed form of the building therefore derives directly from its position on the earth's surface and the geometrical influence of key celestial concepts, a highly appropriate response to function and location. It also works surprisingly well in terms of its immediate context, with the lower level rim of the cone responding to the small scale and model-like qualities of the Altazimuth Pavilion, the sloping glazing and higher level edge on the opposite flank suggesting a transition to the larger scale of the South Building.

With such precise geometries embodied in its form, the construction of the cone has been developed to reflect both its astronomical and sculptural qualities, resulting in the use of a patinated bronze external skin. The primary structural element is a 250mm thick concrete casing that provides both the required physical support, internally and externally, as well as a high level of acoustic isolation for the auditorium below and follows the truncated conical shape of the bronze outer skin.

Bronze is a material that was commonly used in astronomical instruments and is also widely used for the casting of sculptures, particularly those to be placed in outdoor settings. Casting the whole thing on site was not a practical option and therefore the skin was manufactured from a series of 18 curved and tapering 8mm-thick phosphor-bronze segments. Each segment itself is constructed from a number of smaller panels welded together off-site. Depending on their intended location around the conical form, the segments vary in length between 3.7 and 12m, and are supported on a secondary framework of steel members.

The finish is a medium to dark grey, its appearance depending on the prevailing daylight conditions, leavened with subtle undertones of greens, blues and earth colours. As a result of the patination process it has a dappled or blotchy effect that suggests the tiny and infinitely variable bursts of light visible in the night sky. In the centre of the highest part of the cone's casing, on the axis aligned directly with the North Star, a thin observation slot, running from top to bottom, forms the only visible interruption to the smooth casing, and on a clear night should provide a useful sighting aid for interested visitors keen to pinpoint this focal point of celestial movement.

Set amid a generous expanse of green Chinese granite paving, the planetarium's cone sits cool and inscrutable, somewhat sinister in its otherworldly precision, in marked contrast to its parkland surroundings and the adjoining sequence of historic buildings. Underneath the geometric precision of the exterior however, future generations will be able to explore and learn more about the awesome infinities of space and gain a better insight into the wonders of the universe.

NEW ROYAL BATH THERMAL SPA, BATH, SOMERSET

Architect: Grimshaw Architects

Three or four years in the life of a Roman city should seem like a mere flash of time. For Bath's new Royal Spa, it seems as if an age has passed from what appeared to be its practical completion to the day when it could first open its doors. This project has had to endure a catalogue of disputes, delays and technical misfortunes in the process from inception to completion, which has occupied almost a decade.

Grimshaw originally won the design competition for the spa in 1997, it was to cost approximately £19m, and work started on site in September 2002. Early delays were caused over concerns about the impact of construction on the natural hot spring sources, which have played a crucial role in the history of the city. These fears were resolved, but further problems were encountered with defects in the paintwork and a number of troublesome leaks, which led to disputes between the client, contractor and design team. The dispute escalated, legal action was invoked, and the relationships deteriorated to the point where the original contractor was dismissed and an independent investigation into the faults was performed.

During the standoff it became widely accepted that, from the outside at least, Grimshaw's stone and glass insertion slotted into its historic surroundings with ease and sensitivity. Given that the building is located in the heart of a World Heritage site and that the work involved the use and adaptation of several listed buildings, this was no mean achievement.

The new building crams a substantial amount of accommodation onto its tight city centre location, which was created by the demolition of the Beau Street baths in 1998. The main entrance is located in the Grade 1 listed buildings of Nos. 7 and 8 Bath Street, the largest of these being a handsome three storey building of Bath stone with a concave façade in the classical Bath style, with a tall open colonnade running along its base; one of two such buildings that back onto the site of the new building.

The disposition of the key components of the accommodation is ordered and controlled, but thanks to some imaginative spatial arrangements, it does result in some memorable internal spaces. The bulk of the new building's accommodation is housed within a four-square stone-clad block, three storeys in height, largely untroubled by fenestration other than for a series of neat rows of tiny porthole windows arranged around the central axis on the exposed sides.

The block's considerable mass is supported by four chunky double-height tapering columns, expanding into oversized spreading mushroom-like heads that spread across the soffit until they almost touch. More striking is the fact that these columns all emerge out of a large free-form pool, known as The Minerva Bath, which is situated at lower ground level. The space around the pool extends as far as the site boundary, where solid storey high panels line the walls to maintain privacy. The pool surrounds extend beyond the profile of the 'box' overhead, so the space expands upwards around the perimeter, leaving the central box in midair as it were, perched on its four columns. Clever use of pool lighting and the water 'current' system available help create a unique and dramatic undercroft pool environment.

On the outer corner of the site stands a tall, fat stone-clad cylinder, housing a spiral staircase that connects the intermediate floor levels and winds around a large central services duct rising from the basement to the roof. Its smooth stone cladding is punctuated at intervals by bands of the same small porthole windows used in the core block, providing a measure of daylight to the internal stair.

The lowest floor of the central cube, which is roughly a half-storey up from the main entrance, contains the changing rooms. The main vertical circulation core occupies the gap between the face of the new block and the rear of the buildings on Bath Street. Bathers therefore first ascend to the changing rooms and then either descend via stairs or lift to the main spa pool below or ascend to the other facilities at the upper levels. Though lacking the convenience of a single level arrangement, it is clearly the result of the cramped nature of the available site and the need to house several very different functions.

The floor above the changing rooms is devoted to a gym and an array of massage and treatment rooms. The gym occupies a central square space defined by the four columns, a square within a square. In the space between the core's outer wall and the inner gym wall, radiused enclosures fan out from each column, their extent defined by the perimeter of the spreading mushroom column heads, with each resulting three quarter circle divided on the diagonal, providing eight separate massage rooms.

The floor above this provides a suite of steam rooms, at which point the increasingly noticeable influence of an underlying futuristic starship aesthetic becomes more apparent. Here the plan again derives directly from the replicated arrangement of four mushroom columns. A full-height clear glazed circular steam room is centred on each column, its size determined by the extent of the mushroom head; a ceiling mounted movement-activated shower provides a cascade in the centre of the space, and the grids of tiny portholes in the external walls punctuate the enclosure with brilliant spots of natural light.

All of these events however are but a prelude to the building's real showpiece. Ascend via the lifts or stairs to the top floor, proceed through the doors, and there is revealed a superb rooftop pool with the cityscape of Bath set all around and the tower of Bath Abbey as a stunning focal point for the views of the surrounding hills. At this level the stone clad central core sits as a raised plinth above the terrace below, with a minimalist clear glass balustrade lining its perimeter. The pool follows the square plan form of the core, with generous corners softening the geometry and offering a subtle memory of the tiers of mushroom headed columns stacked up below. This is a superb spot from which to enjoy the heated waters for which Bath is famous, and at dusk or nightfall, when the Abbey is illuminated and the stars begin to shine, it can take on a quite magical quality.

That such delights have at last been realised should be some recompense for those who have been embroiled in the new spa's long and troubled procurement, knowing that the heart of the city will undoubtedly be strengthened by this bold, modern and imaginative addition to Bath's world renowned architectural heritage.

NATIONAL COLD WAR EXHIBITION, RAF COSFORD, SHROPSHIRE

Architect: Feilden Clegg, Bradley Architects

It was not until the horrors of Hiroshima and Nagasaki were perpetrated on the unsuspecting Japanese towards the end of World War II that the implications of nuclear weaponry became apparent to the world. The threat of attack by an atomic bomb became the driving force behind the western world's development of sophisticated weapons systems in the decades that followed the end of the war. Ensuring both some degree of early warning of impending attack and the threat of monstrous retaliation were the key strategies of the major powers. The Cold War period was characterised by the uneasy standoff between the USA and Russia, engendered by the threat of mutual annihilation.

This new museum commemorates the period, with an exhibition not only of military hardware, but also of more commonplace objects associated with contemporary life. Alongside those fearsome expressions of nuclear deterrence, such as Britain's V-bombers and various deadly missiles, one can find the Mini, the Beetle and the Trabant, as well as other artefacts of social history. The emphasis however is on the military aspects of the Cold War, including tanks and armoured vehicles, and, as befits an RAF museum, a dominant assembly of 17 different aircraft, some grounded, others suspended and made airborne, all crammed together in dynamic and implausibly close formation.

All these items are housed within a huge sculptural hangar-like building characterised by enormous sweeps of silver metal cladding generated by a clever juxtaposition of two triangulated volumes either side of a central spine. The dynamic thrust of the building derives from its plan, which sets the alignment of the spine wall on the diagonal of a parallelogram shape, generating two triangular floor plates that in turn appear to have slipped part of the way past each other on either side of the spine. The exhibition floor is split across these two triangular areas and two levels, as the building takes advantage of the change in ground level across the site.

The spine is a hollow, steel framed construction approximately 3m in thickness and 25m high, extending to an overall length of 135m. The framing has been omitted across the central section to leave a substantial void, which is spanned by a steel framed lattice that supports the continuous ridge level roof-lights and maintenance walkway. The volume is generated from the triangular plan of each half. Where the apex of each triangle meets the wall of the spine, the cladding is in a vertical plane, and continues out to the end of the spine wall. At the opposing base end of the triangle the cladding slopes outwards, having turned from a wall face into a roof, a deep truss supporting the angled edge of the cladding in a straight line between the ridge and the outer corner of the triangle. Between the two positions the roof plane is a constantly changing complex curve, created by joining the ridge of the spine and the angled outer edge of the triangle with a series of evenly spaced straight-line trusses. This creates a surface that is known as a hyperbolic parabaloid, and the form is duplicated on each side of the spine to generate a dynamic external form enclosing an interior of cathedral-like proportions.

In a further twist of complexity, the outer corner of each of the triangular forms has been raised above ground level, to provide headroom over a much greater proportion of the floor area than if the roof had fallen consistently to the ground. This device creates a low triangular sliver of glazed wall elevation at the foot of each sweeping roof and results in an irregular four-sided end elevation.

The roof covering itself is a galvanised structural steel deck seated on trays fixed to the primary structural trusses and framework, which supports 160mm of glass fibre quilt insulation, a vapour control membrane and an external cladding of an aluminium standing seam roof system; ideal for forming the sinuous three dimensional curves of the roof profile. The constantly varying curves of the silver grey finish reflect the light according to the angle of inclination and position of the sun so that the elevations are rarely uniform in appearance.

Internally, the upper gallery overlooks the lower-level section of the museum and the extending bridge link provides a useful high-level viewpoint for the aircraft suspended in the lower space. Tucked under the front section of the upper gallery are an auditorium and classrooms, together with mechanical plant room and lavatories. Finishes are simple and robust and bright colours are by and large restricted to the exhibits and stands. Given the subject matter, there is an appropriate suggestion of austerity in the untreated and rusty steelwork of the spine framing and trusses. Floors are hardened concrete and the exposed soffits of the decking panels show their grey galvanised finish. Each end elevation is filled with a series of removable translucent PVC fabric panels, supported by and tensioned against intermediate tapering triangulated posts spanning from ground level to the underside of the end truss. Translucent to allow daylight to flood in from each end, both they and the posts can be removed when weather conditions are suitable to permit individual aircraft to be taken in and out.

This is a dynamic and exciting building which provides a stimulating environment for its exhibits with admirable economy and efficiency. For a total outlay of £12.5m the museum provides an opportunity for the public to get to grips with some of the most charismatic artefacts from the Cold War period and demonstrates the perversity of the world's deadliest weapons, whose primary function was to keep the peace.

AWARDS

RIBA AWARDS 2006

The Stirling Prize – The New Area Terminal, Barajas Airport, Madrid; Richard Rogers Partnership

THE STIRLING SHORTLIST

Idea Store, Whitechapel, London; Adjaye Associates

National Assembly for Wales, Cardiff; Richard Rogers Partnership

Brick House, London; Caruso St John

Evelina Children's Hospital, London; Hopkins Architects

Phaeno Science Centre, Wolfsburg, Germany; Zaha Hadid Architects

RIBA SPECIAL AWARDS

The Manser Medal – Holly Barn; Knox Bavan Architects LLP

The Stephen Lawrence Prize – Wrap House, London W4; Alison Brooks Architects

The RIBA Sustainability Award – Heelis, Office for the National Trust, Swindon; Feilden Clegg Bradley

The RIBA Inclusive Design Award – Idea Store, Whitechapel, London E1; Adjaye Associates

Crown Estate Conservation Award – National Gallery East Wing and Central Portico Ph 1; Dixon Jones Ltd with Purcell Miller Tritton

RIBA Client of the Year Award – Royal Botanic Gardens, Kew

The Lubetkin Prize – Southern Cross Station, Melbourne, Australia; Grimshaw (working within the Grimshaw Jackson Joint Venture)

ART

Ruth Maclennan

ARTS FUNDING CRISIS

In March 2007 Prime Minister Tony Blair signed off with a surprising and uplifting speech to cultural leaders insisting that the arts in Britain were going through a golden age. He highlighted the strength of the British film industry, the popularity of the country's museums and the link between dynamism in the arts and the nation as a whole. Blair also promised an end to 'boom and bust' arts funding. However, the Labour golden age seemed more like the age of austerity a month later, when the government made a shock announcement that the Grants for the Arts budget was to be cut by a third. Grants for the Arts, as opposed to revenue funding, is the backbone of public funding for individual artists, as well as institutional projects. The funding was a healthy £83m in 2006–7, but shrunk to £54m in 2007–8. Further reductions are set to leave an emaciated £30m budget by 2009. Mysteriously, a search for 'cuts' on the Arts Council's website results in the following message: 'Sorry – no matches. Try something else.'

The reason for this *volte-face* is the redistribution of funding from the arts and sport, much of it provided by the good causes fund of the National Lottery, to fill the financial black hole otherwise known as the 2012 Olympics. The new prime minister, Gordon Brown, has not revealed his position on the arts, but his iron grip during his decade at the Treasury does not give much ground for optimism. Bloodied, but unbowed by this news, a group of artists responded quickly to the challenge and held an alternative Olympiad on 26 May on Hackney Marshes – 'Grunts for the Arts' – with competitions including the High Heel 100m, the Celebrity Sack Race and Durational Knitting Sprints. The handbag-hurling contest was a reported favourite.

While many people are justifiably angry that the 2012 Olympics are sapping public funding and causing council tax rises in London, the Games are not all bad news for the arts. Regeneration of the East End has closed some studio buildings for redevelopment and major art projects have already begun. An 'Olympic Artists Symposium' was hosted by SPACE, the East London artists' studios organisation, together with the Museum of London to discuss and showcase artists involved in, or affected by the Olympics.

Lottery funding aside, another major subsidy source for artists is academic research grants, in particular by the Arts and Humanities Research Council. Art schools and universities, desperate to increase their research standing to protect their own funding, have been eager to recruit artist-researchers who score precious research points for the institutions with their every exhibition. The criteria for research points are erratic and parochial to say the least. Under the scoring system, points can be gained for exhibiting in a small commercial gallery but not in a major international touring show; and from an article in an obscure peer-reviewed journal, but not a review in a national newspaper. The Research Assessment Exercise system is coming to an end in 2008. Suddenly, three-year research posts are shrinking in number, and few are being advertised beyond 2008.

Art education and art schools are huge money-spinners in the UK, with thousands of students from Europe and further afield competing for places at iconic institutions such as Goldsmiths and Central Saint Martins. Although there are no figures available, the income and jobs generated by art education in Britain are likely to be greater than those produced by the rest of the domestic contemporary art world combined. Beyond the art school, there is clearly a hunger for learning about art as well as the more straightforward accumulation of cultural capital through collecting it. Every museum and public gallery has a major education programme: Tate offers courses in art appreciation and critical theory, and the organisers of the Frieze Art Fair have expanded their repertoire of talks and screenings, cementing the fair's standing as the cultural event of the year.

PRIVATE FOUNDATIONS

While the Arts Council faces severe cuts, and publicly funded art spaces are threatened with slashed budgets, the relatively new phenomenon of the private foundation has gone from strength to strength. The veteran, Charles Saatchi, is still on the scene, although the exhibition of his collection of American art at the Royal Academy in 2006 *USA Today*, did not cause the stir of 1997's *Sensation*. The Saatchi Gallery was to open in new premises in the Duke of York's HQ on the King's Road in November. In the meantime there is Saatchi online, which allows anyone to register and show their work on the site.

The Wellcome Trust opened the year's biggest new venue on Euston Road. Founder Henry Wellcome, who made his fortune in pharmaceuticals and was a prolific and eclectic collector of all things medical and odd founded the trust in 1936. Part of his extraordinary private collection is elegantly installed in the exhibition *Medicine Man,* alongside a temporary exhibition, *The Heart,* and a permanent exhibition, *Medicine Now*. Contemporary works of art commissioned by the trust hang alongside medical specimens (a whale's heart, the complete sequence of the human genome) and historical works. The building itself has been expensively refurbished to house a library, the obligatory café and shop, lecture theatre and screening room. Many of the original features of the dour old building have been retained, but the overall effect is more welcoming and light.

Other thriving foundations include the critically acclaimed Parasol Unit, now two years old and housed on the edge of Hoxton, next door to the Victoria Miro Gallery, and the Louise T. Blouin Foundation, which opened its luxurious new art space in Notting Hill this year with an exhibition of new work by James Turrell.

MAJOR EXHIBITIONS AROUND THE WORLD

In 2007 four of the biggest art world events opened over a single busy week in June: the Venice Biennale, the Art Basel fair, Documenta 12 and the Münster Sculpture Projects. The whirlwind tour of openings and mass guzzling of contemporary art by the art world's frequent flyers was clearly exhausting, even for the most party-hardened among them. The intense networking and clamour for party invitations left both an enormous combined carbon footprint and some very sore heads.

The 52nd Venice Biennale opened on 10 June, to run until 21 November. Tracey Emin occupied the British pavilion with *Borrowed Light*, a rather disappointing showing of neons, embroideries, sculpture and drawings as well as a set of never-before-seen paintings from 1990 titled *Abortion Watercolours*. Emin is only the second woman to represent Britain, after Rachel Whiteread a decade ago. Despite lashings of media hype, there was a distinct feeling that she hadn't pulled the rabbit out of a hat this time. The French pavilion proved to be the festival's big success with Sophie Calle's *Take Care of Yourself*. Calle asked 107 women of different professions to interpret through their own expertise (be it dancing or psychoanalysis) a break-up letter she had been sent by an ex-boyfriend. Despite using her personal life to explore experiences, the artist's approach is open and collaborative, risky and playful, and all about communication. Emin provided a useful counterpoint, as she has exploited her own personal life with equal frankness, but on this occasion seemed stuck in repeating her own familiar tropes.

Scotland had its own exhibition, entitled *Venice and Scotland 2007* at the Palazzo Zenobio, in the Dorsoduro district of Venice. The artists, assembled by the senior curator of the Scottish National Gallery of Modern Art, included Charles Avery, Henry Coombes, Louise Hopkins, Rosalind Nashashibi, Lucy Skaer and Tony Swain. Oddly perhaps, the Ukrainian pavilion, curated by Peter Doroshenko (an American Ukrainian who runs the Baltic Centre for Contemporary Art in Gateshead) featured work by Mark Titchner, last year nominated for the Turner prize, and photographer and video artist Sam Taylor-Wood.

Over in Kassel, a rather non-descript town in Germany, Documenta, billed as the '100 day museum', rolled out for the first time since 2002. First initiated in 1955 by artist and educator Arnold Bode, Documenta 12 (16 June–23 September 2007) was directed by Roger M. Buergel, an international curator and exhibition organiser, and art historian Ruth Noack. Their broad and encompassing aim was 'to show art from the most various regions of the world and in all conceivable media.' The theme of the exhibition followed three *leitmotifs* devised by the curators: 'Is modernity our antiquity? What is bare life? What is to be done?' They are sufficiently vague as to be interpretable in whatever way appealed and the project capitalised on this: 100 publications around the world were asked to consider and publish articles on the *leitmotifs*. The curators chose their favourites for the online printable magazine, *Documenta 12*. British art on show in Documenta included John McCraken's minimalist sculptures, and Mary Kelly's recent recollection of a 1970s performance.

MAJOR SHOWS IN BRITAIN

The most exciting exhibition of the year – if not the decade – was *Citizens and Kings: Portraits in the Age of Revolution, 1760–1830*, held at the Royal Academy from February to April. The exhibition explored the connection between politics and representation at a time of revolution in Europe and America but went beyond exploring the political context to examine the effects of the enlightenment on portraiture, social attitudes and ways of seeing. The transformation in Europe from the *Ancien Régime* to the revolutionary period, subsequent Napoleonic rule, and then to the restoration, was shown not just in the changing styles of royal portraiture, but also the growing interest in representing the humble citizen.

The construction of the unfamiliar new roles of authority and subject in America were fascinatingly realised in paintings by Copley, Gilbert Stuart's portraits of George Washington and Houdon's terracotta bust of Benjamin Franklin. The exhibition brought together an extraordinary array of paintings and sculptures by 90 artists, including many of the most remarkable portraits of rulers, hung together in an outstanding first gallery: Jean-Auguste-Dominique Ingres' *Napoleon I on the Imperial Throne* (1806), Goya's *Ferdinand VII in Royal Robes* (*c.*1815), Reynolds' *George III* and *Queen Charlotte* (1779–80) and Sir Thomas Lawrence's flamboyant *George IV* (1806). The naked statue of an ageing and sinuous Voltaire with an amused expression by Jean-Baptiste Pigalle (1776) is strikingly modern in its directness, if not the Grecian drapes and mask at his feet.

The subject of the National Gallery's autumn blockbuster was Diego Velazquez (18 October 2006–21 January 2007). In addition to healthy receipts and some heaving rooms, the exhibition brought together almost half of the world's surviving works, including a number from the Prado in Madrid, and received sparkling reviews. *Renoir Landscapes 1865–83,* also at the National, demonstrated a more unfamiliar aspect of the popular impressionist's painting, and included several works from the early 1880s when he travelled to the south of France, Italy and North Africa.

Despite a strong 2006–7, the National Gallery is facing a funding crisis as it contemplates raising £200m to save three major works in its collection, which are currently on long-term loan to the gallery. The works – Nicolas Poussin's *Sacraments* (1639, 1644–8), owned by the Duke of Rutland; Titian's celebrated *Portrait of a Young Man* (*c.*1515), owned by Lord Halifax; and a sketch by Rubens for his *Apotheosis of King James in Whitehall* (1629–30), which has been in the collection of the family of Lord Hampden for two centuries – would each fetch significant sums, given the current buoyancy of the market. This is becoming an increasingly familiar situation for British galleries, though there are some positive precedents: the National itself saved Raphael's *Madonna of the Pinks* (*c.*1506–7) three years ago for £22m and Tate raised over £550,000 from the public in just five weeks to keep Turner's *Blue Rigi* watercolour. There is an argument for changing the law on allowing major artworks to be sold abroad, although this implies an obvious and thorny double standard, as Britain houses many treasures which it has no automatic right to own, from Europe in particular.

Tate Britain held a major exhibition of Hogarth's paintings, drawings and prints, from February to April, with reproductions of the broadsheets in which some of the latter originally appeared, thus enabling visitors to leaf through them and imagine the world to which they belonged. The exhibition reinforced the notion that political satire is perhaps more jaundiced and less moral today than that depicted by Hogarth.

Another highlight was the exhibition *How We Are*, the first major survey of photography at the Tate. Alongside familiar names (including Henry Fox Talbot, Julia Margaret Cameron, David Bailey and Tom Hunter), were albums, books, postcards and medical photographs. Although the show brought together an extraordinary array of still images from the past 150 years, the curatorial premise of the exhibition somewhat jarred. The notion that photographs can represent anything other than reality was unchallenged, and the thematic groupings of the works were unimaginative, serving only to underline the many clichés about British society – its earnest multi-culturalism, comfortable suburban living and burgeoning appetite for consumerism.

Downriver at Tate Modern, popular exhibitions included a Gilbert and George retrospective, and an excellent exhibition showing links between the paintings and films of Salvador Dalí, and the deep influence of cinema on his approach to painting and subject matter. Carsten Höller's slide, *Test Site,* in the Turbine Hall captured both public and media interest, generating huge queues and several injuries in the process. The current exhibition in the Turbine Hall is *Global Cities,* a transfer from the 2006 Venice Biennale of Architecture. The exhibition's premise was the statistic that 50 per cent of the world's population now lives in cities. It compares the state of ten global cities, from economic, demographic and ecological perspectives. The content was varied enough, with statistics and graphs, aerial photographs, and architectural proposals. Artists' works, some newly commissioned for the exhibition, are inserted between the information, and provide a welcome microscopic look among the sweeping vistas. Richard Wentworth's discreetly positioned videos of yellow lines being painted on the roads, and aeroplane jet streams, are especially enjoyable in their non-didactic, yet poignant resonance. The subject is vital, yet the global view that this exhibition offers was too general and failed to give any nuanced political or social context for the state of our cities.

Dalí also appeared at the Victoria and Albert Museum in the popular exhibition *Surreal Things.* The show played down the radical nature of surrealist politics and aesthetics, preferring to see the movement as a mere style. The exhibition's highlight was a rare chance to see the work of the underrated Leonora Carrington, who is still alive and working. Tate Liverpool showed a retrospective of Pop artist and Beatle album cover illustrator, Peter Blake, alongside *Centre Of The Creative Universe: Liverpool And The Avant-Garde.*

The season at the Institute of Contemporary Art (ICA) was dominated by conscience-raising exhibitions such as *Memorial to the Iraq War,* in which 26 artists were invited to make proposals for a memorial. The results were neither daring or controversial, but the question itself is important, and the ICA is one of the few places to have raised it. The following exhibition *Insider Art,* featuring work by prison inmates and those in psychiatric care, seemed to suggest the ICA is determined to place art with politics at the heart of its programme.

NEW TRENDS

The last year saw a rejuvenation of live events and performance. There are several reasons for this. Traditionally, performance art was seen as a stand against the commodification of art as object. However in the current climate and, perhaps somewhat more cynically, it could be interpreted as a response to the problem of overproduction and the inability of individuals to keep up with it. Tate Modern is building an extension behind the Turbine Hall, which is to be a dedicated performance space, guaranteeing further live events in the future. In addition, for this year's Manchester International Festival, the curators Hans Ulrich Obrist and Philippe Parreno have invited artists to produce an unmediated piece of art in front of a live audience in just 15 minutes.

There has also been a notable trend for curators from public art institutions to move to private galleries. Senior curator Emma Dexter left Tate to become director of exhibitions at the Timothy Taylor Gallery to coincide with the gallery's move to larger premises. Ben Tuffnell (formerly at Tate Britain) went to Haunch of Venison, and Gregor Muir (also from Tate Modern) to Hauser and Wirth while the outgoing director of the National Gallery, Charles Saumarez Smith, is scheduled to depart for the Royal Academy.

NEW VENTURES

Rich Mix, a new venue in Bethnal Green, East London, opened with the aim of becoming a 'cultural flagship for the capital and, in particular, the ethnic communities of East London,' said Ken Livingstone, Mayor of London. Art institutions will only even attempt to serve this 'regenerative' purpose if properly financed in the future as well as the outset. Other new facilities include the BFI Southbank (replacing the National Film Theatre), opened in the spring in the refurbished building behind the NFT that used to house the Museum of the Moving Image; the Middlesbrough Institute of Modern Art, now housed in a stunning building by Dutch architect Erick van Egeraat, and the ongoing expansion of the British Museum, following a remarkable year which saw record visitor figures of 4.9 million, a rise of 400,000 on 2005. The museum is building an extension to enable it to take larger touring exhibitions, which it struggles to accommodate at the moment. The complex will also include a new conservation centre for the museum's collection and will be used as a training resource for conservators from around the world. Architects Rogers Stirk Harbour and Partners have been appointed and private donors are being sought.

The success of Frieze Art Fair continued, and has spawned a new season: 'Frieze Week', with all the capital's galleries putting on special exhibitions and events to lure the international collectors and dealers who descend on London and Regent's Park. Meanwhile, Zoo Art Fair, a non-profit organisation that shows younger galleries (of up to four-years-old) is also doing well. The number of galleries in the capital is constantly rising – evidenced by the increased number of listings pages in *Time Out.*

MONEY, MONEY, MONEY

The May sales in New York set a record high – the boom boomed again – with Sotheby's turning a record $254.9m (£123m), only to be surpassed by Christie's the following night, which scored $384.6m (£187m). At Sotheby's, contemporary British artists Cecily Brown and Glenn Brown sold well, with Brown's *The Marquess of Breadlabane* (2000) going for $734,000 (£356,000). *The Architect's Home in the Ravine* by Scottish artist Peter Doig, represented by Victoria Miro, doubled its estimate and sold for $3.6m (£1.7m) while Doig's *White Canoe* (1991) sold in February for five times its estimate at $11.2m (£5.4m). Meanwhile at Christie's, Damien Hirst's *Lullaby Spring,* a stainless-steel cabinet filled with 6,136 painted bronze-cast pills, reached $7.4m (£3.6m) only to be sold again in June, in London for £9.65m, the highest price for the sale of a living artist's work. Eastern European and Asian buyers were particularly significant in both the New York and London sales.

In London, the June sales also achieved record prices,

cementing the city's place among the world's most important art markets. The weak dollar means that Americans are keen to sell in the capital and the subsequent greater selection attracts oil-rich buyers from Eastern Europe. In total, the Sotheby's London sales of contemporary art raised over £97m, and combined with Impressionist and Modern art, more than £153m. Christie's sales of post-war and contemporary art raised a total of £92.2m and with the Modern and Impressionist art, £141.5m.

Another sign of the contemporary art boom and the close interaction between galleries and auction houses was Christie's acquisition of the London commercial gallery Haunch of Venison. The headquarters of the gallery is in London, with other branches in Zurich and Berlin, and it is opening a new gallery in New York. Founders Harry Blain and Graham Southern have said they will continue to run the gallery. It remains to be seen how the purchase will affect the relationship between artist and auction house. The latter gathers art from collectors, while dealers often obtain works directly from artists and sell them privately to clients who might not patronise auction houses. This new development suggests a desire to make money in a bull market, but also for the houses to gain more control over the progress of an artist's work prices.

The most striking and, given the soaring market, perhaps the most appropriate new piece of art unveiled this year was by Damien Hirst. A platinum skull set with 8,601 diamonds, *For the Love of God* went on show at London's White Cube Gallery. If the media buzz was inevitable, the length of queues to see his latest artefact were more surprising. The skull came from a shop in Islington, but had not yet found a new home at the time of publication, perhaps weighed down by the £50m price tag which seemed like a direct challenge to the mega-rich new breed of art collectors, with its ostentatious show of diamonds and a hefty dose of religiosity. Could Hirst be the Fabergé of the 21st century?

PRIZES, COMMISSIONS AND SPONSORSHIP

The 2006 Turner Prize – so-called, say some wags, because everyone gets a turn – was won by Tomma Abts for her carefully constructed abstract small 1950s-style paintings. This year's Turner Prize nominees were Zarina Bhimji, Nathan Coley, Mike Nelson and Mark Wallinger, with the latter the early favourite. Wallinger's *State Britain* at Tate Britain reproduces Brian Haw's protest outside the houses of parliament, complete with weather-beaten banners, notes and stuffed toys. By luck (and perhaps a bit of number crunching), Wallinger's work is displayed half inside, half outside the exclusion zone which was established when parliament passed the undemocratic Serious Organised Crime and Police Act prohibiting unauthorised demonstrations within a kilometre radius of Parliament Square. The Turner Prize exhibition will take place at Tate Liverpool this year in recognition of the city's status as European Capital of Culture in 2008.

DEATHS

Sol LeWitt the major minimalist artist, famous for his wall paintings, died this year, aged 78. Founder and director of Eta (Empowering the Artist), Deborah Rawson, died suddenly at the age of 44. She was a passionate supporter of art, pioneering projects that allowed artists the time and space to produce new work, for twenty years.

BROADCASTING

Steve Clarke

TELEVISION

The year 2006–7 was a tumultuous one for broadcasters. Forecasters continued to predict that television was living on borrowed time as the internet, especially video-sharing websites such as YouTube, emerged to challenge traditional broadcast organisations, all of whom increased their own web-based activities. Yet while statistics suggested that young people were spending less time watching TV, the medium's power to generate controversy – and huge viewing figures for the right programmes – remained. It was too early to tell how broadband-delivered TV services like BT Vision would fare.

Arguably the year's biggest broadcasting row came in January when 45,000 people complained to the communications regulator, OFCOM, over what they regarded as racist bullying in *Celebrity Big Brother,* shown by Channel 4. The victim was a Bollywood actress Shilpa Shetty, then largely unknown in the UK. The row's intensity led to calls for the resignation of the station's most senior executives, while no lesser figure than the prime minister-in-waiting, Gordon Brown, was drawn into the furore during a state visit to India.

Channel 4, in common with the BBC, ITV, Five and the breakfast station, GMTV, gained further unwelcome publicity when, in February, it was reported that premium phone line competitions on the daytime show, *Richard and Judy,* were cheating viewers. 'Every day an average of 15,000 viewers pay £1 a time to enter the programme's popular daily competition, You Say, We Pay', observed *The Mail on Sunday*. 'But emails leaked to this newspaper reveal that the husband and wife team encourage thousands of viewers to do so after the potential winners have already been chosen.'

GMTV's managing director Paul Corley was forced to resign as it emerged the broadcaster had swindled an estimated £35m over two years from audiences in phone-in competitions. Even the BBC's once squeaky-clean flagship children's show, *Blue Peter,* was caught up in the row as it became clear that the show had misled viewers by faking a phone-in competition winner when a technical problem prevented callers getting through. There was worse to come. In June Five was fined £300,000 by OFCOM for faking winners in *Brainteaser* and, more shockingly, the BBC was fined for the first time in its history when the regulator imposed a £50,000 penalty for the *Blue Peter* incident.

A RIGHT ROYAL ROW AT THE BEEB

This was only the start of the BBC's problems during the summer that rapidly escalated into the corporation's worst crisis since the Hutton inquiry. The trigger was the BBC1 autumn press launch when station controller Peter Fincham showed a tape of a new documentary, *A Year with the Queen,* in which it appeared that the monarch had walked out of a photoshoot 'in a huff'. It soon emerged that the clip had been edited to change the chronology of events; the sequence was actually filmed before the shoot.

There were demands for Fincham's resignation from an outraged press and the BBC immediately apologised to Buckingham Palace. The documentary's makers, RDF Media, in turn apologised to the BBC. RDF's chief creative officer, Stephen Lambert, confessed he was responsible for editing the sequence out of chronological order. Embarrassingly for the BBC, the incident sparked an internal inquiry, which led to admissions of misleading viewers in six other programmes – including *Comic Relief,* where competition winners were faked.

The crisis of trust may turn out to be a watershed in the relationship between television broadcasters and their audiences; several opinion polls indicated that these episodes had eroded trust between viewers and TV stations. Some commentators said it was wrong to conflate the scandals over rigged phone TV quizzes operated by commercial channels, the row over doctored editing in the Queen documentary and other incidents involving dubious editing practices. Veteran TV chief, Dawn Airey, however, was in no doubt that something was amiss. She told *Broadcast* magazine: 'It's all symptomatic of the same thing: misrepresentation. It's not a storm in a teacup. This is a big kick up the arse for the industry. Nobody should mislead anybody and when premium phone lines are involved, that's theft.'

The BBC once again had to grapple with economies when, in January, the government confirmed that future licence fee increases would no longer be pegged to inflation. The BBC director-general, Mark Thompson, expressed 'real disappointment' at the increase, reportedly engineered by Gordon Brown during the end of his long reign as Chancellor of the Exchequer. The complex formula led to the fee being raised from £131.50 to £135.50 from April 2007, with a maximum of £151.20 by 2012. Negotiations had taken longer than anticipated due to the government's refusal to take the BBC's costings at face value.

Some commentators argued that the corporation's case was damaged by the sudden exit of Michael Grade, who resigned in November, poached by rival ITV. His departure was potentially wounding for the BBC as he was due to take over as head of the new BBC Trust, set up to replace the BBC board of governors. The trust was designed to introduce a more 'arm's length' method of ensuring the corporation was accountable to audiences. The BBC attracted more negative publicity during the year when two of its senior presenters, newsreader Moira Stuart and *Crimewatch*'s Nick Ross, were axed. The corporation denied all charges of sexism and ageism.

ITV BOOSTED BY GRADE'S ARRIVAL

Michael Grade's return to ITV represented a much-needed morale boost for the stricken channel, whose often-criticised chief executive, Charles Allen, finally departed in October. Grade's defection left the BBC without a chairman for several months as a shortage of high-profile candidates delayed the appointment of businessman Michael Lyons until April.

The digital revolution continued to gather pace during the year under review. With the digital switchover due to commence in the autumn of 2007, OFCOM was pleased to report in June that more than 80 per cent of UK homes were watching digital TV. Cable TV was relaunched in January under the Virgin Media banner. Its marketing push was derailed by a bitter row with BSkyB over how much it should pay to carry Sky channels. Unable to resolve the dispute, Virgin Media subscribers found themselves minus a number of Sky channels, including Sky One.

The spat between BSkyB, controlled by Rupert Murdoch's News Corp, and Virgin became more significant following BSkyB's £1bn purchase of a 17.9 per cent stake in ITV. This made Murdoch, who for many years wanted to own a chunk of British terrestrial TV, ITV's biggest single shareholder. As the year unfolded, a number of regulators, including OFCOM and the Competition Commission, began investigations into whether BSkyB's position was too powerful and posed a threat to plurality. While regulators were worried over Sky's market dominance, juries at the TV BAFTAs awarded the broadcaster its first ever prizes at the event – for the special effects-laden Christmas drama *Hogfather* and the documentary *Ross Kemp on Gangs.*

During the year all the main British broadcasters launched so-called on-demand services which allowed audiences to watch shows on the internet after their original transmission date. The most high profile of these was the BBC's iPlayer, which made its debut in July. The BBC director-general, Mark Thompson, hailed the development as a seminal moment for the corporation. He said: 'This is as big a redefinition of what broadcasting can be as the first colour broadcasts.' It remains to be seen how popular these services turn out to be and whether the prediction of BBC new media head, Ashley Highfield, that 10 per cent of all BBC TV viewing will take place via the iPlayer by 2009, is accurate.

LIFE ON MARS – DRAMA FROM A DIFFERENT PLANET

If the emerging world of digital technology was gradually changing people's relationships with television, much of the viewing menu felt traditional. The main soap operas, *EastEnders* – rumoured to be on the verge of adding a fifth weekly episode – *Coronation Street* and *Emmerdale* continued their perennial hold over the ratings charts. BBC1's medical soap *Casualty* celebrated its 20th anniversary in the autumn, while *Casualty* spin-off show, *Holby City,* itself spawned its own spin-off in the spring, *Holby Blue.* But critics found little to praise in the show, despite being written by acclaimed TV dramatist Tony Jordan.

The outstanding BBC drama series of the year was *Life On Mars,* which returned for a second and final run. Starring John Simm as time travelling detective Sam Tyler, critics lavished praise on the programme. When the final episode was screened in April *The Times'* Andrew Billen wrote: '*Life On Mars* was impressive in every way. John Simm as Tyler and Philip Glenister as Hunt helped to create characters at least as memorable as Barlow and Watt from *Z Cars.*' Over on ITV1 another drama that stood out from the pack was *Housewife 49,* written by and starring Victoria Wood as a middle-aged Lancashire housewife recovering from a nervous breakdown at the beginning of the Second World War. Wood was rewarded with two BAFTA awards.

In the autumn two of ITV1's heaviest hitting dramas, *Cracker* and *Prime Suspect,* returned for new cases. Sceptics suggested the revivals only emphasised the channel's difficulty in creating new shows capable of matching these crime classics, but Helen Mirren, making her last appearance as Jane Tennison, received a warm reception from critics.

Following a difficult previous year, the period under review represented what may turn out to be a sustained recovery for ITV1. The appointment of the television veteran Michael Grade as the broadcaster's new executive chairman was a fillip, but improvement in programming and performance pre-dated Grade's arrival in January. ITV1's biggest hit of the year, an unashamedly retro variety show, *Britain's Got Talent,* was commissioned prior to Grade's joining. Nonetheless in March, during one of his first public appearances in his new role, Grade admitted that ITV was 'shedding viewers at an alarming rate', and needed urgently to act to sort out the 'lacklustre' shows. But Grade offered no comfort for the children's TV lobby. During the year ITV stopped making children's shows, claiming it no longer made commercial sense and dropped children's programming from their traditional weekday afternoon slots in favour of quizzes and drama repeats, generating more advertising revenue in the process.

Reviewers welcomed a trilogy of Jane Austen adaptations, screened during the spring, as a sign that ITV1 was moving in the right direction. Billie Piper's role as Fanny Price in *Mansfield Park* was praised, while the other two productions, *Northanger Abbey* and *Persuasion,* also provided some genteel, though hardly adventurous Sunday evening entertainment. Much the same could also be said of Stephen Fry's new drama, *Kingdom.* He played a virtuous county solicitor working in a sleepy Norfolk town, and in doing so, charmed audiences. *Kingdom* may have been bland but the ratings were good and the show will return for a second series.

DOCTOR WHO UPSTAGES ROBIN HOOD

Doctor Who scored again for BBC1 as actress Freema Agyeman replaced Billie Piper as the Time Lord's assistant. The Doctor continued to (re)generate big audiences on Saturday evenings. In general, the previously problematic Saturday night slot proved successful for the BBC's flagship channel. For many viewers a high point of the late summer schedule was *How Do You Solve A Problem Like Maria?,* in which amateur performers competed for the role of Maria in a new Andrew Lloyd Webber production of *The Sound of Music,* making an unlikely TV star out of the theatre impresario.

One new show that failed to live up to the hype was an £8m revival of Robin Hood, shown during the autumn, and starring Jonas Armstrong as the Sherwood Forest outlaw. Not even the presence of Keith Allen as the Sheriff of Nottingham could persuade viewers to tune in en masse to the 13-part series.

BBC1's adaptation of *Jane Eyre,* starring Ruth Wilson as the eponymous heroine and Toby Stephens as Mr Rochester, got off to a slow start for some critics but as the piece got into its stride, many Brontë fans approved. Wrote Judith Woods in *The Daily Telegraph*: 'So what if it had been sexed up for modern audiences? We haven't got all evening to hang about decoding elliptical 19th-century demonstrations of drawing room concupiscence.' Quite. BBC1 was less successful with an ambitious contemporary political thriller *The State Within,* which failed to gain a big audience. *Five Days,* however, the story of a young mother's abduction, excited both audiences and critics. *The Independent's* Thomas Sutcliffe praised the direction: 'Otto Bathurst has a good eye for the queasiness of the CCTV landscape, the way those black-and-white monitors quarter the world into crime scenes in waiting.'

Despite talk of reinvestment in drama by BBC2, the

channel failed to compete effectively against its most direct rival, Channel 4. Not even a revival of the iconic *This Life,* renamed *This Life +10,* scored. There were lukewarm reviews for the much-anticipated *Maxwell* starring David Suchet. A. A. Gill, writing in *The Sunday Times,* opined: 'The only person who stood out as being believable and three-dimensional was Betty, his wife, played by Patricia Hodge.'

Channel 4, in contrast, was acclaimed for several of its politically charged, single dramas including *Longford, Death of a President, The Road to Guantanamo* and *Low Winter Sun,* and another Iraq war drama, *The Mark of Cain.* The acting of Jim Broadbent, cast as the devout Catholic politician, Lord Longford, was one of the small screen dramatic highlights of the year. Drama of a very different kind, the US import *Ugly Betty,* gave the station a Friday night hit. In *The Observer* Phil Hogan described the show, based on a form of Latin American soap opera known as *telenovela,* as an 'odd hybrid of styles – sitcom gags, soap plotting, pantomime villains but America Ferrara is a hoot as Betty Suarez'.

Reality TV in all its various guises remained a mainstay of channel controllers' schedules – but often the hype surrounding a new format backfired. A new BBC2 reality show, *The Verdict,* saw a jury of celebrities, including convicted felon Lord Archer, sit in judgment of a footballer's mock-trial for rape, the trivialisation of which managed to offend both human rights groups and critics. In the spring, *The Apprentice* successfully transferred from BBC2 to BBC1 and gave audiences a surprise winner as Simon Ambrose beat favourite Kristina Grimes. ITV1's attempt to replicate the success of *The Apprentice* produced an identikit model in *Tycoon,* with *Dragons Den* star Peter Jones assuming the mantle of Sir Alan Sugar. It proved to be an embarrassing failure, pulling in only two million viewers, and was soon relegated from its prime-time slot. BBC1's attempt to revive *Castaway,* one of the first wave of reality shows, also flopped, but a new Channel 4 reality format, *The Secret Millionaire,* was a winner at the Rose d'Or festival. In the programme wealthy people give up their ordinary successful lives to live undercover in a deprived community in order to find people they can help. Another stunt to divert jaded viewers, or public service television?

BIG BROTHER – C4 FORCED TO SAY SORRY

As for *Big Brother* itself, commentators believed that the row over *Celebrity Big Brother* in January exposed serious flaws in Channel 4's management, as well as raising old questions regarding how far programme makers are prepared to go in the name of entertainment.

Many viewers were not only angry that fellow contestants bullied Shilpa Shetty, but also furious that, as racist behaviour is contrary to the rules of *Big Brother,* the producers did not intervene earlier. OFCOM forced Channel 4 to apologise for the incident. However, the real and lasting effect of the highly public row over *Celebrity Big Brother* is the damage done to the broadcaster's standing as a public service institution. *The Guardian*'s media editor Matt Wells said: 'Creatively, *Big Brother* is defunct: a tired format revived every year only by producers' attempts to foster ever more extreme conflict.' Perhaps the most damaging comment came from culture secretary, Tessa Jowell, who said it was 'racism presented as entertainment' – in other words, that producers had deliberately provoked a racial conflict. Channel 4, of course, denied the charge but as the broadcaster approaches its 25th anniversary in November, there is a feeling that the tide of public opinion is running against the broadcaster, which had to live with declining revenue and falling audiences – down around one percentage point year-on-year. This was despite the prevalence of *Big Brother* and *Big Brother* spin-off shows in its schedules.

In the documentary genre the clear winner was BBC2's *Andrew Marr's History of Britain,* a surprisingly fresh take on a familiar subject. Channel 4's *The Great Global Warming Swindle,* made by Martin Durkin, looked like an own goal for the broadcaster. The film refuted the scientific consensus that global warming was man-made causing the *Financial Times* to comment: 'Not so long ago, the venerable David Attenborough on the Beeb was telling us that human-driven global warming was real and was coming for us. So that was settled. Now Channel 4, like a dissident schoolboy, is scoffing at the old boy's hobbyhorse and I don't know what to believe.' Generating even more controversy was Channel 4's *Diana – The Witnesses In The Tunnel* because there were claims it would include 'graphic images' of the dying princess. In fact the film was responsibly made. Other documentaries that stood out during the year under review included BBC2's *Stephen Fry – The Secret Life of a Manic Depressive* and *Rain In My Heart,* a film about alcoholism by the veteran TV director Paul Watson, also aired by BBC2.

Another seasoned filmmaker who created waves was Molly Dineen. She contributed *The Lie of The Land* examining the life of ordinary farmers in contemporary Britain, to Channel 4 in May. A. A. Gill wrote in *The Sunday Times:* 'Television . . . treats non-professionals like awkward cripples holding up the gurgling flow of light and sound. When you see ordinary, rough-edged folk given space, treated with respect, it looks like revelation.' Howard Goodall's *How Music Works* was also a success for Channel 4.

One of the most keenly observed developments on BBC1 was the return of current affairs flagship *Panorama* to a prime-time Monday evening slot. Fronted by Jeremy Vine, the reinvented format, reduced by ten minutes to a half-hour programme, received mixed reactions. Ex-*Panorama* reporter Tom Mangold, writing in *The Independent,* said he was disappointed by evidence of what he regarded as the programme 'dumbing down'. '*Panorama* is gradually being tugged down the populist road. The programme seems over-managed by chiefs but doesn't even have its own desperately needed investigations editor to prevent further public humiliations. The few good, exciting and, yes, worthy programmes now shine as rare exceptions.' However, the 'populist road' did result in more viewers – an average increase of 700,000 a week. One episode did achieve notoriety, as clips from an investigation into the scientology cult, conducted by reporter John Sweeney, showed him dramatically losing his temper.

Five, struggling against tough competition, finally entered the digital age by launching two spin-off channels in the autumn: lifestyle service Five Life, and a station dedicated to American shows, Five US. Generally, Five continued to improve the quality of its programmes. There was praise for edgy drama, *Kitchen,* starring Eddie Izzard, the travel show *Paul Merton in China,* and the cheeky sitcom, *Respectable,* set in a suburban brothel. Successful poaching of veteran Australian teen soap *Neighbours* from the BBC in the spring gave the channel a welcome boost.

It was not a vintage year for new comedy, but ITV1 was at last investing in the genre again. One of most successful shows was a welcome revival of Granada TV's *The Royle Family* in a special edition, 'Queen of Sheba', shown as part of the BBC1 Christmas schedule. The quality of the writing and acting won widespread praise. Other highlights included the fourth series of Channel 4's *Peep Show* and a promising new BBC3 sitcom *Gavin and Stacey*, which offered an antidote to the comedy of humiliation perfected by such performers as Ricky Gervais. There were mixed reviews for a new high-profile BBC1 comedy, *Jam and Jerusalem,* written by Jennifer Saunders and featuring a strong female cast including Sue Johnston, Joanna Lumley and Dawn French. The highest audience for a sitcom during the period under review was achieved by French's final bow in *The Vicar of Dibley*. A Christmas special in which Geraldine finally gets hitched was watched by almost 11.5 million viewers, a huge audience in the emerging digital age.

RADIO

As the digital revolution rolled on in television, radio too was undergoing big changes. 'Radio is no longer something that comes out of a dear little box', observed Gillian Reynolds in *The Daily Telegraph* in December. More and people listen to radio via digital TVs, computers, mobile phones and MP3 players. Regardless of how the audience was tuning in, the BBC was a stronger force than ever. In the first quarter of 2007 BBC Radio achieved a record listening share of 56 per cent and the corporation's biggest-ever lead over the commercial opposition – a remarkable 13 per cent. There were record audiences for four of the BBC's five digital-only stations, particularly 6Music, whose audience grew by 40 per cent year-on-year. If the station can sustain a growth rate on this scale, 6Music will overtake Radio 3 within four years.

Central to the BBC's dominance was the continuing success of Radio 2, unchallenged as the country's most popular radio station. As if to emphasise the network's desire to win over more younger listeners, during the period under review Radio 2 signed the ubiquitous and controversial comic Russell Brand, formerly a presenter at 6Music, to front a new late-night Saturday show. Brand was singled out as an important entertainment phenomenon 'because he has come to symbolise a new generation of talent that has built its following on the web', according to *The Guardian.* Commercial rivals, not for the first time, claimed Radio 2 was trying too hard to be fashionable and demanded that the new BBC regulator, the Trust, draw up a tighter remit for the station. Drive-time presenter Chris Evans cemented his place on the schedule with an average of 4.8 million listeners tuning in per week. Evans was feted at the 25th annual Sony Radio Awards, winning the radio personality of the year prize for the second year in a row.

TERRY WOGAN – A PLUG TOO MANY

Arguably Radio 2's popularity was a double-edged sword for the BBC as, on more than one occasion during 2006–7, regulators censured the station. In April listeners complained at the language of guest Jack Dee; OFCOM concluded Radio 2 was in breach of broadcasting codes and the BBC apologised for the 'completely inappropriate' use of language. In June veteran Terry Wogan was ticked off by the BBC for excessively plugging his UKTV Gold chat show on Radio 2's *Wake Up To Wogan.* The warning came after a listener had already complained about the presenter's repeated promotional references to his autobiography, *Mustn't Grumble.* Another embarrassing incident occurred when a spoof on *The Jeremy Vine Show* announced that the Soham double murderer Ian Huntley was dying in prison. Despite being labelled as a spoof some listeners mistook it for a real news report and complained. Once again, the BBC apologised.

There was controversy of a different nature when in January Radio 2 axed the long-running *Your Hundred Best Tunes* series. Some listeners feared the move would lead to less light music on the network, especially since Radio 3 was dispensing with the services of its only series dedicated to the genre – Brian Kay's Thursday show. The host of the replacement Radio 2 programme, *Melodies For You,* was gardening presenter Alan Titchmarsh. A former presenter of *Melodies For You,* Sheridan Morley, died in February. Radio 2 controller Lesley Douglas described Morley as one of the 'great characters' of her station.

There was widespread praise for Bob Dylan's *Theme Time Radio Hour,* broadcast by Radio 2 and 6Music. It was the first time the legendary rock performer had hosted a radio show. Originally available only to subscription radio listeners in the US, the BBC bought the UK rights. Each week the records featured by Dylan were based on a single theme, such as weather or drinking. The music encompassed an eclectic mix of musical styles from the pre-rock 'n' roll era to the present. The programme was nominated for a Broadcasting Press Guild award but was beaten by Radio 4's satirical phone-in *Down The Line.* Radio 2 concerts featuring Bruce Springsteen and Coldplay were also praised.

Radio 1's fortunes were in ascendance too. This was a considerable achievement since changes in listening habits sparked by the emergence of digital media affected young audiences most acutely. In its annual report the BBC noted there was increasing consumption of Radio 1 via online, digital TV and mobile media. Much of Radio 1's appeal was due to the success of Chris Moyles' breakfast show, which broke through the 7 million listener barrier in 2007. This was only 800,000 less than the audience for Wogan on Radio 2. Moyles' appeal was further evidenced by his iTunes chart-topping podcast. During the spring the show achieved 800,000 downloads a month.

TOO MUCH STREET-CRED FOR OFCOM

During the year OFCOM upheld complaints against both Chris Moyles and fellow Radio 1 DJ Scott Mills for bad language; there was even the threat of a financial penalty against offending DJs by the regulator. Moyles' style continued to divide – *The Sunday Times* columnist Paul Donovan was aghast to see Moyles nominated as one of the 25 greatest broadcasters of all time and described the DJ as 'a coarse buffoon'.

Musical highlights of the Radio 1 year included the premiere of Damon Albarn's *The Good, The Bad and The Queen* performed live as part of the new Electric Proms season. Another memorable moment was Noel Gallagher performing a one-man show in a listener's living room, one of over 300 sessions of Radio 1's Live Lounge performances.

It was a remarkable year for John Humphrys on Radio 4, who chalked up two decades as a *Today* presenter in January. His live broadcasts from Iraq in the autumn won widespread acclaim. The reports from Basra, where he interviewed members of the British army undertaking reconstruction work, marked Humphrys' return to frontline reporting. Additionally the broadcaster reported from his native south Wales marking the 40th anniversary of the Aberfan tragedy. *The Guardian* described Humphrys' report as 'a minor masterpiece of memorable imagery'. The presenter's Radio 4 series, *Humphrys In Search of God,* in which he interviewed three religious leaders including Rowan Williams, the Archbishop of Canterbury, also delighted listeners and reviewers. It even won over an initially sceptical Gillian Reynolds, *The Daily Telegraph*'s radio critic who wrote 'If I mistrusted the premise of this series when it began, the cumulative experience of listening to it and thinking about it has been unexpectedly rich. I have a sneaking suspicion Humphrys may have found it so, too.' Humphrys was duly voted journalist of the year at the Sony Awards for his reporting from Iraq.

The danger of journalists working in war-torn communities was brought home by the kidnapping of the BBC's Gaza correspondent Alan Johnston in March. The reporter spent 114 days in captivity before he was released. 'The last 16 weeks have been the very worst of my life,' he said. 'I was in the hands of people who were dangerous and unpredictable. I literally dreamt many times of being free and always woke up back in that room.'

The year's Reith lecturer, economist Jeffrey Sachs, was praised by Paul Donovan in *The Sunday Times* for returning the lectures to form and delivering addresses that were 'of real value and importance'. There was praise too for the arrival of Martha Kearney as the presenter of *The World At One* following the death of Nick Clarke in November. Writing on *The Guardian's* website Elisabeth Mahoney described Kearney's debut as 'smooth and polished'. There were many tributes to Clarke, who had presented *The World At One* every weekday for 13 years. Radio 4 controller Mark Damazer said: 'We have lost a supreme champion of Radio 4 – and the BBC. We owe him much.'

THE ARCHERS – AN EVERYDAY STORY FOR WEBHEADS

In November *The Archers* broadcast its 15,000th episode. The storyline involving a sensational romance between Ruth Archer and conman Sam generated huge interest. In the build-up during October 1.8 million people visited the show's website. On New Year's Day a BBC4 *Arena* documentary celebrated the milestone. Among the contributors were former *Archers* editor Liz Rigbey, who said the job was 'like being put in charge of one of the stately homes of England'.

The new presenter of *Desert Island Discs,* Kirsty Young, continued to divide opinion. In *The Daily Telegraph* Michael Henderson said it was time to ditch the format, but the programme, bolstered by a marketing campaign, posted a record audience in May of 2.9 million, helping Radio 4 overall to reach its highest audience share of 12 per cent. *Desert Island Discs*' high-profile castaways included Ricky Gervais, Yoko Ono and former BBC director-general Greg Dyke. Outstanding documentaries on Radio 4 during the year were Tom Mangold's *Driven by Oil* and two history programmes, *The Invention of Childhood* and *The Making of Modern Medicine.*

Radio 3 had a difficult year. In February controller Roger Wright overhauled the schedules axing five weekday afternoon programmes: *Stage and Screen, Voices, Choral Evensong, Brian Kay's Light Programme* and *Jazz Legends. Choral Evensong* moved to Sundays and Rob Cowan was given a new breakfast show, praised by Ivan Hewett in *The Daily Telegraph*: 'He sounds as classless as Terry Wogan, but without the sarcasm or oiliness. This is important because classical music itself has a "tone" that is very often posh.' However, in *The Guardian* blog Stephen Moss complained that the changes were 'a ragbag'. The number of listeners was down to around 1.9 million, according to figures published in May, but it was too early to assess the impact of the changes on audience behaviour.

Following on from *The Beethoven Experience,* Radio 3 presented various complete works in 2006–7 including weeks dedicated to Tchaikovsky and Stravinsky, and Wilfred Owen's complete war poems in November. Wagner's *Ring Cycle* was broadcast in its entirety over 18 hours with simultaneous translation on digital platforms. Drama highlights included Harold Pinter starring in a new version of his play *The Homecoming.* In June one of BBC Radio's most gifted champions, former network radio head and controller of Radio 2 and 4, David Hatch, died.

COMMERCIAL RADIO – SIGNS OF AN UPTURN

Following another financially challenging year for commercial radio, there were signs in July that at last prospects for the sector were improving. A trading statement issued by Britain's largest private radio operator, GCap Media, owner of Classic FM and London's Capital Radio, indicated that the advertising trend was 'encouraging'. Company chief executive Ralph Barnard added: 'Our brand portfolio has been streamlined, audiences are being built at all our major stations and we are investing where we can see attractive returns. Encouragingly, we are beginning to see signs of improvement in advertising revenues, despite an uncertain outlook for consumer confidence.'

Another positive sign was an announcement, also in July, that Guardian Media Radio Group was investing an additional £1m to encourage creativity in programme making. The group runs 11 stations across the UK including Smooth. On Christmas Day GCap launched digital station theJazz, Britain's first new national radio station for more than four years. Station managing director Darren Henley said: 'We feel we are filling a hole in the landscape and we hope to do for jazz what Classic FM has already done for classical music.' Critics responded favourably to the newcomer praising it for playing music from a wide range of jazz styles, but there were concerns that it might repeat the expensive mistakes of Jazz FM, which after running up losses was eventually re-launched as Smooth.

Earlier in the year harsh trading conditions saw advertising revenues at Chrysalis, owner of London station Heart, dip by 9 per cent. In the summer Chrysalis Radio was sold for £170m to a new investment group, Global Radio, led by the former ITV chief, Charles Allen. The cost of running digital stations was a cause for concern by the commercial sector, who applied pressure on OFCOM to announce a date for the switchover to a digital signal. GCap's Ralph Barnard told the Radio Festival in July: 'We need a very clear road map to going digital. If you can't see the route from where we are today to the ultimate switch-over date, then you can forget about digital radio in the UK. Commercial radio cannot afford to keep shovelling millions of pounds into a bottomless pit that is digital.' But with an estimated 150 million analogue sets in use, no date was forthcoming.

There was optimism in some quarters that Channel 4's imminent arrival on the UK radio scene might help commercial radio to fight back against the BBC. In July

OFCOM awarded a licence to run a group of new digital stations – starting in the summer of 2008 – to 4 Digital Group. The newcomer plans to launch a rival to Radio 4.

Critics praised the commercial sector's UK Music Week project that took place in the spring. Playlists were divided into six musical genres – pop, easy listening, gold, dance/urban, rock and classical – on a station by station basis. 'There is much to applaud in this, even though some stations are not taking part', wrote Paul Donovan in *The Sunday Times.* Guest presenters included Ricky Gervais and Denise Van Outen. A live Stereophonics concert broadcast simultaneously across 145 stations launched the event. Paul Robinson in *The Guardian* saw the event's significance: 'It is easy to dismiss UK Music Week as the stuff that Radio 1 does every day, but for commercial radio it is innovative and groundbreaking. It is also quite a feat of organisation to bring so many commercial stations together to share "event" programming which individually they would not be able to attempt.' Following a dismal showing at the Sony Awards, commercial radio certainly needs to raise its game.

BUSINESS AND FINANCE

Timothy Hindle

BROWN IN, BROWNE OUT

It was the year of BIBO – Brown in, Browne out. On 27 June 2007 Gordon Brown took over as Labour prime minister from Tony Blair after a decade spent as Chancellor of the Exchequer in the shadow of his once close colleague, whilst on 1 May John Browne (Baron Browne of Madingley) resigned from the chairmanship of BP, after a decade spent at the helm of a company that he steered from near-disaster to great success and the fabled promise of going 'Beyond Petroleum'.

Initially the new prime minister seemed set to remain at least as close to business and businessmen as his predecessor, although in his last budget as chancellor he imposed new taxes on companies and air travel. Controversially, he appointed Digby Jones, a former director-general of the Confederation of British Industry (CBI) and a fierce opponent of the minimum wage, to be a minister in his first government. Jones, who shortly afterwards was created a life peer and became Lord Jones of Birmingham, declined to actually join the Labour Party.

Brown also courted controversy by appointing Damon Buffini, the managing partner of a private-equity group Permira, as an adviser on a range of issues. During the year, the trade unions became increasingly hostile to private equity (*see* below), perceiving it as an old-fashioned asset stripper only too eager to lay off workers without due compensation. A *Financial Times* (*FT*) survey of large private-equity deals, however, did suggest that over time they were more likely to be net creators of jobs than their destroyers.

John Browne stepped down after it was revealed that he had lied to a high court judge about where he had met his former lover, Jeff Chevalier. The case arose over an attempt by Browne to prevent a Sunday newspaper from printing Chevalier's memoirs. The judge said he was not prepared to make allowances for a man who 'refers to the various honours he has received when asking the court to prefer his account of what took place'. By resigning, Browne sacrificed his place in the company's performance-related share plan – at a personal loss of up to £12m. A week later he gave up another top post when he resigned from the board of the investment bank Goldman Sachs.

It was not a good year for BP in other respects either. Oil prices rose around the world when the company was compelled to shut its vast Alaskan production facilities after leaks had been discovered in its corroding pipeline system as it snaked across the American state's pristine snow. There were also severe delays in restarting one of BP's Mexican oil platforms, after its operation had been seriously disrupted by a hurricane.

Most damaging of all, however, in November 2006 BP finally settled a civil case arising from a fatal blast in 2005 which killed 15 people at its Texas City refinery. In January, a report by a committee headed by James Baker, a former US treasury secretary, severely criticised the company's safety record. America's Chemical Safety and Hazard Investigation Board subsequently blamed 'safety deficiencies at all levels of the BP Corporation' for the Texas City explosion. The letters 'BP' seemed to stand more for 'Browne's Pitfalls' than 'Beyond Petroleum'.

BP's arch-rival, Royal Dutch Shell, which Browne's early strategic successes had thrown into the shade, was able to shine again. The Anglo-Dutch giant reported the biggest annual profit ever recorded by a UK-listed company – of £12.52bn – largely because of higher output and a strong oil price. Nevertheless, not everything went the company's way. It was forced to sell a chunk of a highly promising stake in the massive Sakhalin-2 project in eastern Russia to a state-controlled national group, Gazprom. The UK's expulsion of four Russian diplomats in the wake of the murder in London in 2006 of Alexander Litvinenko, an exiled former KGB agent, did not augur well for further involvement of UK companies in the exploitation of Russia's considerable natural resources.

OTHER NEW FACES AT THE TOP

Lord Browne was succeeded at the head of BP by Tony Hayward, a former boss of the company's exploration division. Mr Hayward quickly said that he intended to keep a lower profile than his predecessor. Other companies with new bosses included two big banks: Barclays, where Marcus Agius took over from Matthew Barrett, and HSBC, where Michael Geoghegan took over as CEO from Stephen Green, who moved up to become chair. Perhaps the most unlikely new face at the top of British industry was that of Cynthia Carroll, appointed head of Anglo-American, a massive South African mining company now quoted and headquartered in London. An American by birth (and a former senior executive at the Canadian company Alcan), Ms Carroll was the first woman and the first non-South African to run the male-dominated mining business. Weeks after her appointment, the Oppenheimer family, who founded the Anglo-American group, sold a stake worth US$800m (£394m) to a Chinese magnate, Larry Yung.

A further demonstration of the growing internationalisation of the executive suite came with the award of a knighthood to Carlos Ghosn. Born in Brazil to Lebanese parents, the ex-boss of the Japanese car company Nissan (and now CEO of the French car company Renault) was knighted for services to the British car industry. Among those services was the investment of £2.3bn in building Britain's biggest car factory – the Nissan plant in Sunderland.

Rewards for those at the top continued to rise sharply – both the pay of top executives and the fees of non-executives. A survey found that in 2005 the chief executives of companies in the FTSE index were paid 98 times as much as the typical UK employee – that was two-and-a-half times the same multiple five years earlier.

Bonuses to those working in London's financial sector were also at record levels, although the recipients of these rewards had shifted westwards. The hedge-fund and private-equity businesses, where some of today's highest earnings are to be found, have moved out of the City of London and are for the most part now based in Mayfair and the West End of London. The head of Goldman Sachs' London-based 'exotic-derivatives desk' – Moroccan-born Driss Ben-Brahim – was reported to have received an annual bonus in the region of £50m for 2006 alone. It is one of the financial markets' stranger quirks that should the investors in Ben-Brahim's exotic derivatives subsequently lose all the money that he helped them to make in 2006 (and exotic derivatives are by definition risky), he will not personally sacrifice any of the exotic bonus that he made, because of their (temporary) gains.

GAP GROWING

The increasing divide between the highly paid and the poorly paid is global, and even provoked comment from US President George W. Bush during the year. It was also the main topic at the eye-catching Davos meeting of highly paid industrialists and politicians held at the Swiss mountain resort in January.

The less well paid were disinclined to be ruffled by differences in relative pay, since pay rises across the board were at record levels in 2006. This raised fears of inflation to come and encouraged the Bank of England to push interest rates up to a five-year high. The pensions regulator cast a dark shadow over the future welfare of employees, however, when he said that the full cost of honouring corporate pension schemes was £440bn more than the current value of companies' pension-fund assets. Life expectancy is still increasing in Britain, but the ability of retirees to enjoy their extended retirement may not be.

Britons, on average, work longer hours than workers in other EU countries, but the nation is becoming slightly less workaholic. Britons in general were working one hour less per week than they were 15 years ago. From 6 October 2006 they could go on doing so unimpeded if they so wished, until their statutory retirement age. Age discrimination legislation came into effect outlawing companies' early retirement rules. Despite this, equality in the workplace still seemed a distant prospect. A Department of Trade and Industry survey found that 80 per cent of women employed in the financial services industry claimed that they had experienced unfair treatment (such as discrimination, bullying or sexual harassment) in the workplace.

CAPITAL AFFAIRS

Despite one survey showing London to be the most expensive large city in the world and another finding it to be the second most expensive (after Moscow), Britain's capital continued to attract foreigners. Some big American investment banks, such as Merrill Lynch and Lehman Brothers, moved more of their operations and top officers to the city. For them the move, mostly from New York, was particularly expensive since in 2007 sterling hit a 26-year high against the dollar (at over US$2 to the pound). A few foreign investors were deterred by the currency risk. Honda said it would not make a further substantial investment in its UK car plant because of the financial uncertainty caused by the UK's refusal to join the euro.

London topped the world in the cost of its taxis, trains, restaurants and rent. To some extent boosted by the large bonuses paid to financial-sector workers, the city's house prices rose at an annual rate of 13.3 per cent in the first quarter of 2007, a far steeper rise than in other parts of the country. By mid-2007, the average price of a dwelling in London was over £300,000.

The records were not confined to residential property. Canary Wharf's HSBC Tower was sold to a Spanish company for £1.08bn, the most expensive single office block in Europe at the time. Commercial property investment overall in 2006 was at an all-time high, up some 33 per cent on the figure for the previous year. It was well rewarded; average total returns on UK commercial property were 18 per cent in 2006, according to the Royal Institution of Chartered Surveyors.

MERGERS AND ACQUISITIONS

Pay rises in the financial sector were boosted by an enormous volume of mergers and acquisitions (M&A) during the year – transactions, on which banks earn high fees. Global M&A were worth more than US$1,000bn (£492bn) in the first quarter of 2007, the busiest quarter ever and around 14 per cent more than in the same period of 2006. Much of the activity came from companies buying assets in other countries. UK companies bought £29.52bn-worth of overseas businesses, second only to the USA. Barclays Bank and the Royal Bank of Scotland group found themselves in a long-drawn-out struggle for control of the Dutch bank ABN, a battle that was likely to leave the winner with little change out of £50bn.

At the same time, plenty of UK businesses were taken over by non-UK firms. The 2006 calendar year saw a record inflow of foreign direct investment into the UK, much of it in the shape of takeovers of British companies by foreigners. For example, Reuters was taken over by Canada's Thomson Group, while Hanson, the rump of the once mighty Hanson Trust, was taken over by Germany's HeidelbergCement. Even the London Stock Exchange itself almost ended up in foreign hands, managing to fend off an offer from America's Nasdaq exchange worth £2.7bn, and one from Euronext, a pan-European exchange based in Paris.

Some firms that were already foreign-owned remained so even after a sale. Thames Water, for instance, already owned by a German utility, was bought by an Australian bank. Ford, the American car company, set out to sell its UK luxury brands, Jaguar and Land Rover, after a sale earlier in the year of its Aston Martin business.

British Airports Authority (BAA), owner and manager of Heathrow and Gatwick, Europe's two busiest airports, was bought by a group led by Ferrovial, a Spanish construction company. BAA came under heavy criticism for the long delays at its airports, not wholly caused by increased security checks following terrorist threats to blow up a number of airliners in the mid-Atlantic, en route from Britain to the United States. The Competition Commission said it would investigate BAA's 'monopoly'.

The Body Shop, world famous as a pioneer in the production of ethical goods, was bought by L'Oréal, a giant French cosmetics firm keen to gain from the kudos of the British firm's brand, whilst Liverpool FC emphasised what a big business sport has become by being the seventh English Premier League football club to fall under foreign ownership. It was taken over in February by two American businessmen who already owned ice-hockey teams. Perhaps the most unlikely foreign owner of a top-flight British football club was an Icelandic company WH Holding, which purchased West Ham.

A deal at the end of January demonstrated another interesting feature of the international M&A scene. Corus, the rump of Britain's once mighty steel-making industry, was bought by India's Tata Steel for more than £6bn, a demonstration of a new feature of international takeovers – the involvement of developing countries. Not only was Corus bought by an Indian company, but the underbidder, which just failed to win the battle, was a Brazilian company, Companhia Siderurgica Nacional.

Russian businesses were also very active in Britain. Russian oligarch Oleg Deripaska, owner of 80 per cent of Gaz Group (Russia's largest maker of light commercial vehicles), paid £50m for LDV, a loss-making Birmingham van-maker. He said he wanted it as a base for further acquisitions and joint ventures outside Russia. Meanwhile, in a marked reversal of normal outsourcing practice, an

Indian company (ICICI One Source) actually opened a call centre in Northern Ireland.

The flood of foreign money led to fears of a foreign takeover of UK Plc, fears further stoked by a feeling that the game of cross-border takeovers was not being played on a level playing field. Some felt that Britain opened its doors more widely than other countries. Notably, in November 2006 the United States introduced what became known as an 'evergreen clause' into the takeover of the American company Lucent by a French rival Alcatel. The clause allowed the US government to undo the deal at any time in the future if the company ever breached agreements made with the authorities about security. The deal was particularly sensitive because of Lucent's past (and potential future) work for the Pentagon.

Political changes threatened to throw the playing field further out of kilter. The more protectionist-minded Democrats gained control of the US congress and there was the prospect of a Democrat returning to the White House in 2008. Meanwhile, a new government in France and a new prime minister in Britain left at least a possibility that these two countries too might become more protectionist in the short term.

A joint Harris/*FT* poll taken in mid-2007 suggested that people were now less enamoured by the idea and principles of globalisation than they used to be. In the UK, three times as many people thought globalisation was having a negative effect on the country than those who thought it was positive.

There was a backlash against migrant workers. Amicus, the biggest private sector union, urged the government to impose tighter curbs on work permits to slow the flow of cheaper foreign IT staff taking jobs 'at the expense of resident UK professionals'. Tighter limits were placed on the entry of Bulgarians and Romanians when the two countries joined the EU in January 2007.

THE PRIVATE-EQUITY PHENOMENON

The M&A boom was partly driven by the record volume of private-equity deals. These are the opposite of 'going public'. Managers of big pools of money buy companies (or segments of them), take them out of the public eye, and try to make them perform better before selling them off at, they hope, a huge profit. For some time this business has, as Carl Icahn, a prominent American investor, put it, 'had a walk in the park'. It has provided large returns for investors and large salaries for its employees.

Firms like the Blackstone Group, Carlyle and KKR (Kohlberg Kravis Roberts) took famous names such as Alliance Boots and Burger King out of the quoted sector. Blackstone paid US$1bn (£492m) in cash for the Tussauds Group, which includes Madame Tussaud's and the London Eye, two of the capital city's most popular tourist attractions. Blackstone already owned Alton Towers and Chessington Park, and was set on building up a portfolio of what it saw as undervalued leisure-industry businesses.

But during the year private equity's walk in the park stumbled. First of all, financial regulators got nervous. The Financial Services Authority (FSA) – the industry watchdog for financial services – said in November 2006 that it would look more closely at private-equity deals, since it now considered the collapse of a big buy-out 'inevitable', which could then pose a threat to the economy. Then the private-equity firms themselves started to go public, to cash in their chips as it were, a sure sign that the benefits of going private were diminishing.

The firms also relied in many instances on cheap borrowing and advantageous tax treatment of that borrowing. In both Britain and America money became more expensive over the year, and politicians began to ask uncomfortable questions about the apparently low rate of tax paid by the evidently profitable firms.

CROOKERY

The massive growth of mergers and acquisitions increased the likelihood of (illegal though almost unprovable) insider trading. Anyone who got early wind of a deal could make a big profit in the almost certain knowledge that the share price of the company being acquired would go up once the deal was announced. The FSA calculated that 23.7 per cent of all takeover announcements in 2005 were preceded by share price movements that indicated possible insider trading. That compared with 24 per cent in 2000 and 32.4 per cent in 2004.

But there were almost no successful prosecutions for insider dealing, and other investigations into suspected corporate shenanigans were equally frustrated. In July 2007 it was announced that there would be no prosecutions in the long-running so-called 'cash for peerages' investigation, which involved some businessmen. Also, in the previous December, the Serious Fraud Office had dropped a long-running investigation into allegations of bribery at BAE (formerly British Aerospace) after Saudi officials had demonstrated their displeasure by suspending talks on a £10bn deal for Eurofighter Typhoon aircraft. The investigation was into the company's 20-year-old Al Yamamah arms deal with Saudi Arabia.

There was widespread criticism from the City directed at the government's decision to drop the probe, saying it would undermine the UK's reputation, with considerable long-term costs. The US justice department, however, took up the challenge, launching its own probe into corruption by BAE, which has large interests in America.

SUSTAINABILITY

A main concern of companies during the year was to flaunt their green credentials, even though British business had in fact increased its greenhouse emissions by 3.6 per cent in 2006. In February, a UN report saying that global warming was almost certainly man-made (or at least partially), sparked a host of firms to come out with environmentally friendly products and services.

In March, Walkers Crisps claimed to carry the world's first 'carbon label', indicating to consumers who wanted to know that it needed to emit 75g of carbon dioxide in order to produce and transport 34.5g of crisps 'from seed to store'. Northumbrian Water announced plans to collect methane gas produced by sewage-eating bacteria and use it to make green electricity, while McDonald's said that by the end of 2007 it would be running as many as 155 of its UK delivery trucks on biodiesel made entirely from cooking oil that had been collected from its restaurants.

Firms' annual reports grew lengthier as they included more and more about the extent of their social and environmental responsibility. In April, HSBC's annual report weighed in at 454 pages (1.47kg). Postmen were restricted by Royal Mail in the number that they could carry at any one time.

Meanwhile Britain followed Ireland's example and made smoking illegal in all public places – significantly in restaurants, where Britons are spending twice as much as they did in 1992. UK tobacco sales declined by 2.9 per cent in volume in 2006, but grew by 2.5 per cent in value (to £12.7bn). Datamonitor forecasts that UK sales (by volume) will fall by 16.7 per cent between 2006 and 2011.

CONSERVATION

THE BUILT ENVIRONMENT

Matthew Saunders

REFORM AND LEGISLATION

The year under review was dominated by the projected Heritage Protection Review. The long-anticipated consultation paper by the Department of Culture, Media and Sport (DCMS) and the Welsh Assembly Government was published at Easter 2007. It outlined a number of major reforms. At present historic sites can be protected by the listing of historic buildings, scheduling of archaeological sites and the registration of gardens and battlefields. The paper proposed that the current system should be replaced by a new, simplified registry which would provide 'a single point of information about all nationally designated assets'.

Despite previous plans to abolish Grade II*, the present tripartite regime for the grading of listing (II, II* and I) would remain. As previously trailed in earlier versions of the paper, the statutory responsibility for designating in the new system would pass from the culture secretary to English Heritage (EH). The former would consider appeals against EH decisions.

One of the most far-reaching proposals affects the Local Lists, maintained by local authorities, which are to be given statutory teeth, albeit through a rather cumbersome process. As well as appeals after the process, the paper also promised consultations before listings. To preclude preemptive demolition, there would be a system of interim protection. Further emphasis is placed on Heritage Partnership Agreements for complex assets such as barracks, prisons, hospitals or 'large land holdings with multiple historic and major conservation assets'. The partnerships would bypass the need for seeking consent from local authorities. There is at present a little-used system of negative listing. An owner seeking certainty can approach the government to obtain a certificate of immunity from listing, which lasts for five years. Under the new paper, the government proposes to extend the use of these certificates by allowing them to encompass entire sites rather than individual historic assets. Conservation areas, the principal method by which broader areas are protected, which remain the preserve of local authorities, are to be retained, but the consequent need for conservation area consent would be abolished. Local authorities will also be obliged, rather than merely encouraged, to maintain or have access to, an Historic Environment Record, the new name for the earlier non-mandatory Sites and Monuments Records.

THE HERITAGE LOTTERY FUND

The principal source of money for works to the historic environment remained the Heritage Lottery Fund (HLF), which received the welcome announcement in June 2006 that the government confirmed heritage as a Lottery Good Cause for the ten years beyond the expiry of the current operating licence in 2009. This optimism proved to be shortlived as the DCMS announced it would raid the Good Causes funding to pay for the 2012 Olympics. The HLF had been set to lose £71m under the financing arrangements for the Games, but new figures added a further £90m to this total.

Despite these cutbacks, in its third strategic plan, details of which were published in the summer of 2007, the HLF was still able to announce funding of £180m a year for the period up to 2019. It was also able to confirm that all its present grant regimes would continue with the exception of the Awards for All programme.

Funding was also to continue for places of worship and historic townscapes. Grants in England to 153 Grade I and Grade II* churches and chapels were announced by HLF in March 2007. Beneficiaries included St Lawrence, Mereworth in Kent by Colen Campbell (£716,000) and G. E. Street's masterpiece All Saints at Boyne Hill in Berkshire (£754,000). An announcement in November 2006 confirmed the award of £13m under the Townscape Heritage Initiative to areas of definable historic character and patent social need. These included Long Eaton in Derbyshire (£957,000), the Green in Aberdeen (£1.4m), Stokes Croft in Bristol (£535,000) and Richill in County Armagh (£747,000).

Major grant offers (stage one, unless otherwise stated) in the course of the year included:

- Sefton Park, Liverpool (£4.7m)
- J. M. W. Turner's 1824 watercolour of Hastings Fish Market (£192,565) purchased for Hastings Gallery
- The Roundhouse, Derby (£4.2m) to allow Robert Stephenson's 16 sided-polygon of 1839 to become the centrepiece of Derby College
- The Ted Hughes Centre, Mytholmroyd in West Yorkshire (£1m) to celebrate the life of the Poet Laureate born in the town in 1930
- The Rotunda Museum, Scarborough (£1.8m)
- St Peter's Church, Ipswich, Suffolk (£772,000) to convert the redundant medieval church to a centre for musical and artistic events
- John Clare's Cottage, Helpston, near Peterborough (£1.2m) to restore and open to the public the house where the poet was born in 1793
- The National Embroidery and Textile Centre, Manchester (£995,000) to be created within the former church of St Peter at Ancoats
- The Crescent and Spa, Buxton in Derbyshire (£12.5m) to save the great 18th-century set-piece in the heart of the town
- Penicuik House, Scotland (£1.3m) to consolidate the ruins of the Grade A listed 18th-century mansion
- Malpas Court, Newport, Gwent (£750,000) to rescue a derelict early 19th-century villa as education and community space
- Castle Hill, Dungannon, Northern Ireland (£2.2m)
- Rosslyn Chapel, near Edinburgh (£4.5m) matching a grant from Historic Scotland of £2.2m to rescue one of the most eccentric products of Scottish medieval history
- Ordsall Hall, Salford, Greater Manchester (£4.1m)
- The Museum of Somerset, Taunton Castle (£4.8m)
- The Shire Hall, Monmouth (£3.1m)
- The Poundstock Gildhouse, near Bude, in Cornwall (£349,500) to repair, interpret and make disabled friendly this Grade I listed 15th-century church house
- Watts Gallery, Compton, Surrey (£4.3m)

- Keats House, Hampstead, London (£424,000)
- The Little Angel Theatre, Islington, London (£183,000) the oldest surviving marionette theatre in England

During the second half of 2006 major HLF funded schemes saw the reopening of the Dome Cinema in Worthing; the Temple of Minerva at Hardwick Park, County Durham; Nelson's Monument at Great Yarmouth; St George's Church, Bloomsbury, Hawksmoor's masterpiece where repair and reorientation is now almost complete; Fulham Palace; the former Devonshire Royal Hospital at Buxton in Derbyshire, now the centre of the Buxton Campus of the University of Derby; Saltwell Park, Gateshead which won a number of national awards; the Museum of Childhood at Bethnal Green in East London; Weston Park Museum and Mappin Art Gallery in Sheffield; the relocated county archives and Museum at Woodhorn Colliery in Ashington, County Durham; Birkenhead Park in the Wirral and Shaw House, near Newbury in Berkshire. 2007 reopenings include the Fishbourne Roman Palace in Sussex; Wilberforce House in Hull; St George's Hall, Liverpool; The Royal Festival Hall, London; Cowdray House in Sussex; Stanley Spencer Gallery, Cookham, Berkshire; the Shetland Museum at Lerwick and the Theatre Royal, Bury St Edmunds in Suffolk.

CHURCH OPENINGS AND CLOSURES

One of the largest donations from a private charitable trust was the £2.3m offered by the Collyer Ferguson Trust towards the repair of churches in Kent, including those at New Romney, Stone, Cobham, Headcorn, Cranbrook, Chalke, Mereworth, Swanscombe and St George the Martyr, Ramsgate.

More churches are listed Grade I than any other building type, and 2006–7 promised great things in their protection. An English Heritage 'Inspired' campaign to raise awareness of churches and their needs, continued, albeit in a low-key fashion, while a formal response from the government was awaited. One specific result of government parsimony was redressed in the course of the year when the Wolfson Foundation stepped in to replenish English Heritage's grant scheme for cathedrals. Since 2004 this has been reduced to a mere £1m a year – a very modest amount, given that Canterbury Cathedral alone announced this year that it must raise £50m to pay for repairs necessary to remain open. As a result of Wolfson donation, the level of the grant scheme in 2007–8 has been increased to £1.6m. Recipients included the masonry repair programmes at Hereford and Salisbury and works to the reredos in the Roman Catholic Cathedral at Leeds. Meanwhile, the remit of Andrew Lloyd-Webber's creation, the Open Churches Trust, which closed on 1 December 2006 announcing that its campaign to keep churches open to visitors had been largely won, was passed to the newly announced National Churches Trust. This was declared in June 2007 as the successor to the Historic Churches Preservation Trust (HCPT). The HCPT has been a serious source of grant aid – in 2006 it had awarded 372 grants totalling over £1.5m – but now felt the need to build up attendances within congregations, believing strongly that keeping roofs on buildings alone would not prevent closure.

The predicted avalanche of church closures did not materialise but it was disappointing to learn that diocesan authorities intended to close buildings of the quality and visibility of Brighton's parish church of St Peter designed by Sir Charles Barry. A similar fate befell Thomas Penson's St David's Church of 1843, which dominates Newtown in Powys. The Church of the Holy Cross, Birkenhead in the Wirral, an eccentric work by the most adventurous of all Catholic designers of the 20th century, F. X. Velarde, shut, as did the Grade II* listed Methodist Chapel at Carharrack, near Redruth in Cornwall completed in 1815. Some adventurous new uses were announced with a new community centre planned by Great Yarmouth Borough Council within the Grade II* medieval ruins of St Margaret's, Hopton. At All Saints Hospital at Eastbourne in Sussex, Berkeley Homes gained planning permission for a scheme of conversion which kept the richly appointed chapel of 1867 by Henry Woodyer intact to be run as a community resource.

By far the largest holder of former places of worship, the Churches Conservation Trust, took into care the medieval Yorkshire church at Wensley. Early in 2007 the Friends of Friendless Churches, which celebrated its 50th birthday in 2007, acquired a further English church, Llancillo on the Herefordshire border with Wales, and another one in Wales at Llanfigael on Anglesey. The Historic Chapels Trust, set up to look after the nonconformist heritage, completed one of its biggest building campaigns at the Salem Chapel at East Budleigh in Devon for a cost of £700,000. The Scottish Redundant Churches Trust acquired its fifth church in the shape of Benholm Kirk, important for its 15th-century carved sacrament house and fine memorials from the 17th century. The Welsh Religious Buildings Trust, also with a nonconformist brief, began to publish regular newsletters and announced in its first newsletter the acquisition of three buildings: Libanus, a simple Baptist chapel in Carmarthenshire; the Unitarian Chapel at Trecynon, near Aberdare of 1862; and Bethania in Maesteg of 1908, the work of the famous chapel architect Sir William Beddoes Rees.

THREATS

Among the 125 listed buildings threatened by demolition in the last year were the Church Inn at Whitefield in Bury, Lancashire, a richly appointed gin palace of 1910; the Lifeboat Station at Castle Hill, Tenby in Pembrokeshire; and the very distinctive octagonal auction ring of 1882 at Tow Law in Co. Durham. Demolishing listed buildings is fairly unusual, and most applications lodged with planning authorities were for schemes of conversion. Among these proposals were the creation of the supreme court within the Middlesex Guildhall opposite Westminster Abbey (with removal of the original furniture); the conversion of the former King Edward VII Hospital at Midhurst in West Sussex into housing; the proposed extension of Buile Hall Park at Salford into a hotel; and the creation of a single house within the former chapel at Whitelands College, London.

A number of new heritage attractions opened or reopened in the course of the year, as well as those funded by the HLF. Those reopened after repair included Sudley House, Liverpool and the ancient High House Museum at Thetford in Norfolk. The Wellcome Foundation on London's Euston Road opened its new Medicine Man collection in the summer of 2007 to 'explore the connections between medicine, life and art'. There were some backward steps too. The Heritage Centre at Middleton-in-Teesdale in County Durham, centred largely on the lead mining industry, closed late in 2005 and efforts to reverse that decision in 2006 failed. The comparatively new museum within the Manor House at Bury St Edmunds in Suffolk closed and there were high-profile threats to the Theatre Museum in London's Covent Garden, which finally shut in January 2007, and the William Morris Gallery in Walthamstow, where opening hours there were reduced to weekends only and specialist curatorial posts were abolished.

PUBLICATIONS

During 2006–7 there were important published biographies of the church architect Sir Ninian Comper (Anthony Symondson); Thomas Thomas, the first national architect of Wales (Stephen Hughes); Owen Jones, the 19th-century designer (Carol Flores); Ove Arup (Peter Jones); Inigo Jones (Giles Worsley, published posthumously); James Athenian Stuart (Susan Weber Soros); Louis Osman (Jenny Moore); Colin St John Wilson, the architect to the British Library (Sarah Menin and Stephen Kitt); the architect of SPAN Housing Eric Lyons (Barbara Simms); and John Evelyn by (Gillian Darley). Sir Howard Colvin's *Biographical Dictionary of British Architects 1500–1840* went into a fourth edition in May 2007. English Heritage published a major work on secular wall paintings and also sponsored extremely important works on Catholic architecture in England and Wales: *A Glimpse of Heaven* (Christopher Martin), *Jewish Heritage of England* (Sharman Kadish), and a guidance document on the future of historic suburbs. In December 2006 it began a brand new venture with the *English Heritage Historical Review* looking in depth at some of the properties it owns itself, whilst continuing the annual ritual of the *Buildings at Risk* list and *Heritage Counts.* Important new guidance on the treatment of traditional farm buildings was also forthcoming. The new editions of Pevsner's *Buildings of Britain* guides continued with the revisions of Shropshire, Isle of Wight, Essex and Perth & Kinross, and brand new volumes on Carmarthenshire and Ceredigion. New editions of Worcestershire, Herefordshire and Suffolk are on the horizon. Encouraging news came from the University of Bath: at a time when a number of conservation courses are closing down or finding it difficult to attract students, the university set up a new course on the conservation of historic gardens and cultural landscapes.

The most momentous passing of the year was the death of Sir John Smith in February. He was founder of the Landmark Trust and one of the most generous of all contributors to conservation causes.

CONSERVATION

THE NATURAL ENVIRONMENT

Peter Marren

WILD BOAR TO STAY?

Free-ranging wild boars are lurking in English woods for the first time since the Middle Ages. Boars have been farmed for their meat since the 1980s, with some 40 registered farms by 1998. The perhaps inevitable mass escape happened in 1987 when the retaining fence of a boar farm in Kent was blown down. The animals disappeared into dense woods nearby, and were joined by others two years later. Kent and nearby East Sussex is now home to Britain's largest population of wild boars with several hundred animals. Boars have also escaped from farms in Dorset, Herefordshire, Hampshire and Devon, in the latter case after the fence was deliberately cut by animal activists. The population of wild boars is conservatively estimated at 500 animals (other estimates range up to 1,000) and, despite attempts to shoot them or round them up, they seem to be increasing in number. In the south-east the boars are wary and active only by night, but in Devon the recently escaped boars are often spotted by walkers in the woods and lanes.

Natural England, the new body responsible for conservation, farm stewardship and access, favours 'sustainable management' of England's wild boars, with an option to remove them in places where their impact is 'unacceptable'. A consultation exercise by the Department for Environment, Food and Rural Affairs found the public divided on the issue, with 56 per cent opposed to total eradication. However boars can carry diseases such as swine fever and foot-and-mouth, and can raid agricultural crops as well as gardens. One method of controlling them, mooted recently, is a contraceptive vaccine which interrupts the hormones involved in ovulation. It has been tested on captive wild boar with positive results, and is about to be tried out on free-ranging boars in Herefordshire. However boar experts are doubtful of success. Using bait carries the risk of other animals consuming the vaccine, while catching the animals to vaccinate them would be expensive if not impossible. Perhaps we shall just have to learn to live with wild boars, as do the Germans, French and Spanish.

GREAT BUSTARD BREEDS ON SALISBURY PLAIN

Great Bustards are breeding again in Britain for the first time in 170 years. A male bustard was seen displaying on Salisbury Plain in March 2007, and two months later a female bird was watched incubating a clutch of eggs. Unfortunately the nest was abandoned and the two eggs proved to be infertile. The drama did at least show that the introduced bustards are now old enough and in a sufficiently healthy condition to breed. Further breeding attempts are expected in 2008.

The attempt to re-establish the Great Bustard, one of the world's largest flying birds, began in 2004. Salisbury Plain was chosen for its large area of undisturbed natural grassland interlaced with crops, which is similar to the landscape preferred by the bird in Spain and the Russian steppes, where it still occurs in large numbers. Surplus eggs taken from nests in Russia are hatched locally and fed with a glove puppet to avoid any human contact. Once they are fledged the birds are transported by air to England where, after a month in quarantine, they are released into an open pen on Salisbury Plain. Each bird is fitted with wing-tags and a miniature transmitter to allow its movements to be followed.

In 2006 only nine young birds, less than the project managers had hoped for, were obtained, bringing the total number released to nearly 70. Some of the birds were killed by foxes or were injured crashing into fences, while others disappeared. The behaviour of the survivors is proving unpredictable. While some migrate to neighbouring Dorset for the winter, others stay on the Plain, often foraging close to their release site. Two young males which had vanished reappeared in spring 2007.

Since adult males become sexually mature only after four to five years, the first attempts at breeding were not expected until 2008. So the 2007 pairing can be seen as a spirited trial run. With the cooperation of the Russian authorities the releases are to continue until 2014 when it is hoped that a self-sustaining colony of breeding birds will have been established.

IS THE RED SQUIRREL DOOMED?

Scottish Natural Heritage (SNH) unveiled a £4m plan to conserve red squirrels in the Scottish Highlands, which holds three-quarters of the total numbers of red squirrels in Britain. The plan addresses three problems facing the squirrels: competition with the non-native grey squirrel, fragmentation of the squirrel's woodland habitat, and a fatal disease known as squirrelpox. SNH proposes to prevent the further expansion of the grey into the Highlands by providing funds and incentives for eradicating them by trapping or poison. While it acknowledges that the total eradication of the grey squirrel, however desirable, may not be possible, SNH hopes to establish and maintain twenty key strongholds for the red squirrel.

Professor Stephen Harris, an expert on squirrels, believes that such projects are a waste of money. He points out that there have been many attempts to stamp out the grey squirrel since the 1930s, and all have failed. While the grey squirrel has steadily broadened its range, the red squirrel has retreated to Scotland and a handful of woods near the coast, especially on islands. The grey squirrel helps to eliminate its smaller native rival by spreading the squirrelpox virus and also by stripping the woods of the red squirrels' favourite food, most notably hazelnuts. Ominously a red squirrel infected with the deadly virus was found in Scotland in June 2007. The best hope for red squirrels, says Harris, is on isolated islands such as the Isle of Wight and Arran. Since we probably cannot get rid of the grey squirrel, we might as well learn to love it. As Harris points out, when the red squirrel was more common, it, too, was regarded as a serious forest pest.

VISITORS FROM AFAR

Nearly every year brings a crop of rare vagrant birds, including one or two that are new to Britain, but winter 2006–7 saw the first records of some wildly unlikely species blown thousands of miles off course. The most spectacular was an enormous seabird with a six-foot wingspan found in an exhausted condition on a beach near Burnham-on-Sea. A couple out walking rescued the bird, and, believing it to be an outsized fulmar, took it to the local animal rescue centre. After a night in a pen, the bird was released from cliff tops and not seen again. It was identified afterwards from photographs as an immature yellow-nosed albatross, whose nearest nesting grounds are in the South Atlantic. So, regrettably, a bird that hundreds of birders would have crossed England to see was seen only by its rescuers.

One that did attract birdwatchers in their thousands was a lone long-billed murrelet which visited Dawlish Bay, Devon, for a week in November 2006 and obliged them by swimming close to the pier. This bird nests in eastern Siberia and so had strayed a long way. Another first record was a glaucous-winged gull which turned up on a rubbish dump near Gloucester in December and again at Beddington sewage farm in London the following April. Another first record was a Pacific diver which lingered for nearly a month at Farnham gravel pit in North Yorkshire.

A memorable sight for those who saw it was a flock of 17 glossy ibis in Gloucestershire, the largest number of this bird ever seen in Britain. It was hoped that this east-European bird might stay on to breed for the first time, but the flock dispersed with scattered birds seen as far apart as Cornwall, Sussex and Lancashire. They had probably overshot their usual spring migration route from North Africa.

The winter also saw spectacular 'wrecks' of Leach's storm-petrels. Strong westerly winds had blown hundreds of this rarely seen oceanic bird into bottlenecks along the west coast in areas like the Severn estuary and the Mersey where they could be watched from onshore. Up to 150 birds were seen from various headlands in England and Wales. The bird breeds on isolated islands in the North Atlantic, and normally winters far out at sea.

BRITAIN'S 'RAINFOREST' THREATENED

Conservationists are worried about the rate at which 'brownfield' sites are disappearing under bricks and mortar in the Thames estuary. Despite their urban setting brownfield can be rich in insect life, being open, warm and full of wild flowers. Those along the Thames estuary have been dubbed Britain's 'rainforest' because of their extraordinary and unexpected biodiversity. West Thurrock marshes, for example, lie on fly-ash from a former power-station, yet despite their man-made origins now support more than a thousand insects and spiders, including such exotically named rarities as the distinguished jumping-spider *Sittacus distinguendus*, the brown-banded carder-bee *Bombus humilis* and the saltmarsh shortspur beetle *Anisodactylis poeciliodes*. The charity Buglife claims it is Britain's second-richest site for invertebrates.

Despite their rare bees and spiders, such marshes are considered wasteland by local authorities and lie unprotected and waiting to be developed. At Erith Marshes, for example, planning permission was recently given for a 27-hectare business park over the protests of the London Wildlife Trust and others. West Thurrock marshes, too, are threatened by an application for a Royal Mail distribution centre and lorry park there which is expected to destroy half the site. Among other likely casualties is the rare hump-backed ant *Mymica bessarabica* which casts new light on the happy ant characters used in Royal Mail's advertising. The fight to save West Thurrock marshes is being led by Buglife, the new charity for our beleaguered invertebrates.

A claim from the Mayor of London's office that the City is becoming more wildlife-friendly has been challenged by London Wildlife Trust. Although the number of protected sites has risen slightly, the reality, says the trust, is that 474 hectares of wildlife habitat in the area has disappeared since 2001. For example, two-thirds of London's front gardens have been concreted over in recent years to provide parking spaces, a development which has been linked to the mysterious crash of house sparrows in London. While some well-protected rare species, like peregrine and grey heron, are doing well in London, once common ones like sparrows and skylarks are losing out.

WIND OF CHANGE IN THE HIGHLANDS

If every application to erect giant turbines in the windier parts of Scotland were approved, the country's reputation for grand rugged scenery would take a knocking. Such is the view of the explorer Ranulph Fiennes and it is widely shared. Conservationists are divided about wind turbines, acknowledging their role as sources of clean energy while warning of the potentially devastating consequences of poorly sited, poorly planned wind farms. Scotland's wildlife watchdog, Scottish Natural Heritage, is struggling to keep up with the gale of applications, while the RSPB complains that decisions are being made by local authorities without a proper assessment of environmental impact. While an Environmental Impact Assessment is mandatory for large developments, the planning system allows insufficient time for assessors to determine the flight paths and breeding patterns of birds. They are given months to build a case, but the work needs at least a year and preferably two, say the RSPB.

Among the more controversial applications of the past twelve months is a proposal for wind farms on Dava Moor close to the Cairngorms National Park. Dava Moor is a true wilderness inhabited by eagles, red-throated divers and ravens, all considered to be at risk from collisions. Moreover, such applications, if approved, will result in a national park encircled by wind farms and pylons. Another 22-turbine application for Lochluichart in Easter Ross would, say walkers, be visible from two of Scotland's most popular peaks, An Teallach and Ben Wyvis. Of those already approved the 18-turbine wind farm at Edinbane on Skye lies in an area used by golden eagles, while the 48 turbines to be built on Fallago Rig on the Lammermuirs in Berwickshire will, say objectors, be a massive blot on the landscape.

The most controversial development of them all is on the Isle of Lewis in the Outer Hebrides. The original application, by Lewis Windpower, for 234 giant turbines, was reduced to 181. Although the developers say it avoids damage to a designated Special Area for Conservation, the 100m high turbines will inevitably make a strong impact on the flattish, rolling landscape and big open skies of the island. The RSPB has objected on the grounds of its likely impact on the island's high densities of breeding birds. Some 4,000 other objections were received, mainly from local people. The application was nonetheless approved on the grounds that it would bring new jobs and opportunities to the island, which has a declining population. Objectors now pin their hopes on a petition to the Scottish Executive, whose approval is needed since the development depends on a publicly funded cable link to the mainland.

GRASS POWER

As part of their commitment to carbon-neutral energy, EU energy ministers have agreed to increase the share of biofuels used in petrol and diesel to 10 per cent by 2020. Britain has set its own target for biofuels at 5 per cent by 2010. What this means in practice is that subsidies will be made available for farmers to grow oil-rich plants such as oilseed rape and (more interestingly) willow trees, while markets such as biofuel power stations will be developed. As much as 2.5 million acres could be producing biocrops for fuel, heat and power regeneration by 2020.

This will have an impact on wildlife. In its report, *Bioenergy in the UK*, the Wildlife Trust (along with ten other organisations) warns that more monoculture crops grown for energy production could do more harm than good, damaging wildlife as well as soil and water quality, particularly if, as expected, such crops are grown on land formerly set-aside. The trust calls for a balanced audit of bioenergy's potential and drawbacks, and planning policies that guard against unsuitable developments and changes in land-use.

As scientific understanding improves, many different plants could be used to replace petrol and diesel as fuel. Potentially biofuel could help woodland management by generating a market for low-grade timber. Heather moors, too, could be kept in production if some means could be found to bio-refine its natural oils to make gasoline or a solid fuel.

However, the plant everyone is talking about is a non-native one: elephant grass or *Miscanthus*. This giant grass, which grows up to four metres high, needs surprisingly little fertiliser to produce high yields while harvesting can be done at times of the year when machinery is not being used for other crops. In European trials a hectare of *Miscanthus* yielded up to 12 tonnes. Construction began in 2005 on Britain's first *Miscanthus*-fuelled power plant, at Eccleshall, Staffordshire. To meet the expected demand local farmers are already growing the grass. One farmers' cooperative plans to cultivate 10,000 hectares of it over the next three years. Fields of silvery grass several metres tall may be commonplace in a few years' time. They will certainly make a visual impact, for better or worse, but the ecological impact of elephant grass is harder to assess. If grown as a monoculture in large fields its value for wildlife will be limited.

OTTERS RECOVERED

A two-year survey of otters in Scotland suggests that the animal has almost completely recovered since its numbers fell in the 1960s through contamination with DDT and other chemical pollutants. Some 93 per cent of the 1,300 riverbank and coastal sites examined across Scotland showed signs of otter activity. The recovery of the otter is ascribed to improvements in water quality, resulting in healthy fish stocks as well as a more balanced ecosystem. Even so the otter is not, and probably never will be, a common animal. Its population in Scotland is estimated at around 8,000 animals, about the size of the human population of Oban or Stornoway.

A sure sign that numbers of otters have also increased in England is the increasing number of dead ones on the roads. Otters forage in the centre of conurbations like Birmingham and Newcastle, and, in areas where they are being studied, like North Yorkshire, are still increasing. This has surprised experts. With a limited habitat and specialised feeding habits, otters need to cover a lot of ground, and it often brings them into potentially fatal contact with roads. When food is scarce the animals lose condition by burning up energy hunting in chilly waters. On top of that otters are still accidentally poisoned by chemicals, and also still illegally persecuted, for example, by some fish-farmers. So the otter is actually more common than, theoretically, it should be.

INSECT INVASIONS

Many rare insects and spiders seem to be increasing in range, probably as a result of climate change. Some of these are small and obscure species unlikely to be noticed by anyone except specialists, but not all. The Jersey tiger-moth, for example, is a brightly coloured, day-flying moth which has turned up in gardens in south London and is also spreading along parts of the south coast. Another species attracting notice is the wasp spider, so-named because of its bright yellow and black stripes. It is most easily seen in the autumn when the female spider spins its beautiful orb webs in town gardens. Yet another is the bee-wolf, a large wasp-like creature which preys on honey bees, which it carries slung beneath its body like a helicopter carrying a jeep. Once rather rare and confined to dry places along the south coast, the bee-wolf is now common in sand pits as far north as Yorkshire.

Still more surprising was the appearance in a garden in Shepshed, Leicestershire, of the violet carpenter bee, a spectacularly large, dark-winged bee familiar to holidaymakers in the Mediterranean but unknown in Britain. Other reports of large, menacing-looking violet bees around the country suggest that it is arriving and overwintering in fair numbers. A new bumblebee, so far known only by its Latin name *Bombus hypnorum*, has also turned up in the south and seems to be spreading rapidly. Given that three of our small fauna of bumblebees are extinct, a new one is very welcome.

Less welcome is the processionary moth, so-called because the hairy caterpillars follow-my-leader up tree-trunks and along the ground. The loose hairs of the caterpillar blowing in the wind can cause a rash on sensitive skins, and they have been known to defoliate whole trees. The moth has probably been introduced with nursery plants. Another unwanted intruder is the harlequin ladybird, a large, spotty orange or black beetle. A native of America, the ladybird was released in the Netherlands in an ill-advised attempt to control aphids, flew across the Channel and is now well-established and spreading in Britain. It is a voracious predator with an appetite for other ladybirds when it cannot find aphids. It also overwinters in houses, often in large numbers. It, too, is probably here to stay. Whether our native ladybirds can stand up to it remains to be seen.

SHARK ALERT

Sharks in British waters are being overfished according to a report by the Shark Alliance. For centuries they have been targeted for their meat, fins and oil, as well as for sport fishing. Today, however, fishing technology is more efficient than the sharks' reproductive biology can keep up with. Our larger sharks, such as basking shark, blue shark and porbeagle, mature slowly, live a long time and give birth to a limited number of live young after a long gestation. This makes them vulnerable to over-fishing. Unfortunately the quotas set by the European Union are based on stock estimates in the past and not on today's depleted stocks. Moreover, sharks are often fished illegally. Their fins, in particular, are in demand for the ever-growing food markets of the Far East, where shark's fin soup is a great delicacy.

Our commonest and most commercially important

species, the spurdog or spiny dogfish, was targeted first for its liver oil and later for the fish and chip trade where it was sold as 'rock salmon'. Stocks seemed to hold steady until the 1980s when landings fell to less than half. Today landings have fallen to 17 per cent of their peak levels in British waters and the animal is believed to be endangered.

Another victim of a blind and voracious trade is the porbeagle shark, whose flesh is highly prized. Despite its comparative rarity, porbeagle fishing is unregulated. On both sides of the Atlantic the stocks seem to have crashed to between 10 and 20 per cent of former levels. In 2006 the EU commissioner for fisheries did attempt to impose trade restrictions to give stocks the chance to recover, but was overruled by French and Spanish ministers. Steep declines have also been noted for blue, shortfin mako and common thresher sharks. The Shark Alliance concluded, gloomily, that the industry is governed more by self-interested fishing lobbies than by the arguments of conservationists and scientists.

MOTORWAYS FAST-TRACKED

The government has decided to overhaul the planning system which it regards as too slow and cumbersome for today's needs. At the request of the Treasury and Deputy Prime Minister's Office, the economist Kate Barker examined the relationship between economic growth and planning and came up with a series of detailed proposals to streamline the system and allow applications to be processed more quickly. These were endorsed by the government in a planning white paper published in May 2007. In particular the government proposes to place decisions on 'major infrastructural projects', such as motorways, airports, reservoirs and large windfarms, in the hands of an independent infrastructure planning commission.

Conservation bodies are worried about the implications of fast-tracking major developments. The Council for the Protection of Rural England found some of the recommendations 'disturbing'. The Wildlife Trusts fear it could override provisions for protecting wildlife, such as sites of special scientific interest, and claim it undermines the government's own policies. The white paper would take power away from elected local authorities and place it in the hands of 'the country's most ardent proponents of airports and motorways'. The government's own environmental watchdog, Natural England, gave the white paper a cautiously worded qualified support, trusting that the new commission would be 'empowered to secure the conservation and enhancement of the natural environment through a sustainable development duty'. In more straightforward terms, the Wildlife Trusts say the paper 'paves the way for a multiple assault on our most vulnerable wildlife'.

WOLF TO RETURN?

A paper published by the Royal Society advanced a case for reintroducing wolves to Scotland. It argued, with the support of mathematical models, that a comparatively small number of wolves would create great conservation benefits by reducing the numbers of deer and so helping forests to regenerate naturally. It would also free deer estates from the financial burden of having to cull hinds (female deer). The study estimates that, with 500 wolves roaming in packs across the Highlands, deer numbers would fall to a quarter of the present levels within 50 to 60 years. Hence the introduction of wolves is seen as an ecological solution to the long-standing problem of over stocking (a contention the Deer Commission disputes). The study, says Professor Colin Galbraith of Scottish Natural Heritage, 'is a bit theoretical, but it's quite well done'. However there are legal and practical obstructions to the idea. The moral imperative that a country must reintroduce any native animal hunted to extinction, as the wolf was, scarcely applies if the introduced animal is certain to be shot. 'It would be difficult to ensure that sheep [instead of deer] did not become their preferred prey', said Galbraith.

Meanwhile, frustrated by the lack of progress on reintroducing 'lost mammals' like beaver, lynx and wolf, an underground body calling itself the Wild Beasts Trust claims it has plans to illicitly release six wolves. The body also has plans to release beaver and other animals, as well as introducing sturgeon to Scottish lochs in the hope of starting a home-grown caviar industry. A licence is needed to introduce any foreign animal into Britain.

While the prospect of wild wolves roaming the Highlands is still a long way off, the Scottish Landowners Federation surprisingly supported the idea of reintroducing the Eurasian lynx, now considered to have lived in remote parts of Scotland until the fifteenth century. Wild beast enthusiasts were also surprised when the new environment minister, Michael Russell, said he would support a new attempt to release European beavers in Scotland. Scottish Natural Heritage is now drawing up proposals, this time with a ministerial nod and wink to help the beaver on its way (detailed proposals to introduce beavers to Argyll were thrown out by the Scottish Executive in 2005).

DANCE

Bridie Macmahon

The retirement of Darcey Bussell, the Royal Ballet's best-known and well-loved ballerina, in June 2007 was both mourned and celebrated in the dance world and beyond. Bussell retired at the age of 38 when still at the height of her powers, and the sheer beauty and intensity of her final performances in MacMillan's *Song of the Earth* will stand as the finest possible testament to her talent. She joined Sadler's Wells Royal Ballet in 1987 and moved to the Royal Ballet in 1988 where Kenneth MacMillan saw the potential of her tall, strong body combined with her youthful simplicity and sweetness. She created the leading role of Princess Rose in his *Prince of the Pagodas* at the age of 19 and was immediately promoted to principal dancer. The sheer scale, attack and physicality of her dancing were a major departure from the traditions of the Royal Ballet, but her temperament ensured that they enhanced rather than trampled on what had gone before. And by retiring before any of these essential qualities had diminished, she leaves her audience with images that will never tarnish.

ROYAL APPOINTMENT

Kenneth MacMillan's premature death in 1992 and the departure of David Bintley from his post as the company's resident choreographer in 1993 deprived not only Bussell but a whole generation of Royal Ballet dancers of the opportunity to work creatively with a company choreographer. In December 2006 the Royal's director, Monica Mason, took the bold step of appointing the innovative contemporary choreographer Wayne McGregor as the company's first resident choreographer since Bintley. The appointment came only days after the successful premiere of his new work for the company, *Chroma,* and perhaps sought to build on the spirit of excitement and modernity that the work created. McGregor is not about to turn himself into a classical choreographer, and it is difficult to see how his appointment will further the art of classical dance or develop the talents of the Royal's dancers, but it will undoubtedly use those talents to eye-catching effect. McGregor is quoted as saying that 'I would never see myself as becoming the defining force at the Royal Ballet. It's about widening the net.' This is a modest ambition far removed from the passionate creativity of Ashton and MacMillan, and it is to be hoped that in time a classical choreographer who does have the desire – and the undisputed talent – to become the driving force at the company will emerge. The company also announced the appointment of Barry Wordsworth as music director, a post that had remained vacant for many years, in April 2007. Wordsworth is a former music director of the company and a highly respected ballet conductor; he will combine the job with his roles as music director of Birmingham Royal Ballet and principal conductor of the Brighton Philharmonic Orchestra.

Christopher Wheeldon, a Royal Ballet-trained classical choreographer who also created a successful new work for the company, *DGV,* in November 2006, had left his job as New York City Ballet's resident choreographer in the same month. It had been widely predicted that he and not McGregor would be appointed to the Royal Ballet, and this would have been a much more evolutionary appointment; but Wheeldon has opted instead to form his own company, Morphoses, to be based both in London and in New York and to have at its core what he describes as 20 'kick-ass' dancers. He is openly inspired and influenced in his plans by the great Russian impresario Diaghilev, and aims to bring together creative forces from art forms outside dance to mould an exciting new ballet company. His plans are daring and ambitious but may be exactly what ballet needs at this juncture to revive an art form currently undergoing a crisis of confidence and a dearth of true creativity.

Two other new works were given by the Royal Ballet during the season. Alastair Marriott's *Children of Adam,* based on the book of Genesis and the writings of Walt Whitman, was a sincere and atmospheric but rather derivative work mainly notable for using the blazing emerging talents of the Australian dancer Steven McRae in a leading role. A new version of *The Seven Deadly Sins* was created by William Tuckett in April 2007; handsomely designed by Lez Brotherston, it failed to capture the satire and sophistication of the Brecht/Weill 'sung ballet' and seemed more like a long lingering portrayal of only one of the sins – lust. Martha Wainwright sang the part of 'Anna I' effectively, and Zenaida Yanowsky looked sexily beautiful as 'Anna II'; but the sum of the work was not worthy of the considerable talents that had gone into creating it.

ED'S DEBUT

The rest of the Royal Ballet's season was marked by superb performances in both full-length and one-act works. Most notable was the debut of Edward Watson as Prince Rudolf in MacMillan's *Mayerling.* Watson's portrayal was definitive and seemed to emerge fully-formed, with every aspect of Rudolf's development and decline clearly and agonisingly etched through Watson's body and the strength of his acting. Also outstanding was Ivan Putrov's performance as Pierrot in Glen Tetley's magnificent *Pierrot Lunaire,* created in 1962 and set to Schoenberg. Tetley, an American choreographer who fused classical and contemporary styles in his work to great effect, died in January 2007 at the age of 80.

One of the works created by David Bintley during his stint as the Royal Ballet's resident choreographer was a full-length version of Edmond Rostand's *Cyrano de Bergerac,* in 1991. The work was widely judged to have been unsuccessful, but Bintley, director of Birmingham Royal Ballet since 1995, decided to revisit it and the result was premiered by the Birmingham company in February 2007. This new *Cyrano* had simplified designs by the original designer, Hayden Griffin, and a new score by Carl Davis. The work was a great improvement on the 1991 version and produced excellent leading performances from Robert Parker and Elisha Willis. At the end of the season Parker retired from dancing at the age of only 31; he is making a slightly startling and certainly unusual career change to train as a commercial airline pilot in the USA.

BALLET HOO!

Bintley's company had other good reasons to celebrate during the year. The start of the season saw the culmination of an 18-month long collaboration between the company, local authorities and the Youth at Risk charity that specialises in the care and rehabilitation of disadvantaged young people. Several hundred young people were involved in a project aimed at staging a performance of MacMillan's *Romeo and Juliet* at the Birmingham Hippodrome in September 2006. They were trained by Desmond Kelly and Marion Tait and the final cast included professional dancers only as the leading couple; all other roles were taken by the teenagers who until the previous year had had no experience of ballet or performing and who had faced a whole range of social and personal difficulties. The progress of the project and the final performance were televised under the title *Ballet Changed My Life: Ballet Hoo!* and proved to be inspirational for viewers as well as participants. The performance itself was amazingly technically accomplished and conveyed a power and drama comparable with performances by the world's great companies. Of particular note were Linden (Tybalt), Shireenah (Lady Capulet), Christina (Nurse) and Andy (Friar Lawrence). This was an astonishing achievement for all involved and a tribute to the self-discipline and talents of the performers. A couple of months later a gala was held at the Hippodrome to mark Sir Peter Wright's 80th birthday. The company performed his production of *The Nutcracker* and expressed appropriate gratitude and affection to their illustrious former director.

Ballet Hoo! attracted a high and deserved level of public attention. The art received a torrent of less welcome publicity in December 2006 when Simone Clarke, a principal dancer with English National Ballet, was revealed to be member of the far-right British National Party; protesters subsequently disrupted her performance in *Giselle* at the London Coliseum by shouting abuse at her. The company issued a statement disassociating itself from the political views of its employees, and the row eventually died down. The production of *Giselle* being performed was a welcome revival of Mary Skeaping's beautiful 1971 production, made for the company in its former guise as London Festival Ballet. The company otherwise had a successful year under its new director Wayne Eagling, largely playing safe with its repertory but looking forward to more ambitious plans in 2007–8 when it will premiere a new full-length production of *The Snow Queen* by Michael Corder.

NORTH OF THE BORDER

At Scottish Ballet, Ashley Page continues to develop and challenge his company technically and artistically with a repertoire including his own works and pieces from other choreographers. Balanchine's early masterpiece, *Agon,* was performed by the company for the first time to great acclaim at the Edinburgh Festival in the summer of 2006. In a tribute to the company's founder, Peter Darrell, to mark the 20th anniversary of his death, his powerful 1971 one-act version of *Othello* was brought back into the repertoire for the first time since 1992.

Northern Ballet Theatre, on the other hand, plays strictly to the crowds, and does so with confidence. In September 2006 its director David Nixon mounted a lavish and fast-moving production of *The Three Musketeers,* set to music by Malcolm Arnold; the composer died on the day of its premiere at the age of 84. In February 2007 Nixon launched a new production of *The Sleeping Beauty,* renamed *A Sleeping Beauty Tale* and set in outer space. Set partly to Tchaikovsky's score and partly to other 19th-century Russian music, the production was as daft as it was ambitious.

The last Dance Umbrella under the direction of its founder, Val Bourne, was held in the autumn of 2006; in January 2007 Betsy Gregory formally took over the role of artistic director of this major contemporary dance festival now in its 28th year. The 2006 Umbrella opened at the redeveloped Roundhouse theatre in north London with the London premiere of Merce Cunningham's spectacular work *Ocean.* Set to a score by Andrew Culver and designed to be viewed in the round, *Ocean* uses 14 dancers who are surrounded by the audience which is turn surrounded by 150 musicians. The piece is powerful and enigmatic and served as a fitting finale to Bourne's distinguished career. Another high-profile participant in the festival was The Forsythe Company, formed by the former director of the Frankfurt Ballet, William Forsythe, in 2005. His new company offered the UK premiere of *Three Atmospheric Studies,* based loosely on the war in Iraq. The Michael Clark Company showed an expanded version of Clark's 1992 work *Mmm,* to Stravinsky's reduction of his *Rite of Spring* for piano duet.

SACRED MONSTERS

One of the most interesting collaborations in the field of contemporary dance during the year brought together the French ballet star Sylvie Guillem and the charismatic contemporary dancer and choreographer Akram Khan. The result was *Sacred Monsters,* premiered at Sadler's Wells Theatre in September 2006 and combining the spoken word with music and dance. Although at times this teetered perilously close to pretension, the periodic humour and the inventive dance duets choreographed by Khan were its salvation and the work was ultimately entertaining and absorbing.

Rambert Dance Company mounted a series of attractive new works during the year, including *Stand and Stare,* choreographed eloquently by Darshan Singh Bhuller to Bartok and inspired by the work of L. S. Lowry. Less successful was a 'revival' of Andrée Howard's 1939 work *Lady into Fox* based on David Garnett's strange 1922 novella of the same name. Only the central duet survives from the original work, and Mark Baldwin's new choreography for the rest of the piece does nothing to show why the work was so popular when it was first created.

Visitors to the UK included American Ballet Theatre, in its first London performances for 15 years at Sadler's Wells Theatre in February 2007; La Scala Ballet, which brought Nureyev's production of *The Sleeping Beauty* to the Royal Opera House in July 2007; and the Bolshoi Ballet, in another heavyweight season at the London Coliseum in August 2007.

MARK MORRIS

Amidst the frenetic activity of much of the season under review, it took the American choreographer Mark Morris, bringing his *Mozart Dances* to the Barbican for a few precious performances in July 2007, to articulate the 'still, small voice of calm' at the heart of dance. Set to three Mozart pieces (two piano concertos and the *Double Piano Sonata*), the work is a sublime response to the music and overflows with inventiveness, humour and beauty. As ballet seeks ever higher extensions and ever more extreme physicality, it would do well to note the light and shade, the use of stillness, the slow half-movements and the harmony of Morris's dance-making, which incorporates styles and motifs from all the ages in a unique and timeless expression of the power of dance.

PRODUCTIONS

ROYAL BALLET
Founded 1931 as the Vic-Wells Ballet
Royal Opera House, Covent Garden, London WC2E 9DD

WORLD PREMIÈRES: *Chroma* (Wayne McGregor), 17 November 2006. A one-act work. Music, Joby Talbot and Jack White III; set design, John Pawson; costume design, Moritz Junge. Cast led by Alina Cojocaru and Edward Watson

DGV (Danse à grande vitesse) (Christopher Wheeldon), 17 November 2006. A one-act work. Music, Michael Nyman; design, Jean-Marc Puissant. Cast led by Darcey Bussell and Gary Avis

Children of Adam (Alastair Marriott), 5 March 2007. A one-act work. Music, Christopher Rouse; design, Adam Wiltshire. Cast led by Leanne Benjamin, Johannes Stepanek and Steven McRae

The Seven Deadly Sins (William Tuckett), 26 April 2007. A one-act work. Music, Kurt Weill; design, Lez Brotherston. Cast led by Zenaida Yanowsky and Martha Wainwright

COMPANY PREMIÈRE: *Theme and Variations* (Balanchine, 1947), 5 March 2007. Music, Tchaikovsky; design, Peter Farmer. Cast led by Alina Cojocaru and Johann Kobborg

FULL-LENGTH WORKS FROM THE REPERTOIRE: *Coppélia* (Petipa and Cecchetti with additional choreography by de Valois, 1954), *The Sleeping Beauty* (Petipa, prod. Mason and Newton after de Valois and Sergeyev, 2006), *The Nutcracker* (Ivanov, prod. Wright 1984 with revisions 1999), *La Sylphide* (Bournonville, 1836), *Swan Lake* (Petipa and Ivanov, prod. Dowell 1987), *Onegin* (Cranko, 1965), *Mayerling* (MacMillan, 1978)

ONE-ACT WORKS AND *PAS DE DEUX* FROM THE REPERTOIRE: *Stravinsky Violin Concerto* (Balanchine, 1972), *Voluntaries* (Tetley, 1973), *Sinfonietta* (Kylían, 1978), *The Four Temperaments* (Balanchine, 1946), *Rhapsody* (Ashton, 1980), *Napoli Divertissements* (Bournonville, 1842, staged by Johan Kobborg 2007), *Apollo* (Balanchine, 1928), *La fin du jour* (MacMillan, 1979), *Pierrot Lunaire* (Tetley, 1962), *Checkmate* (de Valois, 1937), *Symphonic Variations* (Ashton, 1946), *Song of the Earth* (MacMillan, 1965)

BIRMINGHAM ROYAL BALLET
Founded 1946 as the Sadler's Wells Opera Ballet
Birmingham Hippodrome, Thorp Street, Birmingham B5 4AU

WORLD PREMIÈRES: *Cyrano* (David Bintley), 7 February 2007. A full-length work. Music, Carl Davis; design, Hayden Griffin. Cast led by Robert Parker and Elisha Willis

Small Worlds (Kit Holder), 2 June 2007. A one-act work. Music, Stravinsky; design, Helen Fownes-Davies. Cast led by Nao Sakuma, Chi Cao, Verginia de Gersigny and Iain Mackay

Take Five (David Bintley), 22 June 2007. A one-act work. Music, Dave Brubeck; design, Jean-Marc Puissant. Cast led by Carol Anne Millar, Robert Parker, Kosuke Yamamoto and Elisha Willis

COMPANY PREMIÈRE: *Stravinsky Violin Concerto* (Balanchine, 1972), 14 February 2007. Music, Stravinsky. Cast led by Elisha Willis, Robert Parker, Nao Sakuma and Iain Mackay

FULL-LENGTH WORKS FROM THE REPERTOIRE: *Romeo and Juliet* (MacMillan, 1965), *The Nutcracker* (Ivanov, prod. Wright, additional choreography by Redmon, 1990), *Coppélia* (Petipa and Cecchetti and Wright, prod. Wright 1995).

A performance of *Romeo and Juliet* was given at the Birmingham Hippodrome on 28 September 2006 with a cast largely comprising disadvantaged young people from the West Midlands; the performance was televised as part of the Channel 4 documentary *Ballet Changed My Life: Ballet Hoo!*

A gala performance of *The Nutcracker* was held at the Birmingham Hippodrome on 25 November 2006 to mark the 80th birthday of Sir Peter Wright.

ONE-ACT WORKS FROM THE REPERTOIRE: *Apollo* (Balanchine, 1928), *Pulcinella* (Brandstrup, 2006), *The Firebird* (Fokine, 1910), *Agon* (Balanchine, 1957), *Symphony in Three Movements* (Balanchine, 1972), *The Four Seasons* (Hindle, 1999), *Nine Sinatra Songs* (Tharp, 1982), *Pineapple Poll* (Cranko, 1951), *The Orpheus Suite* (Bintley, 2004), *The Shakespeare Suite* (Bintley, 1999), *Solitaire* (MacMillan, 1956).

ENGLISH NATIONAL BALLET
Founded 1950 as London Festival Ballet
Markova House, 39 Jay Mews, London SW7 2ES

COMPANY PREMIÈRES: *Sinfonietta Giocosa* (Christopher Hampson, 2006), 20 February 2007. Music, Martinu; design, Bruce French

A Million Kisses to my Skin (David Dawson, 2000), 20 February 2007. Music, Bach; set design, David Dawson; costume design, Yumiko Takeshima. Cast led by Laura Bruña, Daria Klimentová, Agnes Oaks, Erina Takahashi, Thomas Edur, Dmitri Gruzdyev and Fabian Reimair

FULL-LENGTH WORKS FROM THE REPERTOIRE: *Giselle* (Coralli and Perrot revised by Petipa, prod. Skeaping 1971), *Alice in Wonderland* (Deane, 1995), *The Nutcracker* (Hampson, 2002), *The Canterville Ghost* (Tuckett, 2006), *Swan Lake* (Petipa/Ivanov prod. Deane, 1997).

ONE-ACT WORK FROM THE REPERTOIRE: *Melody on the Move* (Corder, 2003)

RAMBERT DANCE COMPANY
Founded 1926 as the Marie Rambert Dancers
94 Chiswick High Road, London W4 1SH

WORLD PREMIÈRES: *Stand and Stare* (Darshan Singh Bhuller), 27 September 2006. Music, Bartok; design, Craig Givens

Transit (Melanie Teall), 11 October 2006. Music, extracts from Eric Serra's soundtrack to the film *Léon*; costumes, Roland Mouret

Verge (Cameron McMillan), 14 November 2006. Score, Elspeth Brooke; costumes, Roland Mouret

Lady into Fox (Mark Baldwin and Amanda Eyles, inspired by the 1939 production by Andrée Howard), 14 November 2006. Music, Benjamin Pope; design, Michael Howells

Anatomica #3 (André Gingras), 23 February 2007. Score, Joseph Hyde; design, Fabrice Serafino

Gran Partita (Karole Armitage), 22 May 2007. Music, Mozart; design, Jean-Marc Puissant

WORKS FROM THE REPERTOIRE: *A Steel Garden* (Bruce, 2005), *Constant Speed* (Baldwin, 2005), *Pond Way* (Cunningham, 1998), *bloom* (Collins, 2006), *Divine Influence* (Joyce, 2006), *Swamp* (Clark, 1986), *Dark Elegies* (Tudor, 1937), *Judgment of Paris* (Tudor, 1938)

RICHARD ALSTON DANCE COMPANY
Founded 1994
The Place, 17 Duke's Road, London WC1H 9AB

WORLD PREMIÈRES: *Brink* (Martin Lawrance), 13 March 2007. Music, Ayuo's *Eurasian tango;* costumes, Peter Todd

Fingerprint (Richard Alston), 13 March 2007. Music, Bach; costumes, Peter Todd

Nigredo (Richard Alston), 5 June 2007. Music, Simon Holt; costumes, Peter Todd

Stealing Poison (Martin Lawrance), 5 June 2007. Music, Mark Bowden; costumes, Peter Todd

Tempt My Better Angel (Darren Ellis), 5 June 2007. Music, Evangelia Rigaki; costumes, Peter Todd

WORKS FROM THE REPERTOIRE: *Red Run* (Alston, 1998), *Devil in the Detail* (Alston, 2006), *About-Face* (Lawrance, 2006), *Volumina* (Alston, 2005).

SCOTTISH BALLET
Founded 1956 as the Western Theatre Ballet
261 West Princes Street, Glasgow G4 9EE

WORLD PREMIÈRE: *Sirocco* (Diana Loosmore), 19 September 2006. Music, Ian Simmonds; design, Scottish Ballet. Dancers, Eve Mutso and Erik Cavallari

COMPANY PREMIÈRES: *Room of Cooks* (Ashley Page, 1997), 19 September 2006. Music, Orlando Gough; design, Jon Morrell after Stephen Chambers. Dancers, Patricia Hines, Paul Liburd and Erik Cavallari

Refurbished Behaviour (Ashley Page, 1985, revised 2005), at the Edinburgh International Festival in August 2006 and then 19 September 2006. Music, Wire. Dancers, Diana Loosmore and Jarkko Lehmus

Agon (Balanchine, 1928), at the Edinburgh International Festival in August 2006 and then 5 October 2007. Music, Stravinsky. Cast led by Eve Mutso and Erik Cavallari

In Light and Shadow (Krzysztof Pastor, 2000), at the Edinburgh International Festival in August 2006 and then 11 April 2007. Music, Bach; design, Tatyana van Walsum. Cast led by Adam Blyde and Patricia Hines

FULL-LENGTH WORK FROM THE REPERTOIRE: *Cinderella* (Page, 2005)

ONE-ACT WORKS FROM THE REPERTOIRE: *Two Pieces for HET* (van Manen, 1997), *The Pump Room* (Page, 2005), *32 Cryptograms* (Page, 2004), *Walking in the Heat* (Page, 1992), *Artifact Suite* (William Forsyth, 2004), *Acrid Avid Jam* (Page, 2003), *divertissements* from *The Nutcracker* (Page, 2003), *Othello* (Darrell, 1971).

AWARDS

CRITICS' CIRCLE NATIONAL DANCE AWARDS 2006

De Valois Award for Outstanding Achievement in Dance – Ivor Guest
Best Male Dancer – Carlos Acosta (Royal Ballet)
Best Female Dancer – Miyako Yoshida (Royal Ballet)
Best Choreography (Classical) – Alexei Ratmansky *(The Bright Stream)* (Bolshoi Ballet)
Best Choreography (Modern) – Wayne McGregor *(Amu)* (Random Dance Company)
Best Choreography (Musical Theatre) – Twyla Tharp *(Movin' Out)*
Emerging Artist (Classical) – Steven McRae (Royal Ballet)
Emerging Artist (Modern) – Alexander Varona
Company Prize for Outstanding Repertoire (Classical) – Les Ballets Trockadero de Monte Carlo
Company Prize for Outstanding Repertoire (Modern) – Phoenix Dance Theatre
Best Foreign Dance Company – Bolshoi Ballet
Working Title Billy Elliot Award – Brad Corben and Joseph Poulton
Dance UK Industry Award – Val Bourne
Audience Award – Northern Ballet Theatre and Independent Ballet Wales

LAURENCE OLIVIER AWARDS 2007 (DANCE)

Best Theatre Choreographer – Javier de Frutos for *Cabaret*
Best New Dance Production – *Chroma* (Royal Ballet)
Outstanding Achievement in Dance – Carlos Acosta for his season at Sadler's Wells Theatre in 2006

THE PLACE PRIZE 2006

Nina Rajarani

FILM

Jonathan Theodore

CREATIVE FATIGUE

2007 was dubbed by many critics the year of the 'threequels', dominated as it was by the third outing of several running Hollywood sagas. *Spiderman 3, Pirates of the Caribbean: At World's End* and *Shrek the Third* were predictably the biggest box-office draws of the year. All of them felt past their best. *Pirates* and *Spiderman* suffered from over-budgeting syndrome, their mammoth viewing times crammed in with extra plotlines and special effects to the detriment of characters and storytelling. *Shrek* disappointed with its lack of the daring or subversive wit of its predecessors, its titular lead no longer a hero fighting for recognition but an adult shirking his responsibilities.

More generally, the year saw an extensive creative plundering of past hits. Cinemas were swamped with spin-offs, sequels and remakes, many of which proved a mixed bag. *Poseidon* and the *The Wicker Man* in particular were a poor homage to their originals, and met with audience apathy and critical disdain. Ageing action heroes were wheeled out of retirement to greater success. In *Die Hard 4*, Bruce Willis plays a balder version of the same underdog policeman, but the threat he faces has gone virtual, a youthful cyber-terrorist threatening to bring the digital infrastructure of the United States to its knees. Sylvester Stallone put on his gloves for one last round as *Rocky Balboa*, enough of a hit to raise the possibility of a *Rambo* revival. But the most exciting reinvigoration of a film franchise came with *Casino Royale*, a new direction for the Bond brand, which backtracked from the CGI-enabled escapades of *Die Another Day* to return to its roots with Ian Fleming's first and most famous 007 novel. Ingenious gadgets and unbelievable settings were largely replaced with blood, grit and violence – notable moments including the agent's cold-blooded first kill, and a torture sequence that disturbs in what it suggests rather than shows. Daniel Craig's take on Bond wowed the waverers who had been concerned with his blonde and craggy looks. A physically realistic hard-man, his brutal and amoral veneer hides a vulnerability gradually exposed as the film moves towards a tragic denouement. Bond may be cinema's most ridiculous icon, but Craig gave a convincing performance of it and is justifiably expected to stay in the role for the foreseeable future.

That cinema – or at least western cinema – seems to be stuck in a rut, must be familiar to regular audiences. Partly this could be due to a lack of imagination, though film piracy is likely to be the biggest factor compromising originality. Worth over $6bn (£3bn) in the USA alone, piracy continues to dent coffers and damage the confidence needed to take creative risks. Its biggest impact is on DVD sales and rentals, long-term sources of revenue on which about eight out of ten films depend to recoup their costs. Broadband and file-sharing networks have shifted the focus of piracy from car boot sale bootlegs to quick and easy downloading, and the industry has so far struggled to respond. Plans to fight back with court action against the network hosts, and alternatives in legal download websites, are still in their early days. How successful the battle proves to be will be seen in years to come, though many pundits see an unavoidable decline in the studio system. In this climate of financial uncertainty one wonders how many daring and original ideas have been shelved for the easy money of a *Saw* sequel.

This is not to say that familiar stories cannot be told with a stab of novelty, particularly when cost-effectiveness is on the agenda. The impact of the digital revolution in cinema was evidenced in *300*, a fictionalised recreation of the Battle of Thermopylae, where 300 Spartans and their king stood to the last man against the massed Persian invaders. Whereas the 1962 film was a completely straightforward re-enactment of the Greek legend, the 2007 adaptation, taken from a graphic novel by Frank Miller (of *Sin City* fame), used lusciously rendered CGI visuals that gave the film a mythic, almost dreamlike quality. It also allowed the epic to be shot at the 'modest' expense of $60m (£30m). What gained the film the greatest attention is the issue of cultural sensitivity, or rather lack of it. The Persian army is variously depicted as an assortment of drugged fanatics, mindless barbarians and misshapen monsters, headed by the piercing-adorned and androgynous Darius, a portrayal which earned the film the outrage and formal condemnation of the Iranian government. Critics were divided on its ideological intentions, some attacking *300* for an air of Western cultural superiority, with others content to enjoy it purely as escapist fantasy. In any event, the film's $450m (£225m) taking was a huge and unexpected success, reviving the future chances of the historical epic after high-profile flops *Troy* and *Alexander* left it with a questionable future.

300 aside, most of the drive to push the artistic envelope came this year from outside the English-language world. *The Science of Sleep*, written and directed by the French Michel Gondry, previously behind *Eternal Sunshine of the Spotless Mind,* was a love tale where the vivid dreams and ponderings of its protagonist, Stephane (Gael Garcia Bernal) are evoked in playfully fantastical sequences that roam through his subconscious. The film's weakness was the lack of a great concept to rival *Eternal Sunshine,* its story a comedic but clichéd tale of unrequited love, the spurner an enigmatic and wholly unsympathetic female lead (Charlotte Gainsbourg). But the flair of the project is unquestionable. Its only rival in this area was *Pan's Labyrinth*, a Spanish surrealist fantasy by Mexican director Guillermo del Toro. Not without vision, Guillermo creates a parable about the Spanish experience of civil war and fascism through the descent of a child, Ofelia (Ivana Baquero) into a mythic underworld populated by nightmarish and otherworldly creatures. This beggars comparison to C. S. Lewis' *The Lion, the Witch and the Wardrobe,* a Christian allegory where children escaped through the eponymous wardrobe from Blitz-era Britain into a fairytale, but *Pan's Labyrinth,* directed by a lapsed catholic, is a much darker yarn. It deals with the aftermath of Franco's victory and a local struggle between a ruthless fascist commander and a rebel movement. The harrowing tone of the real-world scenes finds a match in the unsettling phantasmagoria of the fantasy sequences, though the ending, while bittersweet, ends on an affirmative note of personal triumph.

As evidence of the increasing global profile of foreign-language films, *Pan's Labyrinth* won a clutch of awards internationally, including an Academy award for cinematography, and grossed $80m (£40m) worldwide. In this respect it beat *Curse of the Golden Flower,* the latest martial-arts epic by Zhang Yimou, the director of *Hero* and *House of Flying Daggers,* whose films are now tailored to wow western audiences with sumptuous fantasy versions of ancient China. This time round, however, the lavish sets and costumes were not enough to paper over a lacklustre plot.

The USA saw some artistic dabbling in *Inland Empire,* a three-hour ode to the bizarre by surrealist maestro David Lynch. Loosely a story about the filming of a thriller from a cursed script, it is a nightmarish and incomprehensible tale that frightens and compels in equal measure. Filmed on digital camera for added grit and gloom, it is peppered with weird features, notably a bunny-headed family mouthing banalities on a fantasy sitcom show.

Lynch is often cited as a cult director, but his high-art approach only generates a fraction of the interest of the populist end of that spectrum. The kind of fanatical following a film can generate prior even to appearing in cinemas was evidenced by the *Snakes on a Plane* phenomenon. Starring Samuel L. Jackson (who took the role on condition that the title was kept), it was the biggest example of an internet frenzy preceding a release since *The Blair Witch Project.* The film's ridiculous plot, premise and title gained it a runaway online fanbase whose output included fan fiction, poster art, animation clips and short film parodies based on the same concept. The producers, who bowed to popular demand by adding suggested one-liners to the final cut, complemented this attention. Whether filmmaking-by-fans catches on is uncertain, judging by *Snakes'* disappointing takings, earning only half of its $30m (£15m) expected box-office in the opening weekend. Internet hype has not yet proven to have the reliability of more traditional PR routes.

Another cult-status aspiring failure was *Grindhouse,* a Rodriguez-Tarantino creative indulgence harkening to a film age of simple and graphic values. The 'Grindhouse' phenomenon saw its heyday in the 1960s and 1970s, when relaxed censorship laws gave rise to the titular-named cinemas specialising in exploitation films: pulpy and lurid B-movies featuring wanton levels of sex, violence, drug-use and gore, and set to self-consciously absurd plots featuring freaks, mutants, monsters, and general mayhem. *Grindhouse* was a double bill consisting of feature-length films *Planet Terror* and *Death Proof,* bookended by spoof trailers of the same theme. Despite positive critical responses and a considerable media buzz, it bombed at the box office – an outcome attributed to the film's length, with some cinema-goers leaving after the first feature oblivious (or disinterested) to the fact that a second instalment was to follow. *Grindhouse* may not have been the tour de force for Tarantino that was *Kill Bill,* but audiences were compensated for this by Martin Scorsese's marvellous return to form with *The Departed,* arguably his greatest film since iconic 1990 gangster flick *Goodfellas.* A remake of the 2002 Hong Kong thriller *Infernal Affairs,* it is a bold, brash and violent mob tale. Matt Damon and Leonardo DiCaprio play cops on opposite sides of the law, the former on the gangster Costello's payroll and the latter undercover in said gangster's operation. DiCaprio has fully replaced Robert De Niro as Scorsese's muse and he improves with every film they do together. Here he is utterly convincing as a whirlwind of anger and angst, violent and insecure. Matt Damon mirrors this performance with a bland and passionless creep, conceited and morally bankrupt. Best of all is Jack Nicholson, the head hoodlum who sparkles with the demented charisma of the casual sociopath. One expects he can act like this in his sleep. Widely acclaimed by critics, *The Departed* also proved Scorsese's biggest commercial hit, grossing $300m (£150m) on a $90m (£45m) budget.

POLITICAL THEMES

It is a familiar concept that 9/11 reset the parameters of popular culture as much as it did political discourse. Filmmakers are increasingly drawn to the social and political troubles of humanity, and these themes and insights now pepper the whole spectrum of cinema. Science fiction, long a favourite avenue for escapist thrills, moved into more provocative territory this year with depictions of unsettling futures that may await us. *Children of Men,* directed by Alfonso Cuaron *(Yu Tu Mama Tambien* and *Harry Potter 3),* is set in 2027, and paints a world wracked by incurable global infertility. Following a worldwide descent into anarchy, Britain totters on transformed into an Orwellian parody – a racist and authoritarian state. It is a grim place, imploding under its own weight into mayhem and violence, and doomed by the looming extinction of the human race.

Cuaron's brilliance as a director is to make this nightmarish world entirely plausible by filming his scenes amidst a wealth of background detail, most of which is captured in the stunning single-shot camera sequences he is widely famous for. *Children of Men* takes the viewer on a guided tour of this world, first passing through scenes of London as the new Baghdad and a terrorists' playground, then vast, barbed wire-enclosed detention camps, and finally a raging urban war between the 'fascist-ised' British army and waves of desperate illegal immigrants. Beneath all the bleakness, however, is a moving story of hope and faith, the birth of a child signifying a fresh start for humanity.

Another world overrun by its problems was glimpsed in *A Scanner Darkly.* Adapted from a novel by Philip K. Dick, the visionary writer of *Blade Runner* who used sci-fi settings to explore questions of personal identity, it is a druggy and paranoid nightmare. Set in a near future where America is in an all-out drug war with the hyper-prevalent substance D, it stars Keanu Reeves in a suitably cast role as the blank-eyed Bob Arctor, a deep undercover narcotics agent addicted to D.

Initially filmed on digital camera, *A Scanner Darkly* innovates in its use of digital rotoscoping, a painstaking animation technique whereby computer-generated visuals are painted over the original frames. The shifting and distorted effect this creates adds a hallucinatory quality to the picture, as if experienced through the eyes of the drug-addled protagonist. It is an unsettling world to see. Aside from the horrors of substance D abuse, government and corporations are complicit forces with hazily sinister goals, and the web of duplicity extends to include all the main characters. Everyone is wearing a false persona, and Arctor, burnt-out and losing all grip on reality, turns out to be a puppet in the games of his masters. But as with *Children,* a final message of hope for this world comes through at the end.

Focusing not on tales of the future but the lessons from the past was Clint Eastwood – at 77 still a filmmaking force – who returned to full sombre and expansive form with a double bill of films about the invasion of the

Japanese-occupied island of Iwo Jima at the end of the Second World War. *Flags of our Fathers* details the perspective of those servicemen who planted the Star-Spangled Banner flag on the island and were immortalised in a photo that made them national idols. Eastwood is out to subvert the unthinking patriotism of that war. The photo was carefully staged while the soldiers in it were used as propaganda pawns for the military's bond-raising ventures at home, where, as feted celebrities, they are crushed by the awful burden of survivor's guilt and the distorted tale they are forced to spin. Deconstructing cherished war myths in the heat of the Iraqi chaos was a timely but dangerous move for Clint, and American audiences punished his intentions at the box office. Its paired film, the Japanese-language *Letters from Iwo Jima*, avoided such subversion. Depicting events from the perspective of the Japanese in a sympathising and humanising manner, this impeccably politically correct approach made it a box-office triumph in Japan and earned it a clutch of awards, including Academy award nominations for best picture and best director.

Diverse as the expression of political statement is becoming in cinema, nothing has matched the eviscerating punch of documentary filmmaking. A new brand of outspoken amateur film-makers have turned a critical eye at the West's political and commercial institutions, and have generated numerous controversies and calls for change. Left-wing firebrand Michael Moore ignited the trend three years ago with *Fahrenheit 9/11*, a broadside on the Bush government and its Iraq policy that was loved and loathed in equal measure, and he returned to the fray this year with *Sicko*, a merciless swipe at the US healthcare system, which lacks universal coverage and is dominated by big and – so Moore claims – unscrupulous corporations. Notorious for some of his escapades, Moore pushed the bar with a visit to Cuba where he attempted to get 9/11 rescue workers treatment they struggled to find in the USA (and included in his hunt the medical facilities at Guantanamo Bay). Bold even by his standards, this stunt earned Moore the attention of the US treasury department, investigating the film at the time of publication for a possible violation of the US-Cuban travel embargo. One wonders whether they realise they are doing all his PR for him. The biggest documentary success of the year, however, came from Al Gore with *An Inconvenient Truth*, a hugely popular and much-debated film about the frighteningly accelerating impact of global warming. Though lacking the fiery charisma of Moore, Gore's patiently derived arguments carry their own weight and charm and his case, backed now by an overwhelming scientific consensus, is alarming. Gore has combined the film with a tour of the lecture circuit and his commitment to environmental awareness has earned the famously dour, failed presidential candidate an unlikely celebrity status, culminating in his role in setting up the Live Earth concerts.

THE UK SCENE

British cinema had some notable success stories this year. The biggest proved to be *The Queen*, directed by Stephen Frears, which focused on the interaction between Queen Elizabeth II (Helen Mirren) and Prime Minister Tony Blair (Michael Sheen, familiar as prime minister from his role in TV's *The Deal*, also by Frears). Pieced together from extensive interviews with sources close to both protagonists, the film was regarded as spot-on in many of its characterisations, and Mirren's portrait of the Queen is psychologically interesting enough that the balance struck between conjecture and fact never becomes an issue. Both the leads received adulation for their roles and the film exceeded all box-office expectations to make $120m (£60m) worldwide, as well as Academy awards for best director, screenplay and actress.

Official recognition for UK cinema was otherwise muted. No British films were in the official running at Cannes, prompting the usual cries of Euro-American bias, though Anton Corbijn's *Control*, a biopic of Ian Curtis, the troubled frontman of post-punk northern rock band Joy Division, earned an ecstatic reception. Veteran actor Peter O'Toole, now 82, achieved the dubious record for number of best actor Oscar nominations (8) with his performance in *Venus* as a retired lothario engaging in a platonic but sexually suggestive relationship with a younger woman. He lost out to Forest Whitaker for his portrayal of Idi Amin, the eccentric and paranoid Ugandan dictator, in the widely acclaimed *The Last King of Scotland*.

Bush-bashing had its place in *28 Weeks Later*, an apocalyptic zombie-horror follow up to *28 Days Later* that eschewed the tight focus of the original for a broader parallel on belligerent US foreign policy. Danny Boyle, director of the former film and *Trainspotting*, created the surprisingly good *Sunshine*. Starring an ensemble cast of astronauts entrusted with the tasks of reigniting a dying sun, it was marketed as a sci-fi action thriller in the mould of *Armageddon*, but impressed critics with its dreamy, meditative tone and focus on the psychological dimensions of space travel. *Sunshine* hearkened back to the great philosophical sci-fi classics such as Kubrick's *2001* and Tarkovsky's *Solaris*, a brave approach which failed to earn into commercial success.

On a lighter note was *Hot Fuzz*, an action comedy by the team behind cult stoner TV series *Spaced* and zombie-horror parody *Shaun of the Dead*. Simon Pegg plays a driven and conscientious metropolitan cop, dumped into a sleepy rural village for embarrassing his city peers with his over-achievement. Unfortunately the writing team fell victim to creative indulgence. The humour is heavy-handed, taking the obvious pot-shots at rural life before descending into a slapstick parody of an American action film. The sheer unadulterated fun of the enterprise rubs off, littered with comic allusions to crime, action and horror classics. But the gear-shift between genre parodies reflect the lack of a core substantial concept with the mileage of *Shaun*.

AWARDS

ACADEMY AWARDS 2007

Best Picture – *The Departed* (Martin Scorsese)
Best Director – Martin Scorsese *(The Departed)*
Best Actor – Forest Whitaker *(The Last King of Scotland)*
Best Actress – Helen Mirren *(The Queen)*
Best Supporting Actor – Alan Arkin *(Little Miss Sunshine)*
Best Supporting Actress – Jennifer Hudson *(Dreamgirls)*
Best Animated Feature – *Happy Feet* (George Miller)
Best Documentary – *An Inconvenient Truth* (Al Gore)
Best Foreign Language Film – *The Lives of Others* (Florian Henckel von Donnersmarck)
Best Adapted Screenplay – William Monahan *(The Departed)*
Best Original Screenplay – Michael Arndt *(Little Miss Sunshine)*

CANNES FILM FESTIVAL 2007

Palme d'Or – *4 Months, 3 Weeks and 2 Days* (Cristian Mungiu)

Grand Prix – *Mogari no Mori* (Naomi Kawase)
Best Director – *The Diving Bell and the Butterfly* (Julian Schnabel)
Best Screenplay – *The Edge of Heaven* (Faith Atkin)
Best Actor – Konstantin Lavronenko *(The Banishment)*
Best Actress – Jeon Do-yeon *(Secret Sunshine)*
Jury Prize – *Persepolis* (Marjane Satrapi and Vincent Paronnaud); *Silent Light* (Carlos Reygadas)
60th Anniversary Prize – Gus Van Sant *(Paranoid Park)*

BERLIN FILM FESTIVAL 2007
Golden Bear – *Tuya's Marriage* (Wang Quan'an)
Grand Jury Prize – *The Other* (Ariel Rotter)
Silver Bear for Best Director – Joseph Cedar *(Beaufort)*

VENICE FILM FESTIVAL 2006
Golden Lion – *Sanxia Haoren* (Jia Zhangke)
Grand Jury Prize – *Daratt* (Mahamat Saleh Haroun)

LITERATURE

Nick Rennison

FICTION

In fiction, the prize-winning and the bestselling categories sometimes overlap, but not often. Among the notable prize-winners last year was Kiran Desai, whose novel *The Inheritance of Loss* (Hamish Hamilton) won the Booker prize for 2006. Desai, daughter of the well-known novelist Anita Desai, became, at the age of 35, the youngest woman to have won the prestigious prize, but her novel, the story of a retired Indian judge and his relationship with his orphaned granddaughter, caused controversy – particularly in Kalimpong, the Indian town where much of it is set. Residents objected to alleged stereotyping of Indian people of Nepalese descent in the book. The other books on the Booker shortlist were Kate Grenville's *The Secret River* (Canongate), Hisham Matar's *In the Country of Men* (Viking), M. J. Hyland's *Carry Me Down* (Canongate), Sarah Waters' *The Night Watch* (Virago) and Edward St. Aubyn's *Mother's Milk* (Picador).

2007 saw the award of the second recently established, biennial Booker international prize. It went to the Nigerian writer and author of *Things Fall Apart* and *Anthills of the Savannah*, Chinua Achebe. Chosen from a shortlist which included such luminaries of world literature as Margaret Atwood, Doris Lessing and Philip Roth, Achebe was described by the chair of the judging committee, Elaine Showalter, as the man who 'inaugurated the modern African novel' and 'illuminated the path for writers around the world seeking new words and forms for new realities and societies'. The Booker international prize has now been awarded to two writers. Its very much older brother, the Nobel prize for literature, has been granted to 103 writers since its inauguration in 1901. In 2006 the prize went to the Turkish novelist Orhan Pamuk. It was a blow struck for the freedom of writers everywhere that the author of such richly textured fiction as *The Black Book* and *My Name is Red* should be facing enormous criticism and even potential imprisonment in his own country because of his outspoken comments on Turkish responsibility for the Armenian genocide during the First World War, at a time when he was given the highest honour in world literature.

The Orange prize for fiction, awarded for the best novel by a woman writer in English each year, went in 2007 to Chimamanda Ngozi Adichie for her book *Half of a Yellow Sun* (Fourth Estate), a powerful story set amidst the horrors and upheaval of the civil war in Nigeria in the 1960s. She fought off powerful competition from Kiran Desai's 2006 Booker winner *The Inheritance of Loss*, Rachel Cusk's *Arlington Park* (Faber), Jane Harris' *The Observations* (Faber), Xiaolu Guo's *A Concise Chinese-English Dictionary for Lovers* (Chatto & Windus) and *Digging to America* (Chatto & Windus) by Anne Tyler. The third Orange Broadband award for new writers went to Karen Connelly for her novel *The Lizard Cage* (Harvill Secker), an often harrowing but brilliantly written tale of a political dissident imprisoned by Burma's repressive military dictatorship in the 1990s.

The first year of the Costa Book Awards, formerly the Whitbread Awards, saw the usual wide array of titles come under the scrutiny of the judges. William Boyd's *Restless* (Bloomsbury), the story of a young Russian woman recruited into the British Secret Service on the eve of the Second World War, won the novel award, Linda Newbery's *Set in Stone* (David Fickling) took first place in the children's category, John Haynes' *Letter to Patience* (Seren Books) was the poetry winner and Brian Thompson's *Keeping Mum* (Atlantic Books), an account of an ordinary wartime childhood remembered with unsentimental clarity, was the judges' choice in the biography category. Winner of the first novel award was Stef Penney's *The Tenderness of Wolves* (Quercus), an atmospheric murder mystery set in the icy wastes of northern Canada during the 1860s. The book caused a minor stir when it was revealed that Stef Penney had never visited Canada and had done all her research for the book in the British Library. How, some critics asked, could the novel be deemed properly authentic? Others, more attuned to the power of the imagination, pointed out that Penney had never visited the 1860s either but had still succeeded in recreating the era convincingly for her narrative. Clearly the criticism did little to dent the opinion of the Costa judges that here was a fine novel. *The Tenderness of Wolves* was chosen from the list of category winners as the overall Costa book of the year.

The International Impac Dublin literary award remains the world's most lucrative literary prize for a single work of fiction published in English. Shortlisted authors for the 2007 award included such well-known names as Julian Barnes for *Arthur & George* (Jonathan Cape) and Cormac McCarthy for *No Country for Old Men* (Picador), but the winner was the Norwegian writer Per Petterson for his book *Out Stealing Horses* (Harvill Secker), a stark story of an elderly man recalling the events of a long ago summer in the country which had changed his life. Quite reasonably, the translator of the book, Anne Born, walked away with €25,000 (£16,750) of the €100,000 (£67,000) prize.

Richard and Judy may have faced embarrassment with revelations about their show's use of premium-rate phone lines but its influence on the UK book trade remains strong. The two highest-selling novels on the 2006 bestseller list were Kate Mosse's *Labyrinth* (Orion) and Victoria Hislop's *The Island* (Headline). Both had featured as Richard and Judy Summer Reads during the year. Further down the list, Dan Brown's books continued to sell without any assistance from Richard and Judy but they had sprinkled the magic dust of TV exposure on novels such as Elizabeth Kostova's *The Historian* (Time Warner), Sam Bourne's *The Righteous Men* (HarperCollins) and Dorothy Koomson's *My Best Friend's Girl* (Time Warner) and the chart showed the results. The announcement of the Richard and Judy Summer Reads of 2007 meant that books like Kim Edwards' *The Memory Keeper's Daughter* (Penguin), Simon Kernick's *Relentless* (Corgi) and Kate Morton's *The House at Riverton* (Pan) began to shoot up the bestseller lists.

Some major names in British fiction published new titles in the first half of 2007. Ian McEwan's *On Chesil*

Beach (Jonathan Cape) was a poignant and ironic novella, set in the early 1960s, in which the first sexual encounters of two virginal newlyweds have consequences that reverberate throughout their lives. Graham Swift's *Tomorrow* (Picador) was a similarly subtle and nuanced portrait of a marriage, slowly revealed through the thoughts of a woman lying in bed next to her husband of twenty-five years. *Engleby* (Hutchinson) marked something of a change of style for *Birdsong* author Sebastian Faulks. Instead of the powerful narratives of love and war for which he is best known, Faulks provided readers with a blackly comic tale of a cynical journalist whose carefully constructed persona unravels as his past catches up with him. (In July 2007, it was announced that Faulks would soon tackle another character unlike any about which he has written before. He would be the author of a new James Bond novel, given the imprimatur of the Ian Fleming estate, to be published next year.) Iain Banks' *The Steep Approach to Garbadale* (Little, Brown) revisited a subject the author has examined before (wildly eccentric Scottish families revealing secrets long buried) but did so with his usual panache and narrative brilliance.

Sixty years after the publication of his first novel, American literary icon Norman Mailer was still going strong and still unafraid to tackle the most ambitious of themes. *The Castle in the Forest* (Little, Brown) took as its subject nothing less than the nature of evil as it blended fact and fiction in a story of the emergence of Adolf Hitler from Austrian obscurity to pursue his dreams of power. The Second World War featured in several of the novels published earlier in the year. Justin Cartwright's *The Song Before It is Sung* (Bloomsbury) moved back and forth in time in its narrative of a man struggling to unearth the truth about the friendship between an Oxford professor and a German aristocrat executed for his part in a plot to kill Hitler. *Day* (Jonathan Cape) by A. L. Kennedy was set in 1949 and told the story of the former crewman in a bomber plane, now reduced to appearing as an extra in a POW movie, who finds that participation in a fantasy version of the war unlocks his own memories of what he experienced. In 2003 Peter Ho Davies was chosen as one of *Granta's* best of young British novelists on the strength of his short stories. In 2007 he finally published his first novel. *The Welsh Girl* (Sceptre) was set in the Second World War and focused on an enigmatic relationship between the eponymous heroine and a German POW who escapes from a prison camp in the Welsh hills.

Pat Barker travelled one world war further back in time to a period she has already made her own in the *Regeneration* trilogy. *Life Class* (Hamish Hamilton) was the story of a group of art students torn from their studies at the Slade and pitched into the horrors of Flanders. Marina Lewycka's first novel, eye-catchingly entitled *A Short History of Tractors in Ukrainian*, was one of the surprise successes of 2005. Her second, *Two Caravans* (Fig Tree), investigated the lives of exploited migrant workers in the English countryside with the same blend of black comedy and poignantly exact observation that marked her debut. Lionel Shriver's *The Post-Birthday World* (HarperCollins) provided two alternative versions of its narrative. In one its comfortable middle-class heroine succumbed to the temptation of a passionate affair with (rather improbably) a fiery professional snooker player; in the other she resisted and stayed resentfully faithful to her husband. Khaled Hosseini's *A Thousand Splendid Suns* (Bloomsbury), the follow-up to his bestseller and favourite of book clubs worldwide, *The Kite Runner*, was the story of two Afghan women struggling to survive some of the worst years in their country's turbulent history. It promised to be just as successful as his first novel. Alaa Al Aswany's *The Yacoubian Building* (Fourth Estate) has been the bestselling novel in the Arabic world for the last four years. In 2007 English readers got to see what had made this multi-stranded narrative of the lives of the inhabitants of a Cairo apartment block so popular.

Each year the number of crime and mystery novels seems to grow exponentially. Once known as the Golden Dagger, the most prestigious award in the genre now acknowledges a sponsor in its new name of the Duncan Lawrie Dagger (Duncan Lawrie is a private bank). In 2007 it went to the Australian writer Peter Temple for his novel *The Broken Shore* (Quercus). Much admired down under, Temple can now look forward to a higher profile in the UK.

Alexander McCall Smith took his loveable protagonist, Precious Ramotswe, the first female detective in Botswana, on another outing in *The Good Husband of Zebra Drive* (Polygon). Michael Dibdin's final novel about Italian police detective Aurelio Zen, published a few months after Dibdin's untimely death, had the sadly prophetic title of *End Games* (Faber). In *The One From the Other* (Quercus) Philip Kerr returned for the first time since 1991 to his memorable, Chandleresque detective Bernie Gunther, now struggling to walk the mean streets of Munich in the harsh years immediately after the Second World War. *The Savage Garden* (HarperCollins), by Mark Mills, the story of a Cambridge scholar innocently wading into deep waters in post-war Tuscany, benefited from Richard and Judy's attention to rise up the bestseller lists. Other well-known crime writers contributing their bit to the year's fictional mayhem included Carl Hiaasen (*Nature Girl,* published by Bantam), Nicci French (*Losing You,* published by Michael Joseph), Harlan Coben (*The Woods,* published by Orion) and John Connolly (*The Unquiet,* published by Hodder), whose books cleverly cross over from crime to horror.

J. R. R. Tolkien passed away in 1973 but his publishers remain determined that death will be no impediment to the continued publication of new titles by him. *The Children of Hurin* (HarperCollins) was constructed from manuscripts he left and added new tales to the huge saga of Middle-earth. Other fantasy successes, this time by authors still in the land of the living, included Trudi Canavan's *Voice of the Gods* (Orbit), the latest in her *Age of Five* sequence; *Renegade's Magic* (Voyager), the last of a trilogy by Robin Hobb; and *Into a Dark Realm* (Voyager), second in a new series by Raymond E. Feist. Nearly all fantasy fans were eagerly awaiting the first film adapted from Philip Pullman's magnificent 'His Dark Materials' trilogy, due out in the autumn.

In science fiction, Americans have their Hugos and their Nebulas whereas Brits have the more staidly named British Science Fiction Association award for best novel and the Arthur C. Clarke award. The BSFA award for 2006 went to Jon Courtenay Grimwood for his novel *End of the World Blues* (Gollancz) – and the Arthur C. Clarke for 2007 was won by M. John Harrison's futuristic noir thriller *Nova Swing* (Gollancz). Other big titles were *Black Man* (Gollancz) by Richard Morgan, *The Prefect* (Gollancz) by Alastair Reynolds and *Spook Country* (Viking) by cyberpunk pioneer William Gibson.

NON-FICTION

If prizewinners and bestsellers in fiction are not always the same books then this is even more true of non-fiction.

The most high-profile award in the very broad non-fiction category is the Samuel Johnson prize. As in previous years, the 2007 shortlist consisted of books on a wide range of subjects from the history of mind control (*Brainwash* by Dominic Streatfeild, published by Hodder) to a biography of the pioneering traveller in the Middle East, Gertrude Bell (*Daughter of the Desert* by Georgina Howell, published by Pan Macmillan). The eventual winner was Rajiv Chandrasekaran's *Imperial Life in the Emerald City* (Bloomsbury), a startling piece of reportage which took readers into the surreal world of Baghdad's Green Zone, the walled-off enclave that is headquarters for the Americans in Iraq.

The bestselling non-fiction title in the UK for the year under review, Peter Kay's *The Sound of Laughter*, was always highly unlikely to feature in the Samuel Johnson shortlist but Kay was equally unlikely to be much bothered by its absence. Published in the autumn of 2006, the story of growing up in Bolton, struggling with a succession of low-paid jobs and then turning oneself into the country's most popular comedian had sold 600,000 copies in hardback by the end of the year. It continued to keep tills ringing, in both hardback and paperback format, in the first half of 2007.

Other memoirs could only trail along in Kay's wake but some still sold in substantial numbers. Bill Bryson began one of his travel books 'I come from Des Moines. Somebody had to.' His autobiographical *The Life and Times of the Thunderbolt Kid* (Doubleday) showed just what a 1950s childhood in Des Moines was like. It didn't seem too bad. Almost idyllic, in fact. Probably the most eagerly awaited or over-hyped biography of the first half of 2007 – depending on one's perspective – was *The Diana Chronicles* (Century) by Tina Brown. The queen of the New York media glitterati claimed that her life of the princess of hearts would be revelatory but many reviewers seemed to think it had little new to offer.

The nation's obsession with Diana seems unlikely to fade away in the near future, certainly not while the *Daily Express* continues to devote most of its front pages to conspiracy theories about her death. Publishers look set to keep the relentless stream of Diana books coming for a few years yet.

There were other trends in non-fiction publishing. Richard Dawkins' extraordinarily popular *The God Delusion* was the first of a series of books to attack religion and religious belief. Smiting the Almighty was suddenly all the rage. Christopher Hitchens with *God Is Not Great: The Case Against Religion* (Atlantic) and Sam Harris with *Letter to a Christian Nation* (Bantam) followed where Dawkins had led.

The departure of Tony Blair from Downing Street heralded publication of a number of books assessing his time in office. Geoffrey Wheatcroft's *Yo, Blair!* (Politico's) had a subtitle ('Tony Blair's Disastrous Premiership') which left no doubt of its author's opinions. Others were kinder to Blair (although not very markedly) but the biggest post-Blair book was undoubtedly *The Blair Years* (Hutchinson) by former New Labour 'spinmeister' Alastair Campbell. Political gossip-mongers throughout the nation were probably dismayed by the author's self-censoring announcement that he would not publish anything which might harm Labour's electoral prospects, but Campbell's diaries still revealed much about the workings of government over the last ten years that those doing the governing might have wished to keep secret. Gordon Brown started his premiership by, among other things, publishing not one book but two. *Courage: Eight Portraits* (Bloomsbury) was a tribute to heroes of integrity such as Nelson Mandela, Martin Luther King and Raoul Wallenberg; *Britain's Everyday Heroes* (Mainstream) highlighted ordinary people whose commitment to a cause or a community provided inspiration for all.

One surprising bestseller from the history shelves was H. E. Marshall's *Our Island Story* (Galore Park Publishing). It was surprising because it was first published in 1905. Its account of the nation's history from the perspective of an era less troubled by anxieties about Britain's place in the world clearly struck a chord. Other history books were more up-to-date. In the year that marked the bicentenary of the abolition of the slave trade, William Hague took time out from his duties on the opposition front bench to publish *William Wilberforce* (HarperPress), a weighty and scholarly account of the life of the great anti-slave trade campaigner. Meanwhile, John Major took time out from whatever it is that ex-prime ministers do to write *More Than a Game* (HarperPress), a history of cricket's golden years from the eighteenth century to the outbreak of the Second World War. Simon Sebag Montefiore published *Young Stalin* (Weidenfeld & Nicolson), a chilling portrait of a political monster in the making. Jerry White's *London in the Nineteenth Century* (Jonathan Cape), David Kynaston's *Austerity Britain* (Bloomsbury) and Ben Wilson's *Decency and Disorder* (Faber), a history of Britain as it moved from late Georgian riotous living to Victorian propriety, were all big books on big subjects. The earliest historian of all was in Ryszard Kapuscinski's companion *Travels with Herodotus* (Allen Lane). Kapuscinski, who died in January 2007, was often described as the greatest journalist of his generation and was a master of literary reportage. His last book describes how the Polish writer, a pocket edition of the Greek historian's works in hand, set out as a young man to work as a foreign correspondent in Asia and Africa.

In cookery, it seemed as if the British, once assumed to be as skilful at cooking as they were at, say, ski-jumping, were now the height of fashion. Not only did the best-known cooks in the country remain British-born heroes like Jamie Oliver and Gordon Ramsay, rather than the foreign interlopers of yesteryear, but a swathe of books was published, extolling the delights of traditional British food. Laura Mason's and Catherine Brown's *The Taste of Britain* (HarperCollins) and Marwood Yeatman's *The Last Food of England* were only the biggest and best from a large selection.

Books which claim to explain how society, or some part of it, works in a single memorable phrase will never lack for readers. *The Long Tail* (Random House) by Chris Anderson demonstrated how, in a business world transformed by the internet, the future lies with the 'long tail' of a company's backlist products, presumably good news for stockholding bookshops of whatever kind. Nassim Nicholas Taleb's *The Black Swan* replaced good news with bad by revealing that highly improbable and inherently unpredictable events ('black swans') rule the modern world. Andrew Keen's *The Cult of the Amateur* (Nicholas Brealey) compounded the bad news with his claims that bloggers, YouTubers and other Web 2.0 users were threatening to blur the distinction between professional experts, who know what they are talking about, and amateur enthusiasts, who don't. Critics of the book argued that Keen himself didn't know what he was talking about.

POETRY

Last year's article made the uncontentious prediction that Seamus Heaney's collection *District and Circle* (Faber) would win both the T. S. Eliot prize and the Forward prize for poetry. Our powers of prophecy proved only partially effective. Heaney did indeed win the T. S. Eliot award but the Forward prize for best collection went to the Scottish poet Robin Robertson for his volume entitled *Swithering* (Picador). The prize for best first collection went to Tishani Doshi's *Countries of the Body* (Aark Arts) and Sean O'Brien's 'Fantasia on a Theme by James Wright' was chosen as best single poem. Strong contenders for the T. S. Eliot were Simon Armitage's improbably titled collection *Tyrannosaurus Rex versus the Corduroy Kid* (Faber) and Paul Muldoon's *Horse Latitudes* (Faber).

Other well-known poets had new collections. Helen Dunmore's *Glad of These Times* (Bloodaxe) was her first for six years. John Burnside, with *Gift Songs* (Jonathan Cape), the veteran American poet John Ashbery, with *A Worldly Country* (Carcanet), the Irish poet Eavan Boland with *Domestic Violence* (Carcanet) and Adam Thorpe, also admired as a novelist, with *Birds with a Broken Wing* (Jonathan Cape) made the first half of 2007 a good one for lovers of intelligent and demanding modern verse. The year was also marked by celebrations of the centenaries of two of Britain's greatest twentieth-century poets. Those for W. H. Auden were always likely to overshadow those for fellow 1930s poet Louis MacNeice, also born in 1907, but Faber published new *Collected Poems* for both men and some critics would claim that MacNeice deserves to be rated just as highly as his more famous contemporary.

CHILDREN'S

Only one story can kick off any survey of children's literature in the year. As midnight's witching hour approached on 20 July 2007 there was every sign that the launch of *Harry Potter and the Deathly Hallows* (Bloomsbury), the seventh and final book in the series, would be a bigger event than publication of any of the previous six. Fervent fans camped outside bookshops, sometimes for days, awaiting the moment when they could get their hands on the last instalment of the saga. The British and American publishers struggled to sustain the embargo on the book that they had imposed as an apparently complete transcript of it appeared on the web in the week before official publication. Pottermania once more gripped the nation.

Sales in the UK in the first twenty-four hours after bleary-eyed booksellers, dragged from their beds to man the tills were estimated to have reached the eye-popping figure of 2.7 million, making it easily the world's fastest selling book ever.

With new adventures of the Hogwarts teenager loosed upon the world, it was difficult for other children's or young adults' titles to get much of a look-in, but there were books that succeeded in gaining attention and acclaim, although one had to look a long way down the bestseller lists to find a volume not written by J. K. Rowling. *Tunnels* (Chicken House) by Roderick Gordon and Brian Williams, the latest in Louise Rennison's Georgia Nicholson books, *Luuurve Is a Many Trousered Thing* (HarperCollins), Anthony Horowitz's *Nightrise* (Walker Books) and titles by the prolific writer of horror stories for teenagers, Darren Shan, were among those books which fought a rearguard action against the overwhelming Potter tide.

In 2007 two of the most respected awards in children's literature celebrated major anniversaries. In its seventieth year, the Carnegie Medal went to Meg Rosoff's *Just in Case* (Puffin), an offbeat and occasionally dark tale of an adolescent forced to face dramatic changes in his life and to confront the very real figure of Fate. The slightly less venerable Kate Greenaway Medal, awarded for distinguished illustration in a children's book, reached its golden jubilee year and was won by Mini Grey for *The Adventures of the Dish and the Spoon* (Jonathan Cape).

Michael Rosen, poet, novelist and broadcaster, took over from Jacqueline Wilson as Children's Laureate and will serve two years in the post. According to Shami Chakrabarti, chair of the committee which selected him, Rosen's 'gift for capturing the language and imagination of children on and off the page will make him a wonderful champion for the young and their literature'. Rosen himself said he saw the job as Children's Laureate as being 'an ambassador for fun with books'.

NEWS AND TRENDS

In any year in the book trade there are variants of stories that seem to have been around for decades. This year has seen the recurrence of some popular old chestnuts. One is the tale of publishers turning their noses up when confronted by a classic novel submitted as a new manuscript. This year's variation on that theme was the experience of David Lassman, director of the Jane Austen Festival in Bath, who sent off extracts and synopses from Austen novels to 18 publishers under the pseudonym of Alison Laydee, only to have all the recipients reject them as unpublishable. Potentially more shaming for the publishing industry, only one of the editors who replied seemed to have noticed that the opening sentence, 'It is a truth universally acknowledged, that a single man in possession of a good fortune, must be in want of a wife' had been used in the past. Nearly two hundred years in the past.

Another familiar friend is the story of the much-loved fictional character accused of racism, sexism, homophobia or some other equally undesirable quality. This year, not for the first time, it was Tintin's turn. An edition of *Tintin in the Congo* was lambasted by the Commission for Racial Equality and some bookshops agreed to move the book from their children's sections. Hergé's tufty-haired young hero was the product of a different era but it was difficult to deny that *Tintin in the Congo* did embody some appallingly backward views of black Africans, even for the 1930s when it was written.

On the high street, the year did not seem as if it was going to be a good one and Jeremiahs, as so often in the past, were predicting the demise of traditional bookshops or even the inevitable downfall of the book. Certainly the big-name retailers appeared to struggle. Borders announced that it was putting its UK shops up for sale and concentrating on the US market. Waterstones, despite (or, perhaps, because of) its merger with Ottakar's, looked likely to close a number of its branches. Yet sales of books on the internet continued to rise and even some independent high-street shops, despite all the pressure from Amazon, supermarkets and the big chains, found that, through niche marketing and concentration on local needs, they could thrive as minnows in a sea of increasingly aggressive sharks.

Inevitably, there were losses in the literary world in the period under review. The poet John Heath-Stubbs; Nigel Kneale, creator of the *Quatermass* TV series; the travel writer Eric Newby; children's writer Ursula Moray

Williams; Jack Williamson, the veteran American science fiction writer who had sold his first story to pulp magazines in 1928; William Styron, author of *Sophie's Choice* and *The Confessions of Nat Turner*; Philippa Pearce, the writer of the classic children's novel *Tom's Midnight Garden*; the poet and translator Michael Hamburger; the legendary American writer Kurt Vonnegut; Michael Dibdin, the creator of the Italian police detective Aurelio Zen; Robert Anton Wilson, co-author of the cult classic *The Illuminatus! Trilogy*; and the feminist writer Tillie Olsen, all died in the year under review.

Another of the year's casualties was Lesley Blanch, centenarian author of the 1950s bestseller *The Wilder Shores of Love*. When Blanch was born in 1904, the highlights of the year's publications included Henry James' *The Golden Bowl*, Joseph Conrad's *Nostromo* and Beatrix Potter's *The Tale of Benjamin Bunny*. She had lived to see the rise of internet bookselling and a world in which, from the US and the UK to China and India, every other person seemed to be a *Harry Potter* fan. Books and the book trade seem no more likely to fall into obsolescence in the near future than they did in 1904.

MUSIC

POPULAR MUSIC

Piers Martin

SALES SLUMP

This proved to be another tough year for the music industry as sales of CDs continued to fall. The International Federation of the Phonographic Industry (IFPI) said global CD sales in 2006 slumped to 1.7 billion, compared with 1.9 billion in 2005. The IFPI had hoped that increased global sales of digital music would offset the decline, and while digital sales doubled in 2006, with single track downloads topping 795 million, they failed to compensate for the overall drop in music sales. The IFPI also noted that the recording industry is suffering because of widespread internet piracy and CD copying. It is estimated that there were 20 illegal downloads for every song downloaded legally worldwide, while a survey by market research company NPD Group reported that nearly half of all music acquired by fans last year came from unpaid sources such as file-sharing and CD copying.

In the UK, record companies experienced a challenging 12 months. Figures released by the British Phonographic Industry showed that 6.5 million fewer albums were sold during the first half of 2007 than in the same period in 2006. During this time, digital album sales increased by 2 million, but this failed to make up the shortfall. There was bad news on the high street too, as music retailers faced stiff competition from supermarkets and online stores such as Amazon. Competition between major supermarkets such as Asda and Tesco pushed the average price of a CD below £9 for the first time. As more singles and albums were purchased online, traditional music retailers HMV and Woolworths posted depressing sales figures. HMV announced a 73 per cent slide in profits for 2006, blaming 'profoundly changing markets'. Meanwhile, the well-regarded Fopp chain of record shops became a high-profile victim of the uncertain climate. The company declared itself bankrupt in June, closing all 105 of its stores nationwide at the expense of 700 jobs.

Some commentators attributed the decline in CD sales in part to a new approach to consumerism practised by what cultural analysts have termed 'the Facebook generation'. Like MySpace and Bebo, Facebook is a social networking site that allows users to make friends and share information about themselves, such as tastes in music. Facebook is most popular with 16 to 25-year-olds in the US and UK, and had, in June 2007, an estimated 3.5 million users. This age group is the first to take technology for granted and had its first experience of online music consumerism during the digital download boom of the late-1990s through sites such as Napster. As a consequence, the Facebook generation thinks little of downloading music illegally or swapping music files; in fact, research showed they believe all media should be free and funded by advertising. In order to remain profitable, record companies must devise new ways of attracting this confident, solvent and technology-savvy consumer group. One example of this occurred in May when the social music site Last.fm was bought by US media giant CBS Corporation for $280m (£140m). Founded in London five years ago, Last.fm is a music recommendation platform that allows its active users (15 million in June 2007) to connect with other listeners with similar musical tastes, building communities around music. Listeners are bracketed in a 'neighbourhood' with other like-minded users and can suggest artists or songs to other listeners based on their shared musical tastes. Via a piece of software, Last.fm logs each song played on the user's computer or iPod and constructs a detailed profile of the user from this data. For big media companies seeking younger listeners, this kind of ground-level, word-of-mouth information is highly prized.

CHART REVAMP

The Top 40 hit parade was reinvigorated this year when new rules allowing any download to be eligible for the UK singles chart came into force at the beginning of January. This meant that digital sales of album tracks, B-sides, and classic hits from yesteryear would qualify for the charts alongside the weekly new single releases. Previously, a digital download was only eligible if a physical version of the same song was also available. According to the UK Official Chart Company, downloads have driven sales of UK singles up from 32.3 million in 2004 to more than 62.1 million in 2006.

The most-downloaded single of the year was 'Crazy' by US duo Gnarls Barkley, which sold 397,000 copies. In total, 819,553 copies of 'Crazy' were sold, making it the top-selling single of 2006. In December, *X Factor* winner Leona Lewis sold 139,000 downloads in the first week of release of her debut single, 'A Moment Like This', which went on to become 2006's second-highest seller. The new rules led to some surprising inclusions. In January, Snow Patrol's 'Chasing Cars' single, originally released five months earlier, re-entered the Top Ten. At the end of April, Sheffield indie-rock band Arctic Monkeys found they had a total of 18 tracks in the Top 200. As their acclaimed second album, *Favourite Worst Nightmare*, charted at number one in the albums chart, each of its 12 tracks, plus six from their debut album, charted individually in the singles chart. However, this turned out to be a clerical error by the iTunes webstore.

Nevertheless, the band enjoyed a hugely successful year. With characteristic modesty, they accepted the 2006 Mercury Music Prize for their million-selling debut, *Whatever People Say I Am, That's What I'm Not*, in September. They also scooped gongs for best album and best group at February's Brit Awards and in June headlined the Pyramid stage at the Glastonbury Festival, playing to tens of thousands of muddy revellers on the Friday night. UK sales of *Favourite Worst Nightmare* have so far reached 550,000 copies.

Rihanna, the US R&B singer, scored the longest-running number one single since 1994. Somewhat appropriately, 'Umbrella' topped the UK charts for ten weeks during the nation's wettest summer on record. She became the seventh artist in the history of the chart to score a tenth week at number one, and the first since Wet Wet Wet's 'Love Is All Around' in 1994. Moreover, the infectious track inspired its own umbrella-twirling dance in nightclubs, and a range of umbrellas, the Rihanna collection, was manufactured by optimistic US company Totes.

WINEHOUSE MANIA

The British soul singer Amy Winehouse had a year of highs and lows. The north London star released her Motown-styled second album, *Back To Black*, in October to moderate acclaim. By Christmas, however, her regular appearances in the tabloid press and celebrity gossip sites looking worse for wear after numerous nights out, coupled with the success of her hit single 'Rehab', made her a household name. She was crowned Best Female at the Brits. At the Ivor Novello Awards for songwriting in May, 'Rehab' won the Best Contemporary Song. In the US, *Back To Black* entered the Billboard charts at number seven, the highest new entry for a British female artist in the chart's history, raising Winehouse's celebrity profile on both sides of the Atlantic. *Back To Black* became the UK's fastest-selling album in 2007, with sales approaching 1 million in the first seven months alone. As the garlands stacked up, Winehouse's live performances became increasingly erratic. A tabloid fixture for much of the year, the 24-year-old often appeared inebriated onstage and occasionally cancelled shows. In common with Pete Doherty, the talented Babyshambles frontman who endured a particularly grisly year, Winehouse is mainly known not for her music but for her insalubrious lifestyle.

Much of Winehouse's album was produced by Mark Ronson, the dapper 30-year-old British-born, New York-bred DJ and musician, whose own album *Version* attracted glowing notices in the UK. Consisting of feel-good cover versions performed by an all-star cast, including Winehouse, Lily Allen and Robbie Williams, of hits by Coldplay, The Zutons and The Smiths, among others, *Version* sold 250,000. Ronson also produced a good deal of London ska-pop sensation Lily Allen's *Alright, Still* LP, which sold well over 800,000 copies. Allen, a level-headed 22-year-old, enjoyed a remarkable year and blossomed into an unlikely style icon, designing a dress collection for the New Look fashion chain and trainers for Nike. Her pink dress and sunny demeanour brightened a gloomy Glastonbury. Meanwhile, Allen's protégé, Kate Nash, a flame-haired 20-year-old pianist and singer from London, scored a sizeable hit with her debut single, 'Foundations', and album, *Made Of Bricks*.

2006–7 was a busy year for the formidable US producer Tim Mosley, known to millions of hip-hop and R&B fans as Timbaland. The 36-year-old produced big-selling albums by global pop icons Justin Timberlake *(FutureSex/LoveSounds)* and Nelly Furtado *(Loose)*, which spawned the respective hits 'SexyBack' and 'Promiscuous'. In April, he released his own LP, *Timbaland Presents Shock Value*, though there was little shocking about this collaborative platter involving stars such as Elton John, Dr Dre and Missy Elliott. Timbaland also worked on a handful of tracks on *Volta*, the adventurous sixth album by Icelandic diva Björk, and later assisted Madonna in the studio.

BACK FOR GOOD?

Several bands reunited this year, including a few whose split at the time had been famously acrimonious. Seven or even eight-figure offers from promoters for a reunion tour have a tendency to suddenly mend relationships which broke down long ago. So it was hello again to Genesis (the Phil Collins-fronted version), US indie giants Dinosaur Jr and Smashing Pumpkins, pop-metal legends Van Halen, and British rockers The Verve, who reformed for the second time in their career.

Ten years after they first found fame, the five Spice Girls rather cynically agreed to celebrate girl power once more, putting their faltering solo careers behind them. In February, new wave stadium rockers The Police also reformed, having split in the mid-1980s. Sting, Stewart Copeland and Andy Summers embarked upon an international world tour, named The Police Reunion Tour, which ends in 2008, in celebration of the 30th anniversary of their hit 'Roxanne'. After a decade apart, Manchester heartthrobs Take That announced their return this year – albeit without Robbie Williams, their most charismatic member. By mid-December, the well-drilled four-piece had scored UK number ones for their comeback single 'Patience', fourth album *Beautiful World*, which has sold 1.8 million copies, and their DVD, *The Ultimate Tour – Live In Manchester*. Their Ultimate Tour of the UK's arenas sold out within minutes. 'Patience' won Best Single at the Brits. Rumours concerning Williams' return to the band continue to circulate.

In the absence of new material from Coldplay, the epic indie rock of Snow Patrol's *Eyes Open* was the year's top-selling UK album, shifting 1.9 million copies. *Ta-Dah*, the second album by flamboyant New York disco troupe Scissor Sisters, sold 1.3 million. Its lead single, 'I Don't Feel Like Dancing', hit number one and became the second most-played song on UK radio in 2006, after Gnarls Barkley's ubiquitous 'Crazy'. Other acts to pass the million mark this year included James Blunt-alike singer-songwriter and Brits winner James Morrison, with *Undiscovered*; The Kooks, with *Inside In/Inside Out*; and US rockers The Killers, who modelled their second album, *Sam's Town*, on vintage Bruce Springsteen and later headlined Glastonbury.

Two of the world's most successful recording artists broke the mould this year by bypassing the record industry's traditional distribution and marketing methods. Former Beatle Sir Paul McCartney left EMI and signed a deal with Hear Music, the label owned by US coffee chain Starbucks. This meant his latest album, *Memory Almost Full*, could be bought in thousands of Starbucks branches in more than two dozen countries. The cafés played the album repeatedly on its day of release in June. McCartney, 65, also premiered the first video from the album on YouTube, the popular video sharing website, commenting: 'It's a new world.'

In June, Prince, the 49-year-old American pop star, announced that his latest album, *Planet Earth*, would be given away with copies of *The Mail on Sunday* newspaper after a deal with his distributors, Sony BMG, collapsed. On 15 July in an unprecedented move, an estimated 3 million copies of the album were distributed with the newspaper across the UK. *The Mail On Sunday* paid to press and distribute the album, hoping to make money by selling extra copies of the paper and more advertising. *Planet Earth* soon found its way online where it could be downloaded illegally at no cost. Reasoning that most of his income comes from performing, Prince also decided to give away the album to fans who bought tickets for a 21-night residency in August at London's O2 venue, formerly the ill-fated Millennium Dome.

NEW FACES

A fuller-figured garage rock diva named Beth Ditto became one of the year's most recognisable new stars after the 26-year-old came top of the *NME's* influential annual

'Cool List' in November. Ditto, lesbian frontwoman of the Portland trio The Gossip, quickly made the most of her celebrity status by hosting TV shows and writing an advice column in *The Guardian*. The Gossip's raucous debut, *Standing In The Way Of Control*, sold 150,000 copies. One of the more interesting new bands to emerge this year was an imaginative young London trio called Klaxons. Leading lights of East London's fashion-focused 'new-rave' scene, the band's novel idea of fusing 1990s dance music with a rock sensibility resulted in a debut album, *Myths Of The Near Future*, that sold 270,000 copies. Having coined the term 'new rave' as a joke, Klaxons found themselves at the forefront of a colourful youth movement that quickly spread around the world, influencing fashion, art and pop music at ground level. Several upcoming acts categorised as new rave by an excitable media, such as Brazil's CSS, Justice from France, and London's Simian Mobile Disco, benefited from the exposure. Proof, perhaps, that while the recording industry is in turmoil, pop music is healthier than ever.

AWARDS

BRIT AWARDS 2007

British Male – James Morrison
British Female – Amy Winehouse
British Group – Arctic Monkeys
British Album – Arctic Monkeys, *Whatever People Say I Am, That's What I'm Not*
British Single – Take That, 'Patience'
British Breakthrough Act – The Fratellis
British Live Act – Muse
International Male – Justin Timberlake
International Female – Nelly Furtado
International Group – The Killers
International Album – The Killers, *Sam's Town*
International Breakthrough Act – Orson

MERCURY MUSIC PRIZE 2006

Arctic Monkeys, *Whatever People Say I Am, That's What I'm Not*

NME AWARDS 2007

Best British Band – Muse
Best Album – Arctic Monkeys, *Whatever People Say I Am, That's What I'm Not*
Best Live Band – Kasabian
Best New Band – Klaxons
Best Solo Artist – Jamie T
Best Track – The View, 'Wasted Little DJs'
Best International Band – My Chemical Romance
Best Video – The Killers, 'Bones'
Best Radio Show – Zane Lowe, Radio 1

CLASSICAL MUSIC

Lewis Morgan-Klein

COMMEMORATIONS, CELEBRATIONS AND ANNIVERSARIES

The 2006–7 season was seemingly one of endless commemoration with anniversary celebrations ubiquitous in virtually every concert programme. During the second half of 2006 the festivities in honour of two of classical music's great giants, Mozart (250 years since his birth) and Shostakovich (100), rumbled on inexorably until the dying moments of 2006. It took the cold light of the New Year for critics to realise that the celebrations served the composers rather variably. A sense of commemoration fatigue was evident, leading to many predicting a similar fate for Elgar's 150th birthday later in the year. Anniversary mania has become a symptom of populist 'all-you-can-eat' experiences in classical music, as demonstrated by Radio 3's 'the *Ring* in a day' and the complete works of *x* in one weekend/week/day or entire cycles of Beethoven and Bruckner symphonies at the Edinburgh Festival. Some commentators detected the whiff of cynical marketing around the endless tributes yet fresh ideas and methods of presenting classical music are necessary to attract new listeners.

The first of the season's highlights was provided by a tireless, energetic (and extremely overworked) Valery Gergiev, whose mammoth 2006 survey of Shostakovich's entire symphonic output culminated in December. Gergiev conducted performances at the Barbican by the Mariinsky Orchestra and Chorus, the Vienna Philharmonic, the London Symphony Orchestra (LSO) and the Rotterdam Philharmonic, which earned both great critical acclaim and box office success. Gergiev also found time to bring some of Shostakovich's neglected stage works to the Coliseum and the Proms, all in addition to conducting and directing Wagner's *Ring* at the Millennium Centre in Cardiff. His impeccable artistic standards and idiosyncratic interpretations of Shostakovich were well-recorded. Sakari Oramo, who has worked marvels with the City of Birmingham Symphony Orchestra (CBSO), gave a ferocious reading of Shostakovich's Eighth Symphony in September, utilising the occasion to showcase other Russian composers in the first half of the concert.

A brief overview of some of the Himalayan peaks of the second half of the 'Mozart Year' would have to mention, among others, the efforts of pianists Andras Schiff and Alfred Brendel, Sir Charles Mackerras' concert with the CBSO, the appearance of Ivor Bolton to conduct the Salzburg Mozarteum at the Proms and player/conductor Thomas Zehetmair's concert with his own Northern Sinfonia. But of all of the many outstanding anniversary performances, the best Mozart was to be heard on the piano. Schiff's all-Mozart Prom was remarkable not merely as a triumph of programming, nor just because solo performances at the Proms are exceptionally rare, but because of the obvious depth of Schiff's understanding of Mozart and his capacity to differentiate the inner character of each piece in the programme. Among the best of the LSO's excellent cycle of the Mozart piano concertos was Brendel's November concert, conducted by David Zinman at the Barbican. Brendel's power as an experienced interpreter of Mozart is undiminished; his performance was radiant, despite the odd slip. Piotr Anderszewski, too, did well in some of the Mozart piano concertos with various orchestras, including the Academy of St Martin-in-the-Fields and the Scottish Chamber Orchestra. Thomas Zehetmair's wide-ranging Mozart concert in October displayed the conductor's own virtuosity and versatility, as he swapped his violin for the conductor's baton in Piano Concerto No. 27 and Mozart's *Requiem*. The concert served to underline the Northern Sinfonia's current fine form. Sampling the delicacies of the 2006 centenary celebrations would surely have pleased the two composers they commemorated.

Further anniversary concerts, which marked 150 years since the death of Robert Schumann and 50 years since that of Gerald Finzi, continued in the second half of 2006, albeit on a smaller scale. The 30th anniversary of Sir Benjamin Britten's death was also commemorated by a number of events. The best of these came in December with the Wigmore Hall's *In Memoriam* concerts, which explored the wide range of vocal talent for Britten's songs, while the Belcea Quartet and Endellion Quartet gave an excellent survey of the composer's string works, all of which was capped by the Nash Ensemble under Edward Gardner, who performed Britten's *Serenade for Tenor, Horn and Strings* in the concert hall in which it was premiered. Minimalist composer Steve Reich's 70th birthday was celebrated by a number of events, most notably the LSO's *Phases*, a week-long celebration of many of Reich's works in October 2006, including the premiere of his *Daniel Variations*. Of Reich's contemporaries, Philip Glass turned 70 and John Adams 60 in January 2007. Edinburgh's Queen's Hall staged a Scottish Chamber Orchestra (SCO) concert celebrating both composers and included the UK premiere of Glass' Concerto Grosso, an event which also represented Hannu Lintu's debut as SCO conductor. The orchestra also embarked upon an ambitious Sibelius cycle celebrating 50 years since the composer's death.

Sir Edward Elgar, although replaced by Adam Smith on the reverse of the £20 note, is ever popular in Britain and has been the subject of a series of events in what would have been his 150th year. These concerts are intended to emphasise that there is more to the composer than the last night of the Proms and focus attention on his musical cosmopolitanism. As part of their *Realms of Gold* series, the Nash Ensemble drew attention to some of Elgar's less well-known works alongside those of his English contemporaries. Mark Elder's concert at the Bridgewater Hall with the Hallé may have encouraged those listening to consider the composer's absorption of Richard Wagner by programming the *Sea Pictures* beside the preludes to *Tristan, Parsifal, Die Meistersinger von Nürnberg* and *Der fliegende Holländer*. The LSO's June performance of *The Dream of Gerontius*, conducted by Richard Hickox, was certainly one occasion in which the Wagnerian influence on Elgar was recognisable. Sakari Oramo's CBSO performances of *The Apostles, The Kingdom* and Elgar's violin concerto received much-deserved plaudits as part of the 150th Anniversary Weekend in Birmingham. Finally, the Philharmonia, under the leadership of Sir Andrew Davis, a first-rate Elgarian, embarked on an extensive 18-date tour around the UK between April and June, the standards of which remained high throughout.

MUSICAL HIGHLIGHTS OF SEASON 2006–7

Among the vocal highlights of the last year were recitals given by Christine Brewer, Renée Fleming, Angelina Gheorghiu and Dietrich Henschel. Brewer's luscious, weighty soprano, accompanied by Roger Vignoles, made for a superior Wigmore Hall recital in March 2007. Featured performances included Berg's *Seven Early Songs*, Richard Strauss' *Gesänge des Orients* and Britten's *Poet's Echo* carefully offset with some more folksy Dougherty songs. It was with the Berg, and especially the Strauss, however, where Brewer was truly in her post-romantic element, once again showcasing an opulent voice and great warmth of tone. Fleming's Barbican recital with the Royal Philharmonic Orchestra under Andreas Delfs last December demonstrated the soprano's strengths in a similar repertoire to that of Brewer, where she was equally at home with Mozart, Puccini and an excerpt from Strauss' *Daphne*.

Gheorghiu's Barbican recital with the LPO in May included the usual combination of the glitzy opera arias, which made her name, but the recital was praiseworthy for Gheorghiu's sheer expressive vocal beauty and clarity. Baritone Henschel is a superb artist and his October 2006 recital at the Wigmore Hall demonstrated this forcefully, allowing his listeners a chance to hear his rich, edgy and powerful voice tackle a number of songs by Brahms, including the *Vier Ernste Gesänge*, alongside works by Webern and Gund (the latter a real rarity).

Other worthy piano and instrumental recitals over the 2006–7 season included the first half of Schiff's Schubert series with the Philharmonia, which began in April 2007 at the Queen Elizabeth Hall. Here, Schiff's versatility as an accomplished Schubertian pianist and conductor was evident through his solo piano performances and spirited direction of the orchestra. Part two in December is eagerly awaited. Another treat came in the form of Pollini's well-received June piano recital of works by Chopin and Liszt at the Barbican; particularly striking was his deep comprehension of some of the darker works from Liszt's later period and his ability to convey that darkness and emotional force without making the works sound turgid. Sokolov's recital at the Wigmore in the same month and that by Richard Goode in May also deserve mention to illustrate the wealth of recitals given by leading pianists in the UK over the last year.

This season also featured a number of brilliant orchestral concerts. The BBC National Orchestra of Wales (NOW) provided several highlights with an extremely varied and interesting 2006–7 programme; among the best was a performance of works by neglected 20th-century composers Kurt Weill, Aaron Copland and Roy Harris, conducted by Mark Stringer with David Goode on the organ at St David's Hall in Cardiff in November. The principal guest conductor of the BBC NOW, Jac van Steen, gave an authoritative reading of Prokofiev's Fifth Symphony and, together with Barry Douglas, offered a rousing performance of Bartok's Second Piano Concerto in May. Tadaaki Otaka, the orchestra's conductor laureate, has been able to achieve wonderful playing from the NOW, particularly evident in its performance of Mahler's Fifth Symphony. Conductor Ricardo Muti's March appearance in London to conduct the Philharmonia in a performance of Verdi's *Requiem* at Westminster Cathedral justly received rave reviews and, although some wished that the performance had benefited from concert hall acoustics, the devotional atmosphere seemed to suit both the work and Muti's weighty, architectural reading of the score. Also in March, John Eliot Gardiner gave a memorable concert at the Barbican, featuring the Monteverdi Choir and the English Baroque Soloists playing Haydn's *The Creation*. Noteworthy, again, was the singing of Dietrich Henschel in the role of Simon and the high-quality musicianship, which has become synonymous with Eliot Gardiner's name.

Sir Simon Rattle's trip to the Barbican in May 2007 to conduct the Orchestra of the Age of Enlightenment provided some controversy. The performance of Dvorak's Sixth Symphony and Cello Concerto with Steven Isserlis on period instruments divided the critics. A revelation for some, for others it removed much of Dvorak's trademark romantic grandeur, sometimes considered to be his strong suit. Rattle's swift tempi and poor balance irritated some, while others praised him for a determined rendition full of revisionist clarity. Maybe the best Dvorak, however, came from the BBC Symphony Orchestra under Jiri Belohlavek, whose first year with the orchestra has revealed him to be an ambitious and dynamic chief conductor.

SAD LOSSES AND NEW GAINS

The celebratory atmosphere of the 2006–7 season was deflated by the news of the deaths of some of the musical world's brightest stars. Soprano Elisabeth Schwarzkopf, bass-baritone Thomas Stewart, mezzo-soprano Lorraine Hunt Lieberson and dramatic soprano Astrid Varnay passed away, along with composers Sir Malcolm Arnold and Gian Carlo Menotti. September 2006 saw the death of the distinguished impresario Sir John Drummond, who forged a successful, if at times controversial, career in the British arts scene, rising to the directorship of the Proms, the Edinburgh Festival and Radio 3. But perhaps the best-known musician to have died this year was Mstislav Rostropovich, who was both a great cellist and widely respected conductor, whose artistry inspired many of the greatest composers of the 20th century.

One of most eagerly awaited events of the year was the reopening of the modernised Royal Festival Hall in June 2007, which was marked by a gala weekend featuring the London Philharmonic, the London Sinfonietta, the Orchestra of the Age of Enlightenment and the Philharmonia. Among the celebratory free concerts was a recital of Mozart, Schubert and Beethoven by Alfred Brendel and premieres of new compositions by Harrison Birtwistle and Julian Anderson. Critical reception has been mixed, especially given the public fondness for the nearby Queen Elizabeth Hall, which hosted the Hall's programme during the renovations.

Among the year's new appointments was Jonathan Mills, who replaces Sir Brian McMaster as director of the Edinburgh Festival, Proms director Nicholas Kenyon, who moves to the Barbican, and Radio 3 controller Roger Wright, who replaces Kenyon, in addition to his duties at the BBC. A number of conductors have also taken up important new positions. Valery Gergiev replaced Sir Colin Davis as principal conductor of the LSO in January 2007, Harry Bicket was named as the new artistic director of the English concert, Vladimir Jurowski will succeed Kurt Masur as principal conductor of the London Philharmonic Orchestra at the beginning of the 2007–8 season and Esa-Pekka Salonen, who has already enjoyed several successful engagements with the Philharmonia, will replace Christoph von Dohnányi from the beginning of the 2008–9 season.

THE FESTIVAL SEASON

Although the raft of anniversaries in 2006 exerted an influence on much of the programming for the 112th Proms season, works by other composers were not completely overshadowed. The Berlin Philharmonic's two Proms with its conductor Sir Simon Rattle were highly rated, in particular Prom 65, where the orchestra's unique sound did full justice to Bruckner's Seventh Symphony and the brilliant playing of Frank Peter Zimmermann in Szymanowski's First Violin Concerto was much praised. Far outstripping Rattle, in Prom 70 was Bernard Haitink's astounding rendition of Mahler's Symphony No. 2 with the BBC Symphony Orchestra and Chorus and the London Symphony Chorus. Haitink's command of the work's architecture eschewed the episodic, pyrotechnic approach to Mahler taken by many other conductors. Combined with excellent singers and a world-class orchestra on top form it was the seminal experience of the Proms season.

The consistently outstanding voice of soprano Soile Isokoski's was one of the highlights of the Proms and showed her to be a vocal interpreter of Richard Strauss without parallel. Ivan Fischer gave an excellent performance of Stravinsky's *Rite of Spring* with the Budapest Festival Orchestra and Martyn Brabbins, with the BBC Singers and the Nash Ensemble, conducted a highly acclaimed concert featuring Gyorgy Kurtag's *Songs of Despair and Sorrow* and Morton Feldman's challenging *Rothko Chapel*. Significant premieres at the Proms included performances of Mark-Anthony Turnage's *A Relic of Memory* and James Dillon's *Andromeda*.

As the 2006 Edinburgh International Festival drew to a close with a concert performance of *Die Meistersinger von Nürnberg*, dedicated to its departing director Brian McMaster, visitors could look back on a spectacular few weeks of concerts of the highest quality. The Usher Hall played host to complete cycles of Beethoven and Bruckner Symphonies: the former were conducted almost entirely by Sir Charles Mackerras with the Scottish Chamber Orchestra, whereas the Bruckner was shared out more equally. Mackerras' Beethoven was of a high standard, although the Bruckner symphonies were rather more mixed. The eagerly anticipated visit of the Berlin Philharmonic brought festival-goers an extremely good performance of Szymanowski's demanding Violin Concerto No.1 with violinist Frank Peter Zimmermann and Mahler's Symphony No.4 with the polished soprano of Aberdeen-born Lisa Milne. An unexpected but very welcome surprise was Zimmerman's pre-interval encore of Bach's *Chaconne*.

Meanwhile, the Queen's Hall series played host to a number of outstanding recitals. Piano performances by Steven Osborne and Christian Zacharias were highly regarded and well-attended, but it was the singing which shone brightest. Soile Isokoski, accompanied by Marita Viitasalo, performed songs by Mozart, Schoenberg, Britten, Merikanto and Sibelius with her usual flair and linguistic versatility. Bass-baritone Robert Holl's sonorous, gentle-timbre voice treated the audience to a wonderful performance of three of Schumann's *lieder* cycles, accompanied by Robert Vignoles. Jane Irwin and Andrew Kennedy gave a moving and intense performance of Britten with the Scottish Ensemble under Jonathan Morton. Irwin's resonant, autumnal mezzo-soprano and Kennedy's tenor were divided by Britten's *Lachrymae* for viola and strings, which was performed well. Other vocal talent on offer included Anne Schwanewilms, Simon Keenlyside and Angela Denoke, although the most gorgeous singing came from Jonas Kaufmann. Kaufmann's recital with Helmut Deutsch consisted primarily of some of the Strauss lieder in which the tenor excels, while the first half featured songs by Schubert, Bartok and Britten, representing a fine, well-chosen and well-balanced programme. All of the songs were sung to an extremely high standard, revealing a forceful and intelligent voice with an inbuilt vulnerability that qualifies it so well for lieder, although Kaufman's appearance in the concert performance of *Meistersinger* on the festival's last night showed his versatility; his could be a voice to watch out for in opera. If the festival showed anything, it was that McMaster's successor will certainly have a hard act to follow.

AWARDS

GRAMOPHONE AWARDS 2006

Best of Category (Orchestral) and Record of the Year – Mahler, Symphony No. 6. Berlin Philharmonic Orchestra/Claudio Abbado

Best of Category (Chamber) – Taneyev, *Chamber Music*. Vadim Repin; Ilya Gringolts; Nobuko Imai; Lunn Harrell; Mikhail Pletnev

Best of Category (Solo Vocal) – Schubert *Abendbilder*. Christian Gerhaher; Gerold Huber

Best of Category (Instrumental) – Szymanowski *Piano Works*. Piotr Anderszewski

Best of Category (Contemporary) – Magnus Lindberg, *Clarinet Concerto*. Kari Kriikku, Finnish RSO/Sakari Oramo

Best of Category (Historic Archive) – Wagner, *Siegfried*. Bayreuth Festival/Joseph Keilberth

Editor's Choice - Stanford, *Orchestral Songs*. Gerald Finley, BBC NOW/Richard Hickox

Artist of the Year – Angela Hewitt

Lifetime Achievement – Sir Charles Mackerras

THE CLASSICAL BRIT AWARDS 2007

Album of the Year – Paul McCartney, *Ecce Cor Meum*

Classical Recording of the Year – Berliner Philharmoniker, Sir Simon Rattle. Holst, *The Planets*

Singer of the Year – Anna Netrebko, *Russian Album & Violetta*

Young British Classical Performer – Ruth Palmer; Shostakovich, Violin Concerto No. 1

Soundtrack Composer of the Year – George Fenton, *Planet Earth*

Instrumentalist of the Year – Leif Ove Andsnes, *Horizons*

Contemporary Composer Award – John Adams, *The Dharma at Big Sur/My Father Knew Charles Ives*

Lifetime Achievement Award – Dr Vernon Handley, CBE

OPERA

Elizabeth Forbes

FESTIVALS AND NEW PRODUCTIONS

The celebration of the 250th anniversary of the birth of Mozart continued in the first part of the season. The Royal Opera staged *La finta giardiniera* (literally 'the false lady gardener'), a comic opera dating from 1775 when Mozart was nearly 19. Conductor John Eliot Gardner ensured that the performance made good light entertainment, but the highlight of this part of the season was Donizetti's *La Fille du regiment*, directed by Laurent Pelly, in which Natalie Dessay as Marie and Juan Diego Flóres as Tonio were superb enough to expunge fond memories of Joan Sutherland and Luciano Pavarotti in the same roles in the 1966 production.

Almost equally enjoyable was a double bill of Ravel's *L'Heure espagnole* and Puccini's *Gianni Schicchi*, conducted by music director Antonio Pappano and directed by Richard Jones in March 2007. The presence of Bryn Terfel as Schicchi enhanced, but did not disturb, the immaculate ensemble of Puccini's comic masterpiece. The new production of Debussy's *Pelléas et Mélisande*, conducted by Simon Rattle and with a notably good cast, promised another artistic success. Musically, expectations were completely satisfied, but a nondescript staging, poor sets and truly terrible costumes were a disappointment.

A new *Fidelio*, set during the Spanish Civil War, did not please everyone, but Beethoven's opera was admirably served musically; Pappano conducted with great spirit, Karita Mattila made a quite magnificent Leonora and the Covent Garden chorus was in splendid form. Notable revivals included Thomas Adès' *The Tempest*, with mostly the same fine cast as at the premiere in 2004, while Richard Jones' production of Shostakovich's *Lady Macbeth of Mtsensk* remained as powerful as ever, the first half dominated, as before, by John Tomlinson's tremendous characterisation of Boris Ismailov.

Britten's *Owen Wingrave* was given at the Linbury Studio Theatre. Fourteen members of the City of London Sinfonia played the reduced orchestration extremely well, while the staging and a mainly young cast were also good, but the authority of the original singers, both on television and in the main Covent Garden auditorium, was lacking. It was announced during May that the Royal Opera House had bought the DVD production and distribution company, Opus Arte. Tony Hall, the chief executive, said: 'We are using a commercial operation to reach out to lots of people but we will also put money back into the mother ship.'

English National Opera opened the season with the world premiere of *Gaddafi: A Living Myth*. With music by Steve Chandra Savale and Asian Dub Foundation, text by Shan Khan, directed by David Freeman and designed by Es Devlin, this was a dramatic rather than a musical experience for many people in the audience. In sharp contrast, ENO's contribution to the Mozart anniversary, a new production of *The Marriage of Figaro*, was notably well played and sung. Janacek's *Jenufa*, staged by David Alden, won both opera awards at the 2007 Olivier Awards, the best new opera production and the outstanding achievement in opera, for Amanda Roocroft's Jenufa.

ENO gave the London stage premiere of Philip Glass's *Satyagraha* (dating from 1980) in April 2007. The text, adapted from the *Bhagavada Gita*, was sung in Sanskrit (without surtitles), but the very clear production of Phelim McDermott and a magnificent performance by tenor Alan Oke as the central character, M. K. Gandhi, allowed the audience to follow the outlines of Gandhi's early years in South Africa. The composer attended the first night and appeared pleased with both the performance and his reception.

ENO's new music director, Edward Gardner, conducted the new production of Britten's *Death in Venice*, which was directed by Deborah Warner. Ian Bostridge sang the role of Aschenbach most beautifully, but he lacked dramatic plausibility. In another new staging of Britten's last opera, at the 2007 Aldeburgh Festival, Alan Oke made a more convincing Aschenbach. Back at the Coliseum, Gardner also conducted a fine revival of David McVicar's production of Mozart's *La clemenza di Tito*. The season ended with the musical *Kismet*, whose score is adapted from the music of Borodin. Unfortunately, the singing of a talented cast was ruined by over-amplification.

After a year without a home, Opera North returned to the newly renovated Leeds Grand Theatre. The building adjacent to the theatre has been incorporated into the structure and the restoration of the nearby Assembly Rooms will be ready in 2008. The company opened with a new staging of Verdi's *Rigoletto*, directed by Charles Edwards, followed by a new production of Britten's *Peter Grimes* by Phyllida Lloyd. 2007 is the 400th anniversary of Monteverdi's *Orfeo* and Christopher Alden's staging, with Paul Nilon in the title role, was much appreciated. Revivals included Janacek's *Katya Kabanova*, conducted with great sympathy by music director Richard Farnes.

Scottish Opera offered two full-scale new productions, of Handel's *Tamerlano* and Donizetti's *Lucia di Lammermoor*. Neither was much liked, but revivals of Richard Strauss' *Der Rosenkavalier* and Puccini's *Madama Butterfly*, both directed by David McVicar, were extremely successful. The Edinburgh Festival, under its new artistic director, Jonathan Mills, included three concert performances of Monteverdi's *Orfeo* in honour of the anniversary, a double bill of Purcell's *Dido and Aeneas* with Salieri's *Prima la musica, doppo le parole* and a production of Richard Strauss' *Capriccio*, which deals with the same question as Salieri's opera: which comes first, the words or the music?

Welsh National Opera's first new production of the season was Monteverdi's *The Return of Ulysses*, directed by David Alden. Later, WNO's fine chorus was highlighted by the staging of Mussorgsky's *Khovanshchina*, directed by David Pountney. Revivals included Yannis Kokkos' immensely popular production of Wagner's *Tristan und Isolde*. During the summer of 2007 a double bill of Kurt Weill's opera ballet *The Seven Deadly Sins* with Bartok's *Duke Bluebeard's Castle*, both conducted by WNO's music director Carlo Rizzi, was staged in Cardiff and Birmingham. Rizzi also conducted concert performances of Berlioz' *The Damnation of Faust* in both cities.

Glyndebourne Festival opened with Richard Jones' controversial new production of Verdi's *Macbeth*, which updated Shakespeare's plot to the 1950s with the witches as new-age travellers. However, the vocal and orchestral performances under music director Vladimir Jurowski were universally admired. *Bach's St Matthew Passion* may be 'dramatic' but it is not operatic and patrons were slow to book the new production; on the other hand the revival, for only six performances, of Nikolaus Lehnhoff's staging of Wagner's *Tristan und Isolde* could have sold out the theatre several times over. *Macbeth* was given at the Promenade Concerts at the Royal Albert Hall; other Prom operas were *Götterdämmerung* with the BBC SO and Chorus, and *La Damnation de Faust* with the Boston SO conducted by James Levine.

Taking over as general director of Garsington Opera after the death of its founder, Leonard Ingrams, in 2005, Anthony Whitworth-Jones has followed his predecessor in the matter of repertory. The 2007 programme included early Mozart, rare Rossini and Richard Strauss, all favourites of Ingrams. *Il re pastore* – a 'Serenata' as Mozart called it – dating from 1775, is no masterpiece, but Annilese Miskimmon's production, designed by Dick Bird, fitted into the surrounding gardens so perfectly that the result was pure enchantment. Rossini's *La donna del lago*, based on Walter Scott's poem, 'The Lady of the Lake', and Strauss' *Ariadne auf Naxos* were also very enjoyable.

Grange Park Opera provided a genuine rarity in Prokofiev's *The Gambler*, based on the novel by Dostoyevsky. Finely conducted by André de Ridder, directed and designed with great distinction by David Fielding and extremely well sung and acted by a large cast, the opera is highly dramatic. The scene in the casino, in particular, came across with real passion, as fortunes were lost and won at roulette. Though criticised as unsympathetic, the characters in *The Gambler* are neither black nor white but, like most human beings, varying shades of grey. Verdi's *Falstaff*, another ensemble opera, was also much appreciated in Daniel Slater's amusing, modern-dress production.

Another country house festival, Longborough Opera, near Moreton-in-marsh, Gloucestershire, has lifted the height of its theatre roof and enlarged the pit to hold the 60 players required for a full-scale performance of Wagner's *Das Rheingold*, conducted by Anthony Negus and directed by Alan Privee, Longborough's artistic director. A complete *Ring* cycle is hoped to be built up by 2010. Meanwhile a new production of Tchaikovsky's *Eugene Onegin* and a revival of Mozart's *The Magic Flute* made up the 2007 programme. Almeida offered two premieres, *The Silent Twins* by Errollyn Wallen, based on a true story of two mentally disturbed sisters; and *Folksong Opera* by Orlando Gough, presented by Streetwise Opera, which involves homeless people in its productions.

Opening the 2007 Buxton Festival, the new artistic director, Andrew Greenwood, conducted Donizetti's *Roberto Devereux* with Maria Plazas as Elizabeth I. Offenbach's *Bluebeard*, directed by Annilese Miskimmon, followed, while among several other offerings were Philippe Boesman's *Julie*, based on Strindberg's play *Miss Julie*, presented by Music Theatre Wales, which had given the opera's UK premiere at Brecon in May. There was also Jonathan Dove's *Tobias and the Angel*, a community opera and Jiri Benda's *Romeo and Juliet*, first performed in 1776 but only now receiving its British premiere.

LAST GOODBYES

Stephen Pimlott, opera and theatre director, was appointed OBE in the New Year's Honours; six weeks later he died, aged 56. He started his career as a staff director at English National Opera, then moved to Opera North, worked for Scottish Opera, before returning to ENO. A reliable director of repertory operas, he also staged spectacular productions of works such as Borodin's *Prince Igor* and Monteverdi's *The Coronation of Poppea*, and in 2000 he directed the premiere of Param Vir's *Ion* at the Aldeburgh Festival. In the Queen's Birthday Honours, soprano Emma Kirkby was created DBE, while mezzo Rosalind Plowright and tenor Stuart Burrows received the OBE.

Italian-American composer Gian Carlo Menotti died in February 2007, aged 95. Among his many operas, *The Medium* (1946), *The Consul* (1950) and *Amahl and the Night Visitor* (1951), a TV opera, are best known in the UK. Julian Budden, musicologist and author specialising in 19th-century Italian opera, died in February 2007, aged 82. Joining the BBC in 1951, he worked as music producer, chief radio producer of opera and external music organiser until 1983. Meanwhile he wrote a magnificent three-volume work, *The Operas of Verdi* (1973–81), that dealt not only with the text and music of the operas but also with the operatic life of Italy, France and other European countries in the 19th century.

Edmund Tracey, who died in March 2007 aged 79, began his career as a music critic, then in 1965 he joined Sadler's Wells Opera as a director, responsible for opera planning and the literary texts of the operas performed, many of which he translated. He also edited the programmes for several years. In 1968 SWO moved to the London Coliseum and in 1974 was renamed English National Opera. Among Tracey's translations, Offenbach's *The Tales of Hoffmann*, Verdi's *Aida* and *La traviata*, and Gounod's *Faust* were notable. *The Tales of Hoffmann* and *Faust* were new versions, rather than translations, and were both directed by Colin Graham, becoming hugely successful.

Colin Graham, who died in April 2007 aged 75, first worked as a student ASM at Covent Garden; moving to the English Opera Group, he staged several Britten operas, notably the three church Parables. For Sadler's Wells he first directed two Janacek operas, *Cunning Little Vixen* and *From the House of the Dead*, followed by Britten's *Gloriana* and three new operas by Richard Rodney Bennett, *The Mines of Sulphur* (1965), *Penny for a Song* (1967), for which he wrote the text, and *Victory* (1970). His finest work for ENO was Prokofiev's *War and Peace*, a magnificent production worthy of Tolstoy's original. Graham staged the premiere at Snape Maltings of Britten's *Death in Venice*, which was later transferred to Covent Garden.

For English Music Theatre, successor to EOG, Graham staged premieres of Stephen Oliver's *Tom Jones* and Minoru Miki's Kabuki opera, *An Actor's Revenge*. In the 1980s he became artistic director of the Opera Theater of St Louis. Conductor Bryan Balkwill, who died in February 2007 aged 84, was engaged successively with the New London Opera Company, Glyndebourne, the Wexford Festival and Covent Garden, where he conducted some 200 performances of 16 operas. Becoming joint music director of Sadler's Wells Opera in 1966, he worked frequently with Colin Graham, notably on *A Penny for a Song* and Britten's *Peter Grimes*. Later he worked in the USA.

Elisabeth Schwarzkopf, the German soprano, died in August 2006, aged 90. After singing in Berlin and Vienna, she became a member of Covent Garden Opera from 1948 to 1951. Her repertory included Pamina in *The Magic Flute*, Violetta in *La Traviata*, Mimi in *La bohème*, Gilda in *Rigoletto* and Sophie in *Der Rosenkavalier*, all sung in English. She created Anne Trulove in Stravinsky's *The Rake's Progress* at La Fenice, Venice, in 1951. Her finest roles were Mozart's Countess *(Le nozze di Figaro)*, Donna Elvira *(Don Giovanni)*, Fiordiligi *(Così fan tutte)* and the Marschallin in Strauss' *Der Rosenkavalier*, which she returned to Covent Garden to sing in 1959.

Australian soprano Rosina Raisbeck died in December 2006, aged 90. At first a mezzo, she sang small roles at Covent Garden from 1948 to 1950; becoming a dramatic soprano, she took on Wagner's Ortrud in *Lohengrin* and Senta in *The Flying Dutchman*. In 1959 she sang Senta and Elisabeth in *Tannhäusr* for Sadler's Wells (now English National) Opera, followed by a powerful performance of Kabanicha in Janacek's *Katya Kabanova*. She then returned to Australia. Astrid Varnay, another dramatic Wagnerian soprano, died in September 2006 aged 80. She first sang at Covent Garden in 1948, as Brünnhilde in *Die Walküre* and *Siegfried*, and as Isolde. She returned in 1951 as Richard Strauss' Salome, Verdi's Leonora in *Il trovatore* and Aida; finally in 1968 as Kostelnicka in Janacek's *Jenufa*.

French soprano Régine Crespin died in July 2007, aged 80. Renowned for her Wagner and Strauss roles, she sang the Marschallin in *Der Rosenkavalier* at Glyndebourne and at Covent Garden, where she also sang Tosca, Elsa in *Lohengrin* and Leonore in *Fidelio*. Having sung Mme Lidoine, the new Prioress, in Poulenc's *Dialogues des Carmélites* in Paris, she sang Mme Croissy, the old Prioress, in the same opera at Covent Garden. Jerry Hadley, the American tenor, who died in July 2007 aged 55, sang frequently at Covent Garden, as Fenton in Verdi's *Falstaff*, the Duke in *Rigoletto*, Rodolfo in *La bohème* and the title roles of Offenbach's *Les Contes d'Hoffmann* and Berlioz' *La Damnation de Faust*.

PRODUCTIONS

In the summaries of company activities shown below, the dates in brackets indicate the year that the current productions entered the company's repertory.

ROYAL OPERA
Founded 1946
Royal Opera House, Covent Garden, London WC2E 9DD

PRODUCTIONS FROM THE REPERTORY: *Faust* (2004), *Lady Macbeth of Mtsensk* (2004), *La bohème* (1974), *The Queen of Spades* (2001), *Il trovatore* (2002), *Madama Butterfly* (2003), *Orlando* (2003), *The Tempest* (2004), *Stiffelio* (1993), *Don Giovanni* (2002), *Kat'a Kabanova* (1994), *Tosca* (2006), *Rigoletto* (2001), *Così fan tutte* (1995)

NEW PRODUCTIONS: *La Juive* (Halévy), 19 July 2006. Conductor, Daniel Oren, concert performance at the Barbican. Dennis O'Neill (Eleazar), Marina Poplavskaya (Rachel), Alastair Miles (Cardinal Brogni), Dario Schmunk (Leopold), Nicole Cabell (Princess Eudoxie)

La finta giardiniera (Mozart), 21 September 2006. Conductor, John Eliot Gardner; director, Annika Haller; designer, Herbert Murer. Sophie Koch (Ramiro), Kurt Streit (Don Anchise), Genia Kuhmeier (Violanta/Sandrina), Christopher Maltman (Nardo), Patrizia Biccire (Serpetta), Camilla Tilling (Arminda), Robert Murray (Count Belfiore)

Carmen (Bizet), 8 December 2006. Conductor, Antonio Pappano; director, Francesca Zambello; designer, Tanya McCallin. Anna Caterina Antonacci (Carmen), Norah Ansellem (Micaela), Jonas Kaufmann (Don Jose), Matthew Rose (Zuniga), Ildebrando D'Arcangelo (Escamillo), Elena Xanthoudakis (Frasquita), Viktoria Vizin (Mercedes)

La Fille du Régiment (Donizetti), 11 January 2007. Conductor Bruno Campanella; director/costume designer, Laurent Pelly; set designer, Chantal Thomas. Natalie Dessay (Marie), Juan Diego Flórez (Tonio), Felicity Palmer (La Marquise de Berkenfeld), Alessandro Corbelli (Sulpice), Dawn French (La Duchesse de Crackentorp)

L'Heure Espagnol (Ravel), 30 March 2007. Conductor, Antonio Pappano; director, Richard Jones; set designer, John Macfarlane; costume designer, Nicky Gillibrand. Christine Rice (Concepcion), Christopher Maltman (Ramiro), Bonaventura Bottone (Torquemada), Yann Beuron (Gonzalve), Andrew Shore (Don Inigo Gomez)

Gianni Schicchi (Puccini), 30 March 2007. Conductor, Antonio Pappano; director, Richard Jones; set designer, John Macfarlane; costume designer, Nicky Gillibrand. Bryn Terfel (Schicchi), Saimir Pirgu (Rinuccio), Dina Kuznetsova (Lauretta), Gwynne Howell (Simone), Elena Zillio (Zita), Christopher Purves (Marco), Marie McLaughlin (La Cieca), Joan Rodgers (Nella)

Owen Wingrave (Britten), 23 April 2007 at Linbury Studio Theatre. Conductor, Rory Macdonald; director/set designer, Tim Hopkins; costume designer, Gideon Davey. Jacques Imbrailo (Owen), Steven Page (Coyle), Thomas Walker (Lechmere), Vivian Tierney (Miss Wingrave), Elizabeth Woollett (Mrs Coyle), Jennifer Rhys-Davis (Mrs Julian), Allison Cook (Kate), Richard Berkeley-Steele (General Sir Philip Wingrave)

Pelléas et Mélisande (Debussy), 11 May 2007. Conductor Simon Rattle; director, Stanislav Nordey; set designer, Emmanuel Clolus; costume designer, Raoul Fernandez. Angelika Kirchschlager (Mélisande), Gerald Finley (Golaud), Simon Keenlyside (Pelléas), Robert Lloyd (Arkel), Catherine Wyn-Rogers (Geneviève), George Longworth (Yniold)

Fidelio (Beethoven), 27 May 2007. Conductor, Antonio Pappano; director, Jurgen Flimm; set designer, Robert Israel; costume designer, Florence von Gerkan. Karita Mattila (Leonore), Endrick Wottrich (Florestan), Terje Stensvold (Don Pizarro), Eric Halfvarson (Rocco), Ailish Tynan (Marzelline), Robert Murray (Jacquino), Robert Lloyd (Don Fernando)

Thaïs (Massenet), 27 June 2007, concert performance. Conductor, Andrew Davis. Renee Fleming (Thaïs), Thomas Hampson (Athanael), Joseph Calleja (Nicias), Robert Lloyd (Palemon)

ENGLISH NATIONAL OPERA
Founded 1931
London Coliseum, St Martin's Lane, London WC2N 4BS

PRODUCTIONS FROM THE REPERTORY: *La bohème* (1993), *On the Town* (2005), *La clemenza di Tito* (2006)

NEW PRODUCTIONS: *Gaddafi* (Steve Chandra Savale), 7 September 2006. Conductor, James Morgan; director, David Freeman; designer Es Devlin. Ramon Tikaram (Gaddafi), Sharon Duncan-Brewster (Fatima), Riz Ahmed (Salah Al-Bouzaid), Abdi Gouhad (King Sayyid), Ben Bishop (Mr Mister), Martin Turner (Ronald Reagan)

La traviata (Verdi), 27 September 2006. Conductor,

Jonathan Darlington; director, Conall Morrison; set designer, Francis O'Connor; costume designer, Joan O'Cleary. Emma Bell (Violetta), Dwayne Jones (Alfredo), James Westman (Giorgio Germont), Anne-Marie Gibbons (Flora), Robert Poulton (Marquis), Donald Maxwell (Duphol)

Jenufa (Janacek), 9 October 2006. Conductor Mikhail Agrest; director, David Alden; set designer, Charles Edwards; costume designer, Jon Morrell. Amanda Roocroft (Jenufa), Catherine Malfitano (Kostelnicka), Stuart Skelton (Laca), Paul Charles Clarke (Steva), Iain Patterson (Foreman), Lee Bisset (Carolka)

The Marriage of Figaro (Mozart), 2 November 2006. Conductor, Roland Boer; director, Olivia Fuchs; set designer, Yannis Thavoris; costume designer, Niki Turner. Jonathan Lemalu (Figaro), Marie Arnet (Susanna), Lisa Milne (Countess), Mark Stone (Count), Victoria Simmons (Cherubino), Jonathan Veira (Bartolo), Diana Montague (Marcellina), Stuart Kale (Basilio)

The Gondoliers (Sullivan), 18 November 2006. Conductor, Richard Balcombe; director, Martin Duncan; designer, Ashley Martin-Davis. Geoffrey Dolton (Duke of Plaza Toro), Ann Murray (Duchess of Plaza Toro), David Curry (Marco Palmieri), Toby Stafford-Allen (Giuseppe Palmieri), Rebecca Bottone (Casilda), Sarah Tynan (Gianetta), Stephanie Marshall (Tessa)

Agrippina (Handel), 5 February 2007. Conductor, Daniel Reuss; director, David McVicar; designer, John Macfarlane. Sarah Connolly (Agrippina), Christine Rice (Nerone), Lucy Crowe (Poppea), Reno Troilus (Otho)

Satyagraha (Philip Glass), 5 April 2007. Conductor, Johannes Debus; director, Phelim McDermott; set designer, Julian Crouch; costume designer, Kevin Pollard. Alan Oke (M. K. Gandhi), Elena Xanthoudakis (Miss Schlesen), Janis Kelly (Mrs Nandoo), Jean Rigby (Mrs Alexander), Anne-Marie Gibbons (Kkasturbai), Ashley Holland (Mr Kallenbach), Robert Poulton (Prince Arjuna), James Gower (Parsi Rustomji/Lord Krishna)

Death in Venice (Britten), 24 May 2007. Conductor, Edward Gardner; director, Deborah Warner; set designers, Tom Pye & Jean Kalman; costume designer, Chloe Obolensky. Ian Bostridge (Aschenbach), Peter Coleman-Wright (Traveller/Elderly Fop/Old Gondolier/Hotel Manager/Hotel Barber/Leader of the Players/Voice of Dionysus), Iestyn Davies (Voice of Apollo), Benjamin Paul Griffiths (Tadzio)

Kismet (Borodin, arranged Robert Wright & George Forrest), 27 June 2007. Conductor, Richard Hickox; director, Gary Griffin; designer, Ultz. Michael Ball (Poet), Faith Prince (Lalume), Donald Maxwell (Omar Khayyam), Sarah Tynan (Marsinah), Alfie Boe (The Caliph), Julian Curry (Jawan), Graeme Danby (Wazir), Rodney Clark (Chief of Police)

OPERA NORTH
Founded 1978
Grand Theatre, 40 New Briggate, Leeds LS1 6NU

PRODUCTIONS FROM THE REPERTORY: *The Magic Flute* (2003), *The Elixir of Love* (2000), *Katya Kabanova* (1999)

NEW PRODUCTIONS: *Rigoletto* (Verdi), 7 October 2006. Conductor, Martin André; director/designer, Charles Edwards. Rafael Rojas (Duke of Mantua), Alan Opie (Rigoletto), Henriette Bonde-Hansen (Gilda), Rebecca de Pont Davis (Maddalena/Giovanna), Brindley Sherratt (Sparafucile)

Peter Grimes (Britten), 26 October 2006. Conductor, Richard Farnes; director, Phyllida Lloyd; designer, Anthony Ward. Jeffrey Lloyd-Roberts (Grimes), Giselle Allen (Ellen), Christopher Purves (Balstrode), Alan Oke (Bob Boles), Richard Angas (Swallow), Ethna Robinson (Mrs Sedley), Roderick Williams (Ned Keene)

La Voix humaine (Poulenc), 3 November 2006. Conductor, Paul Watkins; director, Deborah Warner; designer, Tom Pye. Joan Rodgers (Elle)

Orfeo (Monteverdi), 16 February 2007. Conductor, Christopher Moulds; director, Christopher Alden; designer, Paul Steinberg. Paul Nilon (Orfeo), Anna Stephany (Euridice/Speranza), Amy Freston (La Musica), Graeme Broadbent (Caronte), Ashley Catling (Apollo), Andrew Foster-Williams (Pluto), Ann Taylor (La Messaggiera/Proserpina)

Dido and Aeneas (Purcell), 5 May 2007. Conductor, Nicholas Kok; director, Aletta Collins; set designer, Giles Cadle; costume designer, Gabrielle Dalton. Susan Bickley (Dido), Amy Freston (Belinda), James Laing (Spirit), Clarissa Meek (Sorceress)

Performances were given at the Leeds Grand Theatre, and on tour in Salford Quays, Nottingham, London (Sadler's Wells Theatre), Newcastle, Sheffield and Bradford.

SCOTTISH OPERA
Founded 1962
39 Elmbank Crescent, Glasgow G2 4PT

PRODUCTION FROM THE REPERTORY: *Der Rosenkavalier* (1999), *Madama Butterfly* (2000)

NEW PRODUCTIONS: *Die Fledermaus* (Johann Strauss), 6 September 2006. Conductor, Oliver Rundell; director, Lee Blakeley; designer, Adrian Lindord. Kate Valentine (Rosalinde), Damian Thantrey (Eisenstein), Benjamin Segal (Alfred), Gail Johnston (Adéle), Lise Christensen (Orlofsky), Julian Hubbard (Falke), Adrian Powter (Frank)

Tamerlano (Handel), 7 November 2006. Conductor, Christian Curnyn; director, John La Bouchardiere; designer, Gideon Davey. Max Cencic (Tamerlano), Tom Randle (Bajazete), Gail Pearson (Asteria), William Purefoy (Andronico), Jennifer Johnston (Irene), Jonathan Best (Leone)

Lucia di Lammermoor (Donizetti), 18 May 2007. Conductor, Julian Smith; director, John Doyle; designer, Liz Ascroft. Sally Silver (Lucia), Butent Bezduz (Edgardo), Andrew Schroeder (Enrico), Christian Reyes Strappa (Raimondo), Nicholas Ransley (Normanno)

Performances were given in Glasgow, Edinburgh, Stoke on Trent and Aberdeen. *Die Fledermaus* was toured to 19 venues between 6 September and 28 October 2006 and 10 venues between 3 April and 5 May 2007.

WELSH NATIONAL OPERA
Founded 1946
Wales Millenium Centre, Bute Place, Cardiff Bay CG10 5AL

PRODUCTIONS FROM THE REPERTORY: *La bohème* (1984), *Tristan und Isolde* (1993), *Carmen* (1997), *Madama Butterfly* (1979)

NEW PRODUCTIONS: *Il ritorno d'Ulisse in patria* (Monteverdi), 16 September 2006. Conductor, Rinaldo Alessandrini; director, David Alden; set designer, Ian MacNeil; costume designer, Gideon Davey. Sara Fulgoni (Penelope), Elizabeth Vaughan (Ericlea), Sarah Tynan

(Melantho/Juno/Fortune), Andrew Tortise (Eurymachus), Paul Nilon (Ulysses), Geoffrey Dolton (Eumaeus)

Khovanshchina (Mussorgsky), 17 February 2007. Conductor, Lothar Koenigs; director, David Pountney; designer, Johan Engels. Julian Close (Dosifey), Robert Hayward (Ivan Khovansky), Tom Randle (Andrei Khovansky), Peter Hoare (Vasily Golitsyn), Peter Sidhom (Shaklovity), Rosalind Plowright (Marfa), Suzanne Murphy (Susanna)

The Seven Deadly Sins (Weill), 11 May 2007. Conductor, Carlo Rizzi; designer, Jonathan Adams. Marie McLaughlin (Anna I)

Duke Bluebeard's Castle (Bartok), 11 May 2007. Conductor, Carlo Rizzi; director, Willy Decker; designer, Jonathan Adams. Sara Fulgoni (Judith), Andrea Silvestrelli (Duke Bluebeard)

Performances were given in Cardiff and on tour in Swansea, Oxford, Llandudno, Birmingham, Bristol, Southampton, Liverpool, Milton Keynes and Plymouth.

GLYNDEBOURNE FESTIVAL OPERA
Founded 1934
Glyndebourne, Lewes, East Sussex BN8 5UU

The festival ran from May 19 to August 28 2007. *Così fan tutte* (2006), *La Cenerentola* (2005) and *Tristan und Isolde* (2003) were revived.

NEW PRODUCTIONS: *Macbeth* (Verdi), 19 May 2007. Conductor, Vladimir Jurowski; director, Richard Jones; designer, Ultz. Sylvie Valayre (Lady Macbeth), Andrzej Dobber (Macbeth), Stanislav Shvets (Banquo), Peter Auty (Macduff), Bryan Griffin (Malcolm)

St Matthew Passion (Bach), 1 July 2007. Conductor, Richard Egarr; director, Katie Mitchell; designer, Vicki Mortimer. Mark Padmore (Evangelist), Harry Waddington (Christus), Ingela Bohlin (soprano), Sarah Connolly (alto), Andrew Tortise (tenor), Christopher Purves (bass)

The Turn of the Screw (Britten), 1 August 2007. Conductor (Edward Gardner); director; Jonathan Kent; designer, Phil Brown. William Burden (Prologue/Peter Quint), Camilla Tilling (Governess), Ann-Marie Owens (Mrs Grose), Emma Bell (Miss Jessell), Christopher Sladden (Miles), Joanna Songi (Flora)

GLYNDEBOURNE TOURING OPERA
Macbeth (2007), *Albert Herring* (1986) and *L'elisir d'amore* (Donizetti, a new production), were performed from 9 October to 8 December 2007 at Glyndebourne, Woking, Milton Keynes, Norwich, Plymouth, Stoke-on-Trent and London (Sadler's Wells Theatre).

GARSINGTON OPERA
Founded 1989
Garsington Manor, Oxford OX44 9DH

The season ran from 9 June to 9 July 2007.

NEW PRODUCTIONS: *Il re pastore* (Mozart), 9 June 2007. Conductor, Stuart Bedford; director, Annilese Miskimmon; designer, Dick Bird. Cora Burggraaf (Aminta), Lucy Crowe (Elisa), Natasha Jouhl (Tamiri), Iain Paton (Alessandro), Thomas Walker (Agenore)

La donna del lago (Rossini), 12 June 2007. Conductor, David Parry; director, David Alden; designer, Gideon Davey. Carmen Giannattasio (Elena), Colin Lee (Giacomo), Michael Colvin (Roderigo), Alexandra Sherman (Malcolm), Dean Robinson (Douglas)

Ariadne auf Naxos (Richard Strauss), 25 June 2007. Conductor, Elgar Howarth; director, Martin Duncan; designer, Francis O'Connor. Orla Boylan (Ariadne), John Horton Murray (Bacchus), Elizabeth Cragg (Zerbinetta), Wendy Dawn Thompson (Composer), Russell Smythe (Music Master), Daniel Norman (Dancing Master), Quirijn de Lang (Harlequin), Nicholas Sharratt (Brighella), Richard Coxon (Scaramuccio), Andrew Slater (Truffaldino)

GRANGE PARK OPERA
Founded 1998
The Coach House, 12 St Thomas Street, Winchester SO23 9HF

The season ran from 31 May to 15 July 2007.

NEW PRODUCTIONS: *The Gambler* (Prokofiev), 31 May 2007. Conductor, André de Ridder; director/designer, David Fielding. Andrew Shore (The General), Katherine Rohrer (Pauline), Jeffry Lloyd-Roberts (Alexei), Carol Rowlands (Babulenka), Hubert Francis (The Marquis), Doreen Curran (Blanche)

The Magic Flute (Mozart), 1 June 2007. Conductor, Richard Balcombe; director, Stephen Medcalf; designer, Francis O'Connor; Adrian Dwyer (Tamino), Elizabeth Atherton (Pamina), Victoria Joyce (Queen of Night), Jeremy White (Sarastro), David Stout (Papageno), Richard Coxon (Monostatos), Tueta Koco (Papagena)

Falstaff (Verdi), 22 June 2007. Conductor, Stephen Barlow; director, Daniel Slater; designer, Angela Davies. Robert Poulton (Falstaff), Janis Kelly (Alice), William Dazeley (Ford), Claire Ormshaw (Nannetta), Victoria Simmonds (Meg), Anne Marie Owens (Quickly) Andrea Giovannini (Fenton)

Performances were given at The Grange, while *The Magic Flute* and a revival of *I Capuleti e I Montecchi* (Bellini) were also given at Nevill Holt.

ENGLISH TOURING OPERA
Founded 1980 as OPERA 80

Orfeo (Monteverdi), *Dido and Aeneas* (Purcell) and *Jephte* (Carissimi), *Erismena* (Cavalli) and *Tolomeo* (Handel) were toured to Hackney, Cambridge, Exeter, Canterbury, Crawley, Lincoln, York, Snape, Buxton, Ulverston, Malvern and Bath between 6 October and 2 December 2006.

The Seraglio (Mozart), *Eugene Onegin* (Tchaikovsky) and *Spirit of Vienna* (Johann Strauss) were toured to Hackney, Crawley, Tunbridge Wells, Cheltenham, Truro, Snape, Poole, Bexhill-on-Sea, Wolverhampton, Buxton, Sheffield, Kendal, Cambridge, Coventry, Durham and Perth between 15 March and 26 May 2007.

PARLIAMENT

Patrick Robathan

The 2006–7 session of parliament opened with the knowledge that it would be the last with Tony Blair as prime minister. During the 2006 summer recess he had announced that he would stand down within a year. He did not name the actual date but did say that he would be gone before the following year's Trades Union Congress. 'I am not going to set a precise date now,' Blair reported. 'I don't think that's right. I will do that at a future date and I'll do it in the interests of the country and depending on the circumstances of the time.' The session closed with the new prime minister, Gordon Brown, experiencing a 'bounce' in the polls, leading to speculation that he might call a snap election in the autumn.

The fact that he was known to be leaving office did little to enhance Mr Blair's authority within parliament – he was exposed on the usual issues of Iraq, Europe and criminal justice and continued to suffer a series of embarrassing defeats. Strangely, despite the boost in public support for the new prime minister (with one of the first polls of the 2007 summer recess showing Labour had forged a nine-point lead which would double the party's current majority), the first month of Gordon Brown's premiership produced nine small backbench rebellions in the House of Commons, none particularly large or worrying, but which saw 21 MPs defying the party whip. These figures were not especially alarming for the new prime minister as the rebels were from amongst the 'usual suspects', but they were proof that the rebellious behaviour seen under the Blair government had not disappeared with a change of leadership. In addition to these revolts, Mr Brown's first month in power also witnessed a series of compromises over the Corporate Manslaughter and Corporate Homicide Bill, the Offender Management Bill and the Pensions Bill in order to placate backbench rebellions. Without such negotiation, the level of rebellion would certainly have been considerably larger.

GOVERNMENT DEFEATS

Tony Blair's problems began in the spillover period immediately after the 2006 summer recess as he attempted to complete his government's 2005–6 legislative programme. His flagship **POLICE AND JUSTICE BILL** was defeated at report stage in the Lords on 9 October when an amendment to remove clauses giving the secretary of state the power to direct if a police force is failing (given the absence of any objective judgement of failure), moved by Liberal Democrat Baroness Harris of Richmond, was passed by 144 votes to 125, a majority against the government of 19. The following day there were two more defeats when cross bencher Lord Lloyd of Berwick moved an amendment to delete a clause that reforms conditional cautions to allow punishments, including fines, to be part of the conditions, which was passed by 207 votes to 146, a majority of 61. The second defeat was based on an amendment moved by another cross bencher, Lord Ramsbotham, to oppose the merging of the five criminal justice inspectorates (police, prisons, probation, court services and Crown Prosecution Services) into one new Justice, Community Safety and Custody Inspectorate, passed by 211 votes to 98, a majority of 113. In the Commons the government dropped the plans for a so called 'super watchdog' but on 24 October, MPs overturned the block on 'fast-track' extraditions to the US by 320 votes to 263 and their call for extradition only if a trial abroad was in the 'interests of justice' by 313 votes to 272, which included 14 Labour rebels. At consideration of Commons amendments on 1 November, the government suffered two further defeats when an amendment moved by Conservative spokesperson Lord Kingsland, which insisted on removing the USA from being granted a lower threshold of evidence in order to extradite until the treaty has been ratified, was passed by 189 votes to 152. Another amendment was insisting on inserting that the 'forum rules' (from the 1957 European Convention on Terrorism) are incorporated: judges shall not order the extradition of a person if an act was partly committed in the UK unless in the interests of justice. This was passed by 171 votes to 138, a majority of 33. On 6 November MPs again overturned the Lords amendments (by 298 votes to 204) with home secretary John Reid saying that if the treaty was blocked by the amendments it could result in 'very serious offenders and suspected offenders escaping justice'. Attempts by peers to reinstate the amendment the next day failed when the Conservatives withdrew their support and it was defeated by 96 votes to 174.

The government also struggled to get through the **ROAD SAFETY BILL** in the form they wanted, suffering three defeats at consideration of Commons amendments on 1 November with the Lords insisting on: (a) a clause enabling local authorities to ring-fence the spending of money (received from speeding fines) on local road safety measures moved by Conservative Lord Hanningfield (passed by 129 votes to 101, a majority of 28); (b) inserting a clause requiring the government to ensure that new heavy goods vehicles should be fitted with retro-reflective tape but that the government should make regulations by 31 December 2007 moved by Conservative Baroness Hanham (by 112 votes to 96, a majority of 16); (c) removing provision criminalising 'careless driving' moved by Conservative Earl Attlee (by 104 votes to 89, a majority of 15). These were overturned in the Commons.

The government saw a further defeat on the 870-page **COMPANIES BILL** on 2 November when they insisted on their amendment that the Freedom of Information Act should apply to the new oversight bodies created under the bill. It was passed by 116 votes to 104, a majority of 12. This was overturned in the Commons. Also on consideration of Commons amendments, the NHS Redress Bill, where Conservative Earl Howe insisted on requiring that investigations under the redress scheme must be conducted 'in accordance with natural justice [so] the person overseeing the investigation is independent of the body. . .under investigation' and that it be 'confined to the facts', was passed by 149 votes to 133, with a majority of 16. The total number of defeats for the government in the Lords in the 2005–6 session, which ended on 8 November, was 62.

The Queen's speech opening the 2006–7 session of

parliament on 15 November contained proposals for 29 bills for the session (including four carried over from the last session and three that would be introduced in draft) designed to provide security in uncertain times by addressing 'the big issues that will effect generations to come' including climate change, pension reform, mass migration and terrorism. Prime Minister Tony Blair described the theme of the speech as 'taking the long-term decisions necessary to give us security and opportunity in a rapidly changing world.' Conservative leader David Cameron felt 'the only good ideas in the Queen's speech are . . . Conservative proposals, and they are all being implemented by Labour. The Queen's speech should have been about the long term, the national interest, and about trusting people and not centralising power. This was the prime minister's last chance to offer hope for a better society, but instead he chose fear, to try to cover up his failures. It is the politics of fear from a government of failure.' Liberal Democrat leader Sir Menzies Campbell said: 'This is a remarkable parliamentary occasion because the prime minister is introducing a programme of legislation that he will not be in place to complete. I cannot remember any instance of that in recent history. This is truly power without responsibility. There are plans for an 11th education bill, a 12th health and social care bill, an eighth terrorism bill and a 24th criminal justice bill since the prime minister took office in 1997. That leads to the conclusion that after nearly ten years in office the government and the prime minister are still chasing the same elusive goals and headlines. This is a rush from judgment towards legislation. The prime minister is trying to legislate his way into history.'

The Queen's speech was approved after six days of debate on 23 November by 263 votes to 190, a government majority of 73.

By the summer of 2007, the Labour government had suffered 41 defeats in the Lords including the complete loss of the **FRAUD (TRIALS WITHOUT JURY) BILL** on 20 March. The bill, which would have ended trial by jury in complex fraud cases, was not unanimously welcomed in the Commons and saw at least seven Labour MPs vote against second reading on 29 November, with one Bob Marshall-Andrews saying: 'This awful bill deserves short shrift. It's a serious attack on civil liberties, which have been our heritage for 800 years.' Others rebelled at third reading on 25 January, reducing the government's majority to 36 (281 votes to 246). At second reading in the Lords on 20 March, peers effectively killed off the bill by approving a motion (by 216 votes to 143) to delay further debate six months – highly unusual at that stage of a bill's passage through parliament. Leading Labour rebel Baroness Mallalieu, QC, said the bill was fundamentally flawed: 'which, in reality, sticks a knife into the main artery of our criminal justice system.' Attorney-General Lord Goldsmith said: 'This bill is not an attack on the jury system and, however constantly that proposition is repeated, it doesn't make it true. It is ultimately about justice, about ensuring that those who are responsible for fraud on the grander scale can be brought to account. We want the sharks to be caught and not just the minnows.' He also reiterated the government's intention to force the bill through in the next parliamentary session, using the Parliament Act.

The recommendation to site the UK's first super-casino in Manchester has created controversy since the initial announcement by the casino advisory panel on 30 January. On 20 March the House of Lords Merits of Statutory Instruments Committee criticised the selection criteria used to pick the site, and when the legislation came before parliament on 28 March, whilst MPs narrowly approved the proposal (by 274 votes to 250, with a much-reduced government majority of 24), peers rejected the proposal by 123 votes to 120. Liberal Democrat peer Lord Clement-Jones said of forcing the vote and rejecting any government compromise: 'The fact is we have all, step by step, been taken on a path which leads to entirely the wrong conclusion and this is not something we should tolerate.' This vote also meant that plans for 16 smaller casinos around the UK had to be shelved. Speaking after the defeat, culture secretary Tessa Jowell said she wanted time 'to reflect on the outcome' and promised new proposals.

The government's attempts to introduce Home Information Packs (HIPs) which were first mooted in their 1997 election manifesto and which were supposed to make the home-buying process easier and quicker, received a mauling during their progress through parliament. The government had plans for HIPs to become compulsory for all sellers in England and Wales on 1 June 2007 but these were met with a chorus of disapproval, both within and outside parliament. On 1 May Lord Filkin, chair of the House of Lords Merits of Statutory Instruments commitee which scrutinised the legislation, said: 'The comments which we have received from key stakeholder organisations in the housing market are striking in the strength of their criticisms . . . we have rarely seen such widespread opposition to proposals.' Attempts by the Conservatives to defeat the legislation in the Commons on 16 May failed by 306 votes to 234. Conservative housing spokesperson Michael Gove said of the packs: 'They are a test case in how not to legislate. They will do nothing to take the strain out of home-buying and only add cost and complexity to the housing market.' On 22 May, following a successful legal challenge from the Royal Institution of Chartered Surveyors, and the same day as the Lords were due to vote on the legislation, communities and local government secretary Ruth Kelly announced. 'We propose to withdraw the home information pack regulations to clear the way for successful implementation of revised arrangements'. This included a delay until 1 August, when the packs were made compulsory, but only for sales of homes with four or more bedrooms. The Lords went ahead with their vote and defeated the legislation by 186 votes to 160, a majority of 26.

The Lords also inflicted a series of defeats upon the government on the substantive bills included in their legislative programme. On the **MENTAL HEALTH BILL**, the government recorded no less than six defeats, the biggest of which, on 10 January, saw a majority of 106 (225 votes to 119) to insert a clause stating that before being subjected to compulsory treatment it should be a requirement that a patient's mental disorder means their 'ability to make decisions about the provision of medical treatment is significantly impaired'. In the Commons on 19 June the government introduced a series of compromises including a proposal ensuring that any compulsory treatment must be of 'therapeutic benefit' and the bill therefore gained its third reading by 272 to 202 votes, a majority of 70. Health minister Rosie Winterton told MPs that mental health organisations had urged her to back the amendment and that it was a good compromise. As the bill was based on the purpose of medical treatment, 'it does not turn on the likelihood of treatment achieving that purpose'.

The government also suffered five defeats on the **PENSION BILL**, the worst being at committee stage on 6 June when they inserted a new clause to set up a 'lifeboat' fund to enable the financial assistance scheme to compensate pensioners whose retirement savings are lost through occupational schemes (by 181 votes to 126, a majority against the government of 55). Despite some Labour MPs remaining critical of the government's stance, this was overturned on 17 July in the Commons by 303 votes to 253 (with 16 Labour MPs voting against the government). Pensions minister Mike O'Brien described the Lords amendment as 'costly, complex and contradictory' and added that opponents should accept that 'their lifeboat amendment has been holed below the waterline and is sinking fast'. The government only avoided more discussion in the Lords by invoking a ruling that this part of the bill was subject to 'financial privilege'.

The Lords also inflicted defeats on the following bills – Offender Management Bill (six times, the largest by 55 votes on 3 July); Legal Services Bill (six times, the largest by 68 votes on 15 May); Corporate Manslaughter and Corporate Homicide Bill (five times, the largest by 96 votes on 5 February); Statistics and Registration Service Bill (three times, the largest by 63 votes on 2 May); Serious Crime Bill (twice, the largest by 62 votes on 25 April); Greater London Authority Bill (twice, the largest by 18 votes on 19 June); Further Education and Training Bill (twice, the largest by 52 votes on 27 February); and Welfare Reform Bill (once). The government's majority in the Commons overturned most of these.

IRAQ

Prime Minister Tony Blair made several statements on developments in Iraq in his last seven months in office and it was an issue that dominated most of his appearances at Prime Minister's Questions (PMQs). Pressed by Liberal Democrat leader Sir Menzies Campbell on 24 January on proposals to bring the troops home by October, he said: 'For us to set an arbitrary timetable – that is what it is – and it is arbitrary because it is not attached to the conditions in Iraq and simply says that we will pull British troops out in October, come what may – would send the most disastrous signal to the people whom we are fighting in Iraq. Let us remind ourselves why they are there. They are there under a United Nations resolution with the full support of the government of Iraq.' In a statement to the House on 21 February he continued: 'Nobody should doubt that whatever the debates about tactics, the strategy is clear: to bring about enduring change in the Middle East as an indispensable part of our own enduring security. The poisonous ideology that erupted after 9/11 has its roots there, and is still nurtured and supported there. It has chosen Iraq as the battleground. Defeating it is essential. Essential for Iraq. But also, now, for us here in our own country. Self-evidently the challenge is enormous. It is the purpose of our enemies to make it so. But our purpose in the face of their threat should be to stand up to them, to make it clear that however arduous the challenge, the values that they represent will not win, and the values we represent, will.'

On 16 April defence secretary Des Browne updated MPs on events in the Middle East, concentrating on the detention of 15 Royal Navy personnel by Iran and the subsequent handling of the situation by the MOD: 'I take responsibility for what happened . . . I have acted to put it right. I have acted to ensure that we learn the lessons of the whole episode.' On 19 June he reported back on the findings of two inquiries into the incident – on its media handling and the other operational aspects. On 11 June the Conservatives, supported by the Liberal Democrats, instigated a debate on the need for an independent inquiry into the Iraq War, with shadow foreign secretary William Hague declaring: 'This government and future governments need to learn the lessons, and the country needs to be assured that they will have done so. No adequate reason remains for the government to refuse to establish such an inquiry to begin its work in the near future, but there is even less reason for them to disagree with the motion before the House today calling for such an inquiry in principle.' Foreign secretary Margaret Beckett rejected the proposal saying: 'I believe that we also have a responsibility to think very carefully about the signals that we send out from this House today – signals that will be closely followed in Iraq and around the world. It is critical that we do not convey to others the impression that this country's commitment to Iraq is weakening at a critical moment, and that we are about to turn away into a period of self-indulgent introspection.' The motion was defeated by 274 votes to 229, a government majority of 45.

EUROPE

Prime Minister Tony Blair regularly reported back to the Commons on developments in Europe. On 12 March he reported on the European Council summit held in Brussels the previous weekend, which had concentrated on deregulation, liberalising the energy market and binding environmental targets: 'The matters it addressed were all fundamental British objectives and we were able to give the German presidency full and active support. Once again, that shows the significance of strong, constructive and positive engagement in Europe.' On 11 June he gave an account of the G8 summit in Heiligendamm: 'The summit made a real breakthrough on climate change, more progress on Africa and showed again the value to Britain of its transatlantic and European alliances.' Conservative leader David Cameron applauded the prime minister, who he said: 'can take credit for pushing the issues of climate change and poverty up the agenda of the group of most powerful nations in the world. The opposition will always ask the appropriate questions about the delivery of the promises that have been made, but raising the profile of those issues is a genuine achievement for which many have cause to be grateful.'

On 25 June Mr Blair reported on the outcome of the European Summit held in Brussels: 'I made it clear that the concept of a constitutional treaty for Europe had to be abandoned and that we should agree instead a conventional amending treaty like the Nice, Amsterdam and Maastricht treaties and the Single European Act. I also made it clear that the UK had four central demands which had to be met . . . All these guarantees not merely remain in the new treaty, but are reinforced in a new overview article that reaffirms them and has full legal force. For the avoidance of doubt, we also obtained a declaration that sets out the unanimous view of all member states about the meaning of those guarantees.' Conservative leader David Cameron replied: 'In his final days in office, the prime minister has concluded negotiations for which after this week he can never be held accountable, and he has agreed to a transfer of power from Britain to Brussels without the permission of the British people. That will be remembered as one of the most flagrant breaches of any of the promises that he has made.' Even Mr Blair's own backbenchers were less than supportive. Gisela Stuart argued: 'Back in April 2004, the reasons for granting a referendum and making a manifesto commitment were not about constitutional change, but because we should let the people have a say. The prime minister's foreign secretary and minister for Europe now argue that one of the main reasons why we should not have a referendum is that we are a parliamentary democracy – yet the document to which the prime minister signed up at the weekend grants the people of Europe a right that neither national parliaments nor governments have, which is to petition the commission for legislative proposals.'

NORTHERN IRELAND

Perhaps the most lasting legacy of the final Blair year will prove to be the successful restoration of a power-sharing assembly in Northern Ireland. Following the Northern Ireland Act 2006 (rushed through parliament in November), which called for the restoration of devolved government by 26 March or a permanent return to direct rule, the prime minister issued a statement on 4 January expressing confidence that the DUP and Sinn Fein both wanted progress in the restoration of power-sharing and would honour their commitment to the St Andrews agreement. Although this actual deadline was not met, agreement was reached and the Northern Ireland Act 2007 was rushed through both Houses in one day (27 March), allowing for restoration of devolved government to Northern Ireland on 8 May. Mr Blair said: 'In a sense, everything we have done over the last ten years has been a preparation for this moment . . . The people of Northern Ireland have said we want peace and power-sharing and the political leadership has then come in behind that and said we will deliver what people want. What it does mean is people can come together, respecting each other's point of view and share power and make sure politics is only expressed through peaceful and democratic means. And in that it will give the people of Northern Ireland the future they want and give heart to all of us who have wanted this process over the past few years. Now at last we have a date certain for the devolution of power and a remarkable coming together of people who have, for very obvious reasons, been strongly opposed in the past.'

Speaking in the Commons on 9 May, the day after ministers from the four main parties in Northern Ireland took their pledge of office in a ceremony at Stormont, Northern Ireland secretary Peter Hain said: 'I do not think it possible to overestimate the significance of yesterday's events at Stormont. In effect, we witnessed the final resolution of what has for centuries been the most intractable source of political conflict in the whole of Europe, and its significance is not confined to relations within these islands. What happened on 8 May 2007 showed the world how a shared future can emerge from even the most bitterly divided and blood-stricken past – and we must never forget how much misery and suffering that caused.'

The following day Mr Blair announced that he would be stepping down as prime minister on 27 June.

OTHER ISSUES

Despite this undoubted success, the last weeks of the Blair administration did not pass smoothly. There was a series of huge rows over the health service, and especially the Medical Training Application Service, through which junior doctors apply for specialist training posts. In April there were security breaches in the system exposed by the media and health secretary Patricia Hewitt had to come to the House on 1 May to admit that 'there is no doubt that confidence in the applications system has been further damaged by these deplorable security breaches'. The real argument was about whether the system was working in the interests of either doctors or patients, with junior doctors calling for both her and health minister Lord Hunt to resign. On 23 May the Conservatives tabled a motion calling for the health secretary's salary to be cut – a traditional way of showing no confidence in a minister, designed to force her resignation. Conservative health spokesperson Andrew Lansley said: 'NHS staff are angry because of the way in which they have been treated. They are angry because the government are constantly telling them how to do their job, even though the government are incompetent at doing their own. The secretary of state has been responsible for so-called NHS reform, but there is no coherent reform. There is not even competent management, but there are urgent tasks to be done. Even the secretary of state's own colleagues in the government do not believe that she is capable of achieving those things, or that she will be responsible for doing so.' Liberal Democrat health spokesperson Norman Lamb supported the motion: 'The Rt. Hon. Lady is a sacrificial lamb for the failings of the government's stewardship of the National Health Service; others should take their share of the responsibility. The extent to which confidence in this government's stewardship of the NHS has collapsed is remarkable. There has been record investment, which we supported, and some genuine progress has been made, yet both the public and health professionals have lost faith.' Mrs Hewitt countered: 'It is this government who will go on listening to staff and, above all, patients. We will make changes when they need to be made and improve services that still need improvement. We will back the NHS and improve it so that it is the fairest and best service in the world.' In the event the motion was defeated by 282 votes to 219, a government majority of 63.

Another issue to dominate parliament during the year was that of post office closures. Trade and industry secretary Alistair Darling originally published proposals for consultation in December but came to the House on 17 May to outline the final details. He confirmed the closure of 2,500 branches but claimed to be maintaining a national network 'larger than all the UK's banks and building societies put together', to be implemented over an 18-month period from the summer. Mr Darling concluded: 'The majority of people in this country want us to maintain a national network of post offices. I believe that the proposals set out today will do that.' Conservative spokesperson Alan Duncan summed up the proposals: 'What this statement really means is the closure of more than one third of the post office network under this government, countless villages losing their only shop, and millions of vulnerable people losing a service that they depend on. Little or no account will be taken of the needs of the elderly, the disabled or the most disadvantaged, and there is too little appreciation of the dedication of our sub-postmasters, who spend years building up their businesses and serving their communities.' Liberal Democrat Susan Kramer expressed 'regret that the consultation process has not led to a fundamental rethink'.

The problems with the Home Office were also a feature of the parliamentary year. On 13 June home secretary John Reid had to come to the House to make various statements on asylum seekers, counter-terrorism and child sex offenders. Having called the department 'not fit for purpose' when he was appointed, it was perhaps no surprise when Mr Blair announced the department was to be split in two on 29 March, creating a new Ministry of Justice to take control of probation, prisons and prevention of re-offending (replacing the Department for Constitutional Affairs) and a slimmed-down Home Office to concentrate on dealing with terrorism, security and immigration. John Reid praised the proposal: 'The changes outlined today will add capacity to that which is already engaged in the formulation and carrying through of our security and counter-terrorism policy. It will develop a more strategic, inclusive, integrated and capable response to the current threat.' Conservative spokesperson David Davis objected as much to the way the announcement was being 'smuggled out' as to its contents: 'Because of the way in which it has been carried out, this ill-thought-through exercise to create a department of justice and a department of security will actually leave public security undermined and a justice system overwhelmed.' Liberal Democrat spokesperson Nick Clegg felt: 'If the manner in which the announcement has been made is any guide to the manner in which it will be implemented, we are headed for further organisational chaos at the heart of government.'

GORDON BROWN'S LAST BUDGET

On 21 March Gordon Brown presented his eleventh and final budget as chancellor. The main proposals included 2p off the basic rate of income tax (reduced to 20p from April 2008) but with the 10p starter rate abolished and an increase in top-rate threshold to £43,000; corporation tax cut by 2p to 28p from April 2008 but the rate on small companies to be raised to 22p by 2009; car duty for so-called 'gas guzzlers' was up to £300 in 2007 and £400 in 2008, with the least-polluting vehicles to have their duty cut to £35; excise duty on beer and cider up by 1p, wine by 5p, duty on spirits frozen and up by 11p on cigarettes, but the 2p fuel duty rise would be delayed for six months; the inheritance tax threshold was to rise to £350,000 by 2010. He also announced more cash for schools (£74bn by 2010) and hospitals (to rise by £8bn in the current year) with total government spending due to rise to £674bn by 2010–11. There was also an increase from £2bn to £8bn in funding for people who lost their pensions when their employers went bust pre-2005. However, Mr Brown rejected Conservative calls for VAT to be added to airline tickets, saying the proposals had not been considered fully. He commented this was 'a budget to expand prosperity and fairness for Britain's families . . . built on the foundation of the longest period of economic stability and sustained economic growth in our country's history. It is a budget for Britain's families; it is a budget for fairness; it is a budget for the future.'

Conservative leader David Cameron took a different view: 'This chancellor cannot run away from his record. He is the chancellor who has put the tax burden up. The chancellor who has taken one tax down but put 99 up . . . the average family is paying £1,300 more because of his budget decisions.' Liberal Democrat leader Sir Menzies Campbell was similarly critical: 'Sadly, this budget does not quite live up to the auspicious nature of the occasion . . . he has delivered a budget of missed opportunities' and, on abolishing the 10p starting tax rate: 'one could say that we are asking the poor to subsidise the rich. That is an example of the sleight of hand that the chancellor has demonstrated in the past.' Labour chair of the Treasury Select Committee, John McFall, welcomed measures that 'will benefit families, society and business'. Senior Conservative MP John Redwood, however, summed it up as 'a budget based on a central con on the income tax proposition. Most people will feel very let down when they read their newspapers tomorrow and see that they are not better off in the way that the chancellor was perhaps trying to hint with his famous announcement at the end of his speech.' After four days of debate during which shadow chancellor George Osborne suggested that it was 'clear that 3.5 million working families will be worse off as a result of this budget . . . Pretty much anyone earning below £18,000 a year will see their income tax bills rise because of the abolition of the 10p rate, which more than cancels out the cut in the basic rate.' The budget was approved on 27 March by 295 votes to 232, a government majority of 63. The Finance Act, implementing the measures in the budget, received royal assent on 19 July.

FOND FAREWELL

Prime Minister Tony Blair held his last ever PMQs on 27 June, ending his speech with the following: 'I have never pretended to be a great House of Commons man, but I pay the House the greatest compliment I can by saying that, from first to last, I never stopped fearing it. The tingling apprehension that I felt at three minutes to 12 today I felt as much ten years ago, and every bit as acute. It is in that fear that the respect is contained. The second thing that I would like to say is about politics and to all my colleagues from different political parties. Some may belittle politics but we who are engaged in it know that it is where people stand tall. Although I know that it has many harsh contentions, it is still the arena that sets the heart beating a little faster. If it is, on occasions, the place of low skulduggery, it is more often the place for the pursuit of noble causes. I wish everyone, friend or foe, well. That is that. The end.' As he left the chamber for the last time, protocol was ignored and he was clapped out with a standing ovation from all sides of the house.

NEW PM – ALL CHANGE ?

Gordon Brown was appointed as prime minister on 27 June. In his first speech as prime minister, Gordon Brown reiterated his promise to bring about change, stating that he would 'try utmost' to serve the people of Great Britain, leading a 'government of all talents' by appointing non-parliamentarians as ministers. At his second PMQs on 11 July, Mr Brown signified that his would take a different approach from his predecessor and would revisit certain previous Labour policies. He unexpectedly announced a review of the government's policy on casinos that would be 'subject to reflection over the next few months. In September we will have a report that will look at gambling in our country, and at the incidence and prevalence of it and its social effects. I hope that during these summer months, we can look at whether regeneration in the areas for the super-casinos may be a better way of meeting their economic and social needs than the creation of super-casinos.'

A week later, at the next PMQs (18 July) he unveiled a consultation on reclassifying cannabis as part of a review of the entire UK drugs strategy. 'We will be asking the public to comment on new ways in which we can improve drugs education in this country, give support to people undergoing treatment and give support to communities that want to chase out drug dealers. . .the home secretary will consult on whether it is right that cannabis should be moved from class C to class B.' Outside parliament, in his first regular press conference, he also announced that he had ordered a Home Office review of legislation permitting 24-hour drinking.

On Iraq, however, when asked on 4 July about a timetable for withdrawal he said: 'It would be wrong to set a timetable at this stage . . . we have obligations, which we have accepted, both to the United Nations and the Iraqi government, and we are not going to break those obligations at this stage.' Like his predecessor, he was forced to begin three of his first four PMQs by sending condolences to the families and friends of UK servicemen killed in Iraq, 'They died doing important work in the service of their country and our country, and we owe them and others who have lost their lives a deep debt of gratitude.'

NEW STRATEGIES – PRIME MINISTER

In his first month as prime minister Gordon Brown made three significant statements in the Commons, again exhibiting a desire to be seen as breaking with Blair's policies. Announcing the publication of a green paper on constitutional reform on 3 July, he highlighted 12 areas where power held by the executive would be limited or surrendered 'to make for a more open 21st-century British democracy which better serves the British people'. He also announced the creation of a National Security Council (described as 'sending out a clear message that at all times we will be vigilant and we will never yield'), and unveiled a new ministerial code, with a new independent adviser whom the PM will ask to scrutinise ministerial conduct, and called for a public debate on the case for a British Bill of Rights or a written constitution. 'The changes that we propose today and the national debate we now begin are founded on the conviction that the best answer to disengagement from our democracy is to strengthen our democracy. It is my hope that this dialogue of all parties and the British people will lead to a new consensus, a more effective democracy and a stronger sense of shared national purpose.' David Cameron agreed that the 'British system of government and politics needs real and lasting change. The country is too centralised, parliament is too weak, ministers do not give straight answers and people feel shut out of decision making.' Sir Menzies Campbell concurred, 'My starting point is that reform of our constitution is long overdue and. . .the United Kingdom deserves a constitution that is fit for the challenges and standards of contemporary Britain. If we are to restore public confidence in our political system, we must be both innovative and inclusive.'

On 11 July the prime minister broke new ground by announcing a consultation on the draft legislative programme ahead of the Queen's speech: 'I believe that it is right, in the interests of good and open government and public debate, that each year the prime minister make a summer statement to the House so that initial thinking, previously private, can be the subject of widespread and informed public debate. Today, in advance of final decisions, the Leader of the House is publishing details of our initial list of proposed legislative measures, inviting debate on them in both Houses this month and making provision for region-by-region deliberation and responses.' David Cameron felt it was all a gimmick: 'I know that it is meant to be some great constitutional innovation, but most of what he announced sounded rather like the Queen's speech last year, the year before and the year before that – a long list of bills, the same priorities and the same failures, and we have heard it all before.' Sir Menzies Campbell was similarly sceptical: 'I say to the prime minister that we should be concerned about the quality of legislation as much as we are about the quantity. It is worth pointing out that during the past ten years, there have been 382 acts of parliament, including ten health acts, 12 education acts and 29 criminal justice acts, and more than 3,000 new criminal offences have been created. The mantra might have been "Education, education, education", but the reality has been "Legislation, legislation, legislation".'

On 25 July 2007 in his statement on national security Mr Brown outlined his counter-terrorism strategy to MPs – under the proposal Britain would get a 'unified border force'. He also announced a review of the policy on intercepting evidence in court and plans to raise from 28 days the time police can hold suspects without charge. 'Our priority as a government is a Britain strong in security, robust in our resolve, resilient in response, so that as a nation we both defeat terrorism and isolate violent extremism, wherever we confront it and whatever its support. I hope that in doing so, an all-party consensus that will extend into every community of this country is possible, so that together we can create a stronger, safer and more cohesive United Kingdom.' David Cameron gave an indication that such a consensus would indeed emerge: 'This is an area, of course, where we can and will work together.' Sir Menzies Campbell did warn: 'For many of us, consensus cannot be achieved at the expense of principle. The essential test for any proposed new power must always be whether it is necessary, not whether it is desirable or convenient.'

NEW STRATEGIES – MINISTERS

Among the numbers of newly appointed ministers who came to the House during the first three weeks of the Brown regime was the new health secretary, Alan Johnson, who said on the NHS next stage review that 'there will be no further centrally dictated, top-down restructuring to primary care trusts and strategic health authorities for the foreseeable future . . . I have asked Professor Sir Ara Darzi to carry out a wide-ranging review of the NHS. This is a once-in-a-generation opportunity to ensure that a properly resourced NHS is clinically led, patient-centred and locally accountable . . . this will ensure that the service is genuinely led by the needs of patients, providing value to the taxpayer as we move to the next stage of improvement. It will protect the enduring, cherished principles of universal health care, free at the point of need, which lay behind the establishment of the NHS, and ensure that this precious institution continues into the 21st century in ruder health than ever.' Conservative spokesperson Andrew Lansley was underwhelmed: 'I was disappointed by what I heard, and . . . NHS staff, along with the public, will be disappointed . . . Where is the immediate priority that the prime minister promised? Where is the autonomy and accountability that the NHS is calling out for? Where is the leadership and the direction that the NHS so badly needs?' Liberal Democrat spokesperson Norman Lamb felt: 'The statement is surely something of an admission of failure, given that after ten years of the government's stewardship of the NHS, they are still searching a strategic direction.'

On 5 July the new innovation, universities and skills secretary John Denham announced reforms to support students in higher education, with more students from poorer families in England receiving full grants for university living costs. 'These reforms promote aspiration, offer opportunity and provide support to students from hard-working families. They promote the world-class standards of our colleges and universities and help deliver the skills and knowledge that business and society need in a global economy.' Conservative spokesperson David Willetts welcomed the reforms but wondered: 'How can the government achieve their objectives of widening participation if the only lever that they pull changes the maintenance grant, when fundamental improvement in the quality of education at school is the key?' Liberal Democrat spokesperson Sarah Teather praised 'the recognition that the previous system was woefully inadequate.'

Ed Balls was appointed secretary of the new Department for Children, School and Families on 10 July. He outlined his priorities under the slogan 'Every child matters' and added: 'We all have a responsibility to ensure that every child has the chance to develop their talents to the full.' Conservative spokesperson Michael Gove wondered why 'after ten years of a prime minister who promised a relentless focus on "Education, education, education", is such an ambitious agenda still required?'

New local government minister John Healey published the conclusions of the government's review of sub-national economic development and regeneration on 17 July with the 'compelling case' for reform 'to give local authorities and communities greater responsibility and opportunity to boost economic growth in their area; to bring consultation and planning for jobs, homes, investment and the environment closer together at both local and regional levels; and to strengthen public scrutiny and accountability of regional plans and the work of regional development agencies, both in the region and in this House.' This would include scrapping the eight regional assemblies. Conservative spokesperson Eric Pickles said: 'The problem is that these proposals reinforce failure with more failure. It risks creating a regional tyranny of governance with no mandate, no legitimacy and no accountability.' Liberal Democrat Andrew Stunnell was even more scathing: 'This is a severe case of top-down, economic-growth-centred thinking that is some 30 years out of date, with the environment forgotten, democracy overridden and diversity scorned.' This statement was followed by one from minister for women and newly elected deputy leader of the Labour Party Harriet Harman on her priorities, launching a consultation with the Women's National Commission to 'focus on three issues: helping families who care for older and disabled relatives, as well as those bringing up children; tackling violence against women and improving the way in which we deal with women who commit crimes; and empowering black and Asian women to help them as a force for good in their communities.' Conservative spokesperson Theresa May welcomed the sentiment but was 'disappointed by the lack of ambition that has been shown in an area where there is still so much to be achieved' and was concerned that 'not a single part of today's statement is a new policy'.

Incoming work and pensions secretary Peter Hain gave his intentions to publish a green paper on full employment: 'to achieve full employment and the eradication of child poverty, especially at a time when the global forces of economic and demographic change present new and ever greater challenges for our economy and labour market, will require a step change in our reforms . . . reigniting the jobs crusade that started in 1997 and renewing the partnership between government, employers and individuals by focusing now on those who remain furthest from the labour market and on those whose potential is untapped.' Conservative spokesperson Chris Grayling felt that the government's solution was always to 'launch yet another consultation, yet another green paper, yet more legislation and yet more initiatives, but they never actually get the job done.' Liberal Democrat Danny Alexander thought the statement 'misses a huge opportunity to deliver extra help to those people who need it most'. John Denham followed immediately with his own statement on delivering world-class skills in England to 'to raise the nation's skills base, build productivity, increase social inclusion and improve economic competitiveness'. Conservative spokesperson David Willetts shared the government's aims but thought the statement 'does not rise to the challenge of providing an employer-driven, individually focused service to improve the nation's skills'. Stand-in Liberal Democrat spokesperson Stephen Williams agreed, fearing that 'unless the government are willing to back up the statement with action rather than exhortation, the ambitious target of being in the premier league by 2010 will be very hard to achieve'.

Newly appointed justice secretary Jack Straw agreed to revise the way forward for House of Lords reform, with the promise of a white paper 'around the turn of the year' and the aim of completing the job 'in the first couple of years of the next parliament'. Conservative spokesperson Nick Herbert thought that rather than 'finishing the job', 'we remain in precisely the same position: intending reform, but still waiting'. Liberal Democrat spokesperson Simon Hughes added: 'Would it not be logical to get on with the process, rather than slow it down?'

The first-ever female home secretary, Jacqui Smith, laid out the government's new strategy for tackling crime over the next three years on 19 July: 'We have proved that when you tackle unemployment and drug and alcohol misuse, crime comes down. When schools and health services, local authorities, police and neighbours work together, crime comes down. When you are not afraid to make tough choices about enforcing standards of behaviour, crime comes down.' Conservative spokesperson David Davis was sceptical: 'Very few members of the public think that the government's crime policy is a success. If she thinks it a success, heaven help the country when she thinks it a failure.' Nick Clegg of the Liberal Democrats was equally dubious: 'This is not a strategy but a rag-bag of unrelated, minor media initiatives, which ignore the fundamental failure in the government's relentless and shameless populist approach to law and order.'

New housing minister Yvette Cooper promised a green paper on affordable housing, which will set 'a bolder framework for the future but we will achieve our goals only if those at regional and local levels, in the public, private and third sectors, and in local communities, all play their part in supporting the homes we need. Building the sustainable homes needed by young people today and by future generations is a test of our commitment to supporting people's aspirations and to achieving social justice.' Conservative spokesperson Grant Shapps felt this was a plan for the 'sink estates of tomorrow', and on the housing crisis: 'It is vital to end the ham-fisted nature of top-down, Whitehall-driven targets.' The Liberal Democrats' spokesperson Paul Holmes thought the statement 'represents the imposition of yet more central control, with the government dictating what houses will be built, where, by which councils and in partnership with whom'. Transport secretary Ruth Kelly unveiled a seven-year strategy for railways on 24 July, setting out ambitions for 'a railway capable of carrying double the number of passengers and twice the amount of freight by 2030, with modern trains and a network whose reliability and safety are among the best in Europe'. Conservative spokesperson Theresa Villiers laid the blame for Britain's transport problems at the feet of Gordon Brown: 'The truth is that the prime minister cannot blame anyone but himself for the state of our transport system, because the extortionate fare increases for grossly overcrowded trains are his fare increases. The transport broken promises are his broken promises.' Liberal Democrat spokesperson Susan Kramer added: 'The statement has been a disappointment . . . and we consider it to be a missed opportunity.' Minister for children Beverley Hughes planned a new ten-year strategy for children, 'Aim Higher', 'to take the lead in promoting a better appreciation of our nation's young people – our future – and that, through the strategy, we can achieve a transformation of the opportunities young people need to succeed'. Welcoming the strategy, Conservative spokesperson Tim Loughton thought it 'essential that the government do not try to displace parents, but work with them and their children, and acknowledge that in the vast majority of cases it is parents who know best how to bring up their own children'.

Other ministerial statements made in parliament during the first month of Gordon Brown's premiership included an update from home secretary Jacqui Smith on developments in counter-terrorism, following the failed car bombs in London and the unsuccessful car bomb attack at Glasgow Airport at the beginning of July. She praised the reaction of the members of the public: 'The fact that people have been prepared to go about their lives as normally as possible this weekend sends the strongest message to those who wish to destroy our way of life and our freedoms that we will not be intimidated by terror.' On 16 July foreign secretary David Miliband announced that the UK had expelled four Russian diplomats over the failure of the Russian government to hand over the prime suspect in the case of the killing of Alexander Litvinenko. Des Browne, the defence secretary, announced the details of a comprehensive spending review settlement for his department for the next three years (an increase of £7.7bn by 2011) and confirmed the order for two new aircraft carriers on 25 July. 'This significant additional investment shows that the government are determined to ensure that in the years ahead the armed forces maintain their well-earned and much-deserved reputation for being the best armed forces in the world.' Conservative spokesperson Liam Fox warned: 'If there is any sleight of hand in what the government are saying on defence expenditure, it will not be forgiven by our troops in combat or in this House.' On 9 July both communities and local government secretary Hazel Blears and environment secretary Hilary Benn updated members of parliament on the flooding in Yorkshire and then in Central England: 'There will be lessons to be learned, and we will learn them.'

The new prime minister encountered significant opposition to his plans for Europe. On 23 July minister for Europe Jim Murphy published a white paper on the UK's approach to the European Union intergovernmental conference to draw up a reform treaty for the enlarged EU, which he felt 'will achieve the UK's aims and deliver for Britain, and for Europe, the capacity to act more effectively to tackle global challenges together . . . The treaty will allow us to move beyond questions of process, and focus on delivering prosperity and security for our citizens. That is firmly in the interests of the EU, and most definitely in the interests of the UK.' Conservative spokesperson Mark Francois wondered why the government would not stick to their manifesto promise for a referendum on any EU constitution: 'Ministers say that they want more accountability and consultation, so why will they not make themselves accountable and consult the British people? Why should the British people trust the government, when the government will not trust them? So we say, honour our promises, trust the people and let them decide.' Labour backbench unrest continued, Kevin Hopkins added: 'I shall be campaigning strongly for a referendum and believe that my view is shared by millions of Labour supporters and trade unionists throughout Britain.'

The year also included an 18-day suspension for Respect MP George Galloway following a critical report from the Committee on Standards and Privileges. Defending himself, Mr Galloway said: 'Being lectured by the current House of Commons on the funding of political campaigns is like being accused of having bad taste by Donald Trump or being accused of slouching by the hunchback of Notre Dame.' Parliament rose for the summer recess on 26 July, not due to return until the beginning of October, with various backbench MPs, including Labour's David Kidney, calling for 'the House to have a more even pattern of sittings and thus a shorter summer recess'.

PUBLIC ACTS OF PARLIAMENT

Public acts included in this list are those which received the royal assent after 31 August 2006. The date stated after each act is the date on which it came into effect.

Civil Aviation Act 2006 c. 34 (various dates, some to be appointed) makes further provision about civil aviation, including provision about the funding of the Air Travel Trust; and for connected purposes.

Fraud Act 2006 c. 35 (to the extent not already in force 15 January 2007) makes provision for, and in connection with, criminal liability for fraud and obtaining services dishonestly.

Wireless Telegraphy Act 2006 c. 36 (8 February 2007) consolidates enactments about wireless telegraphy.

Parliamentary Costs Act 2006 c. 37 (1 April 2007) consolidates the House of Commons Costs Taxation Act 1847, the House of Lords Costs Taxation Act 1849, the Parliamentary Costs Act 1865, the Parliamentary Costs Act 1867, the Parliamentary Costs Act 1871 and the House of Commons Costs Taxation Act 1879, with amendments to give effect to recommendations of the Law Commission and the Scottish Law Commission.

Violent Crime Reduction Act 2006 c. 38 (various dates, some to be appointed) makes provision for reducing and dealing with the abuse of alcohol; about real and imitation firearms, ammunition, and knives and other weapons; amends the Football Spectators Act 1989 and the Football (Disorder) Act 2000; amends the Sexual Offences Act 2003, the Crime and Disorder Act 1998, s 8, the Children and Young Persons Act 1969, s 23, and the Mobile Telephones (Re-programming) Act 2002; and for connected purposes.

Emergency Workers (Obstruction) Act 2006 c. 39 (8 November 2006) makes it an offence to obstruct or hinder persons who provide emergency services; and for connected purposes.

Education and Inspections Act 2006 c. 40 (various dates, some to be appointed) makes provision about primary, secondary and further education and about training; and food or drink provided on school premises or in connection with the provision of education or childcare; provides for the establishment of an Office for Standards in Education, Children's Services and Skills and the appointment of Her Majesty's Chief Inspector of Education, Children's Services and Skills and makes provision about the functions of that office and that chief inspector; provides for the amendment of references to local education authorities and children's services authorities; amends the Leasehold Reform Act 1967, section 29, in relation to university bodies; and for connected purposes.

National Health Service Act 2006 c. 41 (to the extent not already in force 1 March 2007) consolidates certain enactments relating to the health service.

National Health Service (Wales) Act 2006 c. 42 (to the extent not already in force 1 March 2007) consolidates certain enactments relating to the health service.

National Health Service (Consequential Provisions) Act 2006 c. 43 (to the extent not already in force 1 March 2007) makes provision for repeals, revocations, consequential amendments, transitional and transitory modifications and savings in connection with the consolidation effected by the National Health Service Act 2006 and the National Health Service (Wales) Act 2006.

NHS Redress Act 2006 c. 44 (8 November 2006) makes provision about arrangements for redress in relation to liability in tort in connection with services provided as part of the health service in England or Wales; and for connected purposes.

Animal Welfare Act 2006 c. 45 (various dates, some to be appointed) makes provision about animal welfare; and for connected purposes.

Companies Act 2006 c. 46 (various dates, some to be appointed) reforms company law and restates the greater part of the enactments relating to companies and other business organisations; and about directors' disqualification, business names, auditors and actuaries; amends the Enterprise Act 2002, pt 9; and for connected purposes.

Safeguarding Vulnerable Groups Act 2006 c. 47 (various dates, some to be appointed) makes provision in connection with the protection of children and vulnerable adults.

Police and Justice Act 2006 c. 48 (various dates, some to be appointed) establishes a National Policing Improvement Agency; makes provision about police forces, police authorities and police pensions; about police powers and about the powers and duties of community support officers, weights and measures inspectors and others; about the supply to the police and others of information contained in registers of death; for combating crime and disorder; about certain inspectorates; and about the forfeiture of indecent images of children; provides for the conferring of functions on the Independent Police Complaints Commission in relation to the exercise of enforcement functions by officials involved with immigration and asylum; amends the Extradition Act 2003; makes further provision about the use of live links in criminal proceedings; and for various other purposes connected with police and justice.

Road Safety Act 2006 c. 49 (various dates, some to be appointed) makes provision about road traffic, registration plates, vehicle and driver information, hackney carriages and private hire vehicles, and trunk road picnic areas.

Charities Act 2006 c. 50 (various dates, some to be appointed) provides for the establishment and functions of the Charity Commission for England and Wales and the Charity Tribunal; makes other amendments of the law about charities, including provision about charitable incorporated organisations; public charitable collections and other fund-raising carried on in connection with charities and other institutions; and about the funding of such institutions.

Legislative and Regulatory Reform Act 2006 c. 51 (8 January 2007) enables provision to be made for the purpose of removing or reducing burdens resulting from legislation and promoting regulatory principles; makes provision about the exercise of regulatory functions; about the interpretation of legislation relating to the European Communities and the European Economic Area; makes provision relating to section 2(2) of the European Communities Act 1972.

Armed Forces Act 2006 c. 52 (various dates, some to be appointed) makes provision with respect to the armed forces; and for connected purposes.

Northern Ireland (St Andrews Agreement) Act 2006 c. 53 (various dates) make provision for preparations for the restoration of devolved government in Northern Ireland in accordance with the St Andrews Agreement; as to the consequences of compliance, or non-compliance, with the St Andrews Agreement timetable; amends the Northern Ireland Act 1998; makes provision about district policing partnerships; amends the Education (Northern Ireland) Orders 1997 and 2006; and for connected purposes.

Consolidated Fund Act 2006 c. 54 (19 December 2006) authorises the use of resources for the service of the years ending 31 March 2007 and 31 March 2008 and applies certain sums out of the Consolidated Fund to the service of the years ending 31 March 2007 and 31 March 2008.

Investment Exchanges and Clearing Houses Act 2006 c. 55 (20 December 2006) confers power on the Financial Services Authority to disallow excessive regulatory provision by recognised investment exchanges and clearing houses; and for connected purposes.

Appropriation Act 2007 c. 1 (20 March 2007) authorises the use of resources for the service of the years ending 31 March 2006 and 31 March 2007; applies certain sums out of the Consolidated Fund to the service of the years ending 31 March 2006 and 31 March 2007; and appropriates the supply authorised in this session of parliament for the service of the years ending 31 March 2006 and 31 March 2007.

Planning-Gain Supplement (Preparations) Act 2007 c. 2 (20 March 2007) permits expenditure in preparation for the imposition of a tax on the increase in the value of land resulting from the grant of permission for development.

Income Tax Act 2007 c. 3 (6 April 2007: it applies for income tax purposes for the tax year 2007–08 and subsequent years and for corporation tax accounting periods ending 5 April 2007) restates, with minor changes, certain enactments relating to income tax; and for connected purposes. This act is part of the re-write series.

Northern Ireland (St Andrews Agreement) Act 2007 c. 4 (27 March 2007) modifies the effect of the Northern Ireland (St Andrews Agreement) Act 2006.

Welfare Reform Act 2007 c. 5 (various dates, some to be appointed) makes provision about social security; amends the Vaccine Damage Payments Act 1979; and for connected purposes.

Justice and Security (Northern Ireland) Act 2007 c. 6 (various dates, some to be appointed) makes provision about justice and security in Northern Ireland.

International Tribunals (Sierra Leone) Act 2007 c. 7 (18 June 2007) confers power to make provision in relation to the Special Court for Sierra Leone corresponding to that made in relation to the International Criminal Court by International Criminal Court Act 2001 ss 42–48.

Digital Switchover (Disclosure of Information) Act 2007 c. 8 (18 June 2007) makes provision about the disclosure of certain information for purposes connected with digital switchover.

Rating (Empty Properties) Act 2007 c. 9 (19 July 2007) makes provision for and in connection with the liability of owners of unoccupied hereditaments to a non-domestic rate.

Appropriation (No. 2) Act 2007 c. 10 (19 July 2007) authorises the use of resources for the service of the year ending 31 March 2008; applies certain sums out of the Consolidated Fund to the service of the year ending 31 March 2008; appropriates the supply authorised in this session of parliament for the service of the year ending with 31 March 2008; and repeals certain Consolidated Fund and appropriation acts.

Finance Act 2007 c. 11 (19 July 2007) grants certain duties, to alter others, amends the law relating to the National Debt and the Public Revenue, and makes further provision in connection with finance.

Mental Health Act 2007 c. 12 (various dates, some to be appointed) amends the 1983 act, the Domestic Violence, Crime and Victims Act 2004 and the Mental Capacity Act 2005 in relation to mentally disordered persons; and for connected purposes.

Concessionary Bus Travel Act 2007 c. 13 (day or days to be appointed) makes provision about travel concessions; and for connected purposes.

Vehicle Registration Marks Act 2007 c. 14 (19 July 2007) makes further provision about the retention of vehicle registration marks pending transfer.

Tribunals, Courts and Enforcement Act 2007 c. 15 (various dates, some to be appointed) makes provision about tribunals and inquiries; establishes an Administrative Justice and Tribunals Council; amends the law relating to judicial appointments and appointments to the Law Commission; and the law relating to the enforcement of judgments and debts; makes further provision about the management and relief of debt; makes provision protecting cultural objects from seizure or forfeiture in certain circumstances; amends the law relating to the taking of possession of land affected by compulsory purchase; alters the powers of the high court in judicial review applications; and for connected purposes.

Parliament (Joint Departments) Act 2007 c. 16 (19 July 2007) provides for joint departments of the houses of parliament; and for connected purposes.

Consumers, Estate Agents and Redress Act 2007 c. 17 (various dates, some to be appointed) makes provision for the establishment of the National Consumer Council and its functions; to make provision for the abolition of other consumer bodies; about the handling of consumer complaints by certain providers; and requiring certain providers to be members of redress schemes in respect of consumer complaints; amends the Estate Agents Act 1979; makes provision about the cancellation of certain contracts concluded away from business premises; and for connected purposes.

Statistics and Registration Service Act 2007 c. 18 (day or days to be appointed) establishes and makes provision about the Statistics Board; and about offices and office-holders under the Registration Service Act 1953. The objective is, in part, to monitor official statistics.

Corporate Manslaughter and Corporate Homicide Act 2007 c. 19 (various dates, some to be appointed) creates and makes provision in connection therewith a new offence that, in England, Wales or Northern Ireland is called corporate manslaughter and, in Scotland, corporate homicide.

Forced Marriage (Civil Protection) Act 2007 c. 20 (day or days to be appointed) provides for the protection of individuals in the event of their being forced to enter into marriage without their free and full consent and for protecting individuals who have been forced to enter into marriage without such consent.

WHITE PAPERS

This section provides an outline of a selection of white papers that have been published in the last year. For further information visit www.official-documents.co.uk or www.parliament.uk. Alternatively, visit the websites of individual government departments – *see* Government Departments section.

Legal Aid Reform: The Way Ahead was presented to parliament by the Secretary of State for Constitutional Affairs and the Lord Chancellor in November 2006. The paper argues for the replacement of the current method of assigning and paying for legal aid. The new system outlined in the paper calls for a competitive marketplace where practitioners are able to set the prices they charge, rather than bill at a flat rate for the number of hours worked. The transition period to a market system will be managed by a series of fixed and graduated fees to curb escalation in spending and a panel will be introduced for handling cases with high costs.

The Future of the UK's Nuclear Deterrent was presented to parliament by the Secretary of State for Defence and the Secretary of State for Foreign and Commonwealth Affairs in December 2006. The paper presents the results of a government review into its nuclear weaponry and recommends the construction of three or four new submarines (at a cost of around £15–20bn), working with the USA to extend the life of the Trident D5 missile until the 2040s and – to demonstrate the country's commitment to the Nuclear Non-Proliferation Treaty – a reduction in the number of operationally available warheads to fewer than 160.

The House of Lords: Reform was presented to parliament by the Leader of the House of Commons and the Lord Privy Seal in February 2007. In this paper the government outlines its vision for the future composition of the House of Lords before a free vote in parliament. The House described consists of 50 per cent elected members and 50 per cent appointed members. It is to have no party-political majority; 20 per cent of its members are to be non party-political appointments and are to serve long terms which are non-renewable, with the entry of any possible elected members staggered over three elections; representation of the Church of England is to be maintained and the right of hereditary peers to sit and vote on the basis of their ancestry is to be ended.

Trust, Assurance and Safety – The Regulation of Health Professionals in the 21st Century was presented to parliament by the Secretary of State for Health in February 2007 and explores how the quality of care provided by healthcare workers can be assessed in order to maintain patient trust in the sector. It aims to do this by requiring doctors to apply for relicensing and/or specialist recertification every five years, with similar measures for non-medical healthcare workers. The paper also proposes a system of General Medical Council Affiliates at a local level to speed up the complaints procedure and an overhaul of the medical register to enable more information about health professionals to be made available to the public.

Heritage Protection for the 21st Century was presented to parliament by the Secretary of State for Culture, Media and Sport in March 2007. The paper describes the government's plans to change the ways in which the UK's historical, architectural and archaeological sites are protected. It aims to do this by simplifying the existing classification system, publishing easily available registers of historic buildings and sites in England and Wales and providing the public with more detailed information on how and why sites are chosen for protected status.

A Sea Change was presented to parliament by the Secretary of State for Environment, Food and Rural Affairs in March 2007. The paper outlines plans to streamline and update existing marine legislation to cope with new pressures on environment and wildlife. It aims to establish a central Marine Management Organisation to process forthcoming legislation on planning, licensing and to conservation. The bill also proposes a new system of marine planning to improve interaction between the many different users of the country's marine space.

Meeting the Energy Challenge was presented to parliament by the Secretary of State for Trade and Industry in May 2007 and focuses on what the country must do to reduce carbon dioxide emissions in the UK and abroad and to ensure clean and affordable energy, despite a growing dependence on imported fuel. The main proposals are to promote open and competitive energy markets worldwide; to encourage widespread car fuel efficiency standards; to provide affordable methods of monitoring personal energy consumption; to create energy standards to which new homes must comply; and to assist businesses with the transitional costs of meeting energy targets.

Care Matters – Time for Change was presented to parliament by the Secretary of State for Education and Skills in June 2007. The basis of the paper is the continuing gap in achievement between children in care and children that remain with parents or guardians. The paper proposes a number of methods to improve the quality of life for children in care, including regular OFSTED inspections for local authority departments; piloting regional commissioning units to provide a wider choice of placements; improving training and support for foster parents; prioritising children in care during school admission; funding extra one-to-one tuition for failing children and introducing bursaries for young people who continue into higher education.

SCIENCE AND DISCOVERY

Neil Bone

HONEYBEE GENOME SEQUENCED

Commercially important as both a producer of honey and pollinator of food crops, the honeybee *Apis mellifera* has become the third insect (after the fruit fly *Drosophila*, and the *Anopheles* mosquito) to have its complete DNA sequence (genome) determined. The results of a four-year effort were published in the journals *Science* and *Nature* in October 2006. In total, the honeybee genome comprises 236 million basepairs of DNA, distributed over 16 chromosomes. Sequence analysis has identified 10,157 genes.

Availability of the complete honeybee genome sequence is expected to provide insights to the biology and behaviour of social insects. The community in a hive is differentiated, with a single offspring-producing queen supported by castes of non-reproductive workers and drones. The workers, of which there may be tens of thousands, have much shorter lifespans than the queen and show patterns of gene expression that change in response to the needs of the hive. Analysis also shows that some honeybee genes are regulated in a manner more akin to those of vertebrates than other insect species.

Some genes are highly represented in ways specific to the social lifestyle. For example, an unusually high number (around 165) of odorant-receptor genes have been identified; pheromones released during the waggle dance of returning workers are an important means of conveying information on food sources to other members of the hive.

Researchers have also used the data to trace some of the honeybee's evolutionary history, which suggests that honeybees have evolved at a much slower rate than, for example, flies. The divergence of the honeybee and the fly from a common ancestral insect occurred around 300 million years ago. Detailed analysis suggests that Eurasian honeybees came out of Africa in two separate migrations in the distant past.

ANCESTRAL BEE FOSSIL FOUND

Bees have a complicated family tree, comprising around 16,000 members, and are part of the insect order *Hymenoptera*, which includes bees, wasps, ants and sawflies. An ancestral fossil bee was recently discovered in 100 million-year-old amber from a mine in northern Myanmar. Other known fossil bees date back 55–65 million years ago. *Melittosphex burmensis* was only 3mm-long, but shows branched hairs – unique to bees – on its head, thorax, legs and abdomen and several pollen grains are seen to be trapped among the hairs. It is believed that honeybees evolved from predatory wasps, and played an important part in pollination of the first flowering plants, which evolved in parallel during the Cretaceous period.

DATING THE LAST NEANDERTHALS

Modern humans and their closest hominid relative, the Neanderthals, are believed to have diverged from a common ancestor around half a million years ago. The Neanderthals became widespread in Europe and western Asia until their extinction roughly 30,000 years ago. *Homo neanderthalensis* was adapted to life in a harsh environment dominated by glacial conditions and was characterised by short limbs and a heavy torso. Modern humans spread out from Africa into Europe about 40,000 years ago, competing with the Neanderthals and eventually proving more successful in dealing with changing climatic conditions. Debate continues over how long *Homo sapiens* and *Homo neanderthalensis* coexisted (the interval may have been as little as 2,000 or as long as 10,000 years) and whether there was any genetic intermingling.

Recent findings from Gorham's Cave on Gibraltar provide evidence for the survival of a small Neanderthal population in southern Iberia as recently as 28,000 years ago. Stone tools were found at the cave in the 1940s. A more detailed excavation of the cave interior between 1999 and 2005 using mass spectrometry has revealed that the site was occupied repeatedly over a period of several thousand years. The locality would have provided a refuge from harsher conditions farther north, with a diverse environment of sandy plains, woodland and coastline. Studies of seafloor sediment cores obtained from the region show an abrupt deterioration in climate with a marked temperature drop accompanied by drought conditions, which may conceivably have brought about the Neanderthals' demise.

STEPS TOWARDS A NEANDERTHAL GENOME SEQUENCE

Progress is being made towards reconstructing the entire Neanderthal genome sequence, as reported in parallel papers by two research groups published in *Nature* and *Science* in November 2006. Detailed analysis of the differences between Neanderthal DNA and that of *Homo sapiens* is expected to greatly improve understanding of human evolution.

Neanderthal DNA was recovered from a sample, discovered in 1980 at Vindija Cave, Croatia, and dated to around 38,000 years ago. Although extensively degraded, the DNA was uncontaminated. To reconstruct the sequence, scientists in California targeted specific genes, obtaining around 65,000 basepairs (bp) of sequence data. Using polymerase chain reaction amplification, a group in Leipzig were able to retrieve about a million basepairs of Neanderthal sequence, mostly in the form of short (100–200 bp) fragments. Sequences derived from these were aligned to and compared with the human genome, enabling their identification.

Alignment was also carried out with the chimpanzee genome. On the basis of the accepted 6.5 million year divergence time between human and chimpanzee, the frequency of single base differences in Neanderthal sequences suggests that human and Neanderthal diverged around 516,000 years ago.

ETHIOPIAN FOSSIL FIND THROWS FURTHER LIGHT ON HUMAN EVOLUTION

North-east Ethiopia has been a rich source of hominid fossils that have allowed the early evolution of modern humans to be at least partly mapped out. Among celebrated specimens from the region is the partial *Australopithecus afarensis* skeleton known as Lucy, discovered in 1974. An expedition to the Dikika region discovered an exceptionally well-preserved *A.afarensis* skull and partial skeleton during excavations between 2000 and 2003. The remains, of a three-year-old juvenile female, show that *A.afarensis* had legs adapted for upright, bipedal locomotion, but retained ape-like upper body features (including curved fingers) suited to an arboreal lifestyle. Many of the skeletal details were previously unknown, and the fossil appears to represent an intermediate evolutionary form between chimpanzees and humans.

Named Selam ('peace' in the local language), the fossil was recovered from sandstone beds, and it is thought that her remarkable state of preservation results from drowning and burial during a flash flood 3.3 million years ago. Geological studies suggest the region was a river delta prone to flooding and rapid sedimentation.

BRIGHTEST COMET FOR OVER 40 YEARS

A comet discovered with the 50cm Uppsala Schmidt Telescope at Siding Spring Observatory, Australia, in August 2006 became the brightest since the Sun-grazing C/1965 S1 Ikeya-Seki. C/2006 P1 McNaught reached perihelion (the point of closest approach to the Sun in its orbit) at a distance of 0.17 astronomical units (AU; 1 AU is the mean Sun-Earth distance, 150,000,000 km), well inside the orbit of the planet Mercury. As a first-time visitor to the inner Solar System from the distant surrounding Oort Cloud 'reservoir' of comet nuclei, Comet McNaught proved to be extremely dusty. Forward-scattering of sunlight by micron-sized dust particles in the tail close to the time of perihelion led to a spectacular brightening as the comet passed between the Earth and Sun in line of sight.

Observers in the southern hemisphere had particularly stunning views of the comet's broadly fanned dust tail in early evening skies. The tail showed striations which can be ascribed to distinct interludes of dust emission from active regions (vents) on the comet's rotating nucleus. Calculations show the comet to have been trapped by gravitational perturbations by the planets into an extremely long, narrow elliptical orbit around the Sun. Comet McNaught will next return in approximately 90,000 years.

NEW HORIZONS AT JUPITER

Launched in January 2006, NASA's *New Horizons* spacecraft is on course for its 2015 encounter with Pluto following a successful 'gravitational slingshot' manoeuvre as it flew past Jupiter at a distance of 2.3 million kilometres on 28 February 2007. Having taken only 13 months to reach the giant planet, *New Horizons* was accelerated and is now hurtling outwards at 83,600km/h.

Passage through the Jovian system presented an ideal opportunity to test the spacecraft's instruments, and large amounts of data were collected between January and June 2007. The multicolour visible imaging camera (MVIC) proved its low-light capabilities – essential for operation at Pluto's distance from the Sun – with images of Jupiter's satellite Io. MVIC recorded a plume from the volcano Tvashtar, with ejected material rising over 240km above Io's limb. Images of another satellite, Callisto, were taken using the long-range reconnaissance imager. Jupiter's turbulent atmosphere was imaged by an infrared spectral imager, providing scientists with their first really close views of 'Red Junior', a half-sized version of the planet's Great Red Spot formed by the merger of two long-lasting storm systems in 2000.

FAREWELL XENA, HELLO ERIS

It was the discovery of 2003_{UB313}, a Kuiper Belt object larger than Pluto – that led to Pluto's demotion to the new class of dwarf planets at the International Astronomical Union (IAU) general assembly in 2006. Formerly known by the informal title Xena, 2003_{UB313} has now been officially named by the IAU as Eris, for the Greek goddess of strife and disorder. Its single known satellite has been named after Eris' daughter Dysnomia. As a further blow to Pluto's status, Eris was reported in June 2007 to be 27 per cent larger than the erstwhile outermost planet.

PROBING THE UNIVERSE'S DARK SIDE

Astronomers have long known that the visible material in the Universe accounts for only a small fraction, around 15 per cent, of the total. Studies of the rotation of galaxies, for example, give observed velocities that can only be accounted for by the presence of surrounding 'haloes' of dark matter. The nature of dark matter remains a mystery. Many cosmologists believe it to consist of exotic particles which do not interact via observable electromagnetism. However, studies by an international team in California have mapped out the distribution of dark matter.

The work involved detailed examination of half a million distant galaxies in a patch of sky covering about eight times the area of the Full Moon, using the Hubble space telescope's advanced camera for surveys. Measurements of the degree of distortion (a result of the gravitational lensing effect) in individual galaxy images allowed researchers to determine the presence and quantity of dark matter in the intervening space.

Coupled with lower-resolution data from ground-based telescopes in Chile and Hawaii, the results allow a rough three-dimensional reconstruction of dark matter in the Universe, with a 'look back' time of 9 billion years to when the Universe was only one-sixth of its current age. In line with predictions from cosmological theory, the dark matter distribution changes with time. Initially, the distribution was smooth, later becoming filamentary and then clumpy. Complementary studies show that visible (baryonic) matter concentrates along the dark matter filaments: dark matter provides a gravitational 'skeleton' which determines the distribution of the Universe's visible components – galaxies and clusters of galaxies.

HUBBLE REPRIEVED

Released into Earth orbit from the space shuttle *Discovery* in 1990, the Hubble Space Telescope (HST) has been an essential research instrument for astronomers over the past 17 years. Maintenance of the orbiting observatory has depended on servicing visits carried out by astronauts on four occasions between 1993 and 2002. In the wake of the 2003 *Columbia* accident, future servicing missions were considered too risky, and NASA planned to abandon HST. However, this decision was overturned following protests from astronomers, and in October 2006, NASA announced the reinstatement of servicing mission *SM4*, to be carried out late in 2008.

HST is currently in failing health. The advanced camera for surveys (ACS) – the source of many of the telescope's spectacular images – suffered a critical failure on 27 January 2007. The ACS is now inoperable until *SM4* can effect repairs. During the mission, new gyroscopes, essential for accurately pointing HST, and new batteries will be installed in the hope that HST's operational lifetime can be extended to 2013.

While Hubble has been reprieved, doubts have been cast over the future of another iconic astronomical facility, the Arecibo radio telescope in Puerto Rico. Opened in 1963, the 300m dish is the world's largest single radio telescope. Used for radar imaging of near-Earth asteroids, ionospheric research and other studies, the telescope faces closure in 2011 as the US National Science Foundation looks to cut $30m (£15m) from its astronomy budget.

DOUBTS RAISED OVER 'LUNAR ICE'

Surveys by the NASA *Clementine* and *Lunar Prospector* spacecraft in 1994 and 1998 suggested that permanently shadowed craters in the Moon's polar regions may contain significant reserves of water ice, created by comet impacts in the distant past. The availability of water on the Moon could have important benefits for any planned future manned base. One favoured location might be the 19km-diameter crater Shackleton at 89.54 degrees south, very close to the lunar south pole. The crater depths are always in shadow, while parts of its elevated rim have perpetual sunlight, making it ideal for power generation.

Scientists at Cornell University in New York have made a detailed radar reflection study of Shackleton, using the Arecibo radio telescope as a transmitter and a telescope in West Virginia as receiver. Circular polarisation ratio (CPR) data from Shackleton were compared with those reflected from the similar-sized Schauberger G crater, which is similarly positioned but regularly sunlit and therefore likely to have lost any deposited ice. No differences were found. The study concluded that the CPR patterns from both craters are more consistent with reflection from rough terrain. If water ice is present in Shackleton, it is unlikely to exist in large quantities.

DECODING THE ANTIKYTHERA MECHANISM

Discovered in 1901 in the wreck of a Roman vessel on the seabed between Crete and mainland Greece, the Antikythera mechanism is an ancient astronomical calculator. Other artefacts, including marble figures, pottery, glassware and coins reliably date the wreck to 65 BC. The mechanism, heavily encrusted and partly corroded, consists of bronze gear-wheels and is the earliest-known device to involve such technology.

While its nature as an astronomical calculator has been accepted for some time, the precise details of the purpose and operation of the Antikythera mechanism have until recently been poorly understood. Much has been clarified by a major investigation by British and Greek researchers, the results of which were published in *Nature* in November 2006.

Computer-assisted tomography scanning was used to examine the interior of the major surviving fragment of the mechanism, and X-ray imaging allowed deciphering of much more of the text inscribed on the casing than had previously been accessible. Many of the inscriptions appear to relate to its construction and date the Antikythera Mechanism to 150–100 BC. The researchers believe it to have been mounted in a wooden case, with the gear-train operated by hand.

At least 37 hand-cut gear-wheels were involved in the mechanism and were used to successfully reproduce solar and lunar motions on the sky from a geocentric viewpoint. There are strong indications that the construction was based on a model of lunar motion developed by the Greek astronomer Hipparchus of Rhodes. One ingenious gearing incorporates a pin and slot mechanism that reproduces the variations in the Moon's movements due to its elliptical orbit, as recognised by Hipparchus.

EARLIEST GLIDING-FLIGHT MAMMAL

The fossil record shows that gliding flight, aided by extended membrane structures supported by long limbs, has evolved independently several times among mammals. A newly discovered fossil from the Jurassic Daohugou beds in Inner Mongolia, China, has provided the earliest known example of a gliding mammal, dating back at least 125 million years. By contrast, the earliest bat fossils date to 51 million years ago. A squashed skeleton of *Volaticotherium antiquus* ('ancient flying beast') shows this to have been a squirrel-sized insectivorous mammal adapted for an arboreal lifestyle. The elongated tail and limbs of *V.antiquus* supported a hair-covered patagium (flying membrane), the impression of which is well preserved in the Daohugou fossil.

INFLUENCE OF SUBGLACIAL LAKES ON ANTARCTIC ICE FLOWS

Since their first detection by radar studies in the 1960s, over 150 liquid water lakes have been identified under the thick Antarctic ice sheet. Kept liquid by geothermal heat and the pressure of the overlying ice, many of these are dynamic features with water draining from one region to another. Perhaps the best known of these is Lake Vostok, which covers an area of 15,690 sq. km. The lakes have an important effect on the overlying ice, for example, surface topography of ice above lakes is often unusually flat.

The influence of subglacial lakes on ice movements has been highlighted by the recent discovery of four lakes covering a total of 13,300 sq. km in the Queen Maud Land region of east Antarctica. These are located in an area where the Recovery Glacier ice stream – one of the largest in Antarctica – begins to accelerate in its motion towards the ocean surrounding the continent. Upstream of the lakes, ice moves at 2–3m per year; downstream, motion is up to 50m per year. The flow accelerates as a result of reduced friction between basal ice and the underlying bedrock.

Recent observed reduction of the ice sheet in Greenland may have been a result of subglacial water movements. In the context of increased ice-loss from the polar regions in a warming climate, it may become important to understand more clearly just how hydrological processes influence the rate at which glacial deposits are delivered to the oceans.

GRACE TRACKS GREENLAND ICE-LOSS

The Greenland ice sheet is a significant reservoir of water which, were it to melt in its entirety could raise sea levels by as much as 7m. Release of large volumes of fresh water from this reservoir could also influence ocean currents and affect climate in northwest Europe. New remote-sensing data shows that the rate of ice loss from Greenland has more than doubled between 1996 and 2005. Increased precipitation in the high-altitude interior (due to a greater rate of evaporation from warmer oceans) has been outstripped by loss at Greenland's margins. These findings have been confirmed and quantified by results published in September 2006.

Launched into Earth orbit in March 2002, *GRACE* (gravity recovery and climate experiment) is a joint mission between NASA and the German Aerospace Centre. *GRACE* consists of a pair of satellites separated by 220km. The precise distance between the satellites varies in response to changes in Earth's gravitational field enabling changes in the mass of Greenland ice to be accurately determined. The results show an annual loss rate of 192–258 million tonnes between April 2002 and April 2006, equivalent to a rise in mean sea level of 0.5 ± 0.1mm per year. Most of the ice loss has occurred in southern and south-eastern Greenland, where glacier flows have accelerated. It remains to be seen whether this is a short-term variation or part of a sustained longer trend.

MOST LUMINOUS SUPERNOVA

Supernovae are spectacular events of stellar demise that can briefly outshine their host galaxies. Two types are known. Type I supernovae occur in binary star systems where a white dwarf accumulates so much material from its partner it exceeds the critical limit of 1.4 solar masses and undergoes catastrophic 'nuclear runaway'. Type II supernovae result from core collapse in massive, short-lived stars as these expend their material in nuclear reactions. Rebound from the collapse results in dramatic brightening as the star's outer layers are blasted apart.

A supernova discovered on 18 September 2006 in the galaxy NGC 1260, 240 million light years away in the constellation Perseus, has turned out to be the most intrinsically luminous ever observed. Shining with the equivalent light of 50 billion Suns, SN2006gy was two to three times as luminous as a typical type II supernova. The event's unusual nature was highlighted by the long time (70 days, as opposed to the more usual 20–30) taken to reach peak brightness. Observations of its X-ray emissions from NASA's Chandra space telescope confirmed SN2006gy to be a type II event. The star which exploded may have been 150 times bigger than the Sun, close to its theoretical maximum. Prior to the explosion, it shed a considerable amount of mass into the surrounding space.

The southern star Eta Carinae, 7,500 light years away in our own galaxy, is considered a likely candidate for a similar supernova explosion in the future. During the 19th century it brightened markedly and expelled material now seen as closely surrounding nebulosity.

MORE PLANETARY DISCOVERIES BEYOND THE SOLAR SYSTEM

The search for planets orbiting other stars continues to gather pace, with over 220 identified by the summer of 2007. A new addition to the array of instruments taking part in the search is the French Space Agency's COROT (convection rotation and planetary transits) telescope, launched on 27 December 2006. Weighing 630kg, the 4m-long COROT is built around a 30cm-diameter telescope designed to obtain precise measurements of light output from hundreds of thousands of stars during a 30-month mission. Exoplanets passing in front of (transiting) their host star should be revealed by a small dip in brightness. COROT is also designed to detect oscillations due to stellar pulsation. Its first exoplanet detection was reported early in May 2007.

Gaseous 'hot Jupiters' represent the vast majority of exoplanet discoveries to date, and existing instruments fall a little short of the sensitivity required to detect Earth-sized planets. Progress towards this goal should be made by NASA's *Kepler* satellite mission, due to launch late in 2008. Meanwhile, much excitement surrounded the discovery of a planet orbiting the star Gliese 581, at a distance of 20.5 light years in the constellation Libra, announced in April 2007. Designated Gliese 581c, the planet has a mass five times and a radius 50 per cent greater than that of Earth. Orbiting once every 13 days at a distance of 11 million km from the cool red dwarf primary star, Gliese 581c experiences temperatures in the range from 0 to 40°C.

ANTARCTIC OCEAN BIODIVERSITY REVEALED

While the shallower marine environments around Antarctica have been well explored, little has been known, until recently, about the fauna of the deep Southern Ocean surrounding the continent. Results from the international ANDEEP (Antarctic benthic deep-sea biodiversity) project were published in May 2007, detailing findings from three sampling expeditions to the Weddell Sea undertaken between 2002 and 2005. Environmental data and samples were collected from a variety of settings including the continental slope, channel levees and abyssal plain, with water depths ranging from 748 to 6,348m.

Among the findings were 674 species of isopods (a form of crustacean), 585 of which were previously unknown to science. Among 200 species of polychaete worms, 81 proved to be new discoveries, as were 17 of 76 sponge species collected. Contrary to previous assumptions, the fauna of the ocean depths surrounding Antarctica has been found to be remarkably diverse. Much of this richness appears to be supported by the delivery of nutrient-rich water from melting icebergs carved at the continental margins, encouraging growth of phytoplankton at the base of the food chain.

THE SUN IN THREE DIMENSIONS

With increasing dependence on satellites for communications and other activities, the need for better understanding of the Sun's influence on the near-Earth space environment has become clear. At times of high sunspot activity, coronal mass ejections (CMEs) propagating out from the Sun through interplanetary space can interact with Earth's magnetosphere to generate magnetic storms accompanied by spectacular auroral displays but also presenting hazards to satellites and even to power grid systems at ground-level.

Continuous monitoring of the Sun has been carried out using a number of spacecraft, notably the venerable SOHO (solar and heliospheric observatory) which has operated since 1995. Scientists studying 'space weather' now have, for the first time, the chance to observe CMEs and other events in the Sun's inner atmosphere in three dimensions following the launch of NASA's STEREO (solar terrestrial relations observatory) mission in October 2006.

STEREO consists of two 620kg spacecraft, equipped with coronagraph equipment to record observations of developing CMEs and manoeuvred into solar orbit to trail the Earth. STEREO observations can also be used to triangulate sources of radio noise in the solar atmosphere. First results from the mission, released in April 2007, reveal an unexpected fine structure, moulded by magnetic fields, just above the Sun's surface, possibly indicating an important source of activity further out in the corona. Observations, coordinated with those from SOHO, will continue for two years.

COPY NUMBER THE KEY TO HUMAN DIVERSITY

Completion in 2000 of the 3 billion basepair human genome sequence has provided scientists with a valuable tool for investigation of genetic variation between individuals. The most abundant variations are single nucleotide polymorphisms (SNPs), representing changes at the level of one basepair. More far-reaching however, was the discovery that differences in the number of copies of particular genes may be five to ten times more significant than SNPs.

The HapMap project, the first results of which were published in 2005, led to complete sequencing of genomes from 270 individuals from four human populations from China, Japan, Nigeria and the USA. Further examination of the data revealed 1,447 copy number variable regions (CNVRs), where chromosomal DNA may be duplicated or deleted. CNVRs cover both gene sequences coding for proteins, and regulatory DNA. More than half affect several genes and in stretches that may be a million basepairs long. The identified CNVRs cover around 360 million basepairs – about 12 per cent of the human genome.

GENOME SCREEN REVEALS DISEASE LINKS

The importance of the completed human genome sequence as a resource for medical research was always expected to be enormous. This potential is now starting to be realised as scientists carry out 'data mining', and apply the sequence to studies of common inherited diseases. Coupling the sequence with data from the HapMap project, it is now possible to screen for association between specific inherited single nucleotide polymorphisms, and the susceptibility to disease of individuals who carry them in their genomes. A major piece of research in this area has been carried out by British scientists with results reported in *Nature.*

The study looked for SNPs linked to seven common diseases: rheumatoid arthritis, hypertension, Crohn's disease, coronary artery disease, bipolar disorder and type 1 and type 2 diabetes. For each of these diseases, DNA from 2,000 affected individuals was tested against arrayed sets of the roughly 500,000 identified SNPs in the human genome. A control population of 3,000 unaffected individuals was similarly tested. All 17,000 samples came from white Europeans resident in Great Britain. The screen successfully identified twelve previously known gene associations involved in these diseases. A further twelve unknown genes were also highlighted by their increased SNP representation.

Among novel findings was the role of a gene (*IRGM*), involved in elimination of intracellular bacteria by the process of autophagy, in susceptibility to Crohn's disease, which causes chronic bowel inflammation. A surprise was the likely involvement of another gene, *PTNP2,* in both Crohn's disease and type 1 diabetes, suggesting a previously unsuspected overlap in the pathogenesis of the two inflammatory diseases.

MACAQUE GENOME OPENS UP INVESTIGATION OF HUMAN EVOLUTION

An Old World monkey, the rhesus macaque (*Macaca mulatta*) is one of our closest relatives after the great apes, having diverged from a common ancestor about 25 million years ago. Important in several areas of medical research, the macaque has become the third primate, after human and chimpanzee (*Pan troglodytes*) to have its genome sequence determined. The assembled sequence, totalling 2.87 billion basepairs of DNA, in which around 20,000 genes have been recognised, is arranged in 21 chromosomes. Alignment of DNA sequences for genes represented in both human and macaque shows 93.5 per cent identity.

The close correspondence between human and chimpanzee sequences (the two diverged a comparatively recent 6 million years ago) has presented some difficulties to researchers attempting to determine precisely which changes at DNA level make the two species different. Now having a third, more distant primate for comparison enables a process of genomic triangulation in which ancestral forms of genes are clearly defined.

Interestingly, it becomes apparent that some gene forms that we would associate with disease in humans correspond to the form in macaques which are perfectly healthy: the suggestion is that alterations in lifestyle (dietary changes, for example) have rendered the ancestral form deleterious in humans. Refinements of the genomic triangulation approach can be expected in the next few years, as further primates – notably gorilla, orangutan, gibbon and marmoset – join the burgeoning ranks of the sequenced.

FIRST MARSUPIAL GENOME SEQUENCE

In parallel with the great strides being made in sequencing primates, the field of comparative genomics should also benefit from completion of the first marsupial sequence. A draft sequence for the South American grey short-tailed opossum *Monodelphis domestica,* used for many years as a model laboratory animal for studies in neurobiology and developmental biology, was published in May 2007. Marsupials (metatherians), whose young are born at a very early stage of development, diverged from 'placental' mammals (eutherians) 180 million years ago, but initial analysis of the opossum genome sequence – 3.5 billion basepairs of DNA arranged on nine pairs of chromosomes – shows that of 19,000 protein-coding genes, 15,000 closely correspond with their counterparts in eutheria. Contrary to previous findings, genes for components of a well-developed immune system are present in the opossum. An interesting and perhaps very significant finding is that about 20 per cent of the conserved, non-coding 'junk' DNA in eutherians has arisen since the divergence from a common ancestor. Much of this can be traced to recognisable mobile elements (transposons), suggesting that these play an important part in driving evolutionary processes.

SEA URCHIN SURPRISES

Another organism with a key role in laboratory studies of developmental biology is the sea urchin, which shares a number of embryonic features with vertebrates. A series of papers published in a November 2006 issue of *Science* heralded completion of the genome sequence of the Californian purple sea urchin *Strongylocentrotus purpuratus.* Comprising 814 million basepairs of DNA, this encodes around 23,000 genes, including several formerly thought to be vertebrate innovations. Sequence analysis indicates the presence of orthologues for genes involved, in higher organisms, with hearing, balance and chemical sensing, suggesting that the humble sea urchin may have previously unsuspected sensory capabilities in addition to a remarkably complex immune system.

EARLIEST PLATE TECTONICS REVEALED

The Isua supracrustal belt, a 35km-long by 2.5km-thick geological feature in south-west Greenland, contains some of the oldest known rocks on Earth's surface, which are believed to have solidified from molten lava 3.8 billion years ago. A Norwegian study has revealed evidence that the process of sea-floor spreading – a key element in modern plate tectonics – operated at this early epoch, two billion years earlier than previously thought.

Sea-floor spreading occurs at, for example, the Mid-Atlantic Ridge, slowly pushing Europe and North

America apart as the respective plates of continental crust move over the semi-fluid mantle below. New crust extruded as magma from the underlying mantle emerges at mid-oceanic ridges, spreading laterally to form banded rocks known as ophiolites. The report described the discovery of ophiolites in sheeted dike structures, associated with pillow lava derived formations also characteristic of sea-floor spreading. Evidence has also been found for processes of subduction, where old crust is forced back down into the mantle under continental margins, although this is more ambiguous. It is clear that plate tectonics had become established as a process of creating and recycling Earth's crust as long as 4.6 billion years ago.

STEM CELL BREAKTHROUGH OFFERS HOPE OF BLINDNESS CURE

Macular degeneration affects around 500,000 people in the UK and is most commonly a disease of old age which results in loss of vision caused by the death of photoreceptor cells in the retina. Research on mice offers the hope of future cell transplant therapies to restore sight in patients suffering from macular degeneration and other conditions such as retinitis pigmentosa. In cases of the former, photoreceptors are lost from the retina's outer nuclear layer, leaving the neurons in the inner layer, which connect to the optic nerve, intact. Past attempts to restore visual function using transplanted mature retinal cells have failed as these are unable to connect to the existing neuronal network. Experiments in mice and rats using stem cells derived from brain and retina have also enjoyed limited success, as they fail to integrate into the outer nuclear layer or establish functional neuronal connections.

A breakthrough was reported in *Nature* in November 2006. Using transgenic blind mice, British and US scientists tested the effectiveness of retinal stem cells of differing ages. Progenitor cells were taken from the retinas of mouse embryos and from newborn mice over a range of one to fifteen days. Greatest success in integration of transplanted cells into host retinas and establishment of synaptic connections was found with progenitors from newborn mice aged between three to five days. These progenitor cells were harvested at a time coincident with the peak of production for rods (light-sensitive cells, which differ from the retina's colour-sensitive cones). Examination of the retinas of mice into which cells were successfully transplanted showed that the progenitors indeed went on to produce new rods. Effectiveness of the connection between the transplanted cells and the brainstem was demonstrated by restoration of pupillary constriction in response to stimulation with light.

The key outcome of this research is that timing is critical – harvesting stem cells at just the right developmental stage is vital to successful transplantation and subsequent integration and differentiation in the host retina. An obstacle to the use of this technique in human therapy is that the equivalent retinal stem cells appear during the second trimester of foetal development. This may be overcome by future work on gene expression patterns in laboratory-cultured stem cell lines.

CONTINUED SUCCESS FOR *CASSINI* AT SATURN

In orbit around Saturn since July 2000, the *Cassini* spacecraft is now more than halfway through its four-year mission. As planned, *Cassini*'s orbit has been modified to take it out of Saturn's equatorial plane, with the result that there have been fewer close fly-bys of the numerous satellites. Instead, the craft has produced stunning views of the planet's magnificent ring system seen, as never before, from above and below.

Observations of sunlight scattered through to the rings' unlit face have revealed a lot of fine structure, as have light measurements from stars as the rings pass in front of these from *Cassini's* perspective. The outer 'braided' F-ring has been shown to have multiple filaments, perturbed by embedded moonlets including Prometheus. The B-ring – the largest and densest – shows a remarkable, constantly changing clumpy structure. The space between these clumps is empty.

On the planet itself, *Cassini*'s spectrometer found a vast hexagonal cloud structure, 25,000km across and similar to Earth's polar vortices, at Saturn's north pole. In November 2006, mission scientists announced discovery at the south pole of an 8,000km-diameter storm, with winds up to 560km/h and a hurricane-like structure.

Analysis of data from past encounters suggests that the satellites Tethys and Dione are ejecting material, possibly as a result of cryovolcanism. *Cassini*'s encounters with Saturn's largest satellite, Titan (the second-largest in the Solar System) have continued. In January 2007, results were announced from a close fly-by on 22 July 2006, during which the *Cassini* Titan radar mapper surveyed a 6,130km swath of the satellite's northern regions. At latitudes north of 70 degrees, more than 75 radar-dark patches, ranging from 3 to 70km in diameter, were identified. Their smoothness strongly suggests that these are lakes of liquid methane. The existence of a postulated Titan-wide methane ocean was disproved by results from the *Huygens* probe (which landed on Titan's solid surface in January 2005) and earlier radar surveys. Nevertheless, lakes are perfectly possible, with methane playing a similar role in Titan's dense, nitrogen-rich atmosphere to that of water on Earth. A hydrological cycle with methane rain is also thought to operate on Titan. Several of the lakes identified by *Cassini* have sinuous channels leading into them, similar to features imaged during its descent by the *Huygens* lander. While some of the lakes are full to their apparent shoreline, others are less so, indicating possible seasonal variations – perhaps drying up during a local summer. Further observations in 2009–10 should confirm any seasonal influence on the extent of the lakes.

MARS UNDER CLOSE SCRUTINY

Far beyond their original projected 90-day lifespans, NASA's Mars exploration rovers continue to explore the Red Planet's surface. Since landing in January 2004, *Spirit* at Gusev crater and *Opportunity* in *Meridiani Terra* have covered distances in excess of 7 and 11km respectively. The rovers are showing signs of age – *Spirit* is dragging one of its six wheels and a similar problem has developed with one of *Opportunity's* robot arms. *Spirit* has uncovered a patch of silica-rich soil – providing further evidence for the past presence of water on Mars – while *Opportunity* continues its exploration of the 800m-diameter Victoria crater. Currently, operators are looking for a safe route down into the crater's interior.

On 2 November 2006, NASA's venerable *Mars Global Surveyor* (MGS) which has been orbiting the planet since 1997, was lost, apparently as the result of software problems. MGS has left a sizeable legacy of hundreds of thousands of detailed images of the Martian surface. Analysis of some of these has revealed at least 20 new impact craters, the largest around 50m in diameter, resulting from meteorite strikes. Considerable excitement surrounded the December 2006 announcement of evidence for recent water flows on the Martian surface, found on MGS images. Repeated imaging of kilometre-long gullies on Mars shows changes on timescales of 4–5 years. Bright deposits – thought to be surface frost – are seen in many cases; dust flows, on the other hand, appear dark. The flows in these gullies may be similar in nature to mudflows, and cannot travel far before their liquid content evaporates due to Mars' low atmospheric pressure.

VENUS ORBITER INVESTIGATES ATMOSPHERE OF EARTH'S 'TWIN'

Often described as Earth's twin – in terms of size and mass – Venus is a hostile world with a dense, corrosive atmosphere, and searing surface temperatures due to a runaway greenhouse effect. The ESA's *Venus Express* spacecraft has completed its first year in orbit since arriving at the planet in April 2006. The orbiter discovered a huge double vortex storm over Venus' south pole, and observed the oxygen airglow on the planet's night-side. Detailed analysis has been made of the planet's atmospheric chemistry and temperature profile.

On June 6 2007, *Venus Express* was briefly joined by NASA's *Messenger* probe, en route via several 'gravitational slingshot' manoeuvres to an October 2008 arrival at Mercury. Messenger flew 340km above the Venusian cloud-tops, and recorded more than 630 images and other data. The two spacecraft worked in tandem over a 30-hour period, during which data were also collected by Earth-based observatories and space telescopes in Earth orbit. Like *Mars Express, Venus Express* has had its mission extended to May 2009. With Venus, Mars and Saturn each under continuous scrutiny by orbiting spacecraft, and the *New Horizons* fly-by at Jupiter, there can surely never have been such an intensive period of close-up planetary exploration as we have seen in 2006–7.

THEATRE

Jane Edwardes

Audiences' appetite for a big night out remained undiminished. There are currently twenty-two musicals running in the West End. Last autumn saw an unprecedented number of openings including *Wicked*; *Spamalot*; *Cabaret*; *Caroline, or Change*; *Dirty Dancing*; *Porgy and Bess* and *The Sound of Music*. Of those, *Caroline, or Change* came to the end of its scheduled run, and *The Drowsy Chaperone* and *Porgy and Bess* closed for lack of an audience. The rest appear to have bedded in for the long haul. The revival of *The Sound of Music* attracted the most attention as producer Andrew Lloyd Webber looked to television to find his Maria much to the horror of professional performers. The TV reality show *How do you solve a problem like Maria?* attracted audiences of 8 million on Saturday night as the would-be stars submitted themselves to the criticisms of Lloyd Webber and his colleagues as well as the viewers' votes. The eventual winner was 22 year-old Welsh singer, Connie Fisher, who gained 1.4 million votes. She had, in fact, been to drama school, although like so many actors struggled to find work and was employed by a telesales company when she applied to take part in the show.

The competition created a huge amount of interest and *The Sound of Music* opened with a lot of advance ticket sales. It appeared to spark an interest in musicals among a whole new generation and to increase audiences across the board not just for Rodgers and Hammerstein. Playing at the London Palladium, the production was not without its problems. Simon Shepherd was replaced at the last minute by Alexander Hanson as Captain von Trapp and Fisher's standby was dropped when Fisher announced her determination to perform at all performances. She found, however, that her voice couldn't stand the strain and she was ordered to take time off much to the consternation of those who had followed Fisher's fortunes on TV and arrived at the theatre eager to see her onstage.

Inevitably the success of *How do you solve...* has led to imitations. Later in the year, Lloyd Webber set out on another hunt for a new Joseph in *Any Dream Will Do* for a revival of the Lloyd Webber/Tim Rice musical *Joseph and his Technicolor Dreamcoat* based on the production by the talented Steven Pimlott who sadly died during the year. Again, it was a professional actor who triumphed. In this case Lee Mead who had frequently understudied leading roles in the West End without ever getting to play them himself. Now his time has come.

Wicked was an American import, which arrived with high expectations given its reputation in New York. Based on Gregory Maguire's novel with music and lyrics by Stephen Schwartz, the musical explores the back story to *The Wizard of Oz*. Idina Menzel came over to play Elphaba, the green-skinned young girl who becomes the Wicked Witch of the West – only she's not wicked at all, more a defender of those the Wizard sought to repress. While in contrast, the pretty and spoilt Glinda, isn't always virtuous, especially when her numbskull boyfriend unexpectedly falls for Elphaba's green skin. The musical appealed especially to young girls. In contrast, *Dirty Dancing* is based on the movie that was required viewing for all those women, now in their 30s, who fell in love with Patrick Swayze as teenagers.

Those in search of something completely different piled in to see *Spamalot* based on *Monty Python and the Holy Grail*. This too, like *Wicked*, came from America although its roots dig deep into the history of British comedy. First Tim Curry, and then Simon Russell Beale played King Arthur, who solemnly pretends to ride a horse across the stage to the sound of banging coconuts while he survives encounters with a killer rabbit, abusive French soldiers and Knights who say 'Ni'.

Opening much later in the year, and on an even bigger scale than all its predecessors, was *The Lord of the Rings* at the Drury Lane Theatre Royal. The adaptation of JRR Tolkien's cult book has taken years out of the lives of those involved, including producer Kevin Wallace, director Matthew Warchus, musical director Christopher Nightingale and choreographer Peter Darling. The show first opened in Toronto where it received mixed reviews and was forced to close early. Sharing some of the dogged characteristics of Frodo and his friends, the production team persevered despite questions about whether it was good material for a musical and whether the popularity of the films had made a dramatic success unlikely. But they took stock, raised more money (the budget was £12.5m), tightened the script, re-worked the choreography, and opened in London in June. The reviews have not been helpful and it remains to be seen whether the book's many fans will ignore what they've read and buy tickets to see it regardless.

Caroline, or Change by Tony Kushner and Jeanine Tessori at the National Theatre scooped up several awards. It played on the word 'change' as it examined the relationship between a maid and her mistress's son, who always forgets to take his money out of his pockets, and the arrival of the civil rights movement at the beginning of the '60s in the southern states of America. Tonya Pinkins gave a fantastically powerful performance as the maid who can't quite embrace the changing times in George C. Wolfe's production.

With so many musicals playing in so many theatres, it's not surprising that the straight play had a hard time of it, a situation that most predict is only likely to get worse. Fortunately, there are producers like Sonia Friedman and Max Byam Shaw around who are determined that the play should not be squeezed out altogether. They have become increasingly inventive in their efforts to attract audiences for a different kind of entertainment. American film stars were thinner on the ground this year. Instead it was Daniel Radcliffe *(Equus)*, Maggie Smith *(The Lady from Dubuque)*, Rosamund Pike *(Gaslight)* and Billie Piper *(Treats)* who set the pace. There was huge excitement about the casting of Radcliffe in Peter Shaffer's *Equus* as the boy who unaccountably blinds a stable-full of horses, not least because the part required Radcliffe to remove all his clothes. The thought of Harry Potter naked was too much for some people to bear. Radcliffe performed respectably without ever suggesting he was a great actor in the making. He was up against Richard Griffiths as the psychiatrist who finds himself more in sympathy with primitive societies than with the mundanity of today.

Following the success of *Donkey's Years,* another avenue explored was that of the post-war farce. *See How They Run* with its huge number of vicars – a nostalgic trip back to the days when vicars were intrinsically funny – was quickly followed by *Boeing-Boeing* with its complicated plot involving Bernard, a man who makes himself a master of the airport timetable, as he three-times a trio of airhostesses. Mathew Warchus' production managed to stay airborne with the help of a sensational opening cast including Roger Allam, Frances de la Tour and Mark Rylance as Bernard's gormless old school friend. There was more comedy when Patrick Barlow's version of *The 39 Steps* transferred from the Tricycle into the Criterion Theatre based partly on John Buchan's book and partly on Alfred Hitchcock's film.

The new play that created the most noise was *Frost/Nixon* by Peter Morgan who has become famous for portraying real people on TV from Kenneth Williams to Tony Blair – most of them played by Michael Sheen. *Frost/Nixon,* first seen at the Donmar Warehouse, was Morgan's first play for the stage and focused on the famous TV interviews in which David Frost managed to coax an apology out of ex-president Nixon for his role in the Watergate affair. Morgan showed two men desperately trying to save their careers – at the time Frost's career appeared to be in freefall and he was prepared to spend money he didn't have in order to nail the ex-president. Morgan invents a late night telephone call in which the drunken Nixon points out that they are fighting a battle that only one of them can win. The production transferred into the West End with Sheen as Frost and Frank Langella as Nixon, before crossing the Atlantic to Broadway where Langella won a Tony award.

The RSC was in a festive mood as it emerged from all its troubles of the previous years under the dynamic leadership of Michael Boyd. A large deficit was paid off and planning permission was finally granted to all but re-build of the theatre in Stratford, with a complete re-configuration of the auditorium and the addition of a tower from which visitors will be able to survey the surrounding Warwickshire countryside, where Shakespeare once roamed. While the work goes on, a temporary Courtyard Theatre has been added to the back of the old Other Place. In addition, in April 2006 the company embarked on its most ambitious project ever – staging all the plays and poetry of William Shakespeare. Fifteen of the productions in the complete works were staged by the RSC and the festival was also a platform for international artists such as Peter Stein and Yukio Ninagawa. Companies from Germany, Japan, Poland, South Africa, India, Russia, South America, USA, Italy, China and the Middle East all took part. Joining them were some of the UK's most exciting theatre artists and interpreters of Shakespeare, with companies including Propeller, Kneehigh and Forkbeard Fantasy, all participating. Highlights were Marianne Elliott's production of *Much Ado About Nothing* with an award winning Tamsin Greig as Beatrice and Rupert Goold's production of *The Tempest* with Patrick Stewart. Tim Supple's production of *A Midsummer Night's Dream* consisted of a cast of actors drawn from all over India some of whom had never worked on a Shakespearean play before. The text was partly spoken in English but also in 7 other languages including Bengali and Malayalam. For some the culmination was Trevor Nunn's production of *King Lear* with Ian McKellen as Lear, a man painfully aware of his fading powers. The press was most interested in the fact that McKellen, like Daniel Radcliffe, was stripping off during the storm scene. His fame as Gandalf will surely prove a draw as *Lear* and *The Seagull* tour all over the world next year.

The Royal Court was also celebrating as its 50th anniversary came to an end. The final production of – once again – *The Seagull* was also the end of Ian Rickson's tenure as artistic director. It was one of his finest achievements with Kristin Scott Thomas as Arkadina, a brilliant Katherine Parkinson as Masha, and, improbably, Mackenzie Crook from *The Office* as Konstantin. The play's final moment, when Arkadina was caught in a beam of light just as she lifts her head to hear that her son has shot himself, was unforgettable. Since Dominic Cooke took over the Royal Court, there have been considerable changes. At his opening press conference he announced that there was to be less 'cultural tourism' by which he means the affluent classes coming to the theatre to see plays about the dispossessed. Not that those plays will disappear completely, rather that they will be balanced by plays that explore the ruling classes and are maybe rather more uncomfortable for the Royal Court's audience to watch. Cooke began with a series of little known or first time writers upstairs and, in the case of Mike Bartlett, in the main theatre. For his tense play *My Child* director Sasha Wares and designer Miriam Buether transformed the auditorium of the court into a claustrophobic tunnel in which the audience stood as the actors emerged out of the crowd to tell a painful story of a father who tries to maintain a relationship with his son against all odds. Finally, Cooke himself directed a stinging satire on liberal, affluent America in *The Pain and the Itch* by Bruce Norris. A rich couple, Clay and Kelly, who are very quick to judge others, fail to realise their own hypocrisies. The rot in the family is symbolised by the fact that their five-year-old daughter is suffering from a painful rash and that something is gnawing the avocados. The funniest confrontations are between the eastern-European girlfriend of Clay's brother, who was raped as a child but who shocks Clay and Kelly with her attempts to daub their daughter in make-up, her relish for playing with guns, and, inevitably, by lighting up in the sitting room.

The National had an eventful year. Artistic director Nicholas Hytner was busy leading from the front with productions of *The Alchemist, The Rose Tattoo* (he stepped in when Steven Pimlott died), *The Man of Mode* and *Rafta, Rafta...* . For the last, Ayub Khan-Din adapted Bill Naughton's comedy *All in Good Time* and gave it an Asian spin, locating it in an Indian community in Bolton. Gloriously funny, it was very specifically marketed to the Asian community with considerable success. *The Man of Mode* also used the convention of the arranged marriage to update a Restoration comedy, with Rory Kinnear making his mark once more as the ridiculous fop with a great deal more money than sense.

There was some discussion of the benefits of adapting a novel or film for the stage. Marianne Elliott directed Nicholas Wright's adaptation of *Thérèse Raquin,* a novel that's no stranger to transposition. Elliott struggled to create the claustrophobia of the French bourgeois household on the large Lyttelton stage but her production was memorable for the way that the two guilty lovers choreographically tossed and turned on the floor unable to celebrate their marriage. Katie Mitchell, who had a controversial year, bravely took on the seemingly impossible task of adapting *The Waves,* Virginia Woolf's study of a group of friends from 1893 to the 1930s.

Mitchell illustrated Woolf's dramatic soliloquies by using the actors onstage to create a series of images on screen. Mitchell then went on to direct *The Seagull* which so fractured Chekhov's play, transposing it confusingly into the 1920s, that it was hard to feel any engagement with the characters. Finally, there was her revival of Martin Crimp's 1997 play, *Attempts on Her Life,* in which she once again used video in order to stage Crimp's portrait of our media-saturated culture. That production divided audiences like Marmite, there were those who felt it heralded the future of theatre and others who were bored rigid by the lack of a narrative.

Mitchell is a provocative director. Some love the intellectual rigour and obvious integrity of her work; some wish she would allow the plays to speak more for themselves. The National's third adaptation, *A Matter of Life and Death,* directed by Emma Rice from Kneehigh, provoked quite a storm. It was based on the classic film by Powell and Pressburger, in which an airman during the Second World War should by all accounts have died as he leapt out of his burning plane without a parachute. As he prepares to jump, he makes contact with a radio operator with whom he instantly falls in love. His only problem is that a bureaucratic Heaven is determined to track him down in order to keep their books in order. In the film, Peter pleads that love should triumph over death. In the play, he is rather confronted with the desolation of war illustrated by the First World War in which his father fought, and the bombing of Dresden. If this was a leap too far for some, the company produced some ravishing images on stage. Few will forget the sight of Tristan Sturrock and Lyndsey Marshal swinging gently and erotically on a giant bed, and a game of table tennis in which the players were carried by other performers as they dived in slow motion for the ball in a play in which time is always relative.

The reviews for *Life and Death* prompted a big bust up between Nicholas Hytner and the male critics. The day after the first night he was interviewed by a *Times* reporter and confessed that he had had enough of the 'dead white males' who by and large loathed the show and predicted that the Sunday critics, mostly female, would be kinder. In the event, he was right in that Susannah Clapp in *The Observer* was hugely enthusiastic. Hytner made some ill-judged comments about the misogyny of the 'dead white males' who, he stated, dominated the critical fraternity claiming that Mitchell and Rice were picked on because of their gender. Hytner was heavily criticised by those who felt most under attack – Benedict Nightingale, Michael Billington, Charles Spencer – who are used to dishing it out but clearly didn't like being criticised themselves. The director later withdrew his comments about misogyny but stuck to his guns on the issue of whether the older theatre critics recognised modern references and possessed the same visual literacy as the younger generation. Critics, he felt, should get out more. Good relations were re-established but it was clear that Hytner's criticisms had struck a nerve at a time when critics feel increasingly under threat from the internet and are wondering whether there is any longer a place for the well-informed expert who has devoted his or her life to studying the art form. Hytner himself showed that he was in touch with new developments when he supported Punchdrunk's *Faust* set in an old warehouse in Wapping, in which the audience wandered from floor to floor, haphazardly making contact with a dramatisation of the Faust story transposed to the Bible Belt of America. Many people returned again and again in order to make sure that they saw the full story, and to give themselves time to explore the installations dotted throughout the vast building.

The final major production by the National was a revival of *Philistines* immaculately directed by Howard Davies. Gorky, writing at the same time as Chekhov, caught the political mood just before the 1905 revolution as his young people enthusiastically support the workers while the older people feel that their way of life is being swept away forever. Gorky presented these struggles within a family dominated by Phil Davis as the Steptoe-like father who greedily clings to his possessions while his own children fall into depression and their lodgers welcome the changes. A terrific cast was led by Davis and Rory Kinnear as the son who longs to escape but doesn't quite have it in him.

It was a difficult year for arts funding despite an upbeat speech from Tony Blair at the Tate Modern a few months prior to his departure. Arts organisations are largely pessimistic about the future. In addition, the Arts Lottery Fund has been raided to support the Olympics. Battersea Arts Centre had to fight not to become a victim of Wandsworth's determination to keep its council tax low at the expense of the provision of arts facilities for the locals. It was also impossible to interest the Department of Culture, Media and Sport in the fate of the popular Theatre Museum after the announcement by its parent body, the Victoria and Albert Museum (V&A), that it would close in January 2007, and that the contents would be moved to a new gallery at the V&A in Kensington. Their action followed the news that the Heritage lottery had rejected an application to improve the current site in Covent Garden. Supporters of the museum claim that it has been treated as a poor relation by the parent body, not allowed to raise funds of its own and starved of funds from within. In spite of its difficulties, the Theatre Museum has been able to expand its holdings enormously during its existence, with many items donated on the express understanding that they would form part of an independent Theatre Museum collection. A campaign continues to fight for a separate building.

In contrast, there was great jubilation when the Young Vic reopened on the Cut after two years of Walkabout co-producing 22 shows over 22 months with 20 companies across the UK and internationally. The theatre was first built on The Cut just down the road from the Old Vic, on a bomb-site where 54 people sheltering in a bakery had died during the Second World War. The building was erected at a cost of £60,000 and was intended to last for just five years. For many years the fabric of the theatre had been crumbling, and artistic director David Lan invited Haworth Tompkins to redesign and extend the building to include two small additional theatres as well as adequate backstage facilities for administrative staff, technicians, and performers. Steve Tompkins, who has already had great success with the development of the Royal Court in Sloane Square and two temporary buildings for the Almeida, decided to keep the old butcher's shop and to attach the foyers and small theatres alongside. The £12.5m building, for which Haworth Tompkins has won the inaugural RIBA London Building of the Year award, is contemporary and informal, fashioned out of inexpensive materials in keeping with the theatre's youthful audience. The theatre itself is largely unchanged but has a higher roof in order to provide more technical facilities and a pair of double doors at the back which make it easier to bring scenery in from the workshop and also allow for an opening up of the space during performances if required. Most striking from the outside is Clem Crosby's vast yellow painted mural covered in a metal mesh which changes its appearance according to the time of day, providing a glowing presence on the Cut in the evening when the lights are switched on. The opening production of *Tobias and the Angel*, a community opera by Jonathan Dove and David Lan, was a joyous affair and it featured, alongside professional singers and musicians, choruses and choirs of all ages drawn from the local area.

AWARDS

2007 LAURENCE OLIVIER AWARDS

Best New Musical – *Caroline, or Change*; book and lyrics by Tony Kushner, music by Jeanine Tessori at the National Theatre, Lyttelton

Best Actress in a Musical – Jenna Russell for *Sunday in the Park with George* at Wyndham's Theatre

Best Actor in a Musical – Daniel Evans for *Sunday in the Park with George* at Wyndham's Theatre

Best New Play – *Blackbird* by David Harrower at the Albery

Best New Comedy – John Buchan's *The 39 Steps*; adapted by Patrick Barlow from an original concept by Simon Corble and Nobby Dimon at the Criterion

Best Revival – *The Crucible* by Arthur Miller at the Gielgud

Best Performance in a Supporting Role – Jim Norton for *The Seafarer* at the Cottesloe

Outstanding Achievement in Opera – Amanda Roocroft for her performance in English National Opera's *Jenufa* at the London Coliseum

Best New Opera Production – English National Opera's *Jenufa* at the London Coliseum

Best Director – Dominic Cooke for *The Crucible* at the Gielgud

Outstanding Achievement in an Affiliate Theatre – *Pied Piper* at Theatre Royal, Stratford East

The Society's Special Award – Sir John Tomlinson

Outstanding Musical Production – *Sunday in the Park with George*, music and lyrics by Stephen Sondheim, book by James Lapine at Wyndham's

Best Actor – Rufus Sewell for *Rock 'n' Roll* at the Jerwood Theatre Downstairs at the Royal Court and the Duke of York's

Best Actress – Tamsin Greig for *Much Ado About Nothing* at the Novello

Outstanding Achievement in Dance – Carlos Acosta for his programme of work and his performances at Sadler's Wells

Best New Dance Production – The Royal Ballet's *Chroma* at the Royal Opera House

Best Set Design – *Sunday in the Park with George* designed by David Farley and Timothy Bird at Wyndham's

Best Costume Design – *The Voysey Inheritance* designed by Alison Chitty at the Lyttelton

Best Performance in a Supporting Role in a Musical – Sheila Hancock for *Cabaret* at the Lyric

Best Theatre Choreographer – Javier De Frutos for *Cabaret* at the Lyric

Best Sound Design – *Waves* designed by Gareth Fry at the National Theatre Cottesloe

Best Lighting Design – *Sunday in the Park with George* designed by Natasha Chivers and Mike Robertson at Wyndham's

CRITICS' CIRCLE AWARDS FOR 2006

Best New Play – *Rock 'n' Roll* by Tom Stoppard

Best Actor – Rufus Sewell for *Rock 'n' Roll*

Best Actress – Kathleen Turner for *Who's Afraid of Virginia Woolf*

The John and Wendy Trewin Award for Best Shakespearean Performance – Tamsin Greig for *Much Ado About Nothing*

Best Director – John Tiffany for *Black Watch*

The Peter Hepple Award for Best Musical – *Caroline, or Change* by Tony Kushner/Jeanine Tessori

Most Promising Playwright – Nina Raine for *Rabbit*

Best Designer – Punchdrunk Company for *Faust*

The Jack Tinker Award for Most Promising Newcomer (other than a playwright) – Connie Fisher for *The Sound of Music* and Andrew Garfield for *Citizenship* and *The Overwhelming*

EVENING STANDARD THEATRE AWARDS FOR 2006

Best Play – *Rock 'n' Roll* by Tom Stoppard

Best Actor – Rufus Sewell for *Rock 'n' Roll*

Best Actress – Kathleen Turner for *Who's Afraid of Virginia Woolf*

The Sydney Edwards Award for Best Director – Marianne Elliott for *Pillars of the Community*

Best Musical – *Caroline, or Change*

Best Design – Timothy Bird (projection design) and David Farley (set and costume design) for *Sunday in the Park with George*

The Milton Shulman Award for Outstanding Newcomer – Andrew Garfield for *Beautiful Thing; Burn/Chatroom/Citizenship*; *The Overwhelming*

Special Award – The Tricycle for its pioneering work in political theatre

WEATHER

AVERAGE AND GENERAL MONTHLY VALUES 2006–7

Figures given for 1971–2000 are long-term averages. The rest are total rainfall, mean temperature and total hours of sunshine.

	Rainfall (mm)				*Temperature (°C)*				*Total Sunshine (hrs)*			
	1971–2000	2005	2006	2007	1971–2000	2005	2006	2007	1971–2000	2005	2006	2007
ENGLAND AND WALES												
January	94.4	68	35.0	110.5	3.8	5.7	4.0	6.6	49.4	—	51.0	60.5
February	67.4	50	56.3	100.9	3.9	4.0	3.6	5.8	67.1	—	68.3	70.4
March	73.7	53	88.8	64.5	5.8	6.7	4.6	6.9	101.4	—	99.4	156.3
April	60.8	76	46.0	12.3	7.6	8.6	8.2	10.8	145.6	—	160.3	224.7
May	59.2	45	112.1	110.5	10.7	11.0	11.7	11.6	189.5	—	178.5	174.3
June	66.0	56	24.8	144.3	13.5	15.0	15.4	14.6	177.7	—	240.4	156.9
July	57.5	66.3	43.1		15.9	16.3	19.1		191.3	178.4	287.6	
August	72.1	59.5	90.2		15.7	15.8	15.9		182.0	210.6	151.4	
September	80.3	68.4	74.9		13.2	14.8	16.3		133.7	150.6	157.5	
October	93.1	121.9	117.7		10.0	12.7	12.6		99.8	81.1	95.6	
November	93.5	90.0	110.2		6.5	6.0	7.9		63.8	90.9	93.1	
December	101.7	68.7	129.8		4.7	4.3	6.1		42.7	57.0	45.8	
SCOTLAND												
January	170.5	240	109.1	240.2	2.4	4.4	3.3	4.6	30.8	—	34.4	35.7
February	123.4	110	85.2	131.9	2.5	3.0	3.0	4.1	58.1	—	63.6	61.1
March	138.5	108	136.4	135.0	3.9	5.6	2.5	5.2	87.6	—	73.0	120.2
April	86.2	113	109.3	50.6	5.7	6.7	5.8	8.9	128.2	—	175.4	189.0
May	79.0	115	112.1	135.2	8.6	8.3	8.9	8.8	173.2	—	199.2	191.3
June	85.1	105	72.6	112.0	11.0	12.4	12.7	11.9	153.2	—	189.3	133.8
July	92.1	48.9	70.5		13.0	13.4	15.6		145.0	144.2	195.4	
August	107.4	133.8	96.6		12.8	13.1	13.3		137.5	143.4	116.5	
September	139.7	139.9	149.2		10.6	12.0	13.3		104.4	101.9	112.2	
October	162.6	183.9	195.9		7.9	9.8	9.9		74.5	59.8	69.2	
November	165.9	173.2	240.8		4.7	4.7	6.1		43.2	55.4	52.8	
December	169.6	98.2	262.2		3.1	3.7	4.4		24.7	30.4	38.3	

Source: Data provided by the Met Office

WIND FORCE MEASURES

The Beaufort Scale of wind force has been accepted internationally and is used in communicating weather conditions. Devised originally by Admiral Sir Francis Beaufort in 1805, it now consists of the numbers 0–17, each representing a certain strength or velocity of wind at 10m (33ft) above ground in the open.

Scale No.	*Wind Force*	*mph*	*knots*
0	Calm	1	1
1	Light air	1–3	1–3
2	Slight breeze	4–7	4–6
3	Gentle breeze	8–12	7–10
4	Moderate breeze	13–18	11–16
5	Fresh breeze	19–24	17–21
6	Strong breeze	25–31	22–27
7	High wind	32–38	28–33
8	Gale	39–46	34–40
9	Strong gale	47–54	41–47
10	Whole gale	55–63	48–55
11	Storm	64–72	56–63
12	Hurricane	73–82	64–71
13	–	83–92	72–80
14	–	93–103	81–89
15	–	104–114	90–99
16	–	115–125	100–108
17	–	126–136	109–118

TEMPERATURE, RAINFALL AND SUNSHINE

At selected climatological stations, July 2006 – June 2007

Ht — height of station above mean sea level
°C — mean air temperature
Rain — total monthly rainfall
Sun — monthly total

	Ht	*July 2006*			*August 2006*			*September 2006*			*October 2006*		
	m	*Temp. °C*	*Rain mm*	*Sun hrs*	*Temp. °C*	*Rain mm*	*Sun hrs*	*Temp. °C*	*Rain mm*	*Sun hrs*	*Temp. °C*	*Rain mm*	*Sun hrs*
Lerwick	82	13.4	69.0	146.3	12.9	70.0	106.2	12.5	91.8	50.4	9.6	183.6	77.7
Stornoway	15	14.9	55.4	140.4	13.4	59.6	64.7	14.0	87.2	88.6	11.3	168.6	48.0
Dyce	65	16.9	18.4	199.0	14.4	49.8	81.3	14.1	52.2	122.6	11.1	137.8	69.5
Eskdalemuir	242	16.2	81.0	200.2	13.3	76.2	98.5	13.2	181.6	94.6	9.9	159.2	47.9
Aldergrove	68	17.3	90.0	220.2	14.4	96.0	86.8	14.5	92.6	97.1	11.7	77.4	85.5
Bingley	64	17.9	27.4	—	14.0	151.3	—	14.5	136.0	—	11.0	185.4	—
Valley	10	17.7	10.8	277.8	15.3	88.0	146.6	15.9	77.2	155.1	13.3	123.4	116.4
Coleshill	—	20.0	27.8	—	16.0	68.2	—	16.4	81.2	—	12.4	84.8	—
Skegness	6	18.2	19.9	—	15.4	103.2	—	15.8	92.6	—	11.9	65.2	—
Bristol	42	20.1	58.0	294.4	16.9	48.0	149.1	16.7	69.8	150.5	13.4	85.3	76.0
St Mawgan	103	18.3	33.8	255.1	16.2	52.4	209.7	16.1	44.4	163.3	13.6	115.8	111.8
Hastings	45	20.9	16.5	340.0	17.3	103.6	213.6	18.1	63.6	192.9	15.1	117.6	134.8

	Ht	*November 2006*			*December 2006*			*January 2007*			*February 2007*		
	m	*Temp. °C*	*Rain mm*	*Sun hrs*	*Temp. °C*	*Rain mm*	*Sun hrs*	*Temp. °C*	*Rain mm*	*Sun hrs*	*Temp. °C*	*Rain mm*	*Sun hrs*
Lerwick	82	7.3	204.6	35.0	6.7	165.2	15.6	4.7	194.8	29.3	4.5	153.9	49.6
Stornoway	15	7.7	124.1	28.7	7.1	177.6	15.6	6.1	193.5	18.0	5.9	99.4	51.0
Dyce	65	7.4	68.6	85.0	4.0	29.8	88.0	5.6	48.8	57.0	4.8	114.0	61.7
Eskdalemuir	242	6.1	285.0	40.7	4.0	331.4	29.5	4.8	286.9	37.2	3.5	125.2	59.9
Aldergrove	68	7.2	84.6	73.2	5.9	90.0	50.5	6.1	79.6	56.6	5.2	71.4	70.0
Bingley	64	6.9	145.2	—	5.4	247.2	—	5.5	175.9	—	3.2	77.2	—
Valley	10	10.1	127.6	58.4	8.4	140.0	41.1	8.3	88.8	58.5	6.4	39.6	83.6
Coleshill	—	7.9	53.0	—	6.4	80.6	—	7.1	67.6	—	5.5	86.0	—
Skegness	6	7.2	52.0	—	6.4	35.8	—	6.8	52.8	—	5.8	45.4	—
Bristol	42	8.6	99.4	95.7	7.2	94.6	41.9	7.7	120.2	55.9	6.7	75.9	62.7
St Mawgan	103	10.0	129.1	105.4	8.5	101.7	70.8	8.6	81.8	58.2	8.0	163.0	70.2
Hastings	45	10.5	58.4	128.5	7.7	99.5	54.1	7.6	71.1	79.7	7.2	100.3	79.9

	Ht	*March 2007*			*April 2007*			*May 2007*			*June 2007*		
	m	*Temp. °C*	*Rain mm*	*Sun hrs*	*Temp. °C*	*Rain mm*	*Sun hrs*	*Temp. °C*	*Rain mm*	*Sun hrs*	*Temp. °C*	*Rain mm*	*Sun hrs*
Lerwick	82	5.6	107.7	118.4	7.2	58.6	111.8	7.7	58.6	182.5	10.0	12.4	121.4
Stornoway	15	6.5	116.8	129.6	9.5	53.8	157.6	9.0	143.2	172.9	11.8	35.0	205.5
Dyce	65	6.4	33.8	139.9	10.0	27.0	179.4	9.5	116.2	156.8	11.5	109.0	79.0
Eskdalemuir	242	4.9	137.0	95.1	8.5	40.0	173.8	9.0	146.7	127.0	12.4	137.6	85.6
Aldergrove	68	6.1	46.0	129.6	10.5	18.2	194.5	10.9	44.2	202.2	13.7	93.8	131.4
Bingley	64	5.4	59.6	—	9.4	8.4	—	9.9	91.0	—	13.1	282.6	—
Valley	10	7.6	41.0	149.0	10.9	13.8	227.4	11.8	44.2	203.7	14.8	78.4	169.9
Coleshill	—	6.9	64.0	—	11.7	7.6	—	11.5	19.6	—	15.0	138.0	—
Skegness	6	5.5	33.7	—	9.3	2.5	—	11.0	93.3	—	—	—	—
Bristol	42	7.5	49.4	150.2	12.1	5.4	226.6	12.4	130.8	178.9	15.7	107.2	146.2
St Mawgan	103	8.1	88.7	166.2	11.6	20.2	226.1	12.1	115.6	204.5	14.8	115.4	146.3
Hastings	45	8.7	41.2	193.3	13.0	0.0	277.4	13.3	93.7	204.5	15.9	115.6	206.8

Source: Data provided by the Met Office

METEOROLOGICAL OBSERVATIONS LONDON *(Heathrow)*

Temperature maxima and minima cover the 24-hour period 9 to 9h; mean wind speed is 10m above ground; rainfall is for the 24 hours starting on 9h on the day of entry; sunshine is for the 24 hours. *Source:* the Met Office

JULY 2006

	Temperature Max (°C)	Min (°C)	*Wind* knots	*Rain* mm	*Sun* hrs
Day 1	29.7	16.3	6.1	0.0	11.5
2	32.3	19.1	6.5	0.0	11.7
3	31.4	18.4	6.7	0.0	14.0
4	31.3	18.0	5.9	1.4	9.9
5	21.9	19.0	6.1	2.6	0.8
6	25.4	17.0	9.5	trace	3.3
7	22.8	16.8	8.8	0.2	2.7
8	23.5	13.3	9.9	2.4	4.8
9	23.9	14.6	13.5	trace	4.7
10	23.4	14.1	8.3	1.2	1.0
11	25.2	16.1	6.7	0.0	10.0
12	27.6	12.9	5.5	0.0	14.4
13	23.6	14.4	6.7	0.0	4.3
14	24.0	12.3	10.3	0.0	14.3
15	26.3	13.7	8.8	0.0	11.3
16	30.5	14.3	6.7	0.0	14.1
17	32.7	16.1	4.8	0.0	14.3
18	33.2	17.4	6.4	0.0	14.7
19	35.5	18.9	8.0	trace	12.2
20	31.7	19.6	10.5	0.0	10.4
21	31.7	17.9	6.1	3.2	11.8
22	29.5	19.8	5.9	1.2	3.3
23	26.5	16.7	5.9	trace	3.3
24	30.0	15.7	5.6	0.0	9.5
25	33.0	16.8	6.4	trace	11.9
26	32.7	19.9	6.2	2.0	7.8
27	30.3	19.2	5.2	8.6	6.0
28	29.1	17.3	4.5	0.0	8.5
29	26.7	16.3	12.0	0.4	7.8
30	25.8	17.9	10.1	trace	7.4
31	24.2	16.6	12.9	0.4	4.7

AUGUST 2006

	Temperature Max (°C)	Min (°C)	*Wind* knots	*Rain* mm	*Sun* hrs
Day 1	22.9	14.3	12.5	trace	3.3
2	23.2	13.6	11.3	0.6	5.4
3	21.1	14.1	8.6	0.2	3.8
4	23.0	12.1	4.9	0.0	2.9
5	27.1	14.7	3.8	0.0	10.6
6	28.2	17.2	4.9	trace	3.6
7	23.5	18.8	6.3	0.2	0.0
8	26.1	10.0	5.9	0.4	11.0
9	23.4	14.9	7.7	0.0	6.9
10	21.0	12.4	8.6	0.4	4.2
11	21.7	12.1	8.9	trace	2.6
12	19.0	14.5	8.5	2.2	1.3
13	18.7	13.2	5.1	26.8	0.9
14	19.3	12.0	5.1	0.4	0.2
15	21.9	13.5	6.8	0.0	2.4
16	22.5	11.5	5.5	5.4	4.2
17	24.2	14.7	6.8	6.4	5.7
18	20.9	15.0	7.4	2.2	3.1
19	22.3	14.5	10.0	2.6	7.7
20	20.5	15.3	10.4	0.4	0.6
21	22.6	12.8	7.8	0.4	4.5
22	22.4	10.7	5.9	trace	5.7
23	20.9	15.6	7.8	9.4	0.1
24	21.4	14.6	5.7	0.0	2.2
25	22.7	10.2	5.1	5.0	8.0
26	21.2	13.7	6.2	trace	1.2
27	21.6	12.8	11.0	4.2	10.1
28	20.0	13.2	n/a	0.2	7.0
29	19.4	11.8	8.7	1.4	8.8
30	21.0	9.8	7.9	trace	8.7
31	23.6	15.2	11.2	0.0	3.5

SEPTEMBER 2006

	Temperature Max (°C)	Min (°C)	*Wind* knots	*Rain* mm	*Sun* hrs
Day 1	23.3	14.7	9.7	0.2	4.0
2	20.7	14.3	n/a	1.0	0.0
3	26.6	16.0	n/a	trace	5.7
4	24.7	14.5	n/a	trace	4.3
5	25.7	18.3	n/a	0.0	0.9
6	26.5	17.2	8.2	trace	7.8
7	21.3	13.3	7.6	0.0	10.6
8	21.2	9.8	7.5	0.0	12.2
9	22.7	11.9	7.3	0.0	7.4
10	27.1	11.0	5.0	0.0	11.6
11	30.2	14.0	5.9	1.8	7.3
12	20.9	16.1	4.1	4.6	0.0
13	24.0	16.4	6.6	16.2	3.5
14	20.6	16.8	6.4	2.4	0.6
15	22.4	14.7	7.7	0.0	4.9
16	21.3	15.9	5.3	0.0	0.1
17	24.1	15.4	6.2	trace	8.8
18	21.2	15.2	n/a	trace	5.0
19	20.3	13.0	11.0	0.0	9.0
20	22.9	11.5	12.2	0.0	7.8
21	27.8	16.5	11.9	3.4	9.6
22	18.5	15.8	7.0	15.6	2.1
23	23.5	12.9	6.4	5.0	8.6
24	22.6	16.0	6.1	0.6	6.7
25	19.7	15.4	4.8	5.4	0.1
26	21.3	11.7	5.6	0.0	8.9
27	19.9	12.2	9.4	trace	0.8
28	20.1	15.9	8.4	4.8	0.4
29	19.9	15.9	8.9	5.8	0.6
30	19.4	11.8	8.6	11.4	4.6

OCTOBER 2006

	Temperature Max (°C)	Min (°C)	*Wind* knots	*Rain* mm	*Sun* hrs
Day 1	19.5	15.1	12.0	2.0	4.5
2	18.6	13.3	11.6	6.8	4.7
3	17.3	9.0	7.8	0.2	6.4
4	17.2	7.6	7.2	trace	8.0
5	17.0	7.6	10.0	5.4	0.1
6	18.5	13.0	13.9	4.6	0.8
7	16.8	9.5	10.8	0.0	9.0
8	18.1	9.3	8.3	0.4	5.4
9	21.0	12.8	8.0	0.2	1.6
10	21.5	15.2	6.9	3.2	1.8
11	19.6	14.5	6.2	8.4	0.8
12	18.3	8.6	5.5	0.0	8.7
13	19.2	9.5	3.5	0.4	4.4
14	18.9	9.2	6.3	0.0	2.4
15	17.6	12.6	8.6	0.0	5.2
16	19.5	10.6	6.8	0.2	6.6
17	17.3	10.3	6.4	0.4	0.1
18	18.6	13.5	6.1	2.0	2.2
19	17.8	14.7	11.9	4.2	1.2
20	17.8	13.1	10.5	0.4	4.7
21	18.2	13.1	11.3	0.2	5.0
22	16.2	12.1	10.6	7.4	0.0
23	13.8	10.9	6.8	14.2	0.9
24	15.1	10.9	7.4	0.6	3.6
25	16.7	8.1	8.7	2.6	0.0
26	19.5	12.3	11.6	0.2	2.7
27	15.9	5.9	6.0	0.4	3.5
28	17.3	9.5	9.7	trace	0.0
29	16.4	13.0	5.2	0.0	7.8
30	16.9	10.1	7.6	trace	0.1
31	14.6	11.9	13.0	trace	4.1

NOVEMBER 2006

	Temperature Max (°C)	Min (°C)	*Wind* knots	*Rain* mm	*Sun* hrs
Day 1	10.2	3.7	6.8	0.0	8.3
2	9.7	0.6	4.0	0.0	8.5
3	11.8	-0.4	3.0	0.2	8.2
4	11.9	-0.4	4.3	0.0	7.0
5	13.5	1.5	5.7	0.2	5.5
6	13.0	1.9	2.9	0.2	6.5
7	10.3	3.0	3.2	trace	0.3
8	15.0	5.8	7.7	0.4	0.0
9	11.8	5.3	4.6	0.0	8.0
10	12.8	1.2	6.6	6.8	1.2
11	11.2	5.6	11.7	trace	2.1
12	14.2	6.4	8.8	0.8	2.1
13	16.1	7.9	13.4	trace	1.9
14	14.4	11.1	10.7	1.0	0.0
15	15.4	11.5	11.5	5.6	1.3
16	11.2	10.3	8.0	2.2	0.1
17	13.1	5.4	11.0	19.4	0.7
18	10.5	4.1	8.1	0.0	7.4
19	12.4	1.1	7.8	7.2	6.6
20	13.4	3.5	10.8	3.0	0.6
21	8.5	5.7	11.4	trace	5.3
22	12.8	4.1	9.8	9.8	0.0
23	12.9	6.3	13.4	0.4	4.9
24	15.1	5.7	11.1	7.4	0.1
25	13.6	9.6	12.8	10.4	1.5
26	13.3	7.7	10.5	13.4	0.4
27	14.6	9.2	12.8	7.8	1.5
28	13.1	11.6	9.6	0.2	1.8
29	14.0	5.6	8.1	0.2	4.6
30	11.1	7.5	12.5	1.4	0.6

DECEMBER 2006

	Temperature Max (°C)	Min (°C)	*Wind* knots	*Rain* mm	*Sun* hrs
Day 1	13.9	8.8	11.5	2.4	0.0
2	11.4	9.8	9.3	5.0	1.4
3	11.0	8.2	18.5	0.2	4.6
4	14.7	7.9	14.9	0.8	2.9
5	13.2	8.5	18.5	1.4	0.0
6	11.7	8.4	14.3	7.8	4.6
7	11.7	6.9	18.5	1.8	2.2
8	8.9	6.4	7.6	0.6	0.1
9	8.8	1.9	7.1	trace	5.6
10	12.7	0.1	10.5	3.8	2.1
11	12.5	1.9	13.9	1.8	0.0
12	11.7	3.8	13.4	0.2	1.6
13	12.9	6.4	16.0	trace	0.0
14	13.4	11.6	16.2	trace	0.0
15	12.3	10.8	13.0	5.0	0.0
16	8.3	4.7	6.7	0.2	4.9
17	8.9	0.7	5.2	0.8	5.9
18	8.4	2.8	3.5	0.4	0.0
19	3.8	-0.3	2.3	0.0	0.6
20	1.2	-1.0	1.3	0.2	0.0
21	0.8	-2.3	1.0	0.2	0.0
22	2.3	-2.8	1.0	0.2	0.0
23	5.6	-2.1	4.8	0.0	0.0
24	7.0	2.2	6.8	0.0	0.0
25	6.4	5.5	5.5	0.0	0.0
26	7.2	5.1	3.4	0.2	0.0
27	10.2	3.9	6.2	0.4	0.1
28	11.5	3.9	8.6	trace	1.5
29	13.3	4.7	13.8	9.4	0.0
30	13.1	6.8	17.5	12.2	3.1
31	12.8	7.6	14.6	8.6	0.0

JANUARY 2007

	Max (°C)	Min (°C)	knots	mm	hrs
Day 1	9.7	5.1	14.0	4.2	4.9
2	9.8	3.9	12.2	trace	3.9
3	11.7	3.8	13.5	1.2	0.0
4	10.6	8.0	14.0	trace	2.1
5	12.2	7.4	10.2	0.8	0.1
6	10.5	4.0	6.1	12.2	0.0
7	12.0	5.2	14.8	4.2	0.0
8	13.4	5.5	13.5	0.8	0.1
9	13.8	6.9	19.7	9.4	0.0
10	11.4	10.3	15.0	0.2	2.0
11	13.1	5.1	21.6	2.2	0.4
12	13.4	6.8	16.8	trace	0.0
13	12.0	10.1	14.9	1.8	0.1
14	10.6	4.2	9.6	0.0	5.4
15	11.2	4.6	10.4	0.4	2.1
16	11.9	7.9	11.6	4.8	0.0
17	13.0	10.3	14.4	7.6	1.2
18	14.1	7.5	22.8	1.2	0.1
19	13.6	9.7	15.2	2.0	2.0
20	10.3	8.4	17.8	0.2	3.8
21	8.5	4.7	17.2	0.2	4.7
22	5.9	1.7	10.2	0.4	0.1
23	4.0	0.6	9.0	trace	4.2
24	4.7	-1.9	5.7	1.8	0.1
25	5.1	0.1	5.7	0.2	5.3
26	7.9	-2.6	6.5	0.2	1.3
27	9.8	1.9	6.3	0.0	3.5
28	10.0	4.1	10.0	0.0	2.6
29	10.8	5.4	4.4	trace	0.1
30	8.4	6.9	4.0	0.0	0.0
31	11.1	1.1	7.5	0.0	6.5

FEBRUARY 2007

	Max (°C)	Min (°C)	knots	mm	hrs
Day 1	13.3	3.4	4.7	trace	1.7
2	12.1	5.1	5.6	0.2	3.0
3	10.6	0.2	3.0	0.0	8.1
4	6.9	-1.2	3.9	0.0	3.0
5	5.5	1.0	4.3	trace	0.9
6	6.1	-1.1	3.0	0.0	6.3
7	4.5	-5.2	3.6	1.7	7.8
8	3.9	-2.8	7.2	7.6	0.0
9	6.4	0.1	8.4	5.0	0.0
10	10.1	1.5	7.8	6.0	0.7
11	11.3	5.5	12.0	5.8	2.2
12	10.3	7.5	12.9	4.8	0.1
13	9.4	5.8	11.0	15.6	2.1
14	9.7	6.9	7.0	0.6	2.5
15	11.4	-0.4	9.9	0.2	2.9
16	12.4	5.9	6.9	0.2	0.4
17	11.7	4.1	5.0	trace	3.3
18	8.6	5.4	5.7	0.2	0.0
19	11.2	6.8	8.3	1.0	0.0
20	11.0	7.9	7.1	4.2	0.0
21	12.3	8.1	8.8	0.4	5.9
22	10.2	7.9	9.9	4.0	0.0
23	11.9	7.4	10.3	7.2	1.0
24	11.6	8.3	9.9	5.8	1.0
25	10.7	5.5	8.8	5.6	0.1
26	10.8	6.1	8.8	6.0	3.2
27	12.4	3.6	11.2	6.0	0.0
28	11.2	6.2	18.3	4.8	3.1

MARCH 2007

	Temperature Max (°C)	Min (°C)	*Wind* knots	*Rain* mm	*Sun* hrs
Day 1	10.7	4.9	13.0	0.0	5.4
2	11.7	1.5	8.8	6.4	6.5
3	12.9	4.5	10.0	0.4	6.3
4	12.5	2.8	10.9	10.4	0.0
5	11.9	6.1	16.7	11.6	4.8
6	14.8	7.5	14.9	0.8	4.2
7	12.7	6.1	6.2	trace	5.2
8	13.7	3.4	6.2	1.8	7.9
9	12.8	7.2	9.9	0.4	7.5
10	13.9	4.2	9.5	0.0	6.8
11	16.7	5.2	9.1	0.2	9.8
12	16.7	4.2	5.2	0.0	7.3
13	14.1	5.9	4.6	0.0	7.3
14	14.9	3.3	3.4	0.0	7.7
15	13.2	4.2	5.9	trace	7.0
16	13.7	7.2	8.7	0.0	8.3
17	15.9	8.0	14.0	1.2	3.7
18	9.6	6.9	17.6	1.4	7.5
19	8.4	0.8	10.2	2.6	4.0
20	6.9	1.9	12.3	0.4	2.5
21	8.7	-0.3	7.6	0.2	7.4
22	6.9	-1.4	3.7	0.6	0.0
23	8.1	1.9	8.5	trace	0.1
24	8.3	3.6	9.2	0.2	1.2
25	13.2	6.5	8.4	0.0	2.4
26	15.8	3.9	6.6	0.0	10.9
27	17.7	3.3	3.8	0.0	8.0
28	17.1	4.4	3.4	0.2	8.0
29	9.4	7.1	5.5	1.4	0.1
30	9.5	5.4	7.2	3.6	0.0
31	15.3	6.9	12.2	trace	6.9

APRIL 2007

	Temperature Max (°C)	Min (°C)	*Wind* knots	*Rain* mm	*Sun* hrs
Day 1	17.0	6.3	11.3	0.0	8.6
2	18.5	5.8	9.4	trace	11.1
3	9.6	5.2	8.8	0.2	0.0
4	12.7	1.6	7.5	0.0	6.8
5	20.1	2.0	2.8	0.0	11.8
6	17.9	5.5	4.6	0.0	11.4
7	15.7	4.6	3.8	0.0	7.0
8	18.3	3.8	5.3	0.0	11.5
9	17.6	6.0	4.9	0.0	6.9
10	19.5	11.1	4.3	0.0	6.5
11	18.3	8.5	3.5	0.0	2.7
12	18.7	7.7	5.8	0.0	7.6
13	18.7	8.3	5.4	0.0	5.0
14	23.3	7.8	4.6	0.0	10.3
15	24.7	9.6	3.4	0.0	12.1
16	23.3	11.7	5.2	trace	8.7
17	18.4	11.8	5.4	0.0	6.4
18	16.4	6.5	4.0	0.0	10.2
19	20.8	5.3	5.9	0.0	12.3
20	16.7	8.8	7.7	0.0	4.3
21	19.4	5.8	5.9	0.0	10.7
22	22.2	6.7	n/a	trace	7.1
23	18.4	9.6	9.3	1.0	0.1
24	21.1	11.8	7.9	trace	3.5
25	19.1	13.9	7.5	trace	2.3
26	17.1	10.7	7.4	2.4	3.3
27	17.8	9.7	7.8	0.0	3.4
28	22.9	7.9	8.4	0.0	10.6
29	21.2	8.6	7.6	0.0	9.0
30	20.2	8.6	9.8	0.0	13.4

MAY 2007

	Temperature Max (°C)	Min (°C)	*Wind* knots	*Rain* mm	*Sun* hrs
Day 1	21.5	9.3	10.3	0.0	13.3
2	22.1	8.9	10.4	0.0	13.5
3	15.4	7.4	8.7	trace	6.4
4	17.5	8.6	8.8	0.0	6.9
5	14.9	9.1	5.2	0.0	4.6
6	20.4	8.1	10.8	trace	0.6
7	19.2	13.6	16.8	3.2	5.0
8	20.0	10.3	16.5	trace	4.0
9	15.0	9.9	10.4	4.0	0.0
10	16.8	10.0	13.2	5.8	2.2
11	16.7	8.2	12.5	3.8	3.1
12	17.3	10.0	13.3	7.2	3.3
13	15.3	10.4	8.5	7.0	0.7
14	11.9	11.0	6.9	1.2	1.0
15	16.9	5.7	7.9	1.8	1.2
16	16.2	10.1	7.8	3.0	1.4
17	19.2	12.1	7.1	0.2	1.0
18	21.4	12.7	12.1	trace	6.5
19	18.0	9.3	12.0	trace	8.0
20	19.7	7.1	4.1	trace	7.7
21	16.5	11.6	6.0	0.8	0.0
22	22.1	11.4	4.6	0.0	13.7
23	24.5	10.9	4.3	0.0	12.2
24	25.7	13.8	4.8	0.0	6.8
25	23.3	13.8	5.6	1.2	7.6
26	13.4	10.5	5.8	7.8	0.1
27	12.5	9.3	6.2	23.4	0.0
28	10.1	6.6	n/a	4.4	0.0
29	15.6	4.2	8.1	0.6	6.9
30	17.1	6.1	9.2	4.6	2.9
31	19.6	9.7	8.7	trace	9.0

JUNE 2007

	Temperature Max (°C)	Min (°C)	*Wind* knots	*Rain* mm	*Sun* hrs
Day 1	22.1	10.1	4.9	0.0	8.3
2	24.7	11.5	4.5	0.0	14.0
3	25.0	12.2	4.4	0.0	6.9
4	20.0	12.5	6.2	trace	0.9
5	21.8	11.4	8.2	0.0	13.0
6	17.8	11.2	8.7	trace	4.5
7	18.3	12.3	7.4	trace	0.1
8	21.4	13.1	5.0	0.0	2.7
9	24.9	14.4	3.3	0.0	1.0
10	24.9	15.2	5.6	0.0	12.2
11	21.6	14.3	3.8	0.0	0.1
12	23.7	14.4	7.8	0.0	6.2
13	24.3	12.5	6.1	1.8	7.1
14	22.6	14.9	5.5	4.0	0.1
15	20.9	14.5	9.3	1.8	5.0
16	19.5	13.5	9.5	4.8	4.2
17	21.3	12.4	6.8	1.2	3.3
18	20.6	12.3	8.9	1.4	3.8
19	25.4	11.7	8.7	2.6	7.3
20	22.2	13.9	12.3	0.0	10.1
21	21.1	13.2	10.8	3.8	5.9
22	20.0	13.8	9.2	0.4	2.1
23	20.4	14.4	8.6	3.8	2.8
24	16.6	12.3	7.9	9.4	0.1
25	16.2	11.9	10.0	3.6	2.7
26	17.0	11.2	8.9	0.2	4.5
27	19.6	9.2	9.8	4.6	1.4
28	20.1	7.7	10.5	2.8	3.5
29	n/a	13.0	13.7	5.6	5.9
30	18.3	13.2	8.2	12.0	0.0

SPORTS RESULTS

For 2008 sports fixtures, *see* page 13

ALPINE SKIING

WORLD CUP 2006–7

MEN
Downhill: Didier Cuche (Switzerland), 652pts
Slalom: Benjamin Raich (Austria), 605pts
Giant Slalom: Aksel Lund Svindal (Norway), 416pts
Super Giant Slalom: Bode Miller (USA), 304pts
Overall: Aksel Lund Svindal (Norway), 1,268pts

WOMEN
Downhill: Renate Goetschl (Austria), 705pts
Slalom: Marlies Schild (Austria), 760pts
Giant Slalom: Nicole Hosp (Austria), 490pts
Super Giant Slalom: Renate Goetschl (Austria), 540pts
Overall: Nicole Hosp (Austria), 1,572pts

WORLD CHAMPIONSHIPS 2007
Are, Sweden, February

MEN
Downhill: Aksel Lund Svindal (Norway)
Slalom: Mario Matt (Austria)
Giant Slalom: Aksel Lund Svindal (Norway)
Super Giant Slalom: Patrick Staudacher (Italy)
Super Combined: Daniel Albrecht (Switzerland)

WOMEN
Downhill: Anja Paerson (Sweden)
Slalom: Sarka Zahrobska (Czech Republic)
Giant Slalom: Nicole Hosp (Austria)
Super Giant Slalom: Anja Paerson (Sweden)
Super Combined: Anja Paerson (Sweden)

AMERICAN FOOTBALL

AFC Championship 2006–7: Indianapolis Colts beat New England Patriots 38–34
NFC Championship 2006–7: Chicago Bears beat New Orleans Saints 39–14
XLI Superbowl 2007: Indianapolis Colts beat Chicago Bears 29–17

ASSOCIATION FOOTBALL

LEAGUE COMPETITIONS 2006–7

ENGLAND AND WALES
Premiership
1. Manchester United, 89pts
2. Chelsea, 83pts
3. Liverpool, 68pts
Relegated: Sheffield United, Charlton Athletic, Watford

Championship
1. Sunderland, 88pts
2. Birmingham City, 86pts
Play-off winner and third promotion place: Derby County
Relegated: Southend United, Luton Town and Leeds United

League 1
1. Scunthorpe United, 91pts
2. Bristol City, 85pts
Play-off winner and third promotion place: Blackpool
Relegated: Chesterfield, Bradford City, Rotherham United and Brentford

League 2
1. Walsall, 89pts
2. Hartlepool United, 88pts
3. Swindon Town, 85pts
Play-off winner and fourth promotion place: Bristol Rovers
Relegated: Boston United and Torquay United

Football Conference
1. Dagenham and Redbridge, 95pts
Play-off winner and second promotion place: Morecambe

Welsh Premier League
1. The New Saints (formerly TNS), 76pts
2. Rhyl, 69pts
3. Llanelli, 63pts

Women's Premier League National Division
1. Arsenal, 66pts
2. Everton, 52pts
3. Charlton, 50pts

SCOTLAND
Premier Division
1. Celtic, 84pts
2. Rangers, 72pts
Relegated: Dunfermline

Division 1
1. Gretna, 66pts
Relegated: Ross County, Airdrie United

Division 2
1. Morton, 77pts
Play-off winner and second promotion place: Stirling Albion
Relegated: Forfar Athletic and Stranraer

Division 3
1. Berwick, 75pts
Play-off winner and second promotion place: Queen's Park
Bottom: East Stirling

NORTHERN IRELAND
Premier League
1. Linfield, 71pts
2. Glentoran, 63pts
3. Cliftonville, 61pts

REPUBLIC OF IRELAND
Premier Division: 1. Shelbourne, 62pts; 2. Derry City, 62pts; 3. Drogheda United, 58pts

FRANCE
Ligue 1: 1. Lyon, 81pts; 2. Marseille, 64pts; 3. Toulouse, 58pts

GERMANY
Bundesliga: 1. VFB Stuttgart, 70pts; 2. Schalke 04, 68pts; 3. Werder Bremen, 66pts

ITALY
Serie A: 1. Internazionale, 97pts; 2. Roma, 75pts; 3. Lazio, 62pts

NETHERLANDS
Eredivisie: 1. PSV, 75pts; 2. Ajax, 75pts; 3. AZ, 72pts

SPAIN
Primera Liga: 1. Real Madrid, 76pts; 2. Barcelona, 76pts; 3. Sevilla, 71pts

CUP COMPETITIONS 2006–7

ENGLAND
FA Cup final 2007: Chelsea beat Manchester United 1–0
League Cup final 2007: Chelsea beat Arsenal 2–1
Football League Trophy final 2007: Doncaster beat Bristol Rovers 3–2
FA Vase final 2007: Truro beat Totton 3–1
FA Trophy final 2007: Stevenage beat Kidderminster 3–2
Community Shield 2007: Manchester United beat Chelsea 3–0 on penalties (1–1 after 90 minutes)

WOMEN
FA Cup final 2007: Arsenal beat Charlton Athletic 4–1
Premier League Cup final 2007: Arsenal beat Leeds United 1–0

WALES
FA Wales Cup final 2007: Carmarthen Town beat Afan Lido 3–2
FA Wales Premier Cup final 2007: The New Saints beat Newport County 1–0

SCOTLAND
Scottish Cup final 2007: Celtic beat Dunfermline Athletic 1–0
League Cup final 2007: Hibernian beat Kilmarnock 5–1

NORTHERN IRELAND
Irish Cup final 2007: Linfield beat Dungannon Swifts 3–2 on penalties (2–2 aet)

EUROPE
European Champions League final 2007: AC Milan beat Liverpool 2–1
UEFA Cup final 2007: Sevilla beat Espanyol 3–1 on penalties (2–2 aet)

WORLD PLAYER OF THE YEAR
2006 – Fabio Cannavaro (Italy)
2005 – Ronaldinho (Brazil)
2004 – Ronaldinho (Brazil)
2003 – Zinedine Zidane (France)
2002 – Ronaldo (Brazil)
2001 – Luis Figo (Portugal)
2000 – Zinedine Zidane (France)
1999 – Rivaldo (Brazil)
1998 – Zinedine Zidane (France)
1997 – Ronaldo (Brazil)
1996 – Ronaldo (Brazil)
1995 – George Weah (Liberia)
1994 – Romario (Brazil)
1993 – Roberto Baggio (Italy)
1992 – Marco van Basten (Netherlands)

ATHLETICS

EUROPEAN CROSS COUNTRY CHAMPIONSHIPS
San Giorgio su Legnano, Italy, 10 December 2006

SENIOR MEN (9,950m)
Individual: Mo Farah (Great Britain), 27min 56sec
Team: France, 33pts

JUNIOR MEN (5,975m)
Individual: Andrea Lalli (Italy), 23min 14sec
Team: Italy, 68pts

SENIOR WOMEN (8,030m)
Individual: Tatyana Golovchenko (Ukraine), 25min 17sec
Team: Portugal, 47pts

JUNIOR WOMEN (4,100m)
Individual: Stephanie Twell (Great Britain), 12min 33sec
Team: Great Britain, 21pts

AAA INDOOR CHAMPIONSHIPS
Sheffield, 10–11 February 2007

MEN
60m: Craig Pickering (Milton Keynes), 6.58sec
200m: Rikki Fifton (Victoria Park/Tower Hamlets), 21.06sec
400m: Gareth Warburton (Cardiff), 48.02sec
800m: James Brewer (Cheltenham), 1min 49.03sec
1,500m: Chris Warburton (Nottingham), 3min 56.47sec
3,000m: Mo Farah (Newham/Essex Beagles), 7min 50.86sec
60mH: Andy Turner (Sale), 7.55sec
High jump: Martyn Bernard (unattached), 2.23m
Pole vault: Steve Lewis (Newham/Essex Beagles), 5.50m
Long jump: Bernard Yeboah (Belgrave), 7.50m
Triple jump: Nathan Douglas (Oxford City), 17.19m
Shot: Garrett Johnson (USA), 18.98m

WOMEN
60m: Laura Turner (Harrow), 7.25sec
200m: Kadi-Ann Thomas (Milton Keynes), 23.68sec
400m: Nicola Sanders (Windsor, Slough and Eton), 50.60sec
800m: Marilyn Okoro (Shaftesbury Barnet), 2min 04.39sec
1,500m: Katrina Wootton (Bedford), 4min 17.90sec
3,000m: Lisa Dobriskey (Ashford), 8min 55.22sec
60mH: Sara McGreavy (Sale), 8.03sec
High jump: Jessica Ennis (Sheffield), 1.87m
Pole vault: Kate Dennison (Sale), 4.35m
Long jump: Amy Harris (Birchfield), 6.47m
Triple jump: Ashia Hansen (Birchfield), 13.68m
Shot: Jo Duncan (Woodford Green), 16.45m

ENGLISH NATIONAL CROSS COUNTRY CHAMPIONSHIPS
Sunderland, 10 March 2007

SENIOR MEN (12km)
Individual: Frank Tickner (Wells), 37min 31sec
Team: Leeds City, 162pts

JUNIOR MEN (10km)
Individual: Kevin Deighton (Bridlington), 32min 12sec
Team: Liverpool H, 87pts

SENIOR WOMEN (9.2km)
Individual: Liz Yelling (Bedford and County), 28min 56sec
Team: Winchester and District, 41pts

JUNIOR WOMEN (5km)
Individual: Jessica Sparke (Woodford Green), 17min 03sec
Team: Bristol and West, 73pts

EUROPEAN INDOOR CHAMPIONSHIPS
Birmingham, 2–4 March 2007

MEN
60m: Jason Gardener (Great Britain), 6.51sec
400m: David Gillick (Ireland), 45.52sec
800m: Arnoud Okke (Netherlands), 1min 47.92sec
1,500m: Juan Carlos Higuero (Spain), 3min 44.41sec
3,000m: Cosimo Caliandro (Italy), 8min 02.44sec
60mH: Gregory Sedoc (Netherlands), 7.63sec
4 × 400m: Great Britain, 3min 07.04sec
High jump: Stefan Holm (Sweden), 2.34m
Pole vault: Danny Ecker (Germany), 5.71m
Long jump: Andrew Howe (Italy), 8.30m
Triple jump: Phillips Idowu (Great Britain), 17.56m
Shot: Mikulas Konopka (Slovakia), 21.57m
Heptathlon: Roman Sebrle (Czech Republic), 6,196pts

WOMEN
60m: Kim Gevaert (Belgium), 7.12sec
400m: Nicola Sanders (Great Britain), 50.02sec
800m: Oksana Zbrozhek (Russia), 1min 59.23sec
1,500m: Lidia Chojecka (Poland), 4min 05.13sec
3,000m: Lidia Chojecka (Poland), 8min 43.25sec
60mH: Susanna Kallur (Sweden), 7.87sec
4 × 400m: Belarus, 3min 27.83sec
High jump: Tia Hellebaut (Belgium), 2.05m
Pole vault: Svetlana Feofanova (Russia), 4.76m
Long jump: Naide Gomes (Portugal), 6.89m
Triple jump: Carlota Castrejana (Spain),14.64m
Shot: Assunta Legnante (Italy), 18.92m
Pentathlon: Carolina Kluft (Sweden), 4,944pts

IAAF WORLD CROSS COUNTRY CHAMPIONSHIPS
Mombasa, Kenya, 24 March 2007

SENIOR MEN (12km)
Individual: Zersenay Tadesse (Eritrea), 35min 50sec
Team: Kenya, 28pts

JUNIOR MEN (8km)
Individual: Asbel Kiprop (Kenya), 24min 07sec
Team: Kenya, 10pts

SENIOR WOMEN (8km)
Individual: Lornah Kiplagat (Netherlands), 26min 23sec
Team: Ethiopia, 19pts

JUNIOR WOMEN (6km)
Individual: Linet Barasa (Kenya), 20min 52sec
Team: Kenya, 13pts

LONDON MARATHON
London, 22 April 2007
Men: Martin Lel (Kenya), 2hr 07min 41sec
Women: Zhou Chunxia (China), 2hr 20min 38sec

EUROPEAN CUP SUPER LEAGUE
Munich, Germany, 23–24 June 2007

MEN
100m: Craig Pickering (Great Britain), 10.15sec
200m: Marlon Devonish (Great Britain), 20.33sec
400m: Leslie Djhone (France), 45.54sec
800m: Pawel Czapiewski (Poland), 1min 49.00sec
1,500m: Mehdi Baala (France), 3min 47.36sec
3,000m: Bouabdellah Tahri (France), 7min 51.32sec
5,000m: Monder Rizki (Belgium), 14min 15.46sec
3,000mSt: Filmon Ghirmai (Germany), 8min 38.78sec
110mH: Ladji Doucouré (France), 13.35sec
400mH: Perikilis Iovakis (Greece), 48.35sec
4 × 100m: Great Britain, 38.30sec
4 × 400m: Poland, 3min 01.70sec
High jump: Eike Onnen (Germany), 2.30m
Pole vault: Tim Lobinger (Germany), 5.70m
Long jump: Louis Tsatoumas (Greece), 8.16m
Triple jump: Aleksandr Petrenko (Russia), 17.29m
Shot: Peter Sack (Germany), 20.28m
Discus: Piotr Malachowski (Poland), 66.09m
Hammer: Szymon Ziolkowski (Poland), 77.99m
Javelin: Aleksandr Ivanov (Russia), 82.57m
Points: France 116; Germany 116; Poland 110; Great Britain 101; Russia 93; Greece 70; Ukraine 58.5; Belgium 53.5

WOMEN
100m: Yevgeniya Polyakova (Russia), 11.20sec
200m: Muriel Hurtis-Houairi (France), 22.83sec
400m: Fani Halkia (Greece), 51.85sec
800m: Svetlana Usovich (Belarus), 2min 00.71sec
1,500m: Sylwia Ejdis (Poland), 4min 17.05sec
3,000m: Gulnara Samitova (Russia), 8min 47.92sec
5,000m: Olga Kravtsova (Belarus), 15min 20.35sec
3,000mSt: Katarzyna Kowalska (Poland), 9min 45.35sec
100mH: Yevgeniya Snigur (Ukraine), 12.92sec
400mH: Yuliya Pechonkina (Russia), 42.78sec
4 × 100m: Russia, 42.78sec
4 × 400m: Belarus, 3min 23.67sec
High jump: Yelena Slesarenko (Russia), 2.02m
Pole vault: Monika Pyrek (Poland), 4.65m
Long jump: Eunice Barber (France), 6.73m
Triple jump: Téresa N'Zola (France), 14.69m
Shot: Anna Omarova (Russia), 19.36m
Discus: Franka Dietzsch (Germany), 63.60m
Hammer: Tatyana Lysenko (Russia), 75.86m
Javelin: Christina Obergföll (Poland), 70.20m
Points: Russia 127; France 107; Germany 94.5; Poland 89; Ukraine 81; Belarus 80; Greece 75; Spain 64.5

AAA CHAMPIONSHIPS
Manchester, 28–29 July 2007

MEN
100m: Marlon Devonish (Coventry), 10.31sec
200m: Marlon Devonish (Coventry), 20.79sec
400m: Andrew Steele (Trafford), 45.70sec
800m: Michael Rimmer (Liverpool), 1min 47.06sec
1,500m: Andrew Baddeley (Harrow), 3min 43.25sec
5,000m: Mo Farah (Newham/Essex Beagles), 13min 40.19sec
*10,000m:** Phil Nicholls (Tipton), 28min 40.85sec
3,000mSt: Andrew Lemoncello (Fife), 8min 42.57sec
110mH: Andy Turner (Sale), 13.54sec
400mH: Dale Garland (Channel Islands), 49.79sec
5,000m Walk: Dominic King (Colchester), 20min 57.90sec
High jump: Martyn Bernard (Wakefield), 2.24m
Pole vault: Steve Lewis (Newham/Essex Beagles), 5.61m

Long jump: Chris Tomlinson (Newham/Essex Beagles), 7.99m
Triple jump: Tosin Oke (Woodford Green), 16.59m
Shot: Carl Myerscough (Blackpool), 19.39m
Discus: Emeka Udechuku (Woodford Green), 60.83m
Hammer: Andy Frost (Woodford Green), 71.02m
Javelin: Nick Nieland (Shaftesbury Barnet), 73.95m
Decathlon:† Ben Hazell (Basingstoke), 7,528pts

WOMEN
100m: Jeanette Kwakye (Woodford Green), 11.59sec
200m: Jeanette Kwakye (Woodford Green), 23.66sec
400m: Nicola Sanders (Hounslow), 51.33sec
800m: Jemma Simpson (Newquay), 2min 00.91sec
1,500m: Katrina Wootton (Bedford), 4min 09.57sec
5,000m: Jo Pavey (Exeter), 15min 17.77sec
*10,000m:** Jo Pavey (Exeter), 31min 26.94sec
3,000mSt: Helen Clitheroe (Preston), 9min 47.49sec
100mH: Jessica Ennis (Sheffield), 13.25sec
400mH: Tasha Danvers-Smith (Shaftesbury Barnet), 55.43sec
5,000m walk: Johanna Jackson (Redcar), 22min 03.65sec
High jump: Jessica Ennis (Sheffield), 1.87m
Pole vault: Kate Denniso (Sale), 4.20m
Long jump: Kelly Sotherton (Birchfield), 6.53m
Triple jump: Nadia Williams (Shaftesbury Barnet), 13.58m
Shot: Eva Massey (Belgrave), 16.63m
Discus: Philippa Roles (Sale), 57.83m
Hammer: Zoe Derham (Birchfield), 64.99m
Javelin: Goldie Sayers (Belgrave), 63.02m
Heptathlon:† Phyllis Agbo (Thames Valley Harriers), 5,471pts
* Held at Watford, 30 June 2007
† Held at Stoke, 9–10 June 2007

EUROPEAN CHAMPIONSHIPS
Gothenburg, Sweden, 7–13 August 2006

MEN
100m: Francis Obikwelu (Portugal), 9.99sec
200m: Francis Obikwelu (Portugal), 20.01sec
400m: Marc Raquil (France), 45.02sec
800m: Bram Som (Netherlands), 1min 46.56sec
1,500m: Mehdi Baala (France), 3min 39.02sec
5,000m: Jesus Espana (Spain), 13min 44.70sec
10,000m: Jan Fitschen (Germany), 28min 10.94sec
Marathon: Stefano Baldini (Italy), 2hr 11min 32sec
3,000mSt: Jukka Keskisalo (Finland), 8min 24.89sec
110mH: Stanislav Olijar (Latvia), 13.24sec
400mH: Periklis Iokovakis (Greece), 48.46sec
4 x 100m: Great Britain, 38.91sec
4 x 400m: France, 3min 01.10sec
20km walk: Francisco Fernandez (Spain), 1hr 19min 09sec
50km walk: Yohan Diniz (France), 3hr 41min 39sec
High jump: Andrei Silonov (Russia), 2.26m
Pole vault: Alex Averbukh (Israel), 5.70m
Long jump: Andrew Howe (Italy), 8.20m
Triple jump: Christia Olsson (Sweden), 17.67m
Shot: Ralf Bartels (Germany), 21.13m
Discus: Virgilijus Alekna (Lithuania), 68.67m
Hammer: Ivan Tikhon (Belarus), 81.11m
Javelin: Andreas Thorkildsen (Norway), 88.79m
Decathlon: Roman Sebrle (Czech Republic), 8,526pts

WOMEN
100m: Kim Gevaert (Belgium), 11.06sec
200m: Kim Gevaert (Belgium), 22.68sec
400m: Vanya Stambolova (Bulgaria), 49.85sec
800m: Olga Kotlyarova (Russia), 1min 57.38sec
1,500m: Tatyana Tomashova (Russia), 3min 56.91sec
5,000m: Marta Dominguez (Spain), 14min 56.18sec
10,000m: Inga Abitova (Russia), 30min 31.42sec
Marathon: Ulrike Maisch (Germany), 2hr 30min 01sec
3,000mSt: Alesya Turava (Belarus), 9min 26.05sec
100mH: Susanna Kallur (Sweden), 12.59sec
400mH: Yevgeniya Isakova (Russia), 53.93sec
4 × 100m: Russia, 42.71sec
4 × 400m: Russia, 3min 25.12sec
20km walk: Ryta Turava (Belarus), 1hr 27min 08sec
High jump: Tia Hellebaut (Belgium), 2.03m
Pole vault: Yelena Isinbayeva (Russia), 4.80m
Long jump: Ludmila Kolchanova (Russia), 6.93m
Triple jump: Tatyana Lebedeva (Russia), 15.15m
Shot: Natalya Khoronenko (Belarus), 19.43m
Discus: Darya Pishchalnikova (Russia), 65.55m
Hammer: Tatyana Lysenko (Russia), 76.67m
Javelin: Steffi Nerius (Germany), 65.82m
Heptathlon: Carolina Kluft (Sweden), 6,740pts

WORLD CHAMPIONSHIPS
Osaka, Japan, 25 August–2 September 2007

MEN
100m: Tyson Gay (USA), 9.85sec
200m: Tyson Gay (USA), 19.76sec
400m: Jeremy Wariner (USA), 43.45sec
800m: Alfred Kirwa Yego (Kenya), 1min 47.09sec
1,500m: Bernard Lagat (USA), 3min 34.77sec
5,000m: Bernard Lagat (USA), 13min 45.87sec
10,000m: Kenenisa Bekele (Ethiopia), 27min 05.90sec
Marathon: Luke Kibet (Kenya), 2hr 15min 59sec
3,000mSt: Brimin Kipruto (Kenya), 8min 13.82sec
110mH: Liu Xiang (China), 12.95sec
400mH: Kerron Clement (USA), 47.61sec
4 x 100m: USA, 37.78sec
4 x 400m: USA, 2min 55.56sec
20km walk: Jefferson Perez (Ecuador), 1hr 22min 20sec
50km walk: Nathan Deakes (Australia), 3hr 43min 53sec
High jump: Donald Thomas (Bahamas), 2.35m
Pole vault: Brad Walker (USA), 5.81m
Long jump: Irving Saladino (Panama), 8.57m
Triple jump: Nelson Evora (Portugal), 17.74m
Shot: Reese Hoffa (USA), 22.04m
Discus: Gerd Kanter (Estonia), 68.94m
Hammer: Ivan Tikhon (Belarus), 83.63m
Javelin: Tero Pitkamaki (Finland), 90.33m
Decathlon: Roman Sebrle (Czech Republic), 8,676pts

WOMEN
100m: Veronica Campbell (Jamaica), 11.01sec
200m: Allyson Felix (USA), 21.81sec
400m: Christine Ohuruogu (Great Britain), 49.61sec
800m: Janeth Jepkosgei (Kenya), 1min 56.04sec
1,500m: Maryam Jamal (Bahrain), 3min 58.75sec
5,000m: Meseret Defar (Ethiopia), 14min 57.91sec
10,000m: Tirunesh Dibaba (Ethiopia), 31min 55.41sec
Marathon: Catherine Ndereba (Kenya), 2hr 30min 37sec
3,000mSt: Yekaterina Volkova (Russia), 9min 06.57sec
100mH: Michelle Perry (USA), 12.46sec
400mH: Jana Rawlinson (Australia), 53.31sec
4 x 100m: USA, 41.98sec
4 x 400m: USA, 3min 18.55sec
20km walk: Olga Kaniskina (Russia), 1hr 30min 09sec
High jump: Blanka Vlasic (Croatia), 2.05m
Pole vault: Yelena Isinbayeva (Russia), 4.80m
Long jump: Tatyana Lebedeva (Russia), 7.03m

Triple jump: Yargelis Savigne (Cuba), 15.28m
Shot: Valerie Vili (New Zealand), 20.54m
Discus: Franka Dietzsch (Germany), 66.61m
Hammer: Betty Heidler (Germany), 74.76m
Javelin: Barbara Spotakova (Czech Republic), 67.07m
Heptathlon: Carolina Kluft (Sweden), 7,032pts

BADMINTON

WORLD CHAMPIONSHIPS 2006
Madrid, Spain, September

Men's Singles: Dan Lin (China) beat Chunlai Bao (China) 2–1
Women's Singles: Xingfang Xie (China) beat Ning Zhang (China) 2–0
Men's Doubles: Haifeng Fu and Yun Cai (China) beat Anthony Clark and Robert Blair (Great Britain) 2–0
Women's Doubles: Ling Gao and Sui Huang (China) beat Yili Wei and Yawen Zhang (China) 2–0
Mixed Doubles: Gail Emms and Nathan Robertson (Great Britain) beat Donna Kellogg and Anthony Clark (Great Britain) 2–0

WORLD CHAMPIONSHIPS 2007
Kuala Lumpur, Malaysia, August

Men's singles: Dan Lin (China) beat Dwi Kuncoro Sony (Indonesia) 2–0
Women's singles: Lin Zhu (China) beat Chen Wang (Hong Kong) 2–0
Men's Doubles: Markis Kido and Hendra Setiawan (Indonesia) beat Jung Jae Sung and Lee Yong Dae (Rep. of Korea) 2–0
Women's Doubles: Wei Yang and Jiewen Zhang (China) beat Ling Gao and Sui Huang (China) 2–0
Mixed Doubles: Nova Widianto and Lilyana Natsir (Indonesia) beat Bo Zheng and Ling Gao (China) 2–0

ALL-ENGLAND CHAMPIONSHIPS 2007
Birmingham, March

Men's Singles: Dan Lin (China) beat Yu Chen (China) 2–0
Women's Singles: Xingfang Xie (China) beat Hongyan Pi (France) 2–0
Men's Doubles: Kien Keat Koo and Boon Heong Tan (USA) beat Haifeng Fu and Yun Cai (China) 2–0
Women's Doubles: Yili Wei and Yawen Zhang beat Wei Yang and Jiewen Zhang (China) 2–1
Mixed Doubles: Ling Gao and Bo Zheng (China) beat Donna Kellogg and Anthony Clark (Great Britain) 2–1

ENGLISH NATIONAL CHAMPIONSHIPS 2007
Manchester, February

Men's Singles: Nicholas Kidd beat Nathan Rice 2–0
Women's Singles: Elizabeth Cann beat Jill Pittard 2–0
Men's Doubles: Robert Blair and Anthony Clark beat Chris Langridge and David Lindley 2–0
Women's Doubles: Gail Emms and Donna Kellogg beat Natalie Munt and Joanne Nicholas 2–0
Mixed Doubles: Donna Kellogg and Anthony Clark beat Gail Emms and Nathan Robertson 2–1

SCOTTISH NATIONAL CHAMPIONSHIPS 2007
Perth, February

Men's Singles: Gordon Thomson beat Stuart Gilliland 2–0
Women's Singles: Rita Yuan Gao beat Susan Hughes 2–0
Men's Doubles: Andrew Bowman and Watson Briggs beat David Gilmour and Craig Robertson 2–0
Women's Doubles: Susan Hughes and Rita Yuan Gao beat Imogen Bankier and Emma Mason 2–1
Mixed Doubles: Imogen Bankier and Watson Briggs beat Rita Yuan Gao and Craig Robertson 2–0

WELSH NATIONAL CHAMPIONSHIPS 2007
Wrexham, February

Men's Singles: Raj Popat beat Michael Lewis 2–0
Women's Singles: Rachelle Phillips beat Harriet Johnson 2–1
Men's Doubles: Martyn Lewis and Matthew Hughes beat James Phillips and Joe Morgan 2–1
Women's Doubles: Jo Muggeridge and Rachelle Phillips beat Bethan Higginson and Caroline Harvey 2–0
Mixed Doubles: Jo Muggeridge and Matthew Sprake beat Rachelle Phillips and Joe Morgan 2–0

BASEBALL

American League Championship Series 2006: Detroit Tigers beat Oakland Athletics 4–0
National League Championship Series 2006: St Louis Cardinals beat New York Mets 4–3
World Series 2006: St Louis Cardinals beat Detroit Tigers 4–1

BASKETBALL

BRITISH

MEN
BBL Championship final 2007: Newcastle Eagles beat Scottish Phoenix Rocks 95–82
BBL Trophy final 2007: Plymouth Raiders beat Newcastle Eagles 74–65
BBL Cup final 2007: Guildford Heat beat Scottish Phoenix Rocks 82–79
BBL Champions 2006–7: Guildford Heat

WOMEN
EBL Division 1 2006–7: Sheffield Hatters
EBL Division 1 Play-off final 2006–7: Sheffield Hatters beat Rhondda Rebels 76–63
National Cup final 2007: Sheffield Hatters beat Rhondda Rebels 68–65

USA – NATIONAL BASKETBALL LEAGUE (NBA)
Eastern Conference final 2007: Cleveland Cavaliers beat Detroit Pistons 4–2
Western Conference final 2007: San Antonio Spurs beat Utah Jazz 4–1
NBA final 2007: San Antonio Spurs beat Cleveland Cavaliers 4–0

BOWLS — INDOOR

WORLD CHAMPIONSHIPS 2007
Norfolk, January

Men's Singles: Alex Marshall (Scotland) beat Mervyn King (England) 2–0
Women's Singles: Caroline Brown (Scotland) beat Ellen Falkner (England) 2–0
Men's Pairs: David Gourlay (Australia) and Billy Jackson

(England) beat Jason Greenslade and Robert Weale (Wales) 2–0
Mixed Pairs: Jo Morris and Greg Harlow (England) beat Noreen Stratford (New Zealand) and Ian Bond (England) 2–0

BRITISH ISLES INDOOR BOWLS CHAMPIONSHIPS 2007
Thornaby, March

Singles: Iain McLean (Scotland) beat Nick Donaldson (Channel Islands) 21–14
Pairs: Scotland beat Wales 17–15
Triples: Scotland beat England 16–13
Fours: England beat Scotland 20–16

ENGLISH NATIONAL CHAMPIONSHIPS 2007
Melton Mowbray, April

Singles: Craig Docherty beat Graham Shadwell 21–19
Pairs: Angel beat Blackpool N Hall 28–12
Triples: Exonia beat Egham 19–9
Fours: City of Ely beat Folkestone 24–11
Liberty Trophy (Inter-County Championship) final: Hampshire beat Norfolk 119–118
Champion of Champions: Nick Brett beat Neil Smith 21–4

SCOTTISH NATIONAL CHAMPIONSHIPS 2007
West Lothian, January

Pairs: West Lothian beat Elgin 17–13
Triples: East Lothian beat Arbroath 21–13
Fours: Lanarkshire beat Elgin 22–5

BOWLS — OUTDOOR

BRITISH ISLES CHAMPIONSHIPS 2007
Sighthill, June

Singles: Wales beat Scotland 21–6
Pairs: Ireland beat Wales 19–14
Triples: Scotland beat England 18–16
Fours: England beat Ireland 21–12

ENGLISH NATIONAL CHAMPIONSHIPS 2007
Skegness, August

Singles: Essex C beat Yorkshire B 21–10
Pairs: Kent B beat Buckinghamshire 22–21
Triples: Norfolk A beat Leicestershire A 16–14
Fours: Cumbria B beat Essex B 20–18
Middleton Cup: Devon beat Huntingdonshire 126–112
Champion of Champions: Sam Tolchard beat Raymond Gaskins 21–19

SCOTTISH NATIONAL CHAMPIONSHIPS 2007
Ayr, August

MEN
Singles: Port Glasgow beat Muirhead and Birkhill 21–16
Pairs: Troon Portland beat Blacklands 16–11
Triples: Yoker beat Victoria 16–13
Fours: Overtown Waterloo beat Thornhill 14–9

WELSH NATIONAL CHAMPIONSHIPS 2007
Llandrindod Wells, August

Singles: M. Weaver beat S. Harris 21–14
Doubles: D. Weale and R. Weale beat J. Lewis and G. Maund 23–12
Triples: G. Jones, L. Henderson and M. Selway beat M. Harris, L. Morgans and G. Hughes 22–7
Fours: W. Owen, E. Evans, G. Thomas and A. Howells beat D. Vowles, M. Ackland, A. Meddins and J. Greenslade 22–21

BOXING

PROFESSIONAL BOXING
as at 1 August 2007

WORLD BOXING COUNCIL (WBC) CHAMPIONS
Heavy: Oleg Maskaev (Kazakhstan)
Cruiser: Jean Marc Mormeck (France)
Light-heavy: Chad Dawson (USA)
Super-middle: Mikkel Kessler (Denmark)
Middle: Jermain Taylor (USA)
Super-welter: vacant
Welter: Floyd Mayweather (USA)
Super-light: Junior Witter (Great Britain)
Light: David Diaz (USA)
Super-feather: Juan Manuel Marquez (Mexico)
Feather: Injin Chi (Rep. of Korea)
Super-bantam: Rafael Marquez (Mexico)
Bantam: Hozumi Hasegawa (Japan)
Super-fly: Cristian Mijares (Mexico)
Fly: Daisuke Naito (Japan)
Light-fly: Edgar Sosa (Mexico)
Straw: Eagle Kyowa (Japan)

WORLD BOXING ASSOCIATION (WBA) CHAMPIONS
Heavy: Ruslan Chagaev (Uzbekistan)
Cruiser: Jean Marc Mormeck (France)
Light-heavy: Stipe Drews (Croatia)
Super-middle: Mikkel Kessler (Denmark)
Middle: Felix Sturm (Germany)
Super-welter: Joachim Alcine (Haiti)
Welter: Miguel Cotto (Puerto Rico)
Super-light: Gavin Rees (Great Britain)
Light: Juan Diaz (USA)
Super-feather: Edwin Valero (Venezuela)
Feather: Chris John (Indonesia)
Super-bantam: Celestino Caballero (Panama)
Bantam: Wladimir Sidorenko (Ukraine)
Super-fly: Alexander Munoz (Venezuela)
Fly: Takefumi Sakata (Japan)
Light-fly: Juan Carlos Reveco (Argentina)
Straw: Yukata Niida (Japan)

WORLD BOXING ORGANISATION (WBO) CHAMPIONS
Heavy: Sultan Ibragimov (Russia)
Cruiser: Enzo Maccarinelli (Great Britain)
Light-heavy: Zsolt Erdei (Hungary)
Super-middle: Joe Calzaghe (Great Britain)
Middle: Jermain Taylor (USA)
Super-welter: Sergei Dzindziruk (Ukraine)
Welter: Paul Williams (USA)
Super-light: Ricardo Torres (Colombia)
Light: Juan Diaz (Mexico)
Super-feather: Joan Guzman (Dominican Republic)
Feather: Steve Leuvano (USA)
Super-bantam: Daniel Ponce De Leon (Mexico)

Bantam: Jhonny Gonzalez (Mexico)
Super-fly: Fernando Montiel (Mexico)
Fly: Omar Narvaez (Argentina)
Light-fly: Hugo Cazarez (Mexico)
Straw: Ivan Calderon (Puerto Rico)

INTERNATIONAL BOXING FEDERATION (IBF) CHAMPIONS
Heavy: Wladimir Klitschko (Ukraine)
Cruiser: Steve Cunningham (USA)
Light-heavy: Clinton Woods (Great Britain)
Super-middle: Alejandro Berrio (Colombia)
Middle: Arthur Abraham (Germany)
Super-welter: Cory Spinks (USA)
Welter: Kermit Cintron (USA)
Super-light: Paulie Malignaggi (USA)
Light: Julio Diaz (USA)
Super-feather: Mzonke Fana (South Africa)
Feather: Robert Guerrero (USA)
Super-bantam: Steve Molitor (Canada)
Bantam: vacant
Super-fly: vacant
Fly: Nonito Donaire (Philippines)
Light-fly: Ulises Solis (Mexico)
Straw: Florante Condes (Philippines)

BRITISH CHAMPIONS
Heavy: Danny Williams
Cruiser: John Keaton
Light-heavy: Tony Oakey
Super-middle: Carl Froch
Middle: Howard Eastman
Light-middle: Jamie Moore
Welter: Kevin Anderson
Light-welter: Colin Lynes
Light: Jonathan Thaxton
Super-feather: Carl Johanneson
Feather: John Simpson
Super-bantam: Esham Pickering
Bantam: Ian Napa
Fly: vacant

CHESS

FIDE World Champion 2006: Vladimir Kramnik (Russia)
British Champion 2007: Jacob Aargaard

CRICKET

TEST SERIES

AUSTRALIA V ENGLAND
(Australia won series 5–0)
Brisbane (23–27 November 2006): Australia beat England by 277 runs. Australia 602–9 and 202–1; England 157 and 370
Adelaide (1–5 December 2006): Australia beat England by 6 wickets. England 551–6 and 129; Australia 513 and 168–4
Perth (14–18 December 2006): Australia beat England by 206 runs. Australia 244 and 527–5; England 215 and 350
Melbourne (26–28 December 2006): Australia beat England by an innings and 99 runs. England 159 and 161; Australia 419
Sydney (2–5 January 2007): Australia beat England by 10 wickets. England 291 and 147; Australia 393 and 46–0

ENGLAND V WEST INDIES
(England won series 3–0)
Lord's (17–21 May 2007): England drew with West Indies. England 553–5 and 284–8; West Indies 437 and 89–0
Headingley (25–28 May 2007): England beat West Indies by an innings and 283 runs. England 570–7; West Indies 146 and 141
Old Trafford (7–11 June 2007): England beat West Indies by 60 runs. England 370 and 313; West Indies 229 and 394
Chester-le-Street (15–19 June 2007): England beat West Indies by 7 wickets. West Indies 287 and 222; England 400 and 111–3

ENGLAND V INDIA
(India won series 1–0)
Lord's (19–23 July 2007): England drew with India. England 298 and 282; India 201 and 282–9
Trent Bridge (27–31 July 2007): India beat England by 7 wickets. England 198 and 355; India 481 and 73–3
The Oval (9–13 August 2007): England drew with India. India 664 and 180–6; England 345 and 369–6

ONE-DAY INTERNATIONALS

TRIANGULAR SERIES
Melbourne (12 January 2007): Australia beat England by 8 wickets. England 242–8; Australia 246–2
Hobart (16 January 2007): England beat New Zealand by 3 wickets. New Zealand 205–9; England 206–7
Brisbane (19 January 2007): Australia beat England by 4 wickets. England 155; Australia 156–6
Adelaide (23 January 2007): New Zealand beat England by 90 runs. New Zealand 210; England 120
Adelaide (26 January 2007): Australia beat England by 9 wickets. England 110; Australia 111–1
Perth (30 January 2007): New Zealand beat England by 58 runs. New Zealand 318–7; England 260–8
Sydney (2 February 2007): England beat Australia by 92 runs. England 292–7; Australia 200
Brisbane (6 February 2007): England beat New Zealand by 14 runs. England 270–7; New Zealand 256–8
First final: Melbourne (9 February 2007): England beat Australia by 4 wickets. Australia 252; England 253–6
Second final: Sydney (11 February 2007): England beat Australia by 34 runs (Duckworth/Lewis method). England 246–8; Australia 152–8

ENGLAND V WEST INDIES
Lord's (1 July 2007): England beat West Indies by 79 runs. England 225; West Indies 146
Edgbaston (4 July 2007): West Indies beat England by 61 runs. West Indies 278–5; England 217
Trent Bridge (7 July 2007): West Indies beat England by 93 runs. West Indies 289–5; England 196

TWENTY20 INTERNATIONALS
Sydney (9 January 2007): Australia beat England by 77 runs. Australia 221–5; England 144–9
The Oval (28 June 2007): West Indies beat England by 15 runs. West Indies 208–8; England 193–7
The Oval (29 June 2007): England beat West Indies by 5 wickets. West Indies 169–7; England 173–5

WORLD CUP
West Indies, March–April

Group A

	Matches	*Won*	*Lost*	*Tied*	*Points*	*Net run rate*
Australia	3	3	0	0	6	+3.433
South Africa	3	2	1	0	4	+2.403
Netherlands	3	1	2	0	2	−2.527
Scotland	3	0	3	0	0	−3.793

Group B

	Matches	*Won*	*Lost*	*Tied*	*Points*	*Net run rate*
Sri Lanka	3	3	0	0	6	+3.493
Bangladesh	3	2	1	0	4	−1.523
India	3	1	2	0	2	+1.206
Bermuda	3	0	3	0	0	-4.345

Group C

	Matches	*Won*	*Lost*	*Tied*	*Points*	*Net run rate*
New Zealand	3	3	0	0	6	+2.138
England	3	2	1	0	4	+0.148
Kenya	3	1	2	0	2	−1.194
Canada	3	0	3	0	0	−1.389

Group D

	Matches	*Won*	*Lost*	*Tied*	*Points*	*Net run rate*
West Indies	3	3	0	0	6	+0.764
Ireland	3	1	1	1	3	−0.092
Pakistan	3	1	2	0	2	+0.089
Zimbabwe	3	0	2	1	1	−0.886

Super Eights

	Matches	*Won*	*Lost*	*Tied*	*Points*	*Net run rate*
Australia	7	7	0	0	14	+2.400
Sri Lanka	7	5	2	0	10	+1.483
New Zealand	7	5	2	0	10	+0.253
South Africa	7	4	3	0	8	+0.313
England	7	3	4	0	6	−0.394
West Indies	7	2	5	0	4	−0.566
Bangladesh	7	1	6	0	2	−1.514
Ireland	7	1	6	0	2	−1.730

Semi-finals

Kingston (24 April 2007): Sri Lanka beat New Zealand by 81 runs. Sri Lanka 289–5; New Zealand 208

Gros Islet (25 April 2007): Australia beat South Africa by 7 wickets. South Africa 149; Australia 153–3

Final

Bridgetown (28 April 2007): Australia beat Sri Lanka by 53 runs (Duckworth/Lewis method). Australia 281–4; Sri Lanka 215–8

ENGLAND AND WALES DOMESTIC COMPETITIONS

County Championship 2006, Division 1: Sussex, 242pts; *Relegated:* Nottinghamshire, 153pts; Middlesex, 133.50pts – *Division 2:* Surrey, 262pts; *Promoted:* Worcestershire, 229pts

Pro40 2006, Division 1: Essex, 11pts; *Relegated:* Glamorgan, 7pts; Durham, 6pts; Middlesex, 4pts – *Division 2:* Gloucestershire, 12pts; *Promoted:* Worcestershire, 12pts; Hampshire, 11pts

FP Trophy final 2007: Durham beat Hampshire by 125 runs. Durham 312–5; Hampshire 187

Twenty20 Cup final 2007: Kent beat Gloucestershire by four wickets. Gloucestershire 146–8; Kent 147–6

OTHER INTERNATIONAL DOMESTIC CHAMPIONSHIPS

Australia: Pura Cup final 2006–7: Tasmania beat New South Wales by 421 runs. Tasmania 340 and 460; New South Wales 230 and 149. *Ford Cup final 2006–7:* Queensland beat Victoria by 21 runs. Queensland 274–5; Victoria 253–9. *KFC Twenty20 Cup final 2006–7:* Victoria beat Tasmania by 10 runs. Victoria 160–6; Tasmania 150–8

Bangladesh: National League 2006–7: Dhaka Division, 42pts. *National One-Day League 2006–7:* Dhaka Division, 8pts

India: Irani Trophy final 2006–7: Rest of India beat Uttar Pradesh by 9 wickets. Uttar Pradesh 148 and 166; Rest of India 201 and 115–1. *Ranji Trophy Super League final 2006–7:* Mumbai beat Bengal by 132 runs. Mumbai 320 and 294; Bengal 143 and 339. *Ranji Trophy One-Day final 2006-7:* Mumbai beat Rajasthan by 72 runs. Mumbai 287–6; Rajasthan 215. *Deodhar Trophy 2006–7:* West Zone, 19 pts. *Duleep Trophy final 2006–7:* North Zone beat Sri Lanka A by 8 wickets. North Zone 636–7 and 87–2; Sri Lanka A 296 and 426. *Twenty20 Trophy final 2006–7:* Tamil Nadu beat Punjab by 2 wickets. Punjab 134–8; Tamil Nadu 135–8

New Zealand: State Championship final 2006–7: Northern Districts drew with Canterbury. Northern Districts won title. Canterbury 443–8 and 249–6; Northern Districts 319 and 258–2. *State Shield final 2006–7:* Auckland beat Otago by 5 wickets. Otago 119; Auckland 120–5. *Twenty20 final 2006-7:* Auckland beat Otago by 60 runs. Auckland 211–4; Otago 151

Pakistan: Quaid-e-Azam Trophy final 2006–7: Karachi Urban beat Sialkot by 8 wickets. Karachi Urban 403 and 69–2; Sialkot 183 and 288. *ABN Amro Cup final 2006–7:* Peshawar beat Sialkot by 8 wickets. Sialkot 137; Peshawar 138–2. *Patron's Cup final 2006–7:* National Bank of Pakistan beat Habib Bank by 3 wickets. Habib Bank 203; National Bank of Pakistan 206–7. *Patron's Trophy 2006–7:* Habib Bank. *Twenty20 Cup final 2006–7:* Sialkot beat Karachi by 14 runs. Sialkot 151; Karachi 137–7

South Africa: SuperSport Series 2006–7: Titans, 149.240pts. *Provincial Cup final 2006–7:* KwaZulu Natal beat Northerns by 8 wickets. Northerns 121; KwaZulu Natal 124–2. *Pro20 Series final 2006–7:* Lions beat Cobras by 6 wickets. Cobras 147–9; Lions 148–4. *Provincial Challenge final 2006–7:* Gauteng beat Eastern Province by 95 runs. Gauteng 286 and 345; Eastern Province 333 and 203. *Domestic Championship final 2006–7:* Cobras beat Warriors by 18 runs. Cobras 213–9; Warriors 195

Sri Lanka: Premier League Tournament 2006–7: Colombo, 95.720pts. *Premier Limited Overs Tournament final 2006–7:* Nondescripts beat Moors by 6 wickets. Moors 167; Nondescripts 169–4. *Twenty20 Cup final:* Ragama beat Saracens by 111 runs. Ragama 237–6; Saracens 126

West Indies: Carib Challenge final 2006–7: Trinidad and Tobago beat Barbados by 49 runs. Trinidad and Tobago 304 and 200; Barbados 229 and 226. *KFC Cup final 2006-7:* Trinidad and Tobago beat Windward Islands by 5 runs. Trinidad and Tobago 210-8; Windward Islands 205

Zimbabwe: Logan Cup 2006–7: Easterns. *Inter-Provincial One-Day Competition 2006–7:* Easterns

CURLING

MEN'S WORLD CHAMPIONSHIP 2007
Edmonton, Canada, March–April

Final: Canada beat Germany 8–3

WOMEN'S WORLD CHAMPIONSHIP 2007
Aomori, Japan, March

Final: Canada beat Denmark 8–4

EUROPEAN CHAMPIONSHIPS 2006
Basel, Switzerland, December

Men's final: Switzerland beat Scotland 7–6
Women's final: Russia beat Italy 9–4

CYCLING

Vuelta D'Espana 2006: Alexandre Vinokourov (Kazakhstan)
Tour de France 2007: Alberto Contador (Spain)
Giro d'Italia 2007: Danilo Di Luca (Italy)

WORLD ROAD RACE CHAMPIONSHIPS 2006
Salzburg, Austria, September

MEN
Elite Time Trial: Fabian Cancellara (Switzerland)
Road Race: Paolo Bettini (Italy)

WOMEN
Elite Time Trial: Kristin Armstrong (USA)
Road Race: Marianne Vos (Netherlands)

BRITISH NATIONAL ROAD RACE CHAMPIONSHIPS 2007
Abergavenny, August

MEN
Road Race: David Millar

WORLD TRACK CHAMPIONSHIPS 2007
Palma de Mallorca, Spain, March–April

MEN
Points Race: Joan Llaneras Rosello (Spain)
Olympic Sprint: Theo Bos (Netherlands)
1km Time Trial: Chris Hoy (Great Britain)
Individual Pursuit: Bradley Wiggins (Great Britain)
Scratch Race: Kam-Po Wong (Hong Kong)
Keirin: Chris Hoy (Great Britain)
Team Pursuit: Great Britain
Madison: Franco Marvulli and Bruno Risi (Switzerland)
Team Sprint: France
Omnium: Alois Kankovsky (Czech Republic)

WOMEN
Points Race: Katherine Bates (Australia)
500m Time Trial: Anna Meares (Australia)
Individual Pursuit: Sarah Hammer (USA)
Scratch: Yumari Gonzalez Valdivieso (Cuba)
Keirin: Victoria Pendleton (Great Britain)
Sprint: Victoria Pendleton (Great Britain)
Team Sprint: Great Britain

DARTS

BDO World Championship 2007: Martin Adams (England) beat Phill Nixon (England) 7–6
PDC World Championship 2006–7: Raymond van Barneveld (Netherlands) beat Phil Taylor (England) 7–6

EQUESTRIANISM

Burghley Horse Trials 2006: Lucinda Fredericks (Australia) on Headley Britannia
Badminton Horse Trials 2007: Lucinda Fredericks (Australia) on Headley Britannia
British Open Horse Trials 2007 (Gatcombe Park): Mary King (Great Britain) on Call Again Cavalier

ETON FIVES

Amateur Championship (Kinnaird Cup) final 2007: Tom Dunbar and Peter Dunbar beat James Toop and Matthew Wiseman 3–1
Alan Barber Cup final 2007: Old Olavians beat Old Harrovians 2–1
County Championship final 2007: Kent beat Warwickshire 3–0
Schools' Championship 2007: Shrewsbury beat Highgate 3–0
Preparatory Schools' Tournament 2007: Highgate 1 beat Highgate 2 2–0

FENCING

WORLD CHAMPIONSHIP 2006
Turin, Italy, October

MEN
Individual Foil: Peter Joppich (Germany)
Individual Epée: Lei Wang (China)
Individual Sabre: Stanislav Pozdniakov (Russia)
Team Foil: France
Team Epée: France
Team Sabre: France

WOMEN
Individual Foil: Margherita Granbassi (Italy)
Individual Epée: Timea Nagy (Hungary)
Individual Sabre: Rebecca Ward (USA)
Team Foil: Russia
Team Epée: China
Team Sabre: France

EUROPEAN CHAMPIONSHIPS 2007
Gent, Belgium, July

MEN
Individual Foil: Andrea Baldini (Italy)
Individual Epée: Jerome Jeannet (France)
Individual Sabre: Jorge Pina (Spain)
Team Foil: Germany
Team Epée: Hungary
Team Sabre: Russia

WOMEN
Individual Foil: Eugyenia Lamonova (Russia)
Individual Epée: Laura Flessel-Colovic (France)
Individual Sabre: Ekaterina Fedorkina (Russia)
Team Foil: Hungary

Team Epée: Italy
Team Sabre: France

BRITISH CHAMPIONSHIPS 2007
Sheffield, July

MEN
Individual Foil: Richard Kruse
Individual Epée: Jon Willis
Individual Sabre: Chris Buxton
Team Foil: Sussex House
Team Epée: Haverstock Leon Paul A
Team Sabre: Brentwood

WOMEN
Individual Foil: Anna Bentley
Individual Epée: Mary Cohen
Individual Sabre: Jo Hutchison
Team Foil: Sussex House
Team Epée: LTFC Lawrence
Team Sabre: Scimitar A

GOLF (MEN)

THE MAJOR CHAMPIONSHIPS 2007
US Masters (Augusta, 5–8 April): Zach Johnson (USA), 289
US Open (Oakmont, 14–17 June): Angel Cabrera (Argentina), 285
The Open (Carnoustie, 19–22 July): Padraig Harrington (Ireland), 277
US PGA Championship (Southern Hills, 9–12 August): Tiger Woods (USA), 272

WORLD RANKINGS
as at 1 August 2007

1. Tiger Woods *(USA)*; 2. Jim Furyk *(USA)*; 3. Phil Mickelson *(USA)*; 4. Ernie Els *(South Africa)*; 5. Adam Scott *(Australia)*

PGA EUROPEAN TOUR 2006
Omega European Masters (Crans-Sur-Sierre, France): Bradley Dredge (Wales), 267
Open de Madrid (La Moraleja II): Ian Poulter (England), 266
World Match-Play Championship (Wentworth, England): Paul Casey (England)
WGC American Express Championship (The Grove, England): Tiger Woods (USA), 261
Alfred Dunhill Links Championship (Old Course, St Andrews): Padraig Harrington (Ireland), 271
Mallorca Classic (Pula): Niclas Fasth (Sweden), 275
Volvo Masters (Valderrama, Spain): Jeev Milkha Singh (India), 282

TEAM CHAMPIONSHIPS
Ryder Cup (K Club, Ireland): Europe beat USA, $18\frac{1}{2}$–$9\frac{1}{2}$
WGC Barbados World Cup (Sandy Lane): Germany

EUROPEAN TOUR ORDER OF MERIT 2006
1. Padraig Harrington *(Ireland)*; 2. Paul Casey *(England)*; 3. David Howell *(England)*; 4. Robert Karlsson *(Sweden)*; 5. Ernie Els *(South Africa)*

PGA EUROPEAN TOUR 2007
Champions' Tournament (Sheshan, China): Y. E. Yang (Rep. of Korea), 274
Hong Kong Open (Hong Kong): Jose Manuel Lara (Spain), 265
Mastercard Masters (Huntingdale, Australia): Justin Rose (England), 276
New Zealand Open (Gulf Harbour): Nathan Green (Australia), 279
Alfred Dunhill Championship (Leopard Creek, South Africa): Alvaro Quiros (Spain), 275
South African Airways Open (Humewood): Ernie Els (South Africa), 264
Joburg Open (Royal Johannesburg and Kensington): Ariel Canete (Argentina), 266
Abu Dhabi Golf Championship (Abu Dhabi): Paul Casey (England), 271
Qatar Masters (Doha): Retief Goosen (South Africa), 273
Dubai Desert Classic (Emirates): Henrik Stenson (Sweden), 269
Malaysian Open (Saujana): Peter Hedblom (Sweden), 280
Indonesia Open (Damai Indah): Mikko Ilonen (Finland), 275
WGC – Accenture Match Play (Gallery, Arizona): Henrik Stenson (Sweden)
Johnnie Walker Classic (Blue Canyon, Thailand): Anton Haig (South Africa), 275
Singapore Masters (Laguna National): Wen-chong Liang (China), 277
TCL Classic (Yalong Bay, China): Chapchai Nirat (Thailand), 266
WGC – CA Championship (Doral Resort, Florida): Tiger Woods (USA), 278
Madeira Island Open (Santo da Serra): Daniel Vancsik (Argentina), 270
Estoril Open de Portugal (Quinta da Marinha): Pablo Martin (Spain), 277
China Open (Shanghai Silport): Markus Brier (Austria), 274
Asian Open (Shanghai Pudong): Raphael Jacquelin (France), 278
Open de Espana (Centro Nacional de Golf): Charl Schwartzel (South Africa), 272
Italian Open (Castello di Tolcinasco): Gonzalo Fdez-Castano (Spain), 200
Valle Romano Open de Andalucia (Aloha): Lee Westwood (England), 268
Irish Open (Adare Manor): Padraig Harrington (Ireland), 283
BMW PGA Championship (Wentworth): Anders Hansen (Denmark), 280
Wales Open (Celtic Manor): Richard Sterne (South Africa), 263
BA-CA Open (Fontana, Austria): Richard Green (Australia), 268
Open de St Omer (Aa St Omer, France): Carl Suneson (Spain), 276
BMW International Open (München Nord-Eichenried, Germany): Niclas Fasth (Sweden), 275
Open de France (Le Golf National): Graeme Storm (England), 277
European Open (K Club, Ireland): Colin Montgomerie (Scotland), 269
Scottish Open (Loch Lomond): Gregory Havret (France), 270
Players' Championship of Europe (Gut Kaden, Germany): Andres Romero (Argentina), 269

Russian Open (Le Meridien, Moscow): Per Ulrik Johansson (Sweden), 265
WGC – Bridgestone Invitational (Firestone, USA): Tiger Woods (USA), 272
Scandinavian Masters (Arlandastad, Sweden): Mikko Ilonen (Finland), 274
KLM Masters (Kennemer, the Netherlands): Ross Fisher (England), 268

AMATEUR CHAMPIONSHIPS 2007
British Amateur Championship (Royal Lytham & St Annes): Drew Weaver (USA)
English Amateur Championship (Royal St George's): Daniel Wilett (England)
Brabazon Trophy (English Open Strokeplay) (Forest of Arden): Romain Bechu (France) and Jamie Moul (England) shared the trophy, 281
Scottish Amateur Championship (Prestwick): John Gallagher (Scotland)
Scottish Open Strokeplay (Royal Dornoch): Kevin McAlpine (Scotland), 271
Welsh Amateur Championship (Royal St David's): Llewellyn Matthews (Wales)
Welsh Open Strokeplay (Machynys Peninsular): John Parry (England), 277
Irish Amateur Open Championship (Royal Dublin): Lloyd Saltman (Scotland), 291
Irish Amateur Close Championship (Cork): Shane Lowry (Ireland)
Lytham Trophy (Royal Lytham Golf Club): Lloyd Saltman (Scotland), 279
Berkshire Trophy (The Berkshire): Luke Collins (England), 276

GOLF (WOMEN)

THE MAJOR CHAMPIONSHIPS 2007
Kraft Nabisco Championship (Mission Hills Country Club, USA, 29 March–1 April): Morgan Pressel (USA), 285
US Women's Open (Pine Needles Lodge, 28 June–1 July): Cristie Kerr (USA), 279
LPGA Championship (Bulle Rock, USA, 7–10 June): Suzann Pettersen (Norway), 274
Women's British Open (St Andrews Old Course, Scotland): Lorena Ochoa (Mexico), 287

EUROPEAN LPGA TOUR 2006
Nykredit Masters (Odense, Denmark): Karen-Margrethe Juul (Denmark), 273
Austrian Ladies' Open (Fohrenwald-Wiener): Sophie Gustafson (Sweden), 271
Ladies' English Open (Chart Hills): Cecilia Ekelundh (Sweden), 210
Dubai Ladies' Masters (Emirates): Annika Sorenstam (Sweden), 270

EUROPEAN LPGA TOUR ORDER OF MERIT 2006
1. Laura Davies *(England)*; 2. Gwladys Nocera *(France)*; 3. Annika Sorenstam *(Sweden)*; 4. Sophie Gustafson *(Sweden)*; 5. Veronica Zorzi *(Italy)*

EUROPEAN LPGA TOUR 2007
Ladies' Australian Open (Royal Sydney): Karrie Webb (Australia), 278
ANZ Ladies' Masters (Royal Pines, Australia): Karrie Webb (Australia), 269
Tenerife Ladies' Open (Golf del Sur): Nikki Garrett (Australia), 287
Open de Espana Femenino (Mediterraneo): Nikki Garrett (Australia), 275
Ladies' Swiss Open (Gerre Losone): Bettina Hauert (Germany), 285
Ladies' Italian Open (Parco de Medici): Trish Johnson (England), 273
Northern Ireland Ladies' Open (Hilton Temple Patrick): Lisa Hall (England), 214
KLM Ladies' Open (Eindhovensche, Netherlands): Gwladys Nocera (France), 201
Catalonia Ladies' Masters (Masia Bach, Spain): Ashleigh Simon (South Africa), 208
Open de France (Le Golf d'Arras): Linda Wessberg (Sweden), 277
Ladies' Open de Portugal (Gramacho Pestana): Sophie Giquel (France), 206
Ladies' English Open (Chart Hills): Becky Brewerton (Wales), 209
Evian Masters (Evian Les Bains, France): Natalie Gulbis (USA), 284
Scandinavian TPC (Loddekopinge, Sweden): Catriona Matthew (Scotland), 279
Wales Ladies' Championship of Europe (Machynys Peninsular): Joanne Mills (Australia), 282
SAS Masters (Losby, Norway): Suzann Pettersen (Norway), 204

TEAM CHAMPIONSHIP
Women's World Cup of Golf (Gary Player, South Africa): Paraguay

AMATEUR CHAMPIONSHIPS 2007
British Open Championship (Alwoodley): Carlota Ciganda (Spain)
Ladies' British Open Amateur Strokeplay Championship: (Conwy): Mel Reid (England), 290
English Close Amateur Championship (Littlestone): Naomi Edwards (England)
English Strokeplay Championship: Jodi Ewart (England), 304
Helen Holm (Scottish Open Strokeplay Championship) (Troon): Mel Reid (England), 211
Scottish Ladies Close Amateur Championship (Barassie): Jenna Wilson (Scotland)
Welsh Open Strokeplay (Newport): Heather Macrae (Scotland), 219
Welsh Close Championship (Royal St David's): Breanne Loucks (Wales)
Irish Open Strokeplay Championship (Clandeboye): Stacey Keating (Australia), 225
Irish Close Championship (Lahinch): Karen Delaney (Ireland)

GREYHOUND RACING

2006
The Regency (Hove): Caloona Striker
Pall Mall (Oxford): Seomra Rock
Golden Jacket (Crayford): Greenacre Lin
Grand National (Wimbledon): Suit Man
St Leger (Wimbledon): Ninja Blue

2007
The Regency (Hove): Spiridon Louis
Pall Mall (Oxford): Ballymac Charley
Golden Jacket (Crayford): Walk the Line
Grand National (Wimbledon): Jos Cigar
The Derby (Wimbledon): Westmead Lord

GYMNASTICS

EUROPEAN CHAMPIONSHIPS 2007
Amsterdam, Netherlands, April

MEN
Overall Champion: Maxim Deviatovski (Russia)
Individual Apparatus Champions
Floor: Rafael Martinez (Spain)
Pommel Horse: Krisztian Berki (Hungary)
Still Rings: Olexander Vorobyov (Ukraine)
Vault: Anton Golotsutskov (Russia)
Parallel Bars: Mitja Petkovsek (Slovenia)
High Bar: Fabian Hambuechen (Germany)

WOMEN
Overall Champion: Vanessa Ferrari (Italy)
Individual Apparatus Champions
Floor: Vanessa Ferrari (Italy)
Beam: Yulia Lozhecko (Russia)
Vault: Carlotta Giovannini (Italy)
Asymmetric Bars: Dariya Zgoba (Ukraine)

BRITISH MEN'S CHAMPIONSHIPS 2006
Wigan, November

Overall Champion: Ross Brewer
Individual Apparatus Champions
Floor: Steven Jehu
Pommel Horse: Daniel Keatings
Still Rings: David Massam
Vault: Danny Lawrence
Parallel Bars: Adam Cox
High Bar: David Eaton

BRITISH WOMEN'S CHAMPIONSHIPS 2007
Guildford, July
Overall Champion: Elizabeth Tweddle
Individual Apparatus Champions
Floor: Kayleigh Cooke
Beam: Hannah Clowes
Vault: Marissa King
Asymmetric Bars: Elizabeth Tweddle

HOCKEY

MEN
English Hockey League 2006–7: Premier Division: Reading, 44pts; *Division One:* Havant, 46pts; *National North Division:* Sheffield University Bankers, 53pts; *National South Division:* Old Georgians, 61pts
English Hockey League Indoor Championship final 2007: Canterbury beat East Grinstead 7–6
English Hockey League Cup final 2006–7: Cannock beat East Grinstead 1–0
County Championship final 2007: Cheshire beat Sussex 5–4 on penalties (3–3 aet)

WOMEN
English Hockey League 2006–7: Premier Division: Leicester, 44pts; *Division One:* Poynton, 38pts; *National North Division:* University of Durham, 51pts; *National South Division:* Reading, 60pts
English Hockey League Indoor Championship final 2007: Slough beat Bowden Hightown 7–4
English Hockey League Cup final 2006–7: Bowdon Hightown beat Slough 2–0
County Champions 2007: Cumbria

HORSE RACING

THE FLAT

THE CLASSICS

ONE THOUSAND GUINEAS

(1814) Rowley Mile, Newmarket, for three-year-old fillies

Year	*Winner*	*Betting*	*Owner*	*Jockey*	*Trainer*	*Runners*
2003	Russian Rhythm	12–1	Cheveley Park Stud	K. Fallon	Sir Michael Stoute	19
2004	Attraction	11–2	Duke of Roxburghe	K. Darley	M. Johnston	16
2005	Virginia Waters	12–1	Mrs J. Magnier and M. Tabor	K. Fallon	A. O'Brien	20
2006	Speciosa	10–1	M. H. Sly	M. Fenton	Mrs P. Sly	13
2007	Finsceal Beo	5–4	M. A. Ryan	K. Manning	J. Bolger	21

TWO THOUSAND GUINEAS

(1809) Rowley Mile, Newmarket, for three-year-olds

Year	*Winner*	*Betting*	*Owner*	*Jockey*	*Trainer*	*Runners*
2003	Refuse To Bend	9–2	Moyglare Stud Farms	P. Smullen	D. Weld	20
2004	Haafhd	11–2	Sheikh Hamdan Al Maktoum	R. Hills	B. Hills	14
2005	Footstepsinthesand	13–2	Mrs J. Magnier and M. Tabor	K. Fallon	A. O'Brien	19
2006	George Washington	6–4	Mrs J. Magnier and M. Tabor	K. Fallon	A. O'Brien	14
2007	Cockney Rebel	25–1	P. Cunningham	O. Peslier	G. Huffer	24

THE DERBY

(1780) Epsom, 1 mile and about 4 f, for three-year-olds

The first winner was Sir Charles Bunbury's Diomed in 1780. The owners with the record number of winners are Lord Egremont, who won in 1782, 1804, 1805, 1807, 1826 (also won five Oaks); and the late Aga Khan, who won in 1930, 1935, 1936, 1948, 1952. Other winning owners are: Duke of Grafton (1802, 1809, 1810, 1815); Mr J. Bowes (1835, 1843, 1852, 1853); Sir J. Hawley (1851, 1858, 1859, 1868); the 1st Duke of Westminster (1880, 1882, 1886, 1899); and Sir Victor Sassoon (1953, 1957, 1958, 1960).

The Derby was run at Newmarket in 1915–18 and 1940–5.

Year	*Winner*	*Betting*	*Owner*	*Jockey*	*Trainer*	*Runners*
2003	Kris Kin	6–1	Saeed Suhail	K. Fallon	Sir Michael Stoute	20
2004	North Light	7–2	Exors of the late Lord Weinstock	K. Fallon	Sir Michael Stoute	14
2005	Motivator	3–1	Royal Ascot Racing Club	J. Murtagh	M. Bell	13
2006	Sir Percy	6–1	A. E. Pakenham	M. Dwyer	M. Tregoning	18
2007	Authorized	5–4	Saleh Al Homeizi and Imad Al Sagar	L. Dettori	P. Chapple-Hyam	17

THE OAKS

(1779) Epsom, 1 mile and about 4 f, for three-year-old fillies

Year	*Winner*	*Betting*	*Owner*	*Jockey*	*Trainer*	*Runners*
2003	Casual Look	10–1	W. Farish III	M. Dwyer	A. Balding	15
2004	Ouija Board	7–2	Lord Derby	K. Fallon	E. Dunlop	7
2005	Eswarah	11–4	Sheikh Hamdan Al Maktoum	R. Hills	M. Jarvis	12
2006	Alexandrova	9–4	Mrs J. Magnier and M. Tabor	K. Fallon	A. O'Brien	10
2007	Light Shift	13–2	Niarchos family	T. Durcan	H. Cecil	14

ST LEGER

(1776) Doncaster, 1 mile and about 6 f, for three-year-olds (2006 run at York)

Year	*Winner*	*Betting*	*Owner*	*Jockey*	*Trainer*	*Runners*
2002	Bollin Eric	7–1	Sir Neil and Lady Westbrook	K. Darley	T. Easterby	8
2003	Brian Boru	5–4	Mrs J. Magnier	J. Spencer	A. O'Brien	12
2004	Rule Of Law	3–1	Godolphin	K. McEvoy	Saeed bin Suroor	9
2005	Scorpion	10–11	Mrs J. Magnier and M. Tabor	L. Dettori	A. O'Brien	6
2006	Sixties Icon	11–8	Mrs S. Roy	L. Dettori	J. Noseda	11

RESULTS

CAMBRIDGESHIRE HANDICAP
(1839) Newmarket, 1 mile

2003 Chivalry (4y), G. Duffield
2004 Spanish Don (6y), L. Keniry
2005 Blue Monday (4y), S. Drowne
2006 Formal Decree (3y), J. Spencer

PRIX DE L'ARC DE TRIOMPHE
(1920) Longchamp, 1½ miles

2003 Dalakhani (3y), C. Soumillon
2004 Bago (3y), T. Gillet
2005 Hurricane Run (3y), K. Fallon
2006 Rail Link (3y), S. Pasquier

CESAREWITCH
(1839) Newmarket, 2 miles and about 2 f

2003 Landing Light (8y), P. Eddery
2004 Contact Dancer (5y), R. Ffrench
2005 Sergeant Cecil (6y), A. Munro
2006 Detroit City (4y), J. Spencer

CHAMPION STAKES
(1877) Newmarket, 1 mile and 2 f

2003 Rakti (4y), P. Robinson
2004 Haafhd (3y), R. Hills
2005 David Junior (3y), J. Spencer
2006 Pride (6y), C-P. Lemaire

DUBAI WORLD CUP
(1996) Dubai, 1 mile and 2 f

2004 Pleasantly Perfect (6y), A. Solis
2005 Roses In May (5y), J. Velazquez
2006 Electrocutionist (5y), L. Dettori
2007 Invasor (5y), F. Jara

LINCOLN HANDICAP
(1965) Doncaster, 1 mile

2004 Babodana (4y), P. Robinson
2005 Stream Of Gold (5y), R. Winston
2006 Blythe Knight (6y), G. Gibbons
2007 Very Wise (5y), J. Fanning

JOCKEY CLUB STAKES
(1894) Newmarket, 2 miles and 24 yds

2004 Gamut (5y), K. Fallon
2005 Alkaased (5y), J. Fortune
2006 Shirocco (5y), C. Soumillon
2007 Sixties Icon (4y), L. Dettori

PRIX DU JOCKEY CLUB
(1836) Chantilly, 1½ miles, for three-year-olds

2004 Blue Canari, T. Thulliez
2005 Shamardal, L. Dettori
2006 Darsi, C. Soumillon
2007 Lawman, L. Dettori

ASCOT GOLD CUP
(1807) Ascot, 2 miles and about 4 f

2004 Papineau (4y), L. Dettori
2005 Westerner (6y), O. Peslier
2006 Yeats (5y), K. Fallon
2007 Yeats (6y), M. J. Kinane

IRISH DERBY
(1866) Curragh, 1½ miles, for three-year-olds

2004 Grey Swallow, P. Smullen
2005 Hurricane Run, K. Fallon
2006 Dylan Thomas, K. Fallon
2007 Soldier of Fortune, J. A. Heffernan

ECLIPSE STAKES
(1886) Sandown, 1 mile and about 2 f

2004 Refuse To Bend (4y), L. Dettori
2005 Oratorio (3y), K. Fallon
2006 David Junior (4y), J. Spencer
2007 Notnowcato (5y), R. Moore

KING GEORGE VI AND QUEEN ELIZABETH DIAMOND STAKES
(1952) Ascot, 1 mile and about 4 f

2004 Doyen (4y), L. Dettori
2005 Azamour (4yr), M. J. Kinane
2006 Hurricane Run (4yr), C. Soumillon
2007 Dylan Thomas (4y), J. P. Murtagh

GOODWOOD CUP
(1812) Goodwood, about 2 miles

2004 Darasim (6y), J. Fanning
2005 Distinction (6y), M. J. Kinane
2006 Yeats (5yr), M. J. Kinane
2007 Alegretto (4y), R. Moore

STATISTICS

WINNING FLAT OWNERS 2006	
Godolphin	£1,513,116
Sheikh Hamdan Al Maktoum	1,199,775
Gainsborough Stud	975,908
Cheveley Park Stud	907,458
A. E. Pakenham	811,711
Mrs J. Magnier, M. Tabor and D. Smith	762,110
K. Abdulla	690,032
Mrs S. Roy	528,178
M. Tabor	520,162
Sheikh Ahmed Al Maktoum	499,793

WINNING FLAT TRAINERS 2006	
Sir Michael Stoute	£2,837,612
M. Johnston	1,755,651
B. W. Hills	1,661,573
R. Hannon	1,633,553
A. P. O'Brien	1,585,326
Saeed bin Suroor	1,513,116
M. R. Channon	1,413,557
B. J. Meehan	1,365,779
J. Noseda	1,211,153
K. A. Ryan	1,192,922

WINNING FLAT SIRES 2006	*Races won*	*Stakes*
Danehill by Danzig	64	£1,640,675
Mark of Esteem by Darshaan	52	1,583,381
Sadler's Wells by Northern Dancer	41	1,539,791
Pivotal by Polar Falcon	101	1,224,478
Montjeu by Sadler's Wells	34	1,201,018
Cape Cross by Green Desert	60	1,192,219
Galileo by Sadler's Wells	40	1,072,209
Danehill Dancer by Danehill	61	1,042,322
Indian Ridge by Ahonoora	57	1,026,129
Dansili by Danehill	92	970,745

WINNING FLAT JOCKEYS 2006

	1st	2nd	3rd	Unpl.	Total mts
R. L. Moore	182	147	141	704	1,174
J. P. Spencer	155	113	98	474	840
E. Ahern	140	128	109	779	1,156
R. Winston	136	121	104	620	981
L. Dettori	131	81	73	306	591
N. Callan	129	127	128	644	1,028
S. Sanders	117	105	80	532	834
R. Hughes	113	95	107	489	804
J. Fanning	108	94	99	637	938
P. Hanagan	107	118	101	712	1,038

NATIONAL HUNT

HENNESSY GOLD CUP
(1957) Newbury, 3 miles and about 2½ f

2003 Strong Flow (6y), R. Walsh
2004 Celestial Gold (6y), T. Murphy
2005 Trabolgan (7y), M. Fitzgerald
2006 State of Play (6y), P. Moloney

TINGLE CREEK CHASE
(1957) Sandown, 2 miles

2003 Moscow Flyer (9y), B. Geraghty
2004 Moscow Flyer (10y), B. Geraghty
2005 Kauto Star (5y), M. Fitzgerald
2006 Kauto Star (6y), R. Walsh

KING GEORGE VI CHASE
(1937) Kempton, about 3 miles

2003 Edredon Bleu (11y), J. Culloty
2004 Kicking King (6y), B. Geraghty
2005 Kicking King (7y), B. Geraghty
2006 Kauto Star (6y), R. Walsh

CHAMPION HURDLE
(1927) Cheltenham, 2 miles and about ½ f

2004 Hardy Eustace (7y), C. O'Dwyer
2005 Hardy Eustace (8y), C. O'Dwyer
2006 Brave Inca (8y), T. McCoy
2007 Sublimity (7y), P. Carberry

QUEEN MOTHER CHAMPION CHASE
(1959) Cheltenham, about 2 miles

2004 Azertyuiop (8y), R. Walsh
2005 Moscow Flyer (11y), B. Geraghty
2006 Newmill (8y), A. McNamara
2007 Voy Por Ustedes (6y), R. Thornton

CHELTENHAM GOLD CUP
(1924) 3 miles and about 2½ f

2004 Best Mate (9y), J. Culloty
2005 Kicking King (7y), B. Geraghty
2006 War Of Attrition (7y), C. O'Dwyer
2007 Kauto Star (7y), R. Walsh

GRAND NATIONAL
(1837) Liverpool, 4 miles and about 4 f

2004 Amberleigh House (12y), G. Lee
2005 Hedgehunter (9y), R. Walsh
2006 Numbersixvalverde (10y), N. Madden
2007 Silver Birch (10y), R. Power

BETFRED GOLD CUP
(1957) Sandown, 3 miles and about 5 f

2004 Puntal (8y), D. Howard
2005 Jack High (10y), G. Cotter
2006 Lacdoudal (7y), R. Johnson
2007 Hot Weld (8y), G. Lee

STATISTICS

WINNING NATIONAL HUNT TRAINERS 2006–7

P. F. Nicholls	£2,882,752
J. O'Neill	1,619,583
A. King	1,543,850
D. E. Pipe	1,496,169
P. J. Hobbs	1,386,117
N. J. Henderson	905,886
P. Brown	885,135
Miss V. Williams	872,007
F. Murphy	858,914
N. G. Richards	728,829

WINNING NATIONAL HUNT JOCKEYS 2006–7

	1st	2nd	3rd	Unpl.	Total mts
A. P. McCoy	184	117	97	359	757
R. Johnson	154	138	108	448	848
T. J. O'Brien	107	82	67	300	556
R. Thornton	99	77	66	308	550
T. J. Murphy	98	71	53	320	542
G. Lee	89	98	65	425	677
P. J. Brennan	79	60	62	311	512
N. Fehily	75	65	64	270	474
S. Thomas	73	68	40	281	462
R. Walsh	73	55	40	123	291

The above statistics have been provided by *Timeform*, publishers of the *Racehorses* and *Chasers and Hurdlers* annuals

ICE HOCKEY

MEN'S WORLD CHAMPIONSHIPS 2007
Moscow, Russia, May

Final: Canada beat Finland 4–2

WOMEN'S WORLD CHAMPIONSHIPS 2007
Winnipeg, Canada, April

Final: Canada beat USA 5–1

DOMESTIC COMPETITIONS
Elite League Champions 2006–7: Coventry Blaze
Play-off Champions 2007: Nottingham Panthers
Challenge Cup final 2007: Coventry Blaze beat Sheffield Steelers 9–4

NATIONAL HOCKEY LEAGUE
Stanley Cup final 2006–7: Anaheim Ducks beat Ottawa Senators 4–1

ICE SKATING

WORLD CHAMPIONSHIPS 2007
Tokyo, Japan, March

Men: Brian Joubert (France)
Women: Miki Ando (Japan)
Pairs: Xue Shen and Hongbo Zhao (China)
Ice Dance: Albena Denkova and Maxim Staviski (Bulgaria)

EUROPEAN CHAMPIONSHIPS 2007
Warsaw, Poland, January

Men: Brian Joubert (France)
Women: Carolina Kostner (Italy)
Pairs: Aliona Savchenko and Robin Szolkowy (Germany)
Ice Dance: Isabelle Delobel and Olivier Schoenfelder (France)

BRITISH CHAMPIONSHIPS 2007
Nottingham, January

Men: John Hamer
Women: Jenna McCorkell
Pairs: Stacey Kemp and David King
Ice Dance: Sinead Kerr and John Kerr

JUDO

EUROPEAN CHAMPIONSHIPS 2007
Belgrade, Serbia, April

MEN
Heavyweight (over 100kg): Teddy Riner (France)
Light-heavyweight (100kg): Daniel Hadfi (Hungary)
Middleweight (90kg): Valentyn Grekov (Ukraine)
Welterweight (81kg): Robert Krawczyk (Poland)
Lightweight (73kg): Salamu Mezhidov (Russia)
Junior Lightweight (66kg): Zaza Kedelashvili (Georgia)
Bantamweight (60kg): Ruslan Kishmakhov (Russia)

WOMEN
Heavyweight (over 78kg): Anne Sophie Mondiere (France)
Light-heavyweight (78kg): Stephanie Possamai (France)
Middleweight (70kg): Gevrise Emane (France)
Welterweight (63kg): Lucie Decosse (France)
Lightweight (57kg): Isabel Fernandez (Spain)
Junior Lightweight (52kg): Telma Monteiro (Portugal)
Bantamweight (48kg): Alina Alexandra Dumitru (Romania)

BRITISH OPEN CHAMPIONSHIPS 2007
London, January

MEN
Heavyweight (over 100kg): Kirk Hoffmann (USA)
Light-heavyweight (100kg): Joao Taveira (Portugal)
Middleweight (90kg): Peter Cousins (Great Britain)
Welter (81kg): Hugo Silva (Portugal)
Lightweight (73kg): Matthew Purssey (Great Britain)
Junior Lightweight (66kg): Tiago Lopes (Portugal)
Bantamweight (60kg): Damien Bomboir (Belgium)

WOMEN
Heavyweight (over 78kg): Simone Callender (Great Britain)
Light-heavyweight (78kg): Sian Wilson (Great Britain)
Middleweight (70kg): Sally Conway (Great Britain)
Welter (63kg): Ronda Rousey (USA)
Lightweight (57kg): Valerie Gotay (USA)
Junior Lightweight (52kg): Francesca Durand (USA)
Bantamweight (48kg): Jeanette Rodriguez (USA)

MOTORCYCLING

MOTOGP 2006
Malaysian (Sepang): Valentino Rossi (Italy), Yamaha
Australian (Phillip Island): Marco Melandri (Italy), Honda
Japanese (Motegi): Loris Capirossi (Italy), Ducati
Portuguese (Estoril): Toni Elias (Spain), Honda
Spanish (Valencia): Troy Bayliss (Australia), Ducati
Riders' Championship 2006: 1. Nicky Hayden (USA), Honda, 252pts; 2. Valentino Rossi (Italy), Yamaha, 247pts; 3. Loris Capirossi (Italy), Ducati, 229pts

MOTOGP 2007
Qatari (Losail): Casey Stoner (Australia), Ducati
Spanish (Jerez): Valentino Rossi (Italy), Yamaha
Turkish (Istanbul): Casey Stoner (Australia), Ducati
Chinese (Shanghai): Casey Stoner (Australia), Ducati
French (Le Mans): Chris Vermeulen (Australia), Suzuki
Italian (Mugello): Valentino Rossi (Italy), Yamaha
Catalonian (Barcelona): Casey Stoner (Australia), Ducati
British (Donington Park): Casey Stoner (Australia), Ducati
Dutch (Assen): Valentino Rossi (Italy), Yamaha
German (Sachsenring): Dani Pedrosa (Spain), Honda
US (Laguna Seca): Casey Stoner (Australia), Ducati
Czech (Brno): Casey Stoner (Australia), Ducati

250CC GRAND PRIX 2006
Malaysian (Sepang): Jorge Lorenzo (Spain), Aprilia
Australian (Phillip Island): Jorge Lorenzo (Spain), Aprilia
Japanese (Motegi): Hiroshi Aoyama (Japan), KTM
Portuguese (Estoril): Andrea Dovizioso (Italy), Honda
Spanish (Valencia): Alex De Angelis (San Marino), Aprilia
Riders' Championship 2006: 1. Jorge Lorenzo (Spain), Aprilia, 289pts; 2. Andrea Dovizioso (Italy), Honda, 272pts; 3. Alex De Angelis (San Marino), Aprilia, 228pts

250CC GRAND PRIX 2007
Qatari (Losail): Jorge Lorenzo (Spain), Aprilia
Spanish (Jerez): Jorge Lorenzo (Spain), Aprilia
Turkish (Istanbul): Andrea Dovizioso (Italy), Honda
Chinese (Shanghai): Jorge Lorenzo (Spain), Aprilia
French (Le Mans): Jorge Lorenzo (Spain), Aprilia
Italian (Mugello): Alvaro Bautista (Spain), Aprilia
Catalonian (Barcelona): Jorge Lorenzo (Spain), Aprilia
British (Donington Park): Andrea Dovizioso (Italy), Honda
Dutch (Assen): Jorge Lorenzo (Spain), Aprilia
German (Sachsenring): Hiroshi Aoyama (Japan), KTM
Czech (Brno): Jorge Lorenzo (Spain), Aprilia

125CC GRAND PRIX 2006
Malaysian (Sepang): Alvaro Bautista (Spain), Aprilia
Australian (Phillip Island): Alvaro Bautista (Spain), Aprilia
Japanese (Motegi): Mika Kallio (Finland), KTM
Portuguese (Estoril): Alvaro Bautista (Spain), Aprilia
Spanish (Valencia): Hector Faubel (Spain), Aprilia
Riders' Championship 2006: 1. Alvaro Bautista (Spain), Aprilia, 338pts; 2. Mika Kallio (Finland), KTM, 262pts; 3. Hector Faubel (Spain), Aprilia, 197pts

125CC GRAND PRIX 2007
Qatari (Losail): Hector Faubel (Spain), Aprilia
Spanish (Jerez): Gabor Talmacsi (Hungary), Aprilia
Turkish (Istanbul): Simone Corsi (Italy), Aprilia
Chinese (Shanghai): Lukas Pesek (Czech Republic), Derbi
French (Le Mans): Sergio Gadea (Spain), Aprilia
Italian (Mugello): Hector Faubel (Spain), Aprilia
Catalonian (Barcelona): Tomoyoshi Koyama (Japan), KTM
British (Donington Park): Mattia Pasini (Italy), Aprilia
Dutch (Assen): Mattia Pasini (Italy), Aprilia
German (Sachsenring): Gabor Talmacsi (Hungary), Aprilia
Czech (Brno): Hector Faubel (Spain), Aprilia

ISLE OF MAN TOURIST TROPHY 2007
Senior: John McGuinness (England), Honda
Supersport: Ian Hutchinson (England), Honda

WORLD SUPERBIKES 2006
German (Lausitzring): Race 1 – Yukio Kagayama (Japan), Suzuki; Race 2 – James Toseland (Great Britain), Honda
Italian (Imola): Race 1 – Alex Barros (Brazil), Honda; Race 2 – Troy Bayliss (Australia), Ducati
French (Magny Cours): Race 1 – James Toseland (Great Britain), Honda; Race 2 – Troy Bayliss (Australia), Ducati
Riders' World Championship 2006: 1. Troy Bayliss (Australia), Ducati, 431pts; 2. James Toseland (Great Britain), Honda, 336; 3. Noriyuki Haga (Japan), Yamaha, 326pts

WORLD SUPERBIKES 2007
Qatari (Losail): Race 1 – Max Biaggi (Italy), Suzuki; Race 2 – James Toseland (Great Britain), Honda
Australian (Philip Island): Race 1 – Troy Bayliss (Australia), Ducati; Race 2 – James Toseland (Great Britain), Honda
European (Donington Park): Race 1 – James Toseland (Great Britain), Honda; Race 2 – Noriyuki Haga (Japan), Yamaha
Spanish (Valencia): Race 1 – Ruben Xaus (Spain), Ducati; Race 2 – James Toseland (Great Britain), Honda
Dutch (Assen): Race 1 – James Toseland (Great Britain), Honda; Race 2 – Troy Bayliss (Australia), Ducati
Italian (Monza): Race 1 – Noriyuki Haga (Japan), Yamaha; Race 2 – Noriyuki Haga (Japan), Yamaha
British (Silverstone): Race 1 – Troy Bayliss (Australia), Ducati; Race 2 – James Toseland (Great Britain), Honda
Sammarinese (Misano Adriatico): Race 1 – Troy Bayliss (Australia), Ducati; Race 2 – Troy Bayliss (Australia), Ducati
Czech (Brno): Race 1 – James Toseland (Great Britain), Honda; Race 2 – Max Biaggi (Italy), Suzuki
British (Brands Hatch): Race 1 – James Toseland (Great Britain), Honda; Race 2 – James Toseland (Great Britain), Honda

MOTOR RACING

FORMULA ONE GRAND PRIX 2006
Italian (Monza): Michael Schumacher (Germany), Ferrari
Chinese (Shanghai): Michael Schumacher (Germany), Ferrari
Japanese (Suzuka): Fernando Alonso (Spain), Renault
Brazilian (Interlagos): Felipe Massa (Brazil), Ferrari
Drivers' World Championship 2006: 1. Fernando Alonso (Spain), Renault, 134pts; 2. Michael Schumacher (Germany), Ferrari, 121pts; 3. Felipe Massa (Brazil), Ferrari, 80pts
Constructors' World Championship 2006: 1. McLaren, 128pts; 2. Ferrari, 103pts; 3. BMW, 56pts

FORMULA ONE GRAND PRIX 2007
Australian (Melbourne): Kimi Raikkonen (Finland), Ferrari
Malaysian (Sepang): Fernando Alonso (Spain), McLaren
Bahraini (Sakhir): Felipe Massa (Brazil), Ferrari
Spanish (Barcelona): Felipe Massa (Brazil), Ferrari
Monegasque (Monte Carlo): Fernando Alonso (Spain), McLaren
Canadian (Montreal): Lewis Hamilton (Great Britain), McLaren
US (Indianapolis): Lewis Hamilton (Great Britain), McLaren
French (Magny Cours): Kimi Raikkonen (Finland), Ferrari
British (Silverstone): Kimi Raikkonen (Finland), Ferrari
European (Nurburgring): Fernando Alonso (Spain), McLaren
Hungarian (Hungaroring): Lewis Hamilton (Great Britain), McLaren
Turkish (Istanbul): Felipe Massa (Brazil), Ferrari

INDIANAPOLIS 500 2007
Indianapolis, USA, May
Dario Franchitti (Great Britain), Andretti Green

LE MANS 24-HOUR RACE 2007
Le Mans, France, June
Frank Biela (Germany), Emanuele Pirro (Italy) and Marco Werner (Germany), Audi

MOTOR RALLYING

WORLD RALLY CHAMPIONSHIP 2006
Cypriot: Sebastien Loeb (France), Citroen
Turkish: Marcus Gronholm (Finland), Ford
Australian: Mikko Hirvonen (Finland), Ford
New Zealand: Marcus Gronholm (Finland), Ford
British: Marcus Gronholm (Finland), Ford
Drivers' World Championship 2006: 1. Sebastien Loeb, (France), 112pts; 2. Marcus Gronholm, (Finland), 111pts; 3. Mikko Hirvonen (Finland), 65pts
Manufacturers' World Championship 2006: 1. Ford, 195pts; 2. Citroën, 166pts; 3. Subaru, 106pts

WORLD RALLY CHAMPIONSHIP 2007
Monegasque: Sebastien Loeb (France), Citroen
Swedish: Marcus Gronholm (Finland), Ford
Norwegian: Mikko Hirvonen (Finland), Ford
Mexican: Sebastien Loeb (France), Citroen
Portuguese: Sebastien Loeb (France), Citroen
Argentinian: Sebastien Loeb (France), Citroen
Italian: Marcus Gronholm (Finland), Ford
Greek: Marcus Gronholm (Finland), Ford
Finnish: Marcus Gronholm (Finland), Ford
German: Sebastien Loeb (France), Citroen

BRITISH RALLY CHAMPIONSHIP 2007
Cumbria: Guy Wilks (Great Britain), Mitsubishi
Scottish Borders: Eugene Donelly (Ireland), Subaru
Isle of Mann: Eugene Donelly (Ireland), Subaru

DAKAR RALLY 2007
Cars: Stephane Peterhansel (France), Mitsubishi
Motorcycles: Cyril Despres (France), KTM
Trucks: Hans Stacey (Netherlands), MAN

NETBALL

Superleague 2006-07: Team Bath
Superleague play-off 2007: Team Bath
Challenge Cup final 2006-07: Academy beat Oaksway 59–37

NORDIC EVENTS

BIATHLON WORLD CUP 2006–7

MEN
Overall: Michael Greis (Germany), 794pts

WOMEN
Overall: Andrea Henkel (Germany), 870pts

BIATHLON WORLD CHAMPIONSHIPS 2007
Antholz-Anterselva, Italy, February

MEN
10km sprint: Ole Einar Bjoerndalen (Norway)
12.5km pursuit: Ole Einar Bjoerndalen (Norway)
15km mass start: Michael Greis (Germany)
20km individual: Raphael Poiree (France)
4 × 7.5km relay: Russia

WOMEN
7.5km sprint: Magdalena Neuner (Germany)
10km pursuit: Magdalena Neuner (Germany)
12.5km mass start: Andrea Henkel (Germany)
15km individual: Linda Grubben (Norway)
4 × 6km relay: Germany

MIXED
2 × 6km + 2 × 7.5km relay: Sweden

NORDIC WORLD CUP 2006–7

CROSS COUNTRY
Men: Tobias Angerer (Germany), 1,131pts
Women: Virpi Kuitunen (Finland), 1,510pts

SKI-JUMPING
Adam Malysz (Poland), 1,453pts

NORDIC COMBINED
Hannu Manninen (Finland), 765pts

POLO

Prince of Wales Trophy 2007: Cadenza beat Broncos 11–10
Queen's Cup final 2007: Loro Piana beat Ellerston White 12–11
Warwickshire Cup 2007: Elysian Fields beat Cadenza 9–8
Gold Cup (British Open) final 2007: Lechuza Caracas beat Loro Piana 11–10
Coronation Cup 2007: Chile beat England 9–8

RACKETS

World Doubles Challenge 2007: Neil Smith and Mark Hubbard beat Harry Foster and Mark Hue Williams 5–0
Noel Bruce Cup 2006: Harrow beat Malvern 4–0
British Professional Singles Championship final 2007: Mark Hubbard beat David Makey 3–1
British Open Singles Championship final 2007: Harry Foster beat Guy Smith-Bingham 4–2
British Open Doubles Championship final 2007: Harry Foster and Mark Hue Williams beat Neil Smith and Mark Hubbard 4–1
Amateur Singles Championship final 2006: Harry Foster beat Guy Smith-Bingham 3–2
Amateur Doubles Championship 2007: Harry Foster and Mark Hue Williams beat Tim Cockroft and Charlie Danby 4–1
The Foster Cup final 2006 (public schools' singles championship): William Hopton (Eton) beat Sam Northeast (Harrow) 3–1
Public Schools Doubles 2007: Sam Northeast and Glenn Querl (Harrow) beat William Hopton and Chris Stefanowicz (Eton) 4–2

REAL TENNIS

MEN
IRTPA Championship final 2006 (British Professional Singles Championship): Robert Fahey (Australia) beat Camden Riviere (USA) 3–1
British Open Singles final 2006: Robert Fahey (Australia) beat Steve Virgona (Australia) 3–0
British Open Doubles final 2006: Robert Fahey and Ruaraidh Gunn (Australia) beat Steve Virgona (Australia) and Jon Dawes (Great Britain) 3–0
Henry Leaf Cup final 2007 (public schools' old boys' doubles championship): Canford beat Millfield 2–0
World Doubles Championship 2007: Robert Fahey and Steve Virgona (Australia) beat Tim Chisholm and Camden Riviere (USA) 4–3
National League final 2007: Cambridge beat Petworth 5–2
National Inter-Club Championship final 2007: Petworth House beat Cambridge 3–2

WOMEN
British Open Singles Championship final 2007: Charlotte Cornwallis (Great Britain) beat Alex Garside (Great Britain) 2–0
World Doubles Championship final 2007: Charlotte Cornwallis and Penny Lumley (Great Britain) beat Kate Leeming (Australia) and Sue Haswell (Great Britain) 2–0
World Singles Championship 2007: Charlotte Cornwallis (Great Britain) beat Penny Lumley (Great Britain) 2–0

ROWING

BRITISH CHAMPIONSHIPS 2007
Nottingham, July

MEN
Single sculls: Brendan Crean (Agecroft), 8min 38.60sec
Double sculls: Tideway Scullers, 7min 32.63sec
Quadruple sculls: Tideway Scullers, 6min 54.77sec
Coxless pairs: Leander, 7min, 39.10sec
Coxless fours: Reading University, 7min 23.10sec
Coxed fours: Leander, 7min 10.18sec
Eights: Leander, 6min 31.43sec

WOMEN
Single sculls: Joanne Lyons (Reading University), 9min 10.50sec
Double sculls: Leander, 8min 42.51sec
Quadruple sculls: Tideway Scullers and Mortlake Anglian, 7min 33.88sec
Coxless pairs: Nottingham University and Durham University, 9min 07.49sec
Coxless fours: City of Oxford, 8min 16.41sec
Coxed fours: Thames, 8min 11.80sec
Eights: Oxford Brookes University/Osiris, 7min 30.96sec

HENLEY ROYAL REGATTA 2007

Grand Challenge Cup: Shawnigan Lake and Victoria City (Canada) beat Australian Institute of Sport by 1¼ lengths

Stewards' Challenge Cup: Leander Club and Molesey beat Brentwood College and Shawnigan Lake (Canada) by 2¼ lengths

Queen Mother Challenge Cup: AZS Gdansk and AZS Szczecin (Poland) beat Brentwood College and UVIC (Canada) by ½ length

Silver Goblets and Nickalls' Challenge Cup: R. P. Di Clemente and D. Cech (South Africa) beat A. Penkner and J. Urban (Germany) by 2¾ lengths

Double Sculls Challenge Cup: L. Spik and I. Cop (Slovenia) beat M. Sloma and M. Brzezinski (Poland) by 5 lengths

Diamond Challenge Sculls: A.W. Campbell (Great Britain) beat M. Drysdale (New Zealand) by 1¼ lengths

Remenham Challenge Cup: Dortmund R. C. (Germany) beat Thames R. C. and Leander Club by 1½ lengths

Princess Grace Challenge Cup: South Australian Institute of Sport 'B' beat Hollandia (Netherlands) easily

Princess Royal Challenge Cup: M. Guerette (USA) beat J. C. Goldsack (Great Britain) easily

Ladies' Challenge Plate: Harvard University (USA) beat Molesey B. C. and New York Athletic (USA) by 1 length

Visitors' Challenge Cup: Leander Club beat Reading University and Agecroft R. C. easily

Men's Quadruple Sculls: Leander Club and London R. C. beat Tideway Scullers by ½ length

Thames Challenge Cup: Leander Club beat Agecroft R. C. by 5 lengths

Wyfold Challenge Cup: 1829 Boat Club beat London R. C. 'A' by ⅓ length

Britannia Challenge Cup: York City R. C. beat Henley R. C. 'A' by 1 length

Temple Challenge Cup: University of California, Berkeley (USA) beat Cornell University (USA) by 1¼ lengths

Prince Albert Challenge Cup: University of London 'A' beat Goldie B. C. by 1½ lengths

Princess Elizabeth Challenge Cup: Shrewsbury School beat Brentwood College School (Canada) by 1 foot

Fawley Challenge Cup: Henley R. C. and Maidenhead R. C. beat Peterborough City R. C. and Star Club easily

THE 153RD UNIVERSITY BOAT RACE

Putney–Mortlake, 4 miles, 1 f, 180 yd, 10 April 2007

Cambridge beat Oxford by 1¼ lengths; 17min 49sec

Cambridge have won 79 times, Oxford 73 and there has been one dead heat. The record time is 16min 19sec, rowed by Cambridge in 1998.

OTHER ROWING EVENTS

Wingfield Sculls 2006: Alan Campbell (Tideway Scullers)

Oxford Torpids 2007: Cancelled owing to bad weather

Oxford Summer Eights 2007: Men, Magdalen; *Women,* St Edmund Hall

Head of the River 2007: Men, Abandoned owing to bad weather; *Women,* Marlow, Rebecca, Tideway Scullers, Thames

RUGBY FIVES

National Open Singles Championship final 2006: M. Cavanagh beat H. Buchanan 2–0

National Open Doubles Championship final 2006: H. Buchanan and R. Perry beat P. Bishop and J. Minta 2–0

National Ladies' Singles Championship final 2006: Cancelled

National Ladies' Doubles Championship final 2006: Cancelled

National Club Championship final 2007: Manchester Y Club beat Alleyn Old Boys 93–89

National Schools' Singles Championship final 2007: D. Tristao (St Paul's) beat J. Corbin (St Paul's) 2–1

National Schools' Doubles Championship final 2007: A. Griffiths and A. Ladak (St Paul's II) beat D. Tristao and J. Corbin (St Paul's I) 2–1

Varsity Match 2007: Oxford beat Cambridge 241–187

RUGBY LEAGUE

Challenge Cup final 2007: St Helens beat Catalan Dragons 30–8

Super League Grand Final 2006: St Helens beat Hull FC 26–4

World Club Challenge 2007: St Helens beat Brisbane Broncos 18–14

AMATEUR RUGBY LEAGUE 2006–7

National Conference League Premier Division Grand Final: Skirlaugh beat Leigh Miners Rangers 8–4

Division One: Rochdale Mayfield

Division Two: Waterhead

BARLA National Cup final: Halton Simms Cross beat Ince Rose Bridge 23–8

Varsity Match 2007: Oxford beat Cambridge 20–14

RUGBY UNION

SIX NATIONS' CHAMPIONSHIP 2007

3 February	Rome	France beat Italy 39–3
	London	England beat Scotland 42–20
4 February	Cardiff	Ireland beat Wales 19–9
10 February	London	England beat Italy 20–7
	Edinburgh	Scotland beat Wales 21–9
11 February	Dublin	France beat Ireland 20–17
24 February	Edinburgh	Italy beat Scotland 37–17
	Dublin	Ireland beat England 43–13
	Paris	France beat Wales 32–21
10 March	Edinburgh	Ireland beat Scotland 19–18
	Rome	Italy beat Wales 23–20
11 March	London	England beat France 26–18
17 March	Rome	Ireland beat Italy 51–24
	Paris	France beat Scotland 46–19
	Cardiff	Wales beat England 27–18

Final standings: 1. France, 8pts; 2. Ireland, 8pts; 3. England, 6pts; 4. Italy, 4pts; 5. Wales, 2pts; 6. Scotland, 2pts

EUROPEAN COMPETITIONS 2006–7

Heineken European Cup final: Wasps beat Leicester 25–9

European Challenge Cup: Clermont Auvergne beat Bath 22–16

DOMESTIC COMPETITIONS 2006–7

ENGLAND

Premiership: Gloucester, 71pts

Championship final: Leicester beat Gloucester 44–16

National League: Division 1, Leeds, 123pts; *Division 2,* Esher 115pts; *Division 3* (North), Blaydon, 101pts; (South) Southend, 107pts

National Trophy final: Cornish Pirates beat Exeter Chiefs 19–16

County Championship final: Devon beat Lancashire 27–6
County Shield: Warwickshire beat Somerset 22–8
County Plate: Durham beat Eastern Counties 30–20
125th Varsity Match: Cambridge beat Oxford 15–6

ANGLO-WELSH
EDF Cup final: Leicester beat Ospreys 41–35

CELTIC
Magners League: Neath-Swansea, 64pts

SCOTLAND
Premier League: Division 1, Currie, 67pts; *Division 2,* Stirling County, 82pts; *Division 3,* Haddington, 89pts
Cup final: Watsonians beat Boroughmuir 35–29

WALES
Premiership: Neath, 53pts; *National League:* Division 1 (East), Beddau, 57pts; (West), Bonymaen, 54pts
Cup final: Llandovery beat Cardiff 20–18

IRELAND
All Ireland League: Division 1, Cork Constitution, 60pts; *Division 2,* Old Belvedere, 63pts; *Division 3,* Wanderers, 63pts

SHOOTING

138TH NATIONAL RIFLE ASSOCIATION IMPERIAL MEETING
Bisley, July 2007

Queen's Prize: J. W. E. Lewis, 293.26 v-bulls
Grand Aggregate: D. C. Luckman, 699.93 v-bulls
Prince of Wales Prize: P. J. Chance, 75.12 v-bulls
St George's Vase: J. C. Underwood, 150.24 v-bulls
All Comers' Aggregate: P. Patel, 374.52 v-bulls
Kolapore Cup: Great Britain, 1,190.165 v-bulls
Chancellor's Trophy: Cambridge University, 1,133.106 v-bulls
Musketeers Cup: University of London 'A', 573.54 v-bulls
County Championship Long Range: London, 581.57 v-bulls
Mackinnon Challenge Cup: England, 1,163.118 v-bulls
The Albert: G. V. Barnard, 213.22 v-bulls
Hopton Challenge Cup: C. N. Tremlett, 980.114 v-bulls

SNOOKER

2006–7
Grand Prix (Aberdeen): Neil Robertson (Australia) beat Jamie Cope (England) 9–5
UK Championship (York): Peter Ebdon (England) beat Stephen Hendry (Scotland) 10–6
Masters (Wembley): Ronnie O'Sullivan (England) beat Ding Junhui (China) 10–3
Malta Cup (Portomaso): Shaun Murphy (England) beat Ryan Day (Wales) 9–4
Welsh Open (Newport): Neil Robertson (Australia) beat Andrew Higginson (England) 9–8
China Open (Beijing): Graeme Dott (Scotland) beat Jamie Cope (England) 9–5
World Championship (Sheffield): John Higgins (Scotland) beat Mark Selby (England) 18–13

2007–8
Shanghai Masters (China): Dominic Dale (Wales) beat Ryan Day (Wales) 10–6

SPEED SKATING

WORLD ALL-ROUND CHAMPIONSHIPS 2007
Heerenveen, Netherlands, February

MEN
500m: Erben Wennemars (Netherlands), 35.79sec
1,500m: Erben Wennemars (Netherlands), 1min 45.19sec
5,000m: Sven Kramer (Netherlands), 6min 12.97sec
10,000m: Sven Kramer (Netherlands), 12min 49.88sec

WOMEN
500m: Anni Friesinger (Germany), 38.38sec
1,500m: Ireen Wust (Netherlands), 1min. 54.05sec
3,000m: Ireen Wust (Netherlands), 4min 00.28sec
5,000m: Martina Sablikova (Czech Republic), 6min 49.31sec

EUROPEAN CHAMPIONSHIPS 2007
Collalbo, Italy, January

MEN
500m: Enrico Fabris (Italy), 36.38sec
1,500m: Enrico Fabris (Italy), 1min 44.72sec
5,000m: Sven Kramer (Netherlands), 6min 15.65sec
10,000m: Sven Kramer (Netherlands), 13min 10.44sec

WOMEN
500m: Ireen Wust (Netherlands), 39.51sec
1,500m: Ireen Wust (Netherlands), 1min 56.78sec
3,000m: Martina Sablikova (Czech Republic), 4min 03.52sec
5,000m: Martina Sablikova (Czech Republic), 6min 58.45sec

WORLD SHORT TRACK CHAMPIONSHIPS 2007
Milan, Italy, March

MEN
500m: Charles Hamelin (Canada), 41.449sec
1,000m: Hyun Soo Ahn (Rep. of Korea), 1min 27.177sec
1,500m: Apollo Anton Ohno (USA), 2min 33.793sec
3,000m: Kyung-Taek Song (Rep. of Korea), 4min 52.853sec
5,000m relay: Rep. of Korea, 6min 55.399sec
Overall: Hyun-Soo Ahn (Rep. of Korea), 81pts

WOMEN
500m: Kalyna Roberge (Canada), 45.329sec
1,000m: Sun-Yu Jin (Rep. of Korea), 1min 31.622sec
1,500m: Eun-Ju Jung (Rep. of Korea), 2min 22.303sec
3,000m: Sun-Yu Jin (Rep. of Korea), 5min 44.247sec
3,000m relay: Rep. of Korea, 4min 14.450sec
Overall: Sun-Yu Jin (Rep. of Korea), 89pts

EUROPEAN SHORT TRACK CHAMPIONSHIPS 2007
Sheffield, Great Britain, January

MEN
500m: Thibaut Fauconnet (France), 42.864sec
1,000m: Nicola Rodigari (Italy), 1min 27.518sec
1,500m: Nicola Rodigari (Italy), 2min 17.297sec
3,000m: Pieter Gysel (Belgium), 4min 50.819sec
5,000m relay: Germany, 7min 03.185sec
Overall: Nicola Rodigari (Italy), 102pts

WOMEN
500m: Evgenia Radanova (Bulgaria), 44.595sec
1,000m: Evgenia Radanova (Bulgaria), 1min 33.235sec
1,500m: Stephanie Bouvier (France), 2min 28.915sec
3,000m: Evgenia Radanova (Bulgaria), 5min 26.155sec
3,000m relay: Germany, 4min 26.940sec
Overall: Evgenia Radanova (Bulgaria), 102pts

SQUASH RACKETS

MEN
World Open 2006: David Palmer (Australia) beat Gregory Gaultier (France) 3–2
European Championship 2007: Gregory Gaultier (France) beat Renan Lavigne (France) 3–0
European Team Championship 2007: England beat Netherlands 4–0
British Open 2006: Nick Matthew (England) beat Thierry Lincou (France) 3–2
British National Championship 2007: James Willstrop beat John White 3–0

WOMEN
World Team Championship 2006: England beat Egypt 2–0
World Open 2006: Nicol David (Malaysia) beat Natalie Grinham (Australia) 3–2
European Championship 2007: Jenny Duncalf (England) beat Tania Bailey (England) 3–1
European Team Championship 2007: England beat Netherlands 3–0
British Open 2006: Nicol David (Malaysia) beat Rachael Grinham (Australia) 3–0
British National Championship 2007: Jenny Duncalf beat Alison Waters 3–2

SWIMMING

WORLD CHAMPIONSHIPS 2007
Melbourne, Australia, March–April

MEN
50m freestyle: Benjamin Wildman-Tobriner (USA), 21.88sec
100m freestyle: Filippo Magnini (Italy), 48.43sec
200m freestyle: Michael Phelps (USA), 1min 43.86sec
400m freestyle: Tae Hwan Park (Rep. of Korea), 3min 44.30sec
800m freestyle: Oussama Mellouli (Tunisia), 7min 46.95sec
1,500m freestyle: Mateusz Sawrymowicz (Poland), 14min 45.94sec
4 × 100m freestyle relay: United States, 3min 12.72sec
4 × 200m freestyle relay: United States, 7min 03.24sec
50m backstroke: Gerhard Zandberg (South Africa), 24.98sec
100m backstroke: Aaron Peirsol (USA), 52.98sec
200m backstroke: Ryan Lochte (USA), 1min 54.32sec
50m breaststroke: Oleg Lisogor (Ukraine), 27.66sec
100m breaststroke: Brendan Hansen (USA), 59.80sec
200m breaststroke: Kosuke Kitajima (Japan), 2min 09.80sec
50m butterfly: Roland Schoeman (South Africa), 23.18sec
100m butterfly: Michael Phelps (USA), 50.77sec
200m butterfly: Michael Phelps (USA), 1min 52.09sec
200m medley: Michael Phelps (USA), 1min 54.98sec
400m medley: Michael Phelps (USA), 4min 06.22sec
4 × 100m medley relay: Australia, 3min 34.93sec

WOMEN
50m freestyle: Lisbeth Lenton (Australia), 24.53sec
100m freestyle: Lisbeth Lenton (Australia), 53.40sec
200m freestyle: Laure Manaudou (France), 1min 55.52sec
400m freestyle: Laure Manaudou (France), 4min 02.61sec
800m freestyle: Kate Ziegler (USA), 8min 18.52sec
1,500m freestyle: Kate Ziegler (USA), 15min 53.05sec
4 × 100m freestyle relay: Australia, 3min 35.48sec
4 × 200m freestyle relay: USA, 7min 50.09sec
50m backstroke: Leila Vaziri (USA), 28.16sec
100m backstroke: Natalie Coughlin (USA), 59.44sec
200m backstroke: Margaret Hoelzer (USA), 2min 07.16sec
50m breaststroke: Jessica Hardy (USA), 30.63sec
100m breaststroke: Leisel Jones (Australia), 1min 05.72sec
200m breaststroke: Leisel Jones (Australia), 2min 21.84sec
50m butterfly: Therese Alshammar (Sweden), 25.91sec
100m butterfly: Lisbeth Lenton (Australia), 57.15sec
200m butterfly: Jessicah Schipper (Australia), 2min 06.39sec
200m medley: Kathryn Hoff (USA), 2min 10.13sec
400m medley: Kathryn Hoff (USA), 4min 32.89sec
4 × 100m medley relay: Australia, 3min 55.74sec

BRITISH CHAMPIONSHIPS 2007
Manchester, March

MEN
50m freestyle: David Maitre (France), 22.59sec
100m freestyle: Kevin Trannoy (France), 50.33sec
200m freestyle: Daniel Coombs (Loughborough University), 1min 50.24sec
400m freestyle: Dean Milwain (Loughborough University), 3min 52.39sec
1,500m freestyle: Anthony Pannier (France), 15min 23.98sec
400m freestyle relay: Loughborough University, 3min 24.42sec
800m freestyle relay: Loughborough University, 7min 24.11sec
50m backstroke: Benjamin Stasilius (France), 25.94sec
100m backstroke: Benjamin Stasilius (France), 55.62sec
200m backstroke: Benjamin Stasilius (France), 1min 58.81sec
50m breaststroke: Ross Clark (Dun City), 28.75sec
100m breaststroke: Christopher Jones (Swindon), 1min 03.21sec
200m breaststroke: Julien Nicolardot (France), 2min 14.85sec
50m butterfly: Mark Foster (University of Bath), 24.04sec
100m butterfly: Clement Lefert (France), 54.23sec
200m butterfly: Joe Roebuck (Loughborough University), 1min 59.30sec
200m medley: Euan Dale (Loughborough University), 2min 01.92sec
400m medley: Joe Roebuck (Loughborough University), 4min 19.92sec
400m medley relay: Loughborough University, 3min 48.22sec

WOMEN
50m freestyle: Hanna Lorgeril Shcherb (France), 25.67sec
100m freestyle: Hanna Lorgeril Shcherb (France), 56.15sec
200m freestyle: Coralie Balmy (France), 2min 00.24sec
400m freestyle: Coralie Balmy (France), 4min 11.34sec
400m freestyle relay: Ealing, 3min 52.66sec
800m freestyle relay: Ealing, 8min 25.23sec
50m backstroke: Katy Sexton (Portsmouth), 29.70sec

100m backstroke: Katy Sexton (Portsmouth), 1min 02.66sec
200m backstroke: Alexianne Castel (France), 2min 14.20sec
50m breaststroke: Kerry Buchan (South Aberdeen), 32.58sec
100m breaststroke: Kerry Buchan (South Aberdeen), 1min 09.50sec
200m breaststroke: Coralie Dobral (France), 2min 29.16sec
50m butterfly: Ellen Gandy (Beckenham), 27.87sec
100m butterfly: Jemma Lowe (Stockton), 59.78sec
200m butterfly: Jemma Lowe (Stockton), 2min 11.12sec
200m medley: Hannah Miley (Garioch), 2min 15.92sec
400m medley: Hannah Miley (Garioch), 4min 43.50sec
400m medley relay: Ealing, 4min 24.89sec

TABLE TENNIS

WORLD CHAMPIONSHIPS 2007
Zagreb, Croatia, May

Men's Singles: Wang Liqin (China) beat Ma Lin (China) 4–3
Women's Singles: Guo Yue (China) beat Li Xiaoxia (China) 4–3
Men's Doubles: Chen Qi and Ma Lin (China) beat Wang Hao and Wang Liqin (China) 4–2
Women's Doubles: Wang Nan and Zhang Yining (China) beat Guo Yue and Li Xiaoxia (China) 4–0
Mixed Doubles: Guo Yue and Wang Liqin (China) beat Wang Nan and Ma Lin (China) 4–2

EUROPEAN CHAMPIONSHIPS 2007
Belgrade, Serbia, March–April

Men's Singles: Timo Boll (Germany) beat Vladimir Samsonov (Belarus) 4–1
Women's Singles: Jiao Li (Netherlands) beat Xia Lian Ni (Luxembourg) 4–2
Men's Doubles: Timo Boll and Christian Suss (Germany) beat Lucjan Blaszczyk (Poland) and Ruiwu Tan (Croatia) 4–1
Women's Doubles: Svetlana Ganina (Russia) and Viktoria Pavlovich (Belarus) beat Georgina Pota and Krisztina Toth (Hungary) 4–3
Mixed Doubles: Ruta Paskauskiene (Lithuania) and Aleksandar Karakasevic (Serbia) beat Oksana Fadeeva and Fedor Kuzmin (Russia) 4–0
Men's Team: Germany
Women's Team: Hungary

ENGLISH NATIONAL CHAMPIONSHIPS 2007
Sheffield, February

Men's Singles: Paul Drinkhall (Cleveland) beat Alex Perry (Devon) 4–1
Women's Singles: Helen Lower (Staffordshire) beat Kelly Sibley (Warwickshire) 4–1
Men's Doubles: Paul Drinkhall (Cleveland) and Darius Knight (Surrey) beat Alex Perry (Devon) and Terry Young (Berkshire) 3–0
Women's Doubles: Helen Lower (Staffordshire) and Natalie Bawden (Essex) beat Kelly Sibley (Warwickshire) and Joanna Parker (Surrey) 3–0
Mixed Doubles: Kelly Sibley (Warwickshire) and Darius Knight (Surrey) beat Joanna Parker (Surrey) and Paul Drinkhall (Cleveland) 3–0

TENNIS

US OPEN CHAMPIONSHIPS 2006
New York, August–September

Men's Singles: Roger Federer (Switzerland) beat Andy Roddick (USA) 6–2, 4–6, 7–5, 6–1
Women's Singles: Maria Sharapova (Russia) beat Justine Henin-Hardenne (Belgium) 6–4, 6–4
Men's Doubles: Martin Damm (Czech Republic) and Leander Paes (India) beat Jonas Bjorkman (Sweden) and Max Mirnyi (Belarus) 6–7, 6–4, 6–3
Women's Doubles: Nathalie Dechy (France) and Vera Zvonareva (Russia) beat Dinara Safina (Russia) and Katarina Srebotnik (Slovenia) 7–6, 7–5
Mixed Doubles: Martina Navratilova and Bob Bryan (USA) beat Kveta Peschke and Martin Damm (Czech Republic) 6–2, 6–3

AUSTRALIAN OPEN CHAMPIONSHIPS 2007
Melbourne, January

Men's Singles: Roger Federer (Switzerland) beat Fernando Gonzalez (Chile) 7–6, 6–4, 6–4
Women's Singles: Serena Williams (USA) beat Maria Sharapova (Russia) 6–1, 6–2
Men's Doubles: Bob Bryan and Mike Bryan (USA) beat Jonas Bjorkman (Sweden) and Max Mirnyi (Belarus) 7–5, 7–5
Women's Doubles: Cara Black (Zimbabwe) and Liezel Huber (South Africa) beat Chan Yung-Jan and Chuang Chia-Jung (Taiwan) 6–4, 6–7, 6–1
Mixed Doubles: Elena Likhovtseva (Russia) and Daniel Nestor (Canada) beat Victoria Azarenka and Max Mirnyi (Belarus) 6–4, 6–4

FRENCH OPEN CHAMPIONSHIPS 2007
Paris, May–June

Men's Singles: Rafael Nadal (Spain) beat Roger Federer (Switzerland) 6–3, 4–6, 6–3, 6–4
Women's Singles: Justine Henin Hardenne (Belgium) beat Ana Ivanovic (Serbia) 6–1, 6–2
Men's Doubles: Mark Knowles (Bahamas) and Daniel Nestor (Canada) beat Lukas Dlouhy and Pavel Vizner (Czech Republic) 2–6, 6–3, 6–4
Women's Doubles: Alicia Molik (Australia) and Mara Santangelo (Italy) beat Katarina Srebotnik (Slovenia) and Ai Sugiyama (Japan) 7–6, 6–4
Mixed Doubles: Nathalie Dechy (France) and Andy Ram (Israel) beat Katarina Srebotnik (Slovenia) and Nenad Zimonjic (Serbia) 7–5, 6–3

ALL-ENGLAND CHAMPIONSHIPS 2007
Wimbledon, June–July

Men's Singles: Roger Federer (Switzerland) beat Rafael Nadal (Spain) 7–6, 4–6, 7–6, 2–6, 6–2
Ladies' Singles: Venus Williams (USA) beat Marion Bartoli (France) 6–4, 6–1
Men's Doubles: Arnaud Clement and Michael Llodra (France) beat Bob Bryan and Mike Bryan (USA) 6–7, 6–3, 6–4, 6–4
Ladies' Doubles: Cara Black (Zimbabwe) and Liezel Huber (South Africa) beat Katarina Srebotnik (Slovenia) and Ai Sugiyama (Japan) 3–6, 6–3, 6–2
Mixed Doubles: Jelena Jankovic (Serbia) and Jamie Murray (Great Britain) beat Alicia Molik (Australia) and Jonas Bjorkman (Sweden) 6–4, 3–6, 6–1

TEAM CHAMPIONSHIPS
Davis Cup final 2006: Russia beat Argentina 3–2
Federation Cup final 2006: Italy beat Belgium 3–2

VOLLEYBALL

WORLD CHAMPIONSHIPS 2006
Tokyo and Osaka, Japan, November–December

Men's final: Brazil beat Poland 3–0
Women's final: Russia beat Brazil 3–2

YACHTING

AMERICA'S CUP 2007
Valencia, Spain, June–July

Alinghi (Switzerland) beat Team New Zealand 5–2

SPORTS RECORDS

ATHLETICS WORLD RECORDS

as at August 2007

All the world records given below have been accepted by the International Amateur Athletic Federation except those marked with an asterisk* which are awaiting homologation or ratification. Fully automatic timing to 1/100th second is mandatory up to and including 400 metres. For distances up to and including 10,000 metres, records will be accepted to 1/100th second if timed automatically, and to 1/10th if hand timing is used.

MEN

TRACK EVENTS	*hr*	*min*	*sec*
100m			9.74
Asafa Powell (Jamaica) 2007			
200m			19.32
Michael Johnson (USA) 1996			
400m			43.18
Michael Johnson (USA) 1999			
800m		1	41.11
Wilson Kipketer (Denmark) 1997			
1,000m		2	11.96
Noah Ngeny (Kenya) 1999			
1,500m		3	26.00
Hicham El Guerrouj (Morocco) 1998			
1 mile		3	43.13
Hicham El Guerrouj (Morocco) 1999			
2,000m		4	44.79
Hicham El Guerrouj (Morocco) 1999			
3,000m		7	20.67
Daniel Komen (Kenya) 1996			
5,000m		12	37.35
Kenenisa Bekele (Ethiopia) 2004			
10,000m		26	17.53
Kenenisa Bekele (Ethiopia) 2005			
20,000m		56	26.0
Haile Gebrselassie (Ethiopia) 2007			
21,285m	1	00	00.0
Haile Gebrselassie (Ethiopia) 2007			
25,000m	1	13	55.8
Toshihiko Seko (Japan) 1981			
30,000m	1	29	18.8
Toshihiko Seko (Japan) 1981			
Marathon	2	04	55
Paul Tergat (Kenya) 2003			
110m hurdles (1.07m)			12.88
Liu Xiang (China) 2006			
400m hurdles (0.97m)			46.78
Kevin Young (USA) 1992			
3,000m steeplechase		7	53.63
Saif Saaeed Shaheen (Qatar) 2004			

RELAYS	*min*	*sec*
4 × 100m		37.40
USA, 1992, 1993		
4 × 200m	1	18.68
USA, 1994		
4 × 400m	2	54.20
USA, 1998		
4 × 800m	7	02.43*
Kenya, 2006		
4 × 1,500m	14	38.8
Federal Republic of Germany, 1977		

FIELD EVENTS	*m*	*ft*	*in*
High jump	2.45	8	0½
Javier Sotomayor (Cuba) 1993			
Pole vault	6.14	20	1¾
Sergei Bubka (Ukraine) 1994			
Long jump	8.95	29	4½
Mike Powell (USA) 1991			
Triple jump	18.29	60	0¼
Jonathan Edwards (GB) 1995			
Shot	23.12	75	10¼
Randy Barnes (USA) 1990			
Discus	74.08	243	0
Jürgen Schult (GDR) 1986			
Hammer	86.74	284	7
Yuriy Sedykh (USSR) 1986			
Javelin	98.48	323	1
Jan Zelezny (Czech Rep.) 1996			
Decathlon†	9,026pts		
Roman Sebrle (Czech Rep.) 2001			

† Ten events comprising 100m, long jump, shot, high jump, 400m, 110m hurdles, discus, pole vault, javelin, 1500m

WALKING (TRACK)	*hr*	*min*	*sec*
20,000m	1	17	25.6
Bernard Segura (Mexico) 1994			
29,572m	2	00	00.0
Maurizio Damilano (Italy) 1992			
30,000m	2	01	44.1
Maurizio Damilano (Italy) 1992			
50,000m	3	40	57.9
Thierry Toutain (France) 1996			

WOMEN

TRACK EVENTS	*hr*	*min*	*sec*
100m			10.49
Florence Griffith-Joyner (USA) 1988			
200m			21.34
Florence Griffith-Joyner (USA) 1988			
400m			47.60
Marita Koch (GDR) 1985			
800m		1	53.28
Jarmila Kratochvilova (Czechoslovakia) 1983			
1,500m		3	50.46
Qu Yunxia (China) 1993			
1 mile		4	12.56
Svetlana Masterkova (Russia) 1996			
3,000m		8	06.11
Wang Junxia (China) 1993			
5,000m		14	16.63
Meseret Defar (Ethiopia) 2007			
10,000m		29	31.78
Wang Junxia (China) 1993			
Marathon	2	15	25
Paula Radcliffe (GB) 2003			
100m hurdles (0.84m)			12.21
Yordanka Donkova (Bulgaria) 1988			

400m hurdles (0.76m)		52.34
Yuliya Pechonkina (Russia) 2003		
3,000m steeplechase	9	01.59
Gulnara Samitova (Russia) 2004		

RELAYS	*min*	*sec*
4 × 100m		41.37
GDR, 1985		
4 × 200m	1	27.46
USA, 2000		
4 × 400m	3	15.17
USSR, 1988		
4 × 800m	7	50.17
USSR, 1984		

FIELD EVENTS	*m*	*ft*	*in*
High jump	2.09	6	10¼
Stefka Kostadinova (Bulgaria) 1987			
Pole vault	5.01	16	5¼
Yelena Isinbayeva (Russia) 2005			
Long jump	7.52	24	8¼
Galina Chistyakova (USSR) 1988			
Triple jump	15.50	50	10¼
Inessa Kravets (Ukraine) 1995			
Shot	22.63	74	3
Natalya Lisovskaya (USSR) 1987			
Discus	76.80	252	0
Gabriele Reinsch (GDR) 1988			
Hammer	78.67*	258	1
Tatyana Lysenko (Russia) 2007			
Javelin (new implement in 1999)	71.70	235	3
Osleidys Menendez (Cuba) 2005			
Heptathlon†		7,291pts	
Jackie Joyner-Kersee (USA) 1986			

† Seven events comprising 100m hurdles, shot, high jump, 200m, long jump, javelin, 800m

ATHLETICS NATIONAL (UK) RECORDS

as at August 2007

Records set anywhere by athletes eligible to represent Great Britain and Northern Ireland

MEN

TRACK EVENTS	*hr*	*min*	*sec*
100m			9.87
Linford Christie, 1993			
Dwain Chambers, 2002			
200m			19.87
John Regis, 1994			
400m			44.36
Iwan Thomas, 1997			
800m		1	41.73
Sebastian Coe, 1981			
1,000m		2	12.18
Sebastian Coe, 1981			
1,500m		3	29.67
Sebastian Coe, 1985			
1 mile		3	46.32
Steve Cram, 1985			
2,000m		4	51.39
Steve Cram, 1985			
3,000m		7	32.79
David Moorcroft, 1982			
5,000m		13	00.41
David Moorcroft, 1982			
10,000m		27	18.14
Jon Brown, 1998			
20,000m		57	28.7
Carl Thackery, 1990			
20,855m	1	00	00.0
Carl Thackery, 1990			
25,000m	1	15	22.6
Ron Hill, 1965			
30,000m	1	31	30.4
Jim Alder, 1970			
Marathon	2	07	13
Steve Jones, 1985			
3,000m steeplechase		8	07.96
Mark Rowland, 1988			
110m hurdles			12.91
Colin Jackson, 1993			
400m hurdles			47.82
Kriss Akabusi, 1992			

RELAYS	*min*	*sec*
4 × 100m		37.73
GB team, 1999		
4 × 200m	1	21.29
GB team, 1989		
4 × 400m	2	56.60
GB team, 1996		
4 × 800m	7	03.89
GB team, 1982		

FIELD EVENTS	*m*	*ft*	*in*
High jump	2.37	7	9¼
Steve Smith, 1993			
Pole vault	5.80	19	0¼
Nick Buckfield, 1998			
Long jump	8.29*	27	2½
Chris Tomlinson, 2007			
Triple jump	18.29	60	0¼
Jonathan Edwards, 1995			
Shot	21.92	71	11
Carl Myerscough, 2003			
Discus	66.64	218	8
Perris Wilkins, 1998			
Hammer	77.54	254	5
Martin Girvan, 1984			
Javelin	91.46	300	1
Steve Backley, 1992			
Decathlon		8,847pts	
Daley Thompson, 1984			

WALKING (TRACK)	*hr*	*min*	*sec*
20,000m	1	23	26.5
Ian McCombie, 1990			
30,000m	2	19	18
Christopher Maddocks, 1984			
50,000m	4	05	44.6
Paul Blagg, 1990			
26,037m	2	00	00.0
Ron Wallwork, 1971			

WOMEN

TRACK EVENTS	*hr*	*min*	*sec*
100m			11.10
Kathy Cook, 1981			
200m			22.10
Kathy Cook, 1984			
400m			49.43
Kathy Cook, 1984			
800m		1	56.21
Kelly Holmes, 1995			

1,500m		3	57.90
Kelly Holmes, 2004			
1 mile		4	17.57
Zola Budd, 1985			
3,000m		8	22.20
Paula Radcliffe, 2002			
5,000m		14	29.11
Paula Radcliffe, 2004			
10,000m		30	01.09
Paula Radcliffe, 2002			
Marathon	2	15	25
Paula Radcliffe, 2003			
100m hurdles			12.80
Angela Thorp, 1996			
400m hurdles			52.74
Sally Gunnell, 1993			
3,000m steeplechase		9	38.56*
Hattie Dean, 2007			

RELAYS	*min*	*sec*
4 × 100m		42.43
GB team, 1980		
4 × 200m	1	31.57
GB team, 1977		
4 × 400m	3	22.01
GB team, 1991		
4 × 800m	8	23.8
GB team, 1971		

FIELD EVENTS	*m*	*ft*	*in*
High jump	1.95	6	4¾
Diana Elliott, 1982			
Susan Jones, 2001			
Jessica Ennis, 2007			
Pole vault	4.47	14	8
Janine Whitlock, 2002			
Long jump	6.90	22	7¾
Beverley Kinch, 1983			
Triple jump	15.15	49	8½
Ashia Hansen, 1997			
Shot	19.36	63	6¼
Judy Oakes, 1988			
Discus	67.48	221	5
Margaret Ritchie, 1981			
Hammer	68.93	226	1
Lorraine Shaw, 2001			
Javelin (new implement)	65.05*	213	5
Goldie Sayers, 2007			
Heptathlon			6,831pts
Denise Lewis, 2000			

* Awaiting ratification

SWIMMING WORLD RECORDS

AS AT AUGUST 2007

MEN	*min*	*sec*
50m freestyle		21.64
Alexander Popov, Russia		
100m freestyle		47.84
Pieter van den Hoogenband, the Netherlands		
200m freestyle	1	43.86
Michael Phelps, USA		
400m freestyle	3	40.08
Ian Thorpe, Australia		
800m freestyle	7	38.65
Grant Hackett, Australia		
1,500m freestyle	14	34.56
Grant Hackett, Australia		
50m breaststroke		27.18
Oleg Lisogor, Ukraine		
100m breaststroke		59.13
Brendan Hansen, USA		
200m breaststroke	2	08.50
Brendan Hansen, USA		
50m butterfly		22.96
Roland Schoeman, South Africa		
100m butterfly		50.40
Ian Crocker, USA		
200m butterfly	1	52.09
Michael Phelps, USA		
50m backstroke		24.80
Thomas Rupprath, Germany		
100m backstroke		52.98
Aaron Peirsol, USA		
200m backstroke	1	54.32
Ryan Lochte, USA		
200m medley	1	54.98
Michael Phelps, USA		
400m medley	4	06.22
Michael Phelps, USA		
4 × 100m freestyle relay	3	12.46
USA		
4 × 200m freestyle relay	7	03.24
USA		
4 × 100m medley relay	3	30.68
USA		

WOMEN	*min*	*sec*
50m freestyle		24.13
Inge de Bruijn, the Netherlands		
100m freestyle		53.30
Britta Steffen, Germany		
200m freestyle	1	55.52
Laure Manaudou, France		
400m freestyle	4	02.13
Laure Manaudou, France		
800m freestyle	8	16.22
Kate Ziegler, USA		
1,500m freestyle	15	42.54
Janet Evans, USA		
50m breaststroke		30.31
Jade Edmistone, Australia		
100m breaststroke	1	05.09
Leisel Jones, Australia		
200m breaststroke	2	20.54
Leisel Jones, Australia		
50m butterfly		25.46
Therese Alshammar, Sweden		
100m butterfly		56.61
Inge de Bruijn, the Netherlands		
200m butterfly	2	05.40
Jessicah Schipper, Australia		
50m backstroke		28.16
Leila Vaziri, USA		
100m backstroke		59.44
Natalie Coughlin, USA		
200m backstroke	2	06.62
Krisztina Egerszegi, Hungary		
200m medley	2	09.72
Wu Yanyan, China		
400m medley	4	32.89
Katie Hoff, USA		
4 × 100m freestyle relay	3	35.22
Germany		
4 × 200m freestyle relay	7	50.09
USA		
4 × 100m medley relay	3	55.74
Australia		

TIME AND SPACE

ASTRONOMY

TIME MEASUREMENT AND CALENDARS

TIDAL PREDICTIONS

ASTRONOMY

The following pages give astronomical data for each month of the year 2008. There are four pages of data for each month. All data are given for 0h Greenwich Mean Time (GMT), ie at the midnight at the beginning of the day named. This applies also to data for the months when British Summer Time is in operation (for dates, *see* below).

The astronomical data are given in a form suitable for observation with the naked eye or with a small telescope. These data do not attempt to replace the *Astronomical Almanac* for professional astronomers.

A fuller explanation of how to use the astronomical data is given on pages 1269–71.

CALENDAR FOR EACH MONTH

The calendar for each month comprises dates of general interest plus the dates of birth or death of well-known people. For key religious, civil and legal dates *see* page 9. For details of flag-flying days *see* page 23. For royal birthdays *see* pages 23 and 24–5. Public holidays are given in italics. *See* also pages 10 and 11.

Fuller explanations of the various calendars can be found under Time Measurement and Calendars.

The zodiacal signs through which the Sun is passing during each month are illustrated. The date of transition from one sign to the next, to the nearest hour, is given under Astronomical Phenomena.

JULIAN DATE

The Julian date on 2008 January 0.0 is 2454465.5. To find the Julian date for any other date in 2008 (at 0h GMT), add the day-of-the-year number on the extreme right of the calendar for each month to the Julian date for January 0.0.

SEASONS

The seasons are defined astronomically as follows:

Spring from the vernal equinox to the summer solstice
Summer from the summer solstice to the autumnal equinox
Autumn from the autumnal equinox to the winter solstice
Winter from the winter solstice to the vernal equinox

The time when seasons start in 2008 (to the nearest hour) are:

Northern Hemisphere

Vernal equinox	March 20d 06h GMT
Summer solstice	June 21d 00h GMT
Autumnal equinox	September 22d 16h GMT
Winter solstice	December 21d 12h GMT

Southern Hemisphere

Autumnal equinox	March 20d 06h GMT
Winter solstice	June 21d 00h GMT
Vernal equinox	September 22d 16h GMT
Summer solstice	December 21d 12h GMT

The longest day of the year, measured from sunrise to sunset, is at the summer solstice. The longest day in the United Kingdom will fall on 20 June in 2008.

The shortest day of the year is at the winter solstice. The shortest day in the United Kingdom will fall on 21 December in 2008.

The equinox is the point at which day and night are of equal length all over the world.

In popular parlance, the seasons in the northern hemisphere comprise the following months:

Spring	March, April, May
Summer	June, July, August
Autumn	September, October, November
Winter	December, January, February

BRITISH SUMMER TIME

British Summer Time is the legal time for general purposes during the period in which it is in operation (*see also* pages 1273–4). During this period, clocks are kept one hour ahead of Greenwich Mean Time. The hour of changeover is 01h Greenwich Mean Time. The duration of Summer Time in 2008 is from March 30 01h GMT to October 26 01h GMT.

JANUARY 2008

FIRST MONTH, 31 DAYS. *Janus*, god of the portal, facing two ways, past and future

1	*Tuesday*	The UK joined the EEC with Ireland and Denmark, bringing the number of members to nine 1973	day 1
2	*Wednesday*	Gilbert Murray, British diplomat b. 1866 Henry Booth, English politician d. 1694	2
3	*Thursday*	Clement Attlee, British prime minister b. 1883 Herbert Morrison, British statesman b. 1888	3
4	*Friday*	Burma gained independence from the United Kingdom 1948	4
5	*Saturday*	Konrad Adenauer, German chancellor b. 1876 Juan Carlos, king of Spain b. 1938	5
6	*Sunday*	King Richard II b. 1367 Yahya Ayyash, Palestinian leader d. 1996	6
7	*Monday*	Millard Fillmore, US president b. 1800 Hirohito Michinomiya, emperor of Japan d. 1989	week 1 day 7
8	*Tuesday*	James Craig, prime minister of Northern Ireland b. 1871 François Mitterrand, president of France d. 1996	8
9	*Wednesday*	Richard Nixon, US president b. 1913 Napoleon III, emperor of France d. 1873	9
10	*Thursday*	Harold Macmillan became prime minister of Britain 1957	10
11	*Friday*	John A. Macdonald, prime minister of Canada b. 1815 Zenko Suzuki, prime minister of Japan b. 1911	11
12	*Saturday*	Hermann Goering, German Nazi leader b. 1893 Leopoldo Galtieri, president of Argentina d. 2003	12
13	*Sunday*	Henry II, king of Castile b. 1334 Chiang Ching-kuo, Chinese statesman d. 1988	13
14	*Monday*	Anthony Eden, British prime minister d. 1977 Frederick IX, king of Denmark d. 1972	week 2 day 14
15	*Tuesday*	Gamal Nasser, president of Egypt b. 1918 Martin Luther King Jr, US political activist b. 1929	15
16	*Wednesday*	Johannes Rau, German politician b. 1931 Laurent Kabila, president of the DR Congo d. 2001	16
17	*Thursday*	David Lloyd-George, British prime minister b. 1863 Benjamin Franklin, American statesman b. 1706	17
18	*Friday*	John Tyler, US president d. 1862 Hugh Gaitskell, British politician d. 1963	18
19	*Saturday*	Indira Gandhi became the first female prime minister of India 1966	19
20	*Sunday*	Herbert Bowden, British politician b. 1905 King George V d. 1936	20
21	*Monday*	Louis XVI, king of France d. 1793 Vladimir Lenin, Russian revolutionary d. 1924	week 3 day 21
22	*Tuesday*	Queen Victoria d. 1901 Lyndon B. Johnson, US president d. 1973	22
23	*Wednesday*	Richard Nixon announced a peace deal between the USA and Vietnam after a decade of conflict 1973	23
24	*Thursday*	Winston Churchill, British prime minister d. 1965 Caligula, Roman emperor d. AD 41	24
25	*Friday*	Paul-Henri Spaak, prime minister of Belgium b. 1899 Eduard Shevardnadze, Georgian politician b. 1928	25
26	*Saturday*	The Republic of India was proclaimed with Rajendra Prasad as president 1950	26
27	*Sunday*	Wilhelm II, German emperor b. 1859 Rauf Denktash, Turkish-Cypriot politician b. 1924	27
28	*Monday*	King Henry VII b. 1457 King Henry VIII d. 1547	week 4 day 28
29	*Tuesday*	William McKinley, US president b. 1843 King George III d. 1820	29
30	*Wednesday*	Franklin D. Roosevelt, US president b. 1882 Mahatma Gandhi, Indian leader d. 1948	30
31	*Thursday*	Guy Fawkes was executed for his involvement in the Gunpowder Plot 1606	31

ASTRONOMICAL PHENOMENA

d	*h*	
3	00	Earth at perihelion (147 million km.)
5	03	Venus in conjunction with Moon. Venus 7°N.
7	10	Jupiter in conjunction with Moon. Jupiter 4°N.
9	16	Mercury in conjunction with Moon. Mercury 0°.3N.
20	00	Mars in conjunction with Moon. Mars 1°S.
20	17	Sun's longitude 300° ♒
22	05	Mercury at greatest elongation E. 19°
25	04	Saturn in conjunction with Moon. Saturn 3°N.
28	21	Mercury at stationary point
30	23	Mars at stationary point

MINIMA OF ALGOL

d	*h*	*d*	*h*	*d*	*h*
1	15.2	13	02.5	24	13.8
4	12.1	15	23.3	27	10.6
7	08.9	18	20.2	30	07.4
10	05.7	21	17.0		

CONSTELLATIONS

The following constellations are near the meridian at

	d	*h*		*d*	*h*
December	1	24	January	16	21
December	16	23	February	1	20
January	1	22	February	15	19

Draco (below the Pole), Ursa Minor (below the Pole), Camelopardus, Perseus, Auriga, Taurus, Orion, Eridanus and Lepus

THE MOON

Phases, Apsides and Node	*d*	*h*	*m*
● New Moon	8	11	37
☽ First Quarter	15	19	46
○ Full Moon	22	13	35
☾ Last Quarter	30	05	03
Apogee (405,298km)	3	08	11
Perigee (366,455km)	19	08	41
Apogee (404,493km)	31	04	27

Mean longitude of ascending node on January 1, 330°

THE SUN

s.d. 16′.3

Day	Right Ascension h m s	Dec. – ° ′	Equation of time m s	Rise 52° h m	Rise 56° h m	Transit h m	Set 52° h m	Set 56° h m	Sidereal time h m s	Transit of First Point of Aries h m s
1	18 43 12	23 04	−3 04	8 08	8 31	12 03	15 59	15 35	6 40 08	17 17 02
2	18 47 37	22 59	−3 33	8 08	8 31	12 04	16 00	15 37	6 44 04	17 13 06
3	18 52 02	22 54	−4 01	8 08	8 31	12 04	16 01	15 38	6 48 01	17 09 10
4	18 56 26	22 48	−4 29	8 08	8 30	12 05	16 02	15 39	6 51 57	17 05 14
5	19 00 50	22 42	−4 56	8 07	8 30	12 05	16 03	15 41	6 55 54	17 01 18
6	19 05 14	22 36	−5 23	8 07	8 29	12 06	16 04	15 42	6 59 50	16 57 23
7	19 09 37	22 29	−5 50	8 07	8 29	12 06	16 06	15 44	7 03 47	16 53 27
8	19 14 00	22 21	−6 16	8 06	8 28	12 06	16 07	15 45	7 07 43	16 49 31
9	19 18 22	22 13	−6 42	8 06	8 28	12 07	16 08	15 47	7 11 40	16 45 35
10	19 22 44	22 05	−7 07	8 05	8 27	12 07	16 10	15 48	7 15 37	16 41 39
11	19 27 05	21 56	−7 32	8 05	8 26	12 08	16 11	15 50	7 19 33	16 37 43
12	19 31 25	21 47	−7 56	8 04	8 25	12 08	16 13	15 52	7 23 30	16 33 47
13	19 35 45	21 37	−8 19	8 03	8 24	12 09	16 14	15 53	7 27 26	16 29 51
14	19 40 05	21 27	−8 42	8 03	8 23	12 09	16 16	15 55	7 31 23	16 25 55
15	19 44 23	21 16	−9 04	8 02	8 22	12 09	16 17	15 57	7 35 19	16 21 59
16	19 48 41	21 06	−9 25	8 01	8 21	12 10	16 19	15 59	7 39 16	16 18 03
17	19 52 59	20 54	−9 46	8 00	8 20	12 10	16 20	16 01	7 43 12	16 14 08
18	19 57 15	20 43	−10 06	7 59	8 18	12 10	16 22	16 03	7 47 09	16 10 12
19	20 01 31	20 30	−10 25	7 58	8 17	12 11	16 24	16 05	7 51 06	16 06 16
20	20 05 46	20 18	−10 44	7 57	8 16	12 11	16 25	16 07	7 55 02	16 02 20
21	20 10 01	20 05	−11 02	7 56	8 14	12 11	16 27	16 09	7 58 59	15 58 24
22	20 14 14	19 52	−11 19	7 55	8 13	12 11	16 29	16 11	8 02 55	15 54 28
23	20 18 27	19 38	−11 35	7 53	8 11	12 12	16 30	16 13	8 06 52	15 50 32
24	20 22 39	19 24	−11 51	7 52	8 10	12 12	16 32	16 15	8 10 48	15 46 36
25	20 26 50	19 10	−12 06	7 51	8 08	12 12	16 34	16 17	8 14 45	15 42 40
26	20 31 01	18 55	−12 20	7 50	8 07	12 12	16 36	16 19	8 18 41	15 38 44
27	20 35 11	18 40	−12 33	7 48	8 05	12 13	16 38	16 21	8 22 38	15 34 48
28	20 39 20	18 25	−12 45	7 47	8 03	12 13	16 39	16 23	8 26 35	15 30 53
29	20 43 28	18 09	−12 57	7 45	8 02	12 13	16 41	16 25	8 30 31	15 26 57
30	20 47 35	17 53	−13 08	7 44	8 00	12 13	16 43	16 27	8 34 28	15 23 01
31	20 51 42	17 37	−13 18	7 43	7 58	12 13	16 45	16 29	8 38 24	15 19 05

DURATION OF TWILIGHT (in minutes)

Latitude	*52°*	*56°*	*52°*	*56°*	*52°*	*56°*	*52°*	*56°*
	1 January		*11 January*		*21 January*		*31 January*	
Civil	41	47	40	45	38	43	37	41
Nautical	84	96	82	93	80	90	78	87
Astronomical	125	141	123	138	120	134	117	130

THE NIGHT SKY

Mercury is unsuitably placed for observation during the first half of the month but thereafter emerges from the evening twilight to be visible low in the south-western sky at the end of evening civil twilight, until the last couple of days of the month. During this period its magnitude fades from −0.8 to +0.9.

Venus, magnitude −4.0, is a brilliant object in the south-eastern sky before dawn, though the duration of its period of visibility shortens noticeably during the month.

Mars, just past opposition, is a brilliant evening object in the southern sky as soon as it gets dark and still easily visible for several hours after midnight. Mars is in retrograde motion in Taurus until the 30th when it resumes its direct motion. During January its magnitude fades from −1.5 to −0.6. The waxing gibbous Moon passes only 1 degree north of the planet on the night of the 19th–20th.

Jupiter is not visible at first but is gradually emerging from the morning twilight. It may be detected during the last few days of the month, very low above the south-eastern horizon about half an hour before sunrise. Its magnitude is −1.9. Jupiter is in the constellation of Sagittarius. Venus can be used as an aid to finding Jupiter during the last few days of January as it moves eastwards towards Jupiter, being less than 2 degrees from that planet on the 31st.

Saturn, magnitude +0.4, is retrograding in Leo, and by the end of the month is visible from the mid-evening when it rises above the eastern horizon right through until dawn. The Moon, just after Full, passes 3 degrees south of the planet on the morning of the 25th. The rings of Saturn are now closing, and as a result, the planet is not quite as bright as it was in the previous two oppositions. The south pole is presented towards the Earth, but the far side of the rings no longer appears clear of the body of the planet.

THE MOON

Day	R.A.		Dec.	Hor. Par.	Semi-diam.	Sun's Co-Long.	PA of Br. Limb	Ph.	Age	Rise 52°		Rise 56°		Transit		Set 52°		Set 56°	
	h	m	°	′	′	°	°	%	d	h	m	h	m	h	m	h	m	h	m
1	12	58	−10.3	54.5	14.9	183	112	44	22.3	1	16	1	26	6	29	11	29	11	17
2	13	42	−15.4	54.2	14.8	195	110	34	23.3	2	28	2	43	7	11	11	42	11	25
3	14	28	−19.8	54.1	14.7	207	106	26	24.3	3	41	4	03	7	55	11	59	11	36
4	15	17	−23.4	54.1	14.7	220	101	18	25.3	4	54	5	22	8	41	12	22	11	53
5	16	08	−26.1	54.3	14.8	232	95	11	26.3	6	05	6	39	9	31	12	54	12	19
6	17	01	−27.6	54.6	14.9	244	87	6	27.3	7	07	7	45	10	23	13	38	13	00
7	17	56	−27.9	54.9	15.0	256	76	2	28.3	7	59	8	35	11	16	14	37	14	01
8	18	51	−26.7	55.4	15.1	268	51	0	29.3	8	37	9	08	12	10	15	48	15	18
9	19	46	−24.2	55.8	15.2	281	286	0	0.5	9	05	9	29	13	01	17	07	16	43
10	20	39	−20.4	56.3	15.3	293	261	2	1.5	9	25	9	43	13	51	18	28	18	11
11	21	30	−15.6	56.8	15.5	305	253	7	2.5	9	41	9	53	14	38	19	49	19	39
12	22	19	−10.0	57.3	15.6	317	248	13	3.5	9	54	10	00	15	24	21	09	21	05
13	23	07	−3.9	57.8	15.7	329	246	21	4.5	10	05	10	06	16	09	22	30	22	32
14	23	55	+2.4	58.2	15.9	341	245	30	5.5	10	17	10	13	16	55	23	53	—	
15	0	44	+8.8	58.7	16.0	354	246	41	6.5	10	30	10	20	17	44	—		0	00
16	1	36	+14.8	59.1	16.1	6	249	52	7.5	10	46	10	30	18	36	1	19	1	33
17	2	31	+20.1	59.4	16.2	18	253	63	8.5	11	08	10	45	19	32	2	48	3	09
18	3	30	+24.3	59.7	16.3	30	259	74	9.5	11	39	11	08	20	33	4	18	4	47
19	4	33	+27.1	59.8	16.3	42	266	84	10.5	12	25	11	49	21	37	5	41	6	18
20	5	38	+28.0	59.8	16.3	54	275	91	11.5	13	31	12	54	22	41	6	50	7	27
21	6	43	+27.0	59.6	16.2	66	284	97	12.5	14	52	14	21	23	42	7	38	8	10
22	7	45	+24.2	59.2	16.1	79	302	100	13.5	16	20	15	57	—		8	11	8	35
23	8	43	+20.0	58.6	16.0	91	88	100	14.5	17	47	17	32	0	38	8	33	8	51
24	9	37	+14.8	57.9	15.8	103	107	97	15.5	19	10	19	01	1	29	8	50	9	01
25	10	27	+9.0	57.2	15.6	115	113	93	16.5	20	29	20	26	2	16	9	02	9	08
26	11	13	+3.0	56.4	15.4	127	115	87	17.5	21	45	21	47	3	00	9	13	9	14
27	11	58	−2.9	55.7	15.2	139	116	79	18.5	22	58	23	06	3	42	9	24	9	20
28	12	42	−8.6	55.1	15.0	151	115	71	19.5	—		—		4	23	9	35	9	25
29	13	27	−13.9	54.6	14.9	164	113	62	20.5	0	11	0	24	5	05	9	47	9	33
30	14	13	−18.5	54.3	14.8	176	110	52	21.5	1	25	1	44	5	48	10	02	9	42
31	15	00	−22.5	54.2	14.8	188	106	43	22.5	2	38	3	04	6	34	10	23	9	56

MERCURY

Day	R.A.		Dec.	Diam.	Phase	Transit		5° high 52°		5° high 56°	
	h	m	°	″	%	h	m	h	m	h	m
1	19	20	−24.3	5	97	12	42	15	35	14	55
3	19	35	−23.8	5	96	12	48	15	46	15	08
5	19	49	−23.3	5	94	12	54	15	57	15	22
7	20	02	−22.6	5	93	13	00	16	09	15	36
9	20	16	−21.8	5	90	13	06	16	22	15	51
11	20	29	−21.0	5	88	13	11	16	34	16	06
13	20	42	−20.0	6	84	13	16	16	47	16	20
15	20	55	−19.0	6	80	13	20	16	59	16	34
17	21	06	−17.9	6	75	13	24	17	10	16	48
19	21	17	−16.8	6	68	13	26	17	20	16	59
21	21	26	−15.6	7	61	13	27	17	28	17	09
23	21	33	−14.5	7	53	13	26	17	34	17	17
25	21	39	−13.5	8	43	13	23	17	37	17	21
27	21	42	−12.7	8	34	13	18	17	36	17	21
29	21	43	−12.0	9	24	13	09	17	31	17	16
31	21	40	−11.6	9	15	12	58	17	22	17	07

VENUS

Day	R.A.		Dec.	Diam.	Phase	Transit		5° high 52°		5° high 56°	
	h	m	°	″	%	h	m	h	m	h	m
1	15	59	−18.5	15	76	9	20	5	41	6	05
6	16	24	−19.7	14	78	9	25	5	55	6	22
11	16	50	−20.8	14	79	9	31	6	09	6	38
16	17	16	−21.6	13	81	9	37	6	22	6	53
21	17	42	−22.1	13	82	9	44	6	33	7	06
26	18	09	−22.4	13	83	9	51	6	42	7	15
31	18	35	−22.4	13	84	9	58	6	49	7	22

MARS

Day	R.A.		Dec.	Diam.	Phase	Transit		5° high 52°		5° high 56°	
	h	m	°	″	%	h	m	h	m	h	m
1	5	59	+26.9	15	100	23	14	7	16	7	39
6	5	52	+27.0	15	99	22	47	6	49	7	12
11	5	45	+27.0	15	98	22	21	6	22	6	46
16	5	40	+26.9	14	98	21	56	5	57	6	21
21	5	36	+26.8	13	97	21	33	5	34	5	57
26	5	34	+26.8	13	96	21	12	5	11	5	34
31	5	34	+26.7	12	95	20	52	4	50	5	13

SUNRISE AND SUNSET

	London		*Bristol*		*Birmingham*		*Manchester*		*Newcastle*		*Glasgow*		*Belfast*	
	0° 05′	*51° 30′*	*2° 35′*	*51° 28′*	*1° 55′*	*52° 28′*	*2° 15′*	*53° 28′*	*1° 37′*	*54° 59′*	*4° 14′*	*55° 52′*	*5° 56′*	*54° 35′*
d	*h m*	*h m*	*h m*	*h m*	*h m*	*h m*	*h m*	*h m*	*h m*	*h m*	*h m*	*h m*	*h m*	*h m*
1	8 06	16 01	8 16	16 12	8 18	16 04	8 25	16 00	8 31	15 48	8 47	15 53	8 46	16 08
2	8 06	16 02	8 16	16 13	8 18	16 05	8 25	16 01	8 31	15 50	8 47	15 54	8 46	16 09
3	8 06	16 04	8 16	16 14	8 18	16 06	8 25	16 02	8 31	15 51	8 47	15 56	8 46	16 10
4	8 06	16 05	8 15	16 15	8 18	16 07	8 24	16 03	8 31	15 52	8 47	15 57	8 45	16 12
5	8 05	16 06	8 15	16 16	8 17	16 08	8 24	16 05	8 30	15 53	8 46	15 58	8 45	16 13
6	8 05	16 07	8 15	16 17	8 17	16 10	8 24	16 06	8 30	15 55	8 46	16 00	8 45	16 14
7	8 05	16 08	8 15	16 19	8 17	16 11	8 23	16 07	8 29	15 56	8 45	16 01	8 44	16 16
8	8 04	16 10	8 14	16 20	8 16	16 12	8 23	16 09	8 29	15 58	8 44	16 03	8 44	16 17
9	8 04	16 11	8 14	16 21	8 16	16 14	8 22	16 10	8 28	15 59	8 44	16 04	8 43	16 19
10	8 03	16 12	8 13	16 23	8 15	16 15	8 22	16 11	8 27	16 01	8 43	16 06	8 42	16 20
11	8 03	16 14	8 13	16 24	8 15	16 17	8 21	16 13	8 26	16 02	8 42	16 08	8 41	16 22
12	8 02	16 15	8 12	16 25	8 14	16 18	8 20	16 15	8 26	16 04	8 41	16 09	8 41	16 23
13	8 01	16 17	8 11	16 27	8 13	16 20	8 19	16 16	8 25	16 06	8 40	16 11	8 40	16 25
14	8 01	16 18	8 10	16 28	8 12	16 21	8 18	16 18	8 24	16 07	8 39	16 13	8 39	16 27
15	8 00	16 20	8 10	16 30	8 11	16 23	8 18	16 19	8 23	16 09	8 38	16 15	8 38	16 28
16	7 59	16 21	8 09	16 31	8 11	16 24	8 17	16 21	8 22	16 11	8 37	16 17	8 37	16 30
17	7 58	16 23	8 08	16 33	8 10	16 26	8 16	16 23	8 21	16 13	8 36	16 18	8 36	16 32
18	7 57	16 24	8 07	16 35	8 09	16 28	8 15	16 24	8 19	16 14	8 35	16 20	8 35	16 34
19	7 56	16 26	8 06	16 36	8 08	16 29	8 13	16 26	8 18	16 16	8 33	16 22	8 34	16 36
20	7 55	16 28	8 05	16 38	8 07	16 31	8 12	16 28	8 17	16 18	8 32	16 24	8 32	16 37
21	7 54	16 29	8 04	16 40	8 05	16 33	8 11	16 30	8 16	16 20	8 31	16 26	8 31	16 39
22	7 53	16 31	8 03	16 41	8 04	16 35	8 10	16 32	8 14	16 22	8 29	16 28	8 30	16 41
23	7 52	16 33	8 02	16 43	8 03	16 36	8 09	16 33	8 13	16 24	8 28	16 30	8 28	16 43
24	7 51	16 35	8 00	16 45	8 02	16 38	8 07	16 35	8 11	16 26	8 26	16 32	8 27	16 45
25	7 49	16 36	7 59	16 46	8 00	16 40	8 06	16 37	8 10	16 28	8 25	16 34	8 25	16 47
26	7 48	16 38	7 58	16 48	7 59	16 42	8 04	16 39	8 08	16 30	8 23	16 36	8 24	16 49
27	7 47	16 40	7 57	16 50	7 58	16 43	8 03	16 41	8 07	16 32	8 21	16 38	8 22	16 51
28	7 45	16 42	7 55	16 52	7 56	16 45	8 02	16 43	8 05	16 34	8 20	16 41	8 21	16 53
29	7 44	16 43	7 54	16 53	7 55	16 47	8 00	16 45	8 04	16 36	8 18	16 43	8 19	16 55
30	7 43	16 45	7 52	16 55	7 53	16 49	7 58	16 47	8 02	16 38	8 16	16 45	8 18	16 57
31	7 41	16 47	7 51	16 57	7 52	16 51	7 57	16 49	8 00	16 40	8 14	16 47	8 16	16 59

JUPITER

Day	*R.A.*	*Dec.*	*Transit*	*5° high*	
				52°	*56°*
	h m	° ′	*h m*	*h m*	*h m*
1	18 13.1	−23 14	11 32	8 31	9 07
11	18 23.0	−23 11	11 02	8 01	8 37
21	18 32.8	−23 05	10 32	7 30	8 06
31	18 42.2	−22 58	10 03	6 59	7 34

Diameters – equatorial 32″ polar 30″

SATURN

Day	*R.A.*	*Dec.*	*Transit*	*5° high*	
				52°	*56°*
	h m	° ′	*h m*	*h m*	*h m*
1	10 42.8	+9 58	4 02	21 40	21 35
11	10 41.7	+10 08	3 22	20 59	20 54
21	10 39.9	+10 20	2 40	20 17	20 12
31	10 37.7	+10 36	1 59	19 34	19 28

Diameters – equatorial 19″ polar 17″

Rings – major axis 44″ minor axis 5″

URANUS

Day	*R.A.*	*Dec.*	*Transit*	*10° high*	
				52°	*56°*
	h m	° ′	*h m*	*h m*	*h m*
1	23 07.3	−6 28	16 25	20 42	20 29
11	23 08.6	−6 20	15 47	20 05	19 52
21	23 10.1	−6 10	15 09	19 28	19 15
31	23 11.8	−5 59	14 31	18 52	18 39

Diameter 4″

NEPTUNE

Day	*R.A.*	*Dec.*	*Transit*	*5° high*	
				52°	*56°*
	h m	° ′	*h m*	*h m*	*h m*
1	21 31.0	−15 00	14 49	18 10	17 44
11	21 32.3	−14 54	14 10	17 33	17 07
21	21 33.7	−14 48	13 33	16 56	16 30
31	21 35.1	−14 41	12 55	16 19	15 54

Diameter 2″

FEBRUARY 2008

SECOND MONTH, 28 or 29 DAYS. *Februa*, Roman festival of Purification

1	*Friday*	Boris Yeltsin, president of the Russian Federation b. 1931 Shahabuddin Ahmed, president of Bangladesh b. 1930		32
2	*Saturday*	The US supreme court convened for the first time 1790		33
3	*Sunday*	Robert Gascoyne-Cecil, British prime minister b. 1830 Woodrow Wilson, US president d. 1924		34
4	*Monday*	Slavery was banned in the French Republic 1794	week 5 day	35
5	*Tuesday*	Robert Peel, British prime minister b. 1788 Andreas Papandreou, prime minister of Greece b. 1919		36
6	*Wednesday*	Queen Anne b. 1665 Ronald Reagan, US president b. 1911		37
7	*Thursday*	Thomas More, English statesman b. 1478 Daniel Malan, prime minister of South Africa d. 1959		38
8	*Friday*	Yaroslav II, grand prince of Vladimir b. 1191 Mary I, queen of Scotland d. 1587		39
9	*Saturday*	Garrett Fitzgerald, prime minister of Ireland b. 1926 Yuri Andropov, Soviet leader d. 1984		40
10	*Sunday*	Harold Macmillan, British prime minister b. 1894 Maurice Schumann, French statesman d. 1998		41
11	*Monday*	Nelson Mandela was released from prison after 27 years 1990	week 6 day	42
12	*Tuesday*	Francis II, Holy Roman emperor b. 1768 Lady Jane Grey d. 1554		43
13	*Wednesday*	Francis Pym, British politician b. 1922 Catherine Howard, queen consort of Henry VIII d. 1542		44
14	*Thursday*	Rafik Hariri, prime minister of Lebanon d. 2005 Yusuf Salman Yusuf, Iraqi communist leader d. 1949		45
15	*Friday*	H. H. Asquith, British prime minister d. 1928 Henry Hunt, British politician d. 1835		46
16	*Saturday*	Fidel Castro was sworn in as premier of Cuba 1959		47
17	*Sunday*	William III, king of the Netherlands b. 1817 Geronimo, Native American leader d. 1909		48
18	*Monday*	Queen Mary I b. 1516 Kublai Khan, Mongol and Chinese emperor d. 1294	week 7 day	49
19	*Tuesday*	Alvaro Obregon, president of Mexico b. 1880 Deng Xiaoping, Chinese leader d. 1997		50
20	*Wednesday*	Hundreds were killed in election violence in Assam, north-east India 1983		51
21	*Thursday*	Robert Mugabe, president of Zimbabwe b. 1924 Malcolm X, US civil rights campaigner d. 1965		52
22	*Friday*	George Washington, US president b. 1732 Jean-Bédel Bokassa, ruler of the Central African Republic b. 1921		53
23	*Saturday*	Konstantin Päts, president of Estonia b. 1874 William McMahon, prime minister of Australia b. 1908		54
24	*Sunday*	Joe Lieberman, US politician b. 1942 Joseph I, king of Portugal d. 1777		55
25	*Monday*	Néstor Kirchner, president of Argentina b. 1950 William IV, grand duke of Luxembourg d. 1912	week 8 day	56
26	*Tuesday*	Ferdinand I, king of Bulgaria b. 1861 Levi Eshkol, prime minister of Israel d. 1969		57
27	*Wednesday*	The German parliamentary building, the Reichstag, was set on fire 1933		58
28	*Thursday*	Robin Cook, British politician b. 1946 Olof Palme, prime minister of Sweden d. 1986		59
29	*Friday*	Morarji Desai, prime minister of India b. 1896 Carlos Romero, president of El Salvador b. 1924		60

ASTRONOMICAL PHENOMENA

d	*h*	
1	12	Jupiter in conjunction with Venus. Jupiter 0°.6S.
4	06	Jupiter in conjunction with Moon. Jupiter 4°N.
4	12	Venus in conjunction with Moon. Venus 4°N.
6	18	Mercury in inferior conjunction
7	02	Mercury in conjunction with Moon. Mercury 5°N.
7	04	Annular eclipse of Sun
11	02	Neptune in conjunction
16	08	Mars in conjunction with Moon. Mars 2°S.
19	03	Mercury at stationary point
19	07	Sun's longitude 330° ♓
21	03	Total eclipse of Moon
21	10	Saturn in conjunction with Moon. Saturn 3°N.
24	10	Saturn at opposition
26	18	Venus in conjunction with Mercury. Venus 1°S.

MINIMA OF ALGOL

d	*h*	*d*	*h*	*d*	*h*
2	04.3	13	15.6	25	02.8
5	01.1	16	12.4	27	23.7
7	21.9	19	09.2		
10	18.7	22	06.0		

CONSTELLATIONS

The following constellations are near the meridian at

	d	*h*		*d*	*h*
January	1	24	February	15	21
January	16	23	March	1	20
February	1	22	March	16	19

Draco (below the Pole), Camelopardalis, Auriga, Taurus, Gemini, Orion, Canis Minor, Monoceros, Lepus, Canis Major and Puppis

THE MOON

Phases, Apsides and Node	*d*	*h*	*m*
● New Moon	7	03	44
☽ First Quarter	14	03	33
○ Full Moon	21	03	30
☾ Last Quarter	29	02	18
Perigee (370,256km)	14	00	56
Apogee (404,403km)	28	01	25

Mean longitude of ascending node on February 1, 329°

THE SUN

s.d. 16′.2

Day	Right Ascension			Dec. –		Equation of time		Rise 52°		Rise 56°		Transit		Set 52°		Set 56°		Sidereal time			Transit of first point of Aries		
	h	*m*	*s*	°	′	*m*	*s*	*h*	*m*	*h*	*m*	*h*	*m*	*h*	*m*	*h*	*m*	*h*	*m*	*s*	*h*	*m*	*s*
1	20	55	48	17	20	−13	27	7	41	7	56	12	14	16	47	16	32	8	42	21	15	15	09
2	20	59	53	17	03	−13	35	7	39	7	54	12	14	16	49	16	34	8	46	17	15	11	13
3	21	03	57	16	46	−13	43	7	38	7	52	12	14	16	50	16	36	8	50	14	15	07	17
4	21	08	00	16	28	−13	50	7	36	7	50	12	14	16	52	16	38	8	54	10	15	03	21
5	21	12	03	16	11	−13	56	7	35	7	48	12	14	16	54	16	40	8	58	07	14	59	25
6	21	16	04	15	52	−14	01	7	33	7	46	12	14	16	56	16	43	9	02	04	14	55	29
7	21	20	05	15	34	−14	05	7	31	7	44	12	14	16	58	16	45	9	06	00	14	51	33
8	21	24	06	15	15	−14	09	7	29	7	42	12	14	17	00	16	47	9	09	57	14	47	37
9	21	28	05	14	56	−14	12	7	28	7	40	12	14	17	02	16	49	9	13	53	14	43	42
10	21	32	03	14	37	−14	14	7	26	7	38	12	14	17	03	16	51	9	17	50	14	39	46
11	21	36	01	14	18	−14	15	7	24	7	36	12	14	17	05	16	54	9	21	46	14	35	50
12	21	39	58	13	58	−14	15	7	22	7	34	12	14	17	07	16	56	9	25	43	14	31	54
13	21	43	54	13	38	−14	15	7	20	7	31	12	14	17	09	16	58	9	29	39	14	27	58
14	21	47	50	13	18	−14	14	7	18	7	29	12	14	17	11	17	00	9	33	36	14	24	02
15	21	51	44	12	58	−14	12	7	16	7	27	12	14	17	13	17	02	9	37	33	14	20	06
16	21	55	38	12	37	−14	09	7	14	7	25	12	14	17	15	17	05	9	41	29	14	16	10
17	21	59	32	12	16	−14	06	7	12	7	22	12	14	17	17	17	07	9	45	26	14	12	14
18	22	03	24	11	56	−14	02	7	10	7	20	12	14	17	18	17	09	9	49	22	14	08	18
19	22	07	16	11	34	−13	57	7	08	7	18	12	14	17	20	17	11	9	53	19	14	04	22
20	22	11	07	11	13	−13	51	7	06	7	15	12	14	17	22	17	13	9	57	15	14	00	27
21	22	14	57	10	52	−13	45	7	04	7	13	12	14	17	24	17	16	10	01	12	13	56	31
22	22	18	47	10	30	−13	38	7	02	7	10	12	14	17	26	17	18	10	05	08	13	52	35
23	22	22	36	10	08	−13	31	7	00	7	08	12	13	17	28	17	20	10	09	05	13	48	39
24	22	26	24	9	46	−13	23	6	58	7	06	12	13	17	29	17	22	10	13	02	13	44	43
25	22	30	12	9	24	−13	14	6	56	7	03	12	13	17	31	17	24	10	16	58	13	40	47
26	22	33	59	9	02	−13	05	6	54	7	01	12	13	17	33	17	26	10	20	55	13	36	51
27	22	37	46	8	39	−12	55	6	52	6	58	12	13	17	35	17	28	10	24	51	13	32	55
28	22	41	32	8	17	−12	45	6	50	6	56	12	13	17	37	17	31	10	28	48	13	28	59
29	22	45	18	7	54	−12	34	6	47	6	53	12	12	17	38	17	33	10	32	44	13	25	03

DURATION OF TWILIGHT (in minutes)

Latitude	*52°*	*56°*	*52°*	*56°*	*52°*	*56°*	*52°*	*56°*
	1 February		*11 February*		*21 February*		*31 February*	
Civil	37	41	35	39	34	38	34	37
Nautical	77	86	75	83	74	81	73	80
Astronomical	117	130	114	126	113	124	112	124

THE NIGHT SKY

Mercury passes through inferior conjunction on the 6th and remains too close to the Sun for observation throughout the month.

Venus continues to be visible as a splendid object in the early morning skies, magnitude −3.9, though it will only be seen low above the south-eastern horizon, for a short period of time, just before sunrise.

Mars, its magnitude fading from −0.6 to +0.2 during the month, continues to be visible as an evening object in the south-western quadrant of the sky, in the constellation of Taurus. The waxing gibbous Moon will be seen in the vicinity of the planet on the evenings of the 15th and 16th.

Jupiter, magnitude −1.9, is now emerging from the morning twilight and becoming more easily visible as a brilliant object in the south-eastern sky in the mornings, albeit at a low altitude. Venus passes less than 1 degree north of Jupiter on the 1st.

Saturn reaches opposition on the 24th and thus is visible throughout the hours of darkness. Its magnitude is +0.2.

Zodiacal Light. The evening cone may be observed stretching up from the western horizon, along the ecliptic, after the end of twilight, from the beginning of the month to the 7th and again after the 21st. This faint phenomenon is only visible under good conditions and in the absence of both moonlight and artificial lighting.

THE MOON

Day	R.A.		Dec.	Hor. par.	Semi-diam.	Sun's Co-long.	PA of Br. Limb	Ph.	Age	Rise 52°		Rise 56°		Transit		Set 52°		Set 56°	
	h	m	°	′	′	°	°	%	d	h	m	h	m	h	m	h	m	h	m
1	15	50	−25.5	54.3	14.8	200	101	34	23.5	3	50	4	22	7	23	10	50	10	18
2	16	43	−27.4	54.5	14.8	212	95	25	24.5	4	56	5	33	8	14	11	29	10	52
3	17	37	−28.0	54.9	14.9	224	88	17	25.5	5	52	6	30	9	07	12	23	11	45
4	18	33	−27.3	55.3	15.1	237	81	10	26.5	6	35	7	09	10	00	13	30	12	56
5	19	28	−25.2	55.9	15.2	249	75	5	27.5	7	07	7	34	10	53	14	46	14	20
6	20	22	−21.8	56.5	15.4	261	68	2	28.5	7	30	7	50	11	43	16	08	15	49
7	21	14	−17.2	57.1	15.6	273	43	0	29.5	7	47	8	01	12	32	17	31	17	18
8	22	04	−11.7	57.7	15.7	285	249	1	0.8	8	01	8	10	13	20	18	53	18	47
9	22	54	−5.6	58.2	15.8	298	244	4	1.8	8	13	8	16	14	06	20	16	20	16
10	23	43	+0.9	58.6	16.0	310	243	10	2.8	8	25	8	23	14	53	21	40	21	46
11	0	32	+ 7.4	58.9	16.0	322	244	17	3.8	8	38	8	30	15	41	23	06	23	18
12	1	24	+13.6	59.1	16.1	334	246	26	4.8	8	53	8	39	16	32	—		—	
13	2	18	+19.1	59.2	16.1	346	249	37	5.8	9	12	8	51	17	27	0	34	0	53
14	3	15	+23.5	59.2	16.1	358	255	48	6.8	9	40	9	11	18	25	2	03	2	31
15	4	16	+26.6	59.2	16.1	11	261	60	7.8	10	19	9	44	19	27	3	28	4	03
16	5	20	+28.0	59.1	16.1	23	268	71	8.8	11	16	10	39	20	29	4	40	5	18
17	6	23	+27.5	58.9	16.0	35	276	80	9.8	12	30	11	56	21	30	5	34	6	09
18	7	25	+25.3	58.6	16.0	47	282	89	10.8	13	54	13	28	22	26	6	12	6	39
19	8	23	+21.7	58.2	15.9	59	288	95	11.8	15	21	15	02	23	19	6	37	6	57
20	9	17	+16.9	57.8	15.7	71	292	98	12.8	16	45	16	33	—		6	55	7	09
21	10	08	+11.3	57.2	15.6	83	284	100	13.8	18	05	17	59	0	07	7	09	7	17
22	10	55	+5.4	56.6	15.4	96	120	99	14.8	19	22	19	22	0	52	7	20	7	23
23	11	41	−0.7	56.0	15.3	108	119	96	15.8	20	37	20	42	1	35	7	31	7	29
24	12	26	−6.5	55.5	15.1	120	118	92	16.8	21	51	22	02	2	17	7	42	7	35
25	13	11	−12.0	55.0	15.0	132	117	85	17.8	23	05	23	22	2	59	7	53	7	41
26	13	56	−17.0	54.6	14.9	144	114	78	18.8	—		—		3	42	8	07	7	50
27	14	43	−21.2	54.3	14.8	156	110	69	19.8	0	20	0	42	4	27	8	25	8	02
28	15	33	−24.6	54.2	14.8	168	105	60	20.8	1	33	2	02	5	14	8	50	8	19
29	16	24	−26.9	54.3	14.8	181	99	51	21.8	2	41	3	17	6	04	9	23	8	48

MERCURY

Day	R.A.		Dec.	Diam.	Phase	Transit		5° high 52°		5° high 56°	
	h	m	°	″	%	h	m	h	m	h	m
1	21	38	−11.5	9	12	12	52	17	15	17	01
3	21	31	−11.5	10	6	12	37	16	59	16	45
5	21	23	−11.8	10	2	12	20	16	41	16	26
7	21	14	−12.3	10	1	12	03	16	20	16	05
9	21	04	−12.9	10	2	11	46	7	32	7	48
11	20	56	−13.6	10	6	11	30	7	21	7	37
13	20	49	−14.3	10	11	11	16	7	10	7	28
15	20	44	−14.9	10	16	11	04	7	02	7	21
17	20	41	−15.5	9	22	10	54	6	55	7	15
19	20	40	−16.0	9	28	10	46	6	50	7	10
21	20	42	−16.3	9	33	10	39	6	46	7	07
23	20	45	−16.6	8	38	10	35	6	43	7	04
25	20	49	−16.7	8	43	10	31	6	40	7	02
27	20	55	−16.8	8	47	10	29	6	38	7	00
29	21	01	−16.7	8	51	10	28	6	37	6	58
31	21	09	−16.5	7	55	10	28	6	35	6	56

VENUS

Day	R.A.		Dec.	Diam.	Phase	Transit		5° high 52°		5° high 56°	
	h	m	°	″	%	h	m	h	m	h	m
1	18	41	−22.4	12	85	9	59	6	50	7	23
6	19	07	−22.0	12	86	10	06	6	54	7	26
11	19	34	−21.4	12	87	10	13	6	56	7	26
16	20	00	−20.6	12	88	10	19	6	55	7	24
21	20	26	−19.5	12	89	10	25	6	53	7	19
26	20	51	−18.1	11	90	10	31	6	49	7	12
31	21	16	−16.6	11	91	10	36	6	43	7	04

MARS

Day	R.A.		Dec.	Diam.	Phase	Transit		5° high 52°		5° high 56°	
	h	m	°	″	%	h	m	h	m	h	m
1	5	34	+26.7	12	95	20	48	4	46	5	09
6	5	35	+26.6	11	94	20	29	4	27	4	50
11	5	37	+26.5	11	93	20	12	4	09	4	32
16	5	40	+26.5	10	92	19	56	3	53	4	16
21	5	45	+26.4	10	92	19	41	3	37	4	00
26	5	50	+26.3	9	91	19	27	3	23	3	45
31	5	57	+26.2	9	91	19	14	3	09	3	31

SUNRISE AND SUNSET

	London		*Bristol*		*Birmingham*		*Manchester*		*Newcastle*		*Glasgow*		*Belfast*	
	0° 05′	*51° 30′*	*2° 35′*	*51° 28′*	*1° 55′*	*52° 28′*	*2° 15′*	*53° 28′*	*1° 37′*	*54° 59′*	*4° 14′*	*55° 52′*	*5° 56′*	*54° 35′*
d	*h m*	*h m*	*h m*	*h m*	*h m*	*h m*	*h m*	*h m*	*h m*	*h m*	*h m*	*h m*	*h m*	*h m*
1	7 40	16 49	7 50	16 59	7 50	16 53	7 55	16 51	7 58	16 42	8 12	16 49	8 14	17 01
2	7 38	16 50	7 48	17 01	7 49	16 55	7 53	16 53	7 57	16 44	8 11	16 51	8 12	17 03
3	7 37	16 52	7 46	17 02	7 47	16 57	7 52	16 54	7 55	16 46	8 09	16 54	8 10	17 05
4	7 35	16 54	7 45	17 04	7 45	16 58	7 50	16 56	7 53	16 49	8 07	16 56	8 09	17 07
5	7 33	16 56	7 43	17 06	7 44	17 00	7 48	16 58	7 51	16 51	8 05	16 58	8 07	17 09
6	7 32	16 58	7 42	17 08	7 42	17 02	7 46	17 00	7 49	16 53	8 03	17 00	8 05	17 11
7	7 30	17 00	7 40	17 10	7 40	17 04	7 45	17 02	7 47	16 55	8 01	17 02	8 03	17 14
8	7 28	17 01	7 38	17 12	7 38	17 06	7 43	17 04	7 45	16 57	7 59	17 04	8 01	17 16
9	7 27	17 03	7 36	17 13	7 37	17 08	7 41	17 06	7 43	16 59	7 56	17 07	7 59	17 18
10	7 25	17 05	7 35	17 15	7 35	17 10	7 39	17 08	7 41	17 01	7 54	17 09	7 57	17 20
11	7 23	17 07	7 33	17 17	7 33	17 12	7 37	17 10	7 39	17 03	7 52	17 11	7 55	17 22
12	7 21	17 09	7 31	17 19	7 31	17 14	7 35	17 12	7 37	17 05	7 50	17 13	7 53	17 24
13	7 19	17 11	7 29	17 21	7 29	17 16	7 33	17 14	7 35	17 08	7 48	17 15	7 51	17 26
14	7 17	17 12	7 27	17 23	7 27	17 17	7 31	17 16	7 33	17 10	7 46	17 18	7 49	17 28
15	7 16	17 14	7 25	17 24	7 25	17 19	7 29	17 18	7 30	17 12	7 43	17 20	7 47	17 30
16	7 14	17 16	7 24	17 26	7 23	17 21	7 27	17 20	7 28	17 14	7 41	17 22	7 44	17 32
17	7 12	17 18	7 22	17 28	7 21	17 23	7 25	17 22	7 26	17 16	7 39	17 24	7 42	17 34
18	7 10	17 20	7 20	17 30	7 19	17 25	7 23	17 24	7 24	17 18	7 36	17 26	7 40	17 36
19	7 08	17 22	7 18	17 32	7 17	17 27	7 21	17 26	7 22	17 20	7 34	17 28	7 38	17 38
20	7 06	17 23	7 16	17 33	7 15	17 29	7 18	17 28	7 19	17 22	7 32	17 31	7 36	17 40
21	7 04	17 25	7 14	17 35	7 13	17 31	7 16	17 30	7 17	17 24	7 29	17 33	7 33	17 42
22	7 02	17 27	7 12	17 37	7 11	17 33	7 14	17 32	7 15	17 26	7 27	17 35	7 31	17 44
23	7 00	17 29	7 10	17 39	7 09	17 34	7 12	17 34	7 12	17 28	7 25	17 37	7 29	17 47
24	6 58	17 31	7 07	17 41	7 07	17 36	7 10	17 36	7 10	17 31	7 22	17 39	7 26	17 49
25	6 55	17 32	7 05	17 42	7 04	17 38	7 07	17 38	7 08	17 33	7 20	17 41	7 24	17 51
26	6 53	17 34	7 03	17 44	7 02	17 40	7 05	17 40	7 05	17 35	7 17	17 44	7 22	17 53
27	6 51	17 36	7 01	17 46	7 00	17 42	7 03	17 42	7 03	17 37	7 15	17 46	7 19	17 55
28	6 49	17 38	6 59	17 48	6 58	17 44	7 01	17 44	7 00	17 39	7 12	17 48	7 17	17 57
29	6 47	17 39	6 57	17 50	6 56	17 46	6 58	17 46	6 58	17 41	7 10	17 50	7 15	17 59

JUPITER

Day	*R.A.*	*Dec.*	*Transit*	*5° high*	
				52°	*56°*
	h m	*° ′*	*h m*	*h m*	*h m*
1	18 43.1	−22 57	10 00	6 56	7 31
11	18 52.1	−22 47	9 29	6 24	6 59
21	19 00.6	−22 37	8 58	5 52	6 26
31	19 08.4	−22 26	8 27	5 19	5 52

Diameters – equatorial 33″ polar 31″

SATURN

Day	*R.A.*	*Dec.*	*Transit*	*5° high*	
				52°	*56°*
	h m	*° ′*	*h m*	*h m*	*h m*
1	10 37.4	+10 37	1 55	19 29	19 24
11	10 34.7	+10 55	1 13	18 46	18 40
21	10 31.7	+11 14	0 30	18 02	17 56
31	10 28.7	+11 32	23 44	17 18	17 12

Diameters – equatorial 20″ polar 18″
Rings major axis 45″ minor axis 6″

URANUS

Day	*R.A.*	*Dec.*	*Transit*	*10° high*	
				52°	*56°*
	h m	*° ′*	*h m*	*h m*	*h m*
1	23 12.0	−5 58	14 27	18 48	18 35
11	23 13.8	−5 45	13 50	18 12	17 59
21	23 15.9	−5 33	13 13	17 36	17 24
31	23 17.9	−5 19	12 35	17 00	16 48

Diameter 4″

NEPTUNE

Day	*R.A.*	*Dec.*	*Transit*	*10° high*	
				52°	*56°*
	h m	*° ′*	*h m*	*h m*	*h m*
1	21 35.3	−14 40	12 51	9 27	9 52
11	21 36.7	−14 33	12 13	8 48	9 13
21	21 38.2	−14 26	11 35	8 09	8 34
31	21 39.7	−14 18	10 57	7 30	7 55

Diameter 2″

MARCH 2008

THIRD MONTH, 31 DAYS. *Mars*, Roman god of battle

1	*Saturday*	The USA tested the most explosive bomb produced to date, at Bikini in the Pacific ocean 1954	61
2	*Sunday*	Mikhail Gorbachev, Soviet leader b. 1931 Horace Walpole, English politician d. 1797	62
3	*Monday*	The German-Russian treaty of Brest-Litovsk was signed 1918	week 9 day 63
4	*Tuesday*	Robert Mugabe became Zimbabwe's first black prime minister 1980	64
5	*Wednesday*	Zhou Enlai, Chinese premier b. 1898 Joseph Stalin, Soviet leader d. 1953	65
6	*Thursday*	Francesco Guicciardini, Italian statesman b. 1483 Philip Yorke, English politician d. 1764	66
7	*Friday*	Ghulam Nabi Azad, Indian politician b. 1949 Aristide Briand, prime minister of France d. 1932	67
8	*Saturday*	Juvénal Habyarimana, president of Rwanda b. 1937 King William III d. 1702	68
9	*Sunday*	Ernest Bevin, British politician b. 1881 Jules Mazarin, Italian-born politician d. 1661	69
10	*Monday*	Alexander III, tsar of Russia b. 1845 Jan Masaryk, Czechoslovak diplomat d. 1948	week 10 day 70
11	*Tuesday*	191 people were killed and over 1,500 injured in three train station explosions in Madrid 2004	71
12	*Wednesday*	John Abbott, prime minister of Canada b. 1821 Zoran Djindjic, prime minister of Serbia d. 2003	72
13	*Thursday*	Charles Grey, British prime minister b. 1764 Alexander II, tsar of Russia d. 1881	73
14	*Friday*	Mustafa Barzani, Kurdish nationalist activist b. 1903 Karl Marx, German revolutionary d. 1883	74
15	*Saturday*	Andrew Jackson, US president b. 1767 Julius Caesar, emperor of Rome d. 44 BC	75
16	*Sunday*	Pat Nixon, US first lady b. 1912 Austen Chamberlain, British politician d. 1937	76
17	*Monday*	Margaret Bondfield, British politician b. 1873 Ramon Magsaysay, president of the Philippines d. 1957	week 11 day 77
18	*Tuesday*	The Tolpuddle Martyrs were sentenced to transportation to Australia 1834	78
19	*Wednesday*	Adolf Eichmann, German Nazi officer b. 1906 Arthur Balfour, British prime minister d. 1930	79
20	*Thursday*	Abdul Hamid I, sultan of the Ottoman empire b. 1725 King Henry IV d. 1413	80
21	*Friday*	Benito Juárez, president of Mexico b. 1806 Guadalupe Victoria, president of Mexico d. 1843	81
22	*Saturday*	Cheddi Jagan, president of Guyana b. 1918 A. K. Gopalan, Indian Communist leader d. 1977	82
23	*Sunday*	Benito Mussolini founded the Fascist movement in Milan, Italy 1919	83
24	*Monday*	Union of English and Scottish crowns after Queen Elizabeth I's death 1603	week 12 day 84
25	*Tuesday*	Joachim Murat, king of Naples b. 1767 Frederick I, king of Sweden d. 1751	85
26	*Wednesday*	Xenophon Zolotas, prime minister of Greece b. 1904 Cecil Rhodes, coloniser of Rhodesia d. 1902	86
27	*Thursday*	James McNeill, Irish politician b. 1869 Michael Joseph Savage, prime minister of New Zealand d. 1940	87
28	*Friday*	Neil Kinnock, British politician b. 1942 Frank Baker, Australian politician d. 1939	88
29	*Saturday*	John Major, British prime minister b. 1943 Barthelemy Boganda, prime minister of the Central African Republic b. 1959	89
30	*Sunday*	Censu Tabone, president of Malta b. 1913 Léon Blum, French statesman d. 1950	90
31	*Monday*	The Greater London Council was abolished 1986	week 13 day 91

ASTRONOMICAL PHENOMENA

d	*h*	
3	02	Jupiter in conjunction with Moon. Jupiter 4°N.
3	11	Mercury at greatest elongation W. 27°
5	14	Mercury in conjunction with Moon. Mercury 0°.2N.
5	19	Venus in conjunction with Moon. Venus 0°.2S.
8	20	Uranus in conjunction
15	03	Mars in conjunction with Moon. Mars 2°S.
19	14	Saturn in conjunction with Moon. Saturn 2°N.
20	06	Sun's longitude 0° ♈
24	13	Venus in conjunction with Mercury. Venus 1°N.
30	18	Jupiter in conjunction with Moon. Jupiter 3°N.

MINIMA OF ALGOL

d	*h*	*d*	*h*	*d*	*h*
1	20.5	13	07.8	24	19.1
4	17.3	16	04.6	27	15.9
7	14.1	19	01.4	30	12.7
10	10.9	21	22.2		

CONSTELLATIONS

The following constellations are near the meridian at

	d	*h*		*d*	*h*
February	1	24	March	16	21
February	15	23	April	1	20
March	1	22	April	15	19

Cepheus (below the Pole), Camelopardalis, Lynx, Gemini, Cancer, Leo, Canis Minor, Hydra, Monoceros, Canis Major and Puppis

THE MOON

Phases, Apsides and Node	*d*	*h*	*m*
● New Moon	7	17	14
☽ First Quarter	14	10	46
○ Full Moon	21	18	40
☾ Last Quarter	29	21	47
Perigee (366,323km)	10	21	31
Apogee (405,058km)	26	20	07

Mean longitude of ascending node on March 1, 327°

THE SUN

s.d. 16′.1

Day	Right Ascension *h m s*	Dec. ° ′	Equation of time *m s*	Rise 52° *h m*	Rise 56° *h m*	Transit *h m*	Set 52° *h m*	Set 56° *h m*	Sidereal time *h m s*	Transit of first point of Aries *h m s*
1	22 49 03	−7 31	−12 22	6 45	6 51	12 12	17 40	17 35	10 36 41	13 21 07
2	22 52 48	−7 09	−12 10	6 43	6 48	12 12	17 42	17 37	10 40 37	13 17 12
3	22 56 32	−6 46	−11 58	6 41	6 46	12 12	17 44	17 39	10 44 34	13 13 16
4	23 00 16	−6 23	−11 45	6 39	6 43	12 12	17 46	17 41	10 48 31	13 09 20
5	23 03 59	−5 59	−11 32	6 36	6 41	12 11	17 47	17 43	10 52 27	13 05 24
6	23 07 42	−5 36	−11 18	6 34	6 38	12 11	17 49	17 45	10 56 24	13 01 28
7	23 11 24	−5 13	−11 04	6 32	6 35	12 11	17 51	17 48	11 00 20	12 57 32
8	23 15 06	−4 49	−10 50	6 30	6 33	12 11	17 53	17 50	11 04 17	12 53 36
9	23 18 48	−4 26	−10 35	6 27	6 30	12 10	17 55	17 52	11 08 13	12 49 40
10	23 22 29	−4 02	−10 19	6 25	6 28	12 10	17 56	17 54	11 12 10	12 45 44
11	23 26 10	−3 39	−10 04	6 23	6 25	12 10	17 58	17 56	11 16 06	12 41 48
12	23 29 51	−3 15	−9 48	6 20	6 22	12 10	18 00	17 58	11 20 03	12 37 53
13	23 33 31	−2 52	−9 32	6 18	6 20	12 09	18 02	18 00	11 24 00	12 33 57
14	23 37 12	−2 28	−9 15	6 16	6 17	12 09	18 03	18 02	11 27 56	12 30 01
15	23 40 51	−2 04	−8 59	6 14	6 15	12 09	18 05	18 04	11 31 53	12 26 05
16	23 44 31	−1 41	−8 42	6 11	6 12	12 09	18 07	18 06	11 35 49	12 22 09
17	23 48 10	−1 17	−8 24	6 09	6 09	12 08	18 09	18 08	11 39 46	12 18 13
18	23 51 49	−0 53	−8 07	6 07	6 07	12 08	18 10	18 10	11 43 42	12 14 17
19	23 55 28	−0 29	−7 49	6 04	6 04	12 08	18 12	18 12	11 47 39	12 10 21
20	23 59 07	−0 06	−7 32	6 02	6 01	12 07	18 14	18 14	11 51 35	12 06 25
21	0 02 46	+0 18	−7 14	6 00	5 59	12 07	18 15	18 17	11 55 32	12 02 29
22	0 06 24	+0 42	−6 56	5 57	5 56	12 07	18 17	18 19	11 59 29	11 58 33
23	0 10 03	+1 05	−6 38	5 55	5 54	12 06	18 19	18 21	12 03 25	11 54 38
24	0 13 41	+1 29	−6 20	5 53	5 51	12 06	18 21	18 23	12 07 22	11 50 42
25	0 17 19	+1 53	−6 01	5 50	5 48	12 06	18 22	18 25	12 11 18	11 46 46
26	0 20 58	+2 16	−5 43	5 48	5 46	12 06	18 24	18 27	12 15 15	11 42 50
27	0 24 36	+2 40	−5 25	5 46	5 43	12 05	18 26	18 29	12 19 11	11 38 54
28	0 28 15	+3 03	−5 07	5 43	5 40	12 05	18 28	18 31	12 23 08	11 34 58
29	0 31 53	+3 26	−4 49	5 41	5 38	12 05	18 29	18 33	12 27 04	11 31 02
30	0 35 31	+3 50	−4 30	5 39	5 35	12 04	18 31	18 35	12 31 01	11 27 06
31	0 39 10	+4 13	−4 13	5 37	5 32	12 04	18 33	18 37	12 34 58	11 23 10

DURATION OF TWILIGHT (in minutes)

Latitude	52°	56°	52°	56°	52°	56°	52°	56°
	1 March		*11 March*		*21 March*		*31 March*	
Civil	34	37	34	37	34	37	34	38
Nautical	73	80	73	80	74	81	75	84
Astronomical	112	124	113	125	115	128	120	135

THE NIGHT SKY

Mercury remains too close to the Sun for observation throughout the month.

Venus, magnitude −3.9, continues to be visible as a brilliant object at first, but only visible low in the east-south-eastern sky for a short period before dawn. After the first week of the month the planet will be too close to the Sun for observation.

Mars remains visible in the south-western sky in the evenings, and is still visible well after midnight even by the end of the month. Its magnitude fades during March from +0.2 to +0.8, as it moves steadily eastwards from Taurus into Gemini. During the early hours of the 15th the Moon, at First Quarter, passes 1 degree north of the planet

Jupiter, magnitude −2.0, continues to be visible as a brilliant morning object, low in the south-eastern sky, rising around 1.5 to 2 hours before sunrise. On the morning of the 3rd the thin waning crescent Moon passes south of the planet. On the last two mornings of the month the old waning Moon, just after Last Quarter, will again be seen in the vicinity of Jupiter.

Saturn, magnitude +0.3, is visible above the eastern horizon as soon as darkness falls and remains visible for the greater part of the night. Saturn is in Leo. The rings of Saturn present a beautiful spectacle to the observer armed with a small telescope. The diameter of the minor axis is now only 7 arcseconds, considerably less than the polar diameter of the planet itself. The rings were last at their maximum opening in 2002 and will next appear edge-on in 2009.

Zodiacal Light. The evening cone may be observed stretching up from the western horizon, along the ecliptic, after the end of twilight, from the beginning of the month until the 8th and again after the 22nd. This faint phenomenon is only visible under good conditions and in the absence of both moonlight and artificial lighting.

THE MOON

Day	R.A.		Dec.	Hor. par.	Semi-diam.	Sun's Co-long.	PA of Br. Limb	Ph.	Age	Rise				Transit		Set			
										52°		56°				52°		56°	
	h	m	°	′	′	°	°	%	d	h	m	h	m	h	m	h	m	h	m
1	17	18	−28.0	54.5	14.9	193	93	42	22.8	3	42	4	20	6	56	10	10	9	32
2	18	12	−27.7	55.0	15.0	205	87	32	23.8	4	30	5	06	7	48	11	10	10	35
3	19	07	−26.1	55.5	15.1	217	81	23	24.8	5	06	5	36	8	41	12	23	11	53
4	20	01	−23.2	56.2	15.3	229	76	15	25.8	5	32	5	56	9	32	13	42	13	20
5	20	54	−19.1	57.0	15.5	242	72	9	26.8	5	52	6	09	10	22	15	05	14	49
6	21	45	−13.9	57.7	15.7	254	70	4	27.8	6	07	6	18	11	10	16	28	16	19
7	22	35	−7.9	58.5	15.9	266	74	1	28.8	6	20	6	26	11	58	17	52	17	50
8	23	25	−1.4	59.1	16.1	278	217	0	0.3	6	33	6	32	12	46	19	18	19	21
9	0	16	+5.2	59.5	16.2	290	236	2	1.3	6	45	6	39	13	35	20	45	20	55
10	1	08	+11.7	59.8	16.3	303	241	7	2.3	7	00	6	48	14	26	22	15	22	32
11	2	03	+17.6	59.9	16.3	315	245	14	3.3	7	18	7	00	15	21	23	47	—	
12	3	01	+22.5	59.8	16.3	327	250	23	4.3	7	43	7	17	16	20	—		0	12
13	4	02	+26.0	59.5	16.2	339	257	34	5.3	8	19	7	46	17	21	1	15	1	48
14	5	05	+27.8	59.2	16.1	351	264	45	6.3	9	11	8	33	18	23	2	33	3	10
15	6	09	+27.7	58.8	16.0	4	271	56	7.3	10	19	9	44	19	24	3	32	4	08
16	7	10	+26.0	58.3	15.9	16	278	67	8.3	11	40	11	11	20	21	4	14	4	43
17	8	08	+22.7	57.9	15.8	28	284	77	9.3	13	04	12	43	21	13	4	42	5	04
18	9	03	+18.2	57.4	15.6	40	288	85	10.3	14	27	14	13	22	02	5	01	5	17
19	9	53	+13.0	56.9	15.5	52	290	92	11.3	15	47	15	39	22	47	5	16	5	26
20	10	41	+7.3	56.4	15.4	64	289	97	12.3	17	04	17	01	23	30	5	28	5	33
21	11	26	+1.3	55.9	15.2	77	280	99	13.3	18	19	18	22	—		5	39	5	39
22	12	11	−4.6	55.5	15.1	89	164	100	14.3	19	33	19	41	0	12	5	50	5	45
23	12	55	−10.2	55.0	15.0	101	128	98	15.3	20	47	21	01	0	54	6	01	5	51
24	13	41	−15.3	54.7	14.9	113	121	95	16.3	22	01	22	21	1	36	6	14	5	59
25	14	28	−19.8	54.4	14.8	125	115	90	17.3	23	15	23	42	2	21	6	31	6	09
26	15	17	−23.5	54.2	14.8	137	110	84	18.3	—		—		3	07	6	52	6	25
27	16	08	−26.1	54.1	14.7	149	104	76	19.3	0	26	0	59	3	56	7	22	6	48
28	17	00	−27.6	54.2	14.8	162	98	68	20.3	1	30	2	07	4	47	8	03	7	25
29	17	54	−27.8	54.5	14.9	174	91	59	21.3	2	22	2	59	5	39	8	57	8	20
30	18	48	−26.7	54.9	15.0	186	85	49	22.3	3	03	3	36	6	30	10	03	9	31
31	19	41	−24.3	55.5	15.1	198	80	39	23.3	3	32	3	59	7	21	11	18	10	53

MERCURY

Day	R.A.		Dec.	Diam.	Phase	Transit		5° high			
								52°		56°	
	h	m	°	″	%	h	m	h	m	h	m
1	21	05	−16.6	7	53	10	28	6	36	6	57
3	21	13	−16.4	7	57	10	28	6	35	6	55
5	21	21	−16.1	7	60	10	29	6	33	6	53
7	21	30	−15.7	7	63	10	31	6	32	6	51
9	21	40	−15.2	7	65	10	32	6	30	6	49
11	21	50	−14.6	6	68	10	35	6	28	6	46
13	22	01	−13.9	6	70	10	37	6	27	6	44
15	21	11	−13.1	6	72	10	40	6	25	6	41
17	22	22	−12.3	6	74	10	43	6	22	6	37
19	22	33	−11.3	6	76	10	47	6	20	6	34
21	22	45	−10.3	6	78	10	50	6	18	6	30
23	22	57	− 9.2	6	80	10	54	6	15	6	27
25	23	09	− 8.0	5	82	10	58	6	12	6	23
27	23	21	− 6.8	5	84	11	03	6	10	6	19
29	23	33	− 5.4	5	86	11	07	6	07	6	15
31	23	46	− 4.0	5	88	11	12	6	04	6	11

VENUS

Day	R.A.		Dec.	Diam.	Phase	Transit		5° high			
								52°		56°	
	h	m	°	″	%	h	m	h	m	h	m
1	21	12	−16.9	11	91	10	35	6	44	7	05
6	21	36	−15.2	11	91	10	40	6	38	6	56
11	22	01	−13.3	11	92	10	45	6	30	6	46
16	22	24	−11.2	11	93	10	49	6	22	6	36
21	22	48	−9.0	11	94	10	53	6	13	6	24
26	23	11	−6.7	11	94	10	56	6	04	6	13
31	23	34	−4.4	10	95	10	59	5	54	6	01

MARS

Day	R.A.		Dec.	Diam.	Phase	Transit		5° high			
								52°		56°	
	h	m	°	″	%	h	m	h	m	h	m
1	5	55	+26.3	9	91	19	17	3	11	3	34
6	6	02	+26.2	9	91	19	04	2	58	3	20
11	6	10	+26.1	8	90	18	52	2	45	3	07
16	6	18	+25.9	8	90	18	41	2	33	2	55
21	6	27	+25.8	8	90	18	30	2	21	2	42
26	6	36	+25.6	7	90	18	19	2	09	2	30
31	6	45	+25.3	7	90	18	09	1	57	2	18

SUNRISE AND SUNSET

	London		*Bristol*		*Birmingham*		*Manchester*		*Newcastle*		*Glasgow*		*Belfast*	
	0° 05′	*51° 30′*	*2° 35′*	*51° 28′*	*1° 55′*	*52° 28′*	*2° 15′*	*53° 28′*	*1° 37′*	*54° 59′*	*4° 14′*	*55° 52′*	*5° 56′*	*54° 35′*
d	*h m*	*h m*	*h m*	*h m*	*h m*	*h m*	*h m*	*h m*	*h m*	*h m*	*h m*	*h m*	*h m*	*h m*
1	6 45	17 41	6 55	17 51	6 53	17 47	6 56	17 47	6 56	17 43	7 07	17 52	7 12	18 01
2	6 43	17 43	6 53	17 53	6 51	17 49	6 54	17 49	6 53	17 45	7 05	17 54	7 10	18 03
3	6 41	17 45	6 50	17 55	6 49	17 51	6 51	17 51	6 51	17 47	7 02	17 56	7 08	18 05
4	6 38	17 47	6 48	17 57	6 47	17 53	6 49	17 53	6 48	17 49	7 00	17 58	7 05	18 07
5	6 36	17 48	6 46	17 58	6 44	17 55	6 47	17 55	6 46	17 51	6 57	18 00	7 03	18 09
6	6 34	17 50	6 44	18 00	6 42	17 57	6 44	17 57	6 43	17 53	6 55	18 03	7 00	18 11
7	6 32	17 52	6 42	18 02	6 40	17 58	6 42	17 59	6 41	17 55	6 52	18 05	6 58	18 13
8	6 30	17 53	6 39	18 04	6 38	18 00	6 40	18 01	6 38	17 57	6 50	18 07	6 55	18 15
9	6 27	17 55	6 37	18 05	6 35	18 02	6 37	18 03	6 36	17 59	6 47	18 09	6 53	18 17
10	6 25	17 57	6 35	18 07	6 33	18 04	6 35	18 04	6 33	18 01	6 44	18 11	6 50	18 19
11	6 23	17 59	6 33	18 09	6 31	18 06	6 33	18 06	6 31	18 03	6 42	18 13	6 48	18 20
12	6 21	18 00	6 31	18 10	6 28	18 07	6 30	18 08	6 28	18 05	6 39	18 15	6 45	18 22
13	6 18	18 02	6 28	18 12	6 26	18 09	6 28	18 10	6 26	18 07	6 37	18 17	6 43	18 24
14	6 16	18 04	6 26	18 14	6 24	18 11	6 25	18 12	6 23	18 09	6 34	18 19	6 40	18 26
15	6 14	18 06	6 24	18 16	6 21	18 13	6 23	18 14	6 21	18 11	6 31	18 21	6 38	18 28
16	6 12	18 07	6 21	18 17	6 19	18 14	6 21	18 16	6 18	18 13	6 29	18 23	6 35	18 30
17	6 09	18 09	6 19	18 19	6 17	18 16	6 18	18 17	6 16	18 15	6 26	18 25	6 33	18 32
18	6 07	18 11	6 17	18 21	6 14	18 18	6 16	18 19	6 13	18 17	6 24	18 27	6 30	18 34
19	6 05	18 12	6 15	18 22	6 12	18 20	6 13	18 21	6 11	18 19	6 21	18 29	6 28	18 36
20	6 02	18 14	6 12	18 24	6 10	18 22	6 11	18 23	6 08	18 21	6 18	18 31	6 25	18 38
21	6 00	18 16	6 10	18 26	6 07	18 23	6 08	18 25	6 06	18 23	6 16	18 33	6 23	18 40
22	5 58	18 17	6 08	18 27	6 05	18 25	6 06	18 27	6 03	18 25	6 13	18 35	6 20	18 42
23	5 56	18 19	6 06	18 29	6 03	18 27	6 04	18 29	6 00	18 27	6 11	18 37	6 18	18 44
24	5 53	18 21	6 03	18 31	6 00	18 29	6 01	18 30	5 58	18 29	6 08	18 40	6 15	18 46
25	5 51	18 22	6 01	18 32	5 58	18 30	5 59	18 32	5 55	18 31	6 05	18 42	6 13	18 48
26	5 49	18 24	5 59	18 34	5 56	18 32	5 56	18 34	5 53	18 32	6 03	18 44	6 10	18 49
27	5 46	18 26	5 56	18 36	5 53	18 34	5 54	18 36	5 50	18 34	6 00	18 46	6 08	18 51
28	5 44	18 27	5 54	18 37	5 51	18 36	5 51	18 38	5 48	18 36	5 57	18 48	6 05	18 53
29	5 42	18 29	5 52	18 39	5 48	18 37	5 49	18 39	5 45	18 38	5 55	18 50	6 03	18 55
30	5 40	18 31	5 50	18 41	5 46	18 39	5 47	18 41	5 43	18 40	5 52	18 52	6 00	18 57
31	5 37	18 33	5 47	18 42	5 44	18 41	5 44	18 43	5 40	18 42	5 50	18 54	6 58	18 59

JUPITER

Day	*R.A.*	*Dec.*	*Transit*	*5° high*	
				52°	*56°*
	h m	° ′	*h m*	*h m*	*h m*
1	19 07.7	−22 27	8 30	5 22	5 56
11	19 14.8	−22 16	7 58	4 48	5 21
21	19 21.2	−22 05	7 25	4 14	4 46
31	19 26.6	−21 55	6 51	3 39	4 10

Diameters – equatorial 36″ polar 33″

SATURN

Day	*R.A.*	*Dec.*	*Transit*	*5° high*	
				52°	*56°*
	h m	° ′	*h m*	*h m*	*h m*
1	10 29.0	+11 30	23 48	6 18	6 24
11	10 26.1	+11 48	23 06	5 37	5 44
21	10 23.4	+12 03	22 24	4 57	5 03
31	10 21.0	+12 16	21 42	4 16	4 23

Diameters – equatorial 20″ polar 18″
Rings – major axis 45″ minor axis 7″

URANUS

Day	*R.A.*	*Dec.*	*Transit*	*10° high*	
				52°	*56°*
	h m	° ′	*h m*	*h m*	*h m*
1	23 17.7	−5 21	12 39	8 15	8 27
11	23 19.8	−5 07	12 02	7 36	7 48
21	23 21.9	−4 54	11 25	6 58	7 09
31	23 24.0	−4 41	10 47	6 19	6 31

Diameter 4″

NEPTUNE

Day	*R.A.*	*Dec.*	*Transit*	*10° high*	
				52°	*56°*
	h m	° ′	*h m*	*h m*	*h m*
1	21 39.5	−14 19	11 01	7 34	7 59
11	21 40.9	−14 12	10 23	6 55	7 20
21	21 42.2	−14 06	9 45	6 17	6 41
31	21 43.4	−14 00	9 07	5 38	6 02

Diameter 2″

APRIL 2008

FOURTH MONTH, 30 DAYS. *Aperire,* to open; Earth opens to receive seed.

1	*Tuesday*	Otto von Bismarck, German chancellor b. 1815 George II, king of Greece d. 1947	92
2	*Wednesday*	Jim Allister, Northern Irish politician b. 1953 Georges Pompidou, president of France d. 1974	93
3	*Thursday*	Philip III, king of France b. 1245 Miina Sillanpaa, Finnish politician d. 1952	94
4	*Friday*	Hun Sen, prime minister of Cambodia b. 1951 Zulfikar Ali Bhutto, prime minister of Pakistan d. 1979	95
5	*Saturday*	Georges Danton, French revolutionary d. 1794 Chiang Kai-shek, president of China d. 1975	96
6	*Sunday*	Ian Paisley, Northern Irish politician b. 1926 King Richard I d. 1199	97
7	*Monday*	Gerhard Schroder, German chancellor b. 1944 Alexandre Millerand, president of France d. 1943	week 14 day 98
8	*Tuesday*	Ian Smith, prime minister of Rhodesia b. 1919 Kofi Annan, UN secretary-general b. 1938	99
9	*Wednesday*	Emily Hobhouse, British campaigner b. 1860 Lorenzo de Medici, ruler of Florence d. 1492	100
10	*Thursday*	The Good Friday Agreement was signed at the Northern Ireland peace talks 1998	101
11	*Friday*	George Canning, British prime minister b. 1770 Enver Hoxha, Albanian leader d. 1985	102
12	*Saturday*	James I of England (James VI of Scotland) combined the flags of the two countries 1606	103
13	*Sunday*	Thomas Jefferson, US president b. 1743 Boris Godunov, emperor of Russia d. 1605	104
14	*Monday*	Philip III, king of Spain b. 1578 Ernest Bevin, British politician d. 1951	week 15 day 105
15	*Tuesday*	Il-sung Kim, North Korean leader b. 1912 Pol Pot, prime minister of Cambodia d. 1998	106
16	*Wednesday*	Bonnie Prince Charlie was defeated at the Battle of Culloden 1746	107
17	*Thursday*	Nikita Khrushchev, Soviet leader b. 1894 Sirimavo Bandaranaike, prime minister of Sri Lanka b. 1916	108
18	*Friday*	Adolphe Thiers, president of France b. 1797 Arturo Frondizi, president of Argentina d. 1995	109
19	*Saturday*	Joseph Estrada, president of the Philippines b. 1937 Benjamin Disraeli, British prime minister d. 1881	110
20	*Sunday*	Adolf Hitler, German Nazi leader b. 1889 Pontiac, Native American leader d. 1769	111
21	*Monday*	Queen Elizabeth II b. 1926 François Duvalier, president of Haiti d. 1971	week 16 day 112
22	*Tuesday*	Troops stormed the Japanese embassy in Peru, ending the four-month siege by anti-government rebels 1997	113
23	*Wednesday*	James Buchanan, US president b. 1791 Brian Boru, High King of Ireland d. 1014	114
24	*Thursday*	Stafford Cripps, British politician b. 1889 Oliver Tambo, South African leader d. 1993	115
25	*Friday*	Oliver Cromwell, English political leader b. 1599 King Edward II b. 1284	116
26	*Saturday*	Syrian soldiers withdrew from Lebanon after 29 years 2005	117
27	*Sunday*	Ulysses S. Grant, US president b. 1822 John Trenchard, English politician d. 1695	118
28	*Monday*	Saddam Hussein, president of Iraq b. 1937 Benito Mussolini, prime minister of Italy d. 1945	week 17 day 119
29	*Tuesday*	Jeremy Thorpe, British politician b. 1929 Bernardino Machado, president of Portugal d. 1944	120
30	*Wednesday*	Queen Mary II b. 1662 Renzong, emperor of China d. 1063	121

ASTRONOMICAL PHENOMENA

d	*h*	
2	09	Pluto at stationary point
4	22	Venus in conjunction with Moon. Venus 4°S.
5	08	Mercury in conjunction with Moon. Mercury 5°S.
12	06	Mars in conjunction with Moon. Mars 1°S.
15	17	Saturn in conjunction with Moon. Saturn 2°N.
16	07	Mercury in superior conjunction
19	17	Sun's longitude 30° ♉
27	06	Jupiter in conjunction with Moon. Jupiter 3°N.

MINIMA OF ALGOL

d	*h*	*d*	*h*	*d*	*h*
2	09.5	13	20.8	25	08.1
5	06.3	16	17.6	28	04.9
8	03.2	19	14.4		
11	00.0	22	11.2		

CONSTELLATIONS

The following constellations are near the meridian at

	d	*h*		*d*	*h*
March	1	24	April	15	21
March	16	23	May	1	20
April	1	22	May	16	19

Cepheus (below the Pole), Cassiopeia (below the Pole), Ursa Major, Leo Minor, Leo, Sextans, Hydra and Crater

THE MOON

Phases, Apsides and Node	*d*	*h*	*m*
● New Moon	6	03	55
☽ First Quarter	12	18	32
○ Full Moon	20	10	25
☾ Last Quarter	28	14	12
Perigee (361,093 km)	7	19	23
Apogee (405,921 km)	23	09	23

Mean longitude of ascending node on April 1, 326°

THE SUN

s.d. 16′.0

Day	Right Ascension			Dec. +		Equation of time		Rise 52°		Rise 56°		Transit		Set 52°		Set 56°		Sidereal time			Transit of First point of Aries		
	h	m	s	°	′	m	s	h	m	h	m	h	m	h	m	h	m	h	m	s	h	m	s
1	0	42	49	4	36	−3	55	5	34	5	30	12	04	18	34	18	39	12	38	54	11	19	14
2	0	46	28	4	59	−3	37	5	32	5	27	12	03	18	36	18	41	12	42	51	11	15	18
3	0	50	06	5	22	−3	19	5	30	5	25	12	03	18	38	18	43	12	46	47	11	11	23
4	0	53	46	5	45	−3	02	5	27	5	22	12	03	18	39	18	45	12	50	44	11	07	27
5	0	57	25	6	08	−2	45	5	25	5	19	12	03	18	41	18	47	12	54	40	11	03	31
6	1	01	04	6	31	−2	27	5	23	5	17	12	02	18	43	18	49	12	58	37	10	59	35
7	1	04	44	6	53	−2	11	5	21	5	14	12	02	18	45	18	51	13	02	33	10	55	39
8	1	08	24	7	16	−1	54	5	18	5	12	12	02	18	46	18	53	13	06	30	10	51	43
9	1	12	04	7	38	−1	38	5	16	5	09	12	01	18	48	18	55	13	10	26	10	47	47
10	1	15	44	8	01	−1	21	5	14	5	06	12	01	18	50	18	57	13	14	23	10	43	51
11	1	19	25	8	23	−1	06	5	12	5	04	12	01	18	51	18	59	13	18	20	10	39	55
12	1	23	06	8	45	−0	50	5	09	5	01	12	01	18	53	19	01	13	22	16	10	35	59
13	1	26	47	9	06	−0	35	5	07	4	59	12	00	18	55	19	03	13	26	13	10	32	03
14	1	30	29	9	28	−0	20	5	05	4	56	12	00	18	57	19	05	13	30	09	10	28	08
15	1	34	11	9	50	−0	05	5	03	4	54	12	00	18	58	19	07	13	34	06	10	24	12
16	1	37	53	10	11	+0	10	5	01	4	51	12	00	19	00	19	10	13	38	02	10	20	16
17	1	41	35	10	32	+0	24	4	58	4	49	11	59	19	02	19	12	13	41	59	10	16	20
18	1	45	18	10	53	+0	37	4	56	4	46	11	59	19	03	19	14	13	45	55	10	12	24
19	1	49	01	11	14	+0	51	4	54	4	44	11	59	19	05	19	16	13	49	52	10	08	28
20	1	52	45	11	34	+1	03	4	52	4	41	11	59	19	07	19	18	13	53	49	10	04	32
21	1	56	29	11	55	+1	16	4	50	4	39	11	59	19	09	19	20	13	57	45	10	00	36
22	2	00	14	12	15	+1	28	4	48	4	36	11	58	19	10	19	22	14	01	42	9	56	40
23	2	03	59	12	35	+1	39	4	46	4	34	11	58	19	12	19	24	14	05	38	9	52	44
24	2	07	44	12	55	+1	50	4	44	4	32	11	58	19	14	19	26	14	09	35	9	48	48
25	2	11	30	13	15	+2	01	4	42	4	29	11	58	19	15	19	28	14	13	31	9	44	53
26	2	15	17	13	34	+2	11	4	40	4	27	11	58	19	17	19	30	14	17	28	9	40	57
27	2	19	04	13	53	+2	21	4	38	4	25	11	58	19	19	19	32	14	21	24	9	37	01
28	2	22	51	14	12	+2	30	4	36	4	22	11	57	19	20	19	34	14	25	21	9	33	05
29	2	26	39	14	31	+2	38	4	34	4	20	11	57	19	22	19	36	14	29	18	9	29	09
30	2	30	28	14	49	+2	46	4	32	4	18	11	57	19	24	19	38	14	33	14	9	25	13

DURATION OF TWILIGHT (in minutes)

Latitude	52°	56°	52°	56°	52°	56°	52°	56°
	1 April		*11 April*		*21 April*		*31 April*	
Civil	34	38	35	39	37	42	39	44
Nautical	76	84	79	89	83	96	89	106
Astronomical	120	136	127	147	137	165	152	204

THE NIGHT SKY

Mercury passes through superior conjunction on the 16th and remains too close to the Sun for observation until the last few days of the month, when it becomes visible low in the west-north-western sky at the end of evening civil twilight. During this short period its magnitude fades from −1.2 to −0.9.

Venus is unsuitably placed for observation throughout the month.

Mars continues to be visible in the western sky in the evenings, and even by the end of the month should still be observable for a short while after midnight. Mars remains in the constellation of Gemini, as its magnitude fades during April from +0.8 to +1.2. Towards the end of the month Mars passes 5 degrees south of Pollux. The Moon, approaching First Quarter, is near Mars on the evenings of the 11th and 12th.

Jupiter continues to be visible as a conspicuous morning object and by the end of the month is crossing the meridian around the time of sunrise. Its magnitude is −2.2. The waning gibbous Moon passes 3 degrees south of Jupiter on the morning of the 27th.

Saturn, magnitude +0.5, is still visible as an evening object in the south-western quadrant of the sky until well after midnight. The waxing gibbous Moon passes 3 degrees south of Saturn on the evening of the 15th.

THE MOON

Day	R.A.		Dec.	Hor. Par.	Semi-diam.	Sun's Co-Long.	PA of Br. Limb	Ph.	Age	Rise				Transit		Set			
										52°		56°				52°		56°	
	h	*m*	°	′	′	°	°	%	*d*	*h*	*m*	*h*	*m*	*h*	*m*	*h*	*m*	*h*	*m*
1	20	33	−20.7	56.3	15.3	210	75	30	24.3	3	54	4	14	8	11	12	38	12	19
2	21	24	−16.0	57.1	15.6	223	71	21	25.3	4	11	4	25	8	59	13	59	13	47
3	22	14	−10.4	58.0	15.8	235	70	13	26.3	4	25	4	33	9	46	15	22	15	17
4	23	04	− 4.2	58.9	16.0	247	70	6	27.3	4	38	4	41	10	34	16	47	16	47
5	23	55	+2.5	59.7	16.3	259	76	2	28.3	4	51	4	48	11	22	18	14	18	21
6	0	47	+9.1	60.3	16.4	272	126	0	29.3	5	05	4	56	12	14	19	45	19	59
7	1	42	+15.4	60.6	16.5	284	228	1	0.8	5	22	5	07	13	09	21	19	21	41
8	2	40	+20.8	60.7	16.5	296	242	5	1.8	5	45	5	22	14	08	22	53	23	22
9	3	43	+24.9	60.5	16.5	308	251	12	2.8	6	17	5	47	15	11	—		—	
10	4	47	+27.3	60.1	16.4	320	259	20	3.8	7	05	6	29	16	15	0	18	0	54
11	5	53	+27.7	59.6	16.2	333	267	31	4.8	8	10	7	33	17	17	1	26	2	02
12	6	56	+26.4	58.9	16.0	345	275	42	5.8	9	28	8	57	18	16	2	13	2	45
13	7	55	+23.4	58.2	15.9	357	281	53	6.8	10	52	10	29	19	10	2	45	3	10
14	8	51	+19.2	57.5	15.7	9	286	63	7.8	12	15	11	59	20	00	3	08	3	25
15	9	41	+14.1	56.9	15.5	21	289	73	8.8	13	35	13	26	20	45	3	24	3	35
16	10	29	+8.6	56.3	15.3	34	291	82	9.8	14	52	14	48	21	28	3	37	3	43
17	11	15	+2.8	55.8	15.2	46	291	89	10.8	16	06	16	07	22	10	3	48	3	49
18	11	59	−3.0	55.3	15.1	58	288	94	11.8	17	19	17	26	22	51	3	58	3	55
19	12	43	−8.7	54.9	15.0	70	280	98	12.8	18	33	18	44	23	33	4	09	4	01
20	13	28	−13.9	54.6	14.9	82	250	100	13.8	19	46	20	04	—		4	22	4	09
21	14	14	−18.5	54.3	14.8	94	147	100	14.8	21	00	21	24	0	17	4	37	4	18
22	15	02	−22.4	54.1	14.7	107	122	98	15.8	22	12	22	43	1	03	4	57	4	32
23	15	53	−25.3	54.0	14.7	119	111	94	16.8	23	18	23	54	1	51	5	24	4	53
24	16	45	−27.1	54.0	14.7	131	103	89	17.8	—		—		2	41	6	01	5	25
25	17	38	−27.7	54.2	14.8	143	96	82	18.8	0	15	0	52	3	32	6	50	6	13
26	18	32	−27.0	54.5	14.8	155	89	74	19.8	0	59	1	33	4	23	7	51	7	17
27	19	25	−25.0	54.9	15.0	168	83	66	20.8	1	32	2	01	5	14	9	02	8	34
28	20	16	−21.8	55.5	15.1	180	77	56	21.8	1	57	2	19	6	02	10	18	9	57
29	21	06	−17.6	56.2	15.3	192	73	46	22.8	2	15	2	31	6	50	11	36	11	22
30	21	55	−12.5	57.0	15.5	204	70	36	23.8	2	30	2	40	7	36	12	56	12	48

MERCURY

Day	R.A.		Dec.	Diam.	Phase	Transit		5° high			
								52°		56°	
	h	*m*	°	″	%	*h*	*m*	*h*	*m*	*h*	*m*
1	23	52	−3.3	5	89	11	14	6	03	6	09
3	0	05	−1.8	5	91	11	20	6	00	6	04
5	0	18	−0.2	5	93	11	25	5	57	6	00
7	0	32	+1.5	5	95	11	31	5	54	5	56
9	0	46	+3.2	5	96	11	37	5	52	5	52
11	1	00	+4.9	5	98	11	44	5	49	5	48
13	1	15	+6.7	5	99	11	50	5	47	5	44
15	1	30	+8.5	5	100	11	58	5	45	5	41
17	1	45	+10.3	5	100	12	05	18	30	18	36
19	2	01	+12.1	5	99	12	13	18	48	18	55
21	2	17	+13.9	5	98	12	21	19	05	19	14
23	2	33	+15.6	5	95	12	30	19	23	19	33
25	2	49	+17.2	5	91	12	38	19	40	19	52
27	3	05	+18.7	6	87	12	46	19	56	20	10
29	3	21	+20.0	6	81	12	54	20	11	20	26
31	3	36	+21.2	6	75	13	01	20	25	20	41

VENUS

Day	R.A.		Dec.	Diam.	Phase	Transit		5° high			
								52°		56°	
	h	*m*	°	″	%	*h*	*m*	*h*	*m*	*h*	*m*
1	23	39	−3.9	10	95	11	00	5	52	5	59
6	0	01	−1.5	10	96	11	03	5	43	5	47
11	0	24	+1.0	10	96	11	06	5	33	5	35
16	0	47	+3.4	10	97	11	09	5	23	5	24
21	1	09	+5.8	10	98	11	12	5	14	5	12
26	1	32	+8.2	10	98	11	15	5	05	5	02
31	1	55	+10.5	10	98	11	19	4	57	4	51

MARS

Day	R.A.		Dec.	Diam.	Phase	Transit		5° high			
								52°		56°	
	h	*m*	°	″	%	*h*	*m*	*h*	*m*	*h*	*m*
1	6	47	+25.3	7	90	18	07	1	55	2	16
6	6	57	+25.0	7	90	17	57	1	43	2	04
11	7	08	+24.7	7	90	17	48	1	32	1	52
16	7	18	+24.3	6	90	17	39	1	20	1	40
21	7	29	+23.9	6	90	17	30	1	08	1	27
26	7	40	+23.4	6	90	17	21	0	56	1	15
31	7	51	+22.9	6	91	17	12	0	44	1	02

SUNRISE AND SUNSET

	London				*Bristol*				*Birmingham*				*Manchester*				*Newcastle*				*Glasgow*				*Belfast*			
	0°05′		*51°30′*		*2°35′*		*51°28′*		*1°55′*		*52°28′*		*2°15′*		*53°28′*		*1°37′*		*54°59′*		*4°14′*		*55°52′*		*5°56′*		*54°35′*	
d	*h*	*m*	*h*	*m*	*h*	*m*	*h*	*m*	*h*	*m*	*h*	*m*	*h*	*m*	*h*	*m*	*h*	*m*	*h*	*m*	*h*	*m*	*h*	*m*	*h*	*m*	*h*	*m*
1	5	35	18	34	5	45	18	44	5	41	18	43	5	42	18	45	5	38	18	44	5	47	18	56	5	55	19	01
2	5	33	18	36	5	43	18	46	5	39	18	44	5	39	18	47	5	35	18	46	5	44	18	58	5	53	19	03
3	5	31	18	38	5	41	18	48	5	37	18	46	5	37	18	49	5	32	18	48	5	42	19	00	5	50	19	05
4	5	28	18	39	5	38	18	49	5	34	18	48	5	35	18	50	5	30	18	50	5	39	19	02	5	48	19	07
5	5	26	18	41	5	36	18	51	5	32	18	50	5	32	18	52	5	27	18	52	5	37	19	04	5	45	19	09
6	5	24	18	43	5	34	18	53	5	30	18	51	5	30	18	54	5	25	18	54	5	34	19	06	5	43	19	11
7	5	22	18	44	5	32	18	54	5	28	18	53	5	27	18	56	5	22	18	56	5	31	19	08	5	40	19	12
8	5	19	18	46	5	29	18	56	5	25	18	55	5	25	18	58	5	20	18	58	5	29	19	10	5	38	19	14
9	5	17	18	48	5	27	18	58	5	23	18	56	5	23	19	00	5	17	19	00	5	26	19	12	5	35	19	16
10	5	15	18	49	5	25	18	59	5	21	18	58	5	20	19	01	5	15	19	02	5	24	19	14	5	33	19	18
11	5	13	18	51	5	23	19	01	5	18	19	00	5	18	19	03	5	12	19	04	5	21	19	16	5	30	19	20
12	5	11	18	53	5	21	19	03	5	16	19	02	5	16	19	05	5	10	19	06	5	19	19	18	5	28	19	22
13	5	08	18	54	5	18	19	04	5	14	19	03	5	13	19	07	5	08	19	08	5	16	19	20	5	26	19	24
14	5	06	18	56	5	16	19	06	5	12	19	05	5	11	19	09	5	05	19	09	5	14	19	22	5	23	19	26
15	5	04	18	58	5	14	19	08	5	09	19	07	5	09	19	10	5	03	19	11	5	11	19	24	5	21	19	28
16	5	02	18	59	5	12	19	09	5	07	19	09	5	06	19	12	5	00	19	13	5	09	19	26	5	18	19	30
17	5	00	19	01	5	10	19	11	5	05	19	10	5	04	19	14	4	58	19	15	5	06	19	28	5	16	19	32
18	4	58	19	03	5	08	19	13	5	03	19	12	5	02	19	16	4	55	19	17	5	04	19	30	5	14	19	34
19	4	56	19	04	5	06	19	14	5	01	19	14	5	00	19	18	4	53	19	19	5	01	19	32	5	11	19	35
20	4	53	19	06	5	04	19	16	4	58	19	16	4	57	19	20	4	51	19	21	4	59	19	34	5	09	19	37
21	4	51	19	08	5	01	19	18	4	56	19	17	4	55	19	21	4	48	19	23	4	56	19	36	5	07	19	39
22	4	49	19	09	4	59	19	19	4	54	19	19	4	53	19	23	4	46	19	25	4	54	19	38	5	04	19	41
23	4	47	19	11	4	57	19	21	4	52	19	21	4	51	19	25	4	44	19	27	4	51	19	40	5	02	19	43
24	4	45	19	13	4	55	19	23	4	50	19	23	4	49	19	27	4	41	19	29	4	49	19	42	5	00	19	45
25	4	43	19	14	4	53	19	24	4	48	19	24	4	46	19	29	4	39	19	31	4	47	19	44	4	58	19	47
26	4	41	19	16	4	51	19	26	4	46	19	26	4	44	19	30	4	37	19	33	4	44	19	46	4	55	19	49
27	4	39	19	18	4	49	19	27	4	44	19	28	4	42	19	32	4	35	19	35	4	42	19	48	4	53	19	51
28	4	37	19	19	4	47	19	29	4	42	19	30	4	40	19	34	4	32	19	37	4	40	19	50	4	51	19	53
29	4	35	19	21	4	46	19	31	4	40	19	31	4	38	19	36	4	30	19	39	4	37	19	52	4	49	19	54
30	4	34	19	23	4	44	19	32	4	38	19	33	4	36	19	38	4	28	19	41	4	35	19	54	4	47	19	56

JUPITER

Day	*R.A.*		*Dec.*		*Transit*		*5° high*			
							52°		*56°*	
	h	*m*	°	′	*h*	*m*	*h*	*m*	*h*	*m*
1	19	27.1	−21	54	6	47	3	35	4	07
11	19	31.3	−21	46	6	12	2	59	3	30
21	19	34.4	−21	41	5	36	2	22	2	53
31	19	36.2	−21	38	4	58	1	44	2	15

Diameters – equatorial 39″ polar 37″

SATURN

Day	*R.A.*		*Dec.*		*Transit*		*5° high*			
							52°		*56°*	
	h	*m*	°	′	*h*	*m*	*h*	*m*	*h*	*m*
1	10	20.8	+12	17	21	38	4	12	4	19
11	10	19.1	+12	26	20	57	3	32	3	39
21	10	17.9	+12	32	20	17	2	52	2	59
31	10	17.4	+12	33	19	37	2	12	2	19

Diameters – equatorial 19″ polar 17″
Rings – major axis 43″ minor axis 7″

URANUS

Day	*R.A.*		*Dec.*		*Transit*		*10° high*			
							52°		*56°*	
	h	*m*	°	′	*h*	*m*	*h*	*m*	*h*	*m*
1	23	24.2	−4	40	10	44	6	15	6	27
11	23	26.1	−4	27	10	06	5	37	5	48
21	23	28.0	−4	16	9	29	4	58	5	09
31	23	29.6	−4	06	8	51	4	20	4	30

Diameter 4″

NEPTUNE

Day	*R.A.*		*Dec.*		*Transit*		*10° high*			
							52°		*56°*	
	h	*m*	°	′	*h*	*m*	*h*	*m*	*h*	*m*
1	21	43.5	−14	00	9	03	5	34	5	58
11	21	44.5	−13	55	8	25	4	55	5	19
21	21	45.3	−13	51	7	46	4	16	4	40
31	21	46.0	−13	48	7	08	3	37	4	01

Diameter 2″

MAY 2008

FIFTH MONTH, 31 DAYS. *Maia*, goddess of growth and increase

1	*Thursday*	Albert I of Habsburg, king of Germany d. 1308 Joseph Goebbels, German Nazi officer d. 1945	122
2	*Friday*	Moshoeshoe II, king of Lesotho b. 1938 Shomu, emperor of Japan d. 756	123
3	*Saturday*	Golda Meir, prime minister of Israel b. 1898 Niccolù Machiavelli, Italian statesman b. 1469	124
4	*Sunday*	Margaret Thatcher became UK's first woman prime minister 1979	125
5	*Monday*	Leopold II, Holy Roman Emperor b. 1747 Natalija Obrenovic, queen of Serbia d. 1941	week 18 day 126
6	*Tuesday*	Tony Blair, British prime minister b. 1953 Maximilien Robespierre, French revolutionary b. 1758	127
7	*Wednesday*	Josip Broz Tito, president of Yugoslavia b. 1892 Eva Peron, first lady of Argentina b. 1919	128
8	*Thursday*	Ali Hassan Mwinyi, president of Tanzania b. 1925 Kamehameha I, king of Hawaii d. 1819	129
9	*Friday*	Glenda Jackson, British politician b. 1936 Aldo Moro, prime minister of Italy d. 1978	130
10	*Saturday*	Nelson Mandela became South Africa's first black president 1994	131
11	*Sunday*	Spencer Perceval, British prime minister d. 1812 William Pitt (the elder), British prime minister d. 1778	132
12	*Monday*	Johan Vilhelm Snellman, Finnish statesman b. 1806 Thomas Wentworth, English statesman d. 1641	week 19 day 133
13	*Tuesday*	Asgeir Asgeirsson, president of Iceland b. 1894 Fridtjof Nansen, Norwegian statesman d. 1930	134
14	*Wednesday*	Eight Communist states signed the Warsaw Pact 1955	135
15	*Thursday*	Prince Klemens Metternich, Austrian statesman b. 1773 Charles VIII, king of Sweden d. 1470	136
16	*Friday*	Mao Zedong launched the Cultural Revolution in the People's Republic of China 1966	137
17	*Saturday*	Hazel R. O' Leary, US politician b. 1937 Charles-Maurice de Talleyrand, French politician d. 1838	138
18	*Sunday*	India detonated its first nuclear weapon 1974	139
19	*Monday*	Nancy Astor, British politician b. 1879 Ho Chi-Minh, Vietnamese statesman b. 1890	week 20 day 140
20	*Tuesday*	Faisal I, king of Iraq b. 1883 Ecgfrith, king of Northumbria d. 685	141
21	*Wednesday*	Mary Robinson, president of Ireland b. 1944 Conrad IV, king of Germany d. 1254	142
22	*Thursday*	Daniel Malan, prime minister of South Africa b. 1874 Giorgio Almirante, Italian politician d. 1988	143
23	*Friday*	The marriage of King Henry VIII to Catherine of Aragon was annulled 1533	144
24	*Saturday*	Jan Smuts, prime minister of South Africa b. 1870 Harold Wilson, British prime minister d. 1995	145
25	*Sunday*	Max Aitken, Canadian-British politician b. 1879 Sunil Dutt, Indian politician d. 2005	146
26	*Monday*	The last public hanging in England took place 1868	week 21 day 147
27	*Tuesday*	Henry Kissinger, US politician b. 1923 Jawaharlal Nehru, prime minister of India d. 1964	148
28	*Wednesday*	William Pitt (the younger), British prime minister b. 1759 King Edward VIII d. 1972	149
29	*Thursday*	King Charles II b. 1630 Erich Honecker, East German leader d. 1994	150
30	*Friday*	Henry Addington, British prime minister b. 1757 Rama VII, king of Siam d. 1941	151
31	*Saturday*	South Africa left the Commonwealth 1961	152

ASTRONOMICAL PHENOMENA

d	*h*	
3	03	Saturn at stationary point
4	20	Venus in conjunction with Moon. Venus 6°S.
6	22	Mercury in conjunction with Moon. Mercury 2°S.
9	12	Jupiter at stationary point
10	14	Mars in conjunction with Moon. Mars 0°.2S.
12	22	Saturn in conjunction with Moon. Saturn 3°N.
14	04	Mercury at greatest elongation E. 22°
20	16	Sun's longitude 60° ♊
24	12	Jupiter in conjunction with Moon. Jupiter 2°N.
26	16	Mercury at stationary point
26	16	Neptune at stationary point

MINIMA OF ALGOL

Algol is inconveniently situated for observation during May

CONSTELLATIONS

The following constellations are near the meridian at

	d	*h*		*d*	*h*
April	1	24	May	16	21
April	15	23	June	1	20
May	1	22	June	15	19

Cepheus (below the Pole), Cassiopeia (below the Pole), Ursa Minor, Ursa Major, Canes Venatici, Coma Berenices, Bootes, Leo, Virgo, Crater, Corvus and Hydra

THE MOON

Phases, Apsides and Node	*d*	*h*	*m*
● New Moon	5	12	18
☽ First Quarter	12	03	47
○ Full Moon	20	02	11
☾ Last Quarter	28	02	57
Perigee (357,777 km)	6	03	12
Apogee (406,398 km)	20	14	11

Mean longitude of ascending node on May 1, 324°

THE SUN

s.d. 15′.8

Day	Right Ascension			Dec. +		Equation of time		Rise 52°		Rise 56°		Transit		Set 52°		Set 56°		Sidereal time			Transit of first point of Aries		
	h	m	s	°	′	m	s	h	m	h	m	h	m	h	m	h	m	h	m	s	h	m	s
1	2	34	17	15	08	+2	54	4	30	4	15	11	57	19	25	19	40	14	37	11	9	21	17
2	2	38	07	15	26	+3	01	4	28	4	13	11	57	19	27	19	42	14	41	07	9	17	21
3	2	41	57	15	43	+3	07	4	26	4	11	11	57	19	29	19	44	14	45	04	9	13	25
4	2	45	48	16	01	+3	13	4	24	4	09	11	57	19	30	19	46	14	49	00	9	09	29
5	2	49	39	16	18	+3	18	4	22	4	07	11	57	19	32	19	48	14	52	57	9	05	33
6	2	53	31	16	35	+3	23	4	21	4	04	11	57	19	34	19	50	14	56	53	9	01	38
7	2	57	23	16	52	+3	27	4	19	4	02	11	57	19	35	19	52	15	00	50	8	57	42
8	3	01	17	17	08	+3	30	4	17	4	00	11	56	19	37	19	54	15	04	47	8	53	46
9	3	05	10	17	24	+3	33	4	15	3	58	11	56	19	39	19	56	15	08	43	8	49	50
10	3	09	04	17	40	+3	35	4	14	3	56	11	56	19	40	19	58	15	12	40	8	45	54
11	3	12	59	17	55	+3	37	4	12	3	54	11	56	19	42	20	00	15	16	36	8	41	58
12	3	16	54	18	11	+3	39	4	10	3	52	11	56	19	43	20	02	15	20	33	8	38	02
13	3	20	50	18	26	+3	39	4	09	3	50	11	56	19	45	20	04	15	24	29	8	34	06
14	3	24	46	18	40	+3	39	4	07	3	48	11	56	19	46	20	05	15	28	26	8	30	10
15	3	28	43	18	54	+3	39	4	06	3	47	11	56	19	48	20	07	15	32	22	8	26	14
16	3	32	41	19	08	+3	38	4	04	3	45	11	56	19	50	20	09	15	36	19	8	22	18
17	3	36	39	19	22	+3	37	4	03	3	43	11	56	19	51	20	11	15	40	16	8	18	23
18	3	40	37	19	35	+3	35	4	01	3	41	11	56	19	53	20	13	15	44	12	8	14	27
19	3	44	37	19	48	+3	32	4	00	3	40	11	56	19	54	20	15	15	48	09	8	10	31
20	3	48	36	20	01	+3	29	3	59	3	38	11	57	19	55	20	16	15	52	05	8	06	35
21	3	52	36	20	13	+3	25	3	57	3	36	11	57	19	57	20	18	15	56	02	8	02	39
22	3	56	37	20	25	+3	21	3	56	3	35	11	57	19	58	20	20	15	59	58	7	58	43
23	4	00	38	20	37	+3	16	3	55	3	33	11	57	20	00	20	21	16	03	55	7	54	47
24	4	04	40	20	48	+3	11	3	54	3	32	11	57	20	01	20	23	16	07	51	7	50	51
25	4	08	43	20	59	+3	06	3	52	3	30	11	57	20	02	20	25	16	11	48	7	46	55
26	4	12	45	21	09	+2	59	3	51	3	29	11	57	20	04	20	26	16	15	45	7	42	59
27	4	16	49	21	19	+2	53	3	50	3	28	11	57	20	05	20	28	16	19	41	7	39	03
28	4	20	52	21	29	+2	45	3	49	3	26	11	57	20	06	20	29	16	23	38	7	35	07
29	4	24	57	21	39	+2	38	3	48	3	25	11	57	20	07	20	31	16	27	34	7	31	12
30	4	29	01	21	48	+2	29	3	47	3	24	11	58	20	08	20	32	16	31	31	7	27	16
31	4	33	07	21	56	+2	21	3	47	3	23	11	58	20	10	20	34	16	35	27	7	23	20

DURATION OF TWILIGHT (in minutes)

Latitude	*52°*	*56°*	*52°*	*56°*	*52°*	*56°*	*52°*	*56°*
	1 May		*11 May*		*21 May*		*31 May*	
Civil	39	44	41	48	44	53	46	57
Nautical	89	106	97	120	106	141	115	187
Astronomical	152	204	176	TAN	TAN	TAN	TAN	TAN

THE NIGHT SKY

Mercury continues to be visible low above the west-north-western horizon at the end of evening civil twilight, until just after the middle of the month. During this period its magnitude fades from −0.8 to +1.1. This evening apparition is the most suitable one of the year for observers in northern temperate latitudes.

Venus remains too close to the Sun for observation throughout the month.

Mars is still visible as an evening object in the western sky, though no longer visible after midnight, even at the beginning of the month. Its magnitude fades slowly from +1.2 to +1.5 during the month. Early in May, Mars moves from Gemini into Cancer.

Jupiter, magnitude −2.5, continues to be visible as a brilliant morning object low in the south-eastern sky. By the end of the month it is becoming visible low on the horizon by midnight. It reaches its first stationary point on the 9th, and then moves retrograde, in the constellation of Sagittarius. The Galilean satellites are readily observable with a small telescope or even a good pair of binoculars provided that they are held rigidly.

Saturn, magnitude +0.7, is still visible as an evening object in the south-western sky in the evenings, though by the end of the month it will not be visible for long after midnight. Saturn reaches its second stationary point on the 3rd, resuming its direct motion.

THE MOON

Day	R.A.		Dec.	Hor. Par.	Semi-diam.	Sun's Co-Long.	PA of Bright Limb	Ph.	Age	Rise				Transit		Set			
										52°		56°				52°		56°	
	h	m	°	′	′	°	°	%	d	h	m	h	m	h	m	h	m	h	m
1	22	44	–6.6	58.0	15.8	216	69	26	24.8	2	43	2	48	8	22	14	17	14	15
2	23	33	–0.3	58.9	16.1	229	69	17	25.8	2	55	2	55	9	09	15	41	15	45
3	0	23	+6.3	59.8.	16.3	241	72	9	26.8	3	09	3	03	9	58	17	09	17	19
4	1	17	+12.7	60.6	16.5	253	79	4	27.8	3	24	3	12	10	52	18	42	18	59
5	2	14	+18.6	61.1	16.6	265	104	1	28.8	3	44	3	26	11	49	20	18	20	43
6	3	16	+23.3	61.3	16.7	278	219	1	0.5	4	13	3	46	12	52	21	50	22	23
7	4	22	+26.4	61.2	16.7	290	248	4	1.5	4	54	4	21	13	58	23	09	23	45
8	5	29	+27.6	60.7	16.6	302	261	9	2.5	5	54	5	17	15	04	—	—	—	—
9	6	36	+26.8	60.1	16.4	314	270	17	3.5	7	10	6	38	16	07	0	07	0	40
10	7	38	+24.2	59.3	16.2	326	278	27	4.5	8	36	8	11	17	04	0	45	1	12
11	8	36	+20.2	58.4	15.9	339	284	38	5.5	10	02	9	44	17	56	1	11	1	31
12	9	29	+15,2	57.5	15.7	351	288	48	6.5	11	24	11	13	18	44	1	30	1	43
13	10	18	+9.7	56.7	15.5	3	291	59	7.5	12	42	12	36	19	28	1	44	1	52
14	11	04	+3.9	56.0	15.3	15	292	69	8.5	13	57	13	56	20	10	1	56	1	58
15	11	48	–1.9	55.4	15.1	28	292	78	9.5	15	10	15	15	20	51	2	07	2	05
16	12	32	–7.5	54.9	15.0	40	290	85	10.5	16	22	16	32	21	32	2	18	2	11
17	13	17	–12.7	54.5	14.9	52	286	91	11.5	17	35	17	51	22	15	2	30	2	18
18	14	02	–17.5	54.3	14.8	64	279	96	12.5	18	49	19	10	23	00	2	44	2	27
19	14	50	–21.5	54.1	14.7	76	265	99	13.5	20	01	20	29	23	47	3	02	2	40
20	15	40	–24.6	54.0	14.7	88	205	100	14.5	21	09	21	43	—	—	3	27	2	58
21	16	31	–26.7	54.0	14.7	101	124	99	15.5	22	09	22	45	0	37	4	01	3	26
22	17	24	–27.5	54.0	14.7	113	105	97	16.5	22	57	23	32	1	28	4	46	4	09
23	18	18	–27.1	54.2	14.8	125	94	92	17.5	23	33	—	—	2	19	5	44	5	09
24	19	11	–25.4	54.5	14.9	137	86	87	18.5	—	—	0	03	3	09	6	52	6	22
25	20	02	–22.5	54.9	15.0	149	80	80	19.5	0	00	0	24	3	58	8	05	7	43
26	20	52	–18.6	55.5	15.1	162	75	71	20.5	0	20	0	37	4	45	9	22	9	05
27	21	40	–13.8	56.1	15.3	174	71	62	21.5	0	35	0	47	5	31	10	39	10	28
28	22	28	–8.3	56.9	15.5	186	68	51	22.5	0	48	0	55	6	15	11	57	11	52
29	23	15	–2.3	57.8	15.7	198	67	41	23.5	1	01	1	02	7	00	13	17	13	18
30	0	03	+4.0	58.7	16.0	211	68	30	24.5	1	13	1	10	7	47	14	40	14	47
31	0	54	+10.3	59.6	16.2	223	70	20	25.5	1	27	1	18	8	36	16	08	16	21

MERCURY

Day	R.A.		Dec.	Diam.	Phase	Transit		5° high			
								52°		56°	
	h	m	°	″	%	h	m	h	m	h	m
1	3	36	+21.2	6	75	13	01	20	25	20	41
3	3	51	+22.2	6	69	13	07	20	38	20	55
5	4	04	+23.1	6	63	13	13	20	48	21	07
7	4	17	+23.8	7	57	13	18	20	57	21	16
9	4	29	+24.3	7	51	13	22	21	04	21	23
11	4	40	+24.7	7	45	13	25	21	08	21	29
13	4	50	+24.9	8	40	13	26	21	11	21	32
15	4	59	+25.1	8	35	13	27	21	12	21	32
17	5	06	+25.1	9	30	13	26	21	10	21	31
19	5	12	+24.9	9	25	13	24	21	07	21	27
21	5	17	+24.7	10	21	13	20	21	01	21	21
23	5	21	+24.4	10	17	13	15	20	54	21	13
25	5	22	+24.0	10	14	13	09	20	44	21	03
27	5	23	+23.5	11	10	13	01	20	33	20	52
29	5	22	+23.0	11	7	12	52	20	21	20	38
31	5	20	+22.4	12	5	12	42	20	07	20	23

VENUS

Day	R.A.		Dec.	Diam.	Phase	Transit		5° high			
								52°		56°	
	h	m	°	″	%	h	m	h	m	h	m
1	1	55	+10.5	10	98	11	19	4	57	4	51
6	2	19	+12.7	10	99	11	22	4	49	4	42
11	2	43	+14.7	10	99	11	27	4	42	4	33
16	3	07	+16.6	10	99	11	31	4	36	4	25
21	3	32	+18.4	10	100	11	36	4	32	4	19
26	3	57	+19.9	10	100	11	42	4	28	4	14
31	4	23	+21.2	10	100	11	48	4	26	4	11

MARS

Day	R.A.		Dec.	Diam.	Phase	Transit		5° high			
								52°		56°	
	h	m	°	″	%	h	m	h	m	h	m
1	7	51	+22.9	6	91	17	12	0	44	1	02
6	8	02	+22.3	6	91	17	04	0	32	0	49
11	8	13	+21.7	5	91	16	55	0	20	0	36
16	8	24	+21.0	5	91	16	47	0	07	0	23
21	8	35	+20.3	5	92	16	38	23	52	0	09
26	8	47	+19.5	5	92	16	30	23	39	23	53
31	8	58	+18.7	5	92	16	22	23	26	23	39

SUNRISE AND SUNSET

	London		*Bristol*		*Birmingham*		*Manchester*		*Newcastle*		*Glasgow*		*Belfast*	
	0° 05′	*51° 30′*	*2° 35′*	*51° 28′*	*1° 55′*	*52° 28′*	*2° 15′*	*53° 28′*	*1° 37′*	*54° 59′*	*4° 14′*	*55° 52′*	*5° 56′*	*54° 35′*
d	*h m*	*h m*	*h m*	*h m*	*h m*	*h m*	*h m*	*h m*	*h m*	*h m*	*h m*	*h m*	*h m*	*h m*
1	4 32	19 24	4 42	19 34	4 36	19 35	4 34	19 39	4 26	19 42	4 33	19 56	4 45	19 58
2	4 30	19 26	4 40	19 36	4 34	19 36	4 32	19 41	4 24	19 44	4 31	19 58	4 42	20 00
3	4 28	19 27	4 38	19 37	4 32	19 38	4 30	19 43	4 22	19 46	4 28	20 00	4 40	20 02
4	4 26	19 29	4 36	19 39	4 30	19 40	4 28	19 45	4 19	19 48	4 26	20 02	4 38	20 04
5	4 24	19 31	4 34	19 41	4 28	19 41	4 26	19 47	4 17	19 50	4 24	20 04	4 36	20 06
6	4 23	19 32	4 33	19 42	4 27	19 43	4 24	19 48	4 15	19 52	4 22	20 06	4 34	20 08
7	4 21	19 34	4 31	19 44	4 25	19 45	4 22	19 50	4 13	19 54	4 20	20 08	4 32	20 09
8	4 19	19 35	4 29	19 45	4 23	19 46	4 20	19 52	4 11	19 56	4 18	20 10	4 30	20 11
9	4 18	19 37	4 28	19 47	4 21	19 48	4 18	19 53	4 09	19 58	4 16	20 12	4 28	20 13
10	4 16	19 39	4 26	19 48	4 19	19 50	4 17	19 55	4 08	19 59	4 14	20 14	4 27	20 15
11	4 14	19 40	4 24	19 50	4 18	19 51	4 15	19 57	4 06	20 01	4 12	20 16	4 25	20 17
12	4 13	19 42	4 23	19 52	4 16	19 53	4 13	19 59	4 04	20 03	4 10	20 18	4 23	20 18
13	4 11	19 43	4 21	19 53	4 14	19 55	4 12	20 00	4 02	20 05	4 08	20 20	4 21	20 20
14	4 10	19 45	4 20	19 55	4 13	19 56	4 10	20 02	4 00	20 07	4 06	20 22	4 19	20 22
15	4 08	19 46	4 18	19 56	4 11	19 58	4 08	20 04	3 58	20 08	4 04	20 24	4 18	20 24
16	4 07	19 48	4 17	19 58	4 10	19 59	4 07	20 05	3 57	20 10	4 02	20 25	4 16	20 25
17	4 05	19 49	4 15	19 59	4 08	20 01	4 05	20 07	3 55	20 12	4 01	20 27	4 14	20 27
18	4 04	19 51	4 14	20 01	4 07	20 02	4 04	20 08	3 53	20 14	3 59	20 29	4 13	20 29
19	4 02	19 52	4 13	20 02	4 05	20 04	4 02	20 10	3 52	20 15	3 57	20 31	4 11	20 30
20	4 01	19 53	4 11	20 03	4 04	20 05	4 01	20 12	3 50	20 17	3 56	20 33	4 10	20 32
21	4 00	19 55	4 10	20 05	4 03	20 07	3 59	20 13	3 49	20 19	3 54	20 34	4 08	20 34
22	3 59	19 56	4 09	20 06	4 01	20 08	3 58	20 15	3 47	20 20	3 52	20 36	4 07	20 35
23	3 57	19 58	4 08	20 07	4 00	20 10	3 56	20 16	3 46	20 22	3 51	20 38	4 05	20 37
24	3 56	19 59	4 06	20 09	3 59	20 11	3 55	20 17	3 44	20 23	3 49	20 39	4 04	20 38
25	3 55	20 00	4 05	20 10	3 58	20 12	3 54	20 19	3 43	20 25	3 48	20 41	4 03	20 40
26	3 54	20 01	4 04	20 11	3 57	20 14	3 53	20 20	3 42	20 26	3 47	20 42	4 01	20 41
27	3 53	20 03	4 03	20 13	3 56	20 15	3 52	20 22	3 40	20 28	3 45	20 44	4 00	20 43
28	3 52	20 04	4 02	20 14	3 55	20 16	3 50	20 23	3 39	20 29	3 44	20 45	3 59	20 44
29	3 51	20 05	4 01	20 15	3 54	20 17	3 49	20 24	3 38	20 31	3 43	20 47	3 58	20 46
30	3 50	20 06	4 00	20 16	3 53	20 19	3 48	20 25	3 37	20 32	3 42	20 48	3 57	20 47
31	3 49	20 07	4 00	20 17	3 52	20 20	3 48	20 27	3 36	20 33	3 41	20 50	3 56	20 48

JUPITER

Day	*R.A.*		*Dec.*		*Transit*		*5° high*			
							52°		*56°*	
	h	*m*	°	′	*h*	*m*	*h*	*m*	*h*	*m*
1	19	36.2	−21	38	4	58	1	44	2	15
11	19	36.7	−21	38	4	19	1	05	1	36
21	19	35.8	−21	41	3	39	0	25	0	57
31	19	33.7	−21	48	2	58	23	41	0	16

Diameters – equatorial 43″ polar 40″

SATURN

Day	*R.A.*		*Dec.*		*Transit*		*5° high*			
							52°		*56°*	
	h	*m*	°	′	*h*	*m*	*h*	*m*	*h*	*m*
1	10	17.4	+12	33	19	37	2	12	2	19
11	10	17.6	+12	31	18	58	1	33	1	40
21	10	18.4	+12	25	18	19	0	54	1	01
31	10	19.9	+12	16	17	42	0	15	0	22

Diameters – equatorial 18″ polar 16″
Rings – major axis 41″ minor axis 7″

URANUS

Day	*R.A.*		*Dec.*		*Transit*		*10° high*			
							52°		*56°*	
	h	*m*	°	′	*h*	*m*	*h*	*m*	*h*	*m*
1	23	29.6	−4	06	8	51	4	20	4	30
11	23	31.0	−3	57	8	13	3	41	3	52
21	23	32.2	−3	49	7	35	3	02	3	13
31	23	33.2	−3	44	6	57	2	23	2	34

Diameter 4″

NEPTUNE

Day	*R.A.*		*Dec.*		*Transit*		*10° high*			
							52°		*56°*	
	h	*m*	°	′	*h*	*m*	*h*	*m*	*h*	*m*
1	21	40.0	−13	48	7	08	3	37	4	01
11	21	46.4	−13	46	6	29	2	58	3	22
21	21	46.6	−13	45	5	50	2	19	2	42
31	21	46.7	−13	45	5	10	1	39	2	03

Diameter 2″

JUNE 2008

SIXTH MONTH, 30 DAYS. *Junius*, Roman *gens* (family)

1	*Sunday*	Robert Cecil, English statesman b. 1563 Ion Antonescu, prime minister of Romania d. 1946	153
2	*Monday*	Constantine II, king of Greece b. 1940 Giuseppe Garibaldi, Italian military campaigner d. 1882	week 22 day 154
3	*Tuesday*	King George V b. 1865 Eisaku Sato, prime minister of Japan d. 1975	155
4	*Wednesday*	C. G. E. Mannerheim, president of Finland b. 1867 Johan Rudolf Thorbecke, Dutch politician d. 1872	156
5	*Thursday*	Joe Clark, prime minister of Canada b. 1939 Ronald Reagan, US president d. 2004	157
6	*Friday*	Sukarno, president of Indonesia b. 1901 Camillo Cavour, Italian statesman d. 1861	158
7	*Saturday*	Queen Elizabeth II's Silver Jubilee procession 1977	159
8	*Sunday*	Barbara Bush, US first lady b. 1925 Harthacanute, king of Denmark and England d. 1042	160
9	*Monday*	Peter I, tsar of Russia b. 1672 Jeanne III, queen of Navarre d. 1572	week 23 day 161
10	*Tuesday*	Prince Philip, the Duke of Edinburgh b. 1921 Hafez al-Assad, president of Syria d. 2000	162
11	*Wednesday*	The UN officially declared a famine in Sudan with over a million people facing starvation 1998	163
12	*Thursday*	George H. W. Bush, US president b. 1924 Masayoshi Ohira, prime minister of Japan d. 1980	164
13	*Friday*	Ban Ki-moon, UN secretary-general b. 1944 Charles Haughey, prime minister of Ireland d. 2006	165
14	*Saturday*	Che Guevara, Argentine revolutionary b. 1928 Frederick Stanley, governor-general of Canada d. 1908	166
15	*Sunday*	King John signed the Magna Carta at Runnymede in Surrey 1215	167
16	*Monday*	Enoch Powell, British politician b. 1912 Imre Nagy, prime minister of Hungary d. 1958	week 24 day 168
17	*Tuesday*	King Edward I b. 1239 Agha Mohammad Khan, shah of Persia d. 1797	169
18	*Wednesday*	Robert Stewart, British foreign secretary b. 1769 John Aislabie, British politician d. 1742	170
19	*Thursday*	Douglas Haig, British military commander b. 1861 Vaclav Klaus, Czech president b. 1941	171
20	*Friday*	John A. Costello, prime minister of Ireland b. 1891 King William IV d. 1837	172
21	*Saturday*	Prince William of Wales b. 1982 Tage Erlander, prime minister of Sweden d. 1985	173
22	*Sunday*	Jerry Rawlings, president of Ghana b. 1947 Armand Fallières, president of France d. 1931	174
23	*Monday*	Gamal Abdel Nasser was elected the first president of the Republic of Egypt 1956	week 25 day 175
24	*Tuesday*	Horatio Kitchener, British statesman b. 1850 Marie François Carnot, president of France d. 1894	176
25	*Wednesday*	Louis Mountbatten, viceroy of India b. 1900 Warren Burger, US chief justice d. 1995	177
26	*Thursday*	Robert Laird Borden, prime minister of Canada b. 1854 Francisco Pizzaro, Spanish conquistador d. 1541	178
27	*Friday*	Charles Stewart Parnell, Irish politician b. 1846 Georgios Papadopoulos, prime minister of Greece d. 1999	179
28	*Saturday*	Chris Hani, South African politician b. 1942 Franz Ferdinand, archduke of Austria d. 1914	180
29	*Sunday*	Pedro Santana Lopes, prime minister of Portugal b. 1956 Ignacy Jan Paderewski, prime minister of Poland d. 1941	181
30	*Monday*	Hitler ordered the assassination of hundreds of Nazis; now known as the Night of the Long Knives 1934	week 26 day 182

ASTRONOMICAL PHENOMENA

d	*h*	
3	17	Venus in conjunction with Moon. Venus 5°S.
4	04	Mercury in conjunction with Moon. Mercury 6°S
7	15	Mercury in inferior conjunction
7	21	Venus in conjunction with Mercury. Venus 3°N.
8	02	Mars in conjunction with Moon. Mars 1°N.
9	04	Venus in superior conjunction
9	07	Saturn in conjunction with Moon. Saturn 3°N.
19	15	Mercury at stationary point
20	13	Jupiter in conjunction with Moon. Jupiter 2°N.
20	20	Pluto at opposition
21	00	Sun's longitude 90° ♋
27	00	Uranus at stationary point

MINIMA OF ALGOL

Algol is inconveniently situated for observation during June

CONSTELLATIONS

The following constellations are near the meridian at

	d	*h*		*d*	*h*
May	1	24	June	15	21
May	16	23	July	1	20
June	1	22	July	16	19

Cassiopeia (below the Pole), Ursa Minor, Draco, Ursa Major, Canes Venatici, Bootes, Corona, Serpens, Virgo and Libra

THE MOON

Phases, Apsides and Node	*d*	*h*	*m*
● New Moon	3	19	23
☽ First Quarter	10	15	04
○ Full Moon	18	17	30
☾ Last Quarter	26	12	10
Perigee (357,249km)	3	13	05
Apogee (406,243km)	16	17	20

Mean longitude of ascending node on June 1, 322°

THE SUN

s.d. 15′.8

Day	Right Ascension			Dec. +		Equation of time		Rise 52°		Rise 56°		Transit		Set 52°		Set 56°		Sidereal time			Transit of first point of Aries		
	h	*m*	*s*	°	′	*m*	*s*	*h*	*m*	*h*	*m*	*h*	*m*	*h*	*m*	*h*	*m*	*h*	*m*	*s*	*h*	*m*	*s*
1	4	37	12	22	05	+2	12	3	46	3	22	11	58	20	11	20	35	16	39	24	7	19	24
2	4	41	18	22	13	+2	02	3	45	3	21	11	58	20	12	20	36	16	43	21	7	15	28
3	4	45	25	22	20	+1	52	3	44	3	20	11	58	20	13	20	38	16	47	17	7	11	32
4	4	49	31	22	27	+1	42	3	43	3	19	11	58	20	14	20	39	16	51	14	7	07	36
5	4	53	39	22	34	+1	32	3	43	3	18	11	59	20	15	20	40	16	55	10	7	03	40
6	4	57	46	22	40	+1	21	3	42	3	17	11	59	20	16	20	41	16	59	07	6	59	44
7	5	01	54	22	46	+1	10	3	42	3	16	11	59	20	17	20	42	17	03	03	6	55	48
8	5	06	02	22	52	+0	58	3	41	3	16	11	59	20	17	20	43	17	07	00	6	51	52
9	5	10	10	22	57	+0	46	3	41	3	15	11	59	20	18	20	44	17	10	56	6	47	57
10	5	14	18	23	01	+0	35	3	40	3	15	12	00	20	19	20	45	17	14	53	6	44	01
11	5	18	27	23	06	+0	23	3	40	3	14	12	00	20	20	20	46	17	18	50	6	40	05
12	5	22	36	23	10	+0	10	3	40	3	14	12	00	20	20	20	46	17	22	46	6	36	09
13	5	26	45	23	13	−0	02	3	40	3	13	12	00	20	21	20	47	17	26	43	6	32	13
14	5	30	54	23	16	−0	15	3	39	3	13	12	00	20	21	20	48	17	30	39	6	28	17
15	5	35	03	23	19	−0	27	3	39	3	13	12	01	20	22	20	48	17	34	36	6	24	21
16	5	39	13	23	21	−0	40	3	39	3	13	12	01	20	22	20	49	17	38	32	6	20	25
17	5	43	22	23	23	−0	53	3	39	3	13	12	01	20	23	20	49	17	42	29	6	16	29
18	5	47	32	23	25	−1	06	3	39	3	13	12	01	20	23	20	50	17	46	25	6	12	33
19	5	51	41	23	26	−1	19	3	39	3	13	12	01	20	23	20	50	17	50	22	6	08	37
20	5	55	51	23	26	−1	32	3	40	3	13	12	02	20	24	20	50	17	54	19	6	04	42
21	6	00	00	23	26	−1	45	3	40	3	13	12	02	20	24	20	51	17	58	15	6	00	46
22	6	04	10	23	26	−1	58	3	40	3	13	12	02	20	24	20	51	18	02	12	5	56	50
23	6	08	19	23	26	−2	11	3	40	3	14	12	02	20	24	20	51	18	06	08	5	52	54
24	6	12	28	23	25	−2	24	3	41	3	14	12	03	20	24	20	51	18	10	05	5	48	58
25	6	16	38	23	23	−2	36	3	41	3	15	12	03	20	24	20	51	18	14	01	5	45	02
26	6	20	47	23	21	−2	49	3	42	3	15	12	03	20	24	20	50	18	17	58	5	41	06
27	6	24	56	23	19	−3	02	3	42	3	16	12	03	20	24	20	50	18	21	54	5	37	10
28	6	29	05	23	16	−3	14	3	43	3	16	12	03	20	24	20	50	18	25	51	5	33	14
29	6	33	14	23	13	−3	26	3	43	3	17	12	04	20	24	20	50	18	29	48	5	29	18
30	6	37	22	23	10	−3	38	3	44	3	18	12	04	20	23	20	49	18	33	44	5	25	22

DURATION OF TWILIGHT (in minutes)

Latitude	52°	56°	52°	56°	52°	56°	52°	56°
	1 June		*11 June*		*21 June*		*31 June*	
Civil	46	58	48	61	49	63	48	61
Nautical	116	TAN	124	TAN	127	TAN	124	TAN
Astronomical	TAN	TAN	TAN	TAN	TAN	TAN	TAN	TAN

THE NIGHT SKY

Mercury passes through inferior conjunction on the 7th but the long duration of twilight means that it remains unsuitably placed for observation throughout the month.

Venus passes through superior conjunction on the 9th, actually passing behind the disk of the Sun, and thus remaining too close to that body for observation throughout June. It is interesting to note that at this conjunction it is exactly halfway between the only two transits of the planet which occur this century – in 2004 and 2012.

Mars, magnitude +1.6, is no longer a conspicuous object, but continues to be visible in the western sky in the evenings. The planet moves from Cancer back into Leo towards the end of the month. It will be noticed that Mars is moving towards Saturn, being only 5 degrees away from it by the end of June, when it will be seen passing less than 1 degree north of Regulus. By the end of the month Mars will not be visible after about 22h. The 4-day-old crescent Moon will be seen approaching the planet on the evening of the 7th, though closest approach will not occur until after both bodies have set.

Jupiter, magnitude −2.7, continues to be visible as a conspicuous object in the night sky, becoming visible above the south-eastern horizon shortly before midnight at the beginning of the month, and two hours earlier by the end of the month. Jupiter is in the constellation of Sagittarius. The Moon, almost full, will be seen in the vicinity of the planet during the night of the 20th and 21st.

Saturn, magnitude +0.9, continues to be visible low in the western sky in the evenings. Saturn is in the constellation of Leo. The waxing crescent Moon is in the vicinity of the planet on the evenings of the 8th and 9th.

THE MOON

Day	R.A.		Dec.	Hor. Par.	Semi-diam.	Sun's Co-Long.	PA of Br. Limb	Ph.	Age	Rise				Transit		Set			
										52°		56°				52°		56°	
	h	m	°	′	′	°	°	%	d	h	m	h	m	h	m	h	m	h	m
1	1	49	+16.3	60.4	16.5	235	75	12	26.5	1	44	1	29	9	31	17	40	18	01
2	2	48	+21.4	61.0	16.6	247	83	5	27.5	2	08	1	45	10	30	19	15	19	44
3	3	52	+25.3	61.3	16.7	260	101	1	28.5	2	42	2	12	11	35	20	42	21	17
4	4	59	+27.3	61.3	16.7	272	205	0	0.2	3	33	2	58	12	42	21	51	22	26
5	6	08	+27.2	61.0	16.6	284	258	2	1.2	4	44	4	09	13	49	22	39	23	09
6	7	14	+25.2	60.4	16.5	296	273	7	2.2	6	09	5	41	14	51	23	11	23	34
7	8	15	+21.5	59.6	16.2	308	281	14	3.2	7	39	7	18	15	47	23	33	23	49
8	9	12	+16.7	58.7	16.0	321	287	23	4.2	9	06	8	52	16	38	23	50	23	59
9	10	03	+11.2	57.7	15.7	333	291	33	5.2	10	27	10	20	17	24	—	—	—	—
10	10	51	+5.3	56.8	15.5	345	293	44	6.2	11	45	11	43	18	08	0	03	0	07
11	11	36	−0.6	56.0	15.3	357	293	54	7.2	12	59	13	02	18	49	0	14	0	13
12	12	21	−6.3	55.3	15.1	10	292	64	8.2	14	12	14	21	19	31	0	25	0	20
13	13	05	−11.7	54.8	14.9	22	290	73	9.2	15	25	15	39	20	13	0	37	0	27
14	13	51	−16.5	54.4	14.8	34	287	81	10.2	16	38	16	58	20	58	0	51	0	35
15	14	38	−20.7	54.1	14.8	46	282	88	11.2	17	51	18	17	21	44	1	08	0	46
16	15	27	−24.0	54.0	14.7	58	276	93	12.2	19	00	19	33	22	33	1	30	1	03
17	16	18	−26.3	54.0	14.7	71	266	97	13.2	20	03	20	39	23	23	2	01	1	28
18	17	11	−27.4	54.1	14.7	83	246	99	14.2	20	55	21	31	—	—	2	43	2	06
19	18	05	−27.3	54.2	14.8	95	142	100	15.2	21	34	22	06	0	15	3	37	3	02
20	18	58	−25.8	54.5	14.8	107	96	98	16.2	22	04	22	29	1	06	4	43	4	12
21	19	50	−23.2	54.8	14.9	119	84	95	17.2	22	25	22	45	1	56	5	56	5	31
22	20	40	−19.5	55.2	15.0	132	77	90	18.2	22	42	22	56	2	43	7	11	6	53
23	21	29	−14.9	55.7	15.2	144	72	84	19.2	22	55	23	04	3	29	8	28	8	16
24	22	16	−9.6	56.3	15.3	156	68	75	20.2	23	08	23	11	4	13	9	45	9	38
25	23	02	−3.7	56.9	15.5	168	67	66	21.2	23	19	23	18	4	57	11	02	11	01
26	23	49	+2.4	57.7	15.7	180	66	56	22.2	23	32	23	25	5	41	12	21	12	26
27	0	38	+8.5	58.4	15.9	193	67	45	23.2	23	47	23	35	6	28	13	44	13	55
28	1	29	+14.4	59.2	16.1	205	70	34	24.2	—	—	23	48	7	19	15	12	15	30
29	2	25	+19.7	59.9	16.3	217	74	23	25.2	0	07	—	—	8	14	16	43	17	08
30	3	25	+24.0	60.5	16.5	229	81	14	26.2	0	35	0	08	9	14	18	12	18	45

MERCURY

Day	R.A.		Dec.	Diam.	Phase	Transit		5° high			
								52°		56°	
	h	m	°	″	%	h	m	h	m	h	m
1	5	19	+22.1	12	4	12	37	19	59	20	16
3	5	16	+21.4	12	2	12	25	19	44	20	00
5	5	12	+20.8	12	1	12	13	19	28	19	43
7	5	07	+20.2	12	0	12	01	19	12	19	26
9	5	03	+19.6	12	1	11	49	4	40	4	26
11	4	58	+19.0	12	1	11	37	4	31	4	18
13	4	55	+18.6	12	3	11	25	4	22	4	09
15	4	52	+18.3	12	5	11	15	4	13	4	00
17	4	50	+18.1	11	8	11	05	4	04	3	52
19	4	49	+18.0	11	11	10	56	3	56	3	44
21	4	49	+18.0	10	14	10	49	3	48	3	36
23	4	50	+18.1	10	18	10	43	3	41	3	29
25	4	53	+18.4	9	21	10	38	3	34	3	22
27	4	57	+18.7	9	26	10	35	3	29	3	16
29	5	03	+19.1	9	30	10	32	3	24	3	11
31	5	09	+19.6	8	35	10	31	3	20	3	06

VENUS

Day	R.A.		Dec.	Diam.	Phase	Transit		5° high			
								52°		56°	
	h	m	°	″	%	h	m	h	m	h	m
1	4	28	+21.5	10	100	11	49	19	13	19	29
6	4	54	+22.5	10	100	11	56	19	25	19	43
11	5	21	+23.3	10	100	12	02	19	37	19	55
16	5	47	+23.7	10	100	12	09	19	47	20	05
21	6	14	+23.9	10	100	12	17	19	55	20	14
26	6	41	+23.8	10	100	12	24	20	01	20	20
31	7	08	+23.4	10	99	12	31	20	05	20	23

MARS

Day	R.A.		Dec.	Diam.	Phase	Transit		5° high			
								52°		56°	
	h	m	°	″	%	h	m	h	m	h	m
1	9	00	+18.6	5	92	16	20	23	24	23	36
6	9	12	+17.7	5	93	16	12	23	10	23	22
11	9	23	+16.8	5	93	16	03	22	57	23	07
16	9	34	+15.8	5	93	15	55	22	43	22	53
21	9	46	+14.8	5	94	15	46	22	29	22	38
26	9	57	+13.8	5	94	15	38	22	15	22	23
31	10	08	+12.7	4	94	15	30	22	01	22	08

SUNRISE AND SUNSET

	London				*Bristol*				*Birmingham*				*Manchester*				*Newcastle*				*Glasgow*				*Belfast*			
	0°05′		*51°30′*		*2°35′*		*51° 28′*		*1°55′*		*52°28′*		*2° 15′*		*53°28′*		*1°37′*		*54°59′*		*4°14′*		*55°52′*		*5°56′*		*54°35′*	
d	*h*	*m*	*h*	*m*	*h*	*m*	*h*	*m*	*h*	*m*	*h*	*m*	*h*	*m*	*h*	*m*	*h*	*m*	*h*	*m*	*h*	*m*	*h*	*m*	*h*	*m*	*h*	*m*
1	3	49	20	08	3	59	20	18	3	51	20	21	3	47	20	28	3	35	20	35	3	39	20	51	3	55	20	49
2	3	48	20	09	3	58	20	19	3	50	20	22	3	46	20	29	3	34	20	36	3	38	20	52	3	54	20	51
3	3	47	20	11	3	57	20	20	3	49	20	23	3	45	20	30	3	33	20	37	3	38	20	54	3	53	20	52
4	3	46	20	11	3	57	20	21	3	49	20	24	3	44	20	31	3	32	20	38	3	37	20	55	3	52	20	53
5	3	46	20	12	3	56	20	22	3	48	20	25	3	44	20	32	3	31	20	39	3	36	20	56	3	51	20	54
6	3	45	20	13	3	55	20	23	3	47	20	26	3	43	20	33	3	31	20	40	3	35	20	57	3	51	20	55
7	3	45	20	14	3	55	20	24	3	47	20	27	3	42	20	34	3	30	20	41	3	34	20	58	3	50	20	56
8	3	44	20	15	3	55	20	25	3	46	20	28	3	42	20	35	3	29	20	42	3	34	20	59	3	49	20	57
9	3	44	20	16	3	54	20	26	3	46	20	29	3	41	20	36	3	29	20	43	3	33	21	00	3	49	20	58
10	3	44	20	16	3	54	20	26	3	45	20	29	3	41	20	37	3	28	20	44	3	33	21	01	3	48	20	59
11	3	43	20	17	3	53	20	27	3	45	20	30	3	40	20	37	3	28	20	45	3	32	21	02	3	48	20	59
12	3	43	20	18	3	53	20	28	3	45	20	31	3	40	20	38	3	28	20	46	3	32	21	02	3	48	21	00
13	3	43	20	18	3	53	20	28	3	45	20	31	3	40	20	39	3	27	20	46	3	31	21	03	3	47	21	01
14	3	43	20	19	3	53	20	29	3	44	20	32	3	40	20	39	3	27	20	47	3	31	21	04	3	47	21	01
15	3	43	20	19	3	53	20	29	3	44	20	32	3	40	20	40	3	27	20	47	3	31	21	04	3	47	21	02
16	3	42	20	20	3	53	20	30	3	44	20	33	3	39	20	40	3	27	20	48	3	31	21	05	3	47	21	02
17	3	42	20	20	3	53	20	30	3	44	20	33	3	39	20	41	3	27	20	48	3	31	21	05	3	47	21	03
18	3	43	20	21	3	53	20	30	3	44	20	34	3	39	20	41	3	27	20	49	3	31	21	06	3	47	21	03
19	3	43	20	21	3	53	20	31	3	44	20	34	3	40	20	41	3	27	20	49	3	31	21	06	3	47	21	03
20	3	43	20	21	3	53	20	31	3	45	20	34	3	40	20	42	3	27	20	49	3	31	21	06	3	47	21	04
21	3	43	20	21	3	53	20	31	3	45	20	34	3	40	20	42	3	27	20	49	3	31	21	06	3	47	21	04
22	3	43	20	22	3	53	20	31	3	45	20	34	3	40	20	42	3	27	20	50	3	31	21	07	3	47	21	04
23	3	44	20	22	3	54	20	31	3	45	20	35	3	40	20	42	3	28	20	50	3	32	21	07	3	48	21	04
24	3	44	20	22	3	54	20	31	3	46	20	35	3	41	20	42	3	28	20	50	3	32	21	07	3	48	21	04
25	3	44	20	22	3	54	20	31	3	46	20	35	3	41	20	42	3	29	20	50	3	33	21	07	3	49	21	04
26	3	45	20	22	3	55	20	31	3	46	20	34	3	42	20	42	3	29	20	49	3	33	21	06	3	49	21	04
27	3	45	20	22	3	55	20	31	3	47	20	34	3	42	20	42	3	30	20	49	3	34	21	06	3	50	21	04
28	3	46	20	21	3	56	20	31	3	48	20	34	3	43	20	42	3	30	20	49	3	34	21	06	3	50	21	04
29	3	46	20	21	3	57	20	31	3	48	20	34	3	43	20	41	3	31	20	49	3	35	21	06	3	51	21	03
30	3	47	20	21	3	57	20	31	3	49	20	34	3	44	20	41	3	32	20	48	3	36	21	05	3	52	21	03

JUPITER

Day	*R.A.*		*Dec.*		*Transit*		*5° high*			
							52°		*56°*	
	h	*m*	°	′	*h*	*m*	*h*	*m*	*h*	*m*
1	19	33.4	−21	48	2	53	23	37	0	12
11	19	29.9	−21	57	2	11	22	55	23	27
21	19	25.5	−22	08	1	27	22	13	22	45
31	19	20.4	−22	20	0	43	21	30	22	03

Diameters – equatorial 46″ polar 43″

SATURN

Day	*R.A.*		*Dec.*		*Transit*		*5° high*			
							52°		*56°*	
	h	*m*	°	′	*h*	*m*	*h*	*m*	*h*	*m*
1	10	20.1	+12	14	17	38	0	11	0	18
11	10	22.2	+12	01	17	01	23	29	23	36
21	10	24.9	+11	45	16	24	22	51	22	57
31	10	28.0	+11	26	15	48	22	13	22	19

Diameters – equatorial 17″ polar 15″

Rings – major axis 39″ minor axis 6″

URANUS

Day	*R.A.*		*Dec.*		*Transit*		*10° high*			
							52°		*56°*	
	h	*m*	°	′	*h*	*m*	*h*	*m*	*h*	*m*
1	23	33.2	−3	43	6	53	2	19	2	30
11	23	33.9	−3	40	6	14	1	40	1	51
21	23	34.2	−3	38	5	35	1	01	1	11
31	23	34.2	−3	38	4	56	0	22	0	32

Diameter 4″

NEPTUNE

Day	*R.A.*		*Dec.*		*Transit*		*10° high*			
							52°		*56°*	
	h	*m*	°	′	*h*	*m*	*h*	*m*	*h*	*m*
1	21	46.7	−13	45	5	06	1	35	1	59
11	21	46.4	−13	46	4	27	0	56	1	20
21	21	46.0	−13	48	3	47	0	17	0	40
31	21	45.5	−13	52	3	07	23	33	0	01

Diameter 2″

JULY 2008

SEVENTH MONTH, 31 DAYS. *Julius* Caesar, formerly *Quintilis*, fifth month of Roman pre-Julian calendar

1	*Tuesday*	Diana Spencer, Princess of Wales b. 1961 Juan Peron, president of Argentina d. 1974	183
2	*Wednesday*	David Owen, leader of the SDP Party b. 1938 Robert Peel, British prime minister d. 1850	184
3	*Thursday*	A US warship shot down an Iranian passenger aircraft, mistaking it for a fighter jet 1988	185
4	*Friday*	Thomas Jefferson, US president d. 1826 John Adams, US president d. 1826	186
5	*Saturday*	Stamford Raffles, British colonial administrator d. 1826 Hugh Shearer, prime minister of Jamaica d. 2004	187
6	*Sunday*	Nicholas I, tsar of Russia b. 1796 King Edward VI d. 1553	188
7	*Monday*	Michael Howard, British politician b. 1941 Talal bin Abdullah, king of Jordan d. 1972	week 27 day 189
8	*Tuesday*	Micheline Calmy-Rey, Swiss politician b. 1945 Fatima Jinnah, Pakistani politician d. 1967	190
9	*Wednesday*	Donald Rumsfeld, US secretary of defence b. 1932 Philip V, king of Spain d. 1746	191
10	*Thursday*	Ahmet Taner Kislali, Turkish politician b. 1939 Hadrian, emperor of Rome d. 138	192
11	*Friday*	Robert the Bruce, king of Scotland b. 1274 Narai, king of Siam d. 1688	193
12	*Saturday*	Lionel Jospin, prime minister of France b. 1937 Douglas Hyde, president of Ireland d. 1949	194
13	*Sunday*	Patrice de MacMahon, president of France b. 1808 Seretse Khama, president of Botswana d. 1980	195
14	*Monday*	Gerald Ford, US president b. 1913 Paul Kruger, South African revolutionary d. 1904	week 28 day 196
15	*Tuesday*	Hassanal Bolkiah, sultan of Brunei b. 1946 Hammer DeRoburt, president of Nauru d. 1992	197
16	*Wednesday*	Trygve Lie, UN secretary-general b. 1896 Nicholas II, tsar of Russia d. 1918	198
17	*Thursday*	Allied leaders held a conference in Potsdam to decide on the future of Germany 1945	199
18	*Friday*	The body of the government weapons expert Dr David Kelly was discovered 2003	200
19	*Saturday*	Francisco Sá Carneiro, prime minister of Portugal b. 1934 Syngman Rhee, president of South Korea d. 1965	201
20	*Sunday*	Miron Cristea, prime minister of Romania b. 1868 Wilhelm, crown prince of Germany d. 1951	202
21	*Monday*	Thomas Penham-Holles, British prime minister b. 1693 Albert Lutuli, South African politician d. 1967	week 29 day 203
22	*Tuesday*	Saddam Hussein's sons, Uday and Qusay Hussein, were killed by US troops in Iraq 2003	204
23	*Wednesday*	Haile Selassie, emperor of Ethiopia b. 1892 Cordell Hull, US secretary of state d. 1955	205
24	*Thursday*	Gibraltar was captured from the Spanish by the British 1704	206
25	*Friday*	Arthur Balfour, British prime minister b. 1848 Engelbert Dollfuss, chancellor of Austria d. 1934	207
26	*Saturday*	Vladimir Meciar, prime minister of Slovakia b. 1942 Sam Houston, president of the Republic of Texas d. 1863	208
27	*Sunday*	The Battle of Ushant between British and French fleets took place 1778	209
28	*Monday*	Jacqueline Onassis, US first lady b. 1929 Thomas Cromwell, English statesman d. 1540	week 30 day 210
29	*Tuesday*	Henry II, count of Champagne b. 1166 William Wilberforce, British politician d. 1833	211
30	*Wednesday*	Hongzhi, emperor of China b. 1470 Bao Dai, emperor of Vietnam d. 1997	212
31	*Thursday*	Maximilian II, Holy Roman Emperor b. 1527 Baudouin I, king of Belgium d. 1993	213

ASTRONOMICAL PHENOMENA

d	*h*	
1	14	Mercury in conjunction with Moon. Mercury 8°S.
1	18	Mercury at greatest elongation W. 22°
3	14	Venus in conjunction with Moon. Venus 2°S.
4	08	Earth at aphelion (152 million km.)
6	16	Mars in conjunction with Moon. Mars 2°N.
6	20	Saturn in conjunction with Moon. Saturn 3°N.
9	08	Jupiter at opposition
10	18	Saturn in conjunction with Mars. Saturn 0°.6N.
17	13	Jupiter in conjunction with Moon. Jupiter 3°N.
22	11	Sun's longitude 120° ♌
29	20	Mercury in superior conjunction

MINIMA OF ALGOL

d	*h*	*d*	*h*	*d*	*h*
3	03.6	14	14.9	26	02.1
6	00.4	17	11.7	28	22.9
8	21.2	20	08.5	31	19.7
11	18.0	23	05.3		

CONSTELLATIONS

The following constellations are near their meridian at

	d	*h*		*d*	*h*
June	1	24	July	16	21
June	15	23	August	1	20
July	1	22	August	16	19

Ursa Minor, Draco, Corona, Hercules, Lyra, Serpens, Ophiuchus, Libra, Scorpius and Sagittarius

THE MOON

Phases, Apsides and Node	*d*	*h*	*m*
● New Moon	3	02	19
☽ First Quarter	10	04	35
○ Full Moon	18	07	59
☾ Last Quarter	25	18	42
Perigee (359,503 km)	1	21	20
Apogee (405,480 km)	14	04	07
Perigee (363,863 km)	29	23	16

Mean longitude of ascending node on July 1, 321°

THE SUN

s.d. 15′.8

Day	Right Ascension			Dec. +		Equation of time		Rise 52°		Rise 56°		Transit		Set 52°		Set 56°		Sidereal time			Transit of first point of Aries		
	h	m	s	°	′	m	s	h	m	h	m	h	m	h	m	h	m	h	m	s	h	m	s
1	6	41	31	23	06	–3	50	3	45	3	19	12	04	20	23	20	49	18	37	41	5	21	26
2	6	45	39	23	02	–4	01	3	45	3	19	12	04	20	23	20	48	18	41	37	5	17	31
3	6	49	47	22	57	–4	13	3	46	3	20	12	04	20	22	20	48	18	45	34	5	13	35
4	6	53	54	22	52	–4	24	3	47	3	21	12	04	20	22	20	47	18	49	30	5	09	39
5	6	58	01	22	46	–4	34	3	48	3	22	12	05	20	21	20	46	18	53	27	5	05	43
6	7	02	08	22	40	–4	45	3	49	3	24	12	05	20	21	20	45	18	57	24	5	01	47
7	7	06	15	22	34	–4	54	3	50	3	25	12	05	20	20	20	45	19	01	20	4	57	51
8	7	10	21	22	27	–5	04	3	51	3	26	12	05	20	19	20	44	19	05	17	4	53	55
9	7	14	26	22	20	–5	13	3	52	3	27	12	05	20	18	20	43	19	09	13	4	49	59
10	7	18	31	22	13	–5	22	3	53	3	28	12	05	20	18	20	42	19	13	10	4	46	03
11	7	22	36	22	05	–5	30	3	54	3	30	12	06	20	17	20	41	19	17	06	4	42	07
12	7	26	40	21	57	–5	38	3	55	3	31	12	06	20	16	20	39	19	21	03	4	38	11
13	7	30	44	21	48	–5	45	3	56	3	32	12	06	20	15	20	38	19	24	59	4	34	16
14	7	34	48	21	39	–5	52	3	57	3	34	12	06	20	14	20	37	19	28	56	4	30	20
15	7	38	50	21	30	–5	58	3	58	3	35	12	06	20	13	20	36	19	32	53	4	26	24
16	7	42	53	21	20	–6	04	4	00	3	37	12	06	20	12	20	34	19	36	49	4	22	28
17	7	46	54	21	10	–6	09	4	01	3	38	12	06	20	11	20	33	19	40	46	4	18	32
18	7	50	56	21	00	–6	13	4	02	3	40	12	06	20	10	20	32	19	44	42	4	14	36
19	7	54	56	20	49	–6	18	4	03	3	42	12	06	20	08	20	30	19	48	39	4	10	40
20	7	58	56	20	38	–6	21	4	05	3	43	12	06	20	07	20	28	19	52	35	4	06	44
21	8	02	56	20	26	–6	24	4	06	3	45	12	06	20	06	20	27	19	56	32	4	02	48
22	8	06	55	20	15	–6	27	4	07	3	46	12	06	20	05	20	25	20	00	28	3	58	52
23	8	10	54	20	02	–6	29	4	09	3	48	12	06	20	03	20	24	20	04	25	3	54	56
24	8	14	51	19	50	–6	30	4	10	3	50	12	07	20	02	20	22	20	08	22	3	51	00
25	8	18	49	19	37	–6	31	4	12	3	52	12	07	20	00	20	20	20	12	18	3	47	05
26	8	22	45	19	24	–6	31	4	13	3	53	12	07	19	59	20	18	20	16	15	3	43	09
27	8	26	42	19	11	–6	30	4	15	3	55	12	07	19	57	20	17	20	20	11	3	39	13
28	8	30	37	18	57	–6	29	4	16	3	57	12	06	19	56	20	15	20	24	08	3	35	17
29	8	34	32	18	43	–6	28	4	18	3	59	12	06	19	54	20	13	20	28	04	3	31	21
30	8	38	27	18	28	–6	26	4	19	4	01	12	06	19	53	20	11	20	32	01	3	27	25
31	8	42	21	18	14	–6	23	4	21	4	03	12	06	19	51	20	09	20	35	57	3	23	29

DURATION OF TWILIGHT (in minutes)

Latitude	52°	56°	52°	56°	52°	56°	52°	56°
	1 July		*11 July*		*21 July*		*31 July*	
Civil	48	61	47	58	44	53	42	49
Nautical	124	TAN	117	TAN	107	146	98	123
Astronomical	TAN	TAN	TAN	TAN	TAN	TAN	182	TAN

THE NIGHT SKY

Mercury passes through superior conjunction on the 29th and remains too close to the Sun for observation throughout the month.

Venus is too close to the Sun for observation during July but will become visible at the beginning of August.

Mars, magnitude +1.7, is now coming to the end of its period of visibility and is only likely to be visible low above the western horizon for the first week or ten days of the month, as the long evening twilight will hinder observation. After this Mars will not be seen again before 2009. On the evening of the 6th the three-day-old crescent Moon can be used to help locate two planets, both of which will be 4 degrees from the Moon's centre. Saturn, the brighter planet, is almost 4 degrees higher than the Moon, and about 1.5 degrees to the right, while Mars is about 2 degrees to the right and below Saturn.

Jupiter, magnitude −2.7, reaches opposition on the 9th and is therefore visible in the southern skies throughout the hours of darkness. As it is in the constellation of Sagittarius it is never at any great altitude. Even from southern England its maximum altitude is only 16 degrees, while from Scotland it is never more than 11 degrees. On the evenings of the 17th and 18th the Full Moon will be in the vicinity of the planet.

Saturn, magnitude +0.9, may still be seen for a short while low in the western sky in the evenings but will soon get lost in the long evening twilight. Mars passes close by around the 6th, see the note for Mars above.

Twilight. Reference to the section above shows that astronomical twilight lasts all night for a period around the summer solstice (ie in June and July), even in southern England. Under these conditions the sky never gets completely dark as the Sun is always less than 18 degrees below the horizon.

THE MOON

Day	R.A.		Dec.	Hor. Par.	Semi-diam.	Sun's Co-Long.	PA of Br. Limb	Ph.	Age	Rise 52°		Rise 56°		Transit		Set 52°		Set 56°	
	h	m	°	′	′	°	°	%	d	h	m	h	m	h	m	h	m	h	m
1	4	30	+26.7	60.9	16.6	242	90	7	27.2	1	16	0	43	10	20	19	30	20	06
2	5	38	+27.5	61.0	16.6	254	103	2	28.2	2	17	1	41	11	27	20	28	21	01
3	6	45	+26.3	60.8	16.6	266	162	0	29.2	3	36	3	04	12	31	21	08	21	34
4	7	49	+23.2	60.3	16.4	278	271	1	0.9	5	06	4	42	13	32	21	35	21	53
5	8	49	+18.7	59.6	16.3	291	284	5	1.9	6	37	6	20	14	26	21	53	22	05
6	9	43	+13.2	58.8	16.0	303	290	11	2.9	8	04	7	54	15	16	22	08	22	14
7	10	34	+7.3	57.9	15.8	315	293	19	3.9	9	25	9	21	16	02	22	20	22	22
8	11	21	+1.2	56.9	15.5	327	294	28	4.9	10	43	10	44	16	45	22	32	22	28
9	12	07	−4.7	56.1	15.3	340	294	38	5.9	11	58	12	05	17	28	22	44	22	35
10	12	52	−10.3	55.4	15.1	352	293	48	6.9	13	12	13	24	18	10	22	57	22	43
11	13	38	−15.4	54.8	14.9	4	291	58	7.9	14	26	14	44	18	54	23	12	22	53
12	14	24	−19.8	54.4	14.8	16	287	67	8.9	15	39	16	03	19	40	23	33	23	08
13	15	13	−23.3	54.2	14.8	29	282	76	9.9	16	50	17	21	20	28	—		23	29
14	16	04	−25.9	54.1	14.7	41	277	83	10.9	17	56	18	31	21	18	0	01	—	
15	16	57	−27.3	54.1	14.7	53	270	90	11.9	18	51	19	28	22	10	0	39	0	03
16	17	50	−27.5	54.3	14.8	65	263	95	12.9	19	35	20	08	23	01	1	29	0	53
17	18	44	−26.3	54.5	14.9	77	254	98	13.9	20	07	20	35	23	52	2	32	1	59
18	19	37	−24.0	54.9	15.0	90	229	100	14.9	20	31	20	52	—		3	43	3	17
19	20	28	−20.4	55.3	15.1	102	86	100	15.9	20	49	21	05	0	40	4	59	4	39
20	21	17	−16.0	55.7	15.2	114	73	97	16.9	21	04	21	13	1	27	6	17	6	03
21	22	05	−10.8	56.2	15.3	126	68	93	17.9	21	16	21	21	2	12	7	34	7	26
22	22	51	−5.0	56.7	15.5	138	65	87	18.9	21	28	21	27	2	56	8	51	8	49
23	23	38	+1.1	57.3	15.6	151	64	79	19.9	21	40	21	34	3	40	10	10	10	13
24	0	26	+7.2	57.8	15.8	163	65	69	20.9	21	54	21	43	4	26	11	30	11	39
25	1	16	+13.1	58.4	15.9	175	67	59	21.9	22	11	21	54	5	14	12	55	13	10
26	2	09	+18.5	58.9	16.1	187	70	48	22.9	22	34	22	10	6	06	14	22	14	45
27	3	06	+22.9	59.5	16.2	199	76	36	23.9	23	08	22	37	7	02	15	50	16	20
28	4	08	+26.1	59.9	16.3	212	82	26	24.9	23	59	23	23	8	04	17	11	17	47
29	5	13	+27.5	60.2	16.4	224	90	16	25.9	—		—		9	08	18	16	18	52
30	6	19	+27.1	60.3	16.4	236	98	8	26.9	1	09	0	34	10	13	19	03	19	32
31	7	23	+24.7	60.1	16.4	248	106	3	27.9	2	33	2	05	11	14	19	34	19	56

MERCURY

Day	R.A.		Dec.	Diam.	Phase	Transit		5° high 52°		5° high 56°	
	h	m	°	″	%	h	m	h	m	h	m
1	5	09	+19.6	8	35	10	31	3	20	3	06
3	5	17	+20.1	8	40	10	32	3	17	3	03
5	5	26	+20.7	7	45	10	33	3	15	3	00
7	5	37	+21.2	7	51	10	36	3	15	2	59
9	5	48	+21.7	7	56	10	40	3	15	2	59
11	6	01	+22.2	6	62	10	45	3	18	3	01
13	6	15	+22.6	6	69	10	52	3	22	3	04
15	6	30	+22.8	6	75	10	59	3	27	3	09
17	6	46	+23.0	6	81	11	07	3	34	3	16
19	7	03	+23.0	6	86	11	17	3	43	3	25
21	7	21	+22.9	5	91	11	26	3	54	3	36
23	7	39	+22.5	5	95	11	37	4	06	3	49
25	7	57	+22.0	5	97	11	47	4	20	4	03
27	8	15	+21.4	5	99	11	57	4	34	4	18
29	8	32	+20.5	5	100	12	07	19	22	19	37
31	8	50	+19.5	5	100	12	16	19	26	19	39

VENUS

Day	R.A.		Dec.	Diam.	Phase	Transit		5° high 52°		5° high 56°	
	h	m	°	″	%	h	m	h	m	h	m
1	7	08	+23.4	10	99	12	31	20	05	20	23
6	7	34	+22.7	10	99	12	38	20	07	20	24
11	8	01	+21.7	10	99	12	44	20	07	20	23
16	8	26	+20.5	10	98	12	50	20	06	20	20
21	8	52	+19.0	10	98	12	56	20	02	20	15
26	9	17	+17.3	10	97	13	01	19	58	20	09
31	9	41	+15.4	10	97	13	06	19	52	20	01

MARS

Day	R.A.		Dec.	Diam.	Phase	Transit		5° high 52°		5° high 56°	
	h	m	°	″	%	h	m	h	m	h	m
1	10	08	+12.7	4	94	15	30	22	01	22	08
6	10	20	+11.6	4	94	15	21	21	47	21	53
11	10	31	+10.4	4	95	15	13	21	32	21	37
16	10	42	+9.3	4	95	15	05	21	18	21	22
21	10	54	+8.1	4	95	14	56	21	03	21	06
26	11	05	+6.8	4	96	14	48	20	49	20	51
31	11	16	+5.6	4	96	14	39	20	34	20	35

SUNRISE AND SUNSET

	London		*Bristol*		*Birmingham*		*Manchester*		*Newcastle*		*Glasgow*		*Belfast*	
	0°05′	*51°30′*	*2°35′*	*51°28′*	*1°55′*	*52°28′*	*2°15′*	*53°28′*	*1°37′*	*54°49′*	*4°14′*	*55°52′*	*5°56′*	*54°35′*
d	*h m*	*h m*	*h m*	*h m*	*h m*	*h m*	*h m*	*h m*	*h m*	*h m*	*h m*	*h m*	*h m*	*h m*
1	3 48	20 21	3 58	20 30	3 50	20 33	3 45	20 41	3 32	20 48	3 37	21 05	3 52	21 03
2	3 48	20 20	3 59	20 30	3 50	20 33	3 46	20 40	3 33	20 47	3 37	21 04	3 53	21 02
3	3 49	20 20	3 59	20 30	3 51	20 32	3 46	20 40	3 34	20 47	3 38	21 04	3 54	21 02
4	3 50	20 19	4 00	20 29	3 52	20 32	3 47	20 39	3 35	20 46	3 39	21 03	3 55	21 01
5	3 51	20 19	4 01	20 29	3 53	20 31	3 48	20 39	3 36	20 46	3 40	21 02	3 56	21 00
6	3 52	20 18	4 02	20 28	3 54	20 31	3 49	20 38	3 37	20 45	3 41	21 01	3 57	21 00
7	3 53	20 18	4 03	20 27	3 55	20 30	3 50	20 37	3 38	20 44	3 43	21 01	3 58	20 59
8	3 53	20 17	4 04	20 27	3 56	20 29	3 51	20 36	3 39	20 43	3 44	21 00	3 59	20 58
9	3 54	20 16	4 05	20 26	3 57	20 29	3 52	20 36	3 40	20 42	3 45	20 59	4 00	20 57
10	3 56	20 15	4 06	20 25	3 58	20 28	3 53	20 35	3 42	20 41	3 46	20 58	4 01	20 56
11	3 57	20 15	4 07	20 24	3 59	20 27	3 55	20 34	3 43	20 40	3 47	20 57	4 03	20 55
12	3 58	20 14	4 08	20 24	4 00	20 26	3 56	20 33	3 44	20 39	3 49	20 56	4 04	20 54
13	3 59	20 13	4 09	20 23	4 01	20 25	3 57	20 32	3 45	20 38	3 50	20 54	4 05	20 53
14	4 00	20 12	4 10	20 22	4 02	20 24	3 58	20 31	3 47	20 37	3 52	20 53	4 07	20 52
15	4 01	20 11	4 11	20 21	4 04	20 23	4 00	20 30	3 48	20 36	3 53	20 52	4 08	20 51
16	4 02	20 10	4 12	20 20	4 05	20 22	4 01	20 28	3 50	20 35	3 55	20 50	4 09	20 49
17	4 04	20 09	4 14	20 19	4 06	20 21	4 02	20 27	3 51	20 33	3 56	20 49	4 11	20 48
18	4 05	20 08	4 15	20 17	4 07	20 20	4 04	20 26	3 53	20 32	3 58	20 48	4 12	20 47
19	4 06	20 06	4 16	20 16	4 09	20 18	4 05	20 25	3 54	20 30	3 59	20 46	4 14	20 45
20	4 07	20 05	4 18	20 15	4 10	20 17	4 06	20 23	3 56	20 29	4 01	20 45	4 15	20 44
21	4 09	20 04	4 19	20 14	4 11	20 16	4 08	20 22	3 57	20 28	4 03	20 43	4 17	20 43
22	4 10	20 03	4 20	20 13	4 13	20 14	4 09	20 21	3 59	20 26	4 04	20 41	4 18	20 41
23	4 11	20 01	4 22	20 11	4 14	20 13	4 11	20 19	4 00	20 24	4 06	20 40	4 20	20 40
24	4 13	20 00	4 23	20 10	4 16	20 12	4 12	20 18	4 02	20 23	4 08	20 38	4 21	20 38
25	4 14	19 59	4 24	20 08	4 17	20 10	4 14	20 16	4 04	20 21	4 09	20 36	4 23	20 36
26	4 16	19 57	4 26	20 07	4 19	20 09	4 15	20 14	4 05	20 19	4 11	20 35	4 25	20 35
27	4 17	19 56	4 27	20 06	4 20	20 07	4 17	20 13	4 07	20 18	4 13	20 33	4 26	20 33
28	4 19	19 54	4 29	20 04	4 22	20 05	4 19	20 11	4 09	20 16	4 15	20 31	4 28	20 31
29	4 20	19 53	4 30	20 02	4 23	20 04	4 20	20 10	4 11	20 14	4 17	20 29	4 30	20 29
30	4 21	19 51	4 32	20 01	4 25	20 02	4 22	20 08	4 12	20 12	4 18	20 27	4 32	20 28
31	4 23	19 49	4 33	19 59	4 26	20 01	4 23	20 06	4 14	20 10	4 20	20 25	4 33	20 26

JUPITER

Day	*R.A.*	*Dec.*	*Transit*	*5° high*	
				52°	*56°*
	h m	° ′	*h m*	*h m*	*h m*
1	19 20.4	−22 20	0 43	3 51	3 18
11	19 14.9	−22 31	23 53	3 05	2 31
21	19 09.5	−22 42	23 09	2 18	1 44
31	19 04.5	−22 51	22 24	1 33	0 58

Diameters – equatorial 47″ polar 44″

SATURN

Day	*R.A.*	*Dec.*	*Transit*	*5° high*	
				52°	*56°*
	h m	° ′	*h m*	*h m*	*h m*
1	10 28.0	+11 26	15 48	22 13	22 19
11	10 31.6	+11 04	15 12	21 36	21 41
21	10 35.5	+10 41	14 37	20 58	21 03
31	10 39.7	+10 15	14 02	20 21	20 26

Diameters – equatorial 16″ polar 15″
Rings – major axis 37″ minor axis 5″

URANUS

Day	*R.A.*	*Dec.*	*Transit*	*10° high*	
				52°	*56°*
	h m	° ′	*h m*	*h m*	*h m*
1	23 34.2	−3 38	4 56	0 22	0 32
11	23 34.0	−3 40	4 16	23 39	23 49
21	23 33.4	−3 44	3 36	22 59	23 09
31	23 32.7	−3 49	2 56	22 19	22 30

Diameter 4″

NEPTUNE

Day	*R.A.*	*Dec.*	*Transit*	*10° high*	
				52°	*56°*
	h m	° ′	*h m*	*h m*	*h m*
1	21 45.5	−13 52	3 07	23 33	0 01
11	21 44.7	−13 56	2 27	22 54	23 18
21	21 43.8	−14 00	1 47	22 14	22 38
31	21 42.9	−14 05	1 07	21 34	21 59

Diameter 2″

AUGUST 2008

EIGHTH MONTH, 31 DAYS. *Augustus*, formerly *Sextilis*, sixth month of Roman pre-Julian calendar

1	*Friday*	Kurmanbek Bakiyev, president of Kyrgyzstan b. 1949 Louis VI, king of France d. 1137	214
2	*Saturday*	Philippe II, regent of France b. 1674 Paul von Hindenburg, president of the Weimar Republic d. 1934	215
3	*Sunday*	Stanley Baldwin, British prime minister b. 1867 James II, king of Scotland d. 1460	216
4	*Monday*	Queen Elizabeth, the Queen Mother b. 1900 William Cecil, English politician d. 1598	week 31 day 217
5	*Tuesday*	C. V. Devan Nair, president of Singapore b. 1923 Frederick North, British prime minister d. 1792	218
6	*Wednesday*	The first atomic bomb was dropped at Hiroshima, Japan 1945	219
7	*Thursday*	Idi Amin ordered that all non-citizen Asians leave Uganda within 90 days 1972	220
8	*Friday*	Emiliano Zapata, Mexican revolutionary b. 1879 George Canning, British prime minister d. 1827	221
9	*Saturday*	Joop den Uyl, prime minister of the Netherlands b. 1919 Romano Prodi, prime minister of Italy b. 1939	222
10	*Sunday*	Herbert Hoover, US president b. 1874 Yahya Khan, president of Pakistan d. 1980	223
11	*Monday*	The constitution of the German Weimar Republic was signed into law 1919	week 32 day 224
12	*Tuesday*	Mohammad Hatta, vice-president of Indonesia b. 1902 Robert Stewart, British politician d. 1822	225
13	*Wednesday*	Fidel Castro, president of Cuba b. 1926 Ikeda Hayato, prime minister of Japan d. 1965	226
14	*Thursday*	Francis I, king of the Two Sicilies b. 1777 Jonathan Clarkson Gibbs, US politician d. 1874	227
15	*Friday*	Napoleon Bonaparte, emperor of France b. 1769 Macbeth, king of Scotland d. 1057	228
16	*Saturday*	The Peterloo Massacre at St. Peter's Fields, Manchester 1819	229
17	*Sunday*	Menelik II, emperor of Ethiopia b. 1844 Rudolph Hess, German Nazi officer d. 1987	230
18	*Monday*	John Russell, British prime minister b. 1792 Genghis Khan, Mongol leader d. 1227	week 33 day 231
19	*Tuesday*	Bill Clinton, US president b. 1946 Augustus, emperor of Rome d. AD 14	232
20	*Wednesday*	Raymond Poincaré, president of France b. 1860 Johan de Witt, Dutch politician d. 1672	233
21	*Thursday*	King William IV b. 1765 Sobhuza II, king of Swaziland d. 1982	234
22	*Friday*	Jomo Kenyatta, prime minister of Kenya d. 1978 Michael Collins, Irish revolutionary d. 1922	235
23	*Saturday*	Louis XVI, king of France b. 1754 William Wallace, Scottish resistance leader d. 1305	236
24	*Sunday*	Charles IX ordered the St Bartholomew's Day Massacre of the Huguenots in France 1572	237
25	*Monday*	Sean O' Kelly, president of Ireland b. 1882 Stanley Bruce, prime minister of Australia d. 1967	week 314 day 238
26	*Tuesday*	Prince Albert, consort of Queen Victoria b. 1819 Louis-Philippe, king of France d. 1850	239
27	*Wednesday*	Lord Mountbatten was killed by a bomb detonated on his boat by the IRA 1979	240
28	*Thursday*	Paul Martin, prime minister of Canada b. 1938 Prince William, son of King George V d. 1972	241
29	*Friday*	Andrew Fisher, prime minister of Australia b. 1862 Eamon de Valera, president of Ireland d. 1975	242
30	*Saturday*	Denis Healey, British chancellor of the exchequer b. 1917 Grigory Semyonov, Russian counter-revolutionary d. 1946	243
31	*Sunday*	Wilhelmina, queen of the Netherlands b. 1880 King Henry V d. 1422	244

ASTRONOMICAL PHENOMENA

d	*h*	
1	10	Total eclipse of Sun
1	16	Mercury in conjunction with Moon. Mercury 1°N.
2	13	Venus in conjunction with Moon. Venus 2°N.
3	11	Saturn in conjunction with Moon. Saturn 3°N.
4	09	Mars in conjunction with Moon. Mars 4°N.
13	15	Jupiter in conjunction with Moon. Jupiter 3°N.
13	17	Saturn in conjunction with Venus. Saturn 0°.2N.
15	08	Neptune at opposition
15	20	Saturn in conjunction with Mercury. Saturn 0°.6N.
16	21	Partial eclipse of Moon
21	16	Venus in conjunction with Mercury. Venus 1°N.
22	18	Sun's longitude 150° ♍
31	02	Saturn in conjunction with Moon. Saturn 4°N.

MINIMA OF ALGOL

d	*h*	*d*	*h*	*d*	*h*
3	16.5	15	03.8	26	15.0
6	13.3	18	00.6	29	11.8
9	10.1	20	21.4		
12	07.0	23	18.2		

CONSTELLATIONS

The following constellations are near their meridian at

	d	*h*		*d*	*h*
July	1	24	August	16	21
July	16	23	September	1	20
August	1	22	September	15	19

Draco, Hercules, Lyra, Cygnus, Sagitta, Ophiuchus, Serpens, Aquila and Sagittarius

THE MOON

Phases, Apsides and Node	*d*	*h*	*m*
● New Moon	1	10	13
☽ First Quarter	8	20	20
○ Full Moon	16	21	16
☾ Last Quarter	23	23	49
● New Moon	30	19	58
Apogee (404,594 km)	10	20	15
Perigee (368,664 km)	26	03	51

Mean longitude of ascending node on August 1, 319°

THE SUN

s.d. 15′.8

Day	Right Ascension			Dec. +		Equation of time		Rise 52°		Rise 56°		Transit		Set 52°		Set 56°		Sidereal time			Transit of first point of Aries		
	h	m	s	°	′	m	s	h	m	h	m	h	m	h	m	h	m	h	m	s	h	m	s
1	8	46	14	17	59	−6	20	4	22	4	04	12	06	19	49	20	07	20	39	54	3	19	33
2	8	50	06	17	43	−6	16	4	24	4	06	12	06	19	48	20	05	20	43	51	3	15	37
3	8	53	58	17	28	−6	11	4	25	4	08	12	06	19	46	20	03	20	47	47	3	11	41
4	8	57	50	17	12	−6	06	4	27	4	10	12	06	19	44	20	01	20	51	44	3	07	45
5	9	01	41	16	56	−6	00	4	28	4	12	12	06	19	42	19	59	20	55	40	3	03	50
6	9	05	31	16	39	−5	54	4	30	4	14	12	06	19	41	19	56	20	59	37	2	59	54
7	9	09	20	16	22	−5	47	4	32	4	16	12	06	19	39	19	54	21	03	33	2	55	58
8	9	13	09	16	06	−5	39	4	33	4	18	12	06	19	37	19	52	21	07	30	2	52	02
9	9	16	57	15	48	−5	31	4	35	4	20	12	05	19	35	19	50	21	11	26	2	48	06
10	9	20	45	15	31	−5	22	4	36	4	22	12	05	19	33	19	48	21	15	23	2	44	10
11	9	24	32	15	13	−5	13	4	38	4	24	12	05	19	31	19	45	21	19	20	2	40	14
12	9	28	19	14	55	−5	03	4	40	4	26	12	05	19	29	19	43	21	23	16	2	36	18
13	9	32	05	14	37	−4	52	4	41	4	28	12	05	19	27	19	41	21	27	13	2	32	22
14	9	35	50	14	19	−4	41	4	43	4	29	12	05	19	25	19	38	21	31	09	2	28	26
15	9	39	35	14	00	−4	30	4	44	4	31	12	04	19	23	19	36	21	35	06	2	24	30
16	9	43	20	13	41	−4	17	4	46	4	33	12	04	19	21	19	34	21	39	02	2	20	35
17	9	47	04	13	22	−4	05	4	48	4	35	12	04	19	19	19	31	21	42	59	2	16	39
18	9	50	47	13	03	−3	51	4	49	4	37	12	04	19	17	19	29	21	46	55	2	12	43
19	9	54	30	12	43	−3	38	4	51	4	39	12	04	19	15	19	26	21	50	52	2	08	47
20	9	58	12	12	24	−3	23	4	53	4	41	12	03	19	13	19	24	21	54	49	2	04	51
21	10	01	54	12	04	−3	09	4	54	4	43	12	03	19	11	19	21	21	58	45	2	00	55
22	10	05	35	11	44	−2	54	4	56	4	45	12	03	19	09	19	19	22	02	42	1	56	59
23	10	09	16	11	23	−2	38	4	57	4	47	12	03	19	06	19	17	22	06	38	1	53	03
24	10	12	57	11	03	−2	22	4	59	4	49	12	02	19	04	19	14	22	10	35	1	49	07
25	10	16	37	10	42	−2	06	5	01	4	51	12	02	19	02	19	12	22	14	31	1	45	11
26	10	20	17	10	21	−1	49	5	02	4	53	12	02	19	00	19	09	22	18	28	1	41	15
27	10	23	56	10	00	−1	32	5	04	4	55	12	01	18	58	19	06	22	22	24	1	37	20
28	10	27	36	9	39	−1	15	5	06	4	57	12	01	18	55	19	04	22	26	21	1	33	24
29	10	31	14	9	18	−0	57	5	07	4	59	12	01	18	53	19	01	22	30	18	1	29	28
30	10	34	53	8	57	−0	39	5	09	5	01	12	00	18	51	18	59	22	34	14	1	25	32
31	10	38	31	8	35	−0	20	5	11	5	03	12	00	18	49	18	56	22	38	11	1	21	36

DURATION OF TWILIGHT (in minutes)

Latitude	52°	56°	52°	56°	52°	56°	52°	56°
	1 August		*11 August*		*21 August*		*31 August*	
Civil	41	49	39	45	37	42	35	40
Nautical	97	121	90	107	84	97	79	90
Astronomical	179	TAN	154	210	139	168	128	148

THE NIGHT SKY

Mercury is unsuitably placed for observation throughout the month, though observers with binoculars or small telescopes might like to attempt an observation using Venus as a guide on the evening of the 21st when Mercury is only about 1 degree below Venus.

Venus, magnitude −3.9, becomes visible as an evening object at the beginning of the month, shortly after sunset, very low above the western horizon. Only under exceptionally good conditions, including a sea horizon, is it likely to be visible from as far north as Scotland.

Mars remains unsuitably placed for observation.

Jupiter, magnitude −2.6, continues to be visible as a conspicuous object in the south-western quadrant of the sky in the evenings. The waxing gibbous Moon passes 3 degrees south of the planet on the 13th. By the end of the month it is not visible after 23h from southern England, while the time is an hour earlier for Scotland.

Saturn is unsuitably placed for observation as it approaches conjunction early next month.

Neptune is at opposition on the 15th, in the constellation of Capricornus. It is not visible to the naked-eye since its magnitude is +7.9.

Meteors. The maximum of the famous Perseid meteor shower occurs on the morning of the 12th and will be best seen from the late evening of the 11th onwards, though there will be interference from the waxing gibbous Moon until shortly before midnight (observers should refer to the moonset times on the next page).

THE MOON

Day	R.A.		Dec.	Hor. Par.	Semi-diam.	Suns Co-Long.	PA of Br. Limb	Ph.	Age	Rise 52°		Rise 56°		Transit		Set 52°		Set 56°	
	h	m	°	′	′	°	°	%	d	h	m	h	m	h	m	h	m	h	m
1	8	24	+20.7	59.8	16.3	261	117	0	28.9	4	04	3	44	12	12	19	56	20	11
2	9	21	+15.6	59.2	16.1	273	287	0	0.6	5	33	5	20	13	04	20	13	20	22
3	10	13	+9.7	58.5	15.9	285	294	3	1.6	6	59	6	52	13	52	20	26	20	30
4	11	03	+3.6	57.7	15.7	297	296	8	2.6	8	20	8	18	14	37	20	38	20	37
5	11	50	−2.6	56.9	15.5	310	297	15	3.6	9	37	9	42	15	21	20	50	20	43
6	12	36	−8.5	56.1	15.3	322	296	23	4.6	10	53	11	03	16	04	21	03	20	51
7	13	22	−13.8	55.4	15.1	334	294	32	5.6	12	09	12	25	16	49	21	17	21	00
8	14	09	−18.5	54.9	15.0	346	291	42	6.6	13	23	13	45	17	34	21	36	21	13
9	14	58	−22.4	54.5	14.8	359	286	52	7.6	14	36	15	05	18	22	22	01	21	32
10	15	48	−25.3	54.3	14.8	11	281	61	8.6	15	44	16	19	19	11	22	35	22	00
11	16	40	−27.1	54.2	14.8	23	276	70	9.6	16	44	17	21	20	02	23	20	22	43
12	17	34	−27.6	54.3	14.8	35	270	78	10.6	17	32	18	07	20	54	—		23	44
13	18	28	−26.9	54.5	14.9	47	264	86	11.6	18	09	18	39	21	45	0	19	—	
14	19	21	−24.8	54.9	15.0	60	258	92	12.6	18	35	18	59	22	35	1	28	0	58
15	20	13	−21.6	55.4	15.1	72	253	96	13.6	18	55	19	13	23	22	2	43	2	20
16	21	03	−17.4	55.9	15.2	84	251	99	14.6	19	11	19	23	—		4	01	3	45
17	21	51	−12.3	56.4	15.4	96	44	100	15.6	19	24	19	31	0	09	5	19	5	09
18	22	39	−6.6	56.9	15.5	108	60	99	16.6	19	36	19	38	0	54	6	38	6	34
19	23	26	−0.5	57.4	15.7	120	61	95	17.6	19	48	19	45	1	38	7	57	7	58
20	0	14	+5.7	57.9	15.8	133	62	89	18.6	20	02	19	53	2	24	9	18	9	25
21	1	04	+11.8	58.3	15.9	145	64	81	19.6	20	18	20	03	3	11	10	42	10	55
22	1	56	+17.3	58.7	16.0	157	67	72	20.6	20	39	20	17	4	02	12	08	12	29
23	2	52	+22.0	59.0	16.1	169	72	61	21.6	21	09	20	40	4	57	13	36	14	04
24	3	52	+25.4	59.2	16.1	181	78	50	22.6	21	52	21	17	5	56	14	58	15	32
25	4	55	+27.3	59.4	16.2	194	85	39	23.6	22	53	22	17	6	58	16	07	16	44
26	5	59	+27.4	59.5	16.2	206	92	28	24.6	—		23	39	8	01	16	59	17	31
27	7	03	+25.7	59.4	16.2	218	99	18	25.6	0	10	—		9	02	17	35	18	00
28	8	03	+22.3	59.3	16.1	230	104	10	26.6	1	37	1	13	9	59	18	00	18	18
29	9	00	+17.6	58.9	16.1	243	108	4	27.6	3	06	2	49	10	53	18	18	18	30
30	9	53	+12.1	58.5	15.9	255	106	1	28.6	4	32	4	22	11	42	18	32	18	38
31	10	44	+6.0	57.9	15.8	267	334	0	0.2	5	54	5	50	12	28	18	45	18	46

MERCURY

Day	R.A.		Dec.	Diam.	Phase	Transit		5° high 52°		5° high 56°	
	h	m	°	″	%	h	m	h	m	h	m
1	8	58	+19.0	5	99	12	20	19	27	19	40
3	9	15	+17.8	5	98	12	29	19	28	19	40
5	9	30	+16.6	5	97	12	37	19	29	19	39
7	9	46	+15.3	5	95	12	44	19	29	19	38
9	10	00	+13.9	5	94	12	51	19	28	19	35
11	10	14	+12.5	5	92	12	57	19	26	19	33
13	10	28	+11.0	5	90	13	02	19	24	19	29
15	10	41	+9.6	5	88	13	07	19	21	19	25
17	10	53	+8.1	5	86	13	11	19	18	19	20
19	11	05	+6.6	5	84	13	15	19	14	19	16
21	11	16	+5.2	5	82	13	19	19	10	19	10
23	11	28	+3.7	6	80	13	22	19	06	19	05
25	11	38	+2.3	6	78	13	24	19	01	18	59
27	11	48	+0.8	6	76	13	27	18	56	18	53
29	11	58	−0.5	6	74	13	29	18	51	18	46
31	12	08	−1.9	6	71	13	30	18	45	18	40

VENUS

Day	R.A.		Dec.	Diam.	Phase	Transit		5° high 52°		5° high 56°	
	h	m	°	″	%	h	m	h	m	h	m
1	9	46	+15.0	10	97	13	06	19	50	19	59
6	10	10	+12.9	10	96	13	10	19	43	19	50
11	10	33	+10.7	10	95	13	14	19	35	19	40
16	10	56	+8.3	10	95	13	17	19	26	19	29
21	11	19	+5.9	11	94	13	20	19	16	19	17
26	11	41	+3.4	11	93	13	23	19	06	19	05
31	12	04	+0.8	11	92	13	26	18	55	18	52

MARS

Day	R.A.		Dec.	Diam.	Phase	Transit		5° high 52°		5° high 56°	
	h	m	°	″	%	h	m	h	m	h	m
1	11	19	+5.3	4	96	14	38	20	31	20	32
6	11	30	+4.1	4	96	14	30	20	16	20	16
11	11	42	+2.8	4	97	14	21	20	01	20	00
16	11	53	+1.5	4	97	14	13	19	47	19	44
21	12	05	+0.2	4	97	14	05	19	32	19	28
26	12	16	−1.2	4	97	13	57	19	17	19	12
31	12	28	−2.5	4	98	13	49	19	02	18	57

SUNRISE AND SUNSET

	London				*Bristol*				*Birmingham*				*Manchester*				*Newcastle*				*Glasgow*				*Belfast*			
	0°05′		*51°30′*		*2°35′*		*51°28′*		*1°55′*		*52°28′*		*2°15′*		*53°28′*		*1°37′*		*54°59′*		*4°14′*		*55°52′*		*5°56′*		*54°35′*	
d	*h*	*m*	*h*	*m*	*h*	*m*	*h*	*m*	*h*	*m*	*h*	*m*	*h*	*m*	*h*	*m*	*h*	*m*	*h*	*m*	*h*	*m*	*h*	*m*	*h*	*m*	*h*	*m*
1	4	24	19	48	4	35	19	58	4	28	19	59	4	25	20	04	4	16	20	08	4	22	20	23	4	35	20	24
2	4	26	19	46	4	36	19	56	4	30	19	57	4	27	20	02	4	18	20	07	4	24	20	21	4	37	20	22
3	4	27	19	44	4	38	19	54	4	31	19	55	4	28	20	01	4	19	20	05	4	26	20	19	4	38	20	20
4	4	29	19	43	4	39	19	53	4	33	19	54	4	30	19	59	4	21	20	03	4	28	20	17	4	40	20	18
5	4	31	19	41	4	41	19	51	4	34	19	52	4	32	19	57	4	23	20	01	4	30	20	15	4	42	20	16
6	4	32	19	39	4	42	19	49	4	36	19	50	4	34	19	55	4	25	19	58	4	32	20	13	4	44	20	14
7	4	34	19	37	4	44	19	47	4	38	19	48	4	35	19	53	4	27	19	56	4	33	20	11	4	46	20	12
8	4	35	19	36	4	45	19	45	4	39	19	46	4	37	19	51	4	29	19	54	4	35	20	08	4	47	20	10
9	4	37	19	34	4	47	19	44	4	41	19	44	4	39	19	49	4	30	19	52	4	37	20	06	4	49	20	08
10	4	38	19	32	4	48	19	42	4	43	19	42	4	40	19	47	4	32	19	50	4	39	20	04	4	51	20	06
11	4	40	19	30	4	50	19	40	4	44	19	40	4	42	19	45	4	34	19	48	4	41	20	02	4	53	20	04
12	4	41	19	28	4	52	19	38	4	46	19	38	4	44	19	43	4	36	19	46	4	43	19	59	4	55	20	01
13	4	43	19	26	4	53	19	36	4	47	19	36	4	46	19	41	4	38	19	43	4	45	19	57	4	57	19	59
14	4	45	19	24	4	55	19	34	4	49	19	34	4	47	19	39	4	40	19	41	4	47	19	55	4	58	19	57
15	4	46	19	22	4	56	19	32	4	51	19	32	4	49	19	37	4	42	19	39	4	49	19	52	5	00	19	55
16	4	48	19	20	4	58	19	30	4	52	19	30	4	51	19	34	4	43	19	37	4	51	19	50	5	02	19	53
17	4	49	19	18	5	00	19	28	4	54	19	28	4	53	19	32	4	45	19	34	4	53	19	48	5	04	19	50
18	4	51	19	16	5	01	19	26	4	56	19	26	4	54	19	30	4	47	19	32	4	55	19	45	5	06	19	48
19	4	53	19	14	5	03	19	24	4	57	19	24	4	56	19	28	4	49	19	30	4	57	19	43	5	07	19	46
20	4	54	19	12	5	04	19	22	4	59	19	22	4	58	19	26	4	51	19	27	4	59	19	40	5	09	19	43
21	4	56	19	10	5	06	19	20	5	01	19	20	4	59	19	23	4	53	19	25	5	01	19	38	5	11	19	41
22	4	57	19	08	5	07	19	18	5	02	19	17	5	01	19	21	4	55	19	23	5	03	19	36	5	13	19	39
23	4	59	19	06	5	09	19	16	5	04	19	15	5	03	19	19	4	56	19	20	5	04	19	33	5	15	19	36
24	5	01	19	03	5	11	19	13	5	06	19	13	5	05	19	17	4	58	19	18	5	06	19	31	5	17	19	34
25	5	02	19	01	5	12	19	11	5	07	19	11	5	06	19	14	5	00	19	15	5	08	19	28	5	18	19	32
26	5	04	18	59	5	14	19	09	5	09	19	08	5	08	19	12	5	02	19	13	5	10	19	26	5	20	19	29
27	5	05	18	57	5	15	19	07	5	11	19	06	5	10	19	10	5	04	19	10	5	12	19	23	5	22	19	27
28	5	07	18	55	5	17	19	05	5	12	19	04	5	12	19	07	5	06	19	08	5	14	19	21	5	24	19	24
29	5	09	18	53	5	19	19	03	5	14	19	02	5	13	19	05	5	08	19	06	5	16	19	18	5	26	19	22
30	5	10	18	50	5	20	19	00	5	16	18	59	5	15	19	03	5	10	19	03	5	18	19	15	5	28	19	20
31	5	12	18	48	5	22	18	58	5	17	18	57	5	17	19	00	5	11	19	01	5	20	19	13	5	29	19	17

JUPITER

Day	*R.A.*		*Dec.*		*Transit*		*5° high*			
							52°		*56°*	
	h	*m*	°	′	*h*	*m*	*h*	*m*	*h*	*m*
1	19	04.0	−22	52	22	20	1	28	0	54
11	18	59.9	−22	59	21	37	0	44	0	09
21	18	56.9	−23	05	20	55	0	01	23	21
31	18	55.1	−23	08	20	14	23	15	22	39

Diameters – equatorial 45″ polar 42″

SATURN

Day	*R.A.*		*Dec.*		*Transit*		*5° high*			
							52°		*56°*	
	h	*m*	°	′	*h*	*m*	*h*	*m*	*h*	*m*
1	10	40.2	+10	13	13	58	20	17	20	22
11	10	44.6	+9	46	13	23	19	40	19	45
21	10	49.2	+9	18	12	49	19	03	19	07
31	10	53.9	+8	50	12	14	18	26	18	30

Diameters – equatorial 16″ polar 14″
Rings – major axis 36″ minor axis 4″

URANUS

Day	*R.A.*		*Dec.*		*Transit*		*10° high*			
							52°		*56°*	
	h	*m*	°	′	*h*	*m*	*h*	*m*	*h*	*m*
1	23	32.6	−3	50	2	52	22	15	22	26
11	23	31.5	−3	57	2	12	21	36	21	46
21	23	30.3	−4	05	1	31	20	56	21	07
31	23	28.9	−4	14	0	51	20	16	20	27

Diameter 4″

NEPTUNE

Day	*R.A.*		*Dec.*		*Transit*		*10° high*			
							52°		*56°*	
	h	*m*	°	′	*h*	*m*	*h*	*m*	*h*	*m*
1	21	42.8	−14	06	1	03	4	31	4	07
11	21	41.7	−14	11	0	22	3	50	3	26
21	21	40.7	−14	17	23	38	3	09	2	44
31	21	39.6	−14	22	22	58	2	28	2	03

Diameter 2″

SEPTEMBER 2008

NINTH MONTH, 30 DAYS. *Septem* (seven), seventh month of Roman pre-Julian calendar

1	*Monday*	Abdur Rahman Biswas, president of Bangladesh b. 1926 Louis XIV, king of France d. 1715	week 35 day 245
2	*Tuesday*	Daniel arap Moi, president of Kenya b. 1924 Dawit II, emperor of Ethiopia d. 1540	246
3	*Wednesday*	Gaston Thorn, president of the EC b. 1928 Edvard Benes, president of Czechoslovakia d. 1948	247
4	*Thursday*	Carlos Romero Barcelo, governor of Puerto Rico b. 1932 Robert Dudley, English statesman d. 1588	248
5	*Friday*	Benita Ferrero-Waldner, Austrian politician b. 1948 Crazy Horse, Native American leader d. 1877	249
6	*Saturday*	11 Israeli hostages, 5 terrorists and a German police officer were killed in the Munich Massacre 1972	250
7	*Sunday*	Queen Elizabeth I b. 1533 Mobutu Sese Seko, president of Zaire d. 1997	251
8	*Monday*	The Former Yugoslav Republic of Macedonia gained independence from Yugoslavia 1991	week 36 day 252
9	*Tuesday*	Susilo Bambang Chinese leader d. 1976	253
10	*Wednesday*	Nicolás Bravo, president of Mexico b. 1786 Taufa'ahau Tupou IV, king of Tonga d. 2006	254
11	*Thursday*	Ferdinand Marcos, president of the Philippines b. 1917 Salvador Allende, president of Chile d. 1973	255
12	*Friday*	H. H. Asquith, British prime minister b. 1852 Steve Biko, South African anti-apartheid activist d. 1977	256
13	*Saturday*	John II Komnenos, Byzantine emperor b. 1087 Charles James Fox, British foreign secretary d. 1806	257
14	*Sunday*	Jacobo Arbenz Guzmán, president of Guatemala b. 1913 Arthur Wellesley, British prime minister d. 1852	258
15	*Monday*	Joseph Lyons, prime minister of Australia b. 1879 Andre Tardieu, prime minister of France d. 1945	week 35 day 259
16	*Tuesday*	Andrew Bonar Law, British prime minister b. 1858 Louis XVIII, king of France d. 1824	260
17	*Wednesday*	Tessa Jowell, British politician b. 1947 Spiro Agnew, US vice-president d. 1996	261
18	*Thursday*	Jorge Sampaio, president of Portugal b. 1939 Dag Hammarskjüld, UN secretary-general d. 1961	262
19	*Friday*	Giuseppe Saragat, president of Italy b. 1898 James Garfield, US president d. 1881	263
20	*Saturday*	Ananda Mahidol, king of Thailand b. 1925 Gareth Williams, British politician d. 2003	264
21	*Sunday*	Girolamo Savonarola, ruler of Florence b. 1452 King Edward II d. 1327	265
22	*Monday*	Anne of Cleves, wife of King Henry VIII b. 1515 Kaarlo Juho Stahlberg, president of Finland d. 1952	week 38 day 266
23	*Tuesday*	Augustus, emperor of Rome b. 63 BC Louis-Joseph Papineau, French-Canadian politician d. 1871	267
24	*Wednesday*	Konstantin Chernenko, Soviet leader b. 1911 Pedro I, emperor of Brazil d. 1834	268
25	*Thursday*	King Harold II defeated Harold Hardrada, king of Norway, at the Battle of Stamford Bridge 1066	269
26	*Friday*	Christian X, king of Denmark b. 1870 James Keir Hardie, British politician d. 1915	270
27	*Saturday*	The Taliban took control of Kabul, Afghanistan, after three days of fighting 1996	271
28	*Sunday*	Augustus Fitzroy, British prime minister b. 1735 Wenceslas I, Duke of Bohemia d. 929	272
29	*Monday*	Robert Clive, British statesman b. 1725 Nguyen Van Thieu, president of South Vietnam d. 2001	week 38 day 273
30	*Tuesday*	Henry Bolingbroke proclaimed himself King Henry IV upon the abdication of Richard II 1399	274

ASTRONOMICAL PHENOMENA

d	*h*	
1	16	Venus in conjunction with Moon. Venus 5°N.
1	21	Mercury in conjunction with Moon. Mercury 3°N.
2	04	Mars in conjunction with Moon. Mars 5°N.
4	02	Saturn in conjunction
8	04	Jupiter at stationary point
8	18	Mars in conjunction with Mercury. Mars 3°N.
9	03	Pluto at stationary point
9	21	Jupiter in conjunction with Moon. Jupiter 3°N.
11	04	Mercury at greatest elongation E. 27°
12	02	Mars in conjunction with Venus. Mars 0°.3S.
13	02	Uranus at opposition
15	02	Venus in conjunction with Mercury. Venus 4°N.
22	16	Sun's longitude 180° ♎
23	11	Mars in conjunction with Mercury. Mars 4° N.
24	07	Mercury at stationary point
27	16	Saturn in conjunction with Moon. Saturn 4°N.
30	10	Mercury in conjunction with Moon. Mercury 1°N.

MINIMA OF ALGOL

d	*h*	*d*	*h*	*d*	*h*
1	08.6	12	19.9	24	07.1
4	05.4	15	16.7	27	03.9
7	02.2	18	13.5	30	00.7
9	23.0	21	10.3		

CONSTELLATIONS

The following constellations are near their meridian at

	d	*h*		*d*	*h*
August	1	24	September	15	21
August	16	23	October	1	20
September	1	22	October	16	19

Draco, Cepheus, Lyra, Cygnus, Vulpecula, Sagitta, Delphinus, Equuleus, Aquila, Aquarius and Capricornus

THE MOON

Phases, Apsides and Node	*d*	*h*	*m*
☽ First Quarter	7	14	04
○ Full Moon	15	09	13
☾ Last Quarter	22	05	04
● New Moon	29	08	12
Apogee (404,254km)	7	14	57
Perigee (368,854km)	20	03	35

Mean longitude of ascending node on September 1, 317°

THE SUN

s.d. 15′.9

Day	Right Ascension h m s	Dec. ° ′	Equation of time m s	Rise 52° h m	Rise 56° h m	Transit h m	Set 52° h m	Set 56° h m	Sidereal time h m s	Transit of first point of Aries h m s
1	10 42 08	+8 13	−0 01	5 12	5 05	12 00	18 46	18 54	22 42 07	1 17 40
2	10 45 46	+7 51	+0 18	5 14	5 07	12 00	18 44	18 51	22 46 04	1 13 44
3	10 49 23	+7 29	+0 37	5 15	5 09	11 59	18 42	18 48	22 50 00	1 09 48
4	10 53 00	+7 07	+0 57	5 17	5 11	11 59	18 40	18 46	22 53 57	1 05 52
5	10 56 37	+6 45	+1 17	5 19	5 13	11 59	18 37	18 43	22 57 53	1 01 56
6	11 00 13	+6 23	+1 37	5 20	5 15	11 58	18 35	18 41	23 01 50	0 58 00
7	11 03 49	+6 00	+1 57	5 22	5 16	11 58	18 33	18 38	23 05 47	0 54 05
8	11 07 25	+5 38	+2 18	5 24	5 18	11 58	18 30	18 35	23 09 43	0 50 09
9	11 11 01	+5 15	+2 39	5 25	5 20	11 57	18 28	18 33	23 13 40	0 46 13
10	11 14 36	+4 53	+3 00	5 27	5 22	11 57	18 26	18 30	23 17 36	0 42 17
11	11 18 12	+4 30	+3 21	5 28	5 24	11 56	18 23	18 27	23 21 33	0 38 21
12	11 21 47	+4 07	+3 42	5 30	5 26	11 56	18 21	18 25	23 25 29	0 34 25
13	11 25 23	+3 44	+4 03	5 32	5 28	11 56	18 19	18 22	23 29 26	0 30 29
14	11 28 58	+3 21	+4 25	5 33	5 30	11 55	18 16	18 19	23 33 22	0 26 33
15	11 32 33	+2 58	+4 46	5 35	5 32	11 55	18 14	18 17	23 37 19	0 22 37
16	11 36 08	+2 35	+5 08	5 37	5 34	11 55	18 12	18 14	23 41 16	0 18 41
17	11 39 43	+2 12	+5 29	5 38	5 36	11 54	18 09	18 11	23 45 12	0 14 45
18	11 43 18	+1 49	+5 51	5 40	5 38	11 54	18 07	18 09	23 49 09	0 10 50
19	11 46 53	+1 25	+6 12	5 41	5 40	11 54	18 05	18 06	23 53 05	0 06 54
20	11 50 28	+1 02	+6 34	5 43	5 42	11 53	18 02	18 04	23 57 02	0 02 58 23 59 02
21	11 54 03	+0 39	+6 55	5 45	5 44	11 53	18 00	18 01	0 00 58	23 55 06
22	11 57 39	+0 15	+7 16	5 46	5 46	11 53	17 58	17 58	0 04 55	23 51 10
23	12 01 14	−0 08	+7 37	5 48	5 48	11 52	17 55	17 56	0 08 51	23 47 14
24	12 04 50	−0 31	+7 58	5 50	5 50	11 52	17 53	17 53	0 12 48	23 43 18
25	12 08 26	−0 55	+8 19	5 51	5 52	11 52	17 51	17 50	0 16 45	23 39 22
26	12 12 02	−1 18	+8 40	5 53	5 54	11 51	17 48	17 48	0 20 41	23 35 26
27	12 15 38	−1 42	+9 00	5 55	5 56	11 51	17 46	17 45	0 24 38	23 31 31
28	12 19 14	−2 05	+9 20	5 56	5 58	11 51	17 44	17 42	0 28 34	23 27 35
29	12 22 51	−2 28	+9 40	5 58	6 00	11 50	17 41	17 40	0 32 31	23 23 39
30	12 26 28	−2 52	+10 00	6 00	6 02	11 50	17 39	17 37	0 36 27	23 19 43

DURATION OF TWILIGHT (in minutes)

Latitude	52°	56°	52°	56°	52°	56°	52°	56°
	1 September		*11 September*		*21 September*		*31 September*	
Civil	35	39	34	38	34	37	34	37
Nautical	79	89	76	85	74	82	73	80
Astronomical	127	147	120	136	116	129	113	125

THE NIGHT SKY

Mercury remains too close to the Sun for observation throughout September even though it is at its greatest eastern elongation on the 11th.

Venus, magnitude −3.9, continues to be visible as a difficult evening object for a very short time after sunset, very low above the western horizon. Although it is farther from the Sun at the end of the month compared with the beginning, its rapid southward motion in declination negates this increase in elongation so that the time available for observation remains almost exactly the same throughout September. It is still unlikely to be glimpsed by observers as far north as Scotland.

Mars continues to be unsuitably placed for observation.

Jupiter continues to be visible as a brilliant object in the south-western sky in the evenings, magnitude −2.4. On the 8th Jupiter reaches its second stationary point and resumes its direct motion, while on the following evening the waxing gibbous Moon passes 3 degrees south of the planet.

Saturn, magnitude +0.9, is still too close to the Sun for observation at first, but gradually becomes visible as a difficult morning object during the last few days of September, low above the eastern horizon before the morning twilight inhibits observation. The thin waning crescent Moon is near the planet on the mornings of the 27th and 28th.

Uranus is at opposition on the 13th, in the constellation of Aquarius. Uranus is barely visible to the naked eye as its magnitude is +5.7, but it is readily located with only small optical aid.

Zodiacal Light. The morning cone may be observed stretching up from the eastern horizon, along the ecliptic, before the beginning of morning twilight, from the beginning of the month until the 13th. This faint phenomenon is only visible under good conditions and in the absence of both moonlight and artificial lighting.

THE MOON

Day	R.A.		Dec.	Hor. Par.	Semi-diam.	Sun's Co-Long.	PA. of Br. Limb	Ph.	Age	Rise 52°		Rise 56°		Transit		Set 52°		Set 56°	
	h	m	°	′	′	°	°	%	d	h	m	h	m	h	m	h	m	h	m
1	11	31	−0.2	57.3	15.6	279	305	2	1.2	7	14	7	15	13	13	18	57	18	53
2	12	18	−6.2	56.6	15.4	292	301	5	2.2	8	31	8	39	13	57	19	09	19	00
3	13	05	−11.9	55.9	15.2	304	298	11	3.2	9	48	10	01	14	41	19	23	19	08
4	13	52	−16.9	55.3	15.1	316	295	18	4.2	11	04	11	23	15	27	19	40	19	20
5	14	41	−21.1	54.8	14.9	328	291	26	5.2	12	18	12	44	16	14	20	02	19	36
6	15	31	−24.4	54.5	14.8	340	286	35	6.2	13	29	14	01	17	03	20	32	20	00
7	16	23	−26.5	54.3	14.8	353	280	45	7.2	14	33	15	09	17	54	21	13	20	37
8	17	16	−27.5	54.3	14.8	5	274	54	8.2	15	26	16	02	18	45	22	06	21	30
9	18	09	−27.2	54.4	14.8	17	268	63	9.2	16	07	16	39	19	36	23	10	22	39
10	19	03	−25.6	54.7	14.9	29	262	72	10.2	16	37	17	03	20	26	–		23	57
11	19	55	−22.8	55.2	15.0	41	257	81	11.2	16	59	17	20	21	14	0	23	–	
12	20	45	−19.0	55.8	15.2	54	254	88	12.2	17	17	17	31	22	01	1	40	1	21
13	21	34	−14.1	56.4	15.4	66	252	94	13.2	17	31	17	40	22	47	2	58	2	46
14	22	23	−8.6	57.1	15.6	78	253	98	14.2	17	44	17	47	23	33	4	17	4	11
15	23	11	−2.5	57.7	15.7	90	275	100	15.2	17	56	17	55	–		5	37	5	36
16	23	59	+3.8	58.3	15.9	102	42	99	16.2	18	09	18	02	0	19	6	59	7	04
17	0	50	+10.0	58.8	16.0	115	56	97	17.2	18	25	18	12	1	06	8	24	8	35
18	1	42	+15.9	59.2	16.1	127	62	91	18.2	18	45	18	25	1	57	9	52	10	09
19	2	38	+20.9	59.4	16.2	139	67	84	19.2	19	12	18	45	2	52	11	21	11	46
20	3	38	+24.7	59.4	16.2	151	74	75	20.2	19	51	19	18	3	50	12	46	13	18
21	4	41	+26.9	59.4	16.2	163	81	64	21.2	20	46	20	10	4	52	14	00	14	36
22	5	45	+27.4	59.3	16.2	175	88	53	22.2	21	58	21	25	5	54	14	57	15	30
23	6	48	+26.1	59.1	16.1	188	95	41	23.2	23	21	22	55	6	55	15	36	16	04
24	7	48	+23.2	58.8	16.0	200	101	30	24.2	–		–		7	53	16	04	16	24
25	8	45	+18.9	58.4	15.9	212	106	21	25.5	0	47	0	28	8	46	16	24	16	38
26	9	38	+13.7	58.1	15.8	224	108	12	26.2	2	12	2	00	9	36	16	39	16	47
27	10	28	+8.0	57.6	15.7	236	109	6	27.2	3	34	3	28	10	22	16	52	16	55
28	11	15	+1.9	57.1	15.6	249	104	2	28.2	4	53	4	52	11	07	17	04	17	02
29	12	02	−4.1	56.6	15.4	261	72	0	29.2	6	10	6	15	11	51	17	16	17	09
30	12	49	−9.9	56.0	15.3	273	322	1	0.7	7	27	7	38	12	35	17	30	17	17

MERCURY

Day	R.A.		Dec.	Diam.	Phase	Transit		5° high 52°		5° high 56°	
	h	m	°	″	%	h	m	h	m	h	m
1	12	12	−2.5	6	70	13	31	18	42	18	36
3	12	21	−3.8	6	68	13	32	18	37	18	30
5	12	30	−5.1	6	65	13	32	18	30	18	22
7	12	38	−6.2	7	63	13	32	18	24	18	15
9	12	46	−7.4	7	60	13	32	18	18	18	08
11	12	53	−8.4	7	57	13	31	18	11	18	00
13	12	59	−9.4	7	53	13	29	18	04	17	52
15	13	05	−10.2	7	50	13	27	17	57	17	44
17	13	10	−11.0	8	46	13	24	17	50	17	36
19	13	14	−11.6	8	42	13	20	17	42	17	27
21	13	17	−12.1	8	37	13	14	17	34	17	19
23	13	18	−12.3	9	32	13	08	17	26	17	11
25	13	19	−12.4	9	26	13	00	17	18	17	03
27	13	17	−12.2	9	20	12	50	17	10	16	55
29	13	14	−11.8	10	15	12	38	17	01	16	47
31	13	09	−11.1	10	9	12	25	16	53	16	40

VENUS

Day	R.A.		Dec.	Diam.	Phase	Transit		5° high 52°		5° high 56°	
	h	m	°	″	%	h	m	h	m	h	m
1	12	08	+0.3	11	92	13	26	18	53	18	50
6	12	30	−2.3	11	91	13	29	18	42	18	37
11	12	53	−4.8	11	90	13	31	18	31	18	23
16	13	15	−7.4	11	89	13	34	18	20	18	10
21	13	38	−9.8	12	88	13	37	18	09	17	57
26	14	01	−12.2	12	87	13	40	17	59	17	43
31	14	24	−14.5	12	86	13	44	17	48	17	30

MARS

Day	R.A.		Dec.	Diam.	Phase	Transit		5° high 52°		5° high 56°	
	h	m	°	″	%	h	m	h	m	h	m
1	12	30	−2.7	4	98	13	47	18	59	18	53
6	12	42	−4.1	4	98	13	40	18	44	18	37
11	12	54	−5.4	4	98	13	32	18	30	18	21
16	13	06	−6.7	4	98	13	24	18	15	18	06
21	13	19	−8.0	4	99	13	17	18	00	17	50
26	13	31	−9.3	4	99	13	10	17	46	17	34
31	13	44	−10.5	4	99	13	03	17	31	17	18

SUNRISE AND SUNSET

	London				*Bristol*				*Birmingham*				*Manchester*				*Newcastle*				*Glasgow*				*Belfast*			
	0°05′		*51°30′*		*2°35′*		*51°28′*		*1°55′*		*52°28′*		*2°15′*		*53°28′*		*1°37′*		*54°59′*		*4°14′*		*55°52′*		*5°56′*		*54°35′*	
d	*h*	*m*	*h*	*m*	*h*	*m*	*h*	*m*	*h*	*m*	*h*	*m*	*h*	*m*	*h*	*m*	*h*	*m*	*h*	*m*	*h*	*m*	*h*	*m*	*h*	*m*	*h*	*m*
1	5	13	18	46	5	23	18	56	5	19	18	55	5	19	18	58	5	13	18	58	5	22	19	10	5	31	19	15
2	5	15	18	44	5	25	18	54	5	21	18	53	5	20	18	56	5	15	18	56	5	24	19	08	5	33	19	12
3	5	17	18	41	5	27	18	51	5	22	18	50	5	22	18	53	5	17	18	53	5	26	19	05	5	35	19	10
4	5	18	18	39	5	28	18	49	5	24	18	48	5	24	18	51	5	19	18	51	5	28	19	03	5	37	19	07
5	5	20	18	37	5	30	18	47	5	26	18	46	5	26	18	48	5	21	18	48	5	30	19	00	5	39	19	05
6	5	21	18	35	5	31	18	45	5	27	18	43	5	27	18	46	5	23	18	46	5	32	18	57	5	40	19	02
7	5	23	18	32	5	33	18	42	5	29	18	41	5	29	18	44	5	24	18	43	5	34	18	55	5	42	19	00
8	5	24	18	30	5	35	18	40	5	31	18	39	5	31	18	41	5	26	18	40	5	36	18	52	5	44	18	57
9	5	26	18	28	5	36	18	38	5	32	18	36	5	33	18	39	5	28	18	38	5	38	18	49	5	46	18	55
10	5	28	18	26	5	38	18	36	5	34	18	34	5	34	18	36	5	30	18	35	5	39	18	47	5	48	18	52
11	5	29	18	23	5	39	18	33	5	36	18	32	5	36	18	34	5	32	18	33	5	41	18	44	5	50	18	50
12	5	31	18	21	5	41	18	31	5	37	18	29	5	38	18	31	5	34	18	30	5	43	18	42	5	51	18	47
13	5	32	18	19	5	42	18	29	5	39	18	27	5	40	18	29	5	36	18	28	5	45	18	39	5	53	18	45
14	5	34	18	16	5	44	18	26	5	41	18	24	5	41	18	26	5	37	18	25	5	47	18	36	5	55	18	42
15	5	36	18	14	5	46	18	24	5	42	18	22	5	43	18	24	5	39	18	23	5	49	18	34	5	57	18	39
16	5	37	18	12	5	47	18	22	5	44	18	20	5	45	18	22	5	41	18	20	5	51	18	31	5	59	18	37
17	5	39	18	10	5	49	18	19	5	46	18	17	5	46	18	19	5	43	18	17	5	53	18	28	6	01	18	34
18	5	40	18	07	5	50	18	17	5	47	18	15	5	48	18	17	5	45	18	15	5	55	18	26	6	02	18	32
19	5	42	18	05	5	52	18	15	5	49	18	13	5	50	18	14	5	47	18	12	5	57	18	23	6	04	18	29
20	5	44	18	03	5	54	18	13	5	51	18	10	5	52	18	12	5	49	18	10	5	59	18	20	6	06	18	27
21	5	45	18	00	5	55	18	10	5	52	18	08	5	53	18	09	5	51	18	07	6	01	18	18	6	08	18	24
22	5	47	17	58	5	57	18	08	5	54	18	05	5	55	18	07	5	52	18	05	6	03	18	15	6	10	18	22
23	5	48	17	56	5	58	18	06	5	56	18	03	5	57	18	04	5	54	18	02	6	05	18	12	6	12	18	19
24	5	50	17	53	6	00	18	03	5	57	18	01	5	59	18	02	5	56	17	59	6	07	18	10	6	13	18	17
25	5	52	17	51	6	02	18	01	5	59	17	58	6	00	18	00	5	58	17	57	6	09	18	07	6	15	18	14
26	5	53	17	49	6	03	17	59	6	01	17	56	6	02	17	57	6	00	17	54	6	11	18	05	6	17	18	12
27	5	55	17	46	6	05	17	56	6	02	17	54	6	04	17	55	6	02	17	52	6	12	18	02	6	19	18	09
28	5	57	17	44	6	07	17	54	6	04	17	51	6	06	17	52	6	04	17	49	6	14	17	59	6	21	18	07
29	5	58	17	42	6	08	17	52	6	06	17	49	6	08	17	50	6	06	17	47	6	16	17	57	6	23	18	04
30	6	00	17	40	6	10	17	50	6	08	17	47	6	09	17	47	6	07	17	44	6	18	17	54	6	25	18	02

JUPITER

Day	*R.A.*		*Dec.*		*Transit*		*5° high*			
							52°		*56°*	
	h	*m*	°	′	*h*	*m*	*h*	*m*	*h*	*m*
1	18	55.0	–23	08	20	09	23	11	22	35
11	18	54.7	–23	09	19	30	22	31	21	56
21	18	55.7	–23	08	18	52	21	53	21	18
31	18	58.2	–23	06	18	15	21	17	20	42

Diameters – equatorial 42″ polar 39″

SATURN

Day	*R.A.*		*Dec.*		*Transit*		*5° high*			
							52°		*56°*	
	h	*m*	°	′	*h*	*m*	*h*	*m*	*h*	*m*
1	10	54.4	+8	47	12	11	5	59	5	55
11	10	59.1	+8	19	11	36	5	27	5	23
21	11	03.8	+7	51	11	01	4	55	4	51
31	11	08.4	+7	23	10	26	4	22	4	19

Diameters – equatorial 16″ polar 14″

Rings – major axis 36″ minor axis 3″

URANUS

Day	*R.A.*		*Dec.*		*Transit*		*10° high*			
							52°		*56°*	
	h	*m*	°	′	*h*	*m*	*h*	*m*	*h*	*m*
1	23	28.8	–4	15	0	47	5	17	5	06
11	23	27.3	–4	24	0	06	4	35	4	24
21	23	25.8	–4	34	23	21	3	54	3	42
31	23	24.4	–4	43	22	40	3	12	3	01

Diameter 4″

NEPTUNE

Day	*R.A.*		*Dec.*		*Transit*		*10° high*			
							52°		*56°*	
	h	*m*	°	′	*h*	*m*	*h*	*m*	*h*	*m*
1	21	39.5	–14	23	22	54	2	24	1	59
11	21	38.6	–14	28	22	13	1	43	1	18
21	21	37.7	–14	32	21	33	1	02	0	37
31	21	37.0	–14	36	20	53	0	22	23	53

Diameter 2″

OCTOBER 2008

TENTH MONTH, 31 DAYS. *Octo* (eighth), eighth month of Roman pre-Julian calendar

1	*Wednesday*	The People's Republic of China was formally established 1949	275
2	*Thursday*	Charles Albert, king of Sardinia b. 1798 William Cavendish, British prime minister d. 1764	276
3	*Friday*	John Ross, Cherokee chief b. 1790 Gustav Stresemann, chancellor of the Weimar Republic d. 1929	277
4	*Saturday*	Ann Widdecombe, British politician b. 1947 Vladimir Yaroslavich, prince of Novgorod d. 1052	278
5	*Sunday*	Eduardo Duhalde, president of Argentina b. 1941 Henry III, Holy Roman Emperor d. 1056	279
6	*Monday*	Gerry Adams, Irish Republican politician b. 1948 Anwar al-Sadat, president of Egypt d. 1981	week 40 day 280
7	*Tuesday*	Fernando Belaunde Terry, president of Peru b. 1912 Alfred Deakin, prime minister of Australia d. 1919	281
8	*Wednesday*	Betty Boothroyd, British politician b. 1929 Willy Brandt, chancellor of West Germany d. 1992	282
9	*Thursday*	Che Guevara, the Marxist revolutionary, was executed by the Bolivian army 1967	283
10	*Friday*	Radu Vasile, prime minister of Romania b. 1942 Édouard Daladier, prime minister of France d. 1970	284
11	*Saturday*	Arthur Phillip, British colonialist b. 1738 Donald Dewar, first minister of Scotland d. 2000	285
12	*Sunday*	Ramsay Macdonald, British prime minister b. 1866 Anthony Berry, British politician d. 1984	286
13	*Monday*	Margaret Thatcher, British prime minister b. 1925 Le Duc Tho, Vietnamese politician d. 1990	week 41 day 287
14	*Tuesday*	King James II of England and Ireland, and VII of Scotland b. 1633 King Harold II d. 1066	288
15	*Wednesday*	Sali Berisha, president of Albania b. 1944 Pierre Laval, prime minister of France d. 1945	289
16	*Thursday*	David Ben-Gurion, Israeli prime minister b. 1886 Marie Antoinette, queen consort of France d. 1793	290
17	*Friday*	John Wilkes, English politician b. 1725 Philip Sidney, English statesman d. 1586	291
18	*Saturday*	Violeta Chamorro, president of Nicaragua b. 1929 Bess Truman, US first lady d. 1982	292
19	*Sunday*	Myeongseong, empress of Korea b. 1851 King John d. 1216	293
20	*Monday*	Henry Temple, British prime minister b. 1784 Charles VI, Holy Roman Emperor d. 1740	week 42 day 294
21	*Tuesday*	Alphonse de Lamartine, French statesman b. 1790 Horatio Nelson, British naval commander d. 1805	295
22	*Wednesday*	US president John F. Kennedy announced the discovery of Soviet nuclear weapons in Cuba 1962	296
23	*Thursday*	Fatmir Sejdiu, president of Kosovo b. 1951 Edward Smith-Stanley, British prime minister d. 1869	297
24	*Friday*	Domitian, emperor of Rome b. AD 51 Jo Grimond, leader of the Liberal Party d. 1993	298
25	*Saturday*	Michael I, king of Romania b. 1921 King George II d. 1760	299
26	*Sunday*	Thorvald Stauning, prime minister of Denmark b. 1873 Alfred, king of Wessex d. 899	300
27	*Monday*	Theodore Roosevelt, US president b. 1858 Athelstan, king of England d. 939	week 43 day 301
28	*Tuesday*	Mahmoud Ahmadinejad, president of Iran b. 1956 Jahangir, ruler of the Mughal Empire d. 1627	302
29	*Wednesday*	Ellen Johnson-Sirleaf, president of Liberia b. 1938 Walter Raleigh, English courtier d. 1618	303
30	*Thursday*	R. B. Sheridan, Irish politician b. 1751 William Cavendish-Bentinck, British prime minister d. 1809	304
31	*Friday*	Norodom Sihanouk, king of Cambodia b. 1922 Michael Stasinopoulos, president of Greece d. 2002	305

ASTRONOMICAL PHENOMENA

d	*h*	
1	00	Mars in conjunction with Moon. Mars 5°N.
1	23	Venus in conjunction with Moon. Venus 5°N.
6	21	Mercury in inferior conjunction
7	08	Jupiter in conjunction with Moon. Jupiter 2°N.
15	20	Mercury at stationary point
22	09	Mercury at greatest elongation W. 18°
23	01	Sun's longitude 210° ♏
25	04	Saturn in conjunction with Moon. Saturn 4°N.
27	12	Mercury in conjunction with Moon. Mercury 7°N.
29	22	Mars in conjunction with Moon. Mars 5°N.

MINIMA OF ALGOL

d	*h*	*d*	*h*	*d*	*h*
2	21.5	14	08.8	25	20.0
5	18.3	17	05.6	28	16.8
8	15.2	20	02.4	31	13.7
11	12.0	22	23.2		

CONSTELLATIONS

The following constellations are near their meridian at

	d	*h*		*d*	*h*
September	1	24	October	16	21
September	15	23	November	1	20
October	1	22	November	15	19

Ursa Major (below the Pole), Cepheus, Cassiopeia, Cygnus, Lacerta, Andromeda, Pegasus, Capricornus, Aquarius and Piscis Austrinus

THE MOON

Phases, Apsides and Node	*d*	*h*	*m*
☽ First Quarter	7	09	04
○ Full Moon	14	20	02
☾ Last Quarter	21	11	55
● New Moon	28	23	14
Apogee (404,758 km)	5	10	37
Perigee (363,802 km)	17	06	17

Mean longitude of ascending node on October 1, 316°

THE SUN

s.d. 16′.1

Day	Right Ascension			Dec. –		Equation of time		Rise 52°		Rise 56°		Transit		Set 52°		Set 56°		Sidereal time			Transit of first point of Aries		
	h	m	s	°	′	m	s	h	m	h	m	h	m	h	m	h	m	h	m	s	h	m	s
1	12	30	05	3	15	+10	19	6	01	6	04	11	50	17	37	17	34	0	40	24	23	15	47
2	12	33	42	3	38	+10	38	6	03	6	05	11	49	17	34	17	32	0	44	20	23	11	51
3	12	37	20	4	01	+10	57	6	05	6	07	11	49	17	32	17	29	0	48	17	23	07	55
4	12	40	58	4	24	+11	16	6	06	6	09	11	49	17	30	17	27	0	52	13	23	03	59
5	12	44	36	4	48	+11	34	6	08	6	12	11	48	17	28	17	24	0	56	10	23	00	03
6	12	48	15	5	11	+11	52	6	10	6	14	11	48	17	25	17	21	1	00	07	22	56	07
7	12	51	54	5	34	+12	09	6	11	6	16	11	48	17	23	17	19	1	04	03	22	52	11
8	12	55	34	5	57	+12	26	6	13	6	18	11	47	17	21	17	16	1	08	00	22	48	16
9	12	59	14	6	19	+12	43	6	15	6	20	11	47	17	19	17	14	1	11	56	22	44	20
10	13	02	54	6	42	+12	59	6	17	6	22	11	47	17	16	17	11	1	15	53	22	40	24
11	13	06	35	7	05	+13	15	6	18	6	24	11	47	17	14	17	09	1	19	49	22	36	28
12	13	10	16	7	27	+13	30	6	20	6	26	11	46	17	12	17	06	1	23	46	22	32	32
13	13	13	58	7	50	+13	45	6	22	6	28	11	46	17	10	17	04	1	27	42	22	28	36
14	13	17	40	8	12	+13	59	6	23	6	30	11	46	17	07	17	01	1	31	39	22	24	40
15	13	21	23	8	34	+14	13	6	25	6	32	11	46	17	05	16	59	1	35	36	22	20	44
16	13	25	06	8	56	+14	26	6	27	6	34	11	45	17	03	16	56	1	39	32	22	16	48
17	13	28	50	9	18	+14	38	6	29	6	36	11	45	17	01	16	54	1	43	29	22	12	52
18	13	32	35	9	40	+14	50	6	30	6	38	11	45	16	59	16	51	1	47	25	22	08	56
19	13	36	20	10	02	+15	02	6	32	6	40	11	45	16	57	16	49	1	51	22	22	05	01
20	13	40	06	10	24	+15	12	6	34	6	42	11	45	16	55	16	46	1	55	18	22	01	05
21	13	43	53	10	45	+15	22	6	36	6	44	11	45	16	53	16	44	1	59	15	21	57	09
22	13	47	40	11	06	+15	32	6	37	6	46	11	44	16	51	16	41	2	03	11	21	53	13
23	13	51	28	11	27	+15	40	6	39	6	49	11	44	16	48	16	39	2	07	08	21	49	17
24	13	55	16	11	48	+15	48	6	41	6	51	11	44	16	46	16	37	2	11	05	21	45	21
25	13	59	06	12	09	+15	56	6	43	6	53	11	44	16	44	16	34	2	15	01	21	41	25
26	14	02	56	12	30	+16	02	6	45	6	55	11	44	16	42	16	32	2	18	58	21	37	29
27	14	06	46	12	50	+16	08	6	46	6	57	11	44	16	40	16	30	2	22	54	21	33	33
28	14	10	38	13	10	+16	13	6	48	6	59	11	44	16	39	16	28	2	26	51	21	29	37
29	14	14	30	13	30	+16	17	6	50	7	01	11	44	16	37	16	25	2	30	47	21	25	41
30	14	18	23	13	50	+16	20	6	52	7	03	11	44	16	35	16	23	2	34	44	21	21	46
31	14	22	17	14	09	+16	23	6	54	7	05	11	44	16	33	16	21	2	38	40	21	17	50

DURATION OF TWILIGHT (in minutes)

Latitude	*52°*	*56°*	*52°*	*56°*	*52°*	*56°*	*52°*	*56°*
	1 October		*11 October*		*21 October*		*31 October*	
Civil	34	37	34	37	34	38	35	39
Nautical	73	80	73	80	74	81	75	83
Astronomical	113	125	112	124	113	124	114	126

THE NIGHT SKY

Mercury passes through inferior conjunction on the 6th and is too close to the Sun for observation until the middle of the month. Thereafter it is visible as a morning object, low in the east-south-eastern sky around the beginning of morning civil twilight. During this time its magnitude brightens from +0.9 to –0.9. On the morning of the 27th the thin waning crescent Moon passes almost 8 degrees south of the planet. This morning apparition is the most suitable one of the year for observers in the British Isles.

Venus, magnitude –4.0, is a brilliant object in the early evenings, though still very low in the south-western sky. For observers in southern England it is visible for about half-an-hour after sunset, by the end of October. It continues to be a very difficult object to observe, even by the end of the month, for observers in Scotland.

Mars remains unsuitably placed for observation.

Jupiter, magnitude –2.2, is still visible in the south-western sky in the early part of the evening. The Moon, at First Quarter, is in the vicinity of the planet on the evenings of the 7th and 8th.

Saturn, magnitude +1.0, is slowly emerging from the morning twilight and becoming visible low above the eastern horizon for a short while, before being lost in the brightening sky before sunrise. On the morning of the 25th the thin waning crescent Moon passes 5 degrees south of the planet. Saturn is still in Leo. Because the rings are slowly closing, before the Earth passes through the ring plane next year, this is the first occasion since 1997 that the planet's magnitude has faded to this level.

THE MOON

Day	R.A.		Dec.	Hor. Par.	Semi-diam.	Sun's Co-Long.	PA of Br. Limb	Ph.	Age	Rise				Transit		Set			
										52°		56°				52°		56°	
	h	m	°	′	′	°	°	%	d	h	m	h	m	h	m	h	m	h	m
1	13	36	−15.1	55.5	15.1	285	305	3	1.7	8	43	9	00	13	20	17	45	17	28
2	14	24	−19.6	55.0	15.0	298	297	7	2.7	9	59	10	22	14	07	18	06	17	42
3	15	14	−23.3	54.6	14.9	310	291	13	3.7	11	12	11	41	14	55	18	33	18	03
4	16	06	−25.8	54.3	14.8	322	285	20	4.7	12	19	12	53	15	45	19	09	18	34
5	16	58	−27.2	54.2	14.8	334	278	28	5.7	13	16	13	52	16	36	19	57	19	21
6	17	52	−27.3	54.2	14.8	346	272	37	6.7	14	02	14	35	17	27	20	56	20	23
7	18	44	−26.1	54.4	14.8	359	266	47	7.7	14	36	15	04	18	17	22	05	21	37
8	19	36	−23.8	54.7	14.9	11	260	56	8.7	15	01	15	24	19	05	23	18	22	57
9	20	27	−20.3	55.3	15.1	23	256	66	9.7	15	20	15	37	19	52	—	—	—	—
10	21	16	−15.9	55.9	15.2	35	253	75	10.7	15	36	15	47	20	38	0	35	0	20
11	22	04	−10.7	56.7	15.4	47	251	83	11.7	15	49	15	55	21	23	1	53	1	43
12	22	51	−4.9	57.5	15.7	59	251	90	12.7	16	02	16	03	22	09	3	12	3	08
13	23	40	+1.3	58.3	15.9	72	254	96	13.7	16	15	16	11	22	56	4	33	4	35
14	0	30	+7.6	59.1	16.1	84	266	99	14.7	16	30	16	20	23	47	5	57	6	05
15	1	23	+13.7	59.7	16.3	96	4	100	15.7	16	48	16	32	—	—	7	25	7	40
16	2	19	+19.2	60.1	16.4	108	54	98	16.7	17	14	16	50	0	41	8	56	9	18
17	3	19	+23.5	60.3	16.4	120	66	93	17.7	17	49	17	19	1	40	10	26	10	56
18	4	23	+26.3	60.2	16.4	132	76	86	18.7	18	40	18	05	2	43	11	47	12	22
19	5	28	+27.3	60.0	16.3	145	84	77	19.7	19	49	19	15	3	47	12	51	13	25
20	6	33	+26.4	59.6	16.2	157	92	67	20.7	21	10	20	42	4	49	13	37	14	05
21	7	35	+23.8	59.1	16.1	169	99	56	21.7	22	35	22	15	5	49	14	08	14	30
22	8	32	+19.8	58.5	15.9	181	104	45	22.7	—	—	23	46	6	43	14	30	14	45
23	9	25	+14.8	58.0	15.8	193	108	34	23.7	0	00	—	—	7	33	14	46	14	56
24	10	15	+9.3	57.4	15.6	205	110	24	24.7	1	21	1	13	8	20	15	00	15	04
25	11	03	+3.4	56.9	15.5	218	110	16	25.7	2	39	2	37	9	04	15	12	15	11
26	11	49	−2.6	56.3	15.4	230	108	9	26.7	3	56	3	59	9	47	15	24	15	19
27	12	35	−8.3	55.9	15.2	242	103	4	27.7	5	11	5	20	10	30	15	37	15	26
28	13	21	−13.6	55.4	15.1	254	89	1	28.7	6	27	6	41	11	15	15	52	15	36
29	14	09	−18.3	55.0	15.0	267	16	0	0.0	7	42	8	02	12	01	16	10	15	49
30	14	58	−22.1	54.6	14.9	279	309	1	1.0	8	56	9	22	12	49	16	35	16	08
31	15	50	−25.0	54.3	14.8	291	294	4	2.0	10	05	10	37	13	38	17	08	16	35

MERCURY

Day	R.A.		Dec.	Diam.	Phase	Transit		5° high			
								52°		56°	
	h	m	°	″	%	h	m	h	m	h	m
1	13	09	−11.1	10	9	12	25	16	53	16	40
3	13	03	−10.0	10	5	12	11	16	45	16	33
5	12	55	−8.7	10	1	11	55	7	15	7	26
7	12	48	−7.3	10	0	11	40	6	52	7	01
9	12	40	−5.8	10	2	11	25	6	29	6	37
11	12	34	−4.4	10	6	11	12	6	08	6	15
13	12	31	−3.3	9	12	11	00	5	51	5	57
15	12	29	−2.5	9	20	10	52	5	38	5	43
17	12	30	−2.0	8	29	10	45	5	29	5	34
19	12	33	−2.0	8	39	10	41	5	25	5	30
21	12	39	−2.3	7	49	10	39	5	24	5	30
23	12	46	−2.8	7	58	10	39	5	27	5	33
25	12	55	−3.6	6	66	10	40	5	32	5	39
27	13	05	−4.6	6	73	10	43	5	40	5	47
29	13	15	−5.7	6	79	10	45	5	49	5	57
31	13	27	−6.9	6	83	10	49	5	59	6	08

VENUS

Day	R.A.		Dec.	Diam.	Phase	Transit		5° high			
								52°		56°	
	h	m	°	″	%	h	m	h	m	h	m
1	14	24	−14.5	12	86	13	44	17	48	17	30
6	14	48	−16.6	12	85	13	48	17	38	17	17
11	15	12	−18.5	13	84	13	53	17	29	17	05
16	15	36	−20.3	13	83	13	58	17	21	16	53
21	16	02	−21.9	13	81	14	03	17	15	16	42
26	16	27	−23.2	13	80	14	09	17	10	16	33
31	16	53	−24.2	14	79	14	15	17	07	16	27

MARS

Day	R.A.		Dec.	Diam.	Phase	Transit		5° high			
								52°		56°	
	h	m	°	″	%	h	m	h	m	h	m
1	13	44	−10.5	4	99	13	03	17	31	17	18
6	13	57	−11.8	4	99	12	56	17	17	17	03
11	14	10	−13.0	4	99	12	49	17	03	16	47
16	14	23	−14.2	4	99	12	43	16	50	16	32
21	14	36	−15.3	4	99	12	36	16	36	16	17
26	14	50	−16.4	4	100	12	30	16	23	16	02
31	15	04	−17.4	4	100	12	25	16	10	15	47

SUNRISE AND SUNSET

	London *0°05′*		*51°30′*		*Bristol* *2°35′*		*51°28′*		*Birmingham* *1°55′*		*52°28′*		*Manchester* *2°15′*		*53°28′*		*Newcastle* *1°37′*		*54°59′*		*Glasgow* *4°14′*		*55°52′*		*Belfast* *5°56′*		*54°35′*	
d	*h*	*m*	*h*	*m*	*h*	*m*	*h*	*m*	*h*	*m*	*h*	*m*	*h*	*m*	*h*	*m*	*h*	*m*	*h*	*m*	*h*	*m*	*h*	*m*	*h*	*m*	*h*	*m*
1	6	01	17	37	6	11	17	47	6	09	17	44	6	11	17	45	6	09	17	42	6	20	17	51	6	26	17	59
2	6	03	17	35	6	13	17	45	6	11	17	42	6	13	17	43	6	11	17	39	6	22	17	49	6	28	17	56
3	6	05	17	33	6	15	17	43	6	13	17	39	6	15	17	40	6	13	17	36	6	24	17	46	6	30	17	54
4	6	06	17	31	6	16	17	41	6	14	17	37	6	16	17	38	6	15	17	34	6	26	17	44	6	32	17	52
5	6	08	17	28	6	18	17	38	6	16	17	35	6	18	17	35	6	17	17	31	6	28	17	41	6	34	17	49
6	6	10	17	26	6	20	17	36	6	18	17	33	6	20	17	33	6	19	17	29	6	30	17	38	6	36	17	47
7	6	11	17	24	6	21	17	34	6	20	17	30	6	22	17	31	6	21	17	26	6	32	17	36	6	38	17	44
8	6	13	17	22	6	23	17	32	6	21	17	28	6	24	17	28	6	23	17	24	6	34	17	33	6	40	17	42
9	6	15	17	19	6	25	17	29	6	23	17	26	6	26	17	26	6	25	17	21	6	36	17	31	6	42	17	39
10	6	16	17	17	6	26	17	27	6	25	17	23	6	27	17	24	6	27	17	19	6	38	17	28	6	43	17	37
11	6	18	17	15	6	28	17	25	6	27	17	21	6	29	17	21	6	29	17	17	6	40	17	26	6	45	17	34
12	6	20	17	13	6	30	17	23	6	28	17	19	6	31	17	19	6	31	17	14	6	42	17	23	6	47	17	32
13	6	21	17	11	6	31	17	21	6	30	17	17	6	33	17	17	6	33	17	12	6	44	17	21	6	49	17	30
14	6	23	17	09	6	33	17	19	6	32	17	14	6	35	17	14	6	35	17	09	6	46	17	18	6	51	17	27
15	6	25	17	06	6	35	17	16	6	34	17	12	6	36	17	12	6	36	17	07	6	49	17	16	6	53	17	25
16	6	26	17	04	6	36	17	14	6	35	17	10	6	38	17	10	6	38	17	04	6	51	17	13	6	55	17	22
17	6	28	17	02	6	38	17	12	6	37	17	08	6	40	17	07	6	40	17	02	6	53	17	11	6	57	17	20
18	6	30	17	00	6	40	17	10	6	39	17	06	6	42	17	05	6	42	17	00	6	55	17	08	6	59	17	18
19	6	32	16	58	6	42	17	08	6	41	17	04	6	44	17	03	6	44	16	57	6	57	17	06	7	01	17	15
20	6	33	16	56	6	43	17	06	6	42	17	01	6	46	17	01	6	46	16	55	6	59	17	03	7	03	17	13
21	6	35	16	54	6	45	17	04	6	44	16	59	6	48	16	59	6	48	16	53	7	01	17	01	7	05	17	11
22	6	37	16	52	6	47	17	02	6	46	16	57	6	50	16	56	6	50	16	50	7	03	16	59	7	07	17	09
23	6	39	16	50	6	48	17	00	6	48	16	55	6	51	16	54	6	52	16	48	7	05	16	56	7	09	17	06
24	6	40	16	48	6	50	16	58	6	50	16	53	6	53	16	52	6	54	16	46	7	07	16	54	7	11	17	04
25	6	42	16	46	6	52	16	56	6	52	16	51	6	55	16	50	6	56	16	44	7	09	16	52	7	13	17	02
26	6	44	16	44	6	54	16	54	6	53	16	49	6	57	16	48	6	59	16	41	7	11	16	49	7	15	17	00
27	6	46	16	42	6	55	16	52	6	55	16	47	6	59	16	46	7	01	16	39	7	14	16	47	7	17	16	58
28	6	47	16	40	6	57	16	50	6	57	16	45	7	01	16	44	7	03	16	37	7	16	16	45	7	19	16	55
29	6	49	16	38	6	59	16	48	6	59	16	43	7	03	16	42	7	05	16	35	7	18	16	43	7	21	16	53
30	6	51	16	36	7	01	16	46	7	01	16	41	7	05	16	40	7	07	16	33	7	20	16	40	7	23	16	51
31	6	53	16	35	7	03	16	45	7	03	16	39	7	07	16	38	7	09	16	31	7	22	16	38	7	25	16	49

JUPITER

Day	*R.A.*		*Dec.*		*Transit*		*5° high*			
							52°		*56°*	
	h	*m*	°	′	*h*	*m*	*h*	*m*	*h*	*m*
1	18	58.2	−23	06	18	15	21	17	20	42
11	19	01.9	−23	01	17	39	20	42	20	07
21	19	06.7	−22	54	17	05	20	09	19	34
31	19	12.6	−22	45	16	32	19	37	19	03

Diameters – equatorial 38″ polar 35″

SATURN

Day	*R.A.*		*Dec.*		*Transit*		*5° high*			
							52°		*56°*	
	h	*m*	°	′	*h*	*m*	*h*	*m*	*h*	*m*
1	11	08.4	+7	23	10	26	4	22	4	19
11	11	12.7	+6	57	9	52	3	49	3	47
21	11	16.9	+6	33	9	16	3	16	3	14
31	11	20.6	+6	11	8	41	2	42	2	41

Diameters – equatorial 16″ polar 15″
Rings – major axis 37″ minor axis 2″

URANUS

Day	*R.A.*		*Dec.*		*Transit*		*10° high*			
							52°		*56°*	
	h	*m*	°	′	*h*	*m*	*h*	*m*	*h*	*m*
1	23	24.4	−4	43	22	40	3	12	3	01
11	23	23.1	−4	51	22	00	2	31	2	19
21	23	21.9	−4	58	21	19	1	50	1	38
31	23	21.0	−5	04	20	39	1	09	0	57

Diameter 4″

NEPTUNE

Day	*R.A.*		*Dec.*		*Transit*		*10° high*			
							52°		*56°*	
	h	*m*	°	′	*h*	*m*	*h*	*m*	*h*	*m*
1	21	37.0	−14	36	20	53	0	22	23	53
11	21	36.4	−14	38	20	13	23	38	23	12
21	21	36.0	−14	40	19	34	22	58	22	32
31	21	35.9	−14	41	18	54	22	18	21	53

Diameter 2″

NOVEMBER 2008

ELEVENTH MONTH, 30 DAYS. *Novem* (nine), ninth month of Roman pre-Julian calendar

1	*Saturday*	Rudolf IV, duke of Austria b. 1339 Mamie Eisenhower, US first lady d. 1979	306
2	*Sunday*	Pat Buchanan, US politician b. 1938 Peter III, king of Aragon d. 1285	307
3	*Monday*	Alfredo Stroessner, president of Paraguay b. 1912 Peter II, king of Yugoslavia d. 1970	week 44 day 308
4	*Tuesday*	Thomas Klestil, president of Austria b. 1932 Yitzhak Rabin, prime minister of Israel d. 1995	309
5	*Wednesday*	Saddam Hussein, former president of Iraq, was sentenced to death 2006	310
6	*Thursday*	Ignacy Paderewski, prime minister of Poland b. 1860 Khai Dinh, emperor of Vietnam d. 1925	311
7	*Friday*	Leon Trotsky, Russian revolutionary b. 1879 Jaja Wachuku, Nigerian statesman d. 1996	312
8	*Saturday*	Nguyen Khanh, prime minister of South Vietnam b. 1927 Vyacheslav Molotov, Soviet politician d. 1986	313
9	*Sunday*	King Edward VII b. 1841 Neville Chamberlain, British prime minister d. 1940	314
10	*Monday*	Screaming Lord Sutch, British politician b. 1940 Mustafa Kemal Ataturk, Turkish revolutionary d. 1938	week 45 day 315
11	*Tuesday*	Daniel Ortega, president of Nicaragua b. 1945 Liliuokalani, queen of Hawaii d. 1917	316
12	*Wednesday*	Sun Yat-sen, president of China b. 1866 Dolores Ibarruri, Spanish Communist leader d. 1989	317
13	*Thursday*	King Edward III b. 1312 Malcolm III, king of Scotland d. 1093	318
14	*Friday*	Prince Charles b. 1948 Miguel I, king of Portugal d. 1866	319
15	*Saturday*	Brazil became a republic when the second and last emperor, Pedro II, was deposed in a military coup 1889	320
16	*Sunday*	Oswald Mosley, British politician b. 1896 King Henry III d. 1272	321
17	*Monday*	Bernard Montgomery, British Army commander b. 1887 Lala Lajpat Raj, Indian politician d. 1928	week 46 day 322
18	*Tuesday*	Russia ratified the Kyoto Protocol on climate change 2004	323
19	*Wednesday*	King Charles I b. 1600 Indira Gandhi, prime minister of India b. 1917	324
20	*Thursday*	Wilfrid Laurier, prime minister of Canada b. 1841 Francisco Franco, prime minister of Spain d. 1975	325
21	*Friday*	Richard Durbin, US senator b. 1944 Garret Hobart, US vice-president d. 1899	326
22	*Saturday*	Charles de Gaulle, president of France b. 1890 John F. Kennedy, US president d. 1963	327
23	*Sunday*	Hjalmar Branting, prime minister of Sweden b. 1860 Sean O'Kelly, president of Ireland d. 1966	328
24	*Monday*	Zachary Taylor, US president b. 1784 Georges Clemenceau, prime minister of France d. 1929	week 47 day 329
25	*Tuesday*	Charles Kennedy, British politician b. 1959 Hastings Banda, president of Malawi d. 1997	330
26	*Wednesday*	Go-Daigo, emperor of Japan b. 1288 Isabella, queen regnant of Castile and Leon d. 1504	331
27	*Thursday*	Alexander Dubcek, leader of Czechoslovakia b. 1921 Clovis I, king of the Franks d. 511	332
28	*Friday*	Women were allowed to vote for the first time in a general election in New Zealand 1893	333
29	*Saturday*	William Tubman, president of Liberia b. 1895 Philip IV, king of France d. 1314	334
30	*Sunday*	Winston Churchill, British prime minister b. 1874 King Edmund II d. 1016	335

ASTRONOMICAL PHENOMENA

d	*h*	
1	08	Venus in conjunction with Moon. Venus 3°N.
2	07	Neptune at stationary point
3	22	Jupiter in conjunction with Moon. Jupiter 2°N.
21	14	Saturn in conjunction with Moon. Saturn 5°N.
21	23	Sun's longitude 240° ♐
25	17	Mercury in superior conjunction
27	16	Uranus at stationary point
27	20	Mercury in conjunction with Moon. Mercury 4°N.
27	22	Mars in conjunction with Moon. Mars 4°N.
29	04	Mars in conjunction with Mercury. Mars 0°.6N.

MINIMA OF ALGOL

d	*h*	*d*	*h*	*d*	*h*
3	10.5	14	21.7	26	09.0
6	07.3	17	18.5	29	05.8
9	04.1	20	15.4		
12	00.9	23	12.2		

CONSTELLATIONS

The following constellations are near their meridian at

	d	*h*		*d*	*h*
October	1	24	November	15	21
October	16	23	December	1	20
November	1	22	December	16	19

Ursa Major (below the Pole), Cepheus, Cassiopeia, Andromeda, Pegasus, Pisces, Aquarius and Cetus

THE MOON

Phases, Apsides and Node	*d*	*h*	*m*
☽ First Quarter	6	04	03
○ Full Moon	13	06	17
☾ Last Quarter	19	21	31
● New Moon	27	16	55
Apogee (405,753 km)	2	05	03
Perigee (358,961 km)	14	10	07
Apogee (406,494 km)	29	17	08

Mean longitude of ascending node on November 1, 314°

THE SUN

s.d. 16′.2

Day	Right Ascension			Dec. –		Equation of time		Rise 52°		Rise 56°		Transit		Set 52°		Set 56°		Sidereal time			Transit of first point of Aries		
	h	m	s	°	′	m	s	h	m	h	m	h	m	h	m	h	m	h	m	s	h	m	s
1	14	26	12	14	29	+16	25	6	55	7	08	11	44	16	31	16	19	2	42	37	21	13	54
2	14	30	07	14	48	+16	26	6	57	7	10	11	44	16	29	16	17	2	46	34	21	09	58
3	14	34	04	15	07	+16	26	6	59	7	12	11	44	16	27	16	14	2	50	30	21	06	02
4	14	38	01	15	25	+16	26	7	01	7	14	11	44	16	26	16	12	2	54	27	21	02	06
5	14	41	59	15	43	+16	25	7	03	7	16	11	44	16	24	16	10	2	58	23	20	58	10
6	14	45	57	16	02	+16	22	7	04	7	18	11	44	16	22	16	08	3	02	20	20	54	14
7	14	49	57	16	19	+16	20	7	06	7	20	11	44	16	21	16	06	3	06	16	20	50	18
8	14	53	57	16	37	+16	16	7	08	7	23	11	44	16	19	16	04	3	10	13	20	46	22
9	14	57	58	16	54	+16	11	7	10	7	25	11	44	16	17	16	02	3	14	09	20	42	26
10	15	02	00	17	11	+16	06	7	12	7	27	11	44	16	16	16	00	3	18	06	20	38	31
11	15	06	03	17	28	+16	00	7	13	7	29	11	44	16	14	15	59	3	22	03	20	34	35
12	15	10	07	17	44	+15	52	7	15	7	31	11	44	16	13	15	57	3	25	59	20	30	39
13	15	14	11	18	00	+15	45	7	17	7	33	11	44	16	11	15	55	3	29	56	20	26	43
14	15	18	16	18	16	+15	36	7	19	7	35	11	44	16	10	15	53	3	33	52	20	22	47
15	15	22	23	18	31	+15	26	7	20	7	37	11	45	16	08	15	52	3	37	49	20	18	51
16	15	26	30	18	46	+15	16	7	22	7	39	11	45	16	07	15	50	3	41	45	20	14	55
17	15	30	38	19	01	+15	04	7	24	7	41	11	45	16	06	15	48	3	45	42	20	10	59
18	15	34	46	19	16	+14	52	7	26	7	43	11	45	16	04	15	47	3	49	38	20	07	03
19	15	38	56	19	30	+14	39	7	27	7	45	11	45	16	03	15	45	3	53	35	20	03	07
20	15	43	06	19	43	+14	25	7	29	7	47	11	46	16	02	15	44	3	57	32	19	59	11
21	15	47	18	19	57	+14	10	7	31	7	49	11	46	16	01	15	42	4	01	28	19	55	15
22	15	51	30	20	10	+13	55	7	32	7	51	11	46	16	00	15	41	4	05	25	19	51	20
23	15	55	43	20	22	+13	39	7	34	7	53	11	47	15	59	15	39	4	09	21	19	47	24
24	15	59	56	20	35	+13	22	7	35	7	55	11	47	15	58	15	38	4	13	18	19	43	28
25	16	04	11	20	47	+13	04	7	37	7	57	11	47	15	57	15	37	4	17	14	19	39	32
26	16	08	26	20	58	+12	45	7	39	7	59	11	47	15	56	15	36	4	21	11	19	35	36
27	16	12	42	21	09	+12	25	7	40	8	00	11	48	15	55	15	35	4	25	07	19	31	40
28	16	16	59	21	20	+12	05	7	42	8	02	11	48	15	54	15	33	4	29	04	19	27	44
29	16	21	16	21	30	+11	44	7	43	8	04	11	48	15	53	15	32	4	33	01	19	23	48
30	16	25	34	21	40	+11	23	7	45	8	06	11	49	15	53	15	32	4	36	57	19	19	52

DURATION OF TWILIGHT (in minutes)

Latitude	52°	56°	52°	56°	52°	56°	52°	56°
	1 November		*11 November*		*21 November*		*31 November*	
Civil	36	40	37	41	38	43	40	45
Nautical	75	84	78	87	80	90	82	93
Astronomical	115	127	117	130	120	134	123	138

THE NIGHT SKY

Mercury is unsuitably placed for observation throughout the month.

Venus continues to be visible as a brilliant object for a short time after sunset, low above the south-western horizon, magnitude –4.1. The thin crescent Moon, only 3 days old, passes 3 degrees south of the planet on the 1st. By the end of the month observers in England will notice that it sets about two hours after sunset. Observers in Scotland should be able to detect the planet for the first time since February.

Mars continues to be unsuitably placed for observation.

Jupiter, magnitude −2.1, is still visible low in the south-western sky in the early evening, though by the end of the month it is lost to view within two hours after sunset. During the evening of the 3rd the waxing crescent Moon passes 3 degrees south of the planet. Venus has been moving rapidly outwards from the Sun and by the end of the month will again be seen about 2 degrees south of Jupiter.

Saturn, magnitude +0.9, is still visible as a morning object in the south-eastern quadrant of the sky. By the end of the month it may be seen rising above the eastern horizon shortly after midnight.

THE MOON

Day	R.A.		Dec.	Hor. Par.	Semi-diam.	Sun's Co-Long.	PA. of Br. Limb	Ph.	Age	Rise				Transit		Set			
										52°		56°				52°		56°	
	h	*m*	°	′	′	°	°	%	*d*	*h*	*m*	*h*	*m*	*h*	*m*	*h*	*m*	*h*	*m*
1	16	42	−26.7	54.1	14.7	303	284	9	3.0	11	06	11	41	14	29	17	51	17	16
2	17	35	−27.1	54.0	14.7	315	276	15	4.0	11	56	12	30	15	20	18	46	18	12
3	18	28	−26.4	54.1	14.7	328	269	22	5.0	12	34	13	04	16	10	19	51	19	22
4	19	20	−24.4	54.3	14.8	340	263	30	6.0	13	02	13	26	16	58	21	02	20	38
5	20	10	−21.3	54.6	14.9	352	258	39	7.0	13	23	13	42	17	44	22	16	21	58
6	20	58	−17.3	55.1	15.0	4	254	48	8.0	13	40	13	53	18	29	23	31	23	19
7	21	45	−12.5	55.8	15.2	16	251	58	9.0	13	54	14	02	19	13	—		—	
8	22	32	−7.1	56.6	15.4	28	249	68	10.0	14	07	14	10	19	58	0	47	0	41
9	23	19	−1.1	57.6	15.7	41	249	77	11.0	14	19	14	17	20	43	2	05	2	04
10	0	08	+5.0	58.5	15.9	53	250	86	12.0	14	33	14	26	21	32	3	26	3	31
11	0	59	+11.2	59.4	16.2	65	255	93	13.0	14	50	14	37	22	24	4	51	5	02
12	1	54	+16.9	60.2	16.4	77	265	98	14.0	15	12	14	52	23	22	6	21	6	39
13	2	53	+21.8	60.8	16.6	89	307	100	15.0	15	43	15	16	—		7	54	8	20
14	3	57	+25.3	61.1	16.6	101	54	99	16.0	16	28	15	55	0	24	9	22	9	55
15	5	04	+27.0	61.0	16.6	113	76	95	17.0	17	32	16	58	1	30	10	37	11	11
16	6	11	+26.7	60.7	16.5	126	87	89	18.0	18	52	18	22	2	36	11	31	12	02
17	7	16	+24.5	60.2	16.4	138	96	81	19.0	20	20	19	57	3	39	12	08	12	32
18	8	17	+20.7	59.5	16.2	150	102	71	20.0	21	47	21	31	4	37	12	34	12	51
19	9	12	+15.9	58.7	16.0	162	107	60	21.0	23	10	23	01	5	30	12	52	13	03
20	10	04	+10.3	57.9	15.8	174	110	49	22.0	—		—		6	18	13	07	13	13
21	10	52	+4.5	57.1	15.6	186	112	38	23.0	0	30	0	26	7	03	13	19	13	20
22	11	38	−1.4	56.4	15.4	198	112	29	24.0	1	46	1	48	7	46	13	32	13	28
23	12	24	−7.1	55.8	15.2	211	110	20	25.0	3	01	3	08	8	29	13	44	13	35
24	13	10	−12.4	55.3	15.1	223	107	13	26.0	4	15	4	28	9	13	13	58	13	44
25	13	57	−17.2	54.9	15.0	235	102	7	27.0	5	30	5	48	9	58	14	16	13	56
26	14	45	−21.2	54.5	14.9	247	93	3	28.0	6	43	7	08	10	45	14	38	14	13
27	15	36	−24.3	54.3	14.8	259	72	1	29.0	7	54	8	24	11	33	15	08	14	37
28	16	28	−26.3	54.1	14.7	272	333	0	0.3	8	58	9	32	12	24	15	48	15	14
29	17	21	−27.0	54.0	14.7	284	289	2	1.3	9	51	10	26	13	15	16	40	16	05
30	18	14	−26.5	53.9	14.7	296	275	5	2.3	10	33	11	04	14	05	17	42	17	11

MERCURY

Day	R.A.		Dec.	Diam.	Phase	Transit		5° high			
								52°		56°	
	h	*m*	°	″	%	*h*	*m*	*h*	*m*	*h*	*m*
1	13	32	−7.6	6	85	10	51	6	04	6	14
3	13	44	−8.8	5	89	10	55	6	15	6	27
5	13	56	−10.1	5	91	10	59	6	27	6	40
7	14	08	−11.4	5	94	11	03	6	39	6	53
9	14	20	−12.7	5	95	11	07	6	51	7	06
11	14	33	−13.9	5	97	11	12	7	03	7	20
13	14	45	−15.1	5	98	11	16	7	15	7	34
15	14	58	−16.3	5	98	11	21	7	28	7	48
17	15	11	−17.4	5	99	11	26	7	40	8	03
19	15	23	−18.4	5	99	11	31	7	52	8	17
21	15	36	−19.4	5	100	11	36	8	05	8	31
23	15	49	−20.3	5	100	11	41	8	17	8	45
25	16	02	−21.2	5	100	11	46	8	29	8	59
27	16	15	−22.0	5	100	11	51	8	40	9	13
29	16	28	−22.7	5	100	11	57	8	52	9	27
31	16	42	−23.4	5	100	12	02	15	01	14	24

VENUS

Day	R.A.		Dec.	Diam.	Phase	Transit		5° high			
								52°		56°	
	h	*m*	°	″	%	*h*	*m*	*h*	*m*	*h*	*m*
1	16	58	−24.4	14	79	14	17	17	06	16	26
6	17	25	−25.1	14	77	14	23	17	07	16	23
11	17	51	−25.5	15	76	14	30	17	10	16	24
16	18	18	−25.6	15	74	14	37	17	16	16	30
21	18	44	−25.3	16	73	14	44	17	25	16	40
26	19	10	−24.8	16	71	14	50	17	37	16	55
31	19	36	−24.0	17	70	14	56	17	51	17	13

MARS

Day	R.A.		Dec.	Diam.	Phase	Transit		5° high			
								52°		56°	
	h	*m*	°	″	%	*h*	*m*	*h*	*m*	*h*	*m*
1	15	07	−17.6	4	100	12	23	16	07	15	45
6	15	21	−18.6	4	100	12	18	15	55	15	30
11	15	35	−19.5	4	100	12	13	15	43	15	17
16	15	50	−20.4	4	100	12	08	15	32	15	04
21	16	05	−21.1	4	100	12	03	15	21	14	51
26	16	20	−21.8	4	100	11	59	15	11	14	39
31	16	36	−22.4	4	100	11	54	15	02	14	28

SUNRISE AND SUNSET

	London		*Bristol*		*Birmingham*		*Manchester*		*Newcastle*		*Glasgow*		*Belfast*	
	0°05′	*51°30′*	*2°35′*	*51°28′*	*1°55′*	*52°28′*	*2°15′*	*53°28′*	*1°37′*	*54°59′*	*4°14′*	*55°52′*	*5°56′*	*54°35′*
d	*h m*	*h m*	*h m*	*h m*	*h m*	*h m*	*h m*	*h m*	*h m*	*h m*	*h m*	*h m*	*h m*	*h m*
1	6 54	16 33	7 04	16 43	7 04	16 37	7 09	16 36	7 11	16 29	7 24	16 36	7 27	16 47
2	6 56	16 31	7 06	16 41	7 06	16 36	7 11	16 34	7 13	16 26	7 26	16 34	7 29	16 45
3	6 58	16 29	7 08	16 39	7 08	16 34	7 12	16 32	7 15	16 24	7 28	16 32	7 31	16 43
4	7 00	16 27	7 10	16 38	7 10	16 32	7 14	16 30	7 17	16 22	7 30	16 30	7 33	16 41
5	7 01	16 26	7 11	16 36	7 12	16 30	7 16	16 28	7 19	16 20	7 33	16 28	7 35	16 39
6	7 03	16 24	7 13	16 34	7 14	16 28	7 18	16 26	7 21	16 19	7 35	16 26	7 37	16 37
7	7 05	16 22	7 15	16 33	7 15	16 27	7 20	16 25	7 23	16 17	7 37	16 24	7 39	16 35
8	7 07	16 21	7 17	16 31	7 17	16 25	7 22	16 23	7 25	16 15	7 39	16 22	7 41	16 34
9	7 08	16 19	7 18	16 29	7 19	16 23	7 24	16 21	7 27	16 13	7 41	16 20	7 43	16 32
10	7 10	16 18	7 20	16 28	7 21	16 22	7 26	16 19	7 29	16 11	7 43	16 18	7 45	16 30
11	7 12	16 16	7 22	16 26	7 23	16 20	7 28	16 18	7 31	16 09	7 45	16 16	7 47	16 28
12	7 14	16 15	7 24	16 25	7 24	16 19	7 30	16 16	7 33	16 08	7 47	16 14	7 49	16 26
13	7 15	16 13	7 25	16 23	7 26	16 17	7 31	16 15	7 35	16 06	7 49	16 12	7 51	16 25
14	7 17	16 12	7 27	16 22	7 28	16 16	7 33	16 13	7 37	16 04	7 51	16 11	7 53	16 23
15	7 19	16 11	7 29	16 21	7 30	16 14	7 35	16 12	7 39	16 03	7 53	16 09	7 55	16 22
16	7 21	16 09	7 30	16 19	7 32	16 13	7 37	16 10	7 41	16 01	7 56	16 07	7 56	16 20
17	7 22	16 08	7 32	16 18	7 33	16 11	7 39	16 09	7 43	15 59	7 58	16 06	7 58	16 19
18	7 24	16 07	7 34	16 17	7 35	16 10	7 41	16 07	7 45	15 58	8 00	16 04	8 00	16 17
19	7 26	16 05	7 35	16 16	7 37	16 09	7 42	16 06	7 47	15 57	8 02	16 03	8 02	16 16
20	7 27	16 04	7 37	16 14	7 39	16 08	7 44	16 05	7 49	15 55	8 04	16 01	8 04	16 14
21	7 29	16 03	7 39	16 13	7 40	16 06	7 46	16 03	7 51	15 54	8 05	16 00	8 06	16 13
22	7 30	16 02	7 40	16 12	7 42	16 05	7 48	16 02	7 52	15 52	8 07	15 58	8 08	16 12
23	7 32	16 01	7 42	16 11	7 44	16 04	7 49	16 01	7 54	15 51	8 09	15 57	8 10	16 10
24	7 34	16 00	7 44	16 10	7 45	16 03	7 51	16 00	7 56	15 50	8 11	15 56	8 11	16 09
25	7 35	15 59	7 45	16 09	7 47	16 02	7 53	15 59	7 58	15 49	8 13	15 55	8 13	16 08
26	7 37	15 58	7 47	16 08	7 48	16 01	7 54	15 58	8 00	15 48	8 15	15 53	8 15	16 07
27	7 38	15 57	7 48	16 08	7 50	16 00	7 56	15 57	8 01	15 47	8 17	15 52	8 16	16 06
28	7 40	15 57	7 50	16 07	7 52	16 00	7 58	15 56	8 03	15 46	8 18	15 51	8 18	16 05
29	7 41	15 56	7 51	16 06	7 53	15 59	7 59	15 55	8 05	15 45	8 20	15 50	8 20	16 04
30	7 43	15 55	7 53	16 05	7 54	15 58	8 01	15 54	8 06	15 44	8 22	15 49	8 21	16 03

JUPITER

Day	*R.A.*	*Dec.*	*Transit*	*5° high*	
				52°	*56°*
	h m	*° ′*	*h m*	*h m*	*h m*
1	19 13.2	−22 44	16 28	19 34	18 59
11	19 20.1	−22 32	15 56	19 03	18 29
21	19 27.8	−22 17	15 24	18 33	18 01
31	19 36.1	−21 59	14 53	18 05	17 33

Diameters – equatorial 35″ polar 33″

SATURN

Day	*R.A.*	*Dec.*	*Transit*	*5° high*	
				52°	*56°*
	h m	*° ′*	*h m*	*h m*	*h m*
1	11 21.0	+6 09	8 37	2 39	2 37
11	11 24.4	+5 50	8 01	2 05	2 03
21	11 27.3	+5 34	7 25	1 30	1 28
31	11 29.6	+5 21	6 48	0 54	0 53

Diameters – equatorial 17″ polar 15″
Rings– major axis 39″ minor axis 1″

URANUS

Day	*R.A.*	*Dec.*	*Transit*	*10° high*	
				52°	*56°*
	h m	*° ′*	*h m*	*h m*	*h m*
1	23 20.9	−5 04	20 35	1 05	0 53
11	23 20.3	−5 08	19 55	0 24	0 13
21	23 19.9	−5 10	19 15	23 41	23 29
31	23 19.8	−5 10	18 36	23 01	22 49

Diameter 4″

NEPTUNE

Day	*R.A.*	*Dec.*	*Transit*	*10° high*	
				52°	*56°*
	h m	*° ′*	*h m*	*h m*	*h m*
1	21 35.9	−14 41	18 50	22 14	21 49
11	21 35.9	−14 41	18 11	21 35	21 10
21	21 36.2	−14 39	17 32	20 56	20 31
31	21 36.8	−14 36	16 53	20 18	19 53

Diameter 2″

DECEMBER 2008

TWELFTH MONTH, 31 DAYS. *Decem* (ten), tenth month of Roman pre-Julian calendar

1	*Monday*	Sebastian Pinera, Chilean politician b. 1949 King Henry I d. 1135	week 48 day 336
2	*Tuesday*	Ibrahim Rugova, president of Kosovo b. 1944 Hernan Cortés, Spanish conquistador d. 1547	337
3	*Wednesday*	Mikhail Gorbachev and George Bush announced the end of the Cold War at the Malta summit 1989	338
4	*Thursday*	Barbara, queen consort of Spain b. 1711 Robert Jenkinson, British prime minister d. 1828	339
5	*Friday*	Martin Van Buren, US president b. 1782 Roy Welensky, African politician d. 1991	340
6	*Saturday*	King Henry VI b. 1421 Joao Goulart, president of Brazil d. 1976	341
7	*Sunday*	Joseph Cook, prime minister of Australia b. 1860 Felix Houphouet-Boigny, president of Côte d'Ivoire d. 1993	342
8	*Monday*	Francis I, Holy Roman emperor b. 1708 Sarit Dhanarajata, prime minister of Thailand d. 1963	week 49 day 343
9	*Tuesday*	Carlo Azeglio Ciampi, president of Italy b. 1920 Edward Hyde, English statesman d. 1674	344
10	*Wednesday*	James I, king of Scotland b. 1394 Franjo Tudman, president of Croatia d. 1999	345
11	*Thursday*	Aquilino Pimentel Jr, Philippine politician b. 1933 Llywelyn the Last, prince of Wales d. 1282	346
12	*Friday*	Kenya became independent from the United Kingdom 1963	347
13	*Saturday*	B. J. Vorster, prime minister of South Africa b. 1915 Hannes Hafstein, prime minister of Iceland d. 1922	348
14	*Sunday*	King George VI b. 1895 George Washington, US president d. 1799	349
15	*Monday*	Nero, emperor of Rome b. AD 37 Sitting Bull, Native American leader d. 1890	week 50 day 350
16	*Tuesday*	The Boston Tea Party in protest against taxation brought in by the British parliament took place 1773	351
17	*Wednesday*	Mackenzie King, prime minister of Canada b. 1874 Harold Holt, prime minister of Australia d. 1967	352
18	*Thursday*	Christina, queen of Sweden b. 1626 Alfonso II, king of Naples d. 1495	353
19	*Friday*	Margaret Thatcher signed an agreement 1984 to return Hong Kong to China in 1997	354
20	*Saturday*	Robert Menzies, prime minister of Australia b. 1894 Émile Loubet, president of France d. 1929	355
21	*Sunday*	Mikheil Saakashvili, president of Georgia b. 1967 Saparmurat Niyazov, president of Turkmenistan d. 2006	356
22	*Monday*	Frank B. Kellogg, US politician b. 1856 Desmond Hoyte, president of Guyana d. 2002	week 51 day 357
23	*Tuesday*	Wesley Clark, NATO military officer b. 1944 Hideki Tojo, prime minister of Japan d. 1948	358
24	*Wednesday*	Hamid Karzai, president of Afghanistan b. 1957 Karl Dünitz, president of Germany d. 1980	359
25	*Thursday*	Anwar Sadat, president of Egypt b. 1918 Nicolae Ceausescu, president of Romania d. 1989	360
26	*Friday*	José Ramos Horta, prime minister of East Timor b. 1949 Harry S. Truman, US president d. 1972	361
27	*Saturday*	Ernesto Zedillo, president of Mexico b. 1951 Hafizullah Amin, president of Afghanistan d. 1979	362
28	*Sunday*	Milton Obote, president of Uganda b. 1924 Queen Mary II d. 1694	363
29	*Monday*	William Gladstone, British prime minister b. 1809 Harold Macmillan, British prime minister d. 1986	week 52 day 364
30	*Tuesday*	Omar Bongo, president of Gabon b. 1935 Saddam Hussein, president of Iraq d. 2006	365
31	*Wednesday*	Bonnie Prince Charlie, claimant to the English throne b. 1720 Léon Gambetta, French statesman d. 1882	366

ASTRONOMICAL PHENOMENA

d	*h*	
1	09	Jupiter in conjunction with Venus. Jupiter 2°N.
1	15	Jupiter in conjunction with Moon. Jupiter 1°N.
1	16	Venus in conjunction with Moon. Venus 0°.8S.
5	22	Mars in conjunction
18	23	Saturn in conjunction with Moon. Saturn 5°N.
21	12	Sun's longitude 270° ♑
22	09	Pluto in conjunction
26	23	Mars in conjunction with Moon. Mars 3°N.
29	04	Mercury in conjunction with Moon. Mercury 0°.6S.
29	09	Jupiter in conjunction with Moon. Jupiter 0°.6N.
31	12	Jupiter in conjunction with Mercury. Jupiter 1°N.
31	18	Saturn at stationary point
31	19	Venus in conjunction with Moon. Venus 3°S.

MINIMA OF ALGOL

d	*h*	*d*	*h*	*d*	*h*
2	02.6	13	13.9	25	01.2
4	23.4	16	10.7	27	22.0
7	20.3	19	07.5	30	18.8
10	17.1	22	04.4		

CONSTELLATIONS

The following constellations are near their meridian at

	d	*h*		*d*	*h*
November	1	24	January	1	20
December	16	21	December	1	22
November	15	23	January	16	19

Ursa Major (below the Pole), Ursa Minor (below the Pole), Cassiopeia, Andromeda, Perseus, Triangulum, Aries, Taurus, Cetus and Eridanus

THE MOON

Phases, Apsides and Node	*d*	*h*	*m*
☽ First Quarter	5	21	26
○ Full Moon	12	16	37
☾ Last Quarter	19	10	29
● New Moon	27	12	22
Perigee (356,564 km)	12	21	45
Apogee (406,596 km)	26	18	03

Mean longitude of ascending node on December 1, 313°

THE SUN

s.d. 16′.3

Day	Right Ascension			Dec.		Equation of time		Rise 52°		Rise 56°		Transit		Set 52°		Set 56°		Sidereal time			Transit of first point of Aries		
	h	*m*	*s*	° (–)	′	*m*	*s*	*h*	*m*	*h*	*m*	*h*	*m*	*h*	*m*	*h*	*m*	*h*	*m*	*s*	*h*	*m*	*s*
1	16	29	53	21	49	+11	01	7	46	8	07	11	49	15	52	15	31	4	40	54	19	15	56
2	16	34	12	21	59	+10	38	7	47	8	09	11	50	15	51	15	30	4	44	50	19	12	00
3	16	38	32	22	07	+10	14	7	49	8	11	11	50	15	51	15	29	4	48	47	19	08	05
4	16	42	53	22	15	+9	50	7	50	8	12	11	50	15	50	15	28	4	52	43	19	04	09
5	16	47	14	22	23	+9	26	7	51	8	14	11	51	15	50	15	28	4	56	40	19	00	13
6	16	51	36	22	31	+9	01	7	53	8	15	11	51	15	49	15	27	5	00	37	18	56	17
7	16	55	58	22	37	+8	35	7	54	8	16	11	52	15	49	15	27	5	04	33	18	52	21
8	17	00	21	22	44	+8	09	7	55	8	18	11	52	15	49	15	26	5	08	30	18	48	25
9	17	04	44	22	50	+7	43	7	56	8	19	11	53	15	49	15	26	5	12	26	18	44	29
10	17	09	07	22	55	+7	16	7	57	8	20	11	53	15	48	15	25	5	16	23	18	40	33
11	17	13	31	23	01	+6	48	7	58	8	21	11	53	15	48	15	25	5	20	19	18	36	37
12	17	17	55	23	05	+6	21	7	59	8	23	11	54	15	48	15	25	5	24	16	18	32	41
13	17	22	20	23	09	+5	53	8	00	8	24	11	54	15	48	15	25	5	28	12	18	28	45
14	17	26	45	23	13	+5	24	8	01	8	25	11	55	15	48	15	25	5	32	09	18	24	50
15	17	31	10	23	16	+4	55	8	02	8	26	11	55	15	49	15	25	5	36	06	18	20	54
16	17	35	36	23	19	+4	26	8	03	8	26	11	56	15	49	15	25	5	40	02	18	16	58
17	17	40	01	23	22	+3	57	8	04	8	27	11	56	15	49	15	25	5	43	59	18	13	02
18	17	44	27	23	24	+3	28	8	04	8	28	11	57	15	49	15	26	5	47	55	18	09	06
19	17	48	53	23	25	+2	58	8	05	8	29	11	57	15	50	15	26	5	51	52	18	05	10
20	17	53	20	23	26	+2	29	8	05	8	29	11	58	15	50	15	26	5	55	48	18	01	14
21	17	57	46	23	26	+1	59	8	06	8	30	11	58	15	51	15	27	5	59	45	17	57	18
22	18	02	13	23	26	+1	29	8	06	8	30	11	59	15	51	15	27	6	03	41	17	53	22
23	18	06	39	23	26	+0	59	8	07	8	31	11	59	15	52	15	28	6	07	38	17	49	26
24	18	11	06	23	25	+0	29	8	07	8	31	12	00	15	52	15	29	6	11	35	17	45	30
25	18	15	32	23	24	−0	01	8	08	8	31	12	00	15	53	15	29	6	15	31	17	41	34
26	18	19	58	23	22	−0	31	8	08	8	31	12	01	15	54	15	30	6	19	28	17	37	39
27	18	24	25	23	19	−1	00	8	08	8	32	12	01	15	55	15	31	6	23	24	17	33	43
28	18	28	51	23	16	−1	30	8	08	8	32	12	02	15	55	15	32	6	27	21	17	29	47
29	18	33	17	23	13	−1	59	8	08	8	32	12	02	15	56	15	33	6	31	17	17	25	51
30	18	37	42	23	09	−2	28	8	08	8	32	12	03	15	57	15	34	6	35	14	17	21	55
31	18	42	08	23	05	−2	57	8	08	8	31	12	03	15	58	15	35	6	39	10	17	17	59

DURATION OF TWILIGHT (in minutes)

Latitude	52°	56°	52°	56°	52°	56°	52°	56°
	1 December		*11 December*		*21 December*		*31 December*	
Civil	40	45	41	47	41	47	41	47
Nautical	82	93	84	96	85	97	84	96
Astronomical	123	138	125	141	126	142	125	141

THE NIGHT SKY

Mercury remains too close to the Sun for observation throughout December.

Venus, magnitude −4.2, is a magnificent object in the early evening sky, low above the south-western horizon. Shortly before sunset on the evening of the 1st the waxing crescent Moon will blot out the light of the planet to naked-eye observers, while observers with telescopes will see an actual occultation. By the end of the month Venus is visible for over three hours after sunset.

Mars passes through conjunction on the 5th and therefore remains unsuitably placed for observation.

Jupiter, magnitude −2.0, is still a bright object in the south-western sky in the early evening, though by the end of the month it is lost to view before the end of evening civil twilight. On the 1st the crescent Moon, barely 4 days old, passes 2 degrees south of the planet. A similar situation occurs on the evenings of the 28th and 29th though this will be a much more difficult event to observe in twilight conditions. Jupiter remains in Sagittarius throughout the month, entering Capricornus in the New Year. Venus is now moving away from Jupiter during the month and by the end of the year is about 20 degrees east of Jupiter.

Saturn, continues to be visible as a morning object and by mid-December may be seen above the eastern horizon before midnight.

Meteors. The maximum of the well-known Geminid meteor shower occurs on the 13th, and will be best seen on the evening of that day, though the full Moon will cause serious interference.

THE MOON

Day	R.A.		Dec.	Hor. Par.	Semi-diam.	Sun's Co-Long.	PA. of Br. Limb	Ph.	Age	Rise				Transit		Set			
										52°		56°				52°		56°	
	h	*m*	°	′	′	°	°	%	*d*	*h*	*m*	*h*	*m*	*h*	*m*	*h*	*m*	*h*	*m*
1	19	06	−24.8	54.0	14.7	308	267	9	3.3	11	04	11	30	14	54	18	51	18	25
2	19	56	−22.1	54.2	14.8	320	260	16	4.3	11	27	11	47	15	40	20	03	19	44
3	20	44	−18.3	54.6	14.9	333	255	23	5.3	11	45	11	59	16	25	21	16	21	03
4	21	31	−13.8	55.0	15.0	345	251	32	6.3	11	59	12	09	17	08	22	30	22	22
5	22	17	−8.7	55.7	15.2	357	249	41	7.3	12	12	12	17	17	51	23	44	23	42
6	23	02	−3.0	56.4	15.4	9	247	51	8.3	12	24	12	24	18	34	—	—	—	—
7	23	48	+2.9	57.3	15.6	21	247	62	9.3	12	37	12	32	19	19	1	01	1	03
8	0	37	+8.8	58.3	15.9	33	249	72	10.3	12	51	12	41	20	08	2	21	2	29
9	1	29	+14.6	59.2	16.1	45	252	81	11.3	13	10	12	54	21	02	3	46	4	01
10	2	25	+19.8	60.1	16.4	58	258	89	12.3	13	36	13	12	22	01	5	16	5	38
11	3	26	+23.9	60.9	16.6	70	267	96	13.3	14	13	13	43	23	06	6	47	7	16
12	4	32	+26.4	61.4	16.7	82	285	99	14.3	15	08	14	33	—		8	10	8	44
13	5	41	+27.0	61.5	16.8	94	49	100	15.3	16	22	15	50	0	13	9	16	9	49
14	6	49	+25.5	61.3	16.7	106	87	97	16.3	17	51	17	25	1	20	10	02	10	29
15	7	53	+22.2	60.8	16.6	118	99	92	17.3	19	22	19	04	2	23	10	34	10	54
16	8	53	+17.5	60.0	16.4	130	106	85	18.3	20	51	20	39	3	20	10	56	11	09
17	9	47	+11.9	59.1	16.1	143	110	75	19.3	22	14	22	09	4	12	11	12	11	20
18	10	38	+6.0	58.2	15.8	155	113	65	20.3	23	34	23	34	4	59	11	26	11	28
19	11	26	−0.1	57.2	15.6	167	114	55	21.3	—	—	—	—	5	44	11	39	11	36
20	12	12	−5.9	56.4	15.4	179	113	44	22.3	0	50	0	56	6	28	11	51	11	44
21	12	58	−11.4	55.7	15.2	191	111	34	23.3	2	05	2	16	7	11	12	05	11	52
22	13	45	−16.3	55.1	15.0	203	108	25	24.3	3	20	3	36	7	56	12	21	12	03
23	14	33	−20.5	54.6	14.9	215	104	18	25.3	4	34	4	56	8	42	12	42	12	18
24	15	23	−23.7	54.3	14.8	228	98	11	26.3	5	45	6	13	9	30	13	09	12	40
25	16	14	−25.9	54.1	14.7	240	91	6	27.3	6	51	7	24	10	20	13	46	13	12
26	17	07	−27.0	54.0	14.7	252	82	2	28.3	7	47	8	22	11	11	14	34	13	59
27	18	00	−26.7	53.9	14.7	264	59	0	29.3	8	32	9	05	12	01	15	33	15	01
28	18	53	−25.3	54.0	14.7	276	290	0	0.5	9	06	9	34	12	50	16	41	16	14
29	19	43	−22.8	54.1	14.8	289	265	2	1.5	9	32	9	54	13	38	17	53	17	32
30	20	32	−19.2	54.4	14.8	301	256	5	2.5	9	51	10	07	14	23	19	06	18	51
31	21	19	−14.8	54.7	14.9	313	251	11	3.5	10	06	10	17	15	06	20	19	20	09

MERCURY

Day	R.A.		Dec.	Diam.	Phase	Transit		5° high			
								52°		56°	
	h	*m*	°	″	%	*h*	*m*	*h*	*m*	*h*	*m*
1	16	42	−23.4	5	100	12	02	15	01	14	24
3	16	55	−23.9	5	99	12	08	15	02	14	22
5	17	09	−24.4	5	99	12	14	15	03	14	22
7	17	23	−24.8	5	99	12	20	15	05	14	22
9	17	36	−25.1	5	98	12	25	15	08	14	24
11	17	50	−25.3	5	97	12	31	15	12	14	27
13	18	04	−25.5	5	96	12	37	15	17	14	31
15	18	18	−25.5	5	95	12	43	15	23	14	37
17	18	32	−25.4	5	94	12	49	15	30	14	45
19	18	45	−25.3	5	93	12	55	15	38	14	54
21	18	59	−25.0	5	91	13	01	15	47	15	04
23	19	13	−24.6	5	89	13	07	15	57	15	16
25	19	26	−24.1	6	86	13	12	16	07	15	28
27	19	39	−23.6	6	83	13	17	16	17	15	40
29	19	51	−22.9	6	79	13	21	16	27	15	53
31	20	03	−22.2	6	74	13	24	16	37	16	05

VENUS

Day	R.A.		Dec.	Diam.	Phase	Transit		5° high			
								52°		56°	
	h	*m*	°	″	%	*h*	*m*	*h*	*m*	*h*	*m*
1	19	36	−24.0	17	70	14	56	17	51	17	13
6	20	01	−23.0	17	68	15	01	18	07	17	32
11	20	26	−21.6	18	66	15	06	18	23	17	52
16	20	49	−20.1	18	64	15	10	18	39	18	12
21	21	12	−18.3	19	62	15	13	18	55	18	32
26	21	34	−16.3	20	60	15	15	19	11	18	51
31	21	56	−14.3	21	58	15	17	19	27	19	09

MARS

Day	R.A.		Dec.	Diam.	Phase	Transit		5° high			
								52°		56°	
	h	*m*	°	″	%	*h*	*m*	*h*	*m*	*h*	*m*
1	16	36	−22.4	4	100	11	54	8	47	9	20
6	16	51	−23.0	4	100	11	50	8	47	9	22
11	17	07	−23.4	4	100	11	46	8	47	9	24
16	17	23	−23.7	4	100	11	43	8	46	9	24
21	17	39	−24.0	4	100	11	39	8	45	9	24
26	17	56	−24.1	4	100	11	36	8	43	9	22
31	18	12	−24.1	4	100	11	33	8	40	9	19

SUNRISE AND SUNSET

	London 0°05′		51°30′		*Bristol* 2°35′		51°28′		*Birmingham* 1°55′		52°28′		*Manchester* 2°15′		53°28′		*Newcastle* 1°37′		54°59′		*Glasgow* 4°14′		55°52′		*Belfast* 5°56′		54°35′	
d	*h*	*m*	*h*	*m*	*h*	*m*	*h*	*m*	*h*	*m*	*h*	*m*	*h*	*m*	*h*	*m*	*h*	*m*	*h*	*m*	*h*	*m*	*h*	*m*	*h*	*m*	*h*	*m*
1	7	44	15	55	7	54	16	05	7	56	15	57	8	02	15	54	8	08	15	43	8	24	15	48	8	23	16	03
2	7	45	15	54	7	55	16	04	7	57	15	57	8	04	15	53	8	09	15	42	8	25	15	47	8	24	16	02
3	7	47	15	53	7	57	16	04	7	59	15	56	8	05	15	52	8	11	15	42	8	27	15	47	8	26	16	01
4	7	48	15	53	7	58	16	03	8	00	15	56	8	07	15	52	8	12	15	41	8	28	15	46	8	27	16	00
5	7	49	15	53	7	59	16	03	8	01	15	55	8	08	15	51	8	14	15	40	8	30	15	45	8	29	16	00
6	7	51	15	52	8	00	16	02	8	03	15	55	8	09	15	51	8	15	15	40	8	31	15	45	8	30	15	59
7	7	52	15	52	8	02	16	02	8	04	15	54	8	10	15	50	8	17	15	39	8	32	15	44	8	31	15	59
8	7	53	15	52	8	03	16	02	8	05	15	54	8	12	15	50	8	18	15	39	8	34	15	44	8	33	15	59
9	7	54	15	51	8	04	16	02	8	06	15	54	8	13	15	50	8	19	15	39	8	35	15	44	8	34	15	58
10	7	55	15	51	8	05	16	01	8	07	15	54	8	14	15	50	8	20	15	38	8	36	15	43	8	35	15	58
11	7	56	15	51	8	06	16	01	8	08	15	54	8	15	15	50	8	21	15	38	8	38	15	43	8	36	15	58
12	7	57	15	51	8	07	16	01	8	09	15	54	8	16	15	49	8	23	15	38	8	39	15	43	8	37	15	58
13	7	58	15	51	8	08	16	01	8	10	15	54	8	17	15	49	8	24	15	38	8	40	15	43	8	38	15	58
14	7	59	15	51	8	09	16	01	8	11	15	54	8	18	15	49	8	25	15	38	8	41	15	43	8	39	15	58
15	8	00	15	51	8	10	16	02	8	12	15	54	8	19	15	50	8	25	15	38	8	42	15	43	8	40	15	58
16	8	01	15	52	8	10	16	02	8	13	15	54	8	20	15	50	8	26	15	38	8	42	15	43	8	41	15	58
17	8	01	15	52	8	11	16	02	8	14	15	54	8	21	15	50	8	27	15	38	8	43	15	43	8	42	15	58
18	8	02	15	52	8	12	16	02	8	14	15	54	8	21	15	50	8	28	15	39	8	44	15	43	8	43	15	58
19	8	03	15	53	8	12	16	03	8	15	15	55	8	22	15	51	8	28	15	39	8	45	15	44	8	43	15	59
20	8	03	15	53	8	13	16	03	8	16	15	55	8	22	15	51	8	29	15	39	8	45	15	44	8	44	15	59
21	8	04	15	53	8	14	16	04	8	16	15	56	8	23	15	52	8	30	15	40	8	46	15	45	8	44	16	00
22	8	04	15	54	8	14	16	04	8	17	15	56	8	23	15	52	8	30	15	40	8	46	15	45	8	45	16	00
23	8	05	15	55	8	14	16	05	8	17	15	57	8	24	15	53	8	30	15	41	8	47	15	46	8	45	16	01
24	8	05	15	55	8	15	16	05	8	17	15	58	8	24	15	53	8	31	15	42	8	47	15	46	8	46	16	01
25	8	05	15	56	8	15	16	06	8	18	15	58	8	25	15	54	8	31	15	42	8	47	15	47	8	46	16	02
26	8	06	15	57	8	15	16	07	8	18	15	59	8	25	15	55	8	31	15	43	8	48	15	48	8	46	16	03
27	8	06	15	58	8	16	16	08	8	18	16	00	8	25	15	56	8	32	15	44	8	48	15	49	8	46	16	04
28	8	06	15	58	8	16	16	09	8	18	16	01	8	25	15	57	8	32	15	45	8	48	15	50	8	46	16	05
29	8	06	15	59	8	16	16	09	8	18	16	02	8	25	15	57	8	32	15	46	8	48	15	51	8	46	16	06
30	8	06	16	00	8	16	16	10	8	18	16	03	8	25	15	58	8	32	15	47	8	48	15	52	8	46	16	07
31	8	06	16	01	8	16	16	11	8	18	16	04	8	25	16	00	8	31	15	48	8	47	15	53	8	46	16	08

JUPITER

Day	*R.A.*		*Dec.*		*Transit*		*5° high*			
							52°		*56°*	
	h	*m*	°	′	*h*	*m*	*h*	*m*	*h*	*m*
1	19	36.1	−21	59	14	53	18	05	17	33
11	19	44.9	−21	39	14	23	17	37	17	06
21	19	54.1	−21	15	13	53	17	10	16	40
31	20	03.6	−20	49	13	23	16	44	16	15

Diameters – equatorial 33″ polar 31″

SATURN

Day	*R.A.*		*Dec.*		*Transit*		*5° high*			
							52°		*56°*	
	h	*m*	°	′	*h*	*m*	*h*	*m*	*h*	*m*
1	11	29.6	+5	21	6	48	0	54	0	53
11	11	31.4	+5	13	6	10	0	17	0	16
21	11	32.5	+5	09	5	32	23	35	23	34
31	11	33.0	+5	09	4	53	22	56	22	55

Diameters – equatorial 18″ polar 16″
Rings – major axis 41″ minor axis 1″

URANUS

Day	*R.A.*		*Dec.*		*Transit*		*5° high*			
							52°		*56°*	
	h	*m*	°	′	*h*	*m*	*h*	*m*	*h*	*m*
1	23	19.8	−5	10	18	36	23	01	22	49
11	23	20.1	−5	08	17	57	22	22	22	11
21	23	20.6	−5	04	17	18	21	44	21	32
31	23	21.5	−4	58	16	40	21	06	20	55

Diameter 4″

NEPTUNE

Day	*R.A.*		*Dec.*		*Transit*		*5° high*			
							52°		*56°*	
	h	*m*	°	′	*h*	*m*	*h*	*m*	*h*	*m*
1	21	36.8	−14	36	16	53	20	18	19	53
11	21	37.5	−14	33	16	15	19	40	19	15
21	21	38.4	−14	28	15	36	19	02	18	37
31	21	39.5	−14	23	14	58	18	24	18	00

Diameter 2″

RISING AND SETTING TIMES

TABLE 1. SEMI-DIURNAL ARCS (HOUR ANGLES AT RISING/SETTING)

Dec.	*Latitude* 0°	10°	20°	30°	40°	45°	50°	52°	54°	56°	58°	60°	*Dec.*
	h m	*h m*	*h m*	*h m*	*h m*	*h m*	*h m*	*h m*	*h m*	*h m*	*h m*	*h m*	
0°	6 00	6 00	6 00	6 00	6 00	6 00	6 00	6 00	6 00	6 00	6 00	6 00	0°
1°	6 00	6 01	6 01	6 02	6 03	6 04	6 05	6 05	6 06	6 06	6 06	6 07	1°
2°	6 00	6 01	6 03	6 05	6 07	6 08	6 10	6 10	6 11	6 12	6 13	6 14	2°
3°	6 00	6 02	6 04	6 07	6 10	6 12	6 14	6 15	6 17	6 18	6 19	6 21	3°
4°	6 00	6 03	6 06	6 09	6 13	6 16	6 19	6 21	6 22	6 24	6 26	6 28	4°
5°	6 00	6 04	6 07	6 12	6 17	6 20	6 24	6 26	6 28	6 30	6 32	6 35	5°
6°	6 00	6 04	6 09	6 14	6 20	6 24	6 29	6 31	6 33	6 36	6 39	6 42	6°
7°	6 00	6 05	6 10	6 16	6 24	6 28	6 34	6 36	6 39	6 42	6 45	6 49	7°
8°	6 00	6 06	6 12	6 19	6 27	6 32	6 39	6 41	6 45	6 48	6 52	6 56	8°
9°	6 00	6 06	6 13	6 21	6 31	6 36	6 44	6 47	6 50	6 54	6 59	7 04	9°
10°	6 00	6 07	6 15	6 23	6 34	6 41	6 49	6 52	6 56	7 01	7 06	7 11	10°
11°	6 00	6 08	6 16	6 26	6 38	6 45	6 54	6 58	7 02	7 07	7 12	7 19	11°
12°	6 00	6 09	6 18	6 28	6 41	6 49	6 59	7 03	7 08	7 13	7 20	7 26	12°
13°	6 00	6 09	6 19	6 31	6 45	6 53	7 04	7 09	7 14	7 20	7 27	7 34	13°
14°	6 00	6 10	6 21	6 33	6 48	6 58	7 09	7 14	7 20	7 27	7 34	7 42	14°
15°	6 00	6 11	6 22	6 36	6 52	7 02	7 14	7 20	7 27	7 34	7 42	7 51	15°
16°	6 00	6 12	6 24	6 38	6 56	7 07	7 20	7 26	7 33	7 41	7 49	7 59	16°
17°	6 00	6 12	6 26	6 41	6 59	7 11	7 25	7 32	7 40	7 48	7 57	8 08	17°
18°	6 00	6 13	6 27	6 43	7 03	7 16	7 31	7 38	7 46	7 55	8 05	8 17	18°
19°	6 00	6 14	6 29	6 46	7 07	7 21	7 37	7 45	7 53	8 03	8 14	8 26	19°
20°	6 00	6 15	6 30	6 49	7 11	7 25	7 43	7 51	8 00	8 11	8 22	8 36	20°
21°	6 00	6 16	6 32	6 51	7 15	7 30	7 49	7 58	8 08	8 19	8 32	8 47	21°
22°	6 00	6 16	6 34	6 54	7 19	7 35	7 55	8 05	8 15	8 27	8 41	8 58	22°
23°	6 00	6 17	6 36	6 57	7 23	7 40	8 02	8 12	8 23	8 36	8 51	9 09	23°
24°	6 00	6 18	6 37	7 00	7 28	7 46	8 08	8 19	8 31	8 45	9 02	9 22	24°
25°	6 00	6 19	6 39	7 02	7 32	7 51	8 15	8 27	8 40	8 55	9 13	9 35	25°
26°	6 00	6 20	6 41	7 05	7 37	7 57	8 22	8 35	8 49	9 05	9 25	9 51	26°
27°	6 00	6 21	6 43	7 08	7 41	8 03	8 30	8 43	8 58	9 16	9 39	10 08	27°
28°	6 00	6 22	6 45	7 12	7 46	8 08	8 37	8 52	9 08	9 28	9 53	10 28	28°
29°	6 00	6 22	6 47	7 15	7 51	8 15	8 45	9 01	9 19	9 41	10 10	10 55	29°
30°	6 00	6 23	6 49	7 18	7 56	8 21	8 54	9 11	9 30	9 55	10 30	12 00	30°
35°	6 00	6 28	6 59	7 35	8 24	8 58	9 46	10 15	10 58	12 00	12 00	12 00	35°
40°	6 00	6 34	7 11	7 56	8 59	9 48	12 00	12 00	12 00	12 00	12 00	12 00	40°
45°	6 00	6 41	7 25	8 21	9 48	12 00	12 00	12 00	12 00	12 00	12 00	12 00	45°
50°	6 00	6 49	7 43	8 54	12 00	12 00	12 00	12 00	12 00	12 00	12 00	12 00	50°
55°	6 00	6 58	8 05	9 42	12 00	12 00	12 00	12 00	12 00	12 00	12 00	12 00	55°
60°	6 00	7 11	8 36	12 00	12 00	12 00	12 00	12 00	12 00	12 00	12 00	12 00	60°
65°	6 00	7 29	9 25	12 00	12 00	12 00	12 00	12 00	12 00	12 00	12 00	12 00	65°
70°	6 00	7 56	12 00	12 00	12 00	12 00	12 00	12 00	12 00	12 00	12 00	12 00	70°
75°	6 00	8 45	12 00	12 00	12 00	12 00	12 00	12 00	12 00	12 00	12 00	12 00	75°
80°	6 00	12 00	12 00	12 00	12 00	12 00	12 00	12 00	12 00	12 00	12 00	12 00	80°

Note: If latitude and declination are of the same sign, take out the respondent directly. If they are of opposite signs, subtract the respondent from 12h.

Table 1 gives the complete range of declinations in case any user wishes to calculate semi-diurnal arcs for bodies other than the Sun and Moon.

Example:

Lat.	Dec.	Semi-diurnal arc
+52°	+20°	7h 51m
+52°	–20°	4h 09m

TABLE 2. CORRECTION FOR REFRACTION AND SEMI-DIAMETER

	m	*m*	*m*	*m*	*m*	*m*	*m*	*m*	*m*	*m*	*m*	*m*	*m*
0°	3	3	4	4	4	5	5	5	6	6	6	7	0°
10°	3	3	4	4	4	5	5	6	6	6	7	7	10°
20°	4	4	4	4	5	5	6	7	7	8	8	9	20°
25°	4	4	4	4	5	6	7	8	8	9	11	13	25°
30°	4	4	4	5	6	7	8	9	11	14	21	—	30°

SUNRISE AND SUNSET

The local mean time of sunrise or sunset may be found by obtaining the hour angle from Table 1 and applying it to the time of transit. The hour angle is negative for sunrise and positive for sunset. A small correction to the hour angle, which always has the effect of increasing it numerically, is necessary to allow for the Sun's semi-diameter (16′) and for refraction (34′); it is obtained from Table 2. The resulting local mean time may be converted into the standard time of the country by taking the difference between the longitude of the standard meridian of the country and that of the place, adding it to the local mean time if the place is west of the standard meridian, and subtracting it if the place is east.

Example– Required the New Zealand Mean Time (12h fast on GMT) of sunset on May 23 at Auckland, latitude 36° 50′ S. (or minus), longitude 11h 39m E. Taking the declination as +20°.6 (page 1235), we find

	h	*m*
New Zealand Standard Time	+ 12	00
Longitude	– 11	39
Longitudinal Correction	+ 0	21
Tabular entry for Lat. 30° and Dec. 20°, opposite signs	+ 5	11
Proportional part for 6° 50′ of Lat.	–	15
Proportional part for 0°.6 of Dec.	–	2
Correction (Table 2)	+	4
Hour angle	4	58
Sun transits (page 1235)	11	57
Longitudinal correction	+	21
New Zealand Mean Time	17	16

MOONRISE AND MOONSET

It is possible to calculate the times of moonrise and moonset using Table 1, though the method is more complicated because the apparent motion of the Moon is much more rapid and also more variable than that of the Sun.

TABLE 3. LONGITUDE CORRECTION

X / *A*	*40m*	*45m*	*50m*	*55m*	*60m*	*65m*	*70m*
h	*m*	*m*	*m*	*m*	*m*	*m*	*m*
1	2	2	2	2	3	3	3
2	3	4	4	5	5	5	6
3	5	6	6	7	8	8	9
4	7	8	8	9	10	11	12
5	8	9	10	11	13	14	15
6	10	11	13	14	15	16	18
7	12	13	15	16	18	19	20
8	13	15	17	18	20	22	23
9	15	17	19	21	23	24	26
10	17	19	21	23	25	27	29
11	18	21	23	25	28	30	32
12	20	23	25	28	30	33	35
13	22	24	27	30	33	35	38
14	23	26	29	32	35	38	41
15	25	28	31	34	38	41	44
16	27	30	33	37	40	43	47
17	28	32	35	39	43	46	50
18	30	34	38	41	45	49	53
19	32	36	40	44	48	51	55
20	33	38	42	46	50	54	58
21	35	39	44	48	53	57	61
22	37	41	46	50	55	60	64
23	38	43	48	53	58	62	67
24	40	45	50	55	60	65	70

The parallax of the Moon, about 57′, is near to the sum of the semi-diameter and refraction but has the opposite effect on these times. It is thus convenient to neglect all three quantities in the method outlined below.

Notation

ϕ = latitude of observer
λ = longitude of observer (measured positively towards the west)
T_{-1} = time of transit of Moon on previous day
T_0 = time of transit of Moon on day in question
T_1 = time of transit of Moon on following day
δ_0 = approximate declination of Moon
δ_R = declination of Moon at moonrise
δ_S = declination of Moon at moonset
h_0 = approximate hour angle of Moon
h_R = hour angle of Moon at moonrise
h_S = hour angle of Moon at moonset
t_R = time of moonrise
t_S = time of moonset

Method

1. With arguments ϕ, δ_0 enter Table 1 on page 1266 to determine h_0 where h_0 is negative for moonrise and positive for moonset.

2. Form approximate times from
$t_R = T_0 + \lambda + h_0$
$t_S = T_0 + \lambda + h_0$

3. Determine δ_R, δ_S for times t_R, t_S respectively.

4. Re-enter Table 1 on page 1266 with
(*a*) arguments ϕ, δ_R to determine h_R
(*b*) arguments ϕ, δ_S to determine h_S

5. Form $t_R = T_0 + \lambda + h_R + AX$
$t_S = T_0 + \lambda + h_S + AX$

where $A = (\lambda + h)$

and $X = (T_0 - T_{-1})$ if $(\lambda + h)$ is negative
$X = (T_1 - T_0)$ if $(\lambda + h)$ is positive

AX is the respondent in Table 3.

Example – To find the times of moonrise and moonset at Vancouver (ϕ = +49°, λ = +8h 12m) on 2008 January 3. The starting data (page 1220) are

T_{-1} = 7h 11m
T_0 = 7h 55m
T_1 = 8h 41m
δ_0 = –22°

1. h_0 = 4h 09m
2. Approximate values
t_R = 3d 07h 55m + 8h 12m + (–4h 09m)
= 3d 11h 58m
t_S = 3d 07h 55m + 8h 12m + (+4h 09m)
= 3d 20h 16m
3. δ_R = –21°.5
δ_S = –22°.8
4. h_R = – 4h 12m
h_S = +4h 04m
5. t_R = 3d 07h 55m + 8h 12m + (–4h 12m) + 8m
= 3d 12h 03m
t_S = 3d 07h 55m + 8h 12m + (+4h 04m) + 24m
= 3d 20h 35m

To get the LMT of the phenomenon the longitude is subtracted from the GMT thus:

Moonrise = 3d 12h 03m – 8h 12m = 3d 03h 51m
Moonset = 3d 20h 35m – 8h 12m = 3d 12h 23m

ECLIPSES 2008

ECLIPSES

During 2008 there will be four eclipses, two of the Sun and two of the Moon. (Penumbral eclipses of the Moon are not mentioned in this section as they are so difficult to observe).

1. An annular eclipse of the Sun on February 7 is visible as a partial eclipse from the western part of the South Pacific Ocean, New Zealand, and eastern Australia. The partial phase begins at 01h 38m and ends at 06h 12m. The path of annularity starts in the South Pacific Ocean and ends in Antarctica. Annularity begins at 03h 20m and ends at 04h 31m. The maximum duration of annularity is 2m 12s.

2. A total eclipse of the Moon on February 21 is visible from central and western Asia, the Indian Ocean, Africa, Europe, the Atlantic Ocean, Iceland, Greenland, the Americas, and the extreme north-east of Asia. The partial phase begins at 01h 43m and ends at 05h 09m. The total phase begins at 03h 00m and ends at 03h 51m.

3. A total eclipse of the Sun on August 1 is visible as a partial eclipse from north-east Canada, northern Europe, and Asia. The partial phase begins at 08h 04m and ends at 12h 38m. The path of totality starts in the northern islands of Canada, and then crosses northern Greenland, Novaya Zemlya and extreme western Mongolia, before ending in China. Totality begins at 09h 21m and ends at 11h 21m. The maximum duration of totality is 2m 27s.

At Greenwich the eclipse begins at 08h 33m and ends at 10h 05m, with a maximum magnitude of 22 per cent, while at Edinburgh the eclipse begins at 08h 24m and ends at 10h 11m, with a maximum magnitude of 35 per cent.

4. A partial eclipse of the Moon on August 16 is visible from Australasia, Asia (except the extreme north-east), the Indian Ocean, Antarctica, Africa, Europe, Iceland, the Atlantic Ocean, the southern tip of Greenland, the north-east of North America, Central America, and South America. The eclipse begins at 19h 35m and ends at 22h 44m. At maximum eclipse 81 per cent of the Moon's surface is obscured.

POSITIONS OF STARS

The positions of heavenly bodies on the celestial sphere are defined by two co-ordinates, right ascension and declination, which are analogous to longitude and latitude on the surface of the Earth. If we imagine the plane of the terrestrial equator extended indefinitely, it will cut the celestial sphere in a great circle known as the celestial equator. Similarly the plane of the Earth's orbit, when extended, cuts in the great circle called the ecliptic. The two intersections of these circles are known as the First Point of Aries and the First Point of Libra. If from any star a perpendicular is drawn to the celestial equator, the length of this perpendicular is the star's declination. The arc, measured eastwards along the equator from the First Point of Aries to the foot of this perpendicular, is the right ascension. An alternative definition of right ascension is that it is the angle at the celestial pole (where the Earth's axis, if prolonged, would meet the sphere) between the great circles to the First Point of Aries and to the star.

The plane of the Earth's equator has a slow movement, so that our reference system for right ascension and declination is not fixed. The consequent alteration in these quantities from year to year is called precession. In right ascension it is an increase of about 3 seconds a year for equatorial stars, and larger or smaller changes in either direction for stars near the poles, depending on the right ascension of the star. In declination it varies between +20″ and −20″ according to the right ascension of the star.

A star or other body crosses the meridian when the sidereal time is equal to its right ascension. The altitude is then a maximum, and may be deduced by remembering that the altitude of the elevated pole is numerically equal to the latitude, while that of the equator at its intersection with the meridian is equal to the co-latitude, or complement of the latitude.

Thus in London (lat. 51° 30′) the meridian altitude of Sirius is found as follows:

	°	′
Altitude of equator	38	30
Declination south	16	43
Difference	21	47

The altitude of Capella (Dec. +46° 00′) at lower transit is:

Altitude of pole	51	30
Polar distance of star	44	00
Difference	7	30

The brightness of a heavenly body is denoted by its magnitude. Omitting the exceptionally bright stars Sirius and Canopus, the twenty brightest stars are of the first magnitude, while the faintest stars visible to the naked eye are of the sixth magnitude. The magnitude scale is a precise one, as a difference of five magnitudes represents a ratio of 100 to 1 in brightness. Typical second magnitude stars are Polaris and the stars in the belt of Orion. The scale is most easily fixed in memory by comparing the stars with Norton's *Star Atlas.* The stars Sirius and Canopus and the planets Venus and Jupiter are so bright that their magnitudes are expressed by negative numbers. A small telescope will show stars down to the ninth or tenth magnitude, while stars fainter than the twentieth magnitude may be photographed by long exposures with the largest telescopes.

MEAN AND SIDEREAL TIME

The length of a sidereal day in mean time is 23h 56m 04s.09. Hence 1h MT = 1h+$9^{s}.86$ ST and 1h ST = 1h − $9^{s}.83$ MT.

Acceleration

h	*m*	*s*	*m*	*s*	*s*
1	0	10	0	00	0
2	0	20	3	02	1
3	0	30	9	07	2
4	0	39	15	13	3
5	0	49	21	18	4
6	0	59	27	23	5
7	1	09	33	28	6
8	1	19	39	34	7
9	1	29	45	39	8
10	1	39	51	44	9
11	1	48	57	49	10
12	1	58	60	00	
13	2	08			
14	2	18			
15	2	28			
16	2	38			
17	2	48			
18	2	57			
19	3	07			
20	3	17			
21	3	27			
22	3	37			
23	3	47			
24	3	57			

Retardation

h	*m*	*s*	*m*	*s*	*s*
1	0	10	0	00	0
2	0	20	3	03	1
3	0	29	9	09	2
4	0	39	15	15	3
5	0	49	21	21	4
6	0	59	27	28	5
7	1	09	33	34	6
8	1	19	39	40	7
9	1	28	45	46	8
10	1	38	51	53	9
11	1	48	57	59	10
12	1	58	60	00	
13	2	08			
14	2	18			
15	2	27			
16	2	37			
17	2	47			
18	2	57			
19	3	07			
20	3	17			
21	3	26			
22	3	36			
23	3	46			
24	3	56			

To convert an interval of mean time to the corresponding interval of sidereal time, enter the acceleration table with the given mean time (taking the hours and the minutes and seconds separately) and add the acceleration obtained to the given mean time. To convert an interval of sidereal time to the corresponding interval of mean time, take out the retardation for the given sidereal time and subtract.

The columns for the minutes and seconds of the argument are in the form known as critical tables. To use these tables, find in the appropriate left-hand column the two entries between which the given number of minutes and seconds lies; the quantity in the right-hand column between these two entries is the required acceleration or retardation. Thus the acceleration for 11m 26s (which lies between the entries 9m 07s and 15m 13s) is 2s. If the given number of minutes and seconds is a tabular entry, the required acceleration or retardation is the entry in the right-hand column above the given tabular entry, eg the retardation for 45m 46s is 7s.

Example – Convert 14h 27m 35s from ST to MT

	h	*m*	*s*
Given ST	14	27	35
Retardation for 14h		2	18
Retardation for 27m 35s			5
Corresponding MT	14	25	12

For further explanation, *see* pages 1271 and 1272.

EXPLANATION OF ASTRONOMICAL DATA

Positions of the heavenly bodies are given only to the degree of accuracy required by amateur astronomers for setting telescopes, or for plotting on celestial globes or star atlases. Where intermediate positions are required, linear interpolation may be employed.

Definitions of the terms used cannot be given here. They must be sought in astronomical literature and textbooks.

A special feature has been made of the times when the various heavenly bodies are visible in the British Isles. Since two columns, calculated for latitudes 52° and 56°, are devoted to risings and settings, the range 50° to 58° can be covered by interpolation and extrapolation. The times given in these columns are Greenwich Mean Times for the meridian of Greenwich. An observer west of this meridian must add his/her longitude (in time) and vice versa.

In accordance with the usual convention in astronomy, + and – indicate respectively north and south latitudes or declinations.

All data are, unless otherwise stated, for 0h Greenwich Mean Time (GMT), ie at the midnight at the beginning of the day named. Allowance must be made for British Summer Time during the period that this is in operation.

PAGE ONE OF EACH MONTH

The calendar for each month is explained on page 1217.

Under the heading Astronomical Phenomena will be found particulars of the more important conjunctions of the Sun, Moon and planets with each other, and also the dates of other astronomical phenomena of special interest.

Times of Minima of Algol are approximate times of the middle of the period of diminished light.

The Constellations listed each month are those that are near the meridian at the beginning of the month at 22h local mean time. Allowance must be made for British Summer Time if necessary. The fact that any star crosses the meridian 4m earlier each night or 2h earlier each month may be used, in conjunction with the lists given each month, to find what constellations are favourably placed at any moment. The table preceding the list of constellations may be extended indefinitely at the rate just quoted.

The principal phases of the Moon are the GMTs when the difference between the longitude of the Moon and that of the Sun is 0°, 90°, 180° or 270°. The times of perigee and apogee are those when the Moon is nearest to, and farthest from, the Earth, respectively. The nodes or points of intersection of the Moon's orbit and the ecliptic make a complete retrograde circuit of the ecliptic in about 19 years. From a knowledge of the longitude of the ascending node and the inclination, whose value does not vary much from 5°, the path of the Moon among the stars may be plotted on a celestial globe or star atlas.

PAGE TWO OF EACH MONTH

The Sun's semi-diameter, in arc, is given once a month.

The right ascension and declination (Dec.) is that of the true Sun. The right ascension of the mean Sun is obtained by applying the equation of time, with the sign given, to the right ascension of the true Sun, or, more easily, by applying 12h to the Sidereal Time. The direction in which the equation of time has to be applied in different problems is a frequent source of confusion and error. Apparent Solar Time is equal to the Mean Solar Time plus the Equation of Time. For example, at 12h GMT on August 8 the Equation of Time is –5m 35s and thus at 12h Mean Time on that day the Apparent Time is 12h – 5m 35s = 11h 54m 25s.

The Greenwich Sidereal Time at 0h and the Transit of the First Point of Aries (which is really the mean time when the sidereal time is 0h) are used for converting mean time to sidereal time and vice versa.

The GMT of transit of the Sun at Greenwich may also be taken as the local mean time (LMT) of transit in any longitude. It is independent of latitude. The GMT of transit in any longitude is obtained by adding the longitude to the time given if west, and vice versa.

LIGHTING-UP TIME

The legal importance of sunrise and sunset is that the Road Vehicles Lighting Regulations 1989 (SI 1989 No. 1796) as amended make the use of front and rear position lamps on vehicles compulsory during the period between sunset and sunrise. Headlamps on vehicles are required to be used during the hours of darkness on unlit roads, on lit roads with a speed limit exceeding 30mph, or whenever visibility is seriously reduced. The hours of darkness are defined in these regulations as the period between half an hour after sunset and half an hour before sunrise.

In all laws and regulations 'sunset' refers to the local sunset, ie the time at which the Sun sets at the place in question. This common-sense interpretation has been upheld by legal tribunals. Thus the necessity for providing for different latitudes and longitudes, as already described, is evident.

SUNRISE AND SUNSET

The times of sunrise and sunset are those when the Sun's upper limb, as affected by refraction, is on the true horizon of an observer at sea-level. Assuming the mean refraction to be 34′, and the Sun's semi-diameter to be 16′, the time given is that when the true zenith distance of

the Sun's centre is 90°+34′+16′ or 90° 50′, or, in other words, when the depression of the Sun's centre below the true horizon is 50′. The upper limb is then 34′ below the true horizon, but is brought there by refraction. An observer on a ship might see the Sun for a minute or so longer, because of the dip of the horizon, while another viewing the sunset over hills or mountains would record an earlier time. Nevertheless, the moment when the true zenith distance of the Sun's centre is 90° 50′ is a precise time dependent only on the latitude and longitude of the place, and independent of its altitude above sea-level, the contour of its horizon, the vagaries of refraction or the small seasonal change in the Sun's semi-diameter; this moment is suitable in every way as a definition of sunset (or sunrise) for all statutory purposes.
(For further information, *see* footnote on page 1271.)

TWILIGHT

Light reaches us before sunrise and continues to reach us for some time after sunset. The interval between darkness and sunrise or sunset and darkness is called twilight. Astronomically speaking, twilight is considered to begin or end when the Sun's centre is 18° below the horizon, as no light from the Sun can then reach the observer. As thus defined twilight may last several hours; in high latitudes at the summer solstice the depression of 18° is not reached, and twilight lasts from sunset to sunrise.

The need for some sub-division of twilight is met by dividing the gathering darkness into four stages.

(1) *Sunrise or Sunset,* defined as above
(2) *Civil twilight,* which begins or ends when the Sun's centre is 6° below the horizon. This marks the time when operations requiring daylight may commence or must cease. In England it varies from about 30 to 60 minutes after sunset and the same interval before sunrise
(3) *Nautical twilight,* which begins or ends when the Sun's centre is 12° below the horizon. This marks the time when it is, to all intents and purposes, completely dark
(4) *Astronomical twilight,* which begins or ends when the Sun's centre is 18° below the horizon. This marks theoretical perfect darkness. It is of little practical importance, especially if nautical twilight is tabulated

To assist observers the durations of civil, nautical and astronomical twilights are given at intervals of ten days. The beginning of a particular twilight is found by subtracting the duration from the time of sunrise, while the end is found by adding the duration to the time of sunset. Thus the beginning of astronomical twilight in latitude 52°, on the Greenwich meridian, on March 11 is found as 06h 23m − 113m = 04h 30m and similarly the end of civil twilight as 17h 58m +34m = 18h 32m. The letters TAN (twilight all night) are printed when twilight lasts all night.

Under the heading The Night Sky will be found notes describing the position and visibility of the planets and other phenomena.

PAGE THREE OF EACH MONTH

The Moon moves so rapidly among the stars that its position is given only to the degree of accuracy that permits linear interpolation. The right ascension (RA) and declination (Dec.) are geocentric, ie for an imaginary observer at the centre of the Earth. To an observer on the surface of the Earth the position is always different, as the altitude is always less on account of parallax, which may reach 1°.

The lunar terminator is the line separating the bright from the dark part of the Moon's disk. Apart from irregularities of the lunar surface, the terminator is elliptical, because it is a circle seen in projection. It becomes the full circle forming the limb, or edge, of the Moon at New and Full Moon. The selenographic longitude of the terminator is measured from the mean centre of the visible disk, which may differ from the visible centre by as much as 8°, because of libration.

Instead of the longitude of the terminator the Sun's selenographic co-longitude (Sun's co-long.) is tabulated. It is numerically equal to the selenographic longitude of the morning terminator, measured eastwards from the mean centre of the disk. Thus its value is approximately 270° at New Moon, 360° at First Quarter, 90° at Full Moon and 180° at Last Quarter.

The Position Angle (PA) of the Bright Limb is the position angle of the midpoint of the illuminated limb, measured eastwards from the north point on the disk. The Phase column shows the percentage of the area of the Moon's disk illuminated; this is also the illuminated percentage of the diameter at right angles to the line of cusps. The terminator is a semi-ellipse whose major axis is the line of cusps, and whose semi-minor axis is determined by the tabulated percentage; from New Moon to Full Moon the east limb is dark, and vice versa.

The times given as moonrise and moonset are those when the upper limb of the Moon is on the horizon of an observer at sea-level. The Sun's horizontal parallax (Hor. par.) is about 9″, and is negligible when considering sunrise and sunset, but that of the Moon averages about 57′. Hence the computed time represents the moment when the true zenith distance of the Moon is 90° 50′ (as for the Sun) minus the horizontal parallax. The time required for the Sun or Moon to rise or set is about four minutes (except in high latitudes).
See also page 1267 and footnote on page 1271.

The GMT of transit of the Moon over the meridian of Greenwich is given; these times are independent of latitude but must be corrected for longitude. For places in the British Isles it suffices to add the longitude if west, and vice versa. For other places a further correction is necessary because of the rapid movement of the Moon relative to the stars. The entire correction is conveniently determined by first finding the west longitude λ of the place. If the place is in west longitude, λ is the ordinary west longitude; if the place is in east longitude λ is the complement to 24h (or 360°) of the longitude and will be greater than 12h (or 180°). The correction then consists of two positive portions, namely λ and the fraction $\lambda/24$ (or $\lambda°/360$) multiplied by the difference between consecutive transits. Thus for Christchurch, New Zealand, the longitude is 11h 31m east, so λ = 12h 29m and the fraction $\lambda/24$ is 0.52. The transit on the local date 5 March 2008 is found as follows:

		d	*h*	*m*
GMT of transit at Greenwich	March	5	10	22
λ			12	29
0.52 × (10h 22m – 9h 32m)				25
GMT of transit at Christchurch		5	23	16
Corr. to NZ Standard Time			12	00
Local standard time of transit	March	6	11	16

As is evident, for any given place the quantities λ and the correction to local standard time may be combined permanently, being here 24h 29m.

Positions of Mercury are given for every second day, and those of Venus and Mars for every fifth day; they may be interpolated linearly. The diameter (Diam.) is given in seconds of arc. The phase is the illuminated percentage of the disk. In the case of the inner planets this approaches 100 at superior conjunction and 0 at inferior conjunction. When the phase is less than 50 the planet is crescent-shaped or horned; for greater phases it is gibbous. In the case of the exterior planet Mars, the phase approaches 100 at conjunction and opposition, and is a minimum at the quadratures.

Since the planets cannot be seen when on the horizon, the actual times of rising and setting are not given; instead, the time when the planet has an apparent altitude of 5° has been tabulated. If the time of transit is between 00h and 12h the time refers to an altitude of 5° above the eastern horizon; if between 12h and 24h, to the western horizon. The phenomenon tabulated is the one that occurs between sunset and sunrise. The times given may be interpolated for latitude and corrected for longitude, as in the case of the Sun and Moon.

PAGE FOUR OF EACH MONTH

The GMTs of sunrise and sunset for seven cities, whose adopted positions in longitude (W.) and latitude (N.) are given immediately below the name, may be used not only for these phenomena, but also for lighting-up times (*see* page 1269 for a fuller explanation).

The particulars for the four outer planets resemble those for the planets on Page Three of each month, except that, under Uranus and Neptune, times when the planet is 10° high instead of 5° high are given; this is because of the inferior brightness of these planets. The diameters given for the rings of Saturn are those of the major axis (in the plane of the planet's equator) and the minor axis respectively. The former has a small seasonal change due to the slightly varying distance of the Earth from Saturn, but the latter varies from zero when the Earth passes through the ring plane every 15 years to its maximum opening half-way between these periods. The rings were last open at their widest extent (and Saturn at its brightest) in 2002; this will occur again in 2017. The Earth passed through the ring plane in 1995–6 and will do so again in 2009.

TIME

From the earliest ages, the natural division of time into recurring periods of day and night has provided the practical time-scale for the everyday activities of the human race. Indeed, if any alternative means of time measurement is adopted, it must be capable of adjustment so as to remain in general agreement with the natural time-scale defined by the diurnal rotation of the Earth on its axis. Ideally the rotation should be measured against a fixed frame of reference; in practice it must be measured against the background provided by the celestial bodies. If the Sun is chosen as the reference point, we obtain Apparent Solar Time, which is the time indicated by a sundial. It is not a uniform time but is subject to variations which amount to as much as a quarter of an hour in each direction. Such wide variations cannot be tolerated in a practical time-scale, and this has led to the concept of Mean Solar Time in which all the days are exactly the same length and equal to the average length of the Apparent Solar Day.

The positions of the stars in the sky are specified in relation to a fictitious reference point in the sky known as the First Point of Aries (or the Vernal Equinox). It is therefore convenient to adopt this same reference point when considering the rotation of the Earth against the background of the stars. The time-scale so obtained is known as Apparent Sidereal Time.

GREENWICH MEAN TIME

The daily rotation of the Earth on its axis causes the Sun and the other heavenly bodies to appear to cross the sky from east to west. It is convenient to represent this relative motion as if the Sun really performed a daily circuit around a fixed Earth. Noon in Apparent Solar Time may then be defined as the time at which the Sun transits across the observer's meridian. In Mean Solar Time, noon is similarly defined by the meridian transit of a fictitious Mean Sun moving uniformly in the sky with the same average speed as the true Sun. Mean Solar Time observed on the meridian of the transit circle telescope of the Royal Observatory at Greenwich is called Greenwich Mean Time (GMT). The mean solar day is divided into 24 hours and, for astronomical and other scientific purposes, these are numbered 0 to 23, commencing at midnight. Civil time is usually reckoned in two periods of 12 hours, designated am (*ante meridiem,* ie before noon) and pm (*post meridiem,* ie after noon), although the 24 hour clock is increasingly being used.

UNIVERSAL TIME

Before 1925 January 1, GMT was reckoned in 24 hours commencing at noon; since that date it has been reckoned from midnight. To avoid confusion in the use of the designation GMT before and after 1925, since 1928 astronomers have tended to use the term Universal Time (UT) or Weltzeit (WZ) to denote GMT measured from Greenwich Mean Midnight.

In precision work it is necessary to take account of small variations in Universal Time. These arise from small irregularities in the rotation of the Earth. Observed astronomical time is designated UT0. Observed time corrected for the effects of the motion of the poles (giving rise to a 'wandering' in longitude) is designated UT1. There is also a seasonal fluctuation in the rate of rotation of the Earth arising from meteorological causes, often called the annual fluctuation. UT1 corrected for this effect is designated UT2 and provides a time-scale free from short-period fluctuations. It is still subject to small secular and irregular changes.

APPARENT SOLAR TIME

As mentioned above, the time shown by a sundial is called

SUNRISE, SUNSET, MOONRISE AND MOONSET

The tables have been constructed for the meridian of Greenwich and for latitudes 52° and 56°. They give Greenwich Mean Time (GMT) throughout the year. To obtain the GMT of the phenomenon as seen from any other latitude and longitude in the British Isles, first interpolate or extrapolate for latitude by the usual rules of proportion. To the time thus found, the longitude (expressed in time) is to be added if west (as it usually is in Great Britain) or subtracted if east. If the longitude is expressed in degrees and minutes of arc, it must be converted to time at the rate of 1° = 4m and 15′ = 1m. A method of calculating rise and set time for other places in the world is given on page 1267.

The GMT at which the planet transits the Greenwich meridian is also given. The times of transit are to be corrected to local meridians in the usual way, as already described.

Apparent Solar Time. It differs from Mean Solar Time by an amount known as the Equation of Time, which is the total effect of two causes which make the length of the apparent solar day non-uniform. One cause of variation is that the orbit of the Earth is not a circle but an ellipse, having the Sun at one focus. As a consequence, the angular speed of the Earth in its orbit is not constant; it is greatest at the beginning of January when the Earth is nearest the Sun.

The other cause is due to the obliquity of the ecliptic; the plane of the equator (which is at right angles to the axis of rotation of the Earth) does not coincide with the ecliptic (the plane defined by the apparent annual motion of the Sun around the celestial sphere) but is inclined to it at an angle of 23° 26′. As a result, the apparent solar day is shorter than average at the equinoxes and longer at the solstices. From the combined effects of the components due to obliquity and eccentricity, the equation of time reaches its maximum values in February (−14 minutes) and early November (+16 minutes). It has a zero value on four dates during the year, and it is only on these dates (approximately April 15, June 14, September 1 and December 25) that a sundial shows Mean Solar Time.

SIDEREAL TIME

A sidereal day is the duration of a complete rotation of the Earth with reference to the First Point of Aries. The term sidereal (or 'star') time is a little misleading since the time-scale so defined is not exactly the same as that which would be defined by successive transits of a selected star, as there is a small progressive motion between the stars and the First Point of Aries due to the precession of the Earth's axis. This makes the length of the sidereal day shorter than the true period of rotation by 0.008 seconds. Superimposed on this steady precessional motion are small oscillations (nutation), giving rise to fluctuations in apparent sidereal time amounting to as much as 1.2 seconds. It is therefore customary to employ Mean Sidereal Time, from which these fluctuations have been removed. The conversion of GMT to Greenwich sidereal time (GST) may be performed by adding the value of the GST at 0h on the day in question (page two of each month) to the GMT converted to sidereal time using the table on page 1268.

Example – To find the GST at August 8d 02h 41m 11s GMT

	h	*m*	*s*
GST at 0h	21	07	30
GMT	2	41	11
Acceleration for 2h			20
Acceleration for 41m 11s			7
Sum = GST =	23	49	08

If the observer is not on the Greenwich meridian then his/her longitude, measured positively westwards from Greenwich, must be subtracted from the GST to obtain Local Sidereal Time (LST). Thus, in the above example, an observer 5h east of Greenwich, or 19h west, would find the LST as 4h 47m 05s.

EPHEMERIS TIME

An analysis of observations of the positions of the Sun, Moon and planets taken over an extended period is used in preparing ephemerides. (An ephemeris is a table giving the apparent position of a heavenly body at regular intervals of time, eg one day or ten days, and may be used to compare current observations with tabulated positions.) Discrepancies between the positions of heavenly bodies observed over a 300-year period and their predicted positions arose because the time-scale to which the observations were related was based on the assumption that the rate of rotation of the Earth is uniform. It is now known that this rate of rotation is variable. A revised time-scale, Ephemeris Time (ET), was devised to bring the ephemerides into agreement with the observations.

The second of ET is defined in terms of the annual motion of the Earth in its orbit around the Sun (1/31556925.9747 of the tropical year for 1900 January 0d 12h ET). The precise determination of ET from astronomical observations is a lengthy process as the requisite standard of accuracy can only be achieved by averaging over a number of years.

In 1976 the International Astronomical Union adopted Terrestrial Dynamical Time (TDT), a new dynamical time-scale for general use whose scale unit is the SI second (*see* Atomic Time, below). TDT was renamed Terrestrial Time (TT) in 1991. ET is now of little more than historical interest.

TERRESTRIAL TIME

The uniform time system used in computing the ephemerides of the solar system is Terrestrial Time (TT), which has replaced ET for this purpose. Except for the most rigorous astronomical calculations, it may be assumed to be the same as ET. During 2008 the estimated difference TT − UT is about 65 seconds.

ATOMIC TIME

The fundamental standards of time and frequency must be defined in terms of a periodic motion adequately uniform, enduring and measurable. Progress has made it possible to use natural standards, such as atomic or molecular oscillations. Continuous oscillations are generated in an electrical circuit, the frequency of which is then compared or brought into coincidence with the frequency characteristic of the absorption or emission by the atoms or molecules when they change between two selected energy levels. Since the 13th General Conference on Weights and Measures in October 1967, the unit of time, the second, has been defined in the International System of units (SI) as 'the duration of 9 192 631 770 periods of the radiation corresponding to the transition between the two hyperfine levels of the ground state of the caesium-133 atom.'

In the UK, the national time scale is maintained by the National Physical Laboratory (NPL), using an ensemble of atomic clocks based on either caesium or hydrogen atoms. In addition the NPL (along with several other national laboratories) has constructed and operates a caesium fountain primary frequency standard, which utilises the cooling of caesium atoms by laser light to determine the duration of the SI second at the highest attainable level of accuracy. Caesium fountain primary standards typically achieve an accuracy of around 1 part in 1,000 000 000 000 000, which is equivalent to one second in 30 million years.

Timekeeping worldwide is based on two closely related atomic time scales that are established through international collaboration. International Atomic Time (TAI) is formed by combining the readings of more than 250 atomic clocks located in about 55 institutes and was set close to the astronomically-based Universal Time (UT) near the beginning of 1958. It was formally recognised in

1971 and since 1988 January 1 has been maintained by the International Bureau of Weights and Measures (BIPM). Civil time in almost all countries is now based on Co-ordinated Universal Time (UTC), which differs from TAI by an integer number of seconds and was designed to make both atomic time and UT available with accuracy appropriate for most users. On 1 January 1972 UTC was set to be exactly 10 seconds behind TAI, and since then the UTC time-scale has been adjusted by the insertion (or, in principle, omission) of leap seconds in order to keep it within ±0.9 s of UT. These leap seconds are introduced, when necessary, at the same instant throughout the world, either at the end of December or at the end of June. The last leap second occurred immediately prior to 0h UTC on 2006 January 1 and was the 23rd leap second. All leap seconds so far have been positive, with 61 seconds in the final minute of the UTC month. The time 23h 59m 60s UTC is followed one second later by 0h 0m 00s of the first day of the following month. Notices concerning the insertion of leap seconds are issued by the International Earth Rotation and Reference Systems Service at the Observatoire de Paris.

The computation of UTC is carried out monthly by the BIPM and takes place in three stages. First, a weighted average known as Echelle Atomique Libre (EAL) is calculated from all of the contributing atomic clocks. In the second stage, TAI is generated by applying small corrections, derived from the results contributed by primary frequency standards, to the scale interval of EAL to maintain its value close to that of the SI second. Finally, UTC is formed from TAI by the addition of an integer number of seconds. The results are published monthly in the BIPM Circular T in the form of offsets at 5-day intervals between UTC and the time scales of contributing organisations.

RADIO TIME-SIGNALS

UTC is made generally available through time-signals and standard frequency broadcasts such as MSF in the UK, CHU in Canada and WWV and WWVH in the USA. These are based on national time-scales that are maintained in close agreement with UTC and provide traceability to the national time-scale and to UTC. The markers of seconds in the UTC scale coincide with those of TAI.

To disseminate the national time-scale in the UK, special signals (call-sign MSF) are broadcast by the National Physical Laboratory. From 2007 April 1 the MSF service, previously broadcast from British Telecom's radio station at Rugby, has been transmitted from Anthorn radio station in Cumbria. The signals are controlled from a caesium beam atomic frequency standard and consist of a precise frequency carrier of 60 kHz which is switched off, after being on for at least half a second, to mark every second. The first second of the minute begins with a period of 500 ms with the carrier switched off, to serve as a minute marker. In the other seconds the carrier is always off for at least one tenth of a second at the start and then it carries an on-off code giving the British clock time and date, together with information identifying the start of the next minute. Changes to and from summer time are made following government announcements. Leap seconds are inserted as announced by the IERS and information provided by them on the difference between UTC and UT is also signalled. Other broadcast signals in the UK include the BBC six pips signal, the BT Timeline ('speaking clock'), the NPL telephone and internet time services for computers, and a coded time-signal on the BBC 198 kHz transmitters which is used for timing in the electricity supply industry. From 1972 January 1 the six pips on the BBC have consisted of five short pips from second 55 to second 59 (six pips in the case of a leap second) followed by one lengthened pip, the start of which indicates the exact minute. From 1990 February 5 these signals have been controlled by the BBC with seconds markers referenced to the satellite-based US navigation system GPS (Global Positioning System) and time and day referenced to the MSF transmitter. Formerly they were generated by the Royal Greenwich Observatory. The NPL telephone and internet services are directly connected to the national time scale.

Accurate timing may also be obtained from the signals of international navigation systems such as the ground-based LORAN-C, or the satellite-based American GPS or Russian GLONASS systems.

STANDARD TIME

Since 1880 the standard time in Britain has been Greenwich Mean Time (GMT); a statute that year enacted that the word 'time' when used in any legal document relating to Britain meant, unless otherwise specifically stated, the mean time of the Greenwich meridian. Greenwich was adopted as the universal meridian on 13 October 1884. A system of standard time by zones is used worldwide, standard time in each zone differing from that of the Greenwich meridian by an integral number of hours or, exceptionally, half-hours or quarter-hours, either fast or slow. The large territories of the USA and Canada are divided into zones approximately 7.5° on either side of central meridians.

Variations from the standard time of some countries occur during part of the year; they are decided annually and are usually referred to as Summer Time or Daylight Saving Time.

At the 180th meridian the time can be either 12 hours fast on Greenwich Mean Time or 12 hours slow, and a change of date occurs. The internationally recognised date or calendar line is a modification of the 180th meridian, drawn so as to include islands of any one group on the same side of the line, or for political reasons. The line is indicated by joining up the following coordinates:

Lat.	*Long.*	*Lat.*	*Long.*
90° S.	180°	48° N.	180°
51° S.	180°	53° N.	170° E.
45° S.	172.5° W.	65.5° N.	169° W.
15° S.	172.5° W.	68° N.	169° W.
5° S.	180°	90° N.	180°

Changes to the date line would require an international conference.

BRITISH SUMMER TIME

In 1916 an Act ordained that during a defined period of that year the legal time for general purposes in Great Britain should be one hour in advance of Greenwich Mean Time. The Summer Time Acts 1922 and 1925 defined the period during which Summer Time was to be in force, stabilising practice until the Second World War.

During World War 2 (1941–5) and in 1947 Double Summer Time (two hours in advance of Greenwich Mean Time) was used for the period in which ordinary Summer Time would have been in force. During these years clocks were also kept one hour in advance of Greenwich Mean Time in the winter. After the war, ordinary Summer Time was invoked each year from 1948–68.

Between 1968 October 27 and 1971 October 31 clocks were kept one hour ahead of Greenwich Mean Time throughout the year. This was known as British Standard Time.

The most recent legislation is the Summer Time Act 1972, which enacted that 'the period of summer time for the purposes of this Act is the period beginning at two o'clock, Greenwich mean time, in the morning of the day after the third Saturday in March or, if that day is Easter Day, the day after the second Saturday in March, and ending at two o'clock, Greenwich mean time, in the morning of the day after the fourth Saturday in October.'

The duration of Summer Time can be varied by Order in Council and in recent years alterations have been made to synchronise the period of Summer Time in Britain with that used in Europe. The rule for 1981–94 defined the period of Summer Time in the UK as from the last Sunday in March to the day following the fourth Saturday in October and the hour of changeover was altered to 01h Greenwich Mean Time.

There was no rule for the dates of Summer Time between 1995–7. Since 1998 the 9th European Parliament and Council Directive on Summer Time has harmonised the dates on which Summer Time begins and ends across member states as the last Sundays in March and October respectively. Under the directive Summer Time begins and ends at 01hr Greenwich Mean Time in each member state. Amendments to the Summer Time Act to implement the directive came into force in 2002.

The duration of Summer Time in 2008 is:
March 30 01h GMT to October 26 01h GMT

MEAN REFRACTION

Alt.	Ref.	Alt.	Ref.	Alt.	Ref.
° ′	′	° ′	′	° ′	′
1 20		3 12		7 54	
	21		13		6
1 30		3 34		9 27	
	20		12		5
1 41		4 00		11 39	
	19		11		4
1 52		4 30		15 00	
	18		10		3
2 05		5 06		20 42	
	17		9		2
2 19		5 50		32 20	
	16		8		1
2 35		6 44		62 17	
	15		7		0
2 52		7 54		90 00	
	14				
3 12					

The refraction table is in the form of a critical table (*see* page 1268).

ASTRONOMICAL CONSTANTS

Solar parallax	8″.794
Astronomical unit	149597870 km
Precession for the year 2008	50″.291
Precession in right ascension	3^s.075
Precession in declination	20″.043
Constant of nutation	9″.202
Constant of aberration	20″.496
Mean obliquity of ecliptic (2008)	23° 26′ 18″
Moon's equatorial hor. parallax	57′ 02″.70
Velocity of light in vacuo per second	299792.5 km
Solar motion per second	20.0 km
Equatorial radius of the Earth	6378.140 km
Polar radius of the Earth	6356.755 km
North galactic pole (IAU standard)	RA 12h 49m (1950.0). Dec.+27°.4 N.
Solar apex	RA 18h 06m Dec. +30°
Length of year (in mean solar days)	
Tropical	365.24219
Sidereal	365.25636
Anomalistic (perihelion to perihelion)	365.25964
Eclipse	346.62003

Length of month (mean values)	*d*	*h*	*m*	*s*
New Moon to New	29	12	44	02.9
Sidereal	27	07	43	11.5
Anomalistic (perigee to perigee)	27	13	18	33.2

THE EARTH

The shape of the Earth is that of an oblate spheroid or solid of revolution whose meridian sections are ellipses not differing much from circles, whilst the sections at right angles are circles. The length of the equatorial axis is about 12,756 km, and that of the polar axis is 12,714 km. The mean density of the Earth is 5.5 times that of water, although that of the surface layer is less. The Earth and Moon revolve about their common centre of gravity in a lunar month; this centre in turn revolves round the Sun in a plane known as the ecliptic, that passes through the Sun's centre. The Earth's equator is inclined to this plane at an angle of 23.4°. This tilt is the cause of the seasons. In mid-latitudes, and when the Sun is high above the Equator, not only does the high noon altitude make the days longer, but the Sun's rays fall more directly on the Earth's surface; these effects combine to produce summer. In equatorial regions the noon altitude is large throughout the year, and there is little variation in the length of the day. In higher latitudes the noon altitude is lower, and the days in summer are appreciably longer than those in winter.

The average velocity of the Earth in its orbit is 30 km a second. It makes a complete rotation on its axis in about 23h 56m of mean time, which is the sidereal day. Because of its annual revolution round the Sun, the rotation with respect to the Sun, or the solar day, is more than this by about four minutes (*see* page 1271–2). The extremity of the axis of rotation, or the North Pole of the Earth, is not rigidly fixed, but wanders over an area roughly 20 metres in diameter.

ELEMENTS OF THE SOLAR SYSTEM

Orb	Mean distance from Sun (Earth = 1)	Mean distance from Sun km 10^6	Sidereal period days	Synodic period days	Incl. of orbit to ecliptic °	Incl. of orbit to ecliptic ′	Diameter km	Mass (Earth = 1)	Period of rotation on axis days
Sun	—	—	—	—	—		1,392,530	332,981	25–35*
Mercury	0.39	58	88.0	116	7	00	4,879	0.0553	58.646
Venus	0.72	108	224.7	584	3	24	12,104	0.8150	243.019*r*
Earth	1.00	150	365.3	—	—		12,756*e*	1.0000	0.997
Mars	1.52	228	687.0	780	1	51	6,794*e*	0.1074	1.026
Jupiter	5.20	778	4,332.6	399	1	18	142,984*e* 133,708*p*	317.83	0.410*e*
Saturn	9.55	1429	10,759.2	378	2	29	120,536*e* 108,728*p*	95.16	0.426*e*
Uranus	19.22	2875	30,684.6	370	0	46	51,118*e*	14.54	0.718*r*
Neptune	30.11	4504	60,191.2	367	1	46	49,528*e*	17.15	0.671
Pluto †	39.80	5954	91,708.2	367	17	09	2,302	0.002	6.387

e equatorial, *p* polar, *r* retrograde, * depending on latitude, † reclassified as a dwarf planet since August 2006

THE SATELLITES

Name		Star mag.	Mean distance from primary km	Sidereal period of revolution d
EARTH				
I	Moon	—	384,400	27.322
MARS				
I	Phobos	11	9,378	0.319
II	Deimos	12	23,459	1.262
JUPITER				
XVI	Metis	17	127,960	0.295
XV	Adrastea	19	128,980	0.298
V	Amalthea	14	181,300	0.498
XIV	Thebe	16	221,900	0.675
I	Io	5	421,600	1.769
II	Europa	5	670,900	3.552
III	Ganymede	5	1,070,000	7.155
IV	Callisto	6	1,883,000	16.689
XIII	Leda	20	11,165,000	240.92
VI	Himalia	15	11,460,000	250.57
X	Lysithea	18	11,717,000	259.20
VII	Elara	17	11,741,000	259.64
XII	Ananke	19	21,276,000	629.77*r*
XI	Carme	18	23,404,000	734.17*r*
VIII	Pasiphae	17	23,624,000	743.68*r*
IX	Sinope	18	23,939,000	758.90*r*
SATURN				
XVIII	Pan	20	133,583	0.575
XV	Atlas	18	137,640	0.602
XVI	Prometheus	16	139,353	0.613
XVII	Pandora	16	141,700	0.629
XI	Epimetheus	15	151,422	0.695
X	Janus	14	151,472	0.695
I	Mimas	13	185,520	0.942
II	Enceladus	12	238,020	1.370
III	Tethys	10	294,660	1.888
XIII	Telesto	19	294,660	1.888
XIV	Calypso	19	294,660	1.888
IV	Dione	10	377,400	2.737
XII	Helene	18	377,400	2.737
V	Rhea	10	527,040	4.518
VI	Titan	8	1,221,850	15.945

Name		Star mag.	Mean distance from primary km	Sidereal period of revolution d
SATURN				
VII	Hyperion	14	1,464,100	21.277
VIII	Iapetus	11	3,560,800	79.330
IX	Phoebe	16	12,944,300	550.48*r*
URANUS				
VI	Cordelia	24	49,750	0.335
VII	Ophelia	24	53,760	0.376
VIII	Bianca	23	59,170	0.435
IX	Cressida	22	61,780	0.464
X	Desdemona	22	62,660	0.474
XI	Juliet	21	64,360	0.493
XII	Portia	21	66,100	0.513
XIII	Rosalind	22	69,930	0.558
XIV	Belinda	22	75,260	0.624
XV	Puck	20	86,000	0.762
V	Miranda	16	129,900	1.413
I	Ariel	14	190,900	2.520
II	Umbriel	15	266,000	4.144
III	Titania	14	436,300	8.706
IV	Oberon	14	583,600	13.463
XVI	Caliban	22	7,231,000	579.5*r*
XX	Stephano	24	8,004,000	676.5*r*
XVII	Sycorax	21	12,179,000	1,283.4*r*
XVIII	Prospero	23	16,256,000	1,992.8*r*
XIX	Setebos	23	17,418,000	2,203.3*r*
NEPTUNE				
III	Naiad	25	48,230	0.294
IV	Thalassa	24	50,070	0.311
V	Despina	23	52,530	0.335
VI	Galatea	22	61,950	0.429
VII	Larissa	22	73,550	0.555
VIII	Proteus	20	117,650	1.122
I	Triton	13	354,760	5.877
II	Nereid	19	5,513,400	360.136
PLUTO				
I	Charon	17	19,600	6.387

Currently the total number of satellites of the outer planets are: Jupiter 62, Saturn 59, Uranus 27, Neptune 13, Pluto 3.

TERRESTRIAL MAGNETISM

The Earth's main magnetic field corresponds approximately to that of a very strong small bar magnet near the centre of the Earth, but with appreciable smooth spatial departures. The origin of the main field is generally ascribed to electric currents associated with fluid motions in the Earth's core. As a result not only does the main field vary in strength and direction from place to place, but also with time. Superimposed on the main field are local and regional anomalies whose magnitudes may in places approach that of the main field; these are due to the influence of mineral deposits in the Earth's crust. A small proportion of the field is of external origin, mostly associated with electric currents in the ionosphere. The configuration of the external field and the ionisation of the atmosphere depend on the incident particle and radiation flux from the Sun. There are, therefore, short-term and non-periodic as well as diurnal, 27-day, seasonal and 11-year periodic changes in the magnetic field, dependent upon the position of the Sun and the degree of solar activity.

A magnetic compass points along the horizontal component of a magnetic line of force. These lines of force converge on the 'magnetic dip-poles', the places where the Earth's magnetic field is vertical. These poles move with time, and their present approximate adopted mean positions are 84.5° N., 126.5° W. and 64.5° S., 137.6° E.

There is also a 'magnetic equator', at all points of which the vertical component of the Earth's magnetic field is zero and a magnetised needle remains horizontal. This line runs between 2° and 12° north of the geographical equator in Asia and Africa, turns sharply south off the west African coast, and crosses South America through Brazil, Bolivia and Peru; it re-crosses the geographical equator in mid-Pacific.

Reference has already been made to secular changes in the Earth's field. The following table indicates the changes in magnetic declination (or variation of the compass). Declination is the angle in the horizontal plane between the direction of true north and that in which a magnetic compass points. Similar, though much smaller, changes have occurred in 'dip' or magnetic inclination. Secular changes differ throughout the world. Although the London observations suggest a cycle with a period of several hundred years, an exact repetition is unlikely.

London		*Greenwich*	
1580	11° 15′ E.	1900	16° 29′ W.
1622	5° 56′ E.	1925	13° 10′ W.
1665	1° 22′ W.	1950	9° 07′ W.
1730	13° 00′ W.	1975	6° 39′ W.
1773	21° 09′ W.	1998	3° 32′ W.
1850	22° 24′ W.		

In order that up-to-date information on declination may be available, many governments publish magnetic charts on which there are lines (isogonic lines) passing through all places at which specified values of declination will be found at the date of the chart.

In the British Isles, isogonic lines now run approximately north-east to south-west. Though there are considerable local deviations due to geological causes, a rough value of magnetic declination may be obtained by assuming that at 50° N. on the meridian of Greenwich, the value in 2008 is 1° 24′ west and allowing an increase of 12′ for each degree of latitude northwards and one of 27′ for each degree of longitude westwards. For example, at 53° N., 5° W., declination will be about 1°24′ + 36′ + 135′, ie 4° 15′ west. The average annual change at the present time is about 10′ decrease.

The number of magnetic observatories is about 180, irregularly distributed over the globe. There are three in Great Britain, run by the British Geological Survey: at Hartland, north Devon; at Eskdalemuir, Dumfries and Galloway; and at Lerwick, Shetland Islands. The following are some recent annual mean values of the magnetic elements for Hartland.

Year	*Declination West* °	′	*Dip or inclination* °	′	*Horizontal intensity nanoTesla (nT)*	*Vertical intensity nT*
1960	9	58.8	66	43.9	18707	43504
1965	9	30.1	66	34.0	18872	43540
1970	9	06.5	66	26.1	19033	43636
1975	8	32.3	66	17.0	19212	43733
1980	7	43.8	66	10.3	19330	43768
1985	6	56.1	66	07.9	19379	43796
1990	6	15.0	66	09.7	19539	43896
1995	5	33.2	66	07.3	19457	43951
2000	4	43.6	66	06.9	19508	44051
2005	3	56.4	66	06.0	19576	44177
2006	3	47.9	66	04.9	19599	44190

As well as navigation at sea, in the air and on land by compass the oil industry depends on the Earth's magnetic field as a directional reference. They use magnetic survey tools when drilling well-bores and require accurate estimates of the local magnetic field, taking into account the crustal and external fields.

MAGNETIC STORMS

Occasionally, sometimes with great suddenness, the Earth's magnetic field is subject for several hours to marked disturbance. During a severe storm in October 2003 the declination at Eskdalemuir changed by over 5° in six minutes. In many instances such disturbances are accompanied by widespread displays of aurorae, marked changes in the incidence of cosmic rays, an increase in the reception of 'noise' from the Sun at radio frequencies, and rapid changes in the ionosphere and induced electric currents within the Earth which adversely affect satellite operations, telecommunications and electric power transmission systems. The disturbances are caused by changes in the stream of ionised particles which emanates from the Sun and through which the Earth is continuously passing. Some of these changes are associated with visible eruptions on the Sun, usually in the region of sun-spots. There is a marked tendency for disturbances to recur after intervals of about 27 days, the apparent period of rotation of the Sun on its axis, which is consistent with the sources being located on particular areas of the Sun.

TIME MEASUREMENT AND CALENDARS

MEASUREMENTS OF TIME

Measurements of time are based on the time taken by the earth to rotate on its axis (day); by the moon to revolve around the earth (month); and by the earth to revolve around the sun (year). From these, which are not commensurable, certain average or mean intervals have been adopted for ordinary use.

THE DAY

The day begins at midnight and is divided into 24 hours of 60 minutes, each of 60 seconds. The hours are counted from midnight up to 12 noon (when the sun crosses the meridian), and these hours are designated am *(ante meridiem)*; and again from noon up to 12 midnight, which hours are designated pm *(post meridiem)*, except when the 24-hour reckoning is employed. The 24-hour reckoning ignores am and pm, numbering the hours 0 to 23 from midnight.

Colloquially the 24 hours are divided into day and night, day being the time while the sun is above the horizon (including the four stages of twilight defined in the Astronomy section). Day is subdivided into morning, the early part of daytime, ending at noon; afternoon, from noon to about 6pm; and evening, which may be said to extend from 6pm until midnight. Night begins at the close of astronomical twilight (*see* the Astronomy section) and extends beyond midnight to sunrise the next day.

The names of the days are derived from Old English translations or adaptations of the Roman titles.

Sunday	Sun	Sol
Monday	Moon	Luna
Tuesday	Tiw/Tyr (god of war)	Mars
Wednesday	Woden/Odin	Mercury
Thursday	Thor	Jupiter
Friday	Frigga/Freyja (goddess of love)	Venus
Saturday	Saeterne	Saturn

THE MONTH

The month in the ordinary calendar is approximately the twelfth part of a year, but the lengths of the different months vary from 28 (or 29) days to 31.

THE YEAR

The equinoctial or tropical year is the time that the earth takes to revolve around the sun from equinox to equinox, ie 365.24219 mean solar days, or 365 days 5 hours 48 minutes and 45 seconds.

The calendar year usually consists of 365 days but a year containing 366 days is called a bissextile (*see* Roman calendar) or leap year, one day being added to the month of February so that a date 'leaps over' a day of the week. In the Roman calendar the day that was repeated was the sixth day before the beginning of March, the equivalent of 24 February.

A year is a leap year if the date of the year is divisible by four without remainder, unless it is the last year of the century. The last year of a century is a leap year only if its number is divisible by 400 without remainder, eg the years 1800 and 1900 had only 365 days but the year 2000 had 366 days.

THE SOLSTICE

A solstice is the point in the tropical year at which the sun attains its greatest distance, north or south, from the Equator. In the northern hemisphere the furthest point north of the Equator marks the summer solstice and the furthest point south – the winter solstice.

The date of the solstice varies according to locality. For example, if the summer solstice falls on 21 June late in the day by Greenwich time, that day will be the longest of the year at Greenwich though it may be by only a second, but it will fall on 22 June, local date, in Japan, and so 22 June will be the longest day there. The date of the solstice is also affected by the length of the tropical year, which is 365 days 6 hours less about 11 minutes 15 seconds. If a solstice happens late on 21 June in one year, it will be nearly 6 hours later in the next (unless the next year is a leap year), ie early on 22 June, and that will be the longest day.

This delay of the solstice does not continue because the extra day in a leap year brings it back a day in the calendar. However, because of the 11 minutes 15 seconds mentioned above, the additional day in a leap year brings the solstice back too far by 45 minutes, and the time of the solstice in the calendar is earlier, in a four-year pattern, as the century progresses. The last year of a century is in most cases not a leap year, and the omission of the extra day puts the date of the solstice later by about 6 hours. Compensation for this is made by the fourth centennial year being a leap year. The solstice has become earlier in date throughout the last century and, because the year 2000 was a leap year, the solstice will get earlier still throughout the 21st century.

The date of the winter solstice, the shortest day of the year, is affected by the same factors as the longest day.

At Greenwich the sun sets at its earliest by the clock about ten days before the shortest day. The daily change in the time of sunset is due in the first place to the sun's movement southwards at this time of the year, which diminishes the interval between the sun's transit and its setting. However, the daily decrease of the Equation of Time causes the time of apparent noon to be continuously later day by day, which to some extent counteracts the first effect. The rates of the change of these two quantities are not equal or uniform; their combination causes the date of earliest sunset to be 12 or 13 December at Greenwich. In more southerly latitudes the effect of the movement of the sun is less, and the change in the time of sunset depends on that of the Equation of Time to a greater degree, and the date of earliest sunset is earlier than it is at Greenwich, eg on the Equator it is about 1 November.

THE EQUINOX

The equinox is the point at which the sun crosses the Equator and day and night are of equal length all over the world. This occurs in March and September.

DOG DAYS

The days about the heliacal rising of the Dog Star, noted from ancient times as the hottest period of the year in the northern hemisphere, are called the Dog Days. Their incidence has been variously calculated as depending on the Greater or Lesser Dog Star (Sirius or Procyon) and their duration has been reckoned as from 30 to 54 days. A generally accepted period is from 3 July to 15 August.

CHRISTIAN CALENDAR

In the Christian chronological system the years are distinguished by cardinal numbers before or after the birth of Christ, the period being denoted by the letters BC (Before Christ) or, more rarely, AC *(Ante Christum),* and AD (*Anno Domini* – In the Year of Our Lord). The correlative dates of the epoch are the fourth year of the 194th Olympiad, the 753rd year from the foundation of Rome, AM 3761 in Jewish chronology, and the 4714th year of the Julian period. The actual date of the birth of Christ is somewhat uncertain.

The system was introduced into Italy in the sixth century. Though first used in France in the seventh century, it was not universally established there until about the eighth century. It has been said that the system was introduced into England by St Augustine (AD 596), but it was probably not generally used until some centuries later. It was ordered to be used by the bishops at the Council of Chelsea (AD 816).

THE JULIAN CALENDAR

In the Julian calendar (adopted by the Roman Empire in 45 BC) all the centennial years were leap years, and for this reason towards the close of the 16th century there was a difference of ten days between the tropical and calendar years; the equinox fell on 11 March of the calendar, whereas at the time of the Council of Nicaea (AD 325), it had fallen on 21 March. In 1582 Pope Gregory ordained that 5 October should be called 15 October and that of the end-century years only the fourth should be a leap year.

THE GREGORIAN CALENDAR

The Gregorian calendar was adopted by Italy, France, Spain and Portugal in 1582, by Prussia, the Roman Catholic German states, Switzerland, Holland and Flanders on 1 January 1583, by Poland in 1586, Hungary in 1587, the Protestant German and Netherland states and Denmark in 1700, and by Great Britain and its Dominions (including the North American colonies) in 1752, by the omission of 11 days (3 September being reckoned as 14 September). Sweden omitted the leap day in 1700 but observed leap days in 1704 and 1708, and reverted to the Julian calendar by having two leap days in 1712; the Gregorian calendar was adopted in 1753 by the omission of 11 days (18 February being reckoned as 1 March). Japan adopted the calendar in 1872, China in 1912, Bulgaria in 1915, Turkey and Soviet Russia in 1918, Yugoslavia and Romania in 1919, and Greece in 1923.

In the same year that the change was made in England from the Julian to the Gregorian calendar, the beginning of the new year was also changed from 25 March to 1 January.

THE ORTHODOX CHURCHES

Some Orthodox churches still use the Julian reckoning but the majority of Greek Orthodox churches and the Romanian Orthodox Church have adopted a modified 'New Calendar', observing the Gregorian calendar for fixed feasts and the Julian for movable feasts.

The Orthodox Church year begins on 1 September. There are four fast periods and, in addition to Pascha (Easter), twelve great feasts, as well as numerous commemorations of the saints of the Old and New Testaments throughout the year.

THE DOMINICAL LETTER

The dominical letter is one of the letters A–G which are used to denote the Sundays in successive years. If the first day of the year is a Sunday the letter is A; if the second, B; the third, C; and so on. A leap year requires two letters, the first for 1 January to 29 February, the second for 1 March to 31 December.

EPIPHANY

The feast of the Epiphany, commemorating the manifestation of Christ, later became associated with the offering of gifts by the Magi. The day was of great importance from the time of the Council of Nicaea (AD 325), as the primate of Alexandria was charged at every Epiphany feast with the announcement in a letter to the churches of the date of the forthcoming Easter. The day was also of importance in Britain as it influenced dates, ecclesiastical and lay, eg Plough Monday, when work was resumed in the fields, fell on the Monday in the first full week after Epiphany.

LENT

The Teutonic word *Lent,* which denotes the fast preceding Easter, originally meant no more than the spring season; but from Anglo-Saxon times, at least, it has been used as the equivalent of the more significant Latin term *Quadragesima,* meaning the 'forty days' or, more literally, the fortieth day. Ash Wednesday is the first day of Lent, which ends at midnight before Easter Day.

PALM SUNDAY

Palm Sunday, the Sunday before Easter and the beginning of Holy Week, commemorates the triumphal entry of Christ into Jerusalem and is celebrated in Britain (when palm is not available) by branches of willow gathered for use in the decoration of churches on that day.

MAUNDY THURSDAY

Maundy Thursday is the day before Good Friday, the name itself being a corruption of *dies mandati* (day of the mandate) when Christ washed the feet of the disciples and gave them the mandate to love one another.

EASTER DAY

Easter Day is the first Sunday after the full moon which happens on, or next after, the 21st day of March; if the full moon happens on a Sunday, Easter Day is the Sunday after.

This definition is contained in an Act of Parliament (24 Geo. II c. 23) and explanation is given in the preamble to the Act that the day of full moon depends on certain tables that have been prepared. These tables are summarised in the early pages of the Book of Common Prayer. The moon referred to is not the real moon of the heavens, but a hypothetical moon on whose 'full' the date of Easter depends, and the lunations of this 'calendar' moon consist of 29 and 30 days alternately, with certain necessary modifications to make the date of its full agree as nearly as possible with that of the real moon, which is known as the Paschal Full Moon.

A FIXED EASTER

In 1928 the House of Commons agreed to a motion for the third reading of a bill proposing that Easter Day shall, in the calendar year next but one after the commencement of the Act and in all subsequent years, be the first Sunday after the second Saturday in April. Easter would thus fall on the second or third Sunday in April, ie between 9 and 15 April (inclusive). A clause in the bill provided that before it shall come into operation, regard shall be had to any opinion expressed officially by the various Christian churches. Efforts by the World Council of Churches to secure a unanimous choice of date for Easter by its member churches have so far been unsuccessful.

ROGATION DAYS
Rogation Days are the Monday, Tuesday and Wednesday preceding Ascension Day and from the fifth century were observed as public fasts with solemn processions and supplications. The processions were discontinued as religious observances at the Reformation, but survive in the ceremony known as 'beating the parish bounds'. Rogation Sunday is the Sunday before Ascension Day.

EMBER DAYS
The Ember Days at the four seasons are the Wednesday, Friday and Saturday *(a)* before the third Sunday in Advent, *(b)* before the second Sunday in Lent, and *(c)* before the Sundays nearest to the festivals of St Peter and of St Michael and All Angels.

TRINITY SUNDAY
Trinity Sunday is eight weeks after Easter Day, on the Sunday following Pentecost (Whit Sunday). Subsequent Sundays are reckoned in the Book of Common Prayer calendar of the Church of England as 'after Trinity'.

Thomas Becket (1118–70) was consecrated Archbishop of Canterbury on the Sunday after Whit Sunday and his first act was to ordain that the day of his consecration should be held as a new festival in honour of the Holy Trinity. This observance spread from Canterbury throughout the whole of Christendom.

MOVEABLE FEASTS TO THE YEAR 2035

Year	*Ash Wednesday*	*Easter*	*Ascension*	*Pentecost (Whit Sunday)*	*Advent Sunday*
2008	6 February	23 March	1 May	11 May	30 November
2009	25 February	12 April	21 May	31 May	29 November
2010	17 February	4 April	13 May	23 May	28 November
2011	9 March	24 April	2 June	12 June	27 November
2012	22 February	8 April	17 May	27 May	2 December
2013	13 February	31 March	9 May	19 May	1 December
2014	5 March	20 April	29 May	8 June	30 November
2015	18 February	5 April	14 May	24 May	29 November
2016	10 February	27 March	5 May	15 May	27 November
2017	1 March	16 April	25 May	4 June	3 December
2018	14 February	1 April	10 May	20 May	2 December
2019	6 March	21 April	30 May	9 June	1 December
2020	26 February	12 April	21 May	31 May	29 November
2021	17 February	4 April	13 May	23 May	28 November
2022	2 March	17 April	26 May	5 June	27 November
2023	22 February	9 April	18 May	28 May	3 December
2024	14 February	31 March	9 May	19 May	1 December
2025	5 March	20 April	29 May	8 June	30 November
2026	18 February	5 April	14 May	24 May	29 November
2027	10 February	28 March	6 May	16 May	28 November
2028	1 March	16 April	25 May	4 June	3 December
2029	14 February	1 April	10 May	20 May	2 December
2030	6 March	21 April	30 May	9 June	1 December
2031	26 February	13 April	22 May	1 June	30 November
2032	11 February	28 March	6 May	16 May	28 November
2033	2 March	17 April	26 May	5 June	27 November
2034	22 February	9 April	18 May	28 May	3 December
2035	7 February	25 March	3 May	13 May	2 December

NOTES

Ash Wednesday (first day in Lent) can fall at earliest on 4 February and at latest on 10 March

Mothering Sunday (fourth Sunday in Lent) can fall at earliest on 1 March and at latest on 4 April

Easter Day can fall at earliest on 22 March and at latest on 25 April

Ascension Day is forty days after Easter Day and can fall at earliest on 30 April and at latest on 3 June

Pentecost (Whit Sunday) is seven weeks after Easter and can fall at earliest on 10 May and at latest on 13 June

Trinity Sunday is the Sunday after Whit Sunday

Corpus Christi falls on the Thursday after Trinity Sunday

Sundays after Pentecost – there are not less than 18 and not more than 23

Advent Sunday is the Sunday nearest to 30 November

EASTER DAYS AND DOMINICAL LETTERS 1500 TO 2035

Dates up to and including 1752 are according to the Julian calendar. For dominical letters in leap years, *see* note below

		1500–1599	1600–1699	1700–1799	1800–1899	1900–1999	2000–2035
March							
d	22	1573	1668	1761	1818		
e	23	1505/16	1600	1788	1845/56	1913	2008
f	24	1611/95	1706/99	1940			
g	25	1543/54	1627/38/49	1722/33/44	1883/94	1951	2035
A	26	1559/70/81/92	1654/65/76	1749/58/69/80	1815/26/37	1967/78/89	
b	27	1502/13/24/97	1608/87/92	1785/96	1842/53/64	1910/21/32	2005/16
c	28	1529/35/40	1619/24/30	1703/14/25	1869/75/80	1937/48	2027/32
d	29	1551/62	1635/46/57	1719/30/41/52	1807/12/91	1959/64/70	
e	30	1567/78/89	1651/62/73/84	1746/55/66/77	1823/34	1902/75/86/97	
f	31	1510/21/32/83/94	1605/16/78/89	1700/71/82/93	1839/50/61/72	1907/18/29/91	2002/13/24
April							
g	1	1526/37/48	1621/32	1711/16	1804/66/77/88	1923/34/45/56	2018/29
A	2	1553/64	1643/48	1727/38	1809/20/93/99	1961/72	
b	3	1575/80/86	1659/70/81	1743/63/68/74	1825/31/36	1904/83/88/94	
c	4	1507/18/91	1602/13/75/86/97	1708/79/90	1847/58	1915/20/26/99	2010/21
d	5	1523/34/45/56	1607/18/29/40	1702/13/24/95	1801/63/74/85/96	1931/42/53	2015/26
e	6	1539/50/61/72	1634/45/56	1729/35/40/60	1806/17/28/90	1947/58/69/80	
f	7	1504/77/88	1667/72	1751/65/76	1822/33/44	1901/12/85/96	
g	8	1509/15/20/99	1604/10/83/94	1705/87/92/98	1849/55/60	1917/28	2007/12
A	9	1531/42	1615/26/37/99	1710/21/32	1871/82	1939/44/50	2023/34
b	10	1547/58/69	1631/42/53/64	1726/37/48/57	1803/14/87/98	1955/66/77	
c	11	1501/12/63/74/85/96	1658/69/80	1762/73/84	1819/30/41/52	1909/71/82/93	2004
d	12	1506/17/28	1601/12/91/96	1789	1846/57/68	1903/14/25/36/98	2009/20
e	13	1533/44	1623/28	1707/18	1800/73/79/84	1941/52	2031
f	14	1555/60/66	1639/50/61	1723/34/45/54	1805/11/16/95	1963/68/74	
g	15	1571/82/93	1655/66/77/88	1750/59/70/81	1827/38	1900/06/79/90	2001
A	16	1503/14/25/36/87/98	1609/20/82/93	1704/75/86/97	1843/54/65/76	1911/22/33/95	2006/17/28
b	17	1530/41/52	1625/36	1715/20	1808/70/81/92	1927/38/49/60	2022/33
c	18	1557/68	1647/52	1731/42/56	1802/13/24/97	1954/65/76	
d	19	1500/79/84/90	1663/74/85	1747/67/72/78	1829/35/40	1908/81/87/92	
e	20	1511/22/95	1606/17/79/90	1701/12/83/94	1851/62	1919/24/30	2003/14/25
f	21	1527/38/49	1622/33/44	1717/28	1867/78/89	1935/46/57	2019/30
g	22	1565/76	1660	1739/53/64	1810/21/32	1962/73/84	
A	23	1508	1671		1848	1905/16	2000
b	24	1519	1603/14/98	1709/91	1859		2011
c	25	1546	1641	1736	1886	1943	

No dominical letter is placed against the intercalary day 29 February, but since it is still counted as a weekday and given a name, the series of letters moves back one day every leap year after intercalation. Thus, a leap year beginning with the dominical letter C will change to a year with the dominical letter B on 1 March

HINDU CALENDAR

The Hindu calendar is a luni-solar calendar of 12 months, each containing 29 days, 12 hours. Each month is divided into a light fortnight (Shukla or Shuddha) and a dark fortnight (Krishna or Vadya) based on the waxing and waning of the moon. In most parts of India the month starts with the light fortnight, ie the day after the new moon, although in some regions it begins with the dark fortnight, ie the day after the full moon.

The new year according to the civil calendar begins in the month of Chaitra (March/April) and ends in the month of Phalgun (March). The 12 months – Chaitra, Vaishakh, Jyeshtha, Ashadh, Shravan, Bhadrapad, Ashvin, Kartik, Margashirsh, Paush, Magh and Phalgun – have Sanskrit names derived from 12 asterisms (constellations). There are regional variations to the names of the months but the Sanskrit names are understood throughout India.

Every lunar month must have a solar transit and is termed pure *(shuddha)*. The lunar month without a solar transit is impure *(mala)* and called an intercalary month. An intercalary month occurs approximately every 32 lunar months, whenever the difference between the Hindu year of 360 lunar days (354 days 8 hours solar time) and the 365 days 6 hours of the solar year reaches the length of one Hindu lunar month (29 days 12 hours).

The leap month may be added at any point in the Hindu year. The name given to the month varies according to when it occurs but is taken from the month immediately following it. There is no leap month in 2008.

The days of the week are called Raviwar (Sunday), Somawar (Monday), Mangalwar (Tuesday), Budhawar (Wednesday), Guruwar (Thursday), Shukrawar (Friday) and Shaniwar (Saturday). The names are derived from the Sanskrit names of the sun, the moon and five planets, Mars, Mercury, Jupiter, Venus and Saturn.

Most fasts and festivals are based on the lunar calendar but a few are determined by the apparent movement of the sun, eg Sankranti and Pongal (in southern India), which are celebrated on 14/15 January to mark the start of the Sun's apparent journey northwards and a change of season.

Festivals celebrated throughout India are Chaitra (the New Year), Raksha-bandhan (the renewal of the kinship bond between brothers and sisters), Navaratri (a nine-night festival dedicated to the goddess Parvati), Dasara (the victory of Rama over the demon army), Diwali (a festival of lights), Makara Sankranti, Shivaratri (dedicated to Shiva), and Holi (a spring festival). British Hindus commonly celebrate the festival of Diwali as the start of the new year instead of observing it at the beginning of Chaitra.

Regional festivals are Durga-puja (dedicated to the goddess Durga (Parvati)), Sarasvati-puja (dedicated to the goddess Sarasvati), Ganesh Chaturthi (worship of Ganesh on the fourth day (Chaturthi) of the light half of Bhadrapad), Ramanavami (the birth festival of the god Rama) and Janmashtami (the birth festival of the god Krishna).

The main festivals celebrated in Britain are Navaratri, Dasara, Durga-puja, Diwali, Holi, Sarasvati-puja, Ganesh Chaturthi, Raksha-bandhan, Ramanavami and Janmashtami.

For dates of the main festivals in 2008, *see* page 9.

JEWISH CALENDAR

The story of the Flood in the Book of Genesis indicates the use of a calendar of some kind and that the writers recognised 30 days as the length of a lunation. However, after the diaspora, Jewish communities were left in considerable doubt as to the times of fasts and festivals. This led to the formation of the Jewish calendar as used today. It is said that this was done in AD 358 by Rabbi Hillel II, though some assert that it did not happen until much later.

The calendar is luni-solar, and is based on the lengths of the lunation and of the tropical year as found by Hipparchus (*c*.120 BC), which differ little from those adopted at the present day. The year AM 5768 (2007–2008) is the 11th year of the 304th Metonic (Minor or Lunar) cycle of 19 years and the 28th year of the 206th Solar (or Major) cycle of 28 years since the Era of the Creation. Jews hold that the Creation occurred at the time of the autumnal equinox in the year known in the Christian calendar as 3760 BC (954 of the Julian period). The epoch or starting point of Jewish chronology corresponds to 7 October 3761 BC. At the beginning of each solar cycle, the Tekufah of Nisan (the vernal equinox) returns to the same day and to the same hour.

The hour is divided into 1,080 minims, and the month between one new moon and the next is reckoned as 29 days 12 hours 793 minims. The normal calendar year, called a Regular Common year, consists of 12 months of 30 days and 29 days alternately. Since 12 months such as these comprise only 354 days, in order that each of them shall not diverge greatly from an average place in the solar year, a 13th month is occasionally added after the fifth month of the civil year (which commences on the first day of the month Tishri), or as the penultimate month of the ecclesiastical year (which commences on the first day of the month Nisan). The years when this happens are called Embolismic or leap years.

Of the 19 years that form a Metonic cycle, seven are leap years; they occur at places in the cycle indicated by the numbers 3, 6, 8, 11, 14, 17 and 19, these places being chosen so that the accumulated excesses of the solar years should be as small as possible.

A Jewish year is of one of the following six types:

Minimal Common	353 days
Regular Common	354 days
Full Common	355 days
Minimal Leap	383 days
Regular Leap	384 days
Full Leap	385 days

The Regular year has alternate months of 30 and 29 days. In a Full year, whether common or leap, Marcheshvan, the second month of the civil year, has 30 days instead of 29; in Minimal years Kislev, the third month, has 29 instead of 30. The additional month in leap years is called Adar I and precedes the month called Adar in common years. Adar II is called Adar Sheni in leap years, and the usual Adar festivals are kept in Adar Sheni. Adar I and Adar II always have 30 days, but neither this, nor the other variations mentioned, is allowed to change the number of days in the other months, which still follow the alternation of the normal 12.

These are the main features of the Jewish calendar, which must be considered permanent because as a Jewish law it cannot be altered except by a Great Sanhedrin.

The Jewish day begins between sunset and nightfall. The time used is that of the meridian of Jerusalem, which is 2h 21m in advance of Greenwich Mean Time. Rules for the beginning of sabbaths and festivals were laid down for the latitude of London in the 18th century and hours for nightfall are now fixed annually by the Chief Rabbi.

JEWISH CALENDAR 5768–9

AM 5768 (768) is a Minimal Leap year of 13 months 51 sabbaths and 383 days.

Month (length)	AM 5768	AM 5769
Tishri 1 (30)	13 September 2007	30 September
Marcheshvan 1 (29)	3 October	30 October
Kislev 1 (29/30)	11 November	28 November
Tebet 1 (29)	10 December	28 December
Shebat 1 (30)	8 January 2008	26 January 2009
**Adar 1* (30/29)	7 February	
†*Adar II* (29)	8 March	
Nisan 1 (30)	6 April	
Iyar 1 (29)	6 May	
Sivan 1 (30)	4 June	
Tammuz 1 (29)	4 July	
Ab 1 (30)	2 August	
Elul 1 (29)	1 September	

* Known as Adar Rishon in leap years
† Known as Adar Sheni in leap years

JEWISH FASTS AND FESTIVALS

For dates of principal festivals in 2008, *see* page 9.

Tishri 1–2	Rosh Hashanah (New Year)
Tishri 3	*Fast of Gedaliah
Tishri 10	Yom Kippur (Day of Atonement)
Tishri 15–21	Succoth (Feast of Tabernacles)
Tishri 21	Hoshana Rabba
Tishri 22	Shemini Atseret (Solemn Assembly)
Tishri 23	Simchat Torah (Rejoicing of the Law)
Kislev 25	Hanukkah (Dedication of the Temple) begins
Tebet 10	Fast of Tebet
†*Adar* 13	§Fast of Esther
†*Adar* 14	Purim
†*Adar* 15	Shushan Purim
Nisan 15–22	Pesach (Passover)
Sivan 6–7	Shavuoth (Feast of Weeks)
Tammuz 17	*Fast of Tammuz
Ab 9	*Fast of Ab

* If these dates fall on the sabbath the fast is kept on the following day
† Adar Sheni in leap years
§ This fast is observed on Adar 11 (or Adar Sheni 11 in leap years) if Adar 13 falls on a sabbath

MUSLIM CALENDAR

The Muslim era is dated from the *Hijrah,* or flight of the Prophet Muhammad from Mecca to Medina, the corresponding date of which in the Julian calendar is 16 July AD 622. The lunar *hijri* calendar is used principally in Iran, Egypt, Malaysia, Pakistan, Mauritania, various Arab states and certain parts of India. Iran uses the solar hijri calendar as well as the lunar hijri calendar. The dating system was adopted about AD 639, commencing with the first day of the month Muharram.

The lunar calendar consists of 12 months containing an alternate sequence of 30 and 29 days, with the intercalation of one day at the end of the 12th month at stated intervals in each cycle of 30 years. The object of the intercalation is to reconcile the date of the first day of the month with the date of the actual new moon.

Some adherents still take the date of the evening of the first physical sighting of the crescent of the new moon as that of the first of the month. If cloud obscures the moon the present month may be extended to 30 days, after which the new month will begin automatically regardless of whether the moon has been seen. (Under religious law a month must have less than 31 days.) This means that the beginning of a new month and the date of religious festivals can vary from the published calendars.

In each cycle of 30 years, 19 years are common and contain 354 days, and 11 years are intercalary (leap years) of 355 days, the latter being called *kabisah.* The mean length of the Hijrah years is 354 days 8 hours 48 minutes and the period of mean lunation is 29 days 12 hours 44 minutes.

To ascertain if a year is common or kabisah, divide it by 30: the quotient gives the number of completed cycles and the remainder shows the place of the year in the current cycle. If the remainder is 2, 5, 7, 10, 13, 16, 18, 21, 24, 26 or 29, the year is kabisah and consists of 355 days.

MUSLIM CALENDAR 1428–9

Hijrah 1428 AH (remainder 18) is a kabisah year. 1429 AH (remainder 19) is a common year. Calendar dates below are estimates based on calculations of moon phases.

Month (length)	1428 AH	1429 AH
Muharram 1 (30)	10 January 2008	29 December
Safar 1 (29)	9 February	28 January 2009
Rabi' I 1 (30)	9 March	
Rabi' II 1 (29)	8 April	
Jumada I 1 (30)	7 May	
Jumada II 1 (29)	6 June	
Rajab 1 (30)	5 July	
Sha'ban 1 (29)	4 August	
Ramadan 1 (30)	2 September	
Shawwal 1 (29)	2 October	
Dhu'l-Qa'da 1 (30)	31 October	
Dhu'l-Hijjah 1 (30/29)	30 November	

MUSLIM FESTIVALS

Ramadan is a month of fasting for all Muslims because it is the month in which the revelation of the *Qur'an* (Koran) began. During Ramadan, Muslims abstain from food, drink and sexual pleasure from dawn until after sunset throughout the month.

The two major festivals are *Eid ul-Fitr* and *Eid ul-Adha.* Eid ul-Fitr marks the end of the Ramadan fast and is celebrated on the day after the sighting of the new moon of the following month. Eid ul-Adha, the festival of sacrifice (also known as the great festival), celebrates the submission of the Prophet Ibrahim (Abraham) to God. Eid ul-Adha falls on the tenth day of Dhu'l-Hijjah, coinciding with the day when those on *hajj* (pilgrimage to Mecca) sacrifice animals.

Other days accorded special recognition are:

Muharram 1	New Year's Day
Muharram 10	Ashura (the day Prophet Noah left the Ark and Prophet Moses was saved from Pharaoh (Sunni), the death of the Prophet's grandson Husain (Shi'ite))
Rabi'u-l-Awwal (Rabi' I) 12	Mawlid ul-Nabi (birthday of the Prophet Muhammad)
Rajab 27	Laylat ul-Isra' wa'l-Mi'raj (The Night of Journey and Ascension)
*Ramadan**	Laylat ul-Qadr (Night of Power)
Dhu'l-Hijjah 10	Eid ul-Adha (Festival of Sacrifice)

* Moveable feast

For dates of the major celebrations in 2008, *see* page 9.

SIKH CALENDAR

The Sikh calendar is a lunar calendar of 365 days divided into 12 months. The length of the months varies between 29 and 32 days.

There are no prescribed feast days and no fasting periods. The main celebrations are Baisakhi Mela (the new year and the anniversary of the founding of the Khalsa), Diwali Mela (festival of light), Hola Mohalla Mela (a spring festival held in the Punjab), and the Gurpurbs (anniversaries associated with the ten Gurus).

For dates of the major celebrations in 2008, *see* page 9.

THAI CALENDAR

Thailand adopted the Suriyakati calendar, a modified version of the Gregorian calendar during the reign of King Rama V in 1888, using 1 April as the first day of the year. In 1940 the date of the new year was changed to 1 January. The years are counted from the beginning of the Buddhist era (BE), which is calculated to have commenced upon the death of the Lord Buddha, taken to have occurred in 543 BC, so AD 2008 is BE 2551. The Chinese system of associating years with one of twelve animals is also in use in Thailand. The Chantarakati lunar calendar is used to determine religious holidays; the new year begins on the first day of the waxing moon in November or, if there is a leap month, in December.

CIVIL AND LEGAL CALENDAR

THE HISTORICAL YEAR

Before 1752, two calendar systems were used in England. The civil or legal year began on 25 March and the historical year on 1 January. Thus the civil or legal date 24 March 1658 was the same day as the historical date 24 March 1659; a date in that portion of the year is written as 24 March 1658/9, the lower figure showing the historical year.

THE NEW YEAR

In England in the seventh century, and as late as the 13th, the year was reckoned from Christmas Day, but in the 12th century the Church in England began the year with the feast of the Annunciation of the Blessed Virgin ('Lady Day') on 25 March, and this practice was adopted generally in the 14th century. The civil or legal year in the

British dominions (exclusive of Scotland) began with Lady Day until 1751. But in and since 1752 the civil year has begun with 1 January. New Year's Day in Scotland was changed from 25 March to 1 January in 1600.

Elsewhere in Europe, 1 January was adopted as the first day of the year by Venice in 1522, German states in 1544, Spain, Portugal and the Roman Catholic Netherlands in 1556, Prussia, Denmark and Sweden in 1559, France in 1564, Lorraine in 1579, the Protestant Netherlands in 1583, Russia in 1725, and Tuscany in 1751.

REGNAL YEARS

Regnal years are the years of a sovereign's reign and each begins on the anniversary of his or her accession, eg regnal year 57 of the present queen begins on 6 February 2008.

The system was used for dating Acts of Parliament until 1962. The Summer Time Act 1925, for example, is quoted as 15 and 16 Geo. V c. 64, because it became law in the parliamentary session which extended over part of both of these regnal years. Acts of a parliamentary session during which a sovereign died were usually given two year numbers, the regnal year of the deceased sovereign and the regnal year of his or her successor, eg those passed in 1952 were dated 16 Geo. VI and 1 Elizabeth II. Since 1962 Acts of Parliament have been dated by the calendar year.

QUARTER AND TERM DAYS

Holy days and saints days were the usual means in early times for setting the dates of future and recurrent appointments. The quarter days in England and Wales are the feast of the Nativity (25 December), the feast of the Annunciation (25 March), the feast of St John the Baptist (24 June) and the feast of St Michael and All Angels (29 September).

The term days in Scotland are Candlemas (the feast of the Purification), Whitsunday, Lammas (Loaf Mass) and Martinmas (St Martin's Day). These fell on 2 February, 15 May, 1 August and 11 November respectively. However, by the Term and Quarter Days (Scotland) Act 1990, the dates of the term days were changed to 28 February (Candlemas), 28 May (Whitsunday), 28 August (Lammas) and 28 November (Martinmas).

RED-LETTER DAYS

Red-letter days were originally the holy days and saints days indicated in early ecclesiastical calendars by letters printed in red ink. The days to be distinguished in this way were approved at the Council of Nicaea in AD 325.

These days still have a legal significance, as judges of the Queen's Bench Division wear scarlet robes on red-letter days falling during the law sittings. The days designated as red-letter days for this purpose are:

Holy and saints days
The Conversion of St Paul, the Purification, Ash Wednesday, the Annunciation, the Ascension, the feasts of St Mark, SS Philip and James, St Matthias, St Barnabas, St John the Baptist, St Peter, St Thomas, St James, St Luke, SS Simon and Jude, All Saints, St Andrew.

Civil calendar (for dates, *see* page 9)
The anniversaries of the Queen's accession, the Queen's birthday and the Queen's coronation, the Queen's official birthday, the birthday of the Duke of Edinburgh, the birthday of the Prince of Wales, St David's Day and Lord Mayor's Day.

PUBLIC HOLIDAYS

Public holidays are divided into two categories, common law and statutory. Common law holidays are holidays 'by habit and custom'; in England, Wales and Northern Ireland these are Good Friday and Christmas Day.

Statutory public holidays, known as bank holidays, were first established by the Bank Holidays Act 1871. They were, literally, days on which the banks (and other public institutions) were closed and financial obligations due on that day were payable the following day. The legislation currently governing public holidays in the UK, which is the Banking and Financial Dealings Act 1971, stipulates the days that are to be public holidays in England, Wales, Scotland and Northern Ireland.

Certain holidays (indicated by * below) are granted annually by royal proclamation, either throughout the UK or in any place in the UK. The public holidays are:

England and Wales
*New Year's Day
Good Friday
Easter Monday
*The first Monday in May
The last Monday in May
The last Monday in August
26 December, if it is not a Sunday
27 December when 25 or 26 December is a Sunday

Scotland
New Year's Day, or if it is a Sunday, 2 January
2 January, or if it is a Sunday, 3 January
Good Friday
The first Monday in May
*The last Monday in May
The first Monday in August
Christmas Day, or if it is a Sunday, 26 December
*Boxing Day – if Christmas Day falls on a Sunday, 26 December is given in lieu and an alternative day is given for Boxing Day

Northern Ireland
*New Year's Day
17 March, or if it is a Sunday, 18 March
Easter Monday
*The first Monday in May
The last Monday in May
*12 July, or if it is a Sunday, 13 July
The last Monday in August
26 December, if it is not a Sunday
27 December if 25 or 26 December is a Sunday
For dates of public holidays in 2008 and 2009, *see* pages 10–11.

CHRONOLOGICAL CYCLES AND ERAS

SOLAR (OR MAJOR) CYCLE

The solar cycle is a period of 28 years in any corresponding year of which the days of the week recur on the same day of the month.

METONIC (LUNAR, OR MINOR) CYCLE

In 432 BC, Meton, an Athenian astronomer, found that 235 lunations are very nearly, though not exactly, equal in duration to 19 solar years and so after 19 years the phases of the Moon recur on the same days of the month (nearly). The dates of full moon in a cycle of 19 years were inscribed in figures of gold on public monuments in

Athens, and the number showing the position of a year in the cycle is called the golden number of that year.

JULIAN PERIOD

The Julian period was proposed by Joseph Scaliger in 1582. The period is 7,980 Julian years, and its first year coincides with the year 4713 BC. The figure of 7980 is the product of the number of years in the solar cycle, the Metonic cycle and the cycle of the Roman indiction ($28 \times 19 \times 15$).

ROMAN INDICTION

The Roman indiction is a period of 15 years, instituted for fiscal purposes about AD 300.

EPACT

The epact is the age of the calendar Moon, diminished by one day, on 1 January, in the ecclesiastical lunar calendar.

CHINESE CALENDAR

A lunar calendar was the sole calendar in use in China until 1911, when the government adopted the new (Gregorian) calendar for official and most business activities. The Chinese tend to follow both calendars, the lunar calendar playing an important part in personal life, eg birth celebrations, festivals, marriages; and in rural villages the lunar calendar dictates the cycle of activities, denoting the change of weather and farming activities.

The lunar calendar is used in Hong Kong, Singapore, Malaysia, Tibet and elsewhere in south-east Asia. The calendar has a cycle of 60 years. The new year begins at the first new moon after the sun enters the sign of Aquarius, ie the new year falls between 21 January and 19 February in the Gregorian calendar.

Each year in the Chinese calendar is associated with one of 12 animals: the rat, the ox, the tiger, the rabbit, the dragon, the snake, the horse, the goat or sheep, the monkey, the chicken or rooster, the dog, and the pig.

The date of the Chinese new year and the astrological sign for the years 2008–11 are:

2008	7 February	Rat
2009	26 January	Ox
2010	14 February	Tiger
2011	3 February	Rabbit

COPTIC CALENDAR

In the Coptic calendar, which is used in parts of Egypt and Ethiopia, the year is made up of 12 months of 30 days each, followed, in general, by five complementary days. Every fourth year is an intercalary or leap year and in these years there are six complementary days. The intercalary year of the Coptic calendar immediately precedes the leap year of the Julian calendar. The era is that of Diocletian or the Martyrs, the origin of which is fixed at 29 August AD 284 (Julian date).

INDIAN ERAS

In addition to the Muslim reckoning, other eras are used in India. The Saka era of southern India, dating from 3 March AD 78, was declared the national calendar of the Republic of India with effect from 22 March 1957, to be used concurrently with the Gregorian calendar. As revised, the year of the new Saka era begins at the spring equinox, with five successive months of 31 days and seven of 30 days in ordinary years, and six months of each length in leap years. The year AD 2008 is 1930 of the revised Saka era.

The year AD 2008 corresponds to the following years in other eras:

Year 2065 of the Vikram Samvat era
Year 1415 of the Bengali San era
Year 1184 of the Kollam era
Year 5109 of the Kaliyuga era
Year 2551 of the Buddha Nirvana era

JAPANESE CALENDAR

The Japanese calendar is essentially the same as the Gregorian calendar, the years, months and weeks being of the same length and beginning on the same days as those of the Gregorian calendar. The numeration of the years is different, based on a system of epochs or periods, each of which begins at the accession of an emperor or other important occurrence. The method is not unlike the British system of regnal years, except that each year of a period closes on 31 December. The Japanese chronology begins about AD 650 and the three latest epochs are defined by the reigns of emperors, whose actual names are not necessarily used:

Epoch
Taisho – 1 August 1912 to 25 December 1926
Showa – 26 December 1926 to 7 January 1989
Heisei – 8 January 1989

The year Heisei 20 begins on 1 January 2008.

The months are known as First Month, Second Month, etc, First Month being equivalent to January. The days of the week are Nichiyobi (Sun-day), Getsuyobi (Moon-day), Kayobi (Fire-day), Suiyobi (Water-day), Mokuyobi (Wood-day), Kinyobi (Metal-day) and Doyobi (Earth-day).

THE MASONIC YEAR

Two dates are quoted in warrants, dispensations, etc, issued by the United Grand Lodge of England, those for the current year being expressed as *Anno Domini* 2008 – *Anno Lucis* 6008. This *Anno Lucis* (year of light) is based on the Book of Genesis 1:3, the 4,000-year difference being derived, in modified form, from *Ussher's Notation,* published in 1654, which places the Creation of the World in 4004 BC.

OLYMPIADS

Ancient Greek chronology was reckoned in Olympiads, cycles of four years corresponding with the periodic Olympic Games held on the plain of Olympia, in Elis, once every four years. The intervening years were the first, second, etc, of the Olympiad, which received the name of the victor at the Games. The first recorded Olympiad is that of Choroebus, 776 BC.

ZOROASTRIAN CALENDAR

Zoroastrians, followers of the Iranian prophet Zarathushtra (known to the Greeks as Zoroaster) are mostly to be found in Iran and in India, where they are known as Parsees.

The Zoroastrian era dates from the coronation of the last Zoroastrian Sasanian king in AD 631. The Zoroastrian calendar is divided into 12 months, each comprising 30 days, followed by five holy days of the Gathas at the end of each year to make the year consist of 365 days.

In order to synchronise the calendar with the solar year of 365 days, an extra month was intercalated once every

120 years. However, this intercalation ceased in the 12th century and the new year, which had fallen in the spring, slipped back to August. Because intercalation ceased at different times in Iran and India, there was one month's difference between the calendar followed in Iran (Kadmi calendar) and that followed by the Parsees (Shenshai calendar). In 1906 a group of Zoroastrians decided to bring the calendar back in line with the seasons again and restore the new year to 21 March each year (Fasli calendar).

The Shenshai calendar (new year in August) is mainly used by Parsees. The Fasli calendar (new year, 21 March) is mainly used by Zoroastrians living in Iran, in the Indian subcontinent, or away from Iran.

ROMAN CALENDAR

Roman historians adopted as an epoch the foundation of Rome, which is believed to have happened in the year 753 BC. The ordinal number of the years in Roman reckoning is followed by the letters AUC *(ab urbe condita)*, so that the year 2008 is 2761 AUC (MMDCCLXI). The calendar that we know has developed from one said to have been established by Romulus using a year of 304 days divided into ten months, beginning with March. To this Numa added January and February, making the year consist of 12 months of 30 and 29 days alternately, with an additional day so that the total was 355. It is also said that Numa ordered an intercalary month of 22 or 23 days in alternate years, making 90 days in eight years, to be inserted after 23 February.

However, there is some doubt as to the origination and the details of the intercalation in the Roman calendar. It is certain that some scheme of this kind was inaugurated and not fully carried out, for in the year 46 BC Julius Caesar found that the calendar had been allowed to fall into some confusion. He sought the help of the Egyptian astronomer Sosigenes, which led to the construction and adoption (45 BC) of the Julian calendar, and, by a slight alteration, to the Gregorian calendar now in use. The year 46 BC was made to consist of 445 days and is called the Year of Confusion.

In the Roman (Julian) calendar the days of the month were counted backwards from three fixed points, or days, and an intervening day was said to be so many days before the next coming point, the first and last being counted. These three points were the Kalends, the Nones, and the Ides. Their positions in the months and the method of counting from them will be seen in the table below. The year containing 366 days was called *bissextilis annus*, as it had a doubled sixth day *(bissextus dies)* before the March Kalends on 24 February – *ante diem sextum Kalendas Martias*, or a.d. VI Kal. Mart.

Present days of the month	*March, May, July, October have thirty-one days*		*January, August, December have thirty-one days*		*April, June, September, November have thirty days*		*February has twenty-eight days, and in leap year twenty-nine*	
1	Kalendis		Kalendis		Kalendis		Kalendis	
2	VI		IV	ante	IV	ante	IV	ante
3	V	ante	III	Nonas	III	Nonas	III	Nonas
4	IV	Nonas	pridie Nonas		pridie Nonas		pridie Nonas	
5	III		Nonis		Nonis		Nonis	
6	pridie Nonas		VIII		VIII		VIII	
7	Nonis		VII		VII		VII	
8	VIII		VI	ante	VI	ante	VI	ante
9	VII		V	Idus	V	Idus	V	Idus
10	VI	ante	IV		IV		IV	
11	V	Idus	III		III		III	
12	IV		pridie Idus		pridie Idus		pridie Idus	
13	III		Idibus		Idibus		Idibus	
14	pridie Idus		XIX		XVIII		XVI	
15	Idibus		XVIII		XVII		XV	
16	XVII		XVII		XVI		XIV	
17	XVI		XVI		XV		XIII	
18	XV		XV		XIV		XII	
19	XIV		XIV		XIII		XI	
20	XIII		XIII		XII	ante Kalendas	X	ante Kalendas
21	XII		XII	ante Kalendas	XI	(of the month	IX	Martias
22	XI	ante Kalendas	XI	(of the month	X	following)	VIII	
23	X	(of the month	X	following)	IX		VII	
24	IX	following)	IX		VIII		*VI	
25	VIII		VIII		VII		V	
26	VII		VII		VI		IV	
27	VI		VI		V		III	
28	V		V		IV		pridie Kalendas	
29	IV		IV		III		Martias	
30	III		III		pridie Kalendas (Maias, Quinctilis, Octobris, Decembris)			
31	pridie Kalendas (Aprilis, Iunias, Sextilis, Novembris)		pridie Kalendas (Februarias, Septembris, Ianuarias)					

* (repeated in leap year)

CALENDAR FOR ANY YEAR 1780–2040

To select the correct calendar for any year between 1780 and 2040, consult the index below

*leap year

1780 N*	1813 K	1846 I	1879 G	1912 D*	1945 C	1978 A	2011 M
1781 C	1814 M	1847 K	1880 J*	1913 G	1946 E	1979 C	2012 B*
1782 E	1815 A	1848 N*	1881 M	1914 I	1947 G	1980 F*	2013 E
1783 G	1816 D*	1849 C	1882 A	1915 K	1948 J*	1981 I	2014 G
1784 J*	1817 G	1850 E	1883 C	1916 N*	1949 M	1982 K	2015 I
1785 M	1818 I	1851 G	1884 F*	1917 C	1950 A	1983 M	2016 L*
1786 A	1819 K	1852 J*	1885 I	1918 E	1951 C	1984 B*	2017 A
1787 C	1820 N*	1853 M	1886 K	1919 G	1952 F*	1985 E	2018 C
1788 F*	1821 C	1854 A	1887 M	1920 J*	1953 I	1986 G	2019 E
1789 I	1822 E	1855 C	1888 B*	1921 M	1954 K	1987 I	2020 H*
1790 K	1823 G	1856 F*	1889 E	1922 A	1955 M	1988 L*	2021 K
1791 M	1824 J*	1857 I	1890 G	1923 C	1956 B*	1989 A	2022 M
1792 B*	1825 M	1858 K	1891 I	1924 F*	1957 E	1990 C	2023 A
1793 E	1826 A	1859 M	1892 L*	1925 I	1958 G	1991 E	2024 D*
1794 G	1827 C	1860 B*	1893 A	1926 K	1959 I	1992 H*	2025 G
1795 I	1828 F*	1861 E	1894 C	1927 M	1960 L*	1993 K	2026 I
1796 L*	1829 I	1862 G	1895 E	1928 B*	1961 A	1994 M	2027 K
1797 A	1830 K	1863 I	1896 H*	1929 E	1962 C	1995 A	2028 N*
1798 C	1831 M	1864 L*	1897 K	1930 G	1963 E	1996 D*	2029 C
1799 E	1832 B*	1865 A	1898 M	1931 I	1964 H*	1997 G	2030 E
1800 G	1833 E	1866 C	1899 A	1932 L*	1965 K	1998 I	2031 G
1801 I	1834 G	1867 E	1900 C	1933 A	1966 M	1999 K	2032 J*
1802 K	1835 I	1868 H*	1901 E	1934 C	1967 A	2000 N*	2033 M
1803 M	1836 L*	1869 K	1902 G	1935 E	1968 D*	2001 C	2034 A
1804 B*	1837 A	1870 M	1903 I	1936 H*	1969 G	2002 E	2035 C
1805 E	1838 C	1871 A	1904 L*	1937 K	1970 I	2003 G	2036 F*
1806 G	1839 E	1872 D*	1905 A	1938 M	1971 K	2004 J*	2037 I
1807 I	1840 H*	1873 G	1906 C	1939 A	1972 N*	2005 M	2038 K
1808 L*	1841 K	1874 I	1907 E	1940 D*	1973 C	2006 A	2039 M
1809 A	1842 M	1875 K	1908 H*	1941 G	1974 E	2007 C	2040 B*
1810 C	1843 A	1876 N*	1909 K	1942 I	1975 G	2008 F*	
1811 E	1844 D*	1877 C	1910 M	1943 K	1976 J*	2009 I	
1812 H*	1845 G	1878 E	1911 A	1944 N*	1977 M	2010 K	

A

	January	*February*	*March*
Sun.	1 8 15 22 29	5 12 19 26	5 12 19 26
Mon.	2 9 16 23 30	6 13 20 27	6 13 20 27
Tue.	3 10 17 24 31	7 14 21 28	7 14 21 28
Wed.	4 11 18 25	1 8 15 22	1 8 15 22 29
Thur.	5 12 19 26	2 9 16 23	2 9 16 23 30
Fri.	6 13 20 27	3 10 17 24	3 10 17 24 31
Sat.	7 14 21 28	4 11 18 25	4 11 18 25

	April	*May*	*June*
Sun.	2 9 16 23 30	7 14 21 28	4 11 18 25
Mon.	3 10 17 24	1 8 15 22 29	5 12 19 26
Tue.	4 11 18 25	2 9 16 23 30	6 13 20 27
Wed.	5 12 19 26	3 10 17 24 31	7 14 21 28
Thur.	6 13 20 27	4 11 18 25	1 8 15 22 29
Fri.	7 14 21 28	5 12 19 26	2 9 16 23 30
Sat.	1 8 15 22 29	6 13 20 27	3 10 17 24

	July	*August*	*September*
Sun.	2 9 16 23 30	6 13 20 27	3 10 17 24
Mon.	3 10 17 24 31	7 14 21 28	4 11 18 25
Tue.	4 11 18 25	1 8 15 22 29	5 12 19 26
Wed.	5 12 19 26	2 9 16 23 30	6 13 20 27
Thur.	6 13 20 27	3 10 17 24 31	7 14 21 28
Fri.	7 14 21 28	4 11 18 25	1 8 15 22 29
Sat.	1 8 15 22 29	5 12 19 26	2 9 16 23 30

	October	*November*	*December*
Sun.	1 8 15 22 29	5 12 19 26	3 10 17 24 31
Mon.	2 9 16 23 30	6 13 20 27	4 11 18 25
Tue.	3 10 17 24 31	7 14 21 28	5 12 19 26
Wed.	4 11 18 25	1 8 15 22 29	6 13 20 27
Thur.	5 12 19 26	2 9 16 23 30	7 14 21 28
Fri.	6 13 20 27	3 10 17 24	1 8 15 22 29
Sat.	7 14 21 28	4 11 18 25	2 9 16 23 30

EASTER DAYS

March 26	1815, 1826, 1837, 1967, 1978, 1989
April 2	1809, 1893, 1899, 1961
April 9	1871, 1882, 1939, 1950, 2023, 2034
April 16	1786, 1797, 1843, 1854, 1865, 1911 1922, 1933, 1995, 2006, 2017
April 23	1905

B (LEAP YEAR)

	January	*February*	*March*
Sun.	1 8 15 22 29	5 12 19 26	4 11 18 25
Mon.	2 9 16 23 30	6 13 20 27	5 12 19 26
Tue.	3 10 17 24 31	7 14 21 28	6 13 20 27
Wed.	4 11 18 25	1 8 15 22 29	7 14 21 28
Thur.	5 12 19 26	2 9 16 23	1 8 15 22 29
Fri.	6 13 20 27	3 10 17 24	2 9 16 23 30
Sat.	7 14 21 28	4 11 18 25	3 10 17 24 31

	April	*May*	*June*
Sun.	1 8 15 22 29	6 13 20 27	3 10 17 24
Mon.	2 9 16 23 30	7 14 21 28	4 11 18 25
Tue.	3 10 17 24	1 8 15 22 29	5 12 19 26
Wed.	4 11 18 25	2 9 16 23 30	6 13 20 27
Thur.	5 12 19 26	3 10 17 24 31	7 14 21 28
Fri.	6 13 20 27	4 11 18 25	1 8 15 22 29
Sat.	7 14 21 28	5 12 19 26	2 9 16 23 30

	July	*August*	*September*
Sun.	1 8 15 22 29	5 12 19 26	2 9 16 23 30
Mon.	2 9 16 23 30	6 13 20 27	3 10 17 24
Tue.	3 10 17 24 31	7 14 21 28	4 11 18 25
Wed.	4 11 18 25	1 8 15 22 29	5 12 19 26
Thur.	5 12 19 26	2 9 16 23 30	6 13 20 27
Fri.	6 13 20 27	3 10 17 24 31	7 14 21 28
Sat.	7 14 21 28	4 11 18 25	1 8 15 22 29

	October	*November*	*December*
Sun.	7 14 21 28	4 11 18 25	2 9 16 23 30
Mon.	1 8 15 22 29	5 12 19 26	3 10 17 24 31
Tue.	2 9 16 23 30	6 13 20 27	4 11 18 25
Wed.	3 10 17 24 31	7 14 21 28	5 12 19 26
Thur.	4 11 18 25	1 8 15 22 29	6 13 20 27
Fri.	5 12 19 26	2 9 16 23 30	7 14 21 28
Sat.	6 13 20 27	3 10 17 24	1 8 15 22 29

EASTER DAYS

April 1	1804, 1888, 1956, 2040
April 8	1792, 1860, 1928, 2012
April 22	1832, 1984

C

	January	*February*	*March*
Sun.	7 14 21 28	4 11 18 25	4 11 18 25
Mon.	1 8 15 22 29	5 12 19 26	5 12 19 26
Tue.	2 9 16 23 30	6 13 20 27	6 13 20 27
Wed.	3 10 17 24 31	7 14 21 28	7 14 21 28
Thur.	4 11 18 25	1 8 15 22	1 8 15 22 29
Fri.	5 12 19 26	2 9 16 23	2 9 16 23 30
Sat.	6 13 20 27	3 10 17 24	3 10 17 24 31

	April	*May*	*June*
Sun.	1 8 15 22 29	6 13 20 27	3 10 17 24
Mon.	2 9 16 23 30	7 14 21 28	4 11 18 25
Tue.	3 10 17 24	1 8 15 22 29	5 12 19 26
Wed.	4 11 18 25	2 9 16 23 30	6 13 20 27
Thur.	5 12 19 26	3 10 17 24 31	7 14 21 28
Fri.	6 13 20 27	4 11 18 25	1 8 15 22 29
Sat.	7 14 21 28	5 12 19 26	2 9 16 23 30

	July	*August*	*September*
Sun.	1 8 15 22 29	5 12 19 26	2 9 16 23 30
Mon.	2 9 16 23 30	6 13 20 27	3 10 17 24
Tue.	3 10 17 24 31	7 14 21 28	4 11 18 25
Wed.	4 11 18 25	1 8 15 22 29	5 12 19 26
Thur.	5 12 19 26	2 9 16 23 30	6 13 20 27
Fri.	6 13 20 27	3 10 17 24 31	7 14 21 28
Sat.	7 14 21 28	4 11 18 25	1 8 15 22 29

	October	*November*	*December*
Sun.	7 14 21 28	4 11 18 25	2 9 16 23 30
Mon.	1 8 15 22 29	5 12 19 26	3 10 17 24 31
Tue.	2 9 16 23 30	6 13 20 27	4 11 18 25
Wed.	3 10 17 24 31	7 14 21 28	5 12 19 26
Thur.	4 11 18 25	1 8 15 22 29	6 13 20 27
Fri.	5 12 19 26	2 9 16 23 30	7 14 21 28
Sat.	6 13 20 27	3 10 17 24	1 8 15 22 29

EASTER DAYS

March 25	1883, 1894, 1951, 2035
April 1	1866, 1877, 1923, 1934, 1945, 2018, 2029
April 8	1787, 1798, 1849, 1855, 1917, 2007
April 15	1781, 1827, 1838, 1900, 1906, 1979, 1990, 2001
April 22	1810, 1821, 1962, 1973

D (LEAP YEAR)

	January	*February*	*March*
Sun.	7 14 21 28	4 11 18 25	3 10 17 24 31
Mon.	1 8 15 22 29	5 12 19 26	4 11 18 25
Tue.	2 9 16 23 30	6 13 20 27	5 12 19 26
Wed.	3 10 17 24 31	7 14 21 28	6 13 20 27
Thur.	4 11 18 25	1 8 15 22 29	7 14 21 28
Fri.	5 12 19 26	2 9 16 23	1 8 15 22 29
Sat.	6 13 20 27	3 10 17 24	2 9 16 23 30

	April	*May*	*June*
Sun.	7 14 21 28	5 12 19 26	2 9 16 23 30
Mon.	1 8 15 22 29	6 13 20 27	3 10 17 24
Tue.	2 9 16 23 30	7 14 21 28	4 11 18 25
Wed.	3 10 17 24	1 8 15 22 29	5 12 19 26
Thur.	4 11 18 25	2 9 16 23 30	6 13 20 27
Fri.	5 12 19 26	3 10 17 24 31	7 14 21 28
Sat.	6 13 20 27	4 11 18 25	1 8 15 22 29

	July	*August*	*September*
Sun.	7 14 21 28	4 11 18 25	1 8 15 22 29
Mon.	1 8 15 22 29	5 12 19 26	2 9 16 23 30
Tue.	2 9 16 23 30	6 13 20 27	3 10 17 24
Wed.	3 10 17 24 31	7 14 21 28	4 11 18 25
Thur.	4 11 18 25	1 8 15 22 29	5 12 19 26
Fri.	5 12 19 26	2 9 16 23 30	6 13 20 27
Sat.	6 13 20 27	3 10 17 24 31	7 14 21 28

	October	*November*	*December*
Sun.	6 13 20 27	3 10 17 24	1 8 15 22 29
Mon.	7 14 21 28	4 11 18 25	2 9 16 23 30
Tue.	1 8 15 22 29	5 12 19 26	3 10 17 24 31
Wed.	2 9 16 23 30	6 13 20 27	4 11 18 25
Thur.	3 10 17 24 31	7 14 21 28	5 12 19 26
Fri.	4 11 18 25	1 8 15 22 29	6 13 20 27
Sat.	5 12 19 26	2 9 16 23 30	7 14 21 28

EASTER DAYS

March 24	1940
March 31	1872, 2024
April 7	1844, 1912, 1996
April 14	1816, 1968

E

	January	*February*	*March*
Sun.	6 13 20 27	3 10 17 24	3 10 17 24 31
Mon.	7 14 21 28	4 11 18 25	4 11 18 25
Tue.	1 8 15 22 29	5 12 19 26	5 12 19 26
Wed.	2 9 16 23 30	6 13 20 27	6 13 20 27
Thur.	3 10 17 24 31	7 14 21 28	7 14 21 28
Fri.	4 11 18 25	1 8 15 22	1 8 15 22 29
Sat.	5 12 19 26	2 9 16 23	2 9 16 23 30

	April	*May*	*June*
Sun.	7 14 21 28	5 12 19 26	2 9 16 23 30
Mon.	1 8 15 22 29	6 13 20 27	3 10 17 24
Tue.	2 9 16 23 30	7 14 21 28	4 11 18 25
Wed.	3 10 17 24	1 8 15 22 29	5 12 19 26
Thur.	4 11 18 25	2 9 16 23 30	6 13 20 27
Fri.	5 12 19 26	3 10 17 24 31	7 14 21 28
Sat.	6 13 20 27	4 11 18 25	1 8 15 22 29

	July	*August*	*September*
Sun.	7 14 21 28	4 11 18 25	1 8 15 22 29
Mon.	1 8 15 22 29	5 12 19 26	2 9 16 23 30
Tue.	2 9 16 23 30	6 13 20 27	3 10 17 24
Wed.	3 10 17 24 31	7 14 21 28	4 11 18 25
Thur.	4 11 18 25	1 8 15 22 29	5 12 19 26
Fri.	5 12 19 26	2 9 16 23 30	6 13 20 27
Sat.	6 13 20 27	3 10 17 24 31	7 14 21 28

	October	*November*	*December*
Sun.	6 13 20 27	3 10 17 24	1 8 15 22 29
Mon.	7 14 21 28	4 11 18 25	2 9 16 23 30
Tue.	1 8 15 22 29	5 12 19 26	3 10 17 24 31
Wed.	2 9 16 23 30	6 13 20 27	4 11 18 25
Thur.	3 10 17 24 31	7 14 21 28	5 12 19 26
Fri.	4 11 18 25	1 8 15 22 29	6 13 20 27
Sat.	5 12 19 26	2 9 16 23 30	7 14 21 28

EASTER DAYS

March 24	1799
March 31	1782, 1793, 1839, 1850, 1861, 1907 1918, 1929, 1991, 2002, 2013
April 7	1822, 1833, 1901, 1985
April 14	1805, 1811, 1895, 1963, 1974
April 21	1867, 1878, 1889, 1935, 1946, 1957, 2019, 2030

F (LEAP YEAR)

	January	*February*	*March*
Sun.	6 13 20 27	3 10 17 24	2 9 16 23 30
Mon.	7 14 21 28	4 11 18 25	3 10 17 24 31
Tue.	1 8 15 22 29	5 12 19 26	4 11 18 25
Wed.	2 9 16 23 30	6 13 20 27	5 12 19 26
Thur.	3 10 17 24 31	7 14 21 28	6 13 20 27
Fri.	4 11 18 25	1 8 15 22 29	7 14 21 28
Sat.	5 12 19 26	2 9 16 23	1 8 15 22 29

	April	*May*	*June*
Sun.	6 13 20 27	4 11 18 25	1 8 15 22 29
Mon.	7 14 21 28	5 12 19 26	2 9 16 23 30
Tue.	1 8 15 22 29	6 13 20 27	3 10 17 24
Wed.	2 9 16 23 30	7 14 21 28	4 11 18 25
Thur.	3 10 17 24	1 8 15 22 29	5 12 19 26
Fri.	4 11 18 25	2 9 16 23 30	6 13 20 27
Sat.	5 12 19 26	3 10 17 24 31	7 14 21 28

	July	*August*	*September*
Sun.	6 13 20 27	3 10 17 24 31	7 14 21 28
Mon.	7 14 21 28	4 11 18 25	1 8 15 22 29
Tue.	1 8 15 22 29	5 12 19 26	2 9 16 23 30
Wed.	2 9 16 23 30	6 13 20 27	3 10 17 24
Thur.	3 10 17 24 31	7 14 21 28	4 11 18 25
Fri.	4 11 18 25	1 8 15 22 29	5 12 19 26
Sat.	5 12 19 26	2 9 16 23 30	6 13 20 27

	October	*November*	*December*
Sun.	5 12 19 26	2 9 16 23 30	7 14 21 28
Mon.	6 13 20 27	3 10 17 24	1 8 15 22 29
Tue.	7 14 21 28	4 11 18 25	2 9 16 23 30
Wed.	1 8 15 22 29	5 12 19 26	3 10 17 24 31
Thur.	2 9 16 23 30	6 13 20 27	4 11 18 25
Fri.	3 10 17 24 31	7 14 21 28	5 12 19 26
Sat.	4 11 18 25	1 8 15 22 29	6 13 20 27

EASTER DAYS

March 23	1788, 1856, 2008
April 6	1828, 1980
April 13	1884, 1952, 2036
April 20	1924

G

	January	*February*	*March*
Sun.	5 12 19 26	2 9 16 23	2 9 16 23 30
Mon.	6 13 20 27	3 10 17 24	3 10 17 24 31
Tue.	7 14 21 28	4 11 18 25	4 11 18 25
Wed.	1 8 15 22 29	5 12 19 26	5 12 19 26
Thur.	2 9 16 23 30	6 13 20 27	6 13 20 27
Fri.	3 10 17 24 31	7 14 21 28	7 14 21 28
Sat.	4 11 18 25	1 8 15 22	1 8 15 22 29

	April	*May*	*June*
Sun.	6 13 20 27	4 11 18 25	1 8 15 22 29
Mon.	7 14 21 28	5 12 19 26	2 9 16 23 30
Tue.	1 8 15 22 29	6 13 20 27	3 10 17 24
Wed.	2 9 16 23 30	7 14 21 28	4 11 18 25
Thur.	3 10 17 24	1 8 15 22 29	5 12 19 26
Fri.	4 11 18 25	2 9 16 23 30	6 13 20 27
Sat.	5 12 19 26	3 10 17 24 31	7 14 21 28

	July	*August*	*September*
Sun.	6 13 20 27	3 10 17 24 31	7 14 21 28
Mon.	7 14 21 28	4 11 18 25	1 8 15 22 29
Tue.	1 8 15 22 29	5 12 19 26	2 9 16 23 30
Wed.	2 9 16 23 30	6 13 20 27	3 10 17 24
Thur.	3 10 17 24 31	7 14 21 28	4 11 18 25
Fri.	4 11 18 25	1 8 15 22 29	5 12 19 26
Sat.	5 12 19 26	2 9 16 23 30	6 13 20 27

	October	*November*	*December*
Sun.	5 12 19 26	2 9 16 23 30	7 14 21 28
Mon.	6 13 20 27	3 10 17 24	1 8 15 22 29
Tue.	7 14 21 28	4 11 18 25	2 9 16 23 30
Wed.	1 8 15 22 29	5 12 19 26	3 10 17 24 31
Thur.	2 9 16 23 30	6 13 20 27	4 11 18 25
Fri.	3 10 17 24 31	7 14 21 28	5 12 19 26
Sat.	4 11 18 25	1 8 15 22 29	6 13 20 27

EASTER DAYS

March 23	1845, 1913
March 30	1823, 1834, 1902, 1975, 1986, 1997
April 6	1806, 1817, 1890, 1947, 1958, 1969
April 13	1800, 1873, 1879, 1941, 2031
April 20	1783, 1794, 1851, 1862, 1919, 1930, 2003, 2014, 2025

H (LEAP YEAR)

	January	*February*	*March*
Sun.	5 12 19 26	2 9 16 23	1 8 15 22 29
Mon.	6 13 20 27	3 10 17 24	2 9 16 23 30
Tue.	7 14 21 28	4 11 18 25	3 10 17 24 31
Wed.	1 8 15 22 29	5 12 19 26	4 11 18 25
Thur.	2 9 16 23 30	6 13 20 27	5 12 19 26
Fri.	3 10 17 24 31	7 14 21 28	6 13 20 27
Sat.	4 11 18 25	1 8 15 22 29	7 14 21 28

	April	*May*	*June*
Sun.	5 12 19 26	3 10 17 24 31	7 14 21 28
Mon.	6 13 20 27	4 11 18 25	1 8 15 22 29
Tue.	7 14 21 28	5 12 19 26	2 9 16 23 30
Wed.	1 8 15 22 29	6 13 20 27	3 10 17 24
Thur.	2 9 16 23 30	7 14 21 28	4 11 18 25
Fri.	3 10 17 24	1 8 15 22 29	5 12 19 26
Sat.	4 11 18 25	2 9 16 23 30	6 13 20 27

	July	*August*	*September*
Sun.	5 12 19 26	2 9 16 23 30	6 13 20 27
Mon.	6 13 20 27	3 10 17 24 31	7 14 21 28
Tue.	7 14 21 28	4 11 18 25	1 8 15 22 29
Wed.	1 8 15 22 29	5 12 19 26	2 9 16 23 30
Thur.	2 9 16 23 30	6 13 20 27	3 10 17 24
Fri.	3 10 17 24 31	7 14 21 28	4 11 18 25
Sat.	4 11 18 25	1 8 15 22 29	5 12 19 26

	October	*November*	*December*
Sun.	4 11 18 25	1 8 15 22 29	6 13 20 27
Mon.	5 12 19 26	2 9 16 23 30	7 14 21 28
Tue.	6 13 20 27	3 10 17 24	1 8 15 22 29
Wed.	7 14 21 28	4 11 18 25	2 9 16 23 30
Thur.	1 8 15 22 29	5 12 19 26	3 10 17 24 31
Fri.	2 9 16 23 30	6 13 20 27	4 11 18 25
Sat.	3 10 17 24 31	7 14 21 28	5 12 19 26

EASTER DAYS

March 29	1812, 1964
April 5	1896
April 12	1868, 1936, 2020
April 19	1840, 1908, 1992

I

	January	*February*	*March*
Sun.	4 11 18 25	1 8 15 22	1 8 15 22 29
Mon.	5 12 19 26	2 9 16 23	2 9 16 23 30
Tue.	6 13 20 27	3 10 17 24	3 10 17 24 31
Wed.	7 14 21 28	4 11 18 25	4 11 18 25
Thur.	1 8 15 22 29	5 12 19 26	5 12 19 26
Fri.	2 9 16 23 30	6 13 20 27	6 13 20 27
Sat.	3 10 17 24 31	7 14 21 28	7 14 21 28

	April	*May*	*June*
Sun.	5 12 19 26	3 10 17 24 31	7 14 21 28
Mon.	6 13 20 27	4 11 18 25	1 8 15 22 29
Tue.	7 14 21 28	5 12 19 26	2 9 16 23 30
Wed.	1 8 15 22 29	6 13 20 27	3 10 17 24
Thur.	2 9 16 23 30	7 14 21 28	4 11 18 25
Fri.	3 10 17 24	1 8 15 22 29	5 12 19 26
Sat.	4 11 18 25	2 9 16 23 30	6 13 20 27

	July	*August*	*September*
Sun.	5 12 19 26	2 9 16 23 30	6 13 20 27
Mon.	6 13 20 27	3 10 17 24 31	7 14 21 28
Tue.	7 14 21 28	4 11 18 25	1 8 15 22 29
Wed.	1 8 15 22 29	5 12 19 26	2 9 16 23 30
Thur.	2 9 16 23 30	6 13 20 27	3 10 17 24
Fri.	3 10 17 24 31	7 14 21 28	4 11 18 25
Sat.	4 11 18 25	1 8 15 22 29	5 12 19 26

	October	*November*	*December*
Sun.	4 11 18 25	1 8 15 22 29	6 13 20 27
Mon.	5 12 19 26	2 9 16 23 30	7 14 21 28
Tue.	6 13 20 27	3 10 17 24	1 8 15 22 29
Wed.	7 14 21 28	4 11 18 25	2 9 16 23 30
Thur.	1 8 15 22 29	5 12 19 26	3 10 17 24 31
Fri.	2 9 16 23 30	6 13 20 27	4 11 18 25
Sat.	3 10 17 24 31	7 14 21 28	5 12 19 26

EASTER DAYS

March 22	1818
March 29	1807, 1891, 1959, 1970
April 5	1795, 1801, 1863, 1874, 1885, 1931, 1942, 1953, 2015, 2026, 2037
April 12	1789, 1846, 1857, 1903, 1914, 1925, 1998, 2009
April 19	1829, 1835, 1981, 1987

J (LEAP YEAR)

	January	*February*	*March*
Sun.	4 11 18 25	1 8 15 22 29	7 14 21 28
Mon.	5 12 19 26	2 9 16 23	1 8 15 22 29
Tue.	6 13 20 27	3 10 17 24	2 9 16 23 30
Wed.	7 14 21 28	4 11 18 25	3 10 17 24 31
Thur.	1 8 15 22 29	5 12 19 26	4 11 18 25
Fri.	2 9 16 23 30	6 13 20 27	5 12 19 26
Sat.	3 10 17 24 31	7 14 21 28	6 13 20 27

	April	*May*	*June*
Sun.	4 11 18 25	2 9 16 23 30	6 13 20 27
Mon.	5 12 19 26	3 10 17 24 31	7 14 21 28
Tue.	6 13 20 27	4 11 18 25	1 8 15 22 29
Wed.	7 14 21 28	5 12 19 26	2 9 16 23 30
Thur.	1 8 15 22 29	6 13 20 27	3 10 17 24
Fri.	2 9 16 23 30	7 14 21 28	4 11 18 25
Sat.	3 10 17 24	1 8 15 22 29	5 12 19 26

	July	*August*	*September*
Sun.	4 11 18 25	1 8 15 22 29	5 12 19 26
Mon.	5 12 19 26	2 9 16 23 30	6 13 20 27
Tue.	6 13 20 27	3 10 17 24 31	7 14 21 28
Wed.	7 14 21 28	4 11 18 25	1 8 15 22 29
Thur.	1 8 15 22 29	5 12 19 26	2 9 16 23 30
Fri.	2 9 16 23 30	6 13 20 27	3 10 17 24
Sat.	3 10 17 24 31	7 14 21 28	4 11 18 25

	October	*November*	*December*
Sun.	3 10 17 24 31	7 14 21 28	5 12 19 26
Mon.	4 11 18 25	1 8 15 22 29	6 13 20 27
Tue.	5 12 19 26	2 9 16 23 30	7 14 21 28
Wed.	6 13 20 27	3 10 17 24	1 8 15 22 29
Thur.	7 14 21 28	4 11 18 25	2 9 16 23 30
Fri.	1 8 15 22 29	5 12 19 26	3 10 17 24 31
Sat.	2 9 16 23 30	6 13 20 27	4 11 18 25

EASTER DAYS

March 28	1880, 1948, 2032
April 4	1920
April 11	1784, 1852, 2004
April 18	1824, 1976

K

	January	*February*	*March*
Sun.	3 10 17 24 31	7 14 21 28	7 14 21 28
Mon.	4 11 18 25	1 8 15 22	1 8 15 22 29
Tue.	5 12 19 26	2 9 16 23	2 9 16 23 30
Wed.	6 13 20 27	3 10 17 24	3 10 17 24 31
Thur.	7 14 21 28	4 11 18 25	4 11 18 25
Fri.	1 8 15 22 29	5 12 19 26	5 12 19 26
Sat.	2 9 16 23 30	6 13 20 27	6 13 20 27

	April	*May*	*June*
Sun.	4 11 18 25	2 9 16 23 30	6 13 20 27
Mon.	5 12 19 26	3 10 17 24 31	7 14 21 28
Tue.	6 13 20 27	4 11 18 25	1 8 15 22 29
Wed.	7 14 21 28	5 12 19 26	2 9 16 23 30
Thur.	1 8 15 22 29	6 13 20 27	3 10 17 24
Fri.	2 9 16 23 30	7 14 21 28	4 11 18 25
Sat.	3 10 17 24	1 8 15 22 29	5 12 19 26

	July	*August*	*September*
Sun.	4 11 18 25	1 8 15 22 29	5 12 19 26
Mon.	5 12 19 26	2 9 16 23 30	6 13 20 27
Tue.	6 13 20 27	3 10 17 24 31	7 14 21 28
Wed.	7 14 21 28	4 11 18 25	1 8 15 22 29
Thur.	1 8 15 22 29	5 12 19 26	2 9 16 23 30
Fri.	2 9 16 23 30	6 13 20 27	3 10 17 24
Sat.	3 10 17 24 31	7 14 21 28	4 11 18 25

	October	*November*	*December*
Sun.	3 10 17 24 31	7 14 21 28	5 12 19 26
Mon.	4 11 18 25	1 8 15 22 29	6 13 20 27
Tue.	5 12 19 26	2 9 16 23 30	7 14 21 28
Wed.	6 13 20 27	3 10 17 24	1 8 15 22 29
Thur.	7 14 21 28	4 11 18 25	2 9 16 23 30
Fri.	1 8 15 22 29	5 12 19 26	3 10 17 24 31
Sat.	2 9 16 23 30	6 13 20 27	4 11 18 25

EASTER DAYS

March 28	1869, 1875, 1937, 2027
April 4	1790, 1847, 1858, 1915, 1926, 1999, 2010, 2021
April 11	1819, 1830, 1841, 1909, 1971, 1982, 1993
April 18	1802, 1813, 1897, 1954, 1965
April 25	1886, 1943, 2038

M

	January	*February*	*March*
Sun.	2 9 16 23 30	6 13 20 27	6 13 20 27
Mon.	3 10 17 24 31	7 14 21 28	7 14 21 28
Tue.	4 11 18 25	1 8 15 22	1 8 15 22 29
Wed.	5 12 19 26	2 9 16 23	2 9 16 23 30
Thur.	6 13 20 27	3 10 17 24	3 10 17 24 31
Fri.	7 14 21 28	4 11 18 25	4 11 18 25
Sat.	1 8 15 22 29	5 12 19 26	5 12 19 26

	April	*May*	*June*
Sun.	3 10 17 24	1 8 15 22 29	5 12 19 26
Mon.	4 11 18 25	2 9 16 23 30	6 13 20 27
Tue.	5 12 19 26	3 10 17 24 31	7 14 21 28
Wed.	6 13 20 27	4 11 18 25	1 8 15 22 29
Thur.	7 14 21 28	5 12 19 26	2 9 16 23 30
Fri.	1 8 15 22 29	6 13 20 27	3 10 17 24
Sat.	2 9 16 23 30	7 14 21 28	4 11 18 25

	July	*August*	*September*
Sun.	3 10 17 24 31	7 14 21 28	4 11 18 25
Mon.	4 11 18 25	1 8 15 22 29	5 12 19 26
Tue.	5 12 19 26	2 9 16 23 30	6 13 20 27
Wed.	6 13 20 27	3 10 17 24 31	7 14 21 28
Thur.	7 14 21 28	4 11 18 25	1 8 15 22 29
Fri.	1 8 15 22 29	5 12 19 26	2 9 16 23 30
Sat.	2 9 16 23 30	6 13 20 27	3 10 17 24

	October	*November*	*December*
Sun.	2 9 16 23 30	6 13 20 27	4 11 18 25
Mon.	3 10 17 24 31	7 14 21 28	5 12 19 26
Tue.	4 11 18 25	1 8 15 22 29	6 13 20 27
Wed.	5 12 19 26	2 9 16 23 30	7 14 21 28
Thur.	6 13 20 27	3 10 17 24	1 8 15 22 29
Fri.	7 14 21 28	4 11 18 25	2 9 16 23 30
Sat.	1 8 15 22 29	5 12 19 26	3 10 17 24 31

EASTER DAYS

March 27	1785, 1842, 1853, 1910, 1921, 2005
April 3	1825, 1831, 1983, 1994
April 10	1803, 1814, 1887, 1898, 1955, 1966, 1977, 2039
April 17	1870, 1881, 1927, 1938, 1949, 2022, 2033
April 24	1791, 1859, 2011

L (LEAP YEAR)

	January	*February*	*March*
Sun.	3 10 17 24 31	7 14 21 28	6 13 20 27
Mon.	4 11 18 25	1 8 15 22 29	7 14 21 28
Tue.	5 12 19 26	2 9 16 23	1 8 15 22 29
Wed.	6 13 20 27	3 10 17 24	2 9 16 23 30
Thur.	7 14 21 28	4 11 18 25	3 10 17 24 31
Fri.	1 8 15 22 29	5 12 19 26	4 11 18 25
Sat.	2 9 16 23 30	6 13 20 27	5 12 19 26

	April	*May*	*June*
Sun.	3 10 17 24	1 8 15 22 29	5 12 19 26
Mon.	4 11 18 25	2 9 16 23 30	6 13 20 27
Tue.	5 12 19 26	3 10 17 24 31	7 14 21 28
Wed.	6 13 20 27	4 11 18 25	1 8 15 22 29
Thur.	7 14 21 28	5 12 19 26	2 9 16 23 30
Fri.	1 8 15 22 29	6 13 20 27	3 10 17 24
Sat.	2 9 16 23 30	7 14 21 28	4 11 18 25

	July	*August*	*September*
Sun.	3 10 17 24 31	7 14 21 28	4 11 18 25
Mon.	4 11 18 25	1 8 15 22 29	5 12 19 26
Tue.	5 12 19 26	2 9 16 23 30	6 13 20 27
Wed.	6 13 20 27	3 10 17 24 31	7 14 21 28
Thur.	7 14 21 28	4 11 18 25	1 8 15 22 29
Fri.	1 8 15 22 29	5 12 19 26	2 9 16 23 30
Sat.	2 9 16 23 30	6 13 20 27	3 10 17 24

	October	*November*	*December*
Sun.	2 9 16 23 30	6 13 20 27	4 11 18 25
Mon.	3 10 17 24 31	7 14 21 28	5 12 19 26
Tue.	4 11 18 25	1 8 15 22 29	6 13 20 27
Wed.	5 12 19 26	2 9 16 23 30	7 14 21 28
Thur.	6 13 20 27	3 10 17 24	1 8 15 22 29
Fri.	7 14 21 28	4 11 18 25	2 9 16 23 30
Sat.	1 8 15 22 29	5 12 19 26	3 10 17 24 31

EASTER DAYS

March 27	1796, 1864, 1932, 2016
April 3	1836, 1904, 1988
April 17	1808, 1892, 1960

N (LEAP YEAR)

	January	*February*	*March*
Sun.	2 9 16 23 30	6 13 20 27	5 12 19 26
Mon.	3 10 17 24 31	7 14 21 28	6 13 20 27
Tue.	4 11 18 25	1 8 15 22 29	7 14 21 28
Wed.	5 12 19 26	2 9 16 23	1 8 15 22 29
Thur.	6 13 20 27	3 10 17 24	2 9 16 23 30
Fri.	7 14 21 28	4 11 18 25	3 10 17 24 31
Sat.	1 8 15 22 29	5 12 19 26	4 11 18 25

	April	*May*	*June*
Sun.	2 9 16 23 30	7 14 21 28	4 11 18 25
Mon.	3 10 17 24	1 8 15 22 29	5 12 19 26
Tue.	4 11 18 25	2 9 16 23 30	6 13 20 27
Wed.	5 12 19 26	3 10 17 24 31	7 14 21 28
Thur.	6 13 20 27	4 11 18 25	1 8 15 22 29
Fri.	7 14 21 28	5 12 19 26	2 9 16 23 30
Sat.	1 8 15 22 29	6 13 20 27	3 10 17 24

	July	*August*	*September*
Sun.	2 9 16 23 30	6 13 20 27	3 10 17 24
Mon.	3 10 17 24 31	7 14 21 28	4 11 18 25
Tue.	4 11 18 25	1 8 15 22 29	5 12 19 26
Wed.	5 12 19 26	2 9 16 23 30	6 13 20 27
Thur.	6 13 20 27	3 10 17 24 31	7 14 21 28
Fri.	7 14 21 28	4 11 18 25	1 8 15 22 29
Sat.	1 8 15 22 29	5 12 19 26	2 9 16 23 30

	October	*November*	*December*
Sun.	1 8 15 22 29	5 12 19 26	3 10 17 24 31
Mon.	2 9 16 23 30	6 13 20 27	4 11 18 25
Tue.	3 10 17 24 31	7 14 21 28	5 12 19 26
Wed.	4 11 18 25	1 8 15 22 29	6 13 20 27
Thur.	5 12 19 26	2 9 16 23 30	7 14 21 28
Fri.	6 13 20 27	3 10 17 24	1 8 15 22 29
Sat.	7 14 21 28	4 11 18 25	2 9 16 23 30

EASTER DAYS

March 26	1780
April 2	1820, 1972
April 9	1944
April 16	1876, 2028
April 23	1848, 1916, 2000

GEOLOGICAL TIME

The earth is thought to have come into existence approximately 4,600 million years ago, but for nearly half this time, the Archean era, it was uninhabited. Life is generally believed to have emerged in the succeeding Proterozoic era. The Archean and the Proterozoic eras are often together referred to as the Precambrian.

Although primitive forms of life, eg algae and bacteria, existed during the Proterozoic era, it is not until the strata of Palaeozoic rocks are reached that abundant fossilised remains appear. Since the Precambrian, there have been three great geological eras:

PALAEOZOIC ('ANCIENT LIFE')

c.542–c.251 million years ago

Cambrian – Mainly sandstones, slate and shales; limestones in Scotland. Shelled fossils and invertebrates, eg trilobites and brachiopods appear, as do the earliest known vertebrates (jawless fish)

Ordovician – Mainly shales and mudstones, eg in north Wales; limestones in Scotland. First fishes

Silurian – Shales, mudstones and some limestones, found mostly in Wales and southern Scotland

Devonian – Old red sandstone, shale, limestone and slate, eg in south Wales and the West Country

Carboniferous – Coal-bearing rocks, millstone grit, limestone and shale. First traces of land-living creatures

Permian – Marls, sandstones and clays. First reptile fossils

There were two great phases of mountain building in the Palaeozoic era: the Caledonian, characterised in Britain by NE–SW lines of hills and valleys; and the later Hercyian, widespread in west Germany and adjacent areas, and in Britain exemplified in E–W lines of hills and valleys.

The end of the Palaeozoic era was marked by the extensive glaciations of the Permian period in the southern continents and the decline of amphibians. It was succeeded by an era of warm conditions.

MESOZOIC ('MIDDLE FORMS OF LIFE')

c.251–c.65.5 million years ago

Triassic – Mostly sandstone, eg in the West Midlands; primitive mammals appear

Jurassic – Mainly limestones and clays, typically displayed in the Jura mountains, and in England in a NE–SW belt from Lincolnshire and the Wash to the Severn and the Dorset coast

Cretaceous – Mainly chalk, clay and sands, eg in Kent and Sussex

Giant reptiles were dominant during the Mesozoic era, but it was at this time that marsupial mammals first appeared, as well as *Archaeopteryx lithographica,* the earliest known species of bird. Coniferous trees and flowering plants also developed during the era and, with the birds and the mammals, were the main species to survive into the Cenozoic era. The giant reptiles became extinct.

CENOZOIC ('RECENT LIFE')

from c.65.5 million years ago

Palaeocene, *Eocene* – The emergence of new forms of life, including existing species; primates appear

Oligocene – Fossils of a few still existing species

Miocene – Fossil remains show a balance of existing and extinct species

Pliocene – Fossil remains show a majority of still existing species

Pleistocene – The majority of remains are those of still existing species

Holocene – The present, post-glacial period. Existing species only, except for a few exterminated by humans

In the last 25 million years, from the Miocene through the Pliocene periods, the Alpine-Himalayan and the circum-Pacific phases of mountain building reached their climax. During the Pleistocene period ice-sheets repeatedly locked up masses of water as land ice; its weight depressed the land, but the locking-up of the water lowered the sea level by 100–200 metres. The glaciations and interglacials of the Ice Age are difficult to date and classify, but recent scientific opinion considers the Pleistocene period to have begun approximately 1.64 million years ago. The last glacial retreat, merging into the Holocene period, was c.10,000 years ago.

HUMAN DEVELOPMENT

Any consideration of the history of humans must start with the fact that all members of the human race belong to one species of animal, ie *Homo sapiens,* the definition of a species being in biological terms that all its members can interbreed. As a species of mammal it is possible to group humans with other similar types, known as the primates. Amongst these is found a sub-group, the apes, which includes, in addition to humans, the chimpanzees, gorillas, orang-utans and gibbons. All lack a tail, have shoulder blades at the back, and a Y-shaped chewing pattern on the surface of their molars, as well as showing the more general primate characteristics of four incisors, a thumb which is able to touch the fingers of the same hand, and finger and toe nails instead of claws. The factors available to scientific study suggest that human beings have chimpanzees and gorillas as their nearest relatives in the animal world. However, there remains the possibility that there once lived creatures, now extinct, which were closer to modern man than the chimpanzees and gorillas, and which shared with modern man the characteristics of having flat faces (ie the absence of a pronounced muzzle), being bipedal, and possessing large brains.

There are two broad groups of extinct apes recognised by specialists. The ramapithecines – the remains of which, mainly jaw fragments, have been found in east Africa, Asia and Turkey – lived about 14 to 8 million years ago, and from the evidence of their teeth it seems they chewed more in the manner of modern humans than the other presently living apes. The second group, the australopithecines, have left more numerous remains amongst which sub-groups may be detected, although the geographic spread is limited to south and east Africa. Living between 5 and 1.5 million years ago, they were closer relatives of modern humans to the extent that they walked upright, did not have an extensive muzzle and had similar types of pre-molars. The first australopithecine remains were recognised at Taung in South Africa in 1924 and named *Australopithecus africanus,* dating between 3.3 and 2.3 million years ago. The most impressive discovery was made at Hadar, Ethiopia, in 1974 when about half a skeleton of *Australopithecus afarensis,* known as 'Lucy', was found. Some 3.2 million years ago, 'Lucy' certainly walked upright.

Also in east Africa, especially at Olduvai Gorge in Tanzania, between c.2.5 and 1.8 million years ago, lived a hominid group which not only walked upright, had a flat face, and a large brain case, but also made simple pebble and flake stone tools. On present evidence these habilines seem to have been the first people to make tools, however crude. This facility is related to the larger brain size and human beings are the only animals to make implements to be used in other processes. These early pebble tool users, because of their distinctive characteristics, have been grouped as a separate sub-species, now extinct, of the genus *Homo* and are known as *Homo habilis* or 'handy man'.

The use of fire, again a human characteristic, is associated with another group of extinct hominids whose remains, about a million years old, are found in south and east Africa, China, Indonesia, north Africa and Europe. Mastery of the techniques of making fire probably helped the colonisation of the colder northern areas and in this respect the site of Vertesszollos in Hungary is of particular importance. *Homo ergaster* in Africa and *Homo erectus* in Asia are the names given to this group of fossils and they relate to a number of famous individual discoveries, eg Solo Man, Heidelberg Man, and especially Peking Man who lived at the cave site at Choukoutien which has yielded evidence of fire and burnt bone.

The well-known group Neanderthal Man, or *Homo neanderthalensis,* is an extinct form of man that lived between about 350,000 and 24,000 years ago, thus spanning the last Ice Age. Indeed, its ability to adapt to the cold climate on the edge of the ice-sheets is one of its characteristic features, the remains being found only in Europe, Asia and the Middle East. Complete neanderthal skeletons were found during excavations at Tabun in Israel, together with evidence of tool-making and the use of fire. Distinguished by very large brains, it seems that neanderthal man was the first to develop recognisable social customs, especially deliberate burial rites. Why the neanderthals became extinct is not clear but it may be connected with the climatic changes at the end of the Ice Ages, which would have seriously affected their food supplies; possibly they became too specialised for their own good.

The shin bone of Boxgrove Man found in 1993 – *Homo heidelbergensis* – and the Swanscombe skull are the best known early human fossil remains found in England. Some specialists prefer to group Swanscombe Man (or, more probably, woman) together with the Steinheim skull from Germany, seeing both as a separate sub-species. There is too little evidence as yet on which to form a final judgement.

Modern humans – *Homo sapiens* – had evolved to our present physical condition and had colonised much of the world by about 40,000 years ago. There are many previously distinguished individual specimens, eg Cromagnon Man, which may now be grouped together as *Homo sapiens*. It was modern humans who spread to the American continent by crossing the landbridge between Siberia and Alaska and thence moved south through North America and into South America. Equally it is modern humans who over the last 40,000 years have been responsible for the major developments in technology, art and civilisation generally.

One of the problems for those studying human fossils is the lack in many cases of sufficient quantities of fossil bone for analysis. It is important that theories should be tested against evidence, rather than the evidence being made to fit the theory. The Piltdown hoax of 1912 (and not fully exposed until the 1970s) is a well-known example of 'fossils' being forged to fit what was seen in some quarters as the correct theory of human evolution.

The discovery of the structure of DNA in 1953 has come to have a profound effect upon the study of human evolution. For example, it was claimed in 1987 that a common ancestor of all human beings was a person who lived in Africa some 200,000 years ago, thus encouraging the 'out of Africa' theory of hominid migration from east Africa to the Middle East and then throughout the world. There is no doubt that the studies based on DNA have vast potential to elucidate further the course of human evolution.

CULTURAL DEVELOPMENT

The Eurocentric bias of early archaeologists meant that the search for a starting point for the development and transmission of cultural ideas, especially by migration, trade and warfare, concentrated unduly on Europe and the Near East. The Three Age system, whereby prehistory was divided into a Stone Age, a Bronze Age and an Iron Age, was devised by Christian Thomsen, curator of the National Museum of Denmark in the early 19th century, to facilitate the classification of the museum's collections. The descriptive adjectives referred to the materials from which the implements and weapons were made and came to be regarded as the dominant features of the societies to which they related. The refinement of the Three Age system once dominated archaeological thought and remains a generally accepted concept in the popular mind. However, it is now seen by archaeologists as an inadequate model for human development.

Common sense suggests that there were no complete breaks between one so-called Age and another, any more than contemporaries would have regarded 1485 as a complete break between medieval and modern English history. Nor can the Three Age system be applied universally. In some areas it is necessary to insert a Copper Age, while in Africa south of the Sahara there would seem to be no Bronze Age at all; in Australia, Old Stone Age societies survived, while in South America, New Stone Age communities existed into modern times. The civilisations in other parts of the world clearly invalidate a Eurocentric theory of human development.

The concept of the 'Neolithic revolution', associated with the domestication of plants and animals, was a development of particular importance in the human cultural pattern. It reflected change from the primitive hunter/gatherer economics to a more settled agricultural way of life and therefore, so the argument goes, made possible the development of urban civilisation. However, it can no longer be argued that this 'revolution' took place only in one area from which all development stemmed. Though it appears that the cultivation of wheat and barley was first undertaken, together with the domestication of cattle and goats/sheep, in the Fertile Crescent (the area bounded by the rivers Tigris and Euphrates), there is evidence that rice was first deliberately planted and pigs domesticated in south-east Asia, maize first cultivated in Central America and llamas first domesticated in South America. It has been recognised in recent years that cultural changes can take place independently of each other in different parts of the world at different rates and different times. There is no need for a general diffusionist theory.

Although scholars will continue to study the particular societies which interest them, it may be possible to obtain a reliable chronological framework, in absolute terms of years, against which the cultural development of any particular area may be set. The development and refinement of radio-carbon dating and other scientific methods of producing absolute chronologies is enabling the cross-referencing of societies to be undertaken. As the techniques of dating become more rigorous in application and the number of scientifically obtained dates increases, the attainment of an absolute chronology for prehistoric societies throughout the world comes closer to being achieved.

GEOLOGICAL TIME

Era	*Period*	*Epoch*	*Dates*	*Evolutionary stages*
Cenozoic	Quaternary	Holocene	9,600 BC –present	Humans
		Pleistocene	1,808,000– 9,600 BC	
	Tertiary	Pliocene	5,332,000– 1,806,000	
		Miocene	23,030,000–5,332,000	
		Oligocene	34–23 Ma*	
		Eocene	–33.9 Ma	
		Palaeocene	–55.8 Ma	
Mesozoic	Cretaceous		145.5–65.5 Ma	
	Jurassic		199.6–145.5 Ma	First birds
	Triassic		251–199.6 Ma	First mammals
Palaeozoic	Permian		299–251 Ma	First reptiles
	Carboniferous		359.2–299 Ma	First amphibians and insects
	Devonian		416–359.2 Ma	
	Silurian		443.7–416 Ma	
	Ordovician		488.3–443.7 Ma	First fishes
	Cambrian		542–488.3 Ma	First invertebrates
Precambrian	Proterozoic		2500–542 M	First primitive life forms, eg algae and bacteria
	Archaean		3800–2500 M	
	Hadean		4500–3800 M	

* Ma = millions of years ago

TIDAL PREDICTIONS

CONSTANTS

The constant tidal difference may be used in conjunction with the time of high water at a standard port shown in the predictions data below to find the time of high water at any of the ports or places listed.

These tidal differences are very approximate and should be used only as a guide to the time of high water at the places below. More precise local data should be obtained for navigational and other nautical purposes.

All data allow high water time to be found in Greenwich Mean Time: this applies to data for the months when British Summer Time is in operation and the hour's time difference should be allowed for. Ports marked * are in a different time zone and the standard time zone difference also needs to be added/subtracted to give local time.

EXAMPLE

Required: time of high water at Stranraer on 2 January 2008. Appropriate time of high water at Greenock

Afternoon tide 2 January	19h 01m
Tidal difference	– 00h 20m
High water at Stranraer	18h 41m

The columns headed 'Springs' and 'Neaps' show the height, in metres, of the tide above datum for mean high water springs and mean high water neaps respectively.

Port		*Diff.*		*Springs*	*Neaps*
		h	*min*	*m*	*m*
Aberdeen	*Leith*	–1	19	4.4	3.4
*Antwerp	*London*	+0	50	5.8	4.8
Ardrossan	*Greenock*	–0	15	3.2	2.6
Ayr	*Greenock*	–0	25	3.0	2.5
Belfast	*London*	–2	47	3.5	3.0
Blackpool	*Liverpool*	–0	10	8.9	7.0
*Boulogne	*London*	–2	44	8.9	7.2
*Calais	*London*	–2	04	7.2	5.9
*Cherbourg	*London*	–6	00	6.4	5.0
Cobh	*Liverpool*	–5	55	4.2	3.2
Cowes	*London*	–2	38	4.2	3.5
Dartmouth	*London*	+4	25	4.9	3.8
*Dieppe	*London*	–3	03	9.3	7.3
Douglas, IoM	*Liverpool*	–0	04	6.9	5.4
Dover	*London*	–2	52	6.7	5.3
Dublin	*London*	–2	05	4.1	3.4
Dun Loaghaire	*London*	–2	10	4.1	3.4
*Dunkirk	*London*	–1	54	6.0	4.9
Fishguard	*Liverpool*	–4	01	4.8	3.4
Fleetwood	*Liverpool*	0	00	9.2	7.3
*Flushing	*London*	–0	15	4.7	3.9
Folkestone	*London*	–3	04	7.1	5.7
Galway	*Liverpool*	–6	08	5.1	3.9
Glasgow	*Greenock*	+0	26	4.7	4.0
Harwich	*London*	–2	06	4.0	3.4
*Le Havre	*London*	–3	55	7.9	6.6
Heysham	*Liverpool*	+0	05	9.4	7.4
Holyhead	*Liverpool*	–0	50	5.6	4.4
*Hook of Holland	*London*	–0	01	2.1	1.7
Hull (Albert Dock)	*London*	–7	40	7.5	5.8
Immingham	*London*	–8	00	7.3	5.8
Larne	*London*	–2	40	2.8	2.5
Lerwick	*Leith*	–3	48	2.2	1.6
Londonderry	*London*	–5	37	2.7	2.1
Lowestoft	*London*	–4	25	2.4	2.1
Margate	*London*	–1	53	4.8	3.9
Milford Haven	*Liverpool*	–5	08	7.0	5.2
Morecambe	*Liverpool*	+0	07	9.5	7.4
Newhaven	*London*	–2	46	6.7	5.1
Oban	*Greenock*	+5	43	4.0	2.9
*Ostend	*London*	–1	32	5.1	4.2
Plymouth	*London*	+4	05	5.5	4.4
Portland	*London*	+5	09	2.1	1.4
Portsmouth	*London*	–2	38	4.7	3.8
Ramsgate	*London*	–2	32	5.2	4.1
Richmond Lock	*London*	+1	00	4.9	3.7
Rosslare Harbour	*Liverpool*	–5	24	1.9	1.4
Rosyth	*Leith*	+0	09	5.8	4.7
*Rotterdam	*London*	+1	45	2.0	1.7
*St Helier	*London*	+4	48	11.0	8.1
*St Malo	*London*	+4	27	12.2	9.2
St Peter Port	*London*	+4	54	9.3	7.0
Scrabster	*Leith*	–6	06	5.0	4.0
Sheerness	*London*	–1	19	5.8	4.7
Shoreham	*London*	–2	44	6.3	4.9
Southampton (1st high water)	*London*	–2	54	4.5	3.7
Spurn Head	*London*	–8	25	6.9	5.5
Stornoway	*Liverpool*	–4	16	4.8	3.7
Stranraer	*Greenock*	–0	20	3.0	2.4
Stromness	*Leith*	5	26	3.6	2.7
Swansea	*London*	–7	35	9.5	7.2
Tees (River Entrance)	*Leith*	+1	09	5.5	4.3
Tilbury	*London*	–0	49	6.4	5.4
Tobermory	*Liverpool*	–5	11	4.4	3.3
Tyne River (North Shields)	*London*	–10	30	5.0	3.9
Ullapool	*Leith*	–7	40	5.2	3.9
Walton-on-the-Naze	*London*	–2	10	4.2	3.4
Wick	*Leith*	–3	26	3.5	2.8
*Zeebrugge	*London*	–0	55	4.8	3.9

PREDICTIONS

The following data are daily predictions of the time and height of high water at London Bridge, Liverpool, Greenock and Leith. The time of the data is Greenwich Mean Time; this applies also to data for the months when British Summer Time is in operation and the hour's time difference should be allowed for. The datum of predictions for each port shows the difference of height, in metres from Ordnance data (Newlyn).

The section was compiled with the assistance of Chris Stephens.

JANUARY 2008 *High Water* GMT

	LONDON BRIDGE				LIVERPOOL (Alfred Dock)				GREENOCK				LEITH			
	*Datum of Predictions 3.20m below				*Datum of Predictions 4.93m below				*Datum of Predictions 1.62m below				*Datum of Predictions 2.90m below			
	hr	*ht m*	*hr*	*ht m*	*hr*	*ht m*	*hr*	*ht m*	*hr*	*ht m*	*hr*	*ht m*	*hr*	*ht m*	*hr*	*ht m*
TU 1	07 12	6.0	19 58	5.9	04 57	7.5	17 20	7.6	06 20	2.9	18 07	3.2	08 43	4.4	21 12	4.5
W 2	08 12	5.7	20 54	5.7	06 00	7.3	18 25	7.4	07 12	2.9	19 01	3.0	09 38	4.3	22 11	4.4
TH 3	09 23	5.6	21 57	5.7	07 09	7.3	19 35	7.4	08 15	2.9	20 06	2.9	10 37	4.3	23 14	4.4
F 4	10 32	5.7	22 58	5.8	08 12	7.6	20 37	7.6	09 23	3.0	21 19	2.9	11 39	4.4	—	—
SA 5	11 32	5.9	23 53	6.0	09 05	7.9	21 29	7.9	10 22	3.1	22 24	3.0	00 16	4.5	12 37	4.6
SU 6	12 24	6.1	—	—	09 50	8.3	22 13	8.2	11 11	3.3	23 15	3.1	01 10	4.7	13 23	4.8
M 7	00 41	6.3	13 11	6.4	10 31	8.6	22 52	8.4	11 52	3.4	23 59	3.1	01 53	4.9	14 03	5.0
TU 8	01 25	6.4	13 53	6.5	11 09	8.8	23 29	8.6	12 28	3.5	—	—	02 32	5.0	14 39	5.1
W 9	02 06	6.5	14 33	6.6	11 46	9.0	—	—	00 40	3.2	13 02	3.6	03 08	5.1	15 14	5.3
TH 10	02 43	6.5	15 12	6.6	00 06	8.7	12 23	9.1	01 20	3.2	13 35	3.6	03 44	5.2	15 48	5.3
F 11	03 19	6.5	15 51	6.7	00 44	8.8	13 01	9.2	01 59	3.2	14 10	3.6	04 20	5.3	16 23	5.4
SA 12	03 55	6.6	16 30	6.7	01 23	8.8	13 41	9.2	02 38	3.3	14 47	3.6	04 58	5.3	17 00	5.4
SU 13	04 31	6.6	17 12	6.7	02 02	8.8	14 22	9.2	03 17	3.3	15 26	3.6	05 38	5.2	17 39	5.3
M 14	05 10	6.7	17 55	6.6	02 44	8.7	15 05	9.0	03 57	3.3	16 08	3.5	06 21	5.1	18 22	5.2
TU 15	05 54	6.6	18 42	6.4	03 29	8.4	15 54	8.8	04 38	3.2	16 53	3.4	07 08	4.9	19 10	5.1
W 16	06 42	6.5	19 34	6.1	04 22	8.1	16 50	8.4	05 22	3.1	17 44	3.3	08 02	4.7	20 09	4.9
TH 17	07 40	6.2	20 36	5.9	05 25	7.8	17 57	8.1	06 11	3.0	18 47	3.1	09 07	4.6	21 24	4.8
F 18	08 52	6.0	21 49	5.7	06 39	7.7	19 12	8.0	07 14	2.9	20 15	3.0	10 19	4.6	22 46	4.8
SA 19	10 13	5.9	23 03	5.8	07 58	7.9	20 32	8.2	08 52	2.9	21 49	3.0	11 30	4.7	—	—
SU 20	11 29	6.1	—	—	09 08	8.4	21 39	8.6	10 14	3.1	23 01	3.1	00 02	4.9	12 36	5.0
M 21	00 09	6.1	12 36	6.4	10 05	8.9	22 35	9.0	11 12	3.3	23 59	3.2	01 08	5.2	13 32	5.2
TU 22	01 07	6.4	13 33	6.7	10 55	9.3	23 24	9.2	12 02	3.5	—	—	02 04	5.4	14 22	5.5
W 23	01 58	6.6	14 25	6.9	11 41	9.6	—	—	00 52	3.3	12 48	3.6	02 52	5.5	15 07	5.6
TH 24	02 45	6.7	15 13	7.0	00 08	9.3	12 24	9.7	01 41	3.3	13 31	3.7	03 36	5.5	15 51	5.7
F 25	03 27	6.8	15 56	7.0	00 50	9.3	13 04	9.6	02 25	3.3	14 11	3.7	04 19	5.5	16 33	5.6
SA 26	04 04	6.8	16 35	6.9	01 28	9.1	13 42	9.4	03 04	3.2	14 49	3.7	05 00	5.3	17 14	5.5
SU 27	04 37	6.7	17 09	6.8	02 04	8.9	14 19	9.1	03 39	3.2	15 26	3.6	05 39	5.1	17 54	5.3
M 28	05 09	6.7	17 42	6.6	02 39	8.6	14 56	8.7	04 12	3.2	16 02	3.5	06 18	4.9	18 35	5.0
TU 29	05 42	6.5	18 15	6.4	03 16	8.2	15 34	8.2	04 46	3.1	16 40	3.4	06 58	4.6	19 19	4.7
W 30	06 20	6.3	18 52	6.1	03 57	7.7	16 18	7.7	05 24	3.0	17 22	3.2	07 43	4.4	20 11	4.4
TH 31	07 06	5.9	19 38	5.8	04 48	7.3	17 15	7.2	06 07	2.9	18 09	2.9	08 36	4.2	21 12	4.2

FEBRUARY 2008 *High Water* GMT

	LONDON BRIDGE				LIVERPOOL (Alfred Dock)				GREENOCK				LEITH			
F 1	08 04	5.5	20 36	5.5	05 58	7.0	18 31	6.9	07 01	2.8	19 06	2.8	09 36	4.1	22 21	4.1
SA 2	09 23	5.3	21 56	5.5	07 25	7.1	20 01	7.0	08 20	2.7	20 19	2.7	10 44	4.2	23 38	4.2
SU 3	10 55	5.5	23 17	5.7	08 38	7.5	21 08	7.5	09 52	2.9	22 01	2.7	11 59	4.4	—	—
M 4	12 00	5.9	—	—	09 30	8.0	21 56	7.9	10 50	3.1	23 03	2.9	00 46	4.5	13 00	4.6
TU 5	00 17	6.1	12 51	6.3	10 13	8.5	22 37	8.4	11 33	3.3	23 48	3.0	01 35	4.7	13 45	4.9
W 6	01 06	6.4	13 35	6.6	10 52	8.9	23 14	8.7	12 09	3.4	—	—	02 13	5.0	14 22	5.1
TH 7	01 49	6.6	14 17	6.7	11 29	9.2	23 51	9.0	00 28	3.1	12 44	3.4	02 49	5.2	14 56	5.4
F 8	02 29	6.6	14 56	6.8	12 06	9.4	—	—	01 07	3.1	13 17	3.5	03 24	5.4	15 29	5.5
SA 9	03 05	6.7	15 34	6.9	00 27	9.1	12 43	9.6	01 43	3.2	13 53	3.6	03 58	5.5	16 02	5.6
SU 10	03 39	6.8	16 13	6.9	01 04	9.3	13 22	9.7	02 19	3.3	14 31	3.6	04 35	5.5	16 38	5.7
M 11	04 15	6.9	16 51	6.8	01 42	9.2	14 01	9.6	02 55	3.3	15 10	3.6	05 13	5.4	17 17	5.6
TU 12	04 52	6.9	17 31	6.7	02 21	9.1	14 42	9.3	03 32	3.4	15 50	3.6	05 55	5.2	18 00	5.4
W 13	05 33	6.9	18 13	6.5	03 02	8.7	15 28	8.9	04 09	3.3	16 32	3.5	06 39	5.0	18 48	5.2
TH 14	06 18	6.6	19 00	6.1	03 50	8.2	16 22	8.3	04 49	3.2	17 18	3.2	07 30	4.7	19 46	4.8
F 15	07 12	6.2	19 57	5.6	04 53	7.7	17 33	7.7	05 34	3.1	18 15	2.9	08 35	4.5	21 07	4.6
SA 16	08 23	5.7	21 19	5.4	06 15	7.3	19 03	7.4	06 28	2.9	19 56	2.7	09 56	4.4	22 40	4.5
SU 17	10 01	5.6	22 48	5.5	07 51	7.5	20 34	7.8	08 21	2.8	22 00	2.8	11 20	4.5	—	—
M 18	11 26	5.9	23 59	5.9	09 05	8.1	21 38	8.3	10 08	2.9	23 04	3.0	00 05	4.7	12 33	4.8
TU 19	12 31	6.4	—	—	10 00	8.8	22 28	8.9	11 06	3.2	23 56	3.2	01 11	5.0	13 28	5.2
W 20	00 57	6.3	13 26	6.8	10 45	9.3	23 11	9.2	11 52	3.4	—	—	02 00	5.3	14 13	5.4
TH 21	01 46	6.7	14 13	7.0	11 26	9.6	23 50	9.3	00 42	3.2	12 36	3.5	02 41	5.4	14 53	5.6
F 22	02 29	6.8	14 55	7.1	12 04	9.7	—	—	01 24	3.3	13 15	3.6	03 19	5.4	15 31	5.7
SA 23	03 06	6.9	15 33	7.0	00 26	9.3	12 40	9.6	02 01	3.2	13 52	3.6	03 54	5.4	16 08	5.6
SU 24	03 39	6.9	16 04	6.9	00 59	9.2	13 14	9.4	02 33	3.2	14 26	3.6	04 29	5.3	16 44	5.5
M 25	04 08	6.8	16 32	6.8	01 31	9.0	13 46	9.1	03 02	3.2	14 58	3.5	05 03	5.1	17 19	5.3
TU 26	04 37	6.8	17 01	6.7	02 02	8.8	14 18	8.8	03 32	3.2	15 32	3.5	05 38	4.9	17 55	5.0
W 27	05 09	6.7	17 33	6.6	02 35	8.4	14 52	8.3	04 04	3.2	16 07	3.3	06 14	4.7	18 36	4.7
TH 28	05 46	6.4	18 09	6.3	03 10	8.0	15 32	7.7	04 39	3.1	16 46	3.1	06 55	4.5	19 24	4.4
F 29	06 28	6.1	18 53	6.0	03 53	7.4	16 22	7.1	05 18	2.9	17 32	2.8	07 44	4.3	20 23	4.1

MARCH 2008 *High Water* GMT

	LONDON BRIDGE						LIVERPOOL (Alfred Dock)						GREENOCK						LEITH					
	*Datum of Predictions 3.20m below						*Datum of Predictions 4.93m below						*Datum of Predictions 1.62m below						*Datum of Predictions 2.90m below					
	hr		*ht m*	*hr*		*ht m*	*hr*		*ht m*	*hr*		*ht m*	*hr*		*ht m*	*hr*		*ht m*	*hr*		*ht m*	*hr*		*ht m*
SA 1	07	19	5.6	19	45	5.6	04	54	6.9	17	35	6.6	06	07	2.7	18	28	2.6	08	45	4.1	21	33	4.0
SU 2	08	25	5.3	20	55	5.3	06	30	6.8	19	24	6.7	07	15	2.6	19	38	2.5	09	58	4.0	22	53	4.1
M 3	10	07	5.3	22	38	5.5	08	06	7.1	20	43	7.2	09	14	2.7	21	41	2.6	11	18	4.2	—		—
TU 4	11	32	5.8	23	49	5.9	09	03	7.8	21	32	7.8	10	22	2.9	22	44	2.8	00	14	4.3	12	29	4.5
W 5	12	25	6.3	—		—	09	47	8.4	22	12	8.4	11	05	3.1	23	27	3.0	01	07	4.7	13	17	4.9
TH 6	00	40	6.3	13	11	6.6	10	26	8.9	22	49	8.9	11	41	3.3	—		—	01	46	5.0	13	55	5.2
F 7	01	24	6.6	13	53	6.9	11	03	9.4	23	26	9.2	00	06	3.1	12	17	3.4	02	22	5.3	14	29	5.5
SA 8	02	04	6.7	14	32	7.0	11	41	9.7	—		—	00	43	3.1	12	53	3.4	02	57	5.5	15	02	5.7
SU 9	02	41	6.9	15	11	7.0	00	02	9.5	12	20	9.9	01	19	3.2	13	32	3.5	03	32	5.6	15	38	5.8
M 10	03	17	7.0	15	49	7.0	00	41	9.6	12	59	9.9	01	55	3.3	14	12	3.6	04	09	5.6	16	16	5.8
TU 11	03	55	7.1	16	28	6.9	01	19	9.5	13	40	9.7	02	31	3.4	14	53	3.6	04	48	5.5	16	58	5.7
W 12	04	34	7.1	17	07	6.7	01	58	9.3	14	22	9.3	03	07	3.5	15	33	3.6	05	30	5.3	17	44	5.5
TH 13	05	16	7.0	17	48	6.4	02	40	8.8	15	09	8.7	03	44	3.4	16	16	3.4	06	15	5.0	18	36	5.1
F 14	06	02	6.6	18	33	6.0	03	29	8.2	16	06	8.0	04	24	3.3	17	03	3.1	07	07	4.7	19	39	4.7
SA 15	06	58	6.0	19	29	5.5	04	34	7.6	17	25	7.3	05	09	3.1	18	03	2.8	08	18	4.4	21	06	4.4
SU 16	08	19	5.6	21	06	5.2	06	08	7.2	19	06	7.2	06	04	2.8	20	29	2.6	09	47	4.3	22	39	4.4
M 17	10	01	5.5	22	35	5.5	07	44	7.5	20	27	7.7	08	20	2.7	21	59	2.8	11	12	4.5	—		—
TU 18	11	17	6.0	23	41	6.0	08	52	8.1	21	24	8.3	09	55	2.9	22	54	3.0	00	03	4.7	12	22	4.8
W 19	12	16	6.5	—		—	09	43	8.7	22	10	8.8	10	49	3.2	23	39	3.2	01	03	5.0	13	14	5.1
TH 20	00	36	6.5	13	07	6.9	10	26	9.2	22	49	9.1	11	33	3.4	—		—	01	46	5.2	13	55	5.4
F 21	01	23	6.8	13	51	7.1	11	04	9.4	23	25	9.2	00	19	3.2	12	14	3.4	02	22	5.3	14	32	5.5
SA 22	02	04	6.9	14	30	7.1	11	39	9.4	23	57	9.2	00	57	3.2	12	52	3.5	02	55	5.3	15	07	5.5
SU 23	02	40	6.9	15	04	6.9	12	12	9.3	—		—	01	29	3.2	13	26	3.4	03	27	5.3	15	42	5.5
M 24	03	12	6.8	15	32	6.8	00	28	9.1	12	44	9.2	01	57	3.3	13	57	3.4	03	58	5.2	16	15	5.3
TU 25	03	40	6.8	15	57	6.7	00	58	9.0	13	14	8.9	02	26	3.3	14	29	3.4	04	30	5.1	16	50	5.2
W 26	04	09	6.7	16	26	6.7	01	28	8.8	13	46	8.6	02	56	3.3	15	02	3.3	05	02	5.0	17	26	4.9
TH 27	04	42	6.6	16	58	6.6	02	00	8.5	14	19	8.2	03	27	3.3	15	37	3.2	05	37	4.8	18	06	4.7
F 28	05	18	6.4	17	35	6.4	02	34	8.1	14	58	7.7	04	00	3.2	16	17	3.0	06	16	4.6	18	51	4.4
SA 29	06	00	6.1	18	18	6.1	03	15	7.6	15	46	7.1	04	37	3.0	17	03	2.8	07	02	4.3	19	46	4.2
SU 30	06	49	5.7	19	09	5.7	04	11	7.1	16	53	6.7	05	23	2.8	17	59	2.6	08	01	4.1	20	52	4.0
M 31	07	50	5.4	20	13	5.4	05	33	6.8	18	34	6.6	06	27	2.6	19	07	2.5	09	14	4.0	22	08	4.1

APRIL 2008 *High Water* GMT

	LONDON BRIDGE						LIVERPOOL (Alfred Dock)						GREENOCK						LEITH					
TU 1	09	10	5.3	21	42	5.4	07	16	7.1	20	01	7.1	08	01	2.6	20	53	2.6	10	33	4.2	23	25	4.3
W 2	10	50	5.7	23	07	5.8	08	21	7.7	20	54	7.8	09	36	2.8	22	09	2.8	11	44	4.5	—		—
TH 3	11	50	6.2	—		—	09	09	8.3	21	37	8.4	10	25	3.0	22	53	3.0	00	24	4.7	12	36	4.9
F 4	00	03	6.2	12	38	6.6	09	51	9.0	22	16	9.0	11	04	3.2	23	32	3.1	01	10	5.1	13	18	5.2
SA 5	00	49	6.6	13	22	6.9	10	32	9.4	22	55	9.4	11	44	3.3	—		—	01	49	5.4	13	56	5.5
SU 6	01	31	6.9	14	04	7.1	11	13	9.8	23	35	9.6	00	10	3.2	12	26	3.4	02	26	5.6	14	33	5.8
M 7	02	12	7.0	14	44	7.1	11	55	9.9	—		—	00	49	3.3	13	09	3.5	03	04	5.7	15	14	5.9
TU 8	02	54	7.2	15	25	7.1	00	15	9.7	12	38	9.9	01	28	3.4	13	54	3.6	03	43	5.7	15	57	5.9
W 9	03	36	7.2	16	05	6.9	00	57	9.6	13	22	9.6	02	07	3.5	14	38	3.6	04	25	5.5	16	43	5.7
TH 10	04	20	7.2	16	47	6.7	01	40	9.3	14	09	9.1	02	46	3.5	15	22	3.4	05	09	5.3	17	34	5.4
F 11	05	06	6.9	17	30	6.4	02	26	8.8	15	00	8.5	03	25	3.5	16	08	3.2	05	58	5.0	18	31	5.0
SA 12	05	58	6.5	18	18	5.9	03	20	8.2	16	02	7.8	04	07	3.3	17	02	2.9	06	56	4.7	19	41	4.7
SU 13	07	01	6.0	19	25	5.5	04	30	7.7	17	24	7.3	04	54	3.1	18	22	2.7	08	13	4.5	21	03	4.5
M 14	08	25	5.7	20	57	5.4	05	58	7.4	18	50	7.3	05	57	2.9	20	24	2.6	09	36	4.5	22	26	4.5
TU 15	09	46	5.9	22	11	5.7	07	19	7.7	20	00	7.7	08	03	2.8	21	36	2.8	10	52	4.6	23	41	4.7
W 16	10	52	6.2	23	12	6.2	08	22	8.1	20	56	8.2	09	26	3.0	22	27	3.0	11	57	4.9	—		—
TH 17	11	49	6.7	—		—	09	14	8.6	21	41	8.6	10	20	3.2	23	10	3.1	00	38	4.9	12	49	5.1
F 18	00	05	6.5	12	38	6.9	09	58	8.9	22	20	8.9	11	05	3.3	23	48	3.2	01	21	5.0	13	30	5.2
SA 19	00	52	6.8	13	21	7.0	10	37	9.0	22	55	9.0	11	45	3.3	—		—	01	56	5.1	14	08	5.3
SU 20	01	34	6.9	14	00	6.9	11	12	9.0	23	27	9.0	00	23	3.2	12	22	3.3	02	28	5.2	14	43	5.3
M 21	02	12	6.8	14	33	6.8	11	44	9.0	23	57	9.0	00	54	3.3	12	56	3.3	02	58	5.2	15	17	5.3
TU 22	02	46	6.7	15	00	6.6	12	15	8.8	—		—	01	24	3.3	13	28	3.3	03	29	5.2	15	51	5.2
W 23	03	16	6.6	15	27	6.6	00	28	8.9	12	46	8.7	01	53	3.4	14	00	3.3	04	00	5.1	16	26	5.0
TH 24	03	46	6.5	15	57	6.6	01	00	8.7	13	19	8.4	02	24	3.4	14	35	3.2	04	33	5.0	17	03	4.9
F 25	04	20	6.5	16	31	6.5	01	33	8.5	13	55	8.1	02	56	3.4	15	12	3.1	05	08	4.8	17	43	4.7
SA 26	04	57	6.3	17	08	6.4	02	09	8.2	14	34	7.8	03	29	3.3	15	53	3.0	05	47	4.6	18	27	4.5
SU 27	05	40	6.2	17	51	6.1	02	52	7.8	15	22	7.3	04	05	3.1	16	39	2.8	06	31	4.5	19	17	4.3
M 28	06	29	5.9	18	42	5.8	03	45	7.4	16	23	7.0	04	49	2.9	17	35	2.7	07	25	4.3	20	17	4.2
TU 29	07	26	5.7	19	41	5.6	04	54	7.2	17	41	6.9	05	49	2.7	18	38	2.6	08	31	4.2	21	25	4.3
W 30	08	35	5.6	20	55	5.6	06	14	7.3	19	03	7.2	07	04	2.7	19	53	2.7	09	46	4.3	22	35	4.4

MAY 2008 *High Water* GMT

	LONDON BRIDGE *Datum of Predictions 3.20m below				LIVERPOOL (Alfred Dock) *Datum of Predictions 4.93m below				GREENOCK *Datum of Predictions 1.62m below				LEITH *Datum of Predictions 2.90m below			
	hr	*ht m*	*hr*	*ht m*	*hr*	*ht m*	*hr*	*ht m*	*hr*	*ht m*	*hr*	*ht m*	*hr*	*ht m*	*hr*	*ht m*
TH 1	09 56	5.8	22 13	5.9	07 26	7.8	20 05	7.8	08 29	2.8	21 12	2.8	10 53	4.6	23 36	4.7
F 2	11 05	6.2	23 17	6.2	08 23	8.3	20 55	8.4	09 34	3.0	22 08	3.0	11 50	4.9	—	—
SA 3	12 00	6.6	—	—	09 13	8.9	21 41	9.0	10 24	3.2	22 53	3.1	00 28	5.1	12 38	5.2
SU 4	00 10	6.6	12 49	6.9	10 00	9.4	22 25	9.4	11 11	3.3	23 37	3.2	01 13	5.3	13 23	5.5
M 5	01 00	6.9	13 35	7.1	10 46	9.7	23 08	9.6	11 59	3.4	—	—	01 55	5.5	14 08	5.7
TU 6	01 47	7.1	14 20	7.1	11 33	9.8	23 53	9.6	00 20	3.4	12 48	3.5	02 37	5.6	14 54	5.8
W 7	02 34	7.2	15 04	7.0	12 20	9.7	—	—	01 04	3.5	13 38	3.5	03 21	5.6	15 43	5.8
TH 8	03 22	7.2	15 48	6.9	00 39	9.5	13 10	9.4	01 47	3.5	14 27	3.4	04 06	5.5	16 34	5.6
F 9	04 11	7.1	16 33	6.7	01 28	9.3	14 01	9.0	02 29	3.6	15 17	3.3	04 55	5.3	17 28	5.4
SA 10	05 02	6.9	17 20	6.4	02 19	8.9	14 55	8.5	03 12	3.5	16 11	3.1	05 48	5.1	18 28	5.1
SU 11	05 58	6.6	18 14	6.1	03 15	8.4	15 56	8.0	03 57	3.4	17 13	2.9	06 50	4.9	19 35	4.8
M 12	07 01	6.2	19 20	5.8	04 21	8.0	17 05	7.6	04 48	3.2	18 28	2.8	08 02	4.7	20 45	4.6
TU 13	08 11	6.1	20 32	5.8	05 32	7.8	18 17	7.5	05 55	3.0	19 47	2.7	09 13	4.7	21 54	4.5
W 14	09 18	6.1	21 37	6.0	06 41	7.8	19 21	7.6	07 23	2.9	20 52	2.8	10 20	4.7	23 01	4.6
TH 15	10 18	6.3	22 36	6.2	07 44	8.0	20 17	7.9	08 42	3.0	21 46	2.9	11 21	4.8	—	—
F 16	11 13	6.5	23 30	6.5	08 38	8.2	21 05	8.2	09 41	3.1	22 31	3.0	00 00	4.7	12 16	4.9
SA 17	12 03	6.7	—	—	09 25	8.4	21 47	8.5	10 29	3.1	23 11	3.1	00 47	4.8	13 02	5.0
SU 18	00 19	6.6	12 48	6.7	10 07	8.5	22 24	8.6	11 12	3.2	23 48	3.2	01 26	4.9	13 42	5.0
M 19	01 04	6.6	13 28	6.7	10 44	8.6	22 58	8.7	11 50	3.2	—	—	02 00	5.0	14 20	5.0
TU 20	01 46	6.6	14 03	6.6	11 19	8.6	23 31	8.8	00 22	3.3	12 25	3.1	02 32	5.0	14 56	5.0
W 21	02 23	6.5	14 34	6.5	11 51	8.5	—	—	00 55	3.4	12 59	3.1	03 03	5.1	15 31	5.0
TH 22	02 57	6.4	15 04	6.5	00 04	8.7	12 25	8.4	01 27	3.4	13 34	3.1	03 36	5.1	16 07	5.0
F 23	03 30	6.4	15 36	6.5	00 38	8.6	13 00	8.3	01 59	3.4	14 11	3.1	04 10	5.0	16 45	4.9
SA 24	04 05	6.3	16 11	6.4	01 14	8.5	13 38	8.2	02 32	3.4	14 51	3.1	04 47	4.9	17 24	4.8
SU 25	04 43	6.3	16 49	6.4	01 53	8.3	14 18	8.0	03 06	3.3	15 33	3.0	05 25	4.8	18 06	4.7
M 26	05 25	6.3	17 31	6.3	02 36	8.1	15 04	7.7	03 43	3.2	16 19	2.9	06 08	4.7	18 52	4.6
TU 27	06 13	6.2	18 19	6.1	03 25	7.9	15 57	7.5	04 25	3.1	17 10	2.9	06 55	4.6	19 44	4.5
W 28	07 06	6.0	19 14	6.0	04 22	7.8	16 59	7.4	05 17	2.9	18 06	2.8	07 51	4.5	20 44	4.5
TH 29	08 06	6.0	20 18	5.9	05 27	7.8	18 07	7.5	06 22	2.9	19 06	2.8	08 55	4.6	21 49	4.6
F 30	09 15	6.0	21 29	6.0	06 32	8.0	19 14	7.9	07 34	2.9	20 12	2.9	10 03	4.7	22 51	4.8
SA 31	10 24	6.2	22 36	6.3	07 36	8.4	20 14	8.3	08 46	3.0	21 18	3.0	11 05	4.9	23 48	5.0

JUNE 2008 *High Water* GMT

	LONDON BRIDGE				LIVERPOOL (Alfred Dock)				GREENOCK				LEITH			
SU 1	11 25	6.5	23 37	6.6	08 35	8.8	21 08	8.8	09 48	3.2	22 16	3.1	12 03	5.1	—	—
M 2	12 20	6.7	—	—	09 31	9.1	21 58	9.2	10 44	3.3	23 08	3.2	00 41	5.2	12 57	5.4
TU 3	00 34	6.8	13 11	6.9	10 25	9.4	22 48	9.4	11 38	3.3	23 57	3.4	01 30	5.4	13 50	5.6
W 4	01 28	7.0	14 00	7.0	11 17	9.5	23 37	9.5	12 33	3.4	—	—	02 17	5.5	14 42	5.7
TH 5	02 20	7.2	14 48	6.9	12 09	9.4	—	—	00 45	3.5	13 29	3.3	03 05	5.6	15 34	5.7
F 6	03 12	7.2	15 36	6.9	00 27	9.5	13 01	9.3	01 32	3.6	14 23	3.3	03 54	5.5	16 27	5.6
SA 7	04 04	7.1	16 23	6.7	01 18	9.3	13 52	9.0	02 17	3.6	15 17	3.2	04 45	5.5	17 21	5.4
SU 8	04 56	7.0	17 12	6.6	02 09	9.1	14 43	8.7	03 02	3.6	16 11	3.1	05 39	5.3	18 16	5.2
M 9	05 49	6.8	18 02	6.4	03 01	8.8	15 36	8.3	03 48	3.5	17 06	3.0	06 36	5.1	19 14	4.9
TU 10	06 43	6.6	18 55	6.2	03 56	8.4	16 31	7.9	04 38	3.3	18 01	2.9	07 37	5.0	20 12	4.7
W 11	07 40	6.3	19 54	6.1	04 53	8.1	17 31	7.6	05 32	3.2	18 55	2.8	08 38	4.8	21 11	4.5
TH 12	08 39	6.2	20 54	6.0	05 55	7.8	18 33	7.5	06 33	3.0	19 51	2.8	09 38	4.7	22 10	4.4
F 13	09 36	6.1	21 54	6.0	06 57	7.7	19 32	7.6	07 40	2.9	20 48	2.8	10 38	4.6	23 09	4.5
SA 14	10 32	6.2	22 51	6.1	07 56	7.7	20 27	7.8	08 47	2.9	21 43	2.9	11 36	4.6	—	—
SU 15	11 24	6.3	23 46	6.3	08 50	7.9	21 14	8.1	09 47	2.9	22 32	3.0	00 05	4.6	12 31	4.7
M 16	12 13	6.4	—	—	09 38	8.0	21 57	8.3	10 37	3.0	23 16	3.1	00 53	4.7	13 19	4.8
TU 17	00 36	6.4	12 57	6.5	10 21	8.2	22 35	8.5	11 20	3.0	23 56	3.3	01 34	4.8	14 01	4.8
W 18	01 22	6.4	13 38	6.5	10 59	8.3	23 12	8.6	11 59	3.0	—	—	02 10	4.9	14 39	4.9
TH 19	02 04	6.4	14 14	6.5	11 35	8.3	23 47	8.7	00 32	3.4	12 37	3.0	02 44	5.0	15 15	5.0
F 20	02 42	6.4	14 49	6.4	12 11	8.3	—	—	01 06	3.4	13 14	3.0	03 19	5.1	15 50	5.0
SA 21	03 18	6.4	15 24	6.4	00 23	8.7	12 47	8.4	01 39	3.4	13 53	3.1	03 54	5.1	16 27	5.0
SU 22	03 54	6.4	15 58	6.4	01 01	8.7	13 24	8.3	02 12	3.4	14 33	3.1	04 30	5.1	17 04	5.0
M 23	04 32	6.4	16 35	6.4	01 39	8.6	14 03	8.3	02 47	3.4	15 14	3.1	05 06	5.0	17 44	4.9
TU 24	05 12	6.4	17 14	6.4	02 20	8.6	14 44	8.2	03 24	3.4	15 57	3.1	05 45	5.0	18 26	4.8
W 25	05 55	6.4	17 57	6.4	03 04	8.5	15 30	8.1	04 04	3.3	16 42	3.0	06 28	4.9	19 13	4.7
TH 26	06 43	6.3	18 46	6.3	03 53	8.4	16 22	7.9	04 49	3.2	17 30	3.0	07 15	4.9	20 06	4.7
F 27	07 37	6.1	19 44	6.2	04 49	8.2	17 22	7.8	05 43	3.1	18 22	2.9	08 10	4.8	21 06	4.6
SA 28	08 39	6.0	20 50	6.1	05 51	8.2	18 29	7.8	06 48	3.0	19 20	2.9	09 16	4.8	22 11	4.7
SU 29	09 47	6.0	22 01	6.1	06 57	8.2	19 37	8.1	08 04	3.0	20 31	2.9	10 28	4.8	23 15	4.8
M 30	10 55	6.2	23 11	6.3	08 06	8.4	20 42	8.4	09 20	3.0	21 45	3.0	11 37	5.0	—	—

JULY 2008 *High Water* GMT

	LONDON BRIDGE				LIVERPOOL (Alfred Dock)				GREENOCK				LEITH			
	*Datum of Predictions 3.20m below				*Datum of Predictions 4.93m below				*Datum of Predictions 1.62m below				*Datum of Predictions 2.90m below			
	hr	*ht m*	*hr*	*ht m*	*hr*	*ht m*	*hr*	*ht m*	*hr*	*ht m*	*hr*	*ht m*	*hr*	*ht m*	*hr*	*ht m*
TU 1	11 57	6.4	—	—	09 12	8.7	21 42	8.9	10 28	3.1	22 48	3.2	00 16	5.0	12 42	5.2
W 2	00 16	6.6	12 54	6.6	10 13	9.0	22 36	9.2	11 30	3.2	23 43	3.3	01 12	5.2	13 41	5.4
TH 3	01 16	6.8	13 47	6.8	11 08	9.2	23 27	9.5	12 28	3.2	—	—	02 04	5.4	14 35	5.6
F 4	02 12	7.0	14 37	6.9	12 00	9.3	—	—	00 33	3.5	13 25	3.2	02 54	5.6	15 26	5.7
SA 5	03 04	7.1	15 25	6.9	00 16	9.6	12 50	9.3	01 21	3.5	14 19	3.2	03 43	5.6	16 16	5.6
SU 6	03 55	7.2	16 11	6.9	01 05	9.5	13 36	9.2	02 07	3.6	15 09	3.2	04 32	5.6	17 04	5.5
M 7	04 42	7.1	16 54	6.8	01 51	9.4	14 21	8.9	02 50	3.6	15 55	3.1	05 21	5.5	17 53	5.2
TU 8	05 28	6.9	17 35	6.7	02 36	9.1	15 04	8.6	03 33	3.6	16 38	3.1	06 11	5.3	18 41	5.0
W 9	06 12	6.7	18 16	6.6	03 20	8.7	15 47	8.1	04 15	3.5	17 18	3.0	07 01	5.1	19 29	4.7
TH 10	06 56	6.4	19 00	6.3	04 06	8.3	16 34	7.7	04 58	3.3	17 58	2.9	07 54	4.9	20 20	4.5
F 11	07 43	6.1	19 52	6.0	04 56	7.8	17 30	7.4	05 43	3.1	18 42	2.8	08 49	4.6	21 13	4.4
SA 12	08 37	5.9	20 56	5.8	05 57	7.4	18 36	7.2	06 33	2.9	19 34	2.8	09 47	4.4	22 10	4.3
SU 13	09 39	5.7	22 07	5.7	07 07	7.2	19 45	7.4	07 33	2.8	20 41	2.8	10 51	4.3	23 14	4.3
M 14	10 41	5.8	23 14	5.8	08 16	7.3	20 44	7.7	08 48	2.7	21 54	2.9	11 58	4.4	—	—
TU 15	11 39	6.0	—	—	09 14	7.6	21 34	8.1	10 05	2.7	22 51	3.1	00 17	4.5	12 57	4.5
W 16	00 11	6.1	12 31	6.3	10 02	7.9	22 17	8.4	11 01	2.8	23 36	3.2	01 10	4.7	13 43	4.7
TH 17	01 02	6.3	13 17	6.5	10 44	8.1	22 56	8.6	11 45	2.9	—	—	01 52	4.9	14 22	4.9
F 18	01 46	6.5	13 58	6.6	11 21	8.3	23 33	8.8	00 14	3.3	12 23	3.0	02 28	5.0	14 57	5.0
SA 19	02 26	6.6	14 37	6.6	11 57	8.5	—	—	00 48	3.4	13 00	3.0	03 03	5.2	15 32	5.1
SU 20	03 04	6.6	15 12	6.5	00 08	8.9	12 32	8.6	01 20	3.4	13 36	3.0	03 37	5.3	16 06	5.2
M 21	03 40	6.6	15 45	6.5	00 44	9.0	13 07	8.7	01 53	3.5	14 14	3.1	04 10	5.3	16 42	5.2
TU 22	04 16	6.6	16 18	6.6	01 21	9.0	13 43	8.7	02 28	3.5	14 52	3.1	04 45	5.3	17 19	5.2
W 23	04 53	6.6	16 54	6.7	01 59	9.0	14 21	8.7	03 05	3.5	15 31	3.2	05 21	5.3	17 59	5.1
TH 24	05 32	6.6	17 33	6.7	02 39	9.0	15 02	8.5	03 44	3.4	16 11	3.2	06 01	5.2	18 43	5.0
F 25	06 15	6.4	18 18	6.6	03 24	8.8	15 48	8.2	04 25	3.3	16 54	3.1	06 45	5.1	19 31	4.8
SA 26	07 03	6.2	19 10	6.3	04 16	8.4	16 45	7.9	05 11	3.2	17 40	3.0	07 37	4.9	20 28	4.7
SU 27	08 01	5.9	20 14	6.0	05 18	8.1	17 54	7.7	06 09	3.0	18 35	2.9	08 43	4.8	21 38	4.6
M 28	09 12	5.7	21 32	5.9	06 30	7.8	19 13	7.7	07 27	2.8	19 48	2.9	10 05	4.7	22 52	4.7
TU 29	10 31	5.8	22 56	6.0	07 52	7.9	20 31	8.1	09 08	2.8	21 27	2.9	11 26	4.8	—	—
W 30	11 42	6.1	—	—	09 08	8.3	21 35	8.7	10 30	3.0	22 40	3.1	00 02	4.9	12 38	5.1
TH 31	00 09	6.3	12 44	6.4	10 09	8.8	22 29	9.2	11 31	3.1	23 35	3.3	01 04	5.2	13 38	5.4

AUGUST 2008 *High Water* GMT

	LONDON BRIDGE				LIVERPOOL (Alfred Dock)				GREENOCK				LEITH			
F 1	01 11	6.7	13 37	6.7	11 01	9.1	23 17	9.5	12 26	3.2	—	—	01 56	5.4	14 28	5.6
SA 2	02 04	7.0	14 25	6.9	11 48	9.3	—	—	00 24	3.5	13 17	3.2	02 43	5.7	15 14	5.7
SU 3	02 53	7.2	15 10	7.0	00 02	9.7	12 32	9.4	01 10	3.6	14 04	3.2	03 27	5.8	15 57	5.6
M 4	03 38	7.2	15 50	7.0	00 45	9.7	13 13	9.3	01 52	3.6	14 46	3.2	04 11	5.8	16 40	5.5
TU 5	04 19	7.2	16 27	7.0	01 25	9.5	13 50	9.0	02 32	3.6	15 23	3.1	04 54	5.7	17 21	5.3
W 6	04 57	7.0	17 00	6.9	02 03	9.2	14 26	8.7	03 09	3.6	15 56	3.1	05 37	5.4	18 02	5.0
TH 7	05 30	6.8	17 33	6.8	02 40	8.8	15 02	8.3	03 45	3.5	16 28	3.1	06 20	5.2	18 44	4.8
F 8	06 02	6.5	18 09	6.5	03 18	8.3	15 40	7.9	04 22	3.4	17 04	3.0	07 06	4.8	19 28	4.5
SA 9	06 38	6.2	18 51	6.1	04 01	7.7	16 27	7.4	05 02	3.1	17 45	2.9	07 57	4.5	20 19	4.3
SU 10	07 21	5.8	19 46	5.7	04 54	7.2	17 31	7.1	05 47	2.9	18 34	2.8	08 57	4.3	21 18	4.2
M 11	08 19	5.5	21 05	5.4	06 10	6.8	19 01	7.0	06 41	2.7	19 38	2.7	10 04	4.1	22 24	4.2
TU 12	09 49	5.4	22 43	5.5	07 45	6.9	20 19	7.4	07 52	2.6	21 18	2.8	11 21	4.2	23 40	4.4
W 13	11 07	5.7	23 48	5.9	08 53	7.3	21 14	7.9	09 45	2.6	22 30	3.0	12 33	4.4	—	—
TH 14	12 06	6.1	—	—	09 43	7.8	21 58	8.4	10 50	2.8	23 15	3.2	00 44	4.6	13 23	4.7
F 15	00 40	6.3	12 55	6.5	10 24	8.2	22 37	8.8	11 32	2.9	23 52	3.3	01 30	4.9	14 01	5.0
SA 16	01 25	6.6	13 38	6.6	11 01	8.5	23 12	9.0	12 08	3.0	—	—	02 07	5.1	14 35	5.2
SU 17	02 05	6.8	14 16	6.7	11 36	8.7	23 46	9.2	00 26	3.4	12 42	3.0	02 41	5.3	15 08	5.3
M 18	02 42	6.8	14 51	6.7	12 09	8.9	—	—	00 58	3.4	13 15	3.1	03 13	5.5	15 41	5.4
TU 19	03 18	6.8	15 24	6.7	00 21	9.3	12 44	9.0	01 32	3.5	13 50	3.2	03 45	5.6	16 16	5.5
W 20	03 53	6.8	15 56	6.8	00 57	9.4	13 19	9.0	02 08	3.5	14 27	3.2	04 19	5.6	16 52	5.4
TH 21	04 28	6.7	16 30	6.9	01 34	9.4	13 55	9.0	02 46	3.6	15 04	3.3	04 56	5.6	17 31	5.3
F 22	05 05	6.7	17 09	6.9	02 14	9.2	14 35	8.8	03 24	3.6	15 42	3.3	05 37	5.5	18 14	5.1
SA 23	05 46	6.5	17 53	6.7	02 58	8.8	15 20	8.4	04 04	3.4	16 23	3.3	06 23	5.2	19 02	4.9
SU 24	06 30	6.1	18 44	6.3	03 50	8.3	16 17	7.8	04 48	3.2	17 08	3.1	07 17	4.9	20 00	4.6
M 25	07 24	5.7	19 48	5.9	04 56	7.7	17 33	7.4	05 42	3.0	18 01	3.0	08 29	4.7	21 17	4.5
TU 26	08 40	5.4	21 17	5.6	06 21	7.4	19 07	7.5	07 05	2.7	19 17	2.8	10 00	4.6	22 41	4.6
W 27	10 17	5.5	22 53	5.8	07 56	7.6	20 30	8.0	09 23	2.7	21 25	2.9	11 27	4.7	23 57	4.9
TH 28	11 32	5.9	—	—	09 07	8.2	21 30	8.7	10 35	3.0	22 34	3.2	12 38	5.1	—	—
F 29	00 04	6.3	12 32	6.4	10 01	8.8	22 18	9.3	11 28	3.1	23 24	3.4	00 56	5.2	13 32	5.4
SA 30	01 02	6.9	13 22	6.8	10 47	9.2	23 02	9.6	12 15	3.2	—	—	01 44	5.5	14 15	5.5
SU 31	01 51	7.2	14 06	7.1	11 29	9.4	23 41	9.8	00 09	3.5	12 58	3.3	02 26	5.7	14 54	5.6

SEPTEMBER 2008 *High Water* GMT

	LONDON BRIDGE						LIVERPOOL (Alfred Dock)						GREENOCK						LEITH					
	*Datum of Predictions 3.20m below						*Datum of Predictions 4.93m below						*Datum of Predictions 1.62m below						*Datum of Predictions 2.90m below					
	hr		*ht m*	*hr*		*ht m*	*hr*		*ht m*	*hr*		*ht m*	*hr*		*ht m*	*hr*		*ht m*	*hr*		*ht m*	*hr*		*ht m*
M 1	02	35	7.3	14	47	7.1	12	07	9.4	—		—	00	51	3.6	13	38	3.2	03	06	5.8	15	32	5.6
TU 2	03	14	7.3	15	23	7.1	00	19	9.7	12	42	9.3	01	30	3.6	14	12	3.2	03	45	5.8	16	10	5.5
W 3	03	49	7.1	15	55	7.0	00	55	9.5	13	15	9.1	02	06	3.6	14	42	3.2	04	24	5.6	16	46	5.3
TH 4	04	19	6.9	16	25	6.9	01	28	9.2	13	47	8.8	02	40	3.6	15	12	3.2	05	03	5.4	17	23	5.1
F 5	04	47	6.8	16	56	6.8	02	01	8.8	14	20	8.5	03	14	3.5	15	44	3.2	05	42	5.1	18	00	4.9
SA 6	05	16	6.6	17	31	6.5	02	36	8.3	14	55	8.0	03	49	3.4	16	19	3.1	06	25	4.8	18	42	4.6
SU 7	05	50	6.3	18	12	6.1	03	15	7.7	15	37	7.5	04	27	3.1	17	00	3.0	07	14	4.5	19	32	4.4
M 8	06	31	6.0	19	01	5.7	04	05	7.1	16	34	7.1	05	11	2.9	17	48	2.8	08	12	4.2	20	32	4.2
TU 9	07	22	5.5	20	06	5.3	05	17	6.6	18	12	6.8	06	07	2.6	18	52	2.7	09	20	4.1	21	42	4.2
W 10	08	36	5.3	22	02	5.2	07	15	6.7	19	49	7.2	07	18	2.5	20	34	2.8	10	37	4.1	22	59	4.3
TH 11	10	32	5.5	23	19	5.7	08	28	7.2	20	46	7.8	09	27	2.6	21	59	3.0	11	58	4.4	—		—
F 12	11	36	5.9	—		—	09	16	7.8	21	30	8.4	10	27	2.8	22	45	3.2	00	09	4.6	12	51	4.7
SA 13	00	11	6.3	12	26	6.4	09	56	8.3	22	08	8.9	11	07	3.0	23	22	3.3	00	58	4.9	13	29	5.1
SU 14	00	56	6.6	13	08	6.6	10	32	8.7	22	43	9.2	11	43	3.1	23	55	3.4	01	36	5.2	14	04	5.3
M 15	01	36	6.8	13	46	6.7	11	06	9.0	23	18	9.5	12	15	3.2	—		—	02	10	5.5	14	38	5.5
TU 16	02	13	6.9	14	21	6.8	11	40	9.2	23	53	9.6	00	30	3.5	12	48	3.2	02	42	5.7	15	11	5.6
W 17	02	50	6.9	14	56	6.9	12	15	9.3	—		—	01	08	3.6	13	24	3.3	03	16	5.8	15	47	5.6
TH 18	03	25	6.9	15	31	7.0	00	31	9.7	12	53	9.3	01	47	3.6	14	01	3.4	03	53	5.8	16	24	5.6
F 19	04	02	6.9	16	10	7.0	01	11	9.6	13	31	9.2	02	27	3.6	14	39	3.5	04	34	5.7	17	05	5.4
SA 20	04	40	6.7	16	51	6.9	01	53	9.2	14	13	8.9	03	08	3.6	15	18	3.5	05	19	5.5	17	49	5.2
SU 21	05	19	6.5	17	37	6.7	02	39	8.7	15	01	8.4	03	49	3.4	15	59	3.4	06	09	5.2	18	40	4.9
M 22	06	03	6.1	18	31	6.2	03	35	8.1	16	01	7.8	04	35	3.2	16	44	3.2	07	09	4.9	19	44	4.6
TU 23	06	57	5.6	19	42	5.7	04	49	7.4	17	26	7.4	05	33	2.9	17	41	3.0	08	29	4.6	21	10	4.5
W 24	08	27	5.3	21	21	5.6	06	26	7.3	19	05	7.6	07	29	2.7	19	13	2.9	10	00	4.6	22	34	4.7
TH 25	10	06	5.5	22	45	6.0	07	53	7.7	20	19	8.2	09	28	2.8	21	16	3.0	11	24	4.8	23	46	5.0
F 26	11	14	6.0	23	49	6.5	08	54	8.3	21	13	8.8	10	26	3.1	22	17	3.3	12	29	5.1	—		—
SA 27	12	09	6.6	—		—	09	43	8.8	21	59	9.3	11	11	3.2	23	04	3.5	00	41	5.3	13	17	5.3
SU 28	00	41	7.0	12	57	6.9	10	25	9.2	22	40	9.6	11	52	3.3	23	47	3.6	01	26	5.6	13	56	5.5
M 29	01	28	7.3	13	40	7.1	11	03	9.3	23	17	9.6	12	30	3.3	—		—	02	05	5.7	14	31	5.5
TU 30	02	09	7.3	14	19	7.1	11	38	9.3	23	51	9.5	00	26	3.6	13	05	3.3	02	43	5.7	15	05	5.5

OCTOBER 2008 *High Water* GMT

	LONDON BRIDGE						LIVERPOOL (Alfred Dock)						GREENOCK						LEITH					
W 1	02	45	7.1	14	54	7.0	12	10	9.2	—		—	01	03	3.6	13	35	3.3	03	20	5.7	15	39	5.4
TH 2	03	16	7.0	15	25	6.9	00	23	9.3	12	41	9.1	01	38	3.6	14	04	3.4	03	56	5.5	16	13	5.3
F 3	03	42	6.8	15	55	6.8	00	55	9.0	13	12	8.8	02	11	3.5	14	35	3.4	04	34	5.3	16	47	5.1
SA 4	04	09	6.7	16	27	6.7	01	27	8.6	13	44	8.6	02	45	3.5	15	08	3.4	05	12	5.0	17	22	4.9
SU 5	04	39	6.6	17	02	6.4	02	02	8.2	14	20	8.2	03	20	3.3	15	43	3.3	05	53	4.8	18	02	4.7
M 6	05	14	6.4	17	43	6.1	02	41	7.7	15	01	7.7	03	59	3.2	16	22	3.2	06	40	4.5	18	49	4.5
TU 7	05	54	6.1	18	30	5.7	03	29	7.2	15	55	7.2	04	44	2.9	17	09	3.0	07	34	4.3	19	48	4.3
W 8	06	42	5.7	19	29	5.4	04	35	6.7	17	13	6.9	05	40	2.7	18	12	2.8	08	39	4.1	21	00	4.2
TH 9	07	46	5.4	20	48	5.3	06	22	6.6	18	59	7.1	06	50	2.6	19	36	2.8	09	51	4.2	22	14	4.3
F 10	09	26	5.3	22	30	5.6	07	46	7.1	20	04	7.7	08	38	2.7	21	10	3.0	11	04	4.4	23	22	4.6
SA 11	10	51	5.7	23	30	6.1	08	37	7.7	20	50	8.3	09	49	2.9	22	02	3.2	12	04	4.8	—		—
SU 12	11	44	6.2	—		—	09	18	8.3	21	30	8.9	10	33	3.1	22	42	3.3	00	14	5.0	12	49	5.1
M 13	00	17	6.6	12	29	6.6	09	56	8.8	22	09	9.3	11	09	3.2	23	21	3.5	00	57	5.3	13	28	5.4
TU 14	01	00	6.8	13	09	6.8	10	32	9.2	22	47	9.6	11	44	3.3	—		—	01	35	5.6	14	05	5.6
W 15	01	41	7.0	13	49	7.0	11	10	9.5	23	27	9.8	00	01	3.6	12	20	3.4	02	11	5.8	14	41	5.7
TH 16	02	20	7.1	14	29	7.1	11	49	9.6	—		—	00	44	3.6	12	58	3.5	02	50	5.9	15	19	5.7
F 17	02	59	7.0	15	11	7.2	00	08	9.8	12	30	9.5	01	28	3.7	13	38	3.6	03	32	5.9	16	00	5.7
SA 18	03	39	6.9	15	55	7.1	00	53	9.6	13	13	9.3	02	12	3.7	14	19	3.6	04	18	5.8	16	43	5.5
SU 19	04	20	6.8	16	41	7.0	01	39	9.2	13	59	8.9	02	57	3.6	15	00	3.6	05	07	5.6	17	31	5.3
M 20	05	02	6.5	17	32	6.6	02	30	8.6	14	52	8.5	03	43	3.4	15	43	3.5	06	02	5.2	18	26	5.0
TU 21	05	49	6.1	18	32	6.2	03	31	8.0	15	57	8.0	04	35	3.1	16	31	3.3	07	07	4.9	19	37	4.7
W 22	06	50	5.7	19	47	5.8	04	48	7.5	17	20	7.7	05	47	2.9	17	33	3.1	08	27	4.7	21	01	4.7
TH 23	08	23	5.5	21	11	5.9	06	15	7.5	18	43	7.8	07	39	2.8	19	11	3.0	09	48	4.7	22	17	4.8
F 24	09	42	5.8	22	21	6.2	07	29	7.8	19	51	8.2	09	04	2.9	20	47	3.1	11	04	4.8	23	23	5.1
SA 25	10	45	6.2	23	20	6.6	08	27	8.3	20	46	8.7	09	59	3.1	21	48	3.3	12	05	5.0	—		—
SU 26	11	38	6.6	—		—	09	16	8.7	21	33	9.0	10	43	3.3	22	36	3.5	00	17	5.3	12	53	5.2
M 27	00	12	6.9	12	27	6.9	09	58	9.0	22	14	9.2	11	22	3.4	23	19	3.5	01	03	5.4	13	31	5.3
TU 28	00	58	7.1	13	11	7.0	10	35	9.1	22	51	9.2	11	58	3.4	23	59	3.6	01	43	5.5	14	06	5.4
W 29	01	39	7.1	13	51	7.0	11	09	9.2	23	24	9.1	12	31	3.5	—		—	02	21	5.5	14	38	5.4
TH 30	02	15	6.9	14	28	6.8	11	40	9.1	23	56	9.0	00	35	3.5	13	02	3.5	02	57	5.4	15	11	5.3
F 31	02	45	6.7	15	01	6.7	12	11	9.0	—		—	01	10	3.5	13	33	3.6	03	34	5.3	15	43	5.3

NOVEMBER 2008 *High Water* GMT

	LONDON BRIDGE *Datum of Predictions 3.20m below				LIVERPOOL (Alfred Dock) *Datum of Predictions 4.93m below				GREENOCK *Datum of Predictions 1.62m below				LEITH *Datum of Predictions 2.90m below			
	hr	*ht m*	*hr*	*ht m*	*hr*	*ht m*	*hr*	*ht m*	*hr*	*ht m*	*hr*	*ht m*	*hr*	*ht m*	*hr*	*ht m*
SA 1	03 11	6.6	15 32	6.5	00 27	8.8	12 44	8.9	01 44	3.5	14 05	3.6	04 10	5.2	16 16	5.2
SU 2	03 38	6.6	16 04	6.5	01 01	8.5	13 18	8.6	02 20	3.4	14 39	3.6	04 48	5.0	16 51	5.0
M 3	04 10	6.6	16 41	6.3	01 37	8.2	13 55	8.3	02 57	3.3	15 14	3.5	05 28	4.8	17 30	4.8
TU 4	04 46	6.4	17 21	6.2	02 17	7.8	14 37	8.0	03 37	3.2	15 52	3.3	06 12	4.6	18 15	4.6
W 5	05 26	6.2	18 07	6.0	03 04	7.4	15 27	7.6	04 22	3.0	16 37	3.1	07 02	4.4	19 08	4.5
TH 6	06 12	5.9	19 01	5.7	04 01	7.1	16 30	7.3	05 15	2.9	17 34	3.0	07 59	4.3	20 12	4.4
F 7	07 09	5.6	20 04	5.6	05 16	6.9	17 46	7.4	06 18	2.8	18 42	2.9	09 04	4.3	21 23	4.5
SA 8	08 20	5.5	21 20	5.7	06 39	7.2	19 00	7.7	07 34	2.8	19 59	3.0	10 10	4.5	22 29	4.6
SU 9	09 44	5.7	22 34	6.0	07 43	7.7	19 58	8.2	08 52	3.0	21 07	3.2	11 11	4.7	23 26	4.9
M 10	10 51	6.1	23 33	6.4	08 33	8.3	20 48	8.8	09 48	3.1	22 00	3.3	12 04	5.0	—	—
TU 11	11 45	6.5	—	—	09 17	8.8	21 34	9.2	10 32	3.3	22 47	3.5	00 15	5.2	12 51	5.3
W 12	00 23	6.8	12 34	6.8	10 00	9.2	22 19	9.6	11 13	3.4	23 35	3.6	01 01	5.5	13 33	5.5
TH 13	01 09	7.0	13 21	7.1	10 43	9.5	23 05	9.7	11 54	3.5	—	—	01 45	5.7	14 14	5.7
F 14	01 54	7.1	14 08	7.2	11 27	9.6	23 52	9.7	00 23	3.6	12 37	3.6	02 30	5.9	14 57	5.7
SA 15	02 38	7.1	14 56	7.2	12 13	9.6	—	—	01 13	3.6	13 21	3.7	03 18	5.9	15 41	5.7
SU 16	03 22	7.0	15 45	7.2	00 41	9.5	13 02	9.5	02 03	3.6	14 04	3.8	04 07	5.8	16 28	5.6
M 17	04 06	6.8	16 36	7.0	01 32	9.2	13 53	9.2	02 53	3.5	14 48	3.7	05 00	5.6	17 19	5.4
TU 18	04 53	6.5	17 30	6.7	02 26	8.7	14 47	8.8	03 45	3.4	15 34	3.7	05 57	5.3	18 17	5.2
W 19	05 44	6.2	18 30	6.4	03 25	8.3	15 48	8.4	04 42	3.2	16 25	3.5	07 01	5.0	19 26	5.0
TH 20	06 46	6.0	19 36	6.2	04 31	7.9	16 56	8.1	05 51	3.0	17 27	3.3	08 10	4.8	20 39	4.9
F 21	07 59	5.9	20 44	6.2	05 43	7.7	18 07	8.0	07 07	2.9	18 42	3.2	09 20	4.7	21 47	4.9
SA 22	09 08	6.0	21 47	6.3	06 51	7.8	19 14	8.1	08 18	3.0	20 01	3.2	10 28	4.7	22 50	5.0
SU 23	10 09	6.2	22 45	6.4	07 52	8.0	20 12	8.3	09 17	3.1	21 08	3.3	11 29	4.8	23 47	5.1
M 24	11 04	6.4	23 37	6.6	08 43	8.3	21 03	8.5	10 06	3.2	22 03	3.3	12 21	4.9	—	—
TU 25	11 55	6.6	—	—	09 28	8.6	21 48	8.7	10 49	3.3	22 50	3.4	00 37	5.1	13 05	5.0
W 26	00 25	6.7	12 43	6.7	10 08	8.8	22 27	8.8	11 28	3.4	23 32	3.4	01 22	5.2	13 42	5.1
TH 27	01 08	6.7	13 26	6.7	10 44	8.9	23 03	8.8	12 04	3.5	—	—	02 03	5.2	14 17	5.2
F 28	01 46	6.6	14 06	6.6	11 18	9.0	23 36	8.7	00 11	3.4	12 38	3.6	02 41	5.2	14 49	5.2
SA 29	02 19	6.5	14 42	6.5	11 51	8.9	—	—	00 48	3.3	13 11	3.6	03 17	5.2	15 21	5.2
SU 30	02 48	6.5	15 16	6.4	00 09	8.6	12 25	8.9	01 24	3.3	13 44	3.7	03 53	5.1	15 55	5.2

DECEMBER 2008 *High Water* GMT

	LONDON BRIDGE				LIVERPOOL (Alfred Dock)				GREENOCK				LEITH			
M 1	03 18	6.5	15 49	6.4	00 44	8.5	13 01	8.7	02 01	3.3	14 18	3.6	04 29	5.0	16 30	5.1
TU 2	03 50	6.5	16 26	6.4	01 21	8.3	13 39	8.6	02 39	3.3	14 53	3.6	05 07	4.9	17 07	5.0
W 3	04 26	6.4	17 05	6.3	02 00	8.1	14 19	8.4	03 19	3.2	15 30	3.5	05 48	4.8	17 48	4.9
TH 4	05 05	6.3	17 48	6.3	02 43	7.9	15 04	8.1	04 02	3.1	16 11	3.3	06 32	4.7	18 33	4.7
F 5	05 48	6.2	18 36	6.1	03 31	7.6	15 55	7.9	04 49	3.0	16 59	3.2	07 21	4.6	19 24	4.7
SA 6	06 38	6.0	19 30	6.0	04 28	7.4	16 55	7.8	05 41	3.0	17 56	3.1	08 17	4.5	20 24	4.6
SU 7	07 38	5.9	20 32	5.9	05 33	7.4	17 59	7.9	06 39	2.9	19 01	3.1	09 19	4.5	21 31	4.7
M 8	08 48	5.9	21 42	6.0	06 41	7.6	19 04	8.2	07 44	3.0	20 12	3.1	10 22	4.7	22 36	4.8
TU 9	10 01	6.1	22 50	6.2	07 45	8.0	20 06	8.5	08 54	3.1	21 19	3.2	11 21	4.9	23 36	5.0
W 10	11 06	6.4	23 49	6.5	08 41	8.5	21 03	8.9	09 54	3.2	22 20	3.4	12 16	5.1	—	—
TH 11	12 05	6.7	—	—	09 34	9.0	21 58	9.3	10 46	3.4	23 16	3.4	00 33	5.3	13 07	5.4
F 12	00 43	6.8	13 01	7.0	10 24	9.4	22 50	9.5	11 35	3.5	—	—	01 26	5.5	13 54	5.5
SA 13	01 34	6.9	13 54	7.1	11 13	9.6	23 42	9.6	00 10	3.5	12 22	3.6	02 18	5.7	14 41	5.7
SU 14	02 22	7.0	14 46	7.2	12 03	9.7	—	—	01 05	3.5	13 08	3.7	03 09	5.8	15 28	5.7
M 15	03 10	6.9	15 38	7.2	00 33	9.5	12 53	9.7	01 59	3.5	13 55	3.8	04 00	5.8	16 17	5.7
TU 16	03 57	6.8	16 30	7.1	01 24	9.4	13 44	9.6	02 52	3.4	14 41	3.8	04 52	5.7	17 09	5.6
W 17	04 44	6.7	17 21	7.0	02 15	9.1	14 34	9.3	03 43	3.4	15 27	3.8	05 45	5.4	18 03	5.4
TH 18	05 33	6.6	18 14	6.7	03 06	8.7	15 26	8.9	04 35	3.3	16 15	3.7	06 41	5.2	19 02	5.2
F 19	06 23	6.4	19 07	6.5	03 59	8.3	16 20	8.5	05 27	3.1	17 07	3.5	07 39	4.9	20 05	5.0
SA 20	07 19	6.2	20 04	6.3	04 56	7.9	17 19	8.1	06 20	3.0	18 02	3.3	08 40	4.7	21 07	4.9
SU 21	08 21	6.0	21 03	6.1	06 00	7.6	18 24	7.8	07 16	3.0	19 03	3.2	09 40	4.5	22 09	4.8
M 22	09 25	6.0	22 01	6.0	07 06	7.6	19 31	7.8	08 18	2.9	20 11	3.1	10 42	4.5	23 11	4.7
TU 23	10 26	6.0	22 58	6.1	08 07	7.8	20 32	7.9	09 20	3.0	21 22	3.1	11 43	4.6	—	—
W 24	11 24	6.2	23 50	6.2	09 00	8.1	21 24	8.1	10 16	3.2	22 23	3.1	00 11	4.7	12 37	4.7
TH 25	12 17	6.3	—	—	09 46	8.4	22 09	8.3	11 04	3.3	23 13	3.1	01 04	4.8	13 23	4.9
F 26	00 38	6.3	13 06	6.4	10 26	8.7	22 49	8.4	11 45	3.5	23 57	3.2	01 49	4.9	14 01	5.0
SA 27	01 22	6.4	13 49	6.5	11 03	8.8	23 24	8.5	12 22	3.5	—	—	02 28	5.0	14 35	5.1
SU 28	02 00	6.4	14 29	6.5	11 39	8.9	23 58	8.6	00 35	3.2	12 57	3.6	03 04	5.1	15 08	5.2
M 29	02 35	6.4	15 04	6.4	12 13	8.9	—	—	01 12	3.2	13 29	3.6	03 38	5.1	15 41	5.2
TU 30	03 07	6.4	15 38	6.4	00 32	8.6	12 49	8.9	01 48	3.2	14 01	3.6	04 12	5.1	16 14	5.2
W 31	03 39	6.4	16 12	6.5	01 08	8.6	13 25	8.9	02 25	3.2	14 35	3.6	04 47	5.1	16 49	5.2

GENERAL REFERENCE

WEIGHTS AND MEASURES

SI UNITS

The Système International d'Unités (SI) is an international and coherent system of units devised to meet all known needs for measurement in science and technology. The system was adopted by the eleventh Conférence Générale des Poids et Mesures (CGPM) in 1960. A comprehensive description of the system is given in *SI The International System of Units* (HMSO). The British Standards that describe the essential features of the International System of Units are *Specifications for SI units and recommendations for the use of their multiples and certain other units* (BS 5555:1993) and *Conversion Factors and Tables* (BS 350, Part 1:1974).

The system consists of seven base units and the derived units formed as products or quotients of various powers of the base units. Together the base units and the derived units make up the coherent system of units. In the UK the SI base units, and almost all important derived units, are realised at the National Physical Laboratory and disseminated through the National Measurement System.

BASE UNITS
Metre (m) = unit of length
Kilogram (kg) = unit of mass
Second (s) = unit of time
Ampere (A) = unit of electric current
Kelvin (K) = unit of thermodynamic temperature
Mole (mol) = unit of amount of substance
Candela (cd) = unit of luminous intensity

DERIVED UNITS
For some of the derived SI units, special names and symbols exist; those approved by the CGPM are as follows:

Hertz (Hz) = unit of frequency
Newton (N) = unit of force
Pascal (Pa) = unit of pressure, stress
Joule (J) = unit of energy, work, quantity of heat
Watt (W) = unit of power, radiant flux
Coulomb (C) = unit of electric charge, quantity of electricity
Volt (V) = unit of electric potential, potential difference, electromotive force
Farad (F) = unit of electric capacitance
Ohm (Ω) = unit of electric resistance
Siemens (S) = unit of electric conductance
Weber (Wb) = unit of magnetic flux
Tesla (T) = unit of magnetic flux density
Henry (H) = unit of inductance
Degree Celsius (°C) = unit of Celsius temperature
Lumen (lm) = unit of luminous flux
Lux (lx) = unit of illuminance
Becquerel (Bq) = unit of activity (of a radionuclide)
Gray (Gy) = unit of absorbed dose, specific energy imparted, kerma, absorbed dose index
Sievert (Sv) = unit of dose equivalent, dose equivalent index
Radian (rad) = unit of plane angle
Steradian (sr) = unit of solid angle

Other derived units are expressed in terms of base units. Some of the more commonly used derived units are the following:

Unit of area = square metre (m^2)
Unit of volume = cubic metre (m^3)
Unit of velocity = metre per second ($m\ s^{-1}$)
Unit of acceleration = metre per second squared ($m\ s^{-2}$)
Unit of density = kilogram per cubic metre ($kg\ m^{-3}$)
Unit of momentum = kilogram metre per second ($kg\ m\ s^{-1}$)
Unit of magnetic field strength = ampere per metre ($A\ m^{-1}$)
Unit of surface tension = newton per metre ($N\ m^{-1}$)
Unit of dynamic viscosity = pascal second (Pa s)
Unit of heat capacity = joule per kelvin ($J\ K^{-1}$)
Unit of specific heat capacity = joule per kilogram kelvin ($J\ kg^{-1}\ K^{-1}$)
Unit of heat flux density, irradiance = watt per square metre ($W\ m^{-2}$)
Unit of thermal conductivity = watt per metre kelvin ($W\ m^{-1}\ K^{-1}$)
Unit of electric field strength = volt per metre ($V\ m^{-1}$)
Unit of luminance = candela per square metre ($cd\ m^{-2}$)

SI PREFIXES
Decimal multiples and submultiples of the SI units are indicated by SI prefixes. These are as follows:

Multiples	*Submultiples*
yotta (Y) × 10^{24}	deci(d) × 10^{-1}
zetta (Z) × 10^{21}	centi (c) × 10^{-2}
exa (E) × 10^{18}	milli (m) × 10^{-3}
peta (P) × 10^{15}	micro (μ) × 10^{-6}
tera (T) × 10^{12}	nano (n) × 10^{-9}
giga (G) × 10^{9}	pico (p) × 10^{-12}
mega (M) × 10^{6}	femto (f) × 10^{-15}
kilo (k) × 10^{3}	atto (a) × 10^{-18}
hecto (h) × 10^{2}	zepto (z) × 10^{-21}
deca (da) × 10	yocto (y) × 10^{-24}

METRIC UNITS

The metric primary standards are the metre as the unit of measurement of length, and the kilogram as the unit of measurement of mass. Other units of measurement are defined by reference to the primary standards.

MEASUREMENT OF LENGTH
Kilometre (km) = 1000 metres
Metre (m) is the length of the path travelled by light in vacuum during a time interval of 1/299 792 458 of a second
Decimetre (dm) = 1/10 metre
Centimetre (cm) = 1/100 metre
Millimetre (mm) = 1/1000 metre

MEASUREMENT OF AREA
Hectare (ha) = 100 ares
Decare = 10 ares
Are (a) = 100 square metres
Square metre = a superficial area equal to that of a square each side of which measures one metre

Square decimetre = 1/100 square metre
Square centimetre = 1/100 square decimetre
Square millimetre = 1/100 square centimetre

MEASUREMENT OF VOLUME
Cubic metre (m^3) = a volume equal to that of a cube each edge of which measures one metre
Cubic decimetre = 1/1000 cubic metre
Cubic centimetre (cc) = 1/1000 cubic decimetre
Hectolitre = 100 litres
Litre = a cubic decimetre
Decilitre = 1/10 litre
Centilitre = 1/100 litre
Millilitre = 1/1000 litre

MEASUREMENT OF CAPACITY
Hectolitre (hl) = 100 litres
Litre (l or L) = a cubic decimetre
Decilitre (dl) = 1/10 litre
Centilitre (cl) = 1/100 litre
Millilitre (ml) = 1/1000 litre

MEASUREMENT OF MASS OR WEIGHT
Tonne (t) = 1000 kilograms
Kilogram (kg) is equal to the mass of the international prototype of the kilogram
Hectogram (hg) = 1/10 kilogram
Gram (g) = 1/1000 kilogram
*Carat (metric) = 1/5 gram
Milligram (mg) = 1/1000 gram

* Used only for transactions in precious stones or pearls

METRICATION IN THE UK
The European Council Directive 80/181/EEC, as amended by Council Directive 89/617/EEC, relates to the use of units of measurement for economic, public health, public safety or administrative purposes in the member states of the European Union. The provisions of the directives were incorporated into British law by the Weights and Measures Act 1985 (Metrication) (Amendment) Order 1994 and the Units of Measurement Regulations 1994; these instruments amended the Weights and Measures Act 1985. Parallel statutory rules amending Northern Ireland weights and measures legislation were made in May 1995.

The general effect of the 1994 and 1995 legislation is to end the use of imperial units of measurement for trade, replacing them with metric units. Imperial units can, however, be used in addition to metric units, as supplementary indications up to and including 31 December 2009.

IMPERIAL UNITS

The imperial primary standards are the yard as the unit of measurement of length and the pound as the unit of measurement of mass. Other units of measurement are defined by reference to the primary standards. Most of these units are no longer authorised for use in trade in the UK – *see* below.

MEASUREMENT OF LENGTH
Mile = 1760 yards
Furlong = 220 yards
Chain = 22 yards
Yard (yd) = 0.9144 metre
Foot (ft) = 1/3 yard
Inch (in) = 1/36 yard

MEASUREMENT OF AREA
Square mile = 640 acres
Acre = 4840 square yards
Rood = 1210 square yards
Square yard (sq. yd) = a superficial area equal to that of a square each side of which measures one yard
Square foot (sq. ft) = 1/9 square yard
Square inch (sq. in) = 1/144 square foot

MEASUREMENT OF VOLUME
Cubic yard = a volume equal to that of a cube each edge of which measures one yard
Cubic foot = 1/27 cubic yard
Cubic inch = 1/1728 cubic foot

MEASUREMENT OF CAPACITY
Bushel = 8 gallons
Peck = 2 gallons
Gallon (gal) = 4.54609 cubic decimetres
Quart (qt) = 1/4 gallon
*Pint (pt) = 1/2 quart
Gill = 1/4 pint
*Fluid ounce (fl oz) = 1/20 pint
Fluid drachm = 1/8 fluid ounce
Minim (min) = 1/60 fluid drachm

MEASUREMENT OF MASS OR WEIGHT
Ton = 2240 pounds
Hundredweight (cwt) = 112 pounds
Cental = 100 pounds
Quarter = 28 pounds
Stone = 14 pounds
*Pound (lb) = 0.453 592 37 kilogram
*Ounce (oz) = 1/16 pound
*†Ounce troy (oz tr) = 12/175 pound
Dram (dr) = 1/16 ounce
Grain (gr) = 1/7000 pound
Pennyweight (dwt) = 24 grains
Ounce apothecaries = 480 grains
Drachm (ʒ1) = 1/8 ounce apothecaries
Scruple (℈1) = 1/3 drachm

* Units of measurement still authorised for use for trade in the UK
† Used only for transactions in gold, silver or other precious metals, and articles made therefrom

PHASING-OUT OF IMPERIAL UNITS IN THE UK
Since 1965 the United Kingdom has been adopting metric weights and measures in response to the adoption of metric units as the international system of measurement. Since 1 January 2000, goods sold loose by weight (mainly fresh foods) are required to be sold in grams and kilograms, and fathoms (for marine navigation), fluid ounces and pints (for beer, cider, water, lemonade and fruit juice), and therms (for gas supply) are unauthorised units of measurement. Retailers can continue to display the price per imperial unit alongside the price per metric unit. Consumers can continue to express in ounces and pounds the quantity they wish to buy. Retailers will weigh out the equivalent quantity in grams and kilograms. The Weights and Measures Units of Measurement Regulations 1995 (Statutory Instrument 1995 No. 1804) require that metric units should be used for all economic, public health, public safety and administrative purposes.

The units of measurement authorised for use in specialised fields are:

Unit	*Field of application*
inch, foot, yard, mile	Road traffic signs, distance and speed measurement
pint	Dispense of draught beer or cider Milk in returnable containers
acre	Land registration
troy ounce	Transactions in precious metals

MEASUREMENT OF ELECTRICITY

Units of measurement of electricity are defined by the Weights and Measures Act 1985 as follows:

ampere (A) = that constant current which, if maintained in two straight parallel conductors of infinite length, of negligible circular cross-section and placed 1 metre apart in vacuum, would produce between these conductors a force equal to 2×10^{-7} newton per metre of length

ohm (Ω) = the electric resistance between two points of a conductor when a constant potential difference of 1 volt, applied between the two points, produces in the conductor a current of 1 ampere, the conductor not being the seat of any electromotive force

volt (V) = the difference of electric potential between two points of a conducting wire carrying a constant current of 1 ampere when the power dissipated between these points is equal to 1 watt

watt (W) = the power which in one second gives rise to energy of 1 joule

kilowatt (kW) = 1000 watts

megawatt (MW) = one million watts

MEASUREMENT OF SOUND

INTENSITY

Decibels are used to measure the power or intensity of sound. Decibel level is calculated on a logarithmic scale as a ratio against a standard power; each increase of 10db on the scale corresponds to ten times the intensity and twice the loudness. Some examples of decibel levels are:

Silence	0 db
Noise level of ordinary conversation	60db
Damage threshold for noise	90db
Noise level of typical streetworks	110db
Pain threshold for noise	130db

FREQUENCY AND PITCH

Frequency is a measure of how many waves or sound waves pass through a medium over a certain period of time. It is measured in Hertz (Hz) (*see* Derived SI Units), and a frequency of one Hz equals one wave, or one vibration every second. The typical range for human hearing is between 20Hz and 20,000Hz.

Frequency is closely linked to pitch, which indicates how high or low a sound is; a high frequency will have a high pitch, and a frequency doubled sounds an octave higher.

WATER AND LIQUOR MEASURES

1 cubic foot = 62.32 lb

1 gallon = 10 lb

1 cubic cm = 1 gram

1000 cubic cm = 1 litre; 1 kilogram

1 cubic metre = 1000 litres; 1000 kg; 1 tonne

An inch of rain on the surface of an acre (43560 sq. ft) = 3630 cubic ft = 100.992 tons

Cisterns: A cistern 4 × 2½ feet and 3 feet deep will hold brimful 186.963 gallons, weighing 1869.63 lb in addition to its own weight

WATER FOR SHIPS

Kilderkin = 18 gallons

Barrel = 36 gallons

Puncheon = 72 gallons

Butt = 110 gallons

Tun = 210 gallons

BOTTLES OF WINE

Traditional equivalents in standard champagne bottles:

Magnum = 2 bottles

Jeroboam = 4 bottles

Rehoboam = 6 bottles

Methuselah = 8 bottles

Salmanazar = 12 bottles

Balthazar = 16 bottles

Nebuchadnezzar = 20 bottles

A quarter of a bottle is known as a *nip*

An eighth of a bottle is known as a *baby*

ANGULAR AND CIRCULAR MEASURES

60 seconds (") = 1 minute (′)

60 minutes = 1 degree (°)

90 degrees = 1 right angle or quadrant

Diameter of circle × 3.1416 = circumference

Diameter squared × 0.7854 = area of circle

Diameter squared × 3.1416 = surface of sphere

Diameter cubed × 0.523 = solidity of sphere

One degree of circumference × 57.3 = radius*

Diameter of cylinder × 3.1416; product by length or height, gives the surface

Diameter squared × 0.7854; product by length or height, gives solid content

* Or, one radian (the angle subtended at the centre of a circle by an arc of the circumference equal in length to the radius) = 57.3 degrees

MILLION, BILLION ETC

Value in the UK		
Million	thousand × thousand	10^6
*Billion	million × million	10^{12}
Trillion	million × billion	10^{18}
Quadrillion	million × trillion	10^{24}

Value in the USA		
Million	thousand × thousand	10^6
*Billion	thousand × million	10^9
Trillion	million × million	10^{12}
Quadrillion	million × billion US	10^{15}

* The American usage of billion (ie 10^9) is increasingly common, and is now universally used by statisticians

NAUTICAL MEASURES

DISTANCE

Distance at sea is measured in nautical miles. The British standard nautical mile was 6080 feet but this measure has been obsolete since 1970 when the international nautical mile of 1852 metres was adopted by the Hydrographic Department of the Ministry of Defence. The cable (600 feet or 100 fathoms) was a measure approximately one-tenth of a nautical mile. Such distances are now expressed in decimal parts of a sea mile or in metres.

Soundings at sea were recorded in fathoms (6 feet). Depths are now expressed in metres on Admiralty charts.

SPEED

Speed is measured in nautical miles per hour, called knots. A ship moving at the rate of 30 nautical miles per hour is said to be doing 30 knots.

Knots	*mph*	*Knots*	*mph*
1	1.1515	9	10.3636
2	2.3030	10	11.5151
3	3.4545	15	17.2727
4	4.6060	20	23.0303
5	5.7575	25	28.7878
6	6.9090	30	34.5454
7	8.0606	35	40.3030
8	9.2121	40	46.0606

TONNAGE

Under the Merchant Shipping Act 1854, the tonnage of UK-registered vessels was measured in tons of 100 cubic feet. The need for a universal method of measurement led to the adoption of the International Convention on Tonnage Measurements of Ships 1969, which measures, in cubic metres, all the internal spaces of a vessel for the gross tonnage and those of the cargo compartments for the net tonnage. The convention has applied since July 1982 to new ships, ships which needed to be remeasured because of substantial alterations, and ships whose owners requested remeasurement. On 18 July 1994 the convention became mandatory.

DISTANCE OF THE HORIZON

The distance to the horizon can be calculated, in metric units, using the equation $D = 3.8373\sqrt{H}$ where D is the distance in kilometres and H is the height of the observer in metres, and in imperial units using the equation $D = 1.3157\sqrt{H}$ where D is the distance in miles and H is the height of the observer in feet. The resulting distances are those following a straight line from the observer to the horizon; it is not the distance along the curvature of the Earth. The difference between these two figures, however, is minimal for heights below 100km (62 miles).

Height in metres (feet)	*Range in km (miles)*
*1.7 (5.6)	5.0 (3.1)
5 (16)	8.6 (5.3)
10 (32.8)	12.1 (7.5)
50 (164)	27.1 (16.8)
100 (328)	38.4 (23.8)
†509 (1,670)	86.6 (53.8)
1,000 (3,281)	121.34 (75.4)
5,000 (16,404)	271.3 (168.5)
‡8,850 (29,035)	361.0 (224.2)
§9,144 (30,000)	366.9 (228.0)

* Average human height in the UK
† Height of the tallest inhabited building (Taipei 101)
‡ Height of Mt Everest
§ Height of cruising aeroplane

TEMPERATURE SCALES

The SI (International System) unit of temperature is the kelvin, which is defined as the fraction 1/273.16 of the temperature of the triple point of water (ie where ice, water and water vapour are in equilibrium). The zero of the Kelvin scale is the absolute zero of temperature. The freezing point of water is 273.15 K and the boiling point (as adopted in the International Temperature Scale of 1990) is 373.124 K.

The Celsius scale (formerly centigrade) is defined by subtracting 273.15 from the Kelvin temperature. The Fahrenheit scale is related to the Celsius scale by the relationships:

temperature °F = (temperature °C × 1.8) + 32
temperature °C = (temperature °F − 32)÷1.8

It follows from these definitions that the freezing point of water is 0°C and 32°F. The boiling point is 99.974°C and 211.953°F.

The temperature of the human body varies from person to person and in the same person can be affected by a variety of factors. In most people body temperature varies between 36.5°C and 37.2°C (97.7–98.9°F).

Conversion between scales

°C	°F	°C	°F	°C	°F
100	212	60	140	20	68
99	210.2	59	138.2	19	66.2
98	208.4	58	136.4	18	64.4
97	206.6	57	134.6	17	62.6
96	204.8	56	132.8	16	60.8
95	203	55	131	15	59
94	201.2	54	129.2	14	57.2
93	199.4	53	127.4	13	55.4
92	197.6	52	125.6	12	53.6
91	195.8	51	123.8	11	51.8
90	194	50	122	10	50
89	192.2	49	120.2	9	48.2
88	190.4	48	118.4	8	46.4
87	188.6	47	116.6	7	44.6
86	186.8	46	114.8	6	42.8
85	185	45	113	5	41
84	183.2	44	111.2	4	39.2
83	181.4	43	109.4	3	37.4
82	179.6	42	107.6	2	35.6
81	177.8	41	105.8	1	33.8
80	176	40	104	*Zero*	32
79	174.2	39	102.2	−1	30.2
78	172.4	38	100.4	−2	28.4
77	170.6	37	98.6	−3	26.6
76	168.8	36	96.8	−4	24.8
75	167	35	95	−5	23
74	165.2	34	93.2	−6	21.2
73	163.4	33	91.4	−7	19.4
72	161.6	32	89.6	−8	17.6
71	159.8	31	87.8	−9	15.8
70	158	30	86	−10	14
69	156.2	29	84.2	−11	12.2
68	154.4	28	82.4	−12	10.4
67	152.6	27	80.6	−13	8.6
66	150.8	26	78.8	−14	6.8
65	149	25	77	−15	5
64	147.2	24	75.2	−16	3.2
63	145.4	23	73.4	−17	1.4
62	143.6	22	71.6	−18	0.4
61	141.8	21	69.8	−19	−2.2

PAPER MEASURES

Printing Paper	*Writing Paper*
5 bundles = 1 bale	480 sheets = 1 ream
2 reams = 1 bundle	20 quires = 1 ream
516 sheets = 1 ream	24 sheets = 1 quire

INTERNATIONAL PAPER SIZES

The basis of the international series of paper sizes is a rectangle having an area of one square metre, the sides of which are in the proportion of 1:√2. The proportions 1:√2 have a geometrical relationship, the side and diagonal of any square being in this proportion. The effect of this arrangement is that if the area of the sheet of paper is doubled or halved, the shorter side and the longer side of the new sheet are still in the same proportion 1:√2. This feature is useful where photographic enlargement or reduction is used, as the proportions remain the same.

Description of the A series is by capital A followed by a figure. The basic size has the description A0 and the higher the figure following the letter, the greater is the number of sub-divisions and therefore the smaller the sheet. Half A0 is A1 and half A1 is A2. Where larger dimensions are required the A is preceded by a figure. Thus 2A means twice the size A0; 4A is four times the size of A0.

SUBSIDIARY SERIES

B sizes are sizes intermediate between any two adjacent sizes of the A series. There is a series of C sizes which is used much less. A is for magazines and books, B for posters, wall charts and other large items, C for envelopes particularly where it is necessary for an envelope (in C series) to fit into another envelope. The size recommended for business correspondence is A4.

Long sizes (DL) are obtainable by dividing any appropriate sizes from the two series above into three, four or eight equal parts parallel with the shorter side in such a manner that the proportion of 1:√2 is not maintained, the ratio between the longer and the shorter sides being greater than √2:1. In practice long sizes should be produced from the A series only.

It is an essential feature of these series that the dimensions are of the trimmed or finished size.

A SERIES

	mm		*mm*
A0	841 × 1189	A6	105 × 148
A1	594 × 841	A7	74 × 105
A2	420 × 594	A8	52 × 74
A3	297 × 420	A9	37 × 52
A4	210 × 297	A10	26 × 37
A5	148 × 210		

BOOK SIZES

Traditional	*mm*	*Modern*	*mm*
Royal Quarto	250 × 320	Crown Royal	210 × 280
Demy Ouarto	220 × 290	Royal	191 × 235
Crown Quarto	190 × 250	Demy	152 × 229
Royal Octavo	150 × 250	C format	143 × 222
Demy Octavo	143 × 222	B format or trade	129 × 198
Large Crown Qctavo	129 × 198	A format	111 × 175

OBSOLETE MEASURES

Length
Cubit, Digit, Ell, Finger, Hand*, League, Palm, Span
* Still in use for measurement of horses

Capacity
Barrel, Bushel, Cask, Hogshead, Tun

Weight
Clove, Mark, Nail, Sack, Tod

Area
Bovate, Carucate, Perch, Virgate

CLOTHING SIZES

MEN'S

Item	*UK*	*USA*	*Europe*
Suits	36	36	46
	38	38	48
	40	40	50
	42	42	52
	44	44	54
	46	46	56
Shirts	12	12	30–31
	12½	12½	32
	13	13	33
	13½	13½	34–35
	14	14	36
	14½	14½	37
	15	15	38
	15½	15½	39–40
	16	16	41
	16½	16½	42
	17	17	43
	17½	17½	44–45
Shoes	6½	7	39
	7	7½	40
	7½	8	41
	8	8½	42
	8½	9	43
	9	9½	43
	9½	10	44
	10	10½	44
	10½	11	45

WOMEN'S

Item	*UK*	*USA*	*Europe*
Clothing	8	6	36
	10	8	38
	12	10	40
	14	12	42
	16	14	44
	18	16	46
	20	18	48
	22	20	50
	24	22	52
Shoes	4	5½	37
	4½	6	37
	5	6½	38
	5½	7	38
	6	7½	39
	6½	8	39
	7	8½	40
	7½	9	40
	8	9½	41

CONVERSION TABLES FOR WEIGHTS AND MEASURES

Bold figures equal units of either of the columns beside them; thus: 1 cm = 0.394 inches and 1 inch = 2.540 cm

LENGTH			AREA			VOLUME			WEIGHT (MASS)		
Centimetres		*Inches*	*Square cm*		*Square in*	*Cubic cm*		*Cubic in*	*Kilograms*		*Pounds*
2.540	**1**	0.394	6.452	**1**	0.155	16.387	**1**	0.061	0.454	**1**	2.205
5.080	**2**	0.787	12.903	**2**	0.310	32.774	**2**	0.122	0.907	**2**	4.409
7.620	**3**	1.181	19.355	**3**	0.465	49.161	**3**	0.183	1.361	**3**	6.614
10.160	**4**	1.575	25.806	**4**	0.620	65.548	**4**	0.244	1.814	**4**	8.819
12.700	**5**	1.969	32.258	**5**	0.775	81.936	**5**	0.305	2.268	**5**	11.023
15.240	**6**	2.362	38.710	**6**	0.930	98.323	**6**	0.366	2.722	**6**	13.228
17.780	**7**	2.756	45.161	**7**	1.085	114.710	**7**	0.427	3.175	**7**	15.432
20.320	**8**	3.150	51.613	**8**	1.240	131.097	**8**	0.488	3.629	**8**	17.637
22.860	**9**	3.543	58.064	**9**	1.395	147.484	**9**	0.549	4.082	**9**	19.842
25.400	**10**	3.937	64.516	**10**	1.550	163.871	**10**	0.610	4.536	**10**	22.046
50.800	**20**	7.874	129.032	**20**	3.100	327.742	**20**	1.220	9.072	**20**	44.092
76.200	**30**	11.811	193.548	**30**	4.650	491.613	**30**	1.831	13.608	**30**	66.139
101.600	**40**	15.748	258.064	**40**	6.200	655.484	**40**	2.441	18.144	**40**	88.185
127.000	**50**	19.685	322.580	**50**	7.750	819.355	**50**	3.051	22.680	**50**	110.231
152.400	**60**	23.622	387.096	**60**	9.300	983.226	**60**	3.661	27.216	**60**	132.277
177.800	**70**	27.559	451.612	**70**	10.850	1147.097	**70**	4.272	31.752	**70**	154.324
203.200	**80**	31.496	516.128	**80**	12.400	1310.968	**80**	4.882	36.287	**80**	176.370
228.600	**90**	35.433	580.644	**90**	13.950	1474.839	**90**	5.492	40.823	**90**	198.416
254.000	**100**	39.370	645.160	**100**	15.500	1638.710	**100**	6.102	45.359	**100**	220.464

Metres		*Yards*	*Square m*		*Square yd*	*Cubic m*		*Cubic yd*	*Metric tonnes*		*Tons (UK)*
0.914	**1**	1.094	0.836	**1**	1.196	0.765	**1**	1.308	1.016	**1**	0.984
1.829	**2**	2.187	1.672	**2**	2.392	1.529	**2**	2.616	2.032	**2**	1.968
2.743	**3**	3.281	2.508	**3**	3.588	2.294	**3**	3.924	3.048	**3**	2.953
3.658	**4**	4.374	3.345	**4**	4.784	3.058	**4**	5.232	4.064	**4**	3.937
4.572	**5**	5.468	4.181	**5**	5.980	3.823	**5**	6.540	5.080	**5**	4.921
5.486	**6**	6.562	5.017	**6**	7.176	4.587	**6**	7.848	6.096	**6**	5.905
6.401	**7**	7.655	5.853	**7**	8.372	5.352	**7**	9.156	7.112	**7**	6.889
7.315	**8**	8.749	6.689	**8**	9.568	6.116	**8**	10.464	8.128	**8**	7.874
8.230	**9**	9.843	7.525	**9**	10.764	6.881	**9**	11.772	9.144	**9**	8.858
9.144	**10**	10.936	8.361	**10**	11.960	7.646	**10**	13.080	10.161	**10**	9.842
18.288	**20**	21.872	16.723	**20**	23.920	15.291	**20**	26.159	20.321	**20**	19.684
27.432	**30**	32.808	25.084	**30**	35.880	22.937	**30**	39.239	30.481	**30**	29.526
36.576	**40**	43.745	33.445	**40**	47.840	30.582	**40**	52.318	40.642	**40**	39.368
45.720	**50**	54.681	41.806	**50**	59.799	38.228	**50**	65.398	50.802	**50**	49.210
54.864	**60**	65.617	50.168	**60**	71.759	45.873	**60**	78.477	60.963	**60**	59.052
64.008	**70**	76.553	58.529	**70**	83.719	53.519	**70**	91.557	71.123	**70**	68.894
73.152	**80**	87.489	66.890	**80**	95.679	61.164	**80**	104.636	81.284	**80**	78.737
82.296	**90**	98.425	75.251	**90**	107.639	68.810	**90**	117.716	91.444	**90**	88.579
91.440	**100**	109.361	83.613	**100**	119.599	76.455	**100**	130.795	101.605	**100**	98.421

Kilometres		*Miles*	*Hectares*		*Acres*	*Litres*		*Gallons*	*Metric tonnes*		*Tons (US)*
1.609	**1**	0.621	0.405	**1**	2.471	4.546	**1**	0.220	0.907	**1**	1.102
3.219	**2**	1.243	0.809	**2**	4.942	9.092	**2**	0.440	1.814	**2**	2.205
4.828	**3**	1.864	1.214	**3**	7.413	13.638	**3**	0.660	2.722	**3**	3.305
6.437	**4**	2.485	1.619	**4**	9.844	18.184	**4**	0.880	3.629	**4**	4.409
8.047	**5**	3.107	2.023	**5**	12.355	22.730	**5**	1.100	4.536	**5**	5.521
9.656	**6**	3.728	2.428	**6**	14.826	27.276	**6**	1.320	5.443	**6**	6.614
11.265	**7**	4.350	2.833	**7**	17.297	31.822	**7**	1.540	6.350	**7**	7.716
12.875	**8**	4.971	3.327	**8**	19.769	36.368	**8**	1.760	7.257	**8**	8.818
14.484	**9**	5.592	3.642	**9**	22.240	40.914	**9**	1.980	8.165	**9**	9.921
16.093	**10**	6.214	4.047	**10**	24.711	45.460	**10**	2.200	9.072	**10**	11.023
32.187	**20**	12.427	8.094	**20**	49.421	90.919	**20**	4.400	18.144	**20**	22.046
48.280	**30**	18.641	12.140	**30**	74.132	136.379	**30**	6.599	27.216	**30**	33.069
64.374	**40**	24.855	16.187	**40**	98.842	181.839	**40**	8.799	36.287	**40**	44.092
80.467	**50**	31.069	20.234	**50**	123.555	227.298	**50**	10.999	45.359	**50**	55.116
96.561	**60**	37.282	24.281	**60**	148.263	272.758	**60**	13.199	54.431	**60**	66.139
112.654	**70**	43.496	28.328	**70**	172.974	318.217	**70**	15.398	63.503	**70**	77.162
128.748	**80**	49.710	32.375	**80**	197.684	363.677	**80**	17.598	72.575	**80**	88.185
144.841	**90**	55.923	36.422	**90**	222.395	409.137	**90**	19.798	81.647	**90**	99.208
160.934	**100**	62.137	40.469	**100**	247.105	454.596	**100**	21.998	90.719	**100**	110.231

THE PERIODIC TABLE OF ELEMENTS

Key	
6	atomic number
Carbon	name of element
C	chemical number
12.01	atomic mass

	Alkali metals I A	Alkaline earth metals II A	III B	IV B	V B	VI B	V II	VIII			I B	II B	III A	IV A	V A	VI A	VII A	Noble gases
			Transition metals										Non-metals					
1	1 Hydrogen **H** 1.01																	2 Helium **He** 4.00
2	3 Lithium **Li** 6.94	4 Beryllium **Be** 9.01											5 Boron **B** 10.81	6 Carbon **C** 12.01	7 Nitrogen **N** 14.01	8 Oxygen **O** 16.00	9 Fluorine **F** 19.00	10 Neon **Ne** 20.18
3	11 Sodium **Na** 22.99	12 Magnesium **Mg** 24.31											13 Aluminium **Al** 26.98	14 Silicon **Si** 28.09	15 Phosphorus **P** 30.97	16 Sulphur **S** 32.07	17 Chlorine **Cl** 35.45	18 Argon **Ar** 39.95
4	19 Potassium **K** 39.10	20 Calcium **Ca** 40.08	21 Scandium **Sc** 44.96	22 Titanium **Ti** 47.88	23 Vanadium **V** 50.94	24 Chromium **Cr** 52.00	25 Manganese **Mn** 54.95	26 Iron **Fe** 55.85	27 Cobalt **Co** 58.93	28 Nickel **Ni** 58.70	29 Copper **Cu** 63.55	30 Zinc **Zn** 65.39	31 Gallium **Ga** 69.72	32 Germanium **Ge** 72.61	33 Arsenic **As** 74.92	34 Selenium **Se** 78.96	35 Bromine **Br** 79.904	36 Krypton **Kr** 83.80
5	37 Rubidium **Rb** 85.47	38 Strontium **Sr** 87.62	39 Yttrium **Y** 88.91	40 Zirconium **Zr** 91.22	41 Niobium **Nb** 92.91	42 Molybdenum **Mo** 95.94	43 Technetium **Tc** 97.91	44 Ruthenium **Ru** 101.07	45 Rhodium **Rh** 102.91	46 Palladium **Pd** 106.4	47 Silver **Ag** 107.87	48 Cadmium **Cd** 112.41	49 Indium **In** 114.82	50 Tin **Sn** 118.71	51 Antimony **Sb** 121.74	52 Tellurium **Te** 127.60	53 Iodine **I** 126.9045	54 Xenon **Xe** 131.29
6	55 Caesium **Cs** 132.91	56 Barium **Ba** 137.33	Lanthanide series (see below)	72 Hafnium **Hf** 178.49	73 Tantalum **Ta** 180.94	74 Tungsten **W** 183.85	75 Rhenium **Ru** 186.21	76 Osmium **Os** 190.23	77 Iridium **Ir** 192.22	78 Platinum **Pt** 195.08	79 Gold **Au** 196.97	80 Mercury **Hg** 200.59	81 Thallium **Tl** 204.38	82 Lead **Pb** 207.2	83 Bismuth **Bi** 208.98	84 Polonium **Po** 209	85 Astatine **At** 210	86 Radon **Rn** 222.02
7	87 Francium **Fr** 223.02	88 Radium **Ra** 226.03	Actinide series (see below)	104 Rutherfordium **Rf** 261.12	105 Dubnium **Db** 262.11	106 Seaborgium **Sg** 236.12	107 Bohrium **Bh** 262	108 Hassium **Hs** 265	109 Meitnerium **Mt** 266	110 Darmstadtium **Ds** 269	111 Roentgenium **Rg** 272							

Rare earth elements															
Lanthanide series	57 Lanthanum **La** 138.91	58 Cerium **Ce** 140.12	59 Praeseodymium **Pr** 140.91	60 Neodymium **Nd** 144.24	61 Promethium **Pm** 144.91	62 Samarium **Sm** 150.36	63 Europium **Eu** 151.96	64 Gadolinium **Gd** 157.25	65 Terbium **Tb** 158.93	66 Dysprosium **Dy** 162.50	67 Holmium **Ho** 164.93	68 Erbium **Er** 167.26	69 Thulium **Tm** 168.93	70 Ytterbium **Yb** 173.04	71 Lutetium **Lu** 174.97
Actinide series	89 Actinium **Ac** 227.03	90 Thorium **Th** 232.04	91 Protactinium **Pa** 231.04	92 Uranium **U** 238.03	93 Neptunium **Np** 237.05	94 Plutonium **Pu** 244.06	95 Americium **Am** 243.06	96 Curium **Cm** 247.07	97 Berkelium **Bk** 247	98 Californium **Cf** 251.08	99 Eisteinium **Es** 252.08	100 Fermium **Fm** 257.10	101 Mendelevium **Md** 258.10	102 Nobelium **No** 259.10	103 Lawrencium **Lr** 260.11

The periodic table arranges the elements into horizontal rows (periods) and vertical columns (groups) according to their atomic number. The elements in a group all have similar properties; across each period, atoms are electropositive (form positive ions) to the left and electronegative to the right. The earliest version of the periodic table was devised in 1869 by Dmitriy Mendeleyev, who predicted the existence of several elements from gaps in the table.

NOBEL PRIZE WINNERS

For prize winners for the years 1901 – 2003, *see* earlier editions of *Whitaker's Almanack*.

The Nobel Prizes are awarded each year from the income of a trust fund established by the Swedish scientist Alfred Nobel, the inventor of dynamite, who died on 10 December 1896 leaving a fortune of £1,750,000. The prizes are awarded to those who have contributed most to the common good in the domain of:

Physics – awarded by the Royal Swedish Academy of Sciences
Chemistry – awarded by the Royal Swedish Academy of Sciences
Physiology or Medicine – awarded by the Karolinska Institute
Literature – awarded by the Swedish Academy of Arts
Peace – awarded by a five-person committee elected by the Norwegian Storting
Economic Sciences (instituted 1969) – awarded by the Royal Swedish Academy of Sciences

The prizes are awarded every year on 10 December, the anniversary of Nobel's death. The first awards were made on 10 December 1901. The Trust is administered by the board of directors of the Nobel Foundation, Stockholm, consisting of five members and three deputy members. The Swedish government appoints a chairman and a deputy chairman, the remaining members being appointed by the awarding authorities.

The awards in the last three years have been distributed as follows:

	2004	*2005*	*2006*
Physics	David J. Gross *(USA)*, H. David Politzer *(USA)*, Frank Wilczek *(USA)*	Roy J. Glauber *(USA)*, John L. Hall *(USA)*, Theodor W. Hänsch *(Germany)*	John C. Mather *(USA)*, George F. Smoot *(USA)*
Chemistry	Aaron Ciechanover *(Israel)*, Avram Hershko *(Israel)*, Irwin Rose *(USA)*	Yves Chauvin *(France)*, Robert H. Grubbs *(USA)*, Richard R. Schrock *(USA)*	Roger D. Kornberg *(USA)*
Physiology or Medicine	Richard Axel *(USA)*, Linda B. Buck *(USA)*	Barry J. Marshall *(Australia)*, J. Robin Warren *(Australia)*	Andrew Z. Fire *(USA)*, Craig C. Mello *(USA)*
Literature	Elfriede Jelinek *(Austria)*	Harold Pinter *(UK)*	Orhan Pamuk *(Turkey)*
Peace	Wangari Maathai *(Kenya)*	IAEA *(Austria)*, Mohamed ElBaradei *(Egypt)*	Grameen Bank *(Bangladesh)*, Muhammad Yunus *(Bangladesh)*
Economics	Finn E. Kydland *(Norway)*, Edward C. Prescott *(USA)*	Robert J. Aumann *(Israel and USA)*, Thomas C. Schelling *(USA)*	Edmund S. Phelps *(USA)*

ABBREVIATIONS AND ACRONYMS

Ψ	seaport

A

A	ampere
AA	Alcoholics Anonymous
	Automobile Association
AAA	Amateur Athletic Association
ABA	Amateur Boxing Association
abbr(ev)	abbreviation
ABM	anti-ballistic missile
abr	abridged
ac	alternating current
a/c	account
AC	*(ante Christum)* before Christ
	Companion, Order of Australia
ACAS	Advisory, Conciliation and Arbitration Service
ACT	Australian Capital Territory
AD	*(anno Domini)* in the year of our Lord
ADB	Asian Development Bank
ADC	Aide-de-Camp
ADC (P)	Personal ADC to The Queen
adj	adjective
Adj.	Adjutant
Adj. Gen.	Adjutant General
ad lib	*(ad libitum)* at pleasure
Adm.	Admiral
adv	adverb
AE	Air Efficiency award
AEM	Air Efficiency Medal
aet	after extra time
AFC	Air Force Cross
AFM	Air Force Medal
AG	Attorney-General
AGM	air-to-ground missile
	annual general meeting
AH	*(anno Hegirae)* in the year of the Hegira
AI	artificial intelligence
AIDS	acquired immune deficiency syndrome
AIM	Alternative Investment Market
alt	altitude
am	*(ante meridiem)* before noon
AM	amplitude modulation
	(anno mundi) in the year of the world
amp	amplifier
AMU	Arab Maghreb Union
ANC	African National Congress
anon	anonymous
ANZAC	Australian and New Zealand Army Corps
AO	Air Officer
	Officer, Order of Australia
AOC	Air Officer Commanding
AONB	area of outstanding natural beauty
APEC	Asia-Pacific Economic Cooperation
apptd	appointed
APR	annual percentage rate
AS	Anglo-Saxon
ASA	Advertising Standards Authority
	Amateur Swimming Association
ASAP	as soon as possible
ASBO	anti social behaviour order
ASEAN	Association of South-East Asian Nations
ASLEF	Associated Society of Locomotive Engineers and Firemen
ASLIB	Association for Information Management
ATC	Air Training Corps
AUC	*(ab urbe condita)* in the year from the foundation of Rome
	(anno urbis conditae) in the year of the founding of the city
AUT	Association of University Teachers
AV	audio-visual
	Authorised Version *(of Bible)*
AVR	Army Volunteer Reserve
AWOL	absent without (official) leave

B

b.	born
	bowled *(cricket)*
BA	Bachelor of Arts
BAA	British Airports Authority
	British Astronomical Association
BAF	British Athletics Federation
BAFTA	British Academy of Film and Television Arts
BAS	Bachelor in Agricultural Science
	British Antarctic Survey
BBA	British Bankers' Association
BBC	British Broadcasting Corporation
BBFC	British Board of Film Classification
BBSRC	Biotechnology and Biological Sciences Research Council
BC	before Christ
	borough council
	British Columbia *(Canada)*
BCH (D)	Bachelor of (Dental) Surgery
BCL	Bachelor of Civil Law
BCOM	Bachelor of Commerce
BD	Bachelor of Divinity
BDA	British Dental Association
BDS	Bachelor of Dental Surgery
BED	Bachelor of Education
BEM	British Empire Medal
BENG	Bachelor of Engineering
BFI	British Film Institute
BFPO	British Forces Post Office
BLIT	Bachelor of Literature
BLITT	Bachelor of Letters
BM	Bachelor of Medicine
	British Museum
BMA	British Medical Association
BMI	body mass index
BMUS	Bachelor of Music
BNFL	British Nuclear Fuels
BOTB	British Overseas Trade Board
Bp	Bishop
BPHARM	Bachelor of Pharmacy
BPHIL	Bachelor of Philosophy
bpm	beats per minute
Br(it)	Britain
	British
Brig	Brigadier
BSC	Bachelor of Science
BSE	bovine spongiform encephalopathy
BSI	British Standards Institution
BST	British Summer Time
Bt.	Baronet
BTEC	Business and Technology Education Council
BTU	British thermal unit
BVMS	Bachelor of Veterinary Medicine and Surgery

C

c.	*(circa)* about
	chapter (Public Acts)
C	Celsius
	centigrade
C.	Conservative
CA	chartered accountant *(Scotland)*
CAA	Civil Aviation Authority
CAB	Citizens' Advice Bureau
CAD	computer-aided design
Cadw	Ancient Monuments Board for Wales
Cantuar:	of Canterbury *(Archbishop)*
CAP	Common Agricultural Policy
Capt	Captain
CARICOM	Caribbean Community and Common Market
Carliol:	of Carlisle *(Bishop)*
CB	Companion, Order of the Bath
CBE	Commander, Order of the British Empire
CBI	Confederation of British Industry

CBSS Council of the Baltic Sea States
CC Chamber of Commerce
city council
Companion, Order of Canada
county council
county court
CCC county cricket club
CCF Combined Cadet Force
CCHEM chartered chemist
CCTA City Colleges for Technology and the Arts
CD Civil Defence
compact disc
Corps Diplomatique
Cdr Commander
Cdre Commodore
CDS Chief of the Defence Staff
CE civil engineer
Common (or Christian) Era
CEFAS Centre for Environment, Fisheries and Aquaculture Science
CENG chartered engineer
CEO chief executive officer
CERN European Organisation for Nuclear Research
Cestr: of Chester *(Bishop)*
CET Central European Time
Common External Tariff
cf *(confer)* compare
CF Chaplain to the Forces
CFC chlorofluorocarbon
CGC Conspicuous Gallantry Cross
CGEOL chartered geologist
CGI computer-generated imagery
CGM Conspicuous Gallantry Medal
cgs centimetre-gramme-second *(system)*
CGS Chief of General Staff
CH Companion of Honour
CHB/M Bachelor/Master of Surgery
CI Channel Islands
Imperial Order of the Crown of India
CIA Central Intelligence Agency
CICA Conference on Interaction and Confidence Building Measures in Asia
Criminal Injuries Compensation Authority
CICAP Criminal Injuries Compensation Appeals Panel
Cicestr: of Chichester *(Bishop)*
CID Criminal Investigation Department
CIE Companion, Order of the Indian Empire
cif cost, insurance and freight
C-in-C Commander-in-Chief
CIPFA Chartered Institute of Public Finance and Accountancy
CIS Commonwealth of Independent States
CJD Creutzfeld-Jakob disease
CLJ Commander, Order of St Lazarus of Jerusalem
CM *(Chirurgiae Magister)* Master of Surgery
CMG Companion, Order of St Michael and St George
CND Campaign for Nuclear Disarmament
c/o care of
CO Commanding Officer
C of E Church of England
COI Central Office of Information
Col. Colonel
cons. consecrated
Cpl. Corporal
CPM Colonial Police Medal
CPRE Council for the Protection of Rural England
CPS Crown Prosecution Service
CPVE Certificate of Pre-Vocational Education
CRE Commission for Racial Equality
CSA Child Support Agency
CSI Companion, Order of the Star of India
CVO Commander, Royal Victorian Order

D

d *(denarius)* penny
d. died
DBE Dame Commander, Order of the British Empire
dc direct current
DC District of Columbia *(USA)*
district council
DCA Department for Constitutional Affairs
DCB Dame Commander, Order of the Bath
D CH *(Doctor Chirurgiae)* Doctor of Surgery
DCL Doctor of Civil Law
DCM Distinguished Conduct Medal
DCMG Dame Commander, Order of St Michael and St George
DCMS Department for Culture, Media and Sport
DCVO Dame Commander, Royal Victorian Order
DD Doctor of Divinity
DDS Doctor of Dental Surgery
DDT dichlorodiphenyl trichloroethane
del *(delineavit)* he/she drew it
DEFRA Department of the Environment, Food and Rural Affairs
DFC Distinguished Flying Cross
DfES Department for Education and Skills
DFID Department for International Development
DFM Distinguished Flying Medal
DfT Department for Transport
DG *(Dei gratia)* by the grace of God
director general
DHA district health authority
DIP ED Diploma in Education
DIP HE Diploma in Higher Education
DIPHS Diploma of the Heraldry Society
DJ disc jockey
DL Deputy Lieutenant
DLIT Doctor of Literature
DLITT Doctor of Letters
DLR Docklands Light Railway
DMUS Doctor of Music
DNA deoxyribonucleic acid
DNB *Dictionary of National Biography*
do *(ditto)* the same
DoH Department of Health
DOS disk operating system
DPH or DPHIL Doctor of Philosophy
DPP Director of Public Prosecutions
Dr Doctor
DRC Disability Rights Commission
DSC Distinguished Service Cross
Doctor of Science
DSM Distinguished Service Medal
DSO Companion, Distinguished Service Order
DTI Department of Trade and Industry
DTP desktop publishing
Dunelm: of Durham *(Bishop)*
DV *(Deo volente)* God willing
DVD digital versatile disc
DVLA Driver and Vehicle Licensing Agency
DWI Drinking Water Inspectorate
DWP Department for Work and Pensions

E

E east
email
Ebor: of York *(Archbishop)*
EBRD European Bank for Reconstruction and Development
EC European Community
ECB England and Wales Cricket Board
ECG electrocardiogram
ECGD Export Credits Guarantee Department

ECOWAS	Economic Community of West African States
ECSC	European Coal and Steel Community
ECU	European Currency Unit
ED	Efficiency Decoration
EEC	European Economic Community
EEG	electroencephalogram
EFA	European Fighter Aircraft
EFTA	European Free Trade Association
eg	*(exempli gratia)* for the sake of example
EIB	European Investment Bank
EMS	European Monetary System
EMU	European Monetary Union
EOC	Equal Opportunities Commission
EPSRC	Engineering and Physical Sciences Research Council
ER	*(Elizabetha Regina)* Queen Elizabeth
ERM	exchange rate mechanism
ERNIE	electronic random number indicator equipment
ESA	European Space Agency
ESP	extra-sensory perception
ESRC	Economic and Social Research Council
est	established estimate
ETA	*(Euzkadi ta Askatasuna)* (Basque separatist organisation)
et al	*(et alibi)* and elsewhere
	(et alii) and others
etc	*(et cetera)* and the other things/and so forth
et seq	*(et sequentia)* and the following
EU	European Union
Euratom	European Atomic Energy Community
Exon:	of Exeter *(Bishop)*

F

f	*(forte)* loud
F	Fahrenheit
	Fellow of
FA	Football Association
FANY	First Aid Nursing Yeomanry
FAO	for the attention of
FAQ	frequently asked questions
FBA	Fellow, British Academy
FBAA	Fellow, British Association of Accountants and Auditors
FBI	Federal Bureau of Investigation
FBS	Fellow, Botanical Society
FBU	Fire Brigades Union
FCO	Foreign and Commonwealth Office
FC	football club
FCA	Fellow, Institute of Chartered Accountants in England and Wales
FCCA	Fellow, Chartered Association of Certified Accountants
FCGI	Fellow, City and Guilds of London Institute
FCIA	Fellow, Corporation of Insurance Agents
FCIARB	Fellow, Chartered Institute of Arbitrators
FCIB	Fellow, Chartered Institute of Bankers
	Fellow, Corporation of Insurance Brokers
FCIBSE	Fellow, Chartered Institution of Building Services Engineers
FCII	Fellow, Chartered Insurance Institute
FCIPS	Fellow, Chartered Institute of Purchasing and Supply
FCIS	Fellow, Institute of Chartered Secretaries and Administrators
FCIT	Fellow, Chartered Institute of Transport
FCMA	Fellow, Chartered Institute of Management Accountants
FCO	Foreign and Commonwealth Office
FCP	Fellow, College of Preceptors
FD	*(Fidei Defensor)* Defender of the Faith
FE	further education
fec	*(fecit)* made this
ff	*(fecerunt)* made this (pl)
	folios following
ff	*(fortissimo)* very loud
FFA	Fellow, Faculty of Actuaries *(Scotland)*
	Fellow, Institute of Financial Accountants
FFAS	Fellow, Faculty of Architects and Surveyors
FFCM	Fellow, Faculty of Community Medicine
FFPHM	Fellow, Faculty of Public Health Medicine
FGS	Fellow, Geological Society
FHS	Fellow, Heraldry Society
FHSM	Fellow, Institute of Health Service Management
FIA	Fellow, Institute of Actuaries
FIBIOL	Fellow, Institute of Biology
FICE	Fellow, Institution of Civil Engineers
FICS	Fellow, Institution of Chartered Shipbrokers
FIEE	Fellow, Institution of Electrical Engineers
FIERE	Fellow, Institution of Electronic and Radio Engineers
FIFA	*(Fédération Internationale de Football Association)* International Federation of Association Football
FIM	Fellow, Institute of Metals
FIMGT	Fellow, Institute of Management
FIMM	Fellow, Institution of Mining and Metallurgy
FINSTF	Fellow, Institute of Fuel
FINSTP	Fellow, Institute of Physics
FIQS	Fellow, Institute of Quantity Surveyors
FIS	Fellow, Institute of Statisticians
FJI	Fellow, Institute of Journalists
FLA	Fellow, Library Association
FLS	Fellow, Linnean Society
FM	Field Marshal
	frequency modulation
FMEDSCI	Fellow, Academy of Medical Sciences
fo	folio
FO	Flying Officer
fob	free on board
FPHS	Fellow, Philosophical Society
FRAD	Fellow, Royal Academy of Dancing
FRAES	Fellow, Royal Aeronautical Society
FRAI	Fellow, Royal Anthropological Institute
FRAM	Fellow, Royal Academy of Music
FRAS	Fellow, Royal Asiatic Society
	Fellow, Royal Astronomical Society
FRBS	Fellow, Royal Botanic Society
	Fellow, Royal Society of British Sculptors
FRCA	Fellow, Royal College of Anaesthetists
FRCGP	Fellow, Royal College of General Practitioners
FRCM	Fellow, Royal College of Music
FRCO	Fellow, Royal College of Organists
FRCOG	Fellow, Royal College of Obstetricians and Gynaecologists
FRCP	Fellow, Royal College of Physicians, London
FRCPATH	Fellow, Royal College of Pathologists
FRCPE *or* FRCPEd	Fellow, Royal College of Physicians, Edinburgh
FRCPI	Fellow, Royal College of Physicians, Ireland
FRCPSYCH	Fellow, Royal College of Psychiatrists
FRCR	Fellow, Royal College of Radiologists
FRCS	Fellow, Royal College of Surgeons of England
FRCSE *or* FRCSED	Fellow, Royal College of Surgeons of Edinburgh
FRCSGLAS	Fellow, Royal College of Physicians and Surgeons of Glasgow

FRCSI	Fellow, Royal College of Surgeons in Ireland
FRCVS	Fellow, Royal College of Veterinary Surgeons
FRECONS	Fellow, Royal Economic Society
FRENG	Fellow, Royal Academy of Engineering
FRGS	Fellow, Royal Geographical Society
FRHISTS	Fellow, Royal Historical Society
FRHS	Fellow, Royal Horticultural Society
FRIBA	Fellow, Royal Institute of British Architects
FRICS	Fellow, Royal Institution of Chartered Surveyors
FRMETS	Fellow, Royal Meteorological Society
FRMS	Fellow, Royal Microscopical Society
FRNS	Fellow, Royal Numismatic Society
FRPHARMS	Fellow, Royal Pharmaceutical Society
FRPS	Fellow, Royal Photographic Society
FRS	Fellow, Royal Society
FRSA	Fellow, Royal Society of Arts
FRSC	Fellow, Royal Society of Chemistry
FRSE	Fellow, Royal Society of Edinburgh
FRSH	Fellow, Royal Society of Health
FRSL	Fellow, Royal Society of Literature
FRTPI	Fellow, Royal Town Planning Institute
FSA	Fellow, Society of Antiquaries
	Financial Services Authority
	Food Standards Agency
FSS	Fellow, Royal Statistical Society
FSVA	Fellow, Incorporated Society of Valuers and Auctioneers
FT	*Financial Times*
FTI	Fellow, Textile Institute
FTII	Fellow, Chartered Institute of Taxation
FZS	Fellow, Zoological Society

G

GATT	General Agreement on Tariffs and Trade
GBE	Dame/Knight Grand Cross, Order of the British Empire
GC	George Cross
GCB	Dame/Knight Grand Cross, Order of the Bath
GCC	Gulf Cooperation Council
GCHQ	Government Communications Headquarters
GCIE	Knight Grand Commander, Order of the Indian Empire
GCLJ	Knight Grand Cross, Order of St Lazarus of Jerusalem
GCMG	Dame/Knight Grand Cross, Order of St Michael and St George
GCSE	General Certificate of Secondary Education
GCSI	Knight Grand Commander, Order of the Star of India
GCVO	Dame/Knight Grand Cross, Royal Victorian Order
GDP	gross domestic product
Gen.	General
GHQ	general headquarters
GLA	Greater London Authority
GM	genetically modified
	George Medal
GMB	General, Municipal, Boilermakers and Allied Trades Union
GMT	Greenwich Mean Time
GNI	gross national income
GNVQ	General National Vocational Qualification
GOC	General Officer Commanding
GP	General Practitioner
Gp Capt.	Group Captain
GSA	Girls' Schools Association
GST	Greenwich Sidereal Time

H

HAC	Honourable Artillery Company
HB	His Beatitude
HBM	Her/His Britannic Majesty('s)
HCF	highest common factor
	Honorary Chaplain to the Forces
HE	Her/His Excellency
	higher education
	His Eminence
HGV	heavy goods vehicle
HH	Her/His Highness
	Her/His Honour
	His Holiness
HIM	Her/His Imperial Majesty
HIP	Home Information Pack
HIV	human immunodeficiency virus
HJS	*(hic jacet sepultus)* here lies buried
HM	Her/His Majesty('s)
HMAS	Her/His Majesty's Australian Ship
HMC	Headmasters' Conference
HMI	Her/His Majesty's Inspector
HML	Her/His Majesty's Lieutenant
HMS	Her/His Majesty's Ship
HMSO	Her/His Majesty's Stationery Office
HNC	Higher National Certificate
HND	Higher National Diploma
Hon.	Honorary
	Honourable
hp	horse power
HP	hire purchase
HQ	headquarters
HR	human resources
HRH	Her/His Royal Highness
HRT	hormone replacement therapy
HSE	Health and Safety Executive
	(hic sepultus est) here lies buried
HSH	Her/His Serene Highness
HST	Hubble Space Telescope
HTML	hypertext mark-up language
HTTP	hypertext transfer protocol
HWM	high water mark

I

I	Island
IAAS	Incorporated Association of Architects and Surveyors
IAEA	International Atomic Energy Agency
IATA	International Air Transport Association
IBF	International Boxing Federation
ibid	*(ibidem)* in the same place
IBRD	International Bank for Reconstruction and Development
ICAO	International Civil Aviation Organisation
ICBM	inter-continental ballistic missile
ICC	International Cricket Council
ICFTU	International Confederation of Free Trade Unions
ICJ	International Court of Justice
ICOMOS	International Council on Monuments and Sites
ICRC	International Committee of the Red Cross
id	*(idem)* the same
IDA	International Development Association
IDD	international direct dialling
ie	*(id est)* that is
IEA	International Energy Agency
IFA	independent financial adviser
IFAD	International Fund for Agricultural Development
IFC	International Finance Corporation
ILO	International Labour Office/Organisation

ILR Independent Local Radio
IMF International Monetary Fund
IMO International Maritime Organisation
inc. incorporated
INLA Irish National Liberation Army
in loc *(in loco)* in its place
INRI *(Iesus Nazarenus Rex Iudaeorum)* Jesus of Nazareth, King of the Jews
inst *(instant)* current month
Interpol International Criminal Police Organisation
IOC International Olympic Committee
IoM Isle of Man
IOU I owe you
IoW Isle of Wight
IQ intelligence quotient
IRA Irish Republican Army
IRB International Rugby Board
IRC International Red Cross
Is Islands
ISA individual savings account
ISBN International Standard Book Number
ISO Imperial Service Order
International Standards Organisation
ISP internet service provider
ISSN International Standard Serial Number
IT information technology
ITN Independent Television News
ITU International Telecommunication Union
ITV Independent Television
IVF in vitro fertilisation
IWC International Whaling Commission

J

J Judge
Justice
JP Justice of the Peace
Jr Junior

K

KBE Knight Commander, Order of the British Empire
KCB Knight Commander, Order of the Bath
KCIE Knight Commander, Order of the Indian Empire
KCLJ Knight Commander, Order of St Lazarus of Jerusalem
KCMG Knight Commander, Order of St Michael and St George
KCSI Knight Commander, Order of the Star of India
KCVO Knight Commander, Royal Victorian Order
KG Knight of the Garter
KGB *(Komitet Gosudarstvennoi Bezopasnosti)* Committee of State Security *(USSR)*
kHz kilohertz
KLJ Knight, Order of St Lazarus of Jerusalem
ko knock out *(boxing)*
KP Knight, Order of St Patrick
KStJ Knight, Order of St John of Jerusalem
Kt. Knight
KT Knight of the Thistle
kV kilovolt
kW kilowatt
kWh kilowatt hour

L

L Liberal
Lab. Labour
Lat. Latitude
lbw leg before wicket *(cricket)*
lc lower case *(printing)*
LCJ Lord Chief Justice
LCM least/lowest common multiple
LD Liberal Democrat
LDS Licentiate in Dental Surgery
LEA Local Education Authority
LHD *(Literarum Humaniorum Doctor)* Doctor of Humane Letters/ Literature
Lib. Liberal
Lic *(Licenciado)* lawyer *(Spanish)*
lit literary
Lit Hum *(Literae Humaniores)* classics course, Oxford University
LITT D Doctor of Letters
LJ Lord Justice
LLB Bachelor of Laws
LLD Doctor of Laws
LLM Master of Laws
LMS local management in schools
LMSSA Licentiate in Medicine and Surgery, Society of Apothecaries
loc cit *(loco citato)* in the place cited
log logarithm
Londin: of London *(Bishop)*
Long. longitude
LRT London Regional Transport
LS *(loco sigilli)* place of the seal
LSA Licentiate of Society of Apothecaries
LSC Learning and Skills Council
Legal Services Commission
lsd *(librae, solidi, denarii)* pounds, shillings and pence
LSE London School of Economics and Political Science
LST Local Sidereal Time
Lt. Lieutenant
LTA Lawn Tennis Association
ltd limited (liability)
LVO Lieutenant, Royal Victorian Order
LW long wave
LWM low water mark

M

M Member
Monsieur
MA Master of Arts
Maj. Major
maj. majority
max maximum
MB *(Medicinae Baccalaureus)* Bachelor of Medicine
MBA Master of Business Administration
MBC Metropolitan Borough Council
MBE Member, Order of the British Empire
MBO management buy-out
MC Master of Ceremonies
Military Cross
MCC Marylebone Cricket Club
MCH(D) Master of (Dental) Surgery
MD managing director
Doctor of Medicine
MDS Master of Dental Surgery
ME Middle English
myalgic encephalomyelitis
MEC Member of Executive Council
MED Master of Education
mega one million times
MEP Member of the European Parliament
MFH Master of Foxhounds
Mgr Monsignor
MI Military Intelligence
micro one-millionth part
milli one-thousandth part
min minimum
minutes
MIT Massachusetts Institute of Technology
MLA Member of Legislative Assembly
Museums, Libraries and Archives Council
MLC Member of Legislative Council
MLITT Master of Letters
Mlle Mademoiselle
MLR minimum lending rate
MM Military Medal
Mme Madame
MMR measles, mumps and rubella (vaccine)
MN Merchant Navy
MO Medical Officer/Orderly
MoD Ministry of Defence
MoJ Ministry of Justice
MoT Ministry of Transport

MP	Member of Parliament
	Military Police
mph	miles per hour
MPHIL	Master of Philosophy
MR	Master of the Rolls
MRC	Medical Research Council
MRSA	methicillin-resistant staphylococcus aureus
MS	manuscript (*pl* MSS)
	Master of Surgery
	multiple sclerosis
MSC	Master of Science
MSP	Member of Scottish Parliament
MUS B/D	Bachelor/Doctor of Music
MV	merchant vessel
	motor vessel
MVO	Member, Royal Victorian Order
MW	medium wave
MWA	Member of the Welsh Assembly

N

N	north
n/a	not applicable
	not available
NAAFI	Navy, Army and Air Force Institutes
NAFTA	North American Free Trade Agreement
NASA	National Aeronautics and Space Administration
NASUWT	National Association of Schoolmasters/Union of Women Teachers
NATFHE	National Association of Teachers in Further and Higher Education
NATO	North Atlantic Treaty Organisation
NB	New Brunswick
nb	*(nota bene)* note well
NCIS	National Criminal Intelligence Service
NCO	non-commissioned officer
NDPB	non-departmental public body
NEB	New English Bible
nem con	*(nemine contradicente)* no one contradicting
NERC	Natural Environment Research Council
nes	not elsewhere specified
NESTA	National Endowment for Science, Technology and the Arts
NFT	National Film Theatre
NFU	National Farmers' Union
NHS	National Health Service
NI	National Insurance
	Northern Ireland
no	*(numero)* number
non seq	*(non sequitur)* it does not follow
Norvic:	of Norwich *(Bishop)*
NP	Notary Public
NRA	National Rifle Association
NS	New Style *(calendar)*
	Nova Scotia
NSPCC	National Society for the Prevention of Cruelty to Children
NSW	New South Wales
NT	National Theatre
	National Trust
	New Testament
	Northern Territory *(Australia)*
NUJ	National Union of Journalists
NUM	National Union of Mineworkers
NUS	National Union of Students
NUT	National Union of Teachers
NVQ	National Vocational Qualification
NWT	Northwest Territory *(Canada)*
NZ	New Zealand

O

OAP	old age pension(er)
OAPEC	Organisation of Arab Petroleum Exporting Countries
OAS	Organisation of American States
Ob *or* obit	died
OBE	Officer, Order of the British Empire
OC	Officer Commanding
ODA	Overseas Development Administration
OE	Old English
	omissions excepted
OECD	Organisation for Economic Cooperation and Development
OED	*Oxford English Dictionary*
OFCOM	Office of Communications
OFGEM	Office of Gas and Electricity Markets
OFM	Order of Friars Minor *(Franciscans)*
OFREG	Office for the Regulation of Electricity and Gas
OFSTED	Office for Standards in Education
OFT	Office of Fair Trading
OFWAT	Office of Water Services
OHMS	On Her/His Majesty's Service
OHP	overhead projector
OIC	Organisation of the Islamic Conference
OM	Order of Merit
ono	or near(est) offer
ONS	Office for National Statistics
op	*(opus)* work
OP	opposite prompt side *(of theatre)*
	Order of Preachers *(Dominicans)*
	out of print *(books)*
op cit	*(opere citato)* in the work cited
OPEC	Organisation of Petroleum Exporting Countries
OPRAF	Office of Passenger Rail Franchising
OPS	Office of Public Service
ORR	Office of the Rail Regulator
OS	Old Style *(calendar)*
	Ordnance Survey
OSA	Order of St Augustine
OSB	Order of St Benedict
OSCE	Organisation for Security and Cooperation in Europe
OStJ	Officer, Order of St John of Jerusalem
OT	Old Testament
OTC	Officers' Training Corps
Oxon	(of) Oxford
	Oxfordshire

P

p	page
p	*(piano)* softly
PA	personal assistant
	Press Association
	public address (system)
PAYE	pay as you earn
PAYG	pay as you go
pc	*(per centum)* in the hundred
PC	personal computer
	Police Constable
	politically correct
	Privy Counsellor
PDSA	People's Dispensary for Sick Animals
PE	physical education
Petriburg:	of Peterborough *(Bishop)*
PFI	Private Finance Initiative
PG	parental guidance
PGA	Professional Golfers Association
PGCE	Postgraduate Certificate of Education
PHD	Doctor of Philosophy
PHLS	Public Health Laboratory Service
PIF	Pacific Islands Forum
pl	plural
PLA	Port of London Authority
plc	public limited company
PLO	Palestine Liberation Organisation
pm	*(post meridiem)* after noon
PM	post mortem
	Prime Minister
PMRAFNS	Princess Mary's Royal Air Force Nursing Service
PO	Petty Officer
	Pilot Officer
	post office
	postal order
POW	prisoner of war
pp	pages
	(per procurationem) by proxy
PPARC	Particle Physics and Astronomy Research Council
PPS	Parliamentary Private Secretary

PR proportional representation
public relations
PRA President of the Royal Academy
pro tem *(pro tempore)* for the time being
prox *(proximo)* next month
PRS President of the Royal Society
PRSE President of the Royal Society of Edinburgh
PS *(postscriptum)* postscript
PSBR public sector borrowing requirement
psc passed staff college
PSV public service vehicle
PTA Parent-Teacher Association
Pte. Private
PTO please turn over

Q

QARANC Queen Alexandra's Royal Army Nursing Corps
QARNNS Queen Alexandra's Royal Naval Nursing Service
QBD Queen's Bench Division
QC Queen's Counsel
QED *(quod erat demonstrandum)* which was to be proved
QGM Queen's Gallantry Medal
QHC Queen's Honorary Chaplain
QHDS Queen's Honorary Dental Surgeon
QHNS Queen's Honorary Nursing Sister
QHP Queen's Honorary Physician
QHS Queen's Honorary Surgeon
Qld Queensland *(Australia)*
QMG Quartermaster-General
QPM Queen's Police Medal
QS quarter sessions
Queen's Scholar
QSO quasi-stellar object (quasar)
Queen's Service Order
quango quasi-autonomous non-governmental organisation
qv *(quod vide)* which see

R

r. *(recto)* on the right-hand page
R *(Regina)* Queen
(Rex) King
RA Royal Academy/Academician
Royal Artillery
RAC Royal Armoured Corps
Royal Automobile Club
RADA Royal Academy of Dramatic Art
RADC Royal Army Dental Corps
RAE Royal Aerospace Establishment
RAEC Royal Army Educational Corps
RAES Royal Aeronautical Society
RAF Royal Air Force
RAM random-access memory
Royal Academy of Music
RAMC Royal Army Medical Corps
RAN Royal Australian Navy
RAOC Royal Army Ordnance Corps
RAPC Royal Army Pay Corps
RAVC Royal Army Veterinary Corps
R&B rhythm and blues
RBG Royal Botanic Garden
RBS Royal Society of British Sculptors
RC Red Cross
Roman Catholic
RCM Royal College of Music
RCN Royal Canadian Navy
RCT Royal Corps of Transport
R&D research and development
RD refer to drawer *(banking)*
Royal Naval and Royal Marine Forces Reserve Decoration
Rural Dean
RDI Royal Designer for Industry
RE Religious Education
Royal Engineers
REM rapid eye movement
REME Royal Electrical and Mechanical Engineers
Rep representative
Republican
Rep. Republic
Revd Reverend
RFL Rugby Football League
RFU Rugby Football Union
RGN Registered General Nurse
RGS Royal Geographical Society
RHA Regional Health Authority
RHS Royal Horticultural Society
RI Rhode Island *(USA)*
Royal Institute of Painters in Watercolours
Royal Institution
RIBA Royal Institute of British Architects
RIP *(requiescat in pace)* may he/she rest in peace
RIR Royal Irish Regiment
RL rugby league
RM Registered Midwife
Royal Marines
RMA Royal Military Academy
RMN Registered Mental Nurse
RMT National Union of Rail, Maritime and Transport Workers
RN Royal Navy
RNIB Royal National Institute for the Blind
RNID Royal National Institute for the Deaf
RNLI Royal National Lifeboat Institution
RNMH Registered Nurse for the Mentally Handicapped
RNR Royal Naval Reserve
RNVR Royal Naval Volunteer Reserve
RNXS Royal Naval Auxiliary Service
RNZN Royal New Zealand Navy
ROC Royal Observer Corps
Roffen: of Rochester *(Bishop)*
ROI Republic of Ireland
Royal Institute of Oil Painters
ROM read-only memory
RoSPA Royal Society for the Prevention of Accidents
RP Received Pronuciation
Royal Society of Portrait Painters
RPA Rural Payments Agency
rpm revolutions per minute
RRC Lady of Royal Red Cross
RSA Royal Scottish Academician
Royal Society of Arts
RSC Royal Shakespeare Company
RSCN Registered Sick Children's Nurse
RSE Royal Society of Edinburgh
RSM Regimental Sergeant Major
RSPB Royal Society for the Protection of Birds
RSPCA Royal Society for the Prevention of Cruelty to Animals
RSV Revised Standard Version *(of Bible)*
RSVP *(répondez, s'il vous plaît)* please reply
RSW Royal Scottish Society of Painters in Watercolours
Rt. Hon. Right Honourable
RTPI Royal Town Planning Institute
RU rugby union
RUC Royal Ulster Constabulary
RV Revised Version *(of Bible)*
RWS Royal Water Colour Society
RYS Royal Yacht Squadron

S

s second *(also* sec)
section (Public Acts)
(solidus) shilling
S south
SA Salvation Army
South Africa
South America
South Australia
SAARC South Asian Association for Regional Cooperation
SAE stamped addressed envelope
Salop Shropshire
SARS severe acute respiratory syndrome

Sarum:	of Salisbury (Bishop)
SAS	Special Air Service
SBS	Small Business Service
	Special Boat Service
SCD	Doctor of Science
SCM	State Certified Midwife
SCO	Shanghai Cooperation Organisation
SDLP	Social Democratic Labour Party
SEAQ	Stock Exchange Automated Quotations system
sec	second (*also* s)
SEN	special educational needs
	State Enrolled Nurse
SERPS	State Earnings Related Pension Scheme
SFO	Serious Fraud Office
SHMIS	Society of Headmasters and Headmistresses of Independent Schools
SI	statutory instrument
	(Système International d'Unités) International System of Units
sic	so written
SIDS	sudden infant death syndrome
sig	signature
	Signor
SJ	Society of Jesus *(Jesuits)*
SLD	Social and Liberal Democrats
SMP	Statutory Maternity Pay
SNP	Scottish National Party
SOCA	Serious Organised Crime Agency
SOE	Special Operations Executive
SOS	save our souls *(distress signal)*
sp	*(sine prole)* without issue
spgr	specific gravity
Sr	Senior
	Sister *(title)*
SRN	State Registered Nurse
SRO	self-regulating organisation
SS	Saints
	steamship
SSC	Solicitor before Supreme Court *(Scotland)*
SSN	standard serial number
SSP	statutory sick pay
SSSI	Site of Special Scientific Interest
STD	*(Sacrae Theologiae Doctor)* Doctor of Sacred Theology
	subscriber trunk dialling
stet	let it stand *(printing)*
STI	sexually transmitted infection
stp	standard temperature and pressure
STP	*(Sacrae Theologiae Professor)* Professor of Sacred Theology
Sub Lt.	sub-lieutenant
SVQ	Scottish Vocational Qualification

T

TA	Territorial Army
TB	tuberculosis
TD	Territorial Decoration
TEC	Training and Enterprise Council
TEFL	teaching English as a foreign language
temp	temperature
	temporary employee
TES	*Times Educational Supplement*
T&G	Transport and General Workers' Union
THES	*Times Higher Education Supplement*
TLS	*Times Literary Supplement*
TNT	trinitrotoluene *(explosive)*
trans.	translated
TRH	Their Royal Highnesses
trs	transpose *(printing)*
TT	Tourist Trophy *(motorcycle races)*
	tuberculin tested
TUC	Trades Union Congress

U

U	Unionist
UAB	unitary awarding body
UAE	United Arab Emirates
uc	upper case *(printing)*
UC	Unitary Council
UCAS	Universities and Colleges Admissions Service
UCATT	Union of Construction, Allied Trades and Technicians
UCL	University College London
UDA	Ulster Defence Association
UDI	Unilateral Declaration of Independence
UDR	Ulster Defence Regiment
UEFA	Union of European Football Associations
UFF	Ulster Freedom Fighters
UFO	unidentified flying object
UHF	ultra-high frequency
UKAEA	UK Atomic Energy Authority
ULTRA	Unrelated Live Transplant Regulatory Authority
UN	United Nations
UNESCO	United Nations Educational, Scientific and Cultural Organisation
UNHCR	United Nations High Commissioner for Refugees
UNICEF	United Nations Children's Fund
UNIDO	United Nations Industrial Development Organisation
UNITA	National Union for the Total Independence of Angola
UNPO	Unrepresented Nations and Peoples Organisation
UPU	Universal Postal Union
US(A)	United States (of America)
USDAW	Union of Shop, Distributive and Allied Workers
USM	Unlisted Securities Market
USSR	Union of Soviet Socialist Republics
UTC	coordinated universal time system
UVF	Ulster Volunteer Force

V

v	*(versus)* against
v.	*(verso)* on the left-hand page
V&A	Victoria and Albert Museum
VA	Vicar Apostolic
	Victoria and Albert Order
VAD	Voluntary Aid Detachment *(nursing)*
VAT	value added tax
VC	Victoria Cross
VCR	video cassette recorder
VD	venereal disease
	Volunteer Officers' Decoration
VDU	visual display unit
Ven.	Venerable
VHF	very high frequency
VIP	very important person
VRD	Royal Naval Volunteer Reserve Officers' Decoration
VSO	Voluntary Service Overseas

W

W	website
	west
WBC	World Boxing Council
WBO	World Boxing Organisation
WCC	World Council of Churches
WEA	Workers' Educational Association
WEU	Western European Union
WFTU	World Federation of Trade Unions
WHO	World Health Organisation
WI	West Indies
	Women's Institute
Winton:	of Winchester *(Bishop)*
WIPO	World Intellectual Property Organisation
WMD	weapons of mass destruction
WMO	World Meteorological Organisation
WO	Warrant Officer
WRAC	Women's Royal Army Corps
WRAF	Women's Royal Air Force
WRNS	Women's Royal Naval Service

WRVS	Women's Royal Voluntary Service
WS	Writer to the Signet
WTO	World Trade Organisation
WWW	World Wide Web
WYSIWYG	what you see is what you get

Y

YHA	Youth Hostels Association
YMCA	Young Men's Christian Association
YWCA	Young Women's Christian Association

INDEX

I

P

U

V

W

STOP PRESS

CHANGES SINCE PAGES WENT TO PRESS

REGIONAL GOVERNMENT

On 3 September, ministers changed the name of the Scottish Executive to the Scottish Government. Research had showed that the term 'Executive' was often confusing or meaningless to members of the public.

EVENTS OF THE YEAR

AFRICA

1 August. A train derailment between the cities of Ilebo and Kananga killed 100 people in DR Congo.

THE AMERICAS

15 August. Over 500 people were killed in Peru by a powerful earthquake that measured 8.0 on the Richter scale. **27 August.** US attorney-general Alberto Gonzales tendered his resignation after months of criticism and allegations of perjury. **4 September.** Preliminary results from the general election in Jamaica predicted a narrow victory for the opposition Jamaica Labour Party; the People's National Party had been in power since 1989. At least 98 people were killed in Honduras and Nicaragua as Hurricane Felix triggered mudslides and flooding.

ASIA

1. August. Monsoon rains devastated parts of India and Bangladesh; by 6 August, 1,200 people had been killed in the two countries and 19 million displaced. **22 August.** President Maumoon Abdul Gayoom of the Maldives won a national referendum on the country's political future; over 60 per cent of the population endorsed the continuation of a presidential system. **25 August.** Twin bomb attacks killed 42 people in the Indian city of Hyderabad. **3 September.** Khaleda Zia, the former president of Bangladesh, was arrested and charged with extortion and corruption.

EUROPE

27 August. Forest fires in Greece, believed to have been started deliberately, killed over 60 people and destroyed thousands of hectares of land. **28 August.** Abdullah Gul was elected president of Turkey after a parliamentary ballot despite opposition from secularists. **5 September.** Police in Germany arrested three men on suspicion of planning a series of terrorist attacks on US facilities in the country.

MIDDLE EAST

15 August. In the deadliest attack since the 2003 coalition invasion, four coordinated bombs exploded in a Yazidi area in northern Iraq, killing at least 250 people. **28 August.** Over 50 people died in Karbala, Iraq, following clashes between rival Shia militias.

OBITUARIES

Pavarotti, Luciano, opera singer, aged 71 – *d.* 6 September 2007, *b.* 12 October 1935

Roddick, Dame Anita, DBE, entrepreneur and environmentalist, aged 64 – *d.* 10 September 2007, *b.* 23 October 1942